facets complete video catalog no.14

Catherine Foley and Milos Stehlik, Editors

Facets Multi-media, Inc.

Distributed by Academy Chicago Publishers

how to use this catalog

HOW TO FIND A VIDEO

Alphabetically
Check the Title Index, which begins on page 478.
If the film or video is a short which is a part of a compilation, check the Short Film Index on page 431.

By director
Check the Director Index, which begins on page 447.

By country or language
Check the Table of Contents or Subject Area Contents on the following pages.

By genre
See the Table of Contents.

Short films
Check the Short Film Index on page 431.

HOW TO PURCHASE A VIDEO

To order any video, laser disc or CD-Rom in this catalog

Mail the order form on page 509 to
Facets Video, 1517 W. Fullerton Avenue
Chicago, IL 60614

Phone Facets Video toll-free
1-800-331-6197
Monday-Friday 9am-8pm CST
Saturday 10am-6pm CST

Fax (24 hours)
1-312-929-5437
(After October 1, 1996, the area code changes to 773.)

e-mail (24 hours)
sales@facets.org

HOW TO RENT A VIDEO

A majority of the videos in this catalog, including many now out-of-print videos, are available for rental-by-mail from
Facets Video Rentals, 1517 W. Fullerton Avenue, Chicago, IL 60614.
To request rent-by-mail information, write, call toll-free (1-800-331-6197) or e-mail rentals@facets.org

THE WHOLE TOON CATALOG AT FACETS

Facets also proudly presents the nation's best collection of animation on video and laser disc in *The Whole Toon Catalog*.
To request a free copy of the Facets Whole Toon Catalog, write
Facets Video, 1517 W. Fullerton Avenue, Chicago, IL 60614.

table of CONTENTS

subject area CONTENTS

INTERNATIONAL CINEMA

recent french
CINEMA

The 317th Platoon
A brilliant evocation of the senselessness of war during the last days of the French occupation of Indochina, based on the director's own experiences of being taken prisoner at Dien Buen Phu. The film tells of the platoon's retreat, focusing on a career soldier and the commanding young lieutenant as they make their way through ambushes, betrayals, rain, jungle, villages, pain, disease and inexorable fatigue to inevitable annihilation. With awesome cinematography by Raoul Coutard. With Jacques Perrin, Bruno Cremer, Pierre Fabre and Manuel Zarzo. French with English subtitles.
VHS: S13224. $59.95.
Pierre Schoendoerffer, France, 1965, 100 mins.

36 Filette
On a Biarritz family vacation, the 14-year old daughter, a very bored teenager, falls in love with an older man, who takes her to discos, seduces and abandons her. Catherine Breillat in her third feature fashions an insightful drama about sexual politics and male hypocrisy. With Jean-Pierre Leaud and Jean-Francois Stevenin. French with English subtitles.
VHS: S12993. $19.98.
Catherine Breillat, France, 1988, 86 mins.

A la Mode
An adorable French romantic comedy tells the rags-to-riches tale of a talented young fashion designer who turns Paris on its ear at the same time that he's winning the hearts of the city's loveliest women. French with English subtitles.
VHS: S23479. $96.98.
Laser: Letterboxed. LD74810. $39.95.
Remy Duchemin, France, 1993, 89 mins.

The Accompanist
Claude Miller's (The Little Thief) haunting tale of the love-hate relationship between a shy, unsophisticated pianist and the charismatic singer she idolizes is set against the backdrop of WWII France and features great performances from Richard Bohringer, Elena Safonova and Romane Bohringer. French with English subtitles.
VHS: S21894. $19.95.
Claude Miller, France, 1993, 101 mins.

Act of Aggression
Catherine Deneuve and Jean-Louis Trintignant star in this diabolical film about a man whose wife is murdered and who is driven to near-insanity until he tries to take revenge by his own hand. A tense, action-packed mystery. French with English subtitles.
VHS: S00016. $59.95.
Gerard Pires, France, 1982, 94 mins.

All the Mornings in the World
This film combines the fervor of passionate music making and young love in 17th century France in the story of cellist Marin Marais and his learning at the hands of teacher/composer Sainte-Colombe. Gerard Depardieu and his son Guillaume star as a musician in different stages of life, who must choose between his devotion to his instructor, his love for this instructor's daughter, and his art. French with English subtitles.
VHS: S20868. $96.95.
Laser: LD74487. $39.99.
Alain Corneau, France, 1992, 110 mins.

Anderson Platoon
One of the great films about Vietnam, directed by Pierre Schoendoerffer, the documentary focuses on an integrated combat unit led by Black West Pointer Lt. Joseph B. Anderson, and captures the tension, anger, hopelessness and pathos of armed conflict. Winner of the Academy Award for Best Documentary Feature.
VHS: S02404. $19.95.
Pierre Schoendoerffer, France, 1967, 65 mins.

Award Winning French Shorts
Three shorts from the 8th International Festival at Oberhausen: Le The a la Menthe, directed by Pierre Kafien, with some French dialog but no subtitles; End of Summer, from the National Film Board of Canada, in French with subtitles and English narration; and Le Poulet, a comedy from Claude Berri. France/Canada, 1962.
VHS: S02583. $29.95.

Barbarella
The film Jane Fonda most wants to forget. On the planet Sogo, where sin is at a discount, Barbarella (Fonda) runs athwart an evil queen (Anita Pallenberg) and her evil henchman (Milo O'Shea), who threaten our heroine's less-than-intact virtue with an overdose of pleasure. But to the rescue flies an oak tree masquerading as an angel (John Phillip Law), and in the end goodness triumphs, sort of. Fonda sheds her clothes, Law flaps his wings, and in general, everyone acts dotty in this film adaptation of the popular French comic strip. Script by Terry Southern, imaginative sets and top-notch camerawork by Claude Renoir.
VHS: S00095. $19.95.
Laser: Widescreen. LD75155. $34.98.
Roger Vadim, France, 1968, 98 mins.

Barocco
Isabelle Adjani and Gerard Depardieu are a terrific couple. Depardieu is a thief who kills a man and takes his place, including his girlfriend. The two plot blackmail and other intrigues that can only go bad. This over-the-top thriller achieves a singular stylistic unity. French with English subtitles.
VHS: S23291. $79.95.
Andre Techine, France, 1976, 102 mins.

The Best Way
Marc, the aggressive athletic director at a boys' summer camp, discovers the drama teacher dressed in women's clothes, and is shocked by his attraction to him. Their tense confrontation results in Marc forcing him to confront his suppressed sexuality. French with English subtitles.
VHS: S00120. $49.95.
Claude Miller, France, 1982, 85 mins.

Between Heaven and Earth
A fable with serious overtones. Carmen Maura plays Maria, an ambitious television journalist who has a series of surreal dreams. She falls into a profound moral and spiritual crisis when she communicates with her unborn child and believes the baby is unprepared and unwilling to be born. A prominent scientist and a young man in her apartment building try to help her decide the child's fate. "Entertaining and provocative, Carmen Maura is great" (Paul Wunder, WBAI Radio). With Jean-Pierre Cassel, Didier Bezace, Samuel Mussen and Andre Delvaux. French with English subtitles.
VHS: S20076. $79.95.
Marion Hansel, France, 1993, 80 mins.

Bim, the Little Donkey and Dream of the Wild Horses
The first film by the director of The Red Balloon, Bim is a delightful story of a lovable donkey who is taken away from a small boy to become the pet of a very rich family. The boy's efforts to get his donkey back lead to all sorts of adventures. Dream of the Wild Horses is a landmark short film by Georges Franju.
VHS: S01691. $29.95.
Albert Lamorisse, France, 1948, 45 mins.

Blue Jeans
A young boy is sent to England to improve his English, where he has his first experience with the opposite sex. When his girl friend takes up with a more experienced young man, the young boy confides in one of his supervisors and is taken advantage of. French with English subtitles.
VHS: S00158. $59.95.
Hugues des Roziers, France, 1978, 80 mins.

By the Blood of Others
Directed by Marc Simenon, the son of the famous mystery novelist, with Mariangela Melato. In a small village, a deranged man is holding two women hostage in an abandoned farmhouse. The whole village faces the problem of how to free the women without spilling blood. More than just a tense mystery, the film is an acute study of moral responsibility and a detailed picture of small-town French provincial life. French with English subtitles.
VHS: S06502. $59.95.
Marc Simenon, France, 1973, 90 mins.

Camille Claudel
Intense performances by Isabelle Adjani and Gerard Depardieu add fire to this adaptation of the family-"authorized" biography of overlooked sculptress Camille Claudel. After years of living with master sculptor Auguste Rodin (Depardieu) as pupil and lover, Claudel fell into a paranoid depression when he left her. Her disapproving family had her committed to a mental institution, where she wasted away for the remaining 30 years of her life. Adjani won a Cesar for her performance in this tragic story. French with English subtitles.
VHS: S12987. $19.98.
Laser: LD70910. $49.99.
Bruno Nuytten, France, 1990, 149 mins.

Chanel Solitaire
This American-French co-production covers the first 40 years of the life of Coco Chanel, the self-made designer who changed the shape of fashion. Starring Marie-France Pisier, Chanel Solitaire interweaves the professional with the personal. With Rutger Hauer, Timothy Dalton, Karen Black and Brigitte Fossey. In English.
VHS: S01509. $19.99.
George Kaczender, France/USA, 1981, 120 mins.

Chasing Butterflies
A whimsical comedy of social decay from one of the least-known masters of world cinema. Set in a cramped French village sealed off from modern life, the contemporary world begins to intrude via radio reports of terrorism, foreigners snapping up property and greedy relatives settling in. Narda Blanchett stars in this formally beautiful yet unsentimentally nostalgic film. French with English subtitles.
VHS: S26463. $79.95.
Otar Iosseliani, France, 1993, 115 mins.

Colonel Chabert
Gerard Depardieu stars as the returning war hero who is not supposed to return. Now he faces another battle at home to claim that which is rightfully his. Honore de Balzac's novel is treated to a lush production. Also features Fanny Ardant, Fabrice Luchini and Andre Dussollier. French with English subtitles.
VHS: S24953. $95.98.
Yves Angelo, France, 1992, 111 mins.

Cyrano de Bergerac
Gerard Depardieu is magnificent as the poetic soldier with the prominent proboscis. Based on the classic play by Rostand in which a 17th century swordsman proves inarticulate only when it comes to expressing his love for his cousin Roxanne face to face. Packed with pageantry, poetry and robust performances. With Anne Brochet, Jacques Weber, and some 2000 extras. French with English subtitles.
VHS: S14784. $19.95.
Laser: LD72215. $49.95.
Jean-Paul Rappeneau, France, 1989, 135 mins.

Dead Tired (Grosse Fatigue)
Carole Bouquet, Michel Blanc, Philippe Noiret and even Roman Polanski appear in this sinister but darkly comic look at the French film industry. Blanc finds himself in a number of comic situations that are completely inexplicable until he discovers that he has a double. This comic feature shows the seamy underside of the glamorous world of film in France. French with English subtitles.
VHS: S27073. $99.99.
Laser: LD75454. $39.95.
Michel Blanc, France, 1994, 85 mins.

Deadly Sanctuary
Banned in Europe, although now it's difficult to tell why, and based on the writings of the Marquis de Sade, with an international cast including Jack Palance, Klaus Kinski, Sylva Koscina, Akim Tamiroff and Mercedes McCambridge. In English.
VHS: S04784. $39.95.
Jess (Jesus) Franco, France/USA, 1970, 93 mins.

Diva
A breathtaking series of visual images in this stylish romantic thriller; at the heart of the film is an opera-intoxicated 18-year-old mail carrier who becomes unwittingly entangled in a web of murder, intrigue and passion. French dialog with English subtitles.
VHS: S00348. $29.95.
Jean-Jacques Beineix, France, 1982, 123 mins.

Dupont Lajoie (Rape of Innocence)
Jean Carmet stars in this tense dramatic film that explores French racism. At a campground where tourists gather, Carnet's character, Lajoie, accidentally kills the girlfriend of his teenage son when he resists his sexual assault. To save his own life he insinuates that Arabs did it, and then begins a hateful campaign of vengeance that has a surprising outcome. French with English subtitles.
VHS: S22680. $59.95.
Yves Boisset, France, 1974, 103 mins.

The Elegant Criminal (L'Elegant Criminel)
Francis Girod's terrifying study of France's most diabolical 19th century serial killer, a charismatic and elusive romantic figure whose constantly shifting persona—poet, thief, killer and hero—thrilled the public. With Daniel Auteuil, Jacques Duby and Jean Davy. French with English subtitles.
VHS: S17706. $19.98.
Francois Girod, France, 1990, 120 mins.

Elle Voit des Nains Partout
A clever adaptation of the Cafe Theatre Show, this is a very modern fairy tale complete with a wild Tom Thumb brought up by the Nuns of Eternal Help, Little Red Riding Hood, who delivers wine for her father's liquor company, and Snow White, who doesn't get to marry Prince Charming. French with English subtitles.
VHS: S00401. $59.95.
Jean-Claude Sussfeld, France, 1983, 83 mins.

Emilienne
A very high-class menage-a-trois, adroitly and erotically treated in this entertaining film from Guy Casaril. English dubbed.
VHS: S04149. $59.95.
Guy Casaril, France, 1977, 95 mins.

Farinelli
Farinelli, an 18th-century castrato, was one of Europe's most acclaimed singers. This lavishly designed, brilliantly costumed film focuses on his troubled artistic and personal life as he conquers the opera world and has women faint in his presence, yet needs his brother to consummate his sexual conquests. Corbiau ingeniously recreates the unique castrato sound by electronically blending a male and female voice; Jeroen Krabbe appears as Friedrich Handel. French with English subtitles.
VHS: S26396. $19.95.
Laser: LD75080. $34.95.
Gerard Corbiau, France/Belgium/Italy, 1995, 115 mins.

Fort Saganne
This lavish recreation of the Foreign Legion genre stars Gerard Depardieu and Catherine Deneuve in one of the most expensive French films ever made. The epic film follows the story of an extraordinary leader denied the fruits of his labor because of his peasant background. He somehow manages to rise to a position of prominence. Just when he can rightly enjoy the benefits of his rank, the murderous Algerian revolt of 1914 occurs. French with English subtitles.
VHS: S21510. $89.95.
Alain Corneau, France, 1984, 180 mins.

Franz
Two women take up residence at a boarding home that had previously been an all-male residence. One interacts with the group, while the other devotes her attentions to a single man at the home, Jacques Brel. A melodrama that entwines the past and present. French with English subtitles.
VHS: S01668. $19.95.
Jacques Brel, France, 1972, 88 mins.

Germinal
Gerard Depardieu stars in this sweeping film based on Emile Zola's masterful novel. A simple but honest and charismatic miner takes on a heroic quest for justice that leads him and his entire community to a fateful end. This tale of unforgivable wrongs stirs the soul. French with English subtitles.
VHS: S22537. $19.95.
Laser: LD74612. $39.95.
Claude Berri, France, 1993, 158 mins.

Grain of Sand
An incisive study of a woman's attempt at independence stars Delphine Seyrig as an unemployed woman in Paris who tries to reconcile her past with her present. Solange isolates herself from the world around her and decides to go back into the past, to a town in Corsica where she believes she will find the only man she has ever loved. Based on a true story, The Grain of Sand (Le Grain de Sable) is a moving film and a stunning directing debut by Pomme Meffre. With Delphine Seyrig, Genevieve Fontanel, Coralie Seyrig and Michel Aumont. French with English subtitles.
VHS: S03718. $59.95.
Pomme Meffre, France, 1984, 90 mins.

The Holes (Les Gaspards)
One day a busload of tourists suddenly sinks into the ground. So do a few buildings, most of the police force, and some of the choicest beauties in Paris. With Philippe Noiret, Charles Denner and Gerard Depardieu. Dubbed in English.
VHS: S14553. $59.95.
Pierre Tchernia, France, 1972, 92 mins.

Icy Breasts
A top-notch suspense thriller starring Alain Delon as a detective trying to prevent his lovely psychotic client, Mirelle Darc, from killing her lovers. A well-tooled thriller with a stunning climax. French with English subtitles.
VHS: S04246. $59.95.
Georges Lautner, France, 1975, 105 mins.

Indochine
Regis Wargnier's epic is set during the French occupation of Southeast Asia in the 1930s. Catherine Deneuve plays a plantation owner who searches for her adopted Vietnamese daughter Camille (Linh Dan Pham) after the young woman falls in love and becomes a communist revolutionary. "This intimate and tautly scripted work interweaves layers of deep affection with stirring historical details of 30s French Indochina, maintaining throughout an unshakable tension of a world about to change" (Toronto Festival of Festivals). Winner of the 1992 Academy Award for Best Foreign Language Film. French with English subtitles.
VHS: S20220. $19.95.
Laser: LD72330. $39.95.
Regis Wargnier, France, 1992, 160 mins.

Invitation au Voyage
The title comes from the poet Baudelaire, the film tells of a young man's plunge into the twilight world of his own desires as he travels the modern landscape. Winner of special honors at the Cannes Film Festival. French with English subtitles.
VHS: S00635. $19.95.
Peter Del Monte, France, 1982, 90 mins.

Jacques Lacan's Psychoanalysis Part One
A priceless document for anyone interested in contemporary thought and analysis. In interviews with Jacques-Alain Miller, Jacques Lacan, the famous French psychoanalyst called by many the French Freud, exposes with unexpected simplicity his most complex theories of the unconscious; the cure, the difference between psychoanalysis and psychotherapy, love and women. "For anyone hoping to understand the institutionalization of Freudian thought and the challenge Lacan represents, this is an essential work." French with English subtitles.
VHS: S18142. $69.95.
Benoit Jacquot, France, 1974, 60 mins.

Jean de Florette
A marvelous tale of greed and intolerance from the novel by Pagnol about a city hunchback who inherits a valuable piece of property in rural France only to have his efforts thwarted by the villainy of his venal neighbor. With Gerard Depardieu, Yves Montand, Daniel Auteuil, Elisabeth Depardieu and Ernestine Mazurownas as little Manon. French with English subtitles. 122 mins.
VHS: S07522. $19.98.
Claude Berri, France, 1987, 122 mins.

Jean de Florette/Manon of the Spring
Together for the first time on laser disc. Jean de Florette is the story of a hunchback farmer battling a drought and struggling against his scheming neighbors. Its sequel, Manon of the Spring, is the story of Jean's daughter Manon, the wild shepherdess, repulsed by the attentions of the remorseful Ugolin. Starring Gerard Depardieu, Yves Montand and Emmanuelle Beart.
Laser: Widescreen. LD74934. $99.99.
Claude Berri, France, 1987, 235 mins.

Josepha
Michel (Claude Brasseur) and Josepha (Miou-Miou) are husband and wife, actor and actress. On a movie location, Josepha has an affair but then decides to re-join her husband in order to "remake" the man she used to love. A critically-acclaimed, poignant examination of passion and anger. English dubbed.
VHS: S00658. $59.95.
Christopher Frank, France, 1983, 100 mins.

L'Amour en Herbe (Budding Love)
Pascal Meynier and Guilhaine Dubos star in this passionate film about forbidden teenage love. When Pascal's character fails at school, his parents realize he has something on his mind. It turns out to be his lovely 17-year-old friend, Martine. Though forbidden to see her, he remains true to his lover until betrayal intervenes. French with English subtitles.
VHS: S22679. $59.95.
Roger Andrieux, France, 1977, 100 mins.

L'Annee des Meduses
The most erotically charged film since *Last Tango*. A love battle between a nymphet (Valerie Kaprisky) and a gigolo (Bernard Giradeau). The combat is fought on the beaches of the South of France. French with English subtitles.
VHS: S05210. $69.95.
Christopher Frank, France, 1984, 110 mins.

L'Etat Sauvage (The Savage State)
This thriller is set in the 1960's in an African nation, which is struggling to create itself after independence from colonial rule. A UNESCO official returns looking for his wife and finds her living with a powerful black minister in the new government. Racial and sexual prejudices are stripped bare, as the fight begins to end this love affair. With Jacques Dutronc, Marie-Christine Barrault and Michel Piccoli. "Brutally frank!" (Kathleen Carroll, *New York Daily News*). French with English subtitles.
VHS: S14988. $59.95.
  Laser: Widescreen. LD71610. $49.95.
Francois Girod, France, 1978, 111 mins.

L'Homme Blesse (The Wounded Man)
The sensitive story of a French teenager and his discovery of his own homosexuality, this film directed by Patrice Chereau received the French Cesar. Henri, the teenager, tries to stop an attack on a man in a public toilet, is given a sexy kiss by the attacker, and discovers that he is strongly attracted to men. French with English subtitles.
VHS: S06588. $79.95.
Patrice Chereau, France, 1984, 90 mins.

La Grande Bouffe (The Great Feed)
Marcello Mastroianni, Philippe Noiret, Ugo Tognazzi and Michel Piccoli star in this strange, depraved comedy which was a 1970's worldwide sensation. The four men—victims of their appetites—retire to a Parisian villa, where they fill their systems with an overload of carnal pleasures until they die in a blow-out of orgiastic over-indulgence. French with English subtitles.
VHS: S26480. $79.95.
Marco Ferreri, France/Italy, 1973, 125 mins.

La Jetee/
An Occurrence at Owl Creek Bridge
One of the most challenging films ever made, Chris Marker's neo-science fiction film is set in a ruined France after World War III, in which a man's vivid childhood experience allows him to travel forward and backward in time. As a grown man, he meets the girl he had glimpsed as a child at the airport, falls in love with her, chooses to remain in the past, but is executed by those who hold power in the future. France, 1962, 29 mins. Also contains *An Occurrence at Owl Creek Bridge*, directed by Robert Enrico and based on a short story by Ambrose Bierce, which tells the tale of a man who is about to be hanged when the rope suddenly snaps and he is able to escape. Unfortunately, his newly found freedom is short-lived. USA, 1962, 27 mins.
VHS: S06274. $39.95.

La Lectrice
The fabulous French actress Miou-Miou has the title role of a woman who makes her living reading to her varied clientele. Playing her role as storyteller with increasing confidence, Miou-Miou becomes teacher, confidant, provocateur and confessor to her clients. A seductive and humorous comedy that has captured the attention of literate movie goers on an international scale. An unusual film directed with a deft, wry touch by Michel Deville. French with English subtitles.
VHS: S10759. $19.98.
Michel Deville, France, 1989, 98 mins.

La Passante
Romy Schneider in a dual role—as Elsa, a German refugee, and as Lina, the wife of a contemporary world leader. A story of two lovers compelled by action, mystery and political drama. With Michel Piccoli and Maria Schell. French with English subtitles.
  VHS: Out of print. For rental only.
  Laser: LD71087. $49.95.
Jacques Rouffio, France, 1983, 106 mins.

La Petite Bande
Told without dialog, but with a brilliant musical score by Edgar Cosma, *La Petite Bande* is a modern fairy tale of seven youngsters who leave London for France and the many adventures they encounter. Music track.
VHS: S00710. $59.95.
Michel Deville, France, 1984, 90 mins.

La Petite Sirene (The Little Mermaid)
The shocking subject matter of this film—a love affair between a 14 year old girl and a 40 year old man—is handled with a great deal of restraint by French director Roger Andrieux. At first the situation is rather innocent, almost funny. But as the movie progresses things take a dangerous turn, and the climax is jolting. The sex scenes are handled with delicacy; more is suggested than shown. Starring Laura Alexis and Philippe Leotard. French with English subtitles.
VHS: S13818. $59.95.
Roger Andrieux, France, 1985, 104 mins.

La Vie Continue
Annie Girardot stars as a middle aged woman struggling with three children after her husband suddenly dies of a heart attack. With Jean-Pierre Cassel. English dubbed.
VHS: S01709. $59.95.
Moshe Mizrahi, France, 1980

Le Complot (The Conspiracy)
Inspired by historical events, Rene Gainville's intelligent political thriller focuses on France's bitter war with Algeria and the group of disenchanted Army officers who opposed DeGaulle's decision to pull out. In a desperate attempt to save the colony, they attempt a coup. Top-notch cast includes Michel Bouquet and Jean Rochefort caught in a cat and mouse game between rebels, politicos and police. French with English subtitles.
VHS: S13281. $29.95.
Rene Gainville, France, 1973, 120 mins.

Le Crabe Tambour
Based on the career of French naval officer Pierre Guillaume and told through the recollections of his fellow officers, *Le Crabe Tambour* covers some 20 years of French history as Guillaume patrolled the Mekong River in Vietnam by boat in the 50's, then, taken prisoner, spent three years in a Vietnamese jail, and finally participated in the unsuccessful 1961 rebellion of French army generals against Charles de Gaulle. Shot by Charles de Gaulle, the film often recalls Joseph Conrad, and is "one of the grandest, most beautiful adventure movies in years...successfully maintains its epic sweep from start to finish" (*N.Y. Times*). French with English subtitles.
VHS: S08513. $59.95.
Pierre Schoendoerffer, France, 1977, 120 mins.

Le Grand Chemin
An enormous hit in France, *Le Grand Chemin* is a bittersweet, heartwarming tale from the producers of *Three Men and a Cradle*. Filmmaker Jean-Loup Hubert casts his own son in the role of a sensitive young boy caught between the bitterness of his divorcing parents. In an isolated village, he befriends a slightly older local girl who stirs his sexual awakening and initiates him into the mysteries of life. "It's a charmer, rich with humor...a terrific movie about childhood," wrote Judy Stone in *The San Francisco Chronicle*. French with English subtitles.
  VHS: Out of print. For rental only.
  Laser: LD71100. $39.95.
Jean-Loup Hubert, France, 1987, 107 mins.

Les Choses de la Vie
A sensitive businessman, injured in an automobile accident, reflects on his wife and his mistress, both of whom he dearly loves. Though a stylishly sophisticated romantic, *Les Choses de la Vie* builds to a deeply moving examination of the fragility of life relationships. "An extraordinary film" (*Le Figaro*). Starring Romy Schneider, Michel Piccoli, Lea Massari. French with English subtitles.
VHS: S12820. $29.95.
Claude Sautet, France, 1970, 90 mins.

Les Miserables
Jean-Paul Belmondo stars as a retired fighter inspired by the Victor Hugo novel. This illiterate boxer does everything he can, at great risk to his own life, to save a desperate Jewish family during the Nazi domination of France. It won a Golden Globe for its grand sweep and epic proportions. French with English subtitles.
  VHS: S27648. $98.99.
  Laser: LD75557. $39.98.
Claude Lelouch, France, 1995, 175 mins.

Les Violons du Bal
The relationship between art and personal sacrifice is explored in Michel Drach's film about a brilliant young filmmaker obsessed with chronicling his family's extraordinary efforts to escape Nazi-occupied France. Marie-Jose Nat, the director's wife, won the Best Actress Award at Cannes. With Jean-Louis Trintignant. French with English subtitles.
VHS: S17927. $29.95.
Michel Drach, France, 1974, 110 mins.

Life Is a Long Quiet River
An understated social comedy about a nurse who takes revenge on her indifferent lover, a married doctor, by switching two newborn babies. The narrative picks up 12 years later, as the two radically different families adjust to the severe changes when the children are returned to their rightful parents. Chatiliez dissects the mores of the two families, the upper middle class Le Quesnoys and the nefarious, criminal Groseilles. With Benoit Magimel, Helene Vincent and Daniel Gelin. French with English subtitles.
VHS: S18931. $79.95.
Etience Chatiliez, France, 1987, 90 mins.

Little Thief
The story of a female teenage delinquent in France who was reformed by the power of the photographic image. Based on a treatment never filmed by the late director Francois Truffaut and completed by Claude Miller. Story mirrors *400 Blows* in tone and subject matter. French with English subtitles.
VHS: S12223. $89.99.
Claude Miller, France, 1989, 100 mins.

Lola
Jacques Demy's *Lola* is a precisely constructed film about love, "with an almost balletic sense of rhythm set against the urban background of Nantes." The beautiful Anouk Aimee plays Lola, a cabaret dancer, who is courted by her childhood friend. But she is still in love with Michel, who had left her with their child when he went off to seek his fortune. After spending the night with another man, Michel reappears, rich, and takes her away. French with English subtitles.
VHS: S10738. $59.95.
Jacques Demy, France, 1961, 91 mins.

Love After Love
Isabelle Huppert stars along with Hippolyte Giradot and Bernard Giraudeau in this complex story of love and sex. A novelist famed for turning her life into salable fiction must confront changing times. As the 70's generation confronts the 90's, this character finds that the expectations of romance and the fundamental needs of love are often contradictory and comic. French with English subtitles.
VHS: S26608. $89.98.
Diane Kurys, France, 1994, 104 mins.

Love and the Frenchwoman
Seven French directors tackle the steamy subject of French women in love in this often witty omnibus film. With a cast of top actors, including Jean-Paul Belmondo, Marie-Jose Nat, Annie Girardot and Martine Carol. Episodes directed by Michel Boisrond, Jean-Paul Le Chanois, Christian-Jaque, Rene Clair, Jean Delannoy, Henri Verneuil and Henri Decoin. France, 1960, 143 mins. English dubbed.
VHS: S00774. $29.95.

Love Songs
Catherine Deneuve and Christopher Lambert star in this bittersweet love story between a married talent agent and her latest singing discovery. When her writer husband leaves Paris for Montreal to cure his writer's block, she finds the time to please herself. With Nick Mancuso and songs by Michel Legrand. Dubbed in French.
VHS: S04625. $79.95.
Elie Chouraqui, France, 1985, 107 mins.

Love Without Pity
Hippo is a modern bohemian, a Belmondo for the 90s, no job, no hopes, no cares—until he meets a beautiful and successful graduate student. Thus begins an obsessive and intensely passionate affair that consumes them both. Set in Paris, *Love without Pity* is a hard-edged, existential romance for today, about an alienated generation facing tomorrow. Starring Hippolyte Girardot and Mireille Perrier. This acclaimed film was writer/ director Eric Rochant's theatrical debut. French with yellow English subtitles.
  VHS: S15271. $79.98.
  Laser: LD71618. $39.95.
Eric Rochant, France, 1991, 95 mins.

Madame Rosa
Simone Signoret stars in the role of a Holocaust survivor forced into prostitution who befriends and shelters the children of the dispossessed, the prostitutes, Jews and Arabs who can no longer provide or care for their children. With Ben Youb, Claude Dauphin and filmmaker Costa-Gavras. French with English subtitles.
VHS: S00794. $59.95.
Moshe Mizrahi, France, 1977, 104 mins.

Mademoiselle
Tony Richardson's film about sexual obsession is based on a screenplay by Jean Genet. Set in a remote French village, the mayor, chief of police and a virginal school teacher played by Jeanne Moreau are unsettled by the appearance of an Italian guest worker and his teenage son. Moreau's sexual longing for the stranger sets in motion a dark *menage* of betrayal. With Ettore Manni, Keith Skinner and Umberto Orsini. French with English subtitles.
VHS: S20401. $19.98.
Tony Richardson, France, 1966, 105 mins.

Mado
"A beautifully made, complex film about the inter-relationship of love and business," wrote Pauline Kael. Romy Schneider stars as the mysterious woman who belongs to no one. Michel Piccoli and Charles Denner also star. French with English subtitles.
VHS: S00796. $59.95.
Claude Sautet, France, 1979, 130 mins.

A Man and a Woman
The 1966 Academy Award winner, a legendary love story starring Jean-Louis Trintignant as a race car driver who falls in love with Anouk Aimee. Stylish, well-acted and visually dynamic. Available only in a dubbed version.
VHS: S02322. $19.98.
Claude Lelouch, France, 1966, 103 mins.

A Man and a Woman—20 Years Later
Twenty years after the release of *A Man and a Woman*, Lelouch reunites Anouk Aimee and Jean-Louis Trintignant. A hit at numerous film festivals during 1986. French with English subtitles.
VHS: S02323. $19.98.
Claude Lelouch, France, 1986, 112 mins.

A Man in Love
Diane Kurys' (*Entre Nous*) most recent film stars Peter Coyote as an actor who comes to Rome to play Cesare Pavese, the Italian poet whose life ended in suicide. On the set of the film, Coyote becomes obsessed with the leading lady (Greta Scacchi, *Coca-Cola Kid*), and they become involved in an overpowering romance which threatens everything else in their lives. Dubbed in English.
VHS: S05852. $19.98.
Diane Kurys, France, 1987, 110 mins.

Manon of the Spring
Emmanuelle Beart is the grown-up, revenge seeking daughter of the kindly hunchback who was destroyed by the greed of his neighbors. Yves Montand and his nephew Daniel Auteuil learn the awful truth of their villainy in the conclusion of a classic tale of misinformation and retribution. From the novel by Pagnol. French with English subtitles. 123 mins.
VHS: S07523. $19.98.
Claude Berri, France, 1987, 113 mins.

Monkey People
(aka Monkey Folks, Le Peuple Singe)
Five years in the making, this fascinating French documentary about the simian world is narrated by actress Susan Sarandon. There are over 120 species in the tropical forests of Asia, Africa and South America, many of which were captured on film by Gerard Vienne. The film deals with social relations among the animals, using tools to acquire food, and playful activities that prove instructive and entertaining.
VHS: S14575. $19.98.
Gerard Vienne, France, 1989, 85 mins.

The Music Teacher
The music of Verdi, Mahler, Schumann, Mozart, Bellini, Schubert and Offenbach is highlighted in this 1989 Academy Award Nominee for Best Foreign Film. Just before World War I a group of opera students gather to compete to settle a grudge between a retired opera star and a wealthy patron. Lots of emotional fireworks. Called "elegant and cultivated" by the *Boston Globe*. With Jose Van Dam, Joachim Dallyroc and Anne Roussel. French with English subtitles.
VHS: S11535. $19.98.
Gerard Corbiau, Belgium/France, 1989, 100 min.

My Father's Glory
An 11-year-old boy spends an enchanting summer in the rugged French countryside with his family. The experience becomes a turning point in his young life and cements his relationship with his father. From the novel by Marcel Pagnol, a gorgeous film starring Philippe Caubere and Nathalie Roussel. French with English subtitles.
VHS: S16035. $19.98.
Yves Robert, France, 1991, 103 mins.

My Life and Times with Antonin Artaud
Gerard Mordillat's intimate portrait of the multifaceted Artaud begins with his release from prison and his return to Paris. This poet, actor, philosopher and all-around man of the theater is viewed through the eyes of Jacques Prevel, Artaud's disciple, pusher and companion. With Sami Frey and Marc Barbet. French with English subtitles.
VHS: S27755. $89.98.
Gerard Mordillat, France, 1995, 93 mins.

My Mother's Castle
In the companion film to *My Father's Glory*, a boy continues his love affair with the wild country of southern France. Through frequent family visits to their summer home, he learns to love and understand his mother's true nature. The heartfelt conclusion to the story by Marcel Pagnol. French with English subtitles.
VHS: S16036. $19.98.
Yves Robert, France, 1991, 117 mins.

Nea
Nea is a story of turbulent erotic passion and a young girl's striving to overcome the hypocrisy and repression of her father's home. 16-year-old Sybille Ashby, the daughter of a wealthy industrialist, has written her first novel, which her publisher believes to be an erotic masterpiece. But to complete it, Sybille convinces the publisher to initiate her sexually. French with English subtitles.
VHS: S00921. $59.95.
Nelly Kaplan, France, 1976, 100 mins.

Next Summer
A star-studded French romantic drama which features Claudia Cardinale, Fanny Ardant, Philippe Noiret, Marie Trintignant and Jean-Louis Trintignant in the story of an imaginary family in which family frustrations vie with passions, and the quest for power and beauty. A big hit in France. French with English subtitles.
VHS: S06012. $69.95.
Nadine Trintignant, France, 1984, 120 mins.

Next Year If All Goes Well
Isabelle Adjani and Thierry Lhermitte star as two lovers struggling to overcome their own problems and ambitions in a charming, romantic comedy. English dubbed.
VHS: S01502. $19.95.
Jean-Loup Hubert, France, 1983, 95 mins.

Noir et Blanc
Claire Devers' first critically-acclaimed film tracks the sado-masochistic relationship between a bleached-out accountant and a black masseur. As the masochism of Antoine, the unremarkable young man who is the accountant, grows evermore dependent, the film tracks the relationship to its horrifying climax. French with English subtitles.
VHS: S23599. $79.95.
Claire Devers, France, 1989, 89 mins.

Notorious Nobodies (Illustres Inconnus)
Winner of the Camera Award, *Notorious Nobodies*, wrote filmmaker Costa-Gavras, "attempts to describe for us the struggle of men and women around the world to save what is most precious to them: their dignity...neither a plea nor a denunciation but rather an original cinema of exceptional quality, a tragedy about human destiny." Comprised of eight individual stories taking place on the same day in far-flung corners of the globe, *Notorious Nobodies* is "a chronicle of emotions and images of an era, with horror made banal, abrasive humor, and above all, hope dotted throughout. *Notorious Nobodies* is a report both impartial and exhilarating, a film which is humble and ambitious." The eight sequences of the film are set in Prague, Munich, Paris, Vietnam, Geneva, Montevideo, Zaire and France. French with English subtitles.
VHS: S07822. $59.95.
Stanislav Stanojevic, France, 1986, 102 mins.

One Deadly Summer
Psychological thriller features Isabelle Adjani as a mysterious woman who returns to her mother's village to seek revenge on three men who had beaten and raped her mother years before. French with English subtitles.
VHS: S03313. $59.95.
Jean Becker, France, 1983, 134 mins.

Overseas
A stylistically audacious first feature by the talented French actress Brigitte Rouan. Set in the late 40s, *Overseas* traces that opposite fortunes of three wealthy sisters living in French occupied North Africa at the onset of the Algerian war. With Nicole Garcia, Rouan, Marianne Basler and Philippe Galland.
VHS: S16859. $19.98.
Brigitte Rouan, France, 1990, 98 mins.

Paris Vu Par (Six in Paris)
This omnibus film from the major figures of the French New Wave (Jean-Luc Godard, Claude Chabrol, Eric Rohmer, Jean Douchet, Jean Rouch and Jean-Daniel Pollet) offers a series of witty, wry vignettes about contemporary Paris. Godard's work, *Une Femme Est une Femme*, is about a young woman who dispatches letters to her two lovers and is concerned she mixed up the contents. With Joanna Shimkus, Nadine Ballot, Barbet Schroeder, Micheline Dax, Claude Melki, Chabrol and Stephane Audran. French with English subtitles. France, 1964, 98 mins.
VHS: S19543. $69.95.

Peppermint Soda
Diane Kurys' autobiographical first feature charts the adventures of two carefree sisters, Anne (Elenore Klarwein), a shy misfit, and Frederique (Odile Michel), a free-spirited extrovert, during the socially turbulent Paris of the early 60s. Living with their divorced Jewish mother, the girls shuttle between a rigid, claustrophobic school and awkward holidays with their father. The film is a harsh, unsentimental look at adolescence, with the 60s setting serving primarily to define the social and political context of the girls' rites of passage" (*Time Out*). With Anouk Ferjac, Michel Puterflam, Yves Renier and Robert Rimbaud. French with English subtitles.
VHS: S19416. $79.95.
Diane Kurys, France, 1977, 97 mins.

Peril

Michel Deville's acclaimed French film is the story of a wealthy industrialist family which hires a musician to give lessons to their precocious daughter. But the wife seduces the young man and soon becomes the pawn in a deadly game of lust. French with English subtitles.
VHS: S01010. $19.95.
Michel Deville, France, 1985, 100 mins.

A Pure Formality

Gerard Depardieu faces off against director Roman Polanski in this unsettling mystery from the director of *Cinema Paradiso*. Depardieu plays a man accused of a murder that he doesn't remember committing. He and Polanski play a deadly game of deceptions, distortions and lies where a series of unexpected flashbacks finally reveal the unforseen truth about this intriguing case. With a brilliant performance from Polanski. French with English subtitles.
VHS: S26990. $96.99.
Laser: LD75437. $39.95.
Giuseppe Tornatore, France, 1994, 107 mins.

Queen Margot

Winner of five Cesar Awards, Patrice Chereau's stylish, realistic adaptation Alexander Dumas' tale is set during the Catholic-Protestant wars of 16th-century France. Isabelle Adjani plays Margot, the unwilling daughter of Catherine de Medici (Virna Lisi in a Cannes Festival-winning role), who is married to Protestant leader King Henry of Navarre (Daniel Auteuil). In the film Chereau creates a non-stop series of betrayals, intrigues, plots, poisonings, love affairs and executions as Margot falls for a common soldier (Vincent Perez). French with English subtitles.
VHS: S25051. $96.98.
Patrice Chereau, France, 1994, 144 mins.

Red Kiss

Nadia (Charlotte Valandrey) is fifteen, full of life, and loves the poet Apollinaire, cemeteries, Scarlett O'Hara, and...Stalin. Her parents are Jewish immigrants from Poland. Nadia and her parents believe that the revolution is imminent, that the best doctors come from the USSR and that Soviet children are paid to go to school. At a demonstration, Nadia meets Stephane (French heartthrob Lambert Wilson) and through him discovers another life, another world. French with English subtitles.
VHS: S12992. $19.98.
Vera Belmont, France, 1985, 110 mins.

Rendez Vous

Andre Techine's (*Scene of the Crime*) sexy, stylish melodrama stars Juliette Binoche (*Hail Mary, Unbearable Lightness of Being*) as an actress on a "rendezvous" with destiny, who projects a carnality that drives men wild. The obsessive passion culminates in her relationship with a self-destructive lover. "Sizzles with eroticism." French with English subtitles.
VHS: S11634. $29.95.
Andre Techine, France, 1985, 82 mins.

Rendez-Moi Ma Peau

A modern-day witch loses most of her magical power, but has just enough to mess up the lives of two strangers when she transposes their personalities. The fun begins as a detective tracks down Zora the witch, while Jean-Pierre and Marie are trapped inside each other's bodies. French with English subtitles.
VHS: S01105. $59.95.
Patrick Schulmann, France, 1981, 82 mins.

Return of Martin Guerre

Dramatization of an extraordinary imposture that took place in the 16th century and became a legend; the husband leaves his family and years later, returns. He re-integrates himself into the family and community, but then serious doubts spring up about his identity—is he the real Martin Guerre? With Gerard Depardieu, Nathalie Baye. French with English subtitles.
VHS: S01107. $29.95.
Daniel Vigne, France, 1983, 123 mins.

Salut d'Artiste (Salute the Artist)

A comedy about two second-rate actors who are trying to make it in the cinema and theater in Paris. Nicolas is 45; he doesn't lack work, but the roles he gets are invariably bottom-drawer. So he continues to dream about stardom as he accepts anything that pays the bills—commercials, even dubbing parrots' voices in cartoons. His friend Clement, faced with similar frustration, ends up giving up acting and taking an executive job. Directed by Yves Robert and starring Marcello Mastroianni and Francoise Fabian. French with English subtitles.
VHS: S13592. $29.95.
Yves Robert, France, 1974, 96 mins.

Sartre by Himself (Sartre par Lui Meme)

A revealing documentary portrait of the existentialist philosopher and writer. The film offers a conversational feast for anyone with an interest in 20th century philosophy, the intellectual ferment of post-war Paris, or the vibrant personalities of Sartre and his long-time friend, Simone de Beauvoir. French with English subtitles.
VHS: S11594. $99.95.
A. Astruc/M. Contat, France, 1979, 190 mins.

Savage Nights

Cloaked in controversy because its maker and star, Cyril Collard, died of AIDS just days after the film won the coveted Cesar (French Oscar) award, *Savage Nights* is a story of passion and love in the age of HIV. A bisexual photographer finds his life is shared by those he loves in a way that many would find unforgivable. The film provokes and astonishes with its singular perspective; it is all the more incendiary by being rooted in real life. French with English subtitles.
VHS: S22530. $94.99.
Cyril Collard, France, 1993, 126 mins.

Scandal Man

Maurice Ronet plays a photographer who becomes involved in a sensational story when he photographs the daughter of an American Ku Klux Klan leader embracing a black man at a nightclub. French with English subtitles.
VHS: S01964. $19.95.
Richard Balducci, France, 86 mins.

Scene of the Crime

Catherine Deneuve is a strikingly beautiful widow in a tiny French hamlet. She unexpectedly comes across a sexual outlaw played by Danielle Darrieux. This escaped convict brings her to a new sexual awareness in this lyrically paced film. French with English subtitles.
VHS: S25032. $24.95.
Andre Techine, France, 1987, 90 mins.

The Scent of Green Papaya

A moving and undeniably brilliant film by the talented Vietnamese-exile filmmaker Tran Anh Hung, set in 1951 and centered on a young woman who becomes a servant for a turbulent family. The film follows in exquisitely lyrical detail the quiet beauty and stoically accepted hardships of her life as, ten years later, she starts a love affair with her next employer. Shot entirely on a Paris soundstage, this, says critic Roger Ebert, "is a film to cherish." Vietnamese with English subtitles.
VHS: S23925. $19.95.
Laser: LD74799. $34.95.
Tran Anh Hung, Vietnam/France, 1993, 104 mins.

Secret Obsession

Ben Gazzara and Julie Christie star in this dramatic love story set in North Africa and Europe. Ben has an illegitimate son that he won't acknowledge, who grows up to fall in love with Julie Christie, who is already Ben's lover. Talk about a family affair. In English.
VHS: S08069. $79.95.
Ridha Behi, France/Tunisia, 1988, 84 mins.

Seven Deadly Sins

Several French and Italian filmmakers, among them Eduardo De Filippo, Yves Allegret, Georges Lacombe and Roberto Rossellini, create separate vignettes that illustrate the dangers and provocations of the seven vices, suffused with a caustic, black wit. With Michele Morgan, Francoise Rosay, Gerard Philipe, and Isabelle Miranda. French and Italian with English subtitles. 1953, 127 mins.
VHS: S18030. $29.95.

Simone de Beauvoir

A candid portrait of a remarkable woman. Simone de Beauvoir discusses her political views, the student uprisings of 1968, sexual fidelity, aging and death. Interwoven with interviews are archival photographs and footage of the events, both personal and historical, that have shaped her thinking. French with English subtitles.
VHS: S08606. $59.95.
M. Ribowska/J. Dayan, France, 1982, 110 mins.

A Simple Story

Romy Schneider, in her French Academy Award performance, plays a successful industrial designer disturbed by intangible doubts brought on with the approach of middle age. At the crossroads of her life she must balance her career, a teenage son, an ex-husband, a boyfriend and her peers. French with English subtitles.
VHS: S01205. $59.95.
Claude Sautet, France, 1978, 100 mins.

Sincerely Charlotte

A wonderful directing debut by Huppert, this bittersweet, offbeat, romantic drama stars her sister, Isabelle Huppert, as a rock singer who is fingered for the murder of her boyfriend. She escapes with her former (now married) lover Mathieu across the countryside of France. French with English subtitles.
VHS: S02974. $19.95.
Caroline Huppert, France, 1986, 92 mins.

Soldier Duroc...It's Your Party

The story of a love-hungry French soldier who crosses German enemy lines in 1944 France to visit his fiancee, only to be trapped by the German soldiers. With Pierre Tornade, Robert Webber, Michel Galabru. French with English subtitles.
VHS: S01225. $39.95.
Michel Serard, France, 95 mins.

Sorceress

An intriguing film about the clash between a dedicated healer and a pursuer of heretics. Truffaut protege and longtime friend Suzanne Schiffman makes her directorial debut with a convincing period piece that raises timely questions on the role of the church and its oppression of women. At once a theological discourse and a story well told, this film illuminates challenges made toward Christianity as early as the Middle Ages.
English Language Version.
VHS: S17691. $29.95.
Subtitled Version.
VHS: S12672. $29.95.
Suzanne Schiffman, France, 1988, 98 mins.

Soviet Spy

Docudrama written by Hans Otto Meissner, Chief of Protocol at the German Embassy in Tokyo during World War II. Story concerns the case of Richard Sorge, a German journalist hanged as a spy in 1944 for warning Moscow that German armies would attack the Soviets. French with English subtitles. France, 1961, 130 mins.
VHS: S01671. $19.95.

Starting Place

Robert Kramer achieved notoriety with his 1969 documentary, *People's War*. After 24 years he returns with a documentary that continues to explore the same subjects and once again reveals the other side of Vietnamese society, rarely seen in this country. It is provocative and elegiac at the same time, reflecting a perspective altered in part by the passing of time and the reasoned expectations of an older, more sober outlook. France/Great Britain/Vietnam, 1993, 80 mins.
VHS: S27649. $39.95.

Tartuffe

In his first directorial effort, Gerard Depardieu (*Green Card, Cyrano*) breathes new life into Moliere's classic stage masterpiece about religious and sexual hypocrisy. The dazzling cast includes Depardieu, his wife Elizabeth, and renowned classical actor Francois Perier. Based on a stage production directed by Jacques Lasalle of the Theatre National de Strasbourg. "The best production of *Tartuffe* I've seen" (Stanley Kauffmann). French with English subtitles.
VHS: S13590. $79.95.
Gerard Depardieu, France, 1984, 140 mins.

Tatie Danielle

Meet the meanest old lady on earth. She's Auntie—"Tatie"—Danielle, a demanding and manipulative woman who must be waited on hand and foot. When she moves in with her great nephew, he and his wife hope that "Tatie" will be the grandmother the children never had. It doesn't take long, however, for this cantankerous old lady to make everyone's life hell. A clever and darkly hilarious work from director Etienne Chatliez. French with English subtitles.
VHS: S15585. $19.98.
Laser: LD75270. $34.98.
Etienne Chatiliez, France, 1991, 114 mins.

Therese

Alain Cavalier's acclaimed film follows Therese, a 15-year-old girl from provincial France, as she becomes a Carmelite nun and battles with doubts of her faith in the convent. Based on the journal of Therese, published as *Story of a Soul*. The actual Therese was canonized in 1925 and became known as "The Little Flower of Jesus". French with English subtitles.
VHS: S07309. $39.95.
Alain Cavalier, France, 1986, 100 mins.

This Special Friendship

A 16-year-old boy becomes infatuated with a young classmate at a strict Jesuit boarding school. "A masterpiece...shocking in the best sense of the word" (L.A. Times). A sensitively directed film with a bravura performance by Didier Haudepin. French with English subtitles.
VHS: S01333. $49.95.
Jean Delannoy, France, 1964, 99 mins.

This Sweet Sickness

A Hitchcockian study of erotic intrigue is freely adapted from a Patricia Highsmith novel. The practical, quiet loner David (Gerard Depardieu) builds an elaborate mountain chalet to seduce Lise (Dominique Laffin), a married woman with whom he's fallen obsessively in love. David rejects the legitimate and honest love of Juliette (Miou-Miou), with tragic repercussions. Former Truffaut and Godard protege Claude Miller charts these emotions with sureness of touch. With Claude Pieplu and Christian Clavier. French with English subtitles.
VHS: S19294. $24.98.
Claude Miller, France, 1977, 107 mins.

Tom and Lola

These beautiful children have damaged immune systems that force them to remain isolated in hermetically sealed plastic bubbles. This isolation cannot inhibit their beguiling spirit, a spirit that manifests itself in a bold bid to free themselves from this claustrophobic environment. French with English subtitles.
VHS: S21543. $69.95.
Bertrand Arthuys, France, 1994, 98 mins.

Un Coeur en Hiver

Claude Sautet's 13th feature is loosely based on Lermontov's novel *A Hero of Our Time*. Two violin makers (Daniel Auteuil and Andre Dussollier) are affected when a beautiful violinist (Emmanuelle Beart) enters their lives. The film addresses the question of whether Auteuil is able to reconcile his cold, rigid nature with his deep, emotional attraction to Beart. With Elizabeth Bourgine, Myriam Boyer, Brigitte Catillon, and Maurice Garrel as a brilliant music teacher. French with English subtitles.
VHS: S20208. $19.98.
Laser: LD72327. $34.98.
Claude Sautet, France, 1991, 100 mins.

Uranus

From Claude Berri, the director of *Jean de Florette* and *Manon of the Spring*. Gerard Depardieu stars in this controversial adaptation of the French novel about a flawed Renaissance man, a poet, philosopher and hustler, entangled with individual heroism, sexual politics and collaboration with the Nazi occupation forces during World War II. French with English subtitles.
VHS: S17401. $89.99.
Laser: LD75278. $34.98.
Claude Berri, France, 1990, 100 mins.

A Very Curious Girl

Nelly Kaplan's sensational sex comedy, with Bernadette Lafont as the town 'loose girl' who, tired of enduring physical and sexual exploitation, begins to charge for her services, accumulating power she never imagined, and 'gets back at her clients' for what they have done unto her. French with English subtitles.
VHS: S01410. $29.95.
Nelly Kaplan, France, 1971, 105 mins.

Vincent, Francois, Paul & the Others

A lyrical homage to male friendship featuring outstanding performances by Yves Montand, Michel Piccoli and Gerard Depardieu. The three men find their friendship sustains them through a series of middle-age crises. "An extraordinary movie fugue on the theme of friendship. Sautet's style is one of the great pleasures of modern movie-going," wrote *The Washington Post*. French with English subtitles.
VHS: S01417. $29.95.
Claude Sautet, France, 1977, 113 mins.

Voyage en Douce

Geraldine Chaplin and Dominique Sanda star in this graceful film about two women who decide to take charge of their lives. Fed up with the men they know, they set off on a journey. In the lush countryside of Southern France they share jokes, meals, and erotic daydreams. French with English subtitles.
VHS: S22443. $79.95.
Michel Deville, France, 1981, 97 mins.

The Wanderer

Alain Fournier's classic novel, *Le Grand Meaulnes*, is interpreted by Albiococco with fantastic imagery and stunning color—in a remarkable recreation of a child's memories and examination of his transition from romantic, idealistic youth to clear-eyed adult. With Jean Blaise and Brigitte Fossey. "Heartbreaking...Romantic" (L.A. Times). French with English subtitles.
VHS: S15273. $29.95.
Jean-Gabriel Albicocco, France, 1967, 108 mins.

We Were One Man

A simple French farmer and a wounded, abandoned German soldier are ultimately united in an openly sexual relationship in this award-winning French film. French with English subtitles.
VHS: S01437. $49.95.
Philippe Vallois, France, 1980, 90 mins.

Weapons of the Spirit

Between 1940 and 1944, a small village in the mountains of France, Le Chambon, became Europe's most effective haven for Jews, saving 5,000 men, women and children from the Holocaust. In this extraordinary documentary by Pierre Sauvage, who was born and protected in this peaceful village, the director shares this heartwarming story of the poor farming village of French Protestants who, under the eyes of the German occupation forces and the Vichy government, resisted the violence through the "weapons of the spirit." French with English subtitles.
VHS: S12461. $90.00.
Pierre Sauvage, France/USA, 1986, 91 mins.

A Woman at Her Window

Romy Schneider plays an aristocratic woman immersed in the despotic world of Greece circa 1936, who pursues shallow affairs with her noble counterparts (Philippe Noiret). When she rescues a political activist (Victor Lanoux) she falls in love and is transformed by new passions. French with English subtitles.
VHS: S21757. $79.95.
Pierre Granier-Deferre, France, 1977, 110 mins.

CUTTING EDGE FRENCH FILMMAKERS

Baxter

Beware of the dog who thinks! Before *Look Who's Talking* took Hollywood by storm, *Baxter* came out of the kennel in France with his unique perspective on the strange behavior of the human animal. Shuttled from master to master, Baxter disagrees with an old woman, finds himself charged to the newlywed couple across the way, and ends up with a young master who is obsessed with Hitler. French with English subtitles.
VHS: S16685. $19.98.
Laser: CLV/CAV. LD72047. $39.95.
Jerome Boivin, France, 1991, 82 mins.

Chocolat

Claire Denis takes the viewer on an emotional and strikingly visual memory trip back to the colonial Africa of her youth. In her directorial debut, she spins an engaging tale of a small white girl growing up in Cameroon on the isolated compound of her French official father and her lonely gorgeous mother. With Guilia Boschi, Issach de Bankole, Francois Cluzet and Cecile Ducasse. French with English subtitles.
VHS: S11534. $19.98.
Claire Denis, France, 1988, 105 mins.

Dr. Petiot

Michel Serrault stars in this macabre tale of a doctor who lured desperate Jews into a trap. They sought to escape Nazi-controlled France, but this doctor tricked them and murdered them in his own private crematorium and then stole their belongings. Based on the true story of a French physician. French with English subtitles.
VHS: S21511. $29.95.
Christian de Chalonge, France, 1990, 102 mins.

Field of Honor

During the Napoleonic Wars a French farm boy takes the place of the son of a rich family and begins to rethink the bargain when the bullets start to fly. Chris Campion is the young soldier trying to survive the Prussian advance. An intriguing tale of war, irony, and the people caught between the armies, directed with great sensitivity by Jean-Pierre Denis, one of the most talented young French filmmakers. French with English subtitles.
VHS: S10758. $19.98.
Jean-Pierre Denis, France, 1987, 87 mins.

Franck Goldberg: Sampler

A compilation of short films that includes: "Red Souvenir"—a documentary-style look at kids in New York; "No Sellout"—a rap music video based on Malcolm X's speeches; "Lynch"—the story of the police killing of a young graffiti artists in the New York subway; "Promised Land"—an examination of the purposeless violence of the U.S. as seen by this French video artist.
VHS: S07126. $39.95.
Franck Goldberg, France, 1985-86, 60 mins.

The Hairdresser's Husband

An acclaimed, quirky film about erotic obsession from the director of *Monsieur Hire*. Antoine (Jean Rochefort) is a middle-aged man whose life-long ambition to marry a hairdresser is fulfilled in his tender relationship with the beautiful and graceful Matila (Anna Galiena). With Henri Hocking and Maurice Chevit. French with English subtitles.
VHS: S18680. $19.95.
Laser: LD75204. $34.98.
Patrice Leconte, France, 1990, 84 mins.

In the Land of the Deaf

A unique and privileged look inside the world of deaf people. A teacher, a woman treated for mental illness because of her deafness, and a newly wed deaf couple offer compelling portraits from a community estimated to comprise 130 million people worldwide in a film which is revealing, moving and often funny. French and French Sign Language with English subtitles.
VHS: S25993. $79.95.
Nicolas Philibert, France, 1994, 99 mins.

La Femme Nikita

A stylish punk thriller from director Luc Besson (*Subway, The Big Blue*) in which a French street junkie (played by the beautiful Anne Parillaud) is arrested and threatened with life imprisonment. She is then allowed to leave if she agrees to go to work for the French secret police as an assassin. This suspenseful film is highlighted by Besson's stylishly decorous visual compositions and innate sense of dramatic pacing. Also starring Tcheky Karyo and Jeanne Moreau. French with English subtitles.
VHS: S14530. $19.95.
Laser: Widescreen. LD75217. $34.98.
Luc Besson, France, 1991, 117 mins.

The Lacemaker

Isabelle Huppert shot from minor actress to international star with a mesmerizing performance as a young woman incapable of escaping anonymity. This acclaimed and beautiful film by Swiss director Claude Goretta is a sad twist on the Cinderella story as Huppert is swept away by Francois, a rich, handsome young student. At first, he is captivated by her graceful movements and enticed by her virginity. But their romance is short-lived; he soon breaks with her and brings about her mental collapse. French with English subtitles.
VHS: S12953. $79.95.
Claude Goretta, Switzerland/France, 1977, 107 mins.

Marquis

An audacious rendering of the political, social and sexual manners of the *ancien regime* and the class division and social disruption that produced the French Revolution. Adapted from the writings of the Marquis de Sade, Henri Xhonneux and Roland Topor brilliantly wittily film uses elaborate puppets in human form to act out erotic and sexual decadence. "Elegantly naughty with wry, intellectual satire. The film plays out all manner of human desire" (J. Hoberman). French with English subtitles.
VHS: S18104. $29.95.
Henri Xhonneux, France, 1989, 85 mins.

Monsieur Hire

A disturbing and finely crafted thriller about obsession and responsibility. Michel Blanc stars as a reclusive tailor who enjoys watching Sandra Bonnaire undress across the courtyard. When a murder is committed, his peculiarities make him a suspect. Based on a novel by Georges Simeon. With Luc Thuillier and Andre Wilms. Be prepared to be affected. French with English subtitles.
VHS: S13672. $19.98.
Patrice Leconte, France, 1989, 81 mins.

No Fear, No Die

Starring Issach de Bankole, Alex Descas and Jean-Claude Brialy, this film explores a sordid underworld of gambling and desire centered around an illegal cock-fighting club. Two immigrants supply the birds and train them, but the arrangement breaks down when the club owner's mistress (Solveig Dommartin) becomes involved in these murky dealings. From the director of *Chocolat.* French with English subtitles.
VHS: S20785. $29.95.
Claire Denis, France, 1993, 97 mins.

The Professional

Jean Reno, of *La Femme Nikita,* Gary Oldman and Danny Aiello star in this hyper fast thriller from French filmmaker Luc Besson in his American debut. A hitman develops an unexpected bond with an orphaned 12-year-old girl. Saddled with this casualty of the business, her father was intimately involved in illicit activity, *The Professional* still manages to keep up a breakneck pace.
VHS: S24663. $19.95.
Laser: LD74902. $34.95.
Luc Besson, USA, 1994, 84 mins.

Sand and Blood

With the spectacular landscapes of Southern France as her backdrop, director Jeanne Labrune creates a dazzling, sensual film focusing on eroticism and human intimacy. Using the mystique of bullfighting as a stepping stone to broader issues, Labrune explores the friendship between Francisco, a gifted matador, and Manuel, a cultivated doctor and musician. French with English subtitles.
VHS: S12465. $79.95.
Jeanne Labrune, France, 1987, 101 mins.

Son of the Shark

This highly acclaimed French film won the International Critics Prize at the Venice Film Festival. It is based on a true story, and follows a pair of inseparable young brothers. Abandoned by their parents, they terrorize their hometown with acts of desperate violence. Yet some mystical bond keeps this shocking pair oddly in sync. A brilliant feature from one of France's hottest young director-stars. French with English subtitles.
VHS: S26279. $89.98.
Agnes Merlet, France, 1994, 85 mins.

Special Police

This story of intrigue, political scandal, and murder centers on a young woman, Carole Bouquet, as she tries to solve the mystery of her brother's death. A computer expert who works for the police, played by Richard Berry, decides to help her. As they begin to uncover the truth dangerous forces are revealed that threaten them. French with English subtitles.
VHS: S20759. $29.95.
Michel Vianey, France, 1985, 92 mins.

Subway

Besson's stylish, neo-punkish thriller takes its place in the subterranean corners of the Paris subway, as Fred, a casual thief and cool rebel, is on the run. Underground, he encounters a motley collection of subway denizens; a huge European hit, and an intriguing underworld journey. English dubbed.
VHS: S01276. $29.95.
Luc Besson, France, 1985, 104 mins.

Toto the Hero

Winner of the Camera d'Or at the 1991 Cannes Film Festival, this witty and audacious debut film by Belgian director Jaco Van Dormael concerns Thomas, who is convinced he was exchanged at birth with his neighbor Alfred and subsequently condemned to lead an anonymous, insignificant life. Appearing as "Toto le Heros", the invented secret agent of his adolescence, Thomas undergoes a fantastic odyssey to track Alfred down and uncover his true identity. With Michel Bouquet, Mireille Perrier and Jo de Backer. French with English subtitles.
VHS: S18544. $94.95.
Laser: LD75277. $34.98.
Jaco Van Dormael, Belgium/France/Germany, 1991, 90 mins.

Alphaville

Eddie Constantine is Lemmy Caution, inter-galactic private eye, in this bravura mix of comic strip, science fiction and film noir in what is ultimately a new style of cinema in which form and content are identical. Lemmy sets out to dispose of diabolical scientist Leonard von Braun (a.k.a. Leonard Nosferatu) from Alphaville, the futuristic city run by an electronic brain, where love has been banished. A film in which poetry mixes freely with pulp to create a new dimension, a new cinematic reality. French with English subtitles.
VHS: S07702. $29.95.
Laser: LD75075. $49.95.
Jean-Luc Godard, France, 1965, 100 mins.

Band of Outsiders

Claude Brasseur, Sami Frey and Anna Karina plan to steal money hidden in a house where Karina works, but the robbery is messed up and murder is the result. Godard's thriller is set in the fringe world of *Breathless*—the world of outsiders. Most of the film takes place in a suburb of Paris, and Godard has transformed it into a setting of beauty and poignancy. Godard's three characters are "trembling on the edge of crime…dancing on the edge of the volcano" (Richard Roud). French with English subtitles.
VHS: S00093. $29.95.
Jean-Luc Godard, France, 1964, 97 mins.

Breathless

The landmark French New Wave film by Godard features Jean-Paul Belmondo as a small-time hood on the run from the law, having an affair with an American girl in Paris (Jean Seberg). A film which owes much to American film noir and yet revolutionized the world of film. Remastered. French with English subtitles.
VHS: S08698. $24.95.
Laser: CLV. LD71507. $49.95.
Jean-Luc Godard, France, 1959, 89 mins.

Comment Ca Va? (How Is It Going?)

Co-directed by Anne-Marie Mieville, Jean-Luc Godard's work—combining video and film—is a fascinating dialectic on the dissemination and processing of information, both literary and visual. Two workers of a communist newspaper strike out to make a film and video about the meaning of the printing plant. One of the workers, Odette (Mieville), has strange ideas about content and form and how the film should be made. *Comment ca va?* is a formally brilliant work about the transmission of ideas by the major media. French with English subtitles.
VHS: S19232. $59.95.
Jean-Luc Godard/A.-M. Mieville, France, 1976, 76 mins.

Contempt

Based on the novel by Alberto Moravia, featuring Brigitte Bardot as the wife of film producer Jack Palance making a film directed by Fritz Lang (who plays himself in the film) is, in Godard's words, the story of men cut off from themselves, from the world, from reality. They try to clumsily rediscover the light, but are trapped on a dark stage. French with English subtitles.
VHS: S00266. $19.95.
Jean-Luc Godard, France, 1964, 99 mins.

First Name: Carmen

An important recent film by Jean-Luc Godard; in this gun-crazy romance, Godard re-examines not only his own previous attitudes, but the entire *femme fatale* tradition of Western culture. Based freely on the novel by Prosper Merimee and the opera by Bizet, the film is a cool depiction of a sexually explicit romance between a policeman and a beautiful young woman who leads him into a life of crime and humiliation. With Myriem Roussel, Maruschka Detmers, Jacques Bonnaffre. French with English subtitles.
VHS: S09355. $29.95.
Jean-Luc Godard, France, 1983, 85 mins.

Godard/Truffaut Shorts

A short film by Jean-Luc Godard made prior to his release of *Breathless* entitled *All the Boys Are Called Patrick,* and a short film by Francois Truffaut, *Les Mistons,* a charming evocative film about the arousal of sexual feelings in a group of young boys on summer holiday. French with English subtitles.
VHS: S01777. $29.95.
Godard/Truffaut, France, 1957

Ici et Ailleurs (Here and Elsewhere)

Jean-Luc Godard initiated his radical video period with this startling film that combines videotape and film, enabling him to superimpose more than two images simultaneously. Made as part of the "Dziga Vertov group", with Jean-Pierre Gorin and Anne-Marie Mieville, the film was commissioned by the Palestinians and originally titled *Until Victory.* The film's original purpose was to examine life in the Palestinian camps. But following the defeat of the Palestine army in the Six Day War, *Ici et Ailleurs* was radically transformed, becoming a meditation on how cinema records history. Godard, Gorin and Mieville contrast a French family ("Here") with an impressionistic portrait of Palestine ("Elsewhere") reflected and transmitted by television, books and pictures. French with English subtitles.
VHS: S19231. $59.95.
Jean-Luc Godard, France/Switzerland, 1970/1976

King Lear

Struggling to re-interpret his famous relative's tragic tale of passion and madness, the young William Shakespeare, Jr. the Fifth encounters a bewildering array of bizarre personalities and cryptic, ritualistic imagery. A surreal examination of The Bard's most powerful drama, from one of the avant-garde's most adventurous filmmakers. Featuring Burgess Meredith, Molly Ringwald, Woody Allen, Norman Mailer and Peter Sellars.
VHS: S16475. $24.95.
Jean-Luc Godard, France, 1987, 91 mins.

Le Gai Savoir

Two alien beings, brought together in an empty earth space, are exposed to our culture via its popular images—a compelling experiment that not only foreshadows the use of these images in Godard's later films but also explains precisely why these images are the building blocks of any film. As Godard explains at the end, "This film is not and cannot be an attempt to explain cinema or embody its object, but merely suggests effective ways to achieve it. This is not the film that should be made, but if a film is to be made it must follow some of the paths shown here." With Jean-Pierre Leaud and Juliet Berto. French with English subtitles.
VHS: S15378. $29.95.
Jean-Luc Godard, France, 1965, 96 mins.

Le Petit Soldat

The debut feature of Anna Karina, and Godard's second feature, this film was banned in France for its razor-sharp reflection of the Algerian war in a politically divided nation. Michel Subor is a French secret agent on an assassination mission. The film's depiction of brutality and torture, used by both sides in this bloody war, infuriated both the Left and the Right. French with English subtitles.
VHS: S08091. $29.95.
Jean-Luc Godard, France, 1960, 88 mins.

Les Carabiniers

One of the important early-period films from Jean-Luc Godard; a parable about the stupidity and ugliness of war. The story revolves around two gullible clodhoppers who set out to fight for their king in exchange for "all the treasures in the world." French with English subtitles.
VHS: S05327. $29.95.
Jean-Luc Godard, France, 1985, 107 mins.

A Married Woman

Godard managed to infuriate Charles de Gaulle with this frank document of a Parisian romantic triangle. Macha Meril is the young wife and mother in love with her husband and her lover. She doesn't want to decide between them because, quite frankly, she enjoys the attention of both. French with English subtitles.
VHS: S00829. $29.95.
Jean-Luc Godard, France, 1964, 94 mins.

Masculine Feminine

A film about the children of Marx and Coca Cola directed by the child of Brecht and Hollywood. Two young lovers attempt to communicate throughout 15 discontinuous, contrapuntal vignettes. Dancing between precision and improvisation, this is one of Godard's most complex films, representing both a search for tenderness and a disheartening foray into the Sex War. With Jean-Pierre Leaud, Chantal Goya, and Catherine-Isabelle Duport. French with English subtitles.
VHS: S00830. $29.95.
Jean-Luc Godard, France, 1966, 103 mins.

My Life to Live

"One of the most beautiful, touching and original films by Godard, an extremely complex blend of social document, theatricality and interior drama…" (Georges Sadoul). A film in 12 episodes, with Anna Karina the salesgirl in a record shop, who can't pay her rent, is evicted by her landlady, becomes a prostitute. "It triumphs because it is intelligent, discreet, delicate to the touch. It both edifies and gives pleasure because it is about what is most important…the nature of our humanity" (Susan Sontag). French with English subtitles.
VHS: S00907. $19.95.
Jean-Luc Godard, France, 1962, 85 mins.

Numero Deux

Jean-Luc Godard brilliantly mixes video and film, set in the director's Grenoble studio. The action unfolds on two television monitors. Godard secured the money for the film claiming the project was a remake of *Breathless.* The elusive plot essentially concerns the marital discord—set off by the wife's infidelity—between a young working-class couple (Sandrine Battistella and Pierre Oudry) who live in a claustrophobic, high rise apartment complex. The film, made in collaboration with Anne-Marie Mieville, is a dialectic on the relationship of sex and money. "I think it's something like a masterpiece. *Numero Deux* is among the most visually compelling films Godard has ever made. He uses his video monitors to invent a dozen new ways of splitting the screen or layering the image. Compared to it, every other movie in town is just a cavity on the screen" (J. Hoberman, *The Village Voice*). With Alexandre Rignault and Rachel Stefanopoli. French with English subtitles.
VHS: S19233. $59.95.
Jean-Luc Godard, France/Switzerland, 1976, 88 mins.

Oh Woe Is Me (Helas Pour Moi)

Gerard Depardieu meets Jean-Luc Godard in this gentle Godard fable in which divinity touches everyday life. Godard transposes to Switzerland the Greek myth in which Zeus inhabited Amphitryon's body to seduce a man's wife, with surprising results. Godardian touches like titles on the screen, townspeople who function as a theatrical chorus and music from Bach, Beethoven and Tchaikovsky make this a cerebral but passionate exploration of constancy and cinema. French with English subtitles.
VHS: S26336. $89.95.
Jean-Luc Godard, France, 1994, 84 mins.

Paris Vu Par (Six in Paris)

This omnibus film from the major figures of the French New Wave (Jean-Luc Godard, Claude Chabrol, Eric Rohmer, Jean Douchet, Jean Rouch and Jean-Daniel Pollet) offers a series of witty, wry vignettes about contemporary Paris. Godard's work, *Une Femme Est une Femme,* is about a young woman who dispatches letters to her two lovers and is concerned she mixed up the contents. With Joanna Shimkus, Nadine Ballot, Barbet Schroeder, Micheline Dax, Claude Melki, Chabrol and Stephane Audran. French with English subtitles. France, 1964, 98 mins.
VHS: S19543. $69.95.

Pierrot le Fou

One of the high points of 20th century cinema. Ravishing and moving, the story features Jean-Paul Belmondo as Ferdinand, who one evening leaves his wife in the middle of a boring party. He meets a girl with whom he was in love five years earlier, and who is involved with a gang of criminals. After Ferdinand finds a dead man in her room, they leave Paris for a deserted island. One of Godard's most poetic films, full of the anguish of love, aptly summarized in his own words over the first images of the film, "At the age of fifty, Velasquez no longer painted precise objects; he painted what lay between precise objects." The final murder-suicide sequence on the island is one of the most brilliant Godard has ever created. French with English subtitles.
VHS: S10739. $59.95.
Jean-Luc Godard, France, 1965, 110 mins.

Rogopag

The title reflects four brilliant European directors who contributed short films to this collection: Roberto Rossellini, Jean-Luc Godard, Pier Paolo Pasolini and Ugo Gregoretti. *Virginity,* by Rossellini, is a comic essay on the distinctions between illusion and reality. Orson Welles stars in Pasolini's *La Ricotta,* a satire about the debasement of religion. This film caused Pasolini to be charged and sentenced to prison for "insulting the religion of [Italy]." *The New World,* by Godard, offers a chilling view of Paris after a nuclear war. And in Gregoretti's *The Range Grown Chicken,* a family suffers the ravages of brain-washing consumerism. France/Italy, 1962, 122 mins. French and Italian with English subtitles.
VHS: S23995. $79.95.

Sympathy for the Devil

The Rolling Stones rehearse "Sympathy for the Devil" as a white revolutionary tries to commit suicide when her boyfriend switches to Black Power in this singular and daring film originally called *One Plus One.* The film, tackling the themes of growth and revolution, is envisioned as a collage which the viewer is challenged to "edit" himself. With The Rolling Stones, Anne Wiazemsky and Iain Quarrier.
VHS: S22456. $29.95.
Jean-Luc Godard, France, 1970, 92 mins.

Weekend

"End of Cinema, end of world," read the titles at the conclusion of Godard's 1967 apocalyptic film *Weekend.* Godard himself described the work as both "a film found on the junk heap," and "a film lost in the cosmos." Presenting a dark, comic vision of the end of capitalist society, *Weekend* reflects the turmoil and chaos of the late sixties better than any Hollywood film from that era. It also stands as the climax to the first phase of Godard's filmmaking career, before he turned to the making of more experimental Marxist films after the social upheavals of 1968. With Mirielle Darc and Jean-Pierre Leaud. French with English subtitles.
VHS: S14572. $79.95.
Jean-Luc Godard, France, 1967, 105 mins.

A Woman Is a Woman

"I conceived this film within the framework of a neo-realist musical: *an absolute contradiction,* but that's the way I wanted to make the film," said Godard. Godard's closely-knit texture of small bistros, striptease joints, political suspicion and conjugal wavering is constantly violated in its naturalistic surface, not just by the comic turns of the plot, but by Godard's reminders not only that the film is a performance, but that the projected images are themselves illusory: "The film has a beauty that is brash and pathetic, like splintered colored glass, fragments that somehow compose a picture while refusing to hold together: musical, sad, uproarious, definitely frail" (Edgardo Cozarinsky). French with English subtitles.
VHS: S08090. $59.95.
Jean-Luc Godard, France, 1961, 85 mins.

La Jetee

Chris Marker's landmark film is set in postnuclear Paris. The story concerns an astronaut who travels back through time to realize a brief affair with a woman he once glimpsed. With the exception of a haunting shot of the woman blinking, the entire film is composed with still photographs and isolated shots. French with English subtitles.
VHS: S18956. $19.95.
Chris Marker, France, 1962, 29 mins.

La Jetee/ An Occurrence at Owl Creek Bridge

One of the most challenging films ever made, Chris Marker's neo-science fiction film is set in a ruined France after World War III, in which a man's vivid childhood experience allows him to travel forward and backward in time. As a grown man, he meets the girl he had glimpsed as a child at the airport, falls in love with her, chooses to remain in the past, but is executed by those who hold power in the future. France, 1962, 29 mins. Also contains *An Occurrence at Owl Creek Bridge,* directed by Robert Enrico and based on a short story by Ambrose Bierce, which tells the tale of a man who is about to be hanged when the rope suddenly snaps and he is able to escape. Unfortunately, his newly found freedom is short-lived. USA, 1962, 27 mins.
VHS: S06274. $39.95.

Le Joli Mai

Chris Marker's great cinema-verite study of Paris in May, 1962, the month the Algerian War came to an end and France was at peace for the first time since 1939. The first part, "Prayer from the Top of the Eiffel Tower," is about personal happiness and ambition; the second, "The Return of Fantomas," concerned with social and political issues and the relationships of people to each other. A very moving, "personal and ironic film aided by Pierre Lhomme's superb handling of the 'living camera' " (Georges Sadoul). French with English subtitles.
VHS: S05325. $29.95.
Chris Marker, France, 1962, 180 mins.

Sans Soleil

An audacious and remarkable work from the brilliant essayist and poet Chris Marker, *Sans Soleil* visually interprets a series of letters from a wandering cameraman, based on his travels and experiences from West Africa to Tokyo as he searches for purpose, identity and self-definition through his observations, rituals, speculations, passions and predicaments. "As entertaining as *Zelig,* as visionary as *Blade Runner*" (Jim Hoberman, *Village Voice*). In English.
VHS: S18422. $69.95.
Chris Marker, France, 1983, 100 mins.

MAURICE PIALAT

A Nos Amours
Winner of France's Cesar Award for Best Film of 1983, *A Nos Amours* is a powerful, moving study of a working-class girl of 15 who enters a series of casual sexual relationships while looking for the love she has been denied at home. French with English subtitles.
VHS: S00012. $19.95.
Maurice Pialat, France, 1983, 110 mins.

Loulou
French heartthrob Gerard Depardieu and Isabelle Huppert star in this acclaimed film by Maurice Pialat. Huppert plays Nelly, a married woman who meets Loulou (Depardieu), a charming, leather-jacketed stud in a crowded Paris disco. She can't resist his lustful style and returns home with him. Loulou turns out to be as passionate in bed as on the dance floor, and they embark on a free-wheeling relationship that is a mixture of unabashed eroticism and authentic romance. French with English subtitles.
VHS: S12196. $79.95.
Maurice Pialat, France, 1980, 110 mins.

Police
Gerard Depardieu is a tough French cop who becomes a little too attached to his work. He finds the fine line between cop and criminal is blurred when he meets drug dealer Sophie Marceau. In *Police*, director Maurice Pialat (*Loulou*) subverts the mainstream thriller genre for a personal film that deliberately works against all conventional expectations. A wonderfully spontaneous and authentic film. French with English subtitles.
VHS: S14571. $79.95.
Maurice Pialat, France, 1985, 113 mins.

Under the Sun of Satan
A work of great subtlety and tremendous assurance, the film stars Depardieu in his perhaps most astonishing performance, as a tortured country priest who feels unworthy of God's love. Depardieu's priest encounters the young and beautiful Mouchette, played by Sandrine Bonnaire, who lives in a small town and is a murderess who unwittingly shapes the priest's life. A brilliant new film from one of France's most uncompromising directors. French with English subtitles.
VHS: S10868. $79.95.
Maurice Pialat, France, 1987, 101 mins.

Van Gogh
Maurice Pialat's bold biography of Vincent Van Gogh. The film concentrates on the final three months of Van Gogh's life, the period he spent in Arles. Pialat painstakingly captures the artist's daily life and the private demons that plagued him. Stripped of melodrama, the film offers a different interpretation of Van Gogh's "madness." With Alexandra London, Gerard Sety, Bernard Le Coq, Corrine Bourdona and Elsa Zylberstein. French with English subtitles.
VHS: S19333. $19.95.
Maurice Pialat, France, 1991, 155 mins.

JACQUES RIVETTE

Divertimento
The cast of Rivette's *La Belle Noiseuse*, Emmanuelle Beart, Jane Birkin and Michel Piccoli, star in this further meditation on the nature of artistic creation. An artist, seemingly past his prime, finds new inspiration in a young woman who inspires him with both her beauty (as expressed through her body) and her soul. French with English subtitles.
VHS: S23997. $89.95.
Jacques Rivette, France/Switzerland, 1990, 126 mins.

La Belle Noiseuse
Jacques Rivette's ambitious masterpiece explores the artistic process in terms of both its transcendent power and its potential for exploitation and destructiveness. The core of the film is the confrontation between Frenhofer, a renowned but inactive painter, and a model (played by Emmanuelle Beart). It begins in wary hostility, escalates into a pitched battle of wills, and ends as a true collaboration, each driving the other to dangerous limits. "One of the finest films ever made about art" (Gene Siskel, *Chicago Tribune*). Winner of the Grand Jury Prize at the Cannes Film Festival. Cinematography by William Lubtchansky. With Michel Piccoli and Bernard Dufour. French with English subtitles.
VHS: S20304. $89.95.
Jacques Rivette, France/Switzerland, 1990, 240 mins.

The Nun (La Religieuse)
Initially banned by the French government, this brilliant adaptation of Diderot's classic 18th century novel explores the moving tale of Suzanne Simonin (Anna Karina, in perhaps her finest screen performance), a 16-year-old girl who is forced by her parents to enter a convent against her will. Unable to bear the hypocrisy and oppression which characterize her new life, Suzanne becomes desperate for freedom. Her attempts first land her in another convent, which, though quite different, is equally constraining. Based on the novel by Diderot. French with English subtitles.
VHS: S13606. $59.95.
Jacques Rivette, France, 1965, 155 mins.

Paris Belongs to Us
Shot on weekends, with no money and no sets, with actors donating their time and Chabrol providing left-over film stock, this film concerns a group of amateurs who come together in Paris to stage a performance of Shakespeare's *Pericles*. But sexual and political tensions develop, their composer dies, the producer kills himself and a fascist conspiracy seems to be lurking in the background. The result of Rivette's two-year struggle is a work of total originality and inventiveness, of amazing depth and independence of vision. French with English subtitles.
VHS: S07472. $59.95.
Jacques Rivette, France, 1958-60, 124 mins.

RAUL RUIZ

The Golden Boat
This quirky, funny and violent film combines the antics of a homeless, compulsive assassin named Austin, who is desperately in love with a Mexican soap opera star and accompanied by Israel, a philosophy student and part time rock critic for the *Village Voice*, with the fringe of the New York underground. Filmed with the help of the Kitchen, it also includes appearances by such downtown figures as Jim Jarmusch, Vito Acconci, John Zorn, the Wooster Group, and even Annie Sprinkle.
VHS: S18968. $59.95.
Raul Ruiz, USA/Luxembourg/Hong Kong, 1990, 88 mins.

Hypothesis of the Stolen Painting
One of the most important films of the seventies, *The Hypothesis of the Stolen Painting* began as a documentary on writer Pierre Klossowski but soon became, in Ruiz's words, "a fiction about theory." A pompous art collector offers a new history of western art through a guided tour of a fantastic gallery of "living images," all created by the "forgotten" artist, Tonnerr. As our guide drones away about aspects of his collection, the human figures begin to smirk and fidget, emphasizing their play-acting and introducing a new level of spectating into the narrative. Structured as a kind of never-ending detective thriller, Ruiz's film is a daring, fascinating meditation on the relationship between words and images, between works of art and their description or interpretation. Photographed by Sacha Vierny. French with English subtitles.
VHS: S15343. $59.95.
Raul Ruiz, France, 1978, 67 mins.

Life Is a Dream
"If Raul Ruiz wrote novels or poems, he would be a literary celebrity on the short list for the Nobel Prize," said Georgia Brown in *The Village Voice* about this prolific filmmaker of a seemingly unlimited imagination. *Life Is a Dream* is loosely based on the classic play of the same title by Calderon de La Barca. It is a baroque mix of revolutionary politics, pop culture and semiotics that features a Chilean revolutionary using Calderon's play as a mnemonic device. French with English subtitles.
VHS: S26501. $59.95.
Raul Ruiz, France, 1986, 100 mins.

On Top of the Whale
Shot in five languages (one of them imaginary), this film concerns a European anthropological expedition to Patagonia. The ethnologists set out to study a tribe of Indians which now consists of merely two surviving members who speak a strange language made up of only a few phrases (different meanings are produced by varying the inflections). A humorous and intellectual film written and directed by Raul Ruiz, one of the most inventive filmmakers working in Europe today, *On Top of the Whale* is filled with audacious visual ideas, and its cold and misty Northern images often recall Murnau. English, Spanish, French, Dutch and German with English subtitles.
VHS: S13521. $59.95.
Raul Ruiz, Netherlands, 1982, 93 mins.

BERTRAND TAVERNIER

The Clockmaker
Tavernier's debut film, in which Philippe Noiret is the clockmaker whose existence is shattered by the news that his son has been accused of a political murder. Tavernier invests the film with details from the cultural to the personal and domestic. French with English subtitles.
VHS: S00250. $59.95.
Bertrand Tavernier, France, 1975, 105 mins.

Coup de Torchon
Cordier is the only police officer in a small 1938 West African town. He is ridiculed by the local pimps and cuckolded by his wife while his mistress is beaten by her husband. Driven to the brink, he takes revenge on all his enemies. From Jim Thompson's novel *POP 1280*, this darkly funny picture stars Philippe Noiret and Isabelle Huppert. French with English subtitles.
VHS: S00275. $29.95.
Laser: LD75025. $49.95.
Bertrand Tavernier, France, 1981, 128 mins.

Daddy Nostalgie
Dirk Bogarde and Jane Birkin star as a father and daughter who must work through their relationship to arrive at a position of mutual respect and understanding. The painful realization that time is running out makes this scenario all the more compelling. French with English subtitles.
VHS: S20687. $29.98.
Bertrand Tavernier, France, 1990, 105 mins.

Judge and the Assassin
A provocative look at madness and society. In France of the late 19th century, a demented and violent ex-sergeant goes on a rampage of brutal rapes and murders. Philippe Noiret is the clever but ruthless judge who masterminds the capture and interrogation of the murderer, while French comic actor Michel Galabru is the sly psychopath. "Bertrand Tavernier challenges the viewer's reactions, weighing the moral hypocrisy of a self-serving judge against the acts of an insanely murderous victim" (PFA notes). French with English subtitles.
VHS: S11633. $29.95.
Laser: Widescreen. Side 3 CAV. LD71609. $59.95.
Bertrand Tavernier, France, 1975, 100 mins.

L.627
The gritty world of Parisian drug culture is revealed in Tavernier's cinema verite style film. L.627 is the name of the special undercover drug squadron in Paris. But Tavernier is not interested in a simple "take" on the hazardous life of a drug cop. He explores the rivalries and loyalties, and the emotional deprivation that becomes a part of a policeman's life as he struggles to balance truth, justice and love in an alien urban world. French with English subtitles.
VHS: S24378. $79.95.
Bertrand Tavernier, France, 1992, 145 mins.

Life and Nothing But
Bertrand Tavernier once again explores the awful legacy of war. Set in 1920, this powerful drama unfolds in post World War I France—a country devastated both physically and spiritually. It tells the story of two women of differing backgrounds who are looking for the missing men they love. Along the way they encounter two French officers, one detailed to identify the dead and the other assigned to choose a body to be honored as France's unknown soldier. Tavernier turns his film into an incredibly moving journey through the postwar landscape of France, touching on the deep psychological scars which the conflict has left behind. With Philippe Noiret, Sabine Azema and Pascale Vidal. French with English subtitles.
VHS: S14787. $79.98.
Bertrand Tavernier, France, 1989, 135 mins.

Mississippi Blues
Tavernier and Parrish approach the Mississippi Delta through its townspeople and its music—Delta Blues and gospel. They explore their own knowledge of this world—Tavernier's from reading Faulkner and Mark Twain, Parrish's from his intimate knowledge of the South. And they skillfully link the drama with such questions as the relationship of the church to politics, and the relationship of music to the life in the Mississippi Delta.
VHS: S09244. $29.95.
Parrish/Tavernier, USA/France, 1983, 101 mins.

Round Midnight
Bertrand Tavernier's exquisite homage to jazz—the moving story of a black jazz musician in 1959 Paris, struggling to create the bebop sound. With an Oscar for Herbie Hancock's score, one of the most critically acclaimed films of 1986. English dialog.
VHS: S03495. $19.98.
Laser: LD70669. $29.98.
Bertrand Tavernier, France, 1986, 132 mins.

Spoiled Children
Bertrand Tavernier's autobiographical work about a famous filmmaker (Michel Piccoli) who escapes the disruptions of his home life by renting an apartment in a sleek, highrise building. He is immediately drawn into an obsessive affair with a much younger woman (Christine Pascal) who quickly entangles him in a tenants' fight over the brutal behavior of the landlord. "The film carries the weight of Tavernier's convictions about the injustices everyone is forced to contest, domestically and at work" (*Time Out*). With Michel Aumont, Gerard Jugnot and Arlette Bonnard. French with English subtitles.
VHS: S19460. $79.95.
Bertrand Tavernier, France, 1977, 113 mins.

BERTRAND BLIER

Buffet Froid
Filled with black humor, Blier's highly original thriller features Gerard Depardieu. Structured as an absurdly hilarious nightmare, the film's logic is twisted and stark: what do you do if you've been unemployed for six months, your wife has disappeared, and you find yourself looking at your own knife sticking out of the belly of a fellow subway passenger—and you can't remember how it got there? French with English subtitles.
VHS: S08257. $59.95.
Bertrand Blier, France, 1980, 95 mins.

Get Out Your Handkerchiefs
Raoul is a doting husband who thinks the best way to pick up his wife's spirits is with an affair. But a menage-a-trois with a bewildered stranger doesn't work, and finally hope arrives with a precocious 13-year-old Christian who achieves the seemingly impossible. An Academy Award winner for "Best Foreign Film". With Gerard Depardieu, Patrick Dewaere, Carole Laure and Michel Serrault. French with English subtitles.
VHS: S00494. $59.95.
Bertrand Blier, France, 1978, 109 mins.

Menage
This black comedy is a brilliant sexual farce. The charismatic, gay thief Bob (Gerard Depardieu) coolly insinuates himself into the troubled lives of Antoine (Michel Blanc) and Monique (Miou-Miou). The film is redolent with Blier's characteristic wit, energy and sexual daring. French with English subtitles.
VHS: S16945. $89.95.
Bertrand Blier, France, 1986, 84 mins.

Too Beautiful for You
Gerard Depardieu stars as a successful car dealer obsessed with his plain temporary secretary much to the displeasure of his stunningly beautiful wife. Bertrand Blier directs this dark comedy that also stars Josiane Balasko and Carole Bouquet. Expect the unexpected in this artful and painfully funny look at adultery. French with English subtitles.
VHS: S13673. $19.98.
Laser: LD71629. $39.95.
Bertrand Blier, France, 1988, 91 mins.

ALAIN RESNAIS

Hiroshima Mon Amour
From the beginning, in which the love-making of a French actress (Emmanuelle Riva) and a Japanese architect (Eiji Okada) is intercut with newsreel footage of Hiroshima's atomic holocaust and its aftermath, the couple's painful walk through the reconstructed city, Resnais' film recaptures both the pain and the richness of the war. French with English subtitles.
VHS: S00571. $29.95.
Alain Resnais, France, 1959, 91 mins.

La Guerre Est Finie
This great film by Alain Resnais, scripted by Jorge Semprun, stars Yves Montand, Genevieve Bujold, Ingrid Thulin and Michel Piccoli. Resnais shifts between reality and Montand's mental states in an incisive portrait of an aging Spanish revolutionary who is imprisoned by his past as he confronts the failure of his ideas. Resnais explores Montand's insecurities through his relationships with two very different women (Thulin and Bujold). French with English subtitles.
VHS: S23758. $29.95.
Alain Resnais, France, 1966, 120 mins.

Last Year at Marienbad
The strange geometry of a romantic triangle marks the beginning of this elegant, labyrinthine puzzle. Written by French New Wave novelist Alain Robbe-Grillet and from the director of *Hiroshima, Mon Amour*, *Last Year at Marienbad* is a film classic, the subject of myriad interpretations. Starring Delphine Seyrig, Giorgio Albertazzi, and Sacha Pitoeff. French with English subtitles. New presentation in videoscope.
VHS: S00730. $29.95.
Alain Resnais, France, 1961, 90 mins.

Mon Oncle d'Amerique
Three middle class French drifters, each convinced they lack definition and excitement, dream about the imaginary and mythic "American Uncle," cross a behavioral scientist who instills in them a sense of wonder and excitement and the mystery of the unknown. The film is structured like a riddle, "one which proves that surrealism lives" (*Time Out*). With Gerard Depardieu, Nicole Garcia, Roger Pierre and Marie Dubois. French with English subtitles.
VHS: S02141. $79.95.
Alain Resnais, France, 1980, 126 mins.

Muriel
One of the most interesting films from Alain Resnais, a bold and beautiful film, in which Resnais takes an incident from provincial life, the reunion of a middle-aged woman and her old lover at Boulogne. Out of the trivia of everyday life and its anxieties, he creates a mosaic masterpiece that probes the themes of time and memory, and the relationship between personal conscience and public consciousness (the references to the Algerian War). With Delphine Seyrig, Jean-Pierre Kerien, Nina Klein. Music by Hans Werner Henze. French with English subtitles.
VHS: S02079. $59.95.
Alain Resnais, France, 1963, 115 mins.

Night and Fog
Alain Resnais's masterpiece documentary about German concentration camps. Using his preoccupations with time and memory, Resnais has constructed a wrenching study of guilt, French complicity and ultimate responsibility. Resnais revisits the sites, now overgrown with green grass and studded with silence. A cinematic landmark. Cinematography by Sacha Vierny. French with English subtitles.
VHS: S00930. $24.95.
Alain Resnais, France, 1955, 32 mins.

Stavisky
With *Stavisky*, director Alain Resnais has crafted an extraordinarily beautiful and sophisticated film that requires intense concentration but yields tremendous rewards. The story is that of a French swindler and conman extraordinaire, whose financial manipulations in the 30s brought on riots that helped to topple a government. With Jean-Paul Belmondo, Anny Duperey, Charles Boyer and Gerard Depardieu. Photographed by Sacha Vierny, with a musical score by Stephen Sondheim. French with English subtitles.
VHS: S14986. $59.95.
Alain Resnais, France, 1974, 117 mins.

CLAUDE CHABROL

Betty
Claude Chabrol's masterful tale of alienation stars Stephane Audran as a mysterious woman living in an elegant Versailles hotel, who takes in Marie Trintignant, a wife running away from an emotionless middle class marriage. Set in a world of casual affairs and ice-cold betrayals, *Betty* is a suspenseful, moving psychological study. French with English subtitles.
VHS: S21503. $89.95.
Claude Chabrol, France, 1993, 103 mins.

Blood Relative
The great French director Claude Chabrol directed this Canadian production, which stars Donald Sutherland, Stephane Audran, Donald Pleasance and David Hemmings. The situation is an incestuous relationship which leads to deadly consequences. Chabrol directs with a masterly, cool and detached style that results in a first-rate thriller. Filmed in English.
VHS: S11482. $19.95.
Claude Chabrol, Canada, 1983, 101 mins.

Bluebeard
Charles Denner (*The Man Who Loved Women*) tries a different approach to the female of the species in an earlier film directed by Claude Chabrol. As the famous French lady-killer, he dispatches a bevy of international beauties. With Michele Morgan, Hildegard Knef, and Danielle Darrieux. Dubbed in English.
VHS: S03859. $59.95.
Claude Chabrol, France, 1963, 108 mins.

Club Extinction
Previously known as *Dr. M*, *Club Extinction* is Chabrol's masterful reworking of Fritz Lang's *Dr. Mabuse* scripts. In 21st century Berlin an epidemic of bizarre deaths is sweeping through the city, and a steady stream of propaganda fills the air. Each death serves to further excite Dr. M, who directs the subliminal madness from a hidden fortress above the city. One man, the assassin, stands between freedom and mass destruction. Starring Alan Bates, Jennifer Beals, and Andrew McCarthy.
VHS: S13718. $89.95.
Claude Chabrol, France/Germany, 1989, 105 mins.

The Eye of Vichy
Claude Chabrol strips the mask off a forbidden chapter of French history, the Vichy regime, in this controversial documentary which touches the sensitive subject of French complicity and collaboration with the Nazis during World War II. French with English subtitles.
VHS: S27610. $59.95.
Claude Chabrol, France, 1993, 110 mins.

Horse of Pride

"Too poor that I am to possess another animal, at least 'the horse of pride' will always have a stall in my stable," said Breton peasant Alain Le Goff to his grandson Pierre Jakez-Helias, who grew up to write the best-selling novel, *Horse of Pride*. Director Claude Chabrol was drawn to the story, a calendar of Breton ways and customs from 1905-1920 centering around one family's struggles to rise on the social ladder. The film addresses the Breton's fascination with fantasy through both the energies of the young boy, Pierre, who wishes to carry the daydreams of his loved ones into reality, and the Celtic tradition of storytelling with its emphasis on the sensational, the dramatic, and the intensity of imagination. With Jacques Dufilho and Bernadette Lesache. French with English subtitles.
VHS: S09571. $59.95.
Claude Chabrol, France, 1980, 120 mins.

L'Enfer

Claude Chabrol is in top form in this top-notch thriller—the study of deranged jealousy—based on a script by Henri-Georges (*Diabolique*) Clouzot. Paul Cluzet plays the owner of a small hotel who has everything—a beautiful wife, a new son, and a successful business located on a serene lake. But then he hears voices and begins to question his wife's fidelity, which begins a downward spiral into madness. With Emmanuelle Beart. French with English subtitles.
VHS: S25816. $89.98.
Claude Chabrol, France, 1994, 100 mins.

La Rupture

One of Claude Chabrol's best films: a taut, diabolical thriller about a woman (Stephane Audran) who leaves her drug-addicted husband (Jean-Claude Drouot) after he violently attacks their child while in a schizophrenic haze. His aristocratic parents hire a brutal private detective (Jean-Pierre Cassel) to turn up incriminating evidence in order to discredit her in a child custody suit. With Michel Bouquet, Catherine Rouvel and Jean Carmet. French with English subtitles.
VHS: S19461. $24.95.
Claude Chabrol, France/Italy/Spain, 1970, 124 mins.

Le Beau Serge

Claude Chabrol's first, great film—one of the landmarks of the French New Wave. Produced on a miniscule budget in the natural setting in Sardent, Francois (Jean-Claude Brialy) is convalescing in his native village to find his childhood friend (Gerard Blain) a drunkard in a bad marriage, and after an affair with Bernadette Lafont, interferes in Serge's life only to finally accept reality and understand. French with English subtitles.
VHS: S03509. $29.95.
Claude Chabrol, France, 1958, 97 mins.

Le Boucher

A first rate psychological thriller from Claude Chabrol about the evolving relationship of a beautiful school teacher and a serial murderer. "In Chabrol's films, the relationships are plotted with a mathematical precision that does not rule out surprising developments" (Roy Armes). With Stephane Audran, Antonio Passalia, Mario Beccaria and Pasquale Ferone. French with English subtitles.
VHS: S16929. $24.95.
Laser: CLV. LD72051. $39.95.
Claude Chabrol, France/Italy, 1969, 90 mins.

Les Biches

In Chabrol's New Wave set-piece, Federique is a rich and fashionable lesbian who encounters a young, bohemian sidewalk artist called Why. They escape together to St. Tropez for Christmas where Why ends up in bed with the young architect, Paul. Tension between the three escalates when they co-habit Federique's villa. As Paul's affections lean toward Federique, Why begins a jealous transformation that culminates in a deadly conclusion. French with English subtitles.
VHS: S16167. $24.95.
Claude Chabrol, France, 1968, 104 mins.

Les Bonnes Femmes (The Good Girls)

Bernadette Lafont, Clotilde Joano, Stephane Audran and Lucille Saint-Simon star as four working girls in Paris in this brilliant New Wave thriller by Claude Chabrol. What they hope to find is love, but each ends up in the hands of a killer. As always, Chabrol is interested more in the milieu which supports his characters than in the suspense, as he gives us an intimate look at ordinary lives full of boredom and vague dreams. Cinematography by the great Henri Decae. French with English subtitles.
VHS: S26901. $24.95.
Claude Chabrol, France, 1960, 105 mins.

Les Cousins

One of the great Chabrol early films; Charles (Gerard Blain), a student from the provinces, comes to Paris to live with his sophisticated, bullying cousin Paul, falls in love with Florence, but she becomes Paul's mistress. During their examinations, Paul passes effortlessly while Charles fails, and Charles accidentally kills Paul after trying to kill him. An ingenious, brilliant portrayal of student life in Paris, with great cinematography by Henri Decae. French with English subtitles.
VHS: S04906. $79.95.
Claude Chabrol, France, 1958, 110 mins.

Madame Bovary

The classic 19th century novel by Gustave Flaubert has been masterfully adapted to the screen by veteran filmmaker Claude Chabrol. Isabelle Huppert occupies the erotic title role of Emma Bovary, the unhappily married woman who wants more out of life. With Christophe Malavoy, Jean Yanne, Lucas Belvaux and Christiane Minazolli. French with English subtitles.
VHS: S16504. $14.98.
Laser: LD71454. $39.98.
Claude Chabrol, France, 1991, 130 mins.

Paris Vu Par (Six in Paris)

This omnibus film from the major figures of the French New Wave (Jean-Luc Godard, Claude Chabrol, Eric Rohmer, Jean Douchet, Jean Rouch and Jean-Daniel Pollet) offers a series of witty, wry vignettes about contemporary Paris. Godard's work, *Une Femme Est une Femme*, is about a young woman who dispatches letters to her two lovers and is concerned she mixed up the contents. With Joanna Shimkus, Nadine Ballot, Barbet Schroeder, Micheline Dax, Claude Melki, Chabrol and Stephane Audran. French with English subtitles. France, 1964, 98 mins.
VHS: S19543. $69.95.

Piece of Pleasure

Chabrol's dark vision of the complexities of modern marriage. A story of a couple whose marriage is eroding because of the tyrannical will of the husband. French with English subtitles.
VHS: S01029. $59.95.
Claude Chabrol, France, 1976, 100 mins.

Story of Women

An almost perfect film; Claude Chabrol bases his Venice Film Festival award-winning film on the true story of the last woman to be guillotined in France, at the onset of WWII. Isabelle Huppert delivers a stunning, riveting performance as the wife-abortionist who, despite the compromises she makes for the sake of a "better" life, is redeemed as a true individual at the end. A brilliant film from the hands of a true master. French with English subtitles.
VHS: S12990. $29.95.
Claude Chabrol, France, 1988, 112 mins.

Ten Days' Wonder

Claude Chabrol's elegant transposition of an Ellery Queen thriller—a situation of mental aberration, adultery and blackmail. Featuring Orson Welles, Marlene Jobert, Michel Piccoli and Anthony Perkins, the film is notable for its plumbing the psychological depths of the Oedipal complex within the confines of a terrific thriller. In English.
VHS: S07462. $24.95.
Laser: CLV/CAV. LD72056. $39.95.
Claude Chabrol, France, 1971, 101 mins.

This Man Must Die

One of Chabrol's great Hitchcockian thrillers; a writer's young son is struck by a hit-and-run driver, and he searches for the murderer. Chance leads him to the killer's beautiful sister, whom he seduces—a stalking cat and mouse game ensues which ends in a startling climax. English dubbed.
VHS: S01332. $59.98.
Claude Chabrol, France, 1970, 112 mins.

Wedding in Blood

Claude Chabrol offers up another case of murder and marital dissatisfaction. Michel Piccoli has a chronically ill wife who hates to be touched. Stephane Audran has an uncaring politician for a spouse. Each has a plan to be free to make love in the woods.
VHS: S04385. $19.95.
Claude Chabrol, France/Italy, 1974, 98 mins.

LOUIS MALLE

Alamo Bay

A powerful drama based on actual events on the Texas Gulf coast detailing the conflicts between local shrimp fishermen and Vietnamese refugees. With Ed Harris and Amy Madigan from director Louis Malle. Music by Ry Cooder.
VHS: S00026. $79.95.
Louis Malle, USA, 1985, 99 mins.

Atlantic City

Burt Lancaster delivers a stunning performance as the seemingly washed-up gangster, with Susan Sarandon as his lost-soul companion. A moving portrait of American dreams, contained in the small-world milieu of the slums and the gambling palaces of Atlantic City. Based on the screenplay by John Guare.
VHS: S00073. $14.95.
Louis Malle, Canada/USA, 1981, 101 mins.

Au Revoir les Enfants (Goodbye, Children)

Louis Malle returns to the days of German occupation during World War II to recount the story of the friendship between two schoolboys, one Jewish and the other Catholic. A winner of many awards including Best Picture in France. Familiar themes are explored. Subtitled.
VHS: S08496. $19.98.
Laser: LD70846. $39.95.
Louis Malle, France, 1988, 104 mins.

Calcutta

Louis Malle transforms this recording of his trip through India's great city from a simple travelogue into an intense examination of the minute details that make up the lives of those he encounters. An awesome tapestry emerges, one that joins such disparate strands as Moslems and Hindus, or the protests of a former government official and the building of a skyscraper without modern equipment. English narration.
VHS: S22466. $29.95.
Louis Malle, France, 1976, 99 mins.

Damage

French director Louis Malle's adaptation of Josephine Hart's novel about an upper class Parliament member (Jeremy Irons) who has an affair with an ethereal French woman (Juliette Binoche) who is about to be married to Irons' son (Rupert Graves). Miranda Richardson co-stars as Irons' long-suffering wife. This unrated version contains the excised material the MPAA found objectionable enough to warrant an NC-17 rating.
VHS: S18607. $19.95.
Laser: LD72184. $49.95.
Louis Malle, Great Britain/USA, 1992, 111 mins.

Elevator to the Gallows

A Hitchcock-like romantic thriller from director Louis Malle (*Atlantic City*, *Au Revoir les Enfants*) which features a terrific early performance by French superstar Jeanne Moreau as a woman waiting for her lover to return from committing the "perfect crime." Malle sets old Hollywood film noir formulas to new rhythms in what is one of the first films of the French New Wave. Original jazz score by the late great Miles Davis. French with English subtitles.
VHS: S15394. $69.95.
Louis Malle, France, 1957, 87 mins.

The Fire Within

Louis Malle's painful and devastating portrait of dissolution and self-destruction, capturing the final two days of a wealthy French writer visiting his friends, following his release from a mental asylum. Brilliantly scored by Erik Satie, the film has a harsh, bleak beauty and despair. With Maurice Ronet, Lena Skerla, Yvonne Clech and Hubert Deschamps. French with English subtitles.
VHS: S17697. $69.95.
Louis Malle, France, 1963, 108 mins.

The Lovers

A landmark of both French cinema and screen eroticism, *The Lovers* stars Jeanne Moreau as a stylish provincial wife whose shallow life changes when she meets an unpretentious young man. The film caused a furor of protest when it was first released; today its tender sensuality and genuine feeling for passion are a welcome relief. Henri Decae's magical photography and Brahm's Second Quartet create an atmosphere of luminous romanticism. French with English subtitles.
VHS: S16078. $69.95.
Louis Malle, France, 1958, 89 mins.

May Fools

A well-to-do family gathers to divide the spoils of a country estate after the death of the ancient matriarch. Michel Piccoli and Miou-Miou star in this satiric portrait of a family and a nation in conflict. With Bruno Carette, Harriet Walter, Dominique Blanc and Michel Duchaussoy. Set during the summer of 1968. French with English subtitles.
VHS: S13675. $19.98.
Laser: LD71621. $39.95.
Louis Malle, France, 1990, 105 mins.

Murmur of the Heart

Louis Malle directed this affectionate story of a young man's coming of age. When a 14-year-old boy from a bourgeois home is sent to a sanitarium for his health, he learns that mother knows best. A comic and, at the time, quite scandalous motion picture. With Benoit Ferreux as the rambunctious kid and Lea Massari as his sensuous mom. Also Daniel Gelin, Marc Winocourt and Michel Lonsdale. Watch for the dinner tennis match. French with English subtitles.
VHS: S11533. $19.98.
Louis Malle, France/Germany/Italy, 1971, 118 mins.

My Dinner with Andre

Nearly two hours of dinner conversation between New York avant-garde theatre director Andre Gregory and playwright Wallace Shawn becomes a fascinating dialog about the meaning of life, a bizarre and entertaining satirical comedy, and one of the most highly praised films of 1982.
VHS: Out of print. For rental only.
Laser: LD71246. $39.95.
Louis Malle, USA, 1981, 110 mins.

Pretty Baby

Director Malle has taken a taboo subject, child prostitution, and created a film of humanity and beauty. Brooke Shields plays a young girl in 1917 New Orleans; Keith Carradine is a photographer obsessed with the red light district bewitched by Shields. With Susan Sarandon.
VHS: S01053. $19.95.
Laser: LD75341. $29.98.
Louis Malle, USA, 1978, 109 mins.

Vanya on 42nd Street

Louis Malle returns to the characters of his *My Dinner with Andre* in this very cinematic filming of Andre Gregory's staging of Chekhov's *Uncle Vanya*, in a run-down Broadway theatre for a small, private audience. Wallace Shawn and Julianne Moore star in the melancholy drama, using the new translation by David Mamet. The performances are outstanding, and quite surprisingly, this becomes first-rate Chekhov.
VHS: S25658. $19.95.
Laser: LD74988. $34.95.
Louis Malle, USA, 1994, 119 mins.

Very Private Affair

Brigitte Bardot and Marcello Mastroianni star in this tale about the trials of movie stardom. A beautifully filmed story by the director of *My Dinner with Andre* and *Atlantic City*. English dialog.
VHS: S01411. $19.98.
Louis Malle, USA, 1962, 94 mins.

Viva Maria

Louis Malle's bawdy, irreverent work about two beautiful entertainers and anarchists (Jeanne Moreau and Brigitte Bardot) who become entangled in the Mexican revolution. With George Hamilton, Gregor Von Rezzori and Paulette Dubost. French with English subtitles.
VHS: S20402. $19.98.
Louis Malle, France/Italy, 1965, 119 mins.

Zazie dans le Metro

Called "an exceedingly funny picture…funny in a bold, delicate, freakish, vulgar, outrageous, and occasionally nightmarish way…From start to finish, the picture is crammed with sight gags and preposterous photographic stunts. *Zazie* is a film like *Alice in Wonderland*; *Zazie* is a foul-mouthed little cynic, age 11, who comes to Paris for a weekend with her uncle (Philippe Noiret), a female impersonator, and nobody and nothing are quite what they seem" (Pauline Kael). From Louis Malle, the director of *Murmur of the Heart*. French with English subtitles.
VHS: S12991. $69.95.
Louis Malle, France, 1960, 85 mins.

ERIC ROHMER

Chloe in the Afternoon

In *Chloe in the Afternoon*, the last of Eric Rohmer's *Moral Tales* series, Frederic (Bernard Verley) is a married man who fantasizes about the women he sees on the street. When he runs into Bohemian Chloe (Zouzou), an old friend, during his afternoon lunch, he discovers that he may be too squeamish to actually cheat on his wife. "A formal, elegant examination of someone puzzled by marital fidelity, *Chloe in the Afternoon* is a wonderfully cool and lucid expression of the twists and turns of its hero's thoughts." French with English subtitles.
VHS: S06832. $19.98.
Eric Rohmer, France, 1972, 97 mins.

Claire's Knee

Eric Rohmer's most popular work, a vibrant, luscious comedy which focuses on the temptations of a diplomat who visits his childhood home just before he is married to a woman with whom he has lived for six years. Charming and sunny sex comedy. With Jean-Claude Brialy, Lawrence De Monaghan. French with English subtitles.
VHS: S04875. $19.98.
Eric Rohmer, France, 1970, 105 mins.

Four Adventures of Reinette and Mirabelle

In many ways, Rohmer's most offbeat film since 1978's *Perceval*. The film centers on the relationship between two young women: Reinette, a naive but talented painter from the provinces, and Mirabelle, a worldly Parisian student who meets Reinette during summer vacation and invites her to share an apartment during the upcoming school year. The narrative is partitioned into the four segments of the title, each one yielding a graceful epiphany and playing upon a central theme of the perils of idealism. A delightful comedy enhanced by Rohmer's customary richness of characterization. French with English subtitles.
VHS: S13577. $69.95.
Eric Rohmer, France, 1989, 95 mins.

Full Moon in Paris

A headstrong young woman (Pascale Ogier) moves out of her devoted love and takes her own apartment in Paris in order to "experience" loneliness—instead, she juggles various lovers. A continuing investigation by Rohmer of the morality of love and sex. French with English subtitles.
VHS: S00474. $24.95.
Eric Rohmer, France, 1985, 101 mins.

My Night at Maud's

The third in Rohmer's series of moral tales, the story of Jean-Louis, a devout Catholic who, arriving to start a new job at Clermont-Ferrand, meets an attractive and intelligent divorcee. The next day, Jean-Louis meets a young Catholic woman to whom he is immediately attracted, but when he makes advances to her they are rejected. French with English subtitles.
VHS: S04871. $19.98.
Eric Rohmer, France, 1969, 110 mins.

Paris Vu Par (Six in Paris)

This omnibus film from the major figures of the French New Wave (Jean-Luc Godard, Claude Chabrol, Eric Rohmer, Jean Douchet, Jean Rouch and Jean-Daniel Pollet) offers a series of witty, wry vignettes about contemporary Paris. Godard's work, *Une Femme Est une Femme*, is about a young woman who dispatches letters to her two lovers and is concerned she mixed up the contents. With Joanna Shimkus, Nadine Ballot, Barbet Schroeder, Micheline Dax, Claude Melki, Chabrol and Stephane Audran. French with English subtitles. France, 1964, 98 mins.
VHS: S19543. $69.95.

A Tale of Springtime

Eric Rohmer initiates a new cycle, *Tales of the Four Seasons*, with this film about the romantic entanglements between Jeanne, a beautiful philosophy teacher, and Natacha, a younger woman who invites Jeanne to stay at her father's apartment. Natacha tries to manipulate an affair between Jeanne and her father, to get rid of her father's young lover, whom she despises. With Anne Teyssedre, Hugues Quester and Florence Darel. French with English subtitles.
VHS: S18459. $79.98.
Eric Rohmer, France, 1989, 112 mins.

Tale of Winter

Charlotte Very, Michel Voletti, Herve Furic, and Frederic Van Dren Dreissche are cast in this bubbling romantic comedy from Eric Rohmer. Very plays a woman unhappy with her two current lovers. In the pursuit of simplicity, she begins a torrid affair with an old flame. French with English subtitles.
VHS: S26144. $89.95.
Eric Rohmer, France, 1994, 114 mins.

AGNES VARDA

Cleo from 5 to 7

Ninety minutes, exactly, in the life of the singer Corinne Marchant, as she waits for the results of a medical test for cancer, and meets a young soldier about to leave for the Algerian war. Because of the anticipation, every trivial incident takes on a new significance. "Produced mainly in the streets of Paris, this is a moving poem of love and death" (Georges Sadoul). With Cordine Marchand, Antoine Bourseiller. French with English subtitles.
VHS: S03510. $79.95.
Agnes Varda, France/Italy, 1961, 90 mins.

Jacquot de Nantes

Agnes Varda's loving tribute to her late husband, Jacques Demy, begins in Nantes in 1938 with a boy obsessed with movies. This 8-year-old makes puppets for little operettas. As he grows older his obsession never dies, even though his father makes him study mechanics. A number of happy childhood events animate this captivating film about a man who grows up and yet retains a youthful delight in fantasy that shapes his enduring vision and makes him a master of the French musical. French with English subtitles.
VHS: S20738. $19.95.
Agnes Varda, France, 1991, 118 mins.

Le Bonheur

A beautiful, elegant, romantic film that explores the issue of a man who is trying to love two women. Jean-Claude Drouot plays a happily married carpenter who wants his wife to accept that he can love his mistress at the same time. Controversial because of its exploration of morality and because Drouot's real-life family play his wife and children. Agnes Varda's daring is to explore the nature of relationship from a woman's point of view. French with English subtitles.
VHS: S16188. $29.95.
Agnes Varda, France, 1965, 87 mins.

Lion's Love

Varda's journey into American 60's culture is a comment on the margins of Hollywood with Ragni and Rado (*Hair*) and Warhol's Viva as a menage a trois awaiting discovery and fame in an indifferent Hollywood. Varda also weaves in other material—Michael McClure's avant-garde theatre piece *The Beard*, Shirley Clarke's film experiments and TV news. A film made in response to (or acceptance of) the 60's American social, political and cultural upheavals.
VHS: S22467. $39.95.
Agnes Varda, USA, 1969, 115 mins.

Vagabond

Agnes Varda's extraordinarily bleak account of a young woman's death and life. In a breathtaking performance, Sandrine Bonnaire (*A Nos Amours*) is Mona, a waif who drops out of Parisian society to wander the southwest French countryside, exploring the open spaces and implicit freedom absent in her life. In the opening scene, her body is discovered frozen. Varda expertly recounts her life, carefully dissecting French society. French with English subtitles.
VHS: S02982. $24.95.
Agnes Varda, France, 1986, 105 mins.

FRANCOIS TRUFFAUT

The 400 Blows

One of the landmarks of cinema, which introduced the character of Antoine Doinel, played by Jean-Pierre Leaud, to the world, as the 12-year-old boy left to his own devices in an indifferent adult world. An uncompromising film, winner of innumerable awards. French with English subtitles.
VHS: S00006. $29.95.
Laser: LD70800. $59.95.
Francois Truffaut, France, 1959, 97 mins.

The Bride Wore Black

Francois Truffaut's stylish and suspenseful homage to Hitchcock stars a stone-faced Jeanne Moreau tracking down and killing (each in a unique way) the five men responsible for her husband's accidental death. A very odd and dark film, it contains many masterful stylistic flourishes and is further highlighted by an eerie, atmospheric musical score from Bernard Herrmann. Beautifully photographed by Raoul Coutard. French with English subtitles.
VHS: S14805. $19.95.
Laser: LD72165. $34.95.
Francois Truffaut, France, 1968, 107 mins.

Confidentially Yours

This double tribute to Hitchcock and *film noir* pictures a small town that is overtaken by a series of brutal murders. The first suspect is real estate agent Jean-Louis Trintignant. Fanny Ardant, his secretary, believes he is being framed and sets out to solve the mystery. French with newly translated English subtitles.
VHS: S00263. $29.95.
Laser: CLV. LD72100. $49.95.
Francois Truffaut, France, 1983, 110 mins.

Day for Night

Truffaut's love poem to the movies and movie-making features Truffaut playing a director who struggles to complete a film while at the same time handling the emotional problems of staff and crew. Funny and bittersweet, *Day for Night* provides insights into the movie process. Oscar winner for Best Foreign Picture, with Jean-Pierre Leaud, Jacqueline Bisset. English dubbed.
VHS: S00308. $59.95.
Francois Truffaut, France, 1973, 116 mins.

Fahrenheit 451

Truffaut's first English-language production stars Julie Christie and Oskar Werner. Based on Ray Bradbury's masterpiece about a future without books, Werner plays a fireman in charge of burning books who meets a schoolteacher (Christie) who dares to read. In original English language.
VHS: S00425. $59.95.
Laser: LD70028. $34.98.
Francois Truffaut, France, 1966, 112 mins.

Francois Truffaut: 25 Years, 25 Films

This documentary offers a comprehensive overview of Truffaut's career. Added attractions include his first film, *Les Mistons*, interviews with Truffaut discussing his work, the theatrical trailers of nine films, Jean-Pierre Leaud's audition for *The 400 Blows* and Steven Spielberg's discussion of Truffaut's acting role as the scientist in *Close Encounters of the Third Kind*. With commentary by Truffaut scholar and biographer Annette Insdorf.
Laser: LD71929. $39.95.

Francois Truffaut: Stolen Portraits

A brilliant documentary which provides new insights and revelations. Full of extensive clips and in-depth interviews with dozens of Truffaut's collaborators and friends, including Gerard Depardieu, Eric Rohmer, Marcel Ophuls, Claude Chabrol, Jacques Rivette, Truffaut's daughter and Truffaut's former wife, Madeleine Morgenstern, this remarkable film shines new light on the psychological motivations of Truffaut's life and on his filmmaking career. French with English subtitles.
VHS: S26965. $89.98.
Serge Toubiana/Michel Pascal, France, 1993, 93 mins.

Godard/Truffaut Shorts

A short film by Jean-Luc Godard made prior to his release of *Breathless* entitled *All the Boys Are Called Patrick*, and a short film by Francois Truffaut, *Les Mistons*, a charming evocative film about the arousal of sexual feelings in a group of young boys on summer holiday. French with English subtitles.
VHS: S01777. $29.95.
Godard/Truffaut, France, 1957

Jules and Jim

Truffaut's famous love triangle stars Henri Serre as Jim and Oskar Werner as Jules, both in love with Catherine (Jeanne Moreau). Their free-wheeling friendship is suspended when Jules marries Catherine and takes her back to Germany. The two friends are separated by World War I, and when they meet again after the war, Catherine changes partners. One of the films that justifies the invention of the movies. Photography by Raoul Coutard; music by Georges Delerue. French with English subtitles.
VHS: S00663. $29.95.
Laser: LD71069. $59.95.
Francois Truffaut, France, 1961, 105 mins.

Last Metro

Truffaut's poignant, compelling drama, set in Nazi-occupied Paris, unfolds in the Theatre Montmartre, as a group of actors rehearse. But everyone harbors a secret. Catherine Deneuve visits her exiled Jewish husband; the leading man is a member of the Resistance. Touching and tense.
VHS: S00724. $29.95.
Laser: LD71522. $69.95.
Francois Truffaut, France, 1980, 135 mins.

Love on the Run

The latest episode in the life of Truffaut's hero Antoine Doinel begins with our protagonist newly divorced in his thirties and awaiting publication of his first novel. Doinel's incurable romanticism and complicated affairs of the heart make for a funny and bittersweet conclusion With Jean-Pierre Leaud, Marie-France Pisier. French with newly translated English subtitles.
VHS: S00778. $29.95.
Francois Truffaut, France, 1979, 95 mins.

The Man Who Loved Women

More than a comedy of the sexes, this is a touching exploration of the many faces of love. Truffaut's story is of Bertrand Morane, an intelligent and sensitive man who writes his memoirs, remembering all the women he has loved. Starring Charles Denner and featuring Brigitte Fossey, Nathalie Baye and Leslie Caron. English dubbed.
VHS: S00818. $19.98.
Francois Truffaut, France, 1977, 119 mins.

Mississippi Mermaid

Jean-Paul Belmondo plays a wealthy industrialist living on the island of La Reunion, who orders a bride by mail and receives, in place of his intended, the beautiful Catherine Deneuve and a flimsy (but apparently acceptable) explanation. The imposter soon absconds with his bank account and leads him into a murky drama of missing persons and murder. What comes out of this strange mix is a surprisingly powerful adult love story. French with English subtitles.
VHS: S14806. $19.99.
Laser: LD72126. $39.98.
Francois Truffaut, France, 1969, 123 mins.

Shoot the Piano Player

Charles Aznavour is the skilled concert pianist whose role in his wife's suicide has made him hide from life by playing in a bistro. But life and love refuse to pass him by, and inevitably he is drawn back into feeling once again. The film includes many touches of light humor, including Truffaut's homage to American gangster films. French with English subtitles.
VHS: S01192. $29.95.
Laser: LD70461. $49.95.
Francois Truffaut, France, 1960, 80 mins.

Small Change

Small Change presents the viewer with ten boys and girls whose adventures illustrate the different stages of passage from early childhood to adolescence. Some episodes are funny, some serious, some sheer fantasy. Together they animate the notion that childhood is often perilous but also full of grace. French with English subtitles.
VHS: S01216. $19.99.
Laser: LD72156. $34.98.
Francois Truffaut, France, 1976, 106 mins.

The Soft Skin

Truffaut's New Wave classic is a study of a man's first incident of infidelity. Pierre Desailly is the successful publisher who, while often separated from his wife because of business, meets a younger flight attendant, and has an affair. With legendary skill and acute sensitivity, Truffaut rips the mask off the lies, suspicions and guilt that lead to the disintegration of ordinary marriages. French with newly translated English subtitles.
VHS: S01224. $29.95.
Francois Truffaut, France, 1964, 120 mins.

Story of Adele H.

In 1863, the beautiful young daughter of the world-famous writer Victor Hugo crosses the Atlantic in desperate pursuit of the man she believes is her fiance, her lover, her destiny. For months and years she waits for him, harasses him, throws herself in his path. Finally, her intensity gives way to madness. Truffaut called this film the autopsy of a passion. French with English subtitles.
VHS: S01259. $19.99.
Laser: LD71510. $34.98.
Francois Truffaut, France, 1975, 97 mins.

Two English Girls

Based on the only other novel by Henri-Pierre Roche, the author of *Jules and Jim*, the situation is reversed as two sisters are in love with the same man at the turn of the century. Leaud is the young Parisian convalescing at the seaside. Extraordinary mood photography by Almendros. French with English subtitles.
VHS: S01382. $29.95.
Laser: Includes 24 minutes of restored footage. LD72445. $69.95.
Francois Truffaut, France, 1971, 108 mins.

The Wild Child

The Wild Child is based on a remarkable journal, the 1806 memoirs of a French physician, a certain Jean Itard. The record begins in 1798, when a child is found living in the forest like an animal. Dr. Itard sets for himself the task of educating this child who is totally alien to civilization. Shot in austere black and white, the film achieves a depth of vision treating anew love, freedom, the nature of childhood and childhood's end. French with English subtitles.
VHS: S14810. $19.99.
Laser: LD75540. $39.98.
Francois Truffaut, France, 1970, 85 mins.

The Woman Next Door

Fanny Ardant and Gerard Depardieu star as former tempestuous lovers now married to other people who suddenly find themselves living next door to one another. Truffaut masterfully guides the couple through a maze of confused feelings, steering them toward their final encounter. French with newly translated English subtitles.
VHS: S01477. $29.95.
Francois Truffaut, France, 1981, 106 mins.

ROBERT BRESSON

Diary of a Country Priest

The story of an ailing priest who believes he has failed. Pauline Kael said: "*Diary of a Country Priest* is one of the most profound emotional experiences in the history of the cinema." French with English subtitles.
VHS: S19932. $59.95.
Laser: LD75413. $39.99.
Robert Bresson, France, 1951, 116 mins.

L'Argent

The subject of *L'Argent* is materialism, specifically the consequences of the passing of a counterfeit 500-franc note which initiates a chain reaction of corruption and moral error leading to a truly terrifying climax. *L'Argent* is one of Bresson's most perfect works; its subject and form are inseparable; every action leaves a trace, nothing is superfluous. With Christian Patey, Sylvie Van Den Elsen, Michel Briquet and Caroline Lang. French with English subtitles.
VHS: S20302. $79.95.
Robert Bresson, France/Switzerland, 1983, 82 mins.

The Ladies of the Bois de Boulogne (Les Dames du Bois de Boulogne)

This rarely-seen second feature by Bresson was co-scripted by Jean Cocteau based on an anecdote in a novel by Diderot. Two sophisticated women, Helene and Jean, agree to remain friends even when their ardor for one another has died. Helene good naturedly introduces her ex-lover Jean to a new woman and everything seems fine as a new romance begins. But this woman harbors a mysterious past that threatens to unsettle everything. Maria Casares stars in a rigorous, intense film remarkable for Cocteau's layered dialog. French with English subtitles.
VHS: S24045. $59.95.
Robert Bresson, France, 1944, 83 mins.

Lancelot of the Lake

Robert Bresson's masterpiece is set in the last days of the age of chivalry. As the Knights return to King Arthur's Court after a doomed quest for the Holy Grail, they are torn apart by jealousies and rivalries, at the center of which is Lancelot and his relationship with Guinevere. Told in Bresson's austere style, with rich colors and stark images, the film becomes a hypnotic study in the loss of faith, in which reality stands in sharp relief to the spiritual. With Luc Simon, Laura Duc Condominas and Humbert Balsan. French with English subtitles.
VHS: S23284. $79.95.
Robert Bresson, France/Italy, 1975, 80 mins.

A Man Escaped

A perfect film, based on the true story of a French Resistance fighter's escape from a Gestapo prison. In Bresson's hands, the narrative of the prison escape just hours before he is executed becomes a transcendental meditation on the meaning of freedom and existence told in light and shadows. "I would like to show this miracle: an invisible hand over the prison, directing what happens…the film is a mystery…The Spirit breathes where it will," said Bresson. Struck from a beautiful, newly mastered print. French with English subtitles.
VHS: S06464. $69.95.
Robert Bresson, France, 1956, 102 mins.

Mouchette

"Bresson constructs a drama of extraordinary tension and adventure," wrote *The New York Times*. "The adventure leads to escape from life, to a moment when nature and the supernatural meet in a fleeting intimation of grace so powerful that even an awareness of what the camera cannot show us is happiness enough." A 14-year-old friendless schoolgirl, Mouchette, lives with her alcoholic bootleg father, and her mother is dying. She is more sensitive than anyone around her and thus, paradoxically, less able to communicate. Based on the novel *La Nouvelle Histoire de Mouchette* by Georges Bernanos, Mouchette, says Bresson, "is found everywhere: wars, concentration camps, tortures, assassinations." French with English subtitles.
VHS: S06465. $59.95.
Robert Bresson, France, 1960, 80 mins.

Une Femme Douce (A Gentle Woman)

Bresson's first film in color, which introduced 20-year-old Dominique Sanda to the world in a haunting transposition of Dostoevsky's story *A Gentle Creature*. Sanda plays the role of a young woman who marries a pawn broker (Guy Frangin) but finds she cannot bring herself to adapt her life to his, and so leaps to her death from a Paris balcony. We—like the husband—don't really know the reason why. As the young woman, Sanda delivers a star-making performance, perhaps the most erotic and natural of all of Bresson's heroines. French with English subtitles.
VHS: S26462. $79.95.
Robert Bresson, France, 1969, 87 mins.

BARBET SCHROEDER

Barfly

Mickey Rourke and Faye Dunaway are superb in this film based on Charles Bukowski's novel; Rourke is the gifted back-alley poet who's not afraid to defend his honor or freedom, but whose lust for life has given him a unique sense of love and romance. Faye Dunaway is the woman who's seen the darkest side of life and finds a rebirth through her new-found barroom bard.
VHS: S06587. $19.98.
Laser: LD70517. $34.98.
Barbet Schroeder, France/USA, 1987, 100 mins.

Charles Bukowski Tapes

"It's a gem…an outrageously stimulating and unnerving all-night drinking session with a gutter eloquent barroom philosopher who has made his soul your own…One of the most intimate, revelatory and unsparing glimpses any film or video has ever given us of a writer's life and personality," raved Michael Wilmington in *The Los Angeles Times*. Directed by Barbet Schroeder (*Barfly*), a 4-hour video portrait of the renegade poet of contemporary literature.
VHS: S08117. $100.00.
Barbet Schroeder, USA/France, 1987, 240 mins.

General Idi Amin Dada

"I knew he had star quality," director Barbet Schroeder said, tongue-in-cheek, about the notorious Ugandan dictator he had just finished documenting with his camera. Audiences howled at the inadvertently comic antics of the infamous "Big Daddy"—and Amin, in turn, threatened to kill Schroeder if cuts weren't made in the film. See for yourself.
VHS: S13908. $59.95.
Barbet Schroeder, France, 1975, 113 mins.

Kiss of Death

Nicolas Cage and David Caruso are cast in this compelling, effective and superbly acted thriller loosely based on the 1947 film noir classic of the same name. Caruso is a tough ex-con who becomes a police informant. Unfortunately, the criminal underworld is no place to make friends, as Cage's character proves with his violent, psychotic behavior. Samuel L. Jackson is also featured.
VHS: S26293. $96.98.
Laser: LD75071. $39.98.
Barbet Schroeder, USA, 1994, 100 mins.

Koko: A Talking Gorilla

Schroeder's up-close look at a gorilla trained by a Stanford University psychologist to communicate via sign language captures the excitement, charm and controversy surrounding this groundbreaking project. This documentary is as absorbing as it is funny, raising basic questions about conditioning, intelligence, language, as well as the boundaries of humanity itself. Photographed by Nestor Almendros. French and English with English subtitles.
VHS: S13911. $59.95.
Barbet Schroeder, France, 1978, 81 mins.

Maitresse

Gerard Depardieu is a Parisian burglar who one day breaks into a flat which turns out to be the working quarters of Ariane (Bulle Ogier), a professional sadist who serves as dominatrix over a stable of wealthy masochists. Rather than turn him in she convinces him to stay on as her assistant, and the two eventually become lovers. Incidentally, Ariane's customers (all masked) are played by well-heeled Parisian masochists who paid a great deal of money for the privilege of appearing in the film. Not a bad way to finance a movie. French with English subtitles.
VHS: S13910. $59.99.
Barbet Schroeder, France, 1976, 112 mins.

More

The film that catapulted Barbet Schroeder to worldwide fame, *More* is the tender tale of a free-spirited young couple in the late '60s whose open lifestyle leads them down a tragic path. Soundtrack by Pink Floyd. English, French, Spanish and German with English subtitles.
VHS: S13909. $59.95.
Barbet Schroeder, France, 1969, 110 mins.

Reversal of Fortune

Jeremy Irons won an Oscar for his wickedly suave performance as accused socialite Claus von Bulow. The Danish born aristocrat goes from the society page to the front page when his rich American wife suspiciously falls into a coma. The comatose Sunny—played by Glenn Close—narrates much of the film, which also stars Ron Silver as the dynamic appeal lawyer Alan Dershowitz. Based on the book by Dershowitz that was brilliantly adapted for the screen by Nicholas Kazan.
VHS: S13923. $19.95.
Barbet Schroeder, USA, 1990, 112 mins.

Single White Female

Barbet Schroeder directed this brooding psychological thriller about a fashion designer (Bridget Fonda) whose enigmatic roommate (Jennifer Jason Leigh) begins to appropriate her life with frightening ease. With Steven Weber and Peter Friedman.
VHS: S18007. $19.95.
Barbet Schroeder, USA, 1992, 107 mins.

Tricheurs (Cheaters)

A slick drama about gambling neurotics and the clever electronic swindle they engineer at the roulette wheel. Steve Baes, a professional gambler on the international casino circuit, was the real-life inspiration for many of the film's incidents and details, and he also worked on the screenplay. Directed by Barbet Schroeder (*Reversal of Fortune*). French with English subtitles.
VHS: S13912. $69.95.
Barbet Schroeder, France, 1984, 95 mins.

The Valley Obscured by Clouds

A handful of dropouts and dreamers set out to find New Guinea's uncharted valley of the gods; they end up experiencing an odyssey of sexual and spiritual discovery that changes their lives. Photographed by the illustrious Nestor Almendros (*Days of Heaven*), and featuring a musical score by Pink Floyd. French with English subtitles.
VHS: S13913. $59.99.
Barbet Schroeder, France, 1972, 106 mins.

JEAN ROUCH

Le Jaguar
Part fiction, part documentary and part social commentary, *Jaguar* is the story of three young men from the savannah of Niger who leave their homeland to seek wealth and adventure on the coast and in the cities of Ghana. Filmed in the 1950s when no portable synchronized sound equipment was available, Jean Rouch had the main characters of the film improvise a narrative while they viewed the footage which in itself was improvised. The resulting soundtrack consists of remembered dialog, joking and exclamations, and questions and explanations about the action on screen. The three young men, a herdsman, a fisherman and their friend, travel for a month to the coast of Ghana and eventually part to take jobs in the cities. Successful but homesick, they return to Niger; they have become *jaguars* with a knowledge of life in the modern city. English narration.
VHS: $10730. $350.00.
Jean Rouch, France/Niger, 1954, 96 mins.

Les Maitres Fous
Jean Rouch's quintessential film documents the ceremony of a West African religious movement, the Hauku, which was widespread in Niger and Ghana from the 20s to the 50s. In 1954, Rouch was asked by a small group in Ghana to film their annual ceremony in which the participants would enter into a trance and become possessed by a variety of spirits associated with the western colonial powers. Today, *Les Maitres Fous* remains as one of the great works of ethnographic cinema. English narration.
VHS: $10728. $200.00.
Jean Rouch, France/Ghana, 1955, 35 mins.

The Lion Hunters
Filmed in the savannahs of northern Niger and Mali over a seven year period in the 50s and 60s, *The Lion Hunters* follows the Gao hunters on several hunts and explores the relationships between the Songhay tribes and the Fulani herdsmen. When lions raid the cattle of the Fulani herdsmen, the Fulani request the Songhay chiefs to send Gao hunters to their aid. Although lions kill only sick or injured cattle, they will occasionally kill a healthy cow. The Gao are able to determine which lion is responsible since they know each lion's individual characteristics and habits. One of the most important works of Jean Rouch's career. English narration.
VHS: $10729. $300.00.
Jean Rouch, France/Mali, 1965, 68 mins.

Paris Vu Par (Six in Paris)
This omnibus film from the major figures of the French New Wave (Jean-Luc Godard, Claude Chabrol, Eric Rohmer, Jean Douchet, Jean Rouch and Jean-Daniel Pollet) offers a series of witty, wry vignettes about contemporary Paris. Godard's work, *Une Femme Est une Femme*, is about a young woman who dispatches letters to her two lovers and is concerned she mixed up the contents. With Joanna Shimkus, Nadine Ballot, Barbet Schroeder, Micheline Dax, Claude Melki, Chabrol and Stephane Audran. French with English subtitles. France, 1964, 98 mins.
VHS: $19543. $69.95.

MARCEL OPHULS

Hotel Terminus:
The Life and Times of Klaus Barbie
Marcel Ophuls' award-winning documentary spans 70 years and three continents. Culled from 120 hours of interviews, it traces the 40-year-manhunt for Nazi war criminal Klaus Barbie, the ruthless SS interrogator known as "The Butcher of Lyon." "A shocking, unforgettable film" (Ebert and Siskel). Winner of the Academy Award for Best Documentary and the International Critics Prize at the Cannes Film Festival. Original English-language version (includes French, German and Spanish footage subtitled in English). 2 cassettes.
VHS: $10756. $29.98.
Marcel Ophuls, France/USA, 1988, 267 mins.

A Sense of Loss
Ophuls' (*Sorrow and the Pity*) landmark film about northern Ireland probes the living roots of hatred in family folklore, in schools, on the streets. In the process, *A Sense of Loss* reveals the human terms of Ireland's civil warfare.
VHS: $01178. $59.95.
Marcel Ophuls, France/USA, 1972, 135 mins.

Sorrow and the Pity
Marcel Ophuls' monumental documentary covering the German occupation of France during World War II. Through poignant interviews and stark newsreel footage, Ophuls creates a sense of living history. "A magnificent epic on the themes of collaboration and resistance. There's nothing comparable to [it]" (Pauline Kael). English dubbed.
VHS: $01233. $59.95.
Marcel Ophuls, France, 1972, 260 mins.

JEAN-JACQUES ANNAUD

The Bear
A rare and wonderful animal adventure story for adults. Based on the novel *The Grizzly King* by Michigan author James Oliver Curwood, Annaud tells the story of an orphaned cub and the wounded kodiak bear who grudgingly befriends the distant relative. They encounter hunters, packs of trained dogs and other dangers and learn to trust each other. With Jack Wallace and Tcheky Karyo as the humans and starring Bart and Douce as the bears. Filmed on location in the Italian Dolemite mountains.
VHS: $12209. $14.95.
Jean-Jacques Annaud, France, 1988, 93 mins.

The Lover
Jean-Jacques Annaud adapts Marguerite Duras' autobiographical novel *L'Amant*: political, social and class tensions and sexual role-playing refracted through an erotic relationship between a beautiful French girl (Jane March) and her older, elegant, aristocratic Chinese lover (Tony Leung). The film is set in French-occupied Indochina during the 1920s. This is the uncut, unrated European version that was initially rated NC-17. Original dialog.
VHS: $18520. $19.98.
Laser: LD71870. $39.98.
Jean-Jacques Annaud, France/Great Britain, 1991, 113 mins.

The Name of the Rose
Sean Connery and F. Murray Abraham star in this intriguing tale, based on the popular novel by Umberto Eco, about mysterious killings related to forbidden books during a period of the Inquisition.
VHS: Out of print. For rental only.
Laser: LD72307. $34.99.
Jean-Jacques Annaud, Germany/Italy/France, 1986, 128 mins.

Quest for Fire
Eighty thousand years ago the Cro-Magnon equivalents of the Three Stooges set out to find fire. On the way they locate Rae Dawn Chong and invent the missionary position. Less serious than intended, this prehistorical epic does have its moments.
VHS: $04597. $69.98.
Jean-Jacques Annaud, Canada/France, 1981, 100 mins.

FRENCH COMEDY

A Pain in the A..
Jacques Brel and Lino Ventura star in this story of a hired killer who becomes entangled in the life of a suicidal shirt salesman while trying to fulfill a contract on a Mob informer. Funny and original. French with English subtitles.
VHS: $00987. $59.95.
Edouard Molinaro, France, 1973, 90 mins.

Alberto Express
An absurdist comedy about the strange predicament of Alberto, a man nearing 40 and broke, whose family's byzantine rules stipulate he must remunerate his parents for the money spent on his upbringing. In this black comedy about the bonds fractured over family and money, Alberto must find the means to pay off his family or risk losing his forthcoming child. With Sergio Castellitto, Nino Manfredi, Marie Trintignant, Michel Aumont and Jeanne Moreau. French and Italian with English subtitles.
VHS: $18859. $19.98.
Arthur Joffe, France/Italy, 1991, 90 mins.

Bandits
Claude Lelouch's comedy thriller about a criminal's return to society. He's bent on finding the culprits responsible for his wife's murder and the estrangement of his daughter. "A gem [that is] effortlessly charming, intelligent and sophisticated" (*New York Post*). With Jean Yanne, Marie-Sophie L., Patrick Bruel and Corrine Marchand. French with English subtitles.
VHS: $19729. $19.98.
Claude Lelouch, France, 1986, 98 mins.

Barjo
A wacky French farce based on the novel by Philip K. Dick, *Barjo* is the "slightly psychotic" story of young, underdeveloped Barjo, who lives near his sister Fanfan, waiting for the UFOs. When he accidentally burns down his house, he moves in with Fanfan, discovers sex, and quietly drives Fanfan's husband insane. Nutty, off-the-wall comedy from the director of *Baxter*. French with English subtitles.
VHS: $20424. $89.98.
Jerome Boivin, France, 1992, 85 mins.

Belmondo Is the Swashbuckler
An action-adventure comedy, starring Jean-Paul Belmondo as the swashbuckler who out-Errols Errol Flynn in a colorful, wild and action-packed romp through the French Revolution. French with English subtitles.
VHS: $04449. $59.95.
Jean-Paul Rappeneau, France, 1975, 100 mins.

The Brain
Gerard Oury's light, French, romantic comedy stars David Niven as a charismatic thief who devises the daring robbery of a train carrying NATO cash. The other players are Jean-Paul Belmondo, Bourvil, Eli Wallach, Silvia Monti and Fernand Valois.
VHS: $16888. $19.95.
Gerard Oury, France, 1969, 100 mins.

Cartouche
An 18th century cooper's son (Jean-Paul Belmondo) becomes a quick-witted and gallant thief in this hilarious spoof of swashbucklers from Philippe de Broca (*King of Hearts*). He and his friends take over the crime syndicate in Paris, and eventually dedicate themselves to avenging the death of their co-leader, Venus. With Claudia Cardinale, Odile Versois and Philippe Lemaire. French with English subtitles.
VHS: $16186. $29.95.
Philippe de Broca, France/Italy, 1964, 115 mins.

The Cat (Le Chat)
Jean Gabin and Simone Signoret star as a couple whose love has turned to hate after 25 years of marriage. Julien (Jean Gabin) lavishes love on his cat, inciting jealousy in his wife. An award winner at the Chicago International Film Festival and the Berlin Film Festival. French with English subtitles.
VHS: $00221. $59.95.
Pierre Granier-Deferre, France, 1975, 88 mins.

Cross My Heart
A French comedy which became a cult hit. Martin (Nicolas Parodi) conceals his mother's death to avoid the soulless French social services or anonymous orphanage. His classmates enter into a pact to withhold the information from the authorities and tension is established through their intricate efforts to preserve all signs of normalcy. "A comic essay on the desperate ingenuity of youth" (*Time Magazine*). Cinematography by Jean-Claude Saillier. With Sylvain Copans, Cecilia Rouaud and Delphine Gouttman. French with English subtitles.
VHS: $18860. $19.98.
Jacques Fansten, France, 1990, 105 mins.

The Daydreamer (Le Distrait)
From the filmmaker of *Tall Blonde Man With One Black Shoe*, a zany comedy in which Pierre Richard plays an absent-minded advertising man, bumbling through an ad agency and reducing it to a shambles. French with English subtitles.
VHS: $03990. $59.95.
Pierre Richard, France, 1977, 90 mins.

Dear Detective (Tendre Poulet)
Annie Girardot and Philippe Noiret star in this comic thriller about a madcap female police detective. She is investigating the mysterious circumstances surrounding the murders of three senate deputies. Despite this somber focus there is still time for big laughs and even romance. French with English subtitles.
VHS: $22036. $59.95.
Phillipe de Broca, France, 1977, 90 mins.

Delicatessen
Imagine the Coen brothers remaking Terry Gilliam's *Brazil* on speed and you get the idea of this film, set in a vaguely post-nuclear Paris. The action unfolds in a decaying building, where a war breaks out between a group of innocents, cannibals and militant vegetarians. French with English subtitles. With Dominique Pinon (*Diva*), Laure Dougnac and Claude Dreyfus.
VHS: $18069. $89.98.
Laser: LD75125. $24.98.
Jean-Marie Jeunet/Marc Caro, France, 1991, 95 mins.

Delusions of Grandeur
A delightful fast-paced comedy of royal intrigue set in 17th century Spain. Louis de Funes is the evil, all-powerful minister of the King of Spain, and Yves Montand is his clever servant. French with English subtitles.
VHS: $00321. $59.95.
Gerard Oury, France, 1976, 85 mins.

Et la Tendresse?...Bordel!
Between a sex crazed criminal, a happily unemployed intellectual, and a young, timid romantic evolve three couples, and three different attitudes toward love. Offering profound criticisms of heterosexual relationships, this is the hilarious film that launched Patrick Schulmann's career. Dubbed in English.
VHS: $00417. $69.95.
Patrick Schulmann, France, 1979, 97 mins.

Et la Tendresse?...Bordel! #2
A delirium of humor describes the relationship between a color blind painter and radio personality in this, Schulmann's third feature. With Diane Bellego, Christian Francois and Fabrice Luchini. French with English subtitles.
VHS: $16190. $69.95.
Patrick Schulmann, France, 1983, 100 mins.

Extenuating Circumstances
A well-known judge and his wife find themselves stranded in an unsavory auberge outside Paris, where a gang of criminals live. The couple hide their identities and inadvertently become accepted by the gang. When they try to convert their new friends into respectable citizens, an ex-con whom the judge once sentenced to prison appears to upset their plans. French with English subtitles.
VHS: $20757. $29.95.
Jean Boyer, France, 90 mins.

Fernandel the Dressmaker
Comedy directed by one of France's most prolific directors, starring Fernandel, a leading comic for four decades, famous for his long, horse-like face. French with English subtitles.
VHS: $00375. $34.95.
Jean Boyer, France, 1956

The First Time
Claude Berri's (*Manon of the Spring, Germinal*) breakthrough success stars Alain Cohen and Charles Denner in an uproarious comedy about the traditional rite of passage to manhood, that very first time. A young artist and his buddies are desperate to find girls and maybe even love with endless complications along the way. French with English subtitles.
VHS: $23890. $29.95.
Claude Berri, France, 1967, 83 mins.

Forbidden Fruit
Comic actor Fernandel stars as a simple if lusty country doctor who introduces a pretty young woman into his household as an assistant. Her job is something of a mystery, throwing the doctor's marriage into crisis. This melodrama is based on a novel from George Simenon (*Inspector Maigret*). In English.
VHS: $25925. $24.95.

French Fried Vacation (Les Bronzes)
This comic spoof pokes fun at the idea of Club Med style vacations, where grown adults find themselves in exotic locations in search of sexual adventure. Sometimes it seems that it doesn't matter whom you meet so long as you meet a lot of partners. Recreation takes precedence over rest. French with English subtitles.
VHS: $22035. $59.95.
Patrice Leconte, France, 1978, 90 mins.

Heat of Desire
An adventurous, giddy, madcap comedy which features the beautiful Clio Goldsmith as a sultry young woman who attempts to lure a married intellectual into a shady scam devised by her evil mother and oily lover through an utterly uninhibited marathon of lovemaking. Original title: *Plein Sud*. With Patrick Dewaere, Jeanne Moreau. French with English subtitles.
VHS: $00555. $19.95.
Luc Beraud, France, 1982, 90 mins.

The Infernal Trio
A macabre murder comedy, called "erotic chic" by *Newsweek*, directed by Francis Girod. Michel Piccoli plays a sociopathic lawyer who seduces two sisters (Romy Schneider and Mascha Gomska) and enlists them in a conspiracy to marry and murder victims and defraud their insurance companies. Threatened with exposure, they eliminate the witnesses and destroy the bodies with acid, distracted in the butchery only by their erotic arousal. But when a prospective female victim becomes romantically involved with one of the sisters, the infernal trio must stretch itself into an uneasy quartet. French with English subtitles.
VHS: $10871. $29.95.
Francois Girod, France, 1974, 100 mins.

King of Hearts
Alan Bates stars in this popular cult film as a World War I British soldier involved in the insanity of modern warfare. In the small French village of Marville, the inmates of the local asylum have taken over when the local populace has fled in terror. The soldier finds their company preferable to army life. What is so crazy about that? With Jean-Claude Brialy, Genevieve Bujold, Michel Serrault, Adolfo Celliand and Pierre Brasseur.
VHS: $00680. $19.95.
Laser: Widescreen. LD71078. $49.95.
Philippe de Broca, Great Britain/France/Italy, 1967, 100 mins.

La Cage aux Folles
A gay couple in St. Tropez discover their lives are complicated when the son of one of the men wants to marry into a politically repressive family. Ugo Tognazzi and Michel Serrault are Renato and Albin, the owners of the La Cage aux Folles nightclub, which features a popular revue of female impersonation. This surprise international hit was based on the play by Jean Poiret. With Benny Luke and Michael Galabru as the head of the Union of Moral Order. French with English subtitles.
VHS: $00702. $19.95.
Laser: LD70756. $49.95.
Edouard Molinaro, France, 1979, 91 mins.

La Cage aux Folles II
Renato (Ugo Tognazzi) and Albin (Michel Serrault) of *La Cage aux Folles* return as the proprietor and main attraction of the elegant cabaret, La Cage aux Folles. Albin is offended by Renato's suggestion that he is a bit too mature to impersonate the young Marlene Dietrich of the *Blue Angel*, and an incredible series of comic events ensues. English dubbed.
VHS: $00703. $19.98.
Edouard Molinaro, France, 1981, 99 mins.

La Cage aux Folles III
La Cage aux Folles III, The Wedding. The boys are back! The good news is they will inherit a fortune if they marry, but the bad news is they have 18 months to have a baby. English dubbed.
VHS: $00704. $19.95.
Georges Lautner, France, 1986, 88 mins.

La Chevre (The Goat)
The comedy team of Gerard Depardieu and Pierre Richard, who were so successful in *Les Comperes*, bring to the screen another great French farce. Their travels range from the board rooms of a huge multinational conglomerate to the tropics of Mexico, in search of the chairman of the board's missing accident-prone daughter. French with English subtitles.
VHS: $05209. $69.95.
Francis Veber, France, 1985, 91 mins.

La Discrete
Christian Vincent's sophisticated comedy of manners about Antoine (Fabrice Luchini), a parliamentary aide whose plans to end his current relationship are shattered when he discovers his girlfriend embracing another man. Hurt and deeply resentful, he orchestrates a vengeful plot to seduce every woman he meets, abandon her and record the entries in a journal he will publish. "*La Discrete* is an assured and lyrical testament to the old saying, 'Love conquers all' " (*Toronto Festival of Festivals*). With Judith Henry, Maurice Garrel and Marie Bunuel. French with English subtitles.
VHS: $20301. $89.95.
Christian Vincent, France, 1990, 95 mins.

La Grande Vadrouille
In 1943, three allied parachutists land behind enemy lines and end up creating chaos for the conductor and decorator who find them. The only way for this pair to regain their peaceable existence lies in the return of this troublesome trio to a free zone. French with English subtitles.
VHS: $20756. $29.95.
Gerard Oury, France, 1966, 122 mins.

Mama, There's a Man in Your Bed
From the creator of *Three Men and a Cradle*, this heartwarming film is the story of an unlikely romance between a harried CEO and his financially strapped cleaning woman who is desperately trying to keep her five children from going hungry. Writer/director Coline Serreau has a lot to say about class and color differences in a world none too tolerant of either. Starring Daniel Auteuil, Firmine Richard, Pierre Vernier, and Maxime Leroux. French with English subtitles.
VHS: $13792. $89.99.
Coline Serreau, France, 1989, 111 mins.

The Man in a Raincoat
Fernandel visits a chorus girl who charges for her company, only to have the rendezvous cut short when the woman is murdered while changing her clothes. The innocent-of-murder married man finds his troubles only beginning in this comic-mystery. With John McGiver and Bernard Blier. Dubbed into English. B&W.
VHS: $05696. $29.95.
Julien Duvivier, France/Italy, 1957, 97 mins.

One Wild Moment
An hilarious French farce that takes place during the vacation of a recently divorced 44 year old man looking for his fantasies to come true. When his fantasy is realized in the form of a 17 year old girl, she happens to be the daughter of his best friend. French with English subtitles.
VHS: $00967. $59.95.
Claude Berri, France, 1977, 88 mins.

One Woman or Two

Gerard Depardieu is an absent-minded paleontologist looking for a substantial grant from an eccentric American philanthropist. At the airport he mistakes Sigourney Weaver for Dr. Ruth Westheimer and the misunderstandings are only beginning. It's supposed to be a comedy. French with English subtitles.
VHS: S05301. $19.98.
Daniel Vigne, France, 1985, 95 mins.

The Red Inn (L'Auberge Rouge)

One of the funniest classic French comedies, starring the great Fernandel. An innkeeper and his wife (Francoise Rosay) hatch a murderous plan for their guests. Only the will of God in the form of an intervening priest (Fernandel) can save them. French with English subtitles.
VHS: S26877. $24.95.
Claude Autant-Lara, France, 1951, 95 mins.

Return of the Tall Blond Man with One Black Shoe

Pierre Richard and Mireille Dare are in love on vacation in Rio and yet again the target of comedic espionage. Hit-men "Prince" and "Charming" have the Tall Blond at the top of their list, but he manages to bumble through showers of bullets unharmed. The whole mad melee culminates in a confrontation at the symphony orchestra as the hilarious *Tall Blond Man with One Black Shoe* meets its rip-roaring sequel. French with English subtitles.
VHS: S16170. $19.95.
Yves Robert, France, 1973, 84 mins.

A Royal Affair

In this elegant sexual farce Maurice Chevalier plays a mythic French king visiting Paris, who becomes entangled in a group of slapstick and frenetic events, the exchanging of mistresses and political blackmail. Chevalier performs several songs. French with English subtitles. France, 1950, 100 mins.
VHS: S18171. $24.95.

Senechal the Magnificent

Unable to perform on stage, an actor decides to bring his favorite roles to life—that is, real life. The result is a hilarious string of misunderstandings that end up in court. There he gets a new role, but loses his voice. Fernandel is in top comic form in this comic delight of a film. French with English subtitles.
VHS: S21881. $39.95.
Jean Boyer, France, 1957, 95 mins.

Serious About Pleasure

Jane Birkin stars in this comedy about a romantic trio. Richard Leduc and Michael Lonsdale are the two men who share the love of this woman, despite societal disapproval. On the road a series of quirky adventures tests their patience and Birkin's unexpected pregnancy tests their love. French with English subtitles.
VHS: S22886. $79.95.
Robert Benayoun, France, 1975, 100 mins.

Sheep Has Five Legs

One of the best-loved films of Fernandel. In this film, he plays quintuplets as well as the father of the brood—and also plays the actor Fernandel. A totally, wildly improbable comedy. French with English subtitles.
VHS: S01188. $29.95.
Henri Verneuil, France, 1953, 94 mins.

The Sucker (Le Corniauds)

On his way to a vacation, Antoine Marechal (Bourvil) loses his car in an accident. The offending businessman, Saroyan (famed comic Louis de Funes), gives him a Cadillac so that he can still go on to Italy. Only this car turns Antoine into a smuggler. Antoine is not as naive as he seems however, and he manages to make the most of this ridiculous situation. French with English subtitles.
VHS: S22033. $59.95.
Gerard Oury, France, 1965, 90 mins.

Tall Blond Man with One Black Shoe

A beautifully mastered print of the original French version of Yves Robert's international comedy hit. Rival factions within French intelligence try to pass off a randomly selected dupe as a "superagent." Frizzy-haired Pierre Richard, France's reigning king of comedy, is the concert-violinist turned patsy in love with a very pretty but very married harpist. French with English subtitles.
VHS: S13282. $29.95.
Laser: LD71628. $39.95.
Pierre Richard, France, 1972, 90 mins.

Tall Blond Man with One Black Shoe/ Return of the Tall Blond Man

Two of a pair, this is the French comedy that inspired Hollywood to enlist Tom Hanks as *The Man with One Red Shoe*. Capture the laughs at a discount with this specially packaged 2-pack. French with English subtitles.
VHS: S16169. $49.95.

That Man from Rio

Philippe de Broca's caper comedy is a parody of 60s Cold War thrillers. Jean-Paul Belmondo plays an air force pilot who pursues a double agent and thief from Paris to Rio to dense jungles of the Amazon in search of a valuable statuette. "Fantasy takes over, and Belmondo [outdoes] Fairbanks in agility, Lloyd in cliffhanging, and Bond in indestructibility" (Brenda Davies, *Monthly Film Bulletin*). Music by Georges Delerue. With Jean Servais, Francoise Dorleac, Adolfo Celi and Simone Renant. French with English subtitles.
VHS: S20405. $19.98.
Philippe de Broca, France/Italy, 1964, 120 mins.

Three Men and a Cradle

One of the funniest French films in recent years, an unlikely story of three confirmed bachelors who receive a six-month-old roommate. This little bundle of joy can turn into a big bundle of trouble, and chaos of a hilarious kind ensues. French with English subtitles.
VHS: S02266. $14.98.
Coline Serreau, France, 1985, 100 mins.

Widow Couderc

A fun French thriller with Simone Signoret the provincial widow whose love affairs lead her to fall in love with an escaped murderer, based on a novel by Georges Simenon. With Alain Delon. French with English subtitles.
VHS: S01458. $59.95.
Pierre Granier-Deferre, France, 1974, 92 mins.

french CLASSICS

Abel Gance at Work
Rare production footage showing the creator of *Napoleon* at work—includes footage from *La Roue* and *Napoleon*. 43 mins.
VHS: S13210. $19.95.

Abel Gance's Beethoven
The monumental epic from the director of *Napoleon*, Abel Gance's *Beethoven* offers an extraordinary vision of the romantic artist as a tragic hero. This symphonic film, full of magnificent sequences, features Gance's return to the visual freedom of the silent cinema, while using sound in a daring, expressionistic manner. With Harry Baur, Jean-Louis Barrault, Marcel Dallio. French with English subtitles.
VHS: S13045. $29.95.
Abel Gance, France, 1936, 116 mins.

Adam and Evelyn
Stewart Granger is carefree gambler who must change his ways when a friend dies. Granger is left in charge of a young woman who becomes his daughter. It's a pleasant and cheerful tale of evolving loyalties and maturing tastes. Also features Jean Simmons. French with English subtitles.
VHS: S21562. $24.95.
Harold French, France, 1956, 80 mins.

Adorable Julia
A middle-aged actress decides to take on a younger lover in this humorous sex comedy based on the novel by Somerset Maugham. With Lilli Palmer and Charles Boyer. French with English subtitles.
VHS: S14653. $29.96.
Alfred Weidenmann, France, 1962, 97 mins.

Ali Baba and the Forty Thieves
Ali Baba, played by Fernandel, accidentally discovers the magic hiding place of Abdul and his 40 thieves. With this unexpected treasure he buys a beautiful slave to be his wife, only to find his desires thwarted by the plans of the wronged thieves and the master of his new wife, in this comedy based on the old classic. French with English subtitles.
VHS: S20758. $59.95.
Jacques Becker, France, 92 mins.

Back to the Wall
An entertaining and suspenseful tale of murder and blackmail starring the great Jeanne Moreau as the adulterous wife in the middle of everything. French with English subtitles.
VHS: S14655. $29.95.
Edouard Molinaro, France, 1958, 94 mins.

Battle of Austerlitz
An epic production with an international cast (Claudia Cardinale, Orson Welles, Vittorio de Sica, Jean-Louis Trintignant) as Abel Gance, the director of *Napoleon*, returns to his character for the most important battle of his career—*The Battle of Austerlitz*. French dialog with English subtitles.
VHS: S00101. $24.95.
Abel Gance, France, 1960, 180 mins.

Big Grab
Jean Gabin and Alain Delon star in this adventure story of two criminals planning the heist of a gambling casino. Also known as *Any Number Can Win*. French with English subtitles.
VHS: S01670. $24.95.
Henri Verneuil, France, 1963, 118 mins.

Bim, the Little Donkey and Dream of the Wild Horses
The first film by the director of *The Red Balloon*, *Bim* is a delightful story of a lovable donkey who is taken away from a small boy to become the pet of a very rich family. The boy's efforts to get his donkey back lead to all sorts of adventures. *Dream of the Wild Horses* is a landmark short film by Georges Franju.
VHS: S01691. $29.95.
Albert Lamorisse, France, 1948, 45 mins.

Blood and Roses
Roger Vadim's Italian-made adaptation of Sheridan Le Fanu's *Carmilla*, is a kinky thriller about a young woman's obsession with her family's perverse association with vampires. The source material was later remade as *The Vampire Lovers* and *The Blood-Spattered Bride*. With Mel Ferrer, Elsa Martinelli, Annette Vadim and Marc Allegret.
VHS: S16886. $19.95.
Roger Vadim, Italy, 1961, 74 mins.

Blood of the Beasts (Le Sang des Betes)
Contrasting peaceful views of a Parisian suburb with unflinching scenes from a slaughterhouse, this film is a masterpiece that impacted documentary film practice worldwide. Disturbing in its honesty, it challenges a number of banal conceptions seemingly integral to everyday life. French with English subtitles.
VHS: S24076. $14.95.
Georges Franju, France, 1949, 22 mins.

Bomb for a Dictator
Pierre Fresnay stars in this tense tale about an assassination plot. A fanatical terrorist plots the murder of a South American dictator. His plan involves the bombing of an airliner.
VHS: S23797. $24.95.
Alex Joff, France, 1957, 71 mins.

Bride Is Much Too Beautiful
A very early Bardot vehicle—Brigitte Bardot plays the cover girl who is publicized into a fake romance, but she really loves a photographer. With Micheline Presle, Louis Jourdan. English dubbed.
VHS: S05294. $39.95.
Fred Surin, France, 1957, 90 mins.

The Burning Court
A strange film that deals with a number of weird subjects, including occultism, possession, family curses, etc. An unusual and very interesting foreign horror opus, dubbed in English. With Jean-Claude Brialy.
VHS: S15687. $29.95.
Julien Duvivier, France/Italy/Germany, 1961, 113 mins.

Candide
An updated version of Voltaire's classic novella. A modern Candide questioning nothing, and blithely assuming that everything happens for the best in this best of all possible worlds. Starring Jean-Pierre Cassel, Pierre Brasseur and Dahlia Lavi. Dubbed in English.
VHS: S14632. $29.95.
Norbert Carbonnaux, France, 1960, 90 mins.

Carnival in Flanders
In 1616, in a small town in Spanish-occupied Flanders, the city fathers find out that a detachment of Spaniards is arriving and the men leave town. The women, however, join together to seduce and entertain the soldiers. With a script by Charles Spaak and magnificent sets by Lazare Meerson, *Carnival in Flanders* is not only an enjoyable farce, but a rare example of the work of Feyder, a key filmmaker. French with English subtitles.
VHS: S00215. $29.95.
Jacques Feyder, France, 1935, 95 mins.

Casque d'Or
One of the truly great French films: Jacques Becker's "elegant masterwork is a glowingly nostalgic evocation of the Paris of the Impressionists." Serge Reggiani plays a carpenter who is drawn into the underworld of pimps and thieves and eventually driven to murder because of his great love for Marie, a gangster's moll, in a glowing performance from Simone Signoret. Signoret brings a remarkable sensuality to her role in a film that is filled with sun, open air—a kind of transcendence. French with English subtitles.
VHS: S26579. $29.95.
Jacques Becker, France, 1952, 96 mins.

Charterhouse at Parma
Stendahl's novel of the same name about a young Archbishop in love is adapted for the screen in this film featuring actor Gerard Philipe. When he wishes to break his vows, an ambitious aunt intervenes to insure his continued progress at the Italian court. French with English subtitles.
VHS: S20773. $59.95.

Classic Foreign Shorts—Volume 3: Un Chant d'Amour, Romance Sentimentale
Un Chant d'Amour is Jean Genet's only film, a legendary and long suppressed film masterpiece. "A song of man's love soaring above the sexual ghetto of prison and non-existence" (*Cahiers du Cinema*). 20 mins. *Romance Sentimentale* is usually attributed to Sergei Eisenstein, and although Eisenstein worked on it, it was probably directed by Grigori Alexandrov. Photographed by Tisse and financed by its only player—a wealthy woman who wanted to appear in an Eisenstein film—*Romance Sentimentale* was filmed in Paris during the winter of 1929-30. The film is a somber experimental poem portraying the emotions aroused in a woman (Mara Gitry) by the realization that love is dead. 20 mins.
VHS: S26947. $29.95.

Club des Femmes
Entertaining yet powerful film about the personal life of women who work in a Parisian nightclub, with Danielle Darrieux and Elsa Argal. The *New York Times* identified the film's message as: "Women of the world unite against men's tyranny and chauvinism." French with English subtitles.
VHS: S00254. $29.95.
Jacques Deval, France, 1936, 90 mins.

Colette: Of the Goncourt Academy
A filmed reading and dramatization starring the famed French author and her work, *La Chevre de Monsieur Seguin*. French with English subtitles.
VHS: S02579. $34.95.
Yannick Bellon, France, 1951, 30 mins.

Crainquebille
A great satire based on the classic story by Anatole France, the story of a Parisian street merchant, directed by the legendary Jacques Feyder (*Carnival in Flanders*), and starring Maurice Feraudy. Silent.
VHS: S03170. $17.95.
Jacques Feyder, France, 1923, 50 mins.

Crazy for Love
Brigitte Bardot's first film made for one of France's most prolific directors, Jean Boyer, who turned out over 70 films during his career. It's a comedy about the inheritance of a farm in Normandy. Bourvil co-stars. French with English subtitles.
VHS: S02161. $29.95.
Jean Boyer, France, 1952, 100 mins.

Crime and Punishment
Two of the greatest actors, Harry Baur and Pierre Blanchar, and the master of French poetic realism, Pierre Chenal, join in this masterful adaptation of one of the great works of literature. Hailed worldwide as one of the most imaginative adaptations of Dostoevsky's complex, brooding novel, "Chenal's studio-bound stylization and direction created a feverish climate of airless oppression and suspense. And Blanchar's cat-and-mouse confrontation with the magnificent Harry Baur, as the wily magistrate Porfiry, is one of the great acting setpieces of the French screen" (National Film Theatre). French with English subtitles.
VHS: S09197. $59.95.
Pierre Chenal, France, 1935, 110 mins.

The Crucible
Arthur Miller's dramatic masterpiece; the screenplay and dialogue were written by Jean-Paul Sartre and this French film stars Simone Signoret, Yves Montand and Mylene Demongeot. Set in Salem, Massachusetts, in 1692, the film dramatizes the persecution of witches and serves as a powerful allegory for the anti-communist hysteria of America in the 1950s. French with English subtitles.
VHS: S23571. $39.95.
Raymond Rouleau, France, 1957, 108 mins.

The Days of Our Years
Jean Cocteau, Marcel Achard, Andre Roussin, Georges Auric and Pierre Fresnay contributed to this documentary about the first 50 years of the 20th century. Air and sea exploration, the opening of King Tut's tomb and the first rocket launch are included alongside footage of artists and scientists like Sarah Bernhardt, Renoir, Pablo Picasso, Shaw, Auguste Rodin, Jean-Paul Sartre and Henri Matisse. English narration.
VHS: S22465. $29.95.

Dedee d'Anvers
Simone Signoret plays a popular Antwerp barfly who is being tormented by her brutal bouncer boyfriend (Dalio). A kindly sea captain offers to make life much easier for Dedee but he is killed by the bouncer. It is up to the owner of the bar, Bernard Blier, to help the barfly gain her freedom. French with English subtitles.
VHS: S03751. $29.95.
Yves Allegret, France, 1949, 95 mins.

Devil in the Flesh
The account of a clandestine love affair between an adolescent schoolboy and the discontented wife of a soldier during World War1, from the novel by Raymond Radiguet. "It has the beauty and despair of lovers attempting to save something for themselves in a period of hopeless confusion" (Pauline Kael). English dubbed.
VHS: S03749. $34.95.
Claude Autant-Lara, France, 1947, 112 mins.

Diabolically Yours
Poor Alain Delon has lost his memory. But Senta Berger, who claims to be his wife, says everything will be fine once he is out of the hospital and back at his estate. An intricate thriller involving unnatural accidents, murder plots and a lusting Chinese servant. With Sergio Fantoni and Peter Mosbacher as Kim. The last film of Julien Duvivier (*Tales of Manhattan, Flesh and Fantasy*). In English.
VHS: S09316. $29.95.
Julien Duvivier, France, 1968, 90 mins.

Double Agents
A fascinating tale of espionage, mystery and intrigue, set during the Second World War. German spies stationed in England send a woman to France, her mission to deliver British coastal defense secrets to a Nazi lieutenant. Spellbinding. With Marina Vlady and Robert Hossein. Dubbed in English.
VHS: S04366. $29.95.
Robert Hossein, France-Italy, 1959

Duke of the Derby
Veteran actor Jean Gabin stars as a racetrack handicapper used to a lifestyle in excess of his income, which he derives from his daily betting at the track. French with English subtitles.
VHS: S01669. $29.95.
Gilles Grangier, France, 1962, 83 mins.

End of the World
Astronomer Victor Francen announces to the world the arrival of a comet which will strike and destroy the earth in 30 days in this rarest of all finds, Abel Gance's lost science fiction epic *La Fin du Monde*. Unfortunately the original film, running 105 minutes, has been cut to 54 minutes by the U.S. distributor and a silly prologue has been added. But Gance's ending montage of distortion and destruction of the world is nothing short of dazzling. French with English subtitles.
VHS: S23036. $19.98.
Abel Gance, France, 1930, 54 mins.

Eternal Return
Jean Delannoy's modernized version of the legend of Tristan and Isolde. An enormous commercial success during the worst days of the German occupation of France, the film is based on a script by Jean Cocteau, and is the tragic love story of two friends, Patrice and his Uncle Marc, who share a deep friendship. When Patrice falls in love with Marc's wife Nathalie, the loyalty he feels for his uncle prevents him from telling her of his love, only to find that she returns it. French with English subtitles.
VHS: S04914. $29.95.
Jean Delannoy, France, 1943, 100 mins.

The Fabulous Versailles (Royal Affairs in Versailles)
Shot on location, this stunning recreation of the inhabitants and visitors of Versailles features Orson Welles, Claudette Colbert, Edith Piaf, Sacha Guitry and Jean Marais. Three hundred years of the French monarchy comes to life with such figures as Mme. de Pompadour, Ben Franklin (Welles), Louis XIV (Guitry) and many more. Welles also narrates. Dubbed in English.
VHS: S24011. $14.95.
Sacha Guitry, France, 1954, 103 mins.

Forbidden Games
Rene Clement's beautiful allegory is the story of two children orphaned by the war who build a secret cemetery for animals and steal crosses from the church yard to mark the graves. Wonderfully natural performances from Georges Pojouly, whom Clement discovered in a camp, and Brigitte Fossey create a moving film about the effects of war on children. Winner at the Venice Film Festival and Best Foreign Film Oscar. French with English subtitles.
VHS: S00457. $29.95.
Laser: LD70988. $39.95.
Rene Clement, France, 1952, 90 mins.

Four Bags Full
A serio-comic gem about morality set in wartime Germany. Jean Gabin plays a scoundrel who has to help a compatriot carry a slaughtered pig from a butcher to the Black market under the watchful eyes of the Nazis and the hindrances of their countrymen. With great performances from Gabin, Louis de Funes and Bourvil. French with English subtitles.
VHS: S04843. $29.95.
Claude Autant-Lara, France, 1956, 82 mins.

French Way
Josephine Baker stars in this rare wartime musical comedy. Baker plays Cupid to a would-be Romeo and Juliet while trying to re-open her nightclub. Five extraordinary songs by Baker. French with English subtitles. France, 1940.
VHS: S01627. $34.95.

Gervaise
A perfect example of a polished adaptation of a novel, this one, *L'Assommoir* by Emile Zola. Gervaise is a young woman whose husband becomes an alcoholic after an accident. Notable for a marvelous reconstruction of 19th century Paris. French with English subtitles.
VHS: S00493. $24.95.
Rene Clement, France, 1957, 116 mins.

Grand Melies (Franju) and Melies' Short Films
Famous, stylish docudrama directed by Georges Franju on the life of the pioneering "Magician of the Cinema." With special insights into his early career, how he achieved his spectacular effects and his sad final demise. Featuring Melies' wife (Madame Georges Melies) and son (Andre Melies). Following this rare film we are pleased to present quality recordings of Melies' most famous shorts, including: *The Trip to the Moon, Paris to Monte Carlo, Extraordinary Illusions, The Enchanted Well, The Conquest of the Pole,* and *The Apparition*. English narration. 70 mins.
VHS: S13507. $39.95.

Grisbi (Hands Off the Loot)
Jean Gabin stars in this unorthodox tale as the King of the Parisian underworld. When a gold heist goes bad, the loot is suddenly missing, and there will be no honor among these thieves. The legendary Jeanne Moreau joins Gabin in this thriller/drama. Dubbed.
VHS: S21603. $24.95.
Jacques Becker, France, 1953, 94 mins.

Head Against the Wall
Jean-Pierre Mocky stars as a wild young man in love with Anouk Aimee, who is declared insane and spends time in mental institutions until he escapes and returns to Aimee. A work of strange beauty and power, the first feature by Franju. French with English subtitles.
VHS: S03747. $34.95.
Georges Franju, France, 1958, 98 mins.

Head over Heels
Brigitte Bardot stars as a woman, bored with her marriage, who resumes her career as a model. While on assignment in London she meets a man and is flattered by his attention. Also known as *Two Weeks in September*. From the director of *Sundays and Cybele*. French with English subtitles.
VHS: S01667. $19.95.
Serge Bourguignon, France, 1967, 89 mins.

Is Paris Burning?
The gripping heroism of the Allied Resistance during the Paris liberation of 1944 is depicted in this multi-storied war epic scripted by Francis Ford Coppola and Gore Vidal. The illustrious international cast includes: Jean-Paul Belmondo, Kirk Douglas, Yves Montand, and Orson Welles.
VHS: S13707. $29.95.
Rene Clement, France/USA, 1968, 173 mins.

J'Accuse
One of the great films by Abel Gance (*Napoleon*) and a powerful statement against war. A strange man, obsessed with the horrors of war, calls upon the millions of dead soldiers from World War I to rise from their graves and march upon the cities of the world. With Victor Francen, Jean Max. French with English subtitles.
VHS: S12329. $29.95.
Abel Gance, France, 1938, 127 mins.

Jailbird's Vacation
Lino Ventura stars in this story of two ex-cons who takes jobs as lumberjacks in an isolated sawmill in order to extract revenge. French with English subtitles.
VHS: S02799. $19.95.
Robert Enrico, France, 1965, 125 mins.

Joy House
Rene Clement directed this feature which stars Alain Delon as a playboy on the run who lives by his looks, who seeks refuge in a French mansion run by two American women. Original title: *Love Cage.* Jane Fonda and Lola Albright also star. English language.
VHS: S06598. $39.95.
Rene Clement, France, 1964, 98 mins.

Judex
Franju's homage to early crime serials of Feuilliade. The story is set in 1914 at the castle of a wealthy banker whose many wrongs Judex intends to redress, aided by Cocantin and the Liquorice Kid. In the meantime, the banker's daughter is falling in love with the supersleuth. French with English subtitles.
VHS: S00661. $29.95.
Georges Franju, France, 1963, 103 mins.

Just Another Pretty Face
One of the last appearances of Henri Vidal, the handsome, athletic, leading man in many French films. Vidal plays a detective who solves a jewel smuggling case, and falls in love with a young woman who was involved with the smugglers. French with English subtitles.
VHS: S01675. $19.95.
Marc Allegret, France, 1958, 110 mins.

Juve Contre Fantomas
Made in 1913-14, these short films pitting detective Juve against the criminal master of disguise, Fantomas, were very influential in the Surrealist movement. Silent.
VHS: S00667. $29.95.
Louis Feuillade, France, 1913;+x14, 64 mins.

Killing Game
Jean-Pierre Cassel, Claudine Auger and Michel Duchaussoy star in this early film by Alain Jessua. Cassel and Auger are cartoonists who meet a wealthy playboy who lives out his fantasies through cartoons and hires them to create a comic strip. As they do, he begins to live the comic strip out—but unfortunately, it involves murder.
VHS: S06333. $39.95.
Alain Jessua, France, 1967, 90 mins.

Kiss for a Killer
At the center of this film is a beautiful woman played by Mylene Demongeot, who is destined to drive men mad. She may look innocent but this appearance only makes her true passion—cold-blooded murder—more achievable. It's a thriller based on the best-selling novel, that also stars Henri Vidal and Isa Miranda. Dubbed in English.
VHS: S21604. $24.95.

L'Ecole Buissoniere
A simple account of how a village school teacher with "modern" ideas inspires his charges with a passion for knowledge that eventually spreads to their aroused, suspicious parents. The drama unfolds in the classroom of a provincial school where the gradual expansion of a reluctant child's mind is depicted as tangibly and beautifully as the opening of a flower. A vision of hard-core realism that conveys the importance of children in the community. French with English subtitles.
VHS: S16118. $29.95.
Jean-Paul Le Chanois, France, 1951, 84 mins.

L'Etrange Monsieur Victor
Raimu, Pierre Blanchar and Madeleine Renaud are among the brilliant performers cast in this intriguing drama. The title character is brave and beloved by all. But these admirable qualities do not prevent him from allowing an innocent man to be jailed in his place. When this poor man escapes he is determined that the truth be known. French with English subtitles.
VHS: S25105. $59.95.
Jean Gremillon, France, 1937, 113 mins.

L'Idiot
A great French adaptation of Dostoevsky's novel, with the saintly Prince Mishkin played sensitively by Gerard Philipe and Nastassia by Edwige Feuillere. The first feature from Georges Lampin, a former assistant to Rene Clair. French with English subtitles.
VHS: S26578. $29.95.
Georges Lampin, France, 1946, 98 mins.

La Belle Americaine
Robert Dhry directed and stars in this 60's French comedy adventure about a young working man who happens to have a very expensive car. Comic Louis de Funes lends a first-rate turn as the police station chief. Dubbed in English. Also known by the English-language title *What a Chassis!.*
VHS: S26063. $29.95.
Robert Dhry, France, 1961, 97 mins.

La Chute de la Maison Usher
Though directed by Jean Epstein, this French silent version of the Poe classic is also notable for having given apprenticeship to Luis Bunuel. Henri Langlois of the Cinematheque Francaise wrote, "An absolute mastery of editing and rhythm in which slow motion, super-impressions, moving camera shots, and the mobile camera combine to play a totally ungratuitous role. The lighting of the sets transforms them and imparts a sense of mystery. The actors were merely objects."
VHS: S06223. $59.95.
Jean Epstein, France, 1928

La Maternelle
A compassionate tale of the sad-faced, squalid children of the Paris slums who find daily sanctuary from the ugliness and terror of their home lives at "La Maternelle." The story of a gangly waif named Marie, the film captures the anguish among the spattered flowers of Montmartre. French with English subtitles.
VHS: S16117. $29.95.
Jean Benoit-Levy/Marie Epstein, France, 1933, 83 mins.

Lady Chatterley's Lover
Marc Allegret's version of the D.H. Lawrence novel with Danielle Darrieux as the Lady. Although the film was banned for a number of years by the New York Board of Censors, it is now almost too tasteful in its depiction of Lady Chatterley's sexual awakening. Darrieux delivers a performance of great complexity. French with English subtitles.
VHS: S18172. $24.95.
Marc Allegret, France, 1955, 102 mins.

Lafayette
Michel Le Boyer stars with an all-star international cast, including Orson Welles and Vittorio De Sica, in this biographical film. The great noble Frenchman assisted in the American Revolution and became an outspoken defender of freedom and liberty. He aided the ragged but determined armed forces marshalled by Washington. The relationship between Lafayette and his wife is given special attention in this costume spectacular. Dubbed in English.
VHS: S23991. $24.95.
Jean Dreville, France/Italy, 1963, 84 mins.

The Last Adventure
Alain Delon stars in this story of two friends who are fooled by an insurance scam that almost costs them their lives. When they find the man responsible he tells them about a secret treasure aboard a crashed plane somewhere on the coast of Africa, but their search for riches has unexpected results. French with English subtitles.
VHS: S20771. $59.95.
Robert Enrico, France, 1966, 102 mins.

Le Bourgeois Gentilhomme
Moliere's *Le Bourgeois Gentilhomme,* presented by the Comedie Francaise in the tradition of Commedia Dell'Arte. Music by Jean Baptiste Lully, a contemporary of Moliere's. Lavish costumes, ballets and dances. French with English subtitles.
VHS: S00735. $29.95.
Jean Meyer, France, 1958, 97 mins.

Le Cas du Dr. Laurent
(*The Case of Dr. Laurent*). Jean Gabin delivers a stirring performance as a country doctor who is a dedicated man with an abundance of compassion for his patients in this superb example of the "French cinema of quality."
VHS: S05326. $29.95.
Jean-Paul Le Chanois, France, 1957, 92 mins.

Le Gendarme de St. Tropez
This is the first of a highly popular series featuring the comic antics of gendarme Ludovic Cruchot. His ambitions are at odds with the laid-back atmosphere of the resort St. Tropez, and his hopes are finally dashed when his daughter has just a little too much fun on the beach. French with English subtitles.
VHS: S20770. $59.95.
Jean Girault, France, 1965, 95 mins.

Le Golem: The Legend of Prague
The first sound version of the Jewish folk legend of the rabbi who brings the Golem back to life in order to frighten the emperor was shot on location in Prague and features a first-rate performance from Harry Baur as the Emperor, along with Roger Karl and Charles Dorat. French with English subtitles.
VHS: S14690. $79.95.
Julien Duvivier, France, 1935, 96 mins.

Le Grand Melies: The Great Melies, Father of Fiction Films
This amazing documentary, by Georges Franju, traces the life and artistic innovation of an early film great. Melies saw the transformative power latent in the new possibilities offered by the motion picture. Andre Melies portrays his father George in this highly regarded tribute to the French innovator. French with English subtitles, 25 mins.
VHS: S22512. $39.95.
Georges Franju, France, 1936, 25 mins.

Les Abysses
Based on the actual 1933 French murder case which inspired Jean Genet to write *The Maids, Les Abysses* is an electrifying study of avarice, despair and violence. "The cinema has given us its foremost tragedy" (Jean-Paul Sartre). French with English subtitles.
VHS: S14640. $29.95.
Nico Papatakis, France, 1963, 90 mins.

Les Liaisons Dangereuses
The first—and certainly the best—version of Laclos' novel, with the incredible Gerard Philipe playing Valmont, and Jeanne Moreau, Madame de Merteuil. Directed by Roger Vadim and updated to 1960, Vadim's exploration of free-thinking attitudes and portrait of the corrupt upper-class society is particularly distinguished through the outstanding performances of both Philipe and Moreau. With Jean-Louis Trintignant, Annette Vadim; music by, among others, Thelonious Monk. French with English subtitles.
VHS: S10740. $59.95.
Roger Vadim, France, 1959, 106 mins.

Les Miserables
This faithful adaptation of Victor Hugo's great novel stars Jean Gabin as the escaped convict Jean Valjean, who is pursued by the relentless Police Inspector Javert. A great cast; Gabin, in particular, is superb. With Bernard Blier, Bourvil, Serge Reggiani and Daniele Delorme. English dubbed.
Part I.
VHS: S02573. $29.95.
Part II.
VHS: S02574. $29.95.
Jean-Paul Le Chanois, France, 1957, 210 mins.

The Liars
In this unpretentious, low-keyed mystery a Frenchman, after making his fortune in Africa, returns to Paris, advertises for a wife and is almost taken in (and murdered) by two con artists. Starring Dawn Addams and Jean Servais. French with English subtitles.
VHS: S14641. $29.95.
Edmond T. Greville, France, 1964, 92 mins.

Life Upside Down
This Winner of the Best First Film Award at the Venice Film Festival tells the story of a successful real estate developer (Charles Denner) who withdraws from his perfect life. Between his flighty wife and a round of meaningless events his growing detachment may seem insane at first, but it could also be the only sensible solution. French with English subtitles.
VHS: S20878. $79.95.
Alain Jessua, France, 1965, 115 mins.

Little World of Don Camillo
A priest in a northern Italian town has trouble staying out of mischief in this all-time classic. When the communists are elected to power in the town, he tangles with the mayor of the little hamlet, who is a flag-waving party man. With Fernandel, Gino Cervi. Dubbed in English.
VHS: S13354. $29.95.
Julien Duvivier, France, 1951, 106 mins.

Love of Three Queens
Hedy Lamarr, the voluptuous star of *Ecstasy,* plays an actress who portrays three of the most fascinating women in history. Lamarr is Guenevieve, a saintly countess who tries desperately to save her kingdom; Empress Josephine; and Helen of Troy, the woman whose beauty launched a thousand ships. Massimo Serato is the wealthy nobleman who is hopelessly in love with Lamarr in this stirring drama of passion and pleasure.
VHS: S13667. $29.95.
Marc Allegret, USA, 1954, 80 mins.

Mademoiselle Striptease
Brigitte Bardot stars in this film by Marc Allegret, originally titled *Please! Mr Balzac,* the story of a girl who gets caught up in the theft of rare books, and her subsequent attempts to get herself untangled from the web. The young Brigitte Bardot (the film was made the same year as *And God Created Woman*) is particularly engaging. French with English subtitles.
VHS: S06852. $29.95.
Marc Allegret, France, 1957, 99 mins.

Man from Nowhere
A witty and stylish film by Pierre Chenal, and one of the high points of classic French comedy, *The Man from Nowhere* is based on Luigi Pirandello's novel, *The Late Mathias Pascal.* Pierre Blanchar is the henpecked husband who unexpectedly gets a chance to start a new life. A colorful supporting cast, pungent dialog and Chenal's ironic direction combine in a film which mixes melodrama with satire. "A sparkling comic melodrama. Rich characters, luscious turn-of-the-century landscapes and delightful performances are aided by a screenplay which snaps with one witticism after another" (*Detroit News*). French with English subtitles.
VHS: S09198. $59.95.
Pierre Chenal, France, 1937, 98 mins.

Man in the Silk Hat
A moving tribute to the famous french actor of the silent era, Max Linder, whom Chaplin once called "my professor," directed by his daughter. During his lifetime, Linder made some 400-500 short comedies, and came to America to make his only three feature-length films. With numerous excerpts from Linder's films, this is a loving tribute to one of the giants of comedy. Narrated in English by Maud Linder.
VHS: S04870. $24.95.
Maud Linder, France, 1984, 96 mins.

Maria Chapdelaine
The film from which Jean Gabin rose to prominence, from the director of *Pepe Le Moko* and *Poil de Carotte.* One of Duvivier's first great films, which earned him a reputation for his "poetic realism." French with English subtitles.
VHS: S00824. $29.95.
Julien Duvivier, France, 1934, 75 mins.

Marvelous Melies
A collection of great films by the great pioneer magician of the cinema, Georges Melies: *A Trip to the Moon, Paris to Monte Carlo, The Doctor's Secret, Kingdom of the Fairies, The Enchanted Well* and *Conquest of the North Pole.*
VHS: S05789. $29.95.
George Melies, France, 1960, 60 mins.

Max Linder
By 1910 Max Linder was an internationally popular comic, typically playing a dapper dandy of the idle rich. He developed a slapstick style that anticipated Mack Sennett and Chaplin. His popularity was at its peak in 1914, when he was called up for World War I. With original French titles. Silent.
VHS: S00833. $29.95.
Max Linder, France, 1911-13

Mayerling
The romantic, sumptuous film that established Charles Boyer as a screen idol. Set in Vienna in 1883, Boyer plays the Archduke Rudolf, who is madly in love with Maria Vetsera, played by Danielle Darrieux. An opulent romance with a sharp portrait of the Hapsburg court. French with English subtitles.
VHS: S00837. $29.95.
Anatole Litvak, France, 1936, 91 mins.

Melies III: The Search for Munchhausen
A terrific compilation of trick film fantasies from Melies including *Baron Munchhausen's Dream, The Witch's Revenge, The Infernal Caldron, The Damnation of the Monster,* and *The Terrible Turkish Executioners.* 45 mins.
VHS: S14814. $29.95.

Menilmontant
An important film made by Dimitri Kirsanov in France, a silent film done without titles which "is not a melodrama but an antecedent to neo-realism, portraying life itself with a sensitive use of natural sets and a feeling for poetry and truth" (Georges Sadoul). In the film, a young girl is seduced by a young man who deserts her when she is pregnant. She contemplates suicide, meets her sister who's since become a prostitute, and is reconciled with her again.
VHS: S07466. $39.95.
Dimitri Kirsanov, France, 1926, 27 mins

Modigliani (Montparnasse 19)
Jacques Becker inherited this project from Max Ophuls, who co-wrote the screenplay but died before production started. The film is an examination of the art and dissolute life of the 19th-century French painter Modigliani (Gerard Philipe). The story tracks Modigliani's affairs with British poet Beatrice Hastings (Lilli Palmer) and Jeanne (Anouk Aimee), his mistress and model in the final years of his life. "A quiet masterpiece that ultimately soars to sublimity" (Andrew Sarris). With Gerard Sety, Lino Ventura, Lila Kedrova and Lea Padovani. French with English subtitles.
VHS: S19523. $59.95.
Jacques Becker, France, 1958, 110 mins.

Monkey in Winter
Jean-Paul Belmondo and Jean Gabin tear up the town in this story of a young man who returns to his home to marry the daughter of a crusty old alcoholic who runs the inn. French with English subtitles.
VHS: S01674. $19.95.
Henri Verneuil, France, 1962, 105 mins.

Monsieur Vincent
Winner of an Academy Award as Best Foreign Film, Pierre Fresnay gives the characterization of Vincent de Paul an extraordinarily human, emotional portrayal. Based on a scenario by Jean Anouilh, cinematography by Claude Renoir. French with English subtitles.
VHS: S00874. $29.95.
Maurice Cloche, France, 1947

Moore and Thill in Louise
Grace Moore and Georges Thill star in this adaptation of the Charpentier opera. Between domineering parents and her love, a seamstress finds her life severely hemmed in. Confounded, she throws everything aside and confronts the world. French language.
VHS: S25533. $39.95.
Abel Gance, France, 1938, 83 mins.

More Melies
A second companion volume to *Marvelous Melies,* this further compilation of pioneering primitives from Georges Melies includes *The Inn Where No Man Rests, Spiritualist Photographer, The Magic Lantern, Clockmaker's Dream, The Cook in Trouble, The Bob Kick* (a.k.a. *Mischievous Kid*), *The Oracle of Delphi, Drawing Lesson, Jupiter's Thunderbolt* and *The Mermaid.* B&W, 60 mins.
VHS: S08047. $29.95.

Nana
Charles Boyer and Martine Carol star in this color version of Emile Zola's famous novel about a girl from the slums who becomes a respectable lady and then sets out to humiliate the class which is responsible for her previous misery. French with English subtitles.
VHS: S00915. $34.95.
Christian Jacque, France, 1955, 120 mins.

Napoleon
A masterpiece of world cinema, employing a variety of new techniques, including triple screen and mobile use of the camera by strapping it to a galloping horse. Long thought to be lost, the film has been reconstructed and is presented with a sound track composed by Carmine Coppola.
VHS: S00917. $79.95.
Abel Gance, France, 1927, 235 mins.

Napoleon
Orson Welles, Maria Schell, Yves Montand, and Erich von Stroheim star in Sacha Guitry's classic biography of Napoleon, from his youth as a soldier in the French Army until his exile to the Island of Elba. A monumental production with a cast of thousands, originally shot in Technicolor. English dialog.
VHS: S00918. $59.95.
Laser: LD70061. $89.98.
Sacha Guitry, France, 1955, 115 mins.

The Necklace
Based on the story by Guy de Maupassant. Mathilde Loisel is married to a decent but minor government official. Dreams of a better life are put on hold when she loses a necklace, forcing her into menial work to replace it. Only years later is the shocking meaning behind this necklace revealed. In English. 21 mins.
VHS: S22366. $79.95.

An Occurrence at Owl Creek Bridge
Award winning short film based on a story by Ambrose Bierce about the final moments of a man about to be hung for sabotage during the Civil War. Highly recommended.
VHS: S02247. $19.95.
Robert Enrico, France, 1962, 29 mins.

Panique

A major film by one of the most underrated of early French directors, *Panique* is the story of a vicious young crook who robs and murders an elderly woman in a fairground and then conspires with his girlfriend to put the blame for the crime on a bearded recluse, played by the great actor Michel Piccoli. Based on the novel by Charles Simenon, with a script by one of the great French screenwriters, Charles Spaak, *Panique* ends with a harrowing climax in which Simon is hounded to death by an angry mob. French with English subtitles.
VHS: S07099. $29.95.
Julien Duvivier, France, 1946, 87 mins.

Pantaloons (Don Juan)

French comedian Fernandel is mistaken for Don Juan when he is just the servant of the great lover. Didn't Bob Hope make this movie as the servant of Casanova? The Gallic horse-faced farceur makes a convincing swashbuckler much to the rage of Fernando Rey, as a villainous nobleman. Dubbed in English.
VHS: S05439. $29.95.
John Berry, France, 1956, 95 mins.

Paris 1900

Documentary about life in Paris between 1900 and 1914, largely composed of stills from the Cinematheque Francaise. English narration by Monty Woolley. Alain Resnais worked as assistant production supervisor on the film. French songs sung by Claude Dauphin.
VHS: S02578. $29.95.
Nicole Vedres, France, 1948, 50 mins.

Passion for Life

One of the best films by Jean-Paul Le Chanois, and one of the best performances by Bernard Blier; Blier plays a progressive teacher who introduces new teaching methods into a provincial village school, comes into conflict with the traditional parents, but ends up by winning his fight. With Juliette Faber, Edouard Delmont, music by Joseph Kosma. French with English subtitles.
VHS: S06437. $69.95.
Jean-Paul Le Chanois, France, 1948, 89 mins.

Pathe Freres Vol. 1

A collection of early film fantasies from Pathe Freres, including: *The Red Spectre* (hand colored), the imitation of Melies *Trip to the Moon*; *El Buen Cigario* (attributed by some to Max Linder); *Fantasia Florido, Album Marvilloso, La Ruche Mereilleurs.* 60 mins.
VHS: S05790. $29.95.

Pathe Freres Vol. 2

Ten short films from Pathe Freres, including *The Enchanted House, Pixillation, Posada Mysteriosa, The Invisible Thief, The Yawner, The Poor Coat, Wiffels Wins a Beauty Prize, I Fetch the Bread,* and Zecca's classic *Down in the Deep.* 60 mins.
VHS: S05791. $29.95.

Pattes Blanches (White Paws)

Paul Bernard and Suzy Delair star in this 1949 melodrama, directed by Jean Gremillon, about a reclusive aristocrat ridiculed in the provincial French fishing town where he lives, because of the gaudy white spats he is always so fond of wearing. Adapted from a play by Jean Anouilh. "If Emily Bronte had written *The Postman Always Rings Twice*, the result would be the hard-boiled, Gothic *Pattes Blanches*, an extraordinary French film" (Carrie Rickey, *Philadelphia Inquirer*). French with English subtitles.
VHS: S14987. $59.95.
Jean Gremillon, France, 1987, 92 mins.

The Pearls of the Crown

A groundbreaking film with a sharp, satirical underpinning directed by Sacha Guitry and Christian Jacque has Guitry performing four separate roles, stretched out over four centuries, each character feverishly in pursuit of the four pear-shaped pearls aligning the English royal crown. "It is an amazing and weirdly fascinating condensation of fact and fiction" (*Stage*). With Jacqueline Delubac, Lyn Harding and Jean Louis Barrault. English, French and Italian with English subtitles.
VHS: S17488. $59.95.
Sacha Guitry/Christian Jacque, France/Italy, 1937, 121 mins.

Pepe le Moko

A gem of French cinema with an unbelievable performance by Jean Gabin as Pepe le Moko, a Parisian gangster hiding out in the Algerian Casbah. A menacing atmosphere full of shadows contributes to the image of Pepe as the outsider/hero who falls in love with a Parisian woman, tries to escape with her and finds his path blocked by the police. The spine-tingling ending is classic. With Mireille Balin and Line Noro. French with English subtitles.
VHS: S01007. $29.95.
Julien Duvivier, France, 1936, 95 mins.

Phaedra

Anthony Perkins and Melina Mercouri star in this contemporary remake of Euripides' *Hippolytus*, the ancient Greek play about incest between a mother and her stepson. Dubbed in English.
VHS: S20578. $29.95.
Jules Dassin, USA/Greece, 1961, 116 mins.

Phedre

"To see Marie Bell in *Phedre* is a unique opportunity to experience fully what is French genius," said Andre Malraux. This film adaptation of Racine's great tragedy stars Bell when she was a remarkably well-preserved 68 years old—but a great actress in a great French classic. French with English subtitles.
VHS: S01022. $29.95.
Pierre Jourdan, France, 1968, 92 mins.

Pilgrimage to Rome

Jean Gabin, one of France's most beloved film actors, stars as an unrepentant gangster who upon release from jail sets off, disguised as a priest, to recover his hidden loot in Rome. International terrorists hijack his plane causing a small detour on this pilgrimage to the object of his veneration. French with English subtitles.
VHS: S20772. $59.95.
Jean Girault, France, 1976, 90 mins.

Poil de Carotte

Duvivier's poignant story about "Carrot Top," an unloved young boy mistreated by his mother. Carrot Top's often-absent father remains unaware but the family faces a crisis when the boy tries suicide. A moving, sensitive film with great performances by Robert Lynen, Harry Baur and Catherine Fonteney. French with English subtitles.
VHS: S01043. $29.95.
Julien Duvivier, France, 1931, 90 mins.

Princess Tam Tam

Perhaps the best of her six features, Josephine Baker stars in this exotic Pygmalion-like musical comedy about a French author who goes to North Africa to write a novel, but becomes distracted—then entranced—by a native girl whom he transforms into a "princess." Shot partly on location in Tunisia, *Princess Tam Tam* allows Josephine a chance to display her impish, comedic charm, as well as her erotic and evocative talents. "Josephine Baker…the one and only…astonishing," wrote *The New York Post*. French with English subtitles.
VHS: S10867. $29.95.
Edmond T. Greville, France, 1935, 77 mins.

Prix de Beaute

Louise Brooks' last starring role in a feature, and her only film made in France, is a tragic drama about a young typist who wins an international beauty contest unknown to her jealous fiance. The film, wrote Andrew Sarris in *The Village Voice* "confirms once more that Louise Brooks was one of the most enduringly fascinating women ever to appear in front of the camera." French with English subtitles.
VHS: S10395. $59.95.
Augusto Genina, France/Italy, 1930, 93 mins.

The Proud Ones (Les Orgueilleux)

Highly suggestive of Albert Camus' *The Plague*, Yves Allegret's grim adaptation of Sartre's novel *L'Amour Redempteur* was virtually unknown in this country until Martin Scorsese "discovered" the work, and organized its re-release. Michele Morgan plays an aristocratic French woman traveling through Mexico whose husband dies from a mysterious disease. Stranded in a decaying Mexican coastal town, Morgan falls for a local doctor (Gerard Philipe) who is distraught over his wife's death. With Carlos Moctezuma, Victor Mendoza and Michele Cardone. French with English subtitles.
VHS: S19518. $59.95.
Yves Allegret, France, 1953, 105 mins.

Red Balloon

A classic childhood fantasy with appeal for viewers of every age. This is a story of Pascal, a French boy who befriends a red balloon which follows him everywhere. A touching allegory of the magic powers of love and friendship. No dialog.
VHS: S01098. $14.95.
Albert Lamorisse, France, 1956, 34 mins.

Red Balloon/White Mane

Albert Lamorisse's *Red Balloon* is a priceless classic about a young boy's friendship with a red balloon. 1956, 38 mins. His *White Mane* explores man's relationship to nature; it chronicles the efforts of bandits to capture a wild white stallion, and a young boy who rescues him. Winner of the International Grand Prize, Best Short Film, Cannes Film Festival. 1952, 38 mins.
VHS: S18762. $24.95.
Laser: LD70443. $29.95.

Respectful Prostitute

Jean Paul Sartre's famous existential play is adapted for the screen in an English-language version starring Barbara Laage, Ivan Desny and Walter Bryan. A sensitive and compelling look at racial prejudice in America's Deep South, the plot concerns a black man who is shot by a senator's nephew, and a prostitute who is talked into testifying that the murder was committed in defense of an assault.
VHS: S07458. $19.95.
Chas. Brabant/Marcel Pagliero, France, 75 min.

Rififi (Uncut)

Jules Dassin's classic tale, one of the most famous French gangster films ever made, is the story of a gangster who, when sprung from jail, finds his wife living with another man. He returns to his old racket, jewel thievery, and there follows an aftermath of murder, kidnapping and retribution. Steeped in the details of the sleazy Montmartre neighborhood, the film builds incredible suspense, and is particularly famous for its 30-minute, silent bank heist in which the audience is drawn in as participants. This is the complete, 117-minute version, which includes several scenes cut from the film because of sexual or violent content. French with English subtitles.
VHS: S15387. $24.95.
Jules Dassin, France, 1955, 117 mins.

Ruy Blas

Jean Marais plays two roles in Jean Cocteau's adaptation of the Victor Hugo novel. Danielle Darrieux portrays the Queen of Spain in this story of mistaken identity set in the court of Charles II. Revenge and love are the driving forces that set this court aflame with intrigues and romance. French with English subtitles.
VHS: S22034. $59.95.
Pierre Billon, France, 1948, 90 mins.

The Shameless Old Lady

The first feature of theatre designer and director Rene Allio, *The Shameless Old Lady* is an adaptation of Bertolt Brecht's story about a 70-year-old woman who, after 60 years of servitude as dutiful daughter, wife and mother, cuts loose, to the consternation of her stuffy offspring. Madame Bertini, impeccably played by the renowned actress Sylvie, becomes a veritable whirlwind of activity in the final 18 months of her life. French with English subtitles.
VHS: S08124. $39.95.
Rene Allio, France, 1966, 95 mins.

The Sorceress (1956)

A young French engineer is sent to Sweden to build a road. There he encounters an enchanting fairy nymph (Marina Vlady). In reality, she is just a country girl raised in isolation, but the townspeople ostracize her as a witch. These fears spell tragedy for the young love which grows between the Frenchman and the sorceress. French with English subtitles.
VHS: S26874. $69.95.
Andre Michel, France, 1956, 91 mins.

Stormy Waters (Remorques)

Jean Gabin stars as the tough captain of a rescue ship, who has an affair with a beautiful woman (Michele Morgan) he rescues during a fierce gale. Their romance is interrupted when Gabin's wife falls critically ill. English dubbed.
VHS: S01258. $29.95.
Jean Gremillon, France, 1939, 75 mins.

The Story of a Cheat

Sacha Guitry was a seminal influence in French films as an actor, author and producer of over 120 plays, and as a director, screenwriter and actor in 32 movies. Now American audiences can see his work in this classic film. It tells the story of an 11-year-old who discovers that honesty is the best policy. Putting this theory into practice leads to an enchanting tale. Guitry himself is featured. French with English subtitles.
VHS: S22480. $59.95.
Sacha Guitry, France, 1936, 83 mins

Sundays and Cybele

Winner of multiple awards including an Oscar, the moving, intelligently-told account of shell-shocked Hardy Kruger, who finds a source of communication with the outside world through his friendship with the orphaned girl Patricia Gozzi. French with English subtitles.
VHS: S01284. $59.95.
Serge Bourguignon, France, 1962, 110 mins.

Sylvia and the Phantom

An enchanting film that mixes comedy with pathos, the story of a sixteen year old-daughter who has fallen in love with the ghost of her grandmother's lover. The result of this whimsical love affair is a wonderful perspective on first love. French with English subtitles.
VHS: S03308. $24.95.
Claude Autant-Lara, France, 1950, 93 mins.

Tales of Paris

A collection of four short films about Parisian women, made by four talented French directors. Includes *The Tale of Ella*, by Jacques Poitrenaud; *The Tale of Antonia*, by Michel Boisrond; *The Tale of Francoise*, by Claude Barma; and *The Tale of Sophie*, starring Catherine Deneuve, co-written by Roger Vadim, directed by Marc Allegret. France, 1962, 85 mins.
VHS: S15191. $29.95.

Time Out for Love

Michele, beautiful and successful fashion executive, tries to commit suicide when she fears that her affair with Pierre, a race car driver, is on the wane. Things are further complicated when the 19-year-old American girl (played by Jean Seberg) trying to nurse her back to health gets in the middle of things by falling for Pierre herself. Photographed by Raoul Coutard. French with English subtitles.
VHS: S14651. $29.95.
Jean Valere, France, 1961, 93 mins.

Torture of Silence

Released in France as *Mater Dolorosa*, Gance made this picture again in 1932. A melodrama about a doctor who neglects his wife because of his work, and she seeks the company of his best friend. Silent with English subtitles.
VHS: S01364. $24.95.
Abel Gance, France, 1917, 55 mins.

Volpone

Harry Baur plays the raucous old Volpone, Louis Jouvet the shameless, swindling Mosca in this version of the Ben Johnson satire. This was Baur's last film. French with English subtitles.
VHS: S01420. $29.95.
Maurice Tourneur, France, 1939, 95 mins.

Voyage Surprise

A nonsense comedy about a slapstick chase across the beautiful landscape of Haute-Provence, with a script and directed by Pierre Prevert, this film stars Martine Carol and Sioel, in the story of a crazy old man who takes his tourists on a "mystery tour" that collides with a wedding, the police, a brothel, thieves and revolutionaries. French with English subtitles.
VHS: S06440. $79.95.
Pierre Prevert, France, 1946, 108 mins.

Walls of Malapaga

Jean Gabin is a man on the run for killing his mistress. Safely stowed away on a ship, a sudden toothache sends him searching for succor in Genoa. There he meets a lonely waitress with a young daughter. They fall in love, but in this simple tale of desperation and loneliness it may be too late for these sad figures. French with English subtitles.
VHS: S21607. $24.95.
Rene Clement, France/Italy, 1949, 91 mins.

Warrior's Rest

Brigitte Bardot portrays an innocent young woman led to heartbreak by an anarchist student she rescues from suicide and falls in love with. Also known by the title *Love on a Pillow*. French with English subtitles.
VHS: S01673. $19.95.
Roger Vadim, France, 1962, 98 mins.

Will You Dance with Me?

Brigitte Bardot goes undercover as a dance instructor in order to clear her husband of murder charges. With Henri Vidal in the final role of his career. French with English subtitles.
VHS: S01965. $19.95.
Michel Boisrond, France, 1959, 89 mins.

Zou Zou

Also featuring Jean Gabin, who was just on the brink of international success, *Zou Zou* is a Warners-style backstage musical in which a talented Cinderella (in this case a laundress played by Josephine Baker) takes the place of the lead on the opening night and saves the show. Clearly a star vehicle for Baker, she appears at her best here, as a glamorous, larger-than-life sophisticate. Watch for her spectacular rendition of "Haiti" that will remain indelible in everyone's memory. French with English subtitles.
VHS: S10866. $29.95.
Marc Allegret, France, 1934, 92 mins.

MARCEL CARNE

Bizarre Bizarre

A complicated mystery-farce about a group of Victorian Englishmen enmeshed in a web of disguises, lies, murders, romances and all-around intrigue. With a marvelous performance by Michel Simon, a collaboration between director Carne and screenwriter Prevert. French with English subtitles.
VHS: S00134. $29.95.
Marcel Carne, France, 1937, 90 mins.

Children of Paradise

Set in the 1840's, when pantomime and melodrama were at their height on Paris' famed theater street, the Boulevard du Crime, Marcel Carne's delicate yet elaborate portrait of the actors and thieves who made the Boulevard their home has all the passion, intelligence and authority of a truly great work of art. "The *Gone with the Wind* of art films" (Andrew Sarris).
VHS: S14499. $39.95.
Laser: CAV/CLV. Includes interview with Carne, treatment and photos. LD70124. $89.95.
Marcel Carne, France, 1943-45, 188 mins.

Daybreak (Le Jour Se Leve)

Jean Gabin in perhaps the finest role of his career as a factory worker barricaded against the police after a murder. Through a series of flashbacks he thinks over the events that led him to kill. French with English subtitles.
VHS: S00312. $59.95.
Marcel Carne, France, 1939, 87 mins.

Law Breakers

Jacques Brel stars as a judge assigned to investigate the death of a burglary suspect who dies while in police custody. French with English subtitles.
VHS: S01666. $19.95.
Marcel Carne, France, 1971, 107 mins.

Les Visiteurs du Soir

Marcel Carne's charming fantasy, set in the 15th century, and starring Arletty. The devil sends two envoys to a chateau to intervene in the betrothal of a count and a lady, and the male ghost falls in love with Lady Anne. The Devil himself must intervene. The images and sets often have the charm of medieval miniatures, and *Les Visiteurs du Soir* was a considerable success. French with English subtitles.
VHS: S06439. $29.95.
Marcel Carne, France, 1942, 110 mins.

The Marvelous Visit

An inventive adaptation of H.G. Wells' story about a fallen angel who is discovered by a priest and his assistant. The two care for the angel's rehabilitation. The angel wanders into a sleepy village and his eccentric behavior transforms it. With Gilles Kohler, Deborah Berger and Jean-Pierre Castaldi. French with English subtitles.
VHS: S19499. $59.95.
Marcel Carne, France, 1974, 102 mins.

Misty Wharf (Quai des Brumes)

A deserter, Jean Gabin, arrives at the port looking for a ship in which to escape from the police. He has committed a murder during a fit of temper, and while still searching for a likely ship he falls in love with Michele Morgan and her nostalgic beauty. French with English subtitles.
VHS: S21756. $39.95.
Marcel Carne, France, 1938, 90 mins.

RENE CLAIR

A Nous la Liberte

The inspiration for Chaplin's *Modern Times*, an imaginative social satire about a man who escapes from prison and builds a phonograph business with an assembly line every bit as repressive as the prison he escaped from. With elegantly futuristic sets, and a memorable score. French with English subtitles.
VHS: S19455. $29.98.
Rene Clair, France, 1931, 97 mins.

And Then There Were None

A tense adaptation of Agatha Christie's novel in which ten people are inexplicably invited to a remote island, where they are murdered, one by one. With Walter Huston, Barry Fitzgerald, Roland Young and Judith Anderson.
VHS: S07779. $19.95.
Rene Clair, USA, 1945, 98 mins.

Beauties of the Night (Les Belles de Nuit)

A wonderful romantic fantasy from Rene Clair in which a young music teacher escapes his drab life through a world of dreams. Romantic adventures await him every night with beautiful women. Though these dreams start off with enchantment, they end in disaster, forcing him to accept reality and his own true love. Gerard Philipe, Martine Carol, Gina Lollobrigida and Magali Vendeuil star. French with English subtitles.
VHS: S26157. $29.95.
Rene Clair, France, 1952, 89 mins.

Beauty and the Devil (La Beaute du Diable)

Gerard Philipe, Michel Simon and Simone Valere star in an elaborately costumed, romantic drama from Rene Clair. The result is a film which casts an otherworldly shadow on this tale of love and redemption. Mephisto tempts a young man to sell his soul in return for youth, riches and a young gypsy girl. French with English subtitles.
VHS: S26158. $29.95.
Rene Clair, France, 1950, 97 mins.

Crazy Ray

Clair's first feature film reveals the influences of surrealism in the fantastic story of an inventor who discovers a ray which can put people to sleep, and proceeds to put all of Paris under. Silent, English titles.
VHS: S00278. $29.95.
Rene Clair, France, 1922, 60 mins.

The Ghost Goes West

From the mists of the Scottish Highlands, this hilarious fantasy relates the unexpected adventures of an American family when they find their newly purchased castle is haunted by a restless ghost. Starring Robert Donat, Jean Parker and Elsa Lanchester. "It has a dry wit and adroitness of manner that make it delightful" (*New York Times*). Digitally remastered.
VHS: $15055. $19.98.
Rene Clair, Great Britain, 1936, 85 mins.

The Grand Maneuver (Les Grandes Manoeuvres)

Gerard Philipe portrays a handsome dragoon in a pre-World War I garrison town who wagers that a divorcee (Michele Morgan) will fall for his charms. Despite his reputation as a Don Juan, he falls in love, but who would believe him? This romantic comedy is tender, charming and intelligent, all at the same time.
VHS: $23745. $24.95.
Rene Clair, France, 1955, 106 mins.

I Married a Witch

A Salem witch and her sorcerer father come back to haunt the descendant of the Puritan who had them burned. This is a delightful comedy by Thorne Smith (*Topper*) and shows Fredric March and Veronica Lake in top form. This pre-*Bewitched* farce also features Susan Hayward and Robert Benchley.
VHS: $02534. $19.98.
Rene Clair, USA, 1942, 82 mins.

The Italian Straw Hat

Pauline Kael called *The Italian Straw Hat* "one of the funniest films ever made and one of the most elegant as well." Based on an immensely popular farce by Eugene Labiche, the plot is a breezy tale about a bridegroom whose horse has a taste for ladies' hats. Rene Clair substituted sight gags for the clever word play, directed the action at a breakneck pace, and "screwball comedy" was born. This version is transferred from the restored negative, with a newly added musical score by Raymond Alessandrini. Starring Albert Prejean. Silent.
VHS: $16562. $39.95.
Rene Clair, France, 1927, 74 mins.

Le Million

A joy of a musical comedy about two penniless artists who win the lottery and become millionaires. But the lottery tickets are in a coat that is stolen, and then the fun begins. Refreshingly original in use of sound in which the music, dialogue and sound effects were recorded on a single track, and in its stylized action. Totally charming. French with English subtitles.
VHS: $19456. $29.98.
Rene Clair, France, 1931, 81 mins.

Le Voyage Imaginaire

This is one of the rarest Rene Clair films. It follows a group of people who experience a series of surrealistic adventures. Chaplin and Jackie Coogan save the boy gets involved in one episode. It's a valuable example of early silent French cinema.
VHS: $22882. $24.95.
Rene Clair, France, 1925, 62 mins.

Quatorze Juillet

A rarely seen classic. The simple story highlights the romantic adventures of a Parisian taxi driver and a young girl who sells flowers. After meeting on July 14th (Quatorze Juillet, Bastille Day), the two fall in and out of love as the boy gets involved with gangsters and the girl protects him from the law. Starring Anabella and George Rigaud. French with English subtitles.
VHS: $13669. $29.95.
Rene Clair, France, 1932, 85 mins.

Under the Roofs of Paris

Clair's poetic exploration of Parisian life evokes his characters' follies with shabby little garrets, cobblestoned streets, bistros, boudoirs and jails, all recreated within the studio. Also notable is Clair's adventuresome use of music. French with English subtitles.
VHS: $01398. $29.95.
Rene Clair, France, 1929, 95 mins.

HENRI-GEORGES CLOUZOT

Diabolique

The sadistic headmaster of a boys school is murdered by his tremulous wife and vengeful mistress in this classic French thriller. They dump the body, but suddenly the deceased appears in a recent school photograph. The suspense builds to an explosive climax. With Simone Signoret, Vera Clouzot, Paul Meurisse and Charles Vanel. French with English subtitles.
VHS: $00335. $39.95.
Laser: LD70749. $49.95.
Henri-Georges Clouzot, France, 1955, 116 mins.

Jenny Lamour

A fabulous thriller. Suzy Delair plays the music hall girl who believes that she has killed a once old man. Her husband (Bernard Blier) wanted to kill him, but finds him already dead when he arrives. Each hides their experience from the other, and the husband becomes the suspect. Louis Jouvet is brilliant in his role as the world-weary, wise cop. Clouzot creates a brooding atmosphere and etches indelible psychological portraits of trapped, frail human beings. Original title: *Quai des Orfevres*. English dubbed.
VHS: $03748. $29.95.
Henri-Georges Clouzot, France, 1947, 105 mins.

Karajan: Early Images, Vol. 1

In collaboration with the talented French filmmaker Henri-Georges Clouzot (*The Wages of Fear*), conductor Herbert von Karajan launched a series of performance films that attempted to achieve a "visual reinterpretation of a performance." Shot in black and white, this video shows von Karajan in preparation for conducting Beethoven's Fifth symphony, Schumann's Fourth symphony and Dvorak's Ninth symphony, "From the New World."
VHS: $16904. $24.95.
Laser: LD71526. $34.95.
Henri-Georges Clouzot, France/Germany, 1968

Karajan: Early Images, Vol. 2 (1965-66)

An anthology of Herbert von Karajan's work with the Vienna Symphony Orchestra. The highlights are Karajan's rehearsal for Schumann's *Symphony No. 4*, and a performance of Mozart's *Concerto for Violin and Orchestra, No. 5*, with Yehudi Menuhin. The film is directed by the important French filmmaker Henri-Georges Clouzot (*The Wages of Fear*).
VHS: $19894. $29.95.
Laser: LD72002. $34.95.
Henri-Georges Clouzot, France, 89 mins.

Manon

From the novel by Abbe Prevost, this is a modern adaptation of the classic love between Manon Lescaut and the chevalier Des Grieux. The film was set by Clouzot during the German Occupation of France and in the months surrounding D-Day, with Des Grieux a dealer in the Parisian black market and Manon dying in the Palestinian desert. French with English subtitles.
VHS: $03359. $29.95.
Henri-Georges Clouzot, France, 1948, 90 mins.

The Raven (Le Corbeau)

An ingenious, suspenseful thriller, made in wartime occupied France and based on a true story. A small French town is torn asunder by poison pen letters which breed tensions and suicides. The suspects are a doctor, a crippled girl and a sick woman. Ultimately, it is discovered that the criminal is a revered old man. With brilliant performances from Ginette Leclerc and Pierre Fresnay. As the old man says in the film, "You think that goodness is light and darkness is evil. But where is the darkness? Where the light?" French with English subtitles.
VHS: $16563. $59.95.
Henri-Georges Clouzot, France, 1943, 92 mins.

The Wages of Fear

An exercise in terror and suspense, this uncut version stars Yves Montand and Charles Vanel as uncertain comrades—trapped in a South American village—who identify because they are both French and both penniless. Desperate for a job, they agree to drive two trucks filled with nitroglycerine 300 miles over treacherous roads. Basil Wright called this film "the greatest suspense thriller of all time; it is the suspense not of mystery but of Damocles' sword." French with English subtitles.
VHS: $16210. $39.95.
Laser: LD70766. $59.95.
Henri-Georges Clouzot, France, 1953, 148 mins.

JEAN-PIERRE MELVILLE

Bob le Flambeur

An amazing film noir thriller and a film which anticipates the French New Wave with its gritty locations, free-wheeling camera, jump cuts and a musical jazz score. Roger Duchesne plays petty hood and small-time gambler Bob who, newly released from prison, immediately plots to rob the casino at Deauville. Shot between dusk and dawn in Pigalle, this is the quintessential "city at night" film with Bob the kind of a gangster who still has a moral code. Great cinematography by Henri Decae. French with English subtitles.
VHS: $20741. $59.95.
Jean-Pierre Melville, France, 1955, 97 mins.

Le Doulos

A complicated thriller of double and triple crosses, beautiful women and a dark vision of a world in a masterful film noir. Set in the Paris underworld, at the center of which is Jean-Paul Belmondo, a professional informer who maintains his relationship with a police inspector and a burglar just out of jail and afraid he can't hack the criminal life anymore. Famous for its 9½ minute single take—brilliant camerawork from Nicolas Hayer—and terrific performances. With Serge Reggiani, Jean Desailly and Michel Piccoli. French with English subtitles.
VHS: $09905. $59.95.
Jean-Pierre Melville, France, 1962, 108 mins.

Leon Morin, Priest

Jean-Pierre Melville's 1961 French/Italian co-production is set in Nazi-occupied France, and details the fascinating and complex relationship formed between a passionate, anticlerical communist Barny (Emmanuelle Riva) and a disarming, young priest (Jean-Paul Belmondo). Photographed by the great Henri Decae. "An intellectual romance, sharp and witty...with vivid wartime backgrounds" (Leslie Halliwell). French with English subtitles.
VHS: $16985. $59.95.
Laser: Widescreen. LD71601. $49.95.
Jean-Pierre Melville, France/Italy, 1961, 118 mins.

Les Enfants Terribles

A lyrical treatment of Jean Cocteau's perverse tribute to rebellious adolescence. Made in 1949, even today it is one of the most electrifying confrontations of normality by abnormality in the cinema. Paul (Edouard Dermithe) and Elisabeth (Nicole Stephane) are born into such extreme wealth that they are immune to the confines and limits of the real world. Their innocence leads them to self-destruction and to crime. Jean Cocteau's claustrophobic drama is brought to the screen by the great Jean-Pierre Melville in this perverse story of love, death and incest. French with English subtitles.
VHS: $01663. $29.95.
Jean-Pierre Melville, France, 1949, 105 mins.

JEAN VIGO

A Propos de Nice

One of the great works of the cinema, Jean Vigo's "lyrical, violent, and subversive social polemic is full of black humor and biting sarcasm...a short film, but a great one: An example of true cinema, but also an attack on a particular kind of world" (Sadoul). A document with a point of view on the city of Nice, contrasting the hotels with poverty, a film of great contrasts.
VHS: $04841. $24.95.
Jean Vigo, France, 1928, 20 mins.

L'Atalante

The high water mark of French poetic realism, set on a barge plying the Seine. A young barge captain and his bride live on a barge with the eccentric Pere Jules (Michel Simon). With Boris Kauffman's cinematography, which evokes Paris and the Seine with the luminosity of Atget or Cartier-Bresson, and everyday life full of magical moments like Pere Jules' "museum" of exotic marvels and the husband's underwater vision of his lost bride. "May be the greatest film ever made" (Georgia Brown, *The Village Voice*). Initially cut by seven minutes, this version is the fully restored, 89-minute cut. With Dita Parlo, Jean Daste and Michel Simon. French with English subtitles.
VHS: $17696. $69.95.
Jean Vigo, France, 1934, 89 mins.

Zero for Conduct

Based on Vigo's personal childhood experiences, a poetic yet revolutionary portrait of a revolt at a boarding school. Vigo creates a claustrophobic world in which the petty tyrannies of the school regime stand in sharp relief to the tender delirium of the children. Filled with deep psychological insights, this cinematic landmark was banned in France until 1946 on the grounds that it maliciously attacked the French educational system. Music by Maurice Jaubert, photography by Boris Kaufman. With Jean Daste and Louis Lefebvre. French with English subtitles.
VHS: $01500. $29.95.
Jean Vigo, France, 1933, 44 mins.

JEAN RENOIR

Boudu Saved from Drowning

A light comedy as well as a satire on bourgeois lifestyle in France. Michel Simon is Boudu, a scruffy tramp who is saved from his suicide attempt by a bookseller. Boudu insists his rescuer is now responsible for him, and creates chaos in his new home. French with English subtitles.
VHS: $17512. $59.95.
Laser: LD75419. $39.99.
Jean Renoir, France, 1932, 87 mins.

Crime of Monsieur Lange

Based on a scenario of Jacques Prevert, and one of the great films of Jean Renoir, the film sprang from Renoir's belief that the common man, by united action, could overcome tyranny. The head of a small printing press disappears with all the firm's capital. The employees band together, collect some money, and go into business as publishers of the popular novelettes of their neighbor, Monsieur Lange. "The world's greatest...director is Jean Renoir...life is always spilling over a Renoir frame as if the screen were not big enough to encompass all the humanity" (Andrew Sarris, *The Village Voice*). French with English subtitles.
VHS: $05324. $59.95.
Jean Renoir, France, 1936, 90 mins.

Day in the Country

Based on a story by Guy de Maupassant: "An innocent girl comes of age in Jean Renoir's short film. This lyrical tragedy rates with Renoir's greatest... Visually it recaptures the impressionist period" (Pauline Kael). French with English subtitles.
VHS: $19931. $39.95.
Jean Renoir, France, 1935, 40 mins.

Diary of a Chambermaid

Jean Renoir dreamed for ten years about making a film based on the novel by Octave Mirbeau, set in the decadent French upper classes. Paulette Goddard plays the outspoken maid who arouses the enmities of the household. In English.
VHS: $07298. $19.98.
Jean Renoir, USA, 1946, 86 mins.

Elena and Her Men

One of the most important Jean Renoir films, considered by Renoir "une fantasie musicale," the film stars Ingrid Bergman and is a film about the power of love, the power of women, the folly of progress, the beauty of laziness, and the evil of dictators. With Jean Marais, Mel Ferrer, Juliette Greco. French with English subtitles.
VHS: $05992. $59.95.
Jean Renoir, France, 1956, 98 mins.

Elusive Corporal

A story of man's triumph over adversity, set in a P.O.W. camp on the day of the French surrender to Germany in World War II. In many ways an updating of Renoir's 1937 masterpiece *Grand Illusion*. French with English subtitles.
VHS: $17514. $59.95.
Laser: LD71601. $49.95.
Jean Renoir, France, 1962, 109 mins.

French Can Can

"One of the screen's most extraordinarily beautiful displays of late cinematic maturity," said Andrew Sarris about Renoir's film, which stars Jean Gabin as the night club owner who re-discovers the can-can. "Renoir hurls his cancan artists at the viewer, tempting us with the consuming spectacle, which is...inherently kinetic and ineffably voluptuous." French with English subtitles.
VHS: $01662. $59.95.
Jean Renoir, France, 1955, 93 mins.

The Golden Coach

One of the great works of postwar French cinema, Jean Renoir's sublime masterpiece—photographed by his brother Claude—charts the affairs of an 18th-century actress (Anna Magnani) as she travels through colonial Peru with a commedia dell'arte troupe. She is simultaneously pursued by a bullfighter (Ricardo Rioli), a soldier (Paul Campbell) and the Viceroy (Duncan Lamont). With Odoardo Spadaro, Nada Fiorelli and Ralph Truman.
VHS: $19899. $59.95.
Jean Renoir, France/Italy, 1952, 103 mins.

Grand Illusion

A beautifully mastered version of Jean Renoir's great masterpiece, a classic comment on war's fading glory. Set in WW I, the film tells of two French officers captured by German forces. Imprisoned in a prison camp, the two officers encounter Von Rauffenstein, an aristocratic career officer played by von Stroheim. With Jean Gabin, Pierre Fresnay and von Stroheim. French with English subtitles.
VHS: $12469. $29.95.
Laser: LD70373. $89.95.
Jean Renoir, France, 1937, 111 mins.

La Bete Humaine

A psychological drama of murder, revenge, conscience and the eternal triangle, based on a story by Emile Zola. Jean Renoir fills the film with hauntingly beautiful symbolism. French with English subtitles.
VHS: $00700. $39.95.
Jean Renoir, France, 1938, 101 mins.

La Chienne

Jean Renoir's first great sound classic. The scenario is based on a novel by La Foucardiere. It is the story of a cashier who works in a hosiery business and whose sole passion is the painting he does in his spare time. Unhappily married to the widow of a noncommissioned officer who disappeared during the war, he meets a prostitute and becomes tragically involved with her. *La Chienne* combines the best of Renoir's work: the magnificent direction of actors, a subtle and very nuanced portrayal of a rather dubious aspect of French society. French with English subtitles.
VHS: $09570. $59.95.
Jean Renoir, France, 1931, 100 mins.

La Marseillaise

Renoir's remarkable ability to recreate the mood of the past was never more evident than in *La Marseillaise*. A classic tribute to the glory of the French Revolution, the film captures the human values of the struggle as well as the historical perspective. French with English subtitles.
VHS: $17513. $39.95.
Jean Renoir, France, 1938, 131 mins.

Le Petit Theatre de Jean Renoir

Jean Renoir's last film is a return, in some ways, to the humanistic themes of his life, in this theatrical wedding of four separate stories. *Le Dernier Reveillon* (*The Last Christmas Dinner*), is a highly stylized and expanded version of *The Little Matchgirl*; *Le Cireuse Electrique* (*The Electric Floor Waxer*) is a funny comedy sung to music by Joseph Kosma, in which a wife neglects her husband for her vacuum cleaner; *Entr'acte* stars Jeanne Moreau as a turn-of-the-century singer; *Le Roi D'Yvetot* is a story of manners and morals in which a middle-aged man with a seductive young wife is teased by the townspeople who suspect that a man of his age with a young wife must be cuckolded. French with English subtitles.
VHS: $07505. $59.95.
Laser: LD71615. $49.95.
Jean Renoir, France, 1969, 100 mins.

Lower Depths

Another classic statement by Renoir about social and economic classes, this time using a story about an impoverished thief (Jean Gabin) who meets and lives with a Baron (Louis Jouvet). Along the way the Baron discovers the joys of living without material wealth. A feast for the eyes and intellect. French with English subtitles.
VHS: $05857. $29.95.
Jean Renoir, France, 1936, 92 mins.

Madame Bovary

Jean Renoir's French version of Flaubert's great novel stars Valentine Tessier "as an anomalous creature, half swan, half goose. This large woman is not at all what one expects, yet she's surprisingly effective. The sunlight and the spaciousness emphasize Emma's loneliness; she's a middle-class woman with an ample figure, drifting along on romantic daydreams" (Pauline Kael). With Pierre Renoir, Jean's brother, as Charles Bovary, Max Dearly as M. Homais. French with English subtitles.
VHS: $01536. $79.95.
Jean Renoir, France, 1934

Picnic on the Grass

One of the wonders of cinema, Jean Renoir's tribute to French Impressionism and a work of almost overpowering lyricism—as a scientific outing turns into a Bacchanal. Shot at Les Collettes, the Renoir family home near Cannes. French with English subtitles.
VHS: $17515. $59.95.
Jean Renoir, France, 1959, 92 mins.

Renoir Silent Shorts

Includes *Little Match Girl* and *Charleston*, a humorous erotic dance fantasy that scandalized viewers of the time with its provocative sexuality, starring Catherine Hessling. With a jazz score and historical introduction. Silent.
VHS: $03703. $49.95.
Jean Renoir, France, 1926, 30 mins.

The River

Renoir's film about India, a film about British colonialism, a film which Jacques Rivette calls "the only example of a film vigorously reflecting itself (turned upon itself), and in which the narrative structure, the metaphysical themes and the sociological descriptions not only answer one another but are in every way interchangeable." In English.
VHS: $01661. $29.95.
Laser: LD71305. $44.95.
Jean Renoir, India, 1950, 99 mins.

Rules of the Game

One of the great films of all time, a satirical anatomy of polite society, with a mixture of farce and bitterness. Set at a weekend party at the chateau of the rich Marquis de la Chayniest, the story concerns complicated love intrigues. French with English subtitles.
VHS: $04456. $29.95.
Laser: LD70446. $89.95.
Jean Renoir, France, 1939, 90 mins.

The Southerner

One of Renoir's American films, the story of a migrant worker (Zachary Scott) who tries to make a go of it on a farm of his own. English dialog.
VHS: $01236. $19.95.
Jean Renoir, USA, 1945, 91 mins.

Testament of Dr. Cordelier

"A fascinating experiment adapting TV techniques—direct recording, multiple cameras, long takes, thorough pre-rehearsal—to the cinema. The Jekyll and Hyde story transposed to a modern setting affords an excuse for an homage to Renoir's beloved actors, and Jean-Louis Barrault is extraordinary as the evil genius, prancing and twitching like some nightmarish faun on an orgy of destruction. Most of the exteriors were shot on location in the streets of Paris, and the intrusion of this creature lends them a bizarre air of menace" (Tom Milne). French with English subtitles.
VHS: $05328. $29.95.
Jean Renoir, France, 1959, 95 mins.

This Land Is Mine
Charles Laughton is the schoolteacher in occupied Europe, who, put on trial by the Nazis for a murder he did not commit, finds rare courage to defy and defend freedom. One of Renoir's films made in Hollywood. With Maureen O'Hara and George Sanders. English dialog.
VHS: S01331. $49.98.
Jean Renoir, USA, 1943, 103 mins.

Toni
The story of Italian immigrants working in a quarry, of love, murder and betrayal, Renoir's great film is based on an actual incident and shot on location. The film anticipated the Italian neo-realist movement in its near-documentary approach, its use of non-actors in principal roles, in its deep commitment to common people, their lives and struggles. French with English subtitles.
VHS: S01358. $29.95.
Jean Renoir, France, 1934, 83 mins.

Tournament
Silent period spectacle from Renoir, story is set in 1565 when Catherine de Medici attempted to maintain power while balancing between Catholics and Protestants. Silent.
VHS: S03704. $49.95.
Jean Renoir, France, 1929, 90 mins.

MARCEL PAGNOL

Angele
Considered by many to be the finest work of Marcel Pagnol, the film's innovative use of location shooting is an important precursor to neo-realism. Angele combines a melodramatic story of a young girl's seduction, betrayal and redemption by true love with the naturalist settings of Provence. Based on Jean Giono's novel, Un de Baumugnes. With Fernandel, Orane Demazis. French with English subtitles.
VHS: S08258. $59.95.
Marcel Pagnol, France, 1934, 150 mins.

Baker's Wife
The earthy comedy to end all earthy comedies; a young wife leaves her husband for a handsome young shepherd—but tragedy of all French tragedies—she happens to be the baker's wife. The baker, too heartsick to bake, throws the town into panic. And the townspeople organize to cajole, lure, or force the young lady in question away from her lover and back to her husband—so they can get back to their bread. French with English subtitles.
VHS: S00088. $59.95.
Marcel Pagnol, France, 1933, 101 mins.

Cesar
The final film of the trilogy begins twenty years after the first, Marius. Fanny's husband has died and her son is at last told of his true father. Marius and Fanny are reunited at last. French with English subtitles.
VHS: S00223. $39.95.
Marcel Pagnol, France, 1936, 121 mins.

Fanny
The second in the Marcel Pagnol trilogy begun with Marius, in which Marius goes to sea leaving Fanny, his fiancee, pregnant. She in turn marries a sailmaker and rebukes Marius upon his return. Warm comic invention. French with English subtitles.
VHS: S19900. $39.95.
Marc Allegret, France, 1931, 120 mins.

Harvest
A film of utter serenity and great goodness, the story of a scissors grinder and a woman who pass by a deserted town, inhabited by only one man. The woman stays with the man and together they bring new life to the land. Based upon the novel by Jean Giono, featuring Fernandel, Orane Demazis. French with English subtitles.
VHS: S01967. $59.95.
Marcel Pagnol, France, 1937, 128 mins.

Le Schpountz
Fernandel, Charpin and Orane Demazis star in this hilarious comedy about a country bumpkin convinced he is the next great leading man of French film. Once he arrives in Paris, this outsider storms the industry, giving Marcel Pagnol the opportunity to satirize the movie-making industry. French with English subtitles.
VHS: S25107. $59.95.
Marcel Pagnol, France, 1938, 135 mins.

Letters from My Windmill
Three tales from the director of Baker's Wife and Topaze. In the first the devil takes over the body of a dunce and torments a priest at Christmas eve mass. The second documents the troubles that arise when a community of priests make and sell their own wine. And the last is a story of a miller who pretends to compete with a new steam-driven mill. French with English subtitles.
VHS: S01566. $34.95.
Marcel Pagnol, France, 1954, 134 mins.

Marius
The first film of the celebrated Marcel Pagnol trilogy, famous for its dialog and rich humanity. The story introduces Marius who longs to go to sea in spite of his love for Fanny. French with English subtitles.
VHS: S00826. $39.95.
Alexander Korda, France, 1931, 120 mins.

Nais
The horse-faced Fernandel stars in this Marcel Pagnol production, a heartrending love story which crosses the class structures in rural Provence; Nais, a beautiful country girl, is in love with the son of a wealthy family. Fernandel is the hunchback who sacrifices his own love for her in order to give Nais her happiness. French with English subtitles. (For several minutes in this film, subtitles are inadequate.) Very rare film.
VHS: S06480. $34.95.
Fernand Lauterier, France, 1945, 95 mins.

Topaze (1933)
Based on Pagnol's play, this early film chronicles the metamorphosis of a timid and persecuted school teacher. The teacher is fired and finds a new job, where he blindly enters into a business scam. Fernandel, Jacqueline Pagnol and Pierre Larquey star in Pagnol's response to an earlier, less faithful, Hollywood adaptation of his play. French with English subtitles.
VHS: S25104. $59.95.
Louis Gasnier, France, 1933, 92 mins.

Topaze (1951)
The third French version of Pagnol's popular comic play, this time starring Fernandel as the naive schoolteacher who is thrust into the world of wealth, sex and crooked business when he unwittingly becomes a pawn in a wealthy baron's game. French with English subtitles.
VHS: S01660. $59.95.
Marcel Pagnol, France, 1951, 92 mins.

The Well-Digger's Daughter
Touching and hilarious story about a young woman who is seduced and then abandoned, and the unpleasant effect this has on her peasant father. With Raimu, Fernandel and Josette Day. French with English subtitles.
VHS: S01565. $29.95.
Marcel Pagnol, France, 1941, 142 mins.

MAX OPHULS

Caught
A dark and compelling story of a girl married to the wrong man who runs away and falls in love with a struggling young ghetto doctor. Chased down by the husband, she is forced to choose between money and love. Robert Ryan gives a strong performance as the vicious, mentally unstable millionaire husband (based on Howard Hughes). With Barbara Bel Geddes and James Mason as the lovers. Intelligently handled by director Ophuls in his most successful American film.
VHS: S00222. $19.95.
Max Ophuls, USA, 1949, 90 mins.

Earrings of Madame De...
Max Ophuls' powerful romantic tragedy, starring Charles Boyer, Vittorio de Sica, Danielle Darrieux. A spoiled socialite, married to a general, flirts with an amorous diplomat. As the affair escalates, her passion rips through the glittering facade of their privileged existence, plunging them into disaster as they risk everything for love and honor. Newly mastered. French with English subtitles.
VHS: S08999. $24.95.
Laser: LD75543. $49.98.
Max Ophuls, France, 1953, 105 mins.

La Ronde
Love as a bitterly comic merry-go-round. Simone Signoret plays a young whore involved with a young soldier who leaves her, setting off a chain of affairs and partners that ends with Signoret again. Based on the play Reigen by Arthur Schnitzler. French with English subtitles.
VHS: S00711. $29.95.
Laser: LD75027. $49.95.
Max Ophuls, France, 1950, 97 mins.

La Signora di Tutti
The only film that Ophuls made in Italy, La Signora di Tutti features Isa Miranda as Gaby Doriot, a film star at the peak of her popularity with the public and in the depths of despair in her private life. As the film opens, she has attempted suicide. Under ether on the operating table, her life unfolds for her (us) in a series of fragmented flashbacks. A powerful melodrama transcended by sheer stylistic splendor; the visual lyricism of Ophuls' camera movements are at times breathtaking. Italian with English subtitles.
VHS: S01966. $59.95.
Max Ophuls, Italy, 1934, 92 mins.

Le Plaisir
Max Ophuls' ironic, humorous trilogy of De Maupassant short stories stars some of France's greatest stars (Simone Simon, Danielle Darrieux, Jean Gabin, Jean Servais, Madeleine Renaud, Ginette Leclerc, Pierre Brasseur). The three tales are Le Masque, in which an old man rediscovers his youth by wearing a mask; La Maison Telliler, in which a group of prostitutes go on an annual holiday trip to the country; and La Modele, in which an artist who makes mistresses out of his models marries one when she cripples herself while trying to commit suicide. French with English subtitles.
VHS: S00741. $29.95.
Max Ophuls, France, 1952, 94 mins.

Letter from an Unknown Woman
Louis Jourdan is a famed concert pianist who is unaware he has been adored for years by the very shy Joan Fontaine until one very special night of passion that produces a child. Told in a series of flashbacks, Jourdan learns he is a father much too late to do the right thing.
VHS: S07435. $19.95.
Laser: CLV, 1 disc, Criterion. LD71450. $49.95.
Max Ophuls, USA, 1948, 87 mins.

Liebelei
The film which established the reputation for Max Ophuls, based on a play by Arthur Schnitzler; the story of a young lieutenant who is in love with a Viennese girl, and is called to account by a baron who believes him to be the lover of the baroness. The military code requires a duel, the lieutenant is killed, and the girl throws herself out the window in despair. "Ophuls' magical adaptation of Schnitzler's mordant love play is a lament to lost innocence, transported by Ophuls' moving camera into the mystical regions of remembrance" (NY Film Festival). German with English subtitles.
VHS: S07820. $59.95.
Max Ophuls, Germany, 1932, 88 mins.

Lola Montes
Ophuls' opulent biography of the famous 19th-century courtesan whose adventures and love affairs with King Ludwig I, Liszt and a student are told in flashback from a circus ring by the ring master, Peter Ustinov. Brilliant use of color and Cinemascope, breathtaking shots and camera movements; Ophuls conjures up a sublime work that is pure cinema. With Martine Carol, Anton Walbrook, Ivan Desny and Oskar Werner. French with English subtitles.
VHS: S02771. $19.98.
Laser: CLV, widescreen. LD71113. $49.95.
Max Ophuls, France, 1955, 110 mins.

Novotna in The Bartered Bride and The Last Waltz
Novotna, the acclaimed singer from 1930's Europe, stars in both these operas. Smetana's music is beautifully realized in German. Then Oscar Straus' work is presented in English. 76 minutes.
VHS: S25534. $39.95.
Max Ophuls/Leo Mittler, Germany/Czechoslovakia, 1932
Gerald Barry, Great Britain/France, 1935

JEAN COCTEAU

Beauty and the Beast
Jean Cocteau's superb adaptation of Marie Leprince de Beaumont's dark fairy tale is a ferociously inventive and stylized depiction of erotic obsession, about a young woman's discovery of a ravaged soul beneath a monstrous beast. With Jean Marais, Josette Day and Marcel Andre. Cinematography by Henri Alekan. "A sensuously fascinating film, the visual progression of the fable into a dream-world casts its unpredictable spell" (Bosley Crowther).
VHS: S00110. $24.95.
Laser: Cocteau, CAV. LD70865. $89.95.
Jean Cocteau, France, 1946, 93 mins.

Blood of a Poet
The first work of the significant poet, playwright and surrealist Jean Cocteau is one of the most important contributions to early avant-garde cinema—a stunning, primal and powerful work that uses jagged, poetic, harsh and highly personal images, dreams and symbols to reflect an artist's inner life. The work is composed in four illogical, timeless sequences. French with English subtitles.
VHS: S17880. $29.95.
Laser: LD75381. $49.98.
Jean Cocteau, France, 1930, 54 mins.

The Eagle Has Two Heads (L'Aigle A Deux Tetes)
A rarely seen film by Jean Cocteau (Orpheus, Beauty and the Beast) based on his own play. Jean Marais plays the poet/anarchist who falls in love with the queen (Edwige Feuillere) he initially sets out to assassinate in Cocteau's high romantic melodrama. With music by the great Georges Auric. French with English subtitles.
VHS: S23863. $29.95.
Jean Cocteau, France, 1948, 93 mins.

Jean Cocteau: Autobiography of an Unknown
Jean Cocteau, one of the 20th century's greatest eclectic artists, in a definitive portrait completed from archival film. Cocteau relates his experiences from earliest childhood through his life as one of the creative circle in Paris at the turn of the century. In an intense personal narration, he describes his family and the inspiration he drew from his circle of friends including Nijinsky, Diaghilev, Renoir, Picasso, Satie, Chaplin and others. A marvelous portrait of a great artist. 60 mins.
VHS: S07597. $19.95.

Les Parents Terribles (The Storm Within)
This steamy adaptation of Cocteau's own play features Jean Marais as the doting son of a middle-class Parisian family, who falls in love with a young woman (Josette Day), unaware that she is his father's mistress. The riveting psychological drama about the complicated tangle of sexuality, parental rivalry, jealousy and Freudian obsession features a great performance from Marais as a mama's boy in love. French with English subtitles.
VHS: S23864. $29.95.
Jean Cocteau, France, 1948, 98 mins.

Orpheus
Cocteau's famous retelling of the Greek myth, with Jean Marais as Orphee, the successful poet envied and despised, who pushes himself beyond mortality, and Maria Casares as the dark, troubled, passionate Death. A great film. French with English subtitles.
VHS: S00977. $29.95.
Jean Cocteau, France, 1949, 95 mins.

Testament of Orpheus
After 70 years of life and 29 years of filmmaking, Jean Cocteau waves goodbye to films, and this, his last work, is a compendium of his filmic style. We meet Cocteau wandering in the 18th century only to be brought into the 20th where he encounters gypsies, evil omens and the dead poet of Orphee. A great many trick shots and many of Cocteau's collaborators appear in the film: Marais, Leaud, Yul Brynner, Casares. French with English subtitles.
VHS: S01313. $29.95.
Jean Cocteau, France, 1959, 80 mins.

ALBERTO CAVALCANTI

The Life and Adventures of Nicholas Nickleby
Cedric Hardwicke in the Dickens tale of a young boy who tries to save himself and his family from a miserly uncle. Director Cavalcanti was active in the film avant-garde of the 1920's, and gives this film style by paying attention to visual design and lighting.
VHS: S00929. $19.95.
Alberto Cavalcanti, Great Britain, 1947, 105 mins.

Rien Que les Heures
This bold documentary remains a landmark in the tradition of documentary film. The life of Paris is shown over one 24-hour period, including images of the city at work and play. Cinematic effects paint a moody picture resulting in a surrealistic view of this great city. Silent with English intertitles.
VHS: S21080. $19.95.
Alberto Cavalcanti, France, 1926, 45 mins.

Went the Day Well?
Leslie Banks and Elizabeth Allan star in this World War II drama based on a story by Graham Greene. An advance body of German troops secretly occupies a village by posing as Royal Engineers. Eventually they are discovered and a bloody battle follows.
VHS: S23816. $24.95.
Alberto Cavalcanti, Great Britain, 1942, 92 mins.

JACQUES TATI

Gai Dimanche/Swing to the Left
Two rare early short films by Jacques Tati. In Gai Dimanche (French with no subtitles), Tati and the clown Rhum buy a used bus, pick up sight-seers and tour the countryside. In Swing to the Left, Tati plays a farm hand who goes rounds with a professional boxer.
VHS: S04362. $49.95.
Jacques Tati, France, 1931-36

Jour de Fete
The first feature by Jacques Tati. This perceptive and witty village comedy set in Saint-Severe casts Tati as a simple, determined postman trying desperately to modernize his operations, with frightening repercussions. Shot in a splash color format, the film was released in black and white with some hand-tinted color sequences. "Tati was a method, a way of looking at the world to discover comic rhythms never seen before or since in movies" (Vincent Canby). French with English subtitles.
VHS: S18852. $29.95.
Laser: LD70386. $49.95.
Jacques Tati, France, 1949, 76 mins.

Mon Oncle
A masterpiece by the great French comic Jacques Tati which concentrates on young Gerard Arpel and his Uncle Hulot (Jacques Tati) in a house where gadgets overpower everything. Sound effects, minimal dialog contribute to Tati's wry humor. French with English subtitles.
VHS: S00870. $29.95.
Laser: LD71234. $49.95.
Jacques Tati, France, 1956, 114 mins.

Mr. Hulot's Holiday
Jacques Tati's second film introduces M. Hulot (Tati), a genial, eccentric, middle-class French everyman whose vacation at a seaside French resort in Brittany produces one minor catastrophe after another. Tati's intricate juxtaposing of mime and slapstick is so refined, pure and expressive, there's an extraordinary pain, passion and tenderness that produces laughter and heartbreak. With Nathalie Pascaud, Michele Rolla and Louis Perrault. French with English subtitles.
VHS: S00891. $24.95.
Laser: LD71241. $59.95.
Jacques Tati, France, 1952, 91 mins.

Parade
Parade centers around the lives of two small children gradually brought closer together as they wend their way through the activities of a circus. Director Tati appears in the film as Monsieur Loyal, a circus performer, and presents some of his most unique and best known pieces of mime. Loyal is able to transform the mood of the circus into one of celebration and joy through the various music hall numbers weaved throughout the film.
VHS: S13735. $29.95.
Laser: CLV, 1 disc, Criterion. LD70431. $49.95.
Jacques Tati, France, 1974, 85 mins.

Playtime
Called one of the funniest men in the world by the New York Times, Jacques Tati's Playtime is an hilarious comedy and satire on coping with the modern world. For Tati's now-legendary character, M. Hulot, everything seems to be against him—a glass-fronted airport, a new restaurant, even a supermarket. Full of visual gags and inventive use of sound, Playtime is one of the most imaginative and funniest films ever. English dialog.
VHS: S01038. $19.95.
Jacques Tati, France, 1967, 108 mins.

Traffic
Jacques Tati's fifth and final feature, a laugh-filled look at modern society and the automobile, captures the absurdities of human behavior on the street and behind the wheel. Tati's Mr. Hulot is back as an absent-minded inventor trying to transport his ultramodern camper to Amsterdam for an auto show. "Splendidly funny...exuberantly entertaining...Traffic is a hilarious highway odyssey, a panorama that unfolds around Mr. Hulot" (Vincent Canby). English language version. Letterboxed.
VHS: S21383. $79.95.
Jacques Tati, France, 1971, 89 mins.

THE FRENCH LANDSCAPE

Andre Malraux: Les Metaphorses d'Andre Malraux
Made in France in 1986 to commemorate the 10th anniversary of Malraux's death, the film is an eloquent tribute to the remarkable writer, philosopher and artist. The film skillfully combines Malraux's brilliant prose with photographs and archival footage of the places and events which made up his life, including the Far East in the 20's, the Spanish Civil War and the French resistance during WWII. English narration.
VHS: S08607. $200.00.
Marcel Boudu, France, 1986, 90 mins.

Bonjour de Paris
Paris, "La Ville Lumiere"—discover Paris with Marina, a teenager, and her uncle Paul, a true Parisian, as he explains the culture and history of the city by visiting the medieval Notre Dame and Conciergerie, Montparnasse, the contemporary Beaubourg and Defense, as well as other sites. 45 mins.
English Narration.
VHS: S06883. $49.95.
French Narration.
VHS: S06882. $49.95.

Chanel, Chanel
The world of fashion has produced no more charismatic figure than Coco Chanel. Her style was stamped on over half a century of fashion—her life spelling out a new blueprint for simplicity and ease. Top designer Karl Lagerfeld, who became head of the house of Chanel in 1983, has brought back the excitement of fashion that Chanel generated during her prime. Rare archive footage tells the fascinating story of her life. 60 minutes.
VHS: S07624. $29.95.

Edith Piaf: I Regret Nothing
A BBC-produced musical biography of Edith Piaf, the most popular French singer of the 20th century. Extensive footage from Piaf's concerts is included, as well as interviews with those who knew her, such as Charles Aznavour.
VHS: S00936. $29.95.
Michael Houldey, Great Britain, 110 mins.

Edith Piaf: La Vie en Rose
Piaf's life story, told through archival footage and the recollections of her friends, from her beginnings as a street singer to stardom in the *boites* of Paris—a warmly nostalgic video that includes Piaf's singing "La Vie en Rose," "Non, je ne regrette rien," and other favorites.
VHS: S05549. $29.95.

Eternal France
Visit the Normandy Coast and glide along the canals of Alsace to Strasbourg. Wander inside the majestic cathedrals of Reims and Chartres and watch the artistry of glass-makers in Baccarat, the lace-makers in the Auvergne region and the silk painters in Lyon. 50 mins.
VHS: S12273. $24.95.

Floyd on France
The shy and retiring cook extraordinaire Keith Floyd winds his way through six of the great gastronomic and panoramic regions of France. This truly delicious experience includes roasting a sizzling free-range chicken in Provence, and rustling up a delectable omelette in perfectly preserved Perigord. A BBC production. 87 mins.
VHS: S10281. $19.94.

France Nobody Knows
Explore the lesser-known regions of France on this unique tour of the French countryside. Visit Alsace, Savoie, Auvergne, Provence, and the island of Corsica. You'll ride through the Alps, visit a Roman arena, see prehistoric relics. 30 mins.
VHS: S08278. $24.95.

French Singers
Edith Piaf, George Brassens and Maurice Chevalier are each captured in live performances and in rare documentary footage.
VHS: S10590. $29.95.

In Love with Paris
The City of Light and food, fashion, history, art, and shopping. See it all, and capture the spirit of Paris on an unforgettable tour. 50 mins.
VHS: S10766. $24.95.

Jacques Brel
The life and music of the inimitable French composer-singer, the tough Parisian with the guitar who looked life in the eye unflinchingly. There are no June/moon/ spoon lyrics here—Brel lives in the modernity of his music about loving and losing and surviving in love.
VHS: S05550. $39.95.

Jacques Prevert
A portrait of the great poet, playwright and novelist, as Prevert discusses religion, the politics of art, and his work. French *without* English subtitles. 53 mins.
Home Video.
VHS: S06957. $59.95.
Public Performance.
VHS: S09502. $100.00.

Jean Genet
Genet had never accepted an interview before a camera. It is thus an event to see him for the first time, speaking in total liberty about his love of the shadows of prison life, and for the light of Greece, and his involvements with the Black Panthers and other groups; finally, he reveals the birth of his vocation as a writer. French *without* English subtitles.
Home Video.
VHS: S06955. $59.95.
Public Performance.
VHS: S08839. $100.00.

Les Antilles: Guadeloupe and Martinique
These Caribbean islands showcase the rich, atmospheric locales that speak to the social and political heritage of French culture. This is indispensable for class discussion for the Francophone. 60 mins.
French Narration.
VHS: S19781. $35.00.
English Narration.
VHS: S19782. $35.00.

Les Chateaux de la Loire
The history of France comes alive as you tour the magnificent chateaux which dot the Loire. A unique opportunity to examine the splendid interiors and classic architecture of these famous sites. 55 mins. English narration.
VHS: S00003. $49.95.

Les Clips Francophones
Popular music is a highly regarded means to unlocking the barriers of language-learning. These clips, representing the best French artists—M.C. Solaar, Patricia Kaas and King Dady Yod—introduce contemporary language usage ("slang") and cultural styles and attitudes. The lyrics of each song, biographies, grammatical commentary and language exercises are included in each text. 30 mins.
VHS: S19783. $49.95.

Maurice Chevalier
A portrait of the charmer in the straw hat, the most beloved of the song-and-dance men, with archival footage tracing his career from Montmartre to Hollywood, and clips from such films as *The Merry Widow*, *Innocents of Paris* and *Gigi*. Among the many songs Chevalier sings is his signature song, "Louise."
VHS: S10047. $39.95.

Michel Tournier
The hermit of the valley of Chevreuse, who lives in his house "like the snail who secretes his house around him, year by year...a very complex shell," speaks about the themes that are dear to him—the Germany of his youth, Tunisia, photography, the vocation of the writer, and above all, childhood in general, the mystery of which he constantly tries to fathom in his novels, such as *Roi des Aulnes* and *Meteores*. French *without* English subtitles.
Home Video.
VHS: S06958. $59.95.
Public Performance.
VHS: S08831. $100.00.

Moliere
The Royal Shakespeare Company presents Dusty Hughes' version of Mikhail Bulgakov's comedy-drama based on the life of the French playwright. With Anthony Sher as Moliere, a man beset by church and state because of his satire directed at both in *Tartuffe*.
VHS: S00867. $39.98.
Laser: LD71233. $49.95.
Bill Alexander, Great Britain, 1984, 112 mins.

Mont St. Michel
The Cathedral of the Sea has been a site of worship for centuries. Today its collection of religious buildings from the Middle Ages include a treasure of art and architecture. This title, from the series *Spirit of France*, shows the splendor of this unique and holy island. English narration. 56 mins.
VHS: S24935. $29.95.

Montparnasse Revisited
This series captures the history of one of Paris' most colorful and vital districts. The painters, writers, composers, actors, musicians and photographers who made Paris the center of the art world between 1900 and the Second World War defined the avant garde. Together they created modern art as we know it. Each volume is 55 mins. Directed by Matthew Reinders and based on a program by Jean-Marie Drot.
Volume 1: The Brilliant Years, 1900-1914.
VHS: S21041. $29.95.
Volume 2: Artists at War, 1914-1918.
VHS: S21042. $29.95.
Volume 3: Face to Face with Giacometti.
VHS: S21043. $29.95.
Volume 4: A Life in the Day of Man Ray.
VHS: S21044. $29.95.
Volume 5: Who Was Modigliani?
VHS: S21045. $29.95.
Volume 6: The Man Behind Picasso—Daniel-Henry Kahnweiler.
VHS: S21046. $29.95.
Volume 7: Ghosts at the Banquet—The Twenties.
VHS: S21047. $29.95.
Volume 8: Songs and Sentiments—Music Hall.
VHS: S21048. $29.95.
Volume 9: The Composers.
VHS: S21049. $29.95.
Volume 10: Soutine the Obsessed.
VHS: S21050. $29.95.
The Ten-Volume Set.
VHS: S21051. $199.95.

Noel a Paris
Follow a Parisian family as it celebrates the holidays. We participate in a festive dinner, exchange gifts, and continue the celebration throughout New Year's Eve. A wonderful presentation of French tradition and culture. 30 mins.
English Narration.
VHS: S05288. $49.95.
French Narration.
VHS: S05287. $49.95.

Salamandre: Chateaux of the Loire
A study of France's 18 socially important chateaux uses computer animation technology to study the chateau's evolution from feudal fortresses to expansive manors. French and English dialog.
Laser: LD70308. $49.95.

Simone de Beauvoir
This film is the passionate testimony of a half-century of intellectual and political life, the itinerary of a woman who has covered many fields of human endeavor, yet who reveals herself—in the company of her lover, Jean-Paul Sartre—as human and accessible. French *without* English subtitles.
Home Video.
VHS: S06954. $59.95.
Public Performance.
VHS: S08838. $100.00.

Turckhein et Sa Fete du Vin
This show about the fundamental importance of vineyards and wine in French culture reveals the excitement of the various wine fests in the Alsatian village of Turckhein. In French. With transcript and exercises. 30 mins.
VHS: S19805. $39.95.

Versailles
Perhaps the most famous of all royal palaces—built by Louis XIV in the 17th century. Marvel at the Hall of Mirrors, the royal bedchamber, the spectacle of the fountains and the formal gardens. 55 mins. English narration.
VHS: S05279. $69.95.

Visite en France
This cultural video simulates an actual visit to Paris and the surrounding areas by two young students. The sites also include the Loire Valley, and a Son et Lumiere Festival. Various functions such as socializing, greeting, introducing and leaving are incorporated into the conversation, with other vocabulary and expressions related to the various activities attended by the teenagers. Seven 15-minute segments for advanced-beginning-intermediate. 105 mins.
VHS: S09066. $59.95.

BELGIAN CINEMA

Daens
Nominated for an Academy Award for Best Foreign Language Film in 1992, *Daens* is the story of Father Adolph Daens, a Catholic priest who returns to his village after a long absence, to discover his fellow townspeople living in abject poverty. Called by his conscience to speak out against the miserable working conditions in the factories, Father Daens soon finds himself in a head-to-head battle with not only the businessmen and the monarchy, but Catholic Church officials as well. Based on a true story, Father Daens is later elected to Parliament to represent the workers he risked his reputation to champion. With Jan Declier, Antje de Boeck and Gerard Desarthe. Flemish and French with English subtitles.
VHS: S26963. $89.98.
Stijn Coninx, Belgium/France/Netherlands, 1992, 134 mins.

Farinelli
Farinelli, an 18th-century castrato, was one of Europe's most acclaimed singers. This lavishly designed, brilliantly costumed film focuses on his troubled artistic and personal life as he conquers the opera world and has women faint in his presence, yet needs his brother to consummate his sexual conquests. Corbiau ingeniously recreates the unique castrato sound by electronically blending a male and female voice; Jeroen Krabbe appears as Friedrich Handel. French with English subtitles.
VHS: S26396. $19.95.
Laser: LD75080. $34.95.
Gerard Corbiau, France/Belgium/Italy, 1995, 115 mins.

Man Bites Dog
An off-center, mock documentary with a profanely serious thrust about a Belgian documentary crew that impassively follows Ben (Remy Belvaux), a pasty-faced, deadpan serial killer. The film is shot in black and white and composed primarily in hand-held shots, as the filmmakers "profile" their remorseless killer. The corpses mount through the killer's lethal strangulations, shootings and stabbings, though the film is primarily concerned with how the media and society are implicated in the horrendous crimes. French with English subtitles. This is the uncut version.
VHS: S18974. $19.98.
Belvaux/Bonzel/Poelvoorde, Belgium, 1991, 95 mins.

The Music Teacher
The music of Verdi, Mahler, Schumann, Mozart, Bellini, Schubert and Offenbach is highlighted in this 1989 Academy Award Nominee for Best Foreign Film. Just before World War I a group of opera students gather to compete to settle a grudge between a retired opera star and a wealthy patron. Lots of emotional fireworks. Called "elegant and cultivated" by the *Boston Globe*. With Jose Van Dam, Joachim Dallyroc and Anne Roussel. French with English subtitles.
VHS: S11535. $19.98.
Gerard Corbiau, Belgium/France, 1989, 100 min.

CHANTAL AKERMAN

Akermania, Volume One
A collection of shorter works by Chantal Akerman. Includes *Saute ma Ville*, Akerman's first film (1968) which stars the filmmaker at age 18. Also featured is *I'm Hungry, I'm Cold*, the story of two love-struck Belgian girls on the loose in Paris, and the 1972 New York silent experimental film *Hotel Monterey*. French with English subtitles.
VHS: S16298. $19.98.
Chantal Akerman, France, 89 mins.

Eighties
"Goofy hypersophisticated," one critic called it. "Goofy formalism," wrote another. "Goofy deconstruction of the musical." It all adds up, to everyone's delight, to pure, playful pleasure. The first hour, shot on video, is a montage of auditions for parts in a musical comedy. Songs and choreography are rehearsed, repeated, and revised by actors responding to offscreen direction by Akerman. The second part, shot in 35mm, is the wonderful, wholly satisfying pay-off; a musical extravaganza set in a shopping mall. French with English subtitles.
VHS: S12610. $79.95.
Chantal Akerman, Belgium/France, 1983, 85 min.

Je, Tu, Il, Elle
Chantal Akerman's first feature moves like a process or a journey, most likely one from youth into adulthood. Akerman stars as the protagonist of the film, whom we first discover in her apartment compulsively eating raw sugar, reading aloud and rearranging her furniture. She hits the road and after various misadventures finds herself at the home of a woman she loves. The heavy silence underscores themes of estrangement and alienation. With Niels Arestrup and Claire Wauthion. French with English subtitles.
VHS: S12562. $29.95.
Chantal Akerman, France, 1974, 90 mins.

News from Home
"Most simply described, the film is a portrait of Manhattan in which a generally static camera presents a succession of geometrically framed streetscapes—it's a spare and ravishing *city symphony* that takes its cues from Manhattan's own relentless grid" (J. Hoberman).
VHS: S13819. $79.95.
Chantal Akerman, USA/Belgium, 1976, 90 mins.

Night and Day (Nuit et Jour)
Chantal Akerman's daring film about sexual independence concerns one woman's simultaneous relationships with two men. Set over a sweltering Paris summer, the story follows Julie (Guilaine Londez), a beautiful young woman who is involved in a passionate relationship with Jack (Thomas Langmann). Completely isolated from the outside world, with no friends or intimates, they engage in marathon bouts of sex. At night, Jack drives a taxi to support them while Julie walks the Paris streets. Julie is inexorably drawn to Joseph (Francois Negret), a solitary young man who drives Jack's cab during the day. French with English subtitles.
VHS: S19974. $89.98.
Chantal Akerman, France/Belgium, 1991, 91 mins.

Rendezvous d'Anna
One of the most important films of the 70's, Chantal Akerman's "laying bare of grim reality". A woman filmmaker floats around Europe while having encounters with several people, both strangers and intimate partners, that reveal her as a catalyst for commitment. Aurore Clement plays Anna in this minimalist experiment that is perhaps the most accessible of Akerman's films, which evokes human needs, fears and subtleties by concentrating on the spaces in between conversation. With Lea Massari, Helmut Griem, Jean-Pierre Cassel. French with English subtitles.
VHS: S09346. $29.95.
Chantal Akerman, France/Belgium, 1978, 122 mins.

Tout Une Nuit
A hot, steamy summer night. All over the city, it's impossible to sleep. So goes the context of Akerman's film, tension fractured by an explosion of amorous comings and goings. A woman leaves her husband's bed to meet her lover. A little girl runs away from home, her cat in her arms. A man gazes longingly through a window at a woman sitting alone. The film is made entirely of fragments such as these, disregarding narrative content yet evoking the best loved conventions of romantic melodrama. Wonderfully moody location shooting. Cast: Angelo Abazoglou, Natalia Ackerman, Veronique Alain.
VHS: S12561. $29.95.
Chantal Akerman, France/Belgium, 1982, 89 mins.

Window Shopping
This amusing and romantic film combines the simplicity of a 1940s Hollywood musical with a knowing attitude that allows it to strip away some of the squeaky naivete of such films. It's set on one level of a shopping mall where "romance is in the air." Great Fun.
VHS: S13820. $29.95.
Chantal Akerman, France, 1986

SWISS CINEMA

Alpine Fire
One of the stranger brother-sister incest dramas; set in a remote mountain area, the family lives a simple farming life. The son, a deaf-mute, struggles with the "uncontrollable" passions of adolescence. Only his sister understands what he's going through, and in a moment of passion, the siblings begin a torrid and passionate love relationship. Romani with English subtitles.
VHS: S09610. $79.98.
Fredi M. Murer, Switzerland, 1987, 115 mins.

The Boat Is Full
It is the summer of 1942 and the Swiss government, alarmed at the vast numbers of people fleeing Nazi Germany, has set up immigration policies so stringent that they have declared the country "a full lifeboat." Complications arise when a Swiss innkeeper's wife takes in a group of frightened refugees. A haunting film from noted Swiss Filmmaker Markus Imhoof. "Virtually a flawless movie....One I will not soon forget!" (Jeffrey Lyons). French and German with English subtitles.
VHS: S00161. $59.95.
Markus Imhoof, Switzerland, 1980, 100 mins.

Four in a Jeep
Viveca Lindfors, Ralph Meeker and Michael Medwin star in this Berlin Film Festival winner. Vienna is divided among the allied powers, thereby forcing soldiers from the four powers to patrol the streets together. Soon the Russian and American in the group are at odds over a young Austrian woman whose husband has just escaped from a Russian camp.
VHS: S24003. $24.95.
Leopold Lindtberg, Switzerland, 1951, 81 mins.

Journey of Hope
A naive Kurdish family of refugees from Turkey travel to the Swiss border and are forced to cross the Alps at night during the winter. A grueling tale based on fact, it was awarded an Oscar for Best Foreign Language Film. Turkish, Kurdish and German with English subtitles.
VHS: S15418. $19.98.
Laser: LD75210. $34.98.
Xavier Koller, Switzerland, 1990, 111 minutes.

The Last Chance
This innovative Swiss film chronicles the travails of two escaped POW's working their way through Northern Italy to Switzerland. The war in Italy is almost over, but that does not mean everyone they encounter is willing to help these Allied soldiers. E.G. Morrison and John Hoy star in this tense film shot on location in a neo-realist style. English and other languages with English subtitles.
VHS: S23992. $24.95.
Leopold Lindtberg, Switzerland, 1945, 104 mins.

ALAIN TANNER

In the White City
When his ship lands in Lisbon, a disconnected sailor drifts through the streets and twisting alleys of the ghostly "white city," recording himself and his impressions with a Super-8 camera. He settles into a room above a saloon, and soon finds himself in an affair with the barmaid. Keeping a diary on film, he lets his world slip away; his ship leaves port without him, and he sends obscure notes (with some of his film) to his wife in Switzerland. A poignant and beautifully acted film starring Bruno Ganz and Teresa Madruga. French, Portuguese, German and English with subtitles.
VHS: S16499. $79.95.
Alain Tanner, France, 1983, 108 mins.

Jonah Who Will Be 25 in the Year 2000
Alain Tanner's masterpiece; a sensitive, literate and engaging comedy follows eight individuals affected by the political events of 1968. Tanner describes the film as "a dramatic tragi-comedy in political science fiction." Stars Myriam Boyer, Jean-Luc Bideau, Roger Jendly, Jacques Denis and Miou-Miou as a lovely supermarket clerk with no qualms about liberating groceries. French with English subtitles.
VHS: S16679. $79.95.
Alain Tanner, Switzerland, 1976, 115 mins.

La Salamandre
A treat: a journalist and his novelist friend research the story of a girl who was accused of shooting and wounding her uncle. Bulle Ogier delivers a disarming performance as the rare but tough and independent factory worker who confounds the two intellectuals with her inner revolt. Priceless for a scene in which Ogier, now a sales girl in a shoe shop, begins to caress the legs of her customers—funny, absurd, shocking, erotic. A unique film. French with English subtitles.
VHS: S21198. $79.95.
Alain Tanner, Switzerland, 1971, 125 mins.

Messidor
Tanner explores one of his favorite themes—the limitations of freedom—in this totally original mixture of experimentation and melodrama. Clementine Amouroux and Catherine Retore are two young women who hitchhike their way through Switzerland, but even their friendship cannot keep the idyllic odyssey free of fear and violence. French with English subtitles.
VHS: S26464. $79.95.
Alain Tanner, Switzerland/France, 1981, 120 mins.

Shorts
These short English films offer a look at some early work by today's major directors: *Momma Don't Allow* (1956) by Karel Reisz and Tony Richardson, *Nice Time* (1957) by Claude Goretta and Alain Tanner, *Amelia and the Angel* (1958) by Ken Russell and *The Burning* (1967) by Stephen Frears. Total running time 99 mins.
VHS: S22577. $74.95.

DUTCH CINEMA

The Assault
The 1987 winner of the Oscar for Best Foreign Language Picture, Fons Rademakers' epic tale is of a young boy who witnesses the brutal massacre of his family in the final days of World War II. The only survivor, the nightmarish memory haunts him until he uncovers and faces the truth. English dubbed.
VHS: S03573. $79.95.
Fons Rademakers, The Netherlands, 1986, 126 mins.

Crocodiles in Amsterdam
Described as a "slapstick female buddy movie," this Dutch feature stars two friends, Gino and Nina. Though thoroughly different, they manage to wrest friendship from the most inauspicious situations. Nina's rebelliousness and Gino's frivolity place them at each other's mercy, and often in hilarious situations. Dutch with English subtitles.
VHS: S26937. $39.95.
Annette Apon, The Netherlands, 1990, 88 mins.

Dear Boys
A harsh, stylized and feverish piece about dark sexual fantasies and deep romantic longing, the film concerns the romantic and sexual entanglements of a morose, self-absorbed writer and an uninhibited, carefree young man who recklessly pursues thrills and excitement. This groundbreaking, unapologetically gay work is adapted from Gerard Reve's novel. With Hugo Netsers, Hans Dagelet, Bill Van Dijk, and Albert Mol.
VHS: S17444. $69.95.
Paul de Lussanet, The Netherlands, 1980, 90 mins.

Egg
A remarkable film from Holland and one of the gems of the Cannes Film Festival in the year of its release, *Egg* is the story of Johan, a quiet, good-hearted, 35-year-old baker who answers a personal ad from a lonely schoolteacher named Eva. When the woman comes to town after an exchange of many letters, contrary to the expectations of the entire village, she decides to stay. *Egg* is a delightfully deadpan romantic fable in the spirit of Buster Keaton and Jacques Tati. Dutch with English subtitles.
VHS: S12330. $59.95.
Laser: LD70260. $34.95.
Danniel Danniel, The Netherlands, 1988, 58 mins.

The Eye Above the Well
A poetic depiction of life and ritual in the Indian state of Kerala, this unique film, called "a masterpiece" by Luis Marcorelles, features superb performance footage which shows how song, dance, martial arts and religion are passed from one generation to the next. Malayalam with English subtitles.
VHS: S26503. $59.95.
John van der Keuken, The Netherlands, 1988, 94 mins.

For a Lost Soldier
This haunting, true story follows a boy's wartime sexual awakening. It's controversial because this 12-year-old falls in love with a Canadian soldier who is in Holland just at the end of World War II. Ballet star Rudi Van Danzig recreates this memory from his childhood to show how a boy falls in love with his handsome liberator. Dutch with English subtitles.
VHS: S21831. $19.98.
Roeland Kerbosch, The Netherlands, 1993, 95 mins.

The Forbidden Quest
In June 1903 an unremarkable ship called *Holland* departed for Norway. In fact, this ship was secretly headed for the South Pole. Nearly 40 years later, the sole survivor, a ship's carpenter, was finally located in a tiny cottage in Ireland. There, the old man explained how murder, cannibalism and, finally, a spiritual awakening befell the men of that fateful voyage. A harrowing adventure in the tradition of Herman Melville and Joseph Conrad. "Stunning archival footage, an intriguing plot, and a dash of *The Twilight Zone*" (Bill Hoffman, *The New York Post*). Dedicated to Frank Hurley. In English.
VHS: S27563. $59.95.
Peter Delpeut, The Netherlands, 1993, 75 mins.

Fourth Man
Paul Verhoeven's surprise hit is a roller-coaster ride through forbidden sensual pleasure in the context of a kinky thriller. The three men in Christine's past all have one thing in common; they're dead. And when Gerard, seduced by Christine, moves into her life, a grisly series of dreams and visions hints he could be next: the fourth man. English dubbed.
VHS: S00461. $24.95.
Paul Verhoeven, The Netherlands, 1984, 104 mins.

Keetje Tippel
Paul Verhoeven's first international success, the story of a young Dutch girl adrift in 1881 Amsterdam, who rises from a life of poverty and prostitution to become a woman of means, education and attainment. This bawdy, tough, and delightful film is a Cinderella tale for intelligent adults. With the sexy Monique van der Ven and Rutger Hauer. Dutch with English subtitles.
VHS: S08998. $29.95.
Paul Verhoeven, The Netherlands, 1975, 104 mins.

Lyrical Nitrate
An unusual and moving tribute to early cinema constructed from color-tinted and toned nitrate films found deteriorating in the attic of an Amsterdam movie house. Through meticulous restoration, these prints, dating from the earliest years of the century, are shown in the rich and subtle colors in which they were originally exhibited, accompanied by an evocative soundtrack. "The cumulative effect of *Lyrical Nitrate* is a revelation" (*The New York Post*). Dutch intertitles with English subtitles.
VHS: S27564. $59.95.
Peter Delpeut, The Netherlands, 1991, 50 mins.

A Question of Silence
A murder committed by three women, all strangers to each other, leads to a controversial examination of the deep-seated rage—a result of living all their lives in a male-dominated society—which led to the crime. With outstanding performances. Dutch with English subtitles.
VHS: S01081. $59.95.
Marleen Gorris, The Netherlands, 1983, 92 mins.

Rare Dutch and Belgian Experimental Program
Includes five short films: *Mystic Lamb* (11 mins.), *Rain* (10 mins.), *New Earth* (23 mins.), *Bridge* (15 mins.) and *Umbrella* (30 mins.).
VHS: S14922. $29.95.

Rembrandt—1669
The final years of the artist's life and varied career, detailing the tension between his egotistical, self-centered celebrity and the contemplation, insight and emotional refinement of his art. An investigation of a man's art and life, the movie reveals the fascinating process and discoveries Rembrandt was heir to. "A fascinating life, a near perfect union of form and content" (*Variety*). With Frans Stelling, Tom de Koff and Aye Fil. Dutch with English subtitles.
VHS: S17766. $79.95.
Jos Stelling, The Netherlands, 1977, 114 mins.

Spetters (Dubbed)
Violence and tragedy mark this episodic story involving four young people in Holland on a turbulent collision course with their dreams. English dubbed and Dutch with English subtitles.
VHS: S01239. $39.95.
Paul Verhoeven, The Netherlands, 1980, 108 mins.

Spetters (Subtitled)
Dutch filmmaker Paul Verhoeven uses a motorcross championship to explore the homoerotic tensions of three young men, each obsessed with a beautiful, enigmatic hot dog stand owner. Verhoeven combines high melodrama with lurid sex sequences and a heightened visual style that's over-the-top romantic. With Ton Scherpenzeel, Kayak Toon Agterberg and Maarten Spanjer. Cameo appearance by Rutger Hauer. Dutch with English subtitles.
VHS: S18627. $39.95.
Paul Verhoeven, The Netherlands, 1983, 109 mins.

To Play or to Die
Set in a Dutch boys' school, the introverted and shy Kees enters into a psychosexual battle of wills with his handsome tormentor Charel, the leader of the brutal gang that uses fascist sadomasochistic games to exert their power. With Geert Hunaerts and Tjebbo Gerritsma. Dutch with English subtitles.
VHS: S18587. $39.95.
Frank Krom, USA, 1991, 50 mins.

Turkish Delights
A very amusing, uplifting, and tragic story of a couple madly in love. This Academy Award nominee is a study of two free spirits forced to change by the events of their lives. From the director of *The Fourth Man*. English dubbed.
VHS: S01377. $39.95.
Paul Verhoeven, The Netherlands, 1974, 100 mins.

The Vanishing
A young husband descends into the obsessive corners of his mind when his wife Saskia inexplicably vanishes while on holiday in France. This cold-blooded psychological thriller was winner of the 1991 Grand Prize of Dutch Cinema for Best Film. It succeeds the old-fashioned way, by hooking the viewer on the characters and murky undercurrents of the story—seducing us into the midst of a clean, logical nightmare. In the finest tradition of Hitchcock, *The Vanishing* will haunt you long after it is over. "It's unforgettable even if you try to forget it" (*San Francisco Chronicle*). Dutch and French with yellow English subtitles.
VHS: S15444. $19.98.
Laser: LD72197. $39.95.
George Sluizer, The Netherlands, 1991, 107 mins.

recent italian
CINEMA

Acla's Descent into Floristella

Sold into servitude by his parents, 12-year-old Acla must work underground in sulfur mines. Repeatedly beaten by his owner, the threat of sexual abuse is also ever-present. When he runs away, there are dire consequences for both him and his family. The story is based on the social mores and disturbing sexual practices found in 1930's Sicily. Italian with English subtitles.
VHS: S21544. $69.95.
Aurelio Grimaldi, Italy, 1987, 86 mins.

Acqua e Sapone

Comedy based on the adventures of a young woman in the high fashion world in Rome. Complications set in when a handsome janitor (played by Verdone) impersonates her tutor-priest. English title: *Soap and Water*. Italian with English subtitles.
VHS: S00067. $19.95.
Carlo Verdone, Italy, 1983, 100 mins.

Belle Starr

A virtually unclassifiable work by Lina Wertmuller, directed under the pseudonym Nathan Wich. It's a spaghetti western that charts the lawless aggression and sexual anarchy of the notorious bandit queen (Elsa Martinelli). Cinematography by John Alonzo. With Robert Wood, George Eastman, Dan Harrison and Eugene Walter. English dubbed.
VHS: S02190. $59.95.
Lina Wertmuller, Italy, 1979, 90 mins.

Bellissimo: Images of the Italian Cinema

A history of the Italian cinema by Gianfredo Mingozzi, an unprecedented reconstruction of the Italian cinema as a sophisticated art form. This unique film contains clips from the 1940's to the present, including such famous films as *Open City*, *Divorce Italian Style*, *8½* and *Seven Beauties*, and captures the great personalities of Italian filmmaking, including Dino De Laurentiis, Sophia Loren, Bertolucci, Mastroianni, Marco Ferreri, Rossellini, de Sica, Pasolini, Zeffirelli, Fellini, Wertmuller, Monica Vitti, Giancarlo Giannini, and Toto. English and Italian with English subtitles.
VHS: S05170. $29.95.
Gianfranco Mingozzi, Italy, 1987, 110 mins.

Beyond Obsession

From Liliana Cavani (*A Night Porter*) comes this shocker about the strange relationship of a political prisoner (Marcello Mastroianni), his daughter (Eleonora Giorgi) and her obsession with an elusive American (Tom Berenger). With Michel Piccoli. Also known as *Beyond the Door* (1982).
VHS: S17447. $19.95.
Liliana Cavani, Italy, 1982, 116 mins.

Bix

This famed trumpeter revolutionized jazz. In this first-rate musical biography his life and times are recreated based on the known facts. He is seen playing in some of the original locations including spots throughout the Midwest where *Bix* began. Hoagey Carmichael and Pee Wee Russel are just some of the figures seen accompanying him, performing songs like "Dardenella" and "Stardust." In English.
VHS: S20939. $29.95.
Pupi Avati, Italy/USA, 1990, 100 mins.

Bread and Chocolate

Nino Manfredi stars as an Italian immigrant struggling to make a life in the difficult Teutonic world of Switzerland. This comic Everyman finds himself forced into ever more degrading situations, but he never gives up. The result is a comedy with an intense feeling of pathos. With Anna Karina. Italian with English subtitles.
VHS: S27409. $59.95.
Franco Brusati, Italy, 1974, 109 mins.

Brother Sun, Sister Moon

Lavish costume epic depicts the story of St. Francis of Assisi, a man so gentle wild animals would eat from his hand, as he rejects the pomp of the Catholic Church. With some interesting characters working on this production, including Alec Guinness as the Pope, Lina Wertmuller in screenwriting capacity and 60's pop star Donovan supplying the music. English dialog.
VHS: S02623. $14.95.
Franco Zeffirelli, Italy/USA, 1973, 121 mins.

Burn!

Marlon Brando plays Sir William Walker, a cynical freelance secret agent and adventurer hired by the British government to dismantle Portugal's sugar trade monopoly in its Caribbean island colony of Quiemada. "The film soars with the imaginative force of art" (Pauline Kael). English dialog.
VHS: S00192. $19.95.
Laser: CLV. LD70352. $59.95.
Gillo Pontecorvo, Italy, 1970, 112 mins.

Caligula

Bob Guccione's entry into filmmaking was a disaster, but nevertheless, *Caligula* has achieved cult status of sorts. This epic of debauchery in Caligula's Rome stars Peter O'Toole, Malcolm McDowell and John Gielgud. English dialog.
VHS: S05788. $59.95.
Tinto Brass, Italy, 1982, 105 mins.

Caro Diario (Dear Diary)

This magical, virtually indescribable comedy by Nanni Moretti won the Best Director Prize at Cannes and follows the travails of a simple man (Moretti) in search of the true meaning of life. The film's three episodes confront, respectively, the changing character of Rome and of Moretti's generation, the possibility (and impossibility) of solitude, and the nature of truth in medicine. Often hilarious, always original, to say that Moretti is the Italian Woody Allen is to underestimate the pathos which underlies the accuracy of his social observations, the incisiveness of his insights. Don't miss. Italian with English subtitles.
VHS: S23967. $19.98.
Nanni Moretti, Italy, 1994, 100 mins.

Catch As Catch Can

Italy's most successful male model discovers a plot against him—by the animal kingdom. Horses throw him, dogs degrade him, bees sting him and bulls attack him. Soon his best clients grow fearful of using him. Vittorio Gassman in a offbeat Italian comedy. Dubbed in English.
VHS: S04940. $59.95.
Franco Indovina, Italy, 1984, 95 mins.

Christopher Columbus

With the 500th anniversary of his voyage to the Americas comes this historically detailed account of Columbus' discoveries. Gabriel Byrne leads this fascinating story of the life, times and voyages of Columbus. Stars Faye Dunaway, Oliver Reed, Max Von Sydow, Eli Wallach and Nicol Williamson.
VHS: S16039. $19.98.
Alberto Lattuada, Italy, 1985, 128 mins.

Ciao, Professore

This brilliant comedy details the outrageous clash between a strict, no-nonsense teacher and his class of rambunctious, street-smart children. Ultimately it's the teacher who ends up learning more about life from his charges than the other way round. Italian with English subtitles.
VHS: S23107. $96.98.
Laser: LD74806. $39.99.
Lina Wertmuller, Italy, 1993, 91 mins.

Cinema Paradiso

An affectionate salute to the magic of the movies and the individuals who spend their lives in the projection booth. This Italian film received an Oscar for Best Foreign Language Film. Philippe Noiret stars as Alfredo, the projectionist for a small Sicilian village movie palace, who opens up new worlds for one very inquisitive child. With Jaques Perrin, Salvatore Cascio, Pupella Maggio and Marco Leonardi. Italian with English subtitles.
VHS: S12603. $19.98.
Giuseppe Tornatore, Italy, 1989, 125 mins.

The Conviction

Marco Bellocchio's controversial feature starts with a young woman and a professor who are accidentally locked in a museum overnight. This enforced intimacy devolves into a night of love-making. But in the morning the man reveals he had the keys the entire time. The woman, Clair Nebout, accuses him of rape. The question that dominates the court trial is, "Was it coercion or mutual passion?" Italian with English subtitles.
VHS: S23115. $89.98.
Marco Bellocchio, Italy, 1994, 92 mins.

The Cricket

The beautiful Clio Goldsmith gets involved in a triangle—two women living with a singer. The situation becomes complicated when Clio's 17-year-old daughter also moves in. Mother and daughter become rivals in a bizarre erotic entanglement. Italian with English subtitles.
VHS: S00280. $29.95.
Alberto Lattuada, Italy, 1984, 90 mins.

Devil in the Flesh

Although the theme has been done many times, Marco Bellocchio managed to shock the international festival circuit with his notoriously explicit oral sex scene between Maruschka Detmers and Federico Pitzalis. *Devil in the Flesh*, wrote *Variety*, is "paradoxically one of the funniest, lightest works Bellocchio has come up with in some time. Yes, eroticism is a key theme, and thanks to an electrifying performance by Detmers, sparks fly in all directions." Andrea is quietly studying in his last year in high school when Giulia (Detmers) comes into his life.
VHS: S09594. $19.98.
Marco Bellocchio, Italy, 1986, 110 mins.

Ernesto

A lushly mounted, sensitively directed, complex depiction of homosexuality with Martin Halm as the boy who cooly tries anything and Michele Placido as the older, seducing man. "Genuinely erotic…*Ernesto* reconciles the legacies of Pasolini and Fassbinder." Italian with English subtitles.
VHS: S00416. $49.95.
Salvatore Samperi, Italy, 1983, 98 mins.

Everybody's Fine

A bittersweet story of a father's quest to reunite his five grown children in a film from the director of *Cinema Paradiso*. Marcello Mastroianni plays an elderly widower who decides to surprise his children by touring Italy and finding out how they live. Italian with English subtitles.
VHS: S16569. $19.95.
Giuseppe Tornatore, Italy, 1990, 115 mins.

The Eyes, the Mouth

A critically acclaimed tour-de-force; Lou Castel returns to his home to a family traumatized by suicide and unravelling at the seams in a film which re-established Bellocchio as a major world talent. With stunning performances from Castel, Angela Molina and Emmanuelle Riva. Italian with English subtitles.
VHS: S00424. $19.95.
Marco Bellocchio, Italy, 1982, 100 mins.

Flatfoot

Italian comic Bud Spencer stars in this ridiculous comedy about a maverick cop. He suddenly finds himself on the trail of gangsters who are selling drugs to young school kids. Despite this serious issue, there are hilarious situations and plenty of action. French with English subtitles.
VHS: S23891. $29.95.
Steno, Italy, 1971, 93 mins.

The Flavor of Corn

Lorenzo is a handsome, first-year professor with a quiet demeanor. He brings a passion for teaching to his young charges in a small village. As his relationship with his girlfriend deteriorates, he finds himself spending more time with 12-year-old Duilio. Soon Duilio's stepmother is questioning the nature of this amorous friendship. Italian with English subtitles.
VHS: S21545. $69.95.
Gianni Da Campo, Italy, 1994, 89 mins.

Flight of the Innocent

The ten-year-old son of a brutal kidnapper witnesses his entire family's murder at the hands of a rival gang. He escapes only to find himself being hunted by both these relentless killers and the police. The boy's desperate struggle for survival becomes a path to redemption for the crimes of his father. Italian with English subtitles.
VHS: S21034. $92.95.
Laser: LD72409. $34.98.
Carlo Carlei, Italy, 1993, 105 mins.

Forever Mary

Forever Mary tells the story of an idealistic school teacher trying to make a difference in a rigid reform school. The film works in such a traditional, straightforward style that it's easy to overlook its freshness and imagination. Directed by Marco Risi with passion and grace, *Forever Mary* has all the warmth and easy vitality that make Italian films so beguiling, and it affords its durable star Michele Placido one of his richest roles. Italian with English subtitles.
VHS: S15443. $79.95.
Marco Risi, Italy, 1991, 100 mins.

Francesco

Liliana Cavani (*Night Porter*) casts Mickey Rourke as St. Francis of Assisi in this revisionist story of Francis, the son of a rich man, who rejected all that is worldly for a life of poverty. With Helena Bonham Carter.
VHS: S21296. $89.95.
Liliana Cavani, Italy/Britain, 1989, 119 mins.

Henry IV

Pirandello's classic play, directed by Marco Bellocchio (*Fists in the Pocket*), stars Marcello Mastroianni as the aristocrat who falls off a horse and believes himself to be the medieval French Emperor. A fabulous investigation of delusion. With Claudia Cardinale. Italian with English subtitles.
VHS: S04874. $24.95.
Marco Bellocchio, Italy, 1985, 94 mins.

Husbands and Lovers

Julian Sands is cast as an open minded European screenwriter who isn't bothered if wife Joanna Pacula has other lovers. He does get upset, however, when he learns that the brutal Tcheky Karyo is getting rough with his beloved and she doesn't mind. Based on the novel *The Friday Villa* by Albert Moravia. Unrated version. Music by Ennio Morricone. Filmed in English.
VHS: S16578. $19.95.
Mauro Bolognini, Italy, 1991, 94 mins.

The Icicle Thief

Maurizio Nichetti presents an energetic send-up of the 1949 Italian neo-realist masterpiece *The Bicycle Thief* while, at the same time, spoofing the ridiculousness of contemporary television commercials. The writer-director takes on a double acting role as a frustrated filmmaker and a fictional glass factory worker who steals a chandelier for his wife. Complications arise when the boundaries between the two stories collide. With Caterina Sylos Labini, Claudio G. Fava and Heidi Komarek. "This hilarious comedy is everything *The Purple Rose of Cairo* should have been and more" (Jonathan Rosenbaum, *Chicago Reader*). Italian with English subtitles.
VHS: S14456. $19.98.
Maurizio Nichetti, Italy, 1989, 93 mins.

Il Postino (The Postman)

Massimo Troisi stars as a humble postman in a small but beautiful Italian village, whose life is transformed by the simple powers of poetry. Pablo Neruda is poet-living-in-exile who gives this bumbling mailman the right words to seduce the woman of his dreams. Troisi died abruptly after completing this role, turning this touching and deeply felt film into a highly apt but wholly unexpected memorial to his skills as a comic actor. With Maria Grazia Cucinotta and Philippe Noiret. Based on the novel *Burning Patience*, by Antonia Skarmenta. Italian with English subtitles.
VHS: S27378. $99.99.
Laser: LD75509. $39.99.
Michael Radford, Italy, 1995, 108 mins.

In the Name of the Pope-King

In Nome del Papa Re is the recipient of three David de Donatello prizes, and stars Nino Manfredi. Set in 1867 as Italian patriots fight to unify the country and Rome stands alone ruled by the Pope, Monsignor Colobo, a magistrate of the Papal State, is about to resign from his office when young terrorists blow up the barracks of the government troops, and the Monsignor discovers that one of the suspects is his own 20-year-old son. A compelling story of intrigue, political conflict and murder unfolds. Italian with English subtitles.
VHS: S05169. $29.95.
Luigi Magni, Italy, 1985, 115 mins.

Johnny Stecchino

A frenetic comedy directed by and starring Roberto Benigni (*Down by Law* and *Night on Earth*). Playing two roles, Benigni is a shy, nervous bus driver who's seduced by a beautiful Italian mistress (Nicoletta Braschi) to stand in for his nefarious look-alike, Johnny, a corrupt Mafiosi who turned state's evidence. Benigni is like Chaplin on speed—colorful, loopy and insanely funny. With Paolo Banacelli and Franco Volpi. Italian with English subtitles.
VHS: S19058. $19.98.
Laser: CLV. LD72103. $39.99.
Roberto Benigni, Italy, 1991, 100 mins.

Julia and Julia

Kathleen Turner is a troubled American widow living in Trieste, Italy. She's living two lives as she crosses between two realities, one of which features a live husband and the young child she never had. From the director of *Invitation au Voyage*, a bizarre mystery of unexplained passions. With Gabriel Byrne and Sting. In English.
VHS: S06533. $19.98.
Laser: LD71070. $39.98.
Peter Del Monte, Italy, 1987, 98 mins.

The Last Diva

Born in Florence in 1888, Francesca Bertini made her film debut in a 1907 short about a beauty contestant, *Goddess of the Sea*. Exactly 70 years later she starred in Bernardo Bertolucci's *1900* as Burt Lancaster's mother. Temperamental, capricious, willful, egocentric, amazingly elegant and beautiful, Francesca was one of the silver screen's last divas. In this touching, funny and wondrous portrait of a unique woman, scenes from many of her classic films are juxtaposed with interviews of the geniuses of Italian cinema—such as the late Sergio Leone, whose father, Roberto Roberti, directed some of Bertini's finest performances. Italian with English subtitles.
VHS: S14170. $29.95.
Gianfranco Mingozzi, Italy, 1982, 85 mins.

Lucky Luciano

Important film by Francesco Rosi, butchered by the American distributor who also dubbed it and sold it as exploitation. Rosi investigates the final years in the life of the world's most famous mobster, Lucky Luciano, who started the world's greatest crime organization. English dubbed.
VHS: S00783. $9.95.
Francesco Rosi, Italy, 1971, 108 mins.

Malicious

Laura Antonelli gives a tantalizing performance in this bizarre, kinky Italian sex comedy. Antonelli plays a housekeeper for a widow and his three sons, and she quickly becomes the object of lusty affection of every male in the house including the fourteen year old Nino. Director Samperi masterfully combines amusement with a boy's budding sexual awareness and dramatic sequences bordering on danger and erotic passion. English dubbed.
VHS: S00809. $49.95.
Salvatore Samperi, Italy, 1974, 97 mins.

Mediterraneo

Winner of the 1991 Best Foreign Language Academy Award. A small, eight-man battalion is ordered to secure a strategically unimportant Greek island. They are cut off from their superiors and encounter a liberated, magical community of beautiful women, sad-hearted prostitutes, a sympathetic priest and no resistance. With Diego Abatantuono, Claudio Bigagli and Giuseppe Cederna. Italian with English subtitles.
VHS: S18159. $19.98.
Gabriele Salvatores, Italy, 1990, 99 mins.

A Night Full of Rain

Candice Bergen is a feminist. Giancarlo Giannini (*New York Stories*) is a journalist. Their marriage becomes a battle royale of the sexes in this fierce and fun drama which was Lina Wertmuller's first English language film. Shot on location in Italy and San Francisco.
VHS: S13801. $19.98.
Lina Wertmuller, Italy, 1978, 104 mins.

Night Porter

Controversial film about the perverse relationship between a former SS officer in a Nazi concentration camp and a woman, a former inmate at the camp. From one of Italy's few women directors, with Dirk Bogarde and Charlotte Rampling. English dialog.
VHS: S00934. $19.98.
    Laser: LD72308. $29.99.
Liliana Cavani, Italy, 1973, 117 mins.

Open Doors

Gian Maria Volonte stars as a conscientious judge assigned to a notorious murder case in Palermo during the reign of Mussolini. He believes there is more to the story than the self-confessed killer of three is willing to admit—and boy, is he right. Starring Ennio Fantastichini, Renzo Giovampietro and Renato Carpentieri. This rewarding, thoughtful drama was nominated for an Oscar as Best Foreign Language Film. Italian with English subtitles.
VHS: S14786. $79.98.
    Laser: LD71624. $39.95.
Gianni Amelio, Italy, 1989, 109 mins.

Palombella Rossa

Director Nanni Moretti's political comedy about the fate of Italian communism. The action follows a politician who is injured in a car crash and suffers from amnesia. He awakens to find himself about to play an important water polo match. While his teammates negotiate positions and devise strategies, he leaps out of the pool to interview a succession of bureaucrats, partyhacks and militants. "The scope of its concerns, and Moretti's ability to express these in visual terms, is ambitious and accomplished" (Toronto Festival of Festivals). Italian with English subtitles.
VHS: S19975. $19.98.
Nanni Moretti, Italy, 1989, 87 mins.

The Pool Hustlers (Io, Chiara e lo Scuro)

Recent Italian comedy about the fascinating world of big time billiards. A small-time wizard with a stick and balls proves to be a great irritation to the established champion, but still has time for romance. With Francesco Nuti, Giuliana de Sio, and Marcello Loti. Italian with English subtitles.
VHS: S08709. $24.95.
D. Maurizio Ponzi, Italy, 1983, 101 mins.

Profumo di Donna

A blind, middle-aged man, endowed with great serenity, common sense and epicurean knowledge of the pleasures of life, undertakes a journey whose destination is unknown: death or love, solitude or the sweet smell of woman in this comedy drama by Dino Risi. Starring Vittorio Gassmann. Also known as Sweet Smell of Woman. Italian with English subtitles.
VHS: S08780. $69.95.
Dino Risi, Italy, 1975, 103 mins.

Quo Vadis

The Romans of 63 AD revel in a boundless feast of indulgence, romance and mysticism in this recent adaptation of the famous novel by Herman Sinkiewicz. Klaus Maria Brandauer, Frederic Forrest and Max von Sydow star as the Christians take on the Romans. In English.
VHS: S09802. $89.95.
    Laser: LD71288. $59.95.
Franco Rossi, Italy, 1988, 122 mins.

Rorret

An Italian reconsideration of Michael Powell's classic Peeping Tom and several Hitchcock thrillers, this film concerns the shy, anonymous owner of a repertory theater devoted to thrillers and horror movies. Mr. Rorret lives behind the movie screen, documenting the responses of the women watching the films, and begins to stalk them. The film beautifully recreates moments from Hitchcock's Psycho, Dial M for Murder, and Strangers on a Train. "Good, creepy fun" (New York Post).
VHS: S17396. $79.95.
Fulvio Wetzl, Italy, 1987, 105 mins.

Running Away

Sophia Loren and Sydney Penny star as an Italian mother and daughter who flee World War II Rome in hopes of finding safety in the ancestral mountain village. The journey proves perilous and echoes Loren's Oscar-winning role in Two Women. With Robert Loggia, Andrea Occhipinti and Carla Calo. Based on the novel by Alberto Moravia.
VHS: S13271. $89.95.
Dino Risi, Italy/USA, 1989, 101 mins.

The Sleazy Uncle

Franco Brusati's poetic film about an eccentric man, Luca (Vittorio Gassman), whose charm and grace gain the attention of his emotionally rigid, wealthy nephew, Ricardo (Giancarlo Giannini). With wit and sureness of detail, the old man insinuates himself deeper and deeper into the younger man's life. "Outrageous but poetic" (The New York Times). Italian with English subtitles.
VHS: S17363. $89.95.
Franco Brusati, Italy, 1990, 104 mins.

Smugglers

Adventure story of a group of smugglers during the Russian Revolution, who profit from the hardships created by the fighting and must avoid both sides in the conflict. Dubbed in English.
VHS: S04776. $59.95.
Valentino Orsini, Italy, 1975, 110 mins.

Sotto...Sotto

Comedy from Wertmuller commenting on the battle between the sexes, as Oscar's wife tells him she is in love with another. He never suspects it is with her friend Adele. Italian with English subtitles.
VHS: S01234. $19.95.
Lina Wertmuller, Italy, 1984, 104 mins.

The Station

An Italian film about a mysterious woman who's left her fiance and the simple stationmaster who pursues her. With Sergio Rubini, Margherita Buy and Ennio Fantastichini. Cinematography by Alessio Gelsini. Italian with English subtitles.
VHS: S18255. $89.95.
Sergio Rubini, Italy, 1990, 92 mins.

The Story of Boys and Girls

The engagement of two young lovers brings together an intoxicating mix of friends and family. Between the 20 delicious courses and flowing wine, the guests loosen their belts as well as their tongues, spilling family secrets and revealing romantic intrigues. Even the maid gets caught in a lusty tryst that leaves her flushed and rumpled when she serves the next dish. Italian with English subtitles.
VHS: S16525. $19.98.
    Laser: LD72227. $39.95.
Pupi Avati, Italy, 1991, 92 mins.

Summer Night (With Greek Profile, Almond Eyes and Scent of Basil)

Director Lina Wertmuller loves those long titles. She also wrote the rest of the script, which concerns a very rich member of the Italian ruling class who kidnaps a noted terrorist and holds him for ransom. This change of pace leads to smoldering passion on an island estate. With Mariangela Melato and Michele Placido. Italian with English subtitles.
VHS: S05612. $79.95.
Lina Wertmuller, Italy, 1987, 97 mins.

Swept Away

Raffaella, a rich, beautiful, acid-tongued Milanese who has chartered a yacht, and Gennarino, a swarthy Sicilian deckhand, are marooned on an isolated island in the Mediterranean. She is a capitalist for whom the system has paid off; he is a dedicated Communist. Swept Away is the story of their tumultuous courtship, in what one critic described as a "fierce battle of the sexes as witty as it is wise." Letterboxed. Italian with English subtitles.
VHS: S01290. $29.98.
Lina Wertmuller, Italy, 1975, 116 mins.

Tigers in Lipstick

Veteran Italian comedy director Luigi Zampa in an omnibus of seven stories about aggressive women who take advantage of their men. With Ursula Andress, Monica Vitti, Laura Antonelli, Sylvia Kristel, Michele Placido, Roberto (Down by Law) Benigni. In English.
VHS: S07439. $59.95.
Luigi Zampa, Italy, 1979, 83 mins.

Till Marriage Do Us Part

When Laura Antonelli finds out on her wedding night that the groom is actually her brother she must find another way to lose her virginity. A sexual comedic farce that displays the full talents of the lead actress. With Jean Rochefort, Alberto Lionello and Karin Schubert.
VHS: S06875. $29.95.
Luigi Comencini, Italy, 1974, 97 mins.

Tosca's Kiss

The remarkable film by Daniel Schmid, set in the Casa Verdi, the musicians' retirement home set up by Giuseppe Verdi in 1902. Funny, poignant, sensitive, inspiring—"one of the most insightful, life-affirming and just plain entertaining movies." Italian with English subtitles.
VHS: S01365. $39.95.
Daniel Schmid, Italy, 1985, 87 mins.

Tree of the Wooden Clogs

A passionate, moving film, an epic celebration of an Italian family's indomitable spirit, winner of the Grand Prize at the 1978 Cannes Film Festival. The subject of the film is peasant life in northern Italy at the turn of the century, focusing on about a year in the life of three families living on a feudal estate. "A quiet masterpiece" (Newsweek). "The movie, which runs slightly more than three hours, is an accumulation of dozens of experiences of children, adults, old people, village idiots, of harvest times and plantings, of moments of boredom and jealousy, celebrations, fatigue, brief pleasures and mysterious ones. It moves so effortlessly, often with great humor and always with compassion, it seems much shorter than most 90-minute films" (Vincent Canby, New York Times). Italian with English subtitles.
VHS: S12946. $19.98.
Ermanno Olmi, Italy, 1978, 185 mins.

Vito and the Others

A chilling depiction of the street life of the neglected who pass through the extreme poverty of Naples. The realistic, documentary-like plot centers on a 12-year-old boy and his friends, drawn into the netherworld of crime, drugs and prostitution. With Nando Triola, Giovanni Bruno and Mario Lentl. Italian with English subtitles.
VHS: S18752. $69.95.
Antonio Capuano, Italy, 1992, 90 mins.

Volere Volare

Maurizio Nichetti collaborated with animator Guido Manuli in this inventive comedy that blends live action and animation. The story concerns the nervous and complicated romance of a shy special effects technician, Maurizio (Nichetti), and Martina (Angela Finocchiaro), a beautiful actress who dramatizes bizarre sexual fantasies for a group of strange clients. Complications ensue when Maurizio's body is transformed into the form and shape of a cartoon, assuming its own will. With Patrizio Roversi and Mariella Valentini. Italian with English subtitles.
VHS: S19205. $19.98.
    Laser: CLV. LD72102. $39.95.
Maurizio Nichetti/Guido Manuli, Italy, 1991, 92 mins.

When Women Had Tails

Lina Wertmuller co-wrote the screenplay of this slapstick farce about a group of prehistoric cave dwellers. With Senta Berger, Giuliano Gemma, Frank Wolff and Lando Buzzanca. Italian with English subtitles.
VHS: S17734. $29.95.
Pasquale Festa Campanile, Italy, 1970, 110 mins.

Where's Piccone?

A wonderful, very funny film from the Italian comic genius Nanni Loy, starring the incomparable Giancarlo Giannini. The search is on for Pasquale Piccone, who inexplicably vanishes in an ambulance on the way to the hospital. His wife and small-time hustler Giannini team up to discover the mystery and together find that this respectable man has lead a double life. A fantastic, comic voyage into the Neapolitan underworld. Italian with English subtitles.
VHS: S05168. $29.95.
Nanni Loy, Italy, 1985, 110 mins.

BERNARDO BERTOLUCCI

1900

Bernardo Bertolucci's opus, a sweeping, epic achievement which chronicles the rise of Fascism and Socialism in Italy through the interlocking stories of family generations. The stellar cast includes Robert De Niro and Gerard Depardieu as two friends torn apart by the political upheavals in their country, Dominique Sanda, Stefania Sandrelli, Donald Sutherland and Alberto Grimaldi. A work of massive scope, brilliance and power, Pauline Kael said Bertolucci "is trying to make a people's film by drawing on the mythology of the movies, as if it were a collective memory. 1900 is a romantic moviegoer's version of the class struggle—a love poem for the movies as well as for the life of those who live communally on the land." English dialog.
VHS: S06845. $29.95.
Bernardo Bertolucci, Italy, 1977, 245 mins.

Before the Revolution

Bernardo Bertolucci's timelessly lyrical affirmation of youth's rites of passage through love and politics. A young man rejects his middle-class surroundings and struggles with the Communist ideology to which he believes himself committed, only to find that he is too deeply involved with the beauty of life as it was before the revolution. Made when Bertolucci was only 22 years old, Before the Revolution was the revelation of the 1964 New York Film Festival. Italian with English subtitles.
VHS: S07500. $59.95.
Bernardo Bertolucci, Italy, 1962, 110 mins.

The Conformist

Bertolucci equates the rise of Italian fascism with the psychosexual life of his protagonist, for whom conformity becomes an obsession after a traumatic homosexual experience in his youth. A dazzling descent into the nature of corruption of power, with many now-famous sequences and extraordinary cinematography by Vittorio Storaro. With Jean-Louis Trintignant, Dominique Sanda and Stefania Sandrelli. English dubbed.
VHS: S00264. $49.95.
    Laser: LD75355. $29.98.
Bernardo Bertolucci, Italy, 1970, 108 mins.

The Grim Reaper

Rarely since Citizen Kane has a film debut by a director conveyed such promise. Like Rashomon, The Grim Reaper brilliantly explores the many sides to the truth of a brutal murder of a prostitute in a Rome Park. Bernardo Bertolucci delves into the dark underbelly of brute poverty, creating a tense tapestry of behavior and a challenging puzzle which leaves us celebrating life in all is pain, joy and humor. Italian with English subtitles.
VHS: S13280. $29.95.
Bernardo Bertolucci, Italy, 1962, 100 mins.

Last Tango in Paris

Powerful, explosive, erotic, political film that took the world by storm; Maria Schneider and Marlon Brando co-star in this film of love, sex and will. "The most powerfully erotic film ever made," wrote Pauline Kael. "Last Tango is a genuine masterpiece of staggering proportions," said Newsweek. English dialog. Uncut, X-rated version.
VHS: S00727. $19.98.
    Laser: CLV, 2 discs, Criterion. LD70412. $69.95.
    Laser: Letterboxed, MGM. LD71176. $39.98.
Bernardo Bertolucci, Italy, 1974, 129 mins.

Little Buddha

Keanu Reeves and Bridget Fonda star in this sweeping tale of destiny and mysticism. Chris Isaak is a young American boy whose life is transformed forever when he becomes involved with a prince searching for the reincarnation of his beloved teacher. As these different worlds collide, an extraordinary adventure unfolds.
VHS: S22604. $94.99.
    Laser: LD74641. $39.99.
Bernardo Bertolucci, Great Britain, 1994, 123 mins.

Partner

Bertolucci's third feature film is a beautiful, funny adventure that uses sound, silence, music, color and an extremely literary frame of reference to create a two-hour sense of the impression of what it's like to be a romantic in today's world. The screenplay by Bertolucci and Gianni Amico is very freely inspired by Dostoevsky's short novel, The Double, about an ineffectual young man who is taken over—and ultimately driven to madness—by his alter ego, who can do all the things he cannot. Italian with English subtitles.
VHS: S08263. $39.95.
Bernardo Bertolucci, Italy, 1968, 112 mins.

The Sheltering Sky

John Malkovich and Debra Winger star as an unfortunate pair of American tourists adrift in the deserts of North Africa. Bernardo Bertolucci brings this Paul Bowles novel to the screen and tries his best to capture in images, the words and intentions of the author. Vincent Canby called this "Bertolucci's most seductive, most hypnotic movie." With Campbell Scott, Jill Bennett, Timothy Spall and Eric Vu-An.
VHS: S13753. $19.98.
    Laser: LD70674. $39.98.
Bernardo Bertolucci, USA, 1990, 139 mins.

Spider's Stratagem

The breakthrough film of Bertolucci is an extremely atmospheric puzzler, based on a short story by Jorge Luis Borges. A young man visits the provincial town where his anti-Fascist father was assassinated 30 years earlier, and is rejected by the populace at every turn. With Giulio Brogi and Alida Valli, and beautiful cinematography by Vittorio Storaro. Italian with English subtitles.
VHS: S12827. $59.95.
Bernardo Bertolucci, Italy, 1970, 97 mins.

Tragedy of a Ridiculous Man

The seriocomic tale of a sudden kidnapping that jolts a family into togetherness. Ugo Tognazzi portrays the rich Parma dairy farmer forced to sell his possessions to meet the ransom demanded by the terrorist gang holding his son. Bertolucci examines the siege mentality of Italy's leftist brigades and strips the mask off family dynamics hidden behind webs of deceit. "The best Bertolucci movie…in a long time. The best treatment of the generation gap between a father and son that I have yet seen" (Andrew Sarris).
VHS: S13803. $59.99.
Bernardo Bertolucci, Italy, 1981, 116 mins.

TAVIANI BROTHERS

Allonsanfan

Marcello Mastroianni stars in a comic masterpiece making use of bravura lighting and color schemes. Set after Napoleon has fallen in 1816, the film features Martroianni as a disillusioned Jacobin aristocrat released from prison and torn between his revolutionary ideals and comfortable lifestyle. With Laura Betti, Lea Massari. Italian with English subtitles.
VHS: S05167. $29.95.
Paolo & Vittorio Taviani, Italy, 1984, 115 mins.

Fiorile (Wild Flower)

In the orange groves of Italy, the Benedetti family preserves their time-honored ways, including the curse that has followed them for generations. In this provocative tale, greed, lust, romance and forbidden love stalk the unsuspecting members of this clan in a warmly nostalgic look at the process of history. Italian with English subtitles.
VHS: S21211. $19.95.
Paolo & Vittorio Taviani, Italy, 1993, 118 mins.

Kaos

The Taviani Brothers adapted five short stories by Luigi Pirandello to capture the Sicilian landscape "harboring a richness of dramatic tales at once emotional and elemental" (Time Out). With Margarita Lozano, Omero Antonutti and Claudio Bigagli. Italian with English subtitles.
VHS: S17861. $29.98.
Paolo & Vittorio Taviani , Italy, 1984, 187 mins.

Night of the Shooting Stars

This magical film by the Taviani Brothers is set on the night of the Feast of St. Lawrence during the last days of World War II. A woman recalls her beloved and a night years ago when, on another such night, a group of peasants fled through the Tuscan countryside amid exploding shells lighting up the sky instead of stars. The film is a beautiful tapestry of fact, myth and wartime memory, romantic and intense. Italian with English subtitles.
VHS: S00933. $19.98.
Paolo & Vittorio Taviani, Italy, 1982, 106 mins.

MICHELANGELO ANTONIONI

Blow-Up

The classic film questioning the relationship between image and reality; David Hemmings plays a fashion photographer who photographs a woman (Vanessa Redgrave) in a park and later comes to believe that he has actually photographed a murder. Through the photograph, Hemmings is lured out of his life to search for the truth. English dialog.
VHS: S00152. $19.98.
    Laser: CAV, widescreen, 2 discs, Criterion. LD70351. $79.95.
    Laser: Extended play, chapter search, MGM. LD70528. $34.98.
Michelangelo Antonioni, Great Britain, 1966, 111 mins.

Eclipse

The third of Antonioni's great trilogy, with Monica Vitti as the alienated woman among the upper bourgeoisie. A brilliant film, with its stupefying climax of silence, comprised of 58 shots lasting 7 minutes. Italian with English subtitles.
VHS: S00393. $29.95.
Michelangelo Antonioni, Italy, 1966, 123 mins.

Il Grido

Alida Valli and Steve Cochran are featured in the story of a jilted husband who wanders with his daughter from village to village and woman to woman until, after a last gaze at his wife, he falls to his death. Set in the desolate landscapes of Antonioni's own childhood in the Po Valley, the plot "develops no longer explicitly through major events but implicitly in silent interstices between minor events" (Seymour Chatman). A breakthrough work from Antonioni's neo-realist period. Italian with English subtitles.
VHS: S09655. $24.95.
Michelangelo Antonioni, Italy, 1957, 116 mins.

L'Avventura

A film about the fragility of human relationships which established Antonioni as a major talent. A party of rich Italians land on an uninhabited island, and one young woman disappears. "Our drama is non-communication," said Antonioni, "and it is this feeling that dominates the characters in my film." With Monica Vitti. Winner of the Special Jury Award at Cannes. Italian with English subtitles.
VHS: S00696. $29.95.
    Laser: LD70342. $124.95.
Michelangelo Antonioni, Italy, 1960, 145 mins.

La Notte

The second installment of Italian director Michelangelo Antonioni's trilogy. Jeanne Moreau plays a bored, dissatisfied woman who abandons her simple minded husband (Marcello Mastroianni), who in turn attempts to seduce a beautiful, vacant woman (Monica Vitti). Moody, introverted and beautiful, brilliantly photographed by Gianni Di Venanzo. Italian with English subtitles.
VHS: S14850. $19.95.
Michelangelo Antonioni, Italy, 1961, 122 mins.

Red Desert

Antonioni's masterpiece, with the great Monica Vitti playing the neurotic young woman married to an engineer in the industrial wasteland of northern Italy, searching in vain for meaning in life. Antonioni's first film in color—and what color! One of the most important films of the last half of the century. Italian with English subtitles.
VHS: S02080. $29.95.
Michelangelo Antonioni, Italy, 1964 , 116 mins.

Zabriskie Point

Antonioni's portrait of revolutionary America of the 1960's; a disquieting, visually stunning film about two American young people of the 60's, faced with American commercialism, consumerism and the need to find oneself. With Mark Frechette and Daria Halprin. English dialog.
VHS: S01497. $19.98.
Laser: LD70721. $34.98.
Michelangelo Antonioni, USA, 1970, 112 mins.

ETTORE SCOLA

La Nuit de Varennes

This witty and sumptuous approach to the French Revolution takes as its focal point one crucial night in 1791, when Louis XVI and Marie Antoinette flee Paris for the border. Following their carriage is a host of historical and fictional characters, including Casanova (Mastroianni) and Tom Paine (Harvey Keitel). French with English subtitles.
VHS: S00708. $59.95.
Ettore Scola, Italy/France, 1982, 128 mins.

Le Bal

A unique experiment: adapted freely from an enormously successful French stage play, *Le Bal* is a non-talking movie set in a dance hall over a period of 50 years of French history. Through the marathon of waltzes, foxtrots, tangos, boogie steps, twists, cha-chas, rhumbas, the dancers reflect changing styles and mores in an energetic fresco. French with English subtitles.
VHS: S00733. $79.95.
Ettore Scola, Italy/France, 1982, 112 mins.

Macaroni

Marcello Mastroianni and Jack Lemmon star in this film about two World War II buddies who are re-united in Italy amidst a secret, fictitious love affair Antonio has created for his sister with his American friend. In English and some Italian.
VHS: S04955. $79.95.
Laser: LD75346. $29.98.
Ettore Scola, Italy, 1985, 104 mins.

Passione d'Amore

This story of obsessive love between an ugly spinster and a handsome young officer won the Cannes Special Jury Prize in 1981 and is notable for its strong performances from the sensuous Laura Antonelli and Jean-Louis Trintignant. Mad and consumed by desire, this woman manages to overcome the officer's reservations. Steven Sondheim's Tony-award winning musical *Passion* is based on this story. Italian with English subtitles.
VHS: S22231. $24.95.
Ettore Scola, Italy, 1981, 117 mins.

We All Loved Each Other So Much

An affectionate tribute to Italian Cinema (Scola has included footage from DeSica's *Bicycle Thief*, as well as a recreation of *La Dolce Vita*'s fountain scene) as well as a sensitive comedy about the friendship of three men and a woman each has loved. Italian with English subtitles.
VHS: S01435. $29.95.
Ettore Scola, Italy, 1969, 124 mins.

FEDERICO FELLINI

8½

Fellini's great autobiographical masterpiece, the loose portrayal of a film director during the course of making a film and finding himself trapped by his fears and insecurities. Continually inventive with the performance of a lifetime from Marcello Mastroianni as Guido, the director, and from Claudia Cardinale, Anouk Aimee and Sandra Milo. Italian with English subtitles.
VHS: S07140. $59.95.
Laser: Widescreen. **LD70806. $59.95.**
Federico Fellini, Italy, 1963, 138 mins.

Amarcord

A film which breathes freedom—a nostalgic, fantastic and funny reminiscence of growing up in Fellini's home town of Rimini—made, Fellini said, to finish with youth and tenderness. Against the comic background are sets of indelible characters and an omnipresent Fascist state. *Amarcord* breathlessly shifts between the melodramatic, the intimate and the burlesque in what is a deeply personal, shared vision. The images—a peacock flying through the snow, a child on his way to school who encounters cows that the early-morning fog has transformed into monsters—are like icons; unforgettable. Italian with English subtitles.
VHS: S00042. $39.95.
Laser: LD75072. $69.95.
Federico Fellini, Italy, 1974, 127 mins.

Ciao Federico!

A revealing portrait of Fellini at work, directing the actors who populate the unreal world of his *Satyricon*. Immersed in the creative process, Fellini moves through the set, a larger than life embodiment of his characters. English and Italian with English subtitles.
VHS: S00242. $19.95.
Gideon Bachmann, Italy, 1971, 55 mins.

City of Women

Federico Fellini's imaginative voyage into the world of women—or, more accurately, into the world of male fantasies about women, set adrift in the threatening seas of middle-age and feminism. Part apocalyptic joyride, part funhouse, part dream, part vaudeville, *City of Women* stars Marcello Mastroianni in an outlandish work of fantasy and humor. Italian with enhanced English subtitles.
VHS: S11591. $79.95.
Federico Fellini, Italy, 1980, 138 mins.

The Clowns

Fellini's homage to circus clowns is in itself a clownish spoof as it invades the screen with three rings of slapstick, spectacle and sensation. "My films owe an enormous amount to the circus," said Fellini. "For me the clowns were always a traumatic visual experience, ambassadors of a vocation of a showman." This affectionate journey to the root of Fellini's inspiration is comic and magically moving, with one of the best musical scores by the great Nino Rota.
VHS: S00253. $34.95.
Federico Fellini, Italy, 1971, 90 mins.

Fellini Satyricon

Federico Fellini freely adapts the work of Petronius Arbiter in this sexual odyssey through ancient Rome. With an emphasis on spectacle and the grotesque, we follow two young Romans in their pursuit of pleasure and personal survival. With Martin Potter, Hiram Keller, Capucine and Luigi Montefiori as the Minotaur. Letterboxed. Italian with English subtitles.
VHS: S06318. $19.98.
Laser: Widescreen. **LD70979. $124.95.**
Federico Fellini, Italy, 1969, 138 mins.

Fellini's Roma

"A story of a city," to quote Fellini. In *Roma*, Fellini strings together a series of images of Rome, and through his eyes this special city becomes a living, breathing organism. *Roma* is quite possibly Fellini's most avowedly autobiographical film to date—a loving document of his own personal encounter with Rome. Starring Fiona Florence, Britta Barnes, Pia de Doses, Marne Maitland and Peter Gonzales as Fellini at 18. Italian with English subtitles.
VHS: S14807. $19.99.
Laser: LD72120. $49.98.
Federico Fellini, Italy, 1972, 128 mins.

Fellini: A Director's Notebook

In this autobiographical work, the touch of Fellini is everywhere. The film begins with a trip to the set of the never-completed *The Voyage of Mastorna*. Then it shows some of the real elements that inspired the later *Satyricon*, including a subway tour of ancient Rome and some odd characters who might be used in the film. In addition, clips from previous works show Giulietta Massina and Marcello Mastroianni.
VHS: S27768. $29.95.
Federico Fellini, USA/Italy, 1970, 60 mins.

Ginger and Fred

A warm, touching satire not only of television, but of lost hopes and idealism, and of the impossibility of love in the face of blatant commercialism. Giulietta Masina and Marcello Mastroianni are two retired Astaire and Rogers imitators who are reunited after thirty years for a nostalgic TV variety show. Italian with English subtitles.
VHS: S02526. $19.98.
Federico Fellini, Italy, 1986, 128 mins.

I Vitelloni

The young, restless men in a small town on the Adriatic are, each in his own way, discontent. They spend their time pursuing diversion and girls, vaguely dreaming impossible pipe dreams. This brilliant, acid-sharp look at a generation nevertheless reveals Fellini's affection for his characters. The film "is the story of adolescents who cannot see anything more in life than satisfying their animal desires, sleeping, eating, fornication. I was trying to say there is something more, there is always more. Life must have a meaning beyond the animal" (Fellini). Italian with English subtitles.
VHS: S00601. $59.95.
Federico Fellini, Italy, 1953, 104 mins.

Il Bidone

Three small-time crooks run scams on the poor by disguising themselves as priests, in this film that begins as a comedy and turns tragic. When one of them tries to double-cross the others, they beat him up and leave him to die on a stony hillside. In a powerful final sequence, he finds salvation before he dies. With Broderick Crawford, Franco Fabrizi, Giulietta Masina and Richard Basehart. English title: *The Swindle*. Italian with English subtitles.
VHS: S10873. $69.95.
Federico Fellini, Italy, 1955, 92 mins.

Intervista

Fellini's movie combines the film-within-a-film, the essay memoir, a playful recollection of previous works and an eerie conflating of the past and present in this surreal and imaginative distillation of a man's life and work. As Fellini prepares to adapt Kafka's *Amerika*, his every move and gesture is captured by a Japanese documentary crew. The structure allows Fellini to delve into his past, with visits from Marcello Mastroianni and Anita Ekberg and profound remembrances of *La Dolce Vita*. "An enchanting work, a magical mixture of recollection, parody, memoir, satire, self-examination, and joyous fantasy with Fellini himself as the master of ceremonies" (Vincent Canby, *New York Times*). Italian with English subtitles.
VHS: S18583. $89.95.
Federico Fellini, Italy, 1987, 109 mins.

Juliet of the Spirits

"Within a simple, naively romantic narrative frame concerning a wife's desperation over her husband's philanderings, director Federico Fellini has put together an imperial-size fantasy of a physical opulence to make the old Vincente Minnelli musicals look like Army training films," wrote Vincent Canby. Newly mastered from a beautiful print. Italian with English subtitles.
VHS: S11178. $29.95.
Federico Fellini, Italy, 1965, 146 mins.

La Dolce Vita

"A landmark of cinematic social comment," wrote one critic about Fellini's journey through a decadent Rome. Banned by the Church in many countries, the sensationalism of the film often obscured its serious intent. *La Dolce Vita* follows a society journalist (Marcello Mastroianni) through a nightmarish world in which emotions have been destroyed by surface realities, moral conventions and unresolved guilt. With Anita Ekberg, Anouk Aimee, Alain Cuny and Nadia Gray. Italian with English subtitles.
VHS: S00705. $24.95.
Federico Fellini, Italy, 1961, 174 mins.

La Strada

Fellini's masterpiece. Giulietta Masina plays Gelsomina, a tragic waif sold to play clown to travelling show strongman Zampano (Anthony Quinn). "Simplicity itself, *La Strada* is a magical tale and an unbearably painful account of loneliness which will always be associated with the sublimely Chaplinesque Masina…but Quinn, too, is superb, particularly in the final revelation of his own heartbreak and isolation." With Richard Basehart and Aldo Silvani. Italian with English subtitles.
VHS: S00712. $29.95.
Laser: LD71088. $49.95.
Federico Fellini, Italy, 1954, 107 mins.

Nights of Cabiria

The third of Fellini's trilogy of solitude, *Nights of Cabiria* features Giulietta Masina as an impoverished prostitute living on the outskirts of Rome, who is betrayed by her faith in human nature. Winner of the Academy Award for Best Foreign Film, Masina's performance is one of the great performances on film. Italian with English subtitles.
VHS: S18582. $39.95.
Federico Fellini, Italy, 1957, 110 mins.

Spirits of the Dead

Jane and Peter Fonda, Alain Delon, Brigitte Bardot and Terence Stamp are among the stars cast in this adaptation of three Edgar Allan Poe tales. The three episodes are *Metzerngerstein*, directed by Roger Vadim; *William Wilson*, directed by Louis Malle; and Fellini's brilliant *Toby Dammit*. In the first, the Fonda siblings are involved in a macabre tale built around incestuous desire. The middle work concerns a sadistic fiend (Delon) who, among other things, whips the then wildly famous Bardot. Finally, Stamp plays a movie star who loses his head and makes a bet with the devil, whom Fellini portrays, in a brilliant master stroke, as a beautiful little girl in a white dress. French with English subtitles.
VHS: S27647. $59.95.
Roger Vadim/Louis Malle/Federico Fellini, France/Italy, 1968, 117 mins.

Variety Lights

Fellini's first, truly wonderful feature is the story of a group of second-rate theatrical performers on tour. The aging manager of the company falls in love with a newcomer, to the chagrin of his faithful mistress (Giulietta Masina). Though co-directed by Alberto Lattuada, "this is Fellini's film rather than Lattuada's. Already present in his special 'universe': his sense of irony, his baroque qualities, his sympathy for and delight in downtrodden eccentrics, and his portrait of 'bidones' striving comically to find themselves" (Georges Sadoul). Italian with English subtitles.
VHS: S07506. $29.95.
Federico Fellini/A. Lattuada, Italy, 1952, 86 mins.

White Sheik

When a provincial couple go to Rome for their honeymoon, the bride sneaks off to the movie set where her idol, the White Sheik, is making a film. "Perhaps the freshest and the most tender and naturalistic of Fellini's films" (Pauline Kael). Italian with English subtitles.
VHS: S00135. $59.95.
Federico Fellini, Italy, 1952, 86 mins.

PIER PAOLO PASOLINI

Accatone!

A parable of redemption, set in the slums of Rome, Accatone "The Scrounger" (Franco Citti) lives as a thief, beggar and pimp. This is simply one of the most important films of the last 20 years, and a milestone in Italian filmmaking. He's in love with Stella, tries to reform her, but fails. *Accatone*, the debut film of Pier Paolo Pasolini, is notable for "its rough-edged style, its cool, unhysterical portrait of corruption, cruelty, and violence, and its quiet lyricism marked one of the most significant directorial debuts of the sixties." (Georges Sadoul).
VHS: S11153. $39.95.
Pier Paolo Pasolini, Italy, 1961, 120 mins.

Arabian Nights

Pasolini's final film of his Trilogy of Life, *Arabian Nights* is a carnal comic tale following the adventures of a slave girl, Pelligrini, as she rises to power. "Rich, romantic and magnificent! Its graphic sex scenes, which have a dreamy kind of beauty to them, are erotic without being pornographic" (Vincent Canby). Italian with English subtitles.
VHS: S07021. $79.95.
Pier Paolo Pasolini, Italy, 1974, 130 mins.

Canterbury Tales

A film which fits within the context of Pasolini's explorations of bawdy, historical classics (together with *Arabian Nights* and *Decameron*). Pasolini once again seeks out the exotic and controversial aspect of Chaucer's classic. In English.
VHS: S07821. $79.95.
Pier Paolo Pasolini, Italy, 1971, 109 mins.

Decameron

The first part of Pasolini's great trilogy, based on the ribald tales of Boccaccio, which deal with human sensuality and artistic creation. Pasolini has re-fashioned the 100 tales into a collection of 11 sketches that is at the same time erotic, political, humorous and autobiographical. Pasolini himself appears in the role of the painter Giotto, and continues to use non-professional actors because, he said, he was fed up with the traditional cinema's "false language of realism." Italian with English subtitles.
VHS: S08260. $79.95.
Pier Paolo Pasolini, Italy, 1970, 111 mins.

The Gospel According to St. Matthew

Non-actors, rugged Southern Italian landscapes and towns, cinema-verite techniques, expressive close-ups are some of the elements of Pasolini's moving sacred and mythic epic. His Christ is anguished, determined, a peripathetic preacher aware of the afflictions of social injustice, whose miracles are matter-of-fact. Italian with English subtitles.
VHS: S18168. $29.95.
Pier Paolo Pasolini, Italy, 1964, 136 mins.

Hawks and Sparrows

A wildly comic fable, with the great Italian stone-faced clown Toto playing Everyman and Ninetto Davoli, his good natured but empty-headed son. Pasolini uses a comic crow, which philosophizes amusingly and pointedly about the passing scene, as a counterpoint to the performers, representing humanity, as they progress down the road of life. The result is a major Pasolini film and a powerful, tragic fable which shows two delightful innocents caught, like many Italians, between the Church and Marxism. "Complex, mystical and fascinating" (*New York Times*). Italian with English subtitles.
VHS: S12351. $29.95.
Pier Paolo Pasolini, Italy, 1964, 88 mins.

Love Meetings

A witty and sensual investigation of sex in Italy, including impressive appearances by famed author Alberto Moravia and noted psychologist Cesare Musatti, conducted by Pier Paolo Pasolini. Pasolini appears as the interviewer with a wide range of individuals who share their tales of love—prostitution, homosexuality, marital and non-marital liaisons. Italian with English subtitles.
VHS: S12352. $29.95.
Pier Paolo Pasolini, Italy, 1964, 90 mins.

Mamma Roma

Anna Magnani gives a terrific performance in the title role of this key film. It was Pasolini's second feature but it is rarely seen. The story revolves around a former prostitute, played by Magnani, who gets a new chance for a different life. She does her best to help her son, Ettore, get ahead. He is mesmerized, however, by the evils of the big city, so she makes one last desperate attempt to get him a respectable job. Italian with English subtitles.
VHS: S26664. $79.95.
Pier Paolo Pasolini, Italy, 1963, 110 mins.

Medea

Soprano Maria Callas in a dramatic, non-musical interpretation of Euripides' tragedy. "Under Pasolini's direction, Callas becomes a fascinating cinematic presence, brilliant and brutal" (*NY Times*). Italian with English subtitles.
VHS: S00841. $49.95.
Pier Paolo Pasolini, Italy, 1970, 100 mins.

Notes for an African Orestes

One of the landmarks of film, Pier Paolo Pasolini's own diary on his preparations to film a modern-day version of Aeschylus' *Orestes* in Africa has been called by *Village Voice* critic Jim Hoberman, "a key to an understanding of the particular Freudian-Marxist-Christian world-view that was Pasolini's." With footage shot in Uganda and Tanzania, Pasolini scouts remote villages for possible Agammemnons and documents local rituals in a privileged look at the interior of the artistic creative process. Italian with English subtitles.
VHS: S09928. $39.95.
Pier Paolo Pasolini, Italy, 1970, 75 mins.

Oedipus Rex

One of the great films by Pasolini, which adds a prologue and epilogue to the play by Sophocles, was translated by Pasolini. The film adds much psychoanalytic insight to the Sophocles theme; Pasolini's intent was, he said, "to make a kind of completely metaphoric—and therefore mythicized—autobiography; and second, to confront both the problem of psychoanalysis and the problem of the myth." Italian with English subtitles.
VHS: S07333. $29.95.
Pier Paolo Pasolini, Italy, 1967, 110 mins.

Pigsty

A remarkable, late-period work from Pier Paolo Pasolini, *Pigsty* (*I Porcile*) brilliantly interweaves two storylines. In the first, a man wanders a medieval, war-ravaged countryside devouring the weak; in the second, a German youth's profound alienation leads him into a strange relationship with a group of pigs. With Jean-Pierre Leaud, Ugo Tognazzi, Pierre Clementi and Anne Wiazemsky. Italian with English subtitles. Letterboxed.
VHS: S18063. $79.95.
Pier Paolo Pasolini, USA, 1969, 100 mins.

Rogopag

The title reflects four brilliant European directors who contributed short films to this collection: Roberto Rossellini, Jean-Luc Godard, Pier Paolo Pasolini and Ugo Gregoretti. *Virginity*, by Rossellini, is a comic essay on the distinctions between illusion and reality. Orson Welles stars in Pasolini's *La Ricotta*, a satire about the debasement of religion. This film caused Pasolini to be charged and sentenced to prison for "insulting the religion of [Italy]." *The New World*, by Godard, offers a chilling view of Paris after a nuclear war. And in Gregoretti's *The Range Grown Chicken*, a family suffers the ravages of brain-washing consumerism. France/Italy, 1962, 122 mins. French and Italian with English subtitles.
VHS: S23995. $79.95.

Salo: 120 Days of Sodom

An extremely controversial film, the last work by Pier Paolo Pasolini. Loosely based on the book by the Marquis de Sade, Pasolini transplanted the setting to Mussolini's post-Nazi-fascist state of Salo. Pasolini creates a symbolic place where sexual joy and normality are punished while perversion is rewarded. The plot concerns eight fascists who round up 16 teenage boys and girls and, in a secluded villa, submit their hostages to various sadistic ordeals including rape, mutilation and murder. "Pasolini has intended the film to work on many different levels: an illustration of the moral anarchy of absolute power; the debasement of sexuality through violence; an exploration of victims as victimizers. The result is, alternately, surreal, harrowing, depressing, repulsive, and fascinating…a hellish journey through a sick soul." Contains nudity, explicit sexual situations and extreme graphic violence; for mature audiences only. Italian with English subtitles.
VHS: S11717. $89.95.
Laser: CLV. **LD72111. $49.95.**
Pier Paolo Pasolini, Italy, 1975, 115 mins.

Teorema

Pier Paolo Pasolini's breakthrough film, predicated on the theorem that "anything done by the bourgeoisie, however sincere and profound, and noble, is on the wrong track." Into the home of a classic bourgeois family walks in Terence Stamp, a stranger. Each one of the family—mother, father, son, daughter, maid—seeks and finds in the stranger a catalyst for the fulfillment of desire denied within the confines of the family structure. "Liberated thus by a moment of authenticity, each is left, on the visitor's departure, with a personal kind of madness, stripped naked in a symbolic desert." Italian with English subtitles.
VHS: S18193. $79.95.
Pier Paolo Pasolini, Italy, 1968, 93 mins.

Whoever Says the Truth Shall Die

A remarkable film on Pier Paolo Pasolini, poet, political personality, aestheticism and director of such important and controversial films as *Gospel According to St. Matthew* and *Oedipus Rex*. Director Bregstein explores whether Pasolini's murder at age 53 in 1975 was by Pino the Frog, a 17-year-old male prostitute, or an assassination by a group of right-wing fascists. English and Italian with English subtitles.
VHS: S02654. $59.95.
Philo Bregstein, Holland, 1981, 60 mins.

VITTORIO DE SICA

After the Fox

Peter Sellers is Italy's most wanted criminal, the Fox. He devises a scheme to enlist the aid of an entire coastal village to smuggle gold bullion, by posing as a movie director who needs local talent in his new picture. With Britt Eklund and Victor Mature. Script by Neil Simon.
VHS: S04589. $14.95.
Vittorio de Sica, Great Britain/Italy, 1966, 103 mins.

The Bicycle Thief

Perhaps the single most important and moving film of Italian neo-realism, *Bicycle Thief* tells the deceptively simple story of an unemployed man finding work to paste up signs, work requiring a bicycle, which is then stolen. A landmark of cinema. Italian with English subtitles.
VHS: S00128. $69.95.
Laser: Original Italian dialog with English subtitles; analog track contains the English dubbed soundtrack. Includes theatrical trailer and the English dubbed version. **LD70881. $39.95.**
Vittorio de Sica, Italy, 1948, 90 mins.

Bread, Love, and Dreams

Vittorio de Sica stars as a mature marshall posted to a small Italian village. He soon begins to pursue the devilish Frisky (Gina Lollobrigida). Between his accomplished flirting and his determined courting the town is lost in delightful gossip. This warm comedy also features Marisa Merlini and Roberto Risso. Dubbed in English.
VHS: S23985. $24.95.
Luigi Comencini, Italy, 1954, 91 mins.

Children Are Watching Us

With his fifth film, Vittorio de Sica surprised everyone by turning into a vicious critic of society. The film, set among the bourgeoisie, focuses on a marital triangle. The mother of a four-year-old boy leaves her husband for another man; the husband, unable to stand the humiliation, commits suicide. The boy, lonely and unwanted, is sent to an orphanage. The script was written by six scenarists, including Cesare Zavattini, who, through the film, emerged as a driving force in Italian cinema for many years to come. B&W. Italian with English subtitles.
VHS: S02077. $79.95.
Vittorio de Sica, Italy, 1944, 92 mins.

Gold of Naples

Vittorio de Sica directed the four vignettes comprising this famous omnibus film set in the old section of Naples. With a script by Cesare Zavattini, the film exhibits the new style de Sica developed after turning away from neo-realism. *The Racketeer* stars Toto as a poor soul bullied by his wife and children, *Pizza on Credit* stars Sophia Loren as the young wife of a pizza baker, *The Gambler* stars de Sica as a man whose rich wife will not give him money to satisfy his gambling urge, and *Teresa* stars Silvana Mangano as a prostitute trapped into marriage with a strange young gentleman. Italian with English subtitles.
VHS: S06441. $19.95.
Vittorio de Sica, Italy, 1954, 107 mins.

Indiscretion of An American Wife

Neo-realist art film produced by David Selznick, starring Jennifer Jones (Mrs. Selznick) and Montgomery Clift, about a love affair that does not work out. An interesting example of Clift's work.
VHS: S00621. $34.95.
Vittorio de Sica, USA/Italy, 1954, 63 mins.

It Happened in the Park

A story of what goes on during a 24 hour period in the Villa Borghese parks. French with English subtitles.
VHS: S03746. $29.95.
Vittorio de Sica, France/Italy, 1956, 72 mins.

Miracle in Milan

A masterpiece, a key work of Italian neo-realist cinema, a wonderfully inventive and comic film that effectively condemns the inequities that existed for millions of displaced Europeans after World War II. "The rich vein of sly, compassionate humor that Chaplin and Rene Clair used has been tapped by de Sica; the great director has brought up purest gold" (*New York Times*). Grand Award, Cannes Film Festival. Italian with English subtitles.
VHS: S12957. $29.95.
Laser: **LD70419. $49.95.**
Vittorio de Sica, Italy, 1951, 96 mins.

Roof

A masterpiece of neo-realism, the story concerns a young couple who marry against the wishes of the young woman's father and learn that finding an apartment is more difficult than they thought. Italian with English subtitles.
VHS: S01968. $29.95.
Vittorio de Sica, Italy, 1956, 98 mins.

Shoeshine

One of the great films of Italian neo-realism; in Nazi-occupied Rome, two young shoeshine boys get involved in a black market deal in order to raise money for a horse, are caught and sent to prison, and one of them betrays the other. A collaboration between de Sica and the father of neo-realism, Cesare Zavattini, a work of incredible emotion and power. Italian with English subtitles.
VHS: S05869. $79.95.
Vittorio de Sica, Italy, 1946, 90 mins.

Two Women

Sophia Loren won an Academy Award for her portrayal of a mother ravaged by war as she and her 13-year old daughter become the focus of attack by retreating German soldiers. A heartwrenching film—one of the best known—by Vittorio de Sica. Italian with English subtitles.
VHS: S04462. $29.95.
Vittorio de Sica, Italy, 1961, 99 mins.

Umberto D

One of the masterpieces of Italian Neo-Realist cinema— the Italian postwar Renaissance. The story centers on a retired civil servant, living only on his pension, whose best friend is his dog. Unable to survive on his meager income, he sacrifices a part of his pension for his dog, and is evicted by his landlady for non-payment of rent. Italian with English subtitles.
VHS: S01393. $29.95.
Laser: LD70483. $49.95.
Vittorio de Sica, Italy, 1952, 89 mins.

Woman Times Seven

Before Shirley MacLaine discovered she had lived several previous lives she played seven different women in this episodic film comedy. Made in Europe, her co-stars included Peter Sellers, Rossano Brazzi, Vittorio Gassman, Lex Barker, Alan Arkin, Philippe Noiret and Michael Caine. Also Anita Ekberg, Robert Morley and Elsa Martinelli. MacLaine plays widows and wackos and wanton women under the direction of Vittorio De Sica.
VHS: S09314. $59.95.
Vittorio de Sica, USA, 1967, 99 mins.

Yesterday, Today and Tomorrow

Sophia Loren and Marcello Mastroianni star in this Oscar-winning film that contains three different comic stories. Loren is great as the skilled temptress who uses sex to get what she wants, and her striptease remains a steamy, unforgettable film achievement.
VHS: S21220. $29.99.
Vittorio de Sica, Italy, 1964, 119 mins.

ROBERTO ROSSELLINI

Age of the Medici

With a script based on 15th century Florentine texts, this three-part film furthers Rossellini's exploration of the artistic, social, economic and political forces in our modern world. The key figures include Cosimo de Medici, son of an important banker, who saw that the major artistic visions should be allowed free rein as long as they operated under the sponsorship of the Medici. "*The Age of the Medici* is an epic representation of a particular time and space—the extensions of which are timeless and boundless" (Eric Sherman). The three parts are: *Cosimo de Medici*, *The Power of Cosimo*, and *Leon Battista Alberti: Humanism*. One of the major cinematic achievements ever. Available only as a complete, 252 minute set. In English.
VHS: S07384. $149.95.
Roberto Rossellini, Italy, 1973, 252 mins.

Amore

Available for the first time in the original two-part version, *Amore* is Rossellini's homage to the incredible Anna Magnani. In *The Human Voice*, based on Cocteau's one-act drama, Magnani is featured alone onscreen with a telephone, playing to an unseen lover. The interest is centered not so much on her dialog but on her expressive face and her actions—the myriad manifestations of her grief and suffering. *The Miracle*, inspired by a story from Federico Fellini, is a small masterpiece casting Magnani as a simple peasant who must defend her belief that she has given birth to the new Messiah. Condemned by the Catholic League of Decency and banned in several American cities at the time of its release, this inspired film was later praised by the Vatican and upheld in a landmark decision by the U.S. Supreme Court. "Excruciatingly passionate" (Peter Rainer, *L.A. Herald*). Italian with English subtitles.
VHS: S14984. $24.95.
Roberto Rossellini, Italy, 1948, 78 mins.

Blaise Pascal

Generally considered the finest of Rossellini's series of history films, this finely detailed portrait of life in seventeenth century France was described by Rossellini as "the drama of a man who develops scientific thought which is in conflict with the dogmatism of his deep religious faith." Rossellini's portrait of the philosopher/scientist is also a speculation on the nature of knowledge, cultural development, substance, space and time. French with English subtitles.
VHS: S06031. $29.95.
Roberto Rossellini, Italy/France, 1971, 131 mins.

Era Notte a Roma

A major film of Roberto Rossellini: three soldiers, an American, Englishman and Russian, having escaped from a concentration camp during the final months of Rome's occupation, are given refuge in a young woman's loft. She and her fiance survive through various black market schemes. A defrocked priest, Tarcisio, suspects the girl's complicity with Allied soldiers, but is willing to go along with it in return for favors. The woman resists, and Tarcisio causes the scattering of the group and the death of the Russian and several compatriots. In his book on Rossellini, Guarner said that from the point of *Era Notte a Roma* Rossellini no longer merely observed, but began to analyze: "Temporal and spatial leaps occur with utter simplicity and bridge ancient and modern cultures." English, Russian, German and Italian with English subtitles.
VHS: S07383. $79.95.
Roberto Rossellini, Italy, 1960, 145 mins.

Europa 51

A profound and sincere diary of an artist confused by the state of the world around him, this Rossellini film stars Ingrid Bergman as an American society woman living in Rome after the suicide of her son, searching for some meaning in the chaotic, postwar world. She discovers poverty and ends up in an asylum, in one of the major, rarely seen works of Roberto Rossellini. In English.
VHS: S06444. $79.95.
Roberto Rossellini, Italy, 1952, 110 mins.

Fear

Rossellini's last and darkest film, with Ingrid Bergman, shows a marriage stumbling across lines of suspicion, mistrust and fear. The husband of the story attempts blackmailing his wife in an effort to force her into a confession. She tolerates this blackmail because of an abstract guilt over her adulterous actions. Rossellini's visual motifs, darkness and shadows, create the moral muddle through which the characters move. Filmed in English.
VHS: S02951. $79.95.
Roberto Rossellini, Italy, 1954, 84 mins.

Flowers of St. Francis

Rossellini's continuing investigation of the nature of history and myth in the re-telling of the story of St. Francis of Assissi and his band of friars, as they attain perfect harmony with nature. This is the British release version, identical to the original Italian release, 10-15 mins. longer than the original U.S. release. Italian with English subtitles.
VHS: S02076. $79.95.
Roberto Rossellini, Italy, 1950, 75 mins.

General Della Rovere

Rossellini's great moral character study is the story of Emmanuele Bardone, a petty con man, who fleeces his victims until persuaded by the Germans to impersonate a partisan leader. He assumes the admirable qualities of the heroic officer. Italian with English subtitles.
VHS: S00484. $29.95.
Roberto Rossellini, Italy, 1960, 139 mins.

Germany Year Zero

The original edition of Roberto Rossellini's great film—in its German language subtitled version. "The actors were all nonprofessionals. Made in the neo-realist style…his lyrical view of Germany in the immediate postwar period has some magnificent scenes….Among the memorable…are the voice of Hitler on a phonograph among the ruins of the Chancellery, and the death of the hero in a gutted building" (Georges Sadoul).
VHS: S02952. $79.95.
Roberto Rossellini, Germany/Italy, 1947, 75 mins.

Machine to Kill Bad People

One of the rarest and most daring of Rossellini's films. Set shortly after the end of the war, in a small Italian village, a photographer is given a magical camera that has the power to petrify and kill anyone it "shoots." The photographer decides to eliminate all the evil people from the town. But in the process, he learns the difficulty of distinguishing between good and evil. On another level, *Machine to Kill Bad People* is an exploitation of Rossellini's statement that the cinema is unique among the arts because it captures moments of death at work. With Gennaro Pisano, Giovanni Amato and Marilyn Buferd.
VHS: S26382. $29.95.
Roberto Rossellini, Italy, 1948, 80 mins.

Man with a Cross (L'Uomo della Croce)

An extremely rare film by Roberto Rossellini, his third feature, made under the Fascist control of Italy. Basically rejected after the War because of the Fascist content of the film, "Rossellini produces a work which focuses upon the Italian expeditionary forces on the Eastern Front and upon a Catholic chaplain representative of Italy's religious majority…the principal character's humanity and sacrifice seem to prefigure the good-natured priest of *Rome, Open City* who works with leftist Resistance leaders…Rossellini underlines the common humanity in Fascist and Bolshevik alike" (Peter Bonadella, *Italian Cinema from Neo-Realism to Present*). Italian with English subtitles.
VHS: S11170. $69.95.
Roberto Rossellini, Italy, 1943, 76 mins.

Miracle

Brief, sensual and controversial film from Rossellini (source for 1952 Supreme Court case on censorship) starring Anna Magnani as a peasant woman who is convinced she is pregnant with a new Christ child. Based on a story by Federico Fellini, who appears. Italian with English subtitles.
VHS: S00858. $29.95.
Roberto Rossellini, Italy, 1948, 43 mins.

Open City

A beautiful video master, transferred from a new negative, of this key film of Italian Neo-Realism, shot largely during the Nazi occupation of Rome. Two resistance leaders, one a Communist, the other a priest, work toward weakening the German occupation. The cumulative power of Rossellini's feeling for his subject was translated into a visual intensity that makes the picture sometimes almost impossible to watch. With a great performance by Anna Magnani. Italian with English subtitles.
VHS: S13591. $24.95.
Laser: **LD75058. $49.95.**
Roberto Rossellini, Italy, 1945, 103 mins.

Paisan

One of the landmarks of Italian neo-realism; six episodes of the Battle of Italy from 1943-45. Improvised dialog, non-actors, and the story of the people in the War, the film became a cornerstone of postwar Italian cinema, appropriately called, by many critics, a "revelation…It is a people fighting, as others have done so often, against tyranny and their own weakness, against injustice and poverty." Italian with English subtitles.
VHS: S00989. $29.95.
Roberto Rossellini, Italy, 1946, 115 mins.

The Rise of Louis XIV

Italian master Roberto Rossellini works in a documentary-like naturalism to showcase the peculiar antics, mystery and bizarre nature of the extremely unconventional aristocratic French leader. With Jean-Marie Patte, Raymond Jourdan, Silvagni and Katharina Renn. Produced for French television. French with English subtitles.
VHS: S17845. $59.95.
Roberto Rossellini, France, 1966, 100 mins.

Rogopag

The title reflects four brilliant European directors who contributed short films to this collection: Roberto Rossellini, Jean-Luc Godard, Pier Paolo Pasolini and Ugo Gregoretti. *Virginity*, by Rossellini, is a comic essay on the distinctions between illusion and reality. Orson Welles stars in Pasolini's *La Ricotta*, a satire about the debasement of religion. This film caused Pasolini to be charged and sentenced to prison for "insulting the religion of [Italy]." *The New World*, by Godard, offers a chilling view of Paris after a nuclear war. And in Gregoretti's *The Range Grown Chicken*, a family suffers the ravages of brain-washing consumerism. France/Italy, 1962, 122 mins. French and Italian with English subtitles.
VHS: S23995. $79.95.

Seven Deadly Sins

Several French and Italian filmmakers, among them Eduardo De Filippo, Yves Allegret, Georges Lacombe and Roberto Rossellini, create separate vignettes that illustrate the dangers and provocations of the seven vices, suffused with a caustic, dark wit. With Michele Morgan, Francoise Rosay, Gerard Philipe, and Isabelle Miranda. French and Italian with English subtitles. 1953, 127 mins.
VHS: S18030. $29.95.

Stromboli

A beautiful new video print of Rossellini's brilliant and sensual film. It stars the beautiful Ingrid Bergman (then his wife) as a Lithuanian WWII refugee who marries a fisherman on the island of Stromboli to escape internment, then rebels against the rigidity of the island's laws and traditions. "A great film" (Francois Truffaut). Italian with English subtitles.
VHS: S15272. $24.95.
Roberto Rossellini, Italy, 1949, 107 mins.

Vanina Vanini

Based on a story by Stendhal, set in Risorgimento, Italy, in 1824. Vanina Vanini, the daughter of a Roman aristocrat, falls in love with a wounded patriot hiding out in her father's house, nurses him back to health, and naively follows him to northern Italy where she tries to free him of political commitment which separates them in their love. Rossellini's great achievement is to rediscover a historical past spontaneously, accurately, and in all its complexity. With Sandra Milo, Laurent Terzieff. Italian with English subtitles.
VHS: S04907. $29.95.
Roberto Rossellini, Italy, 1961, 113 mins.

Voyage in Italy

Katherine and Alex Joyce are a sophisticated but strained American couple who take a holiday in Italy on family business. While he remains bored and sarcastic, Katherine experiences a physical and psychological awakening in a fresh world of ancient ruins, natural landscapes and temperamentally different people. They come to the edge of breakup before being momentarily reconciled in what many consider to be Rossellini's most influential film. Starring Ingrid Bergman and George Sanders. Also titled *Strangers*.
VHS: S15669. $24.95.
Roberto Rossellini, Italy, 1953, 83 mins.

LUCHINO VISCONTI

Bellissima

Anna Magnani gives an explosive performance as a simple working-class woman who earns extra money as a "nurse," giving cut-price injections to local hypochondriacs. She enters her daughter in a Cinecitta talent competition which seems to offer a chance to solve all her dreams. Ambition becomes obsession, and obsession becomes tragedy, as the mother is conned and the daughter exploited. Italian with English subtitles.
VHS: S00116. $59.95.
Luchino Visconti, Italy, 1952, 108 mins.

Conversation Piece

Burt Lancaster is the rich, isolated professor whose life is shattered when the beautiful Countess Brumonti and her lovely daughter appear at his home. The Professor gradually becomes entangled in the bizarre plots of the Countess and her daughter. English dubbed.
VHS: S00268. $29.95.
Luchino Visconti, Italy, 1974, 112 mins.

The Damned

A gigantic allegory of the rise of Nazism through the decadent Krupp-like family; a baroque film which explores the dark cycles of violence and evil in human history and consciousness with erotic indulgence. With Dirk Bogarde, Ingrid Thulin, Helmut Berger, Charlotte Rampling. English dubbed.
VHS: S00293. $59.95.
Luchino Visconti, Italy, 1969, 154 mins.

Death in Venice

Visconti's adaptation of the classic Thomas Mann novella was a tremendous triumph; Dirk Bogarde plays the aging artist who, in Venice, becomes obsessed with the ideal beauty of a young boy. With stunning cinematography and Visconti's elegant, operatic touch. English dubbed.
VHS: S00316. $59.95.
Luchino Visconti, Italy, 1971, 130 mins.

The Innocent

An elegant, visually beautiful exploration of the constraints of marriage and its disintegration. Featuring a remarkably sensuous performance by Laura Antonelli, and an equally strong performance from Giancarlo Giannini. "*The Innocent* is one of Visconti's most beautiful films" (Vincent Canby). Italian with English subtitles.
VHS: S00625. $29.95.
Luchino Visconti, Italy, 1976, 125 mins.

La Terra Trema

Luchino Visconti's epic saga of Sicilian fishermen remains one of the most important films of Italian neo-realism. Shot entirely on location in Sicily, with the non-actors speaking their own dialect, and hailed as a revelation at the Venice Film Festival, it is a film with "a powerful sense of realism and sense of lyrical grandeur, almost a kind of operatic cinema verite" (Georges Sadoul). Sicilian with English subtitles.
VHS: S03518. $89.95.
Luchino Visconti, Italy, 1948, 161 mins.

Ossessione

One of the great revelations of the cinema: Luchino Visconti's adaptation of James M. Cain's *The Postman Always Rings Twice*, about the tragic love between a wanderer and the wife of an innkeeper, who murder the husband. For long never shown in the U.S., the film had a profound influence on the course of the cinema, beginning the era that would become Italian neo-realism. A masterpiece. Italian with English subtitles.
VHS: S05922. $39.95.
Luchino Visconti, Italy, 1942, 135 mins.

Rocco and His Brothers
Luchino Visconti's brilliant work concentrates on the dramatic clash between two differing value systems—an intellectual belief in the cause of progress and emotional nostalgia for a decaying past. The struggle is played out by two sons, Rocco (Alain Delon), a gentle boy, who is in conflict with Simone (Renato Salvatori), a loutish boxer. Both are in love with Nadia (Annie Girardot), a prostitute, and are bound by old traditions that neither can escape. Considered by many critics to be Visconti's greatest film. Italian with English subtitles.
VHS: S07471. $79.95.
Luchino Visconti, Italy, 1960, 134 mins.

Sandra of a Thousand Delights
In this searing drama, a woman returns to her home town in order to attend a ceremony commemorating her father. He died like millions of Jews in Nazi concentration camps. This trip rekindles a host of unanswered past memories that hint at betrayal, incest, lost love and the haunting possibilities of what might have been. Italian with English subtitles.
VHS: S22464. $39.95.
Luchino Visconti, Italy, 1965, 100 mins.

Senso
One of Luchino Visconti's greatest films—luscious, operatic, and an extraordinary portrait of a decadent and corrupt aristocracy. Set in Venice of 1866, Alida Valli plays an Italian countess who falls in love with an Austrian officer (Farley Granger). When war breaks out, she is torn between her patriotism and her emotional obsession with the officer. Visconti portrays a milieu in which "Livia's seduction and treachery and Franz's cowardice and deceit are an inevitable result of their environment." Italian with English subtitles.
VHS: S09353. $29.95.
Luchino Visconti, Italy, 1955, 115 mins.

White Nights
Mario, a shy young man, meets a mysterious girl, Natalie, weeping as she stands on a canal bridge. She tells him that she loves a sailor who left on a long journey and promised to return in one year; a year has passed and he still hasn't arrived. Gradually, Mario falls in love with the girl and struggles to persuade her that the sailor will never return. Just when he seems to have convinced her, the man from her past does in fact appear. Based on a story by Fyodor Dostoyevsky. With Marcello Mastroianni, Maria Schell and Jean Marais. Italian with English subtitles.
VHS: S13679. $59.95.
Luchino Visconti, Italy, 1957, 107 mins.

SERGIO LEONE

Fistful of Dollars
Leone's sterling spaghetti Western, starring Clint Eastwood as "the man with no name," is a slick remake of Kurosawa's *Yojimbo*, which was itself based on Dashiell Hammett's novel *Red Harvest*. A superlative soundtrack from Ennio Morricone. English dubbed.
VHS: S02177. $19.98.
Laser: LD70570. $34.98.
Sergio Leone, Italy, 1964, 96 mins.

A Fistful of Dynamite
This Sergio Leone epic of a revolution in Mexico is also known under the title *Duck, You Sucker*. It follows the exploits of an Irish terrorist, played by James Coburn, who continuously crosses paths with a Mexican bandit family headed by Rod Steiger. They both like explosives and annoying the government troops. The musical score is by Ennio Morricone. English dialog.
VHS: S03672. $19.98.
Laser: Director's cut, widescreen. LD75542. $49.98.
Sergio Leone, Italy, 1972, 138 mins.

For a Few Dollars More
The second collaboration of Sergio Leone and Clint Eastwood finds Eastwood reluctantly accompanying a mysterious bounty hunter (Lee Van Cleef) to track a vicious killer and his band of outlaw grotesques. Music by Ennio Morricone. With Gian Maria Volonte and Klaus Kinski.
VHS: S02525. $19.98.
Laser: Letterboxed. LD71883. $39.98.
Sergio Leone, Italy/Spain/W. Germany, 1965, 130 mins.

The Good, the Bad and the Ugly
The third—and best—Sergio Leone "Dollars" Western. Set during the Civil War, three men out on the skids search for a treasure chest of the Confederates, each knowing a little about its whereabouts. A great musical score by Ennio Morricone. With Clint Eastwood, Eli Wallach, Lee Van Cleef. A brilliant spaghetti Western and Leone at his best.
VHS: S11553. $29.98.
Laser: LD70587. $39.98.
Sergio Leone, Italy/Spain, 1967, 161 mins.

Once Upon a Time in America
The complete, uncut version of Leone's epic of American criminal life begins with five young men growing up in Brooklyn during the 1920's and the road that leads each of them to becoming powerful Mob bosses. Stars Robert de Niro, James Woods, Elizabeth McGovern, Treat Williams, Tuesday Weld and others, in a film many critics consider the one important film to be released in 1984.
VHS: S00961. $29.98.
Laser: LD71434. $39.98.
Sergio Leone, Italy, 1984, 227 mins.

Once Upon a Time in the West
A great Western by the great Sergio Leone, uncut. Henry Fonda is the ruthless psychopath, Jason Robards the half-breed falsely accused of a terrible slaughter, and Charles Bronson "The Man" who remembers how his brother was savagely tortured. Brilliant direction by Leone achieves a film of epic significance, shot in dazzling Monument Valley locations.
VHS: S00962. $29.95.
Sergio Leone, USA, 1968, 165 mins.

ITALIAN CLASSICS

1860
One of the first modern Italian films, this daring feature is the story of a Sicilian mountaineer who leaves behind his new bride in order to fight with Garibaldi. *1860* was the first Italian film to use actors from real life, and was shot mostly on locations in Sicily where many of Garibaldi's battles took place. A key film in the evolution of Italian neo-realism. Italian with English subtitles.
VHS: S16119. $29.95.
Alessandro Blasetti, Italian, 1933, 72 mins.

Angel in a Taxi
A charming fable with an ingenious premise. A sweet-faced boy named Marietto stars as a clever, mischievous six-year-old in an orphanage who longs for a mother. "Did Jesus choose his own mother?" he asks a nun. She replies in the affirmative—and so Marietto figures that what was good enough for Jesus is good enough for him. Spotting Camilla, a beautiful ballerina, in a magazine, he decides she is to be his parent and runs away to find her. Vittorio De Sica pops up in a trio of small but important disguises: a sympathetic policeman, a harried messenger, and a philosophical taxi driver. Dubbed in English. Italy, 1959, 89 mins.
VHS: S13601. $29.95.

Anna
Anna is a nun on the verge of taking her last vows, whose sinful life as a nightclub entertainer, passion for one man and drive to marry another haunt her. Her old feelings are renewed when her former fiancee is brought to the hospital where she now serves as a nurse after a serious accident. A first-rate performance by Silvana Mangano dominates this powerful drama about the conflict between the flesh and the spirit. With Vittorio Gassman and Raf Vallone. Dubbed in English.
VHS: S26387. $29.95.
Alberto Lattuada, Italy, 1952, 111 mins.

Bandits of Orgosolo
Set in a remote Sardinian village and cast with local non-professional actors, Vittorio de Seta's first feature explores the moral and social cultures unique to the rural cultures of poverty. A shepherd, Michele, must flee an unjust accusation of theft and murder. Forced into the role of an outlaw to survive, he winds up robbing peasants who are as poor as himself. "This is a western from which all the romantic excitement about toughness has been stripped away, and whose characters, instead of being free and wild, have been humiliated deep within themselves by centuries of feudalism." With Michele Cossu and Peppedu Cuccu. English dubbed.
VHS: S00094. $29.95.
Vittorio de Seta, Sardinia, 1961, 98 mins.

Battle of Algiers
Internationally acclaimed, the staggering newsreel-like authenticity of the staged street riots and vital performances of the actors give *Battle of Algiers* a unique dramatic impact on this detailing of the Algerian revolt against the French. French/Algerian with English subtitles.
VHS: S01976. $29.95.
Gillo Pontecorvo, Italy, 1967, 122 mins.

Big Deal on Madonna Street
A hilarious satire on all burglary capers, Mario Monicelli's stylish film is now a classic account of the misadventures of a group of amateurish crooks (Vittorio Gassman, Marcello Mastroianni, Renato Salvatori, Rossana Rory) as they attempt to rob a store. Italian with English subtitles.
VHS: S01657. $29.95.
Mario Monicelli, Italy, 1956, 91 mins.

Bitter Rice
In the dreary rice fields of the Po Valley, a thief on the run meets a hard-working, beautiful girl. Silvana Mangano portrays the seductive rice worker who betrays her comrades in order to steal the thief's loot, a role which rocketed her to international stardom. With Vittorio Gassman, Raf Vallone, Doris Dowling and Lia Corelli. Italian with English subtitles.
VHS: S16185. $29.95.
Giuseppe de Santis, Italy, 1949, 96 mins.

A Bullet for the General
A spaghetti western starring Klaus Kinski and Gian Maria Volonte, both of whom appeared with Clint Eastwood in the Man with No Name movies. This story concerns a band of mercenaries with a mission in a revolution in Mexico. With Martine Beswick, Lou Castel and Jaime Fernandez as the General. Lots of action. English dubbed.
VHS: S06122. $14.95.
Damiano Damiani, Italy, 1967, 95 mins.

Cabiria
The most ambitious and spectacular of the historical epics for which Italy was famous before World War I, *Cabiria* set the standard for big budget, feature-length movies and opened the way for Griffith and DeMille. During the war between Carthage and Rome, a girl—Cabiria—is separated from her parents. In her odyssey through the world of ancient Rome, she encounters an erupting volcano, the barbaric splendor of Carthage, human sacrifice and Hannibal crossing the Alps. Mastered from a 35mm archive print using variable speed projection to match the original hand cranked camera, *Cabiria* features a newly recorded soundtrack from the original 1914 score.
VHS: S06218. $39.95.
Giovanni Pastrone, Italy, 1914, 123 mins.

The Christus
The story of Christ is presented in this silent Italian production that was adapted from a poem by Fausto Salvatore. He most likely based his poem on a much more popular source. Filmed closer to the Holy Land than most Hollywood films on the same subject matter. Silent.
VHS: S04813. $24.95.
Guilio Antamoro, Italy, 1917, 90 mins.

Cyrano de Bergerac
Edmond Rostand's enduring love story is given a unique and beautiful incarnation in this hand-tinted silent classic. Pierre Magnier brings true pathos to the chivalrous lover who dares not reveal his face with its monstrous nose to the woman he loves. Carlo Moser's score captures the excitement of this romantic, action-filled classic. French and English intertitled.
VHS: S27308. $29.95.
Augusto Genina, Italy/France, 1925, 114 mins.

Divorce—Italian Style
The adult comedy sensation that started it all. Marcello Mastroianni, a Sicilian nobleman who, tiring of his fatuous and fawning wife, begins directing his attentions toward his teenage cousin. In an attempt to end his problems once and for all, he devises a plan to catch his wife cheating so he can kill her…but first he must find her a lover! Italian with English subtitles.
VHS: S15951. $79.95.
Pietro Germi, Italy, 1962, 104 mins.

The Easy Life (Il Sorpasso)
A free wheeling comedy about an egotistical braggart (Vittorio Gassman) who has failed at everything he has tried, but who still views life with gusto. He is in love with his fast Lancia car and spends all his time touring around Italy. He takes in hand a meek, repressed law student, played by Jean-Louis Trintignant, and together the two hit the road. "An upper-class *La Dolce Vita*" (*New York Times*). Italian with English subtitles.
VHS: S08784. $69.95.
Dino Risi, Italy, 1963, 105 mins.

Fabiola
An early sound spectacle from Italy of the days of Ancient Rome, focusing on the story of Fabiola, daughter of a Roman senator, who converts to Christianity when her father is killed and his Christian servants accused. With Michel Simon and Henri Vidal. Dubbed in English.
VHS: S14635. $29.95.
Alessandro Blasetti, Italy, 1948, 96 mins.

Fiances (I Fidanzati)
Ermanno Olmi's (*Tree of the Wooden Clogs*) brilliant second feature is the simple story of a young man from Milan who takes a welding job in Sicily which takes him away from his fiancee, because he thinks the separation will be good for their relationship. But loneliness and the strange environment make him turn back to her. Olmi's deep humanism is evident in his moving depiction of the lives of simple people, played by non-professionals. One of the truly great Italian films of the 60's. Italian with English subtitles.
VHS: S26577. $29.95.
Ermanno Olmi, Italy, 1963, 84 mins.

Four Ways Out (La Citta Si Difende)
Gina Lollobrigida stars in this stark, gritty drama co-authored by Federico Fellini. A group of thieves robs a soccer stadium in broad daylight. In hiding, the thieves begin to whither under the pressure of their crimes. Winner of the Best Italian Film at the 1951 Venice Film Festival. Dubbed in English.
VHS: S24014. $24.95.
Pietro Germi, Italy, 1951, 74 mins.

Frate Francisco (Brother Francis of Assisi)
This mammoth, lavish production exemplifies the spectacular Italian historical epics made during the era of silent films. The story is based on the life of the saint. He was born to a life of ease, only to reject everything for a vow of poverty. Alleged to have experienced the stigmata (wounds like those suffered by Christ on the cross), this holy man's spiritual ways remain inspirational. Includes original musical score with sound effects.
VHS: S25866. $24.95.
Guilio Antamoro, Italy, 1927, 75 mins.

Full Hearts and Empty Pockets
The happy-go-lucky adventures of a young, handsome and impoverished gentleman on the loose in Rome. With the kind of luck that only occurs in the Eternal City, he parleys ten lire into a large fortune and a position of power in a seemingly wealthy corporation, becomes the pawn in a struggle between power brokers and blackmailers, and falls in love! With Linda Christian, Gino Cervi, Senta Berger. In English.
VHS: S07508. $29.95.
Camillo Mastrocinque, Germany/Italy, 1963, 88 mins.

The Great War (La Grande Guerra)
A great work by Mario Monicelli, set during the second World War, awarded the Golden Lion at Venice. The two protagonists are cowards whose main concern is to make the best of their humble lives to survive at all costs. Yet at the decisive moment, in a pathetic gesture of heroism and much to their own surprise, they prefer death to treason. "As in his previous comedies, Monicelli created appealing figures of two common Italians at odds with the laws of the world. This time, it is the law of war that crushed them…" (Mira Liehm). Italian with English subtitles.
VHS: S08782. $69.95.
Mario Monicelli, Italy, 1959, 118 mins.

Heart and Soul
Based on the very popular Italian novel *Cuore*, by Edmond de Amicis, this postwar Italian film stars Vittorio De Sica and Maria Mercades in what is a touching portrait of a devoted and philosophical teacher at a boys' school who encounters obstacles, including being suspended for his political beliefs. Italy's answer to *Goodbye Mr. Chips*. Italian with English subtitles.
VHS: S26772. $29.95.
Duilio Coletti, Italy, 1948, 98 mins.

Il Bell'Antonio
Marcello Mastroianni and Claudia Cardinale star in this passionate story of love and sex which was written by Pier Paolo Pasolini and Gino Visentini. Mastroianni plays the dashing Antonio Magnano, who finally relinquishes his bachelorhood and faces the loss of his libido in this ribald satire of marriage, Catholicism and machismo. Italian with English subtitles.
VHS: S20570. $59.95.
Mauro Bolognini, Italy, 1960, 115 mins.

The Iron Crown
A rare work from Mussolini's Italy; critic Mira Liehm writes, "The center of Blasetti's work lay in the mythological films and films with an openly pro-fascist tendency. In the years 1938-1941 he shot a generally overvalued costume tetralogy, which represents a transition between his fascist films and his work after 1942. The most important of this tetralogy…is *The Iron Crown*, a pseudo-historical fantasy based on a naive plot…mixing to create a kind of Italian saga in the style of *Die Niebelungenlied*…Blasetti, the true eclectic, mixed in everything he could think of, including Ariosto and the Grimm Brothers, while his directing drew heavily on early Fritz Lang." Italian with English subtitles.
VHS: S08781. $69.95.
Alessandro Blasetti, Italy, 1941

Kapo
Gillo Pontecorvo (*Battle of Algiers*) directed this moving study of hope and humiliation in Nazi concentration camps. A Jewish family living in Paris during WWII is arrested by the Nazis and shipped to a labor camp where their ordeal begins. "Stark and terrifying" (*Time*). English and some foreign dialog with English subtitles.
VHS: S14638. $29.95.
Gillo Pontecorvo, Italy, 1959, 116 mins.

Laugh for Joy (Risate di Gioia)
Anna Magnani in one of her greatest roles in this moving, bitter story of a film extra in Rome's Cinecitta Studio who is involved with American film executive Fred Clark and con-man Ben Gazzara. A major film by Mario Monicelli (*The Organizer*, *Big Deal on Madonna Street*). Cinemascope. Italian with English subtitles.
VHS: S15182. $59.95.
Mario Monicelli, Italy, 1954, 106 mins.

Les Miserables
This Italian production of Victor Hugo's great novel is notable for its elaborate sets and mounting, with Gino Cervi and Valentina Cortese in leading roles. Mario Monicelli wrote the screenplay. Dubbed in English.
VHS: S13225. $29.95.
Riccardo Freda, Italy, 1952, 119 mins.

Love Everlasting
One of the greatest of the Italian silent film directors is represented by this very rare verismo classic in an era when Italian epic film was capturing the international imagination. Silent.
VHS: S07464. $39.95.
Mario Casserini, Italy, c. 1915

Love in the City
One of the best omnibus films, which brought together the best Italian filmmakers of the 50's. The episodes are: *The Spectator*, by Dino Risi; *When Love Fails*, by Antonioni; *Love Cheerfully Arranged* (also known as *The Matrimonial Agency*), by Fellini; *Paid Love*, by Carlo Lizzani; *The Love of a Mother*, by Zavattini and Maselli and *Italy Turns Around*, by Alberto Lattuada. The inspiration for the film is said to have been Zavattini; particularly notable are the Antonioni episode, in which unsuccessful suicides tell why they blame disappointment in love for trying to end their lives, and the very funny Fellini episode, in which a client (played by Fellini) at a matrimonial agency pretends that he is searching for a wife for a friend who thinks he is a werewolf. 90 mins. Italian with English subtitles.
VHS: S01969. $39.95.

Lure of the Sila
Silvana Mangano, Amedeo Nazzari and Vittorio Gassman star in this sensual tale about unrequited love and passion, revenge and death, set in southern Italy. Gassman, in one of his early appearances, is falsely accused of murder, and years later his sister, now grown up, decides on revenge. Dubbed in English.
VHS: S05602. $29.95.
Duilio Coletti, Italy, 1949, 72 mins.

Musica Proibita
A haunting tale of romance, murder, revenge and fate from the period in Italian cinema just prior to Neo-Realism. The story focuses on the son of an opera tenor who must pay for the sins of his father. Italian with English subtitles.
VHS: S00902. $29.95.
Carlo Campogalliani, Italy, 1943, 93 mins.

Pardon My Trunk
An Italian comedy about a member of a royal family who bestows the unusual gift of a pachyderm to one of his subjects as a suitable reward. The cast includes Vittorio De Sica, Maria Mercader, Nando Bruno and Sabu. When elephants are involved it makes sense to hire Sabu, the elephant boy. English dubbed.
VHS: S06163. $29.95.
Gianni Franciolini, Italy, 1952, 85 mins.

Passionate Thief
Ben Gazzara, Anna Magnani and the famous Italian comic Toto star in this comedy of errors set on New Year's eve. Gazzara and Toto, a pair of plotting pickpockets, have planned an evening of petty larceny. But before they get into the swing of it, Toto's actress friend Anna shows up and proves to be a positive genius for unintentional interference. Dubbed in English.
VHS: S04929. $19.95.
Mario Monicelli, Italy, 1960, 100 mins.

Peddlin' in Society
Clearly inspired by the situation of Moliere's *Would-Be-Gentleman*, *Peddlin' in Society* gives full rein to Anna Magnani's comic talents and Vittorio De Sica's charm. A funny and delightful showcase for both these fine actors. Italian with English subtitles.
VHS: S14644. $29.95.
Gennaro Righelli, Italy, 1947, 90 mins.

The Queen of Sheba
Gino Cervi, Leonora Ruffo, Gino Leurini and Marina Berti are featured in this lavish costume drama set during the reign of King Solomon. There is plenty of desert passion within this plot inspired by the Bible. Intrigues keep the film going, but exotic dancers and a gazelle milk bath have a fascination of their own. Dubbed in English.
VHS: S23990. $24.95.
Pietro Francisi, Italy, 1953, 103 mins.

Rogopag

The title reflects four brilliant European directors who contributed short films to this collection: Roberto Rossellini, Jean-Luc Godard, Pier Paolo Pasolini and Ugo Gregoretti. *Virginity*, by Rossellini, is a comic essay on the distinctions between illusion and reality. Orson Welles stars in Pasolini's *La Ricotta*, a satire about the debasement of religion. This film caused Pasolini to be charged and sentenced to prison for "insulting the religion of [Italy]." *The New World*, by Godard, offers a chilling view of Paris after a nuclear war. And in Gregoretti's *The Range Grown Chicken*, a family suffers the ravages of brain-washing consumerism. France/Italy, 1962, 122 mins. French and Italian with English subtitles.
VHS: S23995. $79.95.

Seduced and Abandoned

One of the funniest Italian films ever—a comedy about the Sicilian code of honor, in which an unexpected chain of events is set in motion against an equally unexpected seduction, with truly hilarious results. With Stefania Sandrelli. Italian with English subtitles.
VHS: S18170. $29.95.
Pietro Germi, Italy, 1963, 118 mins.

The Tenth Victim

In the 21st century, war has been replaced by a survivalist warfare in which computers randomly select "hunters" to prey on "victims," to control overpopulation. Fellini favorite Marcello Mastroianni and sex bomb Ursula Andress are rivals whose showdown is filmed by director Elio Petri as a mass media spectacle.
VHS: S02028. $69.95.
Elio Petri, Italy/USA, 1965, 92 mins.

Time of Indifference

Francesco Maselli's adaptation of Alberto Moravia's novel examines the spiritual malaise and moral decay of an aristocratic family in 20s Italy. With Rod Steiger, Claudia Cardinale, Shelley Winters and Paulette Goddard. In English.
VHS: S19874. $29.95.
Francesco Maselli, Italy, 1964, 84 mins.

Verdi

Pierre Cressoy stars in this dramatization of the life and loves of the famous Italian composer. In color; dubbed in English. Italy, 1953, 80 mins.
VHS: S14670. $29.95.

We the Living

This Italian war-time production of the classic novel of Ayn Rand, the author of *Fountainhead* and *Atlas Shrugged*, is set in Russia of the early 1920's and follows Kira (Alida Valli) as she gradually copes with Russia's sweeping social and ideological changes in the wake of the Revolution. Literally lost for many years, this film was only recently found by Ayn Rand's supporters in Rome, and re-constructed. "One of the most exciting movies to come along in years. A moving epic in the tradition of *Gone with the Wind*" (*Boston Globe*). Italian with English subtitles.
VHS: S09584. $69.99.
Laser: CLV. LD70267. $89.00.
Goffredo Alessandrini, Italy, 1943, 170 mins.

What a Woman!

This comedy stars Charles Boyer as a rakish count who transforms socially-awkward-though-beautiful peasant girl Sophia Loren into a movie star when he secures her picture on the cover of a prestigious magazine. Marcello Mastroianni plays Loren's sophisticated photographer-lover. With Nino Besozzi and Titina De Filippo. English dubbed.
VHS: S19877. $29.95.
Alessandro Blasetti, Italy, 1956, 95 mins.

Where the Hot Wind Blows

"Peyton Place, Italian style!" A fiery Italian soap opera from Jules Dassin, the director of *Never on a Sunday*. Starring tempestuous Gina Lollobrigida, fighting Yves Montand, mysterious Melina Mercouri, and sexy Marcello Mastroianni.
VHS: S01612. $39.95.
Jules Dassin, Italy, 1959, 120 mins.

Woman of Rome

Gina Lollobrigida plays a girl of easy virtue in this film which also stars Daniel Gelin, Franco Fabrizi and Raymond Pellegrin.
VHS: S06854. $34.95.
Luigi Zampa, Italy, 1956, 93 mins.

Women in Prison

In lyric pseudo-documentary style, writer/director/producer Geza von Radvanyi has recreated the humiliation, outrages and sexual frustrations of the women held in detention camps in Italy following the second World War. These women were treated like hardened criminals for the offense of having passports or proper identification. An intense and poignant story. Italian, French and English with English subtitles.
VHS: S14652. $29.95.
Geza von Radvanyi, Italy, 1951, 90 mins.

Women Without Names

Simone Simon stars as a woman trapped in a camp for expatriate women left without documents at the end of World War II. She plots to marry a camp worker and gain her freedom. This drama is notable for its examination of a number of themes then considered quite controversial, including sexuality, lesbianism, abortion and human rights. Italian, French and English dialog with English subtitles.
VHS: S22471. $29.95.
Geza von Radvanyi, Italy, 1949, 94 mins.

SWORD & SANDAL EPICS

Fury of Hercules

Brad Harris plays the title character. He's pumped up and he's not pleased with the way the little people are being treated in a despot's kingdom. He offers his assistance to the lovely Brigitte Corey and her followers. Cast also includes Mara Berni, Carlo Tamberlani, Serge Gainsbourg and Alan Steel.
VHS: S10391. $19.95.
Gianfranco Parolini, USA, 1961, 95 mins.

Giant of Marathon

Steve Reeves and Mylene Demongeot are featured in this sword and sandal spectacle. Reeves is a courageous Greek hero who frustrates an invading Persian army with his muscle-bound antics. This is one of Reeves' best, with cinematography by Mario Bava.
VHS: S23173. $29.95.
Jacques Tourneur, France/Italy, 1960, 90 mins.

Head of Tyrant

Massimo Girotti, Isabelle Corey and Renato Baldini star in this story of deception and lust set in ancient Assyria. A beautiful, innocent, young girl gives herself to a cruel tyrant who has conquered her city. She plans to gain his affection and then decapitate him. Letterboxed.
VHS: S23174. $24.95.
Fernando Cerchiio, Italy, 1959, 83 mins.

Hercules

Steve Reeves stars in the original, uncut spectacle that brings to life the legendary pagan playgrounds of the mystical Mediterranean. The prototype of all the sword and sandal epics.
VHS: S08040. $19.98.
Pietro Francisi, Italy, 1959, 107 mins.

Hercules and the Captive Women

Famed Greek Bodybuilder Hercules (Reg Park) travels to Atlantis and is annoyed by his rude treatment by the sadistic Queen Antinea (Fay Spain). In order to rescue his son he must fight dragons and an army of identical men before removing the island from the map. With Ettore Manni and Marlo Petri and probably some captive women.
VHS: S09130. $29.95.
Vittorio Cottafavi, Italy, 1963, 87 mins.

Hercules in the Haunted World

Reg Park plays Mr. Muscles. He and a buddy go to Hell, literally, to fetch a magical plant that will heal an ailing princess. Once in Hades they encounter Christopher Lee as the evil Lichas, a servant of the god Pluto. Also rock men, seas of lava and nubile maidens in store. With Leonara Ruffo and Giorgio Ardisson.
VHS: S09129. $29.95.
Mario Bava, Italy, 1961, 83 mins.

Hercules Unchained

The Greek hero-god Hercules in further adventures as Steve Reeves once again flexes his muscles in the uncut sequel to *Hercules*.
VHS: S08043. $19.98.
Pietro Francisi, Italy, 1960, 101 mins.

Jason and the Argonauts

Special effects wizard Ray Harryhausen provided the effects for this mythological adventure, which stars Todd Armstrong as the sailor and explorer who returns to the kingdom of Thessaly after a 20-year voyage, to make his rightful claim to the throne, but who must first find the magical fleece. Bernard Herrmann wrote the score.
VHS: S08522. $14.95.
Laser: CAV. LD71557. $99.95.
Don Chaffey, Great Britain, 1963, 104 mins.

Morgan the Pirate

Andre de Toth's exciting costume epic stars Steve Reeves as the madcap adventurer and swashbuckler who pursues the beautiful and seductive Valerie Lagrange. With Lydia Alfonsi and Chelo Alonso.
VHS: S19348. $19.95.
Andre de Toth, Italy, 1961, 95 mins.

Samson

Brad Harris interprets the Biblical role as the strong man with very sensitive hair. Alan Steel is cast as the son of Samson. In this Italian production, the fabled muscle man offers his assistance to the king and confronts many enemies. With Brigitte Corey, Serge Gainsbourg, Carolo Tamberlani and Walter Reeves, who is probably not any relation to George or Steve. In color.
VHS: S10387. $19.95.
Gianfranco Parolini, USA, 1961, 90 mins.

Samson and the 7 Miracles of the World

Considered by many to be one of the great sword and sandal pictures of the 1960s. Samson fights against a murdering horde of Tartar warriors while trying to save the life of a beautiful Chinese princess.
VHS: S15366. $29.95.
Riccardo (Robert Hampton) Freda, France/Italy, 1962, 80 mins.

Spartacus and the Ten Gladiators

Don't look for Kirk Douglas in this Italian sword and sandal epic. Dan Danvidas stars in this spectacle of physical exaggeration in terms of muscular development. In 73 B.C. Spartacus led a revolt against the armies and people of Rome. Rumor has it, he has more than 10 gladiators on his side.
VHS: S10390. $19.95.
Nick Nostro, Italy, 1964, 99 mins.

Terror of Rome Against the Son of Hercules

One of the great Italian gladiator epics, with Marc Forrest strutting his muscles as Poseidon, Son of Hercules, who battles every ferocious beast Caesar pits against him as he struggles to free Rome's captive Christians before they reach the deadly arena. Dubbed in English.
VHS: S04942. $19.95.
Mario Caiano, Italy, 1962, 100 mins.

ITALIAN ISSUES

Alberto Moravia

An in-depth interview with Italy's leading contemporary novelist, as he looks back over his career, discussing his experience of Fascism and the special concern with women that is a hallmark of his writing. Film director Bernardo Bertolucci makes contributions, and specially dramatized readings from Moravia's works are also included. 55 mins.
VHS: S02399. $19.95.

Florence

Robin Williams directs and narrates this journey along the footsteps of Michelangelo through the treasures of Florence: the Medici Palace, Michelangelo's David, as well as the works of Verrocchio, Donatello, Ghilberti's Golden Doors of Paradise, and Brunelleschi's magnificent dome for the Cathedral of Santa Maria del Fiore. Art treasures by Leonardo da Vinci and Botticelli are featured. 50 mins.
VHS: S05049. $19.98.

Florence: Cradle of the Rennaissance

The art and architecture from the hub of the Rennaissance movement continues to impact upon today's modern art scene. This tour is a unique portrait of Florence.
VHS: S16726. $19.98.

Mussolini and I

The true story of the family conflict, intense love and hate, political intrigue and violent death surrounding the fall of Italy's fascist dictator. Bob Hoskins plays Mussolini, with Susan Sarandon and Anthony Hopkins.
VHS: S02370. $19.95.
Alberto Negrin, USA/Italy, 1985, 130 mins.

Nova—Will Venice Survive Its Rescue?

The main square of Venice was submerged under four feet of water in 1966. Since then, the Italian government has been trying to hold back the tides that threaten Venice with increasing frequency. This program examines the controversial effort to save one of the most beautiful cities in the world. 60 mins.
VHS: S11651. $14.98.

Rome

A cultural tour through Rome, narrated by Robin Williams, featuring the art and architecture of the great city, and insights into the ancient world of Rome. Places featured include the Appian Way, the Vatican, the treasures of the Sistine Chapel, The Campidoglio, as well as how Napoleon copied the Roman Forum for the City of Paris. 50 mins.
VHS: S05048. $24.95.

Rome, The Eternal City

Begin your visit to Rome on Palatine Hill, home to emperors, kings and pontiffs. Admire the ruins of the Roman Forum and the colosseum. Go shopping along the Via Condotti, then rest your feet on the Spanish steps. Meet the Romans in Piazza Navona, Campo dei Fiori and at the Trevi Fountain. Tour St. Peter's Basilica, the Sistine Chapel, the Vatican Museums. 55 mins.
VHS: S10771. $24.95.

Vatican City: Art and Glory

There is no other place on the planet that can match the riches of Vatican City. Within its collections there are masterpieces from ancient times, the middle ages and the Renaissance. Only here can one view the Apollo Belvedere, Michelangelo's Sistine Chapel frescoes, and Raphael's masterwork, the School of Athens.
VHS: S24267. $19.98.

Venice: Queen of the Adriatic

Seen through the eyes of artists and architects, this tour of Italy's remarkable "floating" city admires the influence of Venetian culture on western civilization.
VHS: S16725. $19.98.

Vidal in Venice, Part One

Gore Vidal, the celebrated American writer, takes the viewer along the routes of Venice's glorious, mysterious, twisted history. In this beautifully filmed, very personal tour of Venice past and present, Vidal tells about the Venetian people, their Empire, including visits to Crete and Maxos, Venetian strongholds of the past. 55 mins.
VHS: S05050. $29.95.

Vidal in Venice, Part Two

The art treasures, the sumptuous palaces, the literary past, the scandals of yesterday and the touristy Venice of today are all revealed in Vidal's chronicle as he wanders from the canals to the Doge's Palace. 55 mins.
VHS: S05051. $29.95.

Wagner and Venice

Wagner and Venice captures the special relationship that existed between Wagner, as man and composer, and the romantic city of Venice. Narrated by Orson Welles, this remarkable video portrait traces the composer's visits to the legendary city, accompanied by excerpts from Wagner's letters, compositions and poems. Produced by Filmart, Venice, and filmed by Kratky Film, Prague. 30 mins.
VHS: S05171. $29.95.

spanish CINEMA

Against the Wind (Contra El Viento)
Antonio Banderas and Emma Suarez star in this story of obsessive and destructive romantic love. They are brother and sister. Juan (Banderas) takes refuge in an isolated area of Andalusia. His exile from home proves useless however, when his sister decides she must see her true love, her brother. Spanish with English subtitles.
VHS: S23959. $79.95.
Paco Perinan, Spain, 1990, 117 mins.

Belle Epoque
This film won an Oscar as the Best Foreign Language Film in 1994. In this charming romantic comedy, a handsome young soldier flees the Spanish Revolution only to inspire his own sexual revolution. Finding succor in the house of an artist who has four daughters, he proceeds to seduce them all, or is it the other way around? Spanish with English subtitles.
VHS: S22768. $19.95.
Laser: LD74619. $34.95.
Fernando Trueba, Spain, 1992, 109 mins.

Butterfly Wings
This unusual drama about a dysfunctional family registers alternately as sad, horrifying and somber. Carmen hopes her unborn child is a son in order to carry on her husband's name. Guilt and fear prevent her from telling her sensitive and shy six-year-old daughter. The birth of the child triggers a series of nightmarish events. Winner of the Best Picture at the San Sebastian Film Festival. Spanish with English subtitles.
VHS: S20382. $59.95.
Juanma Bajo Ulloa, Spain, 1991, 105 mins.

Colegas
From the director of *El Diputado*, the story of three friends and their transition into adulthood. A crisis comes about when one of the friends becomes pregnant, and the youths resort to street hustling to raise the funds to solve the problem. Spanish with English subtitles.
VHS: S01562. $89.95.
Eloy de la Iglesia, Spain, 117 mins.

Cronica del Alba
Based on a novel by Ramon Sender, *Cronica del Alba* continues the story that Sender started in his novel, *Valentina*. Pepe, the main character, is balancing the time between University studies and a pharmacy lab apprenticeship. Set in 1919 in Zarazoga, Pepe, like all young Spaniards, is caught up in the building tension of the impending rebellion. More in love than ever with the voluptuously grown Valentina, all access to her is now prohibited by her over-protective mother. Spanish with English subtitles.
VHS: S07589. $49.95.
Antonio J. Betancour, Spain, 1982, 82 mins.

Demons in the Garden
Demons in the Garden presents the ironic chronicle of the emotional education in provincial Spain during the post-war Franco years. The film follows the intricate relationships among two feuding brothers and a sister, an overbearing mother and an adopted daughter (stunningly played by Angela Molina) who has given birth to an illegitimate child, fathered by one of the sons, set against a wealth of rich background detail. "This is probably the best film of Aragon's career...a film of great beauty and sensitivity," wrote *Variety*. Spanish with English subtitles.
VHS: S10869. $29.95.
Manuel Gutierrez Aragon, Spain, 1983, 105 min.

Diamond Plaza
Based on the novel by Merce Rodoreda; this film features two opposing characters—the woman, docile and sensitive, the man, domineering yet childish—who are forced to mature when their lives are shattered by a tragic, cruel and violent civil war. Spanish with English subtitles.
VHS: S07733. $59.95.
Francesc Betriu, Spain, 1981, 112 mins.

Don Juan, My Love
It is the eve of All Saints Day and the ghost of Don Juan, the world's most legendary lover, is rising from his grave in a cemetery in Seville, Spain. His soul has been trapped in Purgatory for 450 years, and he is returning to earth to perform a good deed which will free him from his phantom existence. "A breathless bedroom farce!" (*New York Daily News*). With Maria Barranco, Rossy De Palma, and Loles Leon, best known for their roles in Almodovar's *Women on the Verge of a Nervous Breakdown*. Spanish with yellow English subtitles.
VHS: S15545. $19.98.
Antonio Mercero, Spain, 1991, 96 mins.

El Cochecito
A quiet, haunting satire about an old man obsessed with his crippled friend and the motor bike he gets around on, and his family's rejection of his need for freedom and friendship. Winner of the International Critics Prize at the Venice Film Festival. Spanish with English subtitles.
VHS: S04731. $69.95.
Marco Ferreri, Spain, 1961, 81 mins.

El Diputado
A political thriller about a gay man high in the ranks of the Spanish Socialist Party whose love affair with a 16-year-old boy jeopardizes the fate of the nation. The Advocate said the gay love scenes are among the best ever presented in a commercial film. Spanish with English subtitles.
VHS: S00397. $79.95.
Eloy de la Iglesia, Spain, 1983, 111 mins.

El Sacerdote (The Priest)
An early work by Eloy de la Iglesia, this is the shocking story of a troubled priest fighting for his own soul. Father Miguel fights physical and psychic fantasies of sex and suffers from painful memories of a bizarre childhood. Banned at the time of its original release. Spanish with English subtitles.
VHS: S23576. $79.95.
Eloy de la Iglesia, Spain, 1979, 62 mins.

Extramuros
Carmen Maura, famed for her riveting portrayals in *Women on the Verge of a Nervous Breakdown* and *Law of Desire*, plays a nun who is challenged by her irrepressible lesbian desires. Set in a convent during the Spanish Inquisition, the film is not only a depiction of repressed passion, but a sharply critical look at the relationship between the Church and political power as the convent vies for fame and money through the faked visions and stigmata of the lesbian sisters. Spanish with English subtitles.
VHS: S24033. $39.95.
Miguel Picazo, Spain, 1985, 120 mins.

Fortunata y Jacinta
Based on the best-known novel by the great 19th century novelist Benito Perez Galdos, who has been often compared to the Latin equivalent of Flaubert, *Fortunata y Jacinta* is a detailed, keenly observed story of two women who are in love with the same man. Spanish with English subtitles.
VHS: S04609. $39.95.
Angelino Fons, Spain, 1969, 108 mins.

I Don't Want to Talk About It
Marcello Mastroianni stars in Maria-Luisa Bemberg's (*The Official Story*) fairy tale-like film about love. Mastroianni plays a handsome and wealthy European man who picks a rather unlikely object of affection. Bemberg's thought-provoking film poses the question, "How can size matter when it is a question of love?" Spanish with English subtitles.
VHS: S24326. $19.95.
Laser: LD74892. $34.95.
Maria-Luisa Bemberg, Spain, 1994, 102 mins.

I'm the One You're Looking For
Through the exotic streets of Barcelona's underworld, the darker side of love and sexuality comes to life in a taut psychological thriller about a beautiful celebrity model seeking revenge on her family. Vengeful desire becomes an uncontrollable obsession when she teams up with a short-tempered taxi driver and a hot-blooded erotic dancer in her frantic search. Based on a short story by Gabriel Garcia Marquez, who also co-wrote the screenplay. Spanish with English subtitles.
VHS: S13842. $19.98.
Jaime Chavarri, Spain, 1988, 85 mins.

In a Glass Cage
A thriller that redefines the horror film. Written and directed by Agustin Villaronga, the story concerns a Nazi concentration camp doctor and his family living in exile in Spain a few years after the war. After a nasty fall leaves him in need of an iron lung, the Nazi finds his new male nurse an indispensable member of the family. With Gunter Meisner, David Sust and Marisa Paredes as Griselda. Spanish with English subtitles.
VHS: S10734. $79.95.
Agustin Villaronga, Spain, 1986, 110 mins.

In Memoriam
Based on a short story by Adolfo Bioy Casares; Geraldine Chaplin and the great Spanish actor Jose Luis Gomez star in the story of a man who has to come to terms with a past he longed to leave behind, only to find out that his inability to express his feelings has caused a great tragedy. Spanish with English subtitles.
VHS: S07734. $39.95.
Enrique Brasso, Spain, 1976, 96 mins.

La Memoria del Agua
The story of Joseph Fruferman, whose memories of his childhood in Russia and his adult life in France take up the last moments of his life. Images of his mother, late wife and daughter frame these poignant memories in a haunting black and white film in which the narrative is interspliced with documentary fragments. The film centers on the love that makes the impossible possible through its overwhelming power and survives physical death and separation just as water retains its memory even after its molecules separate. Spanish and Russian dialog with English subtitles.
VHS: S27799. $29.95.
Hector Faver, Spain, 1991, 82 mins.

Last Evenings with Teresa (Ultimas Tardes con Teresa)
Based on a novel by Juan Marse; the story of an ill-fated love affair between Teresa, a society girl, and Manolo, an ambitious petty thief. She sees in him an exploited, working class man; for him, she signifies hope. Spanish with English subtitles.
VHS: S07739. $59.95.
Gonzalo Herralde, Spain, 1983, 105 mins.

Lazarillo
This morality tale is set in 17th-century Castile. A fatherless boy is abandoned by his mother and subsequently finds work with a strange succession of employers. A blind beggar, a miserly sacristan, a fake nobleman and even a traveling band of performers all teach him valuable lessons in vanity, cunning, deception and, ultimately, survival. Spanish with English subtitles.
VHS: S21606. $24.95.
Cesar Ardavin, Spain, 1959, 109 mins.

Letters from Alou
Alou is an African immigrant in Spain whose unflagging optimism is unaffected by all the instances of exploitation and discrimination that characterize his new home. This social drama won Best Picture and Best Male Lead at the San Sebastian Film Festival. Spanish, French and Senegalese with English subtitles.
VHS: S20879. $79.95.
Montxo Armendariz, Spain, 1990, 100 mins.

Los Placeres Ocultos
A closeted banker, middle-aged and successful, falls madly in love with a poor but handsome 18-year-old student—with devastating consequences for the young man. Carefully crafted and insightfully scripted, *Los Placeres Ocultos* was the first openly gay film to emerge from Spain following the death of Franco. Virtually unknown to American audiences, this complex updating of *Death in Venice* is among the most powerful affirmations of gay life ever depicted on film. Spanish with English subtitles.
VHS: S11636. $79.95.
Eloy de la Iglesia, Spain, 1977, 97 mins.

Lovers
A sexually provocative film based on actual events in the mid 50s. Set in Franco's post-World War II Spain, the film centers on an intricate, perverse love triangle between a handsome, naive soldier (Jorge Sanz) and his virginal fiance (Maribel Verdu) and a beautiful, widowed landlady (Almodovar regular Victoria Abril). "Steamily entertaining, a sophisticated, highly accomplished work" (Vincent Canby). In Spanish with English subtitles.
VHS: S17972. $19.95.
Vicente Aranda, Spain, 1990, 103 mins.

Marianela
Based on the novel by Benito Perez Galdos, Marianela is the story of a disfigured orphan girl whose only solace is to serve as a guide to a young and handsome blind man, Pablo. When Pablo recovers his eyesight, Marianela's fragile world is shattered. Spanish with English subtitles.
VHS: S03197. $39.95.
Angelino Fons, Spain, 1972, 105 mins.

Miracle in Rome
Called "a small miracle itself" by the *New York Times*, *Miracle in Rome* tells the story of Margarito Duarte, a man whose seven-year-old daughter dies suddenly. Upon visiting her grave twelve years later, Margarito finds his daughter's body just as he had left it. His fellow townspeople call the event a miracle, but the town bishop wants the girl reburied. Based on an original story by Gabriel Garcia Marquez, who also co-wrote the screenplay. Spanish with English subtitles.
VHS: S13511. $19.98.
Lisandro Duque Naranjo, Spain, 1988, 76 mins.

Miracle of Marcelino
The classic, immensely popular film of the 50's, set in a rural area of Spain, an emotionally moving story of a young boy discovering faith. Spanish with English subtitles.
VHS: S06478. $59.95.
Ladislao Vajda, Spain, 1956, 88 mins.

Moonchild
Since ancient times an African tribe has awaited the arrival of a white boy who is the Son of the Moon. David, a 12-year-old European orphan, believes he is that child-god. The result is an unexpected fantasy adventure that is beautifully filmed and magically evocative. Spanish with English subtitles.
VHS: S27612. $59.95.
Agustin Villaronga, Spain, 1989, 80 mins.

Padre Nuestro
This Bunuelian black comedy is a satirical romp about a cardinal (Fernando Rey) who returns to his native village to prepare final arrangements before his death. He reconciles with his atheist brother (Francisco Rabal) though he's torn about acknowledging his illegitimate daughter (Victoria Abril), a notorious local prostitute known as "La Cardenala." "Mr. Rey and Mr. Rabal sing; the two pros give superlative performances full of shadings and surprises" (Walter Goodman). Spanish with English subtitles.
VHS: S19063. $79.95.
Francisco Regueiro, Spain, 1985, 91 mins.

Skyline
Fernando Colombo's unconventional drama about cultural dislocation. The film details the comical day-to-day activities of a resettled Spanish photographer, Gustavo (Antonio Resines), as he attempts to establish his reputation and earn a living in New York. The film has a documentary-style naturalism as Gustavo endures small and private struggles heightened by his unfamiliarity with the language through his determination for self-sufficiency and respect. With Beatriz Perez-Porro, Patricia Cisarano and Jaime Nos. Spanish with English subtitles.
VHS: S01211. $39.95.
Laser: LD71328. $49.95.
Fernando Colombo, Spain, 1983, 90 mins.

Spirit of the Beehive
A landmark Spanish film by Victor Erice, featuring the remarkable Ana Torrent in the story of two little girls growing up after the Spanish Civil War in the countryside. The hypnotic, spellbinding nature of the film is a rare achievement in cinema, as Erice evokes a deep poetry of childhood in a portrait of isolation. Spanish with English subtitles.
VHS: S08104. $29.95.
Victor Erice, Spain, 1973, 95 mins.

Tu Solo
Traditions like bull fighting inevitably depend on venerable institutions. This graceful art is revealed through a true story set in Spain's most prestigious bull fighting school. Students tell their own side of the story, and in a unique tradition, bare all for a nude bullfighting scene.
VHS: S23743. $79.95.
Teo Escamilla, Spain, 1995, 96 mins.

Umbrella for Three (Paraguas Para Tres)
Daniel and Maria are two recently divorced professionals living in modern Spain who happen to run into each other and awful lot. This is a romantic comedy after all, and though it takes a while for it to dawn on them, they are fated to fall in love. Only after a series of comic misadventures do they come to understand the mysteries of chance and love. In Spanish with English subtitles.
VHS: S26277. $59.95.
Felipe Vega, Spain, 1992, 93 mins.

CARLOS SAURA

Ay, Carmela
The always vivacious Carmen Maura, the star of so many films by Pedro Almodovar, plays the title role of an apolitical cabaret performer caught between the combatants of the Spanish Civil War. Maura performs several lively musical numbers in this historical drama directed by Carlos Saura (*Blood Wedding*). With Andres Pajares, Gabino Diego, Miguel Rellan and Maurizio De Razza as the Italian officer in charge of staging a musical revue for a very demanding Fascist audience. In Spanish with English subtitles.
VHS: S15353. $89.99.
Carlos Saura, Spain, 1990, 105 mins.

Blood Wedding
A flamenco ballet version of Federico Garcia Lorca's classic, from the director of *Carmen*. This dramatic story is a duel to the death between the bridegroom and the bride's former lover. Featuring choreographer Antonio Gades, former director of the National Ballet of Spain. Music by Emilio de Diego. Spanish with English subtitles.
VHS: S00150. $24.95.
Carlos Saura, Spain, 1981, 71 mins.

Cria
A beautifully acted, haunting film—Ana, played by Ana Torrent, is the nine-year-old heroine who has an uncanny talent for observing scenes not meant for her eyes. Carlos Saura fashions a film about the darker side of childhood, about superstition, knowledge, and loss of innocence. Spanish with English subtitles.
VHS: S00279. $59.95.
Carlos Saura, Spain, 1977, 115 mins.

Elisa Vida Mia
Fernando Rey won Best Actor at Cannes for his role in this story about a man estranged from his daughter (Geraldine Chaplin). She has returned to help her ailing father and writes his biography. Eventually her own recollections lead to a deeper understanding that enable the two to reunite. Spanish with English subtitles.
VHS: S21758. $59.95.
Carlos Saura, Spain, 1977, 125 mins.

Garden of Delights
One of Carlos Saura's best films; a terrific black comedy starring the great Spanish actor Jose Luis Vasquez as the son of a rich family who, in a car accident, develops amnesia. The spendthrift, greedy family is only concerned with supporting their freewheeling habits. But lost in the amnesia is the number of the Swiss bank account which holds the cash, and so the family has to resort to devious means of psychoanalysis in an attempt to "cure" Jose, and get the bank account number at the same time. Truly a wonderful film. Spanish with English subtitles.
VHS: S07575. $29.95.
Carlos Saura, Spain, 1970, 95 mins.

The Hunt
Made under the repressive regime of Franco's Spain, this brilliant allegory deals with four men rabbit-hunting in the country outside Madrid. As the day passes, the sun gets hotter and petty jealousies spark memories and guilt about the Spanish Civil War. The day ends in violence and a shocking climax as the men's seething anger and hatreds are stripped bare. Also known as *Dispara (Shoot!)*. Spanish with English subtitles.
VHS: S20836. $59.95.
Carlos Saura, Spain, 1965, 87 mins.

Outrage
Antonio Banderas stars as a man who falls passionately in love with a circus sharp shooter. He never suspects that his feelings of devotion are a prelude to the emotional and physical nightmare he will soon enter. It all begins when his lover is raped by three mechanics. Mentally disabled by the attack, she launches a series of vengeful killings and ends up in a bloody showdown with justice. Also known as *Dispara (Shoot!)*. With Francesca Neri, Walter Vidarte and Eulalia Ramon. Spanish with English subtitles.
VHS: S27408. $94.95.
Laser: LD75554. $39.99.
Carlos Saura, Italy/Spain, 1995, 96 mins.

Sevillanas
Seven short flamenco performances, featuring some of Spain's top performers, are collected on this documentary-like work. This film is from the maker of the wildly successful *Carmen*, a dance-laden film featuring spectacular flamenco sequences. In addition to the terrific dance found on this newer work, there is extraordinary music and singing. Spanish with English subtitles.
VHS: S27205. $39.95.
Carlos Saura, Spain, 1992, 55 mins.

The Stilts (Los Zancos)
The Stilts stars Laura del Sol, Fernando Fernan Gomez and Francisco Rabal in a passionate, complex inquiry into the dynamics of the human psyche through the story of a doomed love triangle. Spanish with English subtitles.
VHS: S06843. $24.95.
Carlos Saura, Spain, 1984, 95 mins.

PEDRO ALMODOVAR

Dark Habits
An outrageous comedy from Pedro Almodovar, set in a convent that's falling apart. Mother Superior is feeling low, the youngest nun has been eaten by cannibals, and the convent hasn't saved a soul in years. But a night club singer on the run has taken refuge in the convent, and the nuns throw their wildest party yet. "Hilarious, irreverent fun," wrote *The Village Voice*, "Part Luis Bunuel, part John Waters camp. Lots of laughs." Spanish with English subtitles.
VHS: S08103. $79.95.
Pedro Almodovar, Spain, 1984, 116 mins.

High Heels
Part revenge comedy, thriller and sexual farce, Pedro Almodovar's *High Heels* is a Sirkian melodrama about the bizarre relationship between an aging Spanish movie star and singer (Marisa Paredes) and her daughter, a prominent local television anchor woman (Victoria Abril). Almodovar throws in an acrobatic sex scene, a prison dance number, an on-camera confession, a buried family secret and a final reconciliation. Spanish with English subtitles.
VHS: S16919. $89.95.
Pedro Almodovar, Spain, 1990, 115 mins.

Kika
Pedro Almodovar's offbeat sex farce is the story of Kika, a make-up artist who lives with her lover Ramon, a photographer specializing in women's lingerie. Their maid, Juanita, is madly in love with Kika, while Ramon's stepfather likes to seduce her from time to time. That's only the beginning of the preposterous goings on which really heat up when Pablo, Juanita's brother, an on-the-lam ex-porno star, enters the picture. Spanish with English subtitles.
VHS: S23572. $94.99.
Laser: LD75489. $39.99.
Pedro Almodovar, Spain, 1994, 109 mins.

Labyrinth of Passion
Pedro Almodovar's second feature film features nymphomaniacs, incest victims, transvestites, rock musicians and Iranian fundamentalists living in Madrid. In other words, something for everyone who thinks this filmmaker is the kinkiest and most entertaining modern artist to emerge from the Iberian peninsula since Salvador Dali. Cast includes Cecilia Roth, Helga Line, Marta Fernandez-Mura, Fernando Vivanco and Ruze Neiro as the uncomfortable heir to the Arabian throne. Spanish with English subtitles.
VHS: S12364. $79.95.
Pedro Almodovar, Spain, 1982, 100 mins.

Law of Desire
An entertaining, hedonist film unlike any other. Pablo, the main character, is a filmmaker who lives the high life in Madrid, engaging in casual drugs and homosexual encounters, with the real complications beginning when Pablo brings home Antonio, the government minister's son, who falls madly in love with him. Spanish with English subtitles.
VHS: S06023. $79.95.
Pedro Almodovar, Spain, 1987, 105 mins.

Matador
From Pedro Almodovar, another excursion into the bizarre and offbeat. A retired bullfighter and a female defense attorney find they share similar interests, which happen to be sex and death. His darkest film yet, but filled with madcap characters and wry humor. With Assumpta Serna, Antonio Banderas, Nacho Martinez, Eva Cobo, Chus Lampreave and Carmen Maura. In Spanish with English subtitles.
VHS: S10733. $79.95.
Pedro Almodovar, Spain, 1986, 115 mins.

Pepi, Luci, Bom and Other Girls
Pedro Almodovar announced his stylistic preoccupations and thematic concerns with his first feature after a series of shorts on Super 8 and 16mm. Luci leaves her psychopathic husband for a lesbian affair. He responds by raping Pepi, whose friends, a motley collection of punks and musicians, come to her aid. With Carmen Maura, Eva Siva, Alaska, Felix Rotaeta, Concha. Spanish with English subtitles.
VHS: S16918. $79.95.
Pedro Almodovar, Spain, 1980, 80 mins.

Tie Me Up, Tie Me Down
The controversial hit by Pedro Almodovar about Ricki, who falls in love with Marina, an ex-porn movie star, and proceeds to capture her and tie her up at her own apartment. She is torn between trying to escape and falling in love with him. "Almodovar's theme is not the domination of women, but the strangeness of love and possessiveness. The performances are outstanding. Antonio Banderas is psychopathic and vulnerable, Victoria Abril is fierce and funny" (*Sight and Sound*). Spanish with English subtitles (only R version available).
VHS: S12994. $19.95.
Pedro Almodovar, Spain, 1990, 103 mins.

What Have I Done to Deserve This?
Carmen Maura stars as a housewife and cleaning woman hooked on no-doz who ends up selling one of her sons to a dentist and killing her husband with a ham bone. "An absolutely wonderful black comedy. A small masterpiece," wrote *The New York Times*. Spanish with English subtitles.
VHS: S08102. $79.95.
Pedro Almodovar, Spain, 1985, 100 mins.

Women on the Verge of a Nervous Breakdown
The latest wacky comedy from Pedro Almodovar once again stars Carmen Maura, his perennial leading lady. She plays a popular Spanish actress driven to distraction when her lover leaves for another woman. She knows she can talk him out of leaving if only she can talk directly to him and not deal with the answering machine. A comedy of errors ensues that involve a drugged pitcher of gazpacho, Shiite terrorists and a mental patient who left the asylum too soon. Spanish with English subtitles.
VHS: S10757. $19.98.
Pedro Almodovar, Spain, 1988, 98 mins.

LUIS BUNUEL

Age of Gold
Bunuel's masterpiece extolls love and attacks religion and the social order in an amazing assemblage of images that remain no less provocative today than they were in 1930. Its central metaphor is a couple making love who are continually disturbed by the intrusions of officialdom, police and the Church. It remains one of the most unashamedly erotic films ever made, with a famous toe-sucking sequence. Financed by the Vicomte de Noailles, who gave Bunuel complete freedom and declared it "exquisite and delicious," the film immediately became the object of right-wing extremists and remained unseen for generations because of the Church's threat to excommunicate the Vicomte if the film were distributed. With Gaston Modot, Lya Lys, Max Ernst and Pierre Prevert. French with English subtitles.
VHS: S00024. $29.95.
Luis Bunuel, France, 1930, 62 mins.

Belle de Jour
A masterpiece from Luis Bunuel in which the cool Catherine Deneuve sparkles as a respectable middle class wife with a very contented husband, who finds a day job in a brothel that gives her an outlet for deeper, darker passions. "Bunuel constructs both a clear portrait of the bourgeoisie as degenerate, dishonest and directionless, and an unhysterical depiction of Deneuve's inner fantasy life where she entertains dreams of humiliations galore" (Geoff Andrew). French with English subtitles.
VHS: S26707. $99.99.
Laser: LD75380. $49.98.
Luis Bunuel, France, 1967, 100 mins.

The Criminal Life of Archibaldo de la Cruz
Archibaldo believes a musical box he owned as a youth had the power to kill. He still believes he can kill women and, in fact, confesses to several murders. Bunuel delivers a hilarious portrait of a frustrated sadist who "is an artist...His crimes are his very conscious, aesthetic attempts to revive a delicious sensation" (Raymond Durgnat). With Ernesto Alonso, Miroslava and Rita Macedo. Spanish with English subtitles.
VHS: S18118. $79.95.
Luis Bunuel, Mexico, 1955, 91 mins.

Diary of a Chambermaid
A great Bunuel film in which Bunuel updated the famous Mirabeau novel about the decadent French upper classes of the 19th century to 1928; Jeanne Moreau plays the chambermaid, both demure and cunning, who takes a position in a cheerless chateau, and immediately becomes the newest "objet d'art" for a whole family of perfectly ordinary perverts, from the shoe-fetishist father to the gamekeeper, who is a reactionary and a rapist. French with English subtitles.
VHS: S05990. $24.95.
Luis Bunuel, France, 1964, 97 mins.

Discreet Charm of the Bourgeoisie
Six characters are forever trying to sit down for a meal, but bizarre events—dreams, fantasies, guests, terrorists—interfere. Bunuel's brilliant satire lampoons the church, diplomats, wealthy socialites and radical terrorists and is a pure joy to watch. With Fernando Rey, Delphine Seyrig, Stephane Audran, Bulle Ogier, Jean-Pierre Cassel and Michel Piccoli. French with English subtitles.
VHS: S00345. $24.95.
Luis Bunuel, France, 1972, 100 mins.

El (This Strange Passion)
The psychological study of a man obsessed. A wealthy, middle-aged man marries a young woman and then develops a paranoid obsession with her supposed infidelity. One of the great films from Bunuel's Mexican period, the black humor of *El* failed to be appreciated by critics at the time of its release. It is now considered one of the most representative of Bunuel's personal mythology. Spanish with English subtitles.
VHS: S13680. $59.95.
Luis Bunuel, Mexico, 1952, 88 mins.

El Bruto
A powerful social melodrama which deals with a corrupt landlord who decides he needs a strong-arm man to intimidate his restless tenants. El Bruto, played by Pedro Armendariz, is the thick-headed slaughterhouse worker loyal to the exploiters. Bruto is lusted after by his employer's frustrated wife and at the same time longs for an innocent girl whose father he unfortunately beat to death. Spanish with English subtitles.
VHS: S06934. $24.95.
Luis Bunuel, Mexico, 1952, 83 mins.

The Exterminating Angel
A metaphorically rich and comic film, *Exterminating Angel* is the story of guests invited to an elegant dinner party who find they are unable to leave at the end of the evening. A mysterious force compels them to stay...and stay...and stay. After several days, their well-heeled social facades collapse as hunger, thirst, fear, and boredom send them into a frenzy. Bunuel stated that this film is "a metaphor, a deeply felt, disturbing reflection of the life of modern man, a witness to the fundamental preoccupations of our time." It is certainly one of Bunuel's greatest achievements. Spanish with English subtitles.
VHS: S00422. $39.95.
Luis Bunuel, Mexico, 1962, 95 mins.

Fever Mounts in El Pao
Gerard Philipe's last film, set on an island off the coast of Latin America. Philipe portrays Vazquez, the idealistic secretary to a corrupt and callous governor. When he eventually becomes governor himself, he betrays his humane idealism. Bunuel skillfully blends melodrama with acute political analysis of how systems subvert individuals. English dubbed.
VHS: S00441. $29.95.
Luis Bunuel, Mexico, 1959, 97 mins.

The Great Madcap (El Gran Calavera)
Bunuel's hilarious portrait of the hypocrisy of the middle class centers on the disastrous results of a wealthy man's spendthrift habits and womanizing on his family. An elegant satire on class, sex, advertising and the reverse exploitation of the ruling elite. Spanish with English subtitles.
VHS: S18117. $79.95.
Luis Bunuel, Mexico, 1949, 90 mins.

Illusion Travels by Streetcar
Shot in something like two weeks, to pay grocery bills (one of five features turned out during Bunuel's very active 1952-53 period), *Illusion* tells the story of two young employees of a municipal public transport company in Mexico City—driver and conductor—who get drunk at a local festival and decide to take the girl on one last trip on a train about to be retired from service. This results in a number of hilarious incidents and unexpected adventures. Spanish with English subtitles.
VHS: S13588. $59.95.
Luis Bunuel, Mexico, 1953, 90 mins.

Land Without Bread
An extraordinary film about the impoverished people living in the Las Hurdes region of Spain. Bunuel constructs the film in the manner of a travelogue. The absurdity of the contrast between narration and image results in a vision so powerful the film seems surreal. Plus a classic short film, *Housing Problems*, directed by A. Elton and E. Anstey. Spanish with English subtitles.
VHS: S00720. $29.95.
Luis Bunuel, Spain, 1932, 45 mins.

Los Olvidados
A milestone of filmmaking; Bunuel's great film looks at the lives of young people growing up in the slums of Mexico, and in particular, at the desperately inevitable process by which an older, more corrupt gang leader, Jacob, hounds and destroys the younger, more innocent Pedro, before being destroyed himself. Spanish with English subtitles.
VHS: S09000. $59.95.
Laser: Side 2 CAV. LD71584. $49.95.
Luis Bunuel, Mexico, 1950, 81 mins.

Mexican Bus Ride
Bunuel, in a relaxed, populist mood, presents this story of a young peasant who is forced to leave his bride on their wedding night to travel to the city to finalize his dying mother's will. On his bus journey he encounters a diverse group of passengers in a picaresque adventure which is not without its anarchic and surreal overtones. Spanish with English subtitles.
VHS: S02664. $29.95.
Luis Bunuel, Mexico, 1951, 85 mins.

Milky Way
Luis Bunuel's truly outrageous and very funny satire on the Catholic church and church ritual, and a road movie in its own right. Two tramps on a pilgrimage encounter the Devil, the Virgin Mary, and different arguments about Catholic doctrine. French with English subtitles.
VHS: S06935. $24.95.
Luis Bunuel, France, 1968, 102 mins.

Nazarin
A simple priest tries to live by Christian precepts in one of Luis Bunuel's best—and most unjustly neglected—films. "I am very much attached to Nazarin," said Bunuel. "He is a priest. He could as well be a hairdresser or a waiter. What interests me about him is that he stands by his ideas, that these ideas are unacceptable to society at large, and that after his adventures with prostitutes, thieves and so forth, they lead him to being irrevocably damned by the prevailing social order." With Francisco Rabal, Marga Lopez and Rita Macedo. Spanish with English subtitles.
VHS: S08695. $69.95.
Luis Bunuel, Mexico, 1958, 92 mins.

Phantom of Liberty
One of Bunuel's masterpieces of surrealism, this loosely structured series of anecdotes deals with the concept of freedom. A daisy-chain of characters move through this cinema of dreams and absurdity, demonstrating the cosmic comedy of humans who constantly enslave themselves in order to be free. The lightest and liveliest of Bunuel's films filled with riddles, jokes and outrageous associations ridiculing the power to reason. French with English subtitles.
VHS: S04869. $24.95.
Luis Bunuel, France, 1974, 102 mins.

Simon of the Desert
Bunuel's outrageous satire of the Church has Simon sitting on top of a pillar in the Mexican desert, haunted by the Devil in all forms. Often called the greatest short film of all time, Bunuel's wit has never been more deadly, his surrealist vision never clearer. Spanish with English subtitles.
VHS: S01204. $29.95.
Luis Bunuel, Mexico, 1965, 40 mins.

Susana
Susana is the story of a delinquent girl who escapes from detention and hides out on a remote finca, where she destroys the rigid, uptight family with her immoral scheming. Despite the conventional melodramatic structure, *Susana* displays Bunuel's surreal fascination with the illusion of conventions. Spanish with English subtitles.
VHS: S05991. $24.95.
Luis Bunuel, Mexico, 1951, 87 mins.

That Obscure Object of Desire
A final masterpiece from Bunuel, in which he uses two actresses playing one role to illustrate the unfathomable nature of sexual obsession. Fernando Rey stars. Nominated for two Academy Awards, including Best Foreign Film. French with English subtitles.
VHS: S01314. $29.95.
Laser: LD70472. $49.95.
Luis Bunuel, France, 1976, 100 mins.

Tristana
The stunning Catherine Deneuve is Tristana, a victim of her own captivating beauty who is desired by two men. The first is her lecherous guardian (played by the great Fernando Rey) who, after raising her from a teenager, takes her as his mistress. The other is a young artist (Franco Nero) who wants to marry her but lacks the courage to free her from the corrupt relationship with her guardian. Set in 1920's Spain, *Tristana* is a scathing examination of moral decay viewed through Bunuel's typically dispassionate and ironic eyes. Spanish with English subtitles.
VHS: S15344. $59.95.
Laser: Widescreen. LD75490. $49.95.
Luis Bunuel, Spain, 1970, 98 mins.

Un Chien Andalou/Land Without Bread
Two great early films by Luis Bunuel; *Un Chien Andalou* continues to shock audiences today as it did in 1928; *Land without Bread* is a horrifying account of one of Spain's most desolate regions, a documentary masterpiece made all the more harrowing for its travelogue style.
VHS: S12462. $29.95.
Luis Bunuel, Spain, 1928/32, 42 mins.

Viridiana
Bunuel's outrageous and devastating attack on religion and society. Viridiana, about to take her vows as a nun, takes to the pure Christian life by organizing a haven for a blind man, leper, cripple and beggar. Full of Freudian symbolism, the film ends in a famous orgy of destruction, containing Bunuel's blasphemous scene of the Last Supper. The film that got Bunuel kicked out of Spain. Spanish with English subtitles.
VHS: S01419. $29.95.
Luis Bunuel, Spain, 1961, 90 mins.

A Woman Without Love
Based on a short story by Guy de Maupassant. Set in a decaying mansion, a young wife has a brief secret affair, separates from her lover, and then bears his son. Bunuel makes ample use of the gothic setting in the mansion which is part home, part antiques, part a tomb, in a surrealist plumbing of a bizarre love story. Spanish with English subtitles.
VHS: S06840. $24.95.
Luis Bunuel, Mexico, 1951, 91 mins.

Wuthering Heights
A wonderfully twisted adaption of Charlotte Bronte's famed novel, set in Mexico. Alternatively titled *The Abyss of Passion*, the film was called "a magical example of how an artist of genius can take someone else's classic work and shape it to fit his own temperament without violating it" (Vincent Canby). Spanish with English subtitles.
VHS: S04876. $24.95.
Luis Bunuel, Mexico, 1953, 90 mins.

The Young One
Luis Bunuel's only American film is a powerful work about racism and sexual exploitation. A northern black jazz clarinetist (Bernie Hamilton) fleeing from false rape charges turns up on a small island off the Carolina coast and finds himself being hunted by a game warden (Zachary Scott). The sheriff's racial bigotry flares openly, though he is concealing his own perverse sexual fixation on a beautiful young nymphet (Kay Meersman). "A film that is realistically simple in all its parts, and realistically complex in its total picture of life and people" (Newsweek). With Crahan Denton and Claudio Brook.
VHS: S19462. $59.95.
Luis Bunuel, USA/Mexico, 1960, 95 mins.

SPANISH ISSUES

Barcelona
This city is one of the great Mediterranean cultural centers. Picasso, Miro and Dali all began here. Gaudi, certainly one of the most innovative architects from the turn of the century, added a special touch to Barcelona. This documentary visits some of Gaudi's most famous works, including his unfinished cathedral and Guell Park, as well as other outstanding landmarks in the city, such as the Catalan Museum and early Christian churches. 45 mins.
VHS: S18896. $75.00.

Barcelona: Archive of Courtesy
This video reveals the cultural delights of the capital of Catalonia. The jewel-like architecture of Antonio Gaudi, the art of Joan Miro, and even the contemporary feel of this exciting city make it an unmatched treasure trove of the arts.
VHS: S24265. $19.98.

Cervantes
Horst Buchholz, Gina Lollobrigida, Louis Jourdan, Fernando Rey and Jose Ferrer star in this film based on the life of the author of *Don Quixote*. As a young man, Cervantes left his homeland to become a soldier. The experience was integral to his later artistic development. Dubbed in English. Also known as *Cervantes the Young Rebel*.
VHS: S26876. $24.95.
Vincent Sherman, Spain/France/Italy, 1967, 119 mins.

Cervantes and Friend
Perhaps Spain's greatest author, Cervantes is known worldwide because of his novel *Don Quixote* and its central character. The story of both the author and this memorable old gentleman are revealed in this video. 28 mins.
VHS: S26533. $29.95.

Christmas in Spain
Feliz Navidad! Window shop along Madrid's Plaza Mayor. Join a Spanish family for a special Christmas dinner, and celebrate the Feast of the Three Kings. A wonderful glimpse of Spanish tradition. 30 mins.
English Narration.
VHS: S05263. $49.95.
Spanish Narration.
VHS: S05262. $49.95.

El Escorial and Toledo
Tour the magnificent 16th century palace and monastery built by Phillip II, exhibiting the famous works of Velazquez, Goya and others. Then on to Toledo with its renowned Moorish architecture, the home of El Greco and the legendary fortress of El Alcazar. 40 mins. English narration.
VHS: S05728. $49.95.

"Espana Es..."—
The Sights and Sounds of Modern Spain
This program examines the diversity of contemporary Spain, from the fiesta in Seville to the faster pace in the urban center of Madrid. 28 mins.
VHS: S20276. $29.95.

The Good Fight
It was one of history's most dramatic expressions of international solidarity when 40,000 volunteers from around the world went to fight the armies of Franco, Hitler and Mussolini in the Spanish Civil War of 1936-39. *The Good Fight* tells the story of 3,200 Americans who volunteered to fight on the side of the Spanish Republic. This vivid series of portraits with 12 of the survivors (half the Americans lost their lives in Spain) brings to life the reasons for joining the conflict, and what it was to be a part of a people's army against fascism in the war that was the rehearsal for World War II. An absorbing and passionate account full of humor, pride and deep sorrow, their interviews are illustrated with rare archival footage of the Lincoln Brigade in Spain as well as Hollywood films, songs and newsreels with such notables as Hemingway himself and Henry Fonda. Narrated by Studs Terkel.
VHS: S12206. $69.95.
Laser: CLV. LD71721. $19.98.
Buckner/Dore/Stills, USA, 1984, 98 mins.

Introducing Don Quixote
An introduction to Don Quixote adapted from slide/ film strip shows to video. Covers the role of Miguel Cervantes in Spanish literature, and the essence of Don Quixote. 30 mins.
English Version.
VHS: S06384. $39.95.
Spanish Version.
VHS: S06385. $39.95.

La Gloria de Espana
Once the most powerful nation in the world, witness Spain's Golden Age from the 16th century to the present with its bustling cities and rich countryside. In English and then Spanish. 25 mins. each.
VHS: S05261. $59.95.

La Lengua (The Spanish Language)
Presents an exploration of how the Spanish language came to be such a dominant world language. It explains who speaks Spanish, where and why. English and Spanish as well as Bilingual signs are compared and presented for review and practice. The value of two languages is explained. Spanish and English narration. 55 mins.
VHS: S10320. $59.95.

Loyola, the Soldier Saint
A romantic biography of the founder of the Jesuit movement, this work charts Loyola's brutal war experiences, his spiritual and moral recovery and eventual sainthood. With Raphael Duran. English dubbed.
VHS: S18031. $29.95.
Jose Diaz Morales, Spain/USA, 1952, 93 mins.

Madrid
View the historical splendors of one of the most beautiful cities in Spain. Visit the Plaza Mayor, the Royal Palace and Prado Museum. Then on to modern Madrid with its artists, Flamenco dancers, cafes and bullfights. 57 mins.
English Narration.
VHS: S05260. $49.95.
Spanish Narration.
VHS: S05259. $49.95.

Pamplona/Viva San Fermin
Experience the spectacle, wonder and excitement of Pamplona's traditional running of the Bulls. With a tape script and a teacher's guide. 30 mins.
English Narration.
VHS: S19831. $65.00.
Spanish Narration.
VHS: S19832. $65.00.

Pimpenella: Nuestras Mejores Canciones (Our Favorite Songs)
A concert performance by this acclaimed duo has been captured on videotape. It includes "Ahora Decide", "Valiente", "Solo Tu, Solo Yo", "La Familia" and many more songs. 55 mins.
VHS: S23868. $19.95.

Sabicas: El Maestro de Flamenco
The only video available about the legendary guitarist Agustin Castellon Campos Sabicas, a self-taught child prodigy who became known in Spain as *El Fenomeno*, and who pioneered the use of the flamenco guitar as a solo instrument. This video features four guitar solos played by Sabicas: "Malaguena," "Zapateado del Re," "Sitio de Zaragoza" and "Arabian Dance," as well as a *siguiriya* performed by the late Maria Alba, with guitar accompaniment by Adonis Puertas and vocal accompaniment by Luis Vargas.
VHS: S27204. $49.95.

Salamanca—
The Heart of Spain's Golden Age
Salamanca is as old as Spain itself. Its University, founded in 1223, helped fuel artistic, cultural and educational achievements integral to Spain's Golden Age. The city itself stands as a monument to this historic influence. 30 mins.
VHS: S26534. $32.95.

Seville: Jewel of Andalusia
With its exotic Moorish palaces, ancient Catholic churches and intriguing Jewish neighborhoods this ancient city remains unmatched for its unique sights. There are even ruins from the Visigoth, Greek and Roman invaders.
VHS: S24266. $19.98.

Spain: Everything Under the Sun
Tour the colorful Spanish countryside and see all of her most beautiful cities, including Madrid, Segovia, Avila, Seville, Costa del Sol, and more. 50 mins.
VHS: S05771. $24.95.

Spanish Civil War
A major, unparalleled history of this bloody conflict of the 1930's, a war of belief that claimed three million lives, and featured such men on the front lines as Ernest Hemingway and the famous Abraham Lincoln Brigade. This 6-hour, detailed history of the conflict and the political maneuvers behind it is a remarkable, well-researched portrait of one of the key events of the 20th century. 360 mins. Double cassette.
VHS: S04899. $79.95.

Spanish History—The Heritage of Rome
This program captures the artistic, political, religious and cultural influence of the Roman conquest on Spanish society. 28 mins.
VHS: S20275. $29.95.

Spanish TV Commercials
Spaniards add their own unique approach to advertising in this series of TV commercials. Compare and contrast their ads with ours. Culturally authentic information about Spain is highlighted throughout the film. Includes script.
VHS: S05275. $49.95.

Spanish TV Commercials—Volume 2
A second program of the unique Spanish approach toward commercials, providing an insight into the daily life of the Spanish people. 45 mins.
VHS: S09051. $49.95.

central & south american CINEMA

Alias, La Gringa
This powerful political drama from Peru follows the adventures and escapades of La Gringa, a charismatic criminal who cannot be incarcerated by any jail. Helped by an imprisoned intellectual, he escapes. Determined to aid his accomplice, he returns to prison in disguise and is trapped by a riot and corruption beyond his grasp. Spanish with English subtitles.
VHS: S20383. $59.95.
Alberto Durant, Peru, 1991, 92 mins.

Argentinisima I
Fernando Ayala directed this film inspired by the poetry of Atahualpa Yupanqui, in a film which alternates reality with fantasy, and is based almost entirely on Argentinian folklore. The soundtrack is drawn from various ethnographic music of Argentina, and the film features spectacular scenery of Argentina. With Atahualpa Rupanqui, Mercedes Sosa, Los Chalchaleros, Eduardo Falu, Ariel Ramirez, Jaime Torres. In Spanish *without* English subtitles.
VHS: S04956. $59.95.
F. Ayala/H. Olivera, Argentina, 115 mins.

Barrocco
A visual and musical history of Latin America from the director of *Frida* and *Reed: Insurgent Mexico*. The daring film portrays the birth of Latin American identity through the synthesis of African, Mayan, Aztec and Spanish cultures. "A musical dream that explores the beauty, cruelty and mystery of Latin America through sound and image." (*San Francisco Chronicle*). Spanish with English subtitles.
VHS: S26498. $59.95.
Paul Leduc, Spain/Cuba, 1989, 108 mins.

Black River
Absolute power corrupts absolutely in the Amazonian jungles of Rio Negro. First, a new governor and his ambitious wife (Angela Molina) successfully confront the brutal local chief, but the era they usher in is one of gambling, prostitution and economic exploitation. Frank Ramirez plays the head of security, who grabs control only to initiate a regime of austerity and restriction as madness buries good intentions. Spanish with English subtitles.
VHS: S27737. $59.95.
Atahualpa Lichy, Venezuela/Spain, 1990, 116 mins.

Cabeza de Vaca
A visually spellbinding biography of the Spanish explorer Nunez Cabeza de Vaca, the sole survivor of a 16th-century Spanish shipwreck off the coast of Florida. Cabeza de Vaca discovers the Iguase, a traditional Indian tribe, which allows Cabeza into their tribe. Over the next eight years, he learns about their mysterious culture and becomes a leader of the group. But his former identity catches up with him when a team of Spanish conquistadors return to colonize the Indians. "Bold and imaginative, the film has ambition, freshness, imagination, mystery and exhilarating reach. It has greatness in it" (Jay Carr, *Boston Globe*). With Juan Diego, Daniel Gimenez Cacho and Roberto Sosa. Spanish and Indian with English subtitles.
VHS: S19356. $89.98.
Nicolas Echevarria, Mexico/Spain, 1991, 109 mins.

Camila
A young Catholic socialite from Buenos Aires falls in love and runs away with a young Jesuit priest. The two find temporary happiness in a small provincial village, but eventually they are recognized and ultimately condemned to death without a trial. Spanish with English subtitles.
VHS: S00209. $59.95.
Maria-Luisa Bemberg, Argentina, 1984, 90 mins.

Chicago Latino Cinema Collection: I
The best of contemporary Latin American cinema in six recent feature films as curated in the Chicago Latino Film Festival. The six features in this special collection, each available on a single cassette, are: *Confessing to Laura* (Jaime Osorio Gomez, Colombia); *Tango: Our Dance* (Jorge Zanada, Argentina); *Shoot to Kill* (Carlos Azpurua, Venezuela); *Butterfly Wings* (Juanma Bajo Ulloa, Spain); *Alias, La Gringa* (Alberto Durant, Peru) and *Savage Capitalism* (Andre Klotzel, Brazil). Six-volume set.
VHS: S20598. $299.99.

Chicago Latino Cinema Collection: II
Eight recent Latin American films, including the work of the legendary Argentine director Leopoldo Torre Nilsson and his son, make up this unique retrospective of award-winning contemporary films. Each on a single cassette as well, the eight feature films in this second collection of Latin American cinema are: *Buccaneer Soul* (Carlos Reichenbach, Brazil); *The Love of Silent Movies* (Pablo Torre, Argentina); *Black River* (Atahualpa Lichy, Venezuela/Spain); *We're All Stars* (Felipe Degregori, Peru); *The Day You Love Me* (Sergio Dow, Colombia); *Martin Fierro* (Loepoldo Torre Nilsson, Argentina); *Painted Lips* (*Boquitas Pintadas*) (Leopoldo Torre Nilsson, Argentina) and *The Seven Madmen* (*Los Siete Locos*) (Loepoldo Torre Nilsson, Argentina). Eight-volume set.
VHS: S27831. $349.99.

The City of the Dogs (La Ciudad de los Perros)
A terrific film adaptation of the great South American novel by Mario Vargas Llosa, *The City of Dogs* is the powerful story of a young man's upbringing in the military academy, and eventual disillusionment with both the military structures, the power which they represent, and the system which they enforce. The original title of Llosa's novel was "Time of the Hero." Spanish with English subtitles.
VHS: S04611. $39.95.
Francisco J. Lombardi Pery, 1985, 135 mins.

Confessing to Laura
A gut-wrenching drama from Colombia which is set during a raging civil war in the aftermath of the assassination of liberal leader Jorge Elieser Gaitain in 1948. Three people are trapped in Laura's home during a riot, setting the stage for an intense, unforgettable night. Spanish with English subtitles.
VHS: S20379. $59.95.
Jaime Osorio Gomez, Colombia, 1990, 90 mins.

Crecor de Golpe (Growing Up)
Ubaldo Martinez, Julio Cesar Ludeuna and Cecilia Roth star in this touching story about an orphan who finds the paternal love he needs in an old widower. Spanish with NO subtitles.
VHS: S23922. $24.95.
Sergio Renan, Argentina, 1977, 84 mins.

Crepuscolo
The story of an obsessive passion of a man in love with the wife of his best friend, this classic from the Mexican cinema stars Arturo de Cordova, Gloria Marin and Lilia Michel. In Spanish *without* English subtitles.
VHS: S05919. $39.95.
Julio Bracho, Mexico, 1944, 108 mins.

Cronos
An ingenious alchemist creates a device that grants him eternal life. 400 years later an elderly antique dealer discovers the properties of this unique invention. Though he grows younger every time he uses this device, there is a terrible price to pay. Life after death becomes a bloody promise without end. This film won Grand Prize during Critics' Week at Cannes. Spanish with English subtitles.
VHS: S22127. $19.98.
Guillermo Del Toro, Mexico , 1992, 90 mins.

Cuando Viajan las Estrellas
A Hollywood star comes to Mexico to learn flamenco, but rather learns the ways of the genteel "charro" when she falls in love with one, played by Jorge Negrette, the quintessential singing cowboy, and the most romantic idol of the Golden Age of Mexican cinema. With Raquel Rojas, Joaquin Pardave. In Spanish *without* English subtitles.
VHS: S05920. $39.95.
Alberto Gout, Mexico, 1942, ;+4108 mins.

Cuesta Abajo
Rare musical drama featuring the master of the tango, Carlos Gardel, together with Vicente Padula, Anita Camillo. Spanish *without* English subtitles.
VHS: S06034. $54.95.
John Reinhardt, Argentina, 1934, 65 mins.

Danzon
This sensual, exuberant work by the gifted Mexican director Maria Novaro tells the story of Julia (Maria Rojo), a 40-year-old telephone operator and single mother whose emotional life consists of ballroom dancing. When her dancing partner disappears, Julia undertakes a grueling odyssey to locate him. Her search takes her on an extraordinary inner voyage. "One of the most enchanting surprises of the season" (Andrew Sarris). With Carmen Salinas, Blanca Guerra and Tito Vasconcelos. Spanish with English subtitles.
VHS: S19334. $19.95.
Maria Novaro, Mexico, 1991, 96 mins.

The Day You Love Me
Winner of the Casa de las Americas award for Best Latin American feature, this humorous period film recaptures 1935, the year of Juan Vicente Gomez' dictatorship when Venezuela played host to the great tango singer Carlos Gardel as he presented his film *The Day You Love Me*. Romance and politics clash, exposing the lies, hopes and false dreams of an era on the eve of change as a small city meets, for the first time, the King of the Tango. Spanish with English subtitles.
VHS: S27739. $59.95.
Sergio Dow, Colombia, 1986, 80 mins.

Details of a Duel
One morning a teacher and a butcher leave home to go about their business, which, on this day, includes preparing for death. Contrary to their true natures, one must kill the other by mid-afternoon. Egged on by the clergy, the militia and the town's bureaucrats, a private affair becomes a gladiatorial spectacle. A comedy about escalation, anticipation, and manners, this absurdly inexorable process is the subject of Sergio Cabrera's wry first feature. Spanish with English subtitles.
VHS: S14149. $59.95.
Sergio Cabrera, Columbia, 1989, 97 mins.

Diary of the War of Pigs
Based on the novel by Adolfo Bioy Casares; the generation gap is taken to the extreme by a group of young people who have decided to exterminate all senior citizens in this futuristic vision. One of the great films by the neglected Argentinian film master, Leopoldo Torre Nilsson. Spanish with English subtitles.
VHS: S01124. $59.95.
Leopoldo T. Nilsson, Argentina, 1975, 90 mins.

Don Segundo Sombra
Continuing in the series of adaptations of works from South and Latin American authors, this film is based on an Argentine novel by Riccardo Guiraldes, and is set amidst the life of the Argentine gauchos. Spanish with English subtitles.
VHS: S03199. $59.95.
Manuel Antin, 1969, 110 mins.

Dona Barbara
Based on the 1929 novel by Romulo Gallegos, *Dona Barbara* tells of a dramatic confrontation over land and civil rights, notable for its passionate characterizations.
VHS: S04610. $39.95.
Fernando de Fuentes, Mexico, 1943, 138 mins.

Dona Herlinda and Her Son
A delightful, funny film from Mexico called by David Denby of *New York Magazine* a "sly, deadpan comedy. The ultimate gay homage to mom." Spanish with English subtitles.
VHS: S06022. $79.95.
Jaime H. Hermosillo, Mexico, 1986, 90 mins.

El Compadre Mendoza (Godfather Mendoza)
This rare example of classic Mexican cinema examines the corrupted ideals of the Revolution in the story of an opportunistic landowner who faces the choice of remaining loyal to a general in Zapata's army and being financially ruined or saving his own skin. The character of the general is clearly modeled on Zapata himself. Spanish with English subtitles.
VHS: S26946. $29.95.
Fernando de Fuentes, Mexico, 1933

El Corsario Negro
From the Mexican classic cinema, with fabulous camerawork by the legendary Gabriel Figueroa, in a love, action and adventure story starring Pedro Armendariz and the beautiful Maria Luisa Zea. In Spanish *without* English subtitles.
VHS: S05917. $54.95.
Chano Urueto, Mexico, 1944, 84 mins.

El Dia Que Me Queiras
The tango has always had one voice—the voice is, and has been, the legendary Carlos Gardel. Gardel took an obscure dance born in the brothels of Buenos Aires, sweetened its melody, added lyrics about the life and feelings of a city, culture and people, and gave the tango new dimension. This rare musical drama is one of Gardel's classic films, made in 1935, and stars Rosita Moreno, Tito Lusiardo, Manuel Pelufo. Argentina, 1935, B&W, 95 mins. Spanish *without* English subtitles.
VHS: S05849. $54.95.

El Gran Acontecimiento (The Great Apparition)
The enchanting legend of the Virgin of Guadalupe is brought to life in this animated feature. She is greatly revered both in Mexico, where her shrine is located, and throughout the world. Spanish with NO subtitles.
VHS: S23918. $34.95.

El Grito
The laborers of a sugar plantation face the brutal repression of the ruling power, sacrificing their lives to form the first union in their country, in this powerful film from Peru. Spanish with English subtitles.
VHS: S23477. $39.95.
Alberto Durant, Peru, 1982, 84 mins.

El Muerto
Based on a short story of the same name by Jorge Luis Borges, *El Muerto* traces the life of Benjamin Otalora, in 19th century South America. Otalora, a fugitive, meets the leader of a smuggling ring upon his arrival in Montevideo. The smuggler takes him under his wings, yet when the aging gang leader takes sick, Otalora covertly attempts to claim power within this ring. Spanish with English subtitles.
VHS: S03196. $39.95.
Hector Olivera, Argentina, 1975, 103 mins.

El Mundo del Talisman (The World of the Talisman)
In this animated feature, a brother and sister find a virtual world of booby traps in the planet they inherit. Spanish with NO subtitles. 1987, 80 mins.
VHS: S23912. $24.95.

El Super
A hilarious comedy set in New York, but made by two Cuban exiles. Roberto, a Cuban, has been a building superintendent in New York City for ten years but, from his basement-level point of view, he has eyes only for Cuba or Miami, where it doesn't snow. With humor, compassion and accuracy, the film describes Roberto's dream of returning to his crime-free, snow-free homeland. Spanish with English subtitles.
VHS: S11592. $79.95.
L. Ichaso/O. Jimenez-Leal, USA, 1979, 90 mins.

El Tango en Broadway
Carlos Gardel, Trini Ramos, Blanca Vischer, Vicente Padula, Jaime Davesa star in this rare musical comedy starring the incomparable master of the tango, Carlos Gardel. Spanish *without* English subtitles.
VHS: S05850. $54.95.
Louis Gasnier, Argentina, 1934, 95 mins.

Erendira
Based on a section of Gabriel Garcia Marquez' *One Hundred Years of Solitude*, *Erendira* is an erotic black comedy laden with sexual fantasy, surreal pranks and political allegory. Erendira is a teenage girl exploited as a sexual slave by her greedy grandmother. Spanish with English subtitles.
VHS: S00413. $24.95.
Ruy Guerra, Mexico, 1983, 103 mins.

Fable of the Beautiful Pigeon Fancier
Based on a fragment from his novel *Love in the Time of Cholera*, *Fable of the Beautiful Pigeon Fancier* was conceived and co-written by Nobel Prize winner Gabriel Garcia Marquez. Reteaming Garcia Marquez with director Ruy Guerra (who began his career as an actor, starring in Werner Herzog's masterpiece *Aguirre: Wrath of God*), with whom he'd collaborated on the earlier *Erendira*, *Fable of the Beautiful Pigeon Fancier* tells the story of Orestes, a wealthy factory owner who falls madly in love with a married pigeon breeder. "An elegant Wellesian comedy of fate and manners" (*Los Angeles Times*). Spanish with English subtitles.
VHS: S13692. $19.98.
Ruy Guerra, Mexico/Spain, 1988, 73 mins.

Fabulas de la Selva (Fables of the Green Forest)
Johnny Chuck, Peter Cottontail, Chatterer the Squirrel and all the other characters from Thornton W. Burgess' stories are featured in this animated adaptation of his classic works. Spanish with NO subtitles.
VHS: S23919. $34.95.

Far Away and Long Ago (Alla Lejos y Hace Tiempo)
A poetic rendering of the autobiographical novel by Guillermo Hudson—images of the mystery of the Argentinian pampa, its gauchos, witchcraft and women —perturbing memories that nurtured the writer's childhood. Spanish with English subtitles.
VHS: S07737. $39.95.
Manuel Antin, Argentina, 1974, 91 mins.

Frida
Paul Leduc's widely acclaimed, brilliantly visual tribute to the spirit and determination of Frida Kahlo, who risked her life for her art and love, and became one of the dominant painters of the 20th century. Told in surreal flashbacks reminiscent of her own canvasses, the film remarkably captures the spirit and determination of the woman who made herself into a great artist, a cultural leader, a political activist. With Ofelia Medina, Juan Jose Gurrola, Max Kerlow. Spanish with English subtitles.
VHS: S08997. $29.95.
Paul Leduc, Mexico, 1984, 108 mins.

Funny Dirty Little War
An important film from Hector Olivera, the story is a parable of events in Peronist Argentina. The film is a comedy about rightist Peronists who plot to oust the leftist mayor of the town. But the mayor refuses to budge, and a "funny dirty little war" ensues. Federico Luppi is brilliant as the mayor. Spanish with English subtitles.
VHS: S06841. $24.95.
Hector Olivera, Argentina, 1983, 80 mins.

The Garcia Marquez Collection
A compilation of six feature films based on the stories, chronicles and novels written by Nobel Prize winner Gabriel Garcia Marquez, author of *Love in the Time of Cholera*. Includes *Miracle in Rome*, *Letters from the Park*, *Fable of the Beautiful Pigeon Fancier*, *The Summer of Miss Forbes*, *I'm the One You're Looking For* and *A Very Old Man with Enormous Wings*. All titles are in Spanish with English subtitles.
VHS: S14457. $119.88.

Golden Cockerel (El Gallo de Oro)
Based on a screenplay by Gabriel Garcia Marquez, Carlos Fuentes and Roberto Galvadon, and on a novel by Juan Rulfo. Poor man starts making a fortune with a gamecock, and the greedy owner of the arena, yet their fortune finally severs their relationship. Spanish with English subtitles.
VHS: S07738. $39.95.
Robert Galvadon, Mexico, 1964, 110 mins.

The Green Wall
A breakthrough film from South America, *The Green Wall* is based on Armando Robles Godoy's own experiences of homesteading in the Peruvian jungle. *The Green Wall* is "a bitter and beautiful movie," in which Godoy translates his experience into film poetry rather than flat reportage and uses the physical environment (exquisitely photographed by his cameraman brother, Mario) as a great natural mystery, idyllic but cruel, rich but unyielding to the will of a handsome young settler (Mexican star Julio Aleman, in a vibrant performance) who is determined to survive there with his family. The idyll is broken both by the bureaucracy in far-off Lima, and at the film's end: "The blow comes from the rain forest near their house, where father and son have constructed a mock city of clay as a symbol of the civilized stupidity they sought to escape. The film's final sequence, an almost wordless funeral, is masterful movie making, a haunting glimpse of humanity that lingers in the mind" (Pauline Kael, *The New Yorker*). "A masterpiece!" (Roger Ebert). Spanish with English subtitles.
VHS: S11250. $79.95.
Armando Robles Godoy, Peru, 1970, 110 mins.

In Love
The story of a rebel soldier who dreams of a Mexico in which all are equal. He falls in love with a woman from the privileged class who considers him beneath her social status. Spanish with English subtitles. Mexico, 81 mins.
VHS: S02854. $24.95.

La Boca del Lobo
Hailed by Judy Stone of the *San Francisco Chronicle* as "a powerful drama" and considered by many to be one of the finest films to emerge from Latin and South America in recent years, *La Boca del Lobo* is the study of a bloody encounter between the Peruvian Army and the Maoist Shining Path. Winner of the Grand Prize at the San Sebastian Film Festival. Spanish with English subtitles.
VHS: S12363. $79.95.
Miguel Pereira, Peru, 1989, 100 mins.

La Dama de las Camelias

Based on Alexander Dumas' *Camille*, a novel about the desperate love between a bullfighter and a stage actress, this classic Mexican film stars Maria Felix and Jorge Mistral. Spanish *without English subtitles.*
VHS: S05918. $54.95.
Roberto Gavaldon, Mexico, 1953, 108 mins.

La Discoteca del Amor

Adolfo Aristarain's Argentinian musical comedy in which a funny detective and his clumsy assistant are the odd couple in charge of solving a case of musical piracy. With Cacho Castana, Monica Gonzaga. *In Spanish without English subtitles.*
VHS: S05046. $39.95.
Adolfo Aristarain, Argentina, 1980, 105 mins.

La Hora

Luck suddenly crosses the path of this beggar and with it, the opportunity to help his friends, with a premonition that allows him to see what will happen during the next 24 hours—but he has no idea what will happen in the *final* hour. With Julio Aleman, Diana Ferreti. *In Spanish without English subtitles.*
Mexico, 1987.
VHS: S05047. $79.95.

La Patrilla del Tiempo—1 (Time Patrol—1)

High tech weapons blast the kids from time machine to time machine in this animated feature. Whether they find themselves in prehistoric times or far in the future, it is always a matter of good versus evil. Spanish with NO subtitles. 1986, 95 mins.
VHS: S23916. $34.95.

La Regenta

Based on a novel by Leopoldo Clarin, the story is set in 18th century Spain, and investigates the prejudices of a small town against women. Spanish with English subtitles.
VHS: S03198. $39.95.

La Rosa Blanca

Based on a short story by Bruno Traven, the writer of *Treasure of Sierra Madre*, and one of Mexico's quintessential novelists. Spanish with English subtitles.
VHS: S03200. $39.95.
Roberto Gavaldon, 1960, 100 mins.

La Tigra

Based on the novella by Jose de La Cuadra, this Ecuadorian feature looks at female identity through the eyes of Latin American machismo culture. The Tigress is the myth of woman: beautiful, sexual, powerful and revered. This film may be the best visual equivalent of literary "magical realism" ever filmed, and was awarded the Best Film Prize at the 1990 Cartagena Film Festival. Spanish with English subtitles.
VHS: S26499. $59.95.
Camilo Luzuriaga, Ecuador, 1990, 80 mins.

Let's Go with Pancho Villa (Vamanos con Pancho Villa)

The key work of the godfather of Mexican cinema, Fernando de Fuentes, this remarkable feature is the story of a group of friends who decide to join forces with Pancho Villa. Several die heroic but meaningless deaths, and the last three enter Villa's elite force, Los Dorados, the Golden Ones. Fuentes acutely charts the disillusionment, stagnation and corruption which followed the Revolution in what is clearly a milestone of Latin American cinema. With a remarkable performance from Antonio Fraustio. Spanish with English subtitles.
VHS: S24690. $39.95.
Fernando de Fuentes, Mexcio, 1935, 92 mins.

Like Water for Chocolate

Immensely popular, magical story of a young girl whose cooking is infused with her emotions as she prepares her meals. Unrequited passions, changing political situations and even madness emerge in this highly entertaining, sensual and funny story. Written by Laura Esquivel and directed by her husband.
VHS: S21358. $19.95.
Laser: Letterboxed. LD74638. $39.99.
Alfonso Arau, Mexico, 1992, 105 mins.

Los Hermanos del Hierro

The lives of two boys are predetermined by their embittered mother upon the death of her husband. Her thirst of vengeance would not be quenched until she brought upon them his darkest day of her life. Antonio Aguilar, Julio Aleman, Columba Dominguez star. *In Spanish without English subtitles.*
VHS: S05921. $24.95.
Ismael Rodriguez, Mexico, 1961, 95 mins.

The Love of Silent Movies

Pablo Torre directs this compelling film about a man who can't function in a world outside the lives of the characters he portrays. Ralph de Palma has 15 minutes of fame as a Latin Lover in silent Hollywood films. Thirty years have passed and with them the silent movie era. But de Palma recreates his past glories by paying tribute to silent films each night. Spanish with English subtitles.
VHS: S27736. $59.95.
Pablo Torre, Argentina, 1993, 92 mins.

Macario

The talents of top director Roberto Gavaldon, novelist B. Traven (*The Treasure of Sierra Madre*) and cinematographer Gabriel Figueroa combined to produce this gentle, moving fable on human morality. The title of the film comes from the name of a young peasant, despondent over his inability to provide for his family. On the Day of the Dead, he meets Death, disguised as another peasant, who trades him the power to cure the dying for a portion of turkey. Macario's fame soon spreads around the country, and he soon has a flourishing business—until a local doctor decides to call in The Inquisition. Spanish with English subtitles.
VHS: S11180. $69.95.
Roberto Gavaldon, Mexico, 1958, 91 mins.

Man Facing Southeast

In this critically-acclaimed Argentine film a man named Rantes suddenly appears in a Buenos Aires hospital, expertly playing the organ. But who is he—this man with no recorded identity? Doctor Denis dismisses Rantes' claim of being an alien visitor as a simple case of paranoid delusion. Beatriz, his only visitor, sees him as an intimate and knowing companion. The other patients, intrigued by his mysterious intelligence, see him as their only source of hope. Dubbed.
VHS: S05214. $19.95.
Eliseo Subiela, Argentina, 1986, 105 mins.

Maria Candelaria

"The classic and most memorable of all Mexican films" (B. Rayes Nevares, *The Mexican Cinema*). A poignant story starring Dolores del Rio as a young girl mercilessly persecuted by her townspeople because of her mother's immoral behavior. Spanish with English subtitles.
VHS: S02663. $24.95.
Emilio Fernandez, Mexico, 1945, 99 mins.

Martin Fierro

This riveting film by Leopoldo Torre Nilsson deals with the life of Martin Fierro. Drafted into military service, he is assigned to work for the commander. When he returns home, his wife and family are gone. As he descends into depression, he kills a black man during a drunken fight, and is forced to flee. Together with his friend Cruz, he lives in an Indian encampment in relative safety. Spanish with English subtitles.
VHS: S27740. $59.95.
Leopoldo Torre Nilsson, Argentina, 1968, 135 mins.

Mary My Dearest

A petty thief discovers a former flame who, after once jilting him, has suddenly appeared in his apartment wearing a wedding dress. She fascinates him with magic tricks, persuading him to abandon his life of crime and marry her. They form a vaudeville team whose sexual magnetism is more magical than their threadbare illusions. When Maria's car breaks down, she must turn to an insane asylum for a phone, unleashing an absurd nightmare of entrapment and madness. Co-written from the surreal imagination of Gabriel Garcia Marquez. Spanish with English subtitles.
VHS: S15668. $79.95.
Jaime H. Hermosillo, Mexico, 1983, 100 mins.

Miss Mary

From the director of *Camila*, Julie Christie stars as an English governess in Buenos Aires working for a wealthy family bound by a sense of tradition. Director Maria-Luisa Bemberg weaves broad political events together with intimate personal dramas. English language.
VHS: S03461. $19.95.
Maria-Luisa Bemberg, Argentina, 1986, 100 mins.

Narda or the Summer

Based on the short story by Salvador Elizondo, this Mexican drama is the revealing story of two young men who decide to share a woman during the summer. Narda, however, has plans of her own. She will not belong to either one—both will belong to her. Spanish with English subtitles.
VHS: S23476. $39.95.
Juan Guerrero, Mexico, 1968, 82 mins.

The Official Story

Winner of the Academy Award for Best Foreign Language Film in 1985, this powerful Argentinean feature is the true story of a comfortable middle-class couple and their adopted daughter. As the film progresses, the couple gradually begin to suspect that their daughter may be one of the many Argentinean children separated from their parents as they are detained or tortured and given away. The wife's journey of self-discovery reveals the horrors of the military dictatorship in Argentina. Directed by Luis Puenzo. With great performances from Hector Alterio and Norma Aleandro. Spanish with English subtitles.
VHS: S00949. $19.98.
Luis Puenzo, Argentina, 1985, 112 mins.

Oriane

A taut, Gothic, Latin American romance, winner of the Camera d'Or at the Cannes Film Festival. Marie returns to a rundown Venezuelan house in the jungle where she spent summers as a child. Her return ignites memories of a summer when her adolescent sexual curiosity led to a surprising encounter. "An exotic *Jane Eyre* set in a jungle-choked hacienda" (*Seattle Weekly*). With Doris Wells and Daniela Silverio. Spanish with English subtitles.
VHS: S27801. $29.95.
Fina Torres, Venezuela, 1991, 92 mins.

Painted Lips (Boquitas Pintadas)

This feature about obsessive love deals with a romantically handsome young man in the later stages of tuberculosis who is furiously fought over by four women. The film tells the story as it is recalled after his death by one of the women, who dies 30 years later, finally "cured" of romance. With Alfredo Alcon, Martha Gonzalez and Luisina Brando. Spanish with English subtitles.
VHS: S27741. $59.95.
Leopoldo Torre Nilsson, Argentina, 1975, 120 mins.

The Pearl

Mexican production of the John Steinbeck story about a poor fisherman who finds a beautiful pearl which changes his life. Pedro Armendariz is the bewildered fisherman who finds it hard to believe the changes that happen to himself and his wife.
VHS: S02560. $74.95.
Emilio Fernandez, USA/Mexico, 1947, 77 mins.

The Plague

From the director of *The Official Story*, Luis Puenzo's English-language adaptation of Albert Camus' allegorical novel transposes the setting to an unspecified South American country. The population is under siege by a devastating disease that reduces the city to a claustrophobic hellhole, a prison which no one may leave until the disease has been controlled. Puenzo captures the spiritual drift and harrowing despair of Camus' great existential novel. The international cast includes William Hurt, Jean-Marc Barr, Sandrine Bonnaire, Robert Duvall and Raul Julia. Spanish with English subtitles.
VHS: S19464. $19.98.
Luis Puenzo, Argentina/Spain/France, 1992, 106 mins.

Portrait of Teresa

One of the key Cuban films shot in a fluid style, the film focuses on the stubborn survival of deeply ingrained traditions of machismo and sexism in post-revolutionary society. Teresa, a housewife, incurs the displeasure of her husband because of her involvement in political and cultural groups. Perhaps the most controversial Cuban film to be released in U.S. Spanish with English subtitles.
VHS: S12197. $69.95.
Pastor Vega, Cuba, 1979, 115 mins.

Pubis Angelical

Based on a novel by Manuel (*Kiss of the Spider Woman*) Puig—the poignant story of a dying woman reflecting on her life, intertwining dreams and fantasies of political events with her frustration with the men who stifled her. With Graciella Borges, Alfredo Alcon. Spanish with English subtitles.
VHS: S07740. $39.95.
Raul de la Torre, Argentina, 1983, 117 mins.

Reed: Mexico Insurgente

Paul Leduc's (*Frida Naturelaza Vida*) brilliant first feature focuses on John Reed's experience as an American journalist who covered the Mexican Revolution of 1914. The film shows the Revolution as both mundane and disorganized and poses the question of whether a journalist—surrounded by suffering—can remain an impartial observer. An important milestone in the history of contemporary Latin American cinema, and a powerful, intelligent film. Spanish with English subtitles.
VHS: S25733. $59.95.
Paul Leduc, Mexico, 1971, 106 mins.

Rodrigo D: No Future

A truly powerful film about growing up on the streets in the drug capital of Medelin, Colombia. Shot in quasi-documentary style, many of the young people who appeared in the film are now dead or in jail. In the tradition of *Los Olvidados* and *Pixote*, we meet a variety of young people who will never have to worry about growing old. Spanish with English subtitles.
VHS: S14744. $79.95.
Victor Gaviria, Colombia, 1990, 93 mins.

Romero

Raul Julia gives a compelling performance as the Archbishop of El Salvador, who was murdered for his ability to stir the masses into thoughts of political reform. Oscar Romero was a kind but apolitical churchman until his eyes were opened and he became a powerful voice of the people. With Richard Jordan, Eddie Velez, Tony Plana, Harold Gould and Ana Alicia. A riveting historical lesson from Paulist Pictures. Written by Jon Sacret Young (*Testament*).
VHS: S11582. $29.95.
John Duigan, USA, 1989, 105 mins.

The Roots

This compilation of four short stories by Francisco Gonzales, produced by Manuel Barbachano (*Torero!*), won the International Film Critics Award at Cannes. Includes *The Cows, Our Lady*, *The One-Eyed Boy* and *The Filly*. Spanish with English subtitles.
VHS: S14645. $29.95.
Benito Alazraki, Mexico, 1958, 85 mins.

Santa Sangre

A startling vision of passion and obsession from the creator of *El Topo*. Guy Stockwell stars as Orgo, a sadistic circus master who brutally disfigures his wife after she catches him with another woman. Witness to the horror is their young son, Fenix. Traumatized, he is committed to an asylum. Freed by his armless mother twelve years later, they forge an unholy alliance. He "gives" her his arms, she takes control of his mind. Together they feed a mounting obsession of desire and revenge. Directed and co-written by Alejandro Jodorowsky, *Santa Sangre* is a film of bold and bizarre images, delicately balanced between the theater of the absurd and a circus of horrors. English language version. Available in both R and NC-17 rated versions.
VHS: S13586. $19.98.
Laser: CLV. LD72025. $29.98.
Alejandro Jodorowsky, Mexico/Italy, 1990, 123 mins.

The Seven Madmen (Los Siete Locos)

A daring political thriller set in South America in the 1930s. A failed idealist links up with a strangely assorted group which intends to overthrow the government and install a new regime. But the plan ultimately fails when a military coup beats it to the revolution. With Alfredo Alcon, Norma Aleandro and Thelma Biral. Spanish with English subtitles.
VHS: S27742. $59.95.
Leopoldo Torre Nilsson, Argentina, 1973, 121 mins.

Shattered Cross

Based on the novel by Marcos Aguinis, and winner of the Premio Planeta. A political-ecclesiastical subject of great controversy shapes this film in which a young priest has to face the Church and the Army in order to defend his ideals. With Oscar Martinez, Ana Maria Picchio. Spanish with English subtitles.
VHS: S07735. $59.95.
Mario David, Argentina, 1985, 103 mins.

Shoot to Kill

A mother seeks to clear the damaged reputation of her son when he is murdered during a routine police round-up and condemned as a criminal. She launches a campaign for justice and vindication for her son. "An ambitious suspense thriller which current events in Venezuela make particularly relevant" (*Variety*). Spanish with English subtitles.
VHS: S20381. $59.95.
Carlos Azpurua, Venezuela, 1990, 90 mins.

Summer of Miss Forbes

Written by Nobel prize-winning author Gabriel Garcia Marquez, *The Summer of Miss Forbes* is a wickedly funny black comedy about two children plotting to kill their authoritarian nanny. A biting comedy reminiscent of the work of legendary filmmaker Luis Bunuel, *The Summer of Miss Forbes* was directed by Jaime Humberto Hermosillo, one of Mexico's premier filmmakers. Spanish with English subtitles.
VHS: S13693. $19.98.
Jaime H. Hermosillo, Mex./Spain, 1988, 85 min.

Tango Bar (Carlos Gardel)

Carlos Gardel is teamed up with Rosita Moreno in this 1930's Argentinean musical drama. Spanish *without English subtitles.*
VHS: S06035. $54.95.
John Reinhardt, Argentina, 1935, 58 mins.

Tango: Our Dance

The sensuality and stylized rituals popular with the residents of Buenos Aires are part of the complex art form called the tango. Director Jorge Zanada examines the unique role of this dance within Argentina's social and personal landscape, exploring issues of machismo and passion contained within the dance. With a special appearance by Robert Duvall. Spanish with English subtitles.
VHS: S20380. $59.95.
Jorge Zanada, Argentina, 1988, 71 mins.

Time for Revenge

This political thriller captures a brilliant performance from Federico Luppi as a disenchanted demolition worker who rigs a fake industrial accident in order to get back at his corrupt employers. But the plan fails, and in order to protect himself and the scheme, he goes to extraordinary lengths to fulfill his original goal. Spanish with English subtitles.
VHS: S04872. $24.95.
Adolfo Aristarain, Argentina, 1983, 112 mins.

Times to Come

Reminiscent of *Clockwork Orange* and an Argentine *Blade Runner*, this tense thriller was awarded three prestigious ACE awards—Best Director, Best Actor (Hugo Soto) and Best Supporting Actor (Charly Garcia). Spanish with English subtitles.
VHS: S12361. $79.95.
Gustavo Mosquera, Argentina, 1981

The Track of the Ants

"Halfway between *Koyaanisqatsi* and *Brazil*... Dispensing with story and words, Venezuelan filmmaker Rafael Marziano-Tinoco looks at the life of Caracas much as a disenchanted god might survey an ant hill gone awry" (*Village Voice*). A city symphony with a Latin beat, *The Track of the Ants* focuses on the sprawling tropical metropolis of Caracas, Venezuela. Director Marziano-Tinoco captures both the fading splendor and the brilliant promise of a world continually caught in the crossroads of past and present, nature and civilization. Best Documentary, Philadelphia Film Festival. No dialog.
VHS: S27798. $29.95.
Rafael Marziano-Tinoco, Venezuela/Poland, 1993, 54 mins.

Two to Tango

Don Stroud is a professional assassin sent to Buenos Aires by a secret organization known as "The Company". Down Argentine way he falls for the girlfriend of his target. It takes two to tango when a cold-blooded killer meets a hot-blooded dancer. With Adrienne Sachs, Michael Cavanaugh and Duilio Marzio. Based on the novel *Last Days of the Victim*. In English. Produced by Roger Corman.
VHS: S08510. $79.95.
Hector Olivera, USA/Argentina, 1988, 87 mins.

Veronico Cruz

A fascinating film from Argentina, Miguel Pereira's *Veronico Cruz* shows how the Falklands (Malvinas) war affected the life of an Indian boy from one of Argentina's most remote regions. Awarded the Silver Bear at the Berlin Film Festival, *Veronico Cruz* also received four Condors—Best Picture, Best Director, Best Screenplay and Best Supporting Actor from the Argentine Society of Film Critics. Spanish with English subtitles.
VHS: S12362. $79.95.
Miguel Pereira, Argentina, 1989

A Very Old Man with Enormous Wings

Magical realism and comic confusion blend in a startling film about visions and expectations. Amid the debris of a Columbian cyclone lands an old man with enormous wings, whose seemingly miraculous anatomy attracts the curious and devout from around the world. Silent and disheveled, this fantastical "creature" is housed in a chicken coop as his hosts and the onlookers wait for his heavenly message—which turns out to be a very mixed blessing. Original story by Gabriel Garcia Marquez, who also co-wrote the screenplay. Spanish with English subtitles.
VHS: S13841. $19.98.
Fernando Birri, Cuba/Spain, 1988, 90 mins.

We're All Stars

This wacky comedy of errors takes off when the members of the Huambachano family get a chance to win fame and fortune and to appear as the "family of the week" on the popular TV game show, We're All Stars. The only catch: the television needs the "perfect" family, so the Huambachanos are forced to cover up the family divorce. Winner of Best Picture award at three international film festivals. Spanish with English subtitles.
VHS: S27738. $59.95.
Felipe Degregori, Peru, 1993, 80 mins.

Winter Barracks

Based on a novel by Osvaldo Soriano: a tango singer arrives in a village for a temporary engagement. Soon after, he notices the military repression and is subjected to suffer its brutal consequences. Spanish with English subtitles.
VHS: S07766. $39.95.
Lautaro Murua, Argentina, 1984, 116 mins.

Yanco

Stunningly photographed tale of fantasy and folklore. Yanco is a small Indian boy, considered bewitched because of his hypersensitivity to sound. He flees his village to live on an island and a musical environment. B&W, no dialog, but occasional Spanish with English subtitles.
VHS: S01485. $29.95.
Gonzalez, Mexico, 1960, 85 mins.

TOMAS GUTIERREZ ALEA

Death of a Bureaucrat
With *Death of a Bureaucrat*, Alea pays homage to the history of film comedy—from the anarchic tradition of Bunuel and Vigo, to the satire of Billy Wilder and the physical comedy of silent greats Harold Lloyd and Buster Keaton. The story of a young man's attempt to fight the system is an entertaining and hilarious account of galloping bureaucracy and the tyranny of red tape. An adventurous mix of slapstick farce and paranoid nightmare make this comedy a rich and enjoyable frenzy of laughter. Spanish with English subtitles.
VHS: S13916. $69.95.
Tomas Gutierrez Alea, Cuba, 1966, 87 mins.

Last Supper
A celebrated film from Cuba, photographed with a lush palette, this startlingly beautiful masterpiece is based on an incident from 18th century Cuban history. The film is also a dazzling moral tale of a pious slaveholder who decides to improve his soul and instruct his slaves in the glories of Christianity by inviting 12 of them to participate in a reenactment of the Last Supper. Spanish with English subtitles.
VHS: S12466. $69.95.
Tomas Gutierrez Alea, Cuba, 1976, 101 mins.

Letters from the Park
The enchanting story of two young people too shy to pursue the intimacy they both seek. They independently enlist the help of the local poet to write love letters to each other. The poet writes the letters to make some extra money but also to unburden himself of the unbounded love he feels but for which he has no outlet. When the young woman of the couple becomes the object of his affection, he is confused and faced with a moral and emotional dilemma in this surprising and sweet romance. Based on an original story by Gabriel Garcia Marquez, who also co-wrote the screenplay. Spanish with English subtitles.
VHS: S13510. $19.98.
Tomas Gutierrez Alea, Spain, 1988, 85 mins.

Memories of Underdevelopment
A breakthrough Cuban film, the first Cuban film to be released in the U.S. Set in the 1960's, the film centers on a Europeanized Cuban intellectual, too idealistic (or lazy) to leave for Miami, but too decadent to fit into the new Cuban society. The film is a remarkable demonstration that artistic subtlety, political commitment, and superior entertainment need not be incompatible. Spanish with English subtitles.
VHS: S11593. $69.95.
Tomas Gutierrez Alea, Cuba, 1968, 97 mins.

Strawberry & Chocolate
A sensation from Cuba in which a chance encounter over ice cream between a middle-aged gay man and a young, fervent believer in contemporary Cuban Marxism sets the stage for a funny but serious film about difference and acceptance. Their friendship develops despite official intolerance of homosexuality and it soon withstands that short-sighted policy. This film broke box office attendance records in Cuba and achieved world-wide acclaim. Spanish with English subtitles.
VHS: S26613. $99.99.
Laser: LD75320. $39.98.
Tomas Gutierrez Alea, Cuba, 1994, 104 mins.

Up to a Certain Point
This sly social comedy stars Oscar Alvarez, Mirta Ibarra and Omar Valdes. A married, middle-aged screenwriter is researching the problem of machismo in Cuban society and suddenly falls under the spell of Lina, a strong, self-supporting, young dockworker. Spanish with English subtitles.
VHS: S23285. $79.95.
Tomas Gutierrez Alea, Cuba, 1985, 72 mins.

BRAZILIAN CINEMA

Amor Bandido
A gritty murder mystery from the director of *Dona Flor*, set in the glamorous and seedy Copacabana district of Rio de Janeiro. Christina Ache and Paulo Guarnieri are street people, thrown together by tragedy and eventually torn apart. *Amor* mixes an eerie love triangle of two young lovers and the girl's detective father with the search for a mad killer.
VHS: S12945. $19.98.
Bruno Barreto, Brazil, 1987, 98 mins.

Black God, White Devil
A quintessential film from Brazil's Cinema Novo, this film of immense power from Glauber Rocha is set in the impoverished Northeastern Brazil, and focuses on a poor peasant as he changes from a fanatical preacher into an honorable bandit. A violent yet lyrical portrait of Brazilian society. Portuguese with English subtitles.
VHS: S07299. $79.95.
Glauce Rocha, Brazil, 1964, 102 mins.

Black Orpheus
Marcel Camus' quintessential love story based on the Greek myth of Orpheus and Eurydice is set against the vivid backdrop of carnival in Rio de Janeiro. Orpheus, the streetcar conductor, falls hopelessly in love with Eurydice; winner of the Grand Prize at Cannes as well as an Oscar for Best Foreign Film. Portuguese with English subtitles.
VHS: S00138. $69.95.
Laser: LD70346. $79.95.
Marcel Camus, Brazil, 1958, 103 mins.

Buccaneer Soul
One of Brazil's Cinema Novo's guiding spirits, Carlos Reichenbach, directs this fascinating look at Brazilian love through literature, cinema and music in the story of two friends living through the chaotic 1960's. "One of the most interesting and creative Brazilian filmmakers" (Jonathan Rosenbaum, *Chicago Reader*). Portuguese with English subtitles.
VHS: S27735. $59.95.
Carlos Reichenbach, Brazil, 1993, 116 mins.

Bye Bye Brazil
A small-time travelling sideshow plays over 9,000 miles of backwards Brazil, a mixture of primitivism and progress. One of the most original and entertaining films of recent years, *Bye Bye Brazil* is exotic and exuberant, and often very moving. Portuguese with English subtitles.
VHS: S00198. $19.98.
Carlos Diegues, Brazil, 1980, 110 mins.

The Dolphin
A sensual tale, set on the shores of Brazil, based on the legend of the dolphin-man. On nights with a full moon, a dolphin appears in the form of a handsome young man and seduces women. The local inhabitants are both at odds with and enchanted by the dolphin-man, whose presence scares away the fish, and incites the desires of the town's women and the anxieties of the men. With stunning photography by Pedro Farkas and a strong performance by Cassia Kiss. Portuguese with yellow English subtitles.
VHS: S15546. $19.98.
Walter Lima Jr., Brazil, 1987, 95 mins.

Dona Flor and Her Two Husbands
Funny, sexy and intoxicating! *Dona Flor* is a ribald folktale about a young widow, her respectable new husband, and her dynamic but dead first husband who refuses to stay buried, featuring the sensual Sonia Braga as Dona Flor. Portuguese with English subtitles.
VHS: S00359. $19.98.
Bruno Barreto, Brazil, 1977, 106 mins.

Happily Ever After
A sizzling sexy drama from Bruno Barreto, the director of *Dona Flor and Her Two Husbands*, *Happily Ever After* stars Regina Duarte as a seemingly happy mother who is an interior decorator. By chance, she meets the man of her dreams in a nightclub, who turns out to be a transvestite and a bi-sexual. But Fernanda and Miguel develop a steamy affair, and Miguel takes her on a trip into the criminal underworld, away from the safety of her upper-class existence. Portuguese with English subtitles.
VHS: S06014. $69.95.
Bruno Barreto, Brazil, 1986, 106 mins.

Hour of the Star
The brilliant, critically-acclaimed film by Suzana Amaral, winner at the Berlin Film Festival, based on a novel by Clarice Lispector. The neo-realistic story of a young girl who comes to Sao Paolo from the provinces to find work and love, *Hour of the Star* is an often funny, tragi-comic film, the breakthrough work for Suzana Amaral. Portuguese with English subtitles.
VHS: S04720. $79.95.
Suzana Amaral, Brazil, 1977, 85 mins.

How Tasty Was My Little Frenchman
One of the high points of Brazil's Cinema Novo, this wicked black comedy inspired a furor at Cannes. A French explorer is captured by an Amazon tribe and tries desperately to be accepted by his captors. The tribe feeds him well—only at the end does the Frenchman realize why. A brilliant satire on the Colonialist mentality. French and Tupi with English subtitles.
VHS: S25905. $79.95.
Nelson Pereira dos Santos, Brazil, 1971, 80 mins.

Luzia
Set on the vast and beautiful plains of central Brazil, *Luzia* stars the alluring Claudia Ohana (one of Brazil's biggest box-office stars: *Erendira, Fable of the Beautiful Pigeon Fancier*) as a cowgirl caught in a clash between squatters and the powerful ranch owners. Luzia's extraordinary rodeo skills and incredible beauty attract the attention of the landowners, whose history of marauding returns to gain revenge. Portuguese with yellow English subtitles.
VHS: S15004. $19.98.
Fabio Barreto, Brazil, 1988, 112 mins.

Quilombo
From Carlos Diegues, the director of *Bye Bye Brazil* and *Xica*, comes a handsome tale of revolution and conflict set in the mid-1600's. Disgruntled slaves in northeastern Brazil leave their plantations and form Quilombo de Palmares—their own democratic nation in the jungle. But this doesn't sit well with the Portuguese landowners, who send in their troops to restore control. A sequel of sorts to *Ganga Zumba*, this historical saga is a stirring fusion of folklore, political impact and dynamic storytelling, realized in vibrant tropical colors and set to the pulsing beat of Gilberto Gil's musical score. With Antonio Pompeu, Toni Tornado, and the dazzling Zeze Motta as Dandara the temptress. Portuguese with English subtitles.
VHS: S14573. $79.95.
Carlos Diegues, Brazil, 1984, 114 mins.

Savage Capitalism
Brazil's outrageously dramatic tele-novellas inspire this tale of marital infidelity, national betrayal, public scandal, long lost orphans and of course, forbidden love. When a reporter uncovers the truth behind a company's plans to mine in the interior of Brazil it sets in motion a complex tale. Ecological ruin could result if the primal forces of this passionate land are ignored. Portuguese with English subtitles.
VHS: S21133. $59.95.
Andre Klotzel, Brazil, 1993, 86 mins.

The Story of Fausta
Betty Fari—remembered for her miraculous performance in *Bye Bye Brazil*—is Fausta, a quirky cleaning lady whose voluptuous nature opens the door to a more comfortable life with an elderly widower. From the director of *Dona Flor and Her Two Husbands*. Portuguese with English subtitles.
VHS: S15666. $19.98.
Bruno Barreto, Brazil, 1988, 90 mins.

Terra em Transe
The brief story of this important film by Glauber Rocha is the story of a young poet and journalist who is persuaded by his lover to become involved in the politics of his country..."*Terra em Transe* is perhaps Rocha's most personal film and the most politically committed and polemical film of the Brazilian cinema novo. In Brazil it was attacked as fascist by the academic left and hailed by the extreme left as a revolutionary film ...full of extremely moving and provocative images—including footage from a Rocha documentary, *Maranhao*" (Georges Sadoul). "For me, my most important film...a more profound expression of my life" (Rocha). Portuguese with English subtitles.
VHS: S08783. $69.95.
Glauce Rocha, Brazil, 1966, 112 mins.

Xica
Carlos Diegues' comedy concerns Xica (Zeze Motta), a beautiful black slave who uses her sexual charm and savvy to benefit from Brazil's economic emergence. The film is set in the 18th century, when the fantastic wealth produced from the diamond trade transformed Brazil into a decadent hothouse. Xica ascends to the role of unofficial Empress, gleefully mocking her former masters while stockpiling newly found assets and power. "The film marks Diegues as one of Brazil's most innovative directors, who speaks his piece with exuberance, wit and style" (*San Francisco Chronicle*). With Walmor Chagas, Jose Wilker, Marcus Vinicius and Altair Lima. Portuguese with English subtitles.
VHS: S19417. $79.95.
Carlos Diegues, Brazil, 1976, 109 mins.

CARIBBEAN CINEMA

Belly Pain
This hot, sexy comedy from Kingston, Jamaica, is an authentic pleasure. When a child is bad, people say, "Mother band your belly." But in this case it's "Father band your belly." Mom's having an affair and the daughter is pregnant. Who's having sex with whom? Belly pain can drive you insane with desire or laughter.
VHS: S22213. $29.95.
Carl Ross/Keeling Beckford, Jamaica

Come to Saint Lucia
A look at the cultural and folk life of this attractive Caribbean island. Narrated in English by Von Martin. 25 mins.,
VHS: S06807. $70.00.

Divine Horsemen: The Living Gods of Haiti
Posthumously edited by Teiji and Cherel Ito, a remarkable document of the Rada, Petro and Congo cults of Haiti whose devotees commune with cosmic powers through invocations, voodoo dances and ritual ceremonies. The sound track conveys the power of ritual drumming and singing.
VHS: S00349. $29.95.
Maya Deren, USA, 1947, 50 mins.

Dominican Republic, Cradle of the Americas
A documentary view of the culture, people, and folk life of the Dominican Republic. Columbus loved this island, naming it "Little Spain" (Hispaniola), but before his arrival Indian cultures flourished which left their mark on the everyday lives of the people. From the Arawaks and Taino pre-hispanic Indians of the area to the coming of the Spanish and on up to today's modern life, the Dominican Republic remains a beautiful island with a rich tradition. Directed by Angel Hurtado. English and Spanish narrations by Herbert Morales. 25 mins.
English Narration.
VHS: S06794. $60.00.
Spanish Narration.
VHS: S06795. $60.00.

Haiti: Killing the Dream
The event-filled history of this Caribbean Island is thoroughly documented in this video, starting with the slave revolt that gave it independence from French colonial masters. The story continues into contemporary times, with footage and interviews that reveal such disparate phases as the 1915 occupation of this country by U.S. marines, the rule of Papa Doc Duvalier, and finally the current dispute over the rule of President Aristide. 58 mins.
VHS: S21191. $45.00.

Harder They Come
Jimmy Cliff is Ivan, a country boy who comes to the city to make a record and get his share of that pie up in the sky. But it isn't until he shoots a cop and becomes a fugitive from the law that he gets his sought-after notoriety, proving that you can get it if you really want. The pulsating reggae soundtrack features Cliff, Toots and the Maytels, Desmond Decker. The first genuine Jamaican film.
VHS: S00541. $19.95.
Laser: LD70753. $49.95.
Perry Henzell, Jamaica, 1973, 104 mins.

Islands of the Caribbean
A variety of travel adventures, from nightlife to water sports to shopping, in the Dominican Republic and Puerto Rico. 30 mins.
VHS: S14013. $24.95.

Jamaican Heritage
This film covers the people and cultural aspects of the island's heritage, while not missing any of Jamaica's natural beauty. The music and dance that play such a major role in the life of the people are featured, as well as works of local artists and craftsmen. Directed by Angel Hurtado. Narration in English by Megan Thomas. 25 mins.
VHS: S06783. $70.00.

Krik? Krak!
An innovative feature set in Haiti which blends documentary and fiction scenes to delve into the tormented history of the Black world: Haiti, the terrible experience under Papa Doc Duvalier, and the work of his infamous paramilitary force, the Tontons Macoutes. "Remarkably insightful, original, compassionate picture of the eternal Haiti" (Graham Greene). "Unflinching. Passionate. Creativity and daring in shooting, editing and music are matched by the depth of feeling for the Haitian people" (Jonathan Demme).
VHS: S27807. $29.95.
Vanyoska Gert/Jac Avila, USA/Canada, 78 mins.

Me Yu an' Mi Taxi
This acclaimed comic production includes a dazzling cast of Jamaica's finest comedians, including the master himself—Oliver Samuels. See the full genius of Jamaica's popular theatre in all its fabulous madness.
VHS: S15331. $29.95.

Obeah Wedding
This Jamaican drama tells the story of a middle-class woman who falls victim to a casanova whose only desire is to take advantage of women and then drop them flat. Starring Richard Mullings as Roy Sweetness and Leonie Samuels as Shirley.
VHS: S15333. $29.95.
Jamaica, 1989, 100 mins.

Portrait of the Caribbean
A combined production of the British Broadcasting Corp. and Turner Broadcasting System, this six-hour series looks at the political, cultural and social formation of the region. The program examines the legacy of the area's forefathers—Spain, France, England and parts of Africa. Narrated by Stuart Hall.
Portrait of the Caribbean, Complete Set. 370 mins.
VHS: S19391. $79.95.

Rhythms of Haiti
With a flood of melody and a rainbow of color that engulfs the traveler in a visit to this small but complex Caribbean country, the film captures the folk life as well as tourist aspects of the island. Many of Haiti's artists are shown at work in their natural environment, bringing their landscapes to life. Directed by Angel Hurtado. 25 mins.
English Narration. Roger Wilkison.
VHS: S06792. $70.00.
French Narration. Max Gautier.
VHS: S06793. $70.00.

Son Son
In *Son Son*, a feature from Jamaica, Keith Sheppard was raised by his mother, Karen Clarke, in the ghettoes of Kingston, Jamaica. This young man has an attitude when it comes to finding a job, as suggested by his mother. Ignoring her pleas, he ends up in the streets, where he learns the harsh reality that a life of crime is no easy way to riches.
VHS: S22203. $29.95.

Stepping Razor Red X: The Peter Tosh Story
Tosh was not just a reggae star, but a Rasta visionary, revolutionary, and Jamaican folk hero. Rare concert footage, interviews and narration from Tosh himself make this a special opportunity to understand this legendary musician. From the slums of Kingston, to stardom, to his brutal murder, it's all here.
VHS: S23329. $29.95.
Nicholas Campbell, USA, 1992, 73 mins.

Sugar Cane Alley
Euzhan Palcy's lyrical village drama set in French-occupied 1930s Martinique. The story examines the relationship of a determined, impoverished 11-year-old and his equally difficult and shrewd grandmother, who sacrifices everything for the boy's happiness. With Darling Legitimus, Garry Cadenat, Routa Seck and Joby Bernabe. French with English subtitles.
VHS: S01278. $29.95.
Euzhan Palcy, France, 1984, 107 mins.

THE HISPANIC WORLD

Abuela's Weave
Esperanza's *abuela*, her grandmother, is unmatched in her weaving skills. She shares the gift of traditional Mayan tapestry with her granddaughter. Together they decide to sell their wares in the market, but Abuela's birthmark may frighten away customers. Esperanza must sell their works alone.
VHS: S21884. $44.95.

Adelante Mujeres!
The National Women's History Project presents this unique view on the history of Mexican-American/Chicana women. Beginning with the Spanish Conquest, it documents a host of major events and personalities. This affirmative history employs hundreds of newly available photographs from archives across the continent. 30 mins.
English Version.
VHS: S26514. $125.00.
Spanish Version.
VHS: S26515. $125.00.

Amazonia: Voices from the Rainforest
For over 500 years the native inhabitants of the Amazon have fought against the invasion and destruction of their homeland. This historic devastation has already resulted in the mass extinction of over 700 tribes. In this stunningly filmed work, the people for whom the Amazon has always been home voice both their fears and their hopes. 70 mins.
VHS: S21571. $95.00.

Archeological Yucatan: Mexico
A fascinating travel-view of the legendary ruins of Chichen Itza, Tulum, Uxmal and many other ancient Mayan sites, including visits to Merida, a city of contrasting sights, cultural blends and people.
VHS: S03097. $39.95.

Argentina
Argentina is explored in this documentary, which moves from the Glacier National Park to the desert landscapes, rocky coastline and tropical rain forest. The program also examines the lives of the *gauchos*, Argentina's cowboys. 40 mins.
English Narration.
VHS: S19829. $39.95.
Spanish Narration.
VHS: S19828. $39.95.

Aymaras of Bolivia
With one foot in the world of ancient traditions and the other in contemporary society, the Aymara people of Bolivia straddle centuries. Taped entirely on location in Bolivia, the program looks at a traditional Aymara rite of passage ceremony and the struggle of Aymara women in the capital city of La Paz. Produced by Maryknoll Media. 28 mins.
VHS: S09070. $24.95.

The Aztecs
Established in 1325, Tenochtitlan grew out of religious guidance from the god Huitzilopochtil. Cimalpopoca suffered the burdens of slavery under the lords of Azcapotzalco up to the year 1428, when Itzcoatl gave freedom to his country. Montezuma, Ilhuicamina, Azayacatl, Tizoc and Ahuizotl increased the glory and power of the new Mexican Empire, providing a forum for pursuits in sculpture, architecture and music based around homage for their gods. This is a concise look at the historical and cultural aspects of Aztec society in their varied manifestations. In Spanish, no subtitles. 15 mins.
VHS: S16381. $69.95.

Ballad of Gregorio Cortez

Robert Young's powerful portrayal of the true story of Gregorio Cortez, a turn-of-the-century farmer who kills the sheriff because of a language misunderstanding. One of the most highly acclaimed independent American films of recent years. English and Spanish dialog with English subtitles.
VHS: Out of print. For rental only.
Laser: LD72322. $29.99.
Robert M. Young, USA, 1982, 105 mins.

Barry Lopez

In his books *Arctic Dreams, Of Wolves and Men* and *Crossing Open Ground*, Barry Lopez explores man's role in the natural world. On October 5, 1992, he read his essay "Rediscovery of North America" and spoke to Michael Silverblatt. From the *Lannan Literary Videos* series. 60 mins.
VHS: S27137. $19.95.

Battle for the Falklands

As head of the Argentine military junta, Lieutenant General Leopoldo Galtiere stormed the peaceful Falkland Islands after 150 years of British rule. This program shows how Thatcher struck back, the events, the battles and world reaction. 110 mins.
VHS: S13126. $39.98.

Before the Incas

Machu Picchu represents the pinnacle of Inca civilization. Northern Bolivia belies traces of even earlier cultures that predate the Incas. This program explores the lives of a series of peoples that conquered, occupied, absorbed and replaced their predecessors. Sites like Lake Titicaca, Mochica and Chimu yield their secrets to the modern era in this documentary. 43 mins.
VHS: S22927. $29.95.

Belize

The general patterns of the culture of Belize are shown in this account by the Museum of Modern Art of Latin America. English narration. 20 mins.
VHS: S06769. $60.00.

Bento

A young African-Brazilian leaves his country home to start over in a poor neighborhood in the big city of Sao Paolo. Disadvantages outweigh the opportunities for a young, poor, black Brazilian to be successful. Bento is determined to make life better for himself and his neighbors in an environment where life is a daily struggle to survive. Produced by Maryknoll Media. 14 mins.
VHS: S10838. $24.95.

Bilingual Americans

Explores the "melting pot that never happened" in America, and the bilingual-bicultural nature of American society. Bilingual English-Spanish narration.
VHS: S07431. $59.95.

Brazil: Heart of South America

A video tour of Brazil including Bahia, Rio de Janeiro, the Amazon, the Iguazu Falls, and the beat of Sao Paolo. 55 mins.
VHS: S09878. $24.95.

Building Peace in the Midst of War

An inspiring documentary showing how individuals and communities can make a difference in Central America. This tape includes the moving testimonies of both North Americans and Salvadorans as they talk about humanitarian aid to El Salvador organized by ordinary people who care enough to help. 1988, 30 mins.
VHS: S13967. $75.00.

The Buried Mirror

World-renowned author and diplomat Carlos Fuentes explores the diversity that comprises the Hispanic world. From Spain and Portugal to South and Central America, the Caribbean and the U.S., a whole range of peoples, with specific traditions and histories, make up the entity of Hispanidad.
Program I: The Virgin and the Bull. Fuentes examines the mix of people found in contemporary Latin America. Spanish, Arab, Jewish, Indian and African forebears make for a rich, illustrious and vibrant culture. From the shores of Vera Cruz to Spain, with its flamenco and bull-fighting traditions, this author traces that which defines Latin America. 59 mins.
VHS: S21370. $29.95.
Program II: Conflict of the Gods. Modern Mexico City has revealed the Aztec temples and ruins once thought lost. Carlos Fuentes leads the viewer through an exploration of the Indian world that believed the blond exiled god would return. The meeting of Europe and America was bloody, but there is hope in the union of these traditions. 59 mins.
VHS: S21371. $29.95.
Program III: The Age of Gold. Shortly after the conquest Spain and all of Europe felt the rush of enormous treasures from the New World, including not just gold and silver but chocolate, the tomato and the potato. These gifts transformed a world ambivalent about earthly things. Phillip II lived in a monastic-like cell while Cervantes questioned all values in his work. And yet Native Americans transformed the richness of the Baroque into an American idiom. 59 mins.
VHS: S21372. $29.95.
Program IV: The Price of Freedom. One million Mexicans gather in the Zocalo, the central square of Mexico City, to celebrate El Grito, the cry for independence. Beginning here, Fuentes travels south into the rest of Latin America, sifting through the difficulties and failed promises left in the wake of revolutionary independence. 59 mins.
VHS: S21373. $29.95.

Program V: Unfinished Business. This century has brought enormous changes to the Hispanic communities of the world. Today half a million Mexicans brave border patrols to enter the US in search of Gringo gold. In return they bring Latino gold, the riches of centuries of tradition and change. 59 mins.
VHS: S21374. $29.95.
Complete Set. Five tapes.
VHS: S21375. $99.95.

Burning Rivers

Rich rain forests are chopped down, badly polluted rivers burn and pesticides poison farm workers. All this happens in Guatemala. The social and economic conditions that spawn this nightmare scenario impact the environment. Only when these issues are considered together can a solution be found, one which addresses the unequal distribution of wealth that characterizes this country. 28 mins.
VHS: S21578. $85.00.

Call and Response

Volunteers from the U.S. live in Mexico and Guatemala for a few weeks in Maryknoll's Call and Response Program. This video joins a group of Michigan college students in Oaxaca, Mexico, where they meet and serve a variety of people. 29 mins.
VHS: S15863. $19.95.

Campamento

This documentary was made in a unique place and time. Salvador Allende was the head of a freely elected socialist government in Chile in the 1970's. All that came to an end in a bloody military coup in 1973. In this re-released, award-winning work the efforts of self-determination among slum dwellers are revealed as a unique opportunity cut tragically short by violence. 29 mins.
VHS: S23131. $19.95.

Carlos Fuentes

In this revealing interview with his wife, the Televisa reporter Sylvia Fuentes, Carlos Fuentes speaks of the Hispanic notion of originality and of the function of time in literature. He recalls his youth in the U.S, the affirmation of his identity in that difficult context and his political formation; discusses his major works and reads from *La Region mas Transparente*. Spanish *without* English subtitles.
Home Video.
VHS: S06966. $59.95.
Public Performance.
VHS: S08829. $100.00.

Carlos Fuentes (Lannan Literary Videos)

Mexico's most celebrated novelist reads from *The Death of Artemio Cruz* and *Christopher Unborn*, as well as unpublished manuscripts, in California. It was recorded on October 2, 1989. Lewis MacAdams then interviews this world famous author. From the *Lannan Literary Videos* series. 60 mins.
VHS: S27124. $19.95.

The Colombian Way of Life

Bogota is the focus of this video. Its history, climate, government, geography and rapidly growing population are all examined. The resulting images counteract stereotypes associated with cocaine, coffee and guerilla violence. 24 mins.
VHS: S23709. $129.95.
Laser: LD74790. $149.95.

Colors of Hope

Narrated by Meryl Streep, *Colors of Hope* tells the story of an Argentine family's incredible ability to maintain hope and closeness in spite of the torture and torment which accompanied their years as political prisoners; the moving, true account of hope and perseverance behind such fictionalized accounts as *The Official Story*. Produced by Amnesty International. 1985, 20 mins.
VHS: S06886. $20.00.

Contra Aid—It's Illegal: Karen Parker

A compelling videotaped presentation by attorney Karen Parker, specialist in international law, who charges that U.S. aid to the "contra" forces in Nicaragua violated international and domestic laws.
VHS: S06604. $45.00.
Peggy Pado, USA, 1987, 75 mins.

Cosquin, City of Folklore

A visit to the folklore festival which is celebrated annually in Cosquin, Argentina. Narrated in Spanish by Amelia Bence. 14 mins.
VHS: S06764. $40.00.

Dance of Hope

By Oscar-winning director Deborah Shaffer, *Dance of Hope* features Sting performing his hit song "They Dance Alone" with Peter Gabriel in an Amnesty International concert. This film documents the efforts of relatives of the "disappeared" in Chile to get information on their loved ones from Pinochet's regime. The women involved in the Association for the Relatives of the Detained and Disappeared dance the cueca, Chile's national dance of passion and courtship, alone, to emphasize the loss of their partners. "Haunting in the images of despair, and poignant in a spirit of optimism" (*San Francisco Chronicle*).
VHS: S14147. $19.95.
Deborah Shaffer, USA, 1989, 75 mins.

The Dark Light of Dawn

Commissioned by the Guatemala Human Rights Commission/ U.S.A., this documentary presents a factual overview and moving visual portrait of the recent years of conflict in Guatemala. It traces the manipulation of political power in the country and shows that after the return of civilian rule, military repression has not abated. Human rights violations, especially against the Indian population, are poignantly depicted—and efforts of families to find their "disappeared" relatives are documented.
VHS: S06601. $55.00.
E. Reyes/G. Brown, USA, 1987, 28 mins.

Dateline: San Salvador

For seven years, civil war raged in El Salvador, ravaging the countryside, destroying an already under-developed economy, and placing the country high on the international list of human rights violations. On May 1, 1986, 80,000 Salvadorans, in protest of these conditions, defied the guns of government forces and marched through the streets of their capital, demanding an end to the war. *Dateline: San Salvador* documents this historic march and explores the concerns of the people behind the banners. Spanish with English voice-over.
VHS: S05628. $55.00.
Pamela Cohen, USA, 1987, 28 mins.

David Vinas y Mempo Giardinelli

Subtitled *Senas de exilio*, a liberating discussion about the particular problems of working in exile in this revealing portrait of the writer. Spanish *without* English subtitles. 53 mins.
Home Video.
VHS: S06948. $59.95.
Public Performance.
VHS: S09504. $100.00.

Day of the Dead

The color and spectacle of "The Day of the Dead" rituals and customs are explained by fusing Aztec and European traditions. The celebration is presented in village dances, homes, market places and cemeteries. "A program both entertaining and education and well executed" (*Northeast Newsletter*). 28 mins.
English Narration.
VHS: S19827. $45.00.
Spanish Narration.
VHS: S19826. $45.00.

Death of Che Guevara

In November, 1968, Che Guevara went from Cuba to Bolivia in order to start a new revolutionary movement. But he failed in a dramatic way. This film is an investigation of the capture, and death, of Che Guevara. In Spanish language *without* English subtitles. 92 mins.
VHS: S07906. $59.95.

Destination Nicaragua

A look at Nicaraguan life and the U.S. anti-intervention movement as seen by the citizens who travel to Nicaragua to discover for themselves the people. Narrated by Tyne Daly. "Sobering, encouraging, persuasive" (*L.A. Times*). (For 16mm rentals, call 206-575-1575.)
VHS: S03729. $55.00.
B. Trent/D. Kasper, USA, 1986, 58 mins.

Did They Buy It?: Nicaragua's 1990 Elections

"A fascinating 45-minute video documentary by Chicagoan Bob Hercules, filmed on location with a crew of four, that concentrates largely on the U.S. media coverage of the Nicaraguan elections. What emerges is not only a sharp piece of alternative news coverage that helps to explain the outcome, but also a revealing and multifaceted (and alternately funny and chilling) look at how the U.S. news about Nicaragua actually gets 'created'" (Jonathan Rosenbaum).
VHS: S15192. $29.95.
Bob Hercules, USA, 1991, 45 mins.

Discovering the Music of Latin America

Classical, folk and pre-Columbian all play a large role in the music of Latin America. The many traditions of this diverse region have spawned a rich array of song and dance. 20 mins.
VHS: S23515. $49.95.

The Edge of Hope

A lucid examination of oppression in Mexico, Bolivia, Colombia, and Paraguay. This film documents inequalities between those who work and those who reap the profits in Third World countries. Produced by Maryknoll Media. 24 mins.
VHS: S04924. $24.95.

Egberto Gismonti

Charlie Byrd and Stan Getz pioneered the use of Brazilian rhythms and the bossa nova in American jazz. Brazilian musician Egberto Gismonti lifts the use of these elements to a new plateau, as in this live concert recorded at the 1987 Freiburg Arts Festival. 55 mins.
VHS: S09826. $24.95.

El Crucero

An in-depth picture of a Nicaraguan coffee plantation shot in September 1984 in four different documentary styles. The first section takes a feminist biographical approach, the second a cinema-verite approach, the third uses Brechtian intertitles while a union organizer speaks on the audio track, and the final segment features two women talking while the image depicts a girl carrying a bucket in slow motion.
VHS: S06310. $69.95.
Julia Lesage, USA, 1987, 59 mins.

El Matador

Narrated by Ricardo Montalban, the life of a young bullfighter, Miguel Espinosa Armillita, as he begins his long years of training to become a premier matador. Insights into the traditions, history and culture of Mexico. 59 mins.
English Narration.
VHS: S06835. $49.95.
Spanish Narration.
VHS: S06834. $49.95.

El Salvador: The Seeds of Liberty

The conflict in this embattled land is explored through interviews with military, government and church leaders in El Salvador and the U.S. The film examines the martyrdom of four North American missionaries and the significance of this pivotal event. It contains scenes of the funeral of assassinated Archbishop Romero and interviews with the poor, who relate their tragedies and hopes for a dignified life and a free society. Produced by Maryknoll Media. 28 mins.
VHS: S04925. $24.95.

Empire in the Sun

This colorful documentary explores some of the strange customs, lifestyles, and oddities of the people of Peru. Italian production with English narration. Italy, 1956, 86 mins.
VHS: S10556. $24.95.
Laser: CAV, widescreen. LD70565. $69.98.
Laser: CLV, widescreen. LD70566. $39.98.

Environment Under Fire: Ecology and Politics in Central America

Celebrated for its lush tropical forests, today Central America's natural environment is seriously endangered. More than two-thirds of rain forests have been destroyed and deadly pesticides are being exported from U.S. to Central America. This film explores the issues behind the crisis along with potential solutions. Winner of two major festival awards; produced by the Environmental Project on Central America and the Moving Images Video Project. 28 mins.
VHS: S10888. $75.00.

Epic History of the Mexican Revolution

This is the only documentary of the heroic revolution authorized by the Mexican National Defense Department. Newsreel footage helps create an authentic portrait of the battlefield. In Spanish, no subtitles. 80 mins.
VHS: S16379. $39.95.

Ernesto Cardenal

Ernesto Cardenal is an ordained Catholic priest and revolutionary poet who champions the rights of ordinary Nicaraguans. On January 28, 1991, he read from *Cantico Cosmico* in Los Angeles. The English translations were delivered by Edward Asner and Ruben Martinez (who also interviewed the author). From the *Lannan Literary Videos* series. 60 mins.
VHS: S27130. $19.95.

Festivals and Holidays in Latin America

Celebrations, both religious and secular, reflect the different cultures of the many groups inhabiting Latin America. Bilingual English-Spanish narration.
VHS: S07428. $59.95.

Fiesta

Fiestas are the central expression of honor and tradition in most Mexican small towns. They're designed to celebrate the patron saints through an ethnographic tradition of dance, markets, music and the *charredas* (like rodeos). This film shares how people behave in their time of joy and spontaneity. 22 mins.
VHS: S20238. $29.95.

Flavors of South America

This video takes you to an authentic Peruvian restaurant to observe the customs and practices of local chefs. The program takes a journey into the village markets and countryside to learn about the culture and people of this beautiful country. In Spanish. 56 mins.
VHS: S19823. $29.95.

The Forgotten Village

John Steinbeck wrote the story and script for this moving film about the ancient life of Mexico, the story of the little pueblo of Santiago on the skirts of a hill in the mountains. An extremely moving portrait of life in a Mexican village. Narrated by Burgess Meredith.
VHS: S08785. $39.95.
Herbert Kline, USA, 1941

Gabriel Garcia Marquez

Gabriel Garcia Marquez rarely gives interviews and has never before spoken publicly about his involvement in Latin American cinema, so this exclusive and fascinating interview with him is a considerable coup. This program uses material shot in Colombia and Cuba, archive footage of events in the author's life and clips from films he has worked on. Other interviewees in this program include film directors Ruy Guerra and Fernando Birri, who have both directed films based on Marquez's stories. 59 mins.
VHS: S18388. $19.95.

Grenada Revisited

This video looks back at what precipitated the deployment of over 5,000 U.S. troops to the small Caribbean island and examines the consequences today. Was the 1983 U.S. invasion of Grenada necessary? USA, 1991, 28 mins.
VHS: S15215. $25.00.

Guatemala, Land of Color

A look at the cultural and folk life aspects of one of the most colorful countries in Central America. We begin our tour in the capital of Guatemala City and from there fly inland to the city of Flores, which lies in the jungle and is our entrance to the ancient Mayan city of Tikal. Traversing the labyrinth of paths, the film explores the temples of this highly developed civilization and travels on to the colonial capital of Antigua, changed little since the time of the Spaniards. The film captures the people as they live, work and celebrate their religious holidays. Directed by Angel Hurtado. 25 mins.
English Narration. Renee Channey.
VHS: S06790. $60.00.
Spanish Narration. Ivan Silva.
VHS: S06791. $60.00.

Guatemala: Jeramias and El Salvador: Flor

Two portraits of contemporary youth in two nations in conflict: In *Guatemala*, an Indian teenager is forced to flee from violence in his village. Now in the city, he is torn by bitter memories and adapting to new values. In *El Salvador*, soldiers obliterate Flor's village and kill her uncle and brother. Flor and the rest of her family are re-located to a temporary shelter in the city. As part of a youth group, she now works for a more peaceful society. Produced by Maryknoll Media.
VHS: S06272. $24.95.

Guatemala: When the People Lead

Follows the long and arduous journey home for tens of thousands of Guatemalans who had been living in Mexican refugee camps. Upon their return home, military action threatens their region. 29 mins.
VHS: S23401. $85.00.

The Havana: Cigar of Connoisseurs

The obsession that linked Winston Churchill, John F. Kennedy, Fidel Castro and Groucho Marx begins with Cuban-grown tobacco. These expensive cigars require three to four years of production, all of which goes up in smoke in 45 minutes or less. Shot on location in Cuba, this documentary details the history and tradition of the world's finest cigar. 59 mins.
VHS: S26810. $24.95.

The Healer

An American missionary who works among the Aymara Indians of Peru finds God in an unexpected way. A film of the relationship between the priest and an Indian holy man. Ancient rites and customs of the Aymara are contrasted with traditional rites of Latin American Catholics. Produced by Maryknoll Media. 24 mins.
VHS: S04928. $24.95.

Hispanic Magazine's Guide to Hispanic Excellence

This three-part series offers role models for Latino students. Each 35-minute tape focuses on a specific area of achievement, including *The Leaders, Sports* and *Arts and Entertainment*. This mosaic of excellence comprises Latinos from diverse backgrounds representing different areas of the U.S.
VHS: S21725. $74.85.

Hispanics of Achievement Video Collection

This set compiles compelling biographies of men and women who have contributed to their countries and culture. Figures from South and Central America, Mexico and Spain are included. Period music, historic materials and authoritative opinion make this series an invaluable resource. Each volume is 30 mins.
César Chavez. (1927-1993) Mexican-American labor leader.
VHS: S24449. $39.95.
Ferdinand and Isabella. (1485-1516)/(1451-1504) Spanish monarchs.
VHS: S24452. $39.95.
George Santayana. (1863-1952) Spanish philosopher and poet.
VHS: S24455. $39.95.
Hernan Cortes. (1485-1547) Spanish explorer.
VHS: S24451. $39.95.
Joan Baez. (1941 - Present) Mexican-American folksinger.
VHS: S24447. $39.95.
Juan and Evita Peron. (1895-1974)/(1919-1952) President and First Lady of Argentina.
VHS: S24454. $39.95.
Pablo Neruda. (1904-1973) Chilean poet and diplomat.
VHS: S24453. $39.95.
Pancho Villa. (1878-1923) Mexican revolutionary.
VHS: S24456. $39.95.
Roberto Clemente. (1934-1972) Puerto Rican baseball great.
VHS: S24450. $39.95.
Simon Bolivar. (1783-1830) Latin-American revolutionary.
VHS: S24448. $39.95.
Hispanics of Achievement Video Collection. 10-volume set.
VHS: S24457. $399.50.

Hola Venezuela

Nine short documentaries provide unrehearsed situations of young adults who discuss their lifestyles, values and customs. In Spanish. 60 mins.
VHS: S19822. $39.95.

Honduras, A World into Itself

A look at the folk life and culture of Honduras, the cradle of the ancient Mayan Empire. A panorama of this lovely Central American country, from the ancient ruins of Copan to the bustling cities of today. The film captures the Honduran people in their daily lives, working, playing and surrounded by the natural beauty of their country. The music of the Caramba, the most ancient of American Indian instruments, is heard in the background. Directed by Angel Hurtado, 20 mins.
English Narration. Herbert Morales.
VHS: S06784. $60.00.
Spanish Narration. Marioano Sanchez.
VHS: S06785. $60.00.

Honduras: Carlos and Nicaragua: Balty

Two portraits of contemporary youth coping in nations in conflict. Poverty has not kept Carlos from studying to be a teacher. Through a theatre group, he reaches out to neighbors displaced by war and economic development. Balty is a young medical student who works in a war zone near the Honduran border in Nicaragua. She finds excitement relating her faith to political commitment in a revolutionary society. Produced by Maryknoll Media.
VHS: S06273. $24.95.

I Like It Like That

A remarkable feature set in the Puerto Rican milieu of the Bronx. Rita Moreno, Lauren Velez and Jon Seda star in a hard-edged comedy about a family struggling to keep it all together. The film is a deft mixture of simple drama with humor, in a kind of slum-glamor romanticism that gives humanity to its realistically-drawn characters. Music from the Bario Boyz.
VHS: S24262. $19.95.
Laser: LD74844. $34.95.
Darnell Martin, USA, 1994, 106 mins.

Imagenes Latino Americanas

This video provides intermediate and advanced instruction on comprehension and practical insights into varied lifestyles of modern Latin American societies. Shot on location, the documentary is a starting point for discussions on Latin America. 25 mins.
VHS: S19842. $39.95.

Improper Conduct

Controversial, powerful documentary, a series of interviews with fascinating Cuban intellectuals and homosexuals who have been persecuted under the Castro regime. An indictment of Castro, implicating also those who would turn a blind eye toward repression from the left. Spanish with English subtitles.
VHS: S00614. $79.95.
Nestor Almendros, USA, 1984, 112 mins.

In the Shadow of War/O My People!

In the Shadow of War shows how projects supported by Protestant churches are transforming the life of a community in Nicaragua. Narrated by Glenda Jackson. Directed by J. Reiter and W. Tirando. *O My People!* is a slide show on video telling the story of the suffering in El Salvador using voices of witnesses as well as drawings by children. Directed by J. Friedrich.
VHS: S03953. $95.00.
Reiter/Tirando/Friedrich, USA, 1986, 47 mins.

Incas Remembered

An hour long exploration of the Inca civilization. During their pre-Columbian reign, the Incas developed modern irrigation canals, performed brain surgery and were master builders. Edwin Newman provides the introduction.
VHS: S02155. $24.95.
Peter Jarvis, USA, 1986, 60 mins.

Isabel Allende

The best-selling Chilean author (*La Casa de los Espiritus/ House of the Spirits*) speaks with the Colombian critic Magdalena Garcia Pinto about the extravagant environment that surrounded her youth, and how she created the great novel, "like a tapestry." She speaks of the relationship of Latin American women to feminism, disputing many facile notions on the subject, and affirms the role of a writer as one capable of understanding both sexes. Spanish *without* English subtitles.
Home Video.
VHS: S06963. $59.95.
Public Performance.
VHS: S08840. $100.00.

The Island of Puerto Rico

The diverse regions and peoples of Puerto Rico are profiled in this geographic look at the island. 28 mins.
VHS: S20239. $29.95.

Joan Baez (1941-Present)— Mexican-American Folksinger

From *The Hispanics of Achievement Video Collection*. Includes music, photographs and commentary on the life of the pioneering folk singer and activist. This biography was designed for classroom use. Ages 10+. 30 minutes. Spanish with NO subtitles.
VHS: S24943. $39.95.

Jorge Luis Borges

The great Argentinian writer has an animated dialogue with his young compatriot, the novelist Reina Roffe. With great lucidity, Borges speaks of his work and the aesthetic and philosophical foundations that support it. We see Borges in the cafes and streets of his Buenos Aires and hear him tell unpublished stories of gaucho exploits in the pampa, evoke the avant-garde movements of the first part of the century, and read five of his poems. Spanish *without* English subtitles.
Home Video.
VHS: S06947. $59.95.
Public Performance.
VHS: S08830. $100.00.

Jorge Luis Borges: Borges and I

Weaves together dramatized sequences from Borges' work with a rare interview with Borges at home, an unpretentious apartment overlooking noisy Buenos Aires. The program relates Borges' profoundly original stories to his personal experience and attempts to reconcile the public and private images of this major 20th century writer. 76 mins.
VHS: S04153. $19.95.

Journey of Carlos Fuentes: Crossing Borders

A biography of Carlos Fuentes, filmed in Mexico, Nicaragua and the United States, the camera follows Fuentes on his travels to Aztec ruins, movie sets and war zones. Along the way this writer/diplomat holds forth on art, sex and politics. The film also features readings by Fuentes. 60 min.
VHS: S18387. $19.95.
Joan Saffa, USA, 60 mins.

Juan Carlos Onetti

The Uruguayan writer, creator of *El Astillero* (The Shipyard), speaks with Jorge Ruffinelli about the influence of Faulkner on Latin American letters and about his own obsessive atmospheric writing, and tells several poignant anecdotes about himself in difficult situations. Spanish *without* English subtitles.
Home Video.
VHS: S06952. $59.95.
Public Performance.
VHS: S08836. $100.00.

Juan Goytisolo

The well-known Spanish author has an open dialogue with the Chilean critic and editor Randolph Pope, in which he recalls a childhood dynamited by the Civil War and a youth in open rebellion against the official mythology of Franco's Spain. He discusses the exacerbated state of exile which led him to create the ultimate hyperbole of the traitor "en grande" as paradoxical redeemer of the sclerotic state of the nation. He reads from *Juan Sin Tierra*, *Makbara*, *Senas de Intentidad* and *Paisajes Despues de La Batalla*. Spanish *without* English subtitles.
Home Video.
VHS: S06949. $59.95.
Public Performance.
VHS: S08833. $100.00.

Juan Rulfo

The author of the most important Mexican novel written— *Pedro Parama*—evokes his childhood, with the help of Sylvia Fuentes, in the context of revolutionary Mexico. He describes how a priest's collection of black-listed books introduced him to the world's best writers, as bullets ricocheted through his little town. The presence of death and violence in his fiction is directly related to those difficult years as an orphan. Spanish *without* English subtitles.
Home Video.
VHS: S06965. $59.95.
Public Performance.
VHS: S08835. $100.00.

Julio Cortazar

The author of *Rayuela* (Hopscotch) speaks openly and eloquently with his most rigorous critic, Saul Sosnowski, about the presence of the reader in his fiction and his own trajectory from a kind of literary individualism to a more collective style. He discusses the importance of the Cuban revolution and the tasks he has set for himself as an intellectual in the context of Latin America. He confesses in this last interview before his untimely death in 1986 that he still searches for the "kibbutz of desire, or the center, from which one can imagine, feel and actually live reality in a harmonious manner." Spanish *without* English subtitles.
Home Video.
VHS: S06946. $59.95.
Public Performance.
VHS: S08832. $100.00.

Kids Explore Mexico

The culture, customs and history of Mexico are illustrated in this video aimed at high school students. It makes culture and geography a fun and exciting experience. Lyrics, thought-provoking questions and maps ease class preparation and stimulate class discussion. In English, 34 mins.
VHS: S24790. $49.95.

La Antigua-Guatemala: An American Monument

A documentary on Antigua, the colonial capital of Guatemala. One of the oldest cities in the Americas, it lies in a valley surrounded by volcanoes. Despite volcanic eruptions and earthquakes, it is still much like it would have been found in the days of the early Spaniards. Many of the lovely colonial buildings are preserved, allowing the viewer to go back in history and appreciate the Roman-Arabic architecture that the Spanish have left in Central America. Directed by Angel Hurtado, 25 mins.
English Narration. Renee Channey.
VHS: S06788. $60.00.
Spanish Narration. Andres Morales.
VHS: S06789. $60.00.

La Bamba

The boxoffice success story of Richie Valens (Lou Diamond Phillips), the Mexican-American farm laborer with a string of chart-busting singles who begins his climb to stardom clinging to the love of his girlfriend Donna, strengthened by the perseverance of his mother, and haunted by a growing conflict with his half-brother Bob.
VHS: S07515. $19.95.
Luis Valdez, USA, 1987, 103 mins.

La Conquista

The events leading to Spain's emergence as a superpower in the late 15th century—the expulsion of the Moors, the invention of the printing press, and the discovery of the New World. In English and then Spanish. 25 mins. each.
VHS: S05269. $59.95.

Land of the Conquistadors

Extremadura was a province of Western Spain that was home to such Conquistadores as Cortez, Pizarro, Balboa and Hernando de Soto. This program looks at the historical and social importance of Extremadura to the development of modern Spain. 28 mins.
VHS: S20274. $29.95.

Las Locuras de Porcel y Olmedo Vol. 2

More funny stuff from the genius of Argentine comedy. 76 mins. Spanish *without* English subtitles.
VHS: S08023. $39.95.

Las Nicas and Home Life

Las Nicas is a 45-minute document of interviews with Nicaraguan women, done in 1981 and 1982, in which the women speak about topics of work, sexual politics, religion, family life and social participation. *Home Life* documents a Nicaraguan family in Esteli. Filmmaker is editor of *Jump Cut*. English and Spanish with English subtitles.
VHS: S00722. $69.95.
Julia Lesage, USA, 1985, 72 mins.

The Legend of El Dorado

The myth and reality of gold in the new world as viewed through the pre-Columbian treasures of Bogota's Gold Museum. Pieces from tribes of the Sunu archaeological zone, the Quimbays and the Musicas are featured. Directed by Angel Hurtado, 25 mins.
English Narration.
VHS: S06805. $70.00.
Spanish Narration.
VHS: S06806. $70.00.

Life in Small Hispanic Towns

Between the large metropolitan cities and the rural regions are countless small towns that reflect the history and culture of Latin America. Bilingual English-Spanish narration.
VHS: S07429. $59.95.

Luis J. Rodriguez

Originally from Watts in Los Angeles, Luis J. Rodriguez speaks from a place which is too often ignored. In this video he reads from *The Concrete River*, *Poems Across the Pavement* and *Always Running, La Vida Loca: Gang Days in L.A.* It originally took place on December 8, 1992, in Los Angeles. Michael Silverblatt spoke with this innovative author. From the *Lannan Literary Videos* series. 60 mins.
VHS: S27138. $19.95.

Luis Rafael Sanchez

The author of *La Guaracha del Macho Camacho* and, most recently, *La Importancia de Llamarse Daniel Santos* responds to questions by the great translator Gregory Rabassa. He analyzes the essence of his own novels and speaks of the problems of Caribbean identity in the proximity of the United States. He recites popular poetry and reads from *La Guaracha*. Spanish *without* English subtitles.
Home Video.
VHS: S06964. $59.95.
Public Performance.
VHS: S08843. $100.00.

Luisa Valenzuela

Valenzuela is considered by Carlos Fuentes to be the "crown princess" of Latin American letters. She is a "writer's writer," yet her tales of love in repressive societies—especially her native Argentina—touch upon the basic chords of human emotion. She responds to questions by Magdalena Garcia Pinto and describes the need to "name fears" in order to control and exorcise them. Spanish *without* English subtitles.
Home Video.
VHS: S06871. $59.95.
Public Performance.
VHS: S08842. $100.00.

MacMichael on Nicaragua

Dr. David MacMichael has worked for U.S. government agencies as a specialist in counterintelligence in both Vietnam and El Salvador. This is a dramatic and detailed account of MacMichael's report on Nicaragua, where he travelled extensively and studied the election process for three months.
VHS: S03809. $45.00.
Ian Thiermann, USA, 1984, 30 mins.

The Mambo Kings

Arne Glimcher's adaptation of Oscar Hijueles's Pulitzer prize winning-novel *The Mambo Kings Play Songs of Love* about dreamy innocence and protection of the American Dream in post-war America. The film centers on two young immigrant brothers (Armand Assante and Almodovar regular Antonio Banderas) impassioned reach for fame and recognition as pioneers of the sweet, daring, sexy Mambo music. The film also details various sexual and romantic entanglements. With Cathy Moriarty and Maruschka Detmers.
VHS: S17028. $19.98.
Laser: Widescreen. LD71553. $29.98.
Arne Glimcher, USA, 1992, 104 mins.

Manuel Puig

In this delightful conversation with Reina Roffe, Puig describes his early need to escape the provincial world of his upbringing in the hinterlands of Argentina, and his entire trajectory as a novelist. He discusses and reads from *La Traicion de Rita Hayworth*, *The Buenos Aires Affair*, *Pubis Angelical* and *Sangre de Amor Correspondido*. Spanish *without* English subtitles.
Home Video.
VHS: S06950. $59.95.
Public Performance.
VHS: S08837. $100.00.

Mario Vargas Llosa

Subtitled *Maestro de las voces*, a conversation with the great novelist, author of *City of the Dogs*. Spanish *without* English subtitles. 53 mins.
Home Video.
VHS: S06951. $59.95.
Public Performance.
VHS: S09505. $100.00.

Market Day in a Changing Economy (Latin American Lifestyles)

The traditional market and the role of women in Latin America are explored as the economy of the region develops and expands. Bilingual English-Spanish narration.
VHS: S07427. $59.95.

The Mayan Mystery

This short film recreates the vibrant life once found at the center of great Mayan cities. Striking visuals and an engaging soundtrack sharpen this experience. 18 mins.
VHS: S23717. $49.95.

Memories of a Mexican

A look at the key figures and events of the Mexican Revolution from 1904 to 1924 as described by filmmaker Salvador Toscano. Using archival footage to examine the political and military upheaval that shaped present-day Mexico, the study goes further to depict women's role during this period. 45 mins.
English Version.
VHS: S16374. $39.95.
Spanish Version.
VHS: S16375. $39.95.

Men of Horses

This documentary about the "charros" (Mexican Horsemen) highlights the traditional art of "La Charreria," a colorful rodeo involving various crafts and skills. In Spanish, with no subtitles. 10 mins.
VHS: S16367. $29.95.

A Mexican Colonial Tour

Travel to the most fascinating cities in Mexico. We visit Mexico City, go sightseeing in the Zocalo, shop in the Zona Rosa and visit the museums in Chapultepec. In Cuernavaca, we see the cathedral and the Cuahnahuac Museum which houses Diego Rivera's famous murals. We complete our trip in Taxco, a town famous for its silver. 35 mins.
English Narration.
VHS: S05258. $39.95.
Spanish Narration.
VHS: S05257. $39.95.

Mexican Festivals

Every Mexican village or city has a fiesta, a three- or four-day period when its citizenry express their joy, hopes and optimism about their town and community. English narration. 30 mins.
VHS: S19841. $39.95.

Mexican Market

Just outside Mexico City lies a lively market. Families are seen arriving to prepare for a busy day of selling and bartering. 10 mins.
VHS: S23719. $49.95.

Mexican People and Culture

Designed to present material on the Hispanic peoples of America—their origins and their cultural heritage. Presents an overview of the geography and historical development of modern Mexico and Mexican-Americans and their role in contemporary American life. Bilingual—in both Spanish and English.
VHS: S06740. $59.95.

Mexican Pre-Hispanic Cultures

This program emphasizes pre-Hispanic civilization. The video examines Teotihuacan, the Toltecs, the Aztecs and the Mayas, who pioneered studies in math, astronomy and art. The program also provides an overview of the art, ceramics, sculptures and murals that are collected in Mexican museums. 26 mins.
English Version.
VHS: S20236. $29.95.
Spanish Version.
VHS: S20237. $29.95.

A Mexican Pyramid Tour

Relive history as you tour the fascinating archeological sites of Mexico's past civilizations. You will marvel at the beauty of the Pyramid of the Sun and the pyramids at Mitla. Explore Monte Alban, Chichen Itza and Tulum. As a final stop, we see the famous Museum of Anthropology. 35 mins.
English Version.
VHS: S05256. $39.95.
Spanish Version.
VHS: S05255. $39.95.

Mexican River Cruise

This colorful travel essay follows the voyage of the *Pacific Princess* as she lands at exotic Mexican ports of call including Acapulco, Zihuatanejo-Ixtapa, Puerto Vallarta, Mazatlan and Cabo San Lucas. Claiming fame as the "Love Boat," the *Princess* lives up to her reputation as stops are made at the world's great hotels, restaurants and resorts on route to Los Angeles.
VHS: S15849. $19.95.

The Mexican Way of Life

Mexico has tremendous variety reflected in its landscape and in its people. There are lavish resorts and simple villages. Snow-covered mountains give way to desolate deserts. Even its history reflects the conflicting influences of Native American civilizations and Spanish conquistadors. 23 mins.
VHS: S23710. $129.95.
Laser: LD74791. $149.95.

Mexican Youth Today

This program illustrates the concerns and attitudes of young Mexicans about the fate of their country, the ecology, their futures, goals and ambitions. The program combines interviews with students, commentary from teachers, images of the school, and the students' appreciation for Mexican culture, with a special emphasis on the last day of school. Spanish with English subtitles. 25 mins.
VHS: S20232. $29.95.

Mexico

A fascinating overview of Mexican culture. We explore the most important aspects of its civilization: Indian and Hispanic. Highlights include: bullfights, charros, the Ballet Folklorico, historic sites and pre-Columbian ruins. Delight in the regional dress and costumes of the people. 55 mins.
English Narration.
VHS: S05277. $49.95.
Spanish Narration.
VHS: S05276. $49.95.

Mexico Before Cortez

Many diverse groups built the cities that comprise contemporary Mexico. Artifacts, manuscripts, sculpture and architecture are combined in this film to trace these pre-Colombian peoples. 14 mins.
VHS: S23718. $49.95.

Mexico City—Metropolis in the Mountains

This program studies the consequences of the shifting population rates in Mexico City, where a projected 25 million people will live by the year 2000. It examines the cultural diversity of urban life, emphasizing the city's architectural splendor and grace. 28 mins.
VHS: S20278. $29.95.

Mexico Is...The Sights and Sounds of Modern Mexico

This video reproduces the spirit and energy of the Mexican people, capturing their lives and social behavior in markets, small towns, fiestas, beautiful countryside and ancient history. With limited narration, the film provides an atmospheric sense of contemporary Mexico. 26 mins.
VHS: S20230. $59.95.

Mexico on Video

This video examines the richness of Mexico and looks at pre-Hispanic civilization, the exuberance of mariachis and charros, the floating gardens at Xochimilco, and bullfights. The program highlights Mexico's cultural traditions, the Folkloric Ballet, and murals from leading artist Diego Rivera. 37 mins.
English Version.
VHS: S20234. $29.95.
Spanish Version.
VHS: S20235. $29.95.

Mexico, Journey to the Sun

Discover Mexico, from its ancient ruins and colorful towns to its intriguing nightlife and sunny beaches. 30 mins.
VHS: S14014. $24.95.

Mi Vida Loca: My Crazy Life

Allison Anders' vibrant feature is set in Echo Park, Los Angeles, where best friends Sad Girl and Mousie are now enemies as they have both become pregnant by the same man, Ernesto, a local drug dealer. A gritty slice of life.
VHS: S23484. $95.99.
Laser: LD75229. $34.98.
Allison Anders, USA, 1994, 94 mins.

Miguel Pinero at Magic Gallery

The late, great Nuyorican poet intones his blistering verse at an East Village art show. 1985, 20 mins.
VHS: S10196. $29.95.

Milagro Beanfield War

Robert Redford's personal fable, set in New Mexico, concerns the "war" between a greedy land-developer and a small-time bean farmer. Steeped in the lore of the Chicano culture, the film unabashedly draws on myth and poetic folklore to evoke the regional culture.
VHS: S07293. $14.98.
Laser: LD70056. $34.98.
Robert Redford, USA, 1988, 112 mins.

Modern Puerto Rico

This program explores the dynamic growth and rich beauty of Puerto Rico. The program is first presented in English and then in Spanish. 40 mins.
VHS: S07430. $59.95.

Mysteries of Peru

This two-part program examines two recurring mysteries of Peru. 120 mins.
Tape 1. Who drew the vast figures seen in the Peruvian desert at Nazca, and why?
VHS: S19548. $19.95.
Tape 2. What happened to the ancient civilization that created Peru's vast and undeveloped coastal canals?
VHS: S19549. $19.95.

Neighbors to Nicaragua

Neighbors to Nicaragua tells the story of Project Minnesota/Leon, a sister-state program between Minnesota and the Department of Leon in Nicaragua. Originally set up by church congregations in the Minneapolis area, PML involves people from all walks of life in the day to day life of their counterparts in the sister state. Directed by Gregory Rutchik and Robert Vaaler. 30 minutes.
VHS: S04308. $29.95.

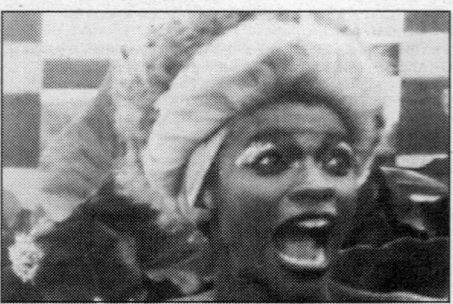

Nicaragua: For the First Time

Examines the Nicaraguan election process in detail by interviewing international observers, electoral experts, all party candidates, and many segments of the population.
VHS: S03730. $95.00.
Cineaccion, USA, 1985, 58 mins.

O My People! El Salvador

Documents the need for change in Central American policy, and pays tribute to the unconquerable human spirit. The story is told in the faces of war victims, etched with both suffering and strength, as voices of the war's witnesses—the displaced and tortured—tell of their horrifying experience in the face of this devastation. Produced by Jim Friedrich. 20 mins.
VHS: S03728. $58.00.

Octavio Paz

A conversation with the critic, novelist and philosopher. Spanish *without* English subtitles. 53 mins.
Home Video.
VHS: S08467. $59.95.
Public Performance.
VHS: S09503. $100.00.

Octavio Paz (Lannan Literary Videos)

Octavio Paz won the Nobel Prize in 1990. He read on October 18, 1988, from *The Collected Poems of Octavio Paz 1957-1987* at Georgetown University in Washington, D.C., with his translator Eliot Weinberger reading the English versions of his poems. Lewis MacAdams interviews this revered Mexican writer in English while Professor Enrico Santi interviews Paz in Spanish. From the *Lannan Literary Videos* series. 60 mins.
VHS: S27114. $19.95.

Old Gringo

From the director of *The Official Story* comes a tale of romance and revolution set in Mexico during the time of Pancho Villa, based on Carlos Fuentes' monumental novel. Jane Fonda stars as an American spinster who takes on a job as a private tutor with a wealthy Mexican family. Timing is everything in a revolution. She meets a handsome rebel general and a bitter but charming old American and guides their destinies. With Burt Lancaster as the title character and Jimmy Smits as General Arroyo.
VHS: S12210. $14.95.
Luis Puenzo, USA, 1989, 119 mins.

The Panama Invasion Revisited

A documentary reviewing the events leading up to the notorious invasion, how the attack was carried out, the resulting casualties, and the impact on life in Panama today. USA, 1991, 28 mins.
VHS: S15216. $25.00.

Paz Si Guerra No

Through narration and Canadian participants, the video is a journey with the International March for Peace across Central America. The march, comprised of 300 individuals from 30 different countries, was organized in support of the Contadora Peace process. Despite being stoned in Costa Rica and rebuffed at the Honduran border, they reached Mexico City, a support of marchers 50,000 strong.
VHS: S03726. $55.00.
Marier/Lucille/Sauriol, Canada, 1986, 59 mins.

Peace Begins Here

Many Americans are concerned about U.S. policy in Central America, but only a small percentage are actively doing something to change it. This provocative video examines the thoughts and motivations of a range of Americans who are taking action. Their personal stories are a powerful inspiration; featured are former Air Force Captain Brian Wilson, who was run over by a train during a protest at Concord Naval Weapons Station, a Presbyterian minister involved in escorting Salvadorans back to their villages, and others. 28 mins.
VHS: S10886. $39.95.

People of the Caribbean

A unique, bi-lingual tape (in Spanish and English) designed to develop concepts regarding the heritage of our minority groups. Highlights the countries that have sent many Black and Spanish-speaking people to the U.S., including Puerto Rico, Dominican Republic, Jamaica, Trinidad and Tobago, Barbados and Cuba. Sound in both English and Spanish.
VHS: S06739. $59.95.

Peru: Inca Heritage

Ruins of the proud Inca people form the backdrop for this video. Peru's contemporary descendants of this ancient civilization are then revealed against these imposing monuments. 17 mins.
VHS: S23714. $49.95.

Photo Album

An original, quirky remembrance of the filmmaker's experiences as a young immigrant from Cuba settling in Boston. This sometimes surreal autobiography stars his real family, and demonstrates Oliver's ability to distinguish between satire and parody. English and Spanish with English subtitles.
VHS: S02906. $29.95.
Enrique Oliver, USA, 1985, 14 mins.

Pictures from a Revolution

A revealing personal document about photojournalist Susan Meiselas, who returned to Nicaragua in 1989, ten years after her groundbreaking photographs on the revolution, to question her subjects and assess the political and social transformation. The film studies the aftermath of events and history, a collision of memory, photography and truth. "Susan Meiselas recalls acts of terrorism and moments of terrible fright" (Vincent Canby).
VHS: S17786. $29.95.
Susan Meiselas/Guzzetti/Rogers, USA, 1991, 92 mins.

Pinatas, Posadas y Pastorelas

Mexico City's neighborhoods are transformed into villages from December 16-25 with the lively and entertaining tradition of *posadas*. See how the religious nature of Mexican life is balanced with Spanish and Indian culture, interweaving customs, theories and modern practices. 25 mins.
English Narration.
VHS: S19840. $49.95.
Spanish Narration.
VHS: S19839. $49.95.

A Place to Call Home

Young people in Veracruz, Mexico face many of the same challenges that young people face in the U.S. Emau—a youth center founded by a Maryknoll priest from New York—offers them friendship, counseling and fun. Look at their lives in the light of *posadas*, the Mexican Christmas commemoration of Mary and Joseph searching out a home for Jesus. 29 mins.
VHS: S15865. $19.95.

Population Explosion and Industrialization (Latin American Lifestyles)

The changes in the environment and society of Latin America are presented as both population and development increases in the 20th century. Bilingual English-Spanish narration.
VHS: S07425. $59.95.

Portrait of Castro's Cuba

This two-part program demystifies Western ideas about living conditions in Castro's Cuba and what its citizenry believes about the last purely Marxist state. The program is "informative, well-focused...a rare peek at modern Cuba" (*Booklist*). 120 mins.
VHS: S19385. $49.95.

Puerto Cabezas: Our Sister City

A unique and remarkable video on Nicaragua, made by two videomakers from Burlington, Vermont. Burlington's sister city is Puerto Cabezas, Nicaragua, a vital port town on the Atlantic Coast. In the video, the vitality, tenacity and hopes of the Miskito Indians and Cosenos emerge through the words of their leaders, the eyes of their children, and their music—the lilting Caribbean beat in Miskito, Spanish, Creole and English.
VHS: S03727. $50.00.
D. Kraft/M. Fishman, USA, 1985, 22 mins.

Puerto Rico: History and Culture

Designed to develop an appreciation of the rich history and cultural traditions of Puerto Rico. In addition to surveying its history from the 15th century to the present, examples are given of the wide variety of cultural and artistic talent in Puerto Rico's tradition. Specifically designed for social studies and foreign language study. Bilingual, presented in both English and Spanish.
VHS: S06741. $59.95.

The Pyramids of the Sun and the Moon

An important film depicting the growth and development of one of the earliest cultures in Mexico. The people of Teotihuacan constructed the Pyramids of the Sun and the Moon with such exact scientific calculation that only recently have modern scientists been able to appreciate their development. Filmed on location in Mexico, this film is a wonderful introduction to pre-Colombian cultures. Directed by Angel Hurtado, 20 mins.
English Narration. Renee Channey.
VHS: S06802. $60.00.
Spanish Narration. Ivan Silva.
VHS: S06803. $60.00.

Qeros: The Shape of Survival

The Qeros Indians live beneath the Peruvian Andes, where they endure rigorous daily struggles with nature in order to survive. The land was formerly occupied by the Incas, who conquered the rival communities. The Qeros take part in elaborate rituals to the Aukis (spirits) to sustain their continued health and safety. 53 mins.
VHS: S20215. $29.95.

Queremos La Paz (We Want Peace)

Nicaraguans from all walks of life speak directly to the people of North America by directly answering the question, "What is your message to the North American people?" This film provides a refreshing glimpse of the Nicaraguan situation and their hopes for the future. "This video is the next best thing to a visit to Nicaragua" (Pete Seeger).
VHS: S03725. $39.00.
Syracuse Alt. Media Netwk., USA, 1986, 33 mins.

A Question of Conscience

On November 16, 1989, uniformed soldiers entered the Jesuit residence on the grounds of El Salvador's Central American University and murdered six priests, their cook and her daughter. This film tells the story behind this brutal massacre. A moving homage to the murdered priests as well as a study of the power of religious commitment. Directed by Ilan Ziv. 43 mins.
VHS: S14733. $39.95.

Raoni

Introduced and narrated by Marlon Brando. Raoni is the forceful and charismatic Chief of the Txucarramae Indians, an Amazonian tribe indigenous to the Brazilian rain forest. He has achieved international recognition as the spokesman for all of Brazil's surviving Indians. *Raoni* focuses on the heroic conflict that pits a lone Indian Chief against the determined rapacity of multinational corporations and short-sighted governments. Nominated for an Academy Award for Best Documentary.
VHS: S10732. $29.95.
Jean-Pierre Dutilleux, France/USA, 1978, 84 mins.

Return of the Maya

A millennium ago the Maya were one of the most advanced civilizations on the planet. Today, after being treated as second class citizens in their own country and being forced into exile from contemporary Guatemala, they are helping uncover the glory of their heritage at the ancient city of Edzna in Mexico. 28 mins.
VHS: S21591. $85.00.

Return to Aguacayo

A dramatic account of 450 displaced Salvadorans who attempt to return to their homes and farming cooperative in the Guazapa region of El Salvador, after having been forced to leave by the army. The unique footage was acquired by a member of a North American religious delegation which went to El Salvador in the hopes of protecting the displaced from attacks by the Armed Forces on their journey home.
VHS: S11492. $35.00.
Celeste Greco, USA, 1987, 18 mins.

Ricardo Montalban's South America

Although poverty and suffering are associated with Latin America, it is a continent rich in culture and beauty. This film is a graphic tour of several countries south of the Panama Canal, capturing dozens of attractive images, but with special emphasis on music and dance. 28 mins.
VHS: S04933. $24.95.

Roses in December

On December 2, 1980, lay missioner Jean Donovan and three American nuns were brutally murdered by members of El Salvador's security forces. With compassion and sensitivity, this film chronicles Jean's brief life—from her affluent childhood in Connecticut, to her decision to volunteer with the Maryknolls in El Salvador, to her tragic death. This award-winning film is an eloquent memorial to a courageous young woman.
VHS: S09442. $39.95.
A. Carrigan/B. Stone, USA, 1982, 56 mins.

Ruben Blades

Robert Mugge's stirring tribute to Ruben Blades, including appearances by Linda Ronstadt and Pete Hamill.
VHS: S05881. $24.95.
Robert Mugge, USA, 1986, 60 mins.

Salsa

The rhythms of salsa, featuring Tito Puente, Charlie Palmieri and Celia Cruz, exploring the connection between salsa and the political and cultural currents in the Latin community. Ruben Blades demonstrates how politics and music work together.
VHS: S08894. $24.95.

School of Assassins

U.S. taxpayers fund some of the worst human rights violators in this hemisphere. Former dictators from throughout South America received their training at the U.S. Army School of the Americas. This documentary reveals the connection between this school and the human rights offenses committed by its graduates in El Salvador. 18 mins.
VHS: S22475. $19.95.

Sentinels of Silence: The Ruins of Ancient Mexico
Filmed almost entirely from helicopter, this documentary presents spectacular views of the seven most important archaeological sites in Mexico: Teotihuacan, Monte Alban, Mitla, Tulum, Palenque, Chichen Itza and Uxmal. Narrated in English by Orson Welles, and in Spanish by Ricardo Montalban. 18 mins.
English Version.
VHS: S16376. $29.95.
Spanish Version.
VHS: S16377. $29.95.

Severo Sarduy
The leader of the avant-garde in Latin America speaks from his estate in Chantilly with the Cuban critic Roberto Gonzalez Echevarria. The range of subjects is great, from Sarduy's humble beginnings as a student and his role as a bard of the provincial Camaguey, to the highly original response to the Cuban revolution embodied in *Gestos* and later in *De Donde son los Cantates*. They explore Sarduy's influential role in introducing such writers as Gabriel Garcia Marquez into the international community from his position at Editions Seuil in Paris, and his relationship to French structuralism. Spanish *without* English subtitles.
Home Video.
VHS: S06962. $59.95.
Public Performance.
VHS: S08841. $100.00.

Shotguns and Accordions
Nationally-aired PBS documentary gives a street-level perspective of the music of the marijuana growing regions of Colombia with a behind-the-scenes tour of the provocative culture. From *Beats of the Heart* series.
VHS: S12607. $19.95.

Si o No?
This program examines the issue of statehood for Puerto Rico: its impact on island life and its consequences for the United States. The program studies the history of the island during the past century, contrasting life on the island and mainland. 28 mins.
VHS: S20279. $29.95.

Simon Bolivar
Maximilian Schell stars as Simon Bolivar, the legendary leader who unites various groups of revolutionaries under his command and in a series of fierce battles proclaims his country's freedom. 120 mins.
VHS: S11111. $49.95.

Sonia Sanchez
This dynamic poet, playwright, activist and teacher stresses African-American unity. On this video she reads from *homegirls & handgrenades* and *Under a Soprano Sky*. Lewis MacAdams then interviews her. This tape was recorded on September 17, 1990, at Georgetown University in Washington, D.C. From the *Lannan Literary Videos* series. 60 mins.
VHS: S27128. $19.95.

The Sounds of Mexico
Mexican music is as diverse and wide-ranging as its geography, and every region has its peculiar rhythms and preferred instruments. This documentary celebrates the richness of the sound and the originality of its voice. In Spanish. 45 mins.
VHS: S19833. $39.95.

Spanish Club: Fiesta!
A live-action video featuring Senora Reyes and her Spanish language club as they explore the meaning of fiesta. The program uses traditional Hispanic songs and stories to teach culture as well as language. For children ages 2-8.
VHS: S21923. $19.95.

Spanish Club: Los Animales!
Senora Reyes and the Spanish Club Kids explore the world of animals in Volume 2 of this series, which uses traditional Hispanic songs and stories for children ages 2-8.
VHS: S21924. $19.95.

Spirit of Samba
Nationally-aired PBS documentary gives a street-level perspective of the black music of Brazil, with a behind-the-scenes tour of the provocative culture. From *Beats of the Heart* series.
VHS: S12606. $19.95.

Stairway to the Mayan Gods
Joseph Campbell wrote the narration for this journey to the ceremonial center of the Mayan Indians of Central America and Mexico. 28 mins.
VHS: S06490. $89.95.

Stairways to the Gods: On the Trail of the Jaguar
The jaguar is the recurrent symbol of the ancient Native American cultures of Central America. Beginning and ending at the sacred pyramid in Tikal, called the Temple of the Great Jaguar, this program follows the symbol of the jaguar across a number of archeological sites, explaining its varied meanings and the light it casts on the peoples of Mesoamerica. 43 mins.
VHS: S22925. $29.95.

Stand and Deliver
Edward James Olmos brings the story of Jaime Escalante and his progress in teaching calculus to unmotivated barrio students to life. An inspirational true-to-life educational miracle set at Garfield High in Los Angeles in 1982. Cast includes Rosana De Soto, Andy Garcia and Lou Diamond Phillips as the gang kid who wants to learn.
VHS: S07925. $14.95.
Laser: LD70683. $24.98.
Ramon Menendez, USA, 1988, 103 mins.

Symphony of Mexico
Symphony of the New World by composer Anton Dvorak provides the rhythm and mood for this fast-paced documentary on modern Mexico. Without words, the program relays the complexities of Mexican culture, bringing the audience on trip that transcends consciousness. 20 mins.
VHS: S16369. $29.95.

Tales from the Latin American Indians
Five magical tales from the Latin American Indians, including *The Magic of the Quetzal Bird*, *The Legend of Mexico City (Eagle and Snake)*, *The Legend of Quezalcoatl* and *The Legend of Loiza*. 30 mins.
English Version.
VHS: S20240. $29.95.
Spanish Version.
VHS: S20241. $29.95.

This Is Mexico
This documentary provides an ideological history of Mexico from ancient times to the present. Images of Indian monuments, dances and dress demonstrate Mexico's rich cultural foundation which then evolved by Spanish influence. This amalgam of culture provides the diverse nature of Mexico today. No narration. 20 mins.
VHS: S16370. $29.95.

This Land Is Our Land
Small family farmers in southern Brazil struggle in grass-roots organizations to gain title to land. Some families are displaced by huge dams, others face bank foreclosures, still others camp out for years in plastic tents to pressure the government to release unused land owned by a small minority. The video contains stories of perseverance, courage and hope in the face of violence and overwhelming odds. Produced by Maryknoll Media. 28 mins.
VHS: S11716. $24.95.

Threads of Tradition
Documents the rebirth of the traditional crafts of weaving and embroidery in the Hispanic culture of southern Colorado. Carding, spinning, dyeing, weaving are shown, as well as many examples of folk art. 14 mins.
VHS: S07637. $29.95.

Tiempo de Morir (A Time to Die)
A prize-winning adaptation of Gabriel Garcia Marquez's short story about a man who must reconcile the past and present when he returns to his village following his release from an 18-year prison stay. Winner of Best Picture and Best Actor awards, Rio de Janeiro Film Festival. Spanish with English subtitles. Mexico. 100 mins. 1989.
VHS: S18656. $79.95.

Touring Mexico
A journey through the clash of climates, cultures and geographical extremes of Mexico, including Mexico City, the Yucatan, the classic Mayan civilization at Uxmal, Chichen Itza, the city of Merida, and the Olmecs of La Venta, the pyramid of Tijan and the mysteries of Monte Alban in Oaxaca. Other features include the City of the Gods at Teotihuacan, the colossi of Tula, the Floating Gardens of Xochimilco and more. 60 mins.
VHS: S09906. $29.95.

Tree of Life
More than just an anthropological documentary, this rare, beautifully made document of the Voladar ritual as performed by the Totonac Indians of Huehuetla, Mexico, brings alive the mythic dimensions of ritual communal celebration. The Voladores (Flyers) ritual is perhaps the oldest surviving dance in the Western Hemisphere, dating back to 500 A.D. It is accompanied by flute and drum music and narration taken from the 15th century Nahuatl poetry.
VHS: S09294. $44.95.

Troubadours: A Musical Performance by Groupo Camayoc
Taped in Esteli, Nicaragua, the program features a unique musical performance by the Nicaraguan folk singing group Camayoc, which means "messenger" in Nahuatl, the language of many Central American indigenous people. They play and sing their own songs and those of Carlos Meija Godoy and Pablo Milanes. Lyrics translated into English by Humberto Estrada.
VHS: S11181. $49.95.
Julia Lesage, USA/Nicaragua, 1987, 49 mins.

TV Commercials
See the innovative approach to advertising in a group of Mexican television commercials that introduce authentic cultural information. 45 mins.
VHS: S19830. $45.00.

Un Dia Cualquiera
This video features daily events in Honduras, including a pick-up soccer game, a party and a wedding, to give viewers the sense and concepts of specific situations. The workbook includes cultural information, oral and written exercises and tests. In Spanish. 30 mins.
VHS: S19820. $49.95.

Unheard Voices
For 10 years civil war raged in El Salvador. Yet rarely do we hear the voices of those who have suffered the most: the children, who make up nearly 1/2 the country's population. Many live in poverty, raised in orphanages or refugee camps. *Unheard Voices* is a poignant, emotional look at these young, forgotten victims. 1990, 16 mins.
VHS: S13966. $55.00.

Victor Hernandez Cruz
The African, Indian and Spanish cultures of Victor Hernandez Cruz's native Puerto Rico infuse his work. He has been the World Heavyweight Poetry champion twice. On this video he reads from *Rhythm, Content and Flavor* and *By Lingual Wholes*. It was recorded in Los Angeles on April 17, 1989. Lewis MacAdams conducted the interview. From the *Lannan Literary Videos* series. 60 mins.
VHS: S27119. $19.95.

Viva La Paz
Documentary about a group of 300 people, from over 40 countries, who travel across Central America in support of dialog and non-military alternatives to the conflicts in the region. A story of citizen diplomacy in action, it offers a unique overview of the distinct but interrelated problems in the five countries and the possibilities for the success of the Central America Peace accord.
VHS: S06605. $55.00.
Kelly Holland, USA, 1987, 58 mins.

Voice of the Voiceless
Over half a million El Salvadoran refugees live in the United States. The war which has driven them here and their struggle to survive amidst poverty and fear of deportation is chronicled in this moving documentary, filmed in the Los Angeles refugee community. 60 mins.
VHS: S04307. $45.00.

War in El Cedro: American Veterans in Nicaragua
A revealing look at the realities of war through the eyes of combat veterans, and an eloquent plea, by those who have been there, to avoid military intervention in the affairs of other countries. Determined to make a positive contribution to a war-torn country, ten American veterans of World War II, Korea and Vietnam travelled to the village of El Cedro to help rebuild a health clinic destroyed by the Contras.
VHS: S11490. $39.95.
Don North, USA, 1987, 50 mins.

We Are Guatemalans
After 12 years in Mexico a group of Guatemalan refugees returned home. Forced to flee the ethnic cleansing of their homeland, this documentary tells a tale of renewed commitment to the future of their country. It centers on the town Cuarto Pueblo and the dramatic ordeals faced by its inhabitants. 28 mins.
VHS: S22474. $19.95.

A Week in the Life of a Mexican Student
Xavier Sierra is a 14-year-old student shown at work, in class and at home in this video. 24 mins.
VHS: S23721. $99.95.

Where Land Is Life
For the indigenous people of Peru's Altiplano, the rugged land around Lake Titanica is more than soil. Centuries of conquest and exploitation have forced the Aymara and Quechua people to give up the land that has sustained them. Today, despite various setbacks, they are reclaiming the land of their birthright, and at the same time rediscovering the traditional methods of agriculture that made this region the breadbasket of Peru. 28 mins.
VHS: S13249. $24.95.

Zocalo—The Heart of Mexico
This program charts 24 hours in the frantic life of Zocalo, Mexico City's central plaza, that mirrors the people, their attitudes, and the cultural, social and life conditions of contemporary Mexico. 23 mins.
VHS: S20233. $59.95.

Zoot Suit
A stylized musical about the arrest of Chicano gang members in Los Angeles in 1942 and the resulting controversial trial. Written and directed by Luis Valdez, based on his own play. Starring Daniel Valdez, Tyne Daly, Mike Gomez, Abel Franco and Edward James Olmos as El Pachuco, the spirit of the Zoot Suit experience.
VHS: S14453. $14.98.
Luis Valdez, USA, 1981, 103 mins.

the german
NEW WAVE

All of Me
Georgette Dee, the famed transvestite cabaret star from Germany, stars as Orlanda. On a concert tour, Orlanda and his/her wife Elisabeth both fall for the same Polish man. This scenario makes for a witty film, and the musical numbers, particularly the title tune, are terrific. German with English subtitles.
VHS: $26867. $39.95.
Bettina Wilhelm, Germany, 1990, 76 mins.

Anita, Dances of Vice
Anita Berber, the notorious "naked" dancer of Berlin of the Weimar era, comes alive in the visions of an old woman who claims to be Anita in Rosa von Praunheim's truly original film. The police commit her to a mental institution where in the old woman's dreams and exchanges with the staff, scenes from Anita's life appear. "Huber is irresistibly funny as the city's pugnacious doyenne of sin," wrote *The Village Voice.* German with English subtitles.
VHS: $09349. $39.95.
Rosa von Praunheim, Germany, 1987, 85 mins

Bagdad Cafe
From Percy Adlon, the director of *Sugarbaby,* an English-language film about a friendship between two women at a desert truck stop motel and diner. One is black and overworked. The other is German and overdressed. A haunting musical score and a top notch supporting cast which includes Jack Palance makes this sweet comedy starring C.C. Pounder and Marianne Sagebrecht a delight. In English.
VHS: $07965. $14.98.
Percy Adlon, USA, 1988, 91 mins.

Black and White as Day and Night
Bruno Ganz stars in this feature, from the director of *Das Boot,* about a man obsessed. Ganz's character devotes himself to computers when he fails at chess. When the machine he works on loses, he becomes determined to best the offending world chess champion himself. Sadly the stress takes an unforeseen toll on his health, leading to a surprise ending. German with English subtitles.
VHS: $23194. $29.95.
Wolfgang Petersen, Germany, 1963, 103 mins.

The Blue Hour
The third feature by Swiss-born Marcel Gisler tells the story of an odd affair between two Berliners: Theo, a hip young callboy, and Marie, his French neighbor. *The Blue Hour* is a look at male prostitution and at gay men who sleep with women. With Andreas Herder, Dina Leipzig and Cyrill Rey-Coquais. German with English subtitles.
VHS: $19446. $39.95.
Marcel Gisler, Germany, 1991, 87 mins.

The Bridge (Die Brucke)
A powerful, deeply moving classic of German cinema. Set in 1945, seven German boys defend an insignificant bridge from an American attack. Based on the autobiographical novel of Manfred Gregor, this searing film was nominated for an Oscar and won a Golden Globe award. Its depiction of futile valor and wasted youth touched audiences the world over. German with English subtitles.
VHS: $26597. $39.95.
Bernhard Wicki, Germany, 1959, 102 mins.

Celeste
From the director of *Bagdad Cafe* and *Sugar Baby* comes one of those rare films to successfully portray the creative and emotional life of an artist. Marcel Proust, the celebrated author of *Remembrance of Things Past,* is seen through the young eyes of Celeste Albaret, who for nine years before the author's death was his cook, companion, secretary, friend and surrogate mother. Award-winning actress Eva Mattes delivers a flawless performance in this stunning and witty love story. Written and directed by Percy Adlon. German with English subtitles.
VHS: $13915. $79.95.
Percy Adlon, Germany, 1981, 107 mins.

Classic Shorts Compilation #13: Lotte Reiniger
Lotte Reiniger was another early pioneer in the development of the animated film. She produced many short films using her technique of animated paper silhouettes. This compilation features five of her animated fairy tales, and a documentary about her work directed by John Isaacs. Includes *Cinderella, The Frog Prince, Hansel and Gretel, Little Chimney Sweep, The Three Wishes,* and *The Art of Lotte Reiniger.* 70 mins.
VHS: $15063. $29.95.

Das Boot (The Boat)
Wolfgang Petersen's gripping work about a German U-boat engaging the British royal fleet, though it's far more important for its narrative tension, claustrophobic use of space, and portrait of men under battle. Taken from Lothar-Guenther Buchheim's novel though in terms of setting, atmosphere and tone, the real source seems closer to Stephen Crane's *The Open Boat.* With Jurgen Prochnow, Herbert Gronemeyer and Klaus Wennemann.
Dubbed Version. 1982, 110 mins.
VHS: $01791. $19.95.
Subtitled Version. German dialog.
VHS: $14834. $39.95.
Laser: 3 sides. LD72444. $39.95.
Wolfgang Petersen, Germany, 1981, 145 mins.

Der Sprinter
In order to please his parents, who are distressed because of his preference for other men, Wieland takes up track and field and is surprised to find himself attracted to a female shot-putter. German with English subtitles.
VHS: $02187. $59.95.
Christopher Boll, W. Germany, 1983, 90 mins.

Dragon Chow
A beautiful and moving film, *Dragon Chow* tells the story of Asian political refugees living on the edge of deportation in the land of economic miracles, West Germany. The film's hero, Shezad, a gentle but resourceful Pakistani, lands a job in a second-rate Chinese restaurant, where he befriends an Oriental waiter named Xiao (Ric Young of *The Last Emperor*). Together they attempt to storm the citadel of Western capitalism by opening a restaurant of their own. German, Urdu and Mandarin with English subtitles.
VHS: $12468. $69.95.
Jan Schutte, Germany, 1987, 75 mins.

Fast Buck
A young man's fascination with love turns to tragedy. German with English subtitles. 90 mins.
VHS: $04775. $59.95.
Renate Stegmuller/Raimund Koplin, Germany, 1983, 95 mins.

Female Misbehavior
Monika Treut's kinky exploration of nonconformist women combines two older short films, *Bondage* (1983), about a sadomasochistic lesbian, and *Annie* (1989), a portrait of former porno star Annie Sprinkle, with two recent documentaries, *Dr. Paglia* and *Max.* The former is a witty send-up of controversial academic Camille Paglia; the latter, a look at a lesbian Native American that shows her transsexual change from woman to man. "Treut is a sexual-political provocateur who in her explorations of the sexual fringe takes us where few filmmakers visit" (*New York Post*).
VHS: $19558. $29.95.
Monika Treut, Germany/USA, 1992, 80 mins.

Film Before Film
A truly unique film by German filmmaker Werner Nekes, who owns one of the world's great collections of primitive motion picture and photographic equipment. In this fascinating documentary, Nekes explores how scientific advances in the 19th century—particularly developments in optics, theories of light, seeing and perception—aided the development of the moving image. But *Film before Film* is not a "documentary" in the traditional sense of the term—it's a great deal of fun and exploration of how moving images function through actual illustration of rare photographic and motion picture equipment. German with English subtitles.
VHS: $08946. $29.95.
Werner Nekes, Germany, 1987, 90 mins.

Flaming Ears
This edgy, sci-fi lesbian fantasy follows the lives of three women: a comic book artist, a performance artist/pyromaniac and and amoral alien who likes lizards. In this cyberdyke movie, love and revenge vie for supremacy amidst violence and ennui in an anti-romantic plea for love of all kinds. German with English subtitles.
VHS: $26936. $39.95.
Angela Hans Sheirl/Ursula Purrer/Dietmar Schipek, Austria, 1991, 84 mins.

Forget Mozart
Beginning in Vienna, Dec. 5, 1791, this German film reconstructs the life and times of the genius composer. As friends and associates gather at his deathbed, the extraordinary arc of his career is laid out, placed in the context of his art and life. He's portrayed as a complicated, difficult artist trying desperately to reconcile his personal life and private obsessions. German with English subtitles.
VHS: $16699. $29.95.
Salvo Luther, Germany, 1986, 93 mins.

Heimat
While America watched *Roots,* Germany watched *Heimat* with the same mixture of pride and shame that held a nation spellbound. The riveting 16-hour film, presented as a 9-tape boxed set, was the sensation of the Munich, London and Venice Film Festivals and a huge hit in France and Germany. It is the incredible interlocking saga of a German family from the end of World War I to 1982. Ambitious, grand, yet very intimate, *Heimat* is an incredible motion picture chronicle—an immersion in the lives, loves and tragedies of the extended Simon family. Shot over two years, the film features 28 leading performers, 140 speaking roles and a cast of 5,000 non-professional actors. German with English subtitles.
VHS: $27403. $149.95.
Edgar Reitz, West Germany, 1984, 924 mins.

Heimat II
"Staggeringly rich….THE SECOND HEIMAT, which runs 25½ hours, forms, with its predecessor, a magnificent, nearly unprecedented 'film novel': a portrait of Germany in the 20th Century with few equals in either film or literature…outlandishly ambitious…an often dazzling success. That [Edgar] Reitz is able to sustain growth and tension, inexorable flow and translucent clarity through the entire vast length, and hold audiences rapt…seems something of a miracle. The story is of Maria's son, Herrmann Simon, and his life in Munich from 1960 to 1970. There, a brilliant young modernist musician and composer, he falls in with an incandescent circle of young students, artists, rebels and lovers—all brought shatteringly to life by Reitz and a splendid cast of actors and musicians…THE SECOND HEIMAT may be the screen's finest portrayal of youth in the 60's" (Michael Wilmington, *Chicago Tribune*). Over 23 hours long. German with clear English subtitles.
VHS: $27808. $249.95.
Edgar Reitz, Germany, 1994, 1416 mins.

I Am My Own Woman
The exceptional life of Eastern-bloc transvestite Charlotte von Mahlsdorf is the subject of this film. Her story symbolizes both political resistance and sexual difference under a repressive regime. It's a documentary with a touch of Brecht that features a true queer free spirit. German with English subtitles.
VHS: $22670. $79.95.
Rosa von Praunheim, Germany, 1993, 91 mins.

Ironhand
Costume adventure story set during the Middle Ages about two friends who grow to serve opposing masters, during a period of conflict between Church and State. German with English subtitles. Germany, 120 mins.
VHS: $04774. $59.95.
Wolfgang Liebeneizer, Germany, 1978, 103 mins.

Jumper
An unusual and disquieting film, in which a collection of tragi-comic characters all seem to lose their footing in the struggle of life without direction. German with English subtitles.
VHS: $02188. $59.95.
Benno Trachtmann, W. Germany, 1985, 90 mins.

Just a Gigolo
Actor David Hemmings directed this post-World War I melodrama starring David Bowie as a veteran looking for work in Berlin. He finds he is best at entertaining lonely older women with too much money. Cast includes Kim Novak, Maria Schell, Sydne Rome, Curt Jurgens, David Hemmings and Marlene Dietrich, who sings the title tune and shows her age. Hemmings debut as director. In English.
VHS: Out of print. For rental only.
Laser: CLV. LD70268. $39.95.
David Hemmings, Germany, 1979, 98 mins.

Killing Cars
Jurgen Prochnow, the captain of *Das Boot,* now plays a brilliant automotive engineer who has designed and built an automobile that runs on cellular energy. This greatly annoys members of the oil cartel and rival gas guzzling car makers. A thriller set in Europe and the Middle East. With Senta Berger, Daniel Gelin and William Conrad as Mahoney. In English.
VHS: $05931. $79.95.
Michael Verhoeven, W. Germany, 1985, 104 min.

Knife in the Head
Bruno Ganz stars as a scientist in this murky political thriller, one of the most interesting films to emerge from the German New Wave. He sets off in search of his estranged wife, but is sidetracked when he loses his speech and memory in a bizarre accident. As the plot develops, a strange and unexpected twist throws him even further off balance. German with English subtitles.
VHS: $20870. $79.95.
Reinhard Hauff, Germany, 1978, 113 mins.

The Last Five Days
In 1943 a young woman (Lena Stolze), part of a group of students who formed a covert opposition group, the White Rose, that decried German crimes, was discovered by the Nazis and sentenced to death. The film explores her confinement, her relationship with a cellmate, the repercussions of her martyrdom, and her heroism and struggle against monumental darkness and depravity. With Lena Stolze and Irm Hermann. German with English subtitles.
VHS: $17632. $79.95.
Percy Adlon, Germany, 1982, 112 mins.

Magdalene
Nastassia Kinski is cast as a 19th century European temptress who turns down a powerful baron and says yes to an idealistic young priest. Some women have duels fought over them; Magdalene has battles fought and history changed to please her. With David Warner, Steve Bond, Franco Nero, Anthony Quayle, Gunter Meisner and Ferdy Mayne.
VHS: $13678. $89.95.
Monica Teuber, Germany, 1988, 89 mins.

Makin' Up
This German film was a surprise hit and won a Student Academy Award. Frenzy is a harried cartoonist who relies on her friend Maischa, a date-crazy person, for inspiration. Maischa has hit a dry patch so in search of inspiration Frenzy must fix Maischa up and inadvertently finds herself on a double date. Includes the short film *The Most Beautiful Breasts in the World.* German with English subtitles.
VHS: $24671. $59.95.
K. Von Garnier/R. Kaufmann, Germany, 1993, 68 mins.

Marianne and Juliane
Barbara Sukowa, Jutta Lampe and Rudiger Vogler star in this drama which chronicles the story of two sisters. One is a left-wing editor, while the other became a communist terrorist who ends up in prison. This film offers a chilling personal account that illustrates the political turmoil that afflicted West Germany in the 1970's. German with English subtitles.
VHS: $21504. $79.95.
Margarethe von Trotta, Germany, 1980, 106 mins.

Me and Him
Griffin Dunne thought he had problems dating in the Big Apple in *After Hours.* That was before he found his male member not only had a mind of its own but a voice as well. Billed as the ultimate buddy picture, this unusual comedy from Doris Dorrie (*Men*) was based on a novel by Alberto Moravia. Cast includes Ellen Greene, Carey Lowell, Kelly Bishop, Craig T. Nelson and Mark Linn-Baker as the voice of Griffin's little friend.
VHS: $11575. $89.95.
Doris Dorrie, USA, 1989, 95 mins.

Mein Krieg (My Private War)
An eerie compilation of home movies and oral histories of six Wehrmacht soldiers who were involved in the Nazi invasion of the former Soviet Union. The images of the war (soldiers swimming in the Black Sea, bombed out landscapes and literally thousands of dead bodies) are contrasted with the soldiers' memories and reminiscences of their experiences. "*Mein Krieg* is annotated only by the veterans themselves as they explicate the material they produced nearly a half-century before" (J. Hoberman, *The Village Voice*).
VHS: $19859. $69.95.
Harriet Eder/Thomas Kufus, Germany, 1990, 90 mins.

Men
Doris Dorrie's runaway hit of a screwball comedy about a businessman (Heiner Lauterbach) who discovers his wife is having an affair with a Bohemian artist. Disguised as the artist's roommate, Lauterbach watches, waits, and plots a strange reversal on the unsuspecting couple. German with English subtitles.
VHS: $20591. $79.95.
Doris Dorrie, Germany, 1985, 99 mins.

Mozart: A Childhood Chronicle
A profound and witty account of Mozart's life from child prodigy to mature composer. "Should not be missed by anyone who has even a passing interest in Mozart," wrote *The New York Times.* German with English subtitles.
VHS: $04730. $79.95.
Klaus Kirschner, Germany, 1976, 224 mins.

My Father Is Coming
An adventurous German woman receives word from her Bavarian father of his intentions to visit her in New York, where she must pull off an elaborate facade of being married and successful. Her gay roommate poses as her husband but complications ensue when a string of bizarre circumstances result in her father's transformation into an underground sexual icon. With Shelly Kastner, Alfred Edel and Annie Sprinkle.
VHS: $18412. $29.95.
Monika Treut, USA/Germany, 1991, 83 mins.

The Nasty Girl
When Sonja investigates the secret past of her home town, she uncovers more than she expected—and more than the townsfolk want revealed. Before she knows it, she is nicknamed "the nasty girl" and her trouble really begins. This provocative comedy about secrets and surprises features a fabulous performance by Lena Stolze and is based on a true story. "One of the best films of the year!" (*Los Angeles Daily News*). German with yellow English subtitles. Presented in letterbox format.
VHS: $15354. $89.99.
Laser: Widescreen. LD75130. $24.98.
Michael Verhoeven, Germany, 1991, 94 mins.

Oppermann Family

Two-cassette mammoth West German TV production based on the novel by Lion Feuchtwanger about the Oppermann family, starting in the Nazi years of 1932, and their attempt to survive in Berlin against the forces of the Hitler regime. German with English subtitles.
VHS: S02005. $99.95.
Egon Monk, Germany, 1982, 238 mins.

Parsifal

Syberberg's (*Our Hitler*) remarkable homage to Richard Wagner, with Edith Clever. Syberberg explores Wagner's last, mystic opera, with a challenging style, using Wagner's face as a set. The actors perform to a recording expressly made for the film. German lyrics with English subtitles.
VHS: S00995. $79.95.
Hans Jurgen Syberberg, Germany, 1982, 255 mins.

Positive

The New York City gay community's response to the AIDS crisis is powerfully documented in *Positive*. Rosa von Praunheim has captured the spirit of activism generated by playwright Larry Kramer, musician and co-founder of People With AIDS Coalition (PWA) Michael Callen, and New York filmmaker and journalist Phil Zwickler. They have chosen to act and speak out, refusing to be "AIDS victims." Having neither the time nor the patience to mince words, their groups, like ACT-UP and Queer Nation, demand a response to the epidemic that has threatened to annihilate them. An immensely important historical document.
VHS: S14152. $29.95.
Rosa von Praunheim/Phil Zwickler, USA, 1990, 80 mins.

The Promise

In this love story the Berlin wall separates two young lovers. They first fall for each other in their teens and their passion stretches over 28 years until the wall no longer presents an obstacle to their joint happiness. It's an epic story about the endurance of love. German with English subtitles.
VHS: S27255. $95.99.
Laser: LD75471. $39.99.
Margarethe von Trotta, Germany, 1995, 115 mins.

Rosa Luxemburg

Rosa Luxemburg's amazing life as a political radical and fiercely independent woman is brought to life in this sweeping biography starring the acclaimed actress Barbara Sukowa. From war and revolution to Luxemburg's tempestuous personal life, including her love affairs and numerous jail sentences, this charismatic figure stayed true to her ideals. German with English subtitles.
VHS: S20595. $79.95.
Margarethe von Trotta, Germany, 1985, 122 mins.

Rosalie Goes Shopping

The wonderfully comic Marianne Sagebrecht plays the calculating German war bride of an Arkansas crop duster. Rosalie Greenspan has 37 credit cards and she isn't afraid of pushing them all over the posted limit. Brad Davis and Judge Reinhold costar in this very original black comedy about achieving the American dream through misrepresentation.
VHS: S12516. $89.95.
Percy Adlon, W. Germany, 1989, 94 mins.

Salmonberries

German director Percy Adlon's political thriller features k.d. lang in her film debut. The story concerns a repressed East German librarian who escapes her oppressive surroundings after her lover is killed trying to scale the Berlin Wall. Devastated and grief stricken, Roswitha (Rosel Zech) travels to Alaska. Trapped in a grim, remote Eskimo outpost, she finds comfort and emotional fulfillment with the sexually ambiguous lang.
VHS: S18844. $29.95.
Percy Adlon, Canada/Germany, 1991, 94 mins.

Schramm

Nekromantik's director Jorg Buttgereit depicts the world of a serial killer in this hypnotizing orgy of sex and violence. It's all seen through the eyes of the killer, Lothar Schramm (Florian Koemer von Gustorf). He is fascinated by a prostitute (Monika M.) and obsessed with death. The result is a well-crafted, surreal vision of love and desire.
VHS: S27510. $29.95.
Jorg Buttgereit, Germany, 90 mins.

Seduction: The Cruel Woman

Pina Bausch dancer Mechtild Grossman plays Wanda, a dominatrix whose troupe services customers and elaborately stages S&M performances in this "stunning" film from German filmmakers Elfi Mikesch and Monika Treut (*Virgin Machine*). Much more important to Mikesch's insinuating camera than the petty tortures are the settings, costumes, and look of each encounter. This is S&M by Avedon, outfits by Dior…By the way, on her off hours, of which there are few, Wanda prefers women. German with English subtitles.
VHS: S12460. $29.95.
E. Mikesch/M. Treut, Germany, 1985, 84 mins.

Silence=Death

This film serves as an important historical document, exploring the reactions of New York's artistic community to the ravages of AIDS. Responses range from David Wojnorowicz' venomous proclamations and paintings, and painter Rafael Gambas' seething indictment of homophobic bigotry, to Keith Haring's nostalgic longing for the days of care-free sex, and Allen Ginsberg's musing upon his shyer attitude about experimenting sexually. Even with the gentler voices, the film's undercurrent is an angry demand for action and recognition. "Best AIDS film to date…" (*The Guardian*).
VHS: S14148. $29.95.
Rosa von Praunheim/Phil Zwickler, USA, 1990, 60 mins.

Street Kid

Peter Kern's story about a 14-year-old street walker and male prostitute who becomes a pawn in a nasty dysfunctional family and their weird games of domination. Filled with stark imagery, powerful performances and a gritty authenticity that "challenges the taboos and constraints of mainstream Hollywood filmmaking." With Winfried Glatzeder, Max Kellerman, Daniel Aminaty and Nicole Weber. German with English subtitles.
VHS: S17778. $69.95.
Peter Kern, Germany, 1991, 89 mins.

Sugarbaby

Percy Adlon's mischievous comedy. An average, overweight mortuary assistant (Marianne Sagebrecht) falls passionately in love with a sweet, good-natured subway station driver (Eisi Gulp). Exploiting his loneliness from his wife's absence, she orchestrates a brief though memorable relationship. With Manuela Denz and Toni Berger. German with English subtitles.
VHS: S01602. $39.95.
Percy Adlon, Germany, 1985, 86 mins.

Swann in Love

Jeremy Irons, Ornella Muti, Alain Delon star in Schlondorff's engrossing, sexy film based on Proust's monumental modern novel, centering on a wealthy gentleman who thrives in the finest circles of high society and risks everything for his erotic obsession. English dialog.
VHS: S01289. $24.95.
Volker Schlondorff, Germany/France, 1984, 110 mins.

Taxi Zum Klo

A smash hit at the Berlin and New York Film Festivals in 1981, *Taxi Zum Klo* is an autobiographical examination of the director's own sexual escapades and fantasies. Frank Ripploh explores every aspect of gay life in Berlin, with hilarious results. German with English subtitles.
VHS: S01304. $79.95.
Frank Ripploh, W. Germany, 1981

Tears in Florence

A love story between a woman who has had a disfiguring auto accident and the man who struck her. As their love blossoms they learn that they are in fact brother and sister. Then the woman discovers she is pregnant. German with English subtitles.
VHS: S02186. $59.95.
Marianne Schafer, Germany, 1982, 90 mins.

Tonio Kroger

A brilliant adaptation of Thomas Mann's 1903 novel about a young writer torn between contradictory desires for security and luxury as well as the carefree, passionate life. Fluid time structure, eerie music, and black and white evoke a dream-like world. German with English subtitles.
VHS: S01360. $29.95.
Rolf Thiele, West Germany, 1965, 92 mins.

Via Appia

A complex film about gay desire and paranoia. A former German steward travels to Rio to find a mysterious man who left a cryptic message, "Welcome to the AIDS Club," following a sexual encounter. "Via Appia, the nickname of a Rio district where male prostitutes hang out, becomes a grim guided tour of the city's gay subculture, its bars, discos, streets and a beach known as the AIDS farm. The documentary-within-the-film-format justifies this material" (Vincent Canby). With Peter Senner, Guilherme de Padua and Yves Jansen. German and Spanish with English subtitles.
VHS: S18693. $39.95.
Jochen Hick, Germany/Brazil, 1992, 90 mins.

Virgin Machine

Called "steamy" by *The San Francisco Chronicle* and "a lesbian Candide…deliriously obscene" by *The San Francisco Examiner*, *Virgin Machine* is an offbeat black and white comedy about a journalist researching romantic love. The study takes her from German endocrinologists to San Francisco's porn industry where she meets Susie Sexpert, a woman who lectures on the relative merits of various strippers and demonstrates dildos the way some women handle tupperware. German with English subtitles.
VHS: S10940. $29.95.
Monika Treut, Germany, 1988, 90 mins.

A Virus Knows No Morals

A black comedy filled with the worst fears, a savagely funny burlesque on the AIDS crisis, irreverent yet deadly serious. Nurses on the night shift roll dice to see which AIDS patient will die next. An epidemic victim is harassed by a reporter on his death bed—he sticks her with a contaminated syringe. The government opens a quarantine called Hell Gay Land. Gay terrorists capture the Minister of Health. An outrageous and yet extremely honest film by von Praunheim, this controversial film shook West Germany. German with English subtitles.
VHS: S09350. $39.95.
Rosa von Praunheim, Germany, 1985, 82 mins.

Wannsee Conference

An acclaimed film that reenacts the fateful January 1942 meeting of the Nazi party and top German officials that set in motion "The Final Solution," the destruction of European Jewry. "It is mesmerizing for seeming to be so commonplace. The *Wannsee Conference* finds a voice for dealing with matters that are, after all, not unspeakable" (Vincent Canby). With Dietrich Mattausch, Gerd Bockmann, Friedrich Beckhaus and Gunter Sporrle. German with English subtitles.
VHS: S07395. $19.95.
Heinz Schirk, Germany, 1984, 87 mins.

Westler: East of the Wall

Before the wall separating East and West Germany came down it divided not just a nation but thousands of families. This film tells a story about the nearly impossible romance between two gay men on opposite sides of the wall. German with English subtitles.
VHS: S24836. $39.95.
Wieland Speck, Germany, 1986, 94 mins.

Whisky and Sofa (Operation Moonlight)

Maria Schell, Carl Michaels and Nadja Gray star in this sparkling romantic comedy. Schell is a beautiful and determined architect who is set on winning a major architectural competition. She even tries to flirt with a rival in order to ensure her success. Naturally this harmless maneuver leads to unforeseen romantic consequences. Dubbed in English.
VHS: S23802. $24.95.
Gunter Grawert, Germany, 1963, 85 mins.

The Wonderful, Horrible Life of Leni Riefenstahl

An exhaustive, infuriating and unforgettable documentary about Leni Riefenstahl at age 90: actress, filmmaker (*Olympia, Triumph of the Will*), propagandist, personal friend of Goebbels and Hitler, photographer, explorer. Filmmaker Ray Mueller confronts Leni as she seeks to remold her image from that of a master propagandist and Nazi to that of a noble and heroic victim of history. Essential viewing. German with English subtitles.
VHS: S23996. $89.95.
Laser: LD75388. $69.99.
Ray Mueller, Germany, 1993, 180 mins.

RAINER W. FASSBINDER

Ali: Fear Eats the Soul

A major film by Fassbinder, *Ali* is the outrageous, touching story of the bumpy love affair between a sixtyish German floorwasher and an inarticulate Arab mechanic barely half her age. A moving romance, a perverse social comedy, a biting drama of racial prejudice, *Ali: Fear Eats the Soul* is all these things, although in Fassbinder's freewheeling vision it is not always easy to tell where one leaves off and another begins. Winner of the International Critics Prize, Cannes Film Festival. German with enhanced English subtitles.
VHS: S11590. $79.95.
Rainer W. Fassbinder, Germany, 1974, 94 mins.

The American Soldier

Fassbinder's homage to Hollywood gangster films is updated for the seventies. Murder is still for sale, but crime is organized by the state, not by the mob. Ricky—hired first by the U.S. to fight in Vietnam, and now by the German police—follows orders to kill: kill soldiers, kill strangers, kill even his girlfriend. Although Ricky wears a soft fedora (as well as a white double-breasted suit), it is Fassbinder who tips his hat, with secondary characters named Walsh and Zimmerman. Stars Karl Scheydt, Fassbinder, Margarethe von Trotta and Kurt Raab. German with English subtitles.
VHS: S16498. $29.95.
Rainer W. Fassbinder, Germany, 1970, 80 mins.

Beware of a Holy Whore

Hanna Schygulla and Rainer Werner Fassbinder are both featured in this film about a doomed film production unit. Both the crew and cast are besieged by every conceivable problem in a luxurious seaside hotel. As they wait for the director to show up and the producer scrambles to procure more cash, they are forced to confront themselves and each other. German with English subtitles.
VHS: S24950. $79.95.
Rainer W. Fassbinder, Germany, 1970, 103 mins.

The Bitter Tears of Petra Von Kant

"A tragi-comic love story disguised as a lesbian slumber party in high-camp drag" (Molly Haskell), the film makes us a witness to the struggles for domination among three lesbians: a successful and "liberated" fashion designer, her contented and silent slave girl, and a sultry but cruel model who ends up making the master her slave. The dynamics of their interrelationships are played out in this claustrophobic, self-contained little world, accompanied only by the music of The Platters and Giuseppe Verdi. A riveting chamber drama of style. With Margit Carstensen, Hanna Schygulla, Eva Mattes and Irm Hermann. German with English subtitles.
VHS: S13914. $29.95.
Rainer W. Fassbinder, Germany, 1972, 124 mins.

Chinese Roulette

A brilliant social satire from the director of *The Marriage of Maria Braun*. When a businessman, his wife, and their lovers are forced by the couple's paraplegic daughter to participate in a rigorous game of truth-telling, latent hatreds within the family are revealed, speeding the way toward the film's shocking climax. Starring Anna Karina and Ulli Lommel. German with English subtitles.
VHS: S12821. $29.95.
Rainer W. Fassbinder, Germany, 1976, 96 mins.

Effi Briest

Fassbinder's masterpiece is the German *Madame Bovary*. Hanna Schygulla plays the inexperienced, beautiful and naive woman who marries a much older Prussian diplomat, falls prey to a charming, shrewd womanizer, and suffers the consequences of an unforgiving society. Beautifully shot in black and white with elegant framing, the film is both a very accurate adaptation of the novel by Theodor Fontane, and a critical re-analysis. With Wolfgang Schenck and Ulli Lommel. German with English subtitles.
VHS: S17620. $79.95.
Rainer W. Fassbinder, Germany, 1974, 140 mins.

Fox and His Friends

A lower-class carnival entertainer professionally known as Fox the Talking Head strikes it rich, after a life of hard knocks, by winning the lottery. His new-found wealth attracts an elegant bourgeois lover, who proceeds to vamp Fox as thoroughly and unthinkingly as Lola Lola or Theda Bara. This ill-fated romance between "the capitalist and the lottery queen" makes for one of Fassbinder's most skillfully wrought films, expertly evoking a brittle, upper-class gay milieu where, as one character puts it, "God's dressed up like Marlene Dietrich, holding his nose." German with English subtitles. Electronically subtitled.
VHS: S06443. $79.95.
Rainer W. Fassbinder, Germany, 1975, 123 mins.

Germany in Autumn

Eleven leading filmmakers collaborated on this protest against Fascist tendencies in West Germany by reflecting on the tragic events of Autumn, 1977, when public official Hanns Martin Schleyer was kidnapped and murdered by the Baader-Meinhof group, whose members mysteriously died in prison. The film's contents range from an elegiac sequence of the burial of the prisoners to newsreel clips of Rommel's cortege and a fictitious argument among TV executives about a controversial production of *Antigone*. In the amazing Fassbinder sequence, he interviews his mother, who first endorses the dictatorship and then physically abuses her boyfriend. The contradictions in the film "belong to one nation: only if all the country's contradictions are together, can you accept this history and understand it" (Alexander Kluge). Screenplay by Heinrich Boll and Peter Steinbach. Directed by Alf Bruseillin, Bernhard Sinkel, Rainer W. Fassbinder, Alexander Kluge, Beate Mainka-Jellinghaus, Maximiliane Mainka, Peter Schubert, Edgar Reitz, Katja Rupe, Hans Peter Cloos and Volker Schloendorff. Germany, 1978, 134 mins.
VHS: S20729. $29.95.
Werner Fassbinder, et al., Germany, 1978, 134 mins.

I Only Want You to Love Me (Ich Will Doch Nur, Dass Ihr Mich Liebt)

Fassbinder's striking tale of a young man's desire to be loved is the story of a man who is saddled with debts and troubled by his unfulfilling home life. In this dark melodrama, his wife and parents seem indifferent to him and to his pain. His unhappy life is significantly altered for the worse when, one night, in a drunken stupor, he kills a bar-keeper, mistaking him for his distant father. German with English subtitles.
VHS: S27665. $29.95.
Rainer W. Fassbinder, West Germany, 1976, 100 mins.

In a Year of Thirteen Moons

One of Fassbinder's most unusual and daring films, *In a Year of Thirteen Moons* stars Erwin Spengler as a man desperately in love with his business partner. He decides to have a sex change operation, becomes Elvira, but this fails to attract the love of his beloved. Instead, the new "she" finds a series of damaging relationships and betrayals. Fassbinder uses harsh color, asymmetrical sets, a dissonant sound track and alternating narrative techniques to evoke the pain of Erwin/Elvira in a film that stretches the boundaries of conventional storytelling. German with English subtitles.
VHS: S23998. $79.95.
Rainer W. Fassbinder, Germany, 1979, 129 mins.

A Man Like Eva

A film based on the life of Rainer Werner Fassbinder, the enfant terrible of the new German cinema. Eva Mattes, one of Fassbinder's own stars, is Fassbinder (in drag) in this film in what Vincent Canby in *The New York Times* called "A stunning performance…a blood-curdling homage…a hypnotic, unorthodox, appropriately paean to Fassbinder, the great German filmmaker who died in 1982." German with English subtitles.
VHS: S06589. $79.95.
Radu Gabrea, Germany, 1983, 92 mins.

The Marriage of Maria Braun

Hanna Schygulla stars in Fassbinder's spectacular weaving of soap opera, comedy, history, politics and social satire into a lucid whole. Maria marries Hermann Braun the night before he is called to the front in WWII Germany. Soon he's believed to be dead, and Maria starts working her way up through the bedrooms of the social elite. When her husband suddenly returns, a fight ensues and she ends up clobbering her lover to death. At the American war trial, Hermann accepts blame and prison sentence, while Maria is left to deal with her uncertain pregnancy and promiscuous nature in this darkly humorous metaphor for the German post-war national spirit. German with English subtitles.
VHS: S01909. $79.95.
Rainer W. Fassbinder, Germany, 1979, 120 mins.

Merchant of Four Seasons

A climax in the prolific career of Rainer Werner Fassbinder. The story, that of a fruit peddler who watches his unexceptional life disintegrate, sounds like a slice-of-life melodrama gone slightly amok, but the treatment is everything; a virtuoso balance of soap opera, social comedy, irony, politics, farce and brilliant ensemble acting. German with English subtitles. With Irm Hermann, Hanna Schygulla.
VHS: S12467. $79.95.
Rainer W. Fassbinder, Germany, 1972, 88 mins.

Mother Kusters Goes to Heaven

A major Fassbinder film. Mother Kusters finds herself suddenly widowed. Her husband was a factory worker who one day goes berserk, killing the boss' son and throwing himself into the machinery. Her daughter, a would-be chanteuse, moves in with a muckraking journalist to further her career. Soon the dead man's life is distorted throughout pages of a cheap tabloid. Fassbinder paints a world where the honest and the good fall prey to a system of corrupt media and politics, a world where only small kindnesses carry relief to overwhelming suffering. German with English subtitles.
VHS: S16695. $79.95.
Rainer W. Fassbinder, Germany, 1975, 108 mins.

Querelle

Brad Davis, Jeanne Moreau and Franco Nero star in Rainer Werner Fassbinder's final film, adapted from Jean Genet's great novel, *Querelle de Brest*. The film focuses on a beautiful but callous and tough young French sailor whose beauty and heartlessness both attract and repell all who meet him. English dialog.
VHS: S01080. $19.95.
Rainer W. Fassbinder, Germany/France, 1982, 106 mins.

Satan's Brew

Kurt Raab stars as a would-be poet and revolutionary whose imagination overreaches his talents. Forced into betrayal, he hurts those around him and ultimately starts to believe that he is the reincarnation of the 19th century German romantic poet Stefan George. This black comedy is a biting satire about the cult of the individual artist. German with English subtitles.
VHS: S24949. $79.95.
Rainer W. Fassbinder, Germany, 1976, 112 mins.

Shadow of Angels (Schatten der Engel)

Rainer Werner Fassbinder collaborated with director Daniel Schmid on this film adaptation of Fassbinder's controversial play *The Garbage, the City and Death*. Much controversy surrounded one character in particular: a Jewish businessman (Klaus Lowitsch), who is always referred to as "the rich Jew." Ultimately, the story is more concerned with the outsider status of this businessman and the prostitute (Ingrid Caven) whom he hires to listen to him (and, on occasion, to perform in a mock wedding ceremony). Both find themselves out of place in a milieu dominated by prostitutes, pimps, corrupt policemen and perverse businessmen. Fassbinder appears as the prostitute's sadistic, gay pimp. German with English subtitles.
VHS: $27664. $29.95.
Daniel Schmid, West Germany/Switzerland, 1976, 105 mins.

The Stationmaster's Wife

Elisabeth Trissenaar is the bored wife whose flamboyant affairs epitomize the fake bourgeois morality and buried social and political resentments within German society. Her pleasant, attentive husband (Kurt Raab) is no match for the succession of oppressive lovers she falls prey to. Fassbinder dramatizes this through a Sirkian deployment of bold, ironic colors, brisk melodrama and tight framing. With Bernard Helfrich, Karl Heinz-von Hassel and Udo Kier. German with English subtitles.
VHS: $18933. $79.95.
Rainer W. Fassbinder, Germany, 1977, 113 mins.

Why Does Herr R. Run Amok?

Herr R., a likable office worker with a family, calmly picks up an ornate lamp one evening and bludgeons to death his wife, child and neighbor. One of Fassbinder's most notorious films, full of brilliant insights into the loneliness of existence, the terrors and anxieties of middle-class life. With Lilith Ungerer, Amadeus Fengler, Franz Maron and Hanna Schygulla. German with English subtitles.
VHS: $20306. $79.95.
Rainer W. Fassbinder, W. Germany, 1969, 87 mins.

WERNER HERZOG

Aguirre: The Wrath of God

"One of the great, mad, passionate, foolhardy masterpieces—as reckless and as brilliant as *Greed* or *Apocalypse Now*" (Roger Ebert). Shot on location in the Amazon, Klaus Kinski is Aguirre searching for El Dorado—the mythical City of Gold. German with English subtitles.
VHS: $00025. $59.95.
Werner Herzog, Germany, 1972, 94 mins.

Fitzcarraldo

Herzog's saga of an impressario's obsession to bring his own opera boat up the Amazon River and over a mountain into Peru where he will have Caruso sing features Klaus Kinski, Claudia Cardinale, in a legendary production made against impossible odds. English dialog.
VHS: $00446. $69.95.
Werner Herzog, Germany, 1982, 157 mins.

Heart of Glass

Werner Herzog's brilliant, sensual, hypnotic film about the magical and desperate attempts of the people in a small village to learn the formula for making special glass, supplied by a wandering herdsman with extraordinary powers. An apocalyptic movie with stunning imagery (cinematography by Jorg Schmidt-Reitwin) that achieves a mystical, surreal power. With Josef Bierbichler, Stefan Guttler, Clemens Scheitz, and Sepp Muller. Music by Popol Vuh. German with English subtitles.
VHS: $17397. $79.95.
Werner Herzog, West Germany, 1976, 94 mins.

Herdsmen of the Sun

Herzog's fascination with the natural world at its most enduringly strange led him to the southern Sahara for *Herdsmen of the Sun*, "a startling anthropological documentary about the nomadic members of the Wodaabe Tribe" (Janet Maslin). Once a year, the men decorate themselves with beads and blue lipstick and festive hats to participate in what amounts to a beauty pageant. French, English and Peul with English subtitles.
VHS: $16054. $59.95.
Werner Herzog, Germany, 1988, 52 mins.

The Mystery of Kaspar Hauser

In 1828, a young man appeared in the town square of Nuremberg, his origins unknown, having apparently been kept in solitary confinement all his life; five years later he was murdered by an unidentified assailant. Kaspar's brief, enigmatic destiny becomes a powerful metaphor for life in Werner Herzog's vision of the extreme edges of existence. Former mental patient Bruno S. delivers a sympathetic and powerful performance. "Herzog achieves a visionary, overcast style" (Pauline Kael, *The New Yorker*). Also known as *Every Man for Himself and God against All*. With Walter Ladengast, Brigitte Mira, Hans Musaus and Willy Semmelrogge. German with English subtitles.
VHS: $20303. $79.95.
Werner Herzog, W. Germany, 1974, 110 mins.

Signs of Life

The breakthrough first feature from Werner Herzog. A young German soldier is stationed on a small Greek island, cut off from the larger traumatic events of the Second World War. The island's beauty tempts him with the promise of peace, but ultimately he cannot accept the potential of this enchanting place. German with English subtitles.
VHS: $26146. $69.95.
Werner Herzog, Germany, 1968, 90 mins.

Stroszek

The adventures of Herzog's alter-ego, Bruno S., continue as a former mental patient and Berlin street singer joins with a whore and an aging eccentric to emigrate to Wisconsin in search of the American dream. "Surprisingly positive, tragicomic, poetic narrative" (Leonard Maltin). With Eva Mattes and Clemens Scheitz. English and German with English subtitles.
VHS: $12826. $79.95.
Werner Herzog, Germany, 1977, 108 mins.

Where the Green Ants Dream

Two tribes of Aborigines, the Wororas and the Riratjingus, preserve their ancient legends, songs and laws of creation in the heart of Australia. They come into conflict with the laws of modern Australia when a large company tries to mine uranium in one of their holy places, the place where the "Green Ants Dream." With Bruce Spence, Wandjuk Marika, Roy Marika. English dialog.
VHS: $07103. $24.95.
Werner Herzog, Germany/Australia, 1985, 99 mins.

Woyzeck

Woyzeck represents one of the most extraordinary events in the history of literature. Written in 1836, just before its author's death at the age of 23, Buchner's drama anticipates by some 50 to 100 years the literary movements of the 20th century. Herzog's version of *Woyzeck* is a film without shadows. This caustic tragedy of an ordinary man's headlong plunge into madness and murder is filmed with a terrible clarity, punctuated by bursts of unexpected lyricism. In the title role, Klaus Kinski delivers a harrowing and unforgettable performance, as stark and unsentimental as the razor with which the hero carries out his chilling destiny. With Eva Mattes. German with English subtitles.
VHS: $12989. $59.95.
Werner Herzog, Germany, 1978, 82 mins.

WIM WENDERS

Faraway, So Close

Otto Sander, Nastassia Kinski, Willem Dafoe and Peter Falk are joined by Lou Reed as himself and a Mikhail Gorbachev look-alike for another angel's view of Berlin. When an angel loses his wings, the temptations of earthly life inevitably tempt Satan and lead to bad memories and gangster inspired violence. English and German with English subtitles.
VHS: $21353. $94.95.
Laser: LD74473. $39.95.
Wim Wenders, Germany, 1993, 146 mins.

Notebook on Cities and Clothes

A provocative documentary by Wim Wenders about high fashion designer Yohji Yamamoto. The film is frequently a passionate and compelling essay about a time (Paris), architecture, language and the creative process. Made during the editing of Wenders' epic *Until the End of the World*. Shot by several cameramen, including Wenders' usual collaborator Robby Muller. Japanese, German, French and English with English subtitles.
VHS: $18192. $59.95.
Wim Wenders, France, 1990, 80 mins.

Paris, Texas

A film by German director Wim Wenders, written by Sam Shepard, photography by Robby Muller, music by Ry Cooder and starring Harry Dean Stanton and Nastassia Kinski! A contemporary story of a man's journey, actual and psychological, to recover his past.
VHS: $00993. $19.98.
Wim Wenders, USA, 1984, 145 mins.

Until the End of the World

Wim Wenders filmed this epic, futuristic drama in fifteen cities in eight countries around the world. The year is 1999. Solveig Dommartin, the enchanting trapeze artist from *Wings of Desire*, pursues William Hurt, who helped himself to stolen money she was guarding for some very nice criminals. She also just might be in love with the mysterious Hurt who is on a secret mission for Max Von Sydow, his even more mysterious father who lives in an underground laboratory in the middle of Australia. Also along for the global chase are boyfriend Sam Neill, and detectives Rudiger Vogler and Ernie Dingo. This ambitious work explores the potential end of the world and the incredible power of our dreams. The tape is presented in a letter-boxed format with Surround Sound and employs state-of-the-art High-Definition video technology.
VHS: $16633. $19.98.
Laser: LD71505. $34.98.
Wim Wenders, France/Germany/Australia, 1991, 178 min.

Wings of Desire

"The first time I saw the film I thought it was a knockout; on second viewing it already seemed a classic," wrote J. Hoberman of Wim Wenders' re-examination of the divided city of Berlin. Damiel, played by Bruno Ganz, is the angel who has grown tired and frustrated at his inability to affect people's lives. When he falls in love with a beautiful trapeze artist, he decides to leave the heavens and enter the mortal world. With incredible cinematography by Henri Alekan, *Wings of Desire* is one of the rare movies of the past decade that actually stretch, break and re-form the boundaries of the medium" (David Denby, *New York Magazine*). German with yellow English subtitles.
VHS: $09593. $19.98.
Wim Wenders, Germany, 1988, 110 mins.

german CLASSICS

Backstairs
A first-rate example of German Expressionist cinema in the story of a maid who is having an affair with a man who disappears one day without warning and leaves her waiting anxiously for a letter from him. With Henry Porten, Fritz Kortner and William Dieterle. Silent.
VHS: S03344. $29.95.
Leopold Jessner, Germany, 1921, 44 mins.

Barcarole
The remarkable Edwige Feuillere stars as a young man who accepts a wager to seduce a married woman. The plot backfires when he finds himself in love and has to accept the penalty of death rather than betray her. An early film in color. German *without* English subtitles.
VHS: S24129. $29.95.
Gerhard Lamprecht, Germany, 1935, 78 mins.

Baron Munchausen
Only the fourth color film made in Germany, *Munchausen* employs a wide range of sensational special effects which amaze and amuse in the recounting of the adventures of the legendary hero Baron von Munchausen. The action ranges from Venice to St. Petersburg to the moon and back, as the Baron (Hans Albers) travels by horse, balloon and cannonball. The film was recently reconstructed by the Friedrich Murnau Foundation. German with English subtitles.
VHS: S00097. $69.95.
Josef von Baky, Germany, 1943, 110 mins.

Berlin, Symphony of a Great City
Walter Ruttmann's great documentary is a dynamic vision of Berlin, unfolding from dawn until midnight. Ruttmann captured the city's expressive poetry by concealing his camera in vans and suitcases to capture a portrait of the city and its people. Music composed and conducted by Timothy Brock, performed by the Olympia Chamber Orchestra. On the same program is *Opus 1*, a ten-minute essay Ruttman shot in 1922.
VHS: S01931. $24.95.
Walter Ruttmann, Germany, 1927, 62 mins.

Black Roses
Near the end of her life, Lilian Harvey asked to see only one of her films, *Black Roses*. A search of the major archives turned up nothing, and she was never again to see her favorite work. Set in 1900's Russia, Harvey (a ballerina) must sleep with the Tsarist governor in order to save the life of her true love. Dennis Hoey also stars. Mastered from the only known nitrate print. Produced in Germany in 1935, and then remade in Germany and Great Britain in 1936.
VHS: S10964. $29.95.
Paul Martin, Germany/Great Britain, 1936, 79 mins.

Blue Light
A painter falls in love with a young girl whom the villagers fear as a witch because only she can reach the dangerous mountain peak. When the painter discovers her secret route, she jumps off a cliff. Riefenstahl's first film as director was shot on location and emphasizes the romantic mysticism of the mountains and the transmuting power of nature. The film so impressed Hitler he asked her to make films for the Nazis. Co-scripted by Bela Balasz. German with English subtitles.
VHS: S00159. $29.95.
Leni Riefenstahl, Germany, 1932, 77 mins.

Blum Affair
An important postwar German film, directed by Erich Engel. On the surface a fast-paced exciting thriller, the film reveals the whole horrible relation of fascism, business and anti-Semitism in Germany of the late 20's. An unemployed man kills an accountant for money. He is caught, brought to a police inspector who, it turns out, served in the same *Freikorps* regiment—the murdered man worked for Blum, a Jewish industrialist, who perhaps knew something of tax fraud at the company. The case becomes a right versus left political drama. With Hans Christian Blech, Gisela Trowe, Kurt Ehrhardt. German with English subtitles.
VHS: S06853. $39.95.
Erich Engel, Germany, 1948, 109 mins.

The Broken Jug
Based on the immensely popular comedy by Heinrich von Kleist about a village judge who has his own sense of dispensing justice during the 18th century, this classic production features Emil Jannings, Angela Salloker and Paul Dahlke, and was adapted by Thea von Harbou. German with English subtitles.
VHS: S24126. $29.95.
Gustav Ucicky, Germany, 1935, 82 mins.

Cabinet of Dr. Caligari
The great Expressionist classic with Werner Krauss as Caligari, the fairground showman who hypnotizes his servant (Conrad Veidt) into committing murder at night. Famous for its distorted painted sets, its grotesque camera angles and its atmospheric horror, this cinematic landmark is now newly mastered from a 35mm archive print with an orchestral score. English intertitles.
VHS: S10765. $29.95.
Laser: LD75516. $49.99.
Robert Wiene, Germany, 1919, 52 mins.

Captain from Koepenick
A big success, this German comedy about a cobbler, who in order to free himself from the dehumanizing effects of petty bureaucracy on the common man impersonates an army officer, is a funny social satire. German with English subtitles.
VHS: S06442. $39.95.
Helmut Kautner, Germany, 1957, 88 mins.

Cesare Borgia
The bloodthirsty reign of Cesare and Lucrezia Borgia is at the center of this long-lost, silent classic film. Conrad Veidt plays one of the descendants of Pope Alexander VI. This ruthless historical character is said to have murdered several people, including his own brother Juan Borgia, and to have committed incest with his sister Lucretia. This careful psychological study of these figures is a thought-provoking examination of greed, lust and evil. Silent with English intertitles.
VHS: S21608. $24.95.
Richard Oswald, Germany, 1923, 83 mins.

Clothes Make the Man
Heinz Ruhmann stars in this Nazi-era feature adapted from a novella by Gottfried Keller about the adventures of a young seamstress in a small town during the Victorian period and her encounters with a tailor who is so well dressed that he's mistaken for a count. Produced in 1940, the film is a rare example of the kind of escapist filmmaking in Nazi Germany. German with English subtitles.
VHS: S24122. $29.95.
Helmut Kautner, Germany, 1940

The Confessions of Felix Krull
Horst Buchholz stars as the charming but devious con-artist who quickly rises in rank as a Parisian hotel employee. A rarely seen adaptation of the famous Thomas Mann novella. Directed by Kurt Hoffman. German with English subtitles.
VHS: S15440. $29.95.
Kurt Hoffman, Germany, 1958, 107 mins.

Congress Dances
Delightful operetta set during the 1815 Congress of Vienna, banned by the Nazis because many of the members of the production crew were Jewish. The film is a fine example of early German sound movie-making. Lilian Harvey plays an ambitious businesswoman who sees potential for financial and romantic opportunities. German with English subtitles.
VHS: S02220. $29.95.
Erik Charell, Germany, 1931, 92 mins.

Day of Freedom—Our Fighting Forces (Tag Der Freiheit)
Leni Riefenstahl (*Triumph of the Will*) directs this propaganda documentary on the armed forces of Nazi Germany. Military parades, lots of flags and leaders. Planes fly in a swastika formation. This short film was thought to have been lost. No dialog or narration. Original music score.
VHS: S05504. $19.95.
Leni Riefenstahl, Germany, 1935, 17 mins.

The Day the Sky Exploded
A science fiction spectacular about a missile that explodes in outer space, causing general chaos and an impromptu asteroid shower. Dubbed in English.
VHS: S14669. $24.95.
Paolo Heusch, Germany, 1957, 80 mins.

Der Untertan (The Subject)
Werner Peters and Erich Nadler star in this rarely seen film from post-war Germany. Directed by Wolfgang Staudte. German with English subtitles.
VHS: S15439. $29.95.
Wolfgang Staudte, Germany, 1951

Devil in Silk
This intense psychological thriller concerns a composer who unknowingly marries a fatally jealous woman. In the end he must try to prove to the police that he is innocent when she turns up dead. Dubbed in English.
VHS: S23800. $24.95.
Rolf Hansen, Germany, 1956, 102 mins.

Diary of a Lost Girl
Louise Brooks appears as an innocent girl whose life collapses when she is made pregnant by her father's young assistant. In this follow-up to *Pandora's Box*, Brooks is just as riveting. Unavailable in the U.S. for over 50 years until its theatrical reissue in 1983, this is the most complete version in existence. Piano and jazz ensemble score.
VHS: S00339. $29.95.
G.W. Pabst, Germany, 1929, 100 mins.

Die Deutsche Wochenschau #1 (The German Weekly Newsreel)
Four newsreels from Nazi Germany are presented in this collection now available on video. Combat footage of the Luftwaffe over Greece and Crete. Winter fighting in Finland and Russia. U-Boats in the North Atlantic. Also fabric being made from waste paper. German with no subtitles. WWII as seen from another viewpoint. Germany, 1941, 50 mins.
VHS: S5500. $24.95.

Die Goldene Stadt
Veit Harlan, the notorious Nazi-era director, and Alfred Braun are responsible for this film about a young girl who lives in a small village and dreams of visiting Prague. Her father won't let her go; he wants her to marry Thomas, a noble German farmer boy. With Krista Soderbaum and Rudolf Prack. One of the most interesting examples of entertainment and propaganda under the Nazis. German *without* English subtitles.
VHS: S24128. $29.95.
Veit Harlan, Germany, 1942

Don Quixote
An extremely rare and beautiful film directed by G.W. Pabst (*The Threepenny Opera*) and based on the Cervantes novel. The film, a British production, was shot in Haute-Provence in France, and features the great Russian actor Feodor Chaliapin as well as George Robey and Sidney Fox. Of particular note are Pabst's sequences of tilting at the windmills.
VHS: S06857. $39.95.
G.W. Pabst, Great Britain/France, 1933, 83 mins.

Ecstasy
This unjustly neglected film has suffered from the notoriety of its nude scene with Hedy Lamarr: the Pope denounced it, Hitler banned it, American distributors censored it and Hedy's millionaire German munitions maker husband tried to buy up all the prints and destroy them. Hedy plays a child bride with an impotent husband who has an affair but refuses to go away with her lover when the husband commits suicide. Notable for its use of location sound and its very stylish, lyrical eroticism and images that beg psychoanalytic interpretation. Minimal English dialog.
VHS: S00394. $19.95.
Gustav Machaty, Germany, 1932, 75 mins.

The Eternal Waltz
A candid, forthcoming and fascinating biography of the brilliant composer Johann Strauss, the so-called Waltz King. This German-made work is set off by its stylish decor, elaborate sets, haunting music and excellent performances from Bernhard Wicki, Hilde Krahl and Annemarie Dueringer. 97 mins.
VHS: S17451. $19.95.
Paul Verhoeven, Germany, 1954, 98 mins.

Fahnen Junker
From bayonet fighting to blasting bunkers, glacier climbing to sniper fire, here is the tough training that molded the leaders of Nazi armies. This original 1943 Nazi film depicts the life at German schools for infantry officers. 17 mins. German with English subtitles.
VHS: S08313. $24.95.

Fortune's Fool
Germany's most famous pre-war actor, Emil Jannings, stars in this film about an uneducated butcher who emerges in the chaotic years after World War I to control the meat-packing industry. Silent.
VHS: S01658. $29.95.
Reinhold Schunzel, Germany, 1923

Friedemann Bach
This war-time, escapist feature is the rather bizarre story of the eldest son of J.S. Bach, Friedemann. He is a gifted musician, but feels so confined by his autocratic family that he ends up wasting his talent. His life ends tragically, in debauchery and penury. With Gustaf Gundgrens and Eugen Klopfer. German with English subtitles.
VHS: S26065. $29.95.
Traugott Muller, Germany, 1941, 100 mins.

Germany Awake
A documentary on the German motion picture and its use as a tool for propaganda, produced by the great German film historian Erwin Leiser. Among the many feature film excerpts included in this film are *Dawn* (1933), *Jew Suss* (1940), *The Rothschilds* (1940), *The Great King* (1942), and others. English commentary and German with English subtitles.
VHS: S03357. $34.95.
Erwin Leiser, Germany, 1968, 90 mins.

Girl from Flanders
Maximilian Schell, Nicole Berger and Gert Frobe star in this anti-war drama. Schell is a lieutenant sickened by the realities of war, who finds solace in a young woman. She is a Belgian who detests the German soldiers in her country until she meets this special man. Dubbed in English.
VHS: S23988. $24.95.
Helmut Kautner, Germany, 1956, 91 mins.

The Golem
Based on the ancient Jewish legend of the clay figure created by Rabbi Loew in the 16th century to defend the Jews in the Prague ghetto against pogrom. In this great classic famous for its extraordinary crowd scenes and painted sets, the Golem falls in love with the Rabbi's daughter, terrorizes the emperor's court and is subdued by an innocent child. "The alternately terrified and exultant crowd at times recalls the flamboyant outlines and disjointed movement of a painting by El Greco" (Lotte Eisner). With Paul Wegener, Albert Steinbruck and Lyda Salmonova. Silent with music track, English titles.
VHS: S00514. $29.95.
Paul Wegener/Carl Boese, Germany, 1920, 118 mins.

Homecoming
Joe May's *The Homecoming* was a big success in America, and much of the credit goes to the visionary producer behind this film, as so many other films of the German Expressionist era, Erich Pommer. The story of the film concerns the escape and arduous trek home of two German POW's from a Russian labor camp. Strong performances from Gustav Frolich (Metropolis) and Lars Hanson, as well as Dita Parlo (L'Atalante) as the young wife who welcomes home the wrong man. Silent with English titles.
VHS: S07756. $29.95.
Joe May, Germany, 1928, 74 mins.

The Island of Bliss
A rare production with sets created by the great Max Reinhardt. Directed by Arthur Kahane, this silent film is presented with an accompanying music track. Germany, 1913.
VHS: S15438. $29.95.

Joyless Street
Famous as the film that brought Greta Garbo to international fame, *Joyless Street* draws a powerful depiction of the deteriorating life of the middle class in Austria during the inflationary years. A landmark of the German silent cinema by one of its greatest talents, the film produces "moments of searing pain, mental anguish, and sheer unblemished beauty" (Paul Rotha, *The Film till Now*). Restored with material from the State Museum Munich and Cinematheque Francaise, this version is longer and closer to the original than any available in the U.S. until now. Piano score.
VHS: S01924. $29.95.
G.W. Pabst, Germany, 1925, 96 min.

Kolberg
Commissioned by the Reich Propaganda Minister to "demonstrate…that a people united at home and at the front will overcome the enemy," this bizarre project is based on the resistance of the city of Kolberg to the advance of Napoleon's armies in 1806 and 1807. As the city's military leaders are willing to capitulate, the Mayor sends his father to ask the Queen of Prussia for help while he organizes the citizens into a militia. Goebbels reportedly hoped that *Kolberg* would rival *Gone with the Wind* in grandeur, and so no expense was spared. Ten thousand uniforms were constructed for the film, 200,000 soldiers were withdrawn from service to take part in battle scenes, and trainloads of salt were sent to create snow for several scenes. Ironically, a few days after *Kolberg* opened in the city of Kolberg, Soviet troops entered the city. German with English subtitles.
VHS: S02254. $79.95.
Veit Harlan, Germany, 1945, 99 mins.

The Love of Jeanne Ney
G.W. Pabst's adaptation of Ilya Ehrenberg's novel about Jeanne Ney (Edith Jehanne), a beautiful young German woman who falls in love with the man (Uno Henning) responsible for her father's murder during the Russian Revolution. They marry and resettle in Paris, where they are hounded by an extortionist (Fritz Rasp). With Brigitte Helm. English intertitles.
VHS: S02193. $24.95.
G.W. Pabst, Germany, 1927, 120 mins.

Ludwig II
A penetrating and lively account of the rise and fall of the Bavarian monarch couched between extremes of dream and illogic, with stunning use of Bavarian locations, landscape and architecture. With O.W. Fischer, Ruth Leuwerik and Marianne Koch. German only, with no English subtitles.
VHS: S17230. $39.95.
Erich Kautner, Germany, 1955, 109 mins.

Luis Trenker
A three-part biography of the German actor, producer, novelist and director, using the occasion of his 95th birthday to portray his first break into films, his political persecution, his Hollywood exile, his return to Germany and his continued involvement in the arts. German *without* subtitles.
Part I. 60 mins.
VHS: S17235. $29.95.
Part II. 60 mins.
VHS: S17236. $29.95.
Part III. 60 mins.
VHS: S17237. $29.95.

Luis Trenker Films
Luis Trenker, one of the most prolific and well-known directors, producers and actors of the German sound era, has remained almost unknown in the West until a "Trenker Revival," at the Telluride Film Festival. This collection of Trenker films is now available in German *without* English subtitles.
Der Berg Ruft. Tonio Carrl, an Italian, and Edward Whymer, an Englishman, both want to be the first to climb the Matterhorn. During one attempt, Whymer has an accident, and Tonia saves his life. Later, during another attempt, Wymer gets to the top a few hours before Tonio, but during the descent, three of Whymer's men are fatally injured and Whymer is accused of cutting the rope to save his life. Again, Tonio comes to his rescue. 1937, 95 mins. German *without* English subtitles.
VHS: S07990. $69.95.
Der Feuerteufel. A historical drama about Prussian and Austrian soldiers who fight against Napoleon. A wood cutter from Kaernten becomes a freedom fighter who battles the French Army and the hatred of his compatriots. 1940, 98 mins. German *without* English subtitles.
VHS: S07991. $49.95.
Der Kaiser von Kalifornien. A Luis Trenker film about the pioneering days of the old American west. The story of the Swiss printer Johann Sutter, who settled as a farmer in unknown California, and on whose land gold was first discovered, starting the California gold rush. 1936, 95 mins. German *without* English subtitles.
VHS: S07985. $49.95.
Der Rebell. Luis Trenker stars in this classic patriotic drama, set in 1809. The freedom-loving mountain dwellers of Tyrol are banding together to fight Napoleon's troops, who have overrun their homeland. When Severin Anderlan, one of their own, comes home from the university, he joins them and fights the oppressors to the bitter end. 92 mins. German *without* English subtitles.
VHS: S07987. $69.95.
Der Sohn der Weissen Berge. Hans Turri, the German skiing champion, also works as an Alpine guide. He trains with his comrades for the coming championships, when, just a few days before the event, an engineer named Milacs hires him as a guide. When Turri returns without Milacs, Turri is suspected of murder. Set in the beautiful Swiss Alps. 1930. German *without* English subtitles.
VHS: S07983. $69.95.
Der Verlorene Sohn. Prodigal son story about Tonio, a native son of the Dolomite mountain region, who is catapulted to New York City at the time of the Great Depression. Just as he hits bottom, an old friend discovers and rescues him. Despite his new-found luxury and the affection of his friend's daughter, Tonio returns to his village, his people, and his girl. 90 mins. German *without* English subtitles.
VHS: S07989. $69.95.
Duell in den Bergen. A suspenseful Alpine drama set in the Dolomites. A border patrol officer is sent to a village in the Dolomites to infiltrate a group of dangerous drug smugglers, and a bitter battle erupts between the police and the villains. German *without* English subtitles. 1950.
VHS: S07984. $69.95.
Flucht in die Dolomiten. Luis Trenker and Marianne Holt star in this drama about Giovanni, a family man, who is under suspicion of having killed his brother. He flees his hometown to work at a construction site high up in the Dolomites. Hard and dangerous work are in store for him, but also temptation in the form of a beautiful local girl. His tribulations end when he returns home and learns that he is cleared of the murder charges. 1955, 87 mins. German *without* English subtitles.
VHS: S07988. $69.95.

Im Banne des Monte Miracolo. The Monte Miracolo is reputed to be a cursed mountain, since up to now all attempts to conquer it have failed and resulted in tragedy and death. When two Dutch men succeed in climbing the bewitched mountain for the first time, the spell seems to be broken. Now two engineers who work in the village also plan to climb the mountain, one of whom is experienced and cautious, the other reckless. 85 mins. German *without* English subtitles.
VHS: S07986. $69.95.

Maedchen in Uniform
Legendary film from the German post-Expressionism period, extremely daring for its time in suggesting lesbianism in the story of a young girl whose identity is choked by the authoritarian boarding school she attends. German with English subtitles.
VHS: S02140. $24.95.
Leontine Sagan, Germany, 1931, 87 mins.

Men Against Tanks/ Engineers to the Front
A Nazi-produced documentary, as German soldiers re-enact combat exploits for this elaborate and frightening film showing how infantrymen battle Soviet armored attacks. In *Engineers to the Front*, German engineer/soldiers—the men who paved the way for the blitzkrieg—lift mines, build bridges and force river crossings under fire. 58 mins. German with English subtitles.
VHS: S08312. $39.95.

Morgenrot
The grim reality of World War I is the subject of this rare film, produced just before Hitler's ascension to power, which tells the story of a German U-boat and its crew in the struggle against the might of England's sea power. An uncertain blend of pacifism and patriotism, the submarine's sinking of a British cruiser leads to sympathy for the lives of the drowned enemy sailors among family members of the U-boat back in Germany, as the film reflects the changing values in post-war Germany. Rudolf Forester and Adele Sandrick star. German *without* English subtitles.
VHS: S07982. $49.95.
Gustav Ucicky, Germany, 1933, 75 mins.

My Song Goes 'Round the World
The British title of *The Joseph Schmidt Story*, this is the last film done in Germany by the prolific director Richard Oswald. Starring Joseph Schmidt and Charlotte Anders. German with English subtitles.
VHS: S02933. $39.95.
Richard Oswald, Germany, 1934

The Old and the Young King
Emil Jannings stars in this elaborate historical drama about the conflict between Frederick William I of Prussia, whose only love is for his army, and his young and brilliant son, Frederick the Great. German with English subtitles.
VHS: S24124. $29.95.
Hans Steinhoff, Germany, 1935, 88 mins.

Olympia: Festival of Beauty
Part Two of Riefenstahl's extraordinary film about the 1936 Olympics. Engrossingly beautiful, the film provides a glimpse of the Nazi mystique and idealization of the youthful male body. English dialog.
VHS: S00955. $19.95.
Leni Riefenstahl, Germany, 1936, 97 mins.

Olympia: Festival of the People
Leni Riefenstahl was given unlimited resources and full artistic freedom to produce this film of the 1936 Olympic Games in Berlin. *Festival of the People* is Part One. Famous sequences include the men's diving competition, Jesse Owen's sprint races and Riefenstahl's use of telephoto lenses and slow motion. English dialog.
VHS: S00956. $19.95.
Leni Riefenstahl, Germany, 1936, 115 mins.

Orphan Boy of Vienna
Wonderful schmaltz in this story of an orphan boy who is fortunate enough to be accepted by the famous Vienna Choir Boys and finds there the maternal love he lacked in the person of Sister Maria. German with English subtitles, 87 mins.
VHS: S03343. $29.95.

Pandora's Box
G.W. Pabst's baroque interpretation of Wedekind's *Lulu* plays is an eerie depiction of erotic obsession and sexual abandon. The action moves between Berlin and London, as Lulu (Louise Brooks), a beautiful, charismatic chorus girl, orchestrates a succession of casual affairs until her fateful encounter with Jack the Ripper. With Fritz Kortner, Franz Lederer and Carl Goetz. Silent with music track. English titles.
VHS: S00990. $24.95.
G.W. Pabst, Germany, 1928, 110 mins.

Paracelsus
An interesting film directed by G.W. Pabst, unfortunately not available in a subtitled version. Paracelsus is named the head physician of Basel and orders the city gates to be closed against the plague. He heals the dancer Fliegenbein of the plague, but the authorities don't approve of his healing methods, seek to arrest him, and Fliegenbein helps Paracelsus escape. German *without* English subtitles.
VHS: S07981. $49.95.
G.W. Pabst, Germany, 1943, 100 mins.

The Phoney American
Also known as *Toller Hecht Auf Krummer Tour* and *It's A Great Life*, William Bendix, Christine Kaufmann and Ron Randell star in this charming comedy about a German orphan raised by a masquerading air force pilot. Bendix is great as a blustery but ultimately kind-hearted sergeant. German with English subtitles.
VHS: S23901. $29.95.
Akos Von Ratony, Germany, 1961, 74 mins.

Rebel Flight to Cuba
This gem is the inspiration behind the 70's Airport disaster/ comedy film. A priest, a minister, a rabbi, an unhappy rich countess, a quibbling couple, a Nazi fugitive and a pregnant woman are just some of the characters that provoke inane subplots and love triangles. The supercool hero even chain smokes. Dubbed in English.
VHS: S22470. $29.95.
Gottfried Reinhardt, Germany, 1959, 90 mins.

Romance in a Minor Key
A wartime feature, this escapist drama stars Marianne Hoppe and Paul Dahlke in the story of a husband who discovers that his wife has somehow acquired a very valuable pearl necklace. A rare example of master filmmaking under the Nazi regime. German with English subtitles.
VHS: S24120. $29.95.
Helmut Kutner, Germany, 1943

Sacred Mountain/White Flame
Two famous short films by director Riefenstahl. Tremendous music and dance sequences, as well as fluid camera shots of idyllic natural settings. Silent with English subtitles. Music track.
VHS: S01146. $34.95.
Leni Riefenstahl, Germany, 1931, 60 mins.

Secrets of a Soul
A professor is driven into a state of terror by a dream in which he attempts to stab his wife, in this remarkable Expressionist feature, which uses Freud's theories of psychoanalysis to depict the professor's dreams. Superimpositions, symbolic images of razors and knives and menacing shadows create a demented world. With Werner Krauss and Jack Trevor. Silent with music track, English intertitles.
VHS: S03701. $19.95.
G.W. Pabst, Germany, 1926, 94 mins.

Shattered
One of the key films of the German *kammerspiel* movement, this silent work chronicles the tragic repercussions of a furtive love affair between a railway worker's daughter (Edith Posca) and her father's apprentice (Werner Krauss). "This grim, small-scale film…is sparse, naturalistic, dealing in a minimum number of characters and observing the unities of time, place and action" (*The Faber Companion to Foreign Films*). With Paul Otto.
VHS: S19598. $39.95.
Lupu Pick, Germany, 1921, 62 mins.

Stop Train 349 (Delay at Marienborn)
Sean Flynn, Jose Ferrer and Nicole Courcel are featured in this thriller. Aboard an American train going from Berlin to the Western Zone is an East German stowaway. The Russians find out and try to stop the train, setting off a battle between the Commies and the good guys.
VHS: S23323. $24.95.
Rolf Hadrich, Germany/Italy/France, 1963, 92 mins.

Street
Classic drama inaugurated an entire series of German films, known as street films, which explore the allures and dangers of city life. Remarkable for its expressionistic lighting, photography, and hallucinatory images of crowds, fireworks, and autos. Silent.
VHS: S01268. $29.95.
Karl Grune, Germany, 1923, 87 mins.

The Student of Prague (1913)
One of the earliest, most important films in the history of silent German cinema, the film incorporates the myths of the Doppelganger, the Faust legend and the shattered mirror image; often considered the first film to incorporate Expressionist means. Silent with English intertitles.
VHS: S01274. $29.95.
Stellan Rye, Germany, 1913, 45 mins.

The Student of Prague (1926)
Conrad Veidt stars in this haunting tale about an unscrupulous student in the mysterious Czech capital. He is intrigued by that which the devil offers him and decides to sell his soul. Germany, 1926, 84 mins. Silent with English intertitles.
VHS: S23850. $24.95.

The Threepenny Opera (1931)
Lotte Lenya plays Jenny in this famous adaptation of Bertolt Brecht/Kurt Weill's play, freely based on John Gay's *Beggar's Opera*. In London at the turn of the century the best friend of a police chief, the bandit Mack the Knife, marries Polly without the knowledge of her father, Peachum, the king of the beggars, and thus starts a conflict between the beggars and the thieves. A newly remastered version. German with English subtitles.
VHS: S21186. $39.95.
G.W. Pabst, Germany, 1931, 114 mins.

The Threepenny Opera (1962)
A lively adaptation of the famous Brecht/Weill musical. This popular version stars Curt Jergens, Gert Frobe, Hildegard Knef and, believe it or not, Sammy Davis, Jr. In English.
VHS: S14661. $29.95.
Wolfgang Staudte, Germany/France, 1962, 124 mins.

Tiefland
Based on the libretto for D'Abert's opera, Riefenstahl directs and plays a gypsy dancer. Filmed largely between 1940 and 1945, Riefenstahl worked slowly to avoid working on any political films. Released successfully in 1954. German with English subtitles.
VHS: S01343. $34.95.
Leni Riefenstahl, Germany, 1940-45, 98 mins.

Triumph of the Will
Enormously controversial film record of a Nazi party solidarity rally at Nuremberg in 1934, crafted by Riefenstahl in her second directorial assignment. A fascinating lesson in the methods used by the Nazis to inspire national support. German with English subtitles.
VHS: S18194. $29.95.
Leni Riefenstahl, Germany, 1936, 80 mins.

Under the Bridge
This 1945 German feature is the story of two bargemen on the River Havel who falls in love with the same woman. With Carl Raddatz, Gustav Knuth and Hannelore Schroth. German with English subtitles.
VHS: S24121. $29.95.
Helmut Kautner, Germany, 1945

Variety
A guided tour through the decadence of postwar Germany, with Emil Jannings as an acrobat, Lya de Putti as his wife, and Werner Krauss, a famous acrobat who seduces the wife and drives the acrobat to suicide. German with English subtitles.
VHS: S01408. $29.95.
E.A. Dupont, Germany, 1925, 79 mins.

Warning Shadows
Directed by Arthur Robinson, an American who lived and worked in Germany during the 1920's, *Warning Shadows* is one of the famous examples of Expressionist cinema. Paul Rotha described the film, which is the story of a count bitterly jealous of his wife, as "a remarkable achievement. Its purely psychological direction, its definite completeness of time and action, its intimate ensemble were new attributes of the cinema. It was a rare instance of complete filmic unity." Extremely rare. Silent with music track.
VHS: S03345. $29.95.
Arthur Robinson, Germany, 1922, 60 mins.

Waxworks
Starring three of Germany's greatest actors of the silent period, *Waxworks* creates a fantastic atmosphere through curiously deformed lighting effects. A poet sees wax figures at a fair and dreams about Jack the Ripper, Ivan the Terrible and an Oriental despot. Silent.
VHS: S01432. $29.95.
Paul Leni, Germany, 1924, 63 mins.

Westfront 1918
The life and death of four German soldiers on the French front during the final months of World War I. One of the finest war films ever made, it has little dialog but tremendous use of natural sounds. German with no subtitles.
VHS: S03702. $29.95.
G.W. Pabst, Germany, 1930, 98 mins.

The White Flame
Leni Riefenstahl, the famed German filmmaker from the Nazi era, also made a number of fascinating silent films. This is one. It falls within that uniquely German genre, the Mountain film, and concerns ski racing. English intertitles.
VHS: S23854. $24.95.
Leni Riefenstahl, Germany, 1921, 30 mins.

White Hell of Pitz Palu
An extremely rare film by G.W. Pabst made at the end of the silent era, and a unique obsession with the German obsession during the 20's with idealized mountain films that "were both brilliant documentaries and first-rate melodramas, with very definite if embryonic propaganda content. They were the inspiration and largely the monopoly of Dr. Arnold Fanck, a former geologist who translated his great passion for the mountains into film….The White Hell of Pitz Palu was the last of the great silent German mountain films, and one of the best and most successful. Most of the film was shot under freezing conditions and other hardships during a five-month location trip to the 12,000 foot high Pitz Palu, in the Bernina group of the Alps" (William Everson). Complete with alternate ending. Silent with English titles. At 24 fps.
VHS: S11450. $24.95.
G.W. Pabst/A. Fanck, Germany, 1929, 95 mins.

Wilhelm Tell
Conrad Veidt stars in this extremely rare, silent German adaptation of the famous story of William Tell, his fight for freedom and his shooting of the apple. William Dieterle, later to become a Hollywood director, appears as an actor in a secondary role. Silent with German and English intertitles.
VHS: S21610. $24.95.

Woman Men Yearn For
A rare and virtually unclassifiable 1928 German silent film with Marlene Dietrich as a beautiful and beguiling temptress. A recently married man falls in love with a woman he sees on a train and gets tangled in a web of murder. With German title cards, though the narrative is simple to follow.
VHS: S17692. $49.95.
Curtis Bernhardt, Germany, 1929

FRITZ LANG

Big Heat
Classic film noir from Fritz Lang. Ruthless criminals, an honest cop, sultry women and a gripping plot are the elements that make up *The Big Heat*. Glenn Ford stars in Lang's best postwar film, with Lee Marvin as a nasty bad guy and a fine performance by Gloria Grahame as his shallow but wily moll.
VHS: S00130. $59.95.
Fritz Lang, USA, 1953, 90 mins.

Cloak and Dagger
Gary Cooper confronts a maze of intrigue behind enemy lines in World War II Nazi Germany. A tense drama with great performances. With Lilli Palmer. English dialog.
VHS: S03502. $59.95.
Laser: LD71456. $29.98.
Fritz Lang, USA, 1946, 106 mins.

Destiny
Lang's first critical success, also known as *Between Two Worlds* or *Beyond the Wall*, an allegory about a confrontation between Death and a girl's love and devotion. Lang here reveals his mastery of the medium, particularly in the architectural design in the film. Silent.
VHS: S00327. $29.95.
Fritz Lang, Germany, 1921, 95 mins.

Dr. Mabuse, the Gambler, Part I
An exciting thriller and social commentary about the evil machinations of the criminal mastermind Mabuse, who in his drive for power manipulates his victims and battles a tenacious investigator. Silent.
VHS: S00363. $29.95.
Fritz Lang, Germany, 1922, 120 mins.

Dr. Mabuse, the Gambler, Part II
Part II, known as *The Inferno*, continues the story of the evil Dr. Mabuse and his attempts on the life of the public prosecutor. The state of upheaval in the world at the time is clearly manifested in the depiction of the police attack on Mabuse's house. Silent.
VHS: S00364. $29.95.
Fritz Lang, Germany, 1922, 122 mins.

Dr. Mabuse, the Gambler, Parts I & II
The set.
VHS: S05400. $59.90.
Fritz Lang, Germany, 1922

The Fatal Passion of Dr. Mabuse
Dr. Mabuse was Lang's super-villain, master of disguise, hypnosis, and deception, who created evil for evil's sake. This Lang's own condensed version of his original two-part epic.
VHS: S05958. $29.95.
Fritz Lang, 1922, Germany, 90 mins.

Fury
Fritz Lang's first Hollywood film after fleeing Nazi Germany is a powerful indictment of mob violence in America. Lang includes some real footage of a 1934 lynching, making *Fury* a frightening document as well as a compelling melodrama. Spencer Tracy portrays a gas station owner who, by a series of coincidences, is accused of a kidnapping and becomes the target of an angry mob which attempts to lynch him and eventually burns down the jailhouse. With Sylvia Sidney and Walter Brennan.
VHS: S15026. $19.98.
Fritz Lang, USA, 1936, 89 mins.

House by the River
One of Lang's favorite themes was the ruinous effect of a man's lust for a woman. In *House by the River*, a man kills his maid and implicates his own brother in the crime. With Louis Hayward and Lee Bowman.
VHS: S00586. $29.95.
Fritz Lang, USA, 1950, 88 mins.

Kriemhilde's Revenge
The second part of Fritz Lang's *Die Nibelungen* focuses on the hero's widow and her attraction to Attila the Hun. Kriemhilde (Margarete Schon) conspires with Attila to invite Gunther (Theodor Loos) and Hagen (Hans Adalbert Schlettow)—her husband's killers—to a banquet that ends up in a bloodbath. Film critic and director Luc Moullet wrote, "The climax is a long battle lasting three-quarters of an hour with encirclements and identical attacks, defenses against the encirclements, and renewed attacks. Lang creates shots with different details and builds a rhythm of variations. It is [at] the same time vehement, dynamic and the opposite." Remastered from a 35mm archive print; organ score.
VHS: S00693. $24.95.
Laser: CLV. LD72004. $29.98.
Fritz Lang, Germany, 1924, 90 mins.

Liliom
Fritz Lang, in his first film in exile from Nazi Germany, teamed up with Franz Waxman and Charles Boyer under the producer Erich Pommer in this rare fantasy, the story of a lowlife carnival barker who is given a second chance to help his family after his own death. The film was released in the U.S. in a version cut by 30 minutes, but this is the un-cut, French release version, un-subtitled, but with the story easy to follow. French with no English subtitles.
VHS: S08336. $39.95.
Fritz Lang, France, 1935, 120 mins.

M
A series of schoolgirls are murdered by a psychopath who terrorizes a large city and is hunted by the police through a network of beggars. Inspired by the real-life "vampire of Dusseldorf," Fritz Lang's great film is one of the key films of German Expressionism. Peter Lorre's performance as the murderer is one of the great screen performances of all time. German with English subtitles.
VHS: S00787. $29.95.
Fritz Lang, Germany, 1931, 95 mins.

Metropolis
A newly mastered version of Fritz Lang's great masterpiece, the first classic of the science fiction genre. His depiction of a giant city controlled by an authoritarian industrialist who lives in a paradise-like garden while the workers live and struggle in subterranean sections of the city was as important for its vision of man in the service of those who control technology as for its implicit and moving social message. "A brilliant piece of expressionist design…with moments of almost incredible beauty and power" (Pauline Kael). Silent with music score.
VHS: S10764. $29.95.
Fritz Lang, Germany, 1926, 90 mins.

Moonfleet
Lang's only feature shot in Cinemascope. Set in Dorset in 1770, a young orphan discovers his guardian is actually a black marketeer who leads a gang of ruthless smugglers. The film is set off by Lang's eye for expressive photography and baroque decor. With Stewart Granger, Jon Whiteley, George Sanders and Joan Greenwood. Letterboxed.
Laser: LD70007. $34.98.
Fritz Lang, USA, 1955, 87 mins.

The Return of Frank James
An early color work by Fritz Lang in his second collaboration with Henry Fonda (*You Only Live Once*), who returns from his role in the 1939 *Jesse James* in this mythic, unsettling and poetic western about a man's determination to avenge his brother's murder. With Gene Tierney, Jackie Cooper and Henry Hull.
VHS: S02368. $14.98.
Fritz Lang, USA, 1940, 92 mins.

Scarlet Street
A great film noir thriller. Edward G. Robinson is the little store cashier who becomes infatuated with and eventually kills a whore (Joan Bennett) and then allows her pimp boyfriend (Dan Duryea) to be executed for the crime. Based on Jean Renoir's *La Chienne* (1931); one of Lang's best works, with brilliant cinematography of New York at night by Milton Krasner.
VHS: S01166. $19.95.
Fritz Lang, USA, 1945, 105 mins.

Secret Beyond the Door
A Freudian psycho-thriller about a husband, obsessed by the connection between architecture and death, who collects rooms where murders have been committed and adds them to his mansion. Fascinating. With Joan Bennett and Michael Redgrave.
VHS: S01172. $19.98.
Fritz Lang, USA, 1948, 99 mins.

Siegfried
The first part of Fritz Lang's *Die Nibelungen*. *Siegfried* concerns one man's heroic efforts to slay an imposing dragon in order to capture the hand of the King's beautiful sister. "*Siegfried* is dominated by architectural structures that often reduce the characters to decorative elements against landscapes or vast buildings. Lang's decorative compositions seem often like frozen bits of life, as if any movement would disturb the geometry" (Georges Sadoul, *Dictionary of Films*). Organ score. Nine of the ten reels of this version were transferred in color from an original tinted print. English intertitles.
VHS: S01198. $24.95.
Laser: CLV. LD72030. $29.98.
Fritz Lang, Germany, 1924, 100 mins.

Spiders
Considered by many to be the real beginning of the golden age of German silent film, Fritz Lang's adventure story is about an organized band of criminals who scheme to dominate the world. Combining a labyrinth of plots with actual exotic locations, Lang succeeded in creating a highly entertaining film, which was reconstructed over a three year period by film historians David and Kimberly Shepard, using original German censorship records and Lang's own instructions for color tinting. Silent with music track.
VHS: S08945. $29.95.
Fritz Lang, Germany, 1919, 137 mins.

Spies (Spione)
Produced just after his epic *Metropolis*, Fritz Lang's *Spies* continues the director's fascination with futuristic technology, expressionistic design and sweeping adventure. Agent #326, Donald Tremaine, leads an army of government operatives in a last ditch effort to destroy the ruthless plans of Haghi, a wheelchair-bound, criminal mastermind whose goal is no less than world domination. Laced with stunning plot twists, seductive femme fatales and an arsenal of imaginative gadgetry, *Spies* was the first true spy movie.
VHS: S01240. $29.95.
Fritz Lang, Germany, 1928, 88 mins.

Testament of Dr. Mabuse
Although confined to a mental institution, the arch-criminal Dr. Mabuse uses his hypnotic powers to operate his plan for world domination. He is finally defeated by Inspector Lohmann (who hunted Peter Lorre in *M* just the year before). Mabuse's mouthing of Nazi platitudes and Lang's depiction of him were too close for comfort, and Joseph Goebbels asked him to change the last reel, offering him leadership of the German film industry. Instead, Lang left his wife (Thea von Harbou, who had by then joined the Nazi party) and fled Germany overnight. German with English subtitles.
VHS: S04915. $24.95.
Fritz Lang, Germany, 1933, 75 mins.

The Thousand Eyes of Dr. Mabuse (Eyes of Evil)
The last film of Fritz Lang spawned more sequels to the character of the master criminal he created in his early films. In this low-budget classic Gert Frobe (*Goldfinger*) is investigating the mysterious murders in the Hotel Luxor in Berlin, which is filled with hidden cameras and two-way mirrors. With Dawn Addams, Peter Van Eyck and Wolfgang Preiss. Dubbed in English. B&W.
VHS: S07075. $39.95.
Fritz Lang, France/Italy/W. Germ., 1960, 103 mins.

Western Union
A great film, and one of the very best Westerns. Fritz Lang directed Robert Young, Randolph Scott, Dean Jagger, Virginia Gilmore in the complex story about the pioneer progress of telegraphic communication across Indian country from Omaha to Salt Lake City. Based on a Zane Grey novel.
VHS: S11192. $39.98.
Fritz Lang, USA, 1941, 90 mins.

Woman in the Moon
Probably the most realistic expedition to the moon prior to 1969, Fritz Lang's great science fiction epic is based on a melodramatic script by Lang and his wife Thea von Harbou. Much of it deals with the conflicts among the crew of the rocket on its way to the Moon. But the real stars are the imaginative sets, special effects and expressive photography, which incorporates work by the pioneer animator Oskar Fischinger, with such prophetic details as multi-stage rockets, weightlessness and the first countdown! Silent with music score, English titles.
VHS: S01476. $29.95.
Fritz Lang, Germany, 1929, 148 mins.

The Woman in the Window
Edward G. Robinson stars as a naive college professor whose research into criminal behavior leads him to a chance acquaintance with a beautiful woman, Joan Bennett, which, in turn, leads to murder and blackmail. This tense melodrama has a sinister feel nicely offset with intriguing psychological motifs and is often seen as a companion piece to Lang's *Scarlet Street*. Raymond Massey is also featured.
VHS: S27749. $19.98.
Fritz Lang, USA, 1944, 99 mins.

FRIEDRICH MURNAU

City Girl
An extremely rare film by Friedrich Murnau, made during his tenure in Hollywood. Originally made as a silent film under the title *Our Daily Bread*, it was shortened by Fox, the producers, and a soundtrack added, then released in 1930 under the title *City Girl*. The film, often compared favorably with *Sunrise*, was shot by Ernest Palmer, and revolves around the intertwined lives of wheat farmers. Silent, music track.
VHS: S02088. $39.95.
Friedrich W. Murnau, USA, 1928, 89 mins.

Faust
Murnau's last German production before going to Hollywood is a lavish one, inspired by Romantic painters like Caspar David Friedrich. Gosta Ekman is the elderly professor who sells his soul to the devil, Emil Jannings plays Mephistopholes and Camilla Horn is Marguerite. This version is mastered from a restored print. Silent with music track, English intertitles.
VHS: S00437. $29.95.
Friedrich W. Murnau, Germany, 1926, 117 mins.

Haunted Castle
An early Expressionist horror/mystery, set in a northern German castle shrouded in a moody atmosphere. The complicated plot involves disguises, jealousies, forbidding dreams and murders. Silent with music track.
VHS: S00547. $34.95.
Friedrich W. Murnau, Germany, 1921, 56 mins.

The Last Laugh
One of the major works of German silent cinema, Murnau's class drama depicts the fall of the respected, aging, hotel doorman (Emil Jannings) of a posh Berlin hotel, who is cruelly stripped of his position and reduced to a bathroom attendant. The film was groundbreaking for its expressive, mobile camera work, which imparts information visually, without subtitles. "The camera on a trolley glides, rises, zooms, or weaves where the story takes it. The camera takes part in the action and becomes a *character* in the drama" (Marcel Carne). With Max Hiller, Maly Delschaft and Hans Unterkirchen.
VHS: S00723. $24.95.
Laser: Includes new orchestral score. LD72446. $49.95.
Friedrich W. Murnau, Germany, 1924, 91 mins.

Nosferatu
One of Murnau's best known films, *Nosferatu*'s eerie telling of the Dracula story was filmed on location in the mountains, towns, and castles of Bavaria. This German Expressionist symphony of horror is brilliantly infused with the subtle tones of nature: both pure and fresh, as well as twisted and sinister. Newly restored and color tinted, this version was remastered from a 35mm negative and includes recently discovered scenes and inter-titles freshly translated from the original German script. At 84 minutes, it is the most complete version available on home video.
VHS: S15038. $29.95.
Laser: LD71827. $39.95.
Laser: CLV. LD72010. $29.98.
Friedrich W. Murnau, Germany, 1922, 84 mins.

Sunrise
Although this was Murnau's first Hollywood film, he scripted it with Carl Mayer while still in Germany. The story concerns the marriage of a peasant couple whose honeymoon in the big city is detoured by a sultry seductress. But the film is neither trite nor melodramatic; Murnau's sets and camera angles imbue the images with a poetic lyricism that reveals the characters' psychological state. Easily his most perfect film, Murnau's *Sunrise* was named the "Greatest film of all time," in a recent *Cahiers du Cinema* Critic's Poll. With George O'Brien, Janet Gaynor and Margaret Livingston.
VHS: S07782. $29.95.
Friedrich W. Murnau, USA, 1927, 97 mins.

Tabu
Filmed entirely in Tahiti, *Tabu* represents an unusual collaboration between legendary directors F.W. Murnau and Robert Flaherty. Combining Flaherty's poetic sense of the native people with Murnau's strong filmic sensibilities, the film tells the story of two lovers doomed by a tribal edict decreeing the beautiful princess as "tabu" to all men. "Murnau is one of the great masters. The beautiful restoration of *Tabu* will enable future generations to enjoy and appreciate his inspiring talent" (Martin Scorsese). Silent with music track.
VHS: S03712. $39.95.
Laser: CLV/CAV. LD71591. $34.95.
Friedrich W. Murnau/Robert Flaherty, USA, 1931, 82 mins.

Tartuffe
F.W. Murnau's (*Nosferatu, Last Laugh*) brilliant adaptation of Moliere's play *Tartuffe* features the great Emil Jannings in a larger-than-life portrait of the classic hypocrite. Silent, English inter-titles, organ score. Carl Mayer adapted Moliere's play for the screen. With Lil Dagover, Luise Hoflich and Werner Krauss as Orgon.
VHS: S26969. $24.95.
Friedrich W. Murnau, Germany, 1925, 70 mins.

GERMAN SIGHTS & SOUNDS

Berlin
This documentary examines the social, political and cultural significance of Berlin, remade in the post-communist, post-Wall atmosphere. With a 64-page travel guide. 60 mins.
English Narration.
VHS: S19844. $39.95.
German Narration.
VHS: S19845. $39.95.

Berlin: Journey of a City
This documentary from the Armed Forces Radio and Television Service tells the story of the city at the epicenter of the Cold War. Beginning with the Allied Occupation in 1945, the film shows the Berlin Airlift and the rise and fall of the infamous Berlin Wall. 60 mins.
VHS: S27636. $19.95.

Best of Nightline: East Germany Opens Its Borders
30 mins.
VHS: S14061. $14.98.

Discover Germany!
A look at Rhineland vineyards, medieval castles, World War II relics, Mad Ludwig's fairy tale castle and Munich's Oktoberfest. 60 mins.
VHS: S23347. $29.95.

Fall of the Berlin Wall
This major symbol of the division between East and West came tumbling down in November 1989. See for yourself history in the making in this West German television documentary that covers the wall's construction and destruction.
VHS: S14002. $59.95.
Peter C. Schmidt, W. Germany, 1990, 49 mins.

German TV Commercials
A collection of TV commercials, prepared by one of the world's leading ad agencies, provides a wonderful insight into contemporary German culture. Features automobile, soap, cereal, cheese, computer and many other products. Includes script. 25 mins.
VHS: S04946. $49.95.

The German Way of Life
Today a new Germany is emerging from the effects of two World Wars and Cold War partition. Germans discuss the effects of this tumultuous history and the role their country played in these momentous events. 25 mins.
VHS: S23706. $129.95.
Laser: LD74788. $149.95.

Germany, A Tapestry of Tradition
West Germany is the land of castles and kings, cathedrals and alpine peaks. Become enveloped in the quiet mystery of the Black forest. Watch a craftsman carve a violin in the village of Mittenwald, and continue on to the awe-inspiring Gothic cathedrals of Wurzburg, Ettal and Nymphenburg. The fairytale castle of Neuschwanstein, built by the eccentric King Ludwig II, comes alive. Join in the Oktoberfest celebration. 55 mins.
VHS: S10769. $24.95.

Illusions
A Brechtian art piece about performance and spectacle by the German chanteuse Ute Lemper. In an intimate concert setting, she performs cabaret songs made famous by Marlene Dietrich and Edith Piaf, including "La vie en rose", "Falling in Love Again" and "Non, je ne regrette rien". 102 mins.
VHS: S19107. $29.95.
Laser: LD71896. $39.95.

Michael Nyman Songbook: Ute Lemper
Filmmaker Volker Schlondorff directs the gifted singer Ute Lemper in her stylish performances of songs by Michael Nyman. The songs are inspired by a letter from Mozart, two texts from Rimbaud and six songs by Paul Celan, the German poet whose themes touch on the moral resonance for a Holocaust survivor. 54 mins.
VHS: S19752. $29.95.
Laser: LD71961. $29.95.
Volker Schlondorff, Germany, 54 mins.

Oktoberfest in Munich
This program provides an opportunity to experience the joy, wonder, laughter, song and community spectacle of Oktoberfest. 30 mins.
English Narration.
VHS: S19855. $65.00.
German Narration.
VHS: S19856. $65.00.

Romantic Road
This magical journey into the world of *Siegfried* and the *Lorelei* offers a compelling introduction to the cultural, artistic and historical significance of traditional German life. 25 mins.
English Narration.
VHS: S19793. $39.95.
German Narration.
VHS: S19792. $39.95.

Then They Came for Me: Intolerance in Modern Germany
Have the horrific excesses of the Third Reich changed Germany into a more tolerant nation? This video shows startling signs of intolerance and suppression unleashed by contemporary upheavals. The end of Communism and the falling of the Berlin Wall have unleashed both hope and fear among Germans, resulting in a growing call for order. 50 mins.
VHS: S26764. $24.95.

AUSTRIAN CINEMA

38: Vienna Before the Fall
Oscar-nominee for Best Foreign Film, "one of the most powerful dramas ever made on the Holocaust...emotionally wrenching, charged with vivid insights" (David Sterritt, *Christian Science Monitor*), an impassioned film about love and political responsibility set against the background of a society on the brink of disaster. With great performances from Sunyi Melles and Tobias Engel. German with English subtitles.
VHS: Out of print. For rental only.
Laser: CLV. LD70266. $39.95.
Wolfgang Gluck, Austria, 1987, 97 mins.

First Love
Based on Turgenev's story, the bittersweet, sensitive study of a 16-year-old boy who becomes infatuated with an impoverished princess during a time of social upheaval. A moving, sensual love story with Schell, Dominique Sanda and John Mouler Brown. English dubbed.
VHS: S00445. $29.95.
Maximilian Schell, Austria, 1966, 90 mins.

The Inheritors
Walter Bannert exposes the terrifying resurgence of neo-fascist groups as 16-year-old Thomas is drawn into a neo-Nazi youth group in contemporary Austria. Winner of numerous Festival prizes, *The Inheritors* is a terrifying psychological study.
Dubbed Version.
VHS: S03952. $19.95.
Subtitled Version.
VHS: Out of print. For rental only.
Walter Bannert, Austria, 1984, 89 mins.

Invisible Adversaries
"A winning combination of sexual frankness and visual wit," wrote J. Hoberman in *The Village Voice*; "Funny, violent, sexual...It makes you reconsider what you and everyone else is doing in life and in art," said Amy Taubin in *Soho Weekly News*. Set in contemporary Vienna, Valie Export's controversial feature has been called a feminist *Invasion of the Body Snatchers*. Anna (Susanne Widl), a Viennese photographer, discovers that extra-terrestrial beings are colonizing the minds of her fellow citizens by raising the human aggression quotient. The outer world immediately becomes disjointed, but the inner world does too, as Anna and her love (Peter Weibel) try to hang onto their deteriorating relationship. A unique and totally original work by Austria's foremost filmmaker, *Invisible Adversaries* is at once philosophical and funny, psychologically revealing and sexually frank—"a witty and visually brilliant essay on gender and experience, culture and environment" (National Film Theatre, London). German with English subtitles.
VHS: S10414. $59.95.
Valie Export, Austria, 1977, 112 mins.

Menschenfrauen
Valie Export's daring film about relationships, *Menschenfrauen* (loosely translated, "humanwomen"), focuses on Franz S., a journalist, and his relationship with four women: the kindergarten nurse Petra, the teacher Gertrude, barmaid Elisabeth and his wife Anna. Franz "doles out honorary pieces of himself to the 'human women' in his seraglio, whispers the same assurances. Eventually, everyone catches on and makes some effort toward independence" (Gary Indiana, *East Village Eye*). "A landmark film...Valie Export achieves in *Menschenfrauen* what Godard strove for but failed in his *Every Man for Himself*—a human view of a woman's place in a man's world...From credits to close, *Menschenfrauen* eludes conventional cinematic vision..." (Seattle Film Festival). German with English subtitles.
VHS: S10416. $59.95.
Valie Export, Austria, 1980, 100 mins.

The Practice of Love
"A dazzling cinematic tour-de-force, combining a thriller narrative with experimental images to tell the story of Judith, a journalist, whose investigation of a murder implicates her two male lovers (an arms dealer and a psychiatrist). Through these relationships, Judith discovers that in a world of male power struggles, love is complicit, marginal or impossible. The film makes a stunningly coherent indictment of male-dominated society." (National Film Theatre, London). Valie Export is "one of the five or six truly original filmmakers working in Europe today who have not been recognized widely and turned into classical 'auteurs,' and this is why each of her films seems initially disturbing, jarring, 'difficult' " (Gary Indiana, *East Village Eye*). German with English subtitles.
VHS: S10415. $59.95.
Valie Export, Austria, 1984, 90 mins.

Requiem for Dominic
Romania, 1989. The anti-communist revolution is erupting into a vicious war. Amid the mob violence, political exile Paul Weiss struggles to learn the fate of a childhood friend, Dominic Paraschiv—only to discover that his wounded comrade has been confined like an animal, accused of the terroristic murder of 80 innocent workers. Based on a true story, this film plunges the viewer into the turbulence of a drama ripped from today's headlines. "The most remarkable political thriller since *Z*" (*Variety*). German with English subtitles.
VHS: S15390. $14.95.
Robert Dornhelm, Austria, 1990, 90 mins.

The Seventh Continent (Der Siebente Kontinent)
This challenging, widely acclaimed film by Austrian filmmaker Michael Haneke is based on a true story. It charts the unusual progress of a family that seems utterly conventional: life holds no challenge or interest for them—they simply go through the motions of living. *The Seventh Continent* unsentimentally records their descent into despair and joint suicide. Modern life emerges as the ultimate culprit in this obsessive tale of extreme indifference. German with English subtitles.
VHS: S26527. $89.95.
Michael Haneke, Austria, 1989, 111 mins.

Symphony in the Mountains
A light romance about a public school teacher who teaches singing and skiing instead of the regular advice of his superiors, falls in love with the sister of one of his students. Featuring songs by the Vienna Boys' Choir. German with English subtitles. Austria, 1935, 75 mins.
VHS: S03356. $49.95.

AUSTRIAN VIEWS

Austria, The Land of Music
Begin your Austrian tour in Salzburg, birthplace of Mozart. Take in the magnificent view of the High Alps outside Heiligenblutt and continue on to Vienna, where coffee houses and elegant shops abound. Attend a concert by the famed Vienna Boys Choir, then travel to the Danube wine district, where the harvest is in progress. 55 mins.
VHS: S10768. $24.95.

Touring Austria
The history, intrigue, romance, opera, festivals, old world grandeur of Austria: the Schoenbrunn and Hofburg palaces, St. Stephen's Cathedral, and the Vienna Boys' Choir. Cruise the Danube, walk the Olympic town of Innsbruck, the Tyrol, the forests and medieval castles of Styria. Glide over the Alps, visit Piber, where the Lippizaner stallions are bred, and gaze at mountainous scenery from the Orient Express. 60 mins.
VHS: S09914. $29.95.

Vienna
Subtitled *The Spirit of the City*, this program explores the character and soul of this amazingly city, a kaleidoscopic vision captured from 20 minutes of motion footage and more than 15,000 still images, and the music of Mozart, Beethoven and Strauss.
Laser: LD70312. $124.95.

Vienna 1900
In 1900 Vienna appeared to be the most carefree place in the world. But beneath this polished surface, the seeds of unrest had been sown by a famous group of disgruntled thinkers including Sigmund Freud, Arnold Schoenberg and Gustav Klimt. *Vienna 1900* explores the lost pleasures of the glittering old empire and the revolution in thought that would change the world forever. 60 mins.
VHS: S11762. $39.95.

scandinavian CINEMA

Babette's Feast
Stephane Audran is Babette, an exiled French cook-housekeeper for a pair of devoutly religious, elderly Danish sisters. When she wins a lottery she asks to prepare a Gallic feast for the women and their friends to show her appreciation. Based on the short story by Karen Blixen (Isak Dinesen). Winner of Academy Award. Danish with English subtitles.
VHS: S08497. $19.98.
Laser: LD70850. $39.95.
Gabriel Axel, Denmark, 1987, 102 mins.

Blueprint for a Million
Gunnar Hellstrom is featured in this surprising portrait about a pair of criminals recently escaped from jail. One of the pair, Erick, realizes he must change his life. Just one last caper should give him the wherewithal to leave crime behind for good. The ending is a surprise to everyone concerned. Dubbed in English.
VHS: S24016. $24.98.
Hasse Ekman, Sweden, 1966, 82 mins.

Children of Nature
Academy Award nominee for Best Foreign Film, *Children of Nature* is an enchanting love story about an elderly farmer, now in an old-age home, who is reunited with his childhood sweetheart. Together, they rekindle the passion of their youth and set off on an incredible adventure. Icelandic with English subtitles.
VHS: S20574. $89.98.
Fridrik Thor Fridriksson, Iceland, 1993, 85 mins.

The Count of the Old Town
Ingrid Bergman plays the role of Elsa Edlund, the daughter of a woman who owns a small bachelor hotel. Against this backdrop of the old city of Stockholm, the film develops as a thriller about the gang of crooks and booze smugglers who hide out at the hotel. See beautiful Ingrid in her early days. Swedish with English subtitles.
VHS: S15065. $19.98.
E. Adolphson/S. Wallen, Sweden, 1935, 104 min.

The Doll
A night watchman has one of the loneliest jobs in the world. In this psychologically unsettling film from Arne Mattson, the watchman-hero decides to liven up his boring hours by borrowing some shapely mannequins from the department store which he guards at night. The other folks in his rooming house take a dim view of this flesh-and-wood romance, however, and tragedy looms as the only alternative." With Per Oscarsson. Swedish with English subtitles.
VHS: S07750. $29.95.
Arne Mattson, Sweden, 1962, 94 mins.

Dollar
Ingrid Bergman stars in this rare pre-war Swedish melodrama about three married couples who are confronted by an American millionairess, Miss Johnstone, with their dishonesty and deceit. Swedish with English subtitles,
VHS: S12448. $19.98.
Laser: CLV/CAV. LD70272. $39.95.
Gustaf Molander, Sweden, 1938, 74 mins.

Dreaming of Rita
A surreal story centered on a young mother named Rita (played by the engaging Marika Lagercrantz), who bears a striking resemblance to the haunting Rita Hayworth. When her mother dies, her widowed father becomes obsessed with finding his lost love, the Rita for whom his daughter was named, who also resembles the Hollywood icon. Mixing comic concepts, this screwball romantic comedy is funny, lyrical, and even contemplative. This film also manages to comment on both child rearing and parental responsibility. Swedish with English subtitles.
VHS: S26797. $59.95.
Jon Lindstrom, Sweden, 1994, 108 mins.

The Element of Crime
Winner at the Cannes Film Festival, and a supremely stylish (and terrifying) thriller. Shot entirely in sepia tone, Michael Elphick plays the cop assigned the Lotto Murders—a diabolical slaughter of little girls. Elphick is a man traumatized by grotesque memories of post-nuke Europe, as in the futuristic nightmare *Blade Runner*, and in his ongoing madness, becomes obsessed with the criminal mind. In English.
VHS: S12279. $79.95.
Lars von Trier, Denmark, 1988, 104 mins.

Elvira Madigan
A modern classic. Elvira (Pia Degermark) is a tightrope artist, and Sixten Sparre (Thommy Berggren), an aristocratic army officer who abandons a promising career for a rapturous affair with Elvira. In the idyllic Swedish countryside they are promptly ostracized for breaking the moral code and the film ends tragically. Lyrical, nostalgic and moving, with beautiful use of Mozart's *Piano Concerto No. 21*. Swedish with English subtitles.
VHS: S00404. $24.98.
Laser: CLV. LD70966. $39.95.
Bo Widerberg, Sweden, 1967, 95 mins.

Emma's Shadow
Emma, the willful and lonely 11-year-old daughter of a cold aristocratic family in the 1930's, runs away by staging her own kidnapping. She stumbles into an unlikely friendship with an ex-convict sewer worker memorably played by Borje Ahlstedt of *Fanny and Alexander*. This story of the deep trust and love which bonds these social opposites is told with spirit and style, while the handsome cinematography richly evokes the period. Danish with English subtitles.
VHS: S14069. $19.98.
Soeren Kragh-Jacobsen, Denmark, 1988, 93 min.

Friends Forever
A teenage boy's sexual confusion becomes a catalyst for change in this tender and unpredictable first feature. Kristian, a shy 16-year-old, is starting a new school. An uncertain conformist, he is irresistibly drawn to the two boys who dominate his class. Henrik, whose unyielding independence defies his androgynous sexual charisma, and Patrick—blond, boisterous and moody—who leads a tyrannical band of troublemakers. The boys' friendship instills self-confidence in Kristian, but their relationship is soon put to the test.
VHS: S15821. $69.95.
Stefan Christian Henszelman, Denmark, 1986, 95 mins.

Girl in a Swing
Meg Tilly plays a mysterious German secretary who captures the interest of Rupert Frazer, a repressed, middle-aged, English antiques dealer. He learns it is always better to know a little something about a potential spouse before you get married.
VHS: S12147. $89.99.
Gordon Hessler, Denmark, 1989, 112 mins.

Good Evening Mr. Wallenberg
A moving and sensitive portrait of Raoul Wallenberg, the heroic Swedish businessman who saved thousands of Jews from extermination in Nazi-dominated Hungary. Despite his amazing courage and luck in his self-appointed mission, his own fate remains a mystery. Swedish with English subtitles.
VHS: S20647. $19.98.
Kjell Grede, Sweden, 115 mins.

Gorilla
This Swedish documentary/drama grafts the story of a white hunter and a beautiful Swedish photographer on to some fascinating documentary footage. See dancing Watusis, pygmies in the jungle, elephants, rhinos, snakes, and the 640-pound gorilla that can sit anywhere it wants. Filmed in the Belgian Congo (now Zaire). Swedish with English subtitles. Sven Nykvist co-directs.
VHS: S05480. $29.95.
Lar Henrik Ottoson, Sweden, 1956, 79 mins.

The Hideaway
A 12-year-old boy who is starved for attention catches a young punk hiding in his basement. The 12-year-old agrees to shelter the older boy and is slowly transformed by the relationship. In the end he must risk everything to save his strange new friend. Danish with English subtitles.
VHS: S24734. $59.95.
Niels Grabo, Denmark, 1993, 70 mins.

House of Angels
A sexy nightclub singer is the sole surviving heir to an old Swedish estate. When she returns to a small town to reclaim her inheritance, her big city ways set the townspeople on edge. This comedy of a black sheep who returns to the fold is a clever tale of love and reversal. Swedish with English subtitles.
VHS: S20737. $19.95.
Colin Nutley, Sweden, 1992, 119 mins.

Hunger
Per Oscarsson gives his greatest performance as Pontus, a starving writer in Norway circa 1890, in Henning Carlsen's filming of a Knut Hamsun novel. Pontus stumbles through the streets in search of his own fantasies. His articles are continually refused by editors, and by autumn he is left penniless and without food. "Every tic, every gesture appears to have been with him for years rather than just assumed for a film part" (Peter Cowie). Winner of the Best Actor Award at the Cannes Film Festival. Swedish with English subtitles.
VHS: S13497. $29.95.
Laser: CLV. LD72050. $39.95.
Henning Carlsen, Sweden, 1966, 100 mins.

I Am Curious—Yellow
The film that scandalized America with its (!) sex and nudity is really a pseudo-Freudian look at the relationship between sex, politics and the body. Lena Nyman is the sociologist trying to get a take on the Swedish class structure while carrying on a passionate affair with a casual visitor to her father's apartment in her bedroom, in front of the Royal Palace, in a tree, on the grass, in a lake. Quintessential 60's nostalgia but a film that broke many taboos and served as a vanguard of liberation. Swedish with English subtitles.
VHS: S00505. $59.95.
Vilgot Sjoman, Sweden, 1968, 95 mins.

I, A Woman
This is the Swedish classic that American couples, in search of cinematic titillation, came flocking to in the 60s. Siv, a gorgeous and restless young woman, revolts against the fanatically religious folks and searches for sexual fulfillment. Dubbed in English.
VHS: S23038. $19.98.
Mac Ahlberg, Sweden, 1966, 80 mins.

Intermezzo
The premiere release of the film that discovered Ingrid Bergman, which took more than 50 years to reach American shores. The romantic drama is the story of a world-famous violinist, whose life is turned upside down when he has an affair with a beautiful, aspiring pianist. When David Selznick saw *Intermezzo*, he brought Ingrid Bergman to Hollywood. Swedish with English subtitles.
VHS: S10881. $19.98.
Laser: LD70269. $39.95.
Gustaf Molander, Sweden, 1936, 91 mins.

June Night
One of Ingrid Bergman's first screen appearances features Bergman as a promiscuous young woman exposed when she becomes the victim of a shooting accident in her small town. Swedish with English subtitles.
VHS: S09356. $19.98.
Laser: CLV/CAV. LD70270. $39.95.
Per Lindberg, Sweden, 90 mins.

The Kingdom
Lars von Trier's audacious and inspired soap opera is set in Copenhagen's Kingdom Hospital, which is ailing. Once a respected site of healing, it has become a carnival of horrors. A restless ghost haunts its corridors crying for redemption. Patients try seances while doctors turn to exorcism and voodoo. Despite these efforts, the terrible secret at the heart of *The Kingdom* remains and continues to ensnare the innocent. This film mixes a range of influences from the erotic to the sardonic in an unforgettable hybrid of comedy and terror. Danish with English subtitles.
VHS: S27595. $99.99.
Laser: LD75556. $89.99.
Lars von Trier, Denmark, 1994, 265 mins.

Ladies on the Rocks
The "buddies" in this very funny road movie are two self-determined women. Aspiring comediennes Micha and Laura pack up their van and tour rural Denmark with their cabaret act. But the show does not sit too well with Micha's rock musician boyfriend nor Laura's bourgeois husband, and domestic problems invariably arise. Danish with English subtitles.
VHS: S16497. $79.95.
Christian Braad Thomsen, Denmark, 1983, 100 mins.

Lakki: The Boy Who Grew Wings
The bittersweet, lyrical adventures of a lonely 14-year-old boy are at the center of this haunting film. Neglected by his father and ignored by his decadent mother, Lakki takes to the streets. There he befriends a punk rocker who brutalizes him. All the while, mysterious feathers sprout from his back until, confronted by a miraculous transformation, he must fight for his sanity. Norwegian with English subtitles.
VHS: S26712. $69.95.
Svend Wam, Norway, 1992, 104 mins.

Lars von Trier: Epidemic
This experimental video by Lars von Trier reveals much of the stylistic vision of the Danish artist/filmmaker who would later go into features with his *Element of Crime* and *Zentropa*. This tape holds part of the *Europa Trilogy*.
VHS: S22583. $74.95.
Lars von Trier, Denmark, 106 mins.

Lily Was Here
A provocative, erotic thriller about a young Dutch woman's descent into crime. Marion Van Trijn stars as the title character, who commits a shocking string of daylight robberies that attracts the attention of the press and the police. With Thom Hoffman, Coen Van Vrijberghe de Coningh, Adrian Brine, Dennis Rudge and Monique Van de Ven. Soundtrack by David A. Stewart of the Eurythmics, featuring the saxophone superstar Candy Duffer. Dubbed in English.
VHS: S16566. $79.95.
Ben Verbong, Netherlands, 1989, 105 mins.

The Littlest Viking
A wacky Icelandic family comedy about a 12-year-old Viking Prince, Sirgard, who takes on fearsome warriors, legendary beasts and far-out characters as he learns about truth, nobility and honor. Dubbed in English.
VHS: S23327. $19.95.
Laser: LD74838. $34.95.
Jorfald/Rasmussen/Bale, Iceland, 1995, 85 mins.

Mazurka (Mazurka Pa Sengekanten)
A Danish sex farce centering on a school dance where, without question, the mazurka will be part of the program. Max, a popular teacher in a boy's school, could be the next dean of students if he gets married and loses his virginity. Those European schools have such strict standards. Dubbed into English. Adults only. Denmark, 1970, 91 mins.
VHS: S05466. $29.95.

Memories of a Marriage
Watch as a lifetime of love unfolds on the screen in this touching Danish love story—a film about the joys and sorrows, victories and defeats, and, above all, the love between a husband and a wife. With Ghita Norby and Frits Helmuth. "A touching portrait of a married life" (*The Wall Street Journal*). "A well crafted and fully realized film" (*New York Post*). Danish with yellow English subtitles.
VHS: S15265. $19.98.
Kaspar Rostrup, Denmark, 1989, 90 mins.

Miss Julie
The definitive version of August Strindberg's riveting play concerning social and sexual domination. Miss Julie is a noblewoman who allows her butler to seduce her after her engagement is broken. With Anita Bjork and Anders Henrikson. Swedish with English subtitles.
VHS: S01720. $29.95.
Alf Sjoberg, Sweden, 1950, 90 mins.

Mozart Brothers
A Swedish opera director—an anguished, divorce-wracked enfant terrible—has a bizarre vision for a production of Mozart's *Don Giovanni*. His efforts to stand the revered opera on its head including destroying the stage in order to install a pool, stripping the opera of its libretto, and freeing the artists of their inhibitions and clothing. Wonderful comic performances in a film that's "witty and uproarious" (*New York Times*). Swedish with English subtitles.
VHS: S10930. $59.95.
Suzanne Osten, Sweden, 1985, 98 mins.

My Life as a Dog
More than just a movie, a phenomenon that has captured the hearts of America. A bright, funny, touching tale of one boy's special growing-up year. Bundled off to a rural village while his ill mother recuperates, young Ingemar finds unexpected adventure with the town's warmhearted eccentrics. Swedish with English subtitles.
VHS: S06240. $19.98.
Laser: Subtitled. LD75232. $34.98.
Lasse Hallstrom, Sweden, 1987, 101 mins.

Only One Night
Ingrid Bergman stars as Eva, the girlfriend of her guardian, Valdemar Moreaux. Their relationship crashes when Eva discovers that she is disgusted by the physical side of love. A Swedish melodrama starring the beautiful young Bergman. Swedish with English subtitles.
VHS: S12449. $19.98.
Laser: LD70273. $39.95.
Gustaf Molander, Sweden, 1937, 87 mins.

Pathfinder
Ruthless invaders disrupt the harmony of living in Lapland about a thousand years ago. A young boy takes on the title role in an attempt to mislead the land pirates who made him an orphan. This Oscar-nominated foreign film is a grand adventure told in an epic visual style. A surprise hit in Norway and this country. In Lapp with English subtitles.
VHS: S13843. $19.98.
Nils Gaup, Norway, 1988, 88 mins.

Pelle the Conqueror
Winner of the Cannes Festival Palme d'Or and the Academy Award for Best Foreign Picture, Bille August's moving film features a remarkable performance by Max von Sydow as the Swedish father who takes his son Pelle to Denmark in search for a new life. In the harsh milieu of the Danish farm, Pelle is inspired by the dreams of those around him, but realising that his father cannot help him fulfill his dream, Pelle sets off for a life of adventure—to conquer the world. Danish with English subtitles.
VHS: S09289. $19.98.
Bille August, Denmark, 1988, 138 mins.

Pretty Boy
In this unflinching and harshly poetic film, the chronicle of a young runaway boy unfolds on the streets of Copenhagen. There he becomes a street hustler. Before the camera, innocence is plundered and finally lost in this compelling exploration of desire. Danish with English subtitles.
VHS: S23290. $69.95.
Carsten Sonder, Denmark, 1993, 87 mins.

Quiet Days in Clichy
Based on Henry Miller's erotic novel written in 1956. Joey, a self-indulgent American choreographer living in Denmark, spends most of his time seducing sexy Parisian girls together with his buddy Cal. "Henry Miller's memoir of friends, women and cheap wine is a relaxed, very sexy outrage..." (Amos Vogel, *Film as a Subversive Art*). With Paul Valjean and Louise White.
VHS: S23039. $19.98.
Jens Jorgen Thorsen, Denmark, 1970, 91 mins.

Remote Control
At the center of this outrageous comedy is a stolen remote control. Soon hostage goldfish, amateur mobsters and a beautiful kidnapee join the plot to thoroughly confound and delight. Between the hoodlum morons and mom everything comes out right in the end. Icelandic with English subtitles.
VHS: S23432. $94.95.
Laser: LD75132. $24.98.
Oskar Jonasson, Iceland, 1992, 85 mins.

Slingshot
This charming coming-of-age film follows the antic travails of a 12-year-old with a special possession. He makes a slingshot from contraband condoms that brings him fame, fortune, and big trouble with the local police. Based on a true story, it won the Swedish Academy Award for Best Picture. Swedish with English subtitles.
VHS: S23326. $19.95.
Laser: LD74755. $34.95.
Ake Sandgren, Sweden, 1993, 102 mins.

Sofie
Liv Ullmann's directorial debut is set in Copenhagen in 1886, and deals with the efforts of Sofie (Karen-Lise Mynster), a beautiful, emotionally sheltered, 28-year-old Jewish woman who longs for independence, to fall in love and get married. Though she is attracted to a charismatic painter (Jesper Christensen), she follows her parents' orders and marries her dull cousin (Torben Zeller). With Erland Josephson and Ghita Norby. Swedish with English subtitles.
VHS: S19972. $79.95.
Liv Ullmann, Sweden, 1992, 142 mins.

Story of Gosta Berling
Greta Garbo in one of her earliest roles. The story follows a pastor, defrocked because of his drinking, as he goes through loves and sorrow. A masterpiece of Scandinavian cinema. Silent.
VHS: S01260. $29.95.
Mauritz Stiller, Sweden, 1924, 93 mins.

Sunday's Children
Ingmar Bergman wrote the screenplay for this haunting film about a 10-year-old boy named Pu. Pu is in the country for the summer with his family. Everything seems peaceful enough until Pu sees his father fighting with his mother. This event inaugurates an emotional time that resonates within all concerned. Swedish with English subtitles.
VHS: S23744. $29.95.
Daniel Bergman, Sweden, 1993, 118 mins.

Swedenhielms
In this classic drama, Ingrid Bergman plays Astrid, the wealthy girlfriend of Bo Swedenhielm, who, together with his aristocratic but impecunious family, is depending on their father winning the Nobel Prize. Swedish with English subtitles.
VHS: S09357. $19.98.
Laser: LD70271. $39.95.
Gustaf Molander, Sweden, 88 mins.

Thomas Graal's Best Child
The comical adventures of Thomas and Bessie are continued in this sequel. The screenwriter has married his secretary who is now acting in his movies. When a child appears in the household the parents are not in agreement as to how to raise a modern youngster. With Victor Sjostrom and Karin Molander. Silent.
VHS: S03707. $29.95.
Mauritz Stiller, Sweden, 1918, 70 mins.

Thomas Graal's Best Film
An astonishingly sophisticated comedy about love and film. Director Stiller was a Russian emigre working in Sweden who discovered Greta Garbo and ultimately went to Hollywood with her. Thomas Graal stars director Victor Sjostrom (The Wind, He Who Gets Slapped). Silent.
VHS: S03706. $29.95.
Mauritz Stiller, Sweden, 1917, 70 mins.

Tong Tana—
A Journey into the Heart of Borneo
Deep within Borneo's lush rainforest, Bruno Manser, a 34-year-old Swiss, has rejected western civilization to live with the nomadic Penan Indians and help them confront the logging companies that threaten their existence. In ten years Borneo's rainforest—the oldest in the world—may be gone forever, and so will be the Penans. Bruno Manser may be one of their last hopes. "A strong environmentalist message...of high artistic order" (Variety). Sweden, 1990, 88 mins.
VHS: S14151. $29.95.

Torment
The budding love between two students, Jan-Erik and Bertha, is threatened by a sadistic Latin teacher nicknamed "Caligula" who torments Jan-Erik in class. When Jan-Erik finds Bertha dead in her room and Caligula hiding in a closet, he accuses him of causing her death. Based on the (first) script by Ingmar Bergman, the character of Caligula was seen as a symbol of Nazism. The film is remarkable for its expressive style and a powerful performance by Mai Zetterling as Bertha. With Alf Kjellin and Stig Olin. Swedish with English subtitles.
VHS: S04913. $19.95.
Alf Sjoberg, Sweden, 1944, 90 mins.

The Treasure of Arne
With Victor Sjostrom, Mauritz Stiller was the most important early Scandinavian director, with a painterly visual style, graphic naturalism and a real affinity for landscape and geography. This film concerns the fate of a 16th century Scottish mercenary, an escaped prisoner, and the damages wrought against wealthy landowner and his family.
VHS: S03708. $19.95.
Mauritz Stiller, Sweden, 1919, 70 mins.

Walpurgis Night
Ingrid Bergman plays a woman who is secretly in love with her married boss. Her boss, it turns out, is also in love with her. This forbidden love soon triggers a murky and melodramatic series of startling events, including abortion, blackmail, murder and suicide. Swedish with English subtitles.
VHS: S15066. $19.98.
Gustaf Edgren, Sweden, 1935, 75 mins.

Witchcraft Through the Ages
A rare and extraordinary film from a little-known master of the silent era. A document of witchcraft from the 15th through the 17th century, the film is reminiscent in style of Bosch, Breughel, Callot and Goya. The film concludes with documented scenes of superstition and cases of possession in 1920. Silent with English subtitles.
VHS: S01471. $29.95.
Benjamin Christensen, Denmark, 1920, 82 mins.

Wolf at the Door
Donald Sutherland brings the later years of artist Paul Gauguin to life in a drama filled with fine art and romantic conquests. This Danish-French co-production is filmed in English and although Anthony Quinn looks more like Gauguin, Max Von Sydow is a dead ringer for August Strindberg.
VHS: S05296. $19.95.
Henning Carlsen, France/Denmark, 1987, 90 mins.

A Woman's Face
Ingrid Bergman depicts the troublesome life of young Anna Holm as a woman who has not only lost both her parents in a fire but was also severely burned and left with terrible facial scars. She descends into a lifestyle of despair and cynical blackmailing schemes. Swedish with English subtitles.
VHS: S15067. $19.98.
Gustaf Molander, Sweden, 1938, 104 mins.

A World of Strangers
Henning Carlsen's adaptation of Nobel prize winning writer Nadine Gordimer's novel demystifies official government reports and media representation to provide a frightening, kaleidoscopic portrait of the faces, events and personalities imprisoned under the iron-clad racial separation laws and fascist ideology of apartheid. Shot surreptitiously on location in South Africa. With Athol Fugard's frequent collaborator Zakes Mokae.
VHS: S17928. $29.95.
Henning Carlsen, South Africa, 1962, 89 mins.

You Are Not Alone
This Danish film honestly explores the boundaries between friendship and love in a boys' school in a film which is full of nuance, gentleness and humor, reminiscent of the early films of Truffaut. Danish with English subtitles.
VHS: S01491. $79.95.
Nielsen & Johansen, Denmark, 1982, 90 mins.

Zentropa
Known in Europe as Europa, this stylistically daring work is set in a bleak, defeated Germany. A young American of German ancestry apprentices as a railway porter. He is seduced by a mysterious heiress whose father owns the line and becomes a pawn in a mysterious web of intrigue and deceit. With Jean Marc Barr, Barbara Sukowa and Eddie Constantine. Narrated by Max von Sydow. English and German with English subtitles.
VHS: S18368. $94.95.
Lars von Trier, Denmark/France/Sweden/Germany, 1991, 112 mins.

INGMAR BERGMAN

After the Rehearsal
Bergman takes a deeply personal look at the theater and its delusions in this spellbinding chamber play. The action of the film takes place on the bare stage after a rehearsal of Strindberg's A Dream Play. Superbly directed and acted, this is a major effort by one of the most renowned directors. Swedish with English subtitles.
VHS: S00022. $19.95.
Ingmar Bergman, Sweden, 1983, 72 mins.

All These Women
A rare comedy for Ingmar Bergman and his first film in color. Music critic Cornelius intends to write a biography of the cellist Felix and tries to gain admittance to the cellist's inner circle—surrounded by women, fountains and fake swans. Full of absurdist barbs, the film stars Bibi Andersson, Eva Dahlbeck, Karin Kavli and Jarl Kulle. Swedish with English subtitles.
VHS: S07499. $29.95.
Ingmar Bergman, Sweden, 1964, 80 mins.

Autumn Sonata
Ingmar Bergman's intense chamber drama was Ingrid Bergman's first Swedish film in almost 40 years and also her last. She plays a famed international concert pianist whose reunion with her daughter quickly deteriorates from euphoria into recriminations over the past. Rivalry, longing and guilt threaten to destroy the bonds that join a mother and her daughter. With Erland Josephson and Gunnar Bjornstrand. Swedish with English subtitles.
VHS: S00078. $39.95.
Laser: Subtitled. LD70848. $49.95.
Ingmar Bergman, Sweden, 1978, 97 mins.

Brink of Life
Superb performances by Eva Dahlbeck, Ingrid Thulin, Bibi Andersson and Max von Sydow mark this study of three women facing childbirth during a 24 hour period in a maternity word. Bergman was awarded the Best Director prize at Cannes for this film. Swedish with English subtitles.
VHS: S00182. $29.95.
Ingmar Bergman, Sweden, 1957, 82 mins.

Cries and Whispers
Ingmar Bergman's anguished, searing examination of the lust, envy, betrayal, love and self-mutilation that passes between four women—three sisters and a family provider—in this sculpted, metaphysical drama. "Bergman uses the women as metaphors for humanity, representing how we respond to anxiety, death, and the visitations of what appears to be a wrathful rather than benevolent God" (James Monaco). With Harriet Andersson, Ingrid Thulin and Liv Ullmann. Cinematography by Sven Nykvist. Swedish with English subtitles.
VHS: S00282. $39.95.
Ingmar Bergman, Sweden, 1972, 91 mins.

Devil's Eye
The Devil dispatches Don Juan to seduce a young, beautiful virgin in one of Bergman's rare comedies. The young girl changes Don Juan's lust to love so that he cannot follow through on his seduction. With Bibi Andersson and Jarl Kulle. Swedish with English subtitles.
VHS: S00331. $29.95.
Ingmar Bergman, Sweden, 1960, 90 mins.

Devil's Wanton
Bergman's sixth film, in which many of his themes and cinematic techniques are in evidence. The story revolves around a set of people adrift in a sea of confusion: a film director, a poet, and a prostitute. Swedish with English subtitles.
VHS: S00333. $29.95.
Ingmar Bergman, Sweden, 1949, 78 mins.

Document: Fanny and Alexander
Beginning on the day before shooting his last feature film and continuing through the wrap, Ingmar Bergman presents the making of Fanny and Alexander. With his brilliant cameraman, Sven Nykvist, and his troupe of actors, Bergman shows how he works behind the camera to shape his singular vision. Swedish with English subtitles.
VHS: S08939. $29.95.
Ingmar Bergman, Sweden, 1985, 105 mins.

Dreams
A study of sexual obsession as two women, the owner of a modeling agency and her top model, both have strange one day affairs with married men while on a photographic outing. Exquisite scenes of austere romanticism and painful irony. Swedish with English subtitles.
VHS: S00373. $24.95.
Ingmar Bergman, Sweden, 1955, 86 mins.

Fanny and Alexander
Bergman's final film, an emotional epic about a year in the lives of two young children, their dreams and impressions, and the eccentric characters who dwell in their glorious mansion. With unparalleled ensemble acting, featuring Erland Josephson, Ewa Froling, Pernila Alwin, and cinematography by Sven Nykvist. Swedish with English subtitles.
VHS: S00431. $29.95.
Ingmar Bergman, Sweden, 1983, 190 mins.

Hour of the Wolf
Max von Sydow portrays an artist living with his wife (Liv Ullmann) on a remote island, haunted by darkness, demons and his imagination, in this effective study of the creative process. Bergman brilliantly uses the eerie landscape to show von Sydow's descent into madness as he is haunted by images of the death of a child. Swedish with English subtitles.
VHS: S17862. $19.98.
Ingmar Bergman, Sweden, 1968, 88 mins.

A Lesson in Love
Ingmar Bergman's "comedy for grownups"—Ernemann, a gynecologist, and his wife meet on a train and pretend not to know each other, as Ernemann tries to "recover" his wife, who has been having an affair with a bombastic sculptor. Swedish with English subtitles.
VHS: S03512. $19.95.
Ingmar Bergman, Sweden, 1954, 95 mins.

The Magic Flute
Quite possibly the best opera adaptation ever put on film, Ingmar Bergman's magical, delightful, enchanting version of Mozart's playful opera, sung in Swedish by a remarkably terrific cast. Bergman and Mozart meeting centuries later, in different mediums, is still a meeting of minds. Swedish with English subtitles.
VHS: S00797. $29.95.
Laser: LD75386. $99.95.
Ingmar Bergman, Sweden, 1973, 134 mins.

The Magician
One of Bergman's most compelling films; Max von Sydow plays the wandering magician with a bag of tricks that turn him from magician to savior, then to con-man and finally to an extraordinary artist. The film has been variously interpreted as an intellectual horror film and as a symbolic self-portrait. With Ingrid Thulin, Gunnar Bjornstrand and Bibi Andersson. Swedish with English subtitles.
VHS: S00799. $29.95.
Ingmar Bergman, Sweden, 1958, 101 mins.

Monika
The young Harriet Andersson is Monika, the sultry teenager who escapes her poverty together with a young man. They camp out on an island off the Swedish coast, exploring their emotions and sensuality, but when summer ends, hunger, pregnancy and boredom drive her back to her old life. "Harriet Andersson gives a memorably moving performance as a self-centered, self-willed, but erotic adolescent" (Georges Sadoul). Swedish with English subtitles.
VHS: S09354. $29.95.
Ingmar Bergman, Sweden, 1952, 82 mins.

Night Is My Future
A moving drama of a musician blinded in an accident, and forced to adjust to a world of darkness. Driven to despair, the musician regains his faith in life by studying to become a church organist and finding the love of a simple woman. Swedish with English subtitles.
VHS: S00931. $29.95.
Ingmar Bergman, Sweden, 1947, 87 mins.

The Passion of Anna
One of Bergman's first works in color is an audacious work about the political, social and sexual interplay of four people on a remote Swedish island, each overcome by associations of guilt, remorse and rage. Sven Nykvist's explosive use of color establishes dramatic texture and conflict. In a Godardian move, the characters frequently break down and discuss the nature of their role. With Max Von Sydow, Liv Ullmann, Bibi Andersson and Erland Josephson. Swedish with English subtitles.
VHS: S17864. $19.98.
Ingmar Bergman, Sweden, 1970, 101 mins.

Persona
Ingmar Bergman's great achievement, a study of madness, breakdown and transference of identity. The story concerns a brilliant actress who unaccountably loses her will to speak and her shifting, intricate and elaborate relationship with the nurse assigned to her rehabilitation. Liv Ullmann is the actress, Harriet Andersson is the nurse. Cinematography by Sven Nykvist. Swedish with English subtitles.
VHS: S17865. $19.98.
Laser: Digital Transfer. LD74926. $34.98.
Ingmar Bergman, Sweden, 1967, 81 mins.

The Ritual
This chamber drama stars Gunnar Bjornstrand, Ingrid Thulin and Anders Ek as members of a small touring company of actors who are trapped in a legal nightmare for an allegedly obscene variety show. A sadistic judge uses the opportunity to ruthlessly examine their personal lives. A brilliant look at the relationship of the artist to society, with a powerful performance from Ingrid Thulin as the unhappy, alcoholic actress. Swedish with English subtitles.
VHS: S26061. $39.95.
Ingmar Bergman, Sweden, 1969, 75 mins.

Sawdust and Tinsel
Ingmar Bergman's profound meditation on art and sexual conflict. Set in turn-of-the-century Sweden and centered on a ragged traveling circus, the plot details the private anguish of the ring master (Ake Gronberg), reunited with his former wife (AnnikaTretow) in a provincial town. Complications erupt when Gronberg's mistress (Harriet Andersson) is seduced by a loquacious actor (Hasse Ekman). With Anders Ek and Gudrun Brost. Swedish with English subtitles.
VHS: S01161. $29.95.
Ingmar Bergman, Sweden, 1953, 83 mins.

Scenes from a Marriage
Liv Ullmann stars in this exploration of the relationship between two people over a 20-year period. "Never before has this extraordinary director and writer explored relationships between the sexes with such compassion and humor. Scenes from a Marriage seems to be the simplest, most lucid, most spare film that Bergman has ever made," wrote Vincent Canby in The New York Times. Roger Ebert calls it "one of the truest, most luminous love stories ever made, an almost-heart-breaking masterpiece." With Erland Josephson.
VHS: S26300. $39.95.
Laser: Widescreen. LD75409. $69.95.
Ingmar Bergman, Sweden, 1974, 168 mins.

Secrets of Women
Ingmar Bergman's exploration of sexual dynamics. Rakel (Anita Bjork), Marta (Maj-Britt Nilsson) and Karin (Eva Dahlbeck) are married to three brothers. While waiting for their arrival at a summer retreat, each woman relates an elaborate incident; Rakel's attempted seduction by a friend; Marta's experiences with a Swedish artist in Paris; and Karin's liberating moments while stuck in an elevator with her husband. Swedish with English subtitles.
VHS: S01175. $39.95.
Ingmar Bergman, Sweden, 1952, 114 mins.

Serpent's Egg
Set in Berlin in 1923, the film is about a Jewish-American trapeze artist (David Carradine) and his sister-in-law (Liv Ullmann), who are entrapped by a mad doctor—a prophet who dreams of what the Nazis will accomplish in the 30's. The screen is filled with powerful images. English dialog.
VHS: S01179. $39.95.
Ingmar Bergman, Germany, 1980, 119 mins.

Seventh Seal
Bergman's powerful allegory of man's search for meaning in life is stunningly visualized. A knight, upon return from the Crusades, plays chess with Death while the Plague ravages medieval Europe. With Max von Sydow, Gunnar Bjornstrand, Bibi Andersson. Swedish with English subtitles.
VHS: S01185. $29.95.
Laser: CAV. LD70453. $79.95.
Laser: C.LV. LD70454. $49.95.
Ingmar Bergman, Sweden, 1956, 96 mins.

The Shame
A brilliant young couple, both violinists, attempt to evade a long-raging civil war and retreat to an island off the coast. The war follows them and they're charged with collaborating with the enemy. A visually spare, emotionally powerful work about hopelessness, betrayal and human weakness. With Liv Ullmann, Max Von Sydow and Gunnar Bjornstrand. Cinematography by Sven Nykvist. Swedish with English subtitles.
VHS: S17863. $24.95.
Ingmar Bergman, Sweden, 1968, 103 mins.

Silence
Part of the Bergman trilogy dealing with the existence of God. Two women are stranded in a remote village where the language is incomprehensible. As one of the women slowly slips into death, the other engages the local barman in a frenzied sexual encounter. Swedish with English subtitles.
VHS: S02773. $24.95.
Ingmar Bergman, Sweden, 1963, 95 mins.

Smiles of a Summer Night
Ingmar Bergman's liveliest work concerns the sexual and romantic roundelay of four couples invited to a country mansion for a summer weekend. "The film is erotic and lyrical, full of blithe spirits brilliantly evoked" (James Monaco). With Gunnar Bjornstrand, Eva Dahlbeck, Ulla Jacobsson and Harriet Andersson. Swedish with English subtitles.
VHS: S01219. $29.95.
Laser: LD70465. $49.95.
Ingmar Bergman, Sweden, 1955, 108 mins.

Summer Interlude

Discovering the diary of a former lover, a ballerina recalls a summer affair with its delirious happiness and tragedy; now a star, she travels back in memory to recapture the pleasure and pain of first love and to purge the memories that have shadowed her own life. "This evocation of past happiness is one of Bergman's most moving films" (Georges Sadoul). Swedish with English subtitles.
VHS: S04912. $29.95.
Ingmar Bergman, Sweden, 1950, 95 mins.

Three Strange Loves

Early Bergman psychological drama follows a husband and wife on a train ride across Germany after the War. As the country struggles to recover the couple ponder the state of their marriage. Swedish with English subtitles.
VHS: S02218. $29.95.
Ingmar Bergman, Sweden, 1949, 88 mins.

Through a Glass Darkly

Powerful psychological study of a young woman's descent into madness. Harriet Andersson plays Karin, who has read that she is an incurable schizophrenic and plunges into a visionary world where God is a spider. With Gunnar Bjornstrand and Max von Sydow. Swedish with English subtitles.
VHS: S01339. $29.95.
Laser: Digital transfer. **LD74974. $49.95.**
Ingmar Bergman, Sweden, 1960, 91 mins.

To Joy

Bergman's seventh film, an examination of the life of a talented violinist who must return to a normal existence after the death of his wife. He receives strength from his son and his music. Music from the works of Mendelssohn and Mozart as well as Beethoven's Ninth Symphony, from which the title is taken. English dubbed.
VHS: S03360. $19.95.
Ingmar Bergman, Sweden, 1950, 93 mins.

The Virgin Spring

Max von Sydow stars in this exploration of a father's revenge for the rape and murder of his daughter. Highly contrasting black and white images evoke an imaginative, medieval world created by cinematographer Sven Nykvist. A stunning work. Swedish with English subtitles.
VHS: S01418. $29.95.
Laser: **LD75073. $49.95.**
Ingmar Bergman, Sweden, 1960, 88 mins.

Wild Strawberries

One of the great films of Bergman, with Victor Sjostrom as the aged Stockholm professor who recollects his past experiences and becomes aware, for the first time, of his failings and shortcomings. With Bibi Andersson, Ingrid Thulin, Gunnar Bjornstrand. Swedish with English subtitles.
VHS: S01462. $29.95.
Laser: **LD70487. $49.95.**
Ingmar Bergman, Sweden, 1957, 95 mins.

Winter Light

Bergman's great film about the meaning of faith features Max von Sydow as a village pastor, empty of faith and desperately unloved, who reveals his bitter failure to offer spiritual consolation to his flock. With Ingrid Thulin, Gunnar Bjornstrand. Swedish with English subtitles.
VHS: S01468. $29.95.
Ingmar Bergman, Sweden, 1962, 80 mins.

JAN TROELL

The Emigrants

Max von Sydow and Liv Ullmann star in this epic pioneer story set during the 1850's. A young Swedish farming family leave their homeland for a new life in America. Realistic in its depiction of the hardships endured by the emigrants in their quest, The Emigrants movingly dramatizes the strength and determination that drove America's early immigrants. Nominated for four Academy Awards. Dubbed in English.
VHS: S20683. $29.99.
Jan Troell, Sweden, 1971, 151 mins.

The New Land

Shot on locations in Wisconsin and Minnesota, The New Land provides a moving portrait of pioneer immigrant life rarely seen in the American cinema: a life of hardship and joys, but also a life which is difficult on the emotional life and stability. The film picks up the story from the ending of The Emigrants to follow the lives of Kristina and Oskar as they try to establish a life in the upper Midwest. With Max Von Sydow and Liv Ullmann. Dubbed in English.
VHS: S20684. $29.99.
Jan Troell, Sweden, 1972, 205 mins.

Zandy's Bride

The American debut of the talented Jan Troell, about the quirky relationship between a shy, reclusive, pioneering peasant (Gene Hackman) and his mail order bride (Liv Ullmann). With Harry Dean Stanton, Eileen Heckart and Susan Tyrrell.
VHS: S18612. $19.98.
Jan Troell, USA, 1974, 116 mins.

AKI & MIKA KAURISMAKI

Amazon

Framed against the backdrop of the Brazilian rain forest, Amazon traces the lives of a failed businessman, (Kari Vaananen), his relationship with a renegade bush pilot (Robert Davi) and his obsession for a beautiful school teacher (Rae Dawn Chong) in a remote outpost. In English.
VHS: S16861. $89.98.
Laser: LD75143. $34.98.
Mika Kaurismaki, USA, 1992, 88 mins.

Ariel

This biting and funny satire is inspired by European black comedies, American road movies and 1930's gangster films. When a Finnish miner loses his job, he is given a huge white Cadillac convertible and embarks on a cross-country trip that leads to a series of unpredictable adventures. Finnish with English subtitles.
VHS: S14067. $79.95.
Aki Kaurismaki, Finland, 1989, 74 mins.

La Vie de Boheme

Kaurismaki succeeds in creating a wonderfully ironic chamber drama about three rebel, eccentric artists—a poet, a painter and a composer. They all live the "bohemian life" in which their friendship and camaraderie are the most valued characteristics, even as each faces the harsh everyday reality of the outer world. Kaurismaki creates a fabulously artificial milieu in a film of gentle and unexpected humor and warmth. French with English subtitles.
VHS: S21117. $89.98.
Aki Kaurismaki, France, 1993, 100 mins.

Leningrad Cowboys Go America

This sublimely absurd road movie chronicles the world tour of the most mediocre polka band in Siberia. Nine musicians, one venal manager and a very determined village idiot leave the tundra for the United States in search of paying gigs. Watch for the cameo by Jim Jarmusch as a used-car dealer. If nothing else you will remember the Cowboys' unique style of dress and grooming. English and Finnish with English subtitles.
VHS: S14785. $19.98.
Laser: Widescreen. **LD71614. $39.95.**
Aki Kaurismaki, Finland, 1989, 78 mins.

The Match Factory Girl

The final part of Aki Kaurismaki's "Proletarian Trilogy" is a bleak portrait of contemporary Helsinki. The tale focuses on Iris (Kati Outinen), a sad-eyed factory woman who seeks the ultimate revenge on the caustic parents who brutalized her and the wealthy architect who sexually humiliated her. With Elina Salo, Esko Nikkari, Vesa Vierikko and Reijo Taipole. Finnish with English subtitles. On the same program is Those Were the Days (1992, 5 mins.), a video of the idiosyncratic Finnish rockers The Leningrad Cowboys.
VHS: S19415. $79.95.
Aki Kaurismaki, Finland, 1989, 70 mins.

Tigrero: A Film That Was Never Made

In 1954, armed with a 16mm camera, film, two cases of vodka and 75 boxes of cigars, director Sam Fuller went to Brazil scouting locations for the action-adventure film Tigrero. Although this Darryl F. Zanuck production was cast with John Wayne, Ava Gardner and Tyrone Power, the film was never shot because of insurance problems. All that remains of Tigrero is Fuller's intriguing footage of the Karaja tribe and their Amazon Rain Forest home. Forty years later, director Mika Kaurismaki ventures back to this location with Fuller and director Jim Jarmusch to talk with the Karaja about the changing world, talk amongst themselves about Fuller's films and the principles of filmmaking, and tell the story of the film that was never made. This film won the International Critics Award at the 1994 Berlin Film Festival.
VHS: S27618. $89.95.
Mika Kaurismaki, Finland/United Germany/Brazil, 1994, 75 mins.

Zombie and the Ghost Train

A black comedy from Mika Kaurismaki. Described as part docu-fiction, part Hamlet-style tragedy and just a bit screwball, this unusual road movie chases after a punk rock band that's never seen, always heard, all the way from Helsinki to Istanbul. Finnish with English subtitles.
VHS: S23429. $59.95.
Mika Kaurismaki, Finland, 1993, 88 mins.

CARL THEODOR DREYER

Day of Wrath

Day of Wrath premiered during the blackest period of Nazi occupation of Denmark. It tells a story of witchcraft in the Denmark of 1623 with great atmospheric intensity, visual beauty, a sense of nature and a sense of anguish. Danish with English subtitles.
VHS: S00311. $29.95.
Carl Theodor Dreyer, Denmark, 1943, 110 mins.

Gertrude

Dreyer's last film, the story of a woman who is unhappily married to a lawyer, meets a famous poet whom she had loved, has an affair with a young composer, and decides to live alone in Paris. Rigorous, poignant, and profound. Danish with English subtitles.
VHS: S00492. $34.95.
Carl Theodor Dreyer, Denmark, 1964, 116 mins.

Leaves from Satan's Book

Dreyer sketches Satan's path through four historical periods, in each as a disrupter of the social forces through already powerful male leaders. Dreyer associates the figure of Christ with female figures, and the photography and composition anticipates his later Passion of Joan of Arc. Silent.
VHS: S03699. $29.95.
Carl Theodor Dreyer, Denmark, 1919, 165 mins.

Master of the House

Also known as Thou Shalt Honor Thy Wife, Dreyer's early morality piece, the story of a spoiled husband who abuses his ordinary wife and mother. Silent with English subtitles.
VHS: S00832. $39.95.
Carl Theodor Dreyer, Denmark, 1925, 118 mins.

Ordet

From the director of Passion of Joan of Arc, Ordet is the story of a theology student who loses his memory and believes he is Christ. Based on a play by Kaj Munk, Ordet is Dreyer's portrayal of the conflict between organized religion and personal belief. Danish with English subtitles.
VHS: S00969. $29.95.
Carl Theodor Dreyer, Denmark, 1955, 126 mins.

Passion of Joan of Arc

One of the most poignant, terrifying and unrelenting emotional historical documents ever filmed. Called an austere masterpiece in reference to the stark sets and extreme close-up photography, Joan of Arc is brilliantly portrayed by Maria Falconetti. Silent.
VHS: S00998. $29.95.
Carl Theodor Dreyer, France, 1928, 114 mins.

Vampyr

Vampyr tells with extraordinary images the nightmarish story of a young man who unwittingly becomes involved with two sisters and their father, all victims of a vampire. Dreyer has transformed LeFanu's horror tale Camilla into an abstract meditation on the theme of death, and his brilliant use of shadow, light, camera movement and settings are as unnerving today as they were upon this sinister film's release 60 years ago. This version is beautifully mastered from a 35mm archive print. "Among the masterpieces of the horror film..." (Carlos Clarens, An Illustrated History of the Horror Film). German with English subtitles.
VHS: S01407. $29.95.
Carl Theodor Dreyer, Denmark, 1931, 75 mins.

VICTOR SJOSTROM

He Who Gets Slapped

This great American silent film, directed by Sweden's Victor Sjostrom, is remarkable both for the performances of Lon Chaney and Norma Shearer and for Sjostrom's incredible lighting effects and use of Expressionist devices. Chaney plays the brilliant scientist who has been cheated out of his discovery and only meets with derision when he tries to claim recognition. Dejected, he becomes a clown with a French traveling circus, and finally exacts a spectacular revenge. With John Gilbert, Tully Marshall, Marc McDermott and Ford Sterling. Silent with music score.
VHS: S19530. $29.95.
Victor Sjostrom, USA, 1924, 85 mins.

Outlaw and His Wife

The great breakthrough film of the Swedish cinema, Victor Sjostrom's 1917 story takes place in Iceland during the 19th century, and is the story of a farmer hunted by the police for a petty crime, who, with his wife, must flee into the hills. Eventually the couple, united by their mutual love, succumb to the brutal forces of nature. This version, restored by Bengt Forslund of the Swedish Film Institute, is accompanied by a full orchestral score, and is tinted in various hues to suggest location and time of day.
VHS: S03705. $29.95.
Victor Sjostrom, Sweden, 1917, 109 mins.

Phantom Chariot

Based on the legend that the coachman of Death must be replaced by the last man to die each year, Sjostrom's film is as famous for its realistic depictions of life in the slums as for its fantasy sequences which make use of double exposures. Silent.
VHS: S01017. $29.95.
Victor Sjostrom, Sweden, 1920

Under the Red Robe

Conrad Veidt, Raymond Massey and Annabella star in this drama about France's notoriously wicked Cardinal Richelieu. A poor soldier is forced to serve the fiend in his conflicts with the protestant Huguenots. Sadly, the soldier falls in love with one of the Cardinal's victims.
VHS: S23814. $24.95.
Victor Sjostrom, Great Britain, 1937, 85 mins.

The Wind

"The Wind is one of the masterpieces of the silent cinema" (Georges Sadoul). Lillian Gish plays a sensitive young girl from Virginia who goes to live with her cousin on the lonely Texas prairie. She survives the threat of an intruder whom she kills in self-defense, a dust storm, and a temporary descent into near madness. The most powerful performance of Gish's career, in which Victor Sjostrom perfectly synthesized the forces of nature and those of human emotion.
VHS: S09283. $29.95.
Victor Sjostrom, USA, 1928, 90 mins.

SCANDINAVIAN WORLD

Finland, Fresh and Original

Begin in the capital city of Helsinki and proceed to visit the neo-classical Senate Square and the striking monument to composer Jean Sibelius; also journey to the unspoiled wilderness of Lapland where reindeer herding is an ongoing tradition. 50 mins.
VHS: S12274. $24.95.

russian CINEMA

Adam's Rib
A contemporary Russian social comedy reminiscent of Chekhov. Set in a crowded flat, the great Irina Churikova plays the stressed-out post-Soviet woman taking care of mute, disabled (but opportunistic) Grandma and her own two daughters. She also tries to deal with her crazed ex-husband and to put a little love into her life, with devastating and hilarious results. A warm, wry comedy. Russian with English subtitles.
VHS: S20826. $89.98.
Vyacheslav Kristofovich, Russia, 1992, 77 mins.

The Anna Akhmatova File
A moving portrait of the extraordinary Soviet poet, Anna Akhmatova. Although her work was banned and went unpublished for 17 years, her poem "Requiem" became the underground anthem for the millions who suffered under Stalin. This unique film, which uses Akhmatova's diaries for text, also includes portraits of Akhmatova's friends and contemporaries—Boris Pasternak, Vladimir Mayakovsky, Mikhail Sostchenko. Russian with English subtitles.
VHS: S13313. $59.95.
Semeon Aranovitch, USSR, 1989, 65 mins.

Autumn Marathon
Andrei is a polite and educated man, an excellent translator of Dostoevsky, and at 45, an established man of letters and college professor. Alla, 25, is genuinely in love with him and Andrei feels perfectly at home in her flat. His official domicile, however, is with Nina, 40, attractive and charming, a good mother, excellent housewife, and in need of Andrei. So, you can see that life is hard for Andrei. This Soviet comedy, scripted by popular playwright Alexander Volodin, is one of the most interesting Soviet films of the last 20 years. Russian with English subtitles.
VHS: S12971. $59.96.
Georgi Daniela, USSR, 1979, 100 mins.

Ballad of a Soldier
Grigori Chukrai's poetic and elegiac war story is one of the major works of post-war Russian cinema, detailing the odd, bemused moments of a soldier's earnest seduction of a country girl while visiting his mother. The film is also devastating at capturing the dread, pain and humiliation of war, and its effects on the people. "The picture flows in such a swift, poetic way that the tragedy of it is concealed by a gentle lyric quality" (*New York Times*). With Vladimir Ivashov and Shanna Prokhorenko. Russian with English subtitles.
VHS: S17516. $59.95.
Grigori Chukrai, Russia, 1959, 89 mins.

Baltic Deputy
An aged scientist is criticized by his colleagues for his support of the Revolution of 1917 and finds friendship and support among the sailors of the Baltic Fleet, who elect him as their deputy to the Petrograd Soviet, in this first-rate psychological drama. Nikolai Cherkassov, in his first major role, gives a brilliant portrayal of the 75-year-old professor although he himself was only 52. Russian with English subtitles.
VHS: S01938. $65.00.
Alexander Zharki/Josef Heifitz, USSR, 1937, 95 mins.

Black & White
Lisa is a young Soviet emigre studying medicine in Manhattan. She meets Roy, an African-American man working as a building superintendent on New York's Lower East Side, and the two fall in love. Their story of passion while living on the edges of Manhattan is ultimately the story of the quest for freedom and identity. With Elena Shevchenko, Gilbert Giles, Patrick Godfrey, Gina Delio, Hayward Boling, Debra Jo Jackson and Stephen Parris. In English.
VHS: S26333. $59.95.
Boris Frumin, USA/Russia, 1991, 96 mins.

The Burglar
Music and the problems of the young share center stage in this "punk" Soviet film. Russian rock star Konstantin Kinchev plays the older of two brothers who defiantly use Leningrad's budding punk culture as a haven for their drunken dad and oppressive society. While much of the narrative rests on the slender shoulders of the younger brother, Kinchev's charismatic musical performance carry the picture's rebel yell against totalitarian tedium. Russian with English subtitles.
VHS: S12966. $59.95.
Valeri Ogorodnikov, USSR, 1988, 101 mins.

Burnt by the Sun
This Academy Award-winning feature (Best Foreign Language Film) is a wonderfully intimate, Chekhovian idyll set in Stalinist Russia which, at its conclusion, packs an explosive political climax. Director Nikita Mikhalkov plays a legendary revolutionary hero living in a dacha outside Moscow with family and friends. Most of the film's complex relationships are seen through the innocent eyes of Mikhalkov's (and the hero's) beautiful daughter in a film that gently reveals the tragedy of living under Stalinism. Russian with English subtitles.
VHS: S26809. $96.99.
Laser: LD75391. $39.95.
Nikita Mikhalkov, Russia, 1994, 134 mins.

Circus
Grigori Alexandrov's daring attempt to import the American musical comedy form into the Soviet Union was conceived by its director as "an eccentric comedy...a real side-splitter." Its star is an American circus artiste who has a black baby—a daring conceit for 1936! The only way she can find happiness is among the Soviet people. Lyubov Orlova is the star in this rare comedy. Russian with English subtitles.
VHS: S27216. $29.95.
Grigori Alexandrov, USSR, 1936, 89 mins.

Close to Eden
Also known as *Urga*, Nikita Mikhalkov's film is set in the vast rolling steppes of inner Mongolia. The young Mongolian shepherd Gombo, his wife Pagma and family live a simple, 19th century existence. Their lives are interrupted a Russian truck driver named Sergei who insinuates himself into their protected lives. Sergei alters the family's traditional perspective when he takes Gombo on a revealing and hilarious trek into the city. Cinematography by Villenn Kaluta. With Badema, Bayaerty, Vladimir Gostukhin and Babushka. Russian and Mongolian with English subtitles.
VHS: S19262. $94.95.
Nikita Mikhalkov, Mongolia/USSR/France, 1991, 118 mins.

Come and See
This towering, cathartic experience, described as "142 minutes of raw emotion," won top prizes at the Moscow and Venice film festivals. The story is based on writer Alex Adamovich's WWII memoirs of SS reprisals against partisans. Set in occupied Byelorussia in 1943, the film follows a raw teenager into the swamps and forests of the border provinces, where he undergoes a hell of atrocities, becoming a middle-aged wreck as he tries to survive the carnage. Remarkable acting, camera work, crowd scenes and direction raise the film far beyond anything comparable as director Elem Klimov manages both a savage beauty and an impassioned elegy in this anti-war film. Russian with English subtitles.
VHS: S12963. $59.95.
Elem Klimov, USSR, 1985, 142 mins.

Commissar
One of the most celebrated Soviet films. In 1967, a Soviet filmmaker told a tale of Jewish life, suffering, bravery and fatalism in a movie about a Red Army commissar who finds herself living with a small-town Jewish family while civil war rages around them. The film, an indictment of anti-Semitism, was Askoldov's first and last feature film. Shortly after its completion, Askoldov was fired and the film locked away. Now finally released, the film's "artistic and emotional impact is formidable...Askoldov has mastered a poetic style" (*Sight and Sound*). Russian with English subtitles.
VHS: S12962. $59.95.
Alexander Askoldov, USSR, 1967-87, 110 mins.

The Cranes Are Flying
A film that marked a radical opening for Soviet cinema; the lighthearted, romantic, lyrical story of a beautiful young girl (Tatiana Samoilova) caught up in the horrors of war. When her fiance (Alexei Batalov) goes off to war, she marries a man whom she does not love and who raped her, is evacuated to Siberia, and after the war, learns of her fiance's death. But she refuses to believe it and waits for his return. A great international success which won the Grand Prix at Cannes. Russian with English subtitles.
VHS: S17517. $59.95.
Mikhail Kalatozov, USSR, 1957, 94 mins.

Creation of Adam
Andrey is a young man who fears his marriage may fall apart because his wife thinks he is gay. A series of events confirm these suspicions as Andrey meets Philip, an enterprising business man who turns his life around. Philip shows Andrey how to love. Russian with English subtitles.
VHS: S26405. $39.95.
Yuri Pavlov, Russia, 1993, 93 mins.

Crime and Punishment
Lev Kulijanov's supremely authentic translation of Dostoevsky's great novel to the screen, with Innokenti Smoktunovsky playing the Police Inspector Porfiry, and Georgi Taratorkin as the impoverished student-murderer Raskolnikov. Perhaps the best performance, however, belongs to Tatyana Bedova as Sonia, the beautiful woman with the power of redemption. Cinemascope. Russian with English subtitles.
VHS: S10718. $29.95.
Lev Kulijanov, USSR, 1970, 220 mins.

Don Quixote
A masterful adaptation of Cervantes' great novel features Nikolai Cherkassov as Quixote, who becomes so impressed with tales of chivalry that he becomes a knight errant, and takes up arms to defend the poor and oppressed. Kozintsev brings to the adaptation a grand sense of color, spectacle and comedy, but preserves Don Quixote's dignity. Russian with English subtitles.
VHS: S01551. $59.95.
Grigori Kozintsev, USSR, 1957, 110 mins.

The Errors of Youth (Wild Oats)
Deemed "too close to 'real' life in the former Soviet Union" and thus banned in 1979, *The Errors of Youth* is the story of Dmitri (Stanislav Zhdanko), a former conscript in the Red Army (now a highly-paid construction worker in Siberia), who finds his love affair disintegrating over the question of children. Disillusioned, he moves to Leningrad, falls into a life of black marketeers, and enters into a marriage of expediency. Director Boris Frumin left the unfinished film behind and emigrated to the United States, and in a historic gesture on Russia's part, was invited back to Leningrad 11 years later to complete the film. With Stanislav Zhdanko, Marina Neyelova and Natalia Varley. Russian with English subtitles.
VHS: S26332. $59.95.
Boris Frumin, USSR, 1978-1989, 87 mins.

Forgotten Tune for the Flute
A funny and warm romantic comedy which was a huge success in the Soviet Union, a satire on the high-ranking class of government officials. Lenny, the main character, is a married man who lives a privileged life. But when he is hospitalized for a minor heart attack, he falls in love with Lida, a sexy nurse, who brings him out of his ordered existence and helps him discover his true personality. Russian with English subtitles.
VHS: S11480. $19.95.
Eldar Ryazanov, USSR, 1987

Freedom Is Paradise
With his mother dead and a missing father that he has never met, 13-year-old Sasha finds himself the unwilling resident of a grim reform school. When Sasha accidentally learns of his father's whereabouts, he sets off on a 1,000 mile odyssey to a gulag-style high security prison. Russian with English subtitles.
VHS: S16260. $69.95.
Sergei Bodrov, USSR, 1989, 75 mins.

Freeze, Die, Come to Life
A brilliant Soviet film about the brutal conditions of life in and around Stalinist labor camps as seen through the eyes of two remarkable children. This first feature by Vitaly Kanevski, who also wrote the screenplay and co-produced the film, is based on some of his own experiences during the eight years he spent growing up outside such a camp. With Pavel Nazarov, Dinara Drukarova, Yelena Popova. Awarded the Camera D'Or for best first film at Cannes. Russian with English subtitles.
VHS: S15941. $19.98.
Vitaly Kanevski, USSR, 1991, 105 mins.

Glasnost Film Festival
This remarkable 12-volume set is a unique opportunity to witness first-hand the contemporary achievements of Soviet filmmakers as they examine a broad range of topics and issues affecting their society.

Glasnost Film Festival Vol. 1: Against the Current and The Wood Goblin. *Against the Current* is a film about ecological crime and how the residents of Kirishi educate themselves to the meaning of citizenship. They are called extremists, but they continue to organize protests of a major synthetic protein plant. "We couldn't breathe, we coughed, we itched, we buried our children...but we can't put up with it any more," a young woman shouts indignantly at a rally. The residents call the illness "Bykov's disease," after the factory's founder, who is now a government minister. Directed by Dmitri Delov, 1988, 27 mins. *The Wood Goblin* focuses on an old man who has lived alone in the woods with a cat and two dogs for 15 years, in a house he built by himself. He commanded a tank company during World War II and after the war was a local Communist Party chief. Fired from his position after a smear campaign, he went away to live in the woods. As he puts it, he "joined the party of the green world," which he now defends against resourceful poachers and woodcutters. Directed by Boris Kustov, 1987, 18 mins. Both films in Russian with English subtitles.
VHS: S11666. $59.95.

Glasnost Film Festival Vol. 2: The Temple. A strikingly beautiful film about the 1000th anniversary of Christianity in Russia and the role of religion in Soviet society, both past and present. The filmmakers interpret the spiritual experience of the nation anew. We attend a holiday celebration at the Trinity-Sergius monastery at Zagorsk, and see how a burned house of worship is restored by an entire community. We talk with a young monk and an 80-year-old parish priest, Nikolai. One Soviet reviewer wrote about this film: "We cannot rewrite history. We can only learn lessons from it." Directed by Vladimir Dyakonov, USSR, 1987, 58 mins. Russian with English subtitles.
VHS: S11667. $59.95.

Glasnost Film Festival Vol. 3: The Tailor and Early on Sunday. *The Tailor* is a sobering look at the spiritual void and disillusionment of the current generation of middle-aged adults. They entered life with faith in their talent, in their destiny, and in love. But by the dawn of the Brezhnev years, they were aged before their time, having lost their preferred work and the opportunity for creative self-realization. Directed by Vladislav Mirzoyan, 1988. 50 mins. *Early on Sunday* is a simple, endearing film. On a Sunday morning in winter, several old village women go to the forest to gather wood. They chop down some sturdy pine trees, build a fire, banter about their life and other things, and finally go home. Their unpretentious observations evoke bursts of laughter, feelings of compassion, and an immense respect for the dignity and patience of these women who are unaware of their own worth. Directed by Murat Mamedov, 1987, 18 mins. Russian with English subtitles.
VHS: S11668. $59.95.

Glasnost Film Festival Vol. 4: Chernobyl and The Bam Zone. *Chernobyl: Chronicle of Difficult Weeks* was made by the first film crew in the disaster zone following the meltdown of the Chernobyl nuclear power plant in 1986. For more than two weeks, they fought for the right to film, then shot continuously for more than three months. A lifeless city. Empty villages. A dead forest. Portions of the film itself are exposed with white blotches—radiation leakage. Various agencies blocked its wider release and Soviet film goers saw the film only after the director's tragic death from radiation poisoning. Directed by Vladimir Shevchenko, 1988, 53 mins. *The Bam Zone: Permanent Residents* is a daring film set in Siberia. The Baikal-Amur Mainline (BAM) Railroad is called the longest monument to the stagnation of the Brezhnev era. "Before filming, we screened miles of BAM films. There were marches and songs, meetings and delegations...But behind the screen, actually, equipment was breaking down, lives were broken and souls became calloused." Directed by Mikhail Pavlov, 1987, 18 mins. Russian with English subtitles.
VHS: S11669. $59.95.

Glasnost Film Festival Vol. 5: Scenes at a Fountain and The Limit. The ironic title of *Scenes* refers to a powerful, rumbling column of fire—the world's largest natural gas fire, which burned over one year on the shores of the Caspian Sea. Flames shot 600 feet high. The film dramatically documents the courageous firemen who risked their lives to cap the howling 600 foot high blaze. Directed by Igor Gonopolsky, 1988, 28 mins. *The Limit* is "a shout of horror about how the terrible catastrophe of drinking condemns a human being." Families are divided, homes are neglected, kids are hungry. A powerful examination of rampant alcoholism in the Soviet Union. Directed by Tatyana Skabard, 1988, 14 mins. Russian with English subtitles.
VHS: S11670. $59.95.

Glasnost Film Festival Vol. 6: And the Past Seems But a Dream and Theatre Square. In 1937, a group of children wrote an idealistic book called "We Are from Igarka." The filmmaker planned to film their touching reunion 50 years later. But a different childhood was revealed than that in the book, "a time that was much more painful than the worst nightmare. It's a film about the collapse of faith, first faith in God, then in Stalin. It's about the slavish need for an idol and the complicated attitudes of people to Stalinism." Directed by Sergei Miroshnichenko. *Theatre Square* focuses on a hunger strike in 1988 staged in Erevan over the disputed Nagorno-Karabkh region, populated by Armenians, but part of the neighboring republic of Azerbaijan. Directed by Grigor Arutnyan, 1988, 28 mins. Russian with English subtitles.
VHS: S11671. $59.95.

Glasnost Film Festival Vol. 7: Black Square and Dialogues. *Black Square* tells the story of Russia's artistic avant-garde from the 1950's to the 1970's, when artists were confronted with semi-official, ideological art. Works could be smashed by bulldozer, flooded with acid, or covered with concrete. *Black Square* is a cinematic appreciation of works only recently allowed to be exhibited, and the story of the artists, many of whom were forced into exile. Directed by Joseph Pasternak, 1988, 56 mins. *Dialogues* features a bacchanal of rock jazz and punk that erupt in an abandoned Leningrad palace. Collective singing, dancing and playing makes the group a community. Directed by Nikolai Obukhovich, 1987, 28 mins. Russian with English subtitles.
VHS: S11672. $59.95.

Glasnost Film Festival Vol. 8: This Is How We Live and Homecoming. A shocking look at the alienation of young people in a daring look at Soviet punks—young people who emulate fascists by wearing swastikas on their sleeves. Directed by Vladimir Oseledchik, 1987, 30 mins. *Homecoming* is a remarkably frank look at the veterans of the Soviet involvement in Afghanistan who return home with unresolved feelings about a demoralizing and unpopular war, not unlike the U.S. involvement in Vietnam. Directed by Tatyana Chubakova, 1987, 17 mins. Russian with English subtitles.
VHS: S11673. $59.95.

Glasnost Film Festival Vol. 9: Marshall Blucher: A Portrait Against the Background of an Epoch. This daring film tries to unlock the riddle of the dramatic 30's in the Soviet Union by studying the fate of the entire country through the biography of one hero. Marshal Vasily Konstantinovich Blucher was one of the best Red Army commanders, a man of irreproachable courage and compassion. Yet in 1938, he was declared an "enemy of the people," and perished in Stalin's torture chambers. Rare archival footage illustrates the excesses of the Stalin era. Directed by Vladimir Eisner, USSR, 1988, 88 mins. Russian with English subtitles.
VHS: S11674. $59.95.

Glasnost Film Festival Vol. 10: The Trial II and Adonis XIV. *The Trial* dramatically chronicles the Stalinist trials of the 30's and 40's, and a court of conscience, putting the epoch of the Stalin personality cult itself on trial. The "Testament" by famed Bolshevik theoretician Nikolai Bukharin, who was executed by Stalin, is revealed here for the first time by his wife Anna. Directed by Igor Belyayev, 1988, 55 mins. *Adonis XIV* is a parable—a goat, its horns ornamented with little bells, leads a herd of sheep, cows and horses to the slaughterhouse. The symbolism was not lost on the censors, who banned the film for over nine years. One director said, "Everyone who sees this short story should look around and ask himself, 'Why did I survive?' " Directed by Bako Sadykov. 1977, 1988, 9 mins. Russian with English subtitles.
VHS: S11675. $59.95.

Glasnost Film Festival Vol. 11: Final Verdict and The Evening Sacrifice. *Final Verdict* is a look at an actual case: a handsome student, on trial, killed a woman and her guest. This remarkable investigation of "in cold blood" tries to understand the motivation behind the tragedy. The killer is a man of intelligence, and during his 20 months on death row discovers he is no longer the person he once was. The film argues the death sentence does not remove the guilt of the killer. Directed by Hertz Frank, 1987, 88 mins. *The Evening Sacrifice* captures the spirit of a crowd. "He placed the camera in the right place and turned it on at the right moment" in this freewheeling example of "underground" filmmaking from the Soviet Union. Directed by Alexander Sokurov, 1987, 17 mins. Russian with English subtitles.
VHS: S11676. $59.95.

Glasnost Film Festival Vol. 12: Are You Going to the Ball? and Tomorrow Is a Holiday. What is the price young athletes pay for their fleeting celebrity? *Are You Going to the Ball?* takes an unprecedented look at one of the Soviet Union's most sacred institutions: its world-famous women's gymnastic team. "It seems to me I gave up all my health for gymnastics," a former champion says in the film, "My entire body is in pain, and now my time is over." Directed by Nadezhda Khvorova, 1987, 28 mins. *Tomorrow Is a Holiday* looks at women whose job is to stuff live chickens into metal containers. The camera observes there is not much difference between the executioners and their victims. The workers' dorms are utilitarian lodgings, sort of containers for people. The women, enraged by their abnormal living conditions, "keep singing songs to avoid crying or swearing." Directed by Sergei Bosukovsky, 1987, 18 mins. Russian with English subtitles.
VHS: S11677. $59.95.

Glasnost Film Festival Complete Set. The complete set of 12 volumes of the Glasnost Film Festival at a special price.
VHS: S11678. $495.00.

The Gorky Trilogy
The renowned Russian film series by director Mark Donskoi, which is based on the autobiography of Maxim Gorky. Here Donskoi re-creates the tone and mood of Gorky's autobiographical stories with an astounding intensity of feeling. "These dramas still retain their vast humanity and optimism, and they remain the best loved of all Soviet films" (David Robinson). Russian with English subtitles. 100 mins. each.
Part 1: *My Childhood.* The first and most famous part of the trilogy depicts Gorky's early life in the 1870's. At the age of four Gorky is placed in the care of his cruel grandfather and loving grandmother. After experiencing the misery of abuse and poverty with his new family, he is forced into the streets and becomes a wandering beggar. 1938.
VHS: S15372. $39.95.

Part 2: My Apprenticeship. In the second part of the trilogy, Gorky begins earning his living at the age of eight. Becoming an apprentice to a bourgeois family that falsely promises him an education, he secretly learns to read on his own and sets off on a series of land and sea voyages. During these excursions Gorky sees that the poverty and misery he has continually suffered are facts of everyday life for most of the Russian people. With this recognition he encounters the seeds of the coming revolution. 1939.
VHS: $15373. $39.95.
Part 3: My Universities. In the final part of his trilogy, Donskoi deals with Gorky's early manhood. At the University Gorky meets several liberal intellectuals and is introduced to their radical politics. Making his first attempts at writing, Gorky joins the revolution and begins to accept his role in this quickly-changing world as a brand new person, washed clean of a painful and stunted past. 1940.
VHS: $15374. $39.95.
Mark Donskoi, USSR, 1938-40

I Am Cuba
The Cuban revolution is at the center of Mikhail Kalatazov's strange, poetic film from 1964 which unites four stories. Originally controversial because of a uniquely Russian view of Cuba, it was not widely seen. Now the film, which features a poem by Yevgeni Yevtushenko, has been re-released to critical acclaim. It offers a uniquely earthy view of Cuba in the early 1960s. Spanish with English subtitles.
VHS: $27339. $79.95.
Laser: LD75464. $69.95.
Mikhail Kalatozov, Cuba/Russia, 1964, 141 mins.

I Was Stalin's Bodyguard
A controversial film that created a storm in Russia by taking the cloak off a violent, repressive era of Soviet history. Filmmaker Semeon Aranovitch found the last surviving personal bodyguard of Josef Stalin, who began to work for him in the 1930's. I Was Stalin's Bodyguard weaves together unprecedented, first-hand testimony with rare footage, including Stalin's home movies. What emerges is a singular portrait of a violent and complex era during which Stalin consolidated his power through brutal repression, yet lead the Soviet Union to victory in World War II. Russian with English subtitles.
VHS: $13312. $59.95.
Semeon Aranovitch, USSR, 1990, 73 mins.

I Worked for Stalin
Semeon Aranovitch's documentary is a brilliant assembly of eyewitness testimony and rare archival photographs and materials. The film records the Machiavellian power plays between Zhdanov, Andreyev, Khrushchev, Malenkov, Suslov and Molotov as they maneuvered for power and prestige to gain the inside track of becoming Stalin's successor. The film is a chilling record of the inner workings of an authoritarian state. Russian with English subtitles.
VHS: $18686. $59.95.
Semeon Aranovitch, USSR, 1990, 67 mins.

Incident at Map Grid 36-80
A Cold War thriller that's a Soviet response to The Hunt for the Red October, about an apocalyptic struggle following a Soviet naval squadron's encounter with a disabled American nuclear submarine. The submarine's computer malfunctions, inadvertently launching its nuclear payload. The film is important for its unprecedented portrait of Soviet military life and its modern technology. Russian with English subtitles.
VHS: $12973. $59.95.
Mikhail Tumanshishvili, USSR, 1983, 85 mins.

Inspector General
Gogol's famous play, performed by members of the Moscow Art Theatre, filmed by Vladimir Petrov. Gogol's work is a satire of provincial corruption in Czarist Russia. An entire town mistakes an illiterate worker for the Czar's Inspector General, and the corrupt officials panic as they believe the man has come to check up on them. Russian with English subtitles.
VHS: $00628. $49.95.
Vladimir Petrov, USSR, 1954, 128 mins.

Interpretation of Dreams
Twentieth-century Russia is the less-than-willing subject of this close psychoanalytic interpretation, inspired by Freud's book of the same name. Archival and newsreel footage, together with commentary employing the psychoanalytic method, offer great insights which clarify such cataclysmic events as the rise of Stalin and the Cold War. This acclaimed film has been called "truly magical and extraordinary." and "an astonishing marriage of Freudian thinking and history." Russian with English subtitles.
VHS: $21132. $29.95.
Andrei Zagdansky, Russia, 1994, 50 mins.

Is It Easy to Be Young
A controversial Soviet documentary, made in 1987, the first look at the punk rock subculture in the Soviet Union. Filmmaker Yuri Podniek captures punks cavorting at a concert, being dragged into court for smashing up a train, and telling the camera about the tender hopes and the drab realities of their lives as hospital orderlies, morticians, and drug-addicted, disillusioned Afghanistan veterans. A powerful, disturbing film. Russian with English subtitles.
VHS: $12967. $59.95.
Yuri Podniek, USSR, 1987, 90 mins.

Jazz Comedy (Jolly Fellows)
Grigori Alexandrov's first musical comedy is the rags-to-fame story of a shepherd boy who reaches lofty heights as a jazz-orchestra conductor. The film belongs to its heroine—Lyubov Orlova—who established herself as the first recognized star of Soviet cinema. Jazz Comedy is also remarkable for the clever camera work of Vladimir Nilsen, who introduced Western camera tricks to Soviet cinema. Russian with English subtitles.
VHS: $27215. $29.95.
Grigori Alexandrov, USSR, 1934, 98 mins.

Jazzman
Good-natured flights of fancy strive to overcome harsh ideological realities in the light-hearted Soviet film, The Jazzman, as a conservatory musician links up with three street musicians. The four try, in the words of the idealogue, to "popularize the monstrous product of a bourgeois culture,"—in other words, to start the first Soviet jazz combo. A charming film with lots of Soviet Dixieland. Russian with English subtitles.
VHS: $12965. $59.95.
Karen Chakhnazarov, USSR, 1983, 95 mins.

Kindergarten
A largely autobiographical memoir directed by poet Yevgeni Yevtushenko, recalling his boyhood years during World War II in Russia while the city of Moscow was being evacuated as the Nazis approached. Told as a picaresque adventure about a little boy who meets carloads of strange characters, the narrative assumes a poetic, experimental form of storytelling as Yevtushenko recreates the overcrowded railroad stations, Nazi planes, black marketeers, women bandits and passengers and villagers. Russian with English subtitles.
VHS: $12974. $59.95.
Yevgeny Yevtushenko, USSR, 1983, 160 mins.

King Lear (Kozintsev)
One of the truly great Soviet films, and possibly the greatest adaptation of Shakespeare to the screen, Grigori Kozintsev's epic adaptation, shot in Lithuania, is a stunningly visual tour-de-force. With screenplay by Boris Pasternak. Russian with English subtitles.
VHS: $03555. $59.95.
Grigori Kozintsev, USSR, 1971, 140 mins.

Lady with the Dog
Based on Chekhov, and directed by the Russian master of Chekhov adaptations, Josef Heifitz, this bittersweet, nostalgic story opens in Yalta at the beginning of the century. A middle-aged bank official on vacation encounters a beautiful young woman named Anna who each day walks her dog along the promenade. They drift into an affair, part, return to their homes and unhappy marriages, but Dmitri is haunted by Anna's memory and the two arrange clandestine meetings, realizing that they are doomed to a life of brief, secret encounters. Russian with English subtitles.
VHS: $01925. $29.95.
Josef Heifitz, USSR, 1960, 86 mins.

Leo Tolstoy
This feature-length film traces the turbulent life of one of the greatest writers of the 19th century, Leo Tolstoy. Follow his life from childhood through his stormy marriage to his death. A vital biography for all who are interested in gaining insight into the driving forces behind Tolstoy's body of work. Russian with English subtitles.
VHS: $13008. $59.95.
Sergei Gerasimov, USSR, 1983, 180 mins.

Lessons at the End of Spring
A young boy's loss of innocence within a pre-perestroika Russian prison is the Kafkaesque premise of this harrowing film. The impressive feature debut of writer-director Oleg Kavun, Lessons at the End of Spring immediately places him at the forefront of Russia's groundbreaking new wave of angry young filmmakers. A landmark in the evolution of Soviet cinema. Mature themes and extensive male nudity. Russian with English subtitles.
VHS: $15495. $69.95.
Olag Kavun, USSR, 1989, 75 mins.

Little Vera
The film that took Russia by storm and then sent a second shock wave when its young star, Natalya Negoda, posed nude for Playboy, declared "a smash hit" by Time Magazine and "Steamy Sex!" by Los Angeles Times. Negoda plays Vera, the sullen, sultry teenager who's torn between her brooding husband and her bitter parents in a dead-end town. With her simmering sensuality and brutal candor, Little Vera is a seductive Russian film that gave the Russians (and Americans) something which they never expected—a truly new sex kitten. Russian with English subtitles.
VHS: $10576. $29.95.
Laser: CLV. LD70262. $39.95.
Vassili Pitchul, USSR, 1988, 135 mins.

Luna Park
A gang of young, tough skinheads make their mark in the chaotic turmoil of post-Communist Russia, where right-wing extremists of all sorts abound. This iron-pumping gang, led by its crazed leader, knows no limits in its terrifying effort to purify the nation. It's a rollercoaster ride of an action film in the tradition of Mad Max. Russian with English subtitles.
VHS: $21196. $89.95.
Pavel Lounguine, Russia, 1992, 107 mins.

Magic Horse
The first cartoon feature film from the Soviet Union, based on one of the most popular children's folk tales, about a boy who befriends a magical horse. With sound dubbed into English.
VHS: $00798. $29.95.
I. Vano, USSR, 1941, 56 mins.

Moscow Does Not Believe in Tears
Vladimir Menshov's melodrama about the cruel anonymity of city life is structured in two parts. The first half is set in 1958, as Menshov charts the interlocking romantic fates of three Russian girls shunned to a workers' dormitory. Tonya (Raisa Ryazanova) finds grace and happiness; Ludmila (Irina Muraveva) is trapped in an unhealthy and oppressive marriage; Katerina (Vera Alentova) is crudely abandoned when her lover discovers she's pregnant. The second half resumes their stories and lives 20 years later. Winner of the 1980 Academy Award for Best Foreign Film. With Alexei Batalov, Alexander Fatiushin and Boris Smorchkov. Russian with English subtitles.
VHS: $19053. $59.95.
Vladimir Menshov, Russia, 1979, 148 mins.

Moscow Parade
Ute Lemper stars in this, the first post-Soviet film about the Stalin era. In 1939, she is a young aristocrat married to a hateful chief of the secret police. His forces have murdered her family but she takes advantage of her marriage to enjoy all the luxuries her present lifestyle allows. When she meets a mysterious man and learns of his plans to paint a horse black, her life is thrown into a whirlwind of change. Russian with English subtitles.
VHS: $21091. $29.95.
Ivan Dykhovichny, Russia, 1993, 103 mins.

New Babylon (Novyi Vavilon)
The Paris Commune of 1871 represents a historic moment that could have led to momentous changes had it succeeded. This early silent Soviet production is based on the events of that often overlooked "forgotten revolution." It dramatizes the fight of the Communards through the story of a young woman caught up in the struggle against the bourgeois. Told in eight parts, this silent epic captures the historic sweep of revolutionary Paris. Includes Dmitri Shostakovich's first film score.
VHS: $27374. $29.95.
Grigori Kozintsev/Leonid Trauberg, USSR, 1929

No Greater Love
The powerful story of a Russian woman who turns her villagers into partisans for revenge against the Germans, who have killed her husband and infant son. An important war-time Soviet film made during the War (1943), the film was dubbed into English by the Soviets. Vera Maretskaya gives an incredible performance as the peasant woman. Dubbed in English.
VHS: $03355. $49.95.
Frederic Ermler, USSR, 1943, 74 mins.

Oblomov
A beautiful adaptation of the famous Ivan Goncharov novel by Nikita (Dark Eyes, Slave of Love) Mikhalkov. Oblomov owns 350 serfs he's never met, and just lies on his back in a St. Petersburg apartment, sleeping, eating, sleeping some more, watching his finances dwindle and whining at his servant for not being sensitive enough. A detailed, beautifully photographed film. Russian with English subtitles.
VHS: $12969. $59.95.
Nikita Mikhalkov, USSR, 1980, 120 mins.

Othello
Russian actor/director Sergei Bondarchuk (War and Peace) stars as the Moor of Venice in this very unusual and compelling Russian adaptation of Shakespeare's great play. The film was awarded the Best Director at the Cannes Film Festival. Dubbed in English.
VHS: $23900. $29.95.
Sergei Yutkevich, Russia, 1955, 108 mins.

The Overcoat
Roland Bykov delivers a moving performance as the poor, degraded clerk in 18th century Russia in this version of Nikolai Gogol's famous short story. Expressionistic in tone, but with a strong dose of realism, it is a commendable adaptation of the story. Russian with English subtitles.
VHS: $00985. $39.95.
Alexei Batalov, USSR, 1962, 73 mins.

Patriots
A remarkable film about divided loyalties in a small Russian town during World War I. The film blends comic, ironic and tragic elements to evoke the eccentric inhabitants of the town, with performances full of spontaneity and remarkably naturalistic use of sound. Yelena Kuzmina stars in a comic role with Nikolai Bogolyubov and Nikolai Kryuchov. "There is something of Chekhov's plays…the concealed and repressed emotions of its characters, the pauses and hints, the circumstances and atmosphere of events, the combination of comic and dramatic elements, all building a profound inner rhythm" (O. Borisov). Russian and German with English subtitles.
VHS: $01939. $59.95.
Boris Barnet, USSR, 1934, 82 mins.

People's Gala Concert
A landmark documentary; Semeon Aranovitch explores the roots of Russian anti-Semitism during Stalin's final years, set around the murder of the brilliant actor Solomon Mikhoels and the case of a group of Russian doctors charged with attempting to poison Stalin. Aranovitch draws on rare archival footage and interviews with survivors and their descendants to relate this untold history. Russian with English subtitles.
VHS: $15824. $79.95.
Semeon Aranovitch, Russia, 1991, 143 mins.

Peter the First Part One
A lavish, spectacular production, the first part covers the early years of the reign of Tsar Peter I. Russian with English subtitles.
VHS: $01552. $59.95.
Vladimir Petrov, USSR, 1937, 95 mins.

Peter the First Part Two
The second part of the lavish biography of Peter the First of Russia. Russian with English subtitles.
VHS: $01553. $59.95.
Vladimir Petrov, USSR, 1938, 104 mins.

Planeta Burg
A foreign sci-fi masterpiece! Cosmonauts land on Venus to find themselves in peril by various alien monstrosities. This appears to be the actual print that Roger Corman used to make parts of the negative to Voyage to the Prehistoric Planet (the film cans are addressed to Roger). Visually stunning. Based on a story by Stanislav Lem. Russian with English subtitles.
VHS: $15370. $29.95.
Pavel Klushantsev, USSR, 1962, 73 mins.

Private Life
Nominated for an Academy Award for Best Foreign Film, Private Life focuses on an executive who loses his perch in the bureaucracy, and finds out what his family and friends really think of him. An acutely observed portrait of hypocrisy in the Soviet middle-class, with vividly drawn observations. With Mikhail Ulyanov, Ita Sanvina and Irena Gubanova. Russian with English subtitles.
VHS: $12968. $59.95.
Yuli Raizman, USSR, 1983, 103 mins.

Rasputin
One of the legendary long-banned Soviet films, Elem Klimov's Rasputin (original title: Agonia) is a brutal look at the self-proclaimed prophet who reveled in decadence, lust and power, and altered the face of the 20th century. Rasputin's madness brought Russia to its feet and sparked the revolution that toppled the throne. "Frenzied semi-delirium…This film's existence has been a legend for nearly a decade," wrote J. Hoberman in The Village Voice. Russian with English subtitles.
VHS: $11472. $59.95.
Elem Klimov, USSR, 1978, 106 mins.

The Red Tent
A virtually unknown but first-rate film by Soviet filmmaker Mikhail Kalatazov, The Red Tent was an international production funded in Italy, and is the tragic story of General Nobile, the heroic Italian who tried to cross the North Pole on a dirigible in the early years of this century. When the dirigible crashed, no one responded to their desperate SOS calls, and the survivors huddled within their makeshift red canvas dwelling and continued to hope. Peter Finch stars as General Nobile, Sean Connery portrays the renowned Arctic explorer Roald Amundsen. In English.
VHS: $07414. $19.95.
Laser: LD75303. $39.98.
Mikhail Kalatazov, 1969, 121 mins.

Revolt of the Fishermen
An extremely rare film: the only cinematic work by the great theater genius Erwin Piscator made in Russia is set on the ship St. Barbara and remarkable for its mixture of naturalism and expressionism. With Alexei Diky, Emma Tseraskaya.
VHS: $24125. $29.95.
Erwin Piscator, Russia, 1935, 60 mins.

Road to Life
Orphaned youths collect into gangs following the turmoil caused by Russia's Revolutionary and Civil wars. Mustafa leads one band sent to be reformed in an experimental program. Despite a caring teacher, change is complicated by new trades and their inescapable criminal pasts. Russian with English subtitles.
VHS: $22473. $39.95.
Nicolai Ekk, Russia, 1931, 100 mins.

Scarecrow
Called the Soviet Lord of the Flies, Scarecrow is a haunting and touching film about a little girl who is ostracized by her cruel classmates. She learns about mob psychology the hard way, registering her bitter comprehension with a luminously expressive face. Russian with English subtitles. With Christula Crbakaita, Yuri Nukulin.
VHS: $12964. $59.95.
Rolan Bykov, USSR, 1985, 101 mins.

Seagull
A sensitive, exquisitely acted version of Chekhov's great play, set in provincial Russia, a penetrating study of the languid melancholia of the residents of an isolated country estate. With Alla Demidova, Lyudmila Savelyeva, Yuri Yakovlev. Russian with English subtitles.
VHS: $01550. $29.95.
Yuri Karasik, USSR, 1971, 99 mins.

Second Circle
Susan Sontag calls Alexander Sokurov "perhaps the most ambitious and original serious filmmaker of his generation." In this film, considered Sokurov's best by many critics, a man confronts his father's death in a society cut off from spiritual values. "Rarely has so much visual and emotional power been generated… the film is extreme in its rigor, subtlety and its sublimity" (Christian Science Monitor). Russian with English subtitles.
VHS: $26495. $59.95.
Alexander Sokurov, Russia, 1990, 90 mins.

The Shooting Party
Emil Lotenau's adaptation of Chekhov's short story about a passive magistrate whose unconsummated desire for a woodsman's daughter leads to a terrifying act of violence, official approval and attempted cover up. The film is related in flashback, as Lotenau deftly explores the judge's turpitude, and by larger extension, the corrupt pre-czarist culture. "So rich in its imagery, to watch [this film] is a fascinating, almost intoxicating experience" (Vincent Canby). With Galina Belyayeva and Oleg Yankovsky. Russian with English subtitles.
VHS: $19066. $79.95.
Emil Loteanu, USSR, 1977, 105 mins.

Siberiade
Russian history over six decades is revealed through the eyes of two opposing families in this epic film. One proletarian family, the Ustyuzhanins, yearns for change, while the aristocratic Solomins desperately cling to their privileged past. These opposing views finally climax in a battle over oil in Siberia. Winner of the 1979 Jury Prize at Cannes. Russian with English subtitles.
VHS: $21541. $79.95.
Andrei Konchalovsky, Russia, 1979, 190 mins.

Sideburns
Yuri Mamin's bitter, dark satire about the rise of fascism and reactionary elements in Russia concerns The Pushkin Club, a right-wing movement, enlisted by the Party to orchestrate "a social cleaning service," charged with eliminating "the scum of Western influence." The film's goal is "to make people laugh at reality before they die of horror," Mamin says. Russian with English subtitles.
VHS: $16737. $59.95.
Yuri Mamin, Russia, 1991, 110 mins.

A Summer to Remember
A small, intimate portrait that recounts the adolescence of a young boy growing up in southern Russia, recalling the relationship with his mother and stepfather, and evoking an innocence and atmosphere he cannot reclaim. The boy's stepfather is played by the excellent Russian filmmaker Sergey Bondarchuk (War and Peace). Russian with English subtitles.
VHS: $01280. $39.95.
Daneba/Talankin, USSR, 1960, 78 mins.

Sword and the Dragon
Beautiful fairytale from Soviet director Alexander Ptushko in which a magic potion and a legendary sword lead a simple farmer into battle against the invading Tugars and their evil leader. Amid galloping hooves and clashing swords, Ilya and his mighty warriors battle to defend their homeland. English dubbed.
VHS: $09194. $19.95.
Alexander Ptushko, USSR, 1960, 81 mins.

Taxi Blues
Pavel Lounguine's first feature is a critique of contemporary Soviet society, captured through the bleak and paternalistic relationship of a hard-drinking, fascist, anti-Semitic taxi driver and a dependent, alcoholic Jewish saxophonist. A French/Soviet co-production with excellent lead performances of Piotr Mamonov and Piotr Zaitchenko. Russian with English subtitles.
VHS: $17398. $89.95.
Pavel Lounguine, Russia/France, 1990, 110 mins.

Tchaikovsky
An opulent biography of the 19th century composer. The film is centered around his antagonistic relationship with his mentor, the pianist Rubenstein, and his long-term benefactor, the Baroness von Meck. The film downplays the composer's homosexuality to develop the tenets of his unhappy marriage. Music arranged and conducted by Dimitri Tiomkin. With Innokenti Smoktunovsky, Antonina Shuranova and Evgeni Leonov. Russian with English subtitles.
VHS: $19056. $59.95.
Igor Talankin, Russia, 1971, 153 mins.

The Theme
Glen Panfilov's daring work was banned by Soviet authorities for eight years. Esenin (Mikhail Ulyanov), a government-approved playwright and functionary, visits his native village for some artistic rejuvenation and falls for a dynamic and brilliant but uncompromising young artist, Sasa (Inna Churikova), who rejects his overtures. Winner of the 1987 Golden Bear winner at the Berlin Film Festival. With Stanislav Lyubshin, Evgeny Vesnik and Sergei Nikonenko. Russian with English subtitles.
VHS: $19054. $59.95.
Gleb Panfilov, Russia, 1979, 98 mins.

The Twelfth Night
Klara Luchko and Alla Larianova star in this masterful Russian adaptation of Shakespeare's great work. All the wit and lyrical humor of this famed play are brilliantly captured in this entertaining and handsome production. Dubbed in English.
VHS: $23906. $29.95.
Yan Fried, Russia, 1956, 88 mins.

Unfinished Piece for a Mechanical Piano
A bittersweet, humorous tapestry of human folly and lost dreams, loosely based on Chekhov's play *Platonov*. The course of the film takes place during a summer day at a decaying summer dacha. The hero had a spoilt love affair and now meets his old girlfriend, married to another. All his passions and frustrations burst out in the open. The film's leisurely atmosphere belies the intensity of the emotional content underneath, with Mikhalkov revealing profound moments of truth. With Alexander Kalyagin, Yelena Solovieva and Yevgey Glushenko. Russian with English subtitles.
VHS: $18694. $59.95.
Nikita Mikhalkov, USSR, 1977, 100 mins.

Viva Castro!
Set in Russia in the 60's, when Fidel Castro was as popular as Elvis Presley was in America, *Viva Castro!* is a brilliant look at Russia's disaffected generation of the young. The year is 1965 and the setting is a small Russian town. Young Kolya's father flees from his home and his family after stealing some coins from a museum, and Kolya's mother is sent to a labor camp as punishment for her husband's crime. Kolya falls in love with his singing teacher, but when his father returns from exile, he becomes involved with his father's nurse. With Pavel Zharkov, Julia Sobolevskaya and Sergey Dontsov. Russian with English subtitles.
VHS: $26331. $59.95.
Boris Frumin, Russia, 1993, 82 mins.

Volga Volga
An unseen miracle of 1930's Soviet cinema, *Volga Volga* is a revelation—a classical musical comedy that catapulted Lyubov Orlova into a Russian mega star. The setting is a giant steamboat making its way up the Volga River. On board is a motley collection of amateur singers and dancers travelling to Moscow to take part in a musical contest. At their center is Lyubov Orlova, featured alongside veteran Meyerhold comedian Igor Ilinsky. A triumphant success upon its release, it remains one of the most important and best-loved films produced by the Soviet regime. Russian with English subtitles.
VHS: $27214. $29.95.
Grigori Alexandrov, USSR, 1937, 90 mins.

War and Peace
The definitive version of Sergei Bondarchuk's epic adaptation of Tolstoy's novel. The story concerns how Napoleon's 1912 Russian invasion affected two upper class families. Winner of the 1968 Best Foreign Language Academy award, the film was shot over five years, with a cast of 10,000 soldiers, nearly 300 sets, 2,000 costumes and production design and art direction culled from more than 40 Russian museums. The film is notable for its gritty authenticity and naturalism and its panoramic social and political portraits, especially the battle of Borodino. Three cassettes. With Ludmila Savelyeva, Vyacheslav Tikhonov and Bondarchuk.
Dubbed in English.
VHS: $07683. $99.95.
Russian with English Subtitles.
VHS: $18466. $99.95.
Sergei Bondarchuk, Russia, 1966/67, 403 mins.

Waterloo
The stirring drama of the historic battle between Napoleon and Wellington, starring Academy Award winner Rod Steiger. The battle itself takes up the last hour of the film and is quite exciting. Also starring Christopher Plummer and Orson Welles. In English.
VHS: $13706. $19.95.
Sergei Bondarchuk, Italy/USSR, 1971, 122 mins.

Window to Paris
This wonderfully inventive, wildly hilarious comedy from Yuri Mamin starts in St. Petersburg, where an impoverished music teacher finds that the closet door of his new one-room apartment opens onto a window on the other side of which lies…Paris! Soon the denizens of the Russian flat are busy transporting themselves (and all the goods they can find) over the Paris rooftops into their St. Petersburg apartment. *Window to Paris* is a sharp, witty and totally original satire. Russian with English subtitles.
VHS: $27083. $96.99.
Yuri Mamin, Russia, 1994, 92 mins.

ANDREI TARKOVSKY

Andrei Rublev
The dazzling and harrowing tale of the 15th century icon painter who survives the cruelties of medieval Russia to create works of art. As bloody Tartar raids, religious brutality, and pagan rites work to quell Rublev's desires and needs, he undertakes a spiritual odyssey that affirms man's ability to transcend adversity. This restored director's cut is presented in letterbox format; Russian with English subtitles.
VHS: $16526. $19.98.
Laser: Uncut, 205 mins. Contains behind-the-scenes production footage. **LD72435. $99.95.**
Andrei Tarkovsky, USSR, 1966, 185 mins.

Directed by Andrei Tarkovsky
It was left to a Polish film crew to document this diary-like last will and testament of the late filmmaker Andrei Tarkovsky. The film was shot in Sweden as Tarkovsky, already ill and in excruciating pain, was directing his final film, *The Sacrifice*. In addition to revealing footage of Tarkovsky at work, the film is a moving look at a major artist at the zenith of his career, concerned as much for the future of mankind as for his art. Swedish and Russian with English subtitles.
VHS: $12972. $59.95.
Michal Leszczylowski, Sweden, 1988, 100 mins.

The Mirror
Tarkovsky's looking glass is not merely cracked but shattered and we see the jagged, jumbled reflections of its shards, images of the director's childhood mixed with fragments of his adult life…a child's wartime exile, a mother's experience with political terror, the breakup of a marriage, life in a country home; all intermingled with slow motion dream sequences and stark newsreel. An essential film whose puzzles provide the key to this intense filmmaker's other works. Russian with English subtitles.
VHS: $13009. $59.95.
Andrei Tarkovsky, USSR, 1985, 101 mins.

My Name Is Ivan
A new print of the first feature film directed by the great Andrei Tarkovsky. This beautiful work, filled with poetic flourishes and an overriding sense of melancholy, immediately placed him in a position of leadership among the young Soviet filmmakers of his era. Set during WW II, it is the story of a young boy who is deprived of his childhood and struggles with the brutal realities of war. The film contains many images that would later become Tarkovsky's trademark, and is a brutally poetic evocation of innocence lost in the face of war. B&W. Russian with English subtitles.
VHS: $14290. $19.98.
Andrei Tarkovsky, USSR, 1962, 84 mins.

Solaris
The release of this remarkable science fiction film marked a milestone in Soviet cinema. *Solaris*, adapted from the science fiction novel by respected Polish writer Stanislav Lem, is one of those rare screen works which improves upon and deepens its literary source. The story deals with a series of expeditions to the planet Solaris—closely examining the ways the various earth scientists interact among themselves and, more importantly, the ways in which they interact with each other's memories. "I find it one of the most original, most poetic, most beautifully paced science-fiction films I've ever seen" (Jonas Mekas, *The Village Voice*). Presented in letterboxed format. Russian with English subtitles.
VHS: $14289. $19.98.
Andrei Tarkovsky, USSR, 1972, 167 mins.

Stalker
In this eerie, hypnotic and highly symbolic work, shot in painterly images that seamlessly move from black and white to color, a fallen meteorite produces the Zone, a blistered wasteland that's only penetrated by special guides called "Stalkers." Tarkovsky's film concerns a three-man expedition into this surreal, frightening region. A powerful, extraordinary cinematic experience that anticipates the dread of Chernobyl. With Alexander Kaidanovsky, Nikolai Grinko, and Anatoli Solonitsin. Russian with English subtitles.
VHS: $16984. $19.98.
Andrei Tarkovsky, Russia, 1979, 161 mins.

SERGEI PARADJANOV

Ashik Kerib
Ashik Kerib is a wandering minstrel, rejected by a powerful merchant to marry his daughter, who travels for one thousand days to finance his wedding. In Paradjanov's hands, it becomes a visual opera of costumes, movement and music, in which surreal framing, icons, pomegranates and other mystical symbols fill a living tableau with images that are simply miraculous. Dedicated to Andrei Tarkovsky, the theme of *Ashik Kerib* is the transforming power of art and the tragedy of the artist. Cinematography by Albert Yavuryan. With Yiur Mgoyan, Veronikia Metonidze and Levan Natroshvili. Azerbaijani and Georgian with English subtitles.
VHS: $19055. $59.95.
Sergei Paradjanov, Russia, 1988, 78 mins.

The Color of Pomegranates
Paradjanov's sublime mosaic on the life, art and spiritual odyssey of the 18th-century Armenian poet Sayat Nova. The film is a collection of images and tableaux that interweave landscapes, villages, costumes, props and music to form a metaphorical history of the Armenian nation. The film "achieves a sort of visionary para-surrealism through the most economical means of gesture, props and texture…A sublime and heartbreaking film" (J. Hoberman, *The Village Voice*). This director's cut repositions the shots and images and restores censored footage. Armenian with English subtitles. On the same program is *Hagop Hovnatanian*, Paradjanov's 12-minute short on the Armenian artist.
VHS: $19064. $79.95.
Sergei Paradjanov, USSR, 1969, 78 mins.

Legend of Suram Fortress
Based on a Georgian legend, the first feature completed by Sergei Paradjanov after being released from prison. The tale hangs on the self-sacrifice of a young man who agrees to be bricked up in a fortress wall in order to make it impregnable against invaders. Paradjanov divides his film into a series of tableaux, once again using minimal dialog and searing imagery in a film of surreal, almost hypnotic power. Georgian with English subtitles.
VHS: $13007. $59.95.
Sergei Paradjanov, USSR, 1984, 100 mins.

Shadows of Forgotten Ancestors
Sergei Paradjanov's masterpiece, a brilliant, epic story of starcrossed lovers set against the ethnographic panorama of the Carpathian Mountains. The film is a visual tour-de-force of symbols, metaphor, lyrical photography and active camera as it interweaves myth and narrative into an elliptical, seamless work of art. Its images "become superimposed on the mind, and will emerge later with a new and more profound meaning, a meaning that escapes logical analysis, that cannot be grasped intellectually, but which calls upon us to respond with feeling" (Robert Walke). With Ivan Nikolaichuk and Larisa Kadochnikova. Ukrainian with English subtitles.
VHS: $07576. $29.95.
Sergei Paradjanov, USSR, 1964, 99 mins.

ANDREI KONCHALOVSKY

Duet for One
A world famous concert violinist played by Julie Andrews finds herself slowly stricken by multiple sclerosis. Andrews shines in an emotional performance as she strives to maintain her marriage and her sense of self-worth. With Max Von Sydow and Alan Bates.
VHS: $03574. $14.95.
Andrei Konchalovsky, USA, 1986, 107 mins.

Inner Circle
Andrei Konchalovsky recreates the terror of the Stalinist years through the eyes of Stalin's personal film projectionist. Tom Hulce stars as Ivan Sanshin, a loyal Communist who screens the latest newsreels and American movies for the man in charge of the Soviet Union, and his close personal friends, without missing a reel change. Lolita Davidovich is memorable as the wife who knows her husband loves Stalin more. With Bob Hoskins as the head of the KGB.
VHS: $16805. $19.95.
Laser: LD71574. $39.95.
Andrei Konchalovsky, USA/USSR, 1991, 134 mins.

Runaway Train
John Voight and Eric Roberts star in this thriller based on a screenplay by Akira Kurosawa, from the director of *Maria's Lovers*. Voight and Roberts play escaped cons in the Northeast wilderness, aboard a speeding train hurtling toward certain derailment.
VHS: $01139. $14.95.
Laser: Letterboxed. **LD72355. $34.98.**
Andrei Konchalovsky, USA, 1985, 112 mins.

Shy People
Andrei Konchalovsky's film is about a chic Manhattan magazine writer and her troubled teenage daughter, who venture deep into the Louisiana bayou, where they find a lot more than their long-lost relatives—violence, mystery and fear.
VHS: $07475. $19.98.
Andrei Konchalovsky, USA, 1987, 119 mins.

Siberiade
Russian history over six decades is revealed through the eyes of two opposing families in this epic film. One proletarian family, the Ustyuzhanins, yearns for change, while the aristocratic Solomins desperately cling to their privileged past. These opposing views finally climax in a battle over oil in Siberia. Winner of the 1979 Jury Prize at Cannes. Russian with English subtitles.
VHS: $21541. $79.95.
Andrei Konchalovsky, Russia, 1979, 190 mins.

EARLY SOVIET CINEMA

Aelita: Queen of Mars
One of the most remarkable discoveries of the Soviet silent cinema, *Aelita* is a stunning big-budget science fiction spectacle. Enormous futuristic sets and radical constructionist costumes were designed by Alexandra Exter to enhance this story of romance, comedy and danger. A Moscow engineer designs a spaceship and travels to Mars to meet the woman who haunts his dreams. He succeeds but finds himself embroiled in a Martian proletarian uprising. *Aelita*, with its exaggerated production design and political undertones, was a profound influence on Fritz Lang's *Metropolis* three years later. Silent, with orchestral score.
VHS: $13826. $29.95.
Yakov Protazanov, USSR, 1924, 113 mins.

Arsenal
A romantic and lyrical masterpiece set during the war of 1914, in the countryside and at the front. *Arsenal* depicts the Revolutionary struggle in Kiev as the arsenal goes on strike and the strikers are defeated. Its great sequences include the symbol of a starving horse, and the death of the Revolutionary hero who, as he struggles forward with open shirt, is riddled with bullets by the Whites. With S. Shavshenko, A. Buchma. Silent with music track, English titles.
VHS: $00069. $29.95.
Alexander Dovzhenko, USSR, 1929, 65 mins.

Bed and Sofa
A landmark of cinema, this brilliant social comedy centers on a menage-a-trois in the midst of a housing shortage in Moscow. The film rejects politics and symbolism for sense of humor and naturalism. It is supposedly based on an episode in the life of the great poet Mayakovsky; Ludmila Semyonova is the extraordinary actress at the center of the triangle. Her decision at the end of the film symbolizes the liberation of women in the new Soviet society.
VHS: $01933. $29.95.
Abram Room, USSR, 1927, 73 mins.

By the Law
Lev Kuleshov's great film—one of the most important films of the silent Soviet period, set in Alaska, where two men are killed in a remote cabin, and the killer is condemned by his two companions. Silent with music. English titles.
VHS: S03553. $39.95.
Lev Kuleshov, USSR, 1926, 90 mins.

Chapayev
A stirring account of a beloved hero of the Russian Revolution, an illiterate Russian who served in Czar's army; after the Revolution, formed his own forces and went on the Red Side, fighting the Whites. Full of incredible images, the film was made from personal experience of the filmmakers. Russian with English subtitles.
VHS: S00231. $49.95.
S. & G. Vassiliev, USSR, 1934, 100 mins.

The Cigarette Girl of Mosselprom
A delightful and boisterous comedy satirizing Soviet life and filmmaking in the 1920's, *The Cigarette Girl of Mosselprom* is the greatest work of director Zhelyabuzhsky, who began as a cameraman with the famous Russ collective. The story follows the exploits of a young woman who is tossed from street vending into the world of movies when she is cast as the lead in a romantic melodrama. Silent, with orchestral score.
VHS: $13821. $29.95.
Yuri Zhelyabuzhsky, USSR, 1924, 78 mins.

Early Russian Cinema: Before the Revolution
An important ten-part video anthology that considers the early thematic, cultural, political and artistic developments of Russian cinema, before the 1917 October Revolution. Music by Neil Brand. Translation by Julian Graffy. "There was the exhilaration of discovery, a vision of marvelous vistas—but also an awesome sense of the vast interior that remains to be explored" (David Robinson, *Sight and Sound*).

Vol. 1: Beginnings. Documentaries like *A Fish Factory in Astrakhan* (1908) preceded the first Russian dramatic production, *Stenka Razin* (Romashkov, 1908). Meanwhile, the Moscow branch of Pathe produced its own version of the film d'art, *Princess Tarankova*, followed with its first of many Chekhov adaptations, *Romance with Double Bass* (Hansen, 1911). 45 mins.
VHS: $17849. $29.95.

Vol. 2: Folklore and Legend. *Drama in a Gypsy Camp* (Siversen, 1908), and the unreleased *Brigand Brothers* (Goncharov, 1912) are typical folklore subjects, while *A 16th Century Russian Wedding* (1909) and *Rusalka* (1910), both directed by the pioneer enthusiast Vasilii Goncharov, show how rapidly Russian cinema espoused national and cultural themes. (55 mins.)
VHS: $17850. $29.95.

Vol. 3: Starewicz's Fantasies. Starewicz's later puppet animation is now better than his brilliant beginnings at the Khazhonkov Studios. He pioneered insect-puppets in *The Ant and the Grasshopper* (1911) before turning to live action fantasy in his version of Gogol's *Christmas Eve* and contributing to the war effort with an anti-German allegory, The Lily of Belgium (1915). 58 mins.
VHS: $17851. $29.95.

Vol. 4: Provincial Variations. Jewish life was one of the exotic subjects covered in provincial films like the Latvian *Wedding Day* (Slovinski, 1912). The remarkably bleak melodrama *Merchant Bashirov's Daughter* (Larin, 1913, set on the Volga) was based on a real murder scandal. (55 mins)
VHS: $17852. $29.95.

Vol. 5: Chardynin's Pushkin. The former touring actor-manager Petr Chardynin made an early name for himself with Pushkin adaptations like *The Queen of Spades* (1910) and *The House of Kolomna* (1913), in which Ivan Mousjoukine played both a dashing officer and a farcical cook in drag. (45 mins.)
VHS: $17853. $29.95.

Vol. 6: Class Distinctions. Despite strict censorship intended to prevent inflammatory material, Goncharov portrayed the hardship of rural life in *The Peasants' Lot* (1912), and an early film by Evgenii Bauer, *The Silent Witnesses* (1914), dealt frankly with servants' views of their masters. (94 mins.)
VHS: $17854. $29.95.

Vol. 7: Evgenii Bauer. The major discovery of the early Russian cinema. In a mere five prolific years, Bauer achieved mastery of several genres, including the social melodrama of *A Child of the Big City* (1913), erotic comedies like *The 1002nd Ruse*, and the psychological gothic drama of *Daydreams*. (95 mins.)
VHS: $17855. $29.95.

Vol. 8: Iakov Protazanov. Protazanov did not shirk controversy or challenge in either his highly successful pre- or post-1917 careers. *The Departure of a Great Old Man* (1912) provoked legal action by the Tolstoy family for its scandalous portrayal of the writer's last days. His *Queen of Spades* starred Mosjoukine in one of his most compelling roles. (104 mins.)
VHS: $17856. $29.95.

Vol. 9: High Society. A panorama of Russian cinema's social impact: *Antosha Ruined by a Corset* (Puchalski, 1916) is a racy, knowing urban comedy; *A Life for a Life* (1916) marked the pinnacle of Bauer's ambition to equal lavish foreign production standards; and *The Funeral of Vera Kholodnaia* (1919) records the vast public response to the early death of Russia's greatest star. (72 mins.)
VHS: $17857. $29.95.

Vol. 10: The End of an Era. Between 1917's two revolutions, cinema reflected new themes, as in Bauer's *The Revolutionary* (1917), but also pursued the traditional subject of thwarted love in what would be his last film, *For Luck* (1917). A fragment *Behind the Screen* (1917) shows the husband-wife stars Mosjoukine and Lisenko on the eve of their departure into exile. (72 mins.)
VHS: $17858. $29.95.

Early Russian Cinema: Complete Set. All 10 volumes of the Early Russian cinema collection at a special price.
VHS: $17859. $250.00.

Earth
A great masterpiece—the fourth and last silent film by Dovzhenko, a lyrical evocation of his native Ukraine, the theme of the life cycle of man developed through constant juxtaposition and intertwining of images of life and death. Ultimately very moving, a film poem of inestimable beauty. Silent with English subtitles.
VHS: $00389. $29.95.
Alexander Dovzhenko, USSR, 1930, 88 mins.

End of St. Petersburg
Commissioned, as was Eisenstein's *Ten Days That Shook the World*, to celebrate the tenth anniversary of the Russian Revolution, *End of St. Petersburg* shows the basic difference in approach between Eisenstein and Pudovkin. Pudovkin concentrates on a peasant who comes to St. Petersburg for a visit and becomes "politicized," believing in strike and revolution. Pudovkin focuses on the individual, with the emotional power of the film emerging from seeing the effects of the Revolution on common people. With Ivan Chuvelyov and Vera Baranovskaya. English titles.
VHS: S00408. $29.95.
Vsevolod Pudovkin, USSR, 1927, 75 mins.

The Extraordinary Adventures of Mr. West in the Land of the Bolsheviks
An inspired satire of America's slanted view of Russia, *Mr. West* is sharply funny as it plays with misconceptions about the Soviet people. A bourgeois American is challenged by his friends to visit those "mad, savage Russians." Once he arrives, he is beset by an onslaught of strange characters and events, thrusting him into a world of danger and intrigue. Soon Mr. West realizes that only through his all-American ingenuity can he survive...then the farce really begins. Silent, with a piano score.
VHS: S03700. $29.95.
Lev Kuleshov, USSR, 1924, 88 mins.

Fall of the Romanov Dynasty
With remarkable historic footage and radical editing, this film stands as a colossal documentary portrait of the collapse of the Czarist regime and the triumphant rise of communist rule. Director Shub, a pioneer in editing and mentor to Sergei Eisenstein (influencing his montage theories), unearthed thousands of films—including personal footage by the Czar's own cameramen—to bring to life a daring and innovative historical drama of the events from 1912 to 1917. Silent, with orchestral score.
VHS: S13822. $29.95.
Esther Shub, USSR, 1927, 90 mins.

Father Sergius
One of the few surviving films from before the October Revolution, *Father Sergius* introduced an anti-religious element into Russian cinema in its realization of Tolstoy's story about an officer who became a monk on the eve of his wedding and suffered tortures of the flesh thereafter. Silent with English subtitles.
VHS: S00435. $29.95.
Yakov Protazanov, USSR, 1917, 81 mins.

Girl with the Hatbox
Moving with the speed and grace of the best American silent comedies, this Russian classic teamed Anna Sten—later a star for Goldwyn in the 1930's—with director Boris Barnet. Sten portrays a working girl who is given a seemingly worthless lottery ticket instead of her wages by her unscrupulous employer. The ticket wins her a fortune, and a madcap chase ensues to possess the ticket—and Anna's love. Silent, with orchestral score.
VHS: S13823. $29.95.
Boris Barnet, USSR, 1927, 67 mins.

Guerilla Brigade
An extremely rare film by Igor Savchenko, the Ukrainian filmmaker who was a contemporary and colleague of both Eisenstein and Dovzhenko. Set during the Civil War, *Guerilla Brigade* is set during the Civil War, and is notable for its poetic and epic depiction of the Ukrainian and Russian people joining together in their struggle. Russian with English subtitles.
VHS: S06898. $69.95.
Igor Savchenko, USSR, 1939, 90 mins.

Happiness
Subtitled "A Tale About a Hapless Mercenary Loser, His Wife, His Well-Fed Neighbor and Also About a Priest, a Nun and Other Old Relics," *Happiness* is a slapstick comedy based on old folklore but changed with (often risque) modern satire. Banned in Russia for 40 years, Medvedkin's film offers a parade of comic oddities, from polka-dotted horses to nuns in see-through tunics. Sergei Eisenstein called *Happiness* "a magnificent film" not only for its sly spoofing of Bolshevik values, but for its ability to incite laughter...even from the dourest revolutionary. Silent, with piano score.
VHS: S13824. $29.95.
Alexander Medvedkin, USSR, 1934, 69 mins.

Mother
Pudovkin's great work depicts an aspect of the abortive 1905 revolt, dramatizing the injustices of Czarist life, but focusing on individuals, on human problems with universal meanings. With an incredible performance by Vera Baranovskaya; one of the landmarks of the history of cinema. Silent with English subtitles.
VHS: S00886. $29.95.
Vsevolod Pudovkin, USSR, 1926, 73 mins.

The Mystery of the Leaping Fish and Chess Fever
Two silent film parodies. One of Sherlock Holmes, the other about the Soviet national pastime. Douglas Fairbanks is the scientific detective Coke Ennyday in the bizarre *Mystery of the Leaping Fish*, written by Tod Browning. The second short is a Russian look at the perils of total devotion to a board game.
VHS: S05686. $29.95.
Pudovkin/Emerson, USA/USSR, 1916-25, 64 mins.

Storm over Asia
Pudovkin's epic of an exploited Mongolian fur trader who becomes involved in the Mongolian uprising against the British during the Civil War period. It is "the film of the destiny of the Occident, although its action takes place in the heart of Asia, on the plateaus of Tibet" (Robert Desnos). Notable for Pudovkin's lyrical/psychological montage which ends in an incredible storm scene which contains "all the dust and debris that Pudovkin could imagine. But how else was Pudovkin to end a film whose attraction for him had been its fable and exotic imagery, except by hyperbole?" (Jay Leyda). With Valeri Inkizhinov, I. Inkizhinov and A. Chistiakov. Silent with music track.
VHS: S01972. $29.95.
Vsevolod Pudovkin, USSR, 1928, 70 mins.

Three Soviet Masters
Three classic short films from the masters of Soviet cinema: Eisenstein, Vertov and Pudovkin. Includes *Behzin Meadow* (30 mins.), *Kino Pravda* (silent, 14 mins.) and *Chess Fever* (silent, 20 mins.).
VHS: S14921. $29.95.

Zvenigora
Ukrainian director Dovzhenko's first major work lyrically captures the entire history of the Ukraine through a series of folk myths stretching from the Viking invasion to the 1919 Civil War. Silent.
VHS: S01970. $29.95.
Alexander Dovzhenko, USSR, 1928, 73 mins.

SERGEI EISENSTEIN

Alexander Nevsky
Sergei Eisenstein's first sound film, with a brilliant music score by Sergei Prokofiev, in a new, meticulous print and new sound recording of this masterpiece. Russian with English subtitles.
VHS: S12949. $29.95.
Sergei Eisenstein, USSR, 1938, 112 mins.

Alexander Nevsky (New Score)
A newly re-mastered, beautiful print of Eisenstein's masterpiece arrives with the famous Prokofiev score newly recorded by the St. Petersburg Philharmonic Orchestra. Russian with English subtitles.
VHS: S24740. $24.98.
Laser: LD75363. $29.98.
Sergei Eisenstein, USSR, 1938, 110 mins.

Battleship Potemkin
Sergei Eisenstein's depiction of the mutiny of the crew of the *Potemkin* during the insurrection of 1905. The bold imagery, stylized composition and powerful rhythmic editing combine to make it a film consistently voted one of the top ten of all time. Silent, with music by N. Kryukov and a brilliant original music score by Edmund Meisel. Digitally remastered.
VHS: S19293. $29.95.
Sergei Eisenstein, USSR, 1925, 65 mins.

Eisenstein
Soviet documentary about the most famous Russian filmmaker, with rare footage of his early life, first films and famous masterpieces, including *Strike*, *Potemkin*, and *Ivan the Terrible*. USSR, 1958, 48 mins.
VHS: S01623. $24.95.

General Line
Begun in 1926 after the completion of *Potemkin*, the film uses what Eisenstein called "polyphonic montage" in which the blacks, whites and grays are used like the sounds and tones of a symphony orchestra. Silent.
VHS: S00485. $29.95.
Sergei Eisenstein, USSR, 1929, 90 mins.

Ivan the Terrible, Part I
Huge close-ups, rich decor and Prokofiev's choral music help make this film one of the great achievements of Russian cinema. In part one, Ivan Grozny is proclaimed Czar of all Russia, but faces treachery within his own family. Russian with English subtitles.
VHS: S00645. $29.95.
Sergei Eisenstein, USSR, 1944, 94 mins.

Ivan the Terrible, Part II
After the great success of *Ivan the Terrible, Part I*, Eisenstein rushed to complete *Part II* of what was to be a trilogy. Eisenstein used color in two sequences to signify psychological meaning. Part II details Ivan's revenge on friends that had denounced him. Russian with English subtitles.
VHS: S00646. $29.95.
Sergei Eisenstein, USSR, 1946, 90 mins.

Que Viva Mexico
Eisenstein's long-lost diamond-in-the-rough, shot by the great Eduard Tisse, and financed by Upton Sinclair. Reconstructed in 1979 by Grigori Alexandrov, the last surviving member of Eisenstein's Mexican team, *Que Viva Mexico* is a silent film narrated in Russian and subtitled in English. Divided into segments: a wedding, a bullfight, a fiesta, a dramatized abortive uprising by peons against feudal masters at the turn of the century. Anyone who has seen the lyrical, ravishing images of Eduard Tisse's *Que Viva Mexico* will revel in the priceless beauty of Eisenstein's incomplete master-work. Russian with English subtitles.
VHS: S12976. $59.95.
Eisenstein/Alexandrov, USSR, 1931, 90 mins.

Secret Life of Sergei Eisenstein
A brilliant documentary on the life and works of the legendary Soviet filmmaker. The film draws on his private memoirs to illustrate a life he described as "intense, joyous, tormented." Weaving together memorable scenes from such masterworks as *Strike*, *Potemkin*, *Alexander Nevsky*, *Ivan the Terrible*, with Eisenstein's sketch books and production notes, the film follows his origins and early career, his sojourns to Europe and the U.S., and his relationships with contemporaries such as Walt Disney, Charlie Chaplin, D.W. Griffith, Pirandello, Brecht, Cocteau, Joyce, Prokofiev and Einstein.
VHS: S12948. $19.95.
Gian Carlo Bertelli, Italy, 1985, 60 mins.

Strike
One of the most original debuts in film history, *Strike* is a brilliant mixture of agit-prop techniques and comic-grotesque stylization in the telling of a factory workers' strike in Czarist Russia in 1912 and the brutal suppression of the strike. Silent.
VHS: S01271. $29.95.
Sergei Eisenstein, USSR, 1924, 75 mins.

Ten Days That Shook the World
Also known as *October*, Eisenstein's famous recreation of the October Revolution during which the Bolsheviks overthrew the Kerensky government. Like his previous work, the film continues Eisenstein's experimental methods. Silent.
VHS: S01306. $29.95.
Sergei Eisenstein, USSR, 1927, 95 mins.

Thunder over Mexico
Also known as *Time in the Sun* and *Eisenstein in Mexico*, this is an edited version of footage from Sergei Eisenstein's unfinished Mexican film, *Que Viva Mexico*. The story has been constructed to focus on the peasant girl and the landowner, and the tragic burial of the two lovers in the sand. Completed by Grigori Alexandrov; cinematography by Eduard Tisse.
VHS: S24123. $29.95.
Sergei Eisenstein, Mexico, 1932

DZIGA VERTOV

Enthusiasm
This tale of coal miners in the Don Basin was made with vivid and unusual use of sound considerably ahead of its time. Upon seeing the film Charles Chaplin wrote: "I would never have believed it possible to assemble mechanical noises to create such beauty. One of the most superb symphonies I have known." English titles.
VHS: S03554. $39.95.
Dziga Vertov, USSR, 1931, 67 mins.

Kino Pravda and Enthusiasm
Two documentaries from the great Soviet polemicist Dziga Vertov, whose avant-garde newsreels known as kino pravda ("film truth") formulated the montage aesthetics of the revolutionary Russian silent cinema of Eisenstein, Kuleshov, Pudovkin and Dovzhenko. Vertov's highly-stylized, non-narrative work produced an anti-formalism which greatly influence Godard.
VHS: S01971. $69.95.
Dziga Vertov, USSR, 1922, 120 mins.

Man with the Movie Camera
Dziga Vertov's masterpiece is an application of "life as it is lived." It makes the cameraman the hero, and is one of the most dynamic experiments with montage; the film also uses trick photography, animation, slow motion and speeded-up shots. It "is a study in film truth on an almost philosophical level...It does deliberately what others try hard to avoid—destroys its own illusions, in the hope that reality will emerge from the process not as a creature of screen illusion but as a liberated spirit" (*Films and Filming*). Silent.
VHS: S00821. $29.95.
Dziga Vertov, USSR, 1928, 69 mins.

Three Songs of Lenin
In this, his last feature film, Vertov paid homage to Russia's great leader with three heartfelt examinations of life in the Soviet Union. "In a Black Prison Was My Face," "We Loved Him" and "In the Great City of Stone" explore the life of Lenin, while showing the effect he had upon the nation and its people. With its exquisite images and masterful editing, *Three Songs of Lenin* paints a living portrait of Vladimir Lenin unequalled by all of the dry rhetoric of history books. Silent, with orchestral score.
VHS: S13825. $29.95.
Dziga Vertov, USSR, 1934, 62 mins.

UKRAINIAN

Harvest of Despair
A documentary about the Ukrainian "terror famine" of 1923-33, which caused the deaths of 7 million people. Using interviews with survivors and scholars to supplement rare photographic evidence, it establishes that the terror famine was deliberately created by the Soviet government as part of Stalin's decades-long effort to destroy the Ukrainian peasantry who resisted collectivization. Academy Award nomination. Canada, 1984, 55 mins.
VHS: S06254. $39.95.

BALTIC

Estonia: A Tale of Two Nations
Estonia is the smallest republic in the USSR, but along with the other two Baltic republics, it is at the forefront of the independence movement sweeping the Soviet Union. This important film shows history in the making. 1990, 45 mins.
VHS: S13955. $95.00.

THROUGH RUSSIAN EYES

7 Up in the Soviet Union
A Soviet variation of Michael Apted's acclaimed documentary series that chronicles the fears and dreams of seven-year-old children. The ethnic tensions, political uncertainty and poverty impacted on 20 Soviet children are dissected in a film called "Unforgettable" (*London Daily Mail*). 70 mins.
VHS: S19243. $19.95.

Andrei Voznesensky
Reading from *An Arrow in the Wall* in Los Angeles on November 19, 1990, this Russian poet made clear why he is revered by so many admirers. Among the translators of his work are such literary figures as W.H. Auden, William Jay Smith and Stanley Kunitz. Poet James Ragan reads from Voznesensky's English translations and also interviews this writer. From the *Lannan Literary Videos* series. 60 mins.
VHS: S27129. $19.95.

Before Gorbachev— From Stalin to Brezhnev
Made in celebration of the 60th anniversary of the October Revolution, this ambitious film documents the history of the USSR for those 60 years, emphasizing progress and the success of communism. 50 mins.
VHS: S12717. $19.98.

Behind Kremlin Walls
Diane Sawyer and Sam Donaldson host this look inside the Soviet symbol of power, including never-before-allowed looks at Lenin's apartments in the Council of Ministers building, the Grand Kremlin Palace, the Terem Palace, treasures and works of art housed in the Armory Palace and more. 60 mins.
VHS: S12290. $19.98.

Best of Nightline: Chernobyl Nuclear Disaster
30 mins.
VHS: S14042. $14.98.

The Black Tulip
Understanding the impact of the Afghan War on Soviet society is essential to an understanding of glasnost and perestroika. *The Black Tulip* is a remarkable look at the human impact of the war on the Soviet people. 1988, 27 mins.
VHS: S13954. $45.00.

Bread and Salt
Jeanne Collachia's documentary skillfully combines the personal and the political as it charts the life of Irina Muraveva, a Soviet woman who renounced her citizenship, gave up her passport and emigrated to the United States in 1986—the year of Gorbachev's political ascension. *Bread and Salt* focuses on Muravyova's return to Russia in 1991, as she experiences the vast social and political restructuring engineered under Gorbachev.
VHS: S19747. $39.95.
Jeanne Collachia, USA, 1991, 95 mins.

Chernobyl
The graphic and otherwise unavailable facts about the after-effects of Chernobyl—the blast site, the people and areas affected, and the questions: What are the statistical risks? Who will develop cancer? Whose children will be mutants? The Chernobyl accident is expected to cause an additional 20,000 to 200,000 deaths in Western Europe.
VHS: S05281. $29.95.

Danylo Shumuk: Life Sentence
Jailed by the Poles, Nazis and Soviets, Shumuk spent more than 42 years in detention for the non-violent expression of his political opinions. This tape is his life-story, and how the efforts of Amnesty International sustained him throughout all of the impossible years. 1987, 27 mins.
VHS: S06892. $20.00.

Discovering Russian Folk Music
Powerful choruses, plaintive songs, swirling dances and magnificent costumes make this musical tradition both beautiful and distinctive. Viewers will delight in this engaging video. 23 mins.
VHS: S23518. $49.95.

Empire of the Red Bear
This three-volume set from the Discovery Channel explores the Russian wilderness which is home to the red bear. It's a landscape of rugged beauty dominated by oversized features, including active volcanoes. 180 mins.
VHS: S25090. $39.95.

Fear and the Muse: The Story of Anna Akhmatova
The great Russian poet is revealed in a video documentary that examines her tragic life in Stalin's Russia, her relationship with poets like Ossip Mandelshtam, and the impact of her poetry, which became a source of strength and inspiration for millions of Russians under Communism. 60 mins.
VHS: S24319. $19.95.

Friends: A Closer Look at the Enemy
Documentary portrait of Betty Petroff, an American teacher/librarian, as she journeys through seven cities in the Soviet Union, eliciting their feelings about the U.S. and the chances for peace in the future. From Leningrad to Red Square, she talks to Soviet citizens of all ages and nationalities to gain their views. Institutional or public performance.
VHS: S06602. $30.00.
G. Shoemaker/B. Petroff, USA, 1987, 30 mins.

From Czar to Stalin
Compiled documentary footage includes World War I, the crowned heads of state in Europe, as well as revolutionary figures in Russia: Lenin, Trotsky and Molotov.
VHS: S03450. $29.98.
Raphael Nussbaum, USA, 1987, 93 mins.

Fun in the U.S.S.R.
Learn how Soviet people spend their weekends. More often than not, what is documented here is the gulf that separates the Soviet people from the Soviet government. A series of whimsical films including *Budget of a Soviet Family* and *Over the Weekend*. 95 mins.
VHS: S12718. $24.98.

Gielgud's Chekhov
Sir John Gielgud hosts and narrates these dramatizations of some of Chekhov's greatest works. 50 minutes each.
Volume 1: *The Fugitive, Desire for Sleep*, and *Rothschild's Violin*.
VHS: S02214. $64.95.
Volume 2: *Volodya* and *The Boarding House*.
VHS: S02215. $64.95.
Volume 3: *The Wallet* and *Revenge*.
VHS: S02216. $64.95.

Golden Domes of Moscow
This rare look at Moscow includes a tour of Red Square, the Kremlin, the Soviet Space Exhibit, a look at a Soviet wedding, the Bolshoi, and even the Russian circus. 30 mins.
VHS: S08279. $24.95.

The House with Knights
The story of a grand apartment building, once the residence of rich and privileged families, which turned into a collective housing unit after the revolution of 1917. Through historical footage and personal interviews with former residents, the incredible story comes alive. Russian with English subtitles. 58 mins.
VHS: S23404. $150.00.

If the People Will Lead

The evolution of freedom in the former Soviet Union was critically influenced by the media. Glasnost ushered in a whole new era of self-expression that could not be reversed even by the coup of 1991. Footage from these troubled times details the growth of freedom. The attempted occupation of a Lithuanian TV station by Soviet soldiers offers a chilling example of the people's courage. 58 mins.
VHS: S21592. $39.95.

Inside Russia

A complete survey of Russia prior to WWII, this rare film was completed only weeks before the German invasion of Russia. Included in the rare footage are sequences on the mountain tribes of the Urals, ancient and modern customs in Tiflis, the oil fields of Bakuk, American machinery in Russian coal mines, the site of the Garden of Eden on the Black sea, the Yalta palaces of the Czar and Grand Duke Dmitri, the Red Square, Maxim Gorky's home, the homes of Tolstoy and Gorky, and much more. Some scratches in print. 75 mins.
VHS: S03351. $49.95.

Joseph Brodsky: A Maddening Space

This unique portrait of Nobel prize-winning poet, essayist and controversial former dissident Joseph Brodsky includes an overview of his troubled life in the Soviet Union, his emigration to the U.S. and his devotion to American literature, and is full of examples of both his poetry and his critical essays. 60 mins.
VHS: S24318. $19.95.

KGB:
The Soviet Sword and Shield of Action

A three-part exploration of the KGB and Soviet intelligence reveals the details of the objectives and means of Soviet intervention around the world. Narrated by Hugh Marlowe, each volume explores the intelligence network of the KGB and its influence and subversive activities. 60 minutes each volume.
Part 1: The Spies.
VHS: S09966. $14.95.
Part 2: The Secrets.
VHS: S09967. $14.95.
Part 3: The Terrorists.
VHS: S09968. $14.95.

The Kremlin

The rich treasures and history of the Kremlin are revealed in this insightful look at the Kremlin, past and present, in the award-winning series produced by Lucy Jarvis. Introduction by Edwin Newman. 60 mins.
VHS: S05317. $24.95.
Laser: LD70295. $39.95.

Lenin and the Bolsheviks

Two enthusiastic profiles are included on this tape of the Revolutionary leader and Soviet hero, Vladimir Ilyich Lenin. These films emphasize the early years—from the first stirrings of the revolutionary spirit to the victory of the Proletariat in 1917. From the *Inside the Soviet Union* series. 60 mins.
VHS: S12708. $19.95.

Life in the Moscow Circus

These neat little films document various aspects of the circus during the past 30 years—going behind the scenes with the traveling circus, unveiling the anticipated big-top circus tents, and following the development of individual performers. 60 mins.
VHS: S12719. $19.98.

Lucky to Be Born in Russia

The sequel to *The Shattered Mirror*, this video relates the human story behind the October 1993 armed confrontation in Moscow, showing the "inner life" of Russian society during this momentous period. The story of a nation searching for a new way as it moves toward an uncertain future. 58 mins.
VHS: S23403. $150.00.

Moscow and Leningrad,
The Crown Jewels of Russia

Journey to Moscow, the soul of Mother Russia and home to eight million of its people. Enter the Kremlin, watch the pageantry of Red Square and see the grandeur of St. Basil's Cathedral. 50 mins.
VHS: S12276. $24.95.

The Moscow Circus:
Animals Under the Big Top

With a cast of more than 6,000 performers and 7,000 animals, the Moscow Circus blends action, live performance and animals.
VHS: S20183. $14.98.

The Moscow Circus:
Dancing Bears and More

The Moscow Circus, which was formed more than 200 years ago by royal decree, blends an astonishing range of animals, fearless tamers and acrobatic entertainers, to stage some amazing physical feats. This program focuses on the theatrical flair of the dancing bears.
VHS: S20182. $14.98.

My Russian Friends

An unprecedented portrait of a people in transition. Using a "verite" camera style with first-person narration, this intimate film confronts political, ideological, and religious issues of concern in the Soviet Union today. 1988, 58 mins.
VHS: S13956. $85.00.

National Geographic Video:
Soviet Circus

A rare opportunity to go behind the scenes of this remarkable circus. Revered as an art form, supported by the government and loved by millions, the Soviet circus thrives today within the confines of a strict society. 60 mins.
VHS: S09277. $19.95.

The New Russian Revolution

Brought to you by the people at CNN, this video document focuses on the failed 1991 hard-line coup in the Soviet Union that temporarily imprisoned President Mikhail Gorbachev and thrust Boris Yeltsin into the world spotlight. USA, 1991, 47 mins.
VHS: S15269. $19.98.

Nicholas and Alexandra

The tragic fate of the last couple in the Russian dynasty is finally exposed to the world. Secrets about their death were maintained by the KGB for decades. This video uses diaries and personal effects from the Imperial Archives to recreate their story. It ends with footage of their woodland grave. 100 mins.
VHS: S25636. $29.95.

Nova—Chernobyl

History's worst nuclear power plant disaster occurred on April 26, 1986 in Chernobyl, USSR. Includes actual footage of the disaster and its aftermath, including Chernobyl as it stands today, as well as opposing views on the long-term health effects of the disaster. 60 mins.
VHS: S11249. $29.98.

Nova—Russian Right Stuff: The Mission

This episode chronicles the arduous training of cosmonauts involved in the Soviet Space Station MIR. 1991, 60 mins.
VHS: S16817. $14.98.

Opiates of the Masses:
Religion in the USSR

The battle between church and state was never more profound than in the Soviet block. This film, made just before the Gorbachev reforms, seems to indicate that the church was winning the battle. 105 mins.
VHS: S12716. $24.98.

Our Russian Front

Lewis Milestone produced this World War II documentary narrated by Walter Huston, dealing with the Russian people's determination against the advancing German Army.
VHS: S10583. $19.95.

Poligon

Thousands of residents living near the Soviet nuclear test site of Semipalatinsk were harmed by ambitious Soviet nuclear arms tests. This extraordinary film, shot just before the fall of USSR, reveals the extent of the damage inflicted on this region as well as the rationale behind the development of ever more deadly arms. The last interview given by Andrei Sakharov is also included. 58 mins.
VHS: S21584. $125.00.

Realms of the Russian Bear

A remarkable television series produced by the BBC in the advent of perestroika, winner of the Sierra Club Centennial Award and several Emmy awards—an unprecedented look at nature and wildlife inside the vast expanses of Russia.
Volume 1: Green Jewel of the Caspian. Visit Astrakhan, the oldest nature reserve on the Volga Delta, where European, Asian and African species of wildlife mingle. 60 mins.
VHS: S22992. $29.98.
Volume 2: The Arctic Frontier. Take a close look at the home of the great white polar bear encompassing one of Russia's most treasured nature preserves—Wrangel Island—where about 10,000 polar bears roam. 60 mins.
VHS: S22993. $29.98.
Volume 3: The Red Deserts. See the abundant wildlife in the deserts of Central Asia, which cover an area larger than the whole of Western Europe and contain a nature reserve that becomes ablaze with color when melting snows bring poppy fields and pistachio groves to life. 60 mins.
VHS: S22994. $29.98.
Volume 4: The Celestial Mountains. Visit the icy peaks of Tian-Shen, the celestial mountains that run for hundreds of miles along the Central Asian Republics and China, where they give shelter to the elusive snow leopard, the rare white-clawed bear, ibex and Marco Polo sheep. 60 mins.
VHS: S22995. $29.98.
Volume 5: Siberia: The Frozen Forest. Siberia is the greatest forest on the planet. Its inhabitants survive temperatures that dip to more than -90° F. It also boasts an immense 6,000-mile expanse of fir and spruce as well as Lake Baikal, the oldest and deepest lake on earth. 60 mins.
VHS: S22996. $29.98.
Volume 6: Born of Fire. The Kamchatka Peninsula is two very different worlds: the Arctic and Southeast Asia in a remote and volatile stretch that is home to some of the most active volcanoes on Earth and where the cool Arctic waters mix with warmer southern currents. 60 mins.
VHS: S22997. $29.98.
Realms of the Russian Bear, Six-Volume Set. Approximately 6 hours.
VHS: S22998. $179.98.

Red Empire

An ambitious account of life inside the former Soviet Union. From the political disruptions and vast changes occasioned by the October Revolution of 1917, the ensuing civil war, this series uncovers top secret documents, archival footage, first hand accounts of the rise and fall of the communist state.
Revolutionaries. This film traces the fall of the imperial Tsar to the opposite fortune of Lenin, the hero of the proletariats.
VHS: S16864. $14.98.
Laser: LD74682. $39.98.
Winners and Losers. The ignominy and massive failure of World War I occasions the outbreak of the Civil War and the political rise of the Communist Party.
VHS: S16865. $14.98.
Class Warriors. Josef Stalin seizes control of the party and enacts a fierce socialist platform.
VHS: S16866. $14.98.
Enemies of the People. Paranoid and possibly off-balanced, Stalin consolidates his power and destroys his "opposition," imprisoning his enemies in gulags, and promoting chaos and anarchy by turning the masses on each other.
VHS: S17685. $14.98.
Patriots. With the outbreak of World War II, the prolonged engagement with the Nazis nearly devastates Soviet society and destroys the empire.
VHS: S16867. $14.98.

Survivors. The defeat of the Axis powers launches the political fortunes of Krushchev, creating the Warsaw Pact, and unleashes the Cold War.
VHS: S16868. $14.98.
Prisoners of the Past. Gorbachev rises to power, issuing a series of radical social and economic reforms.
VHS: S16869. $14.98.
Collector's Set.
VHS: S16870. $99.98.

Red Star Rising:
The Dawn of the Gorbachev Era

The man who has forever changed the fate of the Soviet Union and the world is Mikhail Gorbachev. The complete story via ABC News. 60 mins.
VHS: S12692. $24.98.

Russian People:
Revolution and Evolution

This program explores the history of Russia in the 20th century, and the impact of the changes occurring now under Chairman Gorbachev, as the Soviet Union turns an important corner in the development of their concept of a socialist state. Contains historical material and live footage shot in Moscow, Leningrad and Prague. 45 mins.
VHS: S04166. $39.95.

Sex in the Soviet Union

Ted Koppel, host of ABC's *Nightline*, explores the new sexual mores of the former Soviet Union. Pornography, abortion and prostitution have all exploded because of the headlong rush to enjoy newly found freedoms. 60 mins.
VHS: S23002. $19.98.

The Shattered Mirror

An intimate view of typical Russian life during a period of great social and political change. A remarkable look at the new life, opportunities and challenges that the citizens of Russia now face. Award winner. 58 mins.
VHS: S23402. $150.00.

Solovky Power

Harrowing documentary about the first Soviet prison camp. Aging survivors recall in devastating detail the cruelties and injustice suffered at the hands of their oppressors. Old newsreel footage and recently discovered letters from prisoners further illustrate the bleak conditions. 93 mins.
VHS: S23406. $150.00.

The Soviet Mind

Student views are presented in this program that reveal the impact of tremendous changes across the vast Soviet Union. Social issues and a comparison of capitalism and socialism provoke challenging discussion. 30 mins.
VHS: S23713. $129.95.

Soviet School Day:
Styles in Soviet Education

The film reveals the many faces of Soviet education and the children who participate in it. A Soviet English class discusses Shakespeare and *Catcher in the Rye*, and was produced by the U.S.-USSR Youth Exchange Program.
VHS: S03797. $75.00.
Shirley Ward, USA, 1984, 18 mins.

Soviet Secret Archives

This three-part documentary utilizes rare, never-before-seen footage, personal testimonies and archival materials to relate the evolution of the Red Army. 160 mins.
Red Army Chronicles, Vol. 1. The tragic, brutal history of the Russian Red Army, from the genocidal slaughter of Stalin's top lieutenants during the pre-war purges to the massive casualties they suffered on the Eastern front during the war. 52 mins.
VHS: S19608. $19.95.
Red Navy Chronicles. This documentary probes the extraordinary changes in naval warfare, from Russia's first metal submarine—invented in 1834—through the invention of aircraft carriers and nuclear submarines. 52 mins.
VHS: S19607. $19.95.
The Red Aviator, Vol. 1. This program looks at the profound changes in the development of Russian aviation, from its first full-scale airplane, introduced in 1882, to the World War II-era planes that destroyed 57,000 German aircraft. 52 mins.
VHS: S19606. $19.95.

Soviet Subversion of
the Free World Press

A conversation with Yuri Bezmenov, the former propagandist for the KGB. 90 mins.
VHS: S06492. $59.95.

Soviets on Soviet Jewry

This controversial documentary is intended to explain the Soviet position on Soviet Jews to the outside world. This state-oriented propaganda has biographies on successful Soviet Jews, including a doctor, an engineer and a group of uncensored Jewish poets and writers. The Soviet government warns of the temptation to flee to Israel, but insists that Russia is the "true" homeland. 50 mins.
VHS: S13113. $19.98.

Stalin

An international cast headed by Robert Duvall, authentic Russian locations and superb direction by the Czech emigre Ivan Passer are the hallmarks of this made-for-cable biography of Stalin. The film is an exploration of Stalin's iron-fisted rule. With Jeroen Krabbe, Joan Plowright and Maximilian Schell (as Lenin).
VHS: S18371. $19.98.
Laser: LD74682. $39.98.
Ivan Passer, USA, 1992, 165 mins.

A Taste of Freedom

A chronicle of six weeks in the lives of Sasha and Anya Politkovsky, a prominent TV journalist and his wife, whose daily existence reflects the turmoil and uncertainty of life in contemporary Russia. Russian with English subtitles. 46 min.
VHS: S23405. $150.00.

Ten Days That Shook the World

Not the film by Eisenstein, but a look at the Russian Revolution narrated by Orson Welles. The feelings and events are recreated through a combination of historical footage and interviews with participants in the revolution. 77 mins.
VHS: S09255. $39.95.

Terrorism: The Russian Connection

Ter-ror-ism, n. Use of terror and violence…as a political weapon.—Webster. Andropov, KGB head, becomes Soviet Premier. An Activist Polish Pope is shot by a Turk with Bulgarian connections. US embassies are bombed. Here is the Canadian Broadcasting Company's documentary on the recruitment, training, and techniques of the PLO, other terrorist groups and their Russian connection.
VHS: S03981. $69.95.

Tolstoy

This documentary focuses on the private life of the world-famous author; the descendants of Leo Tolstoy reveal the interesting personal side of the great Russian writer and philosopher.
VHS: S15483. $39.95.

Turgenev's Month in the Country

Suzannah York and Ian McShane star in this fascinating Russian psychological drama of love and passion. England, 90 mins.
VHS: S02752. $74.95.

Video from Russia

Without asking or obtaining permission, an American crew of filmmakers traveled to the Soviet Union and spoke freely with Russian people of all ages and occupations about war, work, friendship and even rock and roll. Translated. English narration by Margot Kidder.
VHS: S02360. $29.95.
Dimitri Devyatkin, USA, 1984, 30 mins.

Vincent Trasov:
My Five Years in a Nutshell

From 1969 to 1974, artist Vincent Trasov assumed the identity of Mr. Peanut to examine identity, persona, anthropomorphism and contemporary mythology. In 1974 he ran for mayor of Vancouver as Mr. Peanut with the support of the artistic community on an art platform: P for performance, E for elegance, A for art, N for nonsense, U for unique and T for talent. He received 5% of the vote, but most of the attention from the media. This is his story. 29 mins.
VHS: S12759. $65.00.

Visions of Russia:
A Granddaughter Returns

A young American college student, video camera in hand, decides to tour the Soviet Union, birthplace of her grandparents. The result is this charming and spontaneous documentary portrait. 29 mins.
VHS: S14693. $34.95.

The Week That Shook the World:
The Soviet Coup

A chronicle that utilizes ABC News' extensive coverage of the attempted Soviet Union coup from August 19-25, 1991. 65 mins.
VHS: S15881. $19.98.

What About the Russians?

"Are the Russians ahead in the nuclear arms race? Why the concern over the MX, the Cruise, the Pershing missiles? Can we trust the Russians to honor a nuclear weapons treaty? How can we end the arms race and maintain our national security?" Government officials including George Kennan, former U.S. ambassador to Russia, Robert McNamara, former Defense secretary, and William Colby, former director of the CIA, discuss these important questions.
VHS: S03803. $45.00.
Thiermann/Verdon-Roe, USA, 1983, 26 mins.

What Soviet Children Are Saying
About Nuclear War

A group of American psychiatrists led by Eric Chivian, M.D., and John Mack, M.D., visited two Soviet Pioneer camps and interviewed Soviet girls and boys aged 10-15. The result is an extraordinary documentary which is informative, refreshing and inspiring.
VHS: S03796. $45.00.
Int'l. Phys. for Prev. Nuc. War, 1983, 22 mins.

When I Think of Russia

An intimate portrait of six exiled Russian artists filmed in New York City. Each considers art not politics their main motive for wanting change. The six discuss their feelings toward art, freedom, the U.S. and U.S.S.R. With Baryshnikov, poet Joseph Brodsky, Victor Korchnoi.
VHS: S01577. $29.95.
Vladmir Rif, USA, 1980, 54 mins.

EASTERN EUROPE/SOVIET UNION

Crossroads of the Cold War

The 1990's are different from the previous decades, and one of the major changes will be in America's role as a world power. After nearly 50 years of a "Cold War" which has dominated world history, the coming decades will reflect many changes. This program is designed to put the topic into a historical perspective and attempt a critical analysis of this process. 28 mins.
VHS: S10782. $29.95.

Fall of Communism

Whereas Communists predicted a Domino effect of nations falling under Communism, what happened was the exact opposite: one by one leftist nations traded in on their politics for a more democratic future. This video covers everything from the crumbling of the Berlin Wall to independence movements in Poland, Lithuania and Mother Russia herself. 80 mins.
VHS: S13179. $19.98.

The Loss of an Enemy

The Cold War was defined by the fear and loathing of an enemy perceived as powerful and intractable. This documentary explores both the history and long-lasting effects of this legacy with the help of numerous experts, including *Time Magazine* correspondent Strobe Talbot and State Department official Richard Burt. 28 mins.
VHS: S21588. $25.00.

polish CINEMA

All Friends Here (Sami Swoi)
A series of comic situations show the history of Pawlak's and Kargul's families. Funny dialogue, clever situations and famous actors make this a winning film for Polish audiences. Polish with English subtitles.
VHS: $26730. $39.95.
Sylwester Checinski, Poland, 1967, 78 mins.

Apple Tree of Paradise
The sequel to *The Girls of Nowopilki* is set in Warsaw after the First World War, when Poland regained her independence. Again, the film follows the lives of the young heroines. Polish with *no* English subtitles.
VHS: $11354. $49.95.
Barbara Sass, Poland, 1985, 112 mins.

Austeria
Early in World War I, a group of Orthodox Jews flee from the Cossack army in Polish Galicia. A secluded country inn becomes their temporary refuge, where emotional attachments, brief love affairs and even a renewed faith in humankind inspire these desperate individuals. From the director of *Joan of the Angels.* Polish with English subtitles.
VHS: $20839. $59.95.
Jerzy Kawalerowicz, Poland, 1988, 110 mins.

Balance
One of the key films of Krzysztof Zanussi, in which the chance meeting with an old friend causes a woman to confront a painful decision: to stay with her husband and child, or to begin a new life with a new partner. With Maja Komorowska, Marek Piwowski, Halina Mikolajska. Polish with English subtitles.
VHS: $11324. $49.95.
Krzysztof Zanussi, Poland, 1974, 99 mins.

Beautiful Stranger
In 1919, during World War I, a young lieutenant confronts the bombastic Rasputin traveling incognito. The General Staff Colonel of the Russian army is impressed with the young man and sends him on a dangerous mission, where he meets a beautiful woman. He must choose between his duty and the woman he loves. Polish with English subtitles.
VHS: $21067. $59.95.
Jerzy Hoffman, Poland, 1993, 84 mins.

The Bermuda Triangle (Trojkat Bermudzki)
Henry, a doctor from Cracow; Ludwig, a popular lawyer from Lodz; and Jarek, the owner of a car repair shop in Gdansk, have known each other for years. Their friendship has been strengthened by their frequent mountain climbing trips; they can count on and trust each other in every situation. Now, as middleaged men, they have money, social position...but also serious troubles. Henry's daughter is being blackmailed, Ludwig is a victim of the intrigue set up by his wife and her lover and Jarek has enormous financial problems. So the three old friends decide to commit what they think is the "perfect" crime in order to get out of their terrible predicaments. Will they succeed? Polish with English subtitles.
VHS: $14234. $49.95.
Wojciech Wojcik, Poland, 1989, 99 mins.

Between the Cup and the Lip
The young, charismatic count Wentzel Croy-Dulmen falls in love with an enigmatic stranger, a beautiful young woman who's the cousin of his grandfather who lives in Poland. His desire for her necessitates a full-scale reconsidering of his thoughts and ideas about Poland. With Jacek Chmielnik and Katarzyna Gnlewkowska. Polish with English subtitles.
VHS: $18084. $49.95.
Zbigniew Kuzminski, Poland, 1987, 114 mins.

Big Deal (Kochaj Albo Rzuc)
The continuing comic adventures of Pawlak and Kargul take on an international cast when the two set off for the world's third largest Polish city, Chicago. Polish with English subtitles.
VHS: $26732. $39.95.

Big-Bang
A UFO lands in a small village and the residents prepare to host the terrestrial, acting as representatives of mankind. With Iga Cembrzynska, Ludwik Benoit. Polish with *no* English subtitles.
VHS: $11359. $39.95.
Andrzej Kondratiuk, Poland, 1986, 98 mins.

The Birthday
The story of a young man in occupied Warsaw whose 23rd birthday falls on the 56th day of the Warsaw Uprising in 1944. With Piotr Lysak, Andrzej Lapicki. Polish with *no* English subtitles.
VHS: $11350. $49.95.
Ewa & Czeslaw Petelski, Poland, 1980, 99 mins.

Black Clouds (Czarne Chmury)
Set in 17th-century Poland, this action packed, cloak-and-dagger series offers riveting adventure. It contains ten episodes on five cassettes. Polish with no subtitles.
VHS: $26738. $99.95.
Andrzej Konic, Poland, 1987, 550 mins.

Border Street
A masterpiece of Polish cinema, a tragedy about the Warsaw ghetto involving an old tailor who tries to save his daughters and others. The film culminates with the Warsaw uprising of 1943, when Jews, with the support of the Polish underground, take up arms and die fighting. With passages of visual brilliance. Polish with English subtitles.
VHS: $00169. $59.95.
Aleksander Ford, Poland, 1948, 101 mins.

Bottom Rock
A contemporary Polish film starring and with the music of Grzegorz Ciechowski, the subject of which is the lack of understanding and hope among young people. Tomasz Hudziec, Jerzy Mercik, Ewa Skibinski star. Polish with English subtitles.
VHS: $12514. $39.95.
Roland Rowinski, Poland, 1987, 83 mins.

By Touch
Two young women, one suffering from cancer and the other a rape victim, seek hope and the will to survive in their friendship in this tautly directed, realistic drama. With Grazyna Szapolowska, Maria Ciunelis. Polish with English subtitles.
VHS: $12359. $49.95.
Magdalena Lazarkiewicz, Poland, 1985, 85 mins.

Caesarian Section
A comedy set in a country hospital, where women compete for the honor of becoming the mother of the millionth inhabitant of the district. Polish with *no* English subtitles.
VHS: $11343. $49.95.
Stanislaw Moszuk, Poland, 1987, 83 mins.

Camouflage (Barwy Ochronne)
Zanussi's sixth film, set in an intellectual milieu, tackles the theme of survival in the rat race, and the extent to which one should bend one's principles. Jakub, the past master at survival, assumes the necessary camouflage: "Survive and you win; perish and you're proved wrong." He engages his colleague, the younger Jaroslaw, in a game which ends in desolation and stalemate. With Zbigniew Zapasiewicz and Piotr Garlicki. Polish with English subtitles.
VHS: $11356. $49.95.
Krzysztof Zanussi, Poland, 1977, 106 mins.

Career of Nikodem Dyzma
A 7-part, 3-cassette series based on a novel by Tadeusz Dolega-Mostowicz about a swindler who through pure coincidence reaches prominent government posts, enjoying the support of the aristocratic and government circles taken in by his image of a strong man. Polish with *no* English subtitles. 3 cassettes.
VHS: $11336. $89.95.
Jan Rybkowski, Poland, 1980, 385 mins.

Casimir the Great
A historical drama that depicts the life of Poland's only king to be dubbed "the Great", for his contribution to the building of the Polish state in the Middle Ages. On two cassettes, in two parts. With Krzysztof Chamiec, Wladyslaw Hancza. Polish with English subtitles.
VHS: $11333. $69.95.

Champion Always Loses
Based on the criminal records of Interpol; two great chess champions in France of the 1930's fall victims to a clever swindle. Polish with *no* English subtitles.
VHS: $11360. $39.95.
Gregorz Lasota, Poland, 1977, 42 mins.

Chatelaine's Daughter
Set during the 1930's, the film focuses on a young journalist who spends his vacation alone in the Mazurian Lake district. One night while camping, a young girl approaches him and asks him to take her to Warsaw. A romance ensues which evolves into an unexpected conclusion. Polish with *no* English subtitles.
VHS: $11358. $39.95.
Marek Nowicki, Poland, 1983, 58 mins.

Cheating Flea
A humorous performance about a cheeky, mischievous flea, based on a poem by Jan Brzechwa. Polish with no subtitles.
VHS: $11295. $39.95.

Children Must Laugh
Aleksandar Ford's powerful documentary, financed by the Jewish labor movement in Poland, is a revealing look at Polish pre-war Jewish life. "Out of the sorrows and shadows of the life of Jewish workers in Poland, a bright ray of hope has come....Hollywood scouts would do well to locate some of the children...[whose] confidence in their ability to 'build a better world' rises above any language barrier" (*The New York Times*). Polish and Yiddish with English narration and subtitles.
VHS: $19534. $54.00.
Aleksandar Ford, Poland/USA, 1935/65, 64 mins.

Citizen P. (Obywatel Piszczuk)
Piszczuk, the hero of Andrzej Munk's *Bad Luck*, appears again, this time striving to adjust to his social environment whatever the price. He yearns to be accepted and appreciated, but always fails. Despite all his hard efforts and good intentions misfortune continues to blight his every move. Starring Jerzy Stuhr. Polish with *no* English subtitles.
VHS: $14235. $49.95.
Andrzej Kotkowski, Poland, 1989, 112 mins.

Colonel Wolodyjowski
A landmark epic, based on the historical trilogy of Henryk Sienkiewicz. Set in the year 1668, at the time of Turkish invasion of Poland's eastern frontier. With Tadeusz Loniski, Magdalena Zawadzka, Daniel Olbrychski. Polish with English subtitles.
VHS: $11329. $49.95.
Jerzy Hoffman, Poland, 1969, 160 mins.

The Comedienne
A nineteenth century costume drama based on a novel by Wladyslaw Reymont. A young and ambitious provincial girl goes to Warsaw to try her talents as an actress. Polish with *no* English subtitles.
VHS: $11335. $69.95.
Jerzy Sztwiernia, Poland, 1986, 225 mins.

Commando (Cichocienni)
This military documentary details the exploits of a brave Polish unit that served with British commandos during World War II. The film follows its training, war-time activities and ultimate fate after 1945. Polish with no subtitles.
VHS: $16822. $29.95.
Marek Widarski, Poland, 73 mins.

Contract
A terrific film by Krzysztof Zanussi. The central characters are Peter, the son of a prominent cardiologist, and Lilka, the daughter of a party dignitary. Their wedding provides a stage for confrontation between their families and friends. With Maja Komorowska and Tadeusz Lomnicki. Polish with *no* English subtitles.
VHS: $11355. $49.95.
Krzysztof Zanussi, Poland, 1980, 114 mins.

The Countess Cosel (Hrabina Cosel)
Jozef Ignacy Kraszewski's novel serves as the basis for this historical romance. It concerns the Countess Cosel's tragic struggle to marry the man she loved, the father of her children, King August II. Polish with English subtitles.
VHS: $26729. $59.95.
Jerzy Antczak, Poland, 1968, 148 mins.

Coup d'Etat
The military coup in Poland waged by Marshal Jozef Pilsudski is the subject of this film. The film covers the history behind this event, from the Autumn of 1925 to the Brzesc Trial in 1931. Polish language only (no subtitles).
VHS: $22210. $39.95.
Ryszard Filipski, Poland, 1981, 158 mins.

Crossed Lines (Gluchy telefon)
A dramatic look at life in Poland at the end of the 1980's. Tomasz is a 30 year old sociologist and former Solidarity activist who now drives a taxi to support himself and his wife and shares an apartment with his in-laws. He is forced to review his hopes and options when he is visited by his old friend Agata, who has spent the last few years abroad. With Hanna Mikuc, Maciej Orlos, Katarzyna Latawiec and Waldemar Kownacki. Polish with English subtitles.
VHS: $16831. $39.95.
Piotr Mikulicki, Poland, 1990, 81 mins.

The Deluge
The action takes place in the 17th century, the turbulent period of the Polish-Swedish war. The plot is woven around the stormy love of the main character in the film, Andrzej Kmicic (played by Daniel Olbrychski), for a young gentlewoman named Olenka. Based on the novel by Nobel prize-winning author Henryk Sienkiewicz, much of this exciting and romantic film was shot in authentic, ancient Polish castles. Nominated for the Best Foreign Language Film Oscar in 1974. Polish with English subtitles.
VHS: $14230. $79.95.
Jerzy Hoffman, Poland, 1973, 185 mins.

The Doll
The emotionally powerful story of an unfulfilled love between a man who is a social climber, and a beautiful but cold woman of aristocratic background, played against a picture of 19th century Poland. Polish *without* English subtitles.
VHS: $11330. $49.95.
Wojciech J. Has, Poland, 1969, 159 mins.

Dr. Judym
Based on a novel by Stefan Zeromski. The hero is a young doctor of low social origin, who sacrifices his love for his work and for helping the poor, at the turn of the century. Polish with English subtitles.
VHS: $11331. $49.95.
Wlodzimierz Haupe, Poland, 94 mins.

Druga Midosc (Second Youth)
After 25 years of marriage, a woman leaves her husband to share her life with a much younger man. She travels for several years, loses all her money, and is left by her new beau. Finally, upon her return to Warsaw, she meets her old husband. Polish with NO subtitles.
VHS: $26653. $24.95.
Michal Waszynski, Poland, 1938, 85 mins.

Dziesieciu z Pawiaka (The Ten from Pawiak)
This is the story of a secret underground organization whose mysterious leader takes on a difficult mission. He resolves to save the lives of his soldiers after they have been sentenced to death. Polish with NO subtitles.
VHS: $26654. $24.95.
Ryszard Ordyriski, Poland, 1931, 90 mins.

Egg-Nog (Kogel Mogel)
Kate dreams of a bright career. She wants to study in town but her father, who owns a large farm, has old-fashioned ideas about a woman's place and tries to arrange a marriage for Kate with successful businessman. Instead, she runs away on her wedding day and begins to face the challenges of life in a big and unfriendly city. Will she go to college, return home, or fall in love? Can one escape from one's destiny? Polish with English subtitles.
VHS: $14233. $49.95.
Roman Zaluski, Poland, 1989, 103 mins.

Enigma Secret
The story of the breaking of the Nazi secret coding machine Enigma, by three Polish mathematicians. Tadeusz Borowski, Piotr Fronczewski, Piotr Garlicki star. Polish with English subtitles.
VHS: $11327. $49.95.
Roman Wionczek, Poland, 1979, 158 mins.

Eve Wants to Sleep (Ewa Chce Spac)
A young woman finds her attempts to secure lodging in the big city frustrated at every turn. The state bureaucracy and the police are the chief culprits. This light comedy was considered quite daring in its time as it is critical of the Polish state. With Barbara Kwiatkowska, Stanislaw Mikulski and Ludwik Benoit. Polish with NO subtitles.
VHS: $26649. $29.95.
Tadeusz Chmielewski, Poland, 1958, 97 mins.

The Faithful River (Wierna Rzeka)
In January 1863, a tragic uprising rocked Poland. This film, based on Stefan Zeromski's novel, shows the heroism which fueled young people at that critical historic moment. It was a struggle that ended for many in death. Polish with English subtitles.
VHS: $26735. $39.95.
Tadeusz Chmielewski, Poland, 1987, 137 mins.

Family Life
One of the key films of the "cinema of moral anxiety." After six years in Warsaw, a design engineer reluctantly returns home to a dilapidated mansion in the country. There he must confront his alcoholic father and a slightly deranged sister, as well as his own life. "At long last, the Polish cinema has a new and important director," wrote Richard Roud. "Very intimate in scale, the film is beautifully acted by Daniel Olbrychski and Jan Kreczmar." Polish with English subtitles.
VHS: $22208. $59.95.
Krzysztof Zanussi, Poland, 1971, 93 mins.

Florian
A young couple in love find themselves involved in a dangerous plot during the First World War. They must hide an ancient church bell of great historical value. The situation appears desperate until the Polish army appears and helps the patriotic couple. Polish with no subtitles.
VHS: $26655. $24.95.
Leonard Buczkowski, Poland, 1938, 90 mins.

Forbidden Songs (Zakazane Piosenki)
This was the first movie made in Poland after World War II; it is the story of the songs sung by all of Warsaw during the German occupation. A stirring tale of the heroic underground fighters, their lives and deaths, and those things which sustained them in their epic struggle for freedom. With Danuta Szaflarska and Jerzy Duszynski. Polish with *NO* English subtitles.
VHS: $15558. $49.95.
Ludwik Starski, Poland, 1947, 100 mins.

Forgotten Melody (Zapomniana Melodia)
The very funny story of love between a young girl and the handsome man who composed a melody for her. With Helena Grossowna and Aleksander Zabczynski. Polish with *NO* English subtitles.
VHS: $15568. $49.95.
Konrad Tom, Poland, 1938, 80 mins.

Fredro for Adults
A unique erotic comedy by Aleksander Fredro, a classic of Polish comedy, produced for the first time by The Syrena Theatre Company in Warsaw in 1988. 72 mins. Polish with *no* English subtitles.
VHS: $11371. $49.95.

General Sosabowski
The exploits of the famed Polish military leader. Born in 1892, Sosabowski commanded the First Land Army also known as "The Children of Warsaw," against the Nazi blitzkrieg in 1939. Polish with no subtitles.
VHS: $16826. $29.95.
E.Z. Szanialawski, Poland, 53 mins.

Girls of Nowopilki
A postwar film version of Pola Gojawiczynska's novel. A lively picture of turn-of-the-century Warsaw as experienced by four young girls. The film begins as the heroines finish primary school and must begin adult life. With Maria Ciunelis, Izabella Drobowitz-Orkisz. Polish with *no* English subtitles.
VHS: $11353. $49.95.
Barbara Sass, Poland, 1985, 94 mins.

Greta
Krzysztof Gruber directed this moving story about a 10-year-old Polish boy who is a fugitive from a labor camp during WWII. As he makes it to a small town he meets a deserter from the German Army. An SS officer identifies the deserter and shoots him. The boy meets Greta, a girl his own age, and invited to her home, late in the evening he meets Greta's father—the SS officer. With Janusz Grabowski, Agnieszka Kruszewska. Polish with English subtitles.
VHS: $09212. $49.95.
Krzysztof Gruber, Poland, 1986, 60 mins.

Gypsies
A cinema-verite documentary produced in Poland during the early 60's, which follows a traveling gypsy caravan across rural Poland. Original synchronous sound with no subtitles. Produced by the Documentary Film Studio.
VHS: $03354. $39.95.
Wladyslaw Slesicki, Poland, 1961, 30 mins.

H. M. Deserters (C. K. Dezerterzy)
This fantastic comedy begins when a bunch of "politically suspected" soldiers of the Austrian-Hungarian empire, whose job it is to guard a camp for Italian POW's, desert from their duties. A long string of adventures soon follows. Polish with *no* English subtitles.
VHS: $14239. $49.95.
Janusz Majewski, Poland, 1986, 166 mins.

Hallo, Fred the Beard (Hallo Szpicbrodka)
A delightful musical comedy. The Red Mill theatre is slowly going to ruin. Fred Kampinos, alias Fred the Beard, suddenly appears to pay all the debts and becomes co-owner. Things get complicated, however, when it is revealed that Fred plans to rob the bank located right next door to the small theatre. Polish with NO English subtitles.
VHS: S15561. $49.95.
Janusz Rzeszewski, Poland, 1978, 98 mins.

His Excellency the Shop Assistant (Jego Ekselencja Subiekt)
A comedy made in 1933 which stars Ina Benita and Eugeniusz Bodo in the story of a shop assistant in a big store who falls in love with the daughter of a VIP. Very funny! Polish with NO English subtitles.
VHS: S15569. $49.95.
Michal Waszynski, Poland, 1933, 85 mins.

Hot Thursday (Goracy Czwartek)
Three 12-year-old friends from a drab mining district accidentally happen upon a plan that could radically improve their lives. A big robbery should grant them the money and success they so desperately crave. In the end, all their hopes don't pan out the way they imagined they would. Polish with English subtitles.
VHS: S26733. $39.95.
Michal Rosa, Poland, 1994, 60 mins.

Hotel Pacific (Zaklete Rewiry)
The action of this film takes places in the 1930s. Roman Boryczko is looking for a job. He eventually finds employment as a dishwasher in the restaurant of the Pacific Hotel and quickly advances through the hotel hierarchy of posts. But the successive stages of his career also prove to be painful lessons in life. Polish with NO English subtitles.
VHS: S15564. $49.95.
Janusz Majewski, Poland, 1975

I Like Bats
A likeable horror story about a beautiful girl—a vampire—who would like to become a human and seeks help from a psychiatrist. Polish with English subtitles.
VHS: S11321. $49.95.
Grzegorz Warchol, Poland, 1985, 90 mins.

Illumination (Iluminacja)
Krzysztof Zanussi's landmark film is a parable about the limits of rationality. A young scientist believes rational analysis can solve everything until he is confronted with an older woman and the accidental death of a close friend. Zanussi deftly mixes dramatic and documentary footage as he "broke new ground in his cryptic, intelligent, ironic and ethical essays on the scientific mind" (Faber Companion to Foreign Films). Polish with English subtitles.
VHS: S26978. $59.95.
Krzysztof Zanussi, Poland, 1973, 91 mins.

In an Old Manor House
Based on a play by the visionary Stanislaw Witkiewicz. The owner of an estate kills his wife after discovering her affair with his son of a previous marriage. Her ghost returns to he manor driving the inhabitants to the verge of insanity in this powerful film. Polish with English subtitles.
VHS: S11319. $49.95.
Andrzej Kotkowski, Poland, 1984, 90 mins.

In Desert and Wilderness (W Pustyni i w Puszczy)
The story of a Polish boy and English girl became the subject of one of the most beautiful adventure books in Polish or perhaps even world literature. Written in 1911 by Henryk Sienkiewicz, the Nobel prize-winning author of Quo Vadis, the tale takes place in the late 19th century, relating the adventures of two kidnapped children who escape and find themselves alone in the middle of uncharted Africa. Polish with English subtitles.
VHS: S14238. $49.95.
Wladyslaw Slesicki, Poland, 1973, 144 mins.

Iron Hand
After a power struggle in the 16th century, Stefan Batory won the Polish crown. His right hand man, Mroczek, began to organize a nationwide network of spies to prevent any activities against his King. This film depicts many characters from this important time in Polish history. Polish with English subtitles.
VHS: S22211. $59.95.
Ryszard Ber, Poland, 1989, 103 mins.

Is Lucyna a Girl? (Czy Lucyna to Dziewczyna?)
This Polish comedy from the 1930s stars Jadwiga Smosarska as Lucyna, a woman in disguise as a man, who gets a job as an engineer. Once instated, she uses her feminine charm to provoke her colleagues. Polish with NO English subtitles.
VHS: S15571. $39.95.
Juliusz Gardan, Poland, 1934, 80 mins.

It'll Be Better (Bedzie Lepiej)
A comic pair of workers from a toy factory in pre-war Lvov are unexpectedly burdened with a nursing job. Great fun! Polish with NO English subtitles.
VHS: S15572. $49.95.
Michal Waszynski, Poland, 1936, 92 mins.

Jadzia
A Polish comedy from 1936 about two companies run by a beautiful woman and handsome man. They engage in a competition which sets off a series of funny events. Polish with no English subtitles.
VHS: S15573. $39.95.
Mieczyslaw Krawicz, Poland, 1936, 92 mins.

Jaguar 1936
Set in Vienna, 1936. A Danish businessman buys a Jaguar at an auto dealership, undaunted by the exorbitant price. Two hours later, he sells it for half the price, giving rise to the suspicion of bank fraud in this detective thriller. Polish with no English subtitles.
VHS: S11361. $39.95.
Gregorz Lasota, Poland, 1977, 53 mins.

Karate Polish Style
A thriller set as two Warsaw artists paint a fresco in the Mazurian Lake District and clash with local thugs. Polish with English subtitles.
VHS: S11320. $49.95.
Jerzy Wojcik, Poland, 1982, 91 mins.

King Boleslaus the Bold (Boleslaw Smialy)
The action of this film is set in 1079, the last year of Boleslaus the Bold's rule. It is the story of conflict between the king and the Bishop of Cracow, a conflict which ended tragically with the bishop's death. Polish with no subtitles.
VHS: S15060. $49.95.
Witold Lesiewicz, Poland, 1972, 105 mins.

Krzyzacy (Knights of the Teutonic Order)
Certainly one of the highest achievements of the 1960 Polish cinema, and a stirring nationalist epic. Based on the classic novel by Henryk Sienkiewicz, Krzyzacy (Knights of the Teutonic Order) is a vivid portrayal of customs and life in medieval Poland, brilliantly directed with epic sweep by Aleksandar Ford. With a cast of thousands, including Andrzej Szalawski and Grazyna Staniszewska. Available in two versions: a Polish-language version with no English subtitles, and an English-dubbed version which is shorter by a half-hour. Color.
Krzyzacy. Polish with English subtitles. 175 mins. 2 cassettes.
VHS: S12354. $59.95.
Knights of the Teutonic Order. English dubbed. 145 mins.
VHS: S12355. $59.95.
Aleksandar Ford, Poland, 1960, 142 mins.

La Cuisine Polonaise (Kuchnia polska)
A Polish pilot returns home after the Second World War with his English wife and young daughter only to be framed and jailed as a spy. When his wife tries to see him freed, a communist government official demands a high personal price. This deeply emotional historical drama covers the years 1940-1950. Polish language version only. No English subtitles. With Krystyna Janda, Krzysztof Kolberger, Piotr Machalica, Zbigniew Zamachowski and Marek Kondrat.
VHS: S16819. $39.95.
Jacek Bromski, Poland, 1991, 108 mins.

Leper (Tredowata)
A moving, melodramatic story of the forbidden love affair between a wealthy young nobleman and the beautiful teacher of a high society girl. The town folk try to destroy the feelings between these two people of different social positions. With Elzbieta Starostecka and Leszek Teleszynski. Polish with English subtitles.
VHS: S15056. $39.95.
Jerzy Hoffman, Poland, 1976, 100 mins.

Little Prince (Ksiazatko)
A young girl is forced to take up a man's disguise in this classic Polish comedy. Karolina Lubienska stars, and the situation gets more complicated when she meets the man of her dreams. Polish with NO English subtitles.
VHS: S15574. $39.95.
T. and S. Szebego, Poland, 1937, 87 mins.

Major Hubal (Hubal)
Legendary Hubal-Major Dobrzanski continued to fight the Nazi occupation of Poland despite the incredible odds against him and his band of soldiers. This war drama is based on a true story. Polish with English subtitles.
VHS: S26734. $39.95.
Bohdan Poreba, Poland, 1973

Man/Woman Wanted (Poszukiwany, Poszukiwana)
A small painting by a relatively unknown local painter disappears from a local museum, prompting a young art historian, afraid that he may be held responsible for it, to disguise himself as a woman and take work as a maid in order to recover the painting. The result is a light-hearted comedy. Wojciech Pokora stars. Polish with English subtitles.
VHS: S14231. $49.95.
Stanislaw Bareja, Poland, 69, mins.

Master and Margarita
A superb adaptation for Polish television of Mikhail Bulgakov's brilliant, troubled novel about Soviet bureaucracy, written during the post-revolutionary years. With Gustaw Holoubek, Zbigniew Zapasiewicz, Anna Dymna. 4 separate cassettes. Polish with English subtitles.
VHS: S12512. $89.95.
Maciej Wojtyszko, Poland, 1990, 373 mins.

Merry Christmas
A comedy set shortly before Christmas, as two men from the countryside go to Warsaw with a truck full of Christmas tress. Polish with no English subtitles.
VHS: S11345. $39.95.
Jerzy Sztwiernia, Poland, 60 mins.

Miners '88 (Gornicy '88)
A history-making documentary, this is a detailed look at the workers' strike at the Manifest Lipcowy mine in Poland in August 1988, the final strike that lead to the breakdown of the old politics in Poland. Polish with no subtitles.
VHS: S16827. $24.95.
Andrzej Piekutowski, Poland, 1988

Miss Ewa's Follies
A musical comedy for children based on a novel by Kornel Makuszynski. The story is set in 1932. Following the departure for China of her physican father, 14-year-old Ewa flees the house of her unfriendly guardians and embarks on a series of "follies"—kind-hearted and wise acts that bring happiness to those involved. Polish with no English subtitles.
VHS: S11296. $39.95.

Most Eligible Bachelor
A comedy about a highlander who is the most eligible bachelor in the village, always seeking a suitable wife. Edward Kusztal stars. Polish with no English subtitles.
VHS: S11344. $49.95.
Janusz Kidawa, Poland, 1982, 80 mins.

Mother Joan of the Angels
One of the landmarks of modern Polish cinema, this gripping adaptation of Aldous Huxley's The Devils of Loudun (like Ken Russell's The Devils), transposes the action to a 17th-century Polish convent, where a priest investigates demonic possession among nuns. But the exorcist finds himself involved in an unavoidable mutual attraction with the Mother Superior. Full of brilliant symbolism, Kawalerowicz weaves a powerful allegory of good vs. evil, chastity vs. eroticism. Polish with English subtitles.
VHS: S22598. $59.95.
Jerzy Kawalerowicz, Poland, 1960, 108 mins.

Nights and Days
A family saga based on a novel by Maria Dabrowska. Set in the second half of the 19th century after the failure of he January 1864 Uprising. The film presents a unique portrait of an oppressed society, exile, and the confiscation of property through the loves and struggles of the Niechcic family. With Jadwiga Baranska, Jerzy Binczycki. Polish with English subtitles.
VHS: S11313. $69.95.
Jerzy Antczak, Poland, 1976, 255 mins.

Oh Charles
A young and handsome engineer divides his free time between his wife and several girl friends, each of whom believes she is his one and only, in this comedy which stars Jan Piechocinski and Dorota Kaminska. Polish with no English subtitles.
VHS: S11342. $49.95.
Roman Zaluski, Poland, 1985, 99 mins.

On the Neman River
A 4-part, 2-cassette epic series based on a novel by Eliza Orseszkowa. A historical love story set in the Grodno area after the January 1863 uprising. With Iwona Pawlak, Antoni Marjanski. Polish with no English subtitles.
VHS: S11337. $69.95.
Kazimierz Kuzminski, Poland, 1980, 280 mins.

Operation Arsenal
A reconstruction of one of the boldest operations performed by the underground Polish Home Army in occupied Warsaw during World War II. The elite "Gray Ranks" freed 25 prisoners who were being transported to the Pawiak prison. With Cezary Morawski, Jan Englert. Polish with no English subtitles.
VHS: S11351. $49.95.
Jan Lomnicki, Poland, 1977, 96 mins.

Peach of a Girl
A musical love story set during the 1930's, with lyrics by Julian Tuwim and Ralph Benatzky and music by Wojciech Gluch. Polish with no English subtitles.
VHS: S11370. $39.95.

The Peasants
Based on a nobel prize-winning novel by Wladyslaw Reymont. Set in a small central Polish village at the beginning of the 20th century, the plot revolves around a father and his son's violent love for the same woman—set against the rich detail of country traditions and folklore. 2 tapes, in two parts. Polish with English subtitles. 184 mins.
VHS: S11332. $69.95.

Personal Search (Rewizja Osobista)
Basia, who is returning from a trip abroad with her young son Peter and beautiful cousin Christine, tries desperately to avoid a search at the Customs desk—yet we do not know what she wants to smuggle. Christine, who is doing her best to avoid a search, as is Christine, who continues her flirting with the young officer. Both ladies, having nearly succeeded in their subterfuge, forget about little Peter—who is hopelessly in love with Christina. Polish with English subtitles.
VHS: S14232. $49.95.
Witold Leszczynski, Poland, 1974, 71 mins.

Pharaoh
One of the most elaborate, detailed, historically accurate epics and a brilliant expose of the use of power. Young Prince Rameses incurs the wrath of the high priest when he takes a Jewish girl as his mistress, and when he succeeds his father as Rameses III, he battles the high priest for economic and military control of Egypt. With George Zelnik, Barbara Bryl and Krystyna Mikolajewska. Unfortunately this (only available) version has been cut by almost 60 minutes. Dubbed in English.
VHS: S04314. $59.95.
Jerzy Kawalerowicz, Poland, 1966, 125 mins.

Poisonous Plants
Robert Glinski directed this taut drama about a disillusioned journalist who searches for a scoop in a devastated, demoralized, contemporary Polish city. With Boguslaw Linda, Katarzyna Figura. Polish with English subtitles.
VHS: S12513. $39.95.
Robert Glinski, Poland, 1975, 70 mins.

Polanicki's Family (Marynia)
This is a film version of the popular Polish television series Polanicki Family. Stan Polanicki is an ambitious young man who meets a lovely young woman called Miss Mary. Her father owes Stan money, but when Stan tries to collect the debt, he discovers his relationship with Miss Mary may suffer. Polish with English subtitles.
VHS: S26979. $39.95.
Jan Rybkowski, Poland, 1983, 104 mins.

Polish Ways (Polskie Drogi)
This film displays a large-scale panorama of an anti-Nazi conspiracy in occupied Poland. It represents an innovative attempt to chart the destinies of Polish life in that troubled time. Immensely popular with audiences, this film helped catapult Kazimierz Kaczor to fame. It contains 11 episodes on 11 cassettes. Polish with no subtitles.
VHS: S26739. $199.95.
Janusz Morgenstern, Poland, 1977, 1026 mins.

Private Investigation (Prywatne Sledztwo)
Rafal, with his wife and two children, are returning home from a weekend trip when a tragic car accident leaves his family dead. After a long hospital stay, where he has seen the police investigation come to an impasse, Rafal decides he will find the hit-and-run killer himself and exact his own revenge. With Roman Wilhelmi and Jan Peszek. Polish with English subtitles.
VHS: S15058. $49.95.
Wojciech Wojcik, Poland, 1986, 99 mins.

The Quack
A melodrama based on a novel by Tadeusz Dolega-Mostowicz, set in Poland of the 1930's. A famous surgeon loses his memory and begins wandering alone through Poland's Eastern frontier. Unbelievable happenings abound, including an intriguing amorous adventure. Polish with English subtitles.
VHS: S11312. $49.95.
Jerzy Hoffman, Poland, 1981, 132 mins.

Rosemary Twig
A musical about the Polish Legions. The story of young soldiers of the first skeleton company formed at Oleandry in 1914, performed by the Rozmaitosci Theatre Company in Warsaw in 1988. Polish with no English subtitles.
VHS: S11369. $39.95.

The Saragossa Manuscript
A cult classic, one of the most interesting films to emerge from Eastern Europe, based on the novel Sanatorium under the Hourglass by Bruno Schultz, this romantic, fantastic and witty tale chronicles the adventures of a Walloon guard under the King of Spain. Something of a Don Juan, this colorful 19th-century character must pass numerous tests to prove his courage, honesty and honor in order to become a member of the powerful Maurentantian family. Polish with English subtitles.
VHS: S22596. $59.95.
Wojciech J. Has, Poland, 1965, 174 mins.

Sarah's House
The men whom beautiful Sarah chooses for her lovers are condemned to physical degradation and annihilation under the spell of her charms. But one day she meets her match in this stylish horror film. Polish with English subtitles.
VHS: S09214. $49.95.
Zygmunt Lech, Poland, 1984, 70 mins.

Sauna
A group of intellectuals and professionals from Poland accidentally meet in a sauna in Helsinki, Finland. As they compare stories they find they face an uncertain future since communism is crumbling at home. It was in that quickly vanishing communist world of Poland that their obscure jargon guaranteed them respect and a livelihood. With Boguslaw Linda, Gabriela Kownacka, Marian Opania, Henryk Bista and Piotr Opania I inni. Polish with NO subtitles.
VHS: S26650. $29.95.
Filip Bajon, Poland, 1992, 90 mins.

Secret Detective
Set in Cracow during 1936; a precious necklace is ingeniously stolen from a famous jeweler. The police in vain try to catch a pair of cheats: a beautiful woman and a sleuth. Polish with no English subtitles.
VHS: S11362. $39.95.
Gregorz Lasota, Poland, 1977, 50 mins.

Serce Matki (Mother's Heart)
Drama unfolds in this early Polish film when two women compete for the same man's attentions. One is the wife, the other is the wife's best friend. When the man unexpectedly dies he leaves behind two grieving woman. There is another unforseen complication. The woman who is not his wife is pregnant. Polish with no subtitles.
VHS: S26656. $24.95.
Michal Waszynski, Poland, 1938, 84 mins.

Siegfried
In 1934, Stefan, an art connoisseur, develops a subtle emotional relationship with homosexual overtones with Siegfried, a young circus acrobat, in this sensitive, daring film. With Gustaw Holoubek, Tomasz Hudziec, Jan Nowicki. Polish with English subtitles.
VHS: S11317. $49.95.
Andrzej Domalik, Poland, 1986, 91 mins.

Sklamalam (I Lied)

A moving love story made in Poland in 1937, the film stars Jadwiga Smosarska and Eugeniusz Bodo in the story of an attractive young woman forced to navigate in a merciless, male-dominated world. Polish *without* subtitles.
VHS: $11684. $29.00.
Mieczysław Krawicz, Poland, 1937, 85 mins.

Special Mission (Misja Specjalna)

A contemporary Polish comedy set in Nazi-occupied Poland. Krzysztof Kowalewski and Dorota Kaminska star in this story about a special mission to intercept a mysterious chest with Himmler's gift to Hitler. Polish with English subtitles.
VHS: $11685. $38.00.
Janusz Rzeszewski, Poland, 1987, 110 mins.

Sportsman Against His Will (Sportowiec Mimo Woli)

A Canadian hockey player is in love with the beautiful Lilly; and their dogs are in love too. A wacky hairstylist is caught in between trying to help all of them. Polish with *NO* English subtitles.
VHS: $15575. $39.95.
Mieczysław Krawicz, Poland, 1939, 80 mins.

The Stranger

Winner of the Best Actress Award at the Gdansk Film Festival, and based on Maria Kuncewiszowa's novel. The film is a psychological study of a woman—a gifted violinist whose talent is wasted—spanning the first three decades of this century. An unhappy love, an unsuccessful marriage and lack of understanding with her daughter together present a moving portrait of unfulfilled dreams. With Ewa Wisniewska. Polish with *no* English subtitles.
VHS: $11338. $49.95.
Ryszard Ber, Poland, 1986, 115 mins.

The Structure of Crystals

Krzysztof Zanussi's debut feature tells the story of a metropolitan member of the scientific elite (Andrzej Zarnecki) who meets with a reclusive old friend (Jan Myslowicz) to convince him to return to the city to resume his work as an important scientist. "It was the first of a series of films [by Zanussi] that look at the scientific community [mainly uncharted territory in the cinema except for science fiction] to make general philosophical points" (*The Faber Companion to Foreign Films*). With Jan Myslowicz, Władysław Jarema and Daniel Olbrychski. Polish with English subtitles.
VHS: $19395. $59.95.
Krzysztof Zanussi, Poland, 1969, 76 mins.

Suspended

Two of Poland's best actors, Krystyna Janda and Jerzy Radziwilowicz, star in this story of a former Polish Home Army officer who is sentenced to death on fabricated charges, escapes from prison, and spend six years in hiding in his fiancee's home during Stalinist times in Poland. Awarded the Best Debut Film Award at the Gdansk Film Festival. Polish with English subtitles.
VHS: $11307. $49.95.
Andrzej Lapicki, Poland, 1986, 92 mins.

Taboo

The talented young Polish director Andrzej Baranski directed this drama about a love triangle set in an austere village. A mother and her daughter are in love with the same man. Polish with English subtitles.
VHS: $11314. $49.95.
Andrzej Baranski, Poland, 1987, 108 mins.

Take It Easy (Nie Ma Mocnych)

After the Second World War, two families settle on adjacent land. Their constant bickering provides a pretext for nonstop laughs. A full 18 years after the war, they still feel passionate about an absurd injustice. Polish with English subtitles.
VHS: $26731. $39.95.
Sylwester Checinski, Poland, 1973, 89 mins.

Teddy-Bear

A comedy from Poland, the story of a divorced couple who compete with each other for the money they share in a joint account in a London bank. With Stanislaw Tym, Bronislaw Pawlik. Polish with *no* English subtitles.
VHS: $11340. $49.95.
Stanislaw Bareja, Poland, 1980, 116 mins.

Thais

In this historical drama, an Alexandrian dancer captures the attention of an ascetic monk. He hopes to save her soul but the very sensuality of her being stands in the way. Anatole France's novel supplies the theme for this beautiful and erotic tale. With Dorota Kwiatkowska, Jerzy Kryszak and Bronislaw Pawlik. Polish with English subtitles.
VHS: $26651. $39.95.
Ryszard Ber, Poland, 1983, 97 mins.

The Tramps (Wloczegi)

Two comic buddies from Lvov take care of a beautiful orphan girl. They make their living singing popular songs that the whole town sings along with them. Watching this film is like taking a journey back to old Lvov. Polish with *NO* English subtitles.
VHS: $15576. $49.95.
Michal Waszynski, Poland, 1939, 99 mins.

The Trial (Proces)

A full-length documentary film about events which took place in 1949-1956 associated with the trial of General Stanislaw Tatar and others. Polish language version. NO subtitles.
VHS: $15061. $49.95.
Krzysztof Lang, Poland, 108 mins.

The Twenties, The Thirties (Lata 20-te, Lata 30-te)

A handsome, young engineer gets himself into trouble when he tries to cheat on his partners. His attempt to ruin them fails as the cabaret he bought in order to lose them money begins to flourish, and the beautiful actress Liza becomes a star. Starring Grazyna Szapolowski and Tomasz Stockinger. Polish with NO subtitles.
VHS: $15059. $49.95.
Janusz Rzeszewski, Poland, 1986, 100 mins.

Ty Co w Ostrej Swiecisz Bramie (Mother Mary Ostrobramska)

A young talented Ryszard is kidnapped by his competitors for information. Prayers offered by his fiance to Mother Mary Ostrobramska magically help him see his beloved and his mother once again. Polish with no subtitles.
VHS: $26657. $24.95.
Jan Nowina Przybylski, Poland, 78 mins.

Upstairs (Pietro Wyzej)

A classic Polish comedy of errors. Two unrelated men with the same name get involved in a string of bizarre and hilarious adventures. Polish with *NO* English subtitles.
VHS: $15577. $39.95.
Leon Trystan, Poland, 1937, 90 mins.

Utan Ksiecia Jozefa (Prince Joseph's Soldier)

During Napoleon's campaign in Poland, a young soldier is accused of desertion. His fiance pleads with the Prince and manages to win him over to her cause. She appeals to Prince Joseph's heart because her cause is love. Polish with no subtitles.
VHS: $26658. $24.95.
Konrad Tom, Poland, 1938, 85 mins.

W Hour

Set in Warsaw on August 1, 1944, when young soldiers from the Home Army units make their last minute preparations for the Warsaw Uprising. Polish with *no* English subtitles.
VHS: $11349. $49.95.
Janusz Morgenstern, Poland, 85 mins.

What Are You Going to Do to Me, If You Catch Me?

The director of a large business tries to save his endangered position by marrying a VIP's daughter, but first he must divorce his current wife, in this recent comedy. Polish with *no* English subtitles.
VHS: $11341. $49.95.
Stanislaw Bareja, Poland, 1978, 107 mins.

Without Love

Ewa, a young and ambitious journalist, seeks to advance her career at any cost. Her methods provoke controversies and one of the stories leads to an unexpected tragedy in this film by Barbara Sass. Polish with English subtitles.
VHS: $11325. $49.95.
Barbara Sass, Poland, 1980, 104 mins.

Woman in the Hat

A young actress begins her career seeking her place in life and on stage. An interesting drama, presenting the contemporary Warsaw artistic community. With Hanna Mikuc, Henryk Machalica. Polish with *no* English subtitles.
VHS: $11357. $49.95.
Stanislaw Rozewicz, Poland, 1984, 116 mins.

Yanosik (Janosik)

Yanosik is a legendary hero of the Tatra Mountains. As the leader of a band of outlaws this mountain robber steals from the rich and helps the poor who are oppressed by the liege lords who rule the countryside. An exciting action film, in the tradition of Robin Hood, full of adventures, fights, duels, pursuits and traps. Polish with English subtitles.
VHS: $14237. $49.95.
Jerzy Passendorfer, Poland, 1973, 144 mins.

YOUNG POLISH DIRECTORS TO WATCH

Baritone

Zbigniew Zapasiewicz stars as a well-known baritone, Taviani, who returns to Poland from abroad for his 50th birthday and promises a grand concert for people in his home town. But shortly before the performance is to begin, he loses his voice. Polish with English subtitles.
VHS: $11311. $49.95.
Janusz Zaorski, Poland, 1985, 100 mins.

Cupid's Bow

A powerful drama about a young married woman who rejects her middle-class conventions and struggles for independence. Set in Cracow after the First World War, the film is based on a novel by Juliusz Kaden Bandrowski, and created a scandal in Poland for its unabashed eroticism. Polish with English subtitles.
VHS: $11318. $49.95.
Jerzy Domaradzki, Poland, 1978, 119 mins.

A Daimler Benz Limousine

On May 5, 1939, in Poznan, two brothers from a Polish-German family steal the car of the Consul General representing the German Reich. This joy ride ends in prison. They are accused of attempted kidnapping and terrorism. One pleads guilty, the other pleads innocent. Now enemies, the two are released and their rivalry takes on a new and cruel dimension. Polish with English subtitles.
VHS: $22212. $59.95.
Filip Bajon, Poland, 1983, 99 mins.

Deja Vu

A period Polish thriller that moves between Chicago and Odessa in 1925. A Chicago mobster and professional hitman is commissioned by the Mafia to track down and kill a traitor who has fled to Odessa. The traitor, Niczypur, uses the newly opened Chicago-Constantinople-Odessa shipping line for an ambitious smuggling operation. The fates of both men will be decided in a violent burst of shoot-outs. With Jerzy Stuhr, Galina Pletrowa, Nikolai Karaczencow and Wladimir Golowin. English, Russian and Polish with English subtitles.
VHS: $19396. $59.95.
Juliusz Machulski, Poland, 1989, 108 mins.

Foul Play

Marek Piwowski directed this detective story, based on a true case from police files, about an armed robbery of a Warsaw department store. A young man is coerced into undercover work for the police, in return for their dropping charges against him. In an interesting twist, the lead roles in the film are played by Olympic Champion boxers Jan Szczepanski and Jerzy Kulej, as the two detectives. Polish with English subtitles.
VHS: $11322. $49.95.
Marek Piwowski, Poland, 1976, 98 mins.

Great Race

One of the most politically daring films to be made in Poland during the 1980's. The subject is a Peace Race, a mass event organized in the spring of 1952. Radek, who runs in the race, wants to win a first prize, and the second wants to win in order to hand a letter to President Bierut, asking for help for his father—a defendant in a political trial. With Tadeusz Bradecki, Krzysztof Pieczynski. Polish with *no* English subtitles.
VHS: $11347. $49.95.
Jerzy Domaradzki, Poland, 1982, 100 mins.

Hero of the Year

Feliks Falk's updating of the story of Danielak, the hero of his film *Top Dog*. Danielak, in a brilliant performance by Jerzy Stuhr, returns to show business after being sacked from his TV job in 1981, with a series of shows titled "Hero of the Year". A brilliant satire on ruthless corruption. Polish with English subtitles.
VHS: $11309. $49.95.
Feliks Falk, Poland, 1985, 115 mins.

Housemaster

An ailing aristocrat and his house master play a clever game of deception in postwar Poland in this showcase for leading Polish actor Tadeusz Lomnicki, who heads the cast. Although made for Polish television, this is a brilliantly directed piece by one of Poland's most interesting filmmakers, Wojciech Marczewski. Polish with English subtitles.
VHS: $12356. $39.95.
Wojciech Marczewski, Poland, 1979, 85 mins.

Interrogation

The 1990 Cannes Film Festival awarded its Best Actress Award to Krystyna Janda for her performance in this intense drama of a woman victimized by a Stalinist government. The film details the horrible abuse of a cabaret singer in 1950's Warsaw who is arrested after a one night stand with a military officer. Originally banned by the Polish government, *Interrogation* is one of the most powerful films to come out of Poland in the last several decades. Polish with English subtitles.
VHS: $14066. $79.95.
Ryszard Bugajski, Poland, 1982, 118 mins.

Issa Valley

Based on the novel by Nobel prize-winning author Czeslaw Milosz; a moving portrait of turn-of-the-century Lithuania, featuring top-notch performances from Anna Dymna, Ewa Wisniewska and Edward Dziewonski. Polish with *no* English subtitles.
VHS: $11339. $49.95.
Tadeusz Konwicki, Poland, 1982, 120 mins.

Kingsize

This allegory made during the communist era in Poland contrasts two imaginary worlds, one made up of dwarves and the other inhabited by people of normal stature. While the dwarves scheme to get ahead in the meager environment of Drawerland, the Kingsize people magically move from one dimension to the next, granting them many privileges, including the company of women. Polish with English subtitles.
VHS: $20841. $59.95.
Juliusz Machulski, Poland, 1988, 108 mins.

Kung-Fu

A film that remained banned for many years, this contemporary drama by Janusz Kijowski is set in the ambiguous moral climate of 1970's Poland. The story focuses on three university friends who begin their careers at the same time. Daniel Olbrychski, Piotr Fronczewski and Andrzej Seweryn star. Polish with English subtitles.
VHS: $11323. $49.95.
Janusz Kijowski, Poland, 1979, 110 mins.

Little Pendulum

From one of the most interesting filmmakers, a key television film which paints a fascinating, tragic and deeply ironic picture of a man's wasted life during the Stalinist period. Janusz Gajos delivers a stunning performance. Polish with *no* English subtitles.
VHS: $11346. $39.95.
Filip Bajon, Poland, 60 mins.

The Magnate

A fascinating film by Filip Bajon, the focus of which is on the downfall of the great aristocratic German family of von Teuss in the context of the social and political situation in Europe in the first half of the 20th century. In the authentic scenery of von Teuss's palace in Pszczyna, southern Poland, the film follows the extravagant life of the old prince and his sons in the refined, if risque, atmosphere of family scandals. 2 cassettes. Polish with *no* English subtitles.
VHS: $11334. $69.95.
Filip Bajon, Poland, 1987, 185 mins.

Masquerade

Janusz Kijowski, one of the boldest members of Poland's film generation of the 1970's, directed this recent film about a famous actor, who, fed up with his popularity, escapes from his conventional career by creating his own theater, without an audience, where the boundary between the real and the imaginary is obscured. Polish with English subtitles.
VHS: $11316. $49.95.
Janusz Kijowski, Poland, 1986, 102 mins.

Mother of Kings

One of the most highly acclaimed Polish films of recent years, the film is the dramatic story about a poor widow charwoman and mother, shown across the span of the worst moments of Poland's history: the Second World War and the Stalinist times. Filmed in black-and-white to incorporate newsreel footage from Stalinist times, the film won the Grand Prix at the Gdansk Festival. Polish with English subtitles.
VHS: $11306. $49.95.
Janusz Zaorski, Poland, 1982, 126 mins.

Pigs

A harrowing film about the extraordinary social and personal transformation within the break up of Poland's communist society, the story focuses on the efforts of two friends, Olo and Franz, former secret police agents, and their attempt to reestablish friends and find their place and identity in the rebuilt state. With Boguslaw Linda, Marek Kondrat and Janusz Gajos. Polish with English subtitles.
VHS: $18244. $49.95.
Wladyslaw Pasikowski, Poland, 1992

The Scoundrel

Taken from actual events, this film concerns a circle of Polish fighters in Lodz, 1910. The film explores the shifting relationship between a terrorist and his bitter enemy. With Adam Ferency, Joanna Trzeplecinska and Boguslaw Linda. Polish with English subtitles.
VHS: $11285. $39.95.
Tomasz Wiszniewski, Poland, 1990, 88 mins.

The Story of Sin (Dzieje Grzechu)

The fourth live-action feature by Walerian Borowczyk, *The Story of Sin* is the first feature made in the filmmaker's native land of Poland, where he began his career as an animator in the fifties. The film is a chronicle of a young girl's progress from her strict Victorian upbringing to a love affair with a young man which soon blossoms into passion, jealousy and a final heroically grotesque self-sacrifice. A celebration of *amour fou*, starring Grazyna Dlugolecka and Jerzy Zelnik. Polish with English subtitles.
VHS: $14236. $49.95.
Walerian Borowczyk, Poland, 1975, 128 mins.

Top Dog

One of the key works of the new Polish cinema of the 1970's, a moral investigation of an ambitious individual who rushes into a tangled web of favor-trading, bribery and slander to eliminate his rivals. The film is set with razor-edged realism and specific detail against an unstylish provincial life which becomes grotesque. Polish with English subtitles.
VHS: $02657. $69.95.
Feliks Falk, Poland, 1978, 115 mins.

Train to Hollywood

A very funny, surreal comedy set in a small Polish town, where a beautiful girl dreams of Marilyn Monroe's career. Will the dining car, where she sells beer, take her straight to Hollywood? Polish with English subtitles.
VHS: $11315. $49.95.
Radoslaw Piwowarski, Poland, 1986, 96 mins.

A Woman and a Woman (Kobieta i Kobieta)

Ryszard Bugajski created this touching film about friendship. It examines a ten-year period in the lives of Barbara and Irena, two very dear friends. Will their friendship survive the numerous professional and personal conflicts they encounter? Only time will tell. With Halina Labonarska and Anna Romantowska. Polish with English subtitles.
VHS: $15057. $49.95.
Ryszard Bugajski, Poland, 1980, 99 mins.

KRZYSZTOF KIESLOWSKI

Blind Chance

The film presents three different biographies of a man's life, using the "what if" formula. Depicted are the possible careers he could have chosen at the turning point in his life, including that of a physician, a political dissident and a party activist. A brave, probing film. Polish with English subtitles.
VHS: $11308. $49.95.
Krzysztof Kieslowski, Poland, 1982, 122 mins.

Blue

Juliette Binoche stars in this provocative thriller, a role for which she won the Cesar Award and the Venice Film Festival Award as best actress. She becomes entangled in a mysterious web of passion and lies after she digs into the past life of her recently and unexpectedly deceased husband. Part One of Kieslowski's acclaimed trilogy, *Three Colors*.
VHS: $21359. $19.95.
Laser: LD75022. $39.99.
Krzysztof Kieslowski, France, 1993, 98 mins.

Camera Buff (Amator)

In Communist Poland, a young father with a movie camera begins to pose a threat when his initial interest in filmmaking is superceded. He intended to photograph his newborn daughter, but suddenly, this newly formed shutterbug is filming everything in sight, including things the authorities would rather not have exposed. One of the key works of modern Polish cinema. Polish with English subtitles.
VHS: $21197. $79.95.
Krzysztof Kieslowski, Poland, 1979, 112 mins.

The Double Life of Veronique

Two remarkably similar women, one in Warsaw and Paris, are acutely aware of each other's existence in this film about the linkage of souls. Veronika is a Polish music student with a beautiful voice and a heart condition. Veronique is a French school teacher paralyzed by doubt. Both roles are played by the beautiful Irene Jacob. Slawomir Idziak's cinematography and Zbigniew Preisner's score are alternately haunting and unforgettable. Polish and French with English subtitles.
VHS: $16928. $89.95.
Laser: LD75182. $34.98.
Krzysztof Kieslowski, Poland/France, 1991, 92 mins.

No End (Without End)

The film's hero, a young libertarian lawyer, dies four days before the film begins, leaving the case of a worker arrested for organizing a strike unresolved. His widow gets involved in the trial while trying to overcome her husband's death but there seems to be no end to his pervasive influence. Krzysztof Kieslowski's powerful portrait of life under martial law in Poland is a film "burning with a passionate engagement with the system" (*Time Out*). With Maria Pakulnis, Aleksander Bardini and Artur Barcis. Polish with English subtitles.
VHS: $20305. $79.95.
Krzysztof Kieslowski, Poland, 1984, 108 mins.

Red

Kieslowski's striking conclusion of his Three Colors trilogy stars Irene Jacob as a model, separated from her lover, who is brought by accident into the life of the aging Jean-Louis Trintignant, retired judge and electronic peeping Tom. As Irene slowly uncovers her lover's secret life, she discovers that her own past is inevitably linked to her destiny. With Jean-Pierre Lorit and Frederique Feder.
VHS: S25606. $19.95.
Laser: Letterboxed. LD75015. $39.99.
Krzysztof Kieslowski, Switzerland, 1994, 99 mins.

Subsidiaries (Personel)

At first glance, the conflicts at the theater seem to be related to the generation gap. Later, discussions between the artists and the technical staff reveal vital differences resulting from irreconcilable moral understandings and socio-political views. Polish with English subtitles.
VHS: S26727. $59.95.
Krzysztof Kieslowski, Poland, 1975, 57 mins.

White

The second part of Kieslowski's Blue-White-Red trilogy, based on the concepts of the French tri-colour. A Polish man's life disintegrates when his new French bride deserts him after only six months. Forced to begin anew, he returns to Poland and plans a clever scheme of revenge against her. Julie Delpy is great as the young wife. French and Polish with English subtitles.
VHS: S23108. $19.95.
Laser: Letterboxed. LD74805. $49.95.
Krzysztof Kieslowski, France/Poland, 1993, 92 mins.

AGNIESZKA HOLLAND

Angry Harvest

Agnieszka Holland's Academy-Award nominated film is a powerful emotional drama set during the German occupation of Poland. The raid on the ghetto, in which a Christian farmer saves a young Jewish woman on the run, and their resulting relationship becomes one of inter-dependent love and ultimate terror that ends in tragedy. A tour-de-force of acting and directing, the film stars Armin Mueller-Stahl, Elisabeth Trissenaar and Wojciech Pszoniak. German with English subtitles.
VHS: S06013. $69.95.
Agnieszka Holland, Germany, 1986, 102 mins.

Europa Europa

The film which took America by storm: Agnieszka Holland's powerful, moving story of a courageous German-Jewish teenager who survived World War II by concealing his identity and living as a Nazi during seven harrowing years through three countries. Based on a true story; a film which changes almost everyone who sees it. "A pure, absurd miracle of history" (New Yorker Magazine). Polish, German with English subtitles.
VHS: S16327. $19.98.
Agnieszka Holland, Poland/France, 1991, 100 mins.

Fever

A gripping political thriller, set in 1905. A group of anarchists plots to assassinate the Russian Tsar's governor in Russian-partitioned Poland. A sensitive script subtly probes the psychological motivations of the anarchists as the bomb is passed among them. Banned for many years by Poland's Communist authorities despite its winning the Grand Prize at the Gdansk Film Festival. With Jan Kanty Pluskiewidz and Barbara Grabowska. Polish with English subtitles.
VHS: S11310. $49.95.
Agnieszka Holland, Poland, 1981, 115 mins.

A Lonely Woman

Agnieszka Holland's last film made in Poland prior to her exile in France—a powerful portrait of a woman raising her child in a small town. Deprived of help and friendship, she is left to her own resources. Will an encounter with a lonely man change her life? Very powerful drama. Polish with English subtitles.
VHS: S11348. $49.95.
Agnieszka Holland, Poland, 1987, 94 mins.

Olivier Olivier

This very unusual story begins when the nine-year-old son of a provincial French family suddenly disappears. Six years later a young man turns up who claims to be the missing youngster, setting off a series of strange reactions from the people he claims as his family. Based, unimaginably, on a true story. With Brigitte Rouan, Jean-Francois Stevenin and Francois Cluzet. French with English subtitles.
VHS: S20708. $19.95.
Laser: LD72381. $34.95.
Agnieszka Holland, France, 1992, 110 mins.

Provincial Actors

This bold first feature is set in the microcosm of a group of actors working in the provinces. While the actors are staging an important Polish play, Liberation, ambition, jealousy and betrayal dominate their inter-personal relations. The leading actor longs for stardom but his dreams have placed his marriage into an impossible situation. Polish with English subtitles.
VHS: S25906. $79.95.
Agnieszka Holland, Poland, 1979, 104 mins.

The Secret Garden

Agnieszka Holland's haunting adaptation of Frances Hodgson Burnett's 1909 classic about an orphaned young girl (Kate Maberly) dispatched to her uncle's remote English estate. With the help of her painfully withdrawn cousin (Heydon Prowse) and a local boy (Andrew Knott), she discovers an enchanting garden. Holland beautifully captures the painful social isolation of childhood. Maggie Smith plays the tyrannical housekeeper.
VHS: S20217. $19.98.
Laser: LD72328. $34.98.
Agnieszka Holland, USA, 1993, 102 mins.

To Kill a Priest

Polish filmmaker-in-exile Agnieszka Holland tells the powerfully realistic story of an activist priest who endured the wrath of the secret police for his secular duties. French heartthrob Christopher Lambert is the political cleric in this story based on the true case of Father Jerzy Popieluszko; Ed Harris is the Communist cop out to get him in. In English.
VHS: S11786. $89.95.
Agnieszka Holland, USA/France, 1988, 117 mins.

Total Eclipse

Leonardo Di Caprio and David Thewlis star in this film based on the affair between Arthur Rimbaud and Paul Verlaine. Rimbaud left a legacy of brilliant poetry and an example of extreme living that inspired contemporary stars like Jim Morrison. Verlaine, a highly regarded writer in his own right, was an older married man when he became infatuated with Rimbaud. This is a grand film about their passion for love and art, a passion finally doomed by madness. Christopher Hampton wrote the screenplay.
VHS: S27617. $96.99.
Laser: LD75553. $39.99.
Agnieszka Holland, Great Britain/France, 1995, 111 mins.

ANDRZEJ WAJDA

Andrzej Wajda Trilogy

Contains A Generation, Kanal and Ashes and Diamonds.
VHS: S20506. $59.95.

Andrzej Wajda, A Portrait

The famed Polish filmmaker speaks candidly about his life and his relationship to his art. This son of a slain Polish cavalry officer fought in the Resistance before he studied painting in Cracow and filmmaking in Lodz. His films include Ashes and Diamonds, Kanal, Man of Marble and Danton. The film has been called an "unforgettable and deeply moving experience." Narrated in English.
VHS: S16821. $29.95.
Ewa Lachnit, Poland, 1989, 76 mins.

Ashes and Diamonds

A brilliant statement from Andrzej Wajda, Ashes and Diamonds illustrates the conflict of idealism and instinct in this story of a young resistance fighter who assassinates the wrong man at the close of World War II. With Zbigniew Cybulski. Polish with English subtitles.
VHS: S00071. $24.95.
Andrzej Wajda, Poland, 1958, 105 mins.

Birch Wood

One of the most beautiful, reflective films of Andrzej Wajda's great career, Birch Wood is the story of two brothers—one seriously ill but full of life, the other a grieving widower, envious of his brother's high spirits in the face of death. Daniel Olbrychski and Olgierd Lukaszewicz star. Polish with English subtitles.
VHS: S11328. $49.95.
Andrzej Wajda, Poland, 1971, 100 mins.

The Conductor

John Gielgud stars as a renowned expatriate Polish conductor who returns home to lead a small, provincial orchestra after a 50-year absence. Though ill and dying Gielgud manages to bring new life to the orchestra, in this sensitive portrayal of a man bent on a final artistic triumph. With Andrej Sewern, winner of the Berlin Film Festival Best Actor Award. English and Polish with English subtitles.
VHS: S20592. $79.95.
Andrzej Wajda, Poland, 1980, 101 mins.

Fury Is a Woman
(The Siberian Lady Macbeth)

Andrzej Wajda shot this extraordinary film in Yugoslavia, during a period of self-imposed political exile. Fury Is a Woman ranks with Akira Kurosawa's Throne of Blood as one of the most successful screen translations of Shakespeare ever made. With Olivera Markovic and Ljuba Tadic. Letterboxed format. Serbian with English subtitles.
VHS: S15510. $59.95.
Andrzej Wajda, Yugoslavia, 1961, 93 mins.

A Generation

Wajda's first feature takes place in 1942 occupied Warsaw, and follows the pursuits of a young man whose life is hardened under the Nazis. When he falls in love with the leader of the Resistance group, he learns to fight back. Stars Tadeusz Lomnicki, Ursula Modrzynska, Zbigniew Cybulski and a very young Roman Polanski. Polish with English subtitles.
VHS: S16189. $24.95.
Andrzej Wajda, Poland, 1954, 90 mins.

Hunting Flies

One of the key films of the Polish film renaissance, this satiric comedy explores the seeming world of emancipated women and emasculated men of Communist Poland. A librarian shares his life and tiny home with his domineering wife. In search of a larger perspective, he has an affair with a beautiful intellectual, who wears fly-shaped glasses. She tries to become the woman behind the great artist. It's a film dedicated to the women of Poland, even as it critiques the relations between the sexes. Polish with English subtitles.
VHS: S23299. $59.95.
Andrzej Wajda, Poland, 1969, 108 mins.

Innocent Sorcerers

This rarely seen film by Andrzej Wajda is reflective of the best of 1960's Polish cinema. The film created a stir with its ironic comic perspective as it focused on young Poles in the 1960's. A bachelor doctor, who is also a jazz musician, can't quite commit himself to his superficial girlfriend. He and his aimless friends find any kind of human contact or emotional commitment a troubling and ultimately uninviting prospect. Polish with English subtitles.
VHS: S22597. $59.95.
Andrzej Wajda, Poland, 1960, 86 mins.

Kanal

Part of the famous Andrzej Wajda trilogy that included A Generation and Ashes and Diamonds. The almost hallucinatory portrait of a group of Polish citizens and patriots who attempt to flee the Nazis through the sewer system of a war-devastated Warsaw. A film of amazing power and rare courage. Polish with English subtitles.
VHS: S02775. $24.95.
Andrzej Wajda, Poland, 1957, 96 mins.

Korczak

Andrzej Wajda's film chronicles the extraordinary efforts of Dr. Janusz Korczak (Wojciech Pszoniak), a pediatrician and author, to protect a group of abandoned children in the Warsaw Ghetto. On Aug. 6, 1942, he refused an offer from the Nazis to spare his life and accompanied 200 orphans of the Warsaw Ghetto to Treblinka. Agnieszka Holland wrote the screenplay; Robby Muller was the cinematographer. Polish with English subtitles.
VHS: S18932. $79.95.
Andrzej Wajda, Poland/France, 1990, 113 mins.

Land of Promise

Based on the novel by Nobel Prize-winner Wladyslav Reymont, Andrzej Wajda's epic film examines the relationships among three industrialists who own a textile factory in Lodz at the turn of the century. The film is an epic about complex class structures; each man represents a different ethnic group: a Pole (Daniel Olbrychski), a German (Andrzej Seweryn) and a Jew (Wojciech Pszoniak). The drama builds to a climax when the overworked, underpaid workers threaten to revolt. With Anna Nehrebecka. Polish with English subtitles.
VHS: S19397. $79.95.
Andrzej Wajda, Poland, 1974, 178 mins.

Layer Cake (Przekladaniec)

Based on Stanislav Lem's novel, this unusual comic film charts the unlucky life of the fictional race car driver Ryszard Fox. After so many accidents and so many internal organ transplants, he is forced to contemplate exactly how much of his body is really his. Polish with English subtitles.
VHS: S26737. $49.95.
Andrzej Wajda, Poland, 1968, 35 mins.

Lotna

Andrzej Wajda, the son of a Polish cavalry officer killed in the Second World War by Germans, made this film as a tribute to the heroic horsemen who faced off against German tanks. It follows the trajectory of an off-white horse which passes among various military officials until it breaks a leg and is shot. Polish with English subtitles.
VHS: S26728. $59.95.
Andrzej Wajda, Poland, 1959, 89 mins.

Maids of Wilko

Andrzej Wajda's adaptation of Jaroslav Iwaszkiewicz's memoirs is set in the late 1920s. Viktor Ruben (Daniel Olbrychski), a World War I veteran and operator of a small factory, reexamines his life following the death of his friend. Returning to the home of his aunt and uncle, he is drawn into a mysterious web of sexual and romantic longing for the five women he was friends with years before. "Wajda...has made an exquisite period piece which lays bare the futility of attempting to resurrect the past" (The Faber Companion to Foreign Films). With Anna Seniuk, Maja Komarowska, Krystyna Zachwatowicz and Christine Pascal. French and Polish with English subtitles.
VHS: S18691. $49.95.
Andrzej Wajda, Poland/France, 1979, 118 mins.

Man of Iron

Made in the center of political events surrounding it, Andrzej Wajda's Man of Iron is a powerful sequel to Man of Marble. The film merges documentary footage of the Solidarity strike into a fictionalized drama of a disillusioned radio producer (Marian Opania) who is ordered to Gdansk to undermine the reputation of one of the leaders of the worker revolt. "An urgent, nervy narrative conveys all the exhilaration and bewilderment of finding oneself on the very crestline of crucial historical change" (Time Out). With Jerzy Radziwilowicz, Krystyna Janda, Irena Byrska and Wieslawa Kosmalska. Winner of the Palme d'Or, 1981 Cannes Film festival. Polish with English subtitles.
VHS: S20403. $19.98.
Andrzej Wajda, Poland, 1981, 152 mins.

Man of Marble

Thirteen years in the making, Wajda's film caused packed houses to rise and sing the Polish national anthem when it finally premiered in Poland in 1977. Denied entrance at Cannes by Polish authorities, it played nonetheless at a commercial theatre there and won the International Critics' Prize. Hailed as "a milestone in Polish cinema" by Variety, Man of Marble is the story of a young filmmaker trying to reconstruct a truthful picture of the Stalinist past, a past obscured by 20 years of shifting propaganda. Polish with English subtitles.
VHS: S12828. $79.95.
Andrzej Wajda, Poland, 1977, 160 mins.

Samson

Andrzej Wajda's profound psychological study of a man who accidentally kills a schoolmate in a brawl and is imprisoned. He is released with the onset of World War II, only to be locked up once more, but in the Warsaw Ghetto. Again he escapes and finds himself trapped, this time in a world of non-Jews where the threat of capture is ever-present. This powerful film makes extraordinary use of naturalistic symbols and a widescreen format. Polish with English subtitles.
VHS: S23300. $59.95.
Andrzej Wajda, Poland, 1961, 119 mins.

The Wedding (Wesele)

A moving drama of Polish destiny, The Wedding is based on a popular nationalistic play (one of the best known literary works in Poland) by Stanislaw Wyspianski about the wedding of a peasant's daughter to a poet. This exceptional work is one of Wajda's most important films; for him it was a synthesis of sorts—a chance to put in one unique metaphor all the ideas and emotions, judgement and love, hate and pride he felt about the country to which he belonged. A landmark in the Polish cinema. Polish with English subtitles.
VHS: S15560. $49.95.
Andrzej Wajda, Poland, 1973, 103 mins.

Without Anesthesia

This contemporary parable offers an unmatched look at the face of Poland before the fall of Communism. A famous Polish foreign correspondent returns home from a successful assignment abroad only to find his marriage and career falling apart. Written by Agnieszka Holland. Polish with English subtitles.
VHS: S22445. $79.95.
Andrzej Wajda, Poland, 1979, 116 mins.

JERZY SKOLIMOWSKI

Hands Up

A legendary film, banned for over a decade in Poland. Jerzy Skolimowski (Moonlighting) directed this probing investigation of a group of young physicians who recall their university days during the Stalinist period while meeting at a class reunion. Originally completed in 1967, the film was not released until 1981 and until the director cut it and added a new color sequence. Polish with English subtitles.
VHS: S11326. $49.95.
Jerzy Skolimowski, Poland, 1967-81, 78 mins.

The Lightship

Jerzy Skolimowski's moody film stars Klaus Maria Brandauer and Robert Duvall in the storm-tossed, suffocating world of a lightship in the age-old struggle between good and evil. The ship's captain must somehow protect his men and his rebellious son against an invading gang led by Duvall, who is both cunning and without scruples.
VHS: S03523. $79.95.
Jerzy Skolimowski, USA, 1986, 87 mins.

The Shout

A spellbinding, occult-tinged tape of mind control and superstitions come true, with a top-notch cast, including Alan Bates, Susannah York, John Hurt and Tim Curry. A surrealistic atmosphere pervades this spine-tingler as a mysterious "shout" kills people in the English countryside. Offbeat, psychological thriller that won the Cannes Film Festival.
VHS: S01197. $29.98.
Jerzy Skolimowski, Great Britain, 1978, 90 mins.

Torrents of Spring

A spectacular cast, including Nastassia Kinski, Timothy Hutton and Valeria Golino, star in this visually beautiful, seductive tale based on a story by Turgenev. Kinski is the wife of a Russian landowner who falls in love with and has a passionate affair with Timothy Hutton. In English.
VHS: S12589. $89.99.
Jerzy Skolimowski, France/Italy, 1989, 100 mins.

ROMAN POLANSKI

Bitter Moon

Roman Polanski's story of two different couples whose wild dreams, fantasies and realities collide on a cruise to Istanbul in a tense game of sexual one-upmanship and menage-a-trois features Hugh Grant, Emmanuelle Seigner, Peter Coyote and Kristin Scott Thomas in a film that's been described as "Love Boat meets Last Tango in Paris."
VHS: S21925. $19.95.
Roman Polanski, France/Britain, 1992, 139 mins.

Chinatown

Jack Nicholson and Faye Dunaway star in Polanski's finely crafted, atmospheric film. What begins as a routine matrimonial snoop job for an average gumshoe mushrooms into a murderous regional and personal scandal told with incredible style, surprises and a gripping narrative line. Outstanding performances by all including John Huston as Dunaway's father and a cameo by Polanski as a great little sleaze.
VHS: S01840. $19.95.
Laser: Widescreen. LD75371. $49.98.
Roman Polanski, USA, 1974, 131 mins.

Cul de Sac

Two failed and wounded gangsters invade the lives of middle-aged milquetoast Donald Pleasance and his nubile young wife (Francoise Dorleac) in Roman Polanski's black comedy. Holding the odd couple hostage, the gangsters become increasingly irrational, and Pleasance is constantly challenged by his wife to take violent action in protest. With superb performances from Jack MacGowran, Lionel Stander, and Jacqueline Bisset.
VHS: S16187. $29.95.
Roman Polanski, Great Britain, 1966, 111 mins.

Death and the Maiden

Sigourney Weaver, Ben Kingsley and Stuart Wilson are featured in this adaptation of Ariel Dorfman's acclaimed play. A woman finally has the opportunity to see justice done for the wrong she suffered. She will go to any extreme—after all, her life was destroyed. It's a knockout psychological thriller.
VHS: S25102. $19.98.
Laser: Widescreen. LD74959. $39.99.
Roman Polanski, France, 1995, 103 mins.

Diary of Forbidden Dreams

A beautiful girl, lost in a remote area of the Italian Riviera, is constantly besieged and trapped into bizarre incidents as she tries to find her way out. Mastroianni is the nobleman of the villa where she takes refuge until she turns into a tiger and attacks. The beautiful Sydne Rome, Roman Polanski and Mastroianni star in this bizarre fantasy, an Alice in Wonderland of the idle European rich. English dialog.
VHS: S00340. $29.95.
Roman Polanski, Italy/Great Britain, 1981, 94 mins.

Fat and the Lean

A brilliant short film by Roman Polanski, made early in his career; a tour-de-force of abstract, existential allegory.
VHS: S09049. $19.95.
Roman Polanski, France, 1964, 20 mins.

Fearless Vampire Killers

Or Pardon Me, Your Teeth Are in My Neck. Roman Polanski directs (and appears in) this cult oddity, a vampire-film spoof that manages both horror and humor. The story involves a professor and his bumbling assistant, who set out to track down a coven of Transylvanian vampires. Cast includes Jack MacGowran, Sharon Tate, Alfie Bass and Terry Downes. This is the restored, original cut.
VHS: S12741. $19.98.
Laser: LD72173. $39.98.
Roman Polanski, USA, 1967, 124 mins.

Frantic
Roman Polanski directs this thriller set in Paris, which finds Harrison Ford more than reasonably concerned when his wife Betty Buckley disappears. A Hitchcock-like plot involves switched luggage and a fetching young courier played by Emmanuelle Seigner. Great scenery and rooftop suspense.
VHS: S07470. $19.98.
  Laser: LD70576. $39.98.
Roman Polanski, USA, 1987, 120 mins.

Knife in the Water
Polanski's debut feature film is an incisive study of three people spending a casual weekend on their yacht. A young man, who joined the couple as a hitchhiker, gradually interferes uncomfortably into the couple's lives, and in a brilliant depiction of inter-personal tensions, tests their marriage. Polish with English subtitles.
VHS: S19406. $39.95.
  Laser: LD70755. $59.95.
Roman Polanski, Poland, 1960, 90 mins.

Macbeth
Roman Polanski's acclaimed version of Shakespeare's *Macbeth* stars Jon Finch as Macbeth in a beautifully nightmarish vision of the great play. English dialog.
VHS: S00789. $19.95.
Roman Polanski, Great Britain, 1976, 139 mins.

Mammals
A brilliant and rarely seen short film by Roman Polanski, at the height of his mastery. This fourth and final of Polanski's short films won the festivals at Oberhausen and Melbourne.
VHS: S08125. $19.95.
Roman Polanski, Poland, 1963, 10 mins.

Pirates
Comic-adventure film about buccaneers who take on a Spanish galleon filled with Aztec gold. Polanski is said to have spent $30 million on the film, of which $10 million was spent on the replica of the ship *Neptune*. Starring Walter Matthau and Charlotte Lewis.
VHS: S01610. $19.95.
Roman Polanski, 1986, 117 mins.

Repulsion
Polanski's first English-language film, a chilling study of madness, stars Catherine Deneuve as a jealously sadistic schizophrenic, terrified of sex. Full of memorable sequences, such as Deneuve's delusions of rape as she sees plaster turn into a clawing hand and walls cracking or overhears the moans of her sister making love. With Yvonne Furneaux and John Fraser.
VHS: S01106. $39.95.
  Laser: Widescreen. LD75387. $99.95.
Roman Polanski, Great Britain, 1965, 105 mins.

Rosemary's Baby
Ira Levin thriller brought to the screen by Roman Polanski, concerning a young wife whose husband becomes involved with a witches' coven. With Mia Farrow and John Cassavetes.
VHS: S02685. $19.95.
Roman Polanski, USA, 1968, 136 mins.

Tenant
Polanski's most autobiographical film is, like *Repulsion*, a journey through the distorted realm of the human mind. Polanski himself plays Trelkovsky, a nebbish file clerk who moves into the apartment of a young suicide, becomes deeply paranoid, certain that the other tenants are trying to drive *him* to suicide. With Isabelle Adjani, Shelley Winters, Lila Kedrova, Melvyn Douglas. English dialog.
VHS: S01308. $49.95.
Roman Polanski, Great Britain, 1976, 126 mins.

Tess
Winner of three Academy Awards, Polanski's interpretation of Thomas Hardy's novel is a beautiful and timeless masterwork destined to be a classic. Nastassia Kinski stars as Tess against the backdrop of a morally rigid Victorian England. The stunning cinematography is unforgettable. English dialog.
VHS: S01311. $29.95.
Roman Polanski, France/Great Britain, 1980, 170 mins.

Two Men and a Wardrobe
Polanski's award winning short is a bitter parable blending slapstick and the absurd, about two men who emerge from the sea carrying a wardrobe. Made while Polanski was a student at the Polish Film School. Also, *The Fat and the Lean*, another Polanski short, this one an attack on government tyranny. Silent.
VHS: S01936. $49.95.
Roman Polanski, Poland, 1958, 35 mins.

What!
After the macabre twists and psychological terror of his English and Hollywood films, Roman Polanski made this sex farce about a beautiful young woman whose temporary stay at an eccentric millionaire's mansion unleashes a series of strange events. A commercial failure on its initial release, the film was cut to 94 minutes and retitled *Diary of Forbidden Dreams*. This letterboxed version restores the excised material. With Marcello Mastroianni, Hugh Griffith, Sydne Rome, Romoli Valli and Polanski, in English.
VHS: S19876. $29.95.
Roman Polanski, Italy, 1973, 113 mins.

POLAND: PAST AND PRESENT

1000 Years of Polish Cavalry (1000 lat jazdy polskiej)
The history of mounted combat in Poland is addressed in this colorful documentary that begins at the battle of Cedynia in 972 A.D. and concludes with the heroic defense against the blitzkrieg of Nazi tanks and planes in 1939. In Polish.
VHS: S16820. $29.95.
E.Z. Szanialawski, Poland, 51 mins.

About Painting (O malarstwie)
A special look at the John Paul II painting collection founded by Janina and Karol Porczynski. Also included are three short films about the state of art in Poland. Polish narration. No English subtitles.
VHS: S16829. $24.95.

As Crosses Are Measure of Freedom (Bo Wolnosc Krzyzami sie Mierzy)
A sensational, deeply moving historical record made in collaboration with and under supervision of the General's closest aide-de-camp: the story of the legendary Polish leader General Anders and the soldiers of the 2nd Corps. English language narration.
VHS: S15578. $39.95.
Krzysztof Szmagier, Poland, 1989, 80 mins.

At Source (U Zrodel)
This tape contains two very interesting documentaries: *100 Days* and *First Test*. Both are about the beginning of the Solidarity movement in Poland, and they include footage from Gdansk and the creation of the Independent Student Society. Polish with NO English subtitles. Poland, 120 mins.
VHS: S15319. $39.95.

At the Bottom of the Hell (Dno piekta)
This documentary describes what happened to captured Polish military officers who were tried in Stalinist courts after World War II. It documents the dire conditions in which they were held and the severity of their sentencing. Polish with no subtitles.
VHS: S16823. $49.95.
Maciej Sienski, Poland, 64 mins.

Best of Kunicka
A recital by the popular Polish singer Halina Kunicka. 98 mins. Polish with *no* English subtitles.
VHS: S11380. $29.95.

Cracow and Its University (Krakow i jego Uniwersytet)
An English language tour of this historically rich Polish city and its more than 600 year old center of learning. You visit the Wawel Castle, the old walls of the city and the famous Cloth House.
VHS: S16828. $24.95.
Fundacia U. Jagiellonskiego, Poland, 1991, 27 mins.

Czeslaw Milosz
Czeslaw Milosz won the Nobel Prize for Literature in 1980. He read from *Selected Poems*, *The Separate Notebooks* and *The Unattainable Earth* in Los Angeles on September 12, 1988. Lewis MacAdams interviewed this poet, novelist, critic and philosopher born in Lithuania. From the *Lannan Literary Videos* series. 60 mins.
VHS: S27113. $19.95.

Fairyland
A series of 12 Polish cartoons for children from popular animation series such as Leon the Fox, Gus and Caesar, Hip-Hop Kangaroo, and Plasticines, from Polish Animation Studios. 110 mins.
VHS: S11291. $39.95.

Far from Poland
A brilliant film: denied a visa to shoot a film in Poland, director Godmilow constructs a film over the bare bones of documentary footage while in New York, resulting in a deft dismemberment of the myth of "documentary truth." The film portrays the birth of the Solidarity movement at the Gdansk shipyards through moving personal testimony and a chilling look at the psychology of a censor.
VHS: S02656. $69.95.
Jill Godmilow, USA, 1984, 106 mins.

Fears
A Polish television special in a 4-part, 2-cassette series about Warsaw cabaret artists in the 1930's. A young actress soon realizes that the price she has to pay for her career is very high. 280 mins. Polish with *no* English subtitles.
VHS: S11352. $69.95.

Fox Leon and Others
A series of short animation pieces for children, a sequel to the compilation *Fairyland*. Polish with *no* English subtitles.
VHS: S11292. $39.95.

Fronczewski—Pietrzak—Smolen Cabaret
A program of songs and sketches originally written for Jan Pietrzak's Warsaw cabaret *Pod Egida*. A delightful and sharp political satire of life in Poland from the 1950's through the early 80's. Polish with *no* English subtitles. 120 mins.
VHS: S11375. $29.95.

In the Silence of the Night
27 of the most beautiful Polish Christmas carols, performed by four choirs and soloists, interestingly enough by choirs from Catholic, Evangelist and Orthodox churches. 90 mins. Polish with *no* English subtitles.
VHS: S11384. $29.95.

Jacek Fedorowicz Cabaret Evening
The leading Polish cabaret satirist, Jacek Fedorowicz, in a cabaret performance satirizing the new political order in Poland. 47 mins.
VHS: S12360. $29.95.

Jan Pietrzak—Mr. Censor
Jan Pietrzak's latest cabaret program, marking his 25 years on the stage, including his now-famous *Zeby Polska byla Polska*. 120 mins. Polish with *no* English subtitles.
VHS: S11374. $49.95.

Jozef Pilsudzki/Road to Independence (Droga do Niepodleglosci)
Two historical documentaries from 1937 and 1935 about Poland's fierce road to independence and the funeral of Marshal Pilsudki. Polish language version. 112 mins.
VHS: S15563. $39.95.

Land of the White Eagle—Part 1
A series of 10-minute films highlighting Poland's history and traditions, her cultural heritage, architecture and landscape. Part 1 of the series visits Gniezno, Zelazowa Wola, Poznan, Pszczyna, the Pieniny and Beskidy mountains and the Eagle Nest trail between Cracow and Czestochowa. Narration in English. 95 mins.
VHS: S11364. $39.95.

Land of the White Eagle—Part 2
Part 2 of the series visits Warsaw, Cracow, Wieliczke salt mine, Marlbork, Torun, Wroclaw, Lodz, and Szczecin. 90 mins. Narration in English.
VHS: S11365. $39.95.

Land of the White Eagle—Part 3
The last in a series of films about Poland, with visits to Czestochowa, Zamosc, Kalwaria Zebrzydowska, Gdansk and Gdynia. 90 mins. In English.
VHS: S11366. $39.95.

Leszek Dlugosz—It Can Be You
A recital of Leszek Dlugosz, the Cracow-based composer and bard. 97 mins. Polish with *no* English subtitles.
VHS: S11379. $29.95.

Let's Cotton Together
A show of popular songs from Lvov performed by the Kalambur Theatre of Wroclaw. Polish with *no* English subtitles. 70 mins.
VHS: S11372. $39.95.

Nothing to Lose
Beginning in 1988, a young filmmaker traveled throughout Poland documenting the growing unrest and organization that led to the end of Communism in Eastern Europe. It is an amazing inside look at the efforts of ordinary people who changed the course of history. 56 mins.
VHS: S21593. $39.95.
Charles Steiner, USA, 1990, 56 mins.

Ordonka
This is the story of the most famous Polish popular singer from the 1930's. Though she became a well-regarded film star and performer, during the Second World War she was also a good samaritan. Includes original footage of *Ordonka*. Polish language narration.
VHS: S22209. $24.95.
Maria Kwiatkowska, Poland, 1993, 50 mins.

Parada Wspomnien
An insightful documentary about the most exciting years in the Solidarity movement, including conspiracy, famous escapes, and more. Polish language version.
VHS: S15565. $29.95.
Bogdan Kosinski/Jacek Petrycki, Poland, 51 mins.

The Pilgrim
An independent documentary made during the first visit of Pope John Paul to Poland in June, 1979. Polish with *no* English subtitles. 80 mins.
VHS: S11367. $29.95.

Poems for Children
Poems for children written by Jan Brzechwa, Jonstanty Ildefons Galczynski and Julian Tuwim, recited by well-known Polish actors. Polish with *no* English subtitles. 64 mins.
VHS: S11294. $39.95.

Poland, A Proud Heritage
Journey to Warsaw, filled with newly restored historical buildings, and gaze at the Royal Castle and Sigmund's Column, the symbol of the city. Sunworship in Gdansk along the Baltic Coast, and experience the serenity of the Bialowieza Forest, Europe's last virgin woodland. Walk through the grounds of Auschwitz, and visit the Jasna Gora monastery, where millions of Poles make an annual pilgrimage to the Black Madonna. 55 mins.
VHS: S10772. $24.95.

Polish Christmas Carols
Traditional Polish Christmas carols and pastorales performed by the Children's Choir from Poniatowa, Halina Frackowiak and Krystyna Pronko. 55 mins. Polish with *no* English subtitles.

Polish Songs
From the battle of Grunwald to September 1939: Polish soldiers' songs down the centuries are performed by the Artistic Ensemble of the Polish Army. 90 mins.
VHS: S12357. $29.95.

Prelude
A 6-part series from Polish television for children and teenagers. A story of four children who, unexpectedly left on their own, have to look after their farm. Total length of the two cassettes, 175 mins. Polish with *no* English subtitles.
VHS: S11363. $69.95.

A Road to Independence (Jozef Pilsudski Droga do Niepodleglosci)
Two documentaries are joined here. One is from 1937, about the Polish road to independence. The other is from 1935 and shows the funeral of Marshal Jozef Pilsudski. B&W. Polish with no subtitles. Poland, 1935-1937, 112 mins.
VHS: S26976. $29.95.

Songs and Dance by Slask (Slask Tanczy i Spiewa)
Slask provides 45 minutes of unparalleled entertainment in this dynamic video. It is the best Polish folk music and dancing available. Colorful scenery from the Karlinek region of Silesia is featured. Poland, 45 mins.
VHS: S26736. $29.95.

Stanislaw Moniuszko— The Haunted Manor
One of the best known operas by Stanislaw Moniuszko, performed at the Grand Theatre in Warsaw. Polish with *no* English subtitles. 135 mins.
VHS: S11368. $39.95.

Sycamore People (Jaworowi ludzie)
A collection of six Polish stories for children, one of which concerns the adventures of *The Sycamore People*. Polish with no subtitles. 60 mins.
VHS: S16830. $24.95.

Tadeusz Drozda Cabaret
Another in the series of videos presenting outstanding Polish cabaret performers. Tadeusz Drozda is the author of the sketches. 105 mins. Polish with *no* English subtitles.
VHS: S11377. $29.95.

Thank You Poles (Dziekujemy Wam Polacy)
The history of the General Maczek Brigade from 1939 to 1945. The exploits of this crack World War II unit are carefully reconstructed using archival documents, photos and films. Also included rare interviews with German Panzer division officers. Polish narration. No English subtitles.
VHS: S16825. $29.95.
Wincenty Ronisz, Poland, 95 mins.

The Theatre of Tadeusz Kantor
A unique documentary on the work of a legendary genius of theatre, Tadeusz Kantor. Filmmaker Denis Bablet traces Kantor's roots as a visual artist in Poland and explores his ingenious methods of designing the props which become living sculptures in his extraordinary theatre productions. The program features rare scenes of Kantor at work with the dedicated actors in his troupe, Cricot 2. In a unique scene, Kantor is on-stage and "conducts" the actors much as a symphony conductor leads an orchestra. Extensive segments from some of Kantor's most famous works, *Wielopole, Wielopole* and *The Dead Class*, are also included. Narrated in English. 144 mins.
VHS: S14812. $59.95.

There Was No Room for You
Christmas Carols from Poland performed by Ewa Bem, Andrzej Hiolski, Bernard Ladysz, Janusz Olejniczak, Irena Santor. 90 mins. Polish with *no* English subtitles.
VHS: S11383. $29.95.

This Is Warsaw (Oto Warszawa)
This recent production looks at the Polish capital city, Warsaw. Both the past and the present are covered in this documentary. English narration.
VHS: S26740. $19.95.
Miroslaw Salicki, Poland, 1994, 30 mins.

Two That Stole the Moon
A four-part animated series for children about twin brothers who run away from home in search of Lazyland. Polish *without* English subtitles.
VHS: S12358. $29.95.
Leszek Gladys, Poland, 1980, 110 mins.

Two Without a Cox
A cabaret program featuring two popular Polish cabaret performers: Janusz Gajos and Krysztof Jaroszynski, with a guest appearance by singer Danua Blazejczyk. Polish with *no* English subtitles.
VHS: S11376. $29.95.

Until in Our Hearts (Dopokiw Sercach Naszych)
This documentary of recent Polish history is based on the memorabilia and letters accumulated in the Polish Institute and Museum in London. Polish with no subtitles. Poland, 1987.
VHS: S16824. $29.95.

White Eagle (Orzel Bialy)
An archival television recording of the Representative Artistic Troupe of the Polish Army, initiated in 1943 as front line theater. Here the group performs a popular program about Polish knights and soldiers, at the Teatr Wielki in Lodz. 115 mins.
VHS: S15559. $39.95.

Wilanow—King Jan III Sobieski Residence (W Wilanowie krola Jana)
This video reveals the opulent baroque home of King Jan III Sobieski. It's a resplendent work of art that was built in honor of the King's wife, Marysienka. Everything from the grand public spaces to the intimate quarters of the royal family and the rooms of the servants are on display in this video. Polish with NO subtitles.
VHS: S26741. $24.95.
Andrzej Lucinski, Poland, 1995, 40 mins.

Wojciech Mlynarski—Lyrical Evening
A recital of lyrical songs written and performed by Wojciech Mlynarski. A variety of songs range from lyrical ballads to love songs and humorous stories. 78 mins. Polish with *no* English subtitles.
VHS: S11378. $29.95.

Workers '80 (Robotnicy '80)

A series of historical film recordings of the strikes in the shipyards of Gdansk in 1980 make up this portrait of the birth of the Solidarity movement and of its leader, Lech Walesa. Polish with no subtitles.
VHS: S26977. $14.95.
Andrzej Zajaczkowski, Poland, 1989, 94 mins.

Zenon Laskowik's Benefit— By the Back Door

A cabaret program of Zenon Laskowik, the star of Polish cabaret. 80 mins. Polish with no English subtitles.
VHS: S11373. $39.95.

CZECH CINEMA

All My Good Countrymen

One of the wonders of the Czech New Wave, *All My Good Countrymen* is also one of the least-known films from this miraculous era of Czech filmmaking. The reason is obvious: completed barely before the Soviet invasion of Czechoslovakia in 1968, it was immediately banned and never shown. Despite this, the film won the Special Jury Prize at the Cannes Film Festival, and stylistically is a work of great lyricism, humor and originality. It weaves magical—and very funny—stories about a group of characters in a small Moravian village, immediately following the socialization of Czechoslovakia in 1948. "The film and the milieu it so precisely evokes are not so much nostalgic as they are powerfully remembered and irrevocably lost....*All My Good Countrymen* reflects the curdled fury of a former true believer" (J. Hoberman, *The Village Voice*). Czech with English subtitles.
VHS: S05252. $59.95.
Vojtech Jasny, Czechoslovakia, 1968, 115 mins.

Boxer and Death

One of the precursor films to the Czech New Wave, this film explores the minds of two men—a prisoner and his keeper—as they try to find fulfillment within the grim confines of a concentration camp. The Nazi commander who has always loved boxing sees a potential in Kopinek, a powerful prisoner who has attempted escape. Czech and German with English subtitles.
VHS: S05893. $29.95.
Peter Solan, Czechoslavakia, 1962, 107 mins.

Closely Watched Trains

An ironic, funny film about a young man on his first job in a small town railroad station, trying to get sexually initiated (in hilarious scenes), who, unwittingly, becomes a tragic hero. Offbeat but tender, *Closely Watched Trains* is a comedy about frustration, eroticism and adventure. Academy Award winner for Best Foreign Picture. With Vaclav Neckar and Jitka Bendova. Czech with English subtitles.
VHS: S00252. $19.98.
Jiri Menzel, Czechoslovakia, 1966, 89 mins.

The Cow

A brilliant achievement from Czech filmmaker Karel Kachyna: the parable about a simple man on a remote mountain top who cares for his ailing mother until he is forced to sell their single cow in order to buy her morphine. The mother dies anyway, but is replaced by a house maid, who in turn is replaced by another woman. This enigmatic fable-like film evokes a sense of hope amidst the most mundane events of an ordinary life in an extraordinary achievement of post-Velvet Revolution Czech cinema. Czech with English subtitles.
VHS: S26411. $89.95.
Karel Kachyna, Czech Republic, 1994, 86 mins.

The Coward

Set in a remote Slovak village during the waning days of World War II, *The Coward* is a probing moral study of heroism. A school teacher and his young wife find a wounded Russian parachutist in their front yard just as the Germans occupy the village; the wife supports the anti-Nazi partisans but her husband collaborates with the Germans. At the end of his humiliation, her husband finds the courage to save his honor and the innocent victims of the Nazis. Czech with English subtitles.
VHS: S27177. $29.95.
Jiri Weiss, Czech Republic, 1962, 113 mins.

Dita Saxova

The moving—and beautifully told—tragic story about an 18-year-old girl living in Prague, who seems beautiful and strong to everyone around her, until, a year later, she commits suicide by jumping off a cliff. Based on a novel by Arnost Lustig, *Dita Saxova* deftly explores the psychological contradictions which motivated her. Czech with English subtitles. B&W.
VHS: S04739. $59.95.
A. Moskalyk, Czechoslovakia, 1967, 98 mins.

Emperor's Nightingale

Full length puppet film notable for puppet design and color, based on the Hans Christian Andersen story. In English.
VHS: S03789. $24.98.
Jiri Trnka, Czechoslovakia, 1948, 67 mins.

Fabulous Adventures of Baron Munchhausen

A masterpiece of animation by Karel Zeman—a fabulous fantasy that mixes live action, antique engravings and animation in a dazzling tour-de-force of fantasy. One of the great works of the cinema. English language version.
VHS: S11474. $29.95.
Karel Zeman, Czechoslovakia, 1965, 75 mins.

The Hard Life of an Adventurer

Karel Stekly (later to become the first Czech to win the Venice Film Festival with *The Strike*) collaborated on the screenplay of this funny send-up of the world of pulp detective stories. A popular mystery writer meets a thief who is a character out of one of his novels. With Otomar Korbelar and Adina Mandlova. Czech with English subtitles.
VHS: S14637. $29.95.
Martin Fric, Czechoslovakia, 1941, 89 mins.

Larks on a String

From director Jiri Menzel (*Closely Watched Trains*) comes a buoyant and lyrical romantic comedy that was banned in Czechoslovakia until the melt-down of the iron curtain in Europe. While serving time for desertion, and taking steps toward re-education, a rag-tag group of workers unite as a young couple in the camp decides to marry. We soon find that even the prison guards can't resist the unlikely romance, as the wedding and on-site honeymoon unfold in a series of hilarious plot twists. With Vaclav Neckar and Jityka Zelenohorska. Czech with yellow English subtitles.
VHS: S15169. $19.98.
Jiri Menzel, Czechoslovakia, 1969, 96 mins.

The Last Butterfly

Tom Courtnay stars in this beautiful film about an actor forced, by a cruel hoax, to perform for the Nazis. Terezin is a model city that should prove to the world how well the Nazis treat imprisoned Jews. When the curtain goes up, however, there is a surprise that no one expected.
VHS: S22890. $19.98.
Karel Kachyna, G.B./Czech Republic, 1994, 106 mins.

Murder Czech Style

Jiri Weiss' *Murder Czech Style* features an endearing performance by Rudolf Hrusinsky as a contented, chubby and slightly clumsy office clerk who gets a shot at true love only to eventually discover that his wife is having a torrid affair with the manager of her husband's company. In a film which is one of the often overlooked masterpieces of the Czech New Wave, Weiss shows "Czech indecisiveness, pettiness and opportunism in a mixture of the imaginary and the real." Czech with English subtitles.
VHS: S27178. $29.95.
Jiri Weiss, Czech Republic, 1966, 90 mins.

My Sweet Little Village

The overbearing Pavek threatens to replace his sidekick, the simple-minded Otik, but he never does. Instead the two continue to work together in this carefully observed portrait of life in a funny little village. Around this Laurel and Hardy-like pair are a group of eccentrics, all bemusedly following their own quirky obsessions. Czech with English subtitles.
VHS: S26207. $59.95.
Jiri Menzel, Czech Republic, 1986, 100 mins.

New Pastures

Early film by Vladimir Cech, who went on to win the Grand Prize at the 1972 Moscow Film Festival for *The Key*. A comedy about three prisoners recently released from jail and their experiences returning home to their small village. Czech with English subtitles.
VHS: S01935. $59.95.
Vladimir Cech, Czechoslovakia, 1962, 92 mins.

Not Angels, But Angels

Young boys in the fast changing world of the Czech Republic find the consumer life is available to them through the sale of their own bodies as prostitutes. This documentary lets them describe their experiences plying the world's oldest trade in a new center for sex tourism. Czech with English subtitles.
VHS: S26404. $39.95.
Wictor Grodecki, Czech Republic, 1994, 80 mins.

On the Comet

Jules Verne's science fiction adventure is brought to life by Czech animator Karel Zeman. Since the early 1950's Zeman has been directing highly imaginative films that combine animation and live action and are marked by their fantastic trick effects. A film for the whole family! English dialog.
VHS: S00958. $24.95.
Karel Zeman, Czechoslovakia, 76 mins.

A Prayer for Katarina Horovitzova

Originally made in 1969, this powerful film based on Arnost Lustig's award-winning novel was confiscated by the Czech Communist government and kept on the shelf for 21 years. This videotape is literally the re-discovered U.S. and world premiere. Awarded the top prize at the Monte Carlo Film and Television Festival and winner of eight other international prizes, it is the story of a beautiful Polish singer and her passion for life, set against the backdrop of the cruel game of trading Jewish lives for those of Nazi officers imprisoned in American jails. With Jiri Adamira, Lenka Fiserova and Cestmir Randa. Czechoslovakia, 1991, 60 mins.
VHS: S13695. $59.95.

Romeo, Juliet and Darkness (Sweet Light in a Dark Room)

Romeo, Juliet and Darkness is a radical departure for Czech filmmaking in its unconventional treatment of the Anne Frank theme in a Czech setting. Pavel, a student, hides Hana, a young Jewish girl, in the attic of his apartment building. He is her only link to the outside world, and their growing trust develops into love, until the two are discovered by Pavel's mother. Weiss' double tragedy of young love and the moral question of responsibility to the Jews during the Nazi occupation is treated with poetic restraint. This film is a powerful condemnation of indifference toward force and terrorism. Also known as *Sweet Light in a Dark Room*. Czech with English subtitles.
VHS: S27179. $29.95.
Jiri Weiss, Czech Republic, 1959, 96 mins.

Summons for the Queen

A mystery involving murder and a black-market network begins with an anonymous tip to the police about a carefree young woman living far beyond her apparent means. Czech and English dialog.
VHS: S01932. $59.95.
Dusan Klein, Czechoslovakia, 1973, 110 mins.

Tereza

Exciting and complicated murder mystery featuring a female police officer, based on the novel by Anna Sedlmaye Rovia and starring Jirina Svorcova. Czech with English subtitles.
VHS: S01934. $69.95.
Pavel Blumenfeld, Czechoslovakia, 1961, 91 min.

Transport from Paradise

An intense psychological drama set in the Terezin ghetto and based on a novel by Arnost Lustig. Directed by Zbynek Brynych (*The Fifth Horseman Is Fear*), what makes the film remarkable is not only its visual dynamism, but the humanization of its characters, which makes it all the more haunting. Czech with English subtitles. B&W.
VHS: S04738. $59.95.
Zbynek Brynych, Czechoslovakia, 1965, 93 min.

Wolf Trap

A landmark in Czech cinema, *Wolf Trap* is set in a small town in Moravia and focuses on a marital triangle. The town veterinarian is married to an older, domineering yet insecure and needful wife. They adopt an orphaned teenage girl. As the veterinarian gradually falls in love with his adopted daughter, director Jiri Weiss brilliantly constructs a psychological prison of middle class life from which there is no escape. Czech with English subtitles.
VHS: S27176. $29.95.
Jiri Weiss, Czech Republic, 1957, 95 mins.

MILOS FORMAN

Amadeus

Milos Forman's adaptation of Peter Shaffer's play is structured as a confession related in flashback, told by the aging court composer, and Mozart's adversary, Salieri (F Murray Abraham). Cinematographer Miroslav Ondricek finds a baroque, expressionist intensity in the Prague locations. Choreography by Twyla Tharp. With Elizabeth Berridge, Simon Callow, Roy Dotrice, Christine Ebersole and Jeffrey Jones. Winner of eight Academy Awards.
VHS: S00041. $14.98.
Laser: LD75367. $44.98.
Milos Forman, USA, 1984, 160 mins.

Competition

Forman's first film combines two short features, *Do We Need All Those Brass Bands?* and *The Audition*. Both films deal with the generation gap, the first in a band competition which can't overcome its tradition, the second a hilarious look at amateur singers auditioning for a role in a Prague cabaret. Forman's style "was simple: focus the eye of the camera as closely as possible on human detail, and then put on the screen everything that turns up as a result of such a microscopic view" (Antonin Liehm). Co-scripted by Ivan Passer. Czech with English subtitles.
VHS: S14634. $29.95.
Milos Forman, Czechoslovakia, 1963, 84 mins.

Firemen's Ball

One of the hallmarks of the Czech New Wave, Milos Forman's anarchic and freewheeling black comedy is a wry and devastating parable about Stalinist authoritarianism. The inventive story concerns the rituals surrounding a small town's celebration of a retiring fire chief and a bizarre beauty pageant as a trenchant commentary about the social and political order. Screenplay by Ivan Passer and Jaroslav Papousek. Cinematography by Miroslav Ondricek. Forman's last Czech film. Czech with English subtitles.
VHS: S00443. $39.95.
Milos Forman, Czechoslovakia, 1967, 73 mins.

Hair

The first musical about the American anti-war movement of the 1960's. Exceptional adaptation of the musical stars Treat Williams as a hippie who meets John Savage, a youth from Oklahoma bound for Vietnam. Forman moves the story beyond the bounds of the stage play to make a strong statement about war. Choreography by Twyla Tharp.
VHS: S03486. $19.98.
Laser: LD71163. $39.98.
Milos Forman, USA, 1979, 121 mins.

Loves of a Blonde

Milos Forman's great comedy is an acute satire of Czech daily life. The film focuses on the relationship of a factory girl and a touring piano player. After spending a night together in a provincial town, she suddenly appears at the doorstep of his parents' house with devastating results. With Hana Brejchova, Josef Sebanek and Vladimir Pucholt. "Compassionate, painfully true and continually beguiling" (*Time Magazine*). Czech with English subtitles.
VHS: S00781. $39.95.
Milos Forman, Czechoslovakia, 1965, 88 mins.

One Flew Over the Cuckoo's Nest

Milos Forman's sharp adaptation of Ken Kesey's anti-authoritarian novel about a shrewd nonconformist (Jack Nicholson) sentenced to an insane asylum who encourages a group of marginal misfits to assert their rights and independence, over the rigid opposition of the head nurse (Louise Fletcher). Cinematography by Haskell Wexler. With Will Sampson, Brad Dourif, Sydney Lassick, Christopher Lloyd, Danny DeVito and Scatman Crothers. Winner of the five top Academy Awards.
VHS: S18973. $14.98.
Milos Forman, USA, 1975, 134 mins.

Ragtime

The lives and loves of a middle class family are set against the scandals and headlines of early 20th-century America. Howard Rollins, Jr., plays the black man involved in murder, Mary Steenburgen is the sweet middle-class woman, and Elizabeth McGovern is the beautiful chorus girl, in Milos Forman's entertaining transposition of the popular best-seller by E.L. Doctorow.
VHS: S01085. $29.95.
Milos Forman, USA, 1983, 155 mins.

Valmont

Milos Forman's adaptation of *Les Liaisons Dangereuses* stars Colin Firth, Annette Bening and Meg Tilly; the script was written by Jean-Claude Carriere, and the cinematography was by Miroslav Ondricek.
VHS: S12418. $14.98.
Laser: LD71390. $29.98.
Milos Forman, USA/France, 1989

JAN NEMEC

Diamonds of the Night

One of the breakthrough films of the Czech New Wave; based on a short story by Arnost Lustig, and brilliantly directed by Jan Nemec; it is the story of two boys who escape from a Nazi transport train, told in a visual, surrealistic style. On the same tape is Nemec/Lustig's short film *A Loaf of Bread*. Czech with English subtitles. B&W.
VHS: S04737. $59.95.
Jan Nemec, Czechoslovakia, 1964, 71 mins.

Oratorio for Prague

One of the most powerful documentaries ever made and a unique document of the Soviet invasion of Czechoslovakia in 1968, *Oratorio for Prague* "is a film so moving that one is near tears from the first moment after the credits appear. The movie was begun as a documentary about the liberalization of Czechoslovakia and then simply continued when the Russian tanks moved in," wrote Renata Adler in *The New York Times*. The only filmed record of the Soviet invasion of Czechoslovakia, the raw footage for *Oratorio for Prague*, when broadcast by television, was seen by more than 600 million people, and became the first information that the Soviet Army had not been "invited" in. Narrated in English.
VHS: S11991. $19.95.
Jan Nemec, Czechoslovakia/France, 1968, 26 mins.

A Report on the Party and the Guests

A miracle of the Czech New Wave, distinguished with being "banned forever" shortly after it was completed. Voted one of the best films of the year by *The New York Times*, it is "an extraordinary allegory...evocative of Kafka or Dostoevsky" (*International Film Guide*). A group of picnickers are led to an elegant banquet, where the "guests" quickly turn collaborators in this brilliant analysis of society and the individual. Czech with English subtitles.
VHS: S05654. $59.95.
Jan Nemec, Czechoslovakia, 1966, 71 mins.

JAN KADAR

Adrift

Jan Kadar's last Czech feature is a brilliant and beautiful film about sexual repression. In the lowlands of the Danube a fisherman rescues a mysterious drowning girl (played by American model Paula Pritchett). The intensity of his feelings conflict with the order of his life as a husband and a father until his passion leads to a tragic climax. Script by Imre Gyongyossy. Czech with English subtitles.
VHS: S23880. $29.95.
Jan Kadar, Czechoslovakia/USA, 1969, 108 mins.

Blue Hotel

From the American Short Story Collection, an adaptation of Stephen Crane's mystery, featuring David Warner and James Keach. Teleplay by Harry Mark Petrakis.
VHS: S00157. $24.95.
Jan Kadar, USA, 1974, 55 mins.

Freedom Road

A made-for-tv movie starring Muhammad Ali as an ex-slave on his way to becoming a U.S. Senator during the Reconstruction Years after the Civil War. Narration by Ossie Davis. Adapted from the Howard Fast novel. With Kris Kristofferson, Ron O'Neal, Barbara O. Jones and Edward Herrmann. Director Jan Kadar's last film.
VHS: S00465. $69.95.
Jan Kadar, USA, 1979, 186 mins.

The Shop on Main Street

A haunting work about the intersecting of the political and personal, developed through the strange yet touching relationship of an elderly Jewish shop owner and a passive carpenter whom the Nazis appoint as her "Aryan controller." Winner of the 1965 Best Foreign Film. With Ida Kaminska and Josef Kroner. "It manages to translate the apocalyptic tragedy of our century into human terms and to do so with laughter and tears, with scorn and passion" (Judith Crist). Slovak with English subtitles.
VHS: S01195. $24.95.
Jan Kadar, Czechoslovakia, 1965, 128 mins.

CZECH REPORT

After the Velvet Revolution

A sobering first-hand look at the impact of democracy on the people of Czechoslovakia after the fall of Communism in 1989. An intimate chronicle of a people and country in transition. 58 mins.
VHS: S23407. $150.00.

Death of Ales Martinu

A disturbing look at the rise in the skinhead movement in the Czech Republic. The film focuses on the story of Ales Martinu, a young Czech skinhead who was killed in a violent confrontation. It vividly illustrates how political changes and economic problems since the fall of Communism have created the climate that breeds fascist movements. 28 mins.
VHS: S23408. $125.00.

Kafka: Nabokov on Kafka

Vladimir Nabokov, widely considered one of the greatest writers of the 20th century, was also a remarkable and legendary professor of literature at Cornell University for many years. Here Vladimir Plummer portrays a witty Nabokov providing entertaining insights into Franz Kafka's perplexing novella *The Metamorphosis*. 30 mins.
VHS: S14263. $24.95.

My Prague Spring

This documentary was filmed in Prague shortly after the fall of Communism. It examines the effects of this historic transformation through the eyes of a young American of Czech descent and his Czech relations, as they come to terms with the values of capitalism. English and Czech with English subtitles.
VHS: S20733. $89.95.
David Mrazek, USA, 1993, 81 mins.

HUNGARIAN CINEMA

Adoption

The breakthrough film for Marta Meszaros (*Diary for All My Children*), a unique mixture of documentary and fictional techniques in the story of Mary, a middle-aged woman, who befriends the younger Julia, who insists on having her child live with her. A film of considerable psychological insight. Hungarian with English subtitles.
VHS: S04726. $69.95.
Marta Meszaros, Hungary, 1975, 89 mins.

After the Revolution

An absurdist peek at the post-Communist Hungarian world. The hero is a writer struggling to complete the great novel, who uses the observations of an extraordinary cat to foment his view of the world. An experimental, tongue-in-cheek feature made in the wake of the cataclysmic political changes in Hungary. Hungarian with English subtitles.
VHS: S15161. $59.95.
Andras Szirtes, Hungary, 1990, 82 mins.

Almanac of Fall

A large, claustrophobic apartment is the setting for this intense chamber-drama from Bela Tarr, one of Europe's most exciting contemporary filmmakers. In this dense setting, the inhabitants of the apartment reveal their darkest secrets, fears, obsessions and hostilities in a style that combines the anguish and existentialism of Bergman with the emotional intensity of Cassavetes. Hungarian with English subtitles.
VHS: S18690. $59.95.
Bela Tarr, Hungary, 119 mins.

The Annunciation

This amazing film, using a cast of children between the ages of 8 and 14, follows the travails of Adam from the Garden of Eden to modern times. Along the way, he becomes a general in Ancient Greece, a Byzantine crusader in Prague, Danton in the French Revolution and a witness to the plague in London. At all times he is tormented and abetted by a young, blond Lucifer. Hungarian with English subtitles.
VHS: S21322. $69.95.
Andras Jeles, Hungary, 1993, 101 mins.

Another Way

Livia, a journalist, is the beautiful, restless wife of an army officer. Eva is a more outspoken reporter. Eva develops an interest in Livia, with whom she shares an office, and begins shyly but doggedly to pursue her. Livia, equally curious at first, becomes frightened but not unreceptive and the two begin to meet frequently at a Budapest cafe where the pianist plays "The Man I Love" as they are swept away by their own flirtation. This wonderfully conceived and finely acted film also digs into deeper issues of political and sexual repression. Hungarian with English subtitles.
VHS: S14097. $59.95.
Karoly Makk, Hungary, 1982, 100 mins.

Bad Guys

A stylistically innovative film from Gyorgy Szomjas, which borrows the conventions of the Western to tell the story of the last days of outlaws in Hungary. In the 1860's, an outlaw and his henchmen hold a reign of terror. But their movement is overtaken by the events of time and a posse is hot on their trail. Hungarian with English subtitles.
VHS: S13344. $69.95.
Gyorgy Szomjas, Hungary, 1979, 93 mins.

Beggar Student

Set in 18th century Cracow, a wonderful Hungarian version of the famous operetta, as General Ollendorf, on the prowl for a brief affair, vows revenge on the lovely Laura, who rejects her by setting up a student to masquerade as the Count Opalinsky. Hungarian with English subtitles.
VHS: S08107. $49.95.
Laszlo Seregi, Hungary, 90 mins.

Cat's Play

The gifted Hungarian filmmaker Karoly Makk (Love) fashions this sharp, observant work about a widowed music teacher's rupture into delusion, obsession and romantic fatalism. The music teacher's ritual weekly dinners with his long-time sweetheart are interrupted by the appearance of the woman's old lover. Hungarian with English subtitles.
VHS: S16930. $59.95.
Karoly Makk, Hungary, 1974, 115 mins.

Cold Days

One of the most important Hungarian films of the 1960's, Andras Kovacs' Cold Days was an extremely courageous theme to tackle at the time, in view of the silence which had, until then, shrouded the Hungarian role in World War II. The film is based on the massacre of several thousand Jewish and Serbian people of Novi Sad in 1942. "The film is structured round the memories and self-justifications of four men involved in the massacre as they await trial in 1946. Each, of course, denies his complicity or responsibility...Many of the images in the film remain unforgettable." Hungarian with English subtitles.
VHS: S13338. $59.95.
Andras Kovacs, Hungary, 1966, 102 mins.

Daniel Takes the Train

This acclaimed feature, structured as a nail-biting thriller, confronts one of the most sensitive political periods, 1956, when Hungarians fought Soviet troops in the streets of Budapest. Daniel, hopelessly in love with Marianne, the girl next door, decides to join his friend on a train headed for the Austrian border. The film, in the words of Variety, captures "the complexities and passions...a tense and grimly funny experience." Hungarian with English subtitles.
VHS: S27800. $29.95.
Pal Sandor, Hungary, 1983, 90 mins.

The Fifth Seal

A haunting story set at the close of World War II in Hungary, this film begins with an unusual premise. A group of friends are arrested when one of them makes a casual remark that offends a commandant. From this chance event a series of daunting tasks emerge that test their commitment to their moral ideals.
VHS: S20618. $59.95.
Zoltan Fabri, Hungary, 1976, 116 mins.

Flowers of Reverie

This prize-winner at the Berlin International Film Festival combines an examination of inner psychological states with the external political turmoil of the Hungarian Revolution (1848-9). A former soldier named Ferenc is imprisoned for his work in the resistance, leading to a tragic outcome. Hungarian with English subtitles.
VHS: S20617. $59.95.
Laszlo Lugossy, Hungary, 1984, 106 mins.

The Girl

An interesting examination of how the overt repression of women in the older pattern of village life has been replaced by the more subtle sexual and economic exploitation inherent in the apparently freer existence of young girls in the contemporary city. A key film from Marta Meszaros. Hungarian with English subtitles.
VHS: S04727. $69.95.
Marta Meszaros, Hungary, 1968, 89 mins.

A Happy New Year!

The frustrations and emptiness of the lives of the professional class are brought into sharp relief in this brilliant comedy set during the course of one New Year's. As the trio of two men and one woman, all chemical engineers, balance their personal and professional lives on New Year's Eve, their future seems hollow, their chance for happiness and fulfillment elusive. Hungarian with English subtitles.
VHS: S18688. $59.95.
Reszo Szoreny, Hungary, 1979, 84 mins.

A Hungarian Fairy Tale

A strange, beautiful and critically-acclaimed film by Gyula Gazdag, A Hungarian Fairy Tale begins at a performance of Mozart's The Magic Flute where a beautiful young woman meets a handsome stranger and, transported by the music, they share one night of love. The son born of this magic night is raised by his mother but at the age of three, must be given a father's name, even a fictitious one, according to Hungarian law. Years later, the engaging Andris sets out to find his "father" as his "father" begins a separate journey. "No less resonant than Wings of Desire" (J. Hoberman, The Village Voice). Hungarian with English subtitles.
VHS: S12365. $89.98.
Gyula Gazdag, Hungary, 1988, 95 mins.

Hungarian Rhapsody

Part of Jancso's proposed trilogy dealing with the relationships between the classes in pre-revolutionary Hungary, Hungarian Rhapsody continues the director's highly symbolic and dynamic style which brought him to fame with his early films. Set in 1911, the film follows Istvan, a nobleman who joins ranks with the peasants in opposition to the ruling class in general, and his statesman brother in particular. With Gyorgy Cserhalmi, Lajos Balaszovits and Gabor Koncz. Hungarian with English subtitles.
VHS: S12509. $59.95.
Miklos Jancso, Hungary, 1983, 101 mins.

Lilly in Love

Christopher Plummer is the successful screenwriter who concocts an ingenious plan to test his wife's infidelity in this U.S.-made comedy by Hungarian filmmaker Karoly (Love) Makk. Maggie Smith is the wife who is courted by her husband, Plummer, in disguise. In English.
VHS: S00756. $79.95.
Karoly Makk, USA, 1985, 104 mins.

The Little Valentino

A brilliant film debut, and one of the most highly acclaimed European films of recent years, this deceptively simple black and white feature anticipates and stylistically surpasses Jim Jarmusch's Stranger than Paradise. The events of the film are concentrated on a single day. The film focuses on Laszlo, a 20-year-old driver's assistant, who spends his day and his money—which he has just stolen—in the aimlessness of everyday life. "It's hard not to be impressed by its on-the-edge assurance" (Chicago Reader). Hungarian with English subtitles.
VHS: S13337. $59.95.
Andras Jeles, Hungary, 1979, 102 mins.

Love

Lili Darvas, the famed stage actress and widow of Ferenc Molnar, portrays a bed-ridden old woman in this emotionally precise drama. Her daughter-in-law, whose husband is in jail as a political prisoner, concocts a fictitious story about his life as a filmmaker in America and forges letters from him filled with Hollywood gossip, which the mother devours as she awaits her son's return. When he is finally sprung from prison, it is too late. Hungarian with English subtitles.
VHS: S13659. $59.95.
Karoly Makk, Hungary, 1971, 92 mins.

Maria's Day

One of the most acclaimed recent Hungarian films, Judit Elek's Maria's Day is set 17 years after the failed revolution of 1848. An aristocratic family gathers at the home of Ignac Czendrey to celebrate his youngest daughter's Name Day. In the course of the one day, the unusual past and present of the Czendrey family are unfolded. The family is related to the revolutionary and legendary poet Sandor Petofi and desperately tries to live up to the Petofi myth. They dream of a heroic new epoch, but while they dream, the mundaneness of the present overcomes them. A powerful and moving film. Hungarian with English subtitles.
VHS: S11289. $59.95.
Judit Elek, Hungary, 1985, 113 mins.

The Midas Touch

Set on the eve of the Russian invasion in 1956, Geza Beremenyi's fable concerns a merchant who's known as the king of the market for his transcendent ability to transform anything he touches into gold. His abilities are questioned when blood flows through the street. Hungarian with English subtitles.
VHS: S13878. $79.95.
Geza Beremenyi, Hungary, 1989, 100 mins.

My Twentieth Century

At the turn of the century, two identical twins grow up and explore their worlds in very opposite ways. The erotic and playful Dora is a soft and self-indulgent contrast to her bomb-throwing revolutionary sister Lili, who was separated from her at birth. The sisters finally cross paths on the famous Orient Express by sleeping with the same confused man. The beautiful Dortha Segda plays both roles in this witty and sensual film from writer/director Ildiko Enyedi. "The most original, one of a kind, film of the year" (American Woman). Hungarian with English subtitles.
VHS: S15264. $19.98.
Laser: LD71560. $49.95.
Ildiko Enyedi, Hungary, 1990, 104 mins.

The Nice Neighbor

Laszlo Szabo stars as a clever but cruel occupant of a Budapest boarding house, one who exercises his exploitative skills to the hilt when the building is torn down and the tenants are allotted new living space. Always playing the role of protector of his fellow tenants, he skillfully manipulates the lot for his own goal: a bigger apartment. Also starring Margit Dayka and Agi Margittay. Hungarian with English subtitles.
VHS: S12510. $59.95.
Zsolt Kezdi-Kovacs, Hungary, 1979, 90 mins.

Nobody's Daughter

This critically acclaimed film follows the tragic life of an eight-year-old orphan girl. Living under a government that sanctions money to foster parents, she finds herself shuffled from family to family; with each move she encounters increasingly brutal abuse. A beautifully acted film which explores an all too real pathos. Hungarian with English subtitles.
VHS: S16500. $59.95.
Lazlo Ranody, Hungary, 1976, 90 mins.

Oh, Bloody Life!

A film of considerable importance from the renowned filmmaker Peter Bacso. Set in the 1950's during the Stalinist era, Bacso's daring film concerns the deportation of Hungarian citizens who have done nothing wrong. Bacso's film is remarkable not only for its courageous depiction of political events, but also for its black comedy. Hungarian with English subtitles.
VHS: S08110. $49.95.
Peter Bacso, Hungary, 1985, 115 mins.

A Priceless Day

From the director of Time Stands Still, this is a thoughtful, ironic rumination on desire and sexual awakening. A 30-year-old kindergarten teacher visits her lover's wife and the two enter a pact to rid themselves of their men. Based on an idea by Peter Zimre. Cinematography by Lajos Koltai. Music by Gyorgy Selmeczi. Cecilia Esztergalyos, Pat Hetenyi and Judit Pogany. Hungarian with English subtitles.
VHS: S18689. $59.95.
Peter Gothar, Hungary, 1980, 87 mins.

Red and the White

One of the most original of films, a haunting work about the absurdity and evil of war. Set in Central Russia during the Civil War of 1918, the story details the constant shifting of power between the White guards and the Red soldiers, first at an abandoned monastery, and later, at a field hospital. Using the wide-screen technique consisting of very long takes and a ceaselessly tracking camera movement, Miklos Jancso has fashioned a brilliant visual style which is truly unique in the history of cinema. Hungarian with English subtitles.
VHS: S08940. $59.95.
Miklos Jancso, Hungary, 1968, 92 mins.

Red Earth

A shrewd satire about Communism, Hungarian style. A bauxite mixer discovers his pigs have unearthed high quality bauxite from his back yard. The troubles start when the village bureaucrats and bauxite prospectors insist the discovery was the result of careful, methodical planning. With Imre Nemeth, Sandor Kocsis, Kalman Toronyi and Ferenc Togh. Hungarian with English subtitles.
VHS: S18687. $59.95.
Laszlo Vitezy, Hungary, 105 mins.

Riddance

A young factory worker pretends to be a student in order to impress the boy with whom she is in love, and his snobbish family, in Marta Meszaros' examination of the class and social tensions which still exist within Hungary. Hungarian with English subtitles.
VHS: S04728. $69.95.
Marta Meszaros, Hungary, 1973, 93 mins.

Round Up

One of the greatest films of Miklos Jancso, the brilliant Hungarian filmmaker. A savage, often ironic epic about the effects of imprisonment, fear and torture, set during the 1848 Hungarian Revolution. Several hundred outlaws are captured and in a cat-and-mouse game forced to reveal active rebels by the Austrian police.
VHS: S18585. $59.95.
Miklos Jancso, Hungary, 1965, 87 mins.

Sindbad

One of the most eloquent, beautiful and truly original films of all time. The subject of the film is an ageing hedonist concerned only with the sensual pleasures of women, food and drink, who now tries to recapture the memory of these vanished delights. Hungarian with English subtitles.
VHS: S04725. $69.95.
Zoltan Huszarik, Hungary, 1971, 98 mins.

Stand Off

A terrific thriller by Gyula Gazdag. 18-year old Zoltan and his younger brother Istvan have taken 16 girls hostage in a dormitory in a student hostel in a Hungarian border town. They demand a flight out of Budapest and a million dollars. "A devastating expression of the frustration of Eastern Europe" (L.A. Times). Intense and powerful performances and a rich musical score. Hungarian with English subtitles.
VHS: S13343. $79.95.
Gyula Gazdag, Hungary, 1989, 97 mins.

Sunday Daughters

A film compared to Truffaut's 400 Blows, set in an institution for teenage girls, directed with verve and compassion by Janosz Rozsa. Juli, a 16-year-old inmate, seems to be moving toward delinquency, and after repeated rejections from her family, escapes. After a close call with death, she survives and her life brightens when an older woman takes her in, but these hopes are smashed when Juli becomes involved with the woman's son. Using non-professional actors, Rozsa delivers stunning performances in a film that is both endearing and probing. Hungarian with English subtitles.
VHS: S11288. $59.95.
Janosz Rozsa, Hungary, 1980, 100 mins.

A Very Moral Night

A spirited turn-of-the-century tale of a poor medical student lodging cheaply and happily in a bordello. When his widowed mother makes a surprise visit, the madam and the girls set about converting the place into a respectable boarding house. Starring Iren Psota, and Margit Makay as the visiting mother. Hungarian with English subtitles.
VHS: S14822. $59.95.
Karoly Makk, Hungary, 1977, 103 mins.

We Never Die

This independently produced Hungarian comedy became a runaway hit; it's full of sharp barbs about life in the neo-Communist universe. The young hero is turned over to his clever uncle "Juicy", who teaches him how to have fun and survive it all with the help of grub, booze and women. The race track or the bedroom are the places best suited to his golden rule, "Don't take life too seriously." Hungarian with English subtitles.
VHS: S22424. $79.95.
Robert Koltai, Hungary, 1994, 90 mins.

The Witness

Peter Bacso's film was banned for more than nine years. Set in 1949, the film is a political satire that mixes forms and styles, symbolism and screwball farce. The story concerns a functionary who's imprisoned and eventually manipulated into providing testimony against his best friend, a government minister on trial for treason. With Ferenc Kallai, Lajos Oze and Zoltan Fabri. Hungarian with English subtitles.
VHS: S18501. $59.95.
Peter Bacso, Hungary, 1968, 110 mins.

ISTVAN SZABO

25, Firemen's Street

An important film by Istvan Szabo with an intricate flashback structure that recalls Resnais. The setting is an old house on the eve of its demolition; during a hot summer night, the numerous inhabitants indulge in dreams and recollections of the events of the past thirty years. Hungarian with English subtitles.
VHS: S04724. $69.95.
Istvan Szabo, Hungary, 1973, 93 mins.

Father

This sensitive, intelligent study of adolescence and maturation focuses on a young man whose defense mechanism consists of idealizing the memory of his dead father. One of the key films of the Hungarian film renaissance, Father is a daring, emotionally charged film. Hungarian with English subtitles.
VHS: S11635. $69.95.
Istvan Szabo, Hungary, 1966, 95 mins.

Hanussen

The third part of Szabo's trilogy (Mephisto, Colonel Redl) stars Klaus Maria Brandauer as a charismatic magician and clairvoyant, whose predictions of the future are uncannily accurate. When the Nazis seize power, he is forced to choose between joining them and standing alone. Brilliantly shot, with a riveting performance by Brandauer, Szabo continues to explore the moral issues which shaped the 20th century. Hungarian and German with English subtitles.
VHS: S12496. $19.95.
Istvan Szabo, Hungary/Germany, 1989

Meeting Venus

Istvan Szabo's first English-language film is the erotic story of an opera star/seductress played by Glenn Close who sets her sights on a young conductor played by Niels Arestrup. The torrid romance is played against the romantic music of Richard Wagner and against the world of opera—full of its bizarre characters, power mongering and power plays, lovers, wives, ex-lovers and ex-wives and unabashed melodrama.
VHS: S16161. $19.98.
Laser: Letterboxed. LD71680. $34.98.
Istvan Szabo, Hungary/France/Great Britain, 1991, 121 mins.

Mephisto

Istvan Szabo's powerful, Academy-Award winning film stars Klaus Maria Brandauer as an actor in pre-war Germany whose quest for success leads him to subordinate everything—political conviction, human relationships, artistic ambition. He is ultimately drawn into a poisonous circle of evil from which he can no longer escape. English dubbed.
VHS: S00848. $19.98.
Istvan Szabo, Hungary, 1981, 132 mins.

HUNGARIAN ISSUES

Hungary, Land of Hospitality

In this land of baroque palaces and cobblestone streets, journey to Budapest and to Lake Balaton, stop in the medieval city of Pecs and tour the renowned Zsolnay porcelain factory. 30 mins.
VHS: S12275. $24.95.

Recsk 1953 Documentary of a Hungarian Secret Labor Camp

This powerful film catalogs the atrocities committed by the Stalinist regime of Hungary. With its release, Recsk received five major European documentary film awards. In Hungarian with English subtitles.
VHS: S16501. $29.95.
L. Gyarmathy/G. Boszormenyi, Hungary, 1989, 100 mins.

Transylvania—The Facts

A call to arms from Hungarian emigres for solidarity and defense of the trampling and destruction of some 15,000 Hungarian villages in Transylvania, the area of Rumania with a significant Hungarian population, this video examines the centuries-old churches, houses, cemeteries as well as the indigenous culture which is in the danger of being annihilated. English version. 30 mins.
VHS: S01981. $19.95.

YUGOSLAV CINEMA

Balkan Express
A very offbeat, funny comedy. The Balkan Express is a band of roving musicians whose music is just cover for their real work as con men. When the Nazis move in, things take a turn for the worse. Outrageously madcap, full of dramatic twists set against the dark horror of the War. English dubbed. Yugoslavia, 1984, 102 mins.
VHS: S00089. $19.95.

Charuga
The spectacular, true story of a Croatian 1920s Robin Hood, a fanatic ex-soldier and Bolshevik who tried to bring the Revolution to Yugoslavia. A visually complex, engrossing, sensual and unsettling action-adventure movie which is also a serious political drama, Charuga began by robbing from the rich and giving to the poor. But as with many self-styled revolutionaries, he soon robs from everyone and keeps it all for himself. Croatian with English subtitles.
VHS: S27795. $29.95.
Rajko Grlic, Croatia, 1991, 108 mins.

The Harms Case
Based on the life and writing of Daniel Harms, a Russian avant-garde poet of the 1920s who has become a cult figure in Yugoslavia, this challenging film is "an alternately hilarious and unsettling portrait...deliriously surrealistic." Serbo-Croatian with English subtitles.
VHS: S26497. $59.95.
Slobodan Pesic, Yugoslavia, 1988, 90 mins.

Hey Babu Riba
"A magic that is special to movies alone. The greatest pleasure in the world is to walk into a movie you never heard of, by a director you never heard of, and then be overwhelmed by beauty and memory and longing," wrote *The New York Post*. The warm and witty portrait of a close-knit group of Belgrade teenagers in Yugoslavia of the 50's, the magic of Jovan Acin's film focuses on four close-knit friends, all in love with the same girl. A cinematic tribute to a lost time and place, *Hey Babu Riba* was the sleeper hit of the London, Miami, Seattle and San Francisco Film Festivals. Serbian with yellow English subtitles.
VHS: S09592. $19.98.
Jovan Acin, Yugoslavia, 1987, 112 mins.

In the Jaws of Life
At the heart of this disarmingly funny and sexy comedy is a middle-aged woman filmmaker, a bit on the chubby side, with a rather confused personal life, who is making a soap opera titled *The Jaws of Life*. The TV soap opera follows the life of a chubby office clerk not unlike the filmmaker. The two stories unfold side by side until the stories begin to converge. "This sex farce is as rueful as it is funny, as earthy as it is politically astute, as cleverly structured as it is unexpected" (*Village Voice*). Croatian with English subtitles.
VHS: S27796. $29.95.
Rajko Grlic, Yugoslavia, 1984, 95 mins.

Melody Haunts My Reverie (You Only Love Once)
Voted as the third best Yugoslav film ever made, and an Official Selection at Cannes, this daring film is the story of an idealistic, young, partisan war hero who becomes a leader in the emerging socialist society of a small Croat village, and finds adjustment to the "new Yugoslavia" extremely difficult. He meets and falls in love with a middle-class ballerina, becomes involved with her bourgeois family and is eventually imprisoned. "A highly sensual romance...as passionate as it is politically catastrophic" (*L.A. Times*). Croatian with English subtitles.
VHS: S27797. $29.95.
Rajko Grlic, Yugoslavia, 1981, 103 mins.

The Secret of Nikola Tesla
Nikola Tesla, one of the leading scientific geniuses of the 19th century, whose experiments with alternating current were crucial in the development of electronic technology, found himself locked in a battle with Thomas Edison, George Westinghouse and financier J.P. Morgan. The source of the conflict was Tesla's radical and visionary theories on wireless sources of energy—which intrigued Westinghouse, enraged the conservative Edison and then repelled the formidable Morgan. This film presents Tesla as a tortured, brilliant and complex man of sometimes maddening crochets and quirks (he claimed to be in communication with beings from outer space), as a drama of psychology and issues, and a mystery. This big-budget U.S.-Yugoslavian co-production stars Orson Welles as J.P. Morgan. In English.
VHS: S10800. $79.95.
Krsto Papic, Yugoslavia/USA, 1980, 120 mins.

That Summer of White Roses
The very talented Yugoslav filmmaker Rajko Grlic directed this international production which stars Tom Conti, Susan George, Rod Steiger. The idyllic summer is disrupted by the arrival of the German Army, in a story of heroism forged by war and love.
VHS: S13030. $19.98.
Rajko Grlic, USA/Yugoslavia, 1989, 98 mins.

Tito and Me
A poignant comedy set in 1950's Belgrade, Zoran is the 10-year-old boy who adores Yugoslavia's leader Marshall Tito and Jasna, a 12-year-old orphan girl. When Jasna goes on a walking tour of Tito's homeland, Zoran follows with hilariously disastrous results. "A funny, beautifully acted family memoir...*Tito and Me* is the work of a sophisticated comic mind" (Vincent Canby, *The New York Times*). Serbo-Croatian with English subtitles.
VHS: S20425. $89.98.
Goran Markovic, Yugoslavia, 1992, 104 mins.

Ward Six
One of the most powerful stories by Anton Chekhov receives a masterful film adaptation in the hands of Lucian Pintilie, one of the world's foremost directors for the stage as well as screen. The story, set at the turn of the century in a provincial Russian town, concerns a doctor who oversees a grotesque mental ward. The only person he meets with any comprehension of life is one of the inmates. The doctor is reported to the authorities by one of the inmates, is judged mad, and the story's two most humane and intelligent men are locked together in Ward No. 6. A subtle, powerful film based on one of the great literary works of Russian literature. Serbian with English subtitles.
VHS: S10009. $59.95.
Lucien Pintilie, Yugoslavia, 1976, 93 mins.

DUSAN MAKAVEJEV

Coca-Cola Kid
Eric Roberts plays a marketing genius sent to boost the Coke company sales in backwoods Australia, only to see his corporate shell penetrated by the gorgeous and very sexy Greta Scacchi. Full of hilarious and memorable scenes, like the kangaroo with an arm in a sling, and a great sex scene full of feathers.
VHS: S00255. $29.98.
Dusan Makavejev, Australia, 1984, 94 mins.

Innocence Unprotected
In 1942 a professional strong man named Dragoljub Aleksic directed and starred in a trite little melodrama titled *Innocence Unprotected*—the first Serbian talkie. Over 20 years later, Dusan Makavejev retrieved the film from the Archives, tinted many of the sequences by hand, and interviewed Aleksic and his co-workers in present day Yugoslavia 1968. The resulting cinematic collage is a funny and daring (in both content and form) mix of a wide variety of film footage—including documentary, narrative, agitprop, and various other bits and pieces of found footage. Serbian with English subtitles.
VHS: S15487. $59.95.
Dusan Makavejev, Yugoslavia, 1968, 78 mins.

Love Affair: Or, the Case of the Missing Switchboard Operator
A key work of Eastern European cinema, *Love Affair* is a radical investigation of the relationship between sex and politics. The story of a young switchboard operator who falls in love with a sanitary worker until she allows herself to be seduced by a younger, more glamorous man. Told through a daring blend of flashbacks and flashforwards and a mix of documentary and fiction. Serbian with English subtitles.
VHS: S02653. $59.95.
Dusan Makavejev, Yugoslavia, 1967, 70 mins.

Man Is Not a Bird
Man Is Not a Bird is a work of genius which takes place in a mining town in eastern Serbia. The central characters are an engineer in one of the factories and a young hairdresser with whom he has an affair. The film "blends actuality with fiction in a manner so unselfconscious as to seem almost natural. Makavejev brings an instinctive poetry to the editing of the film, intercutting brilliantly Beethoven's *Ode to Joy* being performed inside the copper factory, and Jan and Raika making love together with a quiet, feverish urgency" (*International Film Guide*). Serbian with English subtitles.
VHS: S08265. $59.95.
Dusan Makavejev, Yugoslavia, 1966, 80 mins.

A Night of Love
Alfred Molina, Eric Stoltz, Gabrielle Anwar and Camilla Soeberg star in Dusan Makavejev's inventive adaptation of a story by Emile Zola. Originally titled *Manifesto*, the film is full of gentle, erotic irony as a guard (Molina) must protect a king on a visit to his subjects in a small town. A number of revolutionaries will stop at nothing to get the king. Seduction, misguided faith and sheer incompetence combine to produce a wicked, sexy comedy.
VHS: S26402. $89.98.
Dusan Makavejev, Yugoslavia/USA, 1988, 97 mins.

Sweet Movie
The modern cult classic, a hilarious comedy with elements of thriller and horror, "an experience to defy criticism...one of the most challenging, shocking and provocative films of recent years" (Roger Ebert). This daring and totally original film skillfully blends two independent stories with often shocking newsreel footage into a "movie we can't be passive about." The beautiful Carole Laure, winner of the Miss Virginity World contest, is married to Mr. Kapital, a Texas oil billionaire who, instead of consummating their marriage, sterilizes her body with rubbing alcohol. Barely escaping with her life, in Paris Carole has a sexual encounter with El Macho, a rock star at the Eiffel Tower, and ends up in a radical therapy commune. The second story features Anna Prucnal, survivor of The Revolution, now the captain of a boat floating the canals of Amsterdam, whose joyous sexual meeting with a sailor (Pierre Clementi) from the Battleship Potemkin ends up in his murder in a vat of sugar. Pure, unadulterated brilliance, "an audacious attempt...filled with images impossible to forget" (Roger Ebert). English and other languages with English subtitles.
VHS: S10575. $79.95.
Dusan Makavejev, Canada/France, 1975, 97 min.

WR: Mysteries of the Organism
Called "an outrageous, exuberant, marvelous work," by Amos Vogel in *Film Comment* and "a weird and hilarious fantasy...witty and exuberant" by *The New York Times*, *WR: Mysteries of the Organism* is a unique blend of fact and fiction, and Makavejev's landmark film. It deftly juxtaposes the story of the sexual encounter between the beautiful, liberated Milena and a repressed Soviet figure-skating champion with an exploration of the life and theories of psychoanalyst Wilhelm Reich. The "WR" in the film's title stands for either "Wilhelm Reich" or "World Revolution." Makavejev describes it as "a black comedy, political circus, a fantasy on the fascism and communism of human bodies, the political life of human genitals, a proclamation of the pornographic essence of any system of authority and power over others....If you watch for more than five minutes, you become my accomplice." With Dravic, Jagoda Kaloper, Tuli Kupferberg, Jackie Curtis. English and Serbian with English subtitles.
VHS: S11290. $79.95.
Dusan Makavejev, Yugoslavia/USA, 1971, 84 min.

EMIR KUSTURICA

Arizona Dream
Johnny Depp stars as a young drifter who meets a kindred spirit in Faye Dunaway and unexpectedly falls in love. Between their age differences and the reactions of their dysfunctional families, love is put on trial. Jerry Lewis is great as Depp's car dealership huckstering uncle.
VHS: S23859. $19.98.
Emir Kusturica, USA, 1994, 119 mins.

Do You Remember Dolly Bell?
Kusturica's beautifully modulated tale of a young man's entry into adulthood, his loss of virginity in the company of a B-movie stripper and prostitute. Set in the early 60s, Kusturica grafts the pathos of the Eastern European village movie into a complex tale of intrusive cultures, when Western influences such as fashion and rock and roll and the promise of European socialism threatened to roll over traditional customs, practiced rituals and Tito's political reign. With Slavo Stimac, Slobodan Aligrudic and Ljiljana Blagojevic. Serbo-Croatian with English subtitles.
VHS: S18457. $69.95.
Emir Kusturica, Yugoslavia, 1981, 106 mins.

Time of the Gypsies
A potent mix of comedy, drama and the supernatural, Kusturica's amazingly realistic drama set in the heart of the gypsy culture. Perhan, the hero, is telekinetic and is taken to Italy by the "sheik," where he gets a quick education in gypsy survival skills on the streets of Milan. Warm and affectionate, full of comic scenes, with a great gypsy music sound track. With Dvor Dujmovic and Bora Todorovic. Serbo-Croatian and Romany with English subtitles.
VHS: S12744. $19.95.
Emir Kusturica, Yugoslavia, 1990, 136 mins.

When Father Was Away on Business
Kusturica's Cannes-award winning film is a magical portrait of a boy's coming of age in 50's Yugoslavia. As little Malik takes up sleepwalking and experiences his first love, the family knows the real "business" Father is conducting—in a labor camp for his unrepentant Stalinist leanings and his philandering. Serbo-Croatian with English subtitles.
VHS: S15547. $19.98.
Laser: CAV. LD72198. $49.95.
Emir Kusturica, Yugoslavia, 1985, 144 mins.

ROMANIAN CINEMA

The Oak
While Romanian Communism collapses around her, a young woman, the defiant Nela, sets off into the desolate countryside. This apocalyptic road movie, acclaimed at the Cannes Film Festival, evokes a haunting world of extravagant dysfunction and edgy humor. Romanian with English subtitles.
VHS: S20869. $89.95.
Lucien Pintilie, Romania, 1992, 105 mins.

Stone Wedding
Stone Wedding is comprised of two short films based on stories by the classic Romanian writer Igor Agarciceanu, dealing with peasant life and traditions in the Carpathian mountains. Includes *Fefeleaga* (directed by Mircea Veroiu) and *At a Wedding* (directed by Dan Pita). Romanian with English subtitles.
VHS: S14649. $29.95.
Veroiu/Pita, Romania, 1972, 90 mins.

An Unforgettable Summer
An unconventional love story from Lucian Pintilie (*The Oak*), featuring a first-rate performance from Kristin Scott-Thomas (*Bitter Moon, Four Weddings and a Funeral*). A recently married army officer and his bride are sent to an army outpost in a backwoods area. The wife tries to establish a genteel, civilized presence there, but conflicts between the couple and both army personnel and the locals of the remote region cause her efforts to be in vain. French, Romanian and Bulgarian with English subtitles.
VHS: S27200. $89.95.
Lucian Pintilie, Romania, 1994, 82 mins.

GREEK CINEMA

Aunt from Chicago
A wonderful, classic Greek comedy. Aunt Calliope is a naturalized American who returns to Greece to put her brother's house in order. Her four nieces are unmarried, and Aunt Calliope sets to fix it. She remodels their house, changes their clothes, struts them around in bikinis and snares everyone a husband—including herself. A wonderful performance from character actress Georgia Vassiliadou as the Aunt. Greek with English subtitles.
VHS: S26386. $29.95.
Alekos Salekarios, Greece, 1959, 72 mins.

Cannon and Nightingale
"Simple yet complicated, satiric yet poignant, Kambanellis' film is memorable, a milestone of the world cinema" (Film Focus). The film, presented in three short segments, covers periods of the occupation of Greece by German, Italian and British forces. Greek with English subtitles.
VHS: S02665. $39.95.
Kambanellis, Greece, 1966, 90 mins.

Delicanis
Everyone expects a young man living in a village in Crete to become a priest, but he turns out to be the most popular lover on the island. Women of all types, including even his widowed aunt, fall prey to his charms until, shunned by his rural neighbors, he must wander alone from place to place. This comedy recalls old romance stories. Greek with English subtitles. Directed by Manolis Skouloudis.
VHS: S21180. $29.98.

The Enchantress
The first fairy tale from the new Greek cinema, winner of many international awards, a journey in the realm of myth, fear and human invincibility. A 17-year old youth, whom nature has endowed with daring and good looks, sets out from his village to find the Enchantress, a beautiful fairy feared by all. He journeys through an enchanted world inhabited by ghosts, spirits, imps and fairies. The world reveals to viewers, young and old, the power of myth, dreams, and enchantment. Greek with NO subtitles.
VHS: S11993. $59.95.
Manoussos Manoussakis, Greece, 1984, 93 mins.

End of the Game (South Wind)
An important film from the New Greek Cinema; three middle-aged couples, once the pillars of the anti-establishment, now live lives compromised to the lifestyle of the bourgeoisie; on a camping trip, their placidity is disturbed by a young nude girl who throws their complacency in turmoil. Greek with English subtitles.
VHS: S05607. $49.95.
Andreas Thomopoulos, Greece, 1984, 85 mins.

Get an Education, My Son
In this stark satire of contemporary Greek life, a teacher in the countryside must deal with the demands of his job, balancing the conservative educational format of the nation with the desires of his students and family. All this is set against the backdrop of the countryside, which is facing rapid depopulation. Greek with English subtitles. Directed by Thodoros Marangos.
VHS: S21175. $29.98.

Heavy Melon
The study of the development of dignity and consciousness of a young man who leaves his village in order to make his living in Athens. Greek with English subtitles. Greece, 1983, 92 mins.
VHS: S01549. $39.95.

Landscape in the Mist
Theo Angelopoulos' moving portrait of two sad-eyed children who traverse Greece in search of their father is a portrayal of loneliness, disillusionment and betrayal and the vision of a world that is both impersonal and unfeeling. The children's painful odyssey is fraught with terrifying figures, allegorical visions (a hand rising from the sea, a dead white horse outlined in the snow) and self-delusion. With Michalis Zeke, Tania Palaiologou, Eva Kotamanidou and Alika Georgouli. Greek with English subtitles.
VHS: S19542. $79.95.
Theo Angelopoulos, Greece/France/Italy, 1988, 125 mins.

Lysistrata
Aristophanes' ancient Greek play is brought to life in this new adaptation starring Jenny Karezi and Costas Kazakos. Lysistrata is the Athenian woman disgusted by the way men have ruined the country with their endless war. Rallying other women, she proposes that they impose an embargo on sexual relations with men as long as the war lasts. The film liberates the action from the stage, places it on location in the acropolis, and renders Aristophanes' plea in a forceful manner. Contains nudity and strong language. Greek with English subtitles.
VHS: S11718. $39.95.
Yiannis Negrepontis, Greece, 1987, 97 mins.

Man with the Red Carnation
A film which broke all box office records in Greece upon its release, Man with... is a political drama set in the period after the Civil War. It follows the life of Nikos Beloyannis, a fighter in the guerilla underground. With music composed by Mikis Theodorakis. Greek with English subtitles.
VHS: S02666. $39.95.
Nikos Tzimas, Greece, 1982, 110 mins.

Marching On to Glory
Modern Greek mass culture is skewered in this satiric look at the rise of a popular singing star. Though born in a small village, the hero moves to Athens, where fame awaits him. Despite his success this is not an edifying tale, but a cautionary one. Greek with English subtitles.
VHS: S21177. $29.98.

Parangelia
This old tradition stipulates that only those men who have requested a special song can dance as the tune plays. When an underworld figure is interrupted by three policemen during such a dance, he sets out for revenge, acting out all his anger and frustration built up during a lifetime of repression. Greek with English subtitles.
VHS: S21176. $29.98.
Pavlos Tassios, Greece, 1980, 95 mins.

Path of God
The story of a disillusioned young woman who seeks comfort by entering a convent only to find the same exploitation inside the convent as in the outside world. A thriller that involves adultery, false accusations and murder. Greek with English subtitles. Greece, 1984, 88 mins.
VHS: S01548. $39.95.

Red Lanterns
Just before the law closes down a house of prostitution, a number of dramas unfold. Chief among these is the developing romance between a sailor and a prostitute who wants to begin a new life far from the waterfront. Jenny Karezi stars. Greek with English subtitles.
VHS: S23902. $29.95.
Vassilis Georgiadis, Greece, 1963, 85 mins.

Rembetiko
Rembetiko music is a form of Greek urban blues. Rembetiko, winner of the Silver Bear at the Berlin Film Festival, is the story of modern Greece as seen through that music. A highly evocative film which is at once biographical and political. The film's sound is as rich as its color and its characters. Greek with English subtitles.
VHS: S02698. $39.95.
Costas Ferris, Greece, 1983, 101 mins.

Special Request
Based on the true story of Koemtzis, a marginal underworld figure who refused to cooperate with the police during the years of the Junta, and killed two policemen who insulted his brother. He became somewhat of a folk hero while on the run for resisting the dictatorship. "The images, the movement, the poetry all stay with you" (Liberation, Paris). Greek with English subtitles.
VHS: S02667. $39.95.
Pavlos Tassios, Greece, 1980, 96 mins.

When the Greeks
At the turn of the century a young man from a wealthy family is abducted by a group of bandits intent on a hefty ransom. Succeeding in their plan, they must now confront their role in the emerging bourgeois society that contradicts their traditional ways. Greek with English subtitles.
VHS: S21179. $29.98.
Lakis Papastathis, Greece, 1981, 100 mins.

With Glittering Eyes
This is the story of a mass execution in Greece during the Second World War. An old man must decide which of his three sons will survive. It's a tribute to the traditional family and the values of humanism which have always helped the Greek people survive foreign conquerors. Greek with English subtitles.
VHS: S21178. $29.98.
Panos Glikofridis, Greece

MICHAEL CACOYANNIS

Attila 74
Acclaimed as an "extraordinary and devastatingly powerful film," Attila 74 confronts the real-life tragedy of the Turkish invasion of Cyprus in 1974. The film "is history in the making. Remarkably, Cacoyannis manages to sustain at once a passionate engagement and a wide historical view—perhaps because he is seeing events always in terms of people" (Times of London). The film, wrote the L.A. Times, "is at once a deeply personal record and a formal work of art with a structure and a tragic sense of the inevitable, worthy of Euripides." Greek with English subtitles.
VHS: S09196. $59.95.
Michael Cacoyannis, Greece/Cyprus, 1974, 103 mins.

The Girl in Black
The Girl in Black "reveals Elli Lambetti as an actress of truly tragic stature." The story of a young Athenian writer on holiday who falls in love with a girl of impoverished gentility and is unable to respond to her. A disaster provoked by spiteful peasants shocks him into a new awareness of his own involvement in life. "The film has a simplicity and a vibrancy that make it stand out from even the best of foreign films. We experience the emotions and temperament of a new film artist who is trying to find his own way," wrote Pauline Kael. Greek with English subtitles.
VHS: S09550. $59.95.
Michael Cacoyannis, Greece, 1956, 104 mins.

A Matter of Dignity
Cacoyannis creates a cynical portrait of Greek upper class life. A wealthy family is on the verge of bankruptcy, and driven by the paranoid and superficial mother, struggle to maintain a facade of security at the cost of strong family bonds. An exceptional drama that is beautifully acted and typical of Cacoyannis' masterful direction. With Ellie Lambetti, George Pappas and Athena Michaelidou. Greek with English subtitles.
VHS: S12511. $59.95.
Michael Cacoyannis, Greece, 1957, 104 mins.

Stella
Melina Mercouri, in her debut film role as a bouzouki singer and dancer who abhors marriage, defies the rules of conventional morality and pays for a freedom denied her by the men who love her, in Michael Cacoyannis' second film. "Melina Mercouri [is] beautifully controlled... There is a pervasive sense of atmosphere that allows the characters to become an organic part of the streets and the houses used for location (the scene with Stella triumphantly riding an open truck to show the neighbors her lover's gift is among the funniest and best observed) and the folklore material (chiefly bouzouki dances and music by Manos Hatzidakis) is dexterously used to enliven the plot" (International Film Guide). Greek with English subtitles.
VHS: S09551. $59.95.
Laser: LD71341. $29.99.
Michael Cacoyannis, Greece, 1957, 95 mins.

Zorba the Greek
Anthony Quinn is Zorba, a crude, sly, lusty lover of life who passes on his passionate philosophy to a young, inexperienced writer (Alan Bates). Based on the novel by Nikos Kazantzakis, music by Mikis Theodorakis. With Irene Papas and Lila Kedrova.
VHS: S01606. $19.98.
Michael Cacoyannis, Greece, 1964, 142 mins.

COSTA-GAVRAS

Betrayed
Greek director Costa-Gavras investigates white hate groups in America in this controversial drama. Debra Winger stars as a novice FBI undercover agent sent to locate and herself for a political unrest in the heartland. She finds there are two sides to the widower father played by Tom Berenger and both are heavily armed. With John Heard and John Mahoney.
VHS: S09919. $19.98.
Costa-Gavras, USA, 1988

Hanna K.
Costa-Gavras' controversial film shot in Israel, starring Jill Clayburgh as the Israeli attorney who takes on the case of a Palestinian accused of terrorism and gets involved in the personal and political struggle between her and her lover, the district attorney. English dialog.
VHS: S00538. $59.95.
Costa-Gavras, France/USA, 1983, 111 mins.

Missing
Jack Lemmon, Sissy Spacek and John Shea star in Costa-Gavras' political thriller based on the true story of Charles Horman, an American writer who disappears and is killed during the overthrow of Allende's government in Chile. Lemmon is the concerned father whose attempts to learn the truth are stonewalled by bureaucracy and cover-up. English dialog.
VHS: S00862. $24.95.
Costa-Gavras, USA, 1983, 122 mins.

Music Box
Winner of the Silver Bear at the Berlin Film Festival, Costa-Gavras' political thriller stars Jessica Lange as a Chicago attorney defending a Hungarian immigrant (Armin Mueller-Stahl) accused of heinous war crimes more than 50 years ago.
VHS: S12213. $19.95.
Costa-Gavras, USA, 1989, 126 mins.

TURKISH CINEMA

Baba—The Father
Yilmaz Guney (Yol) directed this important Turkish film about a desperately poor boatman who agrees to frame himself for a murder in return for the support of his family. But after 24 years at hard labor, he discovers that his sacrifice has been in vain; his daughter has become a prostitute and his son is one of the murderer's henchmen. A powerfully tragic film. Turkish with English subtitles.
VHS: S15389. $39.95.
Yilmaz Guney, Turkey, 1973, 95 mins.

The Horse
Winner of the prize at the first Tokyo Film Festival, this is an intimate, realistic drama about a father and son confronting the hardships of life in modern Turkey against their own inadequacies, told in lyrical, tragic and compelling fashion reminiscent of The Bicycle Thief. Turkish with English subtitles.
VHS: S04734. $69.95.
Ali Ozgenturk, Turkey, 1982, 116 mins.

The Wall
The final film from the director of Yol, a harsh but sensitive recreation of the 1976 uprising of the destitute and mistreated children in Turkey's central prison in Ankara. Turkish with English subtitles.
VHS: S04733. $69.95.
Yilmaz Guney, Turkey, 1983, 117 mins.

Yol
Winner at the Cannes Film Festival, a powerful film about five Kurdish prisoners given a week's leave to visit their villages; Yol is based on personal experiences of the filmmaker, and is a film about political, religious and sexual oppression. Turkish with English subtitles.
VHS: S01490. $19.95.
Yilmaz Guney, Turkey, 1983, 115 mins.

IRANIAN CINEMA

The Cyclist
A visually sophisticated film which deals with the themes of man's exploitation of man and the inequities between rich and poor. The cyclist is Nassim, an Afghan refugee in need of money to pay his wife's medical expenses. With work difficult to come by, a sleazy promoter suggests he undertake a bicycle marathon. Touting him as the Afghani superman, the huckster wagers that Nassim will circle a small area on the outskirts of town, day and night, for a week. Gamblers, bookies and food vendors gather to watch the desperate cyclist from the sidelines, turning his suffering to their own profit. Winner of the Best Film at the Riminicinema Film Festival. Farsi with English subtitles.
VHS: S27790. $29.95.
Mohsen Makhmalbaf, Iran, 1989, 75 mins.

The Key
Humor, pathos and suspense fill this story of a four-year-old and an infant left home alone while their mother runs out to do some shopping. Young Amir Mohammad has his own ideas about what he wants to do—and watching his baby brother and the meal cooking in the kitchen are not among them. Minor crisis piles on crisis, culminating in the threat of disaster when the cooking pot boils over, dousing the flame on the gas range. As frantic neighbors yell advice to the resourceful youngster, tension mounts. Winner of the award for Best Children's Film at the Berlin Film Festival. Screenplay by Abbas Kiarostami. Farsi with English subtitles.
VHS: S27789. $29.95.
Ebrahim Forouzesh, Iran, 1986, 76 mins.

Life and Nothing More
The film investigates the aftermath of a devastating 1990 earthquake which killed some 50,000 people in northern Iran. This region provided the setting for Kiarostami's Where Is the Friend's Home. Kiarostami's search for the two young actors who played central roles in that film becomes the dramatic source of Life and Nothing More...as a father and son travel to Quoker, the hometown of the two boys, and along the way meet earthquake survivors who desperately and valiantly work to reconstruct their lives."...in many ways the most beautiful and powerful Iranian film I've seen" (Jonathan Rosenbaum, Chicago Reader). Farsi with English subtitles.
VHS: S27792. $29.95.
Abbas Kiarostami, Iran, 1992, 91 mins.

The Need
"One of those rare works in which the perfect rendering of simple elements produces a small, unforgettable masterpiece. The film's two main characters are boys poised between childhood and manhood. Both are poor. The boy through whose eyes we experience the drama has lost his father in the war and seems to have only the bleakest of prospects, until a relative finds him a choice apprentice's position in a print shop. But there is a catch; another boy coveting the spot has also been taken on, with the better of the two getting the permanent job after a trial period. Thus begins a fierce if somewhat covert rivalry that results in workplace sabotage, fighting and then, very surprisingly, friendship" (Godfrey Cheshire, Film Comment). Farsi with English subtitles.
VHS: S27788. $29.95.
Alireza Davudneshad, Iran, 1991, 81 mins.

The Peddler
Shockingly forthright in its view of the social and economic problems of the post-Shah era, The Peddler uses a different cameraman and different style for each of three short tales set among the poor of contemporary Tehran. The first episode follows a kindly but naive couple who want someone to adopt their newborn daughter. The second, an astonishing mix of absurdist comedy and the supernatural, concerns a mentally unstable man who lives with his mother in a ramshackle apartment. The final section draws on the American gangster film to show the last hours of a peddler suspected of betraying his friends. Farsi with English subtitles.
VHS: S27787. $29.95.
Mohsen Makhmalbaf, Iran, 1986, 95 mins.

Where Is the Friend's Home?
A lyrical tale about a traveller searching for his friend's home, who finds himself on an excursion through places and moments of great beauty and wonder. The friends are the schoolmates Ahmad and Mohammad Reza. Mohammad Reza's careless attitude towards his homework has drawn several reprimands from their stern teacher, culminating in the threat of expulsion if he does not do his work. When Ahmad prepares to do his own homework, he finds that he has accidentally picked up Mohammad Reza's notebook. Fearing that his friend will be expelled if he cannot submit his lesson the next day, Ahmad defies his parents and sets out to find his friend's home in the neighboring village. Winner of the Bronze Leopard at the Locarno Film Festival. Farsi with English subtitles.
VHS: S27791. $29.95.
Abbas Kiarostami, Iran, 1989, 90 mins.

ISRAELI CINEMA

The 81st Blow
An historical document made up of footage and stills shot by the Nazis. A compilation of testimony from witnesses who appeared at the Eichmann trial provides a telling narrative. The film's title refers to the story of a Jewish boy in one of the ghettoes, who was struck with 80 blows. He survived and immigrated to Israel, where he found that no one believed his story—which for him was the 81st blow. Academy Award nominee.
VHS: S06570. $79.95.
Jacquot Ehrlich/David Bergman/Haim Gouri, Israel, 1974, 115 mins.

Amazing Grace
A dramatic story is told in this film about the friendship between 18-year-old Jonathon and 30-year-old Thomas. Jonathon places all his hope for happiness in Thomas, who is HIV positive. Winner of the Wolgin Prize at the 1992 Jerusalem Film Festival and Best Film at Turin's Eighth International Gay-Themed Film Festival. Hebrew with English subtitles.
VHS: S22671. $79.95.
Amos Guttman, Israel, 1992, 95 mins.

Atalia
The powerful story, set on kibbutz, of the love between an older woman and a young man. Atalia is a war widow, whose defiant life style is in contradiction to the conventions of kibbutz life. She has become the true outsider, alienated yet psychologically tied to the world of her past, a world she seems unable to leave. Hebrew with English subtitles.
VHS: S15402. $79.95.
Akiva Tevet, Israel, 1985, 90 mins.

Beyond the Walls
Israel's nominee for Best Foreign Film of 1984 is set within the confines of an overcrowded Israeli prison where hatreds and conflicting ideologies come into sharp focus. When a prison official kills a Jew and blames the Arabs the stage is set. Hebrew with English subtitles.
VHS: S00127. $79.95.
Uri Barabash, Israel, 1984, 103 mins.

But Where Is Daniel Wax?
After years of separation, two men, a doctor and a singer return to Israel and meet at a high school reunion. Both men fantasize about their youth and the admiration they held for the class hero, Daniel Wax. A telling commentary on Israeli society, a Jewish version of The Big Chill. Hebrew with English subtitles.
VHS: S12888. $79.95.
Avram Heffner, Israel, 1974, 95 mins.

Cup Final
A political film suffused with humor and wit about an Israeli soldier detained by PLO guerrillas and his shifting relationship with the group's leader, both of whom carry an obsession for the Italian national soccer club. "An uncommon delicacy and wit that's bolstered by the powerful ensemble acting. Like Fuller, Coppola and Kubrick, Eran Riklis brings home the surrealism of war" (The Village Voice). Hebrew with English subtitles.
VHS: S18753. $59.95.
Eran Riklis, Israel, 1992, 107 mins.

Drifting
Controversial Israeli film called "The best gay film ever made," winner of Israeli Oscars for Best Director, Best Actor and Best Cinematography. Hebrew with English subtitles.
VHS: S00376. $69.95.
Amos Guttman, Israel, 1982, 80 mins.

Eagles Attack at Dawn
Rick Jason, Peter Brown and Joseph Shiloal star in this tale of revenge and violence set in the Middle East. An Israeli soldier returns to the prison where he was tortured in order to destroy the sadistic commander of this terrifying place.
VHS: S23889. $29.95.
Menahem Golan, Israel, 1974, 93 mins.

Fictitious Marriage
A high school teacher experiences mid-life crisis when he unexpectedly turns up in Tel Aviv and is mistaken for an Arab laborer. With Shlomo Bar-Aba, Irit Sheleg and Ofra Veingarten. "A human candid camera, an inside look at Israel" (Hadashot). Hebrew with English subtitles.
VHS: S17938. $79.95.
Haim Buzaglo, Israel, 1988, 90 mins.

Hamsin (Eastern Wind)
One of the most highly acclaimed and controversial Israeli films, Daniel Wachsmann's drama focuses on a Jewish landowner and his Arab worker. As the two work to build a ranch in Galilee, tensions flair up over the imminent confiscation of Arab lands, and the "hamsin" (the hot wind of the desert) sends tensions soaring to explosive heights. A powerful contemporary drama. With Shlomo Tarshish and Yasin Shawap. Hebrew with English subtitles.
VHS: S11496. $79.95.
Daniel Wachsmann, Israel, 1983, 90 mins.

Hide and Seek
Now considered a classic of the modern Israeli cinema, this sensitive study of adolescents in the crisis of self-discovery explores the sensitive issue of forbidden love. Can individuals work out their own fate in direct contradiction to a society where only conformity is accepted? Hebrew with English subtitles.
VHS: S06565. $79.95.
Dan Wolman, Israel, 1980, 90 mins.

Hill 24 Doesn't Answer
Four young Zionists are assigned to defend strategic Hill 24 outside Jerusalem, in order to maintain access to the besieged city. Through the diverse personal stories of the defenders, we gain a critical perspective on the birth of Israel and those who risked their lives to ensure the State's survival. "The first major success of the young Israeli cinema is superbly directed" (Georges Sadoul). In English.
VHS: S06566. $79.95.
Thorold Dickinson, Israel, 1955, 101 mins.

House on Chelouche Street
Life in Tel Aviv during the period of British rule is told in terms of the maturing of a young man, Sami, the eldest son of a young widow. The film has an authentic flavor that captures the vigor of the new emerging country. Hebrew with English subtitles.
VHS: S00587. $39.95.
Moshe Mizrahi, Israel, 1973, 111 mins.

Intimate Story
A powerful Israeli drama set on a kibbutz, where Leah and Yaacov are a childless couple failing at childbirth for a second time. Each blames the other for the failure, and the film becomes a powerful metaphor for Israeli society as the supportive atmosphere of the kibbutz is contrasted with its closed community and lack of privacy. Hebrew with English subtitles. With Chava Alberstein and Alex Peleg.
VHS: S11497. $79.95.
Israeli Nadav Levitan, Israel, 1981, 95 mins.

Kuni Lemel in Tel Aviv
A contemporary realization of the story of Kuni Lemel (Mike Burstyn), the Jewish folk hero of the shtetl, about a grandfather's offer to pay his twin grandsons $5 million to marry and return to Israel. The young men are polar opposites, one shy and virtuous, the other outgoing and in love with a shiksa. With Mandy Rice-Davies. Hebrew with English subtitles.
VHS: S17939. $79.95.
Yoel Silberg, Israel, 1977, 90 mins.

Late Summer Blues
A powerful, controversial film from Israel. Drawing on autobiographical details, Late Summer Blues looks at a group of seven 18-year-old men and women during the summer break between their final exams and their induction into Israeli Armed Forces as the War of Attrition at the Suez Canal draws on. This summer holiday will cut short their adolescence. First Prize, Israeli Film Awards. Hebrew with English subtitles.
VHS: S12959. $79.95.
Uri Barabash, Israel, 1987, 101 mins.

Lupo
Lupo is a furniture dealer with an overflowing zest for life who takes on city officials threatening to demolish his neighborhood in order to put up high-rises. A loving comedy. English dialog.
VHS: S00784. $59.95.
Menahem Golan, Israel, 1970, 100 mins.

My Michael
Two intelligent young adults find each other and marry in a divided Jerusalem of the late 1950's. Michael, a responsible and hard-working scientist, is comfortable in the arrangement, in contrast to Hanna, who finds herself unfulfilled by the petit bourgeois life she is leading. Loneliness and fantasy take over in this gentle yet controversial rendering of the novel by Amos Oz. Hebrew with English subtitles.
VHS: S06569. $79.95.
Dan Wolman, Israel, 1975, 90 mins.

Nadia
A teenage girl wants to be a doctor so she enrolls in a good boarding school as the first step toward this career goal. It would be a simple decision, except that this girl is an Arab from a small town in Israel and the school she chooses is Jewish. Resistance and prejudice strike her from all sides, but she perseveres. B&W, Hebrew with English subtitles.
VHS: S26997. $59.95.
Amnon Rubinstein, Israel, 1987, 90 mins.

Noa at Seventeen
It is 1951 and Noa, a seventeen-year old, struggles for personal autonomy as an ideological debate over the future of kibbutz socialism tears her family apart. Should she finish high school or follow her youth movement friends to kibbutz? Will Israel's labor movement follow Moscow blindly or turn its attention to the West? This sophisticated allegory penetrates the very essence of the bond which fused the personal and the political in the early years of the state of Israel. Hebrew with English subtitles.
VHS: S06568. $79.95.
Isaac Yeshurun, Israel, 1982, 86 mins.

Sallah
Arriving from the Orient as an Israeli immigrant, Sallah is full of expectations. Instead, he lands in a ramshackle transit camp that arouses his disgust. He opts to take on the bureaucracy in his own inimitable fashion, with hilarious results. A very humorous satire and Academy Award nominee. Hebrew with English subtitles.
VHS: S12887. $79.95.
Ephaim Kishon, Israel, 1965, 105 mins.

Siege
Set during the Six Day War, this Israeli film, noted for its stark realism, focuses on Tamar, an Israeli woman who loses her husband during the war. Her husband's friends don't want him forgotten, and this forces Tamar to become the ever-grieving widow who, living with her young son, tries to break away from the past, to develop new friends and relationships and establish a new life for herself. With Gilla Almagor and Dahn Ben Amotz. Hebrew with English subtitles.
VHS: S11498. $79.95.
Gilberto Tofano, Israel, 1970, 95 mins.

Take Two
A sexy comedy from Israel. Assi Doron is an Israeli cinematographer who shoots and directs commercials and documentaries. He lives in a luxurious Tel Aviv penthouse where he conducts his nightly love affairs with models and aspiring actresses who are charmed by the tough, arrogant and cynical divorcee. When he is forced to hire a new assistant, he hires a young American woman. But instead of an assistant, he gets a constant critic of his work, and by all rules, the two conflicting personalities should never fall in love. In English.
VHS: S12947. $79.95.
Baruch Dienar, Israel, 1985, 100 mins.

Unsettled Land
Kelly McGillis plays an Austrian doctor who emigrates to Palestine and settles in the Sinai Desert in 1910. With her lover John Shea, she and other Jews attempt to establish a home amidst attacks by hostile Bedouins, inhospitable weather and infighting among the settlers. With Arnon Zadok, Chad Shachar and Christine Boisson. Made on location.
VHS: S08501. $19.95.
Uri Barabash, Israel, 1988, 109 mins.

Wedding in Galilee
An intimate and multi-layered portrait of a Palestinian village under Israeli occupation. The mukhtar of the village wants to hold a traditional wedding for his son, and invites the Israeli military governor as a guest of honor. Beautifully filmed and acted by a cast of non-professionals, the story moves between the alienated grandfather, an angry group of young males prone to violence, an impotent groom and a resourceful bride. Arabic and Hebrew with English subtitles.
VHS: S08938. $24.95.
Michel Kleifi, Israel/Belgium, 1986, 113 mins.

Will My Mother Go Back to Berlin?
Filmmaker Micha Peled's mother escaped Berlin during the Nazi era. She then established herself in Israel. Years later her son travels to the German capital seeking traces of her childhood and returns with a surprise invitation extended to his mother by the mayor of Berlin. Hebrew and German with English subtitles.
VHS: S24715. $59.00.
Micha Peled, Israel/Germany, 60 mins.

Wooden Gun
Set in the tense atmosphere of Tel Aviv of the 1950's, this incisive film focuses on two rival groups of preteens whose behavior, motivated by their interpretations of the concepts of heroism, nationalism and friendship, raise harsh questions. Portrayed are first generation sabras (native-born Israelis) who are separated by a tremendous psychological gap from those who came to Israel from Europe, many of them Holocaust survivors. Hebrew with English subtitles.
VHS: S06567. $79.95.
Han Moshenson, Israel, 1979, 91 mins.

ISRAELI CULTURE

Amatzia: The Bar Kochba Caves
During troubled times, the Jews of ancient Israel often dwelled in artificial limestone underground caves. The Bar Kochba revolt, which was launched against Rome in 132 C.E., was largely waged from such dwelling places. This video takes us down below, where we view an intricate complex of narrow passageways and tunnels—an enlightening look at Israel's lesser known, yet more fascinating archeological sites. Color, 12 mins.
VHS: S15405. $29.95.

Bli Sodot—Without Secrets
Winner of Israeli Emmy Awards, this series is designed to teach Hebrew to children. Alphie, an animated host, and his four human friends employ comic sketches, film clips and animations designed to strengthen listening comprehension, vocabulary, reading and speaking skills. Designed for children of elementary age; each program is approximately 30 mins. In Hebrew.
Intermediate 3/Bet-Dalet/Samech-Ayin.
VHS: S10564. $39.95.
Noon-Kaf/Mem-Zayin/Gimel-Shin.
VHS: S10563. $39.95.
Shin/Resh/Lamed.
VHS: S10565. $39.95.
Tav/Intermediate 1/Bet-Hay.
VHS: S10561. $39.95.
Tet-Kaf/Intermediate 4/Peh-Vav.
VHS: S10565. $39.95.
Tsadi-Kaf/Intermediate 5/Shvah 1.
VHS: S10566. $39.95.

Yud-Peh/Alef-Chet/Intermediate 2.
VHS: S10562. $39.95.
Bli Sodot (Without Secrets), Complete Set Part I—The Consonants. The complete 7-volume set.
VHS: S24295. $179.65.

Bli Sodot (Without Secrets) Part II
Part II of the award-winning series used to teach Hebrew grammar to schoolchildren in Israel. In this section, children are introduced the use of Hebrew vowels. Each program is approximately 30 mins. In Hebrew.
Program 8: Shva II, III, IV.
VHS: S24296. $39.95.
Program 9: Intermediate Shva, Chirik I, II.
VHS: S24297. $39.95.
Program 10: Chirik III, IV, Intermediate Chirik.
VHS: S24298. $39.95.
Program 11: Cholam I, II, III.
VHS: S24299. $39.95.
Program 12: Cholam IV, Intermediate Cholam, Zeireh I.
VHS: S24300. $39.95.
Program 13: Zeireh II, III, IV.
VHS: S24301. $39.95.
Program 14: Intermediate Zeireh, Shuruk I, II.
VHS: S24302. $39.95.
Program 15: Shuruk III, IV, Intermediate Shuruk.
VHS: S24303. $39.95.

The Dhimmis: To Be a Jew in Arab Lands
A comprehensive documentary detailing centuries of persecution endured by Jews living in Arab lands. With rare film footage, photographs, maps and interviews, this is a first-rate overview of Jewish life in the midst of ongoing conflict. 29 mins.
VHS: S14692. $34.95.

The Films of Yaacov Ben Dov: Father of the Hebrew Cinema
These film works are a treasure trove of information about Jewish life in Palestine between 1917 and 1933. Within this Zionist vision of Israel a number of important historical figures are captured. Included are Chaim Wiezman, Winston Churchill, Albert Einstein and more. Prepared by the Spielberg Jewish Film Archive in Jerusalem. 30 mins.
VHS: S23245. $39.95.

The Gevatron—Sing Along
Kibbutz folk singers perform 14 songs on tour. There is also behind-the-scenes footage of these entertainers. Lyrics in Hebrew are translated through English titles. Includes companion booklet. 60 mins.
VHS: S26109. $29.95.

Great Days of History: Exodus and the Birth of Israel
The revelation of the Holocaust did not mean that its survivors would readily be granted asylum in the Promised Land. This riveting chronicle records the dramatic events leading to the establishment of Israel, focusing on Exodus, the clandestine voyage in 1947 of Jewish refugees to Palestine. 55 mins.
VHS: S09436. $29.95.

Homeland
A series of videotapes about the history of the Jewish settlement in the land of Israel in modern times. The series begins in the 19th century and continues through the formation of the modern state of Israel. In Hebrew.
At the Beginning of the Period/Within the Walls of Jerusalem. The first program from Homeland. 44 mins.
VHS: S10567. $39.95.
Crying. A drama which portrays a misfit living in a kibbutz. Also includes an interview with author Aharon Meged. 37 mins.
VHS: S10568. $39.95.

Inside God's Bunker
This is a chilling and detailed portrait of the Jewish settlers in Hebron just before the infamous 1994 massacre. Religious fervor, vigilante actions and ideological indoctrination helped create the atmosphere that exploded into the world's headlines. Hebrew with English narration and subtitles.
VHS: S24716. $59.00.
Micha Peled, Germany/France/Great Britain, 40 mins.

Israel Sings—Sing Along
This musical travelogue of Israel joins the best sights with popular folk songs. It's sung in Hebrew, but English titles translate each song. Includes companion booklet. 60 mins.
VHS: S26108. $29.95.

Israel—This Land Is Yours!
Explore Israel as it is today, its fascinating peoples and historic sites. Visit Masada, Nazareth, Galilee, Jerusalem and more. 28 mins.
VHS: S06696. $29.95.

Israel: A Nation Is Born
This program about the formation of modern Israel examines the 50-year history of the country and its political, cultural and social heritage. Produced by Moreshet Israel, the documentary presents a diversity of voices, including Harry Truman and Bill Clinton, Anwar Sadat and Itzhak Rabin. It is accompanied by commentary from Abba Eban, Israel's elder statesman, who has been an important personal witness to the struggles and hardships. 300 mins.
VHS: S20196. $149.95.

Israel: The Holy Land
Visit the Holy Land and see the historic religious areas as well as the everyday life and excitement that characterizes the people of Israel. See Tel Aviv, Nazareth, Jerusalem, Jericho, and more. 60 mins.
VHS: S05778. $24.95.

Israeli Writers
A series of interviews with contemporary Israeli writers, discussing their literary works. Hebrew without subtitles. Each program approximately 60 mins.
A.B. Yehoshua.
VHS: S10572. $49.95.
Gershom Scholem on S.Y. Agnon.
VHS: S10573. $59.95.
Moshe Shamir.
VHS: S10571. $49.95.

Jerusalem Today: City of Neighborhoods
In the latter half of the 19th century, Jerusalem's inhabitants began to establish their homes beyond the walls of the old city. Since then, scores of neighborhoods have been built. This program examines the Hasidic Beit Ungarin, the Sephardic Ohel Mosche, the Moslem Sheikh Jarach and Talpiot as an example of a garden neighborhood. 29 mins.
VHS: S10600. $29.95.

Jerusalem's Cardo
This journey into the Holy Land roots reveals The Cardo—Jerusalem's ancient, now modern thoroughfare. Walk with Walter Zanger, Israel's favorite tour guide, through the 2000 year-old Roman Gate, on Byzantine paving stones, and in the crusader market. Discover the remnants of a great synagogue and the underground Nea church, the Holy Sepulchre and the multi-level section of the old city. 25 mins.
VHS: S10452. $32.95.

Jerusalem: Musical Celebration
A celebration of the 40th anniversary of the founding of the state of Israel. Master violinist Isaac Stern takes us on a personal tour of Jerusalem while performing popular music for the violin and teaching a class of young children.
VHS: S09862. $39.95.

Jerusalem: Within These Walls
Jerusalem's Old City is a tiny, historic enclave, busy and colorful, the fountainhead of three major religions and home to 26,000 people of profoundly different cultures, living side by side in fragile peace. This National Geographic special is a kaleidoscopic view of the city within a city and its people. 59 mins.
VHS: S04886. $19.95.

Krovim Korvim—Near Ones, Dear Ones
A situation comedy about three Israeli families coping with the daily tension of Israeli life. Recorded before a live audience. Each program is 28 mins. With Yoram Gaon, Hanna Maron, Tiki Dayan and others. In Hebrew.
The Best Become Pilots.
VHS: S10569. $29.95.
Crime and Punishment.
VHS: S10570. $29.95.

Land of Promise
One of Palestine's earliest sound films, Land of Promise utilizes a combination of documentary and travelogue conventions to encourage settlement and investment in the Jewish Homeland. The film portrays Palestine as a land of opportunity for Zionists, a place for fulfilling an ancient dream. English and Hebrew, with narration from David Ross.
VHS: S16316. $72.00.
Juda Leman, Palestine, 1935, 57 mins.

Masada
The story of the siege of 980 Jews who escaped the sacking of Jerusalem by the Romans in 70 A.D. by taking refuge in Herod the Great's winter palace on the mountain of Masada. Made for television, starring Peter O'Toole and Peter Strauss.
VHS: S01717. $19.98.
Boris Sagal, USA, 2000, 131 mins.

Miracle of Survival/The Birth of Israel
This documentary tells the story of the emergent nation of Israel. From the modern military miracle that this country's borders represent, to the continuing everyday survival of the tenacious country, this is a tale of perseverance in the face of the enemy. 60 mins. Includes archival footage.
VHS: S22047. $14.98.

Parpar Nechmad—Lovely Butterfly
This special series designed for children of primary age is entirely in Hebrew, and uses puppets, games, songs and stories to tell children about Jewish holidays and traditions. In elementary Hebrew without subtitles. Each program is 30 mins.
Passover.
VHS: S10455. $29.95.
Chanukah.
VHS: S10456. $29.95.
Purim.
VHS: S10458. $29.95.
Tu B'Shvat.
VHS: S10459. $29.95.
Flowers for the Independence Day.
VHS: S10460. $29.95.

Rabbi Kook
From the series Jews Who Made History, produced in Israel, Rabbi Kook documents the life of the first Chief Rabbi of the state of Israel, from his childhood in Poland through his immigration to Palestine and his involvement with the secular and religious community in Israel. His philosophy of Jewish life made him a symbol for the Religious Zionist movement and on the other end made him enemies within the Orthodox community. 45 mins. English dialog.
VHS: S11596. $29.95.

Shattered Dreams
A massive, chilling, thoughtful and provocative examination of Israel. Born out of the despair of millions as a utopian haven in the desert, Shattered Dreams confronts the realities of Israel today against the background of these utopian beginnings. The film passionately documents what more than 20 years of occupation and expansion have done to the soul of Israel. Provocative and unflinching.
VHS: S12305. $19.98.
Victor Schonfeld, Great Britain, 1988, 173 mins.

The Unafraid
Writer Meyer Levin captured on film the journey of Jews trying to reach Palestine under the watchful British. Levin returned to Israel 30 years later to find out what had become of the courageous travelers. 35 mins.
VHS: S23253. $29.95.

Wall in Jerusalem
Richard Burton narrates this brilliant documentary, which traces the development of Israel into a modern Jewish homeland. Using rare and powerful footage, filmmaker Frederic Rossif documents the earliest settlements, the heavy immigration of the 30's and 40's, the creation of the kibbutz, the Balfour Declaration, relations with the League of Nations, confrontations with the Arabs and the British, the incident with the ship Exodus, the partition, and the Six Days' War.
VHS: S11231. $59.95.
Frederic Rossif, Great Britain, 1972, 91 mins.

A Woman Called Golda
Ingrid Bergman won an Emmy for her splendid performance as Israeli Prime Minister Golda Meir, a former school teacher from Milwaukee, Wisconsin. Judy Davis and Leonard Nimoy play the young Meirs, who immigrate to Palestine and begin work on a Kibbutz. With Anne Jackson, Ned Beatty, Robert Loggia and Barry Foster.
VHS: $10834. $69.95.
Alan Gibson, USA, 1982, 192 mins.

Yearning:
Jerusalem of the 19th Century
The film focuses upon historical developments and changes in Jerusalem of the 19th century, spanning from turn-of-the century Jerusalem, a city on the periphery of the Ottoman Empire, to Allenby's entry into Jerusalem in 1917. 37 mins.
VHS: $10467. $29.95.

Yitzhak Rabin
In this biographical documentary from A&E, the story of Israel's recently assassinated Prime Minister is told in all its complexity. His career paralleled the growth of the state of Israel. Rabin fought for Israeli independence with the Haganah underground army, formulated the Israeli victory in the Six Day War, became Israel's first native-born Prime Minister, and, finally, signed the historic peace treaty with the P.L.O.
VHS: $27211. $19.95.
Bill Harris, USA/Israel, 1995, 50 mins.

MIDEAST: THE CHALLENGE OF CHANGE

17 Days of Terror:
The Hijack of TWA 847
In June of 1985, TWA flight was snatched from its course, and its passengers held hostage for 17 days as the world looked on helplessly. From ABC News. 60 mins.
VHS: $12686. $24.98.

The Aftermath of the War with Iraq
An in-depth look at the political impact and unfinished business of the war with Iraq. This highly informative program examines the underlying political and military goals of the war and their impact on the longer term prospects for stability and peace in the Middle East. USA, 1991, 29 mins.
VHS: $15209. $25.00.

America Held Hostage: The Iran Crisis
From ABC News comes the story of the 444 days that changed history. Fanatic supporters of the Ayatollah stormed the US embassy in Tehran and held 52 people captive for over a year. 60 mins.
VHS: $12687. $24.98.

Amnesty International Report on Iran
A documentary on human rights abuses occurring in Iran today, with a commentary on the domestic and international legal standards contravened by these abuses. 1987, 15 mins.
VHS: $06890. $20.00.

Back to Arafat
The first feature-length documentary about the Armenian genocide. 1.5 million Armenians were killed and an entire people driven from their Turkish homeland. *Back to Arafat* also highlights the aspirations of three generations of Armenians scattered throughout the world, who share the dream of returning to the lands surrounding the holy mountain of Arafat. 100 mins.
VHS: $14734. $50.00.

Behind the Flag
A provocative video documentary featuring perspectives largely absent from mainstream media during the Gulf War. While acknowledging the need to resist Iraqi aggression, the video questions whether war was the best alternative, how the allies conducted the war, how the media reported it, and the costs to the U.S., Iraq, and other countries. USA, 1991, 20 mins.
VHS: $15208. $59.95.

Best of Nightline
Assassination of Egyptian President Anwar Sadat. 70 mins.
VHS: $14023. $14.98.
Colonel Muammar Qaddafi. 30 mins.
VHS: $14034. $14.98.
Flight 847 Hijacked. 60 mins.
VHS: $14035. $14.98.
Iranian Jetliner Shot Down by U.S. 30 mins.
VHS: $14054. $14.98.
Massacre of Marines in Beirut. 30 mins.
VHS: $14025. $14.98.
Qaddafi's Warning. 30 mins.
VHS: $14039. $14.98.
The State of Israel Is Recognized by Palestine. 30 mins.
VHS: $14055. $14.98.
Town Meeting—Holy Land. 30 mins.
VHS: $14053. $14.98.
Yasir Arafat. 30 mins.
VHS: $14048. $14.98.

Bethlehem
Palestinian Christians crafted this documentary about the religious history of this holy city. They begin with the story of Jesus' birth, then explore Bethlehem through archeology, architecture, demographics and legends. 41 mins.
VHS: $23001. $19.98.

Bill Moyers: The Arab World
In this series of conversations with noted scholars, writers and others, Bill Moyers, one of our country's most respected journalists, seeks to clarify the many misconceptions that mar our understanding of the important region stretching from Morocco to Oman. During the course of these discussions, the participants examine the role of religion—and religions—in Arab society, and look back at the historical forces that shaped the modern Arab world. From the PBS series.
Program 1: The Arabs: Who They Are, Who They Aren't.
VHS: $13870. $19.95.
Program 2: The Historic Memory.
VHS: $13871. $19.95.
Program 3: The Image of God.
VHS: $13872. $19.95.
Program 4: The Bonds of Pride.
VHS: $13873. $19.95.

Program 5: Arabs and the West.
VHS: $13874. $19.95.
Complete Set. 5 videotapes.
VHS: $13869. $79.95.

A Chance for Peace
Produced by CNN, the story of the events leading up to the signing of the historic peace treaty between Israel and the Palestinian Liberation Organization. 60 mins.
VHS: $20511. $14.98.

Christians and Christianity in Jerusalem
The site of Jesus' trial and crucifixion, throughout the centuries Jerusalem has drawn both pilgrims and protectors of its holy places. The Christian presence has had a profound influence on the character of the city. The film traces Christianity's link with Jerusalem from the New Testament to the Crusades. 47 mins.
VHS: $10464. $29.95.

Deadly Currents
"The best film I've ever seen on the Middle East" (*Toronto Star*)—a thoughtful documentary about the Israeli-Palestinian conflict which goes far beyond stereotypes to create an amazing portrait of societies at war. *Deadly Currents* delves deeply into the hearts and minds of the men and women behind the rock-throwing mobs, vigilante posses and political figureheads. Arabic and Hebrew with English voice-over and subtitles.
VHS: $27201. $79.95.
Simcha Jacobovici, Canada, 1992, 115 mins.

Death on the Nile:
The Assassination of Anwar Sadat
The Egyptian President turned his back on history and his nation's wishes to pursue peace in the Middle East. He lost his life in the process, cut down by assassin's bullets. From ABC News. 60 mins.
VHS: $12684. $24.98.

Discovering the Music of the Middle East
Islam spread musical traditions from the Middle East as far North as the Balkans. This video introduces a variety of instruments and explains the concepts behind intricate melodic lines and asymmetrical rhythms. 21 mins.
VHS: $23512. $49.95.

Echoes of Conflict
The tensions of the Arab-Israeli conflict are confronted in this showcase of three short films from a new wave of Israeli filmmakers. The titles include *The Movie, Don't Get Involved* and *The Cage*. Witness the turbulence of the Middle East from the perspective of those who face it every day. In Color and B&W. Hebrew with English subtitles.
VHS: $14746. $79.95.
Heller/Weller/Goren, Israel, 1986-89, 91 mins.

Embroidered Canticles
The Matruz is a unique Moroccan-Jewish music which fuses Hebrew and Arabic texts. Andalusian traditions of music and poetry reflecting the centuries-old link between Jewish and Muslim societies are the vital link to this living musical culture. Live performances and interviews with scholars and performers reveal this musical legacy. French, Arabic and Hebrew with English subtitles.
VHS: $23090. $25.00.
Izza Genini, France, 1991, 26 mins.

Farouk: Last of the Pharaohs
An intriguing documentary about Farouk, the last King of Egypt. When he ascended to the throne in 1936, at the age of 16, he was a beloved figure to his country and was expected to accomplish great things. Instead, he became a dissolute playboy, flaunting his love of luxury, huge appetite, gambling and mistresses—all at the expense of his desperately poor countrymen. "Fascinating, frank and fun" (London *Sunday Times*). 50 mins.
VHS: $14516. $29.95.

The Giant Nile
A travelogue that explores the mysteries, beauty, wildlife, landscape, culture and ruins of ancient Egyptian civilization. In this three-part documentary, the viewer is taken on an odyssey of the mind through five countries. 180 mins.
Part One: The Wild River.
VHS: $18276. $19.95.
Part Two: White Nile, Blue Nile.
VHS: $18277. $19.95.
Part Three: Egyptian Journey.
VHS: $18278. $19.95.
Boxed Set. The three-volume, three-hour work is presented in a single, boxed-set edition, including a parchment map.
VHS: $18279. $59.85.

The Gulf Crisis TV Project
The war-maneuvering in the Middle East prompted a group of New York-based TV producers to launch the *Gulf Crisis TV Project*, an effort to put news and views from anti-war activists on television nationwide. The Project contacted 1,000 community groups, from almost every state, to gather videotapes of local activities and demonstrations. The result is this tape, containing four half-hour TV programs entitled "War, Oil and Power;" "Getting Out of the Sand Trap;" "Bring the Troops Home" and "Operation Dissidence." See for yourself! *The Gulf Crisis TV Project* offers another view from America.
VHS: $13775. $29.95.

Inside the West Bank
An in-depth examination of the West Bank, produced as the MPI Video News Magazine, examining the conflict between Israelis and Palestinians in the occupied territories. 90 mins.
VHS: $06545. $19.95.

Israel and the Occupied Territories
This film details Amnesty International's concern with Israel and the Occupied Territories since the *Intifada*. Interviews with human rights lawyers, doctors, prisoners of conscience and others on beatings, lethal shootings, administrative detention and other issues of concern. 21 mins. 1990.
VHS: $12782. $20.00.

Israel vs. the PLO:
The Invasion of Lebanon
Israel's 1982 attempt to obliterate a formidable enemy, the bloody attack on Beirut, and the innocent victims caught in the crossfire. From ABC News. 60 mins.
VHS: $12688. $24.98.

Lifting the Fog:
Intrigue in the Middle East
In this panoramic view, the forces that have shaped this dynamic region are brought clearly into focus. History, religion and politics have traditionally shaped this complex area. Today, oil and geopolitics have only deepened its turbulent mix of influences. 60 mins.
VHS: $22999. $29.98.

A Line in the Sand:
What Did America Win?
Peter Jennings hosts this special presentation that explores the final effects of the Persian Gulf war. 50 mins.
VHS: $15878. $19.98.

Many Through One
In Cairo, Catholics worship in seven different rites that are reminders of Church history, art and tradition. Priests, bishops and lay people explain the practices and beliefs of their respective rites. 29 mins.
VHS: $15861. $19.95.

Mosque
With recent crises in the Middle East, many misconceptions about Islam have invaded the American psyche. But the understanding of 900 million Muslims and their faith is still a mystery to most. This program, filmed in Cairo, introduces a mosque and shows that Muslim believers are not the fanatics that media reports frequently portray. 29 mins.
VHS: $15859. $19.95.

Mysterious Egypt
From the golden mask of King Tutankhamen in Cairo's museum to Tut's burial site in the Valley of the Kings, this film carefully explores all the most important sites of ancient, mysterious Egypt. A delightful selection of breathtaking visuals. 60 mins.
VHS: $15048. $29.95.

Occupied Palestine
"A complex, sensitive and brutally authentic movie, *Occupied Palestine* delivers its message with unnerving sharpness and accuracy. The simple realities of what it means to live under and to resist occupation have never been so clearly presented to a Western audience," wrote Professor Joel Beinin of Stanford University. *Occupied Palestine* is a film reflecting the Palestinian experience of Zionism and resistance to it. Dramatic, contemporary footage is combined with the testimony of Palestinians as well as Zionist settlers and officials, to develop a fresh perspective on a critical international issue. "Quite simply the best film ever made about the Palestine question" (*Middle East Report*).
Home Video.
VHS: $10842. $49.95.
Institutional with public performance rights.
VHS: $10847. $99.95.
David Koff, USA/Israel, 1987, 88 mins.

The Persian Gulf: Images of a Conflict
Sold only as a collectible four-volume set. 6 hours 30 mins. *Volume 1: Prelude to War.* This first program prophetically introduces us to Saddam Hussein in a rare interview with Diane Sawyer which predated the invasion of Kuwait by several weeks. The program then takes us on a time trip through the invasion, the UN resolutions, the debates in both Houses, and the war of words between the US and Iraq—finally culminating in the eventful night of January 16, 1991, when the bombs began to fall. *Volume 2: The Allies Strike.* And now the war begins. Some of the footage contained in this volume has not yet been seen on television and includes reports from Saudi Arabia, Baghdad, and other areas of the Middle East as well as reactions at home. *Volume 3: Saddam Hussein vs. the Coalition behind the Military Strategies.* How was the war really fought? What were Hussein's tactics, and where did he fail? This is an analysis that graphically explains the methodology used to wage one of the most comprehensive wars in history. *Volume 4: A Conversation with General Schwarzkopf.* This is an historic interview, conducted by Barbara Walters, which probes the mind and soul of the man who has achieved almost unprecedented historic military status. No other interview with the General, to date, has proven to disclose so much. This last volume is a fitting conclusion to the entire series.
VHS: $14087. $69.98.

Report from Iraq
Produced by award-winning filmmaker John Koop, this video is a document of the journey of a team of Harvard University doctors, lawyers, and students to Iraq—in the aftermath of the Gulf War. USA, 1991, 22 mins.
VHS: $15212. $59.95.

Sadat
Louis Gosset, Jr., portrays the life and career of Egyptian leader Anwar Sadat. This charismatic man began his political career at the helm of an army, but he is best known today as the man who campaigned hard to bring peace to the Middle East. 193 mins.
VHS: $25754. $24.95.

Sandstorm in the Gulf
This video looks back at the mistakes and miscalculations by our government that contributed to the Gulf War, and looks ahead to the major problems in the Middle East that the War hasn't solved: The Arab-Palestinian-Israeli conflict, arms control, regional security, and the gap between rich and poor nations. A provocative discussion of the politics and history of the region. 25 mins.
VHS: $13932. $29.95.

Sea of Galilee
Journey to the ancient waters of Galilee and visit the locales where the Ministry of Jesus actually occurred. Navigating Galilee's waters and traveling its shores, viewers visit Hamat Gader, the world's oldest synagogue, and the ancient world's second largest hot springs. 25 mins.
VHS: $12301. $24.95.

Secret Egypt: A Trance Journey
Egypt's ancient culture merges disparate influences into a vibrant spiritual whole. Healing trance dances occur in ancient tombs just behind the great pyramids. Rituals of exorcism are performed in tents and on crowded city corners. Even cobras are subject to the influences of these old and unfathomable spiritual ways. This documentary shows a side of Egypt rarely revealed to anyone. 50 mins.
VHS: $26719. $29.95.

The Shifting Sands:
A History of the Middle East
This video gives the background story every family in America should know. Tracing the history of the Middle East over 5,000 years, NBC News uncovers the delicate balance of power that led to the recent conflict in the Gulf. USA, 60 mins.
VHS: $15217. $19.95.

Sites Unseen:
Off the Beaten Track in Jerusalem
A guide to reclusive, obscure and unknown sites of interest in Jerusalem. 45 mins.
VHS: $12907. $39.95.

Stolen Freedom: Occupied Palestine
Casey Kasem (of *America's Top 40* fame) hosts this serious documentary about the plight of the Palestinian people. They have been forced into ghettoes filled with fear and violence. Only the dream of freedom sustains them. 30 mins.
VHS: $23000. $19.98.

Touring Egypt
A fascinating look at Egypt, including walks through the many Cairos of today—the pyramids and Sphinx of Giza, cruising the Nile to Thebes, the Temples of Karnak and Luxor, the temples of Esna and Edfu, Aswan dam and the temple of Isis, the four colossi of Rameses, the Sinai, Suez Canal and the Red Sea, and even El Alamein. 60 mins.
VHS: $09912. $29.95.

Treasures of the Holy Land:
Ancient Art from the Israel Museum
Documents the 1986 Metropolitan Museum of Art exhibition. More than 10,000 years of the Holy Land's history are viewed through the objects on display as Philippe de Montebello, the Museum director, guides the viewer through a rich sampling of artifacts, jewelry, inscriptions, mosaics and household objects. 30 mins.
VHS: $03401. $29.95.

War in the Gulf:
Answering Children's Questions
Peter Jennings and ABC News correspondents, both in the U.S. and in the Middle East, are joined by Operation Desert Storm military speakers to explain the issues of war to children and their parents. 75 mins.
VHS: $22991. $19.98.

YIDDISH & JEWISH CINEMA

Almonds and Raisins: A History of the Yiddish Cinema
Narrated by Orson Welles, this remarkable documentary is a history of the Yiddish cinema, fascinating and funny, a landmark documentary on the whole lost culture of Yiddish film. Between 1927 and 1940, Yiddish filmmakers made over 100 films in Yiddish, expressing the hopes and fears of the immigrant society—dreams of opportunity, assimilation, social betterment, separation from family and failure. *Almonds and Raisins* lovingly captures the ideas and history of the Yiddish cinema and the richness of the Yiddish language.
VHS: $08101. $59.95.
Russ Karel, Great Britain, 1986, 90 mins.

American Matchmaker
(Amerikaner Shadchen)
Edgar G. Ulmer's classic Yiddish film about a dissatisfied man's desire to become a modern day matchmaker after the failure of his most recent marriage, who earmarks for a rival a woman more suited to his own sensibility. With Judith Abarbanel. Yiddish with English subtitles.
VHS: $17937. $69.95.
Edgar G. Ulmer, USA, 1940, 87 mins.

Ashkenaz: Eastern European Jewry
This video offers a nostalgic look at the music of Eastern European Jewry. Yiddish folk songs, liturgical music, Klezmer melodies and even Yiddish theater tunes are all here. The origins of Ashkenazic music are traced with the help of vintage archival footage taken before World War II. 28 mins.
VHS: $21710. $39.95.

Bent Tree
This charming fable, presented in sand animation, is based on the Yiddish folk tune "Oyfn Veg Shteyt A Boym." The story tells of a small child whose mother tries to prevent him from discovering the world and flying away. 4 mins.
VHS: $12884. $16.95.

Cantor's Son
This is a dramatic film based on the life of its star, Moishe Oysher. A youth leaves his home country to join a troupe of traveling performers. Eventually, he lands in America but is barely able to support himself. On a janitorial job, he is "discovered" as having an unusually fine voice and gains immediate fame. Success does not fulfill him though, and he returns, in the end, to the home of his parents. Yiddish with English subtitles.
VHS: $12885. $79.95.
Ilya Motyleff, 1937, 90 mins.

The Dybbuk
Tragedy, conflict and cultural tension among two families are contrasted in this ambitious work inspired by S. Ansky's ethnographic studies of Jews in the Polish-Russian countryside. "Whatever the movie's original intentions, even have dictated that its theme will be read as harbingers of exile and oblivion" (J. Hoberman, *Village Voice*). With Avrom Marevsky, Isaac Samberg and Moshe Lipman. Yiddish with restored English subtitles.
VHS: $18572. $90.00.
Michal Waszynski, Poland, 1937, 123 mins.

East and West
A comedy about urban Jews who dedicate themselves to traditional *shtetl* life. A New York businessman returns with his daughter to Galicia to attend a family wedding. She's drawn to a charismatic young yeshiva scholar who breaks tradition to court her. With Molly Picon, Jacob Kalish and Sidney M. Goldin. "With broad strokes and plenty of self-parody, it raises the issue of modernity." Silent with Yiddish and English intertitles.
VHS: $18573. $72.00.
Sidney M. Goldin/Ivah Abramson, Austria, 1923, 85 mins.

Eli Eli

Long believed lost, this heartwarming musical drama is the classic Yiddish story of a divided family. While Mom and Dad lose the farm, the family is forced to live apart, but they do it with sadness, humor and music. With Esther Feild (*The Yiddish Mama*), Lazar Fried and Muni Serebroff, with songs by Sholom Secunda. Yiddish with English subtitles.
VHS: S04844. $29.95.
Joseph Seiden, USA, 1940, 85 mins.

God, Man and Devil

A pious Torah scribe is seduced by Satan and transformed into a dishonest factory owner who destroys the religious and communal fabric in this adaptation of Jacob Gordin's play. With Mikhal Mikhalesko, Gustav Berger and Berta Gersten. Yiddish with improved English subtitles.
VHS: S18574. $54.00.
Joseph Seiden, USA, 1949, 100 mins.

Green Fields

A restored Yiddish classic, directed by Edgar G. Ulmer. A pastoral romance based on Peretz Hirschbein's legendary tale of a young student who leaves the Yeshiva to wander across the Pale in search of "true Jews." When the orphaned, otherworldly scholar happens upon a family of Jewish peasants who take him in as a boarder and tutor for their children, an interesting juxtaposition of lifestyles ensues. From the National Center for Jewish Film. Yiddish with English subtitles.
VHS: S11648. $72.00.
Edgar G. Ulmer, USA, 1937, 95 mins.

His People

In this early drama, Edward Sloman focuses on two sons, Morris the lawyer and Sammy the prizefighter, in lower Manhattan. As both stray from traditions cherished by their first-generation, Russian-immigrant parents, each learns to preserve the family's self-respect. Alternatively titled *Proud Heart, Common People* and *The Jew*. Silent.
VHS: S16314. $72.00.
Edward Sloman, USA, 1925, 91 mins.

His Wife's Lover (Zayn Vaybs Lubovnik)

A charming Yiddish comedy starring the multi-talented Ludwig Satz, about an actor who disguises himself as an old man in order to test his young fiance's fidelity. With Michael Rosenberg and Lucy Levine. Yiddish with English subtitles.
VHS: S14689. $59.95.
Sidney Goldin, USA, 1931, 77 mins.

Horodok

While visiting relatives in Horodok, a Polish *shtetl* between Minsk and Vilna, the American amateur filmmaker Joseph Shapiro recorded his impressions. As he travels the town on foot, he assembles a pastiche of women at work, schools, markets, farm animals, wooden houses and horse-drawn wagons to create a portrait of the people's poor but pious way. Silent.
VHS: S16315. $30.00.
Joseph Shapiro, Poland, 1930, 11 mins.

Isaac Bashevis Singer in America

Isaac Bashevis Singer stars in this latest issue from the *About the Authors* series. This quintessential Jewish writer shares his 80-plus years of experience through memories and interviews. He is seen in his cluttered New York office and on the streets of the city. Narrated by Judd Hirsch. 60 mins.
VHS: S21233. $24.95.

Isaac Bashevis Singer: Champion of Yiddish Literature

Through a series of frank conversations with the Nobel Laureate, we gain an understanding of his life, his great love and devotion to his mother-tongue, his philosophies of writing as well as religion, and his hopes and aspirations for the future of Yiddish. Includes insightful illustrations by Maurice Sendak. In English. 28 mins.
VHS: S15400. $34.95.

The Jester (Der Purimshpiler)

A romantic comedy, in Yiddish, about a drifter who finds temporary peace when he falls in love with a shoemaker's daughter in a small town. A rare example of Yiddish filmmaking in America. Newly mastered and restored. Yiddish with English subtitles.
VHS: S08951. $79.95.
Joseph Green, USA, 1937, 90 mins.

Jewish Life in Bialystok

Two Polish-Jewish brothers, Shaul and Yizhak Goskind, produced six short films about urban Jewish communities within Poland. This film covers the factories and textile workers, synagogues, parks and libraries of Bialystok. Yiddish with new subtitles. 10 mins.
VHS: S18576. $25.00.

Jewish Life in Cracow

This program looks at Cracow's Jewish quarter, juxtaposing footage of the old and new, the streetcars and horse-drawn carriages, merchants conducting business, sporting activities, games and discussions. The work highlights scenes at the Remu Synagogue and Alte Shul. Yiddish with new English subtitles. 10 mins.
VHS: S18577. $25.00.

Jewish Life in Lvov

The program focuses on the architectural and community landmarks, the Yad Haruzim Trade Union Building, the Old Ghetto, the Modern Temple and the Lazarus Hospital and the Nowosci Theater in Lvov. Yiddish with new English subtitles. 10 mins.
VHS: S18578. $25.00.

Jewish Life in Vilna

This rare film document captures the spirit of Jewish life in pre-World War II Vilna. Lively narration and music accompany film sequences of people engaged in the rituals and realities of daily existence—at work, at play, in the synagogue and in school. Vilna's famous landmarks—the Strashun Library, Shripeshiker Cemetery, YIVO Institute—are among the film's highlights. Yiddish with new English subtitles.
VHS: S12285. $25.00.
Yitzhak Lerner, Poland, 1939, 10 mins.

Jews of Poland

Five cities: Bialystok, Lvov, Krakow, Vilna and Warsaw. Between 1938 and 1939, two filmmakers visited six Jewish communities in Poland to record the vitality of Jewish life. Little did they know that their film would become one of the last visual accounts of a once vibrant world. They have been preserved by the Spielberg Jewish Film Archive in Jerusalem. 50 mins.
VHS: S12896. $49.95.

Jolly Paupers

A restored Yiddish classic. A musical comedy portraying the relentless efforts of two small-town Jews to escape their misery and achieve fame and fortune. In the face of setbacks, community quarrels and even insanity, they refuse to give in to despair. With violent anti-Semitism intensifying in Poland and Nazism looming on the horizon, their satirical monologues provided Jewish audiences with a rare opportunity to escape through laughter. From the National Center for Jewish Film. Yiddish with English subtitles.
VHS: S11649. $54.00.
Warsaw Art Players, Poland, 1937, 62 mins.

The King and the Fool

Solomon Mikhoels and Benjamin Zuskin, the King and the Fool, created the Yiddish Theater in post-revolutionary Moscow. Stalin put an end to their creative efforts. Their story can now be told with the help of interviews from surviving relatives and excerpts from films and plays in which these two performed. 40 mins.
VHS: S23232. $39.95.

Letter to Mother (A Brivele der Mamen)

One of the most famous of Yiddish-language American films, directed by Joseph Green. Set in the Polish Ukraine and New York City, the film traces the break-up of a family due to stress, poverty, the chaos of war, and the difficulties of immigrant life. With Berta Gerstein, Lucy Gehrman. Newly mastered and restored. Yiddish with English subtitles.
VHS: S08949. $72.00.
Joseph Green, USA, 1938, 100 mins.

A Life of Song: A Portrait of Ruth Rubin

A powerful documentary by Cindy Marshall that explores the life of Ruth Rubin, covering her determination to preserve, collect and transmit the vibrant legacy of Yiddish folksongs. "Inspiring to many people who wonder if there is hope that their own minority music will be able to survive in some way" (Pete Seeger). 38 mins.
VHS: S17934. $34.95.

The Light Ahead

Edgar G. Ulmer directed this adaptation by Mendele Mokher Seforim, the grandfather of "19th century modern Yiddish literature," about a weak man's obsession for a blind woman. The film is considered a "penetrating look at shtetl life," and Mendele's "Eastern European Jewish world." With David Opatoshu, Helen Beverly and Isidore Cashier. "Beverly and Opatoshu are perhaps the most beautiful couple in the history of Yiddish cinema" (J. Hoberman, author of *Bridge of Light*). Yiddish with English subtitles.
VHS: S17936. $69.95.
Edgar G. Ulmer, USA, 1939, 94 mins.

Little Mother (Mamele)

Joseph Green directed this Yiddish-language, American-made film about a young girl (the famous Molly Picon) who is left with the responsibilities of tending house for a helpless and ungrateful family of seven. Newly mastered and restored. Yiddish with English subtitles.
VHS: S08950. $79.95.

Mirele Efros

Berta Gersten plays Mirele, a noble, dignified widow and successful businesswoman who comes into conflict with the daughter-in-law she chose for her eldest son. Set in turn-of-the-century Grodno, and based on the Jacob Gordin play. 1938, 80 mins. Yiddish with English subtitles.
VHS: S12886. $79.95.

Mothers of Today (Hayteges Mames)

In this melodrama about a cantor's son gone bad, the promise of American prosperity reveals its downside, that is, the erosion of traditional Jewish values. The cantor's son steals, runs off with a woman of questionable virtue and, worst of all, breaks his mother's heart. Yiddish with English subtitles.
VHS: S26687. $69.95.
Henry Lynn, USA, 1939, 90 mins.

Moving Mountains: The Montreal Yiddish Theatre in the U.S.S.R.

Ina Fichman's remarkable documentary about Dora Wasserman, a Russian-born Jew who returns to her native country, after a 40-year separation, with her talented group of performers to produce the Yiddish play, *Sages of Chelm*.
VHS: S17933. $34.95.
Ina Fichman, Russia, c. 1988, 28 mins.

Nowogrodek

Organized around a visit by Yiddish lexicographer Alexander Harkavy, the activities in Nowogrodek include sporting events, a bustling marketplace, a crowded synagogue courtyard just after Sabbath prayers, the town's fire brigade at work, a children's summer camp and glimpses of the local theater. A lively montage of Poland's medium-sized, Lithuanian-Jewish community. Silent with Yiddish and English intertitles. 1930, 26 mins.
VHS: S16317. $54.00.

Our Children

Suppressed as too Zionist by the Communist Polish government, this film features the comedy team of Dzigan and Schumacher, together with children who survived the Holocaust. The comic actors play all the roles in Sholem Aleichem's *Kasrilevke Brent* (*Kasrilevke Is Burning*). They watch as these orphans perform for them. It's a film that explores what to do with nightmares: should they be remembered or forgotten? Yiddish with new English subtitles.
VHS: S23084. $72.00.
Natan Gross/Shaul Goskind, Poland, 1948, 68 mins.

Overture to Glory

Moishe Oysher stars as the Vilner Balabesi, the cantor who leaves his position as Vilna Cantor in order to seek fame and fortune as an opera star in Warsaw. He feels uncomfortable in his new environment and yearns to return home to his wife, child and community. The film provides a wonderful vehicle for Moishe Oysher's rich cantonal voice. With Helen Beverly and Florence Weiss. "An artistic triumph for the Yiddish motion picture industry." (*New York Herald Tribune*). Yiddish with English subtitles.
VHS: S10256. $79.95.
Max Nosseck, USA, 1940, 85 mins.

Shalom—Songs of Polish Jews

A unique program of songs from the heritage of Polish Jewry, performed in Yiddish and in Hebrew by Slawa Przybylska. 85 mins.
VHS: S11381. $39.95.

The Singing Blacksmith (Yankl der Schmid)

David Pinski's classic story of a blacksmith who sees too many women and drinks far too much liquor. Then he meets Tamare and his life drastically changes, or does it? In this charming story, set in Eastern Europe but shot in New Jersey, we are treated to a quaintly romantic film in the tradition of classic Yiddish comedy-drama. Directed by the esteemed, expressionist master of low-budget Hollywood cinema Edgar G. Ulmer, this film is definitely worth a look. Yiddish with English subtitles.
VHS: S15401. $79.95.
Edgar G. Ulmer, USA, 1938, 95 mins.

Tevye the Dairyman (Tevye der Milkhiker)

This memorable adaptation of Sholem Aleichem's play centers on Tevye, the dairyman, and his daughter Khave, who falls in love with Fedye, the Gentile son of a Ukrainian peasant. Her courtship and marriage pit Tevye's deep-seated faith and loyalty to tradition. Made from a completely restored print. "With all due respect for Zero Mostel and Topol in *Fiddler on the Roof*, it was Maurice Schwartz, the great Yiddish actor/director, who first showed Tevye the Dairyman in his full light as a *mensch* for all seasons. A rare opportunity to see Schwartz in what may have been his most magnificent role" (Judy Stone, *San Francisco Chronicle*). From the National Center for Jewish Film. Yiddish with new English subtitles.
VHS: S12219. $72.00.
Maurice Schwartz, USA, 1939, 96 mins.

Uncle Moses

A historically important adaptation of the Sholom Asch classic, starring legendary Yiddish performer Maurice Schwartz, a driven, unbending despot of his Lower East Side sweatshop who falls in love with the daughter of one of his distraught workers. With Judith Abarbanel and Zvee Scooler. "Immensely entertaining" (*San Francisco Chronicle*). Yiddish with English subtitles.
VHS: S17935. $59.95.
Goldin/Scotto, USA, 1932, 87 mins.

The Vow (Tkies Kaf)

Two friends plan that their unborn children will marry some day. After the friends lose touch with each other, the children, now grown to adulthood, meet and fall in love. Sadly, the father of the boy has already made other plans for his son's future wife. Only the divine intervention of the Prophet Elijah can solve this muddle of human devising. Yiddish with English subtitles.
VHS: S26686. $79.95.
Henryk Szaro, Poland, 1937, 90 mins.

The Yiddish Cinema

A documentary about the vibrant Yiddish film production that flourished in Eastern Europe and the United States between the First and Second World Wars. Employing interviews, music, archival footage and film clips, the program explores the tradition of Yiddish film in expanding culture and language. Narrated by David Mamet.
VHS: S18580. $25.00.
Rich Pontius, USA, 1991, 60 mins.

Yiddish: The Mame-Loshn (The Mother Tongue)

Shot in New York and Los Angeles, this affectionate portrait examines the importance of Yiddish to American Jews today and evokes the language and culture's pleasures through poetry, illustrations, interviews and film clips. Featuring comedian David Steinberg, actor Herschel Bernardi, writers Leo Rosten and Simon Weber, and scholars Joshua Fishman and Saul Goodman.
VHS: S16319. $36.00.
Cordelia Stone/Mary Hardwick, USA, 1980, 58 mins.

Yidl with a Fiddle (Yidl mitn Fidl)

The classic Yiddish language musical comedy. Molly Picon plays a shtetl girl who, disguised as a boy, goes off with her father and a band of traveling musicians into the Polish countryside. Made in pre-war Poland, the film provides a warm rendering of Eastern European Jewish life, made all the more fun and wonderful by Molly Picon's unequaled ability to amuse and entertain. Newly mastered and restored. Yiddish with English subtitles.
VHS: S10258. $72.00.
Joseph Green, Poland, 1936, 92 mins.

Zoll Zeyn (Let It Be)

A documentary that assesses the cultural and linguistic impact of Yiddish in modern day Israel, after the early Zionists established Hebrew as a signifier for hope and recovery. Yiddish with English subtitles.
VHS: S18581. $72.00.
H.M. Broder/F. van der Meulen, Israel, 1989, 135 mins.

THE WORLD OF JUDAISM

Argentina's Jews: Days of Awe

Jews came to Argentina and founded the agricultural community of Moiseville. This video provides a history of Argentinian Jewry, counterbalanced with their current battles with anti-Semitism, assimilation and loss of identity. 55 mins.
VHS: S12890. $34.95.

Benjamin and the Miracle of Hanukkah

Herschel Bernardi narrates this video that explains both the story and the history of Hanukkah. This animation also includes a visit to the site of the Hanukkah miracle and a tale detailing the struggle for religious freedom, told by a Russian emigre. 25 mins.
VHS: S26202. $9.95.

Branching Out: Tracing Your Jewish Roots

Arthur Kurzweil travels to Ellis Island and other sites in this do-it-yourself video about tracing family trees. This genealogist makes the process clear and understandable to any amateur. 30 mins.
VHS: S23249. $39.95.

Bubbe Meises, Bubbe Stories

Ellen Gould wrote and stars in this one-woman show about her two "Bubbes" (Yiddish for grandmothers). It's a heartwarming concoction made up of humorous but emotional tales from the lives of these women who left the old world and struggled to create a life in the new world. 75 mins.
VHS: S26037. $59.95.

Chanuka at Bubbe's

Delightful Muppet-like characters create an irresistible cast in this program explaining the traditions and significance of Chanuka. Great family entertainment. USA.
VHS: S14949. $19.95.

A Chanukah Adventure

Professor Pellah together with his hungry goldfish goes on a mission to publicize the holiday of Chanukah. He assembles a group of young helpers who come up with some great ideas. The Professor's music video is simply priceless and there are segments of public menorah lightings from all over the world. 30 mins.
VHS: S24675. $19.95.

Children Must Laugh

Aleksandar Ford's powerful documentary, financed by the Jewish labor movement in Poland, is a revealing look at Polish pre-war Jewish life. "Out of the sorrows and shadows of the life of Jewish workers in Poland, a bright ray of hope has come…Hollywood scouts would do well to locate some of the children…[whose] confidence in their ability to 'build a better world' rises above any language barrier" (*The New York Times*). Polish and Yiddish with English narration and subtitles.
VHS: S19534. $54.00.
Aleksandar Ford, Poland/USA, 1935/65, 64 mins.

Covenant: People of the Living Law

Theodore Bikel leads a panel of experts who examine the flexibility and subsequent longevity of both the U.S. Constitution and Halacha (Jewish Law). 60 mins.
VHS: S24500. $29.95.

A Day in Warsaw

This kaleidoscopic program brings out the diversity of Warsaw, from the Zamenhof and Nalewki streets that were the centerpiece for the city's 400,000 Jews to its study of ancient and contemporary Jewish architecture, its theaters, cemeteries and other prominent Jewish institutions. Yiddish with new English subtitles. 10 mins.
VHS: S18579. $100.00.

The Discovery

Josh Saviano, teenage star of the hit TV show *The Wonder Years*, is at the center of this video about bar mitzvah. By questioning friends Josh learns about the ceremony, the heritage it represents, and the responsibilities it confers. 60 mins.
VHS: S24503. $29.95.

Dosvedanya Means Good-bye

Roberta Hantgan's film follows the course of Tamara Okun's life. Tamara is a Russian Jew who waited eight years for an exit visa. From Leningrad to Vienna and finally Washington, D.C., this is a story of perseverance, courage and growing awareness of Jewish identity. 30 mins.
VHS: S23258. $34.95.

Falashas

Meyer Levin's classic documentary film study of Ethiopian Jewry in 1973. Levin ventured to Ethiopia to record Jews forgotten by the World. We view Jewish rituals and practices as observed for generations in isolation. An important document which became an international event when the Falashas were air-lifted out of Ethiopia in 1984.
VHS: S06578. $34.95.
Meyer Levin, USA, 1973, 27 mins.

Gefilte Fish

Three generations of women share their individual methods for making Gefilte Fish. 15 mins.
VHS: S12870. $25.95.

Great Cantors of the Golden Age

In 1931, during the Golden Age of *Chazzanut*, the New York film director Joseph Seiden produced *The Voice of Israel*, the only filmed record of some of the most famous cantors from 1910 to 1940. With restored selections from this footage, Dr. Max Wohlberg describes the history and artistry of these unparalleled vocal talents. Featuring Cantors Mordechai Hershman, Adolph Katchko, David Roitman, Yossele Rosenblatt, Joseph Shlisky and Gershon Sirota.
VHS: S16313. $54.00.
Murray E. Simon, USA, 1990, 54 mins.

Great Sadness of Zohara
Nina Menkes combines sound, image and fragments of poetry in this moving film about the journey of a young Jewish woman who is drawn to explore the world of the spirit. Her journey takes her to remote and increasingly desolate regions of the Arab lands—alienating her from the orthodox Jewish community in Israel. This mystical quest culminates in her return to Israel where, indelibly marked, she confronts her loneliness and a devastating sense of exile.
VHS: S07374. $39.95.
Nina Menkes, USA, 1983, 40 mins.

Guilt and Repentance
The major themes of the High Holy Day service are discussed by a panel of eminent Rabbis and scholars. Translations and interpretations of the texts are also included. 60 mins.
VHS: S24506. $29.95.

The Hasidim
A close look at this Jewish sect which originated in Russia in the 1700s and now has settled in neighborhoods in Brooklyn, NY. With Hasidic songs featured on the soundtrack. 29 mins.
VHS: S15534. $45.00.

Hassidism and Questions and Answers on Kabbalah
This tape takes us back to the 18th and 19th centuries and introduces us to information about Hassidism and the teachings of Baal Shem Tov. Tape includes a question and answer session. 119 mins.
VHS: S10518. $49.95.

Hassidut: Hassidic Music
Music is central for the Hassidic community. Famed Rabbi Nahman of Bratslav taught his students that one can pray not only through word but also through song. Filmed in the Hassidic community, beautiful melodies from prayers, celebrations and other significant events are included. 28 mins.
VHS: S21709. $39.95.

Hester Street
Set on the Lower East Side of New York in 1896, Gitl and her son reunite with husband Jake, who had previously immigrated from Russia. Jake has completely embraced America by shedding his ethnic heritage, and is embarrassed when Gitl clings to her old country ways. But in this charming and humorous portrait of the Jewish immigrant experience, Gitl finds a way to become victor instead of victim. Carol Kane was nominated for an Oscar for her portrayal of Gitl. With Stephen Keats.
VHS: S00564. $29.95.
Joan Micklin Silver, USA, 1974, 89 mins.

Hot Bagels: The Hole Story
A personable young bagel baker takes us on a tour through the bagel-making process, from its origins to contemporary methods. 12 mins.
VHS: S12869. $25.95.

I Ask for Wonder: Experiencing God
Prayer, study, ritual, tragedy and good deeds can all be pathways to God. Professors and Rabbis join forces to explain the value of these everyday experiences in the practice of Judaism. 60 mins.
VHS: S24504. $29.95.

Jewish American Patriots
Jewish American Patriots focuses on the largely neglected history of the contributions of Jews in the United States military. From 1644 through Operation Desert Storm, this documentary details the lives of the vast number of American Jews who fought in defense of their country. Dozens of Jewish patriots are highlighted, from George Washington's close friend, Haym Soloman, to the Jewish Veterans of Operation Desert Storm. 60 mins.
VHS: S27244. $29.95.

Jewish Communities of the Middle Ages
The Jewish communities of Babylonia, Spain and Ashkenaz were once sources for rich and varied Jewish life. This video examines each of these important historical Jewish cultures. 30 mins.
VHS: S23247. $39.95.

The Jewish Holidays Video Guide
The Cohen family invites viewers to experience the cycle of the Jewish calendar with their family. They rediscover the history and customs of the holy days, focusing on songs, stories, meals, games, prayers and rituals. Ed Asner, Theodore Bikel, Monty Hall and Judge Wapner are all featured. 90 mins.
VHS: S23010. $29.95.

The Jewish Museum: A Special View
In establishing communities all over the world, Jews have faced the constant challenge of adapting their ancient traditions to other cultures. In *The Jewish Museum*, viewers will see, through the art and artifacts shown, how this challenge has been met for nearly 4,000 years. Based on the collection of the Jewish Museum in New York City. 18 mins.
Home Video.
VHS: S09269. $29.95.
Public Performance.
VHS: S09270. $49.95.

Jewish Soul Music: The Art of Giora Feldman
Once they wandered all over Europe, small bands of Jewish soul musicians, owning neither land nor property. Musical know-how was passed from father to son, their music based on improvisation and musical skill. Giora Feldman is the fourth generation of such musicians, and his life is the story of the revival of Jewish soul music in our times. After 18 years with the Israel Philharmonic, he decided to return to his roots—to become a klezmer, a Jewish soul musician. This is his incredible story. 50 mins.
VHS: S10257. $39.95.

Jews of Djerba
Djerba, an island off the southeast coast of Tunisia, is home for a small and little known Jewish community. Djerbian Jews see their community as a living remnant of the Babylonian Jewish tradition created after the destruction of Solomon's temple over 2500 years ago. 26 mins.
VHS: S12895. $34.95.

A Jumping Night in the Garden of Eden
A wonderful documentary on the klezmer bands, Michael Goldman's film focuses on Kapelye of New York and the Klezmer Conservatory Band in Boston in a depiction of this emotional music of Eastern European Jews. Klezmer music, played at celebrations of Eastern European Jews, provides a vibrant record of cultures, revealing gypsy, Balkan, Turkish influences. And the current klezmer revival signals a reinventing of the past, as three generations of musicians keep klezmer alive. English and Yiddish with English subtitles.
VHS: S09351. $59.95.
Michael Oldman, USA, 1987, 75 mins.

Kabbalah and the Mystics
Go back in time to the mystics of the 16th and 17th centuries. Learn of the nine points and of the Rabbi's Holy Trinity—God, the Torah and Israel. 119 mins.
VHS: S10517. $49.95.

Kaddish
A riveting profile of a young Jewish activist coming to terms with his father's traumatic past during the Holocaust and the legacy of the struggle passed onto him. Yossi Klein is the young man who brings back the memory of his father Zoltan, a radiant and charming Hungarian Jew who escaped the round-up of Jews, hid out, and was spared the horrors of the Holocaust.
VHS: S09352. $39.95.
Steve Brand, USA, 1985, 92 mins.

Keshet ve Anan—Cloud and Rainbow
This series deals with Jewish Holidays, the Jewish calendar and other traditional events, and is primarily designed for children of the elementary and junior high level. Programs are in Hebrew. Each program is approximately 45 mins. Israel, 1989.
New Year and Sukkot.
VHS: S10461. $39.95.
Chanukah.
VHS: S10462. $39.95.
Tu B'Shvat and Purim.
VHS: S10463. $39.95.

Last Jews of Radauti (Song of Radauti)
In this film study of Jews in a small Rumanian town, we meet members of this dwindling community, including the rabbi and shokhet. Observed are the intimate expressions of Jewish life, preparing for the Sabbath, making challah, immersions in the mikveh. 25 mins.
VHS: S12897. $34.95.
Laurence Salzmann, Romania, 25 mins.

Last Journey
Before Nodar Djindjhashvili, a Soviet Jew, left his homeland for the final time, he made an odyssey that took him into 40 communities, spanning 10,000 miles. He recorded Jewish life wherever he found it—in the street, in synagogue, even in cemeteries. What he searches for is the face of Jewish identity. 24 mins.
VHS: S12899. $34.95.

Legendary Voices: Cantors of Yesteryear
In this unique compilation of cantorial greats, we are treated to memorable film recordings of such outstanding voices as David Roitman, Adolph Katchko, Leibele Waldman, Moishe Oysher and Yossele Rosenblatt. A wonderful tribute to a bygone era, and a treasured collector's item for Jewish music lovers everywhere. 45 mins.
VHS: S15406. $49.95.

Lodz Ghetto
This film covers the years 1940-1944 as it chronicles the 200,000 Jews trapped in the Polish ghettos during the German occupation. The film moves from the past and present; the script was developed from the diaries of the survivors and people left behind. Music by Wendy Blackstone. "Your blood turns to ice. To be unmoved by this film is to be made of stone" (*New York Daily News*).
VHS: S17891. $29.95.
Kathryn Taverna/Alan Adelson, USA, 1991

Miracle of Intervale Avenue
This sensitive exploration searches for the secrets of a once thriving Jewish community in the South Bronx that somehow continues despite the decay that surrounds it. The film shows a remarkable reality of Jews, Blacks and Puerto Ricans interacting and helping each other. What makes this film so moving is the cast of vital, complex and moving characters. 65 mins.
VHS: S06576. $59.95.

Morocco: The Music of Moroccan Jews
The Moroccan Jews of North Africa created their own unique musical form of expression by borrowing tunes from their Arab neighbors and adding Hebrew. Filmed in Morocco and Israel, this video focuses on the flavor and the poetry, messianic songs and rhythms that evolved into authentic Moroccan-Jewish music. 28 mins.
VHS: S21708. $39.95.

Now I Know My Aleph Bet
This two-volume set teaches the Hebrew alphabet in a classroom setting through Hebrew songs and Torah tales. Ideal for use in a school setting or at home.
VHS: S24803. $45.00.

An Oasis in Time
Through diaries, journals and personal reminiscences, Jews from many periods and places describe the importance of the Sabbath. There is great value in the age-old practice of one day a week set aside for rest and religious experience. 60 mins.
VHS: S24502. $29.95.

One Word, Many Texts
Edwin Newman hosts this video exploration of the importance placed in text and study within Judaism. Filmed at the Seminary, it shows how traditional texts are read to be relevant for succeeding generations. Includes The Genesis Seminar. 60 min.
VHS: S24499. $29.95.

Operation Moses: A Documentary
The epic story of the rescue, immigration and absorption of Ethiopian Jewry is told in this gripping documentary. Through testimonials and rare footage, we view the saga of a people saved from extinction by the efforts of the World Jewish community. 27 mins.
VHS: S12892. $29.95.

Passover at Bubbe's
Delightful Muppet-like characters create an irresistible cast in this program explaining the traditions and significance of the Passover holiday. USA.
VHS: S14950. $19.95.

A Passover Seder
Elie Wiesel, acclaimed author of over 30 books, shares his own memories and poetic interpretations regarding this holy ceremony. Mark Podwal provides the illustrations for this animated celebration. 30 mins.
VHS: S23945. $14.95.

Passover: Traditions of Freedom
This holiday commemorates the Jew's journey of freedom from the bonds of Egyptian slavery. History, literature, spirituality and even cooking are combined on this important occasion. Elements of the traditions of Passover are examined, including visits to a matzoh factory and a Passover winery, and four seders with Ashkenazic and Sephardic families.
VHS: S23091. $29.95.
John Nathan, USA, 1994, 57 mins.

Pier Marton: Say I'm a Jew
A collage of interviews with Jews who grew up in post war Europe as they describe their experiences. The film progresses from a "memory" of the Holocaust and early self-denial experiences, to a manifesto-like affirmation of Jewish identity. Directed by Pier Marton. 28 mins.
VHS: S13304. $69.95.

Pilgrimage of Remembrance: Jews in Poland Today
Of the three and a half million Jews who lived in Poland on the eve of World War II, only 6,000 remain. Yet, each year, more and more Jews from abroad come to pay homage to the birthplace of their ancestors. Filmed on location in 15 different cities and villages, Yaron Shemer's documentary enables us to see what remains of Jewish life in Poland today, while journeying through what was once a rich and glorious era.
VHS: S15404. $49.95.
Yaron Shemer, Poland, 48 mins.

Rambam Cures the King/ Uncle Pinchey Comes Home
Two informative works constructed in combinations of puppet theater and live action. *Rambam Cures the King* is an engaging work about the Biblical scholar Maimonides, who counsels and provides inspiration from advice influenced by the New Testament. *Rambam* is a thoughtful and serious examination of the Jewish pride, religious persecution and cultural identities. In the contemporary *Uncle Pinchey Comes Home*, a Russian immigrant confronts extreme cultural differences and strange adjustments when he goes to live with his Brooklyn relatives. 60 mins.
VHS: S19241. $9.98.

Regression in Time
Regress in time with Dr. Gelberman to the second century, where he reincarnates himself into his *former life*—the author of the Zokar, Rabbi Simeon bar Yohai. 119 mins.
VHS: S10516. $49.95.

Return to My Shtetl Delatyn
After 61 years, Berl Nachim Lindwer, accompanied by his son and granddaughter, returns to the shtetl he had loved. Formerly in Galicia and now in Poland/Ukraine, Berl walks the streets and views the houses he was never meant to see again. English narration and Dutch with English subtitles. 60 mins.
VHS: S23239. $39.95.

Return to the Jewish Ghetto of Venice
Of the 1300 Jews who lived in Venice before World War II, only ten families remain. Cut to the rhythm of Italian operas, this video combines Venetian textures with a distinctive Jewish tone that captures the life of this much diminished community. 28 mins.
VHS: S23257. $34.95.

Ritual: Three Portraits of Jewish Life
Morning prayer, the Sukkot festival and a brit milah offer three instances where ritual gives meaning and structure to life. This educational video offers learned opinions from Rabbis and religious experts. 60 mins.
VHS: S24498. $29.95.

Routes of Exile: A Moroccan Jewish Odyssey
This compelling look at the remnant of the Jewish community in Morocco provides a new perspective on the current crisis of Jews in a modern Arab state and in the Middle East. Shot on location, the film vividly portrays the ongoing odyssey of a 2,000 year old community whose remarkable journey is still unfolding. 90 mins.
VHS: S06579. $59.95.

Rugrats: A Rugrats Passover
The Rugrats babies are the key characters in this telling of the story of Passover. The Rugrats babies (and even some of the adults) don't seem to understand the manner of celebrating Passover, "a holiday without presents," and participating in a Passover Seder. When Grandpa tells them the story of Moses leading the Hebrews away from the Pharaoh and slavery, everyone finds something to believe in. Animated, 25 mins.
VHS: S27080. $9.98.

The Sabbath Bride
From sundown on Friday until dusk on Saturday, Jews cherish Shabbat as a sanctuary from the stresses and strains of the working week, a legacy passed from one generation to the next, and a symbol of the enduring strength of the Jewish people.
VHS: S16321. $90.00.
Naomi Gryn, Great Britain, 1987, 52 mins.

Saying Kaddish
Tovah Feldschuh, Phyllis Newman and Stephen Pearlman star in this hour-long drama about a Jewish family affirming life in the face of death. An underlying theme emphasizes the importance of community during times of crises. 60 mins.
VHS: S24505. $29.95.

A Secret Space
The story of David Goodman, the son of liberal, secular parents, who stumbles into an abandoned Lower East Side synagogue being reclaimed by a group of spiritual Jews looking for meaning in their lives. To the dismay of his parents, David becomes increasingly interested in his Jewish roots as he is welcomed into the community of worshipers. 80 mins.
VHS: S12868. $79.95.

Sepharad: Judeo-Spanish Music
Five hundred years after the expulsion of Spanish Jewry, the musical heritage of the Sephardim is alive and well. The film focuses on music first sung by Spanish singers in the Middle Ages, lullabies, wedding tunes, synagogue melodies and songs of mourning, performed in the rich traditional style of the Sephardim. 27 mins.
VHS: S21711. $39.95.

The Star, the Castle and the Butterfly
In the Jewish tradition, Prague is known as *ir va'em b'yisrael* or mother in the family of Israel. A city that has nurtured generations of scholars and sages, Prague's Jewish quarter now only hold memories and monuments to a past full of promise and hope. Hugo Gryn visits some of its most evocative sites.
VHS: S16322. $54.00.
Naomi Gryn, Great Britain, 1990, 25 mins.

The Story of Two Synagogues
In Chodorov, Poland, a 17th-century synagogue was decorated with paintings. Through the perspective of the painter, the lives of that place and time are recalled. Then in Curacao, a synagogue from 1732 serves as a bridge to the small but vibrant community of that tropical Carribean island. 17 mins.
VHS: S23259. $29.95.

Tales of the Days of Awe
Judaism has been described as theology in narrative. Dramatic readings of works by I.L. Peretz, Sholom Aleichem and Elie Wiesel demonstrate this thesis. Robert Blumenfeld and Rochelle Oliver read these legends. 60 mins.
VHS: S24507. $29.95.

The Talmud and the Scholar
Rabbi Adin Steinsaltz' modern translation of the Oral Law has brought this text to a new generation of English speakers. In this portrait, his warm and sensitive ways are revealed along with his singular, inspirational perspective. 58 mins.
VHS: S23261. $34.95.

Teiman: Music of Yemenite Jewry
Yemenite Jews have perfected singing and rhythm, drumming and dancing over centuries. World-renowned vocalists Ofra Haza and Noa (Acinoam Nini) are just some of the talented performers who illustrate the Yemeni rhythms that have conquered the world stage. 27 mins.
VHS: S21712. $39.95.

There's No Such Thing as a Chanukah Bush, Sandy Goldstein
A young Jewish girl, confronted with Christmas trees and a friend's Chanukah bush, longs to participate in this custom. Fortunately, her grandfather helps her realize the importance of preserving Jewish customs and appreciating other beliefs when he takes her to an office Christmas party. Ideal for studies in Jewish culture. Named Best Short Dramatic Adaptation of the 1993 Charleston Film Fest. 1993, 23 mins.
VHS: S25712. $295.00.

Voices from Sepharad
Five hundred years after Catholic monarchy expelled Jews from the Iberian peninsula, a changed Spain has begun to acknowledge the cultural riches created by coexistence and the contributions made by Jewish communities during the 15 centuries preceding their exile. In this remarkable seven-part series, *Voices from Sepharad* examines Sephardic Jewry from its roots—with a common language based in the cultures of medieval Spain that nurtured a unique style of poetry, music and folklore—to the modern day Sephardic communities scattered about Europe, North Africa, the Middle East and the Americas who have maintained their Hispanic ties.
VHS: S16810. $180.00.
Solly Wolodarsky, Spain/Israel/France, 1992, 364 mins.

West of Hester Street
With great warmth and humor, *West of Hester Street* interweaves the dramatized events of the movement of Jewish immigrants to Galveston, Texas, with the story of a young Jewish peddler who journeys from Russia to Texas. The late Sam Jaffe narrates the heart-warming story of these pioneers.
VHS: S11230. $39.95.
A. & C. Salzman Mondell, USA, 1983, 58 mins.

Where Is My Child?
This moving tale explores tragedy set against the massive exodus of European Jewry into the United States. With Celia Adler, Anna Lillian and Morris Strassberg. "Inevitably there was a price to be paid in terms of health, family ties and religion" (*Kansas City Jewish Chronicle*).
VHS: S18575. $54.00.
Abraham Left/Harry Lynn, USA, 1937, 92 mins.

Yehuda Amichai
Poems from *Selected Poetry of Yehuda Amichai* were read by this author on March 15, 1989, at Georgetown University in Washington, D.C. Lewis MacAdams interviewed this German-born Jewish poet who often captures the Jewish past in echoes from the Bible. From the *Lannan Literary Videos* series. 60 mins.
VHS: S27117. $19.95.

The Yiddishe Gauchos
This intriguing documentary tells the nearly forgotten tale of how Jewish immigrants to Argentina became a part of that country's ranching culture. These immigrants built schools, hospitals, libraries, theaters and agricultural coops in the wilderness. Narrated by Eli Wallach.
VHS: S23086. $54.00.
Mark Freeman, USA, 1989, 28 mins.

chinese CINEMA

The Blue Kite
Banned by the Chinese government, *The Blue Kite* provides a unique window into contemporary Chinese life and politics. During the Cultural Revolution in China a man called Teitou, his family and his friends all experienced the political and social upheavals that shook a continent. This scathing indictment of life under Chairman Mao was banned along with the filmmaker. Mandarin with English subtitles.
VHS: \$24377. \$79.95.
Laser: Widescreen. LD75374. \$49.98.
Tian Zhuangzhuang, China, 1993, 138 mins.

Breaking with Old Ideas
Produced during the last years of the Cultural Revolution in the People's Republic of China, a product of Mao Tse-Tung's concept of a new world in which all social relationships are transformed. The story concerns the building of a new college for workers and peasants. Chinese with English subtitles.
VHS: S02759. \$59.95.
Li Wen-Hua, China, 1975, 126 mins.

China, My Sorrow
An awestruck 13-year-old boy is arrested by Mao's cultural police for propagating obscene records during the Cultural Revolution. (He composed a love song for a 13-year-old girl.) Isolated in mountain corridors, the young boy befriends another teenage "terrorist" and an elderly Buddhist monk. He imparts on them the need to preserve their family structures and create a greater sense of self. "A deft and oddly lighthearted tribute to the traditions and the spirit of freedom that survived the Cultural Revolution" (Caryn James, *The New York Times*). With Guo Liang Yi and Tieu Quan Nghieu. Mandarin and Shanghaiese with English subtitles.
VHS: S19065. \$79.95.
Dai Sijie, China, 1989, 86 mins.

Crows and Sparrows
The most renowned of China's social commentary films of the 1940s. Jay Leyda called it "a milestone in Chinese film history, worthy to be shown alongside the best of international cinema." The tenants of a Shanghai boarding house struggle valiantly to keep their homes, triumphing when the greedy landlord is forced to flee the advancing Red Army. Completed on the eve of the Communist revolution, the film was saved from Kuyomintang confiscation by being hidden in the film studio ceiling. Mandarin with English subtitles.
VHS: S26491. \$59.95.
Zheng Junli, China, 1949, 111 mins.

Farewell My Concubine
This complex story of passion and political intrigue won the Best Film Award at Cannes and is an ambitious historical epic of China in the 20th century. It follows the enduring friendship between two opera stars in old Beijing. As they prosper, the political upheavals of war and revolution take their toll. When a young prostitute threatens their professional and personal union, it becomes just one of many trials which test the enduring strength of art and love that bind these two men.
VHS: S20736. \$96.95.
Laser: LD74457. \$39.99.
Chen Kaige, China, 1993, 157 mins.

Girl from Hunan
A sweeping portrait of a remote village in turn-of-the-century China struggling to hang on to its feudal traditions. Wedding brings a 12-year-old girl and a breast-fed, two-year-old boy together. As the girl matures, she challenges outlandish ideas of freedom and ends up with an illegitimate child. Her reality is made increasingly complicated as her boy is prepared to marry a few years later, according to tradition. A heightened criticism of feudal attitudes toward women, with a mysterious and affecting focus on the workings of nature; an example of recent Chinese cinema at its finest. Mandarin with English subtitles.
VHS: S15682. \$79.95.
Xie Fei/U Lan, China, 1986, 99 mins.

Go-Masters
A first co-production between Japan and the People's Republic of China, this amazing historical film is the story of a Chinese *go* player who travels to Japan in the 30's, but becomes disillusioned and attempts to escape back home. Set during 1924-1956, the go-master's life with a Japanese master's daughter is doomed as Sino-Japanese hostilities break out, and World War II begins. Grand Prize Winner at the Montreal Film Festival. Japanese and Chinese with English subtitles.
VHS: S07335. \$59.95.
J. Sato/D. Jishun, Japan/China, 1984, 121 mins.

The Horse Thief
The setting is the harsh, barren landscape of Tibet, which on film has a stark beauty not unlike the landscapes of American westerns. Here, amidst a series of tribal and Buddhist rituals captured wordlessly and in great detail, unfolds a tribal drama of theft, ostracism, and terrible retribution. A film of mystical dimensions, *The Horse Thief* is a breathtaking 'Scope epic which concentrates on a primitive way of life and manages to capture it with a surprising degree of sophistication. Mandarin with English subtitles. Full-screen letterbox format.
VHS: S13522. \$59.95.
Tian Zhuangzhuang, China, 1987, 88 mins.

Life on a String
Set in a distant, mythological past, this visually impressive film tells the story of a young boy's search for a possible cure for his blindness. He devotes his life to music and to breaking one thousand strings on a banjo. Chinese with English subtitles.
VHS: S17238. \$79.95.
Chen Kaige, China, 1990, 110 mins.

Mao's Little Red Video
Propaganda shown to the Chinese population during China's Cultural Revolution, intending to encourage the following behind Chairman Mao. 30 mins.
VHS: S13111. \$19.98.

Path of Glory
We follow a bunch of disparate recruits through police training, as they learn to trust each other and work as a team. Familiar enough territory, but this film retains an emphasis on character development, focusing especially on a traumatized former undercover cop who must undergo training a second time, that sets it apart from its companions in the genre. Mandarin with English subtitles. 1980.
VHS: S24185. \$49.95.

Red Firecracker Green Firecracker
A beautiful woman is torn between loyalty to her ancestral heritage and her sensual desire for a rebellious artist. A visually stunning film set against the close of the Ching Dynasty, this tale of forbidden love from award-winning director He Ping ignites the screen with passion. Cantonese with English subtitles.
VHS: S26694. \$99.98.
Laser: LD75383. \$49.98.
He Ping, China, 1994, 117 mins.

Song of China
A rare film, produced in China during 1936, dealing with a cavalcade of families through three generations. The film is timely in that it deals with the universal problem of the generation gap with great sensitivity. Featuring a native Chinese cast and authentic Chinese music on the soundtrack. With English subtitles. China, 1936, 75 mins.
VHS: S14813. \$29.95.

Stage Sisters
Stage Sisters chronicles the fortunes of two actresses in pre-revolutionary China who are separated by money and politics. One accedes to the unscrupulous demands of a wealthy impressario and becomes a famous stage star. The other remains virtuous and joins the revolution. This epic film shows how each lived through the events of civil war and revolution until they are reunited, both on and off the stage. Director Xie Jin has been making films for over 50 years and remains the most popular filmmaker in China. Mandarin with English subtitles.
VHS: S26492. \$59.95.
Xie Jin, China, 1965, 112 mins.

Temptation of a Monk
Joan Chen stars as a beautiful but destructive princess in this epic set in 7th-century China. This story of war, betrayal and merciless revenge is triggered when a general makes a fateful mistake. Now he is relentlessly pursued, as are his mother and his lover (Chen). Based on a book by Lilian Lee, author of *Farewell My Concubine*. Mandarin with English subtitles.
VHS: S26028. \$89.98.
Clara Law, China, 1994, 118 mins.

Wicked City
The wicked city of the title is the rough and tumble world of Hong Kong, only this time it's not gangsters but evil aliens who threaten decent people. The reptoids look ordinary as they work alongside humans but their goal would mean the demise of mankind. Based on the anime hit of the same name, this film blends the style of Hong Kong action films and Japanese sci-fi adventures. Cantonese with English subtitles.
VHS: S26607. \$89.98.
Peter Mak, China, 1995, 88 mins.

Women from the Lake of Scented Souls
At the center of this moving intergenerational family drama is an old legend about two girls. They drowned themselves in a local lake and were said to have flown away as beautiful birds. A contemporary entrepreneur succeeds in business despite her drunken, abusive husband. Now she faces the chore of putting another woman into an unhappy arranged marriage because her mentally ill son desires a wife. Can this older, wiser woman prevent another drowning? Co-winner of the Golden Bear at the 1993 Berlin Film Festival. Mandarin with English subtitles.
VHS: S25832. \$89.95.
Xie Fei, China, 1993, 106 mins.

Women's Story
The plight of Chinese women seen from a woman's point of view. A poignant tale of three peasant women who flee their village to taste freedom in the big city and escape the sexist oppression of rural China. Praised for its feminist viewpoint, Berenice Reynaud calls it "the very stuff every modern woman's life is made of." Special Jury Prize, Paris Women's Film Festival. Mandarin with English subtitles.
VHS: S26493. \$59.95.
Peng Xiaolian, China, 1989, 96 mins.

The Wooden Man's Bride
Two lovers are joined in forbidden love in this tempestuous drama. Kui must deliver a beautiful bride to her new family. While she is en route, kidnappers intervene and before she can reach her husband, he dies. Despite this turn of fortune, she must marry him in effigy, forcing her into an illicit affair with the man she really loves. Mandarin with English subtitles.
VHS: S27753. \$99.99.
Laser: LD75577. \$39.99.
Huang Jianxin, China, 1995, 114 mins.

Yellow Earth
A striking collaboration between two Fifth Generation Chinese filmmakers, director Chen Kaige (*Farewell My Concubine*) and Zhang Yimou (*Raise the Red Lantern*), who photographed the film in deep, stylized colors. Set in spring, 1939, a young soldier researching folk songs enters a small community and gets emotionally entangled with an old man, his 14-year-old daughter and his younger son. The film's conflict is set up by the young woman's attraction to the soldier. With Xue Bai, Wang Xueqi, Tan Tuo and Liu Qiang. Mandarin with English subtitles.
VHS: S19445. \$19.98.
Chen Kaige, China, 1984, 89 mins.

ZHANG YIMOU

Ju Dou
The erotic thriller that China didn't want you to see is now on video. An exquisitely photographed and smartly performed drama of secret love and hidden faces. Trouble closely follows passion when a beautiful young bride is drawn to the handsome, strong nephew of her new husband, an ancient and disagreeable owner of an isolated dye factory. With excellent performances by Gong Li, Li Bao-tan, Li Wei and Zhang Li. Mandarin with English subtitles.
VHS: S15072. \$19.98.
Laser: LD75211. \$34.98.
Zhang Yimou, China/Japan, 1989, 98 mins.

Raise the Red Lantern
The third feature of Zhang Yimou stars the beautiful Gong Li as a 20-year-old college student who leaves school to become the fourth wife of a wealthy, powerful aristocrat. Her presence occasions a series of bitter jealousies and disputes with the three other wives. A fascinating work about sex, oppression and patriarchy. Mandarin with English subtitles.
VHS: S17881. \$19.98.
Zhang Yimou, China/Taiwan, 1991, 125 mins.

Red Sorghum
A visually spectacular film which is a sweeping modern-day fable. The first part tells of a nervous young bride's arrival at a remote provincial winery and her takeover of the family business when her older husband is mysteriously murdered. The second half is a heroic and harrowing drama focused on the brutality of the Japanese during their occupation of China, and on partisan resistance. "The film's exoticism is palpable, almost intoxicating" (David Edelstein, *The Village Voice*). Mandarin with yellow English subtitles.
VHS: S15392. \$79.95.
Zhang Yimou, China, 1987, 91 mins.

The Story of Qiu Ju
In this comedy a woman seeks justice for a simple slight against her husband. Along the way, she encounters a welter of bureaucracy and politesse in this well-observed portrait of contemporary Chinese life. Chinese with English subtitles.
VHS: S20709. \$19.95.
Laser: LD72382. \$34.95.
Zhang Yimou, China, 1993, 100 mins.

To Live
Winner of the 1994 Cannes Palme d'Or, Zhang Yimou's daring political tale of modern China landed him in major difficulties with the Chinese authorities. *To Live* follows a contemporary family across the turbulent face of modern China, from the Japanese invasion through Mao's Great Leap Forward and the Cultural Revolution. The powerful drama is made all the more potent by strong performances from Gong Li. Mandarin Chinese with English subtitles.
VHS: S25900. \$19.98.
Zhang Yimou, China, 1994, 132 mins.

HONG KONG CINEMA

3 Wishes
A priest is denied entry into the afterlife because he has been too good. Instead, the gods order the priest back to Earth to take nine lives, thereby balancing his good deeds. Somehow the priest gets stuck in a peculiar container until an unsuspecting tour conductor sets him free. As a sign of his gratitude, the priest grants him three wishes. Hong Kong, Mandarin with English subtitles.
VHS: S27264. \$49.95.

Aces Go Places II
An extremely likable mixture of Keystone Cops-style slapstick combined with James Bond shenanigans and Cantonese humor, again featuring the fancy-free jewel thief King Kong (Sam Hui). With Sylvia Chang and Carl Mak. Cantonese with English subtitles.
VHS: S13478. \$49.95.
Eric Tsang, Hong Kong, 1983, 100 mins.

Aces Go Places III
(Our Man from Bond Street)
The third in the popular *Aces Go Places* series, featuring handsome Sam Hui as a debonair master thief. Cantonese with English subtitles.
VHS: S14851. \$49.95.
Eric Tsang, Hong Kong, 1982, 94 mins.

Ah Ying
Director Allen Fong's most distinguished work after *Father and Son*. Peter Wang (the director and star of *A Great Wall*) plays a film director trying to start a project in Hong Kong while moonlighting as a lecturer on film. He enters into a Svengali-like relationship with Ah Ying, aspiring actress and fish market vendor. Cantonese with English subtitles.
VHS: S14871. \$49.95.
Allen Fong, Hong Kong, 1983, 110 mins.

Alan & Eric—
Between Hello and Goodbye
The melodrama of two friends (Alan Tam and Eric Tsang) who are reunited after a long separation. Alan is an aspiring singer about to make it big, while Eric has led an unsettled life as a merchant seaman. They decide to run a poultry farm together, but soon a wedge appears between them in the form of Maggie Cheung. It seems they are destined to be separated once again, until they are unexpectedly reunited in San Francisco. Chinese with English subtitles. Hong Kong, 1991.
VHS: S25927. \$49.95.

All About Ah-Long
Chow Yun Fat is a truck driver raising his son alone. This drama is complicated by the return of his former wife. A struggle ensues as the three try to reunify the family. In the end, Chow Yun Fat's character returns to his earlier passion as motorcycle racer for the film's climactic finale. Winner of the 1990 Hong Kong Academy Award for Best Actor. Mandarin with English subtitles.
VHS: S27265. \$49.95.
Johnny To, Hong Kong, 1989, 100 mins.

All for the Winner
"What you see in front of you is not concrete, it's money," explains one of the characters in this spoof of the Hong Kong genre of the gambling movie. Naive Stephen Chow is newly arrived in Hong Kong. His opportunistic uncle quickly discovers that Chow has supernatural powers, such as being able to see through cards and predict the winners of races. His uncle promptly gets him involved in a high stakes gambling tournament, through which the insouciant Chow blithely sails, until love threatens to deprive him of his powers. Chinese with English subtitles. Hong Kong, 1990.
VHS: S25928. \$49.95.

All Men are Brothers—
Blood of the Leopard
One of the best of the period sword epics, lavishly produced and photographed in compositions often resembling Chinese landscape paintings come to life. It's the story of an honest general whose sense of duty allows him to be manipulated by scheming courtiers and ambitious rivals. All the while he resists the aid of his sworn brother, a rough-and-tumble monk. With Tony Leung and Joey Wang. Chinese with English subtitles. Hong Kong, 1993.
VHS: S25929. \$49.95.

All's Well, End's Well
The harmonious life of a family is disrupted by a series of romantic complications in the lives of three brothers in this goofy comedy. First, the long-suffering wife of self-centered Raymond Wong leaves, to be replaced by his new girlfriend, less dedicated to maintaining the house than to spending money. Then radio star Stephen Chow gets knocked on the head, sending him into full Jerry Lewis mode, while a frustrated Maggie Cheung tries to figure out how to end this aggravating condition. Finally, there's the reluctant romance between the swishy Leslie Cheung and his butch, motorcycle-riding cousin. Plenty of Hollywood movies get parodied, including *Ghost*, *Pretty Woman* and *The Terminator*. Chinese with English subtitles. Hong Kong, 1992.
VHS: S25930. \$99.95.

Angel Force
Li Chek Man is a low-ranking woman cop in Hong Kong who finds herself called upon for a secret mission to rescue a fellow agent in Thailand. Her fighting prowess, with the backup of a crack team of warriors, saves the day in this action-packed film, but not before some serious battles are waged. Dubbed in English.
VHS: S22759. \$44.95.
Po-Fa Hwa, Hong Kong, 1994, 95 mins.

The Assassin
A reflective tale taking place over a number of years, set in ancient China, about the making of a hero. Stoic Jimmy Wang (Wang Yu) must weigh his filial obligations and the possibilities of living a normal, happy, domestic life against his duties to his country and his desire to fulfill the heroic destiny he feels lies within him, as he decides whether to assassinate a usurping prime minister. Chinese with English subtitles. Hong Kong, 1985.
VHS: S25932. \$49.95.

Autumn Moon
It all begins when a young Japanese tourist encounters a 15-year-old girl on the streets of Hong Kong. Though the tourist is caught up with shooting video footage and finding bargains, he connects with the girl, in part, because he is also searching for food. Fortunately, the girl's grandmother casts a magic spell that leads the young man into a friendship of deepening intensity with the young woman. Naturally, an erotic interest cannot be avoided. English and Cantonese with English subtitles.
VHS: S26522. \$59.95.
Clara Law, Hong Kong, 1992, 108 mins.

An Autumn's Tale
Director Mabel Cheung attended NYU film school, and this bittersweet romantic drama grew out of her own experiences in Manhattan's lower east side. A naive young woman named Jennifer (Cherie Chung) follows her obnoxious boyfriend from Hong Kong to New York only to find him enjoying the affections of an attractive Chinese-American and planning to move to another city. Jennifer is forced to rely on her rough-edged, and often vulgar, older cousin Sampan (Chow Yun Fat) for companionship and advice. Cantonese with English subtitles.
VHS: S13459. \$49.95.
Mabel Cheung, Hong Kong, 1987, 98 mins.

The Banquet
Produced to raise money for flood victims in China, this is a comedy about a greedy land developer who convinces his father to live with him as part of a scheme to dupe a Kuwaiti prince. The chief entertainment, however, is the parade of Hong Kong stars making cameo appearances, including Gong Li, Leslie Cheung, Stephen Chow, Michael Hui and John Woo. Among those appearing in the story itself are Andy Lau, Jackie Cheung and Samo Hung. Chinese with English subtitles. Hong Kong, 1991.
VHS: $25933. $49.95.

BB30
The title of the movie comes from the license of a doctor's car, stolen by a bungling lawyer (Kenny Bee), who wants to buy the car. The budding romance between the lawyer and the doctor is complicated further when he takes a malpractice suit against her partner and a loan shark starts threatening everyone over a debt owed by the lawyer's cousin. Chinese with English subtitles. Hong Kong, 1990.
VHS: $25934. $49.95.

Beach of the War Gods
Another spin on the *Seven Samurai* tale, this time with Ming Dynasty Chinese villagers, led by an itinerant swordsman played by Jimmy Wang (Wang Yu), banding together to fortify their town and throw back invading Japanese. Chinese with English subtitles.
VHS: $25935. $49.95.
Wang Yu, Hong Kong, 1971

Best Friend of the Cops
Jackie Cheung plays an ex-cop, now a con-man, who dupes a bunch of policemen who are all too ready to be taken in by his scheme. They think they're putting up money to be used as capital in a loan-sharking operation. An off-beat offering in a genre that rarely strays from well-worn paths. Chinese with English subtitles. Hong Kong, 1990.
VHS: $25936. $49.95.

Best of the Best
The story of a policeman in love with the daughter of a gangster, a man who was also once a cop and rival of the hero's father, and who definitely doesn't want his daughter going out with a cop. An above-average mixture of sentiment and violence, filled with a sense of fatalism and funeral images. Chinese with English subtitles.
VHS: $25937. $49.95.
Herman Yau, Hong Kong, 1992

A Better Tomorrow
Kit is an up-and-coming cop, but his brother Ho is a street-hardened criminal. Soon they are both dragged into a savage underworld battle over counterfeit money. Even if Ho wants to go straight, there is a murderous price to pay that forces the brothers into a deadly confrontation.
VHS: $13455. $19.98.
John Woo, Hong Kong, 1986, 90 mins.

A Better Tomorrow—Part III
Chow Yun Fat returns as Mark Gor, the stylish police detective, in this sequel which is actually a prequel. Set in 1974, Gor and his cousin (Tony Leung) want to escape the post-war squalor of Saigon. Unfortunately, both are in love with the same woman (Anita Mui), a gangster moll. This action-filled adventure is loaded with plot twists, outrageously choreographed violent sequences, and a love triangle that leads to tragedy. Also known as *Love and Death in Saigon*. Mandarin with English subtitles.
VHS: $27267. $49.95.
Tsui Hark, Hong Kong, 1989, 114 mins.

Bitter Taste of Blood
A young man trying to escape a life of crime hides out on a farm on an island after refusing "one last job," while he waits for a friend to arrange a passage for him to Taiwan. He seems to find a place on the farm, falling in love with the daughter of the farm's owner. Unfortunately, he cannot escape his past so easily, as his old gang is looking for him and he is harassed by locals resentful of his relationship with the girl. Chinese with English subtitles. Hong Kong, 1986.
VHS: $25938. $49.95.

The Black Wall
Great location shooting in the crowded streets of Hong Kong marks this pessimistic tale of a young man, discontented with the life he is leading, but not knowing how to sever his ties with the gang he has grown up with. Chinese with English subtitles. Hong Kong, 1989.
VHS: $25939. $49.95.

Bloody Hero
A group of outlaws from the mainland are given shelter at a wealthy man's house in Hong Kong, then must flee to the Philippines when a counterfeiting deal goes wrong. Once there, they attempt to double-cross their old benefactor, leading to a bloody confrontation. Chinese with English subtitles.
VHS: $25963. $49.95.
Addy Sung, Hong Kong, 1990

Blue Lightning
After his mother is murdered, a 12-year-old boy must go to live with his estranged father (Danny Lee), an alcoholic ex-cop wallowing in self-pity. Under the influence of the young boy, Lee begins to clean himself up and starts investigating the murder of his ex-wife, assisted by a couple of detectives who have also taken an interest in the boy's welfare, in this glitzy, well-crafted picture. Chinese with English subtitles.
VHS: $25964. $49.95.
Raymond Lee, Hong Kong, 1991

Born Invincible
Some nimble kung-fu in this low-budget flick as a series of students attempt to learn enough to overcome an apparently invisible white-haired villain who has only one vulnerable spot on his body (of which no one knows the location). Chinese with English subtitles. Hong Kong, 1983.
VHS: $25965. $49.95.

Brave Young Girls
Several young women fall into the clutches of gangsters, including an illegal immigrant, a karate champ, and a girl sold into prostitution by her mother. Their only hope lies in cooperating with another woman, a tough cop from Japan pursuing arms smugglers. Chinese with English subtitles. Hong Kong, 1990.
VHS: $25966. $49.95.

The Bride with White Hair
This 1994 Hong Kong Film Award Winner stars Leslie Cheung and Briget Lin in a beautifully filmed story about a pair of star-crossed lovers. Leslie Cheung has several expertly executed sword-play scenes. Mandarin with English subtitles.
Laser: Letterboxed. LD75499. $59.95.
Ronnie Yu, Hong Kong, 1993

Bruce Lee and the Green Hornet
A rare screen test of the martial arts icon and charismatic figure Bruce Lee, on the making of the television series *The Green Hornet*, with three complete, uncut episodes and a short film on the making of Robert Clouzet's *Enter the Dragon*, the actor's fullest and most satisfying work. 90 mins.
VHS: $17577. $19.95.

Bruce Lee Gift Set
The charismatic and kinetic kung fu action star Bruce Lee displays his balletic movements in four different works: *The Chinese Connection*, *Fists of Fury*, *Return of the Dragon* and *Game of Death*.
VHS: $19096. $49.98.

Bruce Lee: The Lost Interview
Martial arts expert Lee became world-renowned for his performances in such Kung-fu classics as *Enter the Dragon*. Now his only interview in English is available. Just after the release of his first film, *The Big Boss*, he spoke in Hong Kong with Canada's premiere journalist Pierre Barton. This is the closest one can get to this extraordinary master. 30 mins.
VHS: $23116. $19.95.

Bullet in the Head
John Woo's epic tale of three friends (Tony Leung, Jackie Cheung and Waise Lee) caught up in the turbulent events of the 1960s in Hong Kong and later, in Vietnam, where the three hope to exploit the anarchy and corruption that prevail, only to find themselves in danger of being overwhelmed by it. Their drama is played out in a country captured by such filmic precedents as *The Deer Hunter*, *Platoon* and *Missing in Action*, seemingly an ideal setting for Woo to explore his themes of loyalty, honor and betrayal. Chinese with English subtitles.
VHS: $20584. $49.95.
John Woo, Hong Kong, 1990

Cageman
A touching, nicely detailed study of a group of long-term inhabitants of a cagehouse, a sort of flophouse where everyone gets an individual cage, little larger than a bed, for themselves. When the building is slated for demolition, the tenants must decide whether to get what compensation they can, or to fight the eviction. The process is complicated by two ambitious local politicians who decide to live for a few days in the cagehouse, now the center of media attention. Chinese with English subtitles. Hong Kong, 1992.
VHS: $25940. $49.95.

Call Girl 1988
A housewife, a runaway and a television star all end up in a call girl ring. This film offers both comedy and serious drama. The male customers search endlessly for satisfaction while the three women reveal the deep sadness involved in their choice of professions. Mandarin with English subtitles.
VHS: $27268. $49.95.
David Lam, Hong Kong, 1988

Casino Raiders
Andy Lau and Alan Tam play lifelong buddies, gamblers trying to leave their former way of life, but they run afoul of some very nasty Japanese gangsters. At the same time, the different paths they have taken away from gambling are forcing them apart. With Rosamund Kwan. Chinese with English subtitles. Hong Kong, 1989.
VHS: $25941. $49.95.

Casino Tycoon II (Part A)
Andy Lau is the general manager of a large casino, adept at balancing the legitimate operations of the casino with the claims of two rival gangs on a part of its profits. When his son is killed, he has to deal with the presence of an unknown rival within his own organization, as well as decide whether to continue his relationship with a beautiful reporter (Joey Wang), or remain with his crippled wife. We are unsure what the *(Part A)* of the title refers to, since the movie is complete—normally it would mean that it was part of a two-tape set. Chinese with English subtitles.
VHS: $25942. $49.95.
Wong Jing, Hong Kong, 1992

Cinema of Vengeance
This documentary on Hong Kong kung fu/action films comments not only on the popular kung fu films of the 1980s but on the entire history of Hong Kong action films. Clips from rare movies and interviews with stars and directors such as Samo Hung, Jackie Chan and Bruce Lee are featured. English and Chinese with English subtitles.
VHS: $27382. $29.95.
Toby Russell, Great Britain, 1994

City Cops
An FBI informant flees the country for Hong Kong where he is sought by a resourceful FBI agent (Cynthia Rothrock), a couple of HK cops, and a lot of gangsters. The fight sequences involving Rothrock distinguish this picture from a mass of similar stories. Mandarin with English subtitles (occasionally cropped).
VHS: $24141. $49.95.
Lau Kar Wing, Hong Kong

City Kids
Gritty tale of two friends growing up on the mean streets of Hong Kong, attempting to overcome the violence and poverty that form their surroundings. One of them wants to go straight, but will loyalty to his troubled childhood pal drag him down? Mandarin with English subtitles.
VHS: $24142. $49.95.
Poon Man Kit, Hong Kong, 1989

City on Fire
Cinema City's answer to *The French Connection* stars Chow Yun Fat as a plain-clothes cop out to bust a syndicate of jewel thieves. Cantonese with English subtitles.
VHS: $13477. $49.95.
Ringo Lam, Hong Kong, 1987, 98 mins.

City Squeeze
A petty and bullying boss hires an attractive public relations officer in an attempt to cheat on his domineering wife, but his plans are complicated when she must work with his put-upon general manager to secure a large contract for the company. The two are drawn together in spite of the comic conflicts thrown in their way. With Kenny Bee. Semi-letterboxed. Mandarin with English subtitles.
VHS: $24143. $49.95.
Clifton C.S. Ko, Hong Kong, 1989

City War
This time the team of Chow Yun Fat and Ti Lung appear on the right side of the law, as a police investigator and a plain-clothes cop who match wits with a vengeful gangster. Cantonese with English subtitles.
VHS: $13469. $49.95.
Sun Chung, Hong Kong, 1989, 100 mins.

Close Escape
Med student finds himself on the run after his brother, unbeknownst to him, rips off stolen diamonds from a mobster, in this above-average crime drama. His friends must locate him before he unwittingly reveals the location of the diamonds. With Aaron Kwok. Mandarin with English subtitles (a bit cropped).
VHS: $24144. $49.95.
Wing Chow, Hong Kong, 1989

A Collection of Chow Yun Fat
Three action-packed films featuring Chow Yun Fat are joined in this video collection. In *Prison on Fire II* a man escapes from prison in order to see his young son. Captured, he must face prison once again, only this time his term is complicated by a new danger. A guard frames him. *Full Contact* follows the story of a gunman double-crossed by a gay villain and a killer. This tale of revenge is tinged with an underlying homoerotic interest. *A Better Tomorrow III* is set in war-ravaged Vietnam. Escape is imperative, but only a gunslinging beauty can help Chow Yun Fat's character leave Vietnam. In Cantonese with English subtitles. The first two are directed by Ringo Lam while the last is directed by Tsui Hark.
VHS: $26517. $79.95.

Comet Butterfly and Sword
This epic battle pits abusive eunuchs against the forces of good. Court intrigues threaten to destroy the Ming Dynasty but a loyal and patriotic farmer, Uncle Lee of the West Wing, teams up with Lady Kao to defeat the forces of chaos. Of course there are plenty of martial arts battles and swordplay on the road to preserving harmony in the Middle Kingdom. Dubbed in English.
VHS: $21828. $49.95.
D J Mike, Hong Kong, 1994

The Contract
Zany Hui Brothers comedy as trio aspires to land contracts for variety shows at TV station. Not so much a plot as a framework on which to hang some fine extended comic sequences. With Michael, Ricky and Samuel Hui. Mandarin with English subtitles (occasionally cropped at edges).
VHS: $24145. $49.95.
Michael Hui, Hong Kong, 1978

Couples, Couples, Couples
Typical romantic comedy about three couples attempting to resolve their difficulties, of course complicating the process along the way. Includes plenty of what passes for humor about AIDS in Hong Kong. Good natured, though. Mandarin with English subtitles (occasionally cropped, but plot easy to follow). 1987.
VHS: $24146. $49.95.

Crocodile Hunter
Andy Lau plays a cop who really should retire, since he's got a bullet lodged in his head. But, no, he's got to come back to track down some dangerous escaped criminals. To make this more difficult, he's saddled with an oafish partner and a couple of obnoxious civilian leads in the case. See chopsticks used as a weapon here. Chinese with English subtitles. Hong Kong, 1989.
VHS: $25943. $49.95.

The Crow
Brandon Lee stars in this exciting and mysterious thriller about a man with strange powers. After a terrible crime, only revenge and justice can drive a man to the extremes that define *The Crow*. Brandon Lee, the son of Bruce Lee, is astounding in this, his last film.
VHS: $22157. $96.98.
Alex Proyas, USA, 1993, 100 mins.

Curry and Pepper
The Starsky and Hutch of Hong Kong cop movies. The irreverent duo battle criminals and their own superiors, but perhaps the biggest test of their friendship comes when they both vie for the attention of a glamorous reporter doing a documentary on them. 1990.
VHS: $24147. $49.95.

The Cyprus Tigers
A trio of happy-go-lucky cops living on Cyprus try to break up a counterfeiting ring headed by a prominent local businessman, while competing with each other and antagonizing their boss. Sure are a lot of Chinese living in Cyprus…Mandarin with English subtitles (occasionally cropped at edges). 1990.
VHS: $24148. $49.95.

Daddy, Father, and Pa Pa
A clever but lonely boy, neglected by his materialistic parents, suddenly finds himself being chased by a criminal gang. Desperate to find him, his mother enlists the aid of two men from her past by telling them that they are each his true father. During the course of the ensuing comic adventures, the three men learn to look beyond their shallow ways. Semi-letterboxed. Mandarin with English subtitles.
VHS: $24149. $49.95.
Clifton C.S. Ko, Hong Kong, 1991

The Dead and the Deadly
Vulgar humor, distinctive local color and amazing martial arts sequences distinguish this story of a young man who experiments with the sorcerer's arts. With Samo Hung and Yuen Biao. Cantonese with English subtitles.
VHS: $13484. $49.95.
Wu Ma, Hong Kong, 1982, 90 mins.

Death by Misadventure: The Mysterious Life of Bruce Lee
An in-depth exploration of the life and death of Bruce Lee, featuring rare footage from his early films. There are numerous television clips of Lee, including Lee with his young son Brandon and Lee breaking boards and demonstrating his famous one-inch punch. Unlike other documentaries on Lee, this film includes details of his death, including interviews with George Lazenby (who was waiting for him the night he died) and his doctor.
VHS: $27381. $29.95.
Toby Russell, Great Britain/Hong Kong, 1994, 90 mins.

Deception
Stylish story of various levels of deception, betrayal and murder among three women. A businesswoman finds herself being blackmailed, but who can she trust to help her? Her longtime associate, about to be left behind as the company moves to Canada, or her unscrupulous stockbroker? Interesting also in that virtually all the major roles are played by women. With Joey Wang. Mandarin with English subtitles. 1989.
VHS: $24150. $49.95.

Diary of the Big Man
Major Hong Kong hunk Chow Yun Fat at his most Cary Grant-like. Chow plays an attractive womanizer with two wives and two households. Of course keeping the two separate is more than a full time job, and when Chow finally slips up, comic complications ensue. Cantonese with English subtitles. Hong Kong.
VHS: $14874. $49.95.

Dragon Fight
Jet Li plays a member of a touring martial arts team stranded in San Francisco when he tries to stop his teammate (C.L.Tu) from defecting. His friend ends up working for organized crime gangs, though, and Li is drawn toward an ultimate confrontation with his former pal. Nice locations and well-staged action with great stunts by Li. Mandarin with English subtitles (occasionally cropped at edges).
VHS: $24152. $49.95.
Billy Tang, Hong Kong, 1989

Dragon: The Bruce Lee Story
An appealing biography of Bruce Lee, the Hong Kong superstar whose mysterious death, at age 33, certified his legend. Jason Scott Lee plays the kung-fu star. With Lauren Holly as Lee's widow Linda.
VHS: $19527. $95.98.
Laser: LD72296. $39.98.
Laser: Widescreen (Lin Ching-Hsai) at LD74836. $69.98.
Rob Cohen, USA, 1993, 119 mins.

Dragons of the Orient
Key martial arts sites, including Shaolin temple, are visited by a group of reporters in this documentary film. Demonstrations of various feats, including sword swallowing, rolling in glass and fire walking, are included. A short history of the mainland Chinese martial arts champion, Jet Li, is also featured. Mandarin with English subtitles.
VHS: $27296. $49.95.
Rocky Law, Hong Kong, 1993

Dream Lovers
This passionate love story, spiced with supernatural elements, alternates between the high fashion/high tech world of contemporary Hong Kong and the mysterious Qin dynasty. When a young orchestra conductor (Chow Yun Fat) meets the daughter of a famous archeologist (Lin Ching-Hsai) at an exhibition of the Qin Emperor's terra cotta army, an affair from the past is reborn and tragedy strikes again. Cantonese with English subtitles.
VHS: $13460. $49.95.
Tony Au, Hong Kong, 1986, 95 mins.

Drunken Tai-Chi
Chen Nu Tsai is the evil boss of Salt Manor. His son, Chen Duo, is a talented fighter who strives for justice. After he harms an opponent, Chen Duo loses his entire family and emerges penniless and alone. Befriended by a top Tai-Chi master, he triumphs by seeking retribution and learning the lesson of gracious generosity. Dubbed in English.
VHS: $22758. $44.95.
Yuang Ho-Ping, Hong Kong, 1994, 95 mins.

Dynamo
Martial arts expert Bruce Li plays a taxi driver who looks like Bruce Lee and also happens to be an expert kung-fu fighter, in this martial arts classic. Dubbed in English. Hong Kong, 81 mins.
VHS: $20571. $39.98.

Enter the Dragon

Bruce Lee is probably the name that comes to mind for most Americans when they think of martial arts action films. Here the stern-faced Lee infiltrates a strange tournament on an island fortress. With John Saxon and Jim Kelly. In English.
VHS: $14867. $49.95.
Laser: LD72261. $34.98.
Robert Clouse, USA, 1973, 97 mins.

Executioners

In a post-nuclear world, water is in short supply. Underworld figures plot to control this precious commodity, but three women stand in their way. These women blaze a trail studded with martial arts feats in their quest to save the world. This sequel to *Heroic Trio* is a must for Hong Kong action and martial arts film enthusiasts. Mandarin with English subtitles.
VHS: $27269. $49.95.
Chiung Siu Tung, Hong Kong, 1993

An Eye for an Eye

When an aging crime boss trying to go legit is framed for a murder, his daughter (Joey Wang) is forced to take over the business. She soon finds herself under the control of the men who framed her father in the first place. Meanwhile, she is loved by two detectives investigating the organization, throwing doubt on their ability to objectively pursue the case. Chinese with English subtitles. Hong Kong, 1990.
VHS: $25931. $49.95.

Fate of Lee Khan

A truly astounding martial arts/historical drama from one of the foremost innovators of the *wu xia pian* genre (swordplay film). Lee Khan must accept his destiny as revolution against the Mongol rulers of the Yuan dynasty swirls around him. Cantonese with English subtitles.
VHS: $13485. $49.95.
King Hu, Hong Kong, 1973, 107 mins.

Fight Back to School

Action-comedy with current Hong Kong favorite Stephen Chow starring as an impetuous cop whose undisciplined behavior earns him one last chance, going undercover as a high school student to recover a stolen pistol, doubly horrible for Chow since he became a cop because he hated school in the first place. The expected misadventures ensue as Chow goes from loathing the school to becoming an all-too-popular fixture there. Mandarin with English subtitles.
VHS: $24153. $49.95.
Gordon Chan, Hong Kong, 1991

Final Victory

Veering from comedy to pathos, this is the story of the unassertive guy who is given the task of watching over his criminal brothers' mistresses while he serves his jail sentence. Things are complicated when he falls in love with one of the women and must cope with the wrath of his brother, soon to be released from prison. Mandarin with English subtitles.
VHS: $24154. $49.95.
Patrick Tam, Hong Kong, 1987

First Time Is the Last Time

Strong, unsensational drama is set in a woman's prison, focusing chiefly on two of the inmates, one in jail for the first time in order to protect her low-life boyfriend, and another, long-term prisoner with the reputation of being a crazy loner, whose story is told in flashback form, the flashbacks rendered in a vivid, kinetic style which contrasts with the subdued colors and control of the prison. Mandarin with English subtitles (sometimes a bit cropped at the edges). 1989.
VHS: $24156. $49.95.

A Fishy Story

Elegant melodrama of an affair between an aspiring starlet (Maggie Cheung) and a cab driver, set against the backdrop of turbulent 60's Hong Kong. Each must choose between the struggle to maintain their relationship and the easier but less fulfilling paths that are offered them. Mandarin with English subtitles (often chopped on right side—no difficulty following the story though).
VHS: $24155. $49.95.
Anthony Chan, Hong Kong, 1990, 99 mins.

Flirting

Seamy tale of adultery and murder, a mix of straight melodrama and exploitation pic about a dispute between two friends over a Thai wife, which leads to dire consequences. Mandarin with English subtitles (sometimes a bit washed out).
VHS: $24157. $49.95.
Lee Tai Hay, Hong Kong, 1988

Flower Drums of Fung Yang

Two lovers are cast out of their village to wander the roads of China. In order to survive, the wife becomes an itinerant singer, until she is kidnapped by bandits terrorizing the region, the leader of whom turns out to be her long-lost brother. Mandarin with English subtitles. 1981.
VHS: $24158. $49.95.

For Your Heart Only

Teen romantic comedy, as a group of exuberant boys takes over the apartment of one of the better-off of the gang and a romance evolves between two classmates. Mandarin with English subtitles.
VHS: $24160. $49.95.

Forbidden Arsenal

Decent action flick, utilizing the popular device of cooperation between characters from Hong Kong, Taiwan and the mainland, in this case three cops, whose cultural misunderstandings make some good comic moments. The action scenes are also good. With Cynthia Khan. Mandarin with English subtitles (sometimes chopped at the sides but no difficulty following the plot). 1991.
VHS: $24161. $49.95.

Fortune Hunters

A gambling master is deserted by his overanxious disciple, who goes to work for the master's ruthless archrival. Soon the protege finds himself facing his former teacher and romantically linked with his teacher's new student, and he must decide which path is the right one. Mandarin with English subtitles. 1987.
VHS: $24162. $49.95.

Full Contact

A Bangkok nightclub bouncer named Jeff is the hero of this action-filled criminal adventure film. Jeff helps his friend Sam escape from a loan shark only to find that Sam has double-crossed him and marked him for death. With both Sam and Mona, Jeff's girlfriend, convinced that Jeff was killed in an explosion, Jeff escapes to Thailand to recuperate and figure out what to do next. His getaway sets the stage for a variety of surprise appearances as he returns to seek his vengeance. Cantonese with English subtitles.
VHS: $27270. $49.95.
Ringo Lam, Hong Kong, 1992, 99 mins.

The Fun, The Luck, and the Tycoon

As a roguish billionaire, Chow Yun Fat is perfect. He manages to bring a light, humorous touch to this comedy about the Lunar New Year. Mandarin with English subtitles.
VHS: $27282. $49.95.
Johnny To, Hong Kong, 1990

God of Gamblers

Chow Yun Fat is the suave, almost telepathic God of Gamblers. A blow to the head dissipates his memory and sends him into a childlike frame of mind. Three small-time hustlers parasitically decide to cash in on this state of affairs, but they eventually grow fond of the former God. When his memory returns, Fat can't remember the three hustlers, but despite this complication, the trio comes to his aid as it becomes clear that he is surrounded by enemies. This comic action film was a huge hit and inspired countless imitations, sequels and parodies. With Andy Lau and Joey Wang. Cantonese with English subtitles.
VHS: $27291. $49.95.
Wong Jing, Hong Kong, 1989, 125 mins.

God of Gamblers II

Chow Yun Fat doesn't appear in this film except as the object of veneration to his disciple, The Knight of Gamblers (Andy Lau). Lau, reprising his role from *God of Gamblers*, is joined by the goofy Saint of Gamblers (Stephen Chiau). In this funny, parodic sequel, the two join forces to thwart a plan that would ruin the God of Gamblers' reputation. Cantonese with English subtitles.
Part A.
VHS: $27292. $49.95.
Part B.
VHS: $28247. $49.95.
Wong Jing, Hong Kong, 1989, 103 mins.

Golden Dart Hero

This action-packed, kung fu adventure film follows the rise of an outlaw called Huang Tianba. When Huang's brother is killed, he seeks revenge but is foiled and captured. Then in a complete reversal from his earlier ways, he devotes himself to the court. There his strength serves him well. Dubbed in English.
VHS: $21830. $49.95.
Li Wenhua, Hong Kong, 1994, 98 mins.

Great Hero from China

Wang Fei Hong is a hero to the Chinese people, who runs a martial arts school. When he decides to destroy the opium drug trade, powerful enemies determine that he must be stopped. Against incredible odds he perseveres, resulting in a series of amazing, all-out martial arts battles. Dubbed in English, 90 mins.
VHS: $22610. $39.95.

Green Snake

Based on an old Chinese fable, this film combines mysticism with romance and climactic battle sequences. Green Snake and Son Ching (Maggie Cheung and Joey Wang) are a pair of snakes who long to be human. Son Ching has been practicing taking human form for 1,000 years and Green Snake for 500 when they are discovered by Fa-Hai, a self-righteous Buddhist monk who finds sin in the snakes' desire to tamper with natural law. In the end, the monk's lack of compassion leads to the destruction of his own ashram and of a nearby town. Cantonese with English subtitles.
VHS: $27271. $49.95.
Tsui Hark, Hong Kong, 1993, 102 mins.

Happy Bigamist

Pleasant romantic comedy. A recently married couple find their lives thrown into turmoil when the husband's first wife, half owner of the house, falls on hard times and is forced to move back. Mandarin with English subtitles.
VHS: $24164. $49.95.

Happy Ghost IV

Teen ghost comedy, as the ghost of a lecherous ancient general keeps interfering in the romantic affairs of the mild-mannered protagonist. Mandarin with English subtitles.
VHS: $24305. $49.97.

Hard Boiled

This film is an action fan's dream. The seamy underworlds of gun smugglers, mobsters and rebel cops collide in this super-fast paced thriller. A police inspector and a mysterious hit man team up to thwart a dastardly plot hatched by ruthless criminals.
Dubbed Version.
VHS: $21500. $19.98.
Laser: LD74629. $124.95.
Subtitled Version. Letterboxed. Cantonese with English subtitles.
VHS: $24848. $19.98.
John Woo, Hong Kong, 1992, 126 mins.

Hard Target

The American debut of Hong Kong action auteur John Woo (*The Killer, Bullet in the Head*) is an operatic reworking of *The Most Dangerous Game*. Set in New Orleans, the story follows a group of aristocrats who brutally attack homeless Vietnam veterans for sport, cruelly orchestrated by a debonair mercenary (Lance Henriksen). Jean-Claude Van Damme plays a sea merchant reluctantly drawn into the mix when a beautiful lawyer (Yancy Butler) enlists his support in tracking down her father. With Wilford Brimley.
VHS: $20181. $49.95.
Laser: LD72326. $34.98.
John Woo, USA, 1993

He Lives by Night

A strangler is stalking the neon streets of nighttime Hong Kong. A couple of detectives and a late-night DJ team up to stop him, or is it her, before the DJ becomes his next victim. Mandarin with English subtitles (often chopped off at edges). 1982.
VHS: $24165. $49.95.

Heart into Hearts

Ad man Alex, facing his impending marriage with trepidation, finds himself drawn to director Joe (Maggie Cheung, in fine form) and must re-evaluate the nature of his relationship with his fiance when they all find themselves in Paris shooting a commercial. Mandarin with English subtitles (occasionally cut off at the ends).
VHS: $24166. $49.95.
Stephen Shin, Hong Kong, 1982

Heartbeat 100

Maggie Cheung is at the center of this peculiar, gory slasher movie and wacky comedy. Cheung is a writer who seeks inspiration for her new screenplay, so she, her sister and a friend travel to a small town that is connected to a recent crime. Instead of inspiration she finds a host of dangers, including haunted houses, corrupt police, a village idiot who carries around poisonous snakes, and his axe-wielding father. When she thinks she witnesses a murder, she decides to investigate on her own, and before long she is helplessly enmeshed in a bizarre concoction that can only lead to mayhem and frustration.
VHS: $27583. $49.95.
Kent Cheng/Lo Kin, Hong Kong, 1986

Hearty Response

An irreverent cop (a breezy Chow Yun Fat) is forced to team up with his boss' rash nephew, who gets him involved with recent illegal immigrant Joey Wang, in a mixture of drama, comedy and intense action scenes. Joey, fearing she might be deported, pretends to believe herself to be Chow's wife, much to his initial irritation, although to his mother's delight. Meanwhile, he continues to chase a drug dealer while she tries to stay clear of a vicious thug involved in her immigration to Hong Kong. Mandarin with English subtitles (sometimes a bit washed out).
VHS: $24168. $49.95.
Low Man, Hong Kong, 1986

Heroic Trio

Three of Hong Kong's biggest female stars, Michelle Yeoh (Khan), Maggie Cheung and Anita Mui, play the leads in this strange tale of competing superheroines thwarting a mysterious series of baby kidnappings, in a comic book style (a la *Batman*). It has been suggested that the film is best read as a political allegory of the three entities of China, Taiwan and Hong Kong having to work together to overcome the many challenges facing them. Mandarin with English subtitles. Letterboxed.
VHS: $24169. $49.95.
Laser: Letterboxed. LD75501. $59.95.
Johnny To, Hong Kong, 1992

How to Pick Girls Up

Three losers pay an obnoxious talk radio personality to teach them how to court women in this exceptionally silly comedy. The radio host, aside from taking every advantage of his new students, is himself guilty of treating his wife in the shabbiest possible manner. When he discovers he is on the verge of losing her, the former losers, along with their girlfriends, intervene to show their teacher the error of his ways. One of the strangest moments in the film is a scene stolen from *A Clockwork Orange*, in which the radio host forces one of the characters to watch scenes from bad kung fu movies in order to cure him of his aggressive behavior. With Maggie Cheung.
VHS: $27584. $49.95.
Wong Jing, Hong Kong, 1988, 97 mins.

The Iceman Cometh

A rip-roaring ride through history with two ancient swordsmen. This thriller comedy includes historic settings in ancient China, promises to be kept to dying martial arts masters, honor to be upheld, special effects, time travel, street life in present-day Hong Kong, a little social commentary, and, of course, good vs. evil. Starring Maggie Cheung and Yuen Biao. Cantonese with English subtitles.
VHS: $14882. $49.95.
Fok Yiu-leung, Hong Kong, 1991, 114 mins.

The Iron-Fisted Monk

One of the earliest directorial efforts of Jackie Chan's pal Samo Hung, who also stars in the film. It's the tale of Shaolin monks who aid villagers to battle the evil Manchus as they swagger through China, raping, looting and pillaging. The mischievous and headstrong Hung, unable to concentrate on his martial arts studies in the temple, sets off on his own to help rid the countryside of the Manchus. Throughout the film he is sometimes aided by his former brethren, the monks, who are more interested in looking out for him than in capturing the Manchus.
VHS: $27585. $49.95.
Samo Hung, Hong Kong, 1976, 87 mins.

It's a Drink! It's a Bomb!

Two scientists have developed a bomb that's disguised as a popular soft drink. One of the scientists is plagued by second thoughts about selling this weapon to the evil Japanese, so he hides the bomb and flees. Unfortunately, he is quickly hunted down and killed, but not before he passes the secret along to three innocent bystanders. The trio quickly team up for comedy, action and romance, as they try to convince the skeptical police that they aren't simply a bunch of loonies (since no evidence of any kind of crime is to be found).
VHS: $27586. $49.95.
David Chung, Hong Kong, 1985, 87 mins.

The Killer

John Woo wrote and directed this brilliant gangster drama set in contemporary Hong Kong. The charismatic Chow Yun Fat stars as an amoral hitman who accidentally blinds a young torch singer, agreeing on a final assignment to pay for her surgery. The other plot is Chow's relationship with a tough, uncompromising cop (Danny Lee), as they battle the Hong Kong underworld. *The Killer* is a high-octane mixture of outlandishly stylized camp and outrageously sensational shoot-outs" (J. Hoberman). Chinese with English subtitles.
VHS: $13457. $19.98.
Laser: Director's cut includes trailers from other John Woo films, deleted scenes, commentary from Woo and a guide to Hong Kong cinema. LD72361. $124.95.
John Woo, Hong Kong, 1989, 102 mins.

Kung Fu the Movie

A feature-length translation of the cult 1970s program about the mysterious, Zen-like actions of Kwai Chang Caine, who gets drawn into an opium plot with an evil warlord (Mako) during the gold rush fever of 1880s California. Brandon Lee, the son of Bruce Lee, co-stars as Caine's adversary. The late Keye Luke appears in flashback as Master Po, Caine's blind instructor.
VHS: $17922. $19.98.
Richard Lang, USA, 1986, 100 mins.

Lady Sun

Traditionally told period piece about a man who marries a spirit, only to lose her when he fails to heed her advice and continues to associate with his old friends, whose doubtful character is made clear when he finds himself wrongfully accused of murder and facing execution. Mandarin with English subtitles (occasionally chopped). 1981.
VHS: $24170. $49.95.

Lai Shi: China's Last Eunuch

Lai Shi, a starving child in a poverty-stricken mountain village, implores his father to "snip it off" so that he may attain wealth and status at the Emperor's Court. Unfortunately, Lai Shi undergoes his transformation just before China's turbulent Twenties. An unnerving yet strangely satisfying mix of detailed historical drama, comedy, and pathos. Cantonese with English subtitles.
VHS: $13466. $49.95.
Chan Tsi-liang, Hong Kong, 1988, 100 mins.

The Last Blood

The bodies fly in locations all around Singapore in this over-the-top action film in which an anti-terrorist expert and a headstrong tourist must cooperate to get a rare blood-type donor to a hospital in time to save an important Buddhist monk and the tourist's girlfriend, all the while pursued by terrorists. With Alan Tam and Andy Lau. Mandarin with English subtitles.
VHS: $24171. $49.95.
Wong Ching, Hong Kong, 1991

Last Hurrah for Chivalry

A variation on the classic 1970's style kung-fu flick, starting out as a routine revenge drama, but bringing in a sense of character missing from most of the genre, and progressively veering from the expected development to question the motivations of its main characters, although with plenty of good action along the way, including a classic scene in which the heroes fight the deadly "sleeping watchman." An early exploration by director John Woo of one of his favorite themes, that of loyalty in a chaotic world. Mandarin with English subtitles (occasionally a bit chopped).
VHS: $24172. $49.95.
John Woo, Hong Kong, 1979

Law or Justice

After a model is raped by a psychotic photographer and he is acquitted thanks to a clever (female) lawyer, her schoolgirl sister tries to get revenge, only to find that the rapist has lured her into a trap. The stage is set for another trial, with the lawyer now having second thoughts about representing her client again. With Joey Wang. Mandarin with English subtitles (positioned low at first). 1989.
VHS: $24173. $49.95.

Legacy of Rage

Fans of the late Brandon Lee who were disappointed by many of his American films will enjoy this action-drama, in which he agrees to help out a friend, only to find himself in jail for murder, while his deceitful buddy becomes obsessed with his girlfriend. The central portion of the film, where Brandon has to learn to cope with being locked up, is especially strong. Mandarin with English subtitles.
VHS: $24174. $49.95.
Ronny Yu, Hong Kong, 1986

Legend of Wisely

A special effects extravaganza in which a group of adventurers journey from Nepal to Egypt to Hong Kong and back again, hot on the trail of a gigantic black pearl stolen from a Himalayan monastery. With Sam Hui, Teddy Robin Kwan and Ti Lung. Cantonese with English subtitles.
VHS: $13464. $49.95.
Teddy Robin Kwan, Hong Kong, 1986, 100 mins.

License to Steal

Two daughters of a master thief enter into deadly competition after one of them, envious of her sister's accomplishments, sets her up and has her imprisoned. With her rival out of the way, the bad sister takes over the family's business to become a ruthless jewel thief, until her sibling gets out of jail and the two head for the inevitable showdown. With Yuen Biao. Mandarin with English subtitles. 1990.
VHS: $24205. $49.95.

Life After Life
Well-made occult thriller about a man who feels he is re-living events from a past life, events which ended up in a murder. It's all bound up with some spooky puppets the man is using as part of a fashion show he is producing, while he attempts to make sense out of the obscure portents he is encountering. Mandarin with English subtitles (occasionally chopped but story followable).
VHS: $24175. $49.95.
Peter Wia-Chuen Yung, Hong Kong, 1981, 88 mins.

Love Soldier of Fortune
An eccentric piano tuner named Antonio Go moves into his ancestral home, only to find it haunted by the ghost of his dead uncle. His uncle was a gifted composer who killed himself over an unrequited love, and in order to help young Go win the object of his affections and avoid his uncle's melancholy fate, the uncle gives his nephew songs he has composed. Unfortunately, the nephew, unsure of himself, sells his uncle's songs to an arrogant and talentless pop singer who claims them as his own. To add insult to injury, the pop singer has designs on popular radio journalist Miss So (Maggie Cheung), apparently the hardest working woman in Hong Kong, who is the same woman Go desires. When Go's uncle suddenly disappears, Go realizes he must depend on his own resources to win the affections of Miss So. Hong Kong, 1988, 91 mins.
VHS: $27587. $49.95.

Love unto Waste
Before *Rouge*, Stanley Kwan captured the hedonism, cynicism and ennui of Hong Kong's smart set. Two Taiwanese women on the make in Hong Kong hook up with a young couple for a drunken night and a casual affair. After one of the group is murdered, the remaining members move toward a new and surprising emotional honesty. Cantonese with English subtitles.
VHS: $13473. $49.95.
Stanley Kwan, Hong Kong, 1986, 97 mins.

Lucky Stars
One of a popular film series featuring the wild adventures of a team of crazy undercover Hong Kong cops. Starring Samo Hung and Alan Tam. Cantonese with English subtitles.
VHS: $14884. $49.95.
Eric Tsang, Hong Kong

The Lunatics
This picture follows with the travails of a social worker who deals with mentally disturbed people, most of whom live on the street and refuse to be admitted to shelters or hospitals for treatment. The dedicated but somewhat worn-down social worker is accompanied on his rounds by a reporter doing a sensationalist story on the mentally ill. The reporter gradually overcomes her preconceived notions about the mentally ill, but not before one of her stories inadvertently sets a tragedy in motion. A strange combination of genuine feeling for the mentally ill and exploitation of them characterizes this movie. The feeling mostly comes about through the generally strong efforts of the cast, including a brief appearance by Chow Yun Fat as one of the street people. Hong Kong, 1986, 87 mins.
VHS: $27588. $49.95.

The Magnificent Butcher
The large Samo Hung is thoroughly engaging as the butcher Wing, a hapless student of legendary martial arts hero Wong Fei Hong. Wing finds himself dragged into an escalating matrix of violence when his sister-in-law is kidnapped by a thuggish student from a rival school. An itinerant and drunken master provides comic relief as he schools Samo in various martial arts techniques. Mandarin with English subtitles.
VHS: $27298. $49.95.
Yuen Woo-Ping, Hong Kong, 1979

Mainland Dundee
Hilarious satire about the three Chinas learning to coexist, personified by a mainland archeologist (Kenny Bee) and his greedy partner sent to Hong Kong, a pragmatic (and greedy) HK native who lets the archeologist live in his apartment, and their neighbor, who still dreams of raising the nationalist flag over the mainland, although his daughter has different intentions toward the young visitor from the People's Republic. Mandarin with English subtitles (occasionally cropped). 1991.
VHS: $24176. $49.95.

The Man from Hong Kong
Pedestrian James Bond-style film about a Hong Kong supercop sent to Australia to nab a criminal, only to get involved in tracking down the mastermind behind a drug-running operation. With Jimmy Wang and George Lazenby (who played Bond in *On Her Majesty's Secret Service*).
VHS: $24179. $49.95.
Brian Trenchard Smith, Australia/Hong Kong, 1975

Master Wong v. Master Wong
Following hard on the heels of the recent spate of movies about Chinese folk hero Wong Fei Hong comes this especially silly entry, in which Wong is portrayed as a naive bumbler in the company of fools. While Wong tries to escape from his reputation as an invincible martial artist, his cohorts are trying to cash in, imposters are springing up, and an unscrupulous promoter wants to manipulate him for his own ends. Mandarin with English subtitles.
VHS: $24177. $49.95.

The Mermaid
Done in a style reminiscent of traditional Chinese opera, this is the story of a 1000-year-old carp who decides to become human for a while, transforming itself into the double of a spoiled heiress, only to fall in love with a scholar who is patiently awaiting the heiress' hand in marriage, leading to massive confusions when the two women appear in the same place at once, even gaining the attention of the gods. Mandarin with English subtitles (occasionally cropped).
VHS: $24178. $49.95.
Kao Li, Hong Kong, 1985

The Middle Man
A Chinese-American Marine is framed for espionage by a Korean gang, and finds himself hunted by the CIA as well as the gang. Luckily for him, his cousin is acrobatic policewoman Cynthia Kahn, who is reluctantly drawn in to rescue her headstrong relative. Chinese with English subtitles. Hong Kong, 1990.
VHS: $25944. $49.95.

The Miracle Fighters
Consistently inventive blend of kung-fu and sorcery, often for humorous effect, as a young martial artist finds refuge with a pair of bickering old sorcerers, who take him on as a joint apprentice, teaching him what he needs to overcome an evil magician in pursuit of him. Mandarin with English subtitles (occasionally cropped).
VHS: $24179. $49.95.
Yuen Woo Ping, Hong Kong, 1981

Mission Kill
A criminal overlord sets out to eliminate the international police team that has interrupted his operations, but a female cop from Hong Kong eludes his team of assassins. She teams up with a Chinese FBI agent to track down the criminal and his henchman, who don't trust each other much either. Mandarin with English subtitles (occasionally washed out or cropped at edges). 1991.
VHS: $24180. $49.95.

The Moon Warriors
Fun period adventure, featuring some nice settings, as a deposed prince (Kenny Bee), fighting his evil brother for the throne, is rescued by a peasant swordsman (Andy Lau). When the prince sends his new friend to escort his betrothed princess (Anita Mui) back to him, the two fall in love. Meanwhile, there's a spy in the prince's camp. Ably directed by martial arts star Samo Hung; also featuring Maggie Cheung. Don't miss the sequences involving Andy Lau's best friend, a killer whale. Chinese with English subtitles.
VHS: $25945. $49.95.
Samo Hung, Hong Kong, 1993

Mr. Possessed
Unfortunately Ridley (Kenny Bee) has been under a curse since childhood: he literally repels women. When he finally meets someone who can be near him (thanks to her Buddhist charm bracelet) and they fall in love, his mother's meddling sets off a chain of spells and counter-spells, culminating in a Poltergeist-like finale of ghosts and magicians. Mandarin with English subtitles (occasionally cropped or washed out).
VHS: $24181. $49.95.
Wang Tsing, Hong Kong, 1988

Mr. Sunshine
Rotund, upbeat Mr. Mak looses his apartment and his job and moves in with a bickering, dysfunctional family (after causing the eldest daughter to loose her job as well), and proceeds to raise their self-esteem and their awareness of others, all the while searching for a job he and the daughter of the family can hold on to for more than a day. Mandarin with English subtitles. 1989.
VHS: $24182. $49.95.

Mr. Vampire
The first of a popular comedy/horror series featuring the Chinese version of a movie vampire, a more corpse-like creature than his Western counterpart. Mr. Vampire sports long purple fingernails and yellow fangs and, when not levitating, hops like a bunny. Stars Ricky Hui. Cantonese with English subtitles.
VHS: $13445. $49.95.
Lau Kun Wai, Hong Kong, 1986, 99 mins.

Mr. Vampire II
Agile martial arts acrobat Yuen Biao stars in this hilarious romp. Learn more vampire lore, including the salutary effects of holding your breath and having on hand a supply of sticky rice and red-inked sutras. Cantonese with English subtitles.
VHS: $13446. $49.95.
Lau Kun Wai, Hong Kong, 1986, 91 mins.

Mr. Vampire III
Richard Ng stars in Lau Koon Wai's third outing with the Chinese spirit world, which, in addition to vampires, offers a bevy of witches and possessed morticians. Cantonese without English subtitles.
VHS: $13447. $49.95.
Lau Kun Wai, Hong Kong, 1987, 95 mins.

Mr. Vampire IV
More laughs and chills as our favorite Chinese vampires return for action in the fourth installment of Lau Koon Wai's popular genre series. Cantonese without English subtitles.
VHS: $13448. $49.95.
Lau Kun Wai, Hong Kong, 1988, 90 mins.

My Beloved
A tale of two lovers forced apart by the man's family once the woman's pregnancy is discovered. She leaves but decides to raise their son by herself. When after a number of years it becomes apparent that the man's new wife cannot bear the child that will continue the family name, they attempt to make the woman turn her child over to them, forcing her to chose between the social advantages her child would enjoy with the well-off family and the intense emotional bond between her and her child. Mandarin with English subtitles.
VHS: $24183. $49.95.
Chu-Huang Chen, Hong Kong, 1988

My Heart Is That Eternal Rose
A woman becomes a gangster's mistress to save her father's life, while her lover must flee the country. Years later they meet again: her father has died and he is a killer doing a job for the gangster. An atmospheric melodrama filled with striking compositions and lurid, tropical colors, tense and melancholy. With Joey Wang, Kenny Bee, Tony Leung. Mandarin with English subtitles (slightly low but readable).
VHS: $24184. $49.95.
Patrick Tam, Hong Kong, 1988

Naughty! Naughty!
Sam Hui (of the Hui Brothers *Mr. Boo* fame) is a charming young man making a living by his wits and other people's money. It takes a beautiful young woman to bring out the good in him—in spite of himself. Cantonese with English subtitles.
VHS: $14859. $49.95.
Lo Wei, Hong Kong, 119 mins.

The New Legend of Shaolin
Jet Li stars in the fantasy film based on a Chinese legend. The Father Superior of the Shaolin Temple decides to destroy a map to a treasure trove before the evil Manchu rulers find out about it and try to steal it. So as not to lose his way to the treasure, the Father Superior has copies of the map tattooed onto the backs of five young masters of Shaolin. Unfortunately, the Manchus *do* find out about the treasure and come looking for the Shaolin masters. Cantonese and Mandarin with English subtitles. 89 minutes each.
Part A.
VHS: $27386. $49.95.
Part B.
VHS: $27387. $49.95.
Wong Jing, Hong Kong

The Occupant
A woman who is writing her dissertation on Chinese superstition moves into an apartment where a popular singing star was the victim of a murder/suicide. Chow Yun Fat is a policeman who, along with a very superstitious car salesman, comes to the aid of the woman when she becomes possessed by the spirit of the singer. Mandarin with English subtitles.
VHS: $27297. $49.95.
Ronnie Yu, Hong Kong, 1984

The Old Master
Don't be misled by the picture of Jackie Chan on the box cover—it's only a reference to his movie *Young Master* and he doesn't appear in this film. Instead, we have the story of an aging master who travels to Los Angeles to teach, but ends up being manipulated into fighting rival schools in a gambling scheme. A loyal student warns him off this scheme and offers him a place to live in return for being taught kung-fu. While the student practices, the master attempts to adjust to American life, including an extended visit to a disco. Mandarin with English subtitles.
VHS: $27287. $49.95.
Joseph Kuo, Hong Kong, 1980

On the Run
Yuen Biao is a detective who loses his police officer wife just as she is about to solve a crime. Betrayed by his fellow officers, Yuen must now rely on a hired killer from Thailand (Pat Ha), who quickly shows herself to be the only person worthy of his trust. Good performances and a well-crafted violent mood give this film a superior sense of suspense and intrigue. Mandarin with English subtitles.
VHS: $27293. $49.95.
Samo Hung, Hong Kong, 1988

Once Upon a Time in China III
Set in China during the last half of the troubled 1800s, this film centers on the evil Empress Dowager and her eunuch, Li Hung Cheung. The two decide to hold a competition of Lion Dance, a form of martial arts. This leads to much chaos and fighting as the different Lion Dance schools prepare for the competition. Meanwhile, Wong Fei-Hong (Jet Li), China's leading Lion Dancer, is busy defending his father's Lion Dance school against a band of gangsters when his girlfriend (Rosamund Kwan) discovers a Russian plot to assassinate the Lion Dancers. Lots of action, including Club-Foot's gravity-defying feats and a fight against the villains on an oil-covered floor. Cantonese with English subtitles.
Part A.
VHS: $27285. $49.95.
Part B.
VHS: $27286. $49.95.
Tsui Hark, Hong Kong, 1993, 102 mins.

Organized Crime & Triad Bureau
Danny Lee stars as a cop who has kidnapped Tung and his girlfriend (played by Cecilia Yip and Anthony Wong), two ringleaders of organized crime. As Lee sets out on his mission to make them pay for their crimes, Yip and Wong are searching for a way out. Chinese with English subtitles.
VHS: $27388. $79.95.
Kirk Wong, Hong Kong, 1993, 91 mins.

Panty Hose Hero
Samo Hung and Alan Tam are two cops who go undercover as homosexuals to catch a serial killer who murders gay men. This scenario allows for some moments of lampooning by ways among the gay men they are trying to save. In addition, there is a violent subplot concerning a drug gang. Mandarin with English subtitles.
VHS: $27281. $49.95.
Samo Hung, Hong Kong, 1990, 99 mins.

Paper Marriage
This Romantic comedy is set in Canada, where an out-of-work and down-on-his-luck Chinese boxer (Samo Hung) accepts a promise of payment to go through a form of marriage with a Hong Kong girl (Maggie Cheung) so she can gain citizenship. When the payment fails to materialize, Samo is forced back into the ring and Maggie even tries mud-wrestling before they ultimately discover their love for each other. Cantonese with English subtitles.
VHS: $13487. $49.95.
Samo Hung, Hong Kong, 102 mins.

Peacock Prince
An archaeological dig disturbs a menacing evil spirit. Only the young Peacock Prince can battle the evil monster Hell King. He sets off for Tokyo and uses a variety of skills including ESP, martial arts and the mastery of Zen to fight back. Also known as *Peacock King* or *Legend of the Phoenix*. Mandarin with English subtitles.
VHS: $27266. $49.95.
Yuen Biao/Nam Lai Choi, Hong Kong, 1987, 86 mins.

Pedicab Driver
Set in Macao and shot in a ravishing, early 20th century period atmosphere, Samo Hung's latest Kung fu effort belongs to the class of ingenious boy-girl romance pictures which Hung has been involved in lately as an actor, such as *Painted Faces* and *Eight Taels of Gold*. In those films, Hung forgoes kung fu for character portrayal. Here, he returns to familiar ground, handling action and lightweight comedy romance with ease. Cantonese with English subtitles.
VHS: $14881. $49.95.
Samo Hung, Hong Kong, 1989, 98 mins.

Peking Opera Blues
Three of the Hong Kong cinema's most popular actresses—Sally Yeh, Cherie Chung, and Lin Ching-Hsai—star in this fast-paced comedy/drama set in turn-of-the-century China. In addition to its stunning art-direction, this film features an assortment of plots and counterplots, assassins, singers, soldiers, and amazing action sequences. Cantonese with English subtitles.
VHS: $13462. $49.95.
Tsui Hark, Hong Kong, 1986, 104 mins.

People's Hero
Ti Lung and Tony Leung star in this thrilling crime drama which borrows liberally from *Dog Day Afternoon*. When two young street punks botch a bank robbery, master criminal Sunny Koo steps in and escalates the theft into a tension-filled hostage situation. Cantonese with English subtitles.
VHS: $13468. $49.95.
Yee Tung-shing, Hong Kong, 1987, 82 mins.

Perfect Match
Comedy and romance as a boss and one of her managers, a toy designer, share a tempestuous relationship, complicated by the reappearance of her ne'er-do-well cousin and rivals within the company. With Andy Lau. Mandarin with English subtitles. 1989.
VHS: $24186. $49.95.

Phantom War
Violent picture about a former Vietnamese soldier who moves to London to be with his longtime love, only to find himself embroiled with warring Chinese gangs and an old enemy from Vietnam. Mandarin with English subtitles. 1990.
VHS: $24187. $49.95.

Pickles Make Me Cry
A low-budget comedy-thriller made in New York by Peter Chow, the Executive Director of Asian Cine-Vision. The title comes from the favorite post love-making snack of William and Jeannie, a young Chinese couple. William and Jeannie also find themselves in something of a pickle when William is shot by a mean Chinatown gang which is trying to extort money from the couple's friends. Cantonese with English subtitles.
VHS: $13479. $49.95.
Peter Chow, USA/Hong Kong, 1988, 85 mins.

Point of No Return
The son and adopted son of an aging hitman, carrying on in their father's footsteps, begin to consider the futility of their way of life once one of them falls in love with the daughter of a policeman, who happens to be their next assignment. With Jackie Cheung and Joey Wang. Mandarin with English subtitles.
VHS: $24188. $49.95.
Guy Y.C. Lai, Hong Kong, 1990

Prison on Fire
A violent prison drama with superstar Chow Yun Fat portraying a cynical gambler serving time for the accidental killing of his adulterous wife. He befriends an innocent and unworldly white collar worker (Leung Ka Fai) who has been framed, and acts as his protector while he adjusts to prison life. Cantonese with English subtitles.
VHS: $13476. $49.95.
Ringo Lam, Hong Kong, 1987, 98 mins.

Revenge of the Tai-Chi Master
During the Ching dynasty a Tai Chi Master discovers that he and his family will suffer annihilation. In response he sends his son away to be raised by a good friend. Twenty years later, the son is grown and sets out for revenge. The only problem is his father's enemy is still powerful and ruthless. Dubbed in English, 90 mins.
VHS: $22609. $39.95.

Road Warriors
An earnest tribute to Hong Kong's unsung heroes, motorcycle traffic cops. In this story, they're trying to stop reckless road racing, especially after the irresponsible son of a publisher runs a school bus off the road, resulting in many casualties. Danny Lee plays the head cop. Mandarin with English subtitles (occasionally cropped).
VHS: $24189. $49.95.
Danny Lee, Hong Kong, 1987

The Roar of the Vietnamese

A violent tale of illegal immigrants being manipulated by criminal gangs, forced to commit crimes in return for supposed passage to the U.S., focusing on a particular group of disparate individuals who bond together under the stress of their situation. More a melancholy action movie than a serious look at the plight of the Vietnamese. Chinese with English subtitles. Hong Kong, 1991.
VHS: $25946. $49.95.

Rose

Maggie Cheung plays Rose, an ace insurance agent beset by insecurities. When a gangster (Roy Cheung) scares away one of her prospective clients, he attempts to make it up to her by taking out a large policy for himself that names Rose as the beneficiary. There is a catch, however: Rose must let him hide out at her place. It doesn't take long for love to develop in this absorbing drama, but the recurring problem of the gangster's violent past is a constant threat to their romantic idyll. Mandarin with English subtitles.
VHS: $27295. $49.95.
Samson Chiu, Hong Kong, 1992, 99 mins.

Rouge

The popular singers/actors Anita Mui and Leslie Cheung are paired in this supernatural love story which alternates between the brothels, theaters and opium dens of Hong Kong in the Thirties, and the cool, detached world of the present day. The ghost of a courtesan appeals to a young journalist to help her find her lost lover who recovered from their joint suicide attempt and thus failed to join her in the spirit world. Cantonese with English subtitles.
VHS: $13465. $49.95.
Stanley Kwan, Hong Kong, 1987, 99 mins.

Royal Tramp

Visually sumptuous parody of Hong Kong's recent swordplay epics, with smart aleck Stephen Chow as the improbably named Wilson Bond, a fast-thinking lowlife who gets caught up in one tangled court intrigue after another, pledging his loyalty to whoever is threatening him at the moment and playing all sides off against each other while trying to figure a way out of the incredible mess he's in. Great fun. Letterboxed. Mandarin with English subtitles (occasionally washed out but otherwise good). 1991.
VHS: $24190. $49.95.

Royal Tramp II

A continuation of the adventures of Wilson Bond, now a big shot friend of the emperor, still being buffeted by the various factions seeking to overthrow the emperor, and still continuing to aggravate his rivals and bluff or squirm his way out of tight situations. Here he's assigned to escort the emperor's sister, about to be married off to form a political alliance with a treacherous prince, in a worthy sequel to the 1991 hit. Mandarin with English subtitles. 1992.
VHS: $24191. $49.95.

Royal Warriors

After three cops (two from Hong Kong and one from Japan) break up an attempt to rescue a prisoner, the rest of the gang vows revenge. This violent action movie is distinguished by its bruising fights and by the presence of martial arts star Michelle Yeoh (Khan), playing one of the three cops. Also known as *In the Line of Duty II*. Chinese with English subtitles. Hong Kong, 1986.
VHS: $25947. $49.95.

Run Tiger Run

"Wacky" and "zany" are the adjectives that best describe this bizarre John Woo comedy, done in a *Pee-Wee's Playhouse* style with strange decor and speeded-up, jerky movements. The plot revolves around the nearly identical appearance of two little boys—one the spoiled heir to a large fortune, whose evil uncle wants to do away with him, the other the son of the diminutive but scrappy Teddy Robin Kwan—and the chaos that ensues when everyone ends up in the rich kid's mansion. Mandarin with English subtitles.
VHS: $24192. $49.95.
John Woo, Hong Kong, 1985

Savior of Soul II

Andy Lau and Rosamund Kwan star in this surreal comedy-adventure in which a trio of adventurers quest for the magical "virgin ice" in a spectacular mountain setting, as well as for a mysterious woman one of the men has dreamed of every night of his life. A strange film in which the outlandish plot developments keep changing the direction you think it's going in. Mandarin with English subtitles.
VHS: $24193. $49.95.

Seaman No. 7

Jimmy Wang plays the title character, a merchant seaman who accidentally kills a man and flees to Japan, ending up in Kobe, where he is taken in by expatriate Chinese, learns Judo, and has to fight off a bunch of drug-running thugs. Low budget, but it's nice to see a different sort of character in a kung-fu flick as Jimmy Wang's earnest seaman tries to figure out how to get by in a foreign country. Mandarin with English subtitles (occasionally cropped and low).
VHS: $24194. $49.95.
Lo Wei, Hong Kong, 1972

Seven Warriors

Villagers hire seven soldiers to help get rid of the bandits who have been raiding them, in this entertaining film that owes more to *The Magnificent Seven* than to *The Seven Samurai*, as characters and even entire scenes are transported from the Old West to 1920's China. With Tony Leung as the leader of the soldiers and Jackie Cheung as one of the band. Mandarin with English subtitles.
VHS: $24195. $49.95.
Terry Tong, Hong Kong, 1989

Seven Years Itch

After seven years of marriage a couple find themselves a bit bored with each other, until the husband goes on a business trip to Singapore and gets mixed up with a pretty hustler who knows a sucker when she sees one. Before long, his wife, his leeching brother-in-law, and his shrill mother-in-law are all involved, and the previously quiet marriage is threatened, especially when the obnoxious Mr. Money appears with the offer to take the wife back with him to the U.S. Mandarin with English subtitles.
VHS: $24196. $49.95.
Johnny To, Hong Kong, 1987

The Seventh Curse

Chow Yun Fat appears as the occultist character Wisely, a character first seen in *Legend of Wisely*. This film offers a heady mixture of fantasy, adventure and the supernatural, featuring demons, monsters, flying killer alien-baby monsters and a spinal cord-eating, walking skeleton. Also known as *Dr. Yeun and Wisely*. Mandarin with English subtitles.
VHS: $27272. $49.95.
Nam Nie Choi, Hong Kong, 1986, 88 mins.

Shanghai 1920

In 1920s Shanghai a Chinese street urchin and the son of a wealthy British trader become fast friends and then become separated. When the Englishman returns years later to start a business, he finds his former friend is now a gangster and their attempts to work together seem destined for failure. The approach of the invading Japanese army to the city throws everyone's lives into confusion, though, and the two find their destinies linked together again. With John Lone. Chinese with English subtitles.
VHS: $27390. $49.95.
Leung Po-Chi, Hong Kong

Skinny Tiger and Fatty Dragon

This entertaining buddy/cop film is the story of two pals busting up a gang of criminals and cheerfully breaking just about all the rules governing police conduct. A series of well-staged fights and chases are lightened by humor, making this a highly enjoyable film. One of the highlights is a chase sequence where the heroes destroy a villain's Mercedes, bit by bit, for the sole purpose of antagonizing the fiend. Samo Hung does a continuous Bruce Lee impression throughout the film, despite or because of the fact that there is absolutely no physical resemblance between the wiry Lee and the portly and often mischievous Hung. Cantonese with English subtitles.
VHS: $27288. $49.95.
Lau Kar Wing, Hong Kong, 1990

Slave of the Sword

In this sexy adventure film the innocent daughter of a masterful artist becomes entwined with murderous prostitutes. When the master retires he makes plans that should save her and his three students, but the pull of intrigue and human nature is too great. Before long the greatest assassination plot imaginable will make use of all their charms. Dubbed in English.
VHS: $21829. $49.95.
Chiu Yan Ping, Hong Kong, 1994

Stunt: A Musical Motion Picture

In this collage of images, representation and meta-reality, the performance artist and stunt man David Leslie orchestrates a spectacular pageant that pays homage to the respective spirits of James Brown, Evel Knievel, Bruce Lee and Julie Andrews. 35 mins.
VHS: $17201. $39.95.

Swordsman

While King Hu is listed as the nominal director of this lavish period epic, the hand of producer Tsui Hark is the dominant influence here. Rousing first entry in the epic *Swordsman* series, carefully detailed, lyrical, and full of fantastic action. Swordsman Ling (Jackie Cheung) and his sidekick "Kiddo" encounter treacherous officials, rebels, and secret sects as the different groups vie to gain possession of a secret scroll stolen from the imperial library. Letterboxed. Mandarin with English subtitles.
VHS: $24197. $49.95.
King Hu, Hong Kong, 1990

Swordsman II

Martial arts star Jet Li takes over the title role in a sequel that's as good as the original, as swordsman Ling continues his adventures in a chaotic world of shifting loyalties and betrayals, the deceiving nature of appearances being exemplified by the evil General Fong, in the midst of transforming himself into a beautiful woman (Briget Lin). With Rosamund Kwan. Mandarin with English subtitles.
VHS: $24198. $49.95.
Ching Siu Tung, Hong Kong, 1991

Sworn Brother

Brutal but well made drama about two brothers operating on different sides of the law but still maintaining a loyalty to each other, the extent of which is tested when the entire family is drawn into danger once the criminal brother is betrayed by his boss. Chinese with English subtitles.
VHS: $25948. $49.95.
Samo Hung, Hong Kong, 1986

The Tai Chi Master

Two monks, friends since childhood, are expelled from the Shaolin monastery for misbehavior. Making their way to the nearest town, one becomes a soldier and the other joins a band of rebels fighting against an oppressive general. The rebel is betrayed by his army friend and can only regain both his sanity and his fighting prowess by rediscovering the Tai-Chi principles of his religious past. Michelle Yeoh is featured in this engaging historical epic. Mandarin with English subtitles.
Part A.
VHS: $27283. $49.95.
Part B.
VHS: $27284. $49.95.
Yuen Woo Ping, Hong Kong, 1993, 92 mins.

Talk to Me, Dicky

Truly ridiculous movie about a couple of detectives tracking down a serial rapist by learning to talk to their penises, which can in turn communicate with the organs of other men, including the rapist. Mandarin with English subtitles. 1992.
VHS: $24199. $49.95.

The Tattoo Connection

A Hong Kong martial arts classic featuring legendary Jim Kelly as a private investigator following the theft of one of the world's biggest diamonds. Dubbed in English.
VHS: $20572. $39.98.
Lee Tse Nam, Hong Kong, 1979, 95 mins.

Teppanyaki

A journey into the strange, silly world of Michael Hui, filled with slapstick, satire and parody. This time he plays a hapless chef attempting to live out his fantasies of escaping to a tropical isle with a pretty stewardess (Sally Yeh). When the chance arises, though, he finds himself accompanied by his bullying wife and father-in-law (and boss), as well as his decrepit father—what would a Michael Hui comedy be without plenty of frustration? Chinese with English subtitles.
VHS: $25949. $49.95.
Michael Hui, Hong Kong, 1983

Thank You Sir

Earnest look at the experiences of a bunch of high school-age cadets in a prestigious police academy. Danny Lee plays the newly appointed deputy commander who tries to bring a more humane approach to training the students, only to run into opposition from other instructors reluctant to change the way things are done. Mandarin with English subtitles.
VHS: $24200. $49.95.
Ivan Lai, Hong Kong, 1989

They Came to Rob Hong Kong

After a violent opening sequence, this turns out to be a silly farce about a group of misfits recruited from mainland China in order to commit a big robbery in Hong Kong. Once they arrive there, however, the group discovers that it is only a pawn in the evil scheme of the master plotter (still coughing up blood after his brawl at the start of the film), and, of course, they band together to foil him. Chinese with English subtitles. Hong Kong, 1989.
VHS: $25950. $49.95.

Those Merry Souls

The nimble Yuen Biao, star of several Jackie Chan action pictures, appears here as a movie stuntman who discovers his late father had been living a secret life. Unbeknownst to him, his father served as a conductor of souls of the newly deceased to the spirit world, and now it is up to Yuen to continue in his father's footsteps. This doesn't sit well with Yuen, who had hoped to live a more ordinary life. With the help of his friends, he attempts to escape his peculiar family legacy. Instead of being an attempt to make a scary ghost picture, this takes a more atmospheric approach, filled with a fondness for Chinese superstition and folklore, as well as plenty of opportunities for Yuen to display his agility. Hong Kong, 1985, 94 mins.
VHS: $27589. $49.95.

The Three Avengers

Bruce Lee stars as Hung Tack, the master of a Kung Fu school in a village plagued by two evil, rich businessmen. These two terrorize Hung and his school, forcing him to battle local gangs. During a fight Hung is spotted by a talent scout and starts a career as a movie star, while his friend, John, is thrown into prison. In the spectacular finale they are reunited doing what they do best, fighting the bad guys. 91 mins. In English.
VHS: $22225. $39.98.

Tiger on the Beat II

Danny Lee takes over the Chow Yun Fat role in this sequel, in which his appropriately named nephew Buffalo arrives in Hong Kong to find a wife, but instead falls for a pretty thief who is being chased by a criminal gang which is after a ring she has stolen from them, leading up to a bruising finale in a bus station. Mandarin with English subtitles.
VHS: $24201. $49.95.
Chia Liang Liu, Hong Kong, 1990

The Tigers

Tony Leung and Andy Lau are part of a quintet of cop buddies in what starts out as a routine action film, but which takes an interesting turn when they keep some money they recover in a drug bust and suddenly find themselves both blackmailed by the gangsters and investigated by the internal affairs unit. The situation becomes increasingly grim as pressure from both sides mounts and there seems to be no way out. Mandarin with English subtitles.
VHS: $24202. $49.95.
Eric Tsang, Hong Kong, 1991

Touch and Go

Hard hitting action with the mild-mannered Samo Hung witnessing a murder and then being pursued by the killers. Things are made worse by a headstrong cop and his reporter sister, who use Samo as a tool for their own purposes, repeatedly putting him in danger. Some great action sequences with the always surprisingly deft Samo, well directed by current favorite Ringo Lam. Mandarin with English subtitles.
VHS: $24203. $49.95.
Ringo Lam, Hong Kong, 1991

Treasure Hunt

Chow Yun Fat is an Americanized CIA agent sent to the Shaolin Temple in mainland China. There he experiences the conflicting pull of modern ways versus ancient Chinese traditions. The plot centers on a psychic link between the CIA agent and a girl held prisoner in the temple. In addition, there are smugglers and agents formulating all kinds of trouble. Filmed on location. Mandarin with English subtitles.
Part A.
VHS: $27300. $49.95.
Part B.
VHS: $28058. $49.95.
Lau Chun-Wai, Hong Kong, 1994

The Valiant Ones

A graceful action film shot almost completely on location, *The Valiant Ones* deals with the preservation of a domestic political force (the Ming Court) against the encroachments of an outside enemy (Japanese pirates) and provides an elemental study of the many facets of the martial arts (displayed by both patriots and pirates). The natural backdrops against which the duel scenes are staged question the relationship between the natural, exterior universe and the mortal (albeit extraordinary) force which is fighting to preserve it. Cantonese with English subtitles.
VHS: $14869. $49.95.
King Hu, Hong Kong

When Taekwondo Strikes

Jhoon Rhee, the father of Taekwondo in the U.S., is featured in this action-packed film. As grandmaster Lee, he takes charge of an underground group of patriots battling the Japanese in occupied Korea. After he is discovered, Lee aided by a Chinese woman and his troupe is forced into a furiously choreographed battle to defend his honor. In English.
VHS: $22226. $59.98.
Huang Feng, Hong Kong, 1973, 95 mins.

Why Me?

This comedy/drama is the story of a young social worker who takes an interest in Big Cat, a large man who thinks he is a child. The social worker wants to bring both Big Cat and his mother, a street vendor, under the protective wing of the Social Services department, but she must first diffuse their mistrust of the government. Chow Yun Fat is featured as the social worker's more experienced supervisor and love interest. Mandarin with English subtitles.
VHS: $27289. $49.95.
Kent Cheng, Hong Kong, 1985

Wild Search

Chow Yun Fat is Mew Mew, a cop investigating an arms smuggling ring. One of the smugglers is killed during a raid, leaving her two children orphaned. Mew Mew becomes infatuated with the orphaned older sister and follows the two children to their rural home. A strong visual sense and a highly kinetic style elevate this film above the standard level of police action films. Cantonese with English subtitles.
VHS: $27294. $49.95.
Ringo Lam, Hong Kong, 1989, 95 mins.

Wing Chun

Michelle Yeoh stars as cross-dressing kung fu innovator Yim Wing Chung, who battles the bandit lords and invents a new kung fu style. Don't miss the "tofu fight" and lesbian foot massage scenes. Chinese with English subtitles.
VHS: $27540. $79.95.
Laser: Letterboxed. LD75500. $59.95.
Yuen Wo Ping, Hong Kong, 1993

Winner Takes All

A young man sets out to avenge the death of his brother by a criminal gang. His flight from an unsuccessful encounter with the gang leads him into the arms of a young woman. She, in turn, becomes the innocent key to the destruction of the gang when they begin a deadly game in which the winner takes all. Starring Alan Tang, Olivia Cheng and Fung Shui Fan. Cantonese with English subtitles.
VHS: $14873. $49.95.
Stanley Siu, Hong Kong, 94 mins.

Witch from Nepal

A man unknowingly inherited a supernatural power from an ancestor, a powerful Nepalese tribal chief, and is hunted by one who wants the power for himself. Cantonese with English subtitles.
VHS: $14857. $49.95.
Ching Siu Ting, Hong Kong, 91 mins.

Wonder Seven

The Wonder Seven is a group of seven highly trained martial artists and undercover government agents stationed in Hong Kong. The seven have all become assimilated into Hong Kong culture when they receive orders that their government is in trouble. They are assigned to steal two computer disks pertaining to a Sino-Japanese deal, but when they complete their assignment, all sorts of mysterious things begin happening. Cantonese and Mandarin with English subtitles. 90 minutes each.
Part A.
VHS: $27384. $49.95.
Part B.
VHS: $27385. $49.95.
Ching Siu Tung, Hong Kong

Zodiac Killers

Pessimistic tale of Chinese living in Tokyo, hoping to beat the intense competition to get ahead in Hong Kong but finding instead that they have few friends and few places to hide when they get involved with Japanese thugs. With Andy Lau. Mandarin with English subtitles. 1991.
VHS: $24204. $49.95.

JACKIE CHAN

The Armour of God
Filmed on location in Yugoslavia, Austria, France and Hong Kong, this fast-moving vehicle for comedy/action star Jackie Chan nearly cost him his life when a relatively simple stunt misfired. Chan plays an adventurer who steals pieces of a prized medieval armour to sell to rich collectors. But these ancient artifacts are also sought by a criminal cult which will stop at nothing to obtain them. When the cult kidnaps Jackie's former love, Jackie comes up with even more spectacular ways to save the armour and the girl. One of Chan's most thrilling and entertaining films (and with him, that's really saying something). Cantonese with English subtitles.
VHS: S14863. $49.95.
Jackie Chan, Hong Kong, 1986, 100 mins.

Bloodpact
Liu Chia Yung stars in this classic Hong Kong action film. Orphaned when his father is killed, a boy seeks shelter in a monastery only to be shunned by its resident Kung-Fu masters. He must learn the art of fighting from a beggar boy and a wiseman. Chan makes a special appearance.
VHS: S27720. $14.99.
Jackie Chan, Hong Kong, 90 mins.

Dragon Lord
In this Jackie Chan kung fu classic, Chan demonstrates the agility, humor and awe-inspiring stunts that made him famous. Jackie and his pals combat a group of smugglers selling Chinese cultural treasures abroad, and at the same time, they compete for the affection of a beautiful village maiden. Mandarin with English subtitles.
VHS: S27299. $49.95.
Jackie Chan, Hong Kong, 1982

Dragons Forever
Childhood friends and frequent collaborators Jackie Chan, Samo Hung and Yuen Biao star in this contemporary comedy with an ecological twist. Big time lawyer Jackie is persuaded to work against a chemical plant, which wants to take over a site used by local fishermen, when he falls for the beautiful cousin of the fishery's owner. In addition to comic bits of kung fu business between the three leads, Dragons boasts an amazing fighting finale with Jackie once again pitted against the formidable "Benny." Cantonese with English subtitles.
VHS: S14875. $49.95.
Samo Hung, Hong Kong, 1988, 88 mins.

Drunken Master
(aka Drunken Monkey in a Tiger's Eye)
Jackie Chan stars as Naughty Panther, the practical joker son of a stern and humorless kung fu master. Jackie's training is given over to his uncle, a mighty fighter with a fearsome reputation. Like Snake in the Eagle's Shadow, Drunken Master is a transitional film in the development of the Jackie Chan screen persona from ersatz Bruce Lee to kung fu comedian. Of this film, Inside Kung Fu proclaimed: "Comedy kung fu has arrived and Jackie is the Chaplinesque champion." Cantonese with English subtitles.
VHS: S14868. $49.95.
Yuen Woo-Ping, Hong Kong, 1978, 90 mins.

The Hand of Death
(aka Countdown in Kung-Fu)
Unremarkable 1970's style kung-fu flick, but notable for being an early effort by renowned director John Woo, and for the presence of Jackie Chan and Samo Hung. Several men band together to protect a messenger, played by Woo, from corrupt Manchus. Mandarin with English subtitles (occasionally chopped on ends).
VHS: S24163. $49.95.
John Woo, Hong Kong, 1975

Heart of the Dragon
Samo Hung plays Jackie Chan's backward younger brother, who believes himself to be seven years old, and spends his time playing with real kids until he witnesses a crime and is pursued by gangsters. More a drama than an action movie, focusing on Jackie's frustrations at having to care for his brother and the hurt and bewilderment of Samo at what he perceives as Jackie's attempts to be rid of him. Mandarin with English subtitles (occasionally cut off at edges).
VHS: S24167. $49.95.
Samo Hung, Hong Kong, 1985

Island of Fire
Violent, lengthy prison movie following the stories of a number of inmates in a corrupt and brutal prison. Tony Leung Ka Fai stars as an undercover cop investigating the reappearance of supposedly dead prisoners as hitmen. The film also features inmates Jackie Chan and Samo Hung and crime bosses Wang Yu and Andy Lau. While borrowing liberally from such U.S. staples as Cool Hand Luke and Bad Boys, this film is held together by its strong cast until its conclusion, a climactic gun battle at a Filipino airport. Chinese with English subtitles.
VHS: S27389. $49.95.
Chu Yen Ping, Hong Kong, 1991

My Lucky Stars
Jackie Chan and Yuen Biao play Hong Kong cops in Japan trying to extradite a notorious criminal. When the Tokyo underworld turns the tables on them, the pair are forced to call for some unconventional reinforcements. With Richard Ng. Cantonese with English subtitles.
VHS: S14862. $49.95.
Samo Hung, Hong Kong, 99 mins.

Painted Faces
Loosely based on the childhood of Samo Hung, Jackie Chan and Yuen Biao (now all martial artists/film stars). This compelling and humorous story shows their training at the Peking Opera School run by Yu Jim-yuen. Cantonese with English subtitles.
VHS: S13481. $49.95.
Alex Law, Hong Kong, 1988, 100 mins.

Project A (Part I)
A period comedy chock full of action and suspense. Jackie Chan plays an honest marine cadet in turn-of-the-century Hong Kong, who must do battle with the smugglers and pirate bands operating on the South China Sea. With Samo Hung and Yuen Biao. Cantonese with English subtitles.
VHS: S13470. $49.95.
Jackie Chan, Hong Kong, 1983, 95 mins.

The Protector
Jackie Chan is a New York cop celebrating his 10th anniversary as an American citizen. The sleazy South Bronx bar where he is sharing an after-shift drink with his partner is raided by a gang of hoodlums. A shoot-out ensues and, in the process, destroys millions of dollars of public property. Now in disgrace, Jackie goes after the gang leader and, in the process, destroys millions of dollars of public property. Now in disgrace, Jackie gets a new partner (Danny Aiello) and a new beat. But where Jackie goes, trouble follows, and the kidnapping of a fashion designer leads Jackie and Danny to Hong Kong and the nastiest drug dealing operation since The French Connection. In English.
VHS: S14854. $49.95.
James Glickenhaus, USA, 1985, 94 mins.

Wheels on Meals
Two young entrepreneurs from Hong Kong (Jackie Chan and Yuen Biao) bring Chinese food to the citizens of Barcelona with the aid of their uniquely customized van. They become involved with a young pickpocket who turns out to be the missing heiress sought by their clumsy private detective pal (Samo Hung). Full of humor, spectacular martial arts scenes, and a bruising final battle between Jackie and bad guy "Benny." Cantonese with English subtitles.
VHS: S14858. $49.95.
Samo Hung, Hong Kong, 1984, 100 mins.

Will of Iron
Jackie is an illustrator with a serious cocaine habit. Even his friend and dealer, Michael, wants him to quit. Even Jackie's marriage to the long-suffering Carol is on the verge of breaking up as a result of his drug problem. The strong-willed Maggie (Maggie Cheung) arrives for a visit, hoping to put an end to all these problems, but instead insults the ruthless gangster behind it all, putting everyone's lives in danger. Mandarin with English subtitles.
VHS: S27290. $49.95.
John Chiang, Hong Kong, 1990

The Young Master
One of Jackie Chan's first films as director/star, it smashed all box office records upon first release and rocketed Jackie to world-wide recognition. This colorful period-comedy follows Jackie as he seeks to restore the honor of his kung fu school and his foster brother. Cantonese with English subtitles.
VHS: S14865. $49.95.
Jackie Chan, Hong Kong, 92 mins.

TAIWANESE CINEMA

Dust in the Wind
A young man sets out to find work in the big city of Taipei so that he can make money to send home and eventually marry his childhood sweetheart. Marked with great sympathy and understanding for its characters and a spare, unhurried style, Dust in the Wind becomes an atmospheric statement on the generation gap and the divide between the village and the city in contemporary Taiwan. From the director of The Time to Live and the Time to Die and A City of Sadness. Taiwanese dialect with English subtitles.
VHS: S14876. $49.95.
Hou Hsiao-hsien, Taiwan, 1987, 109 mins.

Eat Drink Man Woman
Ang Lee's (The Wedding Banquet) winning blockbuster of a movie about food, sex and independence. Master Chef Chu is Taipei's legendary chef whose extraordinary culinary creations are the center piece of the film. His three beautiful daughters are both sexy and rebellious, but Master Chu holds the family together with his Sunday ritual dinners. But as the generations clash, and Master Chu retires, it's the experienced generation that has the final word in a film that's original, funny, surprising—and delectable. Chinese with English subtitles.
VHS: S24824. $19.98.
Laser: LD74957. $39.99.
Ang Lee, Taiwan/USA , 1994, 104 mins.

Flower Love
(aka Love Is Grown with Flowers)
Uneven comedy-drama about a farming village undergoing change, some of the young people wanting to live in the city while others stay on and try to help the older residents adjust to a new scheme to grow flowers to market instead of rice. Mandarin with English subtitles.
VHS: S24159. $49.95.
Tsay Yang-ming, Taiwan, 1989

Outcasts
The most controversial film ever released in Taiwan, Outcasts is the story of teenage boys abandoned by their families because they are gay, and the efforts of an aging photographer to provide a home and family for these young people. Chinese with English subtitles.
VHS: S05987. $49.95.
Yu Kan-Ping, Taiwan, 1986, 102 mins.

Song of the Exile
A memorable film about cultural divisions and alienation. Hueyin is a young Chinese student living in London in 1973. After graduation she returns to Hong Kong because of the job-discrimination she faces in England based on her heritage. Further emotional tensions surface in this touching film after the reunion with her own fragmented family. With Maggie Cheung and Shwu-Fen Chang. Chinese with English subtitles.
VHS: S14745. $79.95.
Ann Hui, Taiwan/China, 1990, 100 mins.

That Day, On the Beach
Generally credited as the film which more than any other marked the launching of the Taiwanese New Wave, That Day, On the Beach mingles the director's own expatriate experience (in the U.S.) with his perceptions of several strata of Taiwanese society. Told in flashbacks, the film begins as two former schoolfriends are reunited after a 13-year separation. One is now a successful concert pianist in Europe; the other has started up a business after the failure of her marriage. The two reminisce about old times, reveal secrets of the past they never dared speak before, and take stock of their present lives. Director Yang weaves several levels of narrative together to create a rich emotional tapestry that reflects the experience of a "lost" generation. Taiwanese dialect with English subtitles.
VHS: S14866. $49.95.
Edward Yang, Taiwan, 1983, 167 mins.

A Time to Live and a Time to Die
Winner of the Golden Bear at the Berlin Film Festival, and directed by one of Asia's most interesting filmmakers, Hou Hsiao-hsien, this film is the story of a family from southern mainland China who migrate to Taiwan in the 1940s to escape financial hardship. Later, they are unable to return and find themselves tragically cut off from their cultural heritage. "Reaches unexpected depths of feeling" (New York Times). Taiwanese with English subtitles.
VHS: S26494. $59.95.
Hou Hsiao-hsien, Taiwan, 1985, 137 mins.

CHINESE CULTURE & POLITICS

Best of Nightline: Student Protest in China
30 mins.
VHS: S14059. $14.98.

China and the Forbidden City
A very special inside look at the mystery, opulence, grandeur, and thousands-year-old history of China's Forbidden City, one of the most opulent treasures of the world. Winner of the Peabody Award. Introduced by Edwin Newman and Lucy Jarvis. 60 mins.
VHS: S05319. $24.95.

China on the March
Written and narrated by Enakashi Bhavani, this documentary is an intriguing chronicle of the turbulent early years of the Communist revolution.
VHS: S15485. $39.95.
Moan Bhavnani, China, 1949-58

China—The Cold Red War
The ideological battles between the US and the USSR were nothing compared to the fierce and inter-communistic battles between the Soviets and the People's Republic of China. 70 mins.
VHS: S12713. $19.98.

The Chinese Way of Life
The People's Republic of China combines ancient ways with thoroughly modern ambitions. Beijing's Forbidden City and the Great Wall are historic sites that continue to draw contemporary tourists. This film offers insights into China's rapidly changing culture. 24 mins.
VHS: S23711. $129.95.

Discovering China and Tibet
Enter the Forbidden City of the Ming Dynasty. Travel to Tibet, a Buddhist culture that remains virtually isolated from the rest of the world. Witness the effects of modernization on the Chinese workplace, a growing industry that has transformed China into an awakening giant. 52 mins.
VHS: S10777. $24.95.

The First Emperor of China
An archeological investigation of the magnificent tomb complex of Qin Shi Huang Di, China's emperor in the third century B.C. The program guides its viewers through the actual excavation, an aerial view of the Great Wall, and a guided tour through the Qin Museum.
Laser: LD70004. $99.95.

Generations: A Chinese Family
A warm and unforgettable portrait of a contemporary Chinese family as they embrace traditions and meet new challenges. Doctor Shen Fasheng, a traditional Chinese doctor, introduces us to his wife, mother, children, and grandchildren. Together they relate their family history, and share with the viewer an intimate glimpse of their daily lives. Produced by Maryknoll Media. 28 mins.
VHS: S04926. $24.95.

I Saw Him in the Rice Field
The inspiring story of Bishop James E. Walsh, among the first U.S. missionaries to arrive in China and last to leave when he was released from a Chinese prison in 1970. His love for the Chinese people began the day he arrived there and endured through 12 years of imprisonment. This film traces the career of this remarkable man. Produced by Maryknoll Media. 28 mins.
VHS: S04929. $24.95.

Ming Garden
Documents the first cultural exchange between the People's Republic of China and the United States, the installation at the Metropolitan Museum of Art of a Ming-style garden courtyard. These gardens are renowned for their unusual rock formations of naturally eroded limestone, elegant wood architectural elements and fired terra cotta brickwork. 30 mins.
VHS: S03400. $29.95.

Moving the Mountain
The momentous events surrounding the Tiananmen Square uprisings of May 1989 are at the center of this moving film by Michael (28 Up, 35 Up) Apted. Part documentary and part dramatization, it captures the feeling of hope and change that inspired the young demonstrators as they sought democracy and confronted a brutal regime. Newsreel footage and powerful personal testimonies of participants in the Tiananmen Square uprisings make this a powerful and compelling film.
VHS: S26863. $99.98.
Laser: LD75418. $39.99.
Michael Apted, USA, 1995, 83 mins.

Religion and Culture in China
China, a growing force in the world scene, has tried to repress all religions. These days, the active practice of religious faith is alive and growing, and its values are clearly in harmony with Chinese culture. Exclusive footage of China provides a background for a discussion of the relationship between faith and culture and the future role of the Catholic church. Produced by Maryknoll Media. 28 mins.
VHS: S06263. $24.95.

The Silk Road: An Ancient World of Adventure
For thousands of years, the fabled Silk Road, as traveled by Marco Polo, was the major link between the people of Europe and the vast riches of mysterious China. Spanning the deserts, grasslands and seas between Rome, Istanbul and the major cities of China, the Silk Road witnessed an ongoing parade of traders and goods, carrying with them their art, religion and culture. The impact of the Silk Road is immeasurable—giants such as Alexander the Great and tyrants like Genghis Khan created our world's history while striding along its path. This first co-production of China Central TV and the outside world was ten years in the making, and produced at a cost exceeding $50 million. Aired to critical acclaim in over 25 countries, it remains the highest rated series in Japan's television history. With a unique soundtrack by Kitaro, the series is available in six separately packaged volumes.
Across the Taklamakan Desert. Be the first foreign visitor in over 75 years to enter an ancient Buddhist city before attempting to cross the Taklamakan Desert, which means "the place from which nothing living returns." After losing your way in 120 degree heat, you will stumble into an ancient ruin, and then risk a night escape across the desert to safety. 55 mins.
VHS: S13407. $29.95.
Glories of Ancient Chang-An. Visit the starting point of the Silk Road, the world's largest city in the 7th century. See the incredible Clay Army of the emperor who united China and built the Great Wall. Buried for almost 2,000 years, the unearthing of the Clay Army was an archeological triumph, and the Silk Road crew were the first foreigners allowed to photograph it. Thrill to the sculptures of the world's largest tomb, enter China's most hallowed Buddhist temple, climb the Great Wall, and examine the hidden underground murals of a legendary princess. 55 mins.
VHS: S13402. $29.95.
In Search of the Kingdom of Lou-Lan. Discover a lost kingdom which vanished into the sands of the desert. Join the first journey in half a century to seek the ruins, in a secure military zone normally forbidden to visitors. You will uncover the Silk Road relics buried over a millenium ago—including a mummy preserved in a secret grave for over 2,000 years. 55 mins.
VHS: S13406. $29.95.
The Art Gallery in the Desert. Tour the world-famous Ma-gao caves, over 30 miles in length, with 3,000 murals and statues—in the middle of the Gobi Desert! Dating from 366 A.D., these caves are a tour-de-force, once-in-a-lifetime dream of art scholars and art lovers alike. 55 mins.
VHS: S13404. $29.95.
The Dark Castle. Encounter a ghost castle in the Gobi Desert, obliterated by Genghis Khan, who exterminated the people who built it. The castle, believed by the Chinese to be cursed, has not been entered for 50 years. You will embark on a Mongol camel journey, cross the desert, and enter the castle gates—alone! 55 mins.
VHS: S13405. $29.95.
Thousand Kilometers Beyond the Yellow River. Cross the Yellow River on a goat-skin raft and gaze in awe at a giant Buddha before entering secret caves never before filmed by a television crew. You will cross the former battlegrounds of the Huns and stroll the streets of a citadel town already hundreds of years old when Marco Polo lived here in the 14th century. 55 mins.
VHS: S13403. $29.95.
The Silk Road (Complete). The complete, six-volume set in a gold-embossed slipcase, at a special price.
VHS: S13408. $149.95.

The Silk Road: Collection Number Two
This second series of six documentaries follows the Silk Road, the overland path to the Far East made famous by Marco Polo. Produced with the cooperation of China Central Television, this mammoth project took over ten years to complete. It dispels the shroud of mystery surrounding the fabled cities and regions of this ancient way.
A Heat Wave Called Turfan. Between the Tian-Shen Mountains and Taklamakan Desert lies a place called the "Land of Fire." In this inhospitable stretch of the Silk Road, mankind has shaped the surroundings in unique and unusual ways. There are the Thousand Buddha Caves with paintings and carvings dating back hundreds of years, the Jiao-ha Castle carved from living rock atop a cliff, and even the Karez, an underground aqueduct system. 55 mins.
VHS: S20881. $29.95.
Journey into Music—South Through the Tian-Shen Mountains. In this segment the customs of the Uighurs are revealed, while the route rises to meet the high mountain pass at Teinmenquan. In the Kysil Caves a trove of Buddhist art can be seen dating from the third century. 55 mins.
VHS: S20883. $29.95.
Khotan—Oasis of Silk and Jade. In the Kun-Lun mountains jade has been mined for centuries, while precious jewels have been sought in the riverbeds below. Weavers continue to ply their ancient trade making rugs. And the Buddhist temple city of Dandan Oilik still stands as a testament to the people who live along this way. 55 mins.
VHS: S20880. $29.95.
Through the Tian-Shen Mountains by Rail. This part of The Silk Road stretches from Turfan over 300 miles of rail to Korla. Along the way you will pass through the notorious, desiccated Gobi Desert. During the construction of the railway, treasures were uncovered from grave mounds hinting at the long history of this remote region. 55 mins.
VHS: S20882. $29.95.
Two Roads to the Pamirs. Kashgar is a Muslim town which can be seen caught up in the riotous celebration greeting the end of Ramadan. Here master craftsmen still transform silk and wood into precious commodities prized the world over. Finally, a Tajik wedding party shows the people of this often overlooked region engaged in an intimate ceremony which everyone can understand and enjoy. 55 mins.
VHS: S20885. $29.95.
Where Horses Fly Like the Wind. Across the Tian-Shen mountains lies the region inhabited by Kazahks (Cossacks), descendants of the Mongols, former rulers of the great Mongol empire. In the West Land are the very horses used by Ghengis Khan and his men. 55 mins.
VHS: S20884. $29.95.
The Silk Road Number Two, Set.
VHS: S20886. $149.95.

japanese CINEMA

The Adventures of a Blind Man (Zato Ichi Skishoyaburi)
The astounding martial arts expert and swordsman samurai Zato Ichi is cornered and outnumbered when he goes to Kasama Town to celebrate the New Year. He uncovers a plot of murder and intrigue that involves the corrupt local magistrate. Japanese with English subtitles.
VHS: S26529. $59.95.
Kimoyoshi Yada, Japan, 1965, 86 mins.

Bad Boys
Susumu Hani's first feature film was almost unanimously praised by critics. Based on a collection of papers written by boys at a reform school, this film was shot on location and acted by real inmates who were, in effect, reliving their own experiences. Adding to the gritty realism is the extensive use of 8mm cameras and hand held shots to photograph scenes as an unobtrusive observer."…among the most talented of the younger generation of film directors from Japan" (Joan Mellen). Japanese with English subtitles.
VHS: S15376. $39.95.
Susumu Hani, Japan, 1960, 90 mins.

Black Lizard
A hilarious caper movie written originally for the stage by Yukio Mishima; the plot concerns a female jewel thief who kidnaps nubile youths and ferries them to a glitzoid secret island. There she turns them into naked love statues—one of them bizarrely played by Mishima himself. Miss Lizard is portrayed by the transvestite actor Akihiro Miwa, who flounces around in an impossible collection of boas and chokers and turns every flourish of her cigarette holder into an over-the-top arabesque. Called "a tale of love, passion, greed and necrophilia" by the *New York Times*, and "Naughty Japanese noir. Like something by Almodovar or John Waters" (*Village Voice*). Japanese with English subtitles.
VHS: S16261. $49.95.
Kinji Fukasaku, Japan, 1968, 90 mins.

The Blind Swordsman's Cane Sword (Kato Ichi Tekka Tabi)
Once again the long suffering but incredibly noble and diligent samurai Zato Ichi is back. Swordplay and martial arts, artfully choreographed, make this a standout in the popular series. Japanese with English subtitles.
VHS: S26530. $59.95.
Kimiyoshi Yasuda, Japan, 1967, 93 mins.

Blind Woman's Curse
Combing a historical yakuza gangster story with horror film atmosphere makes this film a cult favorite. It follows the chain of mysterious events that unfolds when a woman yakuza boss accidentally blinds a woman from a rival gang. Soon violence threatens to engulf everyone in sight. Japanese with English subtitles.
VHS: S26672. $39.95.
Teruo Ishii, Japan, 1970, 83 mins.

Double Suicide
Faithful to the Bunraku puppet theatre tradition for which it was originally written, Shinoda's surrealist, overtly sexual and erotic film concerns Jihei, a merchant of paper products, who has neglected his business because of his relentless pursuit of Koharu, a prostitute. Despite the efforts of both his wife and brother to help him, the business is failing, and a business rival wants to buy out his contract. Based on the play by Chikamatsu Monzaemon. Japanese with English subtitles.
VHS: S07362. $59.95.
Masahiro Shinoda, Japan, 1969, 100 mins.

Family Game
Irreverent, surreal, unpredictable, Morita's film pokes fun at contemporary Japanese ideals—educational achievement, high technology, urban gentility, in the story of a Japanese teenager who has everything money can buy—except grades. Family hires Yoshimoto, a poor but cantankerous college student, whose influence on the family is a combination of Godzilla, Karl Marx and a marine sergeant, waging class war on his natural enemies for the best possible incentive: profit. Japanese with English subtitles.
VHS: S06460. $59.95.
Yoshimitsu Morita, Japan, 1983, 107 mins.

Gate of Hell
An exquisitely stylized tragedy of a warrior's desire for a married noblewoman told in exotic color. Wonderfully choreographed battle scenes, incredible textures and composition. Story is set in 12th century Japan and based on *Rape of Lucrece*. Japanese with English subtitles.
VHS: S00483. $24.95.
Teinosuke Kinugasa, Japan, 1954

Ghost of Yotsuya
This bizarre, spine-tingling, horrifying tale of the supernatural deals with the psychological torture of the inner mind, and stars Shigeru Amachi and Katsuko Wakasugi. Based on a 250-year-old legend, a masterless samurai must shed his wife and marry a younger and wealthier maiden. Japanese with English subtitles.
VHS: S00497. $59.95.
Nobuo Nakagawa, Japan, 1950, 100 mins.

Golden Demon
Koji Shima's breathtaking film about the destructive effect of wealth on society, with the melodramatic tale of star-crossed lovers. An early color film for Japan. Japanese with English subtitles.
VHS: S03305. $29.95.
Koji Shima, Japan, 1953, 95 mins.

Gonza the Spearman
A beautiful film, set in 18th century Japan. The handsome but overly ambitious Gonza is one of the Matsue clan's most talented lancers. Although he is already engaged to the sister of one of his fellow retainers, Gonza agrees to wed the daughter of his lord to better his position. The fiance's infuriated brother plots against Gonza. This classic tale of conflicts between love and honor, duty and devotion, won a Silver Bear at the Berlin Film Festival. Japanese with English subtitles.
VHS: S12204. $79.95.
Masahiro Shinoda, Japan, 1986, 126 mins.

Graves of the Fireflies
Adapted from the story by Akiyuki Nosaka, this portrait of post-war Japanese society before the American occupation deals with Seita and his young sister Setsuko as they try to survive in the ravaged countryside. Japanese with English subtitles.
VHS: S18628. $39.95.

Harikiri
This grim and exquisite film explores the honor in death and the death of honor venerated by the 17th-century samurai. After an unemployed samurai is forced to commit ritual suicide before a feudal lord, his father-in-law returns to the scene, seemingly to commit the same act. Instead this warrior acts out against the cruelly rigid society that enforces such harsh discipline. Japanese with English subtitles.
VHS: S22459. $39.95.
Masaki Kobayashi, Japan, 1962, 135 mins.

Himatsuri
An independent, fortyish lumberjack (Kinya Kitaoji) is outraged by pollution, commercial exploitation and the destruction of wildlife. Believing he's the protector of the mountains through his divine relationship with the goddess of the mountains, he turns to violence against his family to voice his opposition to change and technological intrusion. Awesome sounds and images in a daring film. Japanese with English subtitles.
VHS: S01603. $59.95.
Mitsuo Yanagimachi, Japan, 1985, 120 mins.

Human Condition
One of the great works of Japanese cinema, "this nine and one-half hour long, humanistic anti-war fresco is magnificent, including many forceful scenes that depict the horrors and cruelties of war. Its director, Kobayashi, said, 'I wanted to bring to life the tragedy of men who are forced into war against their will. Kaji is both the oppressor and the oppressed and he learns that he can never stop being an oppressor while he himself is oppressed. Of course I wanted to denounce the crimes of war but I also wanted to show how human society can become inhumane.' " Directed by Masaki Kobayashi, Japan, 1959-61.
Human Condition Part 1 (No Greater Love). The production at mining camps has come to a standstill. Japan is desperate, so Kaji, who believes that war can be won through the hearts and minds of labor, is given authority. 200 mins. B&W. Japanese with English subtitles.
VHS: S08515. $59.95.
Human Condition Part 2 (Road to Eternity). As this sequence opens, Kaji is tortured by the military police for having mistreated the Chinese. Allowed one memorable night with his wife, he is ordered to the front. His records brand him as a "red," and his superiors mistreat him. 180 mins. B&W. Japanese with English subtitles.
VHS: S08516. $59.95.
Human Condition Part 3 (A Soldier's Prayer). Ravaged by hunger and thirst, Kaji awakens to a world gone mad. Surrender? To whom? Americans? Russians? Chiang Kai-shek? Surrendering to avoid needless slaughter, Kaji is force marched to Siberia, where he finds his worst enemy is now a collaborator who brands him a war criminal. Escaping into the wastelands of Siberia, he continues his desperate journey into the ultimate reality of war. 190 mins. B&W. Japanese with English subtitles.
VHS: S08517. $59.95.
Masaki Kobayashi, Japan, 1958-61

The Inland Sea
Lucille Carra's interpretation of critic and author Donald Richie's memoir about growing up in Japan's islands is a private odyssey of the inner and outer landscapes. "Conversational and witty, Donald Richie's voice is beautifully full and the film is quiet and hypnotic" (*Honolulu Star-Bulletin*). Cinematography by Hiro Narita. Score by Toru Takemitsu (*Ran*).
VHS: S18726. $29.95.
Laser: CLV. LD72112. $49.95.
Lucille Carra, Japan, 1992, 57 mins.

Island
Cinematic haiku. A man, his wife and two small boys are the only inhabitants of an island and must, each day, go to the mainland to get their supply of water. The entire story is told without dialog, but rather through visuals, sounds and music. The result is a moving, intensely human allegory for existence with outstanding performances from Nobuko Otowa and Taiji Tonoyama. No dialog.
VHS: S00639. $29.95.
Kaneto Shindo, Japan, 1961, 96 mins.

Kwaidan
Four terrifying tales of the supernatural filmed with visual sensitivity. This is no Japanese monster movie. Rather, it creeps up on you by appealing to human emotions and fears. An Academy Award nominee, this distinctive work is filled with graceful camera movement, unusual colors, haunting sound effects and music. Japanese with English subtitles.
VHS: S00694. $29.95.
Laser: Widescreen. LD71083. $69.95.
Masaki Kobayashi, Japan, 1964, 161 mins.

Late Chrysanthemums
In this adaptation of three Fumiko Hayashi stories, four retired geishas contemplate their past lives and their continuing unequal relationships with men. Filmmaker Mikio Naruse's films center around "women not favored by the traditional family system. They are strong, intelligent women and something in their situation has kept them away from the opportunities for the conventional happy family. They are exiles and they feel their exile keenly" (Audie Bock).
VHS: S17791. $19.98.
Mikio Naruse, Japan, 1954, 101 mins.

Lupine Wolf
An episode from the series "Baby Cart to Hades," the film concerns Itto, a professional assassin, forced to fight his way through medieval Japan as he exterminates every foe in his path. Dubbed in English. Written by Shintaro Katsu, the author of most of the Zatoichi series. Japan, 1988.
VHS: S09037. $59.95.

Masseur Ichi, The Fugitive (Zato Ichi Kyojotabi)
In this martial arts extravaganza the samurai Zato Ichi finds himself trapped between the charms of an old love and his never-ending struggle for survival. Someone has placed a bounty on his head. Japanese with English subtitles.
VHS: S26528. $59.95.
Kimoyoshi Yada, Japan, 1963, 86 mins.

Mistress
A deeply moving exploration of love, betrayal and destiny. Japanese with English subtitles.
VHS: S00863. $19.95.
Shiro Toyoda, Japan, 1953, 106 mins.

Mother (Okasan)
Mikio Naruse's portrait of silent sacrifice and secret strength, the moving story of the Fukuhara family whose business is in ruins, and whose lives are filled with tragedy. But Naruse focuses on the resilience and determination, the inner moral strength of the Japanese during the post-war era, "a gripping image of a nation rising from the ashes." Japanese with English subtitles.
VHS: S06461. $59.95.
Mikio Naruse, Japan, 1952, 98 mins.

The Mystery of Rampo
A famous mystery writer continually pushes the bounds of taste with his fiction in this atmospheric thriller from Japan which is filled with eroticism and suspense. As one of the writer's characters suddenly comes to life, he is pushed into ever more surreal and dangerous situations. Japanese with English subtitles.
VHS: S26861. $99.98.
Laser: LD75415. $39.99.
Kazuyoshi Okuyama, Japan, 1994, 101 mins.

Nanami, First Love
A story of passionate desire and psychological turbulence, a troubled young man abandoned early by his mother seeks the love of a nude model and prostitute, Nanami. Fresh and intriguing visuals, creative camera angles and elaborate montage make for a powerful experience. Japanese with English subtitles.
VHS: S02170. $29.95.
Susumu Hani, Japan, 1968, 104 mins.

Okoge
Misa Shimuzu gives a great performance as the lead character Sayoko, a young women who becomes entwined with two gay men having an affair. The lovers, played by Takehiro Murata and Takeo Nakahara, cannot work out their differences despite the best efforts of Sayoko. It is a story that catalogs the sexual politics of contemporary Japan without moralizing. Japanese with English subtitles.
VHS: S20824. $79.95.
Takehiro Nakajima, Japan, 1992, 120 mins.

Onibaba
A stylish Japanese ghost tale, set in medieval Japan. A peasant woman and her daughter manage an existence by impersonating demons—sexually luring soldiers away from their comrades and murdering them. A warrior manages to save his life by seducing the daughter, but the mother's sorcery conjures up a hideous revenge. Mixing graphic violence with sex, *Onibaba* is an exotic, terrifying, supernatural fantasy. Japanese with English subtitles.
VHS: S08691. $29.95.
Kaneto Shindo, Japan, 1964, 103 mins.

Rikisha-Man
A classic film of unrequited love, starring Toshiro Mifune as a feisty rikisha puller who helps raise a young boy after the father has died, loving the boy's mother from a distance that class cannot cross. Winner of the Venice Film Festival Grand Prize. Japanese dialog with English subtitles.
VHS: S02158. $59.95.
Hiroshi Inagaki, Japan, 1958, 105 mins.

Samurai I
The first part of Hiroshi Inagaki's trilogy about Japan's most notorious 17th century swordfighter, Mushashi Miyamoto (Toshiro Mifune), details his odyssey from farmer to disaffected killer. Having fought on the losing side during the civil war, he returns as a manic outlaw caught between his feelings for a beautiful village girl and a sympathetic Buddhist priest. "The beauty of wooded sequences, several mass battle scenes and other settings is extraordinary" (*Variety*). With Rentaro Mikuni, Karuo Yashigusa and Koji Tsurato. Japanese with English subtitles.
VHS: S18905. $29.95.
Hiroshi Inagaki, Japan, 1954, 92 mins.

Samurai II
In the second part, Miyamoto's technical skills are perfected and his transformation to savage warrior is complete. He undergoes a mythic spiritual quest for inner harmony, disrupted by the presence of a rival samurai and the loss of the woman he loved. With Toshiro Mifune, Koji Tsurata and Sachio Sakai. Japanese with English subtitles.
VHS: S18906. $29.95.
Hiroshi Inagaki, Japan, 1955, 102 mins.

Samurai III
In the final part of this samurai trilogy, Miyamoto resolves the personal and professional tensions in his life, confronting the emotional pain of the two women who love him and the roguish swordsman who challenges his domain. With Toshiro Mifune, Koji Tsuruta, Kaoru Uashigusa and Takashi Shimura. Japanese with English subtitles.
VHS: S18907. $29.95.
Hiroshi Inagaki, Japan, 1956, 105 mins.

Samurai Trilogy: Complete Set
Three-tape set.
VHS: S18908. $69.95.

Shadow of China
A sweeping epic of one man's ascent to power and eventual fall from grace, *Shadow of China* tells the story of a mysterious young tycoon who fights desperately to seize control of Hong Kong—and to hide a past that could destroy him and his empire. Starring John Lone, Sammi Davis, and Vivian Wu, this film, based on the best-selling Japanese novel *Snakehead*, is the English-language film debut by acclaimed Japanese director Mitsuo Yanagimachi. Filmed on location in Hong Kong and Japan. "Elegant, seductive…a modern-day *Casablanca*" (Kevin Thomas, L.A. Times).
VHS: S15074. $9.98.
Mitsuo Yanagimachi, Japan/USA, 1991

She and He
Susumu Hani's first attempt to deal with the theme of women's oppression was this Antonionesque melodrama set in a sterile high rise complex. A woman resident becomes discontent with the empty life she leads with her husband and seeks to make contact with the outside world, so that she may express her inner feelings, which have no outlet within the marriage. When she finally finds a means of expression, her husband's discontent leads to tragedy. A moving story of spiritual rebirth and loss. Japanese with English subtitles.
VHS: S15377. $39.95.
Susumu Hani, Japan, 1963, 110 mins.

The Silk Road
A lavish Japanese epic about warring factions and sacred scrolls in ancient China. More than 100,000 extras were used in the grand scale battle scenes shot on location in the People's Republic of China. Zao Xingte, a failed civil servant, goes west to the kingdom of Xixia, where he is entrusted with a great task that involves a spoiled princess and protecting the hidden library of sacred scriptures. With Koichi Sako, Toshiyuki Nishida and Anna Nakagawa.
VHS: S16712. $89.95.
Laser: LD75258. $34.98.
Junya Sato, Japan, 1988, 99 mins.

Snow Country
Directed by Shiro Toyoda, *Snow Country* focuses on the conflict between Komako, a woman living in the region of northwest Honshu known as the snow country, and Shimamura, a painter in the Nihonga style who feels out of place in Tokyo and wants to escape from the capital, where he only feels alienation. Based on the novel by the same name, *Snow Country* features Ryo Ikebe and Keoko Kishi. Japanese with English subtitles.
   VHS: S08518. $29.95.
   Shiro Toyoda, Japan, 1967, 144 mins.

Summer Vacation: 1999
Romantic and beautifully realized, this film tells the story of four boys who experience the adolescent birth pangs of romantic love, sexual awareness and jealousy. Left behind at boarding school during their vacation, the teenagers' summer idyll is disrupted by the arrival of another youth who seems to reincarnate a dead friend. Delicate and provocative, Kaneko's film creates a haunting image of youth suspended between innocence and experience, androgyny and sexual maturity. Japanese with English subtitles.
   VHS: S13917. $69.95.
   Shusuke Kaneko, Japan, 1988, 90 mins.

The Sword of Doom
The legendary Japanese actor and martial artist Toshiro Mifune stars as the instructor of a brash and revenge-bent young Samurai, played by Tatsuya Nakadai. This action-adventure from Toho Films is presented in Japanese with English subtitles. B&W.
   VHS: S03635. $29.95.
   Laser: Widescreen. **LD75411. $49.95.**
   Kihachi Okamoto, Japan, 1967, 120 mins.

Tetsuo: The Iron Man
A post-punk, Japanese film about a man attacked by a feral woman with a metal hand and his bizarre mutation into a perverse combination of man and machine. It's like Godard remaking *Blue Velvet*. With Tomoroh Taguchi, Nobu Kanaoka and Shinya Tsukamoto. Japanese with English subtitles.
   VHS: S18410. $19.98.
   Laser: LD72348. $39.99.
   Shinya Tsukamoto, Japan, 1989, 67 mins.

Tokyo Decadence
Japanese novelist and filmmaker Ryu Murakami adapts his novel *Topaz*, about a prostitute's (Miho Nikaido) search for redemption. Ai falls under the spell of a charismatic dominatrix and tries desperately to reverse her slide into cocaine dependency and sexual slavery. "Murakami adeptly throws us off balance, with deadpan black humor and a complex politic involving the notion of 'wealth without pride'" (Toronto Film Festival). With Sayoko Amano, Tenmei Kanou and Masahiko Shimada. Japanese with English subtitles.
   VHS: S19176. $29.95.
   Ryu Murakami, Japan, 1991, 112 mins.

Traffic Jam
A young Tokyo couple are at the center of this dark, comic satire. They take their children to visit the husband's faraway parents, but the long road trip proves to be filled with disastrous incidents. Their journey becomes a metaphor for the gap between young Japanese people and their ancestral roots. Japanese with English subtitles.
   VHS: S24731. $79.95.
   Mitsuo Kurotsuchi, Japan, 1991, 108 mins.

Traitors of the Blue Castle
Story of samurai plots against the Shogun features action and swordplay. 1958. 100 minutes. Japanese with English subtitles.
   VHS: S03004. $59.95.

Twenty-Four Eyes
The cost of war is counted in wrecked hopes and wasted human potential in Kinoshita's powerful denunciation of a system that stifles individual growth and transforms personal ambition into unflinching devotion to the state. The films begins in 1928, and follows Miss Oishi, a shockingly modern and progressive Japanese woman, who begins her tenure as an elementary school teacher. To her, the future seems to hold limitless possibilities for her 12 first-grade teachers. But when the story ends, in the late 1940's, this promise has been wrecked by war, poverty, and restrictive tradition. Japanese with English subtitles.
   VHS: S07336. $59.95.
   Keisuke Kinoshita, Japan, 1954, 116 mins.

When a Woman Ascends the Stairs
Hideko Takamine and Tatsuya Nakadai star in this beautiful, ornate drama about a Ginza bar hostess on the eve of her 30th birthday. The films of Japanese master Mikio Naruse were virtually unknown in the United States until the writings of Donald Ritchie and Audie Bock heralded his contributions as the equal of Kurosawa, Ozu or Mizoguchi.
   VHS: S17792. $19.98.
   Mikio Naruse, Japan, 1960, 110 mins.

Zatoichi:
Masseur Ichi and a Chest of Gold
Zatoichi, the blind gambler and masseur, is caught in a cross fire of greed and ambition and must clear his name and his long-time friend, the benevolent *yakuza* chief, who was framed in a gold robbery. Japanese with English subtitles.
   VHS: S17066. $59.95.
   Kazuo Ikehiro, Japan, 1964, 83 mins.

Zatoichi: Masseur Ichi on the Road
As yakuza gangster bosses feud, Ichi ignores their pleas for help because he feels compelled to help a young rich girl on the run. She accidentally injured a powerful lord when he tried to rape her. Her passage is further endangered as rival gangs hope to capture her for ransom. Japanese with English subtitles. 1964, 85 mins.
   VHS: S20857. $59.95.

Zatoichi: The Blind Swordsman and the Chess Expert
A tale of friendship, bravery and discipline, this work details the further adventures of Zatoichi, who befriends a master chess player. Zatoichi gambles all of his money to pay for the medical services of a young woman wounded in a sword fight with Japanese gangsters attempting to rob them. Japanese with English subtitles.
   VHS: S17067. $59.95.
   Kenji Misumi, Japan, 1965, 87 mins.

Zatoichi: The Blind Swordsman and the Fugitives
This samurai drama pits Zatoichi (Shintaro Katsu) against a band of ruffian outlaws. Zatoichi is caught in a sinister web of torture and extortion as local bandits and gangs brutalize the countryside. "The action simply takes your breath away with its speed, surprises and detail" (*The Hawaii Herald*). With Yumiko Nogawa, Kayo Mikimoto and Kyosuke Machida. Japanese with English subtitles.
   VHS: S18911. $59.95.
   Kimiyoshi Yasuda, Japan, 1968, 82 mins.

Zatoichi:
The Blind Swordsman Samaritan
The fight for justice takes on a personal dimension for the famed blind swordsman when his sister Osode sells herself to pay off her brother's gambling debt. This tragic turn of events is the result of an evil plot, designed by a yakuza boss who desires the charming Osode. Zatoichi's crusade for justice has now become a matter of his own family's honor. Japanese with English subtitles. 1968, 84 mins.
   VHS: S20856. $59.95.

Zatoichi:
The Blind Swordsman's Vengeance
Zatoichi (Shintaro Katsu) defends a dying man against a group of young gangsters, when he's entangled in a plan to return some money to an isolated village, now overtaken by a band of guerrillas who must be neutralized. With Shigeru Amachi, Mayumi Ogawa, and Kei Sato. Japanese with English subtitles.
   VHS: S17068. $59.95.
   Tokuzo Tanaka, Japan, 1966, 83 mins.

Zatoichi:
The Life and Opinion of Masseur Ichi
Zatoichi is drawn into an epic revenge match between ruthless gangs in the province Shimosa. When one of the lords tries to enlist Zatoichi's services, the other gang boss hires a savage killer. With Masayo Mari, Ryuzo Shimada, Gen Mitamura and Shigeru Amachi. Japanese with English subtitles.
   VHS: S18909. $59.95.
   Kenji Misumi, Japan, 1962, 96 mins.

Zatoichi: The Return of Masseur Ichi
Masseur Ichi uncovers the crucial secret behind a distinguished lord whom he is hired to massage. Realizing the gravity of the situation, the lord's vassal seeks to silence the blind and seemingly defenseless Ichi. As usual, those who would underestimate this hero pay dearly. Japanese with English subtitles. 1962, 73 mins.
   VHS: S20858. $59.95.

Zatoichi: Zatoichi's Flashing Sword
Fleeing brutal gangsters, Zatoichi is embroiled in a feud between completing yakuza bosses. He declares his allegiance to the benevolent Tsumugi and Yasu responds by raising the stakes, deploying bribery, extortion and murder to gain control of a strategically important river. With Naoko Kubo, Mayumi Nagisa, Ryutaro Gomi and Yutaka Nakamura. Japanese with English subtitles.
   VHS: S18910. $59.95.
   Kazuo Ikehiro, Japan, 1964, 82 mins.

JUZO ITAMI

The Funeral
Juzo Itami's breakthrough Japanese film is a black comedy concerning the rivalries and hypocrisies of a contemporary Japanese family which is called to the funeral of their father. Itami deftly satirizes contemporary Japanese mores and idiosyncracies. Japanese with English subtitles.
   VHS: S07104. $19.98.
   Juzo Itami, Japan, 1986, 112 mins.

Minbo—Or the Gentle Art of Japanese Extortion
Juzo Itami turns his acid humor to Japan's infamous institution—the Yakuza gangs—in this film about a courageous attorney who rallies all of the employees at a hotel in an effort to resist the Yakuza blackmail. After the film was completed, thugs viciously attacked the director, forcing him to go into hiding. A brilliant, satirical look at the underbelly of Japanese modern life. Japanese with English subtitles.
   VHS: S26090. $79.95.
   Juzo Itami, Japan, 1994, 123 mins.

Tampopo
One of the funniest, most enjoyable, satirical comedies is this treasure of a movie the plot of which, loosely, concerns the quest for the perfect Japanese noodle. A mixed-bag of noodle-obsessed men help the heroine of *Tampopo* run the best noodle restaurant in Tokyo, a plan which involves a lot of hilarious madness. Japanese with English subtitles.
   VHS: S07101. $19.98.
   Laser: CLV. **LD72036. $29.98.**
   Juzo Itami, Japan, 1987, 114 mins.

Taxing Woman
Juzo Itami's satiric comedy of ambition, greed and the battle of the sexes. A disarming and dedicated woman tax collector meets her match in a millionaire "love hotel" tycoon and tax-evader extraordinaire. Winner of nine Japanese Academy Awards. Japanese with English subtitles.
   VHS: S08689. $19.98.
   Laser: LD70259. $49.95.
   Juzo Itami, Japan, 1987, 127 mins.

A Taxing Woman's Return
In this rousing follow-up to his 1987 hit, *A Taxing Woman*, Juzo Itami brings back his resourceful and charming heroine, tax inspector Ryoko Itakura (described by Vincent Canby of *The New York Times* as "a far more endearing crime buster than Batman") for another battle of wits against the fat cats and swindlers who thrive in Japan's booming economy. Japanese with English subtitles.
   VHS: S12195. $79.95.
   Juzo Itami, Japan, 1989 127 mins.

SHOHEI IMAMURA

The Ballad of Narayama
Winner of the Grand Prize at the 1983 Cannes Film Festival, *The Ballad of Narayama* is based on one of the most astonishing of all Japanese legends. A century ago in a remote mountain village, local custom dictated that when a person reached 70 years of age, he was taken to Mount Narayama to die. A brilliant film from director Imamura that delivers a vigorous and beautiful affirmation of family, life and death. "A masterpiece of Japanese Cinema to stand beside *Ugetsu*, *Tokyo Story*, or *The Seven Samurai*" (M. Wilmington *LA Weekly*). Japanese with English subtitles.
   VHS: S14498. $29.95.
   Shohei Imamura, Japan, 1983, 129 mins.

Black Rain
A somber, restrained, and very moving story detailing ten years in the life of a family which survived the nuclear bombing of Hiroshima—and the ways in which their bodies and souls were poisoned by the fallout. Filled with haunting images. Japanese with English subtitles. Letterbox format.
   VHS: S14068. $19.98.
   Shohei Imamura, Japan, 1988, 123 mins.

Eijanaika
Called an "historical documentary", *Eijanaika* is "a sprawling, superb-looking period piece charged with Imamura's characteristically fevered eroticism and underplayed black humor. As spectacle, it's stunning in its dynamism and the last half-hour presents one of the most libidinal depictions of a mass uprising since Eisenstein restaged the storming of the Winter Palace. As in *Vengeance Is Mine*, Imamura imbues the cruelty with virtuoso ferocity and an appalling, visionary beauty" (J. Hoberman, *Village Voice*). Japanese with English subtitles.
   VHS: S12205. $79.95.
   Shohei Imamura, Japan, 1981, 151 mins.

Insect Woman
One of Japan's finest actresses, Sachiko Hidari, plays Tome, an impoverished country girl who escapes a brutal existence which includes rape and incest, by fleeing to Tokyo. She proves to be an amoral survivor who fights her way to success as a madam. A dark and often humorous story of sexual exploitation. Japanese with English subtitles.
   VHS: Out of print. For rental only.
   Laser: Widescreen. **LD71561. $49.95.**
   Shohei Imamura, Japan, 1963, 123 mins.

The Pornographers
An exact translation of this film's title would be *The Pornographer—An Introduction to Anthropology*, suggesting, perhaps, Imamura's incomparable wit and perception of the perverse. The bizarre story, almost entirely shot on location, is the story of an Osaka man who makes pornographic films out of a sense of duty to his fellow man. The scenes of him making films are, according to critic/historian Donald Richie, "some of the funniest sequences ever to appear in a Japanese film." Throughout, the film is a technical tour-de-force, the camera constantly taking the role of the voyeur. Japanese with English subtitles.
   VHS: S08697. $29.95.
   Shohei Imamura, Japan, 1966, 92 mins.

Vengeance Is Mine
One of the most strikingly original films of the modern cinema, *Vengeance Is Mine* is an "eclectically horrifying portrait of a psychopathic criminal named Iwao Enokizo…(the film) makes every other film on the *In Cold Blood* theme look like child's play," wrote Tom Allen in *The Village Voice*. Enokizu becomes suspect in the murder of two men who work for the government tobacco monopoly. A nationwide dragnet is set up to capture him, but for 78 days he travels throughout Japan committing fraud, cheating women and taking numerous lives. Japanese with English subtitles.
   VHS: S09959. $39.95.
   Laser: CAV. **LD71391. $89.95.**
   Shohei Imamura, Japan, 1979, 112 mins.

NAGISA OSHIMA

Cruel Story of Youth
Oshima's second feature conveys the pent-up sexuality and disillusionment among Japan's postwar generation. Two lovers live outside the boundaries of their society, performing shakedowns on unsuspecting middle-aged men and speeding away on the angry boy's gleaming motorcycle with the goods. With seemingly disconnected details and stark framings, Oshima creates an atmosphere akin to the French New Wave. Japanese with English subtitles.
   VHS: S16696. $29.95.
   Nagisa Oshima, Japan, 1960, 96 mins.

Empire of Passion (aka In the Realm of Passion)
Oshima follows up his notorious *In the Realm of the Senses* with the story of a peasant woman who, with the help of her lover, kills her husband. Their future hopes wither, however, when the injured party returns from the dead to haunt and endlessly torment them. This sad tale of two lovers consumed by the very passion that they seek is presented to the viewer amidst a somber landscape of embattled moods and emotions, tragic cruelty and overwhelming calm—and the forceful performances and superb photography of this gripping film are unified under Oshima's remarkable lyrical style. *Empire of Passion* earned him the award of Best Director at the 1978 Cannes Film Festival. Starring Kazuko Yoshiyuki, Tatsuya Fuji and Takuzo Kawatani. Japanese with yellow English subtitles.
   VHS: S14574. $19.98.
   Nagisa Oshima, Japan, 1978, 110 mins.

In the Realm of the Senses
A scandal when it was seized by the New York customs and refused entry into the United States, and the sensation of the New York Film Festival, *In the Realm of the Senses* is, in the words of the *Los Angeles Times*, "probably the most thoughtful work of and on eroticism ever created." Explicit in its depiction of sex, and a film about the literally consuming passions of two people, the film is most infamous for its final castration sequence. Japanese with English subtitles.
   VHS: S12222. $19.98.
   Nagisa Oshima, Japan, 1971, 100 mins.

Max Mon Amour
A strange sexual farce, this film shows an unhappy housewife who finds an uncomplicated love in the arms of someone new. Only this strong, silent lover is an ape, a chimpanzee to be more specific. The woman's husband, Higgins the diplomat, is quite understanding and even invites the chimp to move in. It's a comedy of manners with a twist. French with English subtitles.
   VHS: S20740. $89.95.
   Nagisa Oshima, France, 1986, 94 mins.

Merry Christmas Mr. Lawrence
David Bowie delivers a strong performance in Nagisa Oshima's (*In the Realm of the Senses*) apocalyptic tale of a Japanese prison camp during World War II. The film also features To Conti and Ryuichi Sakamoto. English dialog.
   VHS: S00850. $19.95.
   Nagisa Oshima, Japan/Australia, 1983, 124 mins.

The Sun's Burial
Oshima's most blatantly amoral and extravagantly violent version of the juvenile delinquency drama, set in a world of rival teenage gangs, pimps and prostitutes. Set in a hellish Osaka where an exquisitely cruel femme fatale vies for control of the area's most profitable business with the gangs. Japanese with English subtitles.
   VHS: S20596. $79.95.
   Nagisa Oshima, Japan, 1960, 87 mins.

Violence at Noon
After investigating the case history of a rapist, Nagisa Oshima created one of the most effective crime films while transcending the genre. The story unfolds through the recollections of two women—the criminal's wife and one of his victims—strangely united in an effort to protect the rapist from capture. Their despair is linked to that of the rapist himself, and ultimately to the failure of the socialist movement in postwar Japan. Oshima masterfully demonstrates the ways in which the compulsion to crime and self-destruction reflects the pathology of the society in which the criminal and victim lives. With Saeda Kawaguchi, Akiko Koyama, Kei Sato and Matsuhiro Toura. Japanese with English subtitles.
   VHS: S16037. $79.95.
   Nagisa Oshima, Japan, 1966, 100 mins.

KON ICHIKAWA

An Actor's Revenge
A female impersonator in the Kabuki tradition seeks revenge against the villains who caused his parent's death. This complex tale, set in 19th-century Japan, involves numerous plot twists as it blurs the distinctions between illusion and reality. Japanese with English subtitles.
   VHS: S20593. $79.95.
   Kon Ichikawa, Japan, 1963, 114 mins.

Being Two Isn't Easy
A melancholy work about the joys and mysteries of life as experienced by a two-year-old boy, Taro. Taro is thunderstruck by the small (the climbing of stairs) and the significant (space travel). Ichikawa evokes an impressionistic picture of daily life and inter-family conflicts. The film "catches the fantasy and wonder with which a child must gaze" (*Variety*). With Fujko Yamamoto, Eiji Funakoshi and Hiroo Suzuki. Japanese with English subtitles.
   VHS: S20416. $29.95.
   Kon Ichikawa, Japan, 1962, 88 mins.

Burmese Harp
A Japanese army private in Burma is so revolted by the carnage of war that he refuses to return home. Dressed as a Buddhist monk, he remains to bury the dead. The first Japanese film to stress pacifism, *Burmese Harp* is remarkable for its pulsating black and white images and its humanist fervor. Japanese with English subtitles.
   VHS: S00545. $29.95.
   Laser: LD72321. $49.95.
   Kon Ichikawa, Japan, 1956, 116 mins.

Enjo
A superb adaptation of Mishima's novel *Temple of the Golden Pavillion*, this beautifully photographed, disturbing portrait of a man pushed to extremes is the story of innocence betrayed. The young man (played by Ichikawa) comes to post-war Kyoto to become a monk at a cherished Japanese temple. His miserably poor background and his innocence do not prepare him for the pervasive corruption of the urban world, and in a final desperate and violent act, he makes a plea for a fiery purity by setting fire to the holy temple. Japanese with English subtitles.
   VHS: S23756. $79.95.
   Kon Ichikawa, Japan, 1958, 98 mins.

Fires on the Plain
Ichikawa's powerful depiction of the inhumanity of war and passionate cry for sanity. A soldier, part of the retreating Japanese army, is forced to hide in the Philippine jungle, where he finds disease, death and cannibalism. Minimal dialog and intense visual images build to a work of immense power.
   VHS: S00444. $29.95.
   Laser: Widescreen. **LD75074. $49.95.**
   Kon Ichikawa, Japan, 1959, 105 mins.

Makioka Sisters
The Makioka Sisters chronicles the life and affairs of four sisters in 20's Japan. An older, conservative sister tries to continue family traditions and pretensions to status, while the younger sisters discover the new freedoms becoming available to them. This battle over traditional ways is set in marked contrast to social and political changes going on in Japan. Japanese with English subtitles.
   VHS: Out of print. For rental only.
   Laser: CLV. **LD72110. $69.95.**
   Kon Ichikawa, Japan, 1983, 130 mins.

Odd Obsession
An elderly Japanese man with a beautiful young wife finds it difficult to reconcile his feelings of desire with his decreasing potency in this "new interpretation of the love-death theme in which some of the most sordid of human actions are captured by means of the sheerest physical beauty…Erotic obsession is presented with such near-claustrophobic intensity that one longs for outdoor scenes…everything is hidden, secreted away" (Donald Richie). Japanese with English subtitles.
   VHS: S04463. $29.95.
   Kon Ichikawa, Japan, 1960, 96 mins.

Tokyo Olympiad

Utilizing over 100 cameras, the director captures the essence of competition and the beauty of the human form as has never been done before. Ichikawa was commissioned by the Olympic committee to direct a film which would capture the athletic excellence of the event. Not being a sports fan, he chose to present the events in a way which would express the art and beauty involved. Hailed by Gene Siskel as one of his *Top Ten Films I'd Like to See on Video.*
VHS: Out of print. For rental only.
  Laser: CAV, widescreen. LD71371. $99.95.
Kon Ichikawa, Japan, 1964, 170 mins.

Face of Another

Face of Another ascribes metaphysical dimensions to everyday life. A factory worker left faceless by an accident suffers agonies of exile and solitude until he acquires a mask of someone else's face through plastic surgery. Having another face allows him to lead a double life and affords him the chance to seduce his wife as a stranger. Metaphorically, the film treats the chronic anxieties of powerlessness and the small, uniquely Japanese terror of facelessness through nuclear devastation. Japanese with English subtitles.
VHS: S09960. $59.95.
Hiroshi Teshigahara, Japan, 1966, 110 mins.

Rikyu

Teshigahara presents a poignant film exploring the struggle between art and power. Drinking tea was once a casual ritual around which social and diplomatic relationships were practiced. In the 16th Century, Sen-no Rikyu refined the art of the tea ceremony to aesthetic and spiritual heights. His revolutionary ideas brought him to the forefront of Japanese politics when war lord Hideyoshi Toyotomi confided in him as Tea Master, and together they sought what to each was most high: for Rikyu it was beauty, for Hideyoshi, power. Thoughtful performances from Rentaro Mikune, Tsutomu Yamazaki and Yoshiko Mita bring this historical allegory to its tragic close. Japanese with English subtitles.
VHS: S15684. $79.95.
  Laser: CLV. LD71490. $39.95.
Hiroshi Teshigahara, Japan, 1990, 116 mins.

Woman in the Dunes

A woman, confined to a deep pit in the sand dunes, where she is fed by neighbors and forced to clear her house of the threatening sands, is joined by a passing photographer whom the villagers have trapped into sharing her work and bed—forever. This is the situation of Teshigahara's great symbolic and sensual adaptation of Kobo Abe's novel, in which he "builds up the erotic tension…with extreme close-ups that transform the human body into landscape…" (*Oxford Companion to Film*). With Eiji Okada and Kyoko Kishida. Japanese with English subtitles.
VHS: S13589. $24.95.
Hiroshi Teshigahara, Japan, 1964, 123 mins.

Bad Sleep Well

One of Kurosawa's best films, in some ways a prophetic work set in the circles of corporate government and corporations. The film is a black, twisted story of revenge in which a grieving son takes on powerful business and political figures. Set up as a tantalizing thriller, Kurosawa's melodrama is laced with irony and bitter, grotesque humor. Japanese with English subtitles.
VHS: S07334. $24.95.
Akira Kurosawa, Japan, 1959, 135 mins.

Dersu Uzala

Kurosawa's remarkable personal tale of the friendship between a wise old man and a young, Soviet explorer, filmed in the beautiful expanse of Siberia, is a unique story of man's unity with nature, and a powerful testament to faith. Russian dialog with English subtitles.
VHS: S01809. $39.95.
  Laser: Widescreen. LD75028. $69.95.
Akira Kurosawa, Japan, 1980, 124 mins.

Dodes'ka-den

Unforgettable: Kurosawa's blending of fantasy and reality in the story of a group of Tokyo slum dwellers who, cheated by life, survive on illusion and imagination. A passionate affirmation of life, beautifully photographed. The title of the film comes from the sound of the trolleys. Japanese with English subtitles.
VHS: S00351. $29.95.
  Laser: LD75389. $69.99.
Akira Kurosawa, Japan, 1976, 140 mins.

Dreams

From master director Akira Kurosawa (*Rashomon, Kagemusha, Ran*) comes perhaps his most personal film. Eight fascinating episodes dealing with war, childhood fears, the nuclear power question and man's never-ending need to harmonize with nature. Featuring breathtaking visual sequences and Martin Scorsese as Vincent Van Gogh. Japanese with English subtitles.
VHS: S13489. $92.95.
Akira Kurosawa, Japan, 1990, 120 mins.

Drunken Angel

Takashi Shimura plays a doctor who tries to bring about the spiritual and physical recovery of the human debris who live in the ashes of a poor quarter of Tokyo immediately after the war; Toshiro Mifune as an uprooted petty gambler and black-marketeer. One of Kurosawa's classic films in the vein of his love of Dostoevsky. Japanese with English subtitles.
VHS: S00378. $44.95.
Akira Kurosawa, Japan, 1948, 98 mins.

The Hidden Fortress

Set during Japan's feudal wars, this restored version of Akira Kurosawa's drama concerns a gilded princess and her loyal general who undertake a dangerous journey to their homeland, assisted only by a pair of misfits and pursued by warriors and bandits attempting to loot their gold and valuable possessions. Beautifully photographed in widescreen by Ichio Yamazaki. Letterboxed. With Toshiro Mifune, Misa Uehara and Minoru Chiaki. Japanese with English subtitles. With 13 minutes of added footage.
VHS: S00566. $39.95.
  Laser: LD71042. $89.95.
Akira Kurosawa, Japan, 1958, 139 mins.

I Live in Fear

Toshiro Mifune is cast as the aging head of a Tokyo family who is terrified by the prospect of a nuclear war. The industrialist's large family includes a wife, grandchildren and mistresses, and they bicker greedily over the estate as they bring mental incompetence proceedings against the patriarch. Kurosawa transforms this situation into a powerful humanist statement as *I Live in Fear* projects the end of mankind as a result of man's inhumanity to man. With Toshiro Mifune, Eiko Miyuoshi and Takashi Shimura. Japanese with English subtitles.
VHS: S26383. $29.95.
Akira Kurosawa, Japan, 1955, 105 mins.

The Idiot

Drawing from Fyodor Dostoyevsky, Kurosawa transposes this bitter story to postwar Japan. Kameda, a war criminal sentenced to be shot, has been pardoned at the last moment. The shock makes him into an idiot and prone to epileptic fits. Upon release, he is befriended by the strong and tenacious Akama. When they both fall for the beautiful Takeo Nasu, madness becomes a common denominator in this grossly tragic and haunting film. Japanese with English subtitles.
VHS: S15681. $79.95.
Akira Kurosawa, Japan, 1951, 166 mins.

Ikiru

Akira Kurosawa moved outside his usual stylistic preoccupations to make this poetic and emotionally powerful work about a gravely ill, quiet and dignified civil servant who vows to find grace and purpose in his final months, through the building of a public park. It's a thoughtful, contemplative, lyrical work centered by Takashi Shimura's virtuoso performance. With Nobuo Kaneko, Kyoko Seki and Miki Odagiri. Japanese with English subtitles.
VHS: S00608. $39.95.
  Laser: LD70383. $59.95.
Akira Kurosawa, Japan, 1952, 143 mins.

Kagemusha

A masterpiece. Set in 1531 Japan torn by civil strife, *Kagemusha* deals with a mighty Japanese warlord and his commoner look-alike who, after the warlord's death, is used to keep his clan together. Tatsuya Nakadai is superb in the dual role of the war lord and his double, both caught up in the swirl of history as the mighty powers clash in fierce battles and political intrigue. Winner of the Grand Prize at Cannes. Japanese with English subtitles.
VHS: S00668. $29.98.
  Laser: CLV. LD72114. $69.98.
Akira Kurosawa, Japan, 1980, 159 mins.

The Lower Depths

Akira Kurosawa's masterful reworking of the classic play by Maxim Gorky, using foundations of Japanese Noh theatre, set in Edo during the last Tokugawa period. A rare ensemble effect is achieved from the actors in this moving story of a group of destitute people living in a rooming house. Japanese with English subtitles.
VHS: S03513. $24.95.
Akira Kurosawa, Japan, 1957, 125 mins.

Men Who Tread on Tiger's Tail

A very offbeat Kurosawa film, an adaptation of a popular Kabuki drama about a 12th-century lord who is forced to flee his estate with only six dedicated samurai to guard him. He is hunted by his brother, the Shogun, and is ultimately saved by his chief vassal through a clever disguise. The wartime Japanese government banned the film because it didn't extol the concepts of feudalism and obedience; after the war, the Allied Occupation forces banned it for being pro-feudal. Japanese with English subtitles.
VHS: S00847. $39.95.
Akira Kurosawa, Japan, 1945, 60 mins.

No Regrets for Our Youth

An unusual feminist epic saga which focuses on a charming, talented and self-absorbed Japanese woman, Yukie, who is preparing herself for the role of a spoiled, cultured wife. She flirts with two suitors, one a disaffected leftist, the other a right-wing careerist, though she has no personal interest in politics. The earliest personal and first great film by Kurosawa, with a commanding performance by Setsuko Hara as the complex woman whose life unfolds against the backdrop of Japanese militarist society. Japanese with English subtitles.
VHS: S11176. $29.95.
Akira Kurosawa, Japan, 1946, 110 mins.

Quiet Duel

Based on a play by Kazuo Kikuta, this early Kurosawa film concerns an army surgeon who, during a life-saving operation, contaminates himself with syphilis which, at the time, was virtually incurable. Now suffering with the dreaded disease, he is forced to abandon his fiancee but finds the faith to redouble his work to restore people to health, including the man from whom he contracted the disease. With Toshiro Mifune, Takashi Shimura and Miki Sanjko. Japanese with English subtitles.
VHS: S26384. $29.95.
Akira Kurosawa, Japan, 1949, 95 mins.

Rashomon

A cinematic landmark, a brilliant study of the nature of truth. Set in the 12th century. A samurai and his wife are traveling through the woods near Kyoto. They are attacked by a bandit, the wife raped and the husband killed. Four different versions of the incident are told by the participants and a woodcutter who was a witness. Japanese with English subtitles.
VHS: S01092. $29.95.
  Laser: LD70440. $49.95.
Akira Kurosawa, Japan, 1951, 89 mins.

Record of a Living Being

An elderly and wealthy industrialist becomes obsessed with a fear of the atomic bomb. In an attempt to save his family, he pressures them to leave Japan. Their refusal brings about his madness and ruin. Another gripping drama from one of Japan's finest living directors. Japanese with English subtitles. Presented in a slightly letterboxed format (1:1.60).
VHS: S15375. $39.95.
Akira Kurosawa, Japan, 1955, 105 mins.

Red Beard

An offbeat, virtually unaccountable work from the Japanese master Akira Kurosawa, mixing the stylizes soap and the action flick, concerns the legendary doctor called Red Beard who attempts to influence his disciples to turn away from private practice to use their skills on the poor and sick. "The film bowls along magnificently in a weird mixture of genuine emotion, absurdity and poetic fantasy" (*Time Out*). With Toshiro Mifune, as Dr. Gillespie, Yuzo Kayama, Yoshio Tsuchiya.
VHS: S02955. $39.95.
  Laser: LD70444. $69.95.
Akira Kurosawa, Japan, 1965, 185 mins.

Rhapsody in August

This moving drama, set in Nagasaki, explores the trauma of World War II and the aftereffects of the atomic bomb. Four children on a visit to their grandmother in this historic town get invited to Hawaii by their American relations, setting off a chain of painful memories that are finally confronted when an American cousin, Richard Gere, arrives. Japanese with English subtitles.
VHS: S21072. $79.98.
  Laser: LD74469. $39.99.
Akira Kurosawa, Japan, 1991, 98 mins.

Sanjuro

The hero of Kurosawa's *Yojimbo* returns to help a group of very earnest, very green, very young samurai get their clan rid of corruption. As in *Yojimbo*, much of the comic effect comes from imaginative composition and incongruous movement. With Toshiro Mifune. Japanese with English subtitles.
VHS: S01157. $29.95.
  Laser: LD72345. $49.95.
Akira Kurosawa, Japan, 1962, 92 mins.

Sanshiro Sugata

Sanshiro Sugata, like so many of Kurosawa's characters, champions principles against a hostile, established order. In his first film, Kurosawa was already unconventional in style, as the hero advocates the newer art of judo against the traditional and well-entrenched jujitsu masters. Before proving himself, Sanshiro undergoes the long ordeal of learning judo as a discipline in a strikingly visual film extraordinary also for its explosive martial arts choreography. Japanese with English subtitles.
VHS: S03515. $24.95.
Akira Kurosawa, Japan, 1943, 80 mins.

Scandal

Gossip magazines are the target of this film by Kurosawa. A scandal sheet fabricates a romance between Toshiro Mifune, an artist, and a young entertainer. The artist sues the newspaper for libel. But his own lawyer accepts a bribe to ruin the case. *Scandal* is a powerful drama about corruption and redemption. With Mifune, Yoshiko Yamaguchi and Takashi Shimura. Japanese with English subtitles.
VHS: S26385. $29.95.
Akira Kurosawa, Japan, 1950, 105 mins.

Seven Samurai

Set in medieval Japan, Kurosawa's epic centers on a group of impoverished peasants who enlist the protection of seven unemployed samurai to defend their property and harvest from the brutal bandits who terrorize their village. The film is groundbreaking for its visual intensity, stylistic command of movement, space and action, and its expressive emotional range and social criticism. The battle sequences are frightening, devastating and eerie. Cinematography by Asaichi Nakai. With Takashi Shimura, Yoshio Inaba and Toshiro Mifune. Japanese with English subtitles.
VHS: S01182. $34.95.
  Laser: CAV, widescreen. LD70451. $124.95.
  Laser: CLV, widescreen. LD70452. $59.95.
Akira Kurosawa, Japan, 1954, 208 mins.

Stray Dog

A first-rate thriller in which Kurosawa has acknowledged his debt to Georges Simenon. Toshiro Mifune plays rookie Detective Murakami, who loses his gun only to discover that it has fallen into the hands of a killer. Terrified of losing his job, his search takes him into the Tokyo underworld, full of postwar shortages, "divinely hellish under Kurosawa's odd-angled lensing and staccato editing…*Stray Dog* is a Dostoevskian saga of guilt, and expiation, by association" (*Pacific Film Archive*). Japanese with English subtitles.
VHS: S06462. $24.95.
Akira Kurosawa, Japan, 1949, 122 mins.

Throne of Blood

Kurosawa's brilliant interpretation of Shakespeare's *Macbeth* shifts the action to 16th century feudal Japan, where a samurai is motivated by his ambitious wife and spirit to kill his friend. The movie balances stylized action and movement of the Noh theater with the intensity of the American western. Kurosawa and cinematographer Asaichi Nakai create a foreboding atmosphere in the castles and landscape. With Toshiro Mifune, Isuzu Yamada and Minoru Chiaki. Japanese with English subtitles.
VHS: S01338. $39.95.
  Laser: CAV. LD70726. $89.95.
Akira Kurosawa, Japan, 1957, 110 mins.

Yojimbo

Kurosawa's first full-length comedy. Toshiro Mifune is the unemployed samurai warrior who comes to a small village torn apart by two warring factions where he is hired first by one side, then by the other. "Explosively comic and exhilarating," said Pauline Kael. Japanese with English subtitles.
VHS: S01489. $29.95.
  Laser: LD70489. $49.95.
Akira Kurosawa, Japan, 1961, 110 mins.

47 Ronin

Also known as *A Tale of 47 Loyal Retainers of the Genroku Era*, Mizoguchi's two-part film deals with the vengeance of the retainers of Lord Asano in 1703 following his forced hara-kiri. Mizoguchi's film version is based on a Kabuki version of the story by Seika Mayama. "This is a re-discovered wartime saga of noble samurai sentiments and discreet passions. A girding of the spirit is recommended for this wraparound experience in the same way that the best of the long-form classics are to be savored…", wrote Tom Allen and Andrew Sarris in *The Village Voice.* "Mizoguchi has transformed a basic samurai legend of Japanese folklore into an essential historical drama of Japanese cinema. The boxed courtyards and formal gardens of the 18th century are tracking paradises that Mizoguchi's dolly-and-crane shots exploit fully, and the tale of loyal vassals avenging their lord's honor is rendered subtly throughout by a highly disciplined Expressionism."
Part I. 111 mins.
  VHS: S08031. $29.95.
Part II. 108 mins.
  VHS: S08032. $29.95.
Kenji Mizoguchi, Japan, 1942

Chikamatsu Monogatari (Crucified Lovers)

One of the masterworks of Kenji Mizoguchi: in 17th century Japan, the illicit love between a merchant's wife and her servant leads to tragedy. Based on a story by Chikamatsu and derived from a Bunraku play, "it is perhaps Mizoguchi's most intense and concentrated study of social mores in feudal Japan and among his most visually sensuous films" (Georges Sadoul). Japanese with English subtitles.
VHS: S09097. $69.95.
Kenji Mizoguchi, Japan, 1954, 110 mins.

A Geisha

A Geisha is a portrait of geisha life, a document about the rise of feminism in post-war Japan and an examination of the evolving relationship of two women. One is a distinguished geisha (Michiyo Kogure), the other, a 16-year-old novice (Ayako Wakao) whom she is training. Kogure is alarmed by the young woman's romantic delusions. "The film's charm is the compassionate but completely unsentimental way it regards the two women's friendship" (Vincent Canby). Japanese with English subtitles.
VHS: S19544. $69.95.
Kenji Mizoguchi, Japan, 1953, 87 mins.

Life of Oharu

An enduring masterpiece of world cinema, from the director of *Ugetsu. Life of Oharu* is a poignant, exquisitely filmed portrait of a woman victimized by the brutal strictures of 17th century feudal Japan. Mizoguchi shows remarkable insight into the psychology of his female protagonist, and photographs her with slow, graceful, hauntingly beautiful camera movements. Japanese with English subtitles.
VHS: S00753. $59.95.
Kenji Mizoguchi, Japan, 1952, 136 mins.

Osaka Elegy

"In 1936 Mizoguchi made his most brilliant pre-war film, *Osaka Elegy*, shot in 20 days and banned after 1940 for 'decadent tendencies,' a euphemism barely concealing the military government's fear of the radicalism of Mizoguchi's satire of the ruthless, all-pervasive Osaka capitalism. In this film the mature Mizoguchi style emerges for the first time as he creates, entirely through visual means, a balance between the fate of the heroine Ayako and the corrupt, degenerate values of Osaka. The plot concerns the seduction of Ayako, a switchboard operator, by her boss" (Joan Mellen, *The Waves at Genji's Door*). Japanese with English subtitles.
VHS: S09958. $39.95.
Kenji Mizoguchi, Japan, 1936, 84 mins.

Princess Yang Kwei Fei

Kenji Mizoguchi's film about a young servant girl who is transformed into a princess and then destroyed by the shifting loyalties, betrayal and revenge around her. Mizoguchi's use of color, decor and diagonal compositions is fluid and baroque and perfectly reflects the characters' emotional conditions. "One of the most beautiful films ever to treat beauty as a subject" (*Andrew Sarris*). With Masayuki Mori, Machiko Kyo and So Yamamura. Japanese with English subtitles.
VHS: S18421. $79.95.
Kenji Mizoguchi, Japan, 1955, 125 mins.

Sansho the Bailiff

Set in 11th century Japan, the film focuses on a mother who sets off with her two children to find her husband, a former deputy governor, who has been in exile. The family is broken up by a priestess who sells all three to kidnappers, and after many hardships, one of the sons becomes the governor once under Sansho's brutal rule. "Mizoguchi has created a powerful work with strong humanistic overtones. Focusing on the influence the two women in the story have on the hero, the film alternates the idyllic atmosphere of some scenes with the violent cruelty of others" (Georges Sadoul). Japanese with English subtitles.
VHS: S01158. $39.95.
  Laser: LD75422. $69.95.
Kenji Mizoguchi, Japan, 1954, 120 mins.

Sisters of Gion

Often considered to be the best pre-war Japanese film, and Mizoguchi's masterpiece, *Sisters of Gion* is set in the red-light district of Kyoto. The film tells the story of two sisters—the older trained as a geisha in the old tradition, the younger an apprentice devoted to the more progressive ideas. This conflict between the old and the new, wrote Donald Richie in *The Japanese Film*, has become "the protest symbol of modern Japan."
VHS: S03517. $29.95.
Kenji Mizoguchi, Japan, 1936, 69 mins.

Story of the Last Chrysanthemum

Kenji Mizoguchi's chronicle of a Kabuki actor. As the son of a prominent Kabuki family, the young man would be assured eventual fame, but he runs afoul of his father by falling in love with a servant girl, and sets out to make it himself on his own. Contains some of Mizoguchi's most ethereal imagery, as well as some fascinating use of compositions suggestive of Cinemascope before the widescreen process was invented. Japanese with English subtitles.
VHS: S03516. $79.95.
Kenji Mizoguchi, Japan, 1939, 115 mins.

Street of Shame

The last film by the great Mizoguchi, the story of the dreams and problems of a group of prostitutes living in one gaudy Tokyo brothel, with a remarkable performance by the legendary Machiko Kyo. Japanese with English subtitles.
VHS: S01810. $29.95.
Kenji Mizoguchi, Japan, 1956, 88 mins.

Taira Clan Saga

The last great color film by Mizoguchi. Set in the 12th century as the center of power in Japan shifted from feudal nobility to the Buddhist clergy, the story centers on Kiyomori, scion of the Taira clan of swordsmen. At the beginning of the film he quietly acquiesces to his father's authority; at the end he is in open revolt against it. Mizoguchi describes and analyzes this change in a film that is the work of a major artist in full authority. Japanese with English subtitles.
VHS: S10933. $59.95.
Kenji Mizoguchi, Japan, 1955, 90 mins.

Ugetsu

Kenji Mizoguchi's poetic film is set in feudal, war-ravaged, 16th-century Japan and focuses on the opposite fortunes of two peasants who abandon their families to accumulate wealth and prestige and find emptiness and despair. The film is remarkable for its expressive photography, diagonal compositions and uninterrupted takes. With Machiko Kyo and Masayuki Mori. "Scenes of everyday life alternate with those of a dreamlike, erotic intensity. At the end it is difficult to remember where reality stops and hallucination begins" (Newsweek). Japanese with English subtitles. Newly remastered, translated and subtitled print. Presented in original aspect ratio.
VHS: S01390. $24.95.
Laser: LD75412. $49.95.
Kenji Mizoguchi, Japan, 1953, 96 mins.

Utamaro and His Five Women

Mizoguchi's exquisite portrait of the artistic life of Tokyo of the 18th century is a portrait of Edo artist Utamaro (Minnosuke Bando) and his relationship to women. Utamaro stands at the center of the lives of five women who compete for his attention in a film which is remarkably modern for its attitude toward the rights of women. The scenarist, Yoshikata Yoda, stated that the film was an unconscious portrait of Mizoguchi himself. With Kinuyo Tanaka, Kotaro Bando and Hiroko Kawasaki. Japanese with English subtitles.
VHS: S19418. $69.95.
Kenji Mizoguchi, Japan, 1946, 89 mins.

YASUJIRO OZU

An Autumn Afternoon

This profoundly simple and moving film examines changing familial relationships in an increasingly Americanized postwar Tokyo. With his unmistakable and inimitable style, Ozu has created a serenely beautiful film which tells the timeless, moving tale of a father giving up his only daughter in marriage. Both humorous and heartbreaking, An Autumn Afternoon was Ozu's 53rd and last film. Japanese with English subtitles.
VHS: S15393. $69.95.
Yasujiro Ozu, Japan, 1952, 112 mins.

Drifting Weeds

A group of travelling actors visits a town where the leading actor's (Ganjiro Nakamura) ex-mistress lives with their son. Nakamura's present lover (Machiko Kyo) is understandably jealous. Brilliant color cinematography by Kazuo Miyagawa; one of Ozu's great films. "A work of subtle genius" (Film Magazine). Also known as Floating Weeds. Japanese with English subtitles.
VHS: S00377. $29.95.
Laser: LD70983. $44.95.
Yasujiro Ozu, Japan, 1959, 128 mins.

Equinox Flower

When the daughter of a successful business man defies an arranged marriage and runs off with a pianist, the father refuses to give consent. A warm comedy of reconciliation, this film marks Ozu's first use of color. With Shin Saburi, Kinuyo Tanaka, Ineko Arima and Miyuki Kuwano. Japanese with English subtitles.
VHS: S16079. $69.95.
Yasujiro Ozu, Japan, 1958, 118 mins.

Late Spring

In Late Spring, a father feels he is keeping his daughter from marriage; when she is erroneously told that her father is thinking of re-marrying, she agrees to an offer. Late Spring, wrote Donald Richie, is "one of the most perfect, most complete, and most successful studies of character ever achieved in the Japanese cinema." With Setsuko Hara, Chishu Ryu. Japanese with English subtitles.
VHS: S21502. $69.95.
Yasujiro Ozu, Japan, 1949, 107 mins.

Record of a Tenement Gentleman

One of Ozu's most wonderful films, a bittersweet comedy about an abandoned child who manages to create a new surrogate family in an unlikely setting from a very unlikely candidate. The surprise ending only reinforces how carefully this film depicts human emotions. Japanese with English subtitles.
VHS: S25907. $69.95.
Yasujiro Ozu, Japan, 1947, 73 mins.

Tokyo Story

One of the legendary classics of humanist cinema, Tokyo Story tells the simple, sad story of an elderly couple who travel to Tokyo to visit their two married children, only to find themselves politely ushered off to a hot springs resort. "Ozu's technique, as spare and concentrated as a haiku master's verse, transforms the very banalities of the subject into moments of intimacy and beauty seldom captured on film. As always, the themes go beyond the obvious and are conveyed so gently that only afterwards are many apparent." Japanese with English subtitles. With new electronic subtitles.
VHS: S10919. $69.95.
Yasujiro Ozu, Japan, 1953, 139 mins.

JAPANESE ISSUES

Animated Classics of Japanese Literature Collection 1

The first in a series of works that artfully blends animation with timeless classics of Japanese literature. Japanese with English subtitles.
Izu Dancer/The Dancing Girl. This animated film was written by Nobel Prize winner Yasunari Kawabata. In Izu Dancer, a summertime romance develops between a young student and a ballet dancer. But every summer must end. Mori Ohagi's The Dancing Girl tells of the love between a dancer and a businessman whose personal troubles threaten to destroy their devotion.
VHS: S20811. $29.95.
The Harp of Burma, Parts 1 and 2. Though the war is over troops secluded by the rugged terrain of the Burmese mountains continue to fight. Only Private Mizushima can reach them and convince them that all their recent hardships, including casualties, have been borne for naught. Written by Michio Takeyama.
VHS: S20812. $29.95.
Season of the Sun/Student Days/The Graves of the Wild Chrysanthemum. In Shintaro Ishihara's Season of the Sun casual relationships rule Tsugawa's life until he meets the incomparable Eiko. Love holds the promise of redemption but only if Tsugawa can express his desire. Superstitions threaten the important exam results of the dedicated student Kenchicki in Kume Masao's story Student Days. Kenchicki's fervor however, may harm his dreams. In the consecutive feature, The Graves of the Wild Chrysanthemum by Sachio Ito, Tamiko faces an arranged marriage, but longs for another who is not her betrothed. Can love sustain the young pair?
VHS: S20813. $29.95.
A Ghost Story/The Theater of Life. Unwittingly a blind lutist named Houichi places himself in grave danger by performing for the powerful but deceased Heiki family. Their vengeful ways can only be averted if the chief priest acts immediately, in A Ghost Story by Yakumo Koizumi. In Shiro Ozaki's The Theater of Life, Hyokichi learns about courage from his father and applies these important lessons to his adult career.
VHS: S20814. $29.95.
Wandering Days/Growing Up. In Wandering Days by Fumiko Hayashi, a young Fumiko travels from town to town with her parents as they sell medicine. Only Fumiko dreams of another life, that of a great author. Can it become a reality? While in Growing Up (by Ichiyo Higuchi) good friends Shinnoyo and Midori find themselves divided when Shinnoyo joins a rival gang. Their separation is painful but what can be done?
VHS: S20815. $29.95.
Animated Classics of Japanese Literature Collection 1, Complete Set.
VHS: S21005. $119.95.

Animated Classics of Japanese Literature Collection 2

This second installment gives the viewer even more opportunities to discern the true heart of Japan via animated versions of the greatest works of Japanese literature ever written. Subtitled in English.
Sound of the Waves, Parts 1 and 2. In this story by Yukio Mishima, the young fisherman Shinji falls in love with Hatsue shortly after she returns to their island home. Sadly Yasuo's interference disrupts this ideal romance.
VHS: S20816. $29.95.
Sanshiro, The Judoist, Parts 1, 2 and 3. Yano, a master of martial arts, brings together the minor schools of jujitsu to form the art of judo at his own school. The ensuing rivalry between the masters of the jujitsu schools and Yano leads to a bout where Sanshiro, a student of Yano, must prove the superiority of judo. Written by Tsuneo Tomita.
VHS: S20817. $29.95.
The Wind Rises/The Fruit of Olympus. The Wind Rises, by Tatsuo Hori, tells the story of growing love between a writer and a girl in a windswept alpine setting. Can their love provide her with the solace she needs? In Hidemitsu Tanaka's The Fruit of Olympus the Japanese Olympic team is jubilant as they contemplate their entry into the greatest of international competitions. Rivalry threatens to divide them however, just when they need each other most.
VHS: S20818. $29.95.
Asunaro Story/The Story of Koyasu Dog. In Asunaro Story, by Yasushi Inoue, a tragic death teaches the young Ayuta both a powerful lesson in grief and the value of human life. Yukio Togawa's The Story of Koyasu Dog follows a thoroughbred dog through the painful separation from his master which results when he is sent away for medical care. Koyasu's devotion could very well be his undoing.
VHS: S20819. $29.95.
A Walker in the Attic/A Psychological Test/A Red Room. A Walker in the Attic spies on his neighbors through cracks in the ceilings. His eavesdropping is interrupted when a mysterious murder leaves no clues. What exactly does he know? A Psychological Test develops between a crafty student and a famous detective who must prove his guilt. In A Red Room a group of men gather to find inspiration. A new member's sensational plans may offer them the perfect solution in the form of a perfect crime. All three are written by Rampo Edogawa.
VHS: S20820. $29.95.
Animated Classics of Japanese Literature Collection 2, Complete Set.
VHS: S21006. $119.95.

Best of Nightline: Akio Morita

30 mins.
VHS: S14064. $14.98.

Discovering the Music of Japan

Set in a beautiful teahouse, this video shows how three major instruments are used. They are the koto, the samisen and the shakuhachi. Historical information and the contemporary role of these instruments are also explained. 22 mins.
VHS: S23514. $49.95.

Empire of the Rising Sun

A two-volume set which chronicles the Japanese Empire from World War I through the end of World War II and Japan's surrender. 120 mins.
VHS: S09204. $49.95.

The Hidden Japan

Drug addicts, alcoholics and homeless people are considered complete outcasts in Japanese society. They are at times blatantly ignored and considered disposable human beings. This film shows how three Maryknoll Fathers, a Maryknoll Sister and Japanese volunteers are responding to the needs of these social exiles. Maryknollers are also helping to operate a seaport hospitality center in northern Japan for transient foreign sailors. 25 mins.
VHS: S13906. $24.95.

Japan

Jane Seymour examines how Japan's ancient traditions have blended with new technology and modern trends to shape the society and its people today in this four-volume series. Volume 1: The Electronic Tribe focuses on the contrasts between the present day life of factory workers and the inherited religious and rural customs still found in the ordinary home. Volume 2: The Sword and the Chrysanthemum takes a close look at what the West sees as a paradox in Japanese society, as represented by the Samurai warrior, who combined an appreciation of beauty and high culture with fighting aggression. Volume 3: The Legacy of the Shogun looks at the continuing effect of the 17th century Shogun philosophy of hard work, discipline and hierarchy. It also explores the law-abiding nature of contemporary Japan where Tokyo has one of the lowest crime rates in the world. Volume 4: A Proper Place in the World looks at Japan's intervention on the world's stage during the 20th century and its likely future as a world economic superpower. 60 mins. each.
VHS: S16529. $79.98.

Japan: The Island Empire

From the frantic pace of Tokyo to the Great Buddha of Kamakura and the 400-year-old Himeji Castle, this video tour captures the grandeur of Japan. 55 mins.
VHS: S09879. $24.95.

Japanese: Yesterday and Today

Scripted by AP correspondent John Roderick, this two-volume program presents an inside look at Japan. Viewers will learn about the origins of the tea ceremony, Kabuki theater, and haiku poetry as well as about flourishing Japanese industries. Also presented are Japan's prospects for continuing its phenomenal success in the international marketplace. 44 mins.
VHS: S12271. $300.00.

Kendo: The Path of the Sword

Kendo is the original Japanese martial art form. It originates with the sword and the spirit of the warrior. This video shows how practice is performed, the elements of this art including armor and weapons, and the rules governing a match. Interviews help clarify the role of Zen and there is a discussion of the history of this martial art.
VHS: S24860. $29.95.

Kodo: Heartbeat Drummers of Japan

Named after the Japanese word for heartbeat, Kodo is a group of young Asian musicians and dancers who perform traditional and contemporary drumming. 1983, 57 mins.
VHS: S14743. $19.95.

National Geographic Video: Living Treasures of Japan

A tribute to the artists who preserve the richness and beauty of ancient Japanese traditions in a special from National Geographic. 60 mins.
VHS: S07392. $19.95.

Portrait of Japan Complete Set

Known for its consensus culture, Japan remains an enigmatic country beset by contradictions and great accomplishments, according to this four-part documentary. The film examines 20 Japanese men and women, and chronicles their realities, hopes and dreams. 240 mins.
VHS: S19374. $99.95.

ASIAN WORLD

Bali: The Mask of Rangda

Filmed in the remote villages of Bali, this video is an authentic picture of a unique culture. 30 mins.
VHS: S06499. $59.95.

Hong Kong: A Family Portrait

In 1997, the British Crown Colony of Hong Kong, a bustling, capitalistic city, will be returned to the People's Republic of China. This video takes a look at the life of a boat family that has made its home in Hong Kong for more than 100 years, now straddling the gap between the modern world and ancient Chinese customs. A National Geographic production. 60 mins.
VHS: S11654. $19.95.

Impressions of Hong Kong and Macau

Savor the delights of this Queen of the Orient and see why Hong Kong is unique. Visit Macau, steeped in history, and go shopping in some of the world's most diverse marketplaces. 25 mins.
VHS: S10776. $24.95.

Kapalana: Death of a Hawaiian Village

Shot over seven years, this award-winning program contains breathtaking footage of a deadly volcanic eruption that spewed ashes and rained destruction on an isolated village. 48 mins.
VHS: S17222. $29.95.

The Mini Dragons Series

A four-part series studying the men and women striving to raise the "mini dragons," four Pacific Rim countries (Singapore, Taiwan, South Korea and Hong Kong), into competitive international players through increased trade, industrial growth and foreign investment. This program studies the individual communities and cultures as well.
Hong Kong.
VHS: S18065. $29.95.
Singapore.
VHS: S18066. $29.95.
South Korea.
VHS: S18067. $29.95.
Taiwan.
VHS: S18068. $29.95.
Mini Dragons Set. 240 mins.
VHS: S19383. $99.95.

The Mini Dragons Series II

Three one-hour documentaries on rising Asian powers—Thailand, Malaysia and Indonesia. The shows offer detailed tapestry of the people within each country, from the factories to cities and farms. 180 mins.
Indonesia.
VHS: S19372. $29.95.
Malaysia.
VHS: S19371. $29.95.
Thailand.
VHS: S19370. $29.95.
The Mini Dragons Series II: Set.
VHS: S19373. $79.95.

Mystical Malaysia, Land of Harmony

Discover Malaysia, a country of white sand beaches and virgin jungles, a country rich in culture and traditions. Journey to the island of Penang. Travel to Kota Bhary and witness the traditions of batik printing and kite making. Explore the village of Sarawak, home to the headhunters of Borneo. 45 mins.
VHS: S10779. $24.95.

Navigators: Pathfinders of the Pacific

On the remote South Pacific island of Satawal, Mau Piailug is among the last keepers of the ancient secrets of Polynesian navigation. Without instruments or charts, he guides his men aboard their hand-hewn boats on long ocean passages, relying solely on his intricate knowledge of the sea and sky. In The Navigators, Mau presents an intriguing view of his people, still immersed in the communal traditions of their ancestors. Winner of Cine Golden Eagle and American Film Festival. 59 mins.
VHS: S06347. $49.95.

No Longer Colonies: Hong Kong 1997, Macau 1999

As the timetable toward integration with Mainland Communist China continues to move forward, these last European colonies in Asia are filled with a mixture of hope and trepidation. This documentary looks at the history and the prospects of this fascinating region.
VHS: S21849. $19.95.

Peter Jennings Reporting from the Killing Fields

A powerful television special in which Peter Jennings reports from Cambodia about America's continued role in Southeast Asia, and particularly its support for the genocide by the Khmer Rouge. Includes the heated discussion which followed the original ABC TV newscast. 160 mins.
VHS: S12499. $19.98.

Samoa—Culture in Crisis

Modernization threatens traditional values in places like Samoa. The desire for material progress tempts some to abandon traditions. But through the "Kava" ceremony and the presentation of "Fine Mats," local leaders encourage a return to the best aspects of Samoan culture. Produced by Maryknoll Media. 28 mins.
VHS: S04934. $24.95.

Singapore: Crossroads of Asia

Exotic Singapore, the ancient trading port, in a video visit that captures awe-inspiring sights, from the Temple of Heavenly Happines and the Sultan Mosque to the exotic cuisines. 55 mins.
VHS: S09880. $24.95.

Sri Lanka: A Nation in Anguish

A presentation on disappearances and human rights violations committed by the Sri Lankan government, with suggestions for stopping the abuses. Produced by Amnesty International. 18 mins.
VHS: S06891. $20.00.

Taiwan: Exotic Blossom of the Orient

The enchanting island of Taiwan is a land of jade temples, marble cities, sandy beaches. Visit the exquisite National Palace Museum, explore Snake Alley, Tarako Gorge, Wuffeng Temple, and meet the unique people who live here. 50 mins.
VHS: S05763. $24.95.

Touring Korea

Captures the history, legends and drama of the 5,000 year old country, including Chejudo, Korea's own tropical resort, skiing at Dragon Valley, Kyongju, the city of golden treasures, the Mt. Soraksan National Park, the Harvest Moon and Wesak festivals. 60 mins.
VHS: S09909. $29.95.

FILIPINO CINEMA

Macho Dancer

From world-renowned director Lino Brocka comes a story of sex, violence, and political corruption. Abandoned by his American lover, a handsome teenager from the mountains journeys to Manila in an effort to support his family. With a popular call boy as his mentor, Paul enters the glittering world of the "machodancer"—a world of male strippers, prostitution, drugs, sexual slavery, police corruption and murder. Teeming with sex and erotic Oriental beefcake, Macho Dancers is a searing indictment of the hypocrisy and corruption rampant under both the Marcos and Aquino regimes. Uncensored and uncut. Tagalog with English subtitles.
VHS: S14597. $79.95.
Lino Brocka, Philippines, 1988, 136 mins.

Perfumed Nightmare

Called "one of the year's best films" by J. Hoberman in The Village Voice, an enchanting, poignant, and totally original fable by young Philippino filmmaker Kidlat Tahimik, about his awakening to and reaction against American cultural colonialism. Born in 1942 during the Occupation, Tahimik spent the "next 33 typhoon seasons in a cocoon of American dreams." This is his perfumed nightmare: the lotus-land of American technological promise. In his primitive village he worshipped the heroism of the Machine, the sleek beauty of rockets, the efficiency of industrialism. He is the president of his own Werner Von Braun fan club. A bizarre, hallucinatory movie full of dazzling images and outlandish ideas, shot on super 8 for less than $10,000. Winner of the International Critics Award, Berlin Film Festival. English and Tagalog with English subtitles.
VHS: S09300. $59.95.
Kidlat Tahimik, Philippines, 1983, 91 mins.

Rich Boy, Poor Boy

A colleague of the late Filipino director Lino Brocka, Piedro de San Paulo's controversial and banned work rips open the Third World taboo. The story concerns an outlawed relationship between a wealthy, Americanized young man and his strong-willed, quiet farmhand. "Brave and brazen, a bittersweet portrait of friendship and desire" (*Bay Area Reporter*). With Victor Viller, Edwyn Casas, Cristina Ocampo. Tagalog with English subtitles. On the same program is *A Boy Named Cocoy*, about a mountain boy's quest to find a better life in Manila.
VHS: S17777. $59.95.
Piedro de San Paulo, Philippines, 1991, 94 mins.

Turumba

Set in a tiny Philippine village, Tahimik's *Turumba* focuses on one family which traditionally made papier-mache animals to sell during the Turumba religious festivities. When they get a huge order, the whole life of the family is changed, as Tahimik wryly observes the "creation of the proletariat." Tagalog with English subtitles.
VHS: S01379. $59.95.
Kidlat Tahimik, Philippines, 1984, 94 mins.

FILIPINO PERSPECTIVES

Best of Nightline: Marcos & Aquino

60 mins.
VHS: S14041. $14.98.

Filipino Americans: Discovering Their Past for the Future

One of the oldest and most influential Asian communities in the U.S., Filipinos have been in this part of the world since 1587, when they were first brought to California by the Spanish. Ever since then, their contributions have been felt in every spectrum of life on this continent. This is their story. 54 mins.
VHS: S21357. $29.95.

First in the Philippines: A Film History of the Second Oregon Volunteer Regiment

A chronicle of the first U.S. war outside the Western Hemisphere. Assembling contemporary newspaper articles, diaries, letters, unit histories and personal interviews, the film tells of the Oregon volunteer regiment, the first ground force to enter combat in the Spanish-American war in 1898.
VHS: S16461. $29.95.
Robert Koglin, USA, 62 mins.

Philippine Diary

Four vignettes of Philippine life dramatize the conditions which led to the peaceful revolution and which must be improved if the new government is to succeed: the slum dwellers of Manila, the prostitutes near a United States military base, the tenant farmers on the island of Negros, and the peasants bypassed by the march of development on the island of Mindanao. Produced by Maryknoll Media. 28 mins.
VHS: S04932. $24.95.

INDIAN CINEMA

Aashiq

A classical Indian musical with a super cast, directed by India's great showman Raj Kapoor. Stars Kapoor and Padmini. Hindi with English and Arabic subtitles.
VHS: S22173. $39.95.
Raj Kapoor, India, 1967, 156 mins.

The Adversary

A young man, graduated from college, is unable to find meaningful employment. His ensuing hardships and personal grief, magnified by the tense and impersonal setting of Calcutta, make for a most devastating film experience. While at times reminiscent of the emotionally wrenching Italian neo-realist classics, this beautiful film often seems to outstrip them with its overwhelming spiritual perspective and astounding depth of feeling. One of Ray's brilliant masterpieces. Bengali with English subtitles.
VHS: S15380. $39.95.
Satyajit Ray, India, 1971, 110 mins.

Amrapali

The story of a very talented daughter, notable for its excellent picturization of classical Indian dances performed by the talented Vijayantimala. Stars Sunil Dutt and Vijayantimala Omdoa. 1969, 172 mins. Hindi with English and Arabic subtitles.
VHS: S22894. $39.95.

Antarnaad

The films of Shyam Benegal, a major Indian filmmaker, are often social studies of individuals and class structure. *Antarnaad* is the story of changes that occur in the lives of people living in two villages through *Swadhyaya*—a ceremony that involves the study of self. Five people—including a poor fisherman, a smuggler and a widow looking for revenge after the death of her husband—undergo profound changes. With Shabana Azmi, Om Puri, Kulbhushan Kharbanda. Hindi with English subtitles.
VHS: S22169. $39.95.
Shyam Benegal, India, 1992, 160 mins.

Aparajito

The second part of Satyajit Ray's *Apu* trilogy. *Aparajito* follows Apu (Smaran Ghosal) in his intellectual odyssey from the streets of Benares to the promise and optimism of Calcutta, as he begins his college studies. Music by Ravi Shankar. "It's transitional in structure, rather than dramatic, but it's full of insights and revelations" (Pauline Kael). With Pinaki Sen Gupta, Karuna and Kanu Banerji, and Ramani Sen Gupta. Bengali with English subtitles.
VHS: S16957. $24.95.
Satyajit Ray, India, 1957, 108 mins.

Awara

A classical Indian film; an enchanting love story directed by India's greatest showman, Raj Kapoor. The movie presents beautifully the contrast between poor and rich families in India, and is an entertaining mixture full of melodious songs. The story deals with the love of a poor boy for a rich man's daughter. With Raj Kapoor, Nargis, Prithviraj Kapoor. Hindi with English subtitles.
VHS: S22170. $39.95.
Raj Kapoor, India, 1951, 170 mins.

Bandit Queen

Based on the true story of an Indian woman named Phoolan. Sold into marriage at age 11 to a man 20 years her senior, this remarkable woman broke free from convention and misery. She fell in with a group of bandits and inspired a country with her bravery and fearless originality. This Indian outlaw brought a government to its knees. Hindi with English subtitles.
VHS: S27057. $99.98.
Laser: LD75458. $39.95.
Sheekhar Kapur, India, 1994, 119 mins.

Bharamchari

Shammi Kapoor and Rajshree star in this movie for children. A kind-hearted young bachelor takes the responsibility of orphan children. The story includes many songs for children. Hindi with English and Arabic subtitles. India, 1967, 137 mins.
VHS: S22175. $39.95.

Days and Nights in the Forest

An incisive and moving study of four men who leave crowded and cold Calcutta for a brief holiday. At their destination, they will each have different, very unique and personal experiences that will alter their lives—a brief love affair, a cheap sexual experience and true love. By the time they leave, each one has been changed in a radical and unique way. Another insightful examination of the human condition from master director Satyajit Ray. Bengali with English subtitles.
VHS: S15379. $39.95.
Satyajit Ray, India, 1970, 120 mins.

Devi

Satyajit Ray broke radically from his humanist, neo-realist style with this sensual, stylized work about Indian superstitiousness, about a wealthy man who attempts to convince his son's young wife she's an incarnate of the goddess Kali. Bengali with English subtitles.
VHS: S16955. $24.95.
Satyajit Ray, India, 1962, 95 mins.

Dil Deke Dehko

An Indian musical that's both a comedy and a tearjerker. With Shashi Kapoor and Asha Parekh. Hindi with English subtitles. India, 1964, 152 mins.
VHS: S22176. $39.95.

Distant Thunder

A moving dramatization of the effects of famine in India during World War II when the government controlled the food supply in order to feed troops, letting common people starve. The film follows the lives of several individuals including a doctor who humbles himself to survive. Bengali with English subtitles.
VHS: S01547. $44.95.
Satyajit Ray, India, 1974, 92 mins.

Do Ankhen Barah Haath

This award-winning Indian film by V. Shantaram is set in an Indian jail. A kind-hearted superintendent changes the lives of the prisoners. With V. Shantaram and Sandhya. Hindi with English and Arabic subtitles.
VHS: S22177. $39.95.
V. Shantaram, India, 1961, 130 mins.

Genesis

From one of India's most interesting filmmakers, Mrinal Sen, comes a parable of man's exploitation by his fellow man. A weaver and a farmer live peacefully beyond civilization, until a woman comes into their lives. "It brings home the sparseness, beauty and perils of existence," wrote *The New York Times*. Music by Ravi Shankar. Hindi with English subtitles.
VHS: S26502. $59.95.
Mrinal Sen, India, 1986, 105 mins.

God Is My Witness (Khuda Gawah)

Veteran Indian film actor Amitabh Bachchan stars as the noble Badshah Khan in his 85th film role. Khan meets the lovely Benazir (Sridevi) over a game of Buzkashi in Afghanistan, but before he can marry her, he must go to India and avenge Benazir's father's death. "A three-hour opus about love, prison and a man's word of honor…Spectacular!" (Anon Berger, *LA Weekly*). Winner of nine Indian Academy Awards, including Best Director, Best Cinematography and Best Supporting Actor. Featuring Nagarjun and Shilpa Shirodka. Hindi with English subtitles.
VHS: S25883. $49.95.

In Custody

Based on the novel by Anita Desai, this comedy has all the delightful details one expects from a Merchant/Ivory production. Surrounded by wine, women and song, a great poet lives his final days in comic self-indulgence. Then an earnest professor changes everything by interviewing him. Winner, National Film of India, Best Picture and Best Actor—Shashi Kapoor. Hindi with English subtitles.
VHS: S23428. $29.95.
Ismail Merchant, India, 1993, 123 mins.

Kabhi-Kabhi

A musical social drama dealing with middle class family life in India. The movie consists of songs and a strong performance by India's favorite actor, Amitabh Bachchan. With Rakhi Gulzar and Rishi Kapoor. Hindi with English subtitles. Music by Khayam.
VHS: S22172. $39.95.
Yash Chopra, India, 1978, 152 mins.

Mere Hazoor

An interesting Indian feature film about Muslim culture, its lifestyles and "etiquettes." Music by Shankar Jaikrishan. With Reaj Kumar, Mala Sinha and Jetinndra. Hindi with English subtitles.
VHS: S22178. $39.95.
Vinod Kumar, India, 1969, 145 mins.

Mere Jeevan Saathi

A highly unusual film from India: a musical-comedy romance, richly detailing a man's rise to success and sudden downfall. A surreal mosaic of colorful images, with flamboyant camera angles and haunting fantasy sequences. In vivid color! Hindi with English subtitles.
VHS: S00849. $29.95.
Ravee Nagaich, India, 1965, 126 mins.

Mughal-E-Azam

A historical Indian masterpiece, considered one of the mega-productions of the Indian screen. The powerful love story portrays a prince who is willing to leave his throne for the woman he loves. With music and songs. Stars Prithviraj Kapoor, Dilip Kumar, Durka Khote. Music by Nashad. Hindi and Urdu with English subtitles.
VHS: S22171. $39.95.
K. Asif, India, 1960, 182 mins.

Pakeezah

An Urdu-language film which stars Meena Kumari, Raj Kumar and Ashok Kumar in a story set in the Muslim culture of India. Much music and dance. Urdu with English subtitles.
VHS: S22179. $39.95.
Kamaal Amrohi, India, 1975, 173 mins.

Pather Panchali

The opening entry of Satyajit Ray's extraordinary *Apu* trilogy, adapted from the epic novel of Bengali writer B.B. Bandapaddhay, is a fiercely naturalistic, devastating portrait of poverty and despair. Ray uses his considerable storytelling powers of detail, incident and observation to interpret the relationship of a young Bengali boy and his family. The film has an emotional rhythm and a fluid, precise lyricism. Winner of the Jury Prize at the 1956 Cannes Film festival. Music composed and performed by Ravi Shankar. With Kanu Banerji, Karuna Banerji, Uma Da Gupta and Chunibala Devi. Bengali with English subtitles.
VHS: S16956. $24.95.
Satyajit Ray, India, 1955, 112 minutes.

Shree 420

An epic by the talented showman of Indian cinema Raj Kapoor, full of music and dancing. The movie contrasts the poor and the rich in Indian culture and stars Kapoor and Nargis. Music by Shankar Jaikrishan. Hindi with English and Arabic subtitles.
VHS: S22180. $39.95.
Raj Kapoor, India, 1959, 157 mins.

Spices

Spices is a spirited, feminist fable from India, where women have few rights and little power. This story of oppression and rebellion was shot in rural Gujarat with both actual villagers and India's top name stars. It explores a community's reaction to a woman's plight as an impoverished beauty named Sonbai spurns the amorous advances of a local tax collector (called sudebars) and takes refuge in a pepper factory. Few of the villagers have the courage to defend her, least of all its men, who are blind to injustice against women. Sonbai's eventual victory is not simply over the villainous sudebar, but over tyranny itself and the subservience that sustains it. The fiery Sonbai was Smita Patil's (two-time winner of India's National Best Actress Award) last role. Originally titled *Mirch Masala*. Hindi with English subtitles.
VHS: S13652. $29.95.
Ketan Mehta, India, 1986, 98 mins.

Two Daughters

Two wonderfully ironic stories by Ray dealing with the emancipation of women. In the first, a young university graduate rejects his pre-selected bride to marry the village tomboy, who protests. The hero, who does not want to marry a woman he doesn't love, denies the same choice to the girl he does want for his bride. Based on stories by Tagore. With Soumitra Chatterjee, Aparna Das Gupta and Anil Chatterjee. Bengali with English subtitles.
VHS: S04464. $29.95.
Satyajit Ray, India, 1961, 114 mins.

The World of Apu

The final part of Satyajit Ray's *Apu* trilogy, adapted from Bengali writer B.B. Bandapaddhay's epic novel, is a poignant summing up of the earlier films' themes and stylistic preoccupations. Its story traces Apu's leap into adulthood, the consequences of his marriage and birth of his first child. Ray's painterly use of landscape finds a poetry in the incidental, loose textures of daily life. Music by Ravi Shankar. With Soumitra Chatterjee (as Apu), Sharmila Tagore, Alok Chakravarty, and Swapan Mukherji. Bengali with English subtitles.
VHS: S16954. $24.95.
Satyajit Ray, India, 1959, 105 mins.

INDIAN ISSUES

Best of Nightline: Assassination of Indira Gandhi

30 mins.
VHS: S14032. $14.98.

Great Days of History: Gandhi and India's Independence

This documentary presents a portrait of the architect of India's independence and of the techniques of non-violent resistance. The program documents the reasons for the Indian independence movement, the periodic efforts to thwart or throw off British rule and the nature of British reprisals and Gandhi's role in these events. 52 mins.
VHS: S09435. $29.95.

Hindustani Slide: The Indian Classical Guitar of Debashish Bhattacharya

Northern Indian music has recently added the guitar and slide guitar to a rich musical tradition. Debashish has played since the age of three. The master is accompanied by Kumar Bose to reveal the intricacies and purity of this evolving tradition.
VHS: S25059. $24.95.

India, Land of Spirit and Mystique

See the holy city of Varnasi, where pilgrims bathe in the healing waters of the River Ganges. Glide into the past along the canals and lakes of Srinagar. Conclude your visit in Bombay, India's economic hub. 55 mins.
VHS: S10778. $24.95.

Nehru

A fascinating documentary study of the peoples, customs, religions and politics of the "new" India, as told by the descendants of Nehru—the "Father of India."
VHS: S15484. $39.95.
Serge Friendman, USA, 1972

Raga

All the richness of India is in *Raga*. Ravi Shankar returns to Baba, his music guru, after many years of success and acclaim in the West. Indian music had suddenly appeared on the pop scene. And Ravi, who had always wanted to bring his music to the West, is caught up in the whole exuberance of the California sixties music scene. Here we see his popular and triumphant return. Directed by Howard Worth. 95 mins.
VHS: S14716. $19.95.

BUDDHISM & EASTERN RELIGION

The 17th Karmapa's Return to Tsurphu

The Gyalwa Karmapas were the first Tibetan lamas to be acknowledged as reincarnations and represent some of the most important spiritual figures of Tibet. This program studies the spectacle and circumstances behind the 17th Gyalwa Karmapa's triumphant return to his original seat at the Tsurphu monastery in summer of 1992. The film concludes with the Karmapa's enthronement at the Jokhang Temple. 100 mins.
VHS: S18640. $29.95.

Ancient Futures: Learning from Ladakh

A look at the society of Ladakh, a beautiful, ancient culture high in the Western Himalayas, which until recently was a model of sustainable living. Western style development is now threatening their ecological balance and social harmony. A vivid case study of the potentially harmful impact of "progress". 59 mins.
VHS: S23383. $95.00.

Arising from Flames

The Dalai Lama leads the viewer through the basic precepts of his beliefs in a speech he gave at Tucson, Arizona. He describes how to reduce anger and hatred while simultaneously increasing love and forgiveness. His own experiences as an exile from Tibet offer a perfect example of how trying circumstances can be used for positive results. 60 mins.
VHS: S21188. $29.95.

Bhutan: A Himalayan Cultural Diary

A unique story of the people of Bhutan, their religion and the challenge of dealing with the 20th century. A fascinating look at the easternmost country astride the Himalayas. 35 mins.
VHS: S23346. $29.95.

Buddhism and Black Belts

Filmed in Japan, this video explores the connection between Buddhism and daily activity, the historical relationship of Japanese-style martial arts and the meditation-driven ideas and philosophy of Zen Buddhism.
VHS: S18452. $19.95.

A Change of Heart

Ram Dass, aka Dr. Richard Alpert, a Harvard psychologist, received this new name from his guru on a trip to India. In this documentary, the teaching of service that inspired him there becomes valuable to a large audience through excerpts from his ten-week "Reaching Out Course." Interviews with other social activists testify to the effectiveness of this spiritual approach to enlightenment.
VHS: S21299. $29.95.

Exploring the Himalayas, Nepal & Kashmir

This video journey starts in India's state of Kashmir, at Srinagar, on the beautiful Dal Lake, then goes to the ancient trading city of Leh in remote Ladakh and the Annapurna mountains. Raft the Trisuli River, ride the elephant in Chitwan National Park, refuge for the one-horned rhino. Explore the emerald city of Kathmandu, observe the colorful Indra Jatra and meet the engaging Sherpa people living in the shadow of Mt. Everest. 60 mins.
VHS: S12295. $29.95.

Heart of Tibet

This intimate portrait of the 14th Dalai Lama during a visit to Los Angeles reveals His Holiness as a man of simplicity and humor who constantly deals with highly complex ideas and sensitive issues. The program offers a real insight into this remarkable personality, augmented by interviews with the Dalai Lama himself, footage from his visit, and talks with writers, journalists and academicians.
VHS: S15434. $29.95.
David Cherniack, USA, 60 mins.

Himalayan Trekking: Sherpa Expeditions, Nepal

Discover the rugged, remote and stunning high wilderness regions of the Himalayas. Few forms of travel allow close contact with natives and wildlife like trekking. Surprisingly, few treks involve mountaineering ability or specific skills. Local guides strike a path through untamed corners of the world while porters, mules or support vehicles carry the baggage. Walk at your own pace, and enjoy special interests like bird-watching or photography.
VHS: S15845. $19.95.

Kalachakra: The Wheel of Time

This video shows Tibetan Buddhist monks constructing a sand mandala in Ireland according to a 2600-year-old tradition. It is part of the secret Kalachakra initiation rite, which teaches wisdom and compassion. The rite itself is said to affect world peace. 30 mins.
VHS: S26179. $29.95.

Ladakh: In Harmony with the Spirit

Through their belief in tantric Buddism, the people of Ladakh still have strong connections to the psychic energies of gods and demons. This film is a mixture of reality and fiction, history and mythology.
VHS: S16618. $29.95.
Clemens Kuby, USA, 1989, 86 mins.

Mandala: World of Mystic Circle

The mystic uses and scientific possibilities of the mandala are the basis for this examination of the mystic circle used by Tibetan Monks. From a ceremonial dismantling of the sacred Kalachakra mandala to the traces of this eternal pattern found in other historical forms, even in the patterns of matter that make up the universe, this sacred symbol has strange power. 1992, 50 mins.
VHS: S20774. $29.95.

Meaning of Tibetan Buddhist Chanting

Thubtan Pende, an American Buddhist monk who studied in India with the Dalai Lama, explains chanting and Tibetan Buddhist disciplines. Beautiful visuals of Tibetan art, symbolic of the ideas and techniques, are included. 25 mins.
VHS: S18086. $29.95.

Mind in Tibetan Buddhism

With Ole Nydahl. This Tibetan Buddhist master describes the mind as a pure, limitless field where our thoughts create visions which appear objective to us in sleep and death. 30 mins.
VHS: S08641. $29.95.

Mustang: The Hidden Kingdom

The Dalai Lama's personal emissary acts as guide to this legendary place. Then the ancient elephant routes of India and Bhutan are traversed in the *Queen of Elephants*. Both films are from the Discovery Channel.
VHS: S22543. $19.95.

Nepal: Land of the Gods

A journey to the mountain kingdom of Nepal which explores the Bodhisattva ideals of life, death, karma and rebirth in a land where Tantra is an integral part of daily life, with a unique document of the ancient cultures still thriving in Nepal. 62 mins.
VHS: S00922. $29.95.

Ossian: American Boy/Tibetan Monk

Story of a 12-year-old boy who has lived from age four as a monk in a Tibetan Buddhist monastery in Kathmandu, and is thought to be an incarnation of a High Lama. USA, 1984, 27 mins.
VHS: S02099. $19.95.

The Reincarnation of Khensur Rinpoche

A Tibetan monk named Choenzy, living in South India, learns about a young boy in Tibet possessed with uncommon qualities that suggest he may be the reincarnation of his spiritual master, Khensur Rinpoche, a revered figure who died four years earlier. "Between Khensur Rinpoche and me, our relationship goes beyond this present lifetime. It's like his body has changed, but inside, the same consciousness has come" (Choenzy). 62 mins.
VHS: S20214. $29.95.

The Sacred Art of Tibet/ The Visible Compendium

The Sacred Art of Tibet (1972, 28 mins.) was inspired by a gallery showing of unique Tibetan thankas, religious scroll paintings, rupas and other sacred images and artifacts. Jordan set out to present a visual experience of Tibetan Tantric Buddhism, and the resulting film rises above conventional documentary form to become a beautiful and autonomous work of art in its own right. *The Visible Compendium* (1990, 17 mins.) is an animated film that took two years to make and is one of Jordan's most technically refined works to date. It takes the viewer on a trip through idyllic lands where plants smile, an image of a tiger appears in the sun, and nude women wander about comfortably within an enchanted landscape. A beautiful and densely constructed work, rich in enigmatic and allusive images.
VHS: S14552. $59.95.
Larry Jordan, USA, 1972/90, 45 mins.

Sanatan Dharma: Pilgrimage to the Source of Eternal Wisdom

The headwaters to the Mother of India, the Ganges River, are located in the beautiful foothills of the Himalayas. There, Indians and Westerners alike experience the values of truth, simplicity and love that comprise the eternal, universal religion. 43 mins.
VHS: S21230. $29.95.

Tantra

An impressionistic video experience that forsakes all language, plunging the viewer without explanation into the sounds and visual splendor of Tantra (a sect of Hinduism) art and ritual. The result is a hypnotic manifestation of faith and experience in poetic form, an interwoven fabric of sound, color, form, emotion and feeling. Directed by Nik Douglas. 1969, 40 mins.
VHS: S14577. $29.95.

Tantra of Gyuto

The Dalai Lama introduces ancient Tantric rituals that use mantric power to transform consciousness, featuring the harmonic chord-chanting of the Gyuto Lamas. Prefaced by rare footage of Tibet narrated by Francis Huxley. 52 mins.
VHS: S01300. $29.95.

Tibet in Exile

This film documents the tragic plight of Tibet, focusing on the nearly 120,000 Tibetans who have escaped from their remote homeland to live in India and Nepal under the guidance of their leader, the Dalai Lama. The video highlights the story of 10 children smuggled out of Tibet by their relatives.
VHS: S15214. $75.00.
B. Banks/M. McLagan, USA, 1991, 30 mins.

Tibet's Holy Mountain

At the intersection of Tibet, Nepal and India is a 22,000'-high mountain believed to house the throne of the foremost gods of Hinduism and Buddhism. This video shows many religious sites on the route to Mt. Kailish, including the 11th-century Tibetan capital of Guge, and Llahsa, the site of rich decorative arts from the Buddhist tradition. 52 mins.
VHS: S22928. $29.95.

Tibet: A Seed for Transformation

This educational video contains information concerning China's takeover of Tibet and how this may affect the rest of the world. Content includes Tibet's Location, Customs and Culture; China's Nuclear Activities; Human Rights Violations; Environmental Destruction; etc. The soundtrack features chanting by the Dalai Lama and Tibetan monks.
VHS: S14538. $49.95.
Wendy Schofield, USA, 29 mins.

Tibet: The Survival of the Spirit

Shot on location in Tibet without Chinese censorship (although the director was arrested three times while filming), this documentary presents a compelling portrayal of conditions in occupied Tibet today. A journal of the Tibetans' unbreakable will to survive, founded on their religious practices.
VHS: S16617. $29.95.
Clemens Kuby, USA, 1991, 92 mins.

Tibetan Buddhist Meditation

With Ole Nydahl. The Tibetan Buddhist meditation master takes us step by step through the teaching—quieting the mind, focusing on motivations for meditation, and taking refuge in the *Buddha*, *Dharma* and *Sangha*. 30 mins.
VHS: S08642. $29.95.

Tibetan Medicine

Ama Lobsang Dolma, Tibet's first woman doctor, heals both the physical and psychic being by treating the patient rather than the disease. Filmed at the Tibetan Medical Center in the Himalayas. 29 mins.
VHS: S01341. $29.95.

A Trek in Nepal

A group of adventurous Americans experience the rugged natural beauty of trekking in Nepal. Highlights include visits to Sherpa homes, the Namche Bazaar, ancient Buddhist temples and the Himalayas. 28 mins.
VHS: S23349. $29.95.

Walking with the Buddha

As immigrants from Southeast Asia continue to come to the U.S., their influence will undoubtedly grow. Theravad Buddhism, with its emphasis on compassion and meditation, offers an example and challenge to all. Filmed in Thailand, this video looks at the Buddha and his followers.
VHS: S21850. $19.95.

Where Eagles Fly: Portraits of Women in Power

An innovative series focusing on powerful, spiritual women.
Nadia Stepanova, Buryatian Shaman. Stepanova is a Buryatian shaman intent on the revival of ceremonies that were performed in the taiga regions of Siberia north of Mongolia. This area is said to be the birthplace of shamanism at the dawn of civilization. This video captures her spiritual mission. 30 mins.
VHS: S26295. $29.95.
We Will Meet Again in the Land of the Dakini. Doljin Kandro Suren is an 80-year-old Buddhist lama and spiritual guide for thousands from Mongolia and Russia. She resisted the anti-religious policies which demoralized her people and now works to combat their despair through ancient spiritual traditions. Now people the world over can hear her teachings through this video. 30 mins.
VHS: S26183. $29.95.

Zen: In Search of Enlightenment

A revealing look at the Japanese form of Buddhism and the determining element in Japanese character. This program explores Zen—a way of life that stresses discipline and self-abnegation and fosters a single-minded devotion to one's goal. 120 mins.
VHS: S20533. $29.95.

Zen: The Best of Alan Watts

Alan Watts has been hailed as both a Zen master and a leading counterculture figure. Now excerpts from films made between 1965 and 1973 have been culled to bring the best of his teachings to new audiences. It all begins when you can conceive of nature as a metaphor. 60 mins.
VHS: S22970. $29.95.

AFRICAN CINEMA

Faces of Women
Eugenie Cisse Roland, Sidiki Bakaba and Albertine N'Guessan star in this vibrant, adventurous film about contemporary Africa. Two women try to balance the demands of tradition and modern life in their changing world. It's a sensual, joyous combination of raucous comedy and pulsating African music. In indigenous languages and French with English subtitles.
VHS: S22444. $79.95.
Desire Ecare, Ivory Coast, 1985, 105 mins.

Harvest: 3,000 Years
Haile Gerima (*Sankofa*) returned to his native Ethiopia to make this realistic drama set in contemporary Africa. A peasant family struggles to survive under conditions that remain tied to a feudal past, fighting against the demands of a wealthy and uncaring landowner. Gerima's realism puts the story into the broader historical context of the colonialist African legacy. In Amharic with English subtitles.
VHS: S25565. $59.95.
Haile Gerima, Ethiopia, 1976, 150 mins.

Jit
An old-fashioned romantic comedy from Zimbabwe which features the irresistible beat of African jit-jive in the story of UK, determined to win the heart of Sofi, who is closely guarded by her gangster boyfriend. UK's efforts to win Sofi's heart are hilariously hindered by an ancestral spirit. English language.
VHS: S21893. $29.95.
Michael Raeburn, Zimbabwe, 1993, 98 mins.

Kasarmu Ce: This Land Is Ours
A taut West African thriller that draws on Hausa and western storytelling, centering on the efforts of a young man to avenge the murder of his grandfather by a brutal land baron attempting to seize control of the iron-rich village lands. A politically potent and culturally interesting film, *Kasarmu Ce* is a "penetrating, poetic, joyously contemplative thriller set in a rural backdrop" (*West African Magazine*). Hausa with English subtitles.
VHS: S18889. $29.95.
Saddik Balewa, Nigeria, 1991, 84 mins.

La Vie Est Belle (Life Is Rosy)
A farce infused with the Zairian sense of belief in Systeme-D or debrouillardise (the art of hustling for survival), this film explores the rich musical world of Kinshasha. It follows a young man who uses wit and guile to trick his greedy boss, attain the woman he loves, and sing his favorite song ("La Vie Est Belle") on national television. French with English subtitles.
VHS: S27561. $59.95.
Ngangura Mweze/Benoit Lamy, Zaire/Belgium, 1987, 85 mins.

Quartier Mozart
Winner of the *Prix Afrique en Creation* at Cannes in 1992, this humorous and magical tale is filled with the secret antics that enliven a working class neighborhood in Yaounde. A girl takes on the body of a man and learns the true sexual politics of the men around her. In addition, the woman who helps her achieve this transformation metamorphoses herself into Panka, a comic figure who can make a man's penis disappear with a handshake. French with English subtitles.
VHS: S27559. $59.95.
Jean-Pierre Bekolo, Cameroon, 1992, 80 mins.

Tilai
One of the most highly acclaimed contemporary African films. In this troubling drama, a young African man is engaged to the woman he loves until the man's father decides that he should marry this woman himself. This fateful decision forces the young lovers into an illicit affair. On the run, they find tradition and the law will play a large role in their fate. In Moore with English subtitles.
VHS: S26145. $79.95.
Idrissa Ouedraogo, Burkina Faso, 1990, 81 mins.

Touki Bouki (Journey of the Hyena)
Mory and his girlfriend Anta imagine an escape from the difficult life they share in Dakar. Paris is their destination, and, like the heros of French New Wave films, they are utterly alienated from their surroundings. A series of adventures ensues as they plot ways to raise money for their trip, but only one can face up to the reality that awaits them. Wolof with English subtitles.
VHS: S27558. $59.95.
Djibril Diop Mambety, Senegal, 1973, 85 mins.

Wend Kuuni (God's Gift)
The measured rhythms and formal compositions of African oral traditions give shape to this metaphoric tale about Mossi values. A young mute boy, orphaned when his mother refuses to marry, is found and adopted by a village, which names him "Wend Kuuni," or "God's Gift." This remarkable film won a Cesar and numerous other international awards. More with English subtitles.
VHS: S27560. $59.95.
Gaston Kabore, Burkina Faso, 1982, 70 mins.

SOUTH AFRICAN FILMS

7 Up in South Africa
A remarkable work that contrasts the lives, attitudes, fears and hopes of 19 South African children caught in oppressive cycles of political violence, tyranny and authoritarian rule. The film documents their determination and hope in spite of the rigid social and political conditions. "A powerful and deeply disturbing comment on the prospects for change in South Africa. The children introduced here are endearingly open and impish" (*The Guardian*).
VHS: S19244. $19.95.
Angus Gibson, South Africa, 1993, 83 mins.

Come Back, Africa
Under the auspices of making a commercial musical, filmmaker Rogosin made this documentary-style feature on the streets of Johannesburg. *Come Back, Africa* dramatizes the desperate conditions of black Africans under apartheid—not only the squalor of slum living, but the concentrated oppression directed toward breaking up the black family and community.
VHS: S02860. $29.95.
Lionel Rogosin, South Africa, 1960, 83 mins.

Cry Freedom
An intimate, true tragedy set against the upheavals in South Africa. Tells of the friendship of white journalist Donald Woods (Kevin Kline) and black activist Stephen Biko (Denzel Washington), and the subsequent biography of Biko, championing his cause and telling his story to the world.
VHS: S06820. $14.98.
Laser: LD70021. $39.98.
Richard Attenborough, USA, 1987, 157 mins.

Dark City
The oppression and brutality of South Africa's apartheid policies are viewed through the systematic torture of one man committed to the struggle of armed revolution. Shot on location in Zimbabwe and played largely by the members of Johannesburg's Market Theatre. "On one level this is a smoothly paced political thriller, on another a bitter reminder of the whirlwind of violence."
VHS: S18062. $29.95.
Chris Curling, South Africa, 1990, 98 mins.

Dingaka
Early film by the director of *The Gods Must Be Crazy* concerns an attorney who takes the case of a tribesman who is charged with murdering a rival whom he believes killed his daughter. Filmed in Africa, with Stanley Baker and Juliet Prowse.
VHS: S01779. $19.98.
Jamie Uys, Great Britain, 1965, 96 mins.

A Dry White Season
Donald Sutherland is cast as an incredibly naive South African schoolteacher who has trouble believing his black gardener's son would be arrested for no good reason. Set in the historical perspective of violence and unrest in 1976, director Euzhan Palcy (*Sugar Cane Alley*) uses this basically decent man as a symbol of needed political involvement. A powerful film with a first rate cast that includes Janet Suzman, Susan Sarandon, Winston Ntschone, Zakes Mokae and Marlon Brando as a cynical but able liberal lawyer.
VHS: Out of print. For rental only.
Laser: LD70957. $39.98.
Euzhan Palcy, USA, 1989, 97 mins.

Friends
A brilliant debut feature, this is the story of three South African women who find their friendship put to the test by extreme political circumstances. One of the three, a black activist, is involved in a deadly bomb incident. This sets in motion passionate and blinding forces that threaten to destroy the ideals that originally joined them. With Kerry Fox (*An Angel at My Table*). "Fascinating and bold…has a blazing urgency and passion…boasts a thrilling performance by one of the world's great young actresses, New Zealander Kerry Fox" (Michael Wilmington, *Chicago Tribune*).
VHS: S26870. $59.95.
Elaine Proctor, South Africa, 1994, 109 mins.

The Gods Must Be Crazy
An international sensation, one of the highest-grossing foreign films in the U.S. and Europe, Jamie Uys' unlikely comedy is the story of an African bushman who discovers a discarded Coke bottle which ultimately brings him face to face with modern man for the first time. Very heartwarming, entertaining, full of non-stop high-jinks, this story about an innocent bushman's encounter with the 20th century has become one of the cult films of the 1980's.
VHS: S01704. $19.95.
Laser: LD71008. $34.98.
Jamie Uys, South Africa, 1984, 109 mins.

The Gods Must Be Crazy II
Everyone's favorite African Bushman is back in action but this time his mission is personal. When N!Xau finds that his children have been taken for a ride by a pair of unsuspecting poachers, he leaves his village to find them. Along the way he encounters silly white people and other members of the animal kingdom. With Lena Farugia, Hans Strydom and a very tenacious badger.
VHS: S14005. $19.95.
Jamie Uys, USA/Botswana, 1989

The Magic Garden (The Pennywhistle Blues)
An all black cast is featured in this South African musical allegory. Near Johannesburg, a community is affected when some "magic money" is stolen. The film follows those who come in contact with the money from the magic garden. There are many smiles along the way. Filmed in English.
VHS: S05482. $29.95.
Donald Swanson, South Africa, 1960, 63 mins.

Mandela
An HBO film on the life and times of human rights activist Nelson Mandela. Danny Glover and Alfre Woodard star as Nelson and Winnie, a courageous married couple dedicated to opposing the oppression in South Africa. A stirring dramatic reenactment of a man now in his third decade of imprisonment. USA, 1987, 135 mins.
VHS: S06394. $79.95.

Place of Weeping
A powerful human drama of one woman's personal fight for freedom: her bravery, emotional traumas and fight against both the deep-rooted resentment of her people and the violent and oppressive hand of the apartheid system. Starring James Whylie.
VHS: S03037. $19.95.
Darrell Roodt, South Africa, 1986, 90 mins.

Sarafina!
Based on Mbongeni Ngema's classic stage play, Darrell James Roodt's film alternates between stylized dance numbers and a naturalistic depiction of the brutal human rights abuses of apartheid, set during the Soweto uprisings of 1976 and the detainment of Nelson Mandela. Leleti Khumalo is superb in the title role, with Whoopi Goldberg as a fiercely individualistic history teacher who insists her children be taught social responsibilities and acknowledge their African heritage and ritual. With Miriam Makeba, John Kani and Ngema.
VHS: S18248. $94.95.
Darrell Roodt, USA, 1992, 98 mins.

Voices of Sarafina
This Tony-Award nominated musical concerns a South African high school class who create their own play about Nelson Mandela. Part documentary, part Broadway show, the energy is infectious and the songs touch the soul. The music is by Mbogeni Ngema and Hugh Masekela. Cast includes Miriam Makeba, Leleti Khumalo, Pat Miaba and Baby Cele.
VHS: S13315. $29.95.
Nigel Noble, USA, 1988, 90 mins.

AFRICAN SPOTLIGHT

Africa Speaks to the World
At the U.N., a new spotlight has been turned on Africa, but this time by Africans themselves. Acknowledging their mistakes, yet affirming their strengths, they now ask the world's governments and churches to work with them in a new spirit to develop further the many nations on the continent. African leaders from government and church engage in this new dialog, and discuss progress being made, with video input from Tanzania and Zimbabwe. Produced by Maryknoll Media. 28 mins.
VHS: S06269. $24.95.

Africa: Part I
The first two segments of this highly acclaimed series. *Different But Equal* looks at the slave trade in Africa, as Basil Davidson goes back to Africa's origins to show some of the great early civilizations which flourished in Africa; the second segment, *Mastering a Continent*, looks closely at three different communities to examine how African peoples carve out an existence in an often hostile environment. 120 mins.
VHS: S02400. $29.95.

Africa: Part II
The third and fourth segments from the series. In *Caravans of Gold*, Basil Davidson traces the routes of the medieval gold trade which reached from Africa to China and India to Europe; in *Kings and Cities*, the program explores the ways in which African kingdoms functioned as Davidson visits Kano in Nigeria, where a king still holds court in his 15th century palace. 120 mins.
VHS: S02401. $29.95.

Africa: Part III
Segments five and six of the series. *The Bible and the Gun* examines the explorers in Africa, including Stanley and Livingstone and then the missionaries, and finally, men like Cecil Rhodes, who envisioned a diamond-studded empire. *This Magnificent African Cake* looks at the 1800's, when colonialist powers fought over Africa, dramatically altering the face of the continent. 120 mins.
VHS: S02402. $29.95.

Africa: Part IV
Segments seven and eight of Basil Davidson's series. *The Rise of Nationalism* examines the major struggles for African independence—in Ghana, Kenya, Algeria and the Belgian Congo. *The Legacy* looks at Africa in the aftermath of colonial rule, as the continent seeking ways to come to terms with its diverse inheritance. 120 mins.
VHS: S02403. $29.95.

African Ritual and Initiation
Dr. Malidoma Patrice Some explains that during his childhood among the Dagara people, ritual established a link with the worlds of ancestors and spirits. This shaman will lead you to other dimensions of reality. 60 mins.
VHS: S23625. $34.95.

African Safaris
What distinguishes these two videos, which are subtitled "Adventures in Wildlife Observation", is the unique learning approach, looking at animals as does a safari guide, with cues leading the viewer to a better understanding of animal behavior. Consultants include Russell E. Train, founder of the African Wildlife Federation.
Volume 1: Serengeti Migration, Amboseli Elephants. Hundreds of thousands of zebra, wildebeest and Thomson's gazelle follow ancient trails in their annual quest for fresh pasture. Learn how to interpret the cycles that drive animal movements in this guide to the greatest animal migration on earth. Then visit the elephants of Amboseli National Park in Kenya, one of the few parks where elephants have been undisturbed from severe poaching, in an exploration of the behavioral links that bind elephant society. 45 mins.
VHS: S09707. $29.95.
Volume 2: Masai Mara Lions, Virunga Gorillas. The Masai Mara Reserve in Kenya is the best place in the world to see lions in the middle of their summer feasting. The playful side of lions is explored. In Virunga Gorillas, trek to Rwanda into the domain of the endangered mountain gorilla, with dominant silverback males and the warm family community they protect. 45 mins.
VHS: S09708. $29.95.

Belafonte Presents "Fincho"
Harry Belafonte hosts this entertaining look at Nigeria —one primitive village's leap into modern times, in the course of just ten years! 73 minutes.
VHS: S02751. $69.95.

Best of Nightline
Nelson Mandela. 90 mins.
VHS: S14063. $14.98.
South African Debate. 55 mins.
VHS: S14037. $14.98.

Black Man's Land Trilogy, Vol. 1, White Man's Country
Three films on colonialism, nationalism and revolution, called by *The New York Times* "a solid historical document skewed, valuably, to a distinctive African point of view. By affording a forum for black leaders, past and present, it conveys the sense of an enduring dignity that no colonialist rationalizations can eliminate." "A treasure of old stills, buried newsreels, and contemporary interviews, supported by meticulous research and synthesized with the most sensitive acumen. A unique record of what colonialism means in human terms" (Judy Stone, *San Francisco Chronicle*). *White Man's Country* covers the violence of colonial rule, white settlement and African resistance in the story of Kenya, formerly British East Africa, as the British tried to make it a "white man's country" like South Africa or New Zealand. Land was allocated, settlers welcomed, and the "jewel of the British empire," was born. How did Africans confront this process? It was, after all, African land that was taken, African labor that was used to develop it and African taxes that kept the colonial regime solvent. *White Man's Country* combines period photographs and contemporary location footage with the testimony of African and European witnesses, to examine both sides of Europe's "civilizing mission" in Africa. 52 mins.
Home Video.
VHS: S10843. $39.95.
Institutional with public performance rights.
VHS: S10848. $89.95.
David Koff/Anthony Kowarth, Great Britain, 1986

Black Man's Land Trilogy, Vol. 2, Mau Mau
In October 1952 the British government declared a State of Emergency in Kenya. Its object: the defeat of "Mau Mau." In the war that followed, fewer than 40 of 40,000 white settlers were killed while more than 15,000 Africans lost their lives, and hundreds of thousands more were arrested and subjected to a humiliating and often brutal process of "rehabilitation." But what was Mau Mau? A movement based, according to the British Colonial Secretary, on a "perverted nationalism and a sort of nostalgia for barbarism"? Or the Land Freedom Army, an organized political and military response to repression and armed aggression? Using newsreel and previously inaccessible archive footage, and drawing on interviews with participants on both sides, *Mau Mau* examines the myth and reality of Africa's first modern guerrilla war. 52 mins.
Home Video.
VHS: S10844. $39.95.
Institutional with public performance rights.
VHS: S10849. $89.95.
David Koff/Anthony Kowarth, Great Britain, 1986

Black Man's Land Trilogy, Vol. 3, Kenyatta
Jomo Kenyatta's death in 1978 brought to an end a political career that encompassed more than 50 years of African history. Kenyatta entered politics in the mid 1920s and then spent 17 years in exile in Europe. He returned to Kenya in 1946, and was elected President. Arrested in 1952 and imprisoned, he was released in 1961 and two years later became Kenya's first Prime Minister. In power, the man whom Europeans had once reviled as "the leader to darkness and death" was eulogized by them as a pillar of stability. *Kenyatta* weaves archival and contemporary images with interviews with friends and relatives, comrades and opponents, to create a biographical portrait of a key figure in 20th century politics, and a case study of nationalism as a political force in Africa. 52 mins.
Home Video.
VHS: S10845. $39.95.
Institutional with public performance rights.
VHS: S10850. $89.95.
David Koff/Anthony Kowarth, Great Britain, 1986

Earthkeepers
Scientists and environmentalists are warning that if people continue to neglect and abuse the Earth, it might become uninhabitable. Men and women in Kenya and Tanzania are working to reverse growing desertification simply by planting trees. This video shows successful programs of ecological healing done by the people of these east African countries. 28 mins.
VHS: S13907. $24.95.

The Elephants of Timbuktu
Five hundred wild elephants make an extraordinary 600-mile migration annually. Despite this vast undertaking, these animals manage to live in harmony with the nomadic Tuareg people. This video presents an unforgettable Smithsonian Expedition. 50 mins.
VHS: S25868. $24.95.

Eyewitness South Africa
An American TV journalist is assigned to document this dynamic country. Both black and white audiences share his learning experiences as he explores the multi-faceted nation of South Africa. 35 mins.
VHS: S23712. $129.95.

The First World Festival of Negro Arts
In 1966, in Dakar, Senegal, over 2000 people of the African Diaspora convened to celebrate and debate the world-wide renaissance of Black culture. Poets, musicians, painters, dancers, sculptors, intellectuals and political leaders were in attendance. Aime Cesaire and Alione Diop led the debate about "Negritude", a concept first conceived of by Leopold Senghor. 40 mins.
VHS: S24587. $175.00.

Folks Like Us
The Catholic diocese of Bismarck, North Dakota, has sent four people—a priest, a deacon, a nurse and a speech pathologist—to Bura, Kenya. In this documentary studies the team at work and the impact of their project on families and friends back home. 29 mins.
VHS: S15858. $19.95.

From Sunup
The story of women of black Africa, their strength, courage, daily struggles and challenges. A candid, authentic picture of the dawn-to-dusk lives of women in the Third World, produced by a Tanzanian woman, Flora M'mbugu, shot in Tanzania with an all-African crew. Portrays the woman's multiple roles as provider, mother, water-carrier, wood-gatherer, cook and entrepreneur, illustrating that the source of her hope and future lies in women's support of each other. 28 mins.
VHS: S04927. $24.95.

Glimpses of West Africa
An ethnographic video that looks at the geography, culture and people of the West African countries of Cote d'Ivoire, Mali and Senegal. The program contains a transcript and lesson plan. 32 mins.
English Narration.
VHS: S19800. $49.95.
French Narration.
VHS: S19799. $49.95.

Jirimpimbira
Kathleen Arnot's *Tale of Temba* inspired this amusing video about a young African boy whose village is experiencing a difficult drought. An old man gives the boy bones which, together with the magic word *Jirimpimbira*, grant him anything he desires. A misadventure follows which gently points out the folly of greed and selfishness. 25 mins.
VHS: S27535. $9.95.

Karibu
Although the family is probably the most important social unit in East Africa, urbanization draws young people away from their villages to the big cities. Meaning "welcome" in Swahili, *Karibu* examines parishes in Nairobi that are trying to become "welcoming families" for newcomers. 29 mins.
VHS: S15864. $19.95.

Kenya Safari: Essence of Africa
Traverse the jungles of Kenya and see game reserves, Masai villages, a coffee plantation, and more as you see the essence of African life. 45 mins.
VHS: S05776. $24.95.

Kenyan Youth: Preparing for the Future
For youth the world over, hope is the source of energy and direction. From Kenya, a potential Olympic runner, a budding artist and a family of young musicians tell their stories of determination, hard work and dreams of a bright future, demonstrating their varied skills. Produced by Maryknoll media.
VHS: S06271. $24.95.

Learn to Cook the Easy Way with the Kitchen Divas: Preparing an African Feast
The Shelf sisters (author Angela Shelf Medearis and her sister Marcia Shelf), two culinary divas, demonstrate five traditional African dishes that will take the diner from appetizer to desert. It's a an easy guide to challenging but satisfying recipes.
VHS: S27218. $19.95.

Lions of Dakar
Dakar, Senegal, is the center of Afro Pop, the dynamic mix of traditional West African and contemporary American musical rhythms. This documentary charts the city and its musical influences. With performances by Youssou n'Dour, Ismael Lo and Super Diamono. French narration with English subtitles. 50 mins.
VHS: S19797. $49.95.

Mandela: The Man and His Country
Morton Dean narrates this emotional examination of Nelson Mandela, the symbolic head of the anti-apartheid movement, who was recently freed from prison after 27 years by the South African government. Includes interviews with Jesse Jackson and James Michener, plus unforgettable footage shot right after Mandela's release. 50 mins.
VHS: S12291. $19.98.

Masters of the Congo Jungle
Produced in 1960 by the Belgian International Scientific Foundation, this is a chronicle of Henri Storck's two-year exploration of the Belgian Congo. Untouched for centuries by outside civilization, the jungle is now disrupted by the invasion of modern man. Storck captures remnants of the ancient African continent, plant and animal life and regional natives co-existing in the simple grandeur and rhythm of the earth.
VHS: S17448. $19.95.

Nelson Mandela 70th Birthday Tribute
A live tribute concert featuring performances by Sting, George Michael, Eurythmics, Tracy Chapman, Peter Gabriel, the Fat Boys and many more. USA, 117 mins.
VHS: S15308. $14.98.

The New Zimbabwe
Blacks and whites once lived in separate societies in colonial Rhodesia and now hope to work together in the new Zimbabwe. They tell of their aspirations and apprehensions in the early years of independence. This film documents the struggle to build a society based on reconciliation and equality while offering historic insights into the problem of achieving that goal. Produced by Maryknoll Media. 28 mins.
VHS: S04930. $24.95.

Once Upon a Time
In our fast-changing world, Kenyan storytelling traditions are diminished in their ability to pass on legend and wisdom in society. Uncover why the legacy of diviners, healers, poets, storytellers and singers is finding a home with the Church in Africa. 29 mins.
VHS: S15862. $19.95.

Portrait of Africa
Vangelis, Ladysmith Black Mambazo and Miriam Makeba are featured in these beautifully-shot images of Africa from the producers of the Windham Hill series. From Tanzania's sweeping Serengeti to towering Mt. Kilimanjaro, from Kenya's island of Lamu to striking Lake Turkana, the program presents a remarkable array of people, places and wildlife. 58 mins.
VHS: S11194. $29.95.

Project Tanzania: Part 1: A Response Beyond Charity
When dramatic film reports of the Africa famine shocked the world in 1984, a television station in Raleigh, North Carolina looked for some way to help the people of Africa. What developed not only has helped people in the Shunyanga region of Tanzania. It helped North Carolinians understand the meaning of the word "neighbor." Produced by Maryknoll Media. 28 mins.
VHS: S06262. $24.95.

Project Tanzania: Part 2: A Response Beyond Charity
When WRAL-TV in Raleigh, North Carolina asked its viewers to help the people in Tanzania, it also offered those viewers a chance to enrich their lives. This film looks at what's been the impact of Project Tanzania on North Carolinians. Filmed on location and in Raleigh, N.C. Produced by Maryknoll Media. 28 mins.
VHS: S06264. $24.95.

Shooting Africa
Travel with Ian Thomas, a professional wildlife photographer who lives and works in Africa, on a personal safari to photograph the biggest, fastest, fiercest African animals, filming over 30 animals in their natural environment. 30 mins.
VHS: S09916. $21.95.

Something New Out of Africa
Catholic priests are coming from across the Atlantic again, this time from Nigeria to work among African-American Catholics in southern Louisiana and Texas. The priests and their American parishioners describe how this mix of cultures affects their lives and their Catholic faith. Filmed in Nigeria and the United States, 29 mins.
VHS: S15691. $19.95.

Sons of Bwiregi
This film deals with the efforts of Maryknoll Father Ed Hayes to aid the Tanzanian people, torn between old customs and the modern world, to build a future based on their past. When one member of the tribe wants to remarry after the death of his wife, Father Hayes is given the opportunity to show the people that some traditions must change. Produced by Maryknoll Media. 25 mins.
VHS: S04935. $24.95.

South Africa—The Black Red War
Made in 1978, this film analyzes the apartheid system in South Africa from a communist perspective. The violence of the system is exposed through brutal and graphic footage, and the film does much to expose the barbarism of the ruling parties. 60 mins.
VHS: S12715. $19.98.

The Speeches of Nelson Mandela
Nelson Mandela fought apartheid in South Africa for decades, leading to his conviction and imprisonment for sabotage by the South African government. He won the Nobel Peace Prize for his efforts and was released from prison after 27½ years. Speeches from his long career are collected on this video, which show the depth of his struggle and his triumph as the President of South Africa. From *The Speeches Collection*. USA, 1995, 70 mins.
VHS: S27278. $19.98.

Streetmother
Mary Mutahi once gloried in the applause and attention she received as the winner of the title "Miss Nairobi." Now many years later she gives the applause and lots of attention to over 80 youngsters who call her house their home. She is a new mother to these children, once sadly abandoned to the streets of Nairobi. Produced by Maryknoll Media. 25 mins.
VHS: S10839. $24.95.

Wild Rapture
This documentary was shot in Equatorial Africa. It contains very unusual footage depicting the customs and lifestyles of some African peoples.
VHS: S23796. $24.95.
Jaques Dupont, USA, 1950, 68 mins.

Witness to Apartheid
This Emmy Award-winning documentary (Best Direction) was shot clandestinely in South Africa during the 1985 State of Emergency. Its interviews of tortured children and their doctors helped galvanize world wide action to change this unjust system.
VHS: S24586. $180.00.
Sharon Sopher, USA, 1986, 56 mins.

Women in Tanzania
From sunup to sundown, women in Tanzania, East Africa, bear the burden of running the household, raising the children and growing the crops. This program looks at the situation of women in Tanzania from the women's perspectives. Includes discussions by a Tanzanian woman who has studied village life and a woman missioner to Tanzania. Produced by Maryknoll Media. 28 mins.
VHS: S06265. $24.95.

Zambian Safari
A fascinating look at the beauty of Zimbabwe, show on location in South Luangwa and Kafue National parks, featuring the exotic wildlife, plants, birds, people, villages, traditional music and dancing of the land of Victoria Falls, the Zambezi River, and many small villages. 40 mins.
VHS: S05871. $24.95.

VERY SPECIAL

Classic Foreign Shorts—Volume 1
Contains three short films, including the classic take-off on Ingmar Bergman, *The Dove*; *The Existentialist*; and the 1948 short *Loves of Franistan*.
VHS: S09047. $24.95.

Classic Foreign Shorts—Volume 2
Contains Truffaut's early *Les Mistons*; Orson Welles' short *Hearts of Age*; Jean-Luc Godard's *All the Boys Named Patrick*; Roman Polanski's *Fat and the Lean* and *Two Men and a Wardrobe*; and Cavalcanti's *Rien que les Heures*.
VHS: S09048. $24.95.

The Countess
In this Bulgarian *Drugstore Cowboy*, a teenage girl's rebellion through drugs becomes a metaphor for the struggle between individuality and totalitarianism. Prize winner at the Turin, Angers, Troia and Varna Film Festivals, the film is "starkly beautiful and intensely perceptive" (*Philadelphia City Paper*). Bulgarian with English subtitles.
VHS: S26496. $59.95.
Peter Popzlatev, Bulgaria, 1989, 119 mins.

The Jester
This acclaimed Portuguese film, which captured the Grand Prize at the Locarno Film Festival, intertwines excerpts of Alexandre Herculano's classic play *O Bobo*, which chronicles the founding of Portugal's monarchy, with a modern-day drama about Portugal after the loss of Angola, in a brilliant exposition of the rise and fall of empire. Portuguese with English subtitles.
VHS: S26500. $59.95.
Jose Alvaro Morais, Portugal, 1987, 127 mins.

The Sealed Soil (Khak-e Sar Beh Morh)
The first Iranian feature by a woman, Marva Nabili's brave film focuses on a young woman who is confronted with change in pre-revolutionary Iran. She rejects a number of suitors, inviting the displeasure of her family. Soon the rigid orthodoxies of fundamentalist Islamic life prove too much for her and she faces extreme measures (including an exorcism). This film began shooting just before the revolution and had to be smuggled out for completion and distribution. Farsi with English subtitles.
VHS: S26348. $59.95.
Marva Nabili, Iran/USA, 1977, 90 mins.

The Suitors
The first film by a young Iranian living in New York is a high comedy based on culture shock. An Iranian couple in Manhattan sacrifice a sheep in an apartment. The blood drips through the floor onto the head of the super, who calls the police, who misinterpret the idea for a group of terrorists. A SWAT team is dispatched to handle the situation. "An offbeat, intriguing pic…" (*Variety*). Farsi with English subtitles.
VHS: S11996. $59.95.
Ghasem Ebrahimian, USA, 1988, 106 mins.

Why Has Bodhi-Dharma Left for the East?
An aged monk, his young apprentice and an orphan inhabit a remote monastery. This fascinating Korean film by Bae Yong-kyun focuses on their interaction and, in the process, provokes a contemplation on life, death and enlightenment. A solo effort, the film took ten years to complete. Korean with English subtitles.
VHS: S27338. $79.95.
Laser: LD75463. $69.95.
Bae Yong-kyun, Korea, 1989, 135 mins.

OTHER SILENT CINEMA

90 Degrees South: With Scott to the Antarctic
Herbert G. Ponting's chronicle of Captain Robert Scott's heroic and ultimately tragic race for the South Pole was originally released in 1913. Ponting, a renowned still photographer, dedicated his life to the memory of Scott, who died with his entire team on the return trip from the pole after losing the race to Amundsen. Twenty years after his friend's death, Ponting added narration to the film, drawing from Scott's diary entries. This is the deeply personal tribute to the heartbreaking last days of the doomed expedition.
VHS: S16434. $39.95.
Laser: CLV/CAV. LD71592. $29.95.
Herbert G. Ponting, Great Britain, 1933, 72 mins.

Cabiria
The most ambitious and spectacular of the historical epics for which Italy was famous before World War I, *Cabiria* set the standard for big budget, feature-length movies and opened the way for Griffith and DeMille. During the war between Carthage and Rome, a girl—Cabiria—is separated from her parents. In her odyssey through the world of ancient Rome, she encounters an erupting volcano, the barbaric splendor of Carthage, human sacrifice and Hannibal crossing the Alps. Mastered from a 35mm archive print using variable speed projection to match the original hand cranked camera, *Cabiria* features a newly recorded soundtrack from the original 1914 score.
VHS: S06218. $39.95.
Giovanni Pastrone, Italy, 1914, 123 mins.

The Christus
The story of Christ is presented in this silent Italian production that was adapted from a poem by Fausto Salvatore. He most likely based his poem on a much more popular source. Filmed closer to the Holy Land than most Hollywood films on the same subject matter. Silent.
VHS: S04813. $24.95.
Guilio Antamoro, Italy, 1917, 90 mins.

Daughters of Eve
Anny Ondra is the starring vamp in this sultry film. She's a showgirl who specializes in leading men astray. Germany, 1928. Silent with English intertitles.
VHS: S23824. $24.95.

David Copperfield
Charles Dickens' unforgettable tale of an orphan vagabond is touchingly realized in this early, silent, color-tinted film. This is the first feature length adaptation of the literary masterwork.
VHS: S23825. $24.95.
Thomas Bentley, Great Britain, 1913, 55 mins.

Devil's Island
This silent French film from 1926 tells tales of inhumanity set amidst the isolation of the legendary prison Devil's Island. Pauline Frederick and Marion Nixon star. 73 mins.
VHS: S23827. $24.95.

Fabiola
An early sound spectacle from Italy of the days of Ancient Rome, focusing on the story of Fabiola, daughter of a Roman senator, who converts to Christianity when her father is killed and his Christian servants accused. With Michel Simon and Henri Vidal. Dubbed in English.
VHS: S14635. $29.95.
Allessandro Blasetti, Italy, 1948, 96 mins.

Frate Francisco (Brother Francis of Assisi)
This mammoth, lavish production exemplifies the spectacular Italian historical epics made during the era of silent films. The story is based on the life of the saint. He was born to a life of ease, only to reject everything for a vow of poverty. Alleged to have experienced the stigmata (wounds like those suffered by Christ on the cross), this holy man's spiritual ways remain inspirational. Includes original musical score with sound effects.
VHS: S25866. $24.95.
Guilio Antamoro, Italy, 1927, 75 mins.

The Lady of the Lake
This silent British feature captures the exciting adventures and freedom of a young girl (Benita Hume) in Scotland. Loosely based from the period that produced Sir Walter Scott's narrative poem, the story concerns the young girl's saving of the life of the King from outlaws.
VHS: S19531. $29.95.
James A. Fitzpatrick, Great Britain, 1928, 60 mins.

Man in the Silk Hat
A moving tribute to the famous french actor of the silent era, Max Linder, whom Chaplin once called "my professor," directed by his daughter. During his lifetime, Linder made some 400-500 short comedies, and came to America to make his only three feature-length films. With numerous excerpts from Linder's films, this is a loving tribute to one of the giants of comedy. Narrated in English by Maud Linder.
VHS: S04870. $24.95.
Maud Linder, France, 1984, 96 mins.

Max Linder
By 1910 Max Linder was an internationally popular comic, typically playing a dapper dandy of the idle rich. He developed a slapstick style that anticipated Mack Sennett and Chaplin. His popularity was at its peak in 1914, when he was called up for World War I. With original French titles. Silent.
VHS: S00833. $29.95.
Max Linder, France, 1911-13

Moulin Rouge
Made by German director Dupont (*Variety*) after his move to England in 1927, this is a melodrama set in Paris about a young man who becomes infatuated with the Moulin Rouge star whose daughter he is about to marry. Silent.
VHS: S02160. $29.95.
E.A. Dupont, Great Britain, 1929, 90 mins.

She (1911)
H. Rider Haggard wrote the story on which this early and imaginative silent film is based. It involves the discovery of a lost race. James Cruze and Marguerite Snow star.
VHS: S23846. $24.95.
T. Marston/G. Nichols, Great Britain, 1911, 20 mins.

She (1925)
H. Rider Haggard's tale of the immortal Queen Ayesha, "She who must be obeyed," is brought to the screen in this early silent version starring Betty Blythe, Carlyle Blackwell and Mary Odette. Silent with musical score. England, 1925, 57 mins.
VHS: S01636. $24.95.
Leander de Cordova, Great Britain, 1925, 57 mins.

Spartacus
An early Italian silent era spectacle, based on the revolt of the gladiators. Also included on this tape is the rare short, *Uncle Tom's Cabin* (1910). 80 mins.
VHS: S07761. $29.95.

Trapped by the Mormons
A British thriller about a girl from Manchester who is coerced into joining a secret society. Can the proper authorities find and free her before she develops a fixation for living in Utah? Starring Evelyn Brent as Nora Prescott. With Olive Sloane and Olaf Hytten as Elder Marz. Banned in the US for years. Silent.
VHS: S04812. $24.95.
H.B. Parkinson, Great Britain, 1922, 65 mins.

The Wandering Jew
Rudolph and Joseph Schildkraut star in this silent Austrian film adaptation of the legend concerning the Wandering Jew. 1920, 65 mins. English intertitles.
VHS: $23853. $24.95.

What Do Those Old Films Mean?
Noel Burch's remarkable Channel 4 series, discovering the world of silent cinema never before told.

Volume 1: Great Britain 1900-1912—Along the Great Divide. Using extremely rare films, newly scored music and a lively commentary, film historian Noel Burch explores the contradictions in early British cinema between the "gentlemen inventors of the cinema" and film as an entertainment for the poor. Early films in Britain, says Burch, either showed the poor what bright, happy lives their "betters" led, or held up to them their own, usually drunken, depravity. At the same time, the early filmmakers worked in a climate of fear in an era of panic that "the empire was in danger." By examining the earliest classics, like Cecil Hepworth's *Rescued by Rover* and other, much more obscure films, Burch documents the British filmmakers as the earliest pioneers in the techniques of film editing. 26 mins.
VHS: S08682. $29.95.

Volume 2: U.S.A. 1902-1914—Tomorrow the World. Film historian Noel Burch examines early filmmaking in America against the social background of the immigrant masses streaming into the slums, factories and sweatshops of an industrialized America. It was these immigrants who became the earliest patrons of the nickelodeons, in spite of the fact that many of the earliest films depicted non-Americans as ridiculous or loathsome. But when the middle-class discovered the cinema, American movies changed—American film discovered narrative, and at the same time began to censor its own productions, depriving them of social content and criticism. Rare film footage provides the background for this fascinating cinematic and social analysis in this second volume in a remarkable series produced by Britain's Channel Four Television. 26 mins.
VHS: S08683. $29.95.

Volume 3: Denmark 1902-1914—She! Why was Copenhagen the undisputed birthplace of the mature cinema, of psychological realism on the screen, at a time when French or American films were no more than rudimentary melodramas? Film historian Noel Burch examines the Danish silent film phenomenon both from the standpoint of its key figures (the actors Asta Nielsen and Urban Gad, the powerful producer Ole Olsen), and from the social perspective of a Denmark in which women had an advanced position for the time, where feminism was prominent and attitudes toward sexuality liberal. The early Danish cinema was innovative and in such techniques as lighting, camera angles or editing within one and the same scene, they adopted many techniques before the American directors. As the legendary actress Asta Nielsen wrote in her autobiography, "At a time when almost no one considered that films might be an art, I was determined to put all my energies into the artistic potentialities I had discovered in myself during that first film...If I had had a clear awareness of the terrifying world of unscrupulous businessmen who in those days ran the film industry—I would probably not have embarked on that adventure with such enthusiasm." 26 mins.
VHS: S08684. $29.95.

Volume 4: France 1904-1912—The Enemy Below. "One of the most remarkable features of the seventh art is its unanimous appeal to the masses, with none of the intellectual preparation needed for literature or music," wrote Louis Delluc, and in this fascinating program covering the early years of cinema in France, film historian and critic Noel Burch follows the thesis that the appeal of the silent French cinema was the working class. "We were attracted to everything denied us by a moral code laid down by others: luxury, wild parties, the great brass band of vices and the image of woman too, but a woman heroized, elevated to adventuress...a generation of young men fell head over heels in love with Musidora in *Les Vampires*," wrote the poet Louis Aragon. 26 mins.
VHS: S08685. $29.95.

Volume 5: USSR 1926-1930—Born Yesterday. Amid general poverty, social disorder, and the sudden arrival of women in industry, post-Revolutionary Russia was also a period of extraordinary social and cultural experiment. The artists saw art as an instrument of social change, of encouraging new relationships between individuals. The filmmakers and filmmaking groups concentrated on social agitation, on new forms of newsreel, on incorporating into film the great formal experiments of the era. In this fascinating program, film historian Noel Burch focuses on the sexual politics of Soviet cinema—issues such as the collectivization of domestic tasks and child care and the abolition of sexual division of labor in the home. Using rare films which are virtually unknown in the West, Burch provides a unique perspective on this great era of cinema in a climate of virulent change. 26 mins.
VHS: S08686. $29.95.

Volume 6: Germany 1926-1932—Under Two Flags. This volume of *What Do Those Old Films Mean?* focuses on films produced in Germany in the 20's, rarely shown or discussed today. But influenced by the achievements of the young Soviet cinema, the German social workers' movements created the German Workers' Film. Among these early productions were such landmark films as *The Other Side of the Street*, *Our Daily Bread*, *Mother Krausen's Journey to Happiness*, and *Kuhle Wampe*. This remarkable movement for a "populist" cinema in Germany of the Weimar Republic had much in common with similar efforts in other fields of the arts—for example, the art of Kathe Kollwitz. But it was ultimately replaced by the more palatable—and cheerful—films of Billy Wilder and Robert Siodmak, and, ultimately, by the victory of Nazism. 26 mins.
VHS: S08687. $29.95.

Complete Set. Available at a special price.
VHS: S08688. $149.75.

LANGUAGE INSTRUCTION (see also p. 349)

Alles Gute!
This new video course from the Goethe Institut and Inter Nationes will help its readers assimilate the language, culture and daily activities of German-speaking countries. 60 mins.
Lessons 1-4.
VHS: S19846. $55.00.
Lessons 5-8.
VHS: S19847. $55.00.
Lessons 9-12.
VHS: S19848. $55.00.
Lessons 13-16.
VHS: S19849. $55.00.
Lessons 17-20.
VHS: S19850. $55.00.
Lessons 21-26.
VHS: S19851. $55.00.
All Six Guides and Videos.
VHS: S19852. $349.75.

Arc-en-Ciel
The next best thing to being there—total immersion in French, via video. The place is Paris, the characters are four French teenagers and an English friend, who explore realistic situations in Paris. Each of the six episodes is followed by a repetition and display of key expressions. The Video Guide provides a synopsis of each episode. 70 mins.
VHS: S11199. $49.95.

Avantage
This lively collection of 12 mini-programs will strengthen the French language skills of teen-agers. Part I introduces intermediate students to the daily life of French students. Part II explores everyday activities, including a trip to the Ecole du Cirque in Amiens, where film students are trained. Contextualizing grammar and vocabulary makes these lessons both valuable and entertaining.
Part I: Video and Book.
VHS: S19787. $49.95.
Part II: Video and Book.
VHS: S19788. $49.95.
Set of two tapes.
VHS: S19789. $88.00.

Basic Chinese by Video
Pleasure or business travellers will gain a speaking vocabulary of Chinese words and phrases. 90 mins.
VHS: S08277. $74.95.

Basic Hebrew 1 & 2
An introductory course to the Hebrew language, this program is designed to teach Hebrew as a second language. Developed by two professors, *Basic Hebrew* presents vocabulary using live demonstrations, colorful illustrations, graphics, phonetic transcriptions and dramatic scenes with English subtitles. 141 mins. 2 videocassettes and glossary.
VHS: S11595. $95.00.

Chanter pour S'Amuser
This Canadian series involves song, dance and movement to make an impression with young students. Each program introduces vocabulary through movement and songs. *L'Album de Marie-Soleil* concentrates on the parts of the body, animals and prepositions. *Une Journee avec Marie-Soleil* deals with the alphabet, numbers and adjectives. 50 mins.
L'Album de Marie-Soleil.
VHS: S19784. $35.00.
Une Journee avec Marie-Soleil.
VHS: S19785. $35.00.
Chanter pour S'Amuser, Set.
VHS: S19786. $62.00.

Contacto
A video course for teaching Spanish to beginning students. The program, a collaboration between North American and Spanish scholars, features methodologies and teaching practices informed by authoritative language and culture from Spain and the larger Hispanic culture. Important grammar concepts are reviewed and explained on screen with freeze frames and graphics. The text is indexed to each video segment through on-screen video cues. 200 mins.
No. 1: Introduction to Verbs, Articles and Greetings.
VHS: S19766. $39.95.
No. 2: Adverbs, Time and Family Relationships.
VHS: S19767. $39.95.
No. 3: Adjectives, Participles, Interrogatives.
VHS: S19768. $39.95.
No. 4: Reflexives, Indefinites, Possession, Holidays.
VHS: S19769. $39.95.
Pupil's Book.
VHS: S19771. $19.95.
Pupil's Workbook.
VHS: S19773. $11.95.
Teachers Book.
VHS: S19772. $11.95.
Contacto, Set of 4 Videos.
VHS: S19770. $140.00.

Conversations Entre les Jeunes au Sujet des Jeunes
This inventive program offers practical insights into the nature and personality of the French teenager, based on questions most prominently asked by their American contemporaries. The video is organized into various units—fashion, movies, fast food, education and cross cultural attitudes. In French. 120 mins.
VHS: S19806. $39.95.

El Alfabeto Espanol
The role of images in early language acquisition is indisputable. This video combines sound and image to introduce the Spanish alphabet. Useful for native speakers and those learning Spanish for the first time. 17 mins.
VHS: S19819. $49.95.

English Plus
This fast-paced, humorous lesson plan is designed to help students learn the use of spoken, or colloquial, English. The episodes revolve around family, information, food, directions and travel. The booklet contains vocabulary and explanations of each grammatical concept. 62 mins.
VHS: S05988. $59.95.

Ensemble: A Home Video Course for Beginners in French
Designed to provide a survival kit for France. You'll be able to make yourself understood in a variety of situations, and above all, understand what is being said to you. The aim is to equip the viewer to deal with everyday situations. A BBC production. 120 mins.
VHS: S10286. $19.95.

Ensemble: L'Amour de la Vie— An Adventure Story for French Comprehension
This adventure story has been specially designed to develop your skill in understanding simple, everyday French. It also introduces the viewer to many facets of contemporary French life. Filmed entirely on location in southern France and Burgundy, the program follows the exploits of Michel Rolland. Michel has abandoned his studies in favor of the University of Life, and during his odyssey through southern France he takes on a number of jobs and meets a host of French people from different walks of life—each experience providing valuable lessons in French—and in life. A BBC production. 146 mins.
VHS: S10287. $19.94.

Fizz and Martina
This program uses the cartoon characters of two high school classmates to relate task-oriented exercises in the solving of math problems and building Spanish language skills. Contains a teacher's guide, 30 student exercise books and reproducible masters. 60 mins.
VHS: S19774. $179.95.

Functional Readings in Spanish— Signs in a Mexican City
Reading signs in Mexico poses complications for Spanish natives, given the subtle differences in vocabulary and the number of Indian words. This program helps improve "sign-reading" capabilities in Mexico. 28 mins.
VHS: S20277. $29.95.

Grammar Music Videos
These videos teach grammatical skills through comic dialogue and lively music. Each 30-minute program isolates specific fundamentals of Spanish. *Trabajamos Commo Burros* introduces the present tense, *Por Que Me Llama?* explores interrogatives, *Ay Ay Ay* teaches the verb plus infinitive constructions, and *Somos Gente del Mundo* compares ser and estar.
Ay Ay Ay.
VHS: S19816. $49.95.
Por Que?
VHS: S19815. $49.95.
Somos Gente.
VHS: S19817. $49.95.
Trabajamos.
VHS: S19814. $49.95.
Grammar Music Videos, Set.
VHS: S19818. $176.00.

Images de France
A complete course for levels I-III of French, which emphasizes conversational French, cultural aspects of France and its people, and specific grammar topics related to the conversations. The films concentrate on a particular theme and include arrival at the airport, at home, at the cafe, etc. After the initial presentation, a commentator explains what occurred during the sequence and provides an in-depth conversation practice session. All four videos are accompanied by a detailed manual which includes bilingual scripts, tests, notes on grammar topics, and a pronunciation guide. Each program averages 77 mins.
Images de France Level 1, Part 1.
VHS: S09059. $39.95.
Images de France Level 1, Part 2.
VHS: S09061. $39.95.
Images de France Level 1 Viewer's Guide.
VHS: S09062. $5.95.
Images de France Level 2-3, Part 1.
VHS: S09063. $39.95.
Images de France Level 2-3, Part 2.
VHS: S09064. $39.95.
Images de France Level 2-3 Viewer's Guide.
VHS: S09065. $5.95.

Impact
This video allows ESL students to work at their own pace. The 20 teaching units include sections on numbers, interrogatives and present tense. The class will enjoy the upbeat style, interviews and looks at different people and places throughout the world. Workbook included. 60 mins.
VHS: S19843. $49.95.

Kit ou Double
A video notebook composed of six sections about France and French culture designed to help intermediate students. The sections are introduced by puppets. The sections contain specific language goals, created within a realistic cultural or linguistic setting. Each section contains pre-viewing and post-viewing activities and suggestions. 35 mins.
VHS: S19776. $59.95.

Language in Life
Communicating in Life is a two-phased approach to the problems of human communication, starting with a psychological approach based on recent studies in language acquisition patterns. Part Two provides an entertaining and stimulating study of the basic units of speech: nouns and adjectives, verbs and adverbs, using a Buster Keaton-type actor.
VHS: S02206. $64.95.

Language Tapes
A series of five tapes.
Basic Arabic by Video. 90 minutes.
VHS: S02980. $74.95.
Basic English for Hispanics by Video. 90 minutes.
VHS: S02310. $74.95.
Basic English Grammar by Video. 73 minutes.
VHS: S02760. $74.95.
Basic French by Video. 90 minutes.
VHS: S02761. $74.95.
Laser: LD70858. $34.95.
Basic German by Video. 90 minutes.
VHS: S02762. $74.95.
Basic Italian by Video. 90 minutes.
VHS: S02763. $74.95.

Basic Japanese by Video. 90 minutes.
VHS: S02981. $74.95.
Basic Russian by Video. 90 minutes.
VHS: S02864. $74.95.
Basic Spanish by Video. 90 minutes.
VHS: S02764. $74.95.

Las Aventuras de Mafalda
Enjoy Malfalda, Susanita, Felipe, Guille and the rest of the *pandilla* in this hilarious introduction to regional language patterns. With 12 five-minute episodes per video.
Volume 1.
VHS: S19837. $39.95.
Volume 2.
VHS: S19838. $39.95.

Le Tresor d'Histoires Classiques
A set of four tapes, these animated lessons teach history, culture and language in clear French. Intermediate and advanced students will enjoy seeing and hearing works that they have read. Each tape is 50 mins.
VHS: S24791. $73.95.

Living Language
Essential words and phrases in five scenes to everyone who travels: at the airport, at the hotel, on the street, at the restaurant, and at the department store.
Living Language: French. 60 mins.
VHS: S04356. $29.95.
Living Language: German. 90 mins.
VHS: S04358. $29.95.
Living Language: Spanish. 77 mins.
VHS: S04357. $29.95.

Lyric Language French
Students will participate in real life adventures with animated characters from *Family Circus* while building fluency in French in this two-volume set. On-screen lyric titles make singing along easy. Vol. 1 includes the zoo, the supermarket, the seasons and seven other trips. Vol. 2 has ten topics, including the family and the senses. 35 minutes each.
VHS: S24792. $32.90.

Lyric Language French Teacher's Guide
Interactive, entertaining activities reinforce the French vocabulary covered in this video. These activities encourage and motivate students to learn a second language even as they develop multicultural understanding. The Natural Approach and the TPR method engage the viewer in four skill areas.
VHS: S24793. $19.95.

Lyric Language Spanish
Students will participate in real life adventures with animated characters from *Family Circus* while building fluency in Spanish. On-screen lyric titles in Spanish make singing along easy. A two-volume set, Vol. 1 includes the zoo, the supermarket, the seasons and seven other trips. Vol. 2 has nine topics, including the family, the senses and a picnic. 35 minutes each.
VHS: S24788. $45.00.

Lyric Language Spanish Teacher's Guide
Interactive, entertaining activities reinforce the Spanish vocabulary covered in this video. These activities encourage and motivate students to learn a second language even as they develop multicultural understanding. The Natural Approach and the TPR method engage the viewer in four skill areas.
VHS: S24789. $19.95.

Modern Language Instruction
The BBC's specially designed program for quick learning of foreign languages, ideally suited for travelers. Each program contains one video, two audiotapes and two handbooks.
Get By in Italian.
VHS: S19386. $69.95.
Get By in German.
VHS: S19387. $69.95.
Get By in Spanish.
VHS: S19388. $69.95.
Get By in French.
VHS: S19389. $69.95.

Mots Difficiles
A video to teach authentic language and appropriate use of idiomatic expressions to intermediate and advanced French language students, by observing native speakers engaged in realistic, functional dialogs. Rich in scenes and expressions from everyday life. A script is provided.
VHS: S09057. $59.95.

My First Series
These two videos combine easy-to-follow instructions for creative activities with Spanish language instruction. Students will develop new vocabulary and be stimulated into conversation. *My First Activity* demonstrates crafts made from everyday materials, while *My First Cooking* shows some easy fun recipes.
VHS: S24786. $35.95.

Peli the Clown
Beginners will delight in learning Spanish with colorful characters who sing original songs, play games and perform humorous skits. Peli is a great way to introduce a class to Spanish using the Natural Approach. A set of four volumes, each includes an explanatory booklet, suggestions for use and a thematic vocabulary list.
VHS: S24787. $73.95.

Philipp und Sein Bar
This video teaches colors, animals, basic verbs and nouns in German, and is given a humorous note by the interaction of Philipp and the bear. Comprehension is enhanced by the bear's ability to perform many of the tasks which humans carry out easily. The video is divided into sub-units of 5 minutes each. 29 mins.
Philipp und Sein Bar Video.
VHS: S09052. $45.00.
Workbook.
VHS: S09067. $3.95.

Poesie de la Francophonie
For beginning and intermediate levels, this is a collection of 67 poems that represent the French-speaking portions of the world. With selections by Verlaine, Victor Hugo, Jean de La Fontaine, Maurice Careme and Alfred de Musset. 100 mins.
VHS: S19798. $49.95.

Reir, Jugar, Hablar
A new Spanish video for teaching poems, dialogs, activities, games and songs. Created by a dynamic "master" teacher in the New York City school system, who demonstrates her methods with a beginning level FLES Spanish class. An invaluable media tool for teacher training. 70 mins.
VHS: S05282. $44.95.

The Russian Language
A collaboration between top Russian linguists and the St. Petersburg's Documentary Film Studio, this program provides extensive lessons in learning, applying and use of the Russian language, conveyed through the circumstances and events of a fictional American businessman and his various encounters in Russian locations. The video includes an illustrated and colorful textbook and audio cassette of the soundtrack portion to aid the listener and viewer.
VHS: S18446. $99.95.

Say It by Signing
The classic Living Language series special video to help people of all ages communicate with the hearing impaired. 60 minutes.
VHS: S01951. $29.95.

Spanish Emergency Lesson Plans: The Video
Filmed on location in South America, these self-contained lessons provide cultural capsules complete with vocabulary and grammar exercises, joined by on-screen multiple choice exercises on travel, communications and animals. In Spanish. 30 mins.
VHS: S19821. $49.95.

Spot
These animated tales are a valuable educational tool for relating familiar objects and activities viewed by Spot that mirror the experience of his young viewers. 30 mins.
Spot's Adventure—German.
VHS: S19854. $29.95.
Spot's Adventure—Spanish.
VHS: S19825. $29.95.
Spot's First Video—French.
VHS: S19794. $29.95.
Spot's First Video—German.
VHS: S19853. $29.95.
Spot's First Video—Spanish.
VHS: S19824. $29.95.

Survival Spanish
One of the very best language-learning tapes, this ten-lesson conversational course is designed to teach how to "think" in Spanish, offering humor, enthusiasm and real-life situations for business, money, information, restaurants, family, telephone usage and travel. 60 mins.
VHS: S05989. $69.95.

Tell Me Why
This bilingual immersion class teaches the use of content-based materials to learn the subject matter in Spanish. The programs offer a kaleidoscopic range of learning through live-action video, animated slides and charts. 90 mins.
How Things Work.
VHS: S19763. $29.95.
Prehistoric Animals.
VHS: S19762. $29.95.
Tell Me Why, Set.
VHS: S19765. $79.80.

TV und Texte
A valuable language-teaching video about contemporary German society was created to allow students to become active participants. The contents of a news broadcast are broken down, with the difficult words and phrases highlighted for repetition. Written exercises supplement newspaper articles and comprehension questions reveal the amount of learning and text skills being developed. Each unit contains a series of writing and speaking assignments which provide individual and group work. 71-page text with photos, transcripts and an answer key. 50 mins.
VHS: S19790. $49.95.

BRITISH CINEMA

recent british CINEMA

84 Charing Cross Road
A charming adult drama about a 20-year correspondence between a budding New York writer and an English dealer in Antiquarian books. Anne Bancroft and Anthony Hopkins breathe life into this semi-autobiographical film translation of a popular play and novel.
VHS: S04677. $19.95.
David Jones, USA/Great Britain, 1987, 97 mins.

Absolute Beginners: The Musical
When London was starting to swing, they called the first teenagers "Absolute Beginners." David Bowie stars in this film which charts the lives of two lovers who must choose to live by their idealist principles or sell out to get to the top of the fashion world.
VHS: S07699. $14.98.
Julien Temple, Great Britain, 1976, 107 mins.

Absolution
Richard Burton is a strict Catholic school teacher who becomes the victim of a sinister practical joke. A devious mystery written band directed by Anthony Shaffer (Sleuth) that was filmed in 1979, but only recently been made available. With Dominic Guard, Dai Bradley, Andrew Keir and Willoughby Gray.
VHS: S07525. $79.95.
Anthony Shaffer, Great Britain, 1981, 95 mins.

The Advocate
This offbeat, lusty period thriller is set during the (believe it or not) Middle Ages. A brilliant young lawyer is sent to the British countryside where he becomes the center of a complicated series of events involving an accusation of murder, witchcraft, edieval politics and secret societies. Remarkably realistic, The Advocate cleverly bridges ethics with historical drama and the pursuit of justice.
VHS: S24322. $96.98.
  Laser: Widescreen. LD74913. $39.99.
Leslie Megahey, Great Britain, 1994, 102 mins.

An Affair in Mind
Amanda Donohoe and Stephen Dillon star in this gripping psychological thriller produced for the BBC, based on a story by Ruth Rendell. Graham Lanceton is a best-selling novelist who is obsessed with the thoughts of Dru, the rich girl who loves him. From total strangers, they become passionate lovers—the only thing that stands in their way is Dru's husband, Tiny.
VHS: S10437. $19.98.
Michael Baker, Great Britain, 1987, 90 mins.

Afraid of the Dark
The debut film of the talented writer Mark Peploe, a frequent collaborator of Bernardo Bertolucci and Michelangelo Antonioni. This is a dark, nervy, psychological thriller about the real and imagined difficulties of a young child; a nightmare projection of alienation and claustrophobia. With James Fox, Fanny Ardant, Paul McGann and Ben Keyworth as the boy. Cinematography by Bruno De Keyzer. "Chilling; Peploe does something shocking" (Janet Maslin, The New York Times).
VHS: S18008. $19.95.
Mark Peploe, Great Britain, 1991, 91 mins.

An African Dream
Kitty Aldridge plays an English schoolteacher who moves to South Africa in 1906 with her husband. She forms a friendship with an educated native named Katana, much to the displeasure of the local community. When rumors of romantic interest start to surface, tempers flair and actions get out of hand. With John Kani, Dominic Jephcott, John Carson, Richard Haines, Joy Stewart and Lyn Hooker. Filmed in Africa by the director of photography for the Indiana Jones movies.
VHS: S12539. $94.95.
John Smallcombe, Great Britain, 1990, 94 mins.

After Darkness
John Hurt is very concerned about his suicidal schizophrenic younger brother, Julian Sands, in this European thriller. He feels guiltier because he already feels responsible for the death of Julian's twin brother. With Victoria Abril and Pamela Salem.
VHS: S07783. $79.95.
D. Othenin-Girard/S. Buerraz, Switzerland/Great Britain, 1985, 104 mins.

After Pilkington
The calm surface of Oxford academic life is shattered for James Westgate by the sudden reappearance of his childhood sweetheart Penny in this award-winning BBC production. James' intense obsession with Penny draws him into a tangle of misunderstanding, intrigue and murder as their involvement in the mysterious disappearance of Pilkington becomes more than just a re-enactment of their childhood adventures. With Bob Peck (Edge of Darkness) and Miranda Richardson (Dance with a Stranger).
VHS: S10439. $19.98.
Christopher Morahan, Great Britain, 1987, 99 mins.

All Creatures Great and Small
James Herriot's story of a British rural veterinarian, starring Christopher Timothy in a BBC production.
VHS: S01921. $19.98.
Claude Whatham, Great Britain, 1986, 94 mins.

American Friends
An observant social comedy of manners and repression and the collision of sexual awakening and 19th century morality. Set in 1864, a single, middle-aged, Oxford University tutor (Michael Palin), who's studiously avoided romantic relations, encounters two vibrant American women, Caroline Hartley (Connie Booth) and her 17-year-old niece (Trini Alvarado), during his Swiss holiday. He's forced to choose between his long-dormant emotional demands and his academic requirements. With Alfred Molina and David Calder.
VHS: S18996. $92.95.
  Laser: LD75144. $34.98.
Tristam Powell, Great Britain, 1991, 95 mins.

Antonia and Jane
Imelda Staunton and Saskia Reeves star as two grown women who unknowingly envy the lives of each other, in this charming English comedy. With Billy Nighy, Brenda Bruce and Richard Hope.
VHS: S16857. $89.95.
  Laser: LD75147. $34.98.
Beeban Kidron, Great Britain, 1990, 75 mins.

Arch of Triumph
A television remake of Lewis Milestone's adaptation of Erich Maria Remarque's novel. Anthony Hopkins returns to World War II era Paris to exact his revenge on a man who tormented him and the woman he loved. With Leslie-Anne Down and Donald Pleasance.
VHS: S17166. $19.95.
Waris Hussein, Great Britain, 1985, 95 mins.

An Awfully Big Adventure
Hugh Grant, Alan Rickman and Georgina Cates star in this inventive coming-of-age story about a teenage girl obsessed with the theater. This obsession leads her into the very grown-up world of a Liverpool theater company. Secrets, manipulation, menace and sex dominate. Set just after the Second World War, this film is based on Beryl Bainbridge's popular novel by the same title.
VHS: S26710. $19.95.
  Laser: LD75323. $39.98.
Mike Newell, Great Britain, 1995, 113 mins.

BackBeat
Sheryl Lee and Stephen Dorff star in this energetic and exciting drama about a band with a new sound. They are just about to hit it big. In a heady mix of music, youth and love, conflict is inevitable. That's why a band that started out with five members produced only four well-known stars.
VHS: S22079. $94.95.
  Laser: LD74595. $34.95.
Iain Softley, Great Britain, 1993, 100 mins.

Bad Behavior
Les Blair's spirited comedy about a couple whose marriage is fraying around the edges as they prepare to remodel their home. Ellie McAllister (Sinead Cusack) is turning away from her domestic responsibilities and dreams about independence while her husband Gerry (Stephen Rea) is a Walter Mitty-like dreamer who imagines himself as a superhero.
VHS: S20187. $94.95.
  Laser: LD75153. $34.98.
Les Blair, Great Britain, 1993, 103 mins.

Bartleby
Paul Scofield delivers a strong performance as the boss who has empathy with Bartleby, the alienated individual of Herman Melville's novel who is slowly giving up on life. With John McEnery.
VHS: S01550. $29.95.
Anthony Friedman, Great Britain, 1970, 79 mins.

Battle of Britain
Not the documentary, but the all-star recreation of the most decisive battle in history. Michael Caine, Robert Shaw, Christopher Plummer, Sir Laurence Olivier, and Sir Ralph Richardson star in this epic drama complete with amazingly filmed fighting sequences featuring authentic Spitfires, Hurricanes and Heinkels.
VHS: S04769. $19.98.
Guy Hamilton, Great Britain, 1969, 132 mins.

Bawdy Adventures of Tom Jones
Based on one of the classic staples of English literature, the story of Tom Jones, the 18th century playboy, who makes his way through some of England's most prominent bedrooms in his quest for the woman of his dreams.
VHS: S03024. $59.95.
Cliff Owen, Great Britain, 1976, 89 mins.

Beautiful Dreamers
In this warm film, a young doctor befriends Walt Whitman and encounters hostile reaction from the citizens of his small community when he incorporates the poet's philosophy of sexual liberation and individual freedom to treat the mentally ill. With Rip Torn (as Whitman), Colm Feore, Wendel Meldrum, Sheila McCarthy and Colin Fox.
VHS: S17443. $14.95.
  Laser: LD71764. $39.95.
John Kent Harrison, Great Britain, 1991, 108 mins.

Before the Rain
Three intertwined stories are joined in this haunting feature about individuals facing hard choices. Set in the former Yugoslavia and London, it combines ethical and moral quandaries with compelling situations and jarringly striking settings. Academy Award nominee for Best Foreign Language Picture. English and Macedonian with English subtitles.
VHS: S25952. $94.99.
Milcho Manchevski, GB/Macedonia/Fr., 1994, 115 mins.

Bellman and True
A British thriller that is both a detailed character study and a caper film. A meek computer programmer becomes involved in an elaborate bank heist. He soon finds that his associates in crime are no league of gentlemen. With Bernard Hill, Kieren O'Brien, Frances Tomelty, Richard Hope and Ken Bones.
VHS: S08028. $14.98.
Richard Loncraine, Great Britain, 1988, 112 mins.

Bhaji on the Beach
In this warm but hip comedy, a group of women gather for a carefree day on the beach. By nightfall, gossiping, giggling, and arguing over things like battered wives, male strippers, race and sex have brought them closer together. With Peter Cellier, Zohra Segal and Jimmi Harkishin.
VHS: S26920. $96.99.
Gurinder Chadha, Great Britain, 1994, 100 mins.

Billy Liar
From an unsympathetic, working-class family and an insecure dead-end job, Billy Fisher dreams of escape. Free-wheeling Liz (Julie Christie) comes into his life and gives the harassed hero (Tom Courtenay) one possibility to escape.
VHS: S04453. $19.98.
John Schlesinger, Great Britain, 1963, 94 mins.

Black Windmill
Michael Caine stars in this Donald Siegel thriller about a British agent whose son is kidnapped. Caine ruffles the feathers of friend and foe to accomplish the safe return of his flesh and blood. With Janet Suzman, John Vernon, Donald Pleasance, and Delphine Seyrig.
VHS: S07794. $59.95.
Don Siegel, Great Britain, 1974, 106 mins.

Blunt: The Fourth Man
Anthony Hopkins stars as a spy in this taut thriller based on the actual Guy Burgess-Anthony Blunt spy ring. It involved trusted government workers who relied on England's old boy network to rise to the top. Despite their aristocratic upbringing this spy ring sold British secrets to the Soviet Union, undetected for years. Suddenly their secret is out and they must escape.
VHS: S27660. $14.95.
John Glenister, Great Britain, 1992, 86 mins.

Born of Fire
Peter Firth (Equus) is a flautist with a problem. During a London recital he begins to improvise strange melodies. Suzan Crowley is an astronomer who says the music is linked to an upcoming volcanic eruption in Turkey. A tale of the supernatural. With Stefan Kalipha.
VHS: S05222. $79.95.
Jamil Dehlavi, Great Britain/Turkey, 1987, 83 mins.

Breaking Glass
A British drama about a talented young singer and her shot at a show business career. Hazel O'Connor is the rising rock star and Phil Daniels is her youthful manager. With Jon Finch and Jonathan Pryce as a junkie saxophone player. A gritty, tune-filled exploration of the underbelly of success.
VHS: S06121. $49.95.
Brian Gibson, Great Britain, 1980, 93 mins.

Bridge Too Far
A stunning story of one of history's most controversial and disastrous World War II battles, the Allied defeat at Arnhem in 1944. Starring Robert Redford, Michael Caine, Laurence Olivier and Sean Connery. Based on the book by Cornelius Ryan.
VHS: S12426. $29.98.
Richard Attenborough, Great Britain, 1977, 175 mins.

Brimstone and Treacle
A comic drama with rather bizarre underpinnings features Sting (of the group Police) as a handsome young drifter who gradually takes over the lives of a middle class couple and their paralyzed daughter. Music by Police, Go-Go's and Squeeze.
VHS: S01693. $19.98.
Richard Loncraine, Great Britain, 1983, 85 mins.

Britannia Hospital
A day of celebration turns into an apocalyptic nightmare in Lindsay Anderson's biting social satire. The staff of Britannia Hospital is preparing for its 500th anniversary, the visit of the Queen of England. But all is not well, as the gates are mobbed by protesters, the wards overflow with casualties of terrorist bombings, and the unions threaten to strike. With Malcolm McDowell.
VHS: S00183. $19.98.
Lindsay Anderson, Great Britain, 1983, 116 mins.

The Browning Version
Albert Finney plays the disliked British don who suffers humiliation as his wife (Greta Scacchi) carries on an affair with Matthew Modine in this first-rate remake based on the Terrence Rattigan play. Finney delivers a nuanced performance as the teacher who has paid for the sublimation of his feelings by becoming a petty tyrant who is unloved by his wife and finds a fleeting human connection with a young student.
VHS: S23936. $19.95.
  Laser: Widescreen. LD75167. $34.98.
Mike Figgis, Great Britain, 1994, 97 mins.

Burning Secret
Faye Dunaway and Klaus Maria Brandauer star in this exquisitely photographed period drama set in an Austrian sanatorium a few years after World War I. She plays the wife of a diplomat with an ailing young son and Klaus is a dashing war veteran and aristocrat who learns a valuable lesson. With David Eberts as the sensitive youngster.
VHS: S09306. $89.98.
A. Birkin, Great Britain/W. Germany, 1988, 107 mins.

The Bushbaby
When a young woman's plans to smuggle her six-inch pet lemur, "Bushbaby", into the West are mislaid, she enlists the help of her friend Tembo (Louis Gossett Jr.) to guide her and the animal out of the African bush.
VHS: S19034. $19.98.
John Trent, Great Britain, 1970, 100 mins.

Business as Usual
When a store manager is fired from her job for reporting a case of sexual harassment in the work place, the national media rallies to her cause. A contemporary drama starring Glenda Jackson, John Thaw (Inspector Morse on PBS' Mystery series) and Cathy Tyson from Mona Lisa.
VHS: S09142. $89.95.
Lezli-Ann Barrett, Great Britain, 1988, 89 mins.

Buster
Phil Collins plays Buster, a small-time thief with a heart of gold. But his dream of the good life becomes a reality when he pulls off the greatest train robbery in history—$7 million in used bank notes. Off to Acapulco, even paradise has problems, though. And when the money disappears, wife June misses the old way of life and realizes all the money in the world can't take the place of the woman Buster loves. "Two Thumbs Up!" (E&S).
VHS: S09288. $89.99.
David Green, Great Britain, 1988, 102 mins.

Carrington
Emma Thompson gives a terrific performance as Dora Carrington, an unorthodox, androgynous painter from the early 20th century Bloomsbury Group, who passionately loves queer writer Giles Lytton-Strachey (Jonathan Pryce). The highly regarded playwright Christopher Hampton (Les Liaisons Dangereuses) directs this tight, witty and insightful period piece, set amidst the self-conscious world of broken conventions and sexual eccentricities that come to mind whenever the name of the Bloomsbury Group is uttered.
VHS: S27596. $96.99.
  Laser: LD75532. $34.99.
Christopher Hampton, Great Britain, 1995, 116 mins.

Catch Me a Spy
Kirk Douglas stars as Andrej, a Roumanian waiter and secret agent. He hides some microfilm in the luggage of a honeymooning couple in Bucharest and must go to London to retrieve the information, not knowing that he is about to become the bait in a Soviet-British spy exchange. With Marlene Jobert, Trevor Howard and Tom Courtenay.
VHS: S06127. $59.95.
Dick Clement, Great Britain, 1971, 94 mins.

Chariots of Fire
Drama based on a true story of two young men who run in the 1924 Olympics—a Jewish student from Cambridge and a Scottish missionary. Winner of Oscar for Best Picture, as well as Best Musical Score by Vangelis.
VHS: S00228. $19.98.
  Laser: LD70542. $34.98.
Hugh Hudson, Great Britain, 1981, 123 mins.

The Charmer
Nigel Havers is a 1930's con man called Ralph Gorse. Handsome, suave and sophisticated, this charmer is determined to take every opportunity to climb the social ladder. He may very well use every woman in his path. This path however, leads inexorably to graver crimes, including murder.
VHS: S21690. $129.98.
Alan Gibson, Great Britain, 1994, 50 mins.

Children
Ben Kingsley stars as a middle-aged man whose plans to marry recent widow Kim Novak are disturbed by the arrival of seven problematic children that belong to an old college friend. Adding to the drama is the fact that he finds himself growing attached to the eldest teenage daughter. With Geraldine Chaplin, Joe Don Baker and Karen Black. Based on the story by Edith Wharton.
VHS: S16809. $89.95.
Tony Palmer, Great Britain/W. Germany, 1990, 90 mins.

The Clash of the Titans
Portraying the Greek myth, Laurence Olivier is Zeus who sends his mortal son Perseus to face awesome supernatural challenges in pursuit of his destiny. With fantastic effects by Ray Harryhausen which include the taming of Pegasus.
VHS: S16851. $19.98.
  Laser: LD72170. $39.98.
Desmond Davis, Great Britain, 1981, 118 mins.

Comfort and Joy
Bill Forsyth's hilarious, off-beat look at human nature. Bill Paterson plays Alan Bird, a Glasgow radio personality who gets embroiled in a cold war between two feuding Italian ice cream families. Original soundtrack by Mark Knopfler of Dire Straits.
VHS: S00260. $69.95.
Bill Forsyth, Scotland, 1984, 93 mins.

Coming Through
In this biography of D.H. Lawrence the sexual themes of the author are placed in situations taken from his own life. Kenneth Branagh stars as Lawrence with Helen Mirren as Kate, a graduate student that he would seduce. Finally overcome by true love, Lawrence commits himself to choices that lead to scandal and ultimately exile.
VHS: S20808. $29.98.
Peter Barber-Fleming, Great Britain, 1993, 80 mins.

Dark Obsession
Gabriel Byrne stars as a man tormented by jealousy and guilt, who attempts to escape into a world of obsessive, erotic fantasies. His stunning wife, played by Amanda Donohoe, is slowly pulled under by her husband's dark sex games and deepening madness in this story of obsession and retribution. "Steamy, stylish and chilling" (LA Times). "Plenty of sex and intrigue" (Daily Variety).
VHS: S15181. $89.95.
Nick Broomfield, Great Britain, 1991

The Dawning
Anthony Hopkins plays a reluctant 1920s IRA hitman on the loose in the war-ravaged Irish countryside. When he meets a beautiful, confident young woman (Rebecca Pidgeon), he requests her help in a dangerous mission. With Jean Simmons, Trevor Howard and Hugh Grant.
VHS: S18493. $89.98.
Robert Knights, Great Britain, 1988, 97 mins.

Day in the Death of Joe Egg
Director Peter Medak (The Ruling Class) offers a well-done black comedy on the subject of mercy killing. Alan Bates and Janet Suzman are an English couple faced with what to do with their spastic daughter, Jo (Elizabeth Robillard). With Peter Bowles and Sheila Gish. Provocative comedy from playwright Peter Nichols.
VHS: S07583. $69.95.
Peter Medak, Great Britain, 1972, 106 mins.

Day of the Jackal
A superior thriller concerning a plot to assassinate General Charles de Gaulle in Paris. Based on the best selling novel by Frederick Forsyth. Edward Fox is the meticulous hitman assigned to do the job. The top notch cast includes Michel Lonsdale, Delphine Seyrig, Alan Badel, Cyril Cusack and Derek Jacobi. A blueprint for murder.
VHS: S07808. $59.95.
Fred Zinnemann, Great Britain/France, 1973, 143 min.

Deadly Advice
Jane Horrocks stars as Jodie, a teenager who is being driven to an early grave by her pesky mother. Help comes in the form of a book on legendary killers. Soon fiends like Jack the Ripper appear with deadly advice. Jonathan Pryce is also featured as the small town doctor who begins to suspect that something is amiss in this deadly comedy.
VHS: S27754. $99.99.
Laser: LD75578. $39.99.
Mandie Fletcher, Great Britain, 1993, 91 mins.

A Deadly Game
Before the fall of the Berlin Wall, a deadly chess game of espionage raged between the East and West—and no bigger pawn existed than Charlie Muffin (David Hemmings). Returning from East Berlin after a perilous mission, he narrowly avoids a death trap set by his own colleagues. Who will be the pawn when the final move is made?
VHS: S14629. $59.99.
Jack Gold, Great Britain, 1979, 104 mins.

Death on the Nile
Peter Ustinov and Mia Farrow star in this adaptation of Agatha Christie's famous mystery, with Hercule Poirot playing detective games with a dozen or so suspects.
VHS: S04542. $19.98.
John Guillermin, Great Britain, 1978, 135 mins.

Deceivers
Pierce Brosnan (Remington Steele) plays a British officer in the East India Company who uncovers a religious cult of murdering bandits. To secure the facts of the case he disguises himself as a native and joins the band of thugs, without telling anyone but his trusting wife. Well, hello Kali. With Helena Mitchell, Keith Michell and Saeed Jaffrey as Hussein. Filmed on location by Merchant-Ivory productions.
VHS: S08355. $19.98.
Nicholas Meyer, Great Britain, 1988, 100 mins.

The Defense of the Realm
Gabriel Byrne, Greta Scacchi, Denholm Elliott star in David Drury's electrifying thriller. Ex-defense MP in England is caught in a KGB sex scandal, accused of selling national secrets through his mistress. Denholm Elliott, a newspaperman, is the only one who believes he's been framed, but a mysterious heart attack keeps him from revealing what he's learned.
Laser: LD72325. $29.99.
David Drury, Great Britain, 1986, 96 mins.

Distant Voices Still Lives
Director Terence Davies reconstructs the lives of a working class family in Liverpool in postwar England through the use of popular songs. Over 40 hits from the Forties and Fifties illustrate the private history of this family of five. A truly impressive motion picture, impeccably shot and staged, that offers a touch of grandeur to everyday lives. With Freda Dowie, Peter Postlethwait, Angela Walsh, Dean Williams and Lorraine Ashbouren.
VHS: S11529. $89.95.
Terence Davies, Great Britain, 1988, 87 mins.

Doctor and the Devils
Based on an original screenplay by Dylan Thomas, this dramatic thriller concerns two of the most famous villains in the history of English crime. Broom and Fallon begin working for Dr. Thomas Rock providing bodies for his anatomical research.
VHS: S00352. $79.98.
Freddie Francis, Great Britain, 1985, 93 mins.

Doctor Faustus
Richard Burton stars in this retelling of Christopher Marlowe's cautionary tale of an aging scholar who makes a bargain with the Devil. Inquiring minds want to know if Helen of Troy really looked so much like Elizabeth Taylor. Performed by members of the Oxford University Dramatic Society.
VHS: S03943. $19.95.
R. Burton/N. Coghill, Great Britain, 1968, 93 mins.

The Dogs of War
Christopher Walken is a sentimental mercenary in this film of Frederick Forsyth's novel about a plot by a business conglomerate to overthrow an African government for their own profit. With Tom Berenger, Colin Blakely, Paul Freeman and Jobeth Williams. Lots of action and acting.
VHS: S06994. $14.95.
John Irvin, Great Britain, 1980, 102 mins.

Don't Hang Up
Roseanna Arquette and David Suchet play a couple separated by 5000 miles in this comedy featuring the telephone. She's an intense and passionate actress, while he's a tormented but very British playwright. Together they're the phone company's dream couple, in touch only over the wires.
VHS: S20953. $29.95.
Barry Davis, Great Britain, 1990, 84 mins.

Dressmaker
Brilliant performances from two of Britain's greatest actresses, Joan Plowright and Billie Whitelaw, as two sisters locked in a love-hate relationship, highlight this critically-acclaimed film by Jim O'Brien. The sisters' simmering bitterness explodes into the open when their shy 17-year-old niece, whom they have raised since childhood, falls in love with an American G.I.
VHS: S11171. $79.95.
Laser: CLV. LD71589. $39.95.
Jim O'Brien, Great Britain, 1989, 92 mins.

Duellists
Keith Carradine and Harvey Keitel are two officers in Napoleon's army who violently confront each other in a series of savage duels in Ridley Scott's film about passion and honor, based on a story by Joseph Conrad.
VHS: S00379. $19.95.
Ridley Scott, Great Britain, 1977, 110 mins.

Eat the Rich
In direct opposition to the advice of Jonathan Swift, an anarchistic black comedy of questionable taste from the Comic Strip Troupe of Great Britain. All the fun starts to trouble when a motley group of the less-privileged get hungry for the good life. With cameos from Paul McCartney and Koo Stark, music by Motorhead. Cast includes Jimmy Fagg, Lanah Pellay and Nosher Powell.
VHS: S08037. $19.98.
Peter Richardson, Great Britain, 1987, 100 mins.

Edge of Darkness
A powerful mystery set in England focusing on a secret government project which leads to nuclear contamination. With Joe Don Baker, Bob Peck.
VHS: S04954. $29.98.
Martin Campbell, Great Britain, 1986, 157 mins.

Empire State
Docked in a seedy part of London's waterfront, the Empire State harbors a variety of nightclubbers from every walk of life. Ray McAnally ("Cal") is the proprietor of the mysterious realm who is mired in a dirty financial war with a relentless land speculator, Martin Landau.
VHS: S07760. $79.95.
Ron Peck, Great Britain, 1987, 102 mins.

Enchanted April
Mike Newell's wonderfully textured adaptation of Elizabeth von Arnim's 1922 novel about four radically different English women who pool their resources to share the expenses of a breathtaking Italian villa for one month. With Miranda Richardson, Josie Lawrence, Polly Walker and Joan Plowright.
VHS: S18369. $19.95.
Laser: LD75189. $34.98.
Mike Newell, Great Britain, 1991, 93 mins.

The Englishman Who Went up a Hill But Came down a Mountain
Hugh Grant stars as an upstanding surveyor on a mission in this warm comedy. He is sent to an Irish locale to survey the landscape and he makes a startling discovery. Though a certain promontory is a major landmark, it is not, as locally believed, a mountain. It may not be much, but to the local Irish population it is a mountain and they set about making sure it remains classified as such.
VHS: S26709. $99.99.
Laser: LD75321. $39.98.
Christopher Monger, Great Britain, 1995, 96 mins.

Fall from Grace
James Fox, Michael York, Patsy Kensit and Gary Cole star in this chilling tale of espionage and deception. In 1943 Hitler's forces dominate and terrorize Europe. A crack team of British and American intelligence officers undertake a huge gamble. They must convince Hitler of the impossible. Their success could hasten the end of the war. Failure is unthinkable.
VHS: S26521. $69.99.
Waris Hussein, Great Britain, 1994, 240 mins.

Farewell My Lovely
Dick Richards's British version of Raymond Chandler's novel about a private eye's (Robert Mitchum) search for a gangster's girlfriend. With Charlotte Rampling, John Ireland and Sylvia Miles.
VHS: S02144. $19.95.
Dick Richards, Great Britain, 1975, 95 mins.

Fatal Confinement
Joan Crawford stars in this mysterious portrayal of a mother and her daughter, living in seclusion for 15 years. A large corporation pressures her into selling her land for a factory. A tense and volatile drama, reminiscent of Crawford's real-life role as "Mommie Dearest." Paul Berg, Charles Bickford also star.
VHS: S07459. $19.95.
Robert Guest, Great Britain, 1964, 70 mins.

The Favor, the Watch and the Very Big Fish
A small-time photographer (Bob Hoskins) stages an elaborate icon portrait, and the ex-con pianist (Jeff Goldblum) he hires as Christ starts to believe in his own divinity in this whacky comedy. With Natasha Richardson, Michel Blanc and Jean-Pierre Cassel.
VHS: S17342. $92.95.
Laser: LD75194. $34.98.
Ben Lewin, Great Britain/France, 1991, 92 mins.

Feast of July
Embeth Davidtz stars in this engrossing drama set in the 19th-century English countryside. Bella (Davidtz) sets off to find the married man who fathered her stillborn child and ends up in the Wainwright household. Ultimately, she finds more than she bargained for, including a belief in her own resolve which allows her to forge a new life. An exquisitely detailed portrait of a woman's struggle to define and own her life. A Merchant/Ivory production.
VHS: S27523. $99.99.
Laser: LD75548. $39.99.
Christopher Menaul, Great Britain, 1995, 116 mins.

Fish Called Wanda
John Cleese wrote and stars in this hilarious crime caper film set in England. He plays a barrister called Archibald Leach who is seduced by a scheming American seductress (Jamie Lee Curtis) for the whereabouts of the missing loot. Kevin Kline and Michael Palin are also interested. And yes there is a fish named Wanda as well as a woman named Wanda. Not recommended for the owners of small noisy dogs.
VHS: Out of print. For rental only.
Laser: LD74666. $34.98.
Charles Crichton, Great Britain, 1988, 108 mins.

Forbidden Passion—Oscar Wilde— The Movie
Michael Gambon stars as Oscar Wilde—poet, novelist, playwright, scholar, wit—a man of enormous charm and talent, both celebrated and reviled, but living in an illicit triangle of love, passion and deception.
VHS: S05895. $79.95.
Henry Herbert, Great Britain, 1976, 120 mins.

A Foreign Field
Lauren Bacall, Geraldine Chaplin, Jean Moreau and Alec Guiness are all featured in this comedy of undying memory. They reunite at Normandy where they first encountered one another during D-Day. Now 50 years later, old rivalries and even romance are alive once again.
VHS: S21039. $89.98.
Charles Sturridge, Great Britain, 1993, 90 mins.

Four Weddings and a Funeral
Hugh Grant and Andie MacDowell star in this brightly entertaining romantic comedy. The family gatherings of the title offer more than ample opportunity for this unlikely pair, a handsome Brit and a lovely Yank who is already engaged, to slowly get acquainted. After so many weddings what else could they do?
VHS: S21506. $19.95.
Laser: LD74527. $39.95.
Mike Newell, Great Britain, 1994, 117 mins.

Fourth Protocol
An adaptation of the Frederick Forsyth spy novel featuring Michael Caine as a British agent out to foil a Russian plot. The Russians plan to drop a nuclear bomb near an American base in England, thereby destroying their friendly relations.
VHS: S07015. $14.95.
John MacKenzie, Great Britain, 1987, 119 mins.

The Franchise Affair
The Franchise—a secluded mansion inhabited by two secretive women. As moonlight strikes the mansion's attic window, a half-naked young girl flees frantically through the woods. What is the secret of The Franchise? The clue is in the attic....
England, 149 mins.
VHS: S14329. $26.98.

French Lesson
A first feature from Brian Gilbert about an English teen visiting Paris and growing from a vulnerable innocent to a charming, witty, young woman. English and French with English subtitles.
VHS: S00467. $19.98.
Brian Gilbert, Great Britain, 1984, 90 mins.

French Lieutenant's Woman
Harold Pinter wrote the screenplay adapted from John Fowles' novel. A hauntingly beautiful film starring Meryl Streep and Jeremy Irons, about a woman ostracized by Victorian society and abandoned by her lover.
VHS: S00468. $19.95.
Laser: LD70140. $39.98.
Karel Reisz, Great Britain, 1981, 124 mins.

Gandhi
Richard Attenborough's dream project realized in epic style with Ben Kingsley as Gandhi in an Oscar winning performance, and a cast including Candice Bergen, Martin Sheen and John Gielgud.
VHS: S02022. $29.95.
Laser: LD72202. $69.95.
Richard Attenborough, Great Britain, 1982, 187 mins.

The Gathering Storm
Richard Burton stars as Winston Churchill in this historical drama that is set in the pre-war years of 1936-40. Virginia McKenna plays Churchill's wife Clemmie. Based on the writings of this great leader of the 20th century, Burton deals with the abdication of Edward VIII and Neville Chamberlain's appeasement of Hitler's Germany. 1974, 72 mins.
VHS: S06141. $14.95.

Getting Sam Home
A feature film starring Campo, Clegg and Foggy, three lovable elderly rascals from the award-winning British television series, as they answer a last request from Sam to sneak him out of his sick bed. 89 mins.
VHS: S10636. $34.95.

Glass Mountain
Many singers from La Scala appear in the opera sequence of this inspiring film about a British composer who writes an opera about the Italian Alps. With Valentina Cortese and Sebastian Shaw.
VHS: S26381. $29.95.
Henry Cass, Great Britain, 1950, 94 mins.

Gospel According to Vic
Tom Conti and Helen Mirren star in this irreverent Scottish comedy about a very reluctant "miracle man", which was influenced by the films of Bill (Local Hero) Forsyth. "A heaven-sent comedy from Scotland with a delicious performance by Tom Conti," wrote Bob Thomas in Associated Press.
VHS: S03295. $79.95.
Charles Gormley, Great Britain, 1986, 91 mins.

The Great Train Robbery
Sean Connery heads a team of criminals that includes Lesley-Anne Down and Donald Sutherland. They scheme to snatch a fortune in gold from a moving train in 1840's England. Michael Crichton's novel is based on fact. A delightful tongue-in-cheek caper film. Excellent period detail.
VHS: S06993. $19.98.
Michael Crichton, Great Britain, 1979, 111 mins.

The Green Man
This BBC production stars Albert Finney as the alcoholic owner of a countryside inn whose sinister, ghostly tales he conjures up to seduce his female guests turn on him when spirits and apparitions begin to haunt his every move. "Finney pounces with unflagging energy" (The New York Times). With Sarah Berger, Linda Marlowe and Michael Hordern.
VHS: S16860. $24.95.
Laser: CLV. LD72076. $49.95.
Elijah Moshinsky, Great Britain, 1991, 150 mins.

Gregory's Girl
A very funny film from the director of Local Hero and Comfort and Joy, centered on the lives of Glasgow teenagers, specifically Gregory and his girlfriend, Dorothy, who is the new teammate on the soccer team. Quirky, charming, and often very funny, the film is notable for Forsyth's great dialog and ensemble acting.
VHS: S00530. $19.95.
Bill Forsyth, Scotland, 1982, 91 mins.

Gulliver in Lilliput
Based on Jonathan Swift's famous satire, this clever BBC production recounts the adventures of Lemuel Gulliver in the land of the Lilliputians. With Andrew Burt, Elisabeth Sladen, Linda Polan.
VHS: S07179. $19.95.
Barry Letts, Great Britain, 1986, 107 mins.

A Handful of Dust
Evelyn Waugh's satiric novel on the decline of the British empire has been filmed in a very civilized manner. When the decent but very dull James Wilby finds out that his beautiful but cool wife (Kristin Scott Thomas) is having a serious affair with the dashing but penniless Rupert Graves, he goes exploring in South America. With Anjelica Huston and Alec Guinness.
VHS: S08351. $19.95.
Charles Sturridge, Great Britain, 1988, 117 mins.

Handmaid's Tale
Natasha Richardson, Robert Duvall, Faye Dunaway and Elizabeth McGovern star in Volker Schlondorff's stylish adaptation of Margaret Atwood's novel of the not-so-distant future. A fertile woman is forced by her country's government to serve as a Handmaid to the "Commander" and his wife, who has been made sterile by ecological disasters.
VHS: S12766. $19.98.
Volker Schlondorff, Great Britain/USA, 1990, 109 mins.

Hear My Song
A delightful romantic comic adventure based on the exploits of famed Irish tenor Josef Locke. Ned Beatty plays the cautious Irish tax exile being sought by a conniving but well meaning talent booker for a nightclub on the west coast of England. Adrian Dunbar, who co-wrote the script, plays the unemployed club manager, who must redeem himself in the eyes of the woman he loves as well as the community that trusted his judgement.
VHS: S16634. $19.95.
Laser: LD75205. $34.98.
Peter Chelsom, Great Britain, 1991, 104 mins.

Help!
Richard Lester's follow-up to A Hard Day's Night doesn't try to assess the power and impact of the Beatles on popular culture, but creates as many chances and thin narrative lines for the brilliant group to reveal their power. Digitally encoded on Hi-fi, heightening the sharpness of the Beatles' work: "Help," "You're Gonna Lose That Girl," "You've Got to Hide Your Love Away" and "Ticket to Ride." Special Edition contains eight minutes of rare bonus footage.
VHS: S02013. $19.98.
Laser: CAV. LD70376. $79.95.
Laser: CLV. LD70377. $39.95.
Richard Lester, Great Britain, 1965, 98 mins.

Hi-Di-Hi
A holiday camp in the late 50s is the setting for romance, adventure and, most of all, hysterical hijinks. Featuring a lively assortment of original characters, Hi-Di-Hi has been called Britain's answer to Dirty Dancing! From the BBC.
VHS: S11214. $39.98.

Hidden City

Charles Dance is cast as a statistician roped into a mystery by a driven film archivist who discovers a baffling abduction tacked on to the end of a government agricultural film. With Cassie Stuart, Bill Paterson and Tusse Silberg. A stylish thriller set in the film cabinets of the government archives beneath the city streets.
VHS: S08026. $79.95.
Stephen Poliakoff, Great Britain, 1987, 108 mins.

High Spirits

Peter O'Toole stars as an Irish nobleman who schemes to turn his ancestral castle into a popular tourist spot by claiming that it is haunted. Imagine his surprise when he and his guests discover that the castle really is haunted, by quarreling ghosts.
VHS: S08890. $89.95.
Neil Jordan, Great Britain, 1988, 96 mins.

Hitler: The Last Ten Days

Alec Guinness interprets the role of the Fuehrer whose Reich didn't quite last a thousand years. With Berlin in ruins, he gathers his top leaders around him in the bunker and rants a lot. Some days, world domination is not all it is cracked up to be. With Simon Ward, Aldofo Celli, Diane Cilento and Eric Porter.
VHS: S10825. $49.95.
Ennio de Concine, Great Britain/Italy, 1973, 108 mins.

Hope and Glory

John Boorman's critically-acclaimed memory of childhood—moving, funny, bittersweet. The main character, Bill, is a seven-year-old boy, Sarah Miles his ever-tolerant mother who does her best while dad's away at war. While the street is full of rubble, the Luftwaffe is parachuting into the back yard, this is a story of innocence in the face of war—a remarkable portrait of a childhood. On many Ten Best lists, winner of the Golden Globe Award for Best Picture.
VHS: S06364. $14.95.
Laser: LD72302. $29.99.
John Boorman, Great Britain, 1987, 94 mins.

How Many Miles to Babylon

A powerful drama about friendship and loyalty set against the havoc of World War I. Daniel Day-Lewis comes from a wealthy Irish family whose friendship with Christopher Fairbank, a kindred spirit from a lower economic class, ends both of them up in the Army during World War I. Despite their differences in rank, they remain close friends, both become disillusioned with the war, and in an odd twist of irony, one is court-martialed for desertion, the other put in charge of the firing squad. Produced by the BBC.
VHS: S03525. $19.98.
Moira Armstrong, Great Britain, 1986, 106 mins.

Jane Austen's Persuasion

Jane Austen's last novel is superbly realized in this well-acted costume drama. After the end of the Napoleonic Wars, Captain Frederick Wentworth and his former fiance slowly but surely find themselves drawn to each other once again. Set amidst the luxurious trappings of the English upper class, this tale of true love is simply irresistible.
VHS: S27350. $96.99.
Laser: LD75498. $34.95.
Roger Michell, Great Britain, 1995, 104 mins.

Joseph Andrews

Director Tony Richardson (Hotel New Hampshire) adapts another of Henry Fielding's (Tom Jones) attacks on Victorian morals and their inherent hypocrisy. Peter Firth stars as a lowly functionary to Lady Booby (Ann-Margret), whose advances and seductions are rejected in favor of a simple peasant girl. Fielding's novel is purportedly based on Samuel Richardson's Pamela.
VHS: S02538. $49.95.
Tony Richardson, Great Britain, 1977, 99 mins.

Just Like a Woman

Julia Walters and Adrian Pasdar star in this unlikely, comic romance between a suburban housewife and an investment banker who likes to dress in women's clothing. It may be hard to swallow but this charming farce is actually based on a true story. Pasdar does his best to pass as a woman and a charming male lead.
VHS: S25901. $14.98.
Christopher Monger, Great Britain, 1995, 102 mins.

Kitchen Toto

A moving drama about racial tensions and growing up in Kenya in the 1950's. The title refers to a term for a houseboy. A 12-year-old black child is placed with a white family to help around the house. He befriends the 11-year-old son of the white policeman as the Mau Mau's are preparing a violent uprising. With Edwin Mahinda, Bob Peck, Phyllis Logan and Robert Urquhart. A first film written and directed by Kenyan resident Harry Hook.
VHS: S09800. $19.98.
Harry Hook, Kenya/Gr. Britain, 1987, 95 mins.

The Krays

The fascinating, true story of Ronnie and Reggie Kray, England's most famous gangsters, The Krays chronicles the surprising success of the twin "brothers grim" who shared a terrifying taste for blood. Their rise to power and eventual fall from grace is both compelling and horrifying; a chilling portrait of brutal beauty. Starring Gary and Martin Kemp—founding members of the rock group Spandau Ballet.
VHS: S13828. $19.95.
Laser: Chapter stops, digital master; 3 sides. LD75052. $39.95.
Peter Medak, Great Britain, 1990, 119 mins.

Lady Jane

An historical recreation of the nine-day rule of a very minor and very young English monarch. Helena Bonham Carter is impressive in the title role. Cary Elwes is her carefully selected consort. Their romance holds little historical accuracy but it breaks up the parts where one has to wait to hear how the battles came out. With John Wood, Michael Hordern, and many other members of the Royal Shakespeare Company.
VHS: S10829. $79.95.
Laser: LD75301. $39.98.
Trevor Nunn, Great Britain, 1985, 140 mins.

The Lady's Not for Burning

Kenneth Branagh stars in this mystery tale beset by superstition. Branagh is a discharged soldier who must solve the murder of man in order to protect a beautiful woman. She stands accused of witchcraft. The murdered man's body is missing and the townspeople suspect that she has turned him into a dog. Based on the play by respected playwright Christopher Fry. With Bernard Hepton and Cherie Lunghi.
VHS: S26776. $19.95.
Julian Amyes, Great Britain, 1995, 90 mins.

Lamb

Liam Neeson stars as Michael Lamb, a Catholic Brother working at an institution for troubled boys. There he meets 10-year-old Owen Kane, a boy with a series of problems relating both to his disadvantaged past and to the cruel treatment he receives at the hands of the other Brothers at the Home. When Michael Lamb receives an inheritance, he acts on the growing doubts he feels regarding both his faith and the mission of the school where he works. He decides to take Owen to London, setting off a chain of events that leads to tragedy.
VHS: S27055. $89.95.
Colin Gregg, Great Britain, 1995, 110 mins.

Leon the Pig Farmer

Leon, a nice Jewish boy in London, accidentally discovers that he is the product of artificial insemination. Thrown into doubt about his identity, he seeks out his biological father and discovers him to be a Yorkshire pig farmer. After teaching his new family some Yiddish phrases, he is overcome with Jewish guilt (what else!). Starring Mark Frankel, Connie Booth and Janet Suzman.
VHS: S21093. $89.98.
Vadim Jean/Gary Sinyor, Great Britain, 1993, 102 mins.

Let Him Have It

In 1953, Chris Craig, 17, and Derek Bentley, 16, were accused of murdering a South London policeman. The title of the film recalls the fateful words spoken by the unarmed Bentley just prior to a shot fired by his mate in the direction of the police. Director Peter Medak contends the lad was encouraging his friend to surrender the weapon, as this story re-examines a miscarriage of justice. With Christopher Eccleston, Paul Reynolds and Tom Courtenay as the father of the accused.
VHS: S16415. $19.95.
Peter Medak, Great Britain, 1991, 102 mins.

Lifeforce

Patrick Stuart is featured in this genuinely creepy sci-fi horror film about a female vampire. She was dozing in Halley's comet, but once brought back to Earth she awakens to a whole new world of vampiric exploits so vast that the entire planet could be sucked dry.
VHS: S27750. $14.95.
Tobe Hooper, Great Britain, 1985, 101 mins.

Little Dorrit

Christine Edzard's film is a brilliant reworking of the Charles Dickens classic. Brilliant camerawork by Bruno De Keyzer and immaculate sets of John McMillan produce the flavor of Victorian England. Edzard goes to the heart of the novel and makes it new in the story of the pinch-faced, hard-nosed survivor whose belief in herself and in the redemption of humanity forces those about her to survive as well. With an all-star British cast including Alec Guiness, Derek Jacobi, and Sarah Pickering in a brilliant performance as Little Dorrit.
Little Dorrit Part One. Nobody's Fault. The first part is told from Arthur Clenman's point of view.
VHS: S09595. $29.98.
Little Dorrit Part Two. Dorritt's Story. The story is told from Little Dorrit's point of view.
VHS: S09596. $29.98.
Christine Edzard, Great Britain, 1988, 369 mins.

Living Free

The sequel to Born Free continues the story of the Adamsons and their close relationship with Elsa the lioness. Nigel Davenport and Susan Hampshire are the Kenya game wardens who are trusted with the upbringing of three small cubs. Based on the book by Joy Adamson. With Geoffrey Keen.
VHS: S06179. $12.95.
Jack Couffer, Great Britain, 1972, 91 mins.

Local Hero

The delicate ecological balance of a small unspoiled Scottish village is threatened by the plans of a wealthy oilman. Local Hero is a tender, very funny movie about astronomy, a mermaid, a village that wants to get rich and an old man who doesn't. With Burt Lancaster, Peter Riegert.
VHS: S00763. $19.98.
Laser: LD70617. $34.98.
Bill Forsyth, Great Britain, 1983, 111 mins.

London Kills Me

The first film by Hanif Kureishi (My Beautiful Laundrette, Sammy and Rosie Get Laid) concerns a renegade group of drug dealers and the efforts of its confused protagonist to go straight after he's been humiliated. There's a vibrant sexual triangle played out among the three leads, along with a shaded, interesting portrait of atmosphere and local color.
VHS: S17968. $89.98.
Laser: LD75129. $24.98.
Hanif Kureishi, Great Britain, 1991, 107 mins.

The Long Day Closes

Condensed childhood memories of 1940's England are related through elegiac and anecdotal episodes. Like the earlier Distant Voices/Still Lives, this film employs similar techniques but focuses on the mother instead of the father, resulting in a view infiltrated by gentle humor.
VHS: S20710. $19.95.
Terence Davies, Great Britain, 1993, 84 mins.

The Long Good Friday

Bob Hoskins and Helen Mirren star in this gritty but updated gangster film set in London's East End. Hoskins is a cockney hood with big plans. He hopes to enlist foreign help, both underworld and legit, in order to develop the docklands. Of course, his plans can't proceed without a little mob rivalry. Overall, it's a tough, hip thriller.
VHS: S27721. $14.95.
John MacKenzie, Great Britain, 1979, 114 mins.

The Looking Glass War

There may be allusions to Lewis Carroll, but this film is based on John Le Carre's best selling novel of cold war espionage, where Christopher Jones risks all to photograph a rocket in East Berlin. With Ralph Richardson, Anthony Hopkins, Susan George and Pia Degermark.
VHS: S03883. $19.98.
Frank Pierson, Great Britain, 1970, 108 mins.

Lorna Doone

Classic romantic drama set in 17th-century England. A woman named Lorna Doone (Polly Walker), of the bandit Doone family, falls in love with a man from a rival family (Sean Bean), who blames her family for the death of his parents. Love conquers all. Made for British television.
VHS: S20608. $79.98.
Andrew Grieve, Great Britain, 1990, 90 mins.

The Lost Language of the Cranes

A moody BBC adaptation of David Leavitt's novel about family secrets and sexual identity. The film centers on a young man's sexual declaration and its volatile and revealing consequences on the rest of the family. "Graced with subtle, intense performances" (Time Magazine). With Corey Parker, Brian Cox, Eileen Atkins and Angus MacFadyen.
VHS: S18604. $19.98.
Nigel Finch, Great Britain, 1992, 84 mins.

Madame Sousatzka

Shirley MacLaine is magnificent as an aging, highly disciplined London concert piano teacher who resents having her best pupils snatched by greedy musical promoters. Beautiful music and brilliant acting. With Navin Chowdhry, Twiggy, Shabana Azmi and Peggy Ashcroft. Adapted from the novel by Bernice Rubens.
VHS: S09108. $19.95.
John Schlesinger, Great Britain, 1988, 121 mins.

The Madness of King George

Nigel Hawthorne plays the last king ever to rule the North American colonies. He is joined by Helen Mirren (winner of Best Actress Award at Cannes) as the queen and Ian Holm as the Prince of Wales, in this film based on a true story. King George went mad and a variety of cures were brought to bear on this once imposing figure. The result is a tale of maddening cures, political intrigue and overall decline with a touch of British humor. Based on Alan Bennett's play.
VHS: S26268. $19.98.
Laser: LD75069. $39.99.
Nicholas Hytner, Great Britain, 1995, 110 mins.

The Magic Christian

Peter Sellers tries to teach adopted son Ringo Starr about the power and abuses of vast wealth. He will go to outrageous lengths to prove that everyone has their price. With guest stars Raquel Welch, Christopher Lee, John Cleese, Spike Milligan, and Yul Brynner in drag. From the novel by Terry Southern.
VHS: S04244. $14.98.
Laser: CLV. LD72006. $29.98.
Joseph McGrath, Great Britain, 1970, 88 mins.

A Man of No Importance

Albert Finney leads a cast of fine performers in this entertaining and touching story about the conductor of a double decker bus in Ireland. The conductor is fascinated by two things, directing plays (he attempts Oscar Wilde's Salome) and his co-worker, the bus driver.
VHS: S26209. $19.95.
Laser: LD75040. $34.95.
Suri Krishnama, Great Britain, 1994, 98 mins.

Meetings with Remarkable Men

Peter Brook directs this unique search through the Middle East, Central Asia for answers to the question of the meaning of life, based on Gurdjieff's search for hidden knowledge. As a boy, Gurdjieff is influenced by his father, a man of remarkable character, who nurtures his thirst for knowledge while preparing him for a career in medicine and priesthood. But a brush with death and other extraordinary, inexplicable events heighten his sense of wonder about the meaning of man's life, and in hidden ruins, he and his comrades discover ancient scrolls which confirm the existence of a brotherhood with ancient knowledge passed orally from generation to generation. Among those appearing in this extraordinary film are Athol Fugard, Colin Blakely, Terence Stamp.
VHS: S06033. $69.95.
Peter Brook, Great Britain, 1979, 108 mins.

A Mind to Kill

Tension invades a small English seaside town when a brutally murdered girl is found. Police link her body to a previous murder and decide to call in a brilliant university professor for help. The professor also becomes subject to this killer's terror as another fresh body surfaces which turns out to be someone he knew well. Finally, even the police investigator in charge of the case finds that someone he loves could suffer if the madman is not caught soon. With Hywel Bennett, Philip Madoc, Sue Jones-Davies and Nicola Beddoe.
VHS: S26777. $19.98.
Peter Edwards, Great Britain, 1995, 95 mins.

Mirror Crack'd

Agatha Christie's beloved Miss Marple tackles an assembly of all-star suspects in this film version of one of her favorite mystery novels. Angela Lansbury, Elizabeth Taylor and Tony Curtis star.
VHS: S04543. $19.99.
Guy Hamilton, Great Britain, 1980, 105 mins.

Mona Lisa

A moody, expressionist and haunting work by Irish novelist Neil Jordan stars Bob Hoskins as a low-level underground figure caught in a dangerous and intricate game of saving the life of a beautiful prostitute (Cathy Tyson). With Michael Caine, Robbie Coltrane and Clarke Peters.
VHS: S03294. $14.95.
Neil Jordan, Great Britain, 1986, 104 mins.

Monsignor Quixote

Sir Alec Guinness stars as Father Quixote, a parish priest and ancestor of the legendary Don Quixote. It is only a matter of time before he assumes the courage and fury of his demented namesake to "tilt at the windmills" and do battle with evil. England, 118 mins.
VHS: S14627. $59.99.

Murder on The Orient Express

A classic whodunit on a very stylish mode of transportation. Richard Widmark is the type of guy everyone would like to kill and it is up to Albert Finney, as Hercule Poirot, to figure out who did it and why. One of the best Agatha Christie adaptations. Suspects include Lauren Bacall, Sean Connery, Jacqueline Bisset, Anthony Perkins, Vanessa Redgrave, Wendy Hiller, Michael York and Ingrid Bergman—who won an Oscar for her speech about "the little brown babies".
VHS: S10832. $29.95.
Sidney Lumet, Great Britain, 1974, 128 mins.

Naked Civil Servant

John Hurt delivers a compelling performance in the role of Quentin Crisp, based on Crisp's autobiography as a witty homosexual growing up in England of the 30's and 40's through years of intolerance, ostracism and violence. Hurt's tour-de-force performance brings to life Crisp's unique and often sharp wit at once critical of the society as well as of himself.
VHS: S00914. $19.99.
Jack Gold, Great Britain, 1980, 80 mins.

Nicholas and Alexandra

Expensive epic about the final years of the Russian Tsar Nicholas II and Empress Alexandra and their children. Their lavish lifestyle comes to a halt with the rise of Lenin's power, leading to imprisonment and eventual execution. Lavish costume design and beautiful decor in this version based on the biography by Robert Massie. With Tom Baker as Rasputin and Michael Jayson as Nicholas II.
VHS: S03880. $29.95.
Laser: Widescreen. LD75492. $39.95.
Franklin J. Schaffner, Great Britain, 1971, 183 mins.

Nuns on the Run

Eric Idle and Robbie Coltrane decide to leave a life of crime and join a religious order to elude their unsavory pursuers. Sister Superior Janet Suzman thinks the new sisters a bit on the odd side but she does need the help. The disguised crooks also need some help in leaving the country with a bit of cash. Who says comedies about men in women's clothing have to be a drag?
VHS: S12604. $89.98.
Jonathan Lynn, Great Britain, 1990, 92 mins.

O Lucky Man!

Developed from an original treatment by Malcolm McDowell, based on his experiences as a coffee salesman before he became an actor. The subject of the eternal, sometimes very funny, sometimes surreal, circle of human experience—aspiration, energy, wickedness, humor and folly. With Ralph Richardson, Rachel Roberts, Malcolm McDowell.
VHS: S00945. $24.98.
Lindsay Anderson, Great Britain, 1972, 165 mins.

The Object of Beauty

Jake and Tina (played by John Malkovich and Andie MacDowell) are a sexy, jet-setting couple, madly in love and living far beyond their means in a posh London hotel. Confronting a lifestyle-or-death situation, the two plot to collect an insurance payoff after staging the phony theft of Tina's prize sculpture. Unfortunately, Jake and Tina aren't the only crooks in London.
VHS: S14995. $19.98.
Michael Lindsay-Hogg, Great Britain, 1991, 105 mins.

The Old Curiosity Shop

Sir Peter Ustinov, Tom Courtney and James Fox head a superb cast in this film adaptation of a Charles Dickens classic. Young Nell Trent and her grandfather must escape the evil landlord, Quilp. Together they encounter a colorful range of characters that could only be found in 19th-century England.
VHS: S25903. $19.98.
Laser: LD75059. $49.95.
Kevin Connor, Great Britain, 1995, 190 mins.

The Old Man and the Sea

Anthony Quinn stars in this screen adaptation of the Ernest Hemingway classic novel. It is an epic battle of man against nature as waged by a simple but noble fisherman and the young boy who believes in him.
VHS: S24849. $24.98.
Judd Taylor, Great Britain, 1990, 97 mins.

One Russian Summer

John McEnery, as Vadim, holds a grudge against sadistic landowner Oliver Reed. Czarist Russia is on the brink of revolution but the war going on at the Palizyn estate is strictly personal. With Claudia Cardinale and some fancy camerawork. Based on the Lermontov novel.
VHS: S04623. $19.95.
Antonio Calenda, Great Britain/Italy, 1973, 112 mins.

Only Two Can Play

Peter Sellers stars as an ambitious librarian who is willing to seduce the wife of a prominent library board member in order to secure a promotion. Imagine his surprise when he finds that his wife is spending time with a local poet. With Richard Attenborough, Mai Zetterling, Kenneth Griffith and Virginia Maskell. B&W.
VHS: S06072. $69.95.
Sidney Gilliat, Great Britain, 1962, 106 mins.

Orlando

Virginia Woolf's ground-breaking novel about a transsexual from the time of Renaissance England has been transformed into a beautiful film. Tilda Swinton stars with Billy Zane as her romantic American lover while Quentin Crisp reigns as Queen Elizabeth the First.
VHS: S20829. $19.95.
Laser: LD74471. $34.95.
Sally Potter, Great Britain, 1993, 93 mins.

Out of Season

Cliff Robertson and Vanessa Redgrave star in this moody drama about a stranger who returns after twenty years to an English seaside resort and meets a former lover, who now has a daughter almost as old as the number of years he has stayed away. Susan George provides the friction.
VHS: S04667. $19.95.
Alan Bridges, Great Britain, 1975, 90 mins.

Pascali's Island

Ben Kingsley presents another riveting character in this dramatic tale of a Turkish spy on a pre-World War I Greek island. Written and directed by the author of *Fatal Attraction*, this beautifully photographed period piece was shot on location. With Charles Dance and Helen Mirren. A literate and satisfying entertainment. Based on the novel by Barry Unsworth.
VHS: S08934. $19.95.
James Dearden, Great Britain, 1988, 106 mins.

Peter's Friends

Kenneth Branagh's witty comedy uses the structure of John Sayles' *Return of the Secaucus Seven* as six friends, members of an anarchic university theater collective, reunite for a ten-year anniversary over New Year's Eve in the inherited estate of Peter (Stephen Fry) to assess their personal and public successes, failures, family tragedies, heartbreak and romantic and professional disappointments. Sharp performances from Branagh, Emma Thompson and Alphonsia Emmanuel.
VHS: S18725. $19.98.
Laser: LD75239. $34.98.
Kenneth Branagh, Great Britain, 1992, 102 mins.

The Playboys

In this small gem set in an isolated Irish village in the '50s, Robin Wright stars as Tara Maquire, a beautiful, free spirited young woman who steadfastly refuses to name the father of her young child. She's drawn to an itinerant, charming actor (Aidan Quinn), a member of a traveling theater company called The Playboys. Their romance incurs the jealous rage of a drunken police sergeant (Albert Finney) who's obsessed with Tara. With Milo O'Shea.
VHS: S17027. $19.95.
Laser: LD71554. $29.98.
Gilles Mackinnon, Great Britain, 1992, 113 mins.

Playing Away

A team of primarily black West Indians now living in the Brixton area is invited to play a cricket match in a small, very white village outside London. The occasion is Third World Week and this satirical comedy-drama provides laughs and much food for thought about race relations in contemporary England. With Norman Beaton and Robert Urquhart.
VHS: S07171. $14.95.
Horace Ove, Great Britain, 1987, 100 mins.

Plenty

Meryl Streep stars in this David Hare screenplay filmed by Fred Schepisi. Streep is intelligent and sexy in her role as a World War II resistance fighter returning to postwar Britain.
VHS: S01039. $14.95.
Fred Schepisi, Great Britain, 1985, 119 mins.

Priest

Controversial and powerful, this film concerns a young priest overcome by a daunting problem. He must reconcile the contradiction between the tenets of his faith and the desires of his own body. The film is made all the more riveting by its refusal of simple answers. Though spurred by events beyond his control, this priest must ultimately confront the intractable hypocrisy that shrouds homosexuality in the Catholic Church.
VHS: S26884. $99.99.
Laser: LD75445. $39.99.
Antonia Bird, Great Britain, 1995, 98 mins.

The Return of the Musketeers

Richard Lester's boisterous continuation of the popular saga, adapted from Alexandre Dumas' novel *Twenty Years Later*, finds D'Artagnan (Michael York) enlisting the former crew to help save Queen Anne (Geraldine Chaplin) from the evil clutches of Justine (Kim Cattrall)—daughter of the mischievous Milady de Winter. With Oliver Reed, Frank Finlay, C. Thomas Howell, Philippe Noiret and Geraldine Chaplin.
VHS: S19580. $89.98.
Laser: LD71924. $34.98.
Richard Lester, Great Britain/France/Spain, 1989, 101 mins.

The Return of the Native

Joan Plowright and Catherine Zeta Jones are featured in this first rate adaptation of Thomas Hardy's romantic classic. A young woman is torn between her love for two men and the vagaries of fate.
VHS: S24392. $90.98.
Jack Gold, Great Britain, 1994, 99 mins.

Richard III

Sir Ian McKellen leads an all-star cast including Annette Bening, Robert Downey, Jr., Nigel Hawthorne, Maggie Smith and more, in this updated film adaptation of the Shakespeare play. Visually stunning, it was nominated for Academy Awards for art direction and costume design. This film places the story in a fictional but loosely veiled representation of England in the 1930s, where pomp and fascism seem eerily well matched.
VHS: S27707. $99.99.
Laser: LD75566. $34.98.
Richard Loncraine, Great Britain, 1995, 104 mins.

Robin and Marian

Richard Lester continues the high-spirited Robin Hood adventure as Robin regroups the members of his Sherwood Forest band when King John assumes the throne. Sean Connery is Robin Hood; Audrey Hepburn is Marian.
VHS: S03694. $19.95.
Richard Lester, Great Britain, 1976, 112 mins.

The Ruling Class

Peter O'Toole stars as the 14th Earl of Gurney, who happens to believe he is Jesus Christ. An irreverent comedy, *The Ruling Class* is filled with insane ideas and boisterously funny characters. This is the original, uncut version.
VHS: S01137. $39.95.
Peter Medak, Great Britain, 1972, 154 mins.

Running Blind

When British double agent Stuart Wilson is chased through Iceland's savage "Murderer's Country," he teams up with a beautiful woman in a desperate war of survival. England, 120 mins.
VHS: S14332. $49.95.

Sailor Who Fell from Grace with the Sea

Hauntingly erotic film based on a novel by Yukio Mishima, starring Kris Kristofferson as an American seaman whose love affair with Sarah Miles is disturbed by Miles' troubled young son.
VHS: S03449. $19.95.
Lewis John Carlino, Great Britain, 1976, 105 mins.

Scandal

Joanne Whalley-Kilmer and Bridget Fonda sizzle as the underage party girls who topple the Conservative Party in England in the early 60s. When social climbing John Hurt introduces his pretty, young friends to high placed members of government, he never expects a national scandal. He was just trying to be well liked by important people. With Ian McKellen, Britt Ekland and Jeroen Krabbe as Ivanov.
VHS: S10880. $19.95.
Michael Caton-Jones, Great Britain, 1989, 114 mins.

Secret Places

Set in an English girls' boarding school during WW II, this is a sensitive film about growing up—four girls, their first loves, first sex, first discussions, first cigarettes, discussions of life, philosophy, and patriotism—and their "secret places."
VHS: S01173. $79.98.
Zelda Barron, Great Britain, 1985, 98 mins.

The Secret Rapture

Julie Stevenson (*Truly, Madly, Deeply*), Joanne Whalley-Kilmer and Penelope Wilton star in this acclaimed British psychological drama of sibling rivalries, emotional games and ultimate tragedy. Written by noted playwright David Hare (*Damage*), based on his own play.
VHS: S21956. $89.98.
Howard Davies, Great Britain, 1993, 96 mins.

Shadey

A comedy-fantasy-thriller about a man who can read the minds of others and is able to transfer these images to film. He wants to use this gift to finance a sex change operation for himself. With Anthony Sher, Patrick Macnee and Katharine Helmond.
VHS: S04768. $79.98.
Philip Saville, Great Britain, 1985, 106 mins.

Shadow on the Sun

Stefanie Powers is cast in this made-for-TV biography as the adventurous and celebrated Beryl Markham, aviator, author, and woman extraordinaire. She lived life as she pleased, much to the dismay of English society. She romanced royalty, screenwriters and famous African pilots. With Frederic Forrest, James Fox, John Rubinstein, Jack Thompson and Claire Bloom.
VHS: S10983. $29.95.
Tony Richardson, USA/Great Britain, 1988, 192 mins.

Shadowlands

This adaptation of an episode from C.S. Lewis' life stars Anthony Hopkins as the writer, who becomes infatuated with an American woman, Debra Winger. When this author and notorious loner discovers a hitherto unknown quality within himself, the capacity for love, it alters him forever.
VHS: S21137. $19.98.
Richard Attenborough, Great Britain, 1993, 133 mins.

Shirley Valentine

Pauline Collins repeats her award-winning stage role as a dissatisfied British housewife who finds some contentment from an impromptu vacation to Greece. With Tom Conti, Bernard Hill, Joanna Lumley and Julia McKenzie.
VHS: S11736. $14.95.
Laser: LD75256. $34.98.
Lewis Gilbert, Great Britain, 1989, 108 mins.

The Shooting Party

An all-star British cast is featured in this complex film about the personalities, intrigues and conflicts that happen in the course of a weekend shooting party in 1913. James Mason is incredible as the host, presiding over the events with grace and wit. A brilliant look at British class structure in the early years of the century. With James Mason, Dorothy Tutin, John Gielgud and Cheryl Campbell.
VHS: S01193. $19.98.
Alan Bridges, Great Britain, 1984, 108 mins.

Shorts

These short English films offer a look at some early work by today's major directors: *Momma Don't Allow* (1956) by Karel Reisz and Tony Richardson, *Nice Time* (1957) by Claude Goretta and Alain Tanner, *Amelia and the Angel* (1958) by Ken Russell and *The Burning* (1967) by Stephen Frears. Total running time 99 mins.
VHS: S22577. $74.95.

Sid and Nancy

Sid Vicious was punk rock's famous bad boy. Nancy Spungen was a troubled American groupie looking for fame and notoriety. They surprised themselves and the world by falling in love. Director Alex Cox brilliantly conveys their love and euphoria of their love affair to the nightmare that their life became as they plunged into a vortex of drugs and self-delusion. With Gary Oldman and Chloe Webb.
VHS: S02937. $19.98.
Laser: LD72311. $29.99.
Alex Cox, Great Britain, 1986, 101 mins.

Singleton's Pluck

A funny, inventive, bright film—Ian Holm is the single-minded farmer who, frustrated by a British trucking shortage, decides to walk his geese to England. What's funny is that the film is done entirely as a Western, and is full of scathing satire.
VHS: S01208. $19.95.
Richard Eyre, Great Britain, 1984, 89 mins.

Sister My Sister

Two sisters, Julie Walters and Jodhi May, are maids in a small provincial French town in the 1930's. They develop an incestuous passion that grows until it ends in the cold-blooded murder of their mistress and her daughter. The shocking true story is based on real events which inspired Jean Genet's *The Maids*.
VHS: S26287. $94.95.
Laser: LD75414. $39.99.
Nancy Meckler, Great Britain, 1995, 89 mins.

The Spy with the Cold Nose

A British espionage comedy that uses an English bulldog, that has been selected as a good-will gift for the Soviet prime minister, as a method of obtaining secret information. Lionel Jeffries is the British agent with the plan that will work with the cooperation of veterinarian Laurence Harvey. With Daliah Lavi, Denholm Elliott and Paul Ford.
VHS: S06192. $59.95.
Daniel Petrie, Great Britain, 1966, 93 mins.

Stevie

Winner of the 1981 New York Film Critics award, a celebration of love and family, brought to life by Glenda Jackson's remarkable performance. Jackson stars as reclusive poet Stevie Smith, with Mona Washbourne as her doting aunt. Trevor Howard narrates and co-stars.
VHS: S01254. $29.95.
Robert Enders, Great Britain, 1978, 102 mins.

Stormy Monday

The grimy industrial town of Newcastle has a chance for civic improvement if they play ball with American gangster/businessman Tommy Lee Jones. Only jazz club owner Sting and his new handy man Sean Bean don't much care for the Yank's methods. A raw and romantic thriller also starring Melanie Griffith as the very interesting romantic interest.
VHS: Out of print. For rental only.
Laser: LD75265. $34.98.
Mike Figgis, Great Britain, 1988, 93 mins.

Strapless

Blair Brown stars as a workaholic doctor whose sister, Bridget Fonda, forces her to reexamine her life. The sister has not only shown the doctor the importance of romance, but also displays to the doctor a new outlook that courts both spontaneity and danger. Featuring Bruno Ganz (*Wings of Desire*).
VHS: S26286. $19.95.
David Hare, Great Britain, 1990, 99 mins.

Summer House

Jeanne Moreau, Joan Plowright and Julie Walters star in this serious comedy about love, marriage and friendship. A troubled young woman is about to engage in a loveless marriage with an older man. Only one strong, wise woman has the courage to save her from a sad fate. The end is a shocker.
VHS: S25101. $99.95.
Laser: LD75019. $39.99.
Waris Hussein, Great Britain, 1994, 93 mins.

Sunday Bloody Sunday

Nominated for four Academy Awards, *Sunday Bloody Sunday* stars Glenda Jackson, Peter Finch and Murray Head in an unusual love triangle on the rocks. Head plays the enigmatic bisexual involved with both a man and a woman.
VHS: S01283. $19.95.
Laser: LD71182. $49.95.
John Schlesinger, Great Britain, 1971, 110 mins.

The Tall Guy

Jeff Goldblum has the title role as an American actor eking out a living by performing in London. His luck changes when he loses his job as a second banana and falls in love with Kate Lemon, a nurse whose favorite color is orange. With Emma Thompson as the feisty angel of mercy, and Rowan Atkinson as England's most conceited actor.
VHS: S13580. $19.95.
Mel Smith, Great Britain, 1989, 92 mins.

That Sinking Feeling

A preposterous comedy set in Scotland, from the director of *Local Hero* and *Gregory's Girl*. A gang of teenagers invent a hilarious cure for boredom by stealing 100 sinks from a local plumbing warehouse. Forsyth's gift for dialog combined with outstanding performances make this an unforgettable story.
VHS: Out of print. For rental only.
Laser: LD75272. $34.98.
Bill Forsyth, Scotland, 1979, 82 mins.

Thicker Than Water

Theresa Russell and Jonathan Pryce star in this story of murder and psychological terror. A pregnant woman is killed in a car accident. As the husband tries to rebuild his life, he is hampered by the efforts of his deceased wife's identical twin. She is desperate to get her way, using every means at her disposal, including suicide and murder.
VHS: S22870. $19.95.
Marc Evans, Great Britain, 1993, 150 mins.

Tom & Viv

Willem Dafoe plays T.S. Eliot with Miranda Richardson as his first wife. Despite his brilliance as a poet, Elliot could not find personal happiness in his marriage because of an unspeakable secret that ultimately divided these two lovers. This riveting, true story is superbly acted. Richardson was nominated for an Oscar (Best Actress), along with Rosemary Harris (Best Supporting Actress).
VHS: S26035. $99.98.
Laser: LD75064. $39.99.
Brian Gilbert, USA, 1994, 115 mins.

The Trial

Kyle MacLachlan stars as K, the man who unexpectedly finds himself on trial for unnamed crimes. Though confused and unnerved, he resolves to fight an arbitrary and incompetent legal system, resulting in even more troubles, until his life seems hopelessly and irrevocably destroyed. Adapted from Kafka's original book, with Anthony Hopkins and Jason Robards. Screenplay by Harold Pinter.
VHS: S21115. $19.98.
David Jones, Great Britain, 1993, 120 mins.

Turtle Diary

An overlooked film when released, *Turtle Diary* is a romantic comedy starring Glenda Jackson as a children's novelist who seeks inspiration from the beauty and grace of the sea turtle, and Ben Kingsley, who shares her interest in the turtles.
VHS: S01378. $14.98.
John Irvin, Great Britain, 1985, 96 mins.

Unexplained Laughter

Diana Rigg stars as a witty, acid-tongued London journalist taking a vacation with her meek vegetarian friend Elaine Paige. A funny and fast-paced black comedy. England, 85 mins.
VHS: S14333. $49.95.

Unnatural Pursuits

Alan Bates stars as a hilarious, booze-ridden, chain-smoking British playwright in this BBC production. In an all-out effort for success he tours the country with his latest work, experiencing the ignoble process of Americanization at the hands of an L.A. producer (Bob Balaban) and a New York impressario (John Mahoney).
VHS: S22871. $19.95.
Christopher Morahan, Great Britain, 1991, 143 mins.

Utz

George Sluizer's adaptation of Bruce Chatwin's novel about the eccentric passions of Baron Kaspar Joachim von Utz (Armin Mueller-Stahl), who collects decorative Meissen porcelain figures. Set in post-communist Prague, the story follows Marius Fischer (Peter Riegert), a New York-based art dealer, who visits the Baron and discovers that both the porcelain and Utz's housekeeper (Brenda Fricker) have vanished. Fischer and Dr. Vaclav Orlik (Paul Scofield) investigate the disappearance. With Miriam Karlin, Christian Rabe and Jakub Zdenek.
VHS: S19559. $29.95.
George Sluizer, Great Britain/Germany/Italy, 1992, 95 mins.

War of the Buttons

Teen-age boys in two Irish villages engage in an all-out war over common buttons. It's all in play, as the kids will have to be home for supper. *Chariots of Fire* producer David Puttnam and writer Colin Welland are at the helm of this engaging family comedy.
VHS: S27280. $96.99.
John Roberts, Great Britain/Japan, 1995, 95 mins.

Water

Michael Caine follows up his success of *Hannah and Her Sisters* and *Half Moon Street* in this congenial comedy about the commercial and social exploitation of a small Caribbean outpost governed by Caine upon the discovery of a pure mineral water source. With Valerie Perrine, the film is a small satire of economic imperialism, bureaucracy and chic revolutionaries. With appearances by musicians Ringo Starr, George Harrison and Eric Clapton.
VHS: S02632. $29.95.
Dick Clement, Great Britain, 1986, 89 mins.

The Wedding Gift

Jim Broadbent and Julie Walters star as Deric and Diana in this dramatic film about a married couple who overcome tragedy through their devotion to one another. As Diana's health fails she orchestrates a gift of love, a new female companion for her soon-to-be-single husband.
VHS: S22878. $96.98.
Richard Loncraine, Great Britain, 1993, 87 mins.

The Whales of August

Bette Davis and Lilian Gish play aging sisters spending their twilight years in an island cottage on the New England coast. They comb hair, pick berries and chat with visitors Vincent Price, Ann Sothern and Harry Carey Jr. Gish is the sweet sister, Davis the sour and sightless sibling.
VHS: S06275. $14.95.
Laser: LD72316. $29.99.
Lindsay Anderson, USA, 1987, 91 mins.

Where Angels Fear to Tread

Helena Bonham Carter, Judy Davis and Rupert Graves are featured in this lavish adaptation of E.M. Forster's first novel. A British widow falls in love with a young Tuscan man while on vacation in Italy. Unleashed passion leads to heartache for all concerned.
VHS: S21221. $19.95.
Charles Sturridge, Great Britain, 1991, 112 mins.

Whistle Blower

A tense thriller of espionage, spies and counterspies, in which one man's search leads him to the top levels of government intelligence where things are different than they seem and a dark secret world exists that could put out the light of the ordinary world. Michael Caine, James Fox, Nigel Havers and Felicity Dean star. Based on the novel by James Hale.
VHS: S04916. $19.98.
Simon Langton, Great Britain, 1987, 98 mins.

White Mischief

A real life murder mystery set in Kenya during World War II. The wealthy white colonials throw lavish parties, take drugs and take liberties with the more attractive wives. Great costumes and stylish performances grace this tale of decadence and homicide. With Charles Dance, Joss Ackland, Sarah Miles, Geraldine Chaplin, John Hurt, Trevor Howard and Greta Scacchi as Lady Diane, the beauty worth dying over.
Laser: LD72317. $29.99.
Michael Radford, Great Britain, 1988, 107 mins.

Whoops Apocalypse

A black comedy starring Peter Cook, Loretta Swit, Michael Richards and Herbert Lom. Swit plays the first female President of the United States caught in a dispute over an island in the Caribbean. Targets for ridicule include the CIA, the British Royal Family, and atomic bomb misuse. With Rik Mayll and Alexei Sayle.
VHS: S08315. $14.95.
Tom Bussman, USA/Great Britain, 1988

Wild Little Bunch

Based on a true story, this moving film is based on a London slum where a mother struggles to raise 11 children. Beset by pains, she fears her end is near and makes her eldest boy (Jack Wild) promise to take care of his younger brothers. He keeps his promise in the face of many obstacles, and the young boys struggle in an uncaring society.

VHS: $10932. $49.95.
David Hemmings, Great Britain, 1972, 90 mins.

Wings of Fame

A surreal parody on the nature of celebrity. Otakar Votocek's film constructs a strange parallel universe where the afterlife is a hellish sanatorium in which the famous walking dead cavort. Peter O'Toole stars as a pretentious actor who confronts the anonymous, diabolical fan (Colin Firth) who killed him in his bid for recognition and fame.

VHS: $19938. $89.95.
O. Votocek, Great Britain/Czechoslovakia, 1990, 109 mins.

Wish You Were Here

Emily Lloyd gives a spirited and remarkable performance as a young girl growing up in a hurry in post-war England. Her salty language and her sassy behavior are a constant source of irritation to her overbearing father. Based on the early life of Cynthia Payne, the madam of *Personal Services*.

VHS: $06021. $9.95.
David Leland, Great Britain, 1987, 91 mins.

Without a Clue

Michael Caine and Ben Kingsley star in this revisionist comedy about what they claim is the true story of Sherlock Holmes and Dr. Watson. According to Watson, he was the brains that solved all those baffling cases. Holmes was actually a hired actor and a complete fool. With Jeffrey Jones, Lysette Anthony and Paul Freeman as Moriarty. Elementary good fun.

VHS: $09145. $19.98.
Thom Eberhardt, Great Britain, 1988, 108 mins.

A Woman's Guide to Adultery

Rose disapproves of adulterous affairs, and with good reason. Her friends are all entangled in such liaisons, and predictably, the women suffer most. All this foresight fails Rose when she meets a handsome University lecturer. Now she too is trapped by passion that will inevitably lead to great pain for one of the unlucky parties concerned. With Sean Bean, Theresa Russell, Amanda Donohoe and Adrian Dunbar.

VHS: $26774. $24.98.
David Hayman, Great Britain, 1995, 145 mins.

Young Winston

Director Richard Attenborough chronicles the tumultuous rise of one of this century's greatest public figures, and one of its most complex, private men: Winston Churchill, as played by Simon Ward. Also featuring Anne Bancroft and Robert Shaw, *Young Winston* presents a memorable testament to the man and his career.

VHS: $12998. $19.95.
Richard Attenborough, Great Britain, 1972, 157 mins.

Zeppelin

Germany's most dreaded World War I aerial weapon takes to the skies. The mission—bomb England! Interesting special effects highlight this entertaining story of a German-born British aviator emotionally torn by duty and homeland during the war. Starring Michael York and Elke Sommer.

VHS: $13622. $19.98.
Etienne Perier, Great Britain, 1971, 101 mins.

PETER GREENAWAY

26 Bathrooms

The British structuralist Peter Greenaway (*Prospero's Books*) is best known for his pattern-obsessive, symmetrical, intellectual, playful and visually flamboyant features on the nature of the body and art. This short is a brief, comic essay on his larger themes, in short a work about bathrooms and the activities and people inhabiting them.

VHS: $18203. $19.95.
Peter Greenaway, Great Britain, 1993, 30 mins.

The Cook, The Thief, His Wife and Her Lover

Few contemporary filmmakers rival director Peter Greenaway's visual complexity and elaboration. In this style he creates a graphic and layered fable that casts a cynical eye on man's most primal urges: food, lust and violence. A brutal satire on capitalism set predominantly in an exclusive restaurant called "Le Hollandais".

VHS: $13017. $19.95.
Laser: LD75309. $39.98.
Peter Greenaway, Great Britain, 1990, 123 mins.

Death in the Seine

Peter Greenaway's fascinating essay on death and revolution is set in a period between April 1795 and September 1801, when over 300 bodies were pulled from the River Seine in Paris. Two mortuary attendants dutifully noted the condition of each body in great detail, including their clothing, possessions and wounds. This bounty of information is the basis for Greenaway's structuralist speculation on the lives of these corpses and their relationship to the French Revolution.

VHS: $27254. $29.95.
Peter Greenaway, Great Britain, 1994, 44 mins.

Drowning by Numbers

Three generations of women with the same name have rid themselves of their unwanted husbands in the same manner—they drown them. The local coroner, Madgett, agrees to declare the deaths accidental in return for sexual favors. But when things don't go exactly as planned, he devises a final game that could result in the undoing of them all. Another romp through the gutter with director Peter Greenaway (*The Thief, The Cook, His Wife & Her Lover*), characterized by the same sterile beauty that can be found in nearly all of his work.

VHS: $15584. $19.98.
Peter Greenaway, Great Britain, 1991, 121 mins.

Prospero's Books

Peter Greenaway's pattern-obsessed reworking of Shakespeare's *The Tempest* furthers his thematic obsession with numbers and order. Sir John Gielgud is Prospero, the former Duke of Milan who's banished on a magical, isolated island, where he plots his revenge against the men who dethroned him, engages in magic and spectacle, and seeks solace in his collection of extravagantly illustrated books. With Michael Clark, Isabelle Pasco, Erland Josephson and Michael Gambon.

VHS: $17065. $19.95.
Peter Greenaway, Great Britain, 1991, 126 mins.

MIKE LEIGH

Abigail's Party

Mike Leigh's brilliant satire about middle-class English consumerism and appearances, with Alison Steadman's frightening performance as a frantic woman trying to orchestrate an important dinner party, which is interrupted by her husband's untimely heart attack. In this situation, the "unbearable and hopeless fuse to create an explosion of incredible hilarity."

VHS: $17604. $29.95.
Mike Leigh, Great Britain, 1977, 105 mins.

Four Days in July

Mike Leigh's humanism is the hallmark of this BBC television film about the opposite fortunes of two couples in Northern Ireland, one Catholic and one Protestant, both of whom are expecting children. With Brid Brennan, Desmond McAleer, Charles Lawson and Paula Hamilton.

VHS: $17602. $29.95.
Mike Leigh, Great Britain, 1984, 99 mins.

Grown Ups

Mike Leigh's working class comedy about a recently wed couple who must deal with the wife's idiosyncratic sister and their next door neighbor, who was a high school instructor. With Philip Davis, Leslie Manville, Sam Kelly, Lindsay Duncan and Brenda Blethyn.

VHS: $19404. $29.95.
Mike Leigh, Great Britain, 1980, 95 mins.

Hard Labor

This emotionally horrific and yet oddly amusing film is a scathing indictment of classicism and sexism. The grinding daily abuse suffered by a poor elderly woman at the hands of her husband, her children and even her employer illustrate the nature of oppression. Ben Kingsley appears as a hairy but friendly cab driver.

VHS: $21507. $29.95.
Mike Leigh, Great Britain, 1973, 70 mins.

Home Sweet Home

This, the story of three not terribly jolly postmen, centers on Stan, a would-be ladies' man whose wife has left him. Insightful comedy results when Stan compensates for his loneliness by seducing his co-workers' wives. In this unusual film, England emerges as a land of bitter, isolated individuals unconsoled by marriage and pigeonholed by the state.

VHS: $21509. $29.95.
Mike Leigh, Great Britain, 1982, 90 mins.

Kiss of Death

Trevor is a quiet undertaker's assistant. His attempts at romance give shape to a plot characterized by whimsy and a puckish sense of humor. The courtship attempts of this strange misfit must rank among cinema's most funny and awkward expressions of tortured love.

VHS: $21508. $29.95.
Mike Leigh, Great Britain, 1977, 80 mins.

Life Is Sweet

Satirist Mike Leigh is at it again in the London south side with this decidedly bittersweet comedy about the members of a dysfunctional family and their oddball friends. It seems everyone in this film is striving for change. The family tries to balance their differences with alcoholic friends and their short fuses proves a challenge, but they don't forget to laugh a lot along the way.

VHS: $16628. $14.98.
Laser: LD71503. $29.98.
Mike Leigh, Great Britain, 1992, 103 mins.

Naked

This film won in both the Best Film and Best Actor category at the Cannes Film Festival. David Thewlis stars in this funny, erotic and bizarre odyssey, set in the streets of London, that explores the seamy side of desire and longing of post-Thatcherite England.

VHS: $21119. $19.95.
Laser: Includes director's commentary, still photo gallery, trailers and short films. LD74468. $69.95.
Mike Leigh, Great Britain, 1993, 131 mins.

Nuts in May

British filmmaker Mike Leigh has a wonderful sense of rhythms and improvisational textures, and this film recounts the weird adventures of a fierce young couple trying to abide to their strict vegetarian diet, with dangerous repercussions. "Hilarious and appalling" (Vincent Canby). With Roger Sloman, Alison Steadman and Anthony O'Donnell.

VHS: $17603. $29.95.
Mike Leigh, Great Britain, 1976, 84 mins.

Who's Who

Set in a brokerage firm, the movie charts the greed and avarice of some ambitious young traders, each trying to step on top of the other. "In each of [Leigh's] films there comes a transforming moment when the unbearable and the hopeless fuse to create an explosion of recognition of high, incredible hilarity" (Vincent Canby). With Bridget Kane, Simon Chandler, Adam Norton, Philip Davis and Joolia Cappleman.

VHS: $19402. $29.95.
Mike Leigh, Great Britain, 1978, 75 mins.

KEN LOACH

Hidden Agenda

Based loosely on the notorious Stalker case of 1982, involving a British officer who discovered a massive government cover-up, *Hidden Agenda* begins when Kerrigan, the Stalker-like protagonist, travels to Belfast to investigate the killing of an American lawyer who is also an IRA sympathizer. He discovers the murder was committed by the Royal Ulster Constabulary and exposes the cover-up. With Frances McDormand, Brad Dourif and Brian Cox.

VHS: $14295. $19.98.
Ken Loach, Great Britain, 1990, 108 mins.

Ladybird Ladybird

A simply wonderful film from the talented Ken Loach. A small-time singer finds her tough, mostly uneventful life ripped apart by tragedy. A fire destroys her home and severely hurts one of her kids. This incident and a series of problems lead her to lose her children as an unfit mother. Loach's riveting drama is a powerful look at the machinery of the welfare state.

VHS: $26269. $19.98.
Ken Loach, Great Britain, 1994, 102 mins.

Raining Stones

Ken Loach's funny social comedy is set in the British town of Middleton where Bob Williams, survivor, first has his van stolen and then learns the outfit for his daughter Coleen's first communion is going to cost 100 pounds. Among Loach's most accessible films, *Raining Stones* is a bitingly funny comedy that shows the downside to contemporary Britain even as it cleverly reveals the simple humor and tenacity that inspires the average bloke.

VHS: $24861. $89.98.
Ken Loach, Great Britain, 1994, 90 mins.

Riff Raff

Ken Loach directed this first-rate look at the British class system from the bottom up. Stevie is a construction worker whose luck can only improve. His colorful co-workers help keep him from any serious hard labor while Stevie's humor attracts many friends, including an aspiring singer who melts his heart. This down-to-earth comedy shows that being Riff Raff is not so bad.

VHS: $26338. $19.98.
Ken Loach, Great Britain, 1993, 96 mins.

STEPHEN FREARS

Dangerous Liaisons

Nominated for seven Academy Awards, the hottest love affair of 1782 is notable for its sense of style and decor, and strong performances from Glenn Close, John Malkovich and Michele Pfeiffer. A couple of nasty members of 18th century nobility enjoy manipulating the lives and loves of those around them through all kinds of mean-spiritedness. There are three versions of this story available, including *Valmont* and *Liaisons Dangereuses*.

VHS: $09449. $19.98.
Laser: LD70550. $29.98.
Stephen Frears, Great Britain, 1989, 120 mins.

The Grifters

Jim Thompson's novel of love, money and betrayal stars John Cusack as a master of the short con. He must gamble on trusting his dishonest mother or putting his faith in a greedy girlfriend who plays for bigger stakes. Anjelica Huston and Annette Bening were nominated for Oscars for their work, as was director Stephen Frears and scriptwriter Donald E. Westlake. Filmed in the seedier sections of Los Angeles. Don't rent this film for Mother's Day.

VHS: $13830. $19.98.
Stephen Frears, USA, 1990, 114 mins.

Gumshoe

This satire of American film noir detective films from director Frears is filled with adventure, intrigue and laughs. Albert Finney plays a regular schmoe in a London nightclub who decides to become a detective like his movie idols.

VHS: $00535. $69.95.
Stephen Frears, Great Britain, 1971, 85 mins.

Hero

An entertaining movie with equal doses of Preston Sturges and Frank Capra. The story concerns an itinerant, small-time thief (Dustin Hoffman) who saves a group of passengers after a plane crashlands and watches an imposter (Andy Garcia) receive the credit. Geena Davis plays a sharp, ambitious television journalist trying to sort out the confusion.

VHS: $18249. $19.95.
Stephen Frears, USA, 1992, 116 mins.

The Hit

John Hurt is Braddock, the clever, calculating hit man in this clever and entertaining suspense drama. Hurt must transport Terence Stamp, a gangster-turned-informer, to Paris, where he faces execution. "A rollicking black comedy," said *Newsweek*.

VHS: $00575. $14.95.
Stephen Frears, Great Britain, 1985, 97 mins.

My Beautiful Laundrette

The breakthrough film for director Stephen Frears and novelist/filmmaker Hanif Kureishi, about the relationship between a Pakistani innocent (Saeed Jaffrey) and the leader (Daniel Day-Lewis) of a neo-Nazi movement in East London. The first-rate cast includes Roshan Seth, Derrick Branche and Shirley Anne Field.

VHS: Out of print. For rental only.
Laser: CLV, widescreen. LD75107. $39.95.
Stephen Frears, Great Britain, 1986, 97 mins.

Saigon: Year of the Cat

Stephen Frears directed this tale of diplomatic failure and political blindness; playwright David Hare wrote the script. Set in Saigon, Frederic Forrest stars as a man who cannot convince his superiors of the imminent invasion of the Vietcong. As the Vietcong reach Saigon, Forrest and his girlfriend are forced to find their way out before their world goes up in flames.

VHS: $11006. $19.98.
Stephen Frears, Great Britain, 1989, 106 mins.

The Snapper

Stephen Frears' small-town comedy stars Tina Kelleghan as the oldest daughter of a close-knit family, who, when she gets pregnant, refuses to name the father and insists on having the baby. The secret she carries throws the town into turmoil.

VHS: $21886. $96.99.
Laser: LD74531. $39.99.
Stephen Frears, Ireland, 1993, 90 mins.

NICOLAS ROEG

Castaway

Nicolas Roeg directed this sexy, stimulating, often brilliant story of a middle-aged Londoner who advertises for a "wife" to spend a year with him in a remote paradise. But life with the beautiful blonde (Amanda Donohoe) in the idyllic south seas turns out to be a bare-it-all battle of the sexes. With Oliver Reed.

VHS: $05925. $19.95.
Nicolas Roeg, USA, 1987, 118 mins.

Cold Heaven

Nicolas Roeg's film stars Theresa Russell as the unfaithful wife of an American doctor who's found dead on a Mexican vacation. When she returns home, Russell suffers hallucinations that may be connected to her husband's death. With James Russo, Will Patton and Mark Harmon. "Provocative, beautifully edited and lyrically enigmatic" (Jonathan Rosenbaum, *Chicago Reader*).

VHS: $17414. $14.95.
Nicolas Roeg, USA, 1991, 104 mins.

Don't Look Now

Julie Christie and Donald Sutherland star in this beautiful, spellbinding mystery that'll have you on the edge of your seat. When their child drowns in a sudden rainstorm, Sutherland decides to go to Venice for an architectural job and Christie follows. While in Italy, Christie becomes convinced that a mysterious figure in a red raincoat is their beloved child returned from the dead. As the true character of the figure in the red raincoat is revealed, the film creates an atmosphere of terror, fear and ultimate tragedy in a knockout ending. Based on the novel by Daphne du Maurier.

VHS: $00358. $49.95.
Nicolas Roeg, Great Britain, 1974, 110 mins.

Eureka

Another visually stunning film from the director of *Walkabout* and *Don't Look Now*. Gene Hackman stars as a man who has made his fortune in the Canadian wilderness and has retired to a Caribbean island. With Theresa Russell and Mickey Rourke.

VHS: $00418. $14.95.
Nicolas Roeg, Great Britain, 1983, 130 mins.

Full Body Massage

Mimi Rogers and Bryan Brown star in this haunting and erotic tale. She is an art gallery owner who thrives on the finer things in life. One especially indulgent treat she grants herself is a weekly massage with a masseuse named Douglas. When Douglas can't make it one week, Fitch steps in, and suddenly once a week doesn't seem often enough.

VHS: $27428. $89.95.
Nicolas Roeg, USA, 1995, 93 mins.

Heart of Darkness

Based on Joseph Conrad's novel, this film casts John Malkovich in the lead as a character who ends up exploring the edges of his own moral universe in the jungles of Africa. Filmed on location in Belize, with co-stars Tim Roth and James Fox.

VHS: $20776. $92.98.
Laser: LD74489. $39.99.
Nicolas Roeg, USA, 1993, 105 mins.

Man Who Fell to Earth

Nicolas Roeg's stylish classic stars David Bowie as a cosmic visitor to the planet, overwhelmed by capitalist society, human technology and earthly love. This video has now been re-issued with the twenty minutes cut from the original theatrical version fully restored. One of the most mysterious and visually intriguing science fiction films ever made.

VHS: $00815. $69.95.
Nicolas Roeg, Great Britain, 1976, 140 mins.

Performance

Mick Jagger is Turner, a burnt-out rock star, in Roeg's mind-boggling study of consciousness and identity where nothing is true and everything is permitted. Edward Cox co-stars as Chas, a gangster on the run who takes shelter in Turner's home. *Performance* was years ahead of its time, and today remains an audacious and stunning achievement.

VHS: $01009. $19.98.
Laser: LD70652. $29.98.
Nicolas Roeg, Great Britain, 1968, 110 mins.

Sweet Bird of Youth

British stylist Nicolas Roeg (*The Man Who Fell to Earth*) directed this made-for-television adaptation of Tennessee Williams' play about the obsessive relationship between a fading moving star (Elizabeth Taylor) and her ambitious, handsome lover (Mark Harmon). With Rip Torn, Valerie Perrine, Ruta Lee, Kevin Geer and Michael Wilding.

VHS: $20184. $89.95.
Nicolas Roeg, USA, 1989, 95 mins.

Track 29

Theresa Russell stars in another film directed by her much older husband Nicolas Roeg. She plays a bored alcoholic wife of a much older man who is mainly interested in his train set and being spanked by his nurse. She is also visited by a young man who may be the son she gave away before marriage. With Gary Oldman, Christopher Lloyd, Collen Camp, and Sandra Bernhard as the spanking nurse. A bizarre, emotionally charged piece of work.

VHS: $09805. $14.98.
Nicolas Roeg, USA, 1988, 90 mins.

Witches

When young Luke (Jasen Fisher of *Parenthood*) discovers who Miss Ernst (Academy Award winner Anjelica Huston of *Prizzi's Honor*) and her cackling cohorts really are, the adventure of a thousand lifetimes begins. Nicolas Roeg directed this modern fairy tale from a screenplay based on the book by Roald Dahl. It is also one of the last works from the late great Jim Henson (*Sesame Street*, *The Muppet Movie*), who served as executive producer.

VHS: $13440. $19.98.
Laser: LD70708. $24.98.
Nicolas Roeg, USA, 1990, 92 mins.

KEN RUSSELL

Altered States
William Hurt in a dazzling debut as a research scientist on an incredible journey into the inner space of the mind. With Blair Brown and spectacular special effects by Bran Ferren.
VHS: S00038. $14.95.
Laser: LD70501. $29.98.
Ken Russell, Great Britain, 1980, 103 mins.

Boyfriend
Ken Russell adapts the play by Sandy Wilson into an extravagant tribute to Hollywood musicals of the 1930's. Supermodel Twiggy stars as an assistant stage manager who gets her big break when leading lady Glenda Jackson hurts her ankle. With Christopher Gable, Max Adrian, Murray Melvin and Tommy Tune. The show must go on.
VHS: S12232. $19.95.
Laser: LD70532. $39.98.
Ken Russell, Great Britain, 1971, 108 mins.

Crimes of Passion
"You can be as violent as you want in this country, but you talk about sex and everyone reaches for their chastity belts. This picture is about sex and frankness" (Ken Russell). With Kathleen Turner and Anthony Perkins, music by Rick Wakeman.
VHS: S00283. $19.95.
Laser: CLV, widescreen, with original theatrical trailer. LD70930. $49.95.
Ken Russell, Great Britain, 1984, 107 mins.

Dante's Inferno
A neglected film by Kenneth Russell, Dante's Inferno stars Oliver Reed, Judith Paris, and Gala Mitchell. Reed plays the morose and brilliant Dante Gabriel Rosetti. Sensual, prankish, and often drunk, Dante was a gifted poet and painter more concerned with his flamboyant life style than with his literary and artistic output. He drew into his pre-Raphaelite circle some of the most eminent figures of his time; William Morris and his wife Jane, the poet Swinburne, his poetess sister Christina Rosetti, and their critic and champion, John Rustin.
VHS: S11150. $39.95.
Ken Russell, Great Britain, 1968, 90 mins.

The Devils
Oliver Reed is Father Grandier, accused of sorcery by the half-mad nuns of the fortified city of Loudun; Vanessa Redgrave is Sister Jeanne of the Angels, whose own sexual obsession triggers the ferocious events that follow. Based on Aldous Huxley's book.
VHS: S00334. $19.98.
Ken Russell, Great Britain, 1971, 105 mins.

Gothic
Ken Russell recreates a bizarre night at a chateau in Switzerland where Lord Byron, Mary Shelley, Percy Bysshe Shelley and a few friends told scary stories that would later affect their lives. Cast includes Gabriel Byrne, Natasha Richardson and Julian Sands.
VHS: S04624. $14.98.
Ken Russell, Great Britain, 1987, 90 mins.

Isadora
One of Kenneth Russell's achievements has been the popularization of the term "biopic" and indeed, much of Russell's career as the enfant terrible of the British cinema has dealt with films of famous people—Elgar, Liszt, Tchaikovsky, Mahler, among others. This early bio-pic by Russell is an interesting attempt to depict the personality of Isadora Duncan; the film stars Vivien Pickles and Alexei Jawdokimow.
VHS: S07504. $39.95.
Ken Russell, Great Britain, 1966, 67 mins.

Lair of the White Worm
Ken Russell unearths a tale written by Bram Stoker (Dracula) about an ancient pagan snake cult flourishing in the modern English countryside, and adds his own touches of excess and depravity and fun. Can the dashing lord save the beautiful virgin from the unholy clutches of a fiendish but fashionably dressed cult priestess? With Hugh Grant, Catherine Oxenberg, Peter Capaldi and Amanda Donohoe as Lady Sylvia. A forked-tongue-in-cheek horror spoof.
VHS: S09140. $14.98.
Ken Russell, Great Britain, 1988, 90 mins.

Lisztomania
The classical composer as rock superstar, this wild spectacle blends musical genres and cuts across historical generations. Starring Roger Daltry as Franz Liszt, with a guest appearance by Ringo Starr as the Pope. Lots of FUN!
VHS: S00759. $19.98.
Laser: Letterboxed. LD71674. $34.98.
Ken Russell, Great Britain, 1975, 105 mins.

Mahler
A dazzling evocation of the moods, loves and music of one of the foremost composers—Gustav Mahler. By means of flashbacks and dream imagery, the film focuses on the turbulent relationship Mahler had with his beautiful wife. Starring Robert Powell and Georgina Hale, with Mahler's symphonies played by the Concertgebouw Orchestra of Amsterdam.
VHS: S00807. $29.95.
Ken Russell, Great Britain, 1976, 110 mins.

The Music Lovers
Ken Russell's account of the life of Peter Tchaikovsky, a homosexual who sought "salvation" by marrying a persistent admirer who turned out to be a nymphomaniac, shocked many—including the Russian government, which put out its own cleaned-up "official" movie about the man who wrote the 1812 Overture. Russell's film, however, is a sharp and satirical attack on society's hypocrisy and homophobia. Starring Richard Chamberlain and Glenda Jackson.
VHS: S14809. $19.99.
Ken Russell, Great Britain, 1971, 122 mins.

Prisoner of Honor
Richard Dreyfuss stars in this historical reexamination of the infamous "Dreyfus Affair" that kept France in an uproar for over ten years. With Oliver Reed, Jeremy Kemp, Brian Blessed and Peter Vaughn.
VHS: S15605. $89.99.
Laser: LD75241. $34.98.
Ken Russell, USA, 1991, 88 mins.

Salome's Last Dance
British eccentric director Ken Russell pays homage to another flamboyant creative artist, Oscar Wilde, in this colorful adaptation of Wilde's banned play on the last days of John the Baptist as a complete person. Wilde, himself, visits a brothel where his bawdy and symbolic play is performed by members of the house staff. With Glenda Jackson, Stratford Johns, Nicolas Grace, Douglas Hodge and Imogen Millais-Scott as the tantalizing and very spoiled Salome.
VHS: S08232. $89.98.
Ken Russell, Great Britain, 1988, 90 mins.

Shorts
These short English films offer a look at some early work by today's major directors: Momma Don't Allow (1956) by Karel Reisz and Tony Richardson, Nice Time (1957) by Claude Goretta and Alain Tanner, Amelia and the Angel (1958) by Ken Russell and The Burning(1967) by Stephen Frears. Total running time 99 mins.
VHS: S22577. $74.95.

Tommy
Ken Russell's garish and psychedelic handling of The Who's visionary rock opera about a young man named Tommy (Roger Daltry), who retreats into a motionless world after witnessing the murder of his father by his mother (Ann-Margret) and her lover (Oliver Reed). The striking visual compositions and brilliant music (Pete Townsend's landmark lyrics) carry the film. Some excellent performances from non-actors Tina Turner, Eric Clapton and Elton John. Jack Nicholson contributes a great cameo as a specialist assigned to cure Tommy.
VHS: S02920. $14.95.
Ken Russell, Great Britain, 1975, 110 mins.

Valentino
Ken Russell's flamboyant biography of Rudolph Valentino. His masterstroke was the casting of Russian ballet star Rudolf Nureyev in the title role. The screenplay by Russell and Mardik Martin was adapted from the book by Brad Steiger and Chaw Mank. With Leslie Caron, Michelle Phillips, Carol Kane, Felicity Kendal, Huntz Hall and Alfred Marks.
VHS: S20407. $19.98.
Ken Russell, Great Britain, 1977, 127 mins.

Whore
Theresa Russell has the title role in this film about a day in the life of a veteran street prostitute. This raw and raunchy drama seems to exist only to protest the fairy tale presentation of the world's oldest profession in Pretty Woman. With Antonio Fargas, Sanjay, Benjamin Monmouth and Elizabeth Morehead. Crude, lewd and in your face. The star and director are not related.
VHS: S15410. $19.98.
Laser: LD75283. $34.98.
Ken Russell, USA, 1991, 85 minutes

Women in Love
Two sisters, sexually mature and intellectually active, struggle against the confines of a rural English mining town and its rigidly classed layers of society, in this adaptation of D.H. Lawrence's study of sexual uneasiness and doubt. With Alan Bates, Oliver Reed, Glenda Jackson, Jennie Linden.
VHS: S01479. $19.98.
Laser: LD71216. $29.98.
Ken Russell, Great Britain, 1970, 129 mins.

DEREK JARMAN

The Angelic Conversation
Derek Jarman's apocalyptic visualization of 14 Shakespeare sonnets read by actress Judi Dench, capturing the director's characteristic themes: desire, longing, homoeroticism and mysticism. With Paul Reynolds and Phillip Williamson. Music by Coll. "A hypnotically beautiful film" (Time Out).
VHS: S12677. $29.95.
Derek Jarman, Great Britain, 1985, 80 mins.

Blue
Faced by a worsening prognosis, Jarman confronts impending blindness and his own death in this moving and highly unusual work. Conceived as an homage to Yves Klein, its only visual component is a blue screen. The lush narration and beautifully composed sound environment, featuring Fisher Turner's score, chart an emotional landscape transformed by the brutally short life span afforded Jarman because of AIDS.
VHS: S26598. $24.95.
Derek Jarman, Great Britain, 1993, 76 mins.

Caravaggio
Derek Jarman's elegant and extraordinary film on the life of Caravaggio. "Set in a milieu of gamblers and prostitutes, the film evokes the fantasies of rough trade to which the artist supposedly subscribes and then transcends. Jarman's Caravaggio (Nigel Terry) is a cheeky Cockney—but he's ultimately less a character than a vehicle for a series of extraordinary tableaux that reconstruct the original paintings using the dramatic chiaroscuro that Caravaggio pioneered" (J. Hoberman, The Village Voice). With Sean Bean, Garry Cooper and Tilda Swinton.
VHS: S06024. $79.95.
Derek Jarman, Great Britain, 1986, 93 mins.

Derek Jarman Four-Tape Set
Four of Derek Jarman's works have been collected into this unique set: The Angelic Conversation, The Last of England, Jubilee and War Requiem.
VHS: S24263. $89.85.

Edward II
Derek Jarman's adaptation of Christopher Marlowe's 16th century play about Edward II (Steven Waddington), who neglected his beautiful, ambitious wife (Tilda Swinton) to carry out an obsessive, homoerotic relationship with his military lieutenant (Andrew Tiernan). Annie Lennox sings "Every Time We Say Goodbye".
VHS: S17626. $19.95.
Derek Jarman, Great Britain, 1991, 91 mins.

The Garden
Derek Jarman's haunting memoir of his anguish and struggle with AIDS. An examination of his own mortality and the repression of homosexuality, The Garden shifts from the coastal Kent landscapes to the urban decay of contemporary London. The film was shot alternately in Super-8, 16 and 35mm. With Kevin Colins, Roger Cook, Jody Graber and Tilda Swinton.
VHS: S18975. $19.98.
Derek Jarman, Great Britain, 1990, 90 mins.

Jubilee
An angel transports Queen Elizabeth I from the year 1578 to a post-punk, post-Thatcher wasteland where civilization has come to a halt, where bands of teenage girl punks and fascistic police roam the streets; Buckingham Palace is a recording studio, the center of an entertainment empire controlled by media czar Borgia Ginz, who owns everything. The anti-heroes of the film are led by Elizabeth's mirror image, Bod, the murderous leader of a mad household that includes the historian Amyl Nitrate, the sex-obsessed actress Crabs, loving brothers Sphinx and Angel, the artist Viv and their French au pair, Chaos. With Jenny Runacre, Jordan, Little Nell, Toyah Wilcox, music by Brian Eno, Adam and the Ants, Sixousix and the Banshees, Wayne County. "One of the most original, bold and exciting features to have come out of Britain" (Variety).
VHS: S12676. $29.95.
Derek Jarman, Great Britain, 1978, 105 mins.

Last of England
"Wrenchingly beautiful…the film is one of the few commanding works of personal cinema in the late 80's—a call to open our eyes to a world violated by greed and repression, to see what irrevocable damage has been wrought on city, countryside and soul, how our skies, our bodies, have turned poisonous," wrote The Village Voice of Derek Jarman's beautiful film. Synthesizing rock 'n roll, Super-8, gay erotica, old home movies, anti-totalitarian paranoia, Jarman "superimposes an incandescent Belfast over contemporary London …The doomsday rubble landscape… [is] rendered with the imagistic panache of Kenneth Anger and pulverized a la Brakhage. The Last of England is sinister and gorgeous" (J. Hoberman).
VHS: S09555. $29.95.
Derek Jarman, Great Britain, 1987, 87 mins.

Sebastiane
Sebastiane caused riots at the 1977 Locarno Film Festival and became a runaway hit in London. It has "a pretention and perversity about it that are surprisingly appealing in the long run" (Rob Baker, Soho Weekly News). The film tells the highly charged homoerotic story of St. Sebastian. Sebastian spends most of the film tied to the stake, haunted by sexual advances of his commander Severus, and tortured when he refuses him. Newly remastered. Latin with English subtitles.
VHS: S25523. $79.95.
Derek Jarman, Great Britain, 1976, 86 mins.

War Requiem
Derek Jarman's cinematic visualization of Benjamin Britten's celebrated oratorio uses live action and documentary footage from the whole range of 20th century wars. Told as the rueful remembrance of an old soldier, the film is a both faithful and exhilarating visual manifestation of Britten's work. "Complex, beautiful, harrowing and utterly demanding" (Los Angeles Times).
VHS: S13410. $29.95.
Derek Jarman, Great Britain, 1988, 92 mins.

Wittgenstein
Born into the same stressful Central European world which generated Freud, Schoenberg and Hitler, Wittgenstein emerged from Vienna to transform contemporary philosophy. His eccentricity only sharpened his critique of the absurdities of language and other aspects of Western culture. This experimental biographical film shows the stresses which afflicted this closeted homosexual man as he propounded a new philosophical tradition.
VHS: S26599. $79.95.
Derek Jarman, Great Britain, 1993, 75 mins.

TERRY GILLIAM

The Adventures of Baron Munchhausen
Terry Gilliam revives the tall tales of the 17th century German adventurer. John Neville has the title role and little Sarah Polley is his brave assistant as he travels to the Moon and back to save a besieged city. With Eric Idle, Oliver Reed, Uma Thurman, Jonathan Pryce and Robin Williams as the King of the Moon.
VHS: S10978. $19.95.
Laser: CAV, Director's cut. LD71558. $134.95.
Terry Gilliam, Great Britain/Germany, 1989, 126 mins.

Brazil
Terry Gilliam's acclaimed, surrealistic, nightmare vision of a "perfect" future where technology reigns supreme. Spectacular set design, this wildly visual treat stars Jonathan Pryce (as the "Everyman"), with a supporting cast of Robert De Niro and Michael Palin. A chilling black comedy, where 1984 meets A Clockwork Orange, with a script by Tom Stoppard.
VHS: S00177. $19.95.
Laser: LD70018. $39.98.
Terry Gilliam, Great Britain/USA, 1986, 131 mins.

The Fisher King
Terry Gilliam blends romantic comedy with urban angst in this ambitious epic that includes a firebreathing medieval knight running amok in Manhattan. Jeff Bridges stars as a top radio shock jock who loses his job and his self-respect when a faithful listener shotguns a popular yuppie dining spot. Enter Robin Williams as a charming but mentally unstrung, homeless ex-professor of medieval history who sincerely believes the Holy Grail is in New York and needs to be rescued. With Mercedes Ruehl and Amanda Plummer.
VHS: S15711. $19.95.
Laser: LD71180. $99.95.
Terry Gilliam, USA, 1991, 137 mins.

Jabberwocky
Terry Gilliam has Lewis Carroll spinning in his grave with this outrageous interpretation of the Dark Ages as perhaps they should have been. Something evil is lurking in the woods, and Michael Palin with a host of other victims is fated to discover its darkly funny secret.
VHS: S01842. $19.95.
Terry Gilliam, Great Britain, 1977, 101 mins.

Monty Python and the Holy Grail
The legend of King Arthur as interpreted by Monty Python in this irreverent, insanely funny film. Graham Chapman as Arthur convenes the knights to seek the Holy Grail, but things go awry amid medieval pageantry, religious sentiment, transvestism and a man-eating rabbit.
VHS: S00878. $19.95.
Laser: CLV. LD74617. $34.95.
Terry Gilliam, Great Britain, 1974, 95 mins.

Time Bandits
John Cleese, Sean Connery, Shelley Duvall and Michael Palin are among the stars who keep popping up in the strangest of places throughout human history. It seems there are mysterious connections and the Time Bandits are able to jump around. The result is a wild, extravagant adventure that, though quite dark in places, delights everyone.
VHS: S01344. $14.95.
Terry Gilliam, Great Britain, 1981, 110 mins.

PETER WATKINS

Battle of Culloden
A great film by Peter Watkins, based on a re-staging of the 18th century battle in which Bonnie Prince Charlie was defeated. Realistic beyond imagination, despite its historical, epic quality, the film acts as one of the greatest pacifist films ever made.
VHS: S01429. $79.95.
Peter Watkins, Great Britain, 1965, 75 mins.

Edvard Munch
This biographical dramatization of Norway's most famous artist reveals the tumultuous events of his life as recorded in Munch's own memoirs. With stuffy 19th-century Oslo as the background, the creative process of one of the world's foremost expressionist painters emerges. Norwegian and German with English subtitles.
VHS: S20594. $79.95.
Peter Watkins, Norway/Sweden, 1973, 167 mins.

The Journey
Years in the making, filmed in 14 countries, and with a running time of slightly over 14 hours, The Journey, from director Peter Watkins (The War Game, Battle of Culloden), is the most powerful and definitive film to date on the nuclear arms race and the threat of nuclear war. At the heart of this epic, seven-part documentary are Watkins' extended conversations with family groups and cultures around the world: the gripping, personal recollections of survivors of the bombing of Hiroshima and Hamburg during World War II, and the dramatizations of evacuation scenarios by community groups in Norway, the USA, Scotland and Australia. With The Journey Watkins was determined to break down the wall we commonly place between ourselves and the suffering of others; the result is a truly remarkable and uncompromising film. It is composed of seven volumes, which may be purchased individually or as a set.
Volume 1. Includes parts 1, 2 and 3: Citizens in Scotland discuss military expansion in their neighborhood. A Hiroshima survivor begins her recollection of the aftermath of the bombing…. 141 mins.
VHS: S14296. $29.95.
Volume 2. Includes parts 4, 5 and 6: Families from around the world respond to photographic images of Hiroshima. A Norwegian community dramatization of evacuation begins…. 134 mins.
VHS: S14297. $29.95.
Volume 3. Includes parts 7, 8 and 9: Recollections of the bombing of Hamburg during World War II. A woman describes her evacuation of Leningrad during the war…. 128 mins.
VHS: S14298. $29.95.
Volume 4. Includes parts 10, 11 and 12: Women of a Mozambican farming collective discuss the war in their country and its effects on their ability to produce food. Watkins details the amount the U.S. government pays American colleges and universities for their part in nuclear weapons design and production…. 136 mins.
VHS: S14299. $29.95.
Volume 5. Includes parts 13 and 14: An Australian family discusses local media coverage of the nuclear industry in Australia and the protest against it. The New York State evacuation dramatization culminates…. 87 mins.
VHS: S14300. $29.95.
Volume 6. Includes parts 15 and 16: A Korean man describes Japanese treatment of Koreans during World War II. A family demonstrates the personal cost of the MX missile, in bags of groceries…. 104 mins.
VHS: S14301. $29.95.
Volume 7. Includes parts 17, 18 and 19: The Australian community group discusses their experiences, dramatizing life in a bomb shelter. The Norwegian group discusses their experiences as "evacuees." The hundreds of people involved in the production of The Journey are acknowledged in an ingenious, entertaining, 30-minute credit sequence. 138 mins.
VHS: S14302. $29.95.
Complete seven-volume set: 870 mins.
VHS: S16588. $179.85.
Peter Watkins, Sweden/Canada, 1987, 870 mins.

JAMES BOND

Bond 007 Gift Set Volume 1
Sean Connery is featured in all three classic spy thrillers featuring the agent with a license to kill. In Dr. No (1962), 007 must travel to Jamaica to confront a diabolical fiend and beautiful women in swimwear. Then Bond must fight to stay alive as his spirits away key Russian technology in From Russia with Love (1963). Finally, gold represents an evil worth fighting for in Goldfinger. This volume includes Behind-the-Scenes with Goldfinger.
VHS: S26408. $44.92.

Bond 007 Gift Set Volume 2
This volume combines three of the best Sean Connery James Bond films, including *Thunderball* (1965), where Bond tries to prevent a nuclear explosion in Miami, *You Only Live Twice* (1967), the story of a mysterious plot to provoke World War III, and *Diamonds Are Forever* (1971), which is about smuggling from South Africa. This volume also contains *Behind-the-Scenes with Thunderball*.
VHS: $26409. $44.92.

Diamonds Are Forever
This seventh episode of the James Bond series, from the director of *Goldfinger*, stars Sean Connery, Jill St. John and Lana Wood as Plenty O'Toole. The action goes from an L.A. crematorium to the glitter of Las Vegas casinos.
VHS: $00337. $14.98.
Laser: LD70555. $39.98.
Guy Hamilton, USA, 1971, 119 mins.

Dr. No
The first of the phenomenally successful James Bond movies: Sean Connery foils the master criminal Dr. No in the West Indies; Ursula Andress stars.
VHS: $00365. $14.98.
Laser: CLV, 1 disc, Criterion. LD70359. $79.95.
Laser: CLV, MGM. LD72186. $34.98.
Terence Young, Great Britain, 1962, 111 mins.

For Your Eyes Only
The twelfth James Bond adventure, this one starring Roger Moore and an array of gorgeous women. Action-packed, stunt-filled entertainment!
VHS: $00456. $19.98.
Laser: LD70573. $39.98.
John Glen, USA, 1981, 128 mins.

From Russia with Love
The second James Bond film is one of the best, with Lotte Lenya playing the sinister Russian spy, and Sean Connery as Agent 007.
VHS: $05015. $14.98.
Laser: LD70367. $79.95.
Laser: LD72264. $34.98.
Terence Young, Great Britain, 1963, 118 mins.

Goldeneye
Pierce Brosnan is Ian Fleming's James Bond, Agent 007, and he must save the world from disaster yet again. This time the secret code to Goldeneye, a space weapon capable of mass destruction, is about to fall into the wrong hands. Bond must resist the lure of beautiful women, battle amidst outrageous gadgets, and exercise his own license to kill, or the world will be lost. Bono, The Edge and Tina Turner are responsible for the theme song.
VHS: $27651. $104.99.
Laser: LD75558. $44.98.
Martin Campbell, USA, 1995, 130 mins.

Goldfinger
The third of the James Bond films, with Sean Connery as the sophisticated Agent 007 pursuing the ruthless Auric Goldfinger. With Gert Frobe and Honor Blackman as Pussy Galore.
VHS: $00513. $14.95.
Laser: CAV, widescreen, Criterion. LD70370. $79.95.
Laser: CLV, MGM. LD70584. $98.99.
Guy Hamilton, USA, 1964, 108 mins.

License to Kill
James Bond is in Florida for his friend Felix Leiter's marriage, and on the eve of the wedding he and Felix capture South America's most ruthless drug lord. But after a two-million dollar bribe, Sanchez is a free man, and murders the new Mrs. Leifer and feeds Felix to the sharks. The usually cool Bond is beside himself with rage.
VHS: $11265. $19.98.
John Glen, USA, 1989, 135 mins.

Live and Let Die
James Bond pursues the head of a giant heroin operation from harlem to exotic locales in New Orleans and the Caribbean. Moore's first appearance as 007; song by Paul McCartney.
VHS: $07310. $14.95.
Guy Hamilton, Great Britain, 1973, 121 mins.

The Living Daylights
Timothy Dalton's debut as James Bond announced a darker, more introspective agent haunted by failure and the violent necessities of his job. In this sweeping, action packed work, Bond travels through Britain, Eastern Europe, and Afghanistan to track a double dealing Russian general. With Maryan d'Abo as the love interest, Jeroen Krabbe, Joe Don Baker, John Rhys-Davies and Art Malik.
VHS: $27706. $19.95.
Laser: LD70159. $39.98.
John Glen, Great Britain, 1987, 130 mins.

Man with the Golden Gun
Bond plays a deadly game of cat and mouse in the exotic far East, with Roger Moore, Maud Adams, Christopher Lee, Herve Villechaize.
VHS: $07311. $19.95.
Laser: LD70623. $39.98.
Guy Hamilton, Great Britain, 1974, 125 mins.

Moonraker
The world's foremost Special Agent blasts into space as Roger Moore stars in the film that took Agent 007 beyond the stratosphere.
VHS: $07312. $19.95.
Lewis Gilbert, USA, 1979, 126 mins.

Never Say Never Again
Although this is essentially a remake of *Thunderball*, this is a fine film in its own right featuring Sean Connery as James Bond with an all-star cast including Klaus Maria Brandauer, Max von Sydow and Kim Basinger.
VHS: $04389. $14.95.
Laser: LD70638. $39.95.
Irvin Kershner, USA, 1983, 134 mins.

Octopussy
Agent 009 has been killed over an art object stolen from Moscow, and 007 must investigate. His hunt leads him across Cuba, India and Germany, to the secluded palace of the queen of the octopus cult (Maud Adams).
VHS: $07313. $19.95.
Laser: LD70648. $39.95.
John Glen, USA, 1983, 130 mins.

On Her Majesty's Secret Service
Bond's romance, marriage and nonstop action make up the combination of this 6th Bond film starring George Lazenby as Bond, and Diana Rigg and Telly Savalas.
VHS: $07314. $14.98.
Laser: LD70649. $39.98.
Peter Hunt, USA, 1969, 144 mins.

The Sean Connery Collection
The elegant wit, style and grace of Sean Connery, moving from rugged action to romantic appeal, is revealed in this collection of the first three James Bond films, with Terence Young's *Dr. No* and *From Russia with Love* and Guy Hamilton's *Goldfinger*.
Laser: LD71170. $79.98.

Spy Who Loved Me
007 does battle against the arch villain Stromberg and his plans for world destruction. Teaming with a seductive Russian agent, Bond slyly overcomes a persistent, 7-foot-plus, steel-dentured thug played by Richard Kiel to foil the sinister plans of his nemesis. With Roger Moore, Barbara Bach and Curt Jurgens.
VHS: $05659. $19.98.
Lewis Gilbert, Great Britain/USA, 1977, 125 mins.

Thunderball
Sean Connery stars as 007, the secret agent with clever gadgets and a license to kill. He must thwart SPECTRE, a group which is threatening to destroy Miami by an atomic bomb unless a ransom of 100 million pounds is paid. Tom Jones sings the title song.
VHS: $26364. $14.98.
Terence Young, USA, 1965, 125 mins.

You Only Live Twice
The talented novelist Roald Dahl adapted the Ian Fleming original in this expansive and colorful James Bond entry starring Sean Connery as the British spy working undercover in Japan. With Tetsuro Tamba, Akiko Wakabayashi, and Mie Hama.
VHS: $26363. $14.98.
Laser: LD70719. $34.98.
Lewis Gilbert, Great Britain, 1967, 118 mins.

BRITISH CULTURE

75 Golden Years: The Chelsea Flower Show
In 1913, the Royal Horticultural Society moved its Great Spring Show from the Temple Gardens to the Royal Chelsea Hospital. This commemorative video looks back over the last 75 golden years, illustrating the fascinating history with period photographs, music, and film. A BBC production. 40 mins.
VHS: $10284. $19.94.

Ballad to Scotland
This musical journey follows the unmistakable strains of Scottish bagpipes through the glorious panorama of the misty isle. It includes "A Scottish Welcome", "Dance in the Heather" and more. 50 mins.
VHS: $23141. $19.95.

British Military Pageantry
The spectacle of the Royal Tournament and the ceremony of the Changing of the Guard are traditions which lie at the heart of the illustrious British military heritage. 60 mins.
VHS: $23121. $19.95.

The British Way of Life
Geography and historical achievements helped shape the nature of the British people. These elements are explored and interviews from people across Britain help to give context to the endurance of British ways. 23 mins.
VHS: $23707. $129.95.
Laser: LD74789. $149.95.

Chalk-Stream Trout
Trout fishing in the rivers of England and Scotland, including sequences on the raising and stocking of trout, tips on fly fishing and choosing the right fly. 33 mins.
VHS: $15537. $35.00.

The Charm of London
Tour London with Susannah York, and see all the famous and picturesque sights of this historic city. Visit Parliament, St. Paul's, Buckingham Palace, the Tower of London, Harrod's, Piccadilly Circus, and many other interesting spots. 26 mins.
VHS: $05787. $24.95.

Chatsworth
Home to the Duke and Duchess of Devonshire, this stately home also houses a staff of 150 and over 100 pensioners. 500,000 visitors tour its 35,000 acres every year. In this three-part video, the story behind this historic manor is revealed in amazing detail.
VHS: $27104. $69.95.

Commando's Tale
On April 2, 1982, Argentine forces invaded the Falkland Islands in the South Atlantic. Three days later, a British task force set in, putting into motion Britain's biggest military operation since World War II. This program looks at the conflict from the Royal Marines' point of view, using footage and interviews. 82 mins.
VHS: $13129. $29.98.

Diana: The Making of a Princess
In early 1981, when it was announced that Prince Charles would marry a shy, beautiful but anonymous teenager, Diana became famous overnight. This video traces her early life and transition from a kindergarten teacher to one of the most glamorous women of our time. 55 mins.
VHS: $12294. $29.95.

Dragonpark: Sacred Sites of Britain
From neolithic Stone circles and ruins of early Christian churches to contemporary pilgrimage centers, people have been drawn to erect monuments to their beliefs. This documentary explores the mysteries of these monuments, and includes visits to Stonehenge, Avebury, Glastonbury, Iona, Lindisfarne and other sacred centers. 42 mins.
VHS: $07730. $39.95.

Edinburgh Military Tattoo 1987
Music, color, splendor and pageantry are the hallmarks of the Edinburgh Military Tattoo, the world's best-loved military spectacle and the main attraction of Edinburgh, Scotland's annual festival. Set against the atmospheric backdrop of an illuminated Edinburgh Castle, this stirring program provides dazzling displays of military and bagpipe bands. BBC Enterprises. 73 mins.
VHS: $05230. $19.94.

Edward and Mrs. Simpson
This Emmy-Award-winning series is about the king who gave up his throne for the love of a woman, a fairytale all the more romantic because it's true. On two 135-minute cassettes. Total running time: 270 minutes.
VHS: $04540. $29.95.

England, Land of Splendor
The august House of Lords on the Thames in the heart of London, the great cathedrals at Salisbury and Winchester, and great country houses like Blenheim Palace are shown on this video. The Henley Regatta and even views from the Magnificent Lake District are included. 86 mins.
VHS: $21518. $24.95.

English Towns: Chichester, Richmond & Tewkesbury
England has more unspoilt towns than any other country in the world. In this volume, Alex Clifton-Taylor, noted architectural historian, presents some of his own personal favorites. Through his discerning eye, we come to appreciate each town's essential quality and spirit, from Chichester's marvelous use of flint and the "bastard" limestone of Richmond in Yorkshire to the glorious fan-vaulting of Tewkesbury Abbey. 86 mins.
VHS: $10275. $29.95.

An Englishman's Home
This ten-volume series tells the stories of ten historic English houses, and the influential families who built, re-built, preserved and left them as a record of their lives.
Arundel Castle. Home of the Dukes of Norfolk since 1556. The present Duke shows the castle's splendor and explains the family "aura of fatal glory."
VHS: $05551. $29.95.
Breakmore House. A great house filled with exotic treasures, acquired through propitious marriages and licensed privateering.
VHS: $05552. $29.95.
Broadlands. The magnificent house of Lord Mountbatten, where Prince Charles and Diana honeymooned.
VHS: $05558. $29.95.
Chartwell. Winston Churchill's house, filled with history; his daughter, Mary, is the guide.
VHS: $05557. $29.95.
Goodwood House. Still occupied by the descendants of Charles II, this stately home is associated with the famous racecourse.
VHS: $05559. $29.95.
Penshurst Palace. A house with many wings, built at different times with different styles, filled with history dating back to Henry VIII.
VHS: $05560. $29.95.
Stratfield Saye. Filled with mementos of Waterloo, this house was England's gift to the Duke of Wellington after the defeat of Napoleon.
VHS: $05553. $29.95.
Sutton Place. The Tudor mansion occupied by Paul Getty, filled with superb art from ancient Greece to Miro.
VHS: $05555. $29.95.
Uppark. A house of history and legend, a time-capsule of the 18th century, preserved upstairs and downstairs as it was.
VHS: $05554. $29.95.
Wilton. Henry VIII gave Wilton to the first Early of Pembroke; the present Earl shows the magnificent Inigo Jones apartments, paintings by Van Dyck and Rembrandt and other treasures.
VHS: $05556. $29.95.
An Englishman's Home, Set. The complete ten-volume set of *An Englishman's Home* at a package price.
VHS: $05561. $269.95.

Falklands: Task Force South
Shot by a BBC news camera team on board the British flagship, this video documents the British defense of the Falkland Islands during the Argentine invasion. Produced by the BBC. 120 mins.
VHS: $03394. $19.94.

The Heritage of England
This overview of English culture and life examines the influence of English language, law and literature on the shaping of America, from its colonial origins to the present. 28 mins.
VHS: $20273. $29.95.

King Arthur and His Country— Southern England
Learn the story of King Arthur and explore his kingdom— Southern England—as it is today. 25 mins.
VHS: $06694. $19.95.

London: City of Majesty
This program studies London's vast cultural outreach, providing an immediate view of the neighborhood and the communities, the Barbican Theatre, Lloyd's of London, Tower of London, Fleet Street, Sloane Square and the National Portrait Gallery. "When a man is tired of London, he is tired of life; for there is in London all that life can afford" (Samuel Johnson). 48 mins.
VHS: $19171. $19.98.

London: Flower of Cities Allo
The capitol of Britain in a tour of traditional and historic London: St. Paul's Cathedral, the Tower, Buckingham Palace, the House of Parliament, and the museums, theaters, concert halls, shops, restaurants, with spectacular aerial photography of the Thames, Royal Parks, Hampstead Heath and Kew Gardens. 20 mins.
VHS: $07090. $19.95.

Majesty: The History of the British Monarchy
Period images, recreated eyewitness accounts and reenactments shows the remarkable royal history of Great Britain through the centuries. This two-volume set features *The Anglo-Saxons to Elizabeth I* and *16th Century to the House of Windsor*, which offer a complete overview of the triumphs and tribulations of English royalty. 104 mins.
VHS: $27103. $39.95.

Peter Reading
This brilliant English poet's first American reading included selections from *Evagatory* and *Diplopic*. It took place on April 21, 1992, in Los Angeles. He then spoke with Christopher Hitchens and Michael Silverblatt. From the *Lannan Literary Videos* series. 60 mins.
VHS: $27135. $19.95.

Portrait of England: Treasure Houses and Gardens
Stately homes and glorious gardens, and the sounds of Wynton Marsalis in his debut video album as the sole featured artist in this portrait that captures the pastoral vistas, stately homes, castles and gardens that crown Great Britain. 55 mins.
VHS: $11195. $29.95.

Princess and the People
An intimate portrait of Diana, Princess of Wales, who during the first year of her marriage to Prince Charles developed from a shy, rather reluctant celebrity into a confident world figure. Narrated by Richard Whitmore; produced by the BBC. 51 mins.
VHS: $03388. $19.94.

Queen Elizabeth II: 60 Glorious Years
For anyone interested in royalty, this documentary captures the high points of Queen Elizabeth II, as she marries, goes through coronation, and reigns as England's monarch, in this production authorized by Buckingham Palace. 55 mins.
VHS: $05175. $29.95.

Queen Mother
This fascinating retrospective celebrates the ninetieth birthday of one of Great Britain's favorite royal figures—the Queen Mum. From the BBC.
VHS: $12391. $19.94.

Queen's Birthday Parade
A documentary focusing on the annual Trooping of the colours, performed in honor of the British Monarch's birthday by the Household Division, with its seven bands providing stirring military music. Produced by the BBC. 88 mins.
VHS: $03391. $19.94.

The Royal Collection Set
An intimate look at more than 500 years of the British monarchy. The program features sweeping pageantry and spectacle. Christopher Lloyd, the Surveyor of the Queen's Pictures, hosts the program. 180 mins.
VHS: $19365. $99.95.

Royal Family at War
This revealing look at the British Royal family shows how they survived World War II. Group Captain Peter Townsend, the chaperon to both Princess Margaret and Princess Elizabeth, reveals all about these two. He was later involved in a scandal with Princess Margaret. Also includes footage of King George VI's wartime diary. 90 mins.
VHS: $25843. $19.95.

Royal Wedding: H.R.H. the Prince Andrew and Miss Sarah Ferguson
Drawing on the BBC's coverage of the ceremony and procession, an evocation of the color, pageantry and emotion of the Royal wedding, including the full Westminster Abbey service. Produced by the BBC. 100 mins.
VHS: $03387. $19.94.

Royal Windsor and Eton
Windsor Castle has long been a summer residence for the Royal family of Great Britain. In this video you will see it before the disastrous fire of 1992, on the occasion of a royal wedding. Then across the Thames, founding day at Eton, the venerable boy's school, is a chance to witness still more pomp and circumstance. 55 mins.
VHS: $21516. $24.95.

Salute to the Edinburgh Tattoo
Not the oldest of the regular tattoos, but perhaps its most famous. Each year the performances attract audiences totaling a quarter of a million people. The rousing music of the massed pipes and drums and the haunting lament of the lone piper cannot fail to stir the heart of even the most reserved Sassenach. Produced by the BBC. 106 mins.
VHS: $10277. $24.95.

Scotland the Brave
Prince Charles, Colonel in Chief of Scotland's legendary 51st Highland Brigade, leads the Gordon Highlanders as they make their farewell parade appearance in Aberdeen. Highlights of this occasion include crack military precision and patriotic pipe and drum music, the Highlanders' final inspection and their last royal salute. The regimental band also stages a farewell concert to the "Fighting 51st" as well as to the people of Scotland. 1995, 50 mins.
VHS: $27342. $19.95.

Scotland Yard
An inside look at the legendary crime-fighting institution, Scotland Yard, hosted by David Niven.
VHS: $02154. $24.95.
Frank Cvitanovich, USA, 1971, 60 mins.

Scotland Yard's Chamber of Crime

An eerie combination of docudrama and stylized re-enactments that investigates some notorious detective stories and unsolved mysteries, this collection of stories is set in the "The Black Museum," Scotland Yard's official crime museum, and includes Jack the Ripper, the Great Train Robbery and Ruth Ellis, the last woman hanged in Britain. 55 mins.
VHS: S18157. $19.95.

Scotland: World of Difference

Travel "North of the Border" and enter the world of the islands and the beautiful Border country; learn some of the history and legends, visit the people at work and play—fishing, playing golf, playing bagpipes, tossing cabers, making whisky. 25 mins.
VHS: S07088. $19.95.

Touring England

Experience England's rich history and heritage in this acclaimed travel tape which explores London, Windsor Castle, Stonehenge, Bath, Oxford and Cambridge, Warwick, Leeds, Liverpool, Wales and more. 65 mins.
VHS: S11515. $29.95.

Touring Royal Castles & Stately Homes of England

Explore the treasures enclosed in eight of the most splendid homes embraced by 1000 years of English history. Stories of Chippendale furniture, stunning interior design, immaculate landscaping, and magnificent porcelain, gold and silver make up the accouterments of true English nobility. Behind the doors of these stately landmarks, meet the aristocrats and riches of eight British estates. 60 mins.
VHS: S15950. $29.95.

Tower of London: The Official Guide

The Tower of London is an infamous Royal palace, fortress and prison, where many a royal prisoner was kept until they were forced to lose their head. Now it houses the unrivaled collection that comprises the Crown Jewels. All of it is magically accessible to the viewer through this video. 45 mins.
VHS: S21517. $24.95.

Treasure Houses of Britain

John Julius Norwich, The Viscount Norwich, explores some of Great Britain's most magnificent estates in this special series of one-hour films. Each program provides the viewer with unprecedented access to these stately homes and takes the time to explore the history, the collections and their architecture, as well as to introduce them to the current owners, who discuss both the privileges and problems of living in a historic house.
Building for Eternity. Explores the Church of St. Mary the Virgin in Bottesford, Hardwick Hall, Burghley House, Wilton House and Chatsworth. 58 mins.
VHS: S08489. $29.95.
Palaces of Reason and Delight. Features Blenheim Palace, Houghton Hall, Bowhill, Newmark Castle, Drumlanrig Castle, Boughton House, West Wycombe Park, St. Lawrence church in West Wycombe and Syo House. 58 mins.
VHS: S08490. $29.95.
Recapturing the Past. Features Belvoir Castle, Plas Newydd, Penrhyn Castle, Wightwick Manor, Haddon Hall, Lindisfarne Castle. 58 mins.
VHS: S08491. $29.95.

Wales: Heritage of a Nation

The late Richard Burton presents this colorful portrait of his native land; the breathtakingly beautiful Welsh landscapes include mountains and valleys, Roman forts, majestic 13th century castles, ancient abbeys, relics of the early industrial age. 25 mins.
VHS: S07089. $19.95.

Welcome to Britain

A whistle-stop tour through the amazing variety of landscape that characterizes Great Britain. The journey starts and ends amid the sights of London, visits the universities of Oxford and Cambridge, great cathedrals such as Canterbury, York and Salisbury, Edinburgh and the romantic Scottish Highlands, the Lake District and the mountains and castles of Wales; Shakespeare's Stratford-upon-Avon; Devon and South Coast resorts. 20 mins.
VHS: S07087. $19.95.

Westminster Abbey

The most famous Anglican church in the world, home to royal weddings and other great affairs of state. This intriguing journey through nearly a thousand years of history views priceless documents and visits parts of the Abbey never before seen by the public. It is a glorious celebration of a building which traces its story back to Edward the Confessor in the year 1050. Produced by the BBC.
VHS: S12387. $19.94.

The Windsors: A Royal Family

A groundbreaking documentary examining the British royal family through five generations, from the crisis of 1917 through the "annus horribilus" of 1992. The four parts of the film are: *I'm Damned If I'm an Alien, Brothers at War, The Image of a Queen* and *Family Affairs*. Four-volume boxed set. 228 mins.
VHS: S23575. $79.98.

british CLASSICS

1984
Edmond O'Brien defies Big Brother in this effective adaptation of George Orwell's classic novel warning of the dangers of a totalitarian state. Michael Redgrave, Jan Sterling and Donald Pleasance complete the first-rate cast.
VHS: S01520. $29.95.
Michael Anderson, Great Britain, 1956, 88 mins.

21 Days
Graham Greene wrote the adaptation of John Galsworthy's play about a pair of lovers (Laurence Olivier and Vivien Leigh) who share a brief time together before Oliver goes on trial for murder. With Leslie Banks, Hay Petrie, Francis L. Sullivan and Robert Newton.
VHS: S19875. $29.95.
Basil Dean, Great Britain, 1937, 75 mins.

Action for Slander
The British drama concerns the honor of a valiant cavalry officer falsely accused of cheating at cards. When a whisper campaign sullies his good reputation, he goes to court to clear his name. With Clive Brook, Ann Todd, Francis Sullavan and Googie Withers.
VHS: S05704. $29.95.
Tim Whelan, Great Britain, 1938, 84 mins.

Adventures of Sadie
In this hilarious British satire, three love-hungry men are shipwrecked on a deserted island with a very young and voluptuous Joan Collins. Originally titled Our Girl Friday, this film is adapted from a novel by Ernest K. Gann. With George Cole, Kenneth More, Robertson Hare and Hattie Jacques.
VHS: S16225. $19.95.
Noel Langley, Great Britain, 1955, 88 mins.

Adventures of Tartu
Robert Donat stars in this Secret Service drama as Captain Terence Stevenson, who is sent to get the formula for a new poison gas being invented by the Nazis in Czechoslovakia and to blow up the factory that's making it. Donat impersonates Captain Jan Tartu, a member of the Romanian Iron Guard. A first-rate British wartime drama. With Valerie Hobson.
VHS: S26391. $29.95.
Harold S. Bucquet, Great Britain, 1943, 103 mins.

Against the Wind
A high school in World War II-era London is actually a training facility for British spies. When student Andrew (Peter Illing) is kidnapped by the Nazis, the rest of the students come to his rescue. With Robert Beatty, Jack Warner and Simone Signoret in her British film debut.
VHS: S27383. $19.95.
Charles Crichton, Great Britain, 1947, 96 mins.

Alfie
Michael Caine stars as Alfie, a wonderfully shallow womanizer who is desperately trying to figure out what life is all about, in this five-time Oscar nominee satirizing the new British generation.
VHS: S00028. $14.95.
Lewis Gilbert, Great Britain, 1965, 99 mins.

Alphabet Murders
Agatha Christie's famous detective, Hercule Poirot, pursues a lunatic murderer who is choosing his victims in alphabetical order. This curious film from director Frank Tashlin offers an interesting combination of slapstick and whodunit suspense. Starring Tony Randall, Anita Ekberg and Robert Morley.
VHS: S13760. $19.98.
Frank Tashlin, Great Britain, 1965, 90 mins.

Amazing Adventure
Cary Grant inherits two million pounds sterling (English money) but wagers he can live on what he earns by his own toil. Poor guy is suffering from underwork. Employment among the 1937 masses teaches valuable lessons and he meets a nice girl. With Mary Brian.
VHS: S05062. $29.95.
Alfred Zeisler, Great Britain, 1937, 61 mins.

The Amorous Adventures of Moll Flanders
Kim Novak is an ambitious servant girl who loses her virtue to a succession of rich gentlemen, but finally settles for a highwayman. A fine cast romps through 18th century England from bedroom to boudoir, including former Novak spouse Richard Johnson, in this adaptation of the Daniel Defoe novel.
VHS: S16623. $19.95.
Terence Young, Great Britain, 1965, 126 mins.

Anna Karenina
Vivien Leigh plays the title role of Anna, the married woman who gives up everything when she falls in love with the handsome young military officer in this British version of Tolstoy's classic tragedy. With magnificent costumes and sets and support from Ralph Richardson as the cold Karenin.
VHS: S07067. $39.95.
Julien Duvivier, Great Britain, 1948, 110 mins.

Anne of the Thousand Days
Richard Burton and Genevieve Bujold star as King Henry VIII of England and Anne Boleyn in the emotionally charged drama about one of history's most tragic love affairs.
VHS: S04860. $49.95.
Laser: Letterboxed. LD74921. $39.99.
Richard Jarrott, Great Britain, 1969, 146 mins.

The Anniversary
Bette Davis does it again as she creates a memorable screen monster in this adaptation of a play by Bill McIllwraith. The atmosphere is claustrophobic as a demanding mother terrorizes her three grown sons. The three are forced to return home on their parents' wedding anniversary despite the fact that their father is dead. Though they are determined to defy the one-eyed Bette, she has a different scenario in mind.
VHS: S27439. $19.95.
Roy Ward Baker, Great Britain, 1967, 95 mins.

As You Like It
Laurence Olivier and Elisabeth Bergner star in this handsome and fairly faithful translation of the Shakespeare comedy, in which Rosalind (Bergner) and her love Orlando (Olivier) withstand the brutal tactics of her uncle Frederick to secure the throne for her deposed father, Duke Senior.
VHS: S18173. $19.95.
Paul Czinner, Great Britain, 1936, 96 mins.

Bachelor of Hearts
Hardy Kruger is a German exchange student at Cambridge with Sylvia Syms and Ronald Lewis in this hysterical comedy. Kruger's character has troubles both with the English language and the English women around him. There is a great sequence where he tries to date two women at the same time.
VHS: S23780. $24.95.
Wolf Rilla, Great Britain, 1958, 94 mins.

Beachcomber
Charles Laughton and Elsa Lanchester in this adaptation of a Somerset Maugham story about an intelligent but drunken Englishman living in the Dutch East Indies.
VHS: S01878. $29.95.
Erich Pommer, Great Britain, 1938, 87 mins.

Beat Girl
An expose-style melodrama about an architect's teenage daughter, who ends up becoming a big disappointment to her family. With Christopher Lee, Gillian Hills, and Noelle Adam.
VHS: S14654. $29.95.
Edmond T. Greville, Great Britain, 1960, 85 mins.

Beau Brummel
A lavish biography of Napoleon's contemporary George Bryan Brummel (Stewart Granger). A peasant who uses bravery, wit and skill to align himself with the Prince of Wales, Brummel simultaneously seduces a powerful noblewoman (Elizabeth Taylor) engaged to a dull fiance. With Peter Ustinov and Robert Morley.
VHS: S18527. $19.98.
Curtis Bernhardt, Great Britain/USA, 1954, 114 mins.

Belles of St. Trinians
The wild and funny students of St. Trinians engage in a hilarious caper. Alastair Sim is in the dual role of the prim headmistress and her slick bookmaker brother.
VHS: S03782. $19.98.
Frank Launder, Great Britain, 1955, 86 mins.

The Bells Go Down
Tommy Trinder and James Mason star in this tragic but good-humored account of fire fighters in London during the Second World War. Set in the East End, the film also includes on-screen appearances by genuine volunteer members of the Auxiliary Fire Service.
VHS: S23781. $24.95.
Basil Dearden, Great Britain, 1943, 89 mins.

Billy Budd
Herman Melville's classic allegory of treachery, adapted from the stage by Peter Ustinov. With Terence Stamp as the young sailor, and Robert Ryan as Billy Budd's superior, the vicious Claggert.
VHS: S01690. $59.98.
Peter Ustinov, Great Britain, 1962, 123 mins.

Bitter Sweet
Noel Coward story about an elderly woman's memories of a romance with an orchestra leader. With Anna Neagle, Fernand Gravet.
VHS: S02577. $19.98.
Herbert Wilcox, Great Britain, 1933, 76 mins.

Black Roses
Near the end of her life, Lilian Harvey asked to see only one of her films, Black Roses. A search of the major archives turned up nothing, and she was never again to see her favorite work. Set in 1900's Russia, Harvey (a ballerina) must sleep with the Tsarist governor in order to save the life of her true love. Dennis Hoey also stars. Mastered from the only known nitrate print. Produced in Germany in 1935, and then remade in Germany and Great Britain in 1936.
VHS: S10964. $29.95.
Paul Martin, Germany/Great Britain, 1936, 79 mins.

The Blue Lamp
An important British detective film which spawned many imitators, The Blue Lamp tells the tale of a young police officer who must capture the criminal who gunned down his older partner. Starring Dirk Bogarde.
VHS: S14660. $29.95.
Basil Dearden, Great Britain, 1949, 84 mins.

Blue Murder at St. Trinian's
Terry Thomas and Alastair Sim star in this continuation of the antic adventures of England's most troublesome girls' school. Sim is once again the headmistress in drag, and this time he is also in jail. That gives Thomas the chance to lead the girls through misadventures on the continent.
VHS: S23782. $24.95.
Frank Launder, Great Britain, 1958, 86 mins.

The Bobo
Peter Sellers is a matador of little professional accomplishment who exists on cheese sandwiches. He makes a bet to romance a highly sought-after courtesan in order to achieve his dream of singing professionally while bullfighting. Britt Ekland is the object of his desires. She was also Mrs. Sellers at the time. With Rossano Brazzi.
VHS: S14567. $19.98.
Robert Parrish, Great Britain, 1967, 103 mins.

Bonnie Prince Charlie
David Niven and Margaret Leighton star in this costume drama about the legendary 16th-century Prince of Scotland. Beginning in Rome, this film charts the Stuart attempt to wrest control back from the Hanoverian regime.
VHS: S23798. $24.95.
Anthony Kimmins, Great Britain, 1948, 118 mins.

Break in the Circle
A political thriller about an unassuming boat owner who's enlisted by mysterious agents to help a brilliant young scientist escape from communist East Germany. With Forrest Tucker, Eva Bartok, Marius Goring and Guy Middleton.
VHS: S18937. $19.95.
Val Guest, Great Britain, 1957, 69 mins.

Brighton Rock
John Boulting's first-rate postwar gangster drama is set in Brighton and stars Richard Attenborough as Pinkie Brown. The script was written by Terrence Rattigan and Graham Greene and based on Greene's novel. Also known as The Young Scarface.
VHS: S26067. $29.95.
John Boulting, Great Britain, 1947, 92 mins.

Broken Melody
Merle Oberon and John Garrick star in this romantic drama about a successful opera singer who is mistakenly imprisoned and must escape to get back to the woman he loves.
VHS: S14662. $29.95.
Bernard Vorhaus, Great Britain, 1934, 62 mins.

Brothers-in-Law
A zany British comedy starring Ian Carmichael, Terry Thomas and Richard Attenborough in the story of two lawyers who share affections for the same girl, but who both lose out to a third guy.
VHS: S09527. $29.95.
Roy Boulting, Great Britain, 1957, 97 mins.

The Browning Version
Superb acting and an incisive screenplay bring to life the story of an aging and embittered boarding schoolteacher's painful last day of lessons. Once a brilliant scholar, he is now the target of his pupils' ridicule. His cruel wife's affair with a younger colleague only adds to his agony as he awaits a new—albeit undesirable—teaching position.
VHS: S16594. $19.95.
Anthony Asquith, Great Britain, 1951, 90 mins.

Captain's Table
John Gregson is a cargo ship skipper put in charge of a luxury liner and finds he must brush up on his table manners. A British comedy on the high seas with Nadia Gray, Peggy Cummins, Donald Sinden and Maurice Denham. Based on the novel Doctor in the House by Richard Gordon.
VHS: S07911. $19.95.
Jack Lee, Great Britain, 1958, 89 mins.

Captive Heart
An archetypal World War II POW drama with a poetic treatment laced with humor and melodrama. The story focuses on a Czech POW who has stolen the papers of a dead British officer and begins to assume the dead officer's identity.
VHS: S01944. $29.95.
Basil Dearden, Great Britain, 1948, 86 mins.

The Caretaker's Daughter
Hugh Wakefield and Derek Bond are featured in this farce. A jealous wife is deceived by the convoluted stories her husband invents with the help of his friends. The gags that prove he is innocent of infidelity are hilarious.
VHS: S23886. $29.95.
Francis Searle, Great Britain, 1953, 83 mins.

Carry On Admiral
Impersonations and shenanigans abound in this riotous comedy portraying hi-jinx in the Royal Navy. A precursor to the "Carry On" series, the film was originally titled The Ship Was Loaded. With David Tomlinson, Peggy Cummins, Alfie Bass and Ronald Shiner.
VHS: S16226. $19.95.
Val Guest, Great Britain, 1957, 81 mins.

Carry On Nurse
Another hilarious spoof from the "Carry On" masters of comedy, this uproarious sendup of hospital people broke boxoffice records in England. Hilarious madcap comedy.
VHS: S04538. $24.95.
Gerald Thomas, Great Britain, 1960

The Case of the Mukkinese Battle Horn
Before there was "Monty Python" there was "The Goon Show" and England roared with laughter. Now you can too. Peter Sellers and Spike Milligan, two thirds of the BBC radio's resident comic madmen, join together in this free form featurette concerning the disappearance of a prize 9th Century relic and Scotland Yard's attempts to retrieve said item.
VHS: S03652. $19.95.
Joseph Sterling, Great Britain, 1956, 27 mins.

Cash (For Love or Money)
An excellent British comedy about a young man (Robert Donat) who suddenly discovers $100,000 in a sack. Before the film is over Donat learns that money can't buy him peace of mind.
VHS: S14633. $29.95.
Zoltan Korda, Great Britain, 1934, 63 mins.

Cast a Dark Shadow
Lewis Gilbert's adaptation of Janet Green's melodrama about a sly charmer (Dirk Bogarde) who murders women for their inheritance. He finds his match when he marries and plots to kill a former barmaid (Margaret Lockwood). With Kay Walsh, Kathleen Harrison, Robert Flemyng and Mona Washbourne.
VHS: S19861. $29.95.
Lewis Gilbert, Great Britain, 1955, 82 mins.

Catherine the Great
The story of Catherine the Great's turbulent rise to power as a ruler of her empire and her many romances, in a lavish production starring Douglas Fairbanks Jr. and Elizabeth Bergner.
VHS: S03331. $19.95.
Paul Czinner, Great Britain, 1934, 100 mins.

Challenge
Breathtaking photography in the film about the conquest of the Matterhorn co-directed by Luis Trenker, who had worked as a mountain guide until being hired in 1921 to act in the film Marvels of Ski.
VHS: S02244. $19.95.
Luis Trenker/V. Korda, Great Britain, 1938, 77 mins.

The Charge of the Light Brigade
Tony Richardson's historical epic, based in part on Tennyson's poem, about the events that led to British involvement in the Crimean War. Richardson's playfulness and mock grandeur about the horrors of war—highlighted by Richard Williams' animation—are "extravagantly pretty...and some of it is very funny (especially John Gielgud as the whimsical, doddering supreme commander of the British forces, and an undressing sequence with Trevor Howard and Jill Bennett). With David Hemmings, Vanessa Redgrave and Harry Andrews.
VHS: S20388. $19.98.
Tony Richardson, Great Britain, 1968, 130 mins.

Children of the Damned
An accomplished sequel to Village of the Damned, about brilliant and misguided young children and their methodical and ruthless quest for power and control. With Ian Hendry, Alan Badel and Barbara Ferris.
VHS: S17534. $19.98.
Anton Leader, Great Britain, 1964, 90 mins.

A Christmas Carol
Alastair Sim is Scrooge in this wonderful adaptation of Charles Dickens' great story.
VHS: S02660. $19.95.
Brian Desmond Hurst, Great Britain, 1951, 86 mins.

Christopher Columbus
Frederic March is the intrepid Italian explorer who opened up a whole new world to the modern age. After convincing Queen Isabella of Spain to supply patronage, Columbus must brave the uncharted seas in search of his dream—a shorter, more direct route to Asia.
VHS: S21994. $19.95.
David MacDonald, Great Britain, 1949, 104 mins.

Circle of Danger
Ray Milland and Naughton Wayne star in this suspense-filled film about a man who must journey to Britain in order to uncover the mystery surrounding his brother's death. The dead man was part of a special combat unit in World War II.
VHS: S23887. $29.95.
Jacques Tourneur, Great Britain, 1955, 86 mins.

Circus of Fear
Christopher Lee stars in this outstanding psychological drama, released in its uncut 91-minute British release version. Based on an Edgar Wallace story of a murderer amidst the odd people who work in the circus. Re-released as *Psycho-Circus*.
VHS: S08416. $29.95.
John Moxey, Great Britain, 1967, 65 mins.

Citadel
Powerful film about a young idealistic doctor who loses his humanitarian goals and takes up a wealthy practice treating rich hypochondriacs, neglecting his wife and friends in the process. With Ralph Richardson, Rex Harrison and Robert Donat.
VHS: S03452. $24.95.
King Vidor, Great Britain, 1938, 114 mins.

The Clouded Yellow
Trevor Howard stars as a leading British agent opposite a beautiful suspect played by Jean Simmons. Howard's character is fired and tries to get away from his dangerous work, only to find himself embroiled in danger once again by the mysterious beauty. They make a wonderfully glamorous pair of fugitives.
VHS: S24866. $39.95.
Ralph Thomas, Great Britain, 1951, 96 mins.

Clouds over Europe
Laurence Olivier stars as the pilot who helps inspector Ralph Richardson outwit a German spy ring intent on sabotaging Britain's airforce. These two stars bring their wit and charm to a story set in front of an ominous backdrop, Europe poised on the brink of war.
VHS: S21029. $19.98.
Laser: LD75171. $34.98.
Tim Whelan, Great Britain, 1939, 78 mins.

The Colditz Story
Allied prisoners who tried to escape from the Nazis were sent to Colditz, castle turned into an escape-proof fortress by the Third Reich. This film, based on P.C. Reid's book, tells the story of a group of prisoners who tried to escape despite seemingly insurmountable barriers.
VHS: S26481. $14.95.
Guy Hamilton, Great Britain, 1954, 93 mins.

Conspirator
The idyllic marriage of a beautiful and privileged, young American woman (Elizabeth Taylor) is shattered by the devastating admission that her husband (Robert Taylor), an officer in the British Army, is a communist agent. With Honor Blackman and Wilfrid Hyde-White.
VHS: S18521. $19.98.
Victor Saville, Great Britain, 1949, 85 mins.

Contraband Spain
Richard Greene is an American agent who rounds up a pack of smugglers and counterfeiters on the French-Spanish border after his brother is murdered, with the help of singer Anouk Aimee.
VHS: S21563. $24.95.
Philip Gartside, Great Britain, 1955, 82 mins.

Convoy
A chilling World War II film produced by Ealing Studios about the intricate games played out between a German pocket battleship and a British convoy. The only significant film of Pen Tennyson, who was subsequently killed in the war. With Clive Brook, John Clements and Edward Chapman.
VHS: S07070. $19.95.
Pen Tennyson, Great Britain, 1941, 90 mins.

Corridor of Mirrors
Eric Portman, Edna Romney and Christopher Lee are featured in this surreal drama about two soul-crossed lovers. A man fixated on the past falls in love with a woman who resembles one of his Renaissance portraits. Deeply hidden secrets, vengeance and even murder pepper this story of a strange obsession.
VHS: S24006. $24.95.
Terence Young, Great Britain, 1948, 94 mins.

Cotton Queen
Jowly, rotund Will Fyffe, the popular Scottish comedian, and lanky Stanley Holloway, the equally popular British performer, headline this snappy comedy which offers an amusing glimpse of English music-hall style entertainment. Highlights include their drunken shenanigans in an amusement park and an odyssey in an inadvertently stolen police car.
VHS: S13516. $29.95.
Joe Rock, Great Britain, 1937, 80 mins.

Courageous Mr. Penn
Clifford Evans and Deborah Kerr star in this biography about the original Quaker, William Penn. He valiantly fought British persecution until he was permitted to go to America. There he struggled and eventually founded the City of Brotherly Love, Philadelphia. Kerr is magnificent as his converted wife.
VHS: S24005. $24.95.
Lance Comfort, Great Britain, 1941, 88 mins.

The Courtneys of Curzon Street
A multilayered melodrama that covers the years 1900-45 as a charismatic, wealthy, young financier upsets the social balance by falling in love with his housemaid. Also known as *The Courtney Affair*. With Anna Neagle, Michael Wilding, Gladys Young and Coral Browne.
VHS: S18939. $19.95.
Herbert Wilcox, Great Britain, 1947, 112 mins.

Crimes of Stephen Hawke
Tod Slaughter is the title character in this film treatment of one of his Grand Guignol theatrical melodramas. He plays a royal money lender who enjoys breaking the spines of strangers in his off hours. With Eric Portman, Marjorie Taylor and Gerald Berry as Miles Archer. What, no Sam Spade?
VHS: S04043. $29.95.
George King, Great Britain, 1936, 70 mins.

The Cruel Sea
One of the great war films, full of atmospheric detailing which captures the essence of the Battle of the Atlantic.
VHS: S04283. $39.95.
Charles Frend, Great Britain, 1953, 121 mins.

A Cry from the Streets
Max Bygraves stars in this semi-documentary style drama about orphan children in England. Also starring Barbara Murray and Colin Petersen.
VHS: S14668. $29.95.
Lewis Gilbert, Great Britain, 1957, 100 mins.

Cry, the Beloved Country
Based on Alan Paton's excellent novel about the poverty and abuses of the Apartheid Policy in South Africa, this poignant film features powerful performances from Canada Lee, Sidney Poitier and Geoffrey Keen.
VHS: S14783. $69.95.
Zoltan Korda, Great Britain, 1951, 111 mins.

The Dam Busters
Michael Redgrave, Richard Todd and Ursula Jeans are featured in this thrilling World War II yarn. It revolves around an ingenious British plot to sabotage a strategic dam. Suspense, spies and confounding plot twists make this well-crafted film a true crowd-pleaser.
VHS: S23005. $14.95.
Michael Anderson, Great Britain, 1954, 119 mins.

Damn the Defiant!
The commander of a British warship must battle Napoleon's fleet and his own mutinous crew in this thrilling historical adventure. The production, as a whole, shows fine attention to historic detail and stars Alec Guiness and Dirk Bogarde.
VHS: S13573. $14.95.
Lewis Gilbert, Great Britain, 1962, 101 mins.

Dark Journey
Vivien Leigh stars as a double agent during World War I in Stockholm, who becomes involved with the head of German Intelligence, Conrad Veidt.
VHS: S03591. $19.95.
Victor Saville, Great Britain, 1937, 82 mins.

Dark of the Sun
Ruthless mercenaries (Rod Taylor and Jim Brown) venture into the Congo to save refugees trapped by war and upheaval. They also have a reward for this selfless behavior in mind, the recovery of some valuable diamonds. It's a tense drama where the basic human impulses, greed and altruism, come into direct conflict.
VHS: S21016. $19.98.
Jack Cardiff, Great Britain, 1968, 101 mins.

Darling
Landmark British film made during the Kitchen Sink Drama period features Julie Christie as a woman who becomes a prisoner of her own modeling success, leaves her husband for a sexy TV commentator (Laurence Harvey), until she falls restless and falls in love with a jet setter.
Laser: LD70358. $69.95.
John Schlesinger, Great Britain, 1965, 122 mins.

David Copperfield
Robin Phillips, Susan Hampshire, Edith Evans, Michael Redgrave, Laurence Olivier and Richard Attenborough are among the first-rate cast in this adaptation of Charles Dickens' classic tale of a re-discovered orphan. This fine tale is full of more heartrending twists than anything written in our own time.
VHS: S23104. $19.95.
Delbert Mann, Great Britain, 1970, 110 mins.

Dead Lucky
Martin's stab at gambling wins him a fortune—and traps him between a con artist, an assassin, and a mysterious seductress. In gripping conclusion, he becomes both victim and killer. Adapted from the award-winning novel *Lake of Darkness*.
VHS: S14327. $49.95.
Montgomery Tully, Great Britain, 1960, 91 mins.

Dead of Night
Michael Redgrave stars in this spine-tingling suspense classic featuring dreams, premonitions, hallucinations and some well-timed comic breathers. Redgrave is feverishly convincing in the role of the ventriloquist who achieves the ultimate in schizophrenia.
VHS: S00314. $14.95.
Crichton/Cavalcanti, Great Britain, 1955, 104 mins.

Decameron Nights
Joan Fontaine, Joan Collins and Louis Jourdan star in this film adaptation of Boccaccio's classic work, *The Decameron*. Jordan is the author trying to woo Fontaine, who plays a young widow. This is the backdrop for three rather bawdy stories set in a lushly costumed and photographed film.
VHS: S23772. $24.95.
Hugo Fregonese, Great Britain, 1953, 87 mins.

Demi-Paradise
Laurence Olivier stars as a Russian engineer whose preconceived notions about England are changed when he encounters friendship, love and support for his war-torn country. A satirical comedy populated by eccentrics.
VHS: S01626. $29.95.
Anthony Asquith, Great Britain, 1943, 112 mins.

Detective (aka Father Brown)
Alec Guiness is Father Brown in this film adaptation of the beloved character created in G.K. Chesterton's popular mysteries. The eccentric priest has a valuable cross stolen by Peter Finch on a journey from London to Rome. With Joan Greenwood and Bernard Lee. A gem of a mystery, not to be confused with the Frank Sinatra film.
VHS: S07584. $19.95.
Robert Hamer, Great Britain, 1954, 91 mins.

The Devil's Disciple
An adaptation of George Bernard Shaw's satire about the Revolutionary War, with Laurence Olivier as a British officer whose arrival in New England sets off the patriotic fervor of Burt Lancaster and Kirk Douglas.
VHS: S17986. $19.98.
Guy Hamilton, Great Britain, 1959, 83 mins.

Dinner at The Ritz
The hotel, not the cracker. David Niven has his first starring role in this murder mystery about the death of a French banker. The daughter of the banker (Annabella) seeks to clear the family name. The dashing Niven is only too happy to be of assistance. With Paul Lukas and Romney Brent.
VHS: S09830. $19.95.
Harold Schuster, Great Britain, 1937, 77 mins.

Divorce of Lady X
Merle Oberon, Laurence Olivier and Ralph Richardson star in this sophisticated English comedy in which a London barrister allows a pretty lady to spend an "innocent night" in his flat, and finds out that he may be named as a correspondent in a divorce suit.
VHS: S02522. $19.95.
Laser: LD75181. $34.98.
Alexander Korda, Great Britain, 1938, 90 mins.

Doctor at Large
Dirk Bogard stars as Dr. Sparrow, an intern who finds himself trapped in a series of hysterical situations. Between the neurotic women patients of the doctor he interns with and the seductive young wife of another miserly doctor, Dr. Sparrow has his hands full. With Muriel Pavlow, Donald Sinden, James Robertson Justice and Shirley Eaton.
VHS: S06432. $14.95.
Ralph Thomas, Great Britain, 1957, 104 mins.

Doctor at Sea
Sex kitten Brigitte Bardot cruises the high seas as Dirk Bogarde signs on as the ship's doctor, determined to remain a bachelor. Second in the series.
VHS: S06433. $19.98.
Ralph Thomas, Great Britain, 1956, 93 mins.

Dreaming Lips
Elisabeth Bergner gives an enchanting performance as Gaby, married to an orchestra conductor, who falls in love with a world-famous violinist (the young Raymond Massey). A witty, sophisticated tale of illicit romance.
VHS: S05603. $29.95.
Paul Czinner, Great Britain, 1937, 69 mins.

The Drum
The British Army helps an Indian prince to resist his usurping uncle. Armed with a drum, the boy keeps time for the cavalry and helps to save the Raj. Complete with the original theatrical trailer, this exciting adventure stars Sabu.
VHS: S16630. $19.98.
Zoltan Korda, Great Britain, 1938, 104 mins.

Elephant Boy
An early docu-drama about a young boy—the first screen appearance of Sabu—who knows the location of an elephant burial ground.
VHS: S04323. $19.98.
Laser: LD75188. $34.98.
Robert Flaherty/Zoltan Korda, Great Britain, 1937, 80 mins.

Endless Night
Agatha Christie's inimitable style is brought to the screen in this adaptation of her chilling novel, with Hywell Bennett the chauffer who marries a rich American girl (Hayley Mills) and moves into a dream house which turns out to be a nightmare.
VHS: S04544. $14.95.
Bruce Brown, Great Britain, 1966, 96 mins.

Evergreen
Unseen in the United States for 30 years, *Evergreen* is an enchanting film and remains one of the most fondly remembered musicals of the 1930s. Stunning Jessie Matthews became internationally famous for her role in this classic show business tale about a young girl who becomes a stage sensation when she begins masquerading as her long-retired mother. Music and lyrics by Rodgers and Hart.
VHS: S06133. $39.95.
Victor Saville, Great Britain, 1934, 91 mins.

Evil Under the Sun
Peter Ustinov is a delight as Hercule Poirot, Agatha Christie's detective hero. With James Mason, Diana Rigg. England, 102 mins.
VHS: S04545. $19.99.

Fallen Idol
In one of his finest performances, Ralph Richardson plays a butler who is idolized by eight-year-old Bobby Henrey. Drawn into the butler's tangled personal life during a weekend when his parents are away, the boy learns that Richardson is accused of having murdered his wife. Screenplay by Graham Greene from his story *The Basement Room*.
VHS: S00426. $39.95.
Carol Reed, Great Britain, 1948, 92 mins.

Fanny by Gaslight
This romantic melodrama, set in the Victorian era, tells the story of the comely and illegitimate Fanny, who must somehow be saved from the lustful advances of a lascivious Lord. With James Mason.
VHS: S14659. $29.95.
Anthony Asquith, Great Britain, 1944, 108 mins.

Far from the Madding Crowd
John Schlesinger directed this first-rate adaptation of the novel by Thomas Hardy about a tempestuous Dorset girl and her profound influence on three different men—a young cavalry officer, a wealthy landowner and a herdsman. With brilliant performances from Julie Christie, Peter Finch, Terence Stamp, and Alan Bates.
VHS: S11551. $29.95.
Laser: LD70567. $39.98.
John Schlesinger, Great Britain, 1967, 169 mins.

Ferry to Hong Kong
Orson Welles plays the straight-laced ferry boat skipper and Curt Jurgens is the drunken Austrian who are on their way to Macao in this classic comedy.
VHS: S10007. $14.98.
Lewis Gilbert, Great Britain, 1961, 103 mins.

Fighting Pilot
Richard Talmadge and Victor Mace star in this classic adventure film made at a time when talkies were still a novelty. Talmadge is a true warrior who must rescue plans for a secret military aircraft.
VHS: S23774. $24.95.
Noel Mason Smith, Great Britain, 1933, 62 mins.

Fire Down Below
Rita Hayworth declares that "armies have marched over me" but that doesn't deter Robert Mitchum and Jack Lemmon from putting on their hiking boots. Tempers flare in the Caribbean as two smugglers do more than arm wrestle for Rita's company. With Anthony Newley. Filmed in Tobago and London.
VHS: S04748. $19.95.
Robert Parrish, Great Britain, 1957, 116 mins.

Fire over England
Splendid historical spectacle set during the reign of Queen Elizabeth I; dashing young Laurence Olivier plays a daring Englishman who thwarts a Spanish plot against the Queen. Vivien Leigh, Flora Robson and Raymond Massey co-star.
VHS: S00442. $19.95.
Laser: Side 1 CLV. Side 2 CAV. LD71950. $39.95.
William K. Howard, Great Britain, 1937, 89 mins.

Five Golden Hours
Ernie Kovacs is cast as Aldo Bondi, a professional mourner who lives off the generosity of grieving widows. He meets his match when he sincerely falls for broke Italian baroness Cyd Charisse, who has her own ideas about love and money. With Dennis Price, John Le Mesurier, Kay Hammond, Ron Moody and George Sanders as Mr. Bing, the fake lunatic.
VHS: S15897. $19.95.
Mario Zampi, Great Britain/Italy, 1961, 89 mins.

Flame over India
When a Moslem insurgency topples a British fortress in rural India, it's up to a few dignitaries to speed the Maharaja's son to safety. Escaping the fort in a rusty old train, the motley crew faces suspense and adventure, including a traitor in their midst. With Kenneth More, Lauren Bacall and Herbert Lom.
VHS: S16103. $29.95.
J. Lee Thompson, Great Britain, 1959, 130 mins.

Forever and a Day
An all-star British cast unparalleled in the history of motion pictures was assembled for this epic story that spans more than a century—the elaborate tale of a grand old London house and the generations who lived in it from 1804 through the German blitzkrieg of WWII. With Ray Milland, Merle Oberon, Charles Laughton, Claude Rains, Buster Keaton, Ida Lupino, Herbert Marshall, Roland Young and many others, and the directorial talents of Rene Clair, Edmund Goulding, Cedric Hardwicke, Victor Saville, Robert Stevenson and Herbert Wilcox. USA, 1943, 105 mins.
VHS: S12250. $19.95.

Four Sided Triangle
Barbara Payton, once *The Bride of the Gorilla*, finds herself in another fine mess. Two clever scientists are in love with her but she loves only one of them so they make two of her. Two Barbaras should be enough to go around but will they?
VHS: S04091. $29.95.
Terence Fisher, Great Britain, 1953, 81 mins.

Frieda
One of the gems of post-war British filmmaking, an unusually unsentimental drama that makes use of newsreel footage and explores the bitterness of the English people against the Germans within the context of a love story.
VHS: S02171. $29.95.
Basil Dearden, Great Britain, 1947, 98 mins.

Frozen Limits
The best of the films made by the Crazy Gang, a group of three English music hall duos. When the sextet orders fish and chips, it comes wrapped in a 40-year-old newspaper which hawked the discovery of gold in Alaska. The group leaves the big city and heads north, where they find an old prospector who can't quite find his gold mine. A fast-paced comedy.
VHS: S04483. $19.95.
Edward Black, Great Britain, 1939

Funeral in Berlin
Michael Caine stars as British espionage agent Harry Palmer in the second of three films based on the books by Len Deighton. His mission is to assist a Russian defector in the title city. He isn't pleased when the plans change without his knowledge. With Oscar Homolka, Paul Hubschmid and Eva Renzi.
VHS: S10835. $14.95.
Laser: LD75197. $34.98.
Guy Hamilton, Great Britain, 1966, 102 mins.

The Galloping Major
Basil Radford has a scheme to get rich using race horses. Naturally it all goes wrong at first, but after some great laughs the mistaken horse proves its mettle and brings in a happy ending. Includes a cast of great British comics and character actors.
VHS: S23982. $24.95.
Henry Cornelius, Great Britain, 1951, 82 mins.

The Gasbags
The Crazy Gang, a troupe of Brit funnymen, balloons over into enemy territory during World War II. Misadventure follows upon hilarious misadventure, including an attempt by one of the troupe to pass as Hitler. Despite it all, they return home heroes with a secret surprise.
VHS: S23783. $24.95.
Marcel Varnel, Great Britain, 1940, 77 mins.

Gaslight
The first version of Patrick Hamilton's play about an insane criminal who drives his wife crazy in order to find the hidden jewels. Despite its low budget, the film succinctly conveys a sense of madness and evil. MGM supposedly tried to destroy the negative of this original when they made the remake. With Anton Walbrook, Diana Wynyard, Frank Pettingell and Cathleen Cordell.
VHS: S16270. $29.95.
Thorold Dickinson, Great Britain, 1939, 84 mins.

Georgy Girl

An offbeat English comedy of modern day morals, with Lynn Redgrave as the ugly-duckling, and James Mason as the wealthy married man who wants her for his mistress. With a terrific performance from Charlotte Rampling as the violinist-roommate.
VHS: S03299. $19.95.
Silvio Narizzano, Great Britain, 1966, 100 mins.

The Gilded Cage

Alex Nichol, Veronica Hurst and Clifford Evans are cast in this engaging mystery-thriller. A US Air Force officer arrives in London to visit his brother and is immediately immersed in a plot centered around a valuable painting titled The Gilded Cage. Naturally there are mysterious characters and beautiful women scattered amidst the intrigue.
VHS: S24013. $24.95.
John Gilling, Great Britain, 1954, 78 mins.

Girls at Sea

Three young women are stranded on a battleship following a raucous shipboard party, with hilarious consequences. With Guy Rolfe, Ronald Shiner, Alan White and Anne Kimbell.
VHS: S18949. $19.95.
Gilbert Gunn, Great Britain, 1958, 80 mins.

Glory at Sea

Trevor Howard plays the demanding and unpopular commanding officer of a broken-down battleship. The hostile attitudes on deck take a turnabout after a conflict with the Germans proves the ancient battleship is still able to perform. With Richard Attenborough and Sonny Tufts.
VHS: S16107. $29.95.
Compton Bennett, Great Britain, 1952, 90 mins.

The Golden Salamander

Based on the suspenseful adventure novel by Victor Canning, this spirited version is also big on mystery and intrigue. Shot on location in Tunis, it also stars Trevor Howard at his peak as a romantic leading man and then new French star Anouk Aimee.
VHS: S14636. $29.95.
Ronald Neame, Great Britain, 1950, 96 mins.

Great Day

Flora Robson heads a stellar British cast as one of the heroic women who worked day and night for victory in wartime England.
VHS: S12376. $19.98.
Lance Comfort, USA, 1946, 62 mins.

The Great McGonagal

In one of his more outlandish roles, comic genius Peter Sellers, playing Queen Victoria of England, encourages a poor (bad) poet, named Willie McGonagal, to keep on writing. England, 87 mins.
VHS: S15031. $19.95.

Greek Street

An entertaining story of London's Italian quarter by Robert Stevenson. Starring Sari Marizia and Arthur Hambling.
VHS: S15177. $29.95.
Sinclair Hill, Great Britain, 1930, 51 mins.

Green for Danger

A puzzler for both Scotland Yard and the audience as Inspector Cockrill (Alastair Sim) is called in to investigate a murder in a hospital filled with suspicious doctors and staff. Cockrill's interrogation brings them all into question concerning both motive and opportunity and places Cockrill high in the cinema tradition of the droll Yard detective who always gets his man.
VHS: S12955. $19.95.
Sidney Gilliat, Great Britain, 1947, 91 mins.

The Guinea Pig

Richard Attenborough, Bernard Miles and Joan Hickson are featured in this dramatic look at changing educational ideals. A tobacconist's son is admitted to a posh public school as an experiment. The reactions of the staff and the other boys could not have been predicted. Bernard Miles wrote the screenplay.
VHS: S25015. $19.95.
John Boulting, Great Britain, 1948, 97 mins.

Half a Sixpence

Musical based on an H.G. Wells story about a draper's assistant who suddenly inherits a fortune and attempts to move up in society. Starring Tommy Steele and Julia Foster.
VHS: S13785. $19.95.
George Sidney, Great Britain, 1967, 148 mins.

The Happiest Days of Your Life

Alastair Sim and Margaret Rutherford star in this madcap comedy about a group of girls accidentally billeted at a boys school. As the headmaster and headmistress join forces to fend off school inspectors, parents and kids, they find they are well in charge of inspired anarchy.
VHS: S20854. $19.95.
Frank Lauder, USA, 1950, 83 mins.

Harassed Hero

Guy Middleton stars with Evelyn Brook Jones in this comedy about a hapless bachelor who finds himself mixed in with an unsavory lot of counterfeiters. Seriously funny trouble ensues for all concerned.
VHS: S23892. $29.95.
Maurice Elvey, Great Britain, 1954, 72 mins.

The Hasty Heart

Ronald Reagan and Patricia Neal star in this stirring World War II drama about wounded soldiers in a hospital in Burma. They are forced to question many deeply held beliefs when an embittered Scotsman with a few weeks left to live enters their compound.
VHS: S24727. $19.98.
Vincent Sherman, Great Britain, 1949, 101 mins.

The Haunted Strangler

Boris Karloff stars as a novelist who ends up investigating the haunted graves of a prison cemetery when he sets out to prove that the wrong man died for a crime committed 20 years ago.
VHS: S22987. $19.98.
Robert Day, Great Britain, 1958, 81 mins.

Head over Heels

A musical revue about a complicated romantic triangle as a career singer can't distinguish between the two men who are attracted to her. With Jessie Matthews, Robert Flemyng, Louis Borell and Romney Brent.
VHS: S18950. $19.95.
Sonnie Hale, Great Britain, 1937, 81 mins.

Heavens Above

Peter Sellers, Cecil Parker and Ian Carmichael star in this gentle satire about mixed up vicars. Sellers is mistakenly appointed to a rich parish, which is quite a contrast to his last job as a prison minister. The man who didn't get the cushy job, Carmichael, is Sellers' exact opposite. It's a great set-up for humor handled with delicacy.
VHS: S23784. $24.95.
John Boulting, Great Britain, 1963, 105 mins.

The Hill

Sean Connery stars in this tense, unforgiving drama. During World War II, a British stockade in the African desert has a unique torture device. It is a hill over 60 feet high and 210 feet long. Prisoners are forced to climb its steep sides under an unrelenting sun. Rarely has the sadistic nature of the all-male military world been so startlingly captured on celluloid.
VHS: S27573. $19.98.
Sidney Lumet, Great Britain, 1965, 122 mins.

The Horse's Mouth

Alec Guinness delivers a classic performance in this wonderful British comedy based on the novel by Joyce Cary about a non-conformist painter who seeks out bizarre surfaces for his work.
VHS: S04319. $24.95.
Laser: LD70382. $39.95.
Ronald Neame, Great Britain, 1958, 93 mins.

How I Won the War

John Lennon stars in his first solo film performance. A hilarious, surreal collage of battle footage and fast-moving comedy lampooning the absurdity of war. The tenuous plot concerns a troop of British soldiers with a mission to set up a cricket match behind enemy lines in order to impress a visiting V.I.P. Sheer, brilliant lunacy. With Jack MacDowran, Roy Kinnear and Lee Montague.
VHS: S00588. $59.95.
Richard Lester, Great Britain, 1967, 111 mins.

Hue and Cry

An outrageous romp of a movie with Alastair Sim having a field day as he plays a meek detective-story writer who, together with a group of kids, crack a gang of thieves. Terrific British comedy from the same team who made The Lavender Hill Mob.
VHS: S09526. $29.95.
Charles Crichton, Great Britain, 1947, 82 mins.

Hungry Hill

Margaret Lockwood, Dennis Price, Jean Simmons and Cecil Parker star in this costume drama about a wealthy Victorian era family. Despite appearances, the greatness of this Irish family dynasty is built upon generations of treachery. Based on Daphne du Maurier's novel.
VHS: S23894. $29.95.
Brian Desmond Hurst, Great Britain, 1947, 108 mins.

I Am a Camera

An earlier non-musical adaptation of the Christopher Isherwood stories that inspired Cabaret, starring Julie Harris as the outrageous Sally Bowles (Shall we have a drink first or shall we go right to bed?) and Laurence Harvey as Isherwood in pre-Nazi Berlin.
VHS: S00593. $24.95.
Henry Cornelius, Great Britain, 1955, 99 mins.

I Love You, Alice B. Toklas

Corporate lifer Peter Sellers tunes in and drops out in this landmark sixties comedy. "Sellers has never been better" (Leonard Maltin).
VHS: S14569. $19.98.
Laser: LD71474. $34.98.
Hy Averback, USA, 1968, 93 mins.

I Stand Condemned

Laurence Olivier plays a young Russian officer who falls in love with a Russian society girl in 1916. She is engaged to a wealthy contractor who trumps up espionage charges against his younger rival. Olivier looks quite dashing in his uniform and moustache.
VHS: S05068. $29.95.
Anthony Asquith, Great Britain, 1936, 71 mins.

I'm All Right Jack

Britain's great comic talents join forces in this hilariously witty spoof of the absurdities of the labor movement. Starring Peter Sellers and Ian Carmichael, with Richard Attenborough. This is the film that launched Sellers on the road to international stardom. His portrait of a shop steward coming apart at the seams is a masterpiece of characterization.
VHS: S00604. $39.95.
John Boulting, Great Britain, 1969, 101 mins.

If I Were Rich

A clever, witty, Depression-era British drama with Robert Donat as the man who goes through life avoiding paying his bills while waiting for prosperity to return.
VHS: S09213. $29.95.
Zoltan Korda, Great Britain, 1933, 63 mins.

If...

A sometimes shocking portrait of life in a repressive English boarding school. Three non-conforming senior schoolboys revolt against practically everything. Anderson skillfully employs both professional and non-professional actors in building to a shattering, violent climax.
VHS: S00606. $49.95.
Laser: LD75354. $29.98.
Lindsay Anderson, Great Britain, 1969, 111 mins.

The Immortal Battalion (The Way Ahead)

Based on a script by Eric Ambler, with a foreword by Quentin Reynolds, a rousing drama of War—the story of newly recruited civilians who are molded into a hardened battalion of fighting men. With David Niven, Stanley Holloway, Reginald Tate, Peter Ustinov.
VHS: S03058. $19.95.
Carol Reed, Great Britain, 1944, 89 mins.

The Importance of Being Earnest

Oscar Wilde's play took over 57 years to reach the big screen but it was worth the wait. A colorful theatrical film about mating rituals in Great Britain before the turn of the century, when manners and background were more important than the truth. A grand cast includes Michael Redgrave, Joan Greenwood, Margaret Rutherford, Michael Dennison and Edith Evans as Lady Bracknell.
VHS: Out of print. For rental only.
Laser: LD75061. $39.99.
Anthony Asquith, Great Britain, 1952, 95 mins.

Impulse

A young married man gets mixed up with gangsters and an illicit love affair when his wife goes to visit her mother. Starring Arthur Kennedy and Constance Smith.
VHS: S14673. $19.95.
Charles De Latour, Great Britain, 1956, 81 mins.

The Informer

Lars Hanson stars as a man desperate to flee the poverty of Ireland. He turns in an IRA man for cash and runs off to America, but he is haunted by guilt. Based on a novel by Liam O'Flaherty, this film captures the tormented soul of traitor.
VHS: S26987. $24.95.
Arthur Robinson, Great Britain, 1929, 83 mins.

The Inheritance (Uncle Silas)

Jean Simmons and Derrick DeMarney are featured in this suspense-laden thriller. A Victorian girl is sent to her uncle's home after the death of her father. Unfortunately her uncle is more interested in her inheritance than her well-being and she finds herself locked in a desperate struggle to remain alive.
VHS: S23895. $29.95.
Charles Frank, Great Britain, 1947, 90 mins.

The Inn of the Sixth Happiness

A simple English servant girl, played by Ingrid Bergman, travels to China to become a missionary. Based on the true life story of Gladice Alyward, this biography reveals the difficulties she encountered while pursuing the daunting task of founding an orphanage in the 1930's. Her goal was well within reach when political turmoil forced her into an even more heroic role.
VHS: S20705. $19.98.
Laser: LD75379. $49.98.
Mark Robson, Great Britain, 1958, 158 mins.

Innocents in Paris

Alastair Sim, Margaret Rutherford and Christopher Lee are just some of the British stars loaded into this delightful comic romp. Seven different eccentrics are off to France. Crossing the channel, each has a wacky adventure made all the funnier by a stiff upper lip.
VHS: S23112. $24.95.
Gordon Perry, Great Britain, 1953, 60 mins.

Interrupted Journey

Richard Todd and Valerie Harper play an indecisive couple running away together. Suddenly Todd's character gets cold feet and backs out to return to his wife. Unfortunately, the train he is on with his would-be lover crashes shortly thereafter and she dies. The plot contains an even graver twist, transforming this film into a compelling murder mystery.
VHS: S24009. $24.95.
Daniel Birt, Great Britain, 1949, 82 mins.

Ipcress File

First-rate espionage story based on the novel by Len Deighton and the first in a series of Harry Palmer spy mysteries. Michael Caine stars as former petty crook turned myopic secret agent, who gets caught up investigating the disappearances of several noted British scientists. Eerie musical score by John Barry.
VHS: S02944. $14.98.
Sidney J. Furie, Great Britain, 1965, 108 mins

The Iron Duke

Not a statue of John Wayne but the historical film biography of the Duke of Wellington, Arthur Wellesley, who defeated Napoleon's army at Waterloo. The film deals with the years 1815-16 and stars George Arliss as the Iron Duke. With Gladys Cooper, Emlyn Williams, Franklin Dyall and Ellaline Terriss as Duchess Kitty. B&W.
VHS: S07072. $39.95.
Victor Saville, Great Britain, 1935, 80 mins.

Isadora

A terrific portrait of the eccentric, tempestuous American dancer who lived by her own rules, featuring an exceptional performance by Vanessa Redgrave, and co-starring Jason Robards and James Fox as Isadora's famous lovers.
VHS: S00638. $29.95.
Karel Reisz, Great Britain, 1969, 168 mins.

The Italian Job

A British comedy set in Turin about a plan orchestrated by Michael Caine and playwright Noel Coward to steal $4 million in gold bullion pivots on diverting authorities with a complex and unruly "traffic jam." Some delirious action, chase scenes and set pieces and charming, local color.
VHS: S16895. $19.95.
Peter Collinson, Great Britain, 1969, 99 mins.

Jason and the Argonauts

Special effects wizard Ray Harryhausen provided the effects for this mythological adventure, which stars Todd Armstrong as the sailor and explorer who returns to the kingdom of Thessaly after a 20-year voyage, to make his rightful claim to the throne, but who must first find the magical fleece. Bernard Herrmann wrote the score.
VHS: S08522. $14.95.
Laser: CAV. LD71557. $99.95.
Don Chaffey, Great Britain, 1963, 104 mins.

Java Head

Gerrit, the son of a fair-minded seafaring man, is driven from the community by the stern family of the girl he wants to marry, and he's forced to set off on a long sea voyage. With Anna May Wong, Ralph Richardson.
VHS: S09232. $29.95.
J. Walter Ruben, Great Britain, 1934, 82 mins.

Journey for Margaret

A heartbreaking tale about orphaned children trying to survive in a ravaged, bombed out London, based on W.L. White's book as an American correspondent. Robert Young is an American journalist whose life is caught in the crossfire. With Laraine Day, Fay Bainter and Nigel Bruce).
VHS: S17338. $19.98.
W.S. Van Dyke, Great Britain, 1942, 81 mins.

Journey Together

Richard Attenborough and Edward G. Robinson star in this realistic portrayal of American fliers in England during World War I.
VHS: S09532. $29.95.
John Boulting, Great Britain, 1946, 80 mins.

The Jungle Book (Sabu)

Sabu stars as the boy who grew up among the animals and learned to speak their languages in this film based on Rudyard Kipling's tales.
VHS: S01900. $19.95.
Zoltan Korda, USA, 1942, 109 mins.

Khartoum

Charlton Heston vs. Laurence Olivier. Chuck plays British General Charles "Chinese" Gordon. Lord Larry is the Mahdi, the leader of thousands of angry Sudanese tribesmen who would like to remove the colonial influence from their little town. The epic 317 day siege, set in 1885, is well told, with a cast of thousands, some of which include Nigel Green, Alexander Knox, Johnny Sekka and Ralph Richardson as Mr. Gladstone. Narration provided by Leo Genn.
VHS: S12531. $19.98.
Basil Dearden, Great Britain, 1966, 134 mins.

A Kid for Two Farthings

Never underestimate the power of a child's imagination, especially if it's the charming Jonathan Ashmore, who plays Joe in this heartwarming sentimental fantasy from England—the story of a young boy who is convinced that through the powers of a unicorn he can grant the wishes of his mother and friends, who live in a poor part of London.
VHS: S14655. $39.95.
Carol Reed, Great Britain, 1955, 96 mins.

Kiepura in My Song for You

This slight but delightful comedy features Jan Kiepura as an opera singer who sets to work wooing a lovely young woman.
VHS: S24851. $34.95.
Maurice Elvey, Great Britain, 1934, 89 mins.

Kind Hearts and Coronets

A perennial favorite featuring Alec Guinness' famous performance in which he plays eight separate roles in the black comedy of a castoff member of an aristocratic family who sets out to eliminate them all. The sardonic script was written by director Robert Hamer, one of Ealing Studios best writer/directors.
VHS: S00676. $14.98.
Robert Hamer, Great Britain, 1949, 104 mins.

King Solomon's Mines

The original exciting adventure adapted from H. Rider Haggard's famous story of the search for legendary diamond mines in the heart of Africa. Paul Robeson, Cedric Hardwicke and Roland Young star.
VHS: S00682. $39.95.
Laser: LD71696. $34.98.
Robert Stevenson, Great Britain, 1937, 80 mins.

The King's Rhapsody

And exiled king leaves his lover in order to return home to a cold, politically arranged marriage. A classic treatment of the love versus duty theme starring the incomparable Errol Flynn.
VHS: S14658. $29.95.
Herbert Wilcox, Great Britain, 1955, 93 mins.

Kipps
Based on H.G. Wells' satirical comedy about a shopkeeper who inherits a fortune and tries to enter high society. With Michael Redgrave, Diana Wynyard.
VHS: S00683. $29.95.
Carol Reed, Great Britain, 1941, 112 mins.

The Knack…and How to Get It
Richard Lester's chic film set in swinging 60s London about three men (Michael Crawford, Ray Brooks and Donal Donnelly) who occupy the same London house, and a beautiful country girl (Rita Tushingham) who moves in with them. Sexual hijinks abound as the three angle to seduce women, with the charismatic Brooks in the lead as a master of killer charm.
VHS: S20400. $19.98.
Richard Lester, Great Britain, 1965, 84 mins.

Ladies Who Do
In this madcap comedy, a group of cleaning ladies face off against a real estate robber baron who wants to tear down their homes for an office tower complex. Joining forces with a retired colonel, played by Robert Morley, they use stock market secrets from the waste paper baskets they empty to gain some vital economic clout. Peggy Mount also stars.
VHS: S22472. $29.95.
C.M. Pennington Richards, Great Britain, 1963, 90 mins.

Lady in Distress
Also known as *A Window in London*, the intriguing story of a struggling couple who get caught up in an entertaining murder drama. Paul Lukas, Sally Gray and Michael Redgrave star.
VHS: S05383. $24.95.
Herbert Mason, Great Britain, 1939, 59 mins.

Lady L
Peter Ustinov's stylish comedy is adapted from Romain Gary's popular novel, which chronicles the seedy characters and dangerous romantics who inhabit an aristocratic turn-of-the-century Europe. A "film of great wit, urbane elegance, and fast-paced nuttiness" (*The New York Times*). With Paul Newman, David Niven, Sophia Loren and Philippe Noiret.
VHS: S19489. $19.98.
Peter Ustinov, Great Britain, 1965, 107 mins.

Ladykillers
Another wonderfully bizarre comedy from England's Ealing Studios, this starring Alec Guiness as the slightly demented leader of a group of thieves planning their heist in a boarding house while pretending to be a chamber orchestra.
VHS: S00719. $14.98.
Alexander MacKendrick, Great Britain, 1955, 87 mins.

Land of Fury
Jack Hawkins, Glynis Johns and Noel Purcell are confronted with the beauty and dangers of pioneer life in the wilds of New Zealand. The land and the people who have always lived there, the Native Maoris, offer stiff resistance to the settlers' dreams.
VHS: S23896. $29.95.
Ken Annakin, Great Britain, 1954, 82 mins.

Last Days of Dolwyn
A dowager is called upon for help when her Welsh village is slated for extinction as part of a reservoir project. Richard Burtons's first film.
VHS: S14657. $29.95.
Emlyn Williams, Great Britain, 1949, 95 mins.

Last Holiday
Alec Guiness portrays a shy and friendless man who learns he has a fatal illness and vows to enjoy his final days to the fullest. He quits his job, withdraws his savings from the bank, and sets off for a fashionable seaside resort where his life takes an unexpected turn.
VHS: S16593. $39.95.
Henry Cass, Great Britain, 1950, 88 mins.

The Last Reunion
Members of a British bomber crew meet each year at the last request of their dying captain. Eric Portman and Michael Gough lead a fine cast in this eerie, atmospheric ghost story.
VHS: S04068. $29.95.
Leonard Brett, Great Britain, 1955

Late Extra
James Mason's first movie. Alastair Sim, Michael Wilding and Clifford McLaglen also star in this 1935 newspaper drama. Fine acting and tight direction.
VHS: S07397. $29.95.
Albert Parker, Great Britain, 1935, 69 mins.

Lavender Hill Mob
Alec Guinness in one of his most memorable roles, as a shy bank clerk who conspires to steal a million pounds in gold bars from the Bank of England. His plan is to melt down the gold and mold it in the shape of tiny Eiffel Tower souvenirs for resale. Things appear to go well until… Zany, witty and very British, a beloved and classic British comedy.
VHS: S00732. $14.98.
Charles Crichton, Great Britain, 1951, 78 mins.

League of Gentlemen
Eight former soldiers find themselves desperately in need now that the war is over. When they get together it's not to reminisce but to hatch a plan more in keeping with their shady leanings. Robbing a bank seems the perfect solution.
VHS: S14696. $39.95.
Basil Dearden, Great Britain, 1960, 115 mins.

Let's Make Up
A film that combines gritty naturalism with epic spectacle. Set during the London Blitz, a young actress (Anna Neagle) is knocked unconscious during an air raid. She imagines herself as Nell Gwyn, Queen Victoria and her mother. But when she awakens, Neagle must confront the realities of her marriage to a mediocre vaudevillian (Errol Flynn). With Peter Graves, David Farrar and Kathleen Harrison. Alternate title is *Lilacs of the Spring*.
VHS: S19866. $29.95.
Herbert Wilcox, Great Britain, 1954, 94 mins.

Lilacs in the Spring
Anna Neagle, Errol Flynn and Peter Graves are featured in this musical comedy fantasy based on the play *The Glorious Days*, by Henry Purcell. A young woman is knocked out during the London blitz. While asleep she dreams of herself as Nell Gwynn, Queen Victoria and even as her own mother.
VHS: S23785. $24.95.
Herbert Wilcox, Great Britain, 1954, 94 mins.

The Lion in Winter
Peter O'Toole and Katharine Hepburn star in this costume drama concerning royal succession at the English court of Henry II. Based on the successful play, this sumptuous screen version is now transferred to video in a letterbox format, to capture its stunning visual impact, on the occasion of its 25th anniversary.
Laser: LD72304. $34.99.
Anthony Harvey, Great Britain, 1968, 134 mins.

The Living Dead
George Curzon devises a scheme to murder heavily insured people and then bring them back to life. Gerald Du Maurier, the inspector from the Yard, is baffled. Leslie Perrins, his potential son-in-law and a doctor working for the insurance company, helps find the solution.
VHS: S04056. $29.95.
Thomas Bentley, Great Britain, 1936, 63 mins.

Loneliness of the Long Distance Runner
The engrossing story of a rebellious young man chosen to represent his reform school in a track race. A superbly acted film, it also confronts the rigidity of society's mores and institutions. This is a key British film from the 60s directed by Tony Richardson. Starring Tom Courtenay and Michael Redgrave.
VHS: S15359. $19.98.
Laser: LD71675. $34.98.
Tony Richardson, Great Britain, 1962, 103 mins.

Long Haul
Victor Mature stars as an honest American veteran trying to support his English wife in postwar Liverpool. When he stops a phony robbery, he loses his trucking job and falls in with a bad crowd. Not only is he now on the wrong side of the law, he is also on the wrong side of the road. With Gene Anderson, Patrick Allen and British bombshell Diana Dors.
VHS: S15896. $19.95.
Ken Hughes, Great Britain, 1957, 100 mins.

Lord Jim
Lavish adaptation of Joseph Conrad's novel, the existential tale of a seaman in the Far East. With Peter O'Toole, Eli Wallach, James Mason.
VHS: S01711. $19.95.
Richard Brooks, Great Britain, 1965, 154 mins.

Lord of the Flies
Peter Brook's classic adaptation of William Golding's novel about a group of English schoolboys stranded on a desolate island in the aftermath of a nuclear holocaust. Tensions and warfare break out over class grievances and social distinctions. Shot on location in Puerto Rico with nonprofessional actors, Brook images the work as a neo-realistic documentary. With James Aubrey, Tom Chapin and Hugh Edwards.
VHS: S18755. $29.95.
Laser: CLV. LD72099. $49.95.
Peter Brook, Great Britain, 1963, 91 mins.

Lorna Doone
Victoria Hopper, John Loder and Margaret Lockwood are featured in this tale of love set in rural Exmoor. An English farmer falls in love with the daughter of outlaws. Their passion places two very different families into conflict.
VHS: S25700. $19.95.
Basil Dean, Great Britain, 1934, 90 mins.

Love from a Stranger
Basil Rathbone plays a smooth, murdering conman who romances a vacationing American lottery winner to the altar. Ann Harding plays the unsuspecting damsel in distress who learns from a stranger that her hubby is a Bluebeard. Based on Agatha Christie's short story *Philomel Cottage*. A tension-filled game of nerves turns into a deadly game of who's got the poisoned coffee? With Jean Cadell and Bruce Seton. Remade in 1947.
VHS: S09134. $19.95.
Rowland V. Lee, Great Britain, 1937, 86 mins.

Love on the Dole
Deborah Kerr and Clifford Evans star in this story of a British slum family during the Great Depression of the 30s. Based on the novel and play by Walter Greenwood.
VHS: S09531. $29.95.
John Baxter, Great Britain, 1941, 89 mins.

Lucky Jim
Ian Carmichael, Hugh Griffith and Terry Thomas star in this zany comedy about a university professor and a junior lecturer at a British University. Great gags and a keen cast keep this comedy moving.
VHS: S23786. $24.95.
John Boulting, Great Britain, 1957, 95 mins.

The Magic Bow
Stewart Granger stars along with Phyllis Calvert, Cecil Parker and Dennis Price in this biographical film about the youthful violinist and composer Paganini. Roland Pertwee and Norman Ginsbury wrote the screenplay while Yehudi Menuhin provides the violin solos.
VHS: S23897. $29.95.
Bernard Knowles, Great Britain, 1946, 106 mins.

Malta Story
Alec Guinness and Jack Hawkins star in this unique combination of actual wartime footage and reenacted material. The subject is the heroic efforts of the Allied Forces to protect the tiny island of Malta in the Mediterranean.
VHS: S26958. $14.98.
Brian Desmond Hurst, Great Britain, 1953, 98 mins.

Man for All Seasons
Literate, penetrating treatment of the conflict between Thomas More (Paul Schofield) and King Henry VIII (Robert Shaw). Director Zinnemann concentrates on characterization rather than spectacle with superior results. With Orson Welles, Susannah York and Vanessa Redgrave.
VHS: S02639. $19.95.
Laser: Widescreen. LD75496. $44.95.
Fred Zinnemann, Great Britain, 1966, 120 mins.

Man in Grey
The film that boosted James Mason to stardom; an elaborate costume drama which features Phyllis Calbert as a wealthy woman who befriends Margaret Lockwood, a former schoolmate. Years later, Lockwood repays her by trying to steal her husband.
VHS: S05229. $29.95.
Leslie Arliss, Great Britain, 1943, 116 mins.

Man in the White Suit
Alec Guiness plays an unassuming lab assistant who invents a miracle fabric that can be woven into indestructible cloth. Few films have chastized industry so wittily and incisively as this great comedy. There is a Chaplin-like flavor to absurdist scenes pitting a captain of industry against his stubborn young employee.
VHS: S00812. $14.98.
Alexander MacKendrick, Great Britain, 1951, 82 mins.

Man Who Could Work Miracles
An enjoyable and imaginative fantasy scripted by H.G. Wells, starring Roland Young as a recipient of a gift of great powers given by a bored group of aliens who decide to give the power to work miracles to an ordinary fellow to see what happens.
VHS: Out of print. For rental only.
Laser: LD75226. $34.98.
Lothar Mendes, Great Britain, 1937, 82 mins.

The Man Who Never Was
Clifton Webb, Gloria Grahame and Robert Flemyng star in this true and intriguing account of World War II espionage in which the British were able to dupe the Germans into believing that a Mediterranean invasion would take place in Greece instead of Sicily.
VHS: S14135. $19.98.
Ronald Neame, Great Britain, 1955, 102 mins.

Maytime in Mayfair
Anna Neagle and Michael Wilding are featured in this delightful musical comedy about dress designers. In the fashion salons of London intrigues abound, and one of these almost drives the pair apart for good. Fortunately, good spirits prevail.
VHS: S23898. $29.95.
Herbert Wilcox, Great Britain, 1949, 110 mins.

Mill on the Floss
James Mason stars in this adaptation of George Eliot's novel of the scandal that erupts when a young woman spends the night with an engaged man.
VHS: S00856. $19.95.
Tim Whelan, Great Britain, 1936, 80 mins.

Millions Like Us
Patricia Roc, Moore Marriot and Eric Portman are featured in this drama about the impact of war on a family. The title is especially evocative of a situation common in World War II. Even as the hardships piled up at home, everyone was forced to concentrate on the problems afflicting millions more.
VHS: S23806. $24.95.
Sidney Gilliat, Great Britain, 1943, 103 mins.

Mimi
A liberal adaptation of Puccini's *La Boheme*, set in Paris' Latin Quarter, with Gertrude Lawrence as the heroine. Douglas Fairbanks Jr. is the dashing hero. Puccini's melodies are presented in synchronized accompaniment and heard throughout this romantic drama.
VHS: S14642. $29.95.
Paul M. Stein, Great Britain, 1935, 98 mins.

Mine Own Executioner
Burgess Meredith and Kieron Moore star in this tense psychological thriller. An ex-POW is haunted by fears and obsessions that could have deadly consequences. Either the psychiatrist can cure this man or he will kill someone.
VHS: S25016. $19.95.
Anthony Kimmins, Great Britain, 1947, 103 mins.

Moonlight Sonata
Featured appearance by one of the most famous concert pianists of the day, Ignace Jan Paderewski, in this romance set in the household of a Swedish baroness.
VHS: S03752. $34.95.
Lothar Mendes, Great Britain, 1938, 80 mins.

Moonraker
The year is 1651. George Baker and Sylvia Syms star in this historical drama concerning the escape of Charles Stuart during the time of Oliver Cromwell and his "Roundhead" followers. Based on Arthur Watkyn's play.
VHS: S23899. $29.95.
David MacDonald, Great Britain, 1957, 82 mins.

The Mouse That Roared
An inventive satire about the Duchy of Grand Fenwick and its mischievous duchess (Peter Sellers) that boldly declares war against America to boost its economy. Anticipating *Dr. Strangelove*, Sellers also appears as the prime minister and war minister. With Jean Seberg, David Kossoff and William Hartnell.
VHS: S01841. $19.95.
Jack Arnold, Great Britain, 1959, 90 mins.

Murder Ahoy
In this Agatha Christie classic Miss Marple investigates a series of murders aboard a naval cadet training ship. With Margaret Rutherford, Lionel Jeffries, and Stringer Davis.
VHS: S13761. $19.98.
George Pollock, Great Britain, 1964, 74 mins.

Mutiny of the Elsinore
An intrepid reporter boards a ship in search of a story and he gets more than he could possibly have hoped for. Mutiny soon turns this trip into an adventure in which there's little room for objectivity. Starring Paul Lukas and Lyn Harding.
VHS: S21564. $24.95.
Roy Lockwood, Great Britain, 1937, 79 mins.

The Mysterious Island
A rousing adventure adapted from Jules Verne's sequel to *20,000 Leagues under the Sea*. The film charts the strange experiences of a group of escaped Union soldiers marooned on a fantastic island populated by outsized animals. With Michael Craig, Joan Greenwood, Michael Callan and Herbert Lom as Captain Nemo. Special visual effects by Ray Harryhausen.
VHS: S18605. $14.95.
Cy Endfield, Great Britain, 1961, 101 mins.

The Naked Truth
Peter Sellers is a master of disguise in this outrageous comedy. As Nigel Dennis he decides to print a scandalous magazine that reveals the true secrets of several prominent people. They respond to this blackmail with a plot to eliminate this scabrous journalist, but when it fails there is only more scandal to print.
VHS: S21996. $19.95.
Mario Zampi, Great Britain, 1957, 90 mins.

The Nanny
Bette Davis fans will love this taut thriller featuring Davis as a nanny with a murderous bent. A young boy has been accused of drowning his sister, but he insists he is innocent. As he makes his suspicions about the nanny public, murderous schemes develop. This film has terrific suspense and an overall macabre atmosphere.
VHS: S27438. $19.95.
Seth Holt, Great Britain, 1965, 93 mins.

Never Too Late to Mend
Tod Slaughter, the horror man of Europe, plays Squire Meadows, a good church goer and a very strict prison administrator. Based on Charles Reade's 1856 novel about the abominable conditions in English prisons that led Queen Victoria to start penal reforms. With Marjorie Taylor and Jack Livesay. B&W.
VHS: S04042. $29.95.
David MacDonald, Great Britain, 1937

The Night Has Eyes (Terror House)
James Mason stars as a moody music composer living a reclusive life on the Yorkshire Moors. His solitude is interrupted by a curious young woman (Joyce Howard) who suspects Mason of murdering her best friend a year before. Naturally, they fall in love and solve the mystery. B&W.
VHS: S04063. $29.95.
Leslie Arliss, Great Britain, 1942, 79 mins.

Night to Remember
The maiden voyage of the Titanic is meticulously detailed in this remarkable black and white recreation. Based on the best seller by Walter Lord. A great special effects. A memorable ensemble including Kenneth More, Honor Blackman, David McCallum, George Rose and Laurence Naismith as the Captain.
VHS: S06231. $14.98.
Laser: LD74946. $99.95.
Roy Ward Baker, Great Britain, 1958, 123 mins.

Night Train to Munich
British filmmaker Carol Reed's adaptation of Gordon Wellesley's novel *Report on a Fugitive* is a comic suspense thriller about a British intelligence officer (Rex Harrison) who impersonates a Nazi in order to rescue a Czech inventor and scientist who is being detained in Berlin. With Margaret Lockwood, Basil Radford, Naunton Wayne and Paul Henreid.
VHS: S19870. $29.95.
Laser: LD74932. $39.95.
Carol Reed, Great Britain, 1940, 93 mins.

Nightmare
A young woman continually relives the childhood terror of her insane mother stabbing her father to death, in her dreams. At her guardian's home, everything appears normal by day, but come nightfall this past event haunts her. Perhaps the startling vividness of this nightmare is due to more than mere memory. With David Knight, Moira Redmond, Jennie Linden and Brenda Bruce.
VHS: S25570. $14.98.
Freddie Francis, Great Britain, 1963, 83 mins.

Nino Martini in One Night with You
Patricia Roc, Irene Worth and Stanley Holloway join Martini for this madcap comic film about a tenor stranded without identity papers. In this rare treat the wildly flamboyant Italian film world is seen through droll English eyes.
VHS: S24561. $34.95.
Terence Young, Great Britain, 1948, 92 mins.

Non Stop—New York
Anna Lee and John Loder star in this complex and fascinating 1937 mystery which uses a trans-Atlantic air plane ride in a climactic escape from England, three years before such flights existed. Wonderful, tongue-in-cheek mystery about a woman who can provide an alibi for an innocent man who stands accused of murder, but no one will believe her.
VHS: S07399. $29.95.
Robert Stevenson, Great Britain, 1937, 71 mins.

Norman Conquest
Tom Conway, Eva Bartok, Joy Shelton and Ian Fleming are cast in this elaborately plotted thriller. A famed private eye finds himself unwittingly framed by a blond bombshell in a hotel room. Scotland Yard doesn't believe it, even though there is a Nazi smuggler afoot.
VHS: S24017. $24.95.
Bernard Knowles, Great Britain, 1953, 78 mins.

O-Kay for Sound
This Crazy Gang revue comedy of street musicians who are given parts in a drill dressed as city financiers and are then mistaken for the real thing stars Fred Duprez, Enid Taylor and Jimmy Gold.
VHS: S26068. $29.95.
Marcel Varnel, Great Britain, 1937, 86 mins.

The October Man
John Mills and Joan Greenwood are paired in this psychological whodunit. A man finds himself trapped in a deep depression brought on by a head injury. Before he can recover, he is suspected of murdering a girl.
VHS: S25708. $19.95.
Roy Ward Baker, Great Britain, 1948, 91 mins.

Odd Man Out
James Mason is Johnny McQueen, a wounded Irish revolutionary on the run in an unnamed northern Irish city. A classic thriller from filmmaker Carol Reed and an artistic exploration of lower class Gaelic life. The memorable cast includes Robert Newton, Kathleen Ryan, Cyril Cusack and Dan O'Herlihy.
VHS: Out of print. For rental only.
Laser: LD75376. $49.98.
Carol Reed, Great Britain, 1947, 113 mins.

On Approval
Highly amusing, often ingenious comedy starring Clive Brook and Beatrice Lillie, in which two couples spend a holiday on a deserted island home to see if they are suited for each other.
VHS: S00957. $29.95.
Clive Brook, Great Britain, 1944, 80 mins.

Oscar Wilde
Robert Morley, Ralph Richardson and John Neville star in this recreation of the trial where the great Irish-born author was officially disgraced because he desired his own sex. Morley plays Wilde.
VHS: S23807. $24.95.
Gregory Ratoff, Great Britain, 1959, 96 mins.

Paranoiac
Oliver Reed and Janette Scott (*The Day of the Triffids*) star in this murky thriller from Hammer Films. A young heiress is dramatically saved from suicide by a man who claims to be her long lost brother. The two quickly bond, but the woman's other brother, a cruel sadist, remains skeptical, presuming that this newcomer is probably only interested in the vast family fortune. With Sheila Burrell, Alexander Davion and Liliane Brousse.
VHS: S25571. $14.98.
Freddie Francis, Great Britain, 1962, 80 mins.

Passing of the Third Floor Back
A wonderful, ultra-rare, British fantasy. The setting is an old boarding house filled with a variety of people, all with different problems. They're lorded over by an evil, mephisto-like slum lord. The tenants are changed forever by the arrival of a Christ-like stranger who aids them with their problems. A well-thought-out and meaningful storyline about so many of the good and bad aspects of life. Veidt turns in a strong performance as the mysterious stranger in this top-notch British Gaumont production.
VHS: S12327. $29.95.
Berthold Viertel, Great Britain, 1935, 90 mins.

Passport to Pimlico
Wry satire from the Golden Age of British comedy. A group of residents in Pimlico, a London suburb, discover an ancient treaty that ceded their land to the Duke of Burgundy, a discovery that leads to delightful mayhem.
VHS: S01000. $19.98.
Henry Cornelius, Great Britain, 1949, 85 mins.

Petulia
Julie Christie is the title character in this film about the idle rich in San Francisco in the mid-60's. She's a lovely kook who is very attracted to a prominent doctor, played by George C. Scott. A terrific film. With Richard Chamberlain, Shirley Knight and Joseph Cotten.
VHS: S06102. $19.98.
Richard Lester, Great Britain, 1968, 105 mins.

Phantom Fiend
A remake of Alfred Hitchcock's silent classic *The Lodger*, with Ivor Novello recreating his role as a lodger suspected of being Jack the Ripper. England, 70 mins.
VHS: S14675. $29.95.
Maurice Elvey, Great Britain, 1932, 85 mins.

Phantom Ship (Mystery of the Mary Celeste)
Bela Lugosi plays a one-armed seaman with homicidal tendencies who books passage on the ill-fated American sailing vessel *Mary Celeste*. This speculative tale of murder and mayhem was the second production of the newly formed English film company, Hammer Films.
VHS: S03337. $29.95.
Denison Clift, Great Britain, 1935, 80 mins.

The Pickwick Papers
A classic adaptation of Charles Dickens' masterpiece about the members of a fictional English social club, the Pickwick Club, featuring a distinguished English cast including James Hayter, Nigel Patrick.
VHS: S05221. $19.95.
Noel Langley, Great Britain, 1952, 109 mins.

Picture of Dorian Gray
Shane Briant stars in this compelling version of Oscar Wilde's famous story of the young British aristocrat who sinks into the hedonism of London and finds his portrait aging.
VHS: S22986. $29.98.
Glenn Jordan, Great Britain, 1974, 130 mins.

Pimpernel Smith
On the eve of World War II, the most prominent artists and intellectuals are escaping from Germany, aided by a mysterious man who comes out of the shadows, performs his daring and clever rescues, and then vanishes. Filled with many twists, this enjoyable update of the Scarlet Pimpernel character features a charming performance by Leslie Howard.
VHS: S04347. $29.95.
Leslie Howard, Great Britain, 1941, 120 mins.

The Prime Minister
John Gielgud portrays Disraeli, the great British Prime Minister from Victorian times. Despite a lifetime of political successes, he suffered through many personal instances of turmoil and grief. Diana Wynyard and Owen Nares also star.
VHS: S23808. $24.95.
Thorold Dickinson, Great Britain, 1941, 109 mins.

The Prime of Miss Jean Brodie
Maggie Smith, in her Oscar-winning performance, is top-notch as the unconventional, eccentric teacher in an all-girls school in Edinburgh during the 1930s. Miss Brodie's students, the "creme de la creme," adore their teacher, but when they try to shape their lives after Miss Brodie's, disaster ensues. Based on Muriel Spark's novel.
VHS: S10746. $19.98.
Ronald Neame, Great Britain, 1968, 116 mins.

The Prisoner
The original movie-length version of what later became the famous television series. Alec Guinness and Jack Hawkins give superb performances, with Guinness as a cardinal who is arrested and mentally tortured into making a phony confession.
VHS: S09394. $69.95.
Peter Glenville, Great Britain, 1955, 91 mins.

The Prisoner of Corbal
Nils Asther, Hugh Sinclair and Hazel Terry star in this costume drama set during the French Revolution. A lovely young aristocrat escapes Paris disguised as the nephew of a citizen deputy. Corbal seems like the perfect place to hide until the young aristocratic woman is attracted to the local Marquis, forgetting the revolutionary who spirited her to safety.
VHS: S24010. $24.95.
Karl Grune, Great Britain, 1936, 72 mins.

The Private Life of Henry VIII
Charles Laughton gives a tour-de-force performance as the infamous British King Henry, a fat, strutting, arrogant, yet tender, vulnerable and loving man. Politics, statesmanship and international intrigue are just background for the lusty life of the king and his six wives. Also starring Merle Oberon, Robert Donat, and Elsa Lanchester. Digitally remastered.
VHS: S01062. $19.98.
Alexander Korda, Great Britain, 1933, 97 mins.

The Private Secretary
Edward Everett Horton and Alastair Sim star in this amusing comedy set during the Victorian era. Horton is in disguise as a minister hiding from debt collectors. The Church of England is a great place to hide and find laughs as well.
VHS: S23788. $24.95.
Henry Edwards, Great Britain, 1935, 70 mins.

The Promoter
A low-key Ealing comedy adapted from Arnold Bennett's story *The Card*, about a young man's transformation from penniless hustler to provincial power. With his skills for self-promotion, he quickly amasses power and credentials in class-conscious England, though he loses his identity and soul. With Alec Guinness, Glynis Johns, Valerie Hobston and Petula Clark.
VHS: S01978. $39.95.
Ronald Neame, Great Britain, 1952, 88 mins.

The Pumpkin Eater
Harold Pinter wrote the script for this fabulous film based on Penelope Mortimer's novel about a woman (Anne Bancroft) whose middle-class marriage to an unfaithful screenwriter (Peter Finch) spins out of control. With a famous scene of Bancroft having a nervous breakdown in the midst of the Harrods Department Store. James Mason, Cedric Hardwicke and Maggie Smith also star.
VHS: S26447. $19.95.
Jack Clayton, Great Britain, 1964, 118 mins.

Pygmalion
Superlative version of George Bernard Shaw's play, later made as *My Fair Lady*. Leslie Howard excels as the professor, with Wendy Hiller as the Cockney-speaking pupil.
VHS: S01973. $24.95.
Laser: LD71283. $39.95.
Anthony Asquith, Great Britain, 1938, 90 mins.

Rhodes of Africa
Walter Huston, Oscar Homolka and Basil Sydney are featured in this recounting of the famed founder of the Rhodes scholarship fund. In life he was a much-feared representative of the British Empire. This film biography is based on Sarah Gertrude's novel.
VHS: S23809. $24.95.
Berthold Viertel, Great Britain, 1936, 91 mins.

Ring of Bright Water
Fine acting and beautiful cinematography spark this intelligent, heartwarming tale of a man's love for his pet otter. A Disney-like fable for animal lovers, adapted from the bestselling book by Gavin Maxwell. With Bill Travers and Virginia McKenna.
VHS: S14223. $14.98.
Jack Couffer, Great Britain, 1969, 107 mins.

The Rise of Catherine the Great
Alexander Korda returns to his themes of unrequited love and romantic shallowness in this tale of the Empress of Russia and her failing marriage to the Grand Duke (Douglas Fairbanks), while her obsession for an apparently royal madman is vanquished by society and royal indifference.
VHS: S02599. $19.98.
Laser: LD71304. $19.98.
Paul Czinner, Great Britain, 1934, 88 mins.

River of Unrest (Ourselves Alone)
A wily rebel leader leads daring rescues of captured comrades and in general confounds the military might of Great Britain on his home sod of the Emerald Isle. Set before the establishment of the Irish Free State. Cast includes John Loder, John Lodge and Antoinette Cellier. B&W.
VHS: S06187. $29.95.
Brian Desmond Hurst, Great Britain, 1937, 69 mins.

Rocking Horse Winner
One of the most off-beat, startling, disturbing and touching movies of the 50's was also one of the first stories by D.H. Lawrence to be tapped for the movies. The plot is strange and ultimately tragic when a 10-year-old boy learns how to pick winners at the racetrack while riding his own rocking horse, to aid his spendthrift parents out of their endless round of debts. With John Mills, Valerie Hobson, John Howard Davies.
VHS: S12956. $39.95.
Anthony Pelissier, Great Britain, 1950, 91 mins.

Rogue Male
Peter O'Toole stars as an aristocrat with an heroic if dangerous idea: he plans to assassinate Hitler before the world is at war. Despite the failure of his plot, this man is hunted by both the Gestapo and the British police. This thrilling adventure also features Alastair Sim.
VHS: S25522. $19.95.
Clive Donner, Great Britain, 1976

The Romantic Age
Mai Zetterling stars as an art student infatuated with her teacher, who is played by Hugh Williams. This master finds himself hard pressed to resist the charms of his precocious French student.
VHS: S23789. $24.95.
Edmond T. Greville, Great Britain, 1949, 86 mins.

The Runaway Bus
A group of disgruntled passengers, among them several incognito thieves and police detectives, are stranded at the London Airport, and a relief bus driver takes them for an interesting ride. With Margaret Rutherford and Petula Clark. Written and directed by Val Guest.
VHS: S14646. $29.95.
Val Guest, Great Britain, 1954, 78 mins.

Sailing Along
A romantic British musical about a pretty and talented young woman working on a barge who meets the right man and ends up becoming a dancing star. Starring Jessie Matthews and Roland Young.
VHS: S14647. $29.95.
Sonnie Hale, Great Britain, 1938, 90 mins.

School for Scoundrels
Alastair Sim and Terry Thomas are joined by Ian Carmichael in this hysterical spoof of self-improvement techniques. Carmichael goes through a number of Sim's workshops to better himself in a variety of ways. Surprisingly enough these schemes work and Carmichael goes back to show up the ridiculously snooty Thomas.
VHS: S24051. $24.95.
Robert Hamer, Great Britain, 1960, 94 mins.

Scott of the Antarctic
Dramatic rendition of the fateful British expedition to be the first to the South Pole. John Mills is Robert Falcon Scott, English explorer and naval officer, the leader of the 1910 drive, whose heroism has inspired many an English schoolboy. With Christopher Lee, Kenneth More and James Robertson Justice.
VHS: S04052. $14.98.
Charles Frend, Great Britain, 1948, 110 mins.

Scrooge
Sir Seymour Hicks stars as Ebenezer Scrooge in this charming and rather faithful adaptation of Charles Dickens' *A Christmas Carol*. The strength of this tale is in its ability to combine frightening elements like the ghosts with sincere sentiments of goodwill. B&W.
VHS: S27336. $19.95.
Henry Edwards, Great Britain, 1935, 60 mins.

Sea of Sand
Richard Attenborough stars as the commander of a key desert patrol set to sabotage Rommel's fuel supply. Their success could impact the outcome of the historic battle of El Alamein. On the way back to headquarters, their heroism is tested once again by an unforseen Nazi patrol.
VHS: S26959. $14.98.
Guy Green, Great Britain, 1958, 97 mins.

The Sea Shall Not Have Them
A tense British drama about rescuers who try to save the crew of a downed plane, which is hanging on to life by a thread on a rubber raft in the stormy North Seas. With Dirk Bogarde, Michael Redgrave.
VHS: S03720. $39.95.
Lewis Gilbert, Great Britain, 1957, 91 mins.

Seance on a Wet Afternoon
Novelist Bryan Forbes' eerie psychological thriller about a demented woman (Kim Stanley) trapped in a suffocating, childless marriage, who kidnaps a child and devises a scheme to "rescue" the child and claim the ransom. "Consistently intelligent and exciting, the film unerringly illuminates the dangerous areas between private fantasy and public madness" (British Film Institute). With Richard Attenborough, Mark Eden and Patrick Magee.
VHS: S01764. $29.95.
Bryan Forbes, Great Britain, 1964, 116 mins.

Secret Mission
James Mason appears in this early World War II thriller. Four British intelligence officers infiltrate Nazi-occupied France. Their mission is to evaluate German defenses, but their salvation is their cover as champagne merchants.
VHS: S26957. $14.98.
Harold French, Great Britain, 1942, 94 mins.

Seven Sinners (Doomed Cargo)
Also known as *Doomed Cargo*, this comedy-suspense is reminiscent of Alfred Hitchcock, and in particular, *The 39 Steps*. The film stars Edmund Lowe and Constance Cummings, in the story of gunrunners who wreck trains in order to cover up the traces of murder.
VHS: S06856. $14.98.
Michael Balcon, Great Britain, 1936, 70 mins.

The Shadow
A super-rare old dark house thriller. A mysterious figure in black, known only as the shadow, is responsible for a series of blackmailings and cold-blooded murders. The only clue to his identity is a strange oriental gem found in the hand of a dead police inspector. Terrific British chiller. With Henry Kendal, Elizabeth Allan, Sam Livesey.
VHS: S10001. $29.95.
George Cooper, Great Britain, 1936, 63 mins.

Ships with Wings
This World War II film examines the crisis faced by a group of British naval officers who are locked in a struggle with German U-boats for the strategic control in the Atlantic. With John Clements, Ann Todd, Leslie Banks and Hugh Williams.
VHS: S18934. $19.95.
Sergei Nolbandov, Great Britain, 1942, 89 mins.

Sidewalks of London
Charles Laughton puts on quite a show as a busker, or street entertainer, who takes young Vivien Leigh under his wing. Not content with small change from passersby, she dumps her mentor for the stage. With Rex Harrison, Tyrone Guthrie and Larry "Mr. Harmonica" Adler. B&W.
VHS: S05076. $29.95.
Tim Whelan, Great Britain, 1938, 84 mins.

Smallest Show on Earth
A wonderful comedy starring Peter Sellers, Bill Travers, Virginia McKenna, and Margaret Rutherford. A young couple who inherit an old movie house—and a couple of strange movie attendants (Sellers and Rutherford) in the process.
VHS: S07468. $39.95.
Basil Dearden, Great Britain, 1957, 80 mins.

Special British Comedy Boxed Set
Alastair Sim and Trevor Howard star in the comedy thriller *Green for Danger*, about a rash of mysterious deaths at a hospital. In *The Happiest Days of Your Life*, Alastair Sim and Margaret Rutherford try their best to control anarchy in a boy's school accidentally filled with girls. In the third tape, Wendy Hiller and Rex Harrison star in the ironic screen adaptation of George Bernard Shaw's *Major Barbara*. 401 mins.
VHS: S24796. $79.95.

Spitfire
Leslie Howard and David Niven star in this biographical story tracking the development of the famous Spitfire aircraft.
VHS: S03110. $19.98.
Laser: LD75261. $34.98.
Leslie Howard, Great Britain, 1942, 88 mins.

A Spy of Napoleon
Historical drama about the conflict between Emperor Napoleon III and Bismarck of Prussia. Featured is Richard Barthelmess, famous actor during the American silent era in his only British film.
VHS: S02246. $29.95.
Maurice Elvey, Great Britain, 1936, 101 mins.

St. Martin's Lane
Originally released as *Sidewalks of London*, Charles Laughton is the London street entertainer who picks up a waif (Vivien Leigh) and sees her go to stardom, sacrificing his love for her to do so.
VHS: S01555. $49.95.
Tim Whelan, Great Britain, 1938, 84 mins.

Stalag Luft
Stephen Fry stars in this rowdy comic adventure about a prison break at a Nazi P.O.W. camp. His character has an interesting past, 23 escapes and 23 recaptures. Despite these failures, escape is an intriguing possibility, one that could succeed if only he doesn't bungle this one last opportunity. Nicholas Lyndhurst and Geoffrey Palmer also star. 103 mins.
VHS: S24782. $24.95.

The Stars Look Down
Michael Redgrave tries to bring reform to the coal mining industry in Wales. A tough, gripping drama from the novel by A.J. Cronin. With Margaret Lockwood, Evelyn Williams and Cecil Parker. Dangerous working conditions bring real tragedy to light. B&W.
VHS: S02243. $29.95.
Carol Reed, Great Britain, 1939, 104 mins.

Stolen Hours
A stylish remake of *Dark Victory*, about a beautiful, precocious, oil heiress (Susan Hayward) whose decadent lifestyle in the English countryside takes a dramatic turn when she falls in love with a sympathetic doctor (Michael Craig). Cinematography by Harry Waxman. With Diane Baker, Edward Judd and Paul Rogers.
VHS: S19573. $19.98.
Daniel Petrie, Great Britain, 1963, 97 mins.

Storm in a Teacup
A very witty social comedy with Vivien Leigh and Rex Harrison barbing over words, loves and politics in the case of an old lady who refuses to pay for a license for her dog. With Cecil Parker, Ivor Barnard.
VHS: S05177. $29.95.
Victor Saville, Great Britain, 1937, 87 mins.

Sword of Lancelot
Cornel Wilde directs himself as the brave and noble Sir Lancelot in this action-packed return to the days when knights were bold. Brian Aherne is King Arthur and Jean Wallace (Mrs. Wilde) is the beautiful and bewitching Guinevere. How they carry on in Camelot and more.
VHS: S07777. $19.98.
Cornel Wilde, Great Britain, 1963, 116 mins.

A Tale of Two Cities
A richly detailed adaptation of the Charles Dickens novel of turmoil during the French Revolution. Dirk Bogarde, Donald Pleasance, Christopher Lee and Dorothy Tutin star in this epic of the storming of the Bastille, the uncountable deaths by guillotine.
VHS: S12345. $29.98.
Ralph Thomas, Great Britain, 1967, 113 mins.

Taste of Honey
Tony Richardson's landmark British film heralded in so-called "kitchen sink realism" of British films in the 60's. Richardson adapted Shelagh Delaney's play about a young girl who gets pregnant after she leaves home, has an affair with a black sailor, and is cared for by a homosexual friend. Rita Tushingham, Robert Stephens and Dora Bryan star.
VHS: S01302. $19.95.
Tony Richardson, Great Britain, 1961, 100 mins.

That Hamilton Woman
Alexander Korda's rewarding and dense study of obsessive love between British naval baron Lord Admiral Nelson (Laurence Olivier) and Emma Hamilton (Vivien Leigh), a poverty-stricken youth who became an ambassador's wife and Nelson's mistress.
VHS: S02857. $19.98.
Alexander Korda, Great Britain, 1941, 125 mins.

They Who Dare
Dirk Bogarde, Denholm Elliott and Akim Tamiroff portray a group of soldiers working to thwart the Germans in the Aegean. Robert Westerby wrote the screenplay for this tense and engaging wartime thriller.
VHS: S23812. $24.95.
Lewis Milestone, Great Britain, 1954, 100 mins.

The Third Key
Jack Hawkins and Geoffrey Keen star in this exciting mystery about Scotland Yard investigators. A former employee of a safe manufacturer is now a master thief, using his workaday knowledge to gain illicit booty.
VHS: S23905. $29.95.
Charles Frend, Great Britain, 1955, 94 mins.

The Third Man
Graham Greene wrote the script for Carol Reed's film about an American pulp fiction writer's search for the mysterious and enigmatic war profiteer Harry Lime (a wonderful Orson Welles) in post-war Vienna. The film welds German expressionism, British classicism and American B-movie energy and motion. Anton Karas's haunting zither score is nearly as well known as Welles's extraordinary entrance. With Joseph Cotton, Trevor Howard and Bernard Lee. Awardwinning cinematography by Robert Krasker.
VHS: S01327. $24.95.
Laser: LD71366. $39.95.
Carol Reed, Great Britain, 1949, 104 mins.

This England
John Clements and Greta Gynt are at the center of this historical feature about an enduring English village. A journalist learns about five distinct historical periods and the effects of each on this country hamlet, through the contrasting views of both landowner and laborer.
VHS: S25706. $19.95.
David MacDonald, Great Britain, 1942, 84 mins.

Three Cases of Murder
One of the classic omnibus films, *Three Cases of Murder* combines a fantasy, a mystery and a psychological thriller. *In the Picture* is the story of an artist whose spirit resides in a macabre painting; in *You Killed Elizabeth*, two friends are in love with the same woman, one of whom turns up dead; and *Lord Mountdrago* features a stunning performance by Orson Welles as a statesman who is consumed with guilt over the ruin of his opponent.
VHS: S24933. $39.95.
Laser: LD75057. $49.95.
Toye/Eady/O'Ferrall, Great Britain, 1955, 99 mins.

Three Men in a Boat
Laurence Harvey, Jimmy Edwards and David Thomlinson are featured in this light comedy about three men in search of a vacation from the women in their lives. In search of tranquility they set sail on the Thames, where it becomes clear they won't be able to avoid female company at all. Jill Ireland is also featured.
VHS: S23984. $24.95.
Ken Annakin, Great Britain, 1956, 85 mins.

Three Weird Sisters
A terrific Gothic mystery combining the tension of Hitchcock with the color of Dylan Thomas, who wrote the screenplay. Set in Wales, the film concerns a younger brother who returns to his home town, summoned by his sisters, after a mine collapses. The sisters demand he pay for the repairs of the house, he refuses, and the sisters determine to eliminate him. Rich dialog by Thomas, with wonderful performances from Nancy Price, Nova Pilbeam, Raymond Lovell.
VHS: S07480. $34.95.
Daniel Birt, Great Britain, 1948, 83 mins.

Thunder in the City
A smart-mouthed, fast-talking Yankee businessman confronts the very proper but relentlessly shrewd English method of high finance. A sophisticated British satire starring famous American "bad guy" Edward G. Robinson in his first comedy role. With Nigel Bruce.
VHS: S13862. $19.95.
Marion Gering, Great Britain, 1937, 86 mins.

Thursday's Child
Stewart Granger and Sally Ann Howes are joined in this saga about a precocious child star. The result is a disaster for the entire family of the young film actress, at least until she is sent away to boarding school.
VHS: S25701. $19.95.
Rodney Ackland, Great Britain, 1943, 95 mins.

To Paris with Love
Alec Guinness stars as a rich father who takes his unwordly son across the Channel to the City of Lights to learn about life and love and people who live in a different country. A comedy. With Odile Versois, Vernon Gray and Austin Trevor. On your right is the Eiffel Tower.
VHS: S04909. $14.98.
Robert Hamer, Great Britain, 1955, 78 mins.

To Sir, With Love
Sidney Poitier is Mark Thackeray, a novice teacher assigned to a slum school in London's East End. Faced with tough opposition from the disinterested students and the remote school staff, he strives to teach his class what is important to really know in life. With Judy Geeson, Christian Roberts, and Lulu (who sings the title song).
VHS: S01355. $19.95.
Laser: LD75531. $34.95.
James Clavell, Great Britain, 1967, 105 mins.

Tom Brown's Schooldays
A man with revolutionary ideas becomes the headmaster of an exclusive boys' school in England.
VHS: S08364. $29.95.
Gordon Parry, Great Britain, 1940, 81 mins.

Tom Jones
Winner of 4 Academy Awards, including Best Picture, *Tom Jones* is Tony Richardson's adaptation of Henry Fielding's famous novel about a mysteriously abandoned orphan who is adopted by the fussy Squire Allworthy, and thus begins a life of bawdy adventure. An outrageous and lusty comedy of 18th-century English life starring the sexy young Albert Finney. Screenplay by John Osborne.
VHS: S15548. $19.98.
Laser: LD71435. $29.98.
Tony Richardson, Great Britain, 1963, 129 mins.

Tom Thumb
Russ Tamblyn is the miniature forest boy from the famed Grimm Brothers story. He is taken in by a kindly couple, but finds his unusual size an advantage when it becomes necessary to outwit the villainous Terry-Thomas and his evil henchman Peter Sellers.
VHS: S16852. $19.98.
George Pal, Great Britain, 1958, 98 mins.

Tomorrow We Live
John Clements and Greta Gynt star in this engaging drama set in occupied France. Villagers unite to help a spy escape the Nazis so that he can reach Britain.
VHS: S23813. $24.95.
George King, Great Britain, 1942, 85 mins.

Tony Draws a Horse
Cecil Parker and Anne Crawford star in this family-centered farce about a doctor, his wife and their free-spirited young son. While they fight over their son's expressive ability, or lack of discipline, the whole family weighs in with their unsolicited opinions. Meanwhile the boy continues to draw anatomically correct animals.
VHS: S23986. $24.95.
John Paddy Carstairs, Great Britain, 1950, 90 mins.

Tough Guy
Joan Collins stars as the girl friend of an underage hoodlum in London in this violent and controversial film. After Collins gets raped, she is driven to suicide.
VHS: S11110. $19.95.
Lewis Gilbert, Great Britain, 1953, 73 mins.

Train of Events
An ominous grouping of ghastly stories all linked by a terrible train disaster. With Valerie Hobson, John Clements and Peter Finch.
VHS: S14667. $29.95.
Basil Dearden, Great Britain, 1949, 89 mins.

Trans-Atlantic Tunnel
A favorite 1930's disaster movie as Richard Dix fights against human and natural odds to construct an undersea tunnel between Europe and America. Futuristic art deco sets and a top cast including Walter Huston as the U.S. president.
VHS: S01946. $29.95.
Maurice Elvey, Great Britain, 1935, 94 mins.

Treasure Island
Orson Welles and Walter Slezak lend their weight to this retelling of the Robert Louis Stevenson classic tale of sailors, pirates and buried treasure. Welles is great as the gamey eccentric, Long John Silver. It's a great tale for the kid in everyone.
VHS: S23103. $19.95.
John Hough, Great Britain, 1972, 94 mins.

The Trials of Oscar Wilde
Peter Finch and John Fraser star in this story based on the loving relationship between Oscar Wilde and Lord Alfred Douglas. John Furnell's *The Stringed Lute* and Montgomery Hyde's *Trials of Oscar Wilde* provide the literary sources for this intriguing film. Also known as *The Man with the Green Carnation*. With Yvonne Mitchell, Lionel Jeffries and Ian Fleming.
VHS: S26878. $24.95.
Ken Hughes, Great Britain, 1960, 123 mins.

Triple Cross
Christopher Plummer stars as the real-life safe cracker whose skills gave him a second chance. During World War II this skill was so useful that he earned the Triple Cross. Yul Brenner and Romy Schneider also star in this story of spies and betrayal.
VHS: S21012. $19.98.
Terence Young, Great Britain/France, 1967, 126 mins.

Trouble in the Glen
Orson Welles inherits some land in Scotland and does not get on very well with his new neighbors. When he closes a road, displaces some tinkers and upsets a crippled girl, they steal his cow and burn him in effigy. Forrest Tucker, as U.S. Major Lance Lansing, is asked to calm the situation. With Margaret Lockwood and Victor McLaglen. From the writer of *The Quiet Man*.
VHS: S07416. $19.98.
Herbert Wilcox, Great Britain, 1954, 91 mins.

Truth About Women
Laurence Harvey, Julie Harris, Eva Gabor and Wilfrid Hyde-White star in this British soaper about playboy Harvey's endless love affairs.
VHS: S03464. $24.95.
Muriel Box, Great Britain, 1958, 98 mins.

Tunes of Glory
Brilliant performances by Alec Guinness and John Mills as two rival colonels, one replacing the other in the Switzerland regiment. Winner of an Academy Award for Best Screenplay, this is a powerful and moving drama uncovering a clash of wills and ambition.
VHS: S01376. $29.95.
Laser: LD71380. $39.95.
Ronald Neame, Great Britain, 1960, 106 mins.

Undercover
Tom Walls and Michael Wilding star in this compelling drama about Yugoslav partisans. Brothers take different approaches to the Nazi occupation of their country, leading to tension, violence and finally even death.
VHS: S23815. $24.95.
Sergei Nolbandov, Great Britain, 1943, 80 mins.

Up the Creek
Peter Sellers plays an Irish petty officer in the British navy in this service comedy. Made in Hammarscope and black and white. Other distinguished members of the cast include David Tomlinson, Lionel Jeffries and Wilfrid Hyde-White as the Admiral. Not to be confused with the college rafting movie comedy of the same title.
VHS: S06098. $39.95.
Val Guest, Great Britain, 1958, 83 mins.

The VIP's
A glossy account of a group of privileged travelers and interlopers who are stranded in a London airport by fog. The characters include a flamboyant movie producer, a failed businessman, his dedicated secretary and a young woman about to run away with an aging lothario. With Elizabeth Taylor, Richard Burton, Louis Jourdan, Elsa Martinelli and Orson Welles.
VHS: S18526. $19.95.
Anthony Asquith, Great Britain, 1963, 119 mins.

Waltz of the Toreadors
In this robust adaptation of the Jean Anouilh play, Peter Sellers is General Fitzjohn, whose pursuit of a sexy Parisian is thwarted by his put upon wife (Margaret Leighton) and a lecherous doctor. Directed by John Guillermin, the film is a breezy and tasteful comedy of sexual and social morals.
VHS: S02705. $14.98.
Laser: LD75518. $49.95.
John Guillermin, Great Britain, 1962, 100 mins.

The Way Ahead
David Niven, Peter Ustinov and Trevor Howard bring great intensity to this World War II drama. Seven civilians are called to serve their country. Niven must get them into shape for the grueling North African invasion.
VHS: S23956. $19.95.
Carol Reed, Great Britain, 1944, 110 mins.

We Dive at Dawn
John Mills and Eric Portman star in this first-rate World War II submarine saga. Unique for its unusually sensitive characterization of the men on the submarine.
VHS: S10581. $19.95.
Anthony Asquith, Great Britain, 1943, 98 mins.

The Weaker Sex
Ursula Jeans, Cecil Parker and Derek Bond bring realistic portrayals to this fictional account of a widow at home during the trauma of the Second World War. She manages to keep everything running even on the eve of D-Day.
VHS: S25707. $19.95.
Roy Ward Baker, Great Britain, 1949, 89 mins.

When Knights Were Bold
Fay Wray and Jack Buchanan star in this farce about a British nobleman who is having trouble at the manor. Accidentally hit in the head by a suit of armor, he dreams about his illustrious ancestors and learns how to act in a truly noble fashion.
VHS: S23791. $24.95.
Jack Raymond, Great Britain, 1936, 55 mins.

Whiskey Galore
One of the drollest, most amusing British films ever made. Scottish islanders take drastic measures when a cargo of whiskey is marooned off their shore. Also known by the title *Tight Little Island*.
VHS: S02030. $29.95.
Alexander MacKendrick, Great Britain, 1958, 80 mins.

Wicked Lady
Unsatisfied by carnal conquests, her passions drew her into a secret life of crime until she finally took one step too far. With Margaret Lockwood.
VHS: S06543. $19.98.
Leslie Arliss, Great Britain, 1945, 100 mins.

Windom's Way
Peter Finch plays an idealistic doctor stationed on a Far Eastern island that's seething with riots and political unrest, trying to encourage resistance to Communist takeover. One of Finch's most memorable and strongest performances.
VHS: S06431. $29.98.
Ronald Neame, Great Britain, 1958, 108 mins.

The Winslow Boy
Based on the play by Terrence Rattigan, a brilliantly acted courtroom drama with Robert Donat as the barrister who is defending Ronnie Winslow (Neil North) after he has been expelled from school.
VHS: S04559. $19.98.
Anthony Asquith, Great Britain, 1950, 117 mins.

Wrong Arm of the Law
Peter Sellers stars in this funny movie: a trio of cockney men have both the police and the crooks after them because they've been dressing as cops, and confiscating loot from apprehended robbers. With Lionel Jeffries, Bernard Cribbins.
VHS: S04788. $39.95.
Cliff Owen, Great Britain, 1963, 91 mins.

The Years Between
A poignant adaptation of Daphne du Maurier's play about a member of Parliament (Michael Redgrave) who was presumed killed in the war. He turns up unexpectedly in London and discovers his wife (Valerie Hobson) has been elected to replace him and is about to remarry. With Flora Robson, Felix Aylmer and James McKechnie.
VHS: S19878. $29.95.
Compton Bennett, Great Britain, 1946, 100 mins.

Young Wives' Tale
A British social comedy centered around post-war housing shortages. Adapted from the play by Ronald Jeans, the story concerns a playwright and his exuberant wife who are forced to share living quarters with a refined couple. With Joan Greenwood, Nigel Patrick, Derek Farr, Guy Middleton and Audrey Hepburn.
VHS: S19879. $29.95.
Henry Cass, Great Britain, 1951, 79 mins.

Zulu
Michael Caine is featured in this version of British colonial troops under seige by thousands of Zulu warriors, based on a true incident from 1879.
VHS: S01740. $14.95.
Laser: Widescreen. LD70491. $59.95.
Cy Endfield, Great Britain, 1963, 130 mins.

Bridge on the River Kwai
Epic story of British prisoners of war held by the Japanese combines psychological battles of will with gripping action. Winner of seven Oscars including Best Picture and Director. The Oscar for Screenplay went to Pierre Boulle, the novelist who spoke no English, because screenwriters Carl Foreman and Michael Wilson were blacklisted. With William Holden and Alec Guinness. Letterboxed.
VHS: S01785. $19.95.
Laser: Letterboxed. LD72066. $49.95.
David Lean, Great Britain, 1957, 161 mins.

Brief Encounter
Trevor Howard and Celia Johnson play a doctor and a housewife in love with each other but married to other people. Based on Noel Coward's *Still Life*, this is a beautiful and sensitively understated British drama. With Stanley Holloway and Everly Gregg. B&W.
VHS: S06239. $39.95.
David Lean, Great Britain, 1945, 86 mins.

Doctor Zhivago
Lavish Hollywood adaptation of the epic love story set against the Russian Revolution, winner of six Academy Awards. A Russian poet and physician, who wishes to live a quiet, normal life, bears witness to a society in chaos as it struggles to bring forth a new world free from stagnation and oppression. Based on the novel by Boris Pasternak. Sweeping, majestic cinematography on a grand scale. 30th anniversary edition, with 60-minute documentary, trailer and introduction by Omar Sharif. Letterboxed.
VHS: S04332. $24.98.
Laser: LD70561. $99.98.
David Lean, USA/Great Britain, 1965, 176 mins.

Hobson's Choice
Charles Laughton stars in this comedy as a boot shop owner whose despotic manner is challenged when his hot tempered daughter (Brenda de Banzie) decides to marry a meek boot maker played by John Mills. David Lean adapted this farce from one of Britain's most popular plays.
VHS: S02032. $29.95.
Laser: LD75382. $49.98.
David Lean, Great Britain, 1953, 107 mins.

In Which We Serve
Noel Coward stars in this World War II era drama. It follows the life on board a British destroyer as it faces the daily routine of boredom and the constant danger of Nazi U-boats.
VHS: S26960. $14.98.
David Lean, Great Britain, 1942, 115 mins.

Lawrence of Arabia (30th Anniversary Edition)
David Lean's finest achievement is a historically expansive biography of British officer T.E. Lawrence and his military and political victories in the Middle East. The film provides a complex portrait of Lawrence, from his charisma, verve and adventure to his experiments with the dark side of human nature. This 30th Anniversary Edition is presented in its original screen format, with its theatrical trailer, a short on the making of the film and a 32-page booklet. With Peter O'Toole, Alec Guinness, Anthony Quinn and Omar Sharif. Cinematography by Freddie Young.
VHS: S17926. $34.95.
David Lean, Great Britain, 1962, 216 mins.

Lawrence of Arabia (Restored)
A labor of love by Robert A. Harris and Jim Painten and their team of restorers, who have returned nearly 35 minutes to the edited version of the David Lean epic of the exploits of T.E. Lawrence, adventurer and soldier. Peter O'Toole makes a striking impression in his first starring role. The film won seven Oscars. With Alec Guinness, Omar Sharif, Anthony Quinn and Jose Ferrer as the evil Turkish Colonel. Presented in the letterbox format which preserves the wide screen image.
VHS: S10608. $29.95.
Laser: CAV. LD70413. $124.95.
Laser: CLV. LD70414. $69.95.
David Lean, Great Britain, 1962, 216 mins.

Oliver Twist
There have been at least a dozen film versions of this classic tale from Charles Dickens about making the best of a bad situation. This one stars Alec Guiness as Fagin, the ruthless head of a crime school for underprivileged British riffraff. John Howard Davies is Oliver. Little Anthony Newley is his best friend Dodger. With Robert Newton, Kay Walsh and Diana Dors. B&W. A terrific film.
VHS: S06236. $19.98.
Laser: LD75410. $49.95.
David Lean, Great Britain, 1948, 116 mins.

A Passage to India
Judy Davis, Peggy Ashcroft and Victor Banerjee star in this adaptation of E.M. Forster's celebrated novel about the clash of Indian and British cultures and classes in 1920's colonial India.
VHS: S00996. $19.95.
Laser: CLV, widescreen. LD74889. $39.95.
David Lean, Great Britain, 1984, 163 mins.

The Passionate Friends (One Woman's Story)
Claude Rains, Trevor Howard and Ann Todd are superbly cast in this adaptation of an H.G. Wells novel. It all concerns a spurned marriage proposal. After many years the woman who married for money and not for love begins to consider her choice all over again when she meets her old beau.
VHS: S23957. $19.95.
David Lean, Great Britain, 1948, 86 mins.

Ryan's Daughter
Robert Bolt (A Man for All Seasons, The Mission) wrote the screenplay of this long but rewarding study by David Lean about a rich, unsatisfied, married woman (Sarah Miles) who falls for a British soldier (Christopher Jones) during British colonial rule of Ireland. Robert Mitchum is cast as Miles' British school teacher; John Mills is excellent as a crippled mute.
VHS: S02570. $29.95.
Laser: LD70185. $49.98.
David Lean, Great Britain, 1970, 192 mins.

Summertime (Summer Madness)
Katharine Hepburn is a lonely American spinster vacationing in Venice who is swept into a mercurial romance with a charismatic though married local (Rossano Brazzi). "As an aging virgin, [Hepburn is] at the archetype of a Henry James heroine grown old" (Pauline Kael). With Isa Miranda, Darren McGavin, Mari Aldon and Andre Morell.
VHS: S05632. $24.95.
Laser: LD70763. $39.95.
David Lean, Great Britain/USA, 1955, 99 mins.

This Happy Breed
David Lean's version of Noel Coward's play is a cavalcade about an ordinary family living in a suburban house over the course of several decades and generations. Filled with imaginative camera work and color, the film is both beautiful to look at and beautifully played by a winning cast. "It should be gratifying entertainment for those who put their faith in the human heart" (Bosley Crowther).
VHS: S13737. $39.95.
David Lean, Great Britain, 1944, 114 mins.

POWELL/PRESSBURGER

The 49th Parallel
Laurence Olivier heads the cast of this superior World War II movie commissioned by the Ministry of Information in 1940. When six Nazis are separated from their U-Boat in Northern Canada, it's up to the average citizens to stop them from reaching safety. With Eric Portman, Raymond Massey, Leslie Howard, Anton Walbrook and Glynis Johns. B&W.
VHS: S06213. $29.98.
Laser: LD70366. $39.95.
Michael Powell, Great Britain, 1941, 107 mins.

Black Narcissus
Considered one of the most beautiful films ever produced, Black Narcissus is set amidst the awesome grandeur of the Himalayas. Starring Deborah Kerr, this is a haunting emotional film about isolation, spiritual failure and sexual frustration in a convent.
VHS: S00137. $14.98.
Laser: LD70345. $79.95.
Laser: LD70347. $49.95.
Powell/Pressburger, Great Britain, 1947, 100 mins.

A Canterbury Tale
A modern parallel to Chaucer's noted report is the story of the effects of that story's countryside on an American G.I. and three Britishers who find themselves en route to the hallowed cathedral on the same Pilgrims Way taken by travelers some 600 years ago. This rare Michael Powell and Emeric Pressburger film says simple, direct, unaffected and charming things about the venerated traditions of Canterbury, the English and the American Army which "invaded" the area in 1944.
VHS: S12960. $39.95.
Powell/Pressburger, Great Britain, 1948, 97 mins.

Edge of the World
A fascinating early work from British stylist Michael Powell has the visual intensity and gothic romanticism of the Murnau/Flaherty masterpiece Tabu. Shot on the picturesque North Sea isle of Foula, the film centers on a torrid love affair which is disrupted by the harsh disapproval of the woman's father. "Rare for its time, this vigorous location drama in the Flaherty tradition [is]...usually exhilarating" (Leslie Halliwell). With Niall MacGinnis, Belle Chrystal, John Laurie and Finlay Currie.
VHS: S19863. $29.95.
Michael Powell, Great Britain, 1937, 80 mins.

Elusive Pimpernel
David Niven plays Sir Percy Blakeney, the indolent dandy in London, who is also Pimpernel, the leader of a league of young men out to rescue the French aristocrats from the 1792 Terror of Paris. Based on Baroness Orczy's The Scarlet Pimpernel.
VHS: S13736. $39.95.
Powell/Pressburger, Great Britain, 1950, 109 mins.

I Know Where I'm Going
A delightfully unpretentious romantic comedy about a girl who is going to marry for money and who finds her ideas challenged. She runs away and finds true love on a scenic island off the coast of Scotland. With an award-winning performance by Wendy Hiller.
VHS: S12958. $39.95.
Michael Powell, Great Britain, 1946, 91 mins.

Life and Death of Colonel Blimp
From the creators of Red Shoes, this is the drastically cut version of the Powell-Pressburger classic about a pompous British officer who slowly recognizes the limitations of the Empire on the eve of World War II. As social history and satire, this is a brilliant glimpse of the rise and fall of the British monarchy—its antiquated system personified by Clive Candy (Roger Livesey) as he moves from its imperial past (the Boer War) to its destructive future (Suez Canal, India). Deborah Kerr is excellent in three separate roles.
VHS: Out of print. For rental only.
Laser: CLV, 2 discs, Criterion. LD70415. $69.95.
Powell/Pressburger, Great Britain, 1943, 115 mins.

The Lion Has Wings
Michael Powell was one of the three directors of Alexander Korda's documentary exploration of the political, social and military roots which occasioned the outbreak of the second World War. The film focuses on the professionalism and courage of the Royal Air Force. The other directors were Brian Desmond Hurst and Adrian Brunel. With Merle Oberon, Ralph Richardson, June Duprez, Robert Douglas, Anthony Bushell and Brian Worth.
VHS: S19867. $29.95.
Powell/Hurst/Brunel, Great Britain, 1939, 76 mins.

One of Our Aircraft Is Missing
Excellent war melodrama in which the crew of a downed bomber tries to get back to England from its landing place in Holland. From the director of Peeping Tom and Black Narcissus.
VHS: S02590. $39.95.
Michael Powell, Great Britain, 1941, 106 mins.

Peeping Tom
From the director of Red Shoes and Black Narcissus, a classic psychological study of a voyeuristic maniac who murders women while filming them with his 16mm camera. A riveting film in the tradition of Hitchcock. Rarely seen; recommended.
VHS: S01006. $39.95.
Laser: LD72275. $49.95.
Michael Powell, Great Britain, 1960, 88 mins.

Red Shoes
Michael Powell and Emeric Pressburger's classic, beautiful film about a young ballerina (Moira Shearer) and the young composer (Marius Goring) who are taken under the wing of impressario Anton Walbrook.
VHS: S01655. $14.98.
Powell/Pressburger, Great Britain, 1948, 133 mins.

The Small Back Room
The mature and powerful story of crippled munitions expert David Farrar, who is frustrated by his infirmity and the mindless government bureaucracy he must repeatedly contend with during World War II.
VHS: S14529. $39.95.
Powell/Pressburger, Great Britain, 1949, 106 mins.

Tales of Hoffman
Michael Powell and Emeric Pressburger's splendid tale of a poet's amorous adventures. Offenbach's magnificent score and impressive dancing by Moira Shearer and others highlight the pursuit of three women: Olympia is a puppet passed off as a real woman to Hoffman, who sees her torn to pieces before his eyes; a Venetian courtesan, Giulietta, captures Hoffman's mirror image, and his soul; a beautiful singer must remain silent lest she suffer the fate of her mother, who died of consumption.
VHS: S16211. $39.95.
Laser: 2 discs: CAV/CLV. LD71523. $99.95.
Michael Powell, Great Britain, 1951, 124 mins.

SHERLOCK HOLMES

The Abbey Grange
A burnt dog collar provides the clue needed to solve the mysterious murder of Sir Eustace Brackenstall. Starring Jeremy Brett. Granada TV, 55 mins.
VHS: S11703. $24.95.

The Adventures of Sherlock Holmes
Basil Rathbone and Nigel Bruce must outwit the Napoleon of Crime, Dr. Moriarty, in his quest to accomplish the crime of the century. It has to do with the Star of Delhi emerald and the safety of Ida Lupino. With Alan Marshal, E.E. Clive, Henry Stephenson and George Zucco as Moriarty. B&W.
VHS: S06079. $19.98.
Albert Werker, USA, 1939, 82 mins.

The Blue Carbuncle
While Holmes tries to discover the secret behind a precious stone, a man's life hangs in balance. Starring Jeremy Brett. BBC TV, 52 mins.
VHS: S24401. $19.98.

The Boscombe Valley Mystery
The stories of Arthur Conan Doyle are transposed to a contemporary setting, as Watson's fishing holiday is ruined by the shocking declaration of his son's arrest in the murder of a local farmer. With Jeremy Brett as Holmes, Edward Hardwicke as Watson, James Purefoy and Joanna Roth. Granada TV, 50 mins.
VHS: S18154. $24.98.

The Bruce Partington Plans
A young man is brutally murdered. Starring Jeremy Brett. Granada TV, 55 mins.
VHS: S11713. $24.95.

The Cardboard Box
Susan Cushing needs Sherlock Holmes (Jeremy Brett) to find her missing sister. A grisly Christmas gift finally convinces Holmes that he must indeed take on this investigation. Granada TV, 50 mins.
VHS: S27447. $19.98.

The Copper Beeches
Why does Violet Hunter's prospective employer insist that she cut off her hair to take a position at The Copper Beeches as governess? Before too long, Holmes receives a panicked message from the girl. Jeremy Brett plays Holmes. Granada TV, 55 mins.
VHS: S11134. $24.95.

The Creeping Man
A dark, hunched silhouette at her bedroom window and the howling of the family's pet dog has terrified the daughter of an eminent professor. Holmes advises Miss Presbury to keep her door locked as he continues his investigations: "The prowler who looked in on you is no ordinary creature…" Starring Jeremy Brett and Edward Hardwicke. Granada TV, 50 mins.
VHS: S16015. $24.98.

The Crooked Man
Arguing is heard coming from the villa of Colonel James Barclay and his wife Nancy. Then, bloodcurdling screams lead the servants to discover the colonel lies dead. What happened to the Barclays? With Jeremy Brett as Holmes. Granada TV, 55 mins.
VHS: S11133. $24.95.

The Crucifer of Blood
Charlton Heston. You loved him as Moses. You cheered him as Ben Hur. Now you can enjoy the way his mind works as Sherlock Holmes, master detective. The case at hand: a 30-year blood oath which is behind a current crop of ghastly murders. Based on the characters created by A. Conan Doyle and the play by Paul Giovanni. With Richard Johnson as Dr. Watson and Simon Callow as Inspector Lestrade. Also in the cast are Clive Wood, Edward Fox and Susannah Harker as the mysterious Irene St. Claire.
VHS: S15616. $89.98.
Fraser C. Heston, USA/Great Britain, 1991, 105 mins.

The Dancing Men
It seemed like an innocent child's game, but in truth, it may lead to murder. From the acclaimed BBC series starring the incomparable Jeremy Brett as the world's greatest detective. 52 mins.
VHS: S24402. $19.98.

The Devil's Foot
A young woman is found dead, possibly murdered, but there is no trace of injury, sickness or violence. Starring Jeremy Brett. Granada TV, 55 mins.
VHS: S11711. $24.95.

The Disappearance of Lady Frances Carfax
A series of letters from Doctor Watson to Holmes about the enigmatic and mysterious Lady Frances elicits his curiosity, especially when she disappears and Holmes is called in to investigate. Starring Jeremy Brett and Edward Hardwicke. Granada TV, 50 mins.
VHS: S18156. $24.98.

Dressed to Kill
One of the more baffling of the classic Rathbone-Bruce "Holmes" films. Three music boxes, sold at auction, hold the secret to the location of banknote plates stolen from the Bank of England. Expert detection by Holmes solves the almost impossible cipher with the help of bumbling Dr. Watson. USA, 1946, 72 mins.
VHS: S01141. $19.95.

The Dying Detective
Adelaide Savage beseeches Sherlock Holmes (Jeremy Brett) to investigate her husband's cousin, Culverton Smith. Her fears of disaster are confirmed when Victor Savage dies of a rare parasitic fever. This type of illness, oddly enough, happens to be the specialty of the suspicious cousin. Granada TV, 50 mins.
VHS: S27445. $19.98.

The Eligible Bachelor
Jeremy Brett and David Burke star as Holmes and Watson in this story about a missing bride. A young American bride disappears at her wedding breakfast, but Holmes is plagued by nightmares that force him to consider the consequences of any action he might take to solve the mystery of this disappearance. 105 mins.
VHS: S24397. $19.95.

The Empty House
In this companion tape to The Final Problem, Holmes' confrontation with Professor Moriarty may be his last. Starring Jeremy Brett as Holmes. Granada TV, 55 mins.
VHS: S11706. $24.95.

The Final Problem
When the Mona Lisa is stolen from the Louvre in Paris, the French government calls in Holmes to investigate, pitting him against the "Napoleon" of crime, arch criminal Professor Moriarty. With Jeremy Brett as Holmes. Granada TV, 55 mins.
VHS: S11139. $24.95.

The Golden Pince-Nez
Scotland Yard seeks the help of Sherlock Holmes (Jeremy Brett) for a baffling case. The only clue is a golden pince-nez found in the clutches of a murdered young man. It's a mystery that stretches all the way to war-torn St. Petersburg. Granada TV, 50 mins.
VHS: S27443. $19.98.

The Greek Interpreter
Sherlock Holmes' brother Mycroft asks for assistance when Mr. Melas relays to him a mysterious story about a late night visitor. Who was the foreign young man who adamantly refused when Mr. Melas asked him to sign an unknown document? With Jeremy Brett. Granada TV, 55 mins.
VHS: S11135. $24.95.

Hands of a Murderer
Sherlock Holmes (Edward Woodward) and his trusted friend Dr. Watson (John Hillerman) appear to have finally tracked down and captured the devilish Moriarty (Anthony Andrews). A bungling constable lets the fiend escape the gallows and now Holmes and Watson find themselves enmeshed in a series of intrigues and double bluffs that place the fate of England at risk.
VHS: S26775. $24.98.
Stuart Orme, Great Britain, 1995, 97 mins.

The Hound of the Baskervilles (Brett)
What is the weird curse of the Baskerville family? Sir Charles Baskerville is found dead and when Sir Henry Baskerville arrives from America, he finds a death threat waiting for him at his hotel. An escaped killer roams the moors…A woman cries…A dog howls through the night…And Sherlock Holmes is called in to investigate. With Jeremy Brett as Holmes; Granada TV. Please specify Granada TV version. 120 mins.
VHS: S11141. $39.95.
Laser: LD71469. $29.98.

The Hound of the Baskervilles (Cushing)
An eerie rendering of Sir Arthur Conan Doyle's tale made by the Hammer studio. Director Terence Fisher interprets the Baskerville legend, the notorious "hound for hell" that stalks the gilded, secretive family. With Peter Cushing as Holmes, Andre Morell as Watson and Christopher Lee. "The best Sherlock Holmes movie ever made" (Time Out).
VHS: S18479. $19.98.

The Hound of the Baskervilles (Rathbone)
The first of the Basil Rathbone series of Sherlock Holmes films finds Britain's favorite sleuth afoot on the moors of Dartmoor in Devonshire. It seems the Baskerville family is laboring under the curse of a gigantic hound and seeks assistance. Holmes and Watson do their best. With Nigel Bruce, Richard Greene and Chief, a 140-pound Great Dane, as the title character. B&W.
VHS: S06078. $19.98.
Sidney Lanfield, USA, 1939, 80 mins.

The Hound of the Baskervilles (Richardson)
A stylish, well-acted adaptation of Sir Arthur Conan Doyle's story about Sherlock Holmes' investigation of an eerie string of unsolved murders at an English manor. With Donald Churchill, Martin Shaw, Denholm Elliott and Ian Richardson as Holmes.
VHS: S18071. $59.95.
Douglas Hickox, Great Britain, 1983, 100 mins.

The House of Fear
Based on the A. Conan Doyle story The Adventure of the Five Orange Pips, where members of a men's club are being murdered in Scotland. Holmes is summoned to prevent the membership from swindling down to nothing. With Holmes Herbert, Aubrey Mather and Dennis Hoey as Inspector Lestrade. Rathbone and Bruce continue in their most familiar roles. B&W.
VHS: S06083. $19.98.
Roy William Neill, USA, 1945, 69 mins.

The Illustrious Client
Holmes risks his life when he becomes involved with a murdering Austrian baron and the young, wealthy woman who wants to marry him. Can Holmes withstand the evil forces at the baron's command? Starring Jeremy Brett and Edward Hardwicke. Granada TV, 50 mins.
VHS: S16016. $24.98.

The Last Vampyre
Jeremy Brett and David Burke star as the peerless investigators created by Sir Arthur Conan Doyle. In this film villagers begin to suspect that a returned descendant of a family exterminated as vampires is once again causing trouble in their village. 105 mins.
VHS: S24396. $19.95.

The Man with the Twisted Lip
A worried wife consults Sherlock Holmes about her missing husband. Starring Jeremy Brett. Granada TV, 55 mins.
VHS: S11707. $24.95.

The Master Blackmailer
The brilliant Sherlock Holmes (Jeremy Brett) and Doctor Watson (Edward Hardwicke) are enlisted to capture a diabolical blackmailer who has been victimizing a group of Londoners. 120 mins.
VHS: S19930. $24.98.

The Mazarin Stone
Sherlock Holmes (Jeremy Brett) is not at home, so Watson must find the missing Garrideb family member. This person must be found to resolve the last will and testament of the deceased and formerly very wealthy Nathan Garrideb. Coincidentally, or so it seems, someone has stolen the Mazarin Stone, a valuable crown jewel. Granada TV, 50 mins.
VHS: S27444. $19.98.

The Musgrave Ritual
The butler didn't do it—he's dead, and nobody is quite sure why. Starring Jeremy Brett. Granada TV, 55 mins.
VHS: S11704. $24.95.

The Naval Treaty
A secret document disappears and the fate of the future of Europe depends on its retrieval by Sherlock Holmes. Starring Jeremy Brett. BBC TV, 52 mins.
VHS: S24400. $19.98.

The Norwood Builder
Is the young solicitor John McFarlane responsible for the death of the Norwood builder? Why did the builder, until a day before a virtual stranger to McFarlane, want his will suddenly changed to leave everything to McFarlane? Granada TV; with Jeremy Brett as Holmes. 55 mins.
VHS: S11136. $24.95.

The Pearl of Death
Mystery blends with horror in this Sherlock Holmes film based on Doyle's The Six Napoleons. The search is on for the fabled Borgia pearl and a human killing machine that likes to break backs. Starring Rathbone and Bruce. With Evelyn Ankers in several disguises and introducing Rondo Hatton as the Oxton Creeper. B&W.
VHS: S06084. $19.98.
Roy William Neill, USA, 1944, 69 mins.

The Priory School
The Duke of Holdernesse's son is kidnapped from his prestigious preparatory school. Starring Jeremy Brett. Granada TV, 55 mins.
VHS: S11708. $24.95.

The Problem of Thor Bridge
An American gold magnate's governess is being held on charges of shooting his wife, and Holmes is invited to help in the matter. When the American makes an untimely and noisy departure, Holmes is perplexed until Watson suggests a visit to the governess. Starring Jeremy Brett and Edward Hardwicke. Granada TV, 50 mins.
VHS: S16017. $24.98.

The Red Circle
Mrs. Warren asks for Sherlock Holmes (Jeremy Brett) to investigate a strange lodger in her home, a man who never leaves his room. While searching for clues, Holmes finds a former lodger of Mrs. Warren's is dead. An American helps Holmes draw a connection between these two strange occurrences. Granada TV, 50 mins.
VHS: S27446. $19.98.

The Red-Headed League
A mysterious ad calls for all red-headed men to join a league that would pay handsomely for rather nominal services. Pawnbroker Jabez Wilson applies and thinks himself fortunate to get the job until two months later when the league is mysteriously dissolved. With Jeremy Brett as Sherlock Holmes. Granada TV, 55 mins.
VHS: S11138. $24.95.

The Resident Patient
After a corpulent Mr. Blessington sets up doctor Percy Trevelyan in a fashionable practice, his benefactor installs himself at the house as the Resident Patient. When a Russian father and son disappear during a consultation, Holmes and Watson are called in to find out why Mr. Blessington is the most frightened man in town. With Jeremy Brett as Holmes. Granada TV, 55 mins.
VHS: S11137. $24.95.

A Scandal in Bohemia
Starring Jeremy Brett and David Burke, this episode features a distressed King of Bohemia. Naturally the King needs Sherlock Holmes to help him. It seems some indiscretion with a lady could damage the reputation of royalty in Europe. BBC TV, 50 mins.
VHS: S24403. $19.98.

The Scarlet Claw
Holmes and Watson attend an occult convention in Quebec and investigate a mysterious death in the small village of La Morte Rouge. Why anyone would willingly live in a burg called The Red Death is just one more challenge for Basil Rathbone and Nigel Bruce. With Kay Harding and Gerald Hamer. B&W.
VHS: S06082. $19.98.
Roy William Neill, USA, 1944, 74 mins.

The Second Stain
A secret document is stolen from the house of The Secretary for European Affairs. Starring Jeremy Brett. Granada TV, 55 mins.
VHS: S11705. $24.95.

Sherlock Holmes and the Deadly Necklace
Christopher Lee stars as Sherlock Holmes as he and Dr. Watson again battle the evil Moriarty who's after a valuable necklace.
VHS: S09533. $29.95.
Terence Fisher, Great Britain, 1964, 85 mins.

Sherlock Holmes and the Incident at Victoria Falls
Called upon to transport the world's most valuable diamond from Africa to London, the great Sherlock Holmes finds himself in the middle of a murky new mystery that will bring him out of retirement. Romance, murder and mystery in the African jungle, starring Christopher Lee and Patrick Macnee.
VHS: S15583. $89.98.
Bill Corcoran, Great Britain, 1991, 120 mins.

Sherlock Holmes and the Secret Weapon
Dr. Tobel, a Swiss scientist, has invented a new bombsight, and is kidnapped by Holmes' old enemy, Dr. Moriarty. But Dr. Tobel left behind a strange cipher which Holmes will now uncover in a battle of wits. With Basil Rathbone, Nigel Bruce, Lionel Atwill. USA, 1942, 68 mins.
VHS: S01140. $19.95.

Sherlock Holmes and the Spider Woman
This was the first Sherlock Holmes film from Universal with the detective's name out of the title. Gale Sondergaard is the sinister title character who proves a worthy nemesis for Rathbone and Bruce by driving men to commit suicide in their pajamas. With Dennis Hoey as Lestrade. B&W.
VHS: S06085. $19.98.
Roy William Neill, USA, 1944, 62 mins.

Sherlock Holmes and the Voice of Terror
Holmes and Watson are updated to assist in the war against the Nazi menace. Based very loosely on an A. Conan Doyle story, His Last Bow, which involved German spies in WWI. Rathbone and Bruce ferret out a network of saboteurs with the help of Evelyn Ankers. With Thomas Gomez and Reginald Denny. B&W.
VHS: S06080. $19.98.
John Rawlins, USA, 1942, 65 mins.

Sherlock Holmes Faces Death
No nazis in this Rathbone-Bruce film about the mysterious goings on at Hulstone Towers in Northumberland, just plain old fashioned murder. At the ancestral home of the Musgrave family, the secrets of an ancient ritual hold a key to a rash of perplexing deaths. With Dennis Hoey and Hillary Brooke. B&W.
VHS: S06081. $19.98.
Roy William Neill, USA, 1943, 68 mins.

Sherlock Holmes in Washington
The master sleuth goes to the US capitol to find a matchbook that could solve the mystery of the disappearance of a British secret agent. Holmes and Watson see the sights, lecture the FBI and uncover the head of an enemy spy network. With Marjorie Lord, George Zucco and Basil and Nigel as you know who. B&W.
VHS: S06086. $19.98.
Roy William Neill, USA, 1943, 71 mins.

Shoscombe Old Place
Holmes is enlisted to investigate the strange relationship of a brother and sister, a missing creditor and an intricate puzzle whose only clue is a human bone found in a furnace. With Jeremy Brett as Holmes, Edward Hardwicke as Watson and Robin Ellis. Granada TV, 50 mins.
VHS: S18155. $24.98.

The Sign of Four (Brett)
Why after the mysterious disappearance of her father does the beautiful Miss Morstan start receiving each year a present of a rare and lustrous pearl? Who is her mysterious benefactor? Why does this person all of a sudden want to meet her? The mystery builds as Holmes and Watson pursue a priceless hoard of Indian treasure and a murderer. With Jeremy Brett as Holmes. Please specify Granada TV version. 120 mins.
VHS: S11140. $39.95.

The Sign of Four (Richardson)
A superior adaptation of Sir Arthur Conan Doyle's Sherlock Holmes novel about the brilliant detective's face-off with a sinister, one-legged villain and dwarf. Ian Richardson stars as Holmes. With David Healy, Cherie Lunghi, Terence Rigby and Thorley Walters.
VHS: S18070. $59.95.
Desmond Davis, Great Britain, 1983, 100 mins.

The "Silent" Mr. Sherlock Holmes
Two early appearances of Sir Arthur Conan Doyle's immortal creation, Sherlock Holmes. The first, The Copper Beeches (1912), was produced under the personal supervision of Doyle. The Man with the Twisted Lip is one of the few Eille Norwood Holmes silents to survive. Hubert Willis is his Watson. B&W. Silent. USA/Great Britain, 1912-22, 68 mins.
VHS: S05448. $29.95.

Silver Blaze
A highly prized racehorse is abducted, and the horse's trainer is dead. Starring Jeremy Brett. Granada TV, 55 mins.
VHS: S11710. $24.95.

The Six Napoleons
Statues and busts of Napoleon are being smashed all over the London streets. Starring Jeremy Brett. Granada TV, 55 mins.
VHS: S11709. $24.95.

The Solitary Cyclist
A female client of Holmes is kidnapped and he must find her before it's too late. Starring Jeremy Brett. BBC TV, 52 mins.
VHS: S24398. $19.95.

The Speckled Band (Brett)
Holmes must discover a murder weapon that leaves no trace. The survival of a family depends on it. Starring Jeremy Brett. BBC TV, 52 mins.
VHS: S24399. $19.98.

The Speckled Band (Massey)
Raymond Massey in his first film as Sherlock Holmes.
VHS: S03784. $34.95.
Jack Raymond, Great Britain, 1931, 80 mins.

A Study in Scarlet
Reginald Owen stars as Sherlock Holmes in this film based on the A. Conan Doyle story.
VHS: S02591. $34.95.
Edwin L. Marin, USA, 1933

Terror by Night
Sherlock Holmes and the reliable Dr. Watson are engaged to protect the Star of Rhodesia on a train trip to Scotland. Murder and the disappearance of the huge diamond sets Holmes to work. The solution to the railroad robbery and the end of the mayhem is eventual. With Rathbone, Bruce, Alan Mowbray. USA, 1946, 72 mins.
VHS: S01142. $19.95.

The Three Gables
Mary Maberley is grieving the loss of her grandson when a realtor arrives and makes a strange offer to buy her house. A condition of the sale is that she cannot take any of her belongings out of the house. Her lawyer advises her to proceed with care, but it is Sherlock Holmes (Jeremy Brett) who finally unravels the origins of this mysterious offer. Granada TV, 50 mins.
VHS: S27442. $19.98.

The Triumph of Sherlock Holmes
The best of the five Arthur Wontner Holmes films is based on Doyle's Valley of Fear. Wontner looked like the spitting image of Holmes as originally drawn. His Watson was played by Ian Fleming. Not that Ian Fleming. Holmes battles Dr. Moriarty at Birlstone Castle. B&W.
VHS: S05449. $29.95.
Leslie S. Hiscott, Great Britain, 1935, 83 mins.

The Wisteria Lodge
After a murder, Holmes and Watson arrive at the Wisteria Lodge to try and uncover its secret. Starring Jeremy Brett. Granada TV, 55 mins.
VHS: S11712. $24.95.

The Woman in Green
Holmes and Watson are up against the most atrocious crimes since Jack the Ripper. Scotland Yard is baffled, and so is Holmes, until he discovers that behind these crimes is his old nemesis, Dr. Moriarty. With Basil Rathbone, Nigel Bruce, Hillary Brooke. USA, 1945, 68 mins.
VHS: S01143. $19.95.

Young Sherlock Holmes
Story that speculates about the boyhood adventures of the Conan Doyle master sleuth. Includes his introduction to Watson and first case.
VHS: S06298. $19.95.
Barry Levinson, USA, 1985, 109 mins.

british TELEVISION

Absolutely Fabulous Volume One, Part 1
From the BBC, Jennifer Saunders and Joanna Lumley play Edina and Patsy in the biggest British comedy hit since *Fawlty Towers*. They are two 40ish fashionophiles who are out to prove they'll do anything in the name of fun. In this volume they battle with *Fashion, Fat, and France*. 90 mins.
VHS: $25661. $19.98.

Absolutely Fabulous Volume One, Part 2
Edina and Patsy, Jennifer Saunders and Joanna Lumley, are back with mindless over the top and wickedly rich humor in *ISO Tank, Birthday, and Magazine*. 90 mins.
VHS: $25662. $19.98.

Absolutely Fabulous Volume Two, Part 1
Too dumb to know any better and too rich to care, Edina and Patsy, Jennifer Saunders and Joanna Lumley, wend their way through *Hospital, Health, and Morocco*.
VHS: $25663. $19.98.

Absolutely Fabulous Volume Two, Part 2
Even if they could only sober up (or is it settle down?), Edina and Patsy (Jennifer Saunders and Joanna Lumley) would still be the most frighteningly dressed residents of Mayfair. *New Best Friend, Poor and Birth*.
VHS: $25664. $19.98.

Absolutely Fabulous Volume Three, Part 1
Edwina and Patsy's comic misadventures are featured in this collection of three episodes. They represent the final season for this outrageous pair of dimwitted, fast-living, Eurotrash fashion victims. Included are the episodes *Doorhandle, Happy New Year and Sex*. Great Britain, 90 mins.
VHS: $27051. $19.98.

Absolutely Fabulous Volume Three, Part 2
These are the final three episodes of Edwina and Patsy's adventures larger than they should. The episodes *Jealous, Fear and The End* are the last words in comic excess. Great Britain, 90 mins.
VHS: $27052. $19.98.

Agatha Christie's Miss Marple
100 minutes each.
4:50 from Paddington. When a friend decides to visit Miss Marple she has the disagreeable experience of seeing a man strangling a woman in a passing train. Miss Marple sets out to decipher this strange mystery.
VHS: $21162. $19.95.
A Caribbean Mystery. The unflappable Miss Marple goes off to an exclusive resort for a vacation. Just when she is about to become bored among the idle rich, someone is murdered. Now she can do what she does best: outwit the perpetrators of this terrible crime and best the local police.
VHS: $21159. $19.95.
Sleeping Murder. Giles and Gwenda Reed move into their dream house, but this idyll is destroyed by a strange apparition. When Miss Marple discovers the identity of this visitor, she unwittingly provokes the original murderer, placing new victims in danger.
VHS: $21161. $19.95.
The Mirror Cracked from Side to Side. An American movie star goes to the quiet hamlet St. Mary Mead in order to film a new movie. At a party she hosts for the entire village a woman is accidentally poisoned, but it was a mistake. Miss Marple must now investigate the invasion of intrigue from Hollywood that has followed this poor actress.
VHS: $21160. $19.95.
Collector's 4-Video Boxed Set.
VHS: $21163. $79.95.

Agatha Christie's Miss Marple II
Joan Hickson stars as the knitting heroine of this second series of Agatha Christie mysteries.
Agatha Christie's Miss Marple: Murder at the Vicarage. Joan Hickson is Miss Marple, a rather dry old woman with an uncanny sense of justice and a macabre taste for solving crimes. Her investigative powers are suddenly needed in the sleepy country village of St. Mary Mead when a much disliked man is found dead. 100 mins.
VHS: $24232. $19.95.
Agatha Christie's Miss Marple: The Moving Finger. Once again Joan Hickson plays Miss Marple on the trail of murderous intrigue. A rash of poison pen letters is stirring up not only fear but memories of a long forgotten incident many hoped were firmly buried in the past. 100 mins.
VHS: $24233. $19.95.
Agatha Christie's Miss Marple: They Do It with Mirrors. At a rambling country mansion Joan Hickson, as Miss Marple, must contend with a number of off-color incidents. Not only do these events reflect badly on the residents of this great house, but they represent a deadly malice. Only Miss Marple can solve the mystery of the murderer's identity. 100 mins.
VHS: $24234. $19.95.
Agatha Christie's Miss Marple: Nemesis. A cryptic letter sends Miss Marple (Joan Hickson) on a deadly itinerary. Amidst the glorious historic homes she visits there lurks a devious plot fixed on murder. Miss Marple must solve this mystery. 100 mins.
VHS: $24235. $19.95.
Agatha Christie's Miss Marple: At Bertram Hotel. Miss Marple (Joan Hickson) visits her favorite London hotel. Many might find this august setting quite stuffy, but it is just perfect for this sleuth, especially when a murder turns Miss Marple's trip to London into a working vacation. 100 mins.
VHS: $24236. $19.95.
Agatha Christie's Miss Marple II: Collector's Boxed Set. All five videos, each 100 mins.
VHS: $24237. $99.95.

Agatha Christie's Poirot
This witty, imaginative and well acted 10-part series focuses on a string of crimes and murders requiring the attention of Agatha Christie's brilliant detective, the Belgian sleuth Hercule Poirot, brought to vivid, immaculate life by the excellent British actor David Suchet (*The Falcon and the Snowman*).
Four and Twenty Blackbirds.
VHS: $17461. $24.95.
Murder in the Mews.
VHS: $17459. $24.95.
Problem at Sea.
VHS: $17464. $24.95.
The Adventures of the Clapham Cook.
VHS: $17458. $24.95.
The Adventure of Johnnie Waverly.
VHS: $17460. $24.95.
The Dream.
VHS: $17467. $24.95.
The Incredible Theft.
VHS: $17465. $24.95.
The King of Clubs.
VHS: $17466. $24.95.
The Third Floor Flat.
VHS: $17462. $24.95.
Triangle at Rhodes.
VHS: $17463. $24.95.

Archie
The pilot episode of the irreverent and hilarious British comedy program, with John Simpson and Roland Winters. Not the comic strip. On the same program is *The Alan Young Show*.
VHS: $18958. $19.95.

Are You Being Served?
A cast of unbelievably colorful characters make shopping at Grace Brothers a true comic adventure. Their quirky behavior, hilarious banter, and all-round bad manners are on display in two new collections.
Are You Being Served?: Big Brother.
VHS: $15979. $19.98.
Are You Being Served?: Dear Sexy Knickers.
VHS: $15978. $19.98.

Auf Wiedersehen Pet
In the belief that there will be a more rewarding life for them in Germany, three British bricklayers join up with other "down-to-earth" types and set off to find their fortunes. Perhaps the funniest comedy series of the 80's, *Auf Wiedersehen Pet* was hailed by critics and public alike when it premiered on British Television.
Auf Wiedersehen Pet: If I Were a Carpenter... 101 mins.
VHS: $16130. $24.98.
Auf Wiedersehen Pet: The Fugitive... 101 mins.
VHS: $16131. $24.98.

Benny Hill
The British clown prince of comedy in a series of madcap skits and hilarious sketches. Each tape is 55 mins.
Benny Hill's Crazy World!.
VHS: $10345. $19.99.
Benny Hill's Home Video Drive-In.
VHS: $10350. $19.99.
Benny Hill's One Night Video Stand.
VHS: $10349. $19.99.
Benny Hill's Video Follies.
VHS: $10351. $19.99.
Benny Hill's Video Revue.
VHS: $10348. $19.99.
Benny Hill's Video Sideshow.
VHS: $10347. $19.99.
Benny Hill's Video Spotlight.
VHS: $10346. $19.99.

Benny Hill's World: New York
Hill is all over New York, bringing his racy British humor to sites like Central Park, Times Square and the South Street Seaport. He impersonates a rapper and shares that quintessential New York experience, a cab ride. 60 mins.
VHS: $26038. $19.95.

The Best of the Lenny Henry Show
Thrill to revolution, romance, drama and sport with comprehensive comedian Lenny Henry—master of mimicry, devil of disguise. Also starring Frank Bruno, Robbie Coltrane (*Nuns on the Run*) and Dawn French.
VHS: $14514. $19.98.

The Best of the Lovejoy Mysteries
Ian McShane stars as Lovejoy, a charming, handsome, brilliant and thoroughly untrustworthy scoundrel. This disreputable antiques dealer can spot a fake in seconds but he is even more likely to find trouble. The enjoyable British series from A&E includes four episodes, 50 minutes each.
Friends in High Places. Lovejoy agrees to sell an Incan ring for Lady Jane's friend. The question is, which intrigues him more, the ring or its owner?
VHS: $25838. $14.95.
Loveknots. A seemingly ordinary Berber rug is bought for an inflated price at auction. Later this same rug is stolen, leading Lovejoy to suspect something is afoot.
VHS: $25840. $14.95.
Scotch on the Rocks. Lovejoy purchases an 18th-century Scottish commemorative sword from his daughter. Unfortunately, someone else wants it and will do anything to possess it.
VHS: $25839. $14.95.
The Ring. An elaborate scheme should supply Lovejoy with desperately needed cash, except things don't go as planned. Lady Jane finds herself drawn into a game of deception and doesn't even realize it.
VHS: $25841. $14.95.
The Best of the Lovejoy Mysteries, Collector's Boxed Set.
VHS: $25842. $59.95.

The Best of the Two Ronnies
Ronnie Corbett and Ronnie Barker are the Two Ronnies. One is short and dark and the other is taller, whiter and a few pounds larger. They have kept England laughing for years, as well as those who watch public television. Now they are on video and ready to entertain anyone with the price of the rental. England, 1983.
VHS: $05613. $29.98.

The Best of What's Left... Not Only...But Also...
Written by and starring Peter Cook and Dudley Moore, the show is comprised of the best comedy sketches from this famous duo who were an inseparable act during the 60's and 70's. This is their reunion tape.
VHS: $14513. $19.98.

A Bit of Fry and Laurie
Irreverent and sly humor BBC style, literate and self-reflexive, with Stephen Fry and Hugh Laurie (*Jeeves and Wooster*) that's provocative and witty. 89 mins.
VHS: $18876. $19.98.

Black Adder Goes Forth: The Western Front of WWII, 1917
Rowan Atkinson, Tony Robinson, Brian Blessed, Tim McInnerny, Elspet Gray and Peter Cook take the Western Front by storm. Is the 20th Century ready for Black Adder's impudent brand of satire? In two relentless volumes.
Black Adder Goes Forth, Part 1. 100 mins.
VHS: $15974. $14.98.
Black Adder Goes Forth, Part 2. 100 mins.
VHS: $15975. $14.98.

The Black Adder I, Part I
Rowan Atkinson, Tony Robinson, Brian Blessed, Tim McInnerny, Elspet Gray and Peter Cook star in this very popular comedy series. Includes "The Foretelling", "Born to Be King" and "The Archbishop."
VHS: $14511. $14.98.

The Black Adder I, Part II
This irreverent British satire stars Rowan Atkinson, Tony Robinson, Brian Blessed, Tim McInnerny, Elspet Gray and Peter Cook. Includes "The Queen of Spain's Beard", "Witchsmeller Pursuivant" and "The Black Seal."
VHS: $14512. $14.98.

Black Adder II: The 16th Century
Being a Renaissance man is no reason to stop mucking up the pages of history. Edmund is at it again, with his incorrigible exploits tainting two darkly funny volumes. Rowan Atkinson, Tony Robinson, Brian Blessed, Tim McInnerny, Elspet Gray and Peter Cook star in Part 1. Part 2 features Miranda Richardson and Rowan Atkinson.
Black Adder II, Part 1. 100 mins.
VHS: $15972. $14.98.
Black Adder II, Part 2. 100 mins.
VHS: $15973. $14.98.

Black Adder the Third, Part I
Rowan Atkinson stars in this outrageously witty and popular satire, the Blackadder series. In three brilliantly funny episodes set in Regency England, Edmund Blackadder, valet and butler to the phenomenally "mini-brained" Prince Regent, sums up everything from the French Revolution to the British nobility. From the BBC.
VHS: $11212. $14.98.

Black Adder the Third, Part II
This successful series from Britain features three episodes from the scrolls of Blackadder, an English family of cowards and cads, who never seem to get a solid grip on life.
VHS: $12585. $14.98.

Black Adder's Christmas Carol
Rowan Atkinson, Robbie Coltrane and Miranda Richardson star in this farcical adaptation of Dickens's immortal *A Christmas Carol*.
VHS: $17373. $19.98.

Blakes 7
Intergalactic adventure follows an interplanetary resistance group battling for survival against a totalitarian superpower. Roaming a universe of boundless space and restrictive discipline, freedom-fighter Blake and the crew of spaceship *Liberator* lock in combat with the all-powerful forces of the Federation.
Blakes 7, Volume 1. *The Way Back/Space Fall.* 105 mins.
VHS: $16137. $19.98.
Blakes 7, Volume 2. *Cygnus Alpha/Time Squad.* 105 mins.
VHS: $16138. $19.98.
Blakes 7, Volume 3. *The Web/Seek, Locate, Destroy.* 105 mins.
VHS: $16139. $19.98.
Blakes 7, Volume 4. *Mission to Destiny/Duel.* 105 mins.
VHS: $16140. $19.98.
Blakes 7, Volume 5. *Project Avalon/Breakdown.* 105 mins.
VHS: $16141. $19.98.
Blakes 7, Volume 6. *Bounty/Deliverance.* 105 mins.
VHS: $16142. $19.98.
Blakes 7, Volume 7. *Orac/Redemption.*
VHS: $19267. $19.98.
Blakes 7, Volume 8. *Shadow/Weapon.*
VHS: $19268. $19.98.
Blakes 7, Volume 9. *Horizon/Pressure Point.*
VHS: $19269. $19.98.
Blakes 7, Volume 10. *Trial/Killer.*
VHS: $19270. $19.98.
Blakes 7, Volume 11. *Hostage/Countdown.*
VHS: $19271. $19.98.
Blakes 7, Volume 12. *Voices from Past/Gambit.*
VHS: $19272. $19.98.

Blakes 7, Volume 13. *Keeper/Star One.*
VHS: $19273. $19.98.
Blakes 7, Volume 14. *Aftermath/Powerplay.*
VHS: $19274. $19.98.
Blakes 7, Volume 15. *Volcano/Dawn of Gods.*
VHS: $19275. $19.98.
Blakes 7, Volume 16. *Harvest of Kairos/City at Edge of the World.*
VHS: $19276. $19.98.
Blakes 7, Volume 17. *Children of Auron/Rumors of Death.*
VHS: $19277. $19.98.
Blakes 7, Volume 18. *Sarcophagus/Ultraworld.*
VHS: $19278. $19.98.
Blakes 7, Volume 19. *Moloch/Death-Watch.*
VHS: $19279. $19.98.
Blakes 7, Volume 20. *Terminal/Rescue.*
VHS: $19280. $19.98.
Blakes 7, Volume 21. *Power/Traitor.*
VHS: $19281. $19.98.
Blakes 7, Volume 22. *Stardrive/Animals.*
VHS: $19282. $19.98.
Blakes 7, Volume 23. *Headhunter/Assassin.*
VHS: $19283. $19.98.
Blakes 7, Volume 24. *Games/Sand.*
VHS: $19284. $19.98.
Blakes 7, Volume 25. *Gold/Orbit.*
VHS: $19285. $19.98.
Blakes 7, Volume 26. *Warlord/Blake.*
VHS: $19286. $19.98.

Blat
The Russian *Sting*. This cross-cultural comedy pits an Italian-Russian gangster against the British financial establishment, with hilarious results. Robert Hardy stars. Great Britain, 90 mins.
VHS: $14326. $49.95.

Bleak House
Denholm Elliott and Diana Rigg star in Charles Dickens' biting social commentary on 19th century English justice. John Jarndyce (Elliott) rises above a notorious law suit that has devastated others. But tragedy ensues when his young ward becomes obsessed with the labyrinthine case and the intrigue surrounding it. Produced by the BBC.
VHS: $07176. $39.98.
Ross Devenish, Great Britain, 1985, 391 mins.

The Body in the Library
From the BBC Miss Marple series comes another challenging murder mystery from the mind of Agatha Christie. Miss Marple (Joan Hickson) is asked to defend Colonel Bantry's reputation and find someone else responsible for leaving a corpse in a certain room in his country estate.
VHS: $06532. $19.98.
Silvio Narizzano, Great Britain, 1987, 151 mins.

Bread
A BBC comedy regarding the usual things: religion, baby christenings, unrequited love, sexual exploits and prowess. A classic dose of the Liverpool family's trials and tribulations. 85 mins.
VHS: $12631. $29.95.

The Bretts
The Bretts are a fiercely competitive family whose wit and charm have captivated audiences for the entire run of this series. They are the center of London's theater world at a time of unmatched glamour and excitement, the 1920's. Their public triumphs and private traumas, from the star couple at the center of the family to the younger, newer luminaries, offer endless riveting drama. Each set contains 6 episodes of 50 minutes for a total of 5 hours.
Collection 1.
VHS: $22938. $129.98.
Collection 2.
VHS: $22939. $129.98.

Brides of Christ
Brenda Fricker (*My Left Foot*) stars in a searing, award-winning, British drama that captures the restless desperation of a reclusive society and its encounters with the outside world. From student Rosemary's rejection of rigid sexual moral codes to Sister Paul's decision to leave the convent for a radical priest, this is a critically-acclaimed, riveting production. Three tapes in a boxed set. Total length: 300 mins.
VHS: $21903. $59.95.

Brideshead Revisited
The acclaimed BBC series, based on the novel by Evelyn Waugh, on the life of Charles Ryder.
Book I: Chapter 1: Nostalgia for a Vanished Past. Charles meets flamboyant Sebastian Flyte. As the youngest son of the aristocratic Marchmain family, he introduces Charles to a charmed life.
VHS: $06621. $19.98.
Book II: Chapter 2: Home and Abroad. Chapter 3: Shadows Close In. Charles and Sebastian visit the self-exiled Lord Marchmain and his mistress in Venice. Then Charles finally meets the compelling Marchmains. Charles is mesmerized.
VHS: $06622. $19.98.
Book III: Chapter 4: Sebastian Against the World. Chapter 5: Julia Blossoms. Sebastian recognizes that his family is stealing Charles, his only friend. Despairing, he becomes a drunkard and runs away. Meanwhile, his sister Julia blossoms into full womanhood and captivates all.
VHS: $06623. $19.98.
Book IV: Chapter 6: Julia's Marriage. Chapter 7: The Unseen Hook. Julia and Rex Mottram marry despite family disapproval. Lady Marchmain falls ill. Julia asks Charles to find Sebastian and bring him back before his mother dies. Charles finds Sebastian in Morocco, but is shocked at what he finds.
VHS: $06624. $19.98.

Book V: Chapter 8: Brideshead Deserted. Chapter 9: Orphans of the Storm. Charles' and Julia's respective marriages begin to fail. Unexpectedly, they meet again. A torrid love affair ensues. Once again Charles returns to Brideshead Castle—this time as Julia's lover.
VHS: S06625. $19.98.
Book VI: Chapter 10: A Twitch upon the Thread. Chapter 11: Brideshead Revisited. Lord Marchmain returns to Brideshead Castle to die. Displeased with his eldest son, he decides to rewrite his will. A chapter of aristocratic tradition comes to a close.
VHS: S06626. $19.98.
Brideshead Revisited, Giftpack: All the six books with a giftpack for storage.
VHS: S06627. $119.88.

Brother Cadfael

Medieval England provides the perfect gloomy setting for this engaging series of murder mysteries starring acclaimed British actor Sir Derek Jacobi. Jacobi brings the same intensity to this series that he demonstrated in *I, Claudius*. 75 mins. each.
Monk's Hood. The Abbey comes into a great inheritance just as a landowner decides to favor the church, because this patron dies from poison at the abbey itself. In addition to this crime, Cadfael must deal with another problem: the landowner's widow is his childhood sweetheart.
VHS: S23636. $19.95.
One Corpse Too Many. Cadfael has just settled into a new and apparently peaceful existence when he stumbles across a brutal murder. In a city at war, he sets out to find the killer.
VHS: S23633. $19.95.
The Leper of St. Giles. A great wedding is to be held at the abbey but the groom is absent. This powerful Baron mysteriously rode into the night and disappeared. Cadfael must find out who harmed the Baron.
VHS: S23635. $19.95.
The Sanctuary Sparrow. The town's goldsmith is robbed and left for dead, leading Cadfael to set off on a trail cloaked in treachery and murder. Can he succeed in finding the perpetrator before a local witch-hunt turns deadly?
VHS: S23634. $19.95.
Complete Set.
VHS: S23637. $79.80.

Brother Cadfael II

Sir Derek Jacobi stars as a monk with a past who has a passion for solving crimes, in this second series. Once a Crusader, he now uses his skills in botany and medicine to find a host of devilish wrongdoers. Each episode is approximately 75 minutes.
St. Peter's Fair. A disagreeable merchant is murdered, but Cadfael suspects that greed is not the motive for this death. Instead, his worst fears are confirmed as another merchant turns up dead. Cadfael becomes embroiled in a wild chase where his very life is at stake.
VHS: S27393. $19.95.
The Devil's Novice. Though a young man confesses to the murder of a cleric, his admission of guilt is nothing but a lie. He is hiding a family story of cowardice and treachery. Cadfael must uncover this tortuous legacy.
VHS: S27394. $19.95.
The Virgin in the Ice. Cadfael's clumsy but much-loved Novice stands accused of murder and rape. In the desperate search for clues that could save this Novice, Cadfael discovers a renegade band of former Crusaders and a young squire who turns out to be a son he knew nothing about.
VHS: S27392. $19.95.
Brother Cadfael II: Boxed Set. The complete three-volume set.
VHS: S27395. $59.95.

The Buccaneers

Edith Wharton's book of the same name was adapted for this enthralling BBC mini-series. A group of rich American women find love, romance and marriage amidst English high society. New World charms delight the English at first, but a clash of cultures leads to a variety of troubles. This is a heartrending, beautifully produced and costumed production. 288 mins.
VHS: S27064. $59.95.

Butterflies

A BBC comedy about a suburban housewife named Ria with two oafish but lovable sons. Although she's happily married, Ria experiences panic when she looks in the mirror: There's so much left to experience! Enter recent divorcee Leonard, lonely and romantic. 60 mins.
VHS: S12632. $29.95.

Chiller: "Here Comes the Mirror Man"

Gary is a reclusive squatter living in a run down church that is painted entirely black inside. His social worker, Wendy, can't seem to leave him alone and wants to know if Michael was the reason he left the hostel and moved into the church. Oddly, though Gary likes to be alone, he is often seen with Michael. When Wendy is replaced by Anna, Michael's true identity is revealed and the revelation leads to unforeseen terrors.
VHS: S26782. $19.98.
Lawrence Gordon Clark, Great Britain, 50 mins.

Chiller: "Number Six"

Five children have fallen prey to a serial killer influenced by Celtic myth. After butchering each with a Druidic knife, he places the victims behind an old oak tree during a full moon. Now, as another full moon approaches, the only clues are the vestiges of a Celtic settlement and a child's drawing containing a shadowy figure.
VHS: S26784. $19.98.
Lawrence G. Clark/Peter Lover, Great Britain, 50 mins.

Chiller: "Prophecy"

A group of students hold a seance in a dark basement just for kicks. Everyone gets a message "from the Great Beyond," but one, addressed to Frannie, is in Latin. "Non Omnis Moriar" means "I shall not die," and one by one all the participants of the seance die except for Frannie. The mystery deepens when she stays with a family whose motto is "Non Omnis Moriar." It seems they are related to an infamous Satanist who died in the very basement where Frannie first heard this prophetic motto.
VHS: S26780. $19.98.
Lawrence Gordon Clark, Great Britain, 50 mins.

Chiller: "The Man Who Didn't Believe in Ghosts"

A young family move into a Victorian castle in Yorkshire. Mysterious events force the wife to conclude there is a paranormal presence at work in her new home. She flees to London with her son and leaves her doubting husband behind. He has made a career debunking stories of the supernatural. One night, all alone at home, he is forced to confront a mysterious figure who disturbs his sleep.
VHS: S26783. $19.98.
Bob Mahoney, Great Britain, 50 mins.

Chiller: "Toby"

When a young woman's pregnancy fails, she and her husband move to a new home in order to begin again. Just as they seem overwhelmed by the prospect of what might have been, the woman finds that she is pregnant again. Everything seems quite normal, except that the doctors can find no fetus in the woman's swelling body. Madness, or worse still, a manifestation of an otherworldly force, offers the only possible explanation.
VHS: S26781. $19.98.
Bob Mahoney, Great Britain, 50 mins.

Christabel

The acclaimed BBC series written by award-winning playwright Dennis Potter stars Elizabeth Hurley as a beautiful young Englishwoman, married to a young German national. Forced into politics by the events of the rising Nazism around her, *Christabel* is a moving, beautifully produced program about love, hardship, survival and the strength of the individual. Great Britain, 1989, 149 mins.
VHS: S10438. $19.98.

The Complete Black Adder

Finally, all 24 episodes of the hilarious BBC series are available, with new outrageous footage that has never been seen before. Rowan Atkinson's historical and hysterical adventures span the ages for a good laugh.
VHS: S26416. $99.98.

Cool It—Phil Cool

Now meet Phil Cool. The remarkable talent of this new British TV comedian brings you some of the funniest sketches ever. Called "the most flexible face in the business"—watch impressions of the Pope in a fish and chip shop, and Prince Charles interviewing Mick Jagger. 59 mins.
VHS: S10634. $29.95.

The Country Diary of an Edwardian Lady

Pippa Guard stars as Edith Holden, the author who wrote the autobiographical best-seller on which this film is based. Beginning with her idyllic childhood in the British countryside, the film follows Edith through her marriage and her mysterious demise.
VHS: S20809. $26.98.
Dirk Campbell, Great Britain, 90 mins.

Dad's Army

An all-time classic! Join Captain Mainwaring and his bumbling group of British Home Guard at their incompetent best. This cowardly "force of ruthless killers" are always ready to strike terror into the heart of the Wehrmacht. Find them at the Walmington-On-Sea.
Dad's Army: Asleep in the Deep. Messrs. Mainwaring, Wilson and Jones in three hilarious episodes. 83 mins.
VHS: S10622. $29.95.
Dad's Army: Big Guns. 87 mins.
VHS: S16124. $24.98.
Dad's Army: Mum's Army. 87 mins.
VHS: S16125. $24.98.
Dad's Army: The Day the Balloon Went Up. The intrepid Home Guard at their incompetent best in three shows from this classic series. 87 mins.
VHS: S10621. $29.95.
Dad's Army: The Deadly Attachment. 87 mins.
VHS: S16123. $24.98.
Dad's Army: The Two and a Half Feathers. 87 mins.
VHS: S16122. $24.98.

The Dangerous Brothers: World of Danger

Fractured, free spirited and volatile comedy from two of England's most versatile performers, Rik Mayall and Adrian Edmondson (*Drop Dead Fred*). 77 mins.
VHS: S18877. $19.98.

A Dark Adapted Eye

The BBC produced this adaptation of a Ruth Rendell, aka Barbara Vine, murder mystery. Two sisters are engaged in a bitter rivalry. Ultimately their competition ends in murder and execution. This story is adapted from the case of Vera Hillyard, one of the last women to hang in Britain. 150 mins.
VHS: S27745. $19.98.

The Darling Buds of May

An exuberant look at the Larkin family. They're a large, boisterous Kent farmer family with a peculiar tendency to find adventure. With David Jason, Pam Ferris, Philip Franks and Catherine Zeta Jones.
A Breath of French Air. Pop is reluctant to travel to foreign lands for the family's much desired vacation, though Charley convinces everyone France is their ideal destination. With their French primer and the smallest child in tow, everyone loads up the Rolls Royce for a surreal and hilarious road trip to "exotic" locales.
VHS: S19187. $26.98.
Oh! To Be in England. On the eve of the birth of the first grandchild, Pop is considering new lines of business and Charley is trying to forge his way as the family wage earner and provider.
VHS: S19188. $26.98.
A Season of Heavenly Gifts. When Pop witnesses a plane crash in an adjoining field, he agrees to transport the cargo and unwittingly becomes involved in a complex smuggling operation.
VHS: S19190. $26.98.
Stranger at the Gates. A young charismatic stranger arrives seeking work and insinuates himself into the Larkins' home, enchanting the kids with magic tricks.
VHS: S19189. $26.98.
The Darling Buds of May. An unsuspecting tax inspector named Cedric Charlton invades the private space of the Larkins' Kent farm to inquire about Pop's nonexistent accounts.
VHS: S19185. $26.98.

When the Green Woods Laugh. While Pop turns to developing properties for additional income, the rest of the family is preparing for Charley and Mariette's extravagant wedding.
VHS: S19186. $26.98.
The Darling Buds of May, Collection No. 1. This collection contains *The Darling Buds of May*, *When the Green Woods Laugh* and *A Breath of French Air*.
VHS: S19191. $74.98.
The Darling Buds of May, Collection No. 2. This collection contains *Oh! To Be in England*, *Stranger at the Gates* and *A Season of Heavenly Gifts*.
VHS: S19192. $74.98.

The Darling Buds of May: Christmas Is Coming

Christmas is a time of anticipation and joy. In the case of the Darling Buds, Marriette's pregnancy only adds to the holiday spirit. In fact there is so much good cheer in this household that the Bud family decide to share their joy with a family that has less to be thankful for. Based on the nostalgic novels of H.E. Bates, this episode from the British TV series adds a bright cheery look at the holiday season. 50 mins.
VHS: S26778. $19.98.

The Darling Buds of May: Le Grand Weekend

Based on the nostalgic novels of H.E. Bates, this British series looks back at the 1950's. In this episode, the family wins a holiday in Paris. Preparations throw the household into chaos and just as things are bubbling along nicely a hurricane ambles into view. 50 mins.
VHS: S26779. $19.98.

Dennis Potter's Lipstick on Your Collar

Dennis Potter's last television series is still too hot for American television. His previous works for British TV, *The Singing Detective* and *Pennies from Heaven*, were critical and popular triumphs. In this series Potter combines rock 'n' roll daydreams with a story about the Suez crisis. As the War Office agonizes over waning British power, two clerks dream of sexual conquest to the driving new rhythms emanating from America. 120 mins.
VHS: S26696. $59.95.

Dennis Potter: The Last Interview

Potter transformed serious television drama with his insightful works for British TV. *The Singing Detective* and *Pennies from Heaven* were hailed as breakthroughs combining challenging themes with complex characters. Potter's stories went well beyond the usual manipulations found in standard psychological dramas. This interview with Potter, shot shortly before he died, finds him reflecting on both his work and his life. 70 mins.
VHS: S26634. $19.95.

Double Scotch & Wry

Rikki Fulton and the Scotch & Wry team are back in more classic television shows. Supercop, the Rev. I.M. Jolly and Dirty Dickie Dandruff return, as do Alky Broon—the dirtiest barber in Glasgow—and the famous lady missionary, Mrs. Ida Closeshave. 90 mins.
VHS: S10014. $29.95.

Elizabeth R.

Glenda Jackson stars in this Emmy-Award winning television series, first screened on *Masterpiece Theater*. Jackson plays Elizabeth, who became Elizabeth I, one of England's most venerable monarchs. The story begins during the reign of Henry VIII, when he turns from the Catholic Church in search of a male heir through a variety of wives. Despite the arrival of a male heir, it is Elizabeth who triumphs as Queen. 540 mins.
VHS: S25908. $149.98.

The Far Pavilions

Ben Cross and Amy Irving star in an eventful love story set against the backdrop of India during the British Raj. Treachery, intrigue and spectacular battles litter the landscape of this epic series based on M.M. Kaye's best-selling novel. Christopher Lee, Omar Sharif, Rossano Brazzi and Sir John Gielgud are featured. 4-tape boxed set, 320 mins.
VHS: S27397. $89.95.

A Fatal Inversion

In this BBC-produced murder mystery a youthful summer vacation takes a deadly turn. Based on a Ruth Rendell story written under the name of Barbara Vine, it charts the realization among a group of friends that something terribly wrong happened at Wyvis Hall over 12 years ago. 150 mins.
VHS: S27746. $19.98.

Fawlty Towers

John Cleese and Connie Booth wrote and starred in this hilarious television series about a hotel plagued by crisis, chaos and bizarre characters. Each tape has three episodes.
Basil and the Rat. Although Manuel the waiter insists his pet is a Siberian hamster, the health inspector does not agree. Basil vows to solve the problem. With *Communications Problems* and *The Anniversary*. Directed by Douglas Argent. 94 minutes.
VHS: S01892. $14.98.
Kipper and the Corpse. When a guest dies in his sleep, everyone assumes he was killed by the kippers served at breakfast. Basil is concerned with hiding the body so the other guests won't panic. With *Gourmet Night* and *Waldorf Salad*. Directed by J.H. Davies. 90 minutes.
VHS: S01891. $14.98.
The Germans. With Sybil in the hospital, Basil is knocked in the head by a falling moose head and proceeds to tell his German guests the "truth" about their Fatherland. With *Hotel Inspectors* and *A Touch of Class*. Directed by J.H. Davies. 90 minutes.
VHS: S01894. $14.98.
The Psychiatrist. A visiting psychiatrist encounters Basil trying to prove a guest is smuggling women up to his room. With *The Builders* and *The Wedding Party*. Directed by J.H. Davies. 90 minutes.
VHS: S01893. $14.98.
Fawlty Towers: The Complete Set. Four hilarious volumes of the BBC comedy series with John Cleese as the manager of Fawlty Towers. The four episodes are *Basil the Rat*, *The Germans*, *The Kipper and the Corpse*, and *The Psychiatrist*.
VHS: S17378. $54.98.

The Final Cut

Ian Richardson reprises his role as an unflappable British politician in this final part of the deviously funny *House of Cards/To Play the King* series. Richardson stars as Urquhart, a master of manipulation who furthers his own interests with frighteningly adroit abilities. It's a dark comedy that may well explain why politics leads many to despair. 200 mins.
VHS: S27063. $39.98.

Flambards

Early in this century, the young Christina is sent to live with her domineering but disabled Uncle Russel and her cousins Mark and William. They all share Flambards, a decaying but still grand mansion. As the world continues to change around them, these men try to preserve their traditional privileges as best they can, but Christina presents them an irresistible challenge. Each episode is 105 mins.
Episode 1.
VHS: S20792. $26.98.
Episode 2.
VHS: S20793. $26.98.
Episode 3.
VHS: S20794. $26.98.
Episode 4.
VHS: S20795. $26.98.
Episode 5.
VHS: S20796. $26.98.
Episode 6.
VHS: S20797. $26.98.
Complete Set.
VHS: S20798. $139.98.

Fortunes of War

This BBC mini-series launched the working relationship of Kenneth Branagh and Emma Thompson. He plays Guy Pringle, an English university professor who moves to Romania in 1939 with his bride (Emma Thompson). Their academic life in the Balkans brings them in touch with radical anti-fascist movements, the British Secret Service, as well as deposed European royalty on the run.
VHS: S16808. $29.98.
James Cellon-Jones, Great Britain, 1987, 160 mins.

Fundamental Frolics: Not the Nine O'Clock News

This BBC Video presents the bad taste, rock music and outrageous satirical wit of the comedy team. 94 mins.
VHS: S10635. $34.95.

Gallowglass

Ruth Rendell wrote this murder mystery under the pen name Barbara Vine. This BBC adaptation pits two men against each other in a plot centered on a kidnapped Italian princess. One of these men is good, while the other is evil. Their rivalry generates suspense and intrigue. 150 mins.
VHS: S27747. $19.98.

Genghis Cohn

Robert Lindsay, Diana Rigg and Anthony Sher star in this strange comedy about a haunted ex-Nazi. After the war a Nazi concentration camp commandant seeks refuge in a small Bavarian town as a respectable chief of police. There he finds passion in the arms of a kinky widowed baroness, even as he is reminded of his crimes by the apparition of a Jewish comic whom he ordered killed. This comic, "Genghis Cohn," manages to extract a bizarre revenge.
VHS: S26400. $24.95.
Elijah Moshinsky, Great Britain, 1993, 100 mins.

Girls on Top

Sharing a flat is never easy, especially when the people concerned are from vastly different backgrounds. Yet it provides the perfect setting for some of the most respected comediennes to showcase their comic talents. Tracey Ullman, Dawn French, Jennifer Saunders and Ruby Wax play a group of flatmates who don't always see eye-to-eye. 50 mins.
VHS: S16129. $24.98.

Goon Show Movie

The only feature film made by the fabulously funny Goons: Peter Sellers, Spike Milligan and Harry Secombe. This is their version of *Down Among The Z-Men* (also known as *Stand Easy*). England, 1953, 75 mins.
VHS: S00517. $34.95.

Great Expectations

A splendid BBC production of Dickens' famous novel with Gerry Sundquist portraying Pip, the orphan who is smitten by the rich, spoiled Estella. With Stratford Johns, Joan Hickson, Phillip Joseph. 2 parts (5 hours total).
VHS: S07177. $39.98.
Julian Aymes, Great Britain, 1981, 300 mins.

Hancock's Half Hour

Tony Hancock stars and Sid James is featured in this hilarious British television series.
Poison Pen Letters. Three more BBC classics. 90 mins.
VHS: S10629. $29.95.
Radio Ham. Tony welcomes you back to East Cheam with three more episodes.
VHS: S10627. $29.95.
The Bedsitter. The comic genius in three more shows, including *The New Nose*.
VHS: S10628. $29.95.
The Blood Donor. Anthony Hancock—the lad himself—in three classic episodes. 90 mins.
VHS: S10624. $29.95.
The Bowmans. Three more brilliant half-hour comedy gems. 85 mins.
VHS: S10626. $29.95.
The Lift. Three more vintage shows from the BBC's television archives. 90 mins.
VHS: S10625. $29.95.

The Hitchhiker's Guide to the Galaxy

A BBC-television adaptation of Douglas Adams' cult classic about Arthur Dent, a mild-mannered man snatched from Earth prior to its demolition, who takes part in a hyperspace bypass and engages in a journey through space and time with his rescuer and traveling researcher Ford Perfect. Comes in two forms, with the book and without.
Tape (SP mode) and book.
VHS: S18075. $34.98.
Tape only (EP mode).
VHS: S18076. $19.98.
Laser: Contains exclusive, unseen material. LD72434. $59.98.

Hotel Dulac

Anita Brookner's best-selling novel features Anna Massey as the London romance writer whose friends find her guilty of a "serious breach of etiquette," and who is sentenced to a lakefront Swiss hotel during off-season until "she regains her senses." Produced by the BBC.
VHS: S03524. $19.98.
Giles Foster, Great Britain, 1986, 75 mins.

House of Cards

Ian Richardson stars in this British production about corruption among the highest levels of her Majesty's government. Greed and intrigue set the stage for a chilling, puzzling and sinister drama that will delight all thriller fans. Richardson is terrific.
VHS: S26032. $39.98.

The House of Elliot

The BBC devised this charming period television series full of romance, adventure and stunning detail. Two sisters, Beatrice and Evangeline Elliot, struggle to regain the wealth and privilege they were born to but lost. Fashion provides them the opportunity to parlay good taste into wealth and influence, even as British society is transformed around them. Each of the 12 episodes is 50 minutes in length. Six-videotape set.
VHS: S23871. $129.95.

I, Claudius

This famous Masterpiece Theatre series, based on the novel by Robert Graves, has everything: sex, decadence, ambition, insatiable greed, and the fall of the Roman empire.
Complete Set. 7 cassettes.
VHS: S14130. $129.98.

Inspector Morse

A brilliantly acted series that subverts the standard television detective show. Oxford inspector Morse is an eccentric thinker with a keen ability to ferret out clues and signals. "One of the classiest things on television. John Thaw is irresistible as the magnetic but solitary Morse, an Oxford detective with an ear for music, a taste for beer and a nose for sordid crimes" (The Wall Street Journal). With Kevin Whately as Sgt. Lewis.
Absolute Conviction.
VHS: S22070. $19.98.
Dead on Time.
VHS: S22066. $19.98.
Death of Self.
VHS: S22069. $19.98.
Deceived by Flight.
VHS: S19148. $19.98.
Driven to Distraction.
VHS: S19154. $19.98.
Fat Chance.
VHS: S19155. $19.98.
Greeks.
VHS: S22067. $19.98.
Happy Families.
VHS: S22065. $19.98.
Harry Field.
VHS: S22068. $19.98.
Infernal Serpent.
VHS: S19150. $19.98.
Last Bus to Woodstock.
VHS: S19144. $19.98.
Last Seen Wearing.
VHS: S19143. $19.98.
Masonic Mysteries.
VHS: S19152. $19.98.
Promised Land.
VHS: S19153. $19.98.
Second Time Around.
VHS: S19156. $19.98.
Service of All the Dead.
VHS: S19142. $19.98.
Sins of the Fathers.
VHS: S19151. $19.98.
The Dead of Jericho. 105 min.
VHS: S16133. $19.98.
The Ghost in the Machine.
VHS: S19146. $19.98.
The Last Enemy.
VHS: S19147. $19.98.
The Secret of Bay 5B.
VHS: S19149. $19.98.
The Settling of the Sun.
VHS: S19145. $19.98.
The Silent World of Nicholas Quinn. 101 mins.
VHS: S16134. $19.98.
The Wolvercote Tongue.
VHS: S19141. $19.98.

It Ain't Half Hot Mum

From the land of hope and glory! Fall in for a feast of fun as Gloria and the boys in the concert party parade their special brand of army camp in three hilarious episodes. Includes The Jungle Patrol, The Road to Bannu and The Night of the Thugs. 91 mins.
VHS: S16132. $24.98.

Jane Austen's Pride and Prejudice

A first-rate BBC adaptation of the classic Jane Austen comedy of manners. Filmed on the occasion of the 200th anniversary of the novel's writing, this lavishly produced, five-hour, six-cassette production follows the elite of 19th-century English society through games of love and negotiations of marriage. Mrs. Bennet (Alison Steadman) is deeply worried about the fact that all five of her daughters, including the lively Elizabeth (Jennifer Ehle), are as yet unmarried. She plans to convince wealthy neighbor William Collins to marry one of her daughters, but his mischievous friend Fitzwilliam Darcy (Colin Firth) arrives to foul things up. Directed by Simon Langton (Upstairs Downstairs). Featuring a superb soundtrack from composer Carl Davis.
VHS: S27206. $99.95.
Laser: LD75564. $99.99.
Simon Langton, Great Britain, 1995, 300 mins.

Jane Eyre (BBC)

Bronte's famous novel in a remarkable adaptation featuring Timothy Dalton as the mysterious Mr. Rochester, and London stage star Zelah Clarke as the mistreated woman who learns to survive by relying on her independence and intelligence.
VHS: S03527. $24.98.
Julian Aymes, Great Britain, 239 mins.

The Jewel in the Crown

Paul Scott's The Raj Quartet has been brilliantly adapted by Granada Television in this production, a winner of both Golden Globe and Emmy Awards. Now this tale, set during the waning years of the British Empire in India, can be seen in its entirety in eight cassettes, with Dame Peggy Ashcroft, Charles Dance, Geraldine James and Art Malik.
VHS: S02074. $99.95.
Christopher Morahan/Jim O'Brien, Great Britain, 1984, 750 mins.

Jude the Obscure

Thomas Hardy's scathing indictment of Victorian society in a first-rate BBC adaptation. Jude Fawley is the working class stone mason who aspires to the priesthood, but the tragedy of his unrealized ambition is compounded by his tempestuous relationship with Sue Bridehead, herself an outcast for daring to express her sexuality.
VHS: S19090. $79.98.
Hugh David, Great Britain, 1971, 262 mins.

Kevin Turvey Investigates

If one man can be hailed as the jewel among journalists, it must surely be the charismatic Kevin Turvey. He's an ace investigative reporter whose perceptive powers are so limited he backs—quite unwittingly—into genius. Don't miss his exposes on the supernatural, death sex, nasty little sticky things and much, much more. The master of comic digression is played by Rik Mayall (The Young Ones). 44 mins.
VHS: S16126. $24.98.

Last of the Summer Wine

Compo, Clegg and Balamire have a few things in common. They're elderly, unemployed and distinctly delinquent. They spend their lazy days wandering the Yorkshire Dales in this series of highly eccentric escapades from the popular television show. 90 mins.
VHS: S16120. $19.98.

Last of the Summer Wine: Getting Sam Home

Compo, Clegg and Foggy decide that their ailing friend Sam needs one last frolic before he dies. They sneak him out of his sick bed, but find that he is more trouble dead than alive. A relentlessly funny feature based on characters from the comic television series. 89 mins.
VHS: S16121. $24.98.

The Last Place on Earth, Collection Set

This epic race to the South Pole between rival explorers Captain Robert Falcon Scott and Norwegian Roald Amundsen is one of the greatest adventures of the 20th century. In 1911 they crossed over 1500 miles of desolate, frozen waste for different reasons but with the same goal in mind. Both hoped to be the first man at the South Pole. 390 mins.
VHS: S22937. $129.98.

Lillie

A Masterpiece Theater adaptation of the scandalous times of Lillie Langtry, the independent, witty raconteur who upset Edwardian conventions as the first publicly acknowledged mistress of the Prince of Wales and for her flamboyant, active lifestyle and behavior. With Francesca Annis (as Lillie) and Anton Rodgers. A seven-box collector's set running nearly 700 mins.
VHS: S15799. $199.95.

Little Women (BBC)

An enchanting British adaptation of Louisa May Alcott's novel, set during the Civil War, as the four sisters of the March family struggle to grow up without the guiding hand of their loving father.
VHS: S19092. $29.95.
Paddy Russell, Great Britain, 1970, 205 mins.

Love for Lydia

Based on the 1952 novel by H.E. Bates, this enthralling Masterpiece Theater mini-series chronicles the final years of Britain's high-spirited "Careless Twenties" and is an unforgettable portrait of a beautiful and tempestuous woman who personifies the era. Mel Martin gives an exquisite performance as Lydia, who is transformed from a drab and awkward girl into a stunning woman. Seven cassette boxed set, 657 mins.
VHS: S15800. $199.95.

Magic Moments

Jenny Seagrove and John Shea star in the this dramatic battle of wills. She is an executive who convinces Shea to recreate his death-defying act on TV. He agrees as long as she will produce the show herself. This tense and romantic thriller is laced with occult touches and the magic of love. Great Britain, 103 mins.
VHS: S22668. $19.98.

Maid Marian and Her Merry Men

A hip, hilarious retelling of the Robin Hood legend from Maid Marian's point-of-view. She casts quite a different light on the story by showing that Robin Hood was really a wimp who stole all her glory! Kate Lonergan, Wayne Morris and Tony Robinson star in this irreverent spoof with great music—including a reggae theme song. Two episodes.
How the Band Got Together.
VHS: S14264. $14.98.
The Miracle of St. Charlene.
VHS: S14265. $14.95.

The Making of The Hitchhiker's Guide to the Galaxy

A behind-the-scenes on the filmmakers, performers and technicians involved in the filming of The Hitchhiker's Guide to the Galaxy, Douglas Adams' cult novel about an anonymous man marked for interplanetary travel. The program includes an interview with Adams and previously unseen archival footage.
VHS: S19091. $14.98.

The Man from the Pru

Jonathan Pryce and Susannah York star in this murder mystery based on a true story from 1931. Julia Wallace was brutally murdered in her Liverpool home. The public suspected her husband but the courts believed him innocent. Now this beautifully detailed film investigates the lonely, hard world that spawned this as-yet-unsolved mystery.
VHS: S26399. $24.95.
Bob Rohrer, Great Britain, 1989, 90 mins.

Mansfield Park

A lavish treatment of one of the works of Jane Austen by the BBC is now available in this country. In 18th century England an impoverished woman arrives at the estate of her rich uncle, where she is badly treated. Young Fanny Price knows that quality does not come from wealth. She sets out to convince others of that fact. Great Britain, 1986, 261 mins.
VHS: S04671. $24.98.

Mastermind: Great Motor Race

Sam Waterston as an American scientist in London, experimenting with rocket propulsion in 1912. England, 1982, 50 mins.
VHS: S03872. $39.98.

Mastermind: Infernal Device

Sam Waterston, as Professor Quentin E. Deverill, is working on a remote control device and trying to prevent his invention from being used by terrorists plotting to blow up Britain. England, 1982, 49 mins.
VHS: S03873. $39.98.

Merlin of the Crystal Cave

Adapted from Mary Stewart's best-selling novel The Crystal Cave, this swashbuckling adventure and coming-of-age tale is set during the time of King Arthur and focuses on the life and times of Merlin, a young wizard whose mystical powers profoundly impact a kingdom. Great Britain, 1991, 160 mins.
VHS: S20172. $19.98.

Middlemarch

This BBC production of George Elliot's classic tale captures all the passion and disillusionment of the novel. It's an unforgettable tale of blackmail set in a small, 19th-century English village. Stars Rufus Sewell and Juliet Aubrey. 360 mins.
VHS: S26034. $59.98.

Morecambe & Wise Musical Extravaganzas

A host of Britain's best, including Glenda Jackson, Vanessa Redgrave, Cliff Richard and Diana Rigg, join Morecambe and Wise in music and comedy series from their classic BBC comedy series. 60 mins.
VHS: S10012. $19.98.

Morecambe & Wise—Lots More

A collection of sketches from the British TV series starring Eric Morecambe and Ernie Wise. Celebrity guests include Peter Barkworth, Alec Guinness, Glenda Jackson, Peter Vaughan, Gemma Craven, Jill Gascoine and Mick McManus. 50 mins.
VHS: S14496. $22.98.

Morecambe and Wise: Lots and Lots

The TV shows from Eric Morecambe and Ernie Wise are legendary. This collection of their most famous skits features comic delights and special appearances by Glenda Jackson and Eamonn Andrews. 45 mins.
VHS: S22683. $22.98.

A Murder Is Announced

Joan Hickson stars as Agatha Christie's crafty detective, Miss Marple, in the BBC presentation. When a hotel waiter is found shot during the playing of a party game of "murder," Marple suspects the death is not the suicide it appears to be. The movie that answers the question, "who killed Rudi Scherz?"
VHS: S06530. $19.98.
David Giles, Great Britain, 1987, 155 mins.

Murder of a Moderate Man

Denis Quilley stars as an Interpol agent investigating a rash of vicious assassinations set off by the killing of a moderate political leader. Brimming with excitement and foreign intrigue, the chase goes all the way to the Italian Alps. England, 165 mins.
VHS: S14331. $49.95.

The Mystery of Edwin Drood

Based on Charles Dickens' last, unfinished novel, this mystery film shows a corrupt Victorian world dominated by injustice and the resentment it breeds. Edwin Drood vanishes one stormy Christmas Eve. His betrothed, a chaste orphan, joins a choirmaster and a dark young stranger to find the missing man. In this battle between good and evil, passion, lust and intrigue become the weapons of choice.
VHS: S26401. $24.95.
Timothy Forder, Great Britain, 1993, 98 mins.

The New Statesman

A social satire about the unaccountable rise of Alan B'Stard (Rick Mayall), a highly ambitious, conservative MP elected to Parliament when all the opposing candidates mysteriously disappear.
Friends of St. James/Three Line Whipping. Tory MP Alan B'Stard enters into a squalid deal with some politicians of a tiny Caribbean island to export a drug-laced cigarette and get filthy rich in the process. In Three Line Whipping, Alan's erotic intrigues with a French maid cause political problems. He acts out his frustration on an innocent cab driver and events take a dark turn toward the macabre. Directed by Geoffrey Sax. 50 mins.
VHS: S19050. $22.98.
Passport to Freedom/Happiness Is a Warm Guy. In Happiness Is a Warm Guy, B'Stard refines the methods to conceal his tax records and adopt a series of casual affairs in his blind pursuit of power and privilege, dealing in munitions on the side and ruining his political opponents. In Passport to Freedom, B'Stard's wife inherits some money and initiates proceedings to divorce him, though he responds by trying to destroy his wife's female lover. With R.R. Cooper, Marshal Fitzalan and Vivien Heilbron. Directed by Geoffrey Sax. 50 mins.
VHS: S19048. $22.98.
Sex Is Wrong/Waste Not, Want Not. In the first episode, B'Stard is torn between aligning himself with conservative factions trying to ban pornography and his own determination to publish a lewd magazine. What's more, the politically prominent Lady Virginia is pressuring him to publish her expose, "Sex Is Wrong." In Waste Not, Want Not, B'Stard is trying to distance himself from a past transgression, the illegal dumping of nuclear waste. Directed by Geoffrey Sax. 50 mins.
VHS: S19049. $22.98.
The New Statesman, Collection.
VHS: S19051. $59.98.

Northanger Abbey

A BBC adaptation of Jane Austen's novel of erotic attraction, danger and intrigue set in 18th century Bath, a morally decadent society that captures the fancy of Catherine Morland. She's invited by Henry Tilney for a romantic weekend at his estate, Northanger Abbey, where mystery and blood-curdling horror rule the moment. With Peter Finch, Googie Withers, Robert Hardy and Katherine Schlesinger. 90 mins.
VHS: S19180. $24.98.

Oliver Twist

Charles Dickens' classic tale of a young boy's triumph with Ben Rodska as Oliver Twist. A first-rate BBC production. 2 parts (333 minutes total).
VHS: S07178. $39.98.
Gareth Davies, Great Britain, 1985, 333 mins.

One Foot in the Grave: In Lutton Airport No-One Can Hear You Scream

Veteran complainer Victor and his long-suffering wife Margaret return from holiday to find their suburban home trashed—and decide to throw a housewarming party. 89 mins.
VHS: S20502. $19.98.

One Foot in the Grave: Who Will Buy?

A benefit concert gives retired suburbanite Victor Meldrew a chance to warm up his old ventriloquist act, and proves to his wife, Margaret, that whatever can go wrong always does, in this BBC-TV comedy. 89 mins.
VHS: S20501. $19.98.

Open All Hours

One of the last of the corner grocery stores that carry just about everything where you'll find Arkwright, the grasping grocer, and his brow-beaten nephew Granville, who dreams of discovering a world beyond his delivery route. It's also the place where the most amusing neighborhood scandals, romances and adventures are turned into inspired slice-of-life comedy. Stars Ronnie Barker, one half of Britain's internationally popular comedy team, The Two Ronnies.
VHS: S11213. $39.98.

Partners in Crime

This exciting mystery series stars Francesca Annis and James Warwick as Tuppence and Tommy Beresford, two of Agatha Christie's most elegant detectives.
The Ambassador's Boots/The Man in the Mist. In The Ambassador's Boots Tommy and Tuppence delve into diplomatic intrigue as they help an American ambassador unravel a curious incident. In The Man in the Mist, when a famous actress on the eve of marriage draws Tommy and Tuppence into a murder case, it takes them from the high style of a grand hotel to the trail of a policeman's ghost.
Laser: LD70818. $39.95.
The House of Lurking Death/Finessing the King. In The House of Lurking Death chocolates laced with arsenic are a recipe for murder at the grim country mansion of Thurnley Grange. In Finessing the King a cryptic newspaper notice leads to a lovers' rendezvous at a costume ball where the last whispered words of a slain socialite are clues to a deadly puzzle. Tommy and Tuppence investigate.
Laser: LD70816. $39.95.
The Sunningdale Mystery/The Clergyman's Daughter. In The Sunningdale Mystery golf becomes a deadly game when a victim is found on the links, stabbed by a woman's hat pin. In The Clergyman's Daughter Tommy and Tuppence investigate a poltergeist that seems to haunt the house of a cleric's daughter.
Laser: LD70817. $39.95.
The Unbreakable Alibi/The Case of the Missing Lady. In The Unbreakable Alibi love at first sight sparks a strange wager for two ardent detective fans, but their bet soon takes a sinister turn. In The Case of the Missing Lady Tommy and Tuppence help an acclaimed Arctic explorer in his most dangerous search, to find his beautiful fiance, who has disappeared under suspicious circumstances.
Laser: LD70819. $39.95.

A Perfect Spy

From the author of The Russia House, John Le Carre's intricate espionage work is an imaginative thriller about the response of British intelligence when a top member of British Secret Service inexplicably disappears. Peter Egan stars as master spy Magnus Pym, who is enlisted to track down the missing diplomat. "Gripping, sardonic and haunted, the film has the piercing chill of a cloudy autumn day" (The Washington Post). With Dame Peggy Ashcroft. A three-tape set. 376 mins.
VHS: S19913. $79.98.

Pictures

This series is set during the exciting era of silent films. Peter McEnery plays a script writer inspired by the youthful ambitions of an aspiring actress, Wendy Morgan. They are thrown together by a big project but they can't anticipate the ambitions of those around them and their plans for love are threatened by the incessant wheeling and dealing of that bygone era.
Episode 1.
VHS: S20799. $26.98.
Episode 2.
VHS: S20800. $26.98.
Episode 3.
VHS: S20801. $26.98.
Episode 4.
VHS: S20802. $26.98.
Complete Set.
VHS: S20803. $99.98.

Piece of Cake: Complete Set

During World War II, an RAF Hornet Squadron must undergo the rites of passage that will make them seasoned fighter pilots. Their aristocratic CO is arrogant and overconfident. Eventually the concerns of his squadron overtake his attitude as adventure and heartache build toward the climactic battle.
Ian Toynton, Great Britain, 1994, 650 mins.
VHS: S21689. $129.98.

A Pocketful of Rye

Another Agatha Christie BBC production featuring the aging but ever alert Miss Marple. When a London financier is poisoned, the maid seeks out the assistance of Joan Hickson, as the prim and proper sleuth Miss Marple. More bodies are found before the killer is revealed.
Guy Slater, Great Britain, 1987, 101 mins.
VHS: S06531. $19.98.

Poldark

A romance/adventure/epic set in the late 1770's in Cornwall, this film features the beautiful landscapes and historic buildings of old England. It is based on the best-selling book by Winston Graham and tells the story of a man with an iron will whose life shaped the lives of thousands. 12 hours on six cassettes.
VHS: S20626. $149.98.

Porridge

A madcap British comedy based on a highly-regarded television series that stars Ronnie Barker as habitual criminal Norman Stanley Fletcher who miraculously escapes from prison, and the repercussions when he demands to be placed back in line. With Richard Beckinsale, Fulton Mackay, Brian Wilde and Peter Vaughan. Also known as Doing Time.
Dick Clement, Great Britain, 1979, 95 mins.
VHS: S14495. $29.95.

Portrait of a Lady

The story of a spirited young American woman searching for truth. Determined to choose her own destiny, she is brought to England by her Aunt and given every chance to better herself. While seeking freedom, however, she makes some disastrous choices. Richard Chamberlain stars in this classic BBC mini-series based on the Henry James novel. 240 mins.
VHS: S16135. $34.98.

Pride and Prejudice

This BBC production of another popular novel of Jane Austen was filmed on location in the scenic English countryside. The romantic novel of a young woman's adventures and frustrations in acquiring a suitable marriage partner is brought to life by a talented and diverse cast of British actors.
Cyril Coke, Great Britain, 1985, 226 mins.
VHS: S04670. $24.98.

Prime Suspect

In this Emmy Award-winning series, Helen Mirren plays a woman inspector eager to prove that she is as capable as any male police detective. When a young prostitute's body is found, she gets a chance to convince her colleagues of her abilities as she stalks the brutal serial killer responsible. Two cassettes, 230 mins.
VHS: S20827. $79.98.

Prime Suspect 2

In this sequel, Helen Mirren reprises her role as Jane Tennison, a woman detective fighting for respect in a male-dominated police force. As she investigates the murder of a young woman, she faces both community and police pressure to quickly resolve the case because of its racial overtones. Instead, she draws on her ability to solve this daunting case. Two cassettes, 230 mins.
VHS: S20828. $39.95.

Prime Suspect 3

Helen Mirren returns as Detective Jane Tennison, the thoughtful and tenacious woman detective who manages to solve the most complex and troubling cases. In this two tape set, she unravels the mystery surrounding a young boy burned alive. The child was somehow mixed up in a flesh-peddling ring. Now Detective Tennison must confront not only police department rigidity but a seamy underworld as well. Her own personal demons are summoned by this grisly and baffling case.
David Drury, Great Britain, 1995, 205 mins.
VHS: S26929. $39.98.

The Prisoner

The now legendary British television series: 17 segments starring Patrick McGoohan as a retired intelligence agent who finds himself a prisoner on a strange island known as the Village. Produced in 1968. 52 minutes each.
Episode 1: Arrival. Patrick McGoohan resigns his post as an intelligence agent and finds himself at what is known as the Village. He is called Number 6, and is interrogated by Number 2. Directed by Don Chaffey.
VHS: S01055. $29.95.
Episode 2: Chimes of Big Ben. Nadia Gray is brought to the Village under similar circumstances, and is tortured into revealing information. Directed by Don Chaffey.
VHS: S01056. $29.95.
Episode 3: A, B, & C. With Colin Gordon as the new Number 2, a decision is made to extract information from McGoohan by using experimental mind drugs. Directed by Pat Jackson.
VHS: S01054. $29.95.
Episode 4: Free for All. McGoohan is encouraged to run in an election for a new Number 2, and decides to test the system's freedom of speech. Written (under the pen name Paddy Fitz) and directed by Patrick McGoohan.
VHS: S01058. $29.95.
Episode 5: Schizoid Man. The Prisoner is put into a state of hypnosis, brainwashed and given a new identity. Then a double is introduced to the Village. Directed by Pat Jackson.
VHS: S01059. $29.95.
Episode 6: The General. The Villagers are ordered to take part in classes by a professor using a subliminator. Only the Prisoner resists this plan. Directed by Peter G. Scott.
VHS: S01060. $29.95.
Episode 7: Many Happy Returns. The Prisoner seems able to escape, and after several ordeals finds himself in England, where he is interrogated, but not offered an explanation of the Village. Directed by Joseph Seef.
VHS: S01063. $29.95.
Episode 8: Dance of the Dead. McGoohan encounters a former colleague being tortured in order to make him reveal information. Directed by Don Chaffey.
VHS: S01057. $29.95.

Episode 9: Do Not Forsake Me, Oh My Darling. Professor Seltzman has developed a new process which transmits the mind and personality of one man into the body of another. The Professor disappears, and the Prisoner was the last person to see him. Directed by Pat Jackson.
VHS: S02102. $29.95.
Episode 10: It's Your Funeral. The Prisoner is the only one who can stop an assassination plot. In order to defeat the Prisoner, Number 2 sets out on a campaign to discredit him. Directed by Robert Asher.
VHS: S02103. $29.95.
Episode 11: Checkmate. The Village is converted to a chess board, and all the Villagers are to act out a game of chess. The Prisoner takes his position as the Queen's pawn, and plots an escape. Directed by Don Chaffey.
VHS: S02104. $29.95.
Episode 12: Living in Harmony. Originally left unaired during the network run, the Prisoner finds himself in an old Western Township called Harmony, where a judge attempts to make the Prisoner the sheriff of the town. Directed by David Tomblin.
VHS: S02105. $29.95.
Episode 13: Change of Mind. The prisoner is the object of a plan to break him by utilizing new techniques in mind control involving drugs and ultrasonic waves. Directed by Joseph Seef.
VHS: S02106. $29.95.
Episode 14: Hammer into Anvil. The Prisoner creates the impression that he has been sent to spy on Number 2, causing Number 2 to become increasingly paranoid. Directed by Pat Jackson.
VHS: S04964. $29.95.
Episode 15: The Girl Who Was Death. The Prisoner is pitted against a woman who introduces herself as "Death," and seems to be attempting to assassinate him. Directed by David Tomblin.
VHS: S02108. $29.95.
Episode 16: Once upon a Time. Number 2 takes the ultimate step in trying to break the Prisoner: the two are locked in the Embryo Room in a macabre interrogation ritual with the risk of death for the loser. Written and directed by Patrick McGoohan.
VHS: S02109. $29.95.
Episode 17: Fallout. The concluding episode, in which the Prisoner has survived the Embryo Room and is taken to a hidden world beneath the surface of the Village. Here he is faced with his final challenge. Directed by Patrick McGoohan.
VHS: S02110. $29.95.

The Prisoner: Lost Episode

Alternate version of Chimes of Big Ben contains more than two dozen differences including additional scenes and dialog. Thought to have been lost, a print was uncovered in Toronto.
VHS: S03447. $29.95.

Raffles

Raffles and Bunny Manders may seem like an unlikely pair of criminals. Bunny sought out his boyhood hero Raffles, an elegant man at home amidst the turn-of-the-century English aristocracy, precisely because of his sophisticated veneer. It makes the perfect cover that enables them to achieve their wildest criminal fantasies. Each of the six episodes is 52 minutes in length.
VHS: S23754. $129.98.

The Rector's Wife

Set in England's picturesque Cotswald Villages and based on Joanna Trollope's bestseller, this Masterpiece Theater series is the story of Anna Bouverie, a spirited woman struggling to remain dutiful to her family as a life of independence beckons. When she incurs the wrath of the parishioners and her husband, Anna embarks on an intense journey of self-discovery. With Lindsay Duncan, Prunella Scales, Ronald Pickup and Stephen Dillane. 208 mins.
VHS: S23568. $59.95.

Red Dwarf

Described as a "cataclysmic comedy," this critically acclaimed BBC series has gained cult status for its inventive and merciless satire of Dr. Who and other postmodern futuristic programs, combining and merging various genres and situations to create an off-center, sublime comedy of manners.
Red Dwarf I, Part 1: The End. The cataclysmic space comedy saga, winner of the British Science Fiction Award, begins as a radiation leak aboard the space ship Red Dwarf leaves only one apparent survivor, the Chicken Soup Machine Repair Man, Lister. 87 mins.
VHS: S20497. $19.98.
Red Dwarf I, Part 2: Confidence & Paranoia. Lister endures hilarious hallucinations from a space virus. Personifications of his confidence and paranoia begin to battle amidst a rain of herring and exploding mayors. 87 mins.
VHS: S20498. $19.98.
Red Dwarf II, Part 1: Kryten. The crew of the Red Dwarf comes to the rescue of three damsels and an asteroid in distress, then experiences the new game sensation sweeping the solar system. 87 mins.
VHS: S20499. $19.98.
Red Dwarf II, Part 2: Statis Leak. The Red Dwarf goes back in time three million years and revisits the loves of Lister's life, then faces a revolt from the ship's backup computer, Queg 500. 89 mins.
VHS: S20500. $19.98.
Red Dwarf III, Part 1: Marooned & Polymorph. When the Red Dwarf returns to Earth, the crew discovers that time is running backwards. Two crew members find themselves marooned. Finally, Polymorph is loose on the ship, subjecting everyone to a terrifying and gruesome bloodfest.
VHS: S18872. $19.98.
Red Dwarf III, Part 2: Time Slides, Bodyswap & The Last Day. In Time Slides mutated developing liquid allows the crew to step into photographs where they can alter their past. Then in Bodyswap, switched circuits in the ship foment an emergency that can only be solved by the crew switching bodies and genders. In The Last Day, a mechanoid realizes he must face the end of his programmed life and promptly sets off to experience all the pleasures this world has to offer.
VHS: S18873. $19.98.

Red Dwarf IV, Part 1: Camille, DNA & Justice.

The mining vessel Red Dwarf contains a sloppy, whacked-out crew among whom lovesick androids are just part of the problem, in the episode Camille. Later, while floating about in space, they latch on to a vessel that can change the DNA of any living thing, resulting in some very strange creatures. In Justice, world criminals suffer the consequences of their crime, giving the crew cause for concern because of their own hidden histories.
VHS: S18874. $19.98.
Red Dwarf IV, Part 2: White Hole, Dimension Jump & Meltdown. When one of the crew regains her genius level IQ, she powers down the ship and places everyone in danger of disappearing down a White Hole. Then a parallel universe yields a double of the leading crew member via a dimension jump. And in Meltdown, wax figures of famous Earth people have broken free of their programming and are running amok.
VHS: S18875. $19.98.

Reginald Perrin

Leonard Rossiter stars in these episodes of the famous British television series.
The Fall and Rise of Reginald Perrin—1. Reggie makes his escape from the Rat Race. 107 mins.
VHS: S10630. $29.95.
The Fall and Rise of Reginald Perrin—2. Reggie's back in the suburban swim. 120 mins.
VHS: S10631. $29.95.

Reilly: The Ace of Spies

Simply terrific—one of the grandest spy stories ever produced. Based on a true story, Reilly's exploits (which reportedly were the inspiration for James Bond), shook Europe as Reilly—scoundrel, womanizer, legend—uncovers startling information about Russian oil explorations. Sam Neill and Sebastian Shaw star. 80 mins.
VHS: S11007. $19.98.
Laser: LD71298. $39.95.

Reilly: The Ace of Spies Series

Scoundrel. Womanizer. Legend. Sidney Reilly lived by his wits and lived on danger. Now Reilly's escapades are compiled in this special series from the explosive BBC television drama starring Sam Neill as the world's first superspy.
Vol I. It is the early 1900's. Reilly takes on three of his most dangerous and challenging assignments. First he poses as a shipping agent in Manchuria to obtain vital information for the Imperial Japanese Navy, enabling them to sink the entire Russian Pacific Squadron and invade China. A year later, he infiltrates a German shipyard to steal the plans for the deadly new Krupps naval gun. Finally, disguised as a priest, he lies his way aboard a private yacht in Antibes to prevent the French Government from taking control of vast oil deposits recently discovered in British territory. 154 mins.
VHS: S16018. $49.98.
Vol II. 1910. The Czar has ordered the construction of a new Russian fleet, and Reilly hopes to win the contract for his client, a German shipbuilder. Not only will he make a huge personal profit by negotiating the deal, he'll be able to intercept and photograph the drawings of every Russian warship for Britain. Eight years later, Reilly returns to post-Revolutionary Moscow with a daring plan to overthrow Lenin—and install himself as the new leader of the Russian government.
VHS: S16019. $49.98.
Vol III. The 1920's. The Russian Secret Police discover that Reilly is planning to overthrow the Bolsheviks. He narrowly escapes a hail of Bullets and returns to London. There, Reilly and co-conspirator Savinkov join The Trust, a secret organization desperately working to overthrow the Russians. Reilly moves to New York and raises money to support The Trust—until the treachery of one of his employees reveals the group's true nature and evil purpose.
VHS: S16020. $49.98.
Vol IV. Reilly marries Pepita, a beautiful showgirl, but their time together is brief. When Savinkov is killed, Reilly must return to Russia—a dangerous decision that pits him against Stalin. Knowing The Trust is a fraud, he challenges its leaders to prove to the world that they are truly anti-Bolshevik. Stalin learns of the plot, and has Reilly arrested before he can leave the country. Facing imprisonment, torture and certain death, Reilly must rely on the British Government in this thrilling conclusion.
VHS: S16021. $49.98.

Rising Damp

A Dickensian black comedy set in a crumbling boarding house. The landlord, Rigsby, fashions himself an aristocrat, though his manner is mean-spirited, miserly, self-absorbed and prejudiced. With Leonard Rossiter. 150 mins.
All Our Yesterdays/Prowler.
VHS: S19183. $22.98.
Night Out/Charisma.
VHS: S19182. $22.98.
Rooksby/Black Magic.
VHS: S19181. $22.98.
Rising Damp, Collection Set.
VHS: S19184. $59.98.

Rising Damp, Collection Set Series 2

British TV's comedy set in a down-and-out boarding house features some of the most hilarious antics ever located amid English squalor. Leonard Rossiter stars as the landlord in this comedy of gloom.
Permissive Society/Food Glorious Food. When one of Rigsby's boarders, Allen, goes on a blind date, Rigsby betrays a little envy in his criticism. He gets all excited and blames Allan's faltering moral standing on his other boarder Phillip. In the next episode, Rigsby is set off by Ruth's zeal when she starts collecting for famine relief. Despite his worst intentions, Rigsby still manages to contribute something. 50 mins.
VHS: S20804. $22.98.
A Body Like Mine/Moonlight and Roses. When the fitness craze hits Rigsby's home, he is set off balance by everyone's eager embrace of the "body beautiful aesthetic." Then Ruth's new love inspires Rigsby to declare his love for Miss Jones, but it's too little, too late. 50 mins.
VHS: S20805. $22.98.
Perfect Gentleman/Last of the Big Spenders. Rigsby's well-concealed aristocratic demeanor is fully unleashed by the appearance of the courtly Seymour. In the consecutive episode, Rigsby's similarly buried free-spending ways are set loose by the presence of Brenda. This model just happens to like men that aren't afraid to part with their cash.
VHS: S20806. $22.98.
Rising Damp: Complete Set Series 2.
VHS: S20807. $59.98.

Rowan Atkinson in the Amazing Adventures of Mr. Bean

Rowan Atkinson is featured in two episodes from his original British comedy series. This video includes both the pilot episode, Mr. Bean, and the episodes The Return of Mr. Bean and The Library. In these shows, Mr. Bean tries to change on the beach, uses his first credit card and even meets the Royal Family.
VHS: S27053. $19.95.

Rowan Atkinson in the Exciting Escapades of Mr. Bean

Rowan Atkinson inspires more lunatic laughter as Mr. Bean. In The Curse of Mr. Bean, Mr. Bean Goes to Town and The Bus Stop, Atkinson's comic invention attempts to drive a car, dance at disco and swim at a public pool, as well as much more.
VHS: S27054. $19.95.

Rumpole of the Bailey

Part lawyer, part detective, Horace Rumpole is one of the most colorful characters to approach the bench. With his brilliant mind and sly sense of humor, Rumpole's adventures behind the scenes and center stage in the British legal system are a delightful mix of comedy, mystery and courtroom drama.
Rumpole of the Bailey, Vol. 1. Episodes 1 & 2. Rumpole and the Genuine Article. Has an art collector purchased a recently discovered masterpiece or a convincing fake? An embittered artist's jealousy erupts when Rumpole is called to defend him in a celebrated forgery case. Rumpole and the Old Boy Network. The discovery of a brothel in an otherwise respectable London neighborhood draws Rumpole into a web of blackmail and deceit. 104 mins.
VHS: S16028. $49.95.
Rumpole of the Bailey, Vol. 2. Episodes 3 & 4. Rumpole and the Sporting Life. Despite her tearful confession, Rumpole believes the unfaithful wife of a murdered barrister is not the perpetrator, and sets off to find the real killer. Rumpole and the Blind Tasting. The petty jealousies and bits of gossip Rumpole overhears at a high-brow wine tasting party proves useful as he prepares for a case of insurance fraud. 104 mins.
VHS: S16029. $49.95.
Rumpole of the Bailey, Vol. 3. Episodes 5 & 6. Rumpole and the Old, Old Story. Was the partner of a murdered property owner after his valuable land or his wife? Rumpole and Portia. While defending an antique shop owner accused of smuggling illegal weapons, Rumpole discovers a police plot to trap a terrorist. 104 mins.
VHS: S16030. $49.95.
Rumpole of the Bailey, Vol. 4.
VHS: Out of print. For rental only.

The Sandbaggers

Britain's Secret Intelligence Service is often nicknamed The Sandbaggers. Neil Burnside (Roy Marsden) is the Director of Operations for SIS. This former Royal Marine and Sandbagger is dedicated to the service leading him to clash with the powers of the Foreign Office, Westminster and even Downing Street. The entire series is included. 300 mins.
VHS: S21157. $129.98.

Scotch and Wry

The U.K.'s biggest-selling comedy video is now available in the States. Rikki Fulton and the Scotch & Wry team unleash their celebrated outrageous humor from their award-winning series. Meet Supercop, the traffic policeman who keeps failing to make that crucial arrest, the Rev. I.M. Jolly, master of gloom and doom, and Dirty Dickie Dandruff with recipes from his Delicat'messen. 90 mins.
VHS: S10013. $29.95.

Screening Middlemarch

The BBC and the British Film Institute produced this insightful documentary about the adaptation of a 19th century literary classic for television in the 1990's. Conceptualization, packaging and distribution are explored as George Elliot's work is prepared for new audiences. 90 mins.
VHS: S24904. $179.00.

Secret Agent Man

Enjoy the collectible episodes of the British hit spy series starring Patrick McGoohan as British spy John Drake. The entertaining and intelligent scripts developed a cult following, both in Britain and America. 55 minutes each.
Volume 4:
VHS: Out of print. For rental only.
Volume 5.
VHS: Out of print. For rental only.
Volume 6: "The Professionals." John Drake transforms himself into a heavy-drinking, unreliable diplomat to penetrate the social circles in Prague.
VHS: S02131. $19.95.
Volume 7: The Man on the Beach.
VHS: S11127. $19.95.
Volume 8: Dangerous Game.
VHS: S11128. $19.95.

Shadowlands

This BBC production is an intelligent film about British writer C.S. Lewis (Joss Ackland), a notorious loner whose life is radically altered by his obsessive relationship with a beautiful American (Claire Bloom). William Nicholson wrote the screenplay. With David Waller, Rupert Baderman and Rhys Hopkins.
Norman Stone, Great Britain, 1985, 90 mins.
VHS: S17181. $19.95.

Sharpe's

Sean Bean stars in this acclaimed British TV series about the desperate battles fought during the Napoleonic wars in Spain. Bean's character, Richard Sharpe, works under Lord Wellington with a group of men who fight behind enemy lines. Each episode is 100 mins.
Sharpe's Company. Sharpe discovers that he is a father. Now he must save his lover and daughter from the approaching French.
VHS: S24777. $24.95.
Sharpe's Eagles. In this episode Sharpe seeks revenge for a fallen friend. He sets out to capture the French mascot, a carved golden eagle.
VHS: S24776. $24.95.
Sharpe's Enemy. A gang of deserters have taken hold of hostages and demand a hefty ransom. Sharpe is sent with the money only to encounter an old enemy and a dirty trick.
VHS: S24778. $24.95.

Sharpe's Rifles. Sean Bean stars in this action-packed, feature-length film set during the Napoleonic wars in 19th-century Spain. Based on Bernard Cornwell's best-selling novel, Bean is a maverick British officer who has risen in the ranks of Wellington's army because of his bravery. Assumpta Serna plays his lover, the sultry leader of a guerrilla troupe. Filmed on location in England, Portugal and Spain.
VHS: $22667. $24.98.
Sharpe's, The Collection Set. The complete four-episode set.
VHS: $24779. $89.98.

Sharpe's Collection II

The British hero of the Napoleonic wars, Richard Sharpe (Sean Bean), returns for this second installment of dramatic episodes. Once again he leads his men behind enemy lines, fighting the French as well as battling the intrigues spawned by rivalry between men ostensibly on the same side. Based on Bernard Cornwell's best-selling novels. Each video is approximately 100 mins.
Sharpe's Battle. Sharpe must transform the Royal Irish Company, a ceremonial force, into a fighting regiment. The difficulty of this task is deepened by Lord Kiely's wife, a woman who needs help for a personal matter. Meanwhile, false reports of an English massacre in Ireland lead to even more unforeseen troubles.
VHS: $27580. $24.95.
Sharpe's Gold. Aztec gold is at the center of this rollicking episode. Sharpe is detoured by the luster of this treasure and finds that he is not alone. Many are seeking this mythical cache. In the end, complications emanating from a deadly trade of guns for deserters overwhelms key players, including the lovely Ellie, daughter of Admiral Wellington.
VHS: $27579. $24.95.
Sharpe's Honor. Romance adds to the sense of danger in this episode. Sharpe is unwittingly drawn to a pawn of a French spy, the alluring Marquesa Dorada. As a result, Sharpe is drawn into a French plot. Shot on location in the Crimea, Portugal and England.
VHS: $27581. $24.95.
Sharpe's Sword. Sharpe is given a new, dangerous mission. He must protect the trusted spy El Mirador. Unfortunately, Colonel Leroux, an unmatched swordsman, is trying to capture this same spy. When Sharpe is hurt, a lovely, mute woman from a local convent offers Sharpe his only chance for survival.
VHS: $27581. $24.95.
Sharpe's Collection Set.
VHS: $27582. $89.98.

Silas Marner

Ben Kingsley leads a stellar cast including Jenny Agutter in a beautiful evocation of George Eliot's famous novel, shot in the Cotswold Hills of England. Produced by the BBC.
VHS: $03526. $29.98.
Giles Foster, Great Britain, 1986, 92 mins.

Six Wives of Henry VIII

Few television series have attracted as much critical and public acclaim as these six triumphant plays, now preserved on video. Written by six different authors, each play is a lavish and authentic dramatization, produced with style and quality. Binding them together with his magnetic and dignified performance as the mighty monarch is Keith Michell—the definitive Henry VIII. This six-tape collector's set features the stories of Catherine of Aragon, Anne Boleyn, Jane Seymour, Anne of Cleves, Catherine Howard and Catherine Parr.
VHS: $20667. $129.98.

Steptoe and Son

Wilfred Brambell (who played Paul McCartney's grandfather in A Hard Day's Night) is the classic British series that inspired Sanford and Son. The world's most famous rag and bone men clean up in three complete episodes: "Divided We Stand," "The Desperate Hours" and "Porn Yesterday." 90 mins.
VHS: $10015. $29.95.

Steptoe and Son Volume Two

Those battling rag and bone men, Albert and Harold, return in three classic episodes from the famed TV series, "Men of Letters," "Live Now P.A.Y.E. Later" and "Christmas Special 1973." 108 mins.
VHS: $10016. $29.95.

Steptoe and Son: A Star Is Born

Father and son carry on business in each others' pockets and at each other's throats in three more brilliant comedy shows starring Wilfred Brambell as Albert and Harry H. Corbett as Harold.
VHS: $10619. $29.95.

Steptoe and Son: Oh, What a Beautiful Morning

Three more classic gems including Loathe Story and And So to Bed.
VHS: $10620. $29.95.

The Strange Case of the End of Civilization as We Know It

John Cleese utilizes his comic skills in this contemporary detective thriller. Cleese plays the grandson of Sherlock Holmes, an unskilled plotter with an unrivaled reputation for making a mockery of various criminal investigations. The commissioner of police summons him to capture the diabolical genius criminal Professor Moriarty. With Arthur Lowe, Stratford Johns and Connie Booth. 55 mins.
VHS: $19738. $19.95.

Sykes

Eric Sykes and the inhabitants of Sebastopol Terrace appear in three episodes from this insanely popular, long-running British television show. Peter Sellers appears as a guest. 88 mins.
VHS: $10623. $29.95.

Take a Letter Mr. Jones

Rula Lenska is a harried executive in this witty British television series. It centers on an unflappable male secretary who manages to keep the office running smoothly for his female boss. He has to, as she has a seven-year-old daughter depending on her. Two volumes; each contains three episodes, and is 75 mins.
VHS: $25063. $39.95.

Three of a Kind

A triple threat comedy team in a BBC presentation that boasts the talents of Lenny Henry, Tracey Ullman and David Copperfield. Copperfield is no relation to the magician or the fictional character. See a collection of skits, sketches and musical parodies that kept Tracey Ullman employed before her US comedy show. England, 1984, 84 mins.
VHS: $05620. $29.98.

To Play the King

This sequel to House of Cards features Ian Richardson once again lurking about at the highest levels of her Majesty's government. The difference is that this time the stakes are even higher. A magnificent BBC production, 200 mins.
VHS: $26031. $39.98.

A Touch of Frost

David Jason is Inspector Jack Frost, a cop who has no time for legal niceties or delicate sensibilities. Instinct drives this cop to seek justice as best he can. He knows his maverick ways mean he will never advance beyond the rank of detective. But that is a price he is willing to pay. Respect is his ultimate reward. This British television series consists of four tapes, each 102 mins. in length.
VHS: $23755. $74.98.

Two Ronnies: By the Sea and Picnic

Enjoy a double helping of delightful farce in these two irresistible "silent" films from that award-winning British TV comedy team, the Two Ronnies. 80 mins.
VHS: $10632. $29.95.

Two Ronnies: In a Packed Program Tonight

Comedy and musical routines from Ronnie Barker and Ronnie Corbett. A humorous mix of music, quick fire news items and skits and sketches. 59 mins.
VHS: $12634. $29.95.

Up Pompeii: The Legacy

Before Christ there was Senator Ludicrus Sextus, a philandering roue, and his wife Ammonia. But is Ludicrus man enough to meet the curious conditions attached to the inheritance? 90 mins.
VHS: $16127. $24.98.

Up Pompeii: Vestal Virgins

It's Vestal Virgin time in Pompeii…Virgins! In Pompeii?! Can Lurcio the slave find an untouched, fair-skinned maiden or will soothsaying Senna's prophesy of doom come true? Stars Frankie Howerd. 99 mins.
VHS: $16128. $24.98.

Upstairs Downstairs

A classic series from the BBC, Upstairs Downstairs follows the travails of the aristocratic Bellamy Family in Edwardian England. Just as important are the servants who live upstairs. Together they live through the conflicts and traumas of a changing world. This series offers a chance to see how society and the rigid hierarchies of class must evolve as England emerges into a new century where she is no longer preeminent.
Vol. 1: On Trial/For Love of Love.
VHS: $23262. $24.95.
Vol. 2: I Dies from Love/Why Is Her Door Locked.
VHS: $23263. $24.95.
Vol. 3: Guest of Honor/A Special Mischief.
VHS: $23264. $24.95.
Vol. 4: A Change of Scene/Desirous of Change.
VHS: $23265. $24.95.
Vol. 5: The Bolter/A Perfect Stranger.
VHS: $23266. $24.95.
Vol. 6: The Glorious Dead/Facing Fearful Odds.
VHS: $23267. $24.95.
Vol. 7: Wanted, A Good Home/An Old Flame.
VHS: $23268. $24.95.
Collector's Boxed Set.
VHS: $23269. $149.95.

Vendetta for the Saint

Roger Moore is Simon Templar in this televised series based on the character created by Leslie Charteris. A wealthy Robin Hood criminal with oodles of charm and class, he helps out the authorities against the really bad bad guys—like the Italian Mafia, for instance. England, 1968, 98 mins.
VHS: $06097. $59.98.

Victoria Wood: As Seen on TV

Starring and written by the reigning queen of British comedy, Victoria Wood, this tape promises to break new ground in humor in the United Kingdom. With guest stars Julie (Educating Rita) Walters, Duncan Preston, Susie Blake, Celia Immie, and Patricia Routledge.
VHS: $05614. $29.98.
Geoffrey Posner, Great Britain, 1986, 93 mins.

Voyage Round My Father

Laurence Olivier and Alan Bates star in this British television production. Olivier is an eccentric and successful lawyer who goes blind in middle age. Bates is his concerned and baffled son. The script is by John Mortimer. With Jane Asher and Elizabeth Sellars.
VHS: $10613. $89.99.
Alvin Rakoff, Great Britain, 1983, 85 mins.

Watch with Mother

A nostalgic look at BBC children's programs for adults who have not grown up. Join Bill and Ben and the other puppets for adventures in a week's worth of programs. 75 mins.
VHS: $12639. $24.95.

The Woman in Black

This Victorian-era story, starring Adrian Rawlins as a young solicitor, turns deadly with the sighting of a strange woman's apparition. The solicitor must settle the estate of his dead client but this task places him in grave danger as an old curse threatens his sanity.
VHS: $20810. $29.98.
Herbert Wise, Great Britain, 1993, 100 mins.

Yes, Prime Minister: Official Secrets

Three episodes from the BBC comedy series: "Official Secrets," "A Diplomatic Incident" and "A Conflict of Interest." 1987, 89 mins.
VHS: $15977. $19.98.

Yes, Prime Minister: Power to the People

A dead-on satire of English political power, class consciousness and cultural hegemony in this popular BBC production. Created by Anthony Jay and Jonathan Lynn. With Paul Eddington, Nigel Hawthorne and Derek Fowlds. 117 mins.
VHS: $18878. $19.98.

Yes, Prime Minister: The Grand Design/The Ministerial Broadcast/The Smoke Screen

Paul Eddington, Nigel Hawthorne and Derek Fowlds star in this very popular political comedy series from England, currently playing on PBS in all markets. Includes three episodes.
VHS: $14509. $19.98.

Yes, Prime Minister: The Bishop's Gambit

Three episodes from the BBC comedy series: "The Bishop's Gambit," "One of Us" and "Man Overboard." 1986m 91 mins.
VHS: $15976. $19.98.

Yes, Prime Minister: The Key/A Real Partnership/A Victory for Democracy

This popular spoof of British Government stars Paul Eddington, Nigel Hawthorne, and Derek Fowlds. Includes three episodes.
VHS: $14510. $19.98.

Young Ones

This is the popular British television series, featured in this country on MTV, that follows the life and misadventures of a group of young social misfits and deviants. Very funny, very anti-Thatcher, quite lewd. This tape contains three half-hour episodes.
VHS: $12584. $19.98.

The Zero Imperative

This supernatural thriller is the latest thing from the creators of Dr. Who, The Stranger and The Airzone Solution. Colin Baker, Jon Pertwee, Caroline John and others from the original Dr. Who series are featured in this gruesome tale. A psychiatric hospital is suddenly at the center of a mysterious rash of murders. A patient known as Zero is involved, but how? 60 mins.
VHS: $24907. $24.99.

MONTY PYTHON

And Now for Something Completely Different

The first feature film by the Monty Python gang, featuring some of their funniest skits from their TV show, Monty Python's Flying Circus.
VHS: $00048. $19.95.
Laser: Widescreen. LD74614. $34.95.
Ian MacNaughton, Great Britain, 1971

Clockwise

John Cleese is the English head teacher, obsessed with punctuality, as he frantically races to the most important occasion of his life—a meeting of the National Headmaster's Conference. Needless to say, his best laid plans quickly dissolve into a series of epic disasters. Very funny.
VHS: $02973. $14.98.
Christopher Morahan, Great Britain, 1986, 96 mins.

How to Irritate People

Performed before a live audience, John Cleese demonstrates how to bother people so as to unnerve them. "Find out how to pay back job interviewers, movie chatterboxes, garage staff, even bank clerks in the only way they deserve." With support provided by Michael Palin, Graham Chapman, Connie Booth, Gillian Lind and Tim Brooke-Taylor. 65 mins.
VHS: $18133. $19.95.

Life of Brian

Oops, wrong manger! The story of Bethlehem's lesser-known son is a non-stop orgy of assaults, not on anyone's virtue, but on the funny bone. Rich ensemble acting, and animation by Terry Gilliam.
VHS: $00752. $19.98.
Terry Jones, Great Britain, 1979, 94 mins.

Life of Python

A madcap compilation of the remarkable 20-year history of the anarchic and revolutionary British comedy group Monty Python, framed in the voices, anecdotes, personal tales, words, actions and movements of its principal performers. 56 mins.
VHS: $17227. $19.95.

The Missionary

Monty Python performer Michael Palin wrote, co-produced and stars in this ribald comedy about a preacher who's returned from Africa and enlisted to supervise a home for fallen women ("You mean, women who've tripped?"), and becomes entangled in a series of delicate situations. With Maggie Smith, Trevor Howard, Denholm Elliott, Michael Hordern, Graham Crowden and Phoebe Nicholls.
VHS: $02034. $19.95.
Richard Loncraine, Great Britain, 1982, 86 mins.

Monty Python Live at the Hollywood Bowl

The anarchic wit of the British troupe is brought home with a vengeance in this performance film shot in Los Angeles, featuring a series of sketches, improvisations and routines performed by Graham Chapman, John Cleese, Terry Gilliam, Eric Idle, Michael Palin and others.
VHS: $02551. $19.95.
Terry Hughes, Great Britain, 1982, 81 mins.

Monty Python's Flying Circus, Vol. 1

Sixty minutes of Python lunacy includes sketches of "Ministry of Silly Walks," "The Naughty Chemist" and "The Architects Sketch."
VHS: $01914. $19.95.
Ian MacNaughton, Great Britain, 1970, 60 mins.

Monty Python's Flying Circus, Vol. 2

Includes the marvelous skit "The Spanish Inquisition," as well as "The Semaphore Version of Wuthering Heights," "Rat Cuisine" and "The Argument Clinic."
VHS: $01915. $19.95.
Ian MacNaughton, Great Britain, 1970, 59 mins.

Monty Python's Flying Circus, Vol. 3

Another hour of Python fun includes "Village Idiot," "Killer Sheep," "The Travel Agent Sketch" and "The Attila the Hun Show," in which Attila shares his private fears and shows the viewers his bathroom.
VHS: $01916. $19.95.
Ian MacNaughton, Great Britain, 1972, 58 mins.

Monty Python's Flying Circus, Vol. 4

One more hour of zany antics from the Monty Pythons; includes many famous sketches, including "How to Recognize Parts of the Boyd," "Mr. and Mrs. Brian Norris' Ford Popular," "The Farming Club Presents Tchaikovsky," "The Death of Mary Queen of Scots," and "Killer Cars." 60 mins.
VHS: $03301. $19.95.

Monty Python's Flying Circus, Vol. 5

Features the "Spam Sketch," "The Black Eagle," "World Forum," "Flower Arranging," "Gumby Brain Surgery," "Wonderful World of Mollusks," "The Tobacconist," and "The New Royal Navy." 59 mins.
VHS: $03302. $19.95.

Monty Python's Flying Circus, Vol. 6

Monty Python's "Six and Violence" tape featuring the following classic bits: The Conquistador Advertising Agency, The Exchange and Job Mart Interview, Murder Solved by Train Schedules, Dental Appendages, Crackpot Relgions Ltd., How Not To Be Seen, The Adventures of Biggles, Storage Jars, The Show So Far, The Cheese Shop, and Sam Peckinpah's "Salad Days." 58 mins.
VHS: $04882. $19.95.

Monty Python's Flying Circus, Vol. 7

"Pipe Dreams" videocassette, featuring Blackmail (everybody's favorite game show), The Royal Society For Putting Things On Top Of Other Things, Prawn Salad Ltd., The Rude Butcher, Ken Clean-Air-System (The Great White Hope of the British Boxing World), 19th Century English Literature Construction Workers, Olympic Hide & Seek, The Cheap-Laughs From Next Door, and Intergalactic Probe: Algon I. 60 mins.
VHS: $04883. $19.95.

Monty Python's Flying Circus, Vol. 8

The collection of inspired insanity is subtitled "Behind the Eight Ball." Featured bits include "The Queen Will Be Watching", "Intensive Care Unit" and "How to Feed a Goldfish". With John Cleese, Michael Palin, Terry Jones, Graham Chapman, Eric Idle, Terry Gilliam, and others who are paid much less.
VHS: $06825. $19.95.
Ian MacNaughton, Great Britain, 1970-73, 58 mins.

Monty Python's Flying Circus, Vol. 9

Those wacky Britons are back in "Silly Party and Other Favors", a collection of very funny sketches that include "Sorry to Interrupt", "Book of the Month Club" and of course, "Throat Warbler Mangrove". With John, Michael, Terry, Graham, Eric and the other Terry (the American). "It's better than sex," says The New York Times (maybe).
VHS: $06826. $19.95.
Ian MacNaughton, Great Britain, 1970-72, 60 mins.

Monty Python's Flying Circus, Vol. 10

Features such schedules as The Polite Hijacker, Pantomime Horses, Scottish Poetry, Army Recruitment Office, and more. 1970-1972. 60 mins.
VHS: $08113. $19.95.

Monty Python's Flying Circus, Vol. 11

Dirty Vicars, Poofy Judges, and Oscar Wilde Too—includes The Blood Bank, Meet the Gits, and more. 60 mins.
VHS: $08114. $19.95.

Monty Python's Flying Circus, Vol. 12

Presents a major dose of lunacy in sketches like Kamikaze Highlanders, Dennis Moore, The Prejudice Game, Spot the Looney and others. 1973. 60 mins.
VHS: $08115. $19.95.

Monty Python's Flying Circus, Vol. 13

I'm a Lumberjack! includes such classic Python bits as A Spanish Llama Song, Double-Vision Mountaineering, Homicidal Barber, Cinema Talk, Italian Class for Italians, and Mozart's Famous Deaths. 60 mins.
VHS: $09322. $19.95.

Monty Python's Flying Circus, Vol. 14

Chocolate Frogs, Baffled Cats and Other Tasty Treats includes Confuse-a-Cat, Ltd., The Customers Inspector, Animal Debates, A Pitiful Police Raid, The Anchorman Felon, Nauseating Candy Factory, and more. 60 mins.
VHS: $09323. $19.95.

Monty Python's Flying Circus, Vol. 15

Dead Parrots Don't Talk and Other Fowl Plays includes Camel Spotting, You're No Fun Anymore, Corporate Embezzlement, People Who Turn Into Scotsmen, Full Frontal Nudity, The Dead Parrot Sketch, and more. 60 mins.
VHS: $09324. $19.95.

Monty Python's Flying Circus, Vol. 16

A Man with Three Cheeks, or Butt Naught for Me includes the now-classic Flying Sheep; A Man With Three Buttocks; Musical Mice; The Marriage Counselor; Unlike Father, Unlike Son; Boxing for Beliefs and more. 60 mins.
VHS: $09325. $19.95.

Monty Python's Flying Circus, Vol. 17

The Upper-Class Twit Competition includes Flesh-Eating Vegetarians; Bad Movie Ads; The Albatross Vendor; Police Poofs; Me Doctor, You Patient; Historical Impersonations; Confessions of Attila the Hun; Nazi Boarders and more. 60 mins.
VHS: $09326. $19.95.

Monty Python's Flying Circus, Vol. 18

Grab a banana, plum or bunch of grapes and defend yourself against "Killer Fruit," "Despicable Families," "Naughty Complaints" and more. 1970/1973. 60 mins.
VHS: $17613. $19.95.

Monty Python's Flying Circus, Vol. 19

The Pythons practice their art in "Nudge Nudge Wink Wink" and more more funny skits skits. 1970/1973, 60 mins.
VHS: $17614. $19.95.

Monty Python's Flying Circus, Vol. 20

Eric counted up all his fingers and toes to get the title for this one. Includes "Pet Ants," "Dead Poets" and "The Mysterious Michael Ellis." 1970/1973, 60 mins.
VHS: S17615. $19.95.

Monty Python's Flying Circus, Vol. 21

The Pythons get "Scott of the Antarctic," "A License for Eric the 'alibut" and more into one little videocassette. Amazing! 1970/1973, 60 mins.
VHS: S17616. $19.95.

Monty Python's Flying Circus, Vol. 22

The last of the last five Python volumes that will ever, ever be released (goodbye! adieu!) includes three episodes for extra-long lunacy. 1970/1973, 90 mins.
VHS: S17617. $19.95.

Monty Python's Meaning of Life

This savagely satirical film is quite possibly the best of the Monty Python films with its balance of dark, subversive humor and light parodies of God, death, the Empire, Catholicism and gluttony. The film features animation sequences and a short film by Python member Terry Gilliam that bears strong thematic resemblance to his great film, *Brazil*.
VHS: S02550. $19.95.
Laser: LD70058. $34.95.
Terry Jones, Great Britain, 1983, 107 mins.

Parrot Sketch Not Included

Occasioned by its 20th anniversary of Monty Python, this clever program offers a kaleidoscopic look at the sketches, improvs, ramblings, bits and gags of "Python foolery." 75 mins.
VHS: S17228. $19.95.

Personal Services

Julie Walters (*Educating Rita*) winningly plays an English waitress-turned-madam in this fictionalized account of the life of the notorious brothel keeper, Cynthia Payne. She proudly caters to the bizarre tastes of the older gents. Ex-Python Terry Jones directs this naughty but nice comedy-drama about sexual attitudes in England.
VHS: S05172. $79.98.
Terry Jones, Great Britain, 1987, 104 mins.

Pole to Pole

Monty Python regular Michael Palin stars in this madcap adventure about one man's globe-trotting adventures, taken to every corner of the earth, though with a strict caveat: he's forbidden from using any modern means of travel. So he moves around in dog sleds, camels and canoes, with frightening and unpredictable results. Four volumes. 100 mins.
VHS: S17920. $69.95.
Laser: CLV. LD72077. $129.95.

Ripping Yarns

A collection from the BBC series that turns English legends, culture and society inside out. Written by Monty Python's Michael Palin and Terry Jones, starring Palin. Each tape has three episodes.
Ripping Yarns: Tomkinson's Schooldays is a satire on the stuffy, traditional English boarding school complete with bizarre headmaster and cruel school bully. With *Escape from Stalag Luft 112B* and *Golden Gordon.* 90 minutes.
VHS: S01895. $19.98.
More Ripping Yarns: Includes *The Testing of Eric Olthwaite*, about a boy from a mining town in the Depression who gets involved with a seasoned criminal, *Whinfrey's Last Case*, and *Curse of the Claw.* 92 minutes.
VHS: S01896. $19.98.
Even More Ripping Yarns: Roger of the Raj shows how Roger, son of wealthy parents, is posted in India during World War I and grows from a boy to an older boy. With *Murder at Moorstone Manor* and *Across the Andes by Frog.* 90 minutes.
VHS: S01897. $19.98.

Romance with a Double Bass

John Cleese (Monty Python) stars as a bass player scheduled to play in the orchestra at the royal wedding. Arriving early, he takes a quick skinny-dip only to find that the Princess (Connie Booth) has done the same. Hilarious adventure and romance follow.
VHS: S01128. $19.95.
Robert Young, Great Britain, 1974, 40 mins.

The Rutles: All You Need Is Cash

Eric Idle had the brilliant idea to parody the Beatles by creating a story about four young men who get a recording contract because they wear tight pants. Originally filmed as a *Saturday Night Live* skit, the audience response was so positive that Idle and SNL producer Lorne Michaels decided to create a full-length production. George Harrison, Mick Jagger, Paul Simon, John Belushi, Dan Aykroyd, Gilda Radner and Bill Murray are among the musical and comic greats that add to the inspired lunacy. *Sgt. Rutter's Only Darts Club Band* is a highlight that is not to be missed.
VHS: S27693. $19.98.
Eric Idle, Great Britain, 70 mins.

DOCTOR WHO

The Airzone Solution

Colin Baker is joined by three other former *Dr. Who* actors—Peter Davison, Sylvester McCoy and Jon Pertwee—in this feature created by Billy Bags, the producer of *The Stranger.* 65 mins.
VHS: S20912. $24.99.

Arc of Infinity

The Doctor is threatened with certain destruction. This threat also could bring doom to the entire universe. An anti-matter alien wants to bond with the Doctor. All known dimensions could be annihilated as a result. 98 mins.
VHS: S26435. $19.98.

The Ark in Space

In this feature-length space adventure, the Doctor (Tom Baker), Harry and Sarah accidentally arrive on an artificial satellite where the survivors of earth lie in cryogenic suspension waiting to begin life anew. Great Britain, 1975, 90 mins.
VHS: S13727. $19.98.

The Aztecs

The original Doctor, William Hartnell, finds himself in mortal danger when he unexpectedly materializes the TARDIS within an ancient but very much used Aztec temple. Though he and his companions are venerated as gods, they find that they may succumb to temple etiquette and be sacrificed to even more powerful gods. Great Britain, 1964, 100 mins.
VHS: S20783. $19.98.

The Brain of Morbius

Tom Baker stars as Doctor Who, the time-traveling individual who doesn't mind helping the oppressed and downtrodden if it is in the cause of good. >He is capable of moving through both time and space in a craft called the TARDIS, which resembles an English phone booth from the outside. Great Britain, 1984, 59 mins.
VHS: S03869. $19.98.

Castrovalva

In an epic battle with his arch nemesis, the Master, Doctor Who relies on his powers and gifts to gain an advantage, though he's mysteriously unable to conjure up his capacity for regeneration. With Peter Davidson. Great Britain, 1982, 97 mins.
VHS: S19302. $19.98.

The Caves of Androzani

The Doctor's life is saved by the masked Sharaz Jek, who controls all of the precious spectrox on Androzani. But is Jek really his savior? Great Britain, 1984, 101 mins.
VHS: S17377. $19.98.

City of Death

While on vacation in Paris, the Doctor (Tom Baker) is forced to battle a new and unforseen danger. Cracks have begun to tear at the fabric of time itself. The Doctor's nemesis, the sinister Count, is undoubtedly involved. Great Britain, 1979, 100 mins.
VHS: S20781. $19.98.

The Claws of Axos

The Doctor, Jon Pertwee, is on the earth to experience the arriving of the Axons. They come bearing a spectacular gift, but it may be a ruse or, even worse, a trap. 98 mins.
VHS: S27773. $19.98.

The Colin Baker Years

Colin Baker represents the oldest but most youthful appearing Dr. Who because as the Doctor grows older he is reincarnated in ever-younger bodies. This retrospective is filled with interviews and clips that recall Baker's most cherished moments as the sixth Doctor, including his historic debut in Great Britain, 1994, 88 mins.
VHS: S21553. $19.98.

The Curse of Fenric

Transported to Second World War England, Doctor Who battles a curse that summons the wolves of Fenric to usher in a reign of evil. Great Britain, 1991, 104 mins.
VHS: S15350. $19.98.

Curse of Peladon

A secret and indescribably malevolent force is careening along a predetermined course which threatens catastrophe. The entire Galactic Federation could be plunged into a bloody war unless the Doctor can discover the secret behind this mysterious force. 97 mins.
VHS: S26434. $19.98.

Cybermen—The Early Years

These ruthless, cold robots were favorite villains from their very first appearance in 1968. Four full episodes are included: numbers 2 and 4 from *The Moonbase* and numbers 3 and 6 from *The Wheel in Space*. With an introduction by Colin Baker; interviews with Morris Barry, director of many *Doctor Who* episodes; and testimonies from some of the actors who portrayed the evil Cybermen. Great Britain, 1992, 120 mins.
VHS: S18077. $19.98.

The Daemons

Doctor Who investigates the mystery of the Devil's Hump burial mound and discovers a fiendish plot set in motion by his nemesis, the Master. With Jon Pertwee. Great Britain, 1971, 123 mins.
VHS: S19301. $19.98.

The Dalek Invasion of Earth Parts 1 & 2

After the TARDIS sets down in a decaying London of the next century, the Doctor confronts an enemy he thought he vanquished, the Daleks, who currently dominate the Earth. With William Hartnell as the Doctor. Great Britain, 1964, 150 mins.
VHS: S20265. $29.98.

The Daleks

The Doctor has his first terrifying encounter with those mechanized monsters, the Daleks. This original, unedited, two-part classic stars William Hartnell and includes both *The Dead Planet* and *The Expedition* episodes. Great Britain, 174 mins.
VHS: S25750. $29.98.

The Daleks Boxed Set

In this limited edition collection, Doctor Who squares off with his most gifted adversaries, the diabolical Daleks, in a series of programs showcasing the talents and eccentric characterizations of the two actors portraying Doctor Who—William Hartnell and Sylvester McCoy. Great Britain, 1965, 248 mins.
VHS: S19298. $39.98.

Daleks Invasion Earth 2150 AD

Peter Cushing as Doctor Who ends up in London over 200 years in the future where a handful of resistance fighters are waging a guerrilla war against the Daleks. Dr. Who applies his brilliant brain to discovering what the Daleks need from the Earth. Available only in EP mode. Great Britain, 1968, 81 mins.
VHS: S01774. $14.98.

Daleks—The Early Years

A history of the Daleks includes two classic episodes encompassing the Hartnell and Troughton periods. Introduction by Peter Davidson. Great Britain, 1993, 106 mins.
VHS: S19299. $19.98.

The Day of the Daleks

One of the strangest and most intellectually challenging chapters in the Doctor's 25-year history—a classic in its time. Great Britain, 1972, 90 mins.
VHS: S09962. $19.98.

The Deadly Assassin

Doctor Who's arch enemy, The Master, is more deadly than ever in this ultimate showdown. Great Britain, 1976, 90 mins.
VHS: S09963. $19.95.

Death to the Daleks

As a plague spreads throughout the galaxy, a power loss strands Doctor Who (John Pertwee) on Exxilon, the only planet where the antidote to the plague is found. Unfortunately the planet is home to a savagely hostile and degenerate race and the Doctor and Sarah are caught in a struggle between humans, Daleks and Exxilens. Great Britain, 1987, 90 mins.
VHS: S11741. $19.98.

Doctor Who and the Daleks

Pure fun! While Doctor Who (Peter Cushing) is explaining the workings of T.A.R.D.I.S. to his granddaughter, their clumsy friend Ian falls onto the controls, sending them all tumbling through space and time and ending up on the planet of the Daleks. The Daleks hide their bodies in cone-shaped metal encasements and hunt down the peaceful Thals—humans. Doctor Who's mission is to save himself and the Thals from the Daleks. Available only in EP mode.
VHS: S00370. $14.98.
Gordon Flemyng, Great Britain, 1965, 78 mins.

Doctor Who and the Silurians

The Doctor, played by John Pertwee, uncovers more than anyone expected below a top secret atomic research installation. Deep within the shadowy depths lies an unforseen terror. A prehistoric monster threatens to wreak havoc if disturbed in its mysterious lair. 167 mins.
VHS: S25748. $29.98.

The Dominators

Doctor Who joins a handful of desperate Dulcians as they fight an invasion of ruthless Dominators, a battle that threatens even the Earth. This video includes original, unedited black and white footage. Starring Patrick Troughton as the Doctor. Great Britain, 1968, 121 mins.
VHS: S21550. $19.98.

Earthshock

The 1980's brought the universe Peter Davison, the fifth Doctor. In this episode, 26th century Earth hides a system of subterranean caves where a group of geologists has recently been murdered. Androids are guarding the site, but who controls them? Soon the Cybermen make a much feared re-emergence into the light of day. Great Britain, 1982, 99 mins.
VHS: S18078. $19.98.

Enlightenment

The White Guardian's cryptic warning of imminent danger draws Doctor Who into a puzzling contest. Peter Davison is the Doctor who finds himself ensnared in a deadly trap set by the Black Guardian. Great Britain, 1983, 97 mins.
VHS: S21554. $19.98.

The Five Doctors

The legendary 90-minute special is a grand one-time-only union of the first five Doctors as well as a reunion of all of their famous friends, foes and monsters. Great Britain, 1983, 90 mins.
VHS: S09961. $19.98.
Laser: LD74637. $39.98.

Ghost Light

Sylvester McCoy is the time-traveling Doctor in this suspense-filled episode from the long-running BBC television series. An alien ship holds a strange and malevolent cargo. Only the Doctor and his companion can solve the mystery of this dangerous force. 72 mins.
VHS: S27769. $19.98.

The Hartnell Years

Doctor Who's seventh being journeys back in time to glimpse his first incarnation as the anti-hero William Hartnell. Great Britain, 1991, 88 mins.
VHS: S15349. $19.98.

Image of the Fendahl

Tom Baker, as the Doctor, finds himself enmeshed in a fairytale world. Unfortunately the fairytale creature which holds sway in this world is capable of tremendous powers, and that could lead to an ending where everyone does not exactly live happily ever after. 95 mins.
VHS: S27772. $19.98.

Inferno

A top-secret drilling operation has put the entire planet Earth at risk. For the Doctor this operation becomes an unforseen path to a parallel universe. 167 mins.
VHS: S26436. $29.98.

The Invasion

Patrick Troughton stars as the eccentric but fearless space and time traveler. In this episode the disappearance of an eminent scientist draws the Doctor, along with Zoe and Jamie, into a sinister plot. Tobias Vaughn is afoot. 146 mins.
VHS: S25745. $19.98.

The Keeper of Traken

The once solid empire of the Traken begins to disintegrate when the evil Melkur invade their space. With Tom Baker as the Doctor. Great Britain, 1981, 98 mins.
VHS: S20267. $19.98.

Kinda

Peter Davison is the youngest appearing Doctor, which conversely means that he is the oldest. Despite his advancing age he continues to take on troubling forces wherever he goes. In this episode he finds that a planet seemingly like paradise actually contains a deadly, unknown power. 72 mins.
VHS: S27771. $19.98.

The Krotons

Once again with Patrick Troughton portraying Doctor Who, trouble in the Universe threatens another unsuspecting population. The Doctor and Zoe must help the Gonds escape enslavement from the merciless Krotons. But first they must discover the secret behind the mysterious teaching machines. Great Britain, 1969, 91 mins.
VHS: S21552. $19.98.

Logopolis

In this eerie showdown of master intellects, Doctor Who tries to alter the Master's sinister theory to interrupt the causal nexus, destroying the universe's foundation. With Tom Baker. Great Britain, 1981, 99 mins.
VHS: S19300. $19.98.

The Masque of Mandragora

Set in the 15th century, the Doctor (Tom Baker) must conjure up all of his peculiar talents and intuitive skills when he's locked in mortal combat with the mysterious, ancient cult of Demnos. Great Britain, 1976, 99 mins.
VHS: S20268. $19.98.

Mawdryn Undead

The Doctor's capacity for regeneration is put under strain when the Black Guardian earmarks him for assassination. With Peter Davidson as the Doctor. Great Britain, 1983, 99 mins.
VHS: S20269. $19.98.

The Mind Robber

The Doctor and his irreverent crew materialize in a surreal fantasy world overtaken by white robots and fictional monsters that assume staggeringly real proportions. With Patrick Troughton as the Doctor. Great Britain, 1968, 100 mins.
VHS: S20266. $19.98.

More Than 30 Years in the TARDIS

All seven doctors are featured in this informative documentary. The entire history of the series is detailed in a fascinating combination of clips and interviews. 87 mins.
VHS: S26431. $19.98.

The Pertwee Years

John Pertwee portrayed the Doctor in his third incarnation, from 1970 to 1974. This particular form had an inclination for gadgetry and a love for old cars. Pertwee himself narrates this collection, which looks back on scenes from some of his most popular episodes. Included are a behind-the-scenes look at BBC special effects, Pertwee's first appearance as the Doctor, an excerpt from *The Five Doctors*, episode seven from the series *Inferno* and the final episode of *The Daemons*. Great Britain, 1992, 88 mins.
VHS: S17376. $19.98.

Planet of Evil

Tom Baker, one of the most popular Doctors, answers a distress call. Valiant as ever, he responds, though he may regret landing on the Planet of Evil. 94 mins.
VHS: S27770. $19.98.

Planet of the Spiders

Jon Pertwee's final and most suspenseful episode pits him against the deadly spiders from the planet Metebelis. It ultimately boils down to a perilous battle of wits. Fortunately Pertwee is among the most witty of the Doctor's incarnations, who proves more than capable of matching his evil foes. Great Britain, 1974, 150 mins.
VHS: S20779. $19.98.

Pyramids of Mars

Doctor Who and his companion Sara find themselves in 1911 where they meet a professor possessed by an ancient Egyptian god of darkness. He is willing to use robot mummies to help release his controlling master. The Doctor doesn't cooperate with the plot. Great Britain, 1985, 91 mins.
VHS: S03871. $19.98.

Resurrection of the Daleks

The Doctor—in his youthful incarnation, Peter Davison—is trapped with his companions in a time corridor by his most feared enemy, the Daleks. 20th century Earth is the unfortunate setting for the inevitable showdown between these inhuman creatures and the Doctor. Great Britain, 1984, 97 mins.
VHS: S20778. $19.98.

Revenge of the Cybermen

The Doctor (played by Tom Baker) returns to Space Station Nerva to find that his ship, TARDIS, has drifted back a few thousand years in time. The Cybermen attempt to take over TARDIS in order to destroy the planet Voga, where there are extensive gold mines. Great Britain, 1983, 92 mins.
VHS: S00354. $19.98.
Michael Briant, Great Britain, 1983, 92 mins.

Robot

Once again the Earth is under threat, and it's not only a dangerous alien who is to blame. The Doctor, Tom Baker, must fight the hijacker robot threatening the earth with atomic war, if only enfranchised humans will let him. Great Britain, 1975, 99 mins.
VHS: S20780. $19.98.

The Robots of Death

Tom Baker, the most popular of all the doctors on this British tv speculative series, lands on a desert planet loaded with the valuable ore lucanol. The miners are now being killed by formerly friendly robots as they have a new, greedy master. This doesn't sit right with the Doctor. Great Britain, 1986, 91 mins.
VHS: S03870. $19.98.

The Seeds of Death

Patrick Troughton stars as the Doctor in the 21st century and Earth is totally dependent on T-Mat, a revolutionary form of instant travel. When the system breaks down, the Doctor makes a hazardous journey to the relay station only to find it's in the hands of Ice Warriors who plan to invade earth using T-Mat. Great Britain, 1985, 137 mins.
VHS: S11740. $19.98.

Seeds of Doom, Parts 1 & 2

The Krynoid are an alien plant species with a very aggressive sense for violence. They will take over the Earth unless the Doctor can arrest their luxurious but deadly growth. 144 mins.
VHS: S26433. $19.98.

Shada

Originally this 6-part series was not to be completed until Tom Baker, the fourth Doctor Who, stepped in. Now the entire story of the evil Shada is complete. When an artifact from Gallifrey dating back to the time of Rasillon goes missing, retired Timelord Dr. Chronotis calls on the Doctor and Romana to make sure this powerful relic does not fall into the wrong hands. Great Britain, 1979, 110 mins.
VHS: S17374. $19.98.

Silver Nemesis

Go behind the scenes to see how the fascinating episode "Silver Nemesis," from the *Dr. Who* series, was made. Sylvester McCoy is the star of this episode and he will lead fans on this much awaited tour inside one of television's most popular sci-fi series. Great Britain, 1988, 139 mins.
VHS: S21555. $19.98.

The Sontaran Experiment/The Genesis of the Daleks

The Doctor is jettisoned 10,000 years into the future, where he is subjected to a horrifying experiment. In the follow-up *The Genesis of the Daleks*, the Doctor gets involved in a mission from the Timelords. With Tom Baker as the Doctor. Great Britain, 1975, 193 mins.
VHS: S20264. $29.98.

Spearhead from Space

Forbidden to continue his travels through time and space by his fellow time lords, the newly regenerated Doctor (Jon Pertwee) begins his exile on earth and finds himself hurled into one of his most exciting and terrifying adventures. Great Britain, 1970, 92 mins.
VHS: S13728. $19.98.

The Stranger Double Feature: Summoned by Shadows/More Than a Messiah

This science fiction adventure stars Colin Baker and Nicola Bryant from the popular BBC English television series *Dr. Who*. Only this video represents a wholly original concept and story line, based on a project initiated by fans, called "The Stranger and Mrs. Brown." 75 mins.
VHS: S20910. $24.99.

The Stranger: Eye of the Beholder, Part 2

The Stranger revives the tradition of the BBC's greatest science fiction series, *Doctor Who*. Colin Baker, one of the more successful Doctors, is back. In this episode, Solomon Egan and Saul, the materialized terrorists from the Dimensional Web, stumble on a top secret research project called Metaphysic. It promises to open a few minds and no one can be sure of the outcome. 60 mins.
VHS: S26301. $24.99.

The Stranger: In Memory Alone

Colin Baker and Nicola Bryant reprise their roles from *The Stranger*. They are originally famous for their performances as the Doctor and his companion in the wildly popular BBC series, *Dr. Who*. 45 mins.
VHS: S20911. $19.99.

The Talons of Weng-Chiang

Tom Baker is Doctor Who in the heart of Victorian London where he is confronted by a series of bizarre and horrific events. The Doctor not only finds himself battling for his life against the hideously deformed Magnus Greel but also must deal with two other villains. Great Britain, 1988, 141 mins.
VHS: S11742. $19.98.

Terminus

The Black Guardian sabotages the doctor's most valuable asset, the TARDIS. The Doctor, played by Peter Davison, has one last hope. He must rescue a vessel carrying a human cargo of plague victims to ensure he will remain the universe's most respected time traveler. Great Britain, 1983, 99 mins.
VHS: S20782. $19.98.

Terror of the Autons

The Doctor (John Pertwee) finds the Earth in danger. Naturally, it is his most feared enemy, the Master, who is to blame. This fiend has a scheme to destroy humanity. As if that were not enough he also hopes to silence the Doctor forever. 95 mins.
VHS: S25747. $19.98.

Terror of the Zygons

In this thrilling adventure the Doctor (Tom Baker) defends earth from invasion by horrific, transforming aliens. He must vanquish the invading hordes before their reign of terror begins. Great Britain, 1975, 92 mins.
VHS: S13729. $19.98.

The Three Doctors

The three Doctor Whos unite to save the Timelords from an old arch enemy. Great Britain, 1973, 99 mins.
VHS: S15351. $19.98.

Time and the Rani

Unwittingly, the Doctor becomes part of Rani's master plan. She intends to build a time manipulator which will grant her nearly unfathomable powers. 89 mins.
VHS: S26432. $19.98.

The Time Warrior

A terrifying combination of past and future threatens the entire human race and plunges the Doctor (Jon Pertwee) and Sarah into a chilling race against time. Great Britain, 1973, 90 mins.
VHS: S13730. $19.98.

The Tom Baker Years

In late 1974, Tom Baker assumed the character of the Doctor, a role he would maintain for seven years. All his episodes remain in BBC archives, permitting this special collection of excerpted highlights from his most popular adventures to appear together. Double cassette. Great Britain, 1992, 170 mins.
VHS: S18080. $29.98.

The Tomb of the Cybermen

Patrick Troughton portrayed the Doctor's second incarnation in the late 1960's. In this episode, he is joined by his popular assistants Jamie and Victoria as they seek to prevent the re-emergence of the Cybermen, his age-old enemies. They lie harmlessly frozen, but a group of archeologists is poking around and one of them has treacherous plans that could endanger the Universe. Great Britain, 1967, 100 mins.
VHS: S17375. $19.98.

The Trial of the Timelord Boxed Set

A rare edition of the cult British science fiction show, featuring one of the best sagas, as Doctor Who must summon all of his intellectual skills and cunning to defeat a tribunal of timelords accusing him of cosmic interference. Great Britain, 1986, 350 mins.
VHS: S19297. $49.98.

The Troughton Years

A collector's edition of vintage *Doctor Who*. Three rare episodes featuring the Doctor's second incarnation, Patrick Troughton, presented by his successor, Jon Pertwee. Great Britain, 1991, 84 mins.
VHS: S15348. $19.98.

The Twin Dilemma

Is the Doctor's fifth incarnation going to be his last? He no longer seems in control of his powerful mental faculties and has nearly strangled his friend and helper, Peri. The Doctor decides to become a hermit under a dome on a lonely asteroid, but its strange inhabitants don't give him much peace of mind. Where are the original inhabitants, the Gastropods? Great Britain, 1984, 99 mins.
VHS: S18079. $19.98.

The Two Doctors

Colin Baker is now The Doctor, or at least he appears to be, until an earlier incarnation appears, that is Patrick Thornton. As the Doctor follows this image of his past, danger lurks in the shape of the Sontarans. It could mean death for both of them. 132 mins.
VHS: S25749. $19.98.

An Unearthly Child

The first ever televised Doctor Who adventure! The Doctor leads his young granddaughter and a pair of teachers on a quest for fire. Great Britain, 1963, 98 mins.
VHS: S15347. $19.98.

Vengeance on Varos

Colin Baker, the parodoxically younger-looking Doctor, must battle to save the TARDIS. Together with Peri, he journeys to a planet ruled by fear. At the heart of its capital lies the terrifying Punishment Dome. 89 mins.
VHS: S25746. $19.98.

The Visitation/Black Orchid

Once again the Doctor, played by Peter Davison, is enmeshed in a strange and murderous intrigue. Seventeenth-century England is being terrorized by an alien life force, so the Doctor does what is expected. He accepts an invitation to a masked ball knowing that it will lead to danger. 146 mins.
VHS: S27774. $19.98.

The War Games (Parts 1 & 2)

The Aliens have staged a horrifying combat game, pitting soldiers from throughout history against each other. Only the good Doctor can stop the slaughter. Double cassette. Great Britain, 1969, 243 mins.
VHS: S15346. $29.98.

The Web Planet

The deadly Zarbis ensnare the TARDIS, the vehicle key to Doctor Who's time traveling abilities. The Zarbis' hypnotic power has the Doctor trapped in an eerie alien world that he cannot escape. William Hartnell is the Doctor. Great Britain, 1965, 148 mins.
VHS: S21551. $19.98.

IRISH FEATURES

Broth of a Boy

A witty social comedy about an aggressive television producer (Tony Wright) who covers the village's celebration of the world's oldest living man (Barry Fitzgerald). The comic tension springs from Wright's desperate efforts to persuade Fitzgerald to appear on his program. With June Thorburn, Harry Brogan, Eddie Golden and Godfrey Quigley.
VHS: S19860. $29.95.
George Pollock, Ireland, 1958, 77 mins.

Cal

Helen Mirren stars in a performance that earned her the Best Actress Award in Cannes in 1984, in this sensitive love story set in war-torn Northern Ireland. Music score by Dire Straits' Mark Knopfler enshrouds this stark drama haunted by Ulster's numbing violence.
VHS: S00205. $19.98.
Pat O'Connor, Ireland, 1984, 104 mins.

The Crying Game

Irish filmmaker Neil Jordan's film charts a fractured world of deception, abandon and terror. Stephen Rea becomes a reluctant IRA terrorist in exile who ends up protecting a beautiful, mysterious London woman. With Miranda Richardson, Forest Whitaker and the amazing Jaye Davidson. Academy award for best original screenplay (Jordan).
VHS: S18749. $19.98.
Laser: Widescreen. LD75178. $34.98.
Neil Jordan, Great Britain, 1992, 112 mins.

December Bride

In turn-of-the-century Ireland, a woman was expected to live with a stifling sense of decorum. This film concerns a strong-minded woman who went her own way. She has two lovers, brothers who both love her, and this unconventional triangle sets her at odds with the strict, unbending community where she lives because she chose them both. This unconventional film is an acclaimed feature from the Irish film renaissance.
VHS: S26280. $89.98.
Thaddeus O'Sullivan, Ireland, 1993, 90 mins.

The Field

Richard Harris makes his long-awaited return to the screen in this Oscar-nominated portrayal of a man fighting to preserve everything he believes in. Tradition-bound Irishman "Bull" McCabe (Harris) has devoted his life to cultivating a field. When it's put up for auction and might be bought by a wealthy American for development, the resulting conflict has a devastating effect on an entire village. A story of immense power and passion from the writer/director of *My Left Foot*. Also starring Brenda Fricker, Tom Berenger and John Hurt.
VHS: S14975. $19.98.
Jim Sheridan, Ireland, 1990, 113 mins.

In the Name of the Father

Over seven Academy Award nominations testify to the power of this film. Accused of an act of terrorism, a young man finds that not only his whole life is destroyed, but also the lives of those he loves most. From the streets of Belfast to the most hellish British prisons, this film recounts the true story of a man caught in the struggle for Irish independence. With Daniel Day-Lewis and Emma Thompson.
VHS: S21158. $19.98.
Laser: LD72420. $39.98.
Jim Sheridan, Great Britain, 1993, 133 mins.

Into the West

Two young brothers rescue a horse, which turns out to be magical. For their efforts they are rewarded with the adventure of a lifetime. Gabriel Byrne and Ellen Barkin are featured in this heart-warming children's film.
VHS: S21031. $95.98.
Mike Newell, Ireland, 1992, 97 mins.

James Joyce's Women

Fionnula Flanagan stars in episodes of the six women in the literary and personal life of James Joyce. Set at the turn of the century, and based on some of Joyce's writings and diaries, the film has been acknowledged as an erotic investigation of the life of the great writer.
VHS: S00652. $69.95.
Fionnula Flanagan, 1985, 91 mins.

Miracle

A sweetly engaging drama from Neil Jordan, the director of *Mona Lisa*, about two inquisitive teenagers who find out there is more going on in their small Irish coastal town than they ever expected. Beverly D'Angelo stars as a woman of mystery who intrigues newcomers Niall Bryne and Lorraine Pilkington. Filmed on location in the director's home town.
VHS: S15509. $89.98.
Neil Jordan, Ireland, 1991, 100 minutes.

My Left Foot

Distinguished by a brilliant performance from Daniel Day-Lewis, this is a true story about life, laughter and the occasional miracle. Day-Lewis plays Christy Brown, who has cerebral palsy, and whose mother's faith prompts him to paint and write. Nominated for five Academy Awards.
VHS: S12199. $19.98.
Jim Sheridan, Great Britain, 1989, 103 mins.

The Run of the Country

Albert Finney stars in this film about an unlikely romance. A young man escapes his overbearing father and the trauma of his mother's death through an adventurous affair with a spirited woman. Though she appears carefree, her advice finally helps the father and son reconcile.
VHS: S27187. $19.98.
Laser: LD75468. $34.95.
Peter Yates, Ireland, 1995, 116 mins.

Widow's Peak

Mia Farrow, Joan Plowright and Natasha Richardson star in this mysterious comedy about a sexy stranger. The stranger turns an Irish town upside down with her scandalous lies and devious secrets. She must be hiding something, and it could be murder.
VHS: S22665. $19.95.
John Irvin, Ireland/USA, 1994, 98 mins.

IRISH PERSPECTIVES

1641 and the Curse of Cromwell

Tens of thousands of Irish people were mercilessly forced from their lands or massacred at the hands of one of the most hated men in Irish history. These campaigns and the Catholic rebellion of 1641 are sifted through in order to separate myth from the truth. 60 mins.
VHS: S24898. $19.95.

Behind the Mask

A documentary on the Irish Republican Army (IRA) as seen through the eyes of its leading veterans. The documentary examines the personal motivations and actions behind the events of the IRA, the guerilla army, as members speak openly of saturation surveillance, silence, invisibility and anonymity as the IRA's weapons of survival.
VHS: S11599. $29.95.
Frank Martin, USA, 1988, 65 mins.

Charles Haughey's Ireland

Ireland's Prime Minister leads this tour of Ireland, from the Walls of Derry to the charms of County Kerry, to Yeats Country, and Galway of James Joyce, Lady Gregory, W.B. Yeats. Features an open-air concert with Kris Kristofferson, Gaelic football. 60 mins.
VHS: S06656. $29.95.

The Clancy Brothers and Tommy Makem Reunion Concert

The Ulster Hall concert of the Clancy Brothers and Tommy Makem, the rousing Irish acts who strike the perfect balance of traditional folk and highly personal technicians. 60 mins.
VHS: S19207. $24.95.

Derek Mahon

This Irish poet has won the Lannan Poetry Fellowship for his verse. On March 8, 1994, he read from his *Selected Poems* and spoke to Michael Silverblatt. From the *Lannan Literary Videos* series. 60 mins.
VHS: S27145. $19.95.

Dubliners Live

Recorded live at the National Concert Hall in London, an evening of magic and excitement by Ireland's most celebrated folk group, as they are joined by two of the country's best ballad singers, Paddy Reilly and Jim McCann. 75 mins.
VHS: S06650. $29.95.

Eavan Boland

A major Irish poet, Eavan Boland explores the relationship between gender, art and national identity. She read from *In a Time of Violence* and *Outside History* on November 16, 1994, in Los Angeles. She also spoke with poet Eloise Klein Healy, author of *Artemis in Echo Park*. From the *Lannan Literary Videos* series. 60 mins.
VHS: S27149. $19.95.

Far Away from the Shamrock Shore: A History of Irish Music in America

Influences from Irish music and culture have had a lasting impact on contemporary America. Medieval Ireland and contemporary America share common roots. This moving document reveals the continuity of the Irish tradition. Music by the Clancy Brothers & Tommy Makem and Cherish the Ladies is featured. 53 mins.
VHS: S26002. $24.95.

Frank Patterson: Ireland's Golden Voice

Irish music and Ireland's greatest tenor provide the perfect excuse to visit a number of beautiful sights on the Emerald Isle. From Tipperary to Galway, with stops in Dublin and Mayo, and views of many locales, this musical adventure is a great way to experience the best of Irish music. 60 mins.
VHS: S23063. $14.95.

Harp of My Country

The original music of Ireland's greatest national poet, Thomas Moore, recaptured with a 250-piece orchestra and the Ambrosia Chorus Choir, including *Last Rose of Summer*, *The Harp That Once Through Tara's Halls*, *Minstal Boy*, and others. 72 mins.
VHS: S06658. $29.95.

History of Ireland

A unique souvenir of history, scenery and people, bringing together various stages of Irish history starting with ancient Ireland and Newgrange, on through to the Celts, St. Patrick, the Vikings, and more. Shot on location and presented by Brian Munn. 58 mins.
VHS: S09163. $29.95.

Home Away from Home: The Yanks in Ireland

300,000 American servicemen trained and lived in Northern Ireland preparing for battle in World War II. This film documents veterans going back to their "home away from home." Old loves and closely guarded secrets are revealed through interviews and archival footage. 58 mins.
VHS: S26001. $24.95.

Ireland's Emerald Treasures

Journey through gorgeous Ireland and see all the elements of this "Emerald Isle." Begin in Dublin, then on to County Wicklow, Kilkenny, kiss the Blarney Stone, and watch the sun set over Galway Bay. 50 mins.
VHS: S05777. $24.95.

Ireland: A Writer's Island

A beautiful study of Ireland and her most famous writers looking at the rugged beauty of Ireland that has captured the imaginations of Irish artists and writers—including Yeats, Shaw, Joyce, and Wilde—through centuries. 63 mins.
VHS: S12000. $29.95.

Ireland: The Isle of Memories

A visual journey of Ireland, visiting all 32 counties, including Galway, the Aran Islands (where Gaelic is still spoken), Ireland's Holy Mountains, Knock Shrine, Donegal's rugged coastline, Waterford (where the famous crystal is made), and a visit with one of Ireland's best ballad groups, The Barleycorn. 50 mins.
VHS: S06649. $29.95.

An Irish Country Calendar

The four seasons of the year are the focus for this set of videos which reveal eight of Ireland's most gracious country homes. From the misty bogs of County Sligo to the Galty Mountains of Tipperary, this series traces the gentle landscape and climate of the Emerald Isle. Each of the four videos is approximately 50 mins.
VHS: S27427. $79.80.

The Irish Country House

Homes at over 40 locations across Ireland reveal the important history preserved in these magnificent buildings. Whether cherished and preserved or decaying and forlorn, they reveal much about modern Ireland. 58 mins.
VHS: S26000. $24.95.

Irish Homecoming

Irish Americans are shown in this film as they return to Ireland in search of their roots. It is a moving document that reveals the strength of this people's traditions. Music by Clannad, Maura O'Connell and Brian Kennedy is featured. 58 mins.
VHS: S25999. $24.95.

Irish Magic: Irish Music

The roots of the magic of Ireland are found in Irish music, and in this tribute, hosted by actor Sean McGraw and filmed on location in Ireland, appear such performers as The Chieftains, James Galway and Louis Browne, talented performers of the Iileann pipes, Irish harp, accordion and fiddle, as well as tributes to Irish music by Senator Ted Kennedy, novelist Mary Higgins Clark and Michael Burke. 50 mins.
VHS: S06648. $29.95.

Irish Waterways

This three-part series looks at the landscape of Ireland as a rumination on the country's history, culture and national wonder. 180 mins.
Tape 1: Forgotten Locks/Christian Crossing.
VHS: $19550. $19.95.
Tape 2: Viking Invasion/Yesterday's Journey.
VHS: $19551. $19.95.
Tape 3: The Great Race/Endless Road.
VHS: $19552. $19.95.

J.P. Donleavy's Ireland

The witty novelist J.P. Donleavy captures the heart and soul of Ireland. This Discovery Channel video is a cinematic feast which joins the author's words with imagery of enchanting landscapes from the Emerald Isle. 60 mins.
VHS: $25078. $19.95.

Kerry

The Kingdom of Kerry shows an Irish county full of contrasts and color, its craggy coastline fringed by a necklace of sandy beaches and washed by the warm waters of Atlantic's Gulf Stream. 56 mins.
VHS: $11997. $29.95.

Let's Have an Irish Party

Carmel Quinn, Paddy Noonan, Richie O'Shea and John Scott Trotter join in an hour-long of Irish song and dancing. 60 mins.
VHS: S06657. $29.95.

Little Ireland

Ireland's 6000 years of archeological heritage, the range and standards of places to stay, the quality of the food, the festive sounds of Irish music, its unique shopping possibilities, golf courses, and other sporting opportunities, are just some of the experiences that are covered in this program. 60 mins.
VHS: $23064. $14.95.

Man of Aran

One of the masterworks of Robert Flaherty, in which Flaherty's "passionate devotion to the portrayal of human gesture and of a man's fight for his family makes the film an incomparable account of human dignity" (Georges Sadoul). Filmed on the island of Inishmore, it depicts the daily life of people on this isolated island off the coast of Ireland, fishing in their tiny curraghs, the difficulty of their existence, the hunting of a basking shark. A masterpiece.
VHS: S09417. $29.95.
Robert Flaherty, Great Britain, 1934, 76 mins.

Men of Ireland

Set amid the wild Blasket Islands, this film combines ethnographic footage with a story about a medical student who has had too much of life. He finds in the harsh, simple ways of these remote islands a paradise removed from the cares of the modern world.
VHS: $23999. $19.95.
Richard Bird, Ireland, 1938, 62 mins.

Michael Collins: The Shadow of Bealnablath

Beginning with the death of this famous politician and rebel, this documentary traces the role Collins played in Irish history. Dramatic reenactments, photos, old newsreels and interviews explain his role in the great struggle for independence all the way through the civil war that plagued the young republic. 120 mins.
VHS: $21194. $29.95.

Mother Ireland

With historical photographs, political drawings, cartoons and music, this video discovers the unrecorded role of women in Irish history. Censored in Britain, the program features many of Ireland's most prominent women, including the late Mairead Farrell, before she was shot in Gibraltar in 1988. 50 mins.
VHS: $12001. $29.95.

National Geographic Video: Ballad of the Irish Horse

A romantic and moving portrait of the Irish people, and their attachment to the horses on the Emerald Isle.
VHS: S05887. $19.95.

Off Our Knees

1988 marked the 20th anniversary of the continuous mass struggle in the North since the formation of the Civil Rights Movement in Ireland. *Off Our Knees* celebrates the stories and aspirations of the people involved, political activists, working people and human rights campaigners, and demonstrates how and why the basic demands of the Civil Rights Movement have developed into a demand for a United Ireland. 55 mins.
VHS: $11998. $29.95.

The Origins: The Two Traditions in Ireland

The Nationalist and the Unionist traditions are examined from an historic perspective in this intriguing documentary. Myths, fears and beliefs are central to the continuity of both traditions. 30 mins.
VHS: $24896. $14.95.

Out of Ireland

This documentary traces the dramatic sweep of Irish emigration brought on by 19th-century famine. The emigres helped build America. By focusing on ordinary people and their troubled lives this film makes history come alive. 111 mins.
VHS: $26358. $19.95.

Pack Up the Troubles

Can the British government find a solution to the Northern Ireland impasse? In this documentary, extensive interviews with politicians from both sides of this dispute, as well as the relatives of British soldiers who have died there, make a powerful case against continued British involvement. 60 mins.
VHS: $21195. $24.95.

Paddy Reilly Live

An intimate evening of music and song with Ireland's best-loved balladeer, with such favorites as *Spancil Hill, Carrickfergus, The Town I Loved So Well, Fields of Athenry.* 50 mins.
VHS: S06655. $29.95.

The Penal Days

The Penal Laws of post-Cromwellian Ireland were enacted to prevent the legal existence of Irish Catholics. A French Jurist described the Penal Laws as, "... conceived by demons, written in blood, and registered in Hell." 30 mins.
VHS: $24897. $14.95.

Riverdance—The Show

American dancers Michael Flatley and Jean Butler are at the center of this thrilling dance experience. It joins traditional Irish dance and music with the passion of more recent American styles. It is as if a mixture of *Dirty Dancing* with the chemistry of Torvill and Dean were added to Irish folk ways.
VHS: $27643. $24.95.

Robin Williamson in Concert

Robin Williamson is a musician, poet, author, actor, storyteller, raconteur, composer and humanitarian. His String Band, founded in 1965, has had a vital influence on Celtic culture. This concert performance video captures the complete scope of his musical experience.
VHS: $27316. $29.95.

Seamus Heaney

Ireland's complex, violent past informs Seamus Heaney's poetry. He reads from *Selected Poems 1966-1987* and also speaks with Michael Silverblatt for this video. It was recorded on October 15, 1991, in Los Angeles. From the *Lannan Literary Videos* series. 60 mins.
VHS: $27134. $19.95.

The Secret Gardens of Ireland

Though nearly as far north as Moscow, County Kerry, at the western tip of Ireland, contains a treasure of a garden. Established in the late 19th century, it functions as a veritable museum of rare and unique plants. As revealed in this video, it is also a place of great natural beauty. 50 mins.
VHS: $26628. $29.95.

A Sense of Loss

Ophuls' (*Sorrow and the Pity*) landmark film about northern Ireland probes the living roots of hatred in family folklore, in schools, on the streets. In the process, *A Sense of Loss* reveals the human terms of Ireland's civil warfare.
VHS: S01178. $59.95.
Marcel Ophuls, France/USA, 1972, 135 mins.

Song for Ireland

A showcase of the very best in Irish entertainment, filmed on location, featuring Phil Coulter, Mary Black with De Danann, Foster & Allen, the Fureys and Irish mist, hosted by Bryan Murray, and featuring such classics as "The Town I Love So Well," "Sweet Sixteen," "A Song for Ireland." 60 mins.
VHS: S06654. $29.95.

St. Patrick's Cathedral, Dublin

Over 800 years old, the Cathedral named for the patron saint of Ireland stands as a testament to the faith of the Irish people. It has stood witness over the tumultuous history of Ireland. Now this story is revealed by the natural raconteurs who have always flourished in its shadows. 35 mins.
VHS: $26627. $19.95.

St. Patrick: The Living Legend

As the patron saint of Ireland, the man credited with bringing Catholicism to his country, St. Patrick is revered by Irish people the world over. In this documentary, the various traditions and celebrations held in his honor on his day are shown and explained. 52 mins.
VHS: $26626. $19.95.

Stories from Ireland

Eamon Kelly, one of Ireland's most respected actors and master Seanachie (storyteller), draws on the rich Irish storytelling tradition set to the music of Tony McMahon, Kevin Glackin and Paul McGrattan. Kelly, often seen at the Abbey Theatre in Dublin, embellishes old Irish stories with tricks of speech and gesture, in a delightful return to tradition. 60 mins.
VHS: S06652. $29.95.

The Story of the Clancy Brothers and Tommy Makem

The jubilant New York concert by the Clancy Brothers and Tommy Makem offers telling insight into their behavior and performing rituals. The documentary mixes concert material and interviews with Bob Dylan, Mary Travers and Tom Paxton. 60 mins.
VHS: $19208. $24.95.

When Ireland Starved

This extensive documentary charts the most horrific event of modern Ireland's history, the Great Famine in the middle of the 19th century. The effects of this catastrophe have left an indelible mark on this country. Now using archival sketches, many from *The London News*, the scope of this disaster is captured on film. 120 mins.
VHS: $21193. $29.95.

Wolfe Tones On the One Road

The long-awaited, on-location video of these veterans of Irish music at their best. The songs are a compilation of all their hits, including "Boston Rose", "The West's Awake", "The Foggy Dew", "The Zoological Gardens", "On the One Road" and others. 60 mins.
VHS: $12002. $29.95.

australian CINEMA

The Adventures of Priscilla, Queen of the Desert
Terence Stamp returns to the screen in this unlikely farce about three drag queens racing across the Australian outback in order to put on a show. Of course there is more to this film than unbelievably elaborate costumes, campily choreographed lip sync numbers and gay humor. It also tries to say something about love. Great disco numbers from ABBA, Gloria Gaynor, The Village People and Peaches and Herb.
VHS: S24030. $19.95.
Laser: Letterboxed. LD74911. $34.95.
Stephen Elliott, Australia, 1994, 102 mins.

Alice to Nowhere
An Australian drama about murder, kidnapping and survival, starring Rosey Jones and John Waters (*Breaker Morant, Getting of Wisdom*) as Waters sets off on a 350-mile life-or-death trek through the harsh Australian outback. Based on the novel by Evan Green.
VHS: S03754. $59.95.
John Power, Australia, 1986, 210 mins.

All the Rivers Run
Sigrid Thornton and John Waters star in this two-volume blend of adventure, romance and drama about a gutsy, independent woman who forges her own place in the male-dominated society of nineteenth century Australia.
VHS: S04304. $79.95.
George Miller/Pino Amenta, Australia, 1984, 274 mins.

Around the World in 80 Ways
An Australian comedy about a resourceful son who convinces his senile father that he has been around the world although the old man never left his back yard. Through sound effects, props, and makeshift sets he pockets the money for the trip while Dad makes the time of his life. With Philip Quast, Allan Penny, Diana Davidson and Kelly Dingwall.
VHS: S08034. $19.95.
Stephen MacLean, Australia, 1986, 92 mins.

Beyond Innocence
Raymond Radiguet's novel *Devil in the Flesh* is the inspiration for yet another film treatment of a sensuous young woman who attracts the carnal attention of a younger schoolboy. Katia Caballero is Marthe, whose husband is a prisoner-of-war. Keith Smith is Paul, the 17-year-old looking to get beyond innocence. Lots of burning passion is promised.
VHS: S08027. $79.95.
Scott Murray, Australia, 1988, 90 mins.

Bliss
Winner of Australia's Best Picture Award, *Bliss* is an outrageous, surreal comedy about a successful ad executive who suffers a fatal heart attack and returns to view modern life in a new way. He sees how out of touch his family and friends are with nature and each other.
VHS: S00145. $19.95.
Ray Lawrence, Australia, 1985, 112 mins.

Breaker Morant
Edward Woodward is the legendary horsebreaker brought to court martial with two fellow soldiers for a murder committed during the 1901 Boer War. Winner of 10 Australian Awards, and one of the breakthrough Australian films in America.
VHS: S00178. $19.95.
Bruce Beresford, Australia, 1979, 107 mins.

Cane Toads: An Unnatural History
A fat, ugly creature whose sole purpose in life is the pursuit of sexual gratification is rapidly taking over Australia. No, we're not talking about—*Bufo marinus*—was imported to Australia in 1935 in an attempt to rid the country of the Greyback beetle, which was devouring the sugarcane crop. Problem was, the beetle could fly, and the cane toad couldn't. What the cane toad was unusually proficient at, however, was making more cane toads. A very humorous look at a serious problem.
VHS: S14731. $29.95.
Mark Lewis, Australia, 1987, 48 mins.

Country Life
Sam Neill and Greta Scacchi star in this humorous love story. An older man returns to his hometown for a vacation with his young bride. Spring fever takes hold as one by one the men of the small town fall in love with this charming woman. The woman soon realizes she's developed feelings for a young doctor (Neill) that she can't ignore. It's a story where much of the best action happens behind closed doors. With Kerry Fox, John Hargreaves.
VHS: S27302. $99.98.
Laser: LD75475. $39.99.
Michael Blakemore, Australia, 1995, 107 mins.

Crocodile Dundee
The surprise hit of 1986 from Down Under. Paul Hogan plays the Outback's answer to Tarzan but just try to take him to a big city like New York. Lots of wholesome laughs. A "reel" crowd pleaser. >With Linda Kozlowski as the American reporter.
VHS: S03874. $14.95.
Laser: LD75177. $34.98.
Peter Faiman, Australia, 1986, 98 mins.

Crocodile Dundee II
Paul Hogan returns in the role of "Crocodile" Mick Dundee, the Australian hero who speaks politely but carries a big knife. When his American love interest (Linda Kozlowski) is kidnapped by South American drug dealers he rescues her and returns to the land of koalas. The foolish villains track him down on his home turf and learn to regret the decision. Action with a smile.
VHS: S08352. $19.95.
John Cornell, Australia, 1988, 110 mins.

A Cry in the Dark
A riveting, true life human drama from Australia. Meryl Streep and Sam Neill play the parents accused of murdering their infant daughter while on vacation. They claim the baby was snatched from the tent by a dingo, a wild dog native to the continent. Streep has a new look and a new accent and another Oscar nomination.
VHS: S09308. $19.98.
Laser: LD70547. $29.98.
Fred Schepisi, Australia, 1988, 120 mins.

Dead Calm
An Australian thriller that combines murder and mayhem on the high seas. Sam Neill and Nicole Kidman are recovering from a private tragedy by taking a long ocean vacation. They encounter a crazed American and a sinking ship and learn that keeping a lunatic at bay is great therapy for some couples. With Billy Zane as the wacko. Originally a project unfinished by Orson Welles.
VHS: S10612. $19.98.
Laser: Letterboxed. LD74693. $24.98.
Phillip Noyce, Australia, 1989, 97 mins.

Death in Brunswick
Sam Neill stars as an ordinary short order cook who has some serious troubles. He's trying to clean up his act, but first he has to get rid of a body. The problems he encounters along the way are as annoying as they are hilarious. Somehow he manages to come out on top and even meet the girl of his dreams. It's how he gets there that makes all the difference.
VHS: S25567. $96.95.
John Ruane, Australia, 1990, 106 mins.

Death of a Soldier
Based on a true incident during World War II, James Coburn stars as a military lawyer reluctantly defending a confessed psychotic killer of three women in Melbourne.
VHS: S01906. $79.98.
Philippe Mora, Australia/USA, 1985, 93 mins.

Dogs in Space
Michael Hutchence, the lead singer of INXS, heads a cast of youthful performers in this Australian counterculture drama. Alienated youth hang out in a rundown working class neighborhood in Melbourne circa 1978. A provocative look at being down and out down under.
VHS: S06612. $79.98.
Richard Lowenstein, Australia, 1987, 109 mins.

Down Under
Patrick Macnee hosts this adventurous Australian comedy as two Americans find themselves amidst a vast continent they know little about, search for raw gold, and are adopted as sons amongst the aborigines. 1986, 90 mins.
VHS: S10027. $79.95.

Dusty
Bill Kerr stars in this heartwarming Australian story for all ages about the relationship between an old man and a champion sheepdog which is part dingo, part kelpie. Filmed in the Australian bush, this subtle tale of love and companionship is based on a popular children's book written by Frank Dalby Davison. With Carol Burns, Nicolas Holland, Kate Edwards, John Stanton and Noel Trevarthen.
VHS: S15900. $19.95.
John Richardson, Australia, 1982, 88 mins.

The Efficiency Expert
Originally titled *Spottiswoode*, this Australian film is reminiscent of BillForsyth's comedies about cultural and social dislocation. Anthony Hopkins, a demanding efficiency expert, is enlisted to rescue a struggling, family-operated footwear factory, run by a collection of oddballs and eccentrics. With Ben Mendelsohn, Alwyn Kurts and Bruno Lawrence.
VHS: S18765. $94.95.
Laser: LD75187. $34.98.
Mark Joffe, Australia, 1991, 97 mins.

The Everlasting Secret Family
A bizarre and brilliant Australian film that takes us into a fantasy universe of sex and politics. In public the Senator is a popular and powerful politician, happily married with a young son. In private he is a senior member of the "secret family," which controls a world of corruption and sexual manipulation at the highest levels of Australian society.
VHS: S14293. $79.95.
Michael Thornhill, Australia, 1988, 93 mins.

Father
Max Von Sydow is featured in this melodrama about a woman forced to question the very humanity of her father. It begins when she learns of an accusation against him on TV. He is suspected of being a Nazi war criminal. Though she remains convinced her father is innocent, doubts begin to grow.
VHS: S25969. $19.95.
John Power, Australia, 1990, 106 mins.

Fires Within
From the director of *My Brilliant Career* comes a smoldering tale of one man's fight to regain the love of his family and his personal honor. Jimmy Smits stars as Nestor, a Cuban political prisoner who returns after eight years in Castro's prison system to find his wife is now in love with another man. Greta Scacchi and Vincent D'Onofrio complete the triangle of passion that explodes on the streets of Miami in Little Havana. The hot Latin soundtrack is supplied by the Oscar winning Maurice Jarre. 99
VHS: S15047. $99.99.
Gillian Armstrong, USA, 1991, 90 mins.

Flirting
The second part of John Duigan's (*The Year My Voice Broke*) autobiographical trilogy about growing up in the 60s. Danny Embling (Noah Taylor) falls for a beautiful and brilliant young Ugandan woman, Thandiwe Adjewa (Thandie Newton) at a gilded Australian boarding school. "This perceptive and gorgeously acted memory piece may even surpass [the first one] in subtlety, feeling and depth of characterization" (Jonathan Rosenbaum, *Chicago Reader*). With Nicole Kidman.
VHS: S18608. $19.95.
Laser: LD75196. $34.98.
John Duigan, Australia, 1991, 99 mins.

For Love Alone
The sensual story of a young woman's quest for love and creative fulfillment in 1930's Australia, from the producer of *My Brilliant Career*. Tess is the feisty romantic who follows her yearnings to despair and passion.
VHS: S05375. $69.95.
Stephen Wallace, Australia, 1986, 102 mins.

Forty Thousand Horsemen
An Australian World War II movie starring Chips Rafferty, Grant Taylor and Betty Bryant, "the breathtaking beauty from Australia." The fighting Anzacs battle the evil German war machine in the deserts of North Africa. Includes cavalry charges, romance, and lots of horses. Watch where you step.
VHS: S05478. $29.95.
Charles Chauvel, Australia, 1941, 84 mins.

The Fringe Dwellers
Director Bruce Beresford (*Breaker Morant*) investigates the living conditions of the modern Australian Aborigine via the form of daytime drama. Ancient traditions clash with white civilization as we are shown the trials and tribulations of a young, ambitious Aborigine woman named Trilby and her problem-prone family.
VHS: Out of print. For rental only.
Laser: LD70995. $39.95.
Bruce Beresford, Australia, 1987, 96 mins.

Georgia
In this psychological thriller actress Judy Davis portrays two characters, a woman named Georgia, who died under strange circumstances, and her daughter Nina Bailey. Nina, a tough young lawyer, is intrigued when the strange facts surrounding her mother's death suddenly come to light. As Nina digs into the past, similar dangers emerge to threaten her life as well.
VHS: S20646. $19.98.
Ben Lewin, Australia, 1988, 90 mins.

Grievous Bodily Harm
Nominated for four Australian Academy Awards, a baffling thriller which stars Bruno Lawrence. Morris Martin's wife has disappeared, friends say she's dead, but he can see her on a videotape engaging in kinky sex scenes. Morris begins the search amid the rich jet set world of anything goes sex, crooked cops and wealthy professionals with shadowy secrets, and gets trapped in a bizarre series of events which could cause him "grievous bodily harm."
VHS: S08690. $19.95.
Mark Joffe, Australia, 1988, 136 mins.

Ground Zero
An Australian thriller about the secret results of British atomic tests down under in the early 1950's. Colin Friels (Malcolm) is an inquisitive photographer who learns that his father's death was no accident. Jack Thompson is the security man assigned to keep him in line. With Donald Pleasence as a crazy desert hermit with all the answers. Thought provoking and great scenery.
VHS: S09851. $19.95.
M. Pattison/B. Myles, Australia, 1988, 99 mins.

I Live with Me Dad
A homeless father and son who have nothing but each other fight desperately to remain a family in this Australian drama of love, courage, devotion and hope.
VHS: S05896. $79.98.
Paul Maloney, Australia, 1986, 86 mins.

Kangaroo
A critically-acclaimed adaptation of D.H. Lawrence's semi-autobiographical novel follows an idealistic English writer and his wife to Australia, where they hope to find a more tolerant world in which to rebuild their lives. Judy Davis and Colin Friels star.
VHS: S04523. $79.95.
Tim Burstall, Australia, 1985, 110 mins.

Kostas
This early, brilliant film by Paul Cox (*Man of Flowers*) is a poignant and touching examination of a Greek immigrant who falls in love with a socialite, their love threatened by social differences that are put to extreme tests. Autobiographical and very moving.
VHS: S01805. $69.95.
Paul Cox, Australia, 1983, 88 mins.

The Last Days of Chez Nous
Australian director Gillian Armstrong's film about the multilayered relations between men and women in a rambunctious, crowded Sydney flat. A young woman (Kerry Fox), recovering from an unplanned pregnancy and a failed relationship, moves in with her sister (Lisa Harrow), a gifted novelist, who is trying to salvage her relationship with her French husband (Bruno Ganz). The underlying sexual tension erupts when Fox and Ganz eventually give in to their mutual attraction. With Miranda Otto, Kiri Paramore and Bill Hunter.
VHS: S19506. $19.95.
Gillian Armstrong, Australia, 1991, 96 mins.

The Lighthorsemen
An Australian action adventure based on a World War I attack of 800 mounted troops who charged overwhelming forces dug in the desert town of Beersheba in the Middle East. From the director of *Phar Lap*, a different approach to the special relationship some Australian men have with their horses. Improbable but true. With Anthony Andrews, Bill Kerr, Peter Phelps, Jon Blake and Sigrid Thornton.
VHS: S08235. $19.98.
Laser: Widescreen Special Edition, CAV. LD75470. $59.95.
Simon Wincer, Australia, 1988, 115 mins.

Little Women
Louisa May Alcott's classic American novel comes to the screen for the fourth time in a lush production depicting the coming of age of four young women led by a strong matriarch. Set in the 19th century with lavish period costumes and sets, the film stars Academy Award nominee Wynona Rider, Susan Sarandon and Gabriel Byrne.
VHS: S24952. $19.95.
Laser: LD74910. $34.95.
Gillian Armstrong, USA, 1994, 118 mins.

Mad Max Beyond Thunderdome
"A series of films that just keeps getting better and better" (Gene Siskel). Mel Gibson is back as Mad Max, with Tina Turner as the deadly Auntie Entity, the Queen of Bartertown.
VHS: S00793. $14.95.
Laser: LD70619. $34.98.
George Miller, Australia, 1985, 107 mins.

Malcolm
A charming Australian film full of mayhem. Malcolm is a mild-mannered inventor whose new neighbors are a nice couple of professional thieves. When Malcolm combines his ingenuity with his neighbors'criminal aptitude, they pair up to pull off the most outrageous heist ever filmed. "A joy of a movie" (Jeff Lyons).
VHS: S03101. $79.95.
Nadia Tass, Australia, 1986, 86 mins.

Man from Snowy River
A thrilling adventure story set in the Australian frontier of the 1880's, starring Kirk Douglas in a dual role, and highlighted by a climactic chase involving 40 horsemen and over 90 wild stallions.
VHS: S00811. $14.98.
George Miller, Australia, 1982, 104 mins.

Miracle Down Under
Filmed entirely on location in the breathtaking wilds of southern Australia, this feature captures the adventures and conflicts of a rugged group of settlers in the remote bush country during the 1890's. Visions of taming the frontier quickly fade one in summer's drought, until a series of miraculous events rekindles the pioneers' hope.
VHS: S05377. $29.95.
George Miller, Australia, 1987, 101 mins.

Mrs. Soffel
Diane Keaton is a prison warden's wife who falls under the spell of a condemned murderer and aids in his and his brother's dramatic escape. Mel Gibson is the clever and not-so-bad-looking criminal and Matthew Modine is the tag-along brother. Based on a true story set in 1901. With Edward Herrmann and Trini Alvarado. Well directed by Gillian Armstrong (*My Brilliant Career*).
VHS: S06152. $19.99.
Laser: LD72147. $34.98.
Gillian Armstrong, USA, 1984, 113 mins.

Muriel's Wedding
Life is one big comic adventure for Muriel. She leaves Porpoise Spit, her small town home, and her cruel, blonde friends in hopes of finding a new identity in the big city. She changes her name to Mariel, and, along with her best friend Rhonda, discovers eager young men and exciting adventures. Before long Muriel is engaged to be married to a handsome celebrity athlete, but ultimately she must learn that even a dream wedding can't make her a different person.
VHS: S27219. $99.98.
P.J. Hogan, Australia, 1994, 105 mins.

Only the Brave
Two wild teenage girls named Vicki and Alex experiment with everything from drugs and sex to violence and just hanging out. Alex wants to write and finds encouragement, along with a little erotic attention, from her English teacher Kate. Vicki wants to sing like Alex's mother did before she disappeared. Together, these girls explore new boundaries in their friendship until events spiral out of their control. Winner of the Best Feature Film award at the 1994 San Francisco Lesbian and Gay Film Festival.
VHS: S26918. $59.95.
Ana Kokkinos, Australia, 1994, 62 mins.

Patrick
A chilling horror story about a 24-year-old patient in a small hospital who has been in a coma four years and begins to play psychokinetic games with the staff of the hospital.
VHS: S03721. $29.95.
Richard Franklin, Australia, 1978, 96 mins.

Phar Lap
A beautiful and suspenseful movie about adversity, endurance, and the drive to win. *Phar Lap* tells the story of a champion race horse that won 37 races three years capturing the imagination of all of Australia in 1932.
VHS: S01021. $14.98.
Simon Wincer, Australia, 1984, 107 mins.

Prisoners of the Sun

Where does war end and murder begin? That is just one of the questions asked by Australian attorney Bryan Brown at a post-World War II war crimes trial. George Takei (Sulu on *Star Trek*) is cast as the Japanese general under indictment. With Terry O'Quinn as the American political officer who stands between them. It has been called a gripping military drama along the lines of *Breaker Morant*.
VHS: S15099. $89.95.
Laser: LD75242. $34.98.
Stephen Wallace, Australia/USA, 1991, 109 mins.

Proof

Jocelyn Moorhouse's debut film is a psychologically compelling work about a sinister three-way love relationship between a repressed blind photographer (Hugo Weaving), his friend (Russell Crowe) who describes the contents of the photographs, and the photographer's intensely jealous housekeeper (Genevieve Picot). Moorehouse has a brilliant facility for images, rhythms and texture.
VHS: S17710. $19.95.
Jocelyn Moorhouse, Australia, 1991, 90 mins.

Puberty Blues

A funny yet frank look at the coming-of-age of two teenage Australian girls as they learn to cope with growing up on the surfing beaches outside Sydney. From the director of *Tender Mercies*, *Puberty Blues* transcends traditional teen films.
VHS: S01069. $59.95.
Bruce Beresford, Australia, 1981, 86 mins.

Remember Me

Wendy Hughes plays a woman who has everything going well for her until her ex-husband is released from a nine year stay in a psychiatric institute. Then she starts acting crazy. Can her new husband and two children provide her with peace of mind? With Richard Moir and Robert Grubb.
VHS: S07755. $59.95.
Lex Marinos, Australia, 1985, 95 mins.

Return to Snowy River

The Australian scenery and a magnificent herd of horses are once again the focus of this beautifully photographed adventure film. Tom Burlinson and Sigrid Thornton reprise their roles of the daring young horseman and his lady love, but Kirk Douglas, as the disapproving father, has been replaced by Brian Dennehy. Based on the poem by Banjo Paterson.
VHS: S07919. $89.95.
Geoff Burrowes, Australia, 1987, 99 mins.

Road Warrior

Called by Andrew Sarris a "post-apocalyptic adventure yarn of such breathtaking velocity that it would have spun hopelessly out of control without the charismatic hero of Mel Gibson's *Mad Max* at its core," *The Road Warrior* features Gibson as the ultimate anti-hero, battling a gang at the last outpost of civilization. Hair-raising stunts and spectacular chase scenes.
VHS: S01801. $14.95.
Laser: LD70739. $29.98.
George Miller, Australia, 1983, 94 mins.

Robbery Under Arms

Sam Neill (*Omen III*) stars as Captain Starlight, a renegade son of a respected English family who leads an outlaw gang of rustlers and thieves in Australia. With Steven Vidler, Christopher Cummins and Robert Grubb. A re-make of the 1957 film of the same title.
VHS: S06918. $79.95.
Crombie/Hannam, Australia, 1985, 106 mins.

Sirens

Hugh Grant, Sam Neill and Elle MacPherson star in this erotic comedy about a painter, his model and the young vicar who is disturbed by the work they produce together. Though the vicar (Grant) hopes to change this couple, he finds himself seduced by their erotic relationship.
VHS: S22158. $96.98.
John Duigan, Australia, 1994, 102 mins.

Sky Pirates

An Australian fantasy adventure about a daredevil WWII pilot who crashes through a time warp and joins a search for a special stone. John Hargreaves stars as the daring adventurer. Lots of action from Down Under and beyond. With Max Phipps, Meredith Phillips and Bill Hunter.
VHS: S06613. $79.98.
Colin Eggleston, Australia, 1986, 88 mins.

Starstruck

A wacky Australian musical comedy from the director of *My Brilliant Career*, Gillian Armstrong. Jo Kennedy stars as a teenage singing sensation who just knows she has what it takes to be a star if she can just reach the right people. With Ross O'Donovan as her energetic cousin and manager.
VHS: S06193. $19.98.
Gillian Armstrong, Australia, 1982, 95 mins.

Strictly Ballroom

The hit of film festivals in Cannes and Toronto, Baz Luhrmann's Australian film about the subculture of ballroom dancing competitions centers on a 21-year-old maverick dancer who refuses to comply with the rigid rules of the Dance Federation and gets dropped by his partner on the eve of an important dance. Luhrmann's film is an anthropological examination of a vanishing world, a funny and thrilling demystification of backdoor politics and small-scale intrigue. With Paul Mercurio, Tara Morice, Bill Hunter and Pat Thompson.
VHS: S20376. $19.95.
Laser: LD72422. $39.99.
Baz Luhrmann, Australia, 1992, 92 mins.

The Sum of Us

In this gay romantic comedy a young man finds the search for Mr. Right troubled by his busy-body father. Dad is just concerned for a son who seems unable to find that special someone. Altogether it's a light, amiable tale that is darkened by unexpected misfortune. In sunny Australia, however, things always get bright again. Based on David Stevens' play.
VHS: S26443. $29.98.
Laser: LD75085. $39.99.
Kevin Dowling/Geoff Burton, Australia, 1995, 99 mins.

Summer City

Mel (*Mad Max*) Gibson and his wild young friends descend upon a seaside resort for a weekend of surfing and adventure, but when a local girl is seduced she becomes a catalyst in a bizarre chain of events.
VHS: S01279. $19.95.
Christopher Fraser, Australia, 1976, 83 mins.

Sweet Talker

Bryan Brown, the genial star of *FX*, is cast as an ex-con with a bold scheme to raise money from a distressed seaside community by attracting interest in a legendary buried treasure ship. Complications ensue when he becomes emotionally involved with a young boy and his attractive mother, played by Karen Allen. Filmed on location in Australia. To scam or not to be scam, that is the question.
VHS: S15408. $89.98.
Laser: LD75135. $24.98.
Michael Jenkins, Australia, 1991, 91 minutes

Sweetie

A true original—this breakthrough film from Australia's Jane Campion is "as disturbing as Blue Velvet", "an original." Bizarre, often hilarious, *Sweetie* is the story of two very different sisters, the guarded and repressed Kay and the overweight and spontaneous Sweetie.
VHS: S12478. $89.95.
Jane Campion, Australia, 1989, 97 mins.

Test of Love

Based on a true story of a highly intelligent disabled teen who had been misdiagnosed and institutionalized since the age of three in a home for the severely retarded.
VHS: S01505. $69.95.
Gil Brealey, Australia, 1984, 93 mins.

Tim

An engrossing love story; Piper Laurie is the woman who is physically attracted to her gardener who, though handsome, is also slightly retarded. With a great performance from Mel Gibson as the gardener.
VHS: S01736. $39.95.
Michael Pate, Australia, 1979, 108 mins.

A Town Like Alice

Based on Neville Shute's internationally best-selling novel, *A Town Like Alice* follows the lives of Jean Paget and Joe Harman. Meeting in Malaya—she is an attractive young English captive and he is a cheerful Australian POW—they are separated by their captors, and then, by the distance of passing years, finally reunited in the rugged outback of Australia. Starring Bryan Brown and Helen Morse.
VHS: S03463. $29.95.
Laser: LD72256. $69.95.
David Stevens, Australia, 1980, 301 mins.

Vincent

A box office smash, "the most profound exploration of an artist's soul ever to be put on film. In an aesthetic experience verging on an epiphany, [Paul] Cox has sketched from Van Gogh's voluminous letters the portrait of his illustrious countryman and fellow exile not as a mad artist but as an articulate intellectual. Many of the early Van Gogh drawings filmed in Vincent have been generally inaccessible until now and many of the letters were translated from the original Dutch by the director. Hence there are many new facets to the Van Gogh legend that come to life in *Vincent* for the first time" (*Village Voice*). John Hurt is the voice of Van Gogh.
VHS: S12951. $89.95.
Paul Cox, Australia/Holland, 1989, 90 mins.

Warm Nights on a Slow Moving Train

Wendy Hughes plays an attractive schoolteacher who rents her body to lonely male passengers on a weekend train run between Sydney and Melbourne. She needs the money to support her crippled brother's drug habit. Business is good until she meets a beguiling government agent and gets involved in something more dangerous than a social disease. With Colin Friels, Norman Kaye, Grant Tilly and Peter Whitford as "the Steward."
VHS: S10344. $19.95.
Laser: LD71399. $39.95.
Bob Ellis, Australia, 1987, 90 mins.

Waterfront

The sexy Greta Scacchi stars as an Italian immigrant in Australia thrown into a bitter dock workers dispute. Against the odds of language barriers and racial attitudes toward Italians, Greta and union leader Jack Thompson fall in love in a tragic love story.
VHS: S05843. $29.95.
Edward McQ. Mason, Australia, 1987, 284 mins.

We of the Never Never

The true account of life on the Australian frontier based on the journals of a woman pioneer. A moving account of courage, hardship, conflicts, and eventually conquest of the beautiful land of the "never never" of the Aborigines through the power of love.
VHS: S01436. $59.95.
Igor Auzins, Australia, 1982, 90 mins.

Who Killed Baby Azaria

Another version of the story of Lindy Chamberlain and her missing baby Azaria, this was made before *A Cry in the Dark*. She claimed it was taken away by a wild dingo. This mystery-suspense film claims to contain the truth of Australia's most controversial murder trial. As details of the case were still unfolding in 1988, it obviously doesn't tell the whole story. With Elain Hudson, John Hamblin and Max Phipps.
VHS: S09920. $59.95.
Judy Rymer, Australia, 1983, 96 mins.

A Woman's Tale

A haunting work about the demands of a bright, challenging 78-year-old woman (Sheila Florance, in her final performance) to find a grace and dignity in her life, carried out by her relationship with a sympathetic and equally tough nurse (Cox regular Gosia Dobrowlolska). With Norman Kaye, Chris Haywood and Ernest Gray.
VHS: S17882. $79.98.
Paul Cox, Australia, 1991, 93 mins.

Year My Voice Broke

A touching Australian coming-of-age film set in the early 60's in a small Outback community. Young Danny has always had the hots for the independent and beautiful Freya but she prefers the company of older men who are on the run from the law. A fine nostalgic piece about small town secrets and growing up. With Noah Taylor, Loene Carmen and Ben Mendelsohn. Winner of five Australian Film awards including Best Picture.
VHS: S08502. $89.95.
John Duigan, Australia, 1988, 103 mins.

Young Einstein

An intellectually serious slapstick comedy from Australia. Yahoo Serious (born Greg Pead) wrote, directed, produced and stars as the title character in this fictional biography of one of the world's greatest thinkers, had Einstein been born in Tasmania on a little apple farm instead of in Europe. Enjoy his comic exploits as he splits the atom, invents rock and roll and dates Marie Curie. Funny stuff from Down Under. With Jon Howard, Pee Wee Wilson and Odile Le Clezio.
VHS: S11577. $19.95.
Yahoo Serious, Australia, 1989, 90 mins.

PETER WEIR

The Cars That Ate Paris

Australian director Peter Weir's first feature is a delightful black comedy about a small Aussie town that makes its living solely on the visitors they ambush. Inspired, in part, by the driving conditions in Paris, France, Weir's gleefully murderous community is now available in its original uncut version.
VHS: S06069. $19.98.
Peter Weir, Australia, 1974, 91 mins.

Dead Poets Society

Robin Williams gets semi-serious about the written word as he shapes and guides young minds at an Eastern seaboard prep school in the late '50's. The title refers to a secret society of students designed to promote imagination and cultural exchange. With Ethan Hawke, Josh Charles, Sean Leonard, Norman Lloyd and Kurtwood Smith as a disapproving parent.
VHS: S11992. $29.95.
Laser: LD70943. $39.99.
Peter Weir, USA, 1989, 128 mins.

Fearless

Jeff Bridges, Isabella Rossellini and Rosie Perez (in an Oscar-nominated performance) star in this overlooked drama about life-altering experiences. The survivors of a plane crash reach out to each other in an effort to cope with the horrors of death and the accompanying guilt. Also featuring Tom Hulce as a sleazy personal injuries lawyer, and John Turturro.
VHS: S20720. $19.98.
Laser: LD72386. $39.98.
Peter Weir, USA, 1993, 122 mins.

Gallipoli

Adventure story that brings two young men together in the Australian army in 1915, leading to the legendary confrontation between the Australians and Turks at Gallipoli during World War I. From the director of *Last Wave* and *Picnic at Hanging Rock*.
VHS: S00477. $19.95.
Peter Weir, Australia, 1981, 111 mins.

Green Card

The English-speaking debut of French actor Gerard Depardieu, *Green Card* is a sharp comedy of manners, about a repressed horticulturist (Andie MacDowell) who agrees to marry a French musician (Depardieu) and is forced to live with him when immigration authorities check out their backgrounds. They promptly fall in love.
Laser: LD71022. $39.99.
Peter Weir, USA, 1990, 107 mins.

Last Wave

Peter Weir's fourth feature is a visually compelling portrayal of inner hysteria and apocalyptic vision. David Burton (Richard Chamberlain), a Sydney corporate lawyer, is sucked into the whirlpool of events surrounding the mysterious death of an Australian Aborigine when he volunteers to defend those accused of the murder. During the course of the trial, Burton's abstracted dream images begin to reveal strange water-related events in the weather, and concern one of the four Aborigines he is defending.
VHS: S00729. $19.95.
Peter Weir, Australia, 1977, 109 mins.

The Mosquito Coast

Director Peter Weir re-teams with Harrison Ford as they tackle Paul Theroux's novel of an obsessive American inventor who transplants his family to a fictional Central American country which he hopes will welcome a jungle based ice factory. With River Phoenix as the long suffering son and Helen Mirren as the even longer suffering wife.
VHS: S03436. $19.98.
Laser: Letterboxed. LD74481. $34.98.
Peter Weir, USA, 1986, 119 mins.

Witness

Harrison Ford is the cop who runs head-on into the non-violent world of the Amish community in this Academy Award-winning struggle of life and death in which a young Amish woman and her son are caught up in the murder of an undercover narcotics agent.
VHS: S01472. $14.95.
Peter Weir, USA, 1985, 112 mins.

Year of Living Dangerously

Mel Gibson and Sigourney Weaver begin an impassioned love affair intensified by the uncertainties of life in Indonesia on the eve of revolution. Linda Hunt stars as Billy Kwan, a Eurasian cameraman who befriends Gibson.
VHS: S01486. $19.98.
Laser: LD70715. $34.98.
Peter Weir, Australia/USA, 1982, 115 mins.

NEW ZEALAND CINEMA

An Angel at My Table

The true story of one of our century's most gifted writers, *An Angel at My Table* chronicles the life and extraordinary times of Janet Frame. Born in the 1920s, Janet's early years of fairy tales and schoolgirl pranks were tempered by family tragedy. She retreated to her beloved books and began to write poetry and stories. As the years passed her talent grew and so did the challenges to her unique and inspired vision.
VHS: S15620. $19.98.
Laser: CLV. LD72106. $49.95.
Jane Campion, New Zealand, 1991, 157 mins.

Crush

Lane (Marcia Gay Harden) is a reckless driver who inadvertently leaves her friend Christina hospitalized with severe injuries. Fleeing the scene of the crime, she crashes into the lives of a novelist and his teenage daughter Angela. At first she befriends the girl, only to betray this trust by seducing the father. Angela seeks revenge by helping and manipulating Christina to reveal Lane's guilt.
VHS: S21092. $19.98.
Alison MacLean, New Zealand, 1993, 100 mins.

Dead Alive

A strange creature, the Sumatran rat monkey, has bitten an old woman and thereby transformed her into a ghoulish, dead monster who sucks the life out of the living. Her son tries to live a normal life but mom's victims keep on multiplying and, even worse, go on living themselves. Soon a crowd of flesh-hungry monsters is menacing this once-peaceful small town.
VHS: S19240. $14.99.
Laser: LD75180. $34.98.
Peter Jackson, New Zealand, 1992, 85 mins.

Heart of the Stag

Bruno Lawrence (*Smash Palace*) stars as a farmhand who signs on with an isolated sheep ranch and disrupts an incestuous relationship in this offbeat, rather bizarre story. From the director of *Sylvia*.
VHS: S03462. $19.95.
Michael Firth, New Zealand, 1984, 94 mins.

Heavenly Creatures

Peter Jackson's chilling account of two teenage girls who develop an intense emotional and physical relationship, dominated by fantasy, which ultimately leads them to murder, is a stylistically original work. It is remarkable for its insights into the girls' adolescent world of make-believe, as well as the bland suburban world of 1950's New Zealand.
VHS: S24774. $96.98.
Laser: Widescreen. LD74976. $39.99.
Peter Jackson, New Zealand, 1994, 99 mins.

Jack Be Nimble

Alexis Arquette and Sarah Kennedy Smuts are featured in this supernatural thriller about a brother and sister who are split up when their parents abandon them. The brother, Jack, is trapped with a sadistic family. Luckily his sister Dora develops extra-sensory powers that warn her of the dangers faced by her brother.
VHS: S24381. $94.95.
Garth Maxwell, New Zealand, 1994, mins.

Map of the Human Heart

An epic love story between Avik (Jason Scott Lee), an Eskimo, and Albertine (French actress Anne Parillaud), a half-breed, that unfolds in the years 1931-1965. When the lovers are reunited, Avik, a World War II bomber pilot, discovers Albertine is married to Walter Scott (Patrick Bergin), his former protector who saved his life. "A sweeping romance, grand, noble and boldly imaginative" (Jay Carr, *Boston Globe*). With John Cusack, Ben Mendelsohn, Annie Galipeau and Jeanne Moreau.
VHS: S19060. $19.98.
Laser: LD75227. $34.98.
Vincent Ward, New Zealand, 1992, 109 mins.

Meet the Feebles

An adult fantasy film, *Meet the Feebles* relates the events that led up to the infamous "Feebles Variety Massacre," the day that rocked the puppet world. The film, directed by Peter Jackson (*Dead Alive, Heavenly Creatures*), who describes it as "a kind of Roger Rabbit meets Brazil," is set in a contemporary world like ours, with one major difference: there are no human beings. The Feebles' world is entirely populated by puppets—living, breathing, eating puppets with larger-than-life human characteristics and weaknesses…*Meet the Feebles* is a darkly comic satire on greed, lust and jealousy…part satire/soap opera/ musical that is a wildly original feature" (Charles Coleman).
VHS: S26868. $89.95.
Peter Jackson, New Zealand, 1988, 97 mins.

The Mighty Civic

Blending history, fantasy and truth, New Zealand filmmaker Peter Wells weaves a magical spell over the history of old movie palaces. Within this world, showgirls reminisce about their experiences and an usher leads a tour into the secrets of Auckland's Xanadu. The program moves briskly through time, moving from Auckland in the 20s to World War II-era days when American soldiers confronted Kiwi women at the Civic's midnight roof.
VHS: S20216. $29.95.
Peter Wells, New Zealand, 62 mins.

Navigator: A Time Travel Adventure

A highly imaginative epic as a group of medieval villagers, on the verge of being decimated by the bubonic plague, are lead by a visionary boy through the bowels of the earth and end up—in 20th century New Zealand. Called "electrifying….a spellbinder" by *The Rolling Stone*.
VHS: S10721. $59.95.
Vincent Ward, New Zealand, 1988, 101 mins.

Once Were Warriors

The title of Lee Tamahori's breakthrough feature refers to the Maori people and their proud history. Set in an apocalyptic suburban New Zealand landscape, the film focuses on a dysfunctional family. The abused wife struggles to keep her family together despite the brutish and violent ways of her alcoholic husband, which, the filmmaker suggests, is a result of alienation from the authentic (Maori) culture.
VHS: S26282. $19.98.
Laser: LD75060. $49.95.
Lee Tamahori, New Zealand, 1995, 102 mins.

The Piano

Holly Hunter's Oscar-winning performance as a mute woman dedicated to her music takes center stage in this lush drama set in 19th century New Zealand. Harvey Keitel co-stars as the brutish but sensitive man who gives her back what seemed irrevocably lost. A young Anna Paquin more than holds her own with a performance that garnered this new star an Oscar for Best Supporting Actress.
VHS: S20871. $19.98.
Jane Campion, Australia/New Zealand, 1993, 121 mins.

Quiet Earth

A brilliant science-fiction thriller from New Zealand. Bruno Lawrence is the last person on earth, who stumbles upon two more survivors, one a young woman, the other a Maori tribesman. But another disaster is in the making and unless the three can stop it, the human race will be snuffed out.
VHS: Out of print. For rental only.
Laser: LD71287. $34.98.
Geoff Murphy, New Zealand, 1986, 91 mins.

Smash Palace

A breakthrough film from New Zealand; the story of a disintegrating marriage, powerful for its performances, especially that of Bruno Lawrence as the bewildered husband left behind by his bored and discontented wife. Compared by one critic to a cross between *Kramer vs. Kramer* and *Bullitt*.
VHS: Out of print. For rental only.
Laser: LD71330. $39.95.
Roger Donaldson, New Zealand, 1981, 100 mins.

Starlight Hotel

A New Zealand road movie set in the Depression era of 1932. A 13-year-old girl disguises herself as a boy and runs away to find her father. She is assisted by a good looking, socially minded fugitive from justice. The title refers to sleeping out under the open sky. Fine performances by Greer Robson and Peter Phelps.
VHS: S08321. $79.95.
Laser: CLV. LD72034. $29.98.
Sam Pillsbury, New Zealand, 1987, 95 mins.

Tearaway

A very unusual film from New Zealand, the theme of *Tearaway* is adolescent rebellion and and living on the edge, aided by a hip, high-octane rock score.
VHS: S05855. $19.98.
Bruce Morrison, New Zealand/Australia, 1987, 100 mins.

AUSTRALIAN/NEW ZEALAND ISSUES

Australia: Secrets of the Land Down Under

Sample the delights of Sydney, then continue on to Canberra, the Outback of New South Wales, Ayer's Rock, Melbourne, Perth, and the awesome Gold Coast. Australia—the land down under—is a unique and exciting continent; see it all here! 50 mins.
VHS: S05785. $24.95.

The Australian Way of Life

Australians are a largely urban people who paradoxically have access to great, unspoiled wilderness areas. They also enjoy free education and health care in a country that reflects a variety of international influences. 21 mins.
VHS: S23708. $129.95.

The Dreaming Universe

Physicist Fred Wolf maintains that the world of dreams is ontologically real. This entertaining meditation on the nature of human consciousness explores the concept of "dreamtime" originated by Australian Aborigines. 60 mins.
VHS: S23623. $34.95.

National Geographic Video: Australia's Aborigines

Travel to a distant land for a moving and memorable portrait of Australia's aborigines. Meet what may be the last generation of a noble culture that has endured for over 40,000 years. 60 mins.
VHS: S11409. $19.95.

New Zealand Coast to Coast

Explore spectacular New Zealand and see Auckland, Wellington, Christchurch, Queensland, and the amazing beaches, volcanoes, and dense forests that characterize this jewel of the South Pacific. 30 mins.
VHS: S05774. $24.95.

Touring Australia

This tour covers the cities of Melbourne, Sydney and Perth as well as the Kakadu National Park with its Aboriginal art, the inland sea of Lake Eyre, and the Great Barrier Reef. Various, USA, 1987, 48 mins.
VHS: S03327. $29.95.

Touring New Zealand

A land of awesome beauty, this island country with just three million people, 1,200 miles from Australia, is fast becoming one of the most visited destinations in the South Pacific. This fascinating video tour covers over 100 historic, scenic and cultural sites on both of the North and South Islands, including insightful visits to the center of the Maori culture. 70 mins.
VHS: S12293. $29.95.

canadian CINEMA

90 Days

Filmed and acted in almost documentary style, *90 Days* shows the attempt by two men to handle the absurd complications of modern life.
VHS: S04197. $79.98.
Giles Walker, Canada, 1986, 100 mins.

And Hope to Die

Rene Clement (*Purple Noon, Rider on the Rain*) directed this interesting thriller in Canada. Robert Ryan and Jean-Louis Trintignant star in the story of a freelance gangster who has an ingenious plan to steal the sexy and simple-minded kingpin's moll from police custody for a $1 million ransom before she can testify against the Mob. Very stylish. In English.
VHS: S08024. $49.95.
Rene Clement, Canada, 1972, 95 mins.

The Apprenticeship of Duddy Kravitz

Richard Dreyfuss stars as an ambitious Canadian Jew determined to become a success at any price. Based on Mordecai Richler's novel, this powerful comic-drama features an equally able supporting cast. With Jack Warden, Denholm Elliott, Joe Silver, Joseph Wiseman and Micheline Lanctot.
VHS: S06341. $19.95.
Ted Kotcheff, Canada, 1974, 121 mins.

Bay Boy

An autobiographical drama from writer-director Daniel Petrie. Keifer Sutherland stars as an impressionable young man growing up in a tiny Canadian community. Liv Ullmann is cast as his hardworking mother. The time is the 1930s, and local mischief abounds. Cast includes Robert Donat, Matthieu Carriere and Isabelle Mejias. Made on location in Nova Scotia.
VHS: S10468. $79.95.
Daniel Petrie, Canada, 1984, 107 mins.

Black Robe

1634 began the French colonization of Canada through Catholic missions. *Black Robe* tells the story of an extraordinary priest who braved the North American wilderness and extreme cultural difference to carry his message from Europe. An important indictment of the Church's refusal to assimilate other cultures, and the tragic corruption of Native American societies by the West. From the director of *Driving Miss Daisy* and *Breaker Morant*.
VHS: S15868. $94.95.
Laser: LD75159. $34.98.
Bruce Beresford, Canada, 1991, 101 mins.

Blind Trust

A gripping thriller from French Canada concerning the robbery of an armored car. In the tradition of *The Asphalt Jungle*, a small gang of criminals meticulously plan a major heist. An intelligent and well acted crime story with Marie Tifo, Pierre Curzi, Yvan Ponton and Jean-Louis Millette. English dubbed.
VHS: S05892. $79.98.
Yves Simoneau, Canada, 1986, 86 mins.

Blood of the Hunter

Michael Biehn, Gabriel Arcand and Alexandra Vandernoot star in this icy thriller set in the era of the Canadian frontier. A postman sets off across the wilderness, leaving his wife alone. She soon is trapped by a killer tied mysteriously to her husband. Suspense mounts as the postman's mysterious past slowly unravels and the danger to his wife grows.
VHS: S25564. $92.99.
Gilles Carle, Canada, 1994, 92 mins.

The Boys of St. Vincent

A sensitively told story of child molestation within the confines of a Catholic orphanage and the resulting massive cover-up by the Church. Henry Czerny is superb as the tortured Brother Peter Lavin, the stern and difficult guardian who secretly molests his favorite boys. Conspiring to save the reputation of the Catholic-run orphanage, the concerned authorities decide to keep Brother Lavin's actions a secret and bury the case. Now, 15 years later, the victims refuse to remain silent. With Johnny Morina and Brian Dooley.
VHS: S27432. $89.95.
John N. Smith, Canada, 1994, 186 mins.

Candy Mountain

Kevin O'Connor plays an ambitious young musician who goes off on a quest to find the legendary guitar maker Elmore Silk (Harris Yulin). He travels from New York to the wilds of Canada and encounters Tom Waits, David Johansen, Bulle Ogier, Dr. John, Leon Redbone, and others in cameo roles in this entertaining and very odd road movie. Co-directed by Robert (*Pull My Daisy*) Frank and screenwriter Rudy Wurlitzer (*Walker*).
VHS: S08063. $14.98.
Robert Frank/Rudy Wurlitzer, Canada/France/Switzerland, 1987, 90 mins.

Carry On Sergeant

Not to be confused with the British *Carry On* series, which has the same title. This Canadian silent drama concerns a Man of Far North who leaves his wife to fight in World War I. Said to be a controversial and costly film. B&W.
VHS: S04814. $24.95.
Bruce Bairnsfather, Canada, 1928, 09 mins.

Cold Journey

A feature drama about a young Canadian Indian's attempt to find a place for himself. It tells of the cultural shock of an educational system that teaches him to be a white man, and of his attempts to discover a way of life more meaningful to his Indian culture and ancestry. It is a tragic story of unexpected pitfalls and disillusionment that are as cruel as the bitter wind that greets him on his cold and lonely journey. Shot on location with the people of Indian reserves in Saskatchewan and Manitoba.
VHS: S07665. $69.95.
Martin Defalco, Canada, 76 mins.

The Darling Family

In this unconventional feature the glaring inconsistencies and deadening misunderstandings that govern heterosexual intimacy are openly aired. Despite this intense focus, the film has an immediacy that is hard to resist. A young woman who is mystical, emotional and angry confronts the man who made her pregnant. He, by contrast, is practical, reserved and witty. Not surprisingly, the pregnancy is not a disaster for her, but for him it is coming at the worst time. The results are anything but predictable. Linda Griffith wrote the original play and stars opposite Alan Williams in the film.
VHS: S26479. $59.95.
Alan Zweig, Canada, 1994, 85 mins.

Decline of the American Empire

Denys Arcand's critically acclaimed film of sex talk explores the complex and comic relationships between eight Quebec intellectuals who are brought together for a Sunday dinner. Funny, Quebecois drama that was a huge hit on its home ground, a portrait of the Big Chill generation from the perspective of sex. French with English subtitles.
VHS: S03312. $79.95.
Denys Arcand, Canada, 1986, 101 mins.

The Disappearance

Donald Sutherland is a skilled, remorseless contract killer whose difficult assignment is solving the unsolved disappearance of his wife. With Francine Racette, David Hemmings and David Warner.
VHS: S18141. $9.95.
Stuart Cooper, Canada, 1977, 88 mins.

Double Happiness

This warm comedy by Canada's Mina Shum is a witty and charming cross between *The Joy Luck Club* and *The Hollywood Shuffle*. Sandra Oh stars as Jade, a young Chinese woman trying to balance her modern dreams of being an actress while living with her traditionally minded Chinese parents. Jade's parents set themselves on a mission to fix her up with a nice Chinese man, but Jade is already involved in a secret romance with a Caucasian man.
VHS: S27089. $95.99.
Laser: LD75449. $39.99.
Mina Shum, Canada, 1995, 87 mins.

Dr. Bethune

Donald Sutherland stars in this Canadian homage to Dr. Norman Bethune, who fought for medical progress and political justice on three continents, including China. With Helen Mirren and Helen Shaver.
VHS: S20573. $19.98.
Phillip Borsos, Canada, 1992, 115 mins.

Fields of Endless Day

In a series of dramatic and documentary episodes, this film outlines the presence of black people in Canada from the 17th century, when the first explorers first arrived, to the wartime participation and activist groups of the 20th century. The film seeks to uncover the *roots* of Canada's black population by tracing the history of their struggles and triumphs over 375 years. Produced by the National Film Board of Canada.
VHS: S07664. $49.95.
Terence Macartney-Filgate, Canada, 59 mins.

Going Home

A story suppressed for over 70 years; set in North Wales in 1919, thousands of Canadian infantrymen awaited the arrival of homeward bound ships. But they are passed over to accommodate grain shipments, and mutiny mounts among the rank and file.
VHS: S07321. $79.95.
Terry Ryan, Canada, 1986, 100 mins.

Heaven on Earth

Between 1867 and 1914 a multitude of lost and lonely British children were sent to Canada in search of new homes and the love of a family. This film tells the poignant story of how these children coped with a life that was both demanding and often cruel, in a sensitive, compelling film. The film follows the fortunes of five young children, based on factual historical events.
VHS: S10946. $79.95.
Allen Kroeker, Canada, 1988, 100 mins.

Highway 61

This off-center comedy is the second feature by the talented young Canadian independent Bruce McDonald (*Roadkill*). Ostensibly a road movie which takes its title from the mythic Bob Dylan song, the film is about the unlikely adventures of a small-town barber (Don McKellar) who agrees to drive a beautiful, unconventional roadie (Valerie Buhagiar) from Ontario to New Orleans, carrying a corpse she claims is her brother.
VHS: S17071. $89.95.
Bruce McDonald, Canada, 1991, 103 mins.

Home Feeling

The struggle of the residents of a black ghetto in Toronto to form a real community in the face of police, social and institutional perseverance evokes a powerful view of a community that has a positive future despite its image of vandalism, high-density, racial tension, despair and crime. The film focuses intimately on the lives of several of the residents, and their relationship with police, social services and other major institutions. Produced by the National Film Board of Canada.
VHS: S07668. $49.95.
Jennifer Hodge, Canada, 58 mins.

The Housekeeper

Rita Tushingham plays a murdering illiterate who is unstable enough to do it again to protect her secret. She gets a job with a well-to-do Canadian family that eventually gets on her nerves. With great supporting work by Jackie Burroughs. From a novel by Ruth Rendell.
VHS: S04988. $19.98.
Ousama Rawi, Canada, 1986, 102 mins.

I've Heard the Mermaids Singing

A wonderfully whimsical little comedy about imagination and the rude intrusion of reality in the life of an awkward temp worker with a penchant for photography. Sheila McCarthy is Polly and Paule Baillargeon is her new and surprisingly understanding employer. A reel delight from Canada.
VHS: S06046. $19.98.
Patricia Rozema, Canada, 1987, 81 mins.

In Trouble

Julie LaChapelle plays an unhappy woman who finds herself seduced and abandoned and very pregnant. To explain her condition to her three overprotective brothers she invents an imaginary rapist, whom they locate after a diligent manhunt. This leaves Julie in trouble in more ways than the obvious. With Daniel and Donald Pilon.
VHS: S06166. $59.95.
Gilles Carle, Canada, 1967, 82 mins.

Jesus of Montreal

A charismatic actor is hired to punch up the annual Montreal Passion play and discovers he is beginning to take his work far more seriously than he intended. Lothaire Bluteau is truly inspirational in the title role of this award-winning film by Denys Arcand. With Catherine Wilkening, Johanne-Marie Tremblay, Remy Girard and Yves Jacques. French with English subtitles.
VHS: S13674. $19.95.
Denys Arcand, Canada/France, 1989, 118 mins.

Joshua Then and Now

Based on Mordecai (*Apprenticeship of Duddy Kravitz*) Richler's autobiographical novel, the film stars James Woods as Jewish writer Joshua Shapiro at a crucial stage in his life. The film is a realistic depiction of his growing up in the Jewish section of Montreal, with a gangster father (Alan Arkin) and a would-be entertainer mother (Linda Sorensen), who, as a special treat, does striptease for his bar mitzvah. *Joshua* is an often funny and poignant portrait.
VHS: S10760. $79.98.
Ted Kotcheff, Canada, 1985, 118 mins.

The Last Winter

This beautiful, highly acclaimed film concerns a young boy who lives in a wonderful undisturbed country idyll. All his fantasy world, not to mention the world of his everyday life, is set in crisis by his family's impending move to the city. It's a film about learning to accept change that is great for kids and grown-ups alike.
VHS: S26389. $95.99.
Aaron Kim Johnston, Canada, 1989, 103 mins.

Leolo

A French-Canadian coming-of-age film about a boy convinced he was fathered by a tomato. This strange premise sets the mood for a darkly comic fantasy/nightmare with mystical and sexual overtones.
VHS: S20579. $19.95.
Laser: LD74454. $49.99.
Jean-Claude Lauzon, Canada, 1992, 107 mins.

The Lotus Eaters

This coming-of-age film is set on an island off Canada's western coast, a place known for its dreamy, eccentric atmosphere, and a perfect place for Lotus eaters. It brings a ten-year-old sorceress, a teenage love story, two pigs called Mortimer and Ogilvy and a fabled Beatles concert together into a charming, romantic comedy.
VHS: S25951. $79.95.
Paul Shapiro, Canada, 1994, 101 mins.

Love and Human Remains

Thomas Gibson and Mia Kirshner are at the center of this dazzling and twisted thriller. David and Candy were lovers; now they're roommates in search of thrills. Their restless and relentless hunt for new excitement eventually leads them into dangerous waters. Without limits, someone is bound to get hurt. With Matthew Ferguson and Ruth Marshall.
VHS: S26954. $96.99.
Laser: LD75427. $34.95.
Denys Arcand, Canada, 1993, 100 mins.

Loyalties

A marriage is put to the test in a remote village in northern Alberta in this compelling Canadian drama about honesty and human weakness. Kenneth Welsh, Tantoo Cardinal and Susan Wooldridge head a superb cast that finds there is no place far enough to hide from the truth. Strong and memorable performances.
VHS: S06062. $19.95.
Anne Wheeler, Canada, 1986, 98 mins.

Masala

Srinivas Krishna's colorful, independent feature is set in the East Indian community in Toronto. Krishna (played by the director) is traumatized by his parents' deaths and believes he won't live long. "A brash and sprightly Canadian comedy about Indian emigres in Toronto, with musical numbers, erotic dream sequences, exploding airplanes, a blue-skinned Hindu deity who exists mainly on video, a fair amount of farce, and a great deal of satire" (Jonathan Rosenbaum, *Chicago Reader*). With Saeed Jaffrey, Zohra Segal, Sakina Jaffrey and Heri Johal.
VHS: S19728. $19.95.
Srinivas Krishna, Canada, 1991, 105 mins.

Masculine Mystique

What do "real men" think about Feminism? Can they ever learn to adjust to life with a modern woman? This docudrama of four men and their relationships is interwoven in a funny and revealing film. Blue, in his mid-thirties, has spent his adult years searching for the perfect woman, without any luck. Alex, the same age, is married with two children, but says he needs freedom. So he's having an affair. Mort has found someone new but she doesn't want a permanent relationship. And Ashley, devastated by divorce, doesn't want to risk a new commitment. Produced by the National Film Board of Canada.
VHS: S07671. $69.95.
John N. Smith/Giles Walker, Canada, 1984, 87 mins.

Mon Oncle Antoine

Director Claude Jutra's acclaimed, sensitive, breakthrough film of a young boy coming of age in the Canadian backwoods swept the Canadian Academy Awards. Young Benoit slowly becomes aware of the affinities between love, life and death as he works as a stock boy in his uncle Antoine's general store. Since Antoine serves as everything from notary to shopkeeper to undertaker, it is no wonder that Benoit learns about life quickly. French with English subtitles.
VHS: S12954. $39.95.
Claude Jutra, Canada, 1971, 104 mins.

Night Zoo

A French-Canadian crime thriller that won 13 Genie Awards, the equivalent of the U.S. Oscar. Set in Montreal, an ex-con returns to the free world to find his father is dying, his girlfriend is a little crazy and a couple of crooked cops are after the money he has hidden away. Brutal and sensitive. With Gilles Maheu, Roger Le Bel and Lynne Adams. The debut film of Jean-Claude Lauzon.
VHS: S07964. $19.95.
Jean-Claude Lauzon, Canada, 1987, 116 mins.

Obsessed

Kerrie Keane plays a distraught, divorced mother whose young son is struck by a hit and run driver. When the businessman responsible flees from Canada for the safety of the U.S., she starts making the life of Saul Rubinek miserable. Based on the book *Hit and Run* by Tom Alderman. With Alan Thicke, Daniel Pilon and Colleen Dewhurst. A drama with plenty of emotion.
VHS: S10985. $69.95.
Robin Spry, Canada, 1988, 100 mins.

Odyssey of the Pacific (The Emperor of Peru)

Mickey Rooney stars in this children's adventure of a retired railway engineer who is befriended by a trio of youngsters, including a Cambodian refugee who wants to go home by train. A heart warming tale with Monique Mercure, Jean-Louis Roux and Guy Hoffman.
VHS: S07776. $39.95.
Fernando Arrabal, Canada, 1981, 100 mins.

Oh, What a Night

A valentine to 50s romance, freedom and innocence, about two young friends and their first encounters with women, fast cars and music. With Corey Haim, Barbara Williams, Keir Dullea and Robbie Coltrane. A wonderfully evocative soundtrack of Bill Haley, the Penguins, The Monotones and The Dells.
VHS: S17788. $89.95.
Eric Till, Canada, 1992, 90 mins.

Ordinary Magic

A funny adaptation of Malcolm Bosse's novel about Jeffrey (David Fox), an eccentric young dreamer who grew up in India and returns to America to live with his aunt (Glenne Headly) following the death of his parents. With Heath Lamberts, Paul Anka and Ryan Reynolds.
VHS: S20209. $89.95.
Giles Walker, Canada, 1993, 96 mins.

Paper Wedding

This emotionally honest and fiercely intelligent Canadian drama is the movie that *Green Card* should have been. Genevieve Bujold gives one of her best performances as a disillusioned single woman who agrees to marry, in name only, a Chilean political refugee to prevent his deportation. Chilean born actor Manuel Aranguiz is perfectly cast as the grateful husband. The relationship takes an unexpected turn when Canadian immigration officials take an active interest in the case. Shot on location in Quebec. With Dorothe Berryman, Gilbert Sicotte, Jean Mathieu, Monique Lepage and Teo Spychalski as Bujold's married former lover Milosh.
VHS: S15683. $79.95.
Laser: LD71487. $39.95.
Michel Brault, Canada, 1990, 90 mins.

Paris, France

"Feverish eroticism...hot & kinky...goes gleefully over the top" (*The New York Times*). Leslie Hope (*Talk Radio*) stars in this highly erotic film *The New York Post* calls, "a dizzying display of grappling bodies and sizzling hot sex."
VHS: S23862. $14.98.
Gerard Ciccoritti, Canada, 1993, 111 mins.

Princes in Exile

A sensitive, uplifting story about the power of the human spirit. Camp Hawkins is a summer camp for youngsters with life-threatening illnesses. Ryan, a moody 17-year-old, spends his days in his own private world. But when he meets Holly, a fellow camper, he soon learns that love holds the key to many miracles. Winner of the ecumenical prize at the 1990 Montreal World Film Festival.
VHS: S13655. $29.95.
Giles Walker, Canada, 1990, 103 mins.

Salut Victor

This charming tear-jerker follows two older gay men and their budding romance. Victor is gay, and his exuberant spirit inspires Phillipe, a longtime loner, to finally share some of his own unique spirit. French with English subtitles.
VHS: S24834. $39.95.
Anne Claire Poirer, Canada, 1989, 83 mins.

The Savage Woman

Lea Pool's drama about the shifting relationship of a battered woman and a sympathetic engineer who befriends and shelters her from the authorities. As the completion of his water project nears, she must confront the dark and frenzied horror of her past. Named the best feature at the Montreal World Film Festival. With Patricia Tulasne and Matthias Habich. "A steamy sexual odyssey" (*Toronto Globe and Mail*).
VHS: S18407. $39.95.
Lea Pool, Canada, 1991, 100 mins.

September 1939

A Canadian documentary on the Nazi invasion of Poland in September, 1939. Combining Polish newsreels, German propaganda and other rare archival footage, the Blitzkreig (Lightning War) is examined in great detail. Narrated by Frank Willis. See Warsaw reduced to rubble. Canada, 1961, 60 mins.
VHS: S05440. $24.95.

The Sex of the Stars

This charming and lovely film recounts the painful growth experienced by a French Canadian family impacted by divorce and transsexualism. A 12-year-old girl seeks solace in star gazing when her parents divorce and her father becomes a woman. Though the girl tries to recreate the past she finds that her future lies in reconciliation. French with English subtitles.
VHS: S25035. $59.95.
Paule Baillargeon, Canada, 1994, 104 mins.

Souvenir

In 1944, a dashing German soldier and a beautiful French girl fall deeply in love. Now, more than 40 years later, Ernst Kestner (Christopher Plummer), retired and recently widowed, leaves his adopted home in New York and returns to France with his headstrong, estranged daughter (Catherine Hicks) and the fleeting hope of finding the love he left behind. But what they encounter in the french countryside is completely unexpected.
VHS: S09493. $79.95.
Geoffrey Reeve, Canada, 1988, 93 mins.

Special of the Day

Two Canadian chefs prepare a special meal together. Through their collaboration and friendship a special atmosphere arises as they express themselves in the kitchen. Ultimately an entire approach to life is revealed through their work. 24 mins.
VHS: S25049. $19.95.

Straight for the Heart

Lea Pool's erotic feature about a cynical photojournalist who returns to Montreal caught in a lurid sex triangle. After he's simultaneously abandoned by his two lovers, he embarks on a dangerous inner voyage, compensating for his loneliness and despair by photographing the streets, architecture and textures of Montreal. He eventually falls into a tentative and eerie friendship with Quentin, a deaf window washer. "A film filled with visual poetry, a compelling drama [that's] stunningly filmed" (*New York Times*).
VHS: S18408. $39.95.
Lea Pool, Canada, 1988, 92 mins.

Strangers in Good Company

A comedy about eight radically different women in their '70s who are stranded in the Quebec countryside when their bus breaks down. The first feature by the talented documentarian Cynthia Scott, who skillfully depicts these women, a Mohawk, a nonconventional free thinker, a literary lesbian, a nun who's mechanically skilled, and a prodigiously talented blues singer. With Alice Diabo, Constance Garneau, Cissy Meddings and Mary Meigs.
VHS: S16902. $19.95.
Cynthia Scott, Canada, 1990, 101 mins.

Super 8½

Bruce La Bruce is back as a tired porn director with a decided lack of lust. With his career in shambles, a documentary about his former glory days offers him the only respite from his currently bleak and empty life. In this campy send-up of art, porn and rip-offs of classic films, queer icons Vaginal Creme Davis and comic Scott Thompson evoke a world grown weary of intimacy. It's rude and funny.
VHS: S26697. $39.95.
Bruce La Bruce, Canada, 1994, 106 mins.

Tales from the Gimli Hospital

The surreal first feature from Canadian independent Guy Maddin is set in the isolated village of Gimli, Manitoba, at the beginning of the century. Jealousy and madness overtake two men who share a hospital room. In chilling though mocking vignettes, they exchange wild, inventive tales involving pestilence, reckless envy and necrophilia. With Kyle McCullogh, Michael Gottli and Angela Heck.
VHS: S19409. $29.95.
Guy Maddin, Canada, 1987, 72 mins.

Termini Station

Alan King's independent Canadian feature examines the deep emotional bonds between a mother (Colleen Dewhurst) and daughter (the highly accomplished Megan Follows) as they try to cope with family secrets, the father's unexplained death, the mother's alcoholism and the young woman's prostitution. With Gordon Clapp, Debra McGrath, Leon Pownall, Elliott Smith and Norma Dell'Agnese.
VHS: S25970. $19.98.
Allen King, Canada, 1989, 105 mins.

Thirty-Two Short Films About Glenn Gould

In this inventive film, the unique genius of musician Glenn Gould is revealed in a series of dramatic re-enactments, archival footage and film interviews. It rises above the usual biographic movie formulas to capture intimate and revealing details about its elusive subject, who avoided public scrutiny by playing largely in his studio. Colm Feore stars.
VHS: S23677. $19.95.
Laser: LD74759. $34.95.
Francois Girard, Canada, 1993, 94 mins.

The Thrill of It All!

This early work by Norman Jewison (*Moonstruck*) is a hilarious satire of American normalcy and the plastic tendencies of suburbia, soap operas and television commercials. An average woman (Doris Day) becomes an overnight television celebrity despite her husband's (James Garner) objections. The screenplay is by Carl Reiner and Larry Gelbart (*Tootsie*). With Edward Andrews, Elliott Reid, Reginald Owen and ZaSu Pitts.
VHS: S17946. $14.98.
Norman Jewison, USA, 1963, 108 mins.

Tribute

Heartwarming joy as life-of-the-party Jack Lemmon tries to win back his estranged wife and son. A moving drama which also stars Robbie Benson and Lee Remick.
VHS: S14566. $19.98.
Bob Clark, Canada, 1980, 125 mins.

When Night Is Falling

Two women find one another in this sensitive love story. Camille is a repressed Catholic professor currently involved with a man. Her whole life changes, however, when she meets Petra, an enigmatic performer from a visiting circus. Before long, the two women embark on a romance that startles everyone, including themselves, with an unforseen passion.
VHS: S27541. $89.95.
Patricia Rozema, Canada, 1995, 90 mins.

Who Is Killing the Great Chefs of Europe?

A sharp satire with a self-evident plot, with George Segal and Jacqueline Bisset thrown into the mix as travelers trying to solve the string of murders. With a delicious turn by Robert Morley. Also with Jean-Pierre Cassel, Philippe Noiret and Joss Ackland.
VHS: S17380. $19.98.
Ted Kotcheff, Canada, 1978, 112 mins.

Why Shoot the Teacher?

Bud Cort in a warm, amusing story of life on the Canadian prairie during the Depression. Cort plays a shy, awkward teacher from the city who has taken a job in the aptly named town of Bleke, Saskatchewan. With Samantha Eggar.
VHS: S01456. $29.95.
Silvio Narizzano, Canada, 1980, 101 mins.

Winter People

An acclaimed Canadian film by Ted Kotcheff, starring Kelly McGillis, Kurt Russell and Lloyd Bridges, which focuses on an unwed mother who must make a difficult decision when she falls in love with a stranger who's accidentally killed the father of her child.
VHS: S10901. $19.95.
Ted Kotcheff, Canada, 1989, 109 mins.

Wisecracks

Phyllis Diller, Carol Burnett, Whoopi Goldberg, Jenny Jones and other women comics are featured in this behind-the-scenes look at the gritty world of comedy. Women face a tough audience, one filled with unfair and even bigoted expectations, but somehow these woman manage to break the mold and make people laugh at the same time.
VHS: S24564. $19.95.
Gail Singer, Canada, 1994, 93 mins.

Zero Patience

An outrageous movie musical, this films depicts an imaginary love story between 19th-century Victorian writer and explorer Sir Richard Francis Burton and "Patient Zero", the Canadian flight attendant accused by the media of being the man who brought AIDS to North America.
VHS: S22669. $79.95.
John Greyson, Canada, 1993, 100 mins.

ATOM EGOYAN

The Adjuster

Atom Egoyan's fourth feature deals with his recurrent themes of the omnipresence of video, voyeurism, fractured nuclear families and sexual control and domination. Three stories are intercut: Noah is an insurance adjuster who manipulates and controls the clients who've lost their property; his wife Hera is a government film censor who surreptitiously records the objectionable material on video; and an ex-football player and his twisted wife play out elaborate sexual games on the unsuspecting. With Elias Koteas, Arsinee Khanjian and Maury Chaykin.
VHS: S18458. $79.98.
Atom Egoyan, Canada, 1991, 102 mins.

Calendar

Atom Egoyan directs and appears as a photographer in this disturbingly funny film. The photographer is sent to Armenia to take pictures of historic churches. He takes his wife along as a translator but she is sidelined by the depth of her heritage and the charms of her handsome guide.
VHS: S25992. $79.95.
Atom Egoyan, Armenia/Canada, 1993, 75 mins.

Exotica

Atom Egoyan's most accessible film is also one of his best: an obsessive and dangerous love story set in a seedy Toronto night club. An exotic dancer meets a man strangely obsessed with her, especially when she wears a girl's school uniform. Egoyan's complicated plot reveals layer after layer of lust, perversion, sexual abuse and violence in an original vision of the darker side.
VHS: S26373. $99.99.
Laser: Letterboxed. LD75077. $39.99.
Atom Egoyan, Canada, 1995, 103 mins.

Family Viewing

Atom Egoyan's second feature observes a contemporary Canadian family in the crisis mode. Van is upset when he discovers that his childhood movie memories on videotape are being erased to make room for his father's bedroom activities. This prompts him to leave and kidnap his maternal grandmother from the old age home and set up housekeeping in an unused wing of a downtown hotel. A fascinating and very funny study of alienation in a high tech society. With David Hemblen, Aidan Tierney, Gabrielle Rose, Arsinee Khanjian and Selma Kekikian.
VHS: S13268. $19.98.
Atom Egoyan, Canada, 1987, 86 mins.

Next of Kin

Profoundly unhappy with his family life, a young man named Peter (Patrick Tierney) undergoes video therapy with his parents. One day, while at the hospital studying the tapes, he sees the videos of an Armenian family who feel guilty about surrendering their own son, while still an infant, to a foster home. Peter decides to present himself to this family as their long lost son, to finally act out a role different from the one assigned to him in his own life. Filled with haunting images of travel and displacement, *Next of Kin* reveals both a young WASP's response to working class Armenian culture and discourses on the range of roles that life allows us to play.
VHS: S13587. $29.95.
Laser: LD70642. $24.98.
Atom Egoyan, Canada, 1984, 72 mins.

Speaking Parts

A brilliant cinematic jigsaw puzzle. A handsome hotel housekeeper is willing to do anything to advance his film career. Luckily for him, he bears a strong resemblance to a lonely screenwriter's dead brother. A chilly film of obsession, ambition and advances in video technology. With Michael McManus, Arsinee Khanjian.
VHS: S13269. $19.98.
Atom Egoyan, Canada, 1989, 92 mins.

DAVID CRONENBERG

Dead Ringers

David Cronenberg does it again in this psychological horror film starring Jeremy Irons as a pair of disturbed, identical twin gynecologists. A technical and emotional masterpiece that subtly and quite creepily delves into what makes the Mantle brothers tick. With excellent supporting work by Genevieve Bujold. Based loosely on a true story.
VHS: S09841. $19.98.
David Cronenberg, Canada, 1988, 113 mins.

The Dead Zone

Christopher Walken stars in this David Cronenberg film of a Stephen King novel about a man with the ability to read the thoughts of others. This gift is more a curse than a blessing. With Brooke Adams, Tom Skerritt, Herbert Lom and Martin Sheen as a very dangerous political candidate.
VHS: S06130. $19.95.
Laser: LD75359. $29.98.
David Cronenberg, USA, 1983, 104 mins.

The Fly

Cronenberg's *The Fly* is less a remake of the original film than a remake of the original short story about a brilliant scientist who develops a system to transport objects over space and reassemble the molecules in seconds. When an accident fuses his structure with that of a fly, the initial excitement turns to horror as the insect nature begins to exert itself. With an outstanding performance by Jeff Goldblum.
VHS: S02908. $29.98.
Laser: LD70984. $24.98.
David Cronenberg, USA, 1986, 96 mins.

M. Butterfly

Jeremy Irons stars as the French diplomatic functionary seduced by an illusionist from the Beijing Opera. Set in Maoist China and inspired by a true story of espionage, this tale of romance and reversal will surprise even the most jaded viewer. Previously a Broadway hit, the film convincingly portrays the unbelievable facts behind a startling and deceptive facade.
VHS: S20712. $19.98.
Laser: LD72383. $34.98.
David Cronenberg, USA, 1993, 101 mins.

Naked Lunch

David Cronenberg succeeds in filming what many considered unfilmable. He creates a bizarre, drug inspired world based on the once-banned 1959 underground novel by William Burroughs. Peter Weller couldn't be better as a Burroughs-like novelist/junkie who is sent to Interzone on a secret mission by a talking typewriter that transmutes to a roach. With Judy Davis, Julian Sands, Ian Holm and Roy Scheider as Dr. Benway. "A thrilling, astounding, devastating piece of work" (Dave Kehr, *Chicago Tribune*).
VHS: S16382. $94.98.
Laser: LD71581. $39.98.
David Cronenberg, USA, 1991, 117 mins.

Scanners

An explosive tale of mind control and the powers that exist to govern and observe its application. Patrick McGoohan (*The Prisoner*) is the manipulative head of a scientific corporate research facility. His character is called Dr. Ruth. With Stephen Lack and Michael Ironside as the telepathic scanners and Jennifer O'Neill as decoration.
VHS: Out of print. For rental only.
Laser: LD72310. $29.99.
David Cronenberg, Canada, 1981, 104 mins.

Videodrome

Videodrome is a pulsating sci-fi nightmare from macabre master David Cronenberg (*Scanners*) about a world where video can control and alter human life. Featuring a wonderfully sleazy James Woods, and Deborah Harry as a kinky talk-show hostess.
VHS: S01414. $14.98.
David Cronenberg, Canada, 1982, 87 mins.

O CANADA!

Le Quebec

This documentary offers several views of Quebec, detailing the considerable contrast in daily life, from the frenetic pace of Montreal to the reflective and serene forest world of the rural settings. The images and commentaries are meant to spur class discussions. 55 mins.
English Narration.
VHS: S19778. $35.00.
French Narration.
VHS: S19777. $35.00.

Les Jeunes Entrepreneurs

Designed for advanced beginners and students at the intermediate level, this story relates the tale of French-Canadian teenagers who build a robot. Verification of comprehension is made possible by post-viewing activities that stress creativity, listening, speaking, reading and writing. Each video is 25 mins.
A Quel Prix la Publicite?
C'est un Choix Difficile.
VHS: S19802. $29.95.

Un Premier Prix—Perdu, Un Robot

Three Canadian teenagers, determined to win the school science prize, build a robot. Frustrated because it doesn't work, they leave it behind—then the robot takes off. This delightful, live-action story told in simple French is geared to beginning and intermediate French students. 50 mins.
VHS: S05286. $39.95.

AMERICAN FILM

recent american CINEMA

1492: Conquest of Paradise
Ridley Scott's film is considered the definitive historical account of Christopher Columbus' voyages to North America. The film considers Columbus' legacy of colonialism, racism and genocide in the New World. Columbus (French actor Gerard Depardieu) is presented as a visionary scientist with boundless ambitions. With Armand Assante and Sigourney Weaver. Music by Vangelis. The film is letterboxed.
VHS: $18748. $29.95.
Ridley Scott, USA, 1992, 142 mins.

48 Hours
Street-weary cop Nick Nolte springs smart-aleck convict Eddie Murphy for two days in order to capture a mad dog killer. James Remar is the dangerous quarry and Murphy's ex-partner in crime. A violent, comic thriller from Walter Hill. With David Patrick Kelly and Sonny Landham. The redneck bar scene is a classic.
VHS: $02354. $19.95.
Walter Hill, USA, 1982, 97 mins.

9½ Weeks
Mickey Rourke as an advertising man and Kim Basinger as art gallery employee star in a saga of a sexually obsessive relationship with a decided edge toward light sado-masochism. Video contains scenes which are more explicit than the theatrical release.
VHS: $05868. $19.95.
Laser: Letterboxed. LD72335. $34.98.
Adrian Lyne, USA, 1986, 117 mins.

"About Last Night..."
Loosely based on the one-act play by David Mamet, "Sexual Perversity in Chicago," Edward Zwick's film is less a quest for cultural identity than individual choice. Rob Lowe and Demi Moore's apparently innocent liaison becomes a love affair shuttered by convenience and necessity. The film's real power emerges in the performances of Chicagoans James Belushi and Elizabeth Perkins, whose hard-edged cynicism questions the durability of the affair. Co-written by Second City alumnus Tim Kazurinski.
VHS: $02512. $14.95.
Edward Zwick, USA, 1986, 113 mins.

Absense of Malice
Sally Field plays a Miami journalist who writes a story that maligns an innocent man. Paul Newman is the injured party. An intriguing study into the power and privileges of the press written by former reporter Kurt Luedtke. Filmed on location. Strong supporting cast includes Barry Primus, Melinda Dillon, Bob Balaban, Josef Sommer and Wilford Brimley.
VHS: $10373. $19.95.
Sydney Pollack, USA, 1981, 116 mins.

The Accidental Tourist
William Hurt is a travel writer who hates to travel. He also isn't willing to open himself up to what life has to offer until he splits with his wife Kathleen Turner and starts seeing a kookie dog trainer played by Geena Davis. Davis won an Oscar for her performance as Muriel in this film adaptation of the novel by Anne Tyler. Film was also nominated as Best Picture. With Amy Wright and Ed Begley Jr.
VHS: $09412. $19.95.
Laser: LD70495. $29.98.
Lawrence Kasdan, USA, 1988, 125 mins.

The Accused
A stern public prosecutor (Kelly McGillis) takes on a gang-rape case and tries to go simply by the book. But the victim, played powerfully by Jodie Foster (in a performance that earned her an Academy Award), refuses to make things easy, requiring full retribution for what she has suffered. Eventually, they begin to trust one another, and work together to put those responsible behind bars. Based on a notorious real-life case.
VHS: $13708. $19.95.
Laser: LD75116. $24.98.
Jonathan Kaplan, USA, 1988, 110 mins.

Ace Ventura: When Nature Calls
Animal sleuth and hair style freak Ace Ventura returns in this outrageous sequel. Ace and his companion, the monkey Spike, go to Africa to rescue a sacred bat that's been kidnapped. There they manage to baffle an entire continent with their absurd but eminently watchable antics. Starring Jim Carrey as Ace Ventura.
VHS: $27306. $22.98.
Laser: LD75479. $34.98.
Steve Oedekerk, USA, 1995, 94 mins.

Addams Family
Raul Julia, Anjelica Huston, Christopher Lloyd and Christina Ricci head a lively cast of macabre but upbeat characters created by the late cartoonist Charles Addams. The plot concerns foisting a phony Fester on the family in order to find the fabulous hidden Addams fortune. Ace cinematographer Barry Sonnenfeld (Raising Arizona) makes his directorial debut. Nominated for an Oscar for Best Costume Design.
VHS: Out of print. For rental only.
Laser: Widescreen. LD75140. $34.98.
Barry Sonnenfeld, USA, 1991, 102 mins.

Addams Family Values
It is always refreshing to get a new perspective on the endlessly dreary debate of family values. Gomez and Morticia (Raul Julia and Anjelica Huston) have their own contribution to make on this subject. It may disturb or frighten some, but then again what could be more horrible than a close look at someone else's family?
VHS: $20874. $14.95.
Laser: Widescreen. LD75139. $34.98.
Barry Sonnenfeld, USA, 1993, 90 mins.

Advise and Consent
Political drama in which blackmail, suicide and scandal follow the President's appointment of an unpopular Secretary of State. Featuring Henry Fonda, Charles Laughton, Burgess Meredith and Peter Lawford.
VHS: $01994. $29.95.
Otto Preminger, USA, 1962, 142 mins.

The Affair
A black G.I. in England during World War II becomes involved with a confused and lonely married woman. Their affair leads to tragedy when her husband discovers them in the act of love. Now this woman must decide if she can betray everything she has known for a young man from across the ocean. Courtney B. Vance, Ned Beatty and Kerry Fox (An Angel at My Table, Friends) are featured.
VHS: $27150. $94.99.
Paul Seed, USA/Great Britain, 1995, 104 mins.

After the Promise
Mark Harmon stars as an uneducated laborer who loses his four sons to the courts and state authority after his wife dies. Diana Scarwid plays his second wife, who assists him in his struggle to reunite his family. A study in courage and bureaucracy. With Rosemary Dunsmore and Donnelly Rhodes as Dr. Northfield.
VHS: $10618. $19.95.
David Greene, USA, 1987, 93 mins.

Afterburn
An excellent made-for-cable movie stars Laura Dern as the widow of a young fighter pilot who charges the Air Force with initiating a cover up when her husband's plane crashes in Korea, and claims his death was caused by "pilot error." With the help of a craggy, crusading attorney (Robert Loggia), she takes on the military establishment to resurrect her husband's reputation. Based on a true story. With Vincent Spano and Michael Rooker. Music by former Police member Stewart Copeland.
VHS: $17034. $19.98.
Laser: LD75117. $24.98.
Robert Markowitz, USA, 1992, 103 mins.

Against All Odds
Taylor Hackford's stylish remake of the film noir classic Out of the Past stars Jeff Bridges as a former football player sent to a remote Caribbean island to locate the daughter (Rachel Ward) of the team's owner. Ward is enserfed to a sleazy gambler/businessman (James Woods, in a great performance) who's also Bridges' closest friend. A solid cast includes a sinister Richard Widmark, Saul Rubinek and Jane Greer (the female lead in Past) as Ward's mother. Solid title track from Genesis' Phil Collins.
VHS: $02922. $29.95.
Taylor Hackford, USA, 1984, 122 mins.

Against the Wall
Attica is infamous for being the site of a prison uprising where guards were held hostage. While the nation watched, a gripping and deadly drama unfolded, revealing a savage institution that pushed men to the edge. This thriller tells the story of that place and time. Starring Kyle MacLachlan and Samuel L. Jackson, with Harry Dean Stanton.
VHS: $21741. $19.98.
Laser: LD75141. $34.98.
John Frankenheimer, USA, 1993, 115 mins.

Airport
The Arthur Haley bestseller has launched four movies about the personal lives and public danger of traveling by air. This is the first and the best. Burt Lancaster, Dean Martin, Jean Seberg, Helen Hayes, Jacqueline Bisset, Van Heflin, Maureen Stapleton, and Mr. Fixit, George Kennedy, are just a few in this cast hoping for a safe landing in Chicago.
VHS: $03480. $14.95.
George Seaton, USA, 1970, 137 mins.

Alex in Wonderland
Paul Mazursky's second feature is a surreal merging of Fellini's 8½ and Jim McBride's David Holtzman's Diary. The film is an ironic piece about the travails of a young filmmaker (Donald Sutherland) caught in the grip of burnout and artistic frustration. Ellen Burstyn plays Sutherland's long-suffering wife. With Viola Spolin and Jeanne Moreau. Fellini appears briefly.
VHS: $19496. $19.98.
Paul Mazursky, USA, 1970, 110 mins.

Alice in Wonderland
An all-star adaptation of Lewis Carroll's enchanting tale. Cinematography by Fred J. Koenenkamp. Special visual effects by John Dykstra. With Red Buttons, Anthony Newley, Ringo Starr, Telly Savalas, Robert Morley, Sammy Davis Jr., Steve Allen, Steve Lawrence and Edie Gorme.
VHS: $18999. $19.98.
Harry Harris, USA, 1985, 90 mins.

Alice in Wonderland Set
A two-video package containing Alice in Wonderland and Alice Through the Looking Glass.
VHS: $19001. $29.98.
Harry Harris, USA, 1985, 180 mins.

Alice Through the Looking Glass
A continuation of the theme of Alice in Wonderland in a fantasia about life on the reverse side of the mirror, where the plucky, indomitable Alice must stay away from the Jabberwocky. In her quest to return home, Alice runs into a host of eccentric and frightening figures. It's a visually extravagant, feverish ride of fancy and delight. With Ringo Starr, Sally Struthers, Jack Warden, Jonathan Winters, Steve Lawrence, Karl Malden, Beau Bridges and Lloyd Bridges.
VHS: $19000. $19.98.
Harry Harris, USA, 1985, 90 mins.

All Fall Down
Warren Beatty plays the amoral ladies' man Berry-Berry Willant in this adaptation of the James Leo Herlihy novel by playwright William Inge. Eva Marie Saint is just one of the older women who fall for his soulless charm. With Brandon de Wilde as Beatty's admiring little brother. Karl Malden and Angela Lansbury play his alcoholic and possessive parents.
VHS: $16436. $19.98.
John Frankenheimer, USA, 1962, 111 mins.

All Quiet on the Western Front
A television adaptation of Erich Maria Remarque's novel about a group of German soldiers engaged in trench warfare during World War I (first made by Lewis Milestone in 1930). Ernest Borgnine is the determined career soldier responsible for shaping them into fighting men. With Richard Thomas, Patricia Neal, Ian Holm and Donald Pleasance. Contains newly restored footage.
VHS: $07774. $19.95.
Delbert Mann, USA, 1979, 105 mins.

All the President's Men
Superb adaptation of the Woodward-Bernstein book about the events leading to the resignation of Richard Nixon. Quality performances by Dustin Hoffman, Robert Redford and Jason Robards, with Jane Alexander, Martin Balsam, Jack Warden.
VHS: $03362. $19.95.
Alan J. Pakula, USA, 1976, 139 mins.

Always
Critically acclaimed look at marriage, written, directed and featuring Henry Jaglom, about his failed marriage on screen and in real life with ex-wife and co-star Patrice Townsend.
VHS: $00039. $79.95.
Laser: LD70012. $39.98.
Henry Jaglom, USA, 1985, 105 mins.

American Gigolo
International model Lauren Hutton plays the dutiful, decent wife of a state senator with whom Julian (Richard Gere) falls in love. But when a murder is committed and missing jewels are placed in his car, someone is trying to frame him. The film which made a star of Richard Gere.
VHS: $10017. $14.95.
Laser: LD75360. $29.98.
Paul Schrader, USA, 1980, 117 mins.

American Graffiti
A new American classic, which single-handedly started the 60's nostalgia craze. A coming-of-age film that details the lives of several high school teenagers the summer after graduation. Launched the careers of Richard Dreyfuss, Harrison Ford and Suzanne Sommers and established George Lucas as an important new American filmmaker. A perceptive, sweet look at a more innocent time.
VHS: $00044. $14.95.
Laser: LD70013. $34.98.
George Lucas, USA, 1973, 112 mins.

American Me
Edward James Olmos' directorial debut is an ambitious attempt to convey the social, political and personal history of the Mexican Mafia, captured in the expansive life of a ruthless crime lord (Olmos) from his extensive prison stay to his power and influence in the Southwestern Hispanic barrios. It's a well-made, grim and fatalistic account about the allure of crime and the building of community and culture. With William Forsythe, Pepe Serna and Danny De La Paz.
VHS: $18500. $19.95.
Edward James Olmos, USA, 1992, 126 mins.

The American President
Michael Douglas and Annette Bening star in this winning romance set in the White House. President Andrew Shepard (Douglas) is the most popular President in decades. A widower, he is devoted to his daughter, as well as to gun control. Sydney Ellen Wade (Bening) is an environmental lobbyist who can hardly believe her luck when she realizes she is being courted by the number one lobbyist target inside the beltway. Soon, word leaks out and the couple find themselves in the center of a media feeding frenzy where the only thing standing between them and happiness is the approval of the American public. Martin Sheen and Michael J. Fox are featured.
VHS: $27598. $101.99.
Laser: LD75533. $34.95.
Rob Reiner, USA, 1995, 114 mins.

Americathon
The future seems bleak in 1998 America when the entire country teeters on the edge of financial ruin. George Carlin narrates this hilarious yarn about a motley group of public figures who organize a telethon to get Uncle Sam out of debt. Stars a host of familiar faces, including Harvey Korman, John Ritter, Fred Willard, Jay Leno, Zane Buzby, Elvis Costello and Meatloaf.
VHS: $16277. $19.98.
Neal Israel, USA, 1979, 84 mins.

Amongst Friends
The debut film of Rob Weiss charts the complicated relationships of three Jewish friends growing up in the affluent Five Towns section of Long Island, where, as the narrator notes, judges and wiseguys are neighbors. The film is about affluent kids who reject their privileged backgrounds and drift into drugs, graft and robbery. The action follows what happens when one of the friends, following a prison sentence, returns to his neighborhood to discover his friends are beholden to a local gangster. His girlfriend (Mira Sorvino) has patiently awaited his return. With Steve Parlavecchio, Joseph Lindsey and Patrick McGaw.
VHS: $20329. $19.95.
Laser: LD72427. $39.99.
Rob Weiss, USA, 1993, 90 mins.

Anastasia: The Mystery of Anna
Amy Irving stars in this TV-movie about the search for a living Romanov heir. Is Anna Anderson really the daughter of Czar Nicolas II or just an incredibly gifted pretender to the throne? Winner of two Emmy Awards and two Golden Globes. The international cast includes Omar Sharif, Olivia de Havilland, Rex Harrison, Claire Bloom, Edward Fox, Elke Sommer and Susan Lucci. Script by Oscar winner James Goldman (A Lion In Winter) is based on the Peter Knuth book Anastasia: The Riddle of Anna Anderson.
Laser: LD74639. $49.99.
Marvin J. Chomsky, USA, 1986, 200 mins.

And God Created Woman
Rebecca De Mornay stars in Roger Vadim's remake of his own classic tale of the dangers of being born beautiful. Echoing faintly the Bardot version, Vadim transplanted his story to the American Southwest where a sexy ex-con vixen causes trouble for her carpenter husband and her politician lover. With Victor Spano.
VHS: $06864. $14.98.
Roger Vadim, USA, 1988, 98 mins.

Angel City
This powerful piece about social protest and worker exploitation follows the difficulties of migrant workers who are trapped in Angel City, a labor camp where kidnapping and extortion are used to coerce workers. Adapted from the book by Patricia Smith. With Paul Winfield, Jennifer Jason Leigh and Ralph Waite.
VHS: $18812. $19.95.
Philip Leacock, USA, 1980, 100 mins.

Angel Heart
Exotic journey into voodoo, cults, sex and death. A journey of violence and darkness that moves from the streets of New York to the swamps of Louisiana featuring Mickey Rourke, Lisa Bonet, Robert de Niro and Charlotte Rampling.
VHS: $04382. $14.95.
Alan Parker, USA, 1987, 112 mins.

Anguish
Zelda Rubinstein, the diminutive psychic of Poltergeist I, II & III, plays the concerned mother of a disturbed serial killer who removes the eyes of his victims. Michael Lerner is the murderer and Talia Paul, Angel Jove, Cala Pastor and Isabel Garcia-Lorca are some of his potential victims.
VHS: $07098. $79.98.
Bigas Luna, USA, 1988, 89 mins.

Anna
Sally Kirkland gives a wonderful performance as a once famous Czech actress now trying to find work in New York City. She opens her home and heart to a gawky Czech girl who looks just like super-model Paulina Porizkova when she is cleaned up and presentable. A touching variation on All About Eve. Kirkland was nominated for an Oscar.
VHS: $05630. $79.95.
Yurek Bogayevicz, USA, 1987, 101 mins.

Anna Karenina
A recent version of the great Tolstoy novel with Jacqueline Bisset playing Anna, the married wife who sacrifices all for forbidden love. With Christopher Reeve as Count Vronsky and Paul Scofield as Anna's husband, Karenin.
VHS: $12417. $14.95.
Simon Langton, USA, 1985, 96 mins.

Annie O
Fifteen-year-old Annie is the first girl to play on her high school basketball team. Annie is an excellent player (the title of the film comes from her nickname, "Sure Shot Annie," a takeoff on Annie Oakley), rumored to never miss a shot. Annie is elated to be asked to join the varsity team, but her joy is quickly overshadowed by the jealousy her success inspires among her male team players, her brother, her friends, and even her boyfriend. In the end, Annie discovers who her real friends are and learns the power of believing in yourself. With Coco Yares, Chad Willett and Rob Stewart.
VHS: $27303. $89.98.
Laser: LD75476. $39.99.
J. Michael McClary, USA, 1995, 93 mins.

Another 48 Hours
After seven years, Eddie Murphy is released from jail in order to help San Francisco cop Nick Nolte solve a case and to save himself from a manslaughter charge. Lots of action in this sequel that also stars Brion James and Kevin Tighe.
VHS: $21476. $19.95.
Walter Hill, USA, 1990, 96 mins.

Any Wednesday
Jane Fonda is the mistress of Jason Robards and she isn't happy about turning 30 without a band of gold on her finger. She spends a lot of time getting hysterical and all teary in an apartment where the closets are filled with balloons. With Dean Jones and Rosemary Murphy. From the stage play.
VHS: $06101. $19.98.
Robert Ellis Miller, USA, 1966, 109 mins.

Any Which Way You Can
Clint Eastwood stars in this sequel to Every Which Way But Loose, about the comic adventures, fights and romantic pursuits of a Los Angeles trucker who inherits an orangutan. Nominally directed by Eastwood, though actual credit is given to his former stunt advisor, Buddy Van Horn. With Ruth Gordon, Sondra Locke, Geoffrey Lewis, and William Smith.
Laser: LD70505. $29.98.
Buddy Van Horn, USA, 1980, 116 mins.

Anzio
A stellar cast and a large-scale action production distinguish this Hollywood re-telling of the battle of Anzio. Robert Mitchum, Peter Falk, Arthur Kennedy and Earl Holliman are among the stars.
VHS: S10019. $69.95.
Edward Dmytryk, USA/Italy, 1968, 117 mins.

Apollo 13
Tom Hanks, Kevin Bacon, Gary Sinise, Ed Harris and Bill Paxton are just some of the big stars featured in this entertaining but restrained film which examines the declining fortunes of America's space program. Just as everything about outer space appears to be routine, an unforeseen accident rivets the entire planet's attention on the actions of three men. Based on actual events, it builds tension with great precision and power. Letterboxed.
VHS: S26693. $22.98.
Laser: LD75111. $44.98.
Ron Howard, USA, 1995, 140 mins.

Appointment with Death
A posh 1973 tour of the Holy Land turns murderous when a malicious and wealthy dowager is mysteriously poisoned. Each of her fellow high-living tourists had the means to kill her—and a motive. Peter Ustinov stars as Hercule Poirot in this Agatha Christie whodunit. With Lauren Bacall, Carrie Fisher, John Gielgud, Piper Laurie, Hayley Mills.
VHS: S07775. $19.98.
Laser: LD74699. $34.98.
Michael Winner, USA, 1988, 103 mins.

April Morning
Howard Fast's novel is adapted for film in this gripping drama about the causes of the American Revolution. A New England farming family and their friends experience the tyranny of British rule until they finally revolt against the redcoats quartered in their midst.
VHS: S26512. $9.98.
Delbert Mann, USA, 1988, 99 mins.

Arabesque
Gregory Peck and Sophia Loren star in this modern tale of espionage and intrigue in the Middle East and fashionable London. Sophia gets to model many dazzling outfits as she and Peck are pursued by the bad guys. With Alan Badel, Kieron Moore and George Coulouris.
VHS: S07807. $14.95.
Stanley Donen, USA, 1966, 105 mins.

Arctic Blue
Rutger Hauer stars as a viscious killer in this action-packed drama set in the Alaskan wilderness. A plane crash lands, forcing both a lawman (Dylan Walsh) and the accused killer whom he is accompanying to fight for survival together. The elements are fierce, but the adversarial relationship between these men is even more destructive.
VHS: S26208. $96.98.
Laser: LD75039. $34.95.
Peter Masterson, USA, 1995, 95 mins.

The Arrangement
Kirk Douglas plays successful ad executive Eddie Anderson, a man with seemingly everything he needs except piece of mind. When he goes over the edge there is little his understanding wife Deborah Kerr or his classy mistress Faye Dunaway can do to reassemble the Eddie they both knew and loved. With Richard Boone and Hume Cronyn. Based on Elia Kazan's best-selling novel.
VHS: S06115. $19.98.
Elia Kazan, USA, 1969, 125 mins.

Ash Wednesday
Elizabeth Taylor and Henry Fonda star in this film about an aging beauty who tries to rejuvenate her life by changing her looks through plastic surgery.
VHS: S13781. $19.95.
Larry Peerce, USA, 1973, 99 mins.

Assault at West Point
Sam Waterston, Samuel L. Jackson and John Glover star in this costume drama about racial exclusion at the nation's most prestigious military academy. It's a powerful and insightful look at the traditions which still shape our institutions.
VHS: S21141. $92.98.
Harry Moses, USA, 1993, 98 mins.

Assault on a Queen
Crooks dredge up a submarine and use it to hi-jack the vault aboard *H.M.S. Queen Mary*. Rod Serling scripted the film from a novel by Jack Finney. Stars Frank Sinatra, Verna Lisi, Tony Franciosa, Richard Conte and Reginald Denny.
VHS: S16458. $14.95.
Jack Donohue, USA, 1966, 106 mins.

Assault on Precinct 13
John Carpenter's early, and arguably his best film: a tense police drama in which a nearly deserted police station is under siege by a violent street gang. An early urban horror film, notable for its atmosphere and unrelenting tension.
VHS: S09611. $29.95.
Laser: LD74530. $39.99.
John Carpenter, USA, 1976, 90 mins.

At Play in the Fields of The Lord
A cautionary epic adventure filmed on location in the rainforest jungles of Brazil. This exquisitely photographed drama about tests of faith and cultural interference puts the fate of an entire native Indian tribe in the hands of a few American missionaries. Tom Berenger stars as a Cheyenne-American mercenary who decides to join the isolated tribe he has been ordered to destroy. With John Lithgow, Aidan Quinn, Kathy Bates, Daryl Hannah and Tom Waits. Based on the novel by Peter Matthiessen.
VHS: S16033. $14.98.
Laser: LD70291. $44.98.
Hector Babenco, USA, 1991, 186 mins.

Attic
Ray Milland and Carrie Snodgrass star in this superior thriller about a sheltered spinster who revolts against her father, kills him, and escapes to join the isolated attic where the door slams shut and she is locked in the attic forever.
VHS: S08025. $14.98.
George Edwards, USA, 1979, 97 mins.

Avalanche Express
Lee Marvin, Maximilian Schell, Robert Shaw and Linda Evans star in this spy thriller in which the terrors of biological warfare underlie every move. A scientist is lured away to a train ride and his death. All bets are off when the snow begins to fall and these characters find themselves trapped.
VHS: S22509. $19.98.
Mark Robson, USA, 1979, 89 mins.

Avalon
Filmmaker Barry Levinson returns to his home town of Baltimore to tell the fictionalized story of how his family came to America and settled in a section of the city known as Avalon. This multigenerational, episodic drama features strong performances by Armin Mueller-Stahl, Aidan Quinn, Elizabeth Perkins, Joan Plowright and Lou Jacobi as the brother who was gravely insulted when the family didn't wait to cut the Thanksgiving turkey. An affectionate salute to the American immigrant.
VHS: S13754. $19.95.
Barry Levinson, USA, 1990, 126 mins.

Avenging Angel
Sequel to *Angel* starring Betsy Russell as a teenage ex-prostitute now in college working as an undercover cop.
VHS: S03909. $19.95.
R.V. O'Neil, USA, 1985, 93 mins.

Awakenings
The title gives away a few major developments but this Penny Marshall drama still holds a few surprises. Robin Williams stars as a dedicated but painfully reserved research doctor who uncovers a radical form of treatment for a small group of comatose post-encephalitic patients which includes Robert De Niro. Based on the non-fiction account by Dr. Oliver Sacks. With John Heard and Julie Kavner.
VHS: S14479. $19.95.
Laser: LD75528. $39.95.
Penny Marshall, USA, 1990, 121 mins.

Away All Boats!
Jeff Chandler plays a strict captain who must ignite the fighting spirit in his inexperienced crew aboard the WWII destroyer *Belinda*. An exciting, powerful story of battle action in the Pacific Theater. Stars George Nader, Julie Adams, Lex Barker and a bit appearance from Clint Eastwood.
VHS: S16299. $14.95.
Joseph Pevney, USA, 1956, 114 mins.

The Babe
Arthur Hiller's biography of Babe Ruth chronicles his rise from a Baltimore orphanage, his herculean exploits, his aggressively, child-like behavior, his two radically different marriages, and his sudden flameout as a ballplayer who never realized his dream to manage the Yankees. John Goodman plays the Sultan of Swat, with Kelly McGillis, Trini Alvarado, and Bruce Boxleitner. Written by John Fusco (*Crossroads, Thunderheart*) with cinematography by Haskell Wexler.
VHS: S17340. $94.95.
Laser: LD71672. $34.98.
Arthur Hiller, USA, 1992, 115 mins.

Babyfever
Gina (Victoria Foyt) questions the merits of her current safe and secure boyfriend when her dynamic ex returns with an interesting proposition. Thinking she could be pregnant, Gina attends the baby shower of a friend where the women present debate the pros and cons of love, relationships and parenthood in the 1990's.
VHS: S27626. $89.98.
Henry Jaglom, USA, 1995, 110 mins.

The Bachelor
A drama about a shy physician forced to re-examine his life and values in the aftermath of a family tragedy, who opens himself up to new experiences that crystallize in his first significant relationship. With Miranda Richardson, Keith Carradine, Kristin Scott-Thomas, Sarah-Jane Fenton and Max von Sydow. Cinematography by Giuseppe Rotunno. Music by Ennio Morricone.
VHS: S18894. $89.95.
Roberto Faenza, USA/Britain, 1992, 105 mins.

Back in the USSR
A romantic glasnost thriller filmed on many locations in Moscow that are not usually featured on the standard Intourist Bus route. Frank Whaley stars as Archer, a naive American tourist who becomes involved with the Russian criminal underworld through his relationship with Natalya Negoda, the personable star of *Little Vera*. Director Roman Polanski plays Kurilov, the villainous owner of a seedy Soviet nightclub. With Dey Young, Andrew Divof and Brian Blessed as Chazon.
VHS: S16715. $94.98.
Deran Sarafian, USA/USSR, 1991, 89 mins.

Back to the Future
Michael J. Fox is a teenager of the 80's who must travel back in time to make sure his parents meet. One problem is that Mom thinks the son is a lot cuter than his future Dad. Christopher Lloyd is a standout as the scientist who made this all possible. With Lea Thompson and Crispin Glover. Primo frantic entertainment.
Laser: LD74947. $34.98.
Robert Zemeckis, USA, 1985, 116 mins.

Back to the Future II
Michael J. Fox and Christopher Lloyd reprise their roles as Marty McFly and Doc Brown in this new adventure. An exhilarating visit by Marty and the Doc to the year 2015 seemingly resolves a few problems with the future McFly family. But when the two return home, they soon discover someone has tampered with time to produce a nightmarish Hill Valley, 1985. Their only hope is to once again get back to 1955 and save the future.
VHS: S12283. $19.95.
Robert Zemeckis, USA, 1989, 104 mins.

Backdraft
This widescreen edition of Ron Howard's 1991 drama about Chicago firefighters preserves the correct aspect ratio of Mikael Solomon's images. Two brothers (Kurt Russell, William Baldwin) must deal with the psychological fallout of their father's death and deal with the women in their lives (Rebecca De Mornay and Jennifer Jason Leigh). Robert De Niro co-stars as a fire inspector tracking down a vicious arsonist. Some wonderful visual effects from George Lucas's Industrial Light and Magic (ILM). With Scott Glenn, Jason Gedrick, and J.T. Walsh.
VHS: S17438. $19.98.
Laser: Letterboxed. LD71580. $39.98.
Ron Howard, USA, 1991, 135 mins.

Backtrack
When murder is your business, don't fall in love with your work. Milo (Hopper) is an eccentric mob hitman who becomes romantically obsessed with his latest assignment. Jodie Foster is Anne Benton, a successful modern artist who suddenly leaves L.A. for a new life after she witnesses a gangland murder. Some of the other familiar faces in this decidedly offbeat road movie romance include Dean Stockwell, John Turturro, Joe Pesci, Charlie Sheen, Vincent Price and Fred Ward. This is the director's cut and should not be confused with the botched studio version, which Hopper disowns.
VHS: S15693. $19.98.
Dennis Hopper, USA, 1991, 102 mins.

Bad Boys
Sean Penn stars as a Chicago kid in trouble who finds that life in a juvenile detention facility is even harder than life on the streets. His Hispanic arch enemy (Esai Morales) adds more tension to an already unpleasant situation. With Reni Santoni, Ally Sheedy and Eric Gurry.
VHS: S05396. $19.95.
Rick Rosenthal, USA, 1983, 123 mins.

Bad Company
Laurence Fishburne is a CIA operative who must contend with the seductive Ellen Barkin. In this political thriller, Fishburne goes undercover to infiltrate an industrial espionage group. Soon he is confounded by a deadly mix of passion, intrigue and murder.
VHS: S25634. $96.98.
Laser: LD75014. $39.99.
Damian Harris, USA, 1994, 108 mins.

Badlands
Martin Sheen and Sissy Spacek star in a story based on the 1950's murder spree across the Midwestern plains by Charlie Starkweather and his 15-year-old girlfriend, Carol Fugate. A chilling insight into the cold-hearted mind of the sociopath in one of the most stunning directorial debuts in the American cinema. The film, writes British critic Robin Wood, "produces a subtle, idiosyncratic balance between engagement and detachment, complicity and horror."
VHS: S00086. $19.98.
Laser: LD70513. $34.98.
Terence Malick, USA, 1973, 95 mins.

Bail Jumper
Joe is a small town thug and Elaine an ex-con; together they flee Murky Springs, Missouri, in search of an idyllic life in New York City. On the way they're delayed by a series of minor obstacles, including a tornado and a swarm of locusts. But the plagues don't end once they reach their destination. With everything around them falling apart will romance still prevail? "Hip and amusing…a hilarious, nervous odyssey across a vibrant but damaged landscape, something like a traveling *Mystery Train*" (The Film Journal).
VHS: S14998. $79.95.
Christian Faber, USA, 1989, 96 mins.

Ballad of the Sad Cafe
Vanessa Redgrave stars in this adaptation of Carson McCullers' novella and the play by Edward Albee. She plays Miss Amelia, a strong-willed and short-haired woman who runs a profitable moonshine business in a small Southern town. When her ex-husband Keith Carradine returns—up to no good—they settle their differences in a most impressive boxing match. With Rod Steiger, Austin Pendleton and Cork Hubbert as Cousin Lymon.
VHS: S16471. $89.95.
Simon Callow, USA/Great Britain, 1991, 100 mins.

Bang the Drum Slowly
Robert De Niro stars in this perennial favorite about a simple baseball catcher who discovers he is dying. Michael Moriarty, as the pitcher, lends emotional support. A great sports movie and a real tearjerker with a touching performance that signalled the rise of a great actor in De Niro.
VHS: S04325. $14.95.
John Hancock, USA, 1973, 97 mins.

Barnum
Burt Lancaster is cast as Phineas T. Barnum, the illustrious American showman who invented ballyhoo and introduced the word "jumbo" into the American vernacular. This made-for-tv spectacular chronicles the career of the founder of the Greatest Show on Earth is colorfully presented. With Hanna Schygulla as singer Jenny Lind and Sandor Raski as General Tom Thumb.
VHS: Out of print. For rental only.
Laser: LD70856. $39.95.
Lee Phillips, USA, 1988, 100 mins.

Basic Instinct
Paul Verhoeven's highly controversial film about a burnt out homicide detective (Michael Douglas) investigating a string of ice pick murders. Falling for the prime suspect, a smart, beautiful and wealthy bi-sexual novelist (Sharon Stone) could prove fatal. Screenplay by Joe Eszterhas.
VHS: S17400. $19.98.
Paul Verhoeven, USA, 1992, 124 mins.

Basic Instinct (Director's Cut)
Retains the excised footage that received an NC-17 rating and premiered at the 1992 Cannes Film Festival. The special edition features interviews with Verhoeven, Douglas and Stone and a theatrical trailer that was never shown. Shown in the widescreen letterbox format, preserving its original aspect ratio.
VHS: S18251. $24.98.
Paul Verhoeven, USA, 1992, 150 mins.

The Basketball Diaries
Jim Carroll's renowned autobiography about high school, heroin, sex, writing, and, of course, basketball, stars Leonardo DiCaprio as the brooding young Catholic boy struggling to find his voice. Featuring music and a rather amusing cameo by author Jim Carroll. With Bruno Kirby, Lorraine Bracco, and "Marky" Mark Wahlberg.
VHS: S25953. $94.99.
Laser: LD75088. $34.95.
Scott Kalvert, USA, 1995, 102 mins.

Batman Forever
Val Kilmer and Chris O'Donnell star as the crime-fighting duo of Gotham City. They are joined by Tommy Lee Jones, Jim Carrey and Drew Barrymore, who all play unforgettable villains. In this latest Batman film, the Riddler appears with a new invention that steals the very thoughts of its victims. Of course, only Batman and Robin can withstand his fiendish onslaught. Nicole Kidman plays the psychiatrist who tries to get under Batman's skin in a more conventional, romantic way.
VHS: S26486. $19.95.
Laser: LD75097. $39.98.
Taylor Hackford, USA, 1995, 131 mins.

Battle of Neretva
An international cast recreates a major WW II confrontation in Yugoslavia. Partisans must fight Nazi hordes who outnumber them six to one. With Orson Welles, Franco Nero, Yul Brynner, Hardy Kruger, Curt Jurgens and the lovely Sylva Koscina. Originally nearly three hours long.
VHS: S04254. $39.98.
Veljko Bulajic, Yugoslavia/USA/Italy/Germany, 1971, 106 mins.

Battle of the Commandos
Jack Palance leads a group of hardened criminals against a large Nazi cannon installation. He must succeed or D-Day might fail. Curt Jurgens is the German commander, whose job is to keep the big gun in good condition. Sounds like *The Dirty Dozen* meets *The Guns of Navarone*.
VHS: S04251. $39.98.
Umberto Lenzi, USA/Italy, 1971, 94 mins.

Beaches
Bittersweet story of the 30-year friendship between two women, Bette Midler and Barbara Hershey, one of whom is dying of a fatal disease. Above average soaper with several opportunities for Midler to sing; includes her top single, "Wind Beneath My Wings."
VHS: S09790. $89.95.
Garry Marshall, USA, 1988, 123 mins.

Beckett
Richard Burton and Peter O'Toole star in this grand historical drama adapted from the Jean Anouilh play about the tumultuous relationship of an archbishop and a royal monarch in the 12th century. Superb cast includes John Gielgud, Marita Hunt and Felix Aylmer.
VHS: S02638. $59.95.
Peter Glenville, USA, 1964, 148 mins.

The Bedroom Window
Steve Guttenberg learns his affair with Isabelle Huppert, as the boss's wife, can cost him more than his present job, when he volunteers to be a proxy witness against a very disturbed misogynist. Elizabeth McGovern also stars as a spunky crime victim in this lively Hitchcock-like thriller filmed in Baltimore.
VHS: S03683. $14.98.
Curtis Hanson, USA, 1987, 113 mins.

Before Sunrise
Ethan Hawke is a heartbroken young journalist from Texas who invites a beautiful young French student, Julie Delpy, to take a sojourn in Vienna. It leads to a wonderful adventure/romance where the thought that they may never be together again permeates every moment.
VHS: S25616. $19.95.
Laser: LD74972. $34.95.
Richard Linklater, USA, 1995, 101 mins.

Beguiled
Don Siegel's offbeat story is set during the Civil War, and stars Clint Eastwood as a man brought to a girls school to recuperate. At the school, Eastwood only succeeds at stirring up jealousy and hatred. With Geraldine Page.
VHS: S06821. $14.98.
Don Siegel, USA, 1971, 109 mins.

Being Human
Robin Williams stars as a man who has experienced many lifetimes spanning from the Stone Age to the present. This series of vignettes gives Williams the chance to portray characters using his entire range as an actor. History has a way of repeating itself; all we have to do is learn from the past.
VHS: S21682. $19.95.
Laser: LD74493. $39.98.
Bill Forsyth, USA, 1994, 122 mins.

Best Man
Based on Gore Vidal's play and screenplay; an incisive look at the American political process in the story of several presidential candidates who will do virtually anything to get endorsement; a sharp satire on political conventions with dynamite performances from Henry Fonda, Cliff Robertson, Edie Adams, and others.
VHS: S11434. $19.98.
Franklin J. Schaffner, USA, 1964, 102 mins.

Beulah Land
Lesley Ann Warren and Michael Sarrazin star in this TV movie about life in the deep south at the time of the American Civil War. Neighborhood antebellum mansions are also occupied by Eddie Albert, Hope Lange, Paul Rudd and Don Johnson. Based on the novel by Lonnie Coleman.
VHS: S12844. $29.95.
Virgil W. Vogel, USA, 1980, 267 mins.

Beyond Rangoon
Patricia Arquette stars as an American doctor who inadvertently gets caught up in the troubled political intrigues of Myanmar, formerly known as Burma. John Boorman paints this epic drama with broad strokes as he reveals the tragedy of a land in turmoil.
VHS: S27065. $98.99.
Laser: LD75440. $34.95.
John Boorman, USA, 1995, 100 mins.

Big Chill
College friends from the 1960s are re-united at the funeral of a mutual friend who committed suicide, and have to re-examine the twenty years that have passed since the 1960's. Kasdan leads the film to a bittersweet but uplifting conclusion. With Glenn Close, Kevin Kline, Mary Kay Place, Tom Berenger, JoBeth Williams, William Hurt.
VHS: S00129. $19.95.
Laser: LD70344. $49.95.
Lawrence Kasdan, USA, 1983, 105 mins.

Big Girls Don't Cry
Also known as *Step Kids*, this hilarious comedy by Joan Micklin Silver concerns the complications of a young girl's new and eccentric stepfamily. With Hillary Wolf, Griffin Dunne, Margaret Whitton, Adrienne Shelley and David Strathairn.
VHS: S17767. $9.98.
Joan Micklin Silver, USA, 1991, 98 mins.

Biloxi Blues
Neil Simon wrote this film about Eugene Morris Jerome, a young recruit from Brooklyn sent to a Mississippi bootcamp. Christopher Walken is the impossible sergeant, while Matthew Broderick plays the bemused recruit. This is the sequel to Simon's *Brighton Beach Memoirs* and is adapted from a previous stage play.
VHS: S22020. $14.98.
Mike Nichols, USA, 1988, 105 mins.

Birdy
A spellbinding, captivating movie about a Vietnam vet who has come to believe he is a bird, and the efforts of his best friend to break him out of his silence. Part comedy, part drama, totally unlike any movie before.
VHS: S00132. $79.95.
Alan Parker, USA, 1985, 120 mins.

Black and White
Nick Furris and Kim Delgado star in this story of a close friendship between a black man and white man, from their childhood in Newark, through the Korean War and beyond. In the backwoods of the South, kinship turns to horror and forever changes the lives of these two men. Also known as *Lou, Pat and Joe D.*
VHS: S23328. $29.95.
Stephen Vittoria, USA, 1988, 104 mins.

Black Rainbow
Imagine trying to explain you just witnessed a murder that hasn't yet happened. This is the problem facing professional psychic Rosanna Arquette. When she is proven correct, she attracts the attention of a suspicious investigative reporter and a murderer who doesn't want to leave any witnesses in this world or the next. With Jason Robards and Tom Hulce.
VHS: S15449. $89.95.
Mike Hodges, USA, 1991, 103 mins.

Black Widow
Debra Winger and Theresa Russell star in this stylish story about an obsessive investigation of a young woman who seduces, marries and murders wealthy men. With Dennis Hopper, Mary Woronov and a cameo by David Mamet.
VHS: S04339. $19.98.
Laser: CLV. LD72104. $24.98.
Bob Rafelson, USA, 1986, 103 mins.

Blaze
Paul Newman interprets the final years of the notorious Louisiana governor Earl K. Long and his scandalous relationship with stripper Blaze Starr. Lolita Davidovich brings a fair amount of sizzle to the title role but the real concern of the film is the savvy expose on Southern politics and not the sins of the flesh. From the creator of *Bull Durham*, writer-director Ron Shelton.
VHS: S12548. $89.95.
Ron Shelton, USA, 1989, 117 mins.

Blind Fury
Rutger Hauer stars as a blind Vietnam veteran who keeps the son of an old war buddy safe from pursuing mobsters on a cross-country adventure. The ads read "He's lucky he can't see what he's up against." Slapstick humor mixes with graphic violence. Inspired by the Japanese blind swordsman, Zaitochi. With Terry O'Quinn, Lisa Blount, Randall "Tex" Cobb and Meg Foster.
VHS: S14000. $14.95.
Phillip Noyce, USA, 1990, 86 mins.

Blind Justice
Gripping drama about an innocent man tangled in the mechanics of the judicial system. Tim Matheson plays the family man arrested, identified, and jailed for a heinous crime. Based on a true story. With Tim Matheson, Lisa Eichhorn and Mimi Kuzyk.
VHS: S06615. $59.98.
Laser: LD75160. $34.98.
Rod Holcomb, USA, 1986, 94 mins.

Blind Spot
Academy Award winner Joanne Woodward stars with Laura Linney in a film about a seemingly close mother/daughter relationship. Sometimes the intimacy between a mother and her child can obscure the truth, a possibility discovered by Woodward's character in this deeply felt drama.
VHS: S20654. $19.98.
Michael Toshiyuki Uno, USA, 1993, 99 mins.

Blink
Madeleine Stowe and Aidan Quinn are the stars in this sexy thriller centered on a blind musician who regains her sight only to witness a brutal murder. Determined to find the psychotic serial killer who has invaded her dream world, she tracks him down in order to end the hallucinations that now plague her.
VHS: S21139. $19.95.
Michael Apted, USA, 1993, 106 mins.

Blood Money
This heart-pumping mystery thriller, set in Florida and the steamy jungles of Costa Rica, stars Andy Garcia (*The Untouchables*, *Godfather Part III*) and Ellen Barkin (*Sea of Love*). He's a small time bird smuggler; she's an ex-hooker. So what could Contra arms traffickers possibly want from them? Their lives.
VHS: S14093. $79.95.
Jerry Schatzberg, USA, 1988, 95 mins.

Bloodhounds of Broadway
The Roaring Twenties as interpreted by a cast of performers from the Eighties. Four short stories by Damon Runyan are combined in this comic musical salute produced, directed and co-written by the late Howard Brookner. Sometimes this features Madonna, who sings "The Mooch" and "I Surrender, Dear," Matt Dillon, Julie Hagerty, Jennifer Grey, Rutger Hauer, Esai Morales and Randy Quaid.
VHS: S11574. $14.95.
Howard Brookner, USA, 1989, 100 mins.

Blown Away
When an explosion rocks Boston, bomb squad expert Jimmy Dove (Jeff Bridges) dives into action. The evidence points to a bomber more menacing and skilled than any he's ever faced—except one. The possibility that his former mentor, Tommy Lee Jones, is the culprit, sets in motion a plot of revenge and betrayal leading to an explosive confrontation.
VHS: S22903. $19.98.
Laser: LD74622. $44.98.
Stephen Hawkins, USA, 1994, 121 mins.

Blue Chips
Nick Nolte and Shaquille O'Neal combine on-court action with off-court drama to offer a behind-the-scenes look at professional basketball. These two stars from the world of sports and Hollywood bring gritty realism to this story of a coach whose principals are put to the test.
VHS: S21381. $19.95.
Laser: Widescreen. LD75294. $39.98.
William Friedkin, USA, 1994, 108 mins.

Blue Collar
Intense drama and social commentary focusing on the frustrations and fears of auto workers in Detroit featuring Richard Pryor and Harvey Keitel. Music by Jack Nitzsche.
VHS: S04661. $69.95.
Paul Schrader, USA, 1978, 114 mins.

Blue in the Face
Roseanne, Michael J. Fox and Mira Sorvino are just some of the stars featured in this comic continuation of *Smoke*. A series of skits are set in a Brooklyn neighborhood cigar shop which is set to close. Amidst the wacky set-ups, Giancarlo Esposito, Jim Jarmusch, Harvey Keitel, Lou Reed, Lily Tomlin and other celebrities improvise with panache and wit.
VHS: S27691. $99.99.
Laser: LD75572. $39.99.
Wayne Wang/Paul Auster, USA, 1995, 84 mins.

Blue Max
A German airman (George Peppard) becomes a national hero for his courage and skill in World War II dogfights in this spectacularly filmed adventure. James Mason also stars.
VHS: S12163. $19.98.
John Guillermin, USA, 1966, 152 mins.

Blue River
Sam Elliott and Susan Dey are at the heart of this odd dramatic film. Henry Howland (Elliott) is a despotic small town high school principal. He first seduces and then abandons a single mother (Dey), leaving her son hungry for revenge. Howland's hypocritical stance toward the morality of those who look up to him is slowly destroyed by this young man, who cleverly exposes all the secrets hidden away in the village of Blue River.
VHS: S27263. $89.99.
Larry Elikann, USA, 1995, 90 mins.

Blue Sky
Tony Richardson's final film received a belated release despite Jessica Lange's Oscar-winning performance as Carly, which also won her a Golden Globe. Carly is a sultry woman who dreams of glamour. Tommy Lee Jones plays Army Major Hank Marshall. Together they share a passionate roller-coaster marriage. When Hank is thrust into the center of a high level military cover-up, the only person who can save him is Carly.
VHS: S24407. $14.98.
Laser: LD74918. $39.99.
Tony Richardson, USA, 1994, 88 mins.

Blue Steel
Jamie Lee Curtis plays a rookie New York City cop who gets suspended from the force and attracts the romantic attention of a psychotic killer on her first day of work. That's life in the big city for you. With Ron Silver as the nutty stockbroker Eugene. Also in the cast, Clancy Brown, Elizabeth Pena and Louise Fletcher. The look of the film by Kathryn Bigelow (*Near Dark*) is fabulous but don't start counting the number of bullets fired between reloadings.
VHS: S12549. $14.95.
Kathryn Bigelow, USA, 1990, 102 mins.

The Blues Brothers
Jake and Elwood, that is, John Belushi and Dan Aykroyd, bring the characters first seen on *Saturday Night Live* to the streets of Chicago. The plot is a great excuse for fun musical numbers, cop car chases and even the occasional shootout. Carrie Fisher plays a jilted girlfriend packing a big gun. Blues and soul performers Aretha Franklin, Ray Charles, James Brown and Cab Calloway make memorable appearances.
VHS: S22405. $19.95.
John Landis, USA, 1980, 130 mins.

Bob Roberts
Tim Robbins' directorial debut stars Robbins as a right-wing folk singer and political activist who manipulates the media to camouflage a fascist veneer. Framed as a mock documentary covering Roberts' senatorial campaign, the film is a funny, often devastating critique of the political process, the selling out of the media, and the emergence of style over substance. With Giancarlo Esposito, Ray Wise, Gore Vidal and Alan Rickman. Special appearances by John Cusack, Peter Gallagher, Susan Sarandon and James Spader.
VHS: S18464. $19.98.
Tim Robbins, USA, 1992, 102 mins.

Body and Soul
Corruption threatens an honorable young black boxer, played by Leon Isaac Kennedy, at every turn in this dramatic tale. The central question becomes can he resist the destructive influences of the professional boxing world and triumph on the strengths of his own formidable abilities? Muhammad Ali has a cameo.
VHS: S26871. $14.95.
George Bowers, USA, 1981, 100 mins.

Body Bags
An anthology series of three works by John Carpenter and Tobe Hooper. The action is set in a creepy morgue, where people drop in and never leave. The all-star cast includes Robert Carradine, Stacy Keach, Mark Hamill, Deborah Harry, Sheena Easton, David Naughton, Twiggy and David Warner. Cameos by horror auteurs Wes Craven, Sam Raimi, Roger Corman, Hooper and Carpenter.
VHS: S20190. $92.98.
Laser: LD72439. $34.98.
John Carpenter/Tobe Hooper, USA, 1993, 95 mins.

Body Double
Brian De Palma once again pays tribute to Alfred Hitchcock in this tale of an actor involved in a murder where he is the prime witness. Craig Wasson is the voyeuristic thespian. Deborah Shelton is who he likes to watch. But Melanie Griffith, as porn actress Holly Body, is the real star of this twisted thriller.
VHS: S02862. $29.95.
Laser: Letterboxed, Dolby, chapter stops. LD74477. $34.95.
Brian DePalma, USA, 1984, 109 mins.

Body Heat
A sexy, haunting film that echoes the film noir dramas of the 1940's with a flare of irony and passion. Starring William Hurt and Kathleen Turner, it is the directorial debut of Kasdan, who went on to *Big Chill* and *Silverado*.
VHS: S00166. $14.95.
Laser: LD70530. $34.98.
Lawrence Kasdan, USA, 1981, 113 mins.

Bogie
A made-for-tv movie biography of Humphrey Bogart with Kevin O'Connor in the lead role. Ann Wedgeworth is the battling Mayo Methot and Kathryn Harrold is the slinky Lauren Bacall. A behind the scenes look at the personal life of a screen legend directed by Vincent Sherman who worked with the real Bogie on *The Return of Doctor X* in 1939.
VHS: S08495. $12.95.
Vincent Sherman, USA, 1980, 100 mins.

Bonfire of the Vanities
When a Wall Street tycoon takes the wrong exit in a bad neighborhood in the Bronx he becomes the target for scandal and receives a mandatory invitation to appear in court. Tom Hanks stars in this Brian De Palma adaptation of the bestselling Tom Wolfe satire on life in the Big Apple during the 1980's. The all-star cast includes Melanie Griffith, Morgan Freeman, Kim Cattrall, Alan King, F Murray Abraham, and Bruce Willis as the reporter responsible for the whole mess.
VHS: S13721. $19.98.
Brian DePalma, USA, 1990, 126 mins.

The Boost
James Woods and Sean Young star in this film about Lenny, who has everything: a beautiful, passionate, sensual girl; a beautiful house; the best tables in restaurants. Then things begin to crumble. Lenny needs something to get him moving again, and finds The Boost…and it's the beginning of the end. "James Woods is one of the most intense, unpredictable actors in the movies today," said Roger Ebert.
VHS: S09290. $89.99.
Harold Becker, USA, 1988, 95 mins.

The Border
Between the US and Mexico lies a line crossed every day by countless immigrants seeking a better life. It is Jack Nicholson's job to see that they don't cross the border—that is, until he gives into pressure from his wife, Valerie Perrine. Also features Harvey Keitel.
VHS: S21281. $14.98.
Tony Richardson, USA, 1982, 107 mins.

Born on the 4th of July
Tom Cruise performs the true Vietnam experience of Ron Kovic, following his development as an eager, young war volunteer to a paralyzed, embittered veteran. As a youth, and representative of the nation in general, Kovic was inspired by Kennedy's "Ask not what your country can do for you…" speech, but returned from the war to a changed nation and became a vehement and outspoken anti-war demonstrator. With Kyra Sedgwick and Willem Dafoe.
VHS: S12464. $19.95.
Laser: LD70017. $39.98.
Oliver Stone, USA, 1989, 145 mins.

Born to Be Wild
Rick Heller has troubles until he meets a new friend, Katie, a playful 400-pound gorilla. She knows her own mind and even communicates through sign language. Trouble sets in when Katie's owner puts her on display. Now she sorely needs her friend's help.
VHS: S25628. $19.99.
Laser: LD74986. $34.98.
John Gray, USA, 1995, 99 mins.

Born to Win
The unfairly neglected, American debut film of Czech emigre Ivan Passer (*Cutter's Way*) about the seamy underside of urban American life centers on two small-time hustlers, one of whom is a hairdresser suffering from heroin withdrawal. With terrific performances from Robert De Niro and George Segal, Paula Prentiss, Karen Black and Hector Elizondo.
VHS: S17644. $19.99.
Ivan Passer, USA, 1971, 90 mins.

Bound for Glory
The story of Woody Guthrie, America's great folk musician and poet, featuring David Carradine. Winner of two Academy Awards including Best Cinematography by Haskell Wexler, with many of Guthrie's songs, including "This Land Is Your Land" and "Roll On Columbia."
VHS: S00174. $19.98.
Hal Ashby, USA, 1976, 149 mins.

The Bounty
The latest account of that famous shipboard mutiny paints Captain Bligh in a much more sympathetic light. This is only natural as it is based on his own account of the incident. With Anthony Hopkins as the gruff but not that unreasonable captain and hunk Mel Gibson as the fun loving and completely unreliable Mr. Christian. Well made nautical adventure with great South Seas visits. With Daniel Day-Lewis, Edward Fox, Laurence Olivier, Bernard Hill and Liam Neeson.
VHS: S10735. $14.98.
Roger Donaldson, USA, 1984, 130 mins.

Boxing Helena
Julian Sands and Sherilyn Fenn star in this provocative fable of obsession and desire. Taking the title a little too literally, Sand's character tries to contain the object of his interests in a brutally simple way.
VHS: S20599. $95.98.
Laser: LD72428. $39.99.
Jennifer Chambers Lynch, USA, 1993, 107 mins.

The Boys of Cellblock Q
Director Alan Daniels adapts John C. Wall's off-Broadway play and remakes it as a melodrama about the sexual and political corruption in a correction facility for young boys. With Andrew Adams, Lewis Alante, Slade Burrus and Ken Merckx.
VHS: S18246. $39.95.
Alan Daniels, USA, 1992, 85 mins.

Boys on the Side
Whoopi Goldberg, Mary-Louise Parker and Drew Barrymore go on a road trip that careens through a gamut of adventure, but ends in lasting friendship. Though only Whoopi is a lesbian, issues like AIDS and boyfriend hardship make this melodrama a perfect fit for all kinds of girls.
VHS: S25572. $19.98.
Herbert Ross, USA, 1995, 117 mins.

The Brady Bunch
Here's the story of a 70's television show that found new life as a camp cult hit in the 1990's. Shelley Long leads an eerie cast of credible facsimiles in this spoof on the long-running series that mesmerized a nation of vidiots. When the home of the Bradys is threatened by greedy developers, their inane, cheerful attitude comes shining through.
VHS: S25632. $14.95.
Betty Thomas, USA, 1994, 88 mins.

Brainstorm
Directed by special effects wizard Douglas Trumbull, this high-tech movie, with state-of-the-art visual effects, stars Christopher Walken, Louise Fletcher and Natalie Wood (in her last film) in a story about research scientists who perfect a sensory experience device—in the form of a headset—with explosive results.
VHS: S14962. $14.95.
Douglas Trumbull, USA, 1983, 106 mins.

Brannigan
John Wayne plays the title's tough Chicago cop, who is sent to London to bring back fugitive John Vernon. When his prisoner is hijacked, Wayne finds his stay in jolly old England to be extended, much to the dismay of Scotland Yard. With Richard Attenborough, Judy Geeson, Mel Ferrer, Daniel Pilon and Lesley-Anne Down.
VHS: S12139. $19.95.
Douglas Hickox, Great Britain, 1975, 111 mins.

Braveheart
Mel Gibson is Braveheart, the legendary Scottish warrior who battled the English in the 13th century. In this epic film, the very story of independence is brought alive. It's a tale of fierce determination and unforgettable courage with superb battle sequences and a touching love story.
VHS: S27169. $101.99.
Laser: Widescreen, THX. LD75536. $49.95.
Mel Gibson, USA, 1995, 177 mins.

The Breakfast Club
Five teenagers on detention in a suburban school spend a Saturday in the school library and learn to get along. Cheerleader, jock, nerd, street punk and the super shy find harmony after smoking marijuana. The brat pack's finest hour and a half. With Molly Ringwald, Judd Nelson, Emilio Estevez, Anthony Michael Hall and Ally Sheedy.
VHS: S01985. $19.95.
John Hughes, USA, 1985, 97 mins.

Breaking Away
Four college-age friends in Bloomington, Indiana, find some meaning in life when they enter a bicycle race. Script by Steve Tesich won an Oscar. Starring Dennis Christopher, Dennis Quaid, Daniel Stern and Jackie Earle Haley as the "cutters." With Paul Dooley and Barbara Barrie as Christopher's parents.
VHS: S04881. $59.95.
Peter Yates, USA, 1979, 100 mins.

Breathing Lessons
James Garner and Joanne Woodward star in this heartfelt chronicle of an older couple on a short trip. Though they are an odd match—he's a pragmatist and she's inspired if flighty—the road offers them the perfect opportunity to renew their love and commitment for one another. Based on the Pulitzer Prize-winning novel by Anne Tyler.
VHS: S21872. $19.98.
John Erman, USA, 1994, 98 mins.

Bright Angel
Dermot Mulroney embarks on a road trip he will never forget when he offers Lili Taylor a ride from Montana to Wyoming to bail her brother out of jail. This bold, quirky drama features a top notch, eclectic cast that includes Sam Shepard, Valerie Perrine, Burt Young, Sheila McCarthy, Mary Kay Place, Bill Pullman and Delroy Lindo. Based on the short stories by Richard Ford. A real sleeper.
VHS: S15441. $19.98.
Laser: Widescreen. LD75165. $34.98.
Michael Fields, USA, 1991, 94 mins.

Brighton Beach Memoirs
Neil Simon's semi-autobiographical trilogy, transitioned from Broadway to the screen, with Jonathan Silverman as Eugene, the adolescent Simon, growing up in Brooklyn in the 30's, dreaming of girls and writing.
VHS: S03951. $19.95.
Gene Saks, USA, 1986, 108 mins.

Broadcast News
William Hurt, Holly Hunter and Albert Brooks play a tv news reporter, producer and writer in this involving and very funny inside look at the high pressure world of electronic journalism. The recipient of seven Oscar nominations including Best Picture, it also features Robert Prosky, Joan Cusack and Lois Chiles. Written, produced and directed by James L. Brooks (*Terms of Endearment*).
VHS: S07382. $89.98.
James L. Brooks, USA, 1987, 132 mins.

Broadway Bound
Neil Simon wrote this film as the final installment of his trilogy, featuring his alter ego, aspiring writer Eugene Morris Jerome. In this film he tries to leave Brooklyn for good in order to be a comedy writer for a radio show. When left alone, his mother finally decides to do something about his unfaithful father. This touching comic tale is also a moving chronicle of a family in transition.
VHS: S22021. $89.98.
Laser: LD74813. $39.98.
Paul Bogart, USA, 1992, 90 mins.

The Broken Chain
During the Revolutionary War two Iroquois brothers fight to keep their land safe from encroaching European settlers. Pierce Brosnan, Eric Scwheig, Wes Studi and Graham Green form the cast for this moving drama about change and survival in colonial America.
VHS: S21122. $92.98.
Laser: LD74448. $39.99.
Lamont Johnson, USA, 1993, 93 mins.

A Bronx Tale
Robert De Niro is the father of an impressionable boy who is in danger of being seduced by the easy life and fast money he sees on the streets of the Bronx. Sonny, the local mob boss, would find in this youngster a willing accomplice in crime.
VHS: S20655. $19.98.
Laser: Widescreen. LD75295. $39.98.
Robert De Niro, USA, 1993, 122 mins.

Brother John
Sidney Poitier stars as Brother John in a compelling drama set in a small Alabama town. Poitier is the Messiah come back to Earth—except that no one knows that he's come, and that he's black. Wonderful supporting performances by Will Geer, Bradford Dillman and Paul Winfield.
VHS: S06711. $14.95.
James Goldstone, USA, 1972, 94 mins.

The Brothers McMullen
In this romantic comedy, the Best Picture at the 1995 Sundance Festival, three brothers from Long Island confront the unknown territory of love and marriage. After their father dies, their mother returns to Ireland to be with the man she really loves. The three Irish Catholic brothers are left to deal with varying stages of love and marriage, ranging from initial attraction to engagement to the prospect of an extramarital affair. With Edward Burns, Jack Mulcahy, Mike McGlone and Connie Britton.
VHS: S27210. $99.99.
Laser: LD75482. $39.98.
Edward Burns, USA, 1995, 98 mins.

Bugsy
Warren Beatty's attempt to attach Hollywood glamour to the notorious American criminal was nominated for 11 Oscars and took home awards for art direction and best costume design. Beatty imbues East Coast mobster Benjamin "Bugsy" Siegel with an altruistic, pioneer spirit in the building of a casino empire in Las Vegas. Annette Bening is cast as the hard-nosed cutie Virginia Hill. Harvey Keitel and Ben Kingsley were nominated for Oscars, along with Beatty, for their sharp portrayals of famous gangsters. With Elliot Gould, Bebe Neuwirth, Wendy Phillips and Joe Mantegna as George Raft. Script by James Toback.
VHS: S16714. $19.95.
Laser: LD71572. $39.95.
Barry Levinson, USA, 1991, 135 mins.

Bulletproof Heart
Anthony LaPaglia and Mimi Rogers star in this film noir-style love story. A hit man (LaPaglia) sets out to kill his mark, a beautiful socialite who is actually eager to die. Though he is warned that he should steel himself for this assignment (as other men have tried and failed), his own self-doubts and her overwhelming beauty lead to the inevitable—he falls for her in a big way.
VHS: S26370. $93.99.
Mark Malone, USA, 1995, 95 mins.

Bullitt
Cop Steve McQueen spins through San Francisco's streets in a chase that's one of the screen's all-time best. McQueen is the police detective who conceals the death of an underground witness and goes after the killers himself.
VHS: S11614. $19.95.
Laser: LD74689. $24.98.
Peter Yates, USA, 1968, 113 mins.

The Bunker
Anthony Hopkins portrays Adolf Hitler, for which he won an Emmy, in this look at the last days of the Third Reich, based on the book by James P. O'Donnel. Piper Laurie is also featured as Madga Goebbels. Her vital performance was recognized with an Emmy nomination.
VHS: S21030. $19.98.
George Schaefer, USA, 1981, 150 mins.

The 'Burbs
Joe Dante presents a darkly humorous look at suburban living. Neighbors Tom Hanks, Rick Ducommun and Bruce Dern think there is something very odd about the Klopeks, the latest addition to their cul-de-sac community. After all, folks that don't keep up with their yard work might be guilty of devil worship, human sacrifice and lowering property values. With Henry Gibson, Carrie Fisher and Brother Theodore.
VHS: S08710. $14.95.
Joe Dante, USA, 1989, 102 mins.

The Burning Season
Raul Julia stars in this, his final film, as Chico Mendes. He is matched in this gripping biographical film with a supporting cast composed of Edward J. Olmos, Sonia Braga and Nigel Havers. Mendes fought to save the Amazon rain forest with firm conviction. Ultimately his struggle was an inspiration to the entire world.
VHS: S24058. $19.98.
John Frankenheimer, USA, 1994, 123 mins.

Caligula: The Untold Story
Another adaptation chronicling the lurid spectacle of the notorious Roman emperor (played by David Cain Haugton). Directed by David Hills. With Joan McCoy and Laura Gemser.
VHS: S14156. $79.95.

Call of the Wild
Shot in the striking scenery of Finland, and featuring a cast including Charlton Heston and Michele Mercier, this is an epic adaptation of the classic Jack London adventure classic.
VHS: S09165. $19.95.
Ken Annakin, USA, 1972, 100 mins.

Camilla
Jessica Tandy and Bridget Fonda bring their undeniable star power to this warm, funny road movie. They play two strangers who find friendship and fun together despite their differences. It's a comic adventure perfect for all kinds of audiences.
VHS: S25052. $96.98.
Laser: LD74954. $39.99.
Deepa Mehta, USA, 1995, 91 mins.

Canadian Bacon
John Candy is joined by Dan Aykroyd, Rhea Perlman, Kevin Pollak and Bill Nunn in this outrageous comedy satire. Imagine that the U.S. is threatened by a very close, immense neighbor. The country would rally together to defeat the nefarious foe. This scenario is presented to the President of the United States and he decides that in order to ensure his re-election and get those wartime industries humming, he will invade that colossus of the North, Canada.
VHS: S26804. $95.99.
Laser: LD75407. $34.95.
Michael Moore, USA, 1994, 95 mins.

Cancel My Reservation
Bob Hope is a New York talk show host who is so stressed out his doctor tells him to take a vacation. Leaving his wife home, he heads to a ranch in Arizona, where he is implicated in a murder he did not commit.
VHS: S09396. $14.95.
Paul Bogart, USA, 1972, 99 mins.

Candidate
A still refreshing satire based on an original screenplay that grew out of Jeremy Larner's experience in the Eugene McCarthy campaign, with Robert Redford as an idealistic lawyer seeking a Senate seat in California, and Allen Garfield as the sleazy advertising man.
VHS: S01750. $19.98.
Laser: LD71409. $34.98.
Michael Ritchie, USA, 1972, 111 mins.

Cannery Row
Adaptation of John Steinbeck stars Nick Nolte as an ex-baseball player turned marine biologist and Debra Winger as a young runaway. Narration by John Huston, photography by Sven Nykvist, music by Jack Nitzsche.
VHS: S02988. $79.95.
David Ward, USA, 1982, 120 mins.

The Canterville Ghost (Gielgud)
Sir John Gielgud stars as the title spirit in this update of a tale of a cowardly knight who was walled up in the castle and forced to haunt the place until an ancestor would perform a brave deed. Well, the ghost has been waiting for 300 years and his hopes rest on an American cousin played by Ted Wass. Good luck. 1986, 96 mins.
VHS: S04383. $69.95.

The Canterville Ghost (Stewart)
Patrick Stewart is the Oscar Wilde character the Canterville Ghost. Neve Campbell plays the young woman who moves into the Ghost's 400-year-old home and disturbs his sanctuary. Despite this conflict the two team up for laughs and drama, finally dispelling the curse that looms over the ancient pile of Canterville.
VHS: S27597. $99.99.
Laser: LD75550. $39.99.
Syd Macartney, USA, 1995, 91 mins.

Captain America
The eponymous hero returns from the past and gets caught in a superhuman war with his archnemesis, the Red Skull, over control of the planet and the future in this live action adaptation of the popular cartoon hero created by Joe Simon and Jack Kirby.
VHS: S16909. $19.95.
Laser: LD71530. $34.95.
Albert Pyun, USA, 1990

Captain Newman, M.D.
This provocative comedy-drama features Gregory Peck as a dedicated Army psychiatrist who battles the bureaucracy and the macho military mentality on a stateside air base during WWII. With a host of fine performances from Tony Curtis, Angie Dickinson, Bobby Darin, Jane Withers and Robert Duvall. Based on Leo Rosten's bestselling novel.
VHS: S16306. $19.95.
David Miller, USA, 1963, 126 mins.

Carlito's Way
Al Pacino, the star of *Scarface*, is cast as a ruthless Cuban immigrant who finds that the world of 1990's America is still the toughest school of hard knocks. Penelope Ann Miller and Sean Penn also star in this acclaimed film.
VHS: S20692. $19.98.
Laser: Letterboxed. LD72380. $44.98.
Brian DePalma, USA, 1993, 145 mins.

Carnal Knowledge
Jack Nicholson, Ann-Margret, Art Garfunkel and Candice Bergen star in this shattering, bitterly humorous film examining the sexual triumphs and disasters of two American men from college days into their 40's. Written by Jules Feiffer, directed by Mike Nichols.
VHS: S00214. $14.95.
Laser: CLV. LD70126. $49.95.
Mike Nichols, USA, 1971, 96 mins.

Caroline?
Stephanie Zimbalist once solved mysteries on a weekly basis as a television detective on "Remington Steele." Now she plays a very mysterious character in this outstanding Hall of Fame presentation about a young woman who turns up at her wealthy father's mansion 15 years after she was thought to have died in a plane crash. With George Grizzard, Pamela Reed, Patricia Neal, Dorothy McGuire, Shawn Phelan and Jenny Jacobs.
VHS: S16505. $89.98.
Laser: LD71455. $29.98.
Joseph Sargent, USA, 1990, 100 mins.

Casualties of War
Michael J. Fox stars as a new recruit in Vietnam assigned to veteran Sgt. Sean Penn's squad. Fox objects to having a little fun with a captured South Vietnamese woman, his fellow grunts get ugly. With John C. Reilly, Don Harvey, John Leguizamo, Thuy Thu Le and Sam Robards as Chaplain Kirk. Based on a real incident written by Daniel Lang for *New Yorker Magazine*. Script by playwright David Rabe (*Streamers*).
VHS: S16602. $14.95.
Brian DePalma, USA, 1989, 113 mins.

Catch-22
Joseph Heller's modern classic novel about war and its absurdity for the common man stars Alan Arkin, Martin Balsam, Richard Benjamin, Art Garfunkel.
VHS: S01751. $19.95.
Laser: LD75332. $29.98.
Mike Nichols, USA, 1970, 121 mins.

Changes
An alienated youth hits the road and heads for Big Sur. Along the way he meets three women who greatly affect his life. This 60s road movie is highlighted by the music of Judy Collins, Tim Buckley and Neil Young. With Kent Lane, Jack Albertson, Marcia Strassman, Michele Carey and Teri Garr in a small role. The title tune and "Both Sides Now" will be sung.
VHS: S08318. $79.95.
Hall Bartlett, USA, 1969, 93 mins.

Charade
An elegant, sophisticated thriller featuring Audrey Hepburn as the widow of a swindler, Cary Grant as an undercover CIA agent, and a cast of bad guys that includes James Coburn, George Kennedy and Walter Matthau. With a score by Henry Mancini.
VHS: S01752. $19.98.
Stanley Donen, USA, 1963, 113 mins.

Charley Varrick
Walter Matthau stars as a successful bank robber who runs into some uncharacteristic bad luck. He just hit a bank where the mob launders money. Joe Don Baker is on him, determined to make the hit he has been ordered to make. Suspense builds as these two test each other's wits and nerves.
VHS: S21280. $14.98.
Don Siegel, USA, 1973, 111 mins.

Charly
Cliff Robertson won an Oscar for his performance as a mentally retarded patient involved in a program designed to increase his mental capacity by extraordinary levels. With Claire Bloom as his friend and medical advisor. Based on Daniel Keyes' novel, *Flowers for Algernon*. Algernon is a white rodent…who is being tested along with Charly. With Lilia Skala and Dick Van Patten.
VHS: S10935. $19.98.
Ralph Nelson, USA, 1968, 103 mins.

Chasers
Tom Berenger and William McNamara play Navy shore patrol officers who must transfer a dangerous prisoner, the beautiful Erika Eleniak. This comic look at today's coed navy combines great star power and road movie action. Also features Gary Busey.
VHS: S21356. $19.98.
Laser: LD74474. $34.98.
Dennis Hopper, USA, 1994, 102 mins.

Chattahoochee
Gary Oldman is cast as Emmett Foley, a Korean war veteran who was sent to a Florida state mental facility after he shot up his neighborhood for no apparent reason. This grim true story tells the tale of the man responsible for major changes in the care and treatment of the mentally ill. Excellent supporting cast includes Dennis Hopper, Frances McDormand, Pamela Reed, Ned Beatty and M. Emmet Walsh.
VHS: S14001. $19.98.
Mick Jackson, USA, 1989, 97 mins.

Cheyenne Social Club
Gene Kelly directs this bawdy western adventure about an old cowpoke who inherits a brothel in Wyoming and can't decide whether to enjoy himself or close the place down. James Stewart stars as John O'Hanlon, the uncomfortable new owner of the Cheyenne Social Club. Henry Fonda tags along as his talkative saddle buddy Harley Sullivan. With Shirley Jones, Sue Ann Langdon, Jackie Russell and Elaine Devry.
VHS: S16285. $19.98.
Gene Kelly, USA, 1970, 103 mins.

The Children
A leak at the nuclear power plant turns a bus load of children into pint-sized predators with black fingernails capable of frying their victims on contact. Pray you never meet them.
VHS: S14092. $14.95.
Max Kalmanowicz, USA, 1980, 89 mins.

Children of a Lesser God
William Hurt, Marlee Matlin, Piper Laurie and Philip Bosco star in this Academy-Award nominated film, the screen version of a successful Broadway play, with Hurt the special education teacher who falls in love with a troubled deaf woman.
VHS: S03303. $19.95.
Randa Haines, USA, 1986, 119 mins.

Chilly Scenes of Winter
An affectionate, off-beat comedy from director Joan Micklin Silver featuring early film performances by John Heard and Mary Beth Hurt. Based on the novel by Ann Beattie, the film is populated by memorable characters.
VHS: S00234. $19.98.
Joan Micklin Silver, USA, 1979, 96 mins.

China Moon
Ed Harris is Kyle Bodine, a detective who must investigate a murder involving beautiful Rachel Munro (Madeleine Stowe). This sexy and steamy thriller builds an atmosphere of eroticism and danger that threatens to draw in everyone entranced by the allure of *China Moon*.
VHS: S21827. $95.98.
John Bailey, USA, 1994, 99 mins.

China Syndrome
Things really start to rumble when a TV news crew stumbles over an accident at a California nuclear plant. Tempers flare and tensions rise when the piece is pulled and embarrassing questions are asked. With Jane Fonda, Michael Douglas, Jack Lemmon, Wilford Brimley, James Hampton, Peter Donat and James Karen. The title infers a total atomic meltdown that would bore a hole through the Earth all the way to China. A timely and taunt piece of work.
VHS: S10379. $19.95.
Laser: LD75529. $39.95.
James Bridges, USA, 1979, 123 mins.

The Choirboys
The raunchy, hilarious exploits of ten metropolitan policemen in this film based on Joseph Wambaugh's best-selling novel. James Woods, Charles Durning, Louis Gossett Jr., Perry King, Randy Quaid and Burt Young lead a group of rank-and-file L.A. policemen who look for ways to cope with the pressures of their job in offbeat antics.
VHS: S10450. $14.98.
Robert Aldrich, USA, 1977, 120 mins.

Christine
When a teenager (Keith Gordon) buys an old car that needs fixing, it becomes something of an obsession. This harmless tendency turns dangerous when the car responds in kind and becomes a jealous friend. Soon this possessed car is murdering all those who come between it and its owner. Also stars Harry Dean Stanton.
VHS: S22110. $14.95.
Laser: Letterboxed. LD74551. $34.95.
John Carpenter, USA, 1983, 110 mins.

Christmas Coal Mine Miracle
Made-for-tv story based on a true incident of miners trapped by an underground explosion on Christmas Eve. With Kurt Russell.
VHS: S05315. $59.95.
Judd Taylor, USA, 1977, 100 mins.

Christmas Lilies of the Field
Billy Dee Williams stars in this charming sequel to the Academy Award winning *Lilies of the Field*, a sensitive account of a mission's struggle to give a group of orphans a home.
VHS: S09246. $29.95.
Ralph Nelson, USA, 1984, 98 mins.

Christmas Wife
Jason Robards and Julie Harris star in a heartwarming film. Robards plays John Tanner, recently widowed, as he faces his first Christmas alone. He goes to an agency to find someone with whom to share Christmas and meets the shy Iris, who is happy to join him; but there's a secret which, when revealed, changes both their lives forever.
VHS: S11005. $79.99.
David Jones, USA, 1988, 73 mins.

Christopher Columbus: The Discovery
John Glen directs an all-star cast (Marlon Brando, Tom Selleck and Rachel Ward) in a massive international co-production from a story by *Godfather* author Mario Puzo.
VHS: S17707. $19.98.
Laser: LD71800. $39.98.
John Glen, USA, 1992, 121 mins.

Cincinnati Kid
Steve McQueen is terrific in the title role as Eric Stoner, professional poker player. Talk has it, the Kid is the only one good enough to challenge the legendary gambler Edward G. Robinson and win. Place your bets. Among those interested in the results of a certain high stakes game in New Orleans are Karl Malden, Ann-Margret, Tuesday Weld, Joan Blondell, Cab Calloway and Jack Weston. Directed by Norman Jewison, who replaced Sam Peckinpah after he wanted to use Sharon Tate in a nude scene.
VHS: S16443. $19.98.
Norman Jewison, USA, 1965, 104 mins.

Circle of Friends

Chris O'Donnell and Minnie Driver are at the center of this romantic comedy. Bernadette, Eve and Nan are three girlhood friends reunited at college. They all set off on romantic adventures. Bernadette (Driver) falls for the most unlikely candidate: Jack Foley, the big man on campus. As Bernadette's relationship with Jack intensifies, the three women learn some valuable and troublesome lessons about the nature of friendship.
VHS: S25885. $19.98.
Pat O'Connor, USA, 1994, 112 mins.

Citizen Cohn

A complex and powerful, made-for-cable biography of lawyer and conservative activist Roy Cohn, energetically performed by James Woods. Adapted from Nicholas von Hoffman's biography, the film uses an intricate structure, as Cohn, dying from AIDS and denying his homosexuality, details his ambition and lust for power. In the hospital, he's visited by the ghosts of his past: his prosecution of the Rosenbergs, the communist witch hunts in conjunction with Joseph McCarthy, his fierce political battles with the Kennedys and the attempted destabilization of the civil rights movement. With Joe Don Baker, Joseph Bologna, Ed Flanders and Frederic Forrest. "Woods gives a hypnotic, blistering performance" (*Chicago Sun-Times*).
VHS: S18790. $19.98.
Laser: LD75170. $34.98.
Frank Pierson, USA, 1992, 112 mins.

Citizen X

Stephen Rea, Donald Sutherland and Max Von Sydow star in this dramatic HBO production about the most prolific serial killer of all time. It's a chilling, true story of the bungled investigative process that finally pieced together the identity of the dreaded Citizen X. He managed to kill 52 people before he was captured.
VHS: S25053. $19.98.
Chris Gerolmo, USA, 1995, 102 mins.

City Slickers

Billy Crystal, Bruno Kirby and Daniel Stern play three buddies from the Big Apple who each year try to find something new and different to road test their testosterone levels. This vacation it's a cattle drive in the still wild American West. Jack Palance is along for the ride as a trail boss who makes the Marlboro Man look like a wimp. A comic adventure with the emphasis on cute. With Helen Slater, Josh Mostel and Patricia Wettig. Yee hah, little dogies.
VHS: S15173. $19.95.
Laser: Letterboxed. LD74488. $39.99.
Ron Underwood, USA, 1991, 114 mins.

Clara's Heart

Whoopi Goldberg is cast as a caring Jamaican housekeeper who fascinates and inspires young Neil Patrick Harris to improve his attitude and enjoy life. With Kathleen Quinlan, Michael Ontkean, Beverley Todd and Spalding Gray. A sensitive drama with lots of Jamaican music.
VHS: S09167. $14.95.
Laser: LD74690. $24.98.
Robert Mulligan, USA, 1988, 108 mins.

Clarence

Being an angel isn't easy...especially when your name is Clarence Oddbody (Robert Carradine, *Revenge of the Nerds*). The delightfully dizzy guardian angel who saved Jimmy Stewart in *It's a Wonderful Life* is back. And this time he's got the modern world to contend with. An inspiring fantasy for the whole family, *Clarence* proves that with the right spirit, everyone can have a wonderful life.
VHS: S15136. $19.98.
Eric Till, USA, 1990, 92 mins.

Clean and Sober

Michael Keaton gets serious as an options trader with substance abuse and personality problems. He joins a de-tox program to hide out from his boss and the police when his life goes into the dumper. Excellent supporting work by Morgan Freeman and Kathy Baker. From the creator of "Moonlighting" TV show, Glenn Gordon Caron.
VHS: S09923. $19.98.
Glenn Gordon Caron, USA, 1988, 124 mins.

Clean Slate

Dana Carvey stars as M.L. Pogue, a witness to a crime. The problem is he can't remember the details. With his eye-patched pooch and the beautiful femme fatale Valeria Golina, he tries to uncover the forgotten facts that will solve this crime. This fun-filled comedy shows Carvey at his antic best.
VHS: S22126. $19.95.
Mick Jackson, USA, 1994, 107 mins.

Clear and Present Danger

Harrison Ford returns as the CIA agent dedicated to the American way. After the cold war, the enemy is closer to home than before. A presidential advisor is linked to a South American drug cartel. Ford's discovery of this connection sends him into an action adventure/drama where truth must win out over injustice. Anne Archer, Willem Dafoe and James Earl Jones are also featured.
VHS: S23219. $19.98.
Laser: Widescreen. LD75368. $44.98.
Phillip Noyce, USA, 1994, 141 mins.

Cleopatra

Elizabeth Taylor and Richard Burton carry on as one of the most famous romantic couples of the ancient and modern ages. A truly mammoth production filled with spectacle and thousands of extras. With Rex Harrison as Caesar and Roddy McDowall.
VHS: S04586. $29.95.
Joseph L. Mankiewicz, USA, 1963, 251 mins.

The Client

Susan Sarandon and Tommy Lee Jones star in this chilling thriller based on the John Grisham novel. When a rookie lawyer (Sarandon) takes on an overzealous prosecutor (Jones) to protect a young boy, a deadly chain of events is set in play. Soon it's a matter of life and death for everyone involved.
VHS: S22538. $19.98.
Laser: LD74613. $39.98.
Joel Schumacher, USA, 1994, 120 mins.

Cliffhanger

Renny Harlin's vertigo-inducing thriller is set in the Colorado Mountains. The ingenious opening—a group of terrorists hijack a treasury plane in midair but lose $100 million when the plane crashlands in the Rockies—builds up to a wonderfully tense and exciting action pretense. Sylvester Stallone and Michael Rooker play mountain rescue experts who are psychologically scarred by the death of a woman climber. John Lithgow plays the sinister terrorist. With Janine Turner, Paul Winfield, Ralph Waite, Rex Linn, Caroline Goodall, Leon and Michelle Joyner.
VHS: S19873. $99.95.
Renny Harlin, USA, 1993, 118 mins.

Closet Land

Radha Bharadwaj's timely and harrowing drama stars Madeleine Stowe as a children's book author who becomes a political prisoner after a book she writes is deemed subversive. Alan Rickman co-stars.
VHS: S15096. $19.98.
Radha Bharadwaj, USA, 1991, 95 mins.

Clueless

Alicia Silverstone is perfect as Cher, the *Clueless* Beverly Hills teenager who can shop with the best. Longing for something deeper, and a boyfriend as well, Cher manages to skate through a variety of off-putting situations. Though transformed, she manages to come out of it all with her wit and superficiality largely intact.
VHS: S26715. $19.95.
Amy Heckerling, USA, 1995, 97 mins.

Cobb

Tommy Lee Jones is Ty Cobb, perhaps the most disliked baseball hero of all time. Robert Wuhl plays the writer who must try to tell this legend's story, but obnoxious behavior and plain ego stand in the way. Despite it all, the two manage to connect and have some wild times.
VHS: S25654. $19.98.
Ron Shelton, USA, 1994, 129 mins.

Cocktail

Tom Cruise and Bryan Brown are a pair of wild and crazy Manhattan bartenders who rise to the top of their profession. Cruise is young and cocky and Brown is older and sometimes wiser. Elisabeth Shue is the waitress with the trust fund. For those who like a production number with their mixed drinks. Based on the book by Heywood Gould.
VHS: S09154. $89.95.
Roger Donaldson, USA, 1988, 103 mins.

Cocoon

Ron Howard directs a fine batch of Hollywood's senior citizens, who find that the Fountain of Youth is located not far from their Florida retirement community. This new lease on life is provided unintentionally by space aliens led by Brian Dennehy. With Jack Gilford, Hume Cronyn, Jessica Tandy, and Don Ameche as the break-dancing winner of a Best Supporting Actor award.
VHS: S04773. $14.98.
Ron Howard, USA, 1985, 117 mins.

Cold Sassy Tree

Faye Dunaway and Richard Widmark star in this story of a May-December romance that scandalizes the quiet Southern town of Cold Sassy, Georgia, at the turn of the century. Based on the book by Olive Ann Burns.
VHS: S11613. $14.98.
Joan Tewkesbury, USA, 1989, 97 mins.

Color of Night (Director's Cut)

Bruce Willis stars in this super erotic thriller featuring the beautiful Jane March. Willis is a psychologist haunted by his friend and colleague's unexplained murder. Unable to control himself, he is led through passionate intrigues as he tries to find the killer. Includes an extra 15 minutes of controversial, erotic footage. Ruben Blades and Lesley Ann Warren also star.
VHS: S23668. $96.98.
Laser: Letterboxed. LD74808. $39.99.
Richard Rush, USA, 1994, 140 mins.

Colors

Dennis Hopper directs this controversial police story about two partners on an anti-gang patrol in the Los Angeles area. Robert Duvall is the seasoned pro and Sean Penn is cast as the cocky rookie. With Maria Conchita Alonso, Trinidad Silva and many actual members of L.A. street gangs in extra roles.
VHS: S07786. $19.98.
Dennis Hopper, USA, 1988, 120 mins.

Come Along with Me

An adaptation of Shirley Jackson's unfinished novel, starring Estelle Parsons and Silvia Sidney, directed by Joanne Woodward. The plot concerns Mabel Lederer, whose husband, Hughie, passed on. Mabel decides to re-invent herself with a new name and new town, and undertakes a slightly off-center profession: "I dabble in the supernatural."
VHS: S07540. $24.95.
Joanne Woodward, USA, 1986, 60 mins.

Come See the Paradise

English director Alan Parker turns his camera on another infamous American chapter in race relations. The story of the World War II imprisonment of thousands of American citizens with Japanese ancestry is told through the perspective of an Irish-American labor organizer who marries into a Little Tokyo family in Los Angeles. With Dennis Quaid, Tamlyn Tomita, Sab Shimono and Shizu-ko Hoshi. Compelling and questionable.
VHS: S13920. $19.98.
Alan Parker, USA, 1990, 135 mins.

The Comfort of Strangers

Director Paul Schrader returns to the screen with a lurid tale of innocents in jeopardy. English tourists Rupert Everett and Natasha Richardson accept the hospitality of Christopher Walken and Helen Mirren and hope they live to regret it. A stylish exercise written by Harold Pinter.
VHS: S14459. $79.95.
Laser: LD75172. $34.98.
Paul Schrader, USA/Great Britain, 1991, 102 mins.

Coming Home

Jane Fonda, Jon Voight and Bruce Dern star in a powerful drama about the effects of the Vietnam War on the home front. Fonda falls in love with a disabled vet (Voight) while husband Dern is fighting overseas. Good supporting work by Penelope Milford and Robert Carradine.
VHS: S04718. $19.98.
Laser: Chapter search. Includes original trailer. **LD71636. $39.98.**
Hal Ashby, USA, 1978, 127 mins.

The Commitments

Alan Parker directs this joyful musical drama about a talented young group of Dublin musicians from the gritty North Side who try to make good playing American soul music. Robert Arkins stars as the band's resourceful manager Jimmy Rabbitte. He and the rest of The Commitments were chosen from open auditions in Dublin. With Maria Doyle, Dave Finnegan, Johnny Murphy, Dick Massey, Angeline Ball, Bronagh Gallagher, Michael Aherne, Glen Hansard, Felim Gormley, Kenneth McCluskey and Andrew Strong as lead singer Deco Cuffe. Songs include "Mustang Sally", "Try a Little Tenderness" and "In the Midnight Hour". A major delight.
VHS: S15776. $19.98.
Alan Parker, USA/Ireland, 1991, 116 mins.

Compromising Positions

Susan Sarandon and Raul Julia are the stars of this amusing thriller about murder in suburbia. A one-time journalist looks into the death of a seductive dentist. Before long this simple obsession leads to unsuspected perils and quite a few good laughs.
VHS: S23954. $14.95.
Laser: LD75362. $29.98.
Frank Perry, USA, 1985, 99 mins.

Conagher

A moody western adapted from Louis L'Amour's novel about the relationship between a hardened loner and a fiercely independent frontier woman. With Sam Elliott, Katharine Ross and Barry Corbin. Directed by the talented cinematographer Reynaldo Villalobos.
VHS: S18498. $14.98.
Reynaldo Villalobos, USA, 1991, 94 mins.

Conrack

Jon Voight stars as a teacher doing his best to educate a group of underachieving black children who live on an island off the coast of South Carolina. Based on the true story of Pat Conroy and his book *The Water Is Wide*. With Paul Winfield, Madge Sinclair and Hume Cronyn.
VHS: S01856. $59.98.
Martin Ritt, USA, 1974, 107 mins.

Consenting Adults

A seductive murder mystery about an unholy linking between two yuppie couples. A composer and his young wife attempt to inject some life into their dull marriage by experimenting with their beautiful, dangerous neighbors, with catastrophic results. With Kevin Kline, Mary Elizabeth Mastrantonio, Kevin Spacey and Rebecca Miller.
VHS: S18494. $94.95.
Alan J. Pakula, USA, 1992, 109 mins.

Convicts

Robert Duvall, James Earl Jones and Lukas Haas star in this film set on a plantation staffed by convict labor. The owner is violently unpredictable and paranoid, forcing all those around him to confront not only difficult conditions but their own sense of humanity.
VHS: S21149. $29.98.
Peter Materson, USA, 1991, 93 mins.

Cookie

Susan Seidelman looks for the lighter side of organized crime in the New York City area with a family comedy where most of the characters are members of the Family. Peter Falk plays reformed racketeer Dino Capisco. Emily Lloyd is cast as his spunky teenage daughter Cookie, a love-child of Dino's faithful mistress, played by Dianne Wiest. Can father and daughter do business? With Jerry Lewis, Adrian Pasdar and Brenda Vaccaro, script by Nora Ephron and Alice Arden.
VHS: S11663. $14.95.
Susan Seidelman, USA, 1989, 93 mins.

Copycat

Sigourney Weaver and Holly Hunter star, while Harry Connick, Jr., makes his feature-length film debut. A serial killer attempts to destroy a psychiatrist (Weaver) who studies serial killers. Unnerved by this effort, Weaver's character finds that the plot against her is even more insidious than she suspected; it involves an ingenious use of her own research material.
VHS: S27168. $99.99.
Laser: LD75466. $39.98.
Jon Amiel, USA, 1995, 123 mins.

Corrina, Corrina

Whoopi Goldberg and Ray Liotta star in this touching tale of two families joined by love. Ray is a widower in the 1950's who hires a new servant, played by Whoopi. Before long her charm and grace transform this rigid relationship into something that no one had expected. This film contains Don Ameche's last screen appearance.
VHS: S23879. $96.98.
Jessie Nelson, USA, 1994, mins.

The Count of Monte Cristo

An adaptation of Dumas' novel about the charismatic swashbuckler Edmond Dantes (Richard Chamberlain), who was unjustly imprisoned. He assumes a new identity and seeks vengeance on the ruthless man who tried to destroy him. With Tony Curtis, Trevor Howard, Louis Jourdan and Kate Nelligan.
VHS: S18485. $19.98.
David Greene, USA, 1975, 100 mins.

Courtship—An American Romance

Horton Foote's first part of the trilogy of small town love and life that is continued in *One Valentine's Day* and *1918*. Hallie Foote, the author's daughter, heads a cast that includes Amanda Plummer, Steven Hill and William Converse-Roberts. The story is largely autobiographical based on Foote's parents.
VHS: S03602. $79.95.
Howard Cummings, USA, 1986-7, 85 mins.

Cracker: To Be a Somebody

Robbie Coltrane stars as Dr. Eddie Fitzgerald, a combative and enigmatic forensic psychologist who has a nose for crime solving. In this first of the series, an Asian shopkeeper is killed in an apparently racist attack. The killer breaks the pattern however, when one of the investigative team is murdered. Finally the police turn to Fitz for help. 150 mins.
VHS: S26665. $79.95.

Crimes of the Heart

Diane Keaton, Jessica Lange and Sissy Spacek star in Bruce Beresford's adaptation of Beth Henley's Pulitzer-prize winning play about three sisters, re-united after a bizarre incident, struggling to overcome sibling rivalries and the family's reputation.
VHS: S03549. $19.98.
Bruce Beresford, USA, 1986, 105 mins.

Crimson Tide

Denzel Washington and Gene Hackman star in this thriller set aboard a submarine armed with nuclear warheads. An unconfirmed order to launch these weapons sets off a battle for control of the ship. Ultimately, control over the warheads will determine if a battle that could provoke the third world war actually begins.
VHS: S26612. $103.99.
Laser: Widescreen, THX. **LD75370. $44.98.**
Tony Scott, USA, 1995, 116 mins.

Crisis at Central High

Joanne Woodward stars as teacher Elizabeth Huckaby in this vivid recreation of history: the 1957 integration of Little Rock's Central High. A brilliant performance by Woodward; based on Huckaby's own journals. Woodward won an Emmy for her performance.
VHS: S23443. $19.98.
Lamont Johnson, USA, 1981, 125 mins.

Critical Condition

Richard Pryor stars in this comedy that also features Ruben Blades, Joe Dallesandro and Sylvia Miles. Pryor tries to escape the Mafia by pleading insanity. Soon he's longing for the safety of the mental ward after he escapes and is mistaken for a doctor.
VHS: S23953. $14.95.
Laser: LD75296. $29.98.
Michael Apted, USA, 1987, 99 mins.

Cromwell

Richard Harris plays the fiery Oliver Cromwell in this Hollywood story of the 17th century Englishman determined to get England rid of tyrannical rule. Alec Guiness stars as King Charles I.
VHS: S04219. $19.95.
Laser: Widescreen. **LD75493. $39.95.**
Ken Hughes, USA, 1970, 145 mins.

Crooked Hearts

Based on Robert Boswell's critically acclaimed 1987 novel, *Crooked Hearts* is an endearing, insightful look at one family's struggle to come to terms with each other as they start to grow apart. A family secret surfaces in the midst of their seemingly happy environment, and results in tragedy—ultimately forcing them to face each other and the circumstances of their lives with a newfound independence and maturity. Starring Peter Coyote, Cindy Pickett and Jennifer Jason Leigh.
VHS: S14997. $14.95.
Michael Bortman, USA, 1991, 113 mins.

The Crossing Guard

Jack Nicholson and Anjelica Huston star in this dark play on death, revenge and murder. Nicholson aches for the release of a man who killed his daughter while driving under the influence. With his empty life and ruined wife, he has only one goal in mind—making this guy pay.
VHS: S27688. $99.99.
Laser: LD75574. $39.99.
Sean Penn, USA, 1995, 111 mins.

The Crow

Brandon Lee stars in this exciting and mysterious thriller about a man with strange powers. After a terrible crime, only revenge and justice can drive a man to the extremes that define The Crow. Brandon Lee, the son of Bruce Lee, is astounding in this, his last film.
VHS: S22157. $96.98.
Alex Proyas, USA, 1993, 100 mins.

Cruising

Al Pacino and Karen Allen star in this controversial tale of an undercover cop who finds himself fatally attracted to his prey, a killer of gay men in New York's leather scene. Gritty New York locations offer a realistic backdrop to this strange S/M fantasy. Pacino gets his man, only he's no longer sure of what he wants.
VHS: S19447. $19.98.
William Friedkin, USA, 1980, 106 mins.

Cuba

Sean Connery plays a disinterested mercenary who falls for the beautiful Brooke Adams during the defeat of Batista in 1959. With Jack Weston, Hector Elizondo and Chris Sarandon.
VHS: S00286. $14.95.
Richard Lester, USA, 1979, 121 mins.

Cuba Crossing

Stuart Whitman, Robert Vaughn and Raymond St. Jacques are cast in this political thriller about a plot aimed at Fidel Castro. Said to be based on a true story, the film centers on a barkeep/soldier of fortune who is drawn into an assassination for hire scheme.
VHS: S25695. $19.95.
Chuck Workman, USA, 1980, 90 mins.

The Cure
Joseph Mazzello and Brad Renfo are featured in this heartfelt story of a summer filled with a special friendship. They had a dream, but their time together ultimately becomes a treasure which offers more than they had ever hoped for.
VHS: S26465. $98.99.
Laser: LD75092. $34.98.
Peter Horton, USA, 1995, 99 mins.

Curse of the Starving Class
James Woods, Kathy Bates, Randy Quaid and Louis Gossett, Jr. star in this strange film based on Sam Shepard's acclaimed play. A farm family is in trouble and in debt. In addition, they are fully dysfunctional and seemingly good targets for villains like a shady real estate dealer, a slick bar keep and a motorcycle gang. Somehow though, their humanity and humor make it all work.
VHS: S24566. $94.99.
Laser: LD75179. $34.98.
J. Michael McClary, USA, 1994, 102 mins.

Cutter's Way
One of the most original American films of the last decade. Alex Cutter (John Heard) is the Vietnam veteran disfigured in the war. When his best friend Richard Bone (Jeff Bridges) is accused of the murder of a teenage girl, Cutter wants to set off after the real murderer with a vengeance. "A hauntingly powerful work," said New York Magazine.
VHS: S00290. $14.98.
Ivan Passer, USA, 1982, 90 mins.

Cutthroat Island
Geena Davis and Matthew Modine star in this high seas action adventure film. Morgan Adams (Davis) is a pirate who has purchased the handsome, Harvard-educated William Shaw (Modine) to be her slave. Together they try to unravel the secrets of a buried treasure. In their path stands the vicious pirate Dawg Brown (Frank Langella), who forces them into a furious race for the disputed riches of jewels and gold.
VHS: S27548. $99.98.
Renny Harlin, USA, 1995, 118 mins.

D.O.A.
Dennis Quaid is a college professor of literature who finds he has been poisoned, in this remake of the classic Edmond O'Brien film. As there is no antidote he does what he can to find out who has killed him and why. With Meg Ryan, Daniel Stern and Charlotte Rampling. Lots of action and a new use for superglue.
VHS: S07172. $89.95.
R. Morton/A. Jankel, USA, 1988, 98 mins.

Dad
Ted Danson takes a break from the business world where his mother, Olympia Dukakis, is hospitalized, and he finds his dad Jack Lemmon unable to care for himself. From Gary David Goldberg, the creator of TV's Family Ties, a sentimental family drama that goes for heart and funny bone with equal success. With Kathy Baker, Kevin Spacey and Ethan Hawke as the son Danson barely knows.
VHS: S12146. $19.95.
Gary David Goldberg, USA, 1989, 117 mins.

Daisy Miller
Cybill Shepherd is over her head in this screen version of the classic short story by Henry James about an American girl who finds love and tragedy as a tourist in Europe in the 19th century.
VHS: S04317. $14.95.
Peter Bogdanovich, USA, 1974, 92 mins.

Dandy in Aspic
Laurence Harvey plays a Russian double agent posing as a British spy for the past 18 years, who finds his request to return home denied. His life is further complicated when British intelligence assigns him to eliminate his Russian counterpart and friend. With Tom Courtenay, Mia Farrow.
VHS: S09625. $69.95.
Anthony Mann, USA, 1968, 107 mins.

A Dangerous Woman
Debra Winger stars as a mentally disabled woman who becomes attached to Gabriel Byrne. This relationship is doomed when Barbara Hershey enters the picture. A powerful drama that gives Winger plenty of opportunity to display her skills as an actress, particularly when her character violently acts out her deepest feelings.
VHS: S20935. $19.98.
Laser: LD72401. $34.98.
Stephen Gyllenhaal, USA, 1993, 93 mins.

Daniel
Timothy Hutton has the title role in this Sidney Lumet adaptation of the book by E.L. Doctorow concerning a fictionalized account of the infamous Rosenberg executions and the consequences on their children. Mandy Patinkin and Lindsay Crouse star as the parents, Amanda Plummer as Daniel's sister. With Ed Asner and Ellen Barkin.
VHS: S06129. $59.95.
Sidney Lumet, USA, 1983, 130 mins.

Dark Horse
A sensitive story about families directed by David Hemmings focuses on Allie (Ari Meyers), a troubled young woman distraught over her forced relocation after her mother's death. Sentenced to community service on a horse farm, Allie's life is rejuvenated by her friendship with a prize winning horse.
VHS: S16862. $14.98.
David Hemmings, USA, 1992, 98 mins.

Dark Secret of Harvest Home
From the novel Harvest Home by Thomas Tryon (The Other) comes this made-for-tv gothic horror story set in New England. An innocent family moves into a small village and doesn't receive the welcome they deserve. With Bette Davis, Rosanna Arquette, Norman Lloyd, Rene Auberjonois, and David Ackroyd. Originally 200 mins.
VHS: S07799. $59.95.
Leonard Penn, USA, 1978, 118 mins.

Day of the Locust
Nathaniel West's powerful novel about Hollywood in the '30's is faithfully transferred to the big screen. William Atherton is the naive artist who learns that Tinseltown has a heart of tin. With Karen Black, Burgess Meredith, Bo Hopkins, Geraldine Page, Richard A. Dysart, Jackie Earle Haley and Donald Sutherland as the unfortunate Homer.
VHS: S10824. $14.95.
Laser: LD75297. $39.98.
John Schlesinger, USA, 1975, 140 mins.

Day One
A superb television docudrama about the personalities, history, politics and dramatic momentum of how the Manhattan Project—the American project to build the first atomic bomb—ended with the dropping of two bombs on Japan. The drama concentrates on the uneasy collaboration between Gen. Leslie R. Groves (Brian Dennehy), the nuts-and-bolts military commander who orchestrated the massive project, and visionary scientist J. Robert Oppenheimer (John Sayles regular David Strathairn). With Michael Tucker, Hume Cronyn, Richard Dysart, Barnard Hughes, Hal Holbrook and David Ogden Stiers.
VHS: S20285. $89.95.
Joseph Sargent, USA, 1989, 150 mins.

Days of Heaven
An Award winner both at Cannes and in Hollywood, this story follows a trio composed of a fugitive from the Chicago slums (Richard Gere), a shy, rich Texan (Sam Shepard) and a woman (Brooke Adams) caught in a love triangle. Set against the Midwestern wheat fields at the turn of the century, this film is often cited by cinematographers as being one of the most beautifully shot films ever made. Won the Best Oscar for Cinematography.
VHS: S00313. $14.95.
Laser: LD75358. $29.98.
Terence Malick, USA, 1980, 95 mins.

Dazed and Confused
Cult director Richard Linklater (Slacker) takes a hilarious look at the last day of school—and one wild night—in the lives of a group of high school students in 1976 in their nutty return to bongs and bell bottoms, polyester and pukka shells, macrame and mood rings. Music by Aerosmith, Black Sabbath, Alice Cooper, Foghat. "The most slyly funny and dead-on portrait of American teenage life ever made" (Entertainment Weekly).
VHS: S20496. $19.98.
Laser: Letterboxed. LD72291. $34.98.
Richard Linklater, USA, 1993, 103 mins.

Dead Again
Kenneth Branagh, the celebrated director and star of Henry V, proves he can do more than just Shakespeare in his second film behind the camera. He stars as Mike Church, a cynical, American private detective whose latest missing person case is a real doozy. Emma Thompson co-stars as an amnesiac who is tormented by dreams about a murder that occurred before she was born. A stylish whodunit graced by terrific acting, a very smart script and impeccable camerawork. With Derek Jacobi, Andy Garcia, Hanna Schygulla and a very special cameo by Robin Williams.
VHS: S15675. $19.95.
Laser: LD75124. $24.98.
Kenneth Branagh, USA, 1991, 107 mins.

Dead Man Out
Ruben Blades is a dangerous prisoner. Danny Glover is a psychiatrist assigned to find out whether or not his patient is legally sane and thus able to be sentenced to death for his crimes. A compelling HBO movie about truth and consequences. Ink blots will reveal only so much.
VHS: Out of print. For rental only.
Laser: LD70005. $39.95.
Richard Pearce, USA, 1988, 87 mins.

The Dead Pool
Clint Eastwood returns as San Francisco Police Inspector Harry Callahan, for the fifth time. Some deranged person is killing celebrities whose names were listed in a macabre dead pool. When Harry's name is added to the list, he works even harder to catch the killer. With Liam Neeson, Patricia Clarkson and Evan Kim as the latest minority partner of Dirty Harry hoping to stay in one piece until the end of the film.
VHS: S08356. $19.98.
Laser: LD74694. $24.98.
Buddy Van Horn, USA, 1988, 91 mins.

Dead Presidents
A disaffected Vietnam vet turns to crime and finally hits upon a scheme that can change the demeanor of his entire life. Together with his war buddies, he plans to rob an armored car full of "Dead Presidents" (money, that is). In this tightly plotted action film the only color that matters is green.
VHS: S27603. $99.99.
Laser: LD75557. $99.95.
The Hughes Brothers, USA, 1995, 119 mins.

Deadly Obsession
A wacko living in the tunnels under a prestigious college decides to increase his standard of living through blackmail, rat poison and a large hypodermic needle. Coed Denise Adams thought her classes were murder until she met a psychopath named John Doe. Chances are that is not his real name. With Jeffrey Iorio, Martin Haber, Joe Paradise and Darnell Martin. 98
VHS: S12544. $14.98.
Jeno Hodl, USA, 1988, 93 mins.

Dear Brigitte
College professor James Stuart has a genius son who can not only work computers, but also calculate race track odds for enormous profit. But mature I.Q.'s lead to mature desires and the boy wants the woman of his dreams: Brigitte Bardot. With Glynis Johns, Fabian and Billy Mumy as the precocious son.
VHS: S06525. $19.98.
Henry Koster, USA, 1965, 100 mins.

Death Trap
Based on Ira Levin's Broadway hit about a playwright who, after a series of flops, might kill young author Christopher Reeve. A terrific mystery.
VHS: S04333. $69.95.
Sidney Lumet, USA, 1976, 116 mins.

Deer Hunter
Powerful drama that follows a group of friends from a steel town in Pennsylvania through their Vietnam experiences with fine ensemble work from Robert De Niro, Christopher Walken, John Savage, John Cazale and Meryl Streep.
VHS: S02738. $29.95.
Laser: LD70022. $44.98.
Michael Cimino, USA, 1978, 183 mins.

Deliverance
Jon Voight, Burt Reynolds, Ronny Cox and Ned Beatty spend a weekend in the wilds canoeing and trying to avoid inbred, hostile mountain folk in Georgia. Based on the novel by James Dickey, this wilderness nightmare chills to the bone. With Bill McKinney and Herbert Coward.
VHS: S00320. $19.98.
Laser: Letterboxed. LD71676. $34.98.
John Boorman, USA, 1972, 109 mins.

Deranged
When Joyce's husband leaves for a month of business in London, she starts hearing voices—and seeing things. When a masked intruder attacks her, he unleashes in her a frightened little girl tormented by her "special" relationship with Daddy, and a crazed madwoman hungry for revenge.
VHS: S06367. $14.98.
Chuck Vincent, USA, 1987, 85 mins.

The Deserter
Burt Kennedy directed this Italian-Yugoslav cavalry epic about the hostilities between government soldiers and Indians on the Mexican border. With Bekim Fehmiu, Chuck Connors, John Huston, Woody Strode and Richard Crenna.
VHS: S16892. $19.95.
Burt Kennedy, USA, 1971, 100 mins.

Desperado
Spanish heartthrob Antonio Banderas is back as a Mexican desperado in a tongue-in-cheek Western about a guitar player who returns to settle the score with just about anyone he can think of. From the director of El Mariachi. Featuring Hollywood luminaries Steve Buscemi, Cheech Marin, Quentin Tarantino and sultry newcomer Salma Hayek.
VHS: S26989. $98.99.
Laser: LD75438. $39.95.
Robert Rodriguez, USA, 1995, 103 mins.

Destiny Turns on the Radio
James LeGros, Dylan McDermott, Nancy Travis, James Belushi and Quentin Tarantino are featured in this wide-ranging tale that turns on luck. Destiny brings an ex-con, his ex-girlfriend, his superstitious partner and a casino owner together. Destiny, by the way, is a character who turns up in a Las Vegas swimming pool to gamble with all these character's lives.
VHS: S26371. $19.95.
Jack Baran, USA, 1995, 102 mins.

Detonator
Pierce Brosnan, Patrick Stewart and Ted Levine star in this action-packed thriller about a renegade Russian general. The general has threatened the West with a nuclear weapon. Only a special mission led by Brosnan can stop this plot to reignite the cold war. Based on Alistair MacLean's novel.
VHS: S22421. $19.95.
David S. Jackson, USA, 1993, 98 mins.

Dick Tracy
Chester Gould's favorite crime fighter is the subject for a color coded, big budget extravaganza directed by and starring Warren Beatty in the title role. The guy in the bright yellow hat and overcoat is supported by Glenne Headly, Charlie Korsmo and Madonna as the slinky songstress Breathless Mahoney. The forces of evil can be found under pounds of latex and include Dustin Hoffman as Mumbles, William Forsythe as Flattop and Al Pacino as a cross between Richard III and Al Capone.
VHS: S13319. $92.95.
Warren Beatty, USA, 1990, 105 mins.

Diner
Nostalgic, funny, personal memoir of a group of young men in their early 20's, hanging out at their favorite diner in Baltimore, 1959. This was the time of innocence, when sex was something to giggle about but never get, and friendship and loyalty crucial. Mickey Rourke and Daniel Stern are featured.
VHS: S00341. $19.98.
Laser: LD70203. $24.98.
Barry Levinson, USA, 1982, 110 mins.

Dirty Dancing
At a Catskill Mountain resort in 1963 a young woman discovers her hidden talents for moving to the music. Her inspiration is her instructor, the poor and streetwise Johnny Castle. Young Baby (Jennifer Grey) also learns other physical moves with her sensitive hunk, played by Patrick Swayze. A real charmer. With Cynthia Rhodes and Jerry Orbach.
VHS: S06043. $14.98.
Emile Ardolino, USA, 1987, 105 mins.

Dirty Dozen
Very tough, very funny and ultimately very violent film featuring a great all-male cast which includes Lee Marvin, Charles Bronson, John Cassavetes and Robert Ryan as convicts offered amnesty if they go on a suicide mission behind enemy lines during World War II.
VHS: S02348. $19.98.
Laser: LD70557. $39.98.
Robert Aldrich, USA, 1967, 149 mins.

Dirty Harry
Clint Eastwood introduces his most popular character, San Francisco Police Inspector Harry Callahan. He's a tough cop who gets all the dirty jobs. His primary assignment in this film is to stop a psychotic killer named Scorpio. He does. With Andy Robinson, Reni Santoni and John Vernon.
VHS: S00344. $19.98.
Laser: LD71806. $34.98.
Don Siegel, USA, 1971, 102 mins.

Disclosure
Michael Douglas and Demi Moore portray two characters engaged in a deadly battle over sex, power and money. Tom Sanders (Douglas) is married and enjoys his position. It's a comfortable position until his new boss (Moore) decides he's not giving his all. Soon accusations of sexual harassment and even more dire threats drive this thriller into ever graver danger and desperation. Based on the novel by Michael Crichton.
VHS: S24816. $19.98.
Laser: Widescreen. LD74960. $39.99.
Barry Levinson, USA, 1994, 129 mins.

Diving In
An heroic film touching on themes of personal struggle and triumph, Diving In is the story of a talented springboard diver with Olympic dreams who must battle himself to overcome a paralyzing fear of heights. Featuring hot young stars Matt Lattanzi, Matt Adler (Teen Wolf) and Kristy Swanson (Mannequin II).
VHS: S13723. $89.95.
Strathford Hamilton, USA, 1990, 92 mins.

Dog Day Afternoon
This fantastic thriller centers on a bisexual and his buddy, who rob a bank in order to get the cash for a sex change operation for the ring leader's lover. With a first-rate performance by Al Pacino.
VHS: S21858. $19.98.
Laser: LD74523. $39.98.
Sidney Lumet, USA, 1975, 124 mins.

Dog Eat Dog
Three hoodlums steal one million dollars from a bank and hide out on an island in the Adriatic in this camp classic. Stars Jayne Mansfield and Cameron Mitchell.
VHS: S16104. $29.95.
Nazarro/Zugsmith, USA/Germany/Italy, 1963, 84 min.

Dogfight
River Phoenix and Lili Taylor star in this poignant, offbeat romance set in the early 1960's. Just prior to shipping out to Vietnam, four Marine buddies try to find the ugliest women in San Francisco to win a bar bet. After Taylor catches on, Phoenix tries to take her out on a real date to apologize. With Richard Panebianco and a heavily disguised E.G. Dailey as the toothless winner of the dogfight.
VHS: S15529. $19.98.
Nancy Savoca, USA, 1991, 95 mins.

Dolores Claiborne
Kathy Bates and Jennifer Jason Leigh bring star power to this highly successful adaptation of a Stephen King bestseller. In a small New England town a woman is widely believed to have killed her husband. When her aged and mean-spirited employer has a mysterious accident, this woman must face renewed scrutiny and censure. Through it all her love for her only daughter carries her along. This suspenseful melodrama is filled with surprising insights. Letterbox format.
VHS: S26519. $98.99.
Laser: LD75098. $39.95.
Taylor Hackford, USA, 1995, 131 mins.

Dominick and Eugene
A touching story of twin brothers living in Pittsburgh. Ray Liotta is Eugene, the hard working medical student. Tom Hulce is his good natured, mentally slower and older brother Dominick. He works on a garbage truck and gets to find a lot of neat junk. The med student is afraid to leave his brother on his own and take a job in California. Fine performances from both leads. With Jamie Lee Curtis.
VHS: S09822. $19.98.
Robert M. Young, USA, 1988, 96 mins.

Double Crossed
Dennis Hopper stars in this HBO movie about the life and death of Drug Enforcement Agency operative Barry Seal. Can a man who plays both sides of the law be safe on either one? In this case the question is probably moot. With Robert Carradine, Richard Jenkins, G.W. Bailey and Adrienne Barbeau. This true-life drama was awarded two 1991 Ace Awards for best movie/mini-series and best editing in a movie/mini-series.
VHS: S16568. $79.99.
Roger Young, USA, 1991, 111 mins.

Double Edge
Faye Dunaway stars as an ambitious New York journalist given her first international assignment, reporting on the Israeli/Palestinian tensions, and the ensuing moral and ethical consequences of being involved with two men on opposite sides of the political spectrum. "A tough and provocative drama. It's suspenseful, intelligent and emotional" (William Wolf).
VHS: S17889. $19.98.
Amos Kollek, USA, 1991, 85 mins.

Down Came a Blackbird
Raul Julia's final performance is captured in this film which also stars Laura Dern and Vanessa Redgrave. Dern goes undercover at a sanctuary for political prisoners and finds herself kidnapped by military terrorists. Now Julia's character, a professor with a secret past, holds the key to her future.
VHS: S26952. $95.99.
Laser: LD75425. $34.98.
Jonathan Sanger, USA, 1995, 112 mins.

Downhill Racer
Robert Redford stars as a go-for-it member of the U.S. Ski Team, with Gene Hackman as Redford's relentless coach in Michael Ritchie's ski-action picture shot in Europe's Alps.
VHS: S05888. $19.95.
Laser: LD75298. $29.98.
Michael Ritchie, USA, 1969, 102 mins.

Dragon: The Bruce Lee Story
An appealing biography of Bruce Lee, the Hong Kong superstar whose mysterious death, at age 33, certified his legend. Jason Scott Lee plays the kung-fu star. With Lauren Holly as Lee's widow Linda.
VHS: S19527. $95.98.
Laser: LD72296. $39.98.
Laser: Widescreen. LD74836. $69.98.
Rob Cohen, USA, 1993, 119 mins.

Dream Lover
In this sensual thriller, James Spader plays Ray Reardon, an architect who has just met the woman of his dreams, Madchen Amick. Soon this dream becomes a nightmare as this woman's smiling seductive ways are revealed as the means to a horrible end. Unfortunately this is no dream, but a terrifying tale of love gone wrong.
VHS: S22888. $94.99.
Laser: LD74757. $34.95.
Nicholas Kazan, USA, 1993, 103 mins.

Dream of Kings
Anthony Quinn is a respected Greek-American, small-time gambler in Chicago who learns his 12-year-old son (Radames Pera) has a fatal disease. Contrary to his wife's (Irene Papas) constant nagging and disbelief he knows the boy will get better in Greece. From the novel by Harry Mark Petrakis. With Sam Levene, Val Avery and Inger Stevens in her last screen role before her suicide.
VHS: S08126. $59.95.
Daniel Mann, USA, 1969, 107 mins.

Dreamchild
The enchanting, critically-acclaimed story of Alice Hargreaves, the inspiration for Lewis Carroll's *Alice in Wonderland*. On a visit to New York in the 1930's, Alice, now 80 years old, has her early memories brought to life. With Coral Browne and Peter Gallagher.
VHS: S00372. $14.98.
Gavin Millar, USA, 1985, 90 mins.

Driving Miss Daisy
The Pulitzer prizewinning play of Alfred Uhry walked off with four Oscars, including Best Picture and Best Actress. The story concerns the long-term relationship between a strong-willed, elderly, Jewish Southern matron and her accommodating Black chauffeur. Jessica Tandy and Morgan Freeman star in this genteel comedy of bigotry and friendship. With Patti Lupone, Esther Rolle and Dan Aykroyd as Boolie.
VHS: S12524. $19.98.
Laser: LD70562. $24.98.
Bruce Beresford, USA, 1989, 99 mins.

Drop Squad
Eriq La Salle and Vondi Curtis Hall star in this unique thriller about a radical terrorist group. They abduct a black ad executive who sells out his race in a bid for success. Then they apply powerful and sometimes brutal persuasion to win him over to the community's cause. Produced by Spike Lee.
VHS: S24335. $19.98.
Laser: Letterboxed. LD74924. $34.98.
David Johnson, USA, 1994, 88 mins.

Drop Zone
Wesley Snipes stars in this action-packed adventure as a sky diving marshall. His quarry is Gary Busey, a gang leader for a band of techno-terrorists. The story sizzles as Snipes tries to head off this band of violent crazies so they don't succeed in hitting their next target.
VHS: S24873. $19.95.
Laser: LD75369. $44.98.
John Badham, USA, 1994, 101 mins.

Dumb and Dumber
It's a real toss up as to whose character, Jim Carrey or Jeff Daniels, is actually dumber. But it's great fun watching this battle for the last place on the evolutionary ladder. These dimwitted pals travel cross-country to return a suitcase full of cash and somehow manage to outwit everyone who tries to stop them.
VHS: S25655. $19.98.
Peter Farrelly, USA, 1994, 110 mins.

Easy Rider
Counter-culture road movie as Dennis Hopper and Peter Fonda cycle across the Southwest on their way to New Orleans, confronted by violence and bigotry. This film defined an American generation and created a mega-star of Jack Nicholson.
VHS: S01821. $19.95.
Laser: New digital master, widescreen, audio commentary with Peter Fonda and Dennis Hopper. LD75091. $59.95.
Dennis Hopper, USA, 1969, 94 mins.

Eating
Henry Jaglom uses the occasion of a birthday celebration for a discussion about sex, love, relationships, men, politics and self-expression. "A provocative tribute to women—the ideal movie for friends, of whatever sex, to share" (*San Francisco Chronicle*). With Nelly Alard, Frances Bergen, Mary Crosby and Gwen Welles.
VHS: S18437. $89.95.
Laser: LD75184. $34.98.
Henry Jaglom, USA, 1989, 110 mins.

Electra Glide in Blue
Robert Blake stars in this hard edged, well acted story of a pint-sized highway motorcycle patrolman who tries too hard to do the right thing. He finds himself at odds with his superiors, his partner and a van load of roadway hooligans. With Billy Green Bush, Mitchell Ryan, Jeannine Riley and Elisha Cook Jr. Title refers to a motorcycle.
VHS: S06058. $14.95.
James W. Guercio, USA, 1973, 106 mins.

The Electric Horseman
A $12 million thoroughbred horse is missing and Robert Redford, playing a derelict, is riding high. Jane Fonda is strangely attracted to this man on a horse, even if it's not really his mount. Valerie Perrine is also featured in this contemporary film set in Las Vegas.
VHS: S21277. $14.98.
Sydney Pollack, USA, 1979, 120 mins.

Emerald Forest
Story of an American businessman who spends 10 years searching for his son who was captured by a primitive Amazon tribe. A fascinating look at primitive but unique civilization.
VHS: S03906. $14.95.
Laser: LD74464. $39.99.
John Boorman, USA, 1985, 113 mins.

Empire Records
Young, hip and about to be unemployed, the staff at Empire Records are facing all the hilarious travails confronting today's terminally cool. From waiting for stardom as the next best grunge band to shaving, it's all here including the conundrum of virginity—should she or shouldn't she? This is what could happen if you gambled it all away. Liv Tyler stars. Music from Gin Blossoms, The Cranberries, Edwyn Collins and others.
VHS: S27191. $96.99.
Allan Moyle, USA, 1995, 91 mins.

Empty Canvas
The story of a son who breaks away from a repressed existence with his mother (Bette Davis) and pursues a model who wishes nothing more than an affair.
VHS: S04951. $59.95.
Damiano Damiani, USA, 1964, 104 mins.

End of Innocence
Dyan Cannon wrote, directed and stars in the story of a woman trying to survive dealing with her family, her friends and herself. A nervous breakdown triggers a lengthy stay in an expensive rehabilitation center where she meets a variety of supportive patients and learns to cope. With John Heard, George Coe, Lola Mason and the late Rebecca Schaeffer as Cannon at 18.
VHS: S13780. $89.95.
Dyan Cannon, USA, 1990, 102 mins.

The Endless Game
Albert Finney stars as Alec Hillsden, a British intelligence agent, who is determined to discover the truth behind the death of a former colleague, Caroline (Kristin Scott Thomas). They had been lovers once, until she was captured by the KGB, tortured, released and then murdered. George Segal plays a corrupt American agent who is ready to sell his secrets to the highest bidder. But in the world of espionage, facts don't come cheap, and Alec may have to turn traitor to get at the truth. This spy thriller, filmed entirely on location in England, Austria and Finland, was written and directed by Bryan Forbes (*King Rat, International Velvet*) from his best-selling novel.
VHS: S13523. $89.95.
Bryan Forbes, USA, 1989, 123 mins.

Enemies, A Love Story
Ron Silver plays a Holocaust survivor with a serious problem. Three women are in love with him and he is already married to two of them. Paul Mazursky directs this appealing translation of an Isaac Bashevis Singer story set in the boroughs of postwar New York. The film received two Oscar nominations, Anjelica Huston and Lena Olin both for Best Supporting Actress. With Alan King and Margaret Sophie Stein in her U.S. film debut.
VHS: S12421. $19.98.
Paul Mazursky, USA, 1989, 121 mins.

Erik the Viking
Gordon Mitchell stars in this drama of the Norse warrior and his battle-hardened men as they make it to North America and battle the elements, Indians and each other. 1972, 95 mins.
VHS: S11009. $59.95.

Escape from Sobibor
Richard Rashke's compelling book about the largest escape from a Nazi prison camp is successfully adapted by Reginald Rose in this nail-biting thriller. Stars Alan Arkin, Joanna Pacula and Rutger Hauer.
VHS: S22022. $19.98.
Laser: LD75190. $34.98.
Jack Gold, USA, 1987, 120 mins.

Everybody Wins
Nick Nolte and Debra Winger star in a complicated tale involving murder, blackmail, political corruption and the worship of a dead Civil War officer. Set in a small New England town, Nolte plays a highly principled private investigator who has trouble believing his client, who is a known prostitute and a suspected flake. With Jack Warden, Judith Ivey and Will Patton. The script is by Arthur Miller, his first since *The Misfits*.
VHS: S12422. $89.95.
Karel Reisz, USA, 1990, 97 mins.

Excalibur
A serious retelling of the King Arthur legend, visually brilliant. "The imagery is impassioned and has a hypnotic quality. The film is like Flaubert's exotic fantasies—one lush, enraptured scene after another" (Pauline Kael).
VHS: S01754. $19.98.
Laser: Letterboxed. LD71678. $39.98.
John Boorman, USA, 1981, 140 mins.

Execution of Private Slovik
Martin Sheen delivers a powerful performance in the title role of the first American soldier to be sentenced to death for desertion since the Civil War. This true-life World War II drama examines the man and his motives to flee under fire. With Ned Beatty, Mariclare Costello, Matt Clark, Charles Haid and Gary Busey. The script based on the book by William Bradford Huie is written by Richard Levinson and William Link, the creators of *Columbo*.
VHS: S14944. $79.95.
Lamont Johnson, USA, 1974, 120 mins.

Executive Action
While Oliver Stone was making cheap horror movies in Canada, other filmmakers were hard at work debunking the Warren Commission's opinion on the assassination of JFK. Burt Lancaster stars as the disgruntled intelligence agent given the green light to silence the Commander in Chief in Dallas. Robert Ryan and Will Geer play right-wing businessmen who lend their support to the plan. The script by Dalton Trumbo is based on the book by conspiracy theorists Mark Lane and Donald Freed. A low-budget and leisurely effort, but occasionally blood curdling and certainly thought provoking.
VHS: S15825. $19.98.
David Miller, USA, 1973, 91 mins.

Exposure
Peter Coyote plays an American photographer in Brazil who becomes involved in a murder. When he and his girlfriend Amanda Pays have been attacked, he takes knife-fighting lessons from a professional hitman. With Tcheky Karyo, Raul Cortez, Guila Gam and Cassia Kiss.
VHS: S16224. $19.95.
Laser: LD75192. $34.98.
Walter Salles Jr., USA/Brazil, 1991, 105 mins.

Eye of the Needle
Donald Sutherland stars as a steely Nazi assassin on assignment in England during World War II, who finds his mission is complicated by the attentions of a frustrated married woman. With Kate Nelligan and Ian Bannen. From the best-seller by Ken Follett. Tension-filled performances.
VHS: S06059. $14.95.
Richard Marquand, USA, 1981, 112 mins.

Eye on the Sparrow
Mare Winningham and Keith Carradine deliver strong performances in this inspirational true story. They play Ethel and James Lee, a blind-from-birth couple, who must fight the state bureaucracy for the right to legally adopt a child. With Conchata Ferrell, Sandy McPeak, Kaaren Lee and Bianca Rose.
VHS: S15916. $89.98.
John Korty, USA, 1987, 94 mins.

The Eyes of Amaryllis
An adventure tale adapted from Natalie Babbitt's engrossing tale about a young woman who is sent to visit her eccentric grandmother at her coastal beach home as she awaits her husband, lost at sea 30 years earlier. With Ruth Ford, Martha Byrne, and Jonathan Bolt.
VHS: S18513. $14.98.
Frederick King Keller, USA, 1982, 84 mins.

Fabulous Baker Boys
Michelle Pfeiffer, Jeff and Beau Bridges star in this Oscar-nominated film about two cocktail lounge piano players whose career has hit a sour note until they meet chain-smoking Susie Diamond, whose voice and sexy stage presence revitalize the Baker Boys' career as well as cause them to reevaluate their relationships with each other and their music.
VHS: S12004. $14.95.
Steven Kloves, USA, 1989, 116 mins.

The Falcon and the Snowman
Timothy Hutton and Sean Penn are two typical American young men who are willing to sell U.S. government secrets to the Soviets in Mexico in this intriguing account of a true life story. Based on the book by Robert Lindsay. With Lori Singer, Pat Hingle and Dorian Harewood.
VHS: Out of print. For rental only.
Laser: Widescreen. LD74814. $49.99.
John Schlesinger, USA, 1985, 131 mins.

Fallen Angels, Vol. 1
Three stylish film noirs, adapted from hard-boiled 1940s fiction and set in the Los Angeles of the Chandler era. The first volume contains works directed by actor Tom Cruise, Alfonso Cuaron and Jonathan Kaplan (*Love Field*). The films contain an "impeccable polish [that's] bold and intelligent. [The works] are blunt and powerful, like the business end of a snub-nosed pistol" (*The Wall Street Journal*). With Gary Busey, Laura Dern, Peter Gallagher, Diane Lane, Tim Matheson, Isabella Rossellini, Alan Rickman, Nancy Travis and James Woods. 90 mins.
VHS: S19902. $89.98.

Fallen Angels, Vol. 2
The second volume of the gritty, stylish noirs—each centered on tales of deception, betrayal and sexual thrall—are directed by Steven Soderbergh (*sex, lies and videotape*), Phil Joanou (*State of Grace*) and actor Tom Hanks. With Bonnie Bedelia, Gary Oldman, Joe Mantegna, Bruno Kirby and Gabrielle Anwar. 90 mins.
VHS: S19910. $89.98.

Falling Down
Michael Douglas plays the unemployed defense worker who goes on a one-man rampage in Los Angeles. "A wickedly mischievous, entertaining suspense thriller" (Vincent Canby). With Barbara Hershey, Robert Duvall and Tuesday Weld.
VHS: S19206. $19.98.
Laser: LD71897. $34.98.
Joel Schumacher, USA, 1993, 113 mins.

Falling from Grace
John Mellencamp's film about a famous singer who returns to his hometown for his grandfather's 80th birthday and to his past and the woman he left behind. "A funny and touching film" (*Rolling Stone*).
VHS: S17069. $19.95.
John Cougar Mellencamp, USA, 1992, 102 mins.

Family Business
Sean Connery, Dustin Hoffman and Matthew Broderick play three generations of a family of small time New York crooks. When the first caper they pull together goes sour, hard choices must be made concerning blood ties and prison time. Based on the novel by Vincent Patrick. With Rosana DeSoto.
VHS: S12853. $14.95.
Sidney Lumet, USA, 1989, 114 mins.

Far and Away
Ron Howard's epic vision of late 19th century Irish immigrants, with Tom Cruise as an indentured servant to Nicole Kidman, an aristocratic heiress fleeing her rigid, authoritarian father. The couple turns up in Boston, and moves west to take part in the Oklahoma land rush.
VHS: S17737. $19.98.
Ron Howard, USA, 1992, 140 mins.

Fat Man and Little Boy
The story behind the making of the world's first atomic bombs. Paul Newman is cast as the general in charge of completing the project. Dwight Schultz from the A-Team is J. Robert Oppenheimer, the physicist in charge of making the project work. The title refers to the names of the bombs that were dropped on Japan. This historical drama also features John Cusack, Laura Dern and Bonnie Bedelia.
VHS: S11735. $14.95.
Laser: LD75350. $29.98.
Roland Joffe, USA, 1989, 127 mins.

Fatal Attraction (Director's Cut)
The controversial ending the public refused is restored in this widescreen format presentation with an introduction by the director, including personal insights and rehearsal footage. When Anne Archer is out of town for the weekend, husband Michael Douglas involves himself in what he thinks is a harmless affair. Partner Glenn Close misinterprets their casual sex, and reacts by infiltrating the perfect family and trying to break them apart.
VHS: S15709. $29.95.
Adrian Lyne, USA, 1987, 159 mins.

Fatal Vision
Excellent made-for-TV movie based on Joe McGuiness' account of the murder case in which a Marine was accused and convicted of the murder of his wife and daughters. Karl Malden stars as the father-in-law who pursues justice.
VHS: S06404. $69.95.
David Greene, USA, 1984, 200 mins.

Fatherland
Rutger Hauer and Miranda Richardson star in this chilling thriller, packed with action, set in a world where Hitler triumphed. Together they may uncover the secret that allowed the Third Reich to win the war and prosper in a terrible peace. Based on the bestseller by Robert Harris.
VHS: S24567. $19.98.
Christopher Menaul, USA, 1994, 106 mins.

Federal Hill
Nicholas Turturro is at the center of a young, talented cast in this powerful crime drama. Five reckless friends struggle with the hopelessness of an inner city Italian neighborhood in Providence, Rhode Island. An alluring college student, Libby Langdon, comes between two fast friends even as she leads her lover away from a life dominated by gangs. But before he can get away, there is one last scam.
VHS: S25902. $94.99.
Michael Corrente, USA, 1994, 100 mins.

A Few Good Men
Tom Cruise plays a Harvard-educated lawyer assigned to defend two Marines charged with killing another soldier. Jack Nicholson is a career officer with political ambitions whose actions precipitated the crime. With Demi Moore, Kevin Pollak and Kevin Bacon. Letterboxed.
VHS: S18764. $19.98.
Rob Reiner, USA, 1992, 137 mins.

Field of Dreams
Kevin Costner stars as a struggling Iowa farmer who builds a baseball diamond in his corn field so that the ghosts of old players will have somewhere to play ball. This powerful movie fantasy is based on the novel *Shoeless Joe* by W.P. Kinsella and is dedicated to any kid who ever tossed a ball around with his dad. With Amy Madigan, James Earl Jones, Ray Liotta and Burt Lancaster.
VHS: Out of print. For rental only.
Laser: LD70030. $34.98.
Phil Alden Robinson, USA, 1989, 106 mins.

The Fifth Monkey
On a journey to sell four mischievous chimps, a simple peasant (played by Ben Kingsley) shares laughter, danger and heartbreak with the animals…eventually realizing that their friendship is worth more than money. Set in the lush Brazilian tropics, *The Fifth Monkey* is an inspiring and heart-warming tale, brimming with adventure. Great family entertainment.
VHS: S13829. $89.95.
Eric Rochant, USA, 1990, 93 mins.

Finish Line
James Brolin and his son Josh star in this drama about a track coach whose obsession with winning drives his son to take steroids.
VHS: S09876. $79.95.
John Nicolella, USA, 1988, 96 mins.

Fires Within
From the director of *My Brilliant Career* comes a smoldering tale of one man's fight to regain the love of his family and his personal honor. Jimmy Smits stars as Nestor, a Cuban political prisoner who returns after eight years in Castro's prison system to find his wife is now in love with another man. Greta Scacchi and Vincent D'Onofrio complete the triangle of passion that explodes on the streets of Miami in Little Havana. The hot Latin soundtrack is supplied by the Oscar winning Maurice Jarre. 99
VHS: S15047. $89.95.
Gillian Armstrong, USA, 1991, 90 mins.

The Firm
Sydney Pollack's adaptation of John Grisham's best seller stars Tom Cruise as a Harvard-educated tax specialist who joins an impeccable Memphis law firm only to discover it's an elaborate front for the Chicago mob.
VHS: S19512. $19.95.
Laser: Widescreen. LD75310. $39.98.
Sydney Pollack, USA, 1993, 154 mins.

First Knight
Sean Connery, Richard Gere and Julia Ormond star in this costume epic based on the legend of King Arthur. Love and chivalry set the stage for a tempestuous tale. War is nearly overpowered by the personal traumas of the fabled royal love triangle composed of King Arthur, Sir Lancelot and the Lady Guinevere. Featuring Ben Cross and the legendary Sir John Gielgud.
VHS: S26773. $19.95.
Laser: LD75114. $44.95.
Jerry Zucker, USA, 1995, 133 mins.

First to Fight
Chad Everett stars and a young Gene Hackman are featured in this gritty World War II movie. Marriage forces a soldier to reconsider his commitment to fighting. Ultimately the very heat of battle rekindles his courage.
VHS: S24729. $19.98.

First Works
This two-volume series focuses on some of today's hottest directors. They include interviews with these famous filmmakers, their first films, and clips from their blockbuster movies. Volume One contains segments from Taylor Hackford's *Teenage Father*, Spike Lee's *The Answer*, Oliver Stone's *Last Year in Vietnam* and Robert Zemeckis's *Field of Honor*. Roger Corman and Paul Mazursky are also featured. Volume Two features clips from John Carpenter's *Dark Star*, Martin Scorsese's *What's a Nice Girl Like You Doing in a Place Like This?* and *It's Just Not You, Murray*, Susan Seidelman's *And You Act Like One, Too* and John Milius's *Marcello, I'm So Bored*. Richard Donner and Ron Howard are also profiled.
First Works Volume One. 122 mins.
VHS: S26349. $39.95.
First Works Volume Two. 120 mins.
VHS: S26350. $39.95.
First Works Volumes One and Two. 242 mins.
VHS: S26351. $69.95.
Marva Nabili, USA, 1984, 116 mins.

Five Easy Pieces
A classic performance by Jack Nicholson as a classical pianist who has given up his musical career to work in the oil fields. Great supporting work by Karen Black, Susan Anspach, Billy Green Bush and Helena Kallianiotes as a complaining hitchhiker. Classic scene in which Jack finally figures out how to get a simple order of toast.
VHS: S07789. $14.95.
Laser: Widescreen. LD70981. $34.95.
Bob Rafelson, USA, 1970, 96 mins.

The Fixer
John Frankenheimer's "lower depths" adaptation of Bernard Malamud's novel about a Jew who is falsely charged with a crime in Czarist Russia. Alan Bates delivers a deeply moving performance as an individual who stands by his principles when he is detained without a trial and refuses to confess. With Dirk Bogarde, Georgia Brown, Jack Gilford, Hugh Griffith, Elizabeth Hartman and Ian Holm.
VHS: S20389. $19.98.
John Frankenheimer, USA, 1968, 130 mins.

Flashdance
Jennifer Beals stars as a welder by day and interpretive dancer by night, who lives in a huge warehouse and really wants to be a member of the Pittsburgh ballet company. Light on logic but heavy on hot numbers and popular music that started the torn sweatshirt trend of the day. With Michael Nouri, Sunny Johnson and Lilia Skala.
VHS: S01883. $19.95.
Laser: LD75195. $34.98.
Adrian Lyne, USA, 1983, 96 mins.

Flesh and Blood
Rutger Hauer stars in Paul Verhoeven's medieval tale about a mercenary soldier who kidnaps princess Jennifer Jason Leigh away from her husband in this adventure of intrigue and romance. With Tom Burlinson.
VHS: S06822. $14.98.
Paul Verhoeven, USA, 1985, 126 mins.

Flesh and Bone
Dennis Quaid and Meg Ryan star as lovers whose passion may lead to untold dangers. In their ignorance, they unknowingly share a common danger spawned by a deadly secret from the past. James Caan also stars in this romantic thriller.
VHS: S20718. $95.95.
Steven Kloves, USA, 1993, 127 mins.

Flight of the Phoenix
Story of the trials and tensions facing a group of men stranded in the Arabian desert as a result of a plane crash. With James Stewart, Richard Attenborough and Peter Finch.
VHS: S06526. $19.98.
Robert Aldrich, USA, 1966, 147 mins.

The Fool Killer
Twelve-year old runaway George is on a carefree road to adventure when he meets up with an old hobo who tells him a tale of a mythical 8-foot murderer. But George's journey takes a dangerous detour when he suspects that his new-found friend, Milo, a Civil War vet with amnesia, is the real life-wielding killer. With Anthony Perkins, Edward Albert.
VHS: S09668. $19.95.
Servando Gonzalez, USA, 1965, 100 mins.

Fools of Fortune
Set against the turbulent years of the Irish rebellion, *Fools of Fortune* is a compelling drama of one woman's struggle for survival against incredible odds. Starring Mary Elizabeth Mastrantonio, Iain Glen, and Julie Christie. "It is lush and absorbing with superb performances. One of Julie Christie's best performances" (Jeffrey Lyons).
VHS: S14258. $89.95.
Pat O'Connor, USA, 1991, 104 mins.

Forced March
Chris Sarandon plays an actor hired to play a concentration camp inmate for a contemporary film about the Holocaust. He finds his life changed by the experience in ways that surprise him. With Renee Soutendijk, Josef Sommer, Rosalind Cash and Viveca Lindfors. Filmed in Budapest.
VHS: S11725. $89.95.
Rick King, USA, 1989, 104 mins.

Foreign Affairs
A romantic comedy about two trans-Atlantic travelers—a refined, New England teacher (Joanne Woodward) and a gruff, unapologetically persistent suitor (Brian Dennehy)—whose paths repeatedly cross in London. With Stephanie Beacham, Eric Stoltz and Ian Richardson.
VHS: S18786. $89.98.
Jim O'Brien, USA, 1992, 100 mins.

Foreign Student
Robin Givens stars in this tale of obsessive love. A young French student finds himself transferred to a small Southern college in the 1950's. There he is befriended by a star quarterback, and falls in love with a young teacher (Givens). Soon their romance breaks all the rules and taboos.
VHS: S22887. $19.95.
Laser: Wide screen. LD74830. $34.98.
Eva Sereny, USA, 1994, 96 mins.

Forever Lulu
Hanna Schygulla stars as Elaine Hines, a struggling writer whose search for fame and fortune leads to a wacky misadventure of murder and mistaken identity in this offbeat comedy of errors. With Deborah Harry, Alec Baldwin.
VHS: S07318. $79.95.
Amos Kollek, USA, 1987, 104 mins.

Forget Paris
Billy Crystal and Debra Winger star in this charming romantic comedy. Surprisingly, the story gets underway with Crystal searching for his father's body. It seems the corpse was misplaced. Fortunately, this all happens in Paris and as a result it does not take long for a romantic struggle to start between an aggravated son and the airline representative who relays the bad news.
VHS: S26526. $19.95.
Laser: LD75099. $39.95.
Billy Crystal, USA, 1995, 101 mins.

Forgotten Prisoners
A look at the terrifying truth that lies behind the blood-stained walls of a Turkish prison. Ron Silver is Jordan Ford, an American expert in international law who is sent to Turkey by Amnesty International's head of research (Robert Daltrey) to investigate the horrifying stories of brutality in their prisons. What he discovers is that shocking and inhuman torture is routinely practiced on the innocent in the dark, secret underworld of Turkish "justice." USA, 1990, 92 mins.
VHS: S14161. $79.98.
Robert Greenwald, USA, 1990, 92 mins.

Formula
Police detective George C. Scott investigates the murder of an old friend which leads him to billionaire oil magnate Marlon Brando and a secret Nazi formula for synthetic fuel.
VHS: S16444. $19.98.
John G. Avildsen, USA, 1980, 117 mins.

Forrest Gump
Tom Hanks stars as the endearing, naive hero of this unlikely historical film that was nominated for 14 Oscars and won the Academy Awards for Best Picture, Best Actor and Best Director. Through the magic of trick photography, Gump encounters several important figures and plays a hitherto unknown role in the unfolding of current events. Gary Sinise and Sally Field also star.
VHS: S24309. $22.95.
Laser: Widescreen, THX. LD75300. $49.98.
Robert Zemeckis, USA, 1994, 142 mins.

Fort Apache, the Bronx
This tough-talking street melodrama takes a disturbing look at New York's South Bronx at its down and dirty worst. The fine cast includes Paul Newman, Ken Wahl, Ed Asner, Pam Grier and Danny Aiello. It all adds up to an exciting urban nightmare story.
VHS: S07722. $19.98.
Daniel Petrie, USA, 1981, 123 mins.

Four for Texas
Rat Pack members Frank Sinatra and Dean Martin enjoy playing rival con-men competing for control of a profitable river-boat gambling palace anchored in 1870 Galveston. With Anita Ekberg, Ursula Andress, Charles Bronson and a special appearance by the Three Stooges.
VHS: S16290. $19.98.
Robert Aldrich, USA, 1963, 124 mins.

The Fourth Wise Man
Martin Sheen, Alan Arkin and Eileen Brennan star in this drama about one man's search for the Messiah. With Lance Kerwin and Harold Gould.
VHS: S17911. $19.98.
Michael Rhodes, USA, 1979, 72 mins.

Frances
Jessica Lange received an Oscar nomination for her portrayal of Frances Farmer, the intelligent Hollywood actress who was involuntarily committed to a mental institution.
VHS: S04335. $19.95.
Graeme Clifford, USA, 1982, 113 mins.

Frankie and Johnny
Al Pacino and Michelle Pfeiffer star in the comic film adaptation of the 1987 hit stage play *Frankie and Johnny in the Clair de Lune*. Author Terrence McNally opens up his play to include a vast array of supporting characters, but centers on a very persistent short order cook and a world-weary waitress who has heard it all before. With Hector Elizondo, Kate Nelligan, Nathan Lane and Jane Morris.
VHS: S15952. $92.95.
Laser: Widescreen. LD75351. $29.98.
Garry Marshall, USA, 1991, 117 mins.

Frankie Starlight
Matt Dillon, Gabriel Byrne and Anne Parillaud star in this magical story of a young boy growing up with his beautiful mother (Parillaud) and the two men who love her. As a result, he finds himself pulled between their desires. Travelling from Ireland to Texas and back again, this film has a beautiful, sweeping quality that resolves toward a warm and humorous conclusion.
VHS: S27599. $99.99.
Laser: LD75552. $39.99.
Michael Lindsay-Hogg, USA/Ireland, 1995, 100 mins.

French Connection
William Friedkin's edge-of-the-seat thriller about two hard-nosed New York detectives who stumble into an international narcotics smuggling ring. Contains probably the most exciting car chase ever filmed. With an exceptional performance by the always good Gene Hackman, as well as Roy Scheider and Fernando Rey.
VHS: S21861. $14.98.
Laser: LD75484. $39.98.
William Friedkin, USA, 1971, 102 mins.

French Connection 2
New York detective Popeye Doyle goes to Marseilles to crack the heroin ring headed by Frog One. Gene Hackman delivers a first-rate performance. With Fernando Rey and Bernard Fresson.
VHS: S21862. $19.98.
John Frankenheimer, USA, 1975, 118 mins.

French Kiss
Kevin Kline and Meg Ryan star in this light, frothy romantic comedy set in Paris. Ryan is Kate, a woman determined to win back her fiance, who has fallen for someone else. She flies to Paris to find him and instead meets a cunning French con man, Kevin Kline. There is, it seems, a unique magic specific to a genuine French kiss.
VHS: S26388. $19.95.
Laser: LD75079. $39.98.
Lawrence Kasdan, USA, 1995, 111 mins.

French Postcards
Calm down. This feature film chronicles the mostly comical adventures of a small group of American exchange students learning about life and love in Paris. The expatriates for one school year include Blanche Baker, Miles Chapin, David Arshall Grant and Debra Winger. They encounter foreigners like Marie-France Pisier, Mandy Patinkin, Valerie Quennessen and Jean Rochefort. From the writers of *American Graffiti*.
VHS: S10813. $59.95.
Willard Huyck, USA, 1979, 95 mins.

Fresh Horses
Adapted from the Broadway play by Larry Ketron, a rough and tumble romance between a college student in Cincinnati and a young, rural Kentucky woman who is already married to a yahoo who collects guns. With Andrew McCarthy, Molly Ringwald, Ben Stiller, Patti D'Arbanville and author Ketron as an unruly party goer. The title refers to finding new women to replace the ones that don't work out.
VHS: S09141. $89.95.
David Anspaugh, USA, 1988, 105 mins.

Fried Green Tomatoes
A fresh, sentimental adaptation of comedienne Fannie Flagg's novel, which juxtaposes two distinct narratives. The first is a contemporary world about the relationship of an abused, self-loathing woman (Kathy Bates) and a fiercely independent, sharp octogenarian (Jessica Tandy). Tandy interweaves stories of her friendship with a young woman in the pre-World War II South, with intense, heartfelt performances from Mary Stuart Masterson and Mary-Louise Parker.
VHS: S17015. $19.98.
Laser: LD71538. $39.98.
Jon Avnet, USA, 1991, 130 mins.

The Frisco Kid
Gene Wilder is an inexperienced Polish rabbi traveling West in the America of the 1850's to join a waiting congregation in San Francisco. Harrison Ford is the reluctant gunslinger who assists the calamity-prone teacher from the Old Country adjust and survive in the New World.
VHS: S06138. $14.95.
Robert Aldrich, USA, 1979, 119 mins.

From Here to Eternity
Enjoy the steamy remake of this classic love story. Into the cold, controlled, unyielding world of military life comes a story of forbidden sex, unbridled passion and sudden violence. A riveting romance set against the backdrop of World War II. With an all-star cast featuring Natalie Wood, William Devane, Kim Basinger and Steve Railsback.
VHS: S13722. $89.95.
Buzz Kulik, USA, 1979, 110 mins.

From the Hip
Judd Nelson stars as Robin "Stormy" Weathers, a very ambitious young lawyer, in this dramatic comedy that asks him to re-think his yuppie existence. Through scheming and bending the law on his first media attracting case, he is hired to get a possible murderer off the hook. With John Hurt and Elizabeth Perkins.
VHS: S04387. $19.98.
Bob Clark, USA, 1987, 112 mins.

The Fugitive
Harrison Ford stars in this action adventure film about a doctor wrongly accused of a terrible crime. His adversary, played by Tommy Lee Jones, must track this man through a series of incredible settings to uncover the truth behind The Fugitive.
VHS: S20604. $19.98.
Laser: Widescreen. LD72369. $39.98.
Andrew Davis, USA, 1993, 131 mins.

Fugitive Kind
Based on Tennessee Williams' play "Orpheus Descending," Marlon Brando stars as Val Xavier, a drifter from New Orleans whose arrival in Two Rivers, Mississippi, leads to all sorts of commotion. Anna Magnani and Joanne Woodward are just two of the women who enjoy his company.
VHS: S03500. $19.95.
Sidney Lumet, USA, 1959, 119 mins.

Gaby—A True Story
The courageous story of Gabriella Brimmer, a poet and author who overcomes great odds to insure her full rights as a creative human being. Rachel Levin is Gaby. Liv Ullmann is her mother and Norma Aleandro, an Oscar winner for *Official Story*, is her Mexican nanny. A moving tale of love and determination and cerebral palsy.
VHS: S07132. $79.95.
Luis Mandoki, USA, 1987, 94 mins.

Gallant Hours
James Cagney stars as Admiral William F. "Bull" Halsey. Robert Montgomery, who served under Halsey in the Pacific during World War II, directed this impressive war film without showing any scenes of combat. This semi-documentary approach concentrates on the command decisions of Halsey and his Japanese adversary Admiral Hamamoto during a five-week period in late 1942.
VHS: S16438. $19.98.
Robert Montgomery, USA, 1960, 116 mins.

The Gambler
James Caan is a college professor with a compulsive bad habit that is mentioned in the title. He not only puts his money on the line but ultimately his life, his future and his family and friends. The script is by James Toback. With Lauren Hutton, Paul Sorvino, Burt Young and Morris Carnovsky.
VHS: S06140. $19.95.
Karel Reisz, USA, 1974, 114 mins.

Garbo Talks
While Gilbert Rolfe drudges away in an accountant's cubicle, his eccentric mother Estelle joins picket lines on behalf of good causes. But Gilbert rises to the challenge of his life when he learns his mother is dying and wants to meet her idol, Greta Garbo.
VHS: S15250. $19.98.
Sidney Lumet, USA, 1985, 104 mins.

Gas Food Lodging
Allison Anders' depiction of the difficult, complex relationship between a single mother and her two daughters has some graceful, liquid camera work and an excellent performance by Ione Skye as a distracted, promiscuous vixen. Set in a ragged New Mexico town, Anders maps out some tangled relationships while fully exploring post-adolescent and adult sexuality. Adapted from the novel by Richard Peck. Cinematography by Dean Lent. With Brooke Adams, Fairuza Balk and James Brolin.
VHS: S18346. $19.95.
Laser: LD71864. $34.95.
Allison Anders, USA, 1992, 94 mins.

The Gene Krupa Story
Sal Mineo plays the great jazz drummer whose life and career were sidetracked by drugs and fast living. Krupa provides the drum solos himself. Special appearances by song stylist Anita O'Day and musician-band leader Red Nichols. With James Darren and Susan Oliver. B&W.
VHS: S03942. $19.95.
Laser: LD74897. $34.95.
Don Weis, USA, 1960, 101 mins.

George Washington
This three-tape set is based on James Thomas Flexner's biography. All of Washington's dramatic life is seen, from his early manhood through his political career as the father of our nation and on to his retirement at Mount Vernon. Featuring Barry Bostwick and Patty Duke Astin. USA, 1984, 398 mins.
VHS: S20639. $129.98.

George Washington: The Forging of a Nation
In this sequel to *George Washington*, Barry Bostwick and Patty Duke Astin reprise their roles as Mr. and Mrs. George Washington. Washington's career was based on political acumen and charisma. In this film the story of this historic figure continues. 1986, 190 mins.
VHS: S20640. $29.98.

Get Shorty
John Travolta won a Golden Globe for starring in this superbly cast, dark comedy. Gene Hackman, Rene Russo and Danny De Vito round out the crew of Hollywood creatures who surround a Las Vegas hitman. Though this guy is only out to collect on a loan, he fits right in and becomes Hollywood's hottest producer. Even his black gangster clothes mesh perfectly with the L.A. scene.
VHS: S27762. $103.99.
Laser: LD75580. $39.98.
Barry Sonnenfeld, USA, 1995, 105 mins.

The Getaway
Together in life, Kim Basinger and Alec Baldwin now bring the emotional intensity and sexual heat of their union to this exciting thriller. It involves a dangerous deal, a double cross and the ultimate set-up. James Woods also stars.
VHS: S21140. $19.98.
Laser: LD72418. $34.98.
Roger Donaldson, USA, 1993, 115 mins.

Ghost
A romantic-supernatural-fantasy-thriller that seems to have caught on with the movie-going public. Patrick Swayze is murdered but hangs around his old girlfriend to try to warn her that she could be next. With Whoopi Goldberg as the phony spiritualist who finally makes real contact with the other side, and Demi Moore as the lady in danger. Watch for Tony Goldwyn, Rick Aviles, and Vincent Schiavelli as a cranky subway spirit.
VHS: S13653. $14.95.
Jerry Zucker, USA, 1990, 127 mins.

Gift of Love
An adaptation of O. Henry's classic short story *The Gift of the Magi*. Set in early 1900's New York, Marie Osmond stars as a wealthy orphan dutifully resigned to an arranged marriage to "socially acceptable" James Woods. Swiss immigrant Timothy Bottoms captures her heart, however, and she must struggle to please her relatives and herself.
VHS: S13010. $24.95.
Don Chaffey, USA, 1978

Girl Friends
Claudia Weill's breakthrough feature, a bittersweet, true-to-life tale of a young woman learning to make it on her own, and coming to terms with the marriage of her best friend. With Eli Wallach, Melanie Mayron.
VHS: S03714. $19.95.
Claudia Weill, USA, 1978, 88 mins.

The Girl in the Picture
John Gordon Sinclair, the star of Bill Forsyth's *Gregory's Girl*, stars in this light love story about a young photographer forced to try the singles' scene following his break-up with his girlfriend (Irina Brook).
VHS: S02670. $79.98.
Cary Parker, USA, 1985, 90 mins.

The Glory Boys
Rod Steiger and Anthony Perkins star in this thriller about contemporary terrorism. Steiger is an Israeli scientist who is the target of a fanatical group. Perkins is the broken down agent assigned to help him. Together they must fight the assassins known as The Glory Boys.
VHS: S24780. $19.98.
Michael Ferguson, USA, 1984, 78 mins.

Go Tell the Spartans
Burt Lancaster stars as a worried major in charge of a small outpost in Vietnam back when we were there in just an advisory capacity. One of the earliest films about our involvement in Southeast Asia. With Craig Wasson, Marc Singer, Evan Kim, David Clennon, Dolph Sweet and Jonathan Goldsmith. Based on Daniel Ford's novel *Incident at Muc Wa*.
VHS: S00507. $19.98.
Ted Post, USA, 1977, 114 mins.

The Golden Child
In many ways this is Murphy's remake of Chaplin's *The Kid*, except that instead of rescuing a child from the authorities he must rescue a child from the powers of hell. A detective/kung-fu comedy reviled by some as a throw away. However, it's full of action and humor and features an excellent villain in Charles Dance. Murphy's interracial romance in the picture is not exploitative but is shown as perfectly natural.
VHS: S21394. $14.95.
Michael Ritchie, USA, 1986, 96 mins.

Good Morning Vietnam
Robin Williams won an Oscar nomination for Best Actor for the role of the wacky, motor-mouth, military disk jockey Adrian Cronauer. It's 1965 in Saigon and the Armed Forces Radio waves are getting a new sound. With Bruno Kirby and Forest Whitaker. The flip side of war and peace.
VHS: S07165. $29.95.
Laser: LD71011. $39.98.
Barry Levinson, USA, 1987, 121 mins.

Good Mother
Diane Keaton is the title character in this involving story of a divorced woman taken to court in a child custody battle. It seems that her sleep-over boyfriend (Liam Neeson) was a little too free in providing sexual information to her young daughter. With Jason Robards as the stuffy lawyer and Ralph Bellamy and Teresa Wright as the grandparents. Based on the novel by Sue Miller.
VHS: S09925. $89.95.
Leonard Nimoy, USA, 1988, 104 mins.

Goodbye Columbus
Richard Benjamin and Ali MacGraw, in their first starring roles, deal with growing up in an affluent Jewish suburban environment. Based on a novella by Phillip Roth. Benjamin is a discontented Bronx librarian romancing a college girl from suburbia. Sexual politics, spiritual values and material success will be discussed.
VHS: S02852. $19.95.
Larry Peerce, USA, 1969, 105 mins.

Goodbye Girl
Richard Dreyfuss won an Oscar for his role in this Neil Simon comedy about an egotistical looking-for-work actor and the opinionated divorcee with whom he shares an apartment. Marsha Mason is his unwilling roommate. Quinn Cummings is the child who is wise beyond her years. Funny and tender and set in New York City. With Paul Benedict and Barbara Rhoades.
VHS: S08296. $19.98.
Laser: LD70144. $34.98.
Herbert Ross, USA, 1977, 110 mins.

Goonies
When a band of misfit youngsters find a 17th century pirate map, they begin an adventure in a fabulous subterranean world filled with caverns, crooks, skeletons and booby-traps.
VHS: S04390. $14.95.
Laser: LD71142. $34.98.
Richard Donner, USA, 1986, 114 mins.

Gorillas in the Mist
Based on the true story of anthropologist Dian Fossey (Sigourney Weaver), who travels to the African mountains to study gorillas. As this paradise which she describes as "being as close to God as you can get," her interest in gorillas turns into a passion and finally into obsession; trying to save her animals from extinction, she turns to justice and finally revenge.
VHS: S10112. $19.95.
Laser: LD70035. $39.98.
Michael Apted, USA, 1988, 129 mins.

Grand Canyon
Lawrence Kasdan looks at the problems of living in Los Angeles in the '90s and offers a variety of possible alternatives to urban angst. Among them, an uplifting trip to the Grand Canyon. The all-star cast includes Danny Glover, Kevin Kline, Steve Martin, Mary McDonnell, Mary-Louise Parker and Alfre Woodard.
VHS: S16330. $19.98.
Lawrence Kasdan, USA, 1991, 134 mins.

Grand Prix
The famous auto-racing event is the backdrop for personal lives of four top drivers. Spectacular racing sequences are set against the soapsuds of fast cars and fast women. With James Garner, Toshiro Mifune, Yves Montand, Jessica Walter and Eva Marie Saint. Watch out for the curves.
VHS: S03630. $29.99.
Laser: LD70591. $39.97.
John Frankenheimer, USA, 1966, 161 mins.

Gray Lady Down
After a collision, an American nuclear submarine lodges in the neck of an underwater canyon. This rescue film brandishes impressive special effects, with performances from Charlton Heston as the captain, and David Carradine as the designer of an experimental diving craft.
VHS: S16300. $14.95.
David Greene, USA, 1978, 111 mins.

Great Gatsby
Robert Redford and Mia Farrow star in a script by Francis F. Coppola, adapted from the book by F. Scott Fitzgerald about a mysterious man who crashes Long Island society in the 1920's, and the long-lost love he left behind.
VHS: S02652. $14.95.
Laser: LD75384. $35.98.
Jack Clayton, USA, 1974, 144 mins.

Great Imposter
The incredible but true story of the world's greatest masquerader, Ferdinand Waldo Demara, who succeeded in a variety of guises including college professor, Trappist monk and prison warden. Starring Tony Curtis.
VHS: S02939. $59.95.
Robert Mulligan, USA, 1960, 112 mins.

Great Northfield Minnesota Raid
One of Pauline Kael's favorite films; Philip Kaufman's offbeat Western which shows the seamy underbelly of a robbery scheme as Jesse James and Cole Younger join in the heist. An anti-heroic Western featuring Cliff Robertson, Robert Duvall.
VHS: S07296. $14.98.
Philip Kaufman, USA, 1972, 91 mins.

Great Santini
Critically acclaimed sleeper, with a standout performance by Robert Duvall as a career Marine who can only show love "through discipline." Great touches of pathos and humor, with outstanding supporting acting by Blythe Danner and Lisa Jane Persky.
VHS: S07283. $19.98.
Lewis John Carlino, USA, 1979, 116 mins.

Great Waldo Pepper
Robert Redford is a World War I flying ace who barnstorms around the Midwest offering rides for hire and doing fantastic aerial stunts for the amazement of children of all ages. Then he is hired by the movies to fly against his former enemy. With Bo Svenson, Susan Sarandon, Bo Brundin and Margot Kidder.
VHS: S07796. $19.95.
George Roy Hill, USA, 1975, 107 mins.

Greedy
Michael J. Fox, Kirk Douglas and Nancy Travis star in this riotously funny comedy about the perils of inheritance. All kinds of wacky cousins crawl out in search of the millions sure to be left behind when an old uncle appears to be on the verge of passing on. The uncle, Kirk Douglas, finds that he's not a forgotten old man but the very heart of a loving and Greedy clan.
VHS: S22075. $19.98.
Laser: LD74549. $34.98.
Jonathan Lynn, USA, 1994, 113 mins.

Green Berets
Cliched wartime propaganda with Wayne as a Special Forces Colonel out to wipe out the Viet Cong. The only American film in support of the U.S. involvement in the Vietnam War.
VHS: S06977. $19.98.
Laser: Letterboxed. LD74729. $39.98.
John Wayne, USA, 1968, 141 mins.

Gremlins
Director Joe Dante provides the Grinch's version of *It's a Wonderful Life* as an unusual Christmas present multiplies and turns nasty. Filled with cinematic in-jokes and cameo appearances. A young man tries to save his town from complete destruction before his father gets home. With Zack Galligan, Phoebe Cates and Hoyt Axton.
VHS: S01833. $19.98.
Laser: Letterboxed. LD74695. $24.98.
Joe Dante, USA, 1984, 111 mins.

Grizzly
A grizzly of unbearable ferocity preys on the flesh of unsuspecting humans to satisfy his enormous hunger.
VHS: S03263. $14.95.
William Girdler, USA, 1976, 92 mins.

Grumpier Old Men
Walter Matthau and Jack Lemmon are even more prickly and funny in this comic sequel. This time they fight over another woman, Sophia Loren, and contend with unthinkable change, as their bait shop becomes a fashionable restaurant. Ann-Margret also manages to invade the fracas.
VHS: S27763. $103.99.
Laser: LD75581. $39.98.
Howard Deutch, USA, 1995, 101 mins.

A Guide for the Married Woman
Cybill Shepherd stars in this made-for-tv movie about an unsatisfied married woman looking to step out of the relationship for some change-of-pace romance. A light comedy follow up to writer Frank Tarloff's *Guide to the Married Man*. With Barbara Feldon, Eve Arden, Charles Frank, John Hillerman and George Gobel.
VHS: S10034. $59.98.
Hy Averback, USA, 1987, 96 mins.

Guilty by Suspicion
The Hollywood hysteria over the infamous House on Unamerican Activities Committee hearings in the 1950's is grippingly captured in this uncompromising drama. Robert De Niro stars as a successful director whose professional career takes a downward turn when he refuses to name names. The strong supporting cast includes Annette Bening, George Wendt, Patricia Wettig and Martin Scorsese. Sam Wanamaker, a real victim of the blacklist, appears as De Niro's legal advisor.
VHS: S15008. $19.98.
Irwin Winkler, USA, 1991, 105 mins.

Gumshoe Kid
A young man foregoes higher education at Harvard to join the family private detective business. Jeff's first big case is to keep a close watch on a mobster's fiance. Complications ensue. With Jay Underwood (*The Boy Who Could Fly*) as the intrepid Jeff and *Dynasty's* Tracy Scoggins as his first big case. Also Vince Edwards, Arlene Golonka and Pamela Springsteen.
VHS: Out of print. For rental only.
Laser: CLV. LD71723. $19.98.
Joseph Manduke, USA, 1989, 98 mins.

Gypsy
Everything is coming up roses in the big screen biography of legendary entertainer Gypsy Rose Lee. Natalie Wood stars as the child vaudeville performer who finds stardom as the classiest striptease artist on the runway. Rosalind Russell plays the ultimate show biz mom who has difficulty letting her daughters grow up. With Karl Malden, Harvey Korman and Faith Dane. Songs include "You Gotta Have a Gimmick" and "Let Me Entertain You." Music by Julie Styne. Lyrics by Stephen Sondheim. Based on the play by Arthur Laurents and the book *Gypsy: A Memoir* by Gypsy Rose Lee aka Rose Louise Hovick.
VHS: S15840. $19.98.
Mervyn Le Roy, USA, 1962, 149 mins.

The Habitation of Dragons
Academy Award winner Horton Foote wrote the screenplay for this surprising drama featuring Brad Davis. Two lawyer brothers have always found themselves engaged in rivalry. Now, just as one's success seems assured, everything that they always relied upon is about to come undone.
VHS: S24732. $49.98.
Michael Lindsay-Hogg, USA, 1992, 94 mins.

Hanoi Hilton
Michael Moriarty and Paul LeMat as American POW's during Vietnam in a brutal, compelling re-telling of the horrors of prison camps.
VHS: S05971. $14.95.
Laser: Hi-fi, digital. LD74730. $39.98.
Lionel Chetwynd, USA, 1987, 130 mins.

Happy New Year
Peter Falk has a field day in this English language remake of the Claude Lelouch film about a meticulous jewel thief who tries to court a beautiful woman while pulling off the biggest caper of his career. Virtually identical to the earlier 1973 film. Lelouch has a cameo as a train passenger. With Wendy Hughes and Charles Durning.
VHS: S04976. $79.95.
John G. Avildsen, USA, 1987, 86 mins.

Hard Choices
Highly original film that was overlooked upon its release and features an amazing performance by Margaret Klenck as a social worker who gets too close to a juvenile imprisoned and sentenced as an adult. With an appearance by director John Sayles.
VHS: S01860. $19.98.
Rick King, USA, 1984, 90 mins.

Hardware
Dylan McDermott, Stacy Travis, John Lynch and Iggy Pop star in this post-apocalyptic adventure. McDermott lives from trash cans. That's also where he finds his android girlfriend, Travis. She is part of a program that would control population growth by destroying prospective mates.
VHS: S22911. $19.98.
Richard Stanley, USA, 1990, 94 mins.

Harry and the Hendersons
A comic fantasy starring John Lithgow as George Henderson, an easy-going father whose life is suddenly turned upside down when his car hits a real-life Bigfoot at the tail end of a camping trip. Thinking the beast is dead, they take it home, but soon find out the lovable creature is alive and well, and life at the Hendersons becomes a whirlwind of bizarre adventures. With Don Ameche.
VHS: S05248. $89.95.
William Dear, USA, 1987, 111 mins.

Harry and Tonto
Paul Mazursky's poignant drama about an elderly man's cross-country odyssey, featuring remarkable performances by Art Carney and Ellen Burstyn.
VHS: S04337. $19.98.
Paul Mazursky, USA, 1974, 115 mins.

Havana
The capital city of Cuba is the setting for romance and revolution as well as a loose remake of *Casablanca*. Before you can say "Here's looking at you, muchacho", gambler Robert Redford will have to decide whether to get on that boat with Lena Olin or see if her freedom-fighting husband Raul Julia would rather make the trip. With Alan Arkin, Thomas Milian, Tony Plana and an enticing musical score by Dave Grusin.
VHS: S13769. $19.98.
Sydney Pollack, USA, 1990, 145 mins.

Heart Beat
John Heard is Jack Kerouac, the acclaimed author and icon of the Beat Generation, in this narrative film based on Carolyn Cassady's memoirs. Sissy Spacek and Nick Nolte star as Kerouac's California companions Carolyn and Neal Cassady. Together they took chances and struck out toward new frontiers. With Steve Allen and John Larroquette.
VHS: S25871. $19.98.
John Byrum, USA, 1980, 105 mins.

The Heart Is a Lonely Hunter
Alan Arkin stars as John Singer, bringing resourcefulness and resonance to the film adaptation of Carson McCullers' well-received first novel. When his lone friend is institutionalized, Singer's enclosed world explodes in anger and newly-awakened confidence as he comes into contact with a town drunk (Stacy Keach), a young, black activist (Cicely Tyson) and Mick (Sondra Locke), a sympathetic young girl.
VHS: S02533. $19.98.
Robert Ellis Miller, USA, 1968, 124 mins.

Heart of Dixie
Ally Sheedy learns about racism, sexism and rock and roll when she attends college in the Deep South in the late 1950's. Her classmates include the beatnik Phoebe Cates and the Kim Novak of the campus, Virginia Madsen. Treat Williams, as a journalist stringer for the AP, arrives on the scene to enlighten and encourage the headstrong heroine.
VHS: S11532. $79.98.
Martin Davidson, USA, 1989, 96 mins.

Heartburn
Dismissed by many critics, Mike Nichols adapted Nora Ephron's meditation on her brief marriage to Watergate journalist Carl Bernstein by linking the film to questions of love, family and breakdown. Meryl Streep is excellent as Rachel, a magazine journalist whose marriage to Jack Nicholson, a powerful political columnist, is shattered upon revelations of his affair with a diplomat's wife. Ephron adapted her own screenplay. Cast includes Jeff Daniels, Stockard Channing, Maureen Stapleton and John Wood.
VHS: S02628. $19.95.
Mike Nichols, USA, 1986, 109 mins.

Hearts of Fire
From the director of *Jagged Edge* and *Return of the Jedi* comes this rock and roll drama about a rising young singer and her involvement with success and famous musicians. Fiona is the eager young performer who shares a bed with Englishman Rupert Everett and American Bob Dylan. The last film of Richard Marquand.
VHS: S07705. $14.95.
Richard Marquand, USA, 1988, 90 mins.

Heat
Al Pacino and Robert DeNiro are on opposite sides of the law in this searing, blood-spattered film from the originator of *Miami Vice*. Even as Pacino finds his personal life crumbling, he can't control his obsession with an ingenious criminal (DeNiro). Both men find love, only to question its value in the world of guns and honor they both inhabit. Despite these concerns, the film is tense and loaded with action. With Val Kilmer, Tom Sizemore, Diane Venora, Amy Brenneman, Natalie Portman and Jon Voight.
VHS: S27708. $99.99.
Laser: LD75567. $39.98.
Michael Mann, USA, 1995, 172 mins.

Heaven and Earth
Tommy Lee Jones and Joan Chen portray a man and a woman who come together despite their divided loyalties during the Vietnam War. He is a vet who can never forget, while she has seen her country ravaged by a brutal conflict whose effects are still painfully evident today.
VHS: S21086. $19.98.
Laser: LD72413. $39.98.
Oliver Stone, USA, 1993, 142 mins.

Heaven Is a Playground
The game of basketball is showcased in this independent film treatment of the non-fiction book by sportswriter Rick Telander. D.B. Sweeney stars as a white, small town lawyer who moves to Chicago to spend the summer playing basketball with inner city youth. Local talent scout Michael Warren lets him stick around on the condition he help coach a beginning team and handle the legal affairs of a young rising star. With Victor Love, Richard Jordan, Janet Julian and L.A. Clipper star Bo Kimble.
VHS: S15926. $19.95.
Randall Fried, USA, 1991, 111 mins.

The Heidi Chronicles
Jamie Lee Curtis and Tom Hulce star in this screen adaptation of the highly regarded stage play. Penned by Wendy Wasserstein, this play won both the Pulitzer Prize and a Tony Award. The film is the story of Heidi Holland (Curtis), a woman determined to experience life and all its possibilities. Over the course of three decades she fights for the political goals she believes in and manages to develop a successful career. It's a success story with real feminist ideals.
VHS: S27262. $99.98.
Laser: LD75561. $39.95.
Paul Bogart, USA, 1995

Hell in the Pacific
Two men, one American, one Japanese, confront one another on a deserted Pacific island in this feature directed tautly by John Boorman, notable for powerful performances from two top notch actors: Toshiro Mifune and Lee Marvin.
VHS: S12165. $19.98.
John Boorman, USA, 1968, 103 mins.

Henry & June
The story of controversial novelist Henry Miller as seen through the eyes of his lover Anais Nin. Director Philip Kaufman (*The Unbearable Lightness of Being*) once again explores the relationship between the erotic and the literate. With Fred Ward, Maria de Medeiros, and Uma Thurman as June Miller. Richard E. Grant and Kevin Spacey are also to be found hanging around Paris. The first film to receive the NC-17 rating due to its adult nature.
VHS: S13578. $19.95.
Philip Kaufman, USA, 1990, 136 mins.

A Hero Ain't Nothin' but a Sandwich
It takes a real hero to keep a family together. A timely and moving story of an intelligent but alienated ghetto youth's battle with drugs. Based on the popular children's book by Alice Childress. Starring Cicely Tyson, Paul Winfield and impressive young Larry B. Scott.
VHS: S14280. $19.95.
Laser: LD75126. $24.98.
Ralph Nelson, USA, 1978, 107 mins.

Hester Street
Set on the Lower East Side of New York in 1896, Gitl and her son reunite with husband Jake, who had previously immigrated from Russia. Jake has completely embraced America by shedding his ethnic heritage, and is embarrassed when Gitl clings to her old country ways. But in this charming and humorous portrait of the Jewish immigrant experience, Gitl finds a way to become victor instead of victim. Carol Kane was nominated for an Oscar for her portrayal of Gitl. With Stephen Keats.
VHS: S00564. $29.95.
Joan Micklin Silver, USA, 1974, 89 mins.

Hiding Place
Julie Harris stars in this true-life account of a heroic family's imprisonment in a World War II concentration camp for sheltering Jews in Nazi-occupied Holland. Produced by Billy Graham's Evangelistic Foundation.
VHS: S09665. $19.95.
James F. Collier, USA, 1975, 145 mins.

The Hindenburg
George C. Scott and Anne Bancroft star in this drama set during the final flight of the *Hindenberg*. In this version, intrigues related to the rise of the Nazis lead to sabotage, resulting in the famous explosive disaster. The visual and sound effects were awarded Oscars.
VHS: S21767. $19.98.
Robert Wise, USA, 1975, 125 mins.

Hiroshima
This historical feature recreates the situations and decision-making moments that led up to the devastating nuclear blast over Hiroshima. Between Churchill, Truman and Hirohito, a drama of unimaginable proportions unfolds. This film tells the story behind the headlines, where ordinary people find themselves involved in events, the implications of which remain difficult to fathom.
VHS: S26460. $89.98.
Laser: LD75373. $49.98.
R. Spottiswode/K. Kurahara, USA, 1995, 165 mins.

Hobo's Christmas
Barnard Hughes, William Hickey and Gerald McRaney star in this emotional drama of a father's homecoming. After leaving his family to live a hobo's life for 25 years, Chance Grosvenor decides it's time to come home. His best traveling companion, Cincinnati Harold, warns him that his son and the past are memories best left behind. But Chance has to find out for himself.
VHS: S11238. $79.95.
Will MacKenzie, USA, 1987, 94 mins.

Hoffa
Director Danny DeVito, writer David Mamet and actor Jack Nicholson collaborated on this biography of James R. Hoffa. Mamet's screenplay is constructed in a series of flashbacks, built around the mysterious events of Hoffa's 1975 disappearance. The movie is an account of the labor movement, the unholy unions between Hoffa and the Mafia, and his epic battles with former Attorney General Robert Kennedy. The film is held together by Jack Nicholson's brave, gripping performance. With DeVito in a composite role of Hoffa's most loyal lieutenant, Armand Assante and Kevin Anderson.
VHS: S18601. $19.98.
Laser: LD72432. $49.98.
Danny DeVito, USA, 1992, 140 mins.

Hollow Venus: Diary of a Go-Go Dancer
This is the story of Coco Dupree, a young New York performance artist who dances topless in a bar called Paradise. There she meets a mob boss called God, a thug named Richie, and a kept woman known as Desiree. Heather Woodbury stars in this semi-autobiographical glimpse of a netherworld where porn and art mix.
VHS: S22505. $39.95.
Larry Fessenden, USA, 1989, 58 mins.

Home for Christmas
The magic of Christmas is rediscovered by a well-to-do family when an elderly homeless man named Elmer (Mickey Rooney) enters their lives.
VHS: S15089. $79.95.
Peter McCubbin, USA, 1991, 96 mins.

Home for the Holidays
Holly Hunter, Robert Downey, Jr., Dylan McDermott, Anne Bancroft, Claire Danes, Charles Durning, Geraldine Chaplin and Steve Guttenberg are the all-star cast of this family comedy. Hunter was laid off from work, made a pass at her boss, and her daughter's planning to lose her virginity. Just when it seems things can't get any worse for this Chicago art restoration expert, she heads to her parents' house for Thanksgiving. Her brother's gay, her sister and her husband are uptight, her aunt's a drunk and her parents are crazy, but at least it's home.
VHS: S27515. $96.99.
Laser: LD75523. $34.95.
Jodie Foster, USA, 1995, 103 mins.

Homecoming
Made-for-television movie based on characters by Earl Hammer that became the series The Waltons. Starring Patricia Neal, Edgar Bergen and Richard Thomas, with a special appearance by Cleavon Little.
VHS: S01922. $59.98.
Fielder Cook, USA, 1971, 98 mins.

Homework
At the end of his senior year of high school, Tommy finds his education in the form of Diana, a mature woman. His friend Ralph learns the lessons of life from Ms. Jackson. Without knowing what will come of their relationships with these older women, the boys form a rock band as a means to unlimited sexual opportunity. Stars Joan Collins, Michael Morgan, Wings Hauser, Carrie Snodgrass and Betty Thomas.
VHS: S16075. $19.95.
James Beshears, USA, 1982, 90 mins.

Homicide
David Mamet's third feature stars Joe Mantegna as a hardened Baltimore detective whose investigation of a cop-killing drug runner is accidentally interrupted by an anti-Semitic slaying. Confronted by his Jewish heritage, Mantegna must choose between his oath to the police force and his sudden affiliation with the Jewish Mafia. A powerful film which links racism toward Blacks and the still evident hatred of Jews.
VHS: S15928. $19.95.
David Mamet, USA, 1991, 102 mins.

Honor Among Thieves
A tense thriller featuring Charles Bronson as a mercenary locked in a French bank over a weekend with Alain Delon, a doctor. While Bronson's in the bank to rob it, Delon is there to replace misappropriated securities. Both are in constant conflict, and both are ultimately betrayed. In English.
VHS: S04785. $59.95.
Jean Herman, France/USA, 1983, 93 mins.

Hoosiers
Gene Hackman stars as an aging basketball coach who finds a job molding a competitive high school team in a very small town in Indiana in the 1950's. He may be gruff and living under the shadow of a past mistake, but he knows how to produce a winning team. With Barbara Hershey, Sheb Wooley and Dennis Hopper as the town drunk.
VHS: S04526. $14.98.
Laser: LD71046. $19.98.
David Anspaugh, USA, 1986, 114 mins.

Hot Shot
Pele is the main reason to see this lets-go-for-it sports picture that Soccer Match Magazine calls "soccer's answer to The Karate Kid." The Brazilian world champion player is always amazing to watch in action. With Jim Youngs, Mario Van Peebles, David Groh and Billy Warlock.
VHS: S05308. $19.98.
Rick King, USA, 1986, 90 mins.

Hot Spot
Don Johnson drifts into a small Texas town that has two good-looking women and one frequently unattended bank. With Virginia Madsen and Jennifer Connelly as Taylor, Texas' alternatives to watching television. Based on the 1952 novel Hell Hath No Fury by Charles Williams. Steamy stuff indeed.
VHS: S13657. $89.95.
Dennis Hopper, USA, 1990, 120 mins.

House of Cards
In Michael Lessac's debut film, a widowed architect (Kathleen Turner) and her two children return to the United States following an expedition to Central America, where they studied Mayan ruins. The daughter suddenly becomes withdrawn and refuses to speak. Turner tries to discover the roots of her daughter's disorder. She argues with a prominent child psychologist (Tommy Lee Jones)—who diagnoses the girl's condition as a form of autism—over the exact nature of the illness and the correct treatment. With Park Overall, Shiloh Strong, Asha Menina and Michael Horse.
VHS: S19604. $19.98.
Laser: LD75207. $34.98.
Michael Lessac, USA, 1993, 109 mins.

House of Games
David Mamet's acclaimed first feature film, starring Lindsay Crouse as a famed psychiatrist/author whose work draws her into the dangerous but provocative world of a smooth-talking con man, and becomes entwined in a world from which there is no escape. With Joe Mantegna.
VHS: S06327. $19.99.
David Mamet, USA, 1987, 102 mins.

The House of the Spirits
Isabel Allende's magically realist, best-selling novel about an aristocratic Argentinean family is now a lavish film with Meryl Streep, Glenn Close, Jeremy Irons, Winona Ryder and Antonio Banderas. This beautiful epic follows a tempestuous family driven by the conflict between tradition and passion. Ryder is in love but her desires are not fundamental to the family's interest. Only a series of small miracles can solve this impasse.
VHS: S21498. $19.98.
Laser: Widescreen. LD75208. $34.98.
Bille August, USA, 1993, 109 mins.

House on Carroll Street
Kelly McGillis plays a curious researcher for Time Magazine who uncovers an international conspiracy to smuggle in former Nazis and give them the identities of dead Jews. Set in Greenwich Village in 1951, a thriller in the Hitchcock tradition. With Jeff Daniels as the genial FBI agent and Mandy Patinkin as the oily Senator.
VHS: S07528. $19.98.
Peter Yates, USA, 1987, 111 mins.

Household Saints
When the Santangelos, an Italian-American couple, pray for a miracle, their wish is granted, or so they originally think, in the form of a daughter they call Teresa. Tracey Ullman, Vincent D'Onofrio, Lili Taylor and Judith Malina star in this humorous fable of faith, sainthood and sausage.
VHS: S21095. $94.95.
Nancy Savoca, USA, 1993, 124 mins.

Housekeeping
Scottish director Bill Forsyth adapts the novel of Marilynne Robinson about two sisters left in the hands of various relatives after their mother's suicide. Christine Lahti shines as their eccentric aunt Sylvie. With Sara Walker and Andrea Burchill and the great scenery of the Pacific Northwest. A touching lyrical tale.
VHS: S06998. $79.95.
Bill Forsyth, USA, 1987, 117 mins.

How to Make an American Quilt
An all star cast, featuring Winona Ryder, Anne Bancroft, Ellen Burstyn, Kate Nelligan, Kate Capshaw, Samantha Mathis, Jean Simmons, Alfre Woodard and Maya Angelou, gives this romantic comedy heart and verve. A young woman (Ryder) learns about life, love and the power of choices as she hears the life stories of the women in her grandmother's quilting circle and reconsiders her own forthcoming marriage.
VHS: S27522. $99.99.
Laser: LD75524. $39.99.
Jocelyn Moorhouse, USA, 1995, 117 mins.

The Human Factor
A British double agent, Nicol Williamson, faces a dilemma: either he defects to Russia or he dies. Tom Stoppard adapted Graham Greene's acclaimed novel for this stellar cast which includes Robert Morley, Richard Attenborough, Iman, Derek Jacobi and John Gielgud.
VHS: S21165. $19.98.
Otto Preminger, USA, 1979, 115 mins.

Hunchback
Anthony Hopkins, Derek Jacobi and Sir John Gielgud star in this film adaptation of Victor Hugo's masterwork, The Hunchback of Notre Dame. The story is heartrending. An evil arch deacon seeks control over a beautiful gypsy woman. Failing to posses her, he calls Quasimodo into action, and Quasimodo is publicly humiliated. A bond emerges between the Hunchback and the gypsy that is touching and ultimately tragic.
VHS: S22761. $19.98.
Michael Tuchner, USA, 1982, 102 mins.

The Hunger
David Bowie, Catherine Deneuve and Susan Sarandon star in this stylish and moving tale of sophisticated vampires. Deneuve needs new blood in order to keep her 300-year-old lover alive. This film has an erotically charged atmosphere which includes a host of memorable scenes like the lesbian encounters between Deneuve and Sarandon. Ann Magnuson and Willem Dafoe also appear.
VHS: S26970. $19.95.
Tony Scott, USA, 1983, 100 mins.

The Hunt for Red October
Set before Glastnost, a Soviet sub commander takes a prototype out for a test drive and panics both of the super-powers. With Sean Connery as Captain Marko Ramius and Alec Baldwin as CIA analyst Jack Ryan. With Scott Glenn, Sam Neill, Peter Firth and James Earl Jones. Underwater Cat and Mouse.
VHS: S12854. $14.95.
Laser: Letterboxed. LD75311. $39.98.
John McTiernan, USA, 1990, 135 mins.

I Never Sang for My Father
Gene Hackman and Melvyn Douglas star as son and aging father in this sensitive and soul-searching drama. Adapted for the screen from the Robert Anderson play, the subject of responsibility makes for very serious viewing. With Estelle Parsons and Lovelady Powell.
VHS: S04714. $69.95.
Gilbert Cates, USA, 1970, 93 mins.

Iceman
From the director of Chant of Jimmie Blacksmith, Timothy Hutton stars in this drama about a team of researchers in the Artic who find a 40,000 year old man frozen in the ice and bring him back to life.
VHS: S00605. $19.95.
Laser: LD70040. $34.98.
Fred Schepisi, USA, 1984, 101 mins.

If I Ever See You Again
"You Light Up My Life" composer Joseph Brooks directs and stars in this story of a young composer who vows to win the heart of a woman who spurned him years ago. With Joseph Brooks, Shelly Hack and Jimmy Breslin.
VHS: S06713. $69.95.
Joseph Brooks, USA, 1978, 105 mins.

Ike
Robert Duvall is five-star general Dwight D. Eisenhower and Lee Remick is Kay Summersby, his driver. Originally a six-hour mini-series, the action follows this military legend through massive invasions and private affairs. With Dana Andrews and J.D. Cannon.
VHS: S04381. $79.95.
Laser: LD71055. $59.95.
M. Shavelson/B. Sagal, USA, 1978, 196 mins.

Imaginary Crimes
Harvey Keitel stars in this emotional family drama about a troubled relationship between a man and his daughter. When the man does not live up to the expectations of his maturing child, conflict erupts between the two. Ultimately the woman must stand up for her own dreams.
VHS: S24057. $96.99.
Laser: LD74804. $34.98.
Anthony Drazon, USA, 1994, 106 mins.

Immediate Family
James Woods and Glenn Close are a nice married couple from Seattle who want a baby to call their own. Mary Stuart Masterson is a young, unwed, teenage mother-to-be from the Midwest who wants the best for her unborn child. Jonathan Kaplan (Over the Edge) directs this sensitive and fertile drama about the fears and responsibilities of parenting. With Kevin Dillon as the biological father who makes James Woods nervous. Don't let the soap get in your eyes.
VHS: S12125. $89.95.
Jonathan Kaplan, USA, 1989, 94 mins.

Immortal Beloved
Gary Oldman, Jeroen Krabbe and Isabella Rossellini star in this drama about the secret love of composer Ludwig van Beethoven. Unashamedly lush and romantic, though the film rests on scant historic fact, the music and the passion make for a sumptuous entertainment in this grand and beautiful production. The soundtrack is directed by Sir Georg Solti.
VHS: S25540. $19.95.
Laser: LD74952. $39.95.
Bernard Rose, USA, 1994, 121 mins.

The Imported Bridegroom
Pamela Berger adapts Abraham Cahan's novella about a turn-of-the-century, widowed landlord who returns to the old country and becomes involved in the bidding war of a local scholar, with intentions of bringing him back to America to marry his daughter. With Eugene Troobnick, Avi Hoffman, Greta Cowan and Annette Miller. "An endearing film about the immigrant experience" (Boston Globe).
VHS: S17929. $39.95.
Pamela Berger, USA, 1989, 93 mins.

The Impossible Spy
A polished, made-for-cable, spy thriller which chronicles the dramatic split in the life of Eli Cohen (John Shea), an Egyptian-born Jew who built an elaborate cover as a father, husband and businessman. In fact Cohen was a brilliant Israeli agent who infiltrated the top echelon of the Syrian government and secured vital information during the 1967 Six Day War. "A portrait of spies and spying that is as chilling as it is complete" (The New York Times). With Eli Wallach, Michal Bat-Adam, Rami Danon, Sasson Gabray and Chaim Girafi.
Laser: LD71957. $39.95.
Jim Goddard, USA/Britain, 1987, 98 mins.

In a Shallow Grave
Michael Biehn has had his share of tough times in the movies. He battled Arnold Schwarzenegger in The Terminator, aliens in Aliens and Lauren Bacall in The Fan. Now he plays a disfigured WW II veteran who writes love letters to his pre-war sweetheart only to have them delivered by a murderer. With Patrick Dempsey, Michael Beach and Maureen Mueller. Filmed in Virginia. Based on the novel by James Purdy.
VHS: S08316. $19.98.
Kenneth Bowser, USA, 1988, 91 mins.

In Harm's Way
Otto Preminger directed this star-studded World War II epic of naval warfare in the Pacific. John Wayne, Kirk Douglas, Henry Fonda, Dana Andrews, Patricia Neal, Tom Tryon, Larry Hagman, George Kennedy, Carroll O'Connor, Burgess Meredith, Franchot Tone, Slim Pickens and Patrick O'Neal wear uniforms and do brave and noble deeds. War is hell but it's easier to take when it is filmed in Hawaii. B&W. 165 mins.
VHS: S07521. $29.95.
Otto Preminger, USA, 1965, 165 mins.

In the Heat of the Night
Winner of five Oscars including Best Picture, Rod Steiger stars as a red neck sheriff who grudgingly accepts help from Sidney Poitier, a big city detective. Music score by Quincy Jones.
VHS: S03621. $19.95.
Laser: LD74675. $34.98.
Norman Jewison, USA, 1967, 110 mins.

In the Line of Fire
Clint Eastwood stars as a maverick Secret Service agent haunted by his failure to protect John F. Kennedy in Dallas. John Malkovich is a CIA-trained professional assassin whose anger and resentment at American policies results in his chilling determination to kill the President. "This is easily the best American thriller since The Silence of the Lambs" (David Denby). With Rene Russo, Dylan McDermott and Gary Cole.
VHS: S20328. $19.95.
Laser: Letterboxed. LD72332. $39.95.
Wolfgang Petersen, USA, 1993, 127 mins.

Independence Day
From the director of F/X, Robert Mandel's neglected first film is an unsparing and moving profile of an isolated Southwestern town. Mandel counterpoints the drama with his two leads: Kathleen Quinlan, a talented photographer shuttered by provincial custom, and David Keith, an auto racing enthusiast who welcomes the slower lifestyle. In her first film role, Diane Wiest gives a haunting performance as a brutalized wife.
VHS: S04535. $19.98.
Robert Mandel, USA, 1983, 110 mins.

The Indian Runner
Sean Penn's directorial debut is a psychological drama about two brothers in 1968 Nebraska. Joe is a cop who settled down with wife and child; Frank, a recovering Vietnam veteran, lives his life breaking the laws his brother has vowed to uphold. With David Morse, Viggo Mortensen, Dennis Hopper, Charles Bronson and Sandy Dennis.
VHS: S16154. $14.95.
Laser: LD71417. $39.98.
Sean Penn, USA, 1991, 127 mins.

The Infiltrator
Oliver Platt stars in this gripping thriller based on a true story. An American journalist investigates young German skinheads and uncovers a link between these thugs and surviving Nazis. The extent of their evil influence is surprising. This is a dangerous enterprise that places not only his cover at risk, but also his life.
VHS: S26525. $94.99.
John MacKenzie, USA, 1995, 102 mins.

The Innocent
Campbell Scott, Isabella Rossellini and Anthony Hopkins star in this sexy thriller. An aggressive CIA man is forced to confront his young partner when he learns that the younger man has been seduced by a mysterious but beautiful woman. The choice placed before this couple is between deadly secrets and forbidden passions.
VHS: S27413. $99.99.
Laser: LD75507. $39.99.
John Schlesinger, USA, 1995, 119 mins.

Innocent Blood
John Landis balances the gangster movie with black humor. The talented French actress Anne Parillaud stars as a modern day vampire threatening the brutal reign of the local mob, knocking off its members serial style. With Robert Loggia, Anthony LaPaglia and Don Rickles.
VHS: S18222. $19.98.
John Landis, USA, 1992, 113 mins.

Interns
Cliff Robertson and Nick Adams star in this microcosm look at the life and conditions in a big city hospital.
VHS: S05013. $59.95.
David Swift, USA, 1962, 121 mins.

Intersection
Richard Gere is a successful architect whose personal life is on shaky ground. Between his beautiful but aloof wife, played by Sharon Stone, and his sexy, passionate lover, Lolita Davidovich, this man is forced to confront his true feelings when he must cross the intersection.
VHS: S21349. $95.95.
Laser: LD75313. $39.98.
Mark Rydell, USA, 1994, 98 mins.

Interview with the Vampire
Tom Cruise, Brad Pitt, Antonio Banderas, Stephen Rea and Christian Slater are all featured in this stylish adaptation of Anne Rice's runaway bestseller. Lestat is a charming fiend loose in old New Orleans. His hunger sets off a chain of events that span two continents and the gap between the living and the dead.
VHS: S24817. $19.95.
Laser: LD74904. $39.95.
Neil Jordan, USA, 1994, 123 mins.

Invasion of the Space Preachers
The extraterrestrial evangelist, Reverend Lash, has come to Earth to pick the minds and pockets of America on his quest for the ultimate religious experience—Network Television! Brought to you by the Troma Team, the people who brought you The Toxic Avenger.
VHS: S14938. $79.95.
Daniel Boyd, USA, 1990, 100 mins.

Iron Triangle
The human face of war is portrayed in this compassionate drama that views the Vietnam War through the eyes of a veteran American captain (Beau Bridges) and a 17-year-old Vietnamese sniper.
VHS: S08891. $19.95.
Eric Weston, USA, 1989, 91 mins.

Ironweed
Based on the novel by William Kennedy, Hector Babenco's film stars Jack Nicholson and Meryl Streep and is set in 1938 Albany, New York. Francis Phelan, a drifter, returns to Albany to settle matters of conscience after staying away from home for 22 years, and is haunted by visions from his past—his former love Helen, who is a failed singer now living as a bum.
VHS: S06865. $19.98.
Hector Babenco, USA, 1987, 98 mins.

Islander

A coming-of-age tale from the northern waters of the Great Lakes. Inga is an attractive girl of 16 who has grown up in the rough world of commercial fishing on Lake Michigan. Faster than it takes to catch a Coho, she finds childhood a distant memory. A sensitive drama personally recommended by Liv Ullmann. With Kit Wholihan, Jeff Weborg, Julie Johnson and Michael Rock.
VHS: S09871. $79.95.
Nancy Thurow, USA, 1988, 99 mins.

Islands

When Lacey, a punk teenager, is forced to spend the summer with a strange woman (Louise Fletcher), their worlds immediately collide. Unaware that the woman is her real mother, Lacey sees the remote island as a prison. But abrupt and shared dangers suddenly bring Lacey and her mother together, to a new understanding that changes both their lives. 1987, 55 mins.
VHS: S06446. $19.95.

Islands in the Stream

The primary collaborators of Patton re-unite for this adaptation of an unfinished Hemmingway novel. George C. Scott is an alienated and isolated artist who lives in solitude on an island, his fragile paradise shattered by the arrival of three sons—one of whom is subsequently killed in battle.
VHS: S02537. $19.95.
Laser: LD75317. $39.98.
Franklin J. Schaffner, USA, 1977, 110 mins.

Istanbul

Brad Dourif portrays a man cast out from society and haunted by his past, in search of redemption, in an intriguing portrayal of two men playing the game of truth, where one man's adventure is another man's salvation.
VHS: S04346. $59.98.
Marc Didden, USA, 1986, 90 mins.

Jack and His Friends

A satire about Jack (Allen Garfield), a shoe salesman who is thrown out by his unfaithful wife. Jack is promptly kidnapped by a young outlaw couple (Judy Reyes and Sam Rockwell) on the run, who take refuge in Jack's deserted island home. Over a long, decadent weekend, the nature of their relationship subtly changes.
VHS: S19721. $79.95.
Bruce Ornstein, USA, 1992, 93 mins.

Jacknife

Delayed stress syndrome among Vietnam veterans is explored in this heartfelt drama starring Robert De Niro, Kathy Baker and Ed Harris. Based on the play Strange Snow by Stephen Metcalfe, DeNiro and Harris were best buddies until one fateful mission. Now the emotionally crippled Harris doesn't want his war buddy hanging around with his lonely schoolteacher sister. The performances are top notch.
VHS: S10336. $19.98.
David Jones, USA, 1989, 102 mins.

Jacob's Ladder

Don't let the biblical references scare you away. This beautifully photographed metaphysical thriller is more Twilight Zone than Old Testament. Tim Robbins stars as a Vietnam veteran with a serious case of post traumatic stress syndrome. He believes demons are out to get him and the surviving members of his old platoon. With Elizabeth Pena, Matt Craven, Macaulay Culkin, and Danny Aiello as the world's friendliest chiropractor.
VHS: S13717. $19.98.
Adrian Lyne, USA, 1990, 115 mins.

Jade

David Caruso and Linda Fiorentino star in this highly erotic thriller about jealousy, passion and murder. Any man would be furious if he found out his wife was cheating. This film stands out for the gruesome act a cuckolded man performs in his search for vengeance.
VHS: S26988. $98.99.
William Friedkin, USA, 1995, 94 mins.

James A. Michener's Texas

Pulitzer Prize-winner James A. Michener wrote the novel on which this historical drama is based. Maria Conchita Alonso, Patrick Duffy and Stacy Keach are just some of the stars featured in this sweeping epic. It charts the birth of the Lone Star State, where everything—including adventure—is bigger.
VHS: S22423. $19.98.
Laser: LD74831. $39.98.
Richard Lang, USA, 1994, 180 mins.

Jennifer 8

Bruce Robinson's film stars Andy Garcia as a disillusioned cop pursuing a serial killer who preys on blind women. Uma Thurman plays the love interest, a beautiful though emotionally wounded blind woman who is the key to unraveling the killer's identity.
VHS: S18679. $19.95.
Laser: Widescreen. LD75318. $39.98.
Bruce Robinson, USA, 1992, 127 mins.

Jeremiah Johnson

Beautifully shot story of a mountain man surviving winters and learning to live in harmony with Indians features Robert Redford and Will Geer.
VHS: S07495. $19.95.
Laser: LD74705. $34.98.
Sydney Pollack, USA, 1972, 107 mins.

The Jerky Boys: The Movie

One day a couple of losers from Queens make the wrong prank call. Before they know what to do, the mob is after them. Along the way they encounter a number of hilarious adventures. Alan Arkin is great as the mob hitman with the perfect demeanor but lousy aim.
VHS: S26288. $99.97.
Laser: LD75067. $39.99.
James Melkonian, USA, 1995, 81 mins.

JFK (Director's Cut)

The issues opened up by Oliver Stone's award-winning, politically incendiary and audacious reworking of the events, personalities, and alleged government conspiracy in the assassination of President John F. Kennedy are reconsidered with the "director's cut," featuring 17 minutes of additional footage cut from the theatrical release.
VHS: S17877. $24.98.
Laser: Letterboxed. LD71468. $39.98.
Oliver Stone, USA, 1991, 206 mins.

The Jim Rose Circus Sideshow

A look at the freakish sideshow of impresario Jim Rose, who subjects himself and the members of his troupe to astounding feats of bednailing, regurgitation, body piercing, electrocution and worm eating. The program features Bebe the Circus Queen, the Amazing Mr. Lifto, The Torture King, The Enigma and Matt "The Tube" Crowley. "Lollapolozza's human demolition derby" (USA Today).
VHS: S19507. $16.98.

Joe

Peter Boyle is a bigoted hardhat who overreacts to daughter Susan Sarandon's hippie lifestyle. A raw and emotional drama directed by John G. Avildsen (Rocky, The Karate Kid). Think of Archie Bunker with a hunting rifle. With Dennis Patrick, K. Callan and Audrey Caire. America, love it or shoot it.
VHS: S08270. $14.98.
John G. Avildsen, USA, 1970, 107 mins.

Johnny Handsome

A small time criminal gets a new face and a fresh start but how can he forget the crooks who put him in jail and killed his best friend? Mickey Rourke stars in this Walter Hill drama set way down yonder in New Orleans. He goes from looking like the Elephant Man's brother to the spitting image of Mickey Rourke. Great atmosphere and excellent supporting work from Ellen Barkin, Lance Henriksen, Elizabeth McGovern, Forest Whitaker and Morgan Freeman.
VHS: S11766. $14.98.
Walter Hill, USA, 1989, 96 mins.

Johnny Mnemonic

Keanu Reeves stars as a sci-fi courier with a difference. In the future they no longer handcuff couriers to the goods, they plant it in their heads. Reeves is set off on a chase not to protect the goods, but to save his life. It's an overload of suspense. Friends and foes played by Ice-T and Dolph Lundgren are also featured in this debut feature by 1980's art star Robert Longo.
VHS: S26611. $19.95.
Laser: LD75100. $39.99.
Robert Longo, Canada, 1995, 98 mins.

Joni

Based on the best-selling autobiographical book, the true story of Joni Eareckson Tada, starring herself. Inspirational. 75 mins.
VHS: S09792. $19.98.

Journey Back to Oz

An animated sequel to the 1939 classic features the further adventures of Dorothy and her friends. An all-star cast includes the voices of Milton Berle as the Cowardly Lion, Paul Lynde as Pumpkinhead, Mickey Rooney as the Scarecrow, Danny Thomas as the Tin Man, Ethel Merman as the Witch Mombi and Liza Minnelli as Dorothy. Also Margaret Hamilton (the original Wicked Witch of the West) as Auntie Em.
VHS: S10720. $12.98.
Hal Sutherland, USA, 1974, 90 mins.

Joy of Sex

Martha Coolidge (Real Genius) takes the title of a popular sex manual and uses it to front a high school teenage sex comedy. She populates the film with some supporting performers from Valley Girl, like Cameron Dye, Michelle Meyrink and Colleen Camp. Plot concerns a teen virgin who would like to alter that situation before she dies of a fatal disease.
VHS: S06172. $79.95.
Martha Coolidge, USA, 1984, 93 mins.

Judgment in Berlin

In 1978, an East German seeking asylum in the West hijacked a Polish airliner. Martin Sheen plays Judge Herbert Stern, who wrote a book about this volatile and politically sensitive case. With Max Gail, Sean Penn.
VHS: S08133. $29.95.
Leonard Penn, USA, 1988, 92 mins.

Julia

Fred Zinnemann's film adaptation stars Jane Fonda as playwright and author Lillian Hellman and chronicles her deep and involving friendship with Julia (Vanessa Redgrave), a childhood friend. Zinnemann focuses on their intense relationship, which Julia forces by enlisting Hellman's aid to fund an anti-fascist Resistance. Redgrave won a best supporting Oscar. Jason Robards is brilliant in an extended cameo as Dashiell Hammett, Hellman's long-time lover. Film buffs will note a small role by Meryl Streep.
VHS: S02539. $19.98.
Fred Zinnemann, USA, 1977, 118 mins.

K2

Franc Roddam (Quadrophenia) adapts Patrick Meyers' play about a likeable Seattle lawyer (Michael Biehn) and a physicist (Matt Craven) and their struggle to scale the world's most difficult mountain, K2, in northern Pakistan. The stunning location photography is by Gabriel Beristain.
VHS: S17636. $19.95.
Laser: LD75216. $34.98.
Franc Roddam, USA, 1992, 104 mins.

Kalifornia

Dominic Sena's stylish road movie is an unsentimental depiction of madness. A writer (David Duchovny) and his photographer girlfriend (Michele Forbes), are preparing a road trip to research a book about mass murder sites. In order to finance the trip, they reluctantly enlist a white-trash couple (Brad Pitt and Juliette Lewis) to share the expenses. Unbeknownst to them, Pitt is a brutal killer who traps them in a nightmarish journey of dementia, abuse and sexual domination.
VHS: S20219. $19.95.
Dominic Sena, USA, 1993, 116 mins.

Kicking and Screaming

Four young men in their 20s discover there's not much to life after college. It's a scenario rife with comic possibilities, where romance and the trauma of getting on with life seem overwhelming and all-encompassing. When Grover's (Josh Hamilton) retainer-wearing girlfriend Jane (Olivia d'Abo) is accepted at a writing program in Prague, Grover chickens out and stays home with his buddies instead. While his friend Otis (Carlos Jacott) tries and tries again to get on a plane for graduate school and his friend Skippy (Jason Wiles) misses his younger girlfriend Miami (Parker Posey) so much that he re-enrolls in college, Grover confides in perennial student and bartender Chet (Eric Stoltz) and struggles with the pain of love lost.
VHS: S27260. $94.99.
Noah Baumbach, USA, 1995, 96 mins.

Killing Affair

Peter Weller and Kathy Baker star in the tension filled drama about a deadly feud in Appalachia in 1943. Weller shows up at Baker's isolated backwoods home and claims he killed her husband for crimes against Weller's family. With John Glover, Bill Smitrovich and Rhetta Hughes.
VHS: S02935. $79.95.
David Saperstein, USA, 1985, 100 mins.

Killing Fields

An epic story of friendship, combat and survival set within war-torn Cambodia after the victory of the Khmer Rouge. Winner of three Academy Awards, Killing Fields stars Dr. Haing S. Ngor, Sam Waterston and John Malkovich, with music by Mike Oldfield.
VHS: S00674. $19.98.
Laser: LD70607. $29.98.
Roland Joffe, USA, 1984, 142 mins.

Killing Zoe

In the bloody tradition of Reservoir Dogs, this thriller tells a tale of criminals gone worse than bad. An American safecracker goes to Paris to help a buddy with a Bastille Day bank heist. Naturally it goes awry in a totally unexpected way. With Eric Stoltz and Julie Delpy.
VHS: S23117. $14.98.
Laser: LD75215. $34.98.
Roger Avary, USA, 1994, 96 mins.

Kim

Peter O'Toole and Bryan Brown star in this recent adaptation of Rudyard Kipling's adventure novel. An orphan living on his wits in India is befriended by two radically different men. One is a Buddhist monk, while the other is a spy. The only thing these two can agree on is that they both want the boy to follow in their footsteps. John Rhys-Davies is also featured.
VHS: S27621. $19.98.
John Davies, USA, 1984, 150 mins.

King of Marvin Gardens

One of the most unaccountable films of the 70s, Bob Rafelson's feature stars Jack Nicholson and Bruce Dern as two brothers wounded by past failures. Set in Atlantic City, the plot charts their divergent paths to redemption and self-definition. Nicholson retreats into a protective job as a radio performer and Dern pursues a series of get-rich-quick schemes. With Ellen Burstyn and Scatman Crothers.
VHS: S18706. $19.95.
Laser: Chapter stops, digital master. LD75090. $34.95.
Bob Rafelson, USA, 1972, 104 mins.

King of the Gypsies

When Gypsy chief Sterling Hayden is near death he summons his grandson Eric Roberts to lead the tribe. Son Judd Hirsch is annoyed. With Shelley Winters, Annie Potts, and Michael V. Gazzo as part of the clan. Also Susan Sarandon and Brooke Shields, who repeat as mother and daughter. Based on the non-fiction book by Peter Maas. This was Roberts' film debut.
VHS: S10827. $14.95.
Frank Pierson, USA, 1978, 112 mins.

Kingfish: A Story of Huey P. Long

John Goodman is the crooked but charismatic Louisiana politician from the Depression era. To many he was a hero, but to others he was a frightening demagogue. Goodman superbly captures the larger than life quality of this colorful figure.
VHS: S25526. $14.95.
Laser: LD75018. $39.99.
Thomas Schlamme, USA, 1995, 96 mins.

A Kiss Before Dying

Matt Dillon stars in the remake of this popular Ira Levin thriller as a sociopathic killer who will do anything to climb further up the ladder of success. Sean Young plays a pair of twin sisters who sadly discover there is another side to the charming guy they both love. With Diane Ladd, James Russo and Max Von Sydow as the industrialist who loves fishing. Written and directed by the author of Fatal Attraction.
VHS: S14945. $19.95.
James Dearden, USA, 1991, 93 mins.

Kiss of the Spider Woman

One of the finest films of 1985, from the director of Pixote. Featuring an Academy Award winning performance by William Hurt as Molina, and Raul Julia as Valentin, the political prisoner. With the incredible Sonia Braga. Based on the novel by Manuel Puig.
VHS: S00686. $14.98.
Hector Babenco, USA, 1985, 119 mins.

The Klansman

Passions flare and violence erupts when the Ku Klux Klan and militant blacks clash in a backwards Southern town. A violent melodrama that Sam Fuller had a hand in, in the early going. He is still listed as co-scripter but ditched the directing duties. Starring Lee Marvin, Richard Burton, O.J. Simpson and Lola Falana.
VHS: S13703. $19.95.
Terence Young, USA, 1974, 112 mins.

Klute

Jane Fonda stars as the high-priced call girl used as a bait to lure a killer in this suspense-filled mystery. She won the Best Actress Oscar for her compelling character study. With Donald Sutherland, Roy Scheider.
VHS: S11618. $19.98.
Alan J. Pakula, USA, 1971, 114 mins.

Kramer vs. Kramer

Dustin Hoffman must become a single parent when Meryl Streep walks out on their marriage and their young son. A terrific male weepie where Hoffman learns how to make French toast and lots of important parent stuff. With Justin Henry, Jane Alexander. Several Oscars, including Best Picture.
VHS: S03905. $19.95.
Laser: LD72188. $34.95.
Robert Benton, USA, 1979, 104 mins.

Kung Fu the Movie

A feature-length translation of the cult 1970s program about the mysterious, Zen-like actions of Kwai Chang Caine, who gets drawn into an opium plot with an evil warlord (Mako) during the gold rush fever of 1880s California. Brandon Lee, the son of Bruce Lee, co-stars as Caine's adversary. The late Keye Luke appears in flashback as Master Po, Caine's blind instructor.
VHS: S17922. $19.98.
Richard Lang, USA, 1986, 100 mins.

L.A. Law

The feature length, made-for-tv pilot that introduced most of the characters of the popular tv series about the legal profession in Southern California. It all started with a senior partner found face down dead in a plate of beans. With Corbin Bernsen, Harry Hamlin, Susan Dey, Jill Eikenberry and Michael Tucker. USA, 1986, 100 mins.
VHS: S06534. $79.98.

The Labyrinth

Sarah (Jennifer Connelly) wished her baby brother would be taken away by goblins, and her wish came true. The Goblin King has taken the boy off to his castle to be goblinized, and Sarah must now rescue him and face the Wizard-King. Jim Henson's journey into enchantment.
VHS: Out of print. For rental only.
Laser: LD72303. $34.99.
Jim Henson, USA, 1986, 102 mins.

Lady in a Cage

When wealthy widow Olivia de Havilland is trapped in a glass elevator in her mansion, uninvited guests come out of the woodwork. They include a wino, a prostitute and three hooligans—one of which is young James Caan. A very nasty thriller about faulty machinery and freaky people. With Jeff Corey, Ann Sothern, Rafael Campos and Scatman Crothers. B&W.
VHS: S10828. $49.95.
Walter Grauman, USA, 1964, 95 mins.

Lady in Red

Pamela Sue Martin stars as John Dillinger's girlfriend in this Roger Corman production scripted by John Sayles.
VHS: S07014. $69.95.
Lewis Teague, USA, 1979, 93 mins.

Ladyhawke

Matthew Broderick plays an unwilling and unlikely squire to Rutger Hauer's master knight, who labors under a dandy of a curse. He spends his nights as a ferocious beast while his lady love spends her days as a ferocious bird. And you thought the Middle Ages were uncomplicated.
VHS: S04178. $19.98.
Laser: LD74731. $39.98.
Richard Donner, USA, 1985, 121 mins.

The Last Detail

Comedy drama about two career sailors escorting a sailor to the brig, who decide to show the young sailor a good time before he begins his prison sentence. Jack Nicholson is simply marvelous, with Otis Young, Randy Quaid, Michael Moriarty. Screenplay by Robert Towne.
VHS: S02173. $14.95.
Laser: Chapter stops, digital master. LD75089. $34.95.
Hal Ashby, USA, 1973, 105 mins.

Last Exit to Brooklyn

Hubert Selby Jr.'s controversial novel is now a visually arresting and powerfully performed motion picture. The depressed dock area of Brooklyn in the early 1950's serves as a background for anger, violence and forbidden emotions among hookers, drag queens, juvenile delinquents and union organizers. With Stephan Lang, Jerry Orbach, Burt Young, Peter Dobson and Jennifer Jason Leigh as the cold-hearted hooker Tralala.
VHS: S13289. $89.95.
Uli Edel, West Germany/USA, 1990, 102 mins.

The Last Good Time

Armin Mueller-Stahl stars with young Maureen Stapleton and Olivia d'Abo in this unusual love story. Stahl is an aging violinist who finds himself alone with dreams of the past. He happens to meet a young woman, d'Abo, who desperately needs to get away from the streets. Danger, desire and finally even love drive this film toward an unexpected climax.
VHS: S26459. $99.95.
Laser: LD75378. $49.98.
Bob Balaban, USA, 1994, 137 mins.

The Last Movie

Based on the success of Easy Rider, Dennis Hopper was given money to go to Peru and make a movie with his friends. The plot concerns an American movie company making a western. When they leave behind Hopper and lots of their equipment, it is acquired by the local population for unexpected results. The cast includes Peter Fonda, Michelle Phillips, Dean Stockwell, Russ Tamblin, Sylvia Miles, Henry Jaglom, Sam Fuller, Don Gordon, Julie Adams, John Phillip Law and Kris Kristofferson in his screen debut. Bizarre, chaotic and filled with religious symbolism. Also known as Chinchero.
VHS: S10719. $19.95.
Dennis Hopper, USA/Peru, 1971, 108 mins.

Last of the Dogmen

Sociologists Lewis Gates (Tom Berenger) and Lillian Sloan (Barbara Hershey) discover a Native American tribe that history believed had been massacred. For over 100 years, the last surviving Cheyenne Dog Soldiers escaped detection and preserved their culture by hiding out in the wilderness of Montana. Their discovery could spell the end of their way of life. It's a suspense-laden film with an updated Western flavor.
VHS: S27273. $98.99.
Tab Murphy, USA, 1995, 118 mins.

The Last of the Mohicans

James Fenimore Cooper's classic tale of friendship and adventure during the French and Indian War is given a sturdy re-telling in an above average made-for-tv version. It stars Steve Forrest as Hawkeye and features Andrew Prine, Ned Romero and Robert Tessier in this rousing tale of Colonial America.
VHS: S03639. $19.95.
James L. Conway, USA, 1985, 100 mins.

Last of the Red Hot Lovers

This is not a salute to a frankfurter aficionado but another Neil Simon stage comedy being filmed for the movies. Alan Arkin is a restaurateur who seeks the romantic company of three different women, played by Sally Kellerman, Paula Prentiss and Renee Taylor. His biggest fear is that he smells of fish.
VHS: S10819. $19.95.
Gene Saks, USA, 1972, 98 mins.

The Last Outlaw

Mickey Rourke is the ringleader of a gang of desperate bank-robbing outlaws. When they shoot him and leave him for dead it's their first mistake, and maybe their last. The undead desperado is slowly and cautiously hunting down his old gang, one by one. Dermot Mulroney and Steve Buscemi also star.
VHS: S21714. $19.98.
Geoff Murphy, USA, 1994, 90 mins.

The Last Picture Show
Peter Bogdanovich's masterpiece about life in a small Texas town in the early 1950's received six Oscar nominations and swept the supporting actor and actress category. Based on the novel by Larry McMurtry, the all-star cast includes Jeff Bridges, Cybill Shepherd, Timothy Bottoms, Cloris Leachman, Ben Johnson, Ellen Burstyn, Randy Quaid and Eileen Brennan. The town of Anarene was never quite the same after they shut down the Royal theatre.
VHS: S13579. $19.95.
Laser: LD70758. $124.95.
Peter Bogdanovich, USA, 1971, 118 mins.

Last Prostitute
"It was her last chance for innocence, and his first chance for love." Brazilian bombshell Sonia Braga has the title role in this tender coming-of-age story. Co-starring Wil Wheaton, best known for his performance in *Stand by Me*. With David Kaufman, Woody Watson, Dennis Letts and Cotter Smith as Joe. Carmen Culver (*The Thorn Birds*) wrote the script based on the play by William Borden Chase.
VHS: S16025. $89.95.
Lou Antonio, USA, 1991, 93 mins.

The Last Seduction
Linda Fiorentino is a winning temptress who manages to bring ruin to all the men in her life. A scam goes all wrong, but not for Linda, who manages to move on to the next man—or is it victim? Beauty is all the more appealing in an ugly world centered on money and betrayal.
VHS: S24955. $19.95.
Laser: LD74994. $34.95.
John Dahl, USA, 1994, 110 mins.

Last Tycoon
Based on the last F. Scott Fitzgerald novel, an intimate look at the inner workings of a Hollywood studio. Robert De Niro stars as an Irving Thalberg-type producer who wants to accomplish great things and make wonderful pictures. Heavy-weight cast includes Tony Curtis, Robert Mitchum, Jeanne Moreau, Jack Nicholson, Ray Milland, Peter Strauss, Ingrid Boulting and Theresa Russell.
VHS: S10830. $19.95.
Laser: LD75326. $29.98.
Elia Kazan, USA, 1977, 123 mins.

Latino
Wexler's (*Medium Cool*) drama set and shot in Nicaragua. Robert Beltran plays the Chicano Green Beret who is now in the jungles of South America fighting a war that includes innocent civilians among its victims. Slowly, Eddie begins to question what he's doing and why.
VHS: Out of print. For rental only.
Laser: LD71095. $34.98.
Haskell Wexler, USA, 1985, 108 mins.

Le Mans
Steve McQueen shows his skill behind the wheel of automobiles designed to compete in the world-famous, French, 24-hour endurance road race. He plays Michael Delaney, a top driver for the Gulf/Porsche team on the Grand Prix circuit, troubled by the death of a close friend and his own near-fatal accident. Superior racing footage. With Elga Andersen, Siegfried Rauch, Ronald Leigh-Hunt, Jean-Claude Bercq.
VHS: S13299. $39.99.
Lee Katzin, USA, 1971, 106 mins.

Leader of the Band
"Barney Miller's" Steve Landesburg orchestrates this offbeat comedy in which he plays a big city musician who struggles to turn the world's worst high school band into a first-class combo.
VHS: S09285. $14.95.
Nessa Hyams, USA, 1987, 90 mins.

Lean on Me
The story of New Jersey educator Joe Clark. He kicked out the troublemakers in his inner city high school and locked the doors to prevent the drug dealers from coming back in. Morgan Freeman stars as the principal with the baseball bat who made the cover of Time Magazine. With Beverly Todd, Robert Guillaume, and Lynne Thigpen as the disgruntled parent. Another educational miracle film in the tradition of *Stand and Deliver*.
VHS: S10436. $14.95.
John G. Avildsen, USA, 1989, 109 mins.

Leap of Faith
This 90s version of *Elmer Gantry* stars Steve Martin as Jonas Nightengale, a charismatic con man whose traveling ministry conjures up DeMille-like religious spectacles and salvation as an elaborate sting operation complete with Debra Winger. Stranded in a Southwestern farming community, their ideas and principles are tested by actual hardship and pain. With Lolita Davidovich, Lukas Haas and Liam Neeson as a pessimistic sheriff in love with Winger.
VHS: S18766. $19.95.
Laser: Widescreen. LD75219. $34.95.
Richard Pearce, USA, 1992, 110 mins.

Leaving Las Vegas
Nicolas Cage and Elisabeth Shue star in this tender love story of two people living on the far side of hope. Ben Sanderson (Cage) is an alcoholic Los Angeles screenwriter who decides to move to Las Vegas to die. There he meets a prostitute (Shue), equally unapologetic about her own life choices, and together they fall in love. Cage won the Academy Award for his role in this engrossing, complex and beautiful film.
VHS: S27709. $99.99.
Laser: LD75568. $34.98.
Mike Figgis, USA, 1995, 113 mins.

Legends of the Fall
Brad Pitt, Anthony Hopkins and Aidan Quinn star in this beautifully filmed tale about a family in Montana. Tragedy strikes when three brothers find themselves locked in a bitter rivalry over a beautiful woman (Julia Ormond). Based on the novella by Jim Harrison, this film is an elemental tale of family ties, betrayal and love.
VHS: S24815. $19.95.
Laser: LD74905. $39.95.
Edward Zwick, USA, 1994, 133 mins.

Legends of the North
Based on a Jack London classic, this story is set in the frozen north at the end of the 19th century. Randy Quaid stars a deceptive guide who teams up with a man he believes knows the site of a secret lake filled with gold. Tragedy intervenes and the search for Lake Esperanza must continue blindly.
VHS: S24334. $92.99.
Laser: LD75220. $34.98.
Rene Manzor, USA, 1994, 95 mins.

Lemon Sisters
Diane Keaton, Carol Kane and Kathryn Grody star as three childhood friends who find that Atlantic City is not what it used to be. Their hopes of making it big as professional singers is interrupted by healthy doses of reality. With Elliot Gould, Ruben Blades, Aidan Quinn and Matthew Modine.
VHS: S13702. $19.98.
Joyce Chopra, USA, 1990, 93 mins.

Lenny
Bob Fosse brilliantly directs this stark biography of self-destructive, controversial, persecuted comic talent Lenny Bruce. Dustin Hoffman captures all of these contrary emotions in his portrayal of the late 1950's and '60's stand-up comedian. Valerie Perrine stars in the low-key role as Bruce's stripper wife.
VHS: S00743. $19.95.
Bob Fosse, USA, 1974, 112 mins.

Les Miserables
A first-rate adaptation of Victor Hugo's monumental novel about Jean Valjean (Richard Jordan), a low-level thief trying to conceal his past and achieve respectable status despite the hostility and determination of the police chief, Javert (Anthony Perkins), to reveal his full identity. With Cyril Cusack, Claude Dauphin, Sir John Gielgud and Flora Robson.
VHS: S19030. $19.98.
Glenn Jordan, USA, 1978, 123 mins.

Less Than Zero
Bret Easton Ellis' novel of the poverty of spirit and common sense among the children of the rich in the posher areas of Southern California stars Andrew McCarthy, Jami Gertz and Robert Downey Jr. Sex, drugs, music and fashion are touched upon when a college student returns for the holidays to find all his friends have changed.
VHS: S06620. $19.98.
Marek Kanievska, USA, 1987, 100 mins.

Let It Rock
Dennis Hopper, in an effort to upgrade his screen image of playing psychos, drug dealers and alcoholics, is cast as a Hollywood agent/rock promoter who will do anything to make his client a star—including trying to have him killed. With Terrance Robay and Romana Sweeny. Written, produced and directed by Roland Klick.
VHS: S08297. $79.95.
Roland Klick, USA, 1988, 75 mins.

Lethal Weapon
Buddy film featuring Mel Gibson as a borderline psychopath cop and Danny Glover as his family man partner on the trail of a drug ring.
VHS: S05970. $19.98.
Richard Donner, USA, 1987, 110 mins.

Lethal Weapon 2
Mel Gibson and Danny Glover are back as Riggs and Murtaugh, L.A.'s most action-oriented cops. This time the suicidal hunk and the Cosby-clone family man are up against a brutal gang of South African drug smugglers with diplomatic immunity. With Joss Ackland as the smarmy villain. Also Patsy Kensit, Darleen Love and Joe Pesci as a talkative witness in protective custody.
VHS: S11576. $19.98.
Richard Donner, USA, 1989, 113 mins.

Lethal Weapon 3
As could be expected, Murtaugh's (Danny Glover) last week on the police force does not end with only a gold watch. He and partner Riggs (Mel Gibson) uncover a crooked ex-cop who is selling confiscated firearms. The film is non-stop action from beginning to end with comic relief provided by Joe Pesci, who reprises his role from *Lethal Weapon II*.
VHS: S21402. $19.98.
Richard Donner, USA, 1992, 118 mins.

Light of Day
Paul Schrader directed this story of a brother and sister trying to make a go of it at a Cleveland bar, an observant look at ordinary Americans trying to take control of their lives. With Michael J. Fox, Joan Jett, Gena Rowlands.
VHS: S04694. $19.98.
Paul Schrader, USA, 1987, 108 mins.

Light Sleeper
Paul Schrader's film is an investigation of a middle-level drug courier's disintegration. At the center is Willem Dafoe's performance as a former addict who runs drugs for Susan Sarandon. Dafoe attempts to regain his moral balance when he encounters his former girlfriend (Dana Delaney). Ed Lachman was the cinematographer. With David Clennon and Mary Beth Hurt.
VHS: S17969. $19.98.
Paul Schrader, USA, 1992, 103 mins.

Like Father Like Son
Dudley Moore and Kirk Cameron are father and son until by an odd set of events they become son and father. Imagine the fun when a teenager switches bodies with his shorter father who is a respected heart surgeon. Will the son get to operate? Will the father pass the biology final?
VHS: S06920. $89.95.
Rod Daniel, USA, 1987, 101 mins.

Lincoln
Based on the famous historical novel by Gore Vidal, this film stars Sam Waterston as Lincoln and Mary Tyler Moore as his wife. The nation was divided by Lincoln's policies, but his dogged commitment to principle ultimately held the union together. Two-tape set. 190 mins.
VHS: S20638. $89.95.

The Lindbergh Kidnapping Case
Anthony Hopkins and Joseph Cotten star in the controversial account of the kidnapping of the Lindbergh baby. Hopkins, as the kidnapper, Bruno Hauptmann, gives a strong performance.
VHS: S10042. $69.95.
Buzz Kulik, USA, 1976, 105 mins.

Linguini Incident
Rosanna Arquette stars as a kooky but inept escape artist, who waits tables in a trendy NYC nightspot in hopes of making enough money to buy the wedding ring of Mrs. Houdini. When Rosanna decides to rob the eatery she works for, she is joined by her friend, lingerie designer Eszter Balint and bartender David Bowie, who for some reason has to get married before the week is up. With Marlee Matlin, Viveca Lindfors and Buck Henry and Andre Gregory as the restaurant owners who would not rather not pay off a million dollar bet.
Laser: LD72194. $34.95.
Richard Shepard, USA, 1991, 98 mins.

Lip Service
It's bad news for veteran reporter Gil Hutchinson (Paul Dooley) when newcomer Len Burdette (Griffin Dunne) turns his staid morning TV show into a circus. Len's irreverent antics cost Gil his job, but he returns to have his first—and last—laugh.
VHS: S09607. $79.95.
William H. Macy, USA, 1988, 67 mins.

Little Gloria Happy at Last
Emmy Award-winning dramatization based on the best-selling book about the 1934 battle between one of the world's richest women and one of the world's greatest beauties over the custody of ten-year-old heiress Gloria Vanderbilt. With Bette Davis, Angela Lansbury, Maureen Stapleton, Christopher Plummer.
VHS: S05219. $19.95.
Waris Hussein, USA, 1984, 180 mins.

Little Heroes
A spirited young girl and her beloved dog team up to teach an entire town the true meaning of courage. This heartwarming family entertainment stars Raeanin Simpson and "Hoover" as Fuzz. Based on a true story. With Katharine Willis and Keith Christensen.
VHS: S15544. $19.95.
Craig Clyde, USA, 1991, 111 mins.

Little Man Tate
The emotional well being of a child prodigy is the subject of Jodie Foster's accomplished directorial debut. Newcomer Adam Hann-Byrd stars as seven-year-old Fred Tate, an artistic, musical and mathematical genius who worries a lot. Fred would rather have a friend than the correct answer. When his achievements attract the attention of noted educator Diane Wiest, Fred's waitress mom (played by Foster) has to make some hard choices. With Debi Mazar, George Plimpton and Harry Connick Jr.
VHS: S15823. $14.95.
Jodie Foster, USA, 1991, 110 mins.

Little Miss Marker
A remake of the Damon Runyan story that once starred Shirley Temple as the darling child who is left as collateral on a debt that is never going to be paid. With Walter Matthau as the disgruntled bookie, Sara Stimson as the kid and Julie Andrews as the bookie's dame. This fourth telling of the story also features Tony Curtis and Bob Newhart.
VHS: S07802. $49.95.
Walter Bernstein, USA, 1980, 103 mins.

Little Odessa
Two brothers, Tim Roth and Edward Furlong, star in this criminal drama about danger, deceit and family passions. Set amidst the Russian emigre underworld of Queens in New York known as "Little Odessa," this drama captures the gritty urban experience of another new criminal syndicate in the making. Also features Moira Kelly, Vanessa Redgrave and Maximilian Schell.
VHS: S26283. $96.99.
William K. Howard, USA, 1995, 98 mins.

Little Romance
Charming romance about a young American girl living in Paris and running off with a French boy while chaperoned by Laurence Olivier.
VHS: S01820. $14.95.
George Roy Hill, USA, 1979, 108 mins.

Little Women
Louisa May Alcott's classic American novel comes to the screen for the fourth time in a lush production depicting the coming of age of four young women led by a strong matriarch. Set in the 19th century with lavish period costumes and sets, the film stars Academy Award nominee Wynona Rider, Susan Sarandon and Gabriel Byrne.
VHS: S24952. $19.95.
Laser: LD74910. $34.95.
Gillian Armstrong, USA, 1994, 118 mins.

Little Women Gift Set
Louisa May Alcott's classic story, set in the late 19th century, depicts the coming-of-age of four young women led by a strong matriarch. Stars Winona Ryder, Susan Sarandon, Eric Stoltz and Gabriel Byrne. This special gift set includes a sterling silver locket in an enchanting keepsake case and a *Little Women* novelette.
VHS: S26622. $29.95.
Gillian Armstrong, USA, 1994, 118 mins.

The Long Hot Summer
A made-for-tv remake of the William Faulkner story of sexual frustration, greed, and the importance of having a good reputation in the Deep South. It stars Don Johnson, Cybill Shepherd, Judith Ivey, Ava Gardner, William Russ and Jason Robards in an emotional and well-acted drama that features barn burning and unbridled passion.
VHS: S06103. $79.98.
Laser: LD72253. $59.98.
Stuart Cooper, USA, 1985, 200 mins.

Longest Day
With an all-star cast that includes John Wayne, Robert Mitchum, Henry Fonda, Richard Burton and Sean Connery, this epic retelling of the events of D-Day is one of the greatest war films ever made.
VHS: S06537. $24.98.
Laser: LD71114. $69.98.
Ken Annakin, USA, 1962, 180 mins.

Look Who's Talking
A surprise boxoffice hit about an unwed mother looking for the perfect father to help raise little Mikey. The gimmick here is that the baby has help from Bruce Willis to voice his opinions from the first charge of conception all the way through toddlerhood. Kirstie Alley is the mom with a mission. John Travolta is the irresponsible cabdriver who could be Mr. Right. With Olympia Dukakis, Abe Vigoda and George Segal as the biological father.
VHS: S12124. $14.95.
Amy Heckerling, USA, 1989, 96 mins.

Looking for Mr. Goodbar
Diane Keaton stars as an idealistic young teacher caught up in the casual sex atmosphere of the 1970's. Based on the novel by Judith Rossner, this film follows Keaton's aimless exploration of singles bars and the various men that she meets in these quintessentially 70's locales. Of course she regrets it all but not before she meets a young Richard Gere. Tuesday Weld and Tom Berenger are also featured.
VHS: S22511. $39.95.
Richard Brooks, USA, 1977, 136 mins.

Lord of the Flies
Sir William Golding's Pulitzer Prize-winning classic is updated, Americanized and presented in living color. Director Harry Hook (*The Kitchen Toto*) guides 25 novice, young performers through a compelling and dehumanizing adventure. Golding's message of the thin veneer of civilization remains relatively intact despite references to "Alf" and "Miss Piggy". With Bathazar Getty, Chris Furrh and Daniel Pipoly.
VHS: S12523. $19.95.
Laser: LD72305. $49.95.
Harry Hook, USA, 1990, 90 mins.

Lorenzo's Oil
George Miller's film is based on a true story. Nick Nolte and Susan Sarandon portray an economist and a linguist who take on the medical and scientific establishments in their desperate search to find a cure for their son (Zack O'Malley Greenberg), stricken with ALD, a rare, fatal, degenerative brain disorder.
VHS: S18763. $19.98.
Laser: LD71882. $39.98.
George Miller, USA, 1992, 136 mins.

Losing Isaiah
Jessica Lange and Halle Berry star in this wrenching drama about two women locked in a struggle over the same child. It poses tough questions about the most important elements of parenthood. Also featuring Samuel L. Jackson, David Strathairn and Cuba Gooding, Jr.
VHS: S26160. $19.95.
Stephen Gyllenhaal, USA, 1994, 108 mins.

Lost Angels
Hugh Hudson directed this recent feature which stars Donald Sutherland and Adam Horovitz. Set in the suburbs of Los Angeles, the film stars Horovitz as Tim, a high school student who's getting into trouble more than this parents can handle. Unwittingly admitted to a psychiatric hospital for wayward teens, he meets a doctor who sees Tim's bitterness as due to lack of family concern and tries to help him change and move ahead. Featured at the 1989 Cannes Film Festival.
VHS: S10899. $89.98.
Hugh Hudson, USA, 1989, 116 mins.

Lost in Yonkers
Martha Coolidge's evocative adaptation of Neil Simon's Pulitzer Prize-winning play is a war-era tale of two young brothers left in the care of their German grandmother (Irene Worth). The boys fall under the spell of their eccentric, good-natured aunt (Mercedes Ruehl) and their gangster uncle (Richard Dreyfuss).
VHS: S19529. $19.95.
Laser: LD71923. $34.95.
Martha Coolidge, USA, 1993, 112 mins.

Love Affair
Warren Beatty and Annette Bening star in this remake of *An Affair to Remember* as two lovers who, despite their immediate connection, must face the problems of their other romantic attachments. Katharine Hepburn is featured along with Gary Shandling and Pierce Brosnan.
VHS: S24260. $19.98.
Laser: LD74842. $34.98.
Glenn Gordon Caron, USA, 1994, 108 mins.

Lush Life
Forest Whitaker gives a tour-de-force performance as an inspired jazz musician who introduces his best friend, Jeff Goldblum, to the jazz highlife. Wine, women and song make for a heady mix and a powerful film that shows how life and art are connected.
VHS: S21832. $94.95.
Michael Elias, USA, 1993, 106 mins.

Mad Dog and Glory
John McNaughton's drama forges a complicated relationship among three lost souls. A shy Chicago forensics cop (Robert De Niro) derisively named "Mad Dog" inadvertently saves the life of a sullen mobster and loan shark (Bill Murray). His reward is the ambiguous one-week services of Glory (Uma Thurman), a beautiful bartender indentured to the gangster. With David Caruso, Kathy Baker and McNaughton regular Tom Towles.
VHS: S18995. $19.98.
Laser: Letterboxed. LD71890. $34.98.
John McNaughton, USA, 1993, 99 mins.

Mad Love
The ultimate romantic couple, Chris O'Donnell and Drew Barrymore, are featured in this dark and disturbing road movie. Their love seems to make all the sense in the world, but it seems that everyone is against them. Slowly it becomes clear that they have an insurmountable problem, and they learn the hard way that the right choice is rarely the easiest choice, and that sometimes even love is not enough.
VHS: S26614. $99.95.
Laser: LD75319. $39.98.
Antonia Bird, USA, 1995, 96 mins.

Magnificent Adventurer
A saga about Benvenuto Cellini, the famed Florentine sculptor, whose passion for fine arts was matched only by his love for beautiful women and swordplay. With Brett Halsey and Claudia Mori. 1976, 94 mins.
VHS: $11116. $59.95.

The Main Event
Barbra Streisand is a wacky but bankrupt cosmetics executive who finds her finances are dependent upon an over-the-hill boxer played by Ryan O'Neal. The chemistry is apparent from the beginning as Barbra badgers and cajoles the demoralized fighter to perform in the ring. Streisand sings the title song.
VHS: $21929. $14.95.
Howard Zieff , USA, 1979, 105 mins.

Making Love
Michael Ontkean, Kate Jackson and Harry Hamlin star in this film about a love triangle in which two men fall in love. Ontkean is a successful, married doctor who realizes that his perfect marriage has only one problem—he doesn't sexually desire women. Fortunately a young Hamlin is there to show him the way.
VHS: $19448. $69.98.
Arthur Hiller, USA, 1982, 113 mins.

Malice
Alec Baldwin stars in this sexy thriller featuring deception, betrayal and murder. As a gynecologist he reveals a less-than-caring attitude toward a former patient, setting in motion this tense tale of obsessive violence.
VHS: $20719. $95.98.
Laser: LD74458. $39.99.
Harold Becker, USA, 1993, 106 mins.

The Man and the Snake/The Return
Two tales by Ambrose Bierce from the American Short Story collection which capture the mystery and mood of Bierce's writing. Oscar-winning cinematographer Sture Rydman shot both of the tales, which star John Fraser and Andre Morrell, and Peter Vaughan and Rosalie Crutchley. 60 mins.
VHS: $08791. $24.95.

A Man for All Seasons
Charlton Heston directs and stars in this remake of Robert Bolt's historical play about the moral battle between Sir Thomas More and King Henry VIII over the formation of the Church of England. A sweeping epic with Vanessa Redgrave and Sir John Gielgud as Cardinal Wolsey.
VHS: $08228. $79.98.
Charlton Heston, USA, 1988, 120 mins.

Man in the Moon
An emotionally rewarding, coming-of-age story set in the deep South during the 1950's. Reese Witherspoon makes a memorable debut as 14-year-old Dani, an energetic Louisiana tomboy who suddenly discovers the wonder of the boy next door. Unfortunately for her, he also has eyes for her older sister. With Jason London, Emily Warfield, Gail Strickland, Sam Waterston and Tess Harper.
VHS: $16435. $19.98.
Laser: LD71453. $29.98.
Robert Mulligan, USA, 1991, 99 mins.

Man in the Wilderness
This true account concerns a man attacked by a savage grizzly who's left for dead by his cruel superiors during a fur trading expedition in the 1820s. With Richard Harris, John Huston and Percy Herbert.
VHS: $18610. $19.98.
Richard C. Sarafian, USA, 1971, 105 mins.

The Man Without a Face
In his debut film as a director, Mel Gibson adapts the novel by Isabelle Holland and plays the role of a disfigured loner who reluctantly agrees to tutor a fatherless boy (Nick Stahl) so the boy will be admitted into a military prep academy. The two develop an honest and deep relationship which becomes an invaluable lesson in the boy's search for identity, meaning and significance. With Margaret Whitton, Fay Masterson, Gaby Hoffmann, Geoffrey Lewis and Richard Masur.
VHS: $20375. $19.98.
Mel Gibson, USA, 1993, 115 mins.

Marlowe
James Garner stars as Philip Marlowe in this slick update of Raymond Chandler's *The Little Sister*. Marlowe is hired by a nervous young girl to find her missing brother. With a sizzling performance by Rita Moreno as a stripper who helps Garner crack the case.
VHS: $13759. $19.98.
Paul Bogart, USA, 1969, 95 mins.

Mask
Based on a true story, Bogdanovich's account of a courageous teenager who suffers from a disease that enlarged his head, and who searches for love and tries to get his mother (Cher) off drugs.
VHS: $24563. $14.98.
Laser: LD70055. $29.95.
Peter Bogdanovich, USA, 1985, 120 mins.

Matinee
Joe Dante's unjustly neglected feature is a brilliant investigation of Cold War paranoia. Set in a coastal Florida town, John Goodman stars as a William Castle prototype 50s shock producer mounting his fiendish, low grade science fiction classic *Mant!* ("Half man, Half ant, All terror!") during the intense political tension of the Cuban Missile Crisis. The large ensemble cast (including Cathy Moriarty, John Sayles, Dick Miller and some engaging teenage performers) is excellent.
VHS: $18714. $19.98.
Laser: Letterboxed. LD71879. $39.98.
Joe Dante, USA, 1992, 98 mins.

Mayflower Madam
Candice Bergen steps into the role of Sydney Biddle Barrows, the Big Apple socialite with ancestors who arrived in the first boat to Plymouth Rock. She caused quite a stir when arrested for operating an escort service. A made-for-tv movie about how to run the world's oldest profession with a touch of elegance in the 1980's. Based on the book by Barrows, who has a cameo role as a shocked member of New York City society.
VHS: $08500. $19.95.
Lou Antonio, USA, 1988, 100 mins.

Member of the Wedding
Julie Harris gives an exceptional performance as a motherless, 12-year-old girl who is tormented by the awkwardness of adolescence and her struggle toward womanhood. With Ethel Waters and Brandon De Wilde.
VHS: $07001. $69.95.
Fred Zinnemann, USA, 1953, 91 mins.

Memphis
Cybill Shepherd stars as Reeny Purdew, one of three low-down Mississippi Delta drifters with a plan to kidnap the young grandson of a successful black Memphis businessman in 1957. Based on the novel *September September* by Civil War buff Shelby Foote. With John Laughlin, J.E. Freeman, Richard Brooks, Vanessa Bell Calloway, Martin C. Gardner and Moses Gunn. Script by Larry McMurtry, Cybill Shepherd and Susan Rhinehart. From the Canadian director of the riveting armored car heist film, *Pouvoir Intime*.
VHS: $15944. $89.98.
Yves Simoneau, USA, 1992, 92 mins.

Memphis Belle
They've flown 24 missions in their B-17 "Flying Fortress" called the *Memphis Belle*. Now there's just one thing keeping the flyboys from going home to a hero's welcome—mission #25, their most dangerous raid ever. Mathew Modine heads a popular young cast, including Eric Stoltz, Billy Zane, D.B. Sweeney and singer Harry Connick Jr., in this exciting World War II adventure based on a true story. Produced by David Puttnam and Catherine Wyler (whose father William Wyler first told the story of the *Memphis Belle* in a 1944 documentary).
VHS: $13581. $19.98.
Michael Caton-Jones, USA, 1990, 107 mins.

Men Don't Leave
A warmly comic drama from the director of *Risky Business*. Jessica Lange is Beth, totally unprepared for life without her husband. Charming and unpredictable, Beth copes with teenage sons, a new job, and going out on her own.
VHS: $12920. $19.98.
Paul Brickman, USA, 1989, 115 mins.

Mi Vida Loca: My Crazy Life
Allison Anders' vibrant feature is set in Echo Park, Los Angeles, where best friends Sad Girl and Mousie are now enemies as they have both become pregnant by the same man, Ernesto, a local drug dealer. A gritty slice of life.
VHS: $23484. $95.99.
Laser: LD75229. $34.98.
Allison Anders, USA, 1994, 94 mins.

Miami Rhapsody
Sarah Jessica Parker, Antonio Banderas and Mia Farrow are at their best in this light-hearted romantic comedy set in a very contemporary Miami. Parker thinks she is happily engaged until she finds out that every member of her family is involved in an outrageous affair.
VHS: $25633. $96.95.
Laser: LD75013. $39.99.
David Frankel, USA, 1994, 95 mins.

A Midnight Clear
Keith Gordon improves on the promise of *The Chocolate War* with this naturalistic and intelligently made World War II film about a reconnaissance unit, made up of intellectually gifted soldiers, enlisted for a dangerous mission inside the German front near the end of the war. With Kevin Dillon, Gary Sinise, Peter Berg, Ethan Hawke, Frank Whaley and Arye Gross.
VHS: $17624. $19.98.
Laser: LD71775. $34.95.
Keith Gordon, USA, 1991, 107 mins.

Midnight Express
From the director of *Birdy* and Pink Floyd's *The Wall*, Alan Parker's hyper violent and grim portrait of American student Billy Hayes, who was sentenced to 30 years in a Turkish prison for attempting to smuggle hashish into the West. Brad Davis is riveting in the lead role as the frightened Hayes; Paul Smith is memorably brutish as the perversely sadistic chief guard. The Oscar-winning screenplay is by Oliver Stone.
VHS: $02549. $69.95.
Laser: Letterboxed, chapter stops, 3 sides. LD74476. $39.95.
Alan Parker, USA, 1978, 123 mins.

Midnight Run
Robert De Niro plays a bounty hunter assigned to find and return Charles Grodin to a sleazy L.A. bail bondsman. Grodin embezzled millions from the Mob, which he donated to charity, and they want him dead. An entertaining, action-packed, cross-country, serious comedy with Yaphet Kotto, John Ashton, Dennis Farina and the person who wrote this description as an extra in an airport scene. From the Director of *Beverly Hills Cop*.
VHS: $08325. $19.95.
Martin Brest, USA, 1988, 125 mins.

Midway
The tides turned for the Americans when the Japanese attacked the Pacific Island of Midway in 1942. Integrating antique Japanese war films and actual newsreel footage, *Midway* portrays this decisive battle as played out by the familiar faces of Charlton Heston, Henry Fonda, Robert Mitchum, Glenn Ford, James Coburn, Hal Holbrook and Robert Wagner, with Tom Selleck, Pat Morita and Erik Estrada.
VHS: $16302. $19.98.
Jack Smight, USA, 1976, 131 mins.

The Mighty Quinn
Denzel Washington has the title role of a local police chief in Jamaica caught between doing his job and preserving a boyhood friendship. Robert Townsend is Maubee, a petty criminal and island legend who stumbles into an international situation that involves murder and large sums of money. A comic thriller loaded with lots of good music. With James Fox, Sheryl Lee Ralph and M. Emmet Walsh.
VHS: $11203. $89.98.
Carl Schenkel, USA, 1989, 98 mins.

The Migrants
Cloris Leachman, Ron Howard and Sissy Spacek star in this adaptation of Tennessee Williams' great drama. It's a story of a family working hard to achieve the ever-receding American dream. All their hopes come to reside in the fortunes of their son. Sadly, he may not be able to live up to all their expectations. Nominated for six Emmy Awards. 83 mins.
VHS: $21542. $89.95.
Tom Gries, USA, 1974, 83 mins.

Miles from Home
Richard Gere and Kevin Anderson play two Iowa farming brothers who would rather burn their debt-ridden property than turn it meekly over to the bank that eagerly gave them the loans in the first place. This act makes them folk heroes and wanted outlaws. Feature film directing debut of Gary Sinise, a member of the Steppenwolf Theatre Company, as are most of the cast. With John Malkovich, Terry Kinney, Laurie Metcalf, Judith Ivey and Brian Dennehy. A timely contemporary drama.
VHS: $09109. $19.95.
Gary Sinise, USA, 1988, 112 mins.

Mindwalk
Brent Capra's literate and often provocative meditation on ecology and self-preservation. A chance encounter with three distinct professionals (a poet, a physicist and a politician) leads to a lucid and often fascinating conversation about the fate of the earth. With Liv Ullmann, Sam Waterston, John Heard and Ione Skye. Based on Fritjof Capra's book, *The Turning Point*. Music by Philip Glass.
VHS: $18119. $19.95.
Bernt Capra, USA, 1990, 110 mins.

Miracle of the Heart: A Boy's Town Story
Art Carney stars in this made-for-tv movie about an aging priest fighting against forced retirement. The setting is the familiar stomping grounds of Father Flanagan. Mickey Rooney may be gone but kids like Casey Siemaszko are still acting up.
VHS: $04975. $19.95.
Georg Stanford Brown, USA, 1986, 96 mins.

Misery
Academy Award winner for Best Actress Kathy Bates stars as a devoted and deranged fan of unsuspecting author Paul Sheldon (James Caan) in this thriller. From the novel by Stephen King.
VHS: $21809. $19.95.
Laser: LD72450. $39.99.
Rob Reiner, USA, 1993, 107 mins.

Mishima: A Life in Four Chapters
A bold, dramatic film, filmed in three visual styles shifting from the quasi-documentary view of Mishima, Japan's finest postwar author, to black and white flashbacks and highly stylized excerpts from his novels. Fascinating, ambitious, lyrical. English and Japanese with English subtitles.
VHS: $00861. $79.95.
Paul Schrader, USA, 1985, 121 mins.

Miss Firecracker
Holly Hunter is great as a young woman with a questionable reputation who decides to enter a beauty contest. Tim Robbins, Scott Glenn and Mary Steenburgen are just some of the other talented people involved in this fun film. Though it seems hokey at first, a beauty pageant is absolutely the right path to love and popularity available to this woman in her conservative, Southern hometown.
VHS: $26334. $19.98.
Thomas Schlamme, USA, 1988, 102 mins.

Missiles of October
A gripping, true drama about the dark days of the 1960s Cuban missile crisis. Starring Martin Sheen, William Devane.
VHS: $03693. $29.98.
Anthony Page, USA, 1974, 150 mins.

Mission
Two renegade Jesuit priests force the ruling European landowners to climb up a very tall mountain and massacre innocent South American indians. Robert De Niro and Jeremy Irons star in this beautifully photographed, historical drama. With Aidan Quinn.
VHS: $04306. $19.98.
Laser: Letterboxed. LD71201. $39.98.
Roland Joffe, USA, 1986, 126 mins.

Mississippi Burning
Gene Hackman and Willem Dafoe head an FBI investigative team looking to uncover the circumstances surrounding three missing civil rights workers. A powerfully acted and photographed film that blurs historic fact for dramatic effect. With Frances McDormand and Brad Dourif.
VHS: $09573. $19.98.
Alan Parker, USA, 1988, 127 mins.

Mississippi Masala
Moving to the American South in her American debut, the Indian-born, Harvard-educated filmmaker Mira Nair (*Salaam Bombay!*) inverts the Romeo and Juliet story, concerning the forbidden love affair of an entrepreneurial black man (Denzel Washington) and a sheltered, young, Indian woman of their respective families. Brilliantly shot by Ed Lachman, Nair has a marvelous and open way with actors. With Roshan Seth, Charles S. Dutton, and Joe Seneca.
VHS: $17070. $19.95.
Laser: LD72200. $34.95.
Mira Nair, USA, 1991, 110 mins.

Mister Johnson
Bruce Beresford directs this thoughtful and strongly performed study of British colonialism and human relations in Africa. Set in 1923, Pierce Brosnan stars as a district officer assigned to build a road through the bush. The task is accomplished with the help and creative financial calculations of his chief clerk, Mister Johnson. Maynard Eziashi is memorable as the ambitious and unlucky native. With Edward Woodward and Denis Quilley. Based on the novel by Joyce Cary.
VHS: $15407. $19.98.
Bruce Beresford, USA, 1991, 105 mins.

Mistral's Daughter
Judith Krantz's best-selling novel, starting in the 1920's Paris of Chanel and Picasso, to the modeling agencies of 1950's New York, to the contemporary model wars, is a sizzling portrait of glamour life at the top of the world of art and high fashion. With Stacy Keach, Robert Urich, Stefanie Powers, Lee Remick. Total length: 390 mins.
VHS: $04901. $79.95.

Molly Maguires
Sean Connery stars as a leader of the Molly Maguires, a secret society of Irish mine-workers in Pennsylvania in the 1870's who battle their exploitation by mine owners with violence. With Richard Harris and Samantha Eggar.
VHS: $02024. $29.95.
Martin Ritt, USA, 1969, 123 mins.

Mommie Dearest
The outrageous cult movie of the legendary star Joan Crawford, based upon the bestselling book by her adopted daughter Christina Crawford. Faye Dunaway plays Crawford struggling against her inner demons, desperate to be a mother, descending into alcoholism.
VHS: $00869. $19.98.
Laser: LD75385. $35.98.
Frank Perry, USA, 1981, 129 mins.

Money Train
Wesley Snipes and Woody Harrelson are two undercover cops who guard the New York City subway train known as the "Money Train." This action-comedy takes a strange twist when they realize that their work has prepared them for a unique career in crime. Hip, funny and violent, this is a gripping thriller.
VHS: $27507. $101.99.
Laser: LD75522. $34.95.
Joseph Ruben, USA, 1995, 110 mins.

Monkey Trouble
Thora Birch and Harvey Keitel star in this family film about a slightly neglected young girl who befriends a pickpocket monkey. Keitel is the monkey's trainer and owner, who just happens to need his partner for a big heist.
VHS: $22973. $19.98.
Franco Amurri, USA, 1994, 93 mins.

A Month by the Lake
A superb showcase for Vanessa Redgrave as Miss Bentley, an Englishwoman who travels to Italy's Lake Como as she had done for years with her late father before his death. On this particular trip, The Major (Edward Fox), a newcomer to lake Como, appears, and Miss Bentley has a chance at love. Unfortunately, the Major keeps getting distracted by a sexy, young, flirtatious woman (Uma Thurman). Many wonderful repartees result as the two women vie for the attentions of this wealthy bachelor against the backdrop of a luxurious resort. Based on a novel by H.E. Bates.
VHS: $27524. $99.95.
Laser: LD75547. $39.99.
John Irvin, USA, 1995, 91 mins.

Moonlight and Valentino
Elizabeth Perkins stars as Rebecca, a woman who turns to a support network which comprises of her best friend Sylvie (Whoopi Goldberg), her stepmother Alberta (Kathleen Turner) and her sister Lucie (Gwyneth Paltrow) when her husband dies suddenly. Neil Simon's daughter Ellen wrote this serious but humor-filled study of four women responding to grief. Their different approaches are exacerbated when the widow falls for her sexy house painter (played by rock star Jon Bon Jovi).
VHS: $27530. $96.99.
Laser: LD75526. $34.95.
David Anspaugh, USA, 1995, 104 mins.

Moonstruck
The winner of three Oscars, this charming, romantic, ethnic comedy involves a somewhat dowdy Cher involved with two brothers. She's engaged to Danny Aiello but in love with Nicolas Cage. Her parents, Olympia Dukakis and Vincent Gardenia, have their own problems, but wish her the best. Screenplay by John Patrick Shanley (*Five Corners*). Set in Brooklyn.
VHS: $07105. $19.98.
Norman Jewison, USA, 1987, 103 mins.

Morituri
German filmmaker Bernhard Wicki (*The Bridge*) directed this story of a German employed by the British to undertake a dangerous mission aboard a Nazi ship. Marlon Brando and Yul Brynner star.
VHS: $05914. $19.98.
Bernhard Wicki, USA, 1965, 123 mins.

Morning After
Jane Fonda stars as a struggling alcoholic who awakens in a strange bed next to a murdered man, with Jeff Bridges and Raul Julia.
VHS: $03437. $19.98.
Sidney Lumet, USA, 1986, 103 mins.

Moscow on the Hudson
Paul Mazursky (*Unmarried Woman, Blume in Love*) limits the abrupt improvisations that marred Robin Williams' other work, guiding the comedian to his best work as Vladimir, a Russian saxophonist in the Soviet Circus who defects to the West while visiting Bloomingdale's during a New York tour. Maria Conchita Alonso stars as Williams' love interest.
VHS: S02552. $14.95.
Paul Mazursky, USA, 1984, 107 mins.

Mountains of the Moon
Bob Rafelson directed this epic about finding the source of the mysterious River Nile during Victorian England, based on the novel by William Harrison. In an 1854 expedition, two remarkable men, Capt. Richard Burton and Lt. John Speke, embark upon a journey through the wilderness dangerous to both body and soul. The perils of the quest forge a strong bond between the men that one man honors and the other will eventually betray. A powerful adventure.
VHS: S12479. $14.98.
Bob Rafelson, USA, 1990, 140 mins.

Moving
Richard Pryor has just lost his engineering job but has the chance of a lifetime if he can just move 2,000 miles to Boise, Idaho. Predictably, the move is full of comic obstacles. With Beverly Todd and Randy Quaid.
VHS: S21452. $19.98.
Alan Metter, USA, 1988, 89 mins.

Mr. Corbett's Ghost
Circa 1767, New Year's Eve, in a small English town, and Ben Corbett (Paul Scofield) is kept late working by his boss at the apothecary. Ben wishes death upon his employer, and after a mysterious visit from a man who claims to bargain with souls (John Huston), his wish is granted. Now Ben is uncertain about to whom he really belongs, the ghost of his boss or his new master, the Collector of Souls. 1990, 60 mins.
VHS: S13011. $24.95.

Mr. Destiny
James Belushi gets a chance at living his life over when he complains to a magical bartender played by Michael Caine. He soon learns it may be a wonderful life just the way it used to be. With Linda Hamilton, Jon Lovitz, Hart Bochner and Rene Russo. The palatial mansion that serves as Belushi's new home was seen before in *Being There*.
VHS: S13752. $92.95.
James Orr, USA, 1990, 110 mins.

Mr. Frost
He hasn't spoken in two years. No one knows his identity. Officially he doesn't exist...but 24 corpses do. Based on a true story, *Mr. Frost* tests the waters between good and evil, tempting human nature with one irreparable act—murder. With an all-star cast featuring Jeff Goldblum, Alan Bates and Kathy Baker, this eerie thriller exposes the menacing power beneath the surface of a seemingly charming and civilized individual.
VHS: S13537. $89.95.
Phillip Setbon, USA, 1989, 92 mins.

Mr. Jones
Lena Olin plays a successful psychiatrist who gives in to an unprofessional impulse and starts an affair with the charismatic Mr. Jones, played by Richard Gere. This sexy drama tests the limits of professional standards and the irresistible needs of love.
VHS: S20739. $19.95.
Laser: LD72388. $34.95.
Mike Figgis, USA, 1993, 110 mins.

Mr. North
The directorial debut of Danny Huston, son of legendary director John Huston. A Yale graduate's life is suddenly transformed when word gets out that he has miraculous curative powers. Not everyone in the top drawer world of wealthy Rhode Islanders is pleased, however. While some admire him, others want nothing to do with this pleasant faith healer. Set during the 1920s, this film fable is adapted from *Theophilus North* by Thornton Wilder. With Anthony Edwards, Lauren Bacall, Anjelica Huston and Mary Stuart Masterson.
VHS: S26156. $14.98.
Danny Huston, USA, 1988, 90 mins.

Mr. Wonderful
Matt Dillon, Annabella Sciorra, Mary-Louise Parker and William Hurt star in this bittersweet love story about a divorced man who is trying to marry off his ex-wife so he can use her alimony money to start a bowling alley with his buddies.
VHS: S23441. $19.98.
Anthony Minghella, USA, 1993, 99 mins.

Mrs. Soffel
Diane Keaton is a prison warden's wife who falls under the spell of a condemned murderer and aids in his and his brother's dramatic escape. Mel Gibson is the clever and not-so-bad-looking criminal and Matthew Modine is the tag-along brother. Based on a true story set in 1901. With Edward Herrmann and Trini Alvarado. Well directed by Gillian Armstrong (*My Brilliant Career*).
VHS: S06152. $19.99.
Laser: LD72147. $34.98.
Gillian Armstrong, USA, 1984, 113 mins.

Murder in the First
Christian Slater, Kevin Bacon and Gary Oldman star in this courtroom drama. An idealistic lawyer (Slater) takes on the case of a condemned man in Alcatraz (Bacon) and points out the unfair nature of his incarceration. As the story unfolds, their friendship becomes the sole means of keeping their hopes alive.
VHS: S24854. $19.98.
Marc Rocco, USA, 1994, 123 mins.

Murder One
The recreation of a murderous real life crime spree by three escaped prisoners and the younger brother of one of the convicts. Henry Thomas as the little brother tries to phone home for help but the law enforcement officers in Georgia don't take kindly to Yankees murdering the locals. With James Wilder, Stephen Shellen and Errol Slue. A gritty, realistic drama.
VHS: S07917. $79.98.
Graeme Campbell, USA, 1988, 83 mins.

Murphy's Romance
A divorced young mother (Sally Field) and a charming pharmacist (James Garner) spar and fall in love in Martin Ritt's comic love story.
VHS: S00900. $14.95.
Martin Ritt, USA, 1985, 107 mins.

My Antonia
Willa Cather's book has been adapted for the screen in this sensitive film starring Jason Robards, Eva Marie Saint and Neil Patrick Harris. An orphaned boy discovers the mysteries of life and love with a poor immigrant girl.
VHS: S24384. $79.95.
Joseph Sargent, USA, 1994, 92 mins.

My Little Girl
Mary Stuart Masterson stars as Franny, an affluent teen who volunteers to work in a city shelter for disadvantaged girls in Philadelphia. Her enthusiasm is met with scorn but she perseveres to make a difference. With James Earl Jones, Anne Meara and Geraldine Page, in her last role.
VHS: S07139. $79.95.
Connie Kaiserman, USA, 1987, 118 mins.

My Wicked Wicked Ways
Based on the best-selling autobiography of swashbuckling screen idol Errol Flynn, one of Hollywood's all-time most romantic and controversial figures. Duncan Regehr stars as Flynn, along with a supporting cast including Barbara Hershey and Darren McGavin.
VHS: S09933. $59.98.
Don Taylor, USA, 1984, 95 mins.

Nell
Jodie Foster and Liam Neeson star in this bizarre tale about a woman who inhabits her own world. A doctor discovers an isolated woman with a unique pattern of speech. Soon he must fight to keep her free from legal encroachment and the demands of research scientists. Foster won an Academy Award nomination for her role. Natasha Richardson is also featured.
VHS: S25615. $19.98.
Laser: Widescreen. LD74978. $39.99.
Michael Apted, USA, 1995, 113 mins.

The Net
Sandra Bullock stars as a nerdy computer consultant who finds herself trapped in an overwhelming conspiracy. Before she realizes what is happening, she becomes a woman without an identity, fighting villains and battling to save the country. Featuring Dennis Miller and Jeremy Northam.
VHS: S26921. $19.95.
Laser: LD75403. $39.95.
Irwin Winkler, USA, 1995, 114 mins.

Network
A savage satire written by Paddy Chayefsky, looking at the powers behind television programming. With a sizzling performance by Peter Finch (I'm mad as hell and I'm not going to take it anymore) as newscaster Howard Beale, with Faye Dunaway and William Holden.
VHS: S01817. $19.95.
Sidney Lumet, USA, 1976, 116 mins.

Never Talk to Strangers
Antonio Banderas, Rebecca De Mornay, Dennis Miller and Harry Dean Stanton all star in this erotic thriller. De Mornay's character, an aloof psychologist, unexpectedly falls for an odd stranger (Banderas). Though their sexual chemistry seems the prelude to a deeper understanding, it actually leads to danger and death.
VHS: S27307. $98.99.
Laser: LD75480. $34.95.
Peter Hall, USA, 1995, 86 mins.

The New Age
Peter Weller and Judy Davis play a married couple who quit their jobs to open their own boutique. Despite their best efforts, it never really succeeds. The story of their failure provides an amusing and engaging view of the feel-good precepts of "The New Age." Samuel Jackson and Adam West are also featured.
VHS: S23860. $19.98.
Laser: Widescreen. LD74923. $34.98.
Michael Tolkin, USA, 1994, 106 mins.

The New Centurions
An all-star cast in a brilliant episodic adaptation of Joseph Wambaugh's best seller about two rookie cops in Los Angeles who are addicted to danger. Cynical film with good performances and solid storytelling. Starring George C. Scott and Stacy Keach.
VHS: S13574. $14.95.
Richard Fleischer, USA, 1972, 103 mins.

New Jersey Drive
This tough urban tale follows a crew of homeys that live for the thrill of stealing cars. They ride them and sell them to chopshops for cash. A policeman takes a personal interest in stopping their game and the chase turns violent. The odds against survival are great but there's a chance they can get out alive. Music by Queen Latifah, Blak Panta, Heavy D, Naughty by Nature and others.
VHS: S26345. $19.98.
Laser: LD75056. $34.98.
Nick Gomez, USA, 1995, 98 mins.

New Year's Day...Time to Move On
Independent American filmmaker Henry Jaglom once again attempts to examine the nature of contemporary relationships between men and women. He stars as a man in the middle of a mid-life crisis who takes possession of his new apartment only to find the previous tenants—three women—haven't quite moved out. With Gwen Welles, Maggie Jackson, Melanie Winter and Milos Forman.
VHS: S13199. $79.98.
Henry Jaglom, USA, 1989, 90 mins.

New York Nights
Three young and alluring women (Marilyn Chambers, Julia Parton and Susan Napoli), join forces in their quest for the good life in the Big Apple. One is a former model, one is just starting out as an actress, and the third is simply looking for gold. Together they share notes on life, love and the pursuit of happiness through financial security.
VHS: S22539. $89.95.
D. Gary Phelps, USA, 1994, 90 mins.

Nick of Time
Johnny Depp faces off against Christopher Walken in this tense thriller. Walken has kidnapped Depp's young daughter, forcing Depp to comply with a political assassination plot for the ransom. It's a tense standoff where a taut sense of time racing by gives this dilemma added weight.
VHS: S27635. $99.99.
John Badham, USA, 1995, 89 mins.

Night and the City
Irwin Winkler's remake of Jules Dassin's classic 1950 noir stars Robert De Niro as Harry Fabian, a small-time, ambulance-chasing lawyer trying to escape his bleak, anonymous life as a fight promoter in the mob-influenced local boxing circuit. Jessica Lange stars as a bar maid caught in a violent marriage with a dangerous attraction to Fabian. With Cliff Gorman, Alan King, Jack Warden and Eli Wallach.
VHS: S18247. $19.98.
Irwin Winkler, USA, 1992, 104 mins.

The Night of the Following Day
In this chilling adaptation of Lionel White's *The Snatches*, Marlon Brando, together with three associates, orchestrates a daring plan to kidnap a young girl (Pamela Franklin). The plan slowly unravels as each criminal goes slightly mad. "A keenly conducted seminar in the poetics of psychological terror, the film is one of the tensest, toughest thrillers in a long time" (*Time Magazine*). With Richard Boone, Rita Moreno and Jess Hahn.
VHS: S19575. $89.98.
Stuart Cornfield, USA, 1969, 93 mins.

Night Terror
Valerie Harper stars as a housewife who has witnessed the shooting of a highway patrolman.
VHS: S08150. $59.95.
E.W. Swackhamer, USA, 1977, 78 mins.

Nightbreaker
Martin Sheen and Emilio Estevez star in this examination of the U.S. Army's atomic testing of the 1950s, uncovering, in the process, a nuclear nightmare.
VHS: S09599. $79.98.
Peter Markle, USA, 1989, 100 mins.

Nightmare Years
Based on the memoirs of American writer William L. Shirer, and adapted for the screen by Bob Woodward. Sam Waterston and Marthe Keller star in this production shot in Europe detailing the battle to stop Hitler.
VHS: S12191. $89.98.
Anthony Page, USA, 1989, 237 mins.

Nina Takes a Lover
Laura San Giacomo stars as Nina, a young married woman itching for excitement. Her best friend has a lover and seeing them together plants the idea of taking a lover in Nina's head. All it takes is an exciting young British photographer and a series of interviews with a reporter about marriage and infidelity to get Nina going.
VHS: S26800. $95.95.
Alan Jacobs, USA, 1995, 100 mins.

No Drums, No Bugles
A finely wrought drama adapted from a West Virginia story concerning moral convictions and political beliefs. Martin Sheen plays a conscientious objector who avoids military service during the Civil War by hiding in a cave for three years.
VHS: S05173. $19.95.
Clyde Ware, USA, 1971, 85 mins.

Nobody's Fool
Paul Newman, Jessica Tandy and Melanie Griffith are featured in this acclaimed film. It received Academy Award nominations for Best Actor and Best Screenplay. The story follows an older small town scamp leading a comfortable but irresponsible life. Everything changes with the arrival of his estranged son.
VHS: S25719. $19.95.
Robert Benton, USA, 1994, 110 mins.

Nobody's Girls
Cloris Leachman, Esther Rolle and Tanto Cardinal star in this collection of true stories from the Old West about women who used their talents to pioneer long and turbulent lives, from the dry Southwest to the colder climes of Alaska. Whether fighting political battles or simply engaged in making a living, the grit and tenacity of these women is inspiring.
VHS: S25743. $29.95.
Mirra Bank, USA, 1995, 90 mins.

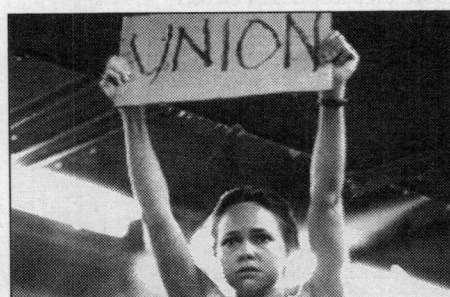

Norma Rae
Sally Fields in her Oscar-winning performance as a spunky Southern mill worker gradually won over to unionization by Ron Leibman as a New York organizer. With Beau Bridges.
VHS: S02343. $19.98.
Laser: LD71257. $34.98.
Martin Ritt, USA, 1979, 117 mins.

Nostradamus
Tcheky Caryo, Rutger Hauer, F. Murray Abraham and Amanda Plummer star in this lavish film about the Western world's most visionary prophet. This monk from the 16th century committed his hellish visions of the future to paper and they have continued to haunt the world with their vividness and their accuracy.
VHS: S24387. $19.95.
Laser: LD74942. $39.99.
Roger Christian, USA, 1994, 118 mins.

Not Without My Daughter
Sally Field stars in the story of a woman, alone with her daughter, who must escape from her husband (Alfred Molina), and from a land where thousands of years of Islamic law makes women a man's personal property. Based on a true story of terror in the volatile Middle East.
VHS: S14101. $14.95.
Brian Gilbert, USA, 1990, 107 mins.

Now and Then
Rosie O'Donnell, Demi Moore, Melanie Griffith and Rita Wilson star in this coming-of-age story. Four women reunite as one of them prepares to give birth, and together they relive the most important summer of their youth. The lessons they learned and the friendships they forged back then have had the strength to carry them through the troubles they've faced in their adult lives. This light comedy has an upbeat and affirming core.
VHS: S27412. $102.99.
Laser: LD75510. $39.99.
Lesli Linka Glatter, USA, 1995, 102 mins.

Nuts
Barbra Streisand is a high priced prostitute arrested for murder. Richard Dreyfuss is the lawyer appointed to defend her. Her wealthy parents, Karl Malden and Maureen Stapleton, would rather have her locked away for mental illness. Will Dreyfuss be able to convince Judge James Whitmore otherwise? A courtroom drama with Eli Wallach as the shrink.
VHS: S06813. $19.98.
Martin Ritt, USA, 1987, 116 mins.

O Pioneers!
The astonishing Jessica Lange stars in this handsome and impeccable adaptation of Willa Cather's turn-of-the-century novel about a fiercely independent young woman who inherits her father's land, earns her family a fortune, though must confront her deep feelings for the visionary and dreamer who's returned with his own demands and ambitions. With John Sayles' regular David Strathairn, Tom Aldredge, Reed Diamond, Heather Graham, and Josh Hamilton.
VHS: S17019. $19.98.
Laser: LD71539. $29.98.
Glenn Jordan, USA, 1991, 100 mins.

Obsession
Cliff Robertson loses his wife and daughter to kidnappers. Years later, on a trip to Florence, he discovers a look-alike of his lost love restoring a church. His interest in life is also restored in this Brian de Palma hommage to Hitchcock. Music by Bernard Herrmann.
VHS: S04660. $59.95.
Brian DePalma, USA, 1976, 98 mins.

Of Mice and Men
In this adaptation of John Steinbeck's novel, set in Depression-era California, John Malkovich and Gary Sinise star as childlike Lennie and his guardian George, who desperately attempt to hold on to a prominent piece of land. With Ray Walston, Casey Siemaszko and Sherilyn Fenn.
VHS: S17923. $19.98.
Laser: LD71839. $34.98.
Gary Sinise, USA, 1992, 114 mins.

An Officer and a Gentleman
Richard Gere is the young recruit who learns that overcoming obstacles will make him a man. Lou Gossett is the drill instructor, Debra Winger, the love interest.
VHS: S01586. $14.95.
Taylor Hackford, USA, 1982, 126 mins.

Oliver Twist
George C. Scott portrays Charles Dickens' most enduring villain in this film adaptation of the famous novel. Oliver suffers all the trepidations of a 19th-century English orphan. His courage and fortitude make him an unforgettable icon of the resiliency of the human spirit. Tim Curry is also featured.
VHS: S21008. $14.98.
Clive Donner, USA, 1982, 88 mins.

On Golden Pond
Henry Fonda and Katharine Hepburn play an aging married couple, Norman and Ethel Thayer, spending a dramatic summer in the woods. Their estranged daughter (Jane Fonda) drops by to clear the air and leave Doug McKeon for them to watch. Three Oscars. Henry Fonda's last film.
VHS: S03479. $14.98.
Mark Rydell, USA, 1981, 110 mins.

Once Around
Richard Dreyfuss and Holly Hunter lead an all-star cast in this critically acclaimed tale of life, love and chance, which examines the way a close-knit Italian-American family is thrown into turmoil when the oldest daughter (Hunter) falls in love with an abrasive and forcefully charming businessman (Dreyfuss). Also starring Gena Rowlands, Laura San Giacomo and Danny Aiello.
VHS: S14256. $19.98.
Lasse Hallstrom, USA, 1991, 114 mins.

One Against the Wind
Set in Nazi-occupied France, Judy Davis plays Mark Lidell, a gilded British aristocrat who risks her standing, family's reputation and life to orchestrate a daring freedom movement for Allied soldiers in this true account. With Sam Neill, Denholm Elliott and Anthony Higgins.
VHS: S18001. $14.98.
Larry Elikann, USA, 1991, 100 mins.

One Day in the Life of Ivan Denisovich
Based on the novel by Alexander Solzhenitsyn, a claustrophobic film set in a Stalinist work camp, with Tom Courtenay as Denisovich, trapped in the oppressive system. "A tribute to the spirit of survival."
VHS: S06851. $79.95.
Caspar Wrede, USA, 1980, 105 mins.

One Night Stand
Ally Sheedy portrays a gutsy yet lonely woman in this bizarre and chilling tale. Even though she seems to know exactly what she desires in a man and how to get it, it may not actually be enough. Her story may well prove the inadequacy of one look, one line, and one night.
VHS: S27252. $92.99.
Talia Shire, USA, 1995

One Trick Pony
A rock-solid songfest of the music world's ups and downs, written by and starring Paul Simon, 1987 Best Album Award winner for his double-platinum album, "Graceland."
VHS: S03496. $14.95.
Robert M. Young, USA, 1980, 98 mins.

Onion Field
A compelling film about an ex-cop who witnesses his partner's murder and is haunted by the slow process of justice. Based on a novel by Joseph Wambaugh, who also wrote the screenplay. With James Savage, James Woods and Ronny Cox.
VHS: S21859. $14.95.
Harold Becker, USA, 1979, 126 mins.

Only You
Robert Downey, Jr., and Marisa Tomei are a dream couple in this Cinderella story for the 1990's. Tomei's character believes in the old fashioned ideals of romantic love, and on a trip to Europe this dream is fulfilled beyond her wildest expectations.
VHS: S23926. $19.95.
Laser: LD74800. $34.95.
Norman Jewison, USA, 1994, 109 mins.

Operation Daybreak
Reinhard "Hangman" Heydrich was Hitler's trusted right-hand man. In Prague during the war, the Czech underground tried to assassinate him. This heroic tale of Czech resistance is the focus of a gripping drama starring Timothy Bottoms, Anthony Andrews and Nicola Pagett.
VHS: S21011. $19.98.
Lewis Gilbert, USA, 1976, 102 mins.

Ordinary People
An intense examination of a family being torn apart by tragedy and tension, *Ordinary People* won four Academy Awards including Best Picture and Director. Featuring Donald Sutherland, Mary Tyler Moore and Timothy Hutton.
VHS: S03261. $19.95.
Robert Redford, USA, 1980, 124 mins.

Orphans
Albert Finney stars in this acclaimed film adaptation of the New York play as Harold, a slick gangster who enters the bleak world of two teenaged orphans to become their unlikely "parent" and change their lives forever. With Matthew Mordine, Kevin Anderson.
VHS: S06607. $79.95.
Alan J. Pakula, USA, 1987, 101 mins.

Orpheus Descending
Based on the Tennessee Williams' classic, Vanessa Redgrave stars as Lady Torrance, a bored housewife rutted in a loveless marriage. Enter handsome young stranger Kevin Anderson, who evokes her long-neglected passion. While they submit to their attraction, Lady's dying husband, too weak himself, enlists the help of his klan to punish the lovers.
VHS: S13263. $79.98.
Peter Hall, USA, 1991, 117 mins.

Other People's Money
Danny DeVito is perfectly cast as Larry the Liquidator, a Wall Street shark who likes nothing better than to buy up small companies and sell them for a healthy profit. Gregory Peck, the highly principled owner of New England Wire and Cable, doesn't want to sell the family business. It is up to the crafty legal mind of Penelope Ann Miller to thwart the corporate takeover. Piper Laurie and Dean Jones are longtime NEW&C employees with agendas of their own. From the long-running play by Jerry Sterner.
VHS: S15724. $19.98.
Norman Jewison, USA, 1991, 101 mins.

The Other Side of the Mountain
Jill Kinmont was an Olympic hopeful until she suffered a skiing accident that left her paralyzed. Marilyn Hassett stars in this true life story of courage and recovery. With Beau Bridges, Dabney Coleman and Belinda J. Montgomery.
VHS: S07806. $59.95.
Larry Peerce, USA, 1975, 101 mins.

The Other Side of the Mountain, Part 2
Jill Kinmont was a shoo-in for the Olympics in downhill skiing until a sporting accident occurred. In Part 2 of her true-life story, she must overcome depression and the death of the man who helped her recover. Features Marilyn Hasset and Timothy Bottoms.
VHS: S21766. $19.98.
Larry Peerce, USA, 1978, 99 mins.

Out of Africa
The autobiographical story of Karen Blixen (pen name Isak Dinesen) and her life on a coffee plantation in Kenya around 1914. Winner of seven Academy Awards, starring Robert Redford, Meryl Streep and Klaus Maria Brandauer.
VHS: S00981. $19.95.
Laser: LD70063. $39.98.
Sydney Pollack, USA, 1985, 161 mins.

Out of the Blue
A stark and realistic portrayal of a young girl, Linda Manz, experiencing the frustrations of small town living and thinking. Her response: rebellion. With Raymond Burr and Dennis Hopper; theme song by Neil Young.
Laser: LD70405. $29.95.
Dennis Hopper, USA, 1984, 94 mins.

Outbreak
Imagine a deadly virus is killing American citizens. Dustin Hoffman and Rene Russo play government scientists sent to prevent a deadly plague. Social, personal crises and governmental indifference (or is it intrigue?) combine to hinder their progress. Ultimately, the fear of contagion cannot match the terror unleashed by sheer murderous desire. Also features Donald Sutherland and Morgan Freeman.
VHS: S26159. $19.98.
Laser: LD75037. $39.98.
Wolfgang Petersen, USA, 1995, 128 mins.

Over the Edge
A disturbing teen drama based on a true incident where alienated suburban youth go on a rampage after being pushed too far by insensitive police and out-of-touch educators. The film debut of Matt Dillon. Other solid performances by Vincent Spano, Pamela Ludwig and Michael Kramer. Co-written by Tim Hunter (*River's Edge*).
VHS: S06162. $14.95.
Jonathan Kaplan, USA, 1979, 91 mins.

The Paper
Michael Keaton, Glenn Close, Randy Quaid and Robert Duvall make up the cast of this fast-paced comedy. The world of newspaper journalism is a place where laughs must be had, even as the truth about the seamier realities of life must be uncovered and delivered to a waiting public.
VHS: S22037. $19.98.
Laser: Widescreen. LD74630. $34.98.
Ron Howard, USA, 1994, 112 mins.

The Paper Chase
The popular drama about a freshman at Harvard Law School who realizes the biggest obstacle to his getting good grades is the brilliant but tough Professor Kingsfield (John Houseman). His problems become intensified when he falls in love with the professor's daughter.
VHS: S07369. $19.98.
James Bridges, USA, 1973, 111 mins.

Paper Moon
Ryan O'Neal stars with his young daughter Tatum in this Oscar-nominated adaptation of Joe David Brown's novel, *Addie Pray*. Ryan poses as a man of God, but he really is on the take. He inadvertently hooks up with an orphan who manages to outdo him in the cons he works for cash. Together they create quite a criminal team. Includes introductory segment with Peter Bogdanovich. Letterboxed.
VHS: S25683. $29.95.
Peter Bogdanovich, USA, 1973, 114 mins.

Paris Trout
Dennis Hopper has the title role in this dramatic tale of crime and prejudice in a small Southern town. With Barbara Hershey as his more liberal wife and Ed Harris as the man looking for the truth. Based on the National Book Award winning novel by Pete Dexter. "Truly powerful" (*New York Post*).
VHS: S14503. $19.98.
Stephen Gyllenhaal, USA, 1991, 98 mins.

Party Girl
Parker Posey is a fresh presence in this new film about a girl living in a non-stop party called her life. This club kid must tone it down if she is to keep her exciting new job and her prospective mate. Inevitably, her formerly wild ways keep intruding into her more sober lifestyle. The result is a comedy for today.
VHS: S27175. $96.96.
Laser: LD75467. $34.95.
Daisy Von Scherler Mayer, USA, 1995, 98 mins.

Passenger 57
Wesley Snipes portrays John Cutter, an ex-government agent, who is coincidentally on the same plane as an evil apprehended terrorist (Bruce Payne) headed to trial in L.A. Unfortunately, some of the terrorist's thugs have also sneaked aboard with plans to hijack the plane. Music by Stanley Clarke.
VHS: S21406. $19.98.
Laser: LD74740. $29.98.
Kevin Hooks, USA, 1992, 84 mins.

Pastime
A classic drama about the game of baseball. William Russ gives an exceptional performance as Roy Dean Bream, an aging relief pitcher playing Class D ball in Central California in the late 1950's. With Glenn Plummer, Noble Willingham, Jeffrey Tambor, Scott Plank and Deirdre O'Connell. Watch for cameos by baseball greats Ernie Banks, Bob Feller, Harmon Killebrew, Bill Mazeroski, Don Newcombe and Duke Snider.
VHS: S16041. $19.95.
Robin Armstrong, USA, 1991, 95 mins.

Patriot Games
Harrison Ford stars in this taut Tom Clancy thriller about a retired CIA analyst who saves his family and an English ambassador from an assassination attempt orchestrated by a rogue faction of the IRA. Ford incurs the vengeance of the lead terrorist when he kills the man's younger brother. With Anne Archer, James Earl Jones, Sean Bean, Samuel L. Jackson, Patrick Bergin, Polly Walker and Richard Harris.
VHS: S17772. $19.95.
Laser: Widescreen. LD75236. $34.98.
Phillip Noyce, USA, 1992, 117 mins.

Paul Bartel's Secret Cinema
Two short early films by the director of *Eating Raoul* and *Lust in the Dust*. The first, entitled *Secret Cinema*, tells the story of a woman who cannot decide whether her life is real or she is a filmed subject; the second is an eight minute short called *Naughty Nurse*.
VHS: S01506. $19.95.
Paul Bartel, USA, 1966, 37 mins.

Pelican Brief
Julia Roberts and Denzel Washington star in this fast-paced thriller adapted from John Grisham's novel about a law student (Roberts) who uncovers a conspiracy that puts her in grave danger. Only one journalist (Washington) has the ability and guts to help her expose this plot. Together they must outwit some of the most powerful men in Washington.
VHS: S21079. $19.98.
Laser: LD72411. $39.98.
Alan J. Pakula, USA, 1993, 141 mins.

Penalty Phase
Peter Strauss stars as a respected judge in this above average tv movie who is faced with releasing a violent killer whose civil rights may have been violated. His decision could affect his upcoming re-election. With Melissa Gilbert, Jane Badler, Milly Perkins and Mitchell Ryan. A riveting drama.
VHS: S07343. $19.95.
Tony Richardson, USA, 1986, 90 mins.

Pennies from Heaven
Based on Dennis Potter's British television series *The Singing Detective*, *Pennies from Heaven* is the unique and stylish story of a Depression-era sheet music salesman, played by Steve Martin, whose own dreary, joyless life is contrasted with the cloying optimism of Tin Pan Alley songs from the period. The stunning, escapist splendor of the 1930's-style musical numbers (set to the original recordings) repeatedly clashes with the bleak circumstances of Martin's real-life existence in this dazzling and intellectually provocative musical—beautifully photographed by Gordon Willis. Newly remastered for video.
VHS: S13970. $19.99.
Laser: MGM. LD71774. $34.98.
Herbert Ross, USA, 1981, 108 mins.

The Perez Family
Alfred Molina, Anjelica Huston, Marisa Tomei and Chazz Palminteri star in this super sexy comedy about family, emigration and love, set amidst the Cuban community in Miami. Molina is finally leaving Cuba after 20 years to join his wife, Huston, but a beautiful woman, Tomei, leads him astray. Twenty years of pent-up passion make this diversion an explosive proposition.
VHS: S26442. $19.98.
Laser: LD75086. $39.99.
Mira Nair, USA, 1995, 135 mins.

Perfect
Rolling Stone investigative reporter John Travolta on the health club scene with Jamie Lee Curtis. From the director of *Mike's Murder*, with Laraine Newman.
VHS: S01008. $14.95.
James Bridges, USA, 1985, 120 mins.

Perfume
A study of passion, betrayal, rivalries and ambition as five beautiful women struggle to form an international cosmetics company and compete in the marketplace.
VHS: S18829. $79.95.
Roland S. Jefferson, USA, 1991, 98 mins.

Permanent Record
When a popular, talented, good looking student jumps off a cliff, he leaves behind a bunch of angry and confused friends. Hardest hit is his best friend, played by Keanu Reeves (*River's Edge*), who wants to hold a memorial service at the high school. With Michelle Meyrink, Pamela Gidley and Alan Boyce as the Jumper.
VHS: S07819. $89.95.
Laser: LD75237. $34.98.
Marisa Silver, USA, 1988, 92 mins.

The Personals
A delightfully fresh film about contemporary relationships in a demanding society. The *L.A. Times* said, "The Personals has everything going for it…amid much humor and not a little anguish, there emerges an acute portrait of modern romance."
VHS: S01014. $24.95.
Laser: LD75238. $34.98.
Peter Markle, USA, 1983, 90 mins.

Picture Windows
This omnibus film is a trilogy of heartrending stories directed by three of Hollywood's most highly acclaimed directors. Alan Arkin stars in *Soir Bleu*, the story of a circus clown in love with his boss' troubled but beautiful wife. The second story, *Song of Songs*, stars Sally Kirkland, Brooke Adams and George Segal in the tale of a baker and the women he loves. Finally, *Language of the Heart* is the story of a young ballerina and her street musician beau. This is an intelligent and highly watchable collection of stories that defy simple formulas and easy solutions.
VHS: S27258. $89.98.
Laser: LD75474. $39.99.
Norman Jewison/Peter Bogdanovich/Jonathan Kaplan, USA, 1995, 95 mins.

Pigeon Feathers
From the pen of Pulitzer Prize-winning author John Updike comes the story of a young man's search through the questions of life and death, and the discovery of living. Christopher Collet and Carole McWilliams star as the mother and son returning to life on a farm and finding some answers to the paradox of living. From the American Short Story Collection. 55 mins.
VHS: S07539. $24.95.

Pink Cadillac
Clint Eastwood is a skip tracer named Tommy Novak assigned to bring in Bernadette Peters for jumping bail. This modern day bounty hunter hadn't planned on falling in love with his spunky quarry or attracting the attention of a nasty white supremacist organization on the West Coast, but stuff happens. With Timothy Carhart, Bill McKinney, and Michael Des Barres as the deadly Alex.
VHS: S11412. $19.98.
Buddy Van Horn, USA, 1989, 121 mins.

Pipe Dreams
Gladys Knight makes her acting debut in this story set against the building of the Alaskan pipeline. Soundtrack is full of songs by Gladys Knight and the Pips. With Stephen Verona, Barry Hankerson, Bruce French.
VHS: S21488. $19.95.
Stephen Verona, USA, 1976, 89 mins.

A Place for Annie
Sissy Spacek, Joan Plowright and Mary-Louise Parker star in this story of courage, compassion and forgiveness. These women are competing to give a home to an abandoned baby. Along the way they learn the true meaning of family as they learn to reconcile their desires with the needs of the baby.
VHS: S22892. $19.98.
John Gray, USA, 1994, 98 mins.

Places in the Heart
Against a Depression-torn background in Waxahachi, Texas, Sally Fields plays a Sheriff's widow who struggles against incredible hardships. With fine performances by John Malkovich, Danny Glover, Ed Harris and Amy Madigan.
VHS: S01034. $19.98.
Laser: LD71276. $34.98.
Robert Benton, USA, 1984, 113 mins.

Platoon
Charlie Sheen goes to Southeast Asia and finds out that war is a very traumatic experience. Giant leeches, killer dope and better-prepared opponents are almost as dangerous to his existence as the other members of his platoon. With Tom Berenger and Willem Dafoe. Oscar for Best Picture.
VHS: S04752. $19.98.
Oliver Stone, USA, 1986, 120 mins.

Portnoy's Complaint
Philip Roth's sexual novel of frustration and self-abuse is now a movie starring Dick Benjamin as Alexander Portnoy. Lee Grant is his Jewish mother and Karen Black is Monkey, his sexual fantasy playmate. Not recommended for the visually impaired—it could give them ideas.
VHS: S04176. $19.95.
Ernest Lehman, USA, 1972, 101 mins.

Portrait of an Artist as a Young Man
This beautiful adaptation of Joyce's autobiographical novel is a faithful portrait of the young author and his coming of age. It portrays Stephen Daedalus and his Irish Catholic upbringing—his confrontation with the tyranny of the church, his sexual guilt and frustration—which start him on the path of rebellion. "Packed with great passages of the Joycean language, and the cast is superb." With Bosco Hogan, T.P. McKenna, John Gielgud.
VHS: S09553. $29.95.
Joseph Strick, USA, 1977, 93 mins.

Positive I.D.
When a woman learns that her brutal rapist is about to be paroled she sets in motion a complicated scheme of retribution. Unable to continue her life as a traumatized housewife whose husband is fooling around, she establishes a new identity. An intelligent and well acted thriller. With Stephanie Rascoe, John Davies, Laura Lane and Steve Fromholtz.
VHS: S07100. $79.90.
Andy Anderson, USA, 1986, 96 mins.

Postcards from America
Based on the writings of the highly regarded artist David Wojnarowicz, this film follows the troubled life of a young gay man. It includes harrowing depictions from America's underside beginning in the 1960's and leading up to the present. This intense film attempts to fathom the terror and anger of a troubled place.
VHS: S26520. $59.95.
Steve McLean, USA, 1994, 95 mins.

Postcards from the Edge
Meryl Streep and Shirley MacLaine star as a disturbed daughter and her overbearing Hollywood mother in this adaptation of the Carrie Fisher novel. Please do not think this is about Carrie Fisher and her mother Debbie Reynolds; that would be jumping to conclusions. This is a fictional work that also includes the talents of Dennis Quaid, Gene Hackman and Richard Dreyfuss. See Tinseltown through the eyes of an insider.
VHS: S13875. $14.95.
Mike Nichols, USA, 1990, 101 mins.

The Postman Always Rings Twice
Adaptation of the James M. Cain novel and remake of the John Garfield/Lana Turner original, about the perfect crime and how the criminals are punished. Jack Nicholson stars as the aimless drifter and Jessica Lange as the hot young wife with the tired old husband.
VHS: S05927. $19.98.
Laser: LD70657. $34.98.
Bob Rafelson, USA, 1981, 123 mins.

Powder
Sean Patrick Flanery stars in this allegory-like tale of an astonishingly pale young man with unusual powers. Though this oddly beautiful young man is taunted by classmates for his startling appearance, he forever transforms the lives of those around him in wholly unexpected and magical ways. With Jeff Goldblum and Mary Steenburgen.
VHS: S27604. $99.99.
Laser: LD75549. $39.99.
Victor Salva, USA, 1995, 112 mins.

Prayer for the Dying
Mickey Rourke, Alan Bates, Bob Hoskins and Liam Neeson bring star power to this thriller. A priest accidentally witnesses an IRA hit, carried out by a man who was fulfilling his last assignment. Now this ordinary bit of everyday violence binds these men in a troubling quandary.
VHS: S26155. $9.99.
Mike Hodges, USA, 1987, 104 mins.

Prelude to a Kiss
Playwright Craig Lucas adapts his prize-winning work about a beautiful, ethereal woman (Meg Ryan) who exchanges souls with a crusty, 80-year-old man (Sydney Walker) on the afternoon of her wedding to a charismatic young editor (Alec Baldwin). A devastating and sharply observed parable about AIDS. With Kathy Bates, Ned Beatty and Patty Duke.
VHS: Out of print. For rental only.
Laser: LD71825. $29.98.
Norman Rene, USA, 1992, 109 mins.

Presumed Innocent
Harrison Ford stars as a prosecuting attorney in Scott Turow's best-selling novel. Charged with the murder of his former mistress and fellow colleague, the circumstantial evidence looks damaging. With Brian Dennehy, Raul Julia, Bonnie Bedelia, Paul Winfield and Greta Scacchi as the victim. A finely crafted whodunit.
VHS: S13656. $14.95.
Laser: LD70658. $29.98.
Alan J. Pakula, USA, 1990, 127 mins.

Pretty in Pink
Molly Ringwald is the school girl from the wrong side of town, Andrew McCarthy the wealthy heartthrob who asks her to the prom. A bittersweet, critically acclaimed love story with an upbeat ending.
VHS: S01523. $19.95.
Laser: LD75342. $29.98.
John Hughes, USA, 1986, 96 mins.

Primal Secrets
Meg Tilly and Ellen Burstyn are superb in this strange psychological thriller. A young artist is engaged by a wealthy socialite to paint a portrait. The artist soon finds herself caught in manipulative machinations behind which murder lurks.
VHS: S25100. $94.95.
Laser: LD75020. $39.99.
Ed Kaplan, USA, 1994, 93 mins.

Prime Time
A funny satire of television and television commercials comprised of black out sketches, like *Grove Tube*, the targets are politics, airline spots, sports programming, with titles such as *The Charles Whitman Invitational* and *The Sexual Deviation Telethon*. With Warren Oates, Kinky Friedman, Harry Shearer, Harris Yulin, George Furth and Fred Dryer. 1980, 75 mins.
VHS: S17446. $19.95.

The Prince of Tides

Barbra Streisand adapts Pat Conroy's expansive novel about Tom Wingo (Nick Nolte), an unemployed Southern football coach and English teacher who goes to New York to care for his suicidal twin sister and becomes involved with Dr. Lowenstein (Streisand), his sister's psychiatrist. Exceptionally well-acted, particularly by Nolte, Kate Nelligan (as Wingo's mother), and Blythe Danner (as Wingo's wife). With Jeroen Krabbe, Melinda Dillon and Jason Gould.
VHS: Out of print. For rental only.
Laser: Criterion. **LD71520. $99.95.**
Barbra Streisand, USA, 1991, 135 mins.

The Princess Bride

A fractured fairy tale from director Rob Reiner which includes a kidnapped beautiful princess, a mysterious pirate, a swordsman with a quest, a lovable giant, comic wizards, and some really nasty villains. With Cary Elwes, Mandy Patinkin, Chris Sarandon, Andre the Giant and Robin Wright as the princess bride.
VHS: Out of print. For rental only.
Laser: CAV. **LD70434. $79.95.**
Laser: CLV. **LD70435. $39.95.**
Rob Reiner, USA, 1987, 101 mins.

Princess Caraboo

Phoebe Cates stars as a charming, exotic princess who transforms the stuffy English aristocracy. Kevin Kline, John Lithgow and Stephen Rea are also featured in this irresistible and romantic live-action fairy tale. It is like a dream come true.
VHS: S24314. $19.95.
Michael Austin, USA, 1994, 96 mins.

The Prisoner of Second Avenue

Jack Lemmon and Anne Bancroft star in this film version of the Neil Simon play about an unemployed executive going through a nervous breakdown. Bancroft is the supporting wife. A comedy with bite. With F. Murray Abraham and Sylvester Stallone in small roles, and Gene Saks, Elizabeth Wilson and Florence Stanley in larger ones.
VHS: S06183. $19.98.
Melvin Frank, USA, 1975, 98 mins.

Private Parts

Legendary cult director Paul Bartel (*Eating Raoul*) delivers his first feature with all the dark comedy and fantastic situations that have turned his films into underground sensations. *Private Parts* plunges us into the foreboding world of a young girl whose adolescent passion for a strange photographer leads her toward a secret that a series of ghastly murders has tried to silence.
VHS: S14960. $19.98.
Paul Bartel, USA, 1972, 86 mins.

Prize

This stylish thriller set in Stockholm stars Paul Newman as a Nobel Prize nominee for literature who becomes involved in international intrigue with physicist Edward G. Robinson just prior to the famous award ceremonies. Based on the novel by Irving Wallace. With Elke Sommer, Diane Baker, Kevin McCarthy and Leo G. Carroll. Watch for the scene where Newman eludes Communist agents by ducking into a nudist convention.
VHS: S16437. $19.95.
Mark Robson, USA, 1963, 135 mins.

The Prodigal

No one knows when the Stuart family started drifting apart. But their American dream has become a nightmare of broken relationships, a conflict of differing goals. When 21-year old Greg returns home from his island hideaway, the conflicts become even more obvious and stressful. With a special appearance by Rev. Billy Graham. USA, 1983, 109 mins.
VHS: S09286. $19.98.
Laser: LD70138. $34.98.

The Prophecy

A Los Angeles cop (Elias Koteas) is joined by an elementary school teacher (Virginia Madsen) for a thrilling showdown with the forces of evil. Christopher Walken is the fallen Gabriel, and he leads his troops into a deadly and mysterious battle that places the fate of the entire planet at his mercy.
VHS: S27498. $99.99.
Laser: LD75520. $39.99.
Gregory Widen, USA, 1995, 97 mins.

The Proud and the Damned

Chuck Connors, Jose Greco and Cesar Romero star in this story of mercenaries and Civil War veterans caught up in a revolution in Latin America.
VHS: S10588. $24.95.
Ferde Grofe, Jr., USA, 1973, 95 mins.

Q & A

Sidney Lumet once again finds corruption in the New York police department. This time Nick Nolte is abusing his power by using his badge to cover up a deliberate murder. Can rookie D.A. Tim Hutton gather all the testimony needed to bring Nolte to justice? With Patrick O'Neal, Armand Assante and Jenny Lumet.
VHS: S12847. $19.98.
Sidney Lumet, USA, 1990, 132 mins.

QB VII

An epic television adaptation of the novel by Leon Uris, the courtroom drama of two men and how they react to the memory of the Holocaust. With strong performances by Anthony Hopkins, Ben Gazzara, Leslie Caron.
Laser: S04395. $139.95.
Tom Gries, USA, 1974, 360 mins.

Quiz Show

Rob Murrow and John Turturro star in this fascinating film based on the real life scandal caused by a television quiz show. A disgruntled ex-champ tells exactly how the show was contrived to make a telegenic newcomer the reigning champ of daytime television.
VHS: S24320. $96.98.
Laser: Letterboxed. **LD74912. $39.99.**
Robert Redford, USA, 1994, 133 mins.

Race with the Devil

Thinking they're going to enjoy a fun and peaceful vacation, two couples witness a bloody sacrifice and are then pursued by the coven of witches responsible for it. With Peter Fonda and Loretta Swit.
VHS: S14793. $14.98.
Jack Starrett, USA, 1975, 88 mins.

Radio Flyer

Set in the '60s, two young brothers (Elijah Wood and Joseph Mazzello) who've just arrived in an anonymous California town with their single mother (Lorraine Bracco) transform their ordinary red wagon into a fantastic machine to escape the rages of their stepfather. With John Heard and Adam Baldwin.
VHS: S16908. $19.95.
Laser: LD71529. $34.95.
Richard Donner, USA, 1992, 114 mins.

Radioland Murders

Director and innovator George Lucas conceived the story for this comic murder mystery starring Mary Stuart Masterson and Brian Benben. When radio station WBN makes its broadcasting debut something goes terribly wrong. As Masterson and Benben team up to find the killer, suspense builds around the possibility of their becoming romantically linked.
VHS: S24323. $19.98.
Mel Slater, USA, 1994, 108 mins.

The Railway Station Man

Adapted from Irish author Julie Johnston's novel, this film is set against a backdrop of violence and terrorism. A woman reeling from the murder of her husband flees to an Irish coastal village and falls in love with an eccentric American builder with a shadowy past. With Julie Christie, Donald Sutherland and John Lynch.
VHS: S18492. $89.98.
Michael Whyte, USA, 1992, 93 mins.

Rain Man

Four Oscars including Best Picture went to this road movie about two brothers who didn't know the other existed until fate tosses them together. The plot may be very similar to the movie comedy *Twins* starring Danny DeVito and Arnold Schwarzenegger but Tom Cruise and Dustin Hoffman look spiffier in their matchup outfits. A sensitive and strongly performed film.
VHS: S09575. $19.98.
Laser: LD70662. $29.98.
Barry Levinson, USA, 1988, 120 mins.

The Rainbow Thief

The stars of *Lawrence of Arabia*, Omar Sharif and Peter O'Toole, are reunited in this whimsical comedy about a petty thief and a displaced heir. Together they may be able to get their hands on a fortune. All they need is roguish wit, a lot of luck and a little magic.
VHS: S26815. $96.99.
Alejandro Jodorowsky, USA, 1990, 87 mins.

Rambling Rose

A rare and intelligent film about sexual attitudes, enlightened behavior and family ties. Laura Dern is inspired as the title character, a beguiling free spirit with a soiled reputation. She finds understanding and a real home while working as a domestic for the Hillyer family in '30s Georgia. With fine performances from Robert Duvall, Diane Ladd, John Heard, David Ogden Stiers and Lukas Haas. Ladd and Dern made Oscar history as the first mother and daughter to be nominated in the same year for acting awards. Based on the novel by Calder Willingham.
VHS: S15692. $14.98.
Laser: LD75131. $24.98.
Martha Coolidge, USA, 1991, 115 mins.

Rampage

William Friedkin's documentary-like exploration of a serial killer's demented psychological condition and the profound moral crisis of an ambitious district attorney personally opposed to capital punishment who's ordered by his superiors to seek the death penalty. Inspired by a California case and the book by William P. Wood. With Michael Biehn, Alex McArthur and Nicholas Campbell.
VHS: S18681. $14.95.
Laser: LD75244. $34.98.
William Friedkin, USA, 1987, 92 mins.

The Rapture

There are six definitions of "rapture" in the dictionary. This provocative thriller, written and directed by Michael Tolkin, tries to encompass them all. Mimi Rogers stars in this unusual drama that tests the religious faith of a born again Los Angeles telephone operator. She embarks on a sensual and spiritual odyssey that culminates in a cataclysm of Biblical proportions. With David Duchovny, Patrick Bauchau, Kimberly Cullum and Will Patton.
VHS: S15925. $19.95.
Michael Tolkin, USA, 1991, 100 mins.

Ratboy

Sondra Locke, who co-starred in six Clint Eastwood films, makes her directorial debut with a curious tale of an odd looking human who is happy to live in a garbage dump. A bittersweet modern fairy tale features Locke, Robert Townsend, Louie Anderson, and Gerrit Graham as the exploiters of the Ratboy.
VHS: S05216. $19.98.
Sondra Locke, USA, 1987, 104 mins.

The Razor's Edge

Bill Murray makes his dramatic debut in this adaptation of W. Somerset Maugham's stirring novel. A returning soldier is disillusioned with Jazz age life and sets off to find the truth in the Himalayas. Home once again, he learns that enlightenment is a difficult passage, particularly when you love someone.
VHS: S24865. $14.95.
John Byrum, USA, 1984, 128 mins.

Real Men

James Belushi is Nick Pirandello, one of the best secret agents in the business. He is assigned to protect a wimpy civilian (John Ritter) who is being used by the government as a decoy in a very important mission concerning extraterrestrials. Lots of action and snappy patter in this spy spoof.
VHS: S06872. $79.98.
Dennis Feldman, USA, 1987, 86 mins.

A Reason to Believe

Allison Smith and Jay Underwood star in this college drama. Charlotte Byrne (Smith) is a sorority girl who has everything—looks, popularity, and the perfect boyfriend (Underwood). She suddenly loses all the things she thought were important when she attends a frat party where one man refuses to take no for an answer. This is the story of how she found the courage to speak out against a system that didn't want to know anything of her pain.
VHS: S27514. $92.99.
Douglas Tirola, USA, 1995, 108 mins.

Reckless

Mia Farrow and Scott Glenn head a cast featuring Mary-Louise Parker, Tony Goldwyn and Stephen Dorff in this surprising Christmastime comedy. Farrow is a woman who cherishes Christmas at home with her family until her husband arranges a deadly surprise. He has hired someone to do her in. Now she must question everything she held dear about family, the holidays and canned mirth.
VHS: S27608. $99.98.
Laser: LD75551. $39.99.
Norman Rene, USA, 1995, 91 mins.

Red Rock West

Nicolas Cage is just an average guy mistaken for a hit man. It's the perfect premise for a film noir thriller. Cage has just blown a chance for a high-paying oil rig job when this mistake occurs. Before he can decide what to do, his supposed target, Lara Flynn Boyle, doubles the offer made on her life by husband J.T. Walsh. Then the real killer, Dennis Hopper, appears.
VHS: S23356. $19.95.
John Dahl, USA, 1993, 98 mins.

Reds

A great American film. At its center, *Reds* is the passionate love affair of legendary journalist and American socialist John Reed (Warren Beatty) and feminist author Louise Bryant (Diane Keaton). Beatty, who co-wrote, produced and directed the film, also crisscrosses the emotional undercurrents with social history: exploring the birth of the American labor movement; the emergence of socialism; a long, beguiling film of exquisite taste and intelligence. The extraordinary cast includes Jack Nicholson as O'Neill, Maureen Stapleton as Goldman, Edward Herrmann as editor Max Eastman and *Being There* author Jerzy Kosinski as bolshevik leader Gregory Zinoviev. Cinematography by the great Vittorio Storaro.
VHS: S02566. $29.95.
Laser: Widescreen. **LD75365. $44.98.**
Warren Beatty, USA, 1981, 195 mins.

Redwood Curtain

A young woman seems to have set all the trauma of her origins in war-ravaged Saigon behind her. Even so, she yearns to discover the truth about her Vietnamese mother and American GI father. They abandoned her before. Can she bear the painful truth she must face in her search for answers?
VHS: S26610. $93.99.
John Korty, USA, 1995, 99 mins.

The Ref

Criminal Dennis Leary has a problem. The couple he has taken hostage, Judy Davis and Kevin Spacey, are driving him nuts. It began as a simple burglary but before it's all over jail would be the best thing that could happen to this thief-turned-victim, as the whole bickering family nags him on to justice.
VHS: S21360. $96.98.
Ted Demme, USA, 1994, 97 mins.

Reflecting Skin

For seven-year old Seth Dove, the world is a very terrifying place. Writer-director Philip Ridley has created a strange and chilling universe on the plains of '50s Idaho where children disappear and death is always in the wind. Jeremy Duncan is unforgettable as the impressionable Seth. Viggo Mortensen co-stars as his older brother Cameron and Lindsay Duncan appears as the mysterious Dolphin Blue, the pale English neighbor widow who may just be a vampire. With David Longworth, Duncan Fraser, Evan Hall and Sherry Bie. This is a powerful film of particular visual splendor and impact.
VHS: S15707. $19.98.
Laser: LD75245. $34.98.
Philip Ridley, USA, 1990, 93 mins.

Reflections in the Dark

Mimi Rogers gives an award-winning performance as a convicted killer in this original psychological thriller. A lone guard becomes privy to her chilling secret and this confidence is so unsettling that it haunts him indefinitely. Billy Zane also stars and John Terry is featured as the husband.
VHS: S26149. $92.98.
Laser: LD75070. $39.99.
Jon Purdy, USA, 1995, 123 mins.

Regarding Henry

Harrison Ford plays a despicable New York lawyer who radically changes his outlook on life after surviving a bullet to the head. This "Capra-esque" formula is not guaranteed so please refrain from trying this technique on any lawyers you may know. With Annette Bening and Miki Allen as the wife and young daughter thankful for the second chance and Bill Nunn as the patient and wise physical therapist.
VHS: S15471. $19.95.
Laser: Widescreen. **LD75246. $34.98.**
Mike Nichols, USA, 1991, 107 mins.

Regina

Anthony Quinn and Ava Gardner return to the screen in this shocking drama of family secrets and personal obsessions. An aging matriarch couple uneasily awaits the homecoming of their only son and his new fiancee. With Ray Sharkey and Anna Karina, in what promises to be a harrowing evening of dinner and discovery.
VHS: S05930. $69.95.
Jean-Yves Prate, USA, 1983, 86 mins.

The Reivers

Based upon William Faulkner's last novel, *The Reivers* is the story of a young man and two adults travelling from small town Mississippi to Memphis. Steve McQueen and Juano Hernandez (*Intruder in the Dust*) star.
VHS: S21403. $14.98.
Mark Rydell, USA, 1969, 107 mins.

Rented Lips

Martin Mull and Dick Shawn are two documentary filmmakers hired to complete a low budget porn film when the first director died under kinky circumstances. Using the same cast they decide to make a musical movie extravaganza instead. With Jennifer Tilly, Robert Downey Jr., Kenneth Mars, Edy Williams and June Lockhart. Script by Martin Mull. From the director of *Greaser's Palace*.
VHS: S07778. $79.95.
Robert Downey, USA, 1988, 82 mins.

Repo Man

First film from the director of *Sid and Nancy*, an outrageous comedy combining the seedy world of auto repossessors and nuclear madness. With Emilio Estevez, Harry Dean Stanton and title song by Iggy Pop. A sleeper.
VHS: S02737. $19.95.
Laser: LD70070. $34.98.
Alex Cox, USA, 1984, 93 mins.

Report to the Commissioner

Rookie cop Michael Moriarty shoots the wrong person and ends up in a stalled elevator with a dangerous criminal. This is the movie that dishes sweating it out. A police melodrama with Richard Gere, Susan Blakely, Vic Taybeck, Tony King, William Devane and Yaphet Kotto.
VHS: S06065. $29.95.
Milton Katselas, USA, 1975, 112 mins.

Resurrection

Edna McCauley experienced clinical death, a journey toward a brightly lit place and then returned to her body with the amazing power of healing. Ellen Burstyn stars as Edna in this touching and unusual drama of faith and the hereafter. With Sam Shepard.
VHS: S03925. $59.95.
Daniel Petrie, USA, 1980, 102 mins.

Reunion

The innocence of youth is shattered by the turbulence of war in this poignant tale of love, friendship, and betrayal. Konradin, an ambassador's son, and Hans, the son of a Jewish doctor, meet in Germany in 1932 and become fast friends. But the carefree days of youth are interrupted by Hitler's rise to power. Hans is sent to America for safety and the boys say farewell forever. Fifty years later, Hans returns to Germany to find his friend and learn the truth about the country he once loved. What he finds will touch your heart. A tense and engrossing drama from director Jerry Schatzberg—expertly scripted by Harold Pinter, and starring Jason Robards.
VHS: S14088. $29.95.
Laser: LD72209. $29.95.
Jerry Schatzberg, USA, 1990, 120 mins.

Revolt of Mother

Based on a short story by Mary E. Wilkins Freeman, the story of two hard-working people of the land, portrayed by Amy Madigan and Jay O. Sanders. While father is going to build a new barn, mother wants a new house—a simple story, set against the rustic backdrop of farming life in New England 1890, the story reveals much about love and respect and the often difficult times between those who strive to build a life together. From the American Short Story Collection. 55 mins.
VHS: S07538. $24.95.

Rich in Love

The collaborators of *Driving Miss Daisy*, director Bruce Beresford and writer Alfred Uhry, are reunited in this tender, Southern, coming-of-age tale about a man (Albert Finney) trying to put together his life when his wife (Jill Clayburgh) unexpectedly leaves him. The story is held together by Kathryn Erbe's tough, tender performance as their confused high school daughter trying to deal with her emerging sexuality. With Piper Laurie, Ethan Hawke and Alfre Woodard.
VHS: S19330. $19.98.
Laser: Letterboxed. **LD71917. $34.98.**
Bruce Beresford, USA, 1992, 105 mins.

Ricochet

Denzel Washington plays a cop who becomes a hero when he gets the bad guy (John Lithgow). Lithgow is a psycho who spends his time in prison plotting his sick revenge.
VHS: S21489. $19.98.
Russell Mulcahy, USA, 1991, 97 mins.

Riders of the Storm (The American Way)

Re-titled from *The American Way*, a lunacy of a movie starring Dennis Hopper as the leader of a band of wild Vietnam veterans who fly the skies endlessly in an old B-29 bomber. Surrealistic and anarchistic, the Vets, after 20 straight years of flight, are ready to discredit Willa Westinghouse, the leading presidential campaigner, who hasn't been completely honest about her background—like the fact that she's really a man. Viciously funny. With Michael J. Pollard, James Aubrey.
VHS: S07168. $14.95.
Maurice Phillips, USA, 1986, 92 mins.

Right Stuff

Long but exhilarating adaptation of Tom Wolfe's account of the U.S. manned space program, with emphasis on test pilot Chuck Yeager, played by Sam Shepard. A contemplation of male mystique, and wonderful observations of the role of the press. With Ed Harris, Dennis Quaid.
VHS: S01116. $29.98.
Laser: LD70665. $39.98.
Philip Kaufman, USA, 1983, 193 mins.

The Right to Remain Silent

Lea Thompson and Robert Loggia star in this edgy comedy featuring appearances by Amanda Plummer, LL Cool J, Laura San Giacomo, Carl Reiner and Christopher Lloyd. Thompson is a rookie cop who processes incoming suspects. All the world in its overwhelming oddness parades before her in this kaleidoscopic view of the human condition.
VHS: S27512. $95.99.
Hubert de la Bouillerie, USA, 1995, 96 mins.

Rising Sun
Philip Kaufman's adaptation of Michael Crichton's novel about two Los Angeles cops, special liaisons to the Japanese, who are investigating the murder of a party girl in the American headquarters of a Japanese conglomerate. Sean Connery plays a mysterious, enigmatic expert on Japan who counsels junior partner Wesley Snipes in the art, skill and traditions of the notoriously insular Japanese society.
VHS: S19605. $95.98.
Laser: Letterboxed. LD72338. $49.98.
Philip Kaufman, USA, 1993, 126 mins.

Ritz
Director Richard Lester (*A Hard Day's Night, Three Musketeers*) keeps the pace fast and furious in this crisp farce about Gaetano Proclo hiding out in a men's bathhouse in New York. With Jack Weston, Rita Moreno, Jerry Stiller and F. Murray Abraham.
VHS: S01118. $19.98.
Laser: LD71475. $34.98.
Richard Lester, USA, 1976, 91 mins.

The River
Australian Mel Gibson (*Mad Max*) and Sissy Spacek provide the emotional force behind this film about a young rural couple's struggle to make a go of it on an impoverished farm. Music by John Williams.
VHS: S01120. $19.95.
Laser: LD70071. $39.98.
Mark Rydell, USA, 1984, 124 mins.

A River Runs Through It
Robert Redford's adaptation of Norman MacLean's autobiographical novella about the tragic lives of two brothers, sons of a Presbyterian minister, and their personal, poetic and scientific fascination with the art of fly fishing. With Craig Sheffer, Brad Pitt, Tom Skerritt and Emily Lloyd.
VHS: S18451. $19.95.
Laser: Letterboxed. LD71866. $39.95.
Robert Redford, USA, 1992, 123 mins.

The River Wild
Meryl Streep stars opposite Kevin Bacon in this suspense-laden adventure film. While on a white-water rafting trip, a family is hijacked by three strangers. Soon Streep is put to the test trying to save her family. David Strathairn is also featured.
VHS: S23927. $19.98.
Laser: THX, Widescreen. LD74920. $39.99.
Curtis Hanson, USA, 1994, 112 mins.

River's Edge
A powerful drama that uses a real incident to convey the hopelessness and hostility barely hidden under the surface of today's teenager. A big kid murders his girlfriend and then brings his friends to view the body. With spooky performances by Crispin Glover and Daniel Roebuck. With Dennis Hopper as the neighborhood crazy.
VHS: Out of print. For rental only.
Laser: LD72309. $29.95.
Tim Hunter, USA, 1987, 99 mins.

The Road to Wellville
Anthony Hopkins is a quack of a doctor who runs a health spa where the likes of Bridget Fonda, Matthew Broderick, John Cusack and Dana Carvey all cross paths. Aside from the wacky cures and contraptions on offer at this turn of the century spa, there are plenty of laughs and even romance in this charming film.
VHS: S24327. $19.95.
Laser: Letterboxed. LD74893. $39.95.
Alan Parker, USA, 1994, 120 mins.

Rob Roy
Liam Neeson and Jessica Lange are at the center of this historical drama with a liberal dose of sex and romance about the legendary Scottish warrior Robert Roy McGregor. He fought off the English and was ultimately destroyed by the force of history, but his story lives on. Tim Roth is terrific as a foppish aristocratic fiend and Jessica Lange gives an outstanding performance.
VHS: S26284. $19.98.
Michael Caton Jones, USA, 1995, 139 mins.

Robin Hood, Prince of Thieves
For the good of all men and the love of one woman Kevin Costner fights to uphold justice by breaking the law. The classic tale of the upstart aristocratic Saxon lord who matches wits and weapons with the debauched and greedy Norman rulers gets a vigorous and liberal retelling for the 90's. With Mary Elizabeth Mastrantonio, Morgan Freeman, Christian Slater and Alan Rickman as the scene stealing Sheriff of Nottingham. Film note: The Merry Men now live in treehouses that look suspiciously like an Ewok village.
VHS: S15011. $24.98.
Kevin Reynolds, USA, 1991, 141 mins.

Robin Hood: The Movie
The swashbuckling legend of Robin Hood unfolds in the 12th Century when the mighty Normans ruled England with an iron fist. Robert Hode (Patrick Bergin, *Sleeping with the Enemy*) is a Saxon nobleman who insults the evil knight Folcanet and is branded an outlaw. Clever and quick witted, he changes his name to Robin Hood and a legend is born. Robin becomes an outlaw hero, celebrated across the land for his dashing heroism. He ambushes tax collectors of the greedy Baron Daguerre, giving the money to the poor. Then, with his true love, Maid Marian (Uma Thurman, *Dangerous Liaisons*), about to be married to Folcanet, Robin and his band of loyal men embark on their boldest adventure yet—to storm the Baron's castle and rescue Marian from a fate worse than death. *Robin Hood: The Movie* is a thrilling medieval adventure filled with action, romance and humor.
VHS: S14229. $89.98.
John Irvin, USA, 1991, 116 mins.

Rocket Gibraltar
Burt Lancaster stars as Levi Rockwell, a writer, professor, comic and lover of the sea who is about to turn 77. In celebration of the event, Levi's four children and eight grandchildren return to his Long Island home. But what begins as a joyful day turns into a surprisingly ironic and moving event as the grandchildren honor Levi's most cherished gift.
VHS: S09984. $14.95.
Daniel Petrie, USA, 1988, 101 mins.

Roman Spring of Mrs. Stone
A predatory gigolo preys upon a vulnerable middle-aged actress seeking love—and willing to pay for it. Vivien Leigh is powerful in this adaptation of Tennessee Williams' novel. With Warren Beatty and Lotte Lenya.
VHS: S05865. $19.98.
Jose Quintero, USA, 1961, 104 mins.

Romeo Is Bleeding
Gary Oldman plays a corrupt cop at the center of a complex tale of love and murder involving three beautiful women, played by Lena Olin, Annabella Sciorra and Juliette Lewis. When he is told to carry out one more criminal task, he chooses the ultimate betrayal and finds that his life is now, more than ever, in grave danger.
VHS: S21142. $94.98.
Laser: LD72419. $34.95.
Peter Medak, USA, 1993, 110 mins.

Roommates
Peter Falk, D.B. Sweeney and Ellen Burstyn are featured in this comedy arising from cramped conditions. Falk plays a gruff old man who comes to stay in his grandson's one-room apartment. Together they explore all the adventures that roommates can, and often must, experience.
VHS: S26203. $99.99.
Laser: LD75065. $39.99.
Peter Yates, USA, 1995, 109 mins.

The Rose
Bette Midler makes her starring debut an event as she lights up the screen in a familiar tale of an entertainer on her way down from the heights of stardom. With Alan Bates, Frederic Forrest and David Keith as the men in her drug- and booze-ridden life. Echoes of Janis Joplin, but the magic is all Midler.
VHS: S05622. $19.98.
Laser: Widescreen. LD74821. $59.98.
Mark Rydell, USA, 1979, 134 mins.

Rosebud
Peter O'Toole and Richard Attenborough star in this adventure-filled thriller, in which a group of Middle-Eastern terrorists hijack a yacht filled with young, rich women. Former New York Mayor John Lindsay is also featured in this film that captures headline topicality in a taut plot.
VHS: S21164. $19.98.
Otto Preminger, USA, 1975, 126 mins.

The Rounders
An adaptation of Max Evans' novel with Henry Fonda and Glenn Ford as amiable bronco busters confronted with the challenge of breaking an ornery horse as they reflect on their life and times. With Edgar Buchanan, Sue Ane Langdon and Hope Holiday.
VHS: S18673. $19.98.
Burt Kennedy, USA, 1964, 85 mins.

Roxanne
Steve Martin successfully updates the story of Cyranno de Bergerac as he plays a small-town fire chief with a big heart and an even larger nose. He falls for Roxanne (Daryl Hannah) but she has eyes only for hunk Rick Rossovich. With Michael J. Pollard, Shelley Duvall and Fred Willard.
VHS: S05318. $14.95.
Fred Schepisi, USA, 1987, 107 mins.

Rubin & Ed
This off-beat, dark and unsettling road movie stars the talented though truly bizarre Crispin Glover with Howard Hesseman as two unruly souls traveling through the desolate Southwest, attempting to bury a cat and make a killing in the real estate market. The other cast members are Karen Black and Michael Green.
VHS: S17020. $89.95.
Trent Harris, USA, 1991, 82 mins.

Running on Empty
A superior family drama about a pair of 60s radicals, still on the run from the FBI, trying to raise a family. Christine Lahti and Judd Hirsch are the concerned parents. River Phoenix is the caring son who dreams of living a life free of constant changes in identity. With Martha Plimpton as the wise and rebellious love interest and Steven Hill as the establishment grandfather. Terrific acting all around.
VHS: S09840. $19.98.
Laser: LD74697. $24.98.
Sidney Lumet, USA, 1988, 116 mins.

Running Scared
Gregory Hines stars with Billy Crystal in this police buddy film set in Chicago. The two begin pursuit of a drug lord just days before they are to retire to Key West. The film is a moderately violent action picture.
VHS: S21396. $14.95.
Laser: Letterboxed. LD74681. $34.98.
Peter Hyams, USA, 1986, 106 mins.

Rush
Jennifer Jason Leigh and Jason Patric burn up the screen as a pair of undercover Texas law enforcement officers and lovers who cross way over the line of self-control in pursuit of drug dealers. With Sam Elliott as their wise control officer, Max Perlich as a tormented small-time dealer and rocker Gregg Allman as the wily target of a major investigation.
VHS: S16629. $19.98.
Laser: LD71504. $39.98.
Lili Fini Zanuck, USA, 1991, 120 mins.

The Russia House
Sean Connery plays a cynical and lonely book publisher living in London, who is coerced by the CIA to aid them in a plot to smuggle out of the Soviet Union a book written by a Russian scientist (Klaus Maria Brandauer) which reveals numerous secrets about the Soviet Defense Program. Along the way he meets and falls in love with the book's Russian editor (Michelle Pfeiffer), who unwittingly becomes a pawn in the dangerous game. Alternating between suspenseful sequences and surprisingly moving emotional scenes, this excellent romantic thriller is intelligently scripted by Tom Stoppard, from the John le Carre novel, and well acted by a superb cast (especially Pfeiffer and Connery). With taut and sensitive direction by Fred Schepisi and beautiful location photography of both Moscow and Leningrad.
VHS: S14243. $14.95.
Fred Schepisi, USA, 1990, 122 mins.

Sabrina
Harrison Ford, Julia Ormand and Greg Kinnear make the perfect love triangle in this updated version of a classic Hollywood romantic comedy. Two rich brothers, one a scion of respectability, the other a playboy, rival each other for the attentions of their servant's daughter, the surprisingly transformed Sabrina.
VHS: S27761. $101.99.
Sydney Pollack, USA, 1995, 127 mins.

Safe Passage
Susan Sarandon and Sam Shepard are paired in this heartrending drama. Mag Singer (Sarandon) is about to start a new life, but an unforseen danger throws her off course. One of her seven sons is at risk, forcing this woman to re-examine all she holds dear.
VHS: S25656. $19.95.
Robert Allen Ackerman, USA, 1994, 98 mins.

The Saint of Fort Washington
Two homeless men, played by Matt Dillon and Danny Glover, grow together in friendship. This compelling drama shows a way of life often ignored by the rest of society. Its warm humor and superb performances challenge stereotypes about the least fortunate among us.
VHS: S22954. $19.98.
Laser: LD72417. $34.98.
Tim Hunter, USA, 1993, 104 mins.

Saturday Night Fever
John Travolta, in his best screen role, is Tony Manero, a paint store employee by day and a disco dancing legend by night. However, the streets of Brooklyn confine this street kid with a dream to better himself. With Karen Lynn Gorney, Donna Pescow and Julie Bocasso. Music by the Bee Gees.
VHS: S02865. $29.95.
Laser: LD75252. $34.98.
John Badham, USA, 1977, 118 mins.

Say Anything...
A wonderfully evocative portrait of a tender and sensitive relationship between a 19-year-old army brat (John Cusack) who loves the class brain (Ione Skye), trying to deal with a very complicated relationship with her father (John Mahoney). A wonderful supporting cast includes Lili Taylor, Amy Brooks and Jason Gould and a great soundtrack.
VHS: S10609. $19.98.
Cameron Crowe, USA, 1989, 100 mins.

Scarecrow
Gene Hackman and Al Pacino star as a pair of drifters on the run from impossible dreams and ex-wives. From the director of *Panic in Needle Park*, Jerry Schatzberg, this is an oddball drama about friendship and survival. With Eileen Brennan, Ann Wedgeworth, Dorothy Tristan and Richard Lynch as a prison bully. Terrific photography by Vilmos Zsigmond.
VHS: S08720. $19.98.
Jerry Schatzberg, USA, 1973, 115 mins.

The Scarlet and the Black
An excellent made for television adaptation of J.P. Gallagher's book, *The Scarlet Pimpernel of the Vatican*, stars Gregory Peck in this fact-based account of a priest who provided sanctuary for escaped allied POWs in Nazi-occupied Rome, pursued by the maniacal Christopher Plummer. Sir John Gielgud is Pope Pius XII. With Barbara Bouchet, Olga Karlatos and Bill Berger.
VHS: S17284. $14.98.
Jerry London, USA, 1983, 156 mins.

The Scarlet Pimpernel
A flamboyant adaptation of two of Baroness Orczy's novels, *The Scarlet Pimpernel* and *Eldorado*, set during the French Revolution. A nobleman conceals his identity to prevent the decadent aristocracy from killing innocent people. With Anthony Andrews, Jane Seymour and Ian McKellen.
VHS: S18487. $19.98.
Clive Donner, USA, 1982, 150 mins.

Scent of a Woman
Martin Brest's entertainment about the curious friendship between a retired, disillusioned, career officer (Al Pacino), who accidentally blinded himself, and a working-class student (Chris O'Donnell) who's hired to care for him during a long weekend holiday. Gabrielle Anwar turns in a stunning performance as a mysterious object of Pacino's affection.
VHS: S19008. $19.98.
Laser: Letterboxed. LD71891. $39.98.
Martin Brest, USA, 1992, 157 mins.

Schindler's List
This Academy Award-winning film tells the story of Oskar Schindler, who saved hundreds of Jews from certain death in Nazi-dominated Europe. Adapted from Thomas Keneally's novel and starring Ben Kingsley, Liam Neeson and Ralph Fiennes. The Collector's Edition includes the novel, a compact disc of the Academy Award-winning score by John Williams and a booklet with an introduction by Steven Spielberg.
Collector's Edition. SLP, letterboxed.
VHS: S21540. $79.95.
Laser: Includes soundtrack, CD and book. LD74526. $139.98.
Full Frame Version.
VHS: S21539. $29.95.
Laser: Letterboxed. LD74525. $49.98.
Steven Spielberg, USA, 1993, 197 mins.

School Ties
A prep school tale of deception and anti-semitism, this story confronts bigotry among America's youth. Set in the Eisenhower era, it tells the story of a boy who would like to get an education through a football scholarship but finds his dream in jeopardy because he is Jewish.
VHS: S20660. $19.95.
Laser: Widescreen. LD75253. $34.98.
Robert Mandel, USA, 1992, 107 mins.

Scream of Fear
Penny Appleby (Susan Strasberg) pays a visit to her father's Riviera resort, although she is told that her father is away on business. Continually terrified by sudden appearances of his ghost, the suspense builds until she finds herself at the edge of a cliff. A terrific chiller.
VHS: S09395. $69.95.
Seth Holt, USA, 1961, 81 mins.

Sea of Love
Someone is killing upscale yuppie males who use the personals to get dates in New York city. Detective Al Pacino is assigned to find the perpetrator even if he has to date some very dangerous women in the interim. With Ellen Barkin as a very likely suspect and John Goodman as Pacino's partner in crime control.
VHS: S11787. $19.95.
Laser: LD70075. $34.95.
Harold Becker, USA, 1989, 113 mins.

Search and Destroy
Dennis Hopper, Christopher Walken, John Turturro, Rosanna Arquette, Griffin Dunne, Illeana Douglas and Ethan Hawke are all featured in this strange story directed by the 1980's art star David Salle. A man with a disastrous life becomes convinced that the answer to all his trouble lies in making a screen epic on a grand scale. It must be fate when he meets a screenwriting receptionist, a karaoke-crazed businessman, and a quick talking street king who all encourage him.
VHS: S26458. $19.98.
Laser: LD75314. $39.98.
David Salle, USA, 1995, 91 mins.

Searching for Bobby Fischer
Joe Mantegna, Laurence Fishburne and Ben Kingsley star in this story about a childhood chess prodigy. In the cutthroat world of professional chess a father and son discover they must learn all the tricks, but only one skill can really help them—their love for one another.
VHS: S21138. $19.98.
Laser: Widescreen. LD75254. $34.98.
Steven Zallman, USA, 1993, 111 mins.

Season of Fear
For the purpose of this film that season is summer. A young man returns to his estranged father's ranch where he engages in a passionate romance with a beguiling woman he later discovers to be his new stepmother. He is drawn into a series of lies and danger. With Michael Bowen, Ray Wise, Clancy Brown, Michael J. Pollard.
VHS: S11204. $79.98.
Douglas Campbell, USA, 1989, 90 mins.

Secret Diary of Sigmund Freud
Offbeat, hilarious spoof of the life and times of the father of modern psychiatry. Bud Cort (*Harold and Maude*) stars as Freud, Carroll Baker as the young Freud's mother, and Klaus Kinski as her lover. With Carol Kane, Marisa Berenson and Dick Shawn.
VHS: S02325. $79.98.
Danford Greene, USA, 1984, 129 mins.

The Secret of My Success
Michael J. Fox takes the New York business world by storm in this breezy comedy of corporate confusion. By taking full advantage of his uncle's company inefficiency and by being lucky, he works both in the mailroom and the exec boardroom. With Helen Slater, Richard Jordan and John Pankow.
VHS: S05316. $19.95.
Herbert Ross, USA, 1987, 110 mins.

The Secret War of Harry Frigg
In 1943, a private engineers the escape of five captured generals. A slick war comedy, starring Paul Newman, John Williams, Sylva Koscina, Andrew Duggan and Tom Bosley.
VHS: S16303. $14.95.
Jack Smight, USA, 1967, 109 mins.

Secrets
Julie Harris stars with Veronica Hamel and Richard Kiley in this stylish, turn-of-the-century, coming-of-age story. Anna Berter is a 14-year-old girl who inhabits a well-ordered world, but behind her family's prosperous and gracious facade lies a scandalous and carefully guarded secret. The secrets of their scandalous past begin to unravel when Halius, a handsome young gentleman, arrives on the scene.
VHS: S27304. $79.98.
Laser: LD75477. $39.99.
Jud Taylor, USA, 1995, 92 mins.

See No Evil, Hear No Evil
The third pairing of Richard Pryor and Gene Wilder has Pryor cast as a deaf man and Wilder as a blind man. The two are being sought by the police and most of the plot revolves around their slapstick attempts to escape. Not up to their previous efforts but the chemistry between the two is still there.
VHS: S21441. $14.95.
Arthur Hiller, USA, 1989, 103 mins.

Seize the Day
Robin Williams plays Tommy Wilhelm in this faithful adaptation of the great Saul Bellow novel of the same title. Nearing 40, a failure, desperately alone and much abused by the society at large, Tommy befriends a shyster, who finds him ripe for the picking. A melancholy tale well told through a weave of past and present. With Robin Williams, Joseph Wiseman, Jerry Stiller, Glenne Headly and Tony Roberts.
VHS: S05714. $29.95.
Laser: LD75563. $39.95.
Fielder Cook, USA, 1986, 93 mins.

Semi-Tough
Burt Reynolds, Kris Kristofferson and Jill Clayburgh star in Michael Ritchie's modern screwball comedy, which deftly tilts the bone-crunching world of pro football with the psyche-jarring "consciousness" movement.
VHS: S15253. $14.95.
Michael Ritchie, USA, 1977, 108 mins.

Separate Peace
Adaptation of John Knowles novel about two school chums during World War II facing adult emotions and motivations.
VHS: S05003. $49.95.
Larry Peerce, USA, 1973, 104 mins.

September 30, 1955
Dennis Quaid made his screen debut in this drama about troubled teens. In a small Arkansas town, college student Jimmy gathers his friends together on the occasion of James Dean's death. Drinking, trouble with the law, and finally tragedy complete this oddly appropriate response to the death of the ultimate teen icon. Featuring Tom Hulce, Lisa Blount and Richard Thomas as Jimmy.
VHS: S26922. $14.98.
James Bridges, USA, 1977, 107 mins.

Serpico
Al Pacino stars in this adaptation of Peter Maas' book about Frank Serpico, the New York cop who exposed corruption within the Department. With John Randolph, Jack Kehoe and F. Murray Abraham.
VHS: S21860. $14.95.
Sidney Lumet, USA, 1973, 130 mins.

Seven
Morgan Freeman and Brad Pitt are two police officers set to work on a baffling, gruesome collection of serial killings. Pitt is new to the big city, while Freeman is getting ready to retire from his hellish occupation. As they track down the murderer they descend into an arena of moral mayhem where the ultimate victim is innocence.
VHS: S27256. $103.99.
Laser: LD75472. $124.95.
David Fincher, USA, 1995, 127 mins.

The Seventh Coin
Set in contemporary Jerusalem, a shrewd Arab boy (Navin Chowdhry) and a beautiful young American tourist (Alexandra Powers) are inadvertently entrusted with a rare, valuable coin dating to the time of King Herod. Instantly drawn to each other, the two are pursued through the maze of ancient architecture and mysterious catacombs by the nefarious Emil Saber (Peter O'Toole), an international terrorist. "O'Toole hits the perfect balance of eccentricity and self-parody" (*Variety*). With John Rhys-Davies and Ally Walker.
VHS: S20218. $92.95.
Laser: LD72329. $39.95.
Dror Soref, USA, 1992, 92 mins.

Shattered
Tom Berenger stars as an amnesia victim who survived driving his Mercedes 560 SL off a California coastline road. Greta Scacchi is the woman who claims to be his wife in this complex thriller from director Wolfgang Petersen. With Joanne Whalley-Kilmer, Corbin Bernsen and Bob Hoskins as the colorful private detective who prefers animals to people. Based on the novel *The Plastic Nightmare* by Richard Neely.
VHS: S15712. $19.98.
Wolfgang Petersen, USA, 1991, 95 mins.

The Shawshank Redemption
Tim Robbins and Morgan Freeman star in this compelling prison drama. A banker who murdered his wife finds himself locked up with hardened criminals. The whole prison suspects he can't last. To everyone's surprise however, he makes common cause with a tough convict resulting in an enduring friendship.
VHS: S24132. $19.95.
Laser: LD74816. $39.95.
Frank Darabont, USA, 1994, 143 mins.

The Shell Seekers
A poignant adaptation of Rosamunde Pilcher's novel about an idiosyncratic widow (Angela Lansbury) who tries to claim some independence from her children after suffering a heart attack. "Lovely, graceful and eloquent" (*Boston Herald*). Screenplay adaptation by playwright James Di Pasquale. With Sam Wannamaker, Christopher Bowen, Anna Carteret, Michael Gough, Patricia Hodge, Denis Quilley, Sophie Ward and Irene Worth.
VHS: S19940. $19.98.
Waris Hussein, USA/Britain, 1989, 100 mins.

Shenandoah
James Stewart gives a great performance as a Virginia farmer during the Civil War who opposes both slavery and warfare until his son is captured and Stewart must act.
VHS: S02740. $19.95.
Laser: LD70078. $34.95.
Andrew V. McLaglen, USA, 1965, 106 mins.

Shoot the Moon
A thoroughly modern vision of marriage featuring Diane Keaton and Albert Finney as a couple whose 15 year marriage is coming apart.
VHS: S01191. $19.99.
Laser: LD72155. $39.98.
Alan Parker, USA, 1981, 124 mins.

Show of Force
Amy Irving stars as a Puerto Rico-based American TV reporter caught up in a government conspiracy that involves the murder of two suspected terrorists. Based on a true incident that occurred in 1978. With Andy Garcia, Robert Duvall and Lou Diamond Phillips as a really creepy police informant.
VHS: S12841. $19.95.
Laser: LD75257. $34.98.
Bruno Barreto, USA, 1990, 93 mins.

Showgirls
Elizabeth Berkley stars as a young girl who goes off to Las Vegas with a dream. She hopes to be a dancer, but instead finds herself sidetracked into the world of lap-dancing. This film's steamy demeanor reveals Las Vegas as a true oasis in the American desert, wholly void of puritanical mores.
VHS: S26951. $96.99.
Laser: LD75424. $49.99.
Paul Verhoeven, USA, 1995, 131 mins.

The Sicilian
Michael Cimino's film of the life and times of a popular Sicilian bandit and folk hero is available only on home video. Will it make more sense? Add a bit more flesh to the many minor characters? Or just show more European extras in vintage clothing? With Christopher Lambert as Guiliano, the title character, Terence Stamp, Joss Ackland and John Turturro. Based on the novel of Mario Puzo.
VHS: S06961. $14.98.
Michael Cimino, USA, 1987, 146 mins.

Siesta
Often compared to David Lynch's *Blue Velvet*, *Siesta* features Ellen Barkin, Martin Sheen, Jodie Foster, Isabella Rossellini and Grace Jones, with a hot soundtrack from Miles Davis. The film is an erotic thriller which journeys into the mind of Claire, a professional stunt woman, whose rendezvous with her Spanish lover becomes a nightmare of madness and violence.
VHS: S06860. $19.95.
Mary Lambert, USA, 1987, 97 mins.

Signs of Life
Beau Bridges, Vincent D'Onofrio and Arthur Kennedy star in this critically-acclaimed, touching film about unique characters in a small town.
VHS: S11556. $19.95.
John David Coles, USA, 1989, 95 mins.

Silence of the North
Oscar-winner Ellen Burstyn stars as the alter ego of Olive Fredrickson, whose autobiographical work was the story of courage and legend, a young widow and her three small children who braved the frontier conditions of Alberta in northern Canada from the early 1900's to the Depression.
VHS: S02602. $59.95.
Laser: Widescreen. LD74948. $34.98.
Allan Winton King, USA, 1981, 94 mins.

Silkwood
Meryl Streep plays Karen Silkwood in this true account of the mysterious circumstances under which Silkwood died while exposing the dangers of plutonium contamination. With Kurt Russell and a wonderful performance by Cher.
VHS: S01202. $19.95.
Laser: LD74833. $49.99.
Mike Nichols, USA, 1983, 131 mins.

Sister, Sister
A southern gothic drama from the writer of *Strange Behavior*, Bill Condon, who makes his directorial debut. Judith Ivey and Jennifer Jason Leigh are two very close siblings who live in a dilapidated Louisiana mansion and harbor a dark secret. Eric Stoltz is the young man with a lot of curiosity.
VHS: S06919. $14.95.
Bill Condon, USA, 1987, 91 mins.

Sitting Ducks
Jaglom's third film, made after *Tracks*, is a comedy about sex, money and vitamins, starring Michael Emil and Zack Norman with Patrice Townsend. Further evidence of real talent in Jaglom.
VHS: S01209. $19.99.
Henry Jaglom, USA, 1983, 88 mins.

Six Degrees of Separation
Stockard Channing, Will Smith and Donald Sutherland star in this unusual drama. John Guare adapted his hit Broadway play about a man pretending to be Sidney Poitier's son who works his way into the lives of a pair of rich Manhattanites. It's a witty and compelling scenario brought convincingly to the screen.
VHS: S21032. $19.98.
Laser: LD72407. $34.98.
Fred Schepisi, USA, 1993, 112 mins.

Slacker
A true sleeper. Richard Linklater's first feature film is a wickedly funny social satire on a new American sub-culture that's inventive, quite bizarre and refreshingly offbeat. Filmed entirely in Austin, Texas, with a cast of hundreds of local residents. The film is a human chain letter: you meet one person and through that person you meet another person, and another …The local characters voice their opinions on a variety of subjects including Madonna's pap smear, the sniper Charles Whitman, and the JFK assassination.
VHS: S16328. $19.98.
Richard Linklater, USA, 1991, 101 mins.

Slaughterhouse Five
Adaptation of Kurt Vonnegut's bizarre fantasy novel follows the story of Billy Pilgrim, who becomes unstuck in time and jumps back and forth in his life with no control. With Michael Sacks and Valerie Perrine. And so it goes.
VHS: S01903. $19.95.
Laser: LD70080. $34.95.
George Roy Hill, USA, 1972, 104 mins.

Sleep with Me
Eric Stoltz, Craig Sheffer and Meg Tilly wind up exploring sex, relationships and each other in this offbeat romantic comedy. Six social events provide the backdrop for this unfolding love triangle between a man, his wife and his best friend. Featuring Quentin Tarantino in a truly silly cameo role.
VHS: S23749. $94.99.
Rory Kelly, USA, 1994, 87 mins.

Sleeping with the Enemy
For Laura (Julia Roberts), Martin Burney appeared to be the man of her dreams. He was handsome, successful and seductively attentive. It wasn't until they were married that she discovered Martin's dark side—compulsive, controlling and dangerously violent. She fakes drowning in a boating accident and relocates to a small midwestern town where she tries to rebuild her life. But Martin soon discovers that Laura is still alive, and he is determined to make her pay for her deceit. Also starring Patrick Bergin (*Mountains of the Moon*) and Kevin Anderson (*In Country*).
VHS: S14228. $19.98.
Joseph Ruben, USA, 1991, 99 mins.

Sleepless in Seattle
Nora Ephron's second film features Tom Hanks as a Seattle architect who grieves over the death of his beautiful wife. His son calls up a national radio show, and prevails on its listeners to help him find a new wife for his father. With Meg Ryan as the new love interest.
VHS: S19513. $19.95.
Laser: LD71921. $34.95.
Nora Ephron, USA, 1993, 104 mins.

The Slender Thread
Anne Bancroft takes an overdose of sleeping pills and phones the crisis clinic for help. It's up to volunteer Sidney Poitier to keep her on the line until the police can trace the call.
VHS: S16457. $14.95.
Sydney Pollack, USA, 1965, 98 mins.

Slither
An ex-con (James Caan), a small-time bandleader (Peter Boyle), his doting wife (Louise Lasser) and a kooky drifter (Sally Kellerman) find themselves being followed while trying to locate a small fortune in embezzled money. They then embark on a chase through a surreal world of trailer camps, bingo halls and laundromats.
VHS: S15247. $19.98.
Howard Zieff, USA, 1973, 92 mins.

Smile
In this terrifically performed and insightfully observed slice of Americana, Michael Ritchie turns his camera on a teen beauty pageant in Santa Rosa, California. Among the contestants are such stars of the future as Melanie Griffith, Annette O'Toole, Collen Camp and Joan Prather. Contest officials include Bruce Dern, Barbara Feldon, Geoffrey Lewis and choreographer Michael Kidd. Title song by Charlie Chaplin. To keep the reactions real, the winner wasn't announced until the camera was rolling.
VHS: S12236. $19.95.
Laser: LD72132. $34.98.
Michael Ritchie, USA, 1975, 113 mins.

Smithereens
This rock movie, capturing the desperation of life in the streets, has become a minor cult classic. Directed by Susan Seidelman (*Desperately Seeking Susan*), *Smithereens* was made on a budget of only $80,000. It also features an appearance by Richard Hell.
VHS: S01220. $29.95.
Susan Seidelman, USA, 1984, 90 mins.

Smoke
A young and lonely bathroom attendant searches for solace in all the wrong places. The film is filled with memories of loves that might have been, from a distant family priest to an absent father.
VHS: S20580. $39.95.
Mark D'Aruia, USA, 1993, 90 mins.

Soldier in the Rain
Steve McQueen and Jackie Gleason star in this bittersweet comedy about friendship and living well in the peacetime Army. Supply Sergeant Eustis Clay sure does admire the way Master Sergeant Maxwell Slaughter operates. With Tony Bill, Tuesday Weld. A tribute to butter brickle ice cream. Script co-written by Blake Edwards.
VHS: S05267. $59.98.
Ralph Nelson, USA, 1963, 87 mins.

Soldier's Tale
Gabriel Byrne and Judge Reinhold star in this tense World War II drama as Allied rivals for the romantic attentions of a French woman of questionable loyalties. Marianne Basler plays Belle, a beautiful woman accused of treason by the French Resistance. Will desire conquer all? Based on the novel by M.K. Joseph.
VHS: S15924. $89.98.
Laser: LD71501. $29.98.
Larry Parr, USA/France, 1991, 96 mins.

Some Folks Call It a Sling Blade
A young reporter hopes to interview a man judged criminally insane for the murder of his own mother. The criminal is about to released after 25 years of incarceration. Between the reporter and this exciting story is a neurotic bureaucrat who tries to protect the strange madman. The film features Molly Ringwald, J.T. Walsh and Billy Bob Thornton. Also included is a behind-the-scenes look at the making of the film.
VHS: S27084. $24.95.
George Hickenlooper, USA, 1995, 45 mins.

Some Kind of Hero
Richard Pryor is cast as a former P.O.W. returning from Vietnam. The world is no longer the place he remembers. His performance as a man dealing with newfound freedom is the saving grace in anotherwise undistinguished film.
VHS: S21450. $14.95.
Laser: LD75334. $29.98.
Michael Pressman, USA, 1982, 97 mins.

Some Kind of Wonderful
Another teenage exploration of alienation and current fashion sense from the John Hughes movie machine. He's farmed out the direction and recycles the plot of *Pretty in Pink* and the result is that it is better the second time around. With Eric Stoltz and Mary Stuart Masterson.
VHS: S04712. $19.98.
Laser: LD75335. $29.98.
Howard Deutch, USA, 1987, 95 mins.

Someone to Love
Orson Welles makes his farewell screen appearance as a one-man Greek chorus in this Henry Jaglom film that takes place in an old theatre on Valentine's Day. A personal comedy about modern relationships finds the director on camera once again asking about commitment and finding the right partner. With Sally Kellerman, Andrea Marcovicci and Jaglom's brother Michael Emil.
VHS: S08236. $79.95.
Laser: LD75259. $34.98.
Henry Jaglom, USA, 1987, 109 mins.

Someone to Watch over Me
When an attractive Manhattan socialite witnesses a brutal murder she is put in the protective custody of a married, good looking cop from another Borough. Sexual tension competes with a maniac killer for screen time. With Tom Berenger, Mimi Rogers and Lorraine Bracco as the cop's wife. A stylish thriller.
VHS: S06996. $14.95.
Ridley Scott, USA, 1987, 106 mins.

Something to Talk About
Julia Roberts stars opposite Dennis Quaid in this comedy about a woman who finds out her husband is playing around. Everything seemed perfect until she discovered he was being unfaithful. Now nothing in the small town where they live will ever be the same again as she goes on a personal rampage to root out the hypocrisy of infidelity. Robert Duvall, Kyra Sedgwick and Gena Rowlands are also featured.
VHS: S26930. $19.95.
Laser: LD75404. $34.98.
Lasse Hallstrom, USA, 1995, 105 mins.

Sometimes a Great Notion
Ken Kesey's powerful dramatic novel of the same name is realized with the help of some great star power, including Paul Newman, Lee Remick, Henry Fonda and Michael Sarrazin. The Northwest is home to the logging industry and the determined people who wrest resources directly from the some of the earth's most beautiful forests.
VHS: S21279. $14.98.
Laser: Widescreen. LD74922. $34.98.
Paul Newman, USA, 1971, 114 mins.

Sommersby
Jon Amiel's remake of Daniel Vigne's *The Return of Martin Guerre* transfers the action from a 16th century French village to post-Civil War American South. Richard Gere is the enigmatic lead figure, a former prisoner of war who turns up following a seven-year absence. With Jodie Foster, Bill Pullman, James Earl Jones and Lee Ermey.
VHS: S19331. $19.95.
Laser: LD71918. $34.98.
Jon Amiel, USA, 1993, 115 mins.

Sophie's Choice
Meryl Streep received an Oscar for her depiction of a Polish Catholic mother who survives the death camp at Auschwitz but not the memories that haunt her in her new life in the United States. Based on the William Styron novel. With Kevin Kline and Peter MacNicol.
VHS: S04600. $14.98.
Alan J. Pakula, USA, 1982, 150 mins.

Sorcerer
William Friedkin's American remake of Henri-Georges Clouzot's classic *The Wages of Fear* concerns four fugitives trapped in a nightmarish Latin American town who agree on a suicidal mission, transporting trucks filled with nitroglycerine, to gain their freedom. With Roy Scheider, Francisco Rabal, Ramon Bieri and Amidou.
VHS: S18998. $19.98.
William Friedkin, USA, 1977, 122 mins.

The Sound and the Silence
Alexander Graham Bell (played by John Bach) was born in Scotland, where his nearly deaf mother (Brenda Fricker) inspired the course of his life's work. This biographical film continues through his greatest creative moments, including the invention of the telephone, the telegraph, and the iron lung.
VHS: S20628. $19.95.
Laser: LD72436. $49.99.
John Kent Harrison, USA, 1993, 93 mins.

Southern Comfort
A group of foolish National Guardsmen find anything but southern hospitality when they go on maneuvers in the Cajun swamps of Louisiana. Walter Hill directs this tale of weekend warriors as a blatant allegory of the Vietnam experience. With Keith Carradine, Powers Booth, Fred Ward, Peter Coyote.
VHS: S04475. $19.95.
Walter Hill, USA, 1981, 106 mins.

Sparkle
Three sisters form a singing group and try to make it big. One of the women, "Sister" (Lonette McKee) falls for a lowlife named "Satin" (Tony King) while the youngest sister, "Sparkle" (Irene Cara) falls for a well-meaning young man, "Stix" (Philip Michael Thomas). Most of the film deals with "Stix" trying to make "Sparkle" a star and with the destructive relationship between "Sister" and "Satin". Also stars Dwan Smith, Mary Alice and Dorian Harewood.
VHS: S21436. $19.98.
Sam O'Steen, USA, 1976, 98 mins.

Speed
Keanu Reeves makes his first appearance as an action hero character in this breakneck adventure film. As a member of an elite swat team, his successes come back to haunt him as a bus is hijacked by a crazed and greedy technical wizard, Dennis Hopper. Sandra Bullock co-stars as the woman who inadvertently gets drawn into the bus ride of her life.
VHS: S22529. $19.98.
Laser: THX sound. LD74611. $34.95.
Jan De Bont, USA, 1994, 115 mins.

Spring Symphony
Nastassia Kinski stars in the story of the passionate romance between the composer Robert Schumann and Clara Wieck, the devoted and brilliant concert pianist who delivered many of his compositions to the world.
VHS: S01243. $79.98.
Peter Schamoni, USA, 1986, 102 mins.

Spy Who Came in from the Cold
Richard Burton is a disillusioned and weary secret agent in this serious espionage drama taken from the novel by John Le Carre. A fine cast under the direction of Martin Ritt includes Claire Bloom, Oskar Werner, Sam Wanamaker, Cyril Cusack, Peter Van Eyck and Michael Hordern. A gripping and realistic thriller. B&W. 105 mins.
VHS: S07520. $19.95.
Laser: LD75263. $34.98.
Martin Ritt, USA, 1966, 105 mins.

St. Elmo's Fire
The new Brat Pack are featured as college kids having their problems. With Demi Moore, Rob Lowe and Emilio Estevez.
VHS: S07433. $19.95.
Joel Schumacher, USA, 1985, 108 mins.

Stacking
Young Megan Follows (*Anne of Green Gables*) is a fourteen year old Montana farm girl trying to hold the family spread together when her father is injured in an accident and her mother would rather be following a photographer on a motorcycle. Follows is a budding new star backed by Frederic Forrest, Christine Lahti, Peter Coyote and Jason Gedrick.
VHS: S06047. $19.98.
Martin Rosen, USA, 1987, 111 mins.

The Stand
Stephen King's epic novel is now an epic film that tells the story of a world devastated by plague. The sad survivors of this catastrophe must face an even greater challenge. Mysteriously they all are drawn together. They find strength in a new community that must make a stand. Gary Sinise, Rob Lowe and Molly Ringwald star.
VHS: S21515. $102.95.
Laser: LD74491. $69.98.
Mick Garris, USA, 1994

Stand by Me
Rob Reiner's skillful adaptation of Stephen King's novella *The Body* is an odyssey of exploration and self-identity as four boys endure a difficult two-day trip to find the body of a dead youth. The film moves freely from adolescent reminiscence to male bonding. The performances by the young actors are uniformly fine—especially Wil Wheaton and River Phoenix; Kiefer Sutherland turns in a scruffy, horrifying caricature of teenage nihilism. Richard Dreyfuss and Evanston's John Cusack turn in cameo roles.
VHS: S02909. $19.95.
Laser: LD75530. $39.95.
Rob Reiner, USA, 1986, 89 mins.

Stanley and Iris
Two-time Academy Award winners Jane Fonda and Robert De Niro triumph in this warm and wonderful romance. Forty-year-old Stanley can neither read nor write. Co-worker Iris learns his secret and becomes his teacher, but when romance unexpectedly blooms they find that love isn't so easy to read. From the director and writers (Harriet Frank Jr. and Irving Ravetch) who teamed on *Hud* and *Norma Rae*.
VHS: S13971. $19.99.
Martin Ritt, USA, 1990, 107 mins.

Star 80
The story of Playmate of the Year Dorothy Stratten and her tragic murder is brought to the screen in a mesmerizing, no holds barred manner. Yet the real focus is on her snake oil husband, played by Eric Roberts (who was robbed of a deserved Oscar nomination). Mariel Hemingway (with breast implants) is the unfortunate Dorothy.
VHS: S04181. $19.98.
Laser: LD74716. $34.98.
Bob Fosse, USA, 1983, 104 mins.

Stars and Bars
This isn't about celebrities with a drinking problem. The title refers to the flag of the Confederate States of America. Daniel Day-Lewis plays an English art expert who journeys to modern day Georgia to buy a Renoir from eccentric Harry Dean Stanton. The trip is complicated by gangsters, natural disasters and the flower of Southern womanhood. With Laurie Metcalf, Glenne Headly, Keith David, Joan Cusack and Spalding Gray. From the novel by William Boyd.
VHS: S07707. $19.95.
Pat O'Connor, USA, 1988

The Stars Fell on Henrietta
Robert Duvall stars with Aidan Quinn, Frances Fisher and Brian Dennehy in this inspiring drama. A stranger stumbles across a family trapped on a bleak Texas farm during the Depression. Somehow, through his own self-confidence, he turns their lives around and gives them hope.
VHS: S27190. $96.99.
Laser: LD75469. $34.98.
James Keach, USA, 1995, 110 mins.

State of Grace
Sean Penn stars as an Irish tough, who together with his mob buddies Ed Harris and Gary Oldman, falls on hard times. This forces them to work as contract killers for the Italians. Between this comedown and the shrinking of their home turf, an intense urban story of desperation and violence emerges.
VHS: S22510. $14.98.
Phil Joanou, USA, 1990, 134 mins.

Staying Together
Lee Grant directs this episodic saga of the McDermott family. When their dad decides to sell the family fried chicken business, his three sons are not happy to learn that they weren't even consulted. A detailed and sentimental exploration of male bonding, family loyalties and small-town life. With Sean Astin, Tim Quill, Dermot Mulroney, Daphne Zuniga, Melinda Dillon, Stockard Channing, Jim Haynie and Dinah Manoff.
VHS: S11722. $89.95.
Lee Grant, USA, 1989, 91 mins.

Stealing Home
Mark Harmon takes a sentimental journey in this nostalgic drama about a minor league baseball player who is summoned home to dispose of the ashes of his former free-spirited baby sitter with whom he shared a life-long bittersweet friendship. With Jodie Foster, William McNamara.
VHS: S09488. $19.95.
Laser: LD74698. $24.95.
Steven Kampmann, USA, 1988, 98 mins.

Steel Magnolias
In a small town in Louisiana, a local beauty parlor serves as the center for good times and gossip for six Southern women. A showcase for Hollywood actresses Sally Field, Shirley MacLaine, Dolly Parton, Olympia Dukakis, Julie Roberts and Daryl Hannah. Can you find the real daughters of the South in this picture? The title refers to the character of these fine examples of Southern womanhood. Based on the popular autobiographical play by Robert Harling.
VHS: S12420. $19.95.
Herbert Ross, USA, 1989, 118 mins.

Stella
Bette Midler is the latest actress to take on the role of the Olive Higgins Prouty heroine who sacrifices her own happiness in order that her daughter will have a better life. The contemporary setting detracts from the plausibility of the circumstances, but Midler is a wow as the barmaid who did it her way. With Stephen Collins, John Goodman and Marsha Mason.
VHS: S12852. $89.98.
John Erman, USA, 1990, 109 mins.

The Stepfather
This may look like your average mad slasher movie, but don't be misled by the packaging. This exploration of a deranged man just trying to find and maintain the perfect American family is several cuts above the usual shlock. Terry O'Quinn is mesmerizing in the title role. Script by Donald Westlake. A real chiller.
VHS: Out of print. For rental only.
Laser: LD72312. $29.99.
Joseph Ruben, USA, 1987, 89 mins.

Steppenwolf
Max von Sydow and Dominique Sanda star in this adaptation of Herman Hesse's classic novel about a man's internal struggle to find peace within himself. "A lush cinematic landscape, engagingly real yet properly symbolic" (Anne Hanley).
VHS: S02979. $59.95.
Fred Haines, USA, 1974, 105 mins.

Sterile Cuckoo
Offbeat tale of awakening love with Liza Minnelli and Wendell Burton. A "surprisingly gentle, surprisingly good film" (Pauline Kael). Based on the novel by John Nichols.
VHS: S02609. $49.95.
Laser: LD75337. $29.98.
Alan J. Pakula, USA, 1970, 107 mins.

The Stoned Age
In this 1970's party film, two dudes go cruisin' for hot babes and find them as well as a whole lot more. Before long they are at the jammingest party ever. The soundtrack includes Blue Oyster Cult, Black Sabbath, Ted Nugent, Foghat and Deep Purple. Michael Kopelow, China Kantner and Renee Griffen star.
VHS: S22866. $94.95.
Laser: LD75264. $34.98.
James Melkonian, USA, 1993, 90 mins.

The Story Lady
Jessica Tandy stars as a woman with an amazing ability to tell stories. When big business tries to commercialize her talents, she reveals an unsuspected strength and fights back. With Ed Begley Jr.
VHS: S20652. $89.95.
Larry Elikann, USA, 1993, 93 mins.

Straight Time
Dustin Hoffman gives a fine, demanding performance as a paroled robber, a man with psycho-sexual relationships with people from the prison world but seemingly unable to maintain relationships with outsiders. Based on the novel *No Beast So Fierce* by Edward Bunker, an ex-convict. With Harry Dean Stanton, Gary Busey and Theresa Russell.
VHS: S02610. $19.98.
Ulu Grosbard, USA, 1978, 114 mins.

Strange Days
Ralph Fiennes, Angela Bassett and Juliette Lewis form the tense romantic triangle that drives this futuristic thriller. It's the dawn of a new millennium and a strange technology is unveiled which is capable of transmitting the sensations of people's experiences directly to the human brain, offering the world some startling new possibilities. A series of killings makes the most of this new technology, but the deaths serve only to shield a more diabolical plot.
VHS: S27369. $99.99.
Laser: LD75512. $49.95.
Kathryn Bigelow, USA, 1995, 145 mins.

Stranger
Adolfo Aristarain, one of Argentina's best filmmakers, directed this U.S. thriller about an amnesia patient and her doctor who are caught in a deadly race against time. With Bonnie Bedelia and Peter Riegert.
VHS: S07327. $79.95.
Adolfo Aristarain, USA, 1987, 100 mins.

A Stranger Among Us
Veteran director Sidney Lumet welds together the themes of police procedure and issues of Jewish identity, in this film about a beautiful, though emotionally troubled, New York detective (Melanie Griffith) who goes undercover in a Hassidic community to solve a young man's brutal murder. Complications ensue when she falls for a brilliant, though unavailable, rabbinical student (Eric Thall). With Mia Sara, Jamey Sheridan and John Pankow.
VHS: S18137. $94.95.
Sidney Lumet, USA, 1992, 117 mins.

Strangers When We Meet
Kirk Douglas is a married architect involved with his beautiful married neighbor Kim Novak. Will this interfere with his building a hill-top home for writer Ernie Kovacs? A compelling and well acted drama of infidelity in California with Barbara Rush, Nancy Kovak and Walter Matthau. 117 mins.
VHS: S07675. $19.95.
Richard Quine, USA, 1960, 117 mins.

Strictly Business
Tommy Davidson from *In Living Color* stars as Bobby Johnson, a streetsmart mailroom employee with a strong desire to better himself. Enter Joseph C. Phillips as Wayman Tinsdale III, a love smitten buppie executive who wishes to meet Halle Berry, a tantalizing nightclub hostess. With David Marshall Grant, Jon Cypher, Anne Marie Johnson and Sam Jackson.
VHS: S15987. $19.98.
Kevin Hooks, USA, 1991, 84 mins.

Stuart Saves His Family
Al Franken is Stuart Smalley, the cable-access affirmation expert with firsthand knowledge of a variety of twelve-step programs. In this feature film comedy he must confront the sense of rejection and negative feelings occasioned by the cancellation of his show. His good friend (Laura San Giacomo) helps him through the dysfunctional morass that threatens his life and family.
VHS: S26394. $19.95.
Harold Ramis, USA, 1994, 95 mins.

Sugar Hill
Wesley Snipes stars as a hardened drug dealer who made it big through crime and drugs. Now he wants a new life with a respectable woman, away from Sugar Hill, where he lives with his brother, Michael Wright. As pressures mount he finds that he cannot simply abandon his past or his kin.
VHS: S21256. $96.98.
Leon Ichaso, USA, 1994, 123 mins.

Suicide Battalion/Hell Squad
Two exciting WWII action films in one program! *Suicide Battalion*. American soldiers fighting behind enemy lines in the Philippines are ordered to destroy vital military documents left behind at an abandoned U.S. base. Stars Michael Connors, John Ashley, Jewell Lian and Russ Bender. Directed by Edward L Cahn. 1958, 64 mins. *Hell Squad*. Five American soldiers do their best to survive when they become lost in the Tunisian desert. It won't be easy with enemy patrols, planes and mine fields waiting around every sand dune. Stars Wally Campo, Brandon Carroll, Fred Galvin, Grey Stuart, Leon Schrier and Cecil Addis. Directed by Burt Topper. 1958, 79 mins.
VHS: S16407. $14.95.

Summer to Remember
A deaf boy and a runaway orangutan learn to communicate and enjoy each other's company. The special relationship is jeopardized when the hairier friend is captured by a traveling circus. Can little Toby save his buddy Casey from the cruel circus trainer? With James Farentino, Tess Harper, Bridgette Andersen, Sean Justin Gerlis and C.J. the Orangutan, who is not to be confused with fellow cast member Burt Young. Made-for-TV.
VHS: S08505. $39.95.
Robert Lewis, USA, 1985, 98 mins.

Summer Wishes, Winter Dreams
Joanne Woodward won the New York Critics Award for Best Actress for her portrayal of a woman coming to grips with a mid-life crisis. With Martin Balsam. Music by Johnny Mandel.
VHS: S01281. $19.95.
Gilbert Cates, USA, 1973, 95 mins.

The Sunshine Boys
Neil Simon adapts his own play about two former vaudeville performers who are reluctantly pressed into service for a special television program. A sharp, observant comedy of manners, with superb performances by Walter Matthau and Oscar-winner George Burns.
VHS: S20504. $14.95.
Laser: LD70145. $34.98.
Herbert Ross, USA, 1975, 111 mins.

Sunshine's on the Way
Amy Wright and Scatman Crothers star in this uplifting tale of a dedicated young woman and her dream to rekindle the music in the lives of the folks in the Sugar Hill nursing home. Wright organizes a band of senior citizens including Crothers, as a cranky jazz trombonist, and draws national attention. With Theresa Merritt, Susan Kingsley and Doc Severinsen as himself.
VHS: S10616. $19.95.
Robert Mandel, USA, 1980, 46 mins.

Superman: The Movie
Christopher Reeve is the Man of Steel in this epic adventure of the famed hero of comic books, tv and the Broadway stage, as well as the big screen. From exploding planet to writing for the Daily Planet, the story is told. Special Oscar for special effects. With Margot Kidder, Jackie Cooper, Marlon Brando and Gene Hackman as super villain Lex Luthor.
VHS: S01286. $19.98.
Laser: LD74743. $29.98.
Richard Donner, USA, 1978, 143 mins.

Superman II
Richard Lester directs this fun-filled sequel that features three escapees from the Phantom Zone who have equal powers with the Man of Steel but not an ounce of his moral fiber. Lex Luthor is eager to be of assistance. With Terence Stamp, Valerie Perrine, Sarah Douglas and of course, Christopher Reeve.
VHS: S04004. $19.98.
Laser: LD74744. $29.98.
Richard Lester, USA, 1980, 127 mins.

Suspect
Cher stars as an attorney who becomes involved in a case that takes her outside of the law when juror Dennis Quaid provides information about drug trafficking.
VHS: S08225. $14.95.
Peter Yates, USA, 1988, 101 mins.

Sweet Lies
Sometimes the only way to win the man of your dreams is to cheat. Treat Williams is the romantic quarry of Joanna Pacula and Julianne Phillips. Williams plays an insurance investigator on a case in France. The title song of this comedy about fraud and deception is composed and sung by Robert Palmer.
VHS: S11165. $79.98.
Nathalie Delon, USA, 1987, 101 mins.

Sweet Lorraine
Maureen Stapleton is the proprietress of a run-down Catskill resort hotel called The Lorraine. Her concerned granddaughter is played by Trini Alvarado. A sweet and sentimental comedy-drama heavy on atmosphere and characterization. With Edith Falco and Todd Graff.
VHS: S05312. $79.95.
Steve Gomer, USA, 1987, 91 mins.

Swimming with Sharks
Kevin Spacey and Frank Whaley star in this dazzling, wicked comedy. The vile fun begins as Whaley's character is humiliated, kicked and even spit on all before ten in the morning. It's enough to make a man take up a gun in self-defense.
VHS: S26660. $94.99.
George Huang, USA, 1995, 93 mins.

T Bone n Weasel
The talented B-movie director Lewis Teague (*Piranha*) directs this engrossing road movie about the reluctant pairing of a former convict (Gregory Hines) and a mentally unbalanced hustler (Christopher Lloyd). With Ned Beatty and Rip Torn.
VHS: S18318. $89.98.
Lewis Teague, USA, 1992, 94 mins.

The Taking of Pelham 1 2 3
A sharp thriller about a group of terrorists who commander a New York City subway car and threaten to kill the hostages unless the bankrupt city agrees to pay them $1 million in one hour. Walter Matthau plays a security transit cop tracking their moves. The cast includes Robert Shaw as the head villain, Martin Balsam, Hector Elizondo and Jerry Stiller.
VHS: S17974. $14.95.
Laser: LD71177. $34.98.
Joseph Sargent, USA, 1974, 104 mins.

A Tale of Two Cities
A reworking of Dickens' novel about the French Revolution. Chris Sarandon stars in the dual role of lawyer (and French nobleman) who sacrifices himself to save another man. With Alice Krige, Peter Cushing and Kenneth More.
VHS: S18486. $19.98.
Jim Goddard, USA, 1980, 156 mins.

Talk Radio
Oliver Stone directed this adaptation of Eric Bogosian's hit stage play, which is loosely based on the murder of Denver talk show host Alan Berg by a neo-Nazi group. Stone transplants the setting to Texas, and weaves in a more intricate subplot involving the talk show host's estranged wife.
VHS: S09456. $19.95.
Laser: LD70086. $34.98.
Oliver Stone, USA, 1988, 103 mins.

Tank Girl
Lori Petty is Tank Girl, an armed and well made-up vigilante justice machine for the future. Her goal is to defeat Water and Power, an evil syndicate controlling the world's supply of water. Ice-T and Malcolm McDowell are also featured.
VHS: S25627. $19.98.
Laser: LD74985. $34.98.
Rachel Talalay, USA, 1995, 106 mins.

Tap
Gregory Hines dances up a storm as Max Washington, ex-con and tap dancer extraordinaire. Max must decide between a life of crime or using his talents for the betterment of mankind. With Sammy Davis Jr. as Little Mo and an aging but very active collection of tap legends like Sandman Simms and Harold Nicolaus. Also the performing talents of Suzanne Douglas and Savion Glover. A movie with a lot of heart and a lot of history.
VHS: S08701. $89.95.
Nick Castle, Jr., USA, 1989, 111 mins.

The Teacher
A lurid thriller about a repressed man drawn into a madly passionate affair with an older, experienced woman at the moment a psychopathic killer trails both of them. With Angel Tompkins, Jay North, and Anthony James.
Laser: LD71360. $39.95.
Hikmet Avedis, USA, 1974, 98 mins.

Telefon
Charles Bronson is a KGB agent sent from Moscow to the U.S.A. to prevent a renegade Russian general from starting WWIII by activating sleeper agents all over America. Lots of explosions and an astute use of rattlesnakes in this Don Siegel thriller. With Lee Remick, Donald Pleasance, Tyne Daley and Sheree North.
VHS: S06197. $69.95.
Don Siegel, USA, 1977, 102 mins.

Tell Me a Riddle
Melvyn Douglas and Lila Kedrova play a happily aging couple who have been married for forty years and now she is dying. This sensitive and touching drama is based on the novella by Tillie Olsen. With Brooke Adams, Zalman King, Dolores Dorn and Joan Harris. Lee Grant's feature film debut as a director.
VHS: S06020. $79.95.
Lee Grant, USA, 1980, 94 mins.

Tender Mercies
A gentle film starring Robert Duvall as a hard-luck country singer trying to put his life together with the support of a new family. Written by Horton Foote, directed by the Australian director of *Breaker Morant*.
VHS: S01309. $19.98.
Bruce Beresford, USA, 1982, 93 mins.

The Tenth Man

A fascinating adaptation of Graham Greene's novella. A wealthy French lawyer surrenders his possessions to avoid the Nazi firing squad. The lawyer gets entangled with the dead man's beautiful, heartbroken sister. With Anthony Hopkins, Derek Jacobi, Kristin Scott Thomas and Cyril Cusack.
VHS: S18488. $19.98.
Laser: LD71868. $34.98.
Jack Gold, USA, 1988, 100 mins.

Terminator 2: Judgment Day

At over $100 million, James Cameron's sequel to his popular feature films ever made. Arnold Schwarzenegger is back as the eponymous, time-traveling death machine, only this time he gets to play the "good" guy—meaning that instead of killing everyone in his path he now only injures them seriously. If you can stand the film's pumped-up violence, most of the special effects and stunt sequences are pretty spectacular, and, despite a few attempts at sentimentality which just flat-out fail, the movie functions fairly well as an entertaining roller coaster ride paced with action, fireworks and mild suspense. Written, produced and directed by James Cameron. Also starring Linda Hamilton.
VHS: S15229. $19.98.
James Cameron, USA, 1991, 139 mins.

Terms of Endearment

Winner of five Oscars including Best Picture, the story of the changing relationship between a mother and daughter over the years mixes humor and heartache. A tear-jerker. With Shirley MacLaine, Jack Nicholson and Debra Winger.
VHS: S03916. $19.95.
James L. Brooks, USA, 1983, 132 mins.

That Was Then...This Is Now

S.E. Hinton's novel achieves a sensitive adaptation in this story of two boys raised as brothers who take on the challenges of growing up, and of the street, at the same time. With Emilio Estevez, Craig Sheffer.
VHS: S03619. $79.95.
Laser: LD75327. $29.98.
Christopher Cain, USA, 1985, 102 mins.

Thelma and Louise

An unhappy housewife named Thelma (played by Geena Davis) and her wisecracking waitress friend Louise (Susan Sarandon) embark on a short trip to escape some of the boredom and mild dissatisfaction they feel in their daily lives. But a twist of fate turns their weekend "getaway" into just that, and they soon find themselves fleeing across the American southwest with the police only two steps behind. This "feminist"/buddy/road/adventure movie created quite a sensation when it was first released in 1991, and, surprisingly, it lives up to most of the hype. The excellent cast also includes Harvey Keitel, Michael Madsen, Christopher MacDonald and newcomer Brad Pitt.
VHS: S15283. $19.98.
Ridley Scott, USA, 1991, 127 mins.

They Only Kill Their Masters

A thriller about the chief of an idyllic coastal California community who tries to piece together the details of a strange murder, the death of a young pregnant woman who may have been attacked by her Doberman. With James Garner, Katharine Ross, Hal Holbrook and Peter Lawford.
VHS: S18481. $19.98.
James Goldstone, USA, 1972, 97 mins.

A Thing Called Love

Peter Bogdanovich's underrated drama is set in Nashville and stars River Phoenix, Samantha Mathis, Dermot Mulroney and Sandra Bullock in the story of four singer/songwriters who chase fame and fortune and find "The Thing Called Love." First-rate performances are supported by an all-country soundtrack.
VHS: S20490. $95.98.
Laser: LD75273. $34.98.
Peter Bogdanovich, USA, 1993, 116 mins.

Things Change

A hilariously funny black comedy about the Mafia and mistaken identity from David Mamet. Joe Mantegna is assigned to deliver Mob witness Don Ameche to court to take a phony rap for a bigshot hoodlum. He decides to give the old man a weekend vacation in Lake Tahoe for being such a stand-up guy. Problems occur when Ameche is mistaken for a bigshot hoodlum. With Robert Prosky. Great Fun.
VHS: S09834. $14.95.
David Mamet, USA, 1988, 114 mins.

The Third Solution

If you feel you missed the first two solutions, join the club. Treat Williams stars as a man who uncovers a secret pact between Moscow and the Vatican and is willing to expose the story to the world. This causes a certain level of tension in the international community. Whatever the Kremlin and the Pope had to discuss in private also interests F. Murray Abraham and Danny Aiello.
VHS: S11687. $79.95.
Pasquale Squitieri, USA/Italy, 1989, 113 mins.

This Boy's Life

Scottish director Michael Caton-Jones' somber adaptation of Tobias Wolff's memoirs about growing up in the Pacific Northwest in the 50s. The film is a collection of painful vignettes about the author as a young boy. Toby (Leonardo DiCaprio) and his mother Caroline (Ellen Barkin) stake out a forlorn, nomadic existence as they move from town to anonymous town without desires or expectations. With Robert De Niro and Jonah Blechman.
VHS: S19239. $19.98.
Laser: LD71916. $34.98.
Michael Caton-Jones, USA, 1993, 115 mins.

The Three Musketeers

Charlie Sheen, Kiefer Sutherland, Chris O'Donnell, Oliver Platt, Tim Curry, Rebecca De Mornay and Gabrielle Anwar star in this new, classic version based on the original tale of chivalrous love and camaraderie. It's a swashbuckling, action-packed romp with the immortal honor guard known as The Three Musketeers.
VHS: S21143. $96.98.
Stephen Herek, USA, 1993, 105 mins.

Three Wishes

Patrick Swayze and Mary Elizabeth Mastrantonio star in this tender romantic comedy. Mastrantonio plays a woman with two sons who has been left alone because her husband is missing in the Korean War. She and her sons open their home to a scruffy man with an even scruffier dog and unexpectedly find their lives changed forever.
VHS: S27499. $98.99.
Martha Coolidge, USA, 1995, 115 mins.

Threesome

John Charles, Lara Flynn Boyle and Stephen Baldwin star in this bittersweet reminiscence about dorm life. Once everything seemed fluid and possibilities just presented themselves. This celebrated, sexually adventurous movie shows what happens when three roommates just go with the flow.
VHS: S21681. $19.95.
Laser: LD74492. $34.95.
Andrew Fleming, USA, 1994, 93 mins.

Til Death Us Do Part

Treat Williams proves to be menacing in this true crime thriller based on one of the more difficult cases of Los Angeles District Attorney Vincent Bugliosi, the man who prosecuted Charles Manson. Williams is suspected of several murders, including that of the husband of his flashy blonde lover but the evidence is only circumstantial. Contains deleted footage not shown in the original television movie.
VHS: S16702. $89.95.
Yves Simoneau, USA, 1991, 93 mins.

Time Flies When You're Alive

An intimate portrait of a marriage challenged by cancer. Paul Linke created and performs this one-man show that details his wife's own struggle with the disease. Called "powerful, disturbing and funny" by the San Francisco Chronicle, "A celebration of life" by the New York Times and "something of a sensation" by the Chicago Tribune. You may remember the actor from his role on the TV show Chips.
VHS: S12600. $59.95.
Roger Spottiswoode, USA, 1989, 79 mins.

Tin Men

Richard Dreyfuss and Danny DeVito star as aluminum siding salesmen involved in an escalating feud. Director Barry Levinson cagily captures what life was like in Baltimore in the early 1960's. With Barbara Hershey as the wife caught in the middle and great supporting work from John Mahoney, Jackie Gayle and Stanley Brock as fellow tin men.
VHS: S06200. $19.95.
Barry Levinson, USA, 1987, 112 mins.

To Dance with the White Dog

Hume Cronyn and Jessica Tandy star in this touching love story. Eternal devotion should last beyond just one lifetime, and for these two lovers, magically it does. It all centers on the appearance of mysterious white dog who manages to comfort a lonely widower.
VHS: S21151. $14.98.
Glenn Jordan, USA, 1993, 98 mins.

To Wong Foo, Thanks for Everything! Julie Newmar

Patrick Swayze, Wesley Snipes and John Leguizamo star as beautiful young drag queens out for a jaunt across America. Along the way, they break some hearts, deepen their sense of fashion and even throw a party. This warm comedy is a perfect gender-bending confection. Stockard Channing and Blythe Danner are both featured.
VHS: S27180. $99.99.
Laser: LD75465. $39.98.
Beeban Kidron, USA, 1995, 109 mins.

Tobruk

During the war in North Africa, a British major and some German Jews try to blow up Rommel's fuel supply. A tough and spectacular war adventure, starring Rock Hudson, George Peppard, Nigel Green, Guy Stockwell and Leo Gordon.
VHS: S16304. $14.95.
Arthur Hiller, USA, 1967, 110 mins.

Tomorrow

Robert Duvall gives a dynamite performance as a caretaker who finds himself caring for a pregnant woman who turns up one day at the lumber mill where he works. Based on a story by William Faulkner, and with a script by Horton Foote (Tender Mercies).
VHS: S04782. $59.95.
Joseph Anthony, USA, 1972, 103 mins.

Tomorrow's Child

A fictional drama about the world's first test-tube baby conceived and grown to full term in the laboratory. William Atherton and Stephanie Zimbalist are the concerned parents in this made-for-tv look at modern science at work. With James Shigeta, Ed Flanders, Salome Jens and Bruce Davison.
VHS: S08039. $59.98.
Joseph Sargent, USA, 1982, 100 minus.

Top Gun

Tom Cruise plays a cocky jet pilot in this unabashed recruitment promo for the U.S. Air Force. At a special combat training school he learns new moves and tries them out on a civilian instructor. With Kelly McGillis, Anthony Edwards, Val Kilmer and Tom Skerritt. Into the air junior birdman!
VHS: S04003. $14.95.
Tony Scott, USA, 1986, 110 mins.

Tora! Tora! Tora!

An expensively mounted battle sequence of the bombing of Pearl Harbor takes up half of this super war drama, which recreates the events leading up to and following the "day of infamy." With Jason Robards, Martin Balsam, Joseph Cotten.
VHS: S09452. $19.98.
Fleischer/Masuda/Fukusaku, USA, 1970, 142 mins.

Tough Guys

Burt Lancaster and Kirk Douglas are two old-time master criminals who pulled off the last great train robbery, are released from prison, and face difficulties adjusting to outside life. With Charles Durning, Dana Carvey and Eli Wallach.
Laser: LD71374. $36.99.
Jeff Kanew, USA, 1986, 104 mins.

Tough Guys Don't Dance

Ryan O'Neal and Isabella Rossellini star in this tongue-in-cheek sendup of film noir written and directed by Norman Mailer. Taken from his novel about greed, lust, ambition, and corpses without heads in Provincetown. With Wings Hauser, Debra Sandlund and Lawrence Tierney. The title is a quote from a real life mobster.
VHS: S06061. $19.95.
Norman Mailer, USA, 1987, 110 mins.

Toys

A black comedy about the military industrial complex. A general (Michael Gambon) assumes control of a family toy manufacturer and tries to convert the vast, surreal plant into a state-of-the-art munitions factory. Robin Williams stars as the general's nephew, a dreamy, lost romantic who leads the counterattack against the general to regain control of the family business. With Joan Cusack, Robin Wright and rapper LL Cool J.
VHS: S18602. $19.98.
Barry Levinson, USA, 1992, 121 mins.

Tracks

Dennis Hopper delivers an impressive performance as the decorated, disoriented Vietnam Vet soldier who is escorting home the body of a friend killed in Nam. On the way he encounters a relentless parade of American caricatures.
VHS: S01366. $19.95.
Henry Jaglom, USA, 1974, 90 mins.

Trading Hearts

Raul Julia is an ex-baseball giant who falls head over heels in love with a minor league singer, played by Beverly D'Angelo. Set in the fabulous 50's, this is a timeless tale of shattered dreams and newfound love.
VHS: S09284. $14.95.
Laser: LD75136. $24.98.
Neil Leifer, USA, 1988, 88 mins.

Train Robbers

John Wayne agrees to help widow Ann-Margret retrieve a half-million dollar treasure in stolen gold bullion buried somewhere in the Mexican desert. He enlists the help of saddle buddies Rod Taylor, Ben Johnson, Bobby Vinton, Jerry Gatlin and Christopher George. Together they must face the mysterious Ricardo Montalban and twenty nameless riders who are also intrigued by the expedition.
VHS: S16293. $19.98.
Laser: Letterboxed. LD71807. $34.98.
Burt Kennedy, USA, 1973, 92 mins.

Treasure Island

An all-new production of Robert Louis Stevenson's timeless classic, with Charlton Heston as the infamous pirate captain Long John Silver, Christian Bale as the cabin boy Jim Hawkins, Oliver Reed as Capt. Billy Bones and Christopher Lee as Blind Pew.
VHS: S12299. $79.98.
Fraser C. Heston, USA, 1990, 132 mins.

Trespass

Bill Paxton and William Sadler try to escape from a Black drug gang in an East St. Louis factory. Crack kingpin Ice-T faces off against Ice Cube in a complicated plot that uses a rap soundtrack, video, and much gratuitous violence.
VHS: S21490. $94.98.
Walter Hill, USA, 1992, 101 mins.

Tribes

An intense and occasionally humorous tv-movie about a group of young marine recruits going through basic training. Darren McGavin is the tough-as-leather Drill Instructor. Jan Michael Vincent is the hippie who was drafted. This Emmy award winning script is set in the late '60's. Cast includes Earl Holliman Jr., Danny Goldman and Richard Yniguez.
VHS: S08038. $59.98.
Joseph Sargent, USA, 1970, 74 mins.

Trip to Bountiful

Geraldine Page won the Oscar for Best Actress in this story of an old woman returning to her childhood home in order to embrace memories. But she is trapped inside an apartment and treated like a child by her son, and ultimately escapes and gets a chance to revive her dreams.
VHS: S01811. $19.95.
Laser: LD72314. $29.99.
Peter Masterson, USA, 1985, 105 mins.

Triumph of the Spirit

Willem Dafoe is cast as Salamo Arouch, a Greek Jew who survived the concentration camp at Auschwitz by boxing for the entertainment of the German officers. His true story is designed to be even more poignant by the fact that the movie was made on location in the former death camp. With Robert Loggia, Wendy Gazelle and Edward James Olmos as a wily Gypsy kapo.
VHS: S12212. $89.95.
Robert M. Young, USA, 1989, 115 mins.

Tropic of Cancer

Joseph Strick's rendering of Henry Miller's autobiographical novel. Set in 30s Paris cafe society, Rip Torn is a disaffected American expatriate novelist searching for meaning and purpose and drifting into a succession of erotic adventures. With James Callahan, David Bauer and Laurence Ligneres. Ellen Burstyn gives a small, remarkable performance as Henry's wife June.
VHS: S19025. $19.95.
Joseph Strick, USA, 1970, 87 mins.

The Trouble with Spies

Donald Sutherland stars as Appleton Porter, a secret agent in her Majesty's Secret Service and Britain's least capable investigator since Inspector Clouseau assisted Scotland Yard. An action adventure with comedy and romance with Robert Morley, Ned Beatty, and Lucy Gutteridge as an attractive Soviet agent. 1987, 91 mins.
VHS: S06395. $79.99.

True Confessions

Robert De Niro and Robert Duvall star as conscientious brothers, whose chosen professions—the priesthood and law enforcement—collide in Los Angeles circa 1948. Based on the popular novel by John Gregory Dunne, this underrated crime drama combines corruption within the Catholic Church with a sensational murder mystery. The sturdy supporting cast includes Charles Durning, Ed Flanders, Burgess Meredith, Kenneth McMillan, Rose Gregorio, Dan Hedaya, Louisa Moritz and Cyril Cusack as Cardinal Danaher.
VHS: S16445. $19.98.
Ulu Grosbard, USA, 1981, 108 mins.

True Stories

David Byrne stars in this wacky view of the people and events of Virgil, Texas, population 40,000 and growing, a gleeful glimpse of Americana where the social fabric might be polyester but the hearts are pure gold...and the good times never end. Featuring a cast of unforgettable characters including John Goodman, who has a flashing "Wife Wanted" sign on his front lawn, and a dancin' faith healer. With Annie McEnroe, Swoosie Kurtz and Spalding Gray.
VHS: S03107. $19.98.
Laser: LD74722. $34.98.
David Byrne, USA, 1986, 89 mins.

Truly, Madly, Deeply

A young woman is consumed by grief because of the death of her young lover (Alan Rickman). Just as her despair and anger seem overwhelming, the dead young man shows up on her doorstep. This unique film combines a love story with a decidedly supernatural angle.
VHS: S25516. $19.95.
Anthony Minghella, USA, 1991, 107 mins.

Trusting Beatrice

Irene Jacob (Double Life of Veronique) is the star of this quirky romantic comedy about a mysterious French woman and her adopted Cambodian child. One day they find themselves homeless because their desperate neighbor has burned down their apartment building. As a result they all move in together with the arsonist's odd family. Love somehow also finds a home in these strange, secret-laden surroundings. Also features Steve Buscemi and Mark Evan Jacobs.
VHS: S24210. $19.95.
Cindy Lou Johnson, USA, 1994, 86 mins.

The Turn of the Screw

Lynn Redgrave portrays a young governess who must protect her charges from the menacing spirits of their former governess and her evil lover.
VHS: S02624. $29.98.
Dan Curtis, USA, 1974, 120 mins.

Turning Point

Anne Bancroft and Shirley MacLaine star as two friends and rivals reunited after a number of years apart, Bancroft as the aging ballerina, MacLaine as the one who abandoned her career to raise a family. Superb dance sequences featuring Mikhail Baryshnikov.
VHS: S01828. $19.95.
Laser: LD72274. $39.98.
Herbert Ross, USA, 1977, 119 mins.

The Tuskegee Airmen

Laurence Fishburne stars along with John Lithgow and Cuba Gooding, Jr., in this tale of heroic African-American World War II fighter pilots. Four new recruits are given the mission to help defend American troops from the air, but their mission also has another important goal. Their success could prove that the courage and skills of African-Americans are equal to those of their countrymen.
VHS: S27725. $94.99.
Robert Markowitz, USA, 1994, 52 mins.

Twilight's Last Gleaming

Burt Lancaster is a renegade Air Force general who takes over a Titan missile silo along with Burt Young and Paul Winfield and demands that the US government tell the American people the truth about Vietnam. Charles Durning is the President. Richard Widmark is in charge of a successful outcome to this tense hostage situation. With Melvyn Douglas and Joseph Cotten.
VHS: S06203. $59.98.
Robert Aldrich, USA, 1977, 146 mins.

Twisted Obsession

A screenwriter is uninspired by his current project and decides to back out—that is, until he meets the director's younger sister. An affair ensues in which the writer learns of the unnaturally domineering relationship the director holds with his sibling. Why, and who is dominating whom, becomes the man's obsession. With Jeff Goldblum and Miranda Richardson.
VHS: S12743. $89.95.
Fernando Trueba, USA, 1990, 109 mins.

The Two Jakes
The long awaited sequel to *Chinatown*. Much has changed since Jake's last adventure in sunburnt Los Angeles. The war has come and gone. The city teems with optimism and fast bucks. But the more things change, the more they stay the same. Especially when a routine marital snoop job explodes into a murder that's tied to a grab for oil—and to Jake's own *Chinatown* past. Two-time Academy Award winner Jack Nicholson stars and directs from a script by renowned screenwriter Robert Towne (*Chinatown*, *Tequila Sunrise*).
VHS: $13433. $14.95.
   Laser: Widescreen. LD75329. $29.98.
Jack Nicholson, USA, 1990, 137 mins.

Two Kinds of Love
Ricky Schroder, Lindsay Wagner and Peter Weller star in this drama of a father seeking reconciliation with his son in the face of the mother's death. Based on the novel *There Are Two Kinds of Terrible* by Peggy Mann.
VHS: $06358. $59.96.
Jack Bender, USA, 1983, 100 mins.

Two Worlds of Jennie Logan
Lindsay Wagner stars in this made-for-tv movie as a woman involved in murder, passion, and intrigue in two centuries simultaneously. Based on the novel *Second Sight* by David Williams. The cast includes Marc Singer, Linda Gray, Henry Wilcoxon and Joan Darling. The movie for people who think deja vu is more than a feeling.
VHS: $08494. $14.95.
Frank de Felitta, USA, 1979, 100 mins.

Unbearable Lightness of Being
Czech author Milan Kundera's novel has been transferred to film by director Philip Kaufman (*The Right Stuff*). The emphasis is less on the philosophic debates of love and life and more on epic visualization of passion and revolution. With Englishman Daniel Day-Lewis as the doctor with two life long loves to choose from—French actress Juliette Binoche and Swedish actress Lena Olin. This polyglot cast is supposed to be all Czechs in this English language version that uses hats and mirrors as sexual aides.
VHS: $07757. $19.98.
   Laser: LD71386. $49.95.
Philip Kaufman, USA, 1988, 156 mins.

Uncle Tom's Cabin
An exceptional cast highlights this television interpretation of Harriet Beecher Stowe's incendiary novel about pre-Civil War relations between blacks and whites, epitomized in the brutally racist actions of landowner Simon Legree (Edward Woodward). With Avery Brooks, Phylicia Rashad, Bruce Dern, Kate Burton, Paula Kelly and Kathryn Walker.
VHS: $19683. $9.98.
Stan Lathan, USA, 1987, 110 mins.

Under Suspicion
Liam Neeson and Laura San Giacomo star in this thriller that meshes two unsavory characters in an unforseen murder. Neeson's character uses his own wife to set up phony adultery charges. When she and a prospective mark are murdered, he comes under suspicion. There is, however, another suspect, the beautiful mistress of the dead man. Soon she has trapped Neeson's character in another plot.
VHS: $26285. $19.95.
Simon Moore, USA, 1991, 100 mins.

Under the Biltmore Clock
An American Playhouse presentation of the F. Scott Fitzgerald short story *Myra Meets His Family*. Sean Young plays a social-climbing flapper who is interested in a wealthy young man played by Lenny Von Dohlen. She is thrilled at his invitation to meet his family at the family estate until she meets his family. How will she react to this eccentric bunch could preclude her joining them on a regular basis.
VHS: $10991. $19.95.
Neal Miller, USA, 1985, 90 mins.

Undercover Blues
What's a family to do when confronted by international arms thieves, local New Orleans hoods and a distinct dearth of affordable child care? In this movie Dennis Quaid and Kathleen Turner have fun fighting crime and simultaneously raising a family.
VHS: $20716. $19.95.
   Laser: LD72385. $34.98.
Herbert Ross, USA, 1993, 90 mins.

Unfaithfully Yours
Remake of the Preston Sturges film, featuring Dudley Moore and Nastassia Kinski, in a story of a conductor who plans to murder his wife.
VHS: $01403. $79.98.
Howard Zieff, USA, 1984, 96 mins.

An Unmarried Woman
A compassionate story in which Jill Clayburgh delivers an unsparing self-examination of a woman's individuality, as she attempts to survive alone. With Alan Bates, Michael Murphy.
VHS: $04590. $69.98.
Paul Mazursky, USA, 1978, 122 mins.

Unremarkable Life
Patricia Neal and Shelley Winters co-star in this story of love, life and emotional rebirth. For the past 15 years, Frances (Neal), carefree but obediently naive, has shared her house with her sister Evelyn (Winters), a stern matriarch who finds comfort in her sister's misery. The two women go about their household duties, never changing their routines, until Frances meets a charming widower and a relationship develops. Then she is forced to choose between loyalty to her sister and the only man she may ever love. "Shelley Winters and Patricia Neal do *On Golden Pond* and *The Whales of August* one better."
VHS: $12280. $14.95.
Amin Q. Chaudhri, USA, 1989, 111 mins.

Unstrung Heroes
Andie MacDowell, John Turturro and Michael Richards star in this family comedy. A young man with a rambunctious sense of life is drawn to the very pair of uncles which the entire family finds crazy. It is a film which proves that heroes can be found in even the most unlikely places.
VHS: $27411. $99.99.
   Laser: LD75508. $39.99.
Diane Keaton, USA, 1995, 93 mins.

The Untouchables
Eliot Ness versus Al Capone, and the battlefield is Chicago. Historically flawed and often physically impossible, this film delivers lots of action, fine performances and snappy one-liners. Kevin Costner is Ness, Robert De Niro is Capone and Sean Connery is the Irish beat cop with a plan to make the Windy City a decent place to live. Watch for the *Potemkin* tribute at Union Station.
VHS: $06241. $19.95.
Brian DePalma, USA, 1987, 119 mins.

The Usual Suspects
Stephen Baldwin, Gabriel Byrne, Benicio del Toro, Kevin Pollak and Kevin Spacey star in this inventive crime story as a bunch of guys brought together for a police line-up. Finding themselves alone together after the cops are through with them, they decide to plan a crime. This plot about a multi-million dollar drug deal gets even stranger because somehow, amidst all the intricately placed flashbacks, these eccentric criminals end up causing a catastrophic explosion. Featuring Chazz Palminteri, Pete Postlethwaite and Suzy Amis.
VHS: $27071. $96.99.
   Laser: LD75442. $39.95.
Bryan Singer, USA, 1995, 106 mins.

V.I. Warshawski
Kathleen Turner stars as V.I. Warshawski, a tough-talking, sexy private eye who knows how to use her two most lethal weapons—powerful charm and all the right moves. When she's hired by the 13-year-old daughter of a murder victim, V.I. gets caught up in an action-packed thriller involving murder, money and a ruthless killer. Also starring Jay O. Sanders and Charles Durning.
VHS: $15355. $92.95.
Jeff Kanew, USA, 1991, 89 mins.

Vamping
Fantasy, remembrance and murder combine in this story about a jazz musician who burglarizes a rich widow to get his saxophone out of the pawn shop, only to fall in love with the widow.
VHS: $10098. $59.96.
Frederick King Keller, USA, 1984, 110 mins.

The Verdict
Paul Newman stars as the aging attorney who overcomes his personal failure by taking on a case of medical malpractice and suing a hospital in a tense courtroom examination of medical and legal ethics. Screenplay by David Mamet, based on the novel by Barry Reed. With Charlotte Rampling, James Mason.
VHS: $02344. $19.98.
   Laser: LD71392. $44.98.
Sidney Lumet, USA, 1982, 128 mins.

Vibes
Cyndi Lauper teams up with Jeff Goldblum and Peter Falk in this supernatural South American treasure hunt comedy. Lauper and Goldblum have psychic abilities that con man Falk thinks he can put to good use in Ecuador. With Julian Sands and Googy Gress. Cindy sings "Hole in My Heart" in her feature film debut.
VHS: $10099. $89.95.
Ken Kwapis, USA, 1988, 99 mins.

Virtuosity
Denzel Washington is a cop forced to play a deadly game. Somehow, a composite of 200 serial killers has escaped the cyberworld game he inhabits. Now this killer stalks real victims relying on the intelligence and viciousness of the minds used to create him. Washington's character is made all the more disturbed by an intriguing personal connection to this virtual madman.
VHS: $27004. $98.99.
Brett Leonard, USA, 1995, 107 mins.

The Visitors
James Woods makes his cinematic debut in this tough, suspenseful drama about a Vietnam veteran who cannot escape his past. On his Connecticut farm all appears peaceful until two friends from his soldier days arrive, bringing with them the unburied memories of difficult times.
VHS: $21148. $19.98.
Elia Kazan, USA, 1972, 88 mins.

Voyage of the Damned
In 1939, almost 2,000 refugees from Nazi Germany were on a ship originally bound for Cuba. Refused entry there and everywhere else, these German Jews were forced back to their home, where they faced certain death. The all-star cast includes Faye Dunaway, Max Von Sydow, Orson Welles, James Mason, Lee Grant, Ben Gazzara and Sam Wanamaker.
VHS: $22029. $9.98.
Stuart Rosenberg, USA, 1976, 134 mins.

Wait until Spring Bandini
Joe Mantegna stars as the philandering head of an immigrant Italian family in Colorado in the 1920s. Ornella Muti is the faithful wife who must compete with stylish Faye Dunaway as the rich Mrs. Hildegarde. With Michael Bacall, Daniel Wilson, Alex Vincent and Burt Young as Rocco. Based on the novel by John Fante with music composed by Angelo Badalamenti (*Twin Peaks*). Presented by Francis Ford Coppola.
VHS: $14996. $19.98.
Dominique Deruddere, USA, 1990, 104 mins.

A Walk in the Clouds
Keanu Reeves stars in this openly sentimental love story. The story unfolds at a family-run vineyard in the 1940s. Two people meet on a bus and accidentally end up posing as a married couple. This scenario is meant to fool the young woman's traditionally-minded Mexican parents. Naturally, there are suspicions, but in the end, the charade succeeds. With Anthony Quinn, Aitana Sanchez-Gijon and Giancarlo Giannini.
VHS: $27209. $99.99.
   Laser: LD75481. $39.98.
Alfonso Arau, USA, 1995, 102 mins.

Walk on the Wild Side
Laurence Harvey travels to Louisiana with runaway Jane Fonda, determined to find his long-lost love (Capucine). But he's devastated when he finds out that Capucine has been reduced to working in a brothel run by a ruthless madam (Barbara Stanwyck). Loosely based on a novel by Nelson Algren, with a terrific score by Elmer Bernstein.
VHS: $07337. $69.95.
Edward Dmytryk, USA, 1962, 114 mins.

Walker
Ed Harris inhabits the role of the political adventurer William Walker, an American who invaded Nicaragua in 1855 with 58 men and won a dubious place in history. Director Alex Cox (*Sid and Nancy*) plays the story for political irony and bizarre humor. With Peter Boyle, Rene Auberjonois and Marlee Matlin as Ellen Martin.
VHS: $06922. $79.95.
Alex Cox, USA, 1987, 95 mins.

Wall Street
Oliver Stone invades the stone canyons of the stock market battle zone with the story of a young broker who is willing to do most anything to land the big account. Michael Douglas won an Oscar for his greed is good philosophy. With Charlie Sheen, Martin Sheen, Hal Holbrook, Sean Young and Daryl Hannah.
VHS: Out of print. For rental only.
   Laser: CLV. LD72105. $39.98.
Oliver Stone, USA, 1987, 128 mins.

War of the Roses
Those looking for an historical drama about a bitter civil war in England are going to be disappointed. This conflict is an all-American marital struggle over division of community property. Danny DeVito directs his pal Michael Douglas and Kathleen Turner in a brutal story of a disintegrating marriage. DeVito also takes the part of a lawyer who cautions others not to follow the example of Oliver and Barbara Rose.
VHS: $12347. $14.98.
   Laser: LD72433. $99.98.
Danny DeVito, USA, 1989, 116 mins.

Wargames
Computer kid whiz taps into the Defense Department's master war computer and nearly starts World War III. Slick feature with Matthew Broderick, Dabney Coleman and Ally Sheedy.
VHS: $03494. $19.95.
   Laser: Letterboxed. LD74591. $34.98.
John Badham, USA, 1983, 114 mins.

Warriors
Inventive comic book style story of a gang crossing rivals' turf in a neon underworld New York. Upon its release this film caused a furor because it supposedly started riots in and around theatres where it played. Creative use of color and action, music by Joe Walsh.
VHS: $07497. $19.95.
Walter Hill, USA, 1979, 90 mins.

The Waterdance
This autobiographical work by Neal Jimenez (*River's Edge*) is a tragicomedy about the recovery of a talented young novelist (Eric Stoltz) paralyzed in a mountain climbing accident, and his time in a paraplegic ward at a local hospital. With Wesley Snipes and William Forsythe as two embittered antagonists, Elizabeth Pena, and Helen Hunt as Stoltz's married lover.
VHS: $18116. $92.95.
   Laser: LD71843. $34.95.
Neal Jimenez/Michael Steinberg, USA, 1991, 110 mins.

Waterhole #3
James Coburn, Carroll O'Connor and Bruce Dern are the three Army buddies who rob a fortune in gold, bury it in the desert, and then have their hands full trying to recover it. With Joan Blondell and Margaret Blye.
VHS: $04435. $19.95.
   Laser: Widescreen. LD75304. $39.98.
William A. Graham, USA, 1967, 95 mins.

Waterland
In this age of cynicism and despair, history teacher Tom Crick, played by Academy Award winner Jeremy Irons, inspires his students to embrace the past. Ethan Hawke is the student who learns to see the marvels and mysteries that life holds.
VHS: $21089. $19.98.
Stephen Gyllenhaal, USA, 1992, 94 mins.

Waterworld
Kevin Costner and Dennis Hopper star in this $90-million extravaganza about the doomed planet Earth. The polar ice caps have melted, turning the entire world into a vast oceanic expanse. One little girl could hold the key to saving mankind from a precarious existence on artificial atolls where the threat of pirates is ever present. With Tina Majorino and Jeanne Tripplehorn.
VHS: $26950. $99.99.
   Laser: LD75423. $44.99.
Kevin Reynolds, USA, 1995, 136 mins.

The Way We Were
Sydney Pollack directed this poignant and beguiling love story about two hopelessly opposite people who fall in love, are married and subsequently divorce over the contradictions of their clashing worlds. As he proved with *Out of Africa*, Pollack handles actors exceptionally well. Robert Redford is a conservative screenwriter at the height of the McCarthy paranoia. Barbra Streisand is a left-wing, Jewish radical unable to embrace the social and political privileges of Redford's past. A stunning score from Marvin Hamlisch, as well as a nicely rendered title track from Streisand.
VHS: $02921. $19.95.
   Laser: Chapter stops, 2 sides, theatrical trailer. LD75053. $34.95.
Sydney Pollack, USA, 1973, 118 mins.

Weeds
Nick Nolte stars as a convict who betters himself by forming a prison theater company and then takes the show on the road when he is paroled. Based on the experiences of ex-convict Rick Cluchey. With Rita Taggart as the theatre/food critic who gets him his big break. Inmate actors include Ernie Hudson, Bill Forsythe and Joe Mantegna.
VHS: $06880. $19.98.
John Hancock, USA, 1987, 115 mins.

Welcome Home, Roxy Carmichael
A gentle satire about celebrity and small-town life. An Ohio community anticipates the return of a reclusive star, while a moody, brilliant, though alienated young hipster (Winona Ryder) secretly fantasizes the mysterious woman is her long-lost natural mother. With Jeff Daniels, Laila Robbins, Dinah Manoff and Thomas Wilson Brown.
VHS: $17981. $14.95.
Jim Abrahams, USA, 1990, 98 mins.

What Can I Do?
This highly innovative film follows the fascinating dinner conversation between an elderly, affluent woman and her five dinner guests. It offers a daring exploration of the relationship between viewer, the screen image and a performer.
VHS: $21863. $19.95.
Wheeler Winston Dixon, USA, 1993, 80 mins.

What's Eating Gilbert Grape
Trapped in a small town, Johnny Depp supports his eccentric family, which includes a 500-pound mother, a mentally disabled brother and two problematic sisters. All this is put in jeopardy when he finds new hope in the outsider Juliette Lewis. Co-stars Leonardo Di Caprio and Mary Steenburgen.
VHS: $21210. $19.95.
Lasse Hallstrom, USA, 1993, 118 mins.

When a Man Loves a Woman
Meg Ryan and Andy Garcia star in this drama about a couple facing alcoholism. Through tears and laughter they overcome this challenge to their marriage and their family. Ultimately it brings them closer to each other by forcing them to concentrate on the most important element in their lives, their enduring love.
VHS: $22711. $96.98.
Luis Mandoki, USA, 1993, 126 mins.

When the Whales Came
A highly acclaimed family film with Paul Scofield starring in a poignant drama about co-existing with the whales. It has been 70 years since the people of Samson Island preyed upon a school of narwhal whales, only to be destroyed by a mysterious curse. The last survivor—an enigmatic mystic known only as the Birdman, lives on Bryher, a neighboring island that is about to be visited by those very same whales. If Bryher is to be spared the deadly curse of Samson, it will be up to two trusting children, Daniel and Gracie, to befriend the deaf bird sculptor and learn his ancient secrets. "A whale of a childhood fable" (*New York Post*). Close-captioned.
VHS: $12185. $89.98.
Clive Rees, USA, 1989, 100 mins.

While You Were Sleeping
Sandra Bullock, Bill Pullman and Peter Gallagher star in this film that offers a strange twist on an old comic theme of romantic rivalry. Bullock is a public transportation worker in Chicago who secretly longs for a stranger. One day he is mugged and falls into a coma. By chance Bullock is mistaken as the man's fiance. As she spins stories about their affair the man's brother comes to figure in her actual erotic life. Of course everything changes when the man in the coma wakes up.
VHS: $26397. $103.99.
   Laser: LD75081. $39.99.
Jon Turteltaub, USA, 1995, 103 mins.

White Dawn
Based on James Houston's true story of three sailors separated from their ship in the Arctic during a hunt for polar bear and walrus. Magnificent scenery and intense drama combine for an intriguing film. With Warren Oates, Timothy Bottoms, Lou Gossett, Jr.
VHS: $01450. $19.95.
   Laser: LD75330. $29.98.
Philip Kaufman, USA, 1975, 110 mins.

White Man's Burden
This is the film that takes as its premise the idea that everyone hates John Travolta because he is white. Harry Belafonte stars as Travolta's blithely unconcerned and bigoted boss. In this drama/thriller, all race relations are reversed, with blacks dominating an unequal society where whites do the hardest and most punishing work. Travolta revolts when he loses his job, and forces everyone to reconsider the price of the "White Man's Burden."
VHS: $27525. $99.99.
Desmond Nakano, USA, 1995, 89 mins.

White Nights
Mikhail Baryshnikov stars as a Russian ballet defector who finds himself back in the USSR. Interesting primarily for the excellent dance sequences. With Gregory Hines and Isabella Rossellini.
VHS: $05333. $19.95.
   Laser: Widescreen. LD75494. $39.95.
Taylor Hackford, USA, 1985, 135 mins.

White Palace
James Spader and Susan Sarandon star in this contemporary love story about a younger man and a bolder woman. She's a waitress in a fast food burger joint; he's a rising ad executive. About all they have in common is that they both live in St. Louis and enjoy great sex. Lasting relationships have been built on less. Based on the novel by Glenn Savan.
VHS: $13585. $19.95.
Luis Mandoki, USA, 1990, 103 mins.

White Sands
An invigorating thriller about a small-town sheriff (Willem Dafoe) who impersonates a dead man and becomes entangled in a complex web of FBI sting operations, black market gun runners, Third World guerrillas, and a wealthy socialite drawn to dangerous causes. With Mickey Rourke, Mary Elizabeth Mastrantonio, M. Emmet Walsh, Samuel L. Jackson and an uncredited Mimi Rogers.
VHS: $17036. $19.95.
Roger Donaldson, USA, 1992, 101 mins.

Who'll Stop the Rain
Nick Nolte is the Vietnam vet who can save Tuesday Weld and her husband Michael Moriarty from their own stupidity and the viciousness of Richard Masur, Ray Sharkey and Anthony Zerbe. A thriller about drug smuggling and much more. From Robert Stone's *Dog Soldiers*.
VHS: S06992. $14.95.
Karel Reisz, USA, 1978, 126 mins.

Who's Afraid of Virginia Woolf
Based on Edward Albee's smash hit play; Elizabeth Taylor and Richard Burton star in the story of the love-hate relationship between a middle-aged professor and his vitriolic but seductive wife.
VHS: S01737. $19.98.
Laser: LD70705. $39.98.
Laser: Widescreen. LD71415. $39.98.
Mike Nichols, USA, 1966, 129 mins.

Whose Life Is It Anyway?
Richard Dreyfuss, John Cassavetes and Christine Lahti deliver outstanding performances in this adaptation of the Broadway hit with Dreyfuss as the sculptor paralyzed in an accident, who argues for his right to die. 1981, 118 mins.
VHS: S02863. $79.95.
John Badham, USA, 1981, 118 mins.

Wicked Stepmother
Bette Davis and Barbara Carrera star in this black comedy about witchcraft. When Davis quit production, Carrera was hired by cult director Larry Cohen (*It's Alive*) to complete the film. The plot concerns shrinking victims of a bizarre cult. The cast includes Colleen Camp, David Rasche, Tom Bosley, Richard Moll, Evelyn Keyes and Lionel Stander.
VHS: S11164. $14.95.
Larry Cohen, USA, 1988, 95 mins.

Wide Sargasso Sea
Talented Australian director John Duigan (*Flirting*) adapted Jean Rhys' sensual novel about the first marriage of Rochester (Nathaniel Parker), the brooding English romantic of Charlotte Bronte's *Jane Eyre*, to a beautiful Creole named Antoinette (Karina Lombard). Set in Jamaica during the 1840s, the film pivots on erotic obsession and sexual delusion. "Infinitely romantic, the film's eroticism is real" (Vincent Canby). With Rachel Ward as Antoinette's mentally unbalanced mother, Michael York, Martine Beswicke and Claudia Robinson.
VHS: S19936. $19.95.
John Duigan, USA/Australian, 1992, 100 mins.

Wild Hearts Can't Be Broken
Gabrielle Anwar stars in the inspirational true story of Sonora Walker, a young girl who thrilled thousands of visitors to Atlantic City during the 1930's and 1940's. Even after she was blinded in an accident, she continued to dive off a 40-foot tower into a tank of water on horseback. With Matt Schoeffling, Kathleen York and Cliff Robertson as wild west showman W.F. Carver, a former partner of Wild Bill Cody.
VHS: S15530. $92.95.
Steve Miner, USA, 1991, 88 mins.

Wild Side
Christopher Walken, Joan Chen and Anne Heche star in this steamy, erotic thriller. Heche is a bank executive with a profitable sideline in prostitution. It all seems as safe as money in the bank until she meets a millionaire and his wife (Walken and Chen). Then things devolve into a kinky mess where the most important desire may well be the desire for cold, hard cash. USA, 1995, 96 mins.
VHS: S27511. $95.99.

Wild Women
Hugh O'Brian leads a group of army engineers who recruit female convicts to pose as their spouses on a secret government mission. The wagon train in this made-for-tv western includes Anne Francis, Marie Windsor, Marilyn Maxwell, Sherry Jackson and Cynthia Hull. Head 'em up and move 'em out.
VHS: S08298. $19.98.
Don Taylor, USA, 1980, 90 mins.

Willie and Phil
The year was 1970. Willie and Phil met quite accidentally, coming out of an art house in Greenwich Village. They soon became great friends—sharing the same sense of humor, protesting the war in Vietnam, enjoying the films of Francois Truffaut; they were inseparable. Then one day Willie and Phil met Jeanette. *Willie and Phil* is an insightful comedy about three loving people growing together and apart in the midst of a decade of change. Starring Michael Ontkean, Margot Kidder and Ray Sharkey.
VHS: S15070. $59.98.
Paul Mazursky, USA, 1980, 115 mins.

Wind
A film about the quest for the America's Cup and the intrigue surrounding a brilliant though reluctant sailor's (Matthew Modine) determination to reclaim the honor and respect of a brilliant tactician (Jennifer Grey). With Stallan Skarsgard and Cliff Robertson.
VHS: S18158. $94.95.
Carroll Ballard, USA, 1992, 115 mins.

The Wind and the Lion
When Arab chieftain Sean Connery kidnaps American beauty Candice Bergen and her two small children, President Teddy Roosevelt (Brian Keith) sends in the Marines. Based extremely loosely on a true incident, but filled with bluster, spectacle and romantic horseback rides. Keith is "bully" as the U.S. prez with the big stick.
VHS: S06205. $19.95.
Laser: LD70182. $34.98.
John Milius, USA, 1975, 120 mins.

Winds of War
The best seller by Herman Wouk, adapted for television in a massive, epic production, starring Robert Mitchum, Ali MacGraw, Jan-Michael Vincent, John Houseman, and a cast of thousands. Complete 14-hour, 43-minute version, on seven cassettes, in boxed set.
VHS: S11193. $139.95.
Dan Curtis, USA, 1988, 883 mins.

Winter Kills
Based on the novel by Richard Condon, *Winter Kills* is an ironic farce about the sexual and political firestorms when the younger brother (Jeff Bridges) of a murdered president attempts to solve the case. The film was a financial disaster when it was first released in 1979, re-edited by the studio, and then reissued in its original form in 1983. With Sterling Hayden, Eli Wallach, Richard Boone, Elizabeth Taylor and John Huston as a Joe Kennedy-like player.
VHS: S16911. $14.95.
William Richert, USA, 1979, 97 mins.

Wired
The life and times of comic performer John Belushi as seen through the eyes of reporter Bob Woodward. You may not have realized what a big fan Belushi was of the guy who helped crack the Watergate scandal. With Michael Chiklis and Gary Groomes as Saturday Night Live stars Belushi and Ackroyd. The resemblance is physically good but the story seems written under the influence. With J.T. Walsh as Woodward and Ray Sharkey as a Puerto Rican guardian angel. Includes a powerful anti-drug message.
VHS: S11530. $89.95.
Larry Peerce, USA, 1989, 112 mins.

Witch Hunt
Dennis Hopper, Penelope Ann Miller and Julian Sands bring strange intensity to their roles in this macabre thriller. Hopper is a private eye looking into the death of a murdered movie mogul. But an evil old as time, not to mention a beautiful woman, entertain any chance that this case will be solved easily.
VHS: S24393. $94.99.
Laser: LD75287. $34.98.
Paul Schrader, USA, 1994, 100 mins.

The Witches of Eastwick
Jack Nicholson, Susan Sarandon, Michelle Pfeiffer and Cher star in this loose adaptation of the John Updike novel about three New England women who summon the Devil to spice up their drab small-town lives. Nicholson has the time of his life as the horny Prince of Darkness. With Veronica Cartwright and lots of cherry pits and balloons.
VHS: S06548. $19.98.
Laser: LD74745. $29.98.
George Miller, USA, 1987, 118 mins.

Without Warning: The James Brady Story
The affecting story of James Brady, the second victim of John Hinkley Jr.'s failed assasination attempt of then president Ronald Reagan. It is also the story behind the major national move towards gun control in the United States. USA, 120 mins.
VHS: S15275. $89.95.
Laser: LD75288. $34.98.
Michael Toshiyuki Uno, USA, 1991, 120 mins.

Wolf
Jack Nicholson and Michelle Pfeiffer are featured in this classy werewolf thriller. While driving, an editor accidentally hits a wolf. As he tries to help the dying animal it bites him, triggering a transformation that ups his aggressiveness, particularly when the moon is full. Before long his assertiveness turns deadly.
VHS: S23221. $19.95.
Laser: LD74664. $39.95.
Mike Nichols, USA, 1994, 125 mins.

A Woman at War
Martha Plimpton and Eric Stoltz star in this unnerving, suspense-laden drama about one woman's effort to save the lives of Jews in occupied Belgium. She finds herself alone after her parents are killed by the Gestapo. Now she infiltrates this very organization in order to combat its horrific goals.
VHS: S23861. $92.98.
Edward Bennett, USA, 1994, 115 mins.

Women of Valor
Susan Sarandon stars in this unorthodox story about the women heroines of World War II. Set in 1942 as U.S. troops pull out of the Philippines, several nurses, Sarandon included, refuse to abandon the wounded. Captured and tortured by the Japanese, the POWs struggle for survival in a story based on actual events and real life heroism.
VHS: S08291. $79.95.
Buzz Kulik, USA, 1987, 95 mins.

The World According to Garp
Robin Williams is writer, wrestler and family man T.S. Garp in this George Roy Hill adaptation of the John Irving bestseller. With Glenn Close as his mother, Mary Beth Hurt as his wife and John Lithgow as his transsexual friend who used to play professional football.
VHS: S04472. $19.98.
Laser: LD74738. $39.98.
George Roy Hill, USA, 1982, 136 mins.

World of Suzie Wong
William Holden is the American artist in Hong Kong who falls heavily for Nancy Kwan, his prostitute model. East meets West and both meet a terrific mud slide. A technicolor romance in the infamous Wanchai district where all the B-girls are beautiful. With Sylvia Sims, Michael Wilding and Jacqueline Chan as Gwenny Lee.
VHS: S08273. $19.95.
Richard Quine, USA, 1960, 129 mins.

Wrestling Ernest Hemingway
Robert Duvall and Richard Harris appear to be complete opposites. One is a reserved, retired Cuban barber, while the other is a salty, Irish ex-sea captain. Also features Academy-Award winning actress Shirley MacLaine.
VHS: S21088. $19.98.
Laser: LD72415. $39.98.
Randa Haines, USA, 1993, 123 mins.

The Wrong Man
Jim McBride (*Big Easy*) directs this taut thriller set in steamy Mexico, with John Lithgow as the innocent bystander caught in a web of murder and obsession for the sultry, mysterious Rosanna Arquette. With Kevin Anderson.
VHS: S20523. $19.95.
Laser: LD72359. $34.98.
Jim McBride, USA, 1993, 98 mins.

Yanks
Richard Gere, Vanessa Redgrave, William Devane and Lisa Eichhorn are all featured in this lavish World War II drama about romance between American soldiers and English women. It's a bittersweet tale of hopeless love. During wartime, the threat of eminent death make every moment precious.
VHS: S21276. $14.98.
John Schlesinger, USA, 1979, 139 mins.

You Light Up My Life
In the process of putting her life back in order, a young woman sets out to fulfill elusive dreams of acting and songwriting. Moving performances from Didi Conn and Joe Silver, with Michael Zaslow, Stephen Nathan and Melanie Mayron. Features the familiar Oscar-winning title song.
VHS: S16413. $19.95.
Joseph Brooks, USA, 1977, 90 mins.

Zelly and Me
The story of a young orphan girl and her foreign nanny. Isabella Rossellini is Mademoiselle, or "Zelly", and Alexandra Jones is the child who falls under her spell. A drama of love and growth with Glynis Johns and director David Lynch in an acting role.
VHS: S07679. $79.95.
Tina Rathborne, USA, 1988, 87 mins.

MARTIN SCORSESE

After Hours
An inventive dark comedy, in which all reality seems to be turned upside-down, peopled by a cast including Rosanna Arquette, Teri Garr, Griffin Dunne and Cheech & Chong. Scorsese received Best Director honors at the 1986 Cannes Film Festival for this. Written by Joseph Minion.
VHS: S00021. $19.98.
Laser: LD70497. $34.98.
Laser: Letterboxed, widescreen. LD70498. $34.98.
Martin Scorsese, USA, 1985, 97 mins.

The Age of Innocence
Edith Wharton's Pulitzer Prize-winning novel, set in 1870's New York, is brought to the screen with lavish sets, costumes, and the star power of Daniel Day-Lewis, Michelle Pfeiffer, and Winona Ryder. It is a tale from a time ruled by rigid conventions and moral standards, but love cannot and should not be denied.
VHS: S20666. $19.95.
Laser: LD72377. $39.95.
Martin Scorsese, USA, 1993, 138 mins.

Alice Doesn't Live Here Anymore
A subtle masterpiece that transforms the struggle of one woman into a memorable symbol of liberation and courage. Stars Ellen Burstyn in an Academy Award winning performance, with Kris Kristofferson and Diane Ladd.
VHS: S03481. $19.98.
Laser: LD70500. $34.98.
Martin Scorsese, USA, 1974, 105 mins.

Cape Fear
Robert De Niro was nominated for an Oscar for his role as Max Cady, a vengeful ex-con on the trail of lawyer Nick Nolte, his wife Jessica Lange and their rebellious teenage daughter Juliette Lewis. Based on the John D. MacDonald novel *The Executioners*, and a remake of the 1962 thriller.
VHS: S16329. $19.98.
Laser: Letterboxed. LD71437. $39.98.
Martin Scorsese, USA, 1991, 127 mins.

Casino
Robert DeNiro, Sharon Stone and Joe Pesci are at the center of this glamorous but hard-hitting film about the Mob in Las Vegas. DeNiro stars as Ace Rothstein (based on the life of Frank Rosenthal), a long-suffering professional gambler who is saved from destruction by his childhood pal Nicky Santoro (Joe Pesci). Rothstein marries Ginger McKenna (Stone), a chip hustler and con artist who very nearly destroys Rothstein's friendship with Santori. Despite this film's excesses (or perhaps because of them), the old Mob-dominated gambling town emerges as a twisted but exciting and seductive pleasure ground where a tangible, tense uncertainty underlays all the hype. Based on Nicholas Pileggi's book *Casino: Love and Honor in Las Vegas*.
VHS: S27631. $99.99.
Laser: LD75538. $44.99.
Martin Scorsese, USA, 1995, 179 mins.

Color of Money
Martin Scorsese's acclaimed update of *The Hustler*. Paul Newman returns as the pool-hall wizard Fast Eddie, who pursues his belief that "money won is twice as sweet as money earned." With Tom Cruise and Mary Elizabeth Mastrantonio.
VHS: S03470. $19.95.
Laser: LD70924. $44.99.
Martin Scorsese, USA, 1986, 119 mins.

Goodfellas
Scorsese once again demonstrates his formal brilliance in this impeccably constructed film about three decades of life with the mob. Based on Nicholas Pileggi's best seller *Wiseguy*, *Goodfellas* displays a stunning narrative virtuosity from its first shot to its last. And the actors, especially Joe Pesci and Lorraine Bracco, all give powerful, passionate performances. Don't miss this. Also starring Robert De Niro, Ray Liotta, and Paul Sorvino. Photographed by Michael Ballhaus.
VHS: S14085. $19.98.
Laser: LD70589. $29.98.
Martin Scorsese, USA, 1990, 148 mins.

Italian American/The Big Shave
Two short films from Martin Scorsese. *Italian American* (starring Charles and Catherine Scorsese), shot on location in his parents' little Italy apartment among plastic sofa covers, fancy picture frames, and assorted lamps and figurines, is a funny look at one family's ancestry, their arrival in America, and the successes that followed. In *The Big Shave* a young man nicks himself shaving and a frightening religious experience suddenly develops. It features Scorsese's black humor at an early age, highlighting his preoccupation with religion, suffering and blood (i.e., Catholicism).
VHS: S14497. $24.95.
Martin Scorsese, USA, 1974/1967, 54 mins.

King of Comedy
Robert De Niro is an obsessive stand-up comic performing in front of cardboard cutouts of his idols. Jerry Lewis is a host of a talk show that De Niro desperately wants to be on. Incredibly funny, true-to-life film by Martin Scorsese.
VHS: S00679. $19.95.
Martin Scorsese, USA, 1982, 101 mins.

Last Temptation of Christ
Martin Scorsese's powerful adaptation of the novel by Nikos Kazantzakis. Particularly notable is Willem Dafoe's performance as Christ.
VHS: S09455. $19.95.
Laser: LD70050. $39.98.
Martin Scorsese, USA, 1988, 131 mins.

Last Waltz
One of the greatest concert movies ever made, *Last Waltz* documents the 1976 Thanksgiving night farewell concert given by The Band at the Winterland in San Francisco. With appearances by Bob Dylan, Eric Clapton, Neil Young, Van Morrison and many more!
VHS: S00728. $19.95.
Martin Scorsese, USA, 1978, 117 mins.

Mean Streets
Set in New York's Little Italy, *Mean Streets* follows Harvey Keitel as he slowly climbs into the hierarchy of a local Mafia family. Keenly observed, gritty and violent, this early film by Scorsese clearly foreshadows his later work, and established him as a major American talent. With Robert De Niro, Cesare Danova, Amy Robinson.
VHS: S00840. $19.98.
Laser: LD70626. $34.98.
Martin Scorsese, USA, 1973, 112 mins.

New York, New York
A celebration of the Big Band Era, starring Robert De Niro and Liza Minnelli, as well as Diahnne Abbott, Mary Kay Place and Lionel Stander. Cinematography by Laszlo Kovacs. This is the long version with the intact Minnelli number, "Happy Endings", restored.
VHS: S00927. $29.95.
Laser: LD70641. $92.98.
Martin Scorsese, USA, 1977, 163 mins.

Raging Bull
Robert De Niro gives an incredible performance as Jake LaMotta, the controversial middleweight fighter of the 1940's. *Raging Bull* shows how LaMotta turned his fears into the physical energy needed to become a champion, while destroying his private life. Breathtaking cinematography!
VHS: S01084. $19.95.
Laser: Letterboxed, chapter search. Includes original theatrical trailer. LD71669. $39.98.
Martin Scorsese, USA, 1980, 127 mins.

Taxi Driver
Scorsese's now-classic film with Robert De Niro as the psychotic cabbie driven to violence in an attempt to "rescue" a teenage prostitute (Jodie Foster). With Albert Brooks, Harvey Keitel, Leonard Harris, Peter Boyle and Cybill Shepherd.
VHS: S01303. $14.95.
Laser: CAV. LD70470. $99.95.
Laser: CLV, widescreen. LD70471. $49.95.
Martin Scorsese, USA, 1975, 114 mins.

Who's That Knocking at My Door?
Martin Scorsese's directorial debut (made when he was only 25 years old) is a fascinating, autobiographical story about the relationship between a young, Catholic kid (Harvey Keitel) who still has a lot of ties to the old neighborhood, and the independent college student (Zina Bethune) he falls for. Featuring a strong performance from Keitel in his screen debut.
VHS: S14082. $59.99.
Martin Scorsese, USA, 1968, 90 mins.

ROBERT ALTMAN

Beyond Therapy
Christopher Durang's play about neurotic New Yorkers and their even crazier shrinks is translated to film by Robert Altman. Julie Hagerty and Jeff Goldblum are the patients. Tom Conti and Glenda Jackson are the therapists. With Christopher Guest as Jeff's boyfriend. A movie that needs professional help.
VHS: S05215. $19.95.
Robert Altman, USA, 1987, 93 mins.

Brewster McCloud
Robert Altman's moody parable is virtually unclassifiable. The anti-hero is the virginal young man, Brewster (Bud Cort), who is building a set of wings in order to take flight in the Houston Astrodome. Altman equates flight with freedom, which he renders through a skillful use of aerial photography. "The first American film to apply an appropriate tone and style to the absurdist follies of our time" (Andrew Sarris). With Sally Kellerman, Michael Murphy, William Windom, Shelley Duvall, Rene Auberjonois and Stacy Keach.
VHS: S20408. $19.98.
Laser: LD74669. $34.98.
Robert Altman, USA, 1970, 105 mins.

Caine Mutiny Court-Martial
Robert Altman directs this made-for-tv version of the classic drama based on Herman Wouk's Pulitzer Prize winning novel. Brad Davis stars as Lt. Cmdr. Phillip Queeg, who lost the command of his Navy vessel during a severe typhoon due to his overt concern for missing strawberries. Eric Bogosian plays the sharp military lawyer trying to defend Jeff Daniels from charges of mutiny. With Peter Gallagher, Michael Murphy, Kevin J. O'Connor and Daniel Jenkins.
VHS: S16472. $89.95.
Robert Altman, USA, 1988, 100 mins.

Countdown
James Caan and Robert Duvall landed on the Moon one year before Neil Armstrong, with the help of director Robert Altman. In this effective ensemble performance the lives of the astronauts, their families and their co-workers are realistically portrayed. Only the technology is dated.
VHS: S04183. $19.98.
Robert Altman, USA, 1968, 101 mins.

Fool for Love
The minimalist, barren landscapes energize the smothering, claustrophobic interiors of Sam Shepard's play in this Robert Altman adaptation that stars Shepard and Kim Basinger as formerly obsessive lovers whose fragmented, scarred past is mysteriously connected to an old man (Harry Dean Stanton), who hides out in an abandoned motel. Randy Quaid has a small but quietly effective role as Basinger's befuddled gentleman caller.
VHS: S02261. $14.95.
Robert Altman, USA, 1985, 108 mins.

James Dean Story
Robert Altman co-directed with G.W. George in 1957, the film explores Dean's personal life through interviews with family and friends, as well as Dean's short career. Contains footage from *East of Eden*, a TV public service message, and more.
VHS: S00651. $9.99.
Robert Altman/G.W. George, USA, 1957, 80 mins.

Long Goodbye
A revisionist updating of Raymond Chandler's well-respected novel. Elliott Gould stars as a shabby, unkempt Philip Marlowe helping out an eccentric friend who is accused of murdering his own wife. Altman's strange film continuously borders on parody of the genre. Also starring Sterling Hayden, Mark Rydell, Henry Gibson, Jim Bouton, and Arnold Schwarzenegger and David Carradine in small, cameo roles.
VHS: S13758. $19.98.
Laser: LD70139. $34.98.
Robert Altman, USA, 1973, 112 mins.

M*A*S*H
Donald Sutherland, Elliott Gould and Robert Duvall in the original, superb, classic dark comedy directed with verve by Robert Altman, juxtaposing the horrors of war with the resiliency of the human spirit. Written by Ring Lardner, Jr.
VHS: S02643. $14.98.
Robert Altman, USA, 1970, 116 mins.

McCabe and Mrs. Miller
A brilliant, offbeat drama of frontier life starring Warren Beatty and Julie Christie. This is Altman's personal and poetic interpretation of an American myth, resulting in a truly original Western. Also appearing are Shelley Duvall, Keith Carradine, Michael Murphy and William Devane.
VHS: S00839. $14.95.
Laser: LD74710. $39.98.
Robert Altman, USA, 1971, 120 mins.

Nashville
The recipient of five Academy Award nominations, Robert Altman's *Nashville* is an explosive drama and human comedy that interweaves the lives of 24 major characters during a five day period in the country music capital. A penetrating and multi-level portrait of America starring Keith Carradine, Karen Black, Geraldine Chaplin, Ronee Blakley, Lily Tomlin and Henry Gibson.
VHS: S00919. $29.95.
Robert Altman, USA, 1975, 159 mins.

The Player
Robert Altman's dark valentine to the American movie industry. The plot is absurdly comic, with Tim Robbins as an icy studio executive who receives a series of threatening, anonymous postcards from a screenwriter he abused, setting in motion a murder and seduction. With Greta Scacchi, Whoopi Goldberg, Fred Ward, Peter Gallagher and 59 actors, directors and stars appearing as themselves.
VHS: S18263. $19.98.
Robert Altman, USA, 1992, 123 mins.

Popeye
The legendary anvil-armed sailor is brought to life in this musical version directed by Robert Altman and starring Robin Williams and Shelley Duvall.
VHS: S04703. $14.95.
Robert Altman, USA, 1980, 114 mins.

Quintet
A stark film of survivors during the final ice age, beautifully photographed in wintry Canada, starring Paul Newman, Bibi Andersson and Fernando Rey. A meditation on life and death from Altman (*Nashville, Three Women*).
VHS: S01083. $19.98.
Robert Altman, USA, 1979, 118 mins.

Ready to Wear (Pret-a-Porter)
Marcello Mastroianni, Julia Roberts, Tim Robbins, Kim Basinger, Sophia Loren, Forest Whitaker, Danny Aiello and other stars, including walk-ons like Cher, make this look at the fashion industry a truly unique enterprise. Funny, irreverent and odd, when Aiello donned drag and high fashion models appeared naked, this film created havoc in the sensitive world of fashion.
VHS: S25115. $19.95.
Laser: LD74953. $39.99.
Robert Altman, USA, 1995, 133 mins.

The Room
Robert Altman directed this drama, which stars Linda Hunt, Julian Sands, and Donald Pleasance. A woman dreams and schemes in a small room while her husband ominously creates scenes in glass bottles. When their sinister landlord plots to rent their space to two mysterious visitors, the room becomes a death trap.
VHS: S10900. $79.95.
Robert Altman, USA, 1987, 48 mins.

Secret Honor
Philip Baker Hall's one-man performance of a fictional meditation/monologue about Richard Nixon. "One of the most scathing, lacerating, and brilliant movies... Nixon is portrayed...with such savage intensity, such passion, such scandal, that we cannot turn away" (Roger Ebert).
VHS: Out of print. For rental only.
Laser: CLV. LD71802. $49.95.
Robert Altman, USA, 1984, 85 mins.

Short Cuts
Raymond Carver's short stories are brought to the screen in this Golden Globe winner, employing some of Hollywood's biggest stars. Jack Lemmon, Lyle Lovett, Matthew Modine, Lily Tomlin and Jennifer Jason Leigh are just some of the big names seen in this harrowing portrayal of everyday people living extraordinary lives.
VHS: S20889. $19.95.
Laser: LD74462. $124.95.
Robert Altman, USA, 1993, 189 mins.

Streamers
Based on the controversial play by David Rabe, the film focuses on the lives of 3 young recruits waiting to receive orders to go to Vietnam. They develop close bonds which are shattered when an aggressive and confused inner city black enters their lives, igniting the underlying racial tension and strain of homosexuality that are the volatile undercurrents in the men's relationships.
VHS: S01267. $29.95.
Robert Altman, USA, 1983, 118 mins.

Tanner '88
A collaboration between Robert Altman and writer and cartoonist Gary Trudeau in their demystification of presidential politics and the television-dominated process. The eponymous character (Michael Murphy) is a liberal Senator running for president who embarks on this surreal odyssey through the political landscape. With Gary Hart, Pat Robertson, Bruce Babbitt and Bob Dole.
Tanner, Part I.
Laser: LD71803. $49.95.
Tanner, Part II.
Laser: LD71804. $49.95.
Tanner, Part III.
Laser: LD71805. $49.95.
Three-tape set.
VHS: S07304. $79.95.
Robert Altman, USA, 1988, 360 mins.

That Cold Day in the Park
A 32-year-old Canadian spinster (Sandy Dennis) sees a young man (Michael Burns) as a symbol of the freedom and youth denied her by the Establishment and entices him into her home. They do not speak and she assumes he is mute. Soon, her compassion becomes a dangerous compulsion and she decides to keep him as her own possession. As he fights to keep her fantasy from becoming his reality, the situation becomes nightmarish, in this chilling, early feature by Robert Altman.
VHS: S13250. $14.98.
Robert Altman, USA, 1969, 91 mins.

Thieves Like Us
Robert Altman's colorful adaptation of Edward Anderson's 1937 novel is set in rural Mississippi during the Depression. The story follows a Southern boy (Keith Carradine) who takes part in a prison breakout with two bank robbers (John Schuck and Bert Remsen) and falls in love with the tough Keechie (Shelley Duvall). "Altman finds a sure, soft tone and never loses it. His account of Coca-Cola-swigging young lovers is the most quietly poetic of his films; it's sensuous right from the first pearly-green long shot, and it seems to achieve beauty without artifice" (Pauline Kael, *The New Yorker*). With Louise Fletcher and Tom Skerritt.
VHS: S20406. $19.98.
Robert Altman, USA, 1974, 123 mins.

Wedding
A freewheeling satire on marriage, with a large cast, in the same vein as *Nashville*, although more defined. With Lillian Gish, Carol Burnett, Lauren Hutton, Mia Farrow and Geraldine Chaplin, shot largely in Lake Forest, Illinois.
VHS: S01440. $59.98.
Robert Altman, USA, 1978, 125 mins.

JONATHAN DEMME

Citizen's Band
Originally made to cash in on the CB radio craze, Jonathan Demme's ensemble comedy-drama is a funny, charming film that portrays Paul "Spider" Le Mat as a small-town CB maniac who stages a one-man crusade to clean up the cluttered air waves. In his way is a thoroughly senile father, gorgeous Candy "Electra" Clark, and the evil, menacing, unknown "Blood." There's also a hilarious subplot which involves an over-eager trucker whose two wives from different cities accidentally meet and discover his bigamist schemes.
VHS: S06846. $59.95.
Jonathan Demme, USA, 1977, 98 mins.

Cousin Bobby
Jonathan Demme's documentary about the Rev. Robert Castle, the director's distant cousin, is an audacious home movie that considers the fiery minister's political and religious convictions, his liberation theology, and estrangement from top church leaders as it shows his work and activism in a poverty-stricken, crime-ridden Harlem neighborhood. It's a "lovely, amiably persuasive demonstration of the personal sources of political conviction. That's entertainment" (*The New Yorker*).
VHS: S17495. $59.95.
Jonathan Demme, USA, 1991, 70 mins.

Married to the Mob
Michelle Pfeiffer shines as the recent widow of a Mob hit man who just wants to live a normal non-criminal existence. Matthew Modine is the youthful FBI agent following her every move. A comedy with heart and bullets from Jonathan Demme. With Dean Stockwell, Mercedes Ruehl, Alec Baldwin and Tony Fitzpatrick as the surly immigration officer.
VHS: S08350. $19.98.
Jonathan Demme, USA, 1988, 104 mins.

Melvin and Howard
Winner of the Academy Awards for Best Supporting Actress and Best Original Screenplay, *Melvin and Howard* tells an offbeat story of a chance encounter between Howard Hughes (played by Jason Robards) and an unsuspecting ne'er-do-well named Melvin Dummar. True story or mythic encounter, the result is an original movie.
VHS: S00846. $14.95.
Jonathan Demme, USA, 1980, 95 mins.

Philadelphia
Winner of two Academy Awards, Tom Hanks for Best Actor and Bruce Springsteen for Best Song, this film tells the moving story of a man who must fight not only AIDS but an ignorant and bigoted society. Denzel Washington plays the lawyer who must struggle with his own unfounded fears to fight for justice on behalf of his colleague, Tom Hanks. With Jason Robards, Mary Steenburgen, Antonio Banderas and Joanne Woodward.
VHS: S21120. $19.95.
Laser: LD72416. $39.95.
Jonathan Demme, USA, 1993, 125 mins.

The Silence of the Lambs
Jonathan Demme's impressive entry into the thriller/slasher genre has more than a few interesting things to say about the way many of this country's most brutal mass murderers end up becoming something akin to minor celebrities (with their own television shows, books, newspaper profiles, movies and talk show appearances). In the film's final scene the audience is implicated most directly, as we are prompted to laugh at the gruesome prospect of another impending murder. Pretty dark and unsavory stuff, but along the way Demme manages to orchestrate several brilliant sequences in the midst of his well-structured narrative; and the performances, led by Jodie Foster and Anthony Hopkins, are uniformly excellent.
VHS: S14730. $19.98.
Laser: CLV. LD72108. $99.98.
Jonathan Demme, USA, 1991, 118 mins.

Swimming to Cambodia
Called "hilarious," "audacious," "amazing," *Swimming to Cambodia* is Jonathan Demme's concert film of Spalding Gray's highly successful one-man show. "No contemporary American artist tells better stories than Gray...a very funny, off-the-wall performance," wrote the *Los Angeles Reader*.
VHS: S04740. $14.98.
Laser: Remastered, widescreen, digital transfer. LD75395. $39.95.
Jonathan Demme, USA, 1986, 85 mins.

Swing Shift
Goldie Hawn and Kurt Russell star in this Jonathan Demme film about the rise of the American woman in the war workforce during World War II. While most of the men are at war, the women are at work in the factory building the planes and equipment needed for the war effort. With Christine Lahti, Holly Hunter, Patty Maloney, Susie Bond, Fred Ward, and Ed Harris as Goldie's husband in the Navy.
VHS: S09315. $19.98.
Laser: LD74718. $34.98.
Jonathan Demme, USA, 1984, 100 mins.

Who Am I This Time?
A shorter work from the director of *Melvin and Howard* and *Silence of the Lambs*. Christopher Walken and Susan Sarandon portray the relationship of two actors in a local theater company. Based on a story by Kurt Vonnegut, Jr. with music by John Cale.
VHS: S01455. $24.95.
Jonathan Demme, USA, 1982, 60 mins.

TIM BURTON

Batman
A wealthy, embittered orphan grows up to make the lives of criminals miserable in this big budget boxoffice extravaganza. Michael Keaton is the muscular caped Crusader, Jack Nicholson is his evil and goofily deranged nemesis, the Joker. Gotham City is the place they meet for fun and games. With Kim Basinger as frosting on the cake and Michael Gough as Alfred the butler. The comic book character is not just for kids anymore.
VHS: S10949. $19.98.
Laser: LD70519. $39.98.
Tim Burton, USA, 1989, 130 mins.

Batman Returns
Tim Burton's brooding sequel is notable for Michael Keaton's warrior/hero, Danny DeVito's perverse charm as the nefarious Penguin, and best of all, Michelle Pfeiffer's coiled, pent-up aggression and sexuality as the Catwoman. Daniel Waters wrote the screenplay. Cinematography by Stefan Czapsky and art design by Bo Welch.
VHS: S17494. $19.98.
Laser: LD71768. $39.98.
Tim Burton, USA, 1992, 126 mins.

Beetlejuice
Michael Keaton stars as the title character, a wacko freelance bio-exorcist who removes humans from the homes of troubled ghosts. A peculiar and energetic comedy with Geena Davis and Alec Baldwin as the nice dead people and Jeffrey Jones, Catherine O'Hara and Winona Ryder as the living family that irks them. Cameos by Dick Cavett and Robert Goulet.
VHS: S01824. $14.95.
Tim Burton, USA, 1988, 92 mins.

Ed Wood
Johnny Depp portrays the nearly inconceivable cult film director/cross-dresser Ed Wood in this imaginative biographical film that won an Academy Award for Martin Landau in the role of actor Bela Lugosi, who (in real life) died during the making of one of Wood's notorious films. A truly singular Hollywood achievement about a stranger-than-fiction filmmaker whose atrocious films, like *Plan 9 from Outer Space* and *Glen or Glenda*, have become cult classics. With Patricia Arquette and Bill Murray.
VHS: S24321. $19.98.
Laser: Letterboxed. LD74914. $39.99.
Tim Burton, USA, 1994, 127 mins.

Edward Scissorhands
This touching fable about a quiet boy with sharp, metal shears for hands manages to entertain and amuse while making some sensitive observations about adolescent loneliness and emotional estrangement. With especially poignant performances from Dianne Wiest and Johnny Depp. Also starring Winona Ryder, Alan Arkin, Kathy Baker, Anthony Michael Hall, and Vincent Price as Edward's inventor.
VHS: S13922. $19.98.
Tim Burton, USA, 1990, 100 mins.

Frankenweenie
Young Victor Frankenstein has lost his dog Sparky to a car accident. When his biology teacher makes a dead frog move with electricity, Victor is inspired as only a mad scientist can be. A hilarious satire, evoking the original 1931 *Frankenstein*, from bolts in the sides of Sparky's neck to the "burning castle" scene—here transported to a miniature golf course windmill. The short that launched Tim Burton's career when Paul Reubens enlisted him to direct *Pee-Wee's Big Adventure*, Burton moved on to create *Beetlejuice* and *Edward Scissorhands*.
VHS: S16034. $14.99.
Tim Burton, USA, 1984, 28 mins.

The Nightmare Before Christmas
Produced by Tim Burton and based on a story and characters by him, this feature tells the story of Jack, the central spook who makes Halloween scary. When he decides to change his holiday affiliation, disaster results, turning Christmas into a nightmare.
VHS: S21295. $19.99.
Henry Selick, USA, 1993, 76 mins.

Pee-Wee's Big Adventure
Paul Reubens star as Pee-Wee in a comedy he also helped co-write. The basic premise has Pee-Wee looking for his lost bike, but it's really just a good reason to see this brilliant comic display his virtuosity in some now classic sequences.
VHS: S24845. $19.98.
Tim Burton, USA, 1985, 92 mins.

STANLEY KUBRICK

2001: A Space Odyssey
Light years ahead of its time, *2001: A Space Odyssey* is a spectacular movie that looks even more wondrous as time passes. This 1968 masterpiece reaches the outer limits of interplanetary space while penetrating the depths of man's inner destiny. Based on the novel by Arthur C. Clarke, featuring the music of Richard Strauss. This version is the result of a new digital video transfer and is presented in widescreen letterbox format.
VHS: Out of print. For rental only.
Laser: CAV, Criterion. LD70481. $124.95.
Laser: Deluxe letterboxed, chapter search, MGM. LD70164. $39.98.
Laser: CLV, Criterion. LD70482. $59.95.
Stanley Kubrick, USA, 1968, 139 mins.

2001: A Space Odyssey (25th Anniversary Edition)
Stanley Kubrick's landmark film traces the three stages of man, from evolutionary, predatory animals to futuristic space travelers, astronauts on a mission to Jupiter sabotaged by a malfunctioning computer known as HAL. "A uniquely poetic piece of science fiction that's hypnotically entertaining" (*The New Yorker*). Adapted from Arthur C. Clarke's story *The Sentinel*. With Keith Dullea, Gary Lockwood and William Sylvester. Special visual effects by Douglas Trumbull. Letterboxed.
VHS: S18674. $19.98.
Laser: CAV, 3 discs, with 4-page insert. LD71876. $69.98.
Laser: CLV, 2 discs. LD71877. $39.98.
Stanley Kubrick, USA, 1968, 141 mins.

Barry Lyndon
Kubrick's tenth feature film is a lavish treatment of Thackeray's 18th century novel and features Ryan O'Neal as a conniving rogue and Marisa Berenson as the widowed Lady Lyndon. Kubrick used antique clothes instead of costumes, and all shooting was on authentic locations.
VHS: S01689. $29.98.
Laser: Letterboxed. LD74726. $39.98.
Stanley Kubrick, USA, 1975, 184 mins.

Clockwork Orange
One of the most audaciously conceived films of recent decades, a merciless vision of the near-future based on Anthony Burgess' chilling novel. The New York Times called it a "brilliant, tour-de-force of extraordinary images, music, words and feelings...so beautiful to look at and to hear that it dazzles the senses and the mind."
VHS: S00251. $19.98.
Stanley Kubrick, USA, 1971, 137 mins.

Dr. Strangelove
This great black comedy stars Peter Sellers as the wheelchair-bound nuclear scientist plotting a scheme to attack Russia's nuclear targets with nuclear bombs. Very funny and very frightening, *Dr. Strangelove or: How I Learned to Stop Worrying and Love the Bomb* stars Sterling Hayden as US Air Force Commander Jack D. Ripper, and George C. Scott as Joint Chief of Staff "Buck" Turgidson.
VHS: S00367. $19.95.
Laser: LD70750. $99.95.
Stanley Kubrick, USA, 1963, 101 mins.

Full Metal Jacket
Stanley Kubrick visits Vietnam. Based on the short but powerful novel, *The Short Timers*, by Gustav Hasford. Follow a few Marines from training on Parris Island to fighting in the Tet Offensive. With Matthew Modine, Adam Baldwin, Dorian Harewood, Lee Ermey and Vincent D'Onofrio. War is hell even when filmed in England.
VHS: S07003. $19.98.
Laser: LD70577. $24.98.
Stanley Kubrick, USA, 1987, 116 mins.

Killer's Kiss
A prizefighter rescues a young woman from her gangster lover and, as a result, is marked for death. An intense film-noir thriller that first brought Stanley Kubrick to the world's attention. He not only wrote and directed this independent production, but also photographed it. Starring Frank Silvera and Irene Kane. "Her soft mouth was the road to sin-smeared violence!"
VHS: S14515. $19.98.
Stanley Kubrick, USA, 1955, 67 mins.

The Killing

Stanley Kubrick directed this classic caper film that concerns illegally removing large amounts of cash from a busy racetrack. Sterling Hayden leads his gang of five on a successful heist but then problems occur for which he hadn't planned. Kubrick uses an elaborate and unusual structure of flashbacks to tell his story. With Vince Edwards, Jay C. Flippan, Marie Windsor, Colleen Gray, Elisha Cook Jr., and Timothy Carey as the grinning sharpshooter, Nikki Arane.
VHS: S11223. $19.95.
Laser: LD71075. $39.95.
Stanley Kubrick, USA, 1956, 83 mins.

The Killing/Killer's Kiss

Two early works from Stanley Kubrick that share a great many of the stylistic and thematic concerns of his later work. The first is a brilliant noir about the planning, execution and aftermath of a daring racetrack heist. *Killer's Kiss* is a dark piece about the relationship of a boxer and a working class woman and the deadly implications of obsession.
Laser: LD71857. $39.98.

Lolita

Kubrick's adaptation of Vladimir Nabokov's classic novel captures the author's black humor with ghoulish understatement. James Mason plays the college professor who marries the lonely widow Shelley Winters purely out of lust for her adolescent daughter. With Peter Sellers playing several characters—all delightfully sinister.
VHS: S02545. $19.98.
Laser: LD70760. $59.95.
Stanley Kubrick, USA, 1961, 150 mins.

Paths of Glory

A shattering film from Stanley Kubrick, bringing into focus the insanity of war in the story of French General Macready, who, during World War I, orders his men into a futile mission. When the men fail, Macready selects three soldiers for trial and execution for cowardice. With incredible performances from Kirk Douglas, Ralph Meeker, Adolphe Menjou, George Macready, Wayne Morris, Richard Anderson. One of the high points of the American cinema.
VHS: S11433. $19.97.
Laser: LD70433. $49.95.
Stanley Kubrick, USA, 1957, 86 mins.

The Shining

A real thriller based on a Stephen King novel, with Jack Nicholson going slowly mad and terrorizing his wife Shelley Duvall and their little boy, who has strange powers of ESP. With Scatman Crothers.
VHS: S01189. $19.98.
Laser: LD74736. $39.98.
Stanley Kubrick, USA, 1980, 146 mins.

Spartacus

This edition of Stanley Kubrick's epic classic features additional footage cut from the film's initial release print, plus the complete original overture and extended soundtrack. Kirk Douglas stars as the leader of slaves rebelling against their Roman masters. With Jean Simmons, Laurence Olivier, Tony Curtis, Charles Laughton and Peter Ustinov. The screenplay was written by the legendary Dalton Trumbo, based on a book by Howard Fast. The restored version of this historical spectacle is presented in widescreen letterboxed format.
VHS: S15075. $19.95.
Laser: 3 discs: CLV/CAV. Second soundtrack commentary by Kirk Douglas, Peter Ustinov and others. Includes original storyboards and titles as well as newsreel footage of the film's London premiere. LD70082. $124.95.
Stanley Kubrick, USA, 1960, 196 mins.

CLINT EASTWOOD

Bird

The film biography of Charlie "Bird" Parker. This legend of modern jazz has his life transformed into a cinematic masterpiece under the direction of Clint Eastwood. Forest Whitaker is Charlie. Diane Venora plays Chan, his loving and long-suffering wife. An epic length salute to the man, the myths and the music.
VHS: S09321. $19.98.
Laser: LD70526. $29.98.
Clint Eastwood, USA, 1988, 160 mins.

The Bridges of Madison County

Clint Eastwood and Meryl Streep are perfectly matched as a mature couple who only late in life discover each other. Based on the best-selling novel from Robert James Waller, it begins with a photo of a covered bridge and blossoms into the romance of a lifetime.
VHS: S27504. $103.99.
Laser: LD75521. $39.98.
Clint Eastwood, USA, 1995, 135 mins.

Bronco Billy

Traces the exploits and fantasy adventures of a shoe salesman as he leads a star-crossed group of disparate hustlers and dreamers on the road in pursuit of a traveling show. "Eastwood manages to both undermine and celebrate his character's fantasy life, while offering a few gentle swipes at contemporary America" (*Time Out*). With Sandra Locke, Scatman Crothers and Geoffrey Lewis.
VHS: S18613. $19.98.
Laser: LD74688. $24.98.
Clint Eastwood, USA, 1980, 119 mins.

Clint Eastwood Western Box Set

Clint Eastwood's Western trilogy—the Academy Award-winning *Unforgiven* (1992), *Pale Rider* (1985) and *The Outlaw Josey Wales* (1976)—are available in digitally remastered, letterboxed versions.
Laser: LD71881. $119.98.

The Eiger Sanction

An interesting if flawed Clint Eastwood film about an art history professor and CIA professional assassin who tracks down spies in the Andes.
Laser: Letterboxed. LD70292. $19.98.
Clint Eastwood, USA, 1975, 125 mins.

High Plains Drifter

Clint Eastwood's western about an enigmatic drifter enlisted by a frontier community to protect them from newly released prisoners. Kind of a vigilante force on the prairie type situation, influenced by the Sergio Leone films that came before it. With Verna Bloom and Marianna Hill.
VHS: S20530. $19.95.
Laser: LD71404. $34.98.
Clint Eastwood, USA, 1973, 105 mins.

Outlaw Josey Wales

Clint Eastwood plays a peaceful farmer turned vigilante during the period after the Civil war. Eastwood took over directing from Philip Kaufman who co-scripted.
VHS: S07496. $19.98.
Laser: LD70650. $39.98.
Clint Eastwood, USA, 1976, 135 mins.

Pale Rider

A film in which Eastwood explores the state of the Western genre and his own screen image, mixing action and humor. Eastwood stars as a mysterious avenger aiding gold prospectors. With Michael Moriarty and Carrie Snodgrass.
VHS: S02916. $19.98.
Laser: LD74696. $24.98.
Clint Eastwood, USA, 1985, 116 mins.

A Perfect World

Kevin Costner and Clint Eastwood star in this tale of kidnapping gone awry. Costner plays the would-be kidnapper who is set upon by Eastwood, a determined lawman. With Laura Dern. It's a gripping suspense story with emotional depth.
VHS: S20888. $19.98.
Laser: LD72391. $39.98.
Clint Eastwood, USA, 1993, 138 mins.

Play Misty for Me

Clint Eastwood self-directs in his directorial debut. He plays a late-night radio disc jockey who is haunted by the ultimate obsessive, "will-not-be-ignored," fatal attraction-type groupie Jessica Walter, who is just as scary as can be. A very competent thriller that still delivers lots of surprises and chills.
VHS: S06818. $19.95.
Clint Eastwood, USA, 1971, 102 mins.

The Rookie

Clint Eastwood's inversion of the buddy film; Eastwood plays a craggy police officer paired with an inexperienced rookie (Charlie Sheen), a wealthy kid with a dark past, investigating a pair of flamboyant German car thieves (Raul Julia and Sonia Braga) responsible in the death of his former partner. With Lara Flynn Boyle and Tom Skerritt.
Laser: LD70729. $29.98.
Clint Eastwood, USA, 1990, 121 mins.

Unforgiven

Clint Eastwood's brilliant reconsideration of the American western. Set in the 1880s, a reformed gunman and failed farmer (Eastwood) reluctantly agrees to collect the bounty on two cowboys who slashed a prostitute's face, setting in motion a mythic confrontation with a corrupt sheriff (Gene Hackman), a hired English assassin (Richard Harris) and a dime novelist (Saul Rubinek). With Morgan Freeman and Frances Fisher. Winner of four Academy Awards.
VHS: S18724. $19.98.
Laser: LD71880. $39.98.
Clint Eastwood, USA, 1992, 131 mins.

White Hunter, Black Heart

An adaptation of Peter Viertel's roman a clef about the making of *The African Queen*. Clint Eastwood directs this intelligent and challenging film about obsession, among other things, and also stars in a highly stylized portrayal of John Huston (the director of *The African Queen*). "The year's most masterful and suggestive Hollywood movie" (Jonathan Rosenbaum).
VHS: S13488. $19.98.
Laser: LD70704. $29.98.
Clint Eastwood, USA, 1990, 112 mins.

DAVID LYNCH

Blue Velvet

David Lynch's demystification of American normalcy. Pitched between '40s camp and '80s post-modernism, Lynch alter ego Kyle McLachlan stars as a college student who discovers a severed ear, leading to a strange and perverse odyssey. He alternates between the innocent (Laura Dern) and the mysterious (Isabella Rossellini). Dennis Hopper stars as a dangerous outlaw. With Dean Stockwell.
VHS: Out of print. For rental only.
Laser: LD70529. $29.98.
David Lynch, USA, 1986, 120 mins.

Elephant Man

Based on the true story of John Merrick, who suffered from a rare, physically distorting disease and was rescued from a life as a circus freak by a courageous doctor. With John Hurt as the Elephant Man and Anthony Hopkins as the doctor.
VHS: S01701. $19.95.
David Lynch, USA, 1981, 124 mins.

Hotel Room

A triptych of gothic stories unfolding in room 603 of a Los Angeles hotel, directed by the gifted filmmaker David Lynch in collaboration with novelists Barry Gifford (*Wild at Heart*) and Jay McInerney. The stories are set in three distinct periods, during the 20s, 50s and present. "Creepy and funny, the stories are marvelously absorbing" (*Los Angeles Times*). With Harry Dean Stanton, Glenne Headly, Griffin Dunne, Chelsea Field and Crispin Glover.
VHS: S19335. $89.95.
David Lynch, USA, 1993, 100 mins.

Twin Peaks

The original seven episodes of the cult television series by filmmakers David Lynch and Mark Frost about the surreal, depraved acts unfolding under the small-town textures of the eponymous community. Lynch alter ego Kyle MacLachlan stars as a quirky federal agent investigating the disappearance and murder of a beautiful, popular, high school woman. The eccentric ensemble includes Joan Chen, Ray Wise, Lara Flynn Boyle, Sherilyn Fenn, James Marshall and Piper Laurie.
Twin Peaks, Vol. 1.
VHS: S17547. $14.95.

Twin Peaks, Vol. 2.
VHS: S17548. $14.95.
Twin Peaks, Vol. 3.
VHS: S17549. $14.95.
Twin Peaks, Vol. 4.
VHS: S17550. $14.95.
Twin Peaks, Vol. 5.
VHS: S17551. $14.95.
Twin Peaks, Vol. 6.
VHS: S17552. $14.95.
Twin Peaks, Vol. 7.
VHS: S17553. $14.95.
Twin Peaks Collector's Series #1. Seven videocassettes.
VHS: S15304. $99.95.

Twin Peaks Pilot

See the Peabody Award-winning series pilot of the cult favorite that the entire country was talking about. Plus, witness exclusive, never-before-broadcast sequences solving Laura Palmer's killing. Created by David Lynch and Mark Frost.
VHS: S14532. $14.95.
David Lynch, USA, 1990, 113 mins.

Twin Peaks: Fire Walk with Me

David Lynch's study of the American Dream in this surreal evocation of small-town America. The plot covers the week leading up to the death of Laura Palmer, the beautiful, emotionally scarred woman whose brutal murder set in motion the plot of the television series. With Sheryl Lee, Moira Kelly, David Bowie, Harry Dean Stanton, Ray Wise, James Marshall, Madchen Amick and Kyle MacLachlan.
VHS: S17866. $19.95.
David Lynch, USA, 1992, 135 mins.

Wild at Heart

Based on Barry Gifford's novel about two southern lovers on the run, this film is director David Lynch's (*Blue Velvet*, *Eraserhead*) campiest feature to date. Despite the loopy subtext of references (mostly to Elvis and *The Wizard of Oz*), Lynch manages to present some powerful visual compositions here and gets all-out performances from stars Nicolas Cage and Laura Dern. Also starring Willem Dafoe, Crispin Glover, Diane Ladd, Isabella Rossellini and Harry Dean Stanton. Winner of the Cannes Film Festival's 1990 Palme d'Or.
VHS: S13515. $19.98.
David Lynch, USA, 1990, 125 mins.

ALAN RUDOLPH

Choose Me

Keith Carradine, Genevieve Bujold and Lesley Ann Warren star in this stylish and sexy romance that explores the quirky, ambiguous truths of heterosexual relationships. A cult favorite for its off-center, eccentric look at contemporary love.
VHS: S00237. $19.95.
Alan Rudolph, USA, 1984, 106 mins.

Equinox

Alan Rudolph's film is about the intersecting fates of twins—an introverted auto mechanic and an underworld gangster, both played by Matthew Modine—who were separated at birth. Lara Flynn Boyle plays a fragile young woman whom the good twin is trying to protect. With Tyra Ferrell, Marisa Tomei as a frightened prostitute, and Kevin J. O'Connor.
VHS: S19731. $19.95.
Laser: Letterboxed. LD72440. $34.95.
Alan Rudolph, USA, 1992, 115 mins.

Love at Large

"A pleasingly complex, often comic tale of love as seen through the filter of a detective film noir. A beautiful woman offers private detective Harry (Tom Berenger) a lot of money to tail her lover, but the description she gives of him is vague (tall, blonde hair, smells good). Harry ends up tailing the wrong guy, and now someone is tailing him. Rudolph's highly stylized sets create an 'alternate' world for his action to take place, focusing on his large cast of characters" (Edwin Jahiel). With Annette O'Toole, Kate Capshaw, Elizabeth Perkins and Ann Magneson.
VHS: S12978. $89.95.
Alan Rudolph, USA, 1990, 97 mins.

The Moderns

Alan Rudolph recreates the cafe society of Paris in 1926. Hemingway, Gertrude Stein, and Marcel Duchamp are background figures in this intriguing tale of art forgery and complicated human relationships. With Keith Carradine, Linda Fiorentino, Genevieve Bujold, Wallace Shawn, Geraldine Chaplin and John Lone as the ruthless art collector.
VHS: S07790. $19.98.
Laser: LD72306. $34.99.
Alan Rudolph, USA, 1988, 126 mins.

Mortal Thoughts

Alan Rudolph's characteristically hypnotic thriller in the form of a police interrogation, with Demi Moore playing a New Jersey housewife drawn into events around the murder of her best friend's (Glenne Headly) abusive husband (Bruce Willis). The intricate flashback structure, Elliot Davis's dazzling camera work and fluid ensemble work create a haunting work. With Harvey Keitel as the homicide detective.
VHS: S15113. $19.95.
Alan Rudolph, USA, 1991, 104 mins.

Mrs. Parker and the Vicious Circle

Jennifer Jason Leigh is Dorothy Parker, the legendary, witty writer and Algonquin Roundtable member. Leigh delivers a dazzling—if controversial—performance that captures something of Parker's razor-sharp tongue, romantic escapades, alcoholism and chronic unhappiness. The film is also a unique portrait of a flamboyant literary era. Matthew Broderick and Stephen Baldwin star; produced by Robert Altman.
VHS: S24568. $19.98.
Alan Rudolph, USA, 1994, 124 mins.

Songwriter

Willie Nelson and Kris Kristofferson team up as two country/western singers who band together to outwit a greedy backer. Plenty of good music and good feeling, with Lesley Ann Warren, Rip Torn and Melinda Dillon.
VHS: S01765. $79.95.
Alan Rudolph, USA, 1984, 94 mins.

Trouble in Mind

Kris Kristofferson, Keith Carradine and Genevieve Bujold star in a passionate, highly stylized love triangle in Rain City, a steamy, unlikely place. Haunting score by Mark Isham, sung by Marianne Faithful.
VHS: Out of print. For rental only.
Laser: LD72315. $29.99.
Alan Rudolph, USA, 1986, 111 mins.

ARTHUR PENN

Alice's Restaurant

You can get anything you want in this Arthur Penn film of the song by Arlo Guthrie which was inspired by his arrest for littering in a small New England town. Relive the late sixties where love was free and some churches were used creatively. With Arlo Guthrie, James Broderick and Pat Quinn as Alice.
VHS: S06228. $14.95.
Arthur Penn, USA, 1969, 111 mins.

Bonnie and Clyde

Bank robbers Bonnie Parker and Clyde Barrow probably didn't deserve the cinematic immortality guaranteed by this masterwork directed by Arthur Penn, but were they wouldn't object to being played by Faye Dunaway and Warren Beatty. Also along for the ride on this Depression era crime spree are Gene Hackman, Estelle Parsons and Michael J. Pollard.
VHS: S00168. $19.98.
Laser: LD70531. $34.98.
Arthur Penn, USA, 1967, 111 mins.

The Chase

Marlon Brando and Robert Redford are on opposite ends of the law in this complex film featuring an all star cast. E.G. Marshall, Angie Dickinson, Jane Fonda, and Robert Duvall all play a role in this screen adaptation of Horton Foote's play, penned by Foote and Lillian Hellman. A prisoner (Redford) escapes and is rumored to be back in his hometown, setting everyone on edge. Brando is the sheriff who must make the best of this peculiar set-up.
Laser: LD75534. $39.95.
Arthur Penn, USA, 1966, 135 mins.

Left-Handed Gun

Arthur Penn's first film, a psychological Western starring Paul Newman as Billy the Kid. Penn explores the theme he would frequently return to: the alienated outsider confronted by a hostile society.
VHS: S03435. $14.95.
Arthur Penn, USA, 1957, 102 mins.

Mickey One

A groundbreaking film with Warren Beatty as a pretty tough comic with a nasty problem. He is convinced that the mob is after him, so he hides out in Chicago. Nightclub life has led to some major disappointments so Mickey is desperately searching for some new leads on a different kind of existence. This gritty and absorbing film was shot on location in Chicago. Written by Alan Surgal, with improvised music from Stan Getz.
Laser: LD75093. $39.95.
Arthur Penn, USA, 1965, 93 mins.

The Miracle Worker

Anne Bancroft and Patty Duke won Oscars for their roles in Arthur Penn's version of Annie Sullivan and her pupil, Helen Keller. The dramatic force of the battle between the strong willed Annie and the animal-willed Helen carries this extraordinary film.
VHS: S00860. $24.95.
Laser: LD71175. $34.98.
Arthur Penn, USA, 1962, 107 mins.

The Missouri Breaks

In 1880's Montana, ranchers and cattle rustlers fight over land and livestock. Interesting for the head-to-head meeting of two great big talents, Jack Nicholson and Marlon Brando. From a screenplay by Thomas McGuane.
VHS: S03622. $19.95.
Laser: Widescreen. LD74970. $49.99.
Arthur Penn, USA, 1976, 127 mins.

Penn and Teller Get Killed

A virtually unclassifiable gem from Arthur Penn about postmodern magicians/comedians Penn and Teller, who announce on national television their desire to be killed, and spend the rest of the film avoiding dire fate. Bleak, funny and nihilistic, the movie was permanently shelved and then turned up in a few film festivals. With Penn Jillette, Teller, Caitlin Clarke, Christopher Durang and David Patrick Kelly.
Laser: LD70651. $24.98.
Arthur Penn, USA, 1989, 90 mins.

STEVEN SPIELBERG

Always

A supernatural romance-adventure involving forest firefighting pilots and strong attachments. Richard Dreyfuss, a cocky pilot in love with Holly Hunter, is reluctant to say the words until after he is dead and assigned to act as guardian angel for a rookie flyer. Based on the 1943 romantic fantasy war movie *A Guy Named Joe*. With John Goodman, Brad Johnson and Audrey Hepburn.
VHS: S12230. $19.95.
Steven Spielberg, USA, 1989

Close Encounters of the Third Kind

Intelligent sci-fi story written by Steven Spielberg about a UFO mystery that leads to the first contact by bewildered humans with space aliens. Beautifully shot by Oscar-winning cinematographer Vilmos Zsigmond and wonderfully acted by Richard Dreyfuss, Teri Garr and Melinda Dillon. With a cameo by French film director Francois Truffaut as a kind-hearted and understanding scientist. Music score by John Williams.
VHS: S03482. $14.95.
Laser: Re-edited and expanded special edition. Dolby.
LD74543. $39.95.
Steven Spielberg, USA, 1977, 135 mins.

The Color Purple

Steven Spielberg's magnum opus, with Whoopi Goldberg and Danny Glover, in an adaptation of Alice Walker's seminal book about a poor black woman who overcomes horrible conditions in her life and finally comes out on top. Excellent performances by all make this a better than average story with drama, humor and gentleness shining through.
VHS: S03551. $19.98.
    Laser: CAV. LD70545. $59.98.
    Laser: CLV. LD70546. $29.98.
Steven Spielberg, USA, 1985, 154 mins.

Duel

Dennis Weaver is a traveling businessman who provokes the wrath of a nameless, faceless driver of a diesel truck in the American Southwest. Directed by Steven Spielberg for television, the script is by Richard Matheson. A wild, nerve-crunching ride. Footage added for theatrical release.
VHS: S07809. $14.98.
    Laser: LD72297. $34.98.
Steven Spielberg, USA, 1971, 90 mins.

E.T.

Steven Spielberg's magnum opus—finally on video. An endearing alien, stranded on Earth, befriends a sweet young boy and his lovable siblings, who all help him to find his way back home. One of the most popular and highest grossing movies in history and quickly becoming a children's classic in the league of The Wizard of Oz.
VHS: Out of print. For rental only.
    Laser: LD70026. $59.98.
Steven Spielberg, USA, 1985, 101 mins.

Empire of the Sun

Andrew Sarris thought Spielberg's story of 11-year-old Jim Graham fighting for survival in Shanghai while it was being invaded by the Japanese army was one of the year's best films.
VHS: S07306. $89.95.
Steven Spielberg, USA, 1987, 153 mins.

Hook

The classic J.M. Barrie story of Peter Pan is updated and given the Steven Spielberg treatment. Dustin Hoffman has the title role as the most feared pirate captain in Never Never Land. Robin Williams is the grown-up Pan and Maggie Smith is Granny Wendy. With Bob Hoskins, Julia Roberts and Glenn Close.
VHS: S16626. $19.95.
    Laser: LD71571. $39.95.
Steven Spielberg, USA, 1991, 144 mins.

Indiana Jones and the Last Crusade

Everyone's favorite archeologist adventurer is back in action as Harrison Ford seeks the Holy Grail and the whereabouts of his scholar father Sean Connery. Can he find both and ride off into the sunset before the nasty Nazis cause him wear and tear on another set of clothes? With Julian Glover, Alison Doody, Denholm Elliott, John Rhys-Davies and River Phoenix as young Indiana Jones.
VHS: S11479. $14.95.
Steven Spielberg, USA, 1989, 126 mins.

Indiana Jones and the Temple of Doom

Action-packed, stunt-infested, and with loads of special effects, the long-awaited release of this boxoffice smash (the second in the series) stars Harrison Ford, this time with Kate Capshaw as the female interest, who ended up the new Mrs. Steven Spielberg after the filming. Booming score by John Williams keeps the activity at a fever pitch.
VHS: S01804. $14.95.
    Laser: Widescreen. LD75312. $39.98.
Steven Spielberg, USA, 1984, 118 mins.

Jaws

The original is a chilling movie about a New England shore community terrorized by shark attacks. Three Oscars including music score and editing. Cameo by Peter Benchley, who wrote the novel upon which film was based. Special collector's edition, letterboxed, featuring interviews with Steven Spielberg.
VHS: S03692. $19.98.
    Laser: Letterboxed. LD71438. $149.98.
Steven Spielberg, USA, 1975, 125 mins.

Jurassic Park

Sam Neil, Laura Dern, Jeff Goldblum, and Richard Attenborough star in this sci-fi adventure blockbuster. The recreation of dinosaurs is the concept behind a theme park. Everything seems fine until the science behind this revivifying scheme goes haywire. Life is a dangerous and unpredictable force.
VHS: S21499. $19.98.
    Laser: CLV, letterboxed. LD74528. $49.98.
    Laser: CAV, letterboxed. LD74529. $74.98.
Steven Spielberg, USA, 1993, 126 mins.

Poltergeist

When you build a community over a graveyard and don't move the bodies, expect the kind of problems that plague this typically American suburban family. Moving furniture and floating toys lead to alternative dimensions and the lowering of real estate values. With Craig T. Nelson, JoBeth Williams and Heather O'Rourke. Great special effects. Co-written and produced by Steven Spielberg.
VHS: S04502. $19.95.
    Laser: CAV, special collector's edition. LD74490. $74.98.
Tobe Hooper, USA, 1982, 114 mins.

Raiders of the Lost Ark

Harrison Ford is an adventure-seeking archeologist after rare and well-guarded ancient artifacts. The entertaining Indiana Jones battles Nazi hordes for the sacred Ark of the Covenant and the company of a spunky Karen Allen. Whiz bang thrills and special effects.
VHS: S01882. $14.95.
Steven Spielberg, USA, 1981, 115 mins.

Schindler's List

This Academy Award-winning film tells the story of Oskar Schindler, who saved hundreds of Jews from certain death in Nazi-dominated Europe. Adapted from Thomas Keneally's novel and starring Ben Kingsley, Liam Neeson and Ralph Fiennes. The Collector's Edition includes the novel, a compact disc of the Academy Award-winning score by John Williams and a booklet with an introduction by Steven Spielberg.
Collector's Edition. SLP, letterboxed.
VHS: S21540. $79.95.
    Laser: Includes soundtrack, CD and book. LD74526. $139.98.
Full Frame Version.
VHS: S21539. $29.95.
    Laser: Letterboxed. LD74525. $49.98.
Steven Spielberg, USA, 1993, 197 mins.

We're Back! A Dinosaur's Story

This is the Spielberg story of dinosaurs who escape extinction and come to New York, delighting the children who love these mammoth creatures. Voices from John Goodman, Martin Short, Julia Child, Jay Leno, and Walter Cronkite are featured in this animated film.
VHS: S20627. $24.98.
    Laser: Letterboxed. LD72370. $24.98.
Steven Spielberg, USA, 1992, 78 mins.

JAMES IVORY

Autobiography of a Princess

An East Indian princess, long divorced and living in self-enforced exile in London, invites her father's ex-tutor to an annual tea party, where they watch old movie footage of Royal India. In this tightly written character study, James Mason and Madhur Jaffrey celebrate a happier past, conveying among the finest of their performances. From the renowned filmmaking team of James Ivory and Ismail Merchant.
VHS: S15670. $29.95.
    Laser: CAV. LD71587. $39.95.
James Ivory, India, 1975, 59 mins.

Bombay Talkie

An English female writer of trash novels arrives in India looking for passion and romance. She finds she can meet her goals with affairs with an actor and a poet, but at what cost to the men involved? With Jennifer Kendall and Zia Mohyeddin.
VHS: S03939. $19.95.
James Ivory, Great Britain, 1970, 115 mins.

The Bostonians

A Merchant/Ivory literary adaptation of Henry James' novel. The plot concerns an intriguing sexual triangle. A beautiful though innocent orator (Madeleine Potter) is caught between a stern suffragette (Vanessa Redgrave) and a repressed, upper class lawyer (Christopher Reeve). With Jessica Tandy, Linda Hunt and Wallace Shawn. Adaptation by Ruth Prawer Jhabvala.
VHS: S00171. $19.95.
James Ivory, USA, 1984, 120 mins.

Courtesans of Bombay

An insightful portrait of the compound in Bombay called Pavanpul where young women entertain men who come searching for the escape of eroticism. "By night the caged birds sing in the pleasure palace" (Jan Hoffman).
VHS: S03940. $19.95.
James Ivory, Great Britain/India, 1985, 74 mins.

The Europeans

An European aristocrat and her brash younger brother upset the lives of their Boston cousins upon their arrival, in Merchant/Ivory's adaptation of Henry James' novel. Screenplay by Ruth Prawer Jhabvala. With Lee Remick, Robin Ellis, Tim Woodward, Wesley Addy and Lisa Eichhorn.
VHS: S00419. $19.95.
    Laser: LD71593. $39.95.
James Ivory, USA, 1979, 90 mins.

Heat and Dust

Julie Christie and Greta Scacchi star in this romantically parallel story about a modern Englishwoman and her great aunt. The aunt (Scacchi), a pretty, witty and reckless young wife of a British civil servant in the 20's, innocently succumbs to India, and one of its princes. 60 years later, Christie follows in her footsteps. A very sexy film.
VHS: S00554. $59.95.
James Ivory, Great Britain/USA, 1983, 130 mins.

The Householder

The first collaboration of producer Ismail Merchant, director James Ivory and novelist and screenwriter Ruth Prawer Jhabvala (A Room with a View, Howards End) is this perceptive comedy about the difficulties of a young Indian man trying to adapt to his arranged marriage. It "tells us some eternal truths about the maturity pains a young husband undergoes but also paints a fresh, vivid and pointed picture of an emerging society" (Judith Crist). With Shashi Kapoor, Leela Naidu and Durga Khote.
VHS: S17631. $29.95.
    Laser: CLV. LD72067. $39.95.
James Ivory, Great Britain, 1962, 101 mins.

Howards End

Merchant/Ivory's wonderfully acted, beautifully constructed adaptation of E.M. Forster's novel about the unconventional love, class struggle and hypocrisy of upper class Edwardian England. The film concerns two sisters (Academy Award winner Emma Thompson and Helena Bonham Carter) and their romantic and personal entanglements with aristocratic, wealthy landowners (Anthony Hopkins and Vanessa Redgrave). Cinematography is by Tony Pierce-Roberts. Academy Award-winning screenplay by Ruth Prawer Jhabvala. With James Wilby, Samuel West and Prunella Scales.
VHS: S18519. $94.95.
    Laser: LD71869. $39.95.
James Ivory, Great Britain, 1992, 143 mins.

Hullabaloo over Georgie and Bonnie's Pictures

Georgie owns some ancient paintings that create quite a stir with his friends and houseguests. The artwork inspires the need for possession. The cast for this dramatic comedy set in India includes Peggy Ashcroft, Victor Banerjee, Saeed Jaffrey and Jane Booker.
VHS: S03938. $19.95.
James Ivory, Great Britain, 1980, 83 mins.

Jane Austen in Manhattan

From the creators of Room with a View, James Ivory and Ismail Merchant venture into this satirical arena when rival theater companies plan to mount an obscure script by Jane Austen: one as a handsome period piece; the other a conceptual, avant-garde design. Anne Baxter and Robert Powell star.
VHS: S02335. $59.95.
James Ivory, USA, 1980, 108 mins.

Jefferson in Paris

Nick Nolte and Greta Scacchi star in this detailed period piece. Thomas Jefferson, one of the United States' founding fathers, had a rather impetuous youthful sojourn in Paris, the City of Light. This fact is the basis for a dramatic recreation of his stay there. A mysterious and worldly woman leads him into a steamy love affair, one that forces him to question old allegiances.
VHS: S26204. $99.99.
    Laser: LD75063. $39.99.
James Ivory, USA, 1995, 139 mins.

Maurice

James Ivory directs this sensitive film about the love relationship between two men who meet studying at Cambridge in 1910. Based on the novel by E.M. Forster which was published after his death. That love that dare not speak its name is now a movie. With James Wilby, Hugh Grant, Rupert Graves, Denholm Elliott and Ben Kingsley.
VHS: S06208. $19.98.
    Laser: CAV, widescreen. LD75106. $59.95.
James Ivory, Great Britain, 1987, 135 mins.

Mr. and Mrs. Bridge

Paul Newman and Joanne Woodward are cast as a conservative Kansas City couple whose marriage comes under close scrutiny as the years grow apart. Based on two novels by Evan S. Connell, this finely etched family drama spends its time and energies on life's quieter moments. With Blythe Danner, Simon Callow and Kyra Sedgwick. Woodward was nominated for an Oscar.
VHS: S13876. $19.98.
James Ivory, USA, 1990, 127 mins.

Noon Wine

Katherine Ann Porter's short story about a Swedish immigrant who finds work on a small Texas farm, and through no fault of his own, becomes the focal point of strife. Starring Fred Ward (Remo Williams) and produced by Ismail Merchant and James Ivory (Room with a View).
VHS: S05320. $24.95.
James Ivory, USA, 1984, 60 mins.

Quartet

A James Ivory film based on the book by Jean Rhys, which stars Maggie Smith, Alan Bates, Isabelle Adjani and Anthony Higgins. These fine performers are involved in a 1920's Bohemian drama set in Paris, wherein seduction and decadence are the name of the game. Not to be confused with the film of the same name based on the writing of Somerset Maugham.
VHS: S06184. $19.98.
James Ivory, Great Britain/France, 1981, 101 mins.

Remains of the Day

In this drama, the relationship between a butler and a housekeeper, played by Anthony Hopkins and Emma Thompson, is stifled by the demands of conflicting duties. The household they manage plays host to important political gatherings attended by fascist leaders. Their roles may very well hasten the demise of their country, not to mention their growing affection for one another. Based on the novel by Kazuo Ishiguri.
VHS: S20777. $19.95.
    Laser: LD72389. $39.95.
James Ivory, Great Britain, 1993, 134 mins.

Room with a View

Maggie Smith stars in this acclaimed film, based on the E.M. Forster novel, which evokes the manners and mores of an era. A witty, lush film with Denholm Elliott, Judi Dench and Simon Callow.
VHS: S02767. $19.98.
    Laser: LD71312. $34.98.
James Ivory, Great Britain, 1986, 117 mins.

Roseland

This Merchant/Ivory trilogy centers on romance in the famous New York dance hall, the Roseland Ballroom, and is a gentle, spirited work redolent in the memories, ambitions and idealized preoccupations of the forlorn souls who inhabit its room. With Christopher Walken, Geraldine Chaplin, Teresa Wright and Lilia Skala. Written by Ruth Prawer Jhabvala.
VHS: S01134. $29.95.
    Laser: CLV. LD72068. $39.95.
James Ivory, USA, 1977, 104 mins.

Savages

James Ivory's offbeat look at society, in which a naked band of primitives, disturbed from their sacrifices by a croquet ball, discover a deserted mansion, and begin to "get civilized." But the line between savages and civilization is not that strong.
VHS: S01160. $29.95.
    Laser: LD72069. $39.95.
James Ivory, USA, 1973, 108 mins.

Slaves of New York

The Tama Janowitz novel of the young and terminally trendy in the Big Apple art community stars Bernadette Peters as a funky hat designer who lives with an up and coming artist who mistreats her. Author Janowitz plays her best friend in a few scenes. Cast includes Madeleine Potter, Mary Beth Hurt, Nick Corri, Chris Sarandon and Adam Coleman Howard as Stash Stotz.
VHS: S10611. $89.95.
James Ivory, USA, 1989, 115 mins.

FRANCIS F. COPPOLA

Apocalypse Now (Remastered)

Francis Ford Coppola's Vietnam War epic conveys a madness with parallels to Joseph Conrad's Heart of Darkness. Lieutenant Willard receives orders to seek out a renegade military outpost led by errant officer Colonel Kurtz, and to "terminate his command with extreme prejudice." This newly enhanced version features a remastered soundtrack in Dolby surround sound.
VHS: S00066. $29.95.
Francis F. Coppola, USA, 1979, 153 mins.

Bram Stoker's Dracula

Francis Ford Coppola's adaptation of Stoker's novel emphasizes sexual undertones. Gary Oldman's Dracula is unhinged as he tries to seduce the beautiful Winona Ryder and destroy his rivals. Anthony Hopkins is Van Helsing, the determined doctor obsessed with the count's destruction. With Keanu Reeves, Sadie Frost and Tom Waits.
VHS: S18655. $19.95.
    Laser: Features documentary The Making of Bram Stoker's Dracula. LD71875. $49.95.
Francis F. Coppola, USA, 1992, 126 mins.

The Conversation

Gene Hackman is brilliant as Harry Caul, the surveillance man who becomes the object of surveillance himself. Coppola's great achievement is in evoking an obsessive sense of paranoia as Hackman struggles to free himself from the maze of secrecy and murder. With Cindy Williams, Harrison Ford, Frederic Forrest.
VHS: S00267. $19.95.
    Laser: LD75356. $29.95.
Francis F. Coppola, USA, 1974, 113 mins.

Cotton Club

Francis Ford Coppola exposes the most violent and passionate era America has ever known: the age of jazz and glamour in the kingdom of organized crime. Richard Gere and Diane Lane star, with a guest appearance by Joe Dallesandro.
VHS: S00272. $14.95.
    Laser: LD72324. $34.99.
Francis F. Coppola, USA, 1984, 128 mins.

Dementia 13

Early Francis Ford Coppola cheapie horror film shot in Ireland with some of the cast from Roger Corman's The Young Racers. Gory axe murders in black and white as a scheming woman tries to gain control of her ex-husband's family fortune. With Luana Anders, William Campbell, Mary Mitchell, and Patrick Magee as a mysterious family physician. B&W.
VHS: S18175. $24.95.
Francis F. Coppola, USA, 1963, 81 mins.

Finian's Rainbow

A wily Irishman, his beautiful daughter and a feisty leprechaun come to a magical valley where anything can happen—and does—in this film version of the famous Broadway classic. Fred Astaire and Petula Clark star.
VHS: S04974. $19.98.
    Laser: Letterboxed. LD71141. $39.98.
Francis F. Coppola, USA, 1968, 142 mins.

Gardens of Stone

James Caan is a career soldier assigned to the Burial Detail at the Arlington National Cemetery. It's 1968 and he is getting more business than he would like. A dramatic story of pain and pride in perilous times. With James Earl Jones, Anjelica Huston and D.B. Sweeney.
VHS: S05307. $89.98.
Francis F. Coppola, USA, 1987, 112 mins.

The Godfather

An epic featuring Marlon Brando as the patriarch of the Corleone family, masterfully balanced between the story of family life and the family crime business. With Al Pacino, James Caan, Robert Duvall, Diane Keaton. Based on Mario Puzo's novel. Music by Nino Rota.
VHS: S00509. $29.95.
Francis F. Coppola, USA, 1972, 171 mins.

The Godfather Part II

A companion piece to the original Godfather, this continues the saga of two generations of successive power in the Corleone family. Coppola tells the story of the rise of a young Don Vito, played by Robert De Niro, and the ascension of the new Don Michael, played by Al Pacino.
VHS: S00510. $29.95.
Francis F. Coppola, USA, 1974, 200 mins.

The Godfather Part III

The saga of the Corleone family is continued under the direction of Francis Ford Coppola. This video release contains the director's cut with additional footage not included in its theatrical release. Al Pacino returns in the title role as an aging Italian-American trying very hard to be legit, without success. The plot involves banking with the Vatican, pursuing a career in opera, and killing your enemies. With Diane Keaton, Talia Shire, Andy Garcia, Eli Wallach, Joe Mantegna, Sophia Coppola, Bridget Fonda and George Hamilton in the role for which Robert Duvall asked for too much money.
VHS: S14795. $29.95.
Francis F. Coppola, USA, 1990, 170 mins.

The Godfather Collection

Contains the individual videotapes of The Godfather, The Godfather Part II and The Godfather Part III, packaged together in a special gift box.
VHS: S12851. $69.90.
Francis F. Coppola, USA, 1972-1990, 541 mins.

The Godfather Trilogy: 1901-1980

Director Francis Ford Coppola supervised the reediting of The Godfather, The Godfather Part II and The Godfather Part III into one continuous film. Spanning nearly eight decades, The Godfather Trilogy: 1901-1980 is the chronological telling of the legacy of the Corleone family. As a special bonus, this package also contains The Godfather Family: A Look Inside, a 73-minute program which goes behind the scenes of the epic saga, and a comprehensive 28-page companion booklet as well. Packaged in an elegant, all-leather deluxe gift box. Six-tape set.
VHS: S13534. $199.95.

Hearts of Darkness: A Filmmaker's Apocalypse

A riveting behind-the-scenes look at the making of Francis Ford Coppola's Apocalypse Now. The film combines interviews with documentary footage shot on location in the Philippines by Eleanor Coppola. This is a must-see for anyone with the slightest interest in how Hollywood movies get made. With Martin Sheen, Dennis Hopper, Larry Fishburne, Robert Duvall, Sam Bottoms, Frederic Forrest, George Lucas, John Milius and Francis Ford Coppola. Watch Marlon Brando improvise his lines and eat a bug.
VHS: S16459. $19.95.
Fax Bahr/George Hickenlooper, USA, 1991, 96 mins.

New York Stories

Three major directors, one city. Martin Scorsese, Francis Ford Coppola and Woody Allen offer an omnibus of short films based on life in the Big Apple. Scorsese leads off with *Life Lessons*, in which master painter Nick Nolte puts the moves on art student Rosanna Arquette. *Life with Zoe* is written by Coppola and his daughter Sofia. It tells the story of a precocious little girl who lives in a fancy hotel. Allen tops off the trio with *Oedipus Wrecks*, a comedy about an unmarried middle aged man whose problems with his pushy mother suddenly involve the entire city. With Woody Allen, Mia Farrow, Julie Kavner and Mae Questel, the voice of Betty Boop, as Woody's mom.
   VHS: S11531. $89.95.
   Laser: LD71255. $39.99.
Martin Scorsese/Coppola/Allen, USA, 1988, 123 mins

Outsiders

A powerful film based on a classic S.E. Hinton novel about teen hopes, fears and rebellion. Coppola has brought together an ensemble of young actors including Matt Dillon, Emilio Estevez, Tom Cruise and Ralph Macchio.
   VHS: S00984. $19.98.
   Laser: Letterboxed. LD74713. $34.98.
Francis F. Coppola, USA, 1983, 91 mins.

Peggy Sue Got Married

Francis Ford Coppola returned to the screen in triumphant form in this drama starring Kathleen Turner, who gets the chance to change her life. The mother of two coping with impending divorce, a freak mishap at her high school reunion sends her back in time, giving her a chance to create an entirely new future for herself.
   VHS: Out of print. For rental only.
   Laser: LD71274. $34.98.
Francis F. Coppola, USA, 1986, 103 mins.

The Rain People

Pregnant Long Island housewife (Shirley Knight) leaves home and goes traveling across America. Along the way in this strongly acted, sensitive drama she meets James Caan, Robert Duvall and some lesser known American actors, one of whom owns a pistol.
   VHS: S04179. $19.98.
Francis F. Coppola, USA, 1969, 102 mins.

Rumble Fish

In black and white with color sequences, *Rumble Fish* is a visually stunning adaptation of S.E. Hinton's novel, starring Matt Dillon and Mickey Rourke as brothers trying to break out of their urban trap. With Dennis Hopper, music by Stewart Copeland (Police).
   VHS: S01138. $59.95.
   Laser: Letterboxed. LD74470. $34.98.
Francis F. Coppola, USA, 1983, 94 mins.

Tonight for Sure

Francis Coppola's first film, an exploitation comedy, done while he was attending UCLA. The story centers on two gentlemen trying to stamp out indecency, which gives Coppola the excuse to show a bevy of naked women running through the desert.
   VHS: S01359. $29.95.
Francis F. Coppola, USA, 1961, 66 mins.

Tucker: The Man and His Dream

Jeff Bridges is Preston Tucker, American inventor and the designer of an automobile too many years ahead of its time to succeed against the major car makers in Michigan. A brilliant, touching family drama about a visionary individual whose life director Coppola has been trying to film for years. With Martin Landau, Joan Allen, Frederic Forrest, Mako, Lloyd Bridges and Jay O. Sanders as William Kirby, Tucker's lawyer.
   VHS: S08354. $19.95.
   Laser: Widescreen. LD75137. $24.98.
Francis F. Coppola, USA, 1988, 111 mins.

You're a Big Boy Now

Francis Ford Coppola's second feature film deals with the problems of surviving a sheltered childhood in a large and inviting city like New York. Peter Kastner is the innocent willing to be corrupted by Elizabeth Hartman. Cast includes Karen Black, Julie Harris, Rip Torn, Geraldine Page and Dolph Sweet as a tough cop.
   VHS: S06207. $19.98.
Francis F. Coppola, USA, 1966, 98 mins.

SAM SHEPARD

Far North

Sam Shepard makes his feature film directorial debut with the story of an eccentric Minnesota farming family. Charles Durning is the opinionated patriarch who wants oldest daughter Jessica Lange to shoot the family horse. To shoot or not to shoot, that is but one of the questions raised in this quirk-ridden drama. With Tess Harper, Patricia Arquette, Donald Moffat and Ann Wedgeworth.
   VHS: S09144. $79.98.
Sam Shepard, USA, 1988, 90 mins.

Silent Tongue

River Phoenix in his final screen appearance is joined by Richard Harris, Dermot Mulroney and Alan Bates in this western about honor and love. A young woman, who is half Native American, is kidnapped, setting off a desperate struggle to set her free. Justice can never be silenced.
   VHS: S21104. $19.95.
Sam Shepard, USA, 1993, 101 mins.

american COMEDY

5 Corners
An endearing, offbeat black comedy set in the Bronx in 1962, featuring a top notch ensemble cast including Jodie Foster, Todd Graff, Tim Robbins and John Turturro as Heinz, the ex-con nutcase. This film does show scenes of violence to penguins and math teachers as well as the entertainment possibilities of an elevator shaft.
VHS: S07913. $14.98.
Tony Bill, USA, 1987, 94 mins.

60 Years with Bob Hope
This documentary takes a rare look at the life of the remarkable performer. Includes some exclusive, never-before-seen footage.
USA, 56 mins.
VHS: S15028. $19.95.

Abbott and Costello
Nine feature films showing the zany duo at their wackiest.
Abbott and Costello Meet Dr. Jekyll and Mr. Hyde. You'll laugh your way through the foggy London street as Abbott and Costello take on Boris Karloff in a hilarious spoof of the famed horror classic. Directed by Charles Lamont, USA, 1952, 77 mins.
VHS: S10443. $14.95.
Abbott and Costello Meet Frankenstein. As railroad baggage clerks, Abbott and Costello receive a strange shipment—the not-so-dead remains of Dracula and Frankenstein's monster. Directed by Charles T. Barton, USA, 1948, 83 mins.
VHS: S10440. $14.95.
Laser: LD70010. $34.98.
Abbott and Costello: Africa Screams. Abbott and Costello prove themselves masters of monkeyshines when a treasure map sends them on a slapstick safari through Africa. Directed by Charles T. Barton, USA, 1949, 79 mins.
VHS: S03279. $19.95.
Abbott and Costello: Buck Privates. Abbott and Costello play two dim-witted salesmen who accidentally enlist in the Army and turn it upside down in this hilarious WWII comedy. Directed by Arthur Lubin, USA, 1941, 84 mins.
VHS: S10441. $14.95.
Abbott and Costello: Hit the Ice. Abbott and Costello get mixed up with gangsters, gun molls and gumshoes in one of their funniest, zaniest comedies. Directed by Charles Lamont, USA, 1943, 89 mins.
VHS: S10445. $14.95.
Abbott and Costello: Hold That Ghost. Bud and Lou inherit an abandoned roadhouse belonging to a rubbed-out monster, in one of the funniest Abbott and Costello movies of all time. Directed by Arthur Lubin, USA, 1941, 86 mins.
VHS: S10442. $14.95.
Abbott and Costello: Naughty Nineties. Abbott and Costello keep the laughs flowing on a Mississippi showboat, performing many of their most famous hits, including the hysterical "Who's On First" dialog that has become one of the most popular comedy routines ever captured on film. Directed by Jean Yarborough, USA, 1945, 72 mins.
VHS: S10447. $14.95.
Abbott and Costello: Time of Their Lives. Alternate title: *The Ghost Steps Out.* A ghostly Lou Costello haunts a nervous Bud Abbott in a mansion built during the Revolutionary War. Directed by Charles T. Barton, USA, 1946, 82 mins.
VHS: S10446. $14.95.
Abbott and Costello: Who Done It? Abbott and Costello are would-be radio writers who find themselves involved in real murder during the recording of a "whodunit" play. Directed by Eric C. Kenton, USA, 1942, 77 mins.
VHS: S10444. $14.95.

The Abbott and Costello Collection
The comic misadventures of Abbott & Costello in three of their hits: S. Sylvan Simon's 1942 musical *Rio Rito* and the 1945 *Abbott & Costello in Hollywood,* and Charles Riesner's *Lost in a Harem.*
VHS: S17326. $49.92.

Abbott and Costello Comin' Round the Mountain
Together the famed comic duo are off for the hills, where their antics make them stand out even more. This pair of not very slick city slickers need to do more than don a coonskin cap to fit in. Maybe they should just give up and laugh along with everyone else.
VHS: S21315. $14.98.
Charles Lamont, USA, 1951, 77 mins.

Abbott and Costello Go to Mars
Only the presence of this pair could explain the mix-up. Though they are supposed to be off to Mars according to the title, they actually end up on Venus, where there is a brief appearance by Anita Ekberg. Maybe the escaped gangster on board is to blame.
VHS: S21314. $14.98.
Charles Lamont, USA, 1953, 77 mins.

Abbott and Costello in Hollywood
Here our two zany friends play a pair of barbers who want their own Hollywood barber shop—and to get it, they find themselves in the middle of numerous close shaves. With cameo appearances by Lucille Ball, Rags Ragland and Preston Foster. Look for a young Dean Stockwell in the supporting cast.
USA, 1945, 83 mins.
VHS: S15425. $19.98.

Abbott and Costello in the Foreign Legion
Walter Slezak is the tough sergeant who must whip these two comic mishaps into fighting shape. Can his tough ways succeed against the bumbling antics of these hopelessly funny ne'er-do-wells? With the desert sun beating down on them all, someone has got to give in.
VHS: S21313. $14.98.
Charles Lamont, USA, 1950, 80 mins.

Abbott and Costello Meet the Invisible Man
One of the duo's best works has them playing private detectives who use an invisible potion to help a boxer framed by a notorious mobster. With Nancy Guild, Arthur Franz, and Sheldon Leonard.
VHS: S17260. $14.98.
Charles Lamont, USA, 1951, 82 mins.

Abbott and Costello Meet the Keystone Kops
In this period piece, the famed comic duo confronts one of silent film's most enduring legendary institutions, the Keystone Kops. Fred Clark is great as a conniving producer, proving that Hollywood's evil ways started early. It's a laugh-filled adventure into entertainment history.
VHS: S21312. $14.98.
Charles Lamont, USA, 1955, 75 mins.

Abbott and Costello Meet the Mummy
The two comics are caught in a thick web of intrigue and adventure as they pursue a beautiful villain, a highly valuable tomb and a fiendish mummy that haunts the entire proceedings. With Marie Windsor, Michael Ansara and Dan Seymour.
VHS: S19070. $14.98.
Charles Lamont, USA, 1955, 79 mins.

Abbott and Costello Vol. I Who's on First
What's on second, I don't know…third base. One of this country's classic comedy routines is now available on video. The version presented here is the one perfected on the comedy team's famous television series. Featuring the manager of the *St. Louis Wolves* and much, much more. USA, 60 mins.
VHS: S15027. $19.95.

Abbott and Costello: Mexican Hayride
Adapted from an original Cole Porter musical without the songs, this Abbott and Costello vehicle unfolds south of the border, with the boys desperately tracking down an old mine deed. With John Hubbard, Pedro de Cordoba, and Fritz Field.
VHS: S17259. $14.98.
Charles Barton, USA, 1947, 77 mins.

Adventures in Babysitting
Elizabeth Shue stars as babysitter Chris Parker in this comic nightmare in which a normal suburban babysitter and her three young charges find themselves swept up in a series of outrageous events.
VHS: S06369. $89.95.
Chris Columbus, USA, 1987, 102 mins.

After the Thin Man
William Powell and Myrna Loy recreate their famous roles as Nick and Nora Charles in an adaptation of a Dashiell Hammett story set on Nob Hill in San Francisco. With assists from their faithful dog Asta, and James Stewart.
VHS: S00023. $24.95.
W.S. Van Dyke, USA, 1936, 113 mins.

Air Raid Wardens
A late period Laurel and Hardy World War II comedy. Laurel and Hardy are rejected from the armed services, and get entangled in a German spy ring which is trying to destroy a large munitions factory. With Edgar Kennedy, Jacqueline White, and Donald Meek.
VHS: S17892. $19.98.
Edward Sedgwick, USA, 1943, 67 mins.

Airplane!
A very funny spoof of the airport pictures of the 70's, with a nonstop stream of gags from beginning to end. With Robert Hays, Peter Graves, Robert Stack, Lloyd Bridges, Julie Hagerty.
VHS: S09565. $14.95.
Laser: Remastered. LD75142. $34.98.
J. Zucker/J. Abrahams/D. Zucker, USA, 1980, 88 mins.

All Night Long
Gene Hackman stars in this comedy about middle-age crises. He is a recently demoted drugstore executive who responds by rebelling. He divorces his wife and gets involved with a distant relative while hoping to invent something miraculous. This new career and life lead him into contact with all kinds of creatures of the night. Barbra Streisand, Diane Ladd and Dennis Quaid also star.
VHS: S22031. $7.95.
Jean-Claude Tramont, USA, 1981, 100 mins.

Amazon Women on the Moon
A comedy compilation from five filmmakers of short skits and spoofs on a variety of topics including modern dating, personalized video adult selections, the dangers of social diseases, modern technology and landing on a planet with hostile armed women in charge. With Arsenio Hall, Rosanna Arquette, Carrie Fisher, Griffin Dunne, Steve Forrest and Sybil Danning.
VHS: S05928. $79.95.
J. Landis/J. Dante/P. Horton, USA, 1987, 85 mins.

And God Spoke
This hilarious mockumentary continues in the tradition of *Spinal Tap.* It shows the crazy antics that go on behind the scenes during the filming of a movie based on the Bible. Troubles of all sorts crop up, particularly financial ones. The first commandment of movie-making must be, "Don't Go Over Budget."
VHS: S23114. $92.98.
Laser: LD75146. $34.98.
Arthur Borman, USA, 1994, 82 mins.

And Justice for All
Al Pacino stars as an angry lawyer in a sharply critical black comedy about the contemporary legal system. Written by Barry Levinson and Valerie Curtin. Jack Warden stars as a crazy judge. John Forsythe plays a sadistic member of the bench. With Craig T. Nelson, Christine Lahti, Jeffrey Tambor and Sam Levene. A film that reinforces the notion that Shakespeare had the right idea of what to do with lawyers.
VHS: S10375. $14.95.
Laser: LD75527. $39.95.
Norman Jewison, USA, 1979, 117 mins.

Angels in the Outfield
Danny Glover, Tony Danza and Christopher Lloyd star in this sentimental remake of the story of a preteen boy who prays that the team can win so that he can be reunited with his father.
VHS: S23226. $19.99.
Laser: Letterboxed. LD74809. $39.99.
William Dear, USA, 1994, 105 mins.

Angie
Academy-Award winner Geena Davis is the perfect comedienne for this humorous look at impending motherhood. Her predicament drives friends and family crazy, but she manages to find her way through this situation with laughter and verve, in New York City, no less.
VHS: S21361. $96.98.
Martha Coolidge, USA, 1994, 108 mins.

Angus
In this comic coming-of-age story, Angus is a teen terror who cuts up on the football field but still can't manage to fit in at high school. Luckily, his geeky friend Troy and his chess-playing grandfather are there to help Angus turn a practical joke into an evening of magic. With Kathy Bates, George C. Scott and Rita Moreno, and introducing Charlie Talbert as Angus.
VHS: S27213. $98.99.
Laser: LD75483. $39.98.
Patrick Read Johnson, USA, 1995, 87 mins.

Animal Crackers
The four Marx Brothers in the uproariously funny film based on the George S. Kaufman musical. Groucho introduced the character of Captain Spaulding, whose song became the theme song of "You Bet Your Life."
VHS: S00053. $19.95.
Laser: LD70096. $34.98.
Victor Heerman, USA, 1930, 98 mins.

Animal House
Tasteless but extremely funny, thanks to John Belushi's rowdy depiction of Bluto Blutarsky, chief animal of the Delta fraternity.
VHS: S00055. $19.95.
John Landis, USA, 1978, 109 mins.

Annabel Takes a Tour/Maid's Night Out
A comedy double feature. Lucy plays the wacky Annabel. Then a rich man's son becomes a milkman (also with Lucille Ball).
VHS: S10647. $19.98.
Lew Landers, USA, 1938, 131 mins.

Another Thin Man
William Powell and Myrna Loy re-team for the third screen adventure of Nick and Nora Charles. They are joined by Nick Jr. Will parenthood deter the solving of society murders? Don't be silly. Asta can always babysit. Script by Dashiell Hammett. B&W.
VHS: S03552. $24.95.
W.S. Van Dyke, USA, 1939, 102 mins.

Another You
Richard Pryor and Gene Wilder are paired in this comedy in which Pryor has to do community service after being paroled by caring for Wilder who has just been released from a sanitarium. The two immediately get mixed up in a scam.
VHS: S21477. $19.98.
Maurice Phillips, USA, 1991, 98 mins.

April Fools
An adult romantic comedy about a grown married man who is not acting his age. Jack Lemmon stars as a businessman who is willing to give up everything to spend a little time with Catherine Deneuve. The cast includes Sally Kellerman, Harvey Korman, Peter Lawford, Myrna Loy and Charles Boyer.
VHS: S10934. $19.98.
Stuart Rosenberg, USA, 1969, 95 mins.

Arthur
Arthur, played by actor Dudley Moore, has $750 million in the bank and yet he's drunk and unhappy almost every waking hour of his life. Enter Liza Minnelli. Boy meets girl; boy loses girl; will boy get girl back? Also starring John Gielgud.
VHS: S14564. $19.95.
Laser: Digital. LD74686. $24.98.
Steve Gordon, USA, 1981, 97 mins.

Arthur 2: On the Rocks
Dudley Moore recreates his Oscar-nominated role as tipsy millionaire Arthur Bach, who is swindled out of his fortune by the father of his ex-fiance. Liza Minnelli returns as the devoted ex-wife who must teach Arthur how to be poor. Very funny. 113 mins.
VHS: S08463. $19.98.
Laser: LD70508. $24.98.

At the Circus
The Marx Brothers try to save Wilson's Wonder Circus from a loan shark, a strongman and a midget and find themselves with Margaret Dumont and a gorilla swinging from a trapeze. With Eve Arden.
VHS: S01826. $19.95.
Laser: LD70156. $39.98.
Edward Buzzell, USA, 1939, 87 mins.

At War with the Army
Dean Martin and Jerry Lewis in their first starring vehicle follow in the tradition of previous comedic greats and attempt a service comedy. The title tells all. With Polly Bergen, Mike Kellin and Angela Greene. Watch for the soda machine gag. B&W.
VHS: S05060. $29.95.
Hal Walker, USA, 1950, 93 mins.

Awful Truth
Wildly funny romp which won the Academy Award opens when a battling couple files for divorce. The only hitch seems to be who will get custody of their beloved terrier, Mr. Smith. Cary Grant and Irene Dunne co-star in this very wacky comedy.
VHS: S00083. $19.95.
Leo McCarey, USA, 1937, 92 mins.

Baby Boom
Diane Keaton is J.C. Wiatt, a Harvard MBA grad and a corporate executive known as the Dragon Lady. Her business and personal life are turned upside down when she inherits an infant girl from a deceased cousin she hasn't seen in years. Eventually she moves to Vermont and meets Sam Shepard and starts a business marketing gourmet baby food. With Harold Ramis and Michelle and Kristina Kennedy as Elizabeth.
VHS: S29396. $19.95.
Laser: Chapter search. Includes original theatrical trailer. LD71638. $29.98.
Charles Shyer, USA, 1987, 103 mins.

Bachelor Mother
A department store employee, played buoyantly by Ginger Rogers, discovers an abandoned baby and is quickly mistaken for its mother; the misunderstandings continue as the store owner's son is then thought to be the baby's father. A delightful comedy, also starring David Niven, Charles Coburn and Frank Albertson.
VHS: S02150. $19.95.
Garson Kanin, USA, 1939, 82 mins.

Bank Dick
As a reward for capturing a robber, W.C. Fields is given the job as a bank security guard. A wonderfully funny romp in what is often considered Fields' best film.
VHS: S03323. $29.95.
Laser: LD70014. $34.98.
Eddie Cline, USA, 1940, 74 mins.

Barbarians at the Gate
A hilarious satire about the go go 80s, as greed and narcissism ruled American big business, encompassing a surreal landscape of junk bonds, high rollers and corporate raiders. Based on the book by Bryan Burrough and John Helyar, this HBO film is a witty examination of the personalities, behind-the-scenes intrigue and power plays to acquire RJ Nabisco. "A sharp-toothed satire and there's a smart, sassy cast to bring it to life" (*Houston Post*). Screenplay by Larry Gelbart (*Tootsie*). With James Garner, Jonathan Pryce, Peter Riegert and Joanna Cassidy.
VHS: S19238. $19.98.
Laser: LD75156. $34.98.
Glenn Jordan, USA, 1993, 107 mins.

Barefoot in the Park
Jane Fonda and Robert Redford star in this breezy film adaptation of the Neil Simon comedy about newly weds living in a five-story walk-up apartment. Charles Boyer plays Victor Velasco, their Greenwich Village neighbor and bon vivant. With Mildred Natwick as Fonda's mother.
VHS: S02084. $19.95.
Laser: LD75361. $29.98.
Gene Saks, USA, 1967, 106 mins.

Batteries Not Included
When an unscrupulous real estate developer sends thugs into a deteriorating tenement to get rid of the last five residents, they need nothing short of a miracle to stay where they are. A delightful fantasy starring Jessica Tandy and Hume Cronyn.
VHS: S07294. $19.95.
Matthew Robbins, USA, 1987, 107 mins.

Bedtime Story
In his first comedic role, Marlon Brando joins David Niven to portray two charming scoundrels who prey on wealthy single women, in this lighthearted romantic comedy set on the Riviera. While masquerading as a deposed Middle European prince, Niven's plans to oust his competitor backfires when the brash Brando portrays Niven's dim-witted brother.
VHS: S10449. $14.98.
Ralph Levy, USA, 1963, 99 mins.

Beethoven
Ivan Reitman produced this appealing family comedy that stars the talented deadpan wit Charles Grodin as the father of a family that welcomes the 185-pound dog who slowly asserts his authority and control over the rest of the family. With Bonnie Hunt and Dean Jones. Written by Edmond Dantes and Amy Holden Jones.
VHS: S17341. $24.98.
Brian Levant, USA, 1992, 95 mins.

Being There
Sublimely funny and bitingly satiric comedy featuring Peter Sellers as a simple-minded gardener who knows only what he watches on television. With Shirley MacLaine and Melvyn Douglas.
VHS: S02823. $19.98.
Laser: LD70522. $29.98.
Hal Ashby, USA, 1979, 130 mins.

The Bellboy
Miami Beach's fabled Fountainbleau has a select group of bellboys, including one monumental klutz, Jerry Lewis. No matter how hard he tries, the results are disastrous and ridiculous, whether he's catering to mafiosi or celebrities like Milton Berle.
VHS: S21740. $14.98.
Jerry Lewis, USA, 1960, 72 mins.

Belle of the Nineties
The talented Leo McCarey directs Mae West in this shrewd comedy about a nightclub singer who makes a valiant play for a prize fighter. Music by Duke Ellington Orchestra. West performs "My Old Flame". With Roger Pryor, Johnny Mack Brown and Warren Hymer.
VHS: S18864. $14.98.
Leo McCarey, USA, 1934, 73 mins.

Beverly Hills Cop
The breakthrough film for Eddie Murphy as the Detroit cop who hits L.A. to track down the killers of an old friend. A very clever blend of comedy and action. With Judge Reinhold, Lisa Eilbacher.
VHS: S01839. $19.95.
Laser: LD75158. $34.98.
Martin Brest, USA, 1984, 105 mins.

Beverly Hills Cop 2
Eddie Murphy is back to help out his L.A. buddies and is fast on the track of an illegal arms dealer (Juergen Prochnow) and his hitlady (Brigitte Nielsen) in this sequel.
VHS: S21478. $19.95.
Tony Scott, USA, 1987, 102 mins.

Big
Tom Hanks stars in this fantasy comedy directed by Penny Marshall about a young boy who makes a magic wish and wakes up looking like Tom Hanks. Be careful of what you ask of a carnival mechanical genie. From 12 to 35 overnight, Josh Baskin now gets to play in the adult world and does pretty well for someone without a high school diploma. With Elizabeth Perkins, John Heard and Robert Loggia. This is a fun movie.
VHS: S09821. $14.98.
Laser: Widescreen. LD74820. $49.98.
Penny Marshall, USA, 1988

The Big Broadcast of 1938
Bob Hope stars in this classic early musical farce set on a ship. While the boat races across the Atlantic, Hope sings and laughs it up with an all star cast which includes W.C. Fields, Martha Raye and Dorothy Lamour. The song "Thanks for the Memories" became Hope's signature tune and won an Oscar.
VHS: S25527. $14.98.
Mitchell Leisen, USA, 1938, 91 mins.

Big Mouth
An appropriate title; Jerry Lewis, in his self-directed effort, makes waves as an eccentric fisherman who dives for sunken treasure but winds up being chased by thugs.
VHS: S07340. $69.95.
Jerry Lewis, USA, 1967, 107 mins.

The Big Store
The three Marx brothers disrupt the peace and quiet of a large department store when pilfering causes Margaret Dumont to hire Groucho (as Wolf J. Flywheel) to investigate. With Virginia Grey and Douglas Dumbrille. B&W.
VHS: S06976. $19.95.
Charles Riesner, USA, 1941, 80 mins.

The Big Store/
Abbott and Costello in Hollywood
A zany double feature from two of Hollywood's greatest comedy teams. The first stars the Marx Brothers as bumbling detectives who nearly demolish a department store while trying to prevent a murder. The second follows Abbott and Costello as they try to open a barber shop in Tinsel Town.
Laser: LD71662. $44.98.

Bill and Ted's Excellent Adventure
Keanu Reeves and Alex Winter star in this surprise hit of 1989 as a pair of California teenage chuckleheads who use a time machine to radically improve their grades. It really impresses the teachers when you can produce Socrates, Genghis Khan, Napoleon and Abraham Lincoln for a class presentation. With George Carlin as a most righteous dude from the future. Awesome, to be sure.
VHS: S12538. $14.95.
Stephen Herek, USA, 1989, 90 mins.

Bingo Long Traveling All-Stars and Motor Kings
Comedy-adventure story of a group of barnstorming players in the 1930's Negro Baseball League stars Richard Pryor, Billy Dee Williams and James Earl Jones. Based on the novel by Chicago author William Brashler.
VHS: S05370. $14.98.
John Badham, USA, 1976, 111 mins.

The Bishop's Wife
Romance, laughter and fantasy abound when Cary Grant appears as a blithe spirit in answer to a Bishop's prayers (David Niven). Niven is in desperate need of funds for a new cathedral, and solutions to an array of other problems including his own marital ones. Grant takes over in a supernatural way, restoring faith, hope and love. Teresa Wright was originally cast in the title role but left to have a baby and was replaced by Loretta Young. Digitally remastered.
VHS: S03118. $19.98.
Henry Koster, USA, 1947, 109 mins.

Blank Check
Every kid's fantasy comes true in this Disney comedy. Brian Bonsall is riding his bike when a crook accidentally runs over it. The crook writes a check to cover the damages but forgets to fill in the amount. Would $1 million be enough?
VHS: S21866. $96.98.
Rupert Wainwright, USA, 1993, 93 mins.

Blazing Saddles
Lunatic humor nominally about the "Old West" stars Cleavon Little as the new sheriff in town, Gene Wilder as the Waco Kid, Slim Pickens, Madeline Kahn and Harvey Korman. The gags never stop.
VHS: S01692. $14.95.
Laser: LD74687. $24.98.
Mel Brooks, USA, 1974, 90 mins.

Blondie
The first of 28 feature films adapted from Chic Young's popular comic strip. The films used small, comic episodes to play out the social and family dynamics of the Bumstead clan. On the eve of their fifth anniversary, Dagwood (Arthur Lake) is fired from his job, and his strange behavior has Blondie (Penny Singleton) thinking he's romantically involved with other women. With Jonathan Hale, Larry Simms, Gene Lockhart, Ann Doran and Danny Mummert.
VHS: S20173. $14.95.
Frank Strayer, USA, 1938, 68 mins.

Blondie Has Trouble
Also known as *Blondie Has Servant Trouble*, this witty farce finds the Bumsteads occupying a haunted house rife with supernatural forces and domestic incompetence. With Penny Singleton, Arthur Lake, Larry Simms, Danny Mummert, Jonathan Hale and Arthur Hohl.
VHS: S20178. $14.95.
Frank Strayer, USA, 1940, 70 mins.

Blondie Hits the Jackpot
Blondie wins a killing on a quiz show sponsored by the local radio station, saving Dagwood from having to perform menial labor at a construction site. With Penny Singleton, Arthur Lake, Larry Simms, Danny Mummert, Jonathan Hale and Arthur Hohl.
VHS: S20174. $14.95.
Edward Bernds, USA, 1949, 66 mins.

Blondie in Society
Blondie enters a prize-winning Great Dane in a dog show, which causes problems for Dagwood—whose important business client also has a dog in competition. With Penny Singleton, Arthur Lake, Larry Simms, Jonathan Hale, Danny Mummert, William Frawley and Edgar Kennedy.
VHS: S20176. $14.95.
Frank Strayer, USA, 1941, 75 mins.

Blondie Knows Best
Dagwood causes a lot of problems when he momentarily pretends to be his boss, J.C. Dithers (Jonathan Hale). One of the Three Stooges, Shemp Howard, turns in a hilarious cameo as an eccentric process server. With Penny Singleton, Arthur Lake, Larry Simms, Marjorie Kent, Steven Geray and Jerome Cowan.
VHS: S20175. $14.95.
Abby Berlin, USA, 1946, 69 mins.

Blondie Takes a Vacation
Blondie and her family purchase a failing mountaintop resort, setting in motion a bizarre succession of comic vignettes and madcap anarchy which comes naturally to the Bumstead family. With Penny Singleton, Arthur Lake and Larry Simms.
VHS: S20177. $14.95.
Frank Strayer, USA, 1939, 68 mins.

Blondie's Blessed Event
Biology and madcap farce intersect as Dagwood inadvertently causes a minor sensation during an important convention while Blondie awaits the arrival of a beautiful, bouncing girl. With Penny Singleton, Arthur Lake, Larry Simms, Marjorie Kent, William Frawley and Danny Mummert.
VHS: S20179. $14.95.
Frank Strayer, USA, 1942, 69 mins.

Blues Busters
Huntz Hall stars as Sach Debussy Jones in this tuneful Bowery Boys comedy. Louie's Sweet Shop is turned into a popular night spot when a tonsillectomy makes a surprise singing star out of Hall. This riles local nightclub owner Craig Stevens who sends Adele Jergens to distract the man with the golden throat. With Leo Gorcey, Billy Benedict, Gabriel Dell, and Phyllis Coates.
VHS: S15828. $14.95.
William Beaudine, USA, 1950, 67 mins.

Bob Hope:
America's Ambassador of Comedy
Having entertained U.S. troops for more than 50 years, Bob Hope has become the country's most beloved good-will ambassador. This glorious profile spans the highlights of his career, starting with his early days in vaudeville, to the "Road" films, to his pioneering variety specials for television. Packed with one-liners, world leaders, and history-breaking moments. 40 mins.
VHS: S15842. $14.99.

Boeing Boeing
Tony Curtis is paired opposite a toned-down Jerry Lewis in this elegant farce about an American journalist in Paris juggling multiple relationships, with frantic, madcap results. With Thelma Ritter, Dany Saval and Christine Schmidtmer.
VHS: S17977. $14.95.
Laser: LD75289. $34.98.
John Rich, USA, 1965, 102 mins.

The Bohemian Girl
Laurel and Hardy team up for this monumental comic effort as gypsies who find themselves trapped with a wholly unexpected responsibility. They must raise a young girl despite their limited means. A whimsical short, *Below Zero*, is also included.
VHS: S21534. $19.95.
James W. Horne, USA, 1936, 90 mins.

Bonnie Scotland
Laurel and Hardy in a spoof of the Gary Cooper film *Lives of a Bengal Lancer*.
VHS: S03451. $19.98.
James W. Horne, USA, 1935, 81 mins.

Bonnie Scotland/Pick a Star
The jovial wit and physical humor of Laurel and Hardy are represented in two of their signature works, James Horne's 1935 *Bonnie Scotland*, about their adventures in a Scottish military regiment stationed in India. Edward Sedgwick's (1937) puts the two in the background, focusing on an aspiring young actress (Rosina Lawrence) in search of fame. Includes the theatrical trailers for both films. 157 mins.
Laser: LD71658. $39.98.

Boy Did I Get a Wrong Number
Would Bob Hope lie? A comical farce made by Mr. Ski Nose late in his career that places him between Elke Sommer and Phyllis Diller. Remember this is Phyllis Diller prior to plastic surgery. Who do you think Bob is going to want to get chummy with? Billed as "the picture that gets you where you laugh."
VHS: S11270. $19.95.
George Marshall, USA, 1966, 99 mins.

Boy Meets Girl
A comically inspired satire of Hollywood artifice stars James Cagney and Pat O'Brien as screenwriters who concoct an elaborate scheme to build up the talent and skills of an unborn child whose mother is a commissary waitress. With Marie Wilson, Ralph Bellamy and Ronald Reagan. "It bounces from one hilarious absurdity to another with all the resilience of a rubber ball" (*Monthly Film Bulletin*).
VHS: S19037. $19.98.
Lloyd Bacon, USA, 1938, 86 mins.

Bride Came C.O.D.
Bette Davis, James Cagney, Harry Davenport star in this comedy about a charter pilot who kidnaps an heiress and then crash lands with her in the desert.
VHS: S13393. $19.98.
William Keighley, USA, 1941, 92 mins.

Buck Privates
Abbott and Costello turn the U.S. Army upside down in this hilarious World War II comedy that made them stars. The Andrews Sisters sing "Boogie Woogie Bugle Boy."
VHS: S05924. $14.98.
Arthur Lubin, USA, 1941, 84 mins.

Buck Privates Come Home
This engaging movie has Abbott and Costello returning home, adjusting to civilian life, and caught in a plan to smuggle a young European child into the country. With Tom Brown, Joan Fulton, Nat Pendleton and Beverly Simmons.
VHS: S17262. $14.98.
Charles Barton, USA, 1947, 77 mins.

Bud Abbott and Lou Costello Meet Jerry Seinfeld
Television star Jerry Seinfeld hosts this look at the comic duo famous for skits like "Who's on First?" There are clips, behind-the-scenes footage and interviews with friends and family of these two stars. 46 mins.
VHS: S24390. $14.98.

Bud Abbott and Lou Costello Meet the Killer
The comic duo reveal their sleuthing side in this thriller that features Boris Karloff as a strange hypnotist. Lou is a bellboy who happens upon a corpse. Fortunately, Bud is there to help him through the ensuing wacky hysteria.
VHS: S24389. $14.98.
Charles Barton, USA, 1949, 84 mins.

The Bullfighters
When Laurel and Hardy go South, everyone goes into hysterics over America's favorite pair of stumblebums. USA, 1945, 61 mins.
VHS: S04606. $29.98.

Buona Sera, Mrs. Campbell
It's the eve of a 20th anniversary reunion of an American World War II squadron. A beautiful Italian woman (Gina Lollobrigida), who's collected money from three flyers, each of whom believes he's the father of her child, is thrown into a panic when her daughter insists on her meeting her actual father. With Phil Silvers, Peter Lawford and Telly Savalas.
VHS: S18010. $19.98.
Laser: LD72166. $34.95.
Melvin Frank, USA, 1968, 113 mins.

Cactus Flower
Goldie Hawn won an Oscar for her role as the ditzy salesgirl pursuing philandering dentist Walter Matthau. Based on the Broadway play. Ingrid Bergman plays Matthau's repressed nurse. With Jack Weston, Rick Lenz and Vito Scotti. A comical romp about acting your age and finding someone to love in your own age bracket.
Laser: LD75495. $34.95.
Gene Saks, USA, 1969, 103 mins.

The Caddy
Jerry Lewis is a very shy golfer who pretends to be a caddy because he can't play the game before a crowd. He tries to coach Dean Martin to play as his championship proxy. Expect a lot of dropped clubs. Dino sings "That's Amore". With Donna Reed, Fred Clark and Barbara Bates. B&W.
VHS: S06989. $19.95.
Norman Taurog, USA, 1953, 95 mins.

California Suite
Neil Simon adapts his Broadway play for the movies as he presents four short stories of guests at the Beverly Hills Hotel. Highlight is Maggie Smith and Michael Caine as a bickering British couple in town for the Academy Awards. Other guests include Jane Fonda, Alan Alda, Elaine May, Walter Matthau, Bill Cosby and Richard Pryor. Smith won a best supporting Oscar for her part.
VHS: S10374. $19.95.
Herbert Ross, USA, 1978, 103 mins.

Call Me Bwana
Passing himself off as an expert on African affairs, Bob Hope is unwittingly exploited by the CIA to recover a strategically important space capsule. Edie Adams goes along for the ride, and they encounter a mysterious couple played by Anita Ekberg and Lionel Davies.
VHS: S19561. $19.98.
Gordon Douglas, USA, 1963, 103 mins.

Casanova Brown
A hilarious social comedy about an estranged couple (Gary Cooper and Teresa Wright) who discover that she is pregnant. Cooper orchestrates an elaborate scheme to steal the baby upon learning she wants to put it up for adoption. With Frank Morgan, Anita Louise and Isobel Olsom.
VHS: S19490. $19.98.
Sam Wood, USA, 1944, 94 mins.

Casanova's Big Night
Bob Hope at his funniest, as a timid tailor who impersonates the great lover Casanova. With Joan Fontaine, Audrey Dalton, Basil Rathbone, Raymond Burr.
VHS: S04427. $14.95.
Norman Z. McLeod, USA, 1954, 86 mins.

Catered Affair
Gore Vidal's adaptation of a Paddy Chayefsky comedy about the daughter of a New York taxicab driver whose mother insists on a bigger wedding than the family can afford. Bette Davis stars with Ernest Borgnine and Debbie Reynolds.
VHS: S13394. $19.98.
Richard Brooks, USA, 1956, 93 mins.

Caught in the Draft
This Bob Hope vehicle casts the comedian as a gilded movie star trying desperately to avoid national service. Hope inadvertently enlists himself, with some peculiar and funny consequences. With Dorothy Lamour, Lynne Overman and Eddie Bracken.
VHS: S18548. $14.98.
David Butler, USA, 1941, 82 mins.

Chances Are
When Cybil Shepherd's murdered husband is reincarnated as Robert Downey Jr., she finds herself falling for a mysterious younger man. Downey has little recollection of his past life but he is willing to see what the future will bring. A romantic comedy with a twist set in Washington, D.C. With Ryan O'Neal and Mary Stuart Masterson as the lovelorn best friend and the attractive daughter Downey never had.
VHS: S11167. $14.95.
Emile Ardolino, USA, 1989, 108 mins.

Chasing Laughter
Three Hal Roach comic shorts, featuring Charley Chase, showcase his frenetic, fast-paced style, in *Mum's the Word*, *Tell 'Em Nothing* and *Mama Behave*. With an organ soundtrack by David Knudtsen.
VHS: S19597. $29.95.
Hal Roach, USA, 1926, 60 mins.

Chasing Those Depression Blues
Four comic shorts that must have made them laugh in the '30s. They include *Dental Follies* with Pinky Lee, *Any Day in Hollywood* with Ben Turpin, *Money on Your Life* with Danny Kaye, and *Art in the Raw*, that teams Edgar Kennedy with Franklin Pangborn. B&W. USA, 1933-38, 58 mins.
VHS: S05454. $24.95.

The Cheap Detective
Peter Falk, Ann-Margret, Eileen Brennan, Sid Caesar, Stockard Channing, James Coco, Dom DeLuise, Louise Fletcher, John Houseman, Madeline Kahn and Fernando Lamas are just some of the stars featured in this madcap spoof of 40's style detective stories. A private dick investigates a strange case littered with molls, mysterious women and double-crossing eccentrics. Written by Neil Simon.
Laser: LD75006. $39.95.
Robert Moore, USA, 1978, 92 mins.

Check and Doublecheck
Join Amos and Andy, the most popular radio comedy team of the Thirties, on a hilarious outing in their one and only motion picture. Duke Ellington co-stars in this outrageous comedy and also plays some of his classic tunes.
VHS: S13992. $19.98.
Melville Brown, USA, 1930, 85 mins.

Christmas in Connecticut
Barbara Stanwyck, an unmarried recipe-writer, must whip up a phony family to attend a holiday dinner that is designed to impress her tradition-minded boss (Sidney Greenstreet). Guests at the table include Dennis Morgan, S.Z. "Cuddles" Sakall and Una O'Connor. B&W.
VHS: S04978. $14.98.
Laser: LD70184. $34.98.
Peter Godfrey, USA, 1945, 101 mins.

A Chump at Oxford
Laurel and Hardy earn the opportunity to receive "the finest education money can buy" at Oxford University. They end up getting more than they bargained for as hilarious predicaments ensue.
VHS: S13864. $14.98.
Alfred Goulding, USA, 1940, 63 mins.

Cinderfella
Jerry Lewis transforms the old fable by becoming Cinderfella. In his Bel Air home an evil stepmother and two scheming stepbrothers keep Lewis occupied with housework. Suddenly his life is transformed by the magical appearance of a Fairy Godfather. Can a princess be far behind? This comedy shows Lewis at his best.
VHS: $21738. $14.98.
Jerry Lewis, USA, 1960, 85 mins.

Clipped Wings
The Bowery Boys unknowingly enlist in the Army Air Corps while visiting a chum and discover the women's barracks are off limits. They also discover a nest of Nazi spies much to the FBI's delight. With Leo Gorcey, Huntz Hall, Philip Van Zandt, Todd Karns, Lyle Talbot and June Vincent.
VHS: $15829. $14.98.
Edward Bernds, USA, 1953, 62 mins.

The Cocoanuts
The hilarious, never-before-released first film of the Marx Brothers, shot on a New York sound stage, with some terrific scenes, including the "Why a duck?" routine, a hilarious auction, and a wonderful classic "viaduct" routine. With Groucho, Harpo, Chico and Zeppo.
VHS: $09458. $19.98.
Joseph Santley/Robert Florey, USA, 1929, 96 mins.

Come Blow Your Horn
Bachelor Frank Sinatra decides to stop playing the field in this jaunty screen version of Neil Simon's first stage hit. With Jill St. John, Tony Bill and Molly Picon.
VHS: $15159. $14.95.
Bud Yorkin, USA, 1963, 115 mins.

Coming to America
Eddie Murphy is a spoiled African prince in search of a suitable mate. He begins his search in New York City in the section known as Queens. Where better to find a royal partner? He poses as a poor student and tries to win the heart of a fast food manager's daughter, with comic results. With John Amos, Arsenio Hall and James Earl Jones. Murphy plays several roles in special makeup. How many can you spot?
VHS: $08353. $14.95.
Laser: LD75173. $34.98.
John Landis, USA, 1988, 116 mins.

Copacabana
Groucho Marx and Carmen Miranda! What more needs to be said?
VHS: $00269. $19.98.
Laser: CLV. LD71978. $29.98.
Alfred E. Green, USA, 1947, 91 mins.

Court Jester
Danny Kaye finds himself impersonating a medieval fool in this complicated comedy classic. A plot is afoot to kill the king and that's no joke to a loyal subject. If you were wondering which brew is true, the pellet with the poison is in the vessel with the pestle. Cast includes Glynis Johns, Basil Rathbone, Angela Lansbury, Cecil Parker, Mildred Natwick and John Carradine.
VHS: $10811. $14.95.
Laser: LD75357. $29.98.
N. Panama/M. Frank, USA, 1956, 101 mins.

The Courtship of Eddie's Father
Little Ronny Howard plays Eddie, the son of widower Glenn Ford, who is determined to find a suitable wife for his dad and a wonderful mother for himself. Shirley Jones, Stella Stevens and Dina Merrill play the blonde, redhead and brunette respectively as they each fall prey to Eddie's pint-sized precocity.
VHS: $14556. $19.98.
Vincente Minnelli, USA, 1962, 117 mins.

Cousins
The American version of the 1975 French film Cousin, Cousine from director Jean-Charles Tacchella that proved to be a big hit in the U.S. Ted Danson and Isabella Rossellini play nice people married to mates Sean Young and William Peterson, who are involved in an affair. To get even, they pretend to become involved physically and find much to their surprise they are truly falling in love. A robust family comedy about fidelity. With Lloyd Bridges and Norma Aleandro.
VHS: $10355. $19.95.
Laser: LD75175. $34.98.
Joel Schumacker, USA, 1989, 110 mins.

Cracking Up
This Jerry Lewis comedy is also known as Smorgasbord, the Swedish word that loosely translates as "more food than you should eat at one sitting." Lewis plays Warren Nefron, a most unlucky person when it comes being employed. In a series of flashback sketches he informs his psychiatrist Herb Edelman why he can't hold on to a job. With Foster Brooks, Buddy Lester, Zane Buzby, Dick Butkus, Sammy Davis Jr. and Milton Berle as a female patient.
VHS: $16460. $19.98.
Jerry Lewis, USA, 1983, 91 mins.

Cross My Heart
Martin Short and Annette O'Toole star as two modern singles trying desperately not to screw up what seems like a possible perfect relationship. They are about to embark on the critical third date and each has a pile of personal secrets that include a seven-year-old child and being fired. A very funny comedy with lots of charm.
VHS: $07143. $14.95.
Armyan Bernstein, USA, 1987, 91 mins.

Crossing Delancey
A warm and genuinely witty modern romance. Amy Irving is a bright, single Jewish woman living in New York who is infatuated with a notorious writer (Jeroen Krabbe) and fears she may be settling for less if she becomes involved with a nice man who sells pickles (Peter Riegert). With Sylvia Miles as the matchmaker.
VHS: $09804. $19.95.
Laser: LD74692. $24.98.
Joan Micklin Silver, USA, 1988, 97 mins.

Dance with Me, Henry
In their final film together, Abbott & Costello star in this comedy about an amusement park owner (Costello) who tends to adopt strays—children, animals, and even Uncle Bud, a conniving gambler (Abbott) with some rather substantial racing debts that manage to pull the two of them into the rough realm of gangsters, corruption and gangland murder. USA, 1956, 80 mins.
VHS: $15423. $19.98.

The Daring Young Man
Joe E. Brown stars as a meek weakling who tries to enlist in the armed forces. He soon becomes mixed up with foreign spies and a radio controlled bowling ball that could affect the security of our nation. Silly and great fun. With Marguerite Chapman, William Wright, Roger Clark. USA, 74 mins.
VHS: $15382. $24.95.

Dave
Ivan Reitman's engaging political satire about Dave Kovic (Kevin Kline), the owner of an employment agency, who bears an uncanny resemblance to the president. When the president is felled by a massive stroke, two Machiavellian political players install Kovic as the president's stand-in. With Sigourney Weaver, Frank Langella, Kevin Dunn, Ving Rhames, and Ben Kingsley as the vice president. Capra-esque.
VHS: $19528. $19.98.
Laser: LD71922. $34.98.
Ivan Reitman, USA, 1993, 107 mins.

A Day at the Races
Those zany boys are at it again! Groucho is Dr. Hugo Z. Hackenbush, a veterinarian put in charge of a sanitarium for wealthy hypochondriacs. He gets involved with two from the racetrack: Harpo the jockey and Chico, a vendor of bad racing tips.
VHS: $02594. $19.95.
Laser: LD70553. $25.98.
Sam Wood, USA, 1937, 111 mins.

Dead Heat on a Merry-Go-Round
James Coburn stars as Eli Kotch, a captivating rogue and full-time con man, in this comical crime caper. In prison, Coburn cleverly seduces an attractive psychologist to win parole.
VHS: $09393. $69.95.
Bernard Girard, USA, 1966, 107 mins.

Dead Men Don't Wear Plaid
Steve Martin stars in this Carl Reiner comic salute to the detective movies of the 1940's. As Rigby Reardon, private eye, he is hired to solve a perplexing mystery that holds the fate of Terre Haute, Indiana, in the balance. Martin interacts with old film clips. A great gimmick and fun for film buffs. With Rachel Ward and Carl Reiner.
VHS: $05542. $19.95.
Carl Reiner, USA, 1982, 89 mins.

Dean Martin & Jerry Lewis Comedy Collection
A collection of three Martin & Lewis films: My Friend Irma (1949), Jumping Jacks (1952) and Scared Stiff (1953).
VHS: $18678. $59.85.

Defending Your Life
Yet another masterpiece from America's finest comedic filmmaker, Albert Brooks (Real Life, Modern Romance, Lost in America). Meryl Streep, Lee Grant, Rip Torn and Buck Henry co-star in this hilarious romantic fantasy about judgment in the afterlife. A funny, beautifully conceived and often quite touching film.
VHS: $15052. $19.98.
Albert Brooks, USA, 1991, 112 mins.

Delicate Delinquent
Jerry Lewis, in his first movie without Dean Martin, plays Sidney Pythias, a frightened janitor being terrorized by a youth gang. During a rumble he is mistaken for a gang member and is given to Darren McGavin to straighten out. With Martha Hyer, Richard Bakalyan and Rocky Marciano as himself.
VHS: $12848. $19.95.
Jerry Lewis, USA, 1957, 100 mins.

Desk Set
One of the true wonders of Hollywood—a top notch comedy with sparks between Spencer Tracy as the efficiency expert and Katharine Hepburn as the intelligent researcher in a TV network. Sparks fly as Tracy and Hepburn mix business with pleasure.
VHS: $11561. $19.98.
Laser: LD70945. $19.98.
Walter Lang, USA, 1957, 103 mins.

Devil Dogs of the Air
A screen comedy about the rivalry of two legendary pilots. James Cagney is an irreverent, selfish pilot interested in the Marines who receives instructions from his idol (Pat O'Brien). Both are drawn to the same carefree woman (Margaret Lindsay). "A loud and roughneck screen comedy, both amusing and exciting" (Andre Sennwald).
VHS: $19040. $19.98.
Lloyd Bacon, USA, 1935, 86 mins.

The Devil's Brother
Laurel and Hardy star as bandits who try to rob the most notorious highwayman of them all: Fra Diavolo, the Devil's Brother! Brilliant gags, lavish sets, and sublime music from Auber's operetta. Co-starring Thelma Todd. USA, 1933, 90 mins.
VHS: $15419. $19.98.

Dirty Rotten Scoundrels
Steve Martin and Michael Caine occupy the roles played by Marlon Brando and David Niven in this very faithful and very comic remake of the 1964 comical farce, Bedtime Story. They play a pair of con men on the French Riviera battling to see who can first swindle money from an American soap queen. With Glenne Headly in the Shirley Jones role. Also Barbara Harris as Lady Fanny of Omaha.
VHS: $00400. $19.98.
Laser: CLV. LD71715. $19.98.
Frank Oz, USA, 1988, 110 mins.

Disorderly Orderly
A crazy Frank Tashlin comedy with Jerry Lewis as an orderly who nearly destroys a nursing home. With Glenda Farrell, Susan Oliver, Everett Sloane.
VHS: $04429. $14.95.
Frank Tashlin, USA, 1964, 90 mins.

Distinguished Gentleman
Eddie Murphy portrays a con man who makes his way into the Congress. Once there he develops a sense of responsibility. Murphy shows he can still get a laugh with just a look. Features Lane Smith, Sheryl Lee Ralph, Joe Don Baker and Charles Dutton.
VHS: $21447. $94.95.
Jonathan Lynn, USA, 1992, 122 mins.

Divorce American Style
Dick Van Dyke and Debbie Reynolds are the central couple in this manic comedy featuring Lee Grant, Jason Robards, Van Johnson and Jean Simmons. When a couple opt for divorce, they don't contemplate all the hassles which the single life entails. In the end, after watching the farcical mismatches that unfold around them, they both pick the most unlikely way out.
VHS: $27186. $19.95.
Bud Yorkin, USA, 1967, 109 mins.

Doc Hollywood
Michael J. Fox stars as Dr. Ben Stone, a self-centered, ambitious physician who was on his way to interview for a staff position in the office of a Beverly Hills plastic surgeon until a car accident stranded him in the very small town of Grady, South Carolina. With Julie Warner, Woody Harrelson, David Ogden Stiers and Bridget Fonda.
VHS: $15701. $19.98.
Michael Caton-Jones, USA, 1991, 104 mins.

Don Juan DeMarco
Marlon Brando, Johnny Depp and Faye Dunaway star in this comedy about a man who is either the greatest lover the world has ever known or just a kook. Depp is great as the would be Don Juan, while Brando and Dunaway make a great pair, who are touched by the ravings of this romantic obsessive.
VHS: $26278. $19.98.
Laser: LD75068. $39.99.
Jeremy Leven, USA, 1995, 92 mins.

Down and Out in Beverly Hills
Based on the same source as Renoir's Boudou Saved from Drowning, director Mazursky has transplanted the story to Beverly Hills, starring Richard Dreyfuss and Bette Midler as the couple whose lives are changed with the arrival of Nick Nolte. With Little Richard.
VHS: $00362. $19.95.
Paul Mazursky, USA, 1986, 103 mins.

Dragnet
Dan Aykroyd in the Jack Webb role provides comic parody, featuring Tom Hanks in the Henry Morgan role of side-kick.
VHS: $06037. $14.95.
Tom Mankiewicz, USA, 1987, 106 mins.

Dream a Little Dream
Another body switching comedy. This time golden agers Jason Robards and Piper Laurie are transported by a mystical ceremony into the bodies of two unaware 15-year-olds played by Corey Feldman and Meredith Salenger. Only Feldman knows the truth of the situation. With Harry Dean Stanton, Susan Blakely and Corey Haim as a few of the folks trying to figure out the change in behavior.
VHS: $10339. $89.95.
Marc Rocco, USA, 1989, 99 mins.

Dream Team
Michael Keaton heads an all-star cast in this comedy about four mental patients who are separated from their therapist on the way to a baseball game. A chronic liar with a violent streak, Billy (Michael Keaton) finds himself on the loose in New York City with his fellow group therapy patients Christopher Lloyd (a clean freak), Peter Boyle (a former advertising executive with a Christ complex), and Stephen Furst (a near-catatonic couch potato).
VHS: $10451. $89.95.
Howard Zieff, USA, 1989, 113 mins.

Duchess and the Dirtwater Fox
Goldie Hawn plays a hooker called Duchess and George Segal is a saddle tramp named Fox. Together they romp through the Old West in search of a dollar. A comedy/western for serious followers only.
VHS: $13018. $19.98.
Laser: LD72219. $59.98.
Melvin Frank, USA, 1976, 104 mins.

Duck Soup
The most immortal film of the Marx Brothers! About the small nation of Fredonia, which has given Groucho complete power to restore order. Political satire and madness both. With Margaret Dumont and Louis Calhern.
VHS: $02018. $19.95.
Leo McCarey, USA, 1933, 70 mins.

Dutchess of Idaho
Slipping a fur-lined parka over her trademark bathing suit, Hollywood's favorite mermaid, Esther Williams, hits the snowy slopes of Idaho's famous Sun Valley in this charming light comedy. Along with Van Johnson, Paula Raymond and John Lund, Esther swims and skis her way into romance.
VHS: $16604. $19.98.
Robert Z. Leonard, USA, 1950, 98 mins.

Eating Raoul
Characterized as a "dextrous, beautifully timed, macabre comedy of manners which tackles kinky sex, economics, gourmet cooking, modern marriage, and even cannibalism," by David Chute in Film Comment, Eating Raoul features a married couple who, poor but proud, are bent on destroying the evil that surrounds them in the swinging singles complex in which they live.
VHS: $00392. $19.98.
Paul Bartel, USA, 1981, 90 mins.

Edgar Kennedy Slow Burn Festival
Three gems selected from the many two-reelers of this master of the slow burn. They include Poisoned Ivory, Edgar Hamlet, and A Clean Sweep. Edgar is aggravated by doctors, in-laws and vacuum cleaners in this trio of time-tested laugh-getters. USA, 1934-37, 59 mins.
VHS: $05460. $24.95.

The Egg and I
This movie may have starred Fred MacMurray and Claudette Colbert as a young couple trying to make a living from a chicken farm, but it will always be remembered as the film debut of Ma and Pa Kettle. Marjorie Main and Percy Kilbride kept up the corn pone act for a total of ten films. Amusing comedy based on the bestselling book by Betty MacDonald.
VHS: $03625. $14.98.
Laser: LD70027. $34.98.
Chester Erskine, USA, 1947, 108 mins.

The Errand Boy
Jerry Lewis stars in this madcap comedy about an errand boy who is actually a spy, watching his fellow employees to gauge their efficiency. The only problem is this spy can't do anything without setting off wild mishaps. Even the simplest of tasks, like getting the car washed or eating lunch, leads to disaster.
VHS: $21737. $14.98.
Jerry Lewis, USA, 1961, 95 mins.

The Family Jewels
Jerry Lewis plays seven (count 'em, seven) different roles in this comedy about a little girl with a big inheritance. Donna Butterworth is the little charmer who needs seven Jerry's to act as her guardians. With Sebastian Cabot, Robert Strauss and Anne Baxter.
VHS: $06988. $19.95.
Jerry Lewis, USA, 1965, 100 mins.

Fancy Pants
Bob Hope convinces Lucille Ball that he is a real British lord and she invites him back to New Mexico to meet the locals. A musical comedy remake of Ruggles of Red Gap. With Bruce Cabot, Eric Blore and John Alexander as Teddy Roosevelt. Songs include "Home Cookin'" and the title song.
VHS: $12849. $19.95.
Laser: LD75193. $34.98.
George Marshall, USA, 1950, 92 mins.

Father Goose
Cary Grant and Leslie Caron in a comedy of wits which has Grant protecting Caron and seven schoolgirls on a South Seas island from the Japanese during World War II.
VHS: $02978. $19.95.
Ralph Nelson, USA, 1964, 116 mins.

Father of the Bride
Spencer Tracy is the title character, a successful lawyer who is totally unprepared for the aggravation of a big wedding. Elizabeth Taylor is the apple of his eye scheduled to marry Don Taylor. A perceptive comedy with Joan Bennett, Billie Burke and Leo G. Carroll. B&W.
VHS: $07009. $19.95.
Laser: LD70195. $34.98.
Vincente Minnelli, USA, 1950, 93 mins.

Father Was a Fullback
Fred MacMurray, Maureen O'Hara, Rudy Vallee and Natalie Wood star in this family comedy about a football coach with plenty of worries. Whether on the gridiron, or at home, he needs all his strategic capabilities just to stay ahead of either game.
VHS: $25975. $14.98.
John M. Stahl, USA, 1949, 99 mins.

Father's Little Dividend
The gruff but lovable Spencer Tracy stars in this delightful comedy about the true-to-life family foibles which accompany the birth of a first grandchild. Featuring the same cast as Father of the Bride, one of MGM's most popular films of 1950.
VHS: $15024. $19.98.
Vincente Minnelli, USA, 1951, 83 mins.

Fear of a Black Hat
In this outrageous comedy, documentary filmmaker Nina Blackburn (Kasi Lemmons) infiltrates the world of rap's most controversial band, Fear of a Black Hat. Nina goes behind the scenes at recording studios, on stage, and even "hangs" with them on the street searching for the answer to elusive questions like: Why have all their managers met with tragic, violent deaths? How many rappers are named Ice? And what about those hats?
VHS: $22914. $94.95.
Rusty Cundieff, USA, 1994, 85 mins.

Female
This invigorating comedy was ahead of its time. It portrays the life of the strong-willed, feminist president (Ruth Chatterton) of a car company whose life is jolted by the appearance of a brash, independent nonconformist (George Brent). With Ruth Donnelly, Ferdinand Gottschalk and Douglas Dumbrille.
VHS: $18126. $19.98.
Michael Curtiz, USA, 1933, 60 mins.

american film 137

A Few Moments with Buster Keaton and Laurel & Hardy

Laurel and Hardy are featured in a color short produced by the Department of Agriculture Forest Service. They are reminded by an off-screen voice how important wood is to the war effort. The other two segments feature Buster Keaton doing commercials for "Simon Pure Beer" and performing a silent routine on the Ed Sullivan Show. USA, 1943-63, 17 mins.
VHS: S05432. $9.95.

Fifth Avenue Girl

A "social comedy" with Ginger Rogers as a homeless girl taken in by a disconcerted millionaire, disrupting his entire household. With Franklin Pangborn.
VHS: S10654. $19.98.
Gregory La Cava, USA, 1939, 83 mins.

Flying Deuces

Some of Laurel and Hardy's best routines. They vacation in Paris, where Ollie falls in love, and finding out his girlfriend is the wife of a legionnaire, they join the Foreign Legion. The result? Total mayhem.
VHS: S00453. $19.95.
Edward Sutherland, USA, 1939, 67 mins.

For Auld Lang Syne

Four comic shorts from the '30's featuring four differing views of humor. The Marx Brothers preview *Monkey Business* for theatre owners. Jacques Tati teams with Rhum in *Gai Dimanche* (*Jolly Sunday*), as pickpockets on an outing. Harry Langdon gets in trouble in a seedy bar when he orders milk. And to conclude, a star-studded tribute to Will Rogers. USA/France, 1932-37, 46 mins.
VHS: S05434. $24.95.

Forsaking All Others

Clark Gable is quietly in love with Joan Crawford, even though she is engaged to Robert Montgomery. When her intended leaves her at the altar to marry someone else, Clark makes his move. With Billie Burke, Charles Butterworth, Frances Drake, Rosalind Russell and Arthur Treacher.
VHS: S16449. $19.98.
W.S. Van Dyke, USA, 1934, 83 mins.

Freshman

An unexpectedly wonderful comedy from Andrew Bergman (*The In-Laws*) that concerns the extracurricular and probably illegal education of a young film student played by Matthew Broderick. Marlon Brando steals the movie with a comic send-up of his role in *The Godfather*. He even ice-skates. Also making a good impression are Bruno Kirby, Penelope Ann Miller, Maximilian Schell and Bert Parks. Yes, Bert Parks. One of the few movies daring enough to co-star a komodo dragon.
VHS: S13317. $14.95.
Andrew Bergman, USA, 1990, 102 mins.

Fuller Brush Girl

A reworking of 1948 Red Skelton vehicle tailored for Lucille Ball's frantic gifts about an ambitious saleswoman inadvertently mixed up with some thieves. With Eddie Albert, Jeff Donnell and Jerome Cowan.
VHS: S18857. $19.95.
Lloyd Bacon, USA, 1950, 93 mins.

Fuller Brush Man

Red Skelton is cast as a struggling door-to-door salesman caught in an intricate murder mystery. With Janet Blair, Don McGuire and Adele Jergens.
VHS: S18858. $14.95.
Frank Tashlin, USA, 1948, 93 mins.

The Fuller Brush Man/ The Fuller Brush Girl

Frank Tashlin penned the screenplays for this pair of wacky films. First Red Skelton is the door-to-door salesman who is accused of murdering his ex-boss. Then Lucille Ball takes her turn going house to house selling cosmetics and finds herself entangled in a double murder. Also features Eddie Albert.
Laser: LD75005. $49.95.
S. Sylvan Simon/Lloyd Bacon, USA, 1948/1950, 178 mins.

Funny Bones

Jerry Lewis is the famous father of a man (Oliver Platt) struggling to get out from under his parent's shadow. This scenario makes for a great comedy full of slapstick and warm humor. It all begins when the younger man makes the mistake of going back to his small hometown for inspiration.
VHS: S26205. $99.99.
Laser: LD75066. $39.99.
Peter Chelsom, USA, 1995, 128 mins.

Funny Guys and Gals of the Talkies

Four shorts: *Golf Specialist* starring W.C. Fields, *Pardon My Pups* with Shirley Temple, *Girls Will Be Boys* with Charlotte Greenwood; and *Groucho Marx, Carole Landis*, which is footage from a radio broadcast during which the two sing.
VHS: S04103. $29.95.

The Gazebo

When a television writer (Glenn Ford) is blackmailed by a mysterious figure with compromising photographs of his Broadway star wife (Debbie Reynolds), he kills the man and disposes of the body under his backyard gazebo. Unfortunately, the body refuses to stay dead. With Carl Reiner, John McGiver, Mabel Albertson, Doro Merande and ZaSu Pitts.
VHS: S20203. $19.98.
George Marshall, USA, 1959, 102 mins.

The Geisha Boy

Jerry Lewis is the Great Wooley, a traveling magician entertaining soldiers in the Far East. Along the way he adopts an orphaned Japanese boy and falls in love with a lovely woman. This warm comedy is a great treat.
VHS: S25834. $14.95.
Frank Tashlin, USA, 1958, 98 mins.

General Spanky

Comedy runs wild when Our Gang's Spanky runs his own ragamuffin Civil War Army. Alfalfa and Buckwheat are among the recruits who use clowning tactics instead of military tactics with Union troops approach.
VHS: S14559. $19.98.
Laser: LD74671. $34.98.
Fred Newmeyer, USA, 1936, 73 mins.

The Ghost Breakers

Bob Hope is a radio commentator who inadvertently becomes part of a gothic murder investigation, set in an atmospheric Cuban mansion Paulette Goddard has inherited. With Richard Carlson, Paul Lukas and Anthony Quinn.
VHS: S18546. $14.98.
George Marshall, USA, 1940, 85 mins.

Ghost Chasers

The Bowery Boys break up a phony seance racket. Huntz Hall helped in this endeavor by a real ghost that only he can see. Spooky stuff, starring Leo Gorcey, David Gorcey, Bernard Gorcey, Billy Benedict and Lela Bliss as Margo the Medium.
VHS: S15832. $14.98.
William Beaudine, USA, 1951, 67 mins.

Ghostbusters

Dan Aykroyd and Harold Ramis wrote and star in this wild flick about a manic band of parapsychologists ridding Manhattan of bizarre apparitions. Bill Murray steals the show, Sigourney Weaver goes along for the ride. Cinematography by Laszlo Kovacs.
VHS: S00498. $19.95.
Laser: CAV. LD70368. $99.95.
Laser: CLV. LD70369. $49.95.
Ivan Reitman, USA, 1984, 105 mins.

Girl Can't Help It

Raucous comedy with Jayne Mansfield as the "dumb bombshell" and Edmond O'Brien as her retired racketeer boyfriend. Jayne is trying to get into show biz, Tom Ewell is the comic talent agent helping out. With Fats Domino, The Platters, Gene Vincent.
VHS: S00503. $59.98.
Frank Tashlin, USA, 1956, 99 mins.

A Girl, A Guy and A Gob

A classic Ball comedy where Lucy is caught between a wealthy snob and an amorous sailor. A *Catch-22* of a different color supervised by Harold Lloyd.
VHS: S10648. $19.98.
Richard Wallace, USA, 1940, 91 mins.

Give Me a Sailor

Bob Hope, Betty Grable and Martha Raye are at the center of this complicated romantic farce. Hope loves Grable but needs to enlist the aid of Raye to get Grable's attention. Unfortunately, Hope must agree to help Raye woo her brother, Jack Whiting.
VHS: S25529. $14.98.
Elliott Nugent, USA, 1938, 78 mins.

Gladiator

Mild-mannered Joe E. Brown takes serum which turns him into a major he-man. Full of comic turns with lots of Brown's physical humor and slapstick.
VHS: S08880. $24.95.
Edward Sedgwick, USA, 1938, 65 mins.

The Glass Bottom Boat

Doris Day gets reeled in by handsome fisherman Rod Taylor while moonlighting as a mermaid on Catalina Island. Also starring Dom DeLuise and Paul Lynde.
VHS: S15244. $19.98.
Laser: LD72175. $34.98.
Frank Tashlin, USA, 1966, 110 mins.

A Global Affair

Bob Hope is hilarious as a United Nations official who is saddled with an abandoned child and is promptly seduced by an international bevy of beautiful women who want the child for themselves. With Yvonne DeCarlo, Robert Sterling and John McGiver.
VHS: S19562. $19.98.
Jack Arnold, USA, 1964, 84 mins.

Go West

The Marx Brothers clown around the sagebrush circuit and ride a train where no iron horse has gone before. Groucho is S. Quentin Quale, a con man trying to flimflam the Panello brothers, Rusty (Harpo) and Joe (Chico). With John Carroll and Diana Lewis. B&W.
VHS: S06979. $19.95.
Edward Buzzell, USA, 1940, 81 mins.

Go West, Young Man

Mae West is a privileged movie queen stranded in a desolate farm community who gets entangled with a local (Randolph Scott), despite a film contract that prohibits such a relationship. With Warren William, Alice Brady and Elizabeth Patterson.
VHS: S18867. $14.98.
Henry Hathaway, USA, 1936, 82 mins.

Goin' to Town

A screwball farce with Mae West as an ambitious dance hall girl who wins a husband playing dice and tries to insinuate herself into upper-class society. Features a hilarious rendition of "Samson and Delilah". With Paul Cavanagh, Ivan Lebedeff and Marjorie Gateson.
VHS: S18868. $14.98.
Alexander Hall, USA, 1935, 74 mins.

Going Bananas

David Mendenhall (*Over the Top*) is adopted by a talking chimp (midget-actor Deep Roy) and enlists the aid of Dom DeLuise and Jimmie Walker when his friend is sold to the circus. Filmed in Kenya with some live animals like boa constrictors. With Warren Berlinger and Herbert Lom. Said to be a slapstick safari.
VHS: S09514. $19.95.
Boaz Davidson, USA, 1988, 95 mins.

Good Night, Michelangelo

A charming, sexy comedy about a family of Italian immigrants living under one roof and trying to pursue their loves and ambitions in a strange environment. Eight-year-old Michelangelo learns important lessons about life and growing up by watching his family's hilarious adventures. Starring Kim Cattrall (*Bonfire of the Vanities*) and Giancarlo Giannini (*New York Stories*). Winner—Best Comedy at the Greater Fort Lauderdale Film Festival 1990.
VHS: S13540. $89.98.
Carlo Liconti, USA, 1989, 91 mins.

Goodbye Love

Charlie Ruggles and Sidney Blackmer headline this comedy about a group of henpecked husbands who refuse to pay their alimony and end up in the city jail.
VHS: S14663. $29.95.
H. Bruce Humberstone, USA, 1934, 65 mins.

The Grass Is Greener

Robert Mitchum shakes up the proper English marriage of Cary Grant and Deborah Kerr in this drawing-room comedy of manners and mores. Jean Simmons offers Cary solace. In other words, it's highbrow hanky panky. From the play by Hugh and Margaret Williams. Letterboxed.
VHS: S04241. $19.95.
Laser: LD71859. $34.98.
Stanley Donen, USA, 1960, 105 mins.

Great Guns

Laurel and Hardy get ready for war as they mobilize for merry madness. USA, 1941, 74 mins.
VHS: S04607. $29.98.

The Great Lover

Bob Hope is a reporter assigned to escort a troop of Boy Rangers on an ocean liner to Europe. Aboard are Rhonda Fleming, her dad the Grand Duke, and a murderer who Bob insists is not him. With Roland Young as the card shark and Jim Backus as the detective. A sea worthy comedy. B&W. 80 mins.
VHS: S07585. $14.95.
Alexander Hall, USA, 1949, 80 mins.

Greetings

An early comedy from director Brian De Palma. This free-form series of vignettes stars Robert de Niro, Jonathan Warden, and Gerrit Graham as three counterculture buddies out to avoid the draft and solve the Kennedy assasination. Free love. Greenwich Village. Police brutality. Also Megan McCormick and Allen Garfield. A sequel, *Hi Mom*, followed in 1970.
VHS: S10354. $79.95.
Brian DePalma, USA, 1968, 88 mins.

Groucho Marx—Classic Television

Groucho Marx hosts the 1950 television pilot of *You Bet Your Life*, recorded live with all the bloopers left in. A rare TV document. 60 mins.
VHS: S10593. $29.95.

Groundhog Day

Bill Murray stars as an obnoxious television weatherman caught in a time warp that forces him to relive the day he's stranded in a small Pennsylvania town. Andie MacDowell is Murray's romantic interest, an independent producer. Chris Elliott is a deadpan camera operator.
VHS: S19047. $19.95.
Harold Ramis, USA, 1993, 101 mins.

Grumpy Old Men

Walter Matthau and Jack Lemmon have been a film comedy team since their portrayal of two zany, mismatched friends in the *Odd Couple*. In this film their age-old enmity is put to the test by renewed rivalry over an attractive young widow, Daryl Hannah. Also features Burgess Meredith, Ann-Margret and Buck Henry.
VHS: S21084. $19.98.
Laser: LD72412. $34.98.
Donald Petrie, USA, 1993, 104 mins.

Guest Wife

Determined to impress his sentimental boss, a quick-thinking bachelor (Don Ameche) talks his best friend's bride (Claudette Colbert) into posing as his own wife. When the hoax gets hopelessly out of hand, he nearly ruins the couple's honeymoon and their marriage.
VHS: S12446. $19.98.
Laser: CLV. LD71987. $29.98.
Sam Wood, USA, 1945, 90 mins.

Half Shot at Sunrise

Max Steiner received his first credit as musical director for this classic comedy featuring vaudeville comedians Wheeler and Woolsey. Plenty of slapstick, one-liners and sight gags.
VHS: S04495. $29.95.
Paul Sloane, USA, 1930, 78 mins.

Hands Across the Table

Carole Lombard is a delight opposite Fred MacMurray in this effervescent comedy. It's a charming tale about a manicurist in search of a husband, ideally a rich husband. There are all the usual deceptions of romance and some rather novel ones that keep this film light and amusing.
VHS: S26224. $19.98.
Mitchell Leisen, USA, 1935, 80 mins.

Hardboiled Mahoney

Terence "Slip" Mahoney (Leo Gorcey) is mistaken for a detective in this Bowery Boys comedy from Monogram Pictures. An inquiry on behalf of a mysterious woman uncovers a phony medium and a blackmailing scam. With Huntz Hall, Gabriel Dell, Betty Compson, Teala Loring and Byron Foulger. This was the last Bowery Boys movie for Bobby Jordan.
VHS: S15830. $14.98.
William Beaudine, USA, 1947, 63 mins.

Harold and Maude

Bud Cort is Harold, an introverted suicidal 19 year old; Ruth Gordon is Maude, a spunky 79 year old. They fall in love in this witty romantic comedy. The early scenes in which Harold tries out suicide methods are outstanding. Music by Cat Stevens.
VHS: S00543. $19.95.
Laser: LD75352. $29.98.
Hal Ashby, USA, 1971, 92 mins.

Heathers

This wicked satire, from first-time screenwriter Daniel Waters, takes on high school, adolescent angst, the ironic glorification of teen suicide, homophobia, popularity, football players, funerals, croquet, and just about anything else you can think of. With Winona Ryder and Christian Slater. Quite dark and funny.
VHS: S13691. $19.95.
Laser: CLV, widescreen, with cast interviews. LD75009. $49.95.
Michael Lehmann, USA, 1989, 102 mins.

Her Favorite Patient (aka Bedside Manner)

A romantic comedy with John Carroll as a pilot whose doctor, played by Ruth Hussey, gives him some extra special tender lovin' care.
VHS: S14672. $29.95.
Andrew L. Stone, USA, 1946, 72 mins.

Her First Romance

This delightful romantic comedy features a confusing mix-up involving two sisters, an attractive cousin and her fiance, played by Alan Ladd. Fortunately it ends as a good comedy should, with everyone finding the right mate. Edith Fellows, Wilbur Evans, Judith Linden and Jacqueline Wells are also featured.
VHS: S22600. $19.95.
George Dmytryk, USA, 1940, 77 mins.

Here Come the Co-Eds

Abbott and Costello play two wacky caretakers whose zany antics inject some life and personality into a boring and repressed girls school. With Peggy Ryan, Martha O'Driscoll, June Vincent and Lon Chaney.
VHS: S19072. $14.98.
Jean Yarbrough, USA, 1945, 87 mins.

Here Come the Girls

Bob Hope is the show biz impresario who tries to ward off a deranged killer. With Arlene Dahl, Rosemary Clooney and Tony Martin. Entertainment from the Four Step Brothers.
VHS: S17978. $14.95.
Claude Binyon, USA, 1953, 100 mins.

Here Come the WAVES

This is a wartime comedy that pairs Bing Crosby and Betty Hutton with the U.S. Navy. Together they sing and dance through just about everything, with Bing even using blackface make-up to perform the superhit that became one of his signature tunes, "Accentuate the Positive."
VHS: S21200. $14.98.
Mark Sandrich, USA, 1944, 99 mins.

Here Comes Mr. Jordan

A prizefighter who is also an amateur saxophonist crashes in his private plane and goes to heaven by mistake—this is the setup of this classic fantasy, as when he goes back to Earth, he has to find another body. With Robert Montgomery, Evelyn Keyes, Claude Rains, James Gleason.
VHS: Out of print. For rental only.
Laser: LD71040. $49.95.
Alexander Hall, USA, 1941, 94 mins.

Hey Abbott!

Abbott and Costello were the definitive burlesque comedy team. This retrospective of their work together, hosted by Milton Berle, contains the most famous routines, including *Who's on First*, *Oyster Stew* and *Floogle Street*. Steve Allen and Phil Silvers tell all through hilarious interviews and reminiscences about this legendary pair. 76 mins.
VHS: S15999. $19.98.

High Anxiety

Mel Brooks takes on Alfred Hitchcock in this funny spoof of some of the Master of Suspense's greatest moments. With Brooks, Madeline Kahn, Harvey Korman.
VHS: S04318. $19.98.
Mel Brooks, USA, 1977, 94 mins.

The History of the World, Part One

Mel Brooks turns his special brand of humor on various periods of history including the Stone Age, Biblical times, the Spanish Inquisition and the French Revolution. Cast includes Dom DeLuise, Gregory Hines, Madeline Kahn, Harvey Korman, Cloris Leachman and Brooks himself. Orson Welles narrates. Guaranteed to be funnier than the Black Plague.
VHS: S06147. $14.98.
Mel Brooks, USA, 1981, 92 mins.

Hold Me Thrill Me Kiss Me
Joel Hershman's outlandish comedy features Max Parrish as the handsome drifter Eli fleeing his spurned fiance (a hilarious Sean Young). He falls under the hypnotic spell of a dominatrix stripper (former porn star Andrea Naschak) who imprisons him in a sleazy trailer park, where he promptly falls for the woman's virginal, beautiful sister (Adrienne Shelly). With Diane Ladd, Dr. Timothy Leary and Bela Lehoczky. The eclectic soundtrack features Poi Dog Pondering, The Violent Femmes, Fred Schneider, The Pixies, The Cramps, King Missile and Jazz Butcher.
VHS: S20197. $92.98.
Joel Hershman, USA, 1992, 92 mins.

Hold Your Man
A brisk comedy of manners about the affair between Jean Harlow and Clark Gable, low-rent grifters whose lifestyle and career choices can't diminish their love. With Stuart Erwin and Elizabeth Patterson.
VHS: S17779. $19.98.
Sam Wood, USA, 1933, 87 mins

Hollywood Clowns
Glenn Ford narrates this retrospective of the screen's great comedians, including Buster Keaton, W.C. Fields, The Marx Brothers, Laurel and Hardy, Charlie Chaplin and Danny Kaye. USA, 1979, 49 mins.
VHS: S10036. $29.95.

Hollywood Hot Tubs
When your parents and your probation officer make you get a job…why not work where everybody plays? This highly original cult comedy is an all time favorite. Getting into hot water has never been so much fun!
VHS: S15033. $19.95.
Chuck Vincent, USA, 1984, 105 mins.

Hollywood or Bust
Dean Martin and Jerry Lewis in their last film together, with Jerry playing an obsessed fan who heads West determined to meet his idol. With Anita Ekberg and Pat Crowley.
VHS: S04428. $14.95.
Frank Tashlin, USA, 1956, 95 mins.

The Honeymoon Machine
Steve McQueen and Jim Hutton star as two American sailors in Venice, Italy, who try to access a Navy computer and electronically manipulate the roulette tables. With Paula Prentiss, Jack Mullaney and Dean Jagger. "A series of laugh explosions that recur with happy frequency" (The Hollywood Reporter).
VHS: S18011. $19.98.
Richard Thorpe, USA, 1961, 87 mins.

Honky Tonk
Con artist Candy Johnson (Clark Gable) had been run out of town after town. Then he got wise, went out and got a town of his own: Yellow Creek, Nevada. A lively, lusty, comic-western co-starring sassy Lana Turner.
VHS: S15259. $19.98.
Jack Conway, USA, 1941, 105 mins.

Honolulu
Comic repercussions, confusion and intrigue abound when a matinee idol movie star exchanges identities with a Hawaiian plantation owner. With Eleanor Powell, Robert Young, George Burns and Gracie Allen.
VHS: S18554. $19.98.
Edward Buzzell, USA, 1939, 84 mins.

Hook, Line, and Sinker
The wacky comedy team of Bert Wheeler and Robert Woolsey agree to help an attractive heiress restore a dilapidated old resort hotel, not knowing that bands of rival gangsters have their own corrupt plans for it.
VHS: S13994. $19.98.
Eddie Cline, USA, 1930, 75 mins.

The Horn Blows at Midnight
A rip-roaring comedy starring Jack Benny as Athaniel, an angel sent from Heaven to destroy Earth, where persecution and hatred have soared out of control. Well-cast fantasy that is highly enjoyable.
VHS: S14562. $19.98.
Raoul Walsh, USA, 1945, 78 mins.

Horsefeathers
The four Marx Brothers go to college in this classic comedy written by humorist S.J. Perelman. The new president of Huxley College is Professor Wagstaff (Groucho), and he needs better football players to have a winning team. He can find them in a speakeasy if only he can guess the password. I'll give you a clue. It isn't horsefeathers. B&W.
VHS: S08323. $19.98.
Laser: LD70039. $34.98.
Norman Z. McLeod, USA, 1932, 67 mins.

The Hospital
Paddy Chayefsky wrote this biting black comedy about a modern mega-hospital that strangles its patients—and doctors—in red tape. George C. Scott stars in a ferocious, Oscar-nominated performance.
VHS: S15251. $19.98.
Arthur Hiller, USA, 1971, 102 mins.

Hot Millions
Peter Ustinov is a shrewd hustler and trickster who manipulates a computer to devise a fake company and embezzle millions, in this engaging comedy. With Maggie Smith, Bob Newhart, Karl Malden, Robert Morley and Cesar Romero.
VHS: S20206. $19.98.
Eric Till, USA, 1968, 106 mins.

Hotel Paradiso
In this boulevard farce, Alec Guinness and Gina Lollobrigida are neighbors trying to carry off an improbable affair in a sleazy hotel. The arrival of an eccentric group of fellow guests leads to a series of zany adventures and mixed up identities. Written by Peter Glenville and Jean-Claude Carriere, from the play by Georges Feydeau. Cinematography by Henri Decae. With Robert Morley, Peggy Mount, Douglas Byng, Akim Tamiroff and Robertson Hare.
VHS: S20205. $19.98.
Peter Glenville, USA, 1966, 99 mins.

Houseboat
Cary Grant and Sophia Loren are teamed in this Oscar-nominated romantic comedy about a widower who hires a governess to look after his three unruly children.
VHS: S04430. $14.98.
Laser: LD75353. $29.98.
Melville Shavelson, USA, 1958, 110 mins.

How to Commit Marriage
A strange Bob Hope/Jackie Gleason comedy about a divorcing couple who are shaken by their daughter's announcement she's about to marry a raffish musician. Gleason is the father of the groom with a bizarre plan to exploit the situation to create a hip new band. With Jane Wyman, Tim Matthieson, Joanna Cameron and Tina Louise.
VHS: S18444. $14.95.
Norman Panama, USA, 1969, 95 mins.

How to Marry a Millionaire
Post World War II comedy in which Marilyn Monroe, Betty Grable and Lauren Bacall try to attract rich men to marry, but discover that love is preferable to money.
VHS: S04202. $19.98.
Laser: LD71059. $69.98.
Jean Negulesco, USA, 1953, 96 mins.

How to Murder Your Wife
Jack Lemmon marries Virna Lisi while under the influence and begins to regret the decision. Is it his fault the blonde Italian who popped out of a bachelor party cake was so alluring, at the time, to this famous cartoonist for a man's adventure strip? With Terry-Thomas as his disapproving manservant and Eddie Mayerhof as his henpecked lawyer. A hilarious comedy about mixing marriage with an active imagination.
VHS: S11220. $19.95.
Laser: LD72266. $39.98.
Richard Quine, USA, 1965, 118 mins.

I'll Do Anything
Nick Nolte, Albert Brooks, Julie Kavner and Tracey Ullman are all featured in this romantic comedy about a father who unexpectedly gains custody of his six-year-old daughter. Nolte is the actor and father whose life is thrown completely out of kilter when Hollywood comes knocking, forcing him to be both a good parent and a star.
VHS: S21382. $95.98.
Laser: LD74475. $34.95.
James L. Brooks, USA, 1994, 116 mins.

I'll Take Sweden
In this madcap comedy, Bob Hope prevents his daughter's (Tuesday Weld) marriage to her uncouth boyfriend (Frankie Avalon) by moving the family to Sweden. Hope's plans for domestic tranquility are shattered when Weld falls for a charismatic and devilish Swedish playboy.
VHS: S19563. $19.98.
Fred De Cordova, USA, 1965, 96 mins.

I'm from Hollywood: Andy Kaufman
This program examines the peculiar genius of the late comedian Andy Kaufman, the brilliant, nervous, sometimes unstable actor and comedian whose signature work came on the NBC program Taxi. Features interviews with Marilu Henner, Tony Danza and Kaufman's stand up contemporaries, and footage from Kaufman's television appearances, particularly Late Night with David Letterman. 60 mins.
VHS: S17347. $19.95.

I'm No Angel
A comedy set against a strange backdrop of carnivals and freak shows, about a beautiful lion tamer (Mae West) who pursues a charismatic playboy (Cary Grant). With Edward Arnold, Gertrude Michael and Kent Taylor.
VHS: S18869. $14.98.
Wesley Ruggles, USA, 1933, 87 mins.

I.Q.
Meg Ryan, Tim Robbins and Walter Matthau are joined in this unlikely romantic comedy in which Albert Einstein plays cupid. Matthau is great as the genius matchmaker whose classic formula (one plus one equals two), generates some real chemistry.
VHS: S25653. $96.98.
Fred Schepisi, USA, 1994, 95 mins.

Iceland
A high-style romantic comedy about a Norwegian beauty (Sonja Henie) who becomes the fixation of an American marine (John Payne). Music by Sammy Kaye and his orchestra, featuring the hit song, "There Will Never Be Another You." With Jack Oakie, Sterling Holloway and Osa Massen.
VHS: S20263. $19.98.
H. Bruce Humberstone, USA, 1942, 79 mins.

If It's Tuesday, This Must Be Belgium
A comedy about cultural displacement and Americans abroad. A group of Americans travel through Europe in a series of comic adventures. With Suzanne Pleshette, Norman Fell, Michael Constantine and Peggy Cass.
VHS: S18017. $19.98.
Laser: LD72178. $34.98.
Mel Stuart, USA, 1969, 99 mins.

In Person
In this comedy Ginger Rogers plays a film star who adopts outlandish disguises to avoid throngs of adoring fans and ends up falling in love with someone ignorant of her identity. With George Brent.
VHS: S10652. $19.98.
William A. Seiter, USA, 1935, 87 mins.

In Society
Abbott and Costello play two down-on-their-luck plumbers who are mistaken for gilded aristocrats. With Marion Hutton, Arthur Treacher and Thomas Gomez.
VHS: S19068. $14.98.
Jean Yarbrough, USA, 1944, 75 mins.

In the Navy
In this rollicking nautical musical-comedy, Abbott and Costello are two sailors bound for duty on the high seas. They befriend a singing star and must help him evade an ambitious reporter. Includes musical numbers by The Andrews Sisters.
VHS: S14903. $14.95.
Laser: LD71406. $34.98.
Arthur Lubin, USA, 1941, 85 mins.

The In-Laws
This wild comedy stars Peter Falk as a CIA agent, or at least he claims to be one. Alan Arkin is really a dentist whose daughter is marrying Falk's son. Somehow the comic relationship between these future in-laws leads them into a plot that foils a South American dictator and his counterfeiting schemes.
VHS: S22865. $19.98.
Laser: LD74704. $34.98.
Arthur Hiller, USA, 1979, 103 mins.

Indian Summer
Mike Binder's autobiographical comedy reworks the Secaucus 7/Big Chill genre for Generation X. Eight childhood friends in their 30s return to their idyllic summer camp to rekindle the protective innocence and joy of their post-adolescence, though the messy complications of real life intrude. With Alan Arkin, Diane Lane, Matt Craven and Elizabeth Perkins.
VHS: S19435. $94.95.
Mike Binder, USA, 1993, 97 mins.

Indiscreet
Singin' in the Rain co-director Stanley Donen produced and directed this elegantly sophisticated comedy about a secret love affair between a beautiful actress and a NATO diplomat. The leads are brilliant: Cary Grant is charming, aloof and funny; Ingrid Bergman alluring, mysterious and quixotic. Letterboxed.
VHS: S02641. $19.95.
Stanley Donen, USA, 1958, 100 mins.

International House
W.C. Fields, George Burns and Gracie Allen romp through China when a scientist has created the first television. With Rudy Vallee, Bela Lugosi and Sterling Holloway, and a special appearance by Cab Calloway singing "Reefer Man."
VHS: S01991. $29.95.
A. Edward Sutherland, USA, 1933, 72 mins.

It Could Happen to You
Nicolas Cage, Bridget Fonda and Rosie Perez star in this screwball comedy about the travails of winning big. A cop (Cage) promises a waitress (Fonda) part of his winnings from a lottery ticket when he doesn't have enough cash for a tip. Though she doesn't believe him, he wins and actually makes good on his promise. Perez is great as the wife who can't understand his generosity.
VHS: S23298. $19.95.
Andrew Bergman, USA, 1994, 101 mins.

It Happens Every Spring
A wacky comedy featuring a mild-mannered academic who accidentally uncovers a wood repellent. From this chance discovery he manages to find a career as an unstoppable pitcher. This charming classic laughs at America's favorite springtime preoccupation. With Ray Milland and Ed Begley.
VHS: S20704. $19.98.
Lloyd Bacon, USA, 1949, 87 mins.

It Started in Naples
Clark Gable travels to Italy to bring home his recently orphaned nephew and runs up against the boy's fiery guardian, Sophia Loren. Mama mia, What fun! USA, 1960, 100 mins.
VHS: S15160. $19.95.

It Started with a Kiss
A clear-eyed comedy about romance and class. An Air Force sergeant (Glenn Ford) is transferred to Spain and has to deal with his wife (Debbie Reynolds) and the car he won in a lottery. With Eva Gabor, Harry Morgan and Fred Clark.
VHS: S18018. $19.98.
Melville Shavelson, USA, 1959, 104 mins.

It Started with Eve
Charles Laughton stars with Deanna Durbin in this hilarious misadventure of love and romance. Laughton plays a grumpy old millionaire whose dying wish is to meet the young lady who is engaged to marry his son. Unfortunately, the bride in question is unavailable. Believing his father is not long for this world, the son finds a quick replacement, a hat check girl (Durbin).
VHS: S23282. $19.98.
Henry Koster, USA, 1941, 90 mins.

It's a Joke, Son!
A folksy, down-home comedy that brought radio's popular "Senator Claghorn" (from the Fred Allen Show) to the screen. Starring Kenny Delmar, Una Merkel, June Lockhart and Douglass Dumbrille.
VHS: S14324. $19.98.
Ben Stoloff, USA, 1947, 67 mins.

It's a Mad, Mad, Mad, Mad World
Forty stars and a million laughs in this wild romp featuring a cast of some of America's greatest funnymen: Jimmy Durante, Milton Berle, Spencer Tracy, Sid Caesar, Buddy Hackett, Ethel Merman, Mickey Rooney, Phil Silvers, Jonathan Winters, the Three Stooges and more. A cult classic!
VHS: S02327. $29.98.
Laser: LD70602. $69.98.
Stanley Kramer, USA, 1963, 155 mins.

It's in the Bag
This outrageous comedy-mystery has Fred Allen inheriting five seemingly worthless chairs from his recently-deceased, rich uncle. But once he sells them for much needed cash, Fred discovers his uncle left a huge fortune in the missing furniture. And so, he's off on a hilarious treasure hunt that leads to laughter and lunacy. With Jack Benny.
VHS: S09496. $19.95.
Richard Wallace, USA, 1945, 87 mins.

Jesse James
A superb cast in this highly fictionalized account of the great American outlaw, featuring Tyrone Power as Jesse, Henry Fonda as his brother Frank, and Randolph Scott.
VHS: S02369. $19.98.
Henry King, USA, 1939, 105 mins.

Joe Versus the Volcano
In this well received Hollywood comedy, Tom Hanks stars as a terminally ill man who sets forth on one final tour of the globe. What he finds is mystical adventure and an odd, romantic companion with the island-bound Meg Ryan.
VHS: S12666. $14.95.
John Patrick Shanley, USA, 1990, 106 mins.

Joey Breaker
A hilarious Hollywood movie starring Richard Edson as a smooth-talking agent on the fast track whose priorities are radically altered when he's drawn to a beautiful and mysterious young Jamaican woman (Cedella Marley). Winner of top prize at the Santa Barbara International Film Festival. Cinematography by Joe DeSalvo. With Erik King, Gina Gershon, Phillip Seymour Hoffman and Fred Fondren.
VHS: S19204. $92.95.
Steven Starr, USA, 1993, 92 mins.

Julia Misbehaves
Elegant bravura and unruly, slapstick energy carry this light and charming work about a divorced couple (Greer Garson and Walter Pidgeon) who are reunited on the eve of their daughter's (Elizabeth Taylor) wedding. With Peter Lawford, Cesar Romero and Lucile Watson.
VHS: S18523. $19.98.
Jack Conway, USA, 1949, 99 mins.

Jumping Jacks
Screwball farce and manic comedy in this Dean Martin and Jerry Lewis comedy detailing their destruction of military order and authoritarian rules when they're enlisted into a military paratroop division. With Mona Freeman, Don DeFore and Robert Strauss.
VHS: S18676. $19.95.
Laser: LD75213. $34.98.
Norman Taurog, USA, 1952, 96 mins.

June Bride
Bretaigne Windust directs this sly farce about the romantic dynamics of two young magazine journalists (Bette Davis and Robert Montgomery) sent to cover a traditional wedding to research an article about June Brides. With Fay Bainter, Tom Tully, Barbara Bates, Jerome Cowan, and Debbie Reynolds's film debut.
VHS: S17333. $19.98.
Bretaigne Windust, USA, 1948, 97 mins.

Keep 'em Flying
This wacky escapade takes Abbott and Costello on a high-flying adventure as new recruits in the Army Air Corps. Loaded with wonderful music, daring stunts and great comic routines.
VHS: S14904. $14.98.
Laser: LD71407. $34.98.
Arthur Lubin, USA, 1941, 86 mins.

The Kettles in the Ozarks
It starts as just a simple visit to some kin folk in Mournful Hollow. Uncle Sedge however needs help from Ma Kettle and all her kids with his housekeeper/fiance and the evil scientists that have just bought his entire corn crop. Great laughs and a twisted plot make this another winner in the series with Marjorie Main.
VHS: S24331. $14.98.
Charles Lamont, USA, 1955, 81 mins.

The Kettles on Old MacDonald's Farm
Marjorie Main stars with Parker Fenelly in this the last of the Kettle films. Ma and Pa offer marriage advice to a young couple, a lumber man and the pampered daughter of his boss, John Smith and Gloria Talbott.
VHS: S24333. $14.98.
Virgil W. Vogel, USA, 1957, 82 mins.

Kid from Brooklyn
Remake of Harold Lloyd's The Milky Way works very well for Danny Kaye as a milkman accidentally turned into a prizefighter.
VHS: S03124. $19.98.
Norman Z. McLeod, USA, 1946, 113 mins.

Kisses for My President
Polly Bergen is hailed as the chief in this comic "what if" about the first female president. Fred MacMurray catches plenty of flak as the first Hubby. With Arlene Dahl, Eli Wallach and Edward Andrews.
VHS: S16275. $19.98.
Laser: LD70047. $34.98.
Curtis Bernhardt, USA, 1964, 113 mins.

Ladies' Man
The adventures of an accident-prone confirmed bachelor who gets a job in a women's boarding house for aspiring actresses. He starts out as the handyman but ends up as the ladies' man. Jerry Lewis, Helen Traubel star.
VHS: S12571. $19.98.
Jerry Lewis, USA, 1961, 106 mins.

The Lady Is Willing
A screwball farce with serious overtones about a musical comedy performer (Marlene Dietrich) who adopts a young baby and falls for her simple though charming pediatrician. With Fred MacMurray, Aline MacMahon and Stanley Ridges.
VHS: S19022. $19.95.
Mitchell Leisen, USA, 1942, 91 mins.

The Lady Says No
A delightful comedy about fickle Joan Caulfield who just can't decide if marriage is right for her. Also starring David Niven.
VHS: S14674. $29.95.
Frank Ross, USA, 1951, 80 mins.

Lady Takes a Chance
John Wayne and Jean Arthur star in a hilarious romantic comedy about a New York girl with matrimonial ideas and a rope-shy rodeo rider who yearns for the wide-open spaces.
VHS: S06414. $14.98.
William A. Seiter, USA, 1943, 86 mins.

The Last Remake of Beau Geste
Director, co-screenwriter and performer Marty Feldman may not have made the last version of the classic P.C. Wren novel of life in the Foreign Legion, but he certainly is responsible for the goofiest. Feldman and Michael York play identical twin brothers who join the Legion on a point of honor. With Ann-Margret as the sexy stepmother and Peter Ustinov as the villainous sergeant.
VHS: S06175. $14.95.
Marty Feldman, USA, 1977, 83 mins.

Latin Lovers
A romantic comedy about a wealthy heiress and businesswoman (Lana Turner) searching for authentic romance. With John Lund, Ricardo Montalban, Jean Hagen and Rita Moreno.
VHS: S18660. $19.98.
Mervyn LeRoy, USA, 1953, 104 mins.

Laurel and Hardy and the Family
Four classic comedies explore the joys, frustrations and obligations of family life. Features *Brats, Their First Mistake, Twice Two* and *Perfect Day*. 85 mins.
VHS: S14698. $14.98.

Laurel and Hardy at Work
In this collection of short subjects, the boys are engaged in three different lines of work and fail at all of them. Featuring *Towed in a Hole, Busy Bodies* and *The Music Box*. USA, 1932/1933, 70 mins.
VHS: S13867. $14.98.

The Laurel and Hardy Collection
Order and reason break down in Laurel and Hardy's *The Devil's Brother*, James Horne's 1935 *Bonnie Scotland*, and their compilation work, *Laurel and Hardy's Laughing '20s* (1965).
VHS: S17311. $49.92.

Laurel and Hardy on the Lam
In this quartet of classic comedies, Stan and Ollie try to flee their troubles, but the trouble always seems to catch up to them—hilariously. Featuring *Scram!, Another Fine Mess, One Good Turn* and *Going Bye-Bye!* USA, 1930-1934, 90 mins.
VHS: S13868. $14.98.

Laurel and Hardy Spooktacular
There are screams galore in these four hilarious comedies from Laurel and Hardy. Includes *The Live Ghost, Oliver the Eighth, Laurel and Hardy Murder Case* and *Dirty Work*. 95 mins.
VHS: S14697. $14.98.

Laurel and Hardy's Laughing '20s
This affectionate compilation of the most hilarious highlights from their classic comedy shorts includes perhaps the greatest pie-throwing melee of the silent era. A must for buffs. USA, 1965, 90 mins.
VHS: S15421. $19.98.
Laser: LD70197. $39.98.

Laurel and Hardy, Vol. 1
The manic energy and physical comedy of Laurel and Hardy are collected in this work of shorts, *Duck Soup, Slipping Wives, Feed 'Em and Weep, With Love and Hisses, Sailor Beware* and *Should Married Men Go Home*.
VHS: S07198. $29.95.

Laurel and Hardy: Rare Home Movies
The comedy team visits the homeland of Stan Laurel in this two-part cinema verite. In the first, the pair visits Tynemouth, England, where they amuse the crowd and sightsee. Ollie is shown wearing his glasses. Part 2 finds them in Edinburgh, Scotland, where they visit a castle and a movie theatre. A rare, behind-the-scenes look. 1932, 25 mins.
VHS: S05712. $19.95.

Laurel and Hardy: Stan "Helps" Ollie
Disaster always strikes in these four hysterical shorts when Stan tries to help Ollie. Includes *County Hospital, Me and My Pal, Hogwild* and *Helpmates*. 85 mins.
VHS: S14699. $14.98.

Legends of Comedy
The greatest comedic legends from Hollywood are seen in this series. Early silent films, the movies and radio shows of the 30's and 40's, even the best gags of TV's golden era, are included in this collection of classic antics. It's a history lesson in humor. Three volumes, each 55 minutes long.
Volume I: The Golden Age of Comedy. The keystone cops, Charlie Chaplin and Buster Keaton set a high standard for film comedy during the silent era. With the coming of sound, W.C. Fields, Laurel and Hardy and even the kids from Our Gang continued this tradition in their best works. *Volume I* contains the most memorable gags ever unleashed by these comic entertainers. 55 mins.
VHS: S20860. $24.95.
Volume II: Great Stars of Film and Radio. From the Broadway stage, great stars of slapstick invaded the developing world of film and broadcasting. Mae West, The Marx Brothers, even Jimmy Durante all brought skills honed in front of live audiences to the cinema and radio broadcasts, thereby reaching homes all across America. 55 mins.
VHS: S20861. $24.95.
Volume III: TV Comedy Classics. With the birth of television, live performances could be heard and seen electronically for the first time. Comic pioneers like Burns and Allen, Jackie Gleason and Art Carney, Red Skelton, Sid Caesar and Imogene Coca realized the potential of TV from the start. Their best efforts are collected on this tape. 55 mins.
VHS: S20862. $24.95.
Legends of Comedy, Three-Volume Set.
VHS: S20863. $59.95.

The Lemon Drop Kid
The Lemon Drop Kid is a racetrack con-man who gets in big trouble when he gives a bad tip to a local gangster. Given until Christmas to make up for a $10,000 loss, he hits on a brilliant and ultimately hilarious scheme. He opens an old folks' home as a ruse to license phony Santa Clauses. Bob Hope stars.
VHS: S22762. $14.98.
Sidney Lanfield, USA, 1951, 91 mins.

Let's Make It Legal
An attractive grandmother falls back in love with an old flame, and casually divorces her gambler husband. A comedy where friendship and love aren't always found in the same man. Stars Claudette Colbert, MacDonald Carey, Zachary Scott, Robert Wagner and Marilyn Monroe.
VHS: S16398. $19.98.
Richard Sale, USA, 1951, 77 mins.

Libeled Lady
A crackerjack comedy starring four of Hollywood's finest. Spencer Tracy is a newspaper editor without scruples. Myrna Loy is the society dame he'd like to keep in the headlines. Add in William Powell and Jean Harlow as Tracy's somewhat reluctant accomplices and wait for the fun to begin. A delight in black and white; remade in 1946 as *Easy to Wed*.
VHS: S11728. $19.98.
Jack Conway, USA, 1936, 98 mins.

Life Begins for Andy Hardy/ Andy Hardy's Private Secretary
This double-feature disc offers two of the best works from the Andy Hardy series, George B. Seitz's 1941 *Life Begins for Andy Hardy*, about Andy's cruel lesson when he travels to New York in search of a job, with Mickey Rooney and Judy Garland (her last appearance in the series). The second program is Seitz's *Andy Hardy's Private Secretary*, about Andy's tutorship with Kathryn Grayson (her debut) and the consequences of his failed English test. Features the original theatrical trailer from each film.
Laser: LD71650. $44.98.

Life Stinks
Only Mel Brooks could find laughs in a comedy about the homeless. He directs, co-writes and stars as a greedy billionaire who pretends to be down and out in order to win a bet and acquire the land needed for a new building complex. Lesley Ann Warren is sensational as the streetwise bag lady who helps Brooks with some long overdue attitude adjustment. With Jeffrey Tambor, Rudy De Luca, Stuart Pankin and Howard Morris as Sailor.
VHS: S15433. $14.95.
Laser: LD74676. $34.98.
Mel Brooks, USA, 1991, 93 mins.

Life with Father
Based on the hit Broadway play by Lindsay and Crouse, music by Max Steiner, with William Powell, Irene Dunne and Elizabeth Taylor, set in 1880's New York.
VHS: S00754. $19.95.
Michael Curtiz, USA, 1947, 118 mins.

Little Giant
A rare Bud Abbott and Lou Costello work features the comic duo playing separate roles rather than being paired together. The frantic plot charts the misadventures of Costello as a harried door-to-door vacuum cleaner salesman. Also known as *On the Carpet*. With Brenda Joyce, George Cleveland and Elena Verdugo.
VHS: S19071. $14.98.
William A. Seiter, USA, 1946, 91 mins.

Little Murders
Elliot Gould is the meek photographer roped into marriage with the overly aggressive Marcia Rodd in this hilarious black comedy about modern relationships, urban living and sniping as a form of therapy. With Vincent Gardenia, Elizabeth Wilson, Donald Sutherland and Alan Arkin, who also makes his film debut as a director. A sure fire hit from the pen of Jules Feiffer.
VHS: S07969. $59.98.
Alan Arkin, USA, 1971, 107 mins.

Lonely Guy
Steve Martin stars as a lonely guy in N.Y.C who seeks the advice of fellow lonely guy Charles Grodin. "Get a dog" is usually a good suggestion. Life size cardboard cut-outs of popular celebrities will also brighten up an empty apartment. One day Steve discovers he doesn't have to eat alone, if he can only find what he did with Judith Ivey's phone number. With Robin Douglass, Steve Lawrence, Merv Griffin and Dr. Joyce Brothers. Based on Bruce Jay Friedman's humorous self-help book *The Lonely Guy's Book of Life*.
VHS: S15771. $19.95.
Arthur Hiller, USA, 1984, 91 mins.

Long, Long Trailer
Lucille Ball, Desi Arnaz and Marjorie Main star in this riotous comedy in which a cumbersome travel trailer creates havoc for a newlywed couple (Ball and Arnaz) on their honeymoon.
VHS: S13355. $19.98.
Vincente Minnelli, USA, 1954, 97 mins.

Look Who's Laughing
Lucy and a myriad of stars from radio's Golden Age combine their talents in one hilarious display of lunacy.
VHS: S10649. $19.98.
Allan Dwan, USA, 1941, 79 mins.

Lost in a Harem
This timeless Abbott & Costello comedy is embellished with lavish production numbers, the Big Band swing of Jimmy Dorsey's Orchestra, gorgeous gal-pal Marilyn Maxwell and hit tunes of the time. A hilarious takeoff on the "sons of the desert" genre.
VHS: S15424. $19.98.
Charles Riesner, USA, 1944, 89 mins.

Lost in Alaska
Bud Abbott and Lou Costello are 19th century prospect hunters in Alaska who are supposed to be helping out a friend but end up getting in more trouble. With Mitzi Green, Tom Ewell and Bruce Cabot.
VHS: S19073. $14.98.
Jean Yarbrough, USA, 1952, 76 mins.

Lost in America
Albert Brooks' masterpiece, an existential road film about an obsessive Yuppie couple (Brooks and Julie Hagerty) who drop out when Brooks' character is denied a promotion in an advertising job. Their dreams of absolute freedom are soon shattered when Hagerty loses their life's fortune during a bad run at the Vegas tables.
VHS: S02546. $19.98.
Laser: Letterboxed. LD74708. $34.98.
Albert Brooks, USA, 1985, 91 mins.

Love Happy
Harpo, Chico and Groucho Marx find themselves in a fine mess involving stolen gems hidden in tins of fish. Femme fatale Ilona Massey wants them back and Raymond Burr is willing to do nasty things to see she gets what she wants. Marilyn Monroe has a bit part as a woman who thinks she is being followed. B&W.
VHS: S04249. $19.95.
David Miller, USA, 1949, 85 mins.

Love Is Better Than Ever
Stanley Donen's shrewd romantic comedy about a small-town dance contest winner (Elizabeth Taylor) who visits New York City and falls for a big city lady killer (Larry Parks). With Tom Tully, Josephine Hutchinson and Ann Doran. Cameo by Gene Kelly.
VHS: S18524. $19.98.
Stanley Donen, USA, 1952, 81 mins.

Lucille Ball Redhead Set
Three of Lucy's earliest and funniest comedies: *The Affairs of Annabel, Too Many Girls*, and *You Can't Fool Your Wife*.
VHS: S10690. $59.98.

Lucky Ghost
Black star Mantan Moreland does a crazy, bug-eyed bit in this 1941 comedy successor to *Mr. Washington Goes to Town*.
VHS: S15481. $29.95.
Jed Buell, USA, 1941

Lust in the Dust
Tab Hunter and Divine. *California* magazine said: "Raunchy but irresistible. It would have made John Wayne lose his lunch." Divine's first film away from director John Waters—still decidedly distasteful.
VHS: S00785. $19.95.
Paul Bartel, USA, 1984, 85 mins.

Luv
A neurotic comedy about a romantic triangle involving Jack Lemmon, Elaine May and Peter Falk. Murray Schisgal's three-character hit play has been expanded to include roles for Eddie Mayehoff, Paul Hartman, Severn Darden and a young Harrison Ford. Lots of talk and double-talk and threatening to jump off bridges in the New York City area.
VHS: S10384. $19.95.
Clive Donner, USA, 1967, 95 mins.

Ma and Pa Kettle
Marjorie Main and Percy Kilbride are the original Ma and Pa Kettle. After appearing as ancillary characters with Fred MacMurray and Claudette Colbert in the *The Egg and I*, this hilarious comic duo spawned a whole series of films. This is the first film starring the famous hillbilly pair who, together with their enormous family, face eviction with humor.
VHS: S21306. $14.98.
Charles Lamont, USA, 1949, 75 mins.

Ma and Pa Kettle at Home
Marjorie Main and Percy Kilbride are back in their roles as a hilarious backwoods couple. In this film they try to fix up their run-down shack of a home in order to convince an editor that they deserve a scholarship for their eldest son (Brett Halsey). Naturally there are plenty of gags in this over-the-top comedy.
VHS: S23876. $14.98.
Charles Lamont, USA, 1952, 82 mins.

Ma and Pa Kettle at the Fair
Sending one of their children to college presents a huge problem for Ma and Pa Kettle, whose modest means will need to be augmented for this ambitious plan. So they decide to enter a number of contests at the State Fair with Ma cooking up a storm and Pa trying his hand at horse-racing.
VHS: S21309. $14.98.
Charles Barton, USA, 1952, 78 mins.

Ma and Pa Kettle at Waikiki
Percy Kilbride makes his final appearance as Pa Kettle in this wacky tropical adventure. The Kettles visit an ailing relative's pineapple factory and Pa has a great idea which inadvertently increases production. This happy accident leads to a plot against the Kettles waged by unscrupulous competitors.
VHS: S24332. $14.98.
Lee Sholem, USA, 1952, 79 mins.

Ma and Pa Kettle Back on the Farm
Marjorie Main and Percy Kilbride fight with crooks again, but this time it's because the crooks believe there are uranium deposits buried on their apparently worthless farm. Ma and Pa Kettle manage somehow to save the homestead in this hilarious film.
VHS: S21308. $14.98.
Edward Sedgwick, USA, 1951, 80 mins.

Ma and Pa Kettle Go to Town
In this Ma and Pa Kettle adventure, Marjorie Main and Percy Kilbride get mixed up with some slick city crooks in New York City. Of course, with their country smarts the duo outwits these know-it-all thieves, resulting in one of the best films in this series.
VHS: S21307. $14.98.
Charles Lamont, USA, 1949, 75 mins.

Ma and Pa Kettle on Vacation
On their way to Paris, Ma and Pa (Marjorie Main and Percy Kilbride) are a backwoods couple who find themselves nearly cheated out of a vacation by a spy scheme. Pa unwittingly agreed to deliver a letter, but after getting them into trouble he seems more interested in Paris nightlife than in helping Ma fix this mess.
VHS: S23875. $14.98.
Charles Lamont, USA, 1953, 76 mins.

Mad Miss Manton
Barbara Stanwyck is a screwball socialite who fancies solving murder mysteries. She eventually involves Henry Fonda in a trail of clues combining sleuth and slapstick from start to finish.
VHS: S10656. $19.98.
Laser: CLV. LD71728. $19.98.
Leigh Jason, USA, 1938, 80 mins.

Made in America
Ted Danson and Whoopi Goldberg star in this comedy about a mix-up at a sperm bank. When Goldberg's artificially inseminated child wants to know who her father is, she finds that he's an uncouth used car salesman.
VHS: S21399. $19.98.
Richard Benjamin, USA, 1993, 109 mins.

Mae West Collection: Special Edition Boxed Set
The flamboyance, spectacle and wit of Mae West are showcased in four different films: Archie Mayo's 1932 *Night after Night*, West's debut work; Wesley Ruggles' 1933 *I'm No Angel*; Leo McCarey's 1934 *Belle of the Nineties* and Raoul Walsh's 1936 *Klondike Annie*. Includes liner notes.
Laser: LD71887. $99.98.

Magic Town
James Stewart and Jane Wyman star in this comedy with Stewart as a pollster who finds the perfect average American town and ruins it when the people of the town find out about Stewart's discovery.
VHS: S09146. $19.95.
Laser: CLV. LD72007. $34.98.
William Wellman, USA, 1947, 103 mins.

Making Mr. Right
Susan Seidelman's (*Desperately Seeking Susan*) romantic fantasy about the relationship between a publicist and the android she's been hired to promote, starring John Malkovich and comedienne Ann Magnuson.
VHS: S04905. $19.98.
Susan Seidelman, USA, 1986, 100 mins.

Man Trouble
Director Bob Rafelson, writer Carol Eastman and actor Jack Nicholson are reunited in this absurd comedy about a misogynist owner (Nicholson) of a dog guard agency who's hired by a beautiful woman (Ellen Barkin) for protection. The two become inadvertent pawns of a nasty underworld crime figure.
VHS: S17921. $19.98.
Bob Rafelson, USA, 1992, 100 mins.

The Man Who Came to Dinner
Based on the play by George Kaufman and Moss Hart, this delightful film is a caricature of Alexander Wolcott as the story of an acid-tongued radio celebrity who breaks his hip on a lecture tour. Hilarity ensues as he terrorizes the suburban home where he recuperates. With Bette Davis, Monty Woolley, Ann Sheridan, Jimmy Durante (in a spoof of Harpo Marx) and Reginald Gardiner (in a spoof of Noel Coward).
VHS: S11626. $19.95.
Laser: LD74677. $34.98.
William Keighley, USA, 1941, 112 mins.

March of the Wooden Soldiers
Victor Herbert's operetta *Babes in Toyland* gets the full Laurel and Hardy treatment. This early feature is one of the great comic pair's first successes.
VHS: S23787. $24.95.
Charles Rogers, USA, 1934, 73 mins.

The Marx Bros. Collection
The best of the Marx Brothers in their early films, Sam Wood's *A Night at the Opera* and *A Day at the Races*, and Edward Buzzell's 1939 *At the Circus*.
VHS: S17325. $49.92.

Marx Brothers—In a Nutshell
Gene Kelly narrates this authorized tribute to the Marx Brothers, including special appearances by Dick Cavett, Robert Klein, David Steinberg, George Fenneman and others, and containing classic comedy scenes from some of the Brothers' best, *Duck Soup, Horse Feathers, Animal Crackers, Cocoanuts, Room Service*. 100 mins.
VHS: S11499. $95.95.

The Mask
Jim Carrey breaks into the bigtime with this major comic role. When a bank clerk finds an ancient mask it changes his life, turning him into a super-hero character with unbelievable plastic abilities. It's a great chance for Carrey to use his antic abilities to their fullest advantage, with amazing computer effects that extend his reach even further.
VHS: S23054. $19.98.
Laser: Widescreen, THX sound. LD74807. $39.99.
Chuck Russell, USA, 1994, 100 mins.

Mastermind
Zero Mostel stars as Inspector Hoku in this comic spoof of the Charlie Chan detective movies. His assignment is to protect a robot from various foreign agents. Lots of slapstick and comic car chases. With Bradford Dillman, Jules Munshen and Sorel Brook.
VHS: S12839. $29.95.
Alex March, USA, 1976, 131 mins.

The Matchmaker
Thornton Wilder's classic romp set in turn-of-the-century New York stars Shirley Booth, Shirley MacLaine, Anthony Perkins, and Robert Morse. This highly amusing farce about a middle-aged widower deciding to re-wed is brought off at breakneck speed, with plenty of laughs.
VHS: S13790. $19.95.
Joseph Anthony, USA, 1958, 101 mins.

The Mating Game
A lyrical, funny, no-holds-barred comedy of manners about class and society. Tony Randall plays a repressed IRS agent who descends on a sleepy, backwater farm house to learn about a family's failure to report their taxes. He quickly falls for the eager, seductive daughter (Debbie Reynolds).
VHS: S18019. $19.98.
George Marshall, USA, 1959, 96 mins.

Me and the Colonel
Danny Kaye and Curt Jurgens star in this unique blend of comedy and suspense. On the eve of the Nazi takeover of Paris, an anti-Semitic Polish colonel (Jurgens) is forced to flee in the company of a Jewish refugee (Kaye). Though their interactions are strained at first, under the threat of discovery they learn to rely upon and trust each other.
VHS: S27185. $19.95.
Peter Glenville, USA, 1958, 110 mins.

Meet the Applegates
From the director of *Heathers* comes an environmental black comedy about intelligent insects from the Amazon rain forest who disguise themselves as a typical sit-com family from the 1950s and invade Ohio in the 1990s. The cast includes Ed Begley Jr., Stockard Channing, Glenn Shadix and Dabney Coleman as Aunt Bea.
VHS: S13921. $92.98.
Michael Lehmann, USA, 1991, 90 mins.

Memoirs of an Invisible Man
A special effects bonanza starring funnyman Chevy Chase as a San Francisco stock analyst who takes a nap too close to a secret, off-limits, government-sponsored laboratory.
VHS: S16735. $19.98.
Laser: Letterboxed. LD71810. $29.98.
John Carpenter, USA, 1992, 99 mins.

Merton of the Movies
An adaptation of George S. Kaufman and Marc Connelly's comedy about the early days of Hollywood. The plot concerns a sweet, naive dreamer (Red Skelton) who arrives in Hollywood and is befriended by a stunt double (Virginia O'Brien). She helps him land his first break. With Gloria Grahame, Alan Mowbray and Hugo Haas.
VHS: S19564. $19.98.
Robert Alton, USA, 1947, 83 mins.

MGM's Big Parade of Comedy
An anthology of more than 50 Hollywood actors, directors and stars performing their magic. The compilation encompasses the silent era through the 1940s, and features Laurel and Hardy, the Marx Brothers, Abbott and Costello, as well as Greta Garbo, Clark Gable, Katharine Hepburn and Jean Harlow. "A delight" (*Hollywood Reporter*). 100 mins.
VHS: S17895. $19.98.

Miss Grant Takes Richmond
Lucille Ball stars in this dizzy comedy about a screwball secretary who innocently gets involved with a gang of crooks…and unwittingly reforms them. Co-starring William Holden.
VHS: S14089. $19.95.
Lloyd Bacon, USA, 1949, 87 mins.

Miss Right
William Tepper (*Drive, He Said*) stars in and wrote this sexual comedy about a modern guy looking for Miss Right in Rome. He has to choose from Karen Black, Virna Lisi, Marie-France Pisier, Margot Kidder, Dalilia Di Lazzaro and Clio Goldsmith. Music by Art Garfunkel. Directed by songwriter-performer Paul Williams.
VHS: S06850. $79.95.
Paul Williams, USA, 1988, 98 mins.

Mistress
A hilarious satire about the lower fringes of the film industry, settling on a failed director's (Robert Wuhl) last chance at redemption when his script about a tormented, self-destructive painter is bought by a fading producer (Martin Landau). The problems ensue when each of the ego-driven financiers demands his respective girlfriend be cast in the lead. With Danny Aiello, Robert De Niro, Sheryl Lee Ralph, Laurie Metcalf and in a wonderful cameo, Christopher Walken.
VHS: S18197. $19.98.
Barry Primus, USA, 1992, 109 mins.

Mo' Money
Daman Wayans stars in this comedy about a con man who goes straight—for a while. When he begins work at a credit card company he reverts to his old ways. He then gets sucked into more dangerous scams. This comedy also stars Marlon Wayans and Stacey Dash.
VHS: S21442. $19.95.
Peter Macdonald, USA, 1992, 97 mins.

Modern Romance
Albert Brooks' second feature film as director is a hilarious look at filmmaking, neurotic behavior and preserving a love relationship. Film editor Brooks is crazy about Katharine Harrold—perhaps too crazy. Sometimes stuffed animals as presents work, sometimes they don't. With Bruno Kirby, George Kennedy and Bob Einstein (Albert's real brother).
VHS: S06151. $14.95.
Albert Brooks, USA, 1981, 93 mins.

Monkey Business
The Marx Brothers are stowaways on the high seas who become bodyguards to rival gangsters with the usual hilarious results, courtesy of an S.J. Perelman script and an unending number of Maurice Chevalier impersonations.
VHS: S03322. $19.95.
Laser: LD70057. $34.95.
Norman Z. McLeod, USA, 1931, 77 mins.

Monsieur Beaucaire
A pleasant satire of the French aristocracy and ancien regime with Bob Hope as a court barber sent on a suicidal mission, with strange and unexpected pleasures. With Joan Caulfield, Patric Knowles and Marjorie Reynolds.
VHS: S18550. $14.98.
George Marshall, USA, 1946, 83 mins.

The Moon Is Blue
Hugh Herbert adapted his stage hit, a sexy comedy about a proud, virginal woman. Striking the right pose, actors William Holden and David Niven bring real charm to this light, romantic comedy. Their perfect foil is Academy Award nominee Maggie McNamara.
VHS: S21166. $19.98.
Otto Preminger, USA, 1953, 95 mins.

Moon over Parador
Richard Dreyfuss plays an American actor asked to impersonate an unexpectedly dead Caribbean dictator. On the plus side is the company of the dictator's mistress (Sonia Braga) and the fact that chief of security (Raul Julia) will not kill him if he says yes. Decisions. Decisions. With Jonathan Winters, Dick Cavett, Charo, Sammy Davis, Jr. and director Paul Mazursky as the dictator's mother.
VHS: S08503. $19.95.
Paul Mazursky, USA, 1988, 103 mins.

Mother, Jugs and Speed
A funny comedy-thriller about an L.A. ambulance service that's in hot competition with a rival company. Bill Cosby gets some funny lines from Harvey Keitel, Raquel Welch, Larry Hagman.
VHS: S21487. $79.98.
Peter Yates, USA, 1976, 98 mins.

Mr. Blandings Builds His Dream House
Classic screwball comedy stars Cary Grant and Myrna Loy as a couple who retreat from the city to the country to settle into a serene lifestyle. Of course reality conflicts with their fantasies.
VHS: S03265. $14.98.
H.C. Potter, USA, 1948, 93 mins.

Mr. Hobbs Takes a Vacation
James Stewart and Maureen O'Hara take the family to a seashore summer house. Good-natured fun with idealized parents trying their best to make things right for their children.
VHS: S06528. $19.98.
Henry Koster, USA, 1962, 116 mins.

Mr. Lucky
Wartime drama/comedy with Cary Grant as a gambler out to fleece a charity organization. When he meets society woman Laraine Day he reforms and falls in love. Later became the basis for a TV series.
VHS: S02554. $19.95.
H.C. Potter, USA, 1943, 99 mins.

Mr. Peabody and the Mermaid
William Powell stars in this comical fantasy about a man who catches a blonde Ann Blyth while fishing for something other than a mermaid. He brings his catch of the day home and hides her in the pond at his villa. Lucky Mr. Peabody is rich—she could have ended up in the bathtub. B&W.
VHS: S04243. $19.95.
Irving Pichel, USA, 1948, 89 mins.

Mr. Saturday Night
Billy Crystal stars as a self-destructive comedian whose entire career is chronicled in this compelling drama/comedy. The biting humor is wickedly satisfying. Significantly this is also a poignant portrayal of a rich and complex life. David Paymar plays the manager/brother and Jerry Lewis makes a surprise cameo appearance. Outtakes hosted by Crystal are also included.
VHS: S22030. $19.95.
Billy Crystal, USA, 1992, 118 mins.

Mrs. Doubtfire
Robin Williams camps it up as a cross-dressing nanny when he finds that it's the only way he can continue to see his children every day. His wife, Sally Fields, has thrown him out for his childish behavior, a trait he comes to understand as a failing when seen from the standpoint of a stern old woman.
VHS: S20784. $19.98.
Chris Columbus, USA, 1993, 120 mins.

Mrs. Wiggs of the Cabbage Patch
W.C. Fields costars with ZaSu Pitts, the neighbor of the title character. Pauline Lord is the long suffering Mrs. Wiggs, who must deal with calamity on a regular basis. A melodrama made hilarious with the courting scenes of Fields and Pitts. B&W.
VHS: S05527. $19.95.
Norman Taurog, USA, 1934, 80 mins.

Murder by Death
Truman Capote is at the center of this film featuring a great comic cast. Peter Falk, Alec Guinness, David Niven, Dame Maggie Smith, Peter Sellers, Eileen Brennan, Nancy Walker, James Coco and Elsa Lanchester star as just a few of the detectives (not in an untenable situation by an eccentric millionaire. He has invited the world's best sleuths to solve a murder for one million dollars. It's a great spoof of over-complicated murder mysteries. Written by Neil Simon.
VHS: S26474. $19.95.
Laser: LD74618. $34.95.
Robert Moore, USA, 1976, 95 mins.

My Breakfast with Blassie
This hysterical sendup of *My Dinner with Andre* has received unanimously rave reviews. Exclusively shot for video, it stars the most famous professional wrestler of all time, Fred Blassie, and comedian Andy Kaufman in his final role. 60 mins.
VHS: S05190. $19.95.

My Cousin Vinny
This inventive comedy of manners and class conflicts stars Joe Pesci as a Brooklyn-trained lawyer whose first assignment is going to Alabama to defend his cousin, mistakenly charged with the murder of a convenience store clerk. With some hilarious Oscar-winning work by Marisa Tomei as Pesci's gum-popping, leather clad girlfriend and Fred Gwynne as the presiding judge. With Ralph Macchio and Mitchell Whitfield.
VHS: S17229. $19.95.
Laser: LD72192. $39.98.
Jonathan Lynn, USA, 1992, 120 mins.

My Dear Secretary
Kirk Douglas stars as a writer who can't separate business from pleasure. His latest secretary agrees to marry him despite his irresponsible ways, and they elope to the mountains with hilarious results. Also starring Laraine Day.
VHS: S13845. $19.95.
Charles Martin, USA, 1949, 94 mins.

My Father the Hero
Gerard Depardieu is the father and hero of the title who brings a Gallic charm to this hilarious comedy. A beautiful and sunny resort is the location for this story of love, relationships and the wackier side of family interaction, where a daughter tests the limits of fraternal devotion. Lauren Hutton is also featured.
VHS: S21310. $96.98.
Steve Miner, France/USA, 1993, 90 mins.

My Favorite Blonde
Bob Hope plays a vaudeville performer with his loyal penguin who is manipulated by a beautiful woman into a dangerous and very funny chess game of espionage and intrigue. With Madeleine Carroll, Gale Sondergaard and George Zucco.
VHS: S18549. $14.98.
Sidney Lanfield, USA, 1942, 78 mins.

My Favorite Brunette
A spoof of hard-boiled detective stories as baby photographer Bob Hope is involved with Dorothy Lamour in espionage doings, with Peter Lorre the hit-man.
VHS: S03340. $19.95.
Elliott Nugent, USA, 1947, 87 mins.

My Favorite Wife
Cary Grant has his life complicated when his legally dead wife returns to make him a bigamist. Irene Dunne and Randolph Scott were shipwrecked on an island for eight years, but that shouldn't be an excuse for ending a marriage. Great fun. Remade as *Move Over Darling*. B&W.
VHS: Out of print. For rental only.
Laser: CLV. LD71731. $19.98.
Garson Kanin, USA, 1940, 88 mins.

My Favorite Year
Peter O'Toole delivers a wonderful performance in this story of a young writer who discovers that his favorite swashbuckling hero is actually a womanizing alcoholic who has trouble living up to his image. With Lainie Kazan, Bill Macy, Lou Jacobi.
VHS: S21871. $19.98.
Laser: LD74522. $34.98.
Richard Benjamin, USA, 1983, 92 mins.

My Friend Irma
Adapted from the popular radio series, this is the film debut of Dean Martin and Jerry Lewis, as juice-bar operators on the show business fringe encountering vivacious blonde Marie Wilson and John Lund. With Diana Lynn, Don DeFore and Hans Conried.
VHS: S18675. $19.95.
George Marshall, USA, 1949, 103 mins.

My Geisha
Shirley MacLaine disguises herself as a geisha to win a role in her husband's new film. This delightful comedy was filmed on location in Japan and features an all-star cast, including Yves Montand, Robert Cummings and Edward G. Robinson.
VHS: S14281. $14.95.
Jack Cardiff, USA, 1962, 120 mins.

My Life's in Turnaround
Phoebe Cates, John Sayles and Martha Plimpton are featured in cameos along with Eric Schaeffer and Donald Lardner Ward in this hilarious behind-the-scenes look at movie making. This hit from the San Francisco Film Festival shows how a guy with nothing can come out on top.
VHS: S25846. $89.95.
Eric Schaeffer, USA, 1994, 84 mins.

My Little Chickadee
W.C. Fields meets his match in Mae West in this rollicking, double entendre comedy Western. When Cuthbert J. Twillie takes a gander at Flora Belle Lee, it's lust at first sight. Greasewood City may not survive the barrage of one-liners penned by the stars. With Margaret Hamilton and Joseph Calleia. B&W.
VHS: S03073. $14.98.
Eddie Cline, USA, 1940, 83 mins.

My Man Godfrey
Carole Lombard is the madcap heiress who finds a gentleman-bum (William Powell) on a garbage heap, brings him home to become the butler. The result is a wonderful, eccentric satire of the idle rich as Godfrey tries to bring sanity into their lives.
VHS: S18178. $19.95.
Gregory La Cava, USA, 1936, 93 mins.

My Stepmother Is an Alien
A comedy in which the title character hails from another planet, where it is not considered polite to chew cigarette butts and swill car battery fluid. Kim Basinger is the alien sent by her planet to undo the harm caused by widowed Earth scientist Dan Aykroyd. With Allyson Hannigan and Jon Lovitz and a special tribute to the song stylings of Jimmy Durante.
VHS: S09392. $14.95.
Richard Benjamin, USA, 1988, 94 mins.

Mystic Pizza
The comedy that takes a bite out of the seaside resort of Mystic, Connecticut, home to three young waitresses who decide their futures look as appetizing as yesterday's pizza and decide an overhaul is in order. Feisty Jojo, sexy Daisy and bookworm Kat discover that life has a secret ingredient, that friendship is a spice worth savoring and that romance can be a slice of heaven. With Julia Roberts, Lili Taylor and Annabeth Gish.
VHS: S24739. $14.98.
Donald Petrie, USA, 1988, 100 mins.

Naked Gun
A short-lived tv series is the inspiration for this boxoffice bonanza from the same guys who gave the world *Airplane*. Leslie Nielsen reprises his role as Lt. Frank Drebin, a dim witted but very successful L.A. cop. His latest assignment is to safeguard the Queen of England, but that is not as important as the non-stop puns, in-jokes, rude noises, and just plain silliness that fill the screen. With O.J. Simpson, Priscilla Presley, Ricardo Montalban and a host of cameo appearances.
VHS: S08714. $14.95.
Laser: LD75233. $34.98.
David Zucker, USA, 1988, 125 mins.

Nasty Habits
If Watergate had taken place in a Philadelphia convent instead of the White House is the premise of this satiric black comedy. Glenda Jackson has the Nixon role. Sandy Dennis is perfect as scapegoat Joan Dean. With Geraldine Page, Melina Mercouri, Anne Jackson, Anne Meara, Jerry Stiller, Rip Torn and Eli Wallach as other religious members involved in scandal and coverup. Buying this video is not a mortal sin, but taking pleasure from watching it is.
VHS: S10736. $19.95.
Michael Lindsay-Hogg, USA, 1977, 97 mins.

Never a Dull Moment
When a New York songwriter (Irene Dunne) marries a rodeo star (played by Fred MacMurray), she finds life on his rustic Wyoming ranch more of a challenge than she bargained for. But there's never a dull moment and plenty of good-natured fun.
VHS: S13996. $19.98.
George Marshall, USA, 1950, 89 mins.

Never Give a Sucker an Even Break
W.C. Fields' last starring role finds him in his prime, playing himself making a movie. It's a collection of song, slapstick and sketches that defy description. Filled with famous lines. ("She drove me to drink, the one thing I'm indebted to her for.")
VHS: Out of print. For rental only.
Laser: LD70062. $34.95.
Eddie Cline, USA, 1941, 71 mins.

Never Say Goodbye
Errol Flynn and Eleanor Parker are delightful in this comedy about a young girl's attempts to reunite her divorced parents. Flynn turns on all his most polished charms in order to convince Parker that he truly has changed.
VHS: S22896. $19.98.
James V. Kern, USA, 1946, 97 mins.

Never Wave at a WAC
An over-indulged, wise-cracking Senator's daughter enters the Women's Army Core to be with her boyfriend beau, but she can't get above the rank of private. Stars Rosalind Russell, Marie Wilson, Paul Douglas, Arleen Whelan and Hillary Brooke. Alternatively titled *The Private Wore Skirts*.
VHS: S16553. $19.95.
Norman Z. McLeod, USA, 1952, 87 mins.

A New Leaf
Elaine May at her funniest—she wrote, directed and stars in this now classic comedy about a penniless playboy (Walter Matthau) who plots to marry and then murder the klutzy botanist (May).
VHS: S04432. $34.95.
Elaine May, USA, 1971, 102 mins.

Next Stop, Greenwich Village
Larry Lapinsky is a young man seeking fame and discovering independence in this bittersweet comedy set in 1950s New York. His mother, deftly played by Shelley Winters, is distraught when he leaves his traditional family home in Brooklyn and moves to bohemian Greenwich Village.
VHS: S16686. $59.98.
Paul Mazursky, USA, 1976, 109 mins.

Next Time I Marry
In this excellent comedy, Lucille Ball is heir to a $20 million fortune but is forced to marry a poor ditch digger in order to get it. Worse than that, she must travel cross-country with him in a tiny trailer—a situation loaded with laughs and surprises.
VHS: S13997. $19.98.
Garson Kanin, USA, 1938, 65 mins.

A Night at the Opera
Along with *Duck Soup*, the funniest of the Marx Brothers films, featuring the boys amidst high society. The five minutes in Groucho's stateroom is one of the funniest continuous laugh inducers of film.
VHS: S02365. $19.95.
Laser: CAV, 2 discs, Criterion. LD70424. $79.95.
Laser: CLV, 1 disc, Criterion. LD70425. $39.95.
Laser: CLV, MGM. LD70643. $43.98.
Sam Wood, USA, 1935, 90 mins.

A Night in Casablanca
Groucho, Harpo and Chico involved in a nest of Nazi spies in a Casablanca hotel. One of the later Marx Brothers films, but still a good one, with great one-liners and their characteristic antics.
VHS: S01977. $19.95.
Archie Mayo, USA, 1946, 85 mins.

Nine Months
Hugh Grant is at the lead of an exciting cast in this delightful comedy. Julianne Moore, Joan Cusack, Jeff Goldblum and Robin Williams are all featured. Grant plays a young man who has the best in life. He thinks he has everything until his girlfriend discovers she is pregnant and Grant is forced to consider how his life will change when he becomes a father.
VHS: S26996. $99.99.
Laser: LD75436. $39.98.
Chris Columbus, USA, 1995, 103 mins.

No Man of Her Own
The only film to star legendary lovers Clark Gable and Carole Lombard is a light and funny meditation on avarice and gambling. Gable is a card shark with little conscience, toward neither the men whose money he takes nor the women whose commitment he cannot abide…until he meets the dangerously alluring Lombard.
VHS: S02788. $19.95.
Wesley Ruggles, USA, 1932, 81 mins.

The Noose Hangs High
Working with long-time collaborator Charles Barton, Bud Abbott and Lou Costello play low level window washers mistaken for mob functionaries who are entrusted with $50,000 and given 36 hours to repay the note when the money is inadvertently spent. Features the notorious routine, "Are You There?" With Cathy Downs, Joseph Calleia and Leon Errol.
VHS: S17896. $19.98.
Charles Barton, USA, 1948, 77 mins.

Norman…Is That You?
A comedy of race, class, sex and duplicity. Redd Foxx is heartbroken when his wife flees to Mexico with his brother, turns to his son for comfort and solace, and discovers the young man is homosexual. He is determined to "convert" his son's sexual orientation, or die trying. With Pearl Bailey and Dennis Dugan.
VHS: S20207. $19.98.
George Schlatter, USA, 1976, 92 mins.

Nothing But Trouble
In their last film made for MGM, set during World War II, Laurel and Hardy are household servants who unexpectedly befriend a gilded child king and stand guard when his life is endangered. With Mary Boland and Henry O'Neill. Directed by Sam Taylor, a frequent collaborator of Harold Lloyd.
VHS: S17897. $19.98.
Sam Taylor, USA, 1944, 79 mins.

Nothing Sacred

One of the funniest movies ever made; Carole Lombard is the small-town girl who thinks she is dying until she is turned into the sweetheart of New York City as a newspaper publicity stunt. Fredric March is the reporter who falls in love with Lombard. When he discovers Carole is not dying after all, it's up to him to get her out of the predicament.
VHS: $18188. $19.95.
Laser: CLV. LD72064. $39.95.
William Wellman, USA, 1937, 71 mins.

The Nutty Professor

Jerry Lewis is a mild mannered chemistry professor who follows in the footsteps of Dr. Jekyll and becomes Buddy Love, a heartless lounge lizard and heartbreaker. Considered to be Jerry's best comedy and worthy of the adoration of the French. With Stella Stevens, Howard Morris, Kathleen Freeman and Henry Gibson.
VHS: $06990. $19.95.
Laser: LD75347. $29.98.
Jerry Lewis, USA, 1963, 108 mins.

Odd Couple

Jack Lemmon and Walter Matthau are two divorced buddies who decide to be roommates in this film adaptation of the Neil Simon smash hit play. Felix is neat and Oscar is a slob but you probably already knew that. With Hohn Fiedler, Herb Edelman, Monica Evans and Carole Shelley as the Pigeon Sisters.
VHS: $10820. $19.95.
Gene Saks, USA, 1968, 105 mins.

Off Limits

A small and wispy Bob Hope vehicle about a charming and cunning fight manager (Hope) unexpectedly drafted into the Army. When his prize recruit is denied entrance into the war, Hope reluctantly backs Mickey Rooney, whose greatest asset may be his beautiful aunt, Marilyn Maxwell.
VHS: $02780. $19.95.
George Marshall, USA, 1953, 89 mins.

Once Bitten

Jim Carrey and Lauren Hutton team up in this vampire spoof. Lauren is an unaging member of the living dead who needs fresh, virginal blood to keep young and beautiful. The only problem is that she lives in L.A. It's a good thing that Carrey happens to come along to help her find the only hold-outs in La La land.
VHS: $26276. $14.98.
Dimitri Villard, USA, 1985, 93 mins.

The Out-of-Towners

Jack Lemmon and Sandy Dennis are having the time of their lives in New York City. Unfortunately that time is nothing like the one they expected, where the plane would land on time, their hotel reservations would be held, their luggage would be found and no one would walk off with their money. A New York nightmare disguised as a frantic comedy from Neil Simon. Cast includes Sandy Baron, Anne Meara, Billy Dee Williams and Paul Dooley.
VHS: $10821. $19.95.
Laser: LD75348. $29.98.
Arthur Hiller, USA, 1970, 98 mins.

Outrageous Fortune

Bette Midler and Shelley Long find each other sharing an acting class and the same boyfriend. Peter Coyote is the wonderful lover and the missing man they are willing to travel cross country to find—if the KGB and the FBI stay out of their way. With George Carlin.
VHS: $05212. $24.95.
Arthur Hiller, USA, 1987, 99 mins.

Pack Up Your Troubles

When one of their World War I soldier buddies is killed, Laurel and Hardy resolve to take care of his orphaned little girl. Good fun.
VHS: $13866. $14.98.
George Marshall, USA, 1932, 68 mins.

Paleface

Bob Hope is Painless Potter, a timid dentist on his way west with his bride Jane Russell, who is an undercover government agent out to discover who is selling guns to the Indians. This movie won an Oscar for Best Song and spawned a sequel and a remake with Don Knotts. With Robert Armstrong, Iris Adrian and Jack Searle. In color.
VHS: $07804. $59.95.
Laser: LD70064. $34.98.
Norman Z. McLeod, USA, 1948, 91 mins.

Palooka

Jimmy Durante stars as a hard-nosed fight manager determined to make a champion out of Palooka, a hapless country bumpkin, in this delightful comedy. The fine cast includes James Cagney's look-alike brother, William.
VHS: $13857. $19.95.
Ben Stoloff, USA, 1934, 86 mins.

Pardners

Dean Martin and Jerry Lewis formed one of the zaniest comedy teams ever to come out of Hollywood. In this team effort they take on the Western, with its gunslingers, prospectors and, most importantly, its fast women. It's among these wildly colorful characters that they intend to regain the lost family seat.
VHS: $21135. $14.95.
Norman Taurog, USA, 1956, 90 mins.

Pardon My Sarong— Abbott and Costello

An Abbott and Costello feature set in the South Seas, about two bus drivers marooned on a tropical island, and the confusion that results when Lou is mistaken for a god, and the two get entangled with jewel thieves. With Lionel Atwill, Virginia Bruce, Robert Paige and William Demarest.
VHS: $17257. $14.98.
Erle C. Kenton, USA, 1942, 84 mins.

Parents

A very black comedy about growing up in 1958. Randy Quaid and Mary Beth Hurt play suburban Indiana cannibals trying to teach little Brian Madorsky traditional family values. Sandy Dennis plays the concerned school guidance counselor. Actor Bob Balaban serves up an arty and odd little shocker in his directorial debut.
VHS: $09534. $19.98.
Bob Balaban, USA, 1989, 81 mins.

Paris Holiday

This comedy farce brings together Bob Hope and the great Fernandel as they live for the affections of a beautiful spy, Anita Ekberg. Filmmaker Preston Sturges appears in a cameo role.
VHS: $11113. $19.95.
Gerd Oswald, USA, 1957, 100 mins.

Paris When It Sizzles

A screenwriter on deadline (William Holden) has his secretary act out the various plot ideas in an engaging comedy starring Audrey Hepburn and Noel Coward.
VHS: $04433. $29.95.
Richard Quine, USA, 1964, 110 mins.

The Patsy

When a well-known entertainer dies, his management company will do anything to continue, even drafting a bellhop (Jerry Lewis) to become his replacement. It doesn't matter that the patsy has no talent; he is positively hilarious and ultimately becomes the toast of Hollywood.
VHS: $21739. $14.98.
Jerry Lewis, USA, 1964, 106 mins.

People Are Funny

And kids say the darndest things, too. Yes, friends, Art Linkletter is part of the cast in this salute to big-time radio. Also adding music and laughs are Ozzie Nelson, Jack Haley, Rudy Vallee and Frances Langford. Performances by the Vagabonds.
VHS: $05467. $29.95.
Sam White, USA, 1946, 94 mins.

The Perfect Marriage

A screwball farce about the marriage of airplane factory executive David Niven and fashion editor Loretta Young. On their tenth anniversary, a minor argument escalates into a severe misunderstanding and the two promptly initiate divorce proceedings. Their precocious nine-year-old daughter (Nina Griffith), caught in the middle, tries to bring about a reconciliation. With Eddie Albert, Virginia Field, Jerome Cowan and Rita Johnson.
VHS: $19903. $19.98.
Lewis Allen, USA, 1946, 88 mins.

The Perils of Pauline

Hold tight for this one! It's one harrowing escape after another. Betty Hutton comes on like fireworks in this witty comedy about the former star of the famous 1914 serials. Great songs, a host of comedy superstars, and incredible stunt scenes.
VHS: $13858. $19.95.
George Marshall, USA, 1947, 96 mins.

Pete 'n' Tillie

Walter Matthau and Carol Burnett are cast as the title couple who meet, marry and manage not to kill each other when the going gets rough. Geraldine Page and the script were nominated for an Oscar. With Rene Auberjonois and Henry Jones. Adapted from *Witch's Milk* by Peter de Vries. Warning: this film does contain nude piano playing.
VHS: $10799. $19.98.
Martin Ritt, USA, 1972, 100 mins.

Pick a Star

A Hal Roach production frequently mistaken for a Laurel and Hardy effort actually centers on a small-town girl (Rosina Lawrence) and her extravagant ambition to become a Hollywood star. The film features some highly stylized musical numbers and two brief though funny interludes with Laurel and Hardy. With Mischa Auer and Patsy Kelly.
VHS: $17898. $19.98.
Edward Sedgwick, USA, 1937, 70 mins.

Pillow Talk

Rock Hudson and Doris Day at their best. Doris is a pert interior decorator. Together they share a party line, and a lot more….Tony Randall is very funny, and the dialog is witty—if you find it funny.
VHS: $04840. $14.95.
Michael Gordon, USA, 1959, 102 mins.

Pin-Up Girl

Betty Grable stars as the leggy girl who is in love with a sailor in this wartime vehicle loaded with songs and specialty numbers.
VHS: $09444. $19.98.
H. Bruce Humberstone, USA, 1944, 83 mins.

Plain Clothes

A high school comedy from Martha Coolidge (*Valley Girl*) about a tough cop who goes undercover. Arliss Howard stars as Nick Dunbar, the cop trying to solve the murder of a teacher. With Abe Vigoda, George Wendt, Seymour Cassel, Diane Ladd, Suzy Amis and Robert Stack.
VHS: $07818. $89.95.
Martha Coolidge, USA, 1988, 98 mins.

Planes, Trains and Automobiles

Steve Martin is an uptight ad exec trying to get home to Chicago for Thanksgiving with his family. His flight from New York City is detoured to Wichita and he finds himself saddled with John Candy, a well meaning but very annoying shower curtain salesman. A traveler's nightmare filled with slapstick, intolerance and more modes of transportation than are mentioned in the title.
VHS: $06243. $19.95.
Laser: LD75240. $34.98.
John Hughes, USA, 1987, 93 mins.

Plaza Suite

Walter Matthau is cast in three separate roles in this Neil Simon comedy centered in a New York hotel. He plays a father of the bride, a film producer and a philanderer opposite Lee Grant, Barbara Harris and Maureen Stapleton. All the stories take place in the same room. With Louise Latham as the bride.
VHS: $10823. $19.95.
Laser: LD75339. $29.98.
Arthur Hiller, USA, 1971, 114 mins.

Please Don't Eat the Daisies

A successful drama critic moves his family to the country in this film which inspired the later television series. A family comedy with amusing and mischievous children, and Doris Day singing the title song. Starring David Niven, Doris Day, Janis Paige, and Spring Byington.
VHS: $13645. $19.98.
Laser: LD72129. $34.98.
Charles Walters, USA, 1960, 111 mins.

Police Academy

A very silly comedy about a bunch of misfits who are allowed to train as law enforcement officers when a woman becomes mayor of a nameless metropolitan city. Filmed in Toronto. A huge financial success that has spawned three sequels, so far. With Steve Guttenberg, Bubba Smith, Michael Winslow, David Graf and Kim Cattrall.
VHS: $05094. $14.95.
Hugh Wilson, USA, 1984, 95 mins.

The Positively True Adventures of the Alleged Texas Cheerleader-Murdering Mom

Michael Ritchie's HBO film returns to the themes and style of his 1975 *Smile* in an audacious satire based on actual events. Holly Hunter is Wanda Holloway, a devoted mother who will stop at nothing to ensure her daughter's placement on the cheerleading squad. She contracts the services of her former brother-in-law (Beau Bridges) to murder the mother of a rival cheerleader. With Swoosie Kurtz.
VHS: $19237. $19.95.
Michael Ritchie, USA, 1993, 100 mins.

The President's Analyst

James Coburn has one of his best roles in this wacky comedy as he plays the president's therapist who soon becomes Public Enemy—when he quits his job and ends up with the President's private secrets. With Godfrey Cambridge, Severn Darden, Joan Delaney.
VHS: $04434. $19.95.
Theodore Flicker, USA, 1967, 100 mins.

The Prince and the Showgirl

A romantic comedy pairing Laurence Olivier (who also directed) and Marilyn Monroe. The title pretty much explains it all.
VHS: $03561. $19.98.
Laser: LD72151. $34.98.
Laurence Olivier, USA, 1957, 117 mins.

Princess and the Pirate

Bob Hope in a hilarious send up of swashbuckling. Hope is the egotistical vaudevillian who gets shanghaied by pirates, gets involved with a lovely princess, and ends up leading a band of cutthroats.
VHS: $03126. $19.98.
David Butler, USA, 1944, 94 mins.

Princess Comes Across

Carole Lombard is once again deceiving an attractive young man, Fred MacMurray. Lombard is putting on airs on board a ship and passing as a princess. She is actually hoping for an acting career, but a murder mystery, not to mention a romance, inflect her desires into a wholly unexpected sphere.
VHS: $26225. $19.98.
William K. Howard, USA, 1936, 77 mins.

Private Benjamin

Goldie Hawn is a pampered, rich young woman who decides to take control of her life by joining the army after being widowed. It's a long way from the mall to bootcamp as the young novice soon discovers. Eileen Brennan is great as the tough-as-nails sarge. Also features Albert Brooks.
VHS: $22028. $14.95.
Laser: LD74741. $29.98.
Howard Zieff, USA, 1980, 110 mins.

The Private Navy of Sgt. O'Farrel

Bob Hope stars in this zany comedy as a serviceman who tries to lay his hands on some beer for his men. When that fails and Phyllis Diller turns up instead, Hope sets off to recover the missing alcohol. Heroism is the last thing any one would expect to find in this antic plot, but heroism and lots of laughs are there in the end. Gina Lollobrigida is also featured.
VHS: $23962. $14.98.
Frank Tashlin, USA, 1968, 92 mins.

The Producers

Mel Brooks' hilarious hit about the plot to produce a Broadway bomb titled "Springtime for Hitler." Unfortunately, the play is a smash…so is this film. With Zero Mostel and Gene Wilder.
VHS: Out of print. For rental only.
Laser: LD70436. $59.95.
Mel Brooks, USA, 1968, 88 mins.

Promise Her Anything

Written by William Peter Blatty, this comedy tells of a different sort of possession, namely that of a trouble-making baby. Warren Beatty stars as a "blue film" director who falls for young French widow Leslie Caron in the next flat.
VHS: $16625. $14.95.
Arthur Hiller, USA, 1966, 98 mins.

Real Life

Albert Brooks' highly underrated film about a documentary filmmaker (Brooks) whose invasion of a "typically American family" to record their lives tears apart the nuclear family, exposing deeper and darker truths about contemporary America. Brooks' film is raw in its visual patterns, yet the long, uninterrupted takes established him as a filmmaker of flair and talent. Co-written by Harry Shearer and produced by Penelope Spheeris, whose directing career has recently flourished (*Suburbia*, *The Boys Next Door*).
VHS: $02565. $19.98.
Albert Brooks, USA, 1978, 99 mins.

Reality Bites

Winona Ryder stars in this romantic comedy that looks at the dazed confusion of the generation lost between *The Brady Bunch* and *Melrose Place*. Gainful employment seems to elude everyone trapped here. Ethan Hawke and Ben Stiller also star.
VHS: $21205. $19.98.
Ben Stiller, USA, 1994, 98 mins.

Red Headed Woman

A sexy shopgirl (Jean Harlow) sets her sights on marrying the boss. She succeeds on that count but finds that she still isn't welcome in his social circles. Written by Anita Loos and also starring Lewis Stone and Charles Boyer.
VHS: $13648. $29.98.
Jack Conway, USA, 1932, 79 mins.

The Reluctant Debutante

Real-life marriage partners Rex Harrison and Kay Kendall team up as a pair of British high society members in this sophisticated comedy about a young American girl who comes for a visit only to find she must make her debut to the blue-blood set.
VHS: $15246. $19.98.
Laser: LD72152. $34.98.
Vincente Minnelli, USA, 1958, 97 mins.

Remember the Night

Once again Barbara Stanwyck plays a woman in trouble with the law. Fortunately, the man prosecuting her for a shoplifting offense, Fred MacMurray, decides to take her home over the Christmas holiday. It offers the kind of family experience Stanwyck's character never had before. When the holiday is over, however, there is still the small matter of the trial. Preston Sturges wrote the script for this romantic comedy.
VHS: $26228. $19.98.
Mitchell Leisen, USA, 1940, 94 mins.

Rich Kids

Robert Altman produced this witty and touching comedy which views divorce from the perspective of children. Trini Alvarado and Jeremy Levy star as the two bright New York adolescents who escape the trauma of their parents' divorces in a puppy-love relationship.
VHS: $08132. $59.95.
Robert M. Young, USA, 1979, 97 mins.

Ride 'Em Cowboy—Abbott and Costello

In this blithe, funny merging of musical, comedy and western formats, Abbott and Costello are hot dog vendors traveling the American West, with Ella Fitzgerald and the Merry Macs performing, "A Tisket, A Tasket." With Dick Foran, Anne Gwynne, and Johnny Mack Brown.
VHS: $17261. $14.98.
Arthur Lubin, USA, 1942, 81 mins.

Riding on Air

Joe E. Brown stars as Elmer, a bungling small town newspaper reporter with a knack for doing the wrong thing…and having it turn out right. A delightful comedy based on the Elmer Lane stories by Richard Macaulay.
VHS: $13860. $19.95.
Edward Sedgwick, USA, 1937, 58 mins.

Rio Rita

Abbott & Costello are at their funniest as two city-bound guys who end up in a small Texas town where they are chased by Nazi spies as they try to do a little matchmaking for a new friend. Kathryn Grayson and John Carroll. Songs co-written by Harold Arlen. USA, 1942, 91 mins.
VHS: $15422. $19.98.

Risky Business

An original comedy abut the wild teenager who goes wilder while his parents are out of town. Established Tom Cruise as a star and re-introduced Ray-Bans as cool. With Rebecca De Mornay and Curtis Armstrong.
VHS: $02176. $14.95.
Paul Brickman, USA, 1983, 96 mins.

The Road to Bali

The only color road film of Bing Crosby and Bob Hope, with many guest stars. Hope and Crosby save Dorothy Lamour from an evil princess and the dangers of the jungle. 91 mins.
VHS: $11112. $29.95.
Hal Walker, USA, 1952, 90 mins.

The Road to Hong Kong

The last of the Road movies for Bob Hope and Bing Crosby takes them to the Far East. They play con men who share a rickshaw with Joan Collins. Watch for Peter Sellers and Dorothy Lamour. Also Robert Morley when Bob and Bing get involved in the space program. Color.
VHS: $13216. $19.98.
Laser: LD74483. $34.98.
Norman Panama, USA, 1962, 91 mins.

The Road to Morocco

One of the funniest Hope/Crosby road pictures has Crosby selling Hope to a charismatic, devilish sheik played by Anthony Quinn, as they both pursue the beautiful princess Dorothy Lamour. With Dona Drake, Vladimir Sokoloff, Monte Blue and Yvonne De Carlo.
VHS: $17245. $14.98.
David Butler, USA, 1942, 83 mins.

The Road to Rio

Bob Hope and Bing Crosby are a zany and trouble-prone pair of musicians who stow away on a Brazil-bound liner that includes Dorothy Lamour on its passenger list. She is under the evil hypnotic spell of her evil aunt Gale Sondergaard. Leave it to Bob and Bing to open those eyes to romance and one liners. B&W.
VHS: S06068. $69.95.
Norman Z. McLeod, USA, 1947, 100 mins.

The Road to Singapore

The debut road picture has Crosby and Hope as a couple of frustrated men holding out in Singapore, who've given up women, and then vie for the affections of Dorothy Lamour. With Charles Coburn, Judith Barrett and Anthony Quinn.
VHS: S17247. $14.98.
Victor Schertzinger, USA, 1940, 84 mins.

The Road to Utopia

The best of Bob Hope-Bing Crosby-Dorothy Lamour road movies, and also the funniest. The plot finds the duo posing as a pair of escaped killers in an attempt to find an Alaskan gold mine, with Lamour on board the laugh-packed trek across the Yukon as the rightful heiress to the gold claim. With Robert Benchley as the narrator.
VHS: S06555. $14.98.
Hal Walker, USA, 1946, 90 mins.

The Road to Zanzibar

A charming road picture with intimations of cannibalism and anarchy has Hope and Crosby portraying carnival performers crossing the African jungle with Dorothy Lamour in search of a diamond mine. With Una Merkel and Eric Blore.
VHS: S17246. $14.98.
Victor Schertzinger, USA, 1941, 92 mins.

The Road to Collector's Set

Bob Hope is joined by his regular companions, Bing Crosby and Dorothy Lamour, in this series of road comedies. *The Road to Morocco, The Road to Singapore, The Road to Utopia* and *The Road to Zanzibar* are joined in this boxed set.
VHS: S25530. $49.98.

Romance in Manhattan

New York chorus girl Ginger Rogers helps Czech immigrant Francis Lederer get used to life in the big city in this sentimental comedy. As the title indicates, love isn't far behind.
VHS: S13517. $19.98.
Stephen Roberts, USA, 1934, 78 mins.

Room Service

Marx Brothers farce with Groucho as a bankrupt Broadway producer fighting off famine and eviction from a hotel room. With Lucille Ball, Ann Miller and Donald MacBride.
VHS: S01132. $19.98.
William A. Seiter, USA, 1938, 78 mins.

The Ropin' Fool, With Will Rogers

American humorist Will Rogers demonstrates the grace and skill required for roping, assembled in extracts and never-before-seen outtakes from his 1921 film *The Ropin' Fool*, which has been restored and reedited by his family's estate. Narrated by his son, Will Rogers, Jr. 28 mins.
VHS: S18788. $9.95.

Roxie Hart

Ginger Rogers is Roxie Hart, a 1920's showgirl who, for the sake of publicity, lets herself be photographed as a murderer. This outrageous conceit sets up a delightful comedy starring Adolphe Menjou, George Montgomery and William Frawley.
VHS: S26711. $19.98.
William Wellman, USA, 1942, 75 mins.

Ruggles of Red Gap

A simply wonderful film, with Charles Laughton as a British butler who is "lost" in a poker game by his master, the Duke of Burnstead (Roland Young) to a rough-and-tumble American rancher. Arriving in the U.S., Laughton's stiff upper lip begins to quiver as he is introduced by his new employer as Colonel Ruggles and soon has such notable grand dames of cinematic comedy as Mary Boland, ZaSu Pitts and Maude Eburne vying for his attention.
VHS: S05995. $14.98.
Laser: LD71570. $34.98.
Leo McCarey, USA, 1935, 90 mins.

Saps at Sea

Stan and Ollie find themselves adrift on the high seas along with an escaped killer in this Laurel and Hardy comedy vehicle made in 1940. Harry Langdon was one of the writers.
VHS: S13865. $14.98.
Gordon Douglas, USA, 1940, 57 mins.

Saratoga

In her final film Jean Harlow stars as a determined woman dueling a charismatic gambler over the deed on her family's thoroughbred farm. With Walter Pidgeon, Lionel Barrymore and Hattie McDaniel.
VHS: S17783. $19.98.
Jack Conway, USA, 1937, 92 mins.

Saving Grace

Robert (*Ballad of Gregorio Cortez*) Young's largely misunderstood comedy stars Tom Conti as an unhappy individual who happens to be the Pope. A humorous but touching look at a religious leader trying to come into contact with the real world. With Fernando Rey, Edward James Olmos, Giancarlo Giannini.
VHS: S01812. $14.95.
Robert M. Young, USA, 1986, 112 mins.

Scared Stiff

Dean Martin and Jerry Lewis remake Bob Hope's *Ghost Breakers*, stationed on an eerie Caribbean island inhabited by supernatural forces. With Lizabeth Scott, Carmen Miranda and Dorothy Malone.
VHS: S18677. $19.95.
George Marshall, USA, 1953, 108 mins.

Scenes from the Class Struggle in Beverly Hills

Paul Bartel, the man who gave the world *Death Race 2000, Private Parts* and *Eating Raoul*, now turns his attention to the filthy rich. Jacqueline Bisset heads a cast of unhappy, sex-starved people with money. Can servants Robert Beltran and Ray Sharkey alleviate the problems of Bisset, Mary Woronov and Ed Begley Jr.? With Bartel as a plump diet doctor and Paul Mazursky as a randy ghost.
VHS: S10994. $19.95.
Paul Bartel, USA, 1989, 103 mins.

Scrooged

Bill Murray is a modern TV executive who is mocking Christmas and finds himself reliving the life of Ebenezer Scrooge. With John Forsythe, Carol Kane and David Johansen as the ghosts of his life who provide him with real holiday spirit. Watch for Buddy Hackett and Mary Lou Retton as Scrooge and Tiny Tim in the TV-show-within-the movie production.
VHS: S10980. $14.95.
Laser: LD75343. $29.98.
Richard Donner, USA, 1988, 101 mins.

The Secret Life of Walter Mitty

The irrepressible Danny Kaye stars as a mild-mannered mouse who imagines himself as a number of daredevil heroes, including a gunslinger in the Old West and a Mississippi riverboat gambler. It's the ultimate daydreamer's film based on a story by James Thurber. Can the final film was one of Walter's fantasies in which he's a gunman involved with the Irish Republican Army! Also starring Virginia Mayo, Ann Rutherford and Boris Karloff. "Danny Kaye's funniest" (*Time*). Digitally remastered.
VHS: S02179. $19.98.
Norman Z. McLeod, USA, 1947, 110 mins.

The Senator Was Indiscreet

William Powell wants to be President of the United States. The only thing that may stop him is his own diary, filled with years of political deals and shenanigans. George S. Kaufman's only shot at directing a movie proves to be a success. With Peter Lind Hayes and Ella Raines.
VHS: S04245. $19.95.
George S. Kaufman, USA, 1947, 81 mins.

Send Me No Flowers

Hypochondriac Rock Hudson sincerely believes he's dying so he asks his best friend Tony Randall to help find his wife, Doris Day, a second husband. This third pairing of Hudson, Day and Randall is a breezy farce that includes Paul Lynde as a cemetery plot salesman—"When you're ready, we're ready."
VHS: S03680. $14.95.
Norman Jewison, USA, 1964, 100 mins.

Seven Days Ashore/ Hurry, Charlie, Hurry

Comedy double feature. A sailor has three girls in one port. A husband tries to sneak away on a fishing trip. A fish in the bush is worth three birds in the hand. USA, 1944, 140 mins.
VHS: S10637. $19.98.

Seven Little Foys

Bob Hope's perennial favorite, with Hope playing famous vaudevillian Eddie Foy, with the seven little Foys filling in the action. James Cagney is terrific as George M. Cohan.
VHS: S07013. $14.95.
Melville Shavelson, USA, 1955, 93 mins.

Seven Thieves

Comic caper story of an elderly crook who conceives one last plan to rob a Monte Carlo casino. With Edward G. Robinson, Rod Steiger, Joan Collins and Eli Wallach.
VHS: S13202. $39.98.
Henry Hathaway, USA, 1960, 102 mins.

Sex and the Single Girl

Helen Gurley Brown's phenomenal best seller was translated into a battle of wills between the sexes, with soft core pornographer Tony Curtis attempting to seduce the brilliant and beautiful psychologist Natalie Wood. With Henry Fonda, Mel Ferrer, Fran Jeffries, and Stubby Kaye.
VHS: S15936. $19.98.
Laser: LD71188. $34.98.
Richard Quine, USA, 1964, 114 mins.

Shadow of the Thin Man

The fourth Thin Man finds Nick and Nora working on the murder of a racetrack jockey. The suspects include Barry Nelson, Donna Reed, Alan Baxter and Henry O'Neill. San Levene is the official cop on duty. Dickie Hall plays the growing Nick Jr. William Powell and Myrna Loy are the proud parents.
VHS: S05609. $24.95.
W.S. Van Dyke, USA, 1941, 97 mins.

Shampoo

Warren Beatty stars as a Beverly Hills hairdresser in this satiric comic drama of life in Southern California in the late 60's. Beatty has success in his career and all the women he can handle, but he feels there is more to life than cutting heads. With Julie Christie, Goldie Hawn, Lee Grant and Jack Warden.
VHS: S01885. $19.95.
Laser: CLV, Criterion. LD70762. $34.95.
Hal Ashby, USA, 1975, 109 mins.

She Done Him Wrong

Mae West in a terrific spoof of the gay 1890's, with Mae repeating her stage success in the role of Diamond Lil, and Cary Grant the guy who gets asked to come up and see her sometime—which he does, with volatile results.
VHS: S04521. $14.98.
Lowell Sherman, USA, 1933, 66 mins.

Shirley Temple and Friends

Three classic two-reelers starring Shirley Temple, including *Merrily Yours, What's to Do* and *Dora's Dunkin Donuts*. 90 mins.
VHS: S08446. $29.95.

Shirley Temple's Baby Burlesks

The curly-topped cutie stars at the age of four in five parodies of popular films, with an all-kid cast. *Kid in Africa* finds Shirley as Madam Cradlebait the Missionary, who is saved from the cannibals by *The Pie-Covered Wagon, Polly-Tix in Washington* and *Glad Rags to Riches*, where she sings her first on-screen song. B&W.
VHS: S05438. $24.95.
Charles Lamont, USA, 1934-33, 50 mins.

Shut My Big Mouth

Joe E. Brown is mistaken for a wealthy businessman, foils a stagecoach holdup, is elected Marshall and tries to win a woman's hand by rescuing her father from a band of evil kidnappers. Hilarious fun with Victory Jory, Fritz Feld and Adele Mara. USA, 80 mins.
VHS: S15383. $24.95.

Silent Movie

Mel Brooks' romp about director Mel Funn, a washed-up alcoholic whose comeback is hinged on his ability to solicit stars Paul Newman, Liza Minnelli and Burt Reynolds to appear in a blockbuster silent film. Brooks' alternate send-up/homage of the silent film generation is embellished with comedic undercurrents from his regulars Dom Deluise and Marty Feldman.
VHS: S02603. $19.98.
Mel Brooks, USA, 1976, 88 mins.

Silver Streak

Richard Pryor teams up with Gene Wilder in this story of a white executive on vacation who winds up involved in a murder. Pryor portrays "Grover", who assists Wilder in evading the police and ultimately in catching the bad guys. The film contains the classic scene where Pryor teaches Wilder to be "Black".
VHS: S21439. $14.98.
Laser: Widescreen. LD75485. $39.98.
Arthur Hiller, USA, 1976, 113 mins.

Singles

Set in the world of Seattle's music scene, this romantic comedy features Matt Dillon and Bridget Fonda. Together they and a charming cast explore the trials and tribulations of young love accompanied by the music of bands like Pearl Jam, Soundgarden and Mudhoney.
VHS: S22602. $19.98.
Cameron Crowe, USA, 1992, 99 mins.

Sister Act

Whoopi Goldberg plays a second rate Reno lounge performer whose connections to her mob-tied boyfriend (Harvey Keitel) force her into the rigid authoritarianism of a local convent and its Mother Superior (Maggie Smith). Nothing is ever the same. With Bill Nunn, Kathy Najimy and scene-stealer Mary Wickes.
VHS: S17635. $19.99.
Laser: Letterboxed. LD71824. $29.99.
Emile Ardolino, USA, 1992, 100 mins.

Sister Act II: Back in the Habit

Whoopi Goldberg received the largest paycheck ever for an actress to reprise her role as a nightclub singer and undercover nun in this sequel to the blockbuster *Sister Act*. Most of her supporting cast including Maggie Smith and scene-stealing Kathy Najimy are back as well.
VHS: S21432. $96.98.
Bill Duke, USA, 1993, 107 mins.

Snow White and the Three Stooges

Champion figure skater Carol Heiss makes her film debut in this silly version of the classic fairy tale, enlivened by the ridiculous antics of Moe, Larry and Curly.
VHS: S10741. $14.98.
Walter Lang, USA, 1961, 107 mins.

Son of Paleface

A return of the hit comedy *Paleface* in which Bob Hope embarks on an hysterical venture West to claim an inheritance and crosses the paths of Jane Russell, Roy Rogers and Trigger.
VHS: S07765. $14.95.
Frank Tashlin, USA, 1952, 95 mins.

Song of the Thin Man

The sixth and last of the Thin Man movies with Powell and Loy concerns the murder of a bandleader on a gambling ship. The supporting cast includes Gloria Grahame, Keenan Wynn, Jayne Meadows, Ralph Morgan and Dean Stockwell as Nick, Jr. Asta Jr. plays the role of Asta.
VHS: S05611. $24.95.
Edward Buzzell, USA, 1947, 86 mins.

Sons of the Desert

Laurel and Hardy attend a convention of the fraternal order of the Sons of the Desert without letting their wives know the real reason for their absence from home and hearth. Said to be their best feature. With Charley Chase, Mae Busch and Dorothy Christy. B&W.
VHS: S01904. $14.98.
William A. Seiter, USA, 1933, 69 mins.

Sorrowful Jones

Bob Hope and Lucille Ball star in this comedy based on a Damon Runyan tale about a penny-pinching Broadway bookmaker who "inherits" a five-year-old girl when her father puts the mopper up as a collateral for a bet and never comes back. Easing Hope's entry into reluctant fatherhood is old flame Lucy, a nightclub singer who just happens to be the personal property of gangster Bruce Cabot, who'll do anything to make sure his horse wins a big race.
VHS: S05997. $14.98.
Sidney Lanfield, USA, 1949, 88 mins.

A Southern Yankee

Red Skelton is delightful as Aubrey Filmore, a featherbrained but loveable bellboy who dreams of becoming an agent for the Union Forces' Secret Service during the Civil War. Buster Keaton devised many of the gags in the film.
VHS: S15248. $19.98.
Edward Sedgwick, USA, 1948, 90 mins.

Stand-In

A very funny farce about a timid accountant whose task it is to reorganize a bankrupt Hollywood studio. His on-the-job training is provided by a sexy "stand-in". With Joan Blondell, Leslie Howard, Humphrey Bogart.
VHS: S05863. $19.95.
Tay Garnett, USA, 1937, 90 mins.

Start the Revolution Without Me

Gene Wilder and Donald Sutherland play two sets of twins mixed up at birth who grow to manhood during the French Revolution on opposite sides of the economic spectrum. With Hugh Griffith and Billie Whitelaw as the King and Queen of France. A historical comedy of considerable hilarity. Orson Welles narrates.
VHS: S06194. $19.98.
Bud Yorkin, USA, 1970, 91 mins.

Steal Big, Steal Little

Andy Garcia appears as twin brothers in this comedy. Ruben and Robby were adopted by a rich woman in Santa Barbara. When she dies, the brothers learn that she designated only Ruben as her heir. As a result, legal battles, mayhem and even murder could result from their brotherly rivalry. Alan Arkin also stars.
VHS: S27486. $99.99.
Andrew Davis, USA, 1995, 134 mins.

The Stooge

Dean Martin and Jerry Lewis are a musical comedy team on the stage with a twist. Martin doesn't realize that it is really the Stooge, and not him, that everyone is interested in. In the end they manage to laugh and sing through it all, with scarcely a blip.
VHS: S21136. $14.95.
Hal B. Wallis, USA, 1951, 100 mins.

The Stoogephile Trivia Movie

Stooge appearances from the stage, screen and television, never before released. This tape "answers all the questions about the world's funniest comedy team." 55 mins.
VHS: S09248. $19.95.

Strawberry Blonde

James Cagney stars as a good-hearted dentist who carries a torch for the vacuous Rita Hayworth, not fully appreciating the great wife Olivia de Havilland is.
VHS: S02611. $19.98.
Raoul Walsh, USA, 1941, 97 mins.

The Sure Thing

Rob Reiner's comedy about Walter "Gib" Gibson, a highly-spirited young guy and self-proclaimed junk food addict, who accidentally ends up sharing a ride to California with prim and proper Alison Badbury.
VHS: S04301. $14.95.
Rob Reiner, USA, 1986, 94 mins.

Teacher's Pet

George Seaton directs this quick paced comedy/drama about a cynical, hardboiled newsroom editor (Clark Gable) whose distrust of journalism schools brings considerable consternation to journalism teacher Doris Day. Gig Young received an Oscar nomination for his role as Day's drunken playboy boyfriend.
VHS: S02786. $14.95.
Laser: LD75390. $39.98.
George Seaton, USA, 1958, 120 mins.

Teachers

A black comedy about the state of inner city high schools. The film is grounded in Nick Nolte's brave performance as a brilliant though burnt out history teacher and JoBeth Williams as his former student, now a lawyer, who brings suit on behalf of an exploited student. With Judd Hirsch, Ralph Macchio, Laura Dern, Lee Grant and Allen Garfield.
VHS: S17975. $14.95.
Arthur Hiller, USA, 1984, 106 mins.

Ted & Venus

A quirky comedy directed by and starring Bud Cort as a loopy, cult poet whose erotic obsession leads him on a complicated and strange odyssey. With Carol Kane, James Brolin, Martin Mull, Woody Harrelson and Dr. Timothy Leary.
VHS: S18442. $89.95.
Bud Cort, USA, 1992, 100 mins.

That Touch of Mink

Cary Grant's Rolls Royce splashes water all over Doris Day, a small-town girl alone in the big city. Naturally, they are mutually attracted. He wants to fool around. She wants a ring, first. Can a honeymoon in Bermuda be far behind? With Gig Young, Audrey Meadows and Mickey Mantle. Letterboxed.
VHS: S04248. $19.95.
Laser: LD71860. $34.98.
Delbert Mann, USA, 1962, 99 mins.

They All Laughed

Ben Gazzara stars in this madcap private detective chase around New York City, as he and partner John Ritter follow and are followed by Audrey Hepburn, Patti Hansen and Dorothy Stratten in her last film role. A hilarious romantic comedy!
VHS: S01321. $19.95.
Peter Bogdanovich, USA, 1981, 115 mins.

They Might Be Giants

A funny movie; George C. Scott is the gentleman who believes himself to be Sherlock Homes, and his psychiatrist companion whose real name is Dr. Watson. With Joanne Woodward, Jack Gifford.
VHS: S04966. $59.95.
Anthony Harvey, USA, 1971, 98 mins.

The Thin Man

Dashiell Hammett's 1932 crime thriller-comedy stars William Powell, Myrna Loy, and Asta, the terrier, in the now-classic plot in which the daughter of an inventor hires private eye Nick Charles to get to the bottom of a case.
VHS: S01324. $19.98.
Laser: LD70694. $34.98.
W.S. Van Dyke, USA, 1934, 90 mins.

The Thin Man Goes Home

Nick goes home to Sycamore Springs to visit his parents and wouldn't you know it, a murder occurs. The fifth entry in the film series finds that small towns can be just as deadly as the big city. With Anne Revere as Crazy Mary. Also Donald Meek and Leon Ames and, of course, Myrna Loy as sophisticated Nora Charles.
VHS: S05610. $24.95.
Richard Thorpe, USA, 1944, 100 mins.

The Thin Man Collection

William Powell and Myrna Loy symbolized the witty discourse, light entertainment and wisecracking repartee in the *The Thin Man*. In addition to the title entry, there's *After the Thin Man, Another Thin Man, Shadow of the Thin Man, The Thin Man Goes Home* and *Song of the Thin Man*.
Laser: LD70172. $124.98.

This Could Be the Night
Robert Wise's comedy about a beautiful schoolteacher (Jean Simmons) who goes to work at a nightclub, and sets off a volatile sexual triangle with the club's two mercurial owners (Paul Douglas and Anthony Franciosa). With Joan Blondell, Julie Wilson and ZaSu Pitts.
VHS: S18013. $19.98.
  Laser: LD74684. $34.98.
Robert Wise, USA, 1957, 105 mins.

This Is Spinal Tap: Special Collector's Edition
This rockumentary parody launched a dozen careers, beginning with writer/director Rob Reiner. Reiner stars as documentary filmmaker Marty Di Bergi, who chronicles the latest North American tour of the British glamour-metal band, Spinal Tap. This Special Collector's Edition includes a video of the title song from the "Tap's" new album, *Break Like the Wind*, as well as a video for "Hell Hole" and their greatest-hits commercial, "Heavy Metal Memories."
VHS: S16674. $14.95.
  Laser: LD72313. $29.99.
Rob Reiner, USA, 1984, 93 mins.

Three Broadway Girls
This vintage comedy about three gold-diggers stars Joan Blondell, Madge Evans and Ina Claire. Big spenders in the Big Apple had better watch their p's and q's when these husband hunters are on the loose. With David Manners and Lowell Sherman (who also directed). B&W.
VHS: S05061. $29.95.
Lowell Sherman, USA, 1932, 78 mins.

Three Fugitives
Nick Nolte is an ex-bank robber who is taken hostage by a desperate Martin Short during a botched holdup. Short needs the money to keep his small daughter in a special school. Before too long, the cops are after all three in this American remake of a French comedy. (The original starred Gerard Depardieu and Pierre Richard.) Both versions were directed by Francis Veber. With James Earl Jones and Sarah Rowland Doroff.
VHS: S11168. $89.95.
Francis Veber, USA, 1989, 96 mins.

Three Men and a Baby
The popular boxoffice hit is now available on video. Leonard Nimoy directs Tom Selleck, Ted Danson and Steve Guttenberg as a trio of fun loving single guys who find a baby on the doorstep of their swinging bachelor apartment. Based on the French film *Three Men and a Cradle*. The six-month-old Blair twins, Lisa and Michelle of Kitchener, Ontario, play the baby.
VHS: S07914. $89.95.
Leonard Nimoy, USA, 1987, 102 mins.

Three Men on a Horse
A spirited and reflective comedy about a shy, passive young man with an uncanny ability for picking race horse winners. With Frank McHugh, Sam Levene, Joan Blondell and Teddy Hart. Adapted from the play by George Abbott and John Cecil Holm.
VHS: S17664. $19.98.
Mervyn Le Roy, USA, 1936, 88 mins.

The Three Stooges
The Stooges made over 200 short comedies from 1934 to 1958. Included here are three of the funniest: *Disorder in the Court* (1936), *Sing a Song of Six Pants* (1947) and *Malice in the Palace* (1949). Wonderful madness. USA, 50 mins.
VHS: S02235. $24.95.

The Three Stooges Collection
Six more collections of priceless moments from the career of the Stooges.
All the World's a Stooge and Other Nyuks.
VHS: S11541. $14.95.
Hold That Lion and Other Nyuks.
VHS: S11536. $14.95.
Studio Stooges and Other Nyuks.
VHS: S11540. $14.95.
The Hot Scots and Other Nyuks.
VHS: S11538. $14.95.
The Uncivil War Birds and Other Nyuks.
VHS: S11537. $14.95.
Three Smart Saps and Other Nyuks.
VHS: S11539. $14.95.

The Three Stooges Go Around the World in a Daze
Jules Verne's classic tale of exploration and adventure takes a wacky turn when the Three Stooges team up with the grandson of the original hero. This has some of the best sight gags dreamed up by the Three Stooges.
VHS: S26507. $14.95.
Norman Maurer, USA, 1963, 94 mins.

The Three Stooges Hit Home
New-to-video episodes of Larry, Moe and Curly.
A Ducking They Will Go and Other Nyuks.
VHS: S07999. $14.95.
Ants in the Pantry and Other Nyuks.
VHS: S07998. $14.95.
In the Sweet Pie and Pie and Other Nyuks.
VHS: S08000. $14.95.
Phony Express and Other Nyuks.
VHS: S08001. $14.95.
Playing the Ponies and Other Nyuks.
VHS: S08002. $14.95.
Three Little Twerps and Other Nyuks.
VHS: S07997. $14.95.

The Three Stooges in Orbit
Despotic television producers exhort the Three Stooges to formulate a new concept for a cartoon. Along the way they accidentally launch a scientist's new invention, a rocket that brings them into contact with Martian invaders. Now they must brainstorm to save their TV careers and the world.
VHS: S26510. $14.95.
Edward Bernds, USA, 1962, 87 mins.

The Three Stooges Meet Hercules
A time machine places the comic antics of the Three Stooges into the ancient era. There, they encounter a villainous Hercules but transform him into the hero of myth and legend. This is the film that mixes Hollywood historical epics and zany Stooges magic.
VHS: S26509. $14.95.
Edward Bernds, USA, 1961, 89 mins.

The Three Stooges—More Nyuks
Six more volumes of the uncensored bits of the Three Stooges.
Cookoo Cavaliers and Other Nyuks.
VHS: S09407. $14.95.
From Nurse to Worse and Other Nyuks.
VHS: S09408. $14.95.
Half-Wit's Holiday and Other Nyuks.
VHS: S09409. $14.95.
Idiots Deluxe and Other Nyuks.
VHS: S09410. $14.95.
Nutty But Nice and Other Nyuks.
VHS: S09411. $14.95.
They Stooge to Conga and Other Nyuks.
VHS: S09406. $14.95.

The Three Stooges: Have Rocket Will Travel
This is the very first Three Stooges feature film. It's a hilarious romp through outer space that all begins when the three find themselves accidentally aboard a rocket. Though disaster looms, laughs carry the day, and the Three Stooges become national heroes.
VHS: S26506. $14.95.
David Lowell Rich, USA, 1959, 76 mins.

The Three Stooges: Stop! Look! and Laugh!
This film brings together episodes from earlier Three Stooges shorts. Ventriloquist Paul Winchell and his dummy Jerry Mahoney are featured as the originators of these classic comic bits.
VHS: S26508. $14.95.
Jules White, USA, 1960, 78 mins.

The Three Stooges: The Outlaws
Adam West co-stars in this final Three Stooges feature. It's a broad parody of that great American film genre, the Western. Nothing holds the comic threesome back as they lampoon everything held sacred the world over by John Wayne and Clint Eastwood fans.
VHS: S26511. $14.95.
Norman Maurer, USA, 1964, 88 mins.

Thrill of a Romance
A 22-year-old Esther Williams reaches Hollywood stardom in this light romantic comedy. *Thrill of a Romance* also marks the first leading role for Van Johnson whose boyish charm made him the heartthrob of a wholesome '40s America, and secured four more film roles that he would star in with Williams.
VHS: S16611. $19.98.
Richard Thorpe, USA, 1945, 104 mins.

Throw Momma from the Train
Billy Crystal has two major problems in this slightly black comedy. One is a severe case of writer's block and the other is Owen, who wants his writing instructor to kill his overbearing mother. Danny DeVito is Owen. Oscar nominee Anne Ramsey is the target for termination. Loosely based on Hitchcock's *Strangers on a Train*, only funnier.
VHS: S06448. $19.98.
Danny DeVito, USA, 1987, 88 mins.

To Be or Not to Be
This remake of the 1942 comedy features Mel Brooks and Anne Bancroft as stars of a Polish theater who become involved with invading Nazis.
VHS: S20445. $14.98.
  Laser: LD71370. $34.98.
Alan Johnson, USA, 1983, 108 mins.

Too Far to Go
Michael Moriarty, Blythe Danner and Glenn Close star in this eccentric comedy about a couple who can't resist being cruel to one another. It has all the insight and wit one would expect from a film based on the stories of Pulitzer Prize-winner John Updike. USA, 1995, 98 mins.
VHS: S27500. $89.95.

Tootsie
Dustin Hoffman plays an unemployed actor who dons women's clothing and becomes a great success in a popular tv soap opera. He also falls in love with a female co-star and learns that he has become a better man by pretending to be a woman. With Jessica Lange, Geena Davis, Dabney Coleman and Bill Murray as his amused roommate.
VHS: Out of print. For rental only.
  Laser: LD70765. $124.95.
Sydney Pollack, USA, 1982, 116 mins.

The Toy
A flat-broke reporter must resort to becoming the "toy" of a rich millionaire's son. Richard Pryor portrays the "Toy" while Jackie Gleason is cast as the millionaire. Both turn in good performances but there is something offensive about the whole idea. It would have been more interesting had the two comedians switched roles.
VHS: S21474. $14.95.
Richard Donner, USA, 1982, 99 mins.

Trading Places
Eddie Murphy is the street hustler, Dan Aykroyd the preppie in this blockbuster comedy of manners where the two leads switch lives and see how they adapt. Very funny. Also stars Don Ameche, Ralph Bellamy and Denholm Elliott.
VHS: S02175. $19.95.
John Landis, USA, 1983, 106 mins.

Trouble Along the Way
The Quiet Man has a "new kind of dame to tame" in this riotous and moving comedy about a hopeless college football team that coopts a famous coach to lead their school out of financial straits. The plan works, but the new coach's methods are not quite above board. John Wayne, Donna Reed and Charles Coburn star.
VHS: S15989. $19.98.
  Laser: LD74721. $34.98.
Michael Curtiz, USA, 1953, 110 mins.

The Trouble with Angels
The authority of the church and adolescent rebellion meet head on in Ida Lupino's film about two young thrill seekers (Hayley Mills and June Harding) who continually test the will and fortitude of their Mother Superior, Rosalind Russell, during their stay in a Pennsylvania convent school.
VHS: S16912. $14.95.
Ida Lupino, USA, 1966, 112 mins.

The Tunnel of Love
An adult comedy of manners directed by Gene Kelly, adapted from the long-running play by Joseph Fields and Peter De Vries. A young couple (Doris Day and Richard Widmark) resorts to desperate measures when they're unable to conceive, and encounter bureaucratic confusion when they decide to adopt. With Gig Young and Gia Scala.
VHS: S18014. $19.98.
Gene Kelly, USA, 1958, 98 mins.

Twenty Bucks
This comic portrayal of contemporary America follows the path of a twenty dollar bill as it crosses the divides of race and class which separate the strata of big city life. Linda Hunt, Steve Buscemi and Gladys Knight portray some of the quirky characters encountered on this cash-driven journey.
VHS: S20887. $19.95.
Keva Rosenfeld, USA, 1992, 91 mins.

Unaccustomed As We Are
Stan Laurel and Oliver Hardy join Thelma Todd and Mae Busch for their very first talkie. It has a simple but brilliant premise. Babe (Hardy) brings his friend home for dinner completely unannounced. This sets off a domestic spat rife with comic possibilities. Both the sound version and the simultaneously released, silent intertitled version are included on this video.
VHS: S26812. $16.95.
Lewis R. Foster, USA, 1929, 39 mins.

The Unofficial Dan Quayle Video
A highly unauthorized and naturally funny collection of Quayle's speeches, non sequiturs, misstatements, press conferences and interviews. 27 minutes.
VHS: S16901. $9.99.

Up the Academy (Mad Magazine Presents Up the Academy)
A raunchy comedy about a tenth rate military school where scholarship and discipline are just two of the words that the cadets would have great difficulty spelling. Lead Ron Leibman had his name removed from the film and from all advertising. Barbara Bach and Ralph Macchio didn't.
VHS: S04177. $59.95.
Robert Downey, USA, 1980, 88 mins.

Up the Sandbox
Barbra Streisand stars as a discontented Manhattan housewife and mother of two small children. She's married to professor David Selby and escapes frequently into dreams of Fidel Castro, bombing the Statue of Liberty and traveling to Africa. With Jane Hoffman, Anne Ramsey and Stockard Channing. Filmed in New York and Kenya.
VHS: S07007. $19.98.
  Laser: LD71472. $34.98.
Irvin Kershner, USA, 1972, 97 mins.

Used Cars
"A classic screwball fantasy—a neglected modern comedy that's like a more restless and visually high-spirited version of the W.C. Fields pictures" (Pauline Kael). Hilarious, energetic! With Kurt Russell and Jack Warden in a brilliant double role.
VHS: S01406. $19.95.
  Laser: CLV, chapter stops. LD74995. $34.95.
Robert Zemeckis, USA, 1980, 95 mins.

Used People
This dark-edged comedy is set in Queens, 1969. The film's comic premise considers the aftermath when a Jewish woman (Shirley MacLaine) is courted by an Italian lothario (Marcello Mastroianni) on the afternoon of her husband's funeral. The movie also deals with MacLaine's relationships with her two monstrously unhappy adult daughters, Bibby (Kathy Bates) and Norma (Marcia Gay Harden). With Jessica Tandy and Sylvia Sidney.
VHS: S18603. $19.98.
Beeban Kidron, USA, 1992, 116 mins.

Utopia
The final film of Laurel and Hardy, a French-Italian co-production also known as *Atoll K* or *Robinson Crusoe-Land*. Laurel and Hardy inherit an island which turns out to be valuable as a source of uranium.
VHS: S02236. $29.95.
Leo Joannon, France/USA, 1952, 83 mins.

Valley of the Sun
Lucille Ball stars in this western comedy/drama about an Army scout in conflict with a government agent over the treatment of the Indians. With Cedric Hardwicke and Dean Jagger.
VHS: S10672. $19.98.
George Marshall, USA, 1942, 78 mins.

Viva Max
Peter Ustinov plays a Mexican general who invades Texas and re-takes the Alamo from a crowd of surprised tourists. This contemporary comedy boasts a fine supporting cast which includes John Astin, Pamela Tiffin, Jonathan Winters and Keenan Wynn. Remember the Alamo, once again.
VHS: S04247. $14.98.
Jerry Paris, USA, 1969, 93 mins.

Volunteers
When a spoiled playboy fleeing from a gambling debt joins the Peace Corps, Thailand is not the better for it. Tom Hanks is the jaded American who finds the jungle too primitive and the local bandits a bit on the aggressive side. With Rita Wilson (now Mrs. Tom Hanks), Tim Thomerson and John Candy as a running dog lacky of an imperialist regime. Ask not what this movie can do for you.
VHS: S09517. $19.95.
Nicholas Meyer, USA, 1985, 107 mins.

W.C. Fields—Straight Up
An Emmy Award-winning special tribute to the great Fields, narrated by Dudley Moore, and including classic comedy scenes from *Never Give a Sucker an Even Break*, *My Little Chickadee*, *The Bank Dick*, *The Dentist* and other notable Fields films. 100 mins.
VHS: S11500. $59.95.

W.C. Fields: On Stage, on Screen, on the Air
W.C. Fields at his cynical best in a classic radio rivalry with Charlie McCarthy and later on the golf course. 60 mins.
VHS: S07025. $19.95.

Walk, Don't Run
Cary Grant's last feature film is a briskly moving comedy of manners set against the Tokyo Olympics of 1964. He's a British industrialist with a housing problem both solved and complicated when he moves in with an American athlete and a proper young English woman. A remake of *The More the Merrier*. With Jim Hutton and Samantha Eggar.
VHS: S06070. $69.95.
  Laser: CLV, letterboxed, chapter stops. LD74996. $34.95.
Charles Walters, USA, 1966, 114 mins.

Wayne's World
Penelope Spheeris directs the feature-length adaptation of the *Saturday Night Live* sketch program detailing the comic adventures of two young hipsters who host a postmodern television show on cable-access from their parents' basement in Aurora, Illinois. Mike Myers and Dana Carvey are the ubiquitous Wayne and Garth. Rob Lowe is a sleazy television programmer and Tia Carrere plays the love interest, a gilded rock goddess.
VHS: S17422. $14.95.
Penelope Spheeris, USA, 1992, 95 mins.

We Think the World of You
Gary Oldman and Alan Bates star in this comedy of forbidden triangles in which Frank has fallen in love with Evie, the girl his best friend left behind. And Evie's a real dog (four legs and a wet nose). There's nothing wrong going on—it's just a hilarious case of puppy love. And love isn't easy when the girl you can't get off your mind isn't allowed on your furniture.
VHS: S09208. $19.95.
Colin Gregg, USA, 1988, 94 mins.

We're No Angels
Robert De Niro and Sean Penn star as a couple of affable convicts who disguise themselves as priests in order to escape into the safety of Canada during the Depression. Based very loosely on the 1955 escaped convict comedy starring Humphrey Bogart, Aldo Ray and Peter Ustinov. The remake also features Demi Moore, Wallace Shawn and James Russo. Excellent period detail.
VHS: S12238. $19.95.
Neil Jordan, USA, 1989, 110 mins.

We're Not Married
Six couples find that they were never legally married in this smartly played comedy. Stars Ginger Rogers, Fred Allen, Victor Moore, Paul Douglas, Eve Arden, Marilyn Monroe, David Wayne, Louis Calhern, Zsa Zsa Gabor, Mitzi Gaynor, Eddie Bracken, James Gleason and Jane Darwell.
VHS: S16399. $19.98.
Edmund Goulding, USA, 1952, 85 mins.

Welcome Stranger
Bing Crosby and Joan Caulfield are joined in this romantic comedy about a young doctor. Old doctor Barry Fitzgerald goes on vacation and a brash young upstart is the surprising substitute who takes over his practice.
VHS: S25013. $14.98.
Elliott Nugent, USA, 1947, 107 mins.

What's New Pussycat
Peter O'Toole visits Parisian psychiatrist Peter Sellers for advice on his love life, but soon learns he is dealing with a quack. With Romy Schneider, Capucine, Paula Prentiss and Woody Allen (the scriptwriter) as Victor Shakadopoulos. Title song by Burt Bacharach and Hal David sung by Tom Jones. Watch for chess games by the Seine, comic bed-hopping and go-kart races.
VHS: S13217. $19.98.
  Laser: LD72134. $34.98.
Clive Donner, USA, 1965, 108 mins.

What's Up Doc
Barbra Streisand and Ryan O'Neal star in this Peter Bogdanovich salute to the screwball comedy. She's a nutcase and he's a very absent-minded musicologist. Together they upset quite a few people in San Francisco. With Madeline Kahn, Kenneth Mars and Liam Dunn.
VHS: S04657. $19.98.
  Laser: Includes theatrical trailer. LD71471. $34.98.
Peter Bogdanovich, USA, 1972, 94 mins.

The Wheeler Dealers
A comedy of cultural and social observation about a sardonic Texas oilman (James Garner) who tries his luck in the hostile environs of Wall Street and captures the attention of stock analyst Lee Remick. With Phil Harris, Chill Wills and Jim Backus.
VHS: $18669. $19.98.
Arthur Hiller, USA, 1963, 100 mins.

When Harry Met Sally
Billy Crystal and Meg Ryan are unforgettable as the pair of would be former lovers who simply can't pull away from one another. It's a romantic comedy about two people who have trouble admitting their own feelings, even if it's plain to everyone else that they were made for each other.
VHS: $22603. $14.95.
Rob Reiner, USA, 1989, 96 mins.

Where the Boys Are
A witty comedy about four beautiful young college students in Fort Lauderdale who share a hotel room and are on the make for male companionship. Connie Francis stars and performs the title song. With Paula Prentiss, Yvette Mimieux, George Hamilton and Jim Hutton.
VHS: $18016. $19.98.
Henry Levin, USA, 1960, 100 mins.

Where the Girls Are
This military short humorously exposes the dangers of VD in an unwittingly campy fashion. A young soldier off to Vietnam tries to heed his C.O.'s warning about the dangers of massage parlors, but when letters from his girl back home are interrupted, he succumbs to temptation with disastrous consequences. 23 mins.
VHS: $24007. $14.95.

Where There's Life
Bob Hope is a hapless and previously unknown heir to a small kingdom. The life of this former dog food peddler is hilariously turned around by court intrigues, kidnapping plots and romance. With Signe Hasso and William Bendix.
VHS: $25528. $14.98.
Sidney Lanfield, USA, 1947, 75 mins.

Where Were You When the Lights Went Out?
A comedy about the personal, romantic and social complications of a Hollywood starlet (Doris Day), known for her virtue, who deals with her straying husband and unnerved producer, and the ensuing mayhem during a massive power blackout in Manhattan. With Robert Morse, Terry-Thomas and Patrick O'Neal.
VHS: $18015. $19.98.
Hy Averback, USA, 1968, 94 mins.

Where's Poppa?
Carl Reiner directs this very black comedy about an uptight New York attorney whose social life is constantly being ruined by his senile mother. George Segal is the lawyer at his wits end. Ruth Gordon is the albatross around his neck. With Trish Van Devere as the new girlfriend and Ron Leibman as Segal's brother Sidney who finds Central Park a place of peril and romance while dressed in a gorilla suit. Script by Robert Klane from his novel.
VHS: $01448. $19.95.
Laser: LD71144. $34.98.
Carl Reiner, USA, 1970, 83 mins.

Whistling in Brooklyn
Red Skelton appears as the popular radio criminologist code-named "The Fox" whose efforts to solve a string of bizarre murders involves various forms of deception and his getting entangled with the Brooklyn Dodgers baseball team. With Ann Rutherford, Polly Benedict, Ray Collins and William Frawley.
VHS: $18482. $19.98.
S. Sylvan Simon, USA, 1943, 87 mins.

Whistling in Dixie
Red Skelton is cast as radio sleuth Wally "The Fox" Benton, whose honeymoon with Ann Rutherford is interrupted by the usual murder and mayhem. With George Bancroft and Guy Kibbee.
VHS: $19567. $19.98.
S. Sylvan Simon, USA, 1942, 73 mins.

Whistling in the Dark
The popular radio sleuth self-named "The Fox" is kidnapped by a cult and ordered by their leader to execute the perfect murder to remove the heir who's blocking the cult's receipt of a vast inheritance. With Red Skelton, Conrad Veidt, Ann Rutherford and Virginia Grey.
VHS: $18483. $19.98.
S. Sylvan Simon, USA, 1941, 78 mins.

White Men Can't Jump
Wesley Snipes and Woody Harrelson team up as a couple of hustlers who prey on pick-up basketball players who assume that white men can't jump. The film is a fast paced comedy with fine performances from Snipes and Rosie Perez as Harrelson's girlfriend. Features Tyra Ferrell, Cylk Cozart and Kadeem Hardison.
VHS: $21443. $19.98.
Ron Shelton, USA, 1992, 115 mins.

Who Framed Roger Rabbit?
The winner of four Academy Awards. A razzle dazzle combination of live action and hilarious animation as private eye Eddie Valiant reluctantly takes on a Toon as a client and learns who is playing patty cake with whom in Los Angeles of the late '40's. With Bob Hoskins, Christopher Lloyd, Joanna Cassidy and the voices of Kathleen Turner as Jessica and Charles Fleischer as Roger. Plus many of your favorite animated friends.
VHS: $10337. $22.99.
Laser: LD71209. $39.99.
Robert Zemeckis, USA, 1988, 104 mins.

Who Killed "Doc" Robbin? (Curley and His Gang in the Haunted Mansion)
An Our Gang comedy, of sorts, in color, starring George Zucco as a mad scientist involved in an atomic firing chamber. It explodes and "Fix-It" Dan and Nurse Ann are both suspects. With Virginia Grey and the successors to the Our Gang Kids.
VHS: $10104. $24.95.
Bernard Carr, USA, 1948, 50 mins.

Who's Harry Crumb?
The real question should be why is Harry Crumb so good at coming up with the right answers to all the wrong questions, but that would be too much to put on a movie marquee. John Candy plays a bumbling private detective who has a yen to dress up in various disguises. His current case involves a kidnap and murder plot. With Jeffrey Jones, Barry Corbin and Annie Potts. Pick a suspect.
VHS: $09509. $19.98.
Paul Flaherty, USA, 1989, 89 mins.

Wilder Napalm
This quirky romantic comedy stars Dennis Quaid and Debra Winger. Two brothers fight fires together but battle each other through their innate telekinetic powers over the love of the same woman. The results of this incendiary mix are passionate, and even fiery.
VHS: $20715. $95.95.
Laser: LD72384. $34.95.
Glen Gordon Caron, USA, 1993, 109 mins.

Wise Guys
A comedy from director Brian De Palma. After trying to hoodwink their mob boss, Harry (Danny DeVito) and Moe (Joe Piscopo) go on the run together. The problem is that each has been secretly assigned to rub out the other. "An abundant movie, filled with ideas and gags and great characters. It never runs dry" (Roger Ebert).
VHS: $13973. $19.99.
Brian DePalma, USA, 1986, 100 mins.

The Wistful Widow of Wagon Gap— Abbott and Costello
Abbott and Costello star in this western parody set in the frontier community of Wagon Gap, Montana. Lou accidentally kills a man and is legally obligated to care for his wife and seven children, rising to become sheriff of the town. With Marjorie Main, George Cleveland, Gordon Jones and William Ching.
VHS: $17258. $14.98.
Charles Barton, USA, 1947, 78 mins.

Without Reservations
Claudette Colbert and John Wayne star in this romantic comedy about a famous woman writer who heads for Hollywood and meets a marine on the train who would be ideal for the male lead in her script.
VHS: $13385. $19.98.
Mervyn LeRoy, USA, 1946, 101 mins.

Woman of Distinction
Rosalind Russell is a leading figure in the community as well as Dean of Benton College. She has no time for romance until she meets Ray Milland, a handsome British astronomer. A captivating comedy!
VHS: $01911. $69.95.
Edward Buzzell, USA, 1950, 85 mins.

Woman's World
This terrific 50's comedy/drama features an all star cast. Clifton Webb, Lauren Bacall, Fred MacMurray, Arlene Dahl, Cornel Wilde and June Allyson star as three couples all set in a highly competitive world of corporate advancement. Three men could become general manager, but this promotion is dependent upon which woman is the perfect wife for the job.
VHS: $24577. $19.98.
Jean Negulesco, USA, 1954, 94 mins.

Wonder Man
Danny Kaye plays the dual role of a scholarly bookworm and his twin brother, a song-and-dance man with gangster troubles. When the latter meets up with a fatal bullet, the bookworm takes his place in a nightclub, resulting in hilarious complications. This entertaining film romp won an Academy Award for Best Special Effects in 1945. Digitally remastered.
VHS: $03487. $19.98.
H. Bruce Humberstone, USA, 1945, 97 mins.

Working Girl
Mike Nichols' insightful romantic comedy has an ebullient spirit, carried by Melanie Griffith's hard-edged portrayal of an ambitious secretary caught in corporate games with her vengeful boss (Sigourney Weaver) and the attractive, charismatic lawyer (Harrison Ford) they're both in love with. With strong supporting work from Alec Baldwin and Joan Cusack. Carly Simon performs the Academy Award winning song, "Let the River Run."
VHS: Out of print. For rental only.
Laser: LD71218. $39.98.
Mike Nichols, USA, 1988, 113 mins.

The World of Abbott and Costello
Over 18 films have been mined to compile this video featuring the humor of Abbott and Costello. This is a great introduction to the entire range of their comic work. 75 mins.
VHS: $24391. $14.98.

The World of Henry Orient
George Roy Hill's mischievous comedy about a brilliant, nonconformist pianist (Peter Sellers) whose strange world is turned out of control by two young girls' dangerous infatuation with him. They follow him around New York City, charting his every move and gesture. With Tippy Walker, Merrie Spaeth, Paula Prentiss and Tom Bosley.
VHS: $19568. $19.98.
Laser: LD72208. $34.98.
George Roy Hill, USA, 1964, 106 mins.

Yankee Zulu
Two childhood friends meet 25 years after parting and are forced to "switch" races. From this premise, a hilarious comedy develops that is perfect family viewing. One catastrophe leads to another until a full-fledged farce emerges from the chaos.
VHS: $27508. $95.99.
Gray Hofmeyr, USA/South Africa, 1995, 90 mins.

The Yellow Cab Man
This very funny comedy stars Red Skelton as an accident-prone inventor of safety gadgets forced by economic necessity into driving a cab, with bizarre and unpredictable consequences. With Gloria De Haven, Walter Slezak, Edward Arnold and James Gleason.
VHS: $17900. $19.98.
Jack Donohue, USA, 1950, 85 mins.

Young Frankenstein
Both a spoof of the original and an affectionate tribute to all the horror films of the 1930's. With Gene Wilder as the young Dr. Frankenstein, Marty Feldman as his bizarre laboratory assistant and Peter Boyle as the scatter-brained monster.
VHS: $01495. $19.98.
Laser: LD71223. $34.98.
Mel Brooks, USA, 1974, 106 mins.

Younger and Younger
Donald Sutherland, Lolita Davidovich, Sally Kellerman, Julie Delpy and Linda Hunt star in this offbeat romantic comedy. At the center of the film is a marriage from hell that is transformed into a match made in heaven.
VHS: $24062. $92.95.
Laser: LD74981. $39.99.
Percy Adlon, USA, 1994, 97 mins.

Yours, Mine and Ours
Lucille Ball plays a widow with eight kids who marries Henry Fonda—and his ten kids. The result is unbelievable bedlam, needless to say. With Van Johnson, Tom Bosley.
VHS: $11158. $14.95.
Melville Shavelson, USA, 1968, 111 mins.

Zenobia
Oliver Hardy played in a number of films as a solo comic act. In this classic film he plays Dr. Tibbit, an animal-loving physician who wins the heart of a carnival elephant. Laughing Gravy, a hilarious short starring both Laurel and Hardy, is also included. 93 mins.
VHS: $21533. $19.95.

WOODY ALLEN

Alice
Mia Farrow plays an upscale housewife and lapsed Catholic who visits an old Chinese herbalist for treatment of her bad back and ends up, as the result of a potion, invisible, whereupon she embarks on a series of magical and romantic adventures. With Joe Mantegna and Blythe Danner.
VHS: $14259. $94.98.
Woody Allen, USA, 1990, 106 mins.

Annie Hall
One of Woody Allen's best and funniest films, with Diane Keaton as the sometime object of Woody Allen's affections and expressions of his neurosis. Winner of many Academy Awards. With Allen, Keaton, Paul Simon, Carol Kane.
VHS: $00059. $19.95.
Laser: CLV, Criterion. LD70339. $49.95.
Laser: Deluxe letterboxed edition. Includes original theatrical trailer. LD71506. $34.98.
Woody Allen, USA, 1977, 94 mins.

Another Woman
Gena Rowlands stars in this Woody Allen drama as an accomplished philosophy professor who eventually realizes she has no friends and not much of a personal life. By listening through a vent to the problems of Mia Farrow she regains her humanity. A distinguished cast includes Gene Hackman, Ian Holm, Sandy Dennis, Martha Plimpton, John Houseman, Blythe Danner and Harris Yulin.
VHS: $09156. $19.95.
Woody Allen, USA, 1988, 81 mins.

Bananas
Woody Allen stars as Fielding Mellish, a New York City products tester who finds himself appointed the president of a Latin American country after a revolution. With Louise Lasser, Charlotte Rae, Conrad Bain, and Howard Cosell as himself. Watch for Sylvester Stallone as a subway hoodlum. Music by Marvin Hamlisch.
VHS: $00092. $19.98.
Laser: LD70191. $44.98.
Woody Allen, USA, 1971, 82 mins.

Broadway Danny Rose
Sitting at the Carnegie Deli are some of the Catskills' greatest comics, swapping stories about the infamous, lovable agent Broadway Danny Rose (played by Woody Allen). A brilliant, comedic tribute to show biz from one of the finest comedians of our time. With Mia Farrow and Nick Apollo Forte.
VHS: $00184. $14.98.
Woody Allen, USA, 1984, 86 mins.

Bullets over Broadway
Woody Allen cast Jim Broadbent, John Cusack, Harvey Fierstein, Mary Louise Parker, Rob Reiner, Tracey Ullman and other great actors in this comedy where gangsters collide with Broadway. A young playwright is desperate to get his play produced and goes to the mob for backing. Like any producer, they do whatever they can to preserve and promote their investment, with hilarious results.
VHS: $23963. $96.98.
Laser: Letterboxed. LD74938. $39.99.
Woody Allen, USA, 1994, 95 mins.

Crimes and Misdemeanors
Woody Allen presents two interlocking stories set in New York. One comic, one serious, but both thoughtful. Martin Landau is a prominent, married eye surgeon troubled by the demands of his mistress Anjelica Huston. Woody Allen is a talented but struggling documentary filmmaker in love with co-worker Mia Farrow but saddled with a dead relationship to wife Joanna Gleason. With Alan Alda, Jerry Orbach and Claire Bloom in a strong supporting role.
VHS: $12157. $89.95.
Woody Allen, USA, 1989, 107 mins.

Everything You Always Wanted to Know About Sex (But Were Afraid to Ask)
Maybe not everything, but Woody Allen does offer a generous selection of topics that include bestiality, transvestism, chastity belts, abnormal sexual research, exhibitionism, and the life of a sperm. With Gene Wilder, Lynn Redgrave, Burt Reynolds, Lou Jacobi, John Carradine, Tony Randall and Louise Lasser. Very loosely based on the best-selling book by Dr. David Reuben.
VHS: $03426. $19.98.
Laser: LD70165. $44.98.
Woody Allen, USA, 1972, 87 mins.

Husbands and Wives
Woody Allen's savagely funny comedy traces the opposite fortunes of two parallel marriages through their extended stages of collapse and rejuvenation. A major subplot concerns Allen, playing a novelist and literature professor, getting emotionally involved with a brilliant 20-year-old student (Juliette Lewis). The movie is shot in the form of a cinema verite documentary. With Judy Davis, Mia Farrow, Liam Neeson and Sydney Pollack.
VHS: $18196. $94.95.
Laser: LD71844. $34.95.
Woody Allen, USA, 1992, 107 mins.

Interiors
Diane Keaton, Marybeth Hurt and Kristin Griffith are sisters who try to come to terms with their parents undergo divorce. Called Woody Allen's masterpiece by many critics, Interiors features brilliant performances from Maureen Stapleton, Geraldine Page and E.G. Marshall.
VHS: $00629. $14.95.
Laser: LD70599. $34.98.
Woody Allen, USA, 1978, 92 mins.

Love and Death
The films of Ingmar Bergman and the literature of 19th century Russian authors take a good-natured, comic drubbing at the hands of filmmaker Woody Allen. He plays a nebbish in love with a distant cousin who only agrees to marry him on the condition that he is reasonably sure he will be killed in battle fighting Napoleon. To Diane Keaton's immediate shock, Woody survives by hiding in a loaded cannon. Duels, herring and walks with the Grim Reaper are also featured.
VHS: $01713. $19.98.
Woody Allen, USA, 1975, 82 mins.

Manhattan
Woody Allen's valentine to his favorite city. Vincent Canby called it "the only truly great American film of the 1970's." Middle-aged writer falls in love with high school senior and trouble ensues. Sound familiar? With a fabulous soundtrack of George and Ira Gershwin classics and the contributed talents of Meryl Streep, Diane Keaton, Mariel Hemingway, Michael Murphy and, of course, Woody Allen. Wonderful black and white photography by Gordon Willis.
VHS: $00822. $19.98.
Laser: Deluxe letterboxed, MGM. LD70175. $34.98.
Woody Allen, USA, 1979, 96 mins.

Manhattan Murder Mystery
Woody Allen and Diane Keaton reunited in a wacky mystery about a bored housewife who enlists her skeptical husband in a dangerous murder investigation. With Alan Alda and Anjelica Huston. "What a treat to see Diane Keaton and Woody Allen together again" (Joel Siegel, Good Morning America).
VHS: $20546. $19.95.
Laser: LD72363. $34.95.
Woody Allen, USA, 1993, 107 mins.

Midsummer Night's Sex Comedy
A witty, affectionate film from Woody Allen, a Bergman-esque sexual romp among a large group of friends at a country home at the turn of the century. First-time appearance in an Allen film by Mia Farrow, with ensemble players Jose Ferrer, Julie Hagerty, Tony Roberts and Mary Steenburgen. Photography (as always) by Gordon Willis.
VHS: $00853. $19.98.
Woody Allen, USA, 1982, 88 mins.

Mighty Aphrodite
Miro Sorvino rightly won an Oscar for her portrayal of a prostitute in this warm and comic love story between two unlikely people. Woody Allen is a bumbling sportswriter who searches for the real mother of his adopted son and happens upon an unusual but hilarious set of gags. Helena Bonham Carter is also featured.
VHS: $27689. $99.99.
Laser: LD75575. $39.99.
Woody Allen, USA, 1995, 99 mins.

New York Stories
Three major directors, one city. Martin Scorsese, Francis Ford Coppola and Woody Allen offer an omnibus of short films based on life in the Big Apple. Scorsese leads off with Life Lessons, in which master painter Nick Nolte puts the moves on art student Rosanna Arquette. Life with Zoe is written by Coppola and his daughter Sofia. It tells the story of a precocious little girl who lives in a fancy hotel. Allen tops off the trio with Oedipus Wrecks, a comedy about an unmarried middle aged man whose problems with his pushy mother suddenly involve the entire city. With Woody Allen, Mia Farrow, Julie Kavner and Mae Questel, the voice of Betty Boop, as Woody's mom.
VHS: $11531. $89.95.
Laser: LD71255. $39.99.
Martin Scorsese/Coppola/Allen, USA, 1988, 123 mins

Play It Again, Sam

Woody Allen's first film with Diane Keaton. Allen plays Allen, a fanatical movie buff with an outrageous recurring hallucination: Humphrey Bogart offering tips on how to make it with the ladies. Eventually Allen discovers that there is one woman with whom he can be himself: his best friend's wife. The final scene is a terrific take-off on *Casablanca*, with roaring plane propellers, heavy fog, and Bogart-style trench coats.

VHS: S01037. $19.95.
Laser: LD75349. $29.98.
Herbert Ross, USA, 1972, 86 mins.

Purple Rose of Cairo

Woody Allen at his best, combining tenderly poignant moments with subtle touches of humor, artfully playing fiction against reality to create superb entertainment. A waitress, bored by her drab life, seeks escape in the movies, where the hero of the film, bored with the monotony of playing the same role over and over, jumps from the screen to join her in the real world. With Mia Farrow and Jeff Daniels. Photographed by Gordon Willis.

VHS: S01074. $14.98.
Woody Allen, USA, 1985, 82 mins.

September

Woody Allen's intimate drama set in the last days of summer in a Vermont country house. Starring Mia Farrow, Denholm Elliott and Sam Waterston, the film focuses on the life, relationships, trials and tribulations, mothers and daughters, and what it's like to survive in a complex world of difficult relationships.

VHS: S07341. $89.98.
Woody Allen, USA, 1987, 82 mins.

Shadows and Fog

Woody Allen's adaptation of his unproduced, one-act, 1977 play *Death* grafts the compulsive tendencies of his own persona to the psychological intensity of German expressionism. Shot in a highly textured, black and white photography by Carlo Di Palma and set in a vaguely middle European village against the surreal backdrop of local circus performers, Allen stars as a clerk caught up in the paranoia and hysteria to capture a depraved serial killer. With Kathy Bates, John Cusack, Mia Farrow, Jodie Foster, Julie Kavner, John Malkovich, Kate Nelligan and Lily Tomlin. Madonna has a cameo as a trapeze artist.

VHS: S17630. $89.98.
Woody Allen, USA, 1991, 89 mins.

Sleeper

Sleeper is loaded with hilarious sight gags and brilliant wit as Woody pokes fun at everything from sex to politics to health foods in this look at the future through the eyes of Woody waking up from 200 years of suspended animation. With Diane Keaton.

VHS: S01213. $19.98.
Woody Allen, USA, 1973, 88 mins.

Stardust Memories

Woody Allen plays a troubled filmmaker attending a film seminar weekend where space aliens confide that they enjoyed his earlier funnier movies. He also has to contend with autograph hounds and several neurotic women. Allen indulges himself in his Fellini period. B&W.

VHS: S03885. $14.98.
Woody Allen, USA, 1980, 91 mins.

What's Up Tiger Lilly?

Woody Allen provides the dubbed dialog for a chopped up Japanese sexy-spy thriller where the object of international intrigue is a recipe for egg salad. The results are wild, sophomoric, and hilarious. With music by the Lovin' Spoonful.

VHS: S01445. $19.95.
Woody Allen, USA, 1966, 80 mins.

Zelig

Woody Allen's side-splitting comic documentary and a scathing attack on the shallowness of American culture. Allen plays Leonard Zelig, a man famous for being famous, who has found a way to be the ultimate conformist: he transforms himself into a likeness of whomever he is with. With Mia Farrow, Saul Bellow, Susan Sontag and Bruno Bettelheim.

VHS: S01499. $19.98.
Laser: LD70722. $34.98.
Woody Allen, USA, 1983, 84 mins.

american WESTERNS

8 Seconds
Luke Perry stars as the rodeo celebrity Lane Frost. This world champion was killed in 1990 at the age of 25. In his short lifetime, Frost managed to find a successful career, fame and most importantly, a strong marriage that endured all the trials of the professional rodeo circuit.
VHS: S22159. $19.95.
John G. Avildsen, USA, 1994, 104 mins.

Ace High
Eli Wallach holds the winning hand in this rambunctious spaghetti western about honor (and double dealing) among thieves. Also starring Kevin McCarthy and Terence Hill (playing a character named Cat Stevens).
VHS: S13713. $19.95.
Giuseppe Colizzi, Italy, 1968, 120 mins.

The Alamo (Original)
A big movie spectacle about the defense of the Alamo was directed by (and stars) John Wayne as Davy Crockett, Richard Widmark as Jim Bowie and Laurence Harvey as Will Travis, in a flag-waving, super production aided with a first-rate musical score by Dmitri Tiomkin.
VHS: S04884. $29.98.
Laser: LD70499. $69.95.
John Wayne, USA, 1960, 161 mins.

The Alamo (Restored)
John Wayne produced, directed and starred in this much underrated historical epic now restored with over half an hour of footage unseen since the film's 1960 premiere. With an Academy-Award nominated score by Dimitri Tiomkin, the film chronicles how 185 men banded together in a crumbling adobe mission and held off an army of 7,000 to ensure the ultimate independence of Texas. Stars Richard Widmark, Laurence Harvey, Richard Boone, and the "Duke" as Davy Crockett.
VHS: S16589. $29.98.
John Wayne, USA, 1960, 202 mins.

Allegheny Uprising
John Wayne is re-united with *Stagecoach* star Claire Trevor in this epic 1939 period piece about those who defied the mandates of the English king in the mid 1760's.
VHS: S03244. $14.95.
William A. Seiter, USA, 1939, 80 mins.

Along Came Jones
This Western parody stars Gary Cooper (who performs a couple of musical numbers) as the eccentric cowboy Melody Jones, who gets mistaken for a ruthless killer. Cinematography by Milton Krasner. Music by Charles Maxwell, Arthur Lange and Hugo Friedhofer. With Loretta Young, William Demarest, Dan Duryea and Frank Sully.
VHS: S01866. $19.98.
Stuart Heisler, USA, 1945, 90 mins.

Along the Great Divide
Spectacular scenery highlights this Western featuring Kirk Douglas as a marshall who rescues accused murderer Walter Brennan from a mob and then escorts him to trial.
VHS: S03433. $14.95.
Raoul Walsh, USA, 1951, 88 mins.

Alvarez Kelly
William Holden stars as the cattle driver who sells cattle to the Union army, and is kidnapped by southern rebel Richard Widmark who wants him to steal cattle for the southern cause.
VHS: S03884. $14.95.
Laser: CLV, letterboxed, chapter stops. LD74907. $39.95.
Edward Dmytryk, USA, 1966, 116 mins.

The Americano
Glenn Ford goes South of the Border all the way to Brazil in this western, or is it a southern? He's delivering a shipment of prize bulls under less than friendly circumstances. With Cesar Romero, Abbe Lane, Frank Lovejoy and Ursula Thiess. In color.
VHS: S04220. $19.95.
William Castle, USA, 1955, 85 mins.

Angel and the Badman
One of the best westerns, with Gail Russell trying to make a human being out of gunslinger John Wayne after he is shot and nursed back to health by his pacifist family. With Bruce Cabot and Harry Carey, Sr.
VHS: S15909. $19.98.
Laser: 45th Anniversary edition. LD71498. $34.98.
James Edward Grant, USA, 1947, 100 mins.

Apache
After the surrender of Geronimo, one Apache leader remains unconquered. This pacifist Indian (played by, of all people, Burt Lancaster) learns from the U.S. Cavalry that sometimes fighting is the only way. But his one man fighting crusade for his tribe's rights ends rather surprisingly. Also starring Charles Bronson.
VHS: S13634. $19.95.
Robert Aldrich, USA, 1954, 91 mins.

The Appaloosa
Marlon Brando stars as Matt Fletcher, a man who has tasted all the vice the Wild West has to offer. Seeking a new life, he returns to his quiet border hometown with his prize possession, a beautiful Appaloosa stallion. When this horse is stolen by the ruthless Mexican bandit Chuy (John Saxon), Matt is forced to return to his bloodthirsty ways in order to regain his property and his honor. Also known as *Southwest to Sonora*.
VHS: S27670. $14.95.
Sidney J. Furie, USA, 1966, 99 mins.

Arizona
This classic Western stars Jean Arthur as a tenacious frontierswoman opposed to corruption and greed in the Wild West. William Holden also stars as the man who falls for this determined woman. It's a big story shot on some of the most elaborate sets ever built for a Hollywood western.
VHS: S20987. $14.95.
Wesley Ruggles, USA, 1940, 121 mins.

Arrowhead
Charlton Heston, Jack Palance and Katy Jurado star in this story about enmity between an army scout and an Indian chief, which is resolved in a dramatic combat. Based on the novel by W.R. Burnett.
VHS: S10433. $19.95.
Laser: LD75149. $34.98.
Charles Marquis Warren, USA, 1953, 105 mins.

Bad Lands
A posse gets lost and pinned down in the Arizona desert by a band of rampaging Apaches. A thinly disguised western remake of *The Lost Patrol*, with a cast that includes Noah Beery Jr., Guinn "Big Boy" Williams, Andy Clyde, Douglas Walton, Robert Coote and Robert Barrat as the sheriff in charge.
VHS: S12830. $19.98.
Lew Landers, USA, 1939, 70 mins.

The Badlanders
W.R. Burnett's classic story of urban crime and punishment, *The Asphalt Jungle* is transferred to the Arizona Old West. Ex-cons Alan Ladd and Ernest Borgnine team up with buddy Nehemiah Persoff to rob crooked land baron Kent Smith's gold mine with unexpected results. With Katy Jurado and Claire Kelly as the women who wait for their men to come home rich and alive.
VHS: S16439. $19.95.
Delmer Daves, USA, 1958, 85 mins.

Badman's Territory
Western veteran Randolph Scott plays a U.S. Marshall who goes up against the James brothers and the Daltons. USA, 1946, 79 mins.
VHS: S10666. $19.98.

The Ballad of Little Jo
Suzy Amis is the original cross-dressing cowboy in this new western. She finds that the old West is not a hospitable place for a woman unless she can prove she is as good as any man. Under the circumstances, she more than rises to the occasion.
VHS: S20717. $19.98.
Laser: LD74459. $39.99.
Maggie Greenwald, USA, 1993, 124 mins.

Bandolero!
Personalities clash and sparks fly when the Bishop brothers hit Val Verde, Texas. They fought on opposite sides of the Civil War, now they are on opposite sides of the law. James Stewart is the honest brother, Dean Martin is the bank-robber brother, sentenced to die. With Raquel Welch.
VHS: S06529. $19.98.
Andrew V. McLaglen, USA, 1968, 106 mins.

Battles with Chief Pontiac
Lon Chaney, Jr., Lex Barker and Helen Westcott star in this frontier film about conflicts between the British and Native Americans. Peace talks are sabotaged through the efforts of a colonel leading German troops.
VHS: S23803. $24.95.
Felix E. Feist, USA, 1953, 75 mins.

Bend of the River
Set in 1840s Oregon, with James Stewart as the outlaw who now works as a wagon train scout, and his conflict with Arthur Kennedy, his one-time friend who now hijacks the supplies of the settlers in order to turn profit. With Julia Adams and Rock Hudson.
VHS: S06814. $19.95.
Anthony Mann, USA, 1952, 91 mins.

Big Hand for the Little Lady
A high stakes game of poker is the subject of this tantalizing western adventure that takes place almost entirely in the backroom of a Texas saloon circa 1896. Joanne Woodward is the little lady who sits in when husband Henry Fonda falls ill. Other players include Jason Robards Jr., Charles Bickford, Kevin McCarthy and John Qualen.
VHS: S16288. $19.98.
Fielder Cook, USA, 1966, 94 mins.

Big Jake
An elderly Texas cattleman swings into action when his grandson is kidnapped by bandits. Violent action sequences distinguish this film from others of John Wayne's later period. With Richard Boone and Maureen O'Hara.
VHS: S15984. $14.98.
George Sherman, USA, 1975, 110 mins.

The Big Stampede
When John Wayne was only 25 years old he already possessed a career as an actor inseparable from the history of the western. In this action-packed feature a cattle stampede becomes the dramatic focus for a hard-riding, gun-shooting cadre of cowboys.
VHS: S20948. $19.98.
Tenny Wright, USA, 1932, 63 mins.

The Big Steal
Join a fast-paced chase through Mexico as Robert Mitchum relentlessly tracks the thief of a $300,000 Army payroll; plenty of terrific plot twists highlight this entertaining action-thriller. Also starring the enticing Jane Greer (Mitchum's femme fatale in *Out of the Past*) and the always reliable William Bendix.
VHS: S15101. $19.98.
Don Siegel, USA, 1949, 71 mins.

The Big Trail
An early masterpiece from Raoul Walsh (*High Sierra*), shot in revolutionary 70mm widescreen process, which concerns a difficult odyssey of a wagon train traveling on an Oregon trail. A highly naturalistic western set off by its expressive use of space, decor, landscape and sound. With John Wayne, Marguerite Churchill, Eli Brendel and Tully Marshall. Cinematography by Lucien Andriot and Arthur Edeson.
VHS: S05909. $14.98.
Raoul Walsh, USA, 1930, 121 mins.

Blood on the Moon
Robert Mitchum stars as a gunfighter for hire who sides first with the cattlemen and then the farmers in a range war. Robert Preston is the man who helps him make up his mind. A moody adult western based on a novel by Luke Short. With Barbara Bel Geddes, Tom Tully, Frank Faylen, Tom Tyler and Walter Brennan.
VHS: S12832. $19.98.
Robert Wise, USA, 1948, 88 mins.

Blue
An intriguing cast of B-players enlivens this Western about a quintessential outsider, an American-born, Mexican-raised gunfighter (Terence Stamp) who falls in love and must deal with his past, in the form of the gang controlled by his adoptive father (Ricardo Montalban). With Joanna Pettet, Karl Malden, Joe De Santis and Sally Kirkland.
VHS: S16887. $19.95.
Silvio Narizzano, Italy/USA, 1968, 113 mins.

Blue Steel
John Wayne has to convince a town to stay and fight for their land when a mean bunch of outlaws try to muscle their way in. The bad guys know there is gold to be mined under Main Street but the Duke is willing to offer them blue steel and hot lead for their trouble. B&W.
VHS: S04081. $19.99.
Robert North Bradbury, USA, 1934, 59 mins.

Born in America
A dark western about an undertaker who finds business slow, so he goes into town and instigates a gun brawl to create a few bodies to bury. Starring James Westerfield and Glen Lee.
VHS: S13881. $59.95.
Jose Antonio Boianos, USA, 1990, 90 mins.

The Bounty Man
Clint Walker stars as Kincaid, the very-tall-in-the-saddle bounty hunter after a young killer. The tables are turned when he is pursued by a gang of cutthroats. With Margot Kidder, Richard Basehart, and veteran Western actors John Ericson, Gene Evans and Arthur Hunnicutt. Made for tv.
VHS: S07150. $19.95.
John Llewellyn Moxey, USA, 1972, 74 mins.

Branded
Alan Ladd goes along with an outlaw's scheme to impersonate the long lost son of wealthy rancher Charles Bickford until he finds he really enjoys being part of the family. Some desperados don't like being double-crossed. With Mona Freeman, Milburn Stone and Joseph Calleia. One of Ladd's better roles.
VHS: S12240. $19.95.
Laser: LD75163. $34.98.
Rudolph Mate, USA, 1951, 103 mins.

Bravados
A first-rate Western with Gregory Peck starring as a man in search for four men who raped and killed his wife, and, in the process, discovering the evils inherent in seeking revenge. With Joan Collins, Stephen Boyd.
VHS: S11190. $39.98.
Henry King, USA, 1958, 98 mins.

Breakheart Pass
Charles Bronson plays an undercover Federal agent investigating a murder on a train in the Old West. Based on the novel by Alistair MacLean, who also wrote the script, which features Ben Johnson, Richard Crenna, Jill Ireland, Charles Durning, Ed Lauter and ex-boxer Archie Moore. Avalanches, Indians and lots of red herrings.
VHS: S09158. $19.95.
Tom Gries, USA, 1976, 95 mins.

Broken Arrow
Delmer Daves' melodramatic western is based on a historical incident—the elaborate efforts of a tribe leader and a former military official attempting to broker peace accords between warring Army and Native American factions. Strong acting, location photography and distinct, colorful acting. With James Stewart, Jeff Chandler and Debra Paget.
VHS: S06527. $14.98.
Delmer Daves, USA, 1950, 93 mins.

Broken Lance
A fascinating remake of Joseph Mankiewicz's *House of Strangers*, about a patriarchal rancher's dissolution of his empire, which opens up deep family resentments and tensions. With Spencer Tracy, Robert Wagner and Jean Peters.
VHS: S11191. $14.98.
Edward Dmytryk, USA, 1954, 96 mins.

Buffalo Bill
A wonderfully colorful biography of the famous Man of the West, with a top-notch cast including Maureen O'Hara, Joel McCrea, Linda Darnell, Anthony Quinn.
VHS: S11189. $39.98.
William Wellman, USA, 1944, 90 mins.

Bugles in the Afternoon
Ray Milland stars as an officer of the Seventh Cavalry stripped of his rank over a mysterious feud with a fellow officer. Years later they meet at Little Big Horn. With Forrest Tucker, George Reeves, Helena Carter and Hugh Marlowe, as Milland's nemesis.
VHS: S04293. $14.95.
Roy Rowland, USA, 1952, 85 mins.

The Burning Hills
Half-breed and social outcast Natalie Wood offers a desperate Tab Hunter a hiding place when this cowboy finds himself on the run from a group of notorious gunmen hot on his trail. Together this couple face the unrelenting danger until they can't run anymore.
VHS: S21001. $19.98.
Stuart Heisler, USA, 1956, 94 mins.

Butch and Sundance: The Early Days
A prequel to *Butch Cassidy and the Sundance Kid* finds Tom Berenger and William Katt as the look-alikes for the Newman/Redford roles. Great scenery and pleasant performances. Our heroes deliver needed medical supplies to a mining camp cut off by snow. With Brian Dennehy, Jeff Corey, John Schuck and Jill Eikenberry.
VHS: S07149. $19.98.
Richard Lester, USA, 1979, 111 mins.

Cahill—U.S. Marshall
A late period John Wayne (1973) western casts the Duke as a frontier lawman whose life is unnerved by his son's descent into a life of crime and depravity. With George Kennedy, Gary Grimes, and Neville Brand.
VHS: S16292. $19.98.
Laser: LD74701. $34.98.
Andrew V. McLaglen, USA, 1973, 103 mins.

Canyon of the Missing Men and Wolfheart's Revenge
Canyon is apparently the only Tom Tyler Western which has survived; *Wolfheart* is an enjoyable, breezy western with the dog star and Guinn "Big Boy" Williams. USA, 1930.
VHS: S05979. $49.95.

The Capture
A reformed gunslinger turned detective investigates an episode from his past, to determine if he shot an innocent man. Breathtaking scenery and landscapes with a terrific Mexican shoot-out finale. With Lew Ayres, Teresa Wright, Victor Jory and Duncan Renaldo.
VHS: S17450. $19.95.
John Sturges, USA, 1950, 90 mins.

Cat Ballou
Jane Fonda is the title character in this satirical western with music, that won Lee Marvin an Oscar for riding a drunken horse. She plays a school teacher turned outlaw in a just cause. Nat King Cole and Stubby Kaye are the strolling minstrels and Cat's gang includes Dwayne Hickman, Michael Callan, Tom Nardidi, and of course, Marvin Lee as Kid Shelleen and his evil no-nosed brother. Great fun.
VHS: S10977. $19.95.
Elliot Silverstein, USA, 1965, 96 mins.

Catlow
Louis L'Amour's Western comedy about the opposite fates of two friends: a good-natured marshall (Richard Crenna) with a penchant for trouble and an amoral thief (Yul Brynner) who orchestrates a $2 million gold robbery. "Relaxing, lighthearted entertainment" (*Los Angeles Times*). With Leonard Nimoy, Jo Ann Pflug and Jeff Corey.
VHS: S18670. $19.98.
Sam Wanamaker, USA, 1971, 103 mins.

Chato's Land
Charles Bronson is cast as Pardon Chato, a peaceable half-breed Apache rancher until he is riled by a boorish posse that molests his woman after Chato accidentally shot the local sheriff. With Jack Palance, Richard Basehart, James Whitmore, Simon Oakland, Richard Jordan. Bronson has only 15 lines in this violent western and 13 of them are in Apache. Filmed in Spain but set in New Mexico.
VHS: S12533. $19.98.
Michael Winner, USA, 1972, 100 mins.

Chisum
The Lincoln County War is restaged, this time with John Wayne as John Simpson Chisum, one of the primary historical figures in the conflict. No need to guess which side wins. With Forrest Tucker, Ben Johnson, Andrew Prine, Christopher George and Geoffrey Deuel as Billy the Kid, another historical figure you might have heard about.
VHS: S04972. $14.95.
Laser: Letterboxed. LD74482. $34.98.
Andrew V. McLaglen, USA, 1970, 110 mins.

Chuka
Rod Taylor straps on his six-gun in this hard-hitting tale of a heroic gunslinger trying to make peace between Indians and the soldiers at a nearby fort. An excellent supporting cast featuring Ernest Borgnine, John Mills and James Whitmore.
VHS: S13709. $19.95.
Gordon Douglas, USA, 1967, 105 mins.

Cimarron
The first Western to win an Oscar for Best Picture (the other being Eastwood's *Unforgiven*) stars Richard Dix and Irene Dunne. Based on the popular novel by Edna Ferber, it chronicles the life of a homesteading family from the Oklahoma Land Rush until 1915. Oscar also went for screenplay. With Estelle Taylor and Nance O'Neil.
VHS: S08338. $19.95.
Wesley Ruggles, USA, 1930, 124 mins.

Circus World
John Wayne stars as Matt Masters, the owner of a Wild West Show on a European tour. He is plagued by personal and natural disasters but never gives up. Rita Hayworth and Claudia Cardinale provide some comfort and some pain. With Lloyd Nolan.
VHS: S04515. $29.95.
Henry Hathaway, USA, 1964, 131 mins.

Cold Feet
A goofy contemporary Western about love, revenge and high fashion footwear, scripted by Tom McGuane and Jim Harrison. When the roguish Keith Carradine double-crosses his partners in crime over a horse in Mexico, he finds that the great state of Montana isn't big enough to hide him from their wrath. With Sally Kirkland and Tom Waits as the injured parties and Rip Torn as the curious local lawman. Watch for Jeff Bridges in an unbilled cameo role.
VHS: S11723. $19.95.
Laser: LD70922. $39.95.
Robert Dornhelm, USA, 1989, 94 mins.

Comanche Territory
Maureen O'Hara stars as a conniving frontierswoman who seeks to cheat the Comanche out of land deeded to them by the government. She's only after silver until she meets James Bowie (Carey MacDonald) and his friend the local government official (Will Geer). Before long, her love of Bowie makes her a new woman.
VHS: S23675. $14.98.
Leonard Goldstein, USA, 1950, 76 mins.

Comancheros
Big scale Western about a member of the Texas Rangers who works undercover to foil a notorious gang of outlaws. With Lee Marvin, John Wayne, Stuart Whitman. Last film of Michael Curtiz.
VHS: S05911. $19.98.
Laser: CLV. LD72115. $49.98.
Michael Curtiz, USA, 1961, 107 mins.

Companeros
Jack Palance, Fernando Rey, Franco Nero and Tomas Milian star in this politically-minded Western. A mercenary helps a revolutionary to rescue a pacifist professor and his followers. Palance is great as a wooden-handed killer who lost his hand when he was nailed to a cross—his pet hawk ate it off to save him.
VHS: S23322. $24.95.
Sergio Corbucci, Italy/Spain/Germany, 1970, 105 mins.

Copper Canyon
A vaudeville marksman does some fancy shootin' to protect ex-Confederate miners from their harsh Yankee bosses. Starring Ray Milland and Hedy Lamarr in colorful, change-of-pace roles.
VHS: S13710. $14.95.
Laser: LD75174. $34.98.
John Farrow, USA, 1950, 84 mins.

The Cowboys
John Wayne leads a cattle drive with 11 youngsters and one black cook. He makes the mistake of insulting Bruce Dern, an unemployed psycho riding the range and up to no good. The boys must learn to grow up in a hurry. With Robert Carradine, Roscoe Lee Browne and Colleen Dewhurst.
VHS: S04973. $14.95.
Laser: Letterboxed. LD74485. $39.98.
Mark Rydell, USA, 1972, 128 mins.

Dakota
John Wayne becomes involved with a land war in Fargo, North Dakota. He sides with the wheat farmers against a gang of greedy homesteaders, headed by Ward Bond and Mike Mazurki. Lots of two-fisted action before the cavalry shows up. With Vera Ralston and Walter Brennan as Capt. Bounce. B&W.
VHS: S04891. $19.95.
Laser: LD71576. $34.98.
Joseph Kane, USA, 1945, 82 mins.

Dances with Wolves (Deluxe Collector's Set)
This winner of seven Oscars is now available in a deluxe set that includes *The Making of*, with new footage that documents the filming of this epic Western, plus the book *Dances with Wolves: The Illustrated Story of the Epic Film* and six full-color lobby cards. Kevin Costner stars as the cavalry man who must exist at the intersection of two cultures, one in touch with the land, the other obsessed with owning it at any cost. Available in letterbox format.
VHS: S21362. $79.98.
Kevin Costner, USA, 1992, 250 mins.

Dances with Wolves (Special Expanded Edition)
A troubled Civil War veteran goes West and finds what he's been missing in the lifestyle and hunting grounds of the Lakota Sioux. Kevin Costner stars as Lt. John Dunbar, aka Dances with Wolves, in this epic tribute to how the West was lost for the Native American population. Seven Oscars, including Best Picture and Best Director, were awarded; and the fine cast includes Mary McDonnell, Grahame Greene, Maury Chaykin, and lots of roaming bison. Special thanks should also go to the lovely and talented Moira McLaughlin whose yeoman, behind-the-scenes efforts were instrumental in getting this important film made. Digitally mastered. In English and Lakota.
VHS: S14602. $29.95.
Kevin Costner, USA, 1990, 237 mins.

Daniel Boone
Daniel Boone is both courageous and dashing as he leads a group of pioneer families to the wilderness beyond the Cumberland mountains—battling Indians, nature, and an evil half-breed played by John Carradine. Also starring George O'Brien and Heather Angel.
VHS: S13849. $19.95.
David Howard, USA, 1934, 75 mins.

Daniel Boone Trail Blazer
This historic Western finds Daniel Boone (Bruce Bennett) leading a group of settlers westward into Kentucky. The Native Americans in the area are suspicious and it does not take much for a French renegade and some British redcoats to convince them of the settlers' bad intentions. Boone however, saves the day. Lon Chaney, Jr., is also featured.
VHS: S23771. $24.95.
Albert C. Gannaway, USA, 1956, 75 mins.

Dark Command
John Wayne had one of his better roles as a Federal Marshall in Lawrence, Kansas. Sworn to uphold the law, he puts Roy Rogers on trial for murder. Roy gets off with the aid of Walter Pidgeon, who bullies the jury. Later, during the Civil War, the power-mad Pidgeon returns to try to burn Lawrence to the ground. B&W.
VHS: S04895. $19.98.
Raoul Walsh, USA, 1940, 95 mins.

Deadly Trackers
Richard Harris stars as a peace-loving Texas sheriff until Rod Taylor and his blood-thirsty gang rob the local bank, kill the lawman's wife and kids, and flee to Mexico. Based on "Riata," a short story by director Sam Fuller.
VHS: S16289. $14.95.
Barry Shear, USA, 1973, 104 mins.

Deadwood
A young cowboy is mistaken for Billy the Kid when he rides into a small frontier town teeming with gold-crazed fortune hunters in this classic Western thriller starring Arch Hall Jr.
VHS: S13797. $29.95.
James Landis, USA, 1945, 100 mins.

Death of a Gunfighter
Richard Widmark is an aging gunfighter-turned-town sheriff who doesn't want to give up his badge. A group of concerned citizens hire a younger and hopefully faster gunman to ease Widmark out of office. Lena Horne plays the girlfriend. With John Saxon and Carroll O'Connor.
VHS: S05526. $19.95.
Robert Totten/Don Siegel, USA, 1969, 100 mins.

Denver and Rio Grande
Set in the 1870s, this non-traditional Western is about the frenzied rivalry between two locomotive companies. With Edmond O'Brien, Sterling Hayden, and Dean Jagger.
VHS: S16891. $19.95.
Byron Haskin, USA, 1951, 89 mins.

Desperadoes
Jack Palance is the leader of a band of Southern guerrillas who go on a murderous rampage through Texas after the Civil War. When Palance's son (Vince Edwards) revolts against the viciousness, he winds up battling his own father.
VHS: S07338. $14.95.
Laser: CLV. LD71980. $39.98.
Henry Levin, USA, 1969, 91 mins.

The Desperate Trail
Sam Elliott, Craig Sheffer and Linda Fiorentino bring proven star power to this updated Western about betrayal, abuse and love on the trail to New Mexico. The film is distinguished for its smart direction and it won the Best Director Award at the Hamptons International Film Festival.
VHS: S24553. $89.98.
P.J. Pesce, USA, 1994, 129 mins.

Destry Rides Again
Marlene Dietrich plays Frenchy, the notorious yet sensational cabaret singer. Her rendition of "See What the Boys in the Back Room Will Have" marked her emergence from her mysterious screen personality of the 30's to her raucous personality of the 40's. With James Stewart as the gunslinger without guns, and Brian Donlevy.
VHS: S01988. $14.95.
George Marshall, USA, 1939, 94 mins.

Devil's Canyon
Ex-lawman Dale Robertson finds the territorial Arizona prison a dangerous place to be without his badge. Hardcase con Stephen McNally asks him to come along for luck on the next big breakout. With Robert Keith, Arthur Hunnicut, Jay Flippen and Virginia Mayo as the bandit queen who knows how to operate a Gatling gun. Originally shot in 3-D.
VHS: S12833. $19.98.
Alfred Werker, USA, 1953, 91 mins.

Dodge City
Big scale Western inspired by the exploits of Wyatt Earp, tells the story of an ex-soldier and trail boss who helps clean up the West. This thoroughly enjoyable Western features a nearly definitive barroom brawl and lots of other action, all displayed in the soft, rich tones of early Technicolor. Starring Errol Flynn, Olivia de Havilland, Ann Sheridan and Bruce Cabot.
VHS: S13635. $19.98.
Laser: LD72172. $34.98.
Michael Curtiz, USA, 1939, 104 mins.

Dudes
The modern American west holds dangers for a trio of New York City punks on their way to California. When one of them is killed by an outlaw gang, Jon Cryer and Daniel Roebuck decide that a man's got to do what a man's got to do. Fueled by the spirit of the Old West, they set out to avenge their buddy. With Catherine Mary Stewart and Lee Ving. When you put peyote in your peace pipe anything can happen.
VHS: S08528. $14.95.
Penelope Spheeris, USA, 1988, 90 mins.

Duel at Diablo
A moody western about the inevitable Indian-and-Calvary conflict, with James Garner, Sidney Poitier, Bibi Andersson and Dennis Weaver.
VHS: S18667. $19.98.
Ralph Nelson , USA, 1966, 103 mins.

Duel in the Sun
An epic Western based on the Nevil Shute novel about a half-breed Indian woman who goes to live in the home of a wealthy cattle baron and falls in love with one of his sons. Jennifer Jones, Gregory Peck, Joseph Cotten and Walter Huston star.
VHS: S01579. $19.98.
King Vidor, USA, 1946, 138 mins.

The Duke
A trio of complete features; a must for John Wayne fans. Includes some of his best: *Fort Apache*, *Flying Leathernecks* and *She Wore a Yellow Ribbon*.
VHS: S10687. $59.98.

Eagle Wing
Martin Sheen, Sam Waterston and Harvey Keitel are featured in this Western about an intense rivalry. Sheen is a soldier who has set his sights on a white stallion, an obsession that pits him directly against White Bull (Waterston). From this rivalry, the very destinies of these two men are joined.
VHS: S23958. $19.95.
Anthony Harvey, USA, 1978, 100 mins.

Escape from Fort Bravo
John Sturges' expressive Western, set in 1860s Arizona, delineates two epic battles between captured Southern soldiers and Native Americans. William Holden plays an embittered Union officer caught in the middle.
VHS: S19498. $19.98.
John Sturges, USA, 1953, 98 mins.

Firecreek
This stark western stars James Stewart as a strong but silent sheriff who must protect his town from marauding gangsters led by Henry Fonda. Together these two actors have come to define archetypal frontiersmen. On opposite sides of the law their rivalry creates unforgettable tension.
VHS: S21002. $19.98.
Vincent McEveety, USA, 1968, 104 mins.

Five Card Stud
Dean Martin and Robert Mitchum star in this western tale of revenge and poker. After five men lynch a card cheat, they learn he was not an only child. With Inger Stevens, Roddy McDowall, Whit Bissell, Denver Pyle and Yaphet Kotto as Little George. Mitchum plays a traveling preacher who puts his faith in God and his trust in Samuel Colt.
VHS: S12244. $19.95.
Henry Hathaway, USA, 1965, 122 mins.

Geronimo
Wes Studi portrays the fearless Native American leader who eluded the entire US calvary. In this drama, Oscar winners Gene Hackman and Robert Duvall play the men who would capture this American legend. This western shows that the spirit of freedom which defined the wild west is an ancient tradition.
VHS: S21078. $19.95.
Laser: LD72410. $34.95.
Walter Hill, USA, 1993, 115 mins.

The Good Guys and the Bad Guys
It's an unusual comedy/western mix featuring a retired sheriff played by Robert Mitchum, who must contend with an aging bad guy, George Kennedy. Kennedy is especially ornery because he has been abandoned by his gang for being over-the-hill. Also features David and John Carradine.
VHS: S21003. $19.98.
Burt Kennedy, USA, 1978, 96 mins.

Gore Vidal's Billy The Kid
Another cinematic look at the most notorious and probably most filmed life of an American western outlaw. Said to be taking a hard look at the truth behind the legend. Val Kilmer has the title role and author Gore Vidal has a cameo part. Also in the cast are Julie Carmen, Duncan Regehr, Rene Auberjonais and Wilford Brimley. A feature presentation from the Turner Network Television.
VHS: S10435. $9.98.
William A. Graham, USA, 1989

Gun Fury
Rock Hudson, Donna Reed and Lee Marvin give exceptional performances in this hard-hitting tale of love, lust and revenge in the Old West. Originally shown in 3-D.
VHS: S15051. $14.95.
Raoul Walsh, USA, 1953, 83 mins.

Gun Smugglers/Hot Lead
Tim Holt stars in both these RKO westerns. First Holt trails a gang stealing guns from the Army. In the second he seeks revenge on a group of thieves who murdered his friend. USA, 1949/1951, 121 mins.
VHS: S10667. $19.98.

Gunfight at The O.K. Corral
The Earps vs. the Clantons. Two rival factions in the Arizona town of Tombstone decide to settle their differences in public. The Earps are the ones with the badges. With Burt Lancaster as Wyatt Earp and Kirk Douglas as the tubercular friend Doc Holliday. Also Rhonda Fleming, Earl Holliman, DeForrest Kelly, John Ireland, and Lee Van Cleef.
VHS: S10837. $14.95.
John Sturges, USA, 1957, 122 mins.

The Gunfighter
A western about a psychologically-scarred gunfighter who tries to come to terms with his bloody, violent past. With Gregory Peck, Helen Westcott and Millard Mitchell.
VHS: S07147. $14.98.
Henry King, USA, 1950, 84 mins.

Half Breed
Jack Beutel, the star of Howard Hughes' *The Outlaw*, has the title role of Charlie Wolf. When villain Reed Hadley hears rumors of gold on tribal land, he plots to make friction between the red man and the white. With Barton MacLane, Janis Carter and Robert Young as the mustached gambler with a heart of gold.
VHS: S12834. $19.98.
Stuart Gilmore, USA, 1952, 81 mins.

Hallelujah Trail
A wagon train loaded with whiskey rolls toward Denver, and cavalry officer Burt Lancaster must protect it. Just about every situation ever faced by a Hollywood cowpoke is fair game for this wild western spoof filled with laughs. Also starring Lee Remick and Martin Landau. This version restores footage not seen in 25 years.
VHS: S14098. $29.99.
Laser: LD70593. $39.97.
John Sturges, USA, 1965, 166 mins.

Hang 'em High
Clint Eastwood stars in this gratifying and suspense filled Western about a man who survives his own unjust lynching. Before long the varmints that tried to kill him are picked off one by one against the beautiful but austere scenery of New Mexico's White Sands National Park.
VHS: S24562. $14.95.
Ted Post, USA, 1968, 116 mins.

The Hanging Tree
A melodramatic Western about a young blind girl and her relationship with a mysterious doctor (Gary Cooper) who tries to clean up a frontier gold mining community. With George C. Scott, Maria Schell and Karl Malden.
VHS: S18611. $19.98.
Delmer Daves, USA, 1959, 106 mins.

Hannie Caulder
After a brutal attack by three outlaws who murdered her husband, Raquel Welch learns to shoot a .45, then sets out to exact her revenge. Starring Ernest Borgnine, Strother Martin, and Jack Elam as the bad guys.
VHS: S13711. $19.95.
Burt Kennedy, USA, 1972, 87 mins.

Haunted Gold
John Wayne stars in this classic western, pitting him against the greedy, gold-hungry desperados and ghost town phantoms found on the American frontier. This mystery/thriller builds suspense around a cache of gold haunted by undying greed.
VHS: S20947. $19.98.
Mack V. Wright, USA, 1933, 54 mins.

Hearts of the West
A heart warming salute to 1930's Hollywood and the Poverty Row Western. It stars Jeff Bridges as a naive would-be Western writer who finds that fate has a different part for him to play. Alan Arkin is the maniacal film director who puts Bridges on the other side of the camera. Offbeat and very enjoyable.
VHS: S03673. $19.98.
Howard Zieff, USA, 1975, 103 mins.

Heaven's Gate
One of the most expensive cost-overruns in the history of Hollywood, which shook the industry deep into its pocketbook, Michael Cimino's attempt at an epic Western is a visually impressive film which was, incidentally, a big success in Europe. The plot centers on a group of landowners and cattlemen who attempt to dispose of settling European immigrants by composing a death list.
VHS: S00557. $24.95.
Michael Cimino, USA, 1981, 149 mins.

High Noon
Gary Cooper is the marshall who fights alone for upholding the law when the entire town is paralyzed with fear. Stark settings and shadows heighten the suspense. The most popular film of 1952. With Grace Kelly, Lloyd Bridges, Lon Chaney and Henry Morgan.
VHS: S00567. $19.95.
Laser: CAV. LD70380. $74.95.
Laser: CLV. LD70381. $49.95.
Fred Zinnemann, USA, 1952, 84 mins.

Hombre
One of Martin Ritt's best films, with Paul Newman as an Indian-raised nonconformist who fights hostile racial and social attitudes in the 1880s American West. Photographed by James Wong Howe.
VHS: S18073. $14.98.
Martin Ritt, USA, 1967, 111 mins.

Hondo
One of John Wayne's best performances and films. He is a cavalry scout who comes across a single mother (Geraldine Page) living with her young son in the wilderness. Though an Apache uprising is brewing, Page's character remains unconcerned, forcing Wayne into action. This Western was so successful that it inspired a 1950's television series.
VHS: S22129. $19.98.
John Farrow, USA, 1953, 84 mins.

Hostile Guns
George Montgomery plays Gid McCool, U.S. Marshall. He has orders to transport a wagon full of prisoners in Texas to the state pen. The prisoners have other plans. With Yvonne DeCarlo, Leo Gordon, Pedro Gonzalez and Robert Emhardt. Also Tab Hunter as naive deputy Mike Reno. In color.
VHS: S12241. $14.95.
Laser: LD75206. $34.98.
R.G. Springsteen, USA, 1967, 91 mins.

How the West Was Won
A large-scale epic about three generations of pioneers, with a great cast and brilliant direction by John Ford, George Marshall and Henry Hathaway. With George Peppard, Debbie Reynolds, Carroll Baker, Gregory Peck, Henry Fonda, James Stewart, John Wayne.
VHS: S11555. $29.98.
Laser: LD70595. $39.98.
Ford/Marshall/Hathaway, USA, 1963, 155 mins.

In Old California
John Wayne plays a pharmacist from Boston who heads west dispensing pills and medical elixirs. No, this is not a comedy. The greedy villain (Albert Dekker) almost gets the Duke lynched by adding poison to one of his tonics. Special news from Sutter's Mill halts the necktie party. B&W.
VHS: S04892. $14.98.
William McGann, USA, 1942, 90 mins.

Invitation to a Gunfighter
In this western, a ruthless land baron hires a killer (Yul Brynner) to fight the farmers he's robbed of their land. George Segal is a Confederate soldier who fights for justice.
VHS: S08148. $19.98.
Richard Wilson, USA, 1964, 92 mins.

Jesse James Under the Black Flag
This extremely rare film stars Jesse James, Jr. as Jesse James and Harvey Hoffman as Cole Younger. This is from a reissue version of the 1930's with documentary type narration and is supposedly the true story of Jesse James as told by his son. A true collector's item. Approximately 59 mins.
VHS: S13273. $24.95.

Jubilee Trail
Wagons ho. Two New Yorkers go west just before gold is discovered in California. On the trail the wife finds out her husband has an old flame and an illegitimate child. What is a woman to do in the middle of nowhere? With Vera Ralston, Joan Leslie, Forrest Tucker, John Russell and Pat O'Brien.
VHS: S11403. $14.95.
Joseph Kane, USA, 1954, 103 mins.

Last of the Redmen
A western loosely adapted from James Fenimore Cooper's The Last of the Mohicans that reinterprets the work from the perspective of Hawkeye's companion. The brave warrior, Uncas (Rick Vallin), must decide whether to intervene and help a group of white men and women betrayed by their Iroquois guide (Buster Crabbe) during the French-Indian Wars. With Jon Hall, Michael O'Shea and Evelyn Ankers.
VHS: S18497. $19.95.
George Sherman, USA, 1947, 77 mins.

The Law and Jake Wade
John Sturges' harsh western about the opposite fortunes of two men (Robert Taylor and Richard Widmark) once linked in crime, who now battle for each other's souls. An edgy work written by William Bowers (The Gunfighter). With Patricia Owens and Robert Middleton.
VHS: S17994. $19.98.
John Sturges, USA, 1958, 87 mins.

Law and Order
Who is better at upholding law and order than the star of this film, Ronald Reagan? Marshall Frame Johnson (Reagan) sets off to retirement on his ranch with his sweetheart, Jeannie (Dorothy Malone). Unfortunately, things are never that simple in the Old West, and Marshall Johnson is quickly called back into service to bring justice to the men who murdered his brother.
VHS: S27671. $14.98.
Nathan Juran, USA, 1953, 80 mins.

A Lawless Street
Joseph H. Lewis (Gun Crazy) directed this western about a disillusioned frontier marshall caught in an epic struggle to remove the violent forces from the community and confront his violent past. With Randolph Scott, Angela Lansbury and Warner Anderson.
VHS: S18495. $19.95.
Joseph H. Lewis, USA, 1955, 78 mins.

Lawman
An offbeat western about a brutally efficient U.S. Marshall who enters an unfamiliar community to transport wanted criminals and encounters resistance and hostility. Robert Ryan is superb as a passive lawman. Impressive for its physical depiction of the outlaw frontier, a battered, ruined landscape of corpses and lost souls. With Lee J. Cobb, Robert Duvall and Sheree North.
VHS: S18668. $19.98.
Michael Winner, USA, 1970, 95 mins.

The Legend of Tom Dooley
Michael Landon and Jo Morrow star in this bleak Western based on the famous folk song by the Kingston Trio. Landon is a confederate soldier who accidentally commits a crime because he does not realize the war is over. Running from the law, he elopes with his fiancee, but tragically they cannot escape this turn of events.
VHS: S24059. $11.95.
Ted Post, USA, 1959, 79 mins.

Lone Star
Clark Gable is a Texas cattle baron who locks horns with politician Broderick Crawford. Their feud reaches a fever pitch when Gable falls in love with Crawford's fiancee, played by Ava Gardner.
VHS: S20561. $19.98.
Vincent Sherman, USA, 1951, 94 mins.

Lonely Are the Brave
A terrific study starring Kirk Douglas as a rebellious cowboy who escapes from jail, and is pursued by a posse determined to capture him at all cost. With Gena Rowlands, Walter Matthau.
VHS: S06816. $19.95.
Laser: Letterboxed. LD74927. $34.98.
David Miller, USA, 1962, 107 mins.

Long Riders
Called "the best directed American movie of the year" by David Denby (New York), Long Riders uses four theatrical families to tell the James Brothers' story. The Keach brothers star as Jesse and Frank, the Carradine brothers as the Younger brothers. From the director of The Warriors.
VHS: S02350. $14.95.
Walter Hill, USA, 1980, 100 mins.

Mad at the Moon
A gothic horror Western about a young bride (Mary Stuart Masterson) who discovers a frightening, supernatural secret about her husband, and seeks solace in his charismatic half-brother (Hart Bochner). With Fionna Flanagan, Cec Verrell and Stephen Blake.
VHS: S17787. $89.98.
Laser: LD71830. $29.98.
Martin Donovan, USA, 1992, 100 mins.

Magnificent Seven
Inspired by Kurosawa's Seven Samurai, this is a powerful Western filled with action against the backdrop of beautiful Mexican scenery. Film stars Yul Brynner, Steve McQueen, Charles Bronson, James Coburn, Eli Wallach.
VHS: S00806. $19.95.
John Sturges, USA, 1960, 127 mins.

A Man Alone
Ray Milland directed and stars in this above average Western about a stranger who reports a stage hold-up to the wrong people. When he is framed for the crime by a supposed solid citizen, Milland accidentally finds refuge in the home of the local sheriff who just happens to have a lovely daughter. With Raymond Burr, Lee Van Cleef, Ward Bond and Mary Murphy.
VHS: S11401. $14.95.
Ray Milland, USA, 1955, 96 mins.

Man from Colorado
Glenn Ford and William Holden are reteamed in this psychological western in which the Civil War produces a kill-crazy judge and a sensible law-abiding marshal from a pair of friendly soldiers. Ford plays the over-enthusiastic jurist who doesn't know the meaning of the word prudence. Action and analysis in the Old West. With Edgar Buchanan and Ellen Drew.
VHS: S09112. $14.95.
Henry Levin, USA, 1949, 99 mins.

Man from Laramie
James Stewart stars as a man determined to get frontier justice in this action-packed drama of a man bent on revenge on those who killed his brother. With Donald Crisp, Arthur Kennedy.
VHS: S06546. $14.95.
Anthony Mann, USA, , 1955, 104 mins.

Man from Utah
Low budget western starring a very young John Wayne as a lawman going undercover to catch crooks. The backdrop is the annual rodeo. Great dialog, like "I'm gonna cloud up and rain all over you."
VHS: S12747. $19.98.
Robert North Bradbury, USA, 1934, 57 mins.

Man in the Saddle
Randolph Scott and Joan Leslie star as two mismatched lovers in this Western filled with unrelenting passions. Emotions run high, leading to jealousy, gun battles and ultimately, death. Beautiful cinematography help make this a first-rate Western.
VHS: S24060. $11.95.
Andre de Toth, USA, 1951, 87 mins.

Man of the West
In 1874 Arizona, a reformed gunman (Gary Cooper) is forced to rejoin his ex-boss in order to save himself and other innocent people from harm. Dismissed by critics in 1958, this powerful story deserves another look. It also features an epochal (for a Western) striptease by Julie London.
VHS: S13636. $19.98.
Anthony Mann, USA, 1958, 100 mins.

Man Who Loved Cat Dancing
The Western tale of a defiant woman who leaves her husband and is kidnapped by a band of train thieves, one of whom she comes to love. Starring Burt Reynolds, Sarah Miles and George Hamilton.
VHS: S13637. $19.98.
Richard C. Sarafian, USA, 1973, 114 mins.

Man Without a Star
King Vidor directed this western with Kirk Douglas as the rugged individualist who helps Jeanne Crain keep her ranch land. With Claire Trevor, Richard Boone.
VHS: S06817. $19.95.
King Vidor, USA, 1955, 89 mins.

The Maverick Queen
Barbara Stanwyck plays the title role in this Zane Grey western. As Kit, the tough, wealthy saloon owner, she encourages the attention of Butch Cassidy and the Sundance Kid but falls for an undercover Pinkerton detective played by Barry Sullivan. With Scott Brady, Wallace Ford and Mary Murphy. A dangerous love story.
VHS: S11404. $14.95.
Joseph Kane, USA, 1956, 90 mins.

McLintock! (Restored Producer's Cut)
An engaging period comedy that re-imagines the West as a sexual war zone. John Wayne is cast as a powerful cattle baron whose wife (Maureen O'Hara) returns following a two-year separation, demanding a divorce. Stephanie Powers plays their daughter trapped in the middle. This restored version was supervised by producer Michael Wayne. With Patrick Wayne, Jack Kruschen and Yvonne De Carlo.
VHS: S18683. $19.98.
Andrew V. McLaglen, USA, 1963, 127 mins.

A Minute to Pray, A Second to Die
But how much time for lunch? Alex Cord stars as a pistolero with an annoying problem of occasional short term paralysis. He is on the run from outlaws, bounty hunters, and lawmen who are just waiting for his gun hand to freeze. With Arthur Kennedy, Robert Ryan, Nicoletta Machiavelli and Mario Brega. In English.
VHS: S07153. $19.98.
Franco Giraldi, Italy, 1967, 100 mins.

Miracle in the Wilderness
Kris Kristofferson stars in this uplifting Christmas western based on The Snow Goose, a novella by Paul Gallico. Jericho Adams, a former Indian fighter, has turned to farming to support his wife and their infant child. Trouble brews when they are all captured by a raiding party of Blackfeet who have never heard the story of the Nativity. Kim Cattrall co-stars.
VHS: S15906. $14.98.
Kevin Dobson, USA, 1991, 88 mins.

Montana
Richard Crenna and Gena Rowlands star as a brawling Western couple at odds over the family ranch in Big Sky Country. He wants to sell it to a power company for oil drilling. She wants to keep it in the family. This contemporary Western was written by Larry McMurtry (Lonesome Dove) and filmed on location in Gallatin County, Montana. The hardy supporting cast includes Lea Thompson, Justin Deas, Elizabeth Berridge, Scott Coffey and Darren Dalton.
VHS: S16716. $14.98.
Laser: LD72196. $29.95.
William A. Graham, USA, 1990, 91 mins.

Monte Walsh
This melancholic western, directed by cinematographer William Fraker, features Lee Marvin as he attempts to cope with the opening up of the frontier and the urbanization of the American West. Adapted from the novel by Jack Schaefer (Shane). With Jeanne Moreau, Jack Palance and Mitch Ryan.
VHS: S18072. $14.98.
William Fraker, USA, 1970, 106 mins.

The Naked Spur
Nothing kinky. This hardy western directed by Anthony Mann features James Stewart as a tough bounty hunter in pursuit of Robert Ryan through the rugged terrain of the Rocky Mountains. Filmed on location with Janet Leigh and Ralph Meeker as two of the distractions that keep the determined Stewart on his toes.
VHS: S03674. $19.97.
Anthony Mann, USA, 1953, 93 mins.

Nevada
Gary Cooper, Thelma Todd, William Powell and Philip Strange in this early Paramount Western. Based on Zane Grey's novel, Cooper is a gunslinger redeemed by the love of a good woman. Silent with music track.
VHS: S07274. $24.95.
John Waters, USA, 1927, 55 mins.

Nevada Smith
Loosely based on a Harold Robbins book, this is the story of a cowboy who takes a long and involved revenge on the outlaws who murdered his family. Starring Steve McQueen, Karl Malden, Brian Keith and Suzanne Pleshette.
VHS: S12246. $14.95.
Henry Hathaway, USA, 1966, 131 mins.

New Mexico
A Western about Army soldiers stationed in a remote cavalry outpost which is under siege from Indian attacks. An officer's determination to negotiate a peace settlement erupts into a savage war following the accidental death of an Indian child. With Lew Ayres, Andy Devine, Raymond Burr and Jeff Corey.
VHS: S19869. $29.95.
Irving Reis, USA, 1952, 78 mins.

Northwest Passage
A terrific epic adventure about the enduring hardships and frustrations while opening up new territory in Colonial America, based on the book by Kenneth Roberts. Robert Young and Walter Brennan are the greenhorns who explore under the tutelage and hard whip of Spencer Tracy.
VHS: S11435. $19.98.
Laser: LD71172. $39.98.
King Vidor, USA, 1940, 125 mins.

The Oklahoma Kid
James Cagney is a brutally effective gunman in a power-hungry battle with Humphrey Bogart to avenge the unjust lynching of his father, in this expressive western enhanced by James Wong Howe's photography. Music by Max Steiner. With Rosemary Lane, Donald Crisp and Harvey Stephens.
VHS: S19043. $19.98.
Lloyd Bacon, USA, 1939, 80 mins.

The Oklahoman
Social drama western about the efforts of a sympathetic frontier community doctor to aid an injured Native American and prevent him from being run out of town. With Joel McCrea, Barbara Hale and Brad Dexter.
VHS: S07152. $14.98.
Francis D. Lyon, USA, 1957, 80 mins.

One-Eyed Jacks
Stanley Kubrick was fired by subsequent director/star Marlon Brando during the filming of this neo-classicist Western that deals with familiar themes of betrayal, dislocation and alienation. Brando is Johnny Rio, betrayed by his best friend (Karl Malden); Malden's exploitation of Monterey and forced lock-up of Brando sets the stage for their obsessive hate, which concludes this densely beautiful film.
VHS: S02558. $19.95.
Marlon Brando, USA, 1961, 141 mins.

Only the Valiant
Gregory Peck plays Captain Lance, a brave but unpopular officer who leads a ragged detail of misfits against a superior force of Apaches. For most, it is the last patrol. With Gig Young, Neville Brand, Ward Bond, Barbara Payton and Lon Chaney Jr. as "A-rab".
VHS: S04295. $14.95.
Laser: C.I.V. LD72012. $29.98.
Gordon Douglas, USA, 1951, 105 mins.

Outlaw
Howard Hughes produced this controversial, sexy western about Billy the Kid, Doc Holliday and the gal with the cleavage who's in love. With Walter Huston, Jane Russell and Thomas Mitchell.
VHS: S03342. $19.95.
Howard Hughes, USA, 1943, 103 mins.

Pocket Money
Paul Newman and Lee Marvin team up in this contemporary western about a very unlucky south of the border business venture. Shady businessman Strother Martin sends Newman and Marvin to Mexico for cattle to supply his rodeo with their own money. With Hector Elizondo, Gregory Sierra, Christine Belford, Kelly Jean Peters and Wayne Rogers as Stretch Russell.
VHS: S16291. $14.95.
Stuart Rosenberg, USA, 1972, 102 mins.

Pony Express
Wide-open landscapes and striking physical tableaux are the backdrops to the daring and early (mis)adventures of the Pony Express: Buffalo Bill (Charlton Heston) and Wild Bill (Forrest Tucker) are posed against ruthless criminals and California loyalists to open up the west and link California to the Union.
VHS: S02790. $14.95.
Jerry Hopper, USA, 1953, 101 mins.

Posse (Douglas)
Kirk Douglas produced, directed and starred in this cynical western about an ambitious, politically-minded lawman. As Marshall Howard Nightengale, he figures the capture of the notorious outlaw Jack Strawhorn (Bruce Dern) should win him the higher office. He never counted on Strawhorn's populist appeal or the outlaw's way with words. With Bo Hopkins, Luke Askew, David Canary and James Stacy.
VHS: S12242. $19.95.
Kirk Douglas, USA, 1975, 92 mins.

Posse (Van Peebles)
Mario Van Peebles' unusual Western concerns five Spanish Civil War veterans stationed in Cuba who rebel against their racist colonel (Billy Zane), seize an illegal gold shipment and flee to the American frontier. Posse is a "big, rousing, hip-hopping, trash-talking, dynamite-looking, all-stops-out, rock-the-house comic/epic western. It's killer entertainment" (Michael Wilmington, Los Angeles Times). With Van Peebles, Stephen Baldwin, Charles Lane, Tiny Lister, Tone Loc, Big Daddy Kane and Blair Underwood. Special appearances by Pam Grier, Isaac Hayes, Melvin Van Peebles, Woody Strode and the Hudlin Brothers.
VHS: S19514. $19.95.
Mario Van Peebles, USA, 1993, 109 mins.

Proud Men
A modern day western about the difficult relationship between a father and son as they seek a tentative reconciliation when they learn the father is dying. With Charlton Heston, Peter Strauss and Belinda Balaski.
VHS: S18499. $14.98.
William A. Graham, USA, 1987, 100 mins.

Pursued
Offbeat Western stars Robert Mitchum as a war hero who seeks a man who killed his father years ago in a family feud. With Teresa Wright and Dean Jagger.
VHS: S24109. $14.98.
Laser: C.I.V. LD72017. $49.98.
Raoul Walsh, USA, 1947, 101 mins.

The Quick and the Dead
Sharon Stone and Gene Hackman are paired in this revisionist Western about gunfighting, revenge and justice. Stone is reluctantly forced into violence to satisfy a strange demand made by Hackman. Somehow she also manages to be the sexiest thing in the hot dusty town she visits. Gary Sinise and Leonardo DiCaprio are also featured.
VHS: S25884. $97.95.
Laser: LD75032. $34.95.
Sam Raimi, USA, 1995, 105 mins.

Rachel and the Stranger
William Holden starts paying a bit more attention to his wife, Loretta Young, when stranger Robert Mitchum starts to drop by on a regular basis. This tale of the early west has plenty of wide open spaces for Holden and Mitchum to settle this matter.
VHS: S12835. $19.98.
Laser: C.I.V. LD71735. $19.98.
Norman Foster, USA, 1948, 79 mins.

Ramrod
Joel McCrea and Veronica Lake star in this action packed story of revenge, desire and dominion in the Old West. When the daughter of a powerful cattle baron sets up her own ranch she soon hires a gunslinger to settle the dispute which, soon turns into a bloody range war. With Charles Ruggles, Donald Crisp, Don DeFore, Preston Foster and Lloyd Bridges. B&W.
VHS: S11405. $14.95.
Andre de Toth, USA, 1947, 94 mins.

Rancho Deluxe
A small gem written by Montana writer Thomas McGuane about the off-beat adventures of two modern-day cattle rustlers. The cast includes Jeff Bridges, Sam Waterston, Harry Dean Stanton and Elizabeth Ashley.
VHS: S17995. $19.98.
Frank Perry, USA, 1974, 93 mins.

Randy Rides Alone
Because that's just the kind of hombre he is. And when it comes to tough, John Wayne is one that won't back down to anyone. He's on the trail of a gang that has been robbing the express company. They don't have a chance. With "Gabby" Hayes. B&W.
VHS: S04083. $19.95.
Harry Fraser, USA, 1934, 60 mins.

The Range Feud/Two Fisted Law

Double your Duke, double your sexy pleasure. This double feature presents young John Wayne in two of his earliest roles. *The Range Feud* is a shoot-em-up, wild-west adventure with a newly appointed sheriff who must arrest his brother, Wayne, for murder. In *Two Fisted Law*, Walter Brennan and Alice Faye join Wayne in the tense tale of an unscrupulous swindler and a rancher bent on revenge.
VHS: S15050. $19.95.
David Ross Lederman, USA, 1931, 58 mins.

The Rare Breed

Maureen O'Hara is a fiery woman who must transport a prize bull to a new owner, Brian Keith. James Stewart is the skeptical cowboy she recruits to help her on this arduous journey. There develops a love triangle between O'Hara, Keith and Stewart. This engaging yarn makes the most of Western trappings, star power, and a convincing love interest.
VHS: S23673. $14.98.
Andrew V. McLaglen, USA, 1966, 97 mins.

Rawhide

Not the tv series with Clint Eastwood and Eric Fleming but a rousing, tension-filled Western starring Tyrone Power and Susan Hayward, as just two of a group of people who are held hostage by outlaws in a stagecoach station. With Jeff Corey, Jack Elam, Dean Jagger and Hugh Marlowe. B&W.
VHS: S07151. $19.98.
Henry Hathaway, USA, 1951, 86 mins.

The Redhead from Wyoming

Gun-in-hand, Maureen O'Hara fights a suave promoter (William Bishop) for control of her town with the help of the sheriff (Alex Nichol). Though O'Hara starts as a simple saloon keeper, she soon rises to the challenge and becomes a real frontier hero.
VHS: S23674. $14.98.
Lee Sholem, USA, 1953, 81 mins.

The Return of a Man Called Horse

Richard Harris returns for this high quality sequel to the original *A Man Called Horse*. In this film he helps the Yellow Hand Sioux in their struggle against the United States' white man. Highlights in this Western include a buffalo hunt, a raid on a fort, and a Sun Vow ceremony featuring many braves. Laurence Rosenthal is responsible for the terrific music.
VHS: S27574. $19.98.
Irvin Kershner, USA, 1976, 129 mins.

Return of the Badmen

Randolph Scott is a U.S. Marshall with his hands full when he confronts the Sundance Kid, Billy the Kid, and the Daltons.
VHS: S10670. $19.98.
Ray Enright, USA, 1948, 91 mins.

Return of the Seven

Yul Brenner reprises the role of Chris, the deadly and compassionate hired gun who once again rounds up six more shootists to protect a poor and humble peasant village south of the Border. This first of several sequels to *The Magnificent Seven* features Warren Oates, Claude Akins, Robert Fuller and Emilio Fernandez.
VHS: S03671. $19.98.
Burt Kennedy, USA, 1966, 97 mins.

Ride Him Cowboy

This is the Duke's first movie, the one that turned John Wayne from a prop man into a matinee idol as the ultimate screen cowboy. He had help from his trusty steed, his white horse Duke, whose name came to stand for the honorable cowpoke himself.
VHS: S20949. $19.98.
Fred Allen, USA, 1932, 55 mins.

Riders of the Desert

The Arizona Rangers are about to be disbanded but the wrongdoings of Hashknife Brooks and his outlaw gang present them with one last mission. With Bob Steele, Al "Fuzzy" St. John and George "Gabby" Hayes. Also Gertrude Messenger. Lots of hair-trigger action. B&W.
VHS: S10060. $24.95.
Robert North Bradbury, USA, 1932, 57 mins.

Riders of the Purple Sage

Ed Harris and Amy Madigan play two wildly opposed characters who find hope in each others' differences. Set in the beautiful badlands, it's a Western where a woman abandoned by her friends and neighbors learns to trust a man who lives outside of the law. Based on the best-selling novel by Zane Grey.
VHS: S27261. $99.98.
Laser: LD75562. $39.95.
Charles Haid, USA, 1995, 90 mins.

Riders of the Range/ Storm over Wyoming

In the first part of this double feature, Tim Holt and his companion Chico are framed for murder. In the second they attempt to settle a dangerous range war.
VHS: S10671. $19.98.
Robert North Bradbury, USA, 1949/1950, 122 mins.

Rio Conchos

A stolen shipment of rifles in Post Civil War Texas could revive the Confederacy if the thieves don't all kill each other first. Action and adventure are prominently featured. Cast includes Richard Boone, Stuart Whitman, Antony Franciosa, Edmond O'Brien and Jim Brown in his screen debut.
VHS: S07156. $19.98.
Gordon Douglas, USA, 1964, 107 mins.

River of No Return

Marilyn Monroe's first Western since a bit part in *A Ticket to Tomahawk*. She's a saloon singer being fought over by Robert Mitchum and Rory Calhoun while little Tommy Rettig tries to grow up fast. Lots of white water action and rampaging Indians, too!
VHS: S04201. $19.98.
Laser: Widescreen. LD74811. $39.99.
Otto Preminger, USA, 1954, 91 mins.

Rough Night in Jericho

Set in the lawless Old West, the film stars Dean Martin as a former idealist gone corrupt. He is now a ruthless land baron who controls Jericho, a frontier mining community, and he pressures a local widow (Jean Simmons) to sell off her profitable stagecoach line. With George Peppard, John McIntire, Slim Pickens, Don Galloway and Brad Weston.
VHS: S19515. $14.98.
Laser: Letterboxed. LD74925. $34.98.
Arnold Laven, USA, 1967, 97 mins.

Sagebrush Trail

Big John Wayne, almost before he was shaving, is sent to prison for a murder he didn't commit. The Duke breaks out of the big house to clear his name. In a nice twist, he unknowingly befriends the real killer. Good B western.
VHS: S12745. $19.98.
Sam Nelson, USA, 1943, 58 mins.

Salome Where She Danced

Yvonne De Carlo makes her debut in this complex western drama. International espionage, historic battles, and a love story are highlighted by De Carlo's legendary dance sequences.
VHS: S13852. $19.95.
Charles Lamont, USA, 1945, 90 mins.

San Antonio

A cowboy incurs the jealousy of a saloon owner by showing his attentions to a pretty dance-hall girl. An elaborate Western, with good production values, that climaxes with a battle in the deserted Alamo. Starring Errol Flynn and Alexis Smith.
VHS: S13638. $19.98.
David Butler, USA, 1945, 105 mins.

Savage Wilderness

Victor Mature stars as a fur trapper who tries to stop the Butcher of Shiloh, played by Robert Preston. This army colonel decides to send his men on a suicide mission against determined Native Americans. Courage and strength define these men from America's wild west.
VHS: S20986. $14.95.
Anthony Mann, USA, 1955, 98 mins.

The Scalphunters

Burt Lancaster stars as trapper Joe Bass in this comical western with a satiric bite. When he is forced by a hostile band of Kiowas to trade his pelts for an educated, escaped black slave (Ossie Davis) he immediately regrets the deal. However, when he loses Davis to a band of dishonorable scalp hunters lead by Telly Savalas, then he wants him back. With Shelley Winters, Dabney Coleman, Dan Vadis and Lancaster's circus partner Nick Cravat as Ramon. A rough and tumble tale of ownership and friendship.
VHS: S12537. $19.98.
Sydney Pollack, USA, 1968, 103 mins.

Sea of Grass

Conrad Richter's famous novel about the fierce struggle between open-range cattlemen and their farmer enemies comes to life through the brilliant talents of Katharine Hepburn, Spencer Tracy and Elia Kazan. A beautiful film, with incredible action sequences, *Sea of Grass* was one of the first big-budget Westerns shot on location in New Mexico. Also starring Robert Walker and Melvyn Douglas.
VHS: S15021. $19.98.
Elia Kazan, USA, 1946, 123 mins.

The Seventh Cavalry

Randolph Scott stars along with Barbara Hale in this tale of honor and ignominy on the frontier. Scott is charged with cowardice and sets out to redeem himself. Everything comes to a head with General Custer in the Black Hills.
VHS: S23810. $24.95.
Joseph H. Lewis, USA, 1956, 75 mins.

Shalako

A cowboy guides aristocratic European big game hunters through the wild plains of 1880 New Mexico. The local Native Americans don't understand their idea of pleasure seeking and attack. Starring Sean Connery and Brigitte Bardot, with Stephen Boyd.
VHS: S15986. $14.98.
Edward Dmytryk, USA, 1968, 113 mins.

The Shootist

A farewell to the Western movie by director Siegel (*Killers, Dirty Harry*), in which John Wayne plays a dying gunfighter returning to Carson City for medical attention from James Stewart. With Lauren Bacall and Ron Howard.
VHS: S01194. $14.95.
Laser: LD75333. $29.98.
Don Siegel, USA, 1976, 100 mins.

Showdown

George Seaton's perceptive Western concerns rivalries between childhood friends Chuck Garvis (Rock Hudson) and Billy Massey (Dean Martin). Both men are drawn to the same woman (Susan Clark); she rejects Massey in order to marry Garvis. With Donald Moffat, John McLiam and Ed Begley, Jr.
VHS: S19517. $14.98.
George Seaton, USA, 1973, 99 mins.

Silver River

Raoul Walsh's psychological western about the moral collapse of a disillusioned former army officer who becomes a ruthless and powerful silver baron in a Nevada frontier town during the Civil War. With Errol Flynn, Ann Sheridan, and Thomas Mitchell.
VHS: S18165. $19.98.
Raoul Walsh, USA, 1948, 110 mins.

Silverado

Lawrence Kasdan's intelligent, entertaining western about the formation of a frontier community and the four men (Kevin Kline, Kevin Costner, Danny Glover and Scott Glenn) who take on an evil cabal of corrupt sheriffs and wealthy landowners. The brilliant secondary cast includes Brian Dennehy, an especially fine John Cleese, Linda Hunt and Rosanna Arquette.
VHS: S24585. $19.95.
Laser: LD70462. $99.95.
Lawrence Kasdan, USA, 1985, 132 mins.

Sitting Bull

A western that takes the form of an interrogation. Dale Roberts is an Army officer defending himself against charges of complicity with the Indians. With Mary Murphy, J. Carrol Naish and Iron Eyes Cody.
VHS: S18954. $19.95.
Sidney Salkow, USA, 1954, 105 mins.

Slaughter Trail

Brian Donlevy is a Cavalry officer assigned to bring the murderer of two Navajos to justice. Gig Young plays the outwardly honest rancher who robs stagecoaches on the side. With Virginia Grey, Andy Devine and folksinger Terry Gilkyson as "Singalong". His songs include "Hoof Beat", "Serenade" and "Jittery Deer-Foot Dan".
VHS: S12836. $19.98.
Irving Allen, USA, 1951, 78 mins.

Somewhere in Sonora

Set in old Mexico, this western stars a young John Wayne, who must find a way to save both his old friend and a silver mine. He is forced to join up with a bandit. This classic movie features all the hallmarks that define the western.
VHS: S20950. $19.98.
Mack V. Wright, USA, 1933, 57 mins.

Sons of Katie Elder

The four title characters return for the funeral of their mother only to find that a greedy land baron is after their inheritance. John Wayne, Dean Martin, Earl Holliman and Michael Anderson Jr. take on the dastardly James Gregory and his son Dennis Hopper. Also involved in the range war are Jeremy Slate, George Kennedy, Strother Martin and Paul Fix. A son's got to do what a son's got to do.
VHS: S12245. $19.95.
Henry Hathaway, USA, 1965, 122 mins.

South of St. Louis

A fast-paced western starring Joel McCrea as a cowboy whose ranching days are disrupted by the Civil War. Alexis Smith as Rouge, the dance hall girl, tries to persuade McCrea into running guns for the Rebels. With Zachary Scott, Alan Hale, Victor Jory and Dorothy Malone as the girl he left behind.
VHS: S04294. $14.95.
Ray Enright, USA, 1949, 88 mins.

Springfield Rifle

Gary Cooper stars in this western as an undercover agent who joins a band of lawless desperados. He is seeking the culprits stealing guns from the federal government. Despite this ruse, there can be no doubt that Cooper is Hollywood's most enduring straight shooter.
VHS: S21000. $19.98.
Andre de Toth, USA, 1952, 93 mins.

The Star Packer

Western action with John Wayne as he organizes a group of ranchers to fight off the Shadow and his gang. Probably no relation to the famed radio crime fighter. So leave it to the Duke to know what evil lurks in the hearts of men. With "Gabby" Hayes. B&W.
VHS: S04082. $19.98.
Robert North Bradbury, USA, 1934, 60 mins.

Station West

Film noir goes west in a gritty, witty mix of gumshoe and six-gun. Dick Powell plays a government agent determined to crack a case of murder and hijacked gold. With Jane Greer, Raymond Burr and Agnes Moorehead.
VHS: S03254. $19.98.
Sidney Lanfield, USA, 1948, 80 mins.

The Stranger Wore a Gun

Shot in 3-D, this western stars Randolph Scott, who is in the service of a cold-blooded bandit and must take part in a hold up before returning to his former life. The great secondary cast includes Ernest Borgnine, Lee Marvin, Claire Trevor and Joan Weldon.
VHS: S17031. $19.95.
Andre de Toth, USA, 1953, 83 mins.

Support Your Local Gunfighter

Talented genre director Burt Kennedy directs this amiable and shrewd western about an amoral con man (James Garner) who manipulates a mining dispute by passing off a crazed reprobate (Jack Elman) as a notorious killer. The rogues list of character actors includes Joan Blondell, Harry Morgan, Marie Windsor and Dub Taylor.
VHS: S18671. $19.98.
Burt Kennedy, USA, 1971, 92 mins.

Tall in the Saddle

John Wayne is a woman-hating cavalry officer who takes over as a ranch foreman of a woman-owned ranch in this enjoyable Western. With Ella Raines and Ward Bond.
VHS: S09507. $19.98.
Edwin L. Marin, USA, 1944, 87 mins.

The Tall Men

Clark Gable and Cameron Mitchell sign on to drive cattle for Robert Ryan not knowing how much trouble is waiting for them along the trail. Bad weather, unfriendly native Americans and the presence of Jane Russell, in color, make for an increase of stress in the Old West.
VHS: S06196. $19.98.
Raoul Walsh, USA, 1955, 122 mins.

The Tall T

Randolph Scott does what a man's got to do in this superior western drama based on *The Captive*, a short story by Elmore Leonard. Richard Boone co-stars as Usher, the leader of an outlaw band that is torn between robbing a stagecoach and holding a newlywed couple for ransom. With Maureen O'Sullivan, Henry Silva, Arthur Hunnicutt, John Hubbard and Skip Homeier as Billy Jack.
VHS: S15893. $19.95.
Budd Boetticher, USA, 1957, 78 mins.

The Telegraph Trail

As a heroic government scout, a young John Wayne and his valued steed, the white miracle horse Duke, must combat crooked traders and Native Americans in this early classic western. Movies like these turned the young actor into an international star.
VHS: S20952. $19.98.
Tenny Wright, USA, 1933, 54 mins.

Ten Wanted Men

Not to be confused with *Ten Tall Men* or *Ten Little Indians*, this is a Randolph Scott western. He plays a rancher who has built a vast empire in Arizona and doesn't want trouble. Villain Richard Boone doesn't have the same notions. With Jocelyn Brando, Skip Homeier, Alfonso Bedoya and Leo Gordon. In color.
VHS: S08705. $69.95.
H. Bruce Humberstone, USA, 1955, 80 mins.

Texas Across the River

A genre-defying Western about the epic adventures of three outsiders. A Southern aristocrat (Rosemary Forsyth) on the run from the law crosses paths with two hip "revolutionaries," Sam Hollis (Dean Martin) and his Indian guide (Joey Bishop), as they try to provide safe passage for guns through rugged Comanche territory. With Alain Delon, Rina Marquand, Peter Graves and Andrew Prine.
VHS: S19516. $14.98.
Laser: Letterboxed. LD74928. $34.98.
Michael Gordon, USA, 1966, 101 mins.

Texas Cyclone

An early John Wayne effort casts the Duke as a quiet loner who teams with a mysterious figure to restore peace and order in a frontier community where a widow is besieged by a ruthless gang. With Tim McCoy, Shirley Grey and Wheeler Oakman.
VHS: S18496. $14.95.
David Ross Lederman, USA, 1932, 58 mins.

There Was a Crooked Man

Kirk Douglas and Henry Fonda star in this comic western adventure about hidden treasure and life in an 1880 territorial prison. Prisoner Douglas was used to running things until Fonda, the strict new warden arrived. Douglas then decides the time is right to plan an escape. Fellow prisoners include Warren Oates, Hume Cronyn, John Randolph, Michael Blodgett, C.K. Yang and Burgess Meredith as the Missouri Kid.
VHS: S16286. $14.95.
Laser: Letterboxed. LD71808. $39.98.
Joseph L. Mankiewicz, USA, 1970, 126 mins.

They Came to Cordura

Gary Cooper is assigned to find some heroes in a raid on Pancho Villa that will be given medals in Washington. He selects Van Heflin, Richard Conte, Michael Callan, Dick York and Tab Hunter to be decorated. Rita Hayworth is along to be decorative.
VHS: S04749. $14.95.
Laser: CLV. LD71752. $29.98.
Robert Rossen, USA, 1959, 123 mins.

They Died with Their Boots On

Errol Flynn is a natural choice for the role of the flamboyant George Armstrong Custer, whose military career came to an abrupt halt during the Battle of Little Big Horn in 1876. The Hollywood version may be historically dubious but it does nothing to tarnish the Custer legend. Olivia de Havilland makes her eighth and final screen appearance with Flynn, as Custer's devoted wife Libbie. With Arthur Kennedy, Charley Grapewin, Gene Lockhart and Anthony Quinn as Chief Crazy Horse.
VHS: S01867. $19.95.
Laser: LD71692. $39.98.
Raoul Walsh, USA, 1942, 140 mins.

The Tin Star

Anthony Perkins plays an inexperienced sheriff, a bit too young, who is assisted in taming a wild town by veteran lawman-turned-bounty hunter Henry Fonda.
VHS: S02791. $14.95.
Laser: LD75275. $34.98.
Anthony Mann, USA, 1957, 93 mins.

To the Last Man

A "B" movie classic. A longstanding feud between two frontier families heats up when one clan undertakes cattle rustling. With a host of talent: Randolph Scott, Shirley Temple, Noah Beery Sr., Buster Crabbe and Barton MacLane.
VHS: S04117. $29.95.
Henry Hathaway, USA, 1933, 70 mins.

Tombstone

Kurt Russell, Charlton Heston and Val Kilmer are just some of the stars featured in this blockbuster Western. Its a classic tale of good guys and bad guys fighting it out on the lonely American frontier. Justice must be defended at all costs.
VHS: S21106. $96.98.
Laser: Widescreen. LD74634. $49.99.
George P. Kosmatis, USA, 1993, 130 mins.

True Grit

John Wayne won an Oscar for his portrayal of a one-eyed, overweight lawman named Rooster Cogburn. He is recruited by a tenacious teenage girl to find the killer of her father. Glen Campbell is the handsome Texas Ranger after the same gang. With Robert Duvall, Dennis Hopper, Jeff Corey and Kim Darby as Mattie Ross.
VHS: S05097. $14.95.
Laser: LD75393. $35.98.
Henry Hathaway, USA, 1969, 128 mins.

Tumbleweeds
One of the screen's most famous Westerns, in which William S. Hart plays a rancher who decides to try his luck when the Cherokee strip opens in 1889. He would like to take along the beautiful Barbara Bedford, if she were willing to settle down and become his wife. This version includes an eight-minute introduction by Hart that was added to the film with its reissue in 1939.
VHS: S16503. $19.95.
Laser: CLV. LD72040. $29.98.
King Baggot, USA, 1925, 81 mins.

Under California Stars
Roy Rogers and Trigger star in this color Western with music and action. A group of horse thieves figure they can make more money by stealing one horse if his name is Trigger. Roy and the rest of the folks at the Double R Ranch disagree. With Andy Devine and Jane Frazee.
VHS: S05490. $19.95.
William Witney, USA, 1948, 71 mins.

Valdez Is Coming
A moody western shot in Spain with Burt Lancaster as a victimized Mexican-American lawman who stages a violent crusade against the dictatorial land baron and gunrunner (Jon Cypher) in his quest for justice and redemption. With Susan Clark, Barton Heyman and Richard Jordan.
VHS: S18672. $19.98.
Edwin Sherin, USA, 1971, 90 mins.

Vengeance Valley
Burt Lancaster and Robert Walker are rivals who can't get along in the open spaces of the Old West. They fight indoors as well. Joanne Dru and Sally Forrest are their womenfolk. Hugh O'Brian and John Ireland play supporting hombres. Bring bullets.
VHS: S05071. $29.95.
Richard Thorpe, USA, 1951, 83 mins.

Vera Cruz
This exciting Western, set in 1860 Mexico, features Gary Cooper and Burt Lancaster involved in a plot to overthrow Emperor Maximilian. A lively and entertaining melodrama, Vera Cruz is highlighted by the use of many unusual locations, and its alternating touches of comedy and suspense. Also starring Cesar Romero, Ernest Borgnine, and Charles Bronson.
VHS: S01870. $19.98.
Laser: LD72158. $34.98.
Robert Aldrich, USA, 1953, 94 mins.

The Villain
In this Road Runner-like western, Kirk Douglas is an incompetent outlaw impersonating the human form of Wile E. Coyote, as director Hal Needham attempts to transform the hapless cartoon figure into the stylized landscapes of the American West. With Ann-Margret, Arnold Schwarzenegger, Paul Lynde, Ruth Buzzi and Strother Martin.
VHS: S17032. $19.95.
Hal Needham, USA, 1979, 89 mins.

The Violent Men
Adapted from Donald Hamilton's novel, this dark Western pits evil land baron Edward G. Robinson against the innocent settlers. An excellent cast includes Barbara Stanwyck, Glenn Ford and Brian Keith.
VHS: S17030. $19.95.
Rudolph Mate, USA, 1955, 96 mins.

Virginia City
Hollywood's greatest stars headline this epic Civil War Western. Based on the true story about a group of Southern sympathizers out to smuggle five million dollars in gold from Nevada and bring the loot to Virginia, this swiftly paced yarn boasts spectacular action sequences, sweeping panoramas and a rousing Max Steiner score. Miriam Hopkins is the dance hall girl who helps the rebels set up her Yankee boyfriend. This was Humphrey Bogart and Errol Flynn's only film together. Also stars Randolph Scott.
VHS: S16099. $19.98.
Michael Curtiz, USA, 1940, 121 mins.

The Virginian
Joel McCrea, Brian Donlevy and Sonny Tufts star in this remake of a classic silent-era Western. A Wild West cowboy (McCrea) marries a Wyoming schoolteacher he has rescued from a villainous cattle rustler. When the cowboy is confronted by thieves and finds that he has been betrayed by his closest friend, he knows he must fight for his honor, even if it means losing his new bride. Based on the novel by Owen Wister.
VHS: S27672. $14.98.
Stuart Gilmore, USA, 1946, 90 mins.

War Arrow
Jeff Chandler must end the Kiowa uprisings in Texas, placing him in direct conflict with the officer in charge, John McIntire. There is another element to this rivalry. Maureen O'Hara's husband is a missing cavalry officer, whose absence ultimately places her in a love triangle between these two. It's a western based on an actual historical incident.
VHS: S23676. $14.98.
George Sherman, USA, 1953, 79 mins.

War Wagon
Plenty of action and laughs as John Wayne and Kirk Douglas team up to capture a stagecoach loaded with gold bullion.
VHS: S03535. $14.98.
Burt Kennedy, USA, 1967, 101 mins.

Warlock
Well-paced Western features Richard Widmark, Henry Fonda and Anthony Quinn. A marshal cleans up a town in this unusual turn by Edward Dmytryk.
VHS: S06519. $19.95.
Laser: LD75281. $34.98.
Edward Dmytryk, USA, 1959, 121 mins.

West of the Divide
John Wayne is on the trail of his father's murderer. This time the Duke also searches for his baby brother, who has been missing since dad took the fatal bullet.
VHS: S12748. $19.98.
Robert North Bradbury, USA, 1934, 54 mins.

Wheel of Fortune
Before there was Vanna White, John Wayne took a spin at being a lawyer who gambled he could uncover the killer of a good friend and put an end to political corruption in Temple City. All the Duke needed was 83 minutes. With Frances Dee, Ward Bond and Wallace Ford. B&W.
VHS: S04893. $19.95.
John H. Auer, USA, 1941, 83 mins.

When the Legends Die
A powerful contemporary Western drama about an aging rodeo cowboy (Richard Widmark) training a young American Indian protege (Frederic Forrest). Excellent performances and exciting rodeo action. With Luana Anders, Vito Scotti and Herbert Nelson. An impressive debut by director Stuart Miller.
VHS: S07148. $19.98.
Stuart Millar, USA, 1972, 105 mins.

White Buffalo
Charles Bronson stars as Wild Bill Hickok in this western adventure about an arduous hunt for a great white buffalo. Will Sampson co-stars as Chief Crazy Horse—or is it Capt. Ahab, as there are certain similarities to a certain novel by Herman Melville. With Kim Novak, Jack Warden, Slim Pickens, Clint Walker and John Carradine. Buffalo designed by the same guy who built King Kong, in the remake.
VHS: I1529. $19.98.
J. Lee Thompson, USA, 1977, 97 mins.

Wild Bill
Jeff Bridges and Ellen Barkin star in this Western based on the legendary Wild Bill Hickok. It's a tale of an unmatched gunfighter who singlehandedly stood for justice in a lawless landscape. John Hurt and Keith Carradine are also featured.
VHS: S27690. $99.99.
Laser: LD75565. $34.99.
Walter Hill, USA, 1995, 98 mins.

Wild West
This offbeat comedy follows an urban cowboy and his crew on the perilous road to country and western stardom. They meet a smart, sultry singer with a past. Suddenly, success seems within their grasp. There may even be a romance in the works. Songs from Garth Brooks and Dwight Yokum are included.
VHS: S24957. $92.99.
Laser: LD75285. $34.98.
David Attwood, USA, 1994, 85 mins.

Will Penny
One of the last great Westerns, with unusually deep characterization. Charlton Heston is the tired cowboy who is staked out to die in the desert by a gang of outlaws. Moments before death, he is taken in by a young frontier woman (Joan Hackett) who is heading west with her young son to join her husband. As she nurses him back to health, he has two problems to deal with: he is madly in love with another man's wife and the outlaw gang is on its way to finish him off. With Donald Pleasence, Lee Majors, Bruce Dern.
VHS: S09569. $19.95.
Laser: LD75286. $34.98.
Tom Gries, USA, 1968, 109 mins.

Winchester '73
A major western with James Stewart involved in hunting down a man and his stolen gun through a series of inter-related episodes. With a great shootout among the hills at the end, Leonard Maltin credits this film with reviving the popularity of Westerns during the 1950's. With Shelley Winters, Dan Duryea.
VHS: S06819. $14.98.
Anthony Mann, USA, 1950, 92 mins.

Winds of the Wasteland
John Wayne appears in this early Western, which was made before he became one of the most popular screen cowboys ever known. 1936, 54 mins.
VHS: S26685. $19.95.

Woman of the Town
Sheriff Bat Masterson cleans up Dodge City with his toughness and grit. The only crime he can't stop is letting dance hall belle Dora Hand steal his heart. With Claire Trevor and Barry Sullivan.
VHS: S14754. $19.95.
George Archainbaud, USA, 1943, 90 mins.

Wyatt Earp
Dennis Hopper is the law man who tamed the West, with Dennis Quaid as the cadaverous Doc Holliday. This film offers a dark view of the most metaphysical of American landscapes, the enduring frontier. There men must rely on their own inner strength to define what's right and wrong before they fight for it. Gene Hackman co-stars.
VHS: S22528. $24.98.
Laser: LD74610. $44.98.
Lawrence Kasdan, USA, 1994, 191 mins.

Young Guns
The legend of William H. Bonney, alias Billy the Kid, notorious back-shooter and cult western figure, gets still another shot at cinematic immortality. Emilio Estevez may just be the definitive Billy the Kid. The Lincoln County War is re-fought by juvenile delinquents with guns. With Charlie Sheen, Keifer Sutherland, Lou Diamond Phillips and Brian Keith.
VHS: S10082. $89.95.
Christopher Cain, USA, 1988, 102 mins.

The Young Land
Pat Wayne, Yvonne Craig, Dan O'Herlihy, Ken Curtis and a young Dennis Hopper are all featured in this western about a racist town. Hopper is a young bully who murders a Mexican. Now a sheriff and a judge must convince opposing sides that they will both be served justly by the American legal system.
VHS: S23907. $19.95.
Ted Tetzlaff, USA, 1959, 89 mins.

Yuma
Clint Walker stars in this made-for-TV western as an honest sheriff whose reputation is tarnished by unknown plotters. The always tall-in-the-saddle Walker fights to restore law and order and his good name. With Barry Sullivan, Edgar Buchanan, Kathryn Hays and Morgan Woodward.
VHS: S08299. $19.98.
Ted Post, USA, 1970, 73 mins.

Adventures of the Old West
This six-volume series, hosted by Kris Kristofferson, tells the story of the frontier through archival footage, rare photos, personal diaries, letters, official documents and first hand accounts. Original songs by Kristofferson enliven this engaging exploration of America's past. Each title is 50 mins.
Frontier Justice the Law and the Lawless.
VHS: S22524. $19.98.
Great Chiefs at the Crossroads.
VHS: S22526. $19.98.
Pioneers and the Promised Land.
VHS: S22525. $19.98.
Scouts in the Wilderness.
VHS: S22521. $19.98.
Texas Cowboys and the Trail Drives.
VHS: S22522. $19.98.
The 49ers and the California Gold Rush.
VHS: S22523. $19.98.
Gift Box Set.
VHS: S22527. $99.98.

The Best of the Real West Complete Set
Kenny Rogers is host for this documentary series that combines original footage, authentic diaries, paintings, photos, and expert commentary to reawaken the adventure of that fabled landscape. Wild Bill, The Alamo, Texas Rangers, Wild Women and Sitting Bull are the five topics covered in depth by this collection. Each video is 50 mins.
VHS: S22535. $59.95.

Custer's Last Trooper
This documentary depicts the drama of the Battle of Little Big Horn and the life of General Armstrong Custer. Authentic artifacts, photos and diary excerpts punctuate this historical essay. 1990, 47 mins.
VHS: S16325. $24.95.

Donner Pass: The Road to Survival
A dramatic re-creation of one of the most horrifying episodes from the American frontier: In 1846, a party of American settlers moving from Illinois to California are reduced to cannibalism when they're decimated by blinding snow storms and other natural disasters. With Robert Fuller, Andrew Prine, Michael Callan and John Anderson.
VHS: S17967. $19.95.
James L. Conway, USA, 1978, 100 mins.

Elko: The Cowboy Gathering
Baxter Black, Waddy Mitchell, Riders in the Sky…they're all here to share their love of the cowboy lifestyle. Music and cowboy poetry make this an enjoyable video with great laughs. 60 mins.
VHS: S23124. $19.95.

A Few Men Well-Conducted: The George Rogers Clark Story
This is the story of George Rogers Clark and his courageous frontiersmen, who fought on the Kentucky and Illinois frontier during the American Revolution. 23 mins.
VHS: S06676. $29.95.

Frontier Heritage
James Whitmore narrates this journey through the wilderness telling the story of the people who conquered America's wild frontiers and started to create a new life in these challenging times.
VHS: S05246. $39.95.

Frontier Progress
James Whitmore is the narrator for this second in a two-part look at the building of America in the great western wilderness, a fascinating look at the courage, strength and perseverance of the people who built a nation.
VHS: S05247. $39.95.

Goldrush Country
Hugh O'Brian narrates this documentary about the lure of gold in the American frontier. Period drawings and engravings help illustrate this historical account of the westward expansion of the nation. 18 mins.
VHS: S23730. $49.95.

The Great West Collection
From Texas to Hawaii, Arizona to Canada, the five-part Great West Collection explores a prominent American tradition.
Great Ranches of the West. Join Michael Martin Murphey for a visit to four of the largest and oldest family-owned ranches in America. Includes a stop at Eaton's Dude Ranch, the original 1879 "Dude ranch". 60 mins.
VHS: S16479. $19.95.
My Heroes Have Always Been Cowboys. Working cattle by day and singing around a campfire at night, Waylon Jennings leads this old fashioned roundup in West Texas. A look at the rugged life of real cowboys on a modern ranch against the background of great songs, including Sweet Mother Texas, A Long Time Ago, I've Always Been Crazy and Last Cowboy Song. 60 mins.
VHS: S16478. $19.95.
Ranch Album. Portraying a way of life that is rooted in hard work, family, a love of nature and a hunger for independence, the Ranch Album celebrates the demanding world of ranching—season by season, and generation by generation. 60 mins.
VHS: S16477. $19.95.
The Last Cowboys. Journey to the ranges of Utah and Nevada to discover the true-life legend of the cowboy. At a modern rodeo, the vital skills of yesterday's cowboys are transformed into a popular sport. Includes a visit to Robbers Roost Ranch, where Butch Cassidy, the Sundance Kid and the Hole in the Wall Gang all laid their hats.
VHS: S16476. $19.95.
The Working Cowboy—In Search of the Cowboy Song. Country musician, cowboy poet and rancher Ian Tyson has always found inspiration in the cowboy's life. His search for the cowboy song drives him to many of Canada's great ranches, underscoring the powerful link between true country living and Western music. 60 mins.
VHS: S16480. $19.95.

How the West Was Lost
This compelling documentary series tells the epic story of the struggle over the American West. Witness the tragic plight of five Native American nations: The Navajo, Nez Perce, Apache, Cheyenne and Lakota. 60-100 mins.
Vol. 1: Clash of Cultures/I Will Fight No More Forever.
VHS: S21801. $29.95.

Vol. 2: Always the Enemy/The Only Good Indian Is a Dead Indian.
VHS: S21802. $29.95.
Vol. 3: A Good Day to Die/Kill the Indian, Save the Man.
VHS: S21803. $29.95.
How the West Was Lost, Set.
VHS: S22002. $79.96.

How The West Was Lost II
The story of the American West is compellingly told in this continuation of the documentary series from the Discovery Channel. Two distinct cultures fought for more than just territory. For Native Americans it was a struggle to survive. Four-volume set, each 90 mins.
VHS: S26048. $79.95.

Life and Times of Wyatt Earp
This documentary tells the story of the gambler, bounty hunter, lawman, and Indian fighter who became an American folk hero. 52 mins.
VHS: S20488. $9.95.

Opening the West (1860-1900)
Reconstruction and Westward Expansion are the themes following President Lincoln's courageous efforts to reunite the nation after the bloody fratricide of the Civil War. With the settlement of the lands beyond the Mississippi, the young nation is well on its way toward maturity and a place among the leading countries of the world.
VHS: S03974. $64.95.

Outlaws: The Ten Most Wanted
Featured in the program The Real West, this documentary looks at the myth and culture of the outlaw. Jesse James, Cole Younger and the rest of the villains are examined, with a special interest in explaining their hold on popular American culture. 60 mins.
VHS: S19724. $19.95.

The Real West
An impressionistic look at the life, times and landscape of the American west, examining the intertwining myths, language, culture and texture of the American frontier. Narrated by Gary Cooper. "A fascinatingly authentic look at the West" (New York Times). 60 mins.
VHS: S19247. $19.95.

Story of the American Cowboy
This documentary is a must-see for cowboy fans and those fascinated by the history of the early West. USA, 60 mins.
VHS: S15030. $19.95.

The Untold West
The Wild West is a source of enduring myths and legends that go to the heart of what it is to be an American. But it was also a place where real people, with all their weaknesses and foibles, lived and died. In this series the truth about a number of formerly taboo topics finally comes to light.
Hot on the Trail. The Wild West was home to innumerable tales of passion and desire. Tobacco was packaged with "girlie cards" to use a vice to sell another vice. Even the infamous Calamity Jane had her weaknesses, blazing a trail across 12 husbands. 60 mins.
VHS: S20955. $14.98.
Outlaws, Rebels and Rogues. Were the West's most notorious bad guys really as tough as they seemed? Or were these desperados just desperate for attention, especially from the press? This humorous look at outlaws includes a close look at the most famous of them all, Billy the Kid. 60 mins.
VHS: S20956. $14.98.
The Black West. It's a little known fact, but Afro-American pioneers, farmers, entrepreneurs, cowboys and even outlaws all played a part in the exploration of the Wild West. Will Rogers and Teddy Roosevelt are just some of the white Americans who learned from these nearly forgotten settlers. 60 mins.
VHS: S20957. $14.98.
The Complete Set.
VHS: S20958. $19.98.

The Way West
Ric Burns crafted this six-hour series that chronicles the story of the West from the San Francisco Gold Rush to the Battle of Wounded Knee. Stunning photos, along with paintings, maps and motion pictures, enliven this historic series. Russell Baker narrates and a host of other voices are featured, including F. Murray Abraham, Graham Greene, Wes Studi, Eli Wallach and many others. Four 90-minute videocassettes.
VHS: S24493. $69.95.

West of the Imagination
The West of awesome landscape and fearsome dangers, of Indians, pioneers, outlaws, cowboys, tradesmen, explorers…this six-volume set explores the sweeping story of the American West as seen through the eyes of its mythmakers and mythologizers—the West of the historians with paintbrush, explorers with camera.
Enduring Dreams. The West of our own century, of Grant Wood, Thomas Hart Benton, and the Dust Bowl.
VHS: S05567. $29.95.
Images of Glory. Nature's grandeur, a thirst for adventure, the last Indian wars—the West continued to beckon.
VHS: S05564. $29.95.
Play the Legend. The West of the cowboy stars and circus barkers, of songsmiths and rodeo artists.
VHS: S05566. $29.95.
The Golden Land. The Oregon Trail becomes the westward passage to freedom, gold, adventure and discovery.
VHS: S05563. $29.95.
The Romantic Horizon. The magical landscapes, noble savages and half-wild mountain men of the new continent.
VHS: S05562. $29.95.
The Wild Riders. The working cowboy and how he became a hero of American folklore.
VHS: S05565. $29.95.
West of the Imagination, Complete. The complete six-volume set of West of the Imagination.
VHS: S05568. $169.00.

Wyatt Earp: Justice at the OK Corral
The myths, legends and realities of the Old West come alive in the Real West with Kenny Rogers as the narrator. Through original footage, authentic diaries, paintings, photos and expert commentary, this video will breathe new life into the legend of Wyatt Earp. The two-tape set also includes the documentary Dodge City. Both tapes are 50 mins.
VHS: S21547. $19.95.

literature ON SCREEN

Almos' a Man
Based on the short story by Richard Wright, and starring LeVar Burton, Madge Sinclair, Robert Dogui. From American Short Story Series.
VHS: S01956. $24.95.
Stan Lathan, USA, 52 mins.

Anais Observed
Anais Nin's surrealistic novels, extensive diaries and deep friendships were all formed at the heart of a developing modern consciousness. Her distinct female persona is especially noteworthy for its overall embrace of human diversity. This portrait captures her life and philosophy. D.H. Lawrence, Otto Rank, Henry Miller, Kenneth Anger and Maya Deren are just some of the personalities captured alongside this singular literary artist.
VHS: S26714. $29.95.

The Ballads of Madison County
Robert James Waller's best-selling book, *The Bridges of Madison County*, was the inspiration for this romantic journey. The author introduces you to the landscape and the people of Madison County in both word and song, while interviews reveal the man behind the writer.
VHS: S20838. $14.98.

Barn Burning
Based on the short story by William Faulkner, with a script by Horton Foote, and starring Tommy Lee Jones and Diane Kagan. From American Short Story Series.
VHS: S02133. $24.95.
Peter Werner, USA, 52 mins.

Bernice Bobs Her Hair
Based on the short story by F. Scott Fitzgerald, and featuring Shelley Duvall, Veronica Cartwright and Bud Cort. From American Short Story Series.
VHS: S02065. $24.95.
Joan Micklin Silver, USA, 52 mins.

The Blue Men
Adapted from the short story by Joy Williams, this haunting tale of adolescent isolation features a young boy's experiences while staying with his grandmother on a small summer island. The narrative touches on the need for the boy and his grandmother to come to terms with their past and deal with tragedy. With Estelle Parsons. 45 mins.
VHS: S20387. $24.95.

A Brighter Garden
Emily Dickinson's poems for each of Nature's seasons are read by actress Frances Sternhagen. "Summer" includes the famed "I'm Nobody! Who are you?" Tasha Tudor's cameo watercolor paintings reflect her deep appreciation of Dickinson's 19th century New England. A mutual love of nature is perfectly reflected in Tudor's snowy winter landscapes, the brighter shades of spring and fall, and even moonlit nights.
VHS: S16336. $44.95.

The Cask of Amontillado
Insults between Italian noblemen lead into this charming tale. Montresor seeks revenge on Fortunato by playing on his friend's vanity and love of wine. Soon Fortunato finds himself deep underground in Montresor's cellar in search of the prized amontillado wine. Based on the story by Edgar Allan Poe. 18 mins.
VHS: S23496. $79.95.

Classic Books on Video
A series of introductions to great works of literature. Each tape contains a dramatization of key scenes from the novel, followed by an on-screen discussion and analysis of the meaning and context of the entire work. Each tape is 40 mins.
A Tale of Two Cities.
VHS: S06279. $29.99.
Crime and Punishment.
VHS: S06276. $19.99.
Hamlet.
VHS: S06280. $19.99.
The Iliad.
VHS: S06278. $19.99.
The Scarlet Letter.
VHS: S06277. $19.99.
Thomas Jefferson.
VHS: S06281. $19.99.

Classic Literary Stories, Vol. 1
All The Troubles of the World, from a story by Isaac Asimov, exploring the implications of a world served by an all-knowing, benevolent computer, and *The Bear*, from a story by William Faulkner, based on the second of his short story versions in which a boy confronts the legend and finds the truth of an old bear. 37 mins.
VHS: S05813. $19.95.

Classic Literary Stories, Vol. 2
The Cash of Amontillado, based on a story by Edgar Allan Poe, one of the masterpieces of horror fiction, and *The Necklace*, based on a story by Guy de Maupassant, in which the borrowed necklace is lost, and the couple must mortgage the last ten years of their life. 40 mins.
VHS: S05814. $19.95.

Classic Literary Stories, Vol. 3
The Coup de Grace, based on a short story by Ambrose Bierce, as a Union soldier searches for his childhood friend amid the scattered dead and wounded, and Bierce's *An Occurrence at Owl Creek Bridge*, the great brooding story of a man's life going before him shortly before his execution. 19 mins.,
VHS: S05815. $19.95.

D.P.
Kurt Vonnegut Jr.'s short story is magically transformed in this Emmy Award-winning production starring Stan Shaw, Rosemary Leach and Julius Gordon. In the barren wasteland of post WW II Germany, a lonely black orphan discovers the only other black he has ever seen—the soldier—and dubs him "Papa." 60 mins.
VHS: S05321. $24.95.

Displaced Person
Based on the short story by Flannery O'Connor, with a script by Horton Foote. With Irene Worth, John Houseman, Shirley Stoler. From American Short Story Series.
VHS: S01958. $24.95.
Glenn Jordon, USA, 52 mins.

Ethan Frome
This adaptation of Edith Wharton's 1911 novel is set in the wintry landscapes of New England. Liam Neeson plays the simple farmer trapped in an emotionless marriage with a hypochondriac (Joan Allen). With Patricia Arquette, Tate Donovan as a sympathetic minister, and Katharine Houghton.
VHS: S19287. $94.95.
John Madden, USA, 1992, 99 mins.

The Glorious Romantics
British actress Jean Marsh (*Upstairs, Downstairs*) complements a wonderful ensemble of actors who portray the great poets Keats, Shelley and Byron, as well as other figures from the Romantic period. Excerpts from the poems "Ode on a Grecian Urn", "Love's Philosophy", "Ozymandias" and more are recited in this charming film. Great Britain, 90 mins.
VHS: S23605. $24.95.

Golden Honeymoon
Based on the short story by Ring Lardner, and starring James Whitmore, Teresa Wright and Stephen Elliot. From American Short Story Series.
VHS: S01959. $24.95.
Noel Black, USA, 52 mins.

Great Expectations
Dickens' novel about the powerful benefactor and the poor man whom he transforms into a respected London businessman is realized with a top cast including Michael York, Sarah Miles, James Mason, Anthony Quayle and Robert Morley.
VHS: S19029. $19.98.
Joseph Hardy, USA/Britain, 1974, 124 mins.

Greatest Man in the World
From the American Short Story Collection, an adaptation of James Thurber's story about a flyer who bests Lindbergh's non-stop flying record only to have the glory withheld until he can be transformed into the right kind of hero. With Brad Davis and Carol Kane.
VHS: S00528. $24.95.
Ralph Rosenblum, USA, 1980, 51 mins.

The Hitchhikers
An low-key adaptation of Eudora Welty's tale of the strange happenings in a gothic Southern town when the body of a hitchhiker is discovered brutally murdered on an isolated country road. "A gem of a film" (*Los Angeles Times*). With Richard Hatch and Patty Duke. 30 mins.
VHS: S20386. $24.95.

The Hollow Boy
American Playhouse's *American Short Story Collection* offers this story by Hortense Calisher. It's set in New York City during 1936. A young German immigrant and a Jewish neighbor attempt an uneasy friendship that is further complicated by the troubles of this time. 60 mins.
VHS: S21245. $24.95.

Hooray for Abbie!
This video tribute to Abbie Hoffman features the Abbie memorials from the Summer of 1989—The Palladium New York—plus the picnic at Washington's Crossing. There are fond remembrances by many friends, including Peter Yarrow, Paul Krassner, Allen Ginsberg, Norman Mailer, Jerry Rubin, The Fugs, Bobby Seale, Dave Dellinger, David Amram, Richie Havens and William Kunstler. Also features brother Jack Hoffman and his wife, Anita. 76 mins.
VHS: S21846. $29.95.

Horse Dealer's Daughter
A haunting film, based on the D.H. Lawrence short story, about a young woman's search for identity. Taken for granted by her brothers after the death of her father, she struggles with an uncertain future—discovering her own self worth through the eyes of the young town doctor. 30 mins.
VHS: S14261. $24.95.

I'm a Fool
Based on a short story by Sherwood Anderson, and starring Ron Howard, Santiago Gonzalez, Amy Irving. From American Short Story series.
VHS: S02134. $24.95.
Noel Black, USA, 52 mins.

Jilting of Granny Weatherall
Based on the short story by Katherine Anne Porter, and starring Geraldine Fitzgerald and Lois Smith. From American Short Story series.
VHS: S02003. $24.95.
Randa Haines, USA, 52 mins.

Jolly Corner
From the American Short Story collection: Henry James-based story concerns a haunted house where a man obsessed with his past is able to see what he might have been like had circumstances been different. With Salome Jens and Fritz Weaver.
VHS: S01538. $24.95.
Arthur Barron, USA, 1977, 43 mins.

Lawrenceville Stories: Prodigious Hickey
An adaptation of Owen Johnson's stories set in the Lawrence Prep School, originally published in *Saturday Evening Post*, centers on a charismatic young man, William Hicks, "The Prodigious Hickey," who devises a plan to restore the reputation of his undistinguished roommate. 60 mins.
VHS: S17168. $24.95.

Lawrenceville Stories: The Return of Hickey
The continuation of Owen Johnson's *Saturday Evening Post* stories set in the Lawrence Prep School finds Hickey returning to school following a suspension, where he's promptly entangled with a polished newcomer who threatens his reign as the local powerbroker. 60 mins.
VHS: S17169. $24.95.

Lawrenceville Stories: Beginning of the Firm
In this concluding episode of Owen Johnson's lyrical stories, Hickey reluctantly joins with his rival, "The Tennessee Shad," to impart lessons on humility and order to an insufferably wealthy freshman. "A beguiling, winsome exercise in nostalgic Americana" (*Washington Post*). 60 mins.
VHS: S17170. $24.95.

Lawrenceville Stories: 3-Pack Miniseries
All three stories, *Prodigious Hickey*, *Return of Hickey*, and *Beginning of the Firm*, collected in one package. 180 mins.
VHS: S17171. $64.95.

Love and Other Sorrows
Harold Brodkey's story is adapted for film with actors Christopher Collet and Elizabeth Franz in this episode from the American Playhouse American Short Story Collection. It's about a 16-year-old boy who, over the course of a summer in St. Louis, learns about love and life. This gentle film is entertaining for all ages. 60 mins.
VHS: S21244. $24.95.

The Mystery of Edwin Drood
Based on Charles Dickens' last, unfinished novel, this mystery film shows a corrupt Victorian world dominated by injustice and the resentment it breeds. Edwin Drood vanishes one stormy Christmas Eve. His betrothed, a chaste orphan, joins a choirmaster and a dark young stranger to find the missing man. In this battle between good and evil, passion, lust and intrigue become the weapons of choice.
VHS: S26401. $24.95.
Timothy Forder, Great Britain, 1993, 98 mins.

Norman and the Killer
Adapted from a short story by the American novelist, essayist and playwright Joyce Carol Oates, *Norman and the Killer* concerns the psychological and emotional trauma inflicted upon a young man and his efforts to reconcile his trauma and guilt when he confronts the man responsible for the crime against him. 30 mins.
VHS: S17023. $24.95.

Notes from a Lady at a Dinner Party
Based on a short story by the great American writer Bernard Malamud (*The Fixer*), David Angsten directed this elegant, sordid tale about the casual flirtation and deceptive planning when a young architect carries out his seduction of his mentor's wife at a dinner party. With Yvonne Suhor, Tim Gregory and John Kirk.
VHS: S16193. $29.95.
David Angsten, USA, 25 mins.

An Occurrence at Owl Creek Bridge
Award winning short film based on a story by Ambrose Bierce about the final moments of a man about to be hung for sabotage during the Civil War. Highly recommended.
VHS: S02247. $19.95.
Robert Enrico, France, 1962, 29 mins.

Open Window/Child's Play (Two from Saki)
Hector Hugh Munro was an imaginative writer who wrote some of our most moving and studied short stories under the pen name Saki. Film versions of two of his most famous stories are included in this collection: *The Open Window* and *Child's Play*. Combined running time 39 mins.
VHS: S14262. $24.95.

Parker Adderson Philosopher and The Music School
Based on short stories by Ambrose Bierce and John Updike; *Parker Adderson* stars Harris Yulin and was directed by Arthur Barron; *The Music School* stars Ron Weyand and was directed by John Korty. 52 mins. From American Short Story series.
VHS: S01539. $24.95.

Paul's Case
Based on the short story by Willa Cather, and starring Eric Roberts and Lindsay Crouse. From American Short Story series.
VHS: S01961. $24.95.
Lamont Johnson, USA, 52 mins.

Rappaccini's Daughter
Based on the short story by Nathaniel Hawthorne and starring Kristoffer Tabori and Kathleen Beller. From The American Short Story series.
VHS: S02004. $24.95.
Dezso Magyar, USA, 52 mins.

A Rose for Emily
A sensitive treatment of William Faulkner's short story about a gilded, repressed young Southern woman, whose strict, suffocating father drove her into an ill-suited relationship with a Northern laborer. Narrated by John Houseman. With Anjelica Huston, John Randolph and John Carradine.
VHS: S14449. $24.95.

Sense and Sensibility
The literary inspiration of Jane Austen's first novel comes to the screen in this BBC adaptation. Elinor and Marianne are two sisters out to catch a husband. One is restrained and the other impetuous, yet both find that finding a suitable mate is not such an easy task to complete.
VHS: S04669. $24.98.
Rodney Bennett, Great Britain, 1986, 174 mins.

Soldier's Home
From the American Short Story Collection, an adaptation of Ernest Hemingway's story of a young man's return from World War I finding that one of the hardest parts of war is the coming home. With Richard Backus and Nancy Marchand.
VHS: S01227. $24.95.
Robert Young, USA, 1976, 41 mins.

To Build a Fire
Jack London's short story is brought to life as narrated by Orson Welles. A lone man travels through the wilderness in -75° weather. The stark realism of the images combines with the power of Orson Welles' reading. 56 mins.
VHS: S09399. $29.95.

Two Soldiers
Taken from *Arts and Entertainment Short Story Collection II*, this free spirited adaptation of a William Faulkner story concerns a naive, determined farm boy who leaves his rural surroundings to find the older brother who abandoned him to fight in World War II. "A rural view of American patriotism (that) provides entertaining viewing for general library audiences" (*Book List*). 30 mins.
VHS: S17024. $24.95.

Women & Men—Stories of Seduction
Six big name Hollywood performers star in three separate stories of interaction between the sexes in this made-for-HBO anthology. Adapted from the works of Mary McCarthy, Ernest Hemingway, and Dorothy Parker and directed by Ken Russell, Tony Richardson, and Frederic Raphael. Cast includes James Woods, Melanie Griffith, Beau Bridges, Elizabeth McGovern, Molly Ringwald and Peter Weller. Music by Marvin Hamlisch. USA, 1990, 90 mins.
VHS: S13300. $19.95.

A Year in Provence
Adapted from Peter Mayle's international best seller, the video recounts the first year of Mayle's stay in rustic Provence. Mayle and his wife Annie have abandoned the London rat race to savor the small pleasures and grace of the French way of life, a world characterized by great food, fine wines and a seductive climate. The Mayles explore the charm of the region and meet a group of unconventional characters who complicate their lives with intrigue and misadventures. Four-cassette deluxe boxed set.
VHS: S18970. $59.95.
David Tucker, Great Britain, 1989, 360 mins.

WRITERS & THEIR WORKS

A.M. Klein: The Poet as Landscape
The personality of the century's leading Anglo-Jewish poet, A.M. Klein, is revealed through interviews, selections from his writing, film footage and historical stills. This is the biography of a fascinating but little understood poet; it touches on everything from his lyrical childhood memories to the tragic silence that overtook Klein in his later years. 58 mins.
VHS: S12867. $39.95.

ABC No Rio, Open Mike
Document of young poets and musicians reading at New York Lower East Side gallery's open mike. Matthew Courtney is MC. 1985, 20 mins.
VHS: S10195. $19.95.

Adrienne Rich
This lesbian poet has revolutionized poetry and the cause of woman-centered culture. She reads from *An Atlas of the Difficult World*, *Diving into the Wreck* and speaks with Michael Silverblatt in Los Angeles on May 14, 1992. From the *Lannan Literary Videos* series. 60 mins.
VHS: S27136. $19.95.

Agatha Christie: How Did She Do It?
This program goes in search of clues to the elusive character of Agatha Christie. The detective is Janet Morgan who, in 1982, was asked to write a biography of the woman who has killed off more people than any other author. How did she do it? Why is it that these books, written by this person, transcend every geographical, social and cultural boundary? 55 mins.
VHS: S07598. $39.95.

Allen Ginsberg

As the bard of the Beat Generation, Allen Ginsberg helped revive American poetry in the 1950s. In this video, his reading and musical performance of poems from *Collected Poems 1947-1980* is captured as it was experienced on February 25, 1989. Lewis MacAdams conducted the interview. From the *Lannan Literary Videos* series. 60 mins.
VHS: S27116. $19.95.

Allen Ginsberg Meets Nanao Sakaki

In a quaint East Village poetry performance space called The Gas Station, internationally renowned poets Allen Ginsberg and Nanao Sakaki gathered. There in the winter of 1988 they made great personal and humanistic music. Since the end of World War II, Nanao Sakaki has lived the life of a wandering poet-storyteller.
VHS: S21845. $29.95.

America in Portrait

Selections from the acclaimed PBS series, "Anyone for Tennyson?" Henry Fonda, William Shatner and James Whitmore are featured in readings of great poetry, often on location, including Frost, Sandburg, Holmes, Edgar Lee Masters (*Spoon River Anthology*), Edgar Allan Poe, Emerson and T.S. Eliot. 45 mins.
VHS: S08792. $24.95.

American Lifestyle Series: Writers

This series offers a view of truly great Americans. These lives stand as testament to the virtues and values of individuality, creativity, and leadership. This collection of four videos profiles some of the greatest U.S. writers.
Helen Keller: Voices and Vision in the Soul. Hugh Downs narrates this program celebrating the accomplishments of the deaf, blind, mute woman who dedicated her life to helping those who were, in her words, "less fortunate than myself." 24 mins.
VHS: S23547. $49.95.
Laser: LD74777. $99.95.
Mark Twain's Hartford Home. E.G. Marshall narrates this tour through Twain's Victorian home in Hartford, where he lived for 20 happy and productive years. 24 mins.
VHS: S23548. $49.95.
Laser: LD74778. $99.95.
Carl Sandburg: Poet of the People. Hugh Downs narrates the story of Sandburg's life. He was born to hardworking immigrants and grew up to be a formidable literary figure. His passion for democracy and the wisdom of the people remains vital through his work. 24 mins.
VHS: S23549. $49.95.
Pearl Buck: The Woman, the World, and Two Good Earths. This visit to the home of the Nobel Prize-winning author is hosted and narrated by Hugh Downs. Buck is a sculptor, a pianist, a philanthropist and a mother to nine adopted children. 24 mins.
VHS: S23550. $49.95.
Laser: LD74779. $99.95.

Angel Rama

The peripatetic critic and editor, whom some would describe as the "Edmund Wilson" of Latin America, converses with novelist Mario Szichman about the state of letters in Latin America, the role of Brazil, and the phenomenon of the so-called "boom" of the novel. He analyses the key works and touches on the work of the youngest writers in the post-boom era. Spanish *without* English subtitles.
Home Video.
VHS: S06945. $59.95.
Public Performance.
VHS: S08834. $100.00.

Anne Rice: Birth of the Vampire

Rice is the author and creator of the most popular contemporary fiction series about vampires. Her central character, the vampire Lestat, has become known to millions of readers. In this profile, the story behind the series is revealed through Anne Rice herself. 50 mins.
VHS: S22533. $14.98.

Anne Waldman

Two-time World Heavyweight Poetry Bout champion, Anne Waldman has a reputation as both a poet and consummate performer. In this video she reads from *Helping the Dreamer* and *New and Selected Poems* and also recites from unpublished work. This video was recorded on March 11, 1991, in Los Angeles, and the interview was conducted by Lewis MacAdams. From the *Lannan Literary Videos* series. 60 mins.
VHS: S27131. $19.95.

Anthony Burgess on D.H. Lawrence

This film, commissioned to mark the 1985 centenary of Lawrence's birth, uses both modern and archival footage to evoke the world of one of Britain's most famous writers. Burgess presents his own appraisal of the man whose explicit views on sex made him a controversial figure in his own time and long beyond. 55 mins.
VHS: S02398. $19.95.

Author to Author Video Series

George Garrett discusses literature with a panel of authors and poets. Series guide included.
Contemporary Poets. Rita Dove, Elizabeth Spire and Henry Taylor discuss American poetry. This panel of poets is particularly insightful about the process of creative writing. 40 mins.
VHS: S24110. $210.00.
Contemporary Short Story Writers. Richard Bausch, Madison Smartt Bell and Alan Cheuse comprise a panel of short story writers. They examine their motivations and explain their decision to concentrate on this literary form. 40 mins.
VHS: S24111. $210.00.
First Novelists. Sydney Blair, Cathryn Hankla and Darcey Steinke expound upon their initial writing experiences, particularly their apprenticeships. 40 mins.
VHS: S24113. $210.00.
The Fiction of Mary Lee Settle. Settle explains the background of her novel *Blood Tie*, and discusses her long career as an author. 40 mins.
VHS: S24110. $210.00.
The Modernist Movement in Poetry. James Dickey and R.W.B. Lewis counter recent arguments put forth against both Modernism and T.S. Eliot. 40 mins.
VHS: S24114. $210.00.

The Beat Generation Show

In May 1994, the first Beat Generation Conference took place in New York City. Participants included Ann Charters, Ray Manzarek (Doors keyboard player), Michael McClure, Allen Ginsberg, Gregory Corso, Lawrence Ferlinghetti, Hettie Jones, Ed Sanders (of Fugs fame), Dr. Hunter S. Thompson and many others. Discussions, performances, poetry and music are all featured. 60 mins.
VHS: S23287. $29.95.

Beat Legends: Allen Ginsberg

Ginsberg unleashes a storm of dream visions and poetic polemics, sometimes accompanied by a mini-pump organ, and bracketed with historical background information. He reads *Western Ballad* (the first song he ever wrote), *The Fifth Internationale*, *CIA Dope Calypso*, *Why I Meditate*, *Plutonium Ode* and *Broken Bone Blues*. A series of poems from 1984-1990 is also shown, which includes the work *Dreamed a Long Walk with Henry Kissinger*. 92 mins.
VHS: S21842. $34.95.

Beat Legends: Gregory Corso

Hypnotic, hyperbolic and trigger-happy, the charismatic Corso rolls and flows at the trip of the tongue, here in a historic reading in Greenwich Village, New York, 1991. Corso reads *Flu Ramblings*, *Wreck of the Nordling*, *Amnesia in Memphis*, *Prophesy 1958*, *The Whole Mess*, *Almost* and much more.
VHS: S21840. $29.95.

Bukowski at Bellevue

In the spring of 1970, Charles Bukowski, then little known, packed his overnight bag, locked the door to his tumbledown East Hollywood apartment behind him, and took his first plane ride to the state of Washington to read at Bellevue Community College. This pioneer reading, his fourth ever, was videotaped in black and white. While the technical aspects of the film are shaky, here is Bukowski at the beginning of a great career, reading powerfully and with grit and humor. 60 mins.
VHS: S06897. $45.00.

Burroughs

Brilliant documentary about William S. Burroughs—writer, homosexual, iconoclast. The film examines both Burroughs' career as a foremost 20th century writer, and his personal life including his relationship with his brother, his killing of his wife.
VHS: S00193. $39.95.
Howard Brookner, USA, 1984, 90 mins.

Carolyn Forche (2/12/90)

Reading from *Gathering the Tribes* and *The Country Between Us* along with works in progress, Forche underscores her interest in the brutal events of the 20th century. Recorded in Los Angeles on February 12, 1990, this video includes an interview with the 1990 winner of the Lannan Literary Fellowship, conducted by Lewis MacAdams. From the *Lannan Literary Videos* series. 60 mins.
VHS: S27125. $19.95.

Carolyn Forche (5/24/94)

This Lannan Poetry Fellowship-winner reads the entire text of her work *The Angel of History*. It occurred on May 24, 1994, in Los Angeles. In addition, she spoke to Michael Silverblatt about her enduring concerns with the traumatic events of our time. From the *Lannan Literary Videos* series. 60 mins.
VHS: S27147. $19.95.

The Circle of the Hills

A biography on the life, art and times of Alfred Lord Tennyson, the brilliant Victorian poet whose odyssey—from one of the 11 children born to a poor country cleric to poet laureate—is beautifully rendered. The program features extracts from Tennyson's best works, including his masterpiece, *The Charge of the Light Brigade*. 61 mins.
VHS: S19686. $29.95.

Cittee Cittee Cittee: The Poetry of Herschel Silverman with the Music of Perry Robinson

Herschel Silverman was there at the beginning in the Village. He always hung with the best of the Beat poets. Now he is back with his Beat jazz poems accompanied by jazz clarinetist Perry Robinson. USA, 1995, 45 mins.
VHS: S26943. $29.95.

Conversation with Gwendolyn Brooks

Pulitzer Prize-winning poet Gwendolyn Brooks, whose works eloquently portrayed scenes of city life and the impact of poverty and neglect in the ghetto, talks about the influences of her family life and her unique contribution to American letters. Produced by the Library of Congress. 28 mins.
VHS: S08130. $49.95.

Conversation with Richard Wilbur

Richard Wilbur, Pulitzer Prize-winning poet, reads some of his favorite poems and reminiscences about his life and work with Grace Cavalieri, poet and host of the national radio series, *The Poet and the Poem*. Produced by the Library of Congress. 28 mins.
VHS: S08131. $29.95.

Denise Levertov

Denise Levertov, though born in England, has become an important American poet, essayist, editor and teacher. In this video she reads from *Evening Train* and from some of her unpublished work. The reading took place in Los Angeles on December 7, 1992. Michael Silverblatt also spoke with this winner of the Lannan Literary Award for Poetry. From the *Lannan Literary Videos* series. 60 mins.
VHS: S27144. $19.95.

Ed McBain

A portrait of the famous novelist of *The Blackboard Jungle* and of the immensely popular series of thrillers about the 87th Precinct detective squad. Follows McBain on a nighttime journey through McBain's world, and dramatizes sequences from his novels. 55 mins.
VHS: S02272. $39.95.

Edgar Allan Poe: Architect of Dreams

Poet, short-story writer and critic, Edgar Allan Poe mastered all of these areas, but is perhaps best known for his macabre sensibility. In works like *The Murders in the Rue Morgue* and *The Tell-Tale Heart*, he showed the world a new and strange literary universe. Dave Smith hosts this documentary which looks at Poe's unhappy life and his literary legacy. From the *About the Authors...* series. USA, 1991, 30 mins.
VHS: S27043. $24.95.

Elmore Leonard

We follow Leonard on his travels as he revisits some of the inspirations for his best-selling books. Throughout the film, excerpts from his novels are read by people who have, in one way or another, helped shape his work—a police officer, a bomb disposal expert, a Hollywood producer and his wife. 61 min.
VHS: S18389. $19.95.

Emily Dickinson: "A Certain Slant of Light"

Julie Harris hosts this documentary exploration of the unique American Poet Emily Dickinson. Though she inhabited a rather small town in New England, Dickinson managed to touch an astonishing range of human experience in her poetry. This video shows where and how Dickinson lived, and reveals the astonishing power of her poetry. From the *About the Authors...* series.
VHS: S27042. $24.95.
Jean Mudge, USA, 1977, 30 mins.

Eminent Scholars Series

Distinguished educators and critics in an organized syllabus of documented lectures on modern American literature. Comes complete with study guide. Each tape is 45 minutes.
American Literature of the Thirties. Leslie Fiedler surveys the major and popular writers of the decade, as well as three writers whose works have been unjustly neglected by critics: Henry Roth, Dashiell Hammett and Margaret Mitchell.
VHS: S08196. $230.00.
American Literature of World War II. Prof. George Garrett explains the differences between the world wars which account for the literature they produced and examines the various responses to the harshness of the war in poets and writers such as Randall Jarrell, James Gould Cozzens, James Jones and Norman Mailer.
VHS: S08197. $230.00.
American Literature and Politics. Critic Leslie Fiedler explores the political dimensions of works as diverse as *Huckleberry Finn* and *Gone with the Wind* in this discussion of the relationship of writing and politics in American culture.
VHS: S08200. $230.00.
American Literature of the Twenties. North Carolina State Professor Michael Reynolds discusses the American writers who came of age during the Roaring Twenties: T.S. Eliot, William Faulkner, Ernest Hemingway and F. Scott Fitzgerald.
VHS: S08394. $230.00.
Black American Literature. Professor Valerie Smith surveys the development of Black American literature from the 1890s to the 1930s, examining the achievements of the authors who consolidated the Afro-American literary tradition at the turn of the century, and the poets and novelists of the Harlem Renaissance.
VHS: S08201. $230.00.
Introduction to John Dos Passos' Fiction. Prof. Townsend Luddington explores the cultural and personal causes for Dos Passos' literary and political radicalism, describes his decline as a writer from the 1940s onwards, and his concurrent move toward increasing political conservatism.
VHS: S08174. $230.00.
Introduction to Theodore Dreiser's Fiction. Warner Bertoff surveys Dreiser's six most important novels, from *Sister Carrie* to *An American Tragedy*, distinguishing between the realist and naturalist world views in the fiction.
VHS: S08175. $230.00.
Introduction to William Faulkner's Fiction. Professor Cleanth Brooks examines the society, culture, geography and history of northern Mississippi and how Faulkner incorporated it into his fiction.
VHS: S08176. $230.00.
Introduction to F. Scott Fitzgerald's Fiction. University of South Carolina professor Matthew Bruccoli presents an overview of Fitzgerald's life and work and identifies the chief themes and techniques of Fitzgerald's fiction.
VHS: S08177. $230.00.
Introduction to Ernest Hemingway's Fiction. Noted literary scholar Alfred Kazin describes Hemingway's transformation of the English language into something immediate and direct.
VHS: S08178. $230.00.
Introduction to John Steinbeck's Fiction. Steinbeck biographer Jackson Benson provides an informative and detailed discussion of the author's life, career and views.
VHS: S08179. $230.00.
Introduction to Edith Wharton's Fiction. Wharton's biographer, R.W.B. Lewis, surveys her major works of fiction and her chief theme—the oppression of the individual by society.
VHS: S08181. $230.00.
Introduction to Thomas Wolfe's Fiction. University of North Carolina professor Louis D. Rubin Jr. discusses how Thomas Wolfe's personality dominates his art of recreated memory.
VHS: S08182. $230.00.
Introduction to Richard Wright's Fiction. Prof. Valerie Smith describes Wright's childhood experiences of poverty and oppression which he transmuted into art, particularly his landmark novel, *Native Son*.
VHS: S08183. $230.00.
Introduction to Robert Frost's Poetry. Harvard Professor Helen Vendler shows how Frost's poetry expresses underlying ambiguity and pain.
VHS: S08184. $230.00.
Introduction to T.S. Eliot's Poetry. Princeton Professor A. Walton Liz traces Eliot's career and surveys the early poetry that culminated in *The Wasteland* and *The Four Quartets*.
VHS: S08185. $230.00.
Modern American Novel. Prof. George Garrett provides an informative overview of American fiction from 1910 to 1950, identifying over 60 prominent novelists and commenting on their work.
VHS: S08198. $230.00.
Modern American Poetry. Professor Helen Vendler surveys the ideas and explicates representative poems of the American internationalists (Eliot and Pound), nationalists (Crane, Cullen, Frost, Hughes, Moore and Williams) and Wallace Stevens.
VHS: S08199. $230.00.
Profession of Authorship in America. Prof. Matthew J. Bruccoli corrects the misapprehension that writing books is the way to fame and fortune, in his detailed account of the business of publishing, stressing the effects of marketing considerations, competing media and financial arrangements, and the influence they've had on the course of 20th century American literature.
VHS: S08203. $230.00.
Realism and Naturalism in American Literature. Prof. Michael S. Reynolds explores the influences of modern art, technology and ideas on American culture of the 20's including the contributions made by the new generation of writers—T.S. Eliot, William Faulkner, Fitzgerald, Hemingway.
VHS: S07732. $230.00.
Southern Literary Renaissance. Professor Louis D. Rubin Jr. contends that the defining characteristic of the 20th century South American writers was their sense of history.
VHS: S08202. $230.00.
Understanding Faulkner's As I Lay Dying. Yale Professor Cleanth Brooks explains how Faulkner surprises and challenges the reader by his multiple use of view and unusual mixture of styles.
VHS: S08186. $230.00.
Understanding Hemingway's A Farewell to Arms. Prof. Michael S. Reynolds separates the autobiographical from the fictional in his analysis of the novel's backgrounds and composition.
VHS: S08187. $230.00.
Understanding Steinbeck's Grapes of Wrath. Prof. Jackson Benson clarifies the ideological backgrounds, composition and literary merits of Steinbeck's masterpiece.
VHS: S08188. $230.00.
Understanding Fitzgerald's The Great Gatsby. F. Scott Fitzgerald biographer Matthew Bruccoli explicates Fitzgerald's solution to the problems of fiction structure by means of first-person, secondary character as the narrator.
VHS: S08189. $230.00.
Understanding Wharton's House of Mirth. Yale Professor R.W.B. Lewis examines the composition and themes of Wharton's devastating critique of shallow, hypocritical and materialistic high society of New York during the Gilded Age.
VHS: S08190. $230.00.
Understanding Wolfe's Look Homeward Angel. Professor Louis D. Rubin Jr. describes Wolfe's first novel as autobiographical, not merely told, but imbued with the emotional fervor of a rhetorical high style.
VHS: S08191. $230.00.
Understanding Dreiser's Sister Carrie. Critic Alfred Kazin calls Dreiser the most enduring of American naturalists, and explains the viewpoints that environment and heredity determined human conduct, as exemplified in *Sister Carrie*.
VHS: S08192. $230.00.
Understanding Dos Passos' U.S.A. Prof. Townsend Luddington explains the political thesis and technical innovations, the prophetic and satiric vision of American culture in Dos Passos' trilogy.
VHS: S08193. $230.00.
Understanding Eliot's The Wasteland. Professor A. Walton Liz focuses on Ezra Pound's role as a virtual collaborator in the making of the poem and explores its methods through an examination of key motifs and passages.
VHS: S09904. $230.00.

Eugene O'Neill, Journey into Genius

This episode from the PBS series *American Masters* stars Matthew Modine as the young Pulitzer Prize winning author. O'Neill's plays, *Mourning Becomes Electra*, *The Iceman Cometh* and *Long Day's Journey into Night*, are unmatched achievements in American drama. This film explores the obsessions and demons of the brilliant dramatist. 60 mins.
VHS: S23606. $24.95.

An Evening with Ed Sanders and the Fugs

Poet, publisher, Woodstock freelance writer and musician Ed Sanders performs on this video at St. Marks Poetry Project and Town Hall, New York City, in 1994. Ed accompanies himself on the dulcimer and his electronic tie. A 1989 Fugs tribute to Abbie Hoffman with Sanders, Tuli Kupferberg and Steven Taylor is also included.
VHS: S26944. $29.95.

Fried Shoes, Cooked Diamonds

A joyous reunion of the Beat poets at the Jack Kerouac School of Disembodied Poetics at Naropa Institute in Boulder. With a special narration by Allen Ginsberg, the film shows the warmth and ease of interchange between the poets, as they read their poetry to each other and discuss their thoughts on writing, politics, religion, and the adventure of consciousness. With William Burroughs, Timothy Leary, Allen Ginsberg, Gregory Corso, Diane di Prima, Peter Orlovsky, Meredith Monk, Amiri Baraka, Anne Waldman, Miguel Pinero, Miguel Algarin and Chogyam Trungpa Rinopche.
VHS: S04537. $29.95.
Costanzo Allione, USA, 1978, 55 mins.

Galway Kinnell

Galway Kinnell is a winner of the Pulitzer Prize and of the 1983 American Book Award. In this video, he reads from his books *What a Kingdom It Was*; *Body Rags*; *The Book of Nightmares*; *Mortal Acts, Mortal Wounds*; *The Past* and *Selected Poems* in Los Angeles on April 18, 1988. Lewis MacAdams conducts the interview. From the *Lannan Literary Videos* series. 60 mins.
VHS: S27109. $19.98.

Gang of Souls

Maria Beatty rediscovers the Beat Generation in this fascinating documentary featuring appearances and reminiscences by William S. Burroughs, Allen Ginsberg, Marianne Faithful, John Giorno, Henry Rollins, Lydia Lunch, Jim Carroll, Gregory Corso, Diane DiPrima, Ed Sanders, Anne Waldman and Richard Hell.
VHS: S11995. $29.95.

Gary Snyder

Influenced by Zen and other elements of Eastern culture, this winner of the Pulitzer Prize is one of the United States' most highly regarded poets. He read from *Axe Handles* and *Left Out in the Rain* on December 12, 1988. Lewis MacAdams conducted the interview. From the *Lannan Literary Videos* series. 60 mins.
VHS: S27115. $19.95.

A Gathering of Men
Robert Bly is one of America's leading poets, a modern day troubadour, according to Bill Moyers, who joins Bly in a gathering of men in Austin, Texas. Using poetry, song, fairy tales, mythology and psychology as well as his own life experiences, Bly leads a group of men in exploring their deeper feelings—about themselves, their fathers, their sons and their roles in society. 90 mins.
VHS: S11922. $29.95.

Gertrude Stein: When This You See, Remember Me
This portrait of the famous American writer shows Stein in Paris from 1905 through the 1930's. Her creativity was expressed not only in writing but in influential friendships with a host of major artists. Picasso, T.S. Eliot, Thorton Wilder, James Joyce, Ernest Hemingway and many more relied on her companionship, criticism and support. Home movies of Stein and her longtime lover, Alice B. Toklas, a rare radio interview, and footage of Stein's art collection round out this exciting documentary. 89 mins.
VHS: S26648. $59.95.
Perry Miller Adato, USA, 1970, 89 mins.

Gielgud's Chekhov
Sir John Gielgud hosts and narrates these dramatizations of some of Chekhov's greatest works. 50 minutes each.
Volume 1: *The Fugitive, Desire for Sleep,* and *Rothschild's Violin.*
VHS: S02214. $64.95.
Volume 2: *Volodya* and *The Boarding House.*
VHS: S02215. $64.95.
Volume 3: *The Wallet* and *Revenge.*
VHS: S02216. $64.95.

Gilbert Sorrentino
This innovative and darkly humorous writer has written over 20 books. On this video he reads from his book of stories, *Under the Shadows.* The reading was recorded on March 2, 1993, in Los Angeles. Michael Silverblatt then talked with Sorrentino about his work. From the *Lannan Literary Videos* series. 60 mins.
VHS: S27139. $19.95.

Gore Vidal
Politician, novelist, playwright, moviemaker, society's observer. Vidal talks about his relatives-in-law, the Kennedys, his fellow writers, Hemingway, Capote, Mailer, in Vidal's usual, acerbic candidness, as well as excerpts from his movies, *The Best Man* and *Myra Breckenridge.* 58 mins.
VHS: S06972. $19.95.

Gore Vidal: The Man Who Said No
Gore Vidal, one of America's greatest writers, challenges the American political establishment in his California campaign for the U.S. Senate. A revealing portrait, sprinkled with Vidal's witticisms, in which Vidal says he is running for office out of "rage."
VHS: S00518. $29.95.
Gary Conklin, USA, 1982, 99 mins.

Great Books: Frankenstein: The Making of the Monster
This work examines the issues brought out with the publication of Mary Shelley's *Frankenstein,* and the source of the novel's power and durability. 50 mins.
VHS: S20080. $19.95.

Great Books: Le Morte d'Arthur: The Legend of the King
This program suggests a possible location of Camelot and explores the connection between Sir Thomas Malory's 15th-century masterpiece, *Le Morte d'Arthur* and George Lucas' kinetic and hair-raising *Star Wars* film trilogy. 50 mins.
VHS: S20078. $19.95.

Great Books: Origin of Species: Beyond Genesis
A mythic journey with Charles Darwin on the H.M.S. *Beagle,* during which Darwin developed the theory of the natural selection of the species. 50 mins.
VHS: S20079. $19.95.

Great Books Set
A set of three titles: *Le Morte d'Arthur, Origin of Species* and *Frankenstein.*
VHS: S20081. $49.95.

Hayden Carruth
Hayden Carruth, a winner of a National Critics Circle Book Award, read from his *Collected Shorter Poems* on November 9, 1993, in Los Angeles. Michael Silverblatt also spoke to Carruth about his poetry. From the *Lannan Literary Videos* series. 60 mins.
VHS: S27143. $19.95.

Hemingway in Cuba
The American author Ernest Hemingway is revealed in all his complexity in this detailed portrait. For over 30 years he inhabited an island paradise, eschewing both the public life that often dominates literary figures and his native land. As Hemingway himself wrote, "The country that a novelist writes about is the country of his heart, and the country he knows is in his heart." 30 mins.
VHS: S27565. $19.95.

Henry Miller Odyssey
Miller describes how he saw his era, his peers and himself. Whether at Big Sur, or on jaunts to old hangouts in Brooklyn and Paris, Miller shares his life in this film. Along the way he describes his painful youth and his art. Lawrence Durrell, Anais Nin, Jakov Gimpel and others appear, adding depth to this intriguing portrait.
VHS: S26713. $29.95.

Herman Melville: Consider the Sea
At the age of 20, Herman Melville set sail for the first time. It was a fateful step that ultimately led him to write such nautically inspired works as *Moby Dick* and *Billy Budd.* Richard Wilbur hosts this incisive documentary which looks at both Melville's life and his life work. From the *About the Authors...* series.
VHS: S27045. $24.95.
Jean Mudge, USA, 1981, 30 mins.

Introducing Great Authors
The vibrant worlds of two of America's giant literary figures—Edgar Allan Poe and Mark Twain—are explored. This vivid and informative program also skillfully guides the student through the fascinating world of William Shakespeare and Charles Dickens. In English.
VHS: S06738. $59.95.

Ishmael Reed
Mixing comic fantasy and social commentary, this novelist, poet, dramatist and publisher has broken new literary ground. Works from his *New and Selected Poems* and *The Terrible Threes* were read by him in Venice, California, on May 26, 1989. Lewis MacAdams conducted the interview. From the *Lannan Literary Videos* series. 60 mins.
VHS: S27122. $19.95.

Jack Kerouac's Road
Through photographs, archival film footage, interviews and skillful reconstructions of events, *Jack Kerouac's Road* traces the life of this gifted American writer—with special attention to his many experiences travelling from one end of the U.S. to the other by car—experiences which he wrote down and turned into a romantic epic. "The only ones for me are the mad ones...who burn, burn, burn like fabulous yellow Roman candles" (J. Kerouac). French with English subtitles.
VHS: S13798. $49.95.
Harmenegilde Chiasson, Canada, 1987, 55 mins.

Jack London
An episodic biography of the famed writer produced during World War II. Susan Hayward and Michael O'Shea star.
VHS: S10589. $24.95.
Alfred Santell, USA, 1943, 94 mins.

James Fenimore Cooper's Leatherstocking Tales: I & II
"The true American myth"—D.H. Lawrence. PBS's authentic adaptation of *Leatherstocking Tales* (I & II): *Deerslayer, Pathfinder, Last of the Mohicans, Pioneers,* and *Prairie.* Natty Bumpo (Hawkeye) and Chingachgook, Delaware chief, bring alive the early 1700s, when Americans, French and Huron were fighting for the vast, uncharted wilderness.
Part I.
VHS: S03959. $64.95.
Part II.
VHS: S03960. $64.95.

James Schuyler: Interview/Reading
In this rare interview with the late Pulitzer-Prize-winning poet, Schuyler elegantly discusses his poetic technique. He also muses on the place of the natural world in poetry. A full-length reading is included.
VHS: S22625. $34.95.
Mitch Corber, USA, 1990, 75 mins.

Joseph Heller
Shows the famous American writer at home and on Coney Island, where he grew up, and captures the vitality of his latest novel, *God Knows,* with cleverly dramatized excerpts. 55 mins.
VHS: S02249. $19.95.

Katherine Anne Porter: The Eye of Memory
Joanne Woodward hosts this episode from the PBS series *American Masters.* Porter was one of America's most intriguing authors. Now the unique perspective of this Pulitzer Prize winner is revealed through an in-depth show highlighted by memories from authors Eudora Welty and Robert Penn Warren. 60 mins.
VHS: S23607. $24.95.

Kay Boyle
Reading from *This Is Not a Letter and Other Poems* and *Testament for My Students* in Los Angeles on September 11, 1989, poet Kay Boyle revealed her interest in human rights. Shawn Wong interviews this author of over 30 books. From the *Lannan Literary Videos* series. 60 mins.
VHS: S27120. $19.95.

Kerouac
An award winning docu-drama about the King of the Beat Generation, Jack Kerouac. Rare footage featuring Allen Ginsberg, Lawrence Ferlinghetti, William Burroughs with music by Charles Mingus, Duke Ellington, Zoot Sims.
VHS: S00671. $29.95.
John Antonelli, USA, 1985, 73 mins.

The Language of Life: A Festival of Poets with Bill Moyers
For Bill Moyers, poetry is news of the mind and the heart. This series features a number of poets whose work has hastened a resurgent interest in this literary tradition. Today poetry is often read, sung, and even performed before large and appreciative audiences. Eighteen poets from an array of cultural traditions are represented in this series.
Come Celebrate with Me. Lucille Clifton and David Mara are two poets who reflect on their respective cultural legacies. Together these authors effectively employ humor while offering insightful observations on the past and the present. 58 mins.
VHS: S26588. $24.95.
Here in the Mind. Gary Snyder and Daisy Zamora have forged a weapon for battle from the same powerful force: eloquent and inspiring language. Snyder defends the natural world from shortsighted onslaughts while Zamora speaks to the causes and passions of the Nicaraguan civil war. 58 mins.
VHS: S26591. $24.95.

Love's Confusing Joy. Coleman Barks has dedicated his efforts to the translation of poems by 13th-century Islamic mystic Jelahudden Rumi. These works are alternately ecstatic, wise and hilarious. Surprisingly, Rumi has much to say to a contemporary American audience. 58 mins.
VHS: S26594. $24.95.
Some Can Sing. Robert Hass, Claribel Alegria, and Carolyn Forche are three poets whose works bridge gaps and cross boundaries. Representing a diverse blend of charisma, background and style, these poets transport audiences to new places. 58 mins.
VHS: S26592. $24.95.
Swirl Like a Leaf. Jimmy Santiago, Robert Bly and Marilyn Chin have all pioneered the use of poetry toward greater understanding of the self. Through the exploration of motivations and fears, these writers have found routes to self discovery and personal reconciliation. 58 mins.
VHS: S26590. $24.95.
The Field of Time. Sandra McPherson and Linda McCarriston are courageous artists who have turned potential tragedy into triumph. Both revel in the beauty of love, family and nature through the use of wondrous and passionate words. 58 mins.
VHS: S26593. $24.95.
The Heart of Things. Adrienne Rich, Victor Hernandez Cruz, and Michael S. Harper join Bill Moyers for this discussion about language. All three writers revel in the ability of language to reveal history and culture even as they change the way poetry is heard, read and absorbed. 58 mins.
VHS: S26589. $24.95.
Welcome to the Mainland. African-American poet Sekou Sundiata is joined by Palestinian born Naomi Shihab Nye in this video. Both celebrate vibrant cultural traditions that have contributed mightily to the contemporary American mosaic. This is the opening program of the series and helps sets a tone of openness and diversity. 58 mins.
VHS: S26595. $24.95.
The Language of Life: A Festival of Poets with Bill Moyers Series.
VHS: S26596. $179.95.

Larry Heinemann
Radicalized by a stint in Vietnam, Heinemann went on to write *Paco's Story.* It garnered him a National Book Award. He read from this book on March 12, 1990, in Los Angeles. Ken Lincoln then interviewed this highly regarded author. From the *Lannan Literary Videos* series. 60 mins.
VHS: S27127. $19.95.

The Lectures, Volume 1
Allen Ginsberg, Amiri Baraka, Robert Creeley and Houston A. Baker are the four poets featured. They are also critics who share their state-of-the art philosophies on poetics. Together they address the ever pertinent questions "What is poetry? Where does poetry expound? Expand?"
VHS: S21844. $29.95.

The Life and Times of Allen Ginsberg
William S. Burroughs, Ken Kesey, Abbie Hoffman, Jack Kerouac, Norman Mailer, Joan Baez, Amiri Baraka, Dick Cavett, Timothy Leary and William F. Buckley, Jr., are among the luminaries who provide perspective on Ginsberg, the poet, pacifist and sexual outlaw who collaborated with the filmmaker to provide this compelling scrapbook of a remarkable life.
VHS: S21887. $29.95.
Jerry Aronson, USA, 1993, 82 mins.

Lost Man's River
Peter Matthiessen, naturalist, author and student of Zen, journeys through the wilderness of the Everglades' Ten Thousand Islands. A last frontier, this labyrinth of islands has always been a natural haven for smugglers, gator poachers and notorious characters such as Edgar "Bloody" Watson, the inspiration for Matthiessen's latest novel, *Killing Mister Watson.* Matthiessen returns to the Everglades, where he reflects on the islands that have occupied him for decades.
VHS: S12671. $19.95.
Laser: LD71115. $29.95.

Louise Gluck
Louise Gluck, winner of the 1985 National Book Critics Circle Award, reads excerpts from her books *First Born, Descending Figure, The House on Marshland* and *The Triumph of Achilles* in Los Angeles on April 4, 1988. Lewis MacAdams interviews her. From the *Lannan Literary Videos* series. 60 mins.
VHS: S27108. $19.98.

Lucille Clifton
Lucille Clifton read from *Good Woman: Poems and a Memoir* and *Next: New Poems* in Los Angeles on June 16, 1988. Lewis MacAdams conducted the interview with the former Poet Laureate of Maryland. From the *Lannan Literary Videos* series. 60 mins.
VHS: S27111. $19.95.

Maxwell Anderson: Lost in the Stars
Robert Lansing hosts this look at one of America's most acclaimed dramatists. Maxwell Anderson penned both dramas and comedies, including *What Price Glory?, Key Largo, The Bad Seed* and more. His works capture the essence of the theater. Featuring Helen Hayes and Burgess Meredith. From the *About the Authors...* series. USA, 1990, 60 mins.
VHS: S27044. $24.95.

The Modern World: Ten Great Writers
A ground-breaking series of profiles of ten great 20th-century writers who helped shape literature. Each program examines the author's experiences and includes commentary by noted scholars as well as dramatized excerpts performed by actors from Great Britain's National Theatre and the Royal Shakespeare Company, including David Suchet, Eileen Atkins, Patrick Malahide, Tim McInnerny, Tim Roth, Brian Glover, Michael Gough and Edward Fox.
Vol. 1: Fyodor Mikhailovich Dostoyevsky. Dostoyevsky ushered in modern literature with his novels *Crime and Punishment, Brothers Karamazov* and *The Idiot.* 58 mins.
VHS: S21906. $24.95.
Vol. 2: Henrik Ibsen. Far ahead of his time, Ibsen outraged audiences by stripping away hypocrisy and convention in his plays *Hedda Gabler, A Doll's House* and *Wild Duck.* 58 mins.
VHS: S21907. $24.95.
Vol. 3: Joseph Conrad. The author of *Lord Jim* and *Heart of Darkness* explored political and existential themes. 58 mins.
VHS: S21908. $24.95.
Vol. 4: Luigi Pirandello. In landmark plays like *Enrico IV* and *Six Characters in Search of an Author,* and in a novel and short stories, Pirandello explored the relationship between outward experience and inward reality. 58 mins.
VHS: S21909. $24.95.
Vol. 5: Marcel Proust. Proust's *Remembrance of Things Past* has rightly taken its place as one of the world's literary masterworks. 58 mins.
VHS: S21910. $24.95.

Vol. 6: Thomas Mann. With *Buddenbrooks, The Magic Mountain, Doctor Faustus* and the novella *Death in Venice,* Mann became the leading German author who confronted the spiritual controversies of 20th-century human experience. 58 mins.
VHS: S21911. $24.95.
Vol. 7: James Joyce. Joyce took stream of consciousness to its extremes in *Finnegan's Wake.* David Suchet stars as Leopold Bloom in scenes from Joyce's *Ulysses.* 58 mins.
VHS: S21912. $24.95.
Vol. 8: Virginia Woolf. Woolf's innovative narrative method in *Orlando, To the Lighthouse* and *The Waves* established her as a leading 20th-century novelist. 58 mins.
VHS: S21913. $24.95.
Vol. 9: Thomas Stearns Eliot. In *Prufrock and Other Observations, The Waste Land* and *The Murder in the Cathedral,* Eliot consciously devised a new idiom of expression. Edward Fox, Eileen Atkins and Michael Gough read excerpts from some of Eliot's most famous poems. 58 mins.
VHS: S21914. $24.95.
Vol. 10: Franz Kafka. With such disturbing works as *The Metamorphosis* and *The Trial,* Kafka's name has become synonymous with the sense of alienation when individuals are confronted by faceless and nameless authority. Tim Roth appears as Kafka and as the character Joseph K. from Kafka's *The Trial.* 58 mins.
VHS: S21915. $24.95.
Modern World: Ten Great Writers, Complete Set. The ten-volume set at a reduced price.
VHS: S21916. $199.95.

A Moveable Feast: Profiles of Contemporary American Authors
An enlightened series profiling contemporary American authors and their work in the environments that most influenced them. From the beaches of Hawaii to the streets of New York, this unique collection presents interviews with, readings by, and documentary segments about some of the most vibrant voices in modern American literature—a true banquet of ideas, identities and intelligence. Eight volumes.
Allen Ginsberg: When the Muse Calls, Answer! 30 mins.
VHS: S14765. $19.95.
Joyce Carol Oates: American Appetites. 30 mins.
VHS: S14768. $19.95.
Li-Young Lee: Always a Rose. 30 mins.
VHS: S14770. $19.95.
Sonia Sanchez: Wear the New Day Well. 30 mins.
VHS: S14763. $19.95.
T. Corraghessan Boyle: World's End. 30 mins.
VHS: S14763. $19.95.
T.R. Pearson: A Short History of a Small Place. 30 mins.
VHS: S14769. $19.95.
Trey Ellis: Platitudes. 30 mins.
VHS: S14764. $19.95.
W.S. Merwin: The Rain in the Trees. 30 mins.
VHS: S14767. $19.95.
Complete eight-volume set.
VHS: S14771. $159.60.

Nathalie Sarraute
An insightful portrait of the great French novelist, including discussions of her novels, *Portrait d'un inconnu* and *L'ere du soupcon.* 50 mins. French *without* English subtitles.
Home Video.
VHS: S06953. $59.95.
Public Performance.
VHS: S09501. $100.00.

A Night for Jack: A Celebration in Honor of the Publication of "The Portable Jack Kerouac Reader and Selected Letters"
Readings, performances and reminiscences marked the occasion of this new publication in New York City on March 15, 1995. Ann Charters acted as host for guests Allen Ginsberg, Clark Coolidge, Dave Van Ronk, David Amram, Ed Sanders and Lee Ranaldo of Sonic-Youth. USA, 1995, 120 mins.
VHS: S26941. $29.95.

Norman Mailer
A self-portrait which includes interviews with Mailer's family, and clips from his films, as well as extensive commentary by Mailer about his generation, drugs, power, boxing, and his view of immortality in light of his book about Gary Gilmore, *The Executioner's Song.* 57 mins.
VHS: S02303. $39.95.

Patricia Highsmith
A portrait of the first lady of crime, famous for her creation Tom Ripley, amoral crook and killer. Conversations with Highsmith are combined with dramatizations showing Ripley in a chilling game of fraud, impersonation, murder. 55 mins.
VHS: S02271. $39.95.

Pattiann Rogers
Biological, botanical and zoological details give Pattiann Rogers' poetry an intense sensual and spiritual quality. Works from *Geocentric, The Tattooed Lady in the Garden* and *Splitting and Binding,* as well as unpublished works, were read by Rogers on May 4, 1993, in Los Angeles. Michael Silverblatt also spoke with Rogers about her work. From the *Lannan Literary Videos* series. 60 mins.
VHS: S27140. $19.95.

Paul Bowles in Morocco
Highly acclaimed composer and writer Paul Bowles has lived in Tangier since the 1940s. Conklin "captures some of the ominous tone so brilliantly manipulated by the author...crowded bazaars, snake charmers, religious ecstatics, camel caravans, magnificent oases."
VHS: S01002. $29.95.
Gary Conklin, USA, 1970, 57 mins.

Paul Bowles: The Complete Outsider
Author of the *The Sheltering Sky,* Paul Bowles reveals all in this intimate portrait. Though he was married to the acclaimed writer Jane Bowles, both he and his wife had numerous homosexual affairs. An icon of the Beat Generation, Paul Bowles has inspired many with his disregard for conventional morality, including William Burroughs, who is said to have based *The Naked Lunch* on this iconoclast inhabitant of Morocco.
VHS: S25720. $59.95.
Catherine Warnow/Regina Weinreich, 1993, 57 mins.

Paul West

Paul West recorded this reading of his work in Los Angeles on September 21, 1993. It includes excerpts from *Tenement of Clay, Out of My Depths, Rat Man of Paris* and *Love's Mansion*. In addition, Michael Silverblatt spoke with this winner of the Lannan Literary Fellowship. From the *Lannan Literary Videos* series. 60 mins.
VHS: S27142. $19.95.

Paule Marshall

A MacArthur Fellowship was awarded to this writer from Brooklyn. Her work reflects the West Indian voices she heard as a child. Excerpts from *Daughters* and a discussion with Michael Silverblatt were recorded on April 12, 1994, in Los Angeles. From the *Lannan Literary Videos* series. 60 mins.
VHS: S27146. $19.95.

Philip Levine

Philip Levine is a winner of the 1991 National Book Award. In this video he reads excerpts from his poetry books *Selected Poems, Sweet Will* and *A Walk with Tom Jefferson*. The reading took place in Los Angeles on June 20, 1988. Lewis MacAdams interviewed him. From the *Lannan Literary Videos* series. 60 mins.
VHS: S27112. $19.95.

Poetry by Americans Series

Biographical sketches of four great American poets are collected in this series. Each short also includes a dramatic reading of one of their best regarded poems.
Poetry by Americans: Edgar Allan Poe. Lorne Greene reads "Annabel Lee." 9 mins.
VHS: S23466. $49.95.
Poetry by Americans: James Weldon Johnson. Raymond St. John reads "The Creation." 12 mins.
VHS: S23468. $49.95.
Poetry by Americans: Robert Frost. "Mending Wall" is read by Leonard Nimoy. 10 mins.
VHS: S23467. $49.95.
Poetry by Americans: Walt Whitman. "O Captain! My Captain!" is read by Efram Zimbalist, Jr. 10 mins.
VHS: S23469. $49.95.

The Poetry Hall of Fame

An incredible collection of great writers, great poems and the best of the human spirit.
The Poetry Hall of Fame: Volume One. William Shatner, Vincent Price, LeVar Burton and Valerie Harper join to recite poetry by some of the greatest English language poets. Shakespeare, Marlow, Whitman, Milton, Wadsworth, Longfellow, Coleridge and Frost are just some of the poets included in this video. 58 mins.
VHS: S23600. $24.95.
The Poetry Hall of Fame: Volume Two. Claire Bloom, Henry Fonda, Irene Worth and Jack Lemmon are featured in this video dedicated to poetry. They recite classics from English and American literature by poets Spencer, Keats, Pope, Blake, Yeats, Dickinson and Plath, among many more. 58 mins.
VHS: S23601. $24.95.
The Poetry Hall of Fame: Volume Three. Vincent Price, Henry Fonda, Robert Culp and Ruby Dee recite a collection of enduring poems that span the gamut from Shakespeare to Eliot. Dryden, Bronte, Burns, Tennyson and Dorothy Parker are among the many poets included. 58 mins.
VHS: S23602. $24.95.
The Poetry Hall of Fame: Volume Four. Ruby Dee, Jack Lemmon, Will Geer and Fred Gwynne recite from a large assortment of classic poems. Works by Poe, Swift, Auden, Longfellow, and many more are included. 58 mins.
VHS: S23603. $24.95.
The Poetry Hall of Fame Four-Volume Set.
VHS: S23604. $91.80.

Poetry in Motion

Experience the power and passion as poets perform their own work in this film of electrifying energy. Performances by Jim Carroll, Amiri Baraka, William Burroughs, Ted Berrigan, John Cage, Ed Sanders, Ntozake Shange, Allen Ginsberg.
VHS: S01042. $39.95.
Laser: LD70319. $39.95.
Ron Mann, USA, 1985, 90 mins.

Poetry in Times of War

This is a discussion sparked by the sudden onslaught of the Gulf War. Allen Ginsberg, Anne Waldman, Douglas Oliver, Tuli Kupferberg and D.H. Mellon all participated in this forum held at St. Mark's Poetry Project, New York City, May 1991. 105 mins.
VHS: S21843. $29.95.

Quip with Yip and Friends

A collection of poetry, limericks and light verse as read by Jack Lemmon and Fred Gwynne. The verse is provided by such greats as Ogden Nash, Dorothy Parker, Phyllis McGinley, e.e. cummings, Edgar "Yip" Harburg and others. 45 mins.
VHS: S12819. $24.95.

Ralph Ellison: The Self-Taught Writer

Ralph Ellison's struggle with poverty and segregation as a child shaped his character. Ultimately he rose to world fame with his most popular and insightful novel, *The Invisible Man*. 30 mins.
VHS: S26769. $19.99.

Ray Bremser: The Jazz Poems

Ray Bremser was one of Jack Kerouac's and Bob Dylan's favorite Beat poets. In this rare appearance from 1995, Bremser puts forth one of the best readings of his life. This is a candid documentary that captures the feel of the moment. USA, 1995.
VHS: S26942. $29.95.

Richard Wilbur

A poet, teacher, critic, lyricist and editor, Richard Wilbur was also the second Poet Laureate of the United States. In this video filmed on April 16, 1990, he reads works from *New and Collected Poems* and unpublished manuscripts at the University of California. David St. John interviews the two-time Pulitzer Prize winner. From the *Lannan Literary Videos* series. 60 mins.
VHS: S27123. $19.95.

Richard Wright: Writing Is His Weapon

Born in poverty, Richard Wright rose to become one of the United States' most respected authors. His prolific output was just one of many things that helped him become successful. 30 mins.
VHS: S26768. $19.99.

Robert Creeley

This co-founder of the Black Mountain poetry movement reads poems from his *Collected Poems, 1945-1975* and *Mirrors*, as well as works in progress in this video. Recorded on April 16, 1990, this tape also includes an interview of the poet conducted by Lewis MacAdams. From the *Lannan Literary Videos* series. 60 mins.
VHS: S27126. $19.95.

Robert Duncan Memorial

This is a tribute to a beloved poet, teacher and friend. Many of his contemporary poets as well as his admirers participated. This event was held within the St. Mark's Poetry Project, New York, 1988.
VHS: S21841. $29.95.

Sharon Olds

Sharon Olds' first book, *Satan Says*, won the inaugural San Francisco Poetry Center Award, while her next book, *The Dead and the Living*, won a National Book Critics Circle Award. Ms. Olds read from the latter book and from *The Gold Cell* on April 8, 1991, in Los Angeles. Lewis MacAdams conducted the interview. From the *Lannan Literary Videos* series. 60 mins.
VHS: S27132. $19.95.

Spymaker:
The Secret Life of Ian Fleming

An action-packed adventure based on the real life of the man who created James Bond, with Jason Connery, Kristin Scott Thomas and Joss Ackland. Fleming, born into an aristocratic English family, single-handedly outwits Soviet intelligence, foils an S.S. monster at a glamorous casino, steals the secrets of the German high command, storms an enemy stronghold at impossible odds and still has time for the fastest cars and the most desirable women.
VHS: S12370. $79.98.
Ferdinand Fairfax, USA, 1990, 96 mins.

A Talk with Ann McGovern

The author of *Shark Lady* not only describes her book, she actually goes underwater and explores the sea. From The *"Good Conversation!"* Video Series. 24 mins.
VHS: S27038. $49.98.

A Talk with Avi

The Newbery Award-winner and author of *Nothing But the Truth* and *The True Confessions of Charlotte Doyle* speaks about his life as a writer. From The *"Good Conversation!"* Video Series. 22 mins.
VHS: S27024. $49.98.

A Talk with Betsy Byars

Betsy Byars, author of the Newbery Award-winning *Summer of the Swans*, describes how she came to write this book. She also has many hobbies which she discusses, including her love of aviation. From The *"Good Conversation!"* Video Series. 18 mins.
VHS: S27027. $49.98.

A Talk with Bruce Coville

My Teacher Is an Alien sold over one million copies. Bruce Coville talks about this comic book and his hilarious twin brother "Igor." From The *"Good Conversation!"* Video Series. 22 mins.
VHS: S27029. $49.98.

A Talk with E.L. Konigsburg

The author of the Newbery Award-winning *From the Mixed Up Files of Mrs. Basil E. Frankweiler* is revealed in this candid discussion of reading and writing. From The *"Good Conversation!"* Video Series. 22 mins.
VHS: S27035. $49.98.

A Talk with Jean Craighead George

The author of *Julie of the Wolves* shares her writing techniques. In a rare personal moment, this Newbery Award-winner even talks with her dog, Kimiq. From The *"Good Conversation!"* Video Series. 26 mins.
VHS: S27032. $49.98.

A Talk with Jean Fritz

Homesick: My Own Story, a Newbery honor book, describes the travels and experiences of author Jean Fritz, who grew up in China. From The *"Good Conversation!"* Video Series. 20 mins.
VHS: S27031. $49.98.

A Talk with Jerry Spinelli

The Newbery Award-winning book *Maniac Magee* is discussed by its author, Jerry Spinelli, who also introduces viewers to his pet rat, Daisy. From The *"Good Conversation!"* Video Series. 20 mins.
VHS: S27040. $49.98.

A Talk with Karla Kuskin

Karla Kuskin explains how she combatted adolescent loneliness with a passion for writing and poetry. From The *"Good Conversation!"* Video Series. 25 mins.
VHS: S27036. $49.98.

A Talk with Lee Bennett Hopkins

This noted author and poet describes how he used reading to help him overcome an impoverished childhood. From The *"Good Conversation!"* Video Series. 18 mins.
VHS: S27033. $49.98.

A Talk with Lynne Reid Banks

The author of *The Indian in the Cupboard* hosts an English tea party and discusses her life and her work. From The *"Good Conversation!"* Video Series. 22 mins.
VHS: S27026. $49.98.

A Talk with M.E. Kerr

This popular young author discusses her book *Gentlehands* and explains why she writes under pseudonyms. From The *"Good Conversation!"* Video Series. 22 mins.
VHS: S27034. $49.98.

A Talk with Madeleine L'Engle

In addition to giving young authors useful tips, this Newbery Award-winning author answers questions about her book *A Wrinkle in Time*. From The *"Good Conversation!"* Video Series. 22 mins.
VHS: S27037. $49.98.

A Talk with Matt Christopher

This former semi-pro ball player has written over one hundred popular sports books. In this video he talks about his writing, his family and his days in sports. From The *"Good Conversation!"* Video Series. 18 mins.
VHS: S27028. $49.98.

A Talk with Nancy Willard

Nancy Willard reads aloud from her Newbery Award-winning book *A Visit to William Blake's Inn: Poems for Innocent and Experienced Travelers*. From The *"Good Conversation!"* Video Series. 18 mins.
VHS: S27041. $49.98.

A Talk with Natalie Babbitt

Natalie Babbitt discusses her modern children's classic *Tuck*. In addition, she gives a guided tour through the miniature house she constructed together with her husband. From The *"Good Conversation!"* Video Series. 20 mins.
VHS: S27025. $49.98.

A Talk with Paula Fox

The Slave Dancer won a Newbery Award. In this video, children's author Paula Fox describes the importance of imagination to her work. From The *"Good Conversation!"* Video Series. 24 mins.
VHS: S27030. $49.98.

A Talk with Phyllis Reynolds Naylor

This Newbery Award-winning author reads from her novel *Shiloh* and gives the behind-the-scenes story which describes how it came to be written. From The *"Good Conversation!"* Video Series. 25 mins.
VHS: S27039. $49.98.

Thom Gunn

Born in England, Thom Gunn has lived in Northern California since 1954. His austere poems of love and death testify to his mastery as a poet. In this video he reads from his *Collected Poems* and talks with Wendy Lesser, the founding editor of *The Threepenny Review*. The interview and reading took place on October 18, 1994, in Los Angeles. From the *Lannan Literary Videos* series. 60 mins.
VHS: S27148. $19.95.

Toni Morrison

Toni Morrison has established herself as the leading chronicler of the black experience in America and as one of America's finest novelists. This program focuses on Morrison on the eve of publication of her new novel, *Beloved*, which already won the Pulitzer Prize for fiction. Morrison talks about the problems of dealing with painful material, and of writing about ordinary people whose experiences seem monumentally larger than life. 55 mins.
VHS: S07599. $19.95.

United States of Poetry

Over two hours of recent poems are joined on this two-tape video set. Produced by KQED, Public Television New York, it includes some of the most exciting young poets around. They are placed in a quick-paced and hip format that suits the excitement of the work. Over 50 poets are included, past and present, from writers as diverse as Lord Buckley, Czeslaw Milosz, Amiri Baraka, Jenny Holzer and Elizabeth Barrett Browning. 150 mins.
VHS: S27700. $29.95.

Voices and Visions

This remarkable video series traces the development of the American poetry tradition. Both the life story and the work of major poets are covered in each video. Perfect for the serious student and those who simply love poetry.
Voices and Visions Volume I: Hart Crane, Walt Whitman, Ezra Pound, William Carlos Williams. A look at poet-physician William Carlos Williams, who established a distinctly American poem; at Hart Crane's preoccupation with technology and its human impact; at the controversial Ezra Pound, who became a leader of the Modernist movement and became enmeshed in economic and political ideals during World War II; and at the remarkable Whitman, including the eclectic sources of his poetry. 240 minutes.
VHS: S24315. $69.95.
Voices and Visions Volume II: Emily Dickinson, Marianne Moore, Elizabeth Bishop, Sylvia Plath. Four unique, American women poets are covered in this four-volume set. Period dramatic recreations evoke the domestic context in which Emily Dickinson wrote her metaphysical poetry. Poets and critics explain the "wild decorum" of Marianne Moore's unique style. Exotic documentary footage heightens the magical realism of Elizabeth Bishop's poems and explores her preoccupation with perception and the boundaries of consciousness. And archival footage of the 1950s pop culture chronicles Sylvia Plath's historical environments and the complex relationship between her troubled life and work. 240 minutes.
VHS: S24316. $69.95.
Voices and Visions Volume III: T.S. Eliot, Robert Lowell, Langston Hughes, Robert Frost, Wallace Stevens. Five videos explore these major poets. They trace the career of T.S. Eliot from the bold originality of *Prufrock* to the meditative style of *Four Quartets*. They contain footage of Robert Lowell in his apartment and on anti-war protest marches, intercut with interviews that discuss his use of autobiography as subject matter for poetry. On-location footage in Senegal, France, Kansas and Harlem chronicles the life of Langston Hughes. Through his lyric poems and dramatic narratives, Robert Frost asserts that nature is the clearest window into the human personality. And presentations of the works of Wallace Stevens reveal his sense of imagination as a journey to a new reality. 300 minutes.
VHS: S24317. $89.95.

Voices and Visions: Elizabeth Bishop

Bishop's fanciful but accessible poems betray her interest with perception and the boundaries of consciousness. Exotic documentary footage extends the magical realism of her work. Mary McCarthy and Octavio Paz are among the commentators included in this video. 60 mins.
VHS: S26318. $19.95.

Voices and Visions: Emily Dickinson

Expressing both doubt and joy, Dickinson's poems are compressed and urgent. At times they reflect lucidity and wit or despair and death-obsession. Adrienne Rich, Joyce Carol Oates and others comment on the legacy of this 19th-century female poet who lived largely as a recluse. 60 mins.
VHS: S26317. $19.95.

Voices and Visions: Ezra Pound

Though a driving force of the Modernist movement, Pound's classically poetic voice recalls ancient and medieval sources. His social and political views led to controversy through accusations of treason and the suspicion of madness. Hugh Kenner, Alfred Kazin and Pound himself are seen in this video, discussing the poet and his work. 60 mins.
VHS: S26314. $19.95.

Voices and Visions: Hart Crane

Advanced technology spurred Crane into lyrical language and a literature of ecstasy. This disorderly and lusty poet's frenzy of illumination had a darker, debauched side. His deterioration and suicide could be traced to this conflicted life. Derek Wolcott, Malcolm Cowley and Richard Howard provide commentary. 60 mins.
VHS: S26315. $19.95.

Voices and Visions: Langston Hughes

Scenes of Hughes' travels in Europe and film of him reading his own work make this video an especially personal view of this great African-American writer. He was active in the black artistic and political movements of his time, a fact attested to by James Baldwin, Gwendolyn Brooks and others. 60 mins.
VHS: S26322. $19.95.

Voices and Visions: Marianne Moore

Witty, subversive and precise, Moore's poems evince remarkable clarity of observation. This film traces her life, times and friendships. Her unusual sources and idiosyncratic work depended on both natural science and her vivid imagination. Grace Schulman, Charles Tomlinson and Kenneth Burkes discuss this poet and her work. 60 mins.
VHS: S26319. $19.95.

Voices and Visions: Robert Frost

Though Frost presented a harsh vision of the world, his work achieved startling popularity. This film mixes interviews with Frost, dramatizations of his work, and commentary by Seamus Heaney, Alfred Edwards and Richard Wilbur. 60 mins.
VHS: S26323. $19.95.

Voices and Visions: Robert Lowell

Interviews with Lowell betray his keen interest in contemporary issues, such as racial injustice, cultural decline and nuclear war. This film examines Lowell's autobiographical and historical concerns as well as his mental anguish. Robert Giroux, Robert Hass and novelist Elizabeth Hardwick, Lowell's second wife, speak about the poet and his work. 60 mins.
VHS: S26325. $19.95.

Voices and Visions: Sylvia Plath

Rage, grief and anger mark the poems of this tragic figure's work. Archival footage, including a long interview with Plath herself, helps to explain some of the power and misery which afflicted the young poet. She committed suicide at 30. 60 mins.
VHS: S26320. $19.95.

Voices and Visions: T.S. Eliot

This poet and philosopher lived in London most of his life. There he worked as a publisher and dramatist whose poems confronted the spiritual uncertainty of his generation. Though Stephen Spender, Quentin Bell, Frank Kermode and others speak about his work, Eliot himself reads his own poems in this video. 60 mins.
VHS: S26321. $19.95.

Voices and Visions: Wallace Stevens

This melancholy existentialist was also an insurance executive. His comic and meditative poems elicit meaning and solace from the landscapes he visited, the weather and the conditions of the soul. Harold Bloom, Joan Richardson and James Merrill address the power of Stevens' work. 60 mins.
VHS: S26324. $19.95.

Voices and Visions: Walt Whitman

Walt Whitman pioneered a new American style of poetry that remains highly influential. This tape recreates the sights and sounds that inspired him. Whitman's idealism continues to inspire new generations of writers from the Beat movement onwards. Allen Ginsberg, Galway Kinnell and Donald Hall comment on this democratic, homosexual lover of the human voice. 60 mins.
VHS: S26313. $19.95.

Voices and Visions:
William Carlos Williams

Williams' penetrating work betrays a clean and insightful style focused on concrete particulars. This style reflects his other concerns as a small town pediatrician. Allen Ginsberg, Marjorie Perloff and Hugh Kenner discuss Williams the man and the poet. 60 mins.
VHS: S26316. $19.95.

W.S. Merwin

This winner of the Pulitzer Prize is a poet, playwright, translator and activist. He read from *Selected Poems* and *Rain in the Trees* in Los Angeles on May 16, 1988. Lewis MacAdams conducted the interview. From the *Lannan Literary Videos* series. 60 mins.
VHS: S27110. $19.95.

Walt Whitman and the Civil War

At the age of 42, Walt Whitman began service on the battlefields of the Civil War as a nurse. The experience profoundly changed his life. This video explores the personal transformation he underwent tending the wounded and the dying and its effect on his poetry. Excerpts of some of his greatest works are included. 28 mins.
VHS: S26532. $29.95.

What Happened to Kerouac?

A lively homage to and biography of a difficult and vulnerable individual who happened to be one of the most influential writers of recent history, Jack Kerouac. Contains footage of Kerouac as well as Allen Ginsberg, William Burroughs, Gregory Corso and Lawrence Ferlinghetti.
VHS: S04513. $69.95.
L. MacAdams/R. Lerner, USA, 1985, 96 mins.

Whispers on the Wind

Focusing on the distinct voices of our poetic heritage, this is a collection of verse as read by LeVar Burton, Ruby Dee and Cameron Mitchell. Included are works by D.H. Lawrence, Alexander Pope, DeBose Heyward, Tennessee Williams and James Dickey. 45 mins.
VHS: S12818. $24.95.

Whodunnit:
The Art of the Detective Story
This program takes a look at the popular, perennial art form from its evolution to its history, heroes, characters and conventions. Viewers learn how authors build suspense and clues, present evidence and hold viewer interest. 36 mins.
VHS: $12277. $174.00.

William S. Burroughs:
Commissioner of the Sewers
A portrait of the author who created *Naked Lunch*. With his characteristically dry wit and subtle humor, Burroughs talks about language and other weapons, about the word as a virus, about death and dreams, about travel in time and space. Burroughs also reads from his own work to the visual accompaniment of his paintings and films.
VHS: $16621. $29.95.
Klaus Maeck, USA, 1986, 60 mins.

With a Feminine Touch
Selections from the acclaimed PBS series, "Anyone for Tennyson?" focusing on the work of women poets, including Edna St. Vincent Millay, Emily Dickinson, the Brontes and Sylvia Plath. Valerie Harper, Claire Bloom and Ruby Dee are captured in some of the most memorable poems, often on location. 45 mins.
VHS: $08793. $24.95.

Women and the Beats:
The Beat Generation Show, Volume II
Anne Waldman, Joyce Johnson and Jan Kerouac are just some of the women who helped shape this important literary movement. Readings, interviews and lectures help clarify the value of the contributions made by these women.
VHS: $24312. $29.95.

MARK TWAIN ADAPTATIONS

The Adventures of Huck Finn (Disney)
Stephen Sommers wrote and directed this Disney adaptation of Mark Twain's classic novel about the shifting friendship between Huck Finn (Elijah Wood), an energetic, go-for-broke kid, and Jim (Courtney B. Vance), a runaway slave who is desperately trying to secure his freedom. With Robbie Coltrane, Jason Robards, Ron Perlman and Dana Ivey.
VHS: $19726. $96.95.
Laser: Letterboxed. LD72340. $39.99.
Stephen Sommers, USA, 1993, 108 mins.

The Adventures of Huckleberry Finn
(Hodges/Moore)
A good screen version of the Mark Twain classic, with an engaging Huck Finn (Eddie Hodges) and an excellent Jim (Archie Moore). Other assorted characters are played by Buster Keaton, Tony Randall, John Carradine, and Sterling Holloway.
VHS: $13639. $19.98.
Michael Curtiz, USA, 1960, 107 mins.

The Adventures of Huckleberry Finn
(Rooney)
Mickey Rooney stars as Mark Twain's Huckleberry Finn, with William Frawley and Walter Connolly.
VHS: $03532. $24.95.
Richard Thorpe, USA, 1939, 88 mins.

The Adventures of Mark Twain:
Fredric March
An eccentric biography of the life and art of the American writer and humorist. Fredric March imbues Twain with wit and invention, perfectly appropriating Twain's gestures and rhythms. With Alexis Smith, Donald Crisp, George Barbier and Binnie Barnes.
VHS: $19466. $19.98.
Irving Rapper, USA, 1944, 130 mins.

The Adventures of Tom Sawyer
(Ebsen/Wyatt)
Mark Twain's classic tale of the *Adventures of Tom Sawyer* comes to life in this production, starring Buddy Ebsen, Jane Wyatt and Vic Morrow as Injun Joe. A delightful treat for the entire family.
VHS: $03321. $39.95.
James Neilson, USA, 1973, 76 mins.

The Adventures of Tom Sawyer
(Kelly/Brennan)
Tommy Kelly stars as Tom Sawyer in this excellent David O. Selznick production of the classic Mark Twain story. Co-starring Walter Brennan and May Robson; photographed by James Wong Howe.
VHS: $14224. $14.98.
Laser: LD70812. $39.98.
Norman Taurog, USA, 1938, 91 mins.

A Connecticut Yankee (Will Rogers)
Will Rogers is a radio expert who travels back in time to the court of King Arthur and changes medieval life by introducing telephones, automobiles, hotdogs and advertising. Maureen O'Sullivan and Myrna Loy co-star in this adaptation of Mark Twain's classic. For a scene in which the queen expresses her affection, Will's face was hand-tinted, frame by frame, to show him "blushing."
VHS: $13493. $19.98.
David Butler, USA, 1931, 96 mins.

A Connecticut Yankee
in King Arthur's Court (Bing Crosby)
Bing Crosby is a modern American chap, circa 1949, who loses consciousness and awakes in the Sixth Century with a lot of explaining to do. This third screen version of the Samuel Clemens cautionary tale is an elaborate musical which features the talents of William Bendix, Sir Cedric Hardwicke and Rhonda Fleming in living color.
VHS: $03492. $14.98.
Tay Garnett, USA, 1949, 107 mins.

A Connecticut Yankee in King Arthur's
Court (Westinghouse Studio One)
Boris Karloff plays King Arthur in this live tv adaptation of the Mark Twain classic about a modern New Englander who finds himself back in the days of Camelot. Also in the cast are Thomas Mitchell and Berry Kroeger. Program opening and commercials deleted. USA, 1952, 51 mins.
VHS: $05442. $24.95.

Huckleberry Finn (1974/Musical)
A colorful musical interpretation of Mark Twain's classic text. Jeff East plays Huck, with Paul Winfield as runaway slave Jim.
VHS: $19031. $14.95.
Laser: LD72123. $34.98.
J. Lee Thompson, USA, 1972, 118 mins.

Huckleberry Finn (1975/Howard)
Ron Howard is Huckleberry Finn in this folksy, homespun version of Mark Twain's eternal tale about Huck and Jim's misadventures on the mighty Mississippi. An enjoyable treatment which nonetheless sacrifices the social criticism and darker elements of the classic novel for simple, straightforward storytelling.
VHS: $03556. $14.98.
Robert Totten, USA, 1975, 74 mins.

Innocents Abroad
Mark Twain on his grand tour of the continents, joined by Brooke Adams and David Ogden Stiers. 116 mins.
VHS: $06393. $19.95.

Life on the Mississippi
A film commissioned for public television, another adaptation of an episode from Mark Twain's boyhood collections of growing up in pre-Civil War Missouri. Robert Lansing is a river boat pilot named Horace Bixby who allows young Sam (David Knell) a chance to test his manhood as an apprentice on an arduous journey up the Mississippi River.
VHS: $02544. $19.95.
Peter Hunt, USA, 1980, 115 mins.

Man That Corrupted Hadleyburg
Based on the short story by Mark Twain, and starring Robert Preston, Fred Gwynne and Tom Aldredge. From American Short Story series.
VHS: $01716. $24.95.
Ralph Rosenblum, USA, 52 mins.

Mark Twain's America
This documentary examines the cultural, artistic, political and social transformation in American society captured through the work and art of Mark Twain. Twain's metamorphosis from droll, regional writer to revolutionary literary figure is paralleled by America's rise from frontier society to world power. Narrated by Howard Lindsay. 60 mins.
VHS: $19248. $19.95.

Mark Twain's Connecticut Yankee
A Connecticut Yankee in King Arthur's Court. What does an innocent young citizen of Hartford, Connecticut do when he's plucked up from the 19th Century and plunked down into King Arthur's medieval court? Mark Twain's tale of American ingenuity in Camelot stars Richard Basehart, Roscoe Lee Browne and Paul Rudd in a satirical spectacular.
VHS: $03958. $64.95.

Mark Twain: A Musical Biography
A biography of Mark Twain framed by the tenets of the roadway musical. "An original biographical tribute to Twain, an extravaganza of singing, dancing and acting" (*The New York Times*). 87 mins.
VHS: $17022. $24.95.

Mysterious Stranger
Mark Twain's irreverent fantasy focuses on a printer's apprentice from Missouri who daydreams himself into a medieval European castle and meets a mysterious, magical youth with formidable powers. 89 mins.
VHS: $06154. $19.95.

The Prince and the Pauper
An all-star cast including Errol Flynn, Claude Rains and Barton MacLane was assembled for this story of the young Prince of England who trades places with his look-alike, a street beggar. Based on the story by Mark Twain.
VHS: $01871. $19.98.
Laser: LD72130. $39.98.
William Keighley, USA, 1937, 120 mins.

Private History of
a Campaign That Failed
Mark Twain's fictionalized reminiscences of his brief, inglorious career in the Confederate militia. Pat Hingle stars as the leader of a troop of rangers who panic and react disgracefully when confronted with the realities of battle. 89 mins.
VHS: $10058. $19.95.

Pudd'nhead Wilson
Ken Howard stars as Pudd'nhead Wilson, a lawyer whose humor no one understands, in this adaptation of Mark Twain's classic story that explores the issues of slavery, justice, and mother/son relationships. Filmed in historic Harper's Ferry, West Virginia.
VHS: $01070. $19.95.
Alan Bridges, USA, 1983, 87 mins.

Rascals and Robbers—
The Secret Adventures of
Tom Sawyer and Huck Finn
Patrick Creadon and Anthony Michael Hall are Tom and Huck in this made-for-tv accounting of their lives that Mark Twain did not write. They join a circus, help free a slave and try to stop a con artist named Scree (Anthony James) from bilking their neighbors. Life on the Mississippi just never slows down.
VHS: $04379. $59.98.
Dick Lowery, USA, 1982, 100 mins.

Tom Sawyer
The Mark Twain novel in a musical adaptation features Johnnie Whitaker, Celeste Holmes, Warren Oates and Jodie Foster, set in real Mississippi locations, and with musical direction by John Williams.
VHS: $12430. $19.98.
Don Taylor, USA, 1973, 103 mins.

theatre ON SCREEN

Agnes of God
Meg Tilly stars in the film adaptation of the John Pielmeyer play as a young nun who conceived, delivered and may have murdered a baby within the confines of the convent. Jane Fonda is the sensitive, chain-smoking court appointed psychiatrist sent to find out the truth. Anne Bancroft is the disapproving Mother Superior. A disturbing drama with no easy answers. Sven Nykvist shot the film in Canada.
VHS: $10377. $19.95.
Norman Jewison, USA, 1985, 98 mins.

Ah, Wilderness
A poignant adaptation of Eugene O'Neill's play about early 20th century small-town life, focusing on the confusion and difficulty confronting a young man's leap into adulthood. With Wallace Beery, Lionel Barrymore and Mickey Rooney. Screenplay by Albert Hackett and Francis Goodrich.
VHS: $17656. $19.98.
Clarence Brown, USA, 1935, 101 mins.

All My Sons
A superb cast brings Arthur Miller's critically-acclaimed play of human frailty and guilt to life. Originally produced in the 1940's, this all-new production remains a moving theatrical experience. Joan Allen, Michael Learned, James Whitmore and Aidan Quinn star.
VHS: $04524. $39.95.
John Power, USA, 1986, 122 mins.

Anthony and Cleopatra (Dalton/Redgrave)
Shakespeare's most popular tale of love, war and political intrigues is realized with the star power of Timothy Dalton, Lynn Redgrave, John Carradine and Anthony Geary. History's most famous lovers are magnificently portrayed, bringing their passion and their ultimate dilemma into sharp focus.
VHS: $19414. $59.95.

Antigone
Irene Papas stars in this faithful adaptation of Sophocles' classic tragedy about the descendants of Oedipus. Greek with English subtitles.
VHS: $09874. $39.95.

Antony and Cleopatra (Royal Shakespeare Company/Patrick Stewart)
Patrick Stewart stars in this Royal Shakespeare Company production of Shakespeare's play. 160 mins.
VHS: $19027. $19.98.

As You Like It
Laurence Olivier and Elisabeth Bergner star in this handsome and fairly faithful translation of the Shakespeare comedy, in which Rosalind (Bergner) and her love Orlando (Olivier) withstand the brutal tactics of her uncle Frederick to secure the throne for her deposed father, Duke Senior.
VHS: $18173. $19.95.
Paul Czinner, Great Britain, 1936, 96 mins.

Bacchantes
Euripides' famous Greek play, a provocative look at the turmoil of a dancer's professional and private life, performed by a cast including Tiana Ela, Pierre Brice, Akim Tamiroff. In English.
VHS: $07461. $19.95.
Giorgio Ferroni, Italy/USA, 100 mins.

Balcony
In a brothel of illusion the customers take over real power during a revolution. Madame Irma (Shelley Winters) runs the house of illusion where ordinary people play out their dreams. Outside, a revolution is in progress. For the Police Chief (Peter Falk), the brothel is the rallying point from which he can suppress the revolution. Roger (Leonard Nimoy), leader of the revolution, seeks refuge in the brothel where he poses as his opponent. Based on the play by Jean Genet.
VHS: $09554. $29.95.
Joseph Strick, USA, 1963, 87 mins.

Barnum
A filmed performance of the London production of the international stage hit starring Broadway sensation Michael Crawford. The show traces the legendary P.T. Barnum's career from his humble beginnings as a promoter of side shows to his eventual triumph as the co-founder of the Barnum and Bailey Circus.
VHS: $14294. $29.95.
Terry Hughes, Great Britain, 1990, 113 mins.

Beckett Directs Beckett: Endgame
Samuel Beckett's favorite play was reportedly *Endgame*, his portrait of modern alienation and despair, set in a dystopic, underground universe where nothing makes sense. Made in collaboration with the San Quentin Drama Workshop. With Bud Thorpe, Rick Cluchey and Teresito Garcia Suro. 96 mins.
VHS: $18456. $29.95.

Beckett Directs Beckett: Krapp's Last Tape
A presentation of the San Quentin Drama Workshop, this play about a retired civil servant reviewing his life by listening to reel to reel tapes features Rick Cluchey in the title role. "This is the essential addition; for those meeting him [Beckett] for the first time, there could be no better way to start" (Australian press). 46 mins.
VHS: $18455. $29.95.

Beckett Directs Beckett: Waiting for Godot
In collaboration with the San Quentin Drama Workshop, Samuel Beckett directs his existential parable about two lost souls awaiting a rendezvous that may or may not be imaginary. With Bud Thorpe, Rick Cluchey, Lawrence Held and Alan Mandell. The play has never been "more human, more accessible or more beautiful" (Newsweek). In two acts running 77 and 60 mins.
VHS: $18454. $39.95.

Beckett Directs Beckett Collection
The three-tape set.
VHS: $18143. $89.95.

The Belle of Amherst
Julie Harris stars as the most famous 19th century American woman poet, Emily Dickinson. In this dramatization, her life as a recluse and spinster is recreated to reveal the sources of her poetry. Dickinson was inspired by the humble everyday occurences found in rural America.
VHS: $22940. $59.95.

Building a Character
Creating a foundation for character development can be made simple using this basic formulated approach. Learn to analyze character, discover emotions, and use your body to become a better, more convincing actor. 86 mins.
VHS: $15917. $59.95.

Caesar and Cleopatra
Based on the play by George Bernard Shaw and full of Shaw's indomitable wit; with Claude Rains, Vivien Leigh, Stewart Granger.
VHS: $08268. $14.98.
Gabriel Pascal, Great Britain, 1948, 134 mins.

Cat on a Hot Tin Roof (1958)
Paul Newman and Elizabeth Taylor star in this steamy screen version of Tennessee Williams' famous play about a rich plantation owner, dying of cancer, who finds most of his family fawning all over him for his money. Fine performances from a cast that includes Burl Ives, Madeleine Sherwood and Larry Gates.
VHS: $13776. $19.95.
Richard Brooks, USA, 1958, 108 mins.

Cat on a Hot Tin Roof (1984)
Jessica Lange is Maggie in Tennessee Williams' sexually obsessed melodrama, with Tommy Lee Jones as Brick and Rip Torn as Big Daddy. Made for American Playhouse television.
VHS: Out of print. For rental only.
Laser: LD70541. $34.98.
Jack Hofsiss, USA, 1984, 122 mins.

Chalk Garden
A moving, beautifully acted drama about a teenager (Hayley Mills) who is set on the right path by her governess (Deborah Kerr). With John Mills, Edith Evans.
VHS: $04522. $14.98.
Ronald Neame, Great Britain, 1964, 106 mins.

Clarence Darrow
Henry Fonda in a command performance as the famous Clarence Darrow, the legendary attorney who fought for the rights of individuals. "I urge every man, woman and child interested in justice and America to see this…As for Mr. Fonda, it would be difficult to think of praise too high…It is just plain wonderful," wrote Clive Barnes in *The New York Times*.
VHS: $06091. $39.95.
John Houseman, USA, 1980, 81 mins.

The Connection
The Living Theatre's production of the play by Jack Gelber; a quintessential work of theatre of the 60's, a harrowing depiction of the dope peddling milieu, as the characters wait for the arrival of Cowboy with the heroin. Critics Prize, Cannes.
VHS: $00265. $29.95.
Shirley Clarke, USA, 1961, 105 mins.

Coriolanus—Westinghouse Studio One
A modern dress update of Shakespeare's Roman play that moves the action to Fascist Italy. Written by Worthington Minor, who introduces the play. With Richard Greene, Judith Evelyn, Richard Purdy and Tom Poston of the *Newhart* show. Betty Furness does the commercials. USA, 1951, 60 mins.
VHS: $05435. $24.95.

Creative Drama & Improvisation
The imagination is the most powerful tool accessible to the actor. It enables the actor and comedian to create situations and background information on a character that might not be drawn from life experience otherwise. These exercises and improvisations will assist you in exploring your imagination.
VHS: $15919. $59.95.

Cyrano de Bergerac (Ferrer)
Jose Ferrer won an Academy Award for his role as the classic soldier of fortune with the oversize nose. With Mala Powers.
VHS: $18180. $19.95.
Michael Gordon, USA, 1950, 112 mins.

Cyrano de Bergerac (Jacobi)
The Royal Shakespeare Company's acclaimed production of Rostand's *Cyrano de Bergerac*, translated and adapted by Anthony Burgess, and starring Derek Jacobi as Cyrano.
VHS: $00292. $59.98.
T. Hands/M. Simpson, Great Britain, 1984, 176 mins.

Da
Hugh Leonard's autobiographical play of growing up adopted in a small seacoast town in Ireland. The film version is directed by character actor Matt Clark. Barnard Hughes is the lovable and crusty title character with whom son Martin Sheen has many mixed emotions. A ghost story. A comedy. A celebration of life. With William Hickey.
VHS: $07581. $19.95.
Matt Clark, Ireland/USA, 1988, 102 mins.

Days of Wine and Roses
Piper Laurie and Cliff Robertson star in the Playhouse 90 production of the J.P. Miller play about a couple facing alcoholism.
VHS: $05014. $24.95.
Laser: Letterboxed. LD71200. $34.98.
John Frankenheimer, USA, 1958, 89 mins.

Desire Under the Elms
In Eugene O'Neill's play adapted by Irwin Shaw, a 19th century New England family is beset by greed, lust and family hatred. With Anthony Perkins, Sophia Loren, Burl Ives and Pernell Roberts.
VHS: $00322. $19.95.
Delbert Mann, USA, 1958, 114 mins.

Don't Start Me to Talking…
This adaptation of John O'Neal's one-man play features Junebug, a mythic folk storyteller born out of the civil rights movement of the 60s. Junebug reveals the wisdom of the common people, who, through great ingenuity and resourcefulness, overcome tremendous adversities in order to survive. 45 mins.
VHS: $23301. $29.95.

The Empty Space
Gerald Feil's film documents a 1970 visit by Peter Brook and his Parisian experimental theater group at the Brooklyn Academy of music. It reveals the exercises and techniques used by this acclaimed director which challenge distinctions between actors and the audience. 60 mins.
VHS: $21192. $29.95.

Entertainer
Playwright John Osborne assisted Tony Richardson in the adaptation of his play in this brilliant depiction of the moral, spiritual and professional decline of a bogus entertainer, Archie Rice. Set against the background of the noisy holiday makers pushing past the placard proclaiming the Suez crisis in which Archie's only contact with real life, his son Mick, is to die. "Richardson used large, oppressive close-ups and shock cutting to the point of technical arrogance, but he brought the audience relentlessly face to face with the failure of the sad characters of Archie and his debilitated alcoholic wife, beautifully played by Brenda de Banzie" (Roger Manvell).
VHS: $08261. $19.95.
Tony Richardson, Great Britain, 1960, 97 mins.

Equus
Richard Burton and Peter Firth in the film version of Peter Shaffer's play about a part-time stableboy who has blinded six horses. Burton as the psychiatrist discovers that the boy comes from a repressive family background.
VHS: $00411. $14.95.
Sidney Lumet, USA, 1977, 145 mins.

Fortune and Men's Eyes
A realistic adaptation of John Herbert's play about homosexual life inside a prison cell. Brutal and uncompromising. "A powerful and often shocking film" (Newsweek). With Wendell Burton, Michael Greer and Zooey (David) Hall.
VHS: $17657. $19.98.
Harvey Hart, Canada, 1971, 102 mins.

The Glass Menagerie
Set in depression-era St. Louis, Tennessee Williams' first play is a hallmark of American theatre, and receives a loving production at the hands of director Paul Newman. The familial, tension-ridden triangle receives brilliant performances from Joanne Woodward, John Malkovich, Karen Allen and James Naughton.
VHS: $07142. $19.98.
Laser: LD70032. $39.98.
Paul Newman, USA, 1987, 134 mins.

Glengarry Glen Ross
James Foley's adaptation of David Mamet's Pulitzer prize-winning play about the confidence games and male bravado of a group of Chicago real estate salesmen. The performances are first-rate, with Al Pacino as the silver-tongued, shrewd operator, Jack Lemmon as the one-time kingpin who's fallen on hard times and Ed Harris as an anonymous, grubby loser. Alec Baldwin turns in a terrifying cameo.
VHS: $18465. $19.98.
Laser: Widescreen. LD75198. $34.98.
James Foley, USA, 1992, 100 mins.

Hamlet (Gibson)
Mel Gibson stars as the melancholy Dane in this film adaptation of the Shakespeare classic, directed by Franco Zeffirelli. The distinguished supporting cast includes Glenn Close, Alan Bates, Paul Scofield, Helena Bonham Carter and Ian Holm.
VHS: $14279. $19.98.
Franco Zeffirelli, USA, 135, mins.

Hamlet (Olivier)
Laurence Olivier produces, directs and interprets the title character, a melancholy Dane dealing with a range of feelings for his stepfather, the new King of Denmark. The film won four Oscars and Olivier received his knighthood. Based on a play by William Shakespeare. Cast includes Jean Simmons, Felix Aylmer and Peter Cushing. Don't look for Rosencrantz and Guildenstern. Filmed in glorious black and white.
VHS: $06230. $19.98.
Laser: LD75461. $69.95.
Laurence Olivier, Great Britain, 1948, 153 mins.

Hamlet (Williamson)
A brilliant, Tony Richardson-directed version of Shakespeare's *Hamlet*, starring Nicol Williamson, Gordon Jackson, Anthony Hopkins, Judy Parfitt.
VHS: $07033. $29.95.
Tony Richardson, Great Britain, 1969, 114 mins.

Harold Clurman
A celebration of the art and life of Harold Clurman, producer, director and critic who was a vital force in American theater for 50 years. Introduced and narrated by Meryl Streep, the film contains impassioned and heartfelt remembrances from Roy Scheider, Arthur Miller, Lee Strasberg, Stella Adler, Julie Harris, Elia Kazan and Karl Malden. 55 mins.
VHS: $18732. $39.95.

Henry V (Branagh)
Kenneth Branagh makes his astounding directorial debut and stars in this critically acclaimed adaptation of Shakespeare's rousing play. With Derek Jacobi, Ian Holm, Judi Dench and Paul Scofield. "…a depth and authority seldom encountered these days on stage or in film" (Dave Kehr, *Chicago Tribune*).
VHS: $12590. $29.98.
Kenneth Branagh, Great Britain, 1990, 138 mins.

Henry V (Olivier)
Laurence Olivier won a special Oscar for outstanding achievement as an actor, producer and director in bringing this work of Shakespeare to the screen. A colorful historical spectacle that includes the battle of Agincourt and serves as a stirring patriotic metaphor for England's survival in WWII. With Robert Newton, Leslie Banks, Renee Asherson and Leo Genn.
VHS: $06237. $19.98.
Laser: LD75076. $69.95.
Laurence Olivier, Great Britain, 1944, 137 mins.

Hobson's Choice
Not the English film, but an American adaptation of the classic stage comedy, based on the plight of three young sisters in desperate need of dowries. With Richard Thomas, Lillian Gish and Jack Warden.
VHS: $06359. $59.98.
Gilbert Cates, USA, 1983, 100 mins.

Inspector General
Danny Kaye pulls the wool over the eyes of the town elders when he pretends to be the important Inspector General whom this Russian village anxiously awaits to impress. Based on a story by Gogol. With music. Cast includes Walter Slezak, Elsa Lancaster and Alan Hale.
VHS: $18186. $19.98.
Henry Koster, USA, 1949, 102 mins.

Julius Caesar (Heston/Gielgud)
John Gielgud gives a superior performance as Julius Caesar in this adaptation of Shakespeare's play, also featuring Charlton Heston, Richard Chamberlain, Robert Vaughn and Diana Rigg.
VHS: $01677. $29.95.
Stuart Burge, Great Britain, 1970, 116 mins.

Julius Caesar (MGM/Brando)
Friends, Romans, countrymen—before Marlon Brando wore a motorcycle jacket, he proved to be quite impressive decked out in a toga. Brando plays Mark Antony in this lavish production of the Shakespeare play. The film won an Oscar for set decoration and art direction, and includes such fine actors as James Mason, John Gielgud, Louis Calhern, Edmond O'Brien, Greer Garson, Deborah Kerr and George Macready. The producer was John Houseman.
VHS: $11222. $19.95.
Joseph L. Mankiewicz, USA, 1953, 120 mins.

King Lear (Laurence Olivier)
Critically acclaimed as "a performance as great as anything he has ever done in his illustrious acting career", *King Lear* proved to be Laurence Olivier's final major screen role. The all-star Shakespearean cast includes Diana Rigg as Lear's daughter Regan. Olivier's monumental portrayal of Shakespeare's embittered King Lear is truly a performance for the ages.
VHS: $10709. $29.95.

King Lear (Orson Welles)
A legendary production of Shakespeare's masterpiece, directed by the acclaimed British stage and film director Peter Brook, and starring Orson Welles. Virtually unseen since its broadcast in the mid-1950's, this is a treasure of a lifetime for fans of film, Shakespeare, Welles, theatre.
VHS: $11175. $39.95.

King Lear (Patrick Magee)
A brilliant, lavish production by Thames Television of the Shakespeare tragedy, with Patrick Magee delivering a powerfully complex performance as the aging Lear.
VHS: $12551. $39.99.

The Lady's Not for Burning

Kenneth Branagh stars in this mystery tale beset by superstition. Branagh is a discharged soldier who must solve the murder of man in order to protect a beautiful woman. She stands accused of witchcraft. The murdered man's body is missing and the townspeople suspect that she has turned him into a dog. Based on the play by respected playwright Christopher Fry, this passionate love story is set in a time ruled by irrational fears. With Bernard Hepton and Cherie Lunghi.
VHS: S26776. $19.95.
Julian Amyes, Great Britain, 1995, 90 mins.

Laurence Olivier: A Life

Famed for being camera shy, this legend of film and theater appears for the first time in a comprehensive, candid interview. Key partnerships, both on and offstage, are recalled by Olivier and by his many friends and colleagues. Features Sir John Gielgud, Sir Ralph Richardson, Douglas Fairbanks, Jr., Dame Peggy Ashcroft and Olivier's wife, actress Joan Plowright. 159 mins.
VHS: S16597. $29.95.

The Life and Adventures of Nicholas Nickleby

Thirty-nine actors from the Royal Shakespeare Company are presented in this dramatization of Charles Dickens' masterful tale. From Wackford Squeer's Dotheboys to the itinerant theater troupe of Mr. Vincent Crummies, this set of videos offers nine hours of engrossing viewing pleasure.
VHS: S23877. $149.95.

A Life in the Theater

Jack Lemmon stars as an aging theater actor who finds himself living in an increasingly artificial dream world, in David Mamet's drama of theater, life, age and experience. Matthew Broderick co-stars. Powerful performances highlight this riveting drama.
VHS: S21514. $94.95.
Gregory Mosher, USA, 1993, 78 mins.

Long Day's Journey into Night

Eugene O'Neill's drama of a problem-prone Tyrone family is faithfully brought to the big screen with all the vices and vitriol intact. Ralph Richardson heads a cast that includes Katharine Hepburn, Jason Robards, Jr. and Dean Stockwell.
VHS: S02576. $19.98.
Laser: LD71550. $39.98.
Sidney Lumet, USA, 1962, 170 mins.

Look Back in Anger—Kenneth Branagh

John Osborne's play has had many successful productions featuring great British actors, including Richard Burton and Malcolm McDowell. Now Kenneth Branagh and Emma Thompson are featured in a convincing production that brings alive the fury which inspired a generation of angry young men.
VHS: S24665. $29.98.
David Jones, Great Britain, 1989, 114 mins.

Lysistrata

Aristophanes' ancient Greek play is brought to life in this new adaptation starring Jenny Karezi and Costas Kazakos. Lysistrata is the Athenian woman disgusted by the way men have ruined the country with their endless war. Rallying other women, she proposes that they impose an embargo on sexual relations with men as long as the war lasts. The film liberates the action from the stage, places it on location in the acropolis, and renders Aristophanes' plea in a forceful manner. Contains nudity and strong language. Greek with English subtitles.
VHS: S11718. $39.95.
Yiannis Negrepontis, Greece, 1987, 97 mins.

Macbeth (Evans)

Sir Maurice Evans and Dame Judith Anderson star in Shakespeare's turbulent drama, produced for television. Great Britain, 1954, 103 mins.
VHS: S01650. $19.95.

Macbeth (Jayson)

Thames Television produced this brilliant adaptation of Shakespeare's play with the cast including Michael Jayson, Barbara Lee Hunt, Ralph Nosseck, Richard Warner.
VHS: S12738. $39.99.

Mack the Knife

Raul Julia returns to the role that made him a star on the Broadway stage. He plays Mac Heath, the suave London master criminal and womanizer, in this film adaption of the Bertolt Brecht and Kurt Weill musical *Threepenny Opera*. Cast includes Richard Harris, Julia Migenes, Julie Walters, Clive Revill and Rachel Robertson. Roger Daltry sings the familiar title tune. Filmed in Yugoslavia to save money.
VHS: S12419. $89.95.
Menahem Golan, USA, 1989, 122 mins.

The Madwoman of Chaillot

British filmmaker Bryan Forbes (*The Stepford Wives*) adapts Jean Giradoux's play about an eccentric and possibly deranged woman (Katharine Hepburn) who's convinced the world is no longer worthy of her attention. The all-star cast includes Charles Boyer, Claude Dauphin, Paul Henreid, Giulietta Masina, Richard Chamberlain and Yul Brynner.
VHS: S15934. $19.98.
Laser: LD71187. $39.98.
Bryan Forbes, Great Britain, 1969, 132 mins.

The Mahabharata (1989/166 mins.)

The ground-breaking theatrical experience by Peter Brook based on the ancient Sanskrit story of two families whose warring feud brings civilization to the brink of doom. With a script written by Jean-Claude Carriere and a cast of multi-ethnic and talented actors, this milestone of theatrical performance, according to one reviewer, "accomplishes the seemingly impossible…in terms of modern cinema, it is somewhat of a miracle."
VHS: S20825. $49.95.
Peter Brook, Great Britain, 1989, 166 mins.

The Mahabharata (1992/318 mins.)

Adapted from the sacred 2000-year-old Sanskrit poem *The Great Story of Mankind*, this full-length film adaptation of the milestone theatre piece by an international company directed by Peter Brook captures the epic sweep of an entire world view. 318 mins.
VHS: S13333. $99.95.
Peter Brook, France/Great Britain, 1992, 318 mins.

Maidsplay and Dreiske Discipline Lecture Demonstration

One of the best realizations of theatre on film, this 1983 Hungarian production documents Nicole Dreiske's production of *Maidsplay*, an original theatre piece inspired by Jean Genet's *The Maids* in Budapest. The production utilizes actual information about the two sisters whose extraordinary crime inspired Genet to write *The Maids* and highlights the themes of violence, sex, drugs, jealousy and incest in the story of the two sisters who, employed as maids in the same house, take turns playing the role of their mistress in a secret and bizarre ritual. The second part of the tape illustrates the basic techniques of The Dreiske Discipline as led by Nicole Dreiske in actor workshops in Budapest. Produced by Judit Koszanyi, directed by Ildiko Szabo. A BBS/Mafilm production. In English. Color, 80 mins.
VHS: S03474. $60.00.

Major Barbara

Filmed in war-torn England, Gabriel Pascal's screen version of George Bernard Shaw's famous play is a memorial to the artists who made it and proof that it takes more than bombs to subdue the English wit. The story of a Salvation Army girl, her munitions manufacturing father and her pragmatic scholar fiance, this film version is a triumph—demonstrating Shaw's own words that "the greatest of our evils and the worst of our crimes is poverty." With Rex Harrison and Deborah Kerr.
VHS: S13734. $29.95.
Gabriel Pascal, Great Britain, 1940, 90 mins.

Marat/Sade
(The Persecution and Assassination of Jean-Paul Marat as Performed by the Inmates of the Asylum of Charenton under the Direction of Marquis de Sade)

Peter Weiss' monumental play, in a mesmerizing adaptation directed by the world-famous theater director Peter Brook, in its original production by the Royal Shakespeare Company. The play features Glenda Jackson as a nutcase in the role of Charlotte Chorday, the assassin of Marat. With Ian Richardson, Patrick Magee, Ruth Baker and Freddie Jones. Terrifying and intense.
VHS: S09855. $59.95.
Laser: LD70264. $39.95.
Peter Brook, Great Britain, 1967, 115 mins.

The Marquise

Noel Coward's drawing room comedy unfolds in the mad opulence of the Compte Raoul De Vriac's spacious chateau outside Paris. Set in 1735, the Compte's former mistress, the Marquise Eloise De Kertournel, floors everybody with her announcement she's staying permanently. With Diana Rigg, Richard Johnson and James Villiers. 55 mins.
VHS: S19179. $24.98.

Marty—Goodyear TV Playhouse

Two years before Ernest Borgnine made the movie, Rod Steiger won praise for his portrayal of the lonely, overweight butcher from the Bronx. The live tv drama featured Nancy Marchand, Betsy Palmer and Nehemiah Persoff. From the Golden Age of tv. Commercials deleted. USA, 1953, 51 mins.
VHS: S05517. $19.95.

Master Harold and the Boys

The Broadway hit play by South Africa's eminent playwright Athol Fugard stars Matthew Broderick. USA, 1986, 90 mins.
VHS: S01528. $19.98.

Medea

An intense rendering of Euripides' masterpiece in this famous production which features Dame Judith Anderson, reprising her role from Broadway. With Colleen Dewhurst.
VHS: S18027. $29.95.

Meet Marcel Marceau

Don't expect an opening monologue. The famed French mime lets his body and his features do all the talking he needs. This one-man show consists of nine parts including a special tribute to Harpo Marx, Buster Keaton, Stan Laurel and Charlie Chaplin. Marceau is said to do a voice-over narration to some skits, but hearing is believing. USA, 1965, 52 mins.
VHS: S05518. $24.95.

The Merchant of Venice

Sir Laurence Olivier and Joan Plowright star in Shakespeare's complex tale of jealousy and greed. 131 mins.
VHS: S19028. $19.98.

The Merry Wives of Windsor (Esquire 4+4)

Shakespeare's play about a lover wooing a potentially unfaithful wife. Starring Leon Charles and Gloria Grahame. 160 mins. Two videocassettes.
VHS: S15187. $59.95.

A Midsummer Night's Dream (BBC)

A live BBC production of Shakespeare's play of star-crossed lovers and the influence of supernatural creatures. Benny Hill appears in the role of Bottom. Also in the cast are Anna Massey, Jill Bennett, Cyril Luckham, Patrick Allen and Peter Wyngarde. A comical fantasy. England, 1960's, 111 mins.
VHS: S05520. $29.95.

A Midsummer Night's Dream (Peter Hall)

Peter Hall's delicate and merry adaptation of Shakespeare's enchanting farce about the shifting loyalties and evolving relationships among two pairs of lovers. Their romantic affection is manipulated with the help of Puck, a magic fairy. With Diana Rigg as Helena, David Warner as Lysander, Ian Richardson as Oberon, King of the Fairies, Judi Dench as Tatania, Queen of the Fairies and Ian Holm as Puck.
VHS: S06074. $24.95.
Peter Hall, Great Britain, 1968, 124 mins.

A Midsummer Night's Dream (Reinhardt)

The brilliant German theater director Max Reinhardt adapts his Broadway production of Shakespeare's enchanting and lyrical play about love, companionship, fate and star-crossed affairs. Two opposite pairs of lovers ward off extravagant spells and the supernatural to consummate their transcendent passion. The film is visually intoxicating and dramatically powerful, retaining Shakespeare's words though finding a sublime grace and subtlety to the moods and rhythms. Music by Mendelssohn. Choreography by Bronislawa Nijinska and Anton Grot. With James Cagney, Dick Powell, Olivia de Havilland and Joe E. Brown.
VHS: S01679. $19.98.
Laser: LD71150. $39.98.
Max Reinhardt, USA, 1935, 135 mins.

Miracle in the Rain— Westinghouse Studio One

The love story written by Ben Hecht is slightly marred by noisy stagehands and sloppy camerawork. The writing is said to overcome any defects of live tv. With Jeffrey Lynn and Joy Geffen in a story of a lonely girl and the soldier who went away. USA, 1950, 56 mins.
VHS: S05452. $29.95.

Monster in a Box

This film version of Spalding Gray's acclaimed stage hit follows an hilarious and insightful tale about a writer with a block. Writer's block metamorphoses into a behemoth document that won't go back in the box. Gray is thus set off on an itinerary that includes stops in an Eastern haunted writer's retreat, an L.A. where screenwriters don't write, and a movie set in Nicaragua where he plays a spy.
VHS: S26337. $19.98.
Nick Broomfield, USA, 1992, 90 mins.

Much Ado About Nothing

Kenneth Branagh's energetic, highly cinematic adaptation of Shakespeare's comedy of love is notable for its beautiful Italian locations and first-rate performances from Branagh, Emma Thompson, Michael Keaton, Robert Sean Leonard, Keanu Reeves and Denzel Washington. "Ravishing entertainment" (Vincent Canby, *The New York Times*).
VHS: S20528. $19.95.
Laser: LD72362. $34.95.
Kenneth Branagh, Great Britain, 1993, 110 mins.

'Night Mother

Adaptation of the Pulitzer Prize winning play stars Sissy Spacek and Anne Bancroft as a mother and daughter whose psyches are slowly unveiled to expose their real feelings about the events of their lives together.
VHS: S03466. $79.95.
Tom Moore, USA, 1986, 96 mins.

The Norman Conquests: Living Together

An HBO adaptation of the play by Alan Ayckbourn concerning the amorous adventures of Norman and his romantic entanglements with three sisters. Cast includes Lucie Arnaz, Craig Wasson, Malcolm McDowell, Ken Howard and Leonard Rossiter. The story is noted for its unusual staging. 93 mins.
VHS: S06157. $59.95.

The Norman Conquests: Table Manners

HBO continues the story of Norman and his way with impressing three sisters. Based on the work by British playwright Alan Ayckbourn, the same story is told in the living room, the garden and the dining room. With Lucie Arnaz, Ken Howard, Craig Wasson, Leonard Rossiter and Malcolm McDowell. 108 mins.
VHS: S06159. $59.95.

Oedipus Rex

A landmark production of Sophocles' great tragedy, as directed and filmed by Sir Tyrone Guthrie; performed in masks, as in original Greece; a play and film which retain the primal emotional power of the original.
VHS: S00947. $59.95.
Tyrone Guthrie, Canada, 1956, 90 mins.

Oh Calcutta!

Video taped telecast of the long-running theatrical revue spoofing modern ideas of sex and sensuality, famous primarily for its nudity.
VHS: S02556. $29.95.
G.M. Aucion, USA, 1980, 120 mins.

Oleanna

David Mamet adapted his own provocative and acclaimed stage play that brilliantly explores the issues of sexual harassment. William H. Macy stars as the college professor who is forced to confront the moral and political implications of power, blackmail and revenge on a contemporary college campus when he is accused of sexual harassment.
VHS: S24825. $19.98.
Laser: LD74958. $39.99.
David Mamet, USA, 1994, 90 mins.

On Borrowed Time

A witty adaptation of Lawrence Edward Watkin's dark fable about death. A middle-aged man is trapped in a tree built by his father and son. The cast includes Lionel Barrymore, Cedric Hardwicke and Una Merkel.
VHS: S17660. $19.98.
Harold S. Bucquet, USA, 1939, 99 mins.

Othello

A remarkably successful silent transposition of Shakespeare's great play, featuring great performances from some of German Expressionism's best actors: Emil Jannings, Werner Kraus, Lya de Putti. Moody, elaborate costumes and sets and first-class acting. Silent with English subtitles.
VHS: S00978. $29.95.
Dimitri Buchowetzki, Germany, 1922, 81 mins.

Our Town (1940)

Thornton Wilder's classic American play about life, marriage and death in a small town is transposed to film with William Holden as the boy-next-door George Gibbs, while Oscar nominee Martha Scott and Frank Craven re-create their original Broadway cast roles.
VHS: S00980. $19.95.
Sam Wood, USA, 1940, 89 mins.

Our Town (1977)

Thornton Wilder's Pulitzer prize- and Emmy Award-winning play is brought to the screen by Hal Holbrook, Barbara Bel Geddes, John Houseman, Robby Benson, Ronny Cox and Sada Thompson. Here is the full poignant portrayal of love, life and death in a small American town that has brought pleasure to millions.
VHS: S05624. $74.95.
Franklin J. Schnaffner, USA, 1977, 120 mins.

Our Town (1988)

Thornton Wilder's classic play about life in a small town brings Yankee simplicity to new depths. In this version Eric Stoltz, Penelope Ann Miller, Peter Maloney, Roberta Maxwell, Frances Conroy, James Reborn and Spalding Gray, the noted monologist, portray the rural characters that epitomize the best of rural America. Produced at Lincoln Center for PBS's Great Performances series.
VHS: S24020. $74.95.
Gregory Mosher, USA, 1988

Paradise Now

Shot during the last presentation of *Paradise Now* by The Living Theatre in Brussels, and before 7,000 spectators in Berlin, made on videotape with expressionism coloring, a unique record of this famous play by The Living Theatre, capturing the frenzy of the original.
VHS: S00991. $29.95.
Sheldon Rochlin, USA, 1970, 95 mins.

Paul Robeson

James Earl Jones delivers a powerful performance as Paul Robeson, the legendary actor, singer, and early champion of human rights, a man of peace, whose career was destroyed by the zealots of the Cold War. "Americans need to see this, not because an actor rises to superlative heights…which Jones does, but because it reintroduces Paul Robeson to the American public."
VHS: S06092. $39.95.
Lloyd Richards, USA, 1980, 118 mins.

The Piano Lesson

Charles Dutton and Alfre Woodard star in this film adaptation of August Wilson's Pulitzer Prize-winning play. A brother and sister fight over differing visions of their future. If they sell a piano they could buy a farm, but this piano represents more than money. It is a link to a vibrant tradition. With Courtney Vance, Carl Gordon, Tommy Hollis and Zelda Harris.
VHS: S26143. $14.98.
Lloyd Richards, USA, 1995, 99 mins.

Playhouse 90: Requiem for a Heavyweight

Famous live television drama version of the classic Clifford Odets play with Jack Palance, Ed and Keenan Wynn in feature roles.
VHS: S09547. $19.95.

Playwrights '56

Paul Newman stars in this early television adaptation of Ernest Hemingway's story *The Butler*.
VHS: S10596. $29.95.

Private Conversations/ On the Set of Death of a Salesman

A first-rate documentary produced with PBS that views the collaborative involvement in the highly-praised CBS theatrical play, *Death of a Salesman*, starring Dustin Hoffman and John Malkovich. The film features interviews with playwright Arthur Miller, director Volker Schlondorff and Malkovich that buttress its cinema verite authenticity—a deep focus view on the celebration of the theatre's naturalism.
VHS: S02262. $19.95.
Christian Blackwood, USA, 1986, 82 mins.

Private Lives

A witty adaptation of Noel Coward's play about a high-society, rancorous couple who can neither stay apart nor together, beautifully acted by Norma Shearer, Robert Montgomery and Una Merkel.
VHS: S17662. $19.98.
Laser: LD72337. $34.98.
Sidney Franklin, USA, 1931, 84 mins.

Richard III

Laurence Olivier's third Shakespeare adaptation moves away from the brooding, austere settings of the early works to a delirious Technicolor treatment of the ruthless tyrant who seizes his throne and wages war at Bosworth. With Olivier, Claire Bloom, Ralph Richardson, John Gielgud and Stanley Baker. Remastered. Letterboxed.
VHS: S01680. $24.95.
Laser: LD72285. $99.95.
Laurence Olivier, Great Britain, 1956, 161 mins.

Rime of the Ancient Mariner

Coleridge's epic poem is brought to life in a recital featuring Sir Michael Redgrave, accompanied by images both real and animated. 60 mins.
VHS: S03158. $59.95.

Robbie Burkett: A Line of Balance
A look at the remarkable career of puppeteer Robbie Burkett as he prepares his production of the Gothic musical thriller *Awful Manors*. A behind-the-scenes look at a man who manipulates over 40 marionettes, speaks and sings in 22 different voices, operates special effects all in one spectacular production and still keeps his strings attached.
VHS: S21958. $24.95.
Margaret Mardirossian, Canada, 1992, 58 mins.

Romeo and Juliet (Laurence Harvey)
Laurence Harvey stars in this commanding interpretation of Shakespeare's great tale of star-crossed lovers. Stunningly photographed on location in Italy, Renato Castellani's version stars Susan Shentall and Flora Robson, and the transitions are narrated by Sir John Gielgud.
VHS: S12346. $29.98.
Renato Castellani, Great Britain, 1964, 135 mins.

Romeo and Juliet (Neame/Hasson)
Christopher Neame and Ann Hasson star as the ill-fated lovers in this British production of the classic play. A fresh and inspirational slant. Produced by Thames TV. 180 mins.
Laser: LD72153. $39.98.

Romeo and Juliet (Zeffirelli)
One of the most popular film adaptations of Shakespeare's classic, the recipient of international acclaim and four Academy Award nominations. Starring Olivia Hussey, Leonard Whiting and Michael York, this modern version brings new vitality and fresh insight to the world's most durable love story. English dialog.
VHS: S01130. $24.95.
Franco Zeffirelli, USA/Italy, 1968, 138 mins.

The Rose Tattoo
A happy-go-lucky trucker awakens a widow to life's joys in this flavorful adaptation of a Tennessee Williams play. Starring Burt Lancaster and the brilliant Anna Magnani. Photographed by James Wong Howe.
VHS: S13787. $19.95.
Daniel Mann, USA, 1955, 117 mins.

School for Scandal
A live television adaptation of the classic satire of the morals and manners of 18th century England by Richard Sheridan. Featuring Joan Plowright as Lady Oliver and Felix Aylmer.
England, 1965, 100 mins.
VHS: S01168. $29.95.

Shakespeare by the English Theater Company
Richard II, Henry IV parts 1 and 2 and *Henry the V* follow the story of two powerful dynasties. In this video collection the legendary conflicts of Agincourt and Tewkesbury are rendered into living history.
VHS: S24890. $129.95.

Shakespeare: The Animated Tales
A series of fully-animated, close-captioned videos, each of which abridges one of the Shakespeare plays to 30 minutes. For ages 10 and up.
A Midsummer Night's Dream.
VHS: S21932. $14.95.
Hamlet.
VHS: S21930. $14.95.
Macbeth.
VHS: S21931. $14.95.
Romeo and Juliet.
VHS: S21933. $14.95.
The Tempest.
VHS: S21934. $14.95.
The Twelfth Night.
VHS: S21935. $14.95.

Signals Through the Flames
The Odyssey of the Living Theatre, the courageous, audacious American theatre company which for 35 years occupied the stages and jails of the world. The film gives a unique sense of a company that, said *Newsweek*, "produced more guts, passion and controversy than any other."
VHS: S01199. $29.95.
Sheldon Rochlin, USA, 1983, 97 mins.

Strange Interlude (1932)
A polished adaptation of Eugene O'Neill's Pulitzer prize-winning play about a brilliant young woman's affair with her husband's best friend. With Clark Gable, Norma Shearer and Maureen O'Sullivan.
VHS: S17663. $19.98.
Robert Z. Leonard, USA, 1932, 110 mins.

Strange Interlude (1988)
Eugene O'Neill's play in a production featuring a brilliant cast including Glenda Jackson, David Dukes and Ken Howard. Based on the Broadway production which *The New York Times* called 'theatre and its most powerful...for those interested in serious theatre it is required watching."
VHS: S07348. $29.95.
Philip Barry, USA, 1988, 190 mins.

A Streetcar Named Desire (1951/Director's Cut)
Tennessee Williams' notorious play was censored when adapted for the screen. Now four minutes of the originally cut material have been found and restored to this "director's cut". Marlon Brando, Kim Hunter and Vivien Leigh star in this drama of betrayal, madness and rape.
VHS: S21085. $19.98.
Laser: LD70687. $39.98.
Elia Kazan, USA, 1951, 125 mins.

A Streetcar Named Desire (1984)
A made-for-television adaptation of Tennessee Williams' play about Blanche du Bois (Ann-Margret), the fading descendant of the once prominent Southern aristocracy, who gets entangled in the lives of her sister (Beverly D'Angelo) and her brutal husband, Stanley Kowalski (Treat Williams). With Randy Quaid, Rafael Campos and Erica Yohn.
VHS: S19684. $9.98.
John Erman, USA, 1984, 94 mins.

A Streetcar Named Desire (1995)
Jessica Lange is Blanche DuBois to Alec Baldwin's Stanley Kowalski in this uncut film version of Tennessee Williams' immortal play. Lange won a Golden Globe for her portrayal of the delicate and mad woman who relies "on the kindness of strangers." John Goodman and Diane Lane also star.
VHS: S27744. $79.99.
Glenn Jordan, USA, 1995, 156 mins.

Strindberg's Miss Julie: Royal Shakespeare Company
August Strindberg, "...one of the prime innovators of our time...the impact of his dramatic method reflected in his Miss Julie is probably greater and less acknowledged than any other modern writer. Strindberg struck strongly into O'Neill, Becket and Tennessee Williams...entering the subconscious where sexual encounter has a fight to the death..." (Arthur Miller, N.Y. Times).
VHS: S02006. $79.95.

Summer and Smoke
This vivid adaptation of a Tennessee Williams play tells the story of a spinster who is tortured by her unrequited love for the town's handsome young doctor. Good performances from Geraldine Page, Laurence Harvey, and Rita Moreno. Musical score by Elmer Bernstein.
VHS: S13786. $19.95.
Laser: Widescreen. LD75267. $34.98.
Peter Glenville, USA, 1961, 118 mins.

The Taming of the Shrew (Esquire 4+4)
Shakespeare's story of two sisters, Katherina and Bianca, and their suitors. Starring Franklin Seales and Karen Austin. 117 mins. Two videocassettes.
VHS: S15189. $59.95.

The Taming of the Shrew (Westinghouse Studio)
Seen on live television, and part of the Westinghouse Studio television program. Charlton Heston and Lisa Kirk star in this 1950 modern dress version with Heston wearing sunglasses and downing beer with the boys while Lisa Kirk appears in tight slacks and with a riding whip. Broadcast June 5, 1950. USA, 1950, 60 mins.
VHS: S06987. $24.95.

The Taming of the Shrew (Zeffirelli)
An exquisite mounting of Shakespeare's comic look at male-female relationships stars Richard Burton as Petruchio, the wily gentleman from Verona who travels to Padua to wed Elizabeth Taylor as the fiery Katharina.
VHS: S01681. $19.95.
Franco Zeffirelli, US/Italy, 1967, 127 mins.

Tea and Sympathy
Deborah Kerr, John Kerr and Leif Erickson recreate their Broadway roles in this glossy Vincente Minnelli adaptation of the Robert Anderson play. A sensitive prep school student finds his extracurricular activity with a teacher's wife quite educational. With Edward Andrews, Dean Jones and Darryl Hickman.
VHS: S13190. $19.98.
Vincente Minnelli, USA, 1956, 122 mins.

The Tempest
Shakespeare's classic tale of the fantasy world of spirits, sorcery, monsters, and shipwrecked scheming noblemen is brought to life in a stunning production featuring Efrem Zimbalist Jr., William H. Bassett, Ted Sorel.
VHS: S04203. $59.95.
William Woodman, 127 mins.

That Championship Season
Jason Miller's play, first performed by the New York Shakespeare Festival, takes place at the 24th reunion of the Scranton High School basketball team. Featuring Robert Mitchum, Bruce Dern, Martin Sheen, Stacy Keach and Paul Sorvino.
VHS: S02367. $79.95.
Jason Miller, USA, 1982, 108 mins.

The Theatre of Tadeusz Kantor
A unique documentary on the work of a legendary genius of theatre, Tadeusz Kantor. Filmmaker Denis Bablet traces Kantor's roots as a visual artist in Poland and explores his ingenious methods of designing the props which become living sculptures in his extraordinary theatre productions. The program features rare scenes of Kantor at work with the dedicated actors in his troupe, Cricot 2. In a unique scene, Kantor is on-stage and "conducts" the actors much as a symphony conductor leads an orchestra. Extensive segments from some of Kantor's most famous works, *Wielopole, Wielopole* and *The Dead Class*, are also included. Narrated in English. 144 mins.
VHS: S14812. $59.95.

Theatre of the Iron Curtain
This film provides a behind-the-scenes look at legitimate theatre in the Soviet Union, and gives a concise history to the art. The camera goes inside theatre schools where actors, directors and producers are trained for a life in the theatre. 55 mins.
VHS: S12723. $19.98.

The Three Sisters
Shelley Winters, Sandy Dennis, Geraldine Page, and Kevin McCarthy star in this famed Actor's Studio production of the equally famous Chekhov play.
VHS: S14677. $19.95.
Paul Bogart, USA, 1965, 150 mins.

Torch Song Trilogy
Harvey Fierstein adapted his Broadway hit play about the trials and tribulations of being a sexually active gay urban male in the 1970's for the big screen. He repeats the role of Arnold Beckoff, a drag artiste looking for love. He finds it with Brian Kerwin and Matthew Broderick. Anne Bancroft is Arnold's very Jewish mother and a prime cause of Arnold's frustrated anger.
VHS: S09390. $19.95.
Paul Bogart, USA, 1988, 126 mins.

Toys in the Attic
George Roy Hill's fluent adaptation of Lillian Hellman's Southern gothic play about a repressed young man's return to his New Orleans home town with a child-like wife. Geraldine Page and Wendy Hiller contribute two horrifying performances as the man's overprotective sisters. With Dean Martin and Yvette Mimieux.
VHS: S17665. $19.98.
George Roy Hill, USA, 1963, 90 mins.

Tragedy of Antony and Cleopatra
Shakespeare's most popular tale of two of history's most famous personages. Starring Lynn Redgrave, John Carradine, Timothy Dalton and Anthony Geary.
VHS: S02373. $59.95.
Laser: LD71375. $69.95.
Lawrence Carra, 183 mins.

The Tragedy of King Lear (Esquire 4+4)
Shakespeare's tragedy about an aging king who has chosen to lay aside the care of his kingship and divide his kingdom among his three daughters. Starring Mike Kellen and Darryl Hickman. 182 mins. Two videocassettes.
VHS: S15188. $59.95.
Laser: LD71376. $69.95.

Tragedy of King Richard II
Shakespeare's drama of the self-centered, weak kind. Starring David Birney, Paul Shenar, John Devlin and William Bassett.
VHS: S03011. $59.95.
William Woodman, 172 mins.

Tragedy of Macbeth
Shakespeare's story of murder, greed and untimely death. Starring Jeremy Brett, Piper Laurie, Simon MacCorkindale and Barry Primus.
VHS: S02222. $59.95.
Arthur Allan Seidelman, 151 mins.

Tragedy of Othello the Moor of Venice
Shakespeare's keen understanding of jealousy in love results in perhaps his greatest triumph as a stage play, and his prime example of the tragic hero, Othello. With William Marshall, Ron Moody and Jenny Agutter. With meticulously constructed costumes and an artist's reproduction of the Globe Theater stage. 159 mins.
VHS: S02987. $59.95.

The Tragedy of Romeo and Juliet
Shakespeare's play of star-crossed young love, feuding families and death. Starring Alex Hyde-White and Blanche Baker. 165 mins. Two videocassettes.
VHS: S15186. $59.95.
Laser: LD71377. $69.95.

Two for the Seesaw
Robert Wise's eccentric comedy about the off-beat romantic flourishes and consequences of an unlikely romance between lawyer Robert Mitchum and free spirit Shirley MacLaine. With Edmund Ryan and Elisabeth Fraser.
VHS: S17666. $19.98.
Laser: LD72157. $39.98.
Robert Wise, USA, 1962, 120 mins.

Uncovering Shakespeare: An Update
William F. Buckley, Jr. moderates this panel discussion featuring a wide range of experts who examine the centuries-old question about Shakespeare's authorship. This documentary was awarded the CINE Golden Eagle Award. 161 mins.
VHS: S21927. $149.95.

Vaudeville Videos
Comics, jugglers, animal acts, skaters, famous names and forgotten names, in a nostalgic look at entertainment from the early years of the century. Includes Weber and Fields, George and Gracie, Jack Smith, Smith and Dale. 60 mins.
VHS: S08013. $29.95.

Vincent
On July 29, 1890, Vincent Van Gogh died in his brother Theo's arms. Devastated, Theo was unable to speak at his brother's funeral. One week later, Theo invited an audience of artists and friends to a Paris lecture hall. In this acclaimed one-man drama presented at the Guthrie Theater, Leonard Nimoy portrays the stricken Theo as he finds the words to honor his late brother's memory.
VHS: S16577. $59.95.
Leonard Nimoy/Bonnie Burns, USA, 1981, 88 mins.

Walls in the City
Paula Killen stars in this independent video directed by Jim Sikora and featuring Tony Fitzpatrick, David Yow, Bill Cusak and original music by the Denison-Kimble Trio.
VHS: S21207. $19.98.

The Water Engine
David Mamet wrote this strange exercise about the deceptions of success. Charles Lang (William H. Macy) is a factory worker who invents an engine that runs on water. He expects this device will save him and his sister (Patti Lupone) from poverty. But Lang never understood that betrayal is just another game in the world of business.
VHS: S24733. $49.98.
Steven Schachter, USA, 1995, 89 mins.

William Shakespeare Series
These five 45-minute lectures explore key issues in the works of this great author, including his comedies, tragedies and historical dramas.
Death in Victory: Shakespeare's Tragic Reconciliations. Fresden Bowers.
VHS: S24115. $230.00.
Feuding and Loving in Shakespeare's Romeo and Juliet. George Walton Williams.
VHS: S24116. $230.00.
Hamlet as Minister and Scourge. Fredson Bowers.
VHS: S24117. $230.00.
The Staging of Shakespeare's Plays. George Walton Williams.
VHS: S24118. $230.00.
The Why and How of Poisoning in Shakespeare's Othello. George Walton Williams.
VHS: S24119. $230.00.

Winterset
Burgess Meredith, Eduardo Ciannelli and John Carradine star in this adaptation of a play by Maxwell Anderson, based on the trial of Sacco and Vanzetti. 1936.
VHS: S08424. $29.95.

PERFORMING ARTS INSTRUCTION

The 16mm Camera
The complete overview of the 12 major 16mm camera systems, including detailed examinations of viewing systems, motor types, running speeds, magazine types, camera loading technique, turret types, lenses and lens mounts, camera noise and baffling, claw mechanisms, metering systems, and more. Two-tape set, 195 mins.
VHS: S22754. $299.00.

Acting in Film
A highly revealing and important video series on the technique craft and skill of acting and the differences and allowances that must be considered in film. "I'm not going to look at a movie the same way again....It will probably change the way you look at whatever movie you rented..." (Roger Ebert). 60 mins.
VHS: S18324. $49.95.

Advanced Television Lighting: A Seminar with Bill Millar, BBC-TV
The unedited classroom lectures of Bill Millar, full of invaluable information for students of television lighting.
Introduction to Drama. Preplanning, special lighting problems, extreme low light situations, lighting for a desert scene, and lighting for a moonlight scene are all discussed. 35 mins.
VHS: S22770. $149.00.
A Question of Quality. An examination of the lighting techniques used in several BBC productions, including the creation of a sunset and lighting to mimic the lighting of Rembrandt and Vermeer. 45 mins.
VHS: S22771. $149.00.
Complete Set. The two-volume series.
VHS: S22769. $249.00.

Advanced Voice Workout for the Actor
Voice expert Susan Leigh focuses on the mechanics of breathing and vocal projection for the theater, leading the viewer through a series of simple stretching, yoga and rib awareness exercises in this sequel to *Voice Workout for the Actor*. 40 mins.
VHS: S22843. $99.00.

Animation Games
Award-winning video exploring alternatives to the traditional method of photographing painted, registered cels. Composed of four sections, the first details an overview of animation techniques, followed by segments on puppet, cutout and pixilation animation. 51 mins.
VHS: S22864. $149.00.

The Art of Radio Advertising
An approach to concept development, copywriting, and directing radio ads by two of the medium's most successful producers. Humor and team work are emphasized. 20 mins.
VHS: S22814. $119.00.

Auditioning for the Actor
How to evaluate your own strengths as an actor and how to select material that supports these strengths, pre-audition skills and strategies, performance critiques and more. 46 mins.
VHS: S22839. $119.00.

The Basic Costumer
An introduction to costume research, taking measurements, costume acquisition and maintenance, and approaches to pattern making. Includes a teacher's guide. 73 mins.
VHS: S22852. $119.00.

Basic Field Production: Lighting
An introduction to effective lighting choices for a basic interview shoot, including balancing mixed light sources, setting exposure, monitoring, and more. 24 mins.
VHS: S22751. $149.00.

Basic Field Production: Sound Recording
A step-by-step demonstration of the necessary planning, equipment selection, mixing strategies, test recording and session procedure for an interview shoot. 32 mins.
VHS: S22730. $149.00.

Basic Radio Skills Series
A comprehensive introduction to both the technical and creative aspects of the radio environment.
Basic Radio Skills: Announcing and Presentation. A typical radio day with six announcers on talk, news and music shows providing insights into their formats and their own personal approaches to their shows. 28 mins.
VHS: S22821. $149.00.
Basic Radio Skills: Editing. A presentation of the two audiotape editing techniques: splice editing and dub editing. Examples of voice edits and music dubbing are included. 16 mins.
VHS: S22820. $119.00.
Basic Radio Skills: Radio News. An in-depth view of radio news at work. Topics include news sources, item selection and scripting, preparation for broadcast and much more. 38 mins.
VHS: S22818. $149.00.
Basic Radio Skills: Radio Talkback. Styles and approaches for the live call-in show. A special instructional segment deals with phone operation, delay systems and call dumping. 35 mins.
VHS: S22819. $149.00.
Basic Radio Skills: Radio Writing. Writing for news and current affairs, commercial copywriting and radio comedy writing are covered in detail. Specialists in each area offer their insights. 47 mins.
VHS: S22822. $149.00.
Basic Radio Skills: The Radio Interview. Basic technical skills of the audio interview are covered, emphasizing content, interaction, preparation of the interviewee. By acting out problem situations (often to humorous results) the viewer learns first hand how to handle effective strategies for dealing with them. 20 mins.
VHS: S22823. $149.00.

Basic Radio Skills: The Radio Studio. Introduction to the hardware of the radio studio: the console, microphones, telephone talkback, turntables and CDs, cart players, etc. Cueing, labeling, cleaning and machine care are emphasized. 31 mins.
VHS: $22817. $149.00.
Complete Set. The seven-volume series. 215 mins.
VHS: $22816. $695.00.

Basic Shooting
This video takes the viewer through all the steps needed in order to produce a videotape. From shopping for a camcorder through all the basics, everything is here, including lighting, microphones, lenses and composition. 47 mins.
VHS: $23951. $14.95.

The Being on TV Preview
Watch the highlights of Gwenn Kelly's *Being on TV: The Crash Course* at a minimal cost to help decide if her program is right for you. 7 mins.
VHS: $22804. $10.00.

Being on TV: The Crash Course
Gwenn Kelly teaches what to expect when you go on TV, how to handle yourself in front of the camera, and how to dress and shape your message for a television audience. 30 mins.
VHS: $22803. $249.00.

Blocking a Scene: Basic Staging with Actors
The basic steps in blocking a scene, from script analysis to dividing the scene into working units to developing a floor plan. Includes an exercise from the play *Candida*. 70 mins.
VHS: $22847. $149.00.

Chroma Key Techniques
An introduction to a wide range of chroma key techniques, including interiors, exteriors, and such refinements as casting shadows and reflections onto chroma keyed backgrounds. 30 mins.
VHS: $22739. $149.00.

Combat for the Stage
There is much more to realistic sword and fist fighting than meets the eye. This exciting and safely illustrated lesson provides all the skills needed to understand sword, fist and firearm combat techniques, as well as choreography for stage falls. 96 mins.
VHS: $15920. $59.95.

Combat for the Stage and Screen
David Boushey, founder of the Society of American Fight Directors and the United Stuntmen's Association, presents a three-part guide to producing a dramatically effective fight scene.
Elizabethan Weaponry. Techniques for the rapier, dagger and rapier, courtsword and single dagger, including slow motion analysis of selected fight sequences. 90 mins.
VHS: $22857. $275.00.
Medieval Weaponry. Moves and safe techniques for broadsword, sword and shield, and quarterstaff fighting, including an orientation to the military technology and technique of the period. 90 mins.
VHS: $22856. $275.00.
Unarmed Combat. Techniques for punching, slapping, hair pulling, kneeing, kicking, gouging and head-bashing are all included in this lively and informative tape. 90 mins.
VHS: $22855. $275.00.
Complete Set. The three-tape set. 270 mins.
VHS: $22854. $700.00.

The Complete Camera Clinic
A complete guide to proper adjustment of all of the internal controls of modern three chip or tube video cameras. Included is a 30-page manual and guide. 60 mins.
VHS: $22756. $179.00.

Creative Drama and Improvisation
Rives Collins leads students through theater games and improvisational exercises, giving them invaluable tools for warm-up, rehearsal, self-exploration and character development. 110 mins.
VHS: $22848. $119.00.

A Creative Partnership: The Actor and Director
A guide through the development of the actor/director relationship in the feature film process, from the auditions and screen tests through the rehearsal process and the shoot. 37 mins.
VHS: $22837. $149.00.

Creative Video Techniques
Harry Mathias, author of *Electronic Cinematography*, give an overview of commercial and feature film technique.
The Art of Using Filters. How to select the right filter to create a mood, the use of polarizers, grads, contrast control filters, color filters, and more. 46 mins.
VHS: $22743. $149.00.
Controlling the Image. Alternatives for determining correct exposure, high key, low key and backlighting tips, the value of waveform monitors, and more. 40 mins.
VHS: $22742. $149.00.
Complete Set. The two-volume set.
VHS: $22741. $249.00.

Design—An Introduction
An introduction to scene and prop design and costume and makeup selection for film and video. 18 mins.
VHS: $22731. $119.00.

Designing and Building Your Desktop Video System
A guide to the many options available through desktop video, including selection of a computer platform, peripherals, software, graphics, paint, animation, special effects, video format, video post-production equipment, system configuration, and design. 45 mins.
VHS: $22789. $149.00.

The Directing Process
If you are planning to direct your first play, or wish to expand what you already know, this video supplies all the organizational tools. An all-encompassing overview that furnishes methods from analyzing the script, selecting a successful production and arranging auditions, to staging the action, coordinating designers and directing rehearsals.
VHS: $15918. $59.95.

The Dub
A program covering the breakdown of location sounds, dialogue replacement, track building, the preparation of tracks for a mixing session, and the actual mix itself. 18 mins.
VHS: $22784. $119.00.

An Editing Exercise
An introduction to film and video editing that uses shots from a sequence of a historical drama as its example. Included are a complete shot list and marked script. 15 mins.
VHS: $22786. $149.00.

Editing Techniques: Reducing Time
An introduction to basic time reduction techniques for shooting and editing, including camera movement, jump cuts, exits and entrances, cut-ins, cutaways, parallel action, and visual effects. 10 mins.
VHS: $22785. $149.00.

The Essentials—4000 Series
In-depth instruction in the use of the Toaster 4000 and Toaster System 3.0 from Lee Stranahan, "the world's smartest Toaster Guy".
Toaster CG Essentials. A look at the Toaster CG's text capabilities, including font sizing, color brush loading, and layer options.
VHS: $22794. $59.95.
Video Toaster Essentials. A guide through the Toaster's switcher, digital video effects, set-up functions, chroma FX and luminance keyer. 90 mins.
VHS: $22793. $59.95.

Feature Film Lighting
In a program designed for professionals and students alike, professional D.P. Russell Boyd discusses lighting in technical terms and touches on many common lighting problems, such as lighting for rain and the use of nets. 56 mins.
VHS: $22757. $149.00.

Film Graphics
A classic of film analysis, this tape demonstrates the structural principles inherent in all art forms and features an in-depth, shot-by-shot analysis of a sequence from Sergei Eisenstein's *Potemkin*. 15 mins.
VHS: $22729. $119.00.

Firearm Safety Onstage
This video dispels the myth that just because you're not using live ammunition, you're safe. A must for all administrators, directors, stage managers, actors and students. 45 mins.
VHS: $22851. $119.00.

Fundamentals of Scenic Painting
A look at the basic components of paint, the characteristics and uses of various media, and a wide range of tools and application techniques. Includes five elevations with overlay grids for student projects as well as an eight-page manual and guide. 81 mins.
VHS: $22860. $249.00.

Great Screenwriting
John Truby (Truby's Writers Studio) provides a four-hour video workshop for would-be writers, covering how to make scripts more powerful and commercially viable. Charting, shaping a script and analyzing story structure are demonstrated through examples by legendary screenwriters. 480 mins.
VHS: $22835. $295.00.

The Hold Up: An Editing Exercise
Roger Ebert guides students through the editing process of a bank robbery scene, from the rushes through the fine cut, and demonstrates how different approaches to editing can result in entirely different films. 20 mins.
VHS: $22781. $119.00.

Hollywood Directors and Their Craft
Top male directors John Badham, Clint Eastwood, John Flynn, Delbert Mann, Michael Schultz, Abraham Polonsky and Robert Wise examine their craft and analyze their working methods. 80 mins.
VHS: $22838. $149.00.

How to Use a C-Stand
A quick guide to the proper use of Century Stands, or "C-Stands" as they're called in the industry. 6 mins.
VHS: $22752. $89.00.

Interview Techniques
The development of an interview is developed, from putting the subject at ease to obtaining all the information you need. Also included is the approach for a current affairs interview. 25 mins.
VHS: $22811. $149.00.

Introduction to Floor Managing
An overview of the duties of the floor manager in a multi-camera studio, including the role of the floor manager in establishing mood, cueing, time signals, and more. 25 mins.
VHS: $22737. $149.00.

An Introduction to Puppet Making
Learn the art of puppet making with award winning puppeteer Jim Gamble. Using common household items, Gamble shows how to make an imaginative array of finger, foot, book and rod puppets. He also demonstrates how to create an elaborate marionette puppet. 30 mins.
VHS: $16756. $19.95.

Introduction to Television Lighting
Bob Forster demonstrates how to model three dimensional objects with light, how to create day and evening lighting, color correction alternatives, and more. 20 mins.
VHS: $22753. $149.00.

Kodak Cinematography Master Class Series
Five of the world's finest cinematographers share lighting tips and techniques in a workshop setting.
Lighting Dances with Wolves with Dean Semler. A demonstration of the techniques that won Dean Semler an Academy Award for the cinematography of *Dances with Wolves*. 29 mins.
VHS: $22773. $89.95.
Lighting Dead Poets Society with John Seale. John Seale guides students through the lighting setups he used to create the feel of different times and seasons in *Dead Poets Society*. 28 mins.
VHS: $22774. $89.95.
Location Lighting with Geoff Burton. Geoff Burton emphasizes making the most of natural lighting, and using tungsten lights to imitate nature. 29 mins.
VHS: $22775. $89.95.
Studio Lighting: A Comparative Workshop with Donald McAlpine and Denis Lenoir. Donald McAlpine and Denis Lenoir go back-to-back to show how creative differences in lighting style can change the feel of a scene. 59 mins.
VHS: $22776. $89.95.
Complete Set. The complete 4-program series.
VHS: $22772. $299.00.

Lessons in Visual Language
Peter Thompson narrates this ten-volume series dealing with the language of moving images.
Editing. A lesson in the creative ways in which editing can be used to reconstruct or rearrange spaces and events. 10 mins.
VHS: $22725. $99.00.
Framing. Tips on how the framing of the screen can convey emotion, define relationships, tell a story, and allude to off-screen surroundings. 10 mins.
VHS: $22718. $99.00.
Image and Screen. A discussion of luminosity, definition, grain, and other sensory qualities of the filmed image. 14 mins.
VHS: $22720. $99.00.
Lenses and Perspective. A lesson in how the position of the viewer of the camera is the central factor in the perception of spacial relationships. 9 mins.
VHS: $22722. $99.00.
Movement and Moving the Camera. A discussion of how camera movement should accommodate (but not duplicate) the natural way the human eye moves as it interacts with visual scenes. 11 mins.
VHS: $22723. $99.00.
Music. A look at the evocative and emotive power of music in film, as well as the structure and purpose of the musical score. 16 mins.
VHS: $22727. $99.00.
Orientation of the Camera. How to use the moving image to either orient the viewer to a space or to deliberately disturb and challenge the viewer's senses. 11 mins.
VHS: $22724. $99.00.
Rhythm. A look at natural and mechanical rhythms and how a sense of rhythm can be achieved through editing. 10 mins.
VHS: $22726. $99.00.
Shot Sizes and Framing Faults. This tape defines the basic types of shots and offers suggestions on how to build a sequence using different types of shots. In addition, common framing errors and their psychological impacts are discussed. 9 mins.
VHS: $22719. $99.00.
The Third Dimension. How to use visual cues to define spacial relationships, construct three-dimensional space, and fool the eye, including a number of startling optical illusions. 7 mins.
VHS: $22721. $99.00.
Complete Set. The complete ten-volume set.
VHS: $22728. $795.00.

Lighting in the Real World
An introduction to how lighting gels and diffusion can solve common lighting problems as demonstrated with several carefully produced sample lighting exercises. 65 mins.
VHS: $22755. $119.00.

LightWave 3D—4000 Series
In-depth instruction in the use of LightWave 3D for animation work. Four tapes.
LightWave 3D Camera & Lighting Techniques. Learn about camera and lighting tips, camera motion paths, animating lights, motion envelopes, lens flare tips, and more. 120 mins.
VHS: $22796. $59.95.
LightWave 3D Displacement Mapping, Morphing & Bones. A guide to using LightWave to twist, bend, deform and animate objects in layout. 100 mins.
VHS: $22797. $59.95.
LightWave 3D Essentials. Learn how to create animations, designs and screens and do key framing using LightWave 3D. 120 mins.
VHS: $22795. $59.95.
LightWave 3D Surfaces & Textures. An exploration of LightWave 3D's surface and texture techniques and how to increase your speed by selecting the proper surfaces for your objects. 115 mins.
VHS: $22798. $59.95.
Complete Set. The four-program series.
VHS: $22800. $179.95.

Location Sound Recording
An introduction to various microphone types and pickup patterns, mic selection and operating technique, the special problems of lavaliere mics, and more. 37 mins.
VHS: $22732. $149.00.

Make-Up for Theatre with Ellen Dennis
Taught by Ellen Dennis, professor of Make-Up and Costume Design at Southern Oregon State College; emphasis on how light and shadow work on the facial structure, use of hairpieces, wigs, period make-up, old-age, hair pieces, and fantasy make-up. 2 complete tapes.
Make-Up for Theatre, Part 1. 60 mins.
VHS: $12862. $39.95.
Make-Up for Theatre, Part 2. 60 mins.
VHS: $12863. $39.95.

The Make-Up Workshop
Learn to age an actor's face 40 years, build mustaches and beards, or change facial features entirely. With some practice and a little creativity, this step-by-step instruction on make-up design and application can turn anyone into an expert make-up artist. 104 min.
VHS: $15921. $59.95.

Making a Video Program
A comprehensive overview of the process involved in video production, from scriptwriting to shooting to editing and titling. 49 mins.
VHS: $22734. $149.00.

Making Grimm Movies
In this series of three tapes, the secrets of motion pictures are clearly demonstrated using outtakes from *The Brothers Grimm*. It shows how you can make your own movies using limited resources available locally. Each tape is 20 minutes long and the set comes with the book *The Guide to Making Grimm Movies*.
Part 1: Scriptwriting, Casting, Makeup. In this first tape viewers learn how to write a script and plan their shoot, as well as how to cast actors and dress them appropriately.
VHS: $21215. $19.95.
Part 2: Locations, Set Design, Sound. Scouting locations and making sets are key to filmmaking. Storyboards are one tool that can help achieve the desired look. Sound is another important technical consideration covered in this part.
VHS: $21216. $19.95.
Part 3: Cinematography, Editing, Acting. Cinematography and editing are demystified in this final tape in the set. Directing and acting, originally theatrical techniques, are very different in filmmaking and are fully explained.
VHS: $21217. $19.95.
Complete Set with Study Guide.
VHS: $21218. $49.95.

Mime over Matter
This complete course in Mime offers the knowledge to unravel the mysteries of one of the world's oldest art forms. Entertain your friends and family in no time following the carefully demonstrated instructions. 101 mins.
VHS: $15922. $59.95.

Movement for the Actor
Northwestern University professor Dawn Maura and her students lead you through a series of movement exercises, including stretching, warmups, and dynamic activity keyed to emotion and memory. 20 mins.
VHS: $22844. $119.00.

Multicamera Direction Planning
The planning and production of a multi-camera video shoot, including read-throughs, design, rehearsals, camera planning, camera scripting, technical run-through, and shooting. 30 mins.
VHS: $22738. $149.00.

Multimedia in Education
New uses for multimedia in fields ranging from business to engineering to psychology to interior design, exploring new ways of teaching and learning. 30 mins.
VHS: $22792. $149.00.

Music for Film
A guide to film music production procedures, including timing, synchronization, and click tracks. Hosted by British composer Ron Goodwin. 55 mins.
VHS: $22787. $149.00.

The New Digital Imaging
An examination of new photographic technologies, including computer manipulation of digital images, digital still cameras, use of scanners, new printing systems, and disc-based storage of photographic images. 20 mins.
VHS: $22788. $149.00.

Off-Line Editing
This two-part series offers a thorough introduction to the strategies and techniques for off-line editing.
Off-Line Editing: An Introduction. An introduction to both linear and non-linear editing, control track, time code, blacking, window dubbing, logging, both assembly and insert editing, straight cuts, split ends, and more. 45 mins.
VHS: $22779. $149.00.
Off-Line Editing: Working with Edit Decision Lists. A guide to the EDL, or Edit Decision List, including how to read an EDL, linear and non-linear formats, editing tips, cleaning, tracing, and more. 27 mins.
VHS: $22780. $149.00.
Complete Set. The two-volume set.
VHS: $22778. $249.00.

The Painters Forum Scene Painting Library
Master painter and teacher Lester Polakov hosts this two-part guide to scene painting.
Volume 1: Introduction. A discussion of the tools of scene painting, including customized implements, priming and lining techniques. Includes a 10-page viewer's guide. 18 mins.
VHS: $22862. $59.95.
Volume 2: Trompe L'Oeil. A guide to the mathematically precise "trompe l'oeil" ("fool the eye") technique used to give two-dimensional surfaces the illusion of being three-dimensional. Includes an 18-page viewer's guide. 41 mins.
VHS: $22863. $175.00.

The Pattern Development Video
A must for cutters and drapers. Author and costumer Rosemary Ingham presents the basics of measuring an actor, analyzing the costume sketch, developing a paper pattern and making and fitting a design mock-up. 75 mins.
VHS: S22853. $149.00.

Performing Shakespeare
Expert Kathleen Conlin leads you through a highly physical series of exercises designed to move you from the exploration of specific words and phrases through the development of complete Shakespearean scenes. 75 mins.
VHS: S22840. $149.00.

Personal Performance Techniques
This video shows how to make a more effective presentation by use of visual cues and performance techniques, and how personal appearance, clothing and hairstyle affect your audience. "Show and tell" techniques are demonstrated and stand up examples are included to provide highly useful tips for TV reporters or anyone involved in presenting information. 20 mins.
VHS: S22810. $149.00.

Post Synchronization: The Editor's Role
A guide through dialogue replacement procedures: the original method, the "rock and roll" method, and ADR, or Automatic Dialogue Replacement. 28 mins.
VHS: S22783. $149.00.

Radio Drama
The rehearsal and recording processes of drama for radio are shown in this first-rate production. Valuable for anyone in the dramatic arts. 55 mins.
VHS: S22815. $149.00.

Radio Production: Making a Radio Commercial
The production process of a commercial is amusingly depicted, from working with the client to recording, through the editing process and up to the final mix. 43 mins.
VHS: S22813. $149.00.

The Role of the Assistant Editor
An introduction to basic procedures of the film editing suite, including logging, edge numbers, syncing, coding, shot breakdown, preparation of a cut work print, and more. 45 mins.
VHS: S22782. $149.00.

The Role of the Script Supervisor
A look at the duties of the script supervisor, including both visual and narrative continuity, script timing and script breakdown, notes, and more. 28 mins.
VHS: S22735. $149.00.

Script to Screen
An overview of the differences between scripting for the stage and screenwriting, including an in-depth look at the work in the studio. 30 mins.
VHS: S22733. $149.00.

Setting the Stage
A companion to *The Fundamentals of Scenic Painting*, this three-tape set gives alternate approaches to common scene painting problems and emphasizes specific paint mixing formulas. 48 mins.
VHS: S22861. $119.00.

Shedding Some Light
An overview of common types of lighting units, gels, light boards and accessories, the basic principles of electricity, lighting safety, hanging, focusing, circuiting, and how to lay out and read a light plot. 95 mins.
VHS: S22858. $119.00.

Shurtleff on Acting
Michael Shurtleff, noted casting director and author of the bestselling *Audition*, teaches for the first time on video in a film that speaks to the heart of what it means to be an actor. 60 mins.
VHS: S22849. $149.00.

The Sitcom Seminars
Three U.S. comedy writers and producers (*Roseanne, Designing Women, The Wonder Years, Murphy Brown, Married…With Children*) provide an in-depth course covering every aspect of the sitcom craft.
Dramatic Structure and Comic Development. The comic possibilities of a premise are explored by John Vorhaus from the hero's goals, the rewards of victory and the escalating jeopardy of failure. 29 mins.
VHS: S22830. $79.00.
Sitcom Rules and Forms. The rules for eight different types of sitcoms are mapped out in this informative video hosted by John Vorhaus. 30 mins.
VHS: S22828. $79.00.
Sitcom Story Structure. From introduction to complication to consequence to relevance, the substructure of every successful comedy television program is demonstrated. 21 mins.
VHS: S22829. $59.00.
A Survival Guide for Sitcom Writers. Hosted by Russ Woody (*Murphy Brown*), this informative video provides guides on getting an agent, the art of pitching your ideas, and the shaping of a writer's career. 23 mins.
VHS: S22834. $59.00.
The Production Process: Part 1. Beginning with the dynamics of the writer's and actor's table, rehearsal, through recording and editing of the program, an inside look at early production is explored. 30 mins.
VHS: S22831. $79.00.
The Production Process: Part 2. Norma S. Vela (*Roseanne, Designing Women*) discusses the role of a sitcom's showrunner. A showrunner is responsible for juggling the demands of writers, actors, directors and the network. 23 mins.
VHS: S22832. $59.00.
The Sitcom Writer's Comic Toolbox. John Vorhaus (*The Wonder Years* and *Married…With Children*) defines the characteristics of a good comic premise, the importance of a central character with a comic perspective on the world, and how to balance endearing traits with exaggerated flaws. 36 mins.
VHS: S22826. $79.00.
The Sitcom Writer's Craft. John Vorhaus approaches the mechanics of sitcom writing, the application of the three-act comic structure and the levels of comic conflict. 29 mins.
VHS: S22827. $79.00.

Three In-Depth Case Studies. Three writers provide an inside look at writing for a specific sitcom. The process of writing for *Roseanne, Murphy Brown* and *Married…With Children* is discussed by their writers. 30 mins.
VHS: S22833. $59.00.
What Is Sitcom? Details the necessary ingredients for a good situation comedy. One essential element is emotional truth and honesty. The writers from *Roseanne* and *Murphy Brown* host. 19 mins.
VHS: S22825. $59.00.
Complete Set. 10 program series.
VHS: S22824. $449.00.

So You Want to Be An Actor
Hosted by Jerry Stiller and Anne Meara, this informational program offers telling insights from leading industry professionals and performers on the techniques aspiring actors can utilize to further their professional ambitions. The video treats such important subjects as locating the right theater schools, finding a photographer for the proper portfolio, preparing the right resume and finding an agent to represent you. It offers insights into casting agents, auditions and how to enter the lucrative arena of commercials and soap operas. With appearances by Christopher Walken, Roscoe Lee Browne, Uta Hagen and Michael Storm. 75 mins.
VHS: S19526. $29.95.

Speak for Yourself: A Dynamic Vocal Workout
Voice expert Susan Leigh offers a series of voice and body warm-ups to help build a strong voice, establish focus and concentration while speaking, and expand your vocal capacity and skills. 26 mins.
VHS: S22805. $99.00.

The Stage Fight Director
Master combat choreographer David Boushey leads you through the many combat scenes in a production of *Romeo and Juliet*. Fascinating for drama students and professionals alike. 30 mins.
VHS: S22859. $119.00.

Stella Adler: Awake and Dream
A documentary portrait of Stella Adler, the influential acting teacher and Method guru whose students included Marlon Brando, Robert De Niro, Warren Beatty and Candice Bergen. Narrated by Frank Langella. 56 mins.
VHS: S18730. $39.95.

Studio Seconds: The Assistant Sound Engineer Video
A lively dramatization of the duties of the assistant sound engineer in a beautifully produced program designed for people planning a career in the recording field. 80 mins.
VHS: S22812. $159.00.

The Subject Is Light
Charles Potts demonstrates the "laws of light" that apply to photography and cinematography while using the fundamental shapes found in nature. 44 mins.
VHS: S22750. $149.00.

Teaching Shakespeare: New Approaches from the Folger Shakespeare Library
This videotape, featuring lively and successful ways to teach Shakespeare, draws on Folger's outstanding Shakespearean resources. The production emphasizes language, improvisation, paraphrasing, performance directing and scholarship, and provides an introduction to Shakespeare's world and Elizabethan music. The central idea is that Shakespeare's words were meant to be heard, that understanding comes through performance. 75 mins. Includes Public Performance Rights.
VHS: S09264. $95.00.

Techniques of TV Interviewing
The elements of a successful television interview and what makes an exciting television story are explored. The program is full of cautionary tales and role models, including an entertaining exchange involving Margaret Thatcher trapping an ill-prepared journalist and turning the tables on him. 20 mins.
VHS: S22808. $149.00.

TV Current Affairs Reporting
What makes an exciting television story? Producers of four Australian current affairs programs discuss their views and stress the importance of building stories around visuals. 48 mins.
VHS: S22809. $149.00.

TV Makeup: The Basics
The basics of materials for a makeup kit, makeup technique for both men and women, makeup removal, "quick fix" techniques, makeup hygiene, and more. 30 mins.
VHS: S22736. $149.00.

TV Newsroom: News Gathering
The interlocking roles of the staff of the WHDH newsroom, including assignment editor, producers, news directors, reporters, writers and photographers. Learn how these professionals work against the clock to produce the newsbreaking stories of today. 12 mins.
VHS: S22806. $119.00.

TV Newsroom: News Production
Follows a real day of news gathering and production at a Boston affiliate. Dozens of employees work together to shape the evening newscast. 10 mins.
VHS: S22807. $119.00.

Video Dance/The Video Dance Lectures
In *Video Dance*, we see the end result of a two-week workshop with seven choreographers and six video directors creating "choreography for the camera". *The Video Dance Lectures* traces the path from choreographer to final shooting script and looks at how the viewer's eye experiences dance. 79 mins.
VHS: S22740. $249.00.

Video Editing
This is a step-by-step guide to the techniques and equipment of video editing. Titles, sound and special effects are all explored. In addition this video covers the basics of edit controllers and discusses the future of nonlinear editing possibilities. 42 mins.
VHS: S23952. $14.95.

Video Post Production
An introduction to pre-production planning, time code and user bits use, structuring the off-line edit, digital effects, audio sweetening, digital audio, and more. 28 mins.
VHS: S22777. $149.00.

Video Scriptwriting for Success and Profit
Stewart Jacoby leads you step-by-step through the stages of scriptwriting, including communicating to the client, script development, the treatment, writing and formatting of your script and storyboarding. 45 mins.
VHS: S22836. $99.00.

Voice Workout for the Actor
Voice expert Susan Leigh leads you through full-body relaxation and stretching, and exercises for pitch and resonance, clarity and dynamic control, resulting in a complete voice and body warm-up. 33 mins.
VHS: S22842. $99.00.

What Is Multimedia?
An examination of hardware, software, scripting, interactivity, robotics, and the latest developments in the field of multimedia. 20 mins.
VHS: S22791. $149.00.

"What's the Score?"— Text Analysis for the Actor
Arthur Wagner teaches his method of examining each action of a script in terms of immediate and overall objectives, and then relating these objectives to personal experience. Also, a guide to examining character dynamics and interactions. 85 mins.
VHS: S22841. $179.00.

Where Do I Start: Basic Set Construction
Basic set construction from start to finish, including building supplies and tools, the construction of flats and platforms, assembly of window and door frames, adding hinges, stiffeners, jacks and moldings, and the transport and assembly of the finished set. 72 mins.
VHS: S22850. $119.00.

The Working Actor: Actors on Acting
Four professional actors talk about techniques for making a character come alive, approaches to body movement, methods of research, ways to work with the script, rehearsal techniques and more. 27 mins.
VHS: S22845. $149.00.

The Working Actor: Teachers on Acting
Three acting teachers discuss assisting natural talent to full expression, the power of live performance versus film and television work, and more. 21 mins.
VHS: S22846. $149.00.

Writing for Film
Four top screen writers, including Oscar winner Frank Pierson (*Cool Hand Luke, Dog Day Afternoon*) and David Williamson (*Gallipoli, The Year of Living Dangerously*), discuss the nuts and bolts of their craft. Topics include finding a story, research techniques, character development, dialog, the three-act script structure, plot and subplot, formula scripts, and much more. 52 mins.
VHS: S16542. $149.00.

Writing for Radio
Four expert radio writers talk about their craft, with an emphasis on the writing of radio drama. All participants emphasize the unlimited potential of radio as a medium of the imagination. Topics include the characteristics of a good radio writer; how to work within the limitations of time slots and tight budgets; plot development; the proper use of stage directions in a radio script; the use of music and sound effects, and more. 44 mins.
VHS: S16544. $149.00.

Writing for Television
Four veteran TV writers discuss the components of a successful television script and reveal their own working methods. Topics include telling a story with pictures; creating a character; generating dialog; collaboration and roleplaying; the rewrite process; adapting a novel; researching and developing a major miniseries. 48 mins.
VHS: S16543. $149.00.

movies
ABOUT MOVIES

American Cinema
PBS compiled this 10-part series about American film. Clips from great movies and interviews with some of the most important figures in front of and behind the camera today make this a vital resource for any cineaste. Martin Scorsese, Clint Eastwood, Steven Spielberg, Harrison Ford, Sidney Lumet and Quentin Tarantino are just some of the popular figures who explain the magic of movies. Each of these five videos is 120 mins.
The Film School Generation/The Edge of Hollywood. Out of the tumult of the 1960's a new generation of young filmmakers emerged, who enlivened Hollywood traditions. Today that transformation continues with the growing influence of independent producers.
VHS: $24139. $29.98.
The Hollywood Style/The Star. Production methods magically transform the world in front of the camera. And the star system is a key element of the way films develop and maintain their mesmerizing appeal.
VHS: $24137. $29.98.
Romantic Comedy/Film Noir. These distinctive Hollywood genres present opposing world views. One is light and optimistic while the other sees the darker aspects governing our emotions and actions.
VHS: $24135. $29.98.
The Studio System/Film in the Television Age. This insightful examination of the two critical institutions shaping American film sheds new light on the formation of this popular art form.
VHS: $24136. $29.98.
The Western/The Combat Film. Masculinity has been defined by the movies centered on the iconic West and the enduring experience of Americans at war.
VHS: $24138. $29.98.
American Cinema, Gift Set. The complete ten-episode, five-tape set.
VHS: $24140. $124.98.

Anatomy of a Filmmaker
The great director Otto Preminger is the subject of this documentary featuring interviews with some of the famous stars he worked with, including Frank Sinatra, Vincent Price, James Stewart, Michael Caine, Deborah Kerr and Burgess Meredith. 119 mins.
VHS: $21167. $19.98.

Anthony Quinn: An Original
This is the incredible odyssey of a man who worked at a "thousand jobs" before appearing in a film by Cecil B. De Mille and marrying the director's daughter. Includes numerous clips from his films and interviews with friends like Julie Harris and Tony Franciosa. Narrated by Anthony Quinn. 60 mins.
VHS: $14624. $19.98.

The Art of Illusion—One Hundred Years of Hollywood Special Effects
From the earliest films onwards, special effects have mesmerized audiences. Now some of the best effects are shown and explained in this informative video. Towering infernos, intergalactic battles, the Apollo 13 blastoff, gremlins, and even dinosaurs from *Jurassic Park* are among the illusions found in this video. 50 mins.
VHS: $26455. $14.98.

Audrey Hepburn Remembered
A nostalgic look at Audrey Hepburn, her career as a star and her role as an ambassador for UNICEF is offered in this documentary. Clips from some of her more popular films are included and a glimpse at her more intimate life is evoked by her family and friends. 66 mins.
VHS: $21519. $19.98.

Bacall on Bogart
Lauren Bacall hosts this loving look at the man behind the reel image. Includes outtakes, home movies, film clips and revealing recollections, with guests including Katharine Hepburn and John Huston. 60 mins.
VHS: $09803. $59.98.

Bela Lugosi: The Forgotten King
Examines the man who became Dracula, through footage from some of his famous films and also outtakes, trailers and stills; from his childhood days in Hungary, career on Broadway and the Hollywood era. 55 mins.
VHS: $09423. $19.95.

Best of Nightline
Lucille Ball Dies. 30 mins.
VHS: $14058. $14.98.
Sir Laurence Olivier Dies. 30 mins.
VHS: $14060. $14.98.

Bette Davis
A portrait of the star who was once billed as "the woman who was loved when she should have been whipped." 22 mins.
VHS: $06419. $14.98.

Breaking into Hollywood
Fifteen crucial steps outlined by Hollywood insiders detail a blueprint for a successful acting career. A producer, an editor and a casting director explain such basic first steps as joining the actors union. USA, 1995, 42 mins.
VHS: $26873. $29.95.

Cameramen at War
The story of the British Film Unit newsreel cameramen during both world wars, produced by the British Ministry of Information and compiled by Len Lye. Special highlights include sensational footage from campaigns in France, Norway, and North Africa, as well as over the skies of England. 26 mins.
VHS: $03346. $29.95.

Cameramen Who Dared
Go behind the lens with the incredible documentary filmmakers who risk their lives to get the perfect shot. Discover what drives these professionals to pioneer their cameras where limits are unknown. 60 mins.
VHS: $11410. $19.95.

Carole Lombard
A sentimental journey through the life of one of Hollywood's best-loved stars, including home movies from her marriage to Clark Gable and scenes from her most famous movies. 24 mins.
VHS: $06421. $14.98.

Cary Grant: The Leading Man
Cary Grant was the very essence of a movie star. His deft comic style merged easily with his strength as a leading man. This documentary portrait goes behind the scenes with clips from his greatest films and interviews with friends and associates like Stanley Donen and Deborah Kerr. Narrated by Richard Kiley. 60 mins.
VHS: $14622. $19.98.

Celebrity Propaganda
The Hollywood effort for World War II as many top stars come out for the war effort. Features Frank Sinatra, James Cagney, Bob Hope, and many more.
VHS: $10580. $19.95.

Cowboys of the Saturday Matinee
James Coburn narrates this fond look at Hollywood's best-loved Western heroes, including all the film elements that make Westerns an enduring art form. Classic clips highlight this light-hearted homage. 75 minutes.
VHS: $02472. $14.95.

The Craft of Acting: Auditioning
Allan Miller is a successful actor and teacher. Some of his pupils, including Dustin Hoffman and Meryl Streep, have become huge stars. Here Miller offers useful advice for a variety of auditioning situations both warm and cold, as well as a prepared monologue and even a call back. 43 mins.
VHS: $24899. $119.00.

Cult People
Seven Hollywood favorites share insightful and informative behind-the-scenes stories of their involvement in some of the most popular cult and television classics ever. Included in this 60-minute nostalgic tribute are *The Avengers'* Patrick MacNee, exploitation legend Cameron Mitchell and *Return of the Living Dead II's* James Karen. Also included are interviews with Curtis Harrington, Russ Meyer, Waris Hussein and Michael Sarne. David Del Valle is the host. USA, 1989, 60 mins.
VHS: $12255. $19.95.

Dear Mr. Gable
This MGM documentary presents the fascinating life story of the man who became the symbol of rugged American masculinity. Narrated by Burgess Meredith and featuring remembrances from friends and peers, as well as a parade of film clips and home movies.
VHS: $15257. $14.95.
Nicolas L. Noxon, USA, 1968, 52 mins.

The Divine Garbo
To many she was a goddess: the most glamorous and mysterious movie star the world has ever known. Greta Garbo arrived in Hollywood in 1924 as a frightened 19-year-old Swedish girl and vanished from the screen 16 years later. In that brief period, she made motion picture history. Loaded with film clips from her greatest performances, this documentary is hosted by Glenn Close. USA, 1990, 47 mins.
VHS: $14934. $19.98.

Epic That Never Was
An examination of the story behind why the adaptation of the epic novel *I Claudius*, begun in 1937 by Josef von Sternberg, was never completed. *Epic That Never Was* includes footage shot by von Sternberg, as well as interviews with Robert Graves, Merle Oberon, and Eileen Corbett. England, 80 mins.
VHS: $02811. $39.95.

Errol Flynn: Portrait of a Swashbuckler
The life and art of Errol Flynn is explored in this uncensored documentary that studies his Hollywood work, drawing on footage and interviews with his former wives, friends, children, collaborators and close friends. 50 mins.
VHS: $18134. $19.95.

Evening with Marlene Dietrich
A live stage performance which recreates the finest musical sequences from Dietrich's films, including songs like *Lili Marlene, I Wish You Love, Honeysuckle Rose.* 60 mins.
VHS: $07026. $29.98.

Film Parade
An extremely rare and priceless film record of the history of motion pictures, produced by film pioneer J. Stuart Blackton. Utilizing rare film footage, including sequences from *The Big Parade* and *Steamboat Willie*, this first compilation history of the motion picture includes glimpses of many who played an important part in Blackton's life and career, including Theodore Roosevelt, Mary Pickford, Blanche Sweet, Harold Lloyd and John Lowell.
VHS: $09524. $39.95.
J. Stuart Blackton, USA, 1933

Filmmakers on Their Craft
Burt Lancaster. Beginning with his early days as a circus performer, Lancaster discusses his work with Kirk Douglas on *Gunfight at the OK Corral*, with Alexander MacKendrick on *The Sweet Smell of Success* and with Luchino Visconti on *The Leopard.* 60 mins.
VHS: $16537. $79.00.

Freddie Young. Young talks in technical terms about his work as director of photography on such films as *Dr. Zhivago, Ryan's Daughter, Lord Jim* and *Lawrence of Arabia.* He also reflects on the changes in film technology during his long career. 61 mins.
VHS: $16538. $79.00.
James Stewart. The veteran actor discusses his work with such directors as Frank Capra, John Ford and Alfred Hitchcock. 40 mins.
VHS: $16539. $79.00.
Milos Forman. The Czech director of *Amadeus* and *One Flew Over the Cuckoo's Nest* discusses his approach to filmmaking with Peter Thompson. He compares his working in Eastern Europe under Communism to his work with the Hollywood studio system, and draws some surprising conclusions. 32 mins.
VHS: $16534. $79.00.
Nicholas Roeg. Peter Thompson interviews the director of *Performance, Walkabout* and *The Man Who Fell to Earth* about his role as a visionary filmmaker operating, for the most part, outside the mainstream. 34 mins.
VHS: $16535. $79.00.
Peter Weir. Weir, director of *Witness* and *Picnic at Hanging Rock*, is interviewed by Peter Thompson in 1982, shortly after making *The Year of Living Dangerously.* He talks about his working methods, and about the dark element in his films. 45 mins.
VHS: $16536. $79.00.
Ronald Neame. This program reveals technique and insight into the filmmaking process as understood by legendary director Ronald Neame, who began his career at the end of the silent era with Alfred Hitchcock's *Blackmail.* 105 mins.
VHS: $16540. $179.00.

Flying Saucers over Hollywood
A documentary video on the making of Ed Wood's landmark 1959 disaster movie, *Plan 9 from Outer Space.* The program studies the film's contribution to the genre, with commentary by Sam Raimi, Valda Hansen, Harry Medved and Joe Dante. Narrated by Lee Harris.
VHS: $18258. $24.95.
Mark Patrick Carducci, USA, 1992

Fonda on Fonda
Who else but Jane Fonda, one of the biggest stars in films today, could show her father, Henry Fonda, with such warmth and insight? Henry Fonda's career as an actor spanned decades of motion picture history, from *The Grapes of Wrath* to *On Golden Pond.* Seeing these two stars together sheds light on an important and vital Hollywood family. 47 mins.
VHS: $20877. $14.98.

Forever James Dean
This documentary is part of the 35th Anniversary salute to the star of *East of Eden, Rebel Without a Cause* and *Giant.* It features never-before-seen material, including Dean's soft-drink T.V. commercial. Visit his Indiana hometown and listen to his high school dramatics teacher, friends and associates reminisce about him. Not to be confused with anyone who sells pork sausage.
VHS: $14007. $19.98.
Ara Chekmayan, USA, 1988, 69 mins.

Francois Truffaut: Stolen Portraits
A brilliant documentary which provides new insights and revelations. Includes extensive clips and in-depth interviews with dozens of Truffaut's collaborators and friends, including Gerard Depardieu, Eric Rohmer, Marcel Ophuls, Claude Chabrol, Jacques Rivette, Truffaut's daughter and Truffaut's former wife, Madeleine Morgenstern, this remarkable film shines new light on the psychological motivations of Truffaut's life and on his filmmaking career. French with English subtitles.
VHS: $26965. $89.98.
Serge Toubiana/Michel Pascal, France, 1993, 93 mins.

From Star Wars to Jedi: Making of a Saga
Mark Hamill narrates this homage to George Lucas and the creation of the Star Wars trilogy as he discusses the various themes and the development of the story.
VHS: $12932. $9.98.

Gary Cooper
An honest and insightful look at "the cowboy" and "womanizer" images of the two-time Oscar winner as best actor. 22 mins.
VHS: $06418. $14.98.

Gary Cooper: American Life, American Legend
Superstar and super Gary Cooper fan Clint Eastwood hosts a fascinating tribute to the man who, more than any other screen great, represented the character of America at its best. For over 35 years, the legendary "Coop" lit up the screen with our hopes, our fears, our doubts and our dreams. USA, 1989, 47 mins.
VHS: $14935. $19.98.

Going Hollywood: The War Years
Van Johnson hosts this nostalgic documentary that spotlights Hollywood's on-and-off the screen efforts during World War II. Includes scenes from such films as *To Be or Not to Be, Guadalcanal Diary* and *The More the Merrier* with reminiscences by actors who lived through the era, including Douglas Fairbanks Jr. and Tony Randall. 76 mins.
VHS: $08169. $19.98.

Grace Kelly—The American Princess
Using home movies and moments from her finest films (like *High Noon* and *Dial M for Murder*), and conversations with Jimmy Stewart, Louis Jourdan and Alec Guiness, this is the story of the American movie star who gave up her career to become Her Serene Highness Princess Grace of Monaco. 60 mins.
VHS: $05953. $19.98.

Great Actors of the 20th Century: Vol. 1
Three different movie stars are profiled. James Cagney plays a sensitive professor whose dissatisfaction about his career is altered when he encounters a box of memorabilia. Errol Flynn is a debt-laden gambler who, in order to marry a reluctant heiress, must defeat an expert young marksman in a duel. David Niven is a mad genius who has devoted the last 15 years to writing a book that he believes will transform their lives. 75 mins.
VHS: $19165. $19.95.

Great Actors of the 20th Century: Vol. 2
Three illustrious horror figures display their gifts for fright and mayhem. Boris Karloff takes form as an apparition and communicates a strange message to a sea captain's wife whose determination to solve a puzzle drives her mad. Vincent Price is under siege from Chinese communists trying to brainwash him. Lon Chaney Jr. is a prosperous junkman who teaches his sons about pride, commitment and honor. 75 mins.
VHS: $19166. $19.95.

Great Actors of the 20th Century: Vol. 3
Three matinee idols are faced with agonizing decisions. Douglas Fairbanks antagonizes a mob boss when he tries to transform a thoroughbred into a champion race horse. Ronald Reagan wants to disavow his troubled past, until he encounters the judge whom he regards as responsible for his brother's death. Charles Boyer faces a bleak outlook on Christmas until his relationship with his wife (Maureen O'Sullivan) alters his perspective. 75 mins.
VHS: $19167. $19.95.

Great Actresses of the 20th Century: Vol. 1
Three actresses take a stand and declare their ambitions. Bette Davis must act decisively to save herself and a band of children from a violent blizzard. Joan Fontaine is a cautious observer who awaits meeting her friend's enigmatic groom. Gloria Swanson must decide to sacrifice her career to prolong her life. 75 mins.
VHS: $19168. $19.95.

Great Actresses of the 20th Century: Vol. 2
This program looks at three young actresses on the eve of their breakthrough. Natalie Wood and her siblings find respect and awe for their new father-figure (Charles Boyer) through a complex reign of errors. Joanne Woodward is a disillusioned high school outcast until a mysterious older man (Dick Powell) orchestrates her personal transformation. Angela Lansbury devises an elaborate plan to withhold information about her troubled past. 75 mins.
VHS: $19169. $19.95.

Great Actresses of the 20th Century: Vol. 3
Three actresses at the peak of their craft highlight this video collection. Greer Garson pursues the vicious killer who murdered her fiance. Loretta Young reunites with her estranged son. Ida Lupino is confined to a penthouse with virtually no food and must decipher the contents of a tape recording in order to escape. 75 mins.
VHS: $19170. $19.95.

Great Hollywood Memories: Volume I
Host Gene Kelly takes us on a history tour of motion pictures from the turn of the century until the beginning of sound. USA, 60 mins.
VHS: $15227. $19.95.

Great Hollywood Memories: Volume II
Host Henry Fonda continues the history of motion pictures from the beginning of sound through the fabulous years of the 30s, 40s, 50s and early 60s. USA, 60 mins.
VHS: $15228. $19.95.

Gregory Peck: His Own Man
This tape tells the story of Gregory Peck, a shy and inarticulate boy from a broken family who eventually rose to superstardom. With clips from *To Kill a Mockingbird, MacArthur* and *The Guns of Navarone.* Narrated by Peck himself. 60 mins.
VHS: $14621. $19.98.

Hearts of Darkness: A Filmmaker's Apocalypse
A riveting behind-the-scenes look at the making of Francis Ford Coppola's *Apocalypse Now.* The film combines interviews with documentary footage shot on location in the Philippines by Eleanor Coppola. This is a must-see for anyone with the slightest interest in how Hollywood movies get made. With Martin Sheen, Dennis Hopper, Larry Fishburne, Robert Duvall, Sam Bottoms, Frederic Forrest, George Lucas, John Milius and Francis Ford Coppola. Watch Marlon Brando improvise his lines and eat a bug.
VHS: $16459. $19.95.
Fax Bahr/George Hickenlooper, USA, 1991, 96 mins.

Hedda Hopper's Hollywood
Join Hollywood's most renowned entertainment reporter for an intimate behind-the-scenes visit with the screen's greatest stars as seen in rare film footage. Bob Hope, Gary Cooper, Betty Grable, Ernest Hemingway and many more stars come out to play in their favorite playgrounds. 58 mins.
VHS: $09495. $19.95.

Here's Looking at You, Warner Bros.
An in-house documentary about the origins, growth and glamour of Warner Bros. Narrated by Clint Eastwood, Barbra Streisand, Goldie Hawn, Steven Spielberg and Chevy Chase.
VHS: $18450. $19.95.
Laser: LD71865. $29.98.
Robert Guenette, USA, 1992, 108 mins.

Hollywood Babylon

Past the studio gates, in the Hollywood backlots and behind the scenes are some of Tinsel Town's most desperately held secrets. In this series the lives of 13 highly acclaimed stars are revealed. Witness the shocking truths and the real life costs that fame and fortune bring to those in the limelight. Each tape is 55 mins.
Volume 1: Grace Kelly/Howard Hughes/Marilyn Monroe/William Holden.
VHS: S21876. $24.95.
Volume 2: John Lennon/Errol Flynn/Vivien Leigh/John Belushi.
VHS: S21877. $24.95.
Volume 3: James Dean/Joseph Kennedy & Gloria Swanson/Alfred Hitchcock/Sophia Loren.
VHS: S21878. $24.95.
Complete Set.
VHS: S22001. $59.95.

Hollywood Chronicles: Censorship—The Unseen Cinema/Sex in the Movies

Censorship—The Unseen Cinema examines the struggle for artistic freedom in Hollywood. From sex to drugs to propaganda, Hollywood has always been under fire from those who wish to control the content of films. *Sex in the Movies* looks at the role of sex and sexual innuendo in motion pictures. Sex symbols Theda Bara, Clara Bow, Marilyn Monroe and others helped to fuel the controversy but did not stop Hollywood's portrayal of sex on film. Hosted by Jackie Cooper. USA, 1991, 50 mins.
VHS: S14839. $19.98.

Hollywood Chronicles: In the Beginning/The Studio System Takes Over

In the Beginning is a story as dramatic as the films themselves, an overview of the earliest years of film: meet film mavericks like Carl Laemmle and D.W. Griffith; track the move of motion picture studios from the East Coast to Hollywood. *The Studio System Takes Over* looks at the founding of the major studios—Paramount, 20th Century Fox, United Artists, and MGM. Tour the studios as you learn how smaller studios merged to become the powerhouses of Hollywood. Hosted by Jackie Cooper. USA, 1991, 50 mins.
VHS: S14837. $19.98.

Hollywood Chronicles: Pen & Ink Movies/The Evolution of Sound

Pen & Ink Movies looks at the development of animation in the 20 years before Walt Disney created Mickey Mouse, featuring an interview with Walter Lantz, the creator of Woody Woodpecker. *The Evolution of Sound* is an in-depth review of how the "talkies" came into Hollywood as the Warner Brothers studio revolutionized the industry and the ways in which sound engineering changed over the years. Hosted by Jackie Cooper. USA, 1991, 50 mins.
VHS: S14847. $19.98.

Hollywood Chronicles: Poverty Row/The New Rebels

Poverty Row is the story of the "B" movies, the low budget films and serials of yesteryear. These low budget pictures were the vehicles that launched many actors to stardom and the studios where they worked have a rich history that is unfolded here. *The New Rebels* looks at the maverick directors and producers of Hollywood. D.W. Griffith, Orson Welles, and others are the focus; and some of today's "rebels", like Stanley Kramer and Paul Bartel, are interviewed. Hosted by Jackie Cooper. USA, 1991, 50 mins.
VHS: S14842. $19.98.

Hollywood Chronicles: Publicity Stunts & Coming Attractions/How Movies Are Made

Publicity Stunts & Coming Attractions reviews the outlandish stunts, publicity campaigns, and preview trailers that have been the cornerstone of Hollywood's publicity machine. *How Movies Are Made* explains the movie-making process. From the development of camera techniques to editing to props and costumes, see how the ideas are brought to life. Hosted by Jackie Cooper. USA, 1991, 50 mins.
VHS: S14841. $19.98.

Hollywood Chronicles: Riding into the Sunset/The American Hero

Riding into the Sunset is the story of the most American genre in all the world—the Western. Join Gene Autry as he talks about the rich history of Westerns in Hollywood. *The American Hero* focuses on the actors that have become the "American Hero." The careers of Douglas Fairbanks, Gary Cooper, James Dean and more are examined for the values that they portrayed on the screen. Hosted by Jackie Cooper. USA, 1991, 50 mins.
VHS: S14838. $19.98.

Hollywood Chronicles: Scandal!/Mysteries & Secrets

Scandal! uncovers some of Hollywood's greatest scandals. The Roscoe "Fatty" Arbuckle case, the suicide of Jean Harlow's husband Paul Bern, Errol Flynn's arrest on rape charges, the Communist scare of the 1950's and more are investigated. *Mysteries & Secrets* explores some of Hollywood's still unsolved mysteries. The William Desmond Taylor murder, the murder of Thelma Todd, the death of "Superman" George Reeves, and more are recounted with rare footage and the headlines of the day. Hosted by Jackie Cooper. USA 1991, 50 mins.
VHS: S14835. $19.98.

Hollywood Chronicles: Stereotypes & Minorities/Familiar Faces, Unknown Names

Stereotypes & Minorities is an overview of the treatment of black actors in Hollywood. Actors Della Reese and Nick Stewart offer their insights and reflect on the changing roles of blacks in films. *Familiar Faces, Unknown Names* features the character actors—those supporting players that we recognize but never know who they are. Hosted by Jackie Cooper. USA, 1991, 50 mins.
VHS: S14843. $19.98.

Hollywood Chronicles: The Depression Years/The Silent Witness

The Depression Years centers on the development of musicals, gangster films and the screwball comedy. Escaping the Depression was the theme of this era, and travelogs, cartoons, and newsreels were all staples of the cinematic entertainment of the time. *The Silent Witness* covers the newsreels and their role in bringing the news to the public. Beyond hard news, the newsreel also brought sports and entertainment news to the public. Hosted by Jackie Cooper. USA, 1991, 50 mins.
VHS: S14846. $19.98.

Hollywood Chronicles: The Futurists/The Wizards of the EFX

The Futurists goes where no man has gone before—the realm of science fiction. From *Metropolis* to *Star Trek*, science fiction films have been the mirror of our future and a tantalizing peek into what that future may be. *The Wizards of EFX* explains the mechanics of special effects, those dazzling moments in film that leave the audience asking, "How did they do that?" Learn how it was done with footage from *King Kong*, *Ghostbusters II* and more. Hosted by Jackie Cooper. USA 1991, 50 mins.
VHS: S14836. $19.98.

Hollywood Chronicles: The Great Detectives/The Great Clowns

The Great Detectives does its own detective work as it looks at the famous sleuths of film. Dick Tracy, Bulldog Drummond, Charlie Chan, Sherlock Holmes and more are investigated. *The Great Clowns* will leave you laughing helplessly as Charlie Chaplin, Harold Lloyd, Buster Keaton, Laurel & Hardy, The Marx Brothers and W.C. Fields leave their vaudeville roots behind to come to Hollywood and create their special brands of comedy. Hosted by Jackie Cooper. USA, 1991, 50 mins.
VHS: S14840. $19.98.

Hollywood Chronicles: The Search for God, Grails & Profits/The Nightmare Factory

The Search for God, Grails & Profits looks at the ties between religion and Hollywood, on film and behind-the-scenes. *The Nightmare Factory* creeps through the world of the horror movies and features interviews with Samuel Arkoff and Roger Corman. The careers of Lon Chaney, Bela Lugosi, and other greats are also included. Hosted by Jackie Cooper. USA, 1991, 50 mins.
VHS: S14845. $19.98.

Hollywood Chronicles: Women with Clout/Hollywood's Children

Women with Clout recaps the career of some of the most powerful women in Hollywood—actresses and directors who controlled their own careers. Mary Pickford, Joan Crawford, Lucille Ball and others are highlighted along with some of the most powerful women in Hollywood today. *Hollywood's Children* features the child stars of Hollywood, including host Jackie Cooper and interviews with Hal Roach and Spanky McFarland. Hosted by Jackie Cooper. USA, 1991, 50 mins.
VHS: S14844. $19.98.

Hollywood Dinosaurs

A program that looks at the creation and evolution of the dinosaur or monsters in early silents, cartoons and the science fiction films of the 50s and 60s, with scenes from *The Lost World*, *Godzilla*, *Gorgo* and *King Kong*. 60 mins.
VHS: S18789. $9.99.

Hollywood Goes to War

A collection of short subjects produced by the Office of War Information. *The All Star Bond Rally* features Bob Hope, Frank Sinatra, Harpo Marx and Betty Grable. *Hollywood Canteen Overseas Special* boasts Dinah Shore, Red Skelton, Eddie Cantor and Jimmy Durante. Also included are Kay Francis, Carole Landis, Martha Raye and Mitzi Mayfair, those "Four Jills in a Jeep." And much more. USA, 1945, 41 mins.
VHS: S05507. $24.95.

Hollywood Mavericks

From Erich Von Stroheim to David Lynch, this portrait features rare interview footage with filmmakers, including Coppola, Hopper, Scorsese, Bogdanovich, Schrader, Rudolph and Lynch. 90 mins.
Laser: CLV(1), CAV(2). LD71495. $39.95.

Hollywood on Trial

John Huston narrates this feature-length documentary about the Hollywood Ten who would not cooperate when accused by the House Committee on Un-American Activities of communist activities. Appearances by Ronald Reagan, Otto Preminger, Zero Mostel, and others. 90 mins.
VHS: S09422. $29.95.

Hollywood Scandals and Tragedies

A video scandal sheet of tantalizing truths filled with remembrances of those who fell from grace with the public. criminal trials of the stars, celebrity suicides, murders, Hollywood funerals, graveyards, and Hollywood myths. 90 mins.
VHS: S07473. $79.95.

Hollywood Screenwriters and Their Craft

Hollywood Screenwriters and Their Craft is presented in three separate programs which can be viewed independently. Program one focuses on the origin of ideas, theme and character. Program two addresses strategies for exposition, the point of attack for the individual scene, and the writing of dialog. Program three examines methodology, artistic preparation, and the place of personal philosophy and point of view in a screenwriter's work. Featuring seven top Hollywood screenwriters, including Julius Epstein (*Casablanca*), Lawrence Kasdan (*Body Heat*) and Waldo Salt (*Midnight Cowboy*).
VHS: S16545. $179.00.

Hollywood Without Make-Up

The home movies of Ken Murray contain dozens of the movie capitol's brightest stars. Thirty years of memories of the film greats at work and at play. Famous faces include Marilyn Monroe, Walt Disney, Clark Gable, Clara Bow, the Marx Brothers, Laurel and Hardy, Mae West, Charlie Chaplin, Humphrey Bogart and many, many more.
VHS: S10037. $24.95.
Ken Murray, USA, 1962, 51 mins.

Hollywood's Children

Roddy McDowall narrates this fascinating look at Hollywood and the child star—from Shirley Temple and Jackie Cooper to Deanna Durbin, Judy Garland and Mickey Rooney—their triumphs and growing up. 58 mins.
VHS: S06040. $19.98.

The House That Shadows Built

This early documentary is a history of Paramount Pictures from 1912 to the early sound years of 1932, with many interesting looks at the birth and growth of a major Hollywood studio. 60 mins.
VHS: S26069. $29.95.

Ingrid Bergman: Portrait of a Star

This widely praised video biography centers on the life and accomplishments of Ingrid Bergman, the actress and the woman. Featuring clips from 25 of her greatest films, rare Hollywood screen tests, home movies from the 1940s and much more. Narrated by Sir John Gielgud. 60 mins.
VHS: S14625. $19.98.

Interview with Jonas Mekas

The famed director of the Anthology Film Archives discusses his film work and his newly re-built institution.
VHS: S10205. $19.98.
Jordi Torrent, USA, 1986, 20 mins.

Jack L. Warner: The Last Mogul

Newly available photographs reveal the life story of one of Hollywood's most important producers. Bette Davis, Errol Flynn, James Cagney, Edward G. Robinson, Humphrey Bogart and Bugs Bunny are just some of the stars who called Warner boss. Clips from some of his most successful films are included. 104 mins.
VHS: S26375. $19.95.

James Cagney Scrapbook

James Cagney in his most memorable roles including "Blood on the Sun" and "Time of Our Lives." 60 mins.
VHS: S07024. $19.95.

James Cagney: Top of the World

Michael J. Fox hosts this tribute to one of Hollywood's most enduring legends. It is a documentary which includes scenes from some of Cagney's highly popular movies and interviews with the star himself. 60 mins.
VHS: S20876. $14.98.

James Stewart: A Wonderful Life

Johnny Carson hosts this tribute to the life and art of James Stewart, whose essential goodness, honesty and simplicity shaped one indelible performance after another. The program weaves interviews and documentary footage on the set of Stewart's best films. USA, 1987, 111 mins.
VHS: S19472. $19.98.

Jeanette MacDonald

From the interview program *Person to Person*, Jeanette MacDonald is seen in prevues of many of her films, along with Nelson Eddy.
VHS: S10604. $29.95.

John Wayne: The Duke Lives On, A Tribute

A documentary on the remarkable film career of the legendary American actor. Excellent film clips. USA, 48 mins.
VHS: S10645. $19.98.

Judy Garland Scrapbook

Judy's formative years through the premiere of her screen triumph, *A Star Is Born* 60 mins.
VHS: S07022. $19.95.

Kisses

From the innocent puppy-love pecks of Mickey Rooney and Judy Garland in *Girl Crazy* to the steamy passion erupting between Ingrid Bergman and Humphrey Bogart in *Casablanca*, *Kisses* is an intimate look at the best kisses from nearly 100 years of the movies. Hosted by Lauren Bacall. 1991, 47 mins.
VHS: S15463. $14.98.

The Last Diva

Born in Florence in 1888, Francesca Bertini made her film debut in a 1907 short about a beauty contestant, *Goddess of the Sea*. Exactly 70 years later she starred in Bernardo Bertolucci's *1900* as Burt Lancaster's mother. Temperamental, capricious, willful, egocentric, amazingly elegant and beautiful, Francesca was one of the silver screen's last divas. In this touching, funny and wondrous portrait of a unique woman, scenes from many of her classic films are juxtaposed with interviews of the geniuses of Italian cinema—such as the late Sergio Leone, whose father, Roberto Roberti, directed some of Bertini's finest performances. Italian with English subtitles.
VHS: S14170. $29.95.
Gianfranco Mingozzi, Italy, 1982, 85 mins.

Leading Ladies

Bette Davis, Joan Crawford, Carole Lombard, Barbara Stanwyck are highlighted in this homage to the leading ladies of Hollywood's golden era. 55 mins.
VHS: S06628. $19.95.

Leading Men

Errol Flynn, Gary Cooper, James Stewart and Gary Cooper in a nostalgic re-examination of their screen careers. 55 mins.
VHS: S06629. $19.95.

The Legend of Valentino

A portrait of Rudolph Valentino through his triumphant film career, detailing his on and off-screen romances, to his sudden and shocking death. 71 mins.
VHS: S03137. $24.95.

Legends

A documentary about kitsch focusing on actors and performers who impersonate show business icons such as Marilyn Monroe, Judy Garland and Elvis Presley in their bid for legitimacy and acceptance. 54 mins.
VHS: S18742. $19.98.

Love Goddesses

A sixty year survey of women on the American screen, reflecting with extraordinary accuracy the customs, manners and mores of the times. Featured at the 1980 Cannes Film Festival's retrospective on "Women in American Cinema."
VHS: Out of print. For rental only.
Laser: LD70006. $49.95.
Turell/Ferguson, USA, 1974, 83 mins.

Mae West and the Men Who Knew Her

Dom DeLuise hosts this look at the life of America's legendary sex goddess. She appeared with the greatest stars, including Cary Grant and W.C. Fields. The video includes interviews with many who knew her work, from Anthony Quinn to Rex Reed and director Robert Wise. A fascinating exploration of one of the first blond bombshells. 57 mins.
VHS: S25997. $24.95.

Making of a Legend: Gone with the Wind

A feature-length documentary detailing the making of the classic Civil War drama, including rare footage of the screen tests, Clark Gable's explanation of why he originally didn't want the role of Rhett Butler and a demonstration of how special effects turned Los Angeles into Tara. Narrated by Christopher Plummer. 124 mins.
VHS: S09816. $29.95.
Laser: LD70585. $39.98.

The Making of Short Cuts (Luck, Trust & Ketchup)

Robert Altman's award winning film *Short Cuts* was based on the stories of Raymond Carver and featured a cast that includes Anne Archer, Jennifer Jason Leigh, Jack Lemmon, Matthew Modine, Lily Tomlin and Tim Robbins. This documentary reveals the behind-the-scenes story of their interactions. 94 mins.
VHS: S24367. $19.98.

The Making of the Stooges

Here's an inside look at the Three Stooges—their behind-the-scenes antics, classic routines, and hilarious unreleased footage. You'll see family and friends in candid interviews that reveal the true personal lives of Larry, Moe, Shemp, and Curly Joe—from the birth of the Stooges to their greatest successes. 60 minutes.
VHS: S02486. $19.95.

The Marilyn Files

Former husband and close friend Robert Slatzer presents this dedication to Marilyn Monroe that uncovers the events leading to the tragic night of August 4, 1962. 55 mins.
VHS: S16603. $19.95.

Marilyn Monroe—Beyond the Legend

She scaled the heights few could even dream of—and was one of the loneliest stars. This portrait draws on some of her greatest moments in film, including *The Seven Year Itch* and *Gentlemen Prefer Blondes*, on archival footage, and conversations with some of those who knew her best, including Robert Mitchum, Celeste Holm and Shelley Winters. 60 mins.
VHS: S10046. $19.98.

Marilyn Monroe: Goddess of the Silver Screen

Few public figures have received as much press during or after their lifetimes as Marilyn Monroe. This exploration of her career and personal life reveals the highs and the lows, traversing her childhood, her first screen test, her marriages and divorces, and her most memorable performances. 30 mins.
VHS: S15843. $14.99.

Memories of Hollywood, Vol. 1

Highlights from over 50 films set to the music of Academy Award-winning composers. Includes liner notes that list the stars, films and composers, some of whom include Gene Autry, Shirley Temple, Douglas Fairbanks, Errol Flynn, Olivia de Havilland, Buster Keaton and Bette Davis.
VHS: S14009. $19.95.
Dann Moss, USA, 1990, 47 mins.

MGM: When the Lion Roars

This six-decade chronicle of the great movie studio is loaded with film clips, rarely seen archival footage and fascinating commentary from the stars. A three-part documentary, available in individual volumes, or as a specially packaged deluxe set complete with companion booklet.
Part I: The Lion's Roar (1924-1936). Empire builders Louis B. Mayer and "Boy Wonder" Irving G. Thalberg mastermind the star-making machinery that made MGM the nation's foremost "Dream Factory." From the first film (*He Who Gets Slapped*, 1924) through the transition from silent to talkies, and ending with the death of Thalberg in 1936. 123 mins.
VHS: S16613. $19.98.
Part II: The Lion Reigns Supreme (1936-1946). The busiest years for MGM were the war years, a time of bright family-films that are still familiars. With L.B. Mayer as the sole head of the studio, an "MGM look" is created featuring magnificent costumes and sets. 121 mins.
VHS: S16614. $19.98.
Part III: The Lion in Winter (1946 and Beyond). The Golden Age of the MGM Musical sings, dances and swims up a storm. New Vice President Dore Schary turns out gritty, reality-based hits like *Battleground*, and the Mayer-Schary rift turns the boardroom into a different kind of battleground. 122 mins.
VHS: S16615. $19.98.
MGM: When the Lion Roars. Deluxe packaged set.
VHS: S16616. $59.98.
Laser: LD71502. $69.98.

Michael Caine: Breaking the Mold

Told in Michael Caine's own words, this biography relates the story of one of Britain's most well-respected actors. He rose from humble beginnings and overcame the stigma of his working class accent to become an international star. Clips from his most popular films and comments from fellow actors, friends and family complete this amazing story. 60 mins.
VHS: S21520. $19.98.

Minnelli on Minnelli

Liza Minnelli hosts this impressionistic "home movie" about her father, MGM director Vincente Minnelli. From 1943 to 1963, Minnelli made 30 films, including *Yolanda and the Thief*, *Father of the Bride*, *An American in Paris*, *The Bandwagon* and *Some Came Running*. USA, 1987, 84 mins.
VHS: S19473. $19.98.

Moments:
The Making of Claire of the Moon
A behind-the-scenes documentary about the production history and personal difficulties in the making of *Claire of the Moon*, independent filmmaker Nicole Conn's highly personal and erotically charged lesbian drama. The program looks at rehearsals, professional and creative relations between the primary collaborators and the shaping and cutting of the film. 1992.
VHS: S18773. $39.98.

Movies About Movies
A compilation of comedies about the movie industry: Oliver Hardy makes a rare appearance in a Sennett film, *Crazy to Act*. The great Mack Swain kids movie idols in *A Movie Star*. Sennett himself along with Andy Clude and Vernon Dent appear in *Hollywood Kid*, while Snub Pollard is a temperamental director in *The Dumbell*.. 70 mins.
VHS: S08601. $34.95.

Movies of the '20s
An array of classic silents featuring Chaplin, Keaton, Fairbanks, Barrymore and Lon Chaney. 55 mins.
VHS: S06630. $19.95.

Movies of the '30s
Recalls the films of the Depression era, the horror classics, the award winners, and heroes and heroines of the thirties. 55 mins.
VHS: S06631. $19.95.

Movies of the '40s
Parades past Hollywood pre-war propaganda through "The War to End All Wars". This film subjects director Frank Capra's triumphs and the threat to Hollywood of a new medium: television. 55 mins.
VHS: S06632. $19.95.

Music for the Movies:
Bernard Herrmann
This documentary was nominated for an Academy Award because it so successfully illustrates the importance of music to the movies. Herrmann worked on over 50 films during his career, including the legendary *Citizen Kane*. Though most widely known for his work with Hitchcock on films like *The Man Who Knew Too Much* and *Psycho*, he also collaborated with other great directors, such as Martin Scorsese on *Taxi Driver*. Includes clips from these and other films.
VHS: S26668. $24.98.
Laser: LD75108. $24.98.
Josh Waletzky, USA, 1992, 58 mins.

Music for the Movies: Georges Delerue
Though remembered for his work on French New Wave films like *Shoot the Piano Player* and *Jules and Jim*, Delerue also worked in Hollywood on films such as *Silkwood* and *Steel Magnolias*. This documentary charts Delerue's career with clips from these films and interviews with Oliver Stone and Ken Russell. 60 mins.
VHS: S26667. $24.98.
Laser: LD75110. $24.98.

Music for the Movies:
The Hollywood Sound
During the golden age of Hollywood, from the 1930's to the 1950's, musical accompaniment in American film reached a high point. Based on the achievements of 19th century masters, these scores transformed films into overwhelming sensory experiences. This BBC documentary explains their evolution. Under the direction of John Mauceri, the BBC National Orchestra of Wales performs this tribute to Hollywood films like *Laura* and *Casablanca*.
VHS: S26917. $24.98.
Laser: LD75401. $29.98.
J. Waletzky/M. Smilow, Great Britain, 86 mins.

Music for the Movies: Toru Takemitsu
Charlotte Zwerin directed this documentary about the master composer Takemitsu. In addition to his many concert hall works he has composed music for numerous classic Japanese films, including *Kwaidan*, *Double Suicide*, *Empire of Passion*, *Dodes'kaden*, *Ran*, *Black Rain* and many more. Interviews with directors Oshima, Kurosawa and Teshigahara are featured. 58 mins.
VHS: S26666. $24.98.
Laser: LD75109. $24.98.

Music of the West:
A Tribute to the Singing Cowboys
This program honors the spirit and artistry of the classic Western movie stars, the singing cowboys of the 30s, 40s and 50s. Performers include Rex Allen, Gene Autry, Eddie Dean, Monte Hale, Herb Jeffries, Roy Rogers, Sons of the Pioneers and cowboy sex symbol Dwight Yoakam, Clint Black, Emmylou Harris, Ry Cooder, Dusty Rogers and Jane Withers.
VHS: S19685. $19.98.
Charles Gayton, USA, 1993, 70 mins.

Myrna Loy: So Nice to Come Home To
She wasn't a vamp, a vixen or a victim. She was a grown-up woman, the woman everyone fell in love with back in the 1930s and 40s. With priceless film clips and guest star reminiscences, Kathleen Turner hosts this joyful profile of Myrna Loy, the beloved star whose greatest weapon was a raised eyebrow. USA, 1990, 46 mins.
VHS: S14936. $19.98.
Laser: LD72199. $29.95.

The New Cinema
Robert Frank, Wim Wenders, Chantal Akerman, Emile de Antonio, Paul Morrissey, Midori Kurisaki and Michael Snow are all present in this documentary about independent film and video. Altogether 25 directors from around the world share their insights on this vital art practice. Topics range from personal and collective approaches to filmmaking, to the problems and practicalities involved in the process, to wiser attempts to define the very nature of film itself.
VHS: S25048. $39.95.
Peter Wintonick, Canada, 1983, 100 mins.

Oscar's Greatest Moments: 1971-1991
The Academy of Motion Picture Arts and Sciences presents a compilation of memorable highlights from 21 years of televised Oscar presentations. Hollywood's biggest stars, funniest moments, famous speeches, outrageous fashions, lavish productions, sensational songs and most touching memories. Hosted by Karl Malden. 110 mins.
VHS: S16560. $14.95.
Laser: CLV, chapter stops. LD74890. $29.95.

Person to Person Interviews—Volume 1
A compilation of interviews with Marilyn Monroe, Bogart and Bacall, Bing Crosby, Eddie and Debbie, Louis Armstrong, W.C. Handy, Rube Goldberg and Ella Fitzgerald.
VHS: S10601. $29.95.

Person to Person Interviews—Volume 2
Groucho Marx, Harpo Marx, Dizzy Gillespie, Carol Channing, Fred Astaire, Janet Leigh and Tony Curtis, and Maria Callas are featured in this collection of interviews.
VHS: S10602. $29.95.

The Pin-Ups: A Picture History
of America's Dream Girls
From French Can-Can dancers to today's supermodels, screen sirens to sex kittens, this encyclopedic look at the pin-up reveals the continuing allure of this sturdy tradition. Marilyn Monroe, Betty Grable, Sophia Loren and Brigitte Bardot are just a few of the unforgettable models included in this video. 60 mins.
VHS: S26154. $19.95.
Laser: CLV. LD75101. $34.95.
Jerome Camuzat, USA, 1994, 60 mins.

Premiere of "A Star Is Born"
A who's who of Hollywood is captured showing up for the premiere of the Judy Garland version of *A Star Is Born*. Jack Carson, George Jessel and others interview such luminaries as Tony Curtis, Lauren Bacall, Dean Martin, Hedda Hopper, Elizabeth Taylor, Liberace and his mother, Joan Crawford, Jack Palance, Cesar Romero, James Dean, Kim Novak and, of course, Judy Garland, and many, many others. USA, 1954, 30 mins.
VHS: S05711. $19.95.

Remembering Marilyn
Lee Remick hosts this program about Hollywood's most public yet misunderstood celebrity, with rare footage of "Norma Jean Baker" from her teenage years, never-before-released films of her stormy marriages to Joe DiMaggio and Arthur Miller, and interviews with many who knew her, including Robert Wagner, Robert Mitchum and Gloria Steinem. 48 mins.
VHS: S09929. $14.98.

The Republic Pictures Story
Gene Autry, Roy Rogers and John Wayne headline this star-spangled tribute to the studio that brought America singing cowboys, action-packed cliffhanger serials and futuristic sci-fi fantasies. 114 mins.
Laser: LD71500. $29.98.

Robert Mitchum: The Reluctant Star
At 12 he was riding box cars; by the time he was 15, he was sentenced to a Georgia chain gang. Robert Mitchum got his first acting job because he "looked mean around the eyes", and what followed was film history in the making. Includes film clips and discussions with friends such as Deborah Kerr and Jane Russell. 60 mins.
VHS: S14626. $19.95.

The Search for Haunted Hollywood
A chilling investigation into Hollywood's gothic past and surreal underside, as host John Davidson takes the viewer on a haunted tour of studio backlots, expressive mansions, and eerie grave sites, looking at Tom Mix's haunted house or Mary Pickford's strange dressing room. With Patrick Macnee, Harry Blackstone, Max Maven, Nonie Fagatt and Richard Senate. 90 mins.
VHS: S17982. $59.95.

Sex and Buttered Popcorn
An uncensored look at the era of movie making which had its roots in the tinsel of the carnival, flourishing throughout the twenties to the fifties. Candid looks at such films as: *She Should'a Said No*, *They Wear No Clothes* and *Child Bride*. Hosted by Ned Beatty. "Wild…funny stuff" (Leonard Maltin).
VHS: S14735. $59.95.

Shirley Temple Scrapbook
Shirley Temple's career on and off the screen from her only color film, *The Little Princess* and in "screen magazine" footage of her personal appearances and marriage. 60 mins.
VHS: S07023. $19.95.

Shooting for Black and White
with Allen Daviau and Denis Lenoir
Daviau is a Hollywood DP who shot *E.T.*, *The Color Purple* and more, while *Monsieur Hire* and *Shuttlecock* are two of Lenoir's films. Here these cinematographers provide a storehouse of information by shooting black and white, exploring silent film techniques and the integration of color film with black and white film. 55 mins.
VHS: S24903. $89.95.

Shooting for Drama
with Robby Muller and Peter James
Muller shot *Paris, Texas* and *To Live and Die in LA* among other films, while James is known for his work in *Alive* and *Driving Miss Daisy*. Together these pros provide great technical and aesthetic insights into the art of cinematography, by shooting the same script with startlingly different results. 55 mins.
VHS: S24900. $89.95.

Shooting for Fantasy
with Sacha Vierny and Denis Lenoir
Monsieur Hire and *Shuttlecock* are two of Lenoir's films. Vierny is famed for his work on films like *Hiroshima, Mon Amour* and *The Cook, The Thief, His Wife and Her Lover*. In this video they shoot the same script but rely on differing special effects to create a fantasy world. 55 mins.
VHS: S24902. $89.95.

Shooting for Realism
with Allen Daviau and Sacha Vierny
Daviau is a Hollywood DP who shot *E.T.*, *The Color Purple* and more, while Vierny is a French cinematographer who shot *Hiroshima, Mon Amour* and *The Cook, The Thief, His Wife and Her Lover*. Given the same set-up, they create original images that are compared and explained to reveal cinematographic insights. 55 mins.
VHS: S24901. $89.95.

The Spencer Tracy Legacy
Hosted by Katharine Hepburn, his glamorous co-star and best friend of 25 years, this delightful film delivers a warm, engrossing, personal insight into the life of Hollywood legend Spencer Tracy. This documentary tribute features interviews with Frank Sinatra, Elizabeth Taylor and many more. USA, 1986, 88 mins.
VHS: S15020. $19.98.

Starring Bette Davis: The TV Years
Davis brings her big screen talent to this trio of TV films. She plays an interior designer, a nasty magazine publisher and a theatrical agent. All three roles give her the chance to be both naughty and nice, but the last is especially good. It will remind the devoted fan of *All About Eve*, and features Gary Merrill, Joi Lansing and Jack Albertson. 76 mins.
VHS: S25923. $24.95.

Steve McQueen—Man on the Edge
The story of the reform school kid who became one of Hollywood's biggest paid stars with roles in such films as *Magnificent Seven*, *The Great Escape* and *Bullitt*. Home movies, clips, actors Chuck Norris and Karl Malden recollect McQueen's career. Narrated by James Coburn. 60 mins.
VHS: S05954. $19.98.

Steve McQueen: Man Behind the Wheel
A documentary profile of Steve McQueen, created from behind-the-scenes interviews and production history on two of his films, Peter Yates' *Bullitt* (1968) and Lee H. Katzin's *Le Mans* (1971).
VHS: S18900. $19.95.

Strictly G.I.
A collection of wartime shorts featuring Judy Garland, Harpo Marx, Bob Hope, Frank Sinatra, Betty Grable, Bing Crosby, and many others.
VHS: S10579. $19.95.

Through the Eyes of Forrest Gump
This documentary offers a view of the filmic processes that made this magical movie possible. Sophisticated techniques allowed Tom Hanks to do such amazing things as hug Lyndon B. Johnson. 37 mins.
VHS: S24310. $9.95.

Tribute to Dar Robinson
Dar Robinson was Hollywood's premier stuntman, who never broke a bone during his 19-year stunt career but lost his life in a freak motorcycle accident at the age of 39. Sylvester Stallone, Burt Reynolds, Clint Eastwood and others pay tribute to Robinson; the tape features stunts from *Lethal Weapon*, *Magnum Force*, *Papillon* and other films. 60 mins.
VHS: S12471. $19.98.

Tribute to Hollywood Stuntmen
Christopher Reeve hosts this special starring Mel Gibson, Tom Selleck, Arnold Schwarzenegger and thrilling stunt scenes from *Rambo*, *Red Heat*, *Running Man* and other films. 60 mins.
VHS: S12470. $19.98.

TVTV Looks at the Oscars
Lily Tomlin is your guide to this irreverent, backstage look at Hollywood's annual awards ceremony. Watch Steven Spielberg lose out in his first bid for best director. Join Lily as she buys her acceptance gown, Lee Grant rehearsing her "losing smile" and Michael Douglas planning his nominations sweep. 60 mins.
VHS: S15556. $24.95.

The Universal Story
Richard Dreyfuss leads viewers behind the scenes for a look at the history of one of Hollywood's greatest studios. From horror icons like Bela Lugosi and Boris Karloff to America's sweetheart, Deanna Durbin, to the thrillers of Alfred Hitchcock, Universal has orchestrated the best movie talents. Clips from the work of these earlier figures are joined with material from today. Sections of *E.T. the Extra-Terrestrial*, *Jurassic Park* and *Schindler's List* are featured.
VHS: S27531. $12.95.
Laser: LD75537. $34.98.
David Heeley, USA, 1995, 119 mins.

Victor Sjostrom
Born and raised in Sweden, his movies are classics which influence filmmakers to this day. Chaplin called him "the greatest director in the world." In the States he directed Chaney, Gish and Garbo. Today most Americans only know him as the star of Ingmar Bergman's (his most famous pupil) 1957 *Wild Strawberries*. But his legacy remains— *The Phantom Carriage*, *He Who Gets Slapped* and *The Wind*, to name just a few of his many wonderful films—and this fascinating documentary tells the dramatic story of one of cinema's giants. Swedish with English subtitles.
VHS: S14171. $29.95.
Gosta Werner, Sweden, 1981, 65 mins.

Visions of Light
Cinematography is the art on which all motion pictures are based. In this documentary over 125 unforgettable films are used to tell the story of this evolving art form. This 1993 winner of the New York Film Critics Circle Award will transfix cinephiles with the glory of motion picture photography.
VHS: S20742. $94.98.
Laser: LD71986. $39.99.
Arnold Glassman, USA, 1993, 95 mins.

Vivien Leigh: Scarlett and Beyond
Vivien Leigh, so many years after her death, still remains elusive, never to be fully known; hosted by Jessica Lange and featuring numerous celebrity interview clips, this documentary tribute gives us new insights into the star who captured the greatest woman's role in the history of motion pictures: Scarlett O'Hara in *Gone with the Wind*. USA, 1990, 46 mins.
VHS: S14937. $19.98.

The Voice from the Screen
A look behind the scenes of the Vitaphone sound-film system. This curious demonstration film was made in 1926 and features the Executive Vice President of Bell Telephone Laboratories explaining just how the sound-on-disc system works. Two musicians play a guitar and ukelele duet for the audience one year before *The Jazz Singer*. USA, 1926, 34 mins.
VHS: S06475. $24.95.

We're Off to See the Munchkins
Follow the yellow brick road to Chesterton, Indiana, site of the annual *Wizard of Oz* festival. This documentary tells the history of the beloved film through the perspective of the little people who portrayed the Munchkins. They tell how they first came upon Oz and recall the past glory of MGM. 78 mins.
VHS: S21870. $39.95.

What Do Those Old Films Mean?
Noel Burch's remarkable Channel 4 series, discovering the world of silent cinema never before told.

Volume 1: Great Britain 1900-1912—Along the Great Divide. Using extremely rare films, newly scored music and a lively commentary, film historian Noel Burch explores the contradictions in early British cinema between the "gentlemen inventors of the cinema" and film as an entertainment for the poor. Early films in Britain, says Burch, either showed the poor what bright, happy lives their "betters" led, or held up to them their own, usually drunken, depravity. At the same time, the early filmmakers worked in a climate of fear in an era of panic that "the empire was in danger." By examining the earliest classics, like Cecil Hepworth's *Rescued by Rover* and other, much more obscure films, Burch documents the British filmmakers as the earliest pioneers in the techniques of film editing. 26 mins.
VHS: S08682. $29.95.

Volume 2: U.S.A. 1902-1914—Tomorrow the World. Film historian Noel Burch examines early filmmaking in America against the social background of the immigrant masses streaming into the slums, factories and sweatshops of an industrialized America. It was these immigrants who became the earliest patrons of the nickelodeons, in spite of the fact that many of the earliest films depicted non-Americans as ridiculous or loathsome. But when the middle-class discovered the cinema, American movies changed—American film discovered narrative, and at the same time began to censor its own productions, depriving them of social content and criticism. Rare film footage provides the background for this fascinating cinematic and social analysis in this second volume in a remarkable series produced by Britain's Channel Four Television. 26 mins.
VHS: S08683. $29.95.

Volume 3: Denmark 1902-1914—She! Why was Copenhagen the undisputed birthplace of the mature cinema, of psychological realism on the screen, at a time when French or American films were no more than rudimentary melodramas? Film historian Noel Burch examines the Danish silent film phenomenon both from the standpoint of its key figures (the actors Asta Nielsen and Urban Gad, the powerful producer Ole Olsen), and from the social perspective of a Denmark in which women had an advanced position for the time, where feminism was prominent and attitudes toward sexuality liberal. The early Danish cinema was innovative and in such techniques as lighting, camera angles or editing within one and the same scene, they adopted many techniques before the American directors. As the legendary actress Asta Nielsen wrote in her autobiography, "At a time when almost no one considered that films might be an art, I was determined to put all my energies into the artistic potentialities I had discovered in myself during that first film…If I had had a clear awareness of the terrifying world of unscrupulous businessmen who in those days ran the film industry—I would probably not have embarked on that adventure with such enthusiasm." 26 mins.
VHS: S08684. $29.95.

Volume 4: France 1904-1912—The Enemy Below. "One of the most remarkable features of the seventh art is its unanimous appeal to the masses, with none of the intellectual preparation needed for literature or music," wrote Louis Delluc, and in this fascinating program covering the early years of cinema in France, film historian and critic Noel Burch follows the thesis that the appeal of the silent French cinema was the working class. "We were attracted to everything denied us by a moral code laid down by others: luxury, wild parties, the great brass band of vices and the image of woman too, but a woman heroized, elevated to adventuress…a generation of young men fell head over heels in love with Musidora in *Les Vampires*," wrote the poet Louis Aragon. 26 mins.
VHS: S08685. $29.95.

Volume 5: USSR 1926-1930—Born Yesterday. Amid general poverty, social disorder, an exodus from the rural areas, and the sudden arrival of women in industry, post-Revolutionary Russia was also a period of extraordinary social and cultural experiment. The artists saw art as an instrument of social change, of encouraging new relationships between individuals. The filmmakers and filmmaking groups concentrated on social agitation, on new forms of newsreel, on incorporating into film the great formal experiments of the era. In this fascinating program, film historian Noel Burch focuses on the sexual politics of Soviet cinema—issues such as the collectivization of domestic tasks and child care and the abolition of sexual division of labor in the home. Using rare films which are virtually unknown in the West, Burch provides a unique perspective on this great era of cinema in a climate of virulent change. 26 mins.
VHS: S08686. $29.95.

Volume 6: Germany 1926-1932—Under Two Flags. This volume of *What Do Those Old Films Mean?* focuses on films produced in Germany in the 20's, rarely shown or discussed today. But influenced by the achievements of the young Soviet cinema, the German social workers' movements created the German Workers' Film. Among these early productions were such landmark films as *The Other Side of the Street, Our Daily Bread, Mother Krausen's Journey to Happiness,* and *Kuhle Wampe.* This remarkable movement for a "populist" cinema in Germany of the Weimar Republic had much in common with similar efforts in other fields of the arts—for example, the art of Kathe Kollwitz. But it was ultimately replaced by the more palatable—and cheerful—films of Billy Wilder and Robert Siodmak, and, ultimately, by the victory of Nazism. 26 mins.
VHS: S08687. $29.95.
Complete Set. Available at a special price.
VHS: S08688. $149.75.

When Chicago Was Hollywood

An examination of Chicago's film culture during the silent era when Chicago was the center of the comedy film as well as the all-black-owned silent movie company at the birth of the form in the early 20th century.
VHS: S18901. $19.95.

William Holden: The Golden Boy

This program reveals a charming and unconventional man with a "wild streak" and a compulsion to test himself at every turn. With clips from his best films, such as *Sunset Boulevard, Stalag 17* and *Sabrina.* Narrated by Richard Kiley. 60 mins.
VHS: S14623. $19.98.

Women Who Made the Movies

Little has been publicized about the many contributions women have made to the growth of the motion picture industry. This unique documentary uses rare film clips and stills to trace the careers and works of such filmmakers as Alice Guy-Blache, Ida Lupino, Ruth Ann Baldwin, Leni Riefenstahl, Lois Weber, Cleo Madison and many others who made a lasting contribution to cinema history. 56 mins.
VHS: S15694. $29.95.

Yul Brynner: The Man Who Was King

Eli Wallach, Rita Moreno and director John Frankenheimer are among the professionals who join Brynner's family to discuss the screen legend. Clips from his films *The King and I, The Ten Commandments, The Magnificent Seven* and *Westworld,* among others, show how this Oscar-winner managed to stay on top until the very end. 58 mins.
VHS: S26763. $24.95.

classic american CINEMA

JOHN FORD

Arrowsmith
Ronald Coleman stars as Martin Arrowsmith, a small town doctor and research scientist who goes to work in the West Indies with a serum to halt the plague. Tragedy forces a reevaluation of his career and personal life. Based on Sinclair Lewis' novel.
VHS: S00068. $19.98.
John Ford, USA, 1931, 95 mins.

Drums Along the Mohawk
Claudette Colbert and Henry Fonda are featured in this story of Colonial life in upstate New York during the Revolutionary War.
VHS: S06521. $19.98.
John Ford, USA, 1939, 103 mins.

Fort Apache
Henry Fonda stars as Col. Thursday, assigned to a remote southwestern garrison, determined to develop a reputation as an Indian fighter. John Wayne is the boot-strap veteran who sees folly in this dangerous scheme.
VHS: S03220. $19.95.
John Ford, USA, 1948, 127 mins.

Four Sons
This silent drama represents one of John Ford's earliest efforts. Set in Germany, it tells the story of a mother and her four sons. Three go off to fight a war and meet their fate, but one travels to America, where he establishes a new life. When his brothers are killed he invites his mother to live with him in the new world. With Margaret Mann, James Hall, Earle Foxe and Charles Morton. Also known as Grandma Bernle Learns Her Letters.
VHS: S27372. $19.95.
John Ford, USA, 1928, 100 mins.

The Fugitive
Henry Fonda plays the priest battling an anti-clerical regime in a dictatorial Central American country in this adaptation of the Graham Greene novel The Power and the Glory. With Dolores del Rio, Pedro Armendariz.
VHS: S12018. $19.98.
John Ford, USA, 1948, 99 mins.

Grapes of Wrath
Certainly one of the all-time classics, this adaptation of the John Steinbeck novel of the dust bowl migration from Oklahoma to California stars Henry Fonda as Tom Joad, John Carradine as Casey. The film won the Academy Award for Best Director.
VHS: S00525. $19.98.
Laser: LD71013. $49.98.
John Ford, USA, 1946, 129 mins.

The History of World War II: Battle of Midway
John Ford's documentary on the Battle of Midway, the large-scale naval engagement that irrevocably changed the course of the war, giving the momentum to the American forces. Ford was hurt during the shooting.
VHS: S19677. $19.95.
John Ford, USA, 1943, 18 mins.

The History of World War II: December 7th
John Ford re-staged the Japanese attack on Pearl Harbor by using Hollywood sound stages to approximate the confusion, panic and disorder. Winner of the Academy Award for Best Documentary Production in 1943.
VHS: S19676. $19.95.
John Ford, USA, 1943, 34 mins.

The Horse Soldiers
John Wayne stars as Colonel Marlowe in this John Ford Civil War adventure. The year is 1863 and the war along the Mississippi River has bogged down. Wayne takes a brigade of Union cavalry on a 600-mile raid to stir things up. With William Holden as the pacifist surgeon and Constance Towers as a troublesome plantation owner. Also along for the ride are Hoot Gibson, Strother Martin, Ken Curtis and Denver Pyle.
VHS: S12138. $19.95.
Laser: Chapter search. Includes original theatrical trailer.
LD71664. $34.98.
John Ford, USA, 1858, 119 mins.

How Green Was My Valley
An offscreen narrator reflects on his life and work in John Ford's poetic and beautiful rendering of Welsh village life. Based on the novel by Richard Llewellyn. With Walter Pidgeon, Maureen O'Hara and Roddy McDowall. Winner for Best Picture in 1941.
VHS: S18449. $19.98.
John Ford, USA, 1941, 118 mins.

How the West Was Won
A large-scale epic about three generations of pioneers, with a great cast and brilliant direction by John Ford, George Marshall and Henry Hathaway. With George Peppard, Debbie Reynolds, Carroll Baker, Gregory Peck, Henry Fonda, James Stewart, John Wayne.
VHS: S11555. $29.98.
Laser: LD70595. $39.98.
Ford/Marshall/Hathaway, USA, 1963, 155 mins.

Hurricane
John Ford directed Dorothy Lamour and Jon Hall as two people seeking to escape the vengeance of a relentless policeman on the island of Manikoora. The special storm effects have yet to be topped. With Raymond Massey, C. Aubrey Smith, Thomas Mitchell and John Carradine. Based by the novel by Charles Nordhoff and James Norman Hall.
VHS: S00592. $19.98.
John Ford, USA, 1937, 102 mins.

Judge Priest
John Ford's masterpiece of classic Americana, set in a small southern town in 1890. Will Rogers is funny and touching as the aging judge, and Stepin Fetchit is the original method actor.
VHS: S03012. $14.95.
John Ford, USA, 1934, 84 mins.

Just Pals
John Ford stands out as a director who worked with film throughout the silent era, only to find even greater success with the advent of sound. This silent comedy is one of his earlier works. It follows the story of a town's ne'er-do-well as he encounters a series of misunderstandings. With Buck Jones, Helen Ferguson, William Buckley and George Stone.
VHS: S27373. $19.95.
John Ford, USA, 1920

The Last Hurrah
John Ford directs Spencer Tracy as Frank Skeffington, an Irish-Catholic big city mayor running his toughest political race. Based on the Edwin O'Connor novel. Top notch cast includes Pat O'Brien, Basil Rathbone, Jeffrey Hunter, Jane Darwell, John Carradine, Donald Crisp and Dianne Foster. B&W.
VHS: S06827. $19.95.
John Ford, USA, 1958, 121 mins.

Long Grey Line
Tyrone Power stars in this sentimental John Ford salute to a cherished West Point athletic instructor. Power plays Maher, a rebellious cadet who finds discipline under athletic coach Ward Bond and responsibility by marrying Maureen O'Hara. With Donald Crisp, Robert Francis, Betsy Palmer, Phil Carey, Milburn Stone as John Pershing and Harry Carey Jr. as Dwight Eisenhower.
VHS: S16406. $19.95.
John Ford, USA, 1955, 138 mins.

Long Voyage Home
One of John Ford's most important films, loosely based on stories by Eugene O'Neill, the film focuses on a group of men at sea, set during World War II, and on their dreams and ambitions. With John Wayne, Thomas Mitchell.
VHS: S04415. $19.98.
John Ford, USA, 1940, 101 mins.

Lost Patrol
A classic military adventure that centers on a British patrol, headed by Victor McLaglen, who have lost their way in the Mesopotamian desert during the first World War. One by one their numbers dwindle as unseen Arab adversaries choose their deadly accurate targets. With Wallace Ford, Reginald Denny, Alan Hale, Billy Bevan and Boris Karloff as a religious fanatic. Based on the novel Patrol by Philip MacDonald. This re-issue contains additional footage.
VHS: S03013. $19.98.
John Ford, USA, 1934, 73 mins.

Man Who Shot Liberty Valance
Jimmy Stewart is the big-city bungling lawyer determined to rid the town of Shinbone of its Number One Nuisance: Liberty Valance (Lee Marvin). With John Wayne and Vera Miles. A culminating Ford western, debunking of western mythology.
VHS: S03891. $19.95.
John Ford, USA, 1962, 120 mins.

Mary of Scotland
John Ford directed this lavish historical drama starring Katharine Hepburn as Mary Stuart, the Catholic threat to the English throne. Her death is less a result of politics or religion as Kate risks all for love. With Fredric March, John Carradine and Florence Eldridge as Queen Elizabeth.
VHS: Out of print. For rental only.
Laser: LD71131. $29.98.
John Ford, USA, 1936, 123 mins.

Mister Roberts
World War II comedy drama about a cargo ship and its crew restless for combat action, with Henry Fonda, James Cagney and Jack Lemmon in an Academy Award winning supporting role as Ensign Pulver.
VHS: S02172. $19.98.
Laser: LD75429. $39.98.
John Ford, USA, 1955, 123 mins.

Mogambo
Clark Gable is cast as a great white hunter being pursued by two desirable women in the wilds of Africa. Grace Kelly and Ava Gardner supply Gable with a safari he will never forget. With Donald Sinden, Laurence Naismith and Philip Stainton. A lusty, full-color remake of Red Dust, which also starred Gable.
VHS: S13193. $19.98.
John Ford, USA, 1953, 115 mins.

My Darling Clementine
A genuine American classic, with the climactic shoot-out at the O.K. Corral between Wyatt Earp, Doc Holliday and the vicious Clanton boys. With Henry Fonda, Victor Mature, Walter Brennan, Tim Holt and Linda Darnell.
VHS: S01784. $19.98.
John Ford, USA, 1946, 97 mins.

The Quiet Man
John Ford's lyrical portrait of Ireland revolves around an American prizefighter (John Wayne) who returns to his birthplace to buy back the family cottage and marry the temptress Maureen O'Hara. Just wonderful.
VHS: S15908. $19.98.
Laser: 40th Anniversary edition includes The Making of the Quiet Man. LD71497. $59.98.
John Ford, USA, 1952, 153 mins.

Rio Grande
John Wayne is Lt. Colonel Kirby Yorke in the third of the trilogy of John Ford's films on the U.S. Cavalry. His mission is to cross the Rio Grande into Mexico and put an end to an annoying band of Apaches. On another front he fights to regain the love of his southern wife who hasn't forgiven him for burning down her family plantation during the Civil War. With Maureen O'Hara, Ben Johnson and J. Carrol Naish. B&W. 45th Anniversary Edition; digitally remastered. Includes original trailer and "The Making of Rio Grande," hosted by Leonard Maltin.
VHS: S06186. $19.98.
Laser: CLV. LD72023. $39.98.
John Ford, USA, 1950, 105 mins.

Searchers
Classic John Ford Western starring John Wayne as Ethan Edwards, a Civil War veteran intent on finding the daughters of his murdered brother, who have been captured by the Comanches. With Jeffrey Hunter, Ward Bond and Natalie Wood.
VHS: S01731. $19.98.
Laser: LD70672. $34.98.
John Ford, USA, 1956, 119 mins.

Sergeant Rutledge
John Ford's post-Civil War courtroom drama about a highly decorated black cavalry officer (Woody Strode) on trial for allegedly raping a white woman. Ford employs highly cinematic devices, flashbacks and multiple perspectives to chronicle Strode's accomplishments. With Jeffrey Hunter, Constance Towers and Billie Burke.
VHS: S18609. $19.98.
John Ford, USA, 1960, 118 mins.

Seven Women
John Ford's last film is a stern melodrama about a group of American women operating a Chinese mission in 1935 under the threat of bandits trying to overrun them. The cast includes Anne Bancroft, Flora Robson, Margaret Leighton, Sue Lyon and Betty Field.
Laser: LD70149. $34.98.
John Ford, USA, 1966, 100 mins.

She Wore a Yellow Ribbon
John Ford teamed up with John Wayne as an iron-willed calvary captain who is battling a Cheyenne uprising. An epic film which won the Oscar for its cinematography.
VHS: S03219. $19.95.
John Ford, USA, 1946, 93 mins.

Stagecoach
John Ford at his greatest in a story of nine passengers on a Cheyenne-bound stagecoach, each with a singular reason for the journey, determined to live through the dangerous trip. With John Wayne, Claire Trevor, John Carradine, Andy Devine.
VHS: S01247. $19.98.
Laser: LD74715. $34.98.
John Ford, USA, 1939, 96 mins.

Straight Shooting
John Ford's first feature. A silent western starring Harry Carey as Cheyenne Harry, an outlaw hired by greedy ranchers to drive off the farmers. Harry has a change of heart and fights for the sodbusters. With Hoot Gibson, Vester Pegg and Molly Malone. Silent.
VHS: S04811. $24.95.
John Ford, USA, 1917, 57 mins.

Sun Shines Bright
It is four decades since General Lee surrendered, but Fairfield, Kentucky's proud Judge Priest (Charles Winninger) still has the Confederate spirit in his heart. Though he is up for reelection, his compassionate nature involves him in romantic and racial affairs that threaten his political career.
VHS: S12444. $19.98.
John Ford, USA, 1953, 92 mins.

They Were Expendable
So much for the surprise ending. John Wayne and Robert Montgomery star as P.T. boat commanders in the Philippines when the Japanese bomb Pearl Harbor. They battle enemy cruisers, planes and floating mine fields and still find time for romance while Army nurses like Donna Reed. A gutsy tribute to brave men from director John Ford. Cast includes Ward Bond, Jack Holt, Marshall Thompson and Cameron Mitchell.
VHS: S12141. $19.98.
Laser: LD71158. $39.98.
John Ford, USA, 1945, 136 mins.

Three Godfathers
Just before Christmas, John Wayne, Pedro Armendariz and Harry Carey Sr. rob a bank in Welcome, Arizona and head into the desert to avoid a posse lead by Ward Bond. They encounter an ailing, pregnant woman in a sandstorm and agree to take care of the child they deliver no matter what. The original "three men and a baby" wasn't directed for laughs. Adapted from the story by Peter B. Kyne.
VHS: S12136. $19.95.
Laser: LD71693. $34.98.
John Ford, USA, 1948, 106 mins.

Two by John Ford
James Stewart in Flashing Spikes and John Wayne in Rookie of the Year. Two baseball stories directed by John Ford.
VHS: S15223. $19.98.
John Ford, USA, 90 mins.

Two Rode Together
Jimmy Stewart is the cynical marshall who is hired to rescue pioneers of the west who are being held by the Comanches. With Richard Widmark.
VHS: S03866. $14.95.
John Ford, USA, 1961, 109 mins.

Wee Willie Winkie
Shirley Temple becomes a little soldier in this blend of comedy and adventure based on a story by Rudyard Kipling and directed by John Ford as she earns her stripes when she averts a bloody uprising. With Cesar Romero and Victor McLaglen.
VHS: S09991. $19.98.
John Ford, USA, 1937, 100 mins.

What Price Glory?
James Cagney and Dan Dailey star in John Ford's stirring film about rambunctious soldiers seeing combat in World War I France.
VHS: S14145. $19.98.
John Ford, USA, 1952, 111 mins.

Wings of Eagles
John Wayne stars in the film bio of Navy airman Frank "Spig" Wead, who turned to screenwriting after a serious accident. This John Ford film covers two World Wars and a rocky marriage to Maureen O'Hara. With Dan Dailey, Ken Curtis, Kenneth Tobey and Ward Bond as John Dodge, a film director comically modeled on John Ford.
VHS: S12135. $19.95.
John Ford, USA, 1957, 118 mins.

Young Mr. Lincoln
Henry Fonda stars as Abraham Lincoln during his years of struggle as a beginning lawyer. Considered an American masterpiece by French cinephiles.
VHS: S06523. $19.98.
Laser: LD71225. $39.98.
John Ford, USA, 1939, 100 mins.

SAM FULLER

The Big Red One
Sam Fuller directs in his comeback film this epic story of five fighting men who cut a path from North Africa to Czechoslovakia, based on Fuller's own experiences as a rifleman with the Army's First Infantry Division. A rich, realistic and individual look at war. With Lee Marvin.
VHS: S03528. $19.98.
Sam Fuller, USA, 1980, 114 mins.

China Gate
Sam Fuller's saga of war and romance set in Indochina. Gene Barry stars as part of a multi-national troop engaging in a deadly mission behind enemy lines; a true melodrama with Nat King Cole singing a couple of songs and playing a foreign legionnaire, and a co-starring performance by Angie Dickinson.
VHS: S09623. $19.95.
Sam Fuller, USA, 1957, 97 mins.

Dead Pigeon on Beethoven Street
A strange, very unique, paranoid thriller from Sam Fuller, with Glenn Corbett playing a government agent intent on digging up incriminating evidence that he can use to frame big-time politicians. The film managed to anticipate the murky feeling of the Nixon era with its credible depiction of a government intent on subverting justice.
VHS: S25924. $24.95.
Sam Fuller, USA, 1972, 92 mins.

The Naked Kiss (The Iron Kiss)
A reformed big city prostitute (ably played by Constance Towers) who tries to go the straight and narrow route in small town America finds that beneath the little town's squeaky clean veneer lies perversion and corruption of the highest order. Michael Dante plays a creepy child molester. (Is there any other kind?) One of the best from Fuller and a cult classic.
VHS: S06479. $29.95.
Laser: LD70423. $44.95.
Sam Fuller, USA, 1964, 90 mins.

Pick Up on South Street
A pickpocket inadvertently acquires top-secret microfilm and becomes a target for espionage agents. Starring Richard Widmark and Thelma Ritter. "This lyrical skid-row noir is one of the great movies of the '50s. The Cold War plot pushes McCarthyism to the far side of the moon" (J. Hoberman). Written and directed by Sam Fuller.
VHS: S13608. $19.98.
Sam Fuller, USA, 1953, 80 mins.

Shock Corridor
To catch a killer and win a Pulitzer prize, reporter-hero Johnny Barrett has himself committed to a mental institution. He must find out who killed Sloan in the kitchen by questioning three inmates who witnessed the crime—men driven crazy by the hypocrisies of the American dream relating to racism, anti-communism and the bomb. A complex, wacky masterpiece by one of Hollywood's great directors, Sam Fuller.
VHS: S18328. $29.95.
Laser: LD70458. $49.95.
Sam Fuller, USA, 1963, 101 mins.

Underworld, U.S.A.

Cliff Robertson stars in this Sam Fuller film about a young man who infiltrates a criminal organization to gain revenge for the death of his father. With Dolores Dorn, Beatrice Kay, and Robert Emhardt as a Mob boss. Crime doesn't pay as well as it used to when bullets were cheaper. B&W.
VHS: S06828. $69.95.
Sam Fuller, USA, 1961, 99 mins.

HOWARD HAWKS

Air Force

This is the daring story of a B-17 "flying fortress" and her tough, brave crew who, after setting out on a routine mission, end up becoming WWII heroes. Directed by the great Howard Hawks in the tradition of his own *The Dawn Patrol*.
VHS: S15130. $19.98.
Howard Hawks, USA, 1943, 119 mins.

Ball of Fire

Mild-mannered professor Gary Cooper is hard at work on a new encyclopedia. He finds the help of a brassy nightclub singer, played by Barbara Stanwyck, both invigorating and distracting. With S.Z. Sakall, Oscar Homolka and Leonid Kinskey as interested faculty members and Dan Duryea as trouble. Script by Billy Wilder and Charles Brackett. B&W.
VHS: S03115. $19.98.
Howard Hawks, USA, 1942, 111 mins.

Barbary Coast

Edward G. Robinson shines as a big shot San Francisco saloon owner during the Gold Rush days. Miriam Hopkins is the dance hall queen who attracts his attention. With Joel McCrea, Walter Brennan, Brian Donlevy and Donald Meek. A brawling action adventure from Howard Hawks. Script by Ben Hecht and Charles MacArthur.
VHS: S03116. $19.98.
Howard Hawks, USA, 1935, 91 mins.

Big Sky

Kirk Douglas as a leader of a keelboat crew out to establish a new trading post in the Northwest and upper reaches of the Missouri River. From the director of *Red River* and *The Big Sleep*.
VHS: S02143. $14.98.
Howard Hawks, USA, 1952, 122 mins.

Big Sleep

Humphrey Bogart is Philip Marlowe in this entertaining adaptation of Raymond Chandler's novel. Blackmail, murder, sex and drugs all come into play as the ace detective tries to sort out the guilty parties. Even the author couldn't figure out who killed the chauffeur. With Lauren Bacall, Martha Vickers and Elisha Cook, Jr.
VHS: S09389. $19.95.
Laser: LD70174. $34.98.
Howard Hawks, USA, 1946, 114 mins.

Bringing Up Baby

One of the funniest movies from Hollywood, a classic screwball comedy. Katharine Hepburn is the madcap heiress with her pet leopard "Baby", who falls for an absent-minded zoologist (Cary Grant) and makes a shambles of his life. Briskly paced fun with May Robson, Charlie Ruggles and Barry Fitzgerald supporting the leads.
VHS: S09362. $14.98.
Howard Hawks, USA, 1938, 102 mins.

Ceiling Zero

Howard Hawks' treatment of professionalism and honor, about a brilliant through irresponsible civil airlines pilot (James Cagney) forced to re-evaluate his life when his self-absorption causes a friend's death. "Directed at a breakneck pace which emphasizes its lean fiber and its concentration on the essentials of its theme" (Andrew Sarris). With Pat O'Brien, June Travis, Stuart Erwin and Isabel Jewell.
VHS: S19039. $19.98.
Howard Hawks, USA, 1936, 95 mins.

Come and Get It

Frances Farmer is cast as a beautiful woman desired by both a father and his son in this drama set in the timber country of the Northwest. Walter Brennan made his mark in this film which was based on a novel by Edna Ferber. William Wyler took over direction from Howard Hawks.
VHS: S01537. $19.98.
William Wyler/Howard Hawks, USA, 1936, 99 mins.

Criminal Code

A young man's birthday party turns into a nightmare when he kills a man in self-defense. After a series of twists the D.A. who railroaded him into prison hires the convict years later to be his chauffeur, and through this he meets and falls in love with the D.A.'s daughter. A very well done, early Howard Hawks film. With John Huston, Phillip Holmes, Constance Cummings, and Boris Karloff.
VHS: S07759. $59.95.
Howard Hawks, USA, 1931, 98 mins.

El Dorado

Howard Hawks revisits and revises *Rio Bravo*, with John Wayne squaring off against numerically superior numbers of bad guys while depending on the help of a drunk, a kid and a fussy senior citizen. With Robert Mitchum, James Caan and Christopher George as the villains. Watch carefully for George Plimpton as one of the baddies Wayne ko's in a barroom brawl.
VHS: S12243. $19.95.
Howard Hawks, USA, 1967, 125 mins.

Gentlemen Prefer Blondes

Marilyn Monroe and Jane Russell form a unique duo in *Gentlemen Prefer Blondes*, one of the classic musicals of the 1950's. Two "little girls from Little Rock" seek their fortune in Paris in Anita Loos' story. Featuring Marilyn's rendition of "Diamonds Are a Girl's Best Friend."
VHS: S00487. $19.98.
Howard Hawks, USA, 1953, 92 mins.

His Girl Friday

One of the wittiest Hollywood comedies: Rosalind Russell is the ace reporter ready to quit for marriage, Cary Grant, her editor trying to convince her to stay. An escaped murderer puts Russell's determination to test. Sophisticated comedy from Howard Hawks.
VHS: S00572. $14.95.
Laser: Chapter stops, restored, digital master, theatrical trailer. LD75051. $39.95.
Howard Hawks, USA, 1940, 95 mins.

I Was a Male War Bride

Ann Sheridan portrays a WAC in World War II who marries a French Army Officer (Cary Grant). Though it's a fairly routine scenario for returning American soldiers, this WAC's new spouse baffles the army bureaucracy, leading to a number of funny mishaps, including Grant appearing in drag.
VHS: S21331. $19.98.
Howard Hawks, USA, 1949, 105 mins.

Land of the Pharaohs

A strange work from Howard Hawks, based on a script by William Faulkner and Harry Kurnitz, about the epic construction of the Great Pyramid. With Jack Hawkins, James Robertson Justice, and a smarmy, dark turn by Joan Collins.
VHS: S15930. $19.98.
Laser: LD71186. $34.98.
Howard Hawks, USA, 1955, 106 mins.

Man's Favorite Sport

Rock Hudson is cast as a fishing supply salesman who doesn't know the first thing about what goes in a tackle box. When publicity agent Paula Prentiss enters the handsome phony in a big time fishing contest, he's hooked. With John McGiver, Maria Perschy, Charlene Holt, Roscoe Karns, Regis Toomey and Norman Alden as fishing guide John Screaming Eagle. Based on the story *The Girl That Almost Got Away*.
VHS: S15770. $14.95.
Howard Hawks, USA, 1964, 121 mins.

Only Angels Have Wings

Cary Grant takes center stage as the mail pilot, in Howard Hawks' two-fisted adventure tale set in South America during the 30's. Jean Arthur is the showgirl; with an outstanding performance from Rita Hayworth.
VHS: S07753. $19.95.
Howard Hawks, USA, 1939, 121 mins.

Red Line 7000

One of Howard Hawks' last films. James Caan stars in this feature about the young daredevils of the racing world and the women with whom they are romantically involved. Hawks, himself a former racer, saw the film as an experiment—cutting back and forth among three separate stories about the racetrack. Full of all Hawks' favorite situations and featuring a number of excellent race scenes.
VHS: S13539. $39.95.
Howard Hawks, USA, 1965, 110 mins.

Red River

The classic cattle-drive movie, often cited as one of the best American westerns. John Wayne is Thomas Dunson, a tyrant of the trail who alienates his foster son (Montgomery Clift) and causes a sagebrush mutiny. Plenty of two-fisted Western action in this battle of the wills, and featuring a great supporting cast. With Walter Brennan, Joanne Dru, Harry Carey Jr. and Sr., John Ireland and Shelley Winters.
VHS: S01101. $19.95.
Laser: LD70664. $39.98.
Howard Hawks, USA, 1948, 133 mins.

Rio Bravo

An American classic features John Wayne as a sheriff trying to prevent a killer from escaping or being captured by a group of men determined to handle him on their own terms. With Dean Martin, Angie Dickinson and Walter Brennan.
VHS: S03588. $19.98.
Laser: LD71679. $39.98.
Howard Hawks, USA, 1959, 141 mins.

Rio Lobo

John Wayne is cast as Union Col. Cord >McNally, a tough soldier in the Civil War whose private battles continue when the larger contest is over. A story of revenge, settling scores after the War, this was Hawks' last film.
VHS: S04598. $19.98.
Howard Hawks, USA, 1970, 102 mins.

Scarface

Paul Muni plays Tony Carmonte, an ambitious hood fighting his way up to be the number one gang boss. Produced by Howard Hughes, *Scarface* is regarded as the best and most brutal of the classic gangster films.
VHS: S01163. $19.95.
Laser: LD70074. $34.95.
Howard Hawks, USA, 1932, 90 mins.

Sergeant York

Gary Cooper stars in an Oscar-winning role as Alvin York, a backwoods boy from Tennesee who overcomes his pacifist principles and decides to fight in World War I, with heroic results. Based on a true story, York worked as consultant on the film. An inspiration.
VHS: S01868. $19.98.
Laser: Chapter search. Includes theatrical trailer. LD71642. $39.98.
Howard Hawks, USA, 1941, 134 mins.

Song Is Born

Danny Kaye stars in this lively remake of *Ball of Fire*, once again directed by Howard Hawks. Kaye is cast as a shy professor who hides a gangster's moll wanted for questioning by the authorities. With Virginia Mayo livening up the study hall of fellow bookworm Hugh Herbert and away from tough guy Steve Cochran. With special musical guests Benny Goodman, Louis Armstrong, Lionel Hampton and Tommy Dorsey.
VHS: S15489. $19.98.
Howard Hawks, USA, 1948, 113 mins.

To Have and Have Not

Humphrey Bogart and 19-year old Lauren Bacall in this adaptation of Ernest Hemingway's wartime adventure. William Faulkner contributes to the screenplay. With Bacall's: "You know how to whistle, don't you Steve? You just put your lips together...and blow."
VHS: S01353. $19.95.
Laser: LD70697. $34.98.
Howard Hawks, USA, 1945, 101 mins.

Today We Live

A fascinating collaboration between Howard Hawks and novelist William Faulkner, who adapted his own semi-autobiographical novel about World War I aviation. Gary Cooper plays an American fighter pilot who is caught in battles with the Germans and is attracted to Joan Crawford. With Robert Young, Franchot Tone and Roscoe Karns.
VHS: S19494. $19.98.
Howard Hawks, USA, 1933, 113 mins.

Twentieth Century

Howard Hawks' classic with John Barrymore as the maniacal Broadway director who takes talented starlet Carole Lombard and transforms her into a smashing success adored by the public and press. But when Lombard tires of Barrymore's manic-excessive ways, she heads to Hollywood for even greater stardom, but possibly loses the one good thing in her life—Barrymore. A treasure.
VHS: S07752. $19.95.
Howard Hawks, USA, 1934, 91 mins.

DOUGLAS SIRK

All I Desire

Barbara Stanwyck is a woman of the theater who is driven from a small Wisconsin town by scandal. Now she hopes to return to her estranged family. Her husband (Richard Carlson) is now seeing a school teacher (Maureen O'Sullivan). Aside from this potential love triangle, there is plenty of drama in the form of her previous lover, the man who hastened her original departure from small town life.
VHS: S26227. $19.98.
Douglas Sirk, USA, 1953, 80 mins.

Battle Hymn

Rock Hudson stars in this tale of courage and selflessness, inspired by the true story of an Ohio minister who became a World War II fighter pilot. During the war, U.S. Air Force Colonel Dean Hess (Hudson) accidentally killed 37 orphans in Germany. Rather than return to his ministry in Ohio, he decided to reenlist and ultimately quieted his guilty conscience by founding an orphanage in Korea. Anna Kashfi and Don Duryea also star.
VHS: S27666. $14.98.
Douglas Sirk, USA, 1957, 108 mins.

Imitation of Life

A remake of the original (with Claudette Colbert), underrated director Douglas Sirk's last film draws the audience into an underworld of backstairs, neon gutters and assembly-line chorus-lines, and includes an exploited black maid with a vitally erotic daughter (Susan Kohner) trying to pass for white. With Lana Turner, John Gavin.
VHS: S00611. $14.95.
Douglas Sirk, USA, 1959, 124 mins.

Magnificent Obsession

Douglas Sirk's elegant transposition of Lloyd Douglas' best seller stars Rock Hudson as an irresponsible playboy who causes the widowhood and blindness of a beautiful woman (Jane Wyman). Lavish color photography and Sirk's brilliant mise-en-scene.
VHS: S00805. $14.95.
Douglas Sirk, USA, 1954, 108 mins.

The Tarnished Angels

Robert Stack, Dorothy Malone and Rock Hudson form a romantic triangle set amidst the tumultuous world of air circus performers. Roger Schulman (Stack) is a former World War I flying ace who is now a tormented and dedicated racing pilot. Schulman overlooks his trick parachutist wife Laverne (Malone) for his first love, flying. Burke Devlin (Hudson) is a reporter doing a story on the air circus who quickly becomes more fascinated with Laverne than with his story. This powerful drama, based on William Faulkner's novel *Pylon*, is a complicated exploration of desire and obsession. With Troy Donahue and Jack Carson.
VHS: S27669. $14.98.
Douglas Sirk, USA, 1957, 91 mins.

Written on the Wind

The lurid lifestyles of the very rich and famous are the subject of this box office champ of 1957 from director Douglas Sirk. Robert Stack is the irresponsible son of an oil magnate. Lauren Bacall is his suffering wife. Rock Hudson plays his best friend and Dorothy Malone won an Oscar for her role as the nymphomaniac sister. Classy trash.
VHS: S07144. $14.95.
Douglas Sirk, USA, 1956, 99 mins.

Zu Neuen Ufern

No less than Douglas Sirk directed this rare German feature set in colonial Australia. Zarah Leander plays a singer who is threatened with deportation for the sake of the man she loves, who has stolen money. With Willy Birgel and Viktor Staal; script by Sirk. German *without* English subtitles.
VHS: S24127. $29.95.
Douglas Sirk, Germany, 1937

GEORGE STEVENS

Alice Adams

Katharine Hepburn stars as the young girl snubbed by society because her father lacks money and ambition. Fred MacMurray is the well-bred beau who gets more than he bargained for in this Oscar-nominated treasure.
VHS: S05656. $14.95.
George Stevens, USA, 1935, 99 mins.

Annie Oakley

Barbara Stanwyck stars in this story of a backwoods young woman who proves she is a formidable marksman and is invited to the Buffalo Bill Wild West Show. With Melvyn Douglas and Preston Foster.
VHS: S02145. $19.95.
George Stevens, USA, 1935, 90 mins.

A Damsel in Distress

Fred Astaire has a terrific time dancing and clowning with Burns and Allen in this P.G. Wodehouse story. George and Ira Gershwin wrote the score, and the classics include "A Foggy Day in London Town" and "Nice Work If You Can Get It."
VHS: S03234. $19.95.
George Stevens, USA, 1937, 101 mins.

Diary of Anne Frank

One of literature's most powerful works is translated into a film which won eight Oscars, as it reenacts the harrowing experiences of the Frank family as they are forced to hide from the Nazis.
VHS: S04330. $24.98.
Laser: LD70946. $49.98.
George Stevens, USA, 1959, 151 mins.

George Stevens: A Filmmaker's Journey

An intimate documentary about the Hollywood director, the film weaves interviews, remembrances, on-camera interviews with his collaborators and colleagues, footage from his films and footage he shot during World War II. The interviews include Warren Beatty, Katharine Hepburn, Fred Astaire, Frank Capra and John Huston. "A wonderfully informative tribute, lit together with love, intelligence, wit and, most important of all, a knowledge of film history" (Vincent Canby).
VHS: S18971. $29.95.
Laser: LD71556. $49.95.
George Stevens Jr., USA, 1984, 111 mins.

George Stevens: D-Day to Berlin

Director George Stevens shot this documentary footage which depicts American efforts in Europe during World War II. It includes some of the most extensive color footage available of both the Normandy invasion and the fall of Berlin. This film won 3 Emmy Awards and was originally commissioned by Dwight D. Eisenhower. George Stevens, Jr. narrates. With William Saroyan, Irwin Shaw and Ivan Moffat.
VHS: S26760. $19.98.
Laser: LD75408. $29.99.
George Stevens, USA, 50 mins.

Giant

A film of staggering scale and grandeur detailing the lives of cattleman Rock Hudson and his society wife Elizabeth Taylor and three generations of land-rich Texans. Featuring a stellar performance by James Dean in the last role of his career.
VHS: S00499. $26.98.
Laser: LD70581. $39.98.
George Stevens, USA, 1956, 201 mins.

Greatest Story Ever Told

The ultimate Hollywood Christian epic, with spectacular scenes and cameo appearances by a stable of Hollywood stars, including John Wayne as the Roman officer during Christ's crucifixion, Charlton Heston, Carroll Baker, Max von Sydow, Angela Lansbury, Sidney Poitier, Shelley Winers, Claude Rains and others.
VHS: S11552. $24.98.
Laser: LD70200. $49.98.
George Stevens, USA, 1965, 141 mins.

Gunga Din

The Rudyard Kipling story of the Indian boy who helps the British put down a colonial revolt stars Cary Grant and Douglas Fairbanks, Jr.
VHS: S02023. $19.95.
George Stevens, USA, 1939, 117 mins.

I Remember Mama

Classic screen adaptation of the John Van Druten play stars the immensely talented Irene Dunne as the matriarch of a close-knit Norwegian family living in San Francisco at the turn of the century. The sterling cast of this heartfelt, sentimental drama also includes Barbara Bel Geddes, Oscar Homolka, Philip Dorn and Ellen Corby. B&W.
VHS: S03221. $19.98.
George Stevens, USA, 1948, 134 mins.

Kentucky Kernels

The great slapstick comedy team of Wheeler and Woolsey join forces with Our Gang's Spanky McFarland for a hilarious backwoods adventure in which the zany trio find themselves staring down the barrels of a hillbilly firing squad.
VHS: S13995. $19.98.
George Stevens, USA, 1934, 75 mins.

The More the Merrier

James Coburn won an Oscar for Best Supporting Actor in this hilarious comedy. Jean Arthur is the working-class girl who finds herself in the predicament of having to share an apartment in World War II-era Washington, D.C. with two men—Joel McCrea and Coburn.
VHS: S11744. $19.95.
Laser: CLV. LD74891. $34.95.
George Stevens, USA, 1943, 104 mins.

Penny Serenade

Romantic comedy starring Cary Grant and Irene Dunne as a couple which adopts a child but then encounters tragedy.
VHS: S01940. $19.95.
Laser: CLV. LD72015. $29.98.
George Stevens, USA, 1941, 125 mins.

A Place in the Sun

Based on Theodore Dreiser's *An American Tragedy*, and featuring strong performances from Montgomery Clift, Elizabeth Taylor and Shelley Winters. Monty Clift is the poor boy driven by the lure of wealth, with his success threatened by complications from his simultaneous affairs with factory girl Shelley Winters and socialite Liz Taylor.
VHS: S04663. $19.95.
George Stevens, USA, 1951, 122 mins

Quality Street

When her sweetheart goes off to the Napoleonic wars, Katharine Hepburn decides she must masquerade as her younger niece to win his love. Based on the play by James Barrie, with a radiant performance by Hepburn.
VHS: S05667. $19.98.
George Stevens, USA, 1937, 84 mins.

Shane

George Stevens' legendary rendition of the archetypal Western myth earned six Academy nominations. Alan Ladd stars as the retired gunfighter who comes to the aid of a frontier family and wins the adoration of the family's impressionable young son. With Jack Palance, Van Heflin and Jean Arthur.
VHS: S03316. $14.95.
Laser: LD75344. $29.98.
George Stevens, USA, 1953, 118 mins.

Swing Time
Fred Astaire and Ginger Rogers in a nostalgic film about the high life in Manhattan during the Twenties, when fortunes were made and lost in an evening at the roulette tables. Music by Jerome Kern, lyrics by Dorothy Fields.
VHS: S02151. $14.98.
Laser: CAV. LD70468. $74.95.
Laser: CLV. LD70469. $39.95.
George Stevens, USA, 1936, 103 mins.

Talk of the Town
A wonderful comedy with an intelligent cast, including Jean Arthur, Cary Grant and Ronald Colman. Grant is a fugitive hiding out with unsuspecting professor Colman and landlady Arthur, who tries to convince the legal-minded Colman that there's a human side to all laws.
VHS: S03297. $19.95.
Laser: CLV, chapter stops. LD74997. $39.95.
George Stevens, USA, 1942, 118 mins.

Woman of the Year
Tracy and Hepburn's first film together; Hepburn is the political journalist much too serious about her work, Tracy the sports reporter who teaches her how to enjoy life. Simply terrific.
VHS: S04741. $19.95.
Laser: LD70710. $34.98.
George Stevens, USA, 1942, 118 mins.

WILLIAM WYLER

Ben Hur
Winner of eleven Oscars including Charlton Heston as Best Actor, an epic spectacle concerning a prince of Judea who incurs the wrath of the Roman Empire. The famous chariot race required a year of film preparation and lasts nearly 20 minutes.
VHS: S02517. $29.98.

Laser: LD70524. $49.98.
William Wyler, USA, 1959, 211 mins.

Ben Hur 35th Anniversary Edition
Celebrating the timelessness of this multi-academy award winning film, this new Deluxe Collector's Edition of the classic starring Charlton Heston also includes the documentary *Ben Hur: The Making of an Epic*, narrated by Christopher Plummer, and the original theatrical trailer. Letterbox format.
VHS: S20641. $39.98.
Laser: 5-disk CAV boxed set. LD72371. $99.98.
William Wyler, 1959, USA, 204 mins.

The Best Years of Our Lives
This epic film focuses on the troubles of three World War II servicemen as they try to pick up the threads of their lives after returning home to the States. An insightful portrait of small-town American life and its values. Starring Myrna Loy, Frederic March, Dana Andrews, Virginia Mayo and Teresa Wright. *The Best Years of Our Lives* was named one of the 50 greatest motion pictures of all time by the members of The American Film Institute. Digitally remastered.
VHS: S03117. $19.98.
William Wyler, USA, 1946, 170 mins.

Big Country
Gregory Peck is the retired sea captain who comes to marry Carroll Baker, but is instead thrown into a battle against Burl Ives and his sons over water rights. Ives won an Oscar as the patriarch; Charlton Heston delivers a strong performance as the ranch foreman. A brilliant musical score by Jerome Moross.
VHS: S11554. $29.95.
Laser: Widescreen. LD75030. $79.99.
William Wyler, USA, 1958, 166 mins.

Carrie
Based on Theodore Dreiser's famous satirical novel *Sister Carrie*, Laurence Olivier and Jennifer Jones star in this story of a middle-aged man who risks his marriage and wealth for the love of young beauty. "Graced by one of Olivier's finest screen performances" (Pauline Kael).
VHS: S13791. $19.95.
William Wyler, USA, 1952, 118 mins.

The Children's Hour
Lillian Hellman's classic play about two teachers who are accused of lesbianism by a student receives powerful treatment from Shirley MacLaine, Audrey Hepburn and James Garner.
VHS: S13345. $19.98.
Laser: LD72169. $34.98.
William Wyler, USA, 1961, 107 mins.

Collector
An adaptation of the John Fowles novel by veteran director Wyler (*Jezebel, Dodsworth*) is an effective psychological thriller about a plan by a psychotic Terence Stamp to kidnap and keep an art student, played by Samantha Eggar.
VHS: S01697. $59.95.
William Wyler, USA, 1965, 119 mins.

Come and Get It
Frances Farmer is cast as a beautiful woman desired by both a father and his son in this drama set in the timber country of the Northwest. Walter Brennan made his mark in this film which was based on a novel by Edna Ferber. William Wyler took over direction from Howard Hawks.
VHS: S01537. $19.98.
William Wyler/Howard Hawks, USA, 1936, 99 mins.

Dead End
Humphrey Bogart is the young man who has grown up knowing only one kind of law—his own. Sylvia Sidney is the sensitive young woman who falls for touchy but tender Joel McCrea in this tense film, set on New York's turbulent Lower East Side.
VHS: S03119. $19.95.
Laser: LD70169. $34.98.
William Wyler, USA, 1937, 92 mins.

Desperate Hours
Inspired by actual events, based on Joseph Hayes' novel and the Broadway play, an all-star cast including Humphrey Bogart, Frederic March, Arthur Kennedy, Martha Scott and Gig Young star in this tour-de-force. Bogart is the escaped con who has nothing to lose. March is a suburban Everyman who has everything to lose—his family is held hostage by Bogart. As *The Desperate Hours* tick by, the two men square off in a battle of wills and cunning that tightens into a fear-drenched finale.
VHS: S09566. $14.95.
William Wyler, USA, 1955, 112 mins.

Dodsworth
Sam Dodsworth, a recently retired industrialist, sets off to Europe with his young wife, Fran. In Paris, Fran's yearning for romance leads her into an open flirtation with an attractive gentleman. Tormented by his wife's actions, Dodsworth begins a search for the happiness which seems to have eluded him. With Walter Huston, Mary Astor, Ruth Chatterton and David Niven. Digitally remastered.
VHS: S00355. $19.98.
William Wyler, USA, 1936, 101 mins.

Funny Girl
Barbra Streisand made her Oscar-winning film debut in this epic screen biography of entertainer Fanny Brice. She sings, dances and roller-skates her way to the top of the show business ladder. There is no doubt about it, a star is born, so please don't rain on her parade. With Omar Sharif as gambler and first husband Nicky Arnstein, Anne Francis, Kay Medford, and Walter Pidgeon as Flo Ziegfeld.
VHS: S10976. $19.95.
William Wyler, USA, 1968 155 mins.

The Heiress
William Wyler directed Olivia de Havilland and an all-star cast in this Oscar-winning classic. De Havilland is the homely, awkward girl who falls in love with the dashing fortune hunter. With brilliant performances by Montgomery Clift and Ralph Richardson, musical score by Aaron Copeland. Based on *Washington Square* by Henry James.
VHS: S03533. $14.95.
William Wyler, USA, 1949, 115 mins.

How to Steal a Million
Audrey Hepburn and Peter O'Toole look great in this comedy shot, in part, on location in Paris. Hepburn's dad is a forger of fine art and he is about to be unmasked by experts. To prevent this, Hepburn schemes to steal one of dad's phony works with O'Toole's help so that it will never be examined. Eli Wallach and Charles Boyer co-star.
VHS: S26406. $19.98.
William Wyler, USA, 1966, 127 mins.

Jezebel
Bette Davis won an Oscar for her performance as the tempestuous Southern belle who manipulates the men in her life. Her engagement to Henry Fonda is broken off due to her insensitivity, and when he returns married, her ruthless jealousy explodes.
VHS: S00654. $19.95.
Laser: LD70604. $34.98.
William Wyler, USA, 1938, 105 mins.

The Letter
A masterpiece of suspense and sexual repression, largely due to the muted tension between Bette Davis and James Stephenson. When a woman is accused of murder, her husband and lawyer try to get her off on a self-defense plea, but was it really? Based on the novel by W. Somerset Maugham. Excellent film noir.
VHS: S01757. $19.95.
William Wyler, USA, 1940, 95 mins.

The Love Trap
Laura La Plante stars in this light-hearted farce about a chorus girl determined to marry the nephew of a powerful and respected judge. Naturally, the entire family is against the young couple, but love will find a way, particularly when there is a good deal of money at stake. Neil Hamilton and Robert Ellis are featured.
VHS: S26770. $24.95.
William Wyler, USA, 1929, 71 mins.

Memphis Belle
World War II documentary produced by the U.S. War Department supervised by Lt. Col. William Wyler, director of *Dodsworth* and *Wuthering Heights*.
VHS: S02593. $19.95.
Laser: LD70628. $24.98.
William Wyler, USA, 1944

Mrs. Miniver
The winner of seven Oscars in 1942 was an effective morale boost for all the folks on the home front. Greer Garson and Walter Pidgeon head a middle-class English family under siege and worried about their son in the RAF. Garson later married the actor who played her son, Richard Ney. With Dame May Whitty, Reginald Owen and Teresa Wright.
VHS: S08341. $19.95.
William Wyler, USA, 1942, 134 mins.

Roman Holiday
Stylish production starring Gregory Peck and Audrey Hepburn about a rebellious princess who wishes to discover living on her own. With Eddie Albert as Peck's pal.
VHS: S01763. $19.95.
Laser: LD75249. $34.98.
William Wyler, USA, 1953, 118 mins.

These Three
Boarding school brat Bonita Granville spreads lies about officials Miriam Hopkins, Merle Oberon and Joel McCrea—the man they both love. Excellent acting and superb direction highlight this Lillian Hellman adaptation of her play *The Children's Hour*, re-made, by that name, by Wyler 25 years later.
VHS: S03128. $19.98.
William Wyler, USA, 1936, 93 mins.

Thunderbolt
William Wyler supervised the production. James Stewart introduces and Lloyd Bridges narrates the activities of the 57th fighter group during "Operation Strangle," which destroyed vital supply routes deep behind German lines. Color.
VHS: S03350. $39.95.
Laser: LD70169. $34.98.
William Wyler, USA, 1945, 45 mins.

The Westerner
Gary Cooper is a wandering saddle bum caught up in a range war between homesteaders and cattlemen who squares off with the legendary Judge Roy Bean (Walter Brennan) in West Texas of the 1880's. When the film was released in 1940 critics praised its realistic touches, especially the way it showed gunfighters stopping to reload their pistols in the middle of shootouts—something other westerns had never shown before. Digitally remastered.
VHS: S03129. $19.98.
William Wyler, USA, 1940, 100 mins.

ORSON WELLES

Chimes at Midnight/Falstaff
The final masterpiece from Orson Welles, an austere, haunting work that reaches the greatness of *Kane, Ambersons* and *Touch of Evil*. Based on his 1938 Theater Guild Production, Welles has meticulously assembled the Falstaff parts from Shakespeare's history plays (including *Merry Wives of Windsor*) and thematically linked them with Holinshed's *Chronicles* to explore the full arc of Falstaff's relationship with Prince Hal—moving from grand affection to bitter disillusionment. Featuring the extraordinary montage sequence at the Battle of Shrewsbury, with Welles, John Gielgud and Ralph Richardson supplying Holinshed's narration.
VHS: S02950. $79.95.
Orson Welles, Italy/USA, 1967, 115 mins.

Citizen Kane
Considered by many to be the greatest American film ever made, this is the story of the life of Charles Foster Kane (patterned after William Randolph Hearst), from his humble beginnings to his materialistic, lonely end. A masterpiece. With Orson Welles, Joseph Cotten, Agnes Moorehead and Everett Sloane. Cinematography by Gregg Toland, with a script by Welles and Herman Mankiewicz.
Laser: CAV. LD70355. $124.95.
Laser: CLV. LD70356. $39.95.
Orson Welles, USA, 1941, 119 mins.

Citizen Kane (50th Anniversary Edition)
One of the greatest films ever made is now available in a version painstakingly restored to its original brilliance in honor of the film's 50th anniversary. With Orson Welles, Dorothy Comingore, Everett Sloane, Paul Stewart. Cinematography by Gregg Toland, script by Welles and Herman Mankiewicz.
VHS: S14599. $19.98.
Laser: CAV. LD70745. $124.95.
Laser: CLV. LD70746. $39.95.
Orson Welles, USA, 1941, 119 mins.

Citizen Kane Gift Set (50th Anniversary Edition)
Includes the restored videocassette version of *Citizen Kane*, the "Reflections on *Citizen Kane*" program and *Citizen Kane: The 50th Anniversary Album*, a hardcover book by Harlan Lebo.
VHS: S14601. $49.98.
Orson Welles, USA, 1941

F for Fake
Orson Welles's "magnificent confidence game, a trick, a seduction and an actual act: a buoyant film about forgery and fakery which, beneath our astonished gaze, explodes into wonderment and guilt" (Michael Wilmington, *Chicago Tribune*). Welles's theme of forgery in art focuses on the forger, Elmyr de Hory, as well as Clifford Irving, de Hory's biographer, Howard Hughes, Pablo Picasso and Welles himself. "Alternately superficial and profound, hollow and moving, simple and complex, this film also enlists the services of Oja Kodar, Welles's principal collaborator after the late 60s, as actor, erotic spectacle and co-writer" (Jonathan Rosenbaum, *Chicago Reader*).
VHS: S24864. $39.95.
Laser: Digital transfer. LD75024. $49.95.
Welles/Reichenbach, USA/France/Iran/Germany, 1976, 125 mins.

A Film Genius: Orson Welles Gift Pack
Includes three of Welles' greatest films: *Citizen Kane*, *Journey into Fear* and *The Magnificent Ambersons*. Also includes an 8" x 10" glossy still from each movie.
VHS: S14600. $59.98.

It's All True
Orson Welles went to Brazil, where he hoped to make a film that captured the essence of that beautiful country. Because of disagreements with the studio over the amount of money he spent it was never completed. Now, using footage he shot and combining interviews with actual crew members, this unfinished work and its tale of lost opportunity can at last be told.
VHS: S21350. $92.98.
R. Wilson/M. Meisel/B. Krohn, USA, 1993, 85 mins.

Journey into Fear
Orson Welles and the Mercury Theatre of the Air Players tackle foreign intrigue in this WWII spy drama set in Turkey. Joseph Cotten is the naive American targeted for death who is offered assistance by Turkish policeman Welles. With Agnes Moorehead, Ruth Warrick and Everett Sloane. Welles co-directed (with Norman Foster) and his scenes stand out. B&W.
VHS: S03249. $19.95.
Orson Welles, USA, 1942, 68 mins.

Lady from Shanghai
Welles' great thriller stars Rita Hayworth as the millionairess in a web of intrigue which includes Welles being accused of murder, and concludes in the dazzling climax played out in a hall of mirrors.
VHS: S00715. $19.95.
Orson Welles, USA, 1948, 87 mins.

Macbeth
Orson Welles' *Macbeth* was shot in 23 days on an extremely low budget, yet is memorable for its rhythm, murky atmosphere of evil, and imaginative visualizations.
VHS: S00788. $19.95.
Orson Welles, USA, 1948, 89 mins.

Magnificent Ambersons
Produced, written and directed by Orson Welles, the follow-up film to *Citizen Kane*, and a work of depth and genius. Welles traces the details of a midwestern family's tragedy. From the novel by Booth Tarkington. With Tim Holt, Anne Baxter, Agnes Moorehead.
VHS: S00804. $19.95.
Laser: LD70417. $99.95.
Orson Welles, USA, 1942, 88 mins.

Mr. Arkadin
Also known as *Confidential Report*, Orson Welles' gothic work concerns the suppression of memory and the past. Welles plays an idiosyncratic and flamboyant tycoon who hires a researcher to investigate his elusive past. The man uncovers a string of killings and deaths. It's an elaborate puzzle, shot in a fragmented, elliptical manner. Welles scholar Jonathan Rosenbaum reports as many as eight different versions of the film exist. With Michael Redgrave, Patricia Medina, Paola Mori, Akim Tamiroff, Mischa Auer and Robert Arden.
VHS: S00890. $29.95.
Laser: LD70125. $39.95.
Orson Welles, France/Spain, 1955, 94 mins.

Orson Welles' Ghost Story
While on break from the shooting of *Othello*, Orson Welles starred in this short film. The plot focuses on a young man haunted by two mysterious women whom he drives home one night. Peter Bogdanovich introduces this newly restored version.
VHS: S22183. $19.98.

Othello
Orson Welles' 1952 film is one of the most important of his career. Shot over four years and made on the run, the images literally composed inside the director's head, Welles' virtuoso *Othello* unfolds in flashbacks, detailing the Moor's shifting relationships with Iago (Michael MacLiammoir) and his beautiful young wife, Desdemona (Suzanne Cloutier). With Robert Coote, Fay Compton and Michael Laurence. Art direction by Alexander Trauner. The film has undergone a significant restoration, cleaning up the images and digitally re-recording the soundtrack in stereo, with members of the Chicago Symphony Orchestra and Lyric Opera of Chicago. The voices were electronically isolated to improve the fidelity of the soundtrack.
VHS: Out of print. For rental only.
Laser: LD72284. $99.95.
Orson Welles, Italy/France/USA, 1952, 93 mins.

Scene of the Crime
Orson Welles hosts a trio of intricate and involving mysteries of murder and assorted crimes against humanity. Welles presents a rogue's gallery of celebrity suspects and then will ask the viewer to make their best case before revealing the culprit and the modus operandi. Culled from the television show, at least there shouldn't be any commercials. USA, 1984-85, 74 mins.
VHS: S10063. $19.98.

Stranger
Orson Welles followed his production of *Citizen Kane* and *Magnificent Ambersons* with this thriller. Welles stars as an escaped Nazi war criminal, Loretta Young is his unsuspecting wife, and Edward G. Robinson is the War Crimes inspector who tracks him down.
VHS: S01262. $19.95.
Orson Welles, USA, 1946, 95 mins.

Touch of Evil
A masterpiece! This is a complete, restored version. Welles plays a sleazy corrupt police official in a squalid town on the Mexican border, matching wits with Charlton Heston. With Janet Leigh, Marlene Dietrich and Zsa Zsa Gabor.
VHS: S01990. $19.98.
Laser: LD70091. $34.98.
Orson Welles, USA, 1958, 108 mins.

The Trial
A newly mastered version of Orson Welles' brilliant film (the one he considered his best), a masterful adaptation of Franz Kafka's novel. With Jeanne Moreau, Anthony Perkins, Romy Schneider, Orson Welles. Original English-language version.
VHS: S08696. $39.95.
Orson Welles, France, 1963, 118 mins.

Working with Orson Welles
A documentary of fascinating insights into the work of Orson Welles as captured by his longtime colleague and cinematographer Gary Graver. As Welles dreams of completing *The Other Side of the Wind*, Graver charts the frustration of this dream. Famous directors, actors, producers and friends of Welles, including Peter Bogdanovich, Stacy Keach and John Huston, describe both Welles and his work. With many rare, never-before-seen clips from Welles' unfinished work.
VHS: S26704. $29.95.
Gary Graver, USA, 1994, 97 mins.

ERNST LUBITSCH

Angel
Lady Maria Barker (Marlene Dietrich) has the perfect life: a famous husband (Herbert Marshall), an English manor, and endless travel. But her husband's inattention forces her into a brief affair with a British stranger in Paris (Melvyn Douglas), who knows her only as *Angel*.
VHS: S22184. $14.98.
Ernst Lubitsch, USA, 1937, 91 mins.

Bluebeard's Eighth Wife
Claudette Colbert is the daughter of a poor French aristocrat who attracts a young millionaire (Gary Cooper) on the French Riviera. The attraction is so obvious that they set a date before Colbert finds out that her fiance has been married seven times before. She decides to teach him a lesson in a series of comic situations that often run counter to her intentions. David Niven is also featured in this light-hearted comic romp.
VHS: S24027. $14.98.
Ernst Lubitsch, USA, 1938, 101 mins.

Gypsy Blood
Ernst Lubitsch's first important film, and the second time he directed Pola Negri, who played a role that made her an international star. Notable for its beautiful sets, the story is tentatively based on Bizet's opera *Carmen*, though, as Georges Sadoul points out, it is closer to the original novella by Prosper Merrimee. Silent with music track. Best copy available.
VHS: S02095. $44.95.
Ernst Lubitsch, Germany, 1918, 104 mins.

Heaven Can Wait
Ernst Lubitsch at his best in this wonderful comedy-fantasy, with Don Ameche as the earthly sinner trying to get admitted to Hell by convincing the Devil that his busy love life has earned him damnation. Gene Tierney is beautiful, and the sparks fly. With Charles Coburn, Marjorie Main.
VHS: S11564. $19.98.
Laser: LD71035. $39.98.
Ernst Lubitsch, USA, 1943, 112 mins

Lady Windermere's Fan
Oscar Wilde's comedy of manners, directed by a filmmaker who was a natural to translate its precise nuances to the screen. The scandalous Mrs. Erlynne returns to save her daughter from disgrace in London and sacrifices her own reputation by claiming the fan left by Lady Windermere in the apartment of Lord Darlington. With Ronald Colman, May McAvoy. Silent, B&W, music track.
VHS: S02087. $29.95.
Ernst Lubitsch, USA, 1925, 85 mins.

Marriage Circle
A delightful continental comedy with the visual wit that became known as the Lubitsch touch. Marie Prevost loves nothing more than to entice the husbands of others, while her husband, Adolphe Menjou, is left to his own devices. Silent.
VHS: S01942. $29.95.
Ernst Lubitsch, USA, 1924, 104 mins.

The Merry Widow
Maurice Chevalier must woo Jeanette MacDonald on the orders of the King of Marshovia in this MGM musical directed by Ernst Lubitsch. Based on the operetta by Franz Lehar, a wealthy woman leaves her small country to join the chorus line in Paris. A charming Prince must bring her back to save the economy. With Edward Everett Horton, Una Merkel and Akim Tamiroff.
VHS: S09868. $19.98.
Ernst Lubitsch, USA, 1934, 99 mins.

Ninotchka
"Garbo laughs!"—and indeed, she does, in her first romantic comedy as the dour Soviet official who discovers the pleasures of Paris (and Melvyn Douglas) and must choose between romance and duty. Lubitsch at his best.
VHS: S00935. $19.98.
Ernst Lubitsch, USA, 1939, 108 mins.

One Arabian Night
Elaborate blend of romance, melodrama and comedy that established the reputation of director Lubitsch as well as the star actress Pola Negri, who plays an exotic dancer. Lubitsch himself appears in the film as a hunchback performer in the dancer's troupe. Silent.
VHS: S02169. $29.95.
Ernst Lubitsch, Germany, 1920, 85 mins.

Passion
Pola Negri stars as a young girl who forsakes a life with a man who loves her in order to enter high society, eventually becoming the mistress of King Louis. Silent with music soundtrack.
VHS: S02813. $39.95.
Ernst Lubitsch, USA, 1919, 133 mins.

The Shop Around the Corner
James Stewart and Margaret Sullavan are co-workers in a Budapest notions shop run by Frank Morgan. The employees are actively feuding, not realizing that each is the other's romantic pen-pal. A charming period comedy, later remade as *In the Good Old Summertime*. Silent.
VHS: S04977. $19.98.
Laser: LD70194. $34.98.
Ernst Lubitsch, USA, 1940, 97 mins.

So This Is Paris
A rare film by Ernst Lubitsch, a delightful tale of marital infidelity, starring Monte Blue, Myrna Roy, Ruth Miller. Silent with musical score.
VHS: S06445. $29.95.
Ernst Lubitsch, USA, 1926, 68 mins.

The Student Prince in Old Heidelberg
An extremely rare 1927 film by Ernst Lubitsch stars Ramon Novarro and Norma Shearer in this melodrama of the prince who woos a bar girl. Silent with music track.
VHS: S13400. $29.98.
Ernst Lubitsch, USA, 1927, 102 mins.

That Uncertain Feeling
Elegant, sophisticated comedy from a master, the director of *Ninotchka*. Starring Merle Oberon and Melvyn Douglas as a couple whose marriage has lost its excitement. Oberon's attempts to reawaken the attentions of Douglas are inspired.
VHS: S01316. $29.95.
Ernst Lubitsch, USA, 1941, 83 mins.

To Be or Not to Be
In what might be, in the hands of someone other than Ernst Lubitsch, a contradiction of terms—a witty, delightfully satirical comedy set in Nazi-occupied Warsaw—Jack Benny leads a troupe of ham actors in outsmarting the Gestapo and reducing them to ridiculous rubble. Benny gives an animated, beautifully-paced performance and Carole Lombard stars as his wife in her last screen performance.
VHS: S01350. $19.98.
Ernst Lubitsch, USA, 1942, 102 mins.

BILLY WILDER

The Apartment
Billy Wilder's great film of tears and laughter as Jack Lemmon and Shirley MacLaine wheel and deal over a New York apartment in a comedy of morality. Winner of five Oscars and worth at least 20 more.
VHS: S05880. $19.95.
Laser: LD70506. $39.98.
Billy Wilder, USA, 1960, 125 mins.

Avanti
Jack Lemmon stars in this romantic comedy about an American businessman who goes to Italy for a very special reason, to collect the body of his father. Oddly enough, murder and foul play also play a role in this well-crafted film, proving that love and justice are indeed blind.
VHS: S21022. $19.98.
Billy Wilder, USA, 1972, 144 mins.

Buddy Buddy
Walter Matthau and Jack Lemmon have been famous as the ultimate pair of grumpy old men ever since *The Odd Couple*. Together they star in this black comedy about a hit man who runs into an unshakable stranger. Paula Prentiss and Klaus Kinski are also featured.
VHS: S21024. $19.98.
Billy Wilder, USA, 1982, 98 mins.

Double Indemnity
A great Billy Wilder film in which "every turn and twist is exactly calculated and achieves its effect with the simplest of means; this shrewd, smooth, tawdry thriller is one of the high points of 40s films" (Kael). Raymond Chandler collaborated on the screenplay in adapting James Cain's story. Barbara Stanwyck is the platinum blonde, Fred MacMurray the insurance salesman she ensnares in a plot to kill her businessman-husband and collect on the double-indemnity clause in his policy.
VHS: S02940. $19.95.
Laser: LD70024. $34.98.
Billy Wilder, USA, 1944, 107 mins.

The Emperor Waltz
In this lavish musical, Bing Crosby plays a salesman of record players to the royalty of the Austro-Hungarian empire. Vienna is magically recreated as only Hollywood could imagine it, and there is plenty of froth to go around.
VHS: S21202. $14.98.
Billy Wilder, USA, 1948, 106 mins.

Fedora
Billy Wilder's German-financed production, based on Thomas Tryon's short story about a charismatic producer who tries to lure an actress out of seclusion to star in the film he's preparing. With William Holden, Martha Keller, Henry Fonda and Jose Ferrer.
VHS: S15937. $19.98.
Laser: LD71184. $34.98.
Billy Wilder, Germany, 1978, 114 mins.

Fortune Cookie
When TV cameraman Jack Lemmon is knocked down at a football game, his shyster lawyer advises him to get all he can out of the fortuitous injury. Walter Matthau won an Oscar for his performance as the conniving legal counsel. With Ron Rich, Cliff Osmond, Judi West and Lurene Tuttle. Biting script by A.L. Diamond and the director.
VHS: S13214. $19.98.
Billy Wilder, USA, 1966, 125 mins.

Front Page
Director Billy Wilder tries his luck with the third screen version of the classic Ben Hecht-Charles MacArthur play about journalistic ethics in Chicago during the late 1920's. Jack Lemmon and Walter Matthau star as the retiring star reporter and the scheming editor who doesn't want to lose his best man.
VHS: S16152. $14.98.
Billy Wilder, USA, 1974, 105 mins.

Irma La Douce
When French policeman Jack Lemmon becomes involved with street walker Shirley MacLaine, he finds his days on the beat coming to an end. The Broadway musical set in Paris is played as a straight comedy by Billy Wilder. Cast includes Lou Jacobi, Herschel Bernardi, Joan Shawlee, Hope Holiday and Bill Bixby.
VHS: S02536. $19.98.
Laser: LD71062. $49.95.
Billy Wilder, USA, 1963, 142 mins.

Kiss Me, Stupid
Dean Martin stars as a famous singer who is duped into spending the night in a small town while on his way from Las Vegas to Hollywood by a couple of local hopefuls who want to sell him some of their songs. With Kim Novak.
VHS: S15245. $19.98.
Laser: LD71161. $39.98.
Billy Wilder, USA, 1964, 126 mins.

The Lost Weekend
Billy Wilder's classic drama stars Ray Milland in a sobering study of alcoholism. The winner of Oscars for Best Picture, Director, Actor and Screenplay in 1945. Cast includes Frank Faylen, Howard da Silva, Jane Wyman and Philip Terry. The D.T.'s are in glorious black and white.
VHS: S06869. $19.95.
Billy Wilder, USA, 1945, 100 mins.

Love in the Afternoon
A sophisticated romantic farce from Billy Wilder featuring Audrey Hepburn and Gary Cooper as an American playboy in Paris. Filled with bubbling champagne and gypsy musicians, as well as Maurice Chevalier.
VHS: S00776. $59.98.
Laser: LD72254. $49.98.
Billy Wilder, USA, 1957, 130 mins.

One, Two, Three
James Cagney plays a Coca Cola executive stationed in West Berlin who finds himself in trouble when his boss's daughter marries a fierce young Communist. It's rowdy entertainment co-scripted and directed by Billy Wilder.
VHS: S15254. $19.98.
Billy Wilder, USA, 1961, 110 mins.

The Private Life of Sherlock Holmes
How much would we know if Sherlock Holmes' devoted sidekick, Dr. Watson, actually kept a detailed diary of his times with the most famous detective ever produced within the English literary tradition? In this humorous mystery involving German spies and even the Loch Ness Monster, you'll find out.
VHS: S21023. $19.98.
Billy Wilder, Great Britain, 1970, 125 mins.

Seven Year Itch
A very funny examination of modern sexual mores with Marilyn Monroe and Tom Ewell. *Seven Year Itch* added to the Monroe Mystique with the image of Marilyn standing over the sidewalk grating to catch the breeze of passing subway trains. Screenplay co-written by Billy Wilder.
VHS: S01183. $19.98.
Billy Wilder, USA, 1955, 105 mins.

Some Like It Hot
Perhaps the funniest American film of the 1950's, Tony Curtis and Jack Lemmon play two second rate musicians on the run from the Chicago mob, who take to dressing in drag. Marilyn Monroe plays Sugar, the singer in an all-female band, and Joe E. Brown as an eccentric millionaire in love with Lemmon in drag.
VHS: S01836. $19.98.
Laser: CAV, 3 discs, Criterion. LD70466. $124.95.
Laser: Remastered, MGM. LD71169. $39.98.
Billy Wilder, USA, 1959, 122 mins.

Spirit of St. Louis
James Stewart stars as Charles Lindbergh, hero of the first trans-Atlantic flight. Based on Lindbergh's Pulitzer winning autobiography.
VHS: S02606. $19.98.
Billy Wilder, USA, 1957, 137 mins.

Stalag 17
World War II POW drama stars William Holden in an Oscar performance as a soldier suspected of being a spy when two prisoners are killed trying to escape. Otto Preminger also appears.
VHS: S02608. $19.95.
Billy Wilder, USA, 1953, 120 mins.

Sunset Boulevard
Gloria Swanson is the aging silent film queen, William Holden the struggling writer in this bizarre, dark and desperate portrait of Hollywood. Winner of three Academy Awards, and one of the greatest American films.
VHS: S01285. $14.95.
Laser: LD75268. $34.98.
Billy Wilder, USA, 1950, 110 mins.

Witness for the Prosecution
Agatha Christie's play about a sensational London murder trial features great performances from Charles Laughton as the aging lawyer, and from Tyrone Power, Marlene Dietrich and Elsa Lanchester.
VHS: S01767. $19.98.
Laser: LD71148. $34.98.
Billy Wilder, USA, 1957, 116 mins.

PRESTON STURGES

Beautiful Blonde from Bashful Bend
Betty Grable is the Wild West girl who's an excellent marksman. When her boyfriend starts flirting with another girl, she takes a shot at him, and accidentally hits a judge in the rear end. Absurd predicaments, a brisk script, and terrific performances from Grable, Cesar Romero and Rudy Vallee.
VHS: S09329. $19.98.
Laser: LD72216. $49.98.
Preston Sturges, USA, 1949, 76 mins.

Christmas in July
Zany, madcap film about a clerk in a coffee company who mistakenly believes he has won a $25,000 prize for a new company slogan and begins a shopping orgy. With Dick Powell and Ellen Drew.
VHS: S01753. $29.95.
Preston Sturges, USA, 1940, 67 mins.

The Great McGinty
A tour-de-force which won Sturges an Oscar, this no-kickbacks-barred fable of grafting politicians stars Brian Donlevy as a down-and-out bartender in South America who tells the story of his rise to political power as the two-fisted crony of party leader Akim Tamiroff. Sturges' sharp-eyed dialog explains American politics as "You got to pay somebody to protect you from human greed."
VHS: S05996. $29.95.
Laser: LD70036. $34.98.
Preston Sturges, USA, 1940, 82 mins.

Hail the Conquering Hero
A brilliant comedy, the story of an army reject who is accidentally treated as a hero when he returns to his small-town home. "The energy, the verbal intensity, the rush of Americana and the congestion seen periodically in *Miracle of Morgan's Creek* stagger the senses." With Eddie Bracken, William Demarest, Ella Raines.
VHS: S13020. $29.95.
Preston Sturges, USA, 1944, 101 mins.

Lady Eve
Barbara Stanwyck is the cardshark, Henry Fonda the millionaire scientist who knows more about snakes than about women. "Neither performer has ever been funnier. The film, based on a story by Monckton Hoffe, is full of classic moments and classic lines; it represents the dizzy high point of Sturges' comedy writing."
VHS: S02941. $19.98.
Laser: LD70044. $34.98.
Preston Sturges, USA, 1941, 97 mins.

Miracle of Morgan's Creek
A great—and very, very funny—American film, with Preston Sturges at his best. Betty Hutton plays the small-town girl who becomes pregnant, only she can't remember who the father is, and whether or not they are married. With Eddie Bracken and William Demarest.
VHS: S04431. $34.95.
Preston Sturges, USA, 1944, 98 mins.

The Old Man and the Sea
Spencer Tracy stars as the fisherman in this screen adaptation of Ernest Hemingway's brief novel of the same name. At the center of the story is a struggle between this old Mexican fisherman and a giant marlin. Their exchange sets the stage for ruminations on the heroics of even the most mundane of activities.
VHS: S27632. $19.98.
Laser: LD75824. $34.98.
Preston Sturges, USA, 1958, 86 mins.

Palm Beach Story
"One of the giddiest and most chaotic of Preston Sturges' satiric orgies. The romantic problems of the leads (Joel McCrea and Claudette Colbert) get shoved aside by the secondary characters. Colbert, travelling by train, gets involved with a bunch of drunken millionaires who….stage an informal skeet shoot in the club car and demolish the glassware. Sturges' comic invention soars…" (Pauline Kael).
VHS: S02942. $29.95.
Laser: LD70065. $34.98.
Preston Sturges, USA, 1942, 88 mins.

Sin of Harold Diddlebock
Harold Lloyd is the former football star who has spent 20 years in the bookkeeping department of an ad agency. Having lived a boring life, he goes to the other extreme, and goes on a wild binge of drinking and gambling—a riotous comedy from Sturges.
VHS: S01206. $19.95.
Preston Sturges, USA, 1946, 90 mins.

Sullivan's Travels
Preston Sturges directed this classic tale of a Hollywood director who is fed up with creating fluff and decides to find out what is really happening in America. To research a "serious" film he disguises himself as a bum and goes on the road. Along the way, Joel McCrea as John L. Sullivan (the director) meets Veronica Lake, William Demarest, Porter Hall, Eric Blore and Franklin Pangborn. Still relevant and profound.
VHS: S08507. $19.95.
Laser: LD70084. $34.98.
Preston Sturges, USA, 1941, 91 mins.

Unfaithfully Yours
Rex Harrison is a famous conductor blessed with both a brilliant career and a young wife. This sidesplitting classic comedy by Sturges follows Rex's downfall when his jealous spying on his wife leads him to believe she's having an affair.
VHS: S05019. $59.98.
Preston Sturges, USA, 1948, 105 mins.

NICHOLAS RAY

55 Days at Peking
Nicholas Ray's superb account of the Boxer Rebellion in 1900s China and the fate of the British caught amidst the fighting. Starring Ava Gardner, Charlton Heston, Flora Robson, David Niven and Paul Lukas.
VHS: S05016. $29.95.
Nicholas Ray, USA, 1963, 150 mins.

Born to Be Bad
The original *Variety* review characterized *Born to Be Bad* as an amalgam of "unnatural mother love, delinquent juvenile behavior and strange adult thinking"! Nicholas Ray directed this first-rate drama about a ruthless woman who achieves her goals by manipulating everyone around her. With Robert Ryan and Joan Fontaine. Virtually never shown, a must for all Nick Ray fans.
VHS: S13358. $19.98.
Nicholas Ray, USA, 1950, 94 mins.

Flying Leathernecks
The commander of a fighter squadron (John Wayne) has to sacrifice his men unmercifully, an attitude for which he is hated by the more sensitive executive officer, Robert Ryan. The day comes when the tables are turned and Mr. Sensitivity finds himself wearing John Wayne's shoes. Director Ray breathes new life into this old formula and the air-battle montages are terrific. Produced by Howard Hughes. An updating of *The Dawn Patrol* to the World War II action in the Pacific.
VHS: S03223. $19.98.
Nicholas Ray, USA, 1951, 102 mins.

In a Lonely Place
Humphrey Bogart stars as Dixon Steele, an alcoholic Hollywood screenwriter who is prone to violence and accused of murder. Gloria Grahame provides him with an alibi and additional headaches. A hard hitting, cynical drama directed by Nicholas Ray from the novel by Dorothy B. Hughes. With Frank Lovejoy, Martha Stewart and Jeff Donnell. B&W.
VHS: S09110. $69.95.
Nicholas Ray, USA, 1950, 91 mins.

Johnny Guitar
A camp and cult favorite, and "the most baroque thing I ever attempted" (Ray), *Johnny Guitar* stars Joan Crawford and Sterling Hayden in an explosive film about two women fighting to control a frontier boomtown that is along the line of a new railroad. This film promotes all kinds of arguing among its fans: is it a comment on McCarthyism, a gender-bending satire, or a western parody? It's a fun watch, whatever it is. With a wild Mercedes McCambridge. Theme song sung by Peggy Lee.
VHS: S04474. $19.98.
Nicholas Ray, USA, 1954, 110 mins.

King of Kings
An excellent production of the life of Jesus Christ from the director of *Rebel Without a Cause*. Intelligently told, with many lavishly filmed and deeply moving scenes, including the Sermon on the Mount. Featuring Jeffrey Hunter, Harry Guardino, Rip Torn and Robert Ryan; narration by Orson Welles.
VHS: S02727. $24.98.
Laser: LD70608. $39.97.
Nicholas Ray, USA, 1961, 170 mins.

Knock on Any Door
Humphrey Bogart is the street-bred-kid-turned-lawyer who's defending Nick Romano, accused of killing a cop, in this gritty depiction of life in the 1930's Chicago stockyard district.
VHS: S04392. $59.95.
Nicholas Ray, USA, 1949, 101 mins.

On Dangerous Ground

Robert Ryan, Ida Lupino, Ward Bond star in this film noir as Bond plays the guy out to revenge his daughter's death and Ryan is the hardened cop who falls in love with the blind sister of a mentally defective murderer.
VHS: S12017. $19.98.
Nicholas Ray, USA, 1951, 82 mins.

Party Girl

Glamour mixes with gangland violence in 1930s Chicago! Robert Taylor and the sultry Cyd Charisse star in this absorbing melodrama. Great dance numbers by Ms. Charisse and weird Nick Ray touches.
VHS: S15525. $19.98.
Laser: LD70148. $34.98.
Nicholas Ray, USA, 1958, 99 mins.

Rebel Without a Cause

James Dean stars in this quintessential story of teenage angst and rebellion. The generation gap movie of the 1950's, with a mixture of innocence, hope, despair and disillusionment set against the injustice and insensitivity of the adult world. One of the greats. With supporting parts by Natalie Wood, Sal Mineo, Nick Adams and Dennis Hopper as Goon.
VHS: S01097. $19.98.
Laser: LD70663. $24.98.
Nicholas Ray, USA, 1955, 111 mins.

A Woman's Secret

Maureen O'Hara and Melvyn Douglas star in the story of a movie business agent who builds up and promotes a singer's career and then devises a plot to kill her. First-rate acting and direction from Nicholas Ray.
VHS: S13353. $19.98.
Nicholas Ray, USA, 1949, 85 mins.

SAM PECKINPAH

The Ballad of Cable Hogue

A magnificent tribute to the West that was. It stars Jason Robards, Jr., as an ornery cuss who runs a waterhole for profit and learns a valuable lesson. When progress approaches, get out of the way. With Stella Stevens, David Warner and L.Q. Jones.
VHS: S04194. $14.95.
Laser: LD70514. $39.98.
Sam Peckinpah, USA, 1970, 122 mins.

Bring Me the Head of Alfredo Garcia

Warren Oates stars in this underrated film by Sam Peckinpah, as a seedy piano player south of the border who knows the location of all of the title character, who deflowered the daughter of a wealthy patron. Expect a high body count and excellent character studies from a cast that includes Gig Young, Robert Webber, Isela Vega, Emilio Fernandez and Kris Kristofferson as a mean biker.
VHS: S06057. $19.98.
Sam Peckinpah, USA, 1974, 112 mins.

The Deadly Companions

Sam Peckinpah's first film is a western which stars Brian Keith as a revenge-bent ex-soldier out to find the man who scalped him during the Civil War. Along the way he meets Maureen O'Hara and becomes involved in a cross country funeral procession. With Chill Wills, Strother Martin and Steve Cochran.
VHS: S10025. $19.95.
Laser: CLV. LD71713. $19.98.
Sam Peckinpah, USA, 1961, 90 mins.

The Getaway

Steve McQueen and Ali MacGraw star in this classic, action-packed thriller. Together they tear up the screen, stealing and shooting their way through a plot of intrigue and love. The chemistry between these two stars cannot be beaten in this, the original version of *The Getaway*.
VHS: S04173. $19.98.
Laser: Widescreen. LD74987. $39.98.
Sam Peckinpah, USA, 1975, 123 mins.

Junior Bonner

Steve McQueen has one of his best roles as the title character in this contemporary Western about an ex-rodeo star still making the effort. An entertaining character study from Sam Peckinpah without massive bloodshed. With Robert Preston, Ida Lupino, Joe Don Baker and Ben Johnson.
VHS: S07154. $19.98.
Sam Peckinpah, USA, 1972, 101 mins.

Major Dundee

Peckinpah's lavish Western features Charlton Heston and Richard Harris leading a band of rebel cavalry soldiers in pursuit of Apaches into Mexico. Peckinpah disowned the film, having had it taken away from him by the studio and re-cut by others, but it's still interesting.
VHS: S01714. $19.95.
Laser: Letterboxed, chapter stops. LD74906. $39.95.
Sam Peckinpah, USA, 1965, 134 mins.

The Osterman Weekend

Rutger Hauer, John Hurt, Dennis Hopper and Meg Foster star in this strange thriller about a controversial talk show host recruited by the CIA. He is supposed to expose some friends suspected of working for the KGB, but of course things are not all they seem.
VHS: S21808. $19.98.
Sam Peckinpah, USA, 1983, 98 mins.

Pat Garrett and Billy the Kid

Romantic mythic version of the changing West, James Coburn stars as Pat Garrett, the former outlaw who has put on a badge to work for the cattlemen and hunt down Kris Kristofferson as Billy. Original score by Bob Dylan, featuring support from Jason Robards, Rita Coolidge and Dylan.
VHS: S02366. $19.95.
Laser: LD70183. $39.98.
Sam Peckinpah, USA, 1973, 106 mins.

Ride the High Country

Two aging gunfighters embark on their last adventure, transporting a shipment of gold. Breathtaking photography by Lucien Ballard; with great performances from Randolph Scott and Joel McCrea.
VHS: S04409. $19.98.
Sam Peckinpah, USA, 1962, 94 mins.

Straw Dogs

David (Dustin Hoffman) moves with his English wife to a seemingly peaceful town in Cornwall. The villagers, disdaining David's reticence, begin subtle harassment, growing steadily more violent as David continues to avoid confrontation, until ultimately, in a harrowingly violent scene, he is forced to react. Susan George stars as Amy, his wife. One of the great Peckinpah films.
VHS: S01266. $14.98.
Laser: LD71344. $49.98.
Sam Peckinpah, USA, 1971, 117 mins.

The Wild Bunch (Director's Cut)

An authentic American western classic and Peckinpah's best film. An aging group of outlaws decides to pull off one last heist, led by William Holden, who plays Pike Bishop, leader of The Wild Bunch, with Robert Ryan as Deke Thornton, who once rode with Pike and now faces return to prison. *The Wild Bunch* broke new ground in the realistic depiction of violence on the screen.
VHS: S01459. $19.98.
Laser: Widescreen, CLV. LD70706. $39.98.
Sam Peckinpah, USA, 1969, 127 mins.

JOSEF VON STERNBERG

Anatahan

Anatahan is the last fiercely independent gesture of the cinema's most uncompromising visionary. Von Sternberg narrates this true story of 12 Japanese sailors who, isolated on a jungle island, continue to believe for years that the war is not yet over. When a girl appears on the island, *Anatahan* becomes the spectacle of man's dignity and honor crumbling before the assault of desire. With Akemi Negishi, Tadashi Suganuma. 95 mins.
VHS: S06859. $29.95.
Josef von Sternberg, USA, 1953, 95 mins.

Blonde Venus

Von Sternberg's only Marlene Dietrich film set in the U.S., Dietrich plays an ex-actress who returns to the stage to raise money to treat her husband's rare illness. She meets wealthy playboy Cary Grant, who falls in love with her, complicating her life. Dietrich is the center of three elaborately staged songs including appearing in a gorilla suit for a rendition of "Hot Voodoo."
VHS: S01987. $14.98.
Josef von Sternberg, USA, 1932, 89 mins.

The Blue Angel (English)

The English-language version of Von Sternberg's classic which differs not only in language, but also in some plot variations from the original German version. Marlene Dietrich stars as the cabaret singer Lola Lola, who brings men to her knees. English dialog.
VHS: S00154. $29.95.
Josef von Sternberg, Germany/USA, 1930, 90 mins.

The Blue Angel (German)

Josef von Sternberg's adaptation of Heinrich Mann's novel about a repressed school teacher (Emil Jannings) who is seduced and destroyed by his demonic obsession for nightclub singer Lola Lola (Marlene Dietrich). "The film is striking for its creative use of sound and its impressive recreation of the sleazy atmosphere of cabaret life" (David Cook, *The History of Narrative Film*). With Kurt Gerron, Hans Albers and Eduard von Winterstein. German with English subtitles.
VHS: S10872. $24.95.
Josef von Sternberg, Germany, 1930, 108 mins.

Crime and Punishment

Made in 28 days and shot on the cheap, Josef von Sternberg's adaptation of Dostoyevsky's novel is a psychological potboiler about Raskolnikov (Peter Lorre), a criminal tortured over his murder of a pawnbroker. He is relentlessly pursued by an inventive detective (Edward Arnold). Full of von Sternberg's trademark visual motifs. With Marian Marsh, Tala Birell and Elizabeth Risdon.
VHS: S18856. $19.98.
Laser: LD71885. $34.95.
Josef von Sternberg, USA, 1935, 88 mins.

Dishonored

In this variation of the *Mata Hari* tale, Marlene Dietrich plays a whore who is recruited by a covert spy ring; she's given the code name "X 27" and falls for a rogue agent (McLaglen). "*Dishonored* is to the cinema what Ravel's *La Valse* is to music—the Viennese Waltz disintegrating into the First World War" (Herman J. Weinberg).
VHS: S19078. $14.98.
Josef von Sternberg, USA, 1931, 91 mins.

Docks of New York

George Bancroft stars in a story of a stocker on the docks whose life is changed by saving a suicidal woman. Released at the same time as *The Jazz Singer*, it unfortunately fell to obscurity. It is now recognized as a great, expressive silent film and considered by some film historians to be the greatest film von Sternberg ever made. Silent.
VHS: S03441. $29.95.
Josef von Sternberg, USA, 1928, 60 mins.

Jet Pilot

A curious collaboration between von Sternberg and Howard Hughes which reworks the themes of *Hell's Angels*. John Wayne plays an American pilot who falls for a beautiful Russian aviator (Janet Leigh). Shot in 1950, the film wasn't finished until 1957. Chuck Yeager performed some of the stunt flying.
VHS: S17256. $14.98.
Josef von Sternberg, USA, 1957, 112 mins.

Last Command

Emil Jannings stars as an immigrant Czarist general reduced to working as a Hollywood film extra. Von Sternberg cuts back to the general's time of grandeur to show how far the mighty can fall, and to criticize the status of Hollywood's power hungry moguls. Preston Sturges considered this the only perfect film ever made. Silent.
VHS: S03442. $29.95.
Josef von Sternberg, USA, 1928, 88 mins.

Macao

Three strangers arrive on the infamous island off the south coast of China and are caught up in a web of intrigue and deception. Jane Russell and Robert Mitchum ignite the plot with their famous, passionate rapport. A modern tale of paradise regained and the magical power of love.
VHS: S02870. $19.98.
Josef von Sternberg, USA, 1952, 80 mins.

Morocco

Marlene Dietrich's American debut. Dietrich is an exotic cabaret singer who's stranded in Morocco and slays every man in her path until she's torn between a wealthy French industrialist (Adolphe Menjou) and an attractive American French Foreign Legion soldier (Gary Cooper). "A cinematic pattern, brilliant, profuse, subtle and at almost every turn inventive" (Wilton A. Barrett). With Ullrich Haupt, Juliette Compton and Francis McDonald.
VHS: S02285. $14.98.
Josef von Sternberg, USA, 1930, 97 mins.

Scarlet Empress

Josef von Sternberg's flamboyant biography on the life and reign of Catherine of Russia. The film chronicles her rise from provincial origins to a cold-hearted killer who used her sexuality to seduce, conquer and attain power. "With grotesque statues and gargoyles, Byzantinesque icons and portraits, impossibly magnificent costumes and perhaps the most lavish production ever undertaken, *Scarlet Empress* apotheosized Dietrich as the ultimate symbol of sexual domination and degradation" (David Cook, *The History of Narrative Film*). With John Lodge, Sam Jaffe and Louise Dresser.
VHS: S19077. $14.98.
Josef von Sternberg, USA, 1934, 109 mins.

Shanghai Express

Josef von Sternberg's spellbinding melodrama about a group of passengers on an express train from Peking to Shanghai who are hijacked by a Chinese warlord. The prostitute "Chinese Lily" (Marlene Dietrich) and the British officer (Clive Brook) she once abandoned are thrown together. "From the hypnotic chiaroscuro photography, the incredibly exotic costumes and the lavish production design, von Sternberg created a mythological China where 'dead space' is virtually absent" (David Cook). With Warner Oland, Anna May Wong and Eugene Pallette.
VHS: S19074. $14.98.
Josef von Sternberg, USA, 1932, 84 mins.

The Shanghai Gesture

The Shanghai Gesture has been called "a delirious melodrama of decadence and sexual guilt that uses its Oriental motifs as a cypher for all that is unknown and unknowable. The battle is waged between a Western hypocrite (Walter Huston) and an Eastern pleasure- queen (Ona Munson); the erotic skirmishes occur between the self-willed but helpless heroine (Gene Tierney) and the apathetic object of her passion (Victor Mature, amazing 'Doctor of Nothing,' poet of Shanghai and Gomorrah'); the chief arena is a casino built like a circle of hell, where nothing is left to change. Subversive cinema at its most sublime" (Tony Rayns, *London Time Out*).
VHS: S06319. $29.95.
Josef von Sternberg, USA, 1941, 97 mins.

Underworld

A gangster is rescued from prison by his moll and his right-hand man. But he soon realizes that the two of them are in love, and he must make a tough decision as the police close in. This melodrama, co-written by Ben Hecht and Joseph von Sternberg, was one of the first to look at crime from the gangster's point of view. With George Bancroft and Evelyn Brent. Silent.
VHS: S15286. $49.95.
Josef von Sternberg, USA, 1927, 82 mins.

ERICH VON STROHEIM

Blind Husbands

Stroheim's first film as a director, set in the Alps. Stroheim plays a handsome officer having an affair with the wife of a boring doctor. The world was shocked when the film was first released. Silent, with English subtitles.
VHS: S00144. $29.95.
Erich von Stroheim, USA, 1919, 98 mins.

Foolish Wives

Publicized as the first film to cost a million dollars, praised for its extravagant visual design and condemned for its portrayal of a rogue count's unbridled and often peculiar sexual obsessions. Characteristic of von Stroheim's greatest work, this newly mastered (from a 35mm print) version has been restored to its full 107 minutes by the American Film Institute.
VHS: S02090. $29.95.
Erich von Stroheim, USA, 1922, 107 mins.

Greed

One of the wonders of film, this miracle of filmmaking, made by Erich von Stroheim against the most impossible of odds, stars Gibson Gowland as McTeague, a San Francisco dentist, who marries ZaSu Pitts, the daughter of German immigrants. When Trina (Pitts) becomes greedy, McTeague becomes a drunken tramp and ends up killing her. A powerful, powerful masterpiece. This tape includes a prologue by film historian Kevin Brownlow, who describes the controversy surrounding the original cuts made to the film by the studio.
VHS: S09281. $29.95.
Laser: LD70592. $39.98.
Erich von Stroheim, USA, 1924, 133 mins.

The Man You Loved to Hate

This exciting and historically important look at the bizarre career of Erich von Stroheim features interviews of his wife, associates, and friends. Excerpts from *Blind Husbands, Foolish Wives* and many others help to provide a detailed study of a creative genius whose perverse aberrations regarding women, art and finances made him a Hollywood outcast. NOTE: Certain film clips used in the television version of this film have been omitted due to copyright restrictions.
VHS: S14172. $29.95.
Patrick Montgomery, USA, 1979, 70 mins.

Merry-Go-Round

Count von Hohenegg plans to marry the Minister of War's daughter, but he falls in love with the organ grinder for a merry-go-round. Forced into the original marriage, the Count is severed from his lover first by law, and then by war. The film was originally directed by Erich von Stroheim but he lost the project in a fight with producer Irving Thalberg. With Norman Kerry, Mary Philbin, Cesare Gravina and Dorothy Wallace. Silent with added music track.
VHS: S16109. $19.98.
Rupert Julian/Erich von Stroheim, USA, 1923, 110 mins.

Queen Kelly

With its restoration in 1985, Erich von Stroheim's eighth and final silent film emerged from over 50 years of obscurity to its first official release and worldwide acclaim. As such, it now ranks as one of the great treasures of film history. The collaboration of Gloria Swanson, then Hollywood's greatest star, and financier Joseph Kennedy, the film was near completion when, after three months of production, Swanson closed it down enraged by von Stroheim's excesses. The story, a gothic romance in which a convent girl is seduced by a Prince and inherits a brother in Africa, is told with stunning visual effect.
VHS: S08943. $39.95.
Erich von Stroheim, USA, 1929, 97 mins.

Wedding March

Erich von Stroheim and Fay Wray in a story that proves that the greatest wealth of a marriage is love. Set in pre-World War I Vienna, a prince set to marry a wealthy princess falls in love with a poor woman. Written by von Stroheim. Silent.
VHS: S03443. $29.95.
Erich von Stroheim, USA, 1928, 113 mins.

JOHN HUSTON

Across the Pacific

The director (John Huston) and stars of *The Maltese Falcon* (Humphrey Bogart, Mary Astor, Sydney Greenstreet) are reunited in this brisk World War II adventure about Bogart's attempt to track down spies in Panama, seduce Astor and confront the elegantly vicious Greenstreet.
VHS: S14304. $19.98.
John Huston, USA, 1942, 97 mins.

The African Queen

Inspired casting teamed Bogart and Hepburn in this romantic adventure/comedy set in a war-torn African jungle. Surviving malaria, insects and persistent conflicts of their personalities, they share victory and tender romance.
VHS: S00020. $19.98.
Laser: LD70814. $55.98.
John Huston, USA, 1951, 105 mins.

The African Queen (Commemorative Edition)

John Huston's adaptation of C.S. Forester's novel focuses on the spirited conflict of two resolute individualists, a drunken captain (Humphrey Bogart) and a repressed missionary (Katharine Hepburn), who undertake a dangerous river odyssey in East Africa against the elite German Navy during World War I. Cinematography by Jack Cardiff. Screenplay by James Agee and John Huston (and an uncredited Peter Viertel). With Robert Morley, Peter Bull, Theodore Bikel and Walter Gotell. The film has been digitally remastered and visually restored. The commemorative edition offers a hardcover edition of Hepburn's *The Making of The African Queen* and a copy of the original shooting script.
VHS: S19474. $59.98.
John Huston, USA, 1951, 105 mins.

Annie

Aileen Quinn, Carol Burnett and Albert Finney star in this adaptation of the Broadway hit based on the comic strip. With Tim Curry and Bernadette Peters.
VHS: S01884. $19.95.
John Huston, USA, 1981, 128 mins.

The Asphalt Jungle

John Huston directs this excellent underworld drama about crime and punishment. Five guys pull off a jewelry heist only to be double-crossed by their fence. With Sterling Hayden, Louis Calhern and Marilyn Monroe as Calhern's "niece."
VHS: S03458. $24.95.
Laser: LD70844. $39.95.
John Huston, USA, 1950, 112 mins.

Beat the Devil

An audacious, offbeat comedy with Humphrey Bogart, Gina Lollobrigida and Peter Lorre, and screenplay by Truman Capote, about a motley group of petty thieves and con artists hoping to grab some valuable uranium deposits. With Robert Morley and Jennifer Jones.
VHS: S00107. $24.95.
John Huston, USA, 1953, 92 mins.

The Bible

John Huston directs the first 22 chapters of Genesis and claims the title of the whole book. He also plays Noah. International cast includes Peter O'Toole, Ava Gardner, Franco Nero, Richard Harris and Michael Parks and Ully Bergryd as Adam and Eve. This is one situation where more people read the book and with good reason.
VHS: S04594. $19.98.
Laser: LD70880. $69.98.
John Huston, Italy, 1966, 155 mins.

Casino Royale

Sean Connery, Peter Sellers, David Niven, Woody Allen, Orson Welles, Ursula Andress star in the film based on the first Fleming 007 novel; the farce begins when Bond is persuaded to join the HMSS and take on a mission to stop Le Chiffre from his big winnings supporting the evil organization.
VHS: S00217. $14.95.
Laser: CAV, widescreen. LD74615. $39.95.
John Huston, USA, 1967, 130 mins.

The Dead

The last film of a great American director is a faithful and artful adaptation of a James Joyce story from *The Dubliners*. The screenplay is by his son, Tony Huston. A well-to-do family and their friends gather for a holiday meal and evening of musical entertainment. The revelers include Anjelica Huston, Dan O'Herlihy, Donald McCann, Cathleen Delany, Marie Kern and Donald Donnelly. A short and solemn swan song.
VHS: S07921. $59.98.
John Huston, USA/Ireland, 1987, 95 mins.

The Dubliners

A very moving and uniquely privileged look at the making of the last film of the late, great John Huston—the making of *The Dead* in Ireland. Few filmmakers have had an opportunity to close their illustrious career as well as Huston, and Lillian Sievernich's film captures Huston, already ill, working to complete his dream project of adapting a story from James Joyce's *The Dubliners* as his film, *The Dead*.
VHS: S00947. $29.95.
Lillian Sievernich, USA, 1987, 83 mins.

Fat City

Stacy Keach and Jeff Bridges star in this brilliant John Huston drama about small time boxers. Move over, Rocky. This is the reality of what life is like for guys who punch each other for a living. With Susan Tyrell and Candy Clark. Based on the Leonard Gardner novel.
VHS: S06067. $19.95.
John Huston, USA, 1972, 100 mins.

In This Our Life

Bette Davis stars as a neurotic girl who steals her sister's husband, leaves him in the lurch, dominates her family and finally is killed as she runs from the police. A first-rate melodrama with Charles Coburn, Olivia de Havilland and Frank Craven.
VHS: S11627. $19.95.
John Huston, USA, 1942, 101 mins.

Independence

A short subject directed by John Huston that concerns the historical events that led to the writing and signing of the Declaration of Independence. E.G. Marshall provides the narration. Cast includes Eli Wallach, Anne Jackson and Patrick O'Neal. In color and with liberty and justice for all.
VHS: S06167. $19.95.
John Huston, USA, 1976, 30 mins.

John Huston: The Man, The Movies, The Maverick

Robert Mitchum hosts this special personal tribute to John Huston that is warm, funny, poignant and full of insights into the life of the man who lived life to the fullest. Joined by stars Paul Newman, Lauren Bacall, Michael Caine, Anjelica Huston, Arthur Miller and Evelyn Keyes, Mitchum shares a fond look at the man who made *The Maltese Falcon*, *African Queen*, *The Dead*, *The Misfits* and *Treasure of Sierra Madre*.
VHS: S10743. $29.98.
Laser: LD71564. $29.95.

Juarez

John Huston at his best. Paul Muni is brilliant as the revolutionary Mexican leader who causes the downfall of Emperor Maximilian. With Bette Davis, Brian Aherne, Claude Rains, John Garfield.
VHS: S13395. $19.95.
John Huston, USA, 1939, 132 mins.

Key Largo

Humphrey Bogart goes to visit the widow of an old war buddy (played by Lauren Bacall), and finds himself in a confrontation with Edward G. Robinson. With an Oscar-winning performance from Claire Trevor.
VHS: S01708. $19.95.
Laser: LD70181. $34.39.
John Huston, USA, 1948, 101 mins.

Let There Be Light

Documentary commissioned by the U.S. War Department on the psychiatric treatment of shell-shocked World War II veterans. The film was confiscated upon completion and banned until 1980 in the fear that it would discourage recruitment. Deeply humanitarian and pacifist.
VHS: S00749. $29.95.
John Huston, USA, 1945, 60 mins.

The Life and Times of Judge Roy Bean

Paul Newman is the self-appointed hanging judge, the only law west of the Pecos. He's stern but he is fair. He's also in love with Lily Langtry (Ava Gardner). Watch for Stacy Keach as the Original Bad Bob, the albino gunman. With Roddy McDowall and Victoria Principal.
VHS: S04196. $14.95.
John Huston, USA, 1972, 124 mins.

List of Adrian Messenger

A witty thriller in which George C. Scott must uncover the identity of a murderer who is killing off the heirs to a family fortune. The audience gets in on the fun by trying to identify the stars who are playing disguised roles in the film: Sinatra, Mitchum, Kirk Douglas, Burt Lancaster and Tony Curtis.
VHS: S01710. $19.95.
John Huston, USA, 1963, 98 mins.

The Mackintosh Man

Paul Newman spends most of this film running for his life all over picturesque locations in Ireland. He has been sent to infiltrate a criminal organization headed by James Mason, a high government official. He doesn't seem amused. Screenplay by Walter Hill.
VHS: S04174. $19.95.
John Huston, USA, 1973, 100 mins.

Maltese Falcon

Even if you've seen this film so often that you know all the dialog, it never ceases to amaze. A search for a priceless statuette provides the action in this classic, excellent film favorite. Noir at its best with great actors Humphrey Bogart, Mary Astor, Sydney Greenstreet and Peter Lorre, based on Dashiell Hammet's thriller.
VHS: S00810. $19.95.
Laser: LD70621. $34.98.
John Huston, USA, 1941, 101 mins.

Man Who Would Be King

Grand telling of the Rudyard Kipling classic adventure story of two soldiers of fortune in 19th century India, who set out to conquer lands and make themselves king. Sean Connery and Michael Caine are brilliantly cast.
VHS: S00819. $19.98.
John Huston, USA, 1975, 129 mins.

Misfits

The last film completed by both Marilyn Monroe and Clark Gable, scripted by Monroe's husband at the time, Arthur Miller. Young divorcee Marilyn settles in Reno, first in the boarding house of Thelma Ritter, then in the home and heart of grizzled cowboy Clark Gable. Her tender-hearted ways clash with the macho culture of rodeo, saloons, and wild horse wrangling—leading to a dramatic climax in the barren desert. Featuring fine supporting performances by Eli Wallach and Montgomery Clift.
VHS: S04198. $19.98.
Laser: LD70631. $39.98.
John Huston, USA, 1961, 124 mins.

Moby Dick

John Huston directs Herman Melville's classic tale of a large, albino, water-based mammal and the obsessive sea captain with one real leg. The script is by Ray Bradbury. Gregory Peck stars as Ahab, Richard Basehart is the lucky Ishmael. Other crew members of the Pequod include Leo Genn, Harry Andrews and Frederick Ledebur as Queequeg. Three white whales were used in the filming off the coast of Ireland; two were lost at sea and still frighten the locals.
VHS: S00865. $19.95.
Laser: LD72127. $34.98.
John Huston, USA/Great Britain, 1956, 116 mins.

Moulin Rouge

The colorful story of French painter Henri Toulouse-Lautrec as interpreted by director John Huston. Jose Ferrer is cast as the Parisian artist who may have been short of stature but never of talent. The film won Oscars for its art direction, set decoration and costumes. Return to the exciting and naughty world of Montmartre in the late 19th century. The cast includes Eric Pohlmann, Colette Marchant, Peter Cushing, Christopher Lee and Zsa Zsa Gabor, who was hot stuff in 1952.
VHS: S11216. $19.95.
Laser: LD72128. $39.98.
John Huston, USA, 1952, 123 mins.

Night of the Iguana

Richard Burton, Deborah Kerr and Ava Gardner star in this adaptation of Tennessee Williams' play about a fallen, alcoholic ex-minister, who is self-exiled to Mexico, where he works as a tour guide.
VHS: S04394. $19.98.
Laser: LD72352. $39.98.
John Huston, USA, 1964, 125 mins.

Phobia

A virtually unknown film by John Huston made in Canada, *Phobia* is a tense whodunit which takes place in a unique treatment center. First a bathtub drowning. Then a fatal elevator ride. A lethal snake bite. One by one, phobia-ridden patients are being murdered, and a patient, a jilted lover, or even their doctor (Paul Michael Glaser) could be the killer.
VHS: S09492. $19.95.
John Huston, Canada, 1980, 91 mins.

Red Badge of Courage

Huston's powerful adaptation of Stephen Crane's novel about the horrors of war. Set during the Civil War, the film features strong performances from Audie Murphy and Bill Mauldin.
VHS: S01762. $24.95.
John Huston, USA, 1951, 69 mins.

Reflections in a Golden Eye

Sexual tensions simmer in the heat of a Georgia army base. A sextet of characters, based on Carson McCullers' novel, try to come to grips with their desires. They include Marlon Brando, Elizabeth Taylor, Brian Keith, Julie Harris and Robert Forster as the soldier who likes to ride bareback.
VHS: S04180. $19.98.
John Huston, USA, 1967, 109 mins.

Treasure of the Sierra Madre

Pauline Kael calls this "one of the strongest of all American movies." Three Americans strike it rich and greed takes over. With Humphrey Bogart, Walter Huston, Tim Holt and Robert Blake, based on the novel by B. Traven.
VHS: S01368. $19.95.
Laser: LD70699. $39.98.
John Huston, USA, 1948, 120 mins.

Under the Volcano

Malcolm Lowry's cult classic brought to life by the legendary director John Huston, starring Albert Finney and Jacqueline Bisset. Filmed on location in Mexico, this film has all the beauty and foreboding of the novel, which paints a vivid picture of alcoholism.
VHS: S01399. $79.95.
Laser: LD70093. $34.98.
John Huston, USA, 1984, 112 mins.

The Unforgiven

A powerful western drama about racism and family ties directed by John Huston. Set in Texas in the 1950's, a proud and strongwilled family discovers an adopted daughter might have Indian blood. The cast includes Burt Lancaster, Audrey Hepburn, Lillian Gish, Charles Bickford and Audie Murphy.
VHS: S03670. $19.95.
Laser: LD72271. $39.98.
John Huston, USA, 1960, 123 mins.

Wise Blood

Based on the powerful novel by Flannery O'Connor, *Wise Blood* traces the career of a religious fanatic who attempts to found a church without salvation. An offbeat masterpiece featuring superb performances by Ned Beatty and Harry Dean Stanton.
VHS: S01470. $59.95.
John Huston, USA, 1979, 106 mins.

GEORGE CUKOR

Adam's Rib

Spencer Tracy and Katharine Hepburn in one of their all-time great appearances as married attorneys who find themselves on opposite sides of a murder case in which Judy Holliday is the accused.
VHS: S03456. $19.95.
Laser: LD70202. $49.98.
Laser: LD70336. $39.95.
George Cukor, USA, 1949, 101 mins.

Bhowani Junction

Earthy Ava Gardner is half-English, half-Indian and all woman in George Cukor's spectacular drama of chaos and revolt in post-colonial India. Shot by Frederick A. Young, who was also the cinematographer for *Lawrence of Arabia*.
VHS: S15115. $19.98.
Laser: LD72164. $34.95.
George Cukor, USA, 1956, 109 mins.

A Bill of Divorcement

Katharine Hepburn's screen debut, starring opposite the legendary John Barrymore. This is a charming and poignant romantic comedy about the unexpected homecoming of a former madman.
VHS: S12168. $39.98.
George Cukor, USA, 1932, 70 mins.

Born Yesterday

Judy Holliday won the Best Actress Oscar for her funny role as the dumb blond girlfriend of Broderick Crawford, a corrupt millionaire junk dealer. Brock, a man with social ambitions, is embarassed by Billie's crass behavior and hires a writer, William Holden, to smarten yer up. A classic comedy.
VHS: S03863. $19.95.
George Cukor, USA, 1950, 103 mins.

Camille

Greta Garbo at the peak of her career, as the consumptive courtesan who falls in love with the young nobleman with tragic results. This adaptation of the Alexandre Dumas play and novel, with Lionel Barrymore and Robert Taylor, is beautiful to look at and clearly defines the Garbo magic.
VHS: S03453. $24.95.
George Cukor, USA, 1936, 110 mins.

The Corn Is Green

One of the George Cukor's parting glances was this seamless, old-fashioned and faithful remake of Irving Rapper's 1945 classic, about the intellectual passion and energy a spinster teacher (Katharine Hepburn) brings to a South Wales mining community.
VHS: S15933. $19.98.
George Cukor, USA, 1974, 100 mins.

David Copperfield

Director Cukor assembled a fine cast to portray the assortment of characters who populate Charles Dickens' epic novel. With W.C. Fields, Lionel Barrymore, Maureen O'Sullivan and Basil Rathbone.
VHS: S03003. $19.98.
Laser: LD70552. $39.98.
George Cukor, USA, 1935, 131 mins.

Dinner at Eight

Based on George S. Kaufman and Edna Ferber's Broadway hit, in which an elaborate dinner party reveals a web of intrigue and romance. A classic American comedy. With Marie Dressler, John Barrymore, Wallace Beery, an adorable Jean Harlow, Lionel Barrymore and Lee Tracy.
VHS: S00342. $19.95.
Laser: LD70556. $34.98.
George Cukor, USA, 1933, 111 mins.

A Double Life

Ronald Colman plays a brilliant actor whose stage roles are beginning to affect the rest of his life. In an Oscar winning performance Colman performs *Othello* once too often for his own good. With Signe Hasso, Edmond O'Brien and Shelley Winters.
VHS: S04228. $19.98.
George Cukor, USA, 1947, 103 mins.

Gaslight

Ingrid Bergman won her first Oscar for her stunning role as a susceptible young woman who marries the suave, romantic Charles Boyer, never suspecting he is involved in a murderous scandal in Cukor's electrifying mystery drama.
VHS: S00482. $19.98.
George Cukor, USA, 1944, 113 mins.

Holiday

Katharine Hepburn and Cary Grant are two kindred spirits trapped in a love triangle in this stylish, intelligent adaptation of the play by Philip Barry as Grant confronts the stuffy New York society. Very delightful.
VHS: Out of print. For rental only.
Laser: CLV. LD74616. $34.95.
George Cukor, USA, 1938, 93 mins.

Justine

The mysterious wife of a well-to-do banker becomes involved in 1930's Middle East politics. Director Cukor gets fine performances from his cast, which includes Anouk Aimee, Dirk Bogarde, Philippe Noiret and Michael York.
VHS: S02324. $59.98.
George Cukor, USA, 1969, 115 mins.

Keeper of the Flame

Top-notch reporter Spencer Tracy has come to a small town to investigate the death of Robert Forrest, a national hero. He's determined to get a story, but things change when he falls in love with Forrest's beautiful widow (Katharine Hepburn).
VHS: S15022. $19.98.
George Cukor, USA, 1942, 100 mins.

Les Girls

A delightful romantic musical comedy with a Cole Porter score, starring Gene Kelly, Mitzi Gaynor, and Kay Kendall. A witty story, delightful musical numbers and a very talented cast.
VHS: S00747. $19.98.
Laser: LD70613. $34.97.
George Cukor, USA, 1957, 114 mins.

Let's Make Love

Marilyn Monroe sings "My Heart Belongs to Daddy" in this breezy comedy of billionaires, show business and the truth. Yves Montand, a very wealthy man, learns he is to be satirized in an off-Broadway revue and wants to close the show until he meets Marilyn.
VHS: S04199. $19.98.
George Cukor, USA, 1960, 118 mins.

A Life of Her Own

George Cukor's romantic triangle about a beautiful and ambitious Midwestern woman (Lana Turner) who arrives in New York with hopes of attaining top status as a model, encounters amazing success, and promptly falls for a charismatic married man (Ray Milland). With Tom Ewell, Louis Calhern and Ann Dvorak. Screenplay by Isabel Lennart.
VHS: S18662. $19.98.
George Cukor, USA, 1950, 108 mins.

Little Women

"Endless pleasure no matter how many times you've seen it" (Leonard Maltin). The Louisa May Alcott novel is portrayed on film featuring Katharine Hepburn, Joan Bennett, Frances Dee and Paul Lukas.
VHS: S03008. $19.95.
Laser: LD70137. $34.98.
George Cukor, USA, 1933, 116 mins.

Love Among the Ruins

The late Sir Laurence Olivier teamed with Katharine Hepburn in George Cukor's delightful comedy about an older actress who is hit with a breach of promise suit by a young gigolo. A "civilized" comedy directed with great flair by Cukor.
VHS: S10754. $14.98.
George Cukor, USA, 1974, 100 mins.

My Fair Lady

Alan Jay Lerner and Frederick Loewe's variation of Shaw's *Pygmalion* is turned into an intellectual comedy of manners by expert director George Cukor, who skillfully allows the byplay of co-star Stanley Holloway to co-exist with the primary storyline of Henry Higgins' schooling of Eliza Doolittle. Rex Harrison and Audrey Hepburn (songs dubbed by Marni Nixon) are the leads; Holloway's "Get Me to the Church on Time" steals the show.
VHS: S02345. $24.95.
Laser: LD71247. $44.98.
George Cukor, USA, 1964, 170 mins.

My Fair Lady (Restored)

Audrey Hepburn and Rex Harrison star in this film adaptation of the classic Broadway musical by Lerner and Loewe, based on George Bernard Shaw's *Pygmalion*. Now it has been carefully restored, and even the original soundtracks recorded by Hepburn have been saved. Interviews with all the stars and the original trailer are included in this limited edition.
VHS: S21959. $24.98.
George Cukor, USA, 1964, 170 mins.

Pat and Mike

Katharine Hepburn and Spencer Tracy team up for their seventh film, as a top female athlete and a shady sports promoter. Ruth Gordon and Garson Kanin supplied the script, which features many popular golf and tennis pros, like Babe Didrikson Zaharias and Gussie Moran, in bit parts. Watch for Charles Bronson as a judo trained thug.
VHS: S09151. $19.98.
George Cukor, USA, 1952, 95 mins.

The Philadelphia Story

One of the most hilarious and captivating romantic comedies ever to grace the screen. Katharine Hepburn is caught between her fiance and her charming ex-husband. With a splendid cast, including Cary Grant, James Stewart and Ruth Hussey.
VHS: S01023. $19.95.
Laser: LD70152. $39.98.
George Cukor, USA, 1940, 118 mins.

Romeo and Juliet

Leslie Howard and Norma Shearer play the title roles in Shakespeare's immortal tale of star-crossed lovers. A fabulous production.
VHS: S15654. $19.95.
George Cukor, USA, 1936, 126 mins.

Song Without End

Dirk Bogarde stars in this biographical drama about the tempestuous life and scandalous career of renowned Hungarian pianist Franz Liszt. With Capucine, Genevieve Page, Patricia Morison and Lou Jacobi.
VHS: S16635. $19.95.
King Vidor/George Cukor, USA, 1960, 141 mins.

A Star Is Born

The second version of the story of a young performer's rise to fame as her actor husband's star fades. Garland's genius makes the story effective, with help from a wonderful performance by James Mason.
VHS: S01734. $29.98.
Laser: LD71337. $39.95.
George Cukor, USA, 1954, 154 mins.

Susan and God

Joan Crawford is cast as a society matron who returns from Europe "aflame with the spirit of do-goodism." Her persistent attempts to convert her jaded society chums prove disruptive, but do cause her husband, Fredric March, to sober up. With Rita Hayworth, Ruth Hussey, John Carroll, Rita Quigley, Rose Hobart, Nigel Bruce and Bruce Cabot. Anita Loos wrote the screenplay.
VHS: S16455. $19.98.
George Cukor, USA, 1940, 117 mins.

Sylvia Scarlett

Katharine Hepburn disguises herself as a boy in order to help her father escape from the law in Paris. The two encounter Cary Grant, a con man, and thus begins a weird yet gentle romance.
VHS: Out of print. For rental only.
Laser: LD71355. $24.95.
George Cukor, USA, 1935, 94 mins.

Travels with My Aunt

Based on the Graham Greene novel of the same name, this film features an all-star cast. Maggie Smith, Alec McCowen, Lou Gossett, Jr., and Cindy Williams are all caught up in a European tour with a secret rationale. Though everything seems to be stylish and graceful, the plot centers on an unconventional lady smuggler who brings style and class to the world of hustling and swindling.
VHS: S27575. $19.98.
George Cukor, USA, 1972, 109 mins.

Two-Faced Woman

Greta Garbo stopped making movies after this comedy failed to generate much interest. She plays an insecure ski instructor who must invent and impersonate a vivacious sister to prevent her brand new husband from going back to his more sophisticated old flame. With Melvyn Douglas as the former playboy publisher who enjoys seeing double. Also with Constance Bennett, Roland Young and Ruth Gordon.
VHS: S11731. $19.98.
George Cukor, USA, 1941, 94 mins.

A Woman's Face

Joan Crawford stars as a professional blackmailer with a disfiguring scar whose life is changed by Melvyn Douglas' plastic surgery, which heals her features but not her scarred emotions. With Conrad Veidt.
VHS: S03455. $19.98.
George Cukor, USA, 1941, 107 mins.

The Women

Brilliant, witty comedy with a stellar cast of women: Norma Shearer, Joan Crawford, Rosalind Russell, Mary Boland, Paulette Goddard and Joan Fontaine. No men appear in the film, but men is what the film is all about. Superb American comedy, with perhaps the wittiest dialog ever put on screen. A must-see.
VHS: S01480. $19.95.
George Cukor, USA, 1939, 133 mins.

FRANK CAPRA

Arsenic and Old Lace

Cary Grant stars in this hilarious black comedy about two sweet old ladies who poison lonely old men with elderberry wine, as a kindness. Cary is the confused nephew who has to juggle dead bodies, escaped murderers and an uncle who thinks he's Teddy Roosevelt with a marriage announcement and the police. With Peter Lorre as Dr. Einstein.
VHS: S02351. $19.95.
Laser: CLV, 1 disc, Criterion. LD70340. $39.95.
Frank Capra, USA, 1944, 118 mins.

The Bitter Tea of General Yen

Frank Capra's film concerns an American missionary (Barbara Stanwyck) who is kidnapped by a powerful Chinese warlord and falls prey to his intoxicating spell. With Nils Asther, Toshia Mori and Walter Connolly.
VHS: S19023. $19.95.
Frank Capra, USA, 1932, 89 mins.

Broadway Bill

Lost for over 40 years, *Broadway Bill* is available for the first time on video. An heiress bets she'll find true love at the racetrack and saddles up to a cheery horse trainer. A romantic comedy in true Capra style. Margaret Hamilton and Jason Robards star.
VHS: S15866. $19.95.
Laser: LD75166. $34.98.
Frank Capra, USA, 1934, 100 mins.

Here Comes the Groom

A happy-go-lucky reporter plots and schemes to keep his former fiancee from marrying a millionaire. If he adopts war orphans, will this win her over? Bing Crosby and Jane Wyman star.
VHS: S12570. $19.95.
Frank Capra, USA, 1951, 114 mins.

A Hole in the Head

The last important film of Frank Capra's career, with Frank Sinatra playing a Miami hotel owner on the verge of bankruptcy, who's forced to scramble to raise funds in order to stay in business. With a terrific performance from Edward G. Robinson, Carolyn Jones, Keenan Wynn.
VHS: Out of print. For rental only.
Laser: LD72177. $39.98.
Frank Capra, USA, 1959, 120 mins.

It Happened One Night

Winner of five Academy Awards, this famous screwball comedy stars Clark Gable and Claudette Colbert as two mismatched lovers. Colbert escapes from her millionaire father, who wants to stop her from marrying a worthless playboy.
VHS: S00642. $19.95.
Laser: LD72146. $34.95.
Frank Capra, USA, 1934, 105 mins.

It's a Wonderful Life

James Stewart is George Bailey, trapped in Bedford Falls, until his faith in life is restored by his Guardian Angel in Frank Capra's delightful comedy, nominated for multiple Academy Awards. Donna Reed, Lionel Barrymore, Thomas Mitchell and Beulah Bondi also star.
VHS: S15106. $19.98.
Laser: CAV. LD70387. $89.95.
Laser: CLV. LD71996. $39.98.
Frank Capra, USA, 1946, 160 mins.

Ladies of Leisure

Early Frank Capra social comedy stars Barbara Stanwyck in her debut performance as an ambitious adventuress and careerist who falls for a roguish artist (Robert Graves) who wishes to make a portrait of her. "The climactic sequence is genuinely tense, exciting and visual in the manner of the best silents" (William K. Everson). With Lowell Sherman, Marie Prevost and George Fawcett.
VHS: S18948. $19.95.
Frank Capra, USA, 1930, 98 mins.

Lady for a Day

Frank Capra's romantic fable of a soft-hearted gangster who helps transform an old apple-seller into a perfect lady was nominated for four Academy Awards, and features wonderful performances from Warren William, May Robson, Guy Kibbee, Glenda Farrell. Adapted from a Damon Runyan story, and one of Capra's first great successes.
VHS: Out of print. For rental only.
Laser: CLV. LD70757. $39.95.
Frank Capra, USA, 1933, 88 mins.

Lost Horizon

Frank Capra's hypnotic and perversely appealing adaptation of James Hilton's novel featuring 22 minutes of restored footage that fully explores the psychological implications of Capra's "utopian paradise." Though the material seems foreign to Capra's style and sensibility, it is a work of lost innocence and spiritual redemption. A plane fleeing revolutionary China is highjacked to a mysterious valley in the Himalayas known as Shangri-La. Ronald Coleman stars as a British diplomat who falls for Jane Wyatt. The expansive, post-modern sets and art direction were inspired by the architecture of Frank Lloyd Wright.
VHS: S02919. $19.95.
Frank Capra, USA, 1937, 132 mins.

Meet John Doe

Capra's classic ode to the common man: Gary Cooper is the unemployed worker built into a symbol by a newspaper publisher only to discover he's the object of political ambitions. With Barbara Stanwyck, Edward Arnold, Walter Brennan.
VHS: S00844. $19.95.
Frank Capra, USA, 1941, 123 mins.

Mr. Deeds Goes to Town

One of Frank Capra's best films, shot during the height of the Depression. Gary Cooper plays Longfellow Deeds, who inherits 20 million dollars and wants to spend it on people during the height of the Depression. Jean Arthur plays the city reporter who is captivated by the naive Deeds.
VHS: S11163. $19.95.
Frank Capra, USA, 1936, 115 mins.

Mr. Smith Goes to Washington

James Stewart stars in Frank Capra's famous film as the naive Jeff Smith, appointed a U.S. senator by a corrupt political party machine. Famous for its heroic one-man fillibuster, it is a moving vision of honor amid political squalor.
VHS: S00889. $19.95.
Laser: Restored, 3 sides, digital master, chapter stops.
LD75054. $44.95.
Frank Capra, USA, 1939, 125 mins.

Negro Soldier

Frank Capra supervised this documentary focusing on black participation in World War II. Langston Hughes hailed it as the most remarkable Negro film ever flashed on the American screen.
VHS: S03347. $19.98.
Frank Capra, USA, 1944, 40 mins.

Platinum Blonde

Jean Harlow and Loretta Young face off in this raucous comedy of romance between the haves and have-nots. Robert Williams is a wise-cracking reporter married to the wealthy Harlow, but his distaste for the confinement of "high society" may just give Young a fighting chance.
VHS: S16591. $19.95.
Frank Capra, USA, 1931, 90 mins.

Pocketful of Miracles

Bette Davis stars as an aging apple-seller who poses as a wealthy grande dame in order to have her daughter marry into a legitimately rich family. Others in the talented cast include Glenn Ford, Hope Lange, Peter Falk, and, making her film debut, Ann-Margret.
VHS: S01041. $14.95.
Laser: Letterboxed, 2 disks. LD74590. $49.98.
Frank Capra, USA, 1961, 137 mins.

Riding High

Bing Crosby and Colleen Gray star in this entertaining musical comedy that has the special Capra touch. Crosby is a race horse owner just waiting for his horse to come in, but of course romance won't wait, especially when there's music in the air. This remake of the classic 30's musical *Broadway Bill* is a delightful update.
VHS: S21600. $19.95.
Laser: LD75247. $34.98.
Frank Capra, USA, 1950, 112 mins.

State of the Union

Spencer Tracy stars as an honest industrialist who finds himself in danger of losing his integrity when he is drafted to run for the presidency. With Katharine Hepburn as his steadfast wife, Angela Lansbury, and Van Johnson.
VHS: S01735. $19.98.
Laser: LD70083. $39.98.
Frank Capra, USA, 1948, 122 mins.

The Strong Man

Harry Langdon stars in this wonderful silent comedy, newly restored by Kevin Brownlow and David Gill. A World War I veteran comes to America with a travelling show, hoping to meet the girl whose letters gave him hope at the front. With a new musical score by Carl Davis. 78 mins.
VHS: S10917. $39.99.
Frank Capra, USA, 1926, 78 mins.

That Certain Thing

Frank Capra's first Columbia Picture. It tells the story of Molly Kelly, a hardworking young woman who marries a millionaire, only to be impoverished once again when his dad disinherits the son, thinking her to be a gold-digger. When she starts a successful box lunch business, dad comes around. With Viola Dana and Ralph Graves. Silent.
VHS: S04805. $24.95.
Frank Capra, USA, 1928, 70 mins.

Unchained Goddess

The Goddess of Weather, along with the characters of Wind, Rain and Clouds, helps explain what weather really is. Animated by Shamus Culhane, most famous for his Betty Boop, and directed by Frank Capra. From the Bell Science Collection. 54 mins.
VHS: S16333. $9.95.

You Can't Take It with You

James Stewart, Jean Arthur, Lionel Barrymore and Edward Arnold star in this 1938 Academy Award-winning, nutty comedy. Based on the play by George S. Kaufman and Moss Hart. The scenes in which Barrymore confronts an IRS man by refusing to pay taxes are among the funniest in film.
VHS: Out of print. For rental only.
Laser: LD72145. $39.95.
Frank Capra, USA, 1938, 126 mins.

ALFRED HITCHCOCK

Alfred Hitchcock TV

Two episodes of the infamous Alfred Hitchcock television series are included on this video. *The Chaney Vase* and *The Sorcerer's Apprentice* both have the master's touch. They are not only suspenseful, but they are both introduced by the rotund thriller king himself.
VHS: S27333. $19.95.
Alfred Hitchcock, USA, 52 mins.

The Birds

Sheer terror from the master. *The Birds* is based on a novella by Daphne Du Maurier and was accomplished by nearly 400 trick shots using thousands of birds. With Tippi Hedren, Rod Taylor, Jessica Tandy and Suzanne Pleshette.
VHS: S01845. $19.95.
Laser: LD70015. $39.98.
Alfred Hitchcock, USA, 1963, 119 mins.

Blackmail

Hitchcock's first sound picture, *Blackmail* is the story of a young girl who stabs an artist to death in defense of her honor. Her boyfriend, a Scotland Yard detective, puts the clues together and decides to protect her. But then an unknown blackmailer comes on the scene, and the film builds into a tense, exciting climax. With Anny Ondra, John Longden, Cyril Ritchard.
VHS: S00141. $19.95.
Laser: LD71521. $49.95.
Alfred Hitchcock, Great Britain, 1929, 86 mins.

Bon Voyage & Aventure Malgache

Many great directors were drafted for the Allied effort in World War II. These two shorts were commissioned by the British Ministry of Information and meant to be screened in France upon liberation. Suspenseful dramas of betrayal and murder were not exactly what they had in mind at the ministry however, and these films were never used for their originally stated purpose. 27 and 31 minutes. French with English subtitles.
VHS: S20960. $39.95.
Alfred Hitchcock, Great Britain, 1944, 58 mins.

Champagne

A millionaire father objects to the man his daughter is in love with, and to teach her a lesson he allows his daughter to think he has become bankrupt. The young woman goes to work in a cabaret serving the same champagne the family fortune was based upon. Filled with sight gags. Silent.
VHS: S00225. $19.98.
Alfred Hitchcock, Great Britain, 1928

Dial M for Murder

Grace Kelly, Ray Milland and Robert Cummings star in Alfred Hitchcock's sophisticated study of the perfect crime. Suave (but rotten to the core) Milland frames his wife (icy beauty Grace Kelly) for murder in this twisting and turning, imaginative thriller from the master of suspense. One of the first 3-D feature films of 1954.
VHS: S00336. $19.98.
Laser: LD70554. $34.98.
Alfred Hitchcock, USA, 1954, 123 mins.

Easy Virtue

Alfred Hitchcock's early silent film about the destruction of a woman's life, in which a suicide leads to the heroine's divorce scandal and a sorry end. Silent with musical track.
VHS: S01640. $24.95.
Alfred Hitchcock, Great Britain, 1927, 60 mins.

Family Plot

Hitchcock's last movie is a diabolically funny search for a missing heir, starring Bruce Dern, Barbara Harris, William Devane, and Karen Black.
VHS: S01853. $14.98.
Laser: LD70029. $39.98.
Alfred Hitchcock, USA, 1976, 120 mins.

The Farmer's Wife

A rustic silent comedy from Alfred Hitchcock. Farmer (Jameson Thomas) doesn't know his housekeeper (Lillian Hall-Davies) is willing to take on more responsibilities around the place. In his search for a bride he is overlooking his own backyard. Silent.
VHS: S04089. $19.98.
Alfred Hitchcock, Great Britain, 1928, 97 mins.

Foreign Correspondent

Hitchcock's second American film was a return to the flawless architecture of his best British thrillers. Set in London and Amsterdam during the war, the film is an entertaining blend of suspense and dark humor involving an American reporter sent to cover the European situation. Among the highlights are the attempted murder atop Westminster Cathedral, a brilliant sequence in an isolated Dutch windmill and an assassination scene in pouring rain. With Herbert Marshall, Joel McCrea, Laraine Day.
VHS: S02020. $19.98.
Laser: LD70575. $39.98.
Alfred Hitchcock, USA, 1940, 120 mins.

Frenzy

A great Hitchcock thriller: the wrong man is suspected when his wife is murdered. Full of Hitchcock's humor, the film stars Alec McCowen, Vivien Merchant, Jon Finch.
VHS: S01703. $19.95.
Laser: LD70031. $34.98.
Alfred Hitchcock, Great Britain, 1972, 116 mins.

I Confess

Montgomery Clift plays a priest who hears a murderer's confession and will not violate the sanctity of the confessional even to protect himself. With Anne Baxter and Karl Malden.
VHS: S01705. $19.98.
Laser: LD70597. $34.98.
Alfred Hitchcock, USA, 1953, 95 mins.

Inside Hitchcock

Enter the mind of Alfred Hitchcock, one of the cinema's greatest directors. See clips from his best films and listen to the Master himself discuss his techniques, his actors, his intentions. Notoriously spellbinding!
VHS: S01948. $39.95.
Richard Schickel, USA, 55 mins.

Jamaica Inn

Hitchcock's last film in England before moving to Hollywood. With Charles Laughton in a story set in the eighteenth century about a young Irish girl who moves to Cornwall, England, to set up an inn.
VHS: S18182. $19.95.
Alfred Hitchcock, Great Britain, 1939, 98 mins.

Juno and the Paycock

This almost-never seen film by Alfred Hitchcock is based on the play by Sean O'Casey and the script was written by Hitchcock and his wife Alma Reville. Set in Ireland in the 1920's, the story revolves around the tragedies of a single, poor Dublin family. James Agee called it "a film which completely justifies the talkies." With Satra Allgood, Edward Chapman, Maire O'Neill. One of the very early sound efforts by Hitchcock.
VHS: S06388. $39.95.
Alfred Hitchcock, Great Britain, 1930, 85 mins.

The Lady Vanishes

One of Hitchcock's best British films; Dame May Whitty stars as the kindly old woman who befriends a young English girl on a European train, and then disappears. All her fellow travellers swear she never existed—only the hero, Michael Redgrave, and she together uncover the web of intrigue.
VHS: S23482. $24.95.
Laser: LD71091. $39.95.
Alfred Hitchcock, Great Britain, 1938, 97 mins.

Lifeboat

Riveting war drama, written by John Steinbeck, starring William Bendix and Tallulah Bankhead as survivors of an American vessel torpedoed by a German sub during World War II. The eight are set adrift in a tiny lifeboat and the drama unfolds as they take aboard a stranded Nazi. Another gem from Alfred Hitchcock with his "appearance" coming in a most unusual way.
VHS: S01949. $19.98.
Laser: LD71107. $39.98.
Alfred Hitchcock, USA, 1944, 96 mins.

Lodger

Hitchcock's first major film, about a young tenant suspected by his landlady of being Jack the Ripper. A tense, imaginative thriller that features Hitchcock's first cameo appearance and first use of the innocent man falsely accused. Silent.
VHS: S00764. $29.95.
Alfred Hitchcock, Great Britain, 1926, 65 mins.

Man Who Knew Too Much (1934)

Hitchcock's first version of this film is the story of an ordinary family caught in a web of international intrigue. The film ends in a brilliant tour-de-force of suspense at the Royal Albert Hall in London. With Leslie Banks, Edna Best, Peter Lorre, Nova Pilbeam.
VHS: S18183. $19.95.
Alfred Hitchcock, Great Britain, 1934, 72 mins.

Man Who Knew Too Much (1955)

Hitchcock's brilliant remake of his own 1934 version features James Stewart and Doris Day as an innocent American couple caught up in a web of international intrigue, kidnapping and assassination.
VHS: S00817. $14.98.
Laser: LD70053. $34.95.
Alfred Hitchcock, USA, 1955, 120 mins.

Manxman

Hitchcock's last silent film was an ambitious film about a lovers' triangle in which some of his favorite themes, such as vertigo and moral conflict, begin to develop. Film was shot on the Isle of Man. Silent.
VHS: S00823. $19.98.
Alfred Hitchcock, Great Britain, 1929

Marnie

Sean Connery and Tippi Hendren star in Hitchcock's psychological thriller of a habitual thief (Hendren) and her employer (Connery), who is determined to help her. One of Hitchcock's most interesting films, with a symbolic use of color to represent emotional fears and reactions, with Hendren unable to help herself because of repressed memories and Connery obsessed with the idea of possessing a beautiful criminal.
VHS: S01770. $19.95.
Laser: LD70054. $39.95.
Alfred Hitchcock, USA, 1964, 130 mins.

Mr. and Mrs. Smith

A bouncy, screwball comedy from Hitchcock! With Carole Lombard as a wife who discovers that her marriage is invalid because of a technicality. With Robert Montgomery.
VHS: S00888. $19.95.
Alfred Hitchcock, USA, 1941, 95 mins.

Murder

Herbert Marshall is the actor who serves on a jury at a murder trial and believes the accused woman is innocent in one of Hitchcock's best early British films. With Norah Baring, Phyllis Konstam, Edward Chapman.
VHS: S00896. $19.98.
Alfred Hitchcock, Great Britain, 1930, 108 mins.

North by Northwest

One of Hitchcock's greatest films; Cary Grant plays Roger Thornhill, the suave ad man mistaken for a Federal agent, trapped in a web of intrigue that ends with the classic climax atop Mount Rushmore. Eva Marie Saint is the amorous spy, Leo G. Carroll the FBI man with double-edged tactics, and James Mason and Martin Landau the icily villainous traders in state secrets.
VHS: S00938. $19.98.
Laser: CAV, 3 discs, Criterion. LD70427. $124.95.
Laser: CLV, 2 discs, Criterion. LD70428. $69.95.
Alfred Hitchcock, USA, 1959, 136 mins.

Notorious

One of the greatest, if not the greatest, of Hitchcock's films. A conflict between love and duty drives the action of this thriller set in Rio just after World War II. A beautiful party girl, the daughter of a Nazi traitor, is enlisted by the U.S. government to marry Nazi spy Claude Rains in order to infiltrate his ring. Cary Grant is the U.S. agent sent to aid her, and one of the great screen romances of all time develops. Beautifully shot, the work of the master at the top of his form.
VHS: S04454. $19.98.
Laser: CAV. LD70429. $99.95.
Laser: CLV. LD70430. $49.95.
Alfred Hitchcock, USA, 1946, 102 mins.

Number Seventeen

A dead body in a deserted house found with handcuffs and a gun in its pocket suddenly disappears. That's the beginning of Hitchcock's early thriller, shot almost entirely at night, providing a display of his early camera technique.
VHS: S00943. $19.98.
Alfred Hitchcock, Great Britain, 1932, 64 mins.

Paradine Case

A very little known, but very interesting Alfred Hitchcock film, based on a novel by Robert Hitchens. Gregory Peck is the lawyer who falls in love with the woman (Alida Valli) whom he's defending. With Ethel Barrymore, Charles Laughton.
VHS: S05908. $19.98.
Alfred Hitchcock, USA, 1948, 125 mins.

Psycho

The Classic! Anthony Perkins is Norman Bates and Janet Leigh is Marion Crane in this masterpiece of the macabre by Alfred Hitchcock.
VHS: S01068. $19.95.
Laser: LD70068. $34.98.
Alfred Hitchcock, USA, 1960, 109 mins.

Rear Window

Injured magazine photographer, confined to his apartment because of a broken leg, suspects a murder has been committed in a neighboring flat. Confined to one set, Rear Window is a tour-de-force; James Stewart plays the photographer, Grace Kelly his New York girlfriend, and Raymond Burr the killer.
VHS: S01095. $19.95.
Alfred Hitchcock, USA, 1954, 101 mins.

Rebecca

Hitchcock's first American film, based on a du Maurier gothic romance. With Laurence Olivier and a fine performance by Joan Fontaine as a shy young woman who marries Olivier. Excellent supporting roles by Judith Anderson, George Sanders, Leo G. Carroll and Nigel Bruce.
VHS: S01096. $19.98.
Laser: CAV. LD70441. $124.95.
Laser: CLV. LD70442. $69.95.
Alfred Hitchcock, USA, 1946, 104 mins.

Rich and Strange

Regarded by some as the key film in Hitchcock's career with themes that foreshadow 39 Steps and North by Northwest, Rich and Strange tells the story of a young couple on a world cruise that turns out catastrophically.
VHS: S01112. $19.98.
Alfred Hitchcock, Great Britain, 1932, 83 mins.

The Ring

A story of two prizefighters in love with the same woman, the title refers both to the boxing ring and a wedding band. Silent.
VHS: S01117. $19.98.
Alfred Hitchcock, Great Britain, 1927, 82 mins.

Rope

One of Hitchcock's most daring experiments in suspense and long takes. Farley Granger and John Dall are the two friends who strangle a classmate for intellectual thrills and then proceed to invite his family and mutual friends to dinner—with the body stuffed inside the trunk they use as a buffet table. James Stewart is the teacher who suspects his students. Inspired by the Leopold-Loeb case.
VHS: S01133. $19.95.
Laser: LD70072. $34.95.
Alfred Hitchcock, USA, 1948, 81 mins.

Sabotage

Based on Joseph Conrad's Secret Agent, in which Sylvia Sidney suspects her husband, a theater manager, is keeping something from her—he is a saboteur, planning to explode a bomb in a railroad station. Suspense from start to finish.
VHS: S01144. $19.95.
Laser: LD70447. $34.95.
Alfred Hitchcock, Great Britain, 1936, 76 mins.

Saboteur

Wartime thriller starring Robert Cummings as an aircraft factory worker who witnesses the firebombing of his plant by a Nazi agent, and finds himself accused of the crime. Hitchcock's first film with an entire cast from the U.S.
VHS: S01730. $19.95.
Alfred Hitchcock, USA, 1942, 108 mins.

Secret Agent

Elsa and Dick are British espionage agents during World War I. Sent to Switzerland to find a German spy, they masquerade as husband and wife. The film ends in a climactic train wreck. Peter Lorre is brilliant as the General sent to assassinate the spy.
VHS: S01171. $24.95.
Laser: LD70450. $34.95.
Alfred Hitchcock, Great Britain, 1936, 84 mins.

Shadow of a Doubt

Hitchcock has said that this is his best American film. Joseph Cotten plays the widow-murderer Charley who dodges the police and joins his relatives in a small California town. Although his niece (Teresa Wright) takes him to her heart, she eventually recognizes him as the murderer. Tense, subtle, brilliant Hitchcock.
VHS: S07295. $19.95.
Laser: LD70077. $34.95.
Alfred Hitchcock, USA, 1943, 108 mins.

Skin Game

Skillful adaptation of a stage play, the story is of a feud between the landed gentry and a rising mercantile family—one of Hitchcock's more successful social commentaries.
VHS: S01210. $19.98.
Alfred Hitchcock, Great Britain, 1931, 85 mins.

Spellbound

Gregory Peck stars as the new director of a mental institution, Ingrid Bergman his love interest, who soon discovers that her lover is actually a mental patient and an imposter in Hitchcock's great suspense thriller.
VHS: S01238. $19.95.
Alfred Hitchcock, USA, 1945, 111 mins.

Stage Fright

Another Hitchcock film set within the confines of the theatre as were Murder, 39 Steps and Sabotage. Drama student Jane Wyman envisions the acting challenge of her life trying to prove the innocence of Richard Todd being framed by Marlene Dietrich.
VHS: S01246. $19.98.
Laser: LD74714. $34.98.
Alfred Hitchcock, Great Britain, 1949, 110 mins.

Strangers on a Train

A brilliantly plotted, diabolically humorous suspense thriller about two murders planned by strangers after an accidental meeting. Hitchcock's mise-en-scene is rich in detail and subtle in its insinuations of guilt and homosexuality. With Robert Walker, Farley Granger, Ruth Roman, based on the novel by Raymond Chandler.
VHS: S01265. $19.95.
Laser: LD70686. $24.98.
Alfred Hitchcock, USA, 1951, 101 mins.

Suspicion

Cary Grant and Joan Fontaine in Hitchcock's thriller about a woman who gradually suspects her husband is a murderer. Fontaine won an Oscar for her performance.
VHS: S01287. $19.95.
Alfred Hitchcock, USA, 1941, 99 mins.

The Thirty-Nine Steps

A Canadian leaves London and goes to Scotland in order to find the spy ring that has stabbed a woman to death at his flat. What follows is Hitchcock's most popular British picture; there is suspense, humor, and great technical finesse.
VHS: S18181. $24.95.
Laser: LD70799. $39.95.
Alfred Hitchcock, Great Britain, 1935, 88 mins.

To Catch a Thief

Cary Grant and Grace Kelly star in this suspenseful thriller about an ex-jewel thief who is suspected of a string of new thefts. Set in the French Riviera, the film has spectacular scenery and won three Oscars, including Best Cinematography.
VHS: S01351. $14.95.
Laser: LD75328. $29.95.
Alfred Hitchcock, USA, 1955, 103 mins.

Topaz

Based on Leon Uris' spy novel, Topaz features John Forsythe as a CIA agent who learns of the Cuban missiles from a defecting Russian. He enlists the aid of a French agent to uncover the espionage in a tense Hitchcock thriller.
VHS: S01363. $19.95.
Alfred Hitchcock, USA, 1969, 126 mins.

Torn Curtain

Paul Newman is a famous scientist who goes to an international congress on physics in Copenhagen with his fiancee, Julie Andrews. While there, she mistakenly picks up a message meant for him and discovers that he's defecting to East Berlin.
VHS: S03324. $19.95.
Laser: LD70090. $39.98.
Alfred Hitchcock, USA, 1966, 128 mins.

The Trouble with Harry

Alfred Hitchcock's macabre comedy about the manic efforts of a group of Vermont residents to dispatch a dead body that refuses to stay buried. Framed by the director's usual preoccupation with sin, guilt and redemption, with some excellent performances by Edmund Gwenn, Shirley MacLaine and John Forsythe. Brilliantly photographed by Robert Burks, with an eerie, understated Bernard Herrmann score.
VHS: S01786. $14.98.
Laser: LD70092. $34.98.
Alfred Hitchcock, USA, 1955, 99 mins.

Under Capricorn

An engrossing, often chilling story set in Australia in the early 19th century. Ingrid Bergman gives an excellent performance as a woman married to a respected but seemingly heartless man, driven to the limits of mental and physical endurance and plunged into fear and alcoholism because of the sinister machinations of an unknown enemy. With Joseph Cotten, Margaret Leighton, Michael Wilding.
VHS: S01395. $19.98.
Alfred Hitchcock, USA, 1949, 117 mins.

Vertigo

The elaborately constructed murder story in which an ex-cop who suffers from vertigo is the innocent pawn, is a masterful study of sexual obsession, and one of Hitchcock's best films. With James Stewart, Kim Novak, Barbara Bel Geddes.
VHS: S01795. $19.95.
Laser: LD70094. $39.98.
Alfred Hitchcock, USA, 1958, 95 mins.

The Wrong Man

The true story of a musician for whom a case of mistaken identity becomes a nightmare. With Henry Fonda and Vera Miles, musical score by Bernard Herrmann and screenplay by Maxwell Anderson.
VHS: S04182. $19.98.
Laser: LD70713. $34.98.
Alfred Hitchcock, USA, 1956, 126 mins.

Young and Innocent

Derrick de Marney is a young writer accused of murder. He escapes, meets a girl, and persuades her to help him find evidence that will prove his innocence. Spiced with Hitchcock's wry humor, the film follows the two of them through adventures with tramps, hotel lounges, lime pits, and a web of suspense.
VHS: S01493. $19.95.
Laser: LD71222. $34.95.
Alfred Hitchcock, Great Britain, 1937, 82 mins.

JOSEPH LOSEY

Assassination of Trotsky

Joseph Losey directed this tense drama of the last days of Leon Trotsky, a leader of the Russian Revolution, during his last days in exile in Mexico, and his death at the hands of assassins. Richard Burton delivers a compelling performance as Trotsky. With Alain Delon, Romy Schneider, Valentina Cortese.
VHS: S04943. $19.98.
Laser: CLV. LD71968. $29.98.
Joseph Losey, Great Britain, 1972, 113 mins.

Don Giovanni

Finally on video, this sumptuous production of Mozart's great opera was shot on location in Venice, and is one of the great films of Joseph Losey. Ruggero Raimondi, Kiri Te Kanawa and Teresa Berganza are principal singers, with Lorin Maazel conducting the Paris Opera Orchestra. Sung in Italian with English subtitles.
VHS: S07688. $39.95.
Joseph Losey, Italy/France, 1972, 185 mins.

The Go-Between

Joseph Losey's tense, sexual class drama based on a brilliant script by Harold Pinter. Julie Christie is the upper-class beauty whose passionate, illicit affair with the groundskeeper (Alan Bates) is orchestrated through notes carried by a young boy, the go-between. The film, told largely in flashback through the boy's eyes, is full of nuance and innuendo; a brilliant dissection of sex and class.
VHS: S27183. $19.95.
Joseph Losey, Great Britain, 1971, 118 mins.

Road to the South

Joseph Losey's second French film is the story of a screenplay writer who is the son of Spanish political refugees. He and his wife have long been settled in France, and though he still keeps ties to his native land, he even writes in French. But his son seems to be growing in the opposite direction; he wants to go back to Spain and discover his roots. This politically charged drama deals with the collisions, rivalries and misunderstandings of one family against the backdrop of Spain's political struggles, especially the turbulence during the last year of the Franco dictatorship. Starring Yves Montand and Miou-Miou. French with English subtitles.
VHS: S13658. $29.95.
Laser: LD71627. $49.95.
Joseph Losey, France, 1978, 100 mins.

Sleeping Tiger

Joseph Losey directed this film noir under a pseudonym while in exile in England. The young Dirk Bogarde is a fifties hood with a "sleeping tiger"—desires that must be tamed before they explode into madness. A prominent psychiatrist (Alexander Knox) tries to help Bogarde as the charming delinquent seduces the doctor's wife. B&W.
VHS: S01214. $34.95.
Joseph Losey, Great Britain, 1954, 89 mins.

Steaming

The last film by the great filmmaker Joseph Losey features a stellar female cast of Vanessa Redgrave, Sarah Miles, Diana Dors and Patti Love in an adaptation of the critically-acclaimed play by Nell Dunn. Six women of totally different backgrounds come together on Ladies Day in a London bathhouse. Here, secluded from the male-dominated outside world, they share the most intimate secrets, as they look for fulfillment and fight barriers and loneliness.
VHS: S02776. $19.95.
Joseph Losey, Great Britain, 1984, 102 mins.

Time Without Pity

Director Joseph Losey, blacklisted in the United States during the reign of Joseph McCarthy, creates a tense and threatening atmosphere in this film noir thriller. Michael Redgrave stars as a guilt-ridden alcoholic who has 24 hours to prevent his son, wrongly accused of murder, from being executed. Featuring Peter Cushing and Joan Plowright.
VHS: S24932. $39.95.
Joseph Losey, Great Britain, 1957, 88 mins.

MUSICALS

1776

The hit Broadway musical focuses on the efforts of the Founding Fathers to have the Declaration of Independence ratified. With Ken Howard, William Daniels and Blythe Danner.
VHS: S05859. $19.95.
Laser: Widescreen. LD74898. $44.95.
Peter Hunt, USA, 1972, 150 mins.

42nd Street

The archetypal backstage musical given depth, life and power by the extravagant touch of Busby Berkeley. Warner Baxter is Julian Marsh, the musical-comedy director, who inserts unknown Ruby Keeler into the lead role when star Bebe Daniels suffers a sprained ankle. The first of Berkeley's musicals that established a populist escapism in American entertainment.
VHS: S02326. $19.98.
Laser: LD70493. $34.98.
Lloyd Bacon, USA, 1933, 89 mins.

Actor

A warm, musical look at the roots of actor Paul Muni, written by the award-winning team of Lawrence and Lee (Mame). From a travelling player in the Hungarian countryside to the New York theatre, and then a Hollywood career. USA, 1978, 105 mins.
VHS: S01601. $39.95.

The Affairs of Dobie Gillis

An exuberant musical comedy graced by big-band music, inventive dance numbers and the romantic difficulties of Dobie Gillis (Bobby Van), an inveterate girlwatcher in search of love on his idyllic campus setting. With Debbie Reynolds, Hans Conried, Barbara Ruick and Bob Fosse.
VHS: S20199. $19.98.
Don Weis, USA, 1953, 74 mins.

Alexander's Ragtime Band

In this exuberant musical, with a score by Irving Berlin, Tyrone Power plays an aristocrat who turns his back on his powerful family business to pursue a career as the leader of a ragtime band. Alice Faye plays a singer and Don Ameche is a virtuoso pianist. The numbers include the title track, "Now It Can Be Told," "My Walking Stick" and "I'm Marching Along with Time." With Ethel Merman, Jean Hersholt and Jack Haley.
VHS: S20255. $19.98.
Laser: LD74822. $124.95.
Henry King, USA, 1938, 105 mins.

All That Jazz

Bob Fosse casts Roy Scheider as basically himself in this semi-autobiographical musical extravaganza. He's a talented dancer-choreographer who loves show business, cigarettes and too many other women to keep his marriage intact. With Ann Reinking, Ben Vereen, Leland Palmer and Jessica Lange as the Angel of Death. A prophetic and dazzling film.
VHS: S07558. $19.95.
Bob Fosse, USA, 1979, 123 mins.

An American in Paris

No film can match An American in Paris for all the joy, all the songs, and all the romance in music and dance. Gene Kelly and Leslie Caron star in this movie set to the glorious melodies of George Gershwin, including: "Embraceable You," "Love Is Here to Stay," "I Got Rhythm" and more.
VHS: S00045. $19.95.
Laser: LD70502. $34.98.
Vincente Minnelli, USA, 1951, 102 mins.

Anchors Aweigh

Gene Kelly and Frank Sinatra play two sailors on leave in Hollywood. While setting up his shy friend Clarence (Sinatra), Gene Kelly, as Joe, falls for Kathryn Grayson and also dances with MGM star Jerry the Mouse. Pamela Britton is the girl from Brooklyn. This musical is recommended by Louella Parsons.
VHS: Out of print. For rental only.
Laser: LD70503. $39.98.
George Sidney, USA, 1945, 146 mins.

Andrew Lloyd Webber: The Premiere Collection Encore

A spirited video collection of some of the best known production numbers and scenes from the hit musicals of Andrew Lloyd Webber, including excerpts from Phantom of the Opera, Aspects of Love, Song and Dance, Evita and Requiem. With Sarah Brightman, Jose Carreras, Cliff Richard, Michael Ball and David Essex. 58 mins.
VHS: S18320. $19.95.

Another Evening with Fred Astaire

Fred Astaire joins Barrie Chase for an unforgettable hour of dancing. This is a rare television appearance by America's most suave dancer ever.
VHS: S23883. $29.95.

April in Paris

Doris Day stars as Ethel "Dynamite" Jackson, an energetic singer who is mistakenly invited to participate in a State Department sponsored theatre festival in the City of Lights. Would you believe they were expecting Ethel Barrymore? Stuffy bureaucrat Ray Bolger is assigned to keep a lid on her exuberance. Naturally they fall in love. With Claude Dauphin, Eve Miller and Paul Harvey. Songs include "I'm Going to Rock the Boat," "I'm Gonna Ring the Bell Tonight" and "Give Me Your Lips".
VHS: S15781. $19.98.
David Butler, USA, 1952, 101 mins.

Around the World

Take a foot-stomping, jitter-bugging tour around the world with Kay Kyser and his crazy band as they entertain overseas while foiling some nasty Nazi agents.
VHS: S11603. $19.98.
Allan Dwan, USA, 1943, 80 mins.

Athena

A romantic musical comedy about the parallel fortunes of two couples. A repressed lawyer leaves his snobbish girlfriend to romance an eccentric health fanatic while his best friend, a television singer, attempts to court the woman's equally quirky sister. With Jane Powell, Debbie Reynolds, Edmund Purdom and Vic Damone.
VHS: S18557. $19.98.
Richard Thorpe, USA, 1954, 96 mins.

Babes in Arms
The original "hey gang, let's put on a show" musical with Mickey Rooney and Judy Garland. Based loosely on a Rodgers and Hart musical, these energetic youngsters follow in their vaudeville parents' footsteps. Songs include "Good Morning", "Where and When" and title tune. With Guy Kibbee and Margaret Hamilton. B&W.
VHS: S06116. $19.98.
Laser: LD70510. $34.98.
Busby Berkeley, USA, 1939, 91 mins.

Babes on Broadway
A terrific showcase for the talents of Judy Garland and Mickey Rooney, with Judy's famous "F.D.R. Jones." The story of young hopefuls on Broadway, Mickey and Judy do everything from Carmen Miranda to Sarah Bernhardt imitations. With Donna Reed and Margaret O'Brien.
VHS: S11159. $19.98.
Laser: LD70511. $39.98.
Busby Berkeley, USA, 1941, 118 mins.

Balalaika
This musical comedy romance finds Nelson Eddy at the head of a Cossack regiment pursuing a young Bolshevik (Ilona Massey). Some of the songs that pepper this delightful MGM operetta, set during the Russian Revolution, are "Ride, Cossack, Ride"; "Tanya"; "Beneath the Winter Snows" and "Soldiers of the Czar".
VHS: S20786. $19.98.
Reinhold Schnuzel, USA, 1939, 102 mins.

The Band Wagon
Delightful musical featuring Fred Astaire and Cyd Charisse in a story line that revolves around the difficulties of putting up a Broadway show. Astaire is in top form!
VHS: Out of print. For rental only.
Laser: CLV. LD70516. $34.98.
Vincente Minnelli, USA, 1953, 112 mins.

Barkleys of Broadway
Astaire and Rogers were re-united after a ten-year separation in this tune-filled musical, with dances ranging from ballroom to swing. Songs include "You'd Be Hard to Replace" and "They Can't Take That Away from Me."
VHS: S05384. $19.98.
Laser: LD70518. $34.98.
Charles Walters, USA, 1949, 109 mins.

Because You're Mine
A farce about opera star Mario Lanza, who's drafted and promptly falls in love with the sister (Doretta Morrow) of his commanding officer (James Whitmore). Features the song "The Lord's Prayer." With Jeff Donnell, Spring Byington and Don Porter.
VHS: S17650. $19.98.
Alexander Hall, USA, 1952, 103 mins.

Belle of New York
Fred Astaire is a rich playboy chasing Vera-Ellen, a Bowery mission worker, in this musical. The numbers include "Let a Little Love Come In" and "Naughty But Nice."
VHS: S05385. $19.98.
Laser: LD72201. $39.98.
Charles Walters, USA, 1952, 82 mins.

Belle of New York/I Love Melvin
Two delightful comedies. The first stars Fred Astaire as a fancy-free playboy and Vera-Ellen as a Bowery mission worker set on reforming him. Directed by Charles Walters, USA, 1952, 82 mins. The second stars Debbie Reynolds and Donald O'Connor in a joyous boy-meets-girl musical. Directed by Don Weis, USA, 1953, 77 mins.
Laser: LD71661. $39.98.

Bells Are Ringing
A cheerful musical featuring Judy Holliday in her last film role as the operator at an answering service who gets involved in the lives of her clients. With Dean Martin, Fred Clark.
VHS: S04400. $19.98.
Laser: LD70523. $39.98.
Vincente Minnelli, USA, 1960, 127 mins.

The Benny Goodman Story
Bandleader Benny Goodman gets the Hollywood treatment in this glossy and tune-filled, semi-factual biography. It stars the multi-talented and somewhat look-alike Steve Allen as the bandleader and Donna Reed as the love interest. Goodman himself provides the music for Allen's fingering on the clarinet.
VHS: S03678. $19.95.
Valentine Davies, USA, 1955, 116 mins.

Bert Rigby You're a Fool
A contemporary light musical comedy from Carl Reiner that celebrates the kind of movies Hollywood used to make. Robert Lindsay (the star of Broadway's You're My Girl) has the title role of an English coal miner with a talent for entertaining in the manner of Astaire, Buster Keaton and other greats. He is discovered and sent to be a star in Hollywood and then reality sets in. A gentle and whimsical film. With Anne Bancroft, Jackie Gayle, Robbie Coltrane and Corbin Bernsen.
VHS: S08719. $19.98.
Carl Reiner, USA, 1989, 94 mins.

Best Foot Forward
Lucille Ball invades a military school in this happy-go-lucky Technicolor musical. Non-stop fun and plenty of trouble, along with many lively tunes. With June Allyson and Nancy Walker.
VHS: S15431. $19.98.
Laser: LD71173. $39.98.
Edward Buzzell, USA, 1943, 95 mins.

The Best Little Whorehouse in Texas
Burt Reynolds and Dolly Parton star in this musical version of Chicken Ranch. Music and lyrics by Carol Hall, choreography by Tony Stevens. With Jim Nabors, Dom Deluise and Charles Durning.
VHS: S02739. $19.95.
Colin Higgins, USA, 1982, 115 mins.

Bing—The Sennett Shorts
Bing Crosby became a film star because of his beautiful crooning singing style. This video contains three shorts from 1932-33, which show the young Crosby to great advantage. It includes a version of Crosby's hit "I Surrender Dear."
VHS: S26799. $24.95.
Mack Sennett, USA, 1932-1933, 60 mins.

Birth of the Blues
Bing Crosby and Mary Martin star in this musical about the origins of the actual Original Dixieland Jazz Group. It starts as a simple gig at a nightclub arranged by a wealthy young man and soon leads to massive fame. Jack Teagarden, the trombonist from the actual jazz group, is featured.
VHS: S25010. $14.98.
Victor Schertzinger, USA, 1941, 76 mins.

Bitter Sweet
This Jeanette MacDonald/Nelson Eddy vehicle was a remake of a 1933 British film. A sentimental operetta from MGM set in 1880 Vienna written by Noel Coward. Songs include "I'll See You Again" and "Tokay". With George Sanders, Herman Bing, Ian Hunter and Sig Ruman.
VHS: S09845. $29.95.
W.S. Van Dyke, USA, 1940, 92 mins.

Blue Skies
Over 30 Irving Berlin songs blanket this musical comedy with Fred Astaire and Bing Crosby. Astaire plays a radio personality who relates the story of his rivalry with friend Crosby for the affections of beautiful young lady played by Joan Caulfield.
VHS: S21204. $19.98.
Stuart Heisler, USA, 1946, 104 mins.

Born to Dance
A classic Eleanor Powell musical about a sailor who meets a girl in New York, with songs by Cole Porter, musical direction by Alfred Newman, and terrific performances from Powell, James Stewart, Virginia Bruce, Reginald Gardiner. Oscar nomination for "I've Got You under My Skin".
VHS: S12145. $19.95.
Laser: LD70131. $34.98.
Roy Del Ruth, USA, 1936, 108 mins.

Breakin'
A musical/break dance film which features a limited plot but a lot of great dancing. The film was one of the earliest to capture the spine-crushing athleticism of break dancing. Features Lucinda Dickey, Adolpho "Shabba Doo" Quinones and Michael "Boogaloo Shrimp" Chambers.
VHS: S21408. $79.95.
Joel Silberg, USA, 1984, 87 mins.

Brigadoon
Gene Kelly and Van Johnson are two Americans afoot and lost in the Scottish highlands when they discover the charming village of Brigadoon and the charms of Cyd Charisse as Fiona Campbell. This endearing Lerner-Loewe musical is directed by Vincente Minnelli and features Barry Jones and Elaine Stewart.
VHS: S07158. $19.95.
Laser: Letterboxed. LD74670. $34.98.
Vincente Minnelli, USA, 1954, 108 mins.

Bright Eyes
Shirley Temple is a young orphan at the center of a custody battle and a sensation when she sings "On the Good Ship Lollipop." With James Dunn and Jane Darwell.
VHS: S09990. $19.98.
David Butler, USA, 1934, 90 mins.

Broadway Melody
This early talkie was the first musical to win a Best Picture Oscar. Score by Arthur Freed and Herb Brown. Bessie Love and Anita Page are two sisters dazzled by the lights of the Great White Way. Tunes include "You Were Meant for Me" and "The Wedding of the Painted Doll." With Charles King, Jed Prouty and Mary Doran.
VHS: S08337. $19.98.
Harry Beaumont, USA, 1929, 104 mins.

Broadway Melody of 1936
This engaging musical about a small-town girl with the gifts to match her big-time dreams featured the spectacular talents of Eleanor Powell, and made her an overnight star. Jack Benny also stars. Winner of the 1935 Oscar for Best Dance Direction.
VHS: S15426. $19.98.
Roy Del Ruth, USA, 1935, 110 mins.

Broadway Melody of 1938
An appearance by a youthful Judy Garland singing "Dear Mr. Gable" highlights this big production musical which also features Robert Taylor, Sophie Tucker and Eleanor Powell.
VHS: S02525. $19.98.
Roy Del Ruth, USA, 1937, 113 mins.

Broadway Melody of 1940
Eleanor Powell and Fred Astaire team up in a sparkling musical treasure as the two dancers (Astaire and George Murphy) compete for a job as well as for a beautiful Broadway star. Cole Porter wrote the score.
VHS: S03103. $19.98.
Laser: LD70533. $34.98.
Norman Taurog, USA, 1940, 103 mins.

Broadway Rhythm
This MGM musical is about a young producer trying to woo a beautiful movie star for his new production. He's rejected in favor of a show headed by his father, setting off some fierce rivalries. With George Murphy, Ginny Simms, Lena Horne, Nancy Walker and the three singing contortionists, the Ross Sisters. Music by Tommy Dorsey and his Orchestra and the pianist Hazel Scott.
VHS: S18558. $19.98.
Roy Del Ruth, USA, 1944, 114 mins.

Broadway Serenade
A period musical about the difficulties and tensions in the marriage of a singer (Jeanette MacDonald) and a songwriter (Lew Ayres). With Ian Hunter, Frank Morgan and Rita Johnson.
VHS: S17651. $19.98.
Robert Z. Leonard, USA, 1939, 114 mins.

Bugsy Malone
A musical unlike any other! Bugsy Malone is a gangster musical set in 1929 New York City, a city populated by hoodlums, showgirls and dreamers. The cast has an average age of 12, led by Jodie Foster as Tallulah. Music by Paul Williams, a pint-size himself.
VHS: S00187. $14.95.
Laser: LD75331. $29.98.
Alan Parker, USA, 1976, 94 mins.

By the Light of the Silvery Moon
The sequel to On Moonlight Bay, from the original story by Booth Tarkington, sets the action in the aftermath of World War I, with the young lovers trying to adjust to civilian life. With Doris Day, Gordon MacRae and Mary Wickes.
VHS: S18461. $19.98.
Laser: LD72167. $34.98.
David Butler, USA, 1953, 102 mins.

Bye Bye Birdie
Dick Van Dyke, Ann-Margret and Janet Leigh star in this energetic musical comedy. Conrad Birdie, an Elvis-like entertainer (Jesse Pearson), is going to be drafted into the Armed Forces. Ann-Margret is the small-town Ohio girl chosen to receive one last kiss live on the Ed Sullivan Show. Paul Lynde is the disapproving father.
VHS: S05338. $19.95.
George Sidney, USA, 1963, 112 mins.

Cabaret
Liza Minnelli and Joel Grey give extraordinary performances in Bob Fosse's musical drama that mirrors the decay and decadence of Germany on the eve of Hitler's rise to power. With Marisa Berenson and Michael York.
VHS: S01837. $19.98.
Laser: LD72168. $39.98.
Bob Fosse, USA, 1972, 119 mins.

Cairo
Jeanette MacDonald stars as mysterious actress and singer who manages to confuse a very interested Robert Young. Though Young is working for the U.S. war effort, this film remains a campy romp. After all, this is an MGM musical comedy, where romance is inspired by the exotic backdrop of Cairo.
VHS: S20789. $19.98.
John McClain, USA, 1942, 100 mins.

Calamity Jane
Sassy, entertaining musical featuring Doris Day, Howard Keel and Phil Carey. Day shines as the gun-slingin', dirty, tough and ragged Jane in a cute story with a lively score. The song "Secret Love" was a big hit and won an Oscar.
VHS: S06123. $19.98.
Laser: LD70290. $34.98.
David Butler, USA, 1953, 101 mins.

Camelot
The epic Broadway hit comes alive with stunning performances by Richard Harris and Vanessa Redgrave as King Arthur and Lady Guinevere. Music by Frederick Loewe, lyrics by Alan Jay Lerner, based on the novel by T.H. White. With Franco Nero, David Hemmings.
VHS: S01749. $29.98.
Laser: LD70539. $29.98.
Laser: Widescreen. LD71408. $39.98.
Joshua Logan, USA, 1967, 173 mins.

Can't Stop the Music
A lavish, gay-themed musical that looks at corruption inside the music-publishing industry. The topliners are the 70s act the Village People, each of whom falls madly in love with Valerie Perrine. "It follows that most of the dialogue is gay in-jokes, with the odd music business joke for variety" (Time Out). "YMCA" and "Macho Man" are highlights. With Steve Guttenberg, Tammy Grimes, June Havoc and Barbara Rush.
VHS: S20417. $14.98.
Nancy Walker, USA, 1980, 119 mins.

Can-Can
Frank Sinatra is a roguish lawyer in Paris trying to keep his cafe owner and glamorous sweetheart (Shirley MacLaine) from being jailed for doing a forbidden dance. Maurice Chevalier approves but the younger judge Louis Jourdan is not as gallant. With Juliet Prowse and songs by Cole Porter. Based on the Abe Burrows musical. Ooh-la-la. 130 mins.
Laser: LD70899. $49.98.
Walter Lang, USA, 1960, 130 mins.

Captain January
Shirley Temple is a happy tot being raised by a lighthouse keeper until a prissy truant officer insists she have a proper home. Shirley sings "The Right Somebody to Love," and "At the Codfish Ball."
VHS: S09992. $19.98.
David Butler, USA, 1936, 76 mins.

The Cat and the Fiddle
A buoyant adaptation of the Jerome Kern/Oscar Hammerstein operetta about the complications of a romantic triangle involving a talented composer (Ramon Novarro), a beautiful performer (Jeanette MacDonald) and the man (Frank Morgan) who comes between them. Songs include "The Night Was Made for Love" and "She Didn't Say Yes."
VHS: S17652. $19.98.
William K. Howard, USA, 1934, 90 mins.

The Chocolate Soldier
Nelson Eddy starred with Metropolitan Opera star and movie novice Riise Stevens in this musical that mated Oscar Strauss's title and music to the play The Guardsman, by Ferenc Molnar. They play opera stars. To test his wife's fidelity he romances her in the guise of a Cossack. With Nigel Bruce and Florence Bates. Remade as Lilly in Love.
VHS: S09869. $19.98.
Roy Del Ruth, USA, 1941, 102 mins.

A Chorus Line
Richard Attenborough directs the film version of the long running Broadway hit musical about an audition for a Broadway chorus line. A diverse cast of men and women reveal their past lives and future hopes to a no-nonsense director played by Michael Douglas. Dancers include Janet Jones, Nicole Fosse, Vicki Frederick, and Alyson Reed.
Laser: LD72323. $34.99.
Richard Attenborough, USA, 1985, 113 mins.

A Christmas Carol
Fredric March stars as Scrooge in this musical adaptation of the Dickens classic with the long-suffering, good-hearted Bob Cratchit and his ever-optimistic family converting the miserly ways of the miserable Scrooge. With Basil Rathbone. USA, 1954, 54 mins.
VHS: S00239. $29.95.
Laser: LD70543. $34.98.

Cinderella
Lesley Ann Warren stars in the Rodgers and Hammerstein musical version of the classic. With Ginger Rogers as the Queen, Walter Pidgeon as the fairy godmother, Jo Ann Fleet, and dozens of sparkling musical numbers.
VHS: S01923. $19.98.
Charles Dubin, USA, 1964, 83 mins.

Coal Miner's Daughter
The film biography of country-western superstar Loretta Lynn. Sissy Spacek won an Academy Award for her performance as the little kid from Butcher's Hollow who grew up to entertain millions. With excellent supporting work by Tommy Lee Jones, Levon Helm and Beverly D'Angelo as Patsy Cline.
VHS: S07805. $19.95.
Michael Apted, USA, 1980, 125 mins.

College Swing
This strange musical features a top-heavy cast with George Burns and Gracie Allen, Bob Hope and Jackie Coogan in the light and charming story about Gracie's exhaustive attempts to graduate college. With Martha Raye and Betty Grable.
VHS: S18547. $14.98.
Raoul Walsh, USA, 1938, 86 mins.

Cover Girl
A Jerome Kern/Ira Gershwin musical that traces the rise of a chorus girl to stardom as a cover girl, with classic songs, including "Long Ago and Far Away." With Rita Hayworth, Gene Kelly, Phil Silvers, and Eve Arden.
VHS: S11631. $19.95.
Laser: LD74896. $34.95.
Charles Vidor, USA, 1944, 107 mins.

Daddy Long Legs
Fred Astaire and Leslie Caron dance together and fall in love in this sentimental tale of a globe-trotting playboy who anonymously adopts a French orphan. Thelma Ritter and Fred Clark co-star.
VHS: S14505. $19.98.
Jean Negulesco, USA, 1955, 126 mins.

Dames
Joan Blondell, Ruby Keeler, Dick Powell, ZaSu Pitts and Hugh Herbert star in this classic Warner Brothers musical, distinguished for its Busby Berkeley dance numbers, including "When You Were a Smile on Mother's Lips and a Twinkle in Your Daddy's Eye." The plot (about the backing of a Broadway musical) is almost incidental to the lavish costumes and first-rate production ensembles.
VHS: S07373. $19.98.
Laser: LD70548. $34.98.
Ray Enright, USA, 1934, 90 mins.

Damn Yankees
A baseball fan sells his soul to the Devil for the chance at rejuvenation and the opportunity to play major league ball. The old geezer becomes Tab Hunter and starts winning games for his team. With Ray Walston as the Prince of Darkness and Gwen Verdon as the tantalizing Lola, who we all know gets whatever Lola wants. Adapted and restaged from the Broadway musical; the choreography is by Bob Fosse.
VHS: S11661. $19.98.
Laser: LD70549. $24.98.
G. Abbott/S. Donen, USA, 1958, 110 mins.

Dancing Lady
Joan Crawford gives her all as a young burlesque dancer seeking Broadway fame, romanced along the Great White Way by one-time real life flame Clark Gable and her future husband (Franchot Tone). Fred Astaire is featured in his screen debut.
VHS: S03105. $19.98.
Laser: LD70732. $39.98.
Robert Z. Leonard, USA, 1933, 93 mins.

A Date with Judy
I'll bet she has a wonderful personality. Spunky Jane Powell has the title role with Elizabeth Taylor as her best friend in this MGM technicolor musical. Wallace Beery is Judy's dad, who later dances with Carmen Miranda. Powell is hoping to date Robert Stack and Xavier Cugat plays himself. Songs include "I'm Strictly on the Corny Side" and "It's a Most Unusual Day."
VHS: S08521. $19.98.
Laser: LD74665. $34.98.
Richard Thorpe, USA, 1948, 113 mins.

The Dawn of Sound
Three musicals trace the evolution of the form, capturing its exuberance and style: Charles Riesner's The Broadway Revue of 1929, Harry Beaumont's The Broadway Melody and Show of Shows.
Laser: LD70285. $99.98.

Deep in My Heart
Jose Ferrer leads a galaxy of stars in a spectacular celebration of musical magic in this exuberant rendition of the life and times of Sigmund Romberg. Also starring Gene Kelly, Ann Miller and Cyd Charisse.
VHS: S15430. $19.98.
Laser: LD71155. $39.98.
Stanley Donen, USA, 1954, 132 mins.

The Desert Song
This beautifully staged and produced version of the Broadway musical stars Gordon MacRae and Kathryn Grayson. The entire uncut score of this Sigmund Romberg/Oscar Hammerstein show is sung and danced with all the customary panache from the golden age of the American musical.
VHS: S20658. $19.98.
H. Bruce Humberstone, USA, 1953, 96 mins.

Dimples
Shirley Temple stars with Frank (*Wizard of Oz*) Morgan and the legendary Stepin Fetchit in this heartwarming period musical.
VHS: S05900. $19.98.
William A. Seiter, USA, 1936, 78 mins.

Disney Presents the Best of Broadway Musicals
John Raitt narrates this exciting compilation of excerpts from some of Hollywood's most popular musicals. Performances by Ethel Merman, Florence Henderson, Carol Channing, Julie Andrews, Pearl Bailey and many more are included from such shows as *Hello Dolly*, *Camelot* and *My Fair Lady*.
VHS: S21764. $19.99.
Laser: LD74636. $24.99.

Dixie Jamboree
Francis Langford, Guy Kibbee and Charles Butterworth star in this musical comedy about life on the last great Mississippi showboat. The free and easy life aboard offers the perfect cover for a gangster on the lam.
VHS: S23818. $24.95.
Christy Cabanne, USA, 1945, 69 mins.

Doctor Doolittle
Rex Harrison is the man who can talk to the animals in this epic musical entertainment for children of all ages. Based on the stories of Hugh Lofting. Oscars went to best Song and Special Visual Effects. With Samantha Eggar, Anthony Newley, Geoffrey Holder and the Pushme-Pullyou llamas.
VHS: S07559. $19.98.
Richard Fleischer, USA, 1967, 144 mins.

Doll Face
Vivian Blaine plays a burlesque dancer out to make it big in show business. The musical featured the performing talents of such diverse individuals as Carmen Miranda and Perry Como. Mr. Relaxation sings "Hubba Hubba Hubba". Dennis O'Keefe was the male lead. B&W.
VHS: S05067. $29.95.
Lewis Seiler, USA, 1945, 80 mins.

The Dolly Sisters
Betty Grable and June Haver star as vaudeville sensations who must balance glamorous careers with the demands of romance. After arriving as refugees from Hungary, they quickly begin singing and dancing their way to the top. The Oscar nominated song "I Can't Begin to Tell You" is just one of the many great tunes featured in this film's lavish production numbers. With John Payne.
VHS: S26923. $19.98.
Laser: LD75455. $39.95.
Irving Cummings, USA, 1945, 114 mins.

Down Argentine Way
A fun musical about an American heiress (Betty Grable) and a South American cowboy (Don Ameche), with a big horse race finale—with Carmen Miranda.
VHS: S09445. $19.98.
Irving Cummings, USA, 1940, 94 mins.

Du Barry Was a Lady
Red Skelton imagines himself in the court of King Louis XIV in this entertaining musical which features Lucille Ball, Zero Mostel and Gene Kelly. Music by the Tommy Dorsey Orchestra.
VHS: S01594. $19.98.
Roy Del Ruth, USA, 1943, 101 mins.

Easter Parade
Judy Garland and Fred Astaire team up in an exuberant film featuring the music and lyrics of Irving Berlin. With Ann Miller and Peter Lawford.
VHS: Out of print. For rental only.
Laser: Remastered, MGM. **LD70129. $34.98.**
Charles Walters, USA, 1948, 103 mins.

Easy to Love
Busby Berkeley staged the lavish water sequence in this aqua-musical set against picture postcard perfect Cypress Gardens, Florida. As a reluctant water queen, Esther Williams swims, dives and water-skis her way through a series of romantic entanglements with Van Johnson, Tony Martin and John Bromfield.
VHS: S16605. $19.98.
Charles Walters, USA, 1953, 97 mins.

The Eddy Duchin Story
Scored to the golden oldies of Cole Porter, George and Ira Gershwin, and Hammerstein, this film biography covers the career of the pianist and bandleader of the '30s and '40s. Tyrone Powers stars as Duchin. With Kim Novak, Victoria Shaw and James Whitmore.
VHS: S16412. $19.95.
George Sidney, USA, 1956, 123 mins.

Everybody Sing
A musical extravaganza featuring the talents of 15-year-old Judy Garland one year before she appeared in *The Wizard of Oz*. Teamed up with "funny girl" Fanny Brice, Billie Burke and Allen Jones, Judy turns this lighthearted story about a stage family into a zany, unforgettable masterpiece.
VHS: S15853. $19.98.
Edwin L. Marin, USA, 1938, 91 mins.

The Fabulous Dorseys
A Big Band biography of sorts with the famous musical brothers playing themselves. They argue a lot but the tunes are what's really happening. With Paul Whiteman, Janet Blair, and a jam session with Art Tatum, Ziggy Elman and Charlie Barnet. B&W.
VHS: S18184. $19.95.
Alfred E. Green, USA, 1947, 91 mins.

Fame
A cross-section of young performers at New York's High School for the Performing Arts. With Irene Cara and Anne Meara.
VHS: S05952. $19.98.
Alan Parker, USA, 1980, 133 mins.

Fashions
A snappy comedy with musical numbers directed by Busby Berkeley. William Powell is a con man and Bette Davis is his girlfriend, who aids him in stealing the latest Paris creations.
VHS: S12317. $24.95.
William Dieterle, USA, 1934, 78 mins.

Fiddler on the Roof
The long-running Broadway musical based on the stories of Sholom Aleichem. Starring Topol, Molly Picon, Norman Crane and Leonard Frey. Music by Jerry Bock adapted for the film by John Williams.
VHS: S01702. $29.95.
Laser: LD70568. $39.98.
Norman Jewison, USA, 1971, 169 mins.

The Firefly
The adventures of a Spanish spy during the Napoleonic war are the setting for this extravagant operetta. With Jeannette MacDonald, Allan Jones, Warren William and Billy Gilbert.
VHS: S17653. $19.98.
Robert Z. Leonard, USA, 1937, 131 mins.

First Love
Robert Stack joins Deanna Durbin for her first on-screen kiss in this fairy tale-like movie. It's an update of the *Cinderella* story set in a 1930's musical comedy, only in this instance, Durbin is an orphan who goes to live with an uncle.
VHS: S27011. $19.98.
Henry Koster, USA, 1939, 85 mins.

Flirtation Walk
Frank Borzage directs an engaging musical about a complicated romance between an ambitious Army private (Dick Powell) and a general's daughter (Ruby Keeler) determined to win him. Best number is "Mr. and Mrs. Is the Name." With Pat O'Brien, Ross Alexander and Guinn Williams.
VHS: S18804. $19.98.
Frank Borzage, USA, 1934, 98 mins.

Flower Drum Song
An outstanding cast stars in this screen adaptation of the famous Rodgers and Hammerstein musical about life and love in San Francisco's Chinatown, with Nancy Kwan, James Shigeta.
VHS: S04401. $19.95.
Henry Koster, USA, 1961, 133 mins.

Follow the Fleet
Irving Berlin wrote the score for this big hit musical, which included the now-famous "Let's Face the Music and Dance" number. The supporting cast features Randolph Scott, Betty Grable, Lucille Ball, and Harried Hilliard.
VHS: S03233. $19.95.
Mark Sandrich, USA, 1935, 110 mins.

Footlight Parade
James Cagney plays a stage director who tries to outdo himself with lavish musical numbers. Joan Blondell, Dick Powell, Guy Kibbee and Ruth Donnelly star in this first-rate Warner Brothers musical which features three Busby Berkeley numbers back-to-back: "Honeymoon Hotel," "By a Waterfall" and "Shanghai Lil."
VHS: S03599. $19.98.
Laser: LD70572. $34.98.
Lloyd Bacon, USA, 1933, 104 mins.

Footloose
Kevin Bacon is tops in this musical about a city kid who moves to a small town where dancing has been banned, and battles with the fire-and-brimstone minister in an effort to bring it back. With Lori Singer, John Lithgow.
VHS: S09567. $19.95.
Laser: Widescreen. **LD75299. $39.98.**
Herbert Ross, USA, 1984, 107 mins.

For Me and My Gal
Gene Kelly teams up with Judy Garland in his first film, as a pair of vaudeville entertainers working the small towns on their way to the glamour and rewards of Broadway. Kelly is an opportunist who really pushes the limits of Garland's affection in this Busby Berkeley musical. With George Murphy and Ben Blue.
VHS: S07161. $19.95.
Busby Berkeley, USA, 1942, 100 mins.

For the First Time
Capri is the perfect place for a musical romantic comedy starring Mario Lanza. With the Mediterranean as a backdrop, Mario plays a famous tenor who sings beautifully and falls in love with a lovely deaf girl. Zsa Zsa Gabor also looks right at home in this island paradise.
VHS: S20788. $19.98.
Rudolph Mate, USA/Germany, 1959, 97 mins.

Forbidden Music
A rare film: Jimmy Durante and Richard Tauber star in this original film version of the satirical operetta written for the screen by Oscar Strauss.
VHS: S05178. $29.95.

Funny Face
Fred Astaire and Audrey Hepburn star in this appealing musical from director Stanley Donen. Fred is a fashion photographer who sees Audrey as star material. Set in Paris with music by George and Ira Gershwin. Songs include "How Long Has This Been Going On". With Suzy Parker, Ruta Lee and Kay Thompson.
VHS: S06139. $14.95.
Laser: Widescreen. **LD75364. $44.98.**
Stanley Donen, USA, 1957, 103 mins.

Funny Lady
The sequel to *Funny Girl*. Barbra Streisand continues the show biz bio of Fanny Brice as she becomes a bigger star and meets and marries showman Billy Rose (James Caan). Lots of big production numbers. With Roddy McDowall, Ben Vereen and Omar Sharif as Nicky Arnstein.
VHS: S05095. $19.98.
Herbert Ross, USA, 1975, 137 mins.

A Funny Thing Happened on the Way to the Forum
Richard Lester's fractured adaptation of the Broadway musical hit about a conniving slave in ancient Rome. Featuring comedy legends Zero Mostel (recreating his Tony award-winning role), Phil Silvers, and the great Buster Keaton. Plenty of bawdy fun, with music and lyrics by Stephen Sondheim.
VHS: S02336. $19.99.
Laser: Letterboxed, chapter search. Includes original trailer. **LD71644. $34.98.**
Richard Lester, USA, 1966, 100 mins.

Gay Divorcee
One of Astaire and Rogers' best-loved song-and-dance comedies. Astaire is caught in a case of mistaken identity when Rogers fakes a love affair to win a divorce.
VHS: S03268. $19.98.
Mark Sandrich, USA, 1934, 107 mins.

Gigi
Leslie Caron is the bewitching title character in this dazzling musical that won nine Oscars including Best Picture. Maurice Chevalier sings "Thank Heaven for Little Girls" and doesn't get arrested. Based on a story by Colette, a young girl at the turn of the century is trained in Paris to be a courtesan. With Hermione Gingold and Louis Jourdan.
VHS: S07159. $19.95.
Laser: LD70582. $34.98.
Vincente Minnelli, USA, 1958, 116 mins.

Girl of the Golden West
Jeanette MacDonald and Nelson Eddy go west in this MGM musical about a singing saloon owner and a dashing bandit who can harmonize. Based on the old stage melodrama by David Belasco. Cast includes Walter Pidgeon, Leo Carillo, Buddy Ebsen, Monty Woolley and Noah Beery. Music by Sigmund Romberg and Gus Kahn. Meet you at the pass for a duet.
VHS: S09847. $19.98.
Robert Z. Leonard, USA, 1938, 120 mins.

Girl Rush
Vaudeville troupers are stranded in San Francisco during the gold rush and decide to put on a show in order to lure women to move to this backward mining town. Stars Robert Mitchum, Wally Brown, Alan Carney and Frances Langford.
VHS: S09177. $19.95.
Gordon Douglas, USA, 1944, 65 mins.

Give a Girl a Break
Burton Lane and Ira Gershwin wrote the songs for this sprightly tale of three young hopefuls looking for stardom. It's tough to get a break…until the leading lady walks out and someone has to step in and take her place. Who will it be? Starring Debbie Reynolds, Marge and Gower Champion, and Bob Fosse.
VHS: S14164. $19.98.
Stanley Donen, USA, 1953, 84 mins.

Glenn Miller Story
Jimmy Stewart and June Allyson star as the popular band leader and his wife in this Anthony Mann film bio loaded with swinging music and fine musicians. Performers include Louis Armstrong, Gene Krupa, Frances Langford and members of the original Glenn Miller orchestra. Tunes include "Chattanooga Choo Choo" and "Pennsylvania 6-5000."
VHS: S07810. $19.98.
Laser: LD70033. $34.98.
Anthony Mann, USA, 1954, 116 mins.

Glorifying the American Girl
An early technicolor musical—the only film produced by Florenz Ziegfeld—with Mary Eaton, Eddie Cantor, Helen Morgan, Rudy Vallee and "famous beauties." Numerous production numbers.
VHS: S06226. $49.95.
Millard Webb, USA, 1929, 96 mins.

Going Hollywood
Raoul Walsh's charming musical about a Hollywood love triangle in which a disaffected school teacher (Marion Davies) falls for a young crooner (Bing Crosby). With Fifi D'Orsay, Stuart Erwin and Ned Sparks.
VHS: S18552. $19.98.
Raoul Walsh, USA, 1933, 78 mins.

Going My Way
Irving Berlin's hit with Bing Crosby as the unconventional singing priest who tries to save a poor parish presided by the gruff-but-lovable Barry Fitzgerald. Winner of seven Academy Awards. Fred Astaire co-stars.
VHS: S01534. $19.98.
Laser: LD70034. $34.98.
Leo McCarey, USA, 1944, 101 mins.

Gold Diggers of 1933
A Busby Berkeley extravaganza that is pure entertainment. In addition to Berkeley's chorus girls, there's Joan Blondell, Ginger Rogers (singing "We're in the Money" in pig Latin), Ruby Keeler and Dick Powell. The original and most famous of the "gold digger" films.
VHS: S01769. $19.98.
Laser: LD70583. $34.98.
Mervyn Le Roy, USA, 1933, 98 mins.

Gold Diggers of 1935
A big-scale Busby Berkeley musical that features Dick Powell, Adolphe Menjou, Gloria Stuart, Alice Brady and Glenda Farrell. Notable for its precision numbers, including such classic numbers as "The Words Are in My Heart" and the Oscar-winner "Lullaby of Broadway."
VHS: S11162. $29.95.
Busby Berkeley, USA, 1935, 95 mins.

The Goldwyn Follies
The music of George Gershwin and lyrics of Ira Gershwin, combined with a lavish production, in a romantic musical comedy extravaganza about Hollywood. The many featured stars include Edgar Bergen, Charlie McCarthy, Adolphe Menjou, George Balanchine American Ballet, Zorina, Phil Baker, Bobby Clark and the Goldwyn Girls.
VHS: S03122. $19.98.
George Marshall, USA, 1938, 115 mins.

Good News
June Allyson and Peter Lawford star as college students in the Roaring Twenties. This remake of the 1930 musical finds a student librarian involved with turning a football hero who has eyes for the campus sexpot. With Patricia Marshall, Joan McCracken, and Mel Torme. The script is by Betty Comden and Adolph Green. Songs include "The Varsity Drag" and "The French Lesson."
VHS: S13306. $19.98.
Charles Walters, USA, 1947, 92 mins.

Goodbye, Mr. Chips
A remake of the 1939 film tracing the life of a shy schoolteacher, adapted from James Hilton's novel. With lyrics and music by Leslie Bricusse. With Peter O'Toole, Petula Clark, Michael Bryant and Michael Redgrave.
Laser: LD70588. $39.97.
Herbert Ross, Great Britain, 1969, 151 mins.

Grease
The movie version of a play that got its start in a bus barn in Chicago stars John Travolta and Olivia Newton-John as California high schoolers addicted to being cool. A high energy, tune-filled romp that features such quasi-teens (at the time) as Stockard Channing, Jeff Conaway and Didi Conn. Eve Arden, Sid Caesar and Edd "Kookie" Byrnes play the bona fide adults. "Grease" is the word and the word is fun.
VHS: S08292. $14.95.
Randal Kleiser, USA, 1978, 110 mins.

The Great Rupert
A funny musical-fantasy about a trained squirrel who discovers a suitcase full of money and gives it to the down-and-out Jimmy Durante, who's at his comic best.
VHS: S14671. $29.95.
Irving Pichel, USA, 1950, 86 mins.

The Great Waltz
This cinematic rhapsody captures the spirit of Johann Strauss' music with spirited inventiveness. Splendid back lot recreations of Vienna, inspiring musical arrangements and bravura camerawork shape this overlooked gem. Joseph Ruttenberg's lovely cinematography earned him an Oscar.
VHS: S14312. $19.98.
Laser: LD74486. $34.98.
Julien Duvivier, USA, 1938, 102 mins.

Great Ziegfeld
William Powell plays the title character, Broadway showman Florenz Ziegfeld (1867-1932), in a film that won three Oscars, including Best Picture. The ads read "50 Stars" and "300 Girls" in this nearly three-hour biography packed with some of the stars that Ziegfeld made possible. Fanny Brice, Ann Pennington and Ray Bolger play themselves. Will Rogers and Eddie Cantor were doubled. With Myrna Loy and Luise Rainer as Ziegfeld's wives.
VHS: S08339. $29.95.
Laser: LD70134. $39.98.
Robert Z. Leonard, USA, 1936, 176 mins.

Guys and Dolls
Marlon Brando, Frank Sinatra and Jean Simmons star in Joseph Mankiewicz's quality adaptation of the Broadway hit about the gamblers, missionaries and underworld sinners that populate writer Damon Runyon's cityscapes. Despite the heavyweight top billing, the best performance is Stubby Kaye's Nicely-Nicely and his brilliant rendition of "Sit Down, You're Rocking the Boat."
VHS: S02529. $19.98.
Joseph L. Mankiewicz, USA, 1955, 150 mins.

Gypsy
Unbeatable Bette Midler recreates the infamous backstage mother as Mama Rose, the original driving force behind famous striptease artiste, Gypsy. This film features the original Broadway choreography by Jerome Robbins with music by Jule Styne and Stephen Sondheim.
VHS: S20650. $89.95.
Emile Ardolino, USA, 1993, 150 mins.

Hallelujah
King Vidor's vibrant, colorful musical depicts the hardship and difficulties of daily black life. The film focuses on a poor Southern farmer who becomes a preacher, on his powerful temptations and fate and on the problems of reconciling these two radically different worlds. The work balances traditional black spirituals with numbers by Irving Berlin ("Waiting at the End of the Road" and "Swanee Shuffle". With Daniel L. Haynes, Nina Mae McKinney and William Fontaine.
VHS: S18504. $19.98.
King Vidor, USA, 1929, 90 mins.

Hallelujah, I'm a Bum
S.N. Berman and Ben Hecht wrote the screenplay for this musical entertainment starring Al Jolson. A tramp meets a woman suffering from temporary amnesia. Soon he falls in love with her and resolves to reform his easy-going ways.
VHS: S23819. $24.95.
Lewis Milestone, USA, 1933, 83 mins.

Hank Williams: "The Show He Never Gave"

A speculative biography of Hank Williams. The filmmakers showcase the definitive Hank Williams concert performance, with country singer "Sneezy" Waters impersonating Williams playing an intimate concert at a roadside bar. 86 mins.
VHS: $17318. $24.95.

The Harvey Girls

Judy Garland goes West to work as a waitress in a Fred Harvey railroad restaurant. When she is not serving grub to prominent westerners like John Hodiak, Ray Bolger and Preston Foster, she is probably singing or setting a good example. With Angela Lansbury, Cyd Charisse.
VHS: $04985. $19.95.
George Sidney, USA, 1946, 102 mins.

The Heat's On

Mae West stars as a fading Broadway performer who tries to convince an aging financier to bankroll her bawdy new musical, despite the objections of the man's sister, who runs the Legion of Purity. With Victor Moore, William Gaxton and Almira Sessions.
VHS: $19021. $19.95.
Gregory Ratoff, USA, 1943, 79 mins.

Hello, Dolly!

Barbra Streisand is Dolly Levi, matchmaker extraordinaire, in this Gene Kelly film of the Broadway hit musical. Walter Matthau is Horace Vandergelder, a wealthy, unmarried businessman. Set at the turn of this century, schemes will be hatched and songs will be sung. With Louis Armstrong.
VHS: $02927. $19.98.
Laser: LD71037. $49.95.
Gene Kelly, USA, 1969, 146 mins.

Hello, Frisco, Hello

Alice Faye stars as singer who rises to fame after her saloon-owner boyfriend (John Payne) leaves her for a socialite. As luck would have it, in the world of musical comedies at least, his marriage crumbles, leaving him destitute, until Faye returns to see if he still loves her.
VHS: $21304. $19.98.
H. Bruce Humberstone, USA, 1943, 98 mins.

High Society

One of the best musicals of the fifties! With Bing Crosby, Frank Sinatra, and Grace Kelly, the score written by Cole Porter and played by Louis Armstrong and his Band. *High Society* is highly entertaining and highly recommended!
VHS: $00570. $19.95.
Charles Walters, USA, 1956, 112 mins.

Higher and Higher

Frank Sinatra is the crooning victim of a crazy plot: a bankrupt millionaire tries to pass off his maid as a debutante in order to marry rich boy next door: Frankie! With the beautiful Michele Morgan.
VHS: $11605. $19.98.
Tim Whelan, USA, 1943, 90 mins.

His Butler's Sister

Deanna Durbin goes off to visit her brother (Pat O'Brien) and finds that he is a butler to a Broadway composer (Franchot Tone). Durbin becomes smitten with the handsome composer and takes up residence with the two, posing as a maid. It's a delightful musical comedy. Charles Previn acted as the music director.
VHS: $27012. $19.98.
Frank Borzage, USA, 1943, 94 mins.

Hit the Deck

The Broadway hit of 1927 was filmed twice before this 1955 MGM set sail. Nine major characters mix the ship-shape world of the Navy with other shapes in a Broadway show. Jane Powell is Admiral Walter Pidgeon's daughter, who wants to be in show business like stage starlet Debbie Reynolds. You can be sure the shore patrol will be involved somewhere. With Vic Damone, Ann Miller, Russ Tamblyn, Tony Martin and Alan King.
VHS: $08520. $19.95.
Laser: Letterboxed. LD74673. $34.98.
Roy Rowland, USA, 1955, 112 mins.

Holiday Inn

Song and dance man Bing Crosby decides to run a Connecticut inn which is open only on holidays. Fred Astaire checks in as Bing's rival in love and both sing and dance to a hit-filled Irving Berlin score, including "White Christmas."
VHS: $01533. $19.98.
Laser: LD70038. $34.98.
Mark Sandrich, USA, 1942, 101 mins.

Hollywood Canteen

Will a GI on leave meet his dream girl at the Hollywood Canteen? You bet—especially when Bette Davis, John Garfield, Barbara Stanwyck, Peter Lorre, Ida Lupino, Joan Crawford and over 30 more Hollywood luminaries give him a helping hand. Vibrant wartime entertainment.
VHS: $14316. $19.98.
Laser: Chapter Search. Includes original theatrical trailer. LD71671. $39.98.
Delmer Daves, USA, 1944, 124 mins.

How to Succeed in Business Without Really Trying

Robert Morse is an ambitious window washer who has dreams of climbing the corporate ladder from inside a building for a change. This Broadway musical transfers entertainingly to film form. Songs by Frank Loesser include "The Brotherhood of Man" and "I Believe in You". With Michelle Lee, Anthony Teague, Maureen Arthur and Rudy Vallee as the head of the Worldwide Wicket Company.
VHS: $11733. $19.95.
Laser: LD70596. $39.98.
David Swift, USA, 1967, 121 mins.

I Could Go on Singing

Judy Garland's last motion picture. She plays an American singing star visiting London to top the bill at the London Palladium, where she meets old flame Dirk Bogarde, who is raising the son they had out of wedlock. Will Judy admit to motherhood and rekindle the old emotions, or just find a bottle to crawl inside? With Gregory Phillips as little Matt and Jack Klugman as her manager.
VHS: $09149. $19.98.
Laser: LD74674. $34.98.
Ronald Neame, Great Britain, 1963, 99 mins.

I Dood It

The timeless comedy of Red Skelton is backed by Eleanor Powell's splendid dancing and the Big Band jazz of Jimmy Dorsey and his Orchestra in this madcap tale of a lovesick stage-door Johnny who finds out that masquerades can backfire—spectacularly. Includes a performance by Lena Horne.
VHS: $15429. $19.98.
Vincente Minnelli, USA, 1943, 102 mins.

I Dream of Jeannie

Ray Middleton and Bill Shirley are featured in this fictional biography of the tin pan alley composer Stephen Foster. Though this Irish-American died at a relatively young age, his songs remain standards that everyone knows. "I Dream of Jeannie" is just one of his many lasting works.
VHS: $23820. $24.95.
Allan Dwan, USA, 1952, 90 mins.

I Love Melvin

Donald O'Connor's just a gofer for *Look* magazine. But he promises chorus girl Debbie Reynolds her face will get onto the cover. Seven songs and a million complications later, it all comes true.
VHS: $14165. $19.98.
Don Weis, USA, 1953, 77 mins.

I Married an Angel

Nelson Eddy and Jeanette MacDonald in their last film together. He plays a playboy who sings and is smitten by a heavenly visitor. Based on a Rodgers and Hart musical which was based on a piece by Hungarian Vaszary Janos. Script for the MGM film by Anita Loos. With Janis Carter, Inez Cooper, Edward Everett Horton and Binnie Barnes.
VHS: $09846. $19.98.
W.S. Van Dyke, USA, 1942, 84 mins.

I'll See You in My Dreams

Michael Curtiz's biographical retelling of the amazing career of lyricist Gus Kahn, who wrote more than 800 tunes, including the memorable pop tunes "Makin' Whoopee", "Ain't We Got Fun", "Toot Tootsie", "It Had to Be You" and "Pretty Baby". With Doris Day, Danny Thomas and Frank Lovejoy.
VHS: $18462. $19.98.
Michael Curtiz, USA, 1951, 110 mins.

In the Good Old Summertime

Judy Garland and Van Johnson are feuding shop clerks who unknowingly exchange romantic pen pal letters in this musical adaptation of *Shop Around the Corner*. The score includes "I Don't Care" and "Wait Til the Sun Shines."
VHS: $09940. $29.95.
Robert Z. Leonard, USA, 1949, 102 mins.

Interrupted Melody

Eleanor Parker portrays famed Australian opera singer Marjorie Lawrence in this Oscar-winning film (Best Screenplay). Lawrence made a heroic comeback after being stricken by polio. Glenn Ford and Roger Moore co-star, with Eileen Farrell providing the singing voice of the diva.
VHS: $21170. $19.98.
Curtis Bernhardt, USA, 1955, 106 mins.

It Happened in Brooklyn

Frank Sinatra plays a singing ex-GI back in Brooklyn and ready for love and success. He finds himself sharing an apartment with high school janitor Jimmy Durante instead. Enter snobby Peter Lawford with a song to sell and no voice to sing it. With Kathryn Grayson and Gloria Grahame. Songs include "Time After Time", "Whose Baby Are You?" and "The Song's Gotta Have Heart".
VHS: $13305. $19.98.
Laser: Chapter search. Includes original theatrical trailer. LD71637. $34.98.
Richard Whorf, USA, 1947, 104 mins.

It's a Date

Following her latest stage triumph, Broadway star Kay Francis decides to vacation in Hawaii before tackling her new role. While she's away her daughter (Deanna Durbin) is offered a part in a prize-winning play—which just happens to be the same part her mother is planning to do in the coming season. A charming musical comedy. With S.Z. Sakall and Walter Pidgeon.
VHS: $14317. $29.98.
William A. Seiter, USA, 1940, 103 mins.

It's a Great Feeling

This breezy musical comedy stars Dennis Morgan and Jack Carson as two Hollywood actors about to begin work on a new movie. The problem is finding a director and a leading lady to work with Carson, who has a reputation as a "ham" and "wolf." Enter Doris Day as a young hopeful from the studio commissary whom Carson attempts to turn into a star.
VHS: $14311. $19.98.
David Butler, USA, 1949, 85 mins.

It's Always Fair Weather

Gene Kelly and Cyd Charisse star in this fast-tempoed, toe-tapping musical featuring three WW II buddies who are re-united ten years after their discharge to find they have nothing in common and dislike one another.
VHS: $03600. $19.98.
G. Kelly/S. Donen, USA, 1955, 109 mins.

The Jazz Singer (Crosland)

It's more than a movie; it's history—the first feature-length film with spoken dialog. Audiences at the October 6, 1927 premiere were electrified by what they could now see *and* hear when star Al Jolson, in the film's best-remembered line, proclaimed: "Wait a minute, you ain't heard nothing yet!" Includes Jolson's famous renditions of "Toot Toot Tootsie Goodbye" and "Mammy".
VHS: $04338. $29.98.
Alan Crosland, USA, 1927, 89 mins.

The Jazz Singer (Curtiz)

Danny Thomas and Peggy Lee star in this version of the musical made famous by both Broadway and Hollywood. You'll be touched by the story of a cantor's son who rejects his father's hopes that he will continue the family tradition, to become a show biz performer. "If I Could Be with You" and "Just One of Those Things" are among the memorable songs contained in this musical drama.
VHS: $20657. $19.98.
Michael Curtiz, USA, 1953, 107 mins.

The Jazz Singer (Fleischer)

Neil Diamond is the son a Cantor (Laurence Olivier), who rejects family tradition in order to pursue a career as a popular singer. Of course, this secular lifestyle creates a clash with his father that is only resolved after a great deal of angst. Based on the early successful sound film from the late 1920's.
VHS: $22032. $14.98.
Richard Fleischer, USA, 1980, 115 mins.

Jesus Christ Superstar

The words and music of Tim Rice and Andrew Lloyd Webber find a home on film in this innovative retelling of the life of Christ. This modern approach to the events of 2000 years ago will not please everyone, but what can? With Ted Neeley, Carl Anderson, Josh Mostel and Yvonne Elliman as Mary Magdalene.
VHS: $04920. $29.95.
Laser: Letterboxed, chapter search. LD71579. $34.98.
Norman Jewison, USA, 1973, 103 mins.

Jolson Sings Again

Vibrant and joyous sequel to *The Jolson Story* has Larry Parks reprising his role as Al Jolson at the decline of his film career. He returns to Broadway to discover the minstrel "blackface" phenomenon that created his popularity has lost its appeal. His manager persuades him to perform for GI's overseas—where he falls passionately in love with Army nurse Barbara Hale. With William Demarest.
VHS: $02918. $19.95.
Henry Levin, USA, 1949, 96 mins.

Jolson Story

A sprawling, big musical that records the life of Al Jolson, the controversial entertainer who played to almost exclusively white audiences, in black face, as the lead in "minstrel jazz" productions. The film traces the origins of Jolson's entry into show business and the effects of his enormous popularity. Larry Parks received an Academy Award nomination for his work as Jolson, elevating the standard biopic conventions through excellent use of Jolson's music, including "My Mammy" and "You Made Me Love You."
VHS: $02917. $19.95.
Alfred E. Green, USA, 1946, 129 mins.

Joy of Living

Dashing Douglas Fairbanks Jr. stars in this comedy with Irene Dunne in which Fairbanks opts to "rescue" stage songstress Dunne from her mercenary family. With Eric Blore and Lucille Ball.
VHS: $10653. $19.98.
Tay Garnett, USA, 1938, 91 mins.

Julie Andrews—Broadway: The Making of Broadway, The Music of Richard Rodgers

From the beginning, Richard Rodgers had Julie Andrews in mind for his blockbuster musical *The Sound of Music*. In this video, Andrews sings songs from this Broadway success, as well as works from the later Andrews hit *Victor/Victoria—The Musical*. 50 mins.
VHS: $26490. $29.95.

Jumbo

A razzle-dazzle circus epic starring Doris Day and Stephen Boyd as the romantic duo who sing the sublime music of Rodgers and Hart. Also starring Jimmy Durante and Martha Raye. Busby Berkeley directed the lavish and breathtaking circus scenes.
VHS: $15432. $19.98.
Laser: LD74667. $39.98.
Charles Walters, USA, 1962, 125 mins.

Kid Millions

Eddie Cantor stars in this early color musical comedy. A large inheritance dislodges a rather unimpressive Brooklyn boy by promising him the hope of great wealth. Before long, Cantor is off on an adventure to Egypt in order to collect. Great songs and an early appearance by Lucille Ball make this a must for fans of classic films.
VHS: $24206. $19.98.
Roy Del Ruth, USA, 1934, 90 mins.

King and I

Stern Siamese monarch Brynner is softened by the influence of English governess Kerr as their clashing cultures and personalities give way to an unspoken love. Magnificent performance by Brynner (who won an Oscar) in this sumptuously produced and moving adaptation of the Broadway musical. "Shall We Dance" highlights the Rogers and Hammerstein score.
VHS: $02541. $19.98.
Walter Lang, USA, 1956, 133 mins.

King of Jazz

This vibrant, sparkling piece of celluloid nostalgia takes the form of a lavish jazz revue with music by American giants such as George Gershwin played out against dazzling production numbers featuring Bing Crosby, Paul Whiteman, and John Boles. This was Universal Pictures' first all-Technicolor feature length musical film, and contains the first sound cartoon sequence as well.
VHS: $00681. $19.98.
John M. Anderson, USA, 1930, 93 mins.

Kismet

The perennial fable of poets, lovers and the Arabian nights, based on the Broadway success featuring Howard Keel, Sebastian Cabot, Vic Damone and Ann Blyth. Music adapted from themes by Alexander Borodin.
VHS: $02259. $19.95.
Laser: LD70609. $34.97.
Vincente Minnelli, USA, 1955, 113 mins.

Lady Be Good

Husband and wife songwriting team Robert Young and Ann Sothern find a love song's great way to patch up a marital spat, in this musical with Red Skelton and Eleanor Powell. With music by the Gershwins, Oscar Hammerstein and Jerome Kern. That's one talented couple!
VHS: $14166. $19.98.
Norman Z. McLeod, USA, 1941, 111 mins.

Lady Be Good/Ship Ahoy

Two romantic comedies starring comedian Red Skelton and dancer Eleanor Powell. Norman Z. McLeod's 1941 *Lady Be Good* concerns a husband and wife songwriting team (played by Robert Young and Ann Sothern). Edward Buzzell's 1942 *Ship Ahoy* has the two caught up in international intrigue on a Naval ship. Includes the theatrical trailers for both films. 207 mins.
Laser: LD71657. $44.98.

Lady Sings the Blues

Diana Ross makes her screen debut as Lady Day, the legendary jazz singer Billie Holiday. More soap opera and fine songs than accurate biography but fans of Miss Ross and Billie Holiday will be happy. With Billy Dee Williams, Sid Melton and Richard Pryor as Piano Man. Film received five Oscar nominations.
VHS: $10836. $29.95.
Laser: LD75302. $39.98.
Sidney J. Furie, USA, 1972, 144 mins.

Let Freedom Ring

Ben Hecht wrote the screenplay for this Western starring Nelson Eddy. When he returns to his hometown, Eddy finds it overrun with corruption and promptly sets out to reclaim this frontier outpost. It's an action-filled patriotic film that includes a particularly noteworthy musical number, Eddy singing "The Star Spangled Banner".
VHS: $20791. $19.98.
Jack Conway, USA, 1939, 100 mins.

Let's Dance

Terrific dance numbers by Fred Astaire distinguish this drama as Betty Hutton tries to win her son back from her Back Bay in-laws. With Roland Young, Ruth Warrick.
VHS: $10434. $19.95.
Laser: LD75221. $34.98.
Norman Z. McLeod, USA, 1950, 112 mins.

Li'l Abner

A colorful and fast-paced romp based on the hit Broadway version of Al Capp's beloved cartoon strip. This musical comedy features Julie Newmar, Stella Stevens, and Robert Strauss.
VHS: $13705. $19.95.
Laser: LD75222. $34.98.
Melvin Frank, USA, 1959, 114 mins.

Lili

Leslie Caron is Lili Daurier, a 16-year-old orphan who finds a home with a traveling carnival and befriends a crippled puppeteer. A charming MGM musical based on a story by Paul Gallico. Cast includes Zsa Zsa Gabor, Amanda Blake, Jean-Pierre Aumont and Mel Ferrer as the puppeteer. Bronislau Kaper's score won an Oscar.
VHS: $06178. $19.95.
Charles Walters, USA, 1953, 81 mins.

The Little Colonel

Shirley Temple, Lionel Barrymore and Bill "Bojangles" Robinson star in this toe-tapping musical set in the Old South.
VHS: $05903. $19.98.
David Butler, USA, 1935, 80 mins.

The Little Match Girl

Twiggy and Roger Daltry star in this musical adaptation of the story of Hans Christian Andersen, Denmark's premier storyteller for children of all ages. Discover the true meaning of Christmas. With Natalie Morse as the match girl and lavish songs and lively dancing to entertain and charm the entire family.
VHS: $05521. $29.95.
Michael Oustance, 90 mins.

Little Miss Broadway

Shirley Temple, George Murphy and Jimmy Durante star in this very amusing backstage musical that includes Shirley's classic "Be Optimistic."
VHS: $05904. $19.98.
Irving Cummings, USA, 1938, 71 mins.

Little Nelly Kelly

The first film to feature Judy Garland as a "solo" actress, *Little Nelly Kelly* follows the daughter of an Irish cop who struggles to maintain family unity while making good on the stage. Garland plays both mother and daughter in this heartfelt musical adapted from George M. Cohan's play about Irish pride. With George Murphy and Charles Winninger.
VHS: $15852. $19.98.
Norman Taurog, USA, 1940, 99 mins.

The Little Prince

Antoine de Saint-Exupery's wonderful book is transformed into a musical with songs written by Alan Jay Lerner and Frederick Loewe. 89 mins.
VHS: $06113. $19.95.
Stanley Donen, USA, 1974, 88 mins.

Little Shop of Horrors

The recent re-make of Roger Corman's classic film, adapted from the smash hit Broadway musical. Stars Steve Martin, Christopher Guest and Ellen Greene. With a fabulous Bill Murray performance as the masochistic dental patient.
VHS: $03865. $19.98.
Frank Oz, USA, 1986, 88 mins.

Littlest Rebel

Shirley Temple sings "Polly Wolly Doodle" and taps her way in and out of Civil War trouble with Bill "Bojangles" Robinson.
VHS: $05902. $19.98.
David Butler, USA, 1935, 70 mins.

Look for the Silver Lining

This visually opulent biography of Broadway star Marilyn Miller (June Haver) interweaves stylish vaudeville numbers and engaging musical routines in a look at her life and work. With Ray Bolger, Rosemary DeCamp and Gordon MacRae.
VHS: $19470. $19.98.
David Butler, USA, 1949, 100 mins.

Louisiana Purchase

Irving Berlin's elegant and witty music sets the tone of this funny and lyrical political satire about the legislative process, with Bob Hope as a shrewd Congressman. With Vera Zorina, Victor Moore and Irene Bordoni.
VHS: $18545. $14.98.
Irving Cummings, USA, 1941, 98 mins.

Love Me or Leave Me

Doris Day stars as singer Ruth Etting in the best performance of her career. A serious show biz bio has Doris sing 12 songs and act up a storm opposite James Cagney as her gimpy, overbearing mentor. Day even got top billing. With Cameron Mitchell. Numbers include "You Made Me Love You" and "Ten Cents a Dance".
VHS: $07160. $19.95.
Charles Vidor, USA, 1955, 122 mins.

Lovely to Look At

Red is the color this season. When Red Skelton inherits a Paris fashion house, he and his buddies turn haute couture inside out. This comic musical also stars Kathryn Grayson, Howard Keel and Ann Miller.
VHS: $14167. $19.98.
Mervyn Le Roy, USA, 1952, 105 mins.

The Loves of Carmen

Rita Hayworth and Glenn Ford are re-teamed in living color as the popular Bizet opera gets the Hollywood treatment. Only the plot remains as Rita's sultry charms turn honest men into sunbaked jellyfish. With Victor Jory, Ron Randell and Luther Adler.
VHS: $04675. $19.95.
Laser: LD74895. $34.95.
Charles Vidor, USA, 1948, 99 mins.

Lucky Me

Doris Day stars in this energetic musical set in Miami about an ambitious performer stuck in a third-rate revue show who unexpectedly gets the notice of a Broadway songwriter. With Robert Cummings, Phil Silvers, and Eddie Foy.
VHS: $15783. $19.98.
Jack Donohue, USA, 1952, 100 mins.

Lullaby of Broadway

A bright Warner Bros. melodrama and musical stars Doris Day as a prominent Broadway star who returns to New York and discovers her mother destitute. A sharp cast includes Gene Nelson, Gladys George, Billy de Wolfe and Florence Bates.
VHS: $15722. $19.98.
Laser: LD74709. $34.98.
David Butler, USA, 1951, 92 mins.

Mad About Music

Deanna Durbin stars as a lonely schoolgirl in Switzerland who feels rejected by her movie star father. At first she invents a father to impress her friends and then actually finds a handsome composer to play the part. In the end, despite these problems, Durbin finds even more family than she could have hoped for.
VHS: $27010. $19.98.
Norman Taurog, USA, 1938, 96 mins.

Make a Wish

Basil Rathbone stars as a charming composer who lives across the lake from a boys' camp. He befriends singing prodigy Bobby Breen and finds inspiration for a new operetta when he meets the boy's mother. With Marion Clare, Leon Errol, Donald Meek and Henry Armetta. B&W.
VHS: $06148. $29.95.
Kurt Neumann, USA, 1937, 77 mins.

Mame

America's comedienne, Lucille Ball, as one of the stage and screen's most enduring dames—Auntie Mame. With a musical score by Jerry Herman.
VHS: $03954. $19.98.
Laser: LD70622. $39.98.
Gene Saks, USA, 1974, 132 mins.

Man of La Mancha

The film version of this popular stage musical stars Peter O'Toole as Don Quixote, James Coco as the faithful Sancho Panza and Sophia Loren as Dulcinea. As if that isn't enough, the soaring musical score includes one of the finest songs ever written—"The Impossible Dream." Enjoy!
VHS: $01715. $19.99.
Laser: LD72125. $39.98.
Arthur Hiller, USA, 1972, 129 mins.

Manhattan Merry-Go-Round

Phil Regan, Ann Dvorak and Cab Calloway star in this melodrama in which a gangster takes over a record company and uses his coercive methods on musical groups. Despite his ruthless ways, the gangster is undone by a temperamental opera singer.
VHS: $23821. $24.95.
Charles F. Reisner, USA, 1937, 89 mins.

Maytime

John Barrymore stands between a romance between an opera star and a poverty ridden singer in Paris. He plays the husband/mentor of Jeanette MacDonald, who is fonder of Nelson Eddy. One of their better vehicles. With Sig Ruman, Herman Bing and Rafaela Ottiano. B&W.
VHS: $06978. $19.95.
Laser: LD72143. $39.98.
Robert Z. Leonard, USA, 1937, 132 mins.

Meet Danny Wilson

Frank Sinatra and Shelley Winters star in this romantic musical drama about a singer who becomes involved in backstage intrigues. A roguish success in New York, his move to Hollywood and ever greater success is tarnished by racketeers. Sinatra is eminently believable in the part.
VHS: $21497. $14.98.
Joseph Pevney, USA, 1951, 86 mins.

Meet Me in Las Vegas

Cowpoke Dan Dailey can't lose in Vegas as long as he holds hands with lovely Cyd Charisse. Big, splashy entertainment loaded with guest stars and Vegas glamour. Cameos by Frank Sinatra, Lena Horne, and Debbie Reynolds.
VHS: $14168. $19.98.
Laser: LD72144. $34.98.
Roy Rowland, USA, 1956, 112 mins.

Meet Me in St. Louis

Judy Garland is the classic American teenager in love, in song, in one of the brightest hours of her career. Meet Me in St. Louis is a charming turn-of-the-century album full of magic and memories. 50th Anniversary edition. Newly remastered. Includes a "making of" documentary, interviews with cast and team, a trailer from 1955, and a recreation of a deleted musical number.
VHS: $00845. $19.95.
Vincente Minnelli, USA, 1944, 114 mins.

Melody Cruise

Step aboard a luxury ocean liner with millionaires Charlie Ruggles, Phil Harris and a cargo of laughs as they try to outsmart the fair sex in a rollicking musical comedy.
VHS: $11608. $19.98.
Mark Sandrich, USA, 1932, 75 mins.

The Merry Widow

A classic adaptation of Franz Lehar's opera, with Lana Turner as an attractive, eligible widow courted by the king of Marshovia (Fernando Lamas), who has designs on her vast wealth, though she foils his schemes.
VHS: $18556. $19.98.
Curtis Bernhardt, USA, 1952, 105 mins.

Million-Dollar Mermaid

One of Esther Williams' best—Williams is the leggy swim star, while Annette Kellerman switches between swimming and romancing Victor Mature. Busby Berkeley produced some of the most spectacular dance numbers for this musical.
VHS: $11160. $29.95.
Laser: LD71153. $34.98.
Mervyn LeRoy, USA, 1952, 115 mins.

Minstrel Man

A rare musical showing a side of American entertainment never shown. Benny Fields is a minstrel performer who gives his daughter over to friends to raise after the death of his wife.
VHS: $09581. $29.95.

Moon over Miami

An entertaining musical romance with Betty Grable, her sister Carole Landis and Charlotte Greenwood going fortune hunting in Miami and coming up with more than they bargained for. Includes the title song, "You Started Something."
VHS: $09448. $19.98.
Walter Lang, USA, 1941, 91 mins.

Movie Struck (Pick a Star)

Laurel and Hardy guest star in this Hollywood musical as themselves. They appear in two long sequences which add up to one reel out of the eight. The story concerns a young girl who wants to be in the movies with the help of publicity man Jack Haley. With Rosina Lawrence and Patsy Kelly. B&W.
VHS: $05065. $19.95.
Edward Sedgwick, USA, 1937, 69 mins.

Mr. Music

A remake of Accent on Youth. Bing Crosby stars as a Broadway songwriter who tries to rejuvenate his life, reclaim his youth and use his music as a means of overcoming personal obstacles and career setbacks. With Nancy Olson, Charles Coburn and Ruth Hussey. Cameos by Groucho Marx and Peggy Lee.
VHS: $17980. $14.95.
Richard Hadyn, USA, 1950, 113 mins.

The Music Man

If you are looking for a movie with 76 trombones and trouble in River City, have I got a musical for you. Robert Preston stars as the energetic Professor Harold Hill, a silver-tongued conman willing to separate a small town of Iowans from their money. With Buddy Hackett, Ronny Howard and Shirley Jones as Marian the Librarian.
VHS: Out of print. For rental only.
Laser: Letterboxed. LD74734. $39.98.
Morton Da Costa, USA, 1962, 151 mins.

My Dream Is Yours

Doris Day sings her way to the top of the charts in this buoyant Technicolor musical comedy set in the days of live radio variety shows. Jack Carson plays her hard-working agent, and a live-action/animated sequence features a very special superstar: Bugs Bunny.
VHS: $14318. $29.98.
Michael Curtiz, USA, 1949, 101 mins.

My Sister Eileen

This exuberant musical remake of the 1942 social comedy is a succession of funny vignettes about two young Ohio women adjusting to the severe culture shock of Greenwich Village and trying to retain their innocence. With Betty Garrett, Janet Leigh, Jack Lemmon, Bob Fosse and Kurt Kasznar.
VHS: $18418. $19.95.
Richard Quine, USA, 1955, 108 mins.

Nancy Goes to Rio

A veteran Broadway actress (Ann Sothern) and her talented, stage-struck daughter (Jane Powell) are chasing the same role and the same man—but neither knows what the other is up to. Includes several Gershwin tunes and a stunning performance by Carmen Miranda.
VHS: $15427. $19.98.
Robert Z. Leonard, USA, 1950, 99 mins.

Naughty Marietta (1935)

Jeanette MacDonald and Nelson Eddy appeared together for the first time in this favorite operetta about a princess who runs away to America and falls in love with an Indian scout.
VHS: $00920. $19.95.
Laser: LD70637. $34.98.
W.S. Van Dyke, USA, 1935, 106 mins.

Naughty Marietta (1955)

Patrice Munsel, as Marietta d'Altena, and Alfred Drake, as Captain Warrington, star in this 1955 adaptation of Victor Herbert's operetta Naughty Marietta. The work includes such popular melodies as "Ah!, Sweet Mystery of Life," "Italian Street Song," "I'm Falling in Love with Someone" and "Tramp! Tramp! Tramp!" 78 mins.
VHS: $20374. $39.95.

Neptune's Daughter

Esther Williams and Ricardo Montalban demonstrate there is more to do in a swimming pool than laps, in the MGM aquatic spectacular. They also sing the Oscar winning song "Baby, It's Cold Outside." With Red Skelton and Betty Garnett as the comic relief. Also Xavier Cugat, Keenan Wynn and Mel Blanc. The last one in the pool has to do a car commercial.
VHS: $08519. $19.95.
Laser: LD72148. $34.98.
Edward Buzzell, USA, 1949, 93 mins.

New Faces

A famous Broadway hit which established the careers of Eartha Kitt, Alice Ghostley, Robert Clary, June Carroll, Paul Lynde, Carol Lawrence and Mel Brooks. Eartha Kitt sings the songs that made her famous: "Monotonous," "C'est Si Bon," and "Santa Baby." Alice Ghostley sings "Boston Beguine," and the entire company romps through "Lizzie Borden."
VHS: $04700. $49.95.
Henry Horner, USA, 1954, 98 mins.

New Moon

Jeanette MacDonald and Nelson Eddy meet in the Bayou State, sing some songs and fall in love. The Oscar Hammerstein/Sigmund Romberg score includes "One Kiss," "Stout-Hearted Men" and "Lover Come Back to Me." With Mary Boland, George Zucco and H.B. Warner. Remake of 1930 film.
VHS: $06975. $19.98.
Laser: LD75541. $39.98.
Robert Z. Leonard, USA, 1940, 105 mins.

Night and Day

Cary Grant plays Cole Porter, the composer who thrilled the world for 40 years with his witty, dramatic and memorable songs. Grant and the rest of the cast sing over twenty Porter classics in this Technicolor film that follows Porter from his undergraduate days at Yale to international acclaim.
VHS: $14315. $19.98.
Laser: LD72351. $39.98.
Michael Curtiz, USA, 1946, 128 mins.

No No Nanette

Anne Neagle, Victor Mature, Richard Carlson, Roland Young and ZaSu Pitts star in this second of three versions of the 1925 Broadway musical.
VHS: $08457. $29.95.
Herbert Wilcox, USA, 1940, 96 mins.

Oklahoma!

The Rodgers and Hammerstein epic musical is a classic of immortal songs and fancy steppin'. "Oh What a Beautiful Morning," "The Surrey with the Fringe on Top" and of course, "Poor Jud Is Dead" are performed with gusto by a cast that includes Gordon MacRae, Shirley Jones, Rod Steiger, Eddie Albert and Gloria Grahame as the sassy Ado Annie.
VHS: Out of print. For rental only.
Laser: LD71260. $44.98.
Fred Zinnemann, USA, 1955, 145 mins.

Oliver!

The musical version of Dicken's classic Oliver Twist adds song and dance to the story of a brave lad trying to survive amidst wretched social conditions and dire poverty. With Mark Lester as Oliver and Jack Wild as the Artful Dodger. Ron Moody is Fagin. Also Oliver Reed, Shani Wallis and Hugh Griffith. Six Oscars.
VHS: $00952. $19.95.
Laser: Letterboxed. LD72187. $39.95.
Carol Reed, Great Britain, 1968, 153 mins.

On a Clear Day You Can See Forever

Barbra Streisand and Yves Montand star in this cheerful musical about past lives. A girl visits a psychiatrist to stop smoking but learns that she has had a series of exciting identities in the past. One of these identities becomes a magnet for the psychiatrist's amorous attentions. Alan Jay Lerner wrote the lyrics and music, while the film is based on the Lerner and Burton Lane musical.
VHS: $22027. $14.95.
Vincente Minnelli, USA, 1970, 129 mins.

On an Island with You

Esther Williams and Peter Lawford travel from shimmering swimming pools to shiny dance floors to remote blue lagoons in this South Seas musical romance.
VHS: $16607. $19.98.
Richard Thorpe, USA, 1948, 117 mins.

On Moonlight Bay

A musical essay about turn-of-the-century innocence and joy. This early Doris Day vehicle is taken from Booth Tarkington's Penrod series about the relationship of two brash young innocents. With Gordon MacRae, Billy Gray and Mary Wickes. Songs include "I'm Forever Blowing Bubbles", "Till We Meet Again", and "Cuddle Up a Little Closer".
VHS: $18460. $19.98.
Laser: LD72149. $34.98.
Roy Del Ruth, USA, 1951, 95 mins.

On the Avenue

Dick Powell stars as a producer of a satiric musical show featuring Alice Faye. Faye is impersonating the well-known socialite and heiress, played by Madeleine Carrol. This scenario spawns a romantic plot perfect for musical comedy, with an engaging score provided by Irving Berlin.
VHS: $21301. $19.98.
Roy Del Ruth, USA, 1937, 89 mins.

On the Town

Leonard Bernstein's Broadway musical, a war-era tale about three sailors searching for an adventure in New York City, has been restaged as a concert at London's Barbican Centre. Conducted by Michael Tilson Thomas, this production includes numbers never performed in the show. Based on an idea by Jerome Robbins, the book and lyrics were composed by Betty Comden and Adolph Green. With Tyne Daly, Thomas Hampson, Frederica von Stade and David Garrison.
VHS: $19709. $29.95.
Laser: LD71932. $34.95.

One Hundred Men and a Girl

Deanna Durbin, the daughter of an unemployed musician, decides to persuade the famous conductor Leopold Stokowski to help her launch an orchestra that will employ her widowed father and another 99 out-of-work musicians. Charles Previn's score won an Oscar for his work on this comedy.
VHS: $23281. $19.98.
Henry Koster, USA, 1937, 84 mins.

One Night in the Tropics

A musical interpretation of Earl Derr Biggers' story Love Insurance, with songs by Jerome Kern, Oscar Hammerstein and Dorothy Fields. In their debut roles, Bud Abbott and Lou Costello are peripheral players to a complicated love triangle of Allan Jones, Nancy Kelly and Robert Cummings. The lunatic pair perform some of their "Who's on First?" routine.
VHS: $19069. $14.98.
A. Edward Sutherland, USA, 1940, 82 mins.

One Night of Love

Louis Silver won an Oscar for his score of this big box office success musical about an opera star who revolts against her tough teacher; it solidified the Hollywood careers of its stars, including Lily Pons, Gladys Swarthout, Miliza Korjus.
VHS: $11632. $19.95.
Victor Schertzinger, USA, 1934, 95 mins.

One Touch of Venus

Ava Gardner brightens up the life of Robert Walker, a window dresser, when his statue of the goddess of love becomes flesh. With Eve Arden, Dick Haymes and a few songs.
VHS: $04221. $19.95.
Laser: CLV. LD72011. $34.98.
William A. Seiter, USA, 1948, 82 mins.

Opposite Sex

The musical version of Clare Booth Luce's popular 1936 play The Women adds men and musical numbers. June Allyson is the good wife who must lose hubby Leslie Nielsen to temptress Joan Collins if she doesn't wise up. Those available with advice include Ann Sheridan, Dolores Gray, Ann Miller, Agnes Moorehead, Carolyn Jones and Joan Blondell. The guys include Dick Shawn, Dean Jones, Jim Backus and bandleader Harry James himself.
VHS: $13308. $19.95.
Laser: LD70730. $34.98.
David Miller, USA, 1956, 115 mins.

Orchestra Wives

George Montgomery and Ann Rutherford are newlyweds coping with the strain of life on the road in this big band film that's one of two Glenn Miller musicals from Fox. With Cesar Romero and Jackie Gleason.
VHS: $14507. $19.98.
Archie Mayo, USA, 1942, 98 mins.

Pagan Love Song

Clad in a sarong, her long hair bleached by the sun and skin the color of bronze, Esther Williams plays a half-American, half-Tahitian girl in this lavish island musical from producer Arthur Freed.
VHS: $16608. $19.98.
Robert Alton, USA, 1950, 76 mins.

Paint Your Wagon

Musical set during the gold rush days in California features Lee Marvin and Clint Eastwood as prospectors who share wife Jean Seberg, whom they purchased at an auction.
VHS: $06474. $29.95.
Joshua Logan, USA, 1969, 166 mins.

Pajama Game

Love and labor relations are the subject of this movie version of a tuneful Broadway musical. Doris Day is a union leader at the Sleeptite Pajama Factory, whose bargaining power is affected when she falls for the shop superintendent John Raitt. With Carol Haney, Eddie Foy, Jr., and Barbara Nichols. Songs include "Hernando's Hideaway" and "Steam Heat," by Richard Adler and Jerry Ross. Choreography by Bob Fosse.
VHS: $11660. $19.98.
G. Abbott/S. Donen, USA, 1957, 101 mins.

Pal Joey

One of the great Rodgers and Hart musicals about the fast-talking, womanizing nightclub entertainer who falls in love with one woman while another, richer one, woos him with the lure of his own night club. The songs include "Bewitched, Bothered and Bewildered," "My Funny Valentine," and "The Lady Is a Tramp." With Frank Sinatra, Kim Novak, Rita Hayworth.
VHS: $11630. $19.95.
Laser: LD74894. $34.95.
George Sidney, USA, 1957, 111 mins.

Panama Hattie

Ann Sothern is Panama Hattie, a salt-of-the-earth nightclub singer in love with a pedigreed officer in Canal Zone, Panama. A spirited WWII montage sparkling with the music of Cole Porter and the classic slapstick of Red Skelton.
VHS: $15428. $19.98.
Norman Z. McLeod, USA, 1942, 79 mins.

Peter Pan

This is the 30th anniversary edition of the classic story of eternal youth, starring Mary Martin as Peter, Cyril Ritchard as Hook, and Sondra Lee as Tiger Lily. The original, uncut family musical.
VHS: $12665. $24.95.
Vincent J. Donehue, USA, 1960, 100 mins.

The Phantom of the Opera
Gaston Leroux's 1911 novel is beautifully translated by the Hirshfeld Theater Company in this gothic work about the sinister composer (David Staller) who hides out in the catacombs of a Paris opera house. Raged with guilt, he kidnaps the beautiful and soulful Christine (Elizabeth Walsh). The evocative sets and baroque production establish an eerie mood and discord. "Staller is as impressive as Michael Crawford and...Elizabeth Walsh is warmer, both vocally and emotionally, than Sarah Brightman was on Broadway" (Stephen Holden, *The New York Times*). Music and lyrics by Lawrence Rosen and Paul Schierhorn. Book and adaptation by Bruce Falstein.
VHS: $19748. $24.95.
Ken Kurtz, USA, 1990, 93 mins.

Pippin
Ben Vereen and William Katt star in this filmed account of the Broadway smash, a colorful, bright pastiche of the fable and romantic epic, designed and choreographed by the brilliant Bob Fosse (*Cabaret, All That Jazz*). "An eye-popping extravaganza" (*L.A. Herald Examiner*).
VHS: $04867. $29.95.

The Pirate
Judy Garland mistakes a very limber circus clown for a notorious pirate. Gene Kelly is flattered by her mistaking him for the Black Macoco and tries to win her love. The real pirate is now the respected town mayor. A sumptuous fantasy/parody musical directed by Vincente Minnelli, with songs by Cole Porter.
VHS: $02260. $29.95.
Vincente Minnelli, USA, 1948, 102 mins.

Pirates of Penzance
Linda Ronstadt stars in this modern adaptation of the Gilbert and Sullivan musical, as originally produced by Joseph Papp. With Angela Lansbury, George Rose.
VHS: $04839. $19.98.
Wilford Leach, USA, 1983, 112 mins.

Playmates
The clowns take on the classics when Kay Kyser meets up with John Barrymore, a has-been actor who tries to inject Kyser's wild act with doses of Shakespeare!
VHS: $11606. $19.98.
Cliff Reid, USA, 1941, 96 mins.

Poor Little Rich Girl
One of Shirley Temple's best films finds Temple running away from home to join a vaudeville team. Wonderful musical numbers include "Military Man". With Jack Haley and Alice Faye.
VHS: $07360. $19.98.
Irving Cummings, USA, 1936, 72 mins.

Presenting Lily Mars
Judy Garland as a small town girl who dreams of fame in this adaptation of the Booth Tarkington novel, featuring Tommy Dorsey and His Orchestra, as well as the Bob Crosby Orchestra.
VHS: $03454. $19.98.
Laser: LD71146. $34.98.
Norman Taurog, USA, 1943, 105 mins.

Private Buckaroo
Sparkling entertainment featuring comedy, song, and the sensational trumpet of Harry James. Nostalgic showcase set during World Wor II, with America's favorite singing siblings, The Andrew Sisters, putting on a show for the soldiers.
VHS: $13863. $19.95.
Eddie Cline, USA, 1942, 70 mins.

Rappin'
Mario Van Peebles (*Posse, New Jack City*) stars in this action-musical as an ex-con trying to stay straight. He winds up in conflict with both his landlord and a gang leader. The music is the real focus of this film. Songs include "Snack Attack" and "FU 12".
VHS: $21401. $14.95.
Joel Silberg, USA, 1985, 92 mins.

Rebecca of Sunnybrook Farm
A heartwarming study and a dozen musical numbers including "On the Good Ship Lollipop" in this Shirley Temple favorite.
VHS: $06338. $19.95.
Laser: CLV. LD71737. $19.98.
Allan Dwan, USA, 1938, 80 mins.

Rhapsody in Blue
The life of George Gershwin, perhaps the greatest composer in American history, is depicted in this lavish motion picture. Robert Alda portrays the gifted musician torn between his love for American popular music and his reverence for the great classics.
VHS: $14314. $19.98.
Laser: Two-set set. LD70199. $39.88.
Irving Rapper, USA, 1945, 139 mins.

Rhythm on the Range
Cowboy Bing Crosby meets an heiress played by Frances Farmer. She is out to lose her fiance, an arranged match. It is a simple, engaging love story with plenty of singing from the crooning cowpoke Crosby. Johnny Mercer, Martha Raye and Bob Burns also star.
VHS: $25012. $14.95.
Norman Taurog, USA, 1936, 68 mins.

Rhythm on the River
Bing Crosby and Mary Martin star as struggling songwriters ghostwriting for the evil Basil Rathbone. In this light romantic comedy, their struggle to be recognized takes them through several funny episodes. Billy Wilder had a hand in the script.
VHS: $21199. $14.98.
Victor Schertzinger, USA, 1940, 92 mins.

Rich, Young and Pretty
An opulent MGM musical coming-of-age story about a sheltered young woman (Jane Powell) who experiences freedom and excitement in Paris. Her hopes for a dashing romance with a charismatic Parisian are stifled by her mother (Danielle Darrieux). With Wendell Corey, Vic Damone and Fernando Lamas.
VHS: $18559. $19.98.
Laser: LD71659. $39.98.
Norman Taurog, USA, 1951, 95 mins.

Roberta
Ginger Rogers and Fred Astaire are joined by Irene Dunne in this adaptation of the smash Broadway hit, as Ginger, posing as a mysterious countess, and Fred, a stranded band leader looking for a chance to kick up his heels, set Paris awhirl. Contains the famous Jerome Kern hits "Smoke Gets In Your Eyes" and "Lovely To Look At."
VHS: $03104. $19.95.
William A. Seiter, USA, 1935, 106 mins.

Robin and the 7 Hoods
Frank Sinatra stars as the lead criminal in this gangland musical comedy featuring Bing Crosby, Dean Martin, Sammy Davis, Jr. and Peter Falk. These criminals are trapped in the usual murderous competition, only they manage to make everyone laugh and dance in the process.
VHS: $26865. $14.95.
Gordon Douglas, USA, 1964, 124 mins.

Roman Scandals
Comedian Eddie Cantor leaves behind the realities of the Depression for a fantasy trip to Ancient Rome. Lots of fun and plenty of musical numbers. With Gloria Stuart, Ruth Etting, Edward Arnold and Verree Teasdale. Watch closely for Lucille Ball in the chorus of one of the Busby Berkeley production numbers.
VHS: $15490. $19.98.
Laser: LD75250. $34.98.
Frank Tuttle, USA, 1933, 93 mins.

Romance on the High Seas
This romantic musical comedy introduced the dazzling Doris Day in her first feature role. Playing a talented but unfulfilled nightclub singer, she agrees to take a cruise posing as a wealthy socialite who'd rather stay home and spy on her husband. But it's all spoiled when the private dick (Jack Carson) hired to spy on the vacationing wife falls in love with the beautiful impostor. The musical numbers were directed by the legendary Busby Berkeley.
VHS: $14313. $29.98.
Laser: LD70173. $39.98.
Michael Curtiz, USA, 1948, 99 mins.

Rosalie
Big MGM musical starring Eleanor Powell as a princess involved with a West Point cadet. Cole Porter supplied the tunes, including "In the Still of the Night". With Nelson Eddy, Frank Morgan, Ray Bolger, Billy Gilbert and Edna May Oliver. Filmed in glorious black and white.
VHS: $08093. $19.98.
W.S. Van Dyke, USA, 1937, 122 mins.

Rose Marie (1936)
Jeanette MacDonald is the opera star searching for her fugitive brother (James Stewart), as Royal Canadian Mountie Nelson Eddy is searching for the same man, and the two fall in love. "Indian Call" is one of the great songs in this musical.
VHS: $04403. $19.95.
Laser: LD70668. $34.98.
W.S. Van Dyke II, USA, 1936, 110 mins.

Rose Marie (1954)
Mervyn Le Roy's widescreen remake of W.S. Van Dyke II's 1936 filmed operetta, with choreography by Busby Berkeley. The story concerns a Canadian mountie who falls in love with the woman he's supposed to educate. With Howard Keel, Ann Blyth, Fernando Lamas, Bert Lahr and Marjorie Main. Letterboxed edition.
Laser: LD70168. $34.98.
Mervyn Le Roy, USA, 1954, 115 mins.

Rose of Washington Square
Al Jolson provides a number of his legendary hit songs for this musical set during Prohibition. Alice Faye is a Ziegfeld star and Tyrone Power plays her crooked husband, leading ultimately to a showdown with the law. When he hits the skids, Faye must decide what to do.
VHS: $21305. $19.98.
Gregory Ratoff, USA, 1939, 86 mins.

Royal Wedding
Fred Astaire stars as the brother of Jane Powell, both of them in England to perform for Queen Elizabeth's wedding, and each of them finds their true love. Contains one of the most famous of Astaire's dance sequences—the dance on the ceiling and walls. Songs by Alan Jay Lerner.
VHS: $07366. $19.95.
Laser: LD74680. $34.98.
Stanley Donen, USA, 1951, 93 mins.

Second Chorus
Fred Astaire and Burgess Meredith vie for the attention of Paulette Goddard in this musical which co-stars Artie Shaw. Includes "Sweet Sue" and "Swing Concerto."
VHS: $01941. $19.95.
Laser: CLV. LD72028. $29.98.
H.C. Potter, USA, 1940, 83 mins.

Second Fiddle
An ambitious Hollywood publicist (Tyrone Power) stages a romance between a skating instructor (Sonja Henie) and a romantic Hollywood star (Rudy Vallee), and slowly falls in love with the breathtaking skater. Irving Berlin wrote the music. With Edna May Oliver and Lyle Talbot.
VHS: $20254. $19.98.
Sidney Lanfield, USA, 1939, 86 mins.

Sensations
An all-star musical comedy extravaganza starring Eleanor Powell, W.C. Fields, Cab Calloway, Woody Herman, and Sophie Tucker. Powell plays a publicity agent out to book the best acts of the year.
VHS: $12319. $24.95.
Chuck Vincent, USA, 1945, 85 mins.

Serenade
Mario Lanza stars as a fruit picker who sings his way to a better life as a world-renowned opera singer. Complications arise when two women try to claim his affections. Joan Fontaine and Vincent Price co-star.
VHS: $20659. $19.98.
Anthony Mann, USA, 1956, 121 mins.

Seven Brides for Seven Brothers
When outdoorsman Howard Keel decides to get married, his six younger brothers also get the urge. The musical movie inspiration for the tv series contains many toe-tapping numbers, including Russ Tamblyn dancing with an axe. With Jane Powell, Julie Newmar and Ruta Lee.
VHS: $05096. $19.95.
Laser: LD70673. $34.98.
Stanley Donen, USA, 1954, 103 mins.

Seven Hills of Rome
Out and about among the seven hills, Mario Lanza is a popular American singer at the center of a musical romantic comedy involving a classic switch of affections. When he can't find his jet-setting fiance, he turns to a local girl for comfort. With Peggy Castle and Marisa Allasio.
VHS: $20787. $19.98.
Roy Rowland, USA, 1957, 104 mins.

Shall We Dance
One of the best of the Fred Astaire and Ginger Rogers films, in this one the pair star as a dance team who pose as husband and wife in order to achieve stardom. With a hummable score by George Gershwin.
VHS: $01881. $14.98.
Mark Sandrich, USA, 1937, 116 mins.

Ship Ahoy
A romantic comedy musical about a beautiful dancer on a cruise ship who is enlisted to transport a dangerous package, completely unaware she's duped by foreign agents. With Eleanor Powell, Red Skelton, Bert Lahr and Frank Sinatra in a supporting performance as a shipmate.
VHS: $18555. $19.98.
Edward Buzzell, USA, 1942, 95 mins.

Show Boat
This musical collaboration of Jerome Kern and Oscar Hammerstein captures the heartbreak, excitement and romantic preoccupations on an old line Mississippi show boat. Hammerstein wrote the screenplay, adapted from Edna Ferber's novel. With Irene Dunne, Allan Jones, Helen Morgan, Paul Robeson (who performs "Old Man River") and Charles Winninger. "Sentimental, literary, but oddly appealing" (Graham Greene). Available in two versions, a three-disc collection or a single disc.
Laser: CAV, 3 discs, Criterion. LD70459. $124.95.
Laser: CLV, 1 disc, Criterion. LD70460. $49.95.
James Whale, USA, 1936, 110 mins.

Show Business
An entertaining romp through the transformation of the American musical theater that echoes the true-life story of its star: the legendary showman Eddie Cantor. A valuable record of classic vaudeville acts.
VHS: $11607. $19.98.
Edwin L. Marin, USA, 1944, 92 mins.

Silk Stockings
Cole Porter wrote the lyrics for this funny and energetic musical version of *Ninotchka*. Cyd Charisse is a KGB agent sent to Paris to kidnap a defecting composer. Fred Astaire is the playboy who shows her the charmed side of life in the West. Director Mamoulian's last film.
VHS: $04405. $19.98.
Laser: LD70678. $34.98.
Rouben Mamoulian, USA, 1957, 117 mins.

Singin' in the Rain
Deservedly one of the best-loved movies of all time! An exhilarating and fast-moving musical comedy that traces the transition from silent films to "talkies," starring dancing Gene Kelly and Debbie Reynolds, with Donald O'Connor, Jean Hagen and Rita Moreno.
VHS: $15851. $19.98.
Laser: CAV, 2 discs, Criterion. LD70463. $89.95.
Laser: CLV, 1 disc, Criterion. LD70464. $39.95.
Laser: CLV, MGM. LD70679. $24.98.
Laser: CAV, MGM. LD70680. $39.98.
Gene Kelly/Stanley Donen, USA, 1951, 103 mins.

The Singing Nun
Debbie Reynolds, Greer Garson, Katharine Ross and Agnes Moorehead appear in this comedic tale of a starkly unconventional Belgian nun (Reynolds) trying to reconcile her musical ambitions with her religious calling.
VHS: $17339. $19.98.
Henry Koster, USA, 1966, 97 mins.

Skirts Ahoy!
Esther Williams joins Vivian Blaine and Joan Evans as a trio of Navy Waves on the lookout for love in this frothy musical comedy. Williams sings, dances and sidestrokes her way through ten weeks of boot camp training.
VHS: $16609. $19.98.
Sidney Lanfield, USA, 1952, 109 mins.

The Sky's the Limit
Fred Astaire plays a Flying Tiger pilot on leave in Manhattan and features Johnny Mercer and Harold Arlen songs like "My Shining Hour" and "One for My Baby and One More for the Road." Astaire staged his own dance numbers in this production.
VHS: $03235. $19.98.
Edward H. Griffith, USA, 1943, 101 mins.

Small Town Girl
A romantic comedy about a handsome stranger who's trapped into a marriage proposal when he's drunk, starring Jane Powell, Farley Granger, Bobby Van, Ann Miller, Nat King Cole. Oscar nomination for the song "My Flaming Heart". Busby Berkeley choreographed the numbers.
VHS: $12144. $19.95.
Laser: Chapter search. Includes original theatrical trailer. LD71666. $34.98.
Leslie Kardos, USA, 1953, 93 mins.

Smilin' Through
Jeanette MacDonald stars in this second remake of the 1922 Norma Talmadge vehicle about a man who loses his fiancee on his wedding day and then raises a niece who grows to look exactly like his long-lost love. With Gene Raymond and Brian Aherne. In color and filled with songs like *A Little Love, A Little Kiss* and *Land of Hope and Glory*.
VHS: $08095. $19.98.
Frank Borzage, USA, 1941, 100 mins.

Song o' My Heart
The world's most beloved Irish tenor, John McCormack, in his first feature film, sings more than a dozen songs, including: "Then You'll Remember Me," "I Hear You Calling Me" and "The Rose of Tralee." This complete version of the film has never before been available on home video. The cast also includes the young Maureen O'Sullivan in her motion picture debut.
VHS: $14240. $39.95.
Frank Borzage, USA, 1929, 91 mins.

Song of Norway
A biography of composer Edvard Grieg with versions of his best music. With Florence Henderson, Toralv Maurstad, Christina Schollin and Edward G. Robinson.
VHS: $05972. $59.98.
Andrew L. Stone, 1943, 142 mins.

Song of the Islands
Victor Mature is the new arrival to the Pacific Island paradise, Betty Grable the local girl whom he fights with and romances.
VHS: $09446. $19.98.
Walter Lang, USA, 1942, 75 mins.

Sound of Music
The hills are alive with the sounds of the Von Trapp family in this beloved Rodgers and Hammerstein epic musical. Julie Andrews and Christopher Plummer lead a cast of wholesome warblers through some terrific scenery and memorable songs. Five Oscars including Best Picture.
VHS: $04772. $29.95.
Robert Wise, USA, 1965, 172 mins.

South Pacific (Gaynor)
An enchanting adaptation of the Rodgers and Hammerstein musical, based on James Michener's *Tales of the South Pacific*. A young Navy man falls in love with an Island girl while stationed in the South Pacific. With Mitzi Gaynor and Rossano Brazzi.
VHS: $04406. $19.98.
Joshua Logan, USA, 1957, 150 mins.

South Pacific (London Sessions)
A diverse group of international performers, including Kiri Te Kanawa, Jose Carreras, Sarah Vaughan, Mandy Patinkin, and the London Symphony Orchestra gather in London to record the music from *South Pacific*, the great musical, in a new way. A remarkable performance is the result. England, 1986, 60 mins.
VHS: $01773. $19.98.

Springtime in the Rockies
A musical comedy from Twentieth Century-Fox with an all star cast that includes Betty Grable, John Payne, Carmen Miranda, Jackie Gleason, Cesar Romero, Charlotte Greenwood and Edward Everett Horton. In Technicolor with Harry James and his band. Miranda sings "Chattanooga Choo Choo". Lots of laughs and musical numbers when a Broadway couple go West.
VHS: $09833. $19.95.
Irving Cummings, USA, 1942, 91 mins.

Stand Up and Cheer
Shirley Temple does her best to help cure America's Depression-era blues in this upbeat musical comedy that suggests laughter is the best remedy for despair. James Dunn co-stars and Shirley sings, "Baby, Take a Bow."
VHS: $09995. $19.98.
Hamilton McFadden, USA, 1934, 69 mins.

A Star Is Born
Barbra Streisand and Kris Kristofferson are the leads in this third version. A talented wife whose star is on the rise quickly overshadows her husband as his career fades. Streisand sings "Evergreen", which won an Oscar for Best Song. With Gary Busey, Oliver Clark and Paul Mazursky.
VHS: $07006. $19.95.
Laser: Letterboxed. LD71470. $39.98.
Frank Pierson, USA, 1976, 140 mins.

Star Spangled Rhythm
In this WWII extravaganza Bing Crosby is crowded by a host of famous MGM stars, including Bob Hope, Ray Milland, Veronica Lake, Susan Hayward, Dick Powell, Mary Martin, Cecil B. De Mille and many others. It includes that favorite hit, "That Old Black Magic".
VHS: $21203. $14.98.
George Marshall, USA, 1942, 99 mins.

Star!
Robert Wise's ambitious musical biography of Gertrude Lawrence was a box office failure when first released. The studio cut nearly an hour from its running time and re-released the film under the title *Those Were the Happy Times*. This expressive work, buttressed by 17 songs from Cole Porter, Kurt Weill and George and Ira Gershwin, dramatizes Lawrence's (Julie Andrews) spectacular rise from seedy London vaudeville halls to West End superstar. The emotional focus is played out through her two principal relationships, her friendship with playwright Noel Coward (Daniel Massey) and her marriage to banker Richard Aldrich (Richard Crenna). With John Collin, Robert Reed, Bruce Forsyth, Beryl Reid and Jenny Agutter.
VHS: $19485. $89.98.
Robert Wise, USA, 1968, 175 mins.

Starlight—A Musical Movie

The talented campers at an upstate New York summer camp for the performing arts must put on a show that will raise enough money to head off the impending sale to a villainous real estate developer (William Hickey). Sounds like "Fame" meets "Meatballs". With the talents of Ricki Lake, Victor Cook, Danny Gerard and Tichina Arnold. Winner of the 1988 Ruby Slipper Award for Best Feature. USA, 1988, 78 mins.
VHS: S10069. $79.95.

Stars and Stripes Forever

Clifton Webb is a pure delight as "March King" John Philip Sousa in this entertaining biography of the man who gave the world some of its most stirring music. Co-stars Robert Wagner, Debra Paget and Ruth Hussey.
VHS: S14506. $19.98.
Henry Koster, USA, 1952, 89 mins.

Step Lively

A musical version of *Room Service* with Frank Sinatra and George Murphy. Scored by Cahn and Styne. A young playwright is forced to become the lead in his own play.
VHS: S10641. $19.98.
Tim Whelan, USA, 1944, 89 mins.

Stop the World I Want to Get Off

This hit from the stages of London and Broadway features the well-known musical songs "What Kind of Fool Am I?", "Once in a Lifetime" and "Gonna Build a Mountain". Shot from a live performance.
VHS: S20656. $19.98.

Stormy Weather

Following the revisionist success of *Cabin in the Sky*, the few black entertainers allowed to work consistently were enlisted for this all-black musical that features Lena Horne, Cab Calloway, Fats Waller and Bill Robinson. The affairs and times of some talented war-era entertainers are loosely connected as a storyline to the powerful music, including Waller's "Ain't Misbehavin'" and Horne's title rendition, which provide depth and resonance. Featuring *Casablanca*'s Dooley Wilson.
VHS: S02828. $19.98.
Andrew L. Stone, USA, 1943, 78 mins.

Stowaway

Shirley Temple, Alice Faye, Robert Young star in this musical adventure of a young orphan in China adopted by a bickering young couple. Shirley smooths things over.
VHS: S05901. $19.98.
William A. Seiter, USA, 1936, 86 mins.

Strike Up the Band

Busby Berkeley directs Mickey Rooney and Judy Garland in this lively musical about Mickey trying to get a job with the Paul Whiteman orchestra. Music by the Gershwin brothers, Alan Arthur Freed and Roger Edens. Tunes include the title song and "La Conga". With Larry Nunn, William Tracy and Paul Whiteman.
VHS: S08096. $19.98.
Laser: LD70688. $39.98.
Busby Berkeley, USA, 1940, 120 mins.

The Student Prince

Sigmund Romberg's opera is the basis for this romantic drama about the heir to the throne (Edmund Purdom) given one last fling in Heidelberg, where he falls madly in love with a forlorn barmaid played by Ann Blyth. With John Ericson, Louis Calhern and Edmund Gwenn. Mario Lanza's singing voice is substituted for Purdom's voice.
VHS: S17654. $19.98.
Richard Thorpe, USA, 1954, 107 mins.

Summer Holiday

Warm and winning Americana from Eugene O'Neill's *Ah, Wilderness*. Mickey Rooney plays an eager lad coming of age in an era of Stanley Steamers and nickel beer. This delightful musical also features excellent supporting performances from Walter Huston and Agnes Moorehead.
VHS: S14169. $19.98.
Laser: LD71167. $39.98.
Rouben Mamoulian, USA, 1948, 92 mins.

Summer Stock

A theater troupe lead by Gene Kelly takes over a farm owned by Judy Garland, and Judy falls in love with show business. With Eddie Bracken, Marjorie Main, Phil Silvers.
VHS: S04983. $19.98.
Laser: LD74683. $34.98.
Charles Walters, USA, 1950, 100 mins.

Sun Valley Serenade

Milton Berle and friends hit the slopes of Sun Valley in this lighthearted romance about a musician who adopts a beautiful Norwegian war refugee. The second of two Fox musicals about the great Glenn Miller.
VHS: S14508. $19.98.
H. Bruce Humberstone, USA, 1941, 86 mins.

Sweeney Todd:
Demon Barber of Fleet Street

Stephen Sondheim's smash musical of a murdering barber and the resultant meat pies made by his wife stars Angela Lansbury and George Hearn.
VHS: S02027. $39.98.
Harold Prince, USA, 1984, 139 mins.

Sweet Charity

Shirley MacLaine has the title role in director Bob Fosse's debut musical about the dime-a-dance girl with the heart of gold. This uncut version is based on the Neil Simon play based on Fellini's *Nights of Cabiria*. Highlights of the Cy Coleman-Dorothy Fields score include "If My Friends Could See Me Now" and "Big Spender."
VHS: S03493. $19.95.
Laser: LD70085. $44.98.
Bob Fosse, USA, 1969, 148 mins.

Sweethearts

Jeanette MacDonald and Nelson Eddy play a temperamental couple of theatre stars currently performing a Victor Herbert operetta. Frank Morgan is their manipulating manager. With Ray Bolger, Florence Rice, and Mischa Auer. Script by Dorothy Parker and husband Alan Campbell. An Oscar for cinematography.
VHS: S09870. $19.98.
Laser: LD71691. $34.98.
W.S. Van Dyke, USA, 1938, 120 mins.

Swing High, Swing Low

Carole Lombard and Fred MacMurray star as two entertainers who meet aboard a cruise ship bound for Panama. Musical comedy that includes Dorothy Lamour and Anthony Quinn.
VHS: S01291. $19.98.
Mitchell Leisen, USA, 1937, 95 mins.

Swing It Professor

Pinky Tomlin and Milburn Stone star in this delightful musical comedy. Tomlin is a college music professor who will not permit jazz in his classroom.
VHS: S09583. $29.95.
Marshall Neilan, USA, 1937, 62 mins.

Take Me Out to the Ball Game

Gene Kelly, Frank Sinatra and Jules Munshin are star players for the Wolves. Esther Williams is the new manager of this turn-of-the-century team. The drive for the pennant has never included so many musical numbers. Including "O'Brien to Ryan to Goldberg".
VHS: S04986. $19.95.
Laser: LD70162. $34.98.
Busby Berkeley, USA, 1949, 90 mins.

Tales from Vienna Woods

Magda Schneider, Wolf Albach-Retty and Walter Slezak star in this musical romance featuring music by Johann Strauss. A singing auto mechanic inherits a castle that fails to live up to his initial high expectations. Fortunately there are two women competing for his attention to liven things up. The Vienna Philharmonic Orchestra provides the music for this film set in a Vienna still unharmed by war. German with English subtitles.
VHS: S23987. $24.95.
George Jacoby, Austria, 1937, 82 mins.

Tauber in Blossom Time

Tauber stars as composer Franz Schubert in this musical set in early 19th-century Vienna. He loves a woman who loves someone else and despite these feelings, he helps her win the affections of this other man. Among the great songs used in this film are "Love Lost for Evermore," "Serenade," "Impatience" and "Faith in Spring," all by Schubert.
VHS: S24035. $34.95.
Paul L. Stein, Great Britain, 1934, 87 mins.

Tea for Two

Doris Day is cast as Nanette Carter, an heiress who invests $25,000 in a 1926 Broadway show not knowing that once she has the lead, she doesn't have the money to spend after all, due to a stock market crash. To secure the promised funds, she must say no to every question for the next 48 hours to win a bet. With Gordon MacRae, Gene Nelson, Eve Arden and Billy DeWolfe. Based loosely on the popular musical *No, No Nanette*. Songs include "I Only Have Eyes for You," "Oh Me, Oh My", "I Know That You Know" and "I Want to Be Happy".
VHS: S15782. $19.98.
David Butler, USA, 1950, 98 mins.

The Tender Trap

Julius Jay Epstein (*Casablanca*) adapted the play by Max Schulman and Robert Paul Smith about a shrewd New York agent and notorious lothario (Frank Sinatra) who meets his match in an intelligent and gritty young actress (Debbie Reynolds). Shot in widescreen by Paul Vogel, with a sharp title song by James Van Heusen and lyrics by Sammy Cahn. With David Wayne and Celeste Holm.
VHS: S18012. $19.98.
Laser: LD70147. $34.98.
Charles Walters, USA, 1955, 111 mins.

Thank Your Lucky Stars

Warner Brothers' wartime effort features cameos by many of the studio stars, including Bette Davis singing, Humphrey Bogart, Errol Flynn, Olivia de Havilland and Spike Jones and his City Slickers.
VHS: S02258. $29.98.
David Butler, USA, 1943, 130 mins.

That Girl from Paris

Opera great Lily Pons is a French singer who escapes an impending marriage to join an American swing band. A fun mixture of slapstick, swing music and classic opera.
VHS: S11609. $19.98.
Leigh Jason, USA, 1936, 105 mins.

That Midnight Kiss

Mario Lanza's first screen appearance in this biography of an unknown who gets his first break and enters into a tentative affair. With Kathryn Grayson, Ethel Barrymore, Jose Turbi and Keenan Wynn.
VHS: S17655. $19.98.
Norman Taurog, USA, 1949, 98 mins.

That's Dancing

Gene Kelly, Liza Minnelli, Baryshnikov and Ray Bolger host a look at some of the great dance scenes in Hollywood musicals from *Fred Astaire* films through *West Side Story*.
VHS: S03365. $29.95.
Laser: LD71154. $39.98.
Jack Haley Jr., USA, 1985, 105 mins.

That's Entertainment

A cavalcade of stars host scenes from over 100 MGM musicals, with many cherished moments. Including Fred Astaire, Peter Lawford, Bing Crosby, Gene Kelly, Liza Minnelli, Debbie Reynolds, Frank Sinatra and many others.
VHS: S03329. $19.95.
Laser: CAV. LD70691. $69.98.
Jack Haley, Jr., USA, 1974, 132 mins.

That's Entertainment II

A spectacular sequel that interweaves footage from 75 films featuring some of the best examples of song and dance in the American cinema. Includes sequences of Gene Kelly and Fred Astaire dancing together for the first time in 30 years.
VHS: S01598. $19.95.
Laser: LD70693. $39.98.
Laser: LD71152. $69.98.
Gene Kelly, USA, 1976, 133 mins.

That's Entertainment III

This collection of clips from classic MGM musicals features elaborate production numbers and outtakes of never-before-seen footage. June Allyson, Cyd Charisse, Lena Horne, Gene Kelly, Ann Miller, Debbie Reynolds, Mickey Rooney and Esther Williams are just some of the stars featured in this exciting new collection.
VHS: S22188. $19.98.
Bud Friedgen/Michael J. Sheridan, USA, 1993, 113 mins.

That's Singing

The Best of Broadway—a celebration of American musical comedy, a star-studded Broadway event! USA, 1986, 120 mins.
VHS: S01530. $19.98.

There's No Business Like Show Business

Dan Dailey and Ethel Merman head a performing family that includes Donald O'Connor, Mitzi Gaynor and Johnny Ray. They all like to sing songs by Irving Berlin, and Marilyn Monroe raises everyone's temperature with a sizzling version of "Heat Wave". The script was nominated for an Oscar and the musical numbers are quite energetic. See for yourself why it's like no business you know.
VHS: S07681. $19.98.
Walter Lang, USA, 1954, 117 mins.

They Shall Have Music

Master violinist Jascha Heifetz plays himself in this sincere melodrama about poor kids and classical music. When the inner city music school run by Walter Brennan faces a financial crisis, his students organize a benefit concert. With Joel McCrea, Andrea Leeds, Marjorie Main, Porter Hall and Gene Reynolds. Watch for Diana Lynn as the little girl at the piano.
VHS: S15841. $19.98.
Archie Mayo, USA, 1939, 105 mins.

This is the Army

George Murphy plays Ronald Reagan's father is this topical melange of songs and skits. Also with Joe Louis, Kate Smith and a host of others.
VHS: S02957. $19.95.
Michael Curtiz, USA, 1943, 121 mins.

A Thousand and One Nights

Cornel Wilde stars as Aladdin with Adele Jergens as his love interest. Aladdin is just a poor boy who loves a princess. All that changes when he becomes the owner of a lamp inhabited by a beautiful genie. Despite the genie's own designs on her master she helps reunite Aladdin and the princess. Along the way there is adventure and intrigue in this delightful musical from the golden era of Hollywood.
VHS: S27181. $19.95.
Alfred E. Green, USA, 1945, 92 mins.

Thousands Cheer

All-star World War II musical featuring Gene Kelly, Kathryn Grayson, Judy Garland, Mickey Rooney and a host of others. Glossy, snappy and designed to inspire.
VHS: S01595. $19.98.
Laser: LD70160. $39.98.
George Sidney, USA, 1943, 126 mins.

Three Daring Daughters

When Jeanette MacDonald decides to marry again, Jose Iturbi is not welcomed with open arms by her three daughters, Jane Powell, Anne Todd and Mary Elinor Donahue. But with a little romance, some songs and a cheerful attitude, no problem is insurmountable.
VHS: S20790. $19.98.
Fred M. Wilcox, USA, 1948, 115 mins.

Three Little Words

Famous songwriters Harry Ruby and Bert Kalmar on their climb to fame, with Fred Astaire, Vera-Ellen, Red Skelton, Debbie Reynolds. Songs include "Who's Sorry Now?" and "Thinking of You."
VHS: S05386. $19.98.
Laser: LD71168. $34.98.
Richard Thorpe, USA, 1950, 102 mins.

The Three Musketeers

A spirited musical adaptation of Alexandre Dumas' popular novel combines slapstick farce (with the appearance of the Ritz Brothers), madcap action and romance. Don Ameche plays D'Artagnan and Binnie Barnes is Lady DeWinter. With Lionel Atwill, Miles Mander, Gloria Stuart and Pauline Moore.
VHS: S20253. $19.98.
Allan Dwan, USA, 1939, 73 mins.

Three Smart Girls

Deanna Durbin was introduced as "Universal's new discovery" in this delightful debut that launched her film career. The adventure begins when three lovely, high spirited girls attempt to reunite their mother and father, who divorced a decade ago. Also features Ray Milland.
VHS: S23279. $19.98.
Henry Koster, USA, 1936, 84 mins.

Three Smart Girls Grow Up

This sequel to *Three Smart Girls* finds Deanna Durbin reprising her role as Penny, the youngest of three sisters. This time she is determined to marry off her two older sisters. Robert Cummings and William Lundigan are the lucky fellas subjected to the affections and schemes of the charming sisters.
VHS: S23280. $19.98.
Henry Koster, USA, 1939, 90 mins.

Till the Clouds Roll By

Musical biography of Jerome Kern, the celebrated composer of stage musicals, including *Show Boat* and screenplays such as *Swing Time* and *Lady Be Good*. Starring Robert Walker as Kern, with Judy Garland, Van Johnson and Lena Horne.
VHS: S01597. $19.95.
Laser: LD74685. $39.98.
Richard Whorf, USA, 1946, 137 mins.

Tin Pan Alley

During World War I struggling song writers John Payne and Jack Oakie pair up with the singing Blane Sisters, played by Alice Faye and Betty Grable. Alfred Newman won an Oscar for his delightful musical score making this song-packed musical comedy.
VHS: S21302. $19.98.
Walter Lang, USA, 1940, 94 mins.

The Toast of New Orleans

If you guessed raisin, you're wrong. Mario Lanza sings "Be My Love" and selections from several popular operas as he plays a Cajun fisherman attracted to a society opera star. Kathryn Grayson also lends her voice to the love story of a woman torn between a spectacular voice and the charm of David Niven. With Rita Moreno.
VHS: S04984. $19.98.
Norman Taurog, USA, 1950, 98 mins.

Tonight and Every Night

Rita Hayworth and Janet Blair star in living color as a pair of London musical entertainers who never miss a performance during World War II. Heartaches and the Heinie's bombs will not deter the spirit of these troupers. With Shelley Winters, Lee Bowman.
VHS: S04674. $29.95.
Victor Saville, USA, 1945, 92 mins.

Too Many Girls

Lucille Ball as a madcap heiress who enlivens a small town college with her antics (and wood ticks). Also stars newcomer Desi Arnaz.
VHS: S10642. $19.98.
George Abbott, USA, 1940, 85 mins.

Top Hat

A Fred Astaire and Ginger Rogers classic! A knockout musical featuring a great score by Irving Berlin.
VHS: S01362. $14.98.
Mark Sandrich, USA, 1935, 97 mins.

Two Girls and a Sailor

Terrific musical entertainment set during the war. June Allyson, Gloria de Haven, Van Johnson, Xavier Cugat and his Orchestra, Jimmy Durante, Tom Drake, Lena Horne, Carlos Ramirez, Harry James and his Orchestra, Jose Iturbi, Gracie Allen, Virginia O'Brien star.
VHS: S12143. $19.95.
Laser: LD70154. $39.98.
Richard Thorpe, USA, 1944, 124 mins.

Two Tickets to Broadway

Here's your one ticket to the behind-the-scenes antics of the early days of TV. A handful of young and hopeful singers, dancers and novelty acts all vie for stardom. Janet Leigh, Gloria De Haven, Ann Miller star.
VHS: S11604. $19.98.
Jerry Wald, USA, 1951, 106 mins.

The Unsinkable Molly Brown

Debbie Reynolds is the feisty title character who earns her moniker by surviving a trip on the *Titanic*. Based on the true story of the wealthiest woman in Denver in the late 1800's. Meredith Willson's score includes "Belly up to the Bar, Boys". With Ed Begley and Harve Presnell.
VHS: S07157. $19.95.
Charles Walters, USA, 1964, 128 mins.

The Vagabond Lover

Rudy Vallee is suddenly thrust into the limelight when he impersonates a famous band leader while conducting his college orchestra. Soon the whole world is clamoring for them. Marie Dressler is also featured in this light musical entertainment.
VHS: S23822. $24.95.
Marshall Neilan, USA, 1929, 66 mins.

Waikiki Wedding

Bing Crosby stars in this delightful musical comedy set in Hawaii. Bing is a press agent who has designs on a beautiful young woman, Shirley Ross, the Miss Pineapple Girl. The song "Sweet Leilani" won an Oscar. Martha Raye is also featured.
VHS: S25011. $14.98.
Frank Tuttle, USA, 1937, 99 mins.

Week-End in Havana

Alice Faye finds herself torn between John Payne and Cesar Romero in beautiful old Havana. Faye is stranded there when a cruise ship runs aground and Payne shows up to smooth things over, but it gets a little more serious than that during the warm Caribbean nights. Carmen Miranda brings her exciting nightlife personality to this charming musical comedy.
VHS: S21303. $19.98.
Walter Lang, USA, 1941, 80 mins.

West Side Story

An extravaganza acclaimed for its musical and choreographic expertise. Score by Leonard Bernstein, lyrics by Stephen Sondheim, choreography by Jerome Robbins, starring Natalie Wood (her songs were dubbed by Marni Nixon) and Rita Moreno.
VHS: S01444. $19.98.
Laser: CAV, widescreen. LD70485. $124.95.
Laser: CLV, widescreen. LD70486. $69.95.
Robert Wise/J. Robbins, USA, 1961, 152 mins.

White Christmas

Bing Crosby and Danny Kaye team up as a show biz act, are joined by Rosemary Clooney and Vera-Ellen, and trek off to Vermont for a Christmas holiday. With a classic score by Irving Berlin that includes "Count Your Blessings Instead of Sheep" and, of course, "White Christmas".
VHS: S01585. $14.95.
Michael Curtiz, USA, 1954, 120 mins.

Whoopee

Eddie Cantor became a star in his screen debut in this comedy about a hypochondriac who goes west for his health. Cantor sings "Making Whoopee" and "My Baby Just Cares for Me." With Eleanor Hunt, Paul Gregory, John Rutherford and Ethel Shutta. Musical numbers by Busby Berkeley. Watch for a young Betty Grable in the chorus. Filmed in early Technicolor.
VHS: S03130. $19.98.
Thornton Freeland, USA, 1930 93 mins.

Wiz
The smash Broadway musical based on the L. Frank Baum book features Diana Ross as Dorothy, with a pre-surgical Michael Jackson, Nipsey Russell and Lena Horne.
VHS: S05098. $19.98.
Sidney Lumet, USA, 1978, 133 mins.

Words and Music
This film bio of Richard Rodgers and Lorenz Hart is highlighted by the likes of Judy Garland, Lena Horne, Gene Kelly, Perry Como and Mel Torme performing a treasure-trove of lavish production numbers and show-stopping solos. Don't miss Judy Garland and Mickey Rooney's duet of *I Wish I Were in Love Again*. Starring Tom Drake and Mickey Rooney.
VHS: S15855. $19.98.
Norman Taurog, USA, 1948, 122 mins.

Xanadu
Olivia Newton-John is a muse to a young roller-boogie artist in this contemporary musical. Music by John Ferrar and the Electric Light Orchestra is featured. Gene Kelly is also present but it really is a chance for Olivia to sing and dance amid wild, futuristic sets.
VHS: S21857. $14.98.
Robert Greenwald, USA, 1980, 88 mins.

Yankee Doodle Dandy
James Cagney won a richly deserved Oscar for his red, white an' blue account of the life of George M. Cohan. He sings, he dances, he talks to the president of the United States. Filmed in B&W though two colorized versions exist. With Walter Huston, Joan Leslie, Jeanne Cagney, S.Z. Sakall and Rosemary DeCamp.
VHS: S01835. $14.95.
Laser: LD70714. $39.98.
Michael Curtiz, USA, 1942, 126 mins.

Yentl
Barbra Streisand directs herself in a sweeping entertainment based on the Isaac Bashevis Singer short story about a young woman who disguises herself as a young man in order to study the Talmud. With Amy Irving and Mandy Patinkin.
VHS: S03476. $19.95.
Laser: LD70718. $39.98.
Barbra Streisand, USA, 1983, 134 mins.

Yolanda and the Thief
Fred Astaire dances and romances with Lucille Bremer in this classical musical fantasy. Astaire is a slick con man out to swindle heiress Yolanda by posing as her guardian angel, but his plans go awry when she steals his heart instead.
VHS: S03102. $19.98.
Laser: LD71784. $34.98.
Vincente Minnelli, USA, 1945, 109 mins.

You Were Never Lovelier
Fred Astaire romances the beautiful Rita Hayworth to a Jerome Kern-Johnny Mercer score in this musical classic set in Buenos Aires. Featured songs include "I'm Old Fashioned" and the title song. Great dance numbers.
VHS: S04750. $19.95.
William A. Seiter, USA, 1942, 92 mins.

You'll Never Get Rich
Robert Benchley is the lecherous stage producer with an eye for chorus girl Sheila Winthrop (Rita Hayworth), while his friend Fred Astaire becomes a suitor for Sheila's affections. A musical comedy.
VHS: S04751. $19.95.
Sidney Lanfield, USA, 1941, 88 mins.

You're the Top—The Cole Porter Story
Some of the most unique, romantic and wittiest songs ever written were products of Cole Porter's genius. Clearly one of the greatest composers to date, his wit and sophisticated style are still the standards to which today's composers and lyricists aspire. To commemorate the 100th anniversary of the late Cole Porter's birth, this profile provides an entertaining look at the man who embraced an elite lifestyle—and chronicled the world of high society. Performances include: Fred Astaire and Ginger Rogers, Judy Garland and Gene Kelly, Grace Kelly and Bing Crosby, and many more. 56 mins.
VHS: S14106. $24.95.

Young at Heart
Frank Sinatra steals Doris Day's heart from Gig Young. Both of the young lovers sing. Songs included are "One for My Baby" and "Someone to Watch over Me". 40th anniversary edition. Digitally remastered. Includes original trailer.
VHS: S04514. $19.95.
Gordon Douglas, USA, 1954, 117 mins.

Ziegfeld Follies
Notable for Fred Astaire's only dance with Gene Kelly, this all-star vehicle also features great performances from William Powell, Judy Garland, Lucille Ball, Lena Horne, Fanny Brice, Red Skelton, Cyd Charisse, Edward Arnold, Esther Williams and Virginia O'Brien. Collector's edition. New digital transfer. Includes original theatrical trailer, original overture and exit music.
VHS: S04407. $19.95.
Laser: LD70723. $34.98.
Vincente Minnelli, USA, 1946, 110 mins.

Ziegfeld Girl
One of Hollywood's great, lavish musicals, with James Stewart, Hedy Lamarr, Lana Turner and Judy Garland. The subject is Ziegfeld's girls as Turner, Lamarr and Garland are recruited by him with their lives changed forever. Contains Busby Berkeley's famous number, "You Stepped out of a Dream," and Judy Garland singing "I'm Always Chasing Rainbows."
VHS: S11161. $19.98.
Laser: LD70724. $19.98.
Robert Z. Leonard, USA, 1941, 131 mins.

Zoot Suit
A stylized musical about the arrest of Chicano gang members in Los Angeles and the resulting controversial trial. Written and directed by Luis Valdez, based on his own play. Starring Daniel Valdez, Tyne Daly, Mike Gomez, Abel Franco and Edward James Olmos as El Pachuco, the spirit of the Zoot Suit experience.
VHS: S14453. $14.95.
Luis Valdez, USA, 1981, 103 mins.

BLAKE EDWARDS

10
Dudley Moore is suffering a mid-life crises that he feels can be solved by a romantic interlude with Bo Derek. Julie Andrews, as the mature relationship in Moore's life, is not amused. The movie that made Ravel's *Bolero* a hit record. With Robert Webber, Brian Dennehy, Sam Jones and Dee Wallace.
VHS: S06198. $19.98.
Blake Edwards, USA, 1979, 121 mins.

Blind Date
Bruce Willis makes his starring feature film debut as a serious, corporate-minded young man who makes the mistake of accepting a blind date with Kim Basinger (as a brunette). Under the influence of alcohol she destroys his life and they fall in love. It's a comedy.
VHS: S04672. $14.95.
Blake Edwards, USA, 1987, 95 mins.

Breakfast at Tiffany's
Audrey Hepburn is superb in this dazzling romantic comedy based on Truman Capote's novella. Audrey is the New York playgirl with a secret, determined to marry a Brazilian millionaire, who falls in love with her next-door neighbor, George Peppard.
VHS: S03776. $14.95.
Laser: Widescreen. LD75307. $39.98.
Blake Edwards, USA, 1961, 114 mins.

Breakfast at Tiffany's: Collector's Edition
Audrey Hepburn and George Peppard star in this classic film based on a story by Truman Capote about love in Manhattan. Henry Mancini wrote the score that won an Oscar for this unforgettable comedy. Hepburn is magical as the young woman who achieves her wildest dreams. This version includes the original theatrical trailer.
VHS: S21768. $59.95.
Laser: Widescreen. LD75392. $79.98.
Blake Edwards, USA, 1961, 114 mins.

Curse of the Pink Panther
Shot simultaneously with *Trail of the Pink Panther*, Blake Edwards tries to preserve his popular series by installing Ted Wass, playing "the world's worst detective," to replace Clouseau, who has disappeared. With Joanna Lumley, Herbert Lom, David Niven, Robert Wagner, Capucine, Harvey Korman and Burt Kwouk.
VHS: S20409. $19.98.
Blake Edwards, USA, 1983, 110 mins.

Days of Wine and Roses
Jack Lemmon and Lee Remick star in this harrowing look at the lives of an alcoholic pair. Lemmon is an advertising executive who drags his wife into his hellish habit. Based on J.P. Miller's television play, this film received many Oscar nominations and won an Oscar for Henry Mancini's title song. Also featuring Jack Klugman and Charles Bickford. The video duplicates the experience of a night at the theater, with a Bugs Bunny cartoon (*Martian Through Georgia*), a newsreel, and previews for *Gypsy* and *Rome Adventure*.
VHS: S25896. $19.98.
Blake Edwards, USA, 1962, 138 mins.

The Great Race
1908's New York/Paris auto race zips along in one gear: hilarious! Join Jack Lemmon, Tony Curtis and Natalie Wood. 2,357 pies are thrown before the end credits.
VHS: S14565. $19.98.
Laser: Letterboxed. LD74728. $39.98.
Blake Edwards, USA, 1965, 160 mins.

The Man Who Loved Women
Remake of the Truffaut film features Burt Reynolds and Julie Andrews.
VHS: S05368. $79.95.
Blake Edwards, USA, 1983, 110 mins.

Micki and Maude
Dudley Moore stars in this hilarious comedy about a lovable bigamist. The fun really begins when both wives become pregnant and are delivering in adjoining rooms at the hospital. Several laugh-out-loud scenes.
VHS: S00852. $79.95.
Blake Edwards, Great Britain, 1984, 120 mins.

Operation Petticoat
Cary Grant commands the submarine *Sea Tiger* during WW II and the war is going fine until he meets military con artist Tony Curtis. Then he must rescue and house a detachment of nurses and meet the enemy in a pink painted sub. With Dina Merrill and Arthur O'Connell. Later a tv series. Letterboxed.
VHS: S04242. $19.95.
Blake Edwards, USA, 1959, 120 mins.

The Party
Peter Sellers teams up with Blake Edwards to make a film that does not include a certain French policeman but does provide plenty of comical embarrassments. Sellers is a bumbling Indian actor—the kind with the turbans—who finds his film career might be advanced by attending a posh Hollywood party—if he doesn't destroy his host's home in the process. With Claudine Longet, Denny Miller and Gavin McLeod.
VHS: S11734. $19.98.
Laser: LD71166. $34.98.
Blake Edwards, USA, 1968, 99 mins.

The Perfect Furlough
An early slapstick work from Blake Edwards (*10*) stars Tony Curtis as a smooth Lothario offered a "perfect furlough" from an Arctic outpost to romance a beautiful film star (Linda Cristal). But military psychiatrist Janet Leigh steps in to restore order following a disastrous publicity gimmick and woo Curtis' wavering affection.
VHS: S02787. $19.95.
Blake Edwards, USA, 1958, 93 mins.

The Pink Panther
The film that established director Blake Edwards' slightly subversive point of view and heightened the diversity of Peter Sellers. Sellers is Inspector Clouseau, the perpetually inept detective in pursuit of David Niven, the charming and brilliant cat burglar known as the Phantom. Robert Wagner, Capucine and Claudia Cardinale are along for the ride. Music by Henry Mancini.
VHS: S02328. $14.95.
Laser: LD70655. $34.98.
Blake Edwards, Great Britain, 1964, 118 mins.

The Pink Panther Strikes Again
Inspector Clouseau is back on the job and before the case is solved, expect an avalanche of comic anarchy. The character created by Blake Edwards and brought to amazing life by Peter Sellers must now defeat his former boss, Herbert Lom, who has been driven mad by the luckiest klutz alive. Lom has a gaunt ray gun ready to pulverize the planet from a small castle in Bavaria if Clouseau is not assassinated by the security agents of the entire world. With Lesley-Anne Down, Omar Sharif, Colin Blakely and Burt Kwouk.
VHS: S02329. $19.95.
Laser: LD71641. $34.98.
Blake Edwards, Great Britain, 1976, 103 mins.

Return of the Pink Panther
An assortment of props, including a steam bath, vacuum cleaner, waxed dance room floor and a deliriously deranged monkey are the comic springs for Peter Sellers' jagged rhythm and off-beat versatility. The story is fairly simple: a diamond is stolen and Clouseau is assigned to retrieve it.
VHS: S02331. $14.98.
Blake Edwards, USA, 1974, 113 mins.

Revenge of the Pink Panther
Peter Sellers and Herbert Lom return in the fifth installment of the popular spoof of mastermind police detectives. With the mafia gunning for Inspector Clouseau, he prefers to let them think he is deceased. Living undercover can have its drawbacks, particularly when your servant converts his apartment into a bordello. Watch for the fireworks when Sellers visits Hong Kong. With Dyan Cannon, Robert Loggia, Robert Webber and Burt Kwouk.
VHS: S02333. $19.98.
Laser: LD70204. $34.98.
Blake Edwards, USA, 1978, 99 mins.

S.O.B.
William Holden made his last screen appearance in this film comedy alongside such Hollywood notables as Robert Preston, Shelley Winters, Larry Hagman and Julie Andrews. This bitter send-up of desperate film industry insiders concerns a director who decides to save a multi-million dollar flop by adding a little exposed flesh. In a startling reflection of real life, Andrews, the wife of the director, goes topless.
VHS: S26327. $19.95.
Blake Edwards, USA, 1981, 121 mins.

A Shot in the Dark
Inspector Clouseau has doubts about the guilt of the maid accused of murder in a French chateau. Peter Sellers and Elke Sommer star in this Blake Edwards classic farce co-written by William Peter Blatty. Top notch comedy with plenty of slapstick and fractured English. With George Sanders, Herbert Lom, Tracy Reed, Graham Stark and Burt Kwouk.
VHS: Out of print. For rental only.
Laser: LD70675. $34.98.
Blake Edwards, USA, 1964, 101 mins.

Sunset
Bruce Willis and James Garner play two real life heroes who meet in a fictional setting in Hollywood in the late 1920's. Willis is Tom Mix, rodeo and movie star, and Garner is the legendary lawman Wyatt Earp. Together they team up to solve a murder in a brothel and swap tall tales. With Mariel Hemingway, Kathleen Quinlan, and Malcolm McDowell as the evil English clown prince of comedy.
VHS: S07980. $89.95.
Blake Edwards, USA, 1988, 107 mins.

Trail of the Pink Panther
Following the unexpected death of Peter Sellers, Blake Edwards responded by using the form and structure of Orson Welles' *Citizen Kane* for a new entry in the *Panther* series. When Inspector Clouseau turns up missing, an intrepid television reporter interviews the people from Clouseau's past to create a biographical portrait. Edwards incorporates previously unused material and outtakes. With David Niven, Herbert Lom, Richard Mulligan, Joanna Lumley, Robert Wagner, Capucine and Robert Loggia.
VHS: S02332. $19.98.
Blake Edwards, USA, 1982, 97 mins.

Victor/Victoria
A very funny sexual comedy of errors. Julie Andrews portrays a gay female impersonator, with Robert Preston, James Garner and Lesley Ann Warren. Music by Henry Mancini.
VHS: S01412. $19.95.
Laser: LD70700. $39.98.
Blake Edwards, USA, 1982, 133 mins.

Wild Rovers
Blake Edwards takes a shot at doing a western. He pairs William Holden with Ryan O'Neal, as a couple of down-on-their-luck cowpokes who turn to bank robbing on a whim. They spend the rest of the movie being pursued by Joe Don Baker and Tom Skerritt. This version is nearly 30 minutes longer than the theatrical release.
VHS: S03669. $19.98.
Laser: LD72135. $39.98.
Blake Edwards, USA, 1971, 138 mins.

CECIL B. DE MILLE

The Cheat
A very early film from Cecil B. De Mille; the story of a young society woman (Fanny Ward) who comes under the control of a scheming Asiatic when she is unable to repay the money she borrows from him. With Sessue Hayakawa.
VHS: S06907. $29.95.
Cecil B. De Mille, USA, 1915, 58 mins.

Cleopatra
Claudette Colbert portrays the infamous Queen of the Nile in this Cecil B. De Mille production. Naturally there is a cast of thousands including Warren William, C. Aubrey Smith, Henrey Wilcoxson, Joseph Schildkraut and Gertrude Michael. Opulence abounds. B&W.
VHS: S02669. $39.95.
Cecil B. De Mille, USA, 1934, 95 mins.

The Crusades
Loretta Young and Henry Wilcoxon are involved in a curious love affair at the heart of *The Crusades*. Wilcoxon is Richard the Lion-Hearted, a man forced to marry a woman he has never seen for political reasons, the beautiful Berengaria (Young). As they battle to save Jerusalem from the Saracens, their love falls victim to other threatening perils. The battle scenes are unmatched in their virtuosity.
VHS: S24024. $14.98.
Cecil B. De Mille, USA, 1935, 126 mins.

The Greatest Show on Earth
This Cecil B. De Mille production won best picture in 1952 and is a rousing tribute to life under the Big Top. Against a background of the Ringling Brothers circus, stars Charlton Heston, Cornel Wilde, Betty Hutton, Gloria Grahame, James Stewart and Dorothy Lamour combine to bring love, adventure, spectacle and suspense to the big screen.
VHS: S06146. $29.95.
Cecil B. De Mille, USA, 1952, 147 mins.

King of Kings
Cecil B. De Mille's opulent Hollywoodization of the new testament, with casts of thousands, in its original silent (with music track) re-incarnation. Featured are H.B. Warner, Dorothy Cumming, Ernest Torrence, Joseph Schildkraut and William Boyd. B&W, with the Resurrection sequence in color.
VHS: S03368. $69.95.
Cecil B. De Mille, USA, 1927, 115 mins.

Madam Satan
A surreal musical extravaganza from Cecil B. De Mille about the efforts of a wealthy socialite to win back her husband's affection following his affair with a showgirl. The production numbers include a masquerade party atop a zeppelin. With Kay Johnson, Reginald Denny and Roland Young.
VHS: S18128. $19.98.
Cecil B. De Mille, USA, 1930, 116 mins.

Male and Female
Gloria Swanson plays a spoiled maiden who always gets her way until shipwrecked with her servants—then it's every man for himself! Silent.
VHS: S08331. $19.95.
Cecil B. De Mille, USA, 1919, 110 mins.

Plainsman
Cecil B. De Mille's massive Western with Gary Cooper as Wild Bill Hickok and Jean Arthur as Calamity Jane, full of terrific action and offbeat romance.
VHS: S04520. $14.98.
Laser: LD70067. $34.98.
Cecil B. De Mille, USA, 1936, 115 mins.

Reap the Wild Wind
This is a movie in which John Wayne takes on a giant squid. He plays Captain Jack Stuart, who battles Key West salvage pirates, hurricanes and the wrath of Paulette Goddard. Ray Milland is the sea lawyer trying to clear the Duke's good name. Raymond Massey is the villainous King Cutler. With Susan Hayward, Robert Preston and Hedda Hopper.
VHS: S08504. $14.98.
Cecil B. De Mille, USA, 1942, 123 mins.

Road to Yesterday
An early, silent production by Cecil B. De Mille, in which four train passengers are transported back to the 18th century into previous lives. Starring Joseph Schildkraut and William Boyd.
VHS: S07465. $49.95.
Cecil B. De Mille, USA, 1925, 136 mins.

Samson and Delilah
The unequalled epic style of Cecil B. De Mille in this story of the legendary strongman and the woman who seduces and then betrays him. With Hedy Lamarr and Victor Mature.
VHS: S04340. $29.95.
Cecil B. De Mille, USA, 1951, 127 mins.

Sign of the Cross
Charles Laughton plays a cruelly indifferent Nero, who burns Rome merely to blame the Christians. Meanwhile, Rome's Prefect (Fredric March) falls in love with a beautiful Christian (Claudette Colbert). This lavish costume drama was a sensation upon its release and continues to fascinate audiences with its intense performances and decadent eroticism.
VHS: S24023. $14.98.
Cecil B. De Mille, USA, 1932, 125 mins.

The Spoilers
The first film version of the classic story of gold hunters in the Alaskan wilderness, starring William Farnum and Tom Santschi. Included at the end are clips from *The Squaw Man*, directed by De Mille. Silent with music score.
VHS: S07488. $19.95.
Cecil B. De Mille, USA, 1914, 110 mins.

The Story of Dr. Wassell
Based on the actual experiences of Dr. Corydon M. Wassell, this film tells the true story of the country doctor who won the Navy Cross for humanitarianism. Dr. Wassell (Gary Cooper) and his love (Laraine Day) are tending to wounded American soldiers in Java. When the Japanese invade, Dr. Wassell learns that only those who can walk are going to be evacuated. Remaining behind with his patients, the doctor manages to save many more of his patients than the Navy thought possible.
VHS: S27668. $14.98.
Cecil B. De Mille, USA, 1944, 137 mins.

The Ten Commandments (1923)

Cecil B. De Mille's first treatment of this Biblical epic, with a cast of thousands and imaginative special effects. Follows Moses' life from birth to manhood to slavery to, finally, leading the Jews out of Egypt. Silent.
VHS: S03439. $29.95.
Cecil B. De Mille, USA, 1923, 146 mins.

The Ten Commandments (1956)

De Mille's extravagant spectacle remake of his own epic cost millions, and made Charlton Heston synonymous with Moses.
VHS: S05372. $29.95.
Cecil B. De Mille, USA, 1956, 210 mins.

The Ten Commandments: 40th Anniversary Collector's Edition

One of the most famous screen epics ever made is finally presented on video, fully restored to its original form. This 40th Anniversary edition of *The Ten Commandments* includes the original theatrical trailer (never before seen on video) and is presented uncut, in widescreen format with spectacular Dolby Surround stereo. Enjoy the gaudy, Technicolor splendor of a bearded Charlton Heston parting the Red Sea; see slaves whipped, pyramids built, false idols worshipped.
VHS: S15100. $35.00.
Cecil B. De Mille, USA, 1956, 245 mins.

The Unconquered

Gary Cooper and Paulette Goddard star in this historical epic set in the young English colonies of North America. Goddard is a convict/slave who is freed by Cooper. She is forced back into servitude, however, by an evil gun-runner (Howard Da Silva). War with the Native Americans is soon at hand and Cooper must decide how he feels about Goddard before it is too late. Boris Karloff is featured as Seneca Chief Guyasuta.
VHS: S24025. $14.98.
Cecil B. De Mille, USA, 1947, 127 mins.

Union Pacific

Barbara Stanwyck and Joel McCrea are joined by Robert Preston and Anthony Quinn in this Western about the first transcontinental rail link. The setting and plot provide more than enough justification for gun-toting action and melodramatic twists, making this a sweeping historical spectacle.
VHS: S24026. $14.98.
Cecil B. De Mille, USA, 1939, 136 mins.

Why Change Your Wife

Gloria Swanson, T. Meighan and Bebe Daniels star in this rare De Mille treasure, made before his "pseudo-epic" period. Silent.
VHS: S08332. $29.95.
Cecil B. De Mille, USA, 1920, 100 mins.

RELIGIOUS FEATURES & EPICS

Abraham

Richard Harris and Barbara Hershey star in this version of the timeless story of Abraham, the biblical patriarch. Abraham's love for his son Isaac is tested when his God demands the ultimate sacrifice. This feature-length drama recalls the struggle that faith represents for all people. With Maximillian Schell.
VHS: S22156. $59.98.
Joseph Sargent, USA/Italy, 1993

Barabbas

A stirring adaptation of Nobel prize-winner Par Lagerkvist's novel about the robber set free when Christ was crucified. With Anthony Quinn and Silvana Mangano.
VHS: S04326. $14.95.
Richard Fleischer, USA, 1962, 134 mins.

The Cardinal

Handsomely produced saga about the personal and religious life of a dedicated Catholic priest who rises to the position of Cardinal. Starring Tom Tryon, Romy Schneider, Ossie Davis and John Huston.
VHS: S01996. $29.98.
Laser: LD70902. $59.95.
Otto Preminger, USA, 1963, 175 mins.

Catholics

Winner of the Peabody Award, a moving contemporary drama about the changing attitudes of the Church, adapted from Brian Moore's novel about simple worship in an ancient Irish monastery now threatened with the increasing permissiveness of the Church. With Trevor Howard and Martin Sheen.
VHS: S01607. $39.95.
Jack Gold, USA, 1973, 86 mins.

David and Bathsheba

Gregory Peck and Susan Hayward play the Biblical sinners who were the talk of Jerusalem a few years back. When the king of the Israelites becomes attracted to the red headed wife of one of his best officers, passion clouds the royal judgement and a valuable lesson is learned. With Kieron Moore, James Robertson Justice and Raymond Massey as a disapproving prophet.
VHS: S10325. $19.98.
Henry King, USA, 1951, 116 mins.

Demetrius and the Gladiators

This sword and sandal saga is the sequel to *The Robe* and features Victor Mature—who was Roman centurion Richard Burton's Christian slave in the original. While the Emperor Caligula (Jay Robinson) searches for the mystical robe of Christ, Demetrius endures a test of faith and goes to gladiator school. With Michael Renie, Susan Hayward, Richard Egan, Debra Paget, Anne Bancroft and Ernest Borgnine.
VHS: S10327. $19.98.
Delmer Daves, USA, 1954, 101 mins.

Francesco

Liliana Cavani (*Night Porter*) casts Mickey Rourke as St. Francis of Assisi in this revisionist story of Francis, the son of a rich man, who rejected all that is worldly for a life of poverty. With Helena Bonham Carter.
VHS: S21296. $89.95.
Liliana Cavani, Italy/Britain, 1989, 119 mins.

Jesus of Nazareth

Italian director Franco Zeffirelli's impassioned interpretation of the life of Christ. British novelist Anthony Burgess (*A Clockwork Orange*) wrote the screenplay. With Anne Bancroft, Ernest Borgnine, Valentina Cortese, James Mason, Robert Powell and Olivia Hussey.
VHS: S17908. $69.98.
Franco Zeffirelli, USA, 1977, 279 mins.

Moses

An all-star cast including Burt Lancaster, Anthony Quayle, Ingrid Thulin, Irene Papas, Mariangela Melato star in this epic theatrical adaptation with a screenplay by Anthony Burgess and Vittorio Bonicelli.
VHS: S04593. $19.98.
G. De Bosio, Great Britain/Italy, 1975, 141 mins.

Old Testament

An Italian production starring Brad Harris, a muscular performer with a history of playing roles from the Bible and Greek mythology. The Macabees battle the Roman Legions. Also starring Mara Lane, Susan Paget, John Heston and several Italian actors with anglicized names. Action and adventure and lots of extras in a film that may deviate form the source material. 1963, 88 mins.
VHS: S10388. $19.95.

The Prodigal

A lavish MGM production shot in Cinemascope. Set in 70 B.C., Edmund Purdom plays a gilded farmer who is obsessed with the beautiful Samarra (Lana Turner). Lavish production of the Biblical favorite. With James Mitchell, Louis Calhern and Audrey Dalton.
VHS: S18661. $19.98.
Richard Thorpe, USA, 1955, 115 mins.

Quo Vadis (1951)

"A super-spectacle in all its meaning" (*Variety*). Robert Taylor, Deborah Kerr and a cast of thousands in Rome in 64 A.D. under Nero the mad emperor, played by Peter Ustinov.
VHS: S02564. $24.98.
Laser: LD70161. $39.98.
Mervyn Le Roy, USA, 1951, 291 mins.

Quo Vadis (1988)

The Romans of 63 AD revel in a boundless feast of indulgence, romance and mysticism in this recent adaptation of the famous novel by Herman Sinkiewicz. Klaus Maria Brandauer, Frederic Forrest and Max von Sydow star as the Christians take on the Romans. In English.
VHS: S09802. $89.95.
Laser: LD71288. $59.95.
Franco Rossi, Italy, 1988, 122 mins.

The Robe

Richard Burton won an Oscar nomination for his portrayal of a Roman soldier in charge of the crucifixion of Jesus Christ. The passionate spectacle about the birth of Christianity was the first film made in Cinemascope. Based on the Lloyd C. Douglas novel. With Jean Simmons and Victor Mature.
VHS: S04595. $19.98.
Henry Koster, USA, 1953, 135 mins.

Samson and Delilah

A made-for-tv retelling of the classical Biblical story of a strong man and a deceitful woman. Anthony Hamilton is the brawn and Belinda Bauer the beauty. With Jose Ferrer, Max Von Sydow, Maria Schell and Victor Mature (DeMille's movie Samson) in his tv debut as the muscleman's dad.
VHS: S07004. $19.98.
Lee Phillips, USA, 1984, 96 mins.

Shoes of the Fisherman

International cast in this adaptation of the Morris West novel about the election of the first Russian Pope includes Anthony Quinn as Pope Kiril I, plus John Gielgud, Vittorio De Sica, David Janssen and Oskar Werner.
VHS: S02728. $29.98.
Laser: LD70180. $39.98.
Michael Anderson, USA, 1968, 152 mins.

Sodom and Gomorrah

Don't look for them on any recent maps. The twin cities of sin made so popular by the Bible can only be found in film form in this Robert Aldrich epic made in Europe. A cast of thousands, and some of them are name performers like Stewart Granger, Anouk Aimee, Pier Angeli, Stanley Baker and Rossana Podesta. Said to have vivid scenes of vice, gore and God's wrath.
VHS: S10324. $19.98.
Laser: LD72204. $69.98.
Robert Aldrich, Italy, 1963, 148 mins.

Song of Bernadette

Jennifer Jones received an Oscar for her performance as the 19th century French peasant girl who claimed to speak to the Virgin Mary near her village of Lourdes. Three other Oscars were awarded to this inspirational but lengthy account. With Vincent Price, Lee J. Cobb, Charles Bickford and Gladys Cooper. Linda Darnell appeared, unbilled, as the Blessed Virgin. B&W.
VHS: S15607. $19.98.
Henry King, USA, 1943, 156 mins.

Story of Ruth

Elana Eden stars as the Biblical Ruth, who renounces her beliefs when she discovers the true Christian faith. With Stuart Whitan, Tom Tryon.
VHS: S11738. $29.98.
Henry Koster, USA, 1960, 132 mins.

AMERICAN CLASSICS

12 O'Clock High

Gregory Peck is commander of a US bomber unit during World War II. As the number of missions flown accumulates, he begins to crack under the strain. Well-made character drama with some fine performances.
VHS: S14138. $19.98.
Laser: LD71381. $49.98.
Henry King, USA, 1949, 132 mins.

13 Rue Madeleine

A documentary-style narrative about the attempts of an O.S.S. agent to locate a secret German missile site in France during World War II. Featuring strong performances from James Cagney, Annabella, and Richard Conte. A rough-and-tumble spy adventure from director Henry Hathaway.
VHS: S03915. $19.98.
Henry Hathaway, USA, 1946, 95 mins.

24 Hours in a Woman's Life

Ingrid Bergman plays a bereaved widow trying to escape her sorrow while traveling. At Monte Carlo she meets a desperate young gambler (Rip Torn), rescues him from suicide, and all within the span of 24 hours falls in love, tries to change him and fails.
VHS: S13432. $29.95.
Silvio Narizzano, USA, 1961, 90 mins.

40 Pounds of Trouble

Tony Curtis, Suzanne Pleshette and Phil Silvers star in this romantic comedy about a wild getaway. Curtis plays a recently divorced casino manager who becomes enmeshed with his latest headliner's niece (Pleshette) and a recently abandoned five-year-old. Together these three are off on an adventure as Curtis must avoid detectives sent by his ex-wife.
VHS: S22125. $14.98.
Norman Jewison, USA, 1962, 106 mins.

The 5000 Fingers of Dr. T

This neglected classic tells the fantastic tale of a young boy who so hates taking piano lessons that he dreams his teacher is a cruel genius ruling over a baroque castle where kidnapped boys are sadistically forced to practice the piano over and over again. Screenplay by Dr. Seuss (Theodore Geisel)—his only full-length, live-action feature. Produced by Stanley Kramer.
VHS: S13189. $19.95.
Roy Rowland, USA, 1953, 88 mins.

633 Squadron

Spectacular aerial photography and a pulse-pounding climactic sequence highlight this WWII drama in the air, starring Cliff Robertson as a combat-weary pilot who is sent on a suicide mission. Screenplay by James Clavell.
VHS: S15131. $19.98.
Walter Grauman, USA, 1964, 95 mins.

The 7th Voyage of Sinbad

Ray Harryhausen's special visual effects enliven this spirited fantasy/drama which pits Sinbad against a cruel and sadistic magician who's reduced the beautiful princess Parisa to microscopic size. Full of imagination and verve, with a musical score by Hitchcock's brilliant collaborator, Bernard Herrmann. With Kerwin Mathews, Kathryn Grant, Torin Thatcher and Richard Eyer.
VHS: S16683. $14.95.
Nathan Juran, USA, 1958, 87 mins.

Above and Beyond

This film focuses on the grueling training and personal motives which shaped the pilots who delivered the final blow to Japan by dropping the first atomic bomb. Starring Norman Panama, Robert Taylor and James Whitmore.
VHS: S21013. $19.98.
Melvin Frank, USA, 1952, 122 mins.

Above Suspicion

Fred MacMurray and Joan Crawford are American honeymooners in pre-war Europe who are asked to do British intelligence a favor and help track down a missing agent. Also starring Basil Rathbone as a Nazi agent—a role that shocked and surprised Sherlock Holmes fans.
VHS: S15114. $19.98.
Richard Thorpe, USA, 1943, 90 mins.

Ace of Aces

Richard Dix is an American artist who enlists in World War I against his inner feelings to prove to his girlfriend that he is a patriot and becomes a bloodthirsty fighter pilot in a high flying aerial combat. An early anti-war film.
VHS: S12371. $19.98.
J. Walter Ruben, USA, 1933, 77 mins.

Across the Wide Missouri

Clark Gable plays trapper and fighter Flint Mitchell, a man of action whose marriage to a woman of the Blackfoot tribe leads him to a profound respect for her people. A breathtakingly beautiful epic, filmed in the Colorado Rockies at elevations of 9,000 to 14,000 feet. With Ricardo Montalban, John Hodiak and Adolphe Menjou as a hooch-swigging Frenchman.
VHS: S15256. $19.98.
William Wellman, USA, 1951, 78 mins.

Action in Arabia

George Sanders is a newspaperman who finds himself in treacherous surroundings amid Nazis as he seeks a fellow reporter's murder. Uses stock desert footage shot by Merian C. Cooper and Ernest B. Schoedsack for a film which was never made.
VHS: S10673. $19.98.
Leonide Moguy, USA, 1944, 76 mins.

Action in the North Atlantic

Humphrey Bogart and Raymond Massey head the crew of the S.S. *Seawitch* in this cinematic salute to the Merchant Marines of World War II. A tense and thrilling tribute to unsung sailors—based on a true story.
VHS: S14305. $19.98.
Lloyd Bacon, USA, 1943, 127 mins.

Actors and Sin

Two stories by Ben Hecht: *Actor's Blood*, with Edward G. Robinson as the father of a murdered actress, and *Woman of Sin*, a satire on Hollywood with Robinson playing the second-rate agent.
VHS: S05715. $19.95.
Lee Games/Ben Hecht, USA, 1952, 82 mins.

Adam Had Four Sons

A beautiful young governess keeps a family from destroying itself in this sensitive drama. Ingrid Bergman comes to serve as the governess for Adam's (Warner Baxter) four sons. As the family gets ripped apart, Ingrid keeps it all together.
VHS: S06114. $59.95.
Gregory Ratoff, USA, 1941, 81 mins.

The Admiral Was a Lady

Edmond O'Brien, Wanda Hendrix and Rudy Vallee are featured in this romantic comedy, with some delightful songs. O'Brien and Hendrix are meant for each other but there is one problem: O'Brien and his veteran pals have vowed never to work again. Ex-WAVE Hendrix needs some convincing, leading to great visual gags. The songs "Once Over Lightly" and "Everything That's Wonderful" add to this upbeat story.
VHS: S23779. $24.95.
Albert S. Rogell, USA, 1950, 87 mins.

Adventure

Clark Gable plays the brawling sailor with a girl in every port who is reeled in by Greer Garson in a love story that "does the whole film industry proud" (*Hollywood Reporter*).
VHS: S20557. $19.98.
Victor Fleming, USA, 1946, 125 mins.

Adventure Girl

Joan Lowell's novel *Adventure Girl* was the basis for this early sound film. Lowell narrates this exciting story about her sea voyage and exploration of jungles in Central America.
VHS: S23881. $19.98.
Herman C. Raymaker, USA, 1931, 65 mins.

Adventures of Don Juan

This Errol Flynn swashbuckling vehicle won the Academy Award for costumes and features a score by Max Steiner.
VHS: S02513. $19.98.
Laser: LD70496. $34.97.
Vincent Sherman, USA, 1948, 110 mins.

The Adventures of Marco Polo

Gary Cooper stars as Marco Polo, the intrepid traveler from medieval times. He sets off for the distant Eastern kingdom, th lavish court of Kubla Khan, where intrigues and adventure abound. This is a classic realized with all the pomp and excess that only old Hollywood could muster.
VHS: S20671. $19.98.
Archie Mayo, USA, 1938, 100 mins.

The Adventures of Robin Hood

The most acclaimed screen version of the King of Sherwood Forest. Errol Flynn is Robin Hood to Olivia de Havilland's Maid Marion. Basil Rathbone and Claude Rains are the villains. Action, drama and romance that has satisfied audiences for years.
VHS: S00019. $19.98.
Laser: LD70731. $34.98.
Michael Curtiz, USA, 1938, 102 mins.

Adventures of Smilin' Jack

Zack Moseley's famous comic-strip character comes roaring to life in this action-packed serial. Daredevil stunt pilot Smilin' Jack Martin takes on the air war in China during the darkest days of WWII. 13 thrilling episodes on two cassettes.
VHS: S13014. $24.95.
Ray Taylor, USA, 1943, 90 mins.

Aerial Gunner

World War II action in the Pacific as Chester Morris and Richard Arlen take time out from fighting each other to battle the Japanese. They both love Lita Ward and feel responsible for her kid brother Jimmy Lydon. From training to fighting on enemy-filled islands, this actioner packs a wallop.
VHS: S07066. $39.95.
William H. Pine, USA, 1943, 78 mins.

Affair in Trinidad

Rita Hayworth sizzles in this romantic spy drama of international intrigue also featuring Glenn Ford and Alexander Scourby. Hayworth stars as Chris Emery, a sultry singer-dancer whose life is turned upside down when her husband is murdered by a globe trotting thief.
VHS: S12996. $19.95.
Vincent Sherman, USA, 1952, 98 mins.

An Affair to Remember

Cary Grant and Deborah Kerr star in Leo McCarey's own remake of *Love Affair*. Grant and Kerr are the shipboard lovers who decide to meet after an absence to see if it all still works.
VHS: S11562. $14.98.
Laser: LD70813. $59.98.
Leo McCarey, USA, 1957, 114 mins.

Affairs of Annabel

One of Lucy's funniest comedies. Ball plays a nutty actress kept in line by her scheming press agent.
VHS: S10646. $19.98.
Ben Stoloff, USA, 1938, 68 mins.

Aggie Appleby, Maker of Men

An early film from the director of *Top Hat* and *Shall We Dance*. A comedy of errors occurs when a wimpy society type must take the place of the title character's macho boyfriend. Wynne Gibson stars as Aggie. Charles Farrell is Adoniram Schlump and William Gargan is the brawny Red Branahan. Based on a play by Joseph O. Kesserling. Also known as *Cupid in the Rough*.
VHS: S15773. $19.98.
Mark Sandrich, USA, 1933, 73 mins.

Agony and the Ecstasy

Based on Irving Stone's best-selling biography of Michelangelo this mammoth Hollywood production starring Charlton Heston and Rex Harrison focuses on Michelangelo's painting of the Sistine Chapel.
VHS: S05926. $19.98.
Laser: LD70821. $69.98.
Carol Reed, USA, 1965, 140 mins.

Al Capone

A semi-documentary account of Chicago's most famous gangster, from the beginnings all the way to his arrest and conviction for tax evasion. Featuring a pushed-to-the-limit portrayal by Rod Steiger which at times borders on clever caricature. This film received many enthusiastic reviews at the time of its release.
VHS: S13616. $19.98.
Richard Wilson, USA, 1959, 105 mins.

The Al Jolson Collection

The wit and grand style of master showman Al Jolson is recollected in this collection of eight of his films, from the landmark *The Jazz Singer* to *The Singing Fool, Say It with Songs, Mammy, Big Boy, Wonder Bar, Go Into Your Dance* and *The Singing Kid*.
Laser: LD70143. $149.98.

Alexander the Great
Robert Rossen (*The Hustler*) wrote and directed this biography of the brilliant military strategist and warrior who conquered everything in his path before his death at 33. Photographed by Robert Krasker in Cinemascope, preserved in the letterbox presentation. With Richard Burton, Frederic March, Danielle Darrieux and Claire Bloom.
VHS: S20769. $19.98.
Laser: LD71648. $39.98.
Robert Rossen, USA, 1956, 135 mins.

Algiers
A classic love story that combines adventure and intrigue, starring Charles Boyer as Pepe le Moko, a crook who seeks refuge from the police in the casbah in North Africa. With Hedy Lamarr.
VHS: S00029. $19.95.
John Cromwell, USA, 1938, 95 mins.

Ali Baba and the Forty Thieves
In this colorful, stylized *Arabian Nights* tale, a deposed prince and his band of outlaws seek vengeance on the nefarious Hulagu Khan and the Mongol forces who murdered his father and seized the throne. Cinematography by George Robinson. With Jon Hall, Maria Montez, Scotty Beckett and Turhan Bey.
VHS: S19313. $14.98.
Arthur Lubin, USA, 1943, 87 mins.

All About Eve
Six Oscars were awarded this cynical and entertaining examination of life as it exists on the Broadway theatre scene. Bette Davis glows as the aging star being undermined by her protege Anne Baxter, as Eve Harrington. With George Sanders, Celeste Holm and Marilyn Monroe. A gem.
VHS: S03911. $19.98.
Laser: LD70823. $49.98.
Joseph L. Mankiewicz, USA, 1950, 138 mins.

All Quiet on the Western Front
Classic adaptation of Erich Maria Remarque's anti-war novel has lost little of its impact over the years. The film follows a group of German recruits during World War I from their idealism to disillusionment.
VHS: S01686. $19.95.
Laser: LD70011. $39.98.
Lewis Milestone, USA, 1930, 103 mins.

All the Brothers Were Valiant
Robert Taylor and Stewart Granger are brothers who compete for Ann Blyth in this film adaptation of Ben Ames' novel about New England whalers. It's a romantic adventure set on the high seas, where trust is often a matter of life and death.
VHS: S21014. $19.98.
Richard Thorpe, USA, 1953, 101 mins.

All the King's Men
Broderick Crawford gives a legendary performance as the brawling, bull-headed Southern politician. A riveting thriller about corruption in the political arena, based on the novel by Robert Penn Warren.
VHS: S00033. $19.95.
Laser: LD72160. $34.95.
Robert Rossen, USA, 1949, 109 mins.

All This and Heaven Too
Charles Boyer and Bette Davis star in this story based upon Rachel Field's novel of a scandalous love affair between an aristocrat and servant, set in Paris of the 1840's.
VHS: S03457. $19.98.
Anatole Litvak, USA, 1940, 141 mins.

All Through the Night
Humphrey Bogart is Gloves Donahue, a Broadway big-shot who takes on a Nazi spy ring in this gangster spoof. When the German baker of his favorite cheesecakes is mysteriously murdered, Bogie sets out to find the killer and ends up in the middle of an international plot to blow up an American warship. With Conrad Veidt, Peter Lorre, Karen Verne and Jackie Gleason.
VHS: S16094. $19.98.
Vincent Sherman, USA, 1942, 107 mins.

The Amazing Mr. X (The Spiritualist)
Turhan Bey is a phony spiritualist who teams up with not-so-dead husband in order to deceive the wealthy widow. Lynn Bari is the bereaved young woman driven to seek the "help" of the mystic. This eerie film also includes Richard Carlson and Donald Curtis. B&W.
VHS: S04066. $29.95.
Laser: CLV/CAV. LD72060. $39.95.
Bernard Vorhaus, USA, 1948, 78 mins.

Ambassador Bill
When Will Rogers is appointed U.S. Ambassador to the revolutionary-plagued European kingdom of Sylvania, his down-to-earth ways and homespun wisdom endear him to the Queen and her son. Ray Milland co-stars in this political satire.
VHS: S13494. $19.98.
Sam Taylor, USA, 1931, 68 mins.

America America
This rarely screened classic was originally nominated for four Academy Awards. It's based on the story of acclaimed director Elia Kazan's uncle, who struggled mightily at the turn of the century in order to fulfill his dream of emigrating to America. A moving, powerful story of American immigration.
VHS: S21146. $19.98.
Elia Kazan, USA, 1963, 168 mins.

The Americanization of Emily
William Bradford Huie's novel is brought to the screen with the star power of Julie Andrews, James Garner and James Coburn. Andrews is a nurse in World War II who falls in love with the first victim of the Normandy landing. As the training progresses that the victim, a cynical Garner, was set up by top brass in this role so that an American would be the first casualty. Even so, with these two a touching romance is unavoidable.
VHS: S12235. $19.98.
Laser: LD72116. $34.98.
Arthur Hiller, USA, 1964, 117 mins.

Anastasia
Yul Brynner and Ingrid Bergman star in this strange but engrossing story about Czar Nicholas' missing daughter, Anastasia. Brynner is a general who devises a scheme to collect the last Czar's money by coaching a young woman to pass as his sole surviving heir. As the mystery progresses, however, even he begins to wonder if this woman might actually be the Czarina Anastasia. Bergman won an Oscar for her performance as the confused young woman. Helen Hayes is also featured.
VHS: S26148. $19.98.
Anatole Litvak, USA, 1956, 105 mins.

Anatomy of a Murder
A riveting courtroom drama pitting small town lawyer James Stewart against big city prosecutor George C. Scott in a trial of Ben Gazzara, accused of murdering his wife's rapist. With a brilliant score by Duke Ellington.
VHS: S01525. $19.95.
Otto Preminger, USA, 1959, 160 mins.

Androcles and the Lion
In Chester Erskine's spirited adaptation of the George Bernard Shaw satire, Jean Simmons, Alan Young and Victor Mature star in a film that moves deftly from Shavian pungency and wit to mordant satire. Androcles volunteers to take on the deadly lion, who, it turns out, is indebted to Androcles for removing a thorn from its wounded paw.
VHS: S02598. $29.95.
Chester Erskine, USA, 1952, 98 mins.

Angel on My Shoulder
Paul Muni is a murdered convict given a chance to do even worse when the Devil offers to return him to the land of the living to tarnish the reputation of an honorable judge. A sweet fantasy also starring Claude Rains, Anne Baxter and George Cleveland.
VHS: S09829. $19.95.
Archie Mayo, USA, 1946, 101 mins.

Angels in the Outfield
Paul Douglas, Janet Leigh, and Keenan Wynn star in this tale of baseball fantasy. The Pittsburgh Pirates need a little celestial help to turn a losing season around. Divine intervention puts them on the path to an unforgettable pennant race.
VHS: S21521. $19.98.
Laser: LD75517. $39.98.
Clarence Brown, USA, 1951, 102 mins.

Angels over Broadway
Written and directed by Ben Hecht at his usual breakneck pace, this black comedy tells of a con man (Douglas Fairbanks, Jr.) who undergoes a change of heart and who, with the assistance of a call-girl (Rita Hayworth), helps turn around the life of his mark. An offbeat morality play.
VHS: S01588. $19.95.
Ben Hecht, USA, 1940, 80 mins.

Angels with Dirty Faces
Rocky Sullivan and Jerry Connolly, two tough East Side kids, grow up to be James Cagney and Pat O'Brien, one a crook and the other a priest, but friends all the way to the electric chair and perhaps beyond. With Humphrey Bogart and the Dead End Kids. A top notch melodrama from Warner Brothers.
VHS: S03317. $19.95.
Laser: LD70146. $34.98.
Michael Curtiz, USA, 1938, 97 mins.

The Animal Kingdom
An intellectual publisher (Leslie Howard) suffers from a moral crisis as he tries to keep both a wife (middle-class Myrna Loy) and a mistress (free-spirited Ann Harding). Sophisticated comedy-drama adapted from a successful Broadway play by Philip Barry.
VHS: S13509. $29.95.
Edward H. Griffith, USA, 1932, 95 mins.

Ann Vickers
Sinclair Lewis' classic novel features Irene Dunne as the man-hating head of a detention home for women, with Walter Huston as the army officer who's also the reason why she hates men.
VHS: S03257. $39.95.
John Cromwell, USA, 1939, 76 mins.

Anna and the King of Siam
A lavish adaptation of Margaret Landon's book on Anna Leonowens (the source of the Rogers and Hammerstein musical, *The King and I*), detailing the experiences of an English governess (Irene Dunne) in 19th-century Thailand. The story examines her complicated relationship with the King of Siam. Oscar-winning cinematography by Arthur Miller. Screenplay by Talbot Jennings and Sally Benson. With Rex Harrison (his Hollywood debut), Lee J. Cobb, Linda Darnell, Gale Sondergaard and Mikhail Rasumny.
VHS: S20256. $19.98.
John Cromwell, USA, 1946, 128 mins.

Anna Christie
Garbo in a great role as a disillusioned prostitute, based on Eugene O'Neill's play, who returns to her father, a barge captain, and falls in love with a sailor, only to be rejected when her tarnished past is revealed.
VHS: S00057. $19.98.
Clarence Brown, USA, 1930, 89 mins.

Anna Karenina
Tolstoy's novel is skillfully brought to the screen for the second time with a melancholy Greta Garbo in her first "talkie." *Love*, her silent version, with John Gilbert as Vronsky, did not pay as much attention to authentic costumes and settings as this sound version. With Fredric March as Vronsky and Basil Rathbone as her unfeeling husband.
VHS: S04211. $24.95.
Clarence Brown, USA, 1935, 95 mins.

An Annapolis Story
This romantic drama set during the Korean War finds Kevin McCarthy and John Derek as brothers who are both naval cadets and happen to be after the same woman. With Diana Lynn as the object of their attentions.
VHS: S14144. $19.98.
Don Siegel, USA, 1955, 81 mins.

Another Time Another Place
Lana Turner is a U.S. correspondent in London who has a fling with a married man who then dies in a plane crash. When she recovers from a nervous breakdown, she decides to visit Sean Connery's wife and child. With Barry Sullivan, Glynis Johns and Terrence Longden. Based on the novel by Lenore Coffee.
VHS: S12850. $39.95.
Lewis Allen, USA, 1958, 95 mins.

Anthony Adverse
Magnificent entertainment from the Golden Years of Hollywood. Winner of Four Academy Awards in 1936, and nominated for Best Picture. Starring Fredric March, Olivia de Havilland, and Claude Rains. Film follows March through the time of Napoleon.
VHS: S00063. $19.98.
Mervyn LeRoy, USA, 1936, 135 mins.

Any Number Can Play
Clark Gable is an ailing casino owner who is used to 20-hour days and high-stakes games. But this time, the jackpot is his life. If he doesn't slow down, his enemies will deal him out—or they'll do him in.
VHS: S20558. $19.98.
VHS: S20558. $19.98.
Mervyn LeRoy, USA, 1949, 112 mins.

Arabian Nights
Two brothers fight over possession of the evil Caliph of Baghdad and the liberation of the enslaved Scheherazade. A film notable for its expressive use of color and decor. With Jon Hall, Maria Montez, Sabu, Leif Erickson and Turhan Bey.
VHS: S19311. $14.98.
John Rawlins, USA, 1942, 87 mins.

Arch of Triumph
Charles Boyer and Ingrid Bergman star in this adaptation of Erich Maria Remarque's novel about a refugee doctor and a girl with a past in Paris, just before the Nazi invasion.
VHS: S01687. $19.95.
Lewis Milestone, USA, 1948, 120 mins.

Armored Command
Howard Keel, Tina Louise and Burt Reynolds star in this story of a beautiful Nazi spy who infiltrates an American Army base. An offbeat war drama.
VHS: S14143. $19.98.
Byron Haskin, USA, 1961, 105 mins.

Around the World in Eighty Days
David Niven as Jules Verne's character Phineas Fogg makes a wager he can circumnavigate the globe in four score days. Along the way he meets 40 major stars in cameo appearances and saves Shirley MacLaine from being cooked on an Indian funeral pyre. Lots of Oscars, including Best Picture.
VHS: S06045. $19.98.
Laser: LD70507. $39.98.
Michael Anderson, USA, 1956, 167 mins.

Artists and Models
Comic book artist Dean uses Jerry's dreams as inspiration, sparking one of the zaniest Martin & Lewis laugh fests you've ever seen. With Shirley MacLaine, Eva Gabor and Anita Ekberg joining the fun.
VHS: S15158. $19.95.
Laser: LD75150. $34.95.
Frank Tashlin, USA, 1955, 109 mins.

As You Desire Me
Based on the play by Pirandello, Greta Garbo is married to Erich von Stroheim but she doesn't actually remember marrying the man. Amnesia is not the only problem they have. With Melvyn Douglas, Hedda Hopper and Owen Moore. B&W.
VHS: S13196. $19.95.
George Fitzmaurice, USA, 1932, 71 mins.

As Young As You Feel
An elderly man, resenting retirement at age 65, is determined to alter corporate policy. He impersonates the company president, and saves the firm from bankruptcy. Based on a story by Paddy Chayefsky. Stars Monty Woolley, with a marvelous cast including Marilyn Monroe, Constance Bennett, Thelma Ritter, David Wayne and Jean Peters.
VHS: S16397. $19.98.
Harmon Jones, USA, 1951, 77 mins.

Ask Any Girl
Charles Walters' elegant, witty comedy about an ambitious young advertising executive (Shirley MacLaine) and her determination to find the right man. When everything else fails, she turns to the brilliant older brother (David Niven) of the man she's attempting to seduce, with unpredictable, funny results. With Rod Taylor and Jim Backus.
VHS: S18009. $19.98.
Charles Walters, USA, 1959, 101 mins.

At Sword's Point
A fun remake of *The Three Musketeers* with Cornel Wilde and Maureen O'Hara leading some of the antics, as the sons of the three musketeers rally around the aging queen in order to prevent her daughter's marriage to a villain. Beautiful Technicolor setting.
VHS: S13383. $19.98.
Lewis Allen, USA, 1951, 81 mins.

Audrey Rose
Anthony Hopkins, Marsha Mason and John Beck star in this terrifying tale of soul possession and reincarnation, directed by Robert Wise (*The Day the Earth Stood Still*). A chilling thriller.
VHS: S14961. $14.95.
Robert Wise, USA, 1977, 113 mins.

Auntie Mame
Morton Da Costa's film adaptation of the play by Jerome Lawrence and Robert E. Lee about an abandoned child whose cruel world is awakened to flamboyant dreams and fantasy when he's adopted by an extravagant, unconventional woman. With Rosalind Russell, Forrest Tucker, Fred Clark and Coral Browne.
VHS: S18895. $19.98.
Laser: LD70509. $29.98.
Morton Da Costa, USA, 1958, 144 mins.

Babe Ruth Story
William Bendix stars as the Legendary Babe Ruth in this biography of a baseball player who was considered a saint and the greatest baseball hero of all time. With Claire Trevor and Charles Bickford.
VHS: S11619. $19.98.
Roy Del Ruth, USA, 1948, 107 mins.

Baby Doll
Karl Malden, Eli Wallach and Carroll Baker star in this explosive, provocative drama written by Tennessee Williams. Condemned by the Legion of Decency as well as Time and Variety, *Baby Doll* is not only a work of smoldering screen history, but also artistry.
VHS: S00085. $19.98.
Elia Kazan, USA, 1956, 115 mins.

Baby Face
The amorous adventures of an ambitious working girl who tries to sleep her way to the top. This obviously pre-production Code melodrama is generally fast-paced and features some good performances. Starring Barbara Stanwyck, George Brent, and John Wayne in a coat and tie.
VHS: S13646. $19.98.
Alfred E. Green, USA, 1933, 70 mins.

The Bachelor and the Bobby Soxer
Myrna Loy plays a judge who orders Cary Grant to pay attention to her kid sister, Shirley Temple, who has fallen for Grant. Naturally, the judge's plan backfires.
VHS: S02152. $19.98.
Irving Reis, USA, 1947, 95 mins.

Bachelor Apartment
Lowell Sherman stars, along with a cast of beautiful women (Irene Dunne, Mae Murray, Claudia Dell, Bess Flowers), in the story of a certified ladies man who shuffles his girlfriends back and forth.
VHS: S13360. $19.98.
Lowell Sherman, USA, 1931, 77 mins.

Bachelor in Paradise
Bob Hope plays a writer who conceals his identity in order to collect data on the sexual activities of a California suburban community. Hope is the only bachelor in this antiseptic environment, a land populated by unhappy wives and distracted husbands. Lana Turner plays Hope's love interest. With Janis Paige, Jim Hutton and Paula Prentiss.
VHS: S19560. $19.98.
Jack Arnold, USA, 1961, 109 mins.

Back Door to Heaven
William K. Howard's potent social docu-drama stars Wallace Ford and Stuart Erwin. Ford turns to crime during the depression, and the well-off members of the community discover that it was their lack of concern that was responsible.
VHS: S06905. $29.95.
William K. Howard, USA, 1939, 85 mins.

Back Street
Susan Hayward plays a glamorous, lonely fashion designer who falls for a charismatic businessman (John Gavin), rejects his marriage overtures, and years later, attempts to resume the affair, despite his wife and children. A film notable for its symbolic use of color, European locations and striking musical score. With Charles Drake, Virginia Grey and Reginald Gardiner. Based on the novel by Fannie Hurst.
VHS: S17945. $14.98.
David Miller, USA, 1961, 107 mins.

Back to Bataan
John Wayne is the American leader of Filipino patriots in an action melodrama based on the actual facts which led to General MacArthur's recapture of the islands. Anthony Quinn is the leader of the Philippine Scouts.
VHS: S03243. $19.98.
Edward Dmytryk, USA, 1945, 97 mins.

Background to Danger
Raoul Walsh's gritty noir set in World War II Turkey stars George Raft as a cynical maverick who hires two colorful villains, Nazi Sidney Greenstreet and Turk Peter Lorre, in his efforts to prevent Turkey from aligning its military and political forces with Germany. With Brenda Marshall. WR Burnett adapted Eric Ambler's novel.
VHS: S18502. $19.98.
Raoul Walsh, USA, 1943, 80 mins.

Bad and the Beautiful
The winner of five Oscars captures the underbelly of life in Tinseltown. Kirk Douglas is an ambitious producer with few personal scruples. He manages to upset Lana Turner, Dick Powell, Barry Sullivan, Walter Pidgeon and Gloria Grahame. A powerful and revealing drama from Vincente Minnelli. B&W.
VHS: S07978. $19.95.
Laser: LD70512. $34.98.
Vincente Minnelli, USA, 1952, 118 mins.

Bad Day at Black Rock
Spencer Tracy stops off in a small town to award a medal and finds he is visiting a hotbed of racism and inhospitality. Even with one arm he manages to shake up this sleepy little burg. With Robert Ryan, Lee Marvin, Anne Francis, Ernest Borgnine, Dean Jagger and Walter Brennan.
VHS: S07977. $19.98.
Laser: Widescreen. LD70855. $49.95.
John Sturges, USA, 1954, 81 mins.

The Bad Seed
Patty McCormack is the darling, blonde, pigtailed little girl who simply can't keep herself from murdering her playmates. Nominated for four Academy Awards, this classic chiller also features Nancy Kelly, Eileen Heckart and William Hopper. B&W.
VHS: S02659. $19.98.
Laser: LD71681. $39.98.
Mervyn Le Roy, USA, 1956, 129 mins.

Band of Angels
Based on the best seller by Pulitzer Prize winner Robert Penn Warren, this Civil War era film portrays the romance between a rich plantation owner and a half-caste woman. Clark Gable stars with Sydney Poitier.
VHS: S20686. $19.98.
Raoul Walsh, USA, 1957, 128 mins.

Bare Knees
The quintessential '20s "flapper" movie about free spirited women, the story concerns Billie (Virginia Lee Corbin), whose arrival at her sister's birthday party unleashes a series of a strange and unsettling events. With a full orchestra score. With Donald Keith, Jane Winton, Johnnie Walker, Forest Stanley and Maude Fulton.
VHS: S17489. $19.98.
Erle C. Kenton, USA, 1928, 61 mins.

Barefoot Contessa
Ava Gardner stars as a fiery Latin dancer destined to be a major Hollywood star. Loosely based on the life of Rita Hayworth, this cynical drama uncovers the underbelly of show business and marriage to the upper crust. With Humphrey Bogart as her only true friend. Also starring Edmond O'Brien and Rossano Brazzi.
VHS: S03908. $19.98.
Laser: LD72117. $39.98.
Joseph L. Mankiewicz, USA, 1954, 128 mins.

The Barretts of Wimpole Street
Norma Shearer and Fredric March star as literary giants Elizabeth Barrett and Robert Browning. A delightful mix of romance and poetry.
VHS: S15656. $19.98.
Laser: LD72162. $34.98.
Sidney Franklin, USA, 1934, 110 mins.

Bataan
A picture of war in its true, ugly detail. The story focuses on 13 Americans of various races fighting a suicidal rearguard action to stave off the Japanese offensive in the Philippines in order to allow the retreating Allied forces to make their escape. Stars Robert Taylor, Thomas Mitchell, Robert Walker and Desi Arnaz.
VHS: S02861. $19.98.
Tay Garnett, USA, 1943, 114 mins.

Bathing Beauty
Red Skelton enrolls in a girl's college to be near his swimming-coach wife Esther Williams. A lavish piece of escapist entertainment filled with South American music and spectacular water ballet sequences.
VHS: S14163. $19.98.
Laser: LD72118. $34.98.
George Sidney, USA, 1944, 101 mins.

Battle Circus
Humphrey Bogart is a hard-bitten Army surgeon with a weakness for women and strong liquor. June Allyson is the idealistic combat nurse who wins his love. A gritty and patriotic portrayal of the now familiar M.A.S.H. units, filmed while the war was still raging in Korea.
VHS: S16095. $19.98.
Richard Brooks, USA, 1953, 90 mins.

Battle Cry
Raoul Walsh's hard-hitting, realistic drama of Marine Corps heroism in the Pacific. Based on a novel and screenplay by Leon Uris.
VHS: S10020. $69.95.
Laser: LD70520. $39.98.
Raoul Walsh, USA, 1955, 169 mins.

Battle of the Bulge
An ambitious drama about the last major German counteroffensive for control of the Ardennes in late 1944, with German panzer division commander Robert Shaw engaged in a series of intricate land maneuvers with Allied forces. An excellent ensemble cast includes Henry Fonda, Dana Andrews, George Montgomery and Ty Hardin. The widescreen cinematography is by Jack Hildyard. Screenplay by Philip Yordan, Milton Sperling and John Melson.
VHS: S18606. $19.98.
Laser: LD70521. $39.98.
Ken Annakin, USA, 1965, 167 mins.

Battle Shock
When as artist on vacation is accused of murder in Acapulco, his wife must try to arrange his escape. Ralph Meeker is the suspect when they learn about his shell-shocked related violence. Janice Rule is his devoted wife. With Paul Henreid and Rosenda Monteros.
VHS: S04226. $39.95.
Paul Henreid, USA, 1956, 88 mins.

Battleground
The heroic American defense of a little Belgian town named Bastogne during the Battle of the Bulge. Van Johnson leads a cast of American fighting men in this World War II drama. They include John Hodiak, George Murphy, Marshall Thompson, Don Taylor, James Whitmore, Leon Ames, Richard Jaeckel and Ricardo Montalban as the Hispanic GI who has never seen snow before. Supporting the actors are actual members of the "Screaming Eagles" of the 101st Airborne Division.
VHS: S12536. $19.98.
Laser: LD72163. $34.95.
William Wellman, USA, 1949, 118 mins.

Beau Geste
William Wellman's spectacular version of his adventure classic stars Gary Cooper, Ray Milland, Robert Preston, as the most famous brothers ever to join the foreign legion. Full of wonderful character actors, this is a great adventure from the best of Hollywood.
VHS: S05998. $29.95.
Laser: Encore edition. LD71439. $34.98.
William Wellman, USA, 1939, 114 mins.

Beauty for the Asking
Lucille Ball stars in this film about a woman who is jilted by her money-hungry suitor. But he finds his tables turned when she invents an exclusive beauty cream and he tries to crawl back into her life. With Patrick Knowles.
VHS: S13359. $19.98.
Glenn Tryon, USA, 1939, 68 mins.

Becky Sharp
The first feature photographed in Technicolor, an adaptation of Thackeray's Vanity Fair, in which a hardened orphan wages war on English society as an ambitious social climber. Miriam Hopkins, Frances Dee, Sir Cedric Hardwicke star.
VHS: S00111. $19.95.
Rouben Mamoulian, USA, 1935, 83 mins.

Bedtime for Bonzo
It's Ronald Reagan proving that environment, not heredity, determines a youngster's future. RR decides to bring up a chimpanzee as a human baby in order to prove his theory. A classic in a league all by itself.
VHS: S00114. $14.95.
Fred De Cordova, USA, 1951, 83 mins.

Beggars in Ermine
Lionel Atwill, Betty Furness and George Hayes star in this melodrama from Monogram Pictures. Atwill is the head of a steel mill with social leanings, who is betrayed, and begins to organize all of the beggars of the nation into a financial force. A very unusual social drama.
VHS: S06906. $29.95.
Phil Rosen, USA, 1934, 80 mins.

Behave Yourself
Farley Granger and Shelley Winters are cast as a couple who mistakenly get caught up in gang warfare. A dog follows Granger home and his wife (Winters) thinks it's a present for her. He readily agrees, but finds out this apparently innocent animal has been trained in gangland espionage. Lon Chaney, Jr., is featured as a gangster.
VHS: S23983. $24.95.
George Beck, USA, 1951, 81 mins.

Behind Office Doors
A "power behind the throne" theme is the essence of this story of the executive secretary who is taken for granted. Mary Astor and Ricardo Cortez star in a pre-code outing.
VHS: S04493. $29.95.
Melville Brown, USA, 1932, 82 mins.

Behind the Rising Sun
This World War II drama is about a Japanese diplomat who urges his now Americanized son to join the Japanese army, but suffers a most devastating consequence. Unusual perspective or point of view taken during World War II.
VHS: S10657. $19.98.
Edward Dmytryk, USA, 1943, 89 mins.

Bell, Book and Candle
An attractive young witch (Kim Novak) vows not to use her magic powers but can't help throwing a love spell when she eyes the new man in her building, James Stewart. This screen version of the Broadway play by John Van Druten also features Jack Lemmon and Ernie Kovacs.
VHS: S03903. $19.95.
Richard Quine, USA, 1959, 106 mins.

The Bells of St. Mary's
The sequel to Going My Way finds Bing Crosby as Father O'Malley, with a new assignment at a run-down parish. He finds his methods at odds with those of Sister Superior Ingrid Bergman. Good wholesome fun with a song or two, and a tug at the heart.
VHS: S04224. $19.98.
Laser: CLV. LD71970. $39.98.
Leo McCarey, USA, 1945, 126 mins.

Beloved Enemy
David Niven plays the male secretary to a top British civil servant trying to solve the Irish problem in 1921. Though it was a small part, Niven was noticed in a cast that top-billed Merle Oberon and Brian Aherne as lovers on opposing sides.
VHS: Out of print. For rental only.
Laser: LD75157. $34.98.
H.C. Potter, USA, 1937, 90 mins.

Beneath the 12-Mile Reef
Robert Webb's film follows two people caught up in the business rivalries of two sponge-diving families on Key West. It is best known for its pioneering use of Cinemascope and its experimental underwater footage. Cinematography by Edward Conjager. Music by Bernard Herrmann. With Robert Wagner, Terry Moore, Gilbert Roland, Peter Graves and J. Carrol Naish.
Laser: Letterboxed. LD71951. $39.98.
Robert Webb, USA, 1953, 103 mins.

Berlin Express
A crack squad of police from four nations is called in to save a German statesman from the murderous Nazi underground in this gripping tale of espionage and intrigue. A great thriller from Jacques Tourneur. Merle Oberon and Robert Ryan star.
VHS: S05669. $19.98.
Jacques Tourneur, USA, 1948, 86 mins.

The Bermuda Affair
Kim Hunter stars with Gary Merill and Ron Randell in this tense melodrama. Two pilots are trapped in a failing plane with only one parachute. Suddenly they recount the complicated business dealings and romantic entanglements that governed their life up until this desperate moment.
VHS: S23884. $29.95.
A. Edward Sullivan, USA, 1956, 88 mins.

Best of Andy Hardy
One of the most popular movie series of all time, with Mickey Rooney, Judy Garland, Kathryn Grayson and Ann Rutherford. Rooney is the typical American teenager, Lewis Stone his stern father, Fay Holden his "swell" mother, Cecilia Parker his older sister Marian. Sara Haden is Aunt Millie and Ann Rutherford is Polly, the girlfriend to whom Andy always returns. Winner of a special Oscar for "its achievement in representing the American Way of Life," this MGM series introduced many starlets-later-to-be-stars. Films from a nostalgic era of Hollywood unlikely to return.
Andy Hardy Gets Spring Fever. With Mickey Rooney and Ann Rutherford. Directed by Woodbridge S. Van Dyke, USA, 1939, 88 mins.
VHS: S11441. $19.95.
Andy Hardy Meets Debutante. With Mickey Rooney and Judy Garland. Directed by George B. Seitz, USA, 1940, 86 mins.
VHS: S11439. $19.95.
Laser: LD70198. $49.98.
Andy Hardy's Double Life. With Mickey Rooney and Esther Williams. Directed by George B. Seitz, USA, 1942, 91 mins.
VHS: S11442. $19.95.
Andy Hardy's Private Secretary. With Mickey Rooney and Kathryn Grayson. Directed by George B. Seitz, USA, 1941, 101 mins.
VHS: S11440. $19.95.
Life Begins for Andy Hardy. With Mickey Rooney and Judy Garland.
VHS: S11437. $19.95.
Love Finds Andy Hardy. With Mickey Rooney and Judy Garland.
VHS: S11438. $19.95.

The Best of Everything
Joan Crawford, Hope Lange and Louis Jourdan star in this adaptation of Rona Jaffe's best-selling novel about the world of publishing. It is an engaging yarn mixing passion, ambition and power into an effective story. Crawford is great as the editor who can never seem to find love amidst the witty literary set.
VHS: S26488. $19.98.
Jean Negulesco, USA, 1959, 121 mins.

Best of the Badmen
Robert Ryan plays an ex-Quantrill Raider who would like to forget the Civil War, but devious Yankee detective Robert Preston won't let him in. Preston is after the rewards on Ryan and his friends (the James boys) and their cousins, the Younger brothers. With Lawrence Tierney, Bruce Cabot, Jack Beutel, Tom Tyler, Claire Trevor and Walter Brennan as Doc Butcher.
VHS: S12831. $19.95.
William D. Russell, USA, 1951, 84 mins.

Betrayal from the East
Lee Tracy stars as a carnival barker turned serviceman in a wartime tale of counterespionage, as the Japanese attempt to control the Panama Canal Zone.
VHS: S12372. $19.98.
William Berke, USA, 1944, 82 mins.

The Bette Davis Collection
The wit and energy of Bette Davis are reflected in this collection of five of her finest works: Edmund Goulding's The Old Maid, William Wyler's The Letter, John Huston's In This Our Life, Irving Rapper's Now, Voyager, and Curtis Bernhardt's A Stolen Life. The original theatrical trailer is shown with each film.
Laser: LD70142. $99.98.

Between Heaven and Hell
Robert Wagner, Terry Moore and Buddy Ebsen star in this psychological drama about a self-centered, prejudiced young recruit who comes of age during WWII. Praise has been lavished on the performance of Buddy Ebsen. With Broderick Crawford as the psycho commander.
VHS: S15196. $14.95.
Richard Fleischer, USA, 1956, 94 mins.

Beware My Lovely
Widow Ida Lupino hires Robert Ryan as a handyman, then discovers he is a psychopath. (Don't you hate it when that happens?) A dark and atmospheric thriller that delivers chills and good performances from its talented leads.
VHS: S05670. $19.95.
Laser: LD71814. $29.98.
Harry Horner, USA, 1952, 77 mins.

Beware of Spooks
Joe E. Brown is a cop afraid of his own shadow who gets mixed up with a haunted house, a pretty girl (Mary Carlisle) and some thugs. An outrageous vehicle for Brown's unique comical style. USA, 76 mins.
VHS: S15381. $24.95.

Beyond the Forest
Bette Davis stars as the unhappy wife of a small-town doctor who has an affair with a wealthy man, murders a witness, attempts suicide, and dies of fever. With Davis' famous line, "If I don't get out of here, I'll just die!"
VHS: S13392. $19.98.
King Vidor, USA, 1949, 96 mins.

Beyond Tomorrow
Three spirits disguised as wealthy men spend Christmas with a down and out couple who deserve a little happiness. A sensitive drama with the obvious Biblical overtones. Richard Carlsona and Jean Parker are the couple. With Maria Ouspenskaya, Harry Carey and C. Aubrey Smith in support. B&W.
VHS: S04086. $29.95.
Edward A. Sutherland, USA, 1940, 84 mins.

Big Business Girl
A youthful Loretta Young plays a business-minded career girl on the way to the top, whose boyfriend must sing for his supper. But Loretta finds that the workaday world is not without hazards as she fends off a boss more interested in her time off. Joan Blondell is also featured in this film, made before the adoption of the censoring pre-Production Code.
VHS: S20830. $19.98.
William A. Seiter, USA, 1931, 75 mins.

The Big Chance
John Darrow and Mickey Rooney act in this early film about a crooked boxer. Suddenly the boxer decides he wants to play it straight, but his manager has other ideas. 1933, 60 mins.
VHS: S26678. $19.95.

The Big Hangover
Van Johnson is a talented lawyer with a troubled past and a hilariously fatal allergy to alcohol. Elizabeth Taylor is the object of his affection, the boss's daughter who helps him cope with his perilous condition. With Leon Ames, Edgar Buchanan and Rosemary DeCamp.
VHS: S18528. $19.98.
Norman Krasna, USA, 1950, 82 mins.

The Big House
Wallace Beery gives a great performance as the consummate tough guy in this classic prison drama. Rage and violence are inevitable when 3000 prisoners share a space built for only 1800. This movie stands the test of time, especially since it inspired so many lesser copies. Also features Robert Montgomery.
VHS: S21015. $19.98.
George Hill, USA, 1930, 86 mins.

Big Jim
A quick visit to Cora's grown son turns into an ordeal when Jim insists she stay for awhile. Although he loves his mother, her "business" becomes suspect, and he soon discovers what she really does for a living. With Loretta Young and Bobby Driscoll.
VHS: S16746. $14.95.
Richard Morris, USA, 1954, 30 mins.

Big Jim McLain
Trouble in paradise! John Wayne stars as a special agent for the House Un-American Activities Committee, who must ferret out a Hawaiian-based Communist spy ring. Another right-wing star vehicle for the Duke. This one also features James Arness (Gunsmoke) and some rather exotic locales in pre-statehood Hawaii.
VHS: S13490. $19.98.
Edward Ludwig, USA, 1952, 90 mins.

The Big Knife
Robert Aldrich's brilliant exploration of greed and desperation in Hollywood. The story of blackmail involves movie star Charlie Castle (Jack Palance), his estranged wife (Ida Lupino) and a sleazy, ruthless studio boss (Rod Steiger). Adapted by James Poe from Clifford Odets's play. With Everett Sloane, Jean Hagen, Shelley Winters and Wesley Addy.
Laser: LD71663. $34.98.
Robert Aldrich, USA, 1955, 113 mins.

The Big Lift
Montgomery Clift, Paul Douglas and Cornell Borchers star in this serious drama about the days of and immediately following the Berlin airlift. The concerted efforts of the U.S. Air Force helped stave off disaster when the Russians blocked passage to the Allied Forces' sectors of the divided German Capitol. Danny MacCullough (Clift) is an American GI in love with Frederica (Borchers), a German woman who turns out to be a villain. This film tells the story of GI pilots romancing German women and also dramatizes the tense effects on daily life that occurred as a result of the Soviet blockade.
VHS: S27332. $19.98.
George Seaton, USA, 1950, 120 mins.

Big News
This early sound film stars Robert Armstrong as an ambitious, no-nonsense reporter fired for antagonizing a gangster and subsequently drawn into a murder plot. With Carole Lombard, Tom Kennedy and Warner Richmond.
VHS: S04489. $19.95.
Gregory La Cava, USA, 1929, 75 mins.

The Big Street
A picaresque Damon Runyan tale of a nightclub singer crippled by a ruthless gangster and the selfless devotion of a busboy named Little Pinks, portrayed by Henry Fonda. The blend of comedy and drama gave Lucille Ball one of her finest roles.
VHS: S03251. $19.95.
Irving Reis, USA, 1942, 82 mins.

The Bigamist
Edmond O'Brien plays a traveling salesman who gets bored in Los Angeles and picks up lonely greasy-spoon cook Ida Lupino. When she announces her pregnancy, they marry. The only problem is that O'Brien already has a wife in San Francisco (Joan Fontaine). This film is the only work in which Lupino directs herself.
VHS: S16102. $29.95.
Ida Lupino, USA, 1953, 79 mins.

Bill and Coo
Dean Riesner directed this imaginative, live-action fantasy film cast exclusively with trained birds in an amusing comedy story. Hollywood was so taken with the film they awarded it a special Oscar.
VHS: S01823. $29.95.
Dean Riesner, USA, 1947, 61 mins.

Billie
Patty Duke plays a girl who has it all: talent, charm and "the Beat"—the rock 'n' roll rhythm in her head that has her out-running every boy on the high school track team. Also starring Jim Backus.
VHS: S15241. $19.98.
Laser: LD72260. $34.98.
Don Weis, USA, 1965, 86 mins.

Bird of Paradise
Joel McCrea and Dolores Del Rio star in this South Seas adventure tale about a Polynesian chief who beds his daughter sacrificed to the Volcano god. With a memorable musical score by Max Steiner.
VHS: S00131. $19.95.
King Vidor, USA, 1932, 80 mins.

Birdman of Alcatraz

When is a man rehabilitated? And what determines the dignity of a human being? These are some of the issues raised in this stirring true story about Robert Stroud (brilliantly played by Burt Lancaster), who became one of the world's leading experts on birds while serving a life sentence for murder. Also starring Thelma Ritter, Telly Savalas and Karl Malden.
VHS: S14306. $19.98.
Laser: LD71689. $39.98.
John Frankenheimer, USA, 1962, 143 mins.

Black Arrow

From the novel by Robert Louis Stevenson. The War of the Roses in England is refought by Louis Hayward and George MacReady with the lovely Janet Blair rooting for the heroic Mr. Hayward. Swashbuckling action and adventure set against an involved tale of revenge that produces a considerable number of bodies punctured by the title instrument of death. With Edgar Buchanan.
VHS: S09111. $69.95.
Gordon Douglas, USA, 1948, 76 mins.

Black Book (Reign of Terror)

Robert Cummings, Richard Basehart, Arlene Dahl star in this vivid costume drama of the French Revolution. Cummings goes undercover with revolutionaries who plan to topple the reign of Robespierre.
VHS: S13049. $19.98.
Anthony Mann, USA, 1949, 89 mins.

Black Dragons

Bela Lugosi plays a Nazi plastic surgeon who transforms six Japanese agents into American industrialists. Inspired by an actual "Black Dragon" Japanese society, this is one of the first anti-Japanese WWII films released after Pearl Harbor. Clayton Moore co-stars without his Lone Ranger mask.
VHS: S04007. $19.98.
William Nigh, USA, 1942, 61 mins.

Black Like Me

James Whitmore stars in this classic and controversial drama about a white magazine reporter who changes the color of his skin so he can experience life as a black man.
VHS: S06585. $19.95.
Laser: LD75316. $39.98.
Carl Lerner, USA, 1964, 107 mins.

The Black Orchid

From the director of *Sounder* and *Norma Rae*, an early film from Martin Ritt stars Sophia Loren as a recently widowed wife, whose late gangster husband's sordid activities threaten the balanced family of her new lover, Anthony Quinn. An excellent performance from Ina Balin as a put-upon daughter.
VHS: S02794. $14.95.
Martin Ritt, USA, 1959, 96 mins.

The Black Swan

Tyrone Power stars in the original pirate adventure, winner of the 1942 Oscar for color cinematography. The 17th-century pirate Jamie Waring (Power) is granted a pardon in exchange for clearing the Caribbean and stopping the high-sea piracy of the fighting ship *The Black Swan*. A former officer on the infamous ship, Power rescues the lovely Maureen O'Hara from the evil clutches of George Sanders and Anthony Quinn. Unfortunately, a traitor is undermining Power's work by giving away information of sailings and arrivals. This swashbuckling classic is based on the novel by Rafael Sabatini.
VHS: S27207. $19.98.
Henry King, USA, 1942, 82 mins.

Blackbeard the Pirate

Robert Newton is the evil captain, Linda Darnell the kidnapped noble lady, and Keith Andes the heroic doctor who rescues her. Filmed in three-strip technicolor.
VHS: S03227. $19.98.
Raoul Walsh, USA, 1952, 99 mins.

Blackboard Jungle

Based on the novel by Evan Hunter. Glenn Ford is a teacher trying to survive in the New York City Public School system. His class of juvenile delinquents includes Vic Morrow, Sidney Poitier, Jamie Farr and Paul Mazursky. A serious drama that also launched Bill Haley's "Rock around the Clock." With Anne Francis, John Hoyt, Louis Calhern and Richard Kiley.
VHS: S11215. $19.95.
Laser: LD74668. $34.98.
Richard Brooks, USA, 1955, 101 mins.

Blessed Event

A penetrating account of a Walter Winchell-type newspaper columnist (Lee Tracy) whose restless probing of Broadway and Hollywood personalities threatens his own welfare in this sharp comedy. With Dick Powell, Ned Sparks, Mary Brian and Ruth Donnelly.
VHS: S18124. $19.98.
Roy Del Ruth, USA, 1932, 78 mins.

Blockade

Madeleine Carroll and Henry Fonda star in this romantic drama, directed with verve by William Dieterle, about a farmer during the Spanish Civil War who takes up arms to defend his land. Touted as Hollywood's first serious contribution to international affairs. With Leo Carrillo, John Halliday.
VHS: S11586. $19.95.
William Dieterle, USA, 1938, 84 mins.

Blonde Crazy

James Cagney stars in this "chipper, hardboiled, amusing essay on petty thievery" (*Time*). He plays a likable Depression Era con-man who teams up with Joan Blondell to make sure suckers and their money are soon parted. They pull off a series of daring and often hilariously funny scams...until Blondell marries a society boy. Also starring Ray Milland.
VHS: S15012. $19.98.
Laser: LD71162. $39.98.
Roy Del Ruth, USA, 1931, 79 mins.

Blood Alley

Produced during the height of the Cold War, William Wellman's *Blood Alley* stars John Wayne as he and Lauren Bacall lead a group of Chinese refugees along a dangerous waterway.
VHS: S12497. $19.98.
Laser: Letterboxed. LD74700. $34.98.
William Wellman, USA, 1955, 115 mins.

Blood on the Sun

James Cagney plays a tough newspaper editor in Tokyo in the late 1920's. He learns of a secret Japanese invasion plan from reporters Wallace Ford and Rosemary DeCamp just before they are murdered. When Japanese agents charge him with the killings, Cagney really gets sore. Based on the 1927 Tanaka document scandal. With Robert Armstrong, Jack Holloran, John Emery and several other Caucasian actors in Japanese roles.
VHS: S12902. $19.98.
Laser: CLV. LD71971. $29.98.
Frank Lloyd, USA, 1945, 98 mins.

Blossoms in the Dust

Greer Garson adopts a family of 2000 with her boundless love in this Oscar-nominated Best Picture that's a classic tear jerker. An enormous success, Garson founds an orphanage after she loses her husband and child.
VHS: S13063. $19.98.
Mervyn Le Roy, USA, 1941, 99 mins.

Blowing Wild

Filmed in Mexico, this stars Gary Cooper as an oil man wildcatter pursued by Barbara Stanwyck, who happens to be married to Anthony Quinn. Greed, lust and vengeance in the early 30's.
VHS: S03503. $19.98.
Hugo Fregonese, USA, 1953, 92 mins.

Blue Bird

Shirley Temple searches for the Blue Bird of Happiness in various fantasy lands, only to find it at home, in this imaginative fantasy that was Twentieth Century Fox's answer to *The Wizard of Oz*. With Gale Sondergaard.
VHS: S09993. $19.98.
Walter Lang, USA, 1940, 83 mins.

Blue Dahlia

Alan Ladd and Veronica Lake made their movie careers in film noirs like this. Raymond Chandler's first original screenplay is classic in its simplicity. Johnny Morrison (Ladd) returns from Naval duty to discover his wife has been cheating on him. Soon she is murdered, leaving Johnny as the prime suspect. Now it's up to him—with the help of sultry vixen Joyce Harwood (Lake)—to clear his name. Includes the original theatrical trailer.
VHS: S27353. $14.98.
George Marshall, USA, 1945, 100 mins.

Bluebeard

John Carradine, a clever puppeteer, has a way with women—he does away with them. His eventual downfall is a beautiful and smart dress shop owner (Jean Parker) who senses that something is not quite right about him. Very effective thriller from an often overlooked director.
VHS: S03006. $39.95.
Edgar G. Ulmer, USA, 1944, 74 mins.

The Bogart Collection

Four of Bogart's best works: Raoul Walsh's *High Sierra* (1941), John Huston's *The Maltese Falcon* (1941), Archie Mayo's *The Petrified Forest* (1936) and John Huston's *The Treasure of the Sierra Madre* (1948). The original theatrical trailer of each film is also presented. 476 mins.
Laser: LD71649. $99.98.

Bombardier

A World War II drama of the men being trained to drop, with accuracy, deadly bombs on the enemy. Constructed as a tribute to those men in uniform.
VHS: S10661. $19.98.
Richard Wallace, USA, 1943, 99 mins.

Bombers B-52

Karl Malden and Efrem Zimbalist Jr. star as airmen who are responsible for the backbone of America's cold war defense. When Zimbalist falls in love with a sergeant's daughter, played by Natalie Wood, this wartime story becomes even more tense.
VHS: S21009. $19.98.
Gordon Douglas, USA, 1957, 106 mins.

Bombshell

Jean Harlow stars in this satire on the 1930's Hollywood star machine. Harlow is the much-used star who tires of the games and quits, thoroughly frustrating an unscrupulous publicity agent. Her attempts to start a new life are continually thwarted by the studios and the Hollywood system. With Lee Tracy, Frank Morgan.
VHS: S13357. $19.98.
Victor Fleming, USA, 1933, 96 mins.

Bonjour Tristesse

Set on the beautiful French Riviera, and adapted from the best-selling book by Francoise Sagan. Deborah Kerr and David Niven star in a portrait of love, lust and tragedy as Kerr falls in love with a playboy (Niven), but is unable to cope with his constant philandering. Co-starring Jean Seberg.
VHS: S06999. $69.95.
Otto Preminger, USA, 1958, 94 mins.

Boom Town

Clark Gable plays Big John McMasters and Spencer Tracy is Square John Sand in this manly saga of oil fields and making lots of money. The women in their lives are Claudette Colbert and Hedy Lamarr. Friendships are strained and punches exchanged over the search for black gold and Texas tea. With Frank Morgan, Joe Yule and Chill Wills as Harmony Jones.
VHS: S12532. $19.98.
Jack Conway, USA, 1940, 117 mins.

Boomerang!

Winning Best Director's Honors from the New York Film Critics, this film is a solid thriller based on the facts of a real criminal case. That is the rationale for the docudrama style. The film concerns a D.A. (Dana Andrews) who believes that the man who confessed to killing a minister is actually innocent. Setting out to prove it provokes more trouble than he ever imagined. Playwright Arthur Miller appears in a brief cameo. With Jane Wyatt and Lee J. Cobb.
VHS: S27441. $19.98.
Elia Kazan, USA, 1947, 88 mins.

Boots and Saddles

Gene Autry is a ranch foreman whose boss turns out to be a British youngster. There are also an unscrupulous competitor, a colonel's feisty daughter, a barn fire, and the well meaning blunders of sidekick Smiley Burnette for Autry to contend with. 1937, 53 mins.
VHS: S26679. $19.95.

Boots Malone

William Holden has the title role as a shady agent for racetrack jockeys. His luck changes when he meets Johnny Stewart, a rich, naive 15-year-old who wants to ride for the roses. With Stanley Clements, Carl Benton Reid, Ed Begley Sr., Ralph Dumke and Harry Morgan as Quarter Horse Harry. Filmed on location at racetracks around the country.
VHS: S15894. $19.95.
William Dieterle, USA, 1952, 102 mins.

Born to Kill

A couple of cold-blooded murderers rob a wealthy brother and sister of everything they own by marrying them. An incredibly hard-boiled film noir that is superbly constructed and stars Lawrence Tierney and Claire Trevor.
VHS: S15102. $19.98.
Robert Wise, USA, 1946, 92 mins.

Bowery Buckaroos

The Bowery Boys go west prospecting for gold. Along the way they raise a ruckus in Hangman's Hollow which leads to Leo Gorcey being charged with murder. They also see what they can do to help a nice girl get back her stolen mine. With Huntz Hall, Bobby Jordan, Gabriel Dell, David Gorcey, Jack Norman, Julie Briggs, Iron Eyes Cody and Chief Yowlachi as Chief Hi-Octane.
VHS: S15827. $14.98.
William Beaudine, USA, 1947, 66 mins.

Boys Town

Spencer Tracy won an Oscar for his role as Father Flanagan, the man who believed there is no such thing as a bad boy. Mickey Rooney is around to thoroughly test that theory. A heartwarming and heart-tugging film about the creation of the home for juvenile delinquents. With Addison Richards, Leslie Fenton, Henry Hull and Gene Reynolds. Oscars also went to the writers Dore Schary and Eleanor Griffin.
VHS: S11219. $19.95.
Laser: LD70153. $34.98.
Norman Taurog, USA, 1938, 96 mins.

Boys' Night Out

A group of married men and an independent friend (James Garner), impatient and tired of their dull, suburban comfort, set up a covert New York apartment for their beautiful, shared "mistress" (Kim Novak), unaware they're part of an elaborate social behavior experiment that has gone awry. With Tony Randall, Howard Duff and Janet Blair.
VHS: S20200. $19.98.
Michael Gordon, USA, 1962, 115 mins.

Boys' Reformatory

When two brothers are framed for a crime, the more responsible one (Frankie Darro) takes the rap, is imprisoned, escapes, and relentlessly pursues the criminals responsible for the acts. With Grant Withers, David Durand and Warren McCollum.
VHS: S18946. $19.95.
Howard Bretherton, USA, 1939, 62 mins.

The Bramble Bush

A gothic thriller about a charismatic New England doctor (Richard Burton) who returns to his small-town origins and gets entangled in the mysterious death of his lover's fatally ill husband. Milton Sperling and Philip Yordan adapted the novel by Charles Mergendahl. With Barbara Rush, Jack Carson and Angie Dickinson.
VHS: S20193. $19.98.
Daniel Petrie, USA, 1960, 105 mins.

The Brave One

Written by Dalton Trumbo under a pseudonym after he was blacklisted by the HUAC committee, this rare classic of a boy's struggle to save the life of his pet bull is presented in a letter-box format.
VHS: Out of print. For rental only.
Laser: Widescreen, CLV. LD74746. $39.95.
Irving Rapper, USA, 1956, 100 mins.

Break of Hearts

Stars Katharine Hepburn as a young composer caught in a turbulent marriage to her famous conductor husband, who has been spoiled by success. Charles Boyer plays opposite Ms. Hepburn in this sentimental drama.
VHS: S10658. $19.98.
Philip Moeller, USA, 1935, 78 mins.

A Breath of Scandal

Casablanca director Michael Curtiz fashions this high-spirited costume period piece based on the celebrated Ferenc Molnar play, *Olympia*. Sophia Loren is a widowed, defiant young princess whose amorous plays for American John Gavin invalidate her supposed romantic arrangement with a not-too-bright prince. A good cast includes Maurice Chevalier and Angela Lansbury.
VHS: S02784. $19.95.
Michael Curtiz, USA, 1960, 98 mins.

Bride Wore Red

Joan Crawford is cast as a poor, embittered cabaret singer who accepts the offer of an all-expense paid holiday at a resort in the Tyrolian Alps. There she is wooed by Robert Young, a wealthy playboy and Franchot Tone, a poetic village postman. With Billie Burke, Reginald Owen and George Zucco as Joan's aristocratic benefactor.
VHS: S16447. $19.98.
Dorothy Arzner, USA, 1937, 103 mins.

The Bridge at Remagen

For the Americans, the bridge at Remagen is the link to the heart of the Third Reich; for the retreating Germans, it's the last hope. Starring Robert Vaughan, E.G. Marshall and Ben Gazzara.
VHS: S15127. $19.98.
John Guillermin, USA, 1969, 116 mins.

The Bridges at Toko-Ri

William Holden, Grace Kelly and Mickey Rooney head a fine cast that explores the lives of Navy jet pilots in Korea. Based on the best seller by James Michener, the special effects earned an Oscar. Also in the cast are Fredric March, Earl Holliman and Robert Strauss.
VHS: S06029. $19.95.
Laser: LD75164. $34.98.
Mark Robson, USA, 1954, 103 mins.

British Intelligence

Boris Karloff plays a German spy acting as a butler in the household of an important British war official. Margaret Lindsay is the double-agent out to expose his organization. This is the third film based on the play *Three Faces East*. A 1930 version featured Eric Von Stroheim and Constance Bennett in the same roles. B&W.
VHS: S04022. $29.95.
Terry Morse, USA, 1940, 62 mins.

Brother Orchid

Two of Hollywood's greatest gangsters (Edward G. Robinson and Humphrey Bogart) star in this fish-out-of-water story featuring bare knuckles, one-liners and a wild story twist. A mobster has to hide out in a monastery while he tries to dodge the enemy and regain control of his gang.
VHS: S15521. $19.98.
Lloyd Bacon, USA, 1940, 87 mins.

Brothers Karamazov

Lavish production of the Dostoevsky novel featuring Yul Brynner, Maria Schell, Claire Bloom and Lee J. Cobb. From the director of *Cat on a Hot Tin Roof* and *Lord Jim*.
VHS: S00186. $24.95.
Richard Brooks, USA, 1957, 147 mins.

The Buccaneer

A swashbuckling tale of adventures taking place during the battle of New Orleans, when Andrew Jackson relies on buccaneer Lafitte to help curb or stall the British invasion. Good cast includes Yul Brynner, Charlton Heston, Claire Bloom and Charles Boyer. This also happens to be the only film Anthony Quinn ever directed.
VHS: S13782. $19.98.
Laser: LD75168. $34.98.
Anthony Quinn, USA, 1958, 121 mins.

Bulldog Drummond

Ronald Colman appeared in his first speaking role as the classic adventurer Captain Hugh "Bulldog" Drummond. The ex-war hero is approached to rescue a young woman's uncle from a nursing home. With Joan Bennett, Montagu Love and Lilyan Tashman. The sets by William Cameron Menzies won an Oscar. B&W.
VHS: S00188. $19.98.
F. Richard Jones, USA, 1929, 90 mins.

Bulldog Drummond Series

Double features.
Volume 1: *Bulldog Drummond Escapes.* Bulldog's girl Phyllis has been made the pawn of an international spy ring and only a daring rescue attempt can save her. 1937. 67 mins. *Bulldog Drummond Comes Back.* An old enemy has kidnapped Bulldog's bride-to-be. Bulldog has little time to rescue her and gets involved in an exciting chase through the English countryside. With Ray Milland and John Barrymore. 1937. 59 mins.
VHS: S03080. $29.95.
Volume 2: *Bulldog Drummond's Revenge.* Bulldog's wife-to-be can't be—just yet. Our hero must investigate the mysterious disappearance of a powerful secret weapon. With John Barrymore, John Howard and Louise Campbell. 1937. 55 mins. *Bulldog Drummond's Peril.* The announcements are out, and our hero moves closer to marriage. Among the wedding gifts is a beautiful diamond, one created using a new synthetic process. When the gem is stolen, Bulldog sets off in hot pursuit! 1938. 66 mins.
VHS: S03081. $29.95.
Volume 3: *Bulldog Drummond's Secret Police.* The ultimate adventurer has been hit with some exciting news about a fabulous treasure hidden beneath a medieval castle guarded by a mad killer. John Howard, Heather Angel and H.B. Warner star. 1939. 54 mins. *Bulldog Drummond's Bride.* The big day has finally arrived. Bulldog shall wed the love of his life, putting an end to his rovings of bachelorhood forever. But just for old-times sake, he agrees to help his good friend solve a most difficult case. 1939. 56 mins.
VHS: S03082. $19.98.
Volume 4: *Bulldog Drummond in Africa.* The head of Scotland Yard has been abducted and threatened with certain death. But they didn't count on Bulldog Drummond leading the rescue operation. With John Howard and Heather Angel. 1938. 58 mins. *Arrest Bulldog Drummond.* Bulldog heads for yet another bachelor dinner to celebrate his ever-pending marriage when a villainous international spy confronts and detains him. 1937. 57 mins.
VHS: S03083. $29.95.
Bulldog Drummond, Set
VHS: S26955. $99.95.

Bullets or Ballots

In this colorful classic Edward G. Robinson stars as a tough New York cop who infiltrates the mob from within in order to break it up. Humphrey Bogart provides added interest and danger. Above average gangster yarn.
VHS: S15522. $19.98.
William Keighley, USA, 1938, 82 mins.

Bullfighter and the Lady

While vacationing in Mexico, Chuck Regan is fascinated by both the bullfights and a local beauty. Hoping to arouse her passion, he trains for the ring with a popular matador. But when Chuck's restlessness results in tragedy, his courage is tested in a brutal contest for love, honor and redemption. Budd Boetticher's great film has been restored to its original length, with unforgettable bullfighting sequences and terrific performances from Robert Stack, Joy Page and Gilbert Roland.
VHS: S09667. $19.98.
Laser: LD71577. $34.98.
Budd Boetticher, USA, 1951, 87 mins.

Bureau of Missing Persons

A drama about the case loads from the bureau of missing people, with Lewis S. Stone as a powerful boss who determines everyone's fate, Pat O'Brien as a neurotic cop, and Bette Davis as an enigmatic woman drawn to him. With Allen Jenkins, Ruth Donnelly and Hugh Herbert.
VHS: S17330. $19.98.
Roy Del Ruth, USA, 1933, 73 mins.

But Not for Me

A theatrical manager, played by Clark Gable, must thwart the amorous advances of his young secretary in order to go after the sophisticated Lilli Palmer.
VHS: S13783. $14.95.
Walter Lang, USA, 1959, 105 mins.

Butterfield 8

Elizabeth Taylor won an Oscar for her performance as call-girl Gloria Wandrous, a high class NYC tart who yearns to settle down and find Mr. Right. Based on the 1935 novel by John O'Hara. The title refers to a phone number. With Eddie Fisher, Dina Merrill, Mildred Dunnock, Susan Oliver, Kay Medford and Laurence Harvey as Weston Liggett.
VHS: S09148. $29.95.
Laser: LD70163. $34.98.
Daniel Mann, USA, 1960, 109 mins.

By Love Possessed

Lana Turner is the center of attention in this glossy romantic vehicle. Based loosely on the novel by James Gould Cozzens. Sparks fly when Turner becomes involved with a prominent New England attorney played by Efrem Zimbalist Jr. Cast includes Jason Robards Jr., George Hamilton and Thomas Mitchell.
VHS: S11284. $14.95.
Laser: Chapter search. Includes original trailer. LD71639. $34.98.
John Sturges, USA, 1961, 115 mins.

C-Man

A hard-hitting 1949 crime drama told in a semi-documentary style, starring John Carradine and Dean Jagger. Jagger plays a customs agent on the trail of jewel smugglers.
VHS: S07396. $29.95.
Joseph Lerner, USA, 1949, 75 mins.

The Cabin in the Cotton

"I'd love to kiss ya, but I jest washt ma hair." Michael Curtiz's melodrama about Southern sharecroppers caught in a romantic tangle between the respectable Richard Barthelmess and sexy Southern seductress Bette Davis. With Dorothy Jordan, Henry B. Walthall and Tully Marshall.
VHS: S17331. $19.98.
Michael Curtiz, USA, 1932, 78 mins.

Cabin in the Sky

Minnelli's first chance to direct was by MGM starring an all-black cast. Eddie Anderson (Rochester on the Jack Benny Show) proves to be an outstanding actor, with Ethel Waters as the woman who saves his life, Lena Horne, and an appearance by Louis Armstrong.
VHS: S01747. $19.98.
Laser: LD70538. $34.98.
Vincente Minnelli, USA, 1943, 99 mins.

The Caine Mutiny

Humphrey Bogart, as Captain Philip Francis Queeg, provokes Van Johnson to seize his ship during a typhoon. Van and fellow officer Robert Francis go on trial defended by Jose Ferrer. A top notch cast in a great courtroom drama. Find out what really happened to the strawberries. With Fred MacMurray as a creep.
VHS: S01854. $19.95.
Laser: 3 sides. LD72443. $39.95.
Edward Dmytryk, USA, 1954, 125 mins.

Call It Murder

Originally released as *Midnight*, based on a novel by the same name. The foreman of a jury sends a young woman to the electric chair and pays with pangs of conscience. He is faced with a moral dilemma when his own daughter is arrested for the same crime. An early performance by Humphrey Bogart led to this film being reissued (after he became a star) under this new title.
VHS: S08415. $29.95.

Call Northside 777

James Stewart stars along with Richard Conte and E.G. Marshall in this absorbing, dramatic film. A reporter, going on his own hunch, investigates a murder where he remains convinced that the law has fingered the wrong man. The semi-documentary style employed in this film makes this tale even more compelling.
VHS: S22532. $19.98.
Henry Hathaway, USA, 1948, 111 mins.

Call Out the Marines

Frank Ryan and William Hamilton directed this updating of the Lowe and McLaglen Flagg and Quint comedy; their last film together. It's the story of two marines fighting over seductress Binnie Barnes while trying to unmask a nest of spies.
VHS: S08879. $24.95.
Frank Ryan, USA, 1942, 67 mins.

Call Out the Marines/The Clay Pigeons

Call Out the Marines follows two marines forced by circumstance to become spies. Frank Ryan, USA, 1942, 67 mins. *The Clay Pigeons* has an honest seaman wrongly accused of treason. Richard Fleischer, USA, 1949, 63 mins.
VHS: S10662. $19.98.

The Canterville Ghost

Charles Laughton is trapped as a fearful ghost for 300 years, awaiting a brave deed that will set him free, in the classic tale loosely adapted from Oscar Wilde. A charmer for the whole family. With Margaret O'Brien, Robert Young.
VHS: S13062. $19.98.
Jules Dassin, USA, 1943, 95 mins.

Cape Fear

Robert Mitchum is a sadistic rapist seeking out the lawyer who put him behind bars (played by Gregory Peck). His search ends in a small North Carolina town where he commences a campaign of terror against Peck's family, which the police are powerless to stop. A tense and well-paced suspenser highlighted by Mitchum's riveting portrayal of a shrewd psychopath, and a terrific cat-and-mouse chase through the Southern bayous.
VHS: S14979. $19.95.
Laser: LD70293. $34.98.
J. Lee Thompson, USA, 1962, 106 mins.

Captain Blood

One of the great Hollywood swashbuckling sagas: Errol Flynn and Olivia de Havilland star in the story of a young doctor unjustly condemned to slavery. Bought from the slave ship by Arabella, he escapes and becomes a notorious pirate.
VHS: S01874. $19.98.
Laser: LD71690. $39.98.
Michael Curtiz, USA, 1935, 120 mins.

Captain Horatio Hornblower

Based on the adventure novels of C.S. Forester, Gregory Peck plays a fearless 19th-century sailor who outwits the Spaniards and the French, and marries his admiral's widow. With Virginia Mayo, Robert Beatty, James Robertson Justice and Terence Morgan. One of Peck's personal favorite roles.
VHS: S16734. $19.98.
Laser: LD71514. $34.98.
Raoul Walsh, USA, 1951, 117 mins.

Captain Kidd

Charles Laughton is the ruthless, greedy pirate in this great Hollywood swashbuckler set in the late 17th century. The action-packed plot on the high seas contains typical elements: buried treasure, double-crossing, and even romance. An outstanding pirate movie.
VHS: S00211. $19.95.
Rowland V. Lee, USA, 1945, 82 mins.

Captain Sinbad

The romance, splendor and adventure of *The Arabian Nights* comes to life as Sinbad returns from his latest voyage and discovers that the kingdom of Baristan has been usurped by the evil despot El Kerim.
VHS: S16846. $19.98.
Byron Haskin, USA, 1963, 86 mins.

Captain Sirocco

Louis Hayward and Binnie Barnes star in this costume epic about a deceitful but dashing pirate. The fiend lives two lives, hiding his identity in order to play the fool and the queen's confidant.
VHS: S23885. $29.95.
Edgar G. Ulmer, USA, 1949, 93 mins.

Captains Courageous

Spencer Tracy won the Oscar for Best Actor for his portrayal of Manuel, the Portuguese fisherman who teaches a millionaire's spoiled son human values in this adaptation of Rudyard Kipling's popular story. With Lionel Barrymore, Melvyn Douglas and Mickey Rooney.
VHS: S01788. $19.98.
Laser: LD71159. $34.98.
Victor Fleming, USA, 1937, 118 mins.

Captains of the Clouds

James Cagney plays a daredevil Canadian bush pilot who longs for the chance to prove his valor and service in World War II. His superiors and the military hierarchy at the Royal Canadian Air Force doubt his prowess, though Cagney proves his skills under fire. Music by Max Steiner. With Dennis Morman, Brenda Marshall and George Tobias.
VHS: S19038. $19.98.
Michael Curtiz, USA, 1942, 113 mins.

Career

Nominated for three Academy awards, Joseph Anthony's caustic story of an ambitious young actor's (Tony Franciosa) fanatic quest for fame and celebrity as a Broadway actor. With Dean Martin, Shirley MacLaine, Joan Blackman, and Carolyn Jones in an expressive, startling performance as an alienated talent agent.
VHS: S16889. $19.95.
Laser: LD75169. $34.98.
Joseph Anthony, USA, 1959, 105 mins.

Carnival Story

Anne Baxter stars as a scheming circus performer in Germany. She finds out her fooling with the affections of her fellow performers will affect the timing of a high wire act. With Steve Cochran, Lyle Bettger, George Nader, and Jay C. Flippan as the circus owner.
VHS: S05075. $29.95.
Kurt Newmann, USA, 1954, 95 mins.

Cary Grant (Boxed Set)

These three films demonstrate Mr. Sophistication's remarkable versatility. Includes *The Bachelor and the Bobby Soxer, Gunga Din* and *Suspicion*.
VHS: S10686. $59.98.

Casablanca

The ultimate in the Bogart myth: his Rick Blaine is cynical, tough, hardened by life's misfortunes, yet still sentimental and idealistic. The dialog is full of quotable Bogart lines, the camerawork by Arthur Edeson evocative, the casting inspired. With Ingrid Bergman, Paul Henreid, Claude Rains, Peter Lorre, Sydney Greenstreet.
Laser: CAV, 2 discs, Criterion. LD70353. $99.95.
Laser: CLV, 1 disc, MGM. LD70540. $34.98.
Michael Curtiz, USA, 1943, 102 mins.

Casablanca (50th Anniversary)

The high-water mark of classic American studio filmmaking, this special 50th anniversary edition has been digitally remastered and includes the original theatrical trailer and a documentary on the making of the film. With Humphrey Bogart, Ingrid Bergman, Paul Henreid, Claude Rains, Conrad Veidt, Sydney Greenstreet and Peter Lorre. Music by Max Steiner.
VHS: S17125. $19.98.
Michael Curtiz, USA, 1942, 102 mins.

Cash McCall

James Garner plays a ruthless futures analyst who is irrevocably altered by his attraction to a beautiful young woman (Natalie Wood). Based on the novel by Cameron Hawley. With Nina Foch, Dean Jagger and E.G. Marshall.
VHS: S20194. $19.98.
Joseph Pevney, USA, 1960, 102 mins.

Cass Timberlane

Sinclair Lewis' story of social and political regionalism deals with the marriage of a lonely judge (Spencer Tracy) and a younger woman (Lana Turner) with a troubling past that threatens the social fabric of a Minnesota town. With Zachary Scott, Tom Drake and Mary Astor.
VHS: S18658. $19.98.
George Sidney, USA, 1947, 119 mins.

Cast a Giant Shadow

Set against the backdrop of Israel's drive for an independent statehood, this absorbing historical document stars Kirk Douglas as David "Mickey" Marcus, an American Jew who helped transform the undisciplined Israeli army into an elite fighting force. The all-star cast includes Frank Sinatra, Yul Brynner, Senta Berger and Angie Dickinson.
VHS: S19491. $19.98.
Melville Shavelson, USA, 1962, 142 mins.

The Castilian

Offbeat casting and historical opulence informs this curious piece about the adventurous efforts of a Spanish nobleman to rally a gang of guerrilla fighters against invading Moorish armies. With Cesar Romero, Alida Valli, Frankie Avalon and Broderick Crawford.
VHS: S19006. $19.98.
Javier Seto, USA/Spain, 1963, 128 mins.

Cavalcade

This elegant interpretation of Noel Coward's play won the Best Picture Oscar in 1933. The film traces the opposite fortunes of two families from the turn of the century to the 1930s and the profound personal and political changes they experience. With Diana Wynyard, Clive Brook and Herbert Mundin.
VHS: S18455. $19.98.
Frank Lloyd, USA, 1933, 110 mins.

Cavalry Charge

Ronald Reagan, Rhonda Fleming, Hugh Beaumont and Bruce Bennett star in this Civil War era drama. Reagan and Bennett are brothers divided by their allegiances to opposing sides in The War Between the States. They overcome these differences in order to fight off Native Americans from the Apache tribe enraged by a dishonest trader. Fleming complicates the story with her red hair and green eyes. Also known as *The Last Outpost*.
VHS: S26875. $29.95.
Lewis R. Foster, USA, 1951, 88 mins.

Chain Lightning

Bogie is a heroic barnstormer who made good during WWII in this romantic air show. Riding on his reputation, he must execute daredevil feats with an experimental ultra-high performance jet. Eleanor Parker gives a charmingly understated portrayal of his earth-bound romantic interest. Humphrey Bogart leads Raymond Massey, Richard Whorf and James Brown.
VHS: S16096. $19.98.
Stuart Heisler, USA, 1950, 95 mins.

Chained

Clark Gable and Joan Crawford are two sides of a love triangle in this involving and sophisticated romance from MGM. Fourteen-year-old Mickey Rooney is featured in an unbilled speaking role.
VHS: S15255. $19.98.
Clarence Brown, USA, 1934, 76 mins.

Challenge to Lassie

This pleasant adventure with America's favorite collie involves a dispute over her ownership. Featuring solid performances from Edmund Gwenn, Geraldine Brooks, Reginald Owen, Sara Allgood, and, of course, Lassie.
VHS: S13640. $19.98.
Richard Thorpe, USA, 1949, 76 mins.

The Champ

Jackie Cooper has unflinching faith in his father, a washed-up prize boxer, in this melodrama that features a dynamite performance from Wallace Beery as the fighter.
VHS: S13387. $19.98.
Laser: LD72119. $34.98.
King Vidor, USA, 1931, 87 mins.

Champagne for Caesar

Genius Ronald Colman becomes a national celebrity on a TV quiz show in this terrific spoof. Vincent Price is hilarious as the show's sponsor, a neurotic soap manufacturer. With Celeste Holm.
VHS: S02645. $19.95.
Richard Whorf, U.S.A, 1950, 90 mins.

Champion

Kirk Douglas has the title role in this brutal film about a boxer with a goal and very little humanity. He thinks he can beat anybody, but the Syndicate thinks otherwise. With Arthur Kennedy, Marilyn Maxwell, Ruth Roman and Lola Albright. B&W.
VHS: S04227. $19.95.
Mark Robson, USA, 1949, 99 mins.

The Charge of the Light Brigade

Errol Flynn and Olivia de Havilland star in this epic production about the British involvement in the Crimean War. Adapted from Alfred Tennyson's classic poem.
VHS: S01865. $19.98.
Laser: Chapter search. Includes original theatrical trailer. LD71667. $34.98.
Michael Curtiz, USA, 1936, 115 mins.

Charlie Chan Collection

Seven of Charlie Chan's most intriguing cases, available for the first time on video.
Castle in the Desert. Directed by Harry Lachman, USA, 1942, 62 mins.
Charlie Chan at the Opera. Directed by H. Bruce Humberstone, USA, 1936, 66 mins.
VHS: S09090. $19.98.
Charlie Chan at the Wax Museum. Directed by Lynn Shores, USA, 1940, 63 mins.
VHS: S09091. $19.98.
Charlie Chan in Paris. Directed by Lewis Seller, USA, 1935, 72 mins.
VHS: S09092. $19.98.
Charlie Chan in Rio. Directed by Harry Lachman, USA, 1941, 60 mins.
VHS: S09093. $19.98.
Charlie Chan's Secret.
VHS: S09094. $19.98.
Murder over New York.
VHS: S09095. $19.98.

Charlie Chan: Meeting at Midnight

Charlie Chan (Sidney Toler) must summon all of his intuitive skills to solve a murder and absolve his daughter, a prime suspect in the crime. With Frances Chan, Mantan Moreland and Jacqueline de Wit. Originally released as *Black Magic*.
VHS: S18475. $19.98.
Phil Rosen, USA, 1944, 67 mins.

Charlie Chan: The Chinese Cat

A beautiful young woman requests Rommy Chan's help in finding her father's killer. The investigation leads Charlie (Sidney Toler) into a labyrinth of mazesin search of uncut diamonds. With Benson Fong, Joan Woodbury and Mantan Moreland.
VHS: S18473. $19.98.
Phil Rosen, USA, 1944, 65 mins.

Charlie Chan: The Jade Mask

Charlie Chan (Sidney Toler) examines the circumstances behind the death of a scientist. With Number Four Son and the world's laziest sheriff, Charlie must negotiate a minefield of traps and daggers in the dead man's contraption-filled mansion. With Mantan Moreland, Edwin Luke and Janet Warren.
VHS: S18474. $19.98.
Phil Rosen, USA, 1945, 66 mins.

Charlie Chan: The Scarlet Clue

This unusual movie identifies the killer early on. The story is a satire of 40s radio shows and sophisticated big city farce. With Sidney Toler (as Chan), Mantan Moreland, Benson Fong and Helen Deveraux.
VHS: S18476. $19.98.
Phil Rosen, USA, 1944, 75 mins.

Charlie Chan: The Secret Service

In this espionage thriller, Charlie Chan (Sidney Toler) pursues the killer of a brilliant inventor and the loss of a device instrumental in combating German U-boats. With Benson Fong. Screenplay by George Callahan (*The Babe Ruth Story*).
VHS: S18477. $19.98.
Phil Rosen, USA, 1944, 64 mins.

Charlie Chan: The Shanghai Cobra

Three men are found dead, victims of cobra venom. Charlie's investigation centers on a bank holding government radium enrichment deposits, a failing detective agency and a beautiful secretary. With Sidney Toler, Benson Fong, Mantan Moreland and Walter Fenner.
VHS: S18478. $19.98.
Phil Karlson, USA, 1945, 65 mins.

The Chase

Peter Lorre plays a bodyguard for a rich gangster whose wife is thinking about running away with Robert Cummings. Michele Morgan may love that Bob but racketeer Steve Cochran wants his newly hired chauffeur dead. Based on a Cornell Woolrich short story. B&W.
VHS: S04039. $29.95.
Arthur Ripley, USA, 1946, 86 mins.

China Seas

Clark Gable is the skipper of a Hong Kong freighter that attracts the attention of Chinese pirates. Should he survive their attack, he must make up his mind on whether he loves his mistress or his fiancee more. With Jean Harlow as China Doll and Rosalind Russell as Sybil Barclay. Based on the novel by Crosbie Garstin.
VHS: S08094. $19.98.
Tay Garnett, USA, 1935, 90 mins.

China Sky

Randolph Scott and Ruth Warrick co-star as American doctors who come to the aid of guerilla leader Anthony Quinn fighting the Japanese in war-ravaged China. Based on the novel by Pearl S. Buck.
VHS: S12373. $19.98.
Ray Enright, USA, 1944, 78 mins.

A Christmas Carol

MGM version of the Charles Dickens' classic about a miser who learns to re-think his approach to life. Starring Reginald Owen as Scrooge. He replaced Lionel Barrymore, whose lameness prevented his participation. With Leo G. Carroll, Ann Rutherford and Gene Lockhart. B&W.
VHS: S04980. $19.95.
Edwin L. Marin, USA, 1938, 69 mins.

Christmas Tree

William Holden stars in this sentimental story about the fatally ill, small son of a millionaire widower who is trying to come to terms with his upcoming loss. A tearjerker also known as *When Wolves Cry*. Includes Verna Lisi and Brook Fuller.
VHS: S10725. $19.95.
Terence Young, USA, 1969, 110 mins.

Christopher Strong

Hepburn's first starring role. She's a flyer who falls for Colin Clive, a married man, and eventually kills herself and her unborn baby. One of the rare examples of work by Dorothy Arzner, the first woman director in Hollywood.
VHS: S03247. $19.95.
Dorothy Arzner, USA, 1933, 77 mins.

City for Conquest
James Cagney and an all-star cast dazzle in this powerful film about a poor young boxer and his brother who dream of one day escaping the ghetto. Beautiful production also features a young Elia Kazan in an acting role as a neighborhood friend turned gangster.
VHS: S15523. $19.98.
Anatole Litvak, USA, 1940, 101 mins.

City That Never Sleeps
Gig Young is a Chicago cop involved in adultery, blackmail and murder and he is the good guy. William Talman is Young's buddy who is responsible for the death of several people and trespassing on CTA property. With Mala Powers, Edward Arnold, Marie Windsor and Chill Wills as Sgt. Joe, the Voice of Chicago. B&W.
VHS: S07134. $19.95.
John H. Auer, USA, 1953, 90 mins.

City Without Men
The personal struggles and social drama of a group of women stationed in a boarding house who tirelessly await the release from prison of their husbands. With Linda Darnell, Michael Duane, Sara Allgood and Edgar Buchanan. Screenplay by W.L. River, George Skier and Donald Davis.
VHS: S18951. $19.95.
Sidney Salkow, USA, 1943, 75 mins.

The Clark Gable Collection
Clark Gable's intelligence, vigor and stunning screen presence are the focus in this collection of three films: Frank Lloyd's original (and superior) 1937 Mutiny on the Bounty, W.S. Van Dyke's 1936 San Francisco, and Jack Conway's 1940 Boom Town.
VHS: S17328. $49.92.
Laser: LD71654. $99.98.

The Clock
Judy Garland and Robert Walker star in this classic Minnelli musical about a soldier and an office worker who meet in New York, fall in love and marry, all on his 48-hour furlough. First rate performances from Garland, Walker, James Gleason and Keenan Wynn.
VHS: S13356. $19.98.
Laser: LD70544. $34.97.
Vincente Minnelli, USA, 1945, 91 mins.

Club Havana
This Edgar G. Ulmer effort revolves around the lives of the people who come into the Club Havana, finding love and death—sort of a perverse road show version of Grand Hotel. A must for all Ulmer fans.
VHS: S15360. $29.95.
Edgar G. Ulmer, USA, 1945, 62 mins.

Cobweb
A melancholic work by Vincente Minnelli about the painful disintegration of a psychologist operating a special clinic. With some terrifying performances from Gloria Grahame and Lauren Bacall. With Charles Boyer and Lillian Gish.
Laser: LD70155. $39.98.
Vincente Minnelli, USA, 1955, 124 mins.

Come Back, Little Sheba
Based on the William Inge play, which paints a gripping portrait of a marriage washed up by booze and alienation. Featuring Burt Lancaster and an Oscar and Tony Award-winning, gut-wrenching performance by Shirley Booth. The title refers to Booth's despairing search for her lost dog but, of course, it's symbolic of a whole lot more than that.
VHS: S13789. $19.95.
Daniel Mann, USA, 1952, 99 mins.

The Comedians
Graham Greene adapted his own novel about "Papa Doc" Duvalier's terror campaign in Haiti. The film focuses on the outlawed relationship of a cynical hotel operator (Richard Burton) and his German mistress (Elizabeth Taylor). With Alec Guinness, Peter Ustinov, Lillian Gish, Zakes Mokae, Roscoe Lee Browne and James Earl Jones.
VHS: S18529. $19.98.
Peter Glenville, USA, 1967, 148 mins.

Command Decision
Clark Gable takes a lot of flak as the general in charge of Operation Stitch. Despite heavy losses over Germany he keeps sending more planes to take out a heavily defended jet fighter factory. With Walter Pidgeon, Brian Donlevy, John Hodiak. Bombs away.
VHS: S13311. $19.98.
Laser: Chapter search. Includes original trailer. LD71668. $34.98.
Sam Wood, USA, 1948, 112 mins.

Commandos Strike at Dawn
Paul Muni is dynamic as a simple fisherman living on the coast of Norway, who, after falling in love with Anna Lee, is forced to flee the Nazi invasion by escaping to England, and then returns to his home village as the leader of the British troops against the Germans.
VHS: S07339. $69.95.
John Farrow, USA, 1942, 96 mins.

Compulsion
Orson Welles stars as Clarence Darrow in this true story of the infamous 1924 Leopold-Loeb murder trial, the trial of two wealthy, intellectual, gay Jewish men who plotted and carried out what they thought would be the perfect crime—the kidnapping and murder of a young cousin. Featuring Dean Stockwell, Bradford Dillman and E.G. Marshall.
VHS: S25573. $19.98.
Laser: Widescreen. LD74971. $39.98.
Richard Fleischer, USA, 1959, 103 mins.

Comrade X
A Ninotchka-inspired satire with Clark Gable playing an American correspondent in Moscow who is blackmailed into marrying a die-hard Communist (Hedy Lamarr).
VHS: S20559. $19.98.
King Vidor, USA, 1940, 90 mins.

Conflict
In this taut psychological drama, a killer is brought to bay by a wily psychologist and a nagging conscience. Humphrey Bogart plays a man who plots to kill his wife because his affections have turned to her younger sister. Sydney Greenstreet is the psychiatrist and family friend who uses mind games to release the killer's remorse. Alexis Smith plays Bogart's femme fatale.
VHS: S16097. $19.98.
Curtis Bernhardt, USA, 1945, 86 mins.

Conqueror
John Wayne plays Genghis Khan in this seldom seen adventure produced by Howard Hughes and directed by Dick Powell in his debut behind the camera. Action, adventure and passion of Mongols on the move all filmed near a hot atomic testing site. Cast includes Susan Hayward, Thomas Gomez, Agnes Moorehead, and Pedro Armendariz Jr. In color.
VHS: S07795. $39.95.
Dick Powell, USA, 1956, 111 mins.

Conquest
Greta Garbo is cast as a married Polish countess who delays Napoleon on his march to conquer Russia. Charles Boyer is the Little Corporal who violates his vows of fidelity to Josephine. With Alan Marshall, Henry Stephenson, Leif Erickson and Dame May Whitty. A costume drama with historical relevance.
VHS: S13194. $19.98.
Clarence Brown, USA, 1937, 115 mins.

Consolation Marriage
Pat O'Brien and Irene Dunne are married after they've both been jilted by their spouses, but years later they face the decision of what to do when their former lovers return. Very charming.
VHS: S09459. $19.98.
Paul Sloane, USA, 1931, 82 mins.

Cool Hand Luke
Christ-figure Paul Newman won't let the yard boss crush him in this fine-spirited chain-gang film. Strother Martin, in a supporting role as the chain gang's boss, made the line "what we have here is a failure to communicate" a cultural catch-phrase of the 1960's. George Kennedy won the Best Supporting Actor Oscar as the leader of the chain gang.
VHS: S11615. $19.98.
Laser: LD74727. $39.98.
Stuart Rosenberg, USA, 1967, 126 mins.

Coquette
Mary Pickford's first sound film was adapted from the Broadway play by George Abbott and Ann Preston Bridges. Pickford plays a gilded Southern belle with an unconventional streak who defies her oppressive father by falling for a charismatic though poor man. With Johnny Mack Brown, Matt Moore and William Janney. Pickford won the 1929 Best Actress Academy Award.
VHS: S17924. $19.98.
Sam Taylor, USA, 1929, 75 mins.

The Corn Is Green
Bette Davis is an English school mistress who volunteers to teach the underprivileged young folks in a poor Welsh mining town. She meets with local opposition but is determined to bring the gift of education to her new home. With John Dall, Joan Lorring and Nigel Bruce.
VHS: S06315. $19.95.
Irving Rapper, USA, 1945, 115 mins.

Cornered
Dick Powell re-teams with Murder My Sweet director Edward Dmytryk as he tries to track down the French collaborator responsible for the death of his war bride while he is being kept in a POW camp. The trail leads to a group of former Nazis and their sympathizers in Argentina. A taut thriller.
VHS: S03248. $19.95.
Edward Dmytryk, USA, 1945, 102 mins.

Court-Martial of Billy Mitchell
In the early twenties, an American Army general was court-martialed for accusing the war department of criminal negligence. A dramatic recreation of historical fact is created by stars Gary Cooper, Rod Steiger, Ralph Bellamy and Elizabeth Montgomery.
VHS: S12595. $19.98.
Laser: CLV. LD71979. $29.98.
Otto Preminger, USA, 1955, 100 mins.

Cowboy and the Lady
Gary Cooper is the cowboy. Merle Oberon is the lady. They meet on a blind date after a rodeo in Florida and decide to get married on a steamer bound for Galveston and live on his ranch in Montana. Problems occur when Coop finds out his new bride is the rambunctious daughter of a rising politician who objects to the union. With Walter Brennan, Fuzzy Knight, Patsy Kelly, Henry Kolker and Harry Davenport as Uncle Hannibal. Nominated for three Oscars.
VHS: S16287. $19.98.
H.C. Potter, USA, 1938, 91 mins.

Crack-Up
A respected art critic and historian believes that priceless works of art are being stolen, but everyone else believes he's insane. An exciting thriller starring Pat O'Brien and Claire Trevor.
VHS: S15103. $19.98.
Irving Reis, USA, 1945, 93 mins.

Craig's Wife
The film that rocketed Rosalind Russell to stardom. The dramatic story of a heartless woman (Russell) who has married a kindly man (John Boles) who refuses to see her manipulations.
VHS: S02925. $19.95.
Dorothy Arzner, USA, 1936, 78 mins.

Crash Dive
Two navy men, Tyrone Power and Dana Andrews, find they are on the same side in the naval war against the Axis forces, but in love they must compete for the same woman, Anne Baxter. This drama of rivalry and love set against the backdrop of World War II won an Academy Award for special effects.
VHS: S21071. $19.98.
Archie Mayo, USA, 1943, 105 mins.

Crashout
Six hardened criminals escape from prison and attempt to remain at large. William Bendix heads this dangerous bunch of fugitives from justice. With William Talman, Luther Adler, and Arthur Kennedy as the humane gang member. See how many tough guys elude the intensive manhunt.
VHS: S07136. $19.95.
Lewis R. Foster, USA, 1955, 82 mins.

Crime of Passion
A pessimistic 50s film noir about a famous columnist (Barbara Stanwyck) whose melodramatic rise to the top is complicated by her affair with a detective (Sterling Hayden). With Raymond Burr, Fay Wray and Royal Dano.
VHS: S19571. $19.98.
Gerd Oswald, USA, 1956, 84 mins.

The Crimson Pirate
One of the great swashbuckler films, starring Burt Lancaster and Nick Cravat as buccaneers in the Mediterranean during the 18th century.
VHS: S03431. $19.98.
Laser: LD74691. $24.98.
Robert Siodmak, USA, 1952, 104 mins.

The Crimson Romance
Ben Lyon, Erich von Stroheim and Sari Maritza are featured in this intriguing drama set during World War I. Two American pilots decide to end their unemployment by joining forces with the Germans. Ultimately, a sadistic commanding officer convinces them to rejoin the Allies.
VHS: S23804. $24.95.
David Howard, USA, 1934, 70 mins.

Criss Cross
Interesting film noir study with Burt Lancaster as a petty crook, Yvonne DeCarlo as his ex-wife and Dan Duryea as her shady new boyfriend. With Tony Curtis in his film debut as DeCarlo's dance partner. One of the best sleazy underworld films of the 1940's and remade in 1995 by Steven Soderbergh as The Underneath.
VHS: S08222. $69.95.
Robert Siodmak, USA, 1949, 87 mins.

The Crooked Circle
A comic mystery about a secret agent who goes undercover as a swami to get the goods on the Crooked Circle. Hocus pocus and spirits from beyond are up to no good. With Ben Lyons, ZaSu Pitts, Roscoe Karns, and C. Henry Gordon as Yoganda. James Gleason is a comic cop.
VHS: S04078. $29.95.
H. Bruce Humberstone, USA, 1932, 68 mins.

Crossfire
This tense thriller was shot entirely at night with a style reminiscent of expressionism. A Jew is murdered in a New York hotel, and three ex-soldiers are suspected. Hollywood's first strong statement against anti-Semitism, starring Robert Mitchum, Robert Young and Robert Ryan as the insane veteran with a rabid hatred of Jews. Based on the novel The Brick Foxhole, by Richard Brooks.
VHS: S03582. $19.98.
Edward Dmytryk, USA, 1947, 86 mins.

Crowded Paradise
Hume Cronyn, Frank Silvera and Nancy Kelly are featured in this insightful and unique social drama about Puerto Ricans living on New York's lower East Side. At first a man is happy about coming to New York to be reunited with his girl friend but bigotry and discrimination soon overtake his joy. A film quite daring for its time.
VHS: S23888. $29.95.
Fred Pressburger, USA, 1956, 94 mins.

Cry Danger
Dick Powell is an ex-con named Rocky fresh out of the joint and looking for the people who framed him and a buddy on a charge of murder and robbery. He touches base with Rhonda Fleming, his buddy's wife and Rocky's former girlfriend. He also looks up William Conrad as Castro, a racketeer he suspects of doing him wrong. A taut film noir.
VHS: S07133. $19.95.
Robert Parrish, USA, 1951, 80 mins.

Cry Vengeance
Mark Stevens is after the people responsible for his undeserved time spent in prison. The tough San Francisco detective takes on the gangsters who set him up. With Skip Homeier, Martha Hyer and Joan Vohs. No one kills this guy's wife and child and walks away clean. Directed by the star.
VHS: S07137. $19.95.
Mark Stevens, USA, 1954, 83 mins.

Cry Wolf
As a mysterious scientist, Errol Flynn matches wits with a determined young widow, played by Barbara Stanwyck, who tries to unravel family secrets. They trade insults but there is romance lurking somewhere just beneath all the hostility.
VHS: S22898. $19.98.
Peter Godfrey, USA, 1947, 83 mins.

D-Day, The Sixth of June
An American soldier has a love affair with a married Englishwoman (Dana Wynter) and weeks later finds himself in the uncomfortable position of fighting along side her husband. Robert Taylor and Richard Todd star as the two officers.
VHS: S09453. $19.98.
Henry Koster, USA, 1965, 106 mins.

D.O.A.
Noir classic (remade with Dennis Quaid and Meg Ryan in 1988) concerns an accountant (Edmond O'Brien) who has been poisoned, has only a few days to live, and must find out who poisoned him and why. Surprisingly effective thriller, with music by Dmitri Tiomkin.
VHS: S04664. $19.95.
Rudolph Mate, USA, 1949, 83 mins.

Dance Fools Dance
A lonely Joan Crawford proves her worth as a Chicago reporter by going after gangster Clark Gable in this brisk, dramatic thriller based on the Jake Lingle killing.
VHS: S13647. $19.98.
Harry Beaumont, USA, 1931, 82 mins.

Dance, Girl, Dance
Lucille Ball plays Bubbles as she and Maureen O'Hara go leg-to-leg in a bout of jealous competition for men and attention. Won acclaim for its feminist angles, especially O'Hara's closing speech.
VHS: S10659. $19.98.
Dorothy Arzner, USA, 1940, 89 mins.

The Dancing Pirate
The second feature to ever be shot in 3-strip Technicolor, with songs by Rodgers and Hart, and starring Frank Morgan and Rita Hayworth in the swashbuckling story of a dance teacher who is shanghaied by pirates.
VHS: S05052. $34.95.
Lloyd Corrigan, USA, 1936, 83 mins.

Dangerous
Bette Davis won her first Oscar (and felt it was a belated award from her having lost the previous year) for her portrayal of an alcoholic, once-famous stage actress hell-bent on self-destruction. She undergoes a change of heart when she meets an admiring architect (Franchot Tone) but now has to get rid of an unwanted husband. She's dangerous!
VHS: S11621. $19.98.
Laser: LD70150. $39.98.
Alfred E. Green, USA, 1935, 78 mins.

Dangerous Moonflight
Also known as Suicide Squadron. Anton Walbrook is a concert pianist who decides to join up as a fighter pilot for the British in World War II over the objections of his wife. An action-packed aerial war movie shot over Britain, with a small cameo by Michael Rennie.
VHS: S12374. $19.98.
Brian Desmond Hurst, USA, 1941, 97 mins.

Dangerous Paradise
William Wellman's adaptation of Joseph Conrad's Victory, about a man dissatisfied with society who retreats to a coastal island and is pursued by a band of criminals. With Nancy Carroll, Richard Arlen, Warner Oland and Gustav von Seyffertitz.
VHS: S18947. $19.95.
William Wellman, USA, 1930, 59 mins.

Dangerous When Wet
Esther Williams plays a farmer's daughter who travels to England to swim the English Channel and finds romance with dashing Frenchman Fernando Lamas. She also joins in a delightful water ballet with cartoon favorites Tom and Jerry.
VHS: S16612. $19.98.
Laser: LD71694. $34.98.
Charles Walters, USA, 1953, 96 mins.

Danny Boy
Robert "Buzz" Henry stars in this sentimental story about a Marine mascot's (Danny the Dog) return home after World War II. The famous dog is kidnapped but escapes; later he sees the crooks and attacks them. The crooks press charges, and Danny is sentenced to the gas chamber, but Henry argues that the sentence should be death by firing squad because he was a marine.
VHS: S04494. $29.95.
Terry Morse, USA, 1946, 67 mins.

Daring Game
Lloyd Bridges leads a group of skydiving frogmen on a mission to free the husband and daughter of his former girlfriend. Known as "The Flying Fish", these guys just love a good adventure. With Michael Ansara, Brock Peters and Joan Blackman. In color.
VHS: S04225. $19.98.
Laslo Benedek, USA, 1968, 100 mins.

Dark Corner
When a suave detective is framed for murder for the second time, it's up to his loyal secretary (Lucille Ball) to help untangle the mystery. His best plans go awry when a sinister man in a white suit appears. A classic, intricate 40's film noir, with Mark Stevens, Clifton Webb and William Bendix.
VHS: S10745. $59.98.
Henry Hathaway, USA, 1947, 98 mins.

The Dark Mirror
Olivia De Havilland plays twin sisters, one of whom is probably a psychotic killer. Is it Ruth or is it Terry? Only their psychiatrist knows for sure, and Lew Ayres isn't talking until he's sure he is not in love with a murderer.
VHS: S04234. $19.95.
Robert Siodmak, USA, 1946, 85 mins.

Dark Passage
Humphrey Bogart plays an escaped San Quentin convict who thinks plastic surgery can be his ticket to a new life. While his face is healing he hides out in the San Francisco home of Lauren Bacall, who believes he is an innocent man. The early part of the film, shot from Bogart's point of view, makes for interesting camera work. With Agnes Moorehead, Bruce Bennett and Douglas Kennedy. Based on the novel by David Goodis.
VHS: S01698. $19.95.
Delmer Daves, USA, 1947, 106 mins.

The Dark Past
William Holden is an escaped convict holed up in the home of psychiatrist Lee J. Cobb with his girlfriend and two fellow inmates. Holden is a bit trigger happy and the doctor is willing to see him without an appointment. With Nina Foch, Adele Jergens and Stephen Dunne.
VHS: S06071. $69.95.
Rudolph Mate, USA, 1948, 75 mins.

Dark Victory
Bette Davis in a great role as a head-strong heiress who suddenly learns she has six months to live. After partying hard for a few months, she falls in love with her doctor. A tear-jerker. With Humphrey Bogart, George Brent and Ronald Reagan.
VHS: S00304. $19.95.
Laser: LD70551. $34.98.
Edmund Goulding, USA, 1939, 106 mins.

The Dawn Patrol
Edmund Goulding's remake of Howard Hawks' 1930 film about the deep seated rivalries between World War I Royal Flying Corps pilots stationed in France in 1915. The cast includes Basil Rathbone as the officer and Errol Flynn and David Niven as brave, rugged recruits. With Donald Crisp and Melville Cooper.
VHS: S01873. $19.98.
Edmund Goulding, USA, 1938, 103 mins.

Days of Glory
Gregory Peck makes his film debut as the leader of a handful of Soviet patriots waging guerilla war against the Nazi invaders. With Tamara Toumanova and Alan Reed.
VHS: S12375. $19.98.
Jacques Tourneur, USA, 1943, 86 mins.

Dead Reckoning
Humphrey Bogart stars as a hard-boiled sleuth, a World War II veteran, who's out to solve the murder of his soldier-buddy, a fellow paratrooper who disappeared on his way to Washington to collect a medal. A must for Bogey fans. With Lizabeth Scott and Wallace Ford.
VHS: S06547. $19.95.
John Cromwell, USA, 1947, 100 mins.

Dead Ringer
A dark, grueling thriller stars Bette Davis as twin sisters who harbor deep resentments over a man who once humiliated them, and the efforts of the nefarious, nasty half to achieve vengeance. With Peter Lorre, Karl Malden and George Macready.
VHS: S15931. $19.98.
Laser: LD71183. $34.98.
Paul Henreid, USA, 1964, 115 mins.

Deadline at Dawn
Bill Williams is a sailor in deep trouble. Lola Lane slips him a "mickey" one night. When he's out cold, she gets murdered. With only seven hours of leave left, he seeks a solution with the help of Susan Hayward and Paul Lukas. One of the great film noirs, based on a screenplay by Clifford Odets, based, in turn, on a novel by Cornell Woolrich.
VHS: S03250. $19.95.
Harold Clurman, USA, 1946, 91 mins.

Dear Wife
In this pleasant and dry sequel to *Dear Ruth*, William Holden and Joan Caulfield reprise their roles as newlyweds whose domestic life is clouded by Caulfield's younger sister (Mona Freeman) provoking Holden into a state senator's race—against his new wife's father.
VHS: S02785. $19.95.
Richard Haydn, USA, 1949, 88 mins.

Death Kiss
The cast of Dracula in an exciting murder mystery set in a movie studio, notable for its snappy dialog and clever plotting. With Bela Lugosi, Edward Van Sloan.
VHS: S03332. $39.95.
Edwin L. Marin, USA, 1933, 72 mins.

The Deep Six
Alan Ladd stars as a Naval officer whose wartime duty leads him to question the Quaker faith and its pacifist ethos. To prove his commitment and courage he leads a dangerous shore mission in the Pacific arena. This World War II drama also co-stars James Whitmore and William Bendix.
VHS: S21010. $19.98.
Rudolph Mate, USA, 1957, 105 mins.

Defiant Ones
Sidney Poitier and Tony Curtis were both nominated for Oscars for their controversial roles in this savvy study of racism. They play a pair of decidedly unfriendly convicts who escape shackled at the wrist in the Deep South. Oscars went for screenplay and cinematography. With Lon Chaney Jr., Theodore Bikel, Claude Akins and Cara Williams.
VHS: S09157. $19.95.
Laser: LD71687. $34.98.
Stanley Kramer, USA, 1958, 97 mins.

Desert Rats
Richard Burton leads the hopelessly outnumbered, but stubbornly defiant, Australian 9th Division in their heroic stand against Rommel in North Africa. Directed by Robert Wise, this film co-stars James Mason as Rommel—recreating his role from *The Desert Fox*. Photographed by Lucien Ballard.
VHS: S14136. $19.98.
Robert Wise, USA, 1953, 88 mins.

Designing Woman
George Wells' Academy Award-winning script takes us through the whirlwind marriage of a rough-edged sportswriter and a chic fashion designer, deftly played by Gregory Peck and Lauren Bacall.
VHS: S15242. $19.98.
Laser: Deluxe letterboxed edition. LD70189. $34.98.
Vincente Minnelli, USA, 1957, 118 mins.

Desire
Marlene Dietrich is the "Countess" Madeline, an embezzler of a small fortune. Car trouble foils her getaway until a young tourist, played by Gary Cooper, helps her escape. Once safely away she promptly dumps him, only to realize he has something she desperately wants—the pearls.
VHS: S22185. $14.98.
Frank Borzage, USA, 1936, 96 mins.

Desiree
Marlon Brando stars as Napoleon, Jean Simmons as Desiree, his 17-year-old mistress and the woman he could not conquer, in this larger-than-life historical melodrama. Based on the novel by Anne-Marie Selinko.
VHS: S05913. $19.98.
Henry Koster, USA, 1954, 110 mins.

Desperate
Steve Brodie gets in deep trouble as a hard-driving trucker involved in a robbery, in this drama from RKO's best period. As a witness to a mob crime, he must escape and hide out with his wife. Soon the coppers are on his tail, as well. With Audrey Long, Raymond Burr and Jason Robards.
VHS: S12019. $19.98.
Anthony Mann, USA, 1947, 73 mins.

Desperate Cargo
Ralph Byrd rescues two show girls, Carol Hughes and Julie Duncan, stranded in a Latin American city. On the way home, pirates attack and once again the hero must find a way to save these women. Naturally there is a running love interest, given the exotic setting.
VHS: S23773. $24.95.
William Beaudine, USA, 1941, 69 mins.

Desperate Journey
Five Allied airmen downed in Germany fight and finagle their way back to England in this rousing WWII spirit-lifter starring Errol Flynn and Ronald Reagan. A film that is heavily laden with anti-German propaganda, which makes it interesting to watch today.
VHS: S15128. $19.98.
Raoul Walsh, USA, 1942, 119 mins.

Destination Tokyo
Cary Grant is the captain of the submarine *U.S.S. Copperfin*. His mission is to land a meteorologist in Tokyo Bay. Along the way he must watch out for submarine nets, floating mines and treacherous prisoners-of-war. With John Garfield and Alan Hale. Script by Albert Maltz, later one of the Hollywood Ten.
VHS: S12535. $19.98.
Delmer Daves, USA, 1944, 135 mins.

Detour
One of the great "B" classics: a masterwork by director Ulmer. A young pianist (Tom Neal) hitchhikes across the country and becomes involved in two murders he didn't commit. (He's not the smartest guy.) Femme fatale Ann Savage hops a ride with Neal and practically steals the film as what is surely one of the most unpleasant creatures that has ever graced the silver screen.
VHS: S00328. $19.95.
Edgar G. Ulmer, USA, 1946, 69 mins.

The Devil and Daniel Webster
A simple New England farmer contracts his soul to the devil and needs the intervention of Daniel Webster, a lawyer, to save the town's souls. With Edward Arnold, Walter Huston and Anne Shirley.
VHS: S04331. $24.95.
Laser: Restored version, CLV. LD70127. $49.95.
William Dieterle, USA, 1941, 86 mins.

The Devil and Miss Jones
Do not confuse this delightful comedy about working conditions in a big city department store with the adults-only feature starring Georgina Spelvin. Spunky Jean Arthur stars as the working girl who befriends Charles Coburn, a millionaire in disguise. Good fun. B&W.
VHS: S04256. $19.95.
Sam Wood, USA, 1941, 92 mins.

The Devil at 4 o'Clock
Spencer Tracy is a priest trying, with the aid of three convicts, to evacuate a children's leper hospital in the midst of a volcanic eruption. With Frank Sinatra, Kerwin Mathews.
VHS: S04329. $59.95.
Mervyn LeRoy, USA, 1961, 126 mins.

The Devil's Brigade
William Holden leads the way in an explosive, fact-based story of the formation, training and hell-in-battle exploits of WWII's renowned 1st Special Service Force. A *Dirty Dozen*-style film.
VHS: S15125. $19.98.
David L. Wolper, USA, 1968, 87 mins.

Devotion
The ever-suffering Ann Harding stars as a young woman who disguises herself as a middle-aged governess in order to be with the man she loves. Leslie Howard plays the heartthrob barrister. Based on the novel *A Little Flat in the Temple* by Pamela Wynne. With Robert Williams, O.P. Heggie, Louise Closser Hale and Dudley Digges. Bring your handkerchiefs.
VHS: S15464. $19.98.
Robert Milton, USA, 1931, 84 mins.

Diamond Head
Charlton Heston is the domineering head of a Hawaiian family ruining nearly everyone's life. With Yvette Mimieux and George Chakiris, based on a novel by Peter Gilman.
VHS: S04531. $69.95.
Guy Green, USA, 1962, 107 mins.

Diane
A costume drama set in 16th century France which stars Lana Turner and Roger Moore as the class-torn lovers whose relationships threaten the political divisions fighting for power. With Pedro Armendariz, Marisa Pavan and Sir Cedric Hardwicke.
VHS: S18665. $19.98.
Laser: LD72262. $34.98.
David Miller, USA, 1956, 110 mins.

Dillinger
The story of John Dillinger's notorious career, from street punk to public enemy number one. A slick, fast-paced gangster thriller featuring a fine performance by Lawrence Tierney in the title role. One of the best films to come out of the Monogram Studio.
VHS: S13618. $19.98.
Max Nosseck, USA, 1945, 70 mins.

Diplomaniacs
Bert Wheeler and Robert Woolsey, the goonisest guys this side of the Marx Brothers, represent the Adoopa Indians at the Geneva Conference, leaving confusion and chaos in their wake.
VHS: S11611. $19.98.
William A. Seiter, USA, 1932, 62 mins.

Dishonored Lady
Hedy Lamarr plays a suicidal magazine editor who moves to Greenwich Village and takes up painting on the advice of her shrink. There she falls in love with a scientist who goes out of town for six months. In the meantime she is a chief suspect in the murder of a jeweler. Oh, those career women!
VHS: S05074. $29.95.
Robert Stevenson, USA, 1947, 86 mins.

Disraeli
An adaptation of the long-running play about the British prime minister, a colorful, bright and electric statesman who ruled during the reign of Queen Victoria. With George Arliss, Joan Bennett, Florence Arliss and Anthony Bushnell. Silent with music track.
VHS: S17925. $19.98.
Alfred E. Green, USA, 1929, 87 mins.

Distant Drums
Gary Cooper heads a group of swamp fighters in this serio-comic adventure re-creation of the Seminole Indian War. Filmed on location in the Florida Everglades with Arthur Hunnicutt and Sheb Wooley, this is the last film Coop made before *High Noon*.
VHS: S03504. $19.98.
Laser: LD71457. $29.98.
Raoul Walsh, USA, 1951, 101 mins.

Dive Bomber
A fascinating World War II-era film about the experiments of military flight surgeons to correct pilot "blackout" during strategic flight missions. With Errol Flynn, Fred MacMurray, and Ralph Bellamy. The brilliant aerial photography is by Bert Glennon and Winton C. Hoch.
VHS: S18163. $19.98.
Michael Curtiz, USA, 1941, 133 mins.

Doctor Takes a Wife
Loretta Young and Ray Milland are caught in a matrimonial mayhem when Young, an independent career woman and writer, is snagged into a major publicity snafu and forced to tie the knot with a brainy medical professor in this whimsical comedy.
VHS: S07002. $69.95.
Alexander Hall, USA, 1940, 89 mins.

Don't Go Near the Water
The Navy establishes a public relations unit on a South Sea island to increase recruitment and promote the glamour and wonder of national service. But the men are terrified of the water and spend their time pursuing women, fun and romance. With Glenn Ford, Fred Clark and Gia Scala.
VHS: S20201. $19.98.
Charles Walters, USA, 1957, 107 mins.

Doomed to Die
Boris Karloff continues his role as Mr. Wong, who is called in to investigate the mysterious demise of a shipping magnate. He attracts a variety of suspects which include an ex-chauffeur, a blackmailing general manager and a supposedly drowned Chinese passenger.
VHS: S04020. $29.95.
William Nigh, USA, 1940, 68 mins.

Double Dynamite
Frank Sinatra is the bank clerk falsely accused of stealing when his racetrack winnings are confused with the money taken during a bank robbery. With Jane Russell and Groucho Marx. Also known as *It's Only Money*.
VHS: S09179. $19.95.
Irving Cummings, USA, 1951, 80 mins.

Double Wedding
A strange William Powell and Myrna Loy collaboration that casts them against type as, respectively, an aggressive off-beat, avant-garde artist and an eccentric art designer trying to marry off Loy's sister. With Florence Rice, Edgar Kennedy and Sidney Toler.
VHS: S18802. $19.98.
Richard Thorpe, USA, 1937, 87 mins.

Doubting Thomas
As a traditional husband whose happy home is turned upside down by an amateur acting company, Will Rogers concocts an elaborate scheme to discourage his wife's theatrical ambitions. An appealing star vehicle.
VHS: S13496. $19.98.
David Butler, USA, 1935, 78 mins.

Down to Earth
Rita Hayworth stars as a goddess, a muse to be more precise, who comes to Broadway. She objects to the way the nine muses are portrayed in a play, but is derailed from her plan to halt the production when she falls for the producer. Also features Larry Parks and Edward Everett Horton. Later remade as *Xanadu*.
VHS: S15527. $19.95.
Laser: LD74007. $34.95.
Alexander Hall, USA, 1947, 101 mins.

Dr. Christian Meets the Women
An entry in the popular series based on the experiences of the Canadian doctor who delivered quintuplets in 1935. The doctor (Jean Hersholt) exposes the harmful practices of a sham doctor exploiting women with a diet and physical culture. With Dorothy Lovett, Edgar Kennedy and Rod La Rocque.
VHS: S18940. $19.95.
William McGann, USA, 1940, 68 mins.

Dr. Syn
A great pirate story, with George Arliss, Margaret Lockwood and John Loder in the film adaptation of Russell Thorndyke's novel about the smuggling vicar of Dymchurch.
VHS: S02994. $24.95.
Roy William Neill, USA, 1937, 90 mins.

Dragon Seed
Katharine Hepburn and Walter Huston star in this adaptation of the Pearl Buck novel set in China during the Japanese invasion in the 30s. Hepburn plays the part of a peasant woman who becomes a heroic guerilla fighter against the Japanese.
VHS: S04204. $19.98.
J. Conway/H. Bacquet, USA, 1944, 149 mins.

Dreaming Out Loud
The popular radio team Lum 'n Abner get involved in several capers in this short film. It all happens because they are trying to bring progress to their small hometown.
VHS: S26680. $19.95.
Harold Young, USA, 1940, 65 mins.

Drifting Souls
A young lady marries for money in order to save the life of her father. This early talkie stars Lois Wilson, Theodore Von Eltz and Shirley Grey.
VHS: S15231. $19.95.
Louis King, USA, 1932, 65 mins.

The Duel
Lord Brandt is a ruthless overbearing gambler whose wagers have exceeded his modest pocketbook. To pay off his debts he attempts to blackmail Ann, heir to the Gainsby estate. With Errol Flynn and Ann Stephens.
VHS: S16747. $14.95.
John Lemont, USA, 1957, 30 mins.

Each Dawn I Die
James Cagney is framed and sent to prison, where he meets tough-guy George Raft. In spite of its contrived plot, the film is remarkable for strong performances by a trio of actors—Cagney, Raft and George Bancroft.
VHS: S09391. $19.95.
William Keighley, USA, 1939, 92 mins.

East of Borneo
Rose Hobart stars as a housewife who braves the jungle to find her missing husband. She carefully contrives a plot to free him but meets resistance from the sinister Prince Hashin. A great adventure! With Charles Bickford.
VHS: S13850. $19.95.
George Melford, USA, 1931, 76 mins.

East of Eden
The film that catapulted James Dean to cult status! Adapted from the Steinbeck novel, *East of Eden* is a modern retelling of the Cain and Abel story. Dean shines in an emotionally charged performance as the lost innocent in search of love and acceptance. Also featuring excellent performances by Raymond Massey and Julie Harris.
VHS: S00390. $19.98.
Laser: LD70563. $24.98.
Elia Kazan, USA, 1954, 105 mins.

East Side, West Side
Gracious society matron Barbara Stanwyck wants to save her marriage, but ex-mistress Ava Gardner's back in town, claws unsheathed and ready for combat. Also starring James Mason.
VHS: S15116. $19.98.
Mervyn Le Roy, USA, 1949, 108 mins.

Edge of Darkness
Robert Rossen wrote this compelling World War II drama about the Norwegian resistance movement, centered on a small village's heroic opposition to the Nazi occupation. With Errol Flynn, Ann Sheridan, Walter Huston and Nancy Coleman.
VHS: S18162. $19.98.
Lewis Milestone, USA, 1943, 124 mins.

Edison, the Man
Spencer Tracy ignites the screen with a powerful and touching portrayal of America's most beloved scientific wonder, Thomas Edison. Written by Dore Schary and Hugo Butler, an Oscar-nominated script.
VHS: S15017. $19.98.
Clarence Brown, USA, 1940, 107 mins.

Egyptian
Lavish costumes and sets recreate ancient Egypt at the dawn of monotheism. The struggle for power in a very hot country is the subject of this epic length saga that stars Jean Simmons, Victor Mature and Gene Tierney. Also in the cast are Michael Wilding, Bella Darvi, Edmund Purdom and Peter Ustinov. Be prepared for treachery, outings on the Nile and visits to elaborate royal tombs.
VHS: S10326. $19.98.
Laser: LD72205. $69.98.
Michael Curtiz, USA, 1954, 139 mins.

El Cid
Charlton Heston plays El Cid, the legendary 11th century Spanish hero who drove the Moors from his country, in one of Hollywood's great spectacle epics. Here Mann's visual style has moved from the breathtaking landscapes of his earlier Westerns to a rich expression of decadence. Highly entertaining.
VHS: S04324. $29.95.
Laser: Widescreen. LD74967. $59.99.
Anthony Mann, USA, 1961, 184 mins.

Elephant Walk
The owner of a tea plantation brings back his English wife, who finds the exotic atmosphere strange and turns to a friendly overseer for comfort. Starring Elizabeth Taylor, Peter Finch, and Dana Andrews.
VHS: S13784. $19.95.
William Dieterle, USA, 1954, 103 mins.

Elmer Gantry
Writer/director Richard Brooks' skillful adaptation of the Sinclair Lewis novel is an unsparing attack on a corrupt but charismatic evangelist named Elmer Gantry (Burt Lancaster), whose perverse pursuit of wealth and power tears apart the social and economic fabric of a small, midwestern town. Lancaster won an Oscar; Shirley Jones is brilliantly cast against type as a prostitute.
VHS: S02339. $19.98.
Laser: LD70193. $39.98.
Richard Brooks, USA, 1960, 146 mins.

Employees' Entrance
A quick-witted comedy about a destitute young woman (Loretta Young) who's forced to take a job at a sprawling, emotionally cold department store run by a vindictive and authoritarian executive (Warren William).
VHS: S18125. $19.98.
Roy Del Ruth, USA, 1933, 75 mins.

Enchanted Cottage
A favorite fantasy set in New England, this adaptation of an Arthur Pinero play stars Dorothy McGuire and Robert Young. Two social outcasts, a disfigured war veteran and a homely girl, are magically transformed, becoming young and beautiful, when they fall in love.
VHS: S05657. $19.98.
John Cromwell, USA, 1945, 78 mins.

Enchantment
David Niven and Teresa Wright star in this touching tale of an aging general who recalls the lost love of his life. Includes original theatrical trailer.
VHS: S23438. $19.98.
Irving Reis, USA, 1948, 102 mins.

Enemy Below
Considered one of the best naval war movies ever made, this suspense-packed film follows an American destroyer and a German U-boat in a deadly game of cat and mouse. Robert Mitchum and Curt Jurgens star as rival captains in two powerful performances.
VHS: S12176. $19.98.
Dick Powell, USA, 1957, 98 mis.

Enforcer
Humphrey Bogart is a district attorney up against a murder for profit mob. When his only witness plunges to his death, Bogart must find new evidence. With Zero Mostel.
VHS: S04296. $19.98.
Laser: CLV. LD71982. $29.98.
Bretaigne Windust, USA, 1951, 87 mins.

Ensign Pulver
Wiseacre gob Jack Nicholson trades gags aboard the U.S.S. *Reluctant* with Walter Matthau, Larry Hagman, Burl Ives and more in this zany sequel to *Mister Roberts*.
VHS: S12588. $19.98.
Joshua Logan, USA, 1964, 105 mins.

Escape Me Never
This melodramatic remake of the 1935 Elisabeth Bergner work, adapted from Margaret Kennedy's novel, details the confusion and resultant hysteria of two musician brothers and the diverse women—a small, anonymous waif and a wealthy heiress—with whom they become involved. With Errol Flynn, Ida Lupino and Gig Young.
VHS: S18164. $19.98.
Peter Godfrey, USA, 1947, 104 mins.

Eternally Yours
David Niven stars as "The Great Arturo"—hypnotist, daredevil, magician, and above all, ladies man. He is attracted to the attractive Loretta Young, who becomes his eager stage assistant and wedded wife. They quarrel. She considers marrying Broderick Crawford and then Niven drops back into her life from an airplane.
VHS: S05063. $29.95.
Tay Garnett, USA, 1939, 95 mins.

Evelyn Prentice
Myrna Loy plays the wife of a criminal defense attorney (William Powell). When her lover (Harvey Stephens), who is blackmailing her, turns up dead, Powell must defend his wife on charges of murder. With Una Merkel, Harvey Stephens, Isabel Jewell and Rosalind Russell.
VHS: S20410. $29.98.
William K. Howard, USA, 1934, 80 mins.

Every Day's a Holiday
Mae West stars as a flamboyant confidence woman trapped in the Bowery, who fools a group of suitors into purchasing sections of the Brooklyn Bridge. With Edmund Lowe, Charles Butterworth and Charles Winninger.
VHS: S18866. $14.98.
A. Edward Sutherland, USA, 1937, 79 mins.

Everything Happens at Night
Ray Milland and Robert Cummings are rival American journalists who travel to Switzerland to verify a rumor about the death of a political commentator, and end up falling in love with and fighting over the affections of the man's daughter (Sonja Henie). With Alan Dinehart, Fritz Feld and Jody Gilbert.
VHS: S20260. $19.98.
Irving Cummings, USA, 1939, 77 mins.

Ex-Lady
Bette Davis stars as an unconventional young woman in love with Gene Raymond. "Provocative and sexy" (Leonard Maltin). With Frank McHugh, Claire Dodd and Ferdinand Gottschalk.
VHS: S17332. $19.98.
Robert Florey, USA, 1933, 67 mins.

The Ex-Mrs. Bradford
William Powell is reluctantly reunited with his former wife, Jean Harlow, to investigate a murder, with some surprising results. With James Gleason and Eric Blore.
VHS: S02871. $19.98.
Stephen Roberts, USA, 1936, 80 mins.

Executive Suite
The corporate power struggle, circa 1954, in the big city. William Holden stars as a rising young exec. June Allyson is his supportive wife. Based on the novel by Cameron Hawley. Cast includes Fredric March, Barbara Stanwyck, Louis Calhern, Paul Douglas and Dean Jagger. This is the movie that explains why they call it a rat race. B&W.
VHS: S07976. $19.98.
Robert Wise, USA, 1954, 104 mins.

Exodus
Paul Newman stars as an idealistic freedom fighter in this sweeping saga depicting the struggle to establish the modern state of Israel. Based on the international bestseller by Leon Uris.
VHS: S02338. $24.98.
Laser: Letterboxed. LD71683. $49.98.
Otto Preminger, USA, 1960, 208 mins.

Face in the Crowd
Andy Griffith stars as the hobo who is discovered by Patricia Neal and turned into a TV star in Elia Kazan's perceptive comment on American values, aided by a strong script by Budd Schulberg, who also collaborated with Kazan in *On the Waterfront*.
VHS: S02825. $19.98.
Elia Kazan, USA, 1957, 125 mins.

Fail Safe
One of the what-if-nuclear-war classics, with President Henry Fonda trying to convince the Soviet Premier that the nuclear attack was a mistake.
VHS: S03778. $19.98.
Sidney Lumet, USA, 1964, 111 mins.

Falcon's Adventure/ Armored Car Robbery
In the first episode of this suspense double feature, the Falcon protects a valuable secret formula from slipping into the wrong hands. In the second episode, a police detective chases murderous thieves, even on his days off.
VHS: S10676. $19.98.
William Lester Williams Berke, USA, 1947/1950, 130 mins.

Fall of the Roman Empire
After poisoning the Emperor, his insane son succumbs to apathy and dissipation, allowing Rome to be overrun by pestilence and the Barbarians. An epic spectacle with several exciting action sequences, extremely high production values and some fine acting. The distinguished cast includes Alec Guinness, James Mason, Christopher Plummer, Sophia Loren, Mel Ferrer and Omar Sharif.
VHS: S09309. $29.95.
Anthony Mann, USA, 1964, 187 mins.

The Fallen Sparrow
McKittrick (John Garfield) plays a deadly game of cat and mouse with ruthless Nazi agents who wish to obtain the secret he possesses. Co-starring the radiant Maureen O'Hara.
VHS: S03579. $19.98.
Richard Wallace, USA, 1943, 94 mins.

Fanny
An American remake of the famous film by Marcel Pagnol is beautifully shot on the Marseilles waterfront in the story of a young girl left with a child by a sailor. With Leslie Caron, Maurice Chevalier, Charles Boyer and Horst Buchholz.
VHS: S23481. $19.95.
Joshua Logan, USA, 1961, 129 mins.

Farewell to Arms
The first Hemingway novel to reach the screen, nominated for four Oscars, with riveting performances by Helen Hayes and Gary Cooper as the sweet English nurse and the cynical American ambulance driver who fall in love on the Italian front and are separated by combat and another man's jealousy.
VHS: S00433. $24.95.
Frank Borzage, USA, 1932, 79 mins.

Farmer Takes a Wife
Betty Grable is the girlfriend of the toughest captain on the Erie Canal, who falls in love with a young farmer hired as a boat hand. The farmer gradually brings Grable around to his love of the land in this fun-filled story. With John Carroll, Dale Robertson.
VHS: S09330. $19.98.
Henry Levin, USA, 1953, 80 mins.

Farmer's Daughter
Loretta Young won an Oscar for her performance as the headstrong Swedish girl who fights for a Congressional seat against the man she loves. With Joseph Cotten, Ethel Barrymore.
VHS: S04334. $59.98.
H.C. Potter, USA, 1947, 97 mins.

The Fatal Hour
Boris Karloff, as that case-solving detective Mr. Wong, is asked by Capt. Street to look into the death of a personal friend. Three more deaths occur before the culprit is nabbed just before the final credits. Jewel smuggling is the motive. With Grant Withers as the Captain.
VHS: S04021. $29.95.
William Nigh, USA, 1940, 68 mins.

FBI Story
FBI career man Jimmy Stewart reflects on his life with the bureau. Machine Gun Kelly, the Ku Klux Klan, and even Nazi spy rings are among those who make the foolhardy mistake of tangling with one of J. Edgar Hoover's finest. Directed by Mervyn LeRoy (*I Am a Fugitive from a Chain Gang*).
VHS: S13491. $19.98.
Laser: LD70727. $39.95.
Mervyn LeRoy, USA, 1959, 149 mins.

Federal Agent
William Boyd interrupted his work in the Hopalong Cassidy series to make this clever and fresh work about a government police officer. Note: A short missing sequence has been bridged by a title card.
VHS: S17491. $14.95.
Sam Newfield, USA, 1936, 53 mins.

Fight for the Title
World War II has just begun, and so has Benny Leonard's reign as lightweight boxing champion of the world. His manager's plea not to enlist falls upon deaf ears as the duty cry beckons the young fighter. Stars Michael Landon and George Brenlin.
VHS: S16740. $14.95.
Eric Kenton, USA, 1957, 30 mins.

The Fighting 69th
James Cagney plays the cocky Brooklyn kid who is a member of the legendary Irish-American unit caught in the apocalyptic battles in the European trenches in WW I. "Forget the plot and think of it instead as the human, amusing and frequently gripping record of a regiment marching off to war" (*New York Times*). With Pat O'Brien, George Brent, Jeffrey Lynn and Alan Hale.
VHS: S19041. $19.98.
William Keighley, USA, 1940, 89 mins.

The Fighting Kentuckian
John Wayne and Oliver Hardy battle land grabbers and river pirates in order to protect a small French settlement in Alabama in 1819. Before you start laughing too hard, there may be some historical facts to back up the scenario. With Vera Hruba Ralston and Paul Fix.
VHS: S04239. $19.95.
George Waggner, USA, 1949, 100 mins.

Fighting Seabees
John Wayne is construction chief Wedge Donovan, who helps create a new branch of military service with buddy Dennis O'Keefe. He uses guts and a bulldozer to stop a Japanese attack. With William Frawley, Paul Fix, Duncan Renaldo and Leonid Kinskey. B&W. With Susan Hayward as the love interest. Trivia note: Seabees stands for "construction battalion" and their motto is "Can Do."
VHS: S09843. $19.95.
H. Lydecker/E. Ludwig, USA, 1944, 100 mins.

The Fighting Sullivans
Taken from the true-life account of five brothers, the extraordinarily close-knit Sullivan family disregards military rules and order to ensure each other's safety and protection during the Battle of Guadalcanal. With Anne Baxter, Thomas Mitchell and Ward Bond.
VHS: S18025. $29.95.
Lloyd Bacon, USA, 1944, 110 mins.

Films of John Wayne
This collection of rare short films features Wayne in simple appearances and as a star. *Rookie of the Year* is an early television episode where the Duke plays a hard-hitting newsman. Wayne is also featured in a 1971 commercial and hosts *The Marguerite Piazza Story*. There's even a plug for the Will Rogers Institute. 59 mins.
VHS: S22436. $19.98.

Finger Man
Federal agents persuade a convicted bootlegger to go undercover and blow the lid off the rackets of a top crime boss. Will he live to enjoy the official pardon or will this uneasy informer end up dead meat? With Frank Lovejoy, Forrest Tucker, Peggy Castle, Glenn Gordon and Evelynne Eaton.
VHS: S11398. $19.95.
Harold Schuster, USA, 1955, 82 mins.

Finishing School
A snobbish private school is thrown into chaos when one of the students becomes pregnant. Ginger Rogers co-stars as Cecelia "Pony" Ferris, the spunky roommate of nice girl Frances Dee in this melodrama where anything goes, as long as you don't get caught. With Bruce Cabot, Beulah Bondi and Billie Burke as Dee's neglectful mom.
VHS: S15465. $19.98.
Wanda Tuchock/George Nicholls Jr., USA, 1934, 75 mins.

First Yank in Tokyo
In this World War II adventure an American soldier undergoes plastic surgery to sneak into Japan to contact an imprisoned scientist who holds the secret to the atom bomb. The first American film to deal with the atomic bomb.
VHS: S10663. $19.98.
Gordon Douglas, USA, 1945, 83 mins.

Five Came Back
Lucille Ball and John Carradine are among the passengers of an ill-fated airliner that crashes in a dense African jungle. Colorful character studies make this an interesting one.
VHS: S10677. $19.98.
John Farrow, USA, 1939, 75 mins.

Five Fingers
James Mason stars as a cool-headed supplier of secret information for the Germans during World War II. He manages to steal secrets from his British Government employers without their ever noticing exactly what he is up to. It's a fascinating and suspense-filled account of espionage superbly filmed.
VHS: S21330. $19.98.
Laser: LD75016. $39.99.
Joseph L. Mankiewicz, USA, 1952, 108 mins.

Flame and the Arrow
Burt Lancaster leads the peasants in revolt against the vile Hessian warlord in medieval Lombardy. Colorful action film from the director of *Cat People* and *Curse of the Demon*.
VHS: S03430. $19.98.
Laser: LD70571. $29.98.
Jacques Tourneur, USA, 1950, 88 mins.

Flame of the Barbary Coast
John Wayne plays Duke Fergus, a naive Montana cattleman visiting San Francisco, where he loses his money and his heart. Ann Dvorak is Flaxen Tarry, the flame of the Barbary Coast. She kinda likes the Duke but she likes money a lot better. The San Francisco earthquake also puts in an appearance.
VHS: S04894. $19.95.
Joseph Kane, USA, 1945, 92 mins.

Flames
Johnny Mack Brown, Noel Francis, George Cooper and Marjorie Beebe star in this touching drama. John and Noel find their love nearly destroyed by distrust. When Noel finds herself under distress because of an evil villain, John rescues her from a raging fire. This film depicted many new lifesaving techniques for its time and was made with the L.A. fire department's help.
VHS: S22435. $19.95.
Karl Brown, USA, 1932, 63 mins.

Flamingo Road
Passion and politics collide when a carnival dancer played by Joan Crawford is stranded in a small Southern town run by Sidney Greenstreet. When he frames her for prostitution, she returns to get revenge by any means possible. With Zachary Scott, David Brian and Virginia Huston.
VHS: S16448. $19.95.
Laser: LD72174. $34.98.
Michael Curtiz, USA, 1949, 94 mins.

Flat Top
Sterling Hayden stars in this WW II service drama about the lives and training of those who fly from aircraft carriers. Combat footage of the real thing is successfully integrated into the fictional story. With Richard Carlson, Keith Larson and Bill Phipps.
VHS: S04253. $19.98.
Lesley Selander, USA, 1952, 85 mins.

Flipper
Set in the Florida Keys and starring an incredibly talented dolphin, this adventure is the story of a fisherman's son who befriends a dolphin. With Chuck Connors, Luke Halpin.
VHS: S12427. $19.98.
James B. Clark, USA, 1963, 87 mins.

Flipper's New Adventure
The further exploits of the world's brightest and most personable dolphin. Flipper and Luke Halpin thwart an extortion plot by some escaped convicts, all set against the exotic backdrop of the Bahamas and Key Biscayne. Bring the kids.
VHS: S13641. $19.98.
Leon Benson, USA, 1964, 103 mins.

Flying Tigers
John Wayne helps the people of China fight the Japanese in this rousing war movie set prior to the U.S. entry into World War II. He plays Squadron Leader Jim Gordon, who is at odds with his mercenary buddy (John Carroll) for stealing his Red Cross girlfriend. With Anna Lee, Gordon Jones and Mae Clarke. From Republic Pictures.
VHS: S15910. $19.95.
Laser: 50th Anniversary edition. LD71499. $34.98.
David Miller, USA, 1942, 101 mins.

Follow Me Quietly
A first-rate RKO film noir thriller about a strangler who kills whenever it rains. William Lundigan and Dorothy Patrick star in this short but effective thriller.
VHS: S12014. $19.98.
Richard Fleischer, USA, 1949, 59 mins.

Follow the Boys
Tony West (George Raft) is rejected for the war effort, but hides this news and opts to organize shows that will cheer the troops. Marlene Dietrich, Orson Welles, W.C. Fields, Dinah Shore, The Andrew Sisters, Sophie Tucker, Jeanette MacDonald and many more do their bit as World War II extras.
VHS: S22187. $14.98.
A. Edward Sutherland, USA, 1944, 111 mins.

Footlight Serenade
A champion heavyweight fighter takes a role in a Broadway show and makes a play for one of the dancers (Betty Grable) who, for career reasons, doesn't want it known that she's married. But her husband is also an actor in the show, and watching the lady-killer champ going after his wife leads to some terrific moments.
VHS: S09331. $19.98.
Gregory Ratoff, USA, 1942, 81 mins.

Footsteps in the Dark
Errol Flynn shows his comic flair as a high society investment banker who secretly moonlights as a mystery writer and amateur sleuth in this tongue-in-cheek whodunit. Maintaining a suave wordly exterior while investigating the seamier side of life inevitably leads to some ridiculous juxtapositions.
VHS: S22897. $19.98.
Lloyd Bacon, USA, 1941, 96 mins.

For Whom the Bell Tolls
Gary Cooper, Ingrid Bergman and Katina Patinou all won Oscars for their work in this adaptation of the classic Ernest Hemingway novel. Overall, it won nine Academy Awards, including Best Picture. The story revolves around an American demolition expert who decides that he must fight against the fascists in Spain. Even as civil war rages, a romance grows between him and a beautiful Spanish woman. This restored version includes the original theatrical trailer and music cut from other released versions.
VHS: S26184. $19.98.
Laser: LD75038. $44.98.
Sam Wood, USA, 1943, 166 mins.

Force of Arms
William Holden and Nancy Olson star in this film about a World War II soldier and his lovely young wife. While Holden struggles toward Rome, his wife desperately tries to find out if he is still alive.
VHS: S24730. $19.98.
Michael Curtiz, USA, 1952, 99 mins.

Force of Evil
Film noir featuring John Garfield as an attorney who works for a mobster and finds himself caught in a numbers racket scheme that could bankrupt New York's "numbers banks".
VHS: S04232. $19.98.
Laser: CLV. LD71984. $29.98.
Abraham Polonsky, USA, 1949, 80 mins.

Forever Amber
Linda Darnell, George Sanders and Cornel Wilde star in Darryl Zanuck's "lavish and beautiful" 17th-century swashbuckler. Darnell conquers the king but she can't have the man she really wants, in this opulent drama directed by Otto Preminger.
VHS: S21955. $19.98.
Laser: LD75460. $49.98.
Otto Preminger, USA, 1947, 140 mins.

Forever, Darling
One of America's favorite comedic couples, Lucille Ball and Desi Arnaz, star in this enchanting story of a pair whose marriage gets into trouble. They find some help when her Guardian Angel (James Mason) steps in.
VHS: S15243. $19.98.
Alexander Hall, USA, 1955, 91 mins.

The Forgotten Village
John Steinbeck wrote the story and script for this moving film about the ancient life of Mexico, the story of the little pueblo of Santiago on the skirts of a hill in the mountains. An extremely moving portrait of life in a Mexican village. Narrated by Burgess Meredith.
VHS: S08785. $39.95.
Herbert Kline, USA, 1941

Fountainhead
Based on Ayn Rand's bestseller, the story of a talented architect who is forced to compromise his talents for the woman he loves. With Gary Cooper, Patricia Neal, Raymond Massey.
VHS: S01869. $19.98.
Laser: Chapter search. Includes original trailer. LD71643. $34.98.
King Vidor, USA, 1949, 114 mins.

Four Daughters
Four sisters, four romances—a much-loved melodramatic treat starring Rosemary Lane, Priscilla Lane, Lola Lane and Gale Page. Claude Rains and John Garfield are in the supporting cast. "Sentimental, but it's grand cinema" (New York Times).
VHS: S15652. $19.98.
Michael Curtiz, USA, 1938, 90 mins.

The Four Horsemen of the Apocalypse
The story of three generations of a wealthy Argentine family that is split by the rise of the Nazis in Europe. With Glenn Ford, Lee J. Cobb, Ingrid Thulin and Yvette Mimieux.
VHS: S04205. $19.98.
Vincente Minnelli, USA, 1961, 154 mins.

Four Jacks and a Jill
Four musicians land a new singer for their nightclub act, but she is being pursued by Desi Arnaz, who may or may not be an ousted foreign king seeking refuge in America.
VHS: S11610. $19.98.
Jack Hively, USA, 1941, 68 mins.

Framed
A nightclub hostess from the wrong side of the tracks swears revenge against the police inspector who has killed her father. A suspenseful drama starring Evelyn Brent and William Holden.
VHS: S15104. $19.98.
George Archainbaud, USA, 1930, 68 mins.

Free Soul
Lionel Barrymore won an Oscar for his famous courtroom scene in this story of a hard-drinking lawyer who successfully defends gangster Clark Gable on a murder rap and then discovers that his daughter has fallen in love with him. With Norma Shearer, Leslie Howard.
VHS: S13389. $19.98.
Clarence Brown, USA, 1931, 91 mins.

French Line
Russell's bust was first shown theatrically in this film in 3-D as she plays the wealthy Texas girl in Paris being romanced by Gilbert Roland. Mary McCarty is terrific providing comic interludes to the musical numbers.
VHS: S09180. $19.95.
Lloyd Bacon, USA, 1954, 102 mins.

From Here to Eternity
The talented Fred Zinnemann (Man for All Seasons, Julia) perfectly captures the static isolation and boredom that envelops the military personnel in peacetime Hawaii on the eve of American participation in World War II. Zinnemann counterposes social history with riveting drama: Burt Lancaster is a career soldier who seduces a commander's unattended wife, Deborah Kerr. Montgomery Clift staggers social convention by falling for Donna Reed, a prostitute. Frank Sinatra and Ernest Borgnine add quality performances as bitter rivals. Winner of eight Academy Awards, including best picture and director.
VHS: S02923. $19.95.
Laser: LD72185. $39.98.
Fred Zinnemann, USA, 1953, 118 mins.

Front Page
Produced by Howard Hughes, the classic Ben Hecht/Charles MacArthur story about the newspaper business. When a convict escapes, Hily Johnson, a young reporter about to leave journalism and enter marriage, is drawn back to work. He and Walter Burns, the managing editor, hide the convict in a roll-top desk in the press room in their obsessive search for a sensational story.
VHS: S18174. $19.95.
Lewis Milestone, USA, 1931, 101 mins.

"G" Men
Cast as a "good guy" for the first time in his career, tough-man James Cagney is a federal agent raised by a crime-boss, hot on the trail of America's Ten Most Wanted criminals. A tense, action-packed classic.
VHS: S15524. $19.98.
William Keighley, USA, 1935, 86 mins.

Gabriel over the White House
A Depression-era fable about a second-rate hustler who is elected president and becomes an uncompromising leader who tries to wipe out corruption and facilitate world peace. With Walter Huston, Karen Morley, Franchot Tone and Dickie Moore.
VHS: S18503. $19.98.
Gregory La Cava, USA, 1933, 86 mins.

Gambit
Michael Caine and Shirley MacLaine star in this classic. It's a film about a great heist scheme. Caine hires the mysterious Eurasian MacLaine to help him steal an invaluable piece of sculpture. His mastermind and her daring help pull off a great fun yarn.
VHS: S20486. $19.98.
Ronald Neame, USA, 1966, 109 mins.

Gangster Story
Walter Matthau directed and starred in this early gem about a Mob-connected bank robber who falls in love with a sympathetic woman (Carol Grace). Caught in a vortex of extremes, with both the police and the mob hunting him down, Matthau runs from his past and tries to live a straight, easy life. With Bruce McFarlan and Garrett Wallberg.
VHS: S19864. $29.95.
Walter Matthau, USA, 1960, 65 mins.

The Gangster
The story of a man who falls victim to his slum environment and ends up a vengeful crook in the midst of rival gangs trying to rub each other out. Starring Barry Sullivan, Harry Morgan, Akim Tamiroff and Shelley Winters.
VHS: S13633. $19.98.
Gordon Wiles, USA, 1947, 84 mins.

General Died at Dawn
Clifford Odets supplied the screenplay for this Lewis Milestone action adventure set in Northern China during the turbulent 30's. Gary Cooper is the American soldier-of-fortune carrying money to buy arms for the peasants. He is captured by the powerful General Yang (Akim Tamiroff, who was nominated for an Oscar). A test of nerves and quick thinking follows. With William Frawley, Porter Hall and Madeleine Carroll as the beautiful spy.
VHS: S08506. $14.98.
Lewis Milestone, USA, 1936, 97 mins.

The Gentle Sex
Joan Gates, Joan Greenwood and Lilli Palmer join the ATS. Despite the variations in their backgrounds, they coalesce into a group at training camp. This is especially important when, after being separated, they find themselves posted together again.
VHS: S23805. $24.95.
Leslie Howard, USA, 1943, 92 mins.

Gentleman Jim
Raoul Walsh's biography of boxer Jim Corbett, who rose from an obscure bank clerk to champion fighter, features strong performances from Errol Flynn and Ward Bond as heavyweight champion John L. Sullivan. Entertaining fare.
VHS: S01876. $19.98.
Raoul Walsh, USA, 1942, 104 mins.

Gentleman's Agreement
Moss Hart adapted Laura Z. Hobson's prize-winning novel about a talented journalist (Gregory Peck) who poses as a Jew in order to research a series of articles about anti-Semitism and discovers a dark and disturbing backlash experienced by his family. With Celeste Holm, Dorothy McGuire and John Garfield.
VHS: S14185. $19.98.
Laser: LD72252. $39.98.
Elia Kazan, USA, 1947, 118 mins.

George Washington Slept Here
An adaptation of the George S. Kaufman/Moss Hart play about the ramifications of an urban couple who flee to the country to rehabilitate a run down house. With Jack Benny, Ann Sheridan, Charles Coburn, Hattie McDaniel and Percy Kilbride.
VHS: S17658. $19.98.
William Keighley, USA, 1942, 93 mins.

Ghost and Mrs. Muir
A truly charming, touching fantasy, with a great musical score from Bernard Herrmann. Gene Tierney, Rex Harrison, George Sanders, Edna Best, Vanessa Brown and Natalie Wood star in the story of a lonely widow who is romanced by the ghost of a sea captain in her haunted English cottage.
VHS: S11563. $39.98.
Joseph L. Mankiewicz, USA, 1947, 101 mins.

Gilda
Rita Hayworth has never been more alluring as the pampered wife of a casino owner in South America who has eyes for her husband's new assistant. The second teaming of Glenn Ford and the gorgeous Hayworth, who steams up the screen by removing just her gloves.
VHS: S02167. $19.95.
Charles Vidor, USA, 1946, 110 mins.

Girl Crazy
Mickey Rooney is sent to a small Southwestern school to forget girls, but he meets Judy Garland, and the experiment's over. A great score by George Gershwin, with Judy Garland, Tommy Dorsey and June Allyson.
VHS: S04402. $19.98.
Laser: LD74672. $34.98.
Norman Taurog, USA, 1943, 99 mins.

The Girl from Missouri
Jean Harlow plays a young non-conformist of questionable virtue who tries to charm a millionaire but falls for a playboy (Franchot Tone) who's on to her game. With Lionel Barrymore and Patsy Kelly.
VHS: S17781. $19.98.
Jack Conway, USA, 1934, 72 mins.

The Girl Who Had Everything
A melodramatic remake of the 1933 A Free Soul, about an innocent and beautiful young woman (Elizabeth Taylor) who falls in love with a sullen underground crime boss (Fernando Lamas) defended by her hard-drinking father (William Powell). With Gig Young and James Whitmore.
VHS: S18522. $19.98.
Richard Thorpe, USA, 1953, 69 mins.

The Glass Key
A pretty terrific, fast-moving thriller with Brian Donlevy accused of murder, henchman Alan Ladd trying to bail him out, and Veronica Lake as the mysterious love interest. Akira Kurosawa, according to one source, claims that this film was the inspiration for his Yojimbo. With William Bendix, as the brutal bodyguard; based on a novel by Dashiell Hammett.
VHS: S09457. $14.98.
Stuart Heisler, USA, 1942, 85 mins.

Go for Broke!
When Pearl Harbor is attacked, resentment against the Japanese runs high, especially with Lt. Michael Grayson (Van Johnson), who is assigned to command a Japanese/American combat unit.
VHS: S15132. $19.98.
Robert Pirosh, USA, 1951, 91 mins.

God's Little Acre
Faithful, effective adaptation of Erskine Caldwell's novel about the lusty, violent aspects of life in rural Georgia. With Robert Ryan, Michael Landon and Buddy Hackett.
VHS: S03592. $19.95.
Anthony Mann, USA, 1958, 118 mins.

Golden Earrings
Abraham Polonsky contributed to the screenplay of this intriguing war-era espionage thriller. A British operative (Ray Milland) is aided by a mysterious gypsy (Marlene Dietrich) in a plot to steal a poison gas formula from Nazi Germany.
VHS: S19076. $14.98.
Mitchell Leisen, USA, 1947, 95 mins.

Gone with the Wind
A film beyond criticism, a work that welds together Hollywood classicism and literary adaptation with grace. Victor Fleming is the credited director, though at various times Howard Hawks, George Cukor and Sam Wood helped shape the narrative and rhythm. Ben Hecht worked on the screenplay. William Cameron Menzies was the production designer. With Clark Gable, Vivien Leigh, Leslie Howard, Olivia de Havilland and Hattie McDaniel.
VHS: S00515. $89.98.
Victor Fleming, USA, 1939, 222 mins.

The Good Earth
Pearl Buck's novel of famine and the fight for survival in pre-revolution China was transformed into one of Hollywood's greatest films, featuring excellent performances by Paul Muni and Oscar-winner Best Actress Luise Rainer. The locust plague sequences are still memorable examples of cinematography.
VHS: S02899. $19.98.
Sidney Franklin, USA, 1937, 138 mins.

Good Sam
Gary Cooper is Sam Clayton, an extremely nice guy who is always willing to help out in any way he can. From loaning his car to preventing a suicide, no one has a better friend, but the tables turn when he finds himself with money troubles. With Ann Sheridan, Ray Collins and Joan Lorring. Not to be confused with Good Neighbor Sam.
VHS: S06229. $19.95.
Leo McCarey, USA, 1948, 116 mins.

Goodbye Again
Ingrid Bergman stars in this Parisian melodrama as a middle-aged woman caught in a web of desire. Based on the novel by Francoise Sagan. Can Bergman carry on an affair with both Anthony Perkins and Yves Montand and still respect herself? She loved two men but her heart had only room for one. Sounds like it's time to remodel or break out the hankies.
VHS: S11282. $19.98.
Anatole Litvak, USA, 1961, 120 mins.

Goodbye, Mr. Chips
Robert Donat (in an Oscar-winning performance) and Greer Garson (in her film debut) star in this adaptation of James Hinton's best seller. A shy English schoolmaster falls in love and becomes a better man and teacher for it. A classic from MGM and a nostalgic tribute to the English public school system, the story is set in 1870.
VHS: S00516. $19.98.
Laser: MGM, 1939. LD70166. $34.98.
Sam Wood, USA, 1939, 115 mins.

Goodbye, My Lady
Brandon de Wilde, Walter Brennan and Sidney Poitier star in this unforgettable story of a backwoods boy and his new-found dog. A real tear-jerker.
VHS: S14570. $14.95.
William Wellman, USA, 1956, 95 mins.

Gorgeous Hussy
Joan Crawford stirs up Washington D.C.'s high society as an innkeeper's daughter who proves an inspiration to President Andrew Jackson. She also spices up the lives of a few senators. With Melvyn Douglas, Robert Taylor, Franchot Tone, James Stewart, and Lionel Barrymore as Old Hickory.
VHS: S16450. $19.98.
Clarence Brown, USA, 1936, 103 mins.

The Graduate (25th Anniversary Edition)
Mike Nichols' film in a new, 25th anniversary edition. Dustin Hoffman stars as the naive college graduate who's seduced by the middle-aged Mrs. Robinson (Anne Bancroft) and promptly falls in love with her daughter (Katharine Ross). This special limited edition is presented in its original wide-screen format and features interviews with the original cast and crew.
VHS: S17037. $19.95.
Laser: CAV. LD70371. $99.95.
Mike Nichols, USA, 1967, 106 mins.

Grand Hotel
Greta Garbo's great role as the world-weary ballerina, John Barrymore as the elegant but broke Baron von Geiger, Lionel Barrymore as Otto Kringelein, a dying nobody, Joan Crawford as a stenographer, and Wallace Beery as General Director Preysing.
VHS: S00523. $19.95.
Edmund Goulding, USA, 1932, 112 mins.

The Great Escape
John Sturges' film is based on a true story about the escape from the Stalag Luft North. With Steve McQueen, James Garner, Richard Attenborough, Charles Bronson, James Coburn and Donald Pleasance.
Laser: LD70752. $89.95.
John Sturges, USA, 1962, 173 mins.

Great Flamarion
Dan Duryea co-stars in this outing as a drunken performer in Erich von Stroheim's stage act. The catch is that in the act von Stroheim uses guns and knives, while Duryea stands between him and the girl he loves.
VHS: S06009. $29.95.
Anthony Mann, USA, 1945, 72 mins.

Great Guy
James Cagney swings into action as a dedicated chief of the Bureau of Weights and Measures with an unbending determination to crusade against corruption in the meat business.
VHS: S02992. $29.95.
John G. Blystone, USA, 1936, 75 mins.

Great Kate
The indomitable brilliance of Katharine Hepburn in three of her most popular performances: Bringing up Baby, Morning Glory, and Stage Door.
VHS: S10689. $59.98.

The Great Lie
Bette Davis and Mary Astor are splendid as two bitchy women in this sparkling drama about a determined girl who loses the man she loves. Davis believes he's dead in a plane crash and takes over the baby which his selfish wife doesn't want. With George Brent, Lucille Watson.
VHS: S11625. $19.95.
Edmund Goulding, USA, 1941, 107 mins.

Great Man Votes
The great actor John Barrymore is cast as a once-respected professor who has climbed into a bottle. His stock in the community rises when he is called upon to cast the deciding vote in an aggressive mayoral race. A savvy political comedy with William Demarest, Donald MacBride, Virginia Weidler and Peter Holden.
VHS: S15466. $19.98.
Garson Kanin, USA, 1938, 72 mins.

The Great Man's Lady
Barbara Stanwyck and Joel McCrea star in this melodrama about life in the old days. Stanwyck is the wife of a town founder and rather consciously decides to defer to this great man's glory. As an old widow, the actual story of her husband's life as a pioneer can be told. It seems she significantly influenced and shaped the town with her courage and ability.
VHS: S26229. $19.98.
William Wellman, USA, 1942, 91 mins.

Green Dolphin Street
Lana Turner, Donna Reed and Van Heflin star in this adventurous story of two sisters in 19th century New Zealand who are both after the same man. Academy Award-winning special effects.
VHS: S15123. $19.98.
Laser: LD71695. $39.98.
Victor Saville, USA, 1947, 141 mins.

Green Fire
Grace Kelly stars in this melodramatic love story. The desires of an emerald prospector (Stewart Granger) conflict with his love for this alluring woman. Grace manages a coffee plantation in Colombia, giving this steamy film an exotic and romantic locale.
VHS: S21168. $19.98.
Andrew Marton, USA, 1954, 100 mins.

The Green Glove
Murder, love and mystery yield an entangled web of intrigue in this post-World War II drama. A jewel thief steals a valuable relic from a church and the church sends out a relentless tracker to find it. Starring Glenn Ford.
VHS: S14752. $19.95.
Rudolph Mate, USA, 1952, 88 mins.

Green Mansions
Anthony Perkins plays a young man who went in search of wealth in the jungle in order to fuel his plot for revenge. Once there, however, he discovers love in the shape of Audrey Hepburn. Forgetting his original goal, Perkins must now try to unravel the strange mystery that ensnares this couple.
VHS: S21173. $19.98.
Mel Ferrer, USA, 1959, 104 mins.

The Green Pastures
A heavily criticized adaptation of Marc Connelly's Pulitzer prize-winning stage play that interprets African-American tales of spirituality and oral black storytelling through a collection of vignettes on various Biblical stories and figures. With Rex Ingram, Oscar Polk, Eddie Anderson and Frank Wilson.
VHS: S02528. $19.98.
William Keighley/Marc Connelly, USA, 1936, 90 mins.

The Greta Garbo Collection
The spirit of the Greta Garbo animates four films in this four-disc boxed set of Clarence Brown's Anna Christie, Anna Karenina and Flesh and the Devil, and Ernst Lubitsch's Camille.
Laser: LD70192. $99.98.

Guadalcanal Diary
Based on an eye-witness account of the Marine invasion of the Solomon Islands during World War II, this is war cinema at its most evocative and realistic. First-rate. With Preston Foster, Lloyd Nolan, William Bendix.
VHS: S12164. $19.98.
Lewis Seiler, USA, 1943, 93 mins.

The Guardsman
An adaptation of Molnar's comedy about a jealous husband who tests his wife's fidelity. The film stars the real-life married couple, Alfred Lunt and Lynn Fontanne. With Roland Young, ZaSu Pitts and Herman Bing.
VHS: S17659. $19.98.
Sidney Franklin, USA, 1931, 89 mins.

Guess Who's Coming to Dinner
Stanley Kramer directs this Oscar-winning movie about the reaction to an interracial relationship by the parents of both parties. Spencer Tracy and Katharine Hepburn make their last film together as the liberal but frazzled couple who are a bit uneasy about Katharine Houghton's fiance Sidney Poitier. With Beach Richards, Cecil Kellaway and Roy E. Glenn Sr. Oscars went to Hepburn and the script.
VHS: S13316. $14.98.
Stanley Kramer, USA, 1967, 108 mins.

Guest in the House
Anne Baxter is causing trouble again. This time she is a disturbed girl who upsets the household in which she plays the title character. With Ralph Bellamy, Ruth Warrick, Margaret Hamilton and Jerome Cowan. Said to be a grim melodrama, made even grimmer by being in black and white.
VHS: S05073. $29.95.
John Brahm, USA, 1944, 121 mins.

Guilty of Treason
One of the Cold War Iron Curtain films. Charles Bickford plays Cardinal Mindszenty of Hungary and of his trial after the communist take-over amid the communist state's mistreatment of enemies of the state.
VHS: S06908. $29.95.
Felix E. Feist, USA, 1949, 86 mins.

Gun Crazy
A femme fatale leads a gun-crazy man into a life of crime as they both set off on a spree of armed robbery and murder. A sort of updated Bonnie and Clyde story which has achieved minor cult status. Starring Peggy Cummins and John Dall. Dalton Trumbo wrote the screenplay.
VHS: S13609. $19.98.
Joseph H. Lewis, USA, 1950, 87 mins.

Gung Ho!
Randolph Scott leads an assault on Mackin Island against the Japanese defenders. Lots of action in this fact-based chronicle of Carlson's Raiders. Some of the tough gyrenes participating are Robert Mitchum, Rod Cameron, Noah Beery Jr. and J. Carrol Naish. Watch out for snipers.
VHS: S04250. $19.95.
Ray Enright, USA, 1943, 88 mins.

Guns of Navarone
A first-rate World War II action film about a group of Allied commandos who are plotting to destroy German guns. Winner of an Academy Award for Special Effects. With Gregory Peck, David Niven, Anthony Quinn and Stanley Baker.
Laser: Letterboxed. Includes trailer. LD72447. $49.95.
J. Lee Thompson, USA, 1961, 157 mins.

A Guy Named Joe
Spencer Tracy is a hot shot WWII pilot until he is killed in action. He is sent from Heaven to protect the surviving members of his squadron. In addition to military pointers, he also supplies advice to the lovelorn. With Van Johnson, Irene Dunne, Ward Bond and Lionel Barrymore as the General.
VHS: S07008. $19.98.
Victor Fleming, USA, 1943, 120 mins.

Hairy Ape
William Bendix stars as the title character in this rarely-seen drama by Eugene O'Neill. Susan Hayward co-stars as the spoiled heiress forced to flee Lisbon on Bendix's tramp steamer.
VHS: S06004. $19.95.
Alfred Santell, USA, 1944, 90 mins.

Hans Christian Andersen
The incredibly talented Danny Kaye stars as Hans Christian Andersen, a young cobbler with a special gift for storytelling. A wonderful musical tale that will teach and delight both young and old. "A magnificent production that is sheer poetry on film" (Hollywood Reporter). Digitally remastered.
VHS: S02530. $19.98.
Charles Vidor, USA, 1951, 112 mins.

Happy Landing
Sonja Henie plays a Norwegian figure skater who follows a charismatic band leader (Cesar Romero) to America. Once there, she falls in love with a pilot (Don Ameche). With Ethel Merman, Jean Hersholt and Billy Gilbert.
VHS: S20261. $19.98.
Roy Del Ruth, USA, 1938, 102 mins.

The Harder They Fall
One of Humphrey Bogart's most memorable performances as Eddie Willis, a sportswriter who joins forces with a corrupt boxing promoter and works to dupe the public into believing Toro Moreno (Mike Lane) has a chance at the heavyweight title. With Rod Steiger.
VHS: S05862. $19.95.
Mark Robson, USA, 1956, 109 mins.

Harmon of Michigan
Tom Harmon plays himself in this story about one of the all-time great and legendary football players. Football, American style, has been an obsession for much of this century. This film portrays a more innocent time, before big money and television had completely transformed the sport.
VHS: S20634. $19.95.
Charles Barton, USA, 1941, 65 mins.

Harriet Craig
Joan Crawford was born to play the part of this psychotic and manipulative homemaker. All the household help live in fear of her exacting ways. When the man of the house is set to make a career advancement which requires some major traveling, Crawford springs into action with meticulously planned ferocity. It's a melodrama featuring Joan at her monstrous best.
VHS: S27184. $19.95.
Vincent Sherman, USA, 1950, 94 mins.

Harvey
James Stewart is Elwood P. Dowd, a gentle alcoholic whose best friend is an invisible six foot rabbit. Stewart was nominated for an Oscar for his performance in the screen adaptation of the Pulitzer Prize winning play by Mary Chase. Cast includes Josephine Hull, Peggy Dow, Jesse White, Charles Drake, and Cecil Kellaway as Dr. Chumley of the Chumley Rest Home. See for yourself how an invisible rabbit can add something special to your life.
VHS: S12131. $19.95.
Laser: LD70037. $34.98.
Henry Koster, USA, 1951, 104 mins.

Hat Box Mystery
Tom Neal stars as the proprietor of a struggling detective agency, and Pamela Blake is the beautiful, much-too-inquisitive secretary. While Neal is out of town, Blake is called on to gather incriminating evidence against a cheating wife, only to commit a murder herself.
VHS: S06930. $24.95.
Lambert Hillyer, USA, 1947, 44 mins.

The Haunting
Robert Wise's nerve-jangling adaptation of Shirley Jackson's The Haunting of Hill House centers on a gathering at a Boston mansion. An anthropologist, a disbeliever and two mediums confront the supernatural terror. With Richard Johnson, Claire Bloom, Julie Harris and Lois Maxwell.
VHS: S01561. $19.98.
Laser: LD72121. $34.98.
Robert Wise, USA, 1963, 112 mins.

Having Wonderful Crime
Mystery, mayhem, and mirth are delivered with considerable charm in this crime comedy in which a criminal lawyer and two flaky amateur sleuths investigate the disappearance of a magician. It wasn't part of his act—or was it? With Pat O'Brien and Carole Landis.
VHS: S13993. $19.98.
A. Edward Sutherland, USA, 1945, 70 mins.

Hawaii
Julie Andrews, Max von Sydow and Richard Harris star in this grand adventure of the Hawaiian islands in the 1800's, based on the best-selling book by James Michener.
VHS: S12425. $24.98.
George Roy Hill, USA, 1966, 186 mins.

He Walked by Night
Called "a gritty masterpiece" by filmmaker Erroll Morris. Richard Basehart stars as a psychotic killer mercilessly tracked down by police detectives. Shot in a highly realistic manner with a fantastic final shoot-out in the L.A. drainage tunnel system. Largely directed by an uncredited Anthony Mann.
VHS: S05959. $29.95.
Laser: CLV/CAV. LD72062. $34.95.
Alfred Werker, USA, 1948, 78 mins.

Hell Ship Mutiny
Two murderous smugglers are terrorizing the natives on a South Sea island. Jon Hall plays a noble sea captain who helps the lovely island princess Mareva to rid her domain of the evil criminals. With Peter Lorre, John Carradine, Roberta Haynes and Mike Mazurki.
VHS: S16112. $29.95.
Lee Sholem, USA, 1957, 66 mins.

Hell's Angels
Howard Hughes made his name in Hollywood as the producer-director of this World War I aviation film notable for incredible aerial action scenes and for launching the career of Jean (Do you mind if I change into something more comfortable?) Harlow.
VHS: S00561. $29.95.
Howard Hughes, USA, 1930, 113 mins.

Heroes Die Young
American soldiers go behind enemy lines to pave the way for a devastating air attack on Nazi-held oil fields. This fast-paced film is based on a true story. With Scott Borland and Krika Peters.
VHS: S14141. $19.98.
Gerald S. Shepard, USA, 1960, 76 mins.

Heroes for Sale
Addict, thief, Commie, bum. They called him everything but what he really was: a hero. Hollywood confronted the Depression head-on with this vivid slice-of-life melodrama. Richard Barthelmess stars as a wounded ex-doughboy who overcomes morphine addiction, joblessness and false imprisonment. A powerful, touching winner! Also starring Loretta Young. "A fascinating social document of the early 1930s" (Leonard Maltin).
VHS: S15013. $19.98.
William Wellman, USA, 1933, 71 mins.

High Sierra
Humphrey Bogart stars as Roy "Mad Dog" Earle, a kindhearted gangster from Indiana who runs into serious trouble in the scenic mountains of Northern California. With Ida Lupino, Arthur Kennedy, Henry Hull, Barton MacLane, Cornel Wilde and Joan Leslie as the young woman with the clubfoot. Script by John Huston and W.R. Burnett, based on Burnett's novel.
VHS: S00569. $19.95.
Raoul Walsh, USA, 1941, 100 mins.

His Double Life
A shy but famous artist finds life much easier once he assumes the role of his recently deceased butler. Based on the play "Buried Alive", this first sound version starred Roland Young. Lionel Barrymore did an earlier version and Monty Woolley had the most success ten years later in Holy Matrimony. With Lillian Gish.
VHS: S05064. $29.95.
Arthur Hopkins, USA, 1933, 67 mins.

His Majesty O'Keefe
Coconut oil is the precious lifeblood of 1870s South Seas traders and scalawags. Easy going mariner Burt Lancaster teaches Fiji Island natives how to exploit their natural resources and defend themselves against pirates. With Joan Rice, Andre Morell, Abraham Sofaer, Benson Fong and Archie Savage.
VHS: S16733. $19.98.
Laser: LD71513. $34.98.
Byron Haskin, USA, 1954, 92 mins.

History Is Made at Night
A story of jealousy, divorce, and true love discovered. It transcends all the cliches of its type. Andrew Sarris said, "Not only the most romantic title in the history of the cinema but a profound expression of Borzage's commitment to love over probability."
VHS: S00573. $19.98.
Frank Borzage, USA, 1937, 98 mins.

Hitchhiker
Frank Lovejoy, Edmond O'Brien and William Talman star in a classic film noir directed by Ida Lupino. Talman is an ex-convict who hitches rides, and then robs and kills the driver. A fascinating psychological study, very rare.
VHS: S06909. $19.95.
Ida Lupino, USA, 1953, 71 mins.

Hitler Dead or Alive
A wealthy American doctor's brother is killed by the Nazis, and holds Hitler personally responsible. He offers a $1,000,000 reward for Hitler, dead or alive, and three American gangsters just out of prison take him up on it: Ward Bond, Paul Fix and Warren Hymer.
VHS: S06002. $29.95.
Nick Grinde, USA, 1942, 70 mins.

Holiday in Mexico
The privileged daughter of the Ambassador to Mexico objects to his relationship with a beautiful singer. With Walter Pidgeon, Jane Powell, Ilona Massey and Roddy McDowall.
VHS: S18553. $19.98.
George Sidney, USA, 1946, 127 mins.

Hollywood Revels
From the Follies Theatre in Los Angeles, welcome to the wonderful world of Burlesque. Baggy pants comedians, candy butchers, and of course, a bevy of beautiful gals all eager to disrobe. With Aleene Dupree, Mickey Lotus Wing and Hillary Dawn. Music written and conducted by Billy Rose. USA, 1947, 58 mins.
VHS: S05476. $24.95.

Home from the Hill
George Peppard and George Hamilton receive their screen debuts in Vincente Minnelli's drama about a southern landowner and his conflicts with his sons and wife. With a terrific performance from Robert Mitchum.
VHS: S11436. $19.98.
Vincente Minnelli, USA, 1960, 150 mins.

Home of the Brave
The story of racial abuse against a black soldier in a combat squad in WW II is a hard-hitting drama. James Edwards is the G.I. under fire from his own buddies. With Lloyd Bridges, Steve Brodie, Frank Lovejoy and Jeff Corey as the shrink.
VHS: S04252. $19.98.
Laser: CLV. LD71990. $29.98.
Mark Robson, USA, 1949, 86 mins.

Homecoming
In this World War II romance, Clark Gable plays an egocentric doctor who leaves his wife (Anne Baxter) to work in the European campaign, where he falls for the dedicated and selfless battlefield nurse Lana Turner. With John Hodiak, Ray Collins and Cameron Mitchell.
VHS: S18666. $19.98.
Mervyn LeRoy, USA, 1948, 113 mins.

Hoodlum Empire
When a Mob chieftain's top gun goes legit and threatens to testify, the streets of the big city fill with blood. Can a senate investigation turn up any evidence of criminal wrongdoing? Or have they been scared or bribed into playing ball with organized crime? With Brian Donlevy, Claire Trevor, Forrest Tucker, Vera Ralston and Luther Adler.
VHS: S11399. $19.95.
Joseph Kane, USA, 1952, 98 mins.

The Hoodlum Priest
Irvin Kershner's compelling drama is based on the story of the Rev. Charles Dismas Clark (Don Murray), a controversial Jesuit priest who pursued the rehabilitation of career criminals. The story focuses on his efforts to help a cynical young thief (Keir Dullea).
VHS: S19495. $19.98.
Irvin Kershner, USA, 1961, 102 mins.

Hoosier Schoolboy
Mickey Rooney and Anne Nagel star in this hard-hitting drama about life in a small town. Schockey (Rooney) is a boy from the wrong side of the tracks. His father is the town drunk despite his heroic World War I record. Fortunately a sympathetic young woman arrives who gives Schockey the will to overcome the odds against him.
VHS: S24008. $24.95.
William Nigh, USA, 1937, 63 mins.

The Horizontal Lieutenant
Set during World War II, Jim Hutton plays an inept Army Intelligence officer stationed on a remote Hawaiian Army outpost, whose idyllic life is interrupted when he inadvertently captures a Japanese spy. With Paula Prentiss, Jim Backus, Miyoshi Umeki and Jack Carter.
VHS: S20204. $19.98.
Richard Thorpe, USA, 1962, 90 mins.

Hotel Reserve
James Mason stars in a World War II drama about guests at a resort who try to flush out a Nazi spy who is apparently vacationing among them. Based on the Eric Ambler novel Epitaph for a Spy.
VHS: S12377. $19.98.
Victor Hanbury, USA, 1945, 79 mins.

Houdini
Tony Curtis stars as the great Houdini, a struggling circus performer who emerges as the world's most captivating escape artist. Co-starring Janet Leigh.
VHS: S13704. $19.95.
George Marshall, USA, 1953, 107 mins.

House Across the Bay
George Raft, nightclub owner and small-time hood, sets his eyes on show girl Joan Bennett, nicknames her "Lucky," and rises to the top of the underworld in this film noir melodrama.
VHS: S10038. $39.95.
Archie Mayo, USA, 1940, 88 mins.

House of Strangers
Edward G. Robinson stars in this thoughtful and well-performed melodrama about an Italian-American banker who has rigid control over his three sons until he is arrested for illegal practices. Susan Hayward is the wife who must keep the family together. With Richard Conte and Luther Adler.
VHS: S13200. $39.98.
Joseph L. Mankiewicz, USA, 1949, 101 mins.

The House on 92nd Street
A super thriller, this film introduced a new feeling of realism to Hollywood films through documentary techniques. It uses actual FBI footage to tell a riveting story about the pursuit and capture of a German spy ring. A German-American is approached by the Gestapo but goes to work for the FBI instead. The screenplay won an Academy Award.
VHS: S25524. $19.98.
Henry Hathaway, USA, 1945, 88 mins.

A House Without a Christmas Tree
Brighten up the holiday season with a tender, uplifting story of a father and daughter who discover that love and understanding are the greatest gifts of all. Jason Robards stars.
VHS: S14788. $14.98.
Paul Bogart, USA, 1972, 90 mins.

Howards of Virginia
A historical account of the Revolutionary war, an epic production which features Cary Grant, Martha Scott, Cedric Hardwicke, Alan Marshall, Richard Karlson, and a cast of thousands.
VHS: S03651. $69.95.
Frank Lloyd, USA, 1940, 122 mins.

Hucksters
Clark Gable plays a Madison Avenue adman who gets his hands dirty trying to sell Beautee soap to the American public. Boss Adolphe Menjou encourages Clark to romance socialite Deborah Kerr for his product endorsement. With Ava Gardner, Sydney Greenstreet, Keenan Wynn and Edward Arnold.
VHS: S13192. $19.98.
Laser: LD71688. $34.98.
Jack Conway, USA, 1947, 115 mins.

Hud
Paul Newman is Hud, a man at odds with his father, tradition and himself. Patricia Neal and Melvyn Douglas both won Academy Awards for their roles, as did James Wong for his brilliant cinematography.
VHS: S00590. $14.95.
Laser: Widescreen. LD75305. $39.98.
Martin Ritt, USA, 1962, 112 mins.

Human Comedy
Clarence Brown directed many quality films for MGM, excursions into rural Americana. Human Comedy, based on the story by William Saroyan, stars Mickey Rooney as a telegraph messenger in Ithaca, California, learning the lessons that come from the experience of separation and loss.
VHS: S04206. $24.95.
Laser: LD72267. $34.98.
Clarence Brown, USA, 1943, 117 mins.

Humoresque
An ambitious violinist finds a patron in a rich, unstable woman in this involving drama starring John Garfield, Joan Crawford and Oscar Levant.
VHS: S13346. $19.98.
Jean Negulesco, USA, 1946, 123 mins.

The Hurricane Express
John Wayne stars in this railroad serial, as a son out to avenge the death of his father at the hands of the evil fiend who calls himself the Wrecker. Plenty of action and thrills are provided as the Duke tracks down his chameleon-like foe. With Tully Marshall and Conway Tearle.
VHS: S05491. $24.95.
A. Schaefer/J.P. McGowan, USA, 1932, 223 mins.

The Hustler
Realistic and riveting drama featuring Paul Newman as Fast Eddie Felson, an arrogant pool hustler who is driven to beat Minnesota Fats, played by Jackie Gleason. With fine performances by George C. Scott and Piper Laurie.
VHS: Out of print. For rental only.
Laser: LD71057. $69.98.
Robert Rossen, USA, 1961, 134 mins.

I Am a Fugitive from a Chain Gang
They put his feet and hands in irons, but they couldn't shackle his will. A gripping tale about an innocent man brutally victimized by the criminal justice system. Based on a true story, Fugitive stars the charismatic Paul Muni (Scarface) in the lead role.
VHS: S01706. $19.98.
Laser: Includes original theatrical trailer. LD71508. $34.98.
Mervyn Le Roy, USA, 1932, 93 mins.

I Am the Law
Edward G. Robinson plays dedicated law professor John Lindsay, who uses his students to ferret out corruption in big city politics. A courtroom drama based on a serial by Fred Allhoff in Liberty Magazine. Cast includes Barbara O'Neil, John Beal, Wendy Barrie, Fay Helm, Louis Jean Heydt and Otto Kruger.
VHS: S08703. $69.95.
Alexander Hall, USA, 1938, 83 mins.

I Conquer the Sea
Sexual and family rivalry are the dominant themes of this work about two brothers (Stanley Morner and Dennis Morgan) who work as whalers and who fall madly in love with the same woman (Steffi Duna). With Douglas Walton and George Cleveland.
VHS: S18942. $19.95.
Victor Halperin, USA, 1936, 68 mins.

I Died a Thousand Times
Time may have passed Mad Dog Earle by…but the law has yet to catch up with him. This gritty manhunt thriller is one of the lushest and most expensively mounted gangster movies of the '50s. A rousing color remake of *High Sierra*, written by W.R. Burnett, whose credits include *Little Caesar*, *High Sierra*, *The Asphalt Jungle*, and *The Great Escape*. Starring Jack Palance, Shelley Winters, Lon Chaney Jr. and Dennis Hopper.
VHS: S14083. $59.99.
Stuart Heisler, USA, 1955, 109 mins.

I Live My Life
Joan Crawford plays a bored New York society girl who travels to Greece and meets a young archeologist played by Brian Aherne. He follows her back to the Big Apple to persuade her to give up her cocktail parties and polo ponies and join him digging up old civilizations in the Aegean.
VHS: S16451. $19.98.
W.S. Van Dyke, USA, 1935, 97 mins.

I Love You Again
A quiet, dignified man (Dick Powell) is transformed by amnesia into a shrewd con man. His wife (Myrna Loy), preparing to divorce him, is drawn back into his life.
VHS: S18806. $19.98.
W.S. Van Dyke II, USA, 1940, 99 mins.

I Wake Up Screaming
An entertaining mystery with Betty Grable and Victor Mature implicated in the murder of Betty's sister (Carole Landis) and pursued by a determined cop (Laird Cregar); with a terrific twist ending.
VHS: S09447. $19.98.
H. Bruce Humberstone, USA, 1941, 82 mins.

I Want to Live
Susan Hayward won an Oscar for her portrayal of a prostitute framed for murder and sentenced to the gas chamber. Fine jazz score by Johnny Mandel, featuring Theodore Bikel.
VHS: S03459. $24.95.
Laser: LD72268. $39.98.
Robert Wise, USA, 1958, 122 mins.

I'll Cry Tomorrow
Susan Hayward is superb in this screen bio of singer-actress Lillian Roth, who fought to overcome bad marriages and alcoholism. Based on Roth's autobiography written with Mike Connolly and Gerold Frank. Cast includes Eddie Albert, Ray Danton, Richard Conte, and Jo Van Fleet as Lillian's mother. Hayward sings "Happiness is a Thing Called Joe", "Sing You Sinners" and several other Roth tunes. The costumes won an Oscar.
VHS: S09150. $24.95.
Daniel Mann, USA, 1955, 117 mins.

I've Always Loved You
Frank Borzage's lavish 1946 romantic drama of love and jealousy is filled out with classical music and the talents of Artur Rubenstein. With Philip Dorn and Catherine McLeod.
VHS: S14322. $19.98.
Laser: CLV. LD71993. $29.98.
Frank Borzage, USA, 1946, 117 mins.

Illicit
A racy Barbara Stanwyck prefers her independence no matter how much she loves James Rennie, so she remains illicitly his. Her careless disregard of conventions comprises the kind of theme which could only be filmed in the early 30s, before the Motion Picture Code was enforced and more sensational topics were placed out of bounds. Joan Blondell also stars.
VHS: S20831. $19.98.
Archie Mayo, USA, 1931, 81 mins.

Impact
Leo Popkin produced and Arthur Lubin directed this complicated crime drama with Brian Donlevy as the target of a murder plot. The wrong man is killed but everyone believes it to be Donlevy, who is now hiding. Jason Robards, Charles Coburn, Mae Marsh appear in supporting roles.
VHS: S08418. $29.95.
Arthur Lubin, USA, 1949, 83 mins.

The Impossible Years
David Niven plays a university psychiatrist writing a book about contending adolescent difficulties and encountering insurmountable problems trying to contain the sexual curiosity of his beautiful 17-year-old daughter. "A comedy of the generation gap which didn't bridge it but fell right into it" (Gerald Garrett). With Lola Albright, Chad Everett and Ozzie Nelson.
VHS: S20202. $19.98.
Michael Gordon, USA, 1968, 98 mins.

In Like Flint
Flint returns. This time the super secret agent fights a group of wealthy and powerful female tycoons who have developed a way of brainwashing women through beauty salon hair dryers! With all the women in the world enslaved, they commander the first U.S. space platform and then replace the President with their own surgically reproduced clone.
VHS: S11264. $19.98.
Gordon Douglas, USA, 1967, 114 mins.

In Old Chicago
This quasi-historical melodrama is centered on one of the most enduring urban legends, the cow that kicked over the lamp and started the great Chicago fire over 100 years ago. Alice Brady is Mrs. O'Leary, with Don Ameche as the good son and Tyrone Power as his villianous brother. It's a good thing Tyrone is so bad. We get a chance to follow this cad to all the dives that made old Chicago so interesting.
VHS: S20707. $19.98.
Henry King, USA, 1938, 115 mins.

Indiscreet
Gloria Swanson is surrounded by wonderful art deco scenery in this romantic comedy that has Swanson trying to hide her scarlet past from Ben Lyon.
VHS: S00620. $29.95.
Leo McCarey, USA, 1931, 81 mins.

The Indiscreet Mrs. Jarvis
The checkered past of Brenda Jarvis is conjured up when her husband wants to promote one of his employees and invites him over for dinner. Sam Weston and his wife Helen arrive, and Brenda is shocked to discover that she and Helen shared an apartment long ago, when Brenda was not so "refined." Stars Angela Lansbury.
VHS: S16741. $14.95.
Alan Smithee, USA, 1955, 30 mins.

Inherit the Wind
Social consciousness director Stanley Kramer choreographs this stark and minimalist examination of the famous Scopes Monkey Trial in which highly charged emotional warfare is staked out between science and fundamental religion. The cast is extraordinary: Spencer Tracy is the sly and spirited Darrow-like defense attorney and Frederic March plays the William Jennings Bryan role. The surprise performance is Gene Kelly as a journalist assigned to the case.
VHS: S02341. $19.98.
Laser: LD72122. $39.98.
Stanley Kramer, USA, 1960, 128 mins.

Inside Daisy Clover
Robert Mulligan (*To Kill a Mockingbird*) directed this sour adaptation of Gavin Lambert's novel about a Hollywood starlet's (Natalie Wood) rise and fall. With Robert Redford, Christopher Plummer, Ruth Gordon and Roddy McDowall.
VHS: S15935. $19.98.
Laser: LD71185. $39.98.
Robert Mulligan, USA, 1965, 128 mins.

Inspiration
A modern version of *Sappho*, the enigmatic Garbo is Yvonne, an alluring artist's model in Paris, whose misfortune is her imprudent past, which compels her to leave the man she loves. Starring Robert Montgomery and Lewis Stone.
VHS: S15117. $19.98.
Clarence Brown, USA, 1931, 76 mins.

Internes Can't Take Money
Barbara Stanwyck is the patient of a young doctor played by Joel McCrea. Though the doctor falls in love, his patient has other pressing needs. She must find her daughter. The child was hidden by her criminal husband before he died. Now she will use any means to find the lost girl, even the abilities of the intern.
VHS: S26230. $19.98.
Alfred Santell, USA, 1937, 79 mins.

Intruder in the Dust
A powerful adaptation of William Faulkner's novel about a proud, independent black man who is accused of shooting an unarmed white man in the back. The film concentrates on the search for the actual killer. It depicts the complex racial and class psychology of the South and presents its protagonist in a perspective that was quite rare for its time. Shot largely in Faulkner's home town of Oxford, Mississippi. With Claude Jarman, Jr., David Brian and Juano Hernandez.
VHS: S18505. $19.98.
Clarence Brown, USA, 1949, 87 mins.

Iron Major
Pat O'Brien is the rugged World War I officer in this biography of Frank Cavanaugh, football coach and war hero. A flag-waver to boost morale.
VHS: S12015. $19.98.
Ray Enright, USA, 1943, 82 mins.

Isle of Forgotten Sins
John Carradine and Frank Fenton are divers looking for $3 million in gold that sunk at sea. When they find it, Sidney Toler, as the nefarious ship captain, wants a much bigger share of the loot. A killer monsoon settles the matter. With Gale Sondergaard.
VHS: S04029. $29.95.
Edgar G. Ulmer, USA, 1943, 82 mins.

Istanbul
Cornell Borchers and Errol Flynn bring sophisticated passion to this romantic thriller. Jim Brennan (Flynn) is a flyer who uncovers a smuggling ring's stash of diamonds. Now he and his fiancee (Borchers) must save themselves from the tense international intrigue their discovery unleashes. The on-screen romance between Flynn and Borchers brings added excitement to this tale of espionage. Nat "King" Cole is featured performing his hit single "When I Fall in Love." The film's original theatrical trailer is also included.
VHS: S27352. $14.98.
Joseph Pevney, USA, 1956, 86 mins.

It Means That to Me
Eddie Constantine, complete with trenchcoat, plays a down-on-his-luck reporter who's set up on espionage charges by the government, then hired to transport top secret micro film.
USA, 1963.
VHS: S15363. $29.95.

It's a Dog's Life
The surprise is that the hero and narrator of this story happens to be a dog! Dean Jagger and Edmund Gwenn star in this revealing look at the world of humans through the eyes of man's best friend. Based on the Richard Harding Davis short story, "The Bar Sinister."
VHS: S16843. $19.98.
Hermann Hoffman, USA, 1955, 87 mins.

It's a Great Feeling/ Thank Your Lucky Stars
Two classical all-star Hollywood romps, the first is an ensemble comedy about the crazed efforts of Dennis Morgan, Doris Day and Jack Carson to break an unknown into show business. David Butler's *Thank Your Lucky Stars* is a buoyant and expansive musical with Bette Davis, Humphrey Bogart, Eddie Cantor, Errol Flynn, Ann Sheridan and John Garfield.
Laser: LD70170. $44.98.

It's a Great Life
Dagwood is dispatched to buy a house, returns as the owner of a prize-winning horse, and gets involved in an epic fox hunt. With Penny Singleton, Arthur Lake and Larry Simms.
VHS: S20180. $14.95.
Frank Strayer, USA, 1943, 75 mins.

Ivanhoe
An elaborately staged costume drama based on the novel by Sir Walter Scott, with an all-star cast including Robert Taylor, Elizabeth Taylor, Joan Fontaine, Emlyn Williams and others.
VHS: S03858. $19.98.
Laser: LD72136. $34.98.
Richard Thorpe, USA, 1952, 106 mins.

Jacare
Jack Buck stars in the first feature film shot in the wilds of the Amazon jungle. It is an exciting, suspense-filled adventure story. 1941, 57 mins.
VHS: S23775. $24.95.

The James Cagney Collection
James Cagney's best work is represented in three of his signature films: William Wellman's 1931 *Public Enemy*, Raoul Walsh's 1949 *White Heat* and Michael Curtiz's flamboyant musical biography, *Yankee Doodle Dandy*.
VHS: S17329. $49.92.

Jane Eyre (1934)
Colin Clive is Rochester in this early sound era (the first sound version of the story) Monogram Studio production of Charlotte Bronte's classic novel. Virginia Bruce plays the title role of the English orphan who grows up to be the governess in a moody, mysterious English manor, and her growing love for its equally curious owner.
VHS: S09579. $39.95.
Christy Cabanne, USA, 1934, 67 mins.

Jane Eyre (1944)
Beautiful adaptation of the Charlotte Bronte novel stars Joan Fontaine as the fragile and noble Jane, in love with the brooding, mysterious and tragic Rochester (Orson Welles in a memorable performance), and is set within a romantic, Gothic framework. With a delicious musical score by famed composer Bernard Herrmann. Also features Agnes Moorehead and a young Elizabeth Taylor.
VHS: S18101. $19.98.
Laser: CLV. LD72107. $59.98.

Jayhawkers
In the maelstrom of pre-Civil War Kansas, a government agent infiltrates a vigilante group called the Jayhawks and a battle for power begins. Starring Jeff Chandler, Fess Parker and Nicole Maurey.
VHS: S13712. $19.95.
Melvin Frank, USA, 1959, 100 mins.

The Joan Crawford Collection
Three films starring Joan Crawford: Michael Curtiz's 1945 *Mildred Pierce*, Jean Negulesco's *Humoresque*, and Curtis Bernhardt's 1947 remake of Crawford's earlier *Possessed*.
VHS: S17327. $49.92.

Joan of Arc
Ingrid Bergman and Jose Ferrer star in this lavish Hollywood production based on the play by Maxwell Anderson. One of Bergman's most famous roles.
VHS: S04391. $19.98.
Victor Fleming, USA, 1948, 100 mins.

Joan of Paris
Michele Morgan is a barmaid who sacrifices her life to help five fugitive British airmen escape from Gestapo-controlled Paris.
VHS: S12378. $19.98.
Robert Stevenson, USA, 1941, 91 mins.

The Joe Louis Story
The classic true-life story of Joe Louis, the first great black boxer, who not only defeated his opponents in the ring but helped to battle racism outside the ring as well.
VHS: S06336. $19.95.
Robert Gordon, USA, 1953, 88 mins.

John Paul Jones
This famous Scotsman, when confronted with the prospect of Britons fighting on American soil, took the battle across the ocean to English coastal waters uttering the phrase, "I have not yet begun to fight." Robert Stack stars as the revolutionary hero with Bette Davis as Catherine the Great.
VHS: S20685. $19.98.
John Farrow, 1959, USA, 126 mins.

Johnny Angel
Stars George Raft as a sea captain who hunts down a notorious mob of mutineers which has killed his father and stolen a fortune in gold bullion.
VHS: S10679. $19.98.
Edwin L. Marin, USA, 1945, 80 mins.

Johnny Apollo
An impeccably executed crime melodrama about a powerful Wall Street broker who is convicted and jailed for embezzling, and his son, who resorts to crime to raise money to help his father get out of prison. Directed by Henry Hathaway, and starring Tyrone Power, Dorothy Lamour and Lloyd Nolan.
VHS: S13613. $19.98.
Henry Hathaway, USA, 1940, 93 mins.

Johnny Belinda
Sensitive story of a deaf mute in Nova Scotia and the gentle doctor who recognizes her intelligence and teaches her sign language. Jane Wyman won Best Actress Award for her performance, with Lew Ayres, Agnes Moorehead.
VHS: S03460. $24.95.
Jean Negulesco, USA, 1948, 103 mins.

Johnny Come Lately
James Cagney plays an itinerant reporter who is given a job on a small town newspaper run by Grace George. When he begins to expose graft and corruption, the crooks that run the town get sore. With Margaret Hamilton, Hattie McDaniel, Arthur Hunnicut and Margorie Lord. Music was nominated for an Oscar. George's only screen appearance.
VHS: S12900. $19.98.
Laser: LD71575. $34.98.
William K. Howard, USA, 1943, 97 mins.

Johnny Eager
This late studio gangster film concerns a brutal racketeer (Robert Taylor) who tries to consolidate his power on the local gambling fronts and on the beautiful society woman (Lana Turner) he manipulates in his bid for control. With Van Heflin, Robert Sterling and Edward Arnold.
VHS: S18659. $19.98.
Mervyn LeRoy, USA, 1941, 107 mins.

Johnny One-Eye
A highly unusual crime story based on a Damon Runyon tale about gangsters out to kill each other. Pat O'Brien plays a man desperate to escape his past, whose life is transformed by his emotional attachment to an abandoned young girl and her dog. With Wayne Morris, Dolores Moran and Gayle Reed.
VHS: S19865. $29.95.
Robert Florey, USA, 1950, 80 mins.

Judge Steps Out
Alexander Knox is cast as an unsatisfied Boston judge who walks out on his shrewish wife and finds happiness working a short order cook for cafe owner Ann Sothern. With George Tobias and Sharyn Moffat. Knox co-wrote the screenplay with the director.
VHS: S15467. $19.98.
Boris Ingster, USA, 1947, 91 mins.

Judgment at Nuremberg
Spencer Tracy presides over the trials of German war criminals in this well scripted, star-spangled production. Both Maximillian Schell and writer Abbey Mann won Oscars for this film. With Richard Widmark, Marlene Dietrich, Judy Garland, Montgomery Clift and William Shatner.
VHS: S09918. $29.95.
Laser: LD70605. $39.98.
Stanley Kramer, USA, 1961, 178 mins.

Jungle Cavalcade
Jack Buck goes into the wilds once again. This time he brings back exciting footage of wild animals in conflict.
VHS: S23776. $24.95.
Clyde E. Elliot, USA, 1930, 80 mins.

The Jungle Trap
Living in Africa, Steve Davis thought he'd outrun his past, but when the judge who wrongly sentenced his brother to death and his wife arrive, he seizes the opportunity to take revenge. Stars Ronald Reagan and Barbara Billingsley.
VHS: S16745. $14.95.
Jus Addiss, USA, 1954, 30 mins.

Jupiter's Darling
In ancient Rome, the beautiful Amytis would rather race her chariot than listen to boring speeches from her fiance. But when the mighty general Hannibal and his army prepare to lay siege, she sneaks away to see the barbarian in person.
VHS: S16606. $19.98.
Laser: LD70158. $34.98.
George Sidney, USA, 1955, 96 mins.

Kansas City Confidential
Preston Foster, John Payne, Coleen Gray and Lee Van Cleef are featured in this exciting crime drama. Payne is accused of a crime he didn't commit and goes to excessive measures to prove it.
VHS: S08419. $29.95.
Phil Karlson, USA, 1952, 98 mins.

The Katharine Hepburn Collection
Three works from the four-time Oscar winning actress, two from her golden period, her remarkable collaboration with George Cukor, the 1939 *The Philadelphia Story* and the 1933 adaptation of Louisa May Alcott's *Little Women*, and Jack Conway's reworking of Pearl Buck's novel, *Dragon Seed*.
VHS: S17307. $49.92.

Keep Punching
A fight film with the womanizing gambler and boxer Henry Armstrong almost seduced by the fast life, and an equally fast woman, played by Mae Johnson. An all-black-cast film also featuring an appearance by Canada Lee.
VHS: S06858. $34.95.
John Clein, USA, 1939, 80 mins.

Kelly's Heroes
An entertaining World War II movie about a weird collection of misfits and unconventional American soldiers who penetrate German lines to pull off a complicated gold heist. With Clint Eastwood, Telly Savalas, Don Rickles, Donald Sutherland, Carroll O'Connor and Harry Dean Stanton.
VHS: S27497. $19.95.
Laser: LD70606. $39.98.
Brian G. Hutton, USA, 1970, 145 mins,

Kennel Murder Case
Terrific mystery at a breathless pace; William Powell is S.S. Van Dyke's super-sleuth.
VHS: S03341. $19.95.
Michael Curtiz, USA, 1933, 73 mins.

The Kentuckian
Burt Lancaster stars in and directs this adaptation of Felix Holt's novel. The film concerns a father and son's odyssey from Kentucky to the wild frontier of Texas. With John Carradine, Una Merkel, John McIntire and Walter Matthau (in his debut).
VHS: S17993. $19.98.
Burt Lancaster, USA, 1955, 104 mins.

Kept Husbands
Sparks fly between a blue-collar man and the boss' daughter. Class conflict arises. This "study" of the "kept" society husbands of rich, shallow girls stars Joel McCrea and Dorothy Mackaill, and features Ned Sparks.
VHS: S06007. $29.95.
Lloyd Bacon, USA, 1931, 95 mins.

The Key
William Holden and Sophia Loren star in this wartime story, as Loren, in the relentless wartime struggle, falls into a series of unhappy relationships in which she passes her apartment key from man to man. When she meets Captain Ross, she learns to love and struggles to keep her promise to be true to him.
VHS: S09630. $69.95.
Carol Reed, USA, 1958, 134 mins.

Key to the City
Loretta Young plays the prim and proper Harvard graduate to Clark Gable's former longshoreman as both are arrested in a nightclub brawl and realize just how different they are—but that doesn't stop them from falling in love.
VHS: S20560. $19.98.
George Sidney, USA, 1950, 101 mins.

Keys of the Kingdom
Based on the novel by A.J. Cronin, with a terrific performance from Gregory Peck as the dedicated missionary spreading Christianity in 19th century China. Also starring Vincent Price, Edmund Gwenn and Roddy McDowall as the young missionary.
VHS: S11737. $19.98.
Laser: LD72206. $49.98.
John M. Stahl, USA, 1944, 137 mins.

Kid Galahad
Michael Curtiz (*Casablanca*) directs Bette Davis, Edward G. Robinson and Humphrey Bogart in this gritty film about a gangster's mob who falls for an innocent young heavyweight. With Wayne Morris, Harry Carey and Jane Bryan.
VHS: S17334. $19.98.
Michael Curtiz, USA, 1937, 101 mins.

Killers
A thriller based on the Ernest Hemingway story, *Killers* stars Lee Marvin, John Cassavetes and Angie Dickinson with Ronald Reagan as a wealthy, unscrupulous underworld character.
VHS: S00673. $19.98.
Don Siegel, USA, 1964, 95 mins.

Kim
Rousing action and a terrific performance by Errol Flynn distinguish this adaptation of Rudyard Kipling's tale of 1880s colonialist India, with British soldiers battling the rebelling Indians.
VHS: S00675. $24.95.
Victor Saville, USA, 1950, 113 mins.

The King and Four Queens
Clark Gable is holed up in a desert ghost town whose only inhabitants are four comely young widows and their flinty mother-in-law. With Jo Van Fleet and Eleanor Parker.
VHS: S15260. $19.98.
Raoul Walsh, USA, 1956, 85 mins.

King of the Roaring Twenties— The Story of Arnold Rothstein
The story of the notorious, shrewd gangster and gambler, Arnold Rothstein, who fixed the 1919 World Series. Starring David Janssen, Dianne Foster and Mickey Rooney.
VHS: S13612. $19.98.
Joseph M. Newman, USA, 1961, 106 mins.

King Richard and the Crusaders
An ambitious, historical adaptation of Walter Scott's *The Talisman*, set during the Crusades. Richard Harrison is Saladin, a dreaded historical figure who arrives in England impersonating a nobleman and falls madly in love with Lady Edith (Virginia Mayo). With George Sanders, Laurence Harvey and Robert Douglas.
VHS: S19007. $19.98.
David Butler, USA, 1954, 113 mins.

King's Row
Ronald Reagan's performance and Erich Wolfgang Korngold's score highlight this powerful tale of small-town decadence. With Ann Sheridan and Robert Cummings.
VHS: S15657. $19.98.
Laser: LD71684. $39.98.
Sam Wood, USA, 1942, 127 mins.

The King's Thief
David Niven plays a noble scoundrel enmeshed in overlapping intrigues at the court of King Charles II. The costumes and sets recreate the pageantry of 17th-century England, giving Niven plenty of opportunity to display his swashbuckling talents. Ann Blyth, George Sanders and Roger Moore are also featured.
VHS: S21017. $19.98.
Robert Z. Leonard, USA, 1955, 78 mins.

Kings Go Forth
Frank Sinatra and Tony Curtis are battle-hardened GIs in France who fall for Natalie Wood, the half-black woman who causes them to confront their bigotry.
VHS: S15124. $19.98.
Delmer Daves, USA, 1958, 110 mins.

Kiss Me Deadly
Private dick Mike Hammer foils the attempt of some crooks to steal a crate of radioactive materials but finds himself unable to protect the woman he originally signed on to help. "Art" meets pulp literature in this fast and violent thriller, filled with tilt shots and symbols, which had a major influence on the young directors of the French New Wave. With Ralph Meeker, Cloris Leachman, and Strother Martin. "I don't care what you do to me, Mike—just do it fast!"
VHS: S13756. $19.98.
Laser: LD72139. $34.98.
Robert Aldrich, USA, 1955, 105 mins.

Kiss of Death
Gloomy and atmospheric gangster drama about a captured thief who informs on his own gang and becomes the target of a psychotic killer's revenge. A tense and seamy picture with good Hollywood location shots. With Victor Mature, Brian Donlevy and Richard Widmark in his film debut.
VHS: S13201. $39.98.
Henry Hathaway, USA, 1947, 98 mins.

Kiss Tomorrow Goodbye
No, this isn't about the last performance of *Annie*, but a Jimmy Cagney gangster picture. He's mean. He's tough. And he's very dangerous as Ralph Cotter, criminal and killer. With Ward Bond, Neville Brand, Luther Adler and Barbara Payton. This film was banned in Ohio for brutality.
VHS: S04711. $29.95.
Laser: CLV. LD72003. $29.98.
Gordon Douglas, USA, 1950, 102 mins.

Kitty Foyle
Ginger Rogers snared a Best Actress Oscar for her remarkable portrayal of a working girl who must choose between a life of upper-crust manners with a wealthy aristocrat, or a simple life with a nearly penniless intern.
VHS: S00688. $19.95.
Sam Wood, USA, 1940, 108 mins.

Klondike Annie
A sharp Mae West vehicle adapted from her play *Frisco Kate*. West is an unjustly accused woman hiding from the law, paired with Victor McLaglen and concealing her identity by living in the Yukon as a Salvation Army worker. With Philip Reed, Helen Jerome Eddy and Harry Beresford.
VHS: S18870. $14.98.
Raoul Walsh, USA, 1936, 80 mins.

Knights of the Round Table
Robert Taylor, Ava Gardner and Mel Ferrer star as King Arthur, Guinevere and Lancelot in this film which was MGM's first production done in Cinemascope.
VHS: S04207. $19.95.
Laser: LD70611. $34.98.
Richard Thorpe, USA, 1953, 117 mins.

Knute Rockne All American
Pat O'Brien delivers a winning performance as the legendary Notre Dame football coach Knute Rockne, whose all-star career came to an tragic end in a plane crash. With Donald Crisp, John Qualen, Albert Basserman and future president Ronald Reagan as the immortal Notre Dame star player George Gipp.
VHS: S15659. $19.98.
Lloyd Bacon, USA, 1940, 96 mins.

La Cucaracha
The first three-color, live-action production was this Oscar-winning comic short about a hot-tempered cantina girl out to regain the lost love of a fellow dancer. Lots of music and dancing with Steffi Dunn, Paul Porcasi and Don Alvarado. The triumph of Technicolor. USA, 1934, 21 mins.
VHS: S05698. $19.95.

Ladies of the Chorus
Marilyn Monroe's first sizable role pairs her with Adele Jergens as a mother/daughter burlesque team in this lively film. Differences arise between them when the budding Monroe takes interest in a wealthy young bachelor, and seems headed for the same romantic blunder that mom made.
VHS: S16592. $19.95.
Phil Karlson, USA, 1949, 61 mins.

Ladies They Talk About
Adapted from the play *Women in Prison*, this sharp, Depression-era work stars Barbara Stanwyck as an imprisoned bank robber and Preston Foster as a reformer who falls in love with her. A strong social and political critique of American life. With Lyle Talbot, Lillian Roth and Susan Hayward.
VHS: S18127. $19.98.
William Keighley, USA, 1933, 67 mins.

Lady by Choice
Carole Lombard plays an exotic fan dancer who takes in bag lady May Robson to clean up her show. She plans to turn the downtrodden into a proper lady and use her for a Mother's Day publicity stunt, but Robson has a few acts of her own. The lively sequel to *Lady for a Day*.
VHS: S16590. $19.95.
David Burton, USA, 1934, 78 mins.

Lady for a Night
Joan Blondell stars as the owner of a Mississippi gambling boat who is accused of murder; John Wayne is her saviour.
VHS: S10011. $14.95.
Leigh Jason, USA, 1941, 87 mins.

Lady from Louisiana
John Wayne fights city corruption that taints the local lottery in New Orleans. As a fearless lawyer he romances the daughter of General Mirbeau, the supposed head of a crooked machine, and works for reform in his spare time. With Ona Munson and Ray Middleton.
VHS: S04889. $19.95.
Bernard Vorhaus, USA, 1941, 85 mins.

Lady in Cement
Frank Sinatra returns as Florida detective Tony Rome. When he finds a dead blonde underwater, ex-con Dan Blocker turns up on his doorstep in an unpleasant mood. Raquel Welch plays the pretty rich lady who may have all the answers. With Martin Gabel, Lainie Kazan, Pat Henry, Richard Deacon and Joe E. Lewis as himself.
VHS: S12522. $59.98.
Laser: LD71821. $59.98.
Gordon Douglas, USA, 1968, 93 mins.

The Lady in Question
Rita Hayworth plays the title character, who is on trial for murder in Paris. Brian Aherne is the kindly juror who believes in her innocence and begins to have his doubts when she falls in love with his son (Glenn Ford). A mixture of comedy, romance and drama that marked the first screen pairing of Hayworth and Ford.
VHS: S08704. $19.95.
Charles Vidor, USA, 1940, 81 mins.

Lady in the Lake
This Raymond Chandler mystery, in which a private eye searches for a man's missing wife, turns out to be an interesting experiment in subjective camera work. The camera takes the first-person point of view of detective Philip Marlowe (Robert Montgomery) throughout the film, only allowing us to see his face when he looks in a mirror. With Lloyd Nolan and Audrey Totter.
VHS: S13757. $19.98.
Robert Montgomery, USA, 1946, 103 mins.

Lady Killer
James Cagney shows why he's one of the greats in this live-wire 1933 film that's "a kind of resume of everything he's done to date in the movies" (*New York Evening Post*). Cagney's a New York thug who stumbles into fame as a movie star in L.A. and then discovers his old gang has come to cash in on his celebrity status. "One of Cagney's best" (*Video Review*). Also starring Mae Clarke. (Cagney squashed a grapefruit in her kisser in *Public Enemy*.)
VHS: S15015. $19.98.
Roy Del Ruth, USA, 1933, 77 mins.

Lady of Burlesque
Based on Gypsy Rose Lee's *G String Murders*, an unusual and entertaining mystery-thriller with an unknown strangler at large in the backstage world of a burlesque opera house. With Barbara Stanwyck and Michael O'Shea.
VHS: S03214. $39.95.
William Wellman, USA, 1943, 92 mins.

Lady on a Train
Ralph Bellamy joins Deanna Durbin for this murder mystery with a comic twist. It all begins when a girl sees a violent murder aboard a train. Initially no one believes her, so she must set out to solve the case herself. Fortunately, she has been mistaken for an heiress, which makes this task a little easier, even as it leads to interesting misunderstandings.
VHS: S27013. $19.98.
Charles David, USA, 1945, 95 mins.

Lady Scarface/The Threat
A master criminal and murderer turns out to be a woman. A convict kidnaps and threatens those who locked him away.
VHS: S10680. $19.98.
Frank Woodruff, USA, 1941/1949, 133 mins.

Last Angry Man
The last film of Paul Muni casts him as an idealistic, aging physician who lives in the slums of Brooklyn. Adapted from the novel by Gerald Green with a script by the author; Muni delivers a powerful performance, sentimental and heartfelt. With David Wayne, Luther Adler, Betsy Palmer, Godfrey Cambridge and Billy Dee Williams.
VHS: S09113. $69.95.
Daniel Mann, USA, 1959, 100 mins.

The Last Mile
Preston Foster stars as "Killer" Mears in this prison drama based on the 1929 penal riots in New York. Clark Gable and Spencer Tracy played the same role on the stage. Prologue has a real prison warden speaking against capital punishment. A taunt, tension-filled drama. With Howard Phillips, Paul Fix and Albert J. Smith as the mean guard.
VHS: S05708. $29.95.
Sam Bischoff, USA, 1932, 69 mins.

Last of Mrs. Cheyney
Larceny among the English upper classes is the subject of this breezy Joan Crawford vehicle. She plays Fay Cheyney, a "respectable adventuress" who worms her way into aristocratic house parties in search of expensive jewels. William Powell plays Charles, her phony butler accomplice. With Robert Montgomery, Frank Morgan, Jessie Ralph, Colleen Clare and Nigel Bruce.
VHS: S16452. $19.98.
Richard Boleslawski, USA, 1937, 99 mins.

The Last of the Mobile Hot-Shots
James Coburn, Lynn Redgrave and Robert Hooks star in this tense drama filled with racial and sexual animosities. Three people are stranded by a never-ending rainstorm, in a dilapidated mansion set in the muggy, close atmosphere of the Louisiana Bayou.
VHS: S21147. $19.98.
Sidney Lumet, USA, 1970, 108 mins.

The Last of the Mohicans
In 1757, colonial America is being torn apart by the French and Indian War. When the daughter of a British General is captured, Hawkeye, played by Randolph Scott, is set in action by his desire to free the woman he loves. Based on James Fenimore Cooper's classic novel.
VHS: S21998. $19.95.
George B. Seitz, USA, 1936, 91 mins.

The Last Safari
A late effort from Western director Henry Hathaway (*True Grit*) about an embittered hunter coming to terms with his friend's death when a young couple hire him to guide a safari hunt. With Kaz Garas, Gabriella Licudi and Johnny Sekka.
VHS: S17979. $14.95.
Henry Hathaway, USA, 1967, 111 mins.

Last Time I Saw Paris
Van Johnson returns to the City of Lights right after World War II only to find that some things and people have changed. Loosely based on F. Scott Fitzgerald's *Babylon Revisited*. Among the disillusioned are Elizabeth Taylor, Donna Reed, Eva Gabor and Roger Moore, in his big screen debut.
VHS: Out of print. For rental only.
Laser: LD72140. $34.98.
Richard Brooks, USA, 1954, 116 mins.

The Last Voyage
The harrowing events of a sinking ocean liner, with devastating psychological fallout for the captain (George Sanders), and the desperate attempts of a man (Robert Stack) to save his wife and child. With Edmond O'Brien and Dorothy Malone.
VHS: S17987. $19.98.
Andrew L. Stone, USA, 1960, 87 mins.

Laughing Sinners
In this bleak Depression era work, Joan Crawford is a tense, insecure cafe entertainer in suicidal despair when her lover leaves her. She is saved by the romantic and selfless Salvation Army officer (Clark Gable). With Neil Hamilton, John Mack Brown and Marjorie Rambeau.
VHS: S18805. $19.98.
Harry Beaumont, USA, 1931, 72 mins.

Laura
Otto Preminger's 1944 film noir is a witty murder mystery with an elaborate cast of characters—detective, beautiful woman and cynical reporter—who get entangled in the plot. Joseph La Shelle won an Academy Award for cinematography. With Gene Tierney, Dana Andrews, Clifton Webb and Vincent Price.
VHS: S18074. $19.98.
Laser: LD71096. $39.98.
Otto Preminger, USA, 1944, 85 mins.

Leave Her to Heaven
Gene Tierney received a best actress nomination for her depiction of a jealous woman unable to control her possessive instincts. This film is a delightful, melodramatic wallow in one of nature's basest passions. Vincent Price and Jeanne Crain co-star.
VHS: S23757. $19.98.
Laser: LD74915. $39.99.
John M. Stahl, USA, 1945, 110 mins.

Legend of the Lost
John Wayne is cast as Joe January, the foremost guide to the Sahara desert. He is hired by Rossano Brazzi to lead him to the lost city of Timgad, said to be filled with gold and precious stones. Local slave girl Sophia Loren also wants to join the expedition. A sand dune saga of romance, betrayal, archeology and thirst.
VHS: S12140. $19.98.
Henry Hathaway, USA, 1957, 109 mins.

Les Miserables
A classy staging of Victor Hugo's novel about a small-time thief (Fredric March) fleeing his past. Charles Laughton plays the police chief. Written by W.P. Lipscomb. With Cedric Hardwicke, Rochelle Hudson and Frances Drake.
VHS: S05853. $59.98.
Richard Boleslawski, USA, 1935, 108 mins.

Let 'Em Have It
The newly formed FBI declares war on gangsters and public enemies. At the top of their list is Joe Keeper, an escaped convict. So begins a spectacular manhunt as the Keefer gang tries to stay one step ahead. With Richard Arlen, Virginia Bruce.
VHS: S09631. $14.95.
Sam Wood, USA, 1935, 96 mins.

Let's Sing Again
Henry Armetta delivers a sensitive performance as an opera star who's lost his voice and now works in a traveling show. He adopts Bobby Breen (in his first film) and together they search out the boy's real father.
VHS: S09580. $29.95.
Kurt Neumann, USA, 1936, 70 mins.

A Letter of Introduction
Adolphe Menjou stars as a famous father of a struggling actress who wants to make it on her own. Andrea Leeds is the determined daughter. Other personalities include Charlie McCarthy and Edgar Bergen, George Murphy, Eve Arden and Ann Sheridan.
VHS: S05072. $29.95.
John M. Stahl, USA, 1938, 104 mins.

Letter to Three Wives
Joseph L. Mankiewicz received an Oscar for his direction of three women reacting to a letter sent by the town flirt, who has run off with one of their husbands. With Jeanne Crain, Linda Darnell, Ann Sothern and Kirk Douglas.
VHS: S18097. $19.98.
Joseph L. Mankiewicz, USA, 1949, 103 mins.

License to Kill
Agent Nick Carter is called in when enemy agents attempt to steal a new secret weapon. Starring Eddie Consantine and Daphne Dayle.
VHS: S15362. $29.95.
Henri Decoin, USA, 1964, 100 mins.

Life of Emile Zola
A penetrating drama and social documentary starring Paul Muni as the famous author of *Nana*. The film documents Zola's struggle as a novelist, his long friendship with the painter Cezanne and his impassioned fight against bigotry as evidenced by his role in the Dreyfuss Case.
VHS: S01758. $19.95.
William Dieterle, USA, 1937, 110 mins.

Lilies of the Field
Sidney Poitier won an Oscar for this earnest, well-meaning and quiet work about a black handyman who reluctantly agrees to help a group of emigre East German nuns build a chapel. The heart of the film is the tender and expressive relationship between Poitier and Lilia Skala, who plays the Mother Superior. With Lisa Mann, Isa Crino and Stanley Adams. Music by Jerry Goldsmith. Screenplay by James Poe.
VHS: S13390. $19.98.
Laser: LD72124. $34.98.
Ralph Nelson, USA, 1963, 93 mins.

Lilith
Warren Beatty and Jean Seberg co-star in this drama about the obsessive love between a therapist and his patient.
VHS: S04662. $59.95.
Robert Rossen, USA, 1964, 126 mins.

A Link in the Chain
On the eve of an awards banquet in his honor, Professor Graham's doubts about his illustrious career are put to rest when he opens a musty box of memorabilia. The three students he recalls—a handicapped artist, rebellious debutante and college hero—have learned about kindness and dignity from him, each in a special way. James Cagney stars in a performance both powerful and touching.
VHS: S16749. $19.98.
Larry Marcus, USA, 1955, 30 mins.

A Lion Is in the Streets

An itinerant confidence trickster becomes a self-titled defender of the people when James Cagney takes on "one of his most colorful and meaningful roles." This busy melodrama cleverly exposes the corruption of southern populist politics. Stars Barbara Hale, Anne Francis, Warner Anderson and Lon Chaney, Jr.
VHS: S16276. $19.98.
Laser: LD70048. $34.98.
Raoul Walsh, USA, 1953, 88 mins.

Listen, Darling

Unwilling to let her widowed mother marry just anyone, Pinky Wingate and her pal Buzz take matters into their own hands. They kidnap Dottie and take her for what becomes a cross-country husband hunt. Walter Pidgeon becomes the affable victim of everyone's affections. Starring Judy Garland and Mary Astor.
VHS: S15854. $19.98.
Edwin L. Marin, USA, 1938, 75 mins.

Little Caesar

This archetypal gangster film stars Edward G. Robinson as a small town thug who, along with his cohort, heads for the big city and ruthlessly pushes his way to the top of the mob. A landmark film, this action-packed melodrama is also a probing social commentary on the criminal mind and Depression era America. Director Mervyn LeRoy had such a fascination for the subject that he went so far as to hire three mobsters from Chicago as advisors on the production.
VHS: S14307. $19.98.
Mervyn LeRoy, USA, 1930, 80 mins.

Little Lord Fauntleroy

The enchanting story of a young boy, brought up in Brooklyn, who's discovered to be a long-lost heir and a British Lord. Fine performances by a superb cast, including Freddie Bartholomew, Mickey Rooney, and Delores Costello.
VHS: S13846. $14.98.
John Cromwell, USA, 1936, 102 mins.

Little Men

Cute adaptation of the Louisa May Alcott tale featuring Kay Francis, Jimmy Lydon and William Demarest. Jack Oakie steals the show as a wild con man.
VHS: S05635. $24.95.
Norman Z. McLeod, USA, 1940, 84 mins.

The Little Minister

Based on a play by Sir James Barrie. Katharine Hepburn is the gypsy girl who falls for the new cleric in a small Scottish village, with near-tragic results.
VHS: S03246. $19.95.
Laser: CLV. LD71727. $19.98.
Richard Wallace, USA, 1934, 101 mins.

Little Orphan Annie

Set in a blighted America beset at the height of the Depression, this is an early adaptation of the prize-winning comic strip about a charismatic, charming young orphan who falls into the warm embraces of a lonely, childless millionaire. With Mitzi Green, Edgar Kennedy, May Robson and Buster Phelps. Written by Wanda Tuchock and Tom McNamara.
VHS: S17445. $19.95.
John S. Robertson, USA, 1932, 60 mins.

The Little Princess

Shirley Temple is the pampered daughter of a British officer who's reported killed in action. Refusing to believe he's dead, she haunts army hospitals to find him. Based on the classic riches to rags story by Frances Hodgson Burnett.
VHS: S09996. $19.98.
Laser: CLV. LD72063. $39.95.
Walter Lang, USA, 1939, 93 mins.

Little Red Schoolhouse

Unprepared for the perils of city life, a rebellious young boy falls in with a gang of crooks after running away from home. This delightful adventure follows him through the consequences of his youthful folly.
VHS: S13847. $19.95.
Charles Lamont, USA, 1936, 64 mins.

Little Women

Four New England sisters wage a Civil War battle for a wealthy neighbor's grandson in this adaptation of Louisa May Alcott's story which stars Elizabeth Taylor, Janet Leigh, June Allyson and Margaret O'Brien.
VHS: S13066. $19.98.
Mervyn LeRoy, USA, 1949, 122 mins.

Lives of a Bengal Lancer

Adventure film set in India during the rule of the British, Gary Cooper stars as an officer of troops guarding the Kyber Pass on India's northern border. One of Hollywood's greatest adventure films.
VHS: S01989. $14.98.
Henry Hathaway, USA, 1935, 110 mins.

Lonelyhearts

Montgomery Clift stars as the writer of an advice column who becomes too involved for his own good in the problems of his readers. Adapted from Nathanael West's *Miss Lonelyhearts*. The excellent cast includes Myrna Loy, Robert Ryan, Jackie Coogan and Maureen Stapleton.
VHS: S04212. $19.98.
Vincent J. Donehue, USA, 1958, 101 mins.

The Lost Moment

Robert Cummings is an ambitious publisher in Europe trying to locate the lost love letters of a famous writer. Susan Hayward claims she has access to them, and Bob believes her. With Agnes Moorehead, Eduardo Cianelli. Based on Henry James' *Aspern Papers*. B&W.
VHS: S04223. $19.98.
Laser: CLV. LD72005. $34.98.
Martin Gabel, USA, 1947, 89 mins.

Lost Zeppelin

Ricardo Cortez stars in this adventure tale of explorers in the Antarctic. Fine acting and (for 1930) great special effects from this Tiffany production.
VHS: S10963. $29.95.
Edward Sloman, USA, 1930, 73 mins.

Love Affair

This RKO classic stars Irene Dunne and Charles Boyer, and was later remade as *An Affair to Remember*. It received five Oscar nominations, and featured songs by Harold Arlen and Buddy De Sylva.
VHS: S04491. $29.95.
Leo McCarey, USA, 1939, 87 mins.

Love Crazy

William Powell and Myrna Loy, America's favorite screen couple, are at it again as an old flame appears on their anniversary and sets flames to the wedded bliss. A crazy love story also starring Jack Carson, Gail Patrick and Florence Bates as the classic, bothersome mother-in-law.
VHS: S15118. $19.98.
Jack Conway, USA, 1941, 99 mins.

Love Has Many Faces

But Lana Turner has more dresses. The "Million Dollar" wardrobe by designer Edith Head earned equal billing with co-stars Cliff Robertson and Hugh O'Brian. Filmed in Acapulco, this steamy melodrama tells the story of a wealthy, aging beauty and the beach boys she desires. With Ruth Roman as a target for gigolos and Stephanie Powers as the younger competition from the States.
VHS: S15892. $19.95.
Alexander Singer, USA, 1965, 105 mins.

Love Is a Many Splendored Thing

Set in Hong Kong during the Korean War, Jennifer Jones plays a Eurasian doctor who falls in love with war correspondent William Holden. With Murray Matheson, Torin Thatcher and Keye Luke.
VHS: S18100. $19.98.
Henry King, USA, 1955, 102 mins.

Love Nest

A writer returns from the Army and discovers that his wife has bought a broken-down brownstone apartment building. The couple finds their landlord responsibilities a consuming activity. Stars William Lundigan, June Haver, Frank Fay, Marilyn Monroe, Leatrice Joy, and future TV host Jack Paar.
VHS: S16400. $19.98.
Joseph M. Newman, USA, 1951, 84 mins.

Love on the Run

A romantic and cosmopolitan thriller about the intertwining fates and activities of a gilded heiress (Joan Crawford) in love with a carefree reporter (Clark Gable) who is pursued by spies. With Franchot Tone, William Demarest and Reginald Owen.
VHS: S18803. $19.98.
W.S. Van Dyke II, USA, 1936, 80 mins.

Love Story

Ryan O'Neal and Ali MacGraw star in this melodramatic feast about young students in love who are thwarted by the travails of life. O'Neal's aristocratic heritage is just one of the hardships that almost come between him and his bride. Just when this pair seem to have defied all the odds against them an unforseen complication threatens to destroy everything. It received Oscar nominations for Best Actor, Best Actress, Best Director, Best Picture, and Best Story and Screenplay, and the Oscar for Best Original Score.
VHS: S22406. $14.95.
Laser: LD75345. $29.98.
Arthur Hiller, USA, 1970, 100 mins.

Love with a Proper Stranger

Natalie Wood is pregnant and Steve McQueen is responsible in this tough, urban love story set in New York City. Gritty locations enhance this study in neo-realism with laughs. It doesn't matter if you believe that McQueen is Italian; you will believe he could get Natalie pregnant. With Edie Adams, Herschel Bernardi, Vic Tayback and introducing Tom Bosley. B&W.
VHS: S08271. $19.95.
Laser: LD75224. $34.98.
Robert Mulligan, USA, 1963, 102 mins.

Loved One

Welcome to the lighter side of death, American style. Based on the novel by Evelyn Waugh, Robert Morse plays a naive British writer who takes a crash course in the California funeral industry that includes both human and animal customers. The all-star cast includes Liberace, James Coburn, Milton Berle, Tab Hunter, Robert Morley, Rod Steiger and Jonathan Winters. Written by Christopher Isherwood and Terry Southern.
VHS: S12233. $39.95.
Laser: LD72141. $39.95.
Tony Richardson, USA, 1965, 116 mins.

Lucky Partners

Errand girl Ginger Rogers is blessed with good fortune when she meets artist Ronald Colman and the two win a sweepstakes. They then depart on an imaginary honeymoon.
VHS: S10655. $19.98.
Lewis Milestone, USA, 1940, 100 mins.

Lust for Life

Kirk Douglas is cast as the tormented genius Vincent Van Gogh in this Vincente Minnelli film in full color. Based on the best-selling biographical novel by Irving Stone. Douglas throws himself into the role, but Anthony Quinn walked away with the Oscar as his best friend Gauguin. A first-class production with James Donald, Pamela Brown and Everett Sloane.
VHS: S11218. $19.95.
Laser: LD70618. $39.98.
Vincente Minnelli, USA, 1956, 122 mins.

Lydia

Merle Oberon revisits her youthful loves in this sentimental adaptation of the French film *Carnet de Bal*. With Joseph Cotten and Edna May Oliver.
VHS: S23437. $19.98.
Julien Duvivier, USA, 1941, 104 mins.

Ma Barker's Killer Brood

The true adventures of America's most notorious mother begins in dust-bowl Oklahoma. Barker leads her sons astray and gives advice to such infamous names as Dillinger, Baby Face Nelson and Machine Gun Kelly. The law finally catches up with her at her plush Florida hideout in an action-packed shoot-out. Derived from the tele-series. With Lurene Tuttle, Tris Coffin, Paul Dubov, Nelson Leigh and Myrna Dell.
VHS: S16113. $29.95.
Bill Karn, USA, 1960, 82 mins.

Madame Bovary

Jennifer Jones stars as the Gustave Flaubert heroine who sacrifices her husband and security for love, with tragic consequences. Features the famous ball scene, which is one of the greatest set pieces ever filmed. With James Mason and Louis Jourdan.
VHS: S01847. $19.98.
Laser: LD71686. $34.98.
Vincente Minnelli, USA, 1949, 115 mins.

Madame Curie

The celebrated story of the discovery of radium reunites *Mrs. Miniver's* Greer Garson and Walter Pidgeon. An excellent screen biography in the lush Hollywood tradition.
VHS: S15653. $19.98.
Laser: LD72142. $34.98.
Mervyn LeRoy, USA, 1943, 124 mins.

Madame Sin

A made for television work about a diabolical genius (Bette Davis) who carefully manipulates a retired CIA agent (Robert Wagner) to gain control of the high-tech Polaris Submarine. With Roy Kinnear, Denholm Elliott, and Paul Maxwell.
VHS: S03913. $19.95.
David Greene, USA, 1972, 72 mins.

Madame X (1937)

Gladys George is the woman who is forced by social customs and circumstances to abandon her son, in this adaptation of the novel by Alexandre Bisson. Years later, when Gladys stands trial for murder, she is defended by a son who is unaware of her actual identity. With John Beal, Warren William, Reginald Owen, William Henry and Henry Daniel.
VHS: S20411. $29.98.
Sam Wood, USA, 1937, 71 mins.

Madame X (1966)

Lana Turner stars in the sixth screen version of a fallen woman on trial for killing the blackmailer who would reveal her identity to the son who is unknowingly defending his mother. A time-proven soap opera with John Forsythe, Ricardo Montalban, Burgess Meredith, Keir Dullea and Constance Bennett in her final role.
VHS: S06182. $14.95.
David Lowell Rich, USA, 1966, 100 mins.

Made for Each Other

James Stewart and Carole Lombard star as an appealing married couple battling interfering in-laws, no money, and illness. With Charles Coburn and Louise Beavers.
VHS: S00795. $19.95.
John Cromwell, USA, 1939, 85 mins.

Mademoiselle Fifi

Simone Simon, the star of the original *Cat People*, is once again cast by producer Val Lewton. This time she plays Elizabeth Rousett, a valiant French laundress who stands up to the invading Prussian Army, circa 1870. Filmed in 1944 as an allegory of conditions in Nazi occupied France. With John Emery, Alan Napier, Helen Freeman, Jason Robards Sr. and Kurt Kreuger as the menacing Lt. Von Eyrick. Based on the stories by French novelist Guy de Maupassant.
VHS: S15775. $19.98.
Laser: CLV. LD71729. $19.98.
Robert Wise, USA, 1944, 69 mins.

Madigan

Richard Widmark plays Detective Madigan, who faces a plethora of problems and police commissioner Henry Fonda as well, in this feature film that later became the basis of a long-running TV series. Shot on location in New York and featuring Harry Guardino, Inger Stevens and James Whitmore.
VHS: S21917. $19.98.
Don Siegel, USA, 1968, 101 mins.

The Magic Sword

A rousing sword and sorcery adventure starring Basil Rathbone, Estelle Winwood and Gary Lockwood. Two-headed dragons, giant ogres and magic demons are all part of this epic tale based on the historic legend of Sir George and the Dragon. From the director of *Food of the Gods*.
VHS: S15267. $19.95.
Bert I. Gordon, USA, 1962, 90 mins.

Magnificent Doll

A historical drama by Frank Borzage; Ginger Rogers plays Dolly Madison, Burgess Meredith is President James Madison and David Niven is the enigmatic Aaron Burr.
VHS: S07781. $29.95.
Frank Borzage, USA, 1946, 95 mins.

The Magnificent Yankee

John Sturges' biography of Supreme Court Justice Oliver Wendell Holmes (Louis Calhern) dramatizes his relationship with his devoted, independent wife (Ann Harding). With Eduard Franz, James Lydon and Philip Ober.
VHS: S19469. $19.98.
John Sturges, USA, 1950, 80 mins.

A Majority of One

Rosalind Russell plays a Jewish matron from Brooklyn who slowly but surely falls in love with a Japanese businessman and widower (Alec Guiness). It's a successful translation of the original Broadway play written by Leonard Spigelgass.
VHS: S21324. $19.98.
Mervyn LeRoy, USA, 1962, 149 mins.

Make Haste to Live

Dorothy McGuire and Stephen McNally star. Crystal's new husband, Steve, is a handsome charmer, but what she doesn't know is that he's also a cold-blooded killer. She thinks her nightmare has ended when she runs away and starts a new life. But Steve is dead set on a touching reunion, and when he gets his hands on her, he'll love her to pieces.
VHS: S09669. $19.95.
William A. Seiter, USA, 1954, 90 mins.

Malaya

James Stewart and Spencer Tracy star in this World War II melodrama set in the Pacific. Smuggling rubber is a dangerous part of the Allied war effort, which requires the help of these two extraordinary characters.
VHS: S21018. $19.98.
Richard Thorpe, USA, 1949, 98 mins.

Mambo

A passion for dancing, a longing for fame, and a deep need for love—these are the powerful forces that flame within the heart of sultry Giovanna Masetti (Silvana Mangano), a beautiful young Venetian woman who resents her drab lot as a factory worker and fosters not-so-secret ambitions to be a great and famous dancer. Directed by Robert Rossen, and co-starring Michael Rennie and Shelley Winters.
VHS: S15174. $29.95.
Robert Rossen, USA/Italy, 1954, 94 mins.

A Man Called Peter

Richard Todd delivers a compelling performance as Peter Marshall, who emigrates to the U.S. from Scotland, becomes a pastor, and then the chaplain of the U.S. Senate. With Jean Peters, Marjorie Rambeau.
VHS: S11739. $19.98.
Henry Koster, USA, 1955, 119 mins.

The Man from Monterey

From the annals of early California history comes this tale of love and rivalry starring young John Wayne. This ornate production features elaborate Mexican-style costumes and Spanish-style colonial architecture.
VHS: S20951. $19.98.
Mark V. Wright, USA, 1933, 57 mins.

The Man I Love

Raoul Walsh's absorbing *noir* is set in a sinister Los Angeles nightclub populated by gangsters and hoods, where Ida Lupino is a beautiful seductress who gets caught up with a charismatic mobster (Robert Alda). With Andrea King, Martha Vickers, Bruce Bennett and Alan Hale.
VHS: S19570. $19.98.
Raoul Walsh, USA, 1946, 76 mins.

Man in the Gray Flannel Suit

Gregory Peck plays a Madison Avenue executive caught between his wife's nagging and the news from his wartime mistress back in Europe. Based on the popular novel by Sloan Wilson. The distinguished cast includes Fredric March, Jennifer Jones, Lee J. Cobb, Keenan Wynn and Marisa Pavan as Maria. Produced by Daryl F. Zanuck and written for the screen by Nunnally Johnson.
VHS: S12518. $19.98.
Laser: LD72220. $69.95.
Nunnally Johnson, USA, 1956, 152 mins.

The Man in the Iron Mask

Rousing adventure of twin brothers: one becomes King of France, the other a carefree gay blade raised by D'Artagnan and the Three Musketeers. A fine swashbuckler. With Louis Hayward and Joan Bennett.
VHS: S12778. $19.95.
James Whale, USA, 1939, 110 mins.

Man of a Thousand Faces

James Cagney stars in this film biography of Lon Chaney, the "master of disguise" who overcame a traumatic childhood to use his skills in mime and impersonation to forge an astonishing film career. The film restages many of the actor's signature roles, including *The Hunchback of Notre Dame*, *The Miracle*, and *Phantom of the Opera*. With Roger Smith, Robert Evans, Jim Backus, and Marjorie Rambeau.
VHS: S17016. $14.98.
Joseph Pevney, USA, 1957, 122 mins.

Man on the Eiffel Tower

The first directing effort of Burgess Meredith: a taut psychological thriller set in Paris centering on a battle of wits between a police investigator and a suspected murderer. With Charles Laughton, Burgess Meredith.
VHS: S03593. $19.95.
Burgess Meredith, USA, 1949, 97 mins.

The Man Who Cheated Himself

A film noir about a cynical detective (Lee J. Cobb) who falls for a beautiful femme fatale (Jane Wyatt). The woman kills her husband and convinces Cobb to shield her from the authorities and help cover up her crime. With John Dall and Terry Frost.
VHS: S19868. $29.95.
Felix E. Feist, USA, 1950, 81 mins.

Man with the Golden Arm

Otto Preminger's adaptation of Nelson Algren's psychological portrait of a drug addict trying to go straight stars Frank Sinatra (who received an Oscar nomination for his portrayal), Eleanor Parker, Kim Novak and Darren McGavin.
VHS: S04439. $19.98.
Otto Preminger, USA, 1955, 119 mins.

The Manchurian Candidate

A compelling thriller based on the Richard Condon novel about brain washing American soldiers to serve as assassins in secret global domination. Starring Frank Sinatra, Janet Leigh, Angela Lansbury and Laurence Harvey as the walking time bomb. This tape contains exclusive interviews with Sinatra, director John Frankenheimer and writer George Axelrod.
VHS: S07005. $19.98.
Laser: This deluxe collector's edition is letterboxed, newly digitally remastered and features commentary by John Frankenheimer. **LD70624. $59.98.**
John Frankenheimer, USA, 1962, 126 mins.

Mandarin Mystery

Last of the Republic Ellery Queen mysteries. Here Eddie Quillan, a star from his days of Pathe through the 1970's, portrays the great detective as he tries to recover the Chinese Mandarin stamp. 1936.
VHS: S08420. $29.95.

Manhattan Melodrama
A memorable tale of boyhood friends who end up on opposite sides of the law...and who both fall for the same mysterious woman. With Clark Gable, William Powell and Myrna Loy.
VHS: S15261. $19.98.
W.S. Van Dyke, USA, 1934, 91 mins.

Mannequin
Joan Crawford and Spencer Tracy star is this rags-to-riches soap opera in which a poor girl meets a rich man and does all right for herself. But first she has to dump the small-time chiseler she has already married and try her luck as a high fashion model.
VHS: S16453. $19.98.
Frank Borzage, USA, 1937, 95 mins.

Marie Antoinette
Norma Shearer is the Austrian princess who found being the queen of France had its down side as well. This lavish MGM production combines palace intrigues with political revolution. Robert Morley is a standout as King Louis XVI. Also in the cast: Tyrone Power, John Barrymore, Gladys George, Anita Louise and Joseph Schildkraut. Feel free to eat cake as you watch.
VHS: S11726. $19.98.
W.S. Van Dyke, USA, 1938, 149 mins.

Marie Galante
Spencer Tracy and Ketti Gallian in a story of international intrigue. Fine acting in a spy drama where the principals must stop the bombing of the Panama Canal.
VHS: S07758. $29.95.
Henry King, USA, 1934, 88 mins.

Marine Raiders
Pat O'Brien and Robert Ryan co-star as devil-dogs in action both on and off the battlefields in a fast-paced action drama. Another flag-waver to boost U.S. morale.
VHS: S12379. $19.98.
Harold Schuster, USA, 1943, 90 mins.

Marjorie Morningstar
Natalie Wood and Gene Kelly star in a drama about growing up Jewish and striving to find a place in the entertainment world. Wood gives perhaps the first glimpse of the modern Jewish American Princess. With Ed Wynn, Martin Milner and Carolyn Jones. From the novel by Herman Wouk.
VHS: S04897. $19.95.
Laser: LD71551. $49.98.
Irving Rapper, USA, 1958, 123 mins.

Mark of Zorro
Tyrone Power is fabulous as the son of a California aristocrat who masquerades as the swashbuckling hero who fights evil in this great Hollywood version. With Linda Darnell, Basil Rathbone and Gale Sondergaard. Famous for its incredible swashbuckling ending between Power and Rathbone. Music by Alfred Newman.
VHS: S01857. $19.98.
Rouben Mamoulian, USA, 1940, 93 mins.

Marked Woman
Bette Davis plays a hostess in a clip joint persuaded by special prosecutor Humphrey Bogart to spill the beans on her crooked employer. In the days before the witness relocation program, harsh rewards were often the price of conviction. With Mayo Methot, Lola Lane and Eduardo Ciannelli as Johnny Vanning. B&W.
VHS: S06351. $19.95.
Laser: LD74678. $34.98.
Lloyd Bacon, USA, 1937, 96 mins.

Maroc 7
Set in Morocco, structured around a robbery and murder tale, Maroc 7 concerns a spy's operation to unmask the identity of thief with multiple personalities. With Gene Barry, Cyd Charisse, and Denholm Elliott.
VHS: S16896. $19.95.
Gerry O'Hara, USA, 1967, 92 mins.

Marty
Ernest Borgnine won a well-deserved Oscar for Best Actor as the shy Bronx butcher who finds love. Academy Awards also went for direction, screenplay and Best Picture. With Betsy Blair, Joe De Santis and Esther Minciotti. From the teleplay by Paddy Chayefsky.
VHS: S08340. $14.95.
Laser: Chapter Search. Includes original theatrical trailer. LD71670. $34.98.
Delbert Mann, USA, 1955, 91 mins.

The Master of Ballantrae
Two brothers toss to decide who will join the 1745 rebellion to make Bonnie Prince Charles king of England. "Declare your allegiance—or answer to his blade!" Supreme swashbuckler Errol Flynn stars in this adaptation of the Robert Louis Stevenson novel, filmed on location in Scotland, England's Cornwall and Sicily. With Anthony Steel, Roger Livesey, Beatrice Campbell and Felix Aylmer.
VHS: S16732. $19.98.
Laser: LD71512. $34.98.
William Keighley, USA, 1953, 89 mins.

The Master Race
The Third Reich is crumbling and diehard Nazis decide to disband and rebuild for the next time. George Coulouris, as Von Beck, disguises himself as a Belgian patriot and attempts to live the simple life. With Stanley Ridges, Osa Massen, Nancy Gates, Lloyd Bridges, and Morris Carnovsky as Old Man Bartoc. Made before the war was over.
VHS: S09311. $19.98.
Herbert J. Biberman, USA, 1944, 96 mins.

Mata Hari
Greta Garbo adds her glamour to the tale of the exotic World War I spy. She dances, she flirts, she gives comfort to wounded soldiers. With Ramon Navarro, Lionel Barrymore, Lewis Stone and Karen Morley.
VHS: S13197. $19.98.
George Fitzmaurice, USA, 1932, 90 mins.

The McConnell Story
Alan Ladd roars into combat in the exciting, true story of Captain Joseph McConnell Jr., America's first triple jet ace. Also starring "America's sweetheart," June Allyson, as the fiery test pilot's understanding wife. Newly restored in true surround stereo.
VHS: S13621. $59.95.
Gordon Douglas, USA, 1955, 107 mins.

Medium Cool
Playing on Marshall McLuhan's phrase, "the cool medium," director Wexler uses a TV cameraman as the eyes through which the 1968 Chicago Democratic convention riots are viewed. An idyllic romance is framed by the realities of death, political hypocrisy, race hatred and revolution.
VHS: S00843. $14.95.
Laser: Widescreen. LD75228. $34.98.
Haskell Wexler, USA, 1969, 110 mins.

Meeting at Midnight (aka Black Magic)
Charlie Chan is forced to solve a murder committed during a seance to clear his daughter, whom the police suspect to be the murderer! Starring Sidney Toler and Manton Moreland.
VHS: S13851. $19.95.
Phil Rosen, USA, 1944, 67 mins.

Melody for Three
Fay Wray is a music teacher and mother of a violin prodigy, who is divorced from orchestra conductor Schuyler Standish.
VHS: S05700. $29.95.
Erle C. Kenton, USA, 1941, 67 mins.

Men
Marlon Brando gives a powerful screen debut performance as a World War II vet confined to a wheelchair who is embittered by his condition. With Teresa Wright and Jack Webb, produced by Stanley Kramer.
VHS: S01759. $19.95.
Laser: CLV. LD72008. $34.98.
Fred Zinnemann, USA, 1950, 85 mins.

Men of Boys Town
"There's no such thing as a bad boy," was the motto of Father Edward J. Flanagan, though his axiom was sometimes sorely tested. Spencer Tracy reprises his role as the benevolent priest who devoted his life to caring for abused and abandoned youths.
VHS: S14563. $19.98.
Norman Taurog, USA, 1941, 106 mins.

Men of the Fighting Lady
Jet pilot Van Johnson sling-shots from the deck of an aircraft carrier stationed off Korea in the Sea of Japan. Based on a thrilling true-life story.
VHS: S15126. $19.98.
Andrew Marton, USA, 1954, 82 mins.

Mercy Plane
James Dunn, Frances Gifford, Matt Fain, William Pawley and Harry Harvey star in this action adventure film about a new rescue airplane. When it is stolen, all indications point to the aircraft's pilot, but he is saved by a young woman unknowingly connected to the thieves.
VHS: S24012. $24.95.
Richard Harlan, USA, 1940, 73 mins.

Midnight
Claudette Colbert, Don Ameche and John Barrymore star in this delightful comedy written by Billy Wilder and Charles Brackett. Colbert is a gold-digger unsatisfied with her cabbie boyfriend (Ameche). To her delight a French aristocrat asks her to pose as a Hungarian Countess in order to distract his wife's latest love interest.
VHS: S24029. $14.98.
Mitchell Leisen, USA, 1939, 94 mins.

Midnight Cowboy (25th Anniversary)
The shocking story of Cowboy Joe Buck, played by Jon Voight, made history when it was released 25 years ago. This naive country boy with a horrible secret moves to New York, where the streetwise Ratso Rizzo (Dustin Hoffman) becomes his guide to seamy city life. Together they explore the world of hustling and even visit Warhol's factory, developing a deep friendship in the process. This film won Oscars for Best Picture, Screenplay and Director. Also features Brenda Vaccaro. A 25th Anniversary re-release.
VHS: S21826. $19.98.
Laser: LD74499. $49.98.
John Schlesinger, USA, 1969, 113 mins.

Midnight Lace
Doris Day is being driven mad and her rich industrialist husband, Rex Harrison, doesn't believe her. Suspects threatening Doris' well-being include Roddy McDowall, John Gavin and Herbert Marshall.
VHS: S03550. $59.95.
David Miller, USA, 1960, 108 mins.

Mildred Pierce
Michael Curtiz, who directed Casablanca and Yankee Doodle Dandy, elevates this Joan Crawford vehicle into a perverse and personal exploration of psychological disorder and collapse. Based on the novel by James M. Cain, Crawford won an Oscar as the hard-working mother with the world's most unpleasant, snobby, status-seeking and boyfriend-stealing daughter (Ann Blyth).
VHS: S02340. $19.98.
Laser: LD70630. $34.98.
Michael Curtiz, USA, 1945, 109 mins.

Millie
An adaptation of Donald Henderson's novel of sexual revenge and tragedy about a rejected man who pursues his disinterested lover's daughter, setting in motion a series of grave mishaps. With Helen Twelvetrees, Robert Ames, Lilyan Tashman and Joan Blondell.
VHS: S18941. $19.95.
John Francis Dillon, USA, 1931, 85 mins.

The Miniver Story
This sequel to William Wyler's award-winning Mrs. Miniver confronts the emotional and psychological effects of World War II, as Greer Garson and Walter Pidgeon try to cope with the social and political fraying of their peculiar family dynamics. Toby dreams about America and Judy falls for a married officer as Mrs. Miniver tries to suppress a long suppressed secret. With John Hodiak, Leo Glenn and Cathy O'Donnell.
VHS: S18801. $19.98.
H.C. Potter, USA, 1950, 104 mins.

Miracle of Our Lady of Fatima
Gilbert Roland and Angela Clarke star in this account of the religious miracle witnessed by farm children in the 1910's, in an event that inspired the small community and the world.
VHS: S06535. $19.98.
Laser: LD74732. $34.98.
John Brahm, USA, 1952, 102 mins.

The Miracle of the Bells
Frank Sinatra and Fred MacMurray star as a priest and a press agent who move heaven and earth to get a movie released after the death of its star (Alida Valli). Lee J. Cobb is the stubborn studio exec who needs a miracle to convince him the picture will be accepted by the public. B&W.
VHS: S05217. $19.95.
Irving Pichel, USA, 1948, 120 mins.

Miracle on 34th Street
The transcendent fable about a young girl (Natalie Wood) who doesn't believe in the spirit of Santa Claus, and the kindly department store clerk (Edmund Gwenn) who goes on trial to prove his identity and validity. With Maureen O'Hara, John Payne, Gene Lockhart and Thelma Ritter. "A delightful comedy-fantasy" (Leonard Maltin).
VHS: S00859. $14.98.
Laser: LD72272. $14.98.
George Seaton, USA, 1947, 96 mins.

Miss Sadie Thompson
Rita Hayworth is the bawdy nightclub entertainer stranded on a tropical island during World War II and loving every minute of it, until she encounters Reverend Davidson (Jose Ferrer).
VHS: S04536. $19.95.
Curtis Bernhardt, USA, 1952, 91 mins.

Mission in Morocco
Bruce Reynolds (Lex Barker), an oil firm executive, learns that an employee who discovered oil in the Sahara has been murdered. He sets off for Morocco with his fiancee (Juli Reding), determined to find the stolen microfilm that reveals the location of the precious oil. Their search puts them head to head with a ruthless gang of Middle Eastern thugs, equally determined to find the microfilm. 1959, 79 mins.
VHS: S12447. $19.98.

Monsoon
John Carradine stars as a deep sea diver hired to recover three million dollars in sunken treasure with his buddy, Frank Fenton. Problems arise when Sidney Toler, the ship's captain, wants a bigger cut and fewer partners. With Gale Sondergaard. Also known as Isle of Forgotten Sins.
VHS: S13318. $14.95.
Edgar G. Ulmer, USA, 1943, 77 mins.

The Moon and Sixpence
An adaptation of W. Somerset Maugham's fictional biography of post-impressionist painter Paul Gauguin shows him as he moves to Tahiti. Largely in black and white, with the paintings in color. With George Sanders, Herbert Marshall, Doris Dudley and Eric Blore.
VHS: S18029. $29.95.
Albert Lewin, USA, 1943, 89 mins.

Moonrise
Frank Borzage at his best; primal passions erupt in a small southern town when a handsome young man is branded the son of a killer and tormented by unforgiving townspeople who hung his father. Mercilessly goaded into committing murder himself, the wanted fugitive must confront the consequences of his actions or be condemned to relive his father's brutal fate. With Ethel Barrymore, Lloyd Bridges.
VHS: S09494. $19.95.
Laser: LD71812. $29.98.
Frank Borzage, USA, 1948, 90 mins.

Morning Glory
Katharine Hepburn is the stage-struck young girl who tries to succeed in New York City theatre. Hepburn won her first Best Actress Oscar for her performance. The film also stars Adolphe Menjou and Douglas Fairbanks, Jr.
VHS: S00882. $19.95.
Laser: LD72282. $39.99.
Lowell Sherman, USA, 1933, 73 mins.

The Mortal Storm
Phyllis Bottom's moving novel, set in Nazi Germany, details the trauma faced by a family split over Hitler's rise. James Stewart is a student who falls in love with his professor's daughter, Margaret Sullavan. As the young couple faces the growing threat of Nazism, they decide to leave. Also includes Robert Young and Robert Stack.
VHS: S21171. $19.98.
Frank Borzage, USA, 1940, 100 mins.

Most Dangerous Game
On a jungle island Zaroff, a mad nobleman, tires of hunting big game and stalks men instead. When Bob, Eve and Martin are shipwrecked there, he pursues them relentlessly. Hunter and prey match wits in this classic. Joel McCrea, Fay Wray, Leslie Banks star.
VHS: S00885. $19.95.
Ernest Schoedsack/Pichel, USA, 1932, 62 mins.

Mountain
When a plane goes down in the Alps veteran mountain guide Spencer Tracy wants to see if there are any survivors. His younger brother Robert Wagner wants to loot the remains of the passengers for valuables. With E.G. Marshall, Claire Trevor, and William Demarest. 105 mins.
VHS: S08171. $19.95.
Edward Dmytryk, USA, 1956, 105 mins.

Mr. Moto's Last Warning
Peter Lorre, as that super sleuth of Japanese ancestry, is called to Port Said near the Suez Canal. It seems that George Sanders and Richardo Cortez want to mine shipping lanes for nefarious purposes. Mr. Moto does not allow the plan to succeed. With John Carradine as the unfortunate British agent.
VHS: S18177. $19.98.
Norman Foster, USA, 1939, 71 mins.

Mr. Robinson Crusoe
Lively adventure story finds Douglas Fairbanks betting he can live on a deserted island for a year without any of the luxuries of the civilized world. Filmed in Tahiti.
VHS: S03786. $19.95.
Laser: LD70403. $34.98.
A. Edward Sutherland, USA, 1932, 80 mins.

Mr. Skeffington
Bette Davis marries the title character to prevent him from having her brother prosecuted for embezzling. Claude Rains doesn't hold her to the marriage when the brother dies, and leaves for Europe. Years pass and Bette loses her hair to diphtheria while Mr. Skeffington has Nazi trouble. Lots of heartache in this soap opera.
VHS: S06352. $19.95.
Laser: LD70632. $39.98.
Vincent Sherman, USA, 1944, 145 mins.

Mr. Skitch
Will Rogers portrays a man fallen on hard times who must pack up his family and head for California. Good family entertainment which depicts life on the road during the Depression.
VHS: S13495. $19.98.
James Cruze, USA, 1933, 70 mins.

Mr. Wong in Chinatown
Boris Karloff's third entry in this detective series. A Chinese princess is murdered by a poisoned arrow and the only witness is a mute dwarf (an orientalized Angelo Rossitto) who disappears. Wong is assisted by Police Captain and his reporter-girlfriend.
VHS: S04018. $29.95.
William Nigh, USA, 1939, 70 mins.

Mr. Wong, Detective
Boris Karloff stars as the title character, a famous Oriental detective based in San Francisco. Chemical manufacturers are being killed by poison gas and James Lee Wong is on the case. This series was to challenge Charlie Chan films yet this story was later remade as Docks of New Orleans, a Charlie Chan 1948 release.
VHS: S04017. $29.95.
William Nigh, USA, 1938, 69 mins.

Mrs. Parkington
This lavish historical spectacle covers six decades of the personal fortune and dramatic self-destruction of an American dynasty. An ambitious woman (Greer Garson) marries a powerful though simple man (Walter Pidgeon) and immediately insinuates herself into his family. With Edward Arnold, Gladys Cooper and Agnes Moorehead.
VHS: S18807. $19.98.
Tay Garnett, USA, 1944, 124 mins.

Murder My Sweet
Dick Powell stars as Raymond Chandler's hard-boiled detective, Phillip Marlowe. A complex web of murder, blackmail and double-dealing make it one of the most exciting detective thrillers of the 40s. Also starring Claire Trevor.
VHS: S00898. $19.95.
Edward Dmytryk, USA, 1944, 95 mins.

Music in My Heart
The lovely Rita Hayworth cold-shoulders a millionaire in favor of a lowly nightclub singer. A light, fairy-tale romance. Tony Martin co-stars.
VHS: S15528. $19.98.
Joseph Santley, USA, 1940, 69 mins.

Mutiny on the Bounty (Brando)
Marlon Brando makes a foppish Fletcher Christian in this lavish MGM remake of the classic Nordhoff-Hall tale of rebellion in the South Seas. Trevor Howard is the hard-driving Captain Bligh. Other crew members include Richard Harris, Gordon Jackson, Hugh Griffith, Percy Herbert and Tarita as the daughter of the native chief. Filmed on location in Tahiti.
VHS: S06153. $29.98.
Laser: 1962, Marlon Brando, MGM. LD70633. $39.98.
Lewis Milestone, USA, 1962, 177 mins.

Mutiny on the Bounty (Laughton)
The classic version, starring Charles Laughton in an unforgettable role as Captain Bligh and Clark Gable as Christian. The picture deservedly won the Oscar for the Best Movie of the Year.
VHS: S02714. $19.95.
Laser: 1935, Charles Laughton, MGM. LD70634. $39.98.
Frank Lloyd, USA, 1935, 133 mins.

My Foolish Heart
Based on J.D. Salinger's story Uncle Wiggily in Connecticut, about the romance between Susan Hayward and Dana Andrews, a war hero who makes Hayward, a married woman, pregnant.
VHS: S23439. $19.98.
Mark Robson, USA, 1949, 98 mins.

My Forbidden Past
In 1890s New Orleans, a woman with a tainted past falls in love with a Yankee doctor. Using her wealth in a cold-blooded scheme to win his affections from his wife, the plot explodes in fateful irony.
VHS: S02873. $19.98.
Robert Stevenson, USA, 1951, 72 mins.

My Girl Tisa
An immigrant girl (Lilli Palmer) is determined to save enough money to bring her father to America. When she falls for an aspiring lawyer (Sam Wanamaker), he begs her to let him use her savings for his education. Torn between her father and the man she loves, a series of comic misadventures leaves her on the verge of being deported.
VHS: S12445. $19.98.
Elliott Nugent, USA, 1948, 95 mins.

My Lucky Star
Sonja Henie plays a department store clerk who enrolls in a local college as a publicity stunt. She is promptly pursued by a group of love-obsessed suitors. The film's glorious climax is a stylized ice ballet from *Alice in Wonderland*. With Richard Greene, Buddy Ebsen, Arthur Treacher and Joan Davis.
VHS: $20262. $19.98.
Roy Del Ruth, USA, 1938, 84 mins.

Mysterious Lady
The magnificent Greta Garbo portrays a Russian spy as only she can. Set during World War I, Garbo vamps a handsome Austrian soldier while scheming to keep her occupation top secret. Directed by Fred Niblo (*Ben Hur: A Tale of the Christ*). Silent film with synchronized musical score.
VHS: $13978. $29.95.
Fred Niblo, USA, 1928, 99 mins.

Mysterious Mr. Wong
Bela Lugosi plays the title character who will stop at nothing to obtain the twelve coins of Confucius. Set in New York's Chinatown, Wong is the first madman mandarin to sport a marked slavic accent—but he does have a way with instruments of torture.
VHS: $04000. $29.95.
William Nigh, USA, 1935, 60 mins.

Mystery of Marie Roget
Detective thriller based on a short story by Edgar Allan Poe, a medical examiner investigates the disappearance of a famous actress. With Maria Montez.
VHS: $03785. $34.95.
Phil Rosen, USA, 1942, 60 mins.

The Mystery of Mr. Wong
The largest star sapphire in the world is stolen during a game of charades when the host of a fancy party is shot dead. Boris Karloff, as the effective detective Mr. Wong, just happens to be one of the guests. After several more murders he solves the case.
VHS: $04019. $29.95.
William Nigh, USA, 1939, 68 mins.

The Naked City
Blacklisted filmmaker Jules Dassin directed this key film noir and achieved realistic settings by using actual New York locations. The plot concerns the police department's unrelenting search for the killer of a young girl. Famous for its astonishing denouement on the Williamsburg bridge. With Barry Fitzgerald, Howard Duff and Dorothy Hart.
VHS: $18239. $29.95.
Jules Dassin, USA, 1948, 96 mins.

The Naked Edge
A taut suspense thriller about a woman (Deborah Kerr) who investigates the possibility that her husband (Gary Cooper) is a killer. With Eric Portman, Diane Cilento and Hermione Gingold.
VHS: $17985. $19.98.
Michael Anderson, USA, 1961, 97 mins.

The Naked Jungle
Charlton Heston is a proud and prosperous plantation owner in South America who thinks the time is right for a mail order bride. When Eleanor Parker arrives, he's not satisfied and prepares to ship her back up the Amazon until an army of soldier ants delays his decision. Great special effects by George Pal.
VHS: $06030. $19.95.
Laser: LD75234. $34.98.
Byron Haskin, USA, 1953, 94 mins.

The Naked Maja
A retelling of the torrid love affair between painter Francisco Goya (Anthony Franciosa) and the Duchess of Alba (Ava Gardner), who sponsored his work. With Amedeo Nzaarai, Gino Cervi and Lea Padovani.
VHS: $19569. $19.98.
Henry Koster, USA, 1959, 112 mins.

Nancy Drew Reporter
Bonita Granville stars as America's favorite teenage sleuth. When Nancy wins a newspaper contest, she gets a shot at the crime beat and discovers an innocent woman has been charged with murder. With John Litel as Carson Drew and Frank Thomas as Ned Nickerson, Jr. Based on the characters created by Carolyn Keene.
VHS: $15797. $19.95.
William Clemens/John Langan, USA, 1939, 65 mins.

Navy Blue and Gold
A colorful tale set at the U.S. Naval Academy. Three friends with distinct personalities (the wealthy innocent, the cynical outsider, and the mysterious figure with a complicated past) enter Annapolis and learn about tradition, discipline and honor. With Robert Young, James Stewart, Florence Rice, Billie Burke, Lionel Barrymore and Tom Brown.
VHS: $20415. $29.98.
Sam Wood, USA, 1937, 93 mins.

Never Let Me Go
Clark Gable is featured as a foreign correspondent whose passion leads him to kidnap his Russian bride (Gene Tierney) after she is denied an exit visa to the U.S.
VHS: $20562. $19.98.
Delmer Daves, USA, 1953, 94 mins.

Never Love a Stranger
John Drew Barrymore, the son of John, the father of Drew, stars in this Harold Robbins adaptation of a young hoodlum on the rise. Also in the cast is Steve McQueen, with fourth billing in his second feature film. McQueen had a bit part in *Somebody Up There Likes Me*. Apparently so, for he never had fourth billing again. B&W.
VHS: $04231. $19.95.
Robert Stevens, USA, 1958, 93 mins.

Never on Sunday
Melina Mercouri stars as Illia, the most popular whore on the Greek port city of Piraeus. Director Dassin (her real life husband) stars as Homer, an American self-taught philosopher who tries to raise her above streetwalking. Hilarious, carefree, with great Greek music throughout.
VHS: $01723. $19.98.
Jules Dassin, USA/Greece, 1960, 91 mins.

Never So Few
John Sturges's World War II epic about jungle fighting, its story centers around American soldiers advising Burmese guerrillas, written by blacklisted writer Dalton Trumbo (under the pen name Millard Kaufman), from the novel by Tom Chamales. With Frank Sinatra, Gina Lollobrigida, Peter Lawford, Steve McQueen and Paul Henreid.
Laser: LD71165. $39.98.
John Sturges, USA, 1959, 124 mins.

Next Voice You Hear
God works in mysterious ways. God speaks to mankind on the radio, and the life of Joe Smith American is changed in this Dore Schary MGM tenure film which stars James Whitmore and Nancy Davis in a story of frustrations and answered prayer.
VHS: $13064. $19.98.
William Wellman, USA, 1950, 83 mins.

Niagara
Marilyn Monroe in full Technicolor does her best to upstage one of the Natural Wonders of the World. All that rushing water just can't compete with a tight dress. The plot to drive Joseph Cotten crazy, however, could use a little work. With Jean Peters.
VHS: $04200. $19.98.
Henry Hathaway, USA, 1953, 89 mins.

Night After Night
A glossy melodrama about a worn-down fighter (George Raft) who buys a bar and tries to seduce a gilded society woman (Constance Cummings) but is upstaged by the flamboyant theatrics of Mae West, in her screen debut. Contains the memorable line, "Goodness had nothing to do with it." With Wynne Gibson and Alison Skipworth.
VHS: $18865. $14.98.
Archie Mayo, USA, 1932, 70 mins.

Night Nurse
Barbara Stanwyck, Joan Blondell and Clark Gable are delightfully entertaining in this Pre-Code film full of racy dialog, decadent settings and daring performances. Stanwyck is a private nurse who discovers quite unethical behavior going on at the residence where she and Blondell are employed. And Gable's intent on making sure she keeps her trap shut.
VHS: $15014. $19.98.
William Wellman, USA, 1931, 73 mins.

The Night of the Hunter
Robert Mitchum gives one of his best performances as Harry Powell, a psychotic self-styled preacher who is after the stolen money of a hanged man. Set in a small West Virginia community during the Depression, this is Charles Laughton's only screen credit as a director. He makes the most of the opportunity.
VHS: $04213. $19.98.
Laser: LD70426. $39.95.
Charles Laughton, USA, 1955, 93 mins.

The Night They Raided Minsky's
Britt Ekland stars as a beautiful young Amish woman who leaves her strict family home and comes to New York to become a dancer. While she originally intends to interpret biblical scenes through dance, a series of mishaps lead her to invent another kind of dance—the striptease.
VHS: $15252. $19.98.
William Friedkin, USA, 1968, 99 mins.

No Highway in the Sky
James Stewart is an engineer fighting against imminent disaster in the air. Only fellow passenger Marlene Dietrich and a flight attendant played by Glynis Johns believe him. Together they must make sure the plane does not take off again. This thriller is based on the gripping novel by Nevil Shute.
VHS: $25909. $19.98.
Henry Koster, USA, 1951, 98 mins.

None But the Brave
U.S. Marine Frank Sinatra crash lands on a Pacific atoll during World War II...and discovers it's held by Japanese troops. After some taut action and suspense the enemies eventually make peace. Believe it or not, this anti-war melodrama was directed by Frankie himself.
VHS: $13620. $19.98.
Laser: LD70645. $34.98.
Frank Sinatra, USA, 1965, 106 mins.

None But the Lonely Heart
A genuine film classic which tells the story of a restless wanderer from London's East End slums who settles down to help his cancer-stricken mother. Directed by Clifford Odets, with an Oscar for Ethel Barrymore and a nomination for Cary Grant.
VHS: $03266. $19.98.
Clifford Odets, USA, 1944, 113 mins.

North Star
Ruth Gordon, Walter Huston and Anne Baxter star in this story about Russian peasants resisting Nazi invaders, based upon a Lillian Hellman script.
VHS: $02184. $39.98.
Lewis Milestone, USA, 1943, 105 mins.

North to Alaska
A couple of prospectors are the focus of this brawling adventure story set in the Klondike in the early 1900's. John Wayne, Stewart Granger, Ernie Kovacs, Capucine, Fabian star.
VHS: $05910. $19.98.
Henry Hathaway, USA, 1960, 117 mins.

Northern Pursuit
Set in the awesome snowbound wasteland of Canada, Errol Flynn is the mountie who is ordered to break up a ring of Nazi saboteurs.
VHS: $01875. $19.98.
Raoul Walsh, USA, 1943, 94 mins.

Northwest Outpost
The last film of Nelson Eddy. He plays a cavalry captain entranced by a married Russian aristocrat living in California. But that's okay, because the beautiful Ilona Massey was forced into marrying Count Igor and would welcome a change in men. With Joseph Schildkraut, Hugo Haas and Elsa Lanchester.
VHS: $12901. $19.98.
Allan Dwan, USA, 1947, 91 mins.

Not As a Stranger
Stanley Kramer's flamboyant melodrama about the strains of professional marriage between a doctor (Robert Mitchum) and the nurse (Olivia de Havilland) who supported him through medical school and his troubled past. With Frank Sinatra, Gloria Grahame, Lon Chaney and Harry Morgan.
VHS: $17996. $19.98.
Stanley Kramer, USA, 1955, 136 mins.

Now Voyager
Bette Davis blossoms under the psychiatric care of Claude Rains, only to fall in love with a married man on a South American cruise. Paul Henreid is the romantic stranger who also has a daughter who could benefit from the care of Claude Rains. A first-rate tear-jerker.
VHS: $02900. $19.95.
Irving Rapper, USA, 1942, 117 mins.

Nun's Story
Adaptation of the book by Kathryn Hulme, with Audrey Hepburn cast as the nun who serves in the Belgian Congo and later decides to leave the convent. With Coleen Dewhurst as the maniacal patient, and a cast including Peter Finch, Edith Evans and Peggy Ashcroft.
VHS: Out of print. For rental only.
Laser: LD74735. $39.98.
Fred Zinnemann, USA, 1959, 149 mins.

Objective, Burma!
A taut, thrilling blockbuster of a war melodrama about a group of tough, tight-lipped paratroopers who are dropped into the Burmese jungle to wipe out a Japanese radar station. Starring Errol Flynn.
VHS: $15129. $19.98.
Raoul Walsh, USA, 1945, 142 mins.

Ocean's 11
Frank Sinatra, Dean Martin, Sammy Davis, Jr., Peter Lawford and Angie Dickinson star in this criminal suspense yarn. A gang decides to cash in on five casinos all at once. The only way to do it is with a complicated and elegant scheme for robbery.
VHS: $26864. $14.95.
Lewis Milestone, USA, 1960, 148 mins.

Of Human Bondage
Based on the novel by W. Somerset Maugham, this is a poignant story of self-destructive love, starring Leslie Howard as a young clubfooted medical student, and Bette Davis as the low-class waitress with whom he falls disastrously in love.
VHS: $18176. $19.95.
John Cromwell, USA, 1934, 83 mins.

Of Human Hearts
Clarence Brown's film dramatizes the estrangement between a fervent, small-town preacher and his son. "A curious all-American fable [that is] splendidly made and acted" (Leslie Halliwell). With Walter Huston, James Stewart, Beulah Bondi, Gene Reynolds, Charles Coburn and Guy Kibbee.
VHS: $20413. $29.98.
Clarence Brown, USA, 1938, 100 mins.

The Old Forest
A fascinating short film set in 1937 Memphis, *The Old Forest* focuses on the dilemma faced by a young gentleman when his engagement to a wealthy lady is threatened by the disappearance of a working class woman. A brilliant adaptation of author Peter Taylor's acclaimed short story. USA, 60 mins.
VHS: $15002. $19.98.

The Old Maid
Bette Davis is in quite a fix when her intended is killed in the Civil War and leaves her expecting their child. When the war is over she opens a nursery school in Philadelphia for orphans and has her daughter adopted by a scheming cousin to insure a proper future. A real tear-jerker. With Miriam Hopkins, George Brent, and Donald Crisp. B&W.
VHS: $06316. $19.95.
Edmund Goulding, USA, 1939, 95 mins.

The Old Swimmin' Hole
The joys of small town life are disrupted for young Chris when a lawyer, acting for his evil millionaire grandfather, wants to take him away to be brought up properly in the city. With Jackie Moran, Marcia Mae Jones and Theodore Von Eltz. Gosh, what's a kid to do?
VHS: $05477. $29.95.
Robert McGowan, USA, 1940, 78 mins.

Oliver Twist
Charles Dickens' great story of the workhouse orphan forced into the criminal world of London pickpockets is notable for its strong performances from Dickie Moore, Irvin Pichel and George Arthur.
VHS: $18189. $19.95.
William J. Cowan, USA, 1933, 71 mins.

Omar Khayyam
William Dieterle directs this large scale, medieval period biography of Persia's celebrated poet and patriot. The cast includes Cornel Wilde, Debra Paget, Raymond Massey and Sebastian Cabot.
VHS: $16897. $19.95.
William Dieterle, USA, 1957, 100 mins.

On the Beach
Powerful adaptation of Nevil Shute's novel about the last people on earth, who face certain death from radioactivity. This film became one of the most celebrated anti-nuclear movies of the Fifties. With Gregory Peck, Ava Gardner and Fred Astaire.
VHS: $02557. $19.98.
Stanley Kramer, USA, 1959, 135 mins.

On the Waterfront
Marlon Brando in the archetypal role as ex-fighter Terry Malloy, working for Boss Johnny Friendly (Lee J. Cobb) on the gang-ridden waterfront. The classic American movie of redemption, with a great script by Budd Schulberg.
VHS: Out of print. For rental only.
Laser: LD72070. $34.95.
Elia Kazan, USA, 1954, 108 mins.

Once Upon a Honeymoon
Ginger Rogers is the ex-burlesque queen who thinks she's met her match with an Austrian baron, but news reporter Cary Grant tries to convince her otherwise. Her charming admirer knows what she does not—that her new husband is really a Nazi agent in disguise.
VHS: $05658. $19.95.
Leo McCarey, USA, 1945, 116 mins.

One in a Million
The debut film of Norwegian Olympic skating star Sonja Henie. The story follows the meteoric fortunes of a beautiful skater after her dazzling New York performance catapults her to the top. With Adolphe Menjou, Don Ameche and the Ritz Brothers.
VHS: $20257. $19.98.
Sidney Lanfield, USA, 1936, 94 mins.

One Man's Way
A low-key biography of controversial minister and proselytizer Norman Vincent Peale (Don Murray) examines his relationship with his wife (Diana Hyland), amid accusations of blasphemy because of his unconventional preaching methods. With Veronica Cartwright, Ian Wolfe and Virginia Christine.
VHS: $19471. $19.98.
Denis Sanders, USA, 1963, 105 mins.

One Minute to Zero
Tay Garnett directed this gritty melodrama starring Robert Mitchum, set during the Korean War. Mitchum is a colonel evacuating American civilians, while Ann Blyth, as a United Nations envoy, provides romance.
VHS: $09175. $19.95.
Tay Garnett, USA, 1952, 105 mins.

One Rainy Afternoon
An actor kisses a strange woman in a Parisian movie house and is put on trial as the Kissing Monster. When she pays his bail a scandal erupts and soon every woman in Paris wants to be kissed by a stranger. With Francis Lederer, Ida Lupino, Hugh Herbert and Donald Meek. B&W.
VHS: $08455. $29.95.
Rowland V. Lee, USA, 1936, 78 mins.

Operation CMrossbow
Michael Anderson's superb World War II thriller written by Emeric Pressburger about a group of highly skilled commandos assigned an apparent suicide mission to break up Hitler's secret wartime experiments with rocket weapons, the V-1 and V-2. With George Peppard, Sophia Loren, Trevor Howard, Tom Courtenay and Anthony Quayle. Letterboxed.
VHS: $21021. $19.98.
Laser: LD71660. $39.98.
Michael Anderson, USA, 1965, 116 mins.

The Oscar
A star-studded ensemble cast headed by Stephen Boyd, Jill St. John, Elke Sommer, Milton Berle, Joseph Cotten, Ernest Borgnine and Tony Bennett in the story of Frankie Fane, who makes her way to Hollywood and to an Oscar nomination.
VHS: $20531. $19.95.
Russell Rouse, USA, 1957, 118 mins.

Our Daily Bread
An ordinary urban couple become farmers and, incidentally, host to a collection of drifters who join together and become a unified community. This tale of organic socialism was released independently because the major studios feared its political theme. An exclusive introduction from the director and two newsreels, *California Election News*, which were meant to hurt the socialist campaign of Upton Sinclair, are also included. This collector's version is mastered from the finest print available.
VHS: $00979. $19.95.
King Vidor, USA, 1934, 74 mins.

Our Man Flint
On his first cinematic secret mission, Secret Agent Flint (James Coburn) faces off against the most dangerous weapon of all, the weather. An evil organization called Galaxy has learned how to send icebergs crashing into the Mediterranean to flood whole valleys.
VHS: $11263. $19.98.
Laser: LD71264. $59.98.
Daniel Mann, USA, 1966, 103 mins.

Our Miss Brooks
Eve Arden is a wise-cracking English teacher trying to snag her colleague Mr. Boynton, played by Robert Rockwell. The film is based on the popular TV series, with veteran actors Gale Gordon and Richard Crenna also featured. Crenna singing "It's Magic" is a high point.
VHS: $21344. $37.95.
Al Lewis, USA, 1956, 85 mins.

Our Vines Have Tender Grapes
A tender adaptation of George Victor Martin's novel (by blacklisted writer Dalton Trumbo) of an immigrant Scandinavian family and the difficulties of acceptance and assimilation they encounter when they resettle in a Wisconsin farm community. With Edward G. Robinson, Agnes Moorehead and Margaret O'Brien.
VHS: $18506. $19.98.
Roy Rowland, USA, 1945, 105 mins.

Outpost in Morocco
George Raft, Marie Windsor and Akim Tamiroff star in this drama about Arab rebellion. Raft is a legionnaire sent to quell the troubles in the desert, but he finds himself trapped in a dilemma when he falls for the rebel leader's daughter (Windsor).
VHS: $23777. $24.95.
Robert Florey, USA, 1949, 92 mins.

The Ox-Bow Incident
Superb drama illustrating the terror of mob rule based on the Walter Van Tilburg Clark novel. With Henry Fonda, Dana Andrews, Anthony Quinn.
VHS: $06524. $19.98.
William Wellman, USA, 1943, 75 mins.

Painted Veil
Greta Garbo has difficulties remaining faithful to her husband in this adaptation of the Somerset Maugham novel. Set in the Orient, George Brent plays her lover, Herbert Marshall is the supportive husband. With Keye Luke, Warner Oland and Jean Hersholt.
VHS: S13195. $19.98.
Richard Boleslawski, USA, 1934, 83 mins.

Pandora and the Flying Dutchman
Ava Gardner and James Mason star in this wildly ambitious interpretation of the legend of the Flying Dutchman. On the south coast of Spain, between cocktail parties and costume changes, Gardner vamps for exciting international playboys. Only the mysterious yachtsman Hendrick van der Zee (Mason), none other than the legendary Flying Dutchman, manages to capture her heart. As the legend goes, he is set to wander until he finds a woman willing to make the ultimate sacrifice for love.
VHS: S26992. $19.95.
Laser: LD75435. $49.99.
Albert Lewin, USA, 1950, 123 mins.

Panic in the Streets
Public health officials search for a carrier of the bubonic plague. An Oscar winner for Best Original Story, director Elia Kazan concocts a semi-documentary suspense story set on the New Orleans waterfront. Great location shooting. With Richard Widmark, Barbara Bel Geddes, Paul Douglas and Jack Palance.
VHS: S13203. $39.98.
Laser: LD72319. $39.98.
Elia Kazan, USA, 1950, 96 mins.

Papa's Delicate Condition
In turn of the century Grangeville, Texas, Jackie Gleason is a railroad supervisor whose "delicate condition," a drinking problem, threatens the stable environment of his family and deeply upsets his wife and eldest daughter. A small, likable film about morals and responsibility, as seen through the eyes of Gleason's six-year-old daughter.
VHS: S02781. $19.95.
Laser: LD75235. $34.98.
George Marshall, USA, 1963, 98 mins.

Paris Blues
Martin Ritt's highly personal essay on Americans abroad. The story concerns two expatriate jazz musicians (Paul Newman and Sidney Poitier) who are caught up in the transcendent energy of Paris' Left Bank. Joanne Woodward and Diahann Carroll play their respective romantic interests. The film features a moody, evocative Duke Ellington score. Special appearance by Louis Armstrong. With Serge Reggiani.
VHS: S19492. $19.98.
Martin Ritt, USA, 1961, 98 mins.

Park Avenue Logger
Lloyd Ingraham thinks his son is less than a man and sends him off to a lumber camp to prove his manhood, not knowing he is already a top wrestler. There he exposes some crooked foremen and wins the heart of a beautiful girl by saving her father's lumber operation.
VHS: S21561. $24.95.
David Howard, USA, 1937, 65 mins.

Parrish
Delmer Daves' bittersweet, operatic adaptation of Mildred Savage's novel set on Connecticut's tobacco farms. Troy Donahue plays an ambitious young man who lives with his mother (Claudette Colbert) on an aristocrat's plantation and falls in love with three different women. With Karl Malden, Dean Jagger, Connie Stevens, Diane McBain and Sharon Hugueny.
VHS: S20195. $19.98.
Delmer Daves, USA, 1961, 138 mins.

Passage to Marseilles
Humphrey Bogart dishes out plenty of excitement in this story of five Devil's Island escapees determined to join the fight against the Nazis. Also starring Claude Rains, Peter Lorre and Sydney Greenstreet.
VHS: S02559. $19.98.
Michael Curtiz, USA, 1944, 109 mins.

Patch of Blue
Sidney Poitier befriends a reclusive blind girl in the park on her first day out of the house in 13 years. Elizabeth Hartman doesn't care what color Sidney is because he is just so nice. Shelley Winters won a best supporting Oscar for her role as the mean-spirited prostitute mother. With Ivan Dixon and Wallace Ford. Based on the story Be Ready with Bells and Drums, by Elizabeth Kata.
VHS: S12530. $19.98.
Guy Green, USA, 1965, 105 mins.

Patton
George C. Scott delivers a stirring performance in this classic screen biography of the charismatic and controversial General George S. Patton. Winner of six Academy Awards.
VHS: S03475. $29.95.
Franklin J. Schaffner, USA, 1970, 176 mins.

The Pawnbroker
Rod Steiger won an Academy Award nomination for Best Actor for his performance as The Pawnbroker. Sidney Lumet's powerful film about a New York pawnbroker who has lost all faith in mankind as a result of his imprisonment in Nazi Germany.
VHS: S01004. $19.98.
Sidney Lumet, USA, 1965, 116 mins.

People Will Talk
Cary Grant and Jean Crain star as a doctor and patient in this absorbing comedy/drama. Eventually they get married, but not before everyone has had a chance to gossip—that is, discuss the merits and problems their earlier relationship is likely to bequeath on their matrimonial union.
VHS: S21332. $19.98.
Joseph L. Mankiewicz, USA, 1951, 110 mins.

Period of Adjustment
An early film from George Roy Hill about the difficulties and tensions of a young married couple whose life is thrown out of balance by their friends' unraveling marriage. With Jane Fonda, Tony Franciosa, Jim Hutton and Jack Albertson.
VHS: S17661. $19.98.
George Roy Hill, USA, 1962, 112 mins.

Personal Property
A stylish remake of The Man in Possession, about mistaken identities and poor assumptions, stars Jean Harlow as an impoverished American widow who falls for a poor though immaculate Englishman. Both are in for the ride of their lives. With Robert Taylor, Una O'Connor and Reginald Owen.
VHS: S17784. $19.98.
W.S. Van Dyke II, USA, 1937, 85 mins.

Petrified Forest
Bette Davis is teamed with Humphrey Bogart in this melodrama based on the play by Robert Sherwood, set in the Arizona desert. Bogart, in his first important screen role, holds a writer (Leslie Howard) and a waitress (Davis) hostage in a diner. Tense drama, with great ensemble acting.
VHS: S11624. $19.98.
Archie Mayo, USA, 1936, 83 mins.

Peyton Place
This long-awaited classic was nominated for nine Academy Awards in 1957 (including Best Picture) and has an all star cast that includes Lana Turner, Hope Lange, Arthur Kennedy, Lloyd Nolan and Lorne Greene. It is the soap opera story of life behind closed doors in a small New England town. The photography of the small town and its setting, and a touchingly sympathetic musical score by Franz Waxman, make this romantic melodrama a gem.
VHS: S13725. $39.98.
Mark Robson, USA, 1957, 157 mins.

Phantom Broadcast
A handsome crooner sings a sweet love song on a radio broadcast, in front of a live audience. He's a popular entertainer with a large, loyal following—particularly among the ladies. However, Grant Murdock is not what he seems. He's just a "splendid dummy": the stand-in for Norman Wilder, a hunchback who's fiercely dedicated to music, and who is actually the one with the velvet voice. The plot of this ironic, strikingly plotted drama starts rolling when an attractive, ambitious, but poor young woman, Laura Hamilton, enlists Murdock's advice regarding her fledgling singing career. It is Wilder who encourages her talent, and he becomes upset when he senses the egotistical, womanizing Murdock is about to seduce her. Featuring a soulful, memorable performance by Ralph Forbes and a ravishing Gail Patrick in one of her earliest screen roles.
VHS: S13604. $29.95.
Phil Rosen, USA, 1933, 63 mins.

Phantom of Chinatown
Keye Luke, Lotus Long and Grant Withers are featured in this clever mystery. An archeologist is just about to lecture on his newest discovery. Before he can begin, however, he chokes and dies. Ancient curses and more mundane criminal elements are bound up in this seemingly unsolvable crime.
VHS: S24015. $14.95.
Phil Rosen, USA, 1941, 61 mins.

Phone Call from a Stranger
A plane crash and phone call bring Bette Davis and Gary Merrill together for a moving encounter that spells both tragedy and hope.
VHS: S05915. $19.98.
Jean Negulesco, USA, 1952, 96 mins.

Picture of Dorian Gray
A fabulously eerie film based on Oscar Wilde's famous tale of evil and madness in Victorian London. A vain and wealthy 19th-century Londoner, who values his looks above all else, admires his newly painted portrait so much that he wishes that he will never grow old. His wish is granted and he looks great, but don't check out the picture of him hidden in the attic. With George Sanders and Donna Reed. The picture was painted by famed artist Ivan Albright.
VHS: S01028. $19.98.
Laser: LD70656. $34.98.
Albert Lewin, USA, 1945, 110 mins.

Pinky
Jeanne Crain stars in this powerful drama about a young woman who passes for white in Boston until she goes home to experience life as a black woman in the deep South. It's a compelling indictment of racism and bigotry. Co-starring Ethel Waters and Ethel Barrymore.
VHS: S21300. $19.98.
Elia Kazan, USA, 1949, 102 mins.

Pitfall
An intriguing film noir which stars Dick Powell as a bored husband whose philandering ways bring tragedy to himself and his family. Suspenseful and well acted. With Jane Wyatt, Lizabeth Scott and Raymond Burr.
VHS: S14321. $19.98.
Laser: CLV. LD72016. $29.98.
Andre de Toth, USA, 1948, 85 mins.

Pittsburgh
The beautiful Marlene Dietrich is courted by rivals John Wayne and Randolph Scott in this love triangle of class differences set in the coal and steel business world. With Frank Craven, Louise Allbritton and Shemp Howard.
VHS: S19075. $14.98.
Lewis Seiler, USA, 1942, 91 mins.

Plunder Road
Five guys knock off a train shipment of gold and try to elude capture by the law enforcement agencies in California. They divide the loot and go their separate ways. Some of the gold is actually melted down into car bumpers. A low budget thriller with Gene Raymond, Wayne Morris, Elisha Cook Jr., Staffor Repp, Steven Ritch and Jeanne Cooper.
VHS: S07135. $19.95.
Hubert Cornfield, USA, 1957, 76 mins.

Point Blank
A superior crime thriller starring Lee Marvin as a double-crossed professional criminal out to settle the score with everyone who sold him out and left him for dead. Based on the novel by Donald Westlake writing as Richard Stark. Cast includes Angie Dickinson, Carroll O'Connor, Keenan Wynn, John Vernon and Lloyd Bochner. Wait for the shootout at Alcatraz.
VHS: S08064. $19.98.
Laser: Letterboxed. LD74679. $34.98.
John Boorman, USA, 1967, 89 mins.

Pork Chop Hill
Gregory Peck is in charge of holding an elevated piece of Korean real estate against the onslaught of North Korean and Chinese Communist troops. A stirring tribute to the American fighting man from the director of All Quiet on the Western Front. The fine cast includes Rip Torn, Harry Guardino, Robert Blake, Woody Strode and George Peppard.
VHS: S06066. $19.95.
Lewis Milestone, USA, 1959, 97 mins.

Port of New York
A G-man goes undercover to infiltrate drug smugglers and mobsters in New York. Yul Brynner's screen debut.
VHS: S05866. $29.95.
Laslo Benedek, USA, 1949, 86 mins.

Portrait of Jennie
The haunting story of a love so strong that even time itself could barely contain it. Joseph Cotten is a struggling artist in New York whose life is transformed after meeting a beautiful and mysterious girl (Jennifer Jones). Winner of two Oscars.
VHS: S12169. $19.98.
William Dieterle, USA, 1948, 86 mins.

Possessed (1931)
Joan Crawford plays a back street girl who rejects her small town job as box factory worker to become the mistress of big city lawyer Clark Gable. When he runs for governor, she becomes a topic of scandal. Based on the novel by Edgar Selwyn, The Mirage. Good soaper not to be confused with later Crawford picture of the same title.
VHS: S08097. $24.95.
Clarence Brown, USA, 1931, 76 mins.

Possessed (1947)
Joan Crawford gives a stunning performance as a woman driven mad by obsessive love; many critics at the time believed that her portrayal in this film topped her performance in Mildred Pierce. The outstanding supporting cast includes Van Heflin, Raymond Massey and Geraldine Brooks.
VHS: S15119. $19.98.
Laser: LD70141. $34.98.
Clarence Brown, USA, 1947, 108 mins.

The Postman Always Rings Twice
Lana Turner and John Garfield are the illicit lovers in this James M. Cain thriller, who plot to murder the husband who is standing in the way of a real good time. A classic film noir available in the original black and white. Cast includes Cecil Kellaway, Leon Ames and Hume Cronyn. Remade in 1981.
VHS: S09152. $19.98.
Tay Garnett, USA, 1946, 113 mins.

Pressure Point
Stanley Kramer's prison drama about a psychiatrist (Sidney Poitier) who tries to get inside the head of his most diabolical patient, an inveterate Nazi fascist (Bobby Darin). Intelligent, provocative and fascinating, taken from an actual case file reported in Dr. Robert Lindner's The Fifty-Minute Hour. With Peter Falk, Barry Gordon and Howard Caine.
VHS: S17990. $19.98.
Stanley Kramer, USA, 1962, 88 mins.

Pride and Prejudice
Outstanding adaptation of the Jane Austen novel with a fine cast including Greer Garson, Laurence Olivier and Maureen O'Sullivan.
VHS: S01880. $24.95.
Laser: LD72150. $34.98.
Robert Z. Leonard, USA, 1940, 118 mins.

The Pride and the Passion
A rousing adaptation of C.S. Forester's novel about the Spanish War of Independence (1810). The plot unfolds in the aftermath of Napoleon's invasion of Spain. Cary Grant, Frank Sinatra and Sophia Loren star as counterguerillas trying to transport a huge canon across the country in order to launch a surprise attack.
VHS: S17989. $19.98.
Stanley Kramer, USA, 1957, 132 mins.

Pride of St. Louis
The life of baseball star Dizzy Dean, who injured himself and then became a sports commentator. With Dan Dailey, Joanne Dru, Richard Haydn, Richard Crenna.
VHS: S11620. $19.98.
Harmon Jones, USA, 1952, 93 mins.

Pride of the Bowery
The East Side Kids swagger off to a Civilian Conservation Corps camp where they predictably get into all sorts of trouble. With Leo Gorcey and, of course, the East Side Kids.
VHS: S13859. $19.95.
Joseph H. Lewis, USA, 1941, 60 mins.

Primrose Path
Ginger Rogers plays the girl from the wrong side of the tracks who falls in love with the ambitious Joel McCrea. With a wonderful performance from Marjorie Rambeau as Rogers' prostitute mother.
VHS: S09360. $19.98.
Gregory La Cava, USA, 1940, 120 mins.

Prince Valiant
Prince Valiant steps out of the Sunday comics and onto the screen, in this swashbuckling tale of royalty and rogues set in the time of King Arthur. Starring James Mason, Janet Leigh and Robert Wagner. Photographed by Lucien Ballard.
VHS: S14222. $14.98.
Henry Hathaway, USA, 1954, 100 mins.

Prisoner of Japan
Alan Baxter and Gertrude Michael star in this thought-provoking melodrama based on a story by Edgar G. Ulmer. David Bowman (Baxter) is a philosophical young astronomer who can't bring himself to thwart a Japanese offensive against American ships. This is a film that speaks to the isolationist sentiment prevalent before the bombing of Pearl Harbor.
VHS: S23989. $24.95.
Arthur Ripley, USA, 1942, 65 mins.

Prisoner of Zenda (1937)
The classic costume drama and among Hollywood's best swashbucklers. Ronald Colman is a commoner who is forced to substitute for his look-alike cousin and falls in love with Madeleine Carroll while Douglas Fairbanks, Jr. is Rupert of Hentzau.
VHS: S11444. $29.95.
John Cromwell, USA, 1937, 101 mins.

Prisoner of Zenda (1952)
The tale of the king's double, who is called on to impersonate the king in order to save the crown, features Stewart Granger in a dual role, with Deborah Kerr and James Mason.
VHS: S02561. $29.95.
Richard Thorpe, USA, 1952, 100 mins.

The Private Affairs of Bel Ami
A ruthless schemer (George Sanders) gets ahead by charming prominent women. Angela Lansbury (Manchurian Candidate; Murder, She Wrote) co-stars in this 1947 adaptation of Guy de Maupassant's famous story. "All women take to men who have the appearance of wickedness!"
VHS: S14319. $19.98.
Albert Lewin, USA, 1947, 112 mins.

Private Hell #36
Ida Lupino wrote, starred in and co-produced this taut dramatic tale of two cops who locate stolen money and keep some for themselves. The boys in blue must now face a heavy case of the guilts. With Howard Duff, Steve Cochran and Dean Jagger. B&W.
VHS: S04716. $19.98.
Laser: LD71813. $34.98.
Don Siegel, USA, 1954, 81 mins.

Private Life of Don Juan
Douglas Fairbanks stars in his final film, pursuing a string of beautiful women, including Merle Oberon.
VHS: S08888. $19.98.
Alexander Korda, USA, 1934, 80 mins.

Proud Rebel
A post-Civil War sentimental drama about a Confederate veteran searching for a doctor who can cure his mute son, with father and son playing father and son. The principles are great, the chemistry excellent and Alan Ladd's last film. Also featuring David Ladd and Olivia de Havilland.
VHS: S12567. $19.98.
Laser: LD75243. $34.98.
Michael Curtiz, USA, 1958, 103 mins.

Public Enemy
James Cagney explodes on the screen in one of his most famous roles as a notorious criminal. This is the film with the infamous "grapefruit scene"! With Jean Harlow and Joan Blondell, from the director of the initial version of A Star Is Born and The Ox-Bow Incident.
VHS: S01771. $19.95.
Laser: LD71179. $39.98.
William Wellman, USA, 1931, 83 mins.

The Purchase Price
Barbara Stanwyck is a torch singer who escapes from her racketeering boyfriend, played by Eddie Fields. She enters into a loveless, arranged marriage with a farmer played by Jim Gilson. Though it's quite a switch from her big city life, Stanwyck manages to wrest romance from even these extremely dire circumstances.
VHS: S20832. $19.98.
William Wellman, USA, 1932, 68 mins.

Queen Bee
Joan Crawford is at her evil best in this gothic southern melodrama. Crawford is married to a wealthy mill owner which gives her nearly unlimited power to manipulate and destroy the lives of those around her. The results are achingly tragic. Barry Sullivan and Betsy Palmer also star.
VHS: S26448. $19.95.
Ronald MacDougall, USA, 1955, 95 mins.

Queen Christina
Greta Garbo had one of her finest roles as the 17th century Swedish monarch who gave up her crown for the man she loved. John Gilbert, Garbo's real-life ex-lover and her frequent co-star in silent pictures, made a brief comeback as the dashing Don Antonio. With Ian Keith, C. Aubrey Smith and Lewis Stone. A classic that boasts more than a memorable last shot.
VHS: S11732. $19.98.
Laser: LD70661. $29.98.
Rouben Mamoulian, USA, 1933, 97 mins.

Quicksand
Mickey Rooney finds himself sinking into a mire of violence and criminal activity when he unofficially borrows twenty bucks from the till at the garage where he works. Peter Lorre is around to blackmail the kid into further trouble, all because he wanted to impress a date. B&W.
VHS: S04040. $19.95.
Irving Pichel, USA, 1950, 79 mins.

Racers
Kirk Douglas is in the driver's seat in this high speed drama about a cocky American trying to be number one in the European racing circuit. His attitude and skill may win him races but not very many friends. With Lee J. Cobb, Cesar Romero, Bella Darvi, Gilbert Roland, Katy Jurado. Filmed on location. Vroom. Vroom.
VHS: S13298. $39.95.
Henry Hathaway, USA, 1955, 112 mins.

Racing Luck
William Boyd stars in this film about a dashing young jockey (Boyd) who's framed into working for a rival horse stable. With Barbara Worth, George Ernest, Esther Muir and Dick Curtis.
VHS: S17490. $14.95.
Sam Newfield, USA, 1935, 56 mins.

The Racketeer
Carole Lombard and Robert Armstrong star in this romantic drama in which the heroine agrees to marry a racketeer in order for her true love to further his career as a violinist. Talk about your sacrifices for the sake of happiness. With Hedda Hopper and John Loder.
VHS: S04490. $29.95.
Howard Higgin, USA, 1929, 66 mins.

Rage of Paris
Danielle Darrieux, star of *Mayerling* and *Club des Femmes*, was brought to Hollywood to star opposite Douglas Fairbanks, Jr. in this funny tale of a young French woman adrift in Manhattan.
VHS: S03788. $29.95.
Henry Koster, USA, 1938, 78 mins.

Rain
W. Somerset Maugham's story of Sadie Thompson, who became a classic of stage, screen and literature, with a brilliant performance from Joan Crawford as the cynical prostitute, and Walter Huston as the minister who tries to reform her.
VHS: S01086. $19.95.
Lewis Milestone, USA, 1932, 91 mins.

Rainmaker
Burt Lancaster and Katharine Hepburn star in this entertaining version of the play by N. Richard Nash. Lancaster is a slick talking con-man and Hepburn is the dubious spinster who doubts whether this Starbuck fellow can produce rain for the crops or sunshine for the heart of a tough single lady. With Earl Holliman, Lloyd Bridges and Wendell Corey.
VHS: S07519. $19.95.
Joseph Anthony, USA, 1956, 121 mins.

The Rains Came
Tyrone Power stars as a powerful man in India who falls for the alluring Myrna Loy in this costume melodrama based on the Louis Bromfield novel. It charts the sweeping events that overpower their attraction for one another, and won an Academy Award for special effects recreating an earthquake.
VHS: S21070. $19.98.
Clarence Brown, USA, 1939, 104 mins.

Raintree County
Elizabeth Taylor is the southern belle who gets the man she thinks she wants but then finds life as a schoolmaster's wife boring. A lush MGM production which features Montgomery Clift, Eva Marie Saint, Nigel Patrick, Rod Taylor, Agnes Moorhead, Walter Abel.
VHS: S01087. $29.98.
Laser: LD70187. $39.98.
Edward Dmytryk, USA, 1958, 166 mins.

Random Harvest
Ronald Colman and Greer Garson star in this lavish MGM production of a James Hilton novel about an amnesiac soldier who leaves a mental hospital and is rescued by a music hall entertainer, whom he marries. A car accident restores his memory a few years later and he returns to the aristocratic life he once knew. The second wife (Garson) must bide her time and hope for a happy ending. With Philip Dorn and Susan Peters. B&W.
VHS: S09153. $19.98.
Laser: LD71171. $39.98.
Mervyn LeRoy, USA, 1942, 124 mins.

Rasputin and the Empress
Three members of the Barrymore family—John, Ethel and Lionel—enact the final days of the Czar's reign, when Rasputin (Lionel) cured the Czar's son of hemophilia and exerted tremendous influence over the family. Some impressive sets, decor and costumes. Prince Youssoupoff filed a suit against MGM claiming historical inaccuracies. With Diana Wynyard and Ralph Morgan.
VHS: S18507. $19.98.
Richard Boleslawski, USA, 1933, 133 mins.

The Razor's Edge
W. Somerset Maugham's powerful novel about a flyer who returns from WWI seeking spiritual peace is given a great rendition with Tyrone Power as the flyer, Gene Tierney as his fiancee, and Anne Baxter.
VHS: S03557. $19.98.
Laser: LD72217. $49.98.
Edmund Goulding, USA, 1946, 146 mins.

Real Glory
The Moro Rebellion in the Philippines just after the Spanish-American War is the subject of this action adventure starring Gary Cooper as Doctor Bill Canavon. With the help of soldiers-of-fortune David Niven and Broderick Crawford, Cooper tries to make peace, combat a cholera epidemic, blow up a dam, defend a besieged fort and fall in love with nurse Andrea Leeds. With Reginald Owen, Kay Johnson, Tetsu Komai and Rudy Robles. Watch for Elmo Lincoln, the first screen Tarzan, as a U.S. captain.
VHS: S16446. $19.98.
Henry Hathaway, USA, 1939, 96 mins.

Reckless
Musical star Mona Leslie (Jean Harlow) goes on a bender with a confused aristocrat—and they wake up married. When he commits suicide, Mona is publicly blamed for his death and must fight her way back to Broadway. Also starring William Powell. The story of this film was written by David O. Selznick under the pseudonym of Oliver Jeffries.
VHS: S15120. $19.98.
Victor Fleming, USA, 1935, 97 mins.

The Reckless Way
This story explores the ups and downs of a young lady trying to break into the movies. This early sound film stars Marion Nixon, Kane Richmond and Inez Courtney.
VHS: S15232. $19.95.
Raymond K. Johnson, USA, 1936, 72 mins.

Red Ball Express
Jeff Chandler, Alex Nicol and Sidney Poitier are soldiers running an emergency supply convoy to a group of Patton's tanks that are surrounded by the Nazis. Based on a true story, this film shows the unsung heroism that helped them overcome enemy bombardment and divisiveness in the ranks, caused, in part, by racism.
VHS: S27667. $14.98.
Budd Boetticher, USA, 1952, 84 mins.

Red Dust
Clark Gable runs a rubber plantation in Indochina and finds he is attracted to both of his female visitors. Will he stick with the brazen bad girl Jean Harlow or steal the refined Mary Astor from her ailing husband? Remade by Gable (with Ava Gardner) as *Mogambo* in 1953. Based on the play by William Collison. With Gene Raymond and Donald Crisp.
VHS: S08098. $19.98.
Victor Fleming, USA, 1932, 83 mins.

The Red Menace
Attempting to show the dangers of Communism, this 1949 film, deliberately made with unknown actors, caused quite a stir at the time of its release with its over-the-top McCarthyesque propaganda. Now it all just seems ridiculously funny, and more than a little sad.
VHS: S14320. $19.98.
Laser: CLV. LD72021. $29.98.
R.G. Springsteen, USA, 1949, 87 mins.

Red Pony
John Steinbeck's classic story is brought to life in this tasteful version. A boy escapes his unpleasant family life through his love of a horse. With Robert Mitchum and Myrna Loy. Music by Aaron Copeland.
VHS: S01100. $19.98.
Laser: CLV. LD72022. $39.98.
Lewis Milestone, USA, 1949, 89 mins.

Remedy for Riches
The fourth film in the Dr. Paul Christian series takes a lighter approach as the good doctor investigates a phony geologist and a troublesome chicken. Jean Hersholt also tries to get the town druggist and his nurse back together. Big doin's in River's End, Minnesota. With Warren Hull, Jed Pouty and Walter Catlett.
VHS: S05702. $19.98.
Erle C. Kenton, USA, 1940, 66 mins.

Renegade/Scarlet River
A Texas Ranger defends a beauty accused of murder; a movie cowboy tests his mettle against a real villain.
VHS: S10669. $19.98.
David Howard, USA, 1933/1938, 114 mins.

Requiem for a Heavyweight
Not a remake of the classic starring Anthony Quinn and Jackie Gleason, but the original television playhouse presentation starring Jack Palance as the down and out boxer, Keenan Wynn as the manager and Kim Hunter as the woman who sees beneath the boxer's exterior. Created by Rod Serling.
VHS: S02985. $19.95.
Ralph Nelson, USA, 1956, 89 mins.

Retreat, Hell!
Frank Lovejoy stars in this Korean war drama. General O.P. Smith defies direct orders to retreat from enemy lines, and engages his troops in a bloody battle against the Communist troops in North Korea. With Richard Carlson, Russ Tamblyn, Anita Louise.
VHS: S09632. $19.95.
Joseph H. Lewis, USA, 1952, 95 mins.

The Return of Peter Grimm
The father of a close-knit family returns from the dead to make amends for all the things he did wrong in his lifetime. With good performances from Lionel Barrymore and a talented cast.
VHS: S14162. $19.98.
George Nicholls, USA, 1935, 82 mins.

Return to Paradise
A South Seas story about a wandering nonconformist (Gary Cooper) as he searches for excitement and meaning. When he turns up on an idyllic coastal island, he falls for a beautiful local (Roberta Haynes) and unwittingly gets entangled in a local rebellion. With Barry Jones and Moira MacDonald.
VHS: S19497. $19.98.
Mark Robson, USA, 1953, 100 mins.

Return to Peyton Place
This sizzling sequel picks up where the original all-star hit left off. It examines the impact the novel supposedly made on the small New England town it chose to uncover and in particular the reaction of several inhabitants who feel they have been maligned. The star-studded cast includes: Carol Lynley, Jeff Chandler, Eleanor Parker, Mary Astor, Robert Sterling, and Tuesday Weld. More closets are unlocked; more skeletons fall out—a must for fans of the original.
VHS: S13726. $19.98.
Jose Ferrer, USA, 1961, 122 mins.

Reunion in France
John Wayne is a wounded RAF pilot who seeks the help of Joan Crawford, a French aristocrat who's fallen on hard times. Her mansion has been turned into a coal allotment bureau by the Nazis and she is forced to find employment as a shop girl. She also believes her ex-boyfriend Philip Dorn is working for the enemy. Can she and the Yank flyer escape to England?
VHS: S12137. $19.95.
Jules Dassin, USA, 1942, 104 mins.

Rhapsody
A passionate three-way love triangle between a strong willed woman (Elizabeth Taylor) used to getting what she wants, a violinist (Vittorio Gassman) more interested in his career and a more appreciative and open pianist (John Ericson) who is drawn to her. With Louis Calhern and Michael Chekhov.
VHS: S18525. $19.98.
Charles Vidor, USA, 1954, 115 mins.

Riff Raff
Another Jean Harlow vehicle on the war between the sexes, pitting the tough, no-nonsense Harlow as a cannery worker who falls for an alcoholic fisherman played by Spencer Tracy, a disillusioned drifter trying to find stability. With Joseph Calleia and Mickey Rooney.
VHS: S17780. $19.98.
J. Walter Ruben, USA, 1936, 94 mins.

Riff-Raff
Pat O'Brien and Walter Slezak star in this drama about a thick-skinned adventurer in Panama who is handed a map to valuable oil deposits by a dying man and everyone's out after the map.
VHS: S12021. $19.98.
Ted Tetzlaff, USA, 1947, 80 mins.

Riot in Cell Block 11
Powerful prison drama filmed realistically. Some of those involved in disturbing the peace of this correctional facility include Neville Brand, Emile Meyer, Frank Faylen, Leo Gordon, and Robert Osterloh. Be advised, the media will be manipulated by hardened criminals.
VHS: S04222. $19.95.
Don Siegel, USA, 1954, 80 mins.

Riptide
A Manhattan chorus girl with a lively past enters into loveless marriage with a dour British diplomat. Matters are complicated when the woman's former lover re-emerges and demands her back. With Norma Shearer, Robert Montgomery, Herbert Marshall, Skeets Gallagher, Ralph Forbes and Lilyan Tashman.
VHS: S20414. $29.98.
Edmund Goulding, USA, 1934, 90 mins.

The Rise and Fall of Legs Diamond
The fast and impressive saga of the Roaring '20s crime lord called "Legs" because of his ability to escape law enforcers. Directed by one of the most fascinating unrecognized talents in the American cinema, Budd Boetticher—and featuring the outstanding photography of Lucien Ballard. "A minor classic" (Andrew Sarris).
VHS: S14084. $59.99.
Budd Boetticher, USA, 1960, 101 mins.

Road House
A psychotic owner of a roadhouse becomes insanely jealous when his singer falls in love with his manager, so he decides to frame him for embezzlement. A 40's film noir with all the characters typically cynical or homicidal. Starring Richard Widmark and the luminous Ida Lupino.
VHS: S13615. $19.98.
Jean Negulesco, USA, 1948, 95 mins.

Roaring Twenties
James Cagney stars as a good man turned crook in this recreation of the world of bootleggers, speakeasies and violence; Humphrey Bogart is the gangster who won't let anything stand in his way.
VHS: S05356. $19.95.
Laser: LD70188. $34.98.
Raoul Walsh, USA, 1939, 106 mins.

Romance
Greta Garbo stars as diva Madame Cavallini, a worldly woman who tries to transcend her colorful past in the arms of a devout young clergyman. Co-starring the young Gavin Gordon.
VHS: S15121. $19.98.
Clarence Brown, USA, 1930, 76 mins.

Rome Adventure
When in Rome, Troy Donahue gets romantic—and falls in love with *both* Angie Dickinson and Suzanne Pleshette. This splendidly scenic drama features breathtaking glimpses of Rome, Verona, Pisa and the Italian Alps, plus a luxuriant score by Max Steiner.
VHS: S13802. $19.98.
Laser: LD70735. $39.98.
Delmer Daves, USA, 1962, 119 mins.

Run for Your Money
A political drama focusing on two Welsh miners who go off on a madcap and lavish spending spree in London. With Donald Houston, Meredith Edwards, Moira Lister and Alec Guinness.
VHS: S18944. $19.95.
Charles Frend, USA, 1949, 83 mins.

Run Silent Run Deep
Clark Gable and Burt Lancaster star in one of the better World War II submarine dramas. The crew of the Nerka isn't pleased when their new captain seems obsessed with sinking the Japanese destroyer that lost Gable his last posting in the silent service. With Jack Warden, Brad Dexter, Nick Cravat, Don Rickles as Ruby. Beware of the Bongo straits.
VHS: S13310. $19.98.
Robert Wise, USA, 1958, 93 mins.

Saint Joan
Graham Greene wrote the screenplay based on George Bernard Shaw's drama, and Jean Seberg made her screen debut as Joan of Arc. With a superb performance by John Gielgud as the Earl of Warwick.
VHS: S01995. $19.98.
Otto Preminger, USA, 1957, 110 mins.

Saint's Vacation/Narrow Margin
The Saint seeks a music box containing a secret code. A detective must protect a gangster's wife. USA, 1941/1952, 133 mins.
VHS: S10682. $19.98.

Salome
Rita Hayworth does the dance of the seven veils in order to keep the head of John the Baptist where it belongs. This novel interpretation of the court of King Herod also stars Charles Laughton, Judith Anderson, Stewart Granger, and Alan Badel as the unfortunate prophet. Historically dubious, but it is in Technicolor.
VHS: S04676. $19.95.
William Dieterle, USA, 1953, 105 mins.

Salt of the Earth
Blacklisted during the McCarthy Era, *Salt of the Earth* portrays the true events of Chicano zinc workers on strike in New Mexico. When the mine owners seek a court injunction to forbid picketing, the wives of the strikers take up the battle. A classic.
VHS: S01151. $29.95.
Laser: LD70320. $39.95.
Herbert J. Biberman, USA, 1954, 94 mins.

San Francisco
Clark Gable plays the owner of the saloon, Spencer Tracy is the priest, and Jeanette MacDonald the belle of San Francisco in this lavish production set against the climax of the San Francisco earthquake.
VHS: S04404. $19.98.
W.S. Van Dyke, USA, 1936, 115 mins.

Sand Pebbles
Steve McQueen is superb as a sailor on an American gunboat patrolling the Yangtze river in 1926 China. Explosive entertainment with Vietnam parallels for those who care to pick up on them. Two video cassettes.
VHS: S14139. $29.98.
Robert Wise, USA, 1966, 193 mins.

The Sands of Iwo Jima
One of John Wayne's best films. He plays Sgt. John M. Stryker, who trains his men hard so that they can fight even harder. When these Marines hit the beach, it retreats. With John Agar, Forest Tucker, Richard Jaeckel and Martin Milner. Tarawa and Iwo Jima co-star. Digitally mastered. Contains trailer and *The Making of The Sands of Iwo Jima*. Introduction by Leonard Maltin.
VHS: S04238. $19.95.
Allan Dwan, USA, 1949, 109 mins.

Santa Fe Trail
Young calvary officers Jeb Stuart (Errol Flynn) and George Armstrong (Ronald Reagan) duel militant abolitionist John Brown (Raymond Massey) and fight over the affections of Olivia de Havilland. The film was roundly condemned for its historical misunderstandings. With Alan Hale, Guinn Williams and William Lundigan.
VHS: S01159. $19.98.
Michael Curtiz, USA, 1940, 109 mins.

Saratoga Trunk
Ingrid Bergman is a Creole of unmatched beauty whose Parisian ways beguile all of New Orleans, especially a young Texan oil man played by Gary Cooper. Bergman is the perfect coquette in this beautiful costume drama about the joys and drawbacks of digging for gold. Based on Edna Ferber's novel, for the most part this film is a wonderfully realized work, but it also features Flora Robson as a maid in blackface.
VHS: S27748. $19.98.
Sam Wood, USA, 1945, 135 mins.

Satan Met a Lady
A fascinating rewrite of *The Maltese Falcon* with Bette Davis, Warren William and Alison Skipworth among the band of crooks and a private detective out to find a rare artifact.
VHS: S13396. $19.98.
William Dieterle, USA, 1936, 74 mins.

The Savage Eye
A cinema-verite documentary-style feature about a dissatisfied Los Angeles woman (Barbara Baxley) who undertakes an excursion into the city's eccentric haunts and nightspots. The film presents Los Angeles as a junk heap of faith healers, con men and social climbers. With Gary Merrill and Herschel Bernardi.
VHS: S19871. $29.95.
B. Maddow/J. Strick/S. Meyers, USA, 1959, 68 mins.

Sayonara
Marlon Brando stars as a pilot in postwar Japan who falls in love with a Japanese entertainer in spite of directives to the contrary issued by Occupation Command. Fine supporting performances by Red Buttons, James Garner and Miyoshi Umeki, based on a novel by James Michener.
VHS: S03508. $19.98.
Joshua Logan, USA, 1957, 147 mins.

The Scar (Hollow Triumph)
Fugitive Paul Henreid kills a psychiatrist whom he physically resembles, and then, while impersonating him, finds out the good doctor has committed some crimes of his own. Also starring Joan Bennett and Eduard Franz.
VHS: S14323. $19.98.
Steve Sekely, USA, 1948, 83 mins.

Scaramouche
A Technicolor swashbuckler starring Stewart Granger, Mel Ferrer and Janet Leigh, and set in the French Revolution. Featuring "one of the finest sword battles in movie history" (*The Motion Picture Guide*).
VHS: S14555. $19.98.
Laser: CAV. LD70448. $89.95.
Laser: CLV. LD70449. $39.95.
George Sidney, USA, 1952, 111 mins.

Scarlet Dawn
Douglas Fairbanks Jr. stars as a Russian aristocrat who falls on hard times because of the Communist revolution. With the help of his former servant, Nancy Carroll, he begins a new life in exile, but treachery and politics intervene, leaving these two characters with nothing more certain than their love for each other.
VHS: S20833. $19.98.
William Dieterle, USA, 1932, 76 mins.

The Scarlet Letter
A story of adultery, Puritan attitudes and an unusual love triangle based upon the classic novel by Nathaniel Hawthorne.
VHS: S01164. $19.95.
Robert Vignola, USA, 1934, 69 mins.

The Scarlet Pimpernel
Leslie Howard is the dashing hero who masquerades as a foppish dandy in this entertaining adventure yarn set during the French Revolution. Raymond Massey and Merle Oberon co-star. A lavish production, and an entertaining script by S.N. Behrman and Robert Sherwood.
VHS: S01165. $19.98.
Harold Young, USA, 1934, 98 mins.

Sea Chase
Half of the navies of the world hunt for freighter captain John Wayne and passenger Lana Turner as the German freighter tries to make it back to Germany from Sydney harbor in 1939.
VHS: S12498. $19.98.
Laser: LD70671. $24.98.
John Farrow, USA, 1955, 117 mins.

Sea Fury

Victor McLaglen and Stanley Baker star as competing tugboat captains in this convincing seafaring yarn. Romance, adventure and treasure combine to heighten their rivalry. It makes a potent driving force at the center of an engaging melodrama.
VHS: S23955. $19.95.
Cy Endfield, USA, 1958, 97 mins.

Sea Hawk

Errol Flynn at his finest. He plays an English privateer making life miserable for Spanish galleons in the 16th century, under the authority of Queen Elizabeth I. In the course of his swashbuckling adventures he invades Panama, is captured, enslaved and then escapes to warn England of a secret Spanish Armada. He also finds time to fall in love with the beautiful niece of the Spanish ambassador. With Claude Rains, Brenda Marshall, Flora Robson, Donald Crisp and Alan Hale. Great swordplay and a memorable musical score by Erich Wolfgang Korngold.
VHS: S01863. $19.95.
Michael Curtiz, USA, 1940, 127 mins.

The Sea Wolf

An adaptation of Jack London's work about a fugitive couple (Ida Lupino and John Garfield) on a ship caught in the vice grip between a hardened though gifted sea captain (Edward G. Robinson) and a writer (Alexander Knox) trying to assert intellectual dominance and superiority.
VHS: S18508. $19.98.
Michael Curtiz, USA, 1941, 90 mins.

The Search for Bridey Murphy

A woman under hypnosis remembers a prior life…and death. Based on real-life events that had all of America talking, this mystery stars Teresa Wright and Louis Hayward.
VHS: S14458. $19.95.
Noel Langley, USA, 1956, 84 mins.

The Second Face

A strange film about the inner transformation of Ella Raines, a beautiful young woman who undergoes plastic surgery to repair her scarred face. With Bruce Bennett, Rita Johnson and Jane Darwell.
VHS: S18935. $19.95.
Jack Bernhard, USA, 1950, 77 mins.

Second Woman

A whole community suspects an architect to be responsible for the death of his fiancee. Robert Young stars in this stylish film noir as the young man who must face not only the wrath of his community, but that of his late fiancee's father as well. With his new love (Betsy Drake) he must prove his innocence.
VHS: S07482. $24.95.
James V. Kern, USA, 1951, 90 mins.

The Secret of Santa Vittoria

Anthony Quinn and Anna Magnani star in this hectic comedy about the love of wine. A tiny Italian village does its best to hide its prized possession, a million bottles of wine, from the Nazis. This film has all the elements of a fast-paced farce with plenty of opportunity for a little alcoholic inspiration. Quinn is the central agent of this comic turn, beginning as little more than a helpless alcoholic and ending as hero.
VHS: S27577. $19.98.
Stanley Kramer, USA, 1969, 139 mins.

Separate Tables

A set of one-act dramas exploring love, rejection and reunion. First, "Table by the Window" follows a pair of lovers caught in a whirlwind of lust. Second, "Table Number Seven" shows a woman's love tested when the object of her distant adoration is accused of a terrible crime. With Julie Christie, Alan Bates, Claire Bloom.
VHS: S03769. $59.95.
Delbert Mann, USA, 1958, 98 mins.

September Affair

Talk about your lucky breaks. When a married man and an unmarried female pianist discover they have been listed as dead in a plane crash, they decide to continue their romantic adventure in Florence, Italy. Joseph Cotten and Joan Fontaine are the forbidden lovers who enjoy classical music and each other. With Jessica Tandy and Francoise Rosay.
VHS: S08272. $24.95.
Laser: LD75255. $34.98.
William Dieterle, USA, 1959, 105 mins.

The Set Up

One of the best movies ever made about the seedy world of professional boxing. Robert Ryan stars as Bill "Stoker" Thompson, a proud but aging palooka who really believes he is just one punch away from a big purse. Filmed in real time, this hard-hitting drama still packs a major wallop. The top notch cast includes Audrey Totter, George Tobias, Wallace Ford and Percy Helton. Screenplay based on a narrative poem by Joseph Moncure March.
VHS: S15774. $19.98.
Robert Wise, USA, 1949, 72 mins.

Seven Faces of Dr. Lao

Tony Randall plays six roles in this western fantasy about a traveling circus that has the power to alter lives. Randall plays the ancient Dr. Lao as well as Pan, Medusa, Merlin, Apolonius and the Abominable Snowman. Special effects won an Oscar. With Barbara Eden and Arthur O'Connell.
VHS: S03109. $19.98.
Laser: LD72154. $34.98.
George Pal, USA, 1964, 100 mins.

Seven Miles from Alcatraz/ Flight from Glory

In this adventure double feature two escapees fight ruthless Nazi spies and dare-devil pilots are recruited to fly over the Andes.
VHS: S10664. $19.98.
Edward Dmytryk, USA, 1943, 129 mins.

Seven Sinners

A sexy singer called Bijou Blanche (Marlene Dietrich) is also nicknamed the naval "Destroyer." She quickly seduces a young navy Lieutenant played by John Wayne. A jealous suitor would keep these young lovers apart, but Bijou Blanche proves her resolve by staying true to the man she loves.
VHS: S22186. $14.98.
Tay Garnett, USA, 1940, 87 mins.

The Seventh Cross

1936. Hitler's stormtroopers comb the country side. George Heisler (Spencer Tracy) barely keeps one step ahead, running from town to town, escaping the fate that awaits him. He is finally aided by a friendly farmer (Hume Cronyn) and his gentle wife (Jessica Tandy). Fred Zinnemann's feature film directorial debut.
VHS: S15018. $19.98.
Fred Zinnemann, USA, 1944, 112 mins.

The Shadow of Silk Lennox

Lon Chaney, Jr., Dean Benton and Jack Mulhall star in this engaging story of a troubled nightclub owner. His world begins to crumble when he is fingered by an undercover G-man. USA, 1935, 60 mins.
VHS: S26879. $24.95.

The Shadow of the Eagle

John Wayne stars as a daredevil pilot out to discover the identity of the criminal genius, the Eagle, who threatens corporation execs through skywriting. This 12-chapter serial has the background of a traveling carnival and lots of thrills. With Pat O'Malley and Little Billy the midget.
VHS: S06337. $24.95.
Ford Beebe, USA, 1932, 226 mins.

Shame (Not Wanted)

Ida Lupino produced and co-wrote the script for this film about the once taboo subject of unwed mothers. Ostracism and disillusionment still greet young women who face childbirth and parenthood alone. This earlier film is a revealing example of how things have changed and yet stayed the same.
VHS: S23903. $29.95.
Elmer Clifton, USA, 1949, 94 mins.

She

Lavish sets and a score by Max Steiner are two features that should have helped propel this film to success like that garnered by producer Merian C. Cooper's earlier film, King Kong. Two explorers, Randolph Scott and Nigel Bruce, find a goddess living beneath the frozen Arctic, She Who Must Be Obeyed. This adventure film has great 1930's style. Based on H. Rider Haggard's novel.
VHS: S26457. $24.95.
Irving Pichel/Lansing C. Holden, USA, 1935, 95 mins.

Shining Hour

Director Frank Borzage directs this dramatic tale of four people caught in a web of frustrated passion and family discord. Joan Crawford stars as the night club dancer who marries one brother only to find out she may prefer his younger sibling. With Robert Young, Melvyn Douglas, Fay Bainter, Hattie McDaniel and Margaret Sullavan as the self-sacrificing Judy. Humorist Ogden Nash co-wrote the screenplay.
VHS: S16454. $19.98.
Frank Borzage, USA, 1938, 77 mins.

Ship of Fools

Based on Katherine Anne Porter's acclaimed novel, the interlocking stories tell of passengers on a ship sailing from Mexico to pre-Hitler Germany. With Simone Signoret, Michael Dunn, Vivien Leigh, Lee Marvin and others.
VHS: S07513. $19.95.
Stanley Kramer, USA, 1965, 149 mins.

Shock

Vincent Price stars in this thriller about a group of killers who have to silence a girl who witnessed one of their crimes. With Lynn Bari and Frank Latimore.
VHS: S07365. $19.95.
Alfred Werker, USA, 1946, 70 mins.

The Shopworn Angel

In this remake of the 1928 Richard Wallace film, Margaret Sullavan plays a beautiful showgirl who changes the life of an innocent young soldier (James Stewart) on his way to the war. Waldo Salt's screenplay is adapted from the play by Dana Burnet. With Walter Pidgeon, Hattie McDaniel and Sam Levene.
VHS: S20412. $29.98.
H.C. Potter, USA, 1938, 85 mins.

Show Them No Mercy

A young couple and their baby are kidnapped by thugs and eventually rescued by the FBI. A lively crime-thriller starring Cesar Romero, Rochelle Hudson and Bruce Cabot.
VHS: S13611. $19.98.
George Marshall, USA, 1935, 76 mins.

The Show-Off

Red Skelton plays the quintessential American huckster who meets and woos ingenue Marilyn Maxwell and incurs considerable hostility from her family in the process.
VHS: S19565. $19.98.
Harry Beaumont, USA, 1946, 83 mins.

Shriek in the Night

An absorbing "B" picture starring Ginger Rogers before her roles with Fred Astaire. The story involves the mystery death of a respected philanthropist who plummets from his balcony.
VHS: S01877. $29.95.
Albert Ray, USA, 1933, 92 mins.

The Silver Horde

Jean McCrea, Joel McCrea and Evelyn Brent star in this classic film about a down-on-his-luck miner. He becomes involved in the salmon business, but his spoiled fiancee provides an unexpected complication—her father is an investor in a competing and canned cannery.
VHS: S22599. $19.95.
George Archainbaud, USA, 1930, 80 mins.

The Sin of Madelon Claudet

A first-rate sobber about a mother who must give up everything so that her illegitimate son will have a good life. Helen Hayes won an Academy Award for her tragic portrayal of this woman who pays such a terrible price for the choices she is forced to make in her life.
VHS: S13568. $19.98.
Edgar Selwyn, USA, 1931, 74 mins.

Sinbad the Sailor

A lavishly produced epic telling the story of Sinbad's eighth voyage, starring Douglas Fairbanks. A rousing, old-fashioned adventure.
VHS: S03224. $19.98.
Richard Wallace, USA, 1947, 117 mins.

Since You Went Away

A sweeping panorama of life on the home-front during World War II, seen through the eyes of one family. All-star cast includes Claudette Colbert, Joseph Cotten, Jennifer Jones and Shirley Temple. Nominated for five Academy Awards.
VHS: S12167. $39.98.
John Cromwell, USA, 1944, 180 mins.

Singapore

Fred MacMurray and Ava Gardner are the perfect pair for this melodramatic mix of an exotic smuggler and a seemingly hopeless love affair. MacMurray is a jewel smuggler who hid some contraband pearls in Singapore because it is where he left the memory of his beloved fiancee (Gardner), killed in an air raid. When he returns to collect his fortune, there is a startling surprise reunion when he discovers that Gardner is in fact alive, although she is afflicted by a loss of memory and married to another man (Roland Culver). Includes the original theatrical trailer.
VHS: S27354. $14.98.
John Brahm, USA, 1947, 79 mins.

The Single Standard

It's the incomparable Greta Garbo breaking convention as a society girl with bohemian sensibilities, who has an affair with a local artist. An enjoyable melodrama with fine performances all around. See the radiant and scandalous Garbo in (gasp!) slacks for the first time on screen. Silent film with synchronized musical score.
VHS: S13979. $29.99.
John S. Robertson, USA, 1929, 93 mins.

Sirocco

Humphrey Bogart as a gun-runner in Damascus caught in a web of mystery, romance and intrigue. With Lee J. Cobb, Zero Mostel.
VHS: S02604. $59.95.
Laser: CLV. LD71739. $19.98.
Curtis Bernhardt, USA, 1951, 98 mins.

Sister Kenny

A moving biographical story about the Australian nurse who instigated polio treatment, with Rosalind Russell winning an Oscar nomination for her moving performance.
VHS: S05668. $19.98.
Dudley Nichols, USA, 1946, 116 mins.

The Sisters

Anatole Litvak's expansive tale crosscuts between three sisters, Bette Davis, Anita Louise, and Jane Bryan, and their various romantic entanglements, betrayals and difficulties. The primary story concerns Davis and her philandering husband, Errol Flynn, caught in San Francisco during the 1906 earthquake. With Ian Hunter, Donald Crisp and Beulah Bondi.
VHS: S17335. $19.98.
Anatole Litvak, USA, 1938, 99 mins.

Sixteen Fathoms Deep

Lon Chaney Jr. is billed under his real name, Creighton Chaney, in this early Monogram underwater saga. The dangers of the deep are pitted against those bold enough to discover its secrets. With Sally O'Neil and Maurice Black. Not to be confused with the 1948 remake that also featured Chaney in the cast.
VHS: S04032. $29.95.
Armand Schaefer, USA, 1933, 57 mins.

Skyscraper Souls

A gritty melodrama about passion and greed concerns a ruthless real estate developer (Warren William) who manipulates markets and personalities in order to build a 100-story office building as he tries to balance his personal life, his wife, his lover and the young woman employed by his office. With Maureen O'Sullivan, Hedda Hopper and Anita Page.
VHS: S18130. $19.98.
Edgar Selwyn, USA, 1932, 99 mins.

Slightly Honorable

This murder mystery spoof weaves a funny and suspenseful tale around a tough young lawyer who steps up to put an end to Vincent Cushing (Edward Arnold) and his powerful political machine. With Pat O'Brien and Broderick Crawford.
VHS: S13853. $19.95.
Tay Garnett, USA, 1940, 75 mins.

Smilin' Through

A lavish romantic remake about the strange pattern of events that attends three generations of people caught up in the passion and murky circumstances behind the death of a Victorian woman on the afternoon of her wedding. With Norma Shearer, Leslie Howard, Fredric March and Ralph Forbes.
VHS: S19572. $19.98.
Sidney Franklin, USA, 1932, 97 mins.

Snake Pit

Olivia de Havilland is brilliant as a woman committed to a mental hospital who is pronounced fit to leave before her consultant thinks she's ready.
VHS: S18103. $19.98.
Laser: CLV. LD72113. $49.98.
Anatole Litvak, USA, 1948, 108 mins.

Snows of Kilimanjaro

Based on Ernest Hemingway's short story, Gregory Peck stars as Harry Street, a renowned writer who reflects on his life and loves while lying wounded on the slopes of the East African mountain Kilimanjaro. With Susan Hayward, Ava Gardner, Leo G. Carroll.
VHS: S01223. $19.95.
Henry King, USA, 1952, 109 mins.

So Ends Our Night

Set against the dark reign of Nazi oppression, John Cromwell's film is an excellent adaptation of Erich Maria Remarque's novel Flotsam, about a German refugee's escape and attempted flight. With Fredric March, Glen Ford, Erich von Stroheim and Frances Dee.
VHS: S18032. $29.95.
John Cromwell, USA, 1941, 117 mins.

So Proudly We Hail

Claudette Colbert is joined by Paulette Goddard, Veronica Lake and Barbara Britton in this wartime drama about nurses in the Pacific. They suffer through the worst of the Second World War in order to help and comfort wounded soldiers, even as they combat their own demoralization and fear.
VHS: S24028. $14.98.
Mark Sandrich, USA, 1943, 126 mins.

Soldier of Fortune

When Susan Hayward's photographer husband disappears in Communist China, she turns to American smuggler Clark Gable to bring Gene Barry back alive. He agrees but demands her company as part of the payment. With Michael Rennie as a representative of the Hong Kong police department. Also Alex D'Arcy, Tom Tully, Richard Loo, Victor Sen Yung and Jack Kruschen as assorted Fragrent Harbor riffraff. A love story with a mercenary heart. Based on the novel by Ernest Gann.
VHS: S12520. $39.98.
Edward Dmytryk, USA, 1955, 96 mins.

The Solid Gold Cadillac

Judy Holliday sparkles in this romantic comedy about a seemingly innocent blond stockholder who uncovers corruption in the upper reaches of her company. Not only does she manage to save the firm, but she also catches the eye of a lonely but successful tycoon. Also features Paul Douglas and Fred Clark.
VHS: S26446. $19.95.
Richard Quine, USA, 1956, 99 mins.

Somebody up There Likes Me

Paul Newman Stars in this film bio of boxer Rocky Graziano, from his youth as street hoodlum in NYC through his Army service to the height of this fighting career. A fine lead performance. Also in the cast are Pier Angeli, Eileen Heckart, Sal Mineo, Robert Loggia, and Steve McQueen in a bit part. B&W.
VHS: S07974. $19.98.
Robert Wise, USA, 1956, 113 mins.

Something of Value

Rock Hudson struggles to fight the Mau Mau warriors and still keep his boyhood friendship with Sidney Poitier. It's not going to be easy, but these situations never are. With Wendy Hiller and Dana Wynter. From the novel by Robert Ruark.
VHS: S04208. $24.95.
Richard Brooks, USA, 1957, 113 mins.

Something to Sing About

James Cagney is the two-fisted band leader in this musical melodrama about Hollywood studio life. With William Frawley and Evelyn Daw.
VHS: S03259. $39.95.
Victor Schertzinger, USA, 1937, 94 mins.

Somewhere I'll Find You

A romantic triangle set against a World War II backdrop. Clark Gable is a foreign correspondent pursued by ambitious journalist Lana Turner, who eventually settles for Gable's younger, more sensible brother (Robert Sterling). With Van Johnson, Keenan Wynn and Frank Faylen.
VHS: S18663. $19.98.
Wesley Ruggles, USA, 1942, 117 mins.

Son of Ali Baba

In this Arabian Nights tale, Tony Curtis is a charismatic hero locked in a deadly confrontation with the evil Caliph, who exploits beautiful princess Piper Laurie to obtain Ali Baba's gold shipment. With Susan Cabot and Victor Joy.
VHS: S19312. $14.98.
Kurt Neumann, USA, 1952, 75 mins.

Son of Fury

Tyrone Power leads a stellar cast on an 18th-century adventure to the South Seas with Gene Tierney, Frances Farmer, Roddy McDowall and John Carradine. When Power is rejected by his rich uncle, he sets off to plot his revenge, in a beautiful tropical paradise.
VHS: S21069. $19.98.
John Cromwell, USA, 1942, 98 mins.

Son of Monte Cristo

A big budget Hollywood production full of last minute rescues, clashing sabres and beautifully detailed sets, featuring Clayton Moore, Louis Hayward, Joan Bennett and George Sanders.
VHS: S03078. $19.95.
Rowland V. Lee, USA, 1940, 105 mins.

Song of Love

Katharine Hepburn delivers an unforgettable performance as world-famous concert pianist Clara Wieck. A story of tragedy and eventual triumph, Song of Love includes Wieck's encounters with some of the greatest musicians and composers of her time—Franz Liszt, Johannes Brahms and Robert Schumann.
VHS: S15019. $19.98.
Clarence Brown, USA, 1947, 120 mins.

A Song to Remember
An almost campy portrait of Frederic Chopin, which inspired many remakes, starring Paul Muni, Cornel Wilde and Merle Oberon. A colorful biography which portrays his flight from Poland and liaison with George Sand.
VHS: S01232. $19.95.
Charles Vidor, USA, 1945, 112 mins.

Sorry, Wrong Number
Barbara Stanwyck plays an invalid heiress whose husband is being blackmailed by William Conrad. One day she overhears a plot to murder a woman on a crossed-wire telephone connection. By the time she figures out she is the intended victim it could be too late. With Burt Lancaster, Wendell Corey and Ed Begley Sr. Based on the radio play by Lucille Fletcher.
VHS: S10833. $19.95.
Laser: LD75260. $34.98.
Anatole Litvak, USA, 1948, 89 mins.

Spectre of the Rose
Dame Judith Anderson and Michael Chekhov star in this film set in the glittering world of international ballet, acting as a stage for murder and madness in a gripping suspense thriller. When a young ballerina discovers that her new husband is going insane, she takes him to a secluded hotel. But now they're alone, he's beyond reason, and their last duet is about to reach a terrifying finale. Ben Hecht wrote and directed this unique suspense thriller.
VHS: S09666. $19.95.
Laser: CLV. LD72033. $29.98.
Ben Hecht, USA, 1946, 90 mins.

Speed Reporter
Richard Talmadge stars as a crackerjack reporter out to smash a bogus reform league. With Luana Walters and Richard Cramer.
VHS: S21556. $24.95.
Bernard B. Ray, USA, 1936, 58 mins.

The Spencer Tracy Collection
Three of Spencer Tracy's films are bound in one collection: John Sturges' offbeat 1955 western, *Bad Day at Black Rock*, his Oscar-winning performance in Victor Fleming's 1937 *Captains Courageous*, and his award-winning work in Norman Taurog's 1938 *Boys Town*.
VHS: S17305. $49.92.

The Sphinx
Lionel Atwill stars in a dual role in this Monogram murder mystery. He plays twin brothers, one a deaf mute, the other a criminal mastermind. When a hotshot reporter and a society editor see through the deception, the brothers are forced to act. With Paul Fix and "Gabby" Hayes.
VHS: S04030. $29.95.
Phil Rosen, USA, 1933, 64 mins.

Splendor in the Grass
Natalie Wood and Warren Beatty (in his screen debut) star as two teenage lovers ripped apart by the repressive mentality of their 1920s Kansas town.
VHS: Out of print. For rental only.
Laser: LD71414. $39.98.
Elia Kazan, USA, 1961, 124 mins.

Split Second
Dick Powell's first effort as a director is a taut thriller about escaped convicts who overtake a nearly deserted town and hold its residents captive.
VHS: S10684. $19.98.
Laser: LD75262. $34.98.
Dick Powell, USA, 1953, 86 mins.

The Spoilers
The fourth version of the Rex Beach Klondike adventure about two roguish adventurers, Randolph Scott and John Wayne, fighting over Alaskan landscapes and a sexy, exotic saloon performer (Marlene Dietrich). "It's a well-packaged mixture of saloon brawls, romance and adventure; much [of the movie] was filmed as a silent" (Leslie Halliwell). With Margaret Lindsay, Harry Carey and Richard Barthelmess.
VHS: S19079. $14.98.
Ray Enright, USA, 1942, 87 mins.

Spook Busters
Long before the Ghostbusters were organized, the Bowery Boys learned how to exterminate supernatural pests. In addition to dehaunting an old house, Leo Gorcey and his pals must deal with Douglas Dumbrille as Dr. Coslow, the mad scientist who wants to put the brain of Huntz Hall inside the body of a gorilla. With Charles Middleton, Bobby Jordan, Gabriel Dell, Billy Benedict and Vera Lewis. The first of 25 Bowery Boys movies from director William Beaudine.
VHS: S15831. $14.98.
William Beaudine, USA, 1946, 68 mins.

Spotlight Scandals
Frank Fay, Billy Gilbert and Harry Langdon join forces for this inspiring film about fame and the power of the proverbial comeback. Scandal destroys a vaudevillian, but he teams up with a new partner and creates a Broadway smash. Bonnie Baker and Radio Rogues provide some great musical numbers.
VHS: S23904. $29.95.
William Beaudine, USA, 1943, 69 mins.

St. Benny the Dip
Comic drama about three con men hiding from the authorities by the director of numerous grade Z movies, Edgar G. Ulmer. Starring Dick Haymes and Roland Young.
VHS: S01245. $29.95.
Edgar G. Ulmer, USA, 1951, 81 mins.

Stage Door
A quality adaptation of the stage play by Edna Ferber and George S. Kaufman, Katharine Hepburn and Ginger Rogers are cast in this comedy/drama that centers on the lives of aspiring actresses in a theatrical boarding house. Lucille Ball has a featured role in the film.
VHS: S02607. $19.95.
Gregory La Cava, USA, 1937, 92 mins.

Stage Door Canteen
An all-star cast including Tallulah Bankhead, Katharine Hepburn, George Raft, Ethel Merman, Merle Oberon, Harpo Marx and George Jessel in this romantic drama of a soldier boy and a canteen hostess.
VHS: S03260. $19.95.
Laser: CLV. LD71751. $29.98.
Frank Borzage, USA, 1943, 135 mins.

Stanley and Livingstone
Spencer Tracy lends his abilities to this Hollywood version of the famous reporter sent to find a missing Scottish missionary in Africa. You don't have to presume with Sir Cedric Hardwicke as the latter half of the title role. A grand adventure film with Walter Brennan, Richard Greene, Charles Coburn, Henry Hull and Nancy Kelly as the invented romantic interest. Some of the footage was shot in Africa.
VHS: S12517. $19.98.
Henry King, USA, 1939, 101 mins.

The Star
An impulsive variation on Billy Wilder's *Sunset Boulevard* stars Bette Davis as a faded, one-time award winning actress who must confront the bitter truth her career is over and consider the implications of a new life and identity. With Sterling Hayden, Natalie Wood, and Warner Anderson.
VHS: S15932. $19.98.
Stuart Heisler, USA, 1952, 89 mins.

A Star Is Born
Janet Gaynor and Fredric March star in the first version of *A Star Is Born*, the story of a young girl whose career is on the rise while that of her husband is on the wane. Adolphe Menjou, May Robson and Andy Devine co-star.
VHS: S18187. $19.95.
William Wellman, USA, 1937, 112 mins.

State's Attorney
John Barrymore stars as a flamboyant and ambitious attorney who nearly pays dearly for his arrogance. With Jill Esmond, William Boyd.
VHS: S12013. $19.98.
George Archainbaud, USA, 1931, 79 mins.

Stella Dallas
Barbara Stanwyck has the title role in this moving soap opera about an unrefined but socially ambitious woman who sacrifices all so that her daughter can benefit from her mistakes. Anne Shirley is the perfect daughter with the great future. With John Boles, Alan Hale and Barbara O'Neil. Based on the novel by Olive Higgins Prouty. Remade in 1990 with Bette Midler.
VHS: S02928. $19.98.
King Vidor, USA, 1937, 105 mins.

A Stolen Life
A true showcase for the talents of Bette Davis as a woman living in New England, who deceives her husband by exchanging identities with her dead twin. Glenn Ford stars as the husband.
VHS: S11623. $19.95.
Curtis Bernhardt, USA, 1946, 107 mins.

Story of Louis Pasteur
The life story and struggles of the legendary French scientist receive heroic treatment in this engrossing adaptation, which features a brilliant (and Oscar-winning) performance. Writers Sheridan Gibney and Pierre Collings also received an Oscar.
VHS: S11550. $19.95.
William Dieterle, USA, 1936, 85 mins.

Stranded
When a courageous teacher and her students are stranded in a blizzard, Miss Enter uses every bit of her skill to keep them alive. But as their food and firewood run out, it becomes apparent that the snowplow sent to rescue them may not arrive on time. Stars Bette Davis and Claudia Bryar.
VHS: S16743. $14.95.
Allen Miner, USA, 1957, 30 mins.

The Strange Affair of Uncle Harry
George Sanders takes drastic steps when his domineering sisters interfere with his romance in this engrossing and melodramatic film noir. With Geraldine Fitzgerald and Ella Raines.
VHS: S14325. $19.98.
Laser: CLV. LD72035. $29.98.
Robert Siodmak, USA, 1945, 80 mins.

Strange Cargo
Clark Gable and Joan Crawford star in this offbeat drama about a motley group of convicts who escape from Devil's Island. The catch in this allegorical tale is that one of the passengers is showing strong signs of being a Christ-like figure. With Ian Hunter, Paul Lukas, Albert Dekker and Peter Lorre as M'sier Pig. Condemned by the Catholic League of Decency upon release.
VHS: S11729. $19.98.
Frank Borzage, USA, 1940, 105 mins.

Strange Illusion
One of the great Edgar G. Ulmer's best and rarest films. Warren William and Regis Toomey star in this metaphysical tale of suspicion and murder; oddly enough, an update of *Hamlet*, as William woos the widowed mother of teenager James Lydon.
VHS: S10962. $29.95.
Edgar G. Ulmer, USA, 1945, 80 mins.

Strange Love of Martha Ivers
A complex mystery featuring Van Heflin, Barbara Stanwyck, Kirk Douglas and Lizabeth Scott in which Stanwyck is tied to her husband through his knowledge of a crime she committed a long time ago.
VHS: S05999. $29.95.
Laser: CLV. LD72065. $34.95.
Lewis Milestone, USA, 1946, 117 mins.

The Strange Love of Molly Louvain
Ann Dvorak finds herself an unwed mother in trouble. Her charms lead her from one troublesome man to the next until finally the law must intervene. Even a cynical reporter, Lee Tracy, cannot resist her, though he knows the whole story of crime, infidelity and heartache behind this young woman. Only before the adoption of the pre-Production Code could a theme like this be explored in motion pictures.
VHS: S20834. $19.98.
Michael Curtiz, USA, 1932, 72 mins.

Strange Woman
Hedy Lamarr stars as a sultry and vicious man-killer in this thriller from that legendary master of B grade cinema, Edgar G. Ulmer. Also starring George Sanders, Louis Hayward and June Lockhart.
VHS: S14664. $29.95.
Edgar G. Ulmer, USA, 1946, 89 mins.

Stranger on the Third Floor
Peter Lorre stars in this thriller about a reporter, who having helped send a man to prison in a murder case, becomes convinced of the man's innocence when the murders continue. With John McGuire, Margaret Tallichet, Charles Waldron and Elisha Cook, Jr.
VHS: S02149. $29.95.
Boris Ingster, USA, 1940, 64 mins.

The Strangler
Victor Buono is a mama's boy living in Boston who goes off the deep end and starts strangling women all over the city. An atmospheric thriller starring David McLean and Ellen Corby.
VHS: S14792. $14.98.
Burt Topper, USA, 1964, 89 mins.

The Stratton Story
James Stewart plays the Chicago White Sox ace who refused to allow a tragic accident impair his prominent baseball career. The baseball scenes are remarkably authentic and exciting. Academy Award-winning screenplay by Douglas Morrow and Guy Trosper. With June Allyson, Frank Morgan, Agnes Moorehead and Bill Williams.
VHS: S19467. $19.98.
Sam Wood, USA, 1949, 106 mins.

The Street of Forgotten Women
This exploitative look at prostitution was made after a number of scandals rocked the silent film world. It purports to be an expose, but actually manages to expose plenty of flesh instead. A young girl is seduced into a life of prostitution after being brutalized and even stripped of her underwear. 55 mins.
VHS: S24002. $19.95.
Donald Crisp, USA, 1926, 72 mins.

Street Scene
Realistic account of life in NY tenements adapted from Elmer Rice's play with a score by Alfred Newman.
VHS: S02001. $24.95.
King Vidor, USA, 1931, 80 mins.

Street with No Name
Based on an actual FBI case of an agent uncovering the head of the city mob. Built around a psychopathic character similar to the one Richard Widmark created in *Kiss of Death*. Starring Widmark, Ed Begley, Mark Stevens and Lloyd Nolan.
VHS: S13614. $19.95.
William Keighley, USA, 1948, 93 mins.

Studs Lonigan
Gritty tale of life on Chicago's South Side in the 1920's features Frank Gorshin and an early appearance by Jack Nicholson.
VHS: S02115. $24.95.
Irving Lerner, USA, 1960, 96 mins.

Sudden Fear
Joan Crawford is an heiress, a successful playwright, and the toast of Broadway. Everything points to untold happiness when she meets the ideal man (Jack Palance). Things sour, however, when Crawford realizes that Palance is intent on murdering her and inheriting her fortune. Soon murder and revenge twist her perfect life into a nightmare. Gloria Grahame is also featured as the other woman.
VHS: S26993. $19.95.
Laser: LD75431. $39.99.
David Miller, USA, 1952, 111 mins.

Suddenly
Frank Sinatra heads a team of assassins who plan to gun down the President of the United States as he steps off the train in Suddenly, California, on his way to a fishing trip. It's up to local lawman Sterling Hayden to see that the Chief Exec has a pleasant vacation. Feature withdrawn for many years after JFK slaying.
VHS: S05078. $19.95.
Lewis Allen, USA, 1954, 77 mins.

Suddenly Last Summer
Elizabeth Taylor and Katharine Hepburn received Oscars for their gripping performances of Tennessee Williams' play about the beautiful Catherine, committed to a mental institution, whose aunt tries to influence the young surgeon to lobotomize her.
VHS: S01277. $19.95.
Joseph L. Mankiewicz, USA, 1959, 114 mins.

Summer of '42
A young adolescent discovers love and sex by meeting a beautiful older war-bride in this light nostalgic film about pubescent boyhood. With Gary Grimes, Jerry Houser, and Jennifer O'Neill. Also, a beautiful Oscar-winning score by Michel Legrand.
VHS: S06309. $19.98.
Laser: LD74717. $34.98.
Robert Mulligan, USA, 1962, 102 mins.

A Summer Place
Romantic summer adventures of the idle rich on an island off the coast of Maine. Sandra Dee and Troy Donahue star in a story of "illicit" love that features "one of the best-known romantic songs in movie history." From the best-seller by Sloan Wilson and also starring Dorothy McGuire and Arthur Kennedy.
VHS: S12582. $19.98.
Laser: LD74742. $39.98.
Delmer Daves, USA, 1959, 130 mins.

Sundown
Gene Tierney stars as a native girl who uncovers a Nazi plot in Africa. To make sure the sun never sets on the British empire, Bruce Cabot, George Sanders, Harry Carey, Joseph Calleia and Reginald Gardiner (one of whom is an enemy agent) try to keep a stiff upper lip and keep the region under control. Lots of action and tea.
VHS: S05069. $19.95.
Henry Hathaway, USA, 1941, 91 mins.

Sundowners
Robert Mitchum and Deborah Kerr as sheepherders in 1920's Australia. Attentive, beautiful care to pictorial detail, nominated for five Academy Awards. With Peter Ustinov and Glynis Johns.
VHS: S03010. $14.95.
Laser: LD74737. $39.98.
Fred Zinnemann, USA, 1960, 113 mins.

Sunrise at Campobello
This is a sincere look at the early life of Franklin Delano Roosevelt. His struggle against polio and return to politics is convincingly played by Ralph Bellamy from his Tony Award winning Broadway performance. Greer Garson stars as Eleanor, with Anne Shoemaker, Hume Cronyn and Jean Hagen. From the play by Dore Schary.
VHS: S16278. $19.98.
Laser: LD70049. $39.98.
Vincent J. Donehue, USA, 1960, 144 mins.

Supernatural
Carole Lombard stars along with Randolph Scott and Vivienne Osborne in this engaging thriller about murder and possession. Lombard is an heiress who longs for contact with her dead brother. A spiritualist offers help but in fact has a completely different turn of events planned.
VHS: S26226. $19.98.
Victor Halperin, USA, 1933, 65 mins.

Surprise Package
When American gangster Yul Brenner is deported to Greece, he becomes attached to the crown jewels of a deposed king living in exile. With Mitzi Gaynor, George Coulouris, Eric Pohlmann, Warren Mitchell, Barry Foster and Noel Coward as King Pavel II. Coward also sings the title song in this caper comedy. Based on *A Gift from the Boys* by Art Buchwald.
VHS: S15891. $19.95.
Stanley Donen, USA/Great Britain, 1960, 100 mins.

Susan Lennox: Her Fall and Rise
Greta Garbo runs away from her brutal father, who wants to marry her off to farmer Alan Hale, only to find that handsome engineer Clark Gable rejects her love when he learns of her affair with a carnival owner. She then becomes a professional mistress while she waits for Clark to change his mind. Based on the novel by David Graham Phillips, who was later shot by a disgruntled reader for his depiction of women.
VHS: S13198. $19.98.
Robert Z. Leonard, USA, 1931, 84 mins.

Suzy
In their lone appearance together, Jean Harlow and Cary Grant star in this World War II-era tale about an American chorus girl marooned in London who turns up in Paris and falls for an enigmatic and charismatic playboy (Grant). With Franchot Tone, Lewis Stone and Benita Hume. Some startling aviation sequences, appropriated from the negative of the classic *Hell's Angels*. Written by Dorothy Parker.
VHS: S17782. $19.95.
George Fitzmaurice, USA, 1936, 93 mins.

Svengali
Although George Du Maurier's *Trilby* has been done several times, this 1931 version with John Barrymore stands as the classic against which the others are measured.
VHS: S01288. $24.95.
Archie Mayo, USA, 1931, 82 mins.

Swamp Fire
Johnny Weissmuller, the Olympic champion, is paired with Buster Crabbe in this heroic tale. When Weissmuller, a river boat captain, falls for a beautiful young woman, he must confront her wealthy and powerful father.
VHS: S25699. $19.95.
William H. Pine, USA, 1946, 69 mins.

The Swan
Charles Vidor's remake of *One Romantic Night* stars Grace Kelly as a mythical princess whose attraction to a charismatic crown prince (Alec Guinness) sets the dizzying, frantic plot of romance, fear and loss in motion. Based on the play by Ferenc Molnar. With Louis Jourdan, Agnes Moorehead, and Leo G. Carroll. This laser disc version also contains the short, *The Wedding in Monaco*.
Laser: LD71651. $39.98.
Charles Vidor, USA, 1956, 109 mins.

Sweet Bird of Youth
Paul Newman and Geraldine Page star in this Tennessee Williams drama of ambition, lust and faded glory. When a not-so-young stud hooks up with an aging movie star, he makes the mistake of revisiting his home town. The fine cast includes Shirley Knight, Rip Torn, Mildred Dunnock and Ed Begley, who won an Oscar for his role as the unforgiving town boss.
VHS: S11221. $19.95.
Laser: LD71178. $39.98.
Richard Brooks, USA, 1962, 120 mins.

Sweet Smell of Success
Burt Lancaster is J.J. Hunsecker, a ruthless and powerful New York columnist, and Tony Curtis is the press agent who will do anything to be in his good graces. Scripted by Clifford Odets and Ernest Lehman. A cult film that was quoted in *Diner*. With Martin Milner, Sam Levene and Barbara Nichols.
VHS: S07979. $19.98.
Laser: LD70689. $34.98.
Alexander MacKendrick, USA, 1957, 96 mins.

Sword of Venus
A splashy, swashbuckling film about the exploits of the son of the famous Monte Christo. Starring Robert Clarke and Dan O'Herlihy.
VHS: S14665. $29.95.
Harold Daniels, USA, 1953, 72 mins.

A Tale of Two Cities
For those of you who didn't know, it was the best of times, it was the worst of times and *this* often filmed classic of Charles Dickens stars Ronald Colman. The two cities are Paris and London and the time is the French Revolution. Splendid MGM production. With Basil Rathbone, Elizabeth Allan and Edna May Oliver.
VHS: S02986. $24.95.
Laser: LD71682. $39.98.
Jack Conway, USA, 1935, 121 mins.

Tales of Manhattan
In addition to W.C. Fields, who appears in a hilarious, classic sequence, Ben Hecht's screenplay is brought to life in this episodic movie by a variety of movie idols, including Rita Hayworth, Ginger Rogers, Henry Fonda, Cesar Romero, Charles Laughton, Paul Robeson and more. It is built around a tailcoat that has unexpected effects on a series of different characters.
VHS: S27607. $19.98.
Julien Duvivier, USA, 1942, 106 mins.

Tall Story
Anthony Perkins is a college basketball star who welcomes disaster when he marries a young coed. Don't miss Jane Fonda's hilarious film debut!
VHS: S15991. $19.98.
Joshua Logan, USA, 1960, 91 mins.

Tamango
American expatriate John Berry, a blacklisted director, spent much of the last five decades in Europe. In this frenetic melodrama, with a curious affinity for racial and class exploitation, Curt Jurgens is a sinister Dutch slave trader in love with a beautiful black woman (Dorothy Dandridge) who's trying to suppress a slave revolt led by Tamango (Alex Cressan). With Jean Servais, Roger Hanin and Guy Mairesse.
VHS: S18254. $29.95.
John Berry, USA, 1959, 98 mins.

Tammy and the Bachelor
Debbie Reynolds introduced the Mississippi riverboat girl in this Ross Hunter production about the headstrong woman who falls for a wealthy Southern aristocrat (Leslie Nielsen) and raises his consciousness about class and ideas. With Fay Wray, Sidney Blackmer, Mildred Natwick and Mala Powers.
VHS: S17947. $14.98.
Joseph Pevney, USA, 1957, 89 mins.

Tammy and the Doctor
Sandra Dee is a Southern charmer who makes the pilgrimage to a Los Angeles hospital to begin her training as a nurse, where she promptly unnerves a young intern (Peter Fonda) and throws medicine and hospital rules upside down. With MacDonald Carey, Beulah Bondi, Margaret Lindsay and Reginald Owen.
VHS: S17948. $14.98.
Harry Keller, USA, 1963, 88 mins.

Tango
Franklin Pangborn is featured in this melodrama starring Hermann Bing and Marie Prevost. A chorus girl falls for a rich guy, a setup certain to lead to heartache. Based on a novel by Vida Hurst, this film also features some interesting dance routines.
VHS: S23790. $24.95.
Phil Rosen, USA, 1936, 66 mins.

The Tanks Are Coming
Sam Fuller wrote the story for this engrossing World War II movie about an armored division's trek to Berlin. A ruthless sergeant leads the group through a war-ravaged landscape, showing little mercy for the enemy and his own men. Stars Steve Cochran and Phil Carey.
VHS: S24728. $19.98.
Lewis Seiler, USA, 1951, 91 mins.

Taras Bulba
Yul Brenner and Tony Curtis star in this tale of 16th century Cossack life in the Ukraine. Shot on location in Argentina, this adventure of hard riding and mighty fighters is based on the novel by Nikolai Gogol. With Christine Kaufmann.
VHS: S04214. $19.98.
Laser: LD72133. $39.98.
J. Lee Thompson, USA, 1962, 122 mins.

Targets
The stunning film-making debut of critic-turned-director Peter Bogdanovich about a psychotic sniper and an aging horror movie star (Boris Karloff in his final film).
VHS: S03286. $49.95.
Peter Bogdanovich, USA, 1968, 92 mins.

Tarzan, the Ape Man
The first great Tarzan movie stars Johnny Weissmuller and Maureen O'Sullivan as the King of the Apes and Jane, the beautiful English girl who leaves civilization behind to become his lover. An exciting and romantic family classic.
VHS: S14308. $19.98.
W.S. Van Dyke, USA, 1932, 99 mins.

Task Force
Delmer Daves' well-made, compelling film balances personal drama, the struggles of Naval officer Gary Cooper, and, within a larger historical purpose, the evolution of the aircraft carrier. The narrative is buttressed with authentic combat footage. With Walter Brennan and Jane Wyatt.
VHS: S19493. $19.98.
Delmer Daves, USA, 1949, 116 mins.

Teahouse of the August Moon
Marlon Brando stars as Sakini, an Okinawan interpreter for the U.S. military in this postwar comedy about tradition, progress and red tape. Glen Ford is the officer in charge of building a schoolhouse but the villagers would really prefer a teahouse instead. Based on the Broadway play by John Patrick. With Eddie Albert, Paul Ford, Harry Morgan, Machiko Kyo and Nijiko Kiyokawa as Miss Higa Jiga.
VHS: S12528. $19.98.
Laser: LD71145. $39.98.
Daniel Mann, USA, 1956, 123 mins.

Tell It to the Judge
Rosalind Russell can't quite decide if she wants to be remarry ex-husband Robert Cummings or not in this romantic screwball comedy. Gig Young shows up to make Cummings jealous during a weekend in the Adirondacks. With Marie McDonald, Louise Beavers and Harry Davenport as Judge MacKenzie Meredith. To reconcile or not to reconcile, that is the question.
VHS: S15895. $19.95.
Norman Foster, USA, 1949, 87 mins.

Tender Comrade
Tearjerker in which lady welders (Ginger Rogers and friends) live communally and support each other while their husbands are out fighting World War II. The communal set-up in the film caused this Dmytryk/Trumbo project to be labeled Communist Propaganda by the HUAC in later years.
VHS: S13518. $19.98.
Edward Dmytryk, USA, 1943, 101 mins.

Test Pilot
Clark Gable, Myrna Loy and Spencer Tracy headline this tense drama of the hazardous exploits of a test pilot and their effect on the lives of those who love him.
VHS: S15262. $19.98.
Victor Fleming, USA, 1938, 118 mins.

Texas Carnival
Esther Williams and Red Skelton play a carnival sideshow team mistaken for a pair of Texas multimillionaires at a swank resort hotel in this lively musical. Skelton proves his rank among the screens greatest clowns in an hilarious slapstick performance.
VHS: S16610. $19.98.
Charles Walters, USA, 1951, 97 mins.

That Brennan Girl
An unaccountable, Freudian thriller that examines the consequences of a mother's oppressive behavior on her daughter (Mona Freeman). The plot studies the woman's subsequent coldness and distrust, until her charismatic second husband (James Dunn) helps her recover. With William Marshall, June Duprez and Frank Jenks.
VHS: S18938. $19.95.
Alfred Santell, USA, 1946, 95 mins.

That Certain Woman
Edmund Goulding (*Dark Victory*) directs this fresh, operatic melodrama based on his earlier work *The Trespasser*, about a gangster's widow (Bette Davis) who falls in love with a socially prominent young man (Henry Fonda), while trying to conceal her past.
VHS: S17336. $19.98.
Edmund Goulding, USA, 1937, 96 mins.

That Forsyte Woman
Greer Garson and Errol Flynn in the sumptuous screen version of John Galsworthy's tale of moneyed elite in the Victorian Era.
VHS: S15655. $19.98.
Compton Bennett, USA, 1949, 114 mins.

Theodora Goes Wild
Irene Dunne deviated from her melodramatic roles to star in this comedy opposite Melvyn Douglas. Dunne appears to be an ordinary small town woman with no outward signs that indicate she is in fact the author of a torrid and sexy romance novel. All that changes when her identity is revealed to the priggish townsfolk. Her New York illustrator (Douglas), a suave New Yorker from a prominent family, comes calling. Together they throw aside convention to have the time of their lives.
VHS: S27182. $19.95.
Richard Boleslavsky, USA, 1936, 93 mins.

There Goes Barder
Eddie Constantine plays a sleazy con-man who's hired by a shady ship owner to be a security agent. Suspenseful spy thriller co-starring May Britt. USA, 1964.
VHS: S15364. $29.95.

They Call It Sin
A young Kansas farm girl, Loretta Young, is a composer who finds herself bewildered by the big bad city. Her musical career is about to take off when an old lover re-emerges and destroys her big chance. Tragedy follows but ultimately true love wins out in this romantic melodrama filmed before the pre-Production Code went into effect.
VHS: S20835. $19.98.
Thornton Freeland, USA, 1932, 75 mins.

They Drive by Night
Humphrey Bogart in one of his finest roles! *They Drive by Night* is a riveting social drama about the trucking trade—fast, hard, bitter, and brilliantly realized. The stunning cast includes George Raft, Ann Sheridan and, of course, Ida Lupino.
VHS: S01322. $19.98.
Laser: LD71149. $34.98.
Raoul Walsh, USA, 1940, 97 mins.

They Made Me a Criminal
John Garfield gives a dynamic yet sensitive portrayal of a fugitive boxer who thinks he has murdered a man. Ann Sheridan is the woman who gives him a second chance. Also stars Claude Rains and the Dead End Kids.
VHS: S01637. $24.95.
Busby Berkeley, USA, 1939, 92 mins.

They Meet Again
A doctor attempts to vindicate a bank teller accused of filching $3,000 in this entry of Hersholt's *Dr. Christian* series. With Jean Hersholt, Dorothy Lovett, Robert Baldwin, Barton Yarborough, Anne Bennett and an entertaining jive number by Leon Tyler.
VHS: S05699. $29.95.
Erle C. Kenton, USA, 1941, 67 mins.

They Met in Bombay
Clark Gable and Rosalind Russell star as two thieves who steal each other's hearts in this sparkling international caper. A Japanese invasion gives Russell second thoughts about a life of crime—and gives Gable a chance to be a hero.
VHS: S20563. $19.98.
Clarence Brown, USA, 1941, 93 mins.

They Won't Believe Me
Robert Young and Susan Hayward star in this first-rate suspense drama about a playboy who suddenly finds himself on trial for murder because of his philandering with three women. Full of great twists.
VHS: S02874. $19.98.
Irving Pichel, USA, 1946, 80 mins.

Thief
Ray Milland stars in this unusual film noir/espionage drama set in New York. This film has one unusual touch—there is not one word of spoken dialog. Don't sneeze. With Rita Gam and Martin Gabel.
VHS: S13012. $19.95.
Russell Rouse, USA, 1952, 86 mins.

The Thief of Baghdad
This sound version of *The Thief* is the winner of three Academy Awards. It stars Sabu as the mischievous Abu. When Abu helps the rightful King of Baghdad escape from prison, he finds himself involved in an incredible series of adventures.
VHS: S17379. $19.98.
Alexander Korda, USA, 1940, 106 mins.

Thin Ice
Olympic skating champion Sonja Henie plays a skating teacher at a Swiss Hotel whose relationship with a charming guest has wide-reaching repercussions when she discovers the mysterious man (Tyrone Power) is an internationally prominent prince. With Arthur Treacher, Joan Davis, Alan Hale, Raymond Walburn and Sig Ruman.
VHS: S20258. $19.98.
Sidney Lanfield, USA, 1937, 86 mins.

Thirteenth Guest
A rare example of output from Monogram Pictures, so admired by Godard: in this old house, a dead millionaire and a mystery are to be solved in this chiller starring Ginger Rogers and Lyle Talbot. Recently re-discovered print.
VHS: S02932. $19.95.
Albert Ray, USA, 1932, 70 mins.

Thirty Seconds over Tokyo
Van Johnson leads a valiant crew on an historic bombing raid over Japan just 131 days after Pearl Harbor. Spencer Tracy makes a cameo appearance as Lt. Col. Jimmy Doolittle, the mission's leader, but the real focus is on Johnson and his crew. With Robert Mitchum, Robert Walker, Don DeFore, and Benson Fong as Young Chung. The semi-documentary style script is by Dalton Trumbo. The special effects won an Oscar.
VHS: S13309. $19.98.
Mervyn Le Roy, USA, 1944, 138 mins.

This Gun for Hire
This uncharacteristically dark adaptation of Graham Greene's novel *A Gun for Sale* stars Alan Ladd as a brutally efficient gunman. He's caught in a complicated conspiracy plot involving an undercover agent (Veronica Lake) as he plots revenge against the man (Laird Cregar) who betrayed him. With Robert Preston and Tully Marshall.
VHS: S18997. $14.98.
Frank Tuttle, USA, 1942, 81 mins.

This Property Is Condemned
Natalie Wood, Robert Redford, Charles Bronson and Robert Blake star in this film adaptation of Tennessee Williams' one-act play, set in a Mississippi railroad town, with Wood falling for Redford, the out-of-towner staying in her mama's boarding house.
VHS: S04399. $19.98.
Laser: LD75274. $34.98.
Sydney Pollack, USA, 1966, 110 mins.

Thomas Crown Affair
A bored millionaire, played by Steve McQueen, masterminds the perfect bank robbery and is pursued by a lovely and dogged insurance investigator (Faye Dunaway) determined to catch him. The stylish photography by Haskell Wexler includes the clever use of multiple-image screens.
VHS: S13755. $19.98.
Laser: Letterboxed, chapter search. Includes original theatrical trailer. **LD71646. $34.98.**
Norman Jewison, USA, 1968, 102 mins.

The Thoroughbred
Once a respected horse trainer, Mr. Fitshue now earns a living as a horse consultant to an unscrupulous group of characters. But when his conscience finally catches up with him, Fairbanks runs into a beautiful victim of one of his scams. Stars Douglas Fairbanks, Jr.
VHS: S16744. $14.95.
Harold Huth, USA, 1954, 30 mins.

Those Daring Young Men in Their Jaunty Jalopies
Follows the numerous accidents and slapstick exploits of participants in a 1500 mile car race to Monte Carlo. It's "Monte Carlo or Bust" in this road rally set in the 1920's. Starring Tony Curtis and Dudley Moore.
VHS: S13538. $39.95.
Ken Annakin, USA, 1969, 125 mins.

Those Magnificent Men in Their Flying Machines
From the opening prologue by Red Skelton, who gives a hysterical aviatic history lesson, this comic feature will delight audiences with its story of a gag-filled international airplane race. Sarah Miles, Terry Thomas, Benny Hill and Sam Wanamaker are just some of the comic stars included in this fun-filled movie.
VHS: S21025. $14.98.
Ken Annakin, USA, 1965, 132 mins.

Three Came Home
Claudette Colbert stars as a woman writer who is imprisoned in a Japanese camp during World War II. The deprivation suffered by the internees and the personal anguish experienced by the camp commander, torn between compassion and duty, is explored. With Sessue Hayakawa, Florence Desmond, Patrick Knowles. Based on the story of writer Agnes Newton Keith, with a script by Nunnaly Johnson.
VHS: S13050. $19.95.
Jean Negulesco, USA, 1950, 106 mins.

Three Comrades
F. Scott Fitzgerald adapted Erich Maria Remarque's novel about three German army officers (Robert Taylor, Robert Young and Franchot Tone) who attempt to rebuild their lives in the aftermath of the Armistice. They find meaning in their relationship with an impoverished English woman (Margaret Sullavan), who exercises a magnetic pull over their habits and lives.
VHS: S18509. $19.98.
Frank Borzage, USA, 1938, 98 mins.

Three Faces of Eve
Tour de force by Joanne Woodward as a young woman with multiple personalities and three separate lives. Lee J. Cobb is the psychiatrist who tries to cure her.
VHS: S18098. $19.98.
Laser: Letterboxed. **LD72339. $59.98.**
Nunnally Johnson, USA, 1957, 91 mins.

Three Faces West
John Wayne leads a Dust Bowl community to workable land in Oregon in this contemporary (1940) drama that combines the New West and anti-Nazi sentiments. Wayne is in love with the daughter of a Viennese surgeon (Charles Coburn), who escaped from a concentration camp.
VHS: S10071. $19.95.
Bernard Vorhaus, USA, 1940, 80 mins.

Three Husbands
From the beyond, a playboy sends a letter to three husbands, hinting that one of their wives was a mistress. A haunting follow-up to the Oscar-winning "Letter to Three Wives." With Eve Arden, Ruth Warrick, Jane Darwell.
VHS: S04851. $29.95.
Irving Reis, USA, 1950, 78 mins.

The Three Musketeers (1933)
Three French Foreign Legionnaires, led by John Wayne, battle evil desert warriors under the blazing sun in this entertaining Saturday matinee serial. While tracking down the elusive El Shaitan, leader of the "Circle of Death", this cunning and resourceful team dodges bullets and bayonets, eventually uncovering the desert devil's maniacal plans and his true identity. Also featuring Lon Chaney Jr. USA, 1933, 215 mins.
VHS: S13512. $24.95.

The Three Musketeers (1935)
The original classic swashbuckling adventure featuring Walter Abel as D'Artagnan, and Paul Lukas, Moroni Olson and Onslow Stevens as the Three Musketeers. From a script by Dudley Nichols, with a musical score by Max Steiner.
VHS: S03226. $29.95.
Rowland V. Lee, USA, 1935, 95 mins.

The Three Musketeers (1948)
En Garde! Gene Kelly is a jaunty D'Artagnan in this funny and thrilling swashbuckler based on the classic Dumas story. With an all-star cast, including Lana Turner, June Allyson, and Van Heflin.
VHS: S15658. $19.98.
Laser: LD70695. $39.98.
George Sidney, USA, 1948, 125 mins.

Three on a Match
Three women who were childhood friends meet again in the big city, and the sad melodrama of their lives unfolds. Equal doses of suspense and tragedy are bolstered by good performances from Ann Dvorak, Bette Davis, and Joan Blondell.
VHS: S13649. $19.98.
Mervyn Le Roy, USA, 1932, 64 mins.

Three Secrets
Eleanor Parker, Patricia Neal and Ruth Roman are three women who each suspect that the foster five-year-old boy who survived a plane crash is the son they gave up for adoption. It's no secret that at least two of them must be wrong. With Frank Lovejoy, Leif Erickson and Duncan Richardson as Johnny. B&W.
VHS: S07415. $19.98.
Robert Wise, USA, 1950, 93 mins.

Thunder Road
Robert Mitchum stars as Lucas Doolin, the fastest and luckiest hauler of moonshine in Kentucky. Mitchum wrote the story and the hit song *Whippoorwill*, which is sung by Keely Smith. His 16-year-old son James plays his ardent kid brother. A cult film and the grand daddy of all those "moonshiner vs. revenooer" movies that followed. B&W.
VHS: $10072. $59.95.
Arthur Ripley, USA, 1958, 92 mins.

Till the End of Time
The story of three returning veterans, based on Niven Busch's novel, *They Dream of Time*. Dorothy McGuire plays the disillusioned WWII widow who falls in love. With Robert Mitchum, Guy Madison.
VHS: $09176. $19.95.
Edward Dmytryk, USA, 1946, 105 mins.

A Time for Dying
"The indispensable last piece in an auteurist jigsaw puzzle…a haunting depiction of waste and futility of violence" (Sarris). Withheld from release for over ten years, the film stars Audie Murphy in a story of youthful innocence and foolish bravado. Boetticher's last film.
VHS: $01345. $34.95.
Budd Boetticher, USA, 1969, 73 mins.

The Tip Off
Ginger Rogers drew favorable notices for this early role as Baby Face, the spitfire girlfriend of boxer Robert Armstrong. Eddie Quillan stars as a radio mechanic whose innocent involvement with a gangster's girlfriend puts him a jam until he makes friends with a prizefighter. With Joan Peers and Ralf Harolde as Nick Vatelli.
VHS: $15468. $19.98.
Albert S. Rogell, USA, 1931, 71 mins.

Titanic
Clifton Webb, Barbara Stanwyck and Audrey Dalton star in this gripping re-enactment of the tragic sinking of the *Titanic*. Eyewitness accounts were used as the basis for the Academy Award-winning Best Story and Screenplay. Before this wholly unexpected accident the mammoth ship was set to revolutionize trans-Atlantic travel. Instead 1500 people drowned, celebrities and common folk alike.
VHS: $24133. $19.98.
Laser: LD74940. $39.99.
Jean Negulesco, USA, 1953, 98 mins.

To Hell and Back
Based on his autobiography, Audie Murphy portrays his own experiences which popularized him as the most decorated infantryman in American war history. Excellent battle sequences depict Murphy's breathtaking heroic exploits. Stars Marshall Thompson, Susan Kohner, Charles Drake, Jack Kelly and Gregg Palmer.
VHS: $16305. $14.95.
Jesse Hibbs, USA, 1955, 106 mins.

To Kill a Mockingbird
Gregory Peck won an Oscar for his role of Atticus Finch, the defense lawyer of a black man accused of rape in the American South. Script by Horton Foote from the novel by Harper Lee. A sensitive and powerful drama. Robert Duvall's film debut. Also Brock Peters, and Mary Badham as Scout. B&W.
VHS: $02640. $19.95.
Laser: LD70089. $39.98.
Robert Mulligan, USA, 1962, 129 mins.

To Please a Lady
She's an eat-'em-alive journalist; he's a ruthless racing driver—they're a perfect match! Clark Gable and Barbara Stanwyck star in this movie that's a "thriller from beginning to end" (*Hollywood Reporter*).
VHS: $20564. $19.98.
Clarence Brown, USA, 1950, 91 mins.

To the Shores of Tripoli
Produced during World War II, this memorable war film details the transformation of a spoiled rich boy into a tough and battle-wise Marine. With John Payne, Maureen O'Hara, Randolph Scott.
VHS: $12166. $19.98.
H. Bruce Humberstone, USA, 1942, 85 mins.

The Toast of New York
Edward Arnold is "Jubilee Jim" Fish in this historical drama about the rise to power of one of the tycoons who ruled Wall Street after the Civil War. Cary Grant starred as his friend and eventual rival for the affections of the legendary Frances Farmer.
VHS: $03237. $19.98.
Laser: CLV. LD71742. $19.98.
Rowland V. Lee, USA, 1939, 109 mins.

Tokyo Joe
Humphrey Bogart plays an American war hero in post-war Japan who becomes involved in smuggling and blackmail to protect his wife and child. He flies planes of contraband goods, sits in a hot tub and gets to talk tough—though probably not all at the same time. With Alexander Knox, Florence Marley, Sessue Hayakawa and Jerome Courtland.
VHS: $08702. $69.95.
Stuart Heisler, USA, 1949, 88 mins.

Toll of the Sea
Notable because it was the first feature film to be shot in Technicolor, and one of the few films produced by the Technicolor Company. The film runs 41 minutes, and the final shot was reconstructed using the original two-strip color cameras to film the final sunset.
VHS: $06010. $29.95.

Tom, Dick and Harry
Academy-Award nominee for best screenplay, this classic comedy tells the delightful tale of a daydreaming girl who can't decide which beau she likes best. Ginger Rogers, Burgess Meredith, Alan Marshall, George Murphy star.
VHS: $05665. $19.98.
Garson Kanin, USA, 1941, 86 mins.

Tomorrow Is Forever
Orson Welles and Claudette Colbert star in a fateful drama that bridges two World Wars. When Welles is wounded while fighting the Huns in the First World War, he decides to start over with a new name in a new country. Colbert, thinking herself a widow, marries George Brent and starts a new family that includes six year old Natalie Wood in her debut role.
VHS: $16441. $19.98.
Irving Pichel, USA, 1946, 104 mins.

Tony Rome
Frank Sinatra plays the title character, a Miami-based private detective who becomes involved with blackmail, phony gems, and the unpleasant Kosterman family. The supporting players include Gena Rowlands, Sue Lyon, Simon Oakland, Jill St. John and Richard Conte as Lt. Santini. Watch for Rocky Graziano, Shecky Greene and Deanna Lund in small roles. Based on the novel *Miami Mayhem* by Marvin H. Albert.
VHS: $12521. $59.95.
Gordon Douglas, USA, 1967, 110 mins.

Too Hot to Handle
Rival newsreel cameramen Clark Gable and Walter Pidgeon are invited by aviatrix Myrna Loy to locate her missing brother in the wilds of the Amazon. Adventure, romance and comic quick thinking prevail. With Leo Carillo, Johnny Hinds and Marjorie Main. Not to be confused with movies of the same title starring Jayne Mansfield and Cherie Caffaro.
VHS: $13191. $19.98.
Jack Conway, USA, 1938, 105 mins.

Topaze
John Barrymore is the idealistic and naive Professor Topaze, who finds himself enmeshed in a hilarious and lucrative fraud. Myrna Loy is the sultry kept woman who tempts him.
VHS: $12170. $39.98.
Harry D'Arrast, USA, 1933, 78 mins.

Topkapi
Jules Dassin's imaginative adaptation of Eric Ambler's novel, *The Light of Day*, about a group of sophisticated thieves orchestrating the perfect heist, the gem-strewn dagger from the Topkapi Museum in Constantinople. Peter Ustinov won the 1964 Academy Award for his performance. With Melina Mercouri, Maximilian Schell and Robert Morley.
VHS: $27576. $19.98.
Laser: LD71652. $34.98.
Jules Dassin, USA, 1964, 120 mins.

Topper Returns
A ghoulish romp in a sinister house of thrills. A funny, spooky mystery with Roland Young, Joan Blondell and Carole Landis.
VHS: $03339. $19.95.
Roy Del Ruth, USA, 1941, 87 mins.

Torch Song
Joan Crawford claws her way to the top of the Great White Way and likes the view. Broadway is her oyster until she meets a blind pianist who isn't exactly dazzled by her beauty and moves. With Michael Wilding, Gig Young, Harry Morgan, Marjorie Rambeau and Nancy Gates. Watch for Crawford doing a number in black face.
VHS: $11727. $19.98.
Laser: LD70698. $34.98.
Charles Walters, USA, 1953, 90 mins.

The Torch
Paulette Goddard and Gilbert Roland are featured in this tale of love and war. A Mexican revolutionary restores the rule of law to a small town, but the love of a young, aristocratic woman threatens to break his concentration.
VHS: $25702. $19.95.

Torpedo Run
Glenn Ford plays an obsessed U.S. submarine commander who is out to destroy a Japanese aircraft carrier that was indirectly responsible for the death of his wife and child. With Ernest Borgnine as his sensible second-in-command. Other crew members include Dean Jones, Fred Wayne and L.Q. Jones as Hash Benson. Originally in Cinemascope.
VHS: $12534. $19.98.
Joseph Penney, USA, 1958, 98 mins.

Tower of London
Many mistakenly assume this is a horror work, with the presence of Boris Karloff and Basil Rathbone, though it's actually an historical adaptation that recounts the relationship of the power-obsessed, ruthless Richard III (Rathbone) and his deranged executioner Mord (Karloff). With Barbara O'Neil, Ian Hunter and Vincent Price.
VHS: $17519. $14.98.
Rowland V. Lee, USA, 1939, 92 mins.

The Tracy and Hepburn Collection
Sexual dynamics and role playing infuse the gentle, witty spirit of these three works with Spencer Tracy and Katharine Hepburn, two directed by George Cukor: *Adam's Rib* (1949) and *Pat and Mike* (1952), and George Stevens's 1952 film, *Woman of the Year*.
VHS: $17306. $49.92.

Trader Horn
An Ivory trader, played by Harry Carey, must find the lost daughter of a missionary. Myriad dangers, including inhospitable tribal peoples, stand in the way. Shot largely in the jungles of Africa, this film represents one of the earliest action adventures to use real locations.
VHS: $21019. $19.98.
W.S. Van Dyke II, USA, 1931, 120 mins.

Train
Director John Frankenheimer delivers a World War II drama about an effort to stop retreating Nazis from leaving France with stolen art treasures in 1944. Burt Lancaster stars as a courageous French railroad inspector and member of the French Resistance who is determined to thwart the latest mission of Col. Von Waldheim (Paul Scofield). With Jeanne Moreau, Albert Remy, Wolfgang Preiss and Michel Simon as the stubborn engineer Papa Boule. No models or processed shots were used in the making of this exciting film in which several camera units were destroyed in crashes and explosions. Frankenheimer replaced original director Arthur Penn at Lancaster's request.
VHS: $16442. $19.98.
John Frankenheimer, USA/France/Italy, 1964, 140 mins.

Trapeze
This expressive work directed by Carol Reed (*The Third Man*) is centered around the high-wire Parisian circus. The drama unfolds in the professional and personal rivalry of a curious and intricate three-way love affair among Tony Curtis, Burt Lancaster and Gina Lollobrigida. Shot at the Cirque d'Hiver in Paris.
VHS: $17988. $19.98.
Laser: Letterboxed. LD72354. $34.98.
Carol Reed, USA, 1956, 106 mins.

Treasure Island
Wallace Beery stars as the dreaded pirate Long John Silver, whose love of a small boy, Jackie Cooper, takes the two on a mysterious journey. With John Barrymore as the wandering fugitive Billy Bones.
VHS: $04210. $24.95.
Victor Fleming, USA, 1934, 104 mins.

A Tree Grows in Brooklyn
Peggy Ann Gardner finds that life can be difficult if you are poor and live in Brooklyn at the turn of the century. Adapted from Betty Smith's novel, a fine drama with a splendid cast. With Dorothy McGuire, Joan Blondell, James Dunn, and Lloyd Nolan.
VHS: $05313. $14.98.
Laser: LD71378. $49.98.
Elia Kazan, USA, 1945, 128 mins.

Trilby
The first of many versions of the famous story by George Du Maurier about the mesmerizing Svengali and his beautiful victim. From a beautiful quality print.
VHS: $13274. $19.95.
Maurice Tourneur, USA, 1917, 59 mins.

Try and Get Me
Frank Lovejoy and Lloyd Bridges are two guys down on their luck when they decide to pull off a kidnapping to raise some money. Their victim dies by accident and they try to return to living a normal life. The community demands that the killers be caught and punished. With Richard Carlson, Dabbs Greer, Kathleen Ryan and Adele Jergens. Based on a factual case in California in 1933.
VHS: $07138. $19.95.
Cy Endfield, USA, 1950, 91 mins.

Tulsa
Oil woman Susan Hayward has to fight for her property while involved in wildcat drilling.
VHS: $05967. $19.95.
Stuart Heisler, USA, 1949, 90 mins.

Tundra
A "flying doctor" whose plane crashes near the Arctic Circle must cover over 400 miles with the help of only a knife and a lighter. Along the way spectacular scenery, unrivaled wild life footage and intimate scenes of Eskimo daily life turn this film into an unparalleled portrayal of this Northernmost region of the U.S.
VHS: $21609. $24.95.
Norman Dawn, USA, 1936, 72 mins.

Tuttles of Tahiti
Charles Laughton brings his inestimable charm to the role of Jonas Tuttle, the patriarch of a fun-loving family living in a tropical paradise. The Tuttles as a rule oppose working for a living on general principals and somehow everything turns out alright. With Jon Hall, Florence Bates, Peggy Blake and Mala. Based on the novel *No More Gas* by Charles Nordhoff and James Norman Hall, the authors of *Mutiny on The Bounty*.
VHS: $15469. $19.98.
Charles Vidor, USA, 1942, 91 mins.

Twelve Angry Men
A teenage boy is accused of killing his father, and between him and capital punishment stands just one man. A vivid, shocking courtroom drama with a powerful cast including Henry Fonda, Lee J. Cobb, E.G. Marshall and Jack Warden.
VHS: $11432. $29.95.
Laser: LD70478. $39.95.
Sidney Lumet, USA, 1957, 96 mins.

Two for the Road
Audrey Hepburn and Albert Finney star as a bickering couple travelling through France who stop to reminisce about their twelve years of marriage.
VHS: $18102. $19.98.
Stanley Donen, USA/Great Britain, 1967, 112 mins.

The Two Mrs. Carrolls
In one of his most off-beat film roles, Humphrey Bogart portrays a psychopathic artist who paints his wives as the Angel of Death, and then poisons them. Alexis Smith plays the iciest of femme fatales, and the first Mrs. Carroll to fall victim to his prey. Barbara Stanwyck co-stars as the second Mrs. Carroll, with Nigel Bruce as the bumbling doctor who both drinks and talks too much.
VHS: $16098. $19.98.
Peter Godfrey, USA, 1947, 99 mins.

Two Sisters
Betty Glickstein promises her dying mother that she will care for her younger sister, Sally. From the tender age of 13, Betty sacrifices all to fulfill her promise, even forsaking the prospect of her own family and future happiness. Yiddish with new English subtitles.
VHS: $23085. $72.00.
Ben K. Blake, USA, 1938, 82 mins.

Two Weeks in Another Town
Vincente Minnelli's imaginative translation of Irwin Shaw's novel about a Rome film production, using footage from Minnelli's *The Bad and the Beautiful*. With Kirk Douglas, Edward G. Robinson, Cyd Charisse and George Hamilton.
Laser: LD70733. $39.98.
Vincente Minnelli, USA, 1962, 107 mins.

Two Weeks with Love
But how much time for lunch? Long before *Dirty Dancing*, other families with eligible daughters found romance on vacations to the Catskills. Jane Powell and Debbie Reynolds are the Robinson sisters, Patti and Melba. With Ricardo Montalban and Carleton Carpenter as the men they attract and Louis Calhern and Ann Harding as the concerned parents. Songs include "Abba Dabba Honeymoon", "Row, Row, Row" and "By the Light of the Silvery Moon".
VHS: $13307. $19.98.
Roy Rowland, USA, 1950, 92 mins.

Tycoon
John Wayne portrays an American engineer attempting to build a railroad through the Andes mountains to the coast. Romantic complications ensue when he falls in love with Senorita Laraine Day.
VHS: $03245. $19.95.
Richard Wallace, USA, 127 mins.

U-Boat Prisoner
An American sailor is captured by a Nazi U-Boat during World War II. This gripping tale of imprisonment during war time has the gritty feel of its time. The rousing spirit that helped the country endure the ravages of this war are convincingly portrayed.
VHS: $20635. $19.95.
Lew Landers, USA, 1944, 65 mins.

The Ugly American
Marlon Brando plays Harrison Carter MacWhite, the U.S. Ambassador to Sarkhan, a mythical Southeast Asian country fraught with factional disputes and growing Communist menace. His good intentions only increase the turmoil. Based on the book by Lederer and Burdick.
VHS: $03679. $59.95.
George H. Englund, USA, 1962, 120 mins.

Ultimate Oz (Collector's Edition)
This commemorative, two-video edition offers a digitally remastered, visually restored version of Victor Fleming's 1939 classic, *The Wizard of Oz*, adapted from Frank Baum's classic tale about the Kansas girl (Judy Garland) who is projected into a surreal landscape of magical characters. The film is complemented by a behind-the-scenes documentary, *The Wonderful Wizard of Oz: The Making of a Movie Classic*, that combines interviews, archival footage, outtakes, a reproduction of the original script, the theatrical trailer and the notes. The documentary, directed by Jack Haley, Jr., features interviews with Ray Bolger, Garland, Jack Haley, Margaret Hamilton, King Vidor and Robert Young.
VHS: $19475. $99.98.
Laser: LD71920. $99.98.
Victor Fleming, USA, 1939, 52 mins.

Ulysses
Joseph Strick directed this daring stream-of-consciousness adaptation of James Joyce's great novel which follows Leopold Bloom through the streets and brothels of turn-of-the-century Dublin. The film culminates in the torrentially earthy monologue of his wife Molly. The intimacy of Joyce's language was without precedent in literature, and its flashbacks, dream episodes, sounds and visual montages translate freely into the language of the cinema. "Joyce's great novel becomes a movie masterpiece," said *Life Magazine*.
VHS: $09552. $29.95.
Joseph Strick, USA, 1967, 120 mins.

Uncertain Glory
Errol Flynn plays an escaped criminal whose fate changes at the hands of the Nazis. He is aboard a Paris-bound train that is suddenly derailed. Hostages are taken and amid the hostility Flynn's character must decide exactly what kind of man he is, given the life and death circumstances.
VHS: $22899. $19.98.
Raoul Walsh, USA, 1944, 102 mins.

Uncle Tom's Cabin
An adaptation of Harriet Beecher Stowe's controversial novel about social and racial conditions and black enfranchisement in the pre-Civil War South. When Abraham Lincoln met Stowe, he reportedly told her, "So, you're the little lady who started this big war." With Herbert Lom as the nefarious Simon Legree.
VHS: $18836. $19.95.
Geza von Radvanyi, Fr./Germ./Yugo./It., 1969, 113 mins.

The Undefeated
John Wayne and Rock Hudson star as Yankee and Rebel commanders learning to trust each other as they start new lives immediately after the Civil War. With beautiful views of the Rio Grande.
VHS: $15985. $14.98.
Laser: LD72221. $59.98.
Andrew V. McLaglen, USA, 1969, 119 mins.

Undercurrent
Departing from her more usual, lighthearted roles, Katharine Hepburn "gives a resounding portrayal" (*New York Herald Tribune*) as the unsuspecting wife of a man driven to madness by his thirst for power. A moody suspense thriller with Robert Taylor, Jayne Meadows (in her screen debut) and a young Robert Mitchum.
VHS: $15025. $19.98.
Vincente Minnelli, USA, 1946, 126 mins.

Underwater
Curvaceous Jane Russell and her husband (Richard Egan) embark on an adventurous hunt for sunken treasure in the Caribbean.
VHS: $10660. $19.98.
John Sturges, USA, 1955, 100 mins.

Underworld Story
The story of a reporter who joins the staff of a small town newspaper and begins to uncover corruption. Starring Gale Storm and Herbert Marshall.
VHS: $13610. $19.98.
Cy Endfield, USA, 1950, 90 mins.

The Unholy Three
A remake of the film released five year previously, *The Unholy Three* spins a tale of three circus freaks who turn to murderous crimes. Members of the original cast include Harry Earles and Lon Chaney, who died before the release of this, his only talking role. With Lila Lee, Ivan Linow, Elliott Nugent and John Miljan.
VHS: S16171. $29.95.
Jack Conway, USA, 1930, 74 mins.

Until They Sail
Director Robert Wise and author James Michener paint an evocative and unsettling portrait of World War II New Zealand, with Paul Newman as an American soldier who gets involved in a murder case, insinuating himself into the lives of four sisters—Jean Simmons, Joan Fontaine, Piper Laurie and Sandra Dee.
VHS: S17991. $19.98.
Robert Wise, USA, 1957, 95 mins.

Up the Down Staircase
Academy Award winner Sandy Dennis stars in this compelling drama as a new teacher at an inner city school. Based on the bestseller by Bel Kaufman, it follows this teacher's struggle to make a difference against great odds. Jean Stapleton also makes an appearance.
VHS: S21345. $29.99.
Robert Mulligan, USA, 1967, 124 mins.

Uptown New York
Jack Oakie proves himself to be a dramatic actor of considerable effectiveness as Eddie Doyle, a man whose wife marries him on the rebound from an affair with another man.
VHS: S13848. $19.95.
Victor Schertzinger, USA, 1932, 81 mins.

The Valley of Decision
Set in the 1870's in Pittsburgh, this love story follows the trouble experienced by a young couple from opposite sides of the social spectrum. Gregory Peck is a mill owner who loves the family's maid, Greer Garson. It's adapted from Marcia Davenport's novel and includes Lionel Barrymore and Dean Stockwell.
VHS: S21172. $19.98.
Tay Garnett, USA, 1945, 111 mins.

Vanity Fair
Myrna Loy stars as Becky Sharp in this modern dance version of the Thackeray novel. Billy Bevan and Montagu Love also star.
VHS: S07065. $39.95.
Chester M. Franklin, USA, 1932, 80 mins.

Velvet Touch
Rosalind Russell plays the stage actress who commits the perfect crime. A solid cast including Claire Trevor and Sydney Greenstreet highlights this tight mystery. With an outstanding script by Leo Rosten.
VHS: S09361. $19.98.
John Gage, USA, 1948, 97 mins.

Vikings
Filmed on location in Norway, this rousing saga tells the story of a proud warrior and a stubborn slave who have the same father but completely opposite ways of approaching life. Kirk Douglas and Tony Curtis are the battling half-siblings fighting over the favors of kidnapped English princess Janet Leigh. With James Donald, Frank Thring and Ernest Borgnine as Ragnar, viking lord and wolf bait. Based on the novel by Edison Marshall.
VHS: S12237. $19.95.
Laser: Letterboxed. LD72336. $34.98.
Richard Fleischer, USA, 1958, 114 mins.

The Virgin Queen
Bette Davis is Queen Elizabeth I, jealously in love with Sir Walter Raleigh (Richard Todd) with Joan Collins her rival. Notable for a flamboyant performance by Davis.
VHS: S05916. $19.98.
Henry Koster, USA, 1955, 92 mins.

Viva Villa!
Ben Hecht wrote this biography of the revolutionary Mexican bandit Pancho Villa, whose guerrilla armies ended the bloody suppression of the governing elite. Wallace Beery plays Villa. With Leo Carrillo, Fay Wray and Donald Cook.
VHS: S18510. $19.98.
Laser: LD72159. $34.98.
Jack Conway, USA, 1934, 115 mins.

Von Ryan's Express
Frank Sinatra and Trevor Howard star in this suspenseful drama about a daring mass escape from a POW camp in World War II Italy. This straightforward adventure boasts a strong cast and impressive action sequences.
VHS: S14140. $19.98.
Mark Robson, USA, 1965, 117 mins.

Wait Until Dark
Audrey Hepburn plays a blind woman who is left alone in her apartment, terrorized by a psychotic (Alan Arkin) and a group of men looking for a heroin stash they are sure in there. A tense thriller, based on Frederick Knott's Broadway play.
Laser: LD72448. $34.98.
Terence Young, USA, 1967, 108 mins.

Wake Island
Award-winning Hollywood account of the Battle for Wake Island during World War II in which outnumbered Marines fought Japanese forces for over two weeks. With Brian Donlevy, Robert Preston and William Bendix.
VHS: S06390. $19.95.
John Farrow, USA, 1942, 88 mins.

Wake of the Bounty
Errol Flynn's first film! A rollicking, swashbuckler of an adventure which has never before been available on video. USA, 1935.
VHS: S15285. $24.95.

Wake of the Red Witch
John Wayne finds high adventure, romance and danger in the South Seas as Captain Ralls. Gail Russell, Adele Mara and Gig Young are on Wayne's side. This is the movie where he wrestles the giant octopus. B&W.
VHS: S04240. $19.95.
Edward Ludwig, USA, 1948, 106 mins.

Walk in the Sun
One of the best Hollywood dramas of men at war; follows American infantrymen pursuing objective in Italy during World War II. With Dana Andrews, Richard Conte and Lloyd Bridges.
VHS: S03005. $39.95.
Laser: CLV. LD70258. $39.95.
Lewis Milestone, USA, 1945, 118 mins.

Walk Softly, Stranger
Joseph Cotten takes on an unusual role as a two-timing crook laying low in a small Ohio town. Alida Valli, Jack Paar also star.
VHS: S12020. $19.98.
Robert Stevenson, USA, 1950, 81 mins.

War and Peace
This classic version of the Leo Tolstoy epic masterpiece following a Russian family at the time of Napoleon's invasion stars Audrey Hepburn, Henry Fonda, Mel Ferrer, John Mills, and is a mammoth, sumptuous production.
VHS: S01427. $29.95.
King Vidor, USA, 1956, 208 mins.

War of the Wildcats
This is the movie where the Indians ask John Wayne to take over the oil lease on their tribal land in Oklahoma so that the evil Albert Dekker won't steal the whole operation. The Duke takes on the extra responsibility and tries to win the girl as well. With Martha Scott and Gabby Hayes.
VHS: S04890. $19.95.
Albert S. Rogell, USA, 1943, 102 mins.

Watch on the Rhine
Outstanding performances by Paul Dukas, Bette Davis, Lucille Watson distinguish this adaptation of the famous Lillian Hellman play about a German refugee and his family, who are pursued by Nazi agents in Washington.
VHS: S13397. $19.98.
Herman Shumlin, USA, 1943, 114 mins.

Watch the Birdie
Red Skelton plays three roles (father, son, grandfather) in this madcap adventure involving three beautiful women and two suave crooks. Co-starring Ann Miller.
VHS: S15249. $19.98.
Jack Donohue, USA, 1950, 71 mins.

Waterloo Bridge
Robert Taylor is the American soldier and Vivien Leigh the dancer who meet in war-torn London and fall in love in this well-acted, touching romance. Based on the play by Robert Sherwood.
VHS: S02625. $19.98.
Mervyn LeRoy, USA, 1940, 103 mins.

Way Back Home
Based on a radio serial, this RKO drama deals with the problems of a Maine preacher in a funny depiction of sinister deeds in a small town. With Bette Davis.
VHS: S13384. $19.98.
William A. Seiter, USA, 1932, 81 mins.

We're No Angels
Humphrey Bogart, Peter Ustinov and Aldo Ray star as three escaped convicts from Devil's Island, who come to the aid of a shopkeeper and his family.
VHS: S04322. $19.95.
Michael Curtiz, USA, 1955, 106 mins.

We're Not Dressing
When Bing is a shipwrecked sailor on a deserted island you can be sure plenty of other entertainers will show up to keep him company. Carole Lombard plays the romantic interest, with George Burns and Gracie Allen along as expeditionists, while Ethel Merman is the spurned suitor of a harried Bing Crosby.
VHS: S21201. $14.98.
Norman Taurog, USA, 1934, 77 mins.

The Wedding Night
New York writer Gary Cooper falls in love with a New England farm girl (Anna Sten) in this touching, sentimental romance which also stars Ralph Bellamy and Walter Brennan.
VHS: S23440. $19.98.
King Vidor, USA, 1953, 84 mins.

Weekend at the Waldorf
A glossy American remake of *Grand Hotel*, this episodic collection of vignettes mixes drawing room comedy with slapstick farce. Lana Turner and Ginger Rodgers are pursued by Van Johnson and Walter Pidgeon. With Edward Arnold, Phyllis Thaxter and Keenan Wynn.
VHS: S18664. $19.98.
Robert Z. Leonard, USA, 1945, 130 mins.

Well
Music by Dmitri Tiomkin provides a superb background to this tension-filled drama. Incisive study of crowd psychology, focusing on the effects of townspeople when a black child falls into a deep well. Starring Harry Morgan, Barry Kelley and Christine Larson.
VHS: S13013. $19.95.
Leo Popkin, USA, 1951, 85 mins.

The West Point Story
Doris Day, Gordon MacRae and James Cagney form an unholy union to stage an ambitious musical at West Point. With music and lyrics by Jule Styne and Sammy Cahn. With Gene Nelson and Alan Hale, Jr.
VHS: S18463. $59.99.
Roy Del Ruth, USA, 1950, 107 mins.

When Gangland Strikes
Public Prosecutor Luke Ellis wants to put Mobster Duke Martella behind bars. The chances for conviction dim when Martella finds something scandalous in the crime fighter's past. A hard-boiled tale of a man driven to see justice done, one way or the other. With Raymond Greenleaf, Marie Millar, Anthony Caruso and John Hudson. The remake of *Main Street Lawyer* (1939). B&W.
VHS: S11400. $19.95.
R.G. Springsteen, USA, 1956, 70 mins.

When Ladies Meet
Sophisticated author Joan Crawford is romantically drawn to suave publisher Herbert Marshall even though the cad is a married man. Young hunk Robert Taylor tries to woo her anyway. With Spring Byington, Florence Shirley and Greer Garson. Anita Loos co-wrote the screenplay.
VHS: S16456. $19.98.
Robert Z. Leonard, USA, 1941, 105 mins.

When's Your Birthday?
Astrology mixes with prizefighting in this comedy starring Joe E. Brown as a boxer who can only win when the stars are in the proper conjunction. His star studies also help pick winning horses at the track. With Edgar Kennedy, Marian Marsh and Fred Keating.
VHS: S10101. $29.95.
Harry Beaumont, USA, 1937, 76 mins.

Where Eagles Dare
Clint Eastwood and Richard Burton star in this breakneck paced World War II thriller. An American general is a prisoner of the Nazis. An elite squad of Allied soldiers is sent to free him from the mountain stronghold where he is being kept. Few films can match this movie's sure sense of tension and suspense. Based on Alistair MacClean's acclaimed novel.
VHS: S27606. $14.95.
Brian G. Hutton, USA, 1968, 158 mins.

Where Love Has Gone
A florid melodrama loosely based on the notorious Lana Turner affair about a young woman charged with killing her mother's abusive and tyrannical boyfriend. Joey Heatherton is the young woman; Susan Hayward plays her mother. Greer Garson is a trusting probation officer. Bette Davis camps it up as the matriarchal leader. Adapted from the novel by Harold Robbins.
VHS: S19026. $14.95.
Edward Dmytryk, USA, 1964, 114 mins.

Whistle Stop
Desperation turns passion's flame into deadly obsession when one man tries to piece back together the fragments of his shattered dreams. Ava Gardner and George Raft star.
VHS: S14753. $19.95.
Leonide Moguy, USA, 1946, 85 mins.

White Cargo
While on an expedition, Walter Pidgeon falls madly in love with a beautiful, sarong-clad girl played by Hedy Lamarr. Survival is a constant struggle at the remote jungle plantation where they meet. This steamy and exotic tale brings melodrama to the tropics.
VHS: S21020. $19.98.
Richard Thorpe, USA, 1942, 90 mins.

The White Cliffs of Dover
A visual interpretation of Alice Duer Miller's poem about an Englishman who seduces a beautiful young American woman, conceives a child and dies in combat during the First World War. Their child, a young man, enters the army on the eve of the Second World War. With Irene Dunne, Roddy McDowall, Van Johnson and Dame May Whitty. "A glorious emotional experience in the fine tradition of romantic theatre" (*Hollywood Reporter*).
VHS: S18511. $19.98.
Clarence Brown, USA, 1944, 126 mins.

White Heat
James Cagney gives a masterful performance as the mentally unhinged gangster Cody Jarrett. Edmond O'Brien is the undercover cop who infiltrates the gang, which includes Steve Cochran, Fred Clark, and Virginia Mayo as Cody's unfaithful wife. This is the movie where Cagney learns that bullets and gasoline storage tanks don't mix. A terrific film in black and white. As the ads say, "Cagney is Red Hot in White Heat."
VHS: S09852. $19.95.
Laser: LD70190. $34.98.
Raoul Walsh, USA, 1949, 114 mins.

White Tower
Glenn Ford, Claude Rains, Alida Valli star in this mountaineering drama set in the Alps. Good action sequences.
VHS: S12016. $19.98.
Ted Tetzlaff, USA, 1950, 98 mins.

Wife vs. Secretary
Clark Gable, Jean Harlow and Myrna Loy are drawn into a threatening love triangle when a wife's jealousies overpower her reason. Jimmy Stewart shines in an early supporting role as secretary Harlow's frustrated boyfriend.
VHS: S15122. $19.98.
Clarence Brown, USA, 1936, 88 mins.

The Wild Bunch
When newlywed George Burrel is left alone with his wife's three teenagers, he gains their love and respect through a comedy of errors. As a parent George has no experience, all he can offer is something that has been missing since their father died: guidance. With George Boyer and Natalie Wood. *Not to be confused with the Sam Peckinpah Western.*
VHS: S16748. $14.95.
William A. Seiter, USA, 1955, 30 mins.

The Wild One
Marlon Brando is Johnny, the leader of a vicious biker gang which invades a small, sleepy California town. The leather-jacketed biker seems bent on destruction until he falls for Kathie, a "good girl," whose father happens to be a cop.
VHS: Out of print. For rental only.
Laser: Remastered, 2 sides, side 2 CAV. LD74478. $34.95.
Laslo Benedek, USA, 1954, 79 mins.

Wilson
Winner of five Oscars, this is the brilliant biography of the World War I era President whose League of Nations idea became an obsession. With Alexander Knox, Charles Coburn and Geraldine Fitzgerald. .
VHS: S16099. $19.98.
Henry King, USA, 1944, 145 mins.

The Window
No one believes a highly imaginative boy when he claims to have seen his neighbors commit a brutal murder, in this taut thriller charged with suspense. Based on a story by Cornell Woolrich, with Bobby Driscoll, Barbara Hale and Arthur Kennedy.
VHS: S05664. $19.98.
Ted Tetzlaff, USA, 1949, 64 mins.

Wing and a Prayer
Don Ameche and Dana Andrews star in this outstanding drama about newly-trained pilots aboard a Pacific-based aircraft carrier in the early days of the war. Featuring actual combat footage.
VHS: S15197. $14.98.
Henry Hathaway, USA, 1944, 97 mins.

Winning
Winning is everything for Paul Newman, a determined car racer. Nothing can get in his way, not Joanne Woodward, and certainly not his rival Robert Wagner. This film brings all the excitement and drama of professional racing to the screen.
VHS: S21278. $14.98.
James Goldstone, USA, 1969, 123 mins.

The Winning Team
Ronald Reagan and Doris Day catch baseball fever in this romantic true story. A telephone linesman turns out to become Hall of Fame pitcher Grover Cleveland.
VHS: S15990. $19.98.
Lewis Seiler, USA, 1952, 98 mins.

Winter Meeting
Bretaigne Windust's stylish melodrama about a disillusioned poet (Bette Davis) who falls for a dark, embittered war hero (Jim Davis), setting in motion a comically romantic love triangle and hidden revelations. With Janis Paige, John Hoyt and Florence Bates.
VHS: S17337. $19.98.
Bretaigne Windust, USA, 1948, 105 mins.

Wintertime
Sonja Henie plays a world-champion figure skater whose charisma and marquee value help stave off the closing of an eccentric hotel owned and operated by her uncle. Music by the Woody Herman Orchestra. With Jack Oakie, Cesar Romero, Carole Landis and Cornel Wilde.
VHS: S20259. $19.98.
John Brahm, USA, 1943, 82 mins.

Without Love
In Hepburn and Tracy's third film together, Hepburn plays a Washington D.C. widow who allows scientist Tracy to set up a laboratory in her basement to conduct secret war-time experiments. Both disillusioned with love, they agree to a marriage strictly for convenience. But can romance be far behind? A witty and winning farce. Lucille Ball co-stars as Hepburn's wise-cracking friend.
VHS: S15023. $19.98.
Laser: Chapter search. Includes original theatrical trailer. LD71665. $34.98.
Harold S. Bucquet, USA, 1945, 103 mins.

The Witness
Accused of killing a bank guard and stealing $150,000, Frank Dana's only hope of avoiding death row relies on the testimony of a beautiful mystery woman. Wearing the judge's patience thin with his continued delays, lawyer Mike Donnegan's search for the key witness ends when she seeks him out and gives a surprising testimony. Stars Charles Bronson and Dick Powell.
VHS: S16742. $14.95.
Robert Aldrich, USA, 1953, 30 mins.

Wives Under Suspicion
James Whale's own remake of his *Kiss before the Mirror*, based on the novel by Ladislaus Fodor. A fine cast includes Warren William, Gail Patrick, Ralph Morgan.
VHS: S08425. $29.95.
James Whale, USA, 1938, 75 mins.

Wizard of Oz
Judy Garland, Ray Bolger, Jack Haley, Bert Lahr, Frank Morgan, Margaret Hamilton, Billie Burke and Toto in the land of Oz, in MGM's great, Technicolor fantasy where Judy follows the Yellow Brick Road.
VHS: S09609. $24.95.
Laser: CLV, MGM. LD70709. $24.98.
Laser: CAV, Criterion. LD71215. $99.95.
Victor Fleming, USA, 1939, 101 mins.

Wolf Call
A pleasing, diverting adventure yarn adapted from the Jack London novel. Our suave John Carroll as a frivolous and wealthy playboy who arrives in Radium City with his trusty, heroic dog Smoky to determine the value of his father's pitchblende mine. Things become complicated as he must contend with a conniving mine manager and his cronies—who represent those who are aware of the property's true value.
VHS: S13603. $24.95.
George Waggner, USA, 1939, 60 mins.

World Gone Mad
Tall ships, rolling seas, buried treasures and treachery are all part of this old-fashioned pirate adventure starring Charles Laughton as Captain Kidd. With John Carradine, Randolph Scott and Reginald Owen. 1939, 85 mins.
VHS: S03001. $39.95.

The Wreck of the Mary Deare
A rousing tale of mutiny, disorder and failed reputation. When the captain of the ship is charged with negligence, a sympathetic salvage boat skipper offers aid and comfort. With Gary Cooper, Charlton Heston and Michael Redgrave.
VHS: S17992. $19.98.
Laser: LD72161. $34.98.
Michael Anderson, USA/Great Britain, 1959, 100 mins.

A Yank in the RAF
Tyrone Power, Betty Grable, and actual air combat footage spark this romantic drama about a cocky American flier who joins the RAF to be near the woman he loves. With upbeat musical numbers, this 1941 Oscar-nominee for Special Effects was one of the most popular war movies of its day.
VHS: S14137. $19.98.
Henry King, USA, 1941, 98 mins.

Yellowneck
Lin McCarthy and Bill Mason are the individuals who star in this fascinating story about a group of Civil War deserters who end up stranded in the Florida Everglades and must face starvation and the elements in their efforts to survive. An insightful drama.
VHS: S14666. $29.95.
Robert Hossman, USA, 1955, 83 mins.

You Can't Fool Your Wife
Lucille Ball is a wife separated from her husband by a meddling mother in-law. They meet again at a bachelor, or rather, at a masked party.
VHS: S10640. $19.98.
Ray McCarey, USA, 1940, 69 mins.

Young Bess
In this lavish historical costume drama a young Elizabeth I is played by Jean Simmons, while her real-life husband, Stewart Granger, plays her amorous would-be lover. Charles Laughton and Deborah Kerr co-star. Sparks fly in this tempestuous tale.
VHS: S21169. $19.98.
George Sidney, USA, 1953, 112 mins.

Young Lions
One of the best of the World War II studies, based on a novel by Irwin Shaw, features Marlon Brando as a German officer, and Montgomery Clift as an American soldier. With Dean Martin and Hope Lange.
VHS: S03499. $19.98.
Laser: LD71224. $69.98.
Edward Dmytryk, USA, 1958, 167 mins.

Young Man with a Horn
Kirk Douglas stars in this story based on the life of jazzman Bix Beiderbecke, with Harry James dubbing in the trumpet playing. With Hoagy Carmichael, Lauren Bacall and Doris Day.
VHS: S03432. $19.98.
Laser: LD70720. $34.98.
Michael Curtiz, USA, 1950, 112 mins.

Young Tom Edison
An earnest essay about the American dream in the story of Tom Edison (Mickey Rooney), the greatest American inventor of his era. Rooney's self-effacement, charm and understatement creates a vivid biographical portrait of Edison's early years. With Fay Bainter, George Bancroft, Virginia Weidler and Eugene Pallette.
VHS: S19468. $19.98.
Norman Taurog, USA, 1940, 82 mins.

silent american CINEMA

20,000 Leagues Under the Sea
For the first time on video, the 1916 film version of the Jules Verne classic, newly remastered from an archive print. This landmark film was 1½ years in the making, and was one of the first great special effects spectaculars of the early cinema. The thrilling story of the renegade Captain Nemo and the sea monster he discovers from the submarine Nautilus is as impressive today as it was upon its initial release 75 years ago.
VHS: S15039. $29.95.
Stuart Paton, USA, 1916, 105 mins.

Adventures of Hairbreadth Harry
These rare silent films are fun-filled, short comedy spoofs of the early silent melodramas, produced by Chaplin imitator Billy West. The fast-paced romps are guaranteed to keep you laughing. Includes *Sawdust Baby, Fearless Harry* and *Rudolph's Revenge*. With orchestral music soundtrack. USA, 65 mins.
VHS: S15230. $19.95.

American Aristocracy
Douglas Fairbanks stars in this silent action comedy involving speeding cars, seaplanes and motor cruises.
VHS: S08886. $24.95.
Lloyd Ingraham, USA, 1917, 52 mins.

American Pluck
George Walsh, Wanda Hawley, Sidney De Grey, Frank Leigh, Leo White star.
VHS: S07217. $19.95.
Richard Stanton, USA, 1925, 64 mins.

Anna Christie
Adaptation of Eugene O'Neill's play about a world-weary prostitute's first encounter with her father, a sentimental old seaman. Blanche Sweet in the title role, this version was re-edited in the USSR.
VHS: S04810. $34.95.
John Griffith Wray, USA, 1923, 75 mins.

Annapolis
An early Pathe production about two Navy men who fall for the same girl. Featuring Johnny Mack Brown, Hugh Allan, Jeanette Loff and Maurice Ryan.
VHS: S07235. $19.95.
Christy Cabanne, USA, 1928, 63 mins.

April Fool
An out-of-work pants-presser makes a fortune in the umbrella business and has to give it all up for the happiness of his daughter. One of Baby Peggy Montgomery's few surviving silent films, it includes a piano score. Mary Alden, Raymond Keane and Snitz Edwards also star.
VHS: S22431. $19.95.
Nat Ross, USA, 1926, 63 mins.

Are Parents People?
Betty Bronson, Florence Vidor, Adolphe Menjou and Lawrence Gray star in this Famous Players-Lasky production. Silent with music track.
VHS: S07237. $19.95.
Malcolm St. Clair, USA, 1925, 63 mins.

Babes in the Woods
This intriguing silent film contains a story within a story. A number of fairy tales are joined to yield a lesson for a woman pining after her brother-in-law. This film includes a charming rendition of the *Hansel and Gretel* tale. Francis Parker and Virginia Lee Corbin star along with a cast of children who act out the fairy tales.
VHS: S23823. $24.95.
Charles Franklin, USA, 1917, 44 mins.

The Back Trail
Hoxie was one of the silent screen's most popular cowboy stars, who could ride and fight with the best of them. In this film he is a war veteran afflicted by amnesia. He is induced to break the law and take over his sister's estate, but his memory returns in time for him to foil the real crooks.
VHS: S18903. $19.95.
Clifford Smith, USA, 1924

Barbara Frietchie
Florence Vidor and Edmund Lowe star in what was originally described as "the drama of glorious American womanhood." Silent with music track.
VHS: S07251. $24.95.

Barbarian
The only surviving film of Monroe Salisbury. The drama is set in the north woods, and the film also stars Jane Novak. Decomposition of nitrate original in some scenes. USA, 1921, 52 mins.
VHS: S08854. $19.95.

The Bat
One of the great silent horror films. A maniacal killer dressed in a weird bat-like costume terrorizes a group of people in a shuddery, spooky old house riddled with secret passageways. The use of miniatures and the overall cinematography is stunning for its day.
VHS: S15365. $29.95.
Roland West, USA, 1926, 81 mins.

Battling Bunyon
Wesley Barry, Molly Malone, Frank Campeau, Harry Mann and Chester Conklin star.
VHS: S07239. $19.95.
Paul Hurst, USA, 1925, 63 mins.

Battling Orioles
Glenn Tryon, Blanche Megaffey, Noah Young, Sam Lufkin, Robert Page star.
VHS: S07262. $19.95.
Ted Wilde/Fred Guiol, USA, 1924, 60 mins.

Beast of Babylon Against the Son of Hercules
Gordon Scott stars in this action film from the silent era. It has a wealth of imaginative detail that compensates for its lack of historical accuracy. 98 mins.
VHS: S23150. $24.95.

Beau Brummel
John Barrymore stars in this early silent version of the English dandy and ladies' man.
VHS: S02584. $34.95.
Harry Beaumont, USA, 1924, 80 mins.

Beau Ravel
Thomas Ince produced this story of aged love starring Lewis Stone, Florence Vidor, Lloyd Hughes and William Conklin. Jitter in two short parts of the film.
VHS: S08858. $24.95.
John Griffith Wray, USA, 1921, 70 mins.

Beggars of Life
The curious and melodramatic adventures of an everyday hobo. This rarely seen Wellman film stars Richard Arlen, Wallace Beery and young Louise Brooks in her finest early role outside of Hawks' *A Girl in Every Port*.
VHS: S15287. $49.95.
William Wellman, USA, 1928, 80 mins.

Behind the Front
Wallace Beery and Raymond Hatton star in this drama which was the third highest grossing film of 1926.
VHS: S08847. $24.95.
Edward A. Sutherland, USA, 1926, 65 mins.

The Bellhop/The Noon Whistle
These two comic shorts are classics from the silent era. The first is directed by Larry Semon and Norman Taurog, and stars Semon opposite Oliver Hardy. Stan Laurel then gets his chance to amuse in *The Noon Whistle*.
VHS: S26689. $19.95.

The Bells
Boris Karloff had the best role of his silent film career as a sideshow hypnotist who must use the full power of his extraordinary skills to extract a murderer's confession. Lionel Barrymore is the guilty party. With Lola Todd and Gustav von Seyffertitz.
VHS: S04084. $29.95.
James Young, USA, 1926, 7 reels

Beloved Rogue
A beautiful silent epic romance of medieval France, notable for its art direction and massive sets. With John Barrymore, Conrad Veidt, Marceline Day.
VHS: S05978. $29.95.
Laser: LD70768. $39.95.
Alan Crosland, USA, 1927, 110 mins.

Ben Hur
Ramon Novarro is the title character in the silent version known for its classic chariot race. Novarro races against Francis X. Bushman who plays his sworn enemy Messala. Truly a thrilling race on a colossal set staged by second unit director Reaves Eason. Based on the novel by Lew Wallace, the film also has a sea battle, lepers and a meeting with Jesus Christ.
VHS: S07791. $29.95.
Laser: LD70525. $39.98.
Fred Niblo, USA, 1927, 116 mins.

Betsy Ross
This great historical silent film has a cast that includes Alice Brady, John Bowers, Lillian Cook, Victor Kennard, Eugenie Woodward and many others. It's based on the intriguing story of Quaker Betsy Griscom, who married John Ross and helped fashion the American flag. Orchestral score.
VHS: S22434. $19.95.
Travers Vale, USA, 1919, 58 mins.

Big Parade
John Gilbert learns that war is not a grand and glorious adventure when he barely survives the trenches of World War I. Produced and directed by King Vidor. With Renee Adoree as the French girl who Gilbert teaches how to chew gum. Also Karl Dane, Hobart Bosworth and Tom O'Brien as Bull. A realistic look at modern warfare.
VHS: S07792. $29.95.
Laser: LD70130. $39.98.
King Vidor, USA, 1925, 126 mins.

Bill Fields and Will Rogers
W.C. Fields stars in his first film as a suitor for the affections of a good-looking woman who is willing to settle his difference with a rival over a friendly game of pool. *Pool Sharks* (1915) recreated his famous vaudeville routine. The *Ropin' Fool* features Will Rogers slipping a lasso over anyone or thing within range. USA/Great Britain, 1915-21, 48 mins.
VHS: S05447. $24.95.

The Black Pirate
Now you can enjoy this Douglas Fairbanks, Sr. swashbuckler in the two-strip color process as it was originally shot. Taken from a rare French print, all of the titles have been replaced in English from the U.S. release. This is a true classic from the silent era and a must for every collection. Orchestra scored.
VHS: S05709. $24.95.
Albert Parker, USA, 1926, 104 mins.

Blood and Sand
In one of his most famous roles, Rudolph Valentino portrays a poor boy who works his way up to becoming a famous matador. In the process he marries his childhood sweetheart but falls into the clutches of a beautiful society woman (Nita Naldi). Shining through gloriously in every shot of the film is the astonishing grace that made Valentino one of the most popular stars in the history of the cinema. Also included is a rare Valentino short. Piano score.
VHS: S00147. $29.95.
Fred Niblo, USA, 1922, 87 mins.

Blood and Steel
William Desmond is out to destroy the railroad of his father's enemy in this silent railroad stunt drama.
VHS: S08876. $24.95.
J.P. McGowan, USA, 1925, 65 mins.

Blot
A carefully observed depiction of social values under pressure in small-town America, the story is of a teacher's wife who steals a chicken for her child.
VHS: S03710. $29.95.
Lois Weber, USA, 1921, 79 mins.

Brass
Monte Blue, Marie Prevost, Harry Myers, Irene Rich, Frank Keenan star.
VHS: S07230. $19.95.
Sidney Franklin, USA, 1923, 60 mins.

Braveheart
Silent film star Rod La Rocque is an Indian brave sent East to study law so that he can defend the tribe's fishing rights. At college, Braveheart becomes an outstanding scholar and an all-American football player. Trouble brews when Braveheart is accused of selling game signals to the opposing team. Orchestra score.
VHS: S22012. $19.95.
Alan Hale, USA, 1925, 62 mins.

Broken Hearts of Broadway
Colleen Moore, John Walker, Alice Lake, Tully Marshall, Kate Price star.
VHS: S07223. $24.95.
Irving Cummings, USA, 1923, 85 mins.

Broken Mask
Cullen Landis, Barbara Bedford, Wheeler Oakman star. Silent with music track.
VHS: S07225. $19.95.
James P. Hogan, USA, 1928, 60 mins.

Bronco Billy Anderson
Four short films from the silent Bronco Billy series: *The Making of Bronco Billy, Bronco Billy's Sentence, The Prisoner, Naked Hands*. 62 mins.
VHS: S08874. $24.95.

Burn 'em Up Barnes
With Johnny Hines, Edmund Breese, George Fawcett, Betty Carpenter. Produced by Mastodon Films, USA, 1921, 70 mins.
VHS: S07257. $24.95.

Burning Daylight
Milton Sills, Doris Kenyon, Arthur Stone and "Big Boy" Williams are just some of the silent stars featured in this gripping melodrama. It's based on Jack London's story of an Alaskan real estate mogul who loses everything to a group of San Francisco investment sharks. Silent, with orchestra score.
VHS: S26968. $24.95.
Richard A. Rowland, USA, 1928, 72 mins.

The Busher
Charles Ray stars. USA, 1918, 60 mins.
VHS: S07241. $19.95.

California in '49
Jacques Jaccard and Ben Wilson directed the feature version of this 15-chapter serial, Days of '49, starring Neva Gerber and Edmund Cobb. USA, 1925, 70 mins.
VHS: S08865. $24.95.

California Straight Ahead
A hilarious trip to California is the subject of this early comedy starring Reginald Denny, Gertrude Olmsted and Tom Wilson.
VHS: S07263. $24.95.
Harry Pollard, USA, 1925, 90 mins.

The Call of the Wilderness
Sandow the dog was one of the silent screen's greatest stars. In this nail-biting melodrama he helps his master fight off competing homesteaders. It's a film that brings the phrase "man's best friend" alive. 58 mins.
VHS: S24001. $19.95.

Camille
Rudolph Valentino is at his prime in this silent classic. It's based on a tale that has inspired stage plays, operas and other films. A dying courtesan falls for an innocent young man. Despite her life of ill repute, their love holds the promise of a better life, if only it weren't for that pesky cough.
VHS: S25696. $19.95.
Fred Niblo, USA, 1921, 55 mins.

Campus Nights
Albert Kelly, Raymond McKee, Shirley Palmer, Marie Quillen, Jean Laverty and J.C. Fowler star in this silent film.
VHS: S07268. $24.95.
Albert Kelly, USA, 1929, 70 mins.

Cat and the Canary
One of the great silent ghost stories, the prototype of all haunted house mysteries!
VHS: S00219. $29.95.
Paul Leni, USA, 1927, 126 mins.

Chang
Chang is a revelation, a prototype for Cooper and Schoedsack's *King Kong*, and a terrifically entertaining film in its own right. Shot entirely in Siam, it tells the story of a farmer and his family, who have settled on a small patch of land at the edge of the jungle. They constantly struggle against the wild animals around them—bears, tigers, leopards, and even...changs! Silent, with a new score by Bangkok composer Bruce Gaston.
VHS: S16428. $39.95.
Laser: CLV/CAV. LD72071. $39.95.
Merian Cooper/Ernest Schoedsack, USA, 1927, 67 mins.

Chapter in Her Life
Rare film from one of the first women directors, Lois Weber, who began her directing career in 1913 after success as a concert pianist and actress. Weber specialized in the concerns of women, and *Chapter in Her Life* tells of the paralysis in the household of an embittered aging man and his widowed daughter-in-law who has no where to go.
VHS: S03711. $24.95.
Lois Weber, USA, 1923, 70 mins.

The Charlatan
A woman is poisoned while in a magician's cabinet. In this suspenseful tale, the identity of the murderer and his motive drive an inspired plot. Transferred from the only known original print available. Margaret Livingston, Rockliffe Fellows, Philo McCullough and Anita Garvin are among the principal stars of this silent classic.
VHS: S23308. $24.95.
George Melford, USA, 1929, 63 mins.

Charley's Aunt
Sydney Chaplin portrays the aunt in this classic comedy. Silent with music track.
VHS: S07265. $24.95.
Scott Sidney, USA, 1925, 85 mins.

Cheerful Fraud
Reginald Denny, Gertrude Olmstead, Emily Fitzroy, Gertrude Astor star.
VHS: S07244. $24.95.
William A. Seiter, USA, 1927, 64 mins.

Civilization
Known also as *He Who Returned*, this was one of three pacifist films made in 1916 on the eve of the US entry into World War I. Set in a mythical kingdom, a king declares war on his neighbors to satisfy a lust for power.
VHS: S00246. $29.95.
Thomas Ince, USA, 1916, 80 mins.

Classic Photoplays
Contains *Ben Hur* (1908, 11 mins); *She*, the first film version of the classic Rider Haggard story with Marguerite Snow and James Cruze; and *Two Orphans* (1911), produced by Carl Selig and released a reel at a time with T.J. Kerrigan, Charles Clory and Kathlyn Williams.
VHS: S05284. $19.95.

Claw
Norman Kerry, Claire Windsor, Helene Sullivan star.
VHS: S07205. $19.95.
Sidney Olcott, USA, 1927, 55 mins.

The Clodhopper
An early Charles Ray production. A boy from the sticks is lured by the Broadway footlights.
VHS: S07242. $19.95.
Victor Schertzinger, USA, 1917, 47 mins.

Coast Patrol
Kenneth McDonald, Claire De Lorez and Fay Wray star. Smugglers run into trouble with the Coast Guard. Grainy.
VHS: S07216. $19.95.
Bud Barsky, USA, 1925, 60 mins.

Cobra
Rudolph Valentino stars as a gambler trying to go straight, who messes around with one too many women and ends up involved in a murder. An early effort for Ritz-Carlton, with Nita Naldi, Casson Ferguson, Gertrude Olmstead and Ellen Percy.
VHS: S04799. $29.95.
Joseph Henabery, USA, 1925, 70 mins.

The Comediennes, Volume 1
Delightful comedies by three ladies of the silent screen are joined in this video, including *The Detectress* (1919, Gale Henry), *Cinderella Cinders* (1924, Alice Howell) and *Spanking Breezes* (1926, Alice Day). 58 mins.
VHS: S23316. $19.95.

The Comediennes, Volume 2
Three more comedy shorts featuring the ladies of the silent screen make up this video. In *T'was Henry's Fault* (1919) Elinor Field buys a flivver—not quite what her husband expected. In *A Roman Scandal* (1920) Colleen Moore joins a theatrical troupe over the protests of her boyfriend. In *Her First Flame* (1920) Gale Henry becomes a fireman as women take over men's jobs.
VHS: S23317. $19.95.

Comedy of Max Linder
These early, short, comic films capture the zany innovations of Max Linder, the comic who inspired Charlie Chaplin. Over a dozen shorts show Max fighting against a world heavy with comic possibilities. From ice skates to fly paper, Max struggles just to get a grip on things. Silent with orchestra score. USA, 1905-1913, 105 mins.
VHS: S27322. $24.95.

Coming of Amos
Rod La Rocque and Noah Beery star in this Cecil B. De Mille production. La Rocque is a vacationing Australian in France who rescues Jetta Goudal from the evil Beery.
VHS: S07207. $29.95.
Paul Sloane, USA, 1923, 58 mins.

Conductor
Charles Hines stars as an Irish street car conductor. USA, 1924, 85 mins.
VHS: S07259. $29.95.

Conquering Power
Rudolph Valentino is perfectly cast in this early silent adaptation of Balzac's *Eugenie Grandet*. It is a story of true love that conquers all, including the overreaching power of wealth.
VHS: S25697. $19.95.
Rex Ingram, USA, 1921, 60 mins.

The Count of Monte Cristo
James O'Neill, the father of playwright Eugene O'Neill, stars in this early silent drama based on the classic Alexandre Dumas story of false imprisonment and revenge. A filmed play which demonstrates the histrionic style of his acting. With Murdock McQuarrie and Nance O'Neil.
VHS: S05707. $19.95.
Edwin S. Porter, USA, 1912, 90 mins.

Covered Wagon
An epic western of the silent screen. A cast of 3,000, including 1,000 Native Americans, was employed to bring the Emerson Hough novel to the big screen. Follow the adventures of the Wingate family as they cross the Platte River, witness cattle stampedes, buffalo hunts and Indian attacks. With J. Warren Kerrigan, Lois Wilson, Ernest Torrence and Alan Hale. Westward Ho!
VHS: S12239. $19.95.
Laser: LD75176. $34.98.
James Cruze, USA, 1923, 60 mins.

The Coward
Charles Ray and Frank Keenan star. USA, 1915, 60 mins.
VHS: S07234. $19.95.

Cricket on the Hearth
This silent film is based on Charles Dickens' story of young love. A newlywed couple discovers a sign of good luck as they enter their new home—a cricket on the hearth. Featuring Paul Gerson, Virginia Brown Faire, Paul Moore and Joan Standing. 1923, 68 mins.
VHS: S23109. $24.95.

The Crowd
An ordinary man struggles to maintain his individuality in a heartless city. Featuring James Murray as John, a store clerk, and Eleanor Boardman as his wife Mary. *The Crowd* is one of the most important films of the silent era; its visual innovations still astonish viewers, and the relevance of its theme has only increased over the years" (*Pacific Film Archive*).
VHS: S09279. $29.95.
King Vidor, USA, 1928, 104 mins.

D'Artagnan
A very early version of Dumas' *The Three Musketeers*, with Orrin Johnson and Dorothy Dalton.
VHS: S13320. $29.95.
Thomas Ince, USA, 1916, c. 65 mins.

Daddies
Mae Marsh, Harry Myers, Claire Adams star in this early William A. Seiter production for Warner Brothers.
VHS: S07240. $19.95.
William A. Seiter, USA, 1924, 60 mins.

Dames Ahoy
Glenn Tryon, Helen Wright, Otis Harlan, Eddie Gribon and Gertrude Astor star. Three sailors on shore leave try to find the blonde who tricked one into drawing half his pay. A silent classic with piano music.
VHS: S22428. $19.95.

The Dancing Daughters
It's Joan Crawford in the role that brought her true movie stardom. Joan portrays a free-spirited flapper with a penchant for dancing, sin, and bathtub gin. Anita Page co-stars as the society debutante who tries to steal Joan's betrothed (Johnny Mack Brown). Silent film with synchronized music score and sound effects.
VHS: S13976. $29.99.
Harry Beaumont, USA, 1928, 98 mins.

Dancing Mothers
Alice Joyce, Norm Trevor and Clara Bow, the "It" girl, star in one of Clara Bow's best flapper roles. Silent with musical score.
VHS: S05599. $24.95.
Herbert Brenon, USA, 1926, 85 mins.

Dangerous Hours
One of the first anti-Communist films to be made in Hollywood, produced by Thomas Ince, and starring Lloyd Hughes.
VHS: S11458. $24.95.
Fred Niblo, USA, 1919, 84 mins.

The Deerslayer
Bela Lugosi is featured as a Native American in this silent adaptation of James Fenimore Cooper's novel *The Deerslayer*. It's an inspiring tale from a time when the promise of this continent seemed limitless. 1920, 60 mins.
VHS: S23826. $24.95.

Dick Turpin
Tom Mix portrays the famous English highwayman. Silent with music track.
VHS: S07222. $24.95.
John G. Blystone, USA, 1925, 70 mins.

The Disciple
William S. Hart's stirring saga of love, lust and conflicting emotions, with Hart as Jim Houston, the shootin' Iron Parson, out to rid a prairie town of corruption. Silent with music score.
VHS: S06929. $29.95.
William S. Hart, USA, 1915, 80 mins.

Don Juan
John Barrymore is stunning as the famous lover and adventurer in the court of Lucrezia Borgia in this top-notch swashbuckler. With Mary Astor, Warner Oland, Myrna Loy, Estelle Taylor. Newly mastered. Silent with music track.
VHS: S13399. $29.98.
Laser: LD70558. $39.98.
Alan Crosland, USA, 1926, 126 mins.

Don Q, Son of Zorro
Douglas Fairbanks swashbuckles his way through two roles as both Zorro and his lesser known son Don Q, also known as Cesar de Vega. This silent screen adventure is filled with action and swordplay. With Mary Astor, Donald Crisp, Warner Oland and Jean Hersholt.
VHS: S05479. $24.95.
Laser: CLV. LD71714. $19.98.
Donald Crisp, USA, 1925, 148 mins.

Douglas Fairbanks Box 1
Three films featuring the swashbuckling Douglas Fairbanks, Sr., are joined in this set. *Robin Hood* (Allan Dwan, USA, 1922, 124 mins.), *The Iron Mask* (Allan Dwan, USA, 1929, 73 mins.) and an early technicolor classic, *The Black Pirate* (Albert Parker, USA, 1927, 88 mins.) are silent films that show this early movie star known as "The Great Adventurer." Each film contains plenty of action and riveting suspense.
VHS: S27569. $69.95.
Allan Dwan/Albert Parker, USA, 1922-1929, 285 mins.

Douglas Fairbanks Box 2
The Three Musketeers (Fred Niblo, USA, 1921, 112 mins.), *The Thief of Baghdad* (Raoul Walsh, USA, 1924, 155 mins.) and *The Gaucho* (F. Richard Jones, USA, 1928, 103 mins.) are films which show the grace and agility that made Douglas Fairbanks, Sr., a sensation of the silent screen. This set offers a unique chance to see him at work in costume dramas that once thrilled the world.
VHS: S27570. $69.95.
Fred Niblo/Raoul Walsh/F. Richard Jones, USA, 1921-1928, 370 mins.

Down to Earth
Douglas Fairbanks is a health nut who causes all kinds of problems. USA, 1917.
VHS: S08885. $19.95.

Down to the Sea in Ships
Curtis Pierce, Ada Laycock, Marguerite Courtot, Clara Bow, James Turffer star.
VHS: S07249. $24.95.
Elmer Clifton, USA, 1922, 100 mins.

Drake Case
This rare Universal courtroom drama was made at the very end of the silent era and stars Robert Frasier, Doris Lloyd and Gladys Brockwell. USA, 1929, 56 mins.
VHS: S11457. $19.95.

Drop Kick
A very rare Richard Barthelmess drama of a college football star, with a cameo appearance by John Wayne. USA, 1927.
VHS: S07762. $24.95.

Dynamite Dan
Boris Karloff, Bruce Mitchell, Kenneth McDonald, Frank Rise star. Silent with music track. Grainy.
VHS: S07227. $24.95.
Bruce Mitchell, USA, 1924, 60 mins.

The Eagle
Rudolph Valentino and Vilma Banky star in this story of love and revenge set in old Russia. Valentino plays The Eagle—the leader of a gang of bandits who fight for the poor and oppressed. With brilliant art direction by William Cameron Menzies, directed by Clarence Brown. A new musical score by Carl Davis.
VHS: S10914. $39.99.
Clarence Brown, USA, 1925, 81 mins.

Early Silent Movie Prevues
This hour-long collection features those thrilling shorts always prefaced with the exciting words, "coming soon." Dozens of stars from the silent era can be seen in their most memorable screen moments.
VHS: S23149. $24.95.

Early Westerns #1
A collection of very early silent Westerns, including *Fatherhood of Buck McKee* (1912, released by Vitagraph), *Sherriff of Stone Gulch* (1918, with Ruth Roland), *The Man from Nowhere* (1914, with J. Warren Kerrigan, Vera Sussan, George Perilet), *Man from Tia Juana* (1917, Jack Hoxie), *Four Gun Bandit* (1919, with Pete Morrison), and *Fight It Out* (1920, with Hoot Gibson). Total length: 115 mins.
VHS: S08870. $24.95.

Early Westerns #2
Contains *Get Your Man* (Neal Hart, 23 mins.), *Battling Travers* (Dick Hatton, 26 mins.), *Extra Man and The Milk Fed Lion* (Art Accord, 27 mins.), *The Man with a Punch* (Hoot Gibson, 18 mins.), and *Bashful Whirlwind* (Edmund Cobb, 22 mins.).
VHS: S08871. $24.95.

Ella Cinders
Colleen Moore, Lloyd Hughes, Vera Lewis, Harry Langdon star. Silent with music track.
VHS: S07281. $19.95.
Alfred E. Green, USA, 1926, 60 mins.

Ella Cinders and Mormon Maid
Two rare silents: Colleen Moore as Ella, a delightful Cinderella-goes-to-Hollywood theme; and Mae Murray, in one of her few extant films, is the maid, co-starring with Frank Borzage (!) and villainous Noah Beery. USA, 1925/1917.
VHS: S05981. $24.95.

Episodes of the Hazards of Helen
Produced by Kalem in 1914, this 119 chapter serial did not contain cliff hanger endings. Each episode is a complete story. The first three star Helen Holmes, the last Helen Gibson. Contains Episode #9, Leap from the Water Tower; #31, The Paytrain; #33, In Danger's Path and #63, The Open Track. 56 mins.
VHS: S11462. $19.95.

Evangeline
Delores Del Rio, Roland Drew and Alec B. Frances star in this silent film classic. The bittersweet love story of the title character is based on Henry Wadsworth Longfellow's tale of a woman in search of her lost love. This film's last reel is heavily damaged but the conclusion is intact. Piano score.
VHS: S22895. $14.95.
Edwin Carewe, USA, 1929, 72 mins.

Eve's Leaves
Leatrice Joy, William Boyd, Robert Edeson star in this early De Mille production.
VHS: S07247. $24.95.
Paul Sloane, USA, 1926, 80 mins.

Evolution
Live-action footage is combined with animation in this early silent drama. Produced by the great Max Fleischer.
VHS: S23828. $24.95.
Max Fleischer, USA, 1923, 75 mins.

The Extra Girl
Mabel Normand stars in a comedy about a young woman's attempts to break into the movies. Made after her involvement in the William Desmond Taylor scandal. Story by Mack Sennett. The scene where she unknowingly leads a lion through a movie lot is a classic. With Billy Bevan, Ralph Graves and Vernon Dent.
VHS: S04803. $24.95.
Laser: Extended play CLV. LD71524. $49.95.
F. Richard Jones, USA, 1923, 70 mins.

Eyes of Youth
Vitagraph star Clara Kimball Young at her peak in 1919 as a young girl with a golden heart who must choose between marrying a rich banker, waiting for assistant bank cashier Milton Sills to earn his fortune, pursuing an operatic career or marrying the man she truly loves. Allowed a glimpse into the future, she learns something very intriguing. At the end of the film, a small role is an actor, new to motion pictures in 1919, credited as "Rudolfo Valentino." 85 mins. 1919, silent with music score.
VHS: S06982. $29.95.

Eyes Right!
Francis X. Bushman stars in this drama about life at a military academy. With Fiobelle Fairbanks, Dora Dean and Larry Kent.
VHS: S08859. $19.95.
Louis Ghaudet, USA, 1926, 46 mins.

False Faces
Lon Chaney and Henry B. Walthall star in this silent spy thriller. Lone Wolf is working as a secret agent for the allies. Soon he is on a mission to the US to find a master German spy played by Chaney.
VHS: S25709. $29.95.
Irvin Willat, 1918, USA, 65 mins.

Fighting American
Pat O'Malley, Mary Astor, Raymond Hatton and Warner Oland star in this drama about an uprising in China that is thwarted by an enterprising American. Silent with music score.
VHS: S10363. $19.95.
Tom Forman, USA, 1924, 65 mins.

The Fighting Coward
A shrewd comedy of manners and observation about the emotional and physical transformation of an insecure young man who leaves home and returns as a brave individual. With Cullen Landis, Ernest Torrence, Mary Astor and Noah Beery. Silent with musical score.
VHS: S20052. $19.95.
James Cruze, USA, 1924, 66 mins.

Fighting Eagle
Rod La Rocque, Phyllis Haver, Sam De Grasse, Sally Rand and Clarence Burton star. Silent with music track.
VHS: S07236. $19.95.

The Fighting Legion
Ken assumes the identity of a murdered Texas Ranger in order to root out the killer and understand the killer's motives. The film was originally released in both silent and sound versions, though only the silent version survives. With Ken Maynard and Dorothy Dwan. Silent with musical score.
VHS: S20053. $19.95.
Harry J. Brown, USA, 1930, 69 mins.

Films of Edmund Cobb
Three complete films by Cobb were transferred from mint 9.5mm prints. The first two are from the Cobb Mountie series, *The Courage of Collier* and *Two Fister*. In the Western *Man Tamer*, Walter Brennan makes an appearance in a small role. These silent films include orchestral score. 55 mins.
VHS: S22433. $24.95.

Films of Thomas Ince
Five films by Thomas Ince: *The Invaders*, *The Struggle*, *Drummer of the Eighth*, *Silent Heroes* and *Last of the Line*, made in 1914 and starring Sessue Hayakawa.
VHS: S05413. $29.95.

The Final Extra
This silent drama tells the sordid tale of bootlegging, murder, show business and the cub reporter who is out to save the girl and get the scoop. With Marguerite De La Motte as Ruth, John Miljan as Mervyn LeRoy and Grant Withers as Pat Riley, the eager beaver reporter.
VHS: S05703. $29.95.
James P. Hogan, USA, 1927, 76 mins.

Flesh and Blood
Lon Chaney stars as an escaped convict who swears revenge. With Edith Roberts and De Witt Jennings.
VHS: S03654. $29.95.
Irving Cummings, USA, 1922, 74 mins.

Flesh and the Devil
"The first of the Garbo-Gilbert romances, [this] was quite certainly a box office milestone—and it also represents something of a high-water mark in the sheer elegance and 'bigness' of movies in their most glamorous era...Honor, loyalty, love—strong emotions all of them, are given full expression in a story which permits no facile solutions" (*Classics of the Silent Screen*). Garbo is simply magnificent as the seductive temptress who drives a wedge between two old friends.
VHS: S09280. $29.95.
Clarence Brown, USA, 1927, 103 mins.

Flirting with Fate
Douglas Fairbanks hires a killer to do him in. When things change for the better, he frantically tries to cancel the order. Produced by Triangle.
VHS: S08882. $24.95.
Christy Cabanne, USA, 1916, 51 mins.

The Flying Fool
Pilot Bill returns from the First World War and finds that he must protect his little brother from a formidable new enemy, a woman. When Bill and his brother's girlfriend meet, his own desires enter the picture. She is a smalltown girl, decent and likable. Before long the brothers are engaged in duel in the air to see who wins her affections.
VHS: S18904. $19.95.
Tay Garnett, USA, 1929, 63 mins.

A Fool There Was
Theda Bara's first and most legendary film tells the story of a good man brought down by an irresistable vamp.
VHS: S05983. $24.95.
Frank Powell, USA, 1915

The Forbidden City
Norma Talmadge and Thomas Meigan are at the center of this early tear-jerker about love in a faraway land. A Chinese woman falls in love with a visiting American official, with disastrous consequences.
VHS: S23829. $24.95.
Sidney Franklin, USA, 1918, 55 mins.

Forty-Nine Seventeen
Joseph Girard, Leo Pierson and Jean Hersholt are featured in this silent film set in a Western ghost town. A retired judge sets out on a mission. He intends to restore this eerie remnant from frontier days.
VHS: S23314. $19.95.
Ruth Ann Baldwin, USA, 1917, 61 mins.

The Four Horsemen of the Apocalypse
Rudolph Valentino became a certified star for his work in this film, especially his notorious tango scene. Based on Blasco Ibanez' novel, this is a story of two brothers who end up on opposing sides in World War I. Stark imagery make this unforgettable anti-war film a silent classic.
VHS: S23111. $29.95.
Rex Ingram, USA, 1921, 114 mins.

Free to Love
A roaring twenties American classic, starring the great Clara Bow.
VHS: S06219. $49.95.
Frank O'Connor, USA, 1925, 61 mins.

From the Manger to the Cross
The Kalem Company reenacted their passion play for the camera, resulting in this, the first Biblical epic to be filmed in the Holy Land. In a straightfoward fashion it shows the life of Christ, beginning with the Nativity and ending with the Crucifixion. It includes footage of the Holy Family at the Sphinx and is tinted to match the release prints.
VHS: S25740. $29.95.
Sidney Olcott, USA, 1915, 71 mins.

The Fugitive
(The Taking of Luke McVane)
William S. Hart shoots a man for cheating at cards and is pursued into the desert by a vigilant sheriff. There they meet a pack of bloodthirsty savages. A pretty busy day in the Old West. Hart's twelfth film. With Enid Markey.
VHS: S05488. $24.95.
William S. Hart, USA, 1915, 36 mins.

Galloping Gallagher
A very rare Fred Thomson film, considered lost for many years. USA, 1924, 50 mins.
VHS: S11453. $24.95.

Garden of Eden
Naughty Lubitsch-like comedy with Corinne Griffith, Lowell Sherman, Louise Dresser.
VHS: S05984. $49.95.
Lewis Milestone, USA, 1928

The Gaucho
Against the peaks of the Andes, Douglas Fairbanks confounds corrupt government forces that would impinge on the romantic free lifestyles of the South American cowboys. This lavishly produced work from the early days of technicolor is an inspiring and exciting romp through the Pampas.
VHS: S27571. $24.95.
F. Richard Jones, USA, 1928, 103 mins.

Getting Gertie's Garter

Marie Prevost, Charles Ray and Franklin Pangborn star in this classic comedy from the golden age of silent film. Gertie's ex-fiance tries to recover an embarrassing token of his former love's affection. The trick is that he must do this without alerting either Gertie or his new love.
VHS: S23830. $24.95.
E. Mason Harper, USA, 1927, 74 mins.

The Girl in the Pullman

Marie Prevost and Harrison Ford (not the same guy) are paired in this romantic comedy. After divorcing her husband, a wife begins to reconsider her husband's worth. Then she sets out to regain his affection while he is on a honeymoon with his new wife. 1927, 65 mins.
VHS: S23831. $24.95.

A Girl's Folly

Doris Kenyon stars as a country girl captivated by the magic of moving pictures. When she can't make it as an actress the actor she adores, Robert Warwick, offers her another path to riches. Soon she is faced with a troubling situation when her mother decides to visit her "successful" daughter.
VHS: S23309. $24.95.
Maurice Tourneur, USA, 1917, 60 mins.

Grand Duchess and the Waiter

Adolphe Menjou and Florence Vidor star in this light comic farce. A millionaire could not possibly attract the attentions of a grand duchess, so he must disguise himself as a waiter.
VHS: S23832. $24.95.
Malcolm St. Clair, USA, 1926, 55 mins.

Grass

In 1924, neophyte filmmakers Merian C. Cooper and Ernest Schoedsack joined forces with journalist and sometime spy Marguerite Harrison and set off to film an adventure. They found excitement, danger and unparalleled drama in the migration of the Bakhtiari tribe of Persia. Each year, more than 50 thousand people and half a million animals crossed the snow-covered mountain ranges and torrential rapids to take their herds to pasture. Few have seen Grass outside of archives. This issue is struck from the original negative, with an updated soundtrack by Iranian Gholam Hussein Janati Ataie.
VHS: S16429. $39.95.
Laser: CLV/CAV. Digitally mastered and transferred. LD71815. $34.95.
Merian Cooper/Ernest Schoedsack, USA, 1925, 70 mins.

Hands Up

Raymond Griffith, to save the South, attempts to destroy and divert the gold from a northern mine.
VHS: S07256. $19.95.
Clarence Badger, USA, 1928, 58 mins.

Hawk of the Hills

Allene Ray, Walter Miller, Robert Chandler are featured in this feature version of the 1927 serial. Soft focus.
VHS: S07184. $19.95.
Spencer Gordon Bennett, USA, 1929, 58 mins.

Hawthorne of the USA

This is an amazing find, one of the rarest of the Wallace Reid films known. Lila Lee and Harrison Ford also appear in this story of an expatriate American in Europe. Reid's character wastes his fortune at the gaming tables of Monte Carlo. Then, in search of peace, he finds instead a princess to love and a communist coup. Transferred from a tinted 35mm nitrate print. Orchestra score.
VHS: S23310. $24.95.
James Cruze, USA, 1919, 55 mins.

Heading Home

Legendary baseball player Babe Ruth stars in this homespun version of his life story. Ruth Taylor, William Sheer, Margaret Sedden and many more star in this silent sports film classic. Orchestra score.
VHS: S23311. $24.95.
Lawrence Windom, USA, 1920, 56 mins.

Headless Horseman

Will Rogers is Ichabod Crane in Washington Irving's Legend of Sleepy Hollow. Silent with music track. USA, 1922, 68 mins.
VHS: S07245. $24.95.

Heart of Humanity

Dorothy Philips and Erich von Stroheim star in this silent Canadian production, with Stroheim as a brutal Prussian officer. Silent with music track.
VHS: S07276. $24.95.
Allen Holubar, Canada, 1919, 110 mins.

Heart's Haven

A rare look at the work of actress Claire Adams. Robert McKim and Carl Gantvoort also star.
VHS: S08856. $24.95.
Benjamin B. Hampton, USA, 1922, 61 mins.

Hell's Hinges

William S. Hart, the first great star of the Westerns, plays Blaze Tracy, a notorious outlaw in the town of Hell's Hinges. When a new minister pulls into town, Blaze is transformed by the sight of the minister's daughter. One of the great silent Westerns.
VHS: S01879. $29.95.
William S. Hart, USA, 1916, 65 mins.

Hidden Aces

Charles Hutchinson, Alice Calhoun, Barbara Tennant, James Bradbury Jr. star. Silent with music track.
VHS: S07232. $19.95.
Howard Mitchell, USA, 1927, 62 mins.

His First Command

William Boyd and Dorothy Sebastian star in this romance between a city slicker and the rugged daughter of a cavalryman. Boyd is sent out of Manhattan to manage a ranch in Kansas but he can't keep his mind on his work. He falls for a woman who only is interested in army men, so he enlists.
VHS: S24004. $19.95.
Gregory La Cava, USA, 1929, 60 mins.

His First Flame

They say love is the only fire against which there is no insurance. Hapless Harry Langdon is beset by two types of flames. He tries firefighting to take his mind off women and nearly burns down the fire station. With Vernon Dent and Natalie Kingston.
VHS: S05695. $24.95.
Harry Edwards, USA, 1926, 62 mins.

His Majesty, the American

Douglas Fairbanks arrives at the court of the Kingdom Alaine just in time to become involved in a plot. The king's minister wants to overthrow the king. Marjorie Daw, Frank Campeau and Sam Southern are just some of the silent era stars showcased in this first film from United Artists.
VHS: S23307. $29.95.
Joseph Henabery, USA, 1919, 100 mins.

His People

Rudolph Schildkraut, Kate Price, Virginia Brown Faire and Arthur Lubin star. Silent with music track. USA, 1927, 93 mins.
VHS: S07220. $24.95.

The History of Chase in Film, Volume One: Comedy Chase

A wild and exciting compilation of chase sequences traces the early historical evolution of the film chase. Thrills, gags and suspense are studded throughout these clips, featuring cars, boats, trains and airplanes.
VHS: S27484. $19.95.

Hotel Imperial

Pola Negri and James Hall star in this lavish tale based in Hungary. In 1917, six Hussars find themselves in a frontier town occupied by Russians. Led by Hall, they take refuge in the beautifully appointed Hotel Imperial.
VHS: S23312. $24.95.
Mauritz Stiller, USA, 1927, 84 mins.

Hula

Clara Bow, Clive Brook and Patricia Dupont star in this delightful tale of love and adventure on a South Sea Island.
VHS: S08850. $24.95.
Victor Fleming, USA, 1928, 64 mins.

The Hunchback of Notre Dame

Filled with huge crowd scenes and massive sets recreating medieval Paris, The Hunchback of Notre Dame is one of the greatest spectacles of the silent era. Starring the legendary Lon Chaney as Quasimodo. Digitally remastered.
VHS: S14337. $19.98.
Laser: CLV. LD71992. $29.98.
Wallace Worsley, USA, 1923, 100 mins.

In the Land of the War Canoes

Edward S. Curtis devoted his life to documenting the world of dwindling Native American cultures. In this film, Curtis told a story of love and revenge among the Kwakiutl Indians of Vancouver Island. Curtis spent three years with the Kwakiutl to meticulously recreate their way of life before the white man came. In addition to the magnificent painted war canoes, the film pictures authentic costumes, ceremonial dances and religious rituals. Silent with soundtrack from 1972 restoration.
VHS: S16431. $39.95.
Laser: LD71816. $29.95.
Edward S. Curtis, USA/Canada, 1914, 47 mins.

In the Tentacles of the North

An exciting tale about the extraordinary courage of a young girl who manages to survive when the ship she is traveling on is caught in the frozen Arctic ice. She battles vainly to preserve her sanity. With Caston Glass, Alice Calhoun and Al Roscoe. Silent with orchestral score.
VHS: S20051. $19.95.
Louis Chaudet, USA, 1926, 54 mins.

The Irish Cinderella

Emralila is a poor orphan girl much abused by an old biddy known as the Ulster Crag—half-man, half-bag and all witch. She has two equally abusive daughters. This silent feature with original organ score parallels the poor child with the struggle for Irish independence. A "reel" oddity. With Pattie MacNamara. 1920's, 72 mins.
VHS: S03659. $29.95.

Iron Mask

Alexandre Dumas' exciting novel of fights, spectacle and romance, in the great thrill show of 1929. With Douglas Fairbanks and Margaret de la Motte.
VHS: S03330. $24.95.
Laser: CLV. LD71995. $29.98.
Allan Dwan, USA, 1929

Is Life Worth Living?

Selznick Pictures produced this moral tale in 1921. It teaches about the value of life through a hard luck story concerning a young man wrongly accused of a crime. This copy was made from a beautiful 35mm print and scored with orchestra music of the period. 66 mins.
VHS: S20633. $19.95.

It

Clara Bow stars with Gary Cooper and Elinor Glyn. Silent with music track.
VHS: Out of print. For rental only.
Laser: LD70097. $39.95.
Clarence Badger, USA, 1927, 71 mins.

It's the Old Army Game

This rare Paramount release features the inimitable W.C. Fields as a small town druggist; lovely, young Louise Brooks co-stars as his beautiful daughter. An excellent print of a predominantly unseen film. Organ sound.
VHS: S15512. $29.95.
Edward A. Sutherland, USA, 1926, 75 mins.

Italian

The story of Italian immigrants in the slums of New York, notable for its realism; produced by Thomas Ince, and starring George Beban. Silent with music score. USA, 1915, 78 mins.
VHS: S07487. $24.95.

Jack-Knife Man

This tear-jerker was one of King Vidor's early directorial efforts. A lonely old riverboat man is left a child by a dying mother. The old man carves many toys from wood for the boy and they grow to love one another. The village snoop feels the child would be better off in an orphanage rather than living on the river and the sheriff is sent to try to take the child away. Organ music track.
VHS: S13272. $24.95.
King Vidor, USA, 1920, 70 mins.

Jesus of Nazareth (The Story of the Saviour's Life)

A realistic, thoroughly detailed, dramatic recreation of the life of Christ, from the Anunciation through the Ascension. In between, we view episodes from his infancy and youth, his preachings and miracles and, finally, his betrayal by Judas Iscariot, his delivery before Pontius Pilate, and the Crucifixion. The titles which lucidly describe the proceedings are taken from appropriate descriptive passages in the Bible. Ultimately, Jesus of Nazareth is a religious epic that's as educational as it is stirring. Silent film with an original organ score, shown at its correct projection speed. USA, 1928, 85 mins.
VHS: S13602. $29.95.

Jungle Princess

E.R. Martin directed this feature version of the 15-chapter 1920 serial The Lost City, which features Juanita Hansen, George Chesebro and Frank Clark.
VHS: S08866. $24.95.
E.R. Martin, USA, 1920, 68 mins.

Just Suppose

A prince pretends to be a pauper, but when love strikes and duty calls, complications arise. Richard Barthelmess, Lois Moran and Geoffrey Kerr star.
VHS: S07202. $24.95.
Kenneth Webb, USA, 1926, 90 mins.

Kean

An extremely rare example of the legendary actor Mosjoukine, who stars as the equally famous British stage actor, Edmund Kean. USA, 1922.
VHS: S06222. $49.95.

Kentucky Derby

Reginald Denny, Lillian Rich, Emmett King, Walter McGrail star.
VHS: S07229. $24.95.
King Baggot, USA, 1927, 68 mins.

The Kiss

One of the very last silent films released by MGM, it was also Garbo's last venture before she "talked" in Anna Christie. The Kiss is a classy melodrama co-starring Garbo opposite a handsome and very young Lew Ayres (making his film debut for MGM). Silent film with synchronized musical score.
VHS: S13975. $29.99.
Laser: LD71081. $39.95.
Jacques Feyder, USA, 1929, 89 mins.

Lamb

The first feature starring Douglas Fairbanks, produced by Triangle Film Corporation. Fairbanks plays a man who proves he is not a "lamb" by being ultra-macho.
VHS: S08881. $24.95.
Christy Cabanne, USA, 1915, 60 mins.

The Last of the Mohicans

This silent adaptation of James Fenimore Cooper's novel is set in colonial America during the French and Indian Wars, and pits the fierce warrior Magua (Wallace Beery) against Hawkeye and his adopted brothers, Uncas and Chingachgook. With Barbara Bedford, Albert Roscoe, James Gordon and Boris Karloff.
VHS: S06225. $39.95.
Laser: CLV/CAV. LD72046. $49.95.
Maurice Tourneur/Clarence Brown, USA, 1920, 75 mins.

The Last Outlaw

Gary Cooper, Jack Luden, Betty Jewell and Flash, The Wonder Horse. Silent with music track, with lots of swell action shots on Flash.
VHS: S07275. $19.95.
Arthur Rosson, USA, 1927, 63 mins.

Leatherneck

William Boyd, Alan Hale and Diane Ellis star in this silent story of love and adventure. USA, 65 mins. 1928.
VHS: S08849. $24.95.

Leopard Woman

Louise Glaum, the most famous of the screen vamps, in an epic of passion, intrigue and espionage in the equatorial jungle. USA, 1920, 68 mins.
VHS: S07218. $19.95.

Let 'Er Go Gallegher

Junior Coghlan, Harrison Ford, Elinor Fair, Wade Boteler and Inan Lebedeff star in this adventure with a waif of the streets. Silent with music score.
VHS: S10360. $19.95.
Elmer Clifton, USA, 1928, 57 mins.

The Light of Faith

Lon Chaney and Hope Hampton star in this inspirational movie. In the 30s, the original 1922 silent film was cut down to be shown to Christians.
VHS: S23196. $29.95.
Clarence Brown, USA, 1922, 33 mins.

Lighting Brice

The complete, exciting 15-chapter serial starring Jack Hoxie and Ann Little. USA, 1919, orchestra music. 300 mins.
VHS: S08861. $49.95.

Linda

A young mountain girl (Helen Foster) is forced to marry a much older man. Noah Beery plays the thoughtful husband who tries to cheer his unhappy young wife, while Warner Baxter portrays the dashing young doctor who becomes her lover. This classic silent melodrama is accompanied by a reconstructed orchestra score.
VHS: S22425. $24.95.
Mrs. Wallace Reid, USA, 1929, 75 mins.

Little American

A super-rare Pickford silent. With Jack Holt in a World War I propaganda piece. 1917, 80 mins.
VHS: S08335. $49.95.

Little Annie Rooney

A good Irish girl takes care of her dad and brother. Mary Pickford, William Haines and Walter James star.
VHS: S08852. $24.95.
William Beaudine, USA, 1925, 100 mins.

Little Orphan Annie

Colleen Moore, Thomas Santschi and Harry Lonsdale star in this early film about a delightful young girl who makes the most of being an orphan. Poet James Whitcomb Riley narrates the story to a group of children gathered about him.
VHS: S26771. $14.95.
Colin Campbell, USA, 1918, 57 mins.

Live Wire

Johnny Hines, part of a circus troupe, uses his skills to save a heroine. USA, 1925, 85 mins.
VHS: S07260. $24.95.

Lorna Doone

Madge Bellamy and John Bowers are featured together in this silent film about a young girl. She is kidnapped and taken from her rich parents and then must be raised by bandits in Scotland.
VHS: S23833. $24.95.
Maurice Tourneur, USA, 1922, 65 mins.

Lost Express

A complete steam locomotive and its cargo disappear without a trace in this early railroad drama that stars Helen Holmes and Henry Barrows. Silent with music score.
VHS: S10366. $19.95.
J.P. McGowan, USA, 1926, 48 mins.

The Lost World

Adapted from a short story by Sir Arthur Conan Doyle, this is the classic tale of prehistoric monsters running amok in contemporary London. The real star is special effects virtuoso Willis O'Brien, whose life-like monsters have an astounding authenticity. Wallace Beery plays Professor Challenger, who must devise a way to defeat the raging monsters. This 90-minute version includes the original trailer, O'Brien's earlier works, Prehistoric Poultry, R.F.D. 10,000 B.C. and The Dinosaur and the Missing Link, and a recreation of some of the long-lost footage.
VHS: S19673. $39.95.
Laser: LD70223. $49.95.
Harry O. Hoyt, USA, 1925, 90 mins.

Love 'Em and Leave 'Em

Frank Tuttle directed this delightful and rambunctious story of the roaring Twenties, and Louise Brooks shines in one of her early film roles. Also starring Evelyn Brent and Lawrence Gray. Orchestra scored.
VHS: S15513. $29.95.
Frank Tuttle, USA, 1927, 70 mins.

Love Never Dies

Madge Bellamy and Lloyd Hughes are great in this dramatic silent film about love, revenge and the violence provoked by these two primal forces. Great action scenes and color tinted.
VHS: S23834. $24.95.
King Vidor, USA, 1922, 55 mins.

The Lubin Studios

Lubin Studios, an early producer of silent shorts, gave figures like Pearl White and Oliver Hardy their start in the movies. This video shows works from as early as 1904 that reveal the influence of Edison's films. Perhaps more importantly, there are comic films included in this collection which reveal the developing comic abilities of Oliver Hardy. Music track added.
VHS: S27482. $19.95.

Lucky Devil

Richard Dix, Esther Ralston, Edna May Oliver, Tom Findley and Anthony Jowitt star. Silent with music track.
VHS: S07269. $19.95.
Frank Tuttle, USA, 1925, 63 mins.

Lure of the Range

Dick Hatton stars in this early silent Western filled with terrific comic gags. 1924, 56 mins.
VHS: S23835. $24.95.

Mad Whirl

Myrtle Stedman, Barbara Bedford, Alec B. Francis, Jack Mulhall and May McAvoy star in this William Seiter production. Silent with music track. USA, 1925, 80 mins.
VHS: S07238. $24.95.

Made for Love

A couple falls in love and fall into a tomb in Egypt. Edmund Burns, Paul Sloane and Leatrice Joy star.
VHS: S07226. $19.95.
Paul Sloane, USA, 1926, 65 mins.

Mademoiselle Midnight

This is one of Mae Murray's last surviving films.
VHS: S23836. $24.95.
Robert Z. Leonard, USA, 1924, 70 mins.

Man from Beyond

Harry Houdini, the celebrated escape artist, starred and produced this film in which Artic explorers discover a shipwreck from 1820 and a frozen sailor whom they revive.
VHS: S03787. $24.95.
Burton King, USA, 1922

The Man from Painted Post
A 1917 silent western starring Douglas Fairbanks Sr. who impersonates a sophisticated city man to tackle of a gang of horse rustlers and win the affections of a beautiful young woman.
VHS: S06224. $19.95.
Joseph Henabery, USA, 1917

Man Who Had Everything
Jack Pickford stars in this story of a young man who is given his every wish, and must decide whether it's a blessing or a curse. Silent with music track. USA, 1920, 60 mins.
VHS: S07213. $24.95.

Manhandled
An examination of a shop girl and her man-troubles in the big city. With Gloria Swanson, Tom Moore, Frank Morgan and Ann Pennington. Silent film with musical score.
VHS: S15384. $24.95.
Allan Dwan, USA, 1924

Mantrap
A Famous Players-Lasky production starring Clara Bow as a temptress, Ernest Torrence, Percy Marmont and Tom Kennedy. Silent with music track.
VHS: S07250. $24.95.
Victor Fleming, USA, 1926, 68 mins.

Mark of Zorro
Of the many films made about the legendary Zorro, most consider this to be the best, with its exciting duel sequences, romance and high adventure. Douglas Fairbanks, Marguerite de la Motte and Noah Beery star. Digitally remastered.
VHS: S14441. $24.95.
Laser: CLV. LD71730. $19.98.
Fred Niblo, USA, 1920, 80 mins.

Marked Money
The villains are after a chest with a secret in this Junior Coghlan drama which also stars George Duryea, Virginia Bradford, Tom Kennedy, Bert Woodruff and Jack Richardson. Silent with music score.
VHS: S10361. $19.95.
Spencer Gordon Bennett, USA, 1928, 61 mins.

Married?
Constance Bennett and Owen Moore star in this story of a couple who must marry for a year in order to inherit a large sum of money.
VHS: S07270. $24.95.
George Terwilliger, USA, 1926, 65 mins.

Mary Pickford—The Early Years
A collection of early films featuring the great Pickford, including *Sweet Memories* and clips from *On Account of Milk, Arcadian Maid, Never Again, The Unchanging Sea, Artful Kate* and *In Old Madrid*, which also stars Owen Moore. 65 mins.
VHS: S11454. $19.95.

Matinee Idols: The Gentlemen
A collection of short films from the years 1911-1914, illustrative of the early male stars of the era: Henry B. Walthall (*Love and Charity*), Every Inch a Man (Wallace Reid), *Dawn and Twilight* (Francis X. Bushman), *Under Royal Patronage* (Francis X. Bushman).
VHS: S07586. $19.95.

Matinee Idols: The Ladies
Short films from the years 1912-1913, featuring early female leads: Clara Kimball Young and Helen Costello (*Lulu's Doctor*); Mary Fuller (9th episode of *What Happened to Mary*); Kathleen Williams, Vera Hamilton (*The Girl at the Cupola*); Florence Lawrence (*Flo's Discipline*); Edith Storey (*A Modern Atlanta*); Beverly Bayne and Eleanor Blanchard (*Teaching Hickville to Sing*); Beverly Bayne (*Will-Be-Weds*), and Pearl White (*The Paper Doll*). 120 mins.
VHS: S07418. $29.95.

Matrimaniac
Douglas Fairbanks and Constance Talmadge star in this action-packed comedy about a man determined, against all odds and outside pressures, to marry the girl he wants. USA, 1918, 48 mins.
VHS: S08884. $24.95.

Mickey
Mabel Normand brightens the silent screen in one of her most popular roles. She plays a Western girl sent East to live with unkind relations. They force her to become a domestic, with hilarious and heart-tugging results. With Lew Cody, Minta Durfee and Minnie Ha Ha. Produced by Mack Sennett.
VHS: S04804. $29.95.
F. Richard Jones, USA, 1919, 110 mins.

Midnight Faces
An eerie psychological thriller about a young woman (Francis X. Bushman) who inherits a beachhouse in the Florida everglades and is subjected to a series of unexplained incidents and events. With Rocky Aoki, Jack Perrin and Kathryn McGuire.
VHS: S18945. $19.95.
Bennett Cohn, USA, 1926, 72 mins.

Midnight Girl
Bela Lugosi, screen's elegant villain, in a rare silent role. Lugosi plays Nicholas Harmon, the immensely wealthy patron of music, in love with Mimi, an opera singer. Lugosi's seductive manner is countered by his son's indifference to an arranged marriage into a socially prominent family.
VHS: S04853. $29.95.
Wilfred Noy, USA, 1925, 61 mins.

Midnight Message
Wanda Hawley, Mary Carr, John Fox Jr., Stuart Holmes star. Grainy.
VHS: S07215. $19.95.
Paul Hurst, USA, 1926, 65 mins.

Mistaken Orders
Helen Holmes, Henry Barrows and Hal Waters star. The wrong orders send two trains dashing toward each other. Silent with music score. 52 mins.
VHS: S10365. $19.95.

Mockery
Lon Chaney plays a noble peasant who must protect a countess from the fury of the Russian revolution. With Barbara Belford, Ricardo Cortez and Emily Fitzroy.
VHS: S16183. $29.95.
Benjamin Christensen, USA, 1927, 75 mins.

The Mollycoddle
Douglas Fairbanks and Wallace Beery are featured in this action-filled silent comedy. As a dashing playboy, Fairbanks steals the show and the girl. He vies with a rather distasteful diamond slugger, culminating in a bang-up climax.
VHS: S23838. $24.95.
Victor Fleming, USA, 1920, 63 mins.

Moran of the Lady Letty
A never-seen Valentino film, re-discovered overseas and available with English titles. A dandy is kidnapped and taken hostage aboard a pirate ship.
VHS: S08333. $29.95.
George Melford, USA, 1922, 71 mins.

A Mormon Maid
Mae Murray, Frank Borzage and Noah Beery are cast in this silent tragic film. Polygamy drives a woman to suicide. Then her daughter is faced with the same marriage prospects. As a result, she is forced to flee to her true love.
VHS: S23839. $24.95.
Robert Z. Leonard, USA, 1917, 60 mins.

My Four Years in Germany
This World War I drama is based on the story of Ambassador James W. Gerard, who witnessed many instances of German intrigue and cruelty. With Halbert Brown, Willard Dashiel, Louis Dean, Earl Schenck and George Riddell. Orchestral score.
VHS: S22429. $24.95.
William Knight, USA, 1918, 122 mins.

My Lady of Whims
Clara Bow stars as a spoiled young lady who is constantly spied upon by her father. With Carmelita Geraghty, Betty Baker, Donald Keith. Silent with music track. USA, 1925, 42 mins.
VHS: S07483. $19.95.

Mystery of the Double Cross
The complete, 15-chapter, 1917 Pathe serial with Molly King and Leon Barry. Not the ordinary cliff-hanger, this is presented as a mystery which it challenges you to solve. 6 hours on 3 video cassettes.
VHS: S11459. $49.95.

The Narrow Road/Alias Jimmy Valentine
Alias Jimmy Valentine (1915), by Maurice Tourneur, tells the story of a bank robber who ends up in the real Sing Sing prison. It's an incredibly realistic early feature that makes startling use of deep staging. *The Narrow Road* (1912) represents a rarely seen work by the master, D.W. Griffith, with Mary Pickford as a woman who must keep her husband from a life of crime. From the *Origins of American Films* series, a joint project of the Library of Congress and Smithsonian Video.
VHS: S21263. $34.95.

Nervous Wreck
A hilarious, silent version of *Whoopee*, with Harrison Ford, Phyllis Haver, in a rollicking comedy.
VHS: S05973. $49.95.
Scott Sidney, USA, 1926, 70 mins.

New School Teacher
Gregory La Cava directs this film based on the rustic humor of Irvin S. Cobb, the story of shy Professor Timmins (Chic Sale) and his adventures with young hooligans. When he isn't busy sitting on thumb tacks, and "keeping up with all the dead languages," he is courting the pretty sister of one of the little pranksters. Great vitality from La Cava, with an entertaining performance from Chic Sale. Silent with music score.
VHS: S06984. $19.95.
Gregory La Cava, USA, 1923, 75 mins.

The Nicklehopper
Mabel Normand and Boris Karloff are featured in this silent story about a dance hall hostess. 1926, 30 mins.
VHS: S23840. $24.95.

Night Bird
It's Reginald Denny to the rescue in this low-key comedy. Silent with music track.
VHS: S07264. $19.95.
Fred Newmeyer, USA, 1928, 76 mins.

Night Club
To prove his love for Vera Reynolds, Raymond Griffith hires Wallace Beery as an assassin. Silent with music track.
VHS: S07254. $19.95.
Frank Urson/Paul Iribe, USA, 1925, 62 mins.

Nomads of the North
Lon Chaney Sr. stars as Raoul Challoner, an innocent man on the run from the mounted police in the Great White North. With Lewis Stone as the relentless Cpl. O'Connor and Betty Blythe as Nanette Roland, Raoul's secret love. This silent adventure also features several adorable animals and an impressive forest fire. Silent with music track.
VHS: S16179. $24.95.
David M. Hartford, USA, 1920, 120 mins.

Norma Talmadge Films
This collection includes five early films of the silent era's rough equivalent to Greer Garson. Talmadge made over 250 films in the silent era. Included in this introduction are *Father's Hatband* (1913), *Sawdust & Salome* (1914), *The Helpful Sisterhood* (1914), *John Rance, Gentleman* (1914), and the 51-minute feature *Children of the House*, made under the supervision of D.W. Griffith. USA, 1913-1916, 112 mins.
VHS: S04809. $29.95.

The Notorious Lady
Lewis Stone and Barbara Bedford star in this miraculously preserved print of an early film tragedy. Stone is a British officer who kills a man he finds in his wife's room. Although innocent of any wrong, his wife claims to be guilty in order to save him. Orchestra score.
VHS: S22013. $19.95.
King Baggot, USA, 1927, 79 mins.

The Nut
Douglas Fairbanks is a wacky inventor who finds himself convinced of an interesting theory. His wealthy girlfriend believes he can be improved through contact with the better off.
VHS: S25710. $24.95.
Theodore Reed, USA, 1921, 61 mins.

Officer 444
Francis Ford directed this 10-chapter serial produced in 1926, starring Ben Wilson and Neva Gerber.
VHS: S08862. $39.95.
Francis Ford, USA, 1926, 200 mins.

Old Heidelberg
Dorothy Gish, Wallace Reid and Erich von Stroheim all are featured in this early version of an old story. Based on W. Meyer-Forster's novel and Richard Mansfield's play, this film follows the troubled love affair between a prince and a barmaid.
VHS: S25711. $19.95.
John Emerson, USA, 1915, 35 mins.

Old Ironsides
Adventure and action film set in the southern Mediterranean, based on the 1930 poem by Oliver Wendell Holmes. Wallace Beery and Boris Karloff are members of the merchant marine fighting pirates of Tripoli.
VHS: S03440. $29.95.
James Cruze, USA, 1926, 111 mins.

Oliver Twist
Lon Chaney as Fagin and Jackie Coogan as Oliver star in this Charles Dickens classic of a master criminal who teaches children to steal.
VHS: S11456. $24.95.
Frank Lloyd, USA, 1922, 80 mins.

One Punch O'Day
Billy Sullivan, Jack Herrick and Charlotte Merrian star in this boxing story.
VHS: S07267. $19.95.
Harry J. Brown, USA, 1926, 60 mins.

Open Switch
Helen Holmes, Jack Perrin, Charles Wittaker and Mack Wright star in this action railroad story of stolen express packages. 1925, 50 mins. Silent with music score.
VHS: S10367. $19.95.

Orchids and Ermine
Carey Wilson wrote the screenplay for this silent romantic comedy about a former telephone switchboard operator played by Colleen Moore. A millionaire could be the answer to all her woes if only she could find one suitably rich and handsome.
VHS: S23841. $24.95.
Alfred Santell, USA, 1926, 75 mins.

Our Modern Maidens
Also known as *Our Dancing Daughters*, this silent work about the opulence and energy of the Jazz Age pivots on the romantic and political entanglements of a group of twenties flappers and musicians. With Joan Crawford, Douglas Fairbanks, Jr., Anita Page and Rod La Rocque.
VHS: S18129. $19.98.
Harry Beaumont, USA, 1928, 97 mins.

Outside the Law
Tod Browning wrote, produced and directed this silent criminal drama that features Lon Chaney in three roles. Chaney, as Black Mike, threatens the happiness of the daughter of a former underworld leader now reformed by a Chinese philosopher. With Priscilla Dean, Ralph Lewis and Wheeler Oakman.
VHS: S05705. $24.95.
Tod Browning, USA, 1921, 113 mins.

Pampered Youths
Cullen Landis and Alice Calhoun star in this silent adaptation of Booth Tarkington's *The Magnificent Ambersons*. It's a timeless story of the decline of a once mighty family. 1925, 35 mins.
VHS: S23842. $24.95.

The Patchwork Girl of Oz/ A Florida Enchantment
Novelist Frank Baum produced *The Patchwork Girl* (1914). It's a film about a journey to Oz in search of a spell that turns innocent bystanders to stone. Hal Roach is featured as the cowardly lion while a young Frenchman plays the girl of the title. In *A Florida Enchantment* (1914), magic transforms men into women and women into men, resulting in a film that has an interesting modern edge, even though it was vilified in its time. From the *Origins of American Films* series, a joint project of the Library of Congress and Smithsonian Video.
VHS: S21265. $34.95.

Paths to Paradise
Raymond Griffith, an international jewel thief, attempts to steal a famous diamond. Silent with music track.
VHS: S07255. $19.95.
Clarence Badger, USA, 1925, 62 mins.

The Penalty
Lon Chaney stars as a hateful monster bent on revenge and power in this silent thriller. It all begins when a young boy has both legs amputated. The only problem is that this fearsome operation was wholly unnecessary. 60 mins.
VHS: S25698. $19.95.

Perils of the Rails
One of the best silent action railroad films with many great stunts, featuring Helen Holmes, Edward Hearn and J.P. McGowan. USA, 1925, 61 mins.
VHS: S08875. $24.95.

Phantom Flyer
Al Wilson, Lillian Gilmore, Buck Connors and Billy Red Jones star. Silent with music track.
VHS: S07209. $19.95.
Bruce Mitchell, USA, 1928, 53 mins.

The Phantom of the Opera
Lon Chaney stars in the greatest role of his career as Erik, the love-torn resident of the hidden depths of the Opera House. This 70th anniversary edition has been completely remastered from a 35mm archive print and features the original 2-strip Technicolor masked ball sequence and fantastic score performed by a 60-piece orchestra.
VHS: S01019. $24.95.
Rupert Julian, USA, 1925, 101 mins.

Playing Dead
A Vitagraph production of a Sidney Drew film, in which he orchestrates his own death so that his wife can enter into a relationship with a man he believes she is in love with. With Donald Hall, Harry English, Isadore Marcil and Alice Lake. Silent with piano score.
VHS: S20025. $24.95.
Sidney Drew, USA, 1915, 58 mins.

Pollyanna
Mary Pickford, America's Sweetheart, stars in this silent slapstick comedy based on Eleanor Porter's book. The optimistic girl smiles at everything no matter how troubling it may be. When she is orphaned, a dour aunt takes her in and is soon transformed by the glad girl's good cheer.
VHS: S26688. $19.95.
Paul Powell, USA, 1920, 60 mins.

Poor Little Rich Girl
Mary Pickford in her first appearance as a child in a major film, an enchanting masterpiece of the early American cinema. Pickford, who was 24 at the time, plays Gwendolyn, a rich girl with everything except her parents' love and attention.
VHS: S01047. $19.95.
Maurice Tourneur, USA, 1917, 99 mins.

Power
William Boyd, Alan Hale, Jacqueline Logan, Carole Lombard and Joan Bennett star. Silent with music track.
VHS: S07212. $24.95.
Howard Hughes, USA, 1928, 74 mins.

Power God
Ben Wilson and Neva Gerber star in this complete 15-chapter serial, directed by Francis Ford. Silent with music track. USA, 1927, 330 mins.
VHS: S07186. $49.95.

Pride of the Clan
Extremely rare Mary Pickford film, directed by Maurice Tourneur, with Matt Moore.
VHS: S05974. $49.95.
Maurice Tourneur, USA, 1916, 80 mins.

Primitive Lover
Constance Talmadge, Harrison Ford and Kenneth Harlan star in this delightful silent comedy of a woman who wants more from her marriage.
VHS: S08846. $24.95.
Sidney Franklin, USA, 1916, 67 mins.

Q Ships
The story of a German submarine commander during World War I, and the conflicts he suffers over his morality and his loyalty to his country. Silent with music track.
VHS: S10585. $19.95.
Geoffrey Barkas, USA, 1928, 78 mins.

Queen of the Chorus
An early chorus line melodrama about a woman with a heart of gold who makes the ultimate sacrifice. With Rex Lease, Virginia Brown Faire and Crawford Kent. Silent film with musical score. USA, 1929.
VHS: S15385. $24.95.

Raffles, The Amateur Racksman
John Barrymore plays the debonair society burglar. Silent with music track. USA, 1917, 70 mins.
VHS: S07253. $24.95.

Raggedy Rose
Stan Laurel directed Mabel Normand in this touching Cinderella story.
VHS: S08848. $24.95.
Stan Laurel, USA, 1926, 56 mins.

Railroad Dramas
Three early short films featuring Helen Holmes and Helen Gibson, and featuring railroads: *The Wild Engine, Rival Railroad Plot* and *The Ghost of the Canyon*. 75 mins.
VHS: S08878. $24.95.

Ranson's Folly
A very rare Richard Barthelmess film, this is a period drama set during the Civil War.
VHS: S05975. $49.95.
Sidney Olcott, USA, 1926

The Raven
This rare feature opens with a history of Edgar Allan Poe's ancestors and follows his rise to maturity. Unable to integrate himself into society, Poe turns to alcohol. This crutch inspires his hallucinatory vision and throws him into the world of "The Raven." Although Poe was more accurately addicted to narcotics, this film remains one of the earliest and most eccentric biopics. With Henry B. Walthall and Wanda Howard. Silent with an added music track.
VHS: S15278. $19.95.
Charles J. Brabin, USA, 1915, 80 mins.

Reaching for the Moon
Douglas Fairbanks is a dreamer who becomes king of Vulgaria and discovers royalty can have its down side. As the constant target for assassins and the object of desire of a homely princess, he looks for a way out in this energetic comedic adventure. With Eileen Percy.
VHS: S05694. $29.95.
John Emerson, USA, 1917, 91 mins.

Red Kimono
A woman is forced into an immoral life, compelling her to take drastic measures. She succeeds but only in part and must soon support herself in the only way that she can, as a prostitute. This is a fascinating silent melodrama.
VHS: 23843. $24.95.
Walter Lang, USA, 1925, 70 mins.

Red Signals
Wallace MacDonald, Earle Williams, Eva Novak star. Silent with music track.
VHS: S07228. $24.95.
J.P. McGowan, USA, 1927, 70 mins.

Regeneration
The first feature by the remarkable Raoul Walsh (*High Sierra*, *The Big Trail*), *Regeneration* is an early look at the possibilities of filmmaking, Walsh used gritty New York locations to create a heightened sense of danger and excitement. With Rockliffe Fellows, John McCann, James Marcus and Maggie Weston. Silent with music track.
VHS: S17449. $29.95.
Raoul Walsh, USA

Reggie Mixes In
Douglas Fairbanks and Bessie Love star in this drama of intrigue set in the underworld.
VHS: S08883. $24.95.
Christy Cabanne, USA, 1916, 58 mins.

The Return of Boston Blackie
Corliss Palmer, Raymond Glenn, Rosemary Cooper and Strongheart the dog star in this silent melodrama. Boston Blackie tries to reform a pretty blonde thief with the help of Strongheart. Orchestral score.
VHS: S22430. $19.95.
Harry O. Hoyt, USA, 1927, 58 mins.

Riders of the Purple Sage
Zane Grey's novel is adapted for the screen in this silent film featuring Tom Mix. It's a tale of revenge sought by a man for the sake of his sister, who suffered under Mormonism.
VHS: S23844. $24.95.
Edfrid Bingham, USA, 1925, 63 mins.

Rip Van Winkle
A silent adaptation of the classic tale about a somnambulent man awakened after a 20-year sleep. With Thomas Jefferson. 1914.
VHS: S18898. $19.95.

Risky Business
Vera Reynolds, a society girl, is shown the hardships of a doctor's life by her gold-digging mother in an attempt to stop the marriage. Also included is the great Snub Pollard short, *Sold at Auction*. With ZaSu Pitts, Ethel Clayton. Silent with music score.
VHS: S07484. $24.95.
Alan Hale, USA, 1928, 104 mins.

Robin Hood
In his *The Parade's Gone By*, film critic Kevin Brownlow says, "*Robin Hood*, if not the most flamboyant of Fairbanks' swashbuckling, is certainly the most awe-inspiring. Its center piece is an enormous castle, said to be the largest set ever constructed in Hollywood. Purely on the level of art direction, *Robin Hood* is an unsurpassed and unsurpassable achievement." This full, almost three-hour version is the most complete available.
VHS: S06389. $24.95.
Allan Dwan, USA, 1922, c. 160 mins.

Romola
This rarely-seen Gish film features both of the Gish sisters (Lillian and Dorothy), with Ronald Colman, William Powell, and a new piano score. Silent with musical score.
VHS: S05976. $49.95.
Henry King, USA, 1924, 120 mins.

Rubber Tires
A film that foreshadowed the Depression soon to come, a family moves to California to seek better fortunes, unaware that their car is unique and worth a great deal of money. USA, 1927.
VHS: S02582. $19.95.

Sadie Thompson
The first film version of Somerset Maugham's classic novella, with the creative talents of Raoul Walsh, Gloria Swanson, Lionel Barrymore and art director William Cameron Menzies. A landmark of the silent era, the film's great achievement is the uncompromising translation of Maugham's controversial story of a San Francisco prostitute and a South Pacific reformer. The tragedy of the film is that, for many years, the last scenes were missing from the only existing print. In this version, the final minutes have been carefully restored and the result is one of the most important triumphs of the silent era. Restored by Dennis Doros. Silent with music score.
VHS: S08944. $29.95.
Laser: LD71315. $49.95.
Raoul Walsh, USA, 1928, 97 mins.

Salome
Alla Nazimova, the notorious wife of Rudolph Valentino, directed this controversial version of Salome with its highly stylized acting and sets.
VHS: S08851. $19.95.
Alla Nazimova, USA, 1922, 35 mins.

Salome and Queen Elizabeth
Two very rare silent films; *Salome* stars Alla Nazimova in a bold and bizarre adaptation of Oscar Wilde's play, with Azimova's famous "Dance of the Seven Veils" sequence; *Queen Elizabeth* features the famous Sarah Bernhardt when she was 56 years old. Silent films with music score, 91 mins. total.
VHS: S06932. $29.95.

The Saturday Night Kid
A curious silent work enlivened by the appearance of two skilled performers, Clara Bow and Jean Arthur. USA, 1929.
VHS: S18952. $19.95.

Scarlet Car
Lon Chaney, Franklyn Farnum and Edith Johnson star in this early Chaney film. Trying to hide the fact of embezzlement, Chaney, the teller in a bank, is left for dead. Silent with music score.
VHS: S10370. $24.95.
Joseph De Grasse, USA, 1917, 70 mins.

Selected Shorts #2
Family Life (1924, Mark June and Ruth Hatt); *Why Worry* (1926, George Bunny); *Be My King* (1928, Lupino Lane); *Idle Eyes*, (1928, Ben Turpin). Various, USA, 1924-28, 70 mins.
VHS: S04818. $19.95.

Sex
The beautiful star of a Broadway show seduces a married man in this silent drama. His marriage collapses but the star finds someone else. Eventually all this fooling around brings personal tragedy. With Louise Glaum, William Conklin and Irving Cummings.
VHS: S05433. $29.95.
Fred Niblo, USA, 1920, 94 mins.

Shadows
Lon Chaney, Marguerite de la Motte, Harrison Ford and Walter Long star in this atmospheric and haunting drama set in Urkey, a small fishing village, with Chaney as a Chinaman barred from the village, whom the Reverend Malden (Harrison Ford, no relation) and his wife de la Motte try to convert to Christianity. Silent with music score.
VHS: S05605. $24.95.
Tom Forman, USA, 1922, 85 mins.

The Shamrock and the Rose
Mack Swain and Maurice Costello are cast in this story of feuding families. Even the priest cannot convince these warring clans to forget their differences. 1927, 60 mins.
VHS: 23845. $24.95.

She Goes to War
Humor, tragedy and romance are all part of this World War I tale directed by Henry King and starring Eleanor Boardman and Al St. John.
VHS: S10582. $19.95.
Henry King, USA, 1929, 50 mins.

The Sheik
The original famous version of Rudolph Valentino's romantic melodrama, as Valentino (Sheik Ahmed) rescues a proud English girl (Agnes Ayres) disguised as a slave. The film that made Valentino an international idol.
VHS: S09401. $19.98.
George Melford, USA, 1921, 80 mins.

Shifting Sands
Gloria Swanson appears in an off-beat role as a woman sent to jail for a crime she didn't commit; she is blackmailed by a ring of spies to obtain a set of secret plans. USA, 1918, 52 mins.
VHS: S08855. $19.95.

A Ship Comes In
Rudolph Schildkraut, Louise Dresser, Milton Holmes and Linda Landi star. Silent with music track.
VHS: S07219. $24.95.
William K. Howard, USA, 1928, 70 mins.

Ships of the Night
Frank Moran and Jacqueline Logan star in this tale of the south seas and the search for her fugitive brother. Silent with music score, 1928, 63 mins.
VHS: S10362. $19.95.

Shock
Lambert Hillyer directed this early silent horror-thriller starring Lon Chaney, Virginia Valli and Christine Mayo.
VHS: S04798. $24.95.
Lambert Hillyer, USA, 1923, 85 mins.

Shore Leave
Richard Barthelmess is a reluctant seaman who has been spotted by Dorothy Mackaill, a dressmaker determined to be married. In this romantic comedy she gives her all to land Barthelmess. It's a scenario that always engages the romantically inclined.
VHS: S23148. $24.95.
John S. Robertson, USA, 1925, 90 mins.

The Short Films of Mary Pickford
America's silent sweetheart in several of her most endearing film shorts. Includes *In Old Madrid* (10 mins.), *Lonely Villa* (10 mins.), *Sweet Memories* (10 mins.), *Her First Biscuits* (5 mins.), *Female of the Species* (10 mins.), *100% Canadian* (10 mins.), *New York Hat* (10 mins.), *Violin Maker of Cremona* (10 mins) and *1776 (The Hessian Renegades)* (10 mins.).
VHS: S14929. $29.95.

Show People
"In this delightful satire on Hollywood in the twenties, Marion Davies plays a star-struck country girl who arrives in Hollywood seeking the glamour of the bright lights, only to find herself the lesser half of a slapstick team. Davies proves herself as the comedienne, whether as Peggy Pepper, baptized into show usiness with seltzer sprayed from a siphon bottle, or Peggy Pepoire, motion picture star. Intended as a gentle satire on the career of Gloria Swanson, it pokes fun at other Hollywood luminaries along the way" (*Pacific Film Archive*).
VHS: S09282. $29.95.
King Vidor, USA, 1928, 81 mins.

The Silent Enemy
Based on a 72 volume history of New France written by Jesuit missionaries between 1610 and 1791, this magical reconstruction of Ojibwa life tells of the time before white man settled the Hudson Bay region. The "silent enemy" is hunger that threatens the tribe as they desperately track thunderous caribou herds. Boasting an all-Native cast, the film begins with a moving narrative from Chief Yellow Robe: "This is the story of my people ...look not upon us as actors. We are Indians living once more our old life. Soon we will be gone. Your civilization will destroy us. But by your magic we will live forever." Newly restored from the 35mm nitrate original, with a music score by Massard Kur Zhene.
VHS: S16432. $39.95.
Laser: CLV/CAV. LD72072. $39.95.
H.P. Carver, Canada/USA, 1930, 87 mins.

Silk Husbands and Calico Wives
House Peters and Mary Alden are cast in this story about the ideal marriage, for a man that is. A wife is supposed to love, honor and obey her husband, at least in older silent movies.
VHS: 23847. $24.95.
Alfred E. Green, USA, 1920, 65 mins.

Simba
Journeying to remote and exotic regions, Martin and Osa Johnson produced, wrote and photographed films celebrating the natural wonders and native tribes of Africa, Asia and the South Seas. For *Simba*, they forded crocodile infested rivers, braved stampeding elephants and stared down angry rhinos in order to film lions in their natural habitat, the veldt. Killing only for food or self protection, the Johnsons became two of Africa's first conservationists. Today, *Simba* is considered the highlight of the Johnson's career.
VHS: S16430. $39.95.
Laser: CLV/CAV. LD72073. $39.95.
Martin and Osa Johnson, USA, 1928, 83 mins.

The Sky Pilot
John Bowers, Colleen Moore, David Butler and Harry Todd star in this early silent by the great King Vidor.
VHS: S03783. $29.95.
King Vidor, USA, 1921, 72 mins.

Skyscraper
Adapted from a story by Dudley Murphy by Elliott Clawson and Tay Garnett, and starring William Boyd. A Pathe production by De Mille.
VHS: S07248. $24.95.
Howard Higgin, USA, 1928, 68 mins.

Smith Family Series
The 1920's version of the sit-com, in six short serials produced by Mack Sennett, called *The Smith Family Series: Smith's New Home, Smith's Fishing Trip, Smith's Picnic, Smith's Customer, Smith's Cook* and *Smith's Army Life*. USA, 118 mins.
VHS: S03172. $24.95.

Smouldering Fires
A very rare drama from Clarence Brown, this is a superbly directed triangle with Laura La Plante, Pauline Frederick. Tape comes from British print never seen in the U.S.
VHS: S05977. $24.95.
Clarence Brown, USA, 1924, 100 mins.

The Social Secretary
Norma Talmadge is Mayme, a good looking girl looking for a job without male interference. Disguised as a plain jane, she is hired by a wealthy woman for the title position. Mayme saves the lady's daughter from a villainous count. With Kate Lester, Gladden Jones and Erich von Stroheim as the Buzzard. A comedy.
VHS: S04808. $19.95.
John Emerson, USA, 1916, 56 mins.

Sold for Marriage
Lillian Gish and Walter Long star in this silent film about a young Russian women in distress. She believes her tormentor is dead and escapes to America. 1916, 43 mins.
VHS: 23848. $24.95.

Son of the Sheik
The last film of Rudolph Valentino, a sequel to his big hit, *The Sheik*. Valentino plays the son of the desert warrior and lover who is out to capture the bandits who wronged a poor dancing girl.
VHS: S03071. $19.98.
Laser: CLV. LD70769. $39.95.
George Fitzmaurice, USA, 1926, 68 mins.

Soul of the Beast
Madge Bellamy, Cullen Landis, Noah Beery and Vola Vale star. Madge and her only friend, a circus elephant, are runaways from an abusing stepfather. Silent with music score.
VHS: S10364. $19.95.
John Griffith Wray, USA, 1923, 65 mins.

Soul-Fire
Richard Barthelmess, Bessie Love, Walter Lang and Arthur Metcalf star.
VHS: S07201. $24.95.
John S. Robertson, USA, 1925, 100 mins.

The Spanish Dancer
The legendary Pola Negri plays a fiery gypsy who maneuvers the King (Wallace Beery) into restoring an impoverished nobleman's estates. With Anthony Moreno and Adolphe Menjou.
VHS: S03171. $18.95.
Herbert Brenon, USA, 1923, 55 mins.

Sparrows
Considered to be Mary Pickford's best feature and a super-production of its day, *Sparrows* is an expert blend of thrilling spectacle and hissable villainy. The story concerns a group of orphan children held in virtual slavery on a southern farm surrounded by a treacherous swamp. In the climax, Mollie (Pickford) leads the children to safety after a hair-raising chase through a wilderness filled with alligators and quicksand. Organ score.
VHS: S01744. $29.95.
William Beaudine, USA, 1926, 81 min.

Speed Spook
Auto-racing is the theme of this early silent film starring Johnny Hines, Faire Binney.
VHS: S07258. $29.95.
Charles Hines, USA, 1924, 85 mins.

The Spieler
Renee Adoree and Alan Hale are cast in this silent dramatic film that reveals the seamier side of carnival life. Love, jealousy and murder all play a role in this frank tale.
VHS: 23849. $24.95.
Frank Lloyd, USA, 1928, 70 mins.

Square Shoulders
Junior Coghlan, Louis Wolheim, Anita Louis and Montague Shaw star in this drama set in a military academy. Silent with music score.
VHS: S10359. $19.95.
E. Mason Hopper, USA, 1929, 56 mins.

The Star Prince
The Star Prince falls to earth on a star and is found and reared by a woodcutter. The Prince sets out to find his real mother and survives several adventures involving the wicked witch and the little princess. This film is enacted by children from the Little Players Film Co. of Chicago.
VHS: S22883. $19.95.
Madeline Brandeis, USA, 1918, 54 mins.

Stella Maris
Mary Pickford stars. Silent with music track.
VHS: S07221. $24.95.
Marshall Neilan, USA, 1918, 70 mins.

Stop at Nothing
The only known surviving film of George Larkin, a very popular silent era actor. USA, 1922, 56 mins.
VHS: S08853. $19.95.

Suds
Mary Pickford, America's sweetheart during the silent era, stars in this charming tale of fantasy and young love. Pickford is a cockney laundress who dreams of a finer life until she finds true love with someone from her own station.
VHS: 23851. $24.95.
John Francis Dillon, USA, 1920, 75 mins.

Surrender
Mary Philbin and Ivan Mousjoukine star in this silent epic set in Russia during World War I. A small village is threatened with utter destruction by Russian generals.
VHS: 23852. $24.95.
Edward Sloan, USA, 1927, 75 mins.

Swan
A young woman of noble blood is encouraged by her mother to marry the older crown prince, but she falls in love with her handsome tutor instead. With Frances Howard, Adolphe Menjou, Richardo Cortez and Ida Waterman. Based on the 1922 Ferenc Molnar play about the Hapsburg royal family. Silent with music track.
VHS: S16177. $29.95.
Dimitri Buchowetzki, USA, 1925, 120 mins.

Sweet Adeline
Charles Ray stars. Silent with music track. Hick becomes a big musical star but loses his girlfriend to his brother.
VHS: S07243. $19.95.
Jerome Storm, USA, 1926, 60 mins.

A Tale of Two Cities/ In the Switch Tower
Norma Talmadge was only 14 years old when she was cast as a lead in her first important film, the original screen version of *A Tale of Two Cities*, in 1911. With *In the Switch Tower* from 1915. Silent. USA, 70 mins.
VHS: S03655. $29.95.

Tarzan of the Apes
Elmo Lincoln and Enid Markey star in this first screen version of the classic story.
VHS: S11455. $19.95.
Scott Sidney, USA, 1918, 59 mins.

The Tempest
An officer in the army of the Czar finds his romance with a princess violently interrupted by the Russian revolutionaries. Featuring a brave—though very melodramatic—performance by John Barrymore. Silent, music track.
VHS: S02089. $29.95.
Sam Taylor, USA, 1928, 99 mins.

Ten Nights in a Barroom

This classic film underscores the evil of drinking alcohol. Perhaps its most famous scene is the final fight sequence. William Farnum, Tom Santschi, Patty Lou Lynd, Robert Fraser and other luminaries of the early cinema are featured.
VHS: S23319. $19.95.
William O'Connor, USA, 1931, 72 mins.

Test of Donald Norton

George Walsh, Tyrone Power, Robert Graves and Eugenie Gilbert star. A man raised by Indians is troubled by fears of being half-Indian.
VHS: S07203. $24.95.
B. Reeves Eason, USA, 1926, 85 mins.

These Girls Won't Talk

That's only because these are silent movies. Titles include *Her Bridal Nightmare* with Colleen Moore as a bride whose hubby has been arrested for losing his pants, *The Campus Carmen* with Daphne Pollard and Carole Lombard, and *As Luck Would Have It* with Betty Compson as a daffy dame who wants to be a nurse.
VHS: S05861. $29.95.
Harry Edwards et al., USA, 1918-28, 81 mins.

The Thief of Baghdad

Douglas Fairbanks on a marvelous quest in an Arabian Nights fantasy/adventure with the lovely Julanne Johnston as the princess who rides off with Fairbanks on his magic carpet. From Raoul Walsh, a dynamic, prolific director.
VHS: S01323. $24.95.
Laser: LD70397. $34.98.
Raoul Walsh, USA, 1924, 132 mins.

The Three Musketeers

An early silent version of the famous novel starring Fairbanks with Leon Barry, Marguerite de la Motte, George Siegmann, Adolphe Menjou.
VHS: S08887. $24.95.
Fred Niblo, USA, 1921, 120 mins.

Through the Breakers

Margaret Livingston, Holmes Herbert, Clyde Cook, Natalie Joyce and Frank Hagney star in this tale of lost love on a South Sea Island. Silent with music score. 1928, 55 mins.
VHS: S10369. $19.95.

Tol'able David

In the Appalachian mountains three evil mountain men cause havoc in a small community. After they kill his dog, cripple his brother and cause the death of his father, little David is forced to deal with them when they try to rob the mail wagon. With Richard Barthelmess, Marion Abbott and Warner Richmond. B&W. One hand-tinted sequence.
VHS: S05481. $19.95.
Henry King, USA, 1921, 106 mins.

Tom Mix Short Subjects

Five short films of Tom Mix produced by Carl Selig: *A Bear of a Story, The Stagecoach Driver and the Girl, How Weary Goes Wooing, Using His Brain, Sage Brush Tom.*
VHS: S08872. $24.95.

Tomboy

Lotta Williams, Herbert Rawliston, Harry Gibbon star.
VHS: S07231. $19.95.
David Kirkland, USA, 1924, 64 mins.

Tong Man

Sessue Hayakawa and Helen Eddy star in this rare film. Silent with music track.
VHS: S07233. $19.95.
William Worthington, USA, 1919, 60 mins.

Too Wise Wives

Rare silent-era films by two woman filmmakers: *Too Wise Wives* is an early feature from 1921 by director Lois Weber, which dissects the proper role of a wife among the socially prominent. Her comic short *How Men Propose* (1913) is also included. *Matrimony's Speed Limit* and *A House Divided*, both by Alice Guy-Blache, are two brief comic films about marriage and divorce. From the *Origins of American Films* series, a joint project of the Library of Congress and Smithsonian Video.
VHS: S21267. $34.95.

Traffic in Souls

Unseen for many years, this rare classic tells the story of the turn-of-the-century white slave trade, running rampant in this country at the time. An early social-problem film, it attempted to make the general public aware of this rarely-talked-about problem. A beautiful condition print. Piano scored.
VHS: S15511. $29.95.
George Tucker, USA, 1913, 74 mins.

Trail of the Axe

Dustin Farnum stars in this story of love and adventure in a Northwoods logging camp. USA, 1919, silent with music track, 55 mins.
VHS: S07204. $24.95.

The Train to Happiness

In the new era of freedom enjoyed by Russia, the Jewish Shalom Theater has taken root. Against a backdrop where emergent anti-semitic groups are also exercising their newly found freedom to express themselves, this troupe is bringing Jewish culture to Jews who were previously denied their culture and religion by communism. 57 mins.
VHS: S23231. $39.95.

Unchastened Woman

Theda Bara, Wyndham Standing, Dale Fuller, Eileen Percy star. Silent with music track.
VHS: S07224. $19.95.
James Young, USA, 1925, 52 mins.

Uncle Tom's Cabin (1903 & 1914)

This tape includes the two earliest film versions of Harriet Beecher Stowe's classic tale of slavery. The 1903 version was restored from Library of Congress paper prints. The 1914 version features Sam Lucas—the first black actor to star in a film.
VHS: S15482. $29.95.

Uncle Tom's Cabin (1914)

An early version of the Harriet Beecher Stowe novel of slavery stars Sam Lucas, who was said to be the first black man to have a leading role in films, as Tom, and also has some black stage actors in the cast.
VHS: S11452. $19.95.
William R. Daly, USA, 1914, 54 mins.

The Unholy Three

A ventriloquist, a dwarf and a strong man carry out a series of bizarre crimes which end in murder. The first in a series of off-kilter tales starring Lon Chaney under Browning's direction. With Harry Earles, Victor McLaglen, Mae Busch and Matt Moore. Silent with music track.
VHS: S16172. $29.95.
Tod Browning, USA, 1925, 76 mins.

The Unknown

One of the rare Lon Chaney films—located in France—now with English subtitles. With Joan Crawford and Normand Kerry. Silent with music score.
VHS: S10371. $24.95.
Tod Browning, USA, 1927, 60 mins.

The Untamable

Gladys Walton, Malcolm McGregor, John Sainpolis and Etta Lee star in this film about a woman with a split personality beautifully changing from an innocent lady to a lady who is cruel and campish. A truly unique film from the silent era. Silent with music score.
VHS: S10368. $19.95.
Herbert Blache, USA, 1923, 65 mins.

Until They Get Me

Pauline Atarke and Joe King star in this adventure in the north as a mountie searches for years to get his man. USA, 1918, 58 mins.
VHS: S08857. $24.95.

The Vanishing American

One of the great silent epics. Richard Dix stars in this Zane Grey tale about a modern American Indian who fights the Germans in WWI only to return to find his people being mistreated by a crooked Indian agent (Noah Beery). Filmed partly in Monument Valley. With Lois Wilson as the schoolmarm and plenty of native American history.
VHS: S05489. $49.95.
George B. Seitz, USA, 1915, 148 mins.

Virginian

An early faithful adaptation of the famous book, with Kenneth Harlan, Florence Vidor and Raymond Hatton.
VHS: S08889. $24.95.
Tom Forman, USA, 1923, 74 mins.

Walking Back

Sue Carrol stars. Troubled teenagers go for a joyride and wind up involved in a robbery scheme. Silent with music track.
VHS: S07246. $19.95.
Rupert Julian, USA, 1926, 53 mins.

We're in the Navy Now

After the huge success of their *Behind the Front*, Wallace Beery and Raymond Hatton were teamed up again in another hilarious look at military life. Silent with music score. USA, 1927, 60 mins.
VHS: S07485. $19.95.

Webs of Steele

J.P. McGowan directed Helen Holmes and Andrew Waldro in this railroad action drama. USA, 1925, 55 mins.
VHS: S08877. $24.95.

West of Zanzibar

Lon Chaney stars as a magician turned ivory trader. He rules a jungle monarchy, but lives for just one thing: revenge on the man who left him in his crippled state. Chaney decides the best way to settle the score is to despoil the man's beautiful young daughter. With Walter Huston, Lionel Barrymore and Mary Nolan.
VHS: S16173. $29.95.
Tod Browning, USA, 1928, 63 mins.

West of Zanzibar/The Unholy Three

Two early silent collaborations between Tod Browning and Lon Chaney. *West of Zanzibar* (1928) deals with a man's determination to destroy the man who caused his crippling injury. *The Unholy Three* (1925) is about the underworld activities of a ventriloquist who forms an unholy trinity with a grotesque strongman and midget. Chaney remade the film in 1930, his only talkie.
Laser: LD71858. $39.98.

Where East Is East

Lon Chaney Sr. is Tiger Haynes, a badly scarred trapper who sells wild animals to the circus. Lupe Velez plays Togo, his beloved daughter. Problems develop when she falls in love with the son of a circus owner, who in turn is being romanced by Tiger's vindictive ex-wife. Silent with music track.
VHS: S16176. $29.95.
Tod Browning, USA, 1929, 140 mins.

While the City Sleeps

Lon Chaney stars as a tough city detective totally absorbed in his work who shelters and then falls for an underworld girl. He wants to marry her, but in the end, the inwardly sentimental detective steps aside for the boy she really loves, a small-time crook who says he wants to go straight. One of the few major films in which Chaney did not appear in disguise. With Wheeler Oakman.
VHS: S01449. $29.95.
Jack Conway, USA, 1928

The Whip

Maurice Tourneur directed this rare early feature already showing his mastery of lighting.
VHS: S04807. $24.95.
Maurice Tourneur, USA, 1917, 60 mins.

White Gold

William K. Howard directed this film starring Jetta Goudal, Kenneth Thomson, George Bancroft. Silent with music tack.
VHS: S07252. $24.95.
William K. Howard, USA, 1927, 70 mins.

White Shadows in the South Seas

An alcoholic doctor in Tahiti finds happiness with a native girl, until he is killed by white colonials. This beautifully photographed film carries with it a rocky history, including a number of different directors. David O. Selznick and Robert Flaherty each played a hand, but Van Dyke wound up with the final director's credit. From a book by Frederick J. O'Brien, star Monte Blue and Raquel Torres.
VHS: S16174. $29.95.
W.S. Van Dyke, USA, 1927, 88 mins.

White Sheep

Glen Tryon stars as the weakling of the family, who proves himself at the end.
VHS: S07261. $19.95.
Hal Roach, USA, 1924, 70 mins.

The White Sister

Lillian Gish plays an Italian aristocrat who is driven away from home when her nasty sister alters their father's will following his death. Gish falls in love with an Italian army officer, but when he is reported killed in the war, the broken-hearted girl decides to become a nun. With Ronald Colman and Gail Cane. Silent with music track.
VHS: S16110. $29.95.
Henry King, USA, 1923, 68 mins.

White Tiger

Three international crooks attempt the crime of the century. Hiding out together in a mountain cabin after the deed, their mutual distrust grows daily. With Priscilla Dean, Matt Moore, Raymond Griffith and Wallace Beery. Though rough, this video was transferred from the best print available. Organ score included.
VHS: S22426. $19.95.
Tod Browning, USA, 1923, 81 mins.

Wild and Woolly

Douglas Fairbanks stars in this comic Western as an overzealous aficionado of Western lore, who somehow manages to best both Native Americans and desperados. Eileen Percy, Walter Bytell, Joseph Singleton, Sam De Grasse and Tom Wilson are also featured.
VHS: S22983. $24.95.
John Emerson, USA, 1917, 58 mins.

Wild Orchids

Garbo is bewitching as a married woman caught in a steamy love triangle set in Java. Lewis Stone co-stars as her husband, and Nils Asther appears as the native prince who steals her heart. Silent film with synchronized music score and sound effects.
VHS: S13977. $29.99.
Sidney Franklin, USA, 1928, 119 mins.

Wings

One of the most exciting of the silent dramas, *Wings* was the first film to be awarded the Oscar for Best Picture. Featuring Clara Bow (The IT Girl) and a short appearance by Gary Cooper, the film has incredible aerial battle sequences. Director Wellman makes a humanistic statement as he explores the devastation of World War I.
VHS: S02831. $19.95.
William Wellman, USA, 1927, 139 mins.

Winning the Futurity

Cullen Landis, Clara Horton, Henry Kolker, Pat Harman star.
VHS: S07211. $19.95.
Scott Dunlap, USA, 1926, 70 mins.

Wishing Ring

An extremely rare film from Maurice Tourneur. A light and charming romance.
VHS: S05986. $24.95.
Maurice Tourneur, USA, 1915, 50 mins.

With Byrd at the South Pole

Byrd's establishment of Little America and the spectacular first flight over the South Pole—part publicity stunt, part scientific milestone—marked the end of an era. This film is a remarkable document of courage and achievement. Byrd, his terrier Igloo, and his companions became legends as popular as Lindbergh, Babe Ruth and Valentino. Winner of the Academy Award for Best Cinematography. Silent with music track.
VHS: S16433. $39.95.
Laser: CLV/CAV. LD72074. $39.95.
Joseph Rucker, USA, 1930, 82 mins.

Wizard of Oz

Not the Judy Garland version, but the original silent adaptation of Frank Baum's book, with Larry Semon as Scarecrow, Oliver Hardy as the Tin Man, and Dorothy Dwan as Dorothy, in this very ambitious slapstick comedy. Silent with music track.
VHS: S22097. $29.95.
Larry Semon, USA, 1925, 65 mins.

Wolf Blood

Marguerite Clayton, George Chesebro, Ray Hanford and Roy Watson star in this gothic tale. George is hurt in an accident and Dr. Horton must use a wolf's blood to save him. Unexplained deaths soon follow, leading George to fear that he is becoming a beast. This may well be the forerunner for the classic wolfman films of the 1930's. From a 35mm tinted print.
VHS: S23313. $19.95.
George Chesebro/George Mitchell, USA, 1925, 68 mins.

Wolves of Kultur

A seven chapter condensation of the great early Charles Hutchinson action serial about stolen plans that must be regained. 1918, 182 mins.
VHS: S11460. $39.95.

Woman of Affairs

Greta Garbo and John Gilbert star in this silent romance about a wild rich girl who goes from man to man until she finally kills herself in a car crash. With Lewis Stone, Douglas Fairbanks Jr. Silent with music track.
Laser: Chapter search. Includes original theatrical trailer. LD71645. $34.98.
Clarence Brown, USA, 1928, 90 mins.

Won in the Clouds

Al Wilson, Helen Foster, Frank Rice, George French, Joe Bennett star. Silent with music track.
VHS: S07208. $19.95.
Bruce Mitchell, USA, 1928, 55 mins.

The Worldly Madonna

Clara Kimball Young has two roles in this rare silent film. As Janet, a convent novitiate, she agrees to exchange places with her sister Lucy, a cabaret dancer, who believes she has killed a man. Though shorter than the original version, the complete story has been preserved in this video version. Organ music accompaniment.
VHS: S22427. $19.95.
Harry Garson, USA, 1922, 47 mins.

Yankee Doodle in Berlin

An early Mack Sennett comedy, a spoof of the Kaiser, with Bothwell Browne, Ford Sterling, Mal St. Clair.
VHS: S07266. $19.95.
Richard Jones, USA, 1918, 60 mins.

The Young April

Bessie Love, Joseph and Rudolph Schildkraut and Bryant Washburn star in this silent comedy about a young orphan. Poor in America, a young woman inherits a great deal of money and a title back in her native Belgravia. There she is to wed the reluctant crown prince. While the prince is off on a last wild fling in Paris, he meets the woman he truly wants to marry, only she has a big surprise in store for the reckless prince.
VHS: S24000. $24.95.
Donald Crisp, USA, 1926, 72 mins.

CHARLES CHAPLIN

Burlesque of Carmen

Chaplin's parody of Cecil B. De Mille's 1915 high budget version of *Carmen*, with Edna Purviance and Ben Turpin.
VHS: S00191. $29.95.
Charles Chaplin, USA, 1916, 30 mins.

Chaplin

Starring Robert Downey Jr., this biography traces Charlie Chaplin's career, including his vaudeville beginnings, his complicated relationship with his mentally unbalanced mother (Geraldine Chaplin, playing her grandmother), his discovery by Mack Sennett (Dan Aykroyd), the birth of the one- and two-reel comedies, and his emergence as the popular artist. Cinematography by Sven Nykvist. Screenplay by novelist William Boyd, filmmaker Bryan Forbes and screenwriter William Goldman. With Milla Jovovich, Moira Kelly, Kevin Kline (as Douglas Fairbanks Jr.), Diane Lane (as Paula Goddard), Marisa Tomei (as Mabel Normand), Nancy Travis and James Woods.
VHS: S19052. $19.98.
Laser: Widescreen. LD75308. $39.98.
Richard Attenborough, USA, 1992, 142 mins.

Chaplin Revue

Three great Chaplin shorts: *A Dog's Life* is regarded by many as Chaplin's first masterpiece, in which the Little Tramp rescues a mutt from a dogfight; *Shoulder Arms* is a comedy about men at the front lines during World War I; and *The Pilgrim* centers on an ex-convict posing as a preacher.
VHS: S00227. $19.98.
Charles Chaplin, USA, 1918, 123 mins.

Charlie Chaplin

The film biography of the genius Chaplin features appearances by Stan Laurel and Oliver Hardy, Fatty Arbuckle and Ben Turpin. USA, 105 mins.
VHS: S02098. $69.95.

Charlie Chaplin Early Years I

Chaplin's early work, including *The Immigrant, The Count* and *Easy Street*, in a tape transferred from original nitrate prints.
VHS: S00383. $19.98.
Laser: CLV. LD71973. $29.98.
Charles Chaplin, USA, 1917, 62 mins.

Charlie Chaplin Early Years II

Three Chaplin classics: *The Pawnshop*, in which Charlie—janitor and clerk—causes pandemonium; *The Adventurer*, in which Chaplin is an escaped convict; and *One A.M.*, in which inanimate objects take on a life of their own to disturb Charlie's rest.
VHS: S00384. $19.98.
Laser: CLV. LD71974. $29.98.
Charles Chaplin, USA, 1916-17, 61 mins.

Charlie Chaplin Early Years III

In *The Cure*, Charlie is an alcohol-tippling man-about-town; in *The Floorwalker*, he runs afoul of a store detective on the escalator; in *The Vagabond*, Chaplin is a wandering violinist who rescues a young girl kidnapped by the gypsies.
VHS: S00385. $19.98.
Laser: CLV. LD71975. $29.98.
Charles Chaplin, USA, 1916-17, 64 mins.

Charlie Chaplin Early Years IV

Behind the Screen is Chaplin's amusing satire on Keystone slapstick stars; in *The Fireman*, Chaplin gets involved in an arson plot; and in the famous *The Rink*, Chaplin is a waiter who serves a live cat to a restaurant patron.
VHS: S00386. $19.98.
Laser: CLV. LD71976. $29.98.
Charles Chaplin, USA, 1916, 63 mins.

Charlie Chaplin's Keystone Comedies

Six one-reel comedies from the first year Chaplin appeared in films. In *Making a Living*, his first film, he plays a seedy Englishman. In *The Tramp*, his second, The Tramp is born. *A Busy Day* finds Charlie in drag. *Mabel's Married Life* he shares with Mabel Normand. In *Laughing Gas* he is a porter working for Dr. Pain, a dentist. In *The New Janitor* he prevents a hold-up.
VHS: S05463. $29.95.
Charles Chaplin, USA, 1914, 67 mins.

Circus/Day of Pleasure

Chaplin joins a traveling circus and falls in love with a bareback rider in one of his great comedies; presented with the short *Day of Pleasure*.
VHS: S02636. $19.98.
Charles Chaplin, USA, 1928, 105 mins.

City Lights

One of Chaplin's most highly acclaimed films, a silent film in the era of talkies that demonstrated Chaplin's genius. The Little Tramp falls in love with a beautiful, blind flower girl and sets out to raise money for an operation to cure her.
VHS: S00245. $19.98.
Laser: LD72318. $69.98.
Charles Chaplin, USA, 1931, 86 mins.

Classic Chaplin

An authoritative collection of Chaplin's early work, with each volume containing program notes that provide biographical information on Chaplin's early career. Available in individual volumes, or as a six-pack at a special price.
Charlie Chaplin at Keystone Studios. A side-splitting collection of Chaplin's first films—comedy classics that feature Chaplin's first-ever on-screen appearance as the legendary Little Tramp. Includes *Making a Living*, *Caught in a Cabaret*, *Mabel's Busy Day*, *The Masquerader*, *The Rounders*. 56 mins.
VHS: S12980. $19.98.
Charlie Chaplin at Essanay Studios I. His first films at Essanay Studios show Chaplin developing his legendary style, especially in the classic short *The Tramp*. Also includes *His New Job*, *The Champion*, *A Woman*. 83 mins.
VHS: S12981. $19.98.
Charlie Chaplin at Essanay Studios II. In this second collection from Essanay Studios, Chaplin continues to develop The Little Tramp character, adding more subtlety and pathos to his work. Includes *By the Sea*, *The Bank*, *Shanghaied*, *A Night in the Show*. 63 mins.
VHS: S12982. $19.98.
Charlie Chaplin at Mutual Studios I. Four delightful films from Chaplin's early period with Mutual Studios, these shorts showcase some of his best-loved work: *The Count*, *The Vagabond*, *The Fireman*, *Behind the Screen*. 100 mins.
VHS: S12983. $19.98.
Charlie Chaplin at Mutual Studios II. The second volume from Mutual Studios includes four tour-de-force comedy classics, including Chaplin in a rare solo performance in *One A.M.*. Also in this volume are *The Pawnshop*, *The Floorwalker*, *The Rink*. 97 mins.
VHS: S12984. $19.98.
Charlie Chaplin at Mutual Studios III. In the last volume of films from Mutual Studios, Chaplin gives a brilliant comedic performance as an immigrant, an escaped convict, and a former tramp turned policeman. Includes *The Immigrant*, *The Cure*, *The Adventurer*, *Easy Street*. 101 mins.
VHS: S12985. $19.98.
Charles Chaplin, USA, 1914-1917

The Count and the Adventurer

Charlie Chaplin stars in two two-reel silent comedies. *The Count* (or *The Phoney Nobleman*) finds out-of-work Charlie impersonating Count Broko, who makes a big hit in high society. *The Adventurer* finds Charlie as an escaped convict. With Edna Purviance.
VHS: S05464. $24.95.
Charles Chaplin, USA, 1916-17, 57 mins.

A Countess from Hong Kong

Marlon Brando and Sophia Loren bring glamour to Charlie Chaplin's final film. Loren stars as Natascha, a Russian countess who has lost her fortune and decides to stow away in the stateroom of Ogden, a wealthy American (Brando). Though Ogden resists, he is ultimately dazzled by Natascha, and the antic slapstick situations created by Harvey (Chaplin) only serve to confuse Ogden more. Includes the original theatrical trailer.
VHS: S27351. $14.98.
Charlie Chaplin, USA, 1966, 120 mins.

Emerging Chaplin

Narrated by Douglas Fairbanks Jr., a roller coaster ride featuring Chaplin as the Little Tramp, from his early films to his stint at Mack Sennett's studios to the classics—*Kid Auto Races*, *The Bank*, *The Tramp*, *The Floorwalker*, *The Rink*, *Easy Street*. 30 mins.
VHS: S09424. $19.95.
Charles Chaplin, USA, 30 mins.

Essanay #1

Charlie Chaplin at the Essanay Studios: *His New Job*, *A Night Out*, *The Champion*, *In the Park*, *A Jitney Elopement*.
VHS: S04820. $29.95.
Charles Chaplin, USA, 1915, 101 mins.

Essanay #2

The Tramp, *By the Sea*, *Work*, *A Woman*, *The Bank*.
VHS: S04821. $29.95.
Charles Chaplin, USA, 1915, 102 mins.

Essanay #3

Shanghaied, *A Night in the Show*, *Burlesque on Carmen*, *Police*, *Triple Trouble* (also known as *The Bond*).
VHS: S04822. $29.95.
Charles Chaplin, USA, 118 mins.

The Eternal Tramp

Charlie Chaplin's rise from the impoverished son of London vaudeville performers to acclaim as a pioneer director, actor, writer and comedian. Narrated by Gloria Swanson, with some footage from his rarely screened early works. 55 mins.
VHS: S17763. $14.98.

The Gold Rush

Charlie Chaplin's immortal, icon-making film, which pits Chaplin as the Little Tramp against the elements of the Yukon, ruthless prospectors and the affections of a dance hall girl. This is the film that includes the classic scene of Chaplin eating his leather shoe and shows his wooden cabin precariously balanced on the edge of a cliff. Silent with music track.
VHS: S26489. $19.95.
Laser: CLV. LD70099. $39.95.
Charles Chaplin, USA, 1925, 82 mins.

Great Dictator

Chaplin's first film with dialog displays his boundless talent for both comedy and drama. Features Chaplin in two roles, one of a little Jewish barber facing the constant threat of religious persecution, the second a devastating lampoon of Hitler because of which Hitler banned it in Germany.
VHS: S00527. $19.98.
Charles Chaplin, USA, 1940, 126 mins.

Keystones #1

Charlie Chaplin in early Keystone comedies: *Making a Living*, *Kid's Auto Race*, *Mabel's Strange Predicament*, *Between Showers*, *A Film Johnny*, *Tango Tangles*, *His Favorite Pastime*, *The Star Border*, *Mabel at the Wheel*.
VHS: S04823. $29.95.
Charles Chaplin, USA, c. 1910

Keystones #2

Twenty Minutes of Love, *Caught in a Cabaret*, *Caught in the Rain*, *A Busy Day*, *The Fatal Mallet*, *The Knockout*, *Mabel's Busy Day*, *Mabel's Married Life*.
VHS: S04824. $29.95.
Charles Chaplin, USA, 107 mins.

Keystones #3

Laughing Gas, *The Property Man*, *Face on the Barroom Floor*, *Recreation*, *The Masquerader*, *His New Profession*, *The Rounders*, *The New Janitor*, *Those Love Fangs*, *Dough and Dynamite*.
VHS: S04825. $29.95.
Charles Chaplin, USA, 120 mins.

The Kid/The Idle Class

The Kid was Chaplin's first feature film and features The Tramp taking in an abandoned baby who grows into an impish urchin played by Jackie Coogan. On the same program is *The Idle Class*, a rare short in which The Tramp wreaks havoc on a golf course.
VHS: S00672. $19.98.
Charles Chaplin, USA, 1921, 85 mins.

King in New York

A satire starring Chaplin as a European monarch who flees to New York hoping to win support for his idealistic plans—an end to nuclear weapons and the creation of a utopian country. Unfortunately, he is met with a deaf ear.
VHS: S00677. $19.98.
Charles Chaplin, USA, 1957, 104 mins.

Limelight

Chaplin blends dark comedy and tragedy in the story of an aging music hall comic who's convinced he can no longer move people to laughter. With Chaplin, Claire Bloom, and the great Buster Keaton.
VHS: S00757. $19.98.
Charles Chaplin, USA, 1951, 120 mins.

Modern Times

Charlie Chaplin's silent homage to the human spirit, in which Chaplin is the victim of industrial boom. He plays the factory worker gone looney by the assembly line who falls in love with a down-and-out young lady and tries through various and eccentric means to find a bit of financial peace. A great comedy, and a great film.
VHS: S00866. $19.98.
Charles Chaplin, USA, 1936, 89 mins.

Monsieur Verdoux

Henri Verdoux is the bank teller who marries and subsequently murders wealthy women in order to support his own wife and child. Chaplin's dark comedy was a commercial failure, yet is an ingenious blend of dark comedy and philosophy.
VHS: S00873. $19.98.
Charles Chaplin, USA, 1947, 122 mins.

Rare Chaplin

Three classic Chaplin shorts, taken from original 35mm prints, of Chaplin during his Essanay period. *The Bank* (1915) features Charlie as a cleaner at the bank, struggling with broom and bucket. *Shanghaied* (1915) features Charlie tricked into service on an old tub about to leave port, ignorant that the owners are preparing to dynamite the boat and collect the insurance. And *A Night in the Show* (1915) features Charlie as a dapper gentleman attending the theatre, who romances the pretty girl in the next seat and in the process manages to get into a fight with a trombone. Silent with musical accompaniment.
VHS: S10761. $29.95.
Charles Chaplin, USA, 1915, 90 mins.

The Tramp and a Woman

Charlie Chapin stars in two short, silent comedies. *The Tramp* features Charlie in his best-known character saving a farmer's daughter from ruffians. Pathos mixes with slapstick for the first time. *A Woman* finds Charlie in women's clothes to escape angry suitors. With Billy Armstrong, Charles Insley and Edna Purviance.
VHS: S05469. $24.95.
Charles Chaplin, USA, 1915, 57 mins.

Unknown Chaplin

One of the wonders of television was this British-TV-financed, truly remarkable series, directed by Kevin Brownlow, in which, for the first time, a filmmaker was allowed access to the Chaplin family's private film vaults. The result is stunning: a beautifully produced exploration of the work and life of the great comic genius, using exquisitely restored film footage mixed together with interviews, insightful commentary and the Chaplin family's home movies. Not to be missed. 55 minutes each.
Hidden Treasures. The lost gems of a glittering career revealed for the first time include home movies, early gags that found their way into *The Great Dictator* and *Limelight*, and the rescued opening sequence from *City Lights*, presented with its original music score.
VHS: S12565. $19.99.
My Happiest Years. In his earliest films, Chaplin left no stone unturned—or tripped over—in his search for comic excellence. Included are lost footage, unseen for nearly 70 years, from *The Cure* and *The Immigrant*.
VHS: S12563. $19.99.
The Great Director. Producing his greatest work on a simple back lot and two stages, rare footage reveals Chaplin at work on his biggest career gambles. Lost footage from *The Kid*, *The Gold Rush* and *City Lights*.
VHS: S12564. $19.99.
Unknown Chaplin, 3-Pack.
VHS: S12566. $39.99.

A Woman of Paris

A Woman of Paris is a moving story of love gone awry in the life of a pretty country girl who winds up in Paris as a kept woman. Also contains the short comedy, *Sunnyside*.
VHS: S01478. $19.98.
Charles Chaplin, USA, 1919, 111 mins.

Work and Police

Two silent shorts by Charlie Chaplin. The first has Charlie as a paper-hanger, the second as Convict 999 returning to a life of crime.
VHS: S05465. $29.95.
Charles Chaplin, USA, 1915 & 1916, 81 mins.

Art of Buster Keaton—Box 1

A boxed set of four Keaton features: *The Saphead*, *Three Ages*, *Our Hospitality/Sherlock Jr.* and accompanying short films. Newly mastered.
VHS: S23125. $79.95.
Laser: LD74801. $99.99.

Art of Buster Keaton—Box 2

A boxed set of four Keaton features: *Navigator*, *Seven Chances*, *Go West*, *Battling Butler* and collected short films. Newly mastered.
VHS: S23126. $109.95.
Laser: LD74802. $139.00.

Art of Buster Keaton—Box 3

A boxed set of three Buster Keaton features: *General*, *College* and *Steamboat Bill Jr.*, and assorted shorts. Newly mastered.
VHS: S23127. $79.95.
Laser: LD74803. $99.95.

Battling Butler

A brilliant Buster Keaton comedy about a timid aristocrat who tries to impress his beloved's father by claiming that he is the famous boxer "Battling" Butler. Things are going well until the real Battling Butler shows up and challenges Keaton to a fight. Newly mastered; also contains the Keaton shorts *Haunted House* and *Frozen North*. Silent with music track.
VHS: S05598. $29.95.
Buster Keaton, USA, 1926, 78 mins.

Blacksmith and Balloonatic

Two Buster Keaton rarities: in *The Blacksmith*, Keaton is the local blacksmith apprentice who works the anvil and forge to fry his eggs at lunch; in *The Balloonatic*, Keaton is trapped in a lighter-than-air balloon at an amusement park with expectedly hilarious results. Silent with musical score. USA, c. 1922, 76 mins.
VHS: S01742. $29.95.

Bluebeard Goes to the Moon

A rare and bizarre Keaton film, in which he plays a World War II soldier who is marooned in Italy, where a scientist recruits him for a rocket ship trip to the moon. The special effects are as laughable as the plot, but this is a rare example of Keaton at the end of his career. 65 mins.
VHS: S05799. $39.95.

Boom in the Moon

Not a sequel to the Elizabeth Taylor and Richard Burton film *Boom*, but a comedy starring Buster Keaton in an adventure of lunar lunacy. The classic deadpan comedian could get a laugh just by standing in front of a camera. Discover how he convulsed millions in this little-known comedy that is literally out of this world.
VHS: S06120. $39.95.
Jaime Salvador, USA, 1946, 83 mins.

Buster and Fatty

Fatty Arbuckle, Buster Keaton and Al St. John are featured in all five of these beautifully preserved and rare short films. Included are *Coney Island* (1917), *Butcher Boy* (1917), *Good Night Nurse* (1918), *Out West* (1918) and *Back Stage* (1919). These comic films all have orchestra accompaniment and come from good to excellent prints. USA, 1917-1919, 94 mins.
VHS: S26852. $19.95.

Buster Keaton

Henry Morgan tells you the story of The Great Stone Face from his early childhood to his maturity as one of Hollywood's greatest comics. Included from the Rohauer Collection is seldom-seen footage from such classics as *Fatty at Coney Island*, *Cops*, *Balloonatics*, *Day Dreams* and *The General*.
VHS: S03961. $69.95.

Buster Keaton (1917-22)

Four of Keaton's early great short films: *The Blacksmith*, *Playhouse*, *Balloonatic*, *Cops*, and *The Garage*.
VHS: S04792. $24.95.
Buster Keaton, USA, 1917-22

Buster Keaton Festival Volume 1

Buster stars in three silent shorts: *The Blacksmith*, *Paleface* and *Cops*. All silent with a newly added musical score. USA, c. 1921, 55 mins.
VHS: S01641. $19.95.

Buster Keaton Festival Volume 2

Three rare silent shorts starring Keaton: *The Boat*, *Frozen North* and *Electric House*. All silent with newly added musical score. USA, c. 1921, 55 mins.
VHS: S01642. $19.95.

Buster Keaton Festival Volume 3

Three classic shorts: *Daydreams*, *Balloonatic* and *The Garage* (with Fatty Arbuckle). Silent with new music score. USA, c. 1921, 55 mins.
VHS: S01643. $19.95.

The Buster Keaton Show

Two shows in one! A rare glimpse of Keaton's television appearances in the '50s reveals his dedication in the gym, and his savoir-faire when he ends up in the boxing ring. In another episode, Buster makes an unlikely hero when he catches some crooks with taffy. Includes the original Studebaker commercials.
VHS: S15698. $29.95.

The Buster Keaton Show: Fishing Story & The Collapsible Clerk

The original nitrate prints of these hilarious "talkie" shorts have been locked away since the 50's. Now they are available, featuring Keaton at his best. His dead-pan style makes him a classic comic and one of America's most beloved humorists.
VHS: S21879. $19.95.

Buster Keaton Talkies, Vol. 1

Three films which star Buster Keaton in the sound era: *One Run Elmer*, *The Chemist*, and *Love Nest on Wheels*.
VHS: S05794. $29.95.

Buster Keaton Talkies, Vol. 2

Three more short films featuring Keaton in the sound age: *Grand Slam Opera*, *Tars and Stripes*, and *Three on a Limb*.
VHS: S05795. $29.95.

Buster Keaton Talkies, Vol. 3

Keaton stars in *Blue Blazes*, *Mixed Magic*, and the one-reeler *Allez Oop*.
VHS: S05796. $29.95.

Buster Keaton Talkies, Vol. 6

Keaton stars in *Ditto*, *Jailbait*, and *Palooka from Paducha*.
VHS: S05797. $29.95.

Buster Keaton Talkies, Vol. 7

Two films starring Keaton: *Timid Young Man* and *Hayseed Romance*.
VHS: S05798. $29.95.

Buster Keaton: A Hard Act to Follow

A brilliant three-volume biography of the great Keaton, prepared by film historians Kevin Brownlow and David Gill. Interviews with Keaton and reminiscences of friends and associates, rare footage and clips from many Keaton films in a unique portrait of this great genius of the silent cinema. Available either separately, or as a set.
From Vaudeville to Movies.
VHS: S10248. $19.99.
Star Without a Studio.
VHS: S10249. $19.99.
A Genius Recognized.
VHS: S10250. $19.99.
Buster Keaton, Complete Set.
VHS: S10247. $39.99.

The Cameraman

Buster Keaton at his greatest as a street photographer, enamored of a movie star, who decides to become a newsreel cameraman. Hilarious. Silent with music track.
VHS: S13398. $29.98.
Clyde Bruckman, USA, 1928, 78 mins.

The Cameraman/Spite Marriage

Two Keaton classics on one laserdisc! Gatefold jacket.
Laser: LD71476. $39.98.

College

An incredible demonstration of Keaton's formidable athletic skills in this famous comedy in which he plays the bookish college student who is forced to prove himself a jock in order to get the girl. Famous sequences include Keaton in a decathlon knocking down every single hurdle with precision, being thrown by a hammer rather than throwing it, and finally catapulting himself through a window to save the heroine from her jock admirer. Includes the shorts *The Blacksmith*, *Electric House* and *Hard Luck*. Silent with music track.
VHS: S23034. $19.95.
James W. Horne, USA, 1927, 67 mins.

Doughboys

Buster Keaton re-teams with his collaborator from *The Cameraman*, Edward Sedgwick, in this military comedy about the reluctant army recruit who becomes a certified war hero and local treasure. With Sally Eilers, Cliff Edwards, and Edward Brophy.
VHS: S17893. $19.98.
Edward Sedgwick, USA, 1930, 79 mins.

Free and Easy

Buster Keaton's first sound movie shows Buster's phenomenal rise from a mechanic to iconic movie star. With cameos from Cecil B. De Mille, Lionel Barrymore, Jackie Coogan and Arthur Lange.
VHS: S17894. $19.98.
Edward Sedgwick, USA, 1930, 92 mins.

The General

Considered by many to be the last great comedy of the silent era, and consistently ranked as a masterpiece. Based on a true incident in the Civil War, the "General" is the railroad engine "engineered" by Confederate Army reject Keaton, who is also humiliated by his girlfriend (Marion Mack), who thinks him a coward. When a small company of Union soldiers penetrates behind Confederate lines, Keaton sets off in hot pursuit in one of the truly great chase scenes ever. The scenes were shot on the narrow gauge lines of Oregon and Keaton used less than 50 titles to explain the whole story. Also contains the shorts *The Playhouse* and *Cops.* Newly mastered. Silent with music track.
VHS: S23033. $29.95.
Buster Keaton/Clyde Bruckman, USA, 1927, 76 mins.

Go West

Keaton leaves the Midwest for Arizona on his way to becoming a cowboy named Friendless. He removes a pebble from the foot of an injured cow, Brown Eyes, and they become inseparable. When Brown Eyes is shipped to Los Angeles, Friendless accompanies her with comic results: Keaton and Brown Eyes exploring department stores and beauty parlors. But this is "the most atypical and at the same time one of the most endearing of his [Keaton's] films. With acrobatics and gag comedy at a minimum, he experimented uncharacteristically with a quality of pathos in his depiction of Friendless and his comradeship with a gentle, sweet cow" (David Thomson). Includes the short films *The Scarecrow* and *Paleface.* Newly mastered. Silent with music track.
VHS: S23032. $29.95.
Buster Keaton, USA, 1925, 72 mins.

Great Stone Face—Buster Keaton—Volume 1

Film clips of Keaton's career, three of his early comedies, *The Paleface, Day Dreams* and *The Blacksmith,* as well as, from the early days of television, a show titled *The Silent Partner,* with Keaton, Joe E. Brown and ZaSu Pitts.
VHS: S10606. $29.95.

Great Stone Face—Buster Keaton—Volume 2

One of Keaton's best comedies, *Cops,* plus his television show *Buster Keaton Detective.* In this episode, Keaton performs a classic spoof of Sam Spade in *The Maltese Falcon.*
VHS: S10603. $29.95.

Kovacs & Keaton

Two rare television appearances by master comedians—Kovacs is silent in *Eugene* (1960) as he mimes his way through life, while Keaton in *Wrestling with Trouble* as his buddy get tangled with two real-life wrestlers (1953). USA, 60 mins.
VHS: S01651. $24.95.

The Lovable Cheat

Based on a Balzac play, this independent film features the comic antics of Charlie Ruggles battling against his many creditors. With Fritz Feld and Buster Keaton.
VHS: S14676. $29.95.
Richard Oswald, USA, 1949, 75 mins.

The Misadventures of Buster Keaton

The wacky owner of a sporting goods store moonlights as the director/producer of a small theater. The hilarious Buster Keaton, with his brilliant flair for slapstick, shines in this comedy classic. USA, 65 mins.
VHS: S15032. $19.95.

The Navigator

One of the funniest of Keaton's comedies, in which he runs a deserted ocean liner single-handed. The original script was to have a penniless man and woman marooned on a dead ship in the middle of the Atlantic. But the question arose as to how two penniless people could afford to be on the ship in the first place, and so the screenwriter, Jean Havez, suggested, "I want a rich boy and a rich girl who never had to lift a finger. I put these two beautiful spoiled brats—the two most helpless people in the world—adrift on a ship, all alone. A dead ship. No lights, no steam." Also contains the shorts *The Boat* and *Love Nest.* Newly mastered. Silent with music track.
VHS: S08845. $29.95.
Donald Crisp, USA, 1924, 60 mins.

Old Spanish Custom

Rare sound film of Keaton in which he plays Leander Proudfoot, a sap who is the patsy in a torrid love triangle. Lupita Tovar is also featured.
VHS: S01644. $24.95.
Adrian Brunel, USA, 1936, 58 mins.

Our Hospitality/Sherlock Jr.

Keaton's hilarious satire on the Hatfield-McCoy family feud was his second feature. Brilliantly set against the backdrop of early rail travel in 1831, the film features Keaton as the scion of an old Southern family who carelessly starts dating from a feuding family. In *Sherlock Jr.* Keaton plays a projectionist who is framed for theft by a jealous rival for the hand of a beautiful girl. Contains an astonishing sequence in which Keaton imagines himself to be a detective, and makes his way into the action of the movie he is projecting on screen. This sequence made Keaton an early favorite of the surrealists. Newly mastered. Silent with music track.
VHS: S23030. $29.95.
Buster Keaton, USA, 1923/1924

Parlor, Bedroom and Bath

A rare Keaton film of the sound era in which he proves he was as brilliant as ever; Keaton is a sign-tacker hit by a car outside a mansion, brought in to recover. A very complicated screwball comedy ensues. A rare glimpse of one of comedy's extraordinary talents.
VHS: S00994. $24.95.
Edward Sedgwick, USA, 1931, 73 mins.

Saphead

Keaton plays the pampered son of "The Wolf of Wall Street", who shocks everyone by making a fortune on the stock market, thus winning the girl of his dreams. Keaton's first feature is based on a play, *The New Henrietta,* and clearly foreshadows the comic mayhem in which Keaton's athletic prowess and impeccable timing would create timeless comedy—as he does here, when he creates total upheaval on the stock market trading floor. Includes the shorts *High Sign* and *One Week.* Silent with music track.
VHS: S23029. $29.95.
Herbert Blache, USA, 1920, 70 mins.

Seven Chances

On his 27th birthday lawyer Buster Keaton is told that he will inherit $7 million if he gets married by 7 p.m. that evening. But his own sweetheart rejects him when she discovers the true nature of his affection and he is driven to desperation proposing to anyone in skirts, including a Scotsman. An ad in the paper saves the day and 500 prospective brides show up at the church. A very funny collection of gags culminating in a hilarious chase scene with the bachelor lawyer being pursued by 500 brides straight into a rock slide. Also includes two shorts: *Neighbors* and *The Balloonatic.* Newly mastered. Silent with music track.
VHS: S23031. $29.95.
Edward Sedgwick, USA, 1929, 77 mins.

Sidewalks of New York

A Buster Keaton talkie casts the virtuoso comedian as a lonely New York millionaire who falls for a poor street girl (Anita Page), and tries to prove his worth by reforming her younger brother and transforming their socially neglected neighborhood. With Cliff Edwards, Frank Rowan and Norman Phillips, Jr.
VHS: S19566. $19.98.
Jules White, USA, 1931, 70 mins.

Speak Easily

After his career as a director was destroyed, Buster Keaton played in a series of sound comedies. This is one of his later period works, about a wealthy college instructor who reluctantly bankrolls a third-rate theatrical troupe. With Jimmy Durante, Thelma Todd and Sidney Toler.
VHS: S17899. $19.98.
Edward Sedgwick, USA, 1932, 82 mins.

Spite Marriage

The great Stone Face himself, Buster Keaton, in his final silent film. This backstage comedy is about a tailor's assistant in love with a young actress (Dorothy Sebastian), who marries him to spite someone else. Here Keaton displays his comic genius in some truly inspired slapstick routines. Silent film with synchronized musical score.
VHS: S13974. $29.99.
Edward Sedgwick, USA, 1929, 82 mins.

Steamboat Bill Jr.

Buster Keaton's great comedy, his "most entertaining balance of the instinctual and the cerebral in a tale of father worship, young love, abject humiliation and heroic redemption" (J. Hoberman, *The Village Voice*). Set in the deep South, Keaton plays the city-bred boy who returns to his steamboat captain father and reluctantly joins him in fighting off a rival trying to take over the river. The cyclone finale is as famous as it is hilarious. Newly mastered; also contains two Keaton shorts: *Convict 13* and *Daydreams.* Silent with music track.
VHS: S23035. $29.95.
Charles F. Reisner, USA, 1928, 71 mins.

Three Ages

Keaton's first feature is a spoof of Griffith's *Intolerance.* Keaton and Wallace Beery parody film cliches. In the Stone Age, Keaton arrives on a date on a dinosaur; in ancient Rome Buster is forced into a chariot race in a blizzard. Keaton pokes fun at the incongruity of cinematic history. Newly mastered. Contains the shorts *The Goat* and *My Wife's Relations.* Silent with music track.
VHS: S01335. $29.95.
Buster Keaton/Eddie Cline, USA, 1923

The Villain Still Pursued Her

Buster Keaton is part of the cast in this spoof of melodramas, complete with mustache twisting villain and an innocent harp-playing heroine. Title cards encourage audience participation. Keaton plays the hero's best friend. With Alan Mowbray, Anita Louise, Hugh Herbert and Margaret Hamilton.
VHS: S05459. $29.95.
Eddie Cline, USA, 1940, 68 mins.

What! No Beer?

In his final lead role in an American production, Buster Keaton is teamed with Jimmy Durante as hopeless Prohibition bootleggers drawn into a zany and crazed plot to make a fortune. With Roscoe Ates, Phyllis Barry and John Milijan.
VHS: S17901. $19.98.
Edward Sedgwick, USA, 1933, 66 mins.

HAROLD LLOYD

Films of Harold Lloyd—Volume 1

A collection of early Harold Lloyd shorts including *The Cinema Director* (1916), *Non-Stop Kid* (1918), *Why Pick on Me* (1918), *On the Fire* (1919); *Ring up the Curtain* (1919), *Just Neighbors* (1919), *Haunted Spooks* (1920) and *Never Weaken* (1921). 120 mins.
VHS: S02353. $29.95.

Films of Harold Lloyd—Volume 2

A selection of early work by Harold Lloyd; also featured are Bebe Daniels and Snub Pollard. Includes *All Aboard, Two Gun Gussie, The City Slicker, Why Pick on Me, Ask Father,* and *I'm on My Way.* 75 mins.
VHS: S13208. $24.95.

Films of Harold Lloyd—Volume 3

Films from the years 1919-1921: *Snob Fever, Don't Shove, Pay Your Dues* and *His Royal Slyness,* as well as a film by Harold's brother Gaylord Lloyd, *Dodge Your Debts.* With Bebe Daniels, Snub Pollard and Mildred Harris. 70 mins.
VHS: S13209. $24.95.

Harold Lloyd Comedies Vol. 1

The famous comedian in *All Aboard, The Non-Stop Kid, Ring up the Curtain,* and *Haunted Spooks.* 60 mins.
VHS: S08016. $29.95.

Harold Lloyd Comedies Vol. 2

Harold Lloyd in *I'm on My Way, High and Dizzy, Bashful* and *Never Waken.* 60 mins.
VHS: S08017. $29.95.

Harold Lloyd Comedies Vol. 3

Includes *Spring Fever, Two Gun Gussie, Eastern Westerner,* and *His Royal Slyness.* 60 mins.
VHS: S08018. $29.95.

Harold Lloyd Set

A five-volume set of *Safety Last, Girl Shy, Speedy, Hot Water* and *The Kid Brother.*
VHS: S19909. $149.98.

Harold Lloyd's Comedy Classics

Four greats from a master of the silent era. Lloyd is *The Chef* complete with Rube Goldberg contraptions; *Cinema Director* is influenced by Chaplin; *Two Gun Gussie* has mild mannered Lloyd mistaken as an outlaw; and *I'm on My Way* is a hilarious view of marriage! USA, 1919, 51 mins.
VHS: S00544. $24.95.

Harold Lloyd: Girl Shy

Harold Lloyd plays a small-town man who overcomes his fright of women by writing a controversial book about lovemaking. The film interweaves stylized physical humor with some hypnotic fantasy sequences of Lloyd's sexual experiences. With Jobyna Ralston, Richard Daniels and Carlton Griffin. Silent with musical score.
VHS: S19905. $29.98.
Fred Newmeyer/Sam Taylor, USA, 1924, 65 mins.

Harold Lloyd: Hot Water

An early madcap Harold Lloyd vehicle about the comic repercussions of a young husband who experiences problems with a turkey, his new car and his wife's parents. "This casually structured star comedy [features] brilliant sequences" (Leslie Halliwell). With Jobyna Ralston and Josephine Crowell. Silent with musical score.
VHS: S19907. $29.98.
Fred Newmeyer/Sam Taylor, USA, 1924, 50 mins.

Harold Lloyd: Safety Last

This is Harold Lloyd's best-known work. Its plot concerns the mad-cap adventures of an ambitious young man unleashed in the big city and contains Lloyd's most famous sequence, his scaling a 12-story building as Lloyd furiously hangs onto the hands of an oversize clock. "Lloyd specialized in the 'comedy of thrills'—a bizarre variant of Keystone mayhem in which the protagonist placed himself in real physical danger to elicit shocks of laughter from the audience" (David Cook, *The History of Narrative Film*). With Mildred Davis, Bill Strothers and Noah Young.
VHS: S19904. $29.98.
Fred Newmeyer/Sam Taylor, USA, 1923, 78 mins.

Harold Lloyd: Speedy

Harold Lloyd's final silent film features a stunning trolley car climax. Lloyd plays a young man who orchestrates a master plan to preserve New York City's last horse-drawn trolley, which is owned and operated by his girlfriend's grandfather. With Ann Christy, Bert Woodruff, Brooks Benedict, and in a very funny cameo, Babe Ruth. Silent with musical score.
VHS: S19906. $29.98.
Ted Wilde, USA, 1928, 90 mins.

Harold Lloyd: The Kid Brother

Harold Lloyd's funny reinterpretation of the *Cinderella* tale. The film moved away from the city landscapes of his earlier works to a country setting. Lloyd plays Harold Hickory, the youngest brother in a competitive, all-male family. Hickory suffers from an inferiority complex, though he eventually humiliates the town bully and captures some local crooks, altering the way his father—the local sheriff—looks at him. "This is [Lloyd's] loosest, sweetest and most relaxed comedy. It explores the terrain with more leisure and curiosity than any previous Lloyd vehicles" (Andrew Sarris). Lewis Milestone made substantial contributions to the film. With Jobyna Ralston, Walter James, Leo Willis and Olin Francis.
VHS: S19908. $29.98.
Ted Wilde/J.A. Howe, USA, 1927, 82 mins.

Harold Lloyd: The Third Genius

David Gill and Kevin Brownlow chronicle the life of Harold Lloyd, the great silent comedian who made more movies than Chaplin and Keaton combined. Rare interviews with director Hal Roach and Lloyd's stunt double, Harvey Parry, give dimension to this under-appreciated comic genius. 110 mins.
VHS: S14849. $59.99.

His Royal Slyness and Haunted Spooks

Harold Lloyd stars in a pair of two-reel silent comedies. The first is a send-up of *The Prisoner of Zenda* with Harold offered the throne of Thermosa. In *Haunted Spooks* the bespectacled nice guy helps a southern heiress acquire her inheritance by marrying her and spending the night in a haunted mansion.
VHS: S01743. $29.95.
Hal Roach/Alf Goulding, USA, 1920, 72 mins.

Sin of Harold Diddlebock

Harold Lloyd is the former football star who has spent 20 years in the bookkeeping department of an ad agency. Having lived a boring life, he goes to the other extreme, and goes on a wild binge of drinking and gambling—a riotous comedy from Sturges.
VHS: S01206. $19.95.
Preston Sturges, USA, 1946, 90 mins.

Speedy

A young man tries to save New York City's last horse-drawn trolley, run by his girlfriend's grandfather. Features exciting views of the city, including a trolley chase scene and a cameo appearance from Babe Ruth. This is one of Harold Lloyd's most stylish comedies, and his last silent film. With Ann Christy, Bert Woodruff and Brooks Benedict.
VHS: S16178. $29.95.
Ted Wilde, USA, 1928, 71 mins.

Airplane Comedies

A compilation of early silent comedies all including airplanes of a bygone era, notable for some of the incredible stunts. Includes *Air Pockets* with some rooftop to rooftop escapades, and Larry Semon, Laurel and Hardy, Little Rascals, Ben Turpin, Billy Bevan and Mack Sennett. Silent and sound.
VHS: S08012. $29.95.

All Night Long and Smile Please

Two comic gems produced by Mack Sennett and starring the extraordinary Harry Langdon: *All Night Long,* in which Langdon encounters a burly man leading a gang in a robbery, and *Smile Please,* in which Harry is a small-town photographer and sheriff. A tour-de-force of Sennett stunts and comic bits. USA, 1924, 66 mins.
VHS: S01741. $29.95.

Arbuckle Volume 3

Early Fatty Arbuckle comedies including *Fatty's New Role; Fatty and Mabel at San Diego; Fatty and Mabel's Simple Life; Fatty and Mabel's Smash Day; Mabel Lost; Mabel, Mabel; Fatty and the Law;* and *Fatty's Plucky Pup.* 120 mins.
VHS: S08604. $49.95.

Baby Face Harry Langdon

Two short films which combine the talents of Harry Langdon with writer-director Frank Capra: *Sunday Afternoon,* which poses the question whether in 1864, when Lincoln declared all men free, did he or did he not include husbands; and *Lucky Stars,* in which Langdon is a trusting soul out to become a great physician and taken for a ride by a quack surgeon. 60 mins. total. Silent with music score.
VHS: S06928. $29.95.

Battling Fool

In this light-hearted look at the world of boxing, William Fairbanks enters the ring to restore his loved one's ability to walk. Golden-faced beauty Eve Novak stars as the broken flower. Silent with an added music track.
VHS: S16108. $29.95.
W.S. Van Dyke, USA, 1924, 56 mins.

Ben Turpin #1

A collection of short comedies starring Ben Turpin, including *Clever Dummy, Cross-Eyed Love, Blondes Revenge, Jolly Jilter, Total Loss* and *Keystone Hotel.* USA, 95 mins.
VHS: S04794. $24.95.

Cannonball/Dizzy Heights

Two farces produced by Mack Sennett featuring the walrus-moustached Chester Conklin. In *Cannonball,* Conklin is an inspector at an explosives factory. *Dizzy Heights* features incredible aerial stunts. USA, 1915, 71 mins.
VHS: S02225. $29.95.

Charley Chase and Ben Turpin

Two silent comedies starring Charley Chase produced by Hal Roach: *All Wet* (1924) and *Publicity Pays* (1924), and a Ben Turpin comedy produced by Mack Sennett: *A Clever Dummy* (1917) with Chester Conklin and Wallace Beery. USA, 67 mins.
VHS: S02228. $29.95.

Charley Chase Jimmy Jump Series

Includes *All Wet, Powder and Smoke, Fighting Fluid, Fraidy Cat, Big Red Riding Hood, Rats Knuckles, Young Oldfield, Poor Fish, Ten Minute Egg* and *One of the Family.* Silent with music track, 120 mins.
VHS: S07188. $24.95.

Charley Chase Vol. 1

Features *Stolen Goods, Publicity Pays, All Dolled Up, His Wooden Wedding, There Ain't No Santa Claus, Forgotten Sweeties.* Silent with music track, 120 mins.
VHS: S07189. $24.95.

Charley Chase Vol. 2

Features *A Dog Shy, Mum's The Word, Looking for Sally, Crazy Like a Fox, Bromo and Juliet.* Silent with music track, 110 mins.
VHS: S07190. $24.95.

Comedy Classics of Mack Sennett and Hal Roach

Three silent gems: *Looking for Trouble, Desperate Scoundrel* and *Love Loot and Crash.* 74 minutes.
VHS: S02223. $29.95.

Comedy Shorts #4

Wine, Women and Sauerkraut—20 Legs Under the Sea, Caretaker's Daughter (Charley Chase), *Busy Buddies* (Neal Burns), *Kiddin Kate* (Dorothy Devore), *Eve's Love Letters* (Stan Laurel). Silent with music track, 110 mins.
VHS: S07194. $24.95.

Early Comedies Volume 1

Dash Through the Clouds (1912, Mabel Normand), *Barney Oldfield's Race for Life* (1913, Sennett), *Settled at the Seaside* (1914, Charlie Chase), *A Mud Bath* (1914, Mabel Normand), *Hogan Out West* (1915), *A Desperate Scoundrel* (1915, Ford Sterling), *Love, Loot and Crash* (1915, Chester Conklin), *Teddy at the Throttle* (1916, Gloria Swanson). Music track. 110 mins.
VHS: S07196. $24.95.

Early Comedies Volume 2

Midnight at the Old Mill (Ham and Bud), *Ring up the Curtain* (Harold Lloyd), *At the Ringside* (Snub Pollard), *White Wings* (Stan Laurel), *Don't Shove—All Aboard* (Harold Lloyd), *Noon Whistle—Oranges and Lemons* (Stan Laurel). Silent with music track. 90 mins.
VHS: S07197. $24.95.

Early Comedies Volume 3

A collection of early short comedies including *Tin Type Romance—A Suffragette in Spite of Himself* (1910) starring Marian MacDermoth, *His Second Childhood* (1914, Charlie Murray), *Duces and Dangers* (1917, Larry Semon), *Chief Cook* (1918, Billy West, Oliver Hardy), *Frauds and Frenzies* (Stan Laurel, Larry Semon), *His Day Out* (1918, Billy West, Oliver Hardy), and *Big Game* (1924, Snub Pollard). 110 mins.
VHS: S08868. $24.95.

Eyes of Ben Turpin Are upon You!

Two of the best performances by the incomparable one-eyed clown, Ben Turpin. *Idle Eyes* (1918) has Ben working in a beauty parlor, making a hilarious mess out of cold-cream treatments and egg shampoos. In *Small Town Idol*, produced by Mack Sennett, Turpin is a small-town guy whose worship of movie actresses gets him into a lot of trouble. This is a condensation of the Mack Sennett feature. Silent with musical score. USA, 1918-21.
VHS: S02993. $24.95.

Fatty Arbuckle

A collection of short films starring Fatty Arbuckle including *Mabel and Fatty's Wash Day*, *Fatty and Mabel at the San Diego Exposition*, *Fatty and Mable's Simple Life*, *Fatty's New Role*, *Fatty's Faithful Fido*, *Miss Fatty's Seaside Lovers*, *Tintype Tangle*. All made in the year 1915. 118 mins.
VHS: S07200. $29.95.

Films of Harry Langdon Volume 1

Includes *Saturday Afternoon* and *Soldier Man*. Approximately 57 mins.
VHS: S10035. $24.95.

Films of Harry Langdon Volume 2

Includes *Boob in the Wood*, *Feet of Mud* and *Lucky Star*. Approximately 58 mins.
VHS: S07278. $24.95.

Films of Oliver Hardy

Oliver Hardy alone in a collection of comedies, including *Battle Royal*, *Stationmaster*, *Enough to Do*, *Paperhanger's Helper*, *Kid Speed*, *Hard Boiled Eggs* and *Along Came Auntie*. Various, USA, 1916-27, 110 mins.
VHS: S04790. $24.95.

Films of Stan Laurel Volume 1

Stan Laurel alone in a collection of short comedies, including *Greater Than Sherlock Holmes*, *Pick and Shovel*, *On the Job*, *Mixed Nuts*, *Roughest Africa*, *Half a Man*, *On the Front Page*, and *Should Tall Men Marry?* Various, USA, 1922-27, 110 mins.
VHS: S04791. $24.95.

Films of Stan Laurel Volume 2

Contains *Kill or Cure* (1915), *Oranges and Lemons* (1912), *Man About Town* (1923). 42 mins.
VHS: S11463. $19.95.

Films of Stan Laurel Volume 3

Contains *Roughest Africa* (1930), *House Boat* (1918), *The Soldiers* (1923). 54 mins.
VHS: S11464. $19.95.

Films of Stan Laurel Volume 4

Contains *Smithy* (1924), *Near Dublin* (1924), *Mixed Nuts* (1924). 50 mins.
VHS: S11465. $19.95.

Flying Elephants

Stan Laurel and Oliver Hardy go back to the Stone Age in this Hal Roach comedy. The head caveman decrees that everyone must marry or else. Hardy falls for the most beautiful girl around, and so does a surprisingly effeminate Stan. Before long, the two resort to the crudest and funniest he-man tactics to impress her and attack each other. Roach apparently directed this film but the credit was given to Butler.
VHS: S26811. $9.95.
Frank Butler, USA, 1928, 20 mins.

Forgotten Comedians

A collection of short films by some of silent comedy's very talented, and funny, but now unjustly neglected comedians. Eddie Quillan stars in *The Channel Swimmer*, Walter Heirs in *Wireless Lizzies*, Jack Richardson, Al Alt, and Dixie Lamont in *Show Business*, Mr. and Mrs. Carter De Haven in *Private, Keep Off*, Lionel Barrymore in *Wife Tamers*, and Monte Banks in *Be Reasonable*. Various, USA.
VHS: S04793. $24.95.

His Picture in the Papers

Douglas Fairbanks stars in this comedy about a non-conformist son of a health food tycoon. USA, 1916, 68 mins.
VHS: S03653. $24.95.

Hollywood Spoofs

Featured are *Uncensored Movies* with Will Rogers, *When Quackle Did Hyde* with Charlie Jau, *Mud and Sand* with Stan Laurel, *Howling Hollywood* with Verna Dent, *Big Moments from Big Pictures* with Will Rogers. Silent with music track, 120 mins.
VHS: S07187. $24.95.

Langdon at Sennett

Veteran vaudeville comic Harry Langdon got his start in movies with Mack Sennett. Frank Capra and Harry Edwards wrote and directed Harry through these memorable early comedies including *Remember When*, *Boob in the Woods*, and *Saturday Afternoon*. 55 mins.
VHS: S08602. $29.95.

Larry Semon #1

A collection of short comedies starring Larry Semon: *The Show*, *The Bellhop*, *The Sawmill*, *The Stuntman*, and *The Clodhopper*. Various, USA, 120 mins.
VHS: S04796. $24.95.

Larry Semon #2

A second volume of short comedies starring Larry Semon: *Risk and Roughnecks*, *Her Boyfriend*, *Dome Doctor*, *Sleuth*, *Well, I'll Be The Sportsman*, and *Clodhopper*. Various, USA, 118 mins.
VHS: S04797. $24.95.

Larry Semon #3

Includes the following shorts starring Larry Semon: *Frauds and Frenzies* (1918), *The Grocery Clerk* (1920), *The Bakery* (1921), *The Sportsman* (1925), and *A Simple Sap* (1928). 118 mins.
VHS: S08867. $24.95.

Leap Year

The only feature film of Roscoe "Fatty" Arbuckle to survive both time and scandal. This pleasant comedy was not available in the U.S. until the 1960's. It played Europe in 1921. A rare look at a master of slapstick in action. Give the big guy a chance. USA, 1921, 60 mins.
VHS: S04802. $24.95.

Lloyd and Chase at Keystone

Harold Lloyd is prominently featured in two films: *Miss Fatty's Seaside Lovers* and *Courthouse Crooks*. Charley Chase stars in *Love, Loot and Crash*, and Lloyd is featured in *Luke's Movie Muddle*. 60 mins. Silent with music track.
VHS: S08014. $29.95.

Mabel Normand Comedies, Vol. 1

Mabel Normand is teamed with Fatty Arbuckle in *Fatty and Mabel Adrift*, with Chaplin and Marie Dressler in *Tillie's Punctured Romance*, and in *The Nicklehopper*. Various, USA, 118 mins.
VHS: S04795. $24.95.

Mabel Normand Comedies, Vol. 2

Includes the following Mabel Normand shorts: *Troublesome Secretary* (1911), *Barney Oldfield's Race for Life* (1913), *Mabel's New Hero* (1913), *A Muddy Romance* (1913). 55 mins.
VHS: S11461. $19.95.

Mabel Normand, Vol. 1

This collection, featuring the great comedienne from the silent era, shows the true extent of her talent. She was a worthy equal to the greats of that special time. Includes *The Water Nymph* (1912), *A Strong Revenge* (1913), *The Jazz Band* (1913), *Fatty and Mabel at San Francisco* (1915) and *Anything Goes* (1927). 64 mins.
VHS: S21082. $24.95.

Mack Sennett: The Biograph Years

The evolution of film comedy took a major step forward when part-time actor-director Mack Sennett started directing films at the Biograph Studio. This selection of six comedies shows how Sennett employed Griffith's "Biograph editing" technique and accelerated it for comic effect. Includes: *Happy Jack: A Hero*, *Turning the Tables*, *A Villain Foiled*, *The Baron*, *Dash through the Clouds*, and *The Manicure Lady*. 60 mins.
VHS: S08603. $29.95.

Peck's Bad Boy

An early Jackie Coogan vehicle in which Jackie is always getting into trouble. With Wheeler, Oakman, Doris May.
VHS: S04789. $24.95.
Laser: LD70406. $29.95.
Sam Wood, USA, 1921, 60 mins.

Perfect Clown

Larry Semon, a forgotten comedy star of the 1920's, is in love with a stenographer named Rosie, and is entrusted with $10,000 in cash by his boss. When he arrives to make the deposit at the bank, it's closed, and he panics and ends up on a zany odyssey through the streets of his city. Oliver Hardy appears in a minor role. Silent with music score.
VHS: S06980. $29.95.
Fred Newmeyer, USA, 1925, 72 mins.

The Roaring Road

Wallace Reid is Toodles Waldron, a car salesman who wants to marry the boss's daughter and participate in a race with a locomotive from San Francisco to Los Angeles. Theodore Roberts is his crusty boss. Ann Little is Chub, the sweetheart of Toodles. With those names it has to be a comedy.
VHS: S04801. $24.95.
James Cruze, USA, 1919, 60 mins.

Sawmill and Dome Doctor

Two comedy shorts by Larry Semon, one of the most popular and highest paid comedians of the early 1920's. His screen character had a huge nose, saucer ears, white face with stupid grin and slicked down hair.
VHS: S02230. $29.95.
Larry Semon, USA, 1922, 71 mins.

Seven Years Bad Luck

A film filled with many classic comedy routines by French comedian Max Linder, called "my teacher" by Charles Chaplin. A broken mirror brings about the seven years of bad luck—all at the same time! Linder exhibits expert timing and physical grace.
VHS: S01184. $29.95.
Max Linder, USA, 1920, 85 mins.

Silent Laugh Makers #2

Three shorts: *Coney Island* (1917) with Fatty Arbuckle, Buster Keaton and Al St. John, and two from 1926 featuring Charlie Chase and Oliver Hardy—*Bromo and Juliet* and *Long Flive the King*. Various, USA, 107 mins.
VHS: S02224. $29.95.

Silent Laugh Makers #3

Four short comedies include: *Picking Peaches* with Harry Langdon, *All Tied Up* (1925), *Don't Shove* (1919) with Harold Lloyd, and *Some Baby* (1922) with Snub Pollard. USA, 82 mins.
VHS: S02234. $24.95.

Snub Pollard...A Short But Funny Man

Australian-born Snub Pollard, one of the most prolific of slapstick comedians, in a trip of typically funny Pollard vehicles: *It's a Gift* (1923), in which Pollard plays a hilariously lazy inventor, *Looking for Trouble* in which he instigates a mud fight among a group of civilized gentlemen, and *Mitt the Prince*, in which he dusts a sidewalk which ends up filthier than when he began. 60 mins total, silent with music score.
VHS: S06981. $24.95.

Syd Chaplin at Keystone

Five comedies by Sydney Chaplin including *Gussle's Wayward Path*, *Gussle the Golfer*, *Gussle's Day of Rest*, *Gussle Tied to Trouble*, *Gus' Backward Way*. 60 mins.
VHS: S08015. $29.95.

Teddy at the Throttle

One of the most famous Mack Sennett comedies features Gloria Swanson and Wallace Beery near the start of their careers with Teddy, one of the screen's first animal stars. A superb parody of melodramas and Griffith-style last minute rescues. USA, 1917, 62 mins.
VHS: S02227. $29.95.

The Three Must-Get-Theirs

This rare spoof of the Fairbanks' *The Three Musketeers* is still a delight. It's presented with the original French subtitles, but they do not diminish the enjoyment value of this rare, orchestra-scored film.
VHS: S22432. $19.95.
Max Linder, USA, 1921, 47 mins.

Tillie Wakes Up

Marie Dressler stars in this sequel to Charlie Chaplin's comic feature-length film *Tillie's Punctured Romance*. Dressler reprises her role as a simple girl from the country bewildered by the complicated ways of the big city. 1917, 50 mins.
VHS: S23147. $24.95.

Tillie's Punctured Romance

Historically important as the first feature-length comedy ever produced, *Tillie's Punctured Romance* is perhaps more noteworthy for its teaming of the greatest silent comedians of the day: Charley Chase, Mabel Normand, the Keystone Kops, Marie Dressler and Charlie Chaplin appears in a rare departure from his Little Tramp characterizations. This version is entirely restored with all new intertitles. Includes the Chaplin short, *Mabel's Married Life*.
VHS: S16739. $19.95.
Mack Sennett, USA, 1914, 73 mins.

When Comedy Was King

A hilarious collection of silent comedians, including The Keystone Cops, Charlie Chaplin, Fatty Arbuckle, Laurel and Hardy, Buster Keaton and many, many more. Various, USA, 1987, 81 mins.
VHS: S02830. $19.98.
Laser: LD75282. $34.98.

When the Clouds Roll By

A hilarious spoof starring Douglas Fairbanks and Kathleen Clifford on the then-new science of psychoanalysis. Silent with music score.
VHS: S07489. $24.95.
Victor Fleming, USA, 1919, 77 mins.

The Wild Party

The funny story of a dishy new professor at an all-girls' school and his rocky relationship with a sexy student who thinks college is just a lark. Stars Clara Bow, Fredric March, Shirley O'Hara and Marceline Day.
VHS: S16175. $29.95.
Dorothy Arzner, USA, 1929, 76 mins.

D.W. GRIFFITH

Abraham Lincoln

Griffith's epic biography of Lincoln begins just prior to his ascent to the White House, and features a remarkable performance from Walter Huston as Lincoln. Griffith's remarkable handling of actors results in a believable portrait of the martyred president.
VHS: S00014. $19.95.
Laser: CLV. LD71965. $29.98.
D.W. Griffith, USA, 1930, 84 mins.

America

Griffith's patriotic, historical spectacle about the American Revolution, which combines a love story with events from Virginia to New England. The film is notable for Griffith's recreation of many of the famous battles; with Neil Hamilton, Lionel Barrymore. Silent, music track.
VHS: S02094. $59.95.
D.W. Griffith, USA, 1924, 81 mins.

Avenging Conscience

Griffith's first elaborate feature is notable for its use of double exposures and masks which would later influence the German Expressionist cinema. With Henry B. Walthall, Blanche Sweet. Silent with music track.
VHS: S02091. $39.95.
D.W. Griffith, USA, 1914, 58 mins.

The Birth of a Nation

D.W. Griffith's debut feature is credited with revolutionizing form and content in the cinema. Its epic story assessed the political, social, racial and personal consequences of the Civil War on American life, from the perspective of two families, the Southern Stonemans and the Northern Camerons. The story intersects the personal with the historic and political, Lincoln's assassination, the Reconstruction and the rise of the Ku Klux Klan. This deluxe edition features a 30-minute documentary on the making of the film, with interviews, archival footage and outtakes. Adapted from Thomas Dixon's novel and play *The Clansman*. With Lillian Gish, Mae Marsh, Miriam Cooper and filmmaker Raoul Walsh. Cinematography by Billy Bitzer and Karl Brown.
VHS: S18433. $39.95.
D.W. Griffith, USA, 1914, 187 mins.

Broken Blossoms

D.W. Griffith's pastoral effort set in a Dickensian London about the oppression of a frail young street urchin desperate to escape her bleak circumstances. The young woman falls in love with a sympathetic Chinese missionary, who shields her from her tyrannical and abusive father. "There are stretches of Griffith poetry, a marvelous use of light and shade in cameraman Billy Bitzer's evocation of foggy Limehouse, and a truly unforgettable performance from Lillian Gish" (*Time Out*). With Richard Barthelmess and Donald Crisp. Newly remastered print struck from an archival source.
VHS: S18434. $24.95.
D.W. Griffith, USA, 1919, 90 mins.

Corner in Wheat and Selected Biograph Shorts

A collection of eight one- and two-reel works D.W. Griffith directed from 1909-1913 for the American Mutoscope and Biograph Company that highlighted Griffith's narrative inventions. The other works showcased are *Those Awful Hats*, *The Sealed Room*, *The Unchanging Sea*, *His Trust*, *The New York Hat*, *An Unseen Enemy* and *The Mothering Heart*. Featuring Mary Pickford and Lillian and Dorothy Gish. 118 mins.
VHS: S18431. $24.95.

D.W. Griffith Triple Feature

Mae Marsh, Lillian Gish, Mary Pickford, and Blanche Sweet are among those featured in these three landmark Griffith westerns, including: *The Battle of Elderbush Gulch* (1913), *Lola's Promise* (1912), and *The Goddess of Sagebrush Gulch* (1912). *Elderbush* was considered by Griffith to be the third best film he ever made. It also marked the film debut of beautiful young Lillian Gish.
VHS: S00533. $19.95.
D.W. Griffith, USA, 1912-13, 50 mins.

Dream Street

A follow-up to *Broken Blossoms*, based on material by the same author, featuring Tyrone Power Sr., Ralph Graves and Carol Dempster. A story of two brothers, both in love with the same dancing girl, while a gambler plans to take her for his own.
VHS: S02245. $49.95.
D.W. Griffith, USA, 1921, 148 mins.

Greatest Question

Josephine Crowell, George Nichols and Lillian Gish star. Gish witnessed a murder many years ago and finds it is still haunting her. Silent with music track.
VHS: S07277. $24.95.
D.W. Griffith, USA, 1919, 80 mins.

Griffith Shorts (1908-09)

Short films made by Griffith during 1908-1909: *Crossroads of Life*, *Adventures of Dolly*, *A Calamitous Elopement*, *The Curtain Pole*, *The Jones Have Amateur Theatricals*, *A Drunkard's Reformation*, *What Drink Did*, *Confidence*, *Resurrection*, *Her First Biscuits*, *Violin Maker of Cremona*.
VHS: S04827. $29.95.
D.W. Griffith, USA, 1909-09, 120 mins.

Griffith Shorts (1909)

Griffith films made in 1909: *The Country Doctor*, *The Renunciation*, *Sweet and Twenty*, *The Mended Lute-Sealed Room*, *1776 or the Hassian Renegades*, *Pippa Passes*, *Lines of Whie on a Sullen Sea*, *The Gibson Goddess*, *The Light That Came*.
VHS: S04828. $29.95.
D.W. Griffith, USA, 1909, 110 mins.

Griffith Shorts (1909-1910)

Griffith films from 1909-1910: *A Corner in What*, *Her Terrible Ordeal*, *The Last Deal*, *In the Border States*, *Mugzy's First Sweetheart*, *An Arcadian Maid*, *House with Closed Shutters*, *The Usurer*, *Modern Prodigal*, *The Rose*.
VHS: S04829. $29.95.
D.W. Griffith, USA, 1909-1910, 120 mins.

Griffith Shorts (1909-1911)

Those Awful Hats, *The Son's Return*, *A Strange Meeting*, *Romance of Western Hills*, *Sorrows of the Unfaithful*, *What Shall We Do With Our Old*, *The Long Road*, *Love in the Hills*, *A Woman Scorned*, *With the Enemy's Help*.
VHS: S04838. $29.95.
D.W. Griffith, USA, 1909-1911, 120 mins.

Griffith Shorts (1910-1911)

The Message of the Violin, *The Fugitive*, *Sunshine Sue*, *Winning Back His Love*, *When a Man Loves*, *Two Paths*, *His Trust*, *Fates Turning*, *Fisher Folks*, *Lily of the Tenements*.
VHS: S04830. $29.95.
D.W. Griffith, USA, 1910-1911, 120 mins.

Griffith Shorts (1911)

The Lonedale Operator, *Enoch Arden* (parts 1 and 2), *Primal Call*, *Fighting Blood*, *Bobby The Coward*, *Country Cupid*, *Last Drop of Water*, *As a Boy Dreams*, *The Revenue Man and His Girl*.
VHS: S04831. $29.95.
D.W. Griffith, USA, 1911, 120 mins.

Griffith Shorts (1911-1912)

A Squaw's Love, *Adventures of Billy*, *The Battle*, *Through Darking Vales*, *The Miser's Heart*, *Failure*, *Saved from Himself*, *For His Son*, *The Transformation of Mike*.
VHS: S04832. $29.95.
D.W. Griffith, USA, 1911-1912, 129 mins.

Griffith Shorts (1912, #1)

Sunbeam, *Iola's Promise*, *The Goddess of Sagebrush Gulch*, *A Girl and Her Trust*, *The Female of the Species*, *Lesser Evil*, *A Beast at Bay*, *Lena and the Geese*, *Man's Genesis*, *The Sands o'Dee*.
VHS: S04833. $29.95.
D.W. Griffith, USA, 1912, 120 mins.

Griffith Shorts (1912, #2)

The Narrow Road, *Under Burning Skies*, *One Is Business the Other Crime*, *School Teacher and the Waif*, *A Change of Spirit*, *Unseen Enemy*, *Blind Love*, *Two Daughters of Eve*, *Friends*, *So Near Yet So Far*.
VHS: S04834. $29.95.
D.W. Griffith, USA, 1912, 120 mins.

Griffith Shorts (1912, #3)

Painted Lady, Musketeers of Pig Alley, Massacre, New York Hat, Burglars' Dilemma, The God Within, Telephone Girl and the Lady, Oil and Water.
VHS: S04835. $29.95.
D.W. Griffith, USA, 1912, 120 mins.

Griffith Shorts (1913)

The Unwelcome Guest, Near to the Earth, The Wanderer, House of Darkness, His Mother's Son, Timely Interception, Death's Marathon, Mothering Heart.
VHS: S04836. $29.95.
D.W. Griffith, USA, 1913, 120 mins.

Griffith Shorts (1913-1914)

The Switch Tower, Brute Force, The Reformers, Battle of Elderbrush Gulch, Pathways of Life.
VHS: S04837. $29.95.
D.W. Griffith, USA, 1913-1914, 120 mins.

Hearts of the World

Noel Coward made his first appearance in this story which takes place in a French village during World War I. The film espouses democracy and patriotism, and was a great commercial success. With Lillian Gish, Erich von Stroheim.
VHS: S00552. $19.98.
Laser: CLV. LD71988. $29.98.
D.W. Griffith, USA, 1918

Home Sweet Home

What started out as a one-reeler Griffith later expanded into a feature-length biography of John Howard Payne and his immortal song, "Home Sweet Home." Lillian Gish, Dorothy Gish, Mae Marsh, Blanche Sweet star in this series of vignettes, each illustrating a Payne song.
VHS: S01746. $29.95.
D.W. Griffith, USA, 1914, 62 mins.

Idol Dancer

A drunken Yankee beachcomber befriends a half-caste native girl scorned by the villagers in this Griffith epic set in the South Seas. Richard Barthelmess, Claire Seymour and Creighton Hale star in the film, which ends in a rousing climax. Silent, music track.
VHS: S02092. $29.95.
D.W. Griffith, USA, 1920, 76 mins.

Intolerance

Four separate stories are interwoven: the fall of Babylon, the death of Christ, the massacre of the Hugenots, and a modern drama—all cross-cut and building with enormous energy to a thrilling chase and finale. Far ahead of its time, Griffith created a spectacle which audiences of the day did not accept but which has become a classic of world cinema. This specially packaged double cassette edition of *Intolerance* has been remastered using variable speed projection and color tints to match the original release prints, making it the best version available anywhere. Tinted with organ score.
VHS: S13048. $29.95.
Laser: CAV. LD71052. $69.95.
Laser: CLV. LD71994. $29.98.
D.W. Griffith, USA, 1919, 190 min.

Isn't Life Wonderful

Griffith's last independent production, shot on location in Germany. A compassionate, romantic drama of postwar deprivation that decried the evils that led to the War, and exalted the power of love.
VHS: S00641. $44.95.
D.W. Griffith, USA, 1924

Judith of Bethula

The first four-reel film done in America (approximately 40 minutes), *Judith of Bethula* is a Biblical epic considered a stupendous production in its day. It was expanded to a longer version by Biograph Studios in 1917. Silent with music track.
VHS: S00662. $19.98.
Laser: CLV. LD71999. $29.98.
D.W. Griffith, USA, 1914

Judith of Bethula/Home Sweet Home

D.W. Griffith's biblical epic anticipates the structural elements of *Intolerance* as it interweaves four contrapuntal tales about a beautiful Bethulian widow, Judith, who seduces the Assyrian conqueror Holofernes in order to assassinate him and preserve her city. The film is important for its sweep and technical innovations and dense storytelling. *Home Sweet Home* is considerably different, a fascinating musical biography of John Howard Payne. With Lillian and Dorothy Gish, Mae Marsh, Blanche Sweet and Henry B. Walthall.
VHS: S18436. $24.95.
D.W. Griffith, USA, 1913/14, 118 mins.

Love Flower

One of three pictures Griffith shot for First National, a melodrama about a man who, with his daughter, escapes to a tropical island to elude a police detective. Shot on location in Fort Lauderdale, Florida, and in the Bahamas.
VHS: S00775. $49.95.
D.W. Griffith, USA, 1920, 70 mins.

Mother and the Law

An extremely rare D.W. Griffith film, which was later incorporated into Griffith's famous *Intolerance*, with many of the scenes deleted.
VHS: S11451. $24.95.
D.W. Griffith, USA, 1914, 93 mins.

The Musketeers of Pig Alley and Selected Biograph Shorts

Seven key works from D.W. Griffith's Biograph period are represented, most of them dealing with social themes, class distinctions and pure action. Works include *The Burglar's Dilemma, The Sunbeam, The Painted Lady, One Is Business, The Other Crime, Death's Marathon* and *The Battle at Elderbush Gulch*. With Lillian Gish, Mae Marsh, Blanche Sweet and Donald Crisp. 117 mins.
VHS: S18432. $24.95.

Orphans of the Storm

Two innocent orphans (Lillian and Dorothy Gish) arrive in Paris just prior to the French Revolution and are exploited, separated, and nearly find each other again—until they become involved in the Revolution themselves. A luxurious, large-scale Griffith spectacle. Digitally remastered.
VHS: S14444. $19.98.
Laser: CLV. LD72013. $29.98.
D.W. Griffith, USA, 1921, 190 mins.

Sally of the Sawdust

W.C. Fields' first major film, a classic of circus life, also starring Carol Dempster and Alfred Lunt. Music track.
VHS: S01150. $29.95.
D.W. Griffith, USA, 1925, 124 mins.

The Short Films of D.W. Griffith— Volume 1

Includes four early works by Griffith: *The Battle* (10 mins.), *The Battle at Elderbush Gulch* (10 mins.), *His Trust and His Trust Fulfilled* (28 mins.) and *Her Terrible Ordeal* (10 mins.).
VHS: S14925. $29.95.

The Short Films of D.W. Griffith— Volume 2

Six more early films from the American master: *The Unseen Enemy* (15 mins.), *The Little Tease* (10 mins.), *Man's Genesis* (10 mins.), *Musketeers of Pig Alley* (10 mins.), *The Switchtower* (10 mins.) and *Lonedale Operator* (11 mins.).
VHS: S14926. $29.95.

The Short Films of D.W. Griffith— Volume 3

Two silent shorts by the legendary D.W. Griffith: *The Tunnel Workers* (23 mins.) and *The Girls and Daddy* (26 mins.).
VHS: S14927. $29.95.

The Short Films of D.W. Griffith— Volume 4

Includes three more early short films from Griffith: *Enoch Arden* (20 mins.), *The Transformation of Mike* (20 mins.) and *What Should We Do with Our Old* (10 mins.).
VHS: S14928. $29.95.

Sorrows of Satan

The last major film by D.W. Griffith, in a lavish production originally intended for De Mille. With Carol Dempster, Adolphe Menjou, Ricardo Cortez and an exotic Lya de Putti.
VHS: S08334. $29.95.
D.W. Griffith, USA, 1926, 111 mins.

True Heart Susie

One of the lesser known great films by Griffith, director of *Birth of a Nation* and *Intolerance*, *True Heart Susie* features a superlative performance by Lillian Gish. The story of a childhood romance is told with simple charm and unpretentious style.
VHS: S01375. $29.95.
D.W. Griffith, USA, 1919, 62 mins.

Way Down East

D.W. Griffith's Victorian pastoral stars Lillian Gish as an eager though exploited young woman abandoned by her obsessive, cavalier husband when he learns she's pregnant, who finds temporary comfort and solace with a wealthy, passive, small-town lawyer. The film has two constructs, an evocative portrait of small-town Americana and a suspense melodrama about desire and attraction and despair that attains its climax in the famous ice floe sequence. With Richard Barthelmess, Lowell Sherman and Edgar Nelson.
VHS: S18435. $24.95.
D.W. Griffith, USA, 1920, 149 mins.

White Rose

A very rare D.W. Griffith film. Shot in the bayous of Louisiana, it's a simple, sentimental outlook on life. Mae Marsh and Ivor Novello star in the story of a minister who falls in love with an abandoned and outcast orphan girl.
VHS: S12151. $29.95.
D.W. Griffith, USA, 1923, 120 mins.

television SHOWS

The Abbott and Costello Television Show

Abbott and Costello's television comedy series recaptures the vivid atmosphere of live television during the early 50s. "The show pioneered the use of ensemble cast comedy sketches on live television and the intricate sense of timing reflects those vaudeville origins" (*Washington Post*).
Tape 1. This collection includes *Duck Dinner, Hillary's Birthday, Million Dollar Refund* and *Actors' Home.* 110 mins.
VHS: S19586. $19.95.
Tape 2. This collection includes *Lou's Birthday, Getting a Job, Uncle Bozzo* and *Stolen Skates.* 110 mins.
VHS: S19587. $19.95.
Tape 3. This collection includes *Lou Falls for Ruby, Hillary's Father, Uncle Ruppert* and *Bingo's Troubles.* 110 mins.
VHS: S19588. $19.95.
Tape 4. This collection includes *The Drugstore, Square Meal, $1,000 Prize* and *Wife Wanted.* 110 mins.
VHS: S19589. $19.95.
Tape 5. This collection includes *Police Academy, Charity Bazaar, Killer's Wife* and *Well Oiled.* 110 mins.
VHS: S19590. $19.95.
Tape 6. This collection includes *Wrestling Match, In Society, Lou's Marriage* and *Beauty Contest.* 110 mins.
VHS: S19591. $19.95.

Abraham Lincoln—Westinghouse Studio One

The life and death of the 16th President of the United States comes to live tv. The story by John Drinkwater covers Lincoln from his acceptance of the nomination to Ford's Theatre. With Robert Pastene, Judith Evelyn and a 21-year-old James Dean as a Union soldier sentenced to be shot for sleeping on guard duty.
USA, 1952, 60 mins.
VHS: S05436. $24.95.

Absolutely the Best of the Soupy Sales Show

Before David Letterman there was Soupy Sales and his inventive and charged parody of the talk show format. This collection of his best work, culled from some of his television shows, features the work of his gang of outcasts—White Tooth, Black Fang and Pookie—as well as some of his strange songs, e.g., "Your Brains Fell Out." 60 mins.
VHS: S18138. $19.95.

Aeon Flux

Aeon Flux is the animated heroine first glimpsed on MTV's *Liquid Television.* Four episodes of her surreal exploits in a violent world are captured on this video. Traveling between two warring nations is dangerous enough, but Aeon also must combat her sexy lover, Trevor Goodchild. 120 mins.
VHS: S27616. $14.98.

All Color News—Sampler

A remarkable collection of clips from the New York City feature news program for cable TV. Hard and gritty, this is the early political and socially-oriented work by artists Scott & Beth B, Charlie Ahearn, John Ahearn, and Tom Otterness—now well-known for their other productions.
VHS: S07110. $29.95.
All Color News, USA, 1978, 28 mins.

All My Children: Behind the Scenes

If you have ever wondered what goes on beneath the sheets during those steamy love scenes, then this video offers an unbeatable opportunity. Walt Wiley hosts this candid view of the most famous daytime series. Not only are the workings of this show exposed, but Erica Kane's closet is thrown wide open.
VHS: S22545. $14.98.

Amazing Stories: Book 1

Two great episodes from executive producer Steven Spielberg's acclaimed television series: *The Wedding Ring,* directed by Danny DeVito, and *The Mission,* directed by Spielberg himself. Featuring Kevin Costner, Kiefer Sutherland, Danny DeVito and Rhea Perlman. USA, 70 mins.
VHS: S13827. $79.95.

Amazing Stories: Book 4

Explore the incredible in these three episodes from *Amazing Stories,* the popular series from executive producer Steven Spielberg. Includes *Mirror, Mirror,* directed by Martin Scorsese; *Blue Man Down,* directed by Paul Michael Glaser; and *Mr. Magic,* directed by Donald Petrie. USA, 71 mins.
VHS: S15582. $79.95.

America's Funniest Animal Foul-Ups

Outrageous animals steal the show in this menagerie of mayhem. From the makers of "Foul-Ups, Bleeps and Blunders." Hosted by funnyman and "Tonight Show" regular Kelly Monteith. 30 mins.
VHS: S16332. $9.95.

America's Funniest Kid Foul-Ups

Comedian Kelly Monteith, a frequent guest on *The Tonight Show,* hosts this candid collection of gags and blunders starring the youth of America. Or at least those youngsters whose parents own video camcorders. From the producer of the ABC network hit *Foul-Ups, Bleeps and Blunders* comes the real story about what kindergartners think of being on television. 30 mins.
VHS: S15496. $9.95.

America's Funniest TV Foul-Ups

Some of television's funniest moments have been hidden away... until now. See President Nixon as he attempts to throw out the season's first baseball, car dealer tycoon Cal Worthington being attacked by a two-ton truck, a cooking show that goes up in flames, and other hilarities. Hosted by comedian Kelly Monteith. 30 mins.
VHS: S16331. $9.95.

The Andy Rooney Television Collection

The droll, idiosyncratic voice of Americana, humorist and essayist Andy Rooney offers his vignettes, anecdotes and quirky stories about man, nature, technology and contemporary life in three video programs: *His Minutes, Volumes 1 & 2* and *A Bird's Eye View of America.*
VHS: S19098. $39.98.

Andy Rooney: His Best Minutes, Vol. 1

Andy Rooney's deadpan observations on American institutions, humor, bureaucracy, culture, society, politics and the individual character are collected in this witty assemblage of his *60 Minutes* vignettes, *A Few Minutes with Andy Rooney.* 70 mins.
VHS: S19322. $19.98.

Andy Rooney: His Best Minutes, Vol. 2

A follow-up to the humorist's earlier collection of his *60 Minutes* pieces, quiet, reflective and droll reflections on the American character. 73 mins.
VHS: S19323. $19.98.

Bank on the Stars

Bill Cullen hosts this tv quiz show where contestants watch scenes from newly released films and must answer questions about what they have seen. Films on this program include *Apache* with Burt Lancaster, Jacques Tati's *Mr. Hulot's Holiday,* and *The Caine Mutiny,* with Humphrey Bogart and Van Johnson. Someone ought to bring this show back. USA, 1954, 30 mins.
VHS: S06477. $19.95.

The Bastard: Part I of the Kent Family Chronicles

Andrew Stevens leads an all-star cast in this exciting, sweeping adventure saga based on John Jakes' best-selling American Bicentennial series. Olivia Hussey and Kim Cattrall co-star in this fascinating and compelling drama set against one of the most exciting periods of American history.
VHS: S15277. $29.98.
Lee Katzin, USA, 1978, 189 mins.

Beauty and the Beast

This television series starring Linda Hamilton had a cult following. It placed the fairy tale of *Beauty and the Beast* right under contemporary Manhattan. Romance and fantasy take on a dark perspective, rendering this age-old tale suitable for our times. Each episode is approximately 49 mins.
Episode 1: Once Upon a Time in New York.
VHS: S07437. $14.98.
Episode 2: Terrible Savior.
VHS: S23092. $14.98.
Episode 3: Siege.
VHS: S23093. $14.98.
Episode 4: No Way Down.
VHS: S23094. $14.98.
Episode 5: Masques.
VHS: S23095. $14.98.
Episode 6: The Beast Within.
VHS: S23096. $14.98.
Episode 7: Nor Iron Bars a Cage.
VHS: S23097. $14.98.
Episode 8: Song of Orpheus.
VHS: S23098. $14.98.
Episode 9: Dark Spirit.
VHS: S23099. $14.98.
Episode 10: A Children's Story.
VHS: S23100. $14.98.
Episode 11: An Impossible Silence.
VHS: S23101. $14.98.
Episode 12: Shades of Grey.
VHS: S23102. $14.98.

Beauty and the Beast: Above, Below and Beyond

A sequel to the tremendously popular television series which follows the adventures of Beauty and her Beast. 100 mins.
VHS: S09664. $19.95.

The Bells of Cockaigne & Broadway Trust

James Dean and Gene Lockhart star in *The Bells of Cockaigne* (30 mins.), an Armstrong Circle Theatre television production written by George Lawther. James Dean is a long-suffering dock worker struggling to save enough money to move his family to a warmer climate in the hopes that the dry air will improve his asthmatic son's health. His co-worker Pat (Gene Lockhart) dreams of winning a local newspaper contest and using the prize money to see his native Ireland one last time. *Broadway Trust* (25 mins.) stars Lloyd Bridges in a true story of embezzlement, faith and friendship from the *Crossroads* television series. *Crossroads* was a television series overseen by religious officials, which produced programs based on true stories of the decisions people made when they found themselves at moral crossroads in their lives. B&W. From *The James Dean Collection.*
VHS: S27328. $19.95.
James Sheldon, USA, 1952, 55 mins.

Best of Abbott and Costello Live

A generous helping of the raucous comedy of Bud Abbott and Lou Costello distilled from their live television appearances. This popular comedy team will, of course, be doing their classic hit "Who's on First" as well as enough material to fill nearly an hour with their funny routines that kept America in stitches in the early 1950's. B&W. 58 mins.
VHS: S07526. $19.95.

The Best of Candid Camera

A fun-filled selection from Allen Funt's famous television series.
VHS: S04504. $59.99.

The Best of Ernie Kovacs

The work of the great Ernie Kovacs is now available for the first time on home video. His television career from 1950 to 1962 has been painstakingly researched and collected from over 100 hours of footage to create this series of his best comedy bits. Most of this rare film material has not been seen for decades. Five volumes.
Volume 1. Features classic bits from the early television shows, including the "crazy" 1812 Overture and the "Whom Dunnit" game show.
VHS: S14701. $19.95.
Volume 2. "The Music Show" features the gorilla *Swan Lake* ballet, and a street scene set to Bartok.
VHS: S14702. $19.95.
Volume 3. Featuring material from the final "Eugene" broadcast. Plus the comic Dutch Masters commercials.
VHS: S14703. $19.95.
Volume 4. Featuring Miklos Molnar making "Chicken Molnar" and the best of the oscilloscope gags.
VHS: S14704. $19.95.
Volume 5. Containing material broadcast in January 1962, just after Kovacs death.
VHS: S14705. $19.95.
The complete five-volume set.
VHS: S14706. $99.75.

The Best of Howard and Dave

Snippets of music, news, performance, and plenty of humor fill this collection from the "Howard and Dave Show." These critically acclaimed talk show hosts from California rally an abundance of information and entertainment directly for Gay and Lesbian audiences.
VHS: S15680. $29.95.

Best of On the Road with Charles Kuralt

One of America's premier journalists, Charles Kuralt goes on the road and provides an epic vision of America, its people, cultures, landscapes and diversity in three separate videos: *American Heritage, Seasons of America* and *Unforgettable People.*
VHS: S19097. $49.98.

The Best of Red Green

The PBS cult comedy hit *The Red Green Show* features do-it-yourselfer Red Green (Steve Smith) and his nephew Harold as they host a hilarious round-up of memorable moments from Possum Lodge. Called "...the funniest thing to hit public television since *Monty Python's Flying Circus*" (*Milwaukee Journal*), *The Best of Red Green* features numerous episodes of *Adventures with Bill* and *Handyman Corner.* Includes the seven-minute documentary *The Making of Red Green.* With Pat McKenna and Rick Green.
VHS: S27198. $19.95.
Stephen Benedict/Steve Lambert/Andrew Robertson, USA, 1995, 67 mins.

Best of Spike Jones—Volume 1

An anthology of snippets from his popular TV show produced and edited under the personal supervision of Spike Jones, Jr. Enjoy once again the melodic sounds of cowbells, foghorns, slide whistles and various other musical paraphernalia that were standard issue for Spike and the City Slickers. B&W. 1952-57, 51 mins.
VHS: S10809. $29.95.
Laser: LD75120. $24.98.

Best of Spike Jones—Volume 2

More of the wacky and weird musical renditions of Spike Jones and his band of City Slickers. Ten popular songs are presented with the special Spike touch. See how many you can still identify. Feel free to ring your cowbell at home while you watch this unusual comedy-variety show. B&W. 1952-57, 53 mins.
VHS: S10810. $29.95.
Laser: LD75121. $24.98.

Best of Spike Jones—Volume 3

An all-new hilarious highlights from Spike Jones' popular 50's TV shows. 54 mins.
VHS: S08112. $29.95.

The Best of the 90's Home Video

This collection features some of the best moments from the first season of what is easily the most important and innovative news show on the air, a show that does all the things that television is supposed to do but never does. "The 90's" comes out of Chicago, appearing mainly on local PBS stations; part "60 Minutes," part counterculture documentary, part rock and roll, all experimental and groundbreaking, it presents a truly global and often radical view of world events.
VHS: S13773. $19.95.

The Beverly Hillbillies Go Hollywood

Four episodes of the popular television comedy are seamlessly woven together in this story detailing misadventures and crazy antics when Jed decides to buy a movie studio. Will American movies ever be the same? With Buddy Ebsen, Max Baer Jr. and Donna Douglas. 104 mins.
VHS: S19749. $19.98.

The Bill Dana Show

A classic television series. Dana is cast as Jose Jimenez, a Chaplinesque New York City bellman who represents the ambitions and desires of the American Dream he has turned upside down. He's an everyman with a burning desire to succeed but who has an inopportune tendency to screw up. With his friend Byron Glick (Don Adams), he experiences one strange encounter after another with heartbreaking and ironic consequences. "I rank Dana's Jose Jimenez among the true great original characters in the world scope of show business" (Ed Sullivan).
The Bill Dana Show: Vol. 1.
VHS: S19250. $14.95.
The Bill Dana Show: Vol. 2.
VHS: S19251. $14.95.
The Bill Dana Show: Vol. 3.
VHS: S19252. $14.95.
The Bill Dana Show: Vol. 4.
VHS: S19253. $14.95.
The Bill Dana Show: Vol. 5.
VHS: S19254. $14.95.
The Bill Dana Show: Vol. 6.
VHS: S19255. $14.95.
The Bill Dana Show: Vol. 7.
VHS: S19256. $14.95.
The Bill Dana Show: Vol. 8.
VHS: S19257. $14.95.
The Bill Dana Show: Vol. 9.
VHS: S19258. $14.95.
The Bill Dana Show: Vol. 10.
VHS: S19259. $14.95.
The Collectors Boxed Edition: Vol. 1-5.
VHS: S19260. $59.95.
The Collectors Boxed Edition: Vol. 6-10.
VHS: S19261. $59.95.

Bloopers: Vol. 2

A compilation of special screw-ups never before included in one video. Includes Robin Williams, Henry Winkler, Alan Alda, Elizabeth Taylor and many more. Parental discretion advised. USA, 55 mins.
VHS: S15029. $19.95.

Bosom Buddies, Vol. 1

Tom Hanks was famous as a man in woman's clothing long before he played a gay man in *Philadelphia.* Together with Peter Scolari he waltzed through a number of strange, comic situations in which he and his friend had to explain their presence in drag despite their deeply ingrained heterosexual longings. They just happened to live in a "women only" hotel. Includes the pilot and the aptly titled "Macho Man." 51 mins.
VHS: S25959. $9.95.

Bosom Buddies, Vol. 2

Tom Hanks and Peter Scolari stayed true to form in these episodes that mix gender-bending with humor. Includes "Kip and Sonny's Date" and "Revenge." 51 mins.
VHS: S25960. $9.95.

Bosom Buddies, Vol. 3

Hanks and Scolari keep up the good ruse in "Kip Quits" and "The Hospital." 51 mins.
VHS: S25961. $9.95.

Bosom Buddies, Vol. 4

"There's No Business/Other Than That" and "She's a Wonderful Person" show Tom Hanks and Peter Scolari at their most beautifully comic. 51 mins.
VHS: S25962. $9.95.

The Bowery Boys

An intimate compilation work featuring the madcap charm and flair of *The Bowery Boys,* with interviews with the major players, hilarious outtakes and bloopers, rare archival still photographs and clips of the best programs. With Huntz Hall, Leo Gorcey and Robby Jordan.
VHS: S17554. $14.98.

The Brady Bunch, Vol. 1

It's the lovely story of a lovely lady who was bringing up three very lovely girls 'til one day... This is it—the original 1970's television series. Includes the first episode, "The Honeymoon," and "A Camping We Will Go." 51 mins.
VHS: S25955. $9.95.

The Brady Bunch, Vol. 2

This volume from the original 1970's television series includes the episodes "The Tattletale" and "Law and Disorder." 51 mins.
VHS: S25956. $9.95.

The Brady Bunch, Vol. 3

The episodes "Will the Real Jan Brady Please Stand Up" and "Her Sister's Shadow" effectively encapsulate 1970's sitcom wisdom on sibling rivalry. 51 mins.
VHS: S25957. $9.95.

The Brady Bunch, Vol. 4

"Getting Davy Jones" and "The Subject Was Noses" span the gamut of teenage angst from idol worship to the importance of appearance. 51 mins.
VHS: S25958. $9.95.

Bronco: Death of an Outlaw

This television western with Ty Hardin re-invents the western legend of Pat Garrett and Billy the Kid. The program paints Billy as a respectable family man unfairly prosecuted for past misdeeds by buffalo hunter and "opportunist" Pat Garrett. 1960, 60 mins.
VHS: S16283. $14.98.

Bronco: Shadow of Jesse James

Another piece that demythologizes the west, with its eponymous hero inadvertently crossing paths with the famed outlaws of the time, the vicious Jesse James (played by James Coburn), Cole Younger and Belle Starr. With Ty Hardin (as Bronco).
VHS: S16284. $14.98.

Bruce Lee and the Green Hornet

A rare screen test of the martial arts icon and charismatic figure Bruce Lee, on the making of the television series *The Green Hornet*, with three complete, uncut episodes and a short film on the making of Robert Clouzet's *Enter the Dragon*, the actor's fullest and most satisfying work. 90 mins.
VHS: S17577. $19.95.

Bumbledown/Sound of Maggie

A bitingly satirical puppet show on the life of Ronald Reagan from the people at *Spitting Image*. Directed by Graham C. Williams. Also on the cassette is *The Sound of Maggie*. 76 mins.
VHS: S15183. $24.95.

Bumbledown:
The Life and Times of Ronald Reagan

The character assassinators known as "Spitting Image" target our 43rd President. This puppet show reveals the sometimes painful and always shameful truth, from the moment Ronald opened his mouth to the time he tried to say something that made sense. 38 mins.
VHS: S16115. $14.98.

A Candle for St. Jude

A Westinghouse Studio One presentation, this program tells the story of a ballet troupe in conflict. The prima ballerina is forcing Hilda to change her ballet. Choreography by Ruthanna Boris with Lili Darvas and Tanaquil LeClerq in the cast. Betty Furness hosts the program which is missing its opening and first commercial. USA, 1952, 56 mins.
VHS: S03657. $24.95.

Car 54: Where Are You?

The cult 60's television series, collected in two-episode packs which follow the original air dates.
Car 54: Volume 1. Contains *Who's for Swordfish?* and *Something Nice for Sol*. 50 mins.
VHS: S12126. $14.95.
Car 54: Volume 2. Contains *Home Sweet Sing Sing* and *Change Your Partner*. 50 mins.
VHS: S12127. $14.95.
Car 54: Volume 3. Contains *I Won't Go* and *Muldoon's Star*. 50 mins.
VHS: S12128. $14.95.
Car 54: Volume 4. Contains *Paint Job* and *Love Finds Muldoon*. 50 mins.
VHS: S12129. $14.95.
Car 54 Pre-Pack. Volumes 1-4 of *Car 54* at a special price.
VHS: S12130. $59.98.

Charles Kuralt: American Heritage

From Charles Kuralt's essay on Americana, *On the Road*, this program uses the openness and expanse of the road to look at the evolution of American traditions, culture and society from colonial settlers to the rugged individualists of the Wild West. 60 mins.
VHS: S19320. $19.98.

Charles Kuralt: Seasons of America

Collected from journalist Charles Kuralt's provocative *On the Road* series, this work looks at the year-long celebration of American spectacle and insight, of small-town festivals and social and community traditions. 60 mins.
VHS: S19321. $19.98.

Charles Kuralt: Unforgettable People

A portrait of eccentric and inspiring people discovered by journalist Charles Kuralt on his *On the Road* program. 55 mins.
VHS: S19319. $19.98.

Cheyenne: The Iron Trail

Clint Walker stars as the cryptic drifter. *The Iron Trail* features Dennis Hopper as a ruthless outlaw planning a daring assassination attempt of President Ulysses S. Grant. 1957, 60 mins.
VHS: S16281. $14.98.

Cheyenne: White Warrior

Michael Landon guest starred in this episode of the '50s television western as a white youth brought up by Commanches who becomes the bargaining chip between Apache warriors and the wagon master Cheyenne Bodie. 1958, 60 mins.
VHS: S16282. $14.98.

Chicago Television

A look at the world of live TV in Chicago through clips from Svengoolie, Kukla, Fran and Ollie, Dick Tracy Show, Chicago Cubs, White Sox, Bulls and Blackhawks, complete episodes from Frosty the Snowman to the Mighty Hercules and sights of Chicago including Riverview and the Beatles at Comiskey Park. 120 mins.
VHS: S26083. $14.95.

China Beach

The pilot episode for the popular TV dramatic series about medical care, music and moral dilemma in Southeast Asia. Emmy winning Dana Delaney as McMurphy leads a well chosen cast in this opening barrage of nostalgia that features Nan Woods, Michael Boatman, Robert Riccardo, Brian Wimmer and Chloe Webb. Written and produced by John Sacret Young.
VHS: S12859. $19.98.
Rod Holcomb, USA, 1988, 95 mins.

A Concert in Pantomime

An extremely rare performance featuring Red Skelton and Marcel Marceau. USA, 60 mins.
VHS: S15225. $19.95.

A Conversation with George Burns

An interview with George Burns, conducted by Monty Hall, that traces his Jewish roots and expounds on his philosophy. With selected clips from the Burns and Allen routine that made his reputation. 27 mins.
VHS: S17930. $29.95.

Crosscurrents and C-Man

Two classic episodes from the 1950's are presented as prime examples of television film noir. First up, from *Crosscurrents*, is "The Case of the Forged Passports." Agent Christopher Storm (Gerald Mohr) battles beauties and shady characters in Vienna as he searches for stolen printing plates which are being used to produce forged American passports. Written and directed by Sheldon Reynolds. In the *C-Man* episode, "The Case of the Perfect Gentleman," a nightclub owner gets mixed up with a couple of gangsters, federal agents, the IRS and two women. Written and directed by Robert Sloane.
VHS: S13503. $24.95.

Danger Man

The television series *Danger Man* features Patrick McGoohan as British agent John Drake with plots and world intrigue as he encounters it. This spy drama would later transform into the *Secret Agent* series.
Danger Man Vol. 1: Bury the Dead.
VHS: S11129. $19.95.
Danger Man Vol. 2: Under the Lake.
VHS: S11130. $19.95.
Danger Man Vol. 3: Affair of State.
VHS: S11131. $19.95.
Danger Man Vol. 4: View from the Villa.
VHS: S11132. $19.95.

Dark Shadows 1:
The Resurrection of Barnabas Collins

The popular Gothic TV show is now on video. The first collection includes the first year prelude and then episodes 1-5 of the saga of TV's favorite daytime drama vampire. In the New England community of Collinsport, a courtly bloodsucker really livens up the town. With Jonathan Frid, Joan Bennett, Lara Parker, Grayson Hall and John Carlen. 120 mins.
VHS: S10992. $29.95.

Dark Shadows 2: Three-Pack

The saga of the Collins family continues with episodes 6-20 in this three-pack set of home video gothic drama. Jonathan Frid stars as the tormented vampire revived two hundred years after falling ill to a witch's curse. With Lara Parker as the devilish Angelique. 360 mins.
VHS: S10993. $79.95.

Dark Shadows, Volumes 5-8

Twenty complete episodes from the late 1960's (five episodes per videocassette). Though susceptible to Barnabas' powers, Maggie becomes aware of Barnabas' vampirism and devises a plan to drive a stake through his heart.
VHS: S12694. $79.98.

Dark Shadows, Volumes 9-12

The plot begins to thicken. Maggie Evans has disappeared. Barnabas, still looking for a new lover, sets his evil eye on a new beauty, Victoria Winter. Twenty episodes.
VHS: S12695. $79.98.

Dark Shadows, Volumes 13-16

Twenty complete episodes from the original series, five episodes per volume.
VHS: S12696. $79.98.

Dark Shadows, Volumes 17-20

David Collins begins to understand his family secrets. Twenty episodes.
VHS: S12697. $79.98.

Dark Shadows, Volumes 21-24

David Collins discovers Barnabas' coffin. Dr. Woodward begins an investigation into Barnabas that leads to a startling revelation. Julia Hoffman's experiments to cure Barnabas of his vampirism backfire when Barnabas assumes the appearance of a 175-year old man. 4 individually packaged tapes, 105 mins. each.
VHS: S12288. $79.98.

Dark Shadows, Volumes 25-28

Barnabas is determined to make Victoria his bride, and he enslaves Carolyn to assist him in his romantic plan. Volume 28 includes a flashback sequence; drama takes place in 1795. Twenty episodes.
VHS: S12698. $79.98.

Dark Shadows, Volumes 29-32

The 1795 flashback continues. Vicki is transported back to 1795, where she meets 18th century Collins family members. The 1795 Collinses are puzzled by Vicki's strange behavior and clothing. A youthful and human Barnabas Collins anxiously awaits his marriage to Josette DuPres. Josette's maidservant Angelique wants Barnabas for herself, and is determined to destroy Barnabas' and Josette's relationship through her black magic. 4 individually packaged tapes. Available only as a four-pack.
VHS: S12525. $79.98.

Dark Shadows, Volumes 45-48

The 1795 flashback continues. Victoria Winters is led to the gallows, convicted of witchcraft. After the noose is placed around her neck, she mysteriously reappears at Collinwood in the 20th century. 4 individually packaged tapes.
VHS: S13279. $79.98.

Dark Shadows, Volumes 49-52

Roger Collins marries a beautiful young lady named Cassandra, who is really Angelique in disguise. Julia Hoffman and Dr. Lang experiment to find a permanent cure for Barnabas' vampirism. Cassandra, however, is determined to make Barnabas a creature of the night once more, and she initiates a dream curse that affects everyone at Collinwood. Four individually packaged tapes in the set; five episodes per tape. 105 mins. each cassette.
VHS: S13533. $79.98.

Dark Shadows, Volumes 53-56

Hoping to free himself and the entire Collins family of Angelique's evil schemes, Barnabas Collins hires artist Sam Evans to age Angelique's portrait, causing her to turn into a 200-year-old woman. The man-made creature Adam kidnaps Carolyn Stoddard and hides her in an abandoned farm cellar. Willie Loomis becomes the next victim of Angelique's evil dream curse. The vengeful ghost of Reverend Trask appears at the Old House and bricks up the now-human Barnabas inside the basement wall to die. Four individually packaged tapes in the set; five episodes per tape. 105 mins. each cassette.
VHS: S13567. $79.98.

Dark Shadows, Volumes 57-60

Reverend Trask's ghost captures Cassandra Collins (alias Angelique) and tries to destroy her through an exorcism. Barnabas Collins fears Angelique will return and again curse him as a vampire. Warlock Nicholas Blair arrives at Collinwood, claiming to be Cassandra's brother. Through black magic he returns Angelique to Collinwood in the guise of Cassandra. Professor Stokes warns Victoria Winters that she is the next intended victim of the dream curse. He befriends Adam and learns of the man-made creature's hatred of Barnabas. Four individually packaged tapes in the set; five episodes per tape. 105 mins. each cassette.
VHS: S13536. $79.98.

Dark Shadows, Volumes 61-64

Fearing for Victoria Winter's safety, Barnabas Collins forces Vicki to reveal her nightmare resulting from Angelique's frightening dream curse. Warlock Nicholas Blair causes Angelique to age and vows to destroy her unless she returns the vampire curse to Barnabas. Angelique learns of the mysterious link between Barnabas and Adam. Four individually packaged tapes in the set, with five *Dark Shadows* episodes per tape. 105 mins. per tape.
VHS: S13681. $79.98.

Dark Shadows, Volumes 65-68

Warlock Nicholas Blair brings Angelique back from the dead as a vampire. After handyman Tom Jennings' death, Barnabas and Julia Hoffman seek the identity of the vampire responsible for his demise. Barnabas discovers fang marks on Julia's neck and realizes she is a victim of Tom, who has now risen as one of the living dead. 4 individually packaged tapes. 5 episodes per tape (105 mins. each tape).
VHS: S13840. $79.98.

Dark Shadows, Volumes 69-72

While being held captive in the mausoleum secret room, Maggie begins to remember how Barnabas kidnapped her months before and attempted to turn her into his vampire bride…. Four individually packaged tapes. Five *Dark Shadows* episodes per tape.
VHS: S14475. $79.98.

Dark Shadows, Volumes 73-76

Barnabas Collins and Julia Hoffman succeed in creating Eve, a mate for the man-made Adam, unaware they have reincarnated Danielle Roget, one of the 18th century's most evil women…. Four individually packaged tapes. Five *Dark Shadows* episodes per tape.
VHS: S14474. $79.98.

Dark Shadows, Volumes 81-84

After David and Amy discover Quentin's skeleton in a sealed-off room, the ghosts of Quentin and Beth Chavez appear to the children…. Four individually packaged tapes. Five *Dark Shadows* episodes per tape.
VHS: S14613. $79.98.

Dark Shadows, Volumes 85-88

Barnabas Collins summons the ghost of Peter Bradford to help Barnabas travel back to the 18th century in an attempt to prevent Victoria Winters from hanging as a witch…. Four individually packaged tapes. Five *Dark Shadows* episodes per tape. (105 mins. each tape)
VHS: S14980. $79.95.

Dark Shadows, Volumes 89-92

The mysterious ghost of Beth Chavez leads Chris Jennings to the unmarked grave of a child. Barnabas Collins and Chris discover a pentagram inside the child's coffin. As the ghost of Quentin Collins furthers his control of David Collins and Amy Jennings, the residents at Collinwood realize that the children are possessed by an evil spirit…. 4 videocassettes; 5 episodes per tape.
VHS: S14946. $79.95.

Dark Shadows, Volumes 93-96

In the year 1897, Barnabas finds himself a vampire once again as he is trapped inside his chained coffin after being unexpectedly transported back in time from the 20th century…. 4 individually packaged videos. 5 episodes per tape. Complete set only.
VHS: S15097. $79.98.

Dark Shadows, Volumes 97-100

In 1897, the insane Jenny Collins escapes from the tower room at Collinwood. Barnabas Collins is shocked to find Angelique, who advises him to return to the 20th century…. 4 individually packaged tapes. 5 episodes per tape. Complete set only.
VHS: S15270. $79.98.

Dark Shadows, Volumes 101-104

Quentin Collins and Magda the gypsy discover the mysterious urn which contains the flames of life for Laura Collins, who is a creature of the supernatural—an immortal Phoenix…. 4 individually packaged tapes; 5 episodes per tape (105 mins. each).
VHS: S15608. $79.98.

Dark Shadows, Volumes 105-108

The 1897 flashback continues with Barnabas, Quentin and the rest of the inhabitants of Collinwood. Four individually packaged tapes, five episodes per tape. 420 minutes.
VHS: S15870. $79.98.

Dark Shadows, Volumes 109-112

The Collins family discovers that Barnabas is a vampire as the 1897 flashback continues. Four individually packaged tapes, five episodes per tape. 420 mins.
VHS: S15888. $79.98.

Dark Shadows, Volumes 117-120

Julia travels back in time to 1897, and attempts to save Barnabas, who has been trapped in a basement cell in Collinwood. Four individually packaged cassettes, five episodes per tape. 420 mins.
VHS: S16530. $79.98.

Dark Shadows, Volumes 121-124

The 1897 flashback continues as Barnabas meets the reincarnation of Josette. Four individually packaged cassettes, five episodes per tape. 420 mins.
VHS: S16793. $79.98.

Dark Shadows: Behind the Scenes

This is a complete history of the legendary Gothic drama, tracing its beginnings, development into a national phenomenon, and its vibrant cult afterlife. A must-see for fans. 60 mins.
VHS: S15520. $19.98.

Dark Shadows: Music Videos

This specially compiled videocassette features musical highlights from the original soundtrack of *Dark Shadows* combined with memorable scenes from the classic series. Includes "Quentin's Theme"! 40 mins.
VHS: S15519. $19.98.

Dark Shadows: Vampires & Ghosts

This chilling compilation from the macabre daytime series brings the most frightening moments of that series together on one videotape. Barnabas Collins the vampire and other dark shadows from the Collinwood mansion are featured. 60 mins.
VHS: S26802. $19.98.

Dave Garroway's Wide Wide World

A special show from the '50s taped at Gene Autry's Melody Ranch. With John Wayne, Gary Cooper, Clayton Moore, John Ford and many more stars of the Hollywood Western. 75 mins.
VHS: S15697. $29.95.

Daytime's Greatest Weddings:
All My Children

Susan Lucci, known to millions as the complex and disturbing Erica Kane, hosts this collection of video memories that feature Pine Valley's most romantic couples. Of course, Erica Kane's own unforgettable marital merry-go-round is also featured. 45 mins.
VHS: S22548. $14.98.

Daytime's Greatest Weddings:
General Hospital

This collection of nuptial bliss contains the most historic wedding from daytime television, the wedding of Luke and Laura. Their union even made the cover of Newsweek. Jackie Zeman and Brad Maule (Bobby and Tony Jones) act as hosts.
VHS: S22549. $14.98.

Daytime's Greatest Weddings:
One Life to Live

Erika Slezak (Vicki Buchanan) hosts this dizzying plunge into the romances of daytime's Buchanan family. This collection of unforgettable love vignettes will bring on a flood of reminiscences. 45 mins.
VHS: S22547. $14.98.

Daytime's Most Wanted

ABC's soap operas employ dynamic leading men who romance women for a living, at least on screen. In this video their personal lives are revealed as something completely different. Historical footage also shows the rich romantic evolution of these charismatic screen figures.
VHS: S22546. $14.98.

The Defender

Steve McQueen, Ralph Bellamy, William Shatner and Martin Balsam star in the pilot of this controversial TV series. These original live television broadcasts from 1957 pit attorney Bellamy, who is convinced his client McQueen is guilty, against his own son (Shatner), who believes him innocent. 112 mins.
VHS: S13431. $19.95.

Dennis the Movie Star

Now Dennis is menacing the movies in a hilarious collection of movie exclusives from the top-rated, animated TV series.
VHS: S10753. $19.98.

Dick Tracy

The original Dick Tracy along with his crime busting pals Joe Jitsu, Go Go Gomez, Heap O'Callory, Hemlock Holmes and The Retouchables in this animated TV series based on the comic strip created by Chester Gould. Each volume is 51 mins.
Dick Tracy Volume 1.
VHS: S12500. $12.95.
Dick Tracy Volume 2.
VHS: S12501. $12.95.
Dick Tracy Volume 3.
VHS: S12502. $12.95.
Dick Tracy Volume 4.
VHS: S12503. $12.95.
Dick Tracy Volume 5.
VHS: S12504. $12.95.
Dick Tracy Volume 6.
VHS: S12505. $12.95.

Edward R. Murrow: The Best of Person to Person
This video culls together the best of intimate, freewheeling conversations of legendary journalist Edward R. Murrow, with President and Mrs. Kennedy, Frank Sinatra, Marilyn Monroe, and Marlon Brando. 90 mins.
VHS: S19318. $19.98.

Errol Flynn Theatre
Legendary screen swashbuckler Errol Flynn presents three episodes from his 1956-1957 television series. Besides acting as host, Flynn stars in two of the stories, while the third is a chilling tale of the supernatural. In "The Duel" Flynn is a villainous swordsman. In "The Strange Auction" Flynn co-stars with his wife, Patrice Wymore, and son, Sean Flynn; Patrice buys Errol at an auction. And in "The Sealed Room" a young lady is possessed by the spirit of a dead woman.
VHS: S13426. $29.95.

First Draw Gift Set
The high point of American television westerns is presented in this impressive collection of *Gunsmoke*, *Rawhide* and *Wild, Wild West*.
VHS: S19101. $39.98.

Fishing Trip: I Love Lucy: Deep Sea Fishing and The Honeymooners: Something Fishy
A pair of hilarious fishing expeditions as two of TV's big clowns try to get the big one. 60 mins.
VHS: S12348. $14.98.

Ford Star Jubilee
Noel Coward and Mary Martin star in this live television production of *Together with Music*.
VHS: S10597. $29.95.

Ford Star Jubilee Salute to Cole Porter
A record of the live television salute to Cole Porter, featuring Louis Armstrong, Gordon MacRae, Shirley Jones and Bing Crosby, among others.
VHS: S10598. $29.95.

Four Star Playhouse
This classic television dramatic series was produced by the "Four Stars" who owned the company: Dick Powell, David Niven, Charles Boyer, and Ida Lupino. All of Hollywood's greatest stars appeared on this program, one of the best of television's *Golden Age*.
Volume 1: *The Test* stars Dick Powell and Francis Rafferty; *The Interlude*, Dick Powell and Joanne Woodward.
VHS: S09535. $29.95.
Volume 2: *The Lost Silk Hat* stars Ronald Colman; *Welcome Home*, Dick Powell and David Hart.
VHS: S09536. $29.95.
Volume 3: *The Listener* stars Ida Lupino and Richard Lupono; *The Devil to Pay* features Charles Boyer and Ida Lupino.
VHS: S09537. $29.95.
Volume 4: *Vote of Confidence* features David Niven, Amanda Blake and Chuck Connors; *Tusitala*, David Niven portraying Robert Louis Stevenson.
VHS: S09538. $29.95.
Volume 5: *Girl on the Bridge* features Dick Powell and Coleen Gray; *The Gift* is with Charles Boyer and Maureen O'Sullivan.
VHS: S09539. $29.95.
Volume 6: *Shadowed* stars Dick Powell and Francis Dee; Dick Powell and Barbara Billingsley are featured in *The Gun*.
VHS: S09540. $29.95.
Volume 7: *Girl on the Park Bench* features Joan Fontaine with Craig Stevens; *A Place of His Own*, Charles Boyer and Stacy Harris.
VHS: S09541. $29.95.
Volume 8: *The Adolescent* stars Ida Lupino and Hugh Beaumont; *The Bomb* features David Niven and Margaret Sullavan.
VHS: S09542. $29.95.
Volume 9: *The Bad Streak* features Charles Boyer and Virginia Grey; Beverly Garland and David Niven are in *Touch and Go*.
VHS: S09543. $29.95.
Volume 10: Ida Lupino and George Macready are featured in *House for Sale*; Dick Powell stars in *To Die at Midnight*.
VHS: S09544. $29.95.
Volume 11: Dick Powell and Regis Toomey star in *The Squeeze*; Dick Powell and Dick Foran are in *Detective's Holiday*.
VHS: S09545. $29.95.
Volume 12: Dick Powell and Frances Bergen star in *High Stakes*; Dick Powell, Regis Toomey and Alan Mowbray are featured in *The Stacked Deck*.
VHS: S09546. $29.95.

The Fugitive
The television show starring David Janssen as a doctor falsely charged with killing his wife, who escapes police custody and relentlessly pursues a one-armed man responsible for the act. One of the hallmarks of television, this collection includes the famous final episode.
The Fugitive, Final Episode.
VHS: S17588. $14.95.
The Fugitive, Vol. 1.
VHS: S17578. $24.95.
The Fugitive, Vol. 2.
VHS: S17579. $24.95.
The Fugitive, Vol. 3.
VHS: S17580. $24.95.
The Fugitive, Vol. 4.
VHS: S17581. $24.95.
The Fugitive, Vol. 5.
VHS: S17582. $24.95.
The Fugitive, Vol. 6.
VHS: S17583. $24.95.
The Fugitive, Vol. 7.
VHS: S17584. $24.95.
The Fugitive, Vol. 8.
VHS: S17585. $24.95.
The Fugitive, Vol. 9.
VHS: S17586. $24.95.
The Fugitive, Vol. 10.
VHS: S17587. $24.95.
The Fugitive, Vol. 11. *10,000 Pieces of Silver* and *The Evil Men Do*.
VHS: S26185. $24.95.
The Fugitive, Vol. 12. *The Last Oasis* and *Walls of Knight*.
VHS: S26186. $24.95.
The Fugitive, Vol. 13. *Run the Man Down* and *The Devil's Disciple*.
VHS: S26187. $24.95.
The Fugitive, Vol. 14. *The Other Side of the Coin* and *The One That Got Away*.
VHS: S26188. $24.95.

The Fugitive, Vol. 15. *Nobody Loses All the Time* and *The Ivy Maze*.
VHS: S26189. $24.95.
The Fugitive, Vol. 16. *Stroke of Genius* and *In a Plain Paper Wrapper*.
VHS: S26190. $24.95.
The Fugitive, Vol. 17. *Fatso* and *Stranger in the Mirror*.
VHS: S26191. $24.95.
The Fugitive, Vol. 18. *Man in a Chariot* and *The 2130*.
VHS: S26192. $24.95.
The Fugitive, Vol. 19. *Passage to Helena* and *Dossier on a Diplomat*.
VHS: S26193. $24.95.
The Fugitive, Vol. 20. *Corner of Hell* and *Endgame*.
VHS: S26194. $24.95.
The Fugitive, Boxed Set, Vols. 1-5.
VHS: S17618. $83.95.
The Fugitive, Boxed Set, Vols. 6-10.
VHS: S17643. $83.95.

G.E. Theatre
Ronald Reagan hosts and stars in *The Martyr*, a story of civil war in 1923 Ireland.
VHS: S10595. $29.95.

Golden T.V. Memories of the 50's, Volume 1
A mishmash of programming from the 50's including dramas, westerns, comedy, talent and more. Includes Abbott and Costello, Jack Benny, Ed Wynn and excerpts from *Space Ranger*, *Fu Manchu* and *Arthur Godfrey*. 60 mins.
VHS: S13161. $19.98.

Golden T.V. Memories of the 50's, Volume 2
Includes Groucho Marx, Edward R. Murrow, Jack Lemmon, excerpts from *Robin Hood*, *Scarlet Pimpernel*, *Life with Luigi*, and more. 60 mins.
VHS: S13162. $19.98.

Golden T.V. Memories of the 50's, Volume 3
Includes Robert Shaw, Buster Crabbe, Alan Hale Jr., excerpts from *Howdy Doody*, *Winky Dink and Me*, *The Cisco Kid*, *Biff Baker U.S.A.*, and more. 60 mins.
VHS: S13163. $19.98.

Golf Classic: I Love Lucy: The Golf Game and The Honeymooners: The Golfer
Comedy that's way above par. Riotous "fore" play as TV's two top clowns try to get in the swing of things.
VHS: S12349. $14.98.

Good Night and Good Luck: The Edward R. Murrow Television Collection
Arguably the greatest journalist in the history of American media, Edward R. Murrow traces the social, political and personal tensions in post-war American life, in *The Best of Person to Person*, *The Best of See It Now*, *The McCarthy Years* and *Harvest of Shame*.
VHS: S19099. $69.98.

The Grace Kelly Story
Cheryl Ladd is the young star who becomes a princess. Lloyd Bridges and Diane Ladd are also featured in this dramatic version of the fairy tale life that captivated the entire world. 104 mins.
VHS: S25755. $19.95.

Harvest
James Dean, Dorothy Gish and Ed Begley star in this tragic story of a small town family and the hopes they pin on the coming harvest. From *The James Dean Collection*.
VHS: S27329. $19.95.
James Sheldon, USA, 1953, 53 mins.

Hill Number One
A story of faith and inspiration. Originally broadcast on Easter Sunday in 1951, the enlightening program, about Christ's Passion, is as inspirational today as it was 40 years ago. Starring James Dean, Leif Erickson and Roddy McDowall. 57 mins.
VHS: S14091. $19.95.

The Honeymooners Valentine's Special
The Honeymooners make love, not war, in some of the most hilarious romantic scenes and sketches of Brooklyn's famous foursome. 30 mins.
VHS: S09806. $14.95.

The Honeymooners Hidden Episodes
Total mayhem starring Ralph Kramden, in these never-released episodes of *The Honeymooners* from the Fifties. Jackie Gleason, Art Carney, Audrey Meadows and Joyce Randolph star. Collect them all! 55 minutes each.
Volume 1: "Letter to the Boss," "Suspense," and "Dinner Guest".
VHS: S02853. $29.95.
Volume 2: "Songs and Witty Sayings" and "Norton Moves In".
VHS: S08914. $29.95.
Volume 3: "Christmas Party" and "Forgot to Register".
VHS: S08914. $29.95.
Volume 4: "New Year's Eve Party" and "Two-Family Car".
VHS: S08912. $29.95.
Volume 5: "The Next Champ" and "Expectant Father".
VHS: S08910. $29.95.
Volume 6: "Move Uptown" and "Lucky Number".
VHS: S08908. $29.95.
Volume 7: "The Little Man Who Wasn't There" and "Goodnight Sweet Prince".
VHS: S08906. $29.95.
Volume 8: "My Fair Landlord" and "Income Tax".
VHS: S08905. $29.95.
Volume 9: "Ralph's Sweet Tooth," "Cold," and "Pickles".
VHS: S08903. $29.95.
Volume 10: "Cupid" and "Manager of a Baseball Team".
VHS: S08902. $29.95.

The Honeymooners Lost Episodes
Celebrate the 40th Anniversary of the now legendary television comedy with the release of these remaining lost episodes.
Volume 26. *Boxtop Kid*. Ralph becomes obsessed with entering contests after Alice's sister and brother-in-law win a trip to Europe. Jackie Gleason. *Halloween Party for the Boss*. Ralph assumes that a party being thrown for his boss on Halloween is a costume party in this remake of an earlier skit. 1954, 50 mins.
VHS: S15885. $19.98.

Volume 27. *The People's Choice*. A pair of crooked politicians hand-pick Ralph as their candidate for a local election after he helps capture a notorious killer. *What's the Name*. Ralph and Alice sing in this skit about an actress' name that eludes the Kramdens and Nortons. The song "One of These Days" is featured in this remake of an earlier episode. 1954, 50 mins.
VHS: S15886. $19.98.
Volume 28. *Hero*. Ralph convinces a new kid in the building that he was a star athlete in school. *Manager of the Baseball Team*. Ralph thinks he's going to be manager of the bus company, but his boss has other ideas in this remake of a 1953 episode. 1955/1957, 50 mins.
VHS: S15887. $19.98.

The Honeymooners Lost Episodes: 12-Volume Set
This boxed set comprises 22 *Honeymooners* skits, in their uncut and original format, compiled on 11 cassettes. Also included is a bonus cassette, *History of the Lost Episodes: The First Season*, which examines the development of the characters Ralph, Alice, Ed and Trixie, starting with the earliest *Honeymooners* skits. B&W, approximately 10 hours.
VHS: S26531. $129.98.

The Honeymooners—Honeybloopers!
See the Great One's most riotous on-the-air mishaps—classic foul-ups, props that wouldn't work, scenery that falls down. 52 mins.
VHS: S11126. $19.95.

The Honeymooners: The Best of the Lost Episodes
Two years of the finest work of this groundbreaking, stylistically daring comedy that used a stripped down, psychologically dense naturalism to convey class, social and sexual tensions and make trenchant comments about the American dream is distilled into this single tape. These are works that were unearthed in Jackie Gleason's basement. The frenetic pace, existential wit and comic edge are on view. 30 mins.
VHS: S18597. $14.98.

I Love Lucy
Classic episodes which helped establish Lucy as the First Lady of Television.
I Love Lucy Volume 1. *Lucy Does a TV Commercial*, and *Lucy's Italian Movie*.
VHS: S09600. $14.95.
I Love Lucy Volume 2. *Job Switching*, and *Fashion Show*.
VHS: S09601. $14.95.
I Love Lucy Volume 3. *Lucy Meets Harpo Marx*, and *L.A. at Last!* (with William Holden).
VHS: S09602. $14.98.
I Love Lucy Volume 4. *Lucy Is Enceinte* (Pregnant), and *Lucy Goes to the Hospital*.
VHS: S09603. $14.98.
I Love Lucy Volume 5. The love affair with Lucy continues with two episodes: *Lucy and Bob Hope* in which Lucy dons disguises to get Bob Hope to appear at the Club Babalu, and *Lucy and Superman* in which only the Man of Steel can save Lucy from the jam she's in. 53 mins.
VHS: S11266. $14.98.
I Love Lucy Volume 6. *Pioneer Women* features Lucy and Ethel as a bet leaves them without modern appliances and the apartment in shambles, and in *The Camping Trip*, Lucy and Ricky scheme against each other. 53 mins.
VHS: S11267. $14.98.
I Love Lucy Volume 7. An old washing machine comes between the Ricardos and the Mertzes in *Never Do Business with Friends* and a pair of trashed TV's gives the Ricardos and Mertzes their day in court— against each other—in *The Courtroom*. 53 mins.
VHS: S11268. $14.98.
I Love Lucy Volume 8. A botched magic trick makes Lucy and Ricky a hilariously inseparable couple in *The Handcuffs*, and a shot at show biz puts stars in Lucy's eyes and pie in Ricky's face in *The Ballet*. 53 mins.
VHS: S11269. $14.98.

I Love Lucy
This 90-minute compilation features the best of the *I Love Lucy* show from 1951 to 1952.
Laser: LD70121. $49.95.

I Love Lucy's Zany Road Trip
Struck from the original 35mm prints, this pristine collection of 27 *I Love Lucy* episodes features all of the "California Trip," taking the gang through Tennessee and New Mexico on their way to L.A. Almost 20 shows direct from La La Land feature an abundance of cameos, including John Wayne, Rock Hudson and Harpo Marx among many others. In two specially boxed volumes, with a collectible poster map of their trip inserted with Part 1.
I Love Lucy's Zany Road Trip, Part 1. 360 mins.
VHS: S15980. $49.98.
I Love Lucy's Zany Road Trip, Part 2. 330 mins.
VHS: S15981. $49.98.

I Love Lucy: Adventures in Europe
Seventeen episodes from the classic American sitcom have been seamlessly edited together, providing a marathon of viewing pleasure. Lucy, Ricky, Ethel and Fred inspire laughter throughout this whirlwind tour follows the entire gang on vacation in Europe. 6½ hours are included on three tapes.
VHS: S21713. $69.98.

I Love Lucy: The Very First Show
This pilot revolutionized the nascent television industry when it first appeared. Ever since, the succeeding episodes of this American original have never missed a broadcast day. Lucy and Ricky, not to mention Fred and Ethel, are part of TV history. 45 mins.
VHS: S21007. $12.98.

I Want My MTV
Among the most creative of MTV segments are the quick promos that use everything from live action spots featuring stars like Denis Leary, to the most imaginative, cutting edge animation. They are grouped on this tape so that now you can see favorites like Jimmy the Cab Driver, Toby (the Frank Sinatra impersonator) or Randee of the Redwoods any time. 45 mins.
VHS: S26305. $12.98.

I'm a Fool & The Wild Bunch
Ronald Reagan hosts *I'm a Fool* (26 mins.), a television production based on a Sherwood Anderson short story and starring James Dean, Natalie Wood and Eddie Albert. James Dean is a poor, young stable boy who lies about his position in life to impress Natalie Wood. When he realizes his lie will prevent her from ever being able to find him again he tries to recant, but it's too late. *The Wild Bunch* (31 mins.) stars Natalie Wood and Charles Boyer in a familial comedy of errors. When newlywed George Burrel (Boyer) is left alone with his wife's three teenage children, he's in for a crash course in parenting. Luckily, eldest daughter Louise (Wood) shows him that his love and guidance are both needed and appreciated. From *The James Dean Collection*.
VHS: S27330. $19.95.
Don Medford/William A. Seiter, USA, 1953-1955, 57 mins.

It's Hullabaloo!
Shows of the popular music show from 1965-66 are collected in this set of four volumes. Famous guest hosts like Frankie Avalon, Annette, Soupy Sales and Petula Clark inspire uncontrollable outbreaks of nostalgia. But it's music from The Shangri-Las, Marianne Faithfull, Brenda Lee, The Rolling Stones, The Supremes, Lola Falana, The Everly Brothers, and more that make this collection so worthwhile. Each video is approximately 60 mins.
VHS: S27638. $79.98.

Jack Benny Program
The funniest man who ever lived in Waukegan, Illinois, is remembered in this one hour, two episode B&W presentation from 1958. Joining Jack are Eddie "Rochester" Anderson, Don Wilson and Mel Blanc. If you are lucky Jack might also play his violin. USA, 1958, 60 mins.
VHS: S07801. $29.95.

The Jack Benny Program
Jack Benny was on television from the very beginning. His live variety show presented the perfect showcase for his comedic ability as well as the diverse talents of his assorted guests, many of whom were also legendary stars of film and television. This five-volume set joins some of his most memorable programs together for the first time.
1: *Johnny Carson Guests/Jack Takes Boat to Hawaii*. The *Tonight Show's* Johnny Carson went on to become television's most famous late night television talk show host. In this installment of *The Jack Benny Program* Carson's youthful zany persona is seen at a crucial stage of development, while Jack is off to Hawaii in this famous comic take-off on the perils of travel. 60 mins.
VHS: S20842. $14.98.
2: *The Peter Lorre—Joanie Sommers Show/The Smothers Brothers Show*. Acclaimed entertainers Peter Lorre and Joanie Sommers star in this edition of the *The Jack Benny Program*, giving them a chance to showcase their comic abilities. The Smothers Brothers developed their own successful career in variety television after their appearance with Jack Benny. 60 mins.
VHS: S20843. $14.98.
3: *The Income Tax Show/Jack Adopts a Son*. Jack Benny spoofs the common man's gravest bane—income tax—and its hand servant, the tax man. Then he tackles the difficulties of adoption and the prospect of proving his suitability for fatherhood. 60 mins.
VHS: S20844. $14.98.
4: *Jack on Trial for Murder/Jack Plays Tarzan*. Jack Benny lampoons the legal system, finding laughs in court. When Jack makes fun of that mythic figure Tarzan, the sobriquet "king of the apes" gains unforseen dimensions. 60 mins.
VHS: S20845. $14.98.
5: *Jack Is Kidnapped/The Lucille Ball Show*. Only Jack Benny could have this much fun when captured and held against his will. Once again his quiet humor sneaks up on his adversaries and takes them completely by surprise. Lucille Ball and Jack Benny combine the best that early television has to offer in this installment of his show. 60 mins.
VHS: S20846. $14.98.

Jane Eyre
A Westinghouse Studio One Summer Theatre production of Charlotte Bronte's classic tale of a young governess in peril. This well-done tv version performed live includes Katharine Bard, Kevin McCarthy and Frances Starr in its distinguished cast. USA, 1952, 59 mins.
VHS: S03658. $24.95.

Judy Garland (General Electric Theatre)
Ronald Reagan hosts a musical half-hour with the talented and tragic Judy Garland. She starts off with "I Feel a Song Coming On" and then proceeds to sing as many as possible, time permitting. Joe Bushkin is on piano and Nelson Riddle and his Orchestra provide the rest of the musical accompaniment. USA, 1956, 30 mins.
VHS: S05516. $19.95.

The Legend of the Beverly Hillbillies
A collection of outtakes and comic highlights from the long-running television program. This tape also features interviews with series regulars Buddy Ebsen, Max Baer Jr. and Donna Douglas. 48 mins.
VHS: S19750. $12.98.

The Life of Riley: The Bendix Episodes
Veteran film star William Bendix takes on network television and the role of the ever-bumbling Chester A. Riley. The four episodes are *Riley Engages an Escort*, *Riley Executive Type*, *Riley Steps Out* and *Riley Camps Out*. Hilarious. 90 mins.
VHS: S21900. $14.99.

The Life of Riley: The Gleason Episodes
The TV series which introduced Jackie Gleason as the first Chester A. Riley, blue collar hero. With an incredible supporting cast. The four episodes in this two-volume set are: *Tonsils, Babs and Simon Step Out, Egbert's Chemistry Set* and *The French Professor.* All were originally broadcast in 1949. 90 mins.
VHS: S21899. $14.99.

Little Women
Nancy Marchand stars in this adaptation of Louisa May Alcott's classic tale. Directed by Lela Swift, 60 mins.
VHS: S27334. $19.95.

The Lone Ranger
Three episodes of The Lone Ranger television series, starring Clayton Moore and Jay Silverheels.
Message to Fort Apache. 55 mins.
VHS: S09040. $19.95.
Six Gun Sanctuary. 55 mins.
VHS: S09041. $19.95.

A Long Time Till Dawn
James Dean, Naomi Riordan and Robert Simon star in the Kraft Television Theatre production of Rod Serling's melodrama *A Long Time Till Dawn.* When juvenile delinquent Joe Harris (Dean) is released from prison, he returns home to find his wife, Barbie (Riordan), has left him. In a heartbroken rage he beats up "Pops," the mutual friend who told her to leave him, then flees New York for his father (Simon) and his small-town boyhood home. From *The James Dean Collection.*
VHS: S27331. $19.95.
Dick Dunlop, USA, 1953, 60 mins.

The Lost Stooges
Just when you thought you've heard every nyuk, woop and Hey, Moe, a collection of rare, unbilled walk-ons by Larry, Moe and Curly in MGM feature films, including The Stooges with Clark Gable, Joan Crawford, Jimmy Durante and Robert Montgomery, and (!) their only appearance in Technicolor. 68 mins.
VHS: S12012. $14.98.

The Lou Gehrig Story—Climax
Wendell Corey stars as the Iron Man of the Yankees in this live tv drama from 1956. Documentary footage is integrated skillfully into the drama of a sportsman struck down by a fatal disease. With Jean Hagen, James Gregory and Harry Carey Jr. *Climax* is sponsored by Chrysler Corp. USA, 1956, 60 mins.
VHS: S05441. $24.95.

Lucy and Desi: A Home Movie
Television's most famous couple, Lucille Ball and Desi Arnaz, reveal their intimate family life in this touching documentary. It is a wonderful treasure, told with the help of never-before-seen film clips. Lucie Arnaz, their only daughter, hosts this behind-the-scenes look at two of TV's first superstars. 111 mins.
VHS: S22935. $19.95.

The Man from U.N.C.L.E.
Espionage, Cold War politics and international intrigue defined this superb 60s television series starring Robert Vaughn and David McCallum as the bravura and intellectually daring spies. The show typically attracted leading actors and directors for their involvement. It was set apart by its location shooting, set pieces, writing and production qualities. For the first time, 22 volumes are available on cassette.
The Man from U.N.C.L.E., Vol. 1.
VHS: S17555. $14.98.
The Man from U.N.C.L.E., Vol. 2.
VHS: S17556. $14.98.
The Man from U.N.C.L.E., Vol. 3.
VHS: S17557. $14.98.
The Man from U.N.C.L.E., Vol. 4.
VHS: S17558. $14.98.
The Man from U.N.C.L.E., Vol. 5.
VHS: S17559. $14.98.
The Man from U.N.C.L.E., Vol. 6.
VHS: S17560. $14.98.
The Man from U.N.C.L.E., Vol. 7.
VHS: S17561. $14.98.
The Man from U.N.C.L.E., Vol. 8.
VHS: S17562. $14.98.
The Man from U.N.C.L.E., Vol. 9.
VHS: S17563. $14.98.
The Man from U.N.C.L.E., Vol. 10.
VHS: S17564. $14.98.
The Man from U.N.C.L.E., Vol. 11.
VHS: S17565. $14.98.
The Man from U.N.C.L.E., Vol. 12.
VHS: S17566. $14.98.
The Man from U.N.C.L.E., Vol. 13.
VHS: S17567. $14.98.
The Man from U.N.C.L.E., Vol. 14.
VHS: S17568. $14.98.
The Man from U.N.C.L.E., Vol. 15.
VHS: S17569. $14.98.
The Man from U.N.C.L.E., Vol. 16.
VHS: S17570. $14.98.
The Man from U.N.C.L.E., Vol. 17.
VHS: S17571. $14.98.
The Man from U.N.C.L.E., Vol. 18.
VHS: S17572. $14.98.
The Man from U.N.C.L.E., Vol. 19.
VHS: S17573. $14.98.
The Man from U.N.C.L.E., Vol. 20.
VHS: S17574. $14.98.
The Man from U.N.C.L.E., Vol. 21.
VHS: S17575. $14.98.
The Man from U.N.C.L.E., Vol. 22.
VHS: S17576. $14.98.

Mark of Cain— Westinghouse Studio One
A live tv drama about a young man on parole from Sing Sing who tries to start his life with a clean slate. After seven years in prison his mother and his girlfriend are glad to see him, but his brother is less than warm. With Warren Stevens, Everett Sloane and Mildred Dunnock. USA, 1953, 60 mins.
VHS: S05443. $24.95.

Maverick: Duel at Sundown
Squinting, itchy-trigger badman Clint Eastwood becomes Maverick's rival in romance. This is a glimpse of the stoic grit and wily charm that would become Eastwood's trademark in his later roles. James Garner stars as television's most infamous gambler of the Old West. 1959, 60 mins.
VHS: S16279. $14.98.

Maverick: Shady Deal at Sunny Acres
The con is on when Maverick bamboozles the banker who swindled him. A sparkling crew of rogues and rascals along with his brother all chip in to recover the lost loot. Stars James Garner, Efrem Zimbalist, Jr. and Diane Brewster. 1958, 60 mins.
VHS: S16280. $14.98.

Medusa: Dare to Be Truthful
A dead-on parody of Madonna's 1991 documentary *Truth or Dare,* written and performed by MTV comedian Julie Brown. Brown stars as Medusa, embarking on her *Blonde Leading the Blonde* tour. Featuring the videos "Vague," "Expose Yourself," and "Everybody, Be Excited." With cameos from Bobcat Goldthwait and Chris Elliott.
VHS: S17219. $14.95.

The Mod Squad Lost Pilot
The Teeth of the Barracuda was originally aired as a TV movie of the week in 1968. It explains how this trio of hip, young kids were formed into a police unit known as the Mod Squad. 76 mins.
VHS: S26200. $14.98.

The Mod Squad
Peggy Lipton, Michael Cole and Clarence Williams III are the hippest television series of the 1960's. They bridged the generation gap with their up-to-date fashions, including bell bottom pants and hippie-inspired hairdos, but combined them with hard-edged law-and-order ways.
The Mod Squad, Volume 1. *The Teeth of the Barracuda* and *Mother of Sorrow.*
VHS: S26195. $19.99.
The Mod Squad, Volume 2. *Keep the Faith Baby* and *The Comeback.*
VHS: S26196. $19.99.
The Mod Squad, Volume 3. *A Run for the Money* and *To Linc—With Love.*
VHS: S26197. $19.99.
The Mod Squad, Volume 4. *The Guru* and *A Short Course in War.*
VHS: S26198. $19.99.
The Mod Squad, Volume 5. *The Connection (Part One)* and *The Connection (Part Two).*
VHS: S26199. $19.99.
The Mod Squad Boxed Set—Volumes 1-5.
VHS: S26201. $88.75.

The Monkees: Boxed Set
They sold over 23 million records and went platinum five times. Finally the entire television series featuring this 60's pop group is available in one deluxe box set. All 58 episodes and the pilot, as well as the rarely screened, *33⅓ Monkees Per Revolution* are included.
VHS: S26220. $399.98.

More! Police Squad!
The second collection of three more episodes of the inspired but short-lived tv police comedy. Titles include *Revenge and Remorse, The Butler Did It* and *Testimony of Evil.* Written and co-directed by ZAZ, Jim and David Zucker and pal Jim Abrahams, and starring Leslie Nielsen and Allan North, this is fun for the whole family if your whole family has a sense of humor.
VHS: S08716. $19.95.
Zucker/Abrahams/Zucker, USA, 1982, 75 mins.

MTV's Beavis and Butt-Head: Chicks n' Stuff
Generation X's most articulate spokesmodels, Beavis and Butt-Head, share their innermost thoughts on the opposite sex. This tape has all the bonehead humor and outrageous material fans have come to expect from MTV's biggest animated stars. It includes a whole new episode that has not yet been broadcast. 45 mins.
VHS: S26303. $14.98.

MTV's Beavis and Butt-head: Feel Our Pain
Eight lewd and ridiculous episodes from the destroyers of taste are compiled on this video. Together these two animated characters have managed to lower standards across the nation, casting them into the vaunted circle of cable TV stars. 50 mins.
VHS: S27532. $14.98.

MTV's Beavis and Butt-Head: The Final Judgement
Seven episodes of MTV's animated Generation X losers, Beavis and Butt-Head, are brought together on this video. Everyone from Coach Buzzhead to Principal McVickers is out to get them, but these guys are too dumb to be conquered. 45 mins.
VHS: S25886. $14.98.

MTV's Beavis and Butt-Head: There Goes the Neighborhood
Beavis and Butt-Head torture their neighbor Tom Anderson with classic mindless inanities. These guys are the Three Stooges of the 1990's. 45 mins.
VHS: S23747. $14.98.

MTV's Beavis and Butt-Head: Work Sucks
Only these two animated morons could devise a bunch of get-rich-quick schemes that are worse than poverty. It's scenarios like these that make these guys the undisputed heroes of the slacker generation. 45 mins.
VHS: S23746. $14.98.

MTV's The Best of Liquid TV
This is a collection of experimental and underground animation from the Emmy-Award winning show *Liquid Television.* It's always inventive, challenging and bizarre, the best animation around. 45 mins.
VHS: S23748. $12.98.

MTV's The Head, Volume 1
Jim, the Head, is an animated mutant superhero with too much cranium. This ultra dome is actually home to an alien named Roy. Together the two combine thoughts on saving the planet and the human race from a cruel and dangerous universe. Their adventures are wacky, strange and freakish. 55 mins.
VHS: S26304. $12.98.

Muhammad Ali vs. Zora Folley
From Madison Square Garden, a World Heavyweight Bout fought on March 22, 1967. Don Duphy reports the blow-by-blow. Win Elliot supplies the color commentary. Pre-fight training films and interviews are shown, as is a post-fight interview with Ali and his father. USA, 1967, 68 mins.
VHS: S05455. $29.95.

My Man Norton
From the producer-director of *The Great Gleason* comes this tribute to TV cult figure Ed Norton, the sewer worker who climbed out of a manhole and into the living rooms and hearts of millions of viewers. This compilation of some of the funniest routines performed by actor Art Carney on *The Honeymooners* is hosted by Joyce Randolph, who played Norton's wife, Trixie. With Jackie Gleason and Audrey Meadows, also a new Norton music video.
VHS: S08119. $29.95.
Jeff Forrester, USA, 1988, 50 mins.

My Name Is Bill W.
This Emmy Award-winning Hallmark Hall of Fame production stars James Woods as Bill Wilson, a reformed alcoholic. This maverick confounds the local chapter of Alcoholics Anonymous. Also features James Garner.
VHS: S21775. $19.98.

Mystery of the Riverboat
The Mississippi River and the swamps of Louisiana comprise the setting for mystery, murder and plenty of serial-style heroics. An unusually atmospheric and intelligent chapter play starring Robert Lowery, Eddie Quillan and Lyle Talbot. 13 episodes on two cassettes.
VHS: S13015. $24.95.

The Nativity—Westinghouse Studio One
The story of the first Christmas is presented in a moving live tv musical based on English mystery plays of the 14th and 15th centuries. With Hurd Hatfield, Miriam Wolfe, Paul Tripp and The Robert Shaw Chorale. With Betty Furness as the spokeswoman. USA, 1952, 60 mins.
VHS: S05314. $59.95.

No Time for Sergeants
The original classic stars Andy Griffith as Will Stockdale as he takes on his old sergeant and the practical jokers who share his barrack. From the original live television broadcast of 1955. 60 mins.
VHS: S20487. $19.95.
Laser: LD74712. $34.98.

Of Human Bondage
This Westinghouse Studio One version first played in 1949 and starred Charlton Heston one year prior to the release of his first film, *Dark City.* Heston plays the crippled med student in love with an uncaring waitress. Betty Furness hosts and program includes a commercial for a 12½ inch picture tube tv set. USA, 1949, 60 mins.
VHS: S03656. $24.95.

One for the Road
Morley Safer joins Charles Kuralt in this portrait of the beloved television journalist. The program includes some of the most memorable moments from Kuralt's *Sunday Morning* and *On the Road* reports. 46 mins.
VHS: S21716. $19.95.

The Ox-Bow Incident
Robert Wagner, Cameron Mitchell and Raymond Burr are featured in this classic early television adaptation of the Walter Van Tilburg Clark novel.
VHS: S10594. $29.95.

Patterns
A live television production of Rod Serling's drama about corporate politics and the destruction of individuality. Told from the perspective of Fred Staples (Richard Kiley), a new executive, the plot details the public humiliation of a decent, sensitive man (Ed Begley Sr.) carried out by the ruthless company boss (Orson Welles regular Everett Sloane). With Elizabeth Montgomery. Program includes interviews with cast and crew technicians.
VHS: S18795. $19.95.
Fielder Cook, USA, 1955, 59 mins.

The Patty Duke Show
Eight hilarious shows about identity and confusion with Patty Duke essaying the dual roles of identical cousins.
Laser: LD71147. $49.98.

The Persuaders—London Conspiracy
Tony Curtis and Roger Moore are two playboy adventurers in the television series where they team up to right wrongs and live the good life. In this episode Moore, as Sir Brett Sinclair, must impersonate himself, with Curtis as his phony butler, to foil the London conspiracy. England, 1976, 102 mins.
VHS: S06093. $59.98.

The Persuaders—Mission: Monte Carlo
Tony Curtis and Roger Moore are the Persuaders, a pair of wealthy bon vivants who enjoy disrupting stylish criminal plots in scenic parts of the globe—like Monaco for instance. This British tv series promises action, beautiful women and smart remarks. England, 1975, 96 mins.
VHS: S06094. $59.98.

The Persuaders—Sporting Chance
Roger Moore teams up with Tony Curtis to fight crime and drive very fast sports cars in the television series from England. In this episode the well dressed good guys face sabotage and bribery on the race car circuit. Are the Persuaders up to the challenge? Are you kidding? England, 1976, 102 mins.
VHS: S06095. $59.98.

The Persuaders—The Switch
Roger Moore is Sir Brett Sinclair. Tony Curtis is Danny Wilde. And together they are the Persuaders, playboys who use their time and money to fight crime and have fun. When an old friend turns out to be a professional killer our heroes have their work cut out for them. England, 1977, 102 mins.
VHS: S06096. $59.98.

Peter Gunn
Master filmmaker and comic specialist Blake Edwards, working with his longtime collaborator, composer Henry Mancini, was the force behind this witty and interesting television series about a complex and nervy investigator caught between the sordid, noir backdrop of low-level gangsters and beautiful women. Two episodes on each tape.
Peter Gunn: Death House.
VHS: S17589. $9.95.
Peter Gunn: Lynn's Blues.
VHS: S17592. $9.95.
Peter Gunn: The Comic.
VHS: S17593. $9.95.
Peter Gunn: The Torch.
VHS: S17594. $14.95.

Peter the Great
Based on a Pulitzer prize-winning novel, this lavish production brings the incredible life of Russia's greatest czar to the screen with Maximilian Schell, Vanessa Redgrave, Laurence Olivier and Omar Sharif. 380 mins.
VHS: S20636. $39.95.

Police Squad! Help Wanted!
A compilation of three episodes from the defunct but very funny tv series that inspired the hit movie. From the creative team of Jerry Zucker, Jim Abrahams and David Zucker, who wrote and directed *Airplane* and *Top Secret,* comes this terrific spoof on tv cop shows. With Leslie Nielsen and Allan North as a pair of deadpan L.A. cops. Special guests Florence Henderson and Lorne Greene are announced but never appear.
VHS: S08715. $19.95.
Laser: LD75340. $29.98.
Zucker/Abrahams/Zucker, USA, 1982, 75 mins.

Pontius Pilate— Westinghouse Studio One
Set 15 years after the Crucifixion, the story is told from the Roman governor's point of view. A moving drama that depicts Pilate as a victim of circumstances. With Cyril Ritchard, Geraldine Fitzgerald and Francis L. Sullivan. Performed live. B&W. USA, 1952, 59 mins.
VHS: S05451. $24.95.

Prairie Home Companion: Last Show
The final live performance of Garrison Keillor's unique radio program at the World Theatre in St. Paul, Minnesota from June 13, 1987. With Chet Atkins and Leo Kottke, and all the news from Lake Wobegon. USA, 1987, 114 mins.
VHS: S03756. $29.95.

Prairie Home Companion: The Second Annual Farewell Performance
Garrison Keillor and the APHC cast return for a "second farewell" performance at the Radio City Music Hall on June 4, 1988. Guests include Chet Atkins, Butch Thompson, Leo Kottke, The Everly Brothers and Vince Giordano and the Nighthawks. Also Robin and Linda Williams and the latest news from Lake Wobegon. More fun than an invitation to a hot dinner. 1988.
VHS: S08347. $29.95.

Prime Time Cowboys
These episodes represent the best of both the "adult" and the more adventurous "kid" type of television westerns: from *The Rifleman,* "The Sharpshooter" (the pilot episode, including Chuck Connors, Joan Crawford and Dennis Hopper); from *Sky King,* "Bullet Bait"; from *The Adventures of Kit Carson,* "Roaring Challenge"; and from *The Cisco Kid,* "Heaven for Heavies".
VHS: S13430. $39.95.

The Real World Reunion: Inside Out
Outtakes, excerpts from the original cast tryouts, and profiles of the most popular cast members make this reunion a must for all MTV *Real World* fans. Few know that the original pilot was never aired. This video has scenes from the show that started it all. USA, 1995, 75 mins.
VHS: S27189. $12.98.

The Real World: Vacations
MTV's fascinating at-home glimpse of today's generation pioneered a new documentary-type soap opera. On vacation in Jamaica, Mexico and Hawaii, the casts of some of the best series go all out to have a good time. Of course, there are problems like a bad date at a nude beach and even an unexpected pregnancy. Includes appearances by Heather B. Rachel Campos, Jon Brennan and more. 55 mins.
VHS: S26306. $14.98.

The Ren & Stimpy Show
These irreverent cartoons feature hipsters Ren Hoek, a small though shrewd, asthmatic chihuahua with a violently short fuse, and Stimpy, a lovable though temperamental cat.
Have Yourself a Stinky Little Christmas. Ren and Stimpy satirize the commercialization of holiday fervor as Stimpy goes searching for his lost companion Stinky in this uproarious and completely unsentimental parody. The lunacy is topped off with three inspired vignettes, two Christmas carol videos and the absurd "Yak Shaving Day" tale. 40 mins.
VHS: S19083. $14.98.

In Disguise. Nick's infamous pair of house pets lead kids through animated adventures to surreal places where most adults will surely fear to tread. Three favorite episodes are included, along with the "Secret Video Membership Oath" and the brand new music video "Ren's Pecs". 42 mins.
VHS: S20663. $14.98.

On Duty. More comical and fantastic episodes of inspired comedy by the deranged duo of Ren and Stimpy. The highlights of this collection are their MTV music videos, "Royal Canadian Kiltered Yaksmen Anthem" and "Firedogs."
VHS: S20286. $14.98.

The Classics. This volume presents the original episodes that established the quirky charm of the downtrodden dog and cat. The works include *Space Madness, Untamed World* and *Stimpy's Inventions*, featuring the notorious "Happy Happy Joy Joy." The program also includes the short *Breakfast Tips* and the *Log* commercial. 40 mins.
VHS: S19080. $14.98.

The Stinkiest Stories. The two desperately try to outperform one another in outlandish and offensive material in this absurd collection of "gross, disgusting" material. The volume features *Nurse Stimpy, The Cat That Ate the Golden Hairball* and *Ren's Toothache.* The program concludes with two *Powdered Toastman* vignettes. 40 mins.
VHS: S19082. $14.98.

The Stupidest Stories. Highlights include *Stimpy's Big Day, Robin Hoek* and *The Big Shot*, in which Stimpy composes an insipid poem to win the $47 million contest. The program also has two *Ask Dr. Stupid* vignettes. 40 mins.
VHS: S19081. $14.98.

Rich Little's Robin Hood
It's Rich Little as Groucho Marx portraying Robin Hood in this hilarious romp through Sherwood Forest. Imagine Carol Channing as Maid Marion, John Wayne as Little John…you get the idea. Hilarious comedy from an international impersonator. 60 mins.
VHS: S13796. $14.95.

Ride the Wind
The Cartwright clan is back in action on video. Taken from episodes of the long running classic tv western *Bonanza*, the owners of the Ponderosa battle angry Paiutes and unscrupulous tycoons. Starring Lorne Greene, Dan Blocker and Michael Landon. When Little Joe joins the Pony Express, can his father Ben get him out of serious trouble? In color, 100 mins.
VHS: S11406. $14.95.

The Rifleman
The legendary television program is presented in a two-package, ten-volume series. Chuck Connors is cast as a widower farmer trying to raise his young son (Johnny Crawford) amid a world of bandits and desperados. Some of the actors appearing in guest spots include Dennis Hopper, Warren Oates, Robert Culp, Lee Van Cleef, Agnes Moorehead and James Coburn. Various directors, including Sam Peckinpah, Robert Altman, Arthur Hiller and Richard Donner contributed to the show.
Vol. 1-5.
VHS: S18266. $59.95.
Vol. 6-10
VHS: Out of print. For rental only.

Roe vs. Wade
Winner of multiple Emmys, based on the 1973 court case regarding abortion rights, with Holly Hunter and Amy Madigan. The powerful story concerns Ellen Campbell, desperate to terminate an unwanted pregnancy, who, together with a young attorney, is determined to prove the Texas law forbidding abortion is unconstitutional. Their struggle leads them to the U.S. Supreme Court, where Jane Roe's personal ordeal changes U.S. history.
VHS: S11602. $14.95.
Laser: LD75133. $24.98.
Gregory Hoblit, USA, 1989, 92 mins.

Roy Rogers Show, Vol. 1
Two episodes from the original television series: *Mountain Pirates* (ahoy, Roy! Don't wait for Trigger in this one; Roy chases after outlaws in a daring motorboat pursuit) and *Empty Saddles* (there's more trouble than beans in a chuck wagon when rustlers terrorize Roy and Dale's cattle drive!). 46 mins.
VHS: S12554. $12.95.

Roy Rogers Show, Vol. 2
Two episodes from the original television series: *Smoking Guns* (will happy trails become war paths? Devious prospectors take ore that belongs to a local tribe) and *Sheriff Missing* (meet Roy Rogers, thug; he masquerades as a criminal to outfox villains intent on setting up a gambling parlor). 46 mins.
VHS: S12555. $12.95.

Roy Rogers Show, Vol. 3
Two episodes from the original television series: *The Morse Mixup* (it looks like there's been a murder…and all signs point to Roy as the culprit!) and *High Stakes* (his badge says Marshal but he's really a crook who wants to make sure a key witness never testifies; justice has its day when Roy intervenes). 46 mins.
VHS: S12556. $12.95.

Roy Rogers Show, Vol. 4
Two episodes from the original television series: *Head for Cover* (when revenge-minded robbers come looking for their double-crossing boss, Roy trails the thieves and nabs 'em all!) and *Paleface Justice* (they've readied the hangman's noose for an innocent Indian lad; can Roy come up with proof that will prevent the lynching?). 46 mins.
VHS: S12557. $12.95.

Roy Rogers Show, Vol. 5
Two episodes from the original television series: *Tossup* (the mine is worthless…but can two families come up with gold in their hearts? Roy is peacemaker when a mine dispute erupts into a bitter feud) and *Brady's Bonanza* (jumpin' Geiger Counter! Pat Brady unwittingly sells his claim to a uranium mine for two dollars). 46 mins.
VHS: S12558. $12.95.

Roy Rogers Show, Vol. 6
Two episodes from the original television series: *Fishing for Fingerprints* (it's no fish story; the one that got away will be the criminal himself if Roy and Bullet don't care about for clues) and *Fighting Sire* (a boxing champ is ashamed of his timid son until Roy shows the champ that being a man doesn't mean being a bully). 46 mins.
VHS: S12559. $12.95.

The Rush Limbaugh Video Collectors Set
A three-volume program on radio host and conservative commentator Rush Limbaugh.
VHS: S18274. $49.95.

The Scarlet Letter— Westinghouse Studio One
The classic tale of adultery and retribution in Colonial America is presented on live tv. The cast includes Mary Sinclair, John Baragrey and Richard Purdy. Nathanial Hawthorne's granddaughter is on hand to receive a plaque in his memory. Commercials deleted. USA, 1950, 52 mins.
VHS: S05450. $24.95.

Secrets of the Unknown
This series, produced by ABC News, explores some of the mysteries of our time: Was Jack the Ripper more than one person? Could Ninja warriors transform themselves into panthers and beasts of prey? Hosted by Edward Mulhare.
Dreams & Nightmares.
VHS: S09174. $14.95.
Jack the Ripper.
VHS: S09170. $14.95.
Ninja: Real Story.
VHS: S09172. $14.95.
Pyramids.
VHS: S09173. $14.95.
The Titanic.
VHS: S09169. $14.95.
UFOs.
VHS: S09171. $14.95.

Silver Theatre
Chico Marx stars in a situation comedy called "Papa Romani" on *Silver Theatre* on CBS in 1950. The Romani family has a new telephone installed, which leads to comic complications. With Margaret Hamilton and William Frawley. You'll have to watch the tape to find out if the family is Italian or Gypsy. USA, 1950, 25 mins.
VHS: S10066. $19.95.

Son of the Morning Star
The rise and fall of George Armstrong Custer is ably retold in this epic made-for-tv movie. Gary Cole (*Midnight Caller*) is the brazen cavalry officer whose bid for the Presidency stopped on a grassy slope near the Little Big Horn. Based on the book by Evan S. Connell. With Rosanna Arquette and Dean Stockwell. The title refers to the Indian name given to this controversial boy general.
VHS: S14478. $19.98.
Mike Robe, USA, 1991, 186 mins.

The Sophisticated Gents
The Sophisticated Gents tells the story of nine boyhood friends reunited after 25 years to honor an old coach who helped guide them through their turbulent early years. Though each has been dealt a different hand, all must confront how the complexity of their lives as black men in American society remains in stark, painful contrast to the innocent joy remembered from their boyhood club. Stars Paul Winfield, Rosey Grier, Melvin Van Peebles, Alfre Woodard, Ron O'Neal, Rosalind Cash, Denise Nicholas and Raymond St. Jacques.
VHS: S16541. $89.95.
Harry Falk, USA, 1981, 200 mins.

Spitting Image: The Music Video
A sensational and hilarious musical extravaganza with performances from today's top pop star latex look-alikes. Stars Sting, Michael Jackson, Imelda Marcos, Queen Elizabeth II and many more. Includes "The Chicken Song." 56 mins.
VHS: S16116. $19.98.

Stars in the Eye
The opening of Television City in Hollywood. With Jack Benny, Lucille Ball, Amos & Andy, George Burns and many more. USA, 1952, 60 mins.
VHS: S15224. $19.95.

The Story of "0": The Series
This novel has now been serialized. It tells the story of "O," a beautiful Parisian fashion photographer obsessed with her lover Rene. More than anything she wishes to be his slave. She will do anything to win and keep his love. It all begins in Rene's Rolls Royce. He takes her to a chateau outside Paris, where she must undergo a series of debasing encounters that may drive her to sexual distraction.
The Story of "O": Parts 1, 2 and 3.
VHS: S22497. $179.85.
The Story of "O": Parts 4, 5 and 6.
VHS: S22498. $179.85.
The Story of "O": Parts 7, 8 and 9.
VHS: S22499. $179.85.
The Story of "O": Part 10.
VHS: S22500. $59.95.

The Story of Television
A number of interesting short segments reveal key elements of the history of the television medium. There is a 1950's film explaining how TV works, scenes from the first telecast of Roosevelt at the World's Fair of 1939, and even a conversation between General David Sarnoff (Chair of RCA) and Dr. Vladimir Zworykin, the father of television. 27 mins.
VHS: S24074. $14.95.

Super Heroes
1966 fall TV preview hosted by Batman and Robin. On the same program, *Stamp Day for Superman* with George Reeves.
VHS: S09549. $29.95.

Super TV Bloopers
Rare goofs and outtakes from *Mash, Happy Days, Laverne & Shirley, Peyton Place, The Dick Van Dyke Show* and *You Bet Your Life.*
VHS: S09548. $29.95.

T.V. Classics, Vol. 1: Hollywood Half Hour & Public Defender
Two early live television dramas from the golden age of T.V. broadcasting. This tape includes representative episodes from two of the most popular series. In the first, Joan Leslie accepts a job with madman Vincent Price. In the latter, Public Defender Reed Hadley helps Charles Bronson in his scrape with the law. 52 mins.
VHS: S13151. $19.98.

T.V. Classics, Vol. 2: Howdy Doody & Art Linkletter and the Kids
Everyone's favorite freckled puppet from the 50's teams up with the young pals of Art Linkletter who are saying "the darndest" things. Two episodes. 52 mins.
VHS: S13152. $19.98.

T.V. Classics, Vol. 3: Colonel March of Scotland Yard & Sherlock Holmes
Very early Sherlock Holmes plus Boris Karloff as Inspector March of Scotland Yard. Two episodes from television's earliest crime shows. 52 mins.
VHS: S13153. $19.98.

T.V. Classics, Vol. 4: Arthur Godfrey's Talent Scouts & The Ed Wynn Show
Here, Arthur Godfrey introduces a young Rod McKuen to the public, and the goofy Ed Wynn hosts the Three Stooges. 52 mins.
VHS: S13154. $19.98.

T.V. Classics, Vol. 5: The Burns and Allen Show & Heaven for Betsy
The pilot episode of the long running interplay between George Burns and Gracie Allen. Also, an episode from a short-lived domestic comedy starring Jack Lemmon. 52 mins.
VHS: S13155. $19.98.

T.V. Classics, Vol. 6: Armchair Detective & Public Prosecutor
Two early "whodunit" mysteries designed to involve audience participation—the viewer is asked to solve the mystery. In *Public Prosecutor*, the guessing becomes a game show as a panel of experts offer their choices. 52 mins.
VHS: S13156. $19.98.

T.V. Classics, Vol. 7: Four Star Playhouse & The Stars and The Story
Two high quality mystery programs from the 50's. The first stars Dick Powell as Willie Dante, owner of the San Francisco gambling parlor Dante's Inferno. The second features Peter Lorre tracking down the perpetrator of an art theft. 52 mins.
VHS: S13157. $19.98.

T.V. Classics, Vol. 8: The Jack Benny Show
Two episodes from the stylish programming of Jack Benny featuring two of the 50's biggest stars: Humphrey Bogart and Jayne Mansfield. 52 mins.
VHS: S13158. $19.98.

T.V. Classics, Vol. 9: The Cisco Kid & The Roy Rogers Show
Episodes from the two most popular television westerns, featuring "the Robin Hood of the West" and the Singing Cowboy. 52 mins.
VHS: S13159. $19.98.

T.V. Classics, Vol. 10: The Life of Riley
A rare occasion then and now: a situation comedy with bite and social commentary. Jackie Gleason stars as Riley in two episodes about domestic urban lifestyles. 52 mins.
VHS: S13160. $19.98.

T.V. Party
The best of the long-running New York City cable TV show produced in the early 1980s, features as guests Deborah Harry, David Byrne, Jean-Michel Basquiat, and others—with the T.V. Party Orchestra including Walter Stedding, Chris Stein, Bob Fripp and others. Interview magazine columnist Glenn O'Brien hosted what was called "the tv show that's a cocktail party that is also a political party" with lively guests, great music, late-night behavior and adult situations.
VHS: S07123. $29.95.
Glenn O'Brien, USA, 1980-82, 30 mins.

Tales of Tomorrow
Classic science-fiction from television's Golden Age presented as it was originally telecast, with all the original commercials. Screen legend James Dean stars (in a recently re-discovered episode) as a scientist working with Rod Steiger on an experiment that takes a deadly turn and unleashes "The Evil Within." Plus Henry Jones (*Arachnophobia*) in "The Spider's Web," a chilling tale of what happens to three survivors of a boating accident who wash up on a deserted island that's no tropical paradise. USA, 1952, 60 mins.
VHS: S13520. $19.95.

Ten Little Indians
A live television version of the classic Agatha Christie novel where ten invited guests are systematically bumped off by an unseen hand. Each death corresponds to the circumstances described in a children's poem. With Nina Foch, Barry Jones, Romney Brent, Peter Bathhurst and Kenneth Haigh. And the killer is… 60 mins.
VHS: S04908. $24.95.

This Is Your Life
The story of Stan Laurel and Oliver Hardy as told by Ralph Edwards. 30 minutes.
VHS: S02648. $29.95.

The Thorn Birds
The epic story of Father Ralph and Meggie Cleary, and their forbidden romance. Told in only 486 minutes with a cast that includes Barbara Stanwyck, Jean Simmons, Bryan Brown, Mare Winningham, Earl Holliman, Philip Anglim, Richard Kiley, Christopher Plummer, Ken Howard, Piper Laurie, and of course Richard Chamberlain and the lovely Rachel Ward. Set in Australia and based on the bestselling novel by Colleen McCullough. This popular tv mini-series won six Emmys. Four volume set.
VHS: S14579. $119.99.
Daryl Duke, USA, 1983, 486 mins.

The Three Stooges Comedy Classics
Moe, Larry, Curly and Shemp are comic characters responsible for some of the best and funniest shorts ever made. Eighteen of their best, fifteen with Curly and three with Shemp, are brought together in this boxed set. Over 300 mins.
Laser: LD75083. $99.95.

Thriller
Boris Karloff hosts this collection of the best episodes from the classic 1960's television series, *Thriller*. Some of these creepy stories even include Karloff as an actor. Grim tales like these have an unnatural life all their own, which keeps this series entertaining and frightening.
Masquerade. Tom Poston and Elizabeth Montgomery are a newly wed couple who accept the hospitality of a fiendish family. But the honeymooners prove more than a match for their hapless hosts. Co-stars John Carradine. 50 mins.
VHS: S21491. $12.98.
The Grim Reaper. William Shatner is a greedy young man who discovers the truth behind the legend of the Grim Reaper. This fiend exacts a terrible revenge on the murderous young man. 50 mins.
VHS: S21493. $12.98.
The Prediction. Boris Karloff hosts and stars in this episode of *Thriller*. Karloff is a mentalist who can predict the deaths of people around him. Those who ignore his predictions must face the dire consequences. 50 mins.
VHS: S21494. $12.98.
The Premature Burial. In this episode a wealthy old man is accidentally buried alive. Karloff is the friend that saves him from this grisly fate. When the old man marries again, his new young wife plans to put him back just where Karloff found him. 51 mins.
VHS: S21495. $12.98.
The Terror in Teakwood. In this episode a wife faces a mortal terror when her musician husband desecrates the grave of his arch rival. Revenge and rivalry know no bounds between life and death. 49 mins.
VHS: S21492. $12.98.

Treasures of the Twilight Zone
Six highly sought-after episodes and rare unavailable footage of the anthology show that used science fiction as a startling take off into humans' greatest fears, desires and weaknesses.
VHS: S19100. $29.98.

Trip to Christmas
A traditional look at American Christmas' through the years gleaned from the live Telephone Hour Christmas shows. Hosted by Jane Wyatt, the stars include Earl Wrightson, Lois Hunt, The Lennon Sisters, Lisa Della Casa, Phyllis Curtin and Violette Verdy and Edward Villela dancing the Nutcracker Pas de Deux. 45 mins.
VHS: S08471. $19.95.

TV's Best Adventures of Superman: Volume 1
Three super-classics: *Superman on Earth* (1951) traces the caped hero from his Krypton origins to his first adult adventures on earth. *All That Glitters* (1957) finds Lois Lane and Jimmy Olsen swallowing Kryptonite pills to become like Superman. *Superman* (1941), the first-ever cartoon, pits our hero against a mad scientist and his terrifying ray gun. 63 mins.
VHS: S06246. $29.98.

TV's Best Adventures of Superman: Volume 2
Another trio of stories: *Crime Wave* (1953) asks, "Who's the secret mastermind behind crime in Metropolis?" Superman discovers the incredible answer. In *The Perils of Superman* (1957), the Man of Steel takes on a legion of lead-masked criminals. Finally, in *The Mechanical Monsters* (1941), four decades before "transformers" became a household word, Superman battles an ingenious, rampaging robot army in a cartoon classic. 62 mins.
VHS: S06247. $29.98.

Twilight Zone
The ever-popular TV series with stars including Robert Redford, Agnes Moorehead, William Shatner, Lee Marvin, Burgess Meredith, Jack Klugman and Jonathan Winters.
Twilight Zone Vol. 1. Contains two episodes: *The Invaders* and *Nothing in the Dark.*
VHS: S11918. $14.98.
Laser: D71382. $39.98.
Twilight Zone Vol. 2. Contains two episodes: *Time Enough at Last* and *The Monsters Are Due on Maple Street.*
VHS: S11919. $14.98.
Laser: D71383. $39.98.
Twilight Zone Vol. 3. Contains two episodes: *Nightmare at 20,000 Feet* and *The Odyssey of Flight 33.*
VHS: S11920. $14.98.
Twilight Zone Vol. 4. Contains two episodes: *A Game of Pool* and *Steel.*
VHS: S11921. $14.98.
Twilight Zone Vol. 5. Contains two episodes: *Walking Distance*, about a high-pressured executive who travels back in time; and *Kick the Can*, the story of an old man who tries to convince the other residents of his rest home that they can be young again if they play children's games.
VHS: S14270. $14.98.
Twilight Zone Vol. 6. Contains two episodes: *Mr. Dingle, The Strong*, starring Burgess Meredith and Don Rickles; and *Two*, starring Elizabeth Montgomery and Charles Bronson.
VHS: S14271. $14.98.
Twilight Zone Vol. 7. Contains two eerie tales: *A Passage for Trumpet*, starring Jack Klugman as a loser whose suicide attempt has even failed…or has it? and *The Four of Us Are Dying*, about a man who can change his face to look like anyone he chooses.
VHS: S14272. $14.98.
Twilight Zone Vol. 8. Contains two episodes: *Long Distance Call*, in which a boy talks to his dead Grandma—who wants him to join her—using a toy telephone; and *I Sing the Body Electric*, in which Anne, resentful of her new robot grandma, runs away…straight into the path of an oncoming car.
VHS: S14273. $14.98.

War and Remembrance

A seven-volume, 14-hour set taken from the tv mini-series that is a sequel to "The Winds of War." World War II is covered from December 15, 1941, to July 1943. Includes 44 starring roles and thousands of extras. Centers on Captain "Pug" Henry (Robert Mitchum), his battles and his love life. Highlights include Pearl Harbor, graphic scenes of Nazi atrocities, Stalingrad, North Africa and the fall of Mussolini. USA. 1988, 14 hours total.
VHS: S08230. $139.95.

Wild Palms

Oliver Stone produced this audacious six-hour television series adapted from Bruce Wagner's surreal comic strip. An ambitious senator (Robert Loggia) invents a holographic television channel to program virtual reality. A television executive (James Belushi) is drawn into a sadistic web of murder, intrigue and sexual power. As the principals fight over control of the holographic image, an underground war breaks out and the individuals try desperately to connect their crazed, hyper dreams to their real life experiences. With Dana Delaney, Kim Cattrall, Angie Dickinson and Ernie Hudson. Directed by Peter Hewitt, Keith Gordon, Phil Joanou and Kathryn Bigelow. Two-tape set.
VHS: S19304. $99.98.
Laser: LD74824. $89.99.

Wrestling with Gorgeous George

There were other "sports" on early television, but, for many, television, wrestling and Gorgeous George were almost synonymous; George Raymond Wagner was wrestling's greatest showman during the Fifties. This tape also includes Woodrow Wilson "Woody" Strode (one of the first black wrestlers on television, who later turned to acting, landing roles in four John Ford features), and a "spectacular" all-girl wrestling match.
VHS: S13427. $29.95.

Wuthering Heights—
Westinghouse Studio One

Charlton Heston stars as the moody Heathcliff in this live tv adaptation of the Emily Bronte novel. Passions and tempers flare on the English moors. With Mary Sinclair and Richard Waring. The commercials have been deleted but the story is complete. USA, 1950, 51 mins.
VHS: S05444. $24.95.

Your Show of Shows

The 50s comedy show that showcased leading writing, directing and comedic talents, including writers Woody Allen, Mel Brooks, Carl Reiner and Steve Martin, and performers Sid Caesar, Imogene Coca, Jack Benny and countless others.
Volume 1.
VHS: S16946. $19.95.
Volume 2.
VHS: S16947. $19.95.

independent spirits

independent american
CINEMA

1988

Selected as an outstanding film of the year at the London Film Festival, *1988* "mixes deadly seriousness and high camp, avant-garde aesthetics and transsexual athletics with an atmosphere that is alternately sordid and seductive" (David Harris, *Boston Phoenix*).
VHS: S01625. $59.95.
Richard Schmidt, USA, 1977, 93 mins.

Acid Is Groovy Kill the Pigs

This title is the Manson-like scrawl left at the scene of the *Fatal Vision* murders of a policeman's wife and two kids. It formed the basis of the cop's alibi that crazed hippies had done this horrible crime. In this fantasy the hippie killers come to life.
VHS: S22504. $19.95.
Joe Christ, USA, 1993, 35 mins.

The Age of Insects

Jack Ramey plays a N.Y. doctor conducting mad hormone experiments. A wealthy lingerie manufacturer pays to have his fey son Lance rehabilitated. The doctor's East Indian assistant, Lisa Zane, falls for the young man as she rubs insect enzymes on him. Lance awakens transformed, but not as foreseen.
VHS: S22615. $49.95.
Eric Marano, USA, 1991, 75 mins.

Alan and Naomi

Based on the novel by Myron Levoy, and set in World War II-era Brooklyn, this sensitive film studies the friendship between a brash, young local boy and a troubled French girl traumatized by a dark, grisly experience.
VHS: S16910. $89.95.
Sterling VanWagenen, USA, 1991, 94 mins.

Alice Dropped the Mirror and It Broke

In this experimental narrative a woman filmmaker edits a documentary about four men: a leader, a cowboy, an anarchist and an artist. These superficial representations of male romantic power force Alice into her film. She uncovers their hidden artifice.
VHS: S22647. $39.95.
Penelope Wehrli, USA, 1989, 63 mins.

Alien Nation

A few hundred thousand aliens from another planet are the Earth's new minority group. One of their members (Mandy Patinkin) is teamed with a hardboiled, jaded and bigoted cop (James Caan) to help him solve an important case. An entertaining twist on the cop/buddy movie.
VHS: S22657. $19.95.
Robert Cooney, USA, 1979, 28 mins.

All the Love in the World

Oscar-winning cinematographer Janusz Kaminski (*Schindler's List*) shot this beautiful story of love and murder. Eddy Wluicki is a young man who loves being in love, in a world where such romantic notions fade when confronted by the brutal realities of life. He strikes back at the innocent victims whom he blames for the death of love.
VHS: S21129. $59.95.
Daniel Curran, USA, 1990, 90 mins.

American Blue Note

A truly pleasant slice of life set in 1960. Peter MacNicol stars as Jack "The Sax" Solow, the optimistic leader of a New Jersey jazz quintet looking for fame and fortune but willing to settle for a paying gig. This wry, well judged, independent romantic comedy hits all the right notes. With Trini Alvarado, Louis Guss, Carl Capotorto, Jonathan Walker, Bill Christopher and Tim Guinee.
VHS: S15708. $89.95.
Ralph Toporoff, USA, 1989, 96 mins.

American Fabulous

A highly regarded, independent work about the strange and hypnotic odyssey of its young hero. A nomadic, itinerant writer reflects on his midwestern origins and his travels from New York to Los Angeles. It's a "tour of a wild, low-life gay existence [that's] captivating, hilarious, yet touching. Jeffrey Strouth displays a wit that might conceivably amuse Oscar Wilde" (Kevin Thomas, *Los Angeles Times*).
VHS: S18413. $29.95.
Reno Dakota, USA, 1992, 105 mins.

American Heart

Martin Bell's (*Streetwise*) dramatic debut examines the lifestyles of the socially marginal. Jeff Bridges plays Jack, a convict whose plans of moving to Alaska are thwarted by the appearance of his 14-year-old son, Nick (Edward Furlong). The two settle into a difficult daily existence in a Seattle boarding room as Jack tries desperately to avoid the temptation of the grift, while Nick is attracted to the romantic allure of the streets. Lucinda Jenney contributes a remarkable turn as Jack's battle-scarred girlfriend.
VHS: S19465. $19.98.
Laser: LD75145. $34.98.
Martin Bell, USA, 1992, 113 mins.

American Orpheus

Rick Schmidt's variation of Jean Cocteau's *Orphee*, about the relationship between a young mother and daughter, shattered by the absence of husband and father who abandoned them. "Shot with a lean, composed style, what is particularly striking is its sense of intimacy and simple emotional honesty" (*Seattle International Film Festival*). With Jody Esther, Karen Rodriguez, Curtis Imrie and Willie Boy Walker. Cinematography by Kyle Bergersen.
VHS: S17768. $39.95.
Richard Schmidt, USA, 1992, 93 mins.

American Taboo

Paul Wunderlich is a 30-year-old assistant to his arrogant photographer boss, Michael, whose sexually suggestive fashion photos have made him the buzz of the town. While Michael photographs provocative young women, Paul smolders with desire and contempt. Reacting to a lifetime of sexual repression, Paul takes up his own camera, releasing tightly sealed boxes of childhood memories that culminate in a taboo relationship with the teenaged girl next door. This Academy Award winning film evokes a dream world where fear and love are merged.
VHS: S16335. $49.95.
Steve Lustgarten, USA, 1983, 94 mins.

Approaching Omega

A back-packing expedition is the setting for what the *LA Reader* called "an entertaining and playful manipulation of the conventions of storytelling."
VHS: S01546. $49.95.
John Dorr, USA, 1983

Bad Lieutenant

Abel Ferrara's portrait of a corrupt, self-destructive New York vice lieutenant. In a great performance, Harvey Keitel plays a drug-addicted rogue cop trying to settle his gambling debts while investigating the violent rape of a beautiful young nun. Despite sequences of wrenching horror, especially the cop's verbal humiliation of two New Jersey teenagers, *Bad Lieutenant* achieves a grace and poetic intensity. Cinematography by Ken Kelsch. Screenplay by Abel Ferrara and Zoe Lund. With Victor Argo, Paul Calderone, Leonard Thomas and Frankie Thorn.
VHS: S18912. $19.95.
Laser: LD75154. $34.98.
Abel Ferrara, USA, 1992, 98 mins.

Ballad of Gregorio Cortez

Robert Young's powerful portrayal of the true story of Gregorio Cortez, a turn-of-the-century farmer who kills the sheriff because of a language misunderstanding. One of the most highly acclaimed independent American films of recent years. English and Spanish dialog with English subtitles.
VHS: Out of print. For rental only.
Laser: LD73753. $29.99.
Robert M. Young, USA, 1982, 105 mins.

Barcelona

Taylor Nichols is a sales rep in Barcelona who can't quite master the fast Barcelona scene. His cousin (Christopher Eigeman), however, is an obnoxious Navy man easily at home in this exciting city. That is, before they both become aware of a lingering anti-American sentiment that sends this comic, sexy film off on a violent tangent.
VHS: S23678. $19.98.
Laser: Widescreen. LD74812. $39.99.
Whit Stillman, USA, 1994, 102 mins.

Basement Tape

A series of humorous sketches by Larry Hankin, including his Academy Award nominee *Solly's Diner*.
VHS: S01544. $49.95.

Begotten

A nightmare classic, this film chronicles the strange fate of a godlike thing that dies when it gives birth to a messiah thing. ("Thing" is the only appropriate word that can describe this creature.) There are no names, no dialogue, and no compromises in this bleak tale.
VHS: S23753. $39.95.
E. Elias Merhage, USA, 1991, 78 mins.

Best of the Fests 1988

A film festival in a box! Featured are award-winning shorts from the Ann Arbor, Athens, Chicago International, CINE, Student Academy Awards, New York Expo, and other U.S. film festivals. This "best of" compilation ranges from a mini-documentary about tattoos to a black comedy involving a fat man, a young woman, her baby son—and hot pizza. Includes: *Arcata Brain Closet, A Slice of Life, Sky Heart, The Early Worm, Anna Spilt the Oil, The Mother Art, Cerridwen's Gift, Trust Me* and *Zebu*. 90 mins.
VHS: S13831. $19.95.

Best of the Fests 1989

An eye-opening compilation of award-winning, short films from festivals all over the United States and Canada—including the AFI, Black Maria, Montreal, and Ottawa festivals. With subjects ranging from a parody of the hit TV show "That Girl", to a documentary exploring the realities of the Pamplona bull runs, this tape is a must-see. 10 shorts, including: *That Grip; Breakfast Messages; Goodbye, Grampa; Suelto!; Please Don't Feed the Animals; Feed the Dog; Recurrents; Oregon Country; You Take Care Now* and *Jokers*. 90 mins.
VHS: S13832. $19.95.

Best of the Fests 1990

An outstanding mixed-genre collection of the best recently produced short films. This tape, like the others in the series, is designed to give the viewer an entertaining and powerfully incisive overview of the year's greatest new animation, comedy, documentary, dramatic, and experimental works. 11 short films, including: *Dr. Bed Bug; Geologic Time; The Measurements of Oxford; Rumba; Middle Grays; Song from an Angel; Macha's Curse; No Pain, No Gain; Triangle; An Urban Tragedy* and *Spartacus Rex*. 90 mins.
VHS: S13833. $19.95.

Best of the Fests 1991

A wild compilation featuring award winning shorts from 1991's top international festivals. Includes *Six Point Nine, Why We Fight, Balloon Head, Walls in the Woods, Post No Bills, Wanting for Bridge, In Transit, Harvest Town, Stealing Altitude, Madcap* and *Man Descending*. USA, 90 mins.
VHS: S15543. $19.95.

Best of the New York Underground

This collection of extraordinary films is best for the adventurous. *Queen Mercy, Screaming Chigger Productions, Pleasant Hill USA* and *Rosa Mi Amour* are just four of the films here that focus on odd, even unsavory material. A peep show dancer, child beating, a small town killer, and a graveyard where all is not dead yet are some of the elements explored in these films. 1994, 90 mins.
VHS: S25609. $29.95.

Best of Volcanic Video

Scenes of Bohemian life today are featured in this collection of highlights from a cable access show. Renegade art expression, doc- and mockumentary, downtown and off-off performance are just some of the elements collected in this video.
VHS: S22648. $29.95.
Dave Channon, USA, 1990-93, 100 mins.

The Big Dis

This highly-regarded first feature by Gordon Eriksen and John O'Brien is a funny and trenchant interracial comedy about a young black soldier on weekend leave determined to find easy, anonymous sex, though his world shattered when he's dissed (i.e., "disrespected") by 12 candidates. It's an ambitious first effort shot in textured black and white. "A disarming fast-talking comedy, spiked with street jargon and rap music…with the buzz of authenticity," the *Village Voice* wrote.
VHS: S17104. $59.95.
Eriksen/O'Brien, USA, 1989, 88 mins.

Black Hearts Bleed Red

Subterranean art icon and social menace Joe Coleman stars in this hard-edged but moving and respectful adaptation of Flannery O'Connor's short story about why lonely women should never accept help on the road.
VHS: S22628. $19.95.
Jeri Cain Rossi, USA, 1990, 15 mins.

Blood

"A film about desperation in the New York streets. A funny, bitter look at white, middle-class youth trying to be touch in the trappings of pornography, drugs and quick money. The first punk film. In its stream-of-consciousness way, *Blood* evokes Manhattan street life even more powerfully than Martin Scorsese's *Taxi Driver*. Ms. Krasilovsky brings into camera an array of furtive, frustrated people—e.g., hookers and juvenile delinquents—and allows them to talk about themselves as we watch them in action. As a depiction of contemporary urban despair, *Blood*, more specifically, is an angry, outraged protest of the exploitation of women by men" (Kevin Thomas, *Los Angeles Times*).
VHS: S07772. $29.95.
Alexis Krasilovsky, USA, 1975, 21 mins.

Blue in the Face

Roseanne, Michael J. Fox and Mira Sorvino are just some of the stars featured in this comic continuation of *Smoke*. A series of skits are set in a Brooklyn neighborhood cigar shop which is set to close. Amidst the wacky set-ups, Giancarlo Esposito, Jim Jarmusch, Harvey Keitel, Lou Reed, Lily Tomlin and other celebrities improvise with panache and wit.
VHS: S27691. $99.99.
Laser: LD75572. $39.99.
Wayne Wang/Paul Auster, USA, 1995, 84 mins.

Bodies, Rest & Motion

Michael Steinberg adapts Roger Heden's play about the sexual and social languor of Generation X. Set in an anonymous Arizona wasteland of concrete slabs and decaying landscapes, the film is a chamber drama which follows the turbulent social and sexual relations among four lost souls. The cast of characters includes Nick (Tim Roth), a dissatisfied television salesman; his girlfriend Beth (Bridget Fonda); Carol (Phoebe Cates), Beth's neighbor and friend, and Nick's former lover; and Sid (Eric Stoltz), a casually hip housepainter who becomes infatuated with Beth.
VHS: S19574. $19.95.
Michael Steinberg, USA, 1993, 94 mins.

Body Snatchers

Gabrielle Anwar, Meg Tilly and Forest Whitaker star in this third remake of *Invasion of the Body Snatchers*, the classic science fiction story of aliens who intend to take over the world. The pod people are back with their incredible talent to infiltrate society and pose as normal human beings.
VHS: S21087. $19.98.
Laser: LD72414. $39.98.
Abel Ferrara, USA, 1993, 87 mins.

Borders

A kaleidoscopic survey of the physical, political and moral borders that inhibit the free movement of people and ideas, *Borders* mixes commentary, computer graphics, dramatic fiction, live documentary footage and investigative journalism to present a tremendous range of information. *Borders* tempers its serious and sometimes infuriatingly ludicrous subject matter with the sardonic wit of its interviewees and comic computer art.
VHS: S13336. $29.95.
M. Aldighieri/J. Tripician, USA, 1989, 53 mins.

bottom land

Hailed as "blunt and uncompromising" (*Los Angeles Times*) and "deeply moving" (*Variety*), this is the story of three men in crisis. Stephen Saunders returns home to the family farm and must overcome the doubt and lost love of his son. A powerful, uncompromising, emotionally-stirring, debut feature. Voted Best First Feature.
VHS: S21131. $59.95.
Edward Radtke, USA, 1991, 75 mins.

Break of Dawn

Unsung hero Pedro J. Gonzalez was an immensely popular musician and radio personality in Los Angeles during the Depression. This is the true-life story of a man who lived comfortably until he challenged a powerful and corrupt political system bent on prejudice, and of his controversial trial, which exposed the paranoid hysteria of a city suddenly faced with economic ruin. Mexico's great singer and actor Oscar Chavez stars as Gonzalez. With Maria Rojo and Tony Plana.95
VHS: S12553. $69.95.
Isaac Artenstein, USA, 1988, 100 mins.

Brunch/28

The first of these two shorts is a breezy, animated video of an early morning vignette that is both light and beautiful. It is produced by painter Jill and video artist Carole. *28* is a birthday video that offers a bright comic romp with piquant edges by Carole.
VHS: S22658. $19.95.
Fleischmann Sisters, USA, 1986-1987, 15 mins.

Caligari's Cure

Tom Palazzolo's first narrative feature film is a hilarious take-off of Robert Wiene's 1919 classic, *The Cabinet of Dr. Caligari*. The veteran Chicago filmmaker draws on his memories of Catholic school and adolescent sexual fantasies, reenacted by a zany cast.
VHS: S00207. $39.95.
Tom Palazzolo, USA, 1983, 80 mins.

Candide in the Americas

A video sketch of chapters 10-20 of Voltaire's novel, in which Candide and his faithful servant Cacambo bomb around this best of all possible worlds in an old Chevy. Quiet, curious, this is the German filmmaker's sketch for a feature film.
VHS: S10187. $49.95.
Harold Vogl/Andrew Bergen, USA, 1986, 62 min.

China Girl

A pretty young Italian boy meets a pretty young Chinese girl at a dance in Lower Manhattan. They'd like to continue the relationship but their respective friends and families in Chinatown and Little Italy say not on your life. A modern bloody update of Romeo and Juliet from the sensitive director of *Ms. 45* and *Driller Killer*.
VHS: S06100. $79.98.
Abel Ferrara, USA, 1987, 89 mins.

Chip Lord: Selected Works

A collection of short films by Chip Lord: *Celebrity Author, Bi-Coastal and Executive Air Traveller, Get Ready to March, Abscam (Framed), Three Drugs*, and *AUTO FIRE LIFE*. All of the films deal with media identity and mass media imagery—for example, *Abscam (Framed)* utilized FBI Abscam footage in a tongue-in-cheek re-enactment at the scene of the crime.
VHS: S09576. $19.95.
Chip Lord, USA, 28 mins.

The Church of Shooting Yourself

Selected programs from the public access show *The Church of Shooting Yourself* are featured in this collection. The World Trade Center after the bombing, a Beat reunion at a William Burroughs book signing, a protest against Time-Warner's anti cable-access stance, and even a visit to Jim Morrison's grave are included.
VHS: S22616. $29.95.
Rik Little, USA, 1993, 120 mins.

Citizen Tanya

Raymond Pettibon and Dave Markey co-direct the SLA/Patty Hearst drama in a detonation of 60's counterculture. "A free, sexy, right-on Tanya is forged of the uptight, poor little rich girl Patty over the white hot flame of 400 Amerikan years of bottled up race/sex/black/white fury in the person of Field Marshall Cinque."
VHS: S20527. $19.95.

Clean, Shaven

Peter Greene stars as a man desperately hoping to find his lost daughter. Schizophrenic hallucinations and a rabid policeman complicate this overwhelming task. Detective McNally won't let up because he suspects this strange character is actually a serial killer stalking children. Winner of Best First Feature award at the 1993 Chicago International Film Festival.
VHS: S26938. $89.98.
Lodge Kerrigan, USA, 1993, 80 mins.

Clerks

For the slacker generation life seems to be just a series of dead-end jobs where catering to jerks is the only way to pay the bills. This great, independently-made comedy follows a parade of annoying shoppers helped by two friends. One works at a convenience store and the other at a video shop next door.
VHS: S24576. $96.98.
Laser: Letterboxed. LD74977. $39.99.
Kevin Smith, USA, 1994, 92 mins.

Committed

The striking story of film star/leftist/iconoclast Frances Farmer. In 1935 Farmer was an overnight Hollywood sensation; within ten years she was in a state mental hospital. From stardom to a locked ward to a lobotomy, the film reconstructs a compelling and many-layered look at the life and repression of this culturally defiant woman. "Superbly shot and acted…more subtle than the sledgehammer Hollywood feature—and no less mythic" (J. Hoberman).
VHS: S14154. $29.95.
Sheila McLaughlin/L. Tillman, USA, 1984, 77 mins.

Dance Hall Racket

"Scalley's Dance Emporium" is a place where anything goes. Busty women, knife fights, lascivious dancing, and even a diamond smuggling ring keep the joint jumping. Lenny Bruce plays Scalley's assistant, a man whose talents include planting blades in the bellies of men who get too fresh with the girls. Scripted by Bruce, the film contains many pearls of dialog, such as "If you've got the money, I've got the time." Features his wife Honey Harlow as a bimbo, along with Phil Tucker, Timothy Farreland Sally Marr.
VHS: $16106. $29.95.
Phil Tucker, USA, 1953, 60 mins.

Dangerous Game

Madonna is joined by James Russo and Harvey Keitel in this violent and intense psychodrama. Playing a film director, Keitel pushes his art to ever greater extremes until the violence he creates begins to seep into his real life. Madonna and Russo play the actors who come to embody his darkest visions.
VHS: $21033. $95.98.
Laser: LD72408. $34.98.
Abel Ferrara, USA, 1993, 108 mins.

Desert Spirits

In this experimental feature, two men find themselves stranded in the desert when their car breaks down. They take peyote to kill some time and find themselves in another world, where lizards talk, sensory perception expands and demonic spirits seek their prey.
VHS: $22422. $19.95.
Patrick McGuinn, USA, 1994, 35 mins.

Destroy All Blondes/
The Naked Hipstress/Sick Sick Sister

In the first of these shorts there is a comic account of the lives of the great poohbahs of the early 80's downtown New York scene. Turgid rivalries threaten the very core of hip existence. Then two gorgeous but politically opposed sisters catfight to the death in a shocking expose. This second short features a young David Byrne.
VHS: $22613. $49.95.
Mark Kehoe, USA, 1979-1990, 45 mins.

The Doom Generation

From the maker of *The Living End* comes another installment of violence and sex cooled by stereotypical generation X elan. Two kids meet up with a bleeding dude and set off to terrorize the motorized world. A stop at a convenience store leaves a talking head without its body and a bizarre family murder/suicide, so the three main characters go on the run and all have sex with each other. Can they evade the gang of skinheads?
VHS: $27521. $94.99.
Gregg Araki, USA, 1995, 83 mins.

Doomed Love

Widely-praised feature that won honors in Berlin, the film is a moving psychological drama of obsession—combining elements of romantic mythology and melodrama. Actor and painter Bill Rice stars as a frustrated professor of romantic literature who reaches the end of his rope and resolves to be reunited with his deceased true love.
VHS: $07117. $59.95.
Andrew Horn, USA, 1983, 75 mins.

Dorothy and Alan at Norma Place

A two-hour dramatized biography of literary wit Dorothy Parker; Strawn Bovee stars as Parker, whose private life is traced from her celebrated Algonquin circle heyday in 1920s New York through her alcoholic vegetation in West Hollywood of the 1960s.
VHS: $05873. $49.95.
John Dorr, USA, 1987, 120 mins.

Dr. Jekyll and Ms. Hyde

A myopic visionary, Dr. Jekyll pursues her need for change and power through a labyrinth of falls, fires, transformations and escapes. Hand painted sets and simple effects add to this work's power.
VHS: $22618. $29.95.
J. Kathleen White, USA, 1980, 34 mins.

Duet for Spies/
Frankie Lymon's Nephew Story

Jim Neu's script helps create a symbolic enactment of the covert relationship between power and sex in the first of these two shorts. It's a dark, post-Cold War comedy equating individual and institutional delusions. Then, in the Lymon story, we learn of a young night club singer who just said yes. He lived fast but died slow. Now several of his wives are fighting over his estate.
VHS: $22502. $39.95.
Jacob Burckhardt, USA, 1990-1993, 61 mins.

El Mariachi

This film by 24-year-old director Robert Rodriquez was made for the unbelievable sum of $7,000. Rodriquez playfully evokes Peckinpah, noir westerns and Hitchcock. A maverick loner and mariachi player (Carlos Gallardo) enters a Mexican border town and is instantly confused with a dark, brutally efficient assassin (Reinol Martinez). Spanish with English subtitles.
VHS: $19057. $19.95.
Laser: Special Collector's Edition. LD71892. $49.95.
Richard Rodriquez, USA, 1992, 80 mins.

Emerald Cities

"The film juxtaposes the Santa Claus myth, nuclear war, punk rock, hypnotic self-analysis, psychedelic drugs and video manipulation—you know, all that stuff we usually think about. This is one of the best independent films we've seen all year" (B.D. Rhodewalt, *L.A. Dee Da*).
VHS: $00405. $59.95.
Richard Schmidt, USA, 77 mins.

Enormous Changes at the Last Minute

Based on the short stories of Grace Paley comes a truly touching trilogy of connecting episodes in the lives of three women and the people that come into their lives. The film celebrates real life in its problems and its joys. Top notch cast includes Kevin Bacon, Ellen Barkin and Maria Tucci. Script by John Sayles and Susan Rice.
VHS: $03667. $59.95.
E. Hovde/M. Bank/M. Meyer, USA, 1985, 115 min.

Experience: Perception,
Interpretation, Illusion

This tape features the work of diverse Southern California artists. Each artist creates a 30 to 60 second spot that reflects his or her work and personality. Featuring: Carole Caroompas, Karen Carson, Michael Davis, James Doolin, Ann Page, Scott Grieger, Raul Guerrero, William Leavitt, Jerry McMillan, Michael C. McMillen, Margit Omar, John Outterbridge and John Valadez.
14 mins.
VHS: $14585. $19.95.

Experienced Movers

A video epic—the story of the robbery of an art museum in "Boraxville,"—*X-Movers* savors the interpersonal seaminess of a world of petty thugs and downwardly mobile youth. A story of love and deception, from a play by Evan McHale.
VHS: $07115. $69.96.
Larry Fessenden, USA, 1985, 140 mins.

The Fifth Annual Best of the Fests

This collection of award-winning short films includes *Through an Open Window; The Listener*, created at the Renaissance Experimental Laboratory; *My Birthday Cake*, and *Faith and Patience*, by Sheila Sofian.
VHS: $17873. $19.95.

Film Musicals

Two remarkable films by New York writer and Hollywood emigre Tina L'hotsky. *Barbie* is self-portrait as dark surrealism, with the artist playing a human Barbie who fully nude at home ritually cooks and eats a Barbie doll. *Snakewoman* stars Patti Astor as the woman who conquers Africa as the Snakewoman—shot in a 30's styled adventure story.
VHS: $07118. $39.95.
Tina L'hotsky, USA, 1977, 45 mins.

Floundering

James LeGros, John Cusack, Ethan Hawke, Steve Buscemi and Kim Wayans star in this witty satire about generation X layabouts. After college there is a world just waiting to be explored, and these characters let it wait. Great soundtrack includes Sebadoh, Red House Painters, Drunken Boat and more.
VHS: $24664. $94.95.
Kevin Smith, USA, 1994, 92 mins.

Force of Circumstance

A political thriller, this film follows a Moroccan human rights activist's attempt to thwart a royal envoy. The envoy would buy an historic Virginia estate for his boss, the king. Eric Mitchell, as Boris Major, stars in this film, set in both Casablanca and Washington, D.C. Steve Buscemi and Mark Boone Jr. are featured.
VHS: $22607. $59.95.
Liza Bear, USA, 1990, 89 mins.

Foreigner

Poe's punk thriller stars filmmaker Eric Mitchell as Max Menace, replete with platinum hair, a secret agent who arrives in New York to meet his contact. Patti Astor co-stars as a mysterious blonde in this gritty depiction of New York.
VHS: $00460. $59.95.
Amos Poe, USA, 1978, 90 mins.

Fresh

An electrifying feature about a 12-year-old boy (Sean Nelson) who walks a fine line between attending school and carrying drugs in his drug-infested Brooklyn environment. After witnessing a murder, he must fight for his own survival. A film that's at once powerful and riveting, and one that refuses to make a judgment call on its young protagonist. With Samuel L. Jackson.
VHS: $23480. $96.98.
Laser: Letterboxed. LD74939. $39.99.
Boaz Yakin, USA, 1994, 114 mins.

Fun Down There

Buddy is a young man living with his very ordinary family in upstate New York. Up till now his only source of sexual gratification has been between the covers of *Playgirl* Magazine. Buddy soon leaves the small town and heads off to New York City; during his first week in the East Village Buddy finds a new job, new friends, (safe) sexual adventure and, perhaps, the beginnings of romance.
VHS: $13508. $39.95.
Roger Stigliano, USA, 1988, 89 mins.

Fusion Arts

Solstice events at the Rivington St. Sculpture Garden in NYC (now destroyed) unfold toward a climax consisting of a noise rock concert on the huge junk sculpture by Demo Moe. 1987, 40 mins.
VHS: $22664. $29.95.

Geek Maggot Bingo

Cookie Mueller called this story of a mad doctor and his hunchback assistant a "breath of fresh air, but infected with bats, flies and spawning maggots." Special effects by Ed French. Stars Brenda Bergman and Donna Death.
VHS: $10163. $39.95.
Nick Zedd, USA, 1983, 70 mins.

Gift

A feature co-directed by former Jane's Addiction lead singer Perry Farrell blurs the distinctions between drama and music video, in a film that combines live music with a loose storyline dealing with memory, drug abuse, sex, racism, the cops and the medical profession. The musical numbers include "Step," "Classic Girl," "Ain't No Right" and "Don't Call Me Nigger, Whitey," performed by Farrell and guest performer Ice-T.
VHS: $19725. $19.98.
Perry Farrell/Casey Niccoli, USA, 1992, 80 mins.

God's Police

Australian artist Robert Cooney crafted this indictment of religious bigotry from super-8 footage depicting the Pope in NYC. With Janet Stein, Vivienne Dick and others.
VHS: $22656. $39.95.
Robert Cooney, USA, 1980, 60 mins.

Hangin' with the Homeboys

Four friends from the South Bronx, two black and two Puerto Rican, spend an eventful Friday night in Manhattan. This fresh and funny film, written and directed by Joseph B. Vasquez, has heart and soul and a streetsmart sensibility. With John Leguizamo, Mario Joyner, Doug E. Doug and Nestor Serrano.
VHS: $15822. $19.95.
Joseph B. Vasquez, USA, 1991, 88 mins.

Hearing Voices

An unconventional feature follows Erika (Erika Nagy), a beautiful though emotionally troubled fashion model, who repeatedly falls into abusive relationships. Troubled by a succession of difficult medical complications, she falls for Lee (Stephen Gatta), a sensitive young man who is her doctor's gay lover. The film is "beautiful and rigorous, taking us to places the movies rarely, if ever, have gone" (Kevin Thomas, *Los Angeles Times*).
VHS: $19324. $79.95.
Sharon Greytak, USA, 1989, 87 mins.

Heat and Sunlight

Jealousy and obsession overwhelm a photographer during the final 16 hours of his love affair with a dancer. This independent American film, which won the Grand Prize at the U.S. Film Festival, is an intense look at the darker side of human relationships. "Narratively wild and aesthetically risky, it's an emotionally gritty and raucously tender film, a remarkable feat" (*Hollywood Reporter*). B&W.
VHS: $12822. $29.95.
Rob Nilsson, USA, 1987, 98 mins.

Henry (Portrait of a Serial Killer)

John McNaughton's *Henry*, shot in Chicago using local theatrical talent, places an emphasis on acting, rather than special effects, that's almost unheard of in the psycho-killer genre. As Henry, Michael Rooker "becomes a coarser, working-class James Dean; he has the same shyness, the same vulnerability, but lacks the verbal gifts to express himself even to Dean's degree" (Dave Kehr, *Film Comment*).
VHS: $12829. $19.98.
Laser: LD74643. $29.98.
John McNaughton, USA, 1989, 90 mins.

Home Free All!

A small, intimate film from independent director Stewart Bird about the renewal of a stagnant friendship between childhood friends: Barry is a vague "hippie radical" in search of structure, comfort and family; Al wants to break from the comfort zone of his suburban existence into free and wide open spaces. A quiet contemplation on the implications of choice.
VHS: $02766. $69.95.
Stewart Bird, USA, 1983, 92 mins.

How to Survive

A collection of humorous video sketches written, directed and performed by Larry Hankin. In *Solly's Diner*, Larry plays a down-on-his-luck, penniless drifter trying to get fed. *Time for a Beer* details ways to drink in a bar without money. Three other shorts included.
VHS: $01654. $49.95.
Larry Hankin, USA, 1986

I Am the Cheese

A captivating independent film about a young man's lonely search for his own identity, starring Robert Wagner, Robert MacNaughton and Hope Lange. "Absorbing, brilliant," wrote *The New York Times*.
VHS: $00596. $59.95.
Robert Jiras, USA, 1984, 96 mins.

In Between

A unique exploration of feminine isolation, celebrated at many international film festivals—made by California filmmaker Wade Novy. The subject of the film is an isolated woman (Maggie McOmie), who gets cut off from reality because of her emotional reactions. In a tense study worthy of Antonioni, Novy portrays the woman's increasing sense of withdrawal and anxiety. The film displays great originality in editing, skillfully depicting a shattering, internal emotional state of an individual.
VHS: $03722. $39.95.
Wade Novy, USA, 1980, 30 mins.

In the Land of the Owl Turds

In this off-beat, humorous, and often poignant drama, a lonely, self-absorbed young man attempts to overcome the difficulties often inherent in his search for the ideal woman. Written and directed by and starring Harrod Blank. Produced by Les Blank.
VHS: $02903. $39.95.
Harrod Blank, 1987, 30 mins.

Inside Monkey Zetterland

Los Angeles before the earthquake was already an upside down kind of town. This complicated melodrama/comedy features terrorist boarders, a biker dad, a dysfunctional family, and at the center of it all a neurotic screenwriter named Monkey Zetterland.
VHS: $20735. $92.95.
Laser: LD74452. $39.99.
Jeffery Levy, USA, 1992, 93 mins.

It Don't Pay To Be an Honest Citizen

A mugged filmmaker tries to recover his stolen film and is thereby plunged into the ambiguous currents of the criminal world. This first feature is wryly observed, in part, because of its documentary roots.
VHS: $22608. $39.95.
Jacob Burckhardt, USA, 1985, 85 mins.

Johnny Suede

The debut work of the talented Tom DiCillo, Jim Jarmusch's frequent collaborator (*Stranger Than Paradise*). Brad Pitt stars as a playfully cool hipster living among the ruin and devastation of the Lower East Side. Johnny is trying to make a living as a musician and play out the complicated relationships in his life, in particular a beautiful and sympathetic teacher to whom he can't fully commit.
VHS: $18565. $59.95.
Laser: LD75209. $34.98.
Tom DiCillo, USA, 1991, 97 mins.

Judgment Day Theater:
The Book of Manson

Raymond Pettibon recreates the big bang of End-of-the-World cult projections with Robert Hecker as Charlie Manson and other characters, including Tex Watson, Norman Mailer, Jimi Hendrix, Roman Polanski and Leslie Van Houten.
VHS: $20525. $19.95.

Junior High School

"I'd like to share one of the most delightful experiences I've ever had at the movies," wrote critic Roger Ebert, "...at the U.S.A. Film Festival they screened a 39-minute movie named *Junior High School* and I was completely won over: How could we have anticipated such a completely winning, sunny and wickedly funny experience from a previously unsung film?" An original musical about innocent teenage romance, the film was shot on location at a real high school, with real junior high school kids playing themselves. "I think it's impossible not to be charmed out of your socks with *Junior High School*," wrote Ebert.
VHS: $08264. $14.95.
Wechter/Wankin/Jacobsen, USA, 1979, 39 mins.

Just Another Weekend

Two sisters find more than they bargain for when their escape from December's shop-til-you-drop ritual lands them on the snow covered high country of Colorado. As if family tension weren't high enough with Lisa and Ginny's awkward love affairs in the way, uncovering a property development scam to build condos over a uranium dump sends this wry comedy over the edge. An irrepressible first feature starring the hilarious talents of Justine Madero, Mary Elizabeth Holmes, Rinde Eckert and Jo Harvey Allen.
VHS: $15769. $45.00.
Elizabeth Sher, USA, 1988

Kidnapped

Mitchell's first feature is a stark unedited recreation of Warhol's *Vinyl*. This film purports to be the story of bored terrorists who kidnap a businessman, and shows off a cast and crowd of hip poseurs talking sex, manners and politics.
VHS: $07122. $59.95.
Eric Mitchell, USA, 1978, 60 mins.

Kids

Famed photographer Larry Clark makes his directorial debut with this sensational story of teenage life in Manhattan. Ignoring the challenge posed by AIDS, these kids pursue sex and drugs with no regard for the future in a world as violent as it is hopeless. Justifiably controversial, *Kids* was hailed as "very, very powerful" (Roger Ebert) and denounced as manipulative and exploitative. "The confident visual style and flat, elliptical, near plotless storytelling are tremendously accomplished, yet the same elements...could be seen as a celebration of amorality, as a contrived, romanticized celebration of the death wish" (Ray Pride, *New City*).
VHS: $26956. $96.95.
Larry Clark, USA, 1995, 91 mins.

The Killing Floor

A very powerful, raw film produced for American Playhouse. Shot in Chicago and set against the backdrop of the Chicago stock yards, the film focuses on Frank, recently returned from World War I, who wants a better life and becomes involved in the labor movement. But the pressures of the recession mount, and the stock yards become filled with racial tension. Finally, bloodshed erupts on the streets with the Chicago race riot of 1919. The film has a remarkable documentary feel, and features strong performances from Damien Leake, Alfre Woodard, Moses Gunn, Clarence Felder and Bill Bremer. 1987, 118 mins.
VHS: $10894. $19.95.

King Blank

A sour-spirited, foul-mouthed epic of ennui, this film is set in a motel room at NYC's Kennedy Airport. Over two days an obsessive husband lost in a web of psychotic delusion and his immigrant wife find themselves trapped in a psycho-drama of absurdity. It even features a scene where Ron Vawter forces Gary Indiana to perform fellatio.
VHS: $22627. $49.95.
Michael Oblowitz, USA, 1983, 90 mins.

Landlord Blues

In this quintessentially New York story it's tenant vs. landlord. A sleazy real estate owner is spurred on by the hopes of changing a neighborhood. Fortunately for the people who live there, he's not too clever. Richly ironic, this film maintains an even balance between sadness and humor.
VHS: $22501. $39.95.
Jacob Burckhardt, USA, 1988, 96 mins.

Larry Smith/Apollo Belvedere

Flashbacks and urban paranoia yield a fast-paced schizo portrait in the first of these two short films. In *Apollo*, a foppish, tormented filmmaker inhabits a mock melodrama with his absurdly devoted spouse. Glenn Branca did the audio and Jim Jarmusch was on the crew.
VHS: $22614. $29.95.
Rik Little, USA, 1976-1977, 45 mins.

Laughing Horse

A stranded traveller in the desert finds himself working for an unusual couple as their driver in a search for a mysterious mustang. The trio drive through the Southwest waiting for the unexpected.
VHS: $01543. $49.95.
Michael Blake, USA, 1986

Laws of Gravity

Nick Gomez's first feature was shot in 12 days and made for $38,000. It's a daring excursion into male bravado, the story of the small-time criminal activities of two Bensonhurst hustlers and their strong, determined girlfriends. The plot is motivated by the reappearance of a neighborhood criminal, who turns up with a bag full of handguns and an unexplained source of money. The real star is cinematographer Jean de Segonzac, who shot the entire movie with a hand-held camera. With Peter Greene, Edie Falco, Adam Trese and Arabella Field.
VHS: $18443. $89.95.
Laser: LD74455. $39.99.
Nick Gomez, USA, 1992, 100 mins.

Lighthearted Nation

A video essay that is a delightful look at the Duplex Nursing Home and the contributors to the *Duplex Planet* magazine. The magazine was started by the activities director for the home, and the contributors offer humorous anecdotes and opinions on subjects ranging from their mothers, moon-walking and fortune tellers to having a good attitude in life.
VHS: $14819. $39.95.
Jim McKay, USA, 1989, 60 mins.

A Little Stiff

This delightful romantic comedy charts a film student's unrequited love for an art student. It's a subtle, witty and charming movie that explores a world of student-led Bohemian angst.
VHS: $21513. $39.95.
Caveh Zahedi/Greg Watkins, USA, 1991, 85 mins.

Living in Oblivion

Steve Buscemi heads up an exciting cast featuring James LeGros, Catherine Keener and Dermot Mulroney. This wrenching but comic look at independent filmmaking shows a young filmmaker forced to ponder the inevitable question: Can anything be worth going through the hell of making a low-budget feature film? Winner of the Screenwriting Award at the 1995 Sundance Film Festival.
VHS: $27066. $96.99.
Laser: LD75441. $34.95.
Tom DiCillo, USA, 1995, 92 mins.

The Long Island Four

Based on a true-life incident, the Super-8 feature by the late director was an underground hit. It tells the story of four Nazi saboteurs who landed in the U.S. in 1942 and were captivated by the decadent nightlife of New York City.
VHS: $07116. $59.95.
Anders Grafstrom, USA, 1980, 100 mins.

The Lost Films of Cassandra Stark

The work of Cassandra Stark is poetic and disturbing. This collection reveals the reverent quality of her evolved ritualistic films. She is a protege of Nick Zedd.
VHS: $22629. $29.95.

Love & a .45

Two friends accidentally murder a young girl during a routine robbery. Deciding that his friend is crazy and may kill him next, Watty (Gil Bellows) takes off with his girlfriend, Star (Renee Zellweger). It's a honeymoon on the lam. They are in love, they have a .45, and it's too bad the town they live in is as tough and ruthless as they are. Soundtrack includes music by Meat Puppets, Butthole Surfers and The Jesus and Mary Chain.
VHS: $23994. $94.99.
Laser: LD75223. $34.98.
C.M. Talkington, USA, 1994, 102 mins.

Love Crimes

Patrick Bergin, who played Julia Roberts' sadistic husband in *Sleeping with the Enemy*, continues to abuse women on film, this time in the guise of a famous fashion photographer. Sean Young plays Dana Greenway, an aggressive Atlanta assistant district attorney who goes beyond the scope of her office to play detective. With Arnetia Walker and James Read. Story by Allan Moyle is based on a true-life case in which a man impersonated photographer Richard Avedon in the 1970's. This unrated video contains eight minutes not seen in the theatrical release.
VHS: $16806. $19.98.
Laser: LD71685. $29.98.
Lizzie Borden, USA, 1991 , 85 mins.

Love Show

A live television production by the painter and writer Walter Robinson features painted titles, taped and live skits on the perennial theme: a gem of its kind.
VHS: $10180. $29.95.
Walter Robinson, USA, 1982, 28 mins.

Love, Drugs & Violence

A collection of ten twisted short works, featuring comedy, experimental, and music films. You'll witness a re-edited Nancy Reagan exclaim "Cocaine makes me happy!", naked lovers strapped to trucks in a desperate attempt to consummate their love, a Sunday brunch gone berserk, and much more. 10 shorts, including: *A Trip to the Movies, 12 Pack, Purge, Slap, The Reagans Speak Out on Drugs, Violent, New Shoes, Bust Up, Ain't Gonna Pee in the Cup* and *Horror Brunch!!!*. 60 mins.
VHS: $13837. $19.95.

Lydia Lunch: Malicious Intent

Why We Murder and *Universal Infiltrators* were shot at The Knitting Factory in New York by Richard Kern while *The Beast* was shot at L.A.C.E. in L.A. by Chris Iovenko. Together these works explore a world of anti-social rantings that may inspire anger, violence and more. 90 mins.
VHS: $25608. $29.95.
Richard Kern/Chris Iovenko, USA, 1994, 90 mins.

M/W/F Music Video One

This collection features *Sharp's Downtown NY; Space Party*, with John Sex and Ann Magnuson; *Film Spectators Are Quiet Vampires; Heterosexual Love; No Sell Out; Wedding Show; Concrete People; Rumble; Twenty-eight; Metal Modern Romance; Human Waste* and *Cezanne*. 45 mins.
VHS: $22640. $39.95.

Mac

Actor John Turturro's directing debut. Turturro plays Niccolo Vitelli, a first-generation Italian builder whose uncompromising craftsmanship and insistence on perfection ruptures his friendship with his brothers (Michael Badalucco and Carl Capotorto). With Katherine Borowitz, Ellen Barkin and John Amos.
VHS: $19059. $95.95.
Laser: LD71893. $34.95.
John Turturro, USA, 1992, 117 mins.

Magdalena Viraga

This mysterious and imaginative experimental feature film by Nina Menkes concerns the inner life of a prostitute who is arrested as a murder suspect. Filmed in the bars, dance halls, and churches of east L.A., it is a compelling portrayal of the young woman's psychological journey from passivity to awareness. Menkes uses closeup shots and surreal details, and a text woven with poetry to suggest the emotional numbing and physical torment the woman endures and the effort required to confront the condition of her life.
VHS: $07376. $49.95.
Nina Menkes, USA, 1986, 90 mins.

The Making of the Holland Tunnel Drive-In Billboard

Artist Leni Schwendinger has created a documentary about the process of designing in light for the large billboard next to the Holland Tunnel. The goal was to transform the viewer's perception of the site, creating conditions for new, previously unquestioned meanings to emerge while engaging the viewer's imagination. Approximately 13 mins.
VHS: $14580. $49.95.

A Man, a Woman and a Killer

In part a film about the making of a film, within the framework of a fictional plot involving a hired killer and his victim. A collaboration by Rick Schmidt (*Emerald Cities*) and Wayne Wang (*Chan Is Missing*).
VHS: $00011. $59.95.
Rick Schmidt/Wayne Wang, USA, 75 mins.

Manhattan Naturally and Stories from Brooklyn

A fanciful drama of the sale of Manhattan by naive Indians. *Stories* features painter Paula Collery talking about her native borough.
VHS: $10176. $29.95.
Brian Pierson, USA, 1983, 28 mins.

Mediamystics

This video collection includes *Blue Moon, Soma Sema, Open Sesame, Fungus Eroticus* and *Dervish Machine*. Honed by frequent live gigs, these works fuse tribal and sacred elements, to explore the mystical knowledge of the body in cybertech.
VHS: $22637. $39.95.
Bradley Eros/Jean Liotta, USA, 1988-92, 60 mins.

Medusa Challenger

Joe Mantegna stars in this classic independent film about a mildly retarded young man who helps his uncle (Jack Wallace) sell roses to motorists at a traffic signal. "The clarity of narrative and bittersweet view of human nature of an O. Henry story" (Roger Ebert). ALA selection for young adults.
VHS: $11641. $29.95.
Steven Elkins, USA, 1977, 24 mins.

Metropolitan

Charlie loves Audrey. Audrey loves Tom. Tom loves Serena. Refreshingly original and funny, *Metropolitan* is a wry and witty look at the high-spirited escapades of high society's rich children. A stunning debut for first-time writer-director Whit Stillman and his talented assortment of young, unknown actors. "…ironic, touching, and wickedly funny" (M. McGrady, *News Day*).
VHS: $14278. $19.95.
Whit Stillman, USA, 1990, 98 mins.

Moment to Moment

A rarely seen, independent work from the director of *Putney Swope*, the film begins with twelve men on horseback playing softball, and continues with word games and a train of hilarious vignettes.
VHS: $00868. $59.95.
Robert Downey, USA, 1979, 80 mins.

Morgan's Cake

A film of irony and ribald humor that deals with the mysteries of growing up, *Morgan's Cake* is Rick Schmidt's fourth feature, and is in some ways an homage to Karel Reisz' wacky comedy, *Morgan*. The character in the film is, in fact, named after "Morgan," and confronts problems of absurdly comic proportions: a love affair, divorced parents, draft registration, car payments—as, cut adrift, he must learn to fend for himself.
VHS: $07536. $49.95.
Richard Schmidt, USA, 1987, 87 mins.

The Motorist

"This sad, funny, gorgeous-looking feature-length videotape tracks the end of an American dream," wrote the *East Bay Express* of Chip Lord's video feature. For Lord, the automobile has been an object of distracted desire and metaphorical charge since 1974. That year, with Ant Farm, he buried ten Cadillacs nose-down in a Texas wheat field and called the public sculpture "Cadillac Ranch." The star of *Motorist* is a gray 1962 Ford Thunderbird, behind the wheel the Motorist (played with glib rawness by Richard Marcus) is heading for L.A. and reminiscing about the formative influence of the automobile. He's a third-generation Ford man who spews franchise history while he fills the tank with premium. His almost continuous narrative mixes with tabloid news radio as the Motorist gets lost in the Los Angeles of Repoman on his way to meet a Japanese importer of classic American cars.
VHS: $09578. $59.95.
Chip Lord, USA, 1989, 60 mins.

The Music of Chance

The feature debut of documentary filmmaker Philip Haas (*Money Man*) is an adaptation of Paul Auster's allegorical novel. Mandy Patinkin plays a drifter and failed fireman who stakes a gifted card player (James Spader) in a game with two cagey, eccentric millionaires (Charles Durning and Joel Grey). When they're unable to pay off their debts, Patinkin and Spader are forced to build a wall composed of 15th century stones across a decayed landscape. "This haunting and elegantly made [film has] a sustaining air of mystery" (Janet Maslin, *The New York Times*). With M. Emmet Walsh, Samantha Mathis and Christopher Penn.
VHS: $19939. $19.95.
Laser: LD72229. $34.95.
Philip Haas, USA, 1993, 98 mins.

My Neighborhood

Offbeat, deadpan comedy which stars Kriegman as the owner of a local bar, who indiscriminately invites people he meets on the street in, offers them free drinks, and shows them bizarre videotapes he's made. Gradually, the mood of the film darkens.
VHS: $00909. $60.00.
Mitchell Kriegman, USA, 1982, 28 mins.

My New Gun

Stacy Cochran's colorful farce—set in a claustrophobic New Jersey suburb—details the comic misadventures and curious chain of events which result when a repressed doctor (Stephen Collins) buys his dissatisfied housewife (Diane Lane) a .38 revolver. The troubles start when her mysterious neighbor Skippy (James LeGros)—who harbors a great crush on her—asks to borrow the prized weapon. With Tess Harper, Bill Raymond, Bruce Altman and Maddie Corman.
VHS: $19576. $94.95.
Laser: Letterboxed. LD72356. $34.95.
Stacy Cochran, USA, 1992, 99 mins.

Nadja

In this stylish, supernatural thriller, a pair of twin brother and sister vampires haunt contemporary New York. Their father is killed by the meddling Dr. Van Helsing, but they resolve to fight back. On the prowl amidst New York's extensive nightlife, they attempt to seduce Van Helsing's beloved niece and nephew. Featuring Peter Fonda, Elina Lowensohn, Martin Donovan, Suzy Amisand Galaxy Craze. B&W.
VHS: $27056. $99.98.
Laser: LD75457. $39.95.
Michael Almereyda, USA, 1995, 92 mins.

The Natural History of Parking Lots

What can a father do with a languorous teenage son who hot-wires antique cars even though they inhabit a world of money-choked splendor in L.A.? Dad pays his hot, sexy gun-running older brother $2000 a week to watch out for him. From this set-up it's only a matter of time before all the weird fauna of a hazy, whacked-out L.A. make an appearance.
VHS: $22507. $29.95.
Everet Lewis, USA, 1994, 92 mins.

New York Videos

Jens Jurgenson and Jim Spring create art videos for music television. This selection of their work features some of the most innovative groups from the East Village, such as Bongwater, Pussy Galore, Foetus, John Spencer Blues Exploration, Railroad Jerk and Marin Bisi.
VHS: $22638. $29.95.
Jens Jurgenson/Jim Spring, USA, 1988-93

News News

A lively feature news program based on producer/television pioneer Peter Fend's view of the world. 28 mins.
VHS: $10173. $29.95.

Nice Girls…Films by and About Women

This compilation of award-winning short films is a sometimes challenging, always entertaining look into the lives, and through the lenses, of women today. Whatever you do, don't miss *Nice Girls Don't Do It*—an explicit, celebratory analysis of female ejaculation. This collection includes *Emergence of Eunice, You Take Care Now, Urban Steal, Constant State of Departure, Broken Heart, Social Experiment, New Shoes, A Still Life of Postcards, Another Great Day!, Giving Away* and, of course, *Nice Girls Don't Do It*. USA, 90 mins.
VHS: $15541. $19.95.

Nick Zedd

This is a portrait of no-budget filmmaker and Lower East Side punk icon, Nick Zedd. He is seen popping in and out of some of the area's most historic protests and riots.
VHS: $22652. $49.95.
Clayton Patterson, USA, 1989, 29 mins.

Nick Zedd: Steal This Video

This collection shows why Zedd is one of the most notorious filmmakers around. For *Thrust in Me* Zedd claims he was banned from every screening room in the country. *The Bogus Man, Police State, Whoregasm* and *The Wild World of Lydia Lunch* are all equally outrageous. 90 mins.
VHS: $25607. $29.95.
Nick Zedd, USA, 1994, 90 mins.

Niggernight

Four misguided youths into heavy metal music go on a self-ordained moral crusade, the twisted brainchild of Steve, the group's guru of hate. Stars Brian Cullen, Steve Witting, filmed in Brooklyn.
VHS: $10189. $59.95.
Michael Wolfe, USA, 1981, 20 mins.

Night Tide

The inspiration for *Night Tide* is the last stanza of Poe's "Annabel Lee." A young sailor on leave (Dennis Hopper) falls in love with an orphan girl posing as a mermaid in a California seafront show. Because of childhood fears which remain in her subconscious, she believes that she really is a mermaid. Raymond Durgnat wrote, "A collector's piece for connoisseurs of the offbeat…One is strongly reminded of Fritz Lang, of Aldrich's *Kiss Me Deadly*, of Charles Laughton's *Night of the Hunter*….A classically beautiful example of screen expressionism reconciled with realistic locales." Dennis Hopper stars.
VHS: $07457. $19.95.
Curtis Harrington, USA, 1961, 82 mins.

Nightsongs

This controversial feature by Marva Nabili folllows a Chinese-Vietnamese immigrant who comes to New York to live with her already established family. She works in a sweat shop along with her relatives. At night she writes in a journal about her husband and sons, whom she left behind. This simple story evokes the alienated and difficult world of today's immigrant experience. English and Chinese with English subtitles.
VHS: $26347. $79.95.
Marva Nabili, USA, 1984, 116 mins.

Nitrate Kisses

Unlike any other documentary, this work combines Barbara Hammer's unique experimental film style with archival footage to yield a unique view of overlooked lesbian and gay history. From the era of Nazism to today's AIDS epidemic, this work forces everyone to remember the importance of queer lives without evading any aspect of love, from the physical to the sublime.
VHS: $24031. $39.95.
Barbara Hammer, USA, 1992, 67 mins.

Northern Lights

A breakthrough American independent film, set against the bitter Midwestern winters and the equally brutal economic forces of 1915 America, the story concerns a small farmer who is pitted against the powers that control both commerce and government. A powerful film shot in northern Minnesota, unique for its startling realism. The first independent American feature to win the Camera d'Or Award at Cannes.
VHS: $11239. $19.95.
John Hanson/Rob Nilsson, USA, 1979, 95 mins.

Not Quite Love

Film featurette stars a 10-year-old ghetto waif and prophet seeking love in an alienated metropolis. Shot in the night club ambience, with lots of music, singing and dancing.
VHS: $10185. $29.95.
Schmidlapp/Stedding, USA, 1981-88, 30 mins.

Not Top Gun

Produced by Paper Tiger TV in 1987, this irreverent take-off is a critique of the blockbuster movie *Top Gun* and a satire on its attitudes of militarization and fetishization of high-tech technology.
VHS: $09577. $39.95.
Chip Lord, USA, 1987, 26 mins.

Odd Birds

Jeanne Collachia's period film, set in 1965, is a sensitive study of Joy Chan (Donna Lai Ming Lew), a 15-year-old Chinese-American teenager with burning ambition to become an actress, despite her mother's strong objections. Joy is encouraged by her friend with Brother T.S. Murphy (Michael Moriarty), an idiosyncratic math teacher at a local boys' school. The film has "humanism, validity and compassion that are rare in any film" (Joe Leyden, *Houston Chronicle*). With Nancy Lee, Bruce Gray, Karen Maruyama and Scott Crawford.
VHS: $19746. $19.98.
Jeanne Collachia, USA, 1985, 90 mins.

On the Edge

Called "a thinking man's *Rocky*," Bruce Dern stars as the runner who overcomes virtually all odds. Directed by Rob (*Northern Lights*) Nilsson.
VHS: $01535. $79.95.
Rob Nilsson, USA, 1986, 95 mins.

Oued Nefifik: A Foreign Movie

This comedy of manners is set in a post-colonial setting. A tourist's holiday falls apart in the aftermath of bloody riots in Casablanca, Morocco. Film, TV news and text are mixed in this deconstructed narrative.
VHS: $22606. $29.95.
Liza Bear, USA, 1982, 28 mins.

Panic in the City

A thoroughly strange film about 60s revolutionaries trying to unleash World War III by detonating a bomb in Los Angeles, and a hardened sheriff (Howard Duff) trying to prevent the catastrophe. With Stephen McNally, Nehemiah Persoff and Dennis Hopper.
VHS: $18943. $19.95.
Eddie Davis, USA, 1968, 97 mins.

Photo Album

An original, quirky remembrance of the filmmaker's experiences as a young immigrant from Cuba settling in Boston. This sometimes surreal autobiography stars his real family, and demonstrates Oliver's ability to distinguish between satire and parody. English and Spanish with English subtitles.
VHS: $02906. $29.95.
Enrique Oliver, USA, 1985, 14 mins.

Picture Bride

Tamlyn Tomita stars in this gripping drama based on one woman's journey to a new life spawned by a photograph. Tomita's character travels to Hawaii in order to marry a man whom she has never met, with only a picture to help her find him. Once there, the tropical splendor of Hawaii inspires her toward a passionate romance. Winner of Best Picture Award at Sundance Film Festival.
VHS: $26398. $99.99.
Laser: LD75082. $39.99.
Kayo Hatta, USA, 1995, 95 mins.

Pink Nights

Kevin Anderson is Danny, a shy Chicago high schooler who helps out three beautiful women with a place to live when his mother goes out of town. A wholesome comedy about a platonic menage a quatre. Filmed in Chicago with the music of Phil N the Blanks, Bohemia and Planet Street. With Peri Kaczmarek, Shaun Allen and Jessica Vitkus.
VHS: $07344. $14.95.
Philip Koch, USA, 1985, 87 mins.

The Plot Against Harry

A sleeper of Rip van Winkle dimensions, Michael Roemer's subtly innovative ethnic comedy went over the heads of preview audiences in 1969, sat on a shelf for 20 years, then resurfaced in 1989 to triumphant festival screenings and rave reviews. The central character is Harry Plotnik, a sad-sack Jewish gangster who finds his numbers racket slipping away. Under pressure from well-meaning relatives, Harry makes an erratic effort to go straight, triggering a series of humiliations and small disasters. Rather than partitioning the film's humor into a series of self-enclosed gags, Roemer instead creates a constant and pervasive comic atmosphere, based on sharply observed details, slow build-ups, throw-aways, deadpan reactions, egg-on-face ironies, and a precise sense of anticlimax.
VHS: $13576. $29.95.
Michael Roemer, USA, 1969/89, 81 mins.

Poison

An interwoven trilogy, the film uses three distinct stylistic conventions to explore the writings of Jean Genet, arriving at a profound realization of poison in the human mind, body and soul: A gritty prison drama reveals a homosexual's despair at being constantly confronted by forbidden passions; a campy '50s horror film send-up portrays a scientist's search for the essence of sexuality, and draws a compelling parallel to the HIV crisis when things go awry; and a tabloid mystery criticizes religious sentimentality as it reveals the circumstances surrounding the murder of a wife-beater by his own child, who then flew out the window toward heaven. Winner of the Grand Jury Prize at the Sundance Film Festival.
VHS: $15839. $19.98.
Laser: LD72226. $34.95.
Todd Haynes, USA, 1991, 85 mins.

Police State

The Lower East Side king of sleaze is arrested for being a junkie/faggot by Officer Krupke, Willoughby Sharp. Sadistic Rockets Redglare shows that local police brutality is on par with anything that the world has to offer. Charles Horatio Crowley is also featured.
VHS: $22632. $19.95.
Nick Zedd, USA, 1987, 19 mins.

Polly Perverse Strikes Again!

Subtitled *A Love Story with Sociopathic Tendencies*, Dan Sallitt's film is the campy story of Nick Huxley, out of whose past comes Theresa, "a social disease who sleeps with anything that moves and who has decided that she wants Nick back. Nick, a successful photographer with a stable relationship, is determined to banish Theresa and youthful folly from his life. But neither Nick's girlfriend Arliss, a modern spirit who believes in driving buried emotions out in the open, nor Theresa, who seems to have an unseen power on her side, is willing to let it go at that." With S.A. Griffin, Strawn Bovee, Dawn Wildsmith.
VHS: S04585. $49.95.
Dan Salitt, USA, 1986

Potato Wolf Coleslaw

Extracts from Wolfgang Staehle's *After Art*, Christy Rupp's *Urban Wildlife*, Walter Robinson's *Love Show*, Sally White's varieties and Scott Miller's wrestling special. Produced by the group Potato Wolf. 1983, 58 mins.
VHS: S10178. $49.95.

Potato Wolf Showcase

A sampler of the first year of the artists' cable TV series in black and white features a live performance by Cara Perlman, Kiki Smith, Ellen Cooper, Mitch Corber, Alan Moore, Jim Sutcliffe and others. 58 mins.
VHS: S10177. $49.95.

Potato Wolf Spring 1984

Extracts from George Schifini's *Philosophy*, Albert Di Martino's *Tesla*, Bradley Eros and Aline Mare's *Erotic Psyche*, Corber and White's live wedding, Moore's nightmare theatre, and McFerran's *May 19th*. 1984, 28 mins.
VHS: S10179. $49.95.

Powaqqatsi

Godfrey Reggio's sequel to *Koyaanisqatsi* contrasts modern urban life with images of nature and cultures of the Third World. Once again Philip Glass provides the haunting musical score while Reggio relies on the power of his editing and bravura imagery.
VHS: S12506. $89.95.
Godfrey Reggio, USA, 1988, 97 mins.

Promised Land

Jason Gedrick is a small town basketball player who turns to law enforcement when college doesn't work out. The hopes and dreams of young Americans are tested in this unusual drama about living with less. With Tracy Pollan, Kiefer Sutherland and Meg Ryan, as the very wild, red-haired Bev. The talent shines in this offbeat independent film.
VHS: S07440. $89.98.
Michael Hoffman, USA, 1987, 110 mins.

Putney Swope

A token black accidentally becomes chairman of a conservative ad agency, transforming the firm into "Truth and Soul, Inc." Classic satire from director Robert Downey, featuring Mel Brooks in one of his first film roles.
VHS: S01075. $19.95.
Laser: LD74962. $39.99.
Robert Downey, USA, 1969, 88 mins.

Queen of Diamonds

Nina Menkes' audacious feature is set in contemporary Las Vegas. Menkes' style suggests an American Chantal Akerman, with her painterly, evocative depiction of real time characterized by long takes, natural light and a documentary-style naturalism. Tinka Menkes plays a Vegas blackjack dealer abandoned by her husband. Her life is irrevocably altered by her friendship and caring for a dying old man. "Within this arid emotional landscape the protagonist stands, able to dish out what she receives—anger, boredom, contempt—but threatening to vanish if she is not soon loved. *Queen of Diamonds* is a powerful film which spurns resolution, daring its viewers instead to tune into the psychic frequencies of American alienation" (Jon Stout, Los Angeles Film Forum).
VHS: S18685. $59.95.
Nina Menkes, USA, 1991, 77 mins.

Ramona

A low-key, fresh road movie about a quiet, reflective American (Jason Scott), a free-spirited Mexican woman and an ethereal doll maker named Ramona, who hides in the back of his trunk to get through customs. The three undertake a mythic road trip through the colorful American landscape. "*Ramona* is a blend of drama, sophisticated romance and quirky comedy" (*Cinema*). With Heidi Von Palleske, Cain Devore and Michael David Lally.
VHS: S20378. $89.95.
Jonathan Sarno, USA, 1990, 90 mins.

Raptures of the Deep

A live TV black and white production spoofing Jacques Cousteau; the bathyscaphe discovers undersea psychiatry and merpeople. Includes an advertisement by Peter Fend, and a skit by performance artist and painter Ilona Granet.
VHS: S10174. $29.95.
Alan Moore, USA, 1981, 28 mins.

Red Italy

Second feature by the French-born film director is a Bertolucci-style story of a bored, rich woman looking for romance and adventure. She meets an American G.I., dumps him, and then falls for a Communist worker. Cast includes Jim Lurie and Mitchell himself in a b/w evocation of the post-war nightclub scene.
VHS: S07121. $59.95.
Eric Mitchell, USA, 1979, 55 mins.

Reptile Mind

Dramatization of an anarchist's nightmare—his friends run into lizards. With Bobby G., Kiki Smith, Ellen Cooper, Carol Parkinson and others.
VHS: S10175. $29.95.
Alan Moore, USA, 1982, 28 mins.

Resident Alien

Quentin Crisp, author and professional pansy, has always led a charming, if not charmed, life. While *The Naked Civil Servant* tells of his early and troubled life in Great Britain, this film shows how celebrity in America suited the grand old dame. Fran Lebowitz, Holly Woodlawn, Michael Musto, and other New York scenesters are featured.
VHS: S25103. $79.95.
Jonathan Nossiter, USA, 1990, 85 mins.

Revenge of the Amazons/Metal Madam

Intimate cult secrets and group therapy pseudo sects are featured in this unusual musical. Behind the scenes, a buxom and hysterical Sandy Karbinsky (Janice DeRosa) finds there are unforeseen consequences to joining an all-woman encounter group. Could it be a twist on the world's oldest profession?
VHS: S22612. $39.95.
Mark Kehoe, USA, 1979, 40 mins.

Revolution! A Red Comedy

This independent American satire follows the exploits of a group of would-be student revolutionaries seduced by the bourgeois indulgences of Long Island. "A film that any Marxist—even Zeppo—would appreciate" (*Newsday*). Stars Kimberly Flynn, Christopher Renstrom and Georg Osterman.
VHS: S16296. $69.95.
Jeff Kahn, USA, 1991, 84 mins.

Risk

Direct from its Sundance premiere, this sexy drama stars Karen Sillas as a striking New York City model who poses in the nude. A strange man with a sordid past falls in love with her and his obsession soon transforms her life into a whirlwind of passion, desire and danger.
VHS: S26027. $69.95.
D. Deirdre Fishel, USA, 1994, 94 mins.

Road to Ruin

An updated Sturges-like effort, this Paris-based romantic comedy features Peter Weller as a dashing playboy and international financier who pretends he's broke to determine whether the intentions of his girlfriend (Carey Lowell) are honorable.
VHS: S16863. $14.98.
Monique Annaud, USA, 1992, 94 mins.

Roadside Prophets

This road movie begins when the star, John Doe (formerly of the rock group X), receives the cremated remains of an unknown man. The dead man also left behind an intriguing image of a mythical Nevada town, which inspires John to go off in search of this unlikely shangri-la. A strange kid joins John on his search through back roads, where even stranger people are encountered. Music by the Pogues, the Beastie Boys and John Doe, and an appearance by Timothy Leary are featured.
VHS: S20690. 19.95.
VHS: S20690. $19.95.
Abbe Wool, USA, 1992, 96 mins.

Roadsinger

Independent video work by Gary LeGault, starring the filmmaker as a washed-up entertainer on the come-back trail working small bars and clubs.
VHS: S01545. $49.95.
Gary LeGault, USA, 1986

Ruby in Paradise

Winner of the 1993 Grand Prize at the Sundance Film Festival, this film, starring the beautiful and accomplished Ashley Judd, charts the progress of a woman toward her own personal paradise. Visually stunning cinematography shows the Florida locations to great advantage in this story of one woman's quest for meaning.
VHS: S20711. $19.95.
Victor Nunez, USA, 1993, 115 mins.

Runnin' Kind

Independent filmmaker Max Tash directed this journey of an Ohio-born, middle-class kid who takes off for the underground rock scene of L.A. With David Packer, Pleasant Gehman, Brie Howard, Rosie Flores. Music by The Screaming Sirens.
VHS: S11585. $79.98.
Max Tash, USA, 1989, 100 mins.

Safe

Todd Haynes (*Poison*) directs this unusual, stylish film which stars Julianne Moore (*Vanya on 42nd Street*) as a California suburban housewife who suffers from an insidious modern dilemma. Everything she is surrounded by becomes toxic to her; she is made ill by the poisoned, chemically-laden environment. She seeks refuge in a holistic center in Albuquerque only to discover that the center's magnetic leader has his own personal agenda.
VHS: S26860. $96.99.
Laser: LD75396. $39.95.
Todd Haynes, USA, 1995, 119 mins.

Sex, Drugs, and Rock & Roll

Famed actor/writer Eric Bogosian creates ten different characters set in as many vignettes. Aggressively realized, these raw, thought-provoking mini-dramas startle and surprise the viewer with their power.
VHS: S20688. $19.98.
John McNaughton, USA, 1991, 100 mins.

She Must Be Seeing Things

"A wryly sophisticated comedy…plays like a lesbian homage to *Unfaithfully Yours*," wrote Jay Carr in *The Boston Globe*. Agatha is an international lawyer, Jo a filmmaker. While Jo is on the road with her film, Agatha reads her diary and becomes insanely jealous to the point of dressing up as a man and "shadowing" her. "Groundbreaking in its understated portrayal of sophisticated urban lesbians exploring such dynamics as sex and sexuality, career and commitment, fidelity and companionship. The film gives us characters who are richly realistic and demonstrates that McLaughlin is a complex and refreshingly thoughtful talent…" (*New York Native*).
VHS: S10941. $29.95.
Sheila McLaughlin, USA, 1988, 85 mins.

Signal 7

Sensitive portrayal of two San Francisco cabbies about a long night's journey into self-discovery, following the interactions of two middle-aged taxi drivers cum actors. Title comes from the alert signal that a driver not responding may be in trouble. One of the first features to be shot on video and transferred to film, with interesting visual results.
VHS: S03438. $79.95.
Rob Nilsson, USA, 1985, 92 mins.

Sir Drone

Raymond Pettibon presents the early days of Los Angeles punk rock as an attempt "to break the organic human chain of metaphysical fate. There and then and forever after, music was to be no longer music. Hippies were to be no longer hippies. Everything was instead to be punk."
VHS: S20526. $19.95.

Six Shorts (Pam Payne)

A collection of video motion paintings/visual songs, featuring *Up on the Roof*, about flying lessons from a six-year-old; *Brief Undermode*, a cryptic triptych with Terry Moore; *What We Do*, which illustrates the creative mode; *Octobre*, feminine perception confliction; *Microwave*, in which a child tells how to properly misuse an oven; and *Mira*, a portrait of East 4th Street.
VHS: S22642. $29.95.
Pam Payne, USA, 1988-90, 30 mins.

Sleepwalk

Somewhere between what is real and what is fantastic is the subject of this film by Sara Driver. On the streets of New York a young woman encounters ancient Chinese fairy tales that cannot be explained as ordinary nightmares. With Suzanne Fletcher and Ann Magnuson. Cinematography by Franz Prinzi and Jim Jarmusch. Some days it doesn't pay to read your fortune cookie.
VHS: S10615. $19.95.
Sara Driver, USA/Germany, 1988, 90 mins.

Solo

A wordless, hypnotic masterpiece that follows a climber from a predawn canyon floor to a breathtaking panorama of snow, sky and peaks. Winner of numerous festival awards, including Film Festivals in Moscow, Melbourne and Chicago.
VHS: S01230. $29.95.
Mike Hoover, USA, 1971, 30 mins.

Spanking the Monkey

Jeremy Davies stars as a young man on his way to a prestigious summer internship in Washington, D.C., after finishing his first year of pre-med. He returns to his home town for a weekend visit, to find his mother confined to her bed with a broken leg and his father unwilling and unable to care for her. Forced to delay his internship, he attempts to deal with his incestuous relationship with his mother and the absenteeism of his controlling father.
VHS: S22891. $19.95.
David O. Russell, USA, 1994, 99 mins.

Speed Freaks with Guns

The unregenerate spawn of Nick Zedd, Richard Kern, Tommy Turner, *et al.*, this Texan-come-lately continues to push the borders of bad taste. Sometimes this is an all too real jump into the mind of a psycho killer. Bad humor scarcely affects the manifest atrocities put on the screen by this short feature.
VHS: S22503. $14.95.
Joe Christ, USA, 1991, 30 mins.

Stations of the Elevated

An astonishingly beautiful film about graffiti-covered trains hurtling through a strange urban landscape filled with the debris of a decaying civilization. The music of Charles Mingus counterpoints the recurring visual riffs of the tension-filled imagery.
VHS: S12342. $19.95.
Manfred Kirchheimer, USA, 1980, 45 mins.

Sticky Fingers

A silly and upbeat comedy about two New York female musicians who cannot resist spending a ton of money that is left in their apartment by a frightened drug dealer for safekeeping. Helen Slater and Melanie Mayron are the heavy spenders. With Eileen Brennan and Carol Kane as their neighbors and Danitra Vance and Christopher Guest as their amazed friends. Co-written by Mayron with director Catlin Adams.
VHS: S07793. $89.95.
Catlin Adams, USA, 1988, 89 mins.

Suture

Dennis Haybert, Mel Harris and Michael Harris star in this tense thriller which mixes treachery, passion and mistaken identity. An homage to Hitchcock, the central characters are two brothers. When one brother is set up to be mistaken for the other all the worst of one's deeds come back to haunt them both. "Daringly original! A mind-blowing journey to the outer limits" (*New York Post*).
VHS: S25099. $19.98.
Laser: LD75021. $39.99.
Scott McGehee/David Siegel, USA, 1994, 96 mins.

Sweet Love, Bitter

In this thinly disguised account of the last years in the life of Charlie "Bird" Parker, comedian Dick Gregory produces a diverse performance as Richie "Eagle" Coles, a jazz saxophonist with a genius for friendship and self-destruction. Artist Charles McPherson ghosts for Gregory on the gorgeous score by Billie Holiday's pianist, Mal Waldron.
VHS: S15796. $59.95.
Herbert Danska, USA, 1966, 92 mins.

Testament

Jane Alexander and William Devane star in this dramatic story of a family caught in the aftermath of a nuclear attack. Powerfully yet sensitively written, and acted out in a manner that enables the audience to care for the characters.
VHS: S01312. $14.95.
Laser: LD75338. $29.98.
Lynne Littman, USA, 1983, 90 mins.

They Eat Scum

John Waters liked this "disgusting outlay of cheapness, decadence, nihilism and everyday cannibalism. Nick Zedd's film must rank as something of an ultimate achievement of non-committal, unblinking savagery, a true expression of what used to be called the 'punk ethos'." Stars Donna Death.
VHS: S10162. $39.95.
Nick Zedd, USA, 1979, 70 mins.

Thousand Pieces of Gold

Based on a true story about a young Chinese woman torn from her homeland and forced into a mining town bordello. She escapes that fate by taking in laundry, eventually making her way in the new world and finding love in frontier America with Dennis Dun. Based on a true story.
VHS: S15982. $14.95.
Nancy Kelly, USA, 1991, 105 mins.

Time Expired

A powerful independent short about a convict (Bob Gosse) about to be released from jail who faces choosing between the two loves of his life—his loyal, spirited wife (Edie Falco) or his extravagant transvestite lover (John Leguizamo).
VHS: S18969. $14.95.
Danny Leiner, USA, 1992, 30 mins.

Time of Destiny

Timothy Hutton marries Melissa Leo much to the displeasure of her Basque rancher father. The time is World War II, and Leo's brother William Hurt follows him into combat in Europe for revenge. From the makers of *El Norte*, a melodrama of love, hate and obsession. With Stockard Channing and Megan Follows, music by Ennio Morricone.
VHS: S08168. $19.98.
Gregory Nava, USA, 1988, 118 mins.

Tribulation 99: Alien Anomalies under America

1,000 years ago, an alien race called the Quetzals came to earth and inhabited its hollow center until fallout from A-bombs mutated their genitals to the point that they were forced to mate with snakes for survival. This experimental montage uses phoney tabloid headlines and a frenetic juxtaposition of clips from the press and B-movies to criticize U.S. policy in Latin America since World War II. Seriously cerebral fun daring to emerge out of our conservative times.
VHS: S16027. $19.95.
Craig Baldwin, USA, 1990, 48 mins.

Twins

A comedy of fratricide, this film by the independent director best known for his 1982 graffiti-rap adventure *Wild Style* stars performance artist Michael Smith in a double role as the psychopath Sam seeking to destroy his twin Stan, the policeman. *Twins* is Ahearn's second feature, and he uses a deliberately structured and largely stationary camera technique as a throwback to the era of Keystone comedies and Buster Keaton films.
VHS: S07109. $59.95.
Charlie Ahearn, USA, 1980, 50 mins.

Two Small Bodies

Fred Ward and Suzi Amis star in this psychosexual battle of the sexes. Ward is Lieutenant Brown, a detective who believes Eileen (Amis) has murdered her children. Repulsion and attraction send them spinning in orbit around each other until the boundary between truth and illusion is dissolved.
VHS: S21790. $19.95.
Beth B, USA/Germany, 1994, 85 mins.

Uforia

A New York cult classic; the off-beat satire on evangelism and UFO hysteria. Fred Ward plays a Waylon Jennings look-alike who becomes partners with phony preacher Harry Dean Stanton, while Ward's wacky girlfriend (Cindy Williams) is convinced aliens are about to land and save the world.
VHS: S04859. $59.95.
John Binder, USA, 1986, 92 mins.

Vermont Is for Lovers

This unusual feature has become a cult hit. It's a mix of documentary and romantic comedy about a pair of transplanted New Yorkers who are working out their pre-marital angst in the Vermont countryside. Though the surroundings seem to promise peace and tranquility (as well as long-lived marriages), this couple can't seem to make the final commitment. The result is a charming, funny film which is a razor-sharp look at relationships, the roles of men and women and the institution of marriage.
VHS: S26140. $59.95.
John O'Brien, USA, 1993, 88 mins.

The Videotapes of Elizabeth Sher, Volumes 1-11

I.V. Magazine #1. *I.V. Magazine*—a very creative alternative to the bland network TV magazine shows—combines a pastiche of interviews, humor, satire and music. This edition includes an interview with a policewoman at target practice, a peep behind the scenes at a fantasy phone call service, fashion mutilation set to an industrial score, and more. 60 mins.
VHS: S05674. $45.00.
I.V. Magazine #2. An upbeat amalgam of weird, whimsical and ironic visions, this edition of *I.V. Magazine* includes *Showtime* (with a soundtrack by Minimal Man), an original look at Hong Kong, a chat with a reformed bank robber who lunched with Reagan, ads for products you won't believe exist, and a musical tribute to the roaring 20's featuring a Samurai Tap Dancer. 60 mins.
VHS: S05675. $45.00.
I.V. Magazine #3. A special edition—*Information for People Who Can Take It Straight*—is a full-scale invasion into the computer age conducted by mega-hostess MacDonna. View tips for handypersons and upscale house hunters, the whimsy of computerized martial arts, and an English "industrial music video" set to the tune of tearing velcro, along with computer-animated frenzy in a dumpster with mime Arina Isaacson. 60 mins.
VHS: S05676. $45.00.

What's Inside These Shorts? A witty, humorous series of video-shorts that includes *Juggling*, about the pressures of motherhood and work; *Beat It*, an exercise in frustration; *The Training*, as serious as any potty-training film can be; plus a tongue-in-cheek look at pre-pubescent lust, and a nightmare of a gynecological checkup. 60 mins.
VHS: S05677. $45.00.

Brainwash and Beyond. Explores the parameters of the art-video interface in a charged look at Empty-Vee (MTV), and offers a montage of impressions of contemporary culture, including unusual looks at amusement parks, car washes, and more—with industrial soundtrack works by Phil Hopper. 60 mins.
VHS: S05678. $45.00.

How to Make a Body of Art. Four members of the Arts Community—museum curator, gallery director, art consultant and performance space coordinator—discuss a range of topics from ethics of the art world to some of the tawdry aspects of the art-finance interface. They cover tips on launching art into the marketplace, tax advantages, presentation, and more—in a way that is upbeat with a touch of irreverence. 15 mins.
VHS: S05679. $30.00.

Interviews with Artists: Program 1. A combination of interviews with artists in various media: painter John King; video artist Vee Hotchkin, who talks about her secret of eternal youth; narrative painter M. Louise Stanley; sculptor Tyler Hoare, who replaces the Red Baron with the Sopwith Camel in San Francisco Bay; and members of Survival Research, leading masters of avant-garde irreverence. 45 mins.
VHS: S05680. $39.95.

Interviews with Artists: Program 2. Three minority artists reveal the genesis and motivations behind their art: John Abduljaami, a sculptor, carves poignant stories in wood; painter and printmaker Carmen Lomas Garza shows how her work has evolved; and altar and installation artist Amalia Mesa Bains constructs her personal tribute to Santa Teresa as she begins her "Renunciation"—a five-month fast—and loses 100 pounds. 30 mins.
VHS: S05681. $35.00.

Women by Women. At an historic exhibition of leading Hispanic artists that portrays woman as healer, mother, sister, abuelita, indegena and worker—held at Galeria de la Raza in San Francisco—women artists explain how they have evolved their own individual voices while paying homage to a common cultural and female heritage. 60 mins.
VHS: S05682. $39.95.

Dancing on the Edge of Success: An Interview with Choreographer Margaret Jenkins. Dancer/ choreographer Margaret Jenkins discusses her sources and influences—Merce Cunningham, Martha Graham and Jose Limon among them—and describes her experiences in the early days of modern dance in New York, the building of her own San Francisco company, and the joys and difficulties of keeping it alive. Discussion is interspersed with a view of her dancers rehearsing and developing a new piece in collaboration with Yoko Ono. 30 mins.
VHS: S05683. $35.00.

Interviews with Artists: Program 3. Realist painter Anton Gintner describes the relation of his inner-city Oakland (California) surroundings and love of the blues to his work; puppeteer and mime Arina Isaacson talks about her "family" of archetypal dolls and her hand-building method of working with them; and "Arts Plural" artists Chaarles Amirkhanian and Carol Law explain the interaction between his sound/text and her surrealistic pop slide images in their joint performance. 30 mins.
VHS: S05684. $35.00.

War Dance

This collection of music videos features the San Francisco-based Video Band. "War Dance", "Reagan Commercials" and "California Zones" are just some of the pieces included. 1986, 30 mins.
VHS: S22660. $29.95.

War is Menstrual Envy—Parts I, II and III

Annie Sprinkle, Kembra Phaler, Nick Zedd and Ari Roussimoff star in this singular work. Everything is so alien and yet it all rings true. It's a raw and emotional experience.
VHS: S22633. $39.95.
Nick Zedd, USA, 1991, 80 mins.

Water and Power

Pat O'Neill's striking independent feature deploys a series of technically sophisticated processes, time and multiple exposure photography, to present a kaleidoscopic and enthralling vision of contemporary Los Angeles that is at once surreal and poetic. "An astonishing evocation of Los Angeles. If it is not the greatest film ever made about Los Angeles, it is certainly the most poetic and most profound" (*USA Today Magazine*). Winner of the Grand Prize at the 1989 Sundance Film Festival.
Laser: LD71954. $34.95.
Pat O'Neill, USA, 1989, 55 mins.

Waterworks

Water is a universal symbol. It touches us all on numerous levels from the physical to the unconscious. This tape presents eight California artists and their diverse perceptions of water. Artists featured include: Robbert Flick, Mineko Grimmer, Doug Hall, Michael C. McMillen, Richard Misrach, Nam June Paik with Paul Garriin, Lewis de Soto and Bill Viola. 11 mins.
VHS: S14586. $39.95.

Wax, or the Discovery of the Television Among the Bees

A surreal science fiction thriller and narrative video by David Blair about Jacob Maker, a weapons-guidance expert and beekeeper whose will is manipulated by supernatural images projected onto a television inserted inside his head. The device enables Jacob to enter an alternative universe (created through a dazzling use of computer graphics) of A-bombs (the Trinity nuclear test site), the Gulf War, the desert near Alamorado, New Mexico, the Tower of Babel and the "Garden of Eden." Blair narrates the film in a deadpan manner. "The images obliquely illustrate the narrative, and the constant visual flux often suggests a graphic novel translated into MTV" (Jonathan Rosenbaum, *Chicago Reader*).
VHS: S20284. $29.95.
David Blair, USA, 1990, 85 mins.

The Wedding Show

Not since Miss Vicky and Tiny Tim tied the knot on Carson has the sacrament of marriage been opened up to live TV. But the bride and groom would have it no other way. This actual wedding features a variety of comic episodes.
VHS: S10170. $29.95.
Mitch Corber/Sally White, USA, 1984, 28 mins.

What Happened Was...

Karen Sillas stars in this exciting film that won the Grand Jury Prize at the 1994 Sundance Film Festival. Dating is often an unnerving, albeit exciting and sexy, prospect. Two young office workers venture into the unknown territory of their dreams and desires, which results in a number of startling revelations. The journey into the uncharted territory of erotic fantasies and private thoughts makes for one highly unpredictable romantic encounter.
VHS: S27257. $99.98.
Laser: LD75473. $39.99.
Tom Noonan, USA, 1994, 90 mins.

When Things Get Rough on Easy Street, Ovid and Shorts

This video features dissolving slides of web-like, calligraphic imagery set to stormy music mixes. *Ovid* is made up of scenes from the opera *X-S*, with music by Rhys Chatham. True ambient art video.
VHS: S22641. $49.95.
Joseph Nechvatal, USA, 60 mins.

Where Evil Dwells (The Trailer)

This collaboration is based on the story of the infamous "Satan Teen," Ricky Kasso. He killed himself in jail after he and a friend had been accused of murdering another boy in a satanic ritual on Long Island. This trailer is all that remains of the feature, which was destroyed by fire.
VHS: S22631. $39.95.
Tommy Turner/David Wojnarowicz, USA, 1986, 34 mins.

White Trash at Heart

This is an uproarious romp through the twisted byways of Lynch-land. Shocking and funny, it offers a satire of breakneck pacing and unlimited boundaries.
VHS: S22611. $24.95.
Holly Hardman, USA, 1992, 33 mins.

The Whole World Is Watching—Weatherman '69

Raymond Pettibon, Los Angeles artist, re-captures the drama of the Weathermen as Kim Gordon, playing Bernadine Dohrn, "whip[s] a detention room full of bad boys into a fightin' killin' guerilla band of right-on Nixonslayers."
VHS: S20524. $19.95.

Wide World of Lydia Lunch

An intimate portrait of the hard-bitten no-wave rocker Lydia Lunch. Also contains the shorts *Thrust in Me*, featuring the filmmaker in both male and female roles in collaboration with the cinematographer Richard Kern, *Kiss Me Goodbye* and *Go to Hell*.
VHS: S10164. $39.95.
Nick Zedd, USA, 1983-86, 61 mins.

Wigstock: The Movie

It all began with a bunch of New York drag queens who didn't want to stop partying so they put on a show in Tomkins Square Park—in the daytime. Now it has grown into an annual celebration of queer crossdressers from all over. Underground stars The "Lady" Bunny, Jackie Beat, the Mistress Formica, Lypsinka and Joey Arias are joined by RuPaul, Crystal Waters, Alexis Arquette and Deee-Lite on a trip across a landscape of cosmetic wonders.
VHS: S26862. $99.98.
Laser: LD75417. $39.99.
Barry Shils, USA, 1995, 82 mins.

Wild Flower

Set in the Depression-era South, Diane Keaton directed this evocative piece about a beautiful young woman's emotional and personal awakening, brought out by music, literature, poetry and romance. With Patricia Arquette, Beau Bridges, Susan Blakely, Reese Witherspoon and William McNamara. "Touching and staggeringly beautiful" (*Variety*).
VHS: S17785. $89.95.
Diane Keaton, USA, 1992, 94 mins.

Wild Style

This breakthrough musical feature with style and attitude to spare is a rumination on hip hop: street art, break dancing and rap music. The plot follows the romantic passion of Zoro (Lee Quinones), a South Bronx artist caught up in a turbulent romance with Pink (Sandra Fabara), the queen of the underground graffiti movement. Fab Five Freddy is a playfully hip impressario. "*Wild Style* is easily among the best film musicals of the past half decade" (J. Hoberman). With musical performances by D.J.'s Grand Master Flash, Grand Wizard Theodore, Grand Master Caz and The Cold Crush. The cast includes Patti Astor and Busy Bee.
VHS: S01463. $34.95.
Charlie Ahearn, USA, 1982, 82 mins.

X-Rated: Movieyeur

A movie-length salad with suspense, malice, comedy, screams, commercials, music—just like the real thing. Also includes *Faxion* (1984, 11 mins), a morals tape based on a painting by Balthus, and *Sex*, a vagina story co-starring fingers, nipples, buttocks and a few extras.
VHS: S10186. $49.95.
Franz Villa, USA, 1986, 68 mins.

Yellow Fever/La Fievre Jaune

During an epidemic at the end of the 19th century, soldiers guard a quarantined village. The father of a Cajun family has broken the quarantine to return to his family, soon falls sick with the fever. Hiding his boat, the family tries to keep his presence from quarantine officials. To the authorities, interning the victims means stopping the fever; to the family, it means death. A film from Glen Pitre (*Belizaire the Cajun*). In Cajun French with English subtitles.
VHS: S06503. $89.95.
Glen Pitre, USA, 1979, 30 mins.

Zebrahead

Anthony Drazan's feature debut is a poetic reworking of *Romeo and Juliet*. The film depicts an unlikely romance between battle-scarred, high school teens: Zack (Michael Rappaport), a tough Jewish kid who falls for Nikki (N'Bushe Wright), an independent black woman. With De Shon Castle, Ron Johnson and Ray Sharkey. Cinematography by Maryse Albert. Music by Taj Mahal.
VHS: S18871. $19.95.
Anthony Drazen, USA, 1991, 100 mins.

JOHN CASSAVETES

Big Trouble

Alan Arkin and Peter Falk, the co-stars of *The In-Laws*, are reteamed in a wacky comedy about murder and insurance scams. Arkin is hired by Beverly D'Angelo to knock off her nutty husband Falk. With Paul Dooley, Robert Stack, Richard Libertini and Charles Durning. The last film directed by John Cassavetes.
VHS: S09312. $19.95.
John Cassavetes, USA, 1985, 93 mins.

A Child Is Waiting

John Cassavetes directed this sensitive drama about the care and treatment of special education youngsters. Burt Lancaster is the benevolent but sometimes brusque administrator of a facility for the retarded; Judy Garland wants to help make the lives of the children as full and fun-filled as possible. With Gena Rowlands, Stephen Hill and Bruce Ritchey.
VHS: S11730. $19.98.
Laser: Chapter search. Includes original trailer. LD71640. $34.98.
John Cassavetes, USA, 1963, 102 mins.

Faces/Shadows

Two landmark films which, for many, are the foundation stones of independent American cinema. *Shadows*, John Cassavetes' first film, features two brothers and a sister who move jerkily through their lives as Cassavetes' free-wheeling camera, naturalistic dialog and jump cuts capture their arguments, sexual encounters and parties. With Lelia Goldoni, Ben Carruthers and Hugh Hurd. 1959, 87 mins. *Faces* features Gena Rowlands, John Marley, Lynn Carlin and Seymour Cassel in a riveting account of the events leading to the breakdown of a marriage. The performances are extraordinary in a film which is a legend. 1968, 130 mins.
VHS: S26961. $89.98.
John Cassavetes, USA, 1959/1968, 87/130 mins.

Gloria

John Cassavetes creates a powerful, tension-filled story about an ex-gun moll and showgirl on the run from the mob protecting the son of neighbors who have already been killed by the mob. With Gena Rowlands in an Oscar-nominated performance.
VHS: S00506. $69.95.
John Cassavetes, USA, 1980, 121 mins.

The Killing of a Chinese Bookie

John Cassavetes' unusual gangster drama features Ben Gazzara as the owner of a lurid Los Angeles strip joint who is ordered by the mafia to execute a Chinese gangster to pay off his gambling debts. This is one of Cassavetes' most personal films; it can be read as a ferocious critique of American capitalism and racism. With Seymour Cassel, Timothy Carey, Azizi Johari, Virginia Carrington and Meade Roberts.
VHS: S19263. $89.95.
John Cassavetes, USA, 1976, 109 mins.

Opening Night

John Cassavetes' neglected masterpiece about the nature of performance, art and the complicity between performer and audience. Gena Rowlands is a bitter, insecure actress on the verge of a breakdown. In previews for a play, she is haunted by the accidental death of an obsessive fan. The film was never commercially released until 1991. With Cassavetes, Ben Gazzara, Joan Blondell and Zohra Lampert. Cinematography by Frederick Elmes.
VHS: S18720. $89.95.
John Cassavetes, USA, 1977, 144 mins.

A Woman Under the Influence

John Cassavetes' masterpiece centers on a dysfunctional Los Angeles family; in an astounding performance, Gena Rowlands stars as a tightly-wound woman who loves her children too much, withholds her affection from her husband (Peter Falk), and goes slowly insane by her unrealized expectations. A brilliant, uncompromising work, with strong secondary work by Katherine Cassavetes, Lady Rowlands and Fred Draper.
VHS: S17304. $19.95.
John Cassavetes, USA, 1974, 155 mins.

JOHN SAYLES

Baby, It's You

John Sayles wrote and directed this look back at high school life in New Jersey in the early 1960's. Rosanna Arquette is a bright, middle class Jewish girl who becomes involved with Vincent Spano, an Italian Catholic from a lower economical and social level, who calls himself The Sheik. When she goes off to a fancy college, the Sheik tries his luck in Miami imitating Frank Sinatra. With Matthew Modine, Tracy Pollan and Robert Downey Jr. in small roles.
VHS: S10356. $79.95.
Laser: LD75151. $34.98.
John Sayles, USA, 1983, 105 mins.

City of Hope

John Sayles wrote, directed and played a major role in this provocative drama of political corruption and racial upheaval. Vincent Spano and Joe Morton head an impressive ensemble cast of 31 principal characters. With David Strathairn as Asteroid, the befuddled street person, and Sayles, himself, as the sleazy Carl.
VHS: S16087. $19.95.
Laser: LD71573. $39.95.
John Sayles, USA, 1991, 130 mins.

Eight Men Out

John Sayles brings the saga of the 1919 White Sox World Series scandal to the movie-going public. Based on the book by Eliot Asinof, this is a rich, finely detailed account of the eight players who agreed to throw the World Series for money. A fine cast includes John Cusack, D.B. Sweeney, David Strathairn, Christopher Lloyd, Clifton James, John Mahoney, John Sayles, and Studs Terkel as the reporter who broke the hearts of every kid in America.
VHS: S09820. $19.98.
Laser: LD70962. $39.95.
John Sayles, USA, 1988, 121 mins.

Passion Fish

John Sayles' perceptive and lyrical film unfolds in the atmospheric Louisiana bayou and charts the emotional relationship of two fiercely dependent women—an acerbic, caustic actress (Mary McDonnell) and her idiosyncratic caretaker (Alfre Woodard)—as one attempts to confront her vulnerable past. Sayles' regular David Strathairn contributes a stunning performance as a local who makes the tentative seduction of McDonnell. With Vondie Curtis-Hall and Nora Dunn.
VHS: S18746. $94.95.
John Sayles, USA, 1992, 137 mins.

The Secret of Roan Inish (Island of the Seals)

Magical and unforgettable, this beautiful film, shot on location in Ireland, captures the grandeur of simple lives transformed by fantasy. A young girl must find her missing brother. This simple but vital task sparks a story which brings an Irish legend to life. It involves an enchanted isle inhabited by seals.
VHS: S26620. $98.99.
Laser: LD75113. $34.95.
John Sayles, USA, 1995, 102 mins.

GUS VAN SANT

Drugstore Cowboy

Matt Dillon gives the performance of his career as the drug-addicted criminal who masterminds a series of robberies in the Pacific Northwest. A harsh and decidedly unsentimental look at life on the fringe that deals honestly with the world of controlled substances. A top notch cast includes Kelly Lynch, James LeGros, Heather Graham, James Remar and William Burroughs as Father Tom, the junkie priest. Don't say "no" to this drug movie.
VHS: S11724. $14.98.
Gus Van Sant, USA, 1989, 100 mins.

Even Cowgirls Get the Blues

Uma Thurman, Rain Phoenix, Lorraine Bracco and William Hurt star in this adaptation of Tom Robbins' best-selling novel. Gus Van Sant, director of *Drugstore Cowboy* and *My Own Private Idaho*, brings his remarkable visual style to this high camp road movie set in the early 1970's, about a hitchhiker, free love and lesbian passion. Also features Angie Dickinson, Keanu Reeves, Roseanne Arnold, Crispin Glover, Sean Young and Buck Henry. Music by k.d. lang.
VHS: S22383. $19.95.
Gus Van Sant, USA, 1994, 96 mins.

My Own Private Idaho

In this modern restructuring of the '60s road movie, River Phoenix and Keanu Reeves hustle their way through Seattle, Portland, Idaho and Rome on a quest for River's missing mother. With a meticulous, lyric style, the film combines sprawling landscapes, scenes of passionless sexuality and allusions to Orson Welles' *Chimes at Midnight* as it addresses issues of love, family, politics and homosexuality. A work of great complexity and beauty from the director of *Mala Noche* and *Drugstore Cowboy*.
VHS: S15927. $19.95.
Gus Van Sant, USA, 1991, 102 mins.

To Die For

Nicole Kidman stars as Suzanne Stone, a beautiful but vacuous weather girl whose real talents lie in manipulation, treachery, and self-promotion. Matt Dillon plays the unsuspecting husband who becomes the target of her murder plot. She doesn't plan to do it alone but rather enlists a love-struck teenager to act as assassin. It's the perfect scenario for launching her career as a celebrity. With Joaquin Phoenix and Illeana Douglas.
VHS: S27526. $99.99.
Laser: LD75525. $34.95.
Gus Van Sant, USA, 1995, 107 mins.

THE COEN BROTHERS

Barton Fink

An inside look in the average life of a Hollywood screenwriter as interpreted by the brothers Coen. John Turturro and John Goodman are fellow residents of the Hotel Earle, a very quiet California hotel where the most unusual things happen. Set in 1941, this truly bizarre and scathing period drama won three major awards at the Cannes Film Festival. With Judy Davis, Jon Polito, John Mahoney and Michael Lerner as studio boss Jack Lipnick. Have you got that Barton Fink feeling?
VHS: S15450. $19.98.
Joel Coen, USA, 1991, 116 minutes.

Blood Simple

The first film scripted by the talented Coen brothers. A critically acclaimed thriller set in rural Texas tells the old story of a man who hires a sleazy private eye to kill his wife and her boyfriend. Told in a very imaginative way, it combines chilling suspense with offbeat humor, with double and triple crosses building to a blood-curdling surprise climax. The most inventive and original thriller in years.
VHS: S00149. $14.98.
Laser: LD70016. $34.98.
Joel Coen, USA, 1983, 96 mins.

Hudsucker Proxy

The Coen Brothers' inventive, dazzling (and misunderstood) "comedy of invention" features dynamite performances from Tim Robbins as the fall guy and Jennifer Jason Leigh as the persuasive reporter who falls in love with him in this funny, stylish homage to the movies.
VHS: S21897. $19.98.
Laser: Widescreen. LD74524. $34.98.
Joel Coen, USA, 1993, 112 mins.

Miller's Crossing

A strikingly stylish gangster film. Set in 1929, *Miller's Crossing* is the story of the friendship between Leo (Albert Finney), the city's Irish political boss, and Tom (Gabriel Byrne), Leo's cool, brainy aide. Their friendship is severed when Leo and Tom both fall in love with Verna (Marcia Gay Harden). Tom joins ranks with Leo's foremost enemy and rival for political power, and a bloody gang war erupts. Also starring John Turturro and J.E. Freeman.
VHS: S13607. $19.98.
Joel Coen, USA, 1990, 115 mins.

Raising Arizona

A comedy about parental expectations and criminal activity. Nicolas Cage and Holly Hunter are a childless couple who need a little bundle of joy to make their lives complete. So they borrow one of a group of quintuplets, but complications ensue in this wacky, live-action, road-runner-like farce.
VHS: S04626. $19.95.
Laser: LD71291. $39.98.
Joel Coen, USA, 1987, 94 mins.

QUENTIN TARANTINO

Natural Born Killers

Quentin Tarantino provided the story that sets Woody Harrelson and Juliette Lewis as a deranged couple intently killing their way across the American landscape. It's a unique mix of comic book, sitcom and MTV style, with a deadly serious plot about the nature of crime and murder in an age of mass media and celebrity.
VHS: S23220. $19.98.
Laser: LD74663. $39.98.
Oliver Stone, USA, 1994, 119 mins.

Pulp Fiction

John Travolta, Uma Thurman, Samuel Jackson, Bruce Willis, Harvey Keitel and Rosanna Arquette are all part of the stellar cast of this highly acclaimed film. Two hit men encounter a bizarre series of adventures in a seamy L.A. world of criminals and kooks. The Academy Award-winning screenplay by Quentin Tarantino can't be beat.
VHS: S26211. $19.95.
Laser: CLV, widescreen THX. LD75062. $39.99.
Quentin Tarantino, USA, 1994, 154 mins.

Reservoir Dogs

The debut of Quentin Tarantino employs a novelistic structure to evoke the aftermath of a failed jewelry heist. Lawrence Tierney plays an underworld figure who recruits five criminals to stage a daring mid-afternoon robbery, led by Harvey Keitel. Quickly becoming a cult classic. With Tim Roth, Chris Penn, Steve Buscemi and Michael Madsen as an effective, sadistic creep.
VHS: S18195. $14.95.
Laser: Widescreen. LD75161. $34.98.
Quentin Tarantino, USA, 1992, 99 mins.

True Romance

Tony Scott's stylish variation of the lovers on the run theme, with Christian Slater as a lonely Detroit comic book store clerk who impulsively marries a call girl (Patricia Arquette). After Slater inadvertently steals a suitcase full of cocaine from a vicious pimp (Gary Oldman), he and Arquette travel to Los Angeles, with the mob in feverish pursuit. Screenplay by Quentin Tarantino (Reservoir Dogs). This director's cut features three minutes of footage that was excised in order to secure an R-rating for its theatrical release. With Dennis Hopper, Val Kilmer, Brad Pitt, Christopher Walken, Bronson Pinchot, Saul Rubinek and Michael Rappaport.
VHS: S19941. $19.98.
Laser: Widescreen. LD72251. $39.98.
Tony Scott, USA, 1993, 121 mins.

JON JOST

All the Vermeers in New York

From the tenacious American independent Jon Jost, this visually ravishing, precise and emotionally fluid piece tracks the romantic obsession, emotional desperation, individual expression and tension of a disparate group of New York artists and businessmen. Largely about the conflicts produced between commerce and art, the movie is less a narrative than a collection of vignettes about the textures and off-center rhythms of urban culture. Shot in widescreen, with some wonderfully executed tracking shots, Jost conceived, wrote, photographed and edited this audacious work. With Stephen Lack, French actress Emmanuelle Chaulet and Katherine Bean.
VHS: S17499. $24.98.
Jon Jost, USA, 1990, 87 mins.

Angel City

In a comic, hard-boiled, detective story form, this film by Jon Jost intermixes an examination of the nature of images and their supposed truth with an elaborately detailed social, political and economic critique of the Los Angeles-Hollywood scene.
VHS: S03762. $59.95.
Jon Jost, USA, 1981, 75 mins.

Bell Diamond

A formally exquisite and politically pointed study of an alienated Vietnam veteran set against the backdrop of a bankrupt mining town. Filmed in Butte, Montana, director Jost collaborated with a cast that not only acted improvisationally without written texts, but was largely composed of non-professionals.
VHS: S07368. $69.95.
Jon Jost, USA, 1987, 96 mins.

Chameleon

A day in the life of a Los Angeles drug pusher featuring Bob Glaudini (Angel City). Chameleon is a cautionary tale about the self-destructiveness of American opportunism.
VHS: S07367. $69.95.
Jon Jost, USA, 1990, 90 mins.

Jon Jost's Frameup

America's iconoclastic filmmaker, Jon Jost, turns his attention to two losers, one an ex-con, the other a dizzy waitress, who hit the road. In Jost's tragi-comic tale, they travel over great swaths of the West encountering a host of "all-American" characters in a trenchant and subtle analysis of bonding and loneliness. Howard Swain and Nancy Carlin are a real-life couple who bring these characters to life.
VHS: S23752. $89.98.
Jon Jost, USA, 1993, 91 mins.

Last Chants for a Slow Dance

A feature by Jon Jost which chronicles the aimless wandering of a man named Tom Bates who travels in his truck around Montana. The film weaves the story through his encounters with hitchhikers and people on the road.
VHS: S03763. $69.95.
Jon Jost, USA, 1983, 90 mins.

Plain Talk and Common Sense

A 110-minute essay on the State of the Nation by one of America's leading independent filmmakers—Jon Jost. "Plain Talk and Common Sense (uncommon senses) is Jost's most successful film yet—a movie of expansive negativity that, putting patriotism under erasure, proposes to represent America and then revels in its inability to do so" (J. Hoberman, Village Voice).
VHS: S15190. $69.95.
Jon Jost, USA, 1987, 110 mins.

Rembrandt Laughing

Focuses on a pair of ex-lovers five years after their break-up. In cinema verite fashion, the film follows their daily encounters with friends and associates.
VHS: S16151. $79.95.
Jon Jost, 1989, USA, 100 mins.

Slow Moves

Two drifters meet on the Golden Gate Bridge, start an affair, run into money trouble and drive across the country on a spree which ends when one's gunned down trying to rob a store, in this independent film noir by Jon Jost.
VHS: S03764. $69.95.
Jon Jost, USA, 1984, 93 mins.

Speaking Directly

A unique and powerful film essay mixing autobiography, socio-political observation and reflexive cinema. "In the history of the American avant-garde, Speaking Directly stands as a remarkable achievement: between the currents of pure cinema and committed documentary/fiction" (Ian Christie).
VHS: S06107. $69.95.
Jon Jost, USA, 110 mins.

Stagefright

The most experimental of Jon Jost's feature-length films, Stagefright was shot for German television, and is a daring meditation on cinema, theater, performance and politics. "As long as Jost goes on making more films just as truthful, I don't expect him to win any popularity contests" (Jonathan Rosenbaum).
VHS: S06295. $69.95.
Jon Jost, USA, 1981, 74 mins.

Sure Fire

Tom Blair stars as an aggressive entrepreneur who tries to make a killing in real estate in the small, depressed towns of South-Central Utah, until he finds himself losing his grip, in Jon Jost's acclaimed independent feature. "It's clearly an American masterpiece. Spare and disturbing, but with dark, comic touches…" (Variety). With Kate Dezina, Robert Ernst, Kristi Hager. Letterboxed.
VHS: S20515. $24.98.
Jon Jost, USA, 1993, 86 mins.

HAL HARTLEY

Amateur

Hal Hartley directed this offbeat comedy, which stars Martin Donovan, Isabelle Huppert and Elina Lowensohn as three individuals joined in a love triangle and trapped in a fight for survival. How can an amnesiac, a porn star and a nymphomaniac ex-nun escape ruthless, single-minded corporate killers? That's where the comedy of this stylish film comes in.
VHS: S26700. $96.99.
Laser: LD75112. $39.95.
Hal Hartley, USA/Great Britain/France, 1994, 105 mins.

Surviving Desire

Hal Hartley offers a one-hour program about the affair between an uptight English professor (Martin Donovan) and Sophie (Mary Ward), one of his students, who has a penchant for poetry. The film is quirky, fun and unsettling. On the same program are two Hartley shorts, Theory of Achievement and Ambition, both very funny, Godardian works about art, sex and money.
VHS: S17919. $19.98.
Hal Hartley, USA, 1991, 86 mins.

Trust

She's a smart-mouthed suburban brat. He's a disillusioned computer genius with a hand grenade. Together they embark on a very different, very modern romance in which they both learn a lot about each other, about acceptance, about love, and about trust. This is Hal Hartley's hilarious follow-up to his equally funny and intelligent debut feature, The Unbelievable Truth. "Entertaining! Genuinely eccentric! A Godardian mixture of ardent talk, deadpan hyperbole and unexpected action!" (J. Hoberman, Village Voice).
VHS: S15526. $19.98.
Laser: CLV. LD72039. $29.98.
Hal Hartley, USA/Great Britain, 1991, 107 mins.

The Unbelievable Truth

Robert Burke and Adrienne Shelly star in this twisted black comedy. Burke is an ex-con who falls for the boss's daughter, but she has troubles of her own. Shelly stars as the model whose thoughts continually turn to the coming Armageddon.
VHS: S26110. $19.95.
Laser: LD75138. $24.98.
Hal Hartley, USA, 1990, 100 mins.

JILL GODMILOW

Far from Poland

A brilliant film: denied a visa to shoot a film in Poland, director Godmilow constructs a film over the bare bones of documentary footage while in New York, resulting in a deft dismemberment of the myth of "documentary truth." The film portrays the birth of the Solidarity movement at the Gdansk shipyards through moving personal testimony and a chilling look at the psychology of a censor.
VHS: S02656. $69.95.
Jill Godmilow, USA, 1984, 106 mins.

The Popovich Brothers of South Chicago

This ground-breaking film from Jill Godmilow focuses on a musical group that has been keeping traditional Serbian music alive and well within Chicago's ethnic Serbian community for over 50 years. In this documentary, the importance of old world customs, invigorated by the American values of tolerance and diversity, are reflected in the unique, rousing music of the Popovich Brothers.
VHS: S21130. $29.95.
Jill Godmilow, USA, 1978, 60 mins.

JIM JARMUSCH

Down by Law

Jim Jarmusch's third feature following his immensely successful Stranger Than Paradise stars Tom Waits, John Lurie—and in a treasure of a performance, Roberto Benigni—as a group of escaped convicts in the swamps of Louisiana. A funny, original film featuring brilliant cinematography by the great Robby Muller.
VHS: S03022. $14.98.
Jim Jarmusch, USA, 1986, 95 mins.

Mystery Train

"Jim Jarmusch makes bizarre, minimalist and simpatico road movies, with characters on the edge of pop culture discovering a poetically shabby America. We see the land through the eyes of foreigners, unspoiled but prejudiced by American myths." Three separate but interwoven episodes centered in a rundown Memphis hotel reveal the experiences of non-Americans in America. Two young Japanese lovers travel through town on a rock 'n roll pilgrimage, a newly widowed Italian woman waits for a flight back to Rome while she is visited by the ghost of Elvis, a British man makes some friends, gets drunk and commits murder. "There is no real mystery in Mystery Train. It makes it points on Elvis-worship, restlessness and race relations out front. But there is a mystery about its construction. The leisurely, distancing pace works beautifully" (Edwin Jahiel). 1990, 110 mins.
VHS: S12988. $19.98.
Jim Jarmusch, USA, 1989, 113 mins.

Night on Earth

Jim Jarmusch's film is structured episodically, with the narrative simultaneously unfolding in Los Angeles, New York, Paris, Rome and Helsinki, and concerns the relationship of cab drivers and their passengers. The ensemble cast includes Gena Rowlands, Winona Ryder, Rosie Perez, Giancarlo Esposito, Armin Mueller-Stahl, Beatrice Dalle, Isaach de Bankole, Roberto Benigni, Matti Pellonpaa and Kari Vaananen. Tom Waits composed the music and performs two numbers.
VHS: S17625. $19.95.
Jim Jarmusch, USA, 1991, 125 mins.

JONAS MEKAS

The Brig

The Living Theatre's famous play by Kenneth Brown: hell in a Marine Corps prison in which humiliation and brutality are dished out according to the book, with guards and inmates performing a mad ritual of degradation…a work of art that serves as a metaphor of protest.
VHS: S00181. $29.95.
Jonas Mekas, USA, 1964, 65 mins.

He Stands in a Desert Counting the Seconds of His Life

Shot in 1965, this is part of Mekas' diary films. It includes very little personal material and focuses on sketches of events and people largely outside Mekas' life. Roberto Rossellini, Ken Jacobs, Alberto Cavalcanti, Peter Kubelka, Kenneth Anger, Jackie Onassis, Lee Radziwill, Andy Warhol, P. Adams Sitney, Yoko Ono, Allen Ginsberg and John Lennon are among those seen.
VHS: S25797. $75.00.
Jonas Mekas, USA, 1969, 160 mins.

In Between

Footage from 1964-1968 that did not find its way into the Walden reels is joined in this classic period piece. Mostly centered in New York, it also includes travel footage and appearances by David Wise, Salvador Dali, Allen Ginsberg, Jack Smith, Shirley Clarke, Jane Holzer and more. Mel Lyman plays his banjo on the roof.
VHS: S25795. $75.00.
Jonas Mekas, USA, 1975, 52 mins.

Lost, Lost, Lost

These diary sequences come from 1949-1963. In them Mekas documents his arrival in Brooklyn from Lithuania, his struggle with the exile community, his move to Manhattan, and his involvement with the New York poetry and experimental film scene.
VHS: S25796. $100.00.
Jonas Mekas, USA, 1963, 158 mins.

Notes for Jerome

Footage from three distinct visits to the home of Jerome Hill make up this tribute to him. Mekas visited Hill in 1966 with P. Adams Sitney. He then returned briefly in 1967 and again after Hill's death in 1974. This elegy is dedicated to Hill, who may have felt as much an exile as Mekas did. Music performed by Hill, Taylor Mead, Charles Rydell and others makes up the soundtrack.
VHS: S25799. $75.00.
Jonas Mekas, USA, 1978, 45 mins.

Paradise Not Yet Lost (aka Oona's Third Year)

These scenes from Mekas' film diaries were shot in 1977. It includes many memorable sequences from New York, including a visit to the mother of Maya Deren (Marie Deren), Peter Kubelka's concert, and the St. Patrick's Day Parade. Other sections focus on travel to friends and relatives in Sweden, Lithuania and Austria, and concludes again in New York.
VHS: S25798. $75.00.
Jonas Mekas, USA, 1979, 160 mins.

Reminiscences of a Journey to Lithuania

This diary film begins with footage shot by Mekas in New York in the early 1950's. Then a trip back to his native Lithuanian village in 1971 shows his reaction to the changes experienced by his homeland. Finally a sequence shot in Vienna where Mekas was interned during the war and a trip to Austria end this poetic film experience.
VHS: S25800. $100.00.
Jonas Mekas, USA/Great Britain/Germany, 1971, 82 mins.

Scenes from the Life of Andy Warhol

This collection of footage shot between 1965 and 1982 includes many notables from the factory and other celebrities basking in the glow of Warhol. Nico, Lou Reed, Edie Sedgwick, Peter Orlovsky, John Lennon, Henry Geldzahler, Paul Morrissey, Caroline Kennedy and Mick Jagger are just some of those present in this work from the acclaimed experimental filmmaker Jonas Mekas. Music by the Velvet Underground.
VHS: S25793. $75.00.
Jonas Mekas, USA, 1991, 38 mins.

Zefiro Torna or Scenes from the Life of George Macinuas

Footage of the Fluxus heavy, Macinuas, depicts his family, various Fluxus events, and scenes from his private life. Shot between 1952-1978, it is set to Monteverdi music and Jonas Mekas reading from The Diaries kept during the last years of Macinuas' life.
VHS: S25794. $75.00.
Jonas Mekas, USA, 1992, 35 mins.

STEVEN SODERBERGH

Kafka

Steven Soderbergh's follow-up to sex, lies and videotape is set in a baroque, sinister Prague. Jeremy Irons plays an insurance underwriter who, following a friend's disappearance, gets entangled with a shadowy anarchist group and an unbalanced doctor performing perverse scientific experiments. The cast includes Theresa Russell, Joel Grey, Ian Holm, Jeroen Krabbe, Armin Mueller-Stahl and Alec Guinness.
VHS: S17789. $92.95.
Laser: Widescreen. LD75128. $24.98.
Steven Soderbergh, USA/France/Great Britain, 1991, 100 mins.

King of the Hill

Steven Soderbergh's splendid, realistic tale of growing up during the Depression in St. Louis, based on the memoirs of A.E. Hotchner. The young Jesse Bradford stars as 12-year-old Aaron, whose perseverance and intelligence help him overcome the incredible odds growing up with a family that's falling apart. With Jeroen Krabbe, Lisa Eichhorn, Karen Allen, Spalding Gray and Elizabeth McGovern. "Simply one of the year's best films" (Siskel & Ebert).
VHS: S20548. $19.98.
Laser: Letterboxed. LD72364. $34.98.
Steven Soderbergh, USA, 1993, 102 mins.

sex, lies and videotape

When an old college buddy drops into the lives of a Louisiana yuppie couple, the bonds of matrimony begin to fray. Steve Soderbergh's accomplished feature film debut scored a big win at Cannes and really annoyed Spike Lee. James Spader also won a Best Actor Award at Cannes for his role as the soft-spoken, sensitive visitor. With Peter Gallagher and Andie MacDowell as the former perfect couple and Laura San Giacomo as the lusty sister-in-law.
VHS: S11693. $19.95.
Laser: CAV. LD70456. $124.95.
Laser: CLV. LD70457. $134.98.
Steven Soderbergh, USA, 1989, 100 mins.

The Underneath

In this thriller, a handsome drifter (Peter Gallagher) named Michael Chambers goes home. There he finds that the good looks and the good luck he relied on while traveling may not be worth much. His mother wants to start a new life while his brother is consumed by jealous rage. Chambers hopes to reignite an old flame, but there is a complication there as well. Soon he is transfixed in a treacherous game of emotional turmoil, joining sex, desire and violence.
VHS: S26991. $19.98.
Laser: LD75430. $34.98.
Steven Soderbergh, USA, 1994, 100 mins.

MONTE HELLMAN

Creature from the Haunted Sea

Roger Corman created this and even appears in a cameo in the story of a gangster who tries to cover his tracks by inventing the story of a sea monster.
VHS: S08431. $29.95.
Roger Corman/Monte Hellman, USA, 1960, 76 mins.

Flight to Fury

Jack Nicholson stars as a rugged con man who writes the script and steals the show as a handful of connivers plan to swipe a fortune in diamonds. Based on a story by director/producer Hellman.
VHS: S12587. $19.98.
Monte Hellman, USA, 1964, 73 mins.

Ride in the Whirlwind

Jack Nicholson wrote the screenplay for this unusual western. When three down-and-out cowpokes run into a gang of thieves, they find themselves wanted for a crime they didn't commit. Jack Nicholson, Cameron Mitchell and Millie Perkins star.
VHS: S25626. $29.98.
Monte Hellman, USA, 1965, 83 mins.

Shooting

An unconventional Western starring Warren Oates and Will Hutchins as two former bounty hunters out for revenge, with a powerful, hair-raising finale. With Jack Nicholson and Millie Perkins.
VHS: S06340. $29.98.
Monte Hellman, USA, 1967, 82 mins.

AFRICAN-AMERICAN INDEPENDENTS

Ashes and Embers
This award winning film is the story of a Vietnam veteran who, nearly a decade later, begins to come to terms with his role in the war and his role as a Black person in America. His transformation from an embittered ex-soldier to a strong and confident man is provoked and encouraged by the love and chastisement of his grandmother and friends.
VHS: $13411. $59.95.
Haile Gerima, USA, 1983, 120 mins.

Beat Street
Afrika Bambaata and the Soul Sonic Force, Grand Master Melle Mel and the Furious Five along with salsa king Ruben Blades provide the music in this break dance docudrama. Features Rae Dawn Chong, Leon Grant, Saundra Santiago and Kadeem Hardison.
VHS: $21458. $14.98.
Stan Lathan, USA, 1984, 106 mins.

Big City Blues
Filmed in Chicago, featuring Jim Brewer talking about the links between traditional blues and the new urban sound, as well as performances by Son Seals and harpist Billy Branch.
VHS: $03194. $24.95.
St. Clair Bourne, USA, 28 mins.

Boomerang
Eddie Murphy's first romantic comedy shows him portraying a womanizing advertising executive. The first object of his affections (Robin Givens) is too much for him because of her aggressive approach so he turns to a "nicer" woman (Halle Berry). The cast includes David Allen Grier, Martin Lawrence, Grace Jones, Eartha Kitt, Chris Rock, Tisha Campbell, John Witherspoon and Melvin Van Peebles.
VHS: $21448. $19.95.
Laser: Widescreen. LD75122. $24.98.
Reginald Hudlin, USA, 1992, 118 mins.

Bopha!
Morgan Freeman's directorial debut casts Danny Glover as a South African police officer torn between his duty, his conscience, and his family. This tense drama offers a view inside that troubled country.
VHS: $20614. $95.98.
Laser: LD75162. $34.98.
Morgan Freeman, USA, 1993, 120 mins.

Boyz N The Hood
John Singleton made Oscar history as the first African-American to be nominated as best director. He also became, at age 23, the youngest filmmaker to be so honored for this powerful drama about responsibility and survival. Cuba Gooding Jr. delivers a fine performance as Tre Styles, a young man trying to make the right decisions while dealing with the dangers of living in South Central L.A. With excellent work by rapper Ice Cube, Morris Chestnut and Larry Fishburne as Tre's discerning father.
VHS: $15671. $19.95.
Laser: LD71181. $49.95.
John Singleton, USA, 1991, 107 mins.

Buck and the Preacher
Sidney Poitier's first feature as director. Poitier also plays a wagonmaster on the long trek out West as the wagon train is attacked by white nightriders and encounters a group of slaves freed at the end of the Civil War. With Harry Belafonte as a hustler preacher and Ruby Dee.
VHS: $21479. $19.95.
Sidney Poitier, USA, 1971, 103 mins.

Bush Mama
This landmark of African-American cinema reveals the powerful drama of a black woman now on welfare in the Los Angeles ghetto, trying to care for her daughter after being stranded alone by her man's imprisonment for a crime he didn't commit. Though scripted and professionally acted, the film succeeds in capturing the rich style of ghetto language and humor. Its street scenes, where outbursts of violence assume a fantasy-like power, alternate with fantasy scenes, which gain in reality from the juxtaposition. The narrative is loosely structured, flowing readily from real time to flashback, real life to nightmare. A daring film in concept and execution.
VHS: $15644. $59.95.
Haile Gerima, USA, 1976, 100 mins.

Bustin' Loose
Richard Pryor stars as a con artist enlisted to drive a group of orphans across country. Cicely Tyson co-stars in this comedy. The film captures Pryor, on whose idea the film is based, at the height of his comic power.
VHS: $21449. $14.98.
Oz Scott, USA, 1981, 94 mins.

Car Wash
An ensemble comedy of a typical day at a Los Angeles car wash. The owner is white, the workers mostly black, Spanish and oppressed, but they do seem to have lots to laugh about on the job. Guest stars include Richard Pryor, George Carlin, Professor Irwin Corey and the Pointer Sisters. With Melanie Mayron, Ivan Dixon, Antonio Fargas and Sully Boyar.
VHS: $07800. $59.95.
Michael Schultz, USA, 1976, 97 mins.

Carbon Copy
George Segal plays a secretly Jewish, successful corporate executive whose illegitimate Black son (Denzel Washington) suddenly shows up and reveals Segal for what he is in this film by Michael (Car Wash) Schultz.
VHS: $21480. $14.95.
Michael Schultz, USA, 1981, 91 mins.

Child of Resistance and Hour Glass
Two experimental shorts by Haile Gerima are on this video. Child of Resistance follows a personal transformation inspired by a dream brought on by Angela Davis' incarceration. In Hour Glass, a pro basketball player imagines himself a gladiator before he decides to go home.
VHS: $25566. $39.95.
Haile Gerima, USA, 1972, 57 mins.

Clarence and Angel
When 12-year-old Clarence moves with his family from South Carolina to New York City he finds school can be a major hassle when he can't read. The black kid is befriended by a kung fu crazy Hispanic kid named Angel, who assists him on his road to literacy. Warm and funny. With Darren Brown, Mark Cardova, Cynthia McPherson and Leroy Smith.
VHS: $07131. $59.95.
Robert Gardner, USA, 1980, 75 mins.

The Color of Love
A revolutionary and sexually provocative work that attempts to confront the issues, mixed identity and confusion of interracial relationships while exploring the nature of attraction and taboo sexual themes. 90 mins.
VHS: $18816. $19.95.

Cooley High
This film focuses on several members of the 1964 graduating class of Edwin G. Cooley Vocational High School in Chicago. Director Schultz was intent on presenting black teenagers—their aspirations, exuberance, silliness, awkwardness, and despair—in a more understanding way than any other Hollywood filmmaker had before him. "Cooley High is a landmark movie, one of the year's most important and heartening pictures" (Kevin Thomas, Los Angeles Times).
VHS: $13765. $79.98.
Michael Schultz, USA, 1975, 107 mins.

Cotton Comes to Harlem
Based on the Chester Himes novel. Two Harlem cops suspect a Marcus Garvey-like preacher is advocating a back-to-Africa movement to cover for a much more elaborate scam. With Godfrey Cambridge, Raymond St. Jacques, Calvin Lockhart and Redd Foxx.
VHS: $17976. $14.95.
Ossie Davis, USA, 1970, 97 mins.

Daughters of the Dust
This remarkable first feature by Julie Dash follows three generations of African-American women at the turn of the century, structured around the family's migration from the Sea Island to the mainland. Beautifully shot by Arthur Jaffa, the film is a poetic series of pastoral images, landscapes, sound, ritual, music, colors and voice. The film is steeped in the highly distinctive, traditional oral black storytelling, told through a highly unusual narrative device, related by an unborn child. The images sing. With Cora Lee Day, Alva Rogers, Barbara-O, Turla Hoosier and Kaycee Moore.
VHS: $16913. $24.95.
Julie Dash, USA, 1991, 113 mins.

Deep Cover
Larry Fishburne's first major role is as an undercover cop from the Midwest imported to infiltrate a West Coast drug ring. Jeff Goldblum plays a lawyer who becomes Fishburne's "partner" in drug dealing.
VHS: $21481. $19.95.
Bill Duke, USA, 1992, 106 mins.

Devil in a Blue Dress
Denzel Washington is terrific in this stylish thriller set in 1940s Los Angeles. Private Eye Easy Rawlins (Washington) thought he was being asked to take a relatively simple case that would make him some easy money. He didn't expect it would lead to his being blackmailed by a crooked politician. Rawlins quickly finds himself in a netherworld of suspense and deceit where the devil must be paid. Jennifer Beals is featured.
VHS: $27347. $99.95.
Laser: LD75497. $34.95.
Carl Franklin, USA, 1995, 101 mins.

Disorderlies
The Fat Boys are the stars of this Three Stooges-like comedy about an incompetent hospital staff. As you might expect they also perform a number of songs. The film is an enjoyable combination of rap music and sheer idiocy.
VHS: $21400. $19.98.
Michael Schultz, USA, 1987, 86 mins.

Firehouse
A made-for-television movie about a black fire fighter (Richard Roundtree) who is assigned to an all-white New York City fire station just as an arsonist tries to destroy the black community.
VHS: $18820. $19.95.
Alex March, USA, 1972, 73 mins.

The Five Heartbeats
Robert Townsend's follow-up to Hollywood Shuffle is a moreserious film which follows the career of an African-American musical group, The Five Heartbeats. The group's highs and lows as well as their music are chronicled. Features Townsend, Tressa Thomas, Michael Wright, Harry J. Lennix and Diahann Carroll.
VHS: $21433. $19.98.
Robert Townsend, USA, 1991, 120 mins.

Ganja and Hess
A landmark African-American feature which stars Marlene Clark and Duane Jones, who had previously starred in Night of the Living Dead. Bill Gunn's Ganja and Hess, "once seen as a standard vampire movie, has been reinterpreted as a multi-layered study of conflicts within African-American culture" (Ephraim Katz). Jones plays an anthropologist who contracts a mysterious disease after he is stabbed with an ancient object. The attack makes him immortal but also makes him a vampire.
VHS: $21928. $39.95.
Bill Gunn, USA, 1970, 110 mins.

Ghost Dad
Bill Cosby dies in a cab accident and has only a couple of days to get his finances in order to provide for his children in this family comedy. With Kimberly Russell, Denise Nicholas.
VHS: $21482. $19.98.
Sidney Poitier, USA, 1990, 84 mins.

The Glass Shield
Michael Boatman and Ice Cube star in this intense thriller about a man wrongfully accused of a crime. Ice Cube could be put away for a long time if a rookie cop (Boatman) does not solve a shocking murder case. In the end, Boatman must decide whether to uphold the law or remain loyal to the unspoken code of silencethat shields him from the violent streets. With Lori Petty, Elliott Gould.
VHS: $26953. $99.99.
Laser: LD75426. $39.99.
Charles Burnett, USA, 1995, 110 mins.

Go Tell It on the Mountain
James Baldwin's searing autobiographical novel about the African-American experience follows a family's migration from the rural South to Harlem. At the center of the film is a young man who struggles to understand and earn the approval of his stern, moody stepfather. "A remarkable film, Go Tell It on the Mountain is powerful enough to lift us off the ground. [The film] soars." (The Wall Street Journal). With Paul Winfield, James Bond III, Olivia Cole, Rosalind Cash, Ruby Dee, Linda Hopkins and Alfre Woodard.
VHS: $20385. $69.95.
Stan Lathan, USA, 1984, 97 mins.

Greased Lightning
Richard Pryor plays Wendell Scott, the first U.S. African-American stock car driver in this biographic film most of which was apparently directed by Melvin Van Peebles, but completed and credited to Michael Schultz. With Pam Grier, Cleavon Little, Richie Havens, Beau Bridges.
VHS: $21483. $19.98.
Melvin Van Peebles/Michael Schultz, USA, 1977, 96 mins.

Half Slave, Half Free
Originally released as Solomon Northrup's Odyssey, an emotionally wrenching, true story of a free black man who is kidnapped and placed into slavery in the South, and spends 12 years of his life under various masters. Based on Northrup's memoirs. With Avery Brooks and Mason Adams.
VHS: $01532. $59.95.
Gordon Parks, USA, 1985, 100 mins.

Harlem Nights
Black nightclub owners Richard Pryor and Eddie Murphy team up against the mob and the law in this action comedy. Curiously, Pryor is cast as the more cautious and learned of the two men. Murphy also directed an all-star cast that includes Redd Foxx (with his usual acidic wit), Danny Aiello (Do the Right Thing), Della Reese, Jasmine Guy and Arsenio Hall.
VHS: $21446. $19.95.
Eddie Murphy, USA, 1989, 118 mins.

Higher Learning
Laurence Fishburne, Ice Cube, Jennifer Connelly and Tyra Banks star in this thought-provoking film about diversity on a formerly quiet college campus. Race and sexuality are just some of the issues explored in this troubling drama. Sometimes love and understanding are not enough.
VHS: $25847. $19.95.
Laser: LD75004. $39.95.
John Singleton, USA, 1994, 127 mins.

House Party
One night in East St. Louis, Illinois—the "Blackest city in America"—two teens named Kid and Play decide to take advantage of vacationing parents by throwing a bash, a blow out, a house party. Peppered with hip rap music by these real-life musicians, this is the story of that fateful night and the misadventures of the teens and their friends. A def, Black version of Risky Business.
VHS: $12749. $19.98.
Reginald Hudlin, USA, 1990, 100 mins.

House Party 2: The Pajama Jam
The stars of House Party are back and in college. In order to raise tuition "Kid 'N Play" (Christopher Reid and Christopher Martin) put together a fundraiser. Needless to say, it does not turn out exactly as planned. Features Tisha Campbell, Iman, Queen Latifah and Martin Lawrence.
VHS: $21395. $19.98.
Doug McHenry/George Jackson, USA, 1991, 94 mins.

House Party 3
"Kid N' Play" return for a third House Party. This time Kid is on his way to the altar and Play takes it upon himself to plan the bachelor party of all time. The fiance, Veda, becomes suspicious of Kid's party plans resulting in more madcap madness like that featured in the first two installments. The film also introduces female rappers TLC. Features Christopher Reid and Christopher Martin (aka Kid N' Play), Tisha Campbell, Bernie Mac and Michael Colyar.
VHS: $21386. $19.95.
Eric Meza, USA, 1994, 93 mins.

How U Like Me Now
A young man on the south side of Chicago deals with his social climbing girlfriend. She is overly ambitious while he lacks drive. A sort of romantic comedy with a great script. Features Darnell Williams, Salli Richardson, Daniel Gardner and Raymond Whitefield.
VHS: $21432. $92.95.
Daryll Roberts, USA, 1992, 109 mins.

I Know Why the Caged Bird Sings
An eloquent film based on poet Maya Angelou's memories of the hardships, private joys and public pleasures of growing up in the Depression-era South. Ostracized by the social and racial caste systems of the period, Angelou finds self-expression and fulfillment through writing. Written by Leonora Thuna, Ralph B. Woolsey and Angelou. With Diahann Carroll, Esther Rolle, Ruby Dee, Paul Benjamin, Roger E. Mosley and Constance Good (who plays Maya as a young girl).
VHS: $19890. $19.98.
Fielder Cook, USA, 1979, 100 mins.

In Motion: Amiri Baraka
Called "a brilliantly executed documentary" by The New York Times, a fascinating exploration of the writer and political activist formerly known as Leroi Jones. Following Baraka from his early days as a poet in New York City's Greenwich Village to his present literary and political activities, In Motion: Amiri Baraka is a portrait of a man of singular commitment to social change. Interspersed throughout the film are excerpts from Baraka's powerful play The Dutchman, one of the archetypal literary works of the 1960's, as well as scenes from other Baraka plays.
VHS: $10909. $59.95.
St. Clair Bourne, USA, 1985, 60 mins.

Jason's Lyric
This powerful drama follows the efforts of a young man who seeks to change his life against the overwhelming odds that face him on the street. Love can be a redemptive force. Forest Whitaker, Allen Paine and Bokeem Woodbine star. Music by the Cranberries, Salt 'n' Pepa and others is featured on the soundtrack.
VHS: $23961. $94.95.
Laser: LD74929. $34.95.
Doug McHenry, USA, 1994, 119 mins.

Juice
Cinematographer Ernest Dickerson's (Do the Right Thing, Jungle Fever) directorial debut deals with inner city crime and the search for respect by urban youth. A young D.J. called "Q", is talked into committing a robbery and winds up involved in a murder. The cast includes Omar Epps, Jermaine Hopkins, Tupac Shakur and Samuel L. Jackson.
VHS: $21444. $19.95.
Laser: Widescreen. LD75212. $34.98.
Ernest R. Dickerson, USA, 1992, 95 mins.

Just Another Girl on the I.R.T.
Leslie Harris' debut film is a vivid portrait of the panache of a 17-year-old Brooklyn African-American woman. Ambitious and colorful, she is played by astonishing newcomer named Ariyan Johnson, who portrays a street-tough woman with plans to attend college and study medicine. Harris documents life in the projects, from the unique perspective of a young black woman. With Kevin Thigpen, Jerard Washington and Ebony Jerido.
VHS: $19024. $92.98.
Laser: LD75214. $34.98.
Leslie Harris, USA, 1992, 90 mins.

Krush Groove
Blair Underwood (LA Law, Posse) stars in the first all-rap musical. Musicians featured include Kurtis Blow, The Fat Boys and Sheila E.
VHS: $21404. $14.95.
Laser: LD74707. $34.98.
Michael Schultz, USA, 1985, 95 mins.

Last Dragon
Motown's Berry Gordy produced this musical kung-fu film featuring pop singer Vanity. The plot involves a young kung-fu enthusiast portrayed by Taimak, who fights the evil "Sho-Nuff, Shogun of Harlem". Never mind the mixed-up cultural references—this is primarily a musical. Music by Stevie Wonder, Smokey Robinson, The Temptations and Debarge.
VHS: $21398. $79.98.
Michael Schultz, USA, 1985, 108 mins.

Laurel Avenue
From Carl Franklin, the director of the acclaimed One False Move, this HBO miniseries details the intimate joys, sorrows, hardships and family dynamics of the Arnett family in St. Paul, Minnesota over a long weekend. This bold work, gloriously alive and telling in details, is an intimate look at the conflicts and dreams of an African-American family. "The most emotionally layered look at black life ever presented" (James Wolcott, The New Yorker).
VHS: $20377. $49.99.
Carl Franklin, USA, 1993, 156 mins.

The Learning Tree
A well-intentioned and beautifully photographed film version of Gordon Parks' autobiographical novel set in Kansas in the mid-1920s. Writer-director-producer Parks recreates his teen years in a small town where a young black learns about life. With Kyle Johnson as Newt and Dana Elcar as the Sheriff.
VHS: $03572. $19.98.
Gordon Parks, USA, 1969, 107 mins.

Let's Do It Again
Sidney Poitier and Bill Cosby reprise their roles in this sequel to Uptown Saturday Night. The two men fleece a couple of gamblers in order to build a lodge hall. Features Ossie Davis, Jimmy Walker, John Amos, Denise Nicholas and Calvin Lockhart.
VHS: $21459. $19.98.
Sidney Poitier, USA, 1975, 113 mins.

Love Your Mama
Ruby L. Oliver's debut film has an immediacy and unflinching naturalism in the story of a South side Chicago family that is unhinged by the father's alcoholism, the daughter's pregnancy and the two sons' descent into criminal activities. Carol Hall's tough lead performance as the title player who is desperately trying to hold her family together is graced by an unforced intensity and verve. Oliver was a Chicago day-care operator who spent $1 million of her own money to finance this independent work. "A film of great strength and sincerity" (Dave Kehr, Chicago Tribune). With Audrey Morgan, Andre Robinson, Ernest Raymond and Kearo Johnson.
VHS: $19633. $89.95.
Ruby Oliver, USA, 1989, 94 mins.

Mahogany
Diana Ross plays a poor secretary from Chicago who rises to the height of the international fashion scene. All she needs is the help of Tony Perkins and the love of Billy Dee Williams. Also making the scene are Beah Richards, Jean-Pierre Aumont and Nina Foch. Sing, Diana, sing. With direction supplied by Motown Records exec Berry Gordy.
VHS: $10831. $14.95.
Berry Gordy, USA, 1976, 109 mins.

Menace II Society
This stylized inner-city gangster drama is the debut film of Allan and Albert Hughes, 21-year-old fraternal twins. Set in a claustrophobic Watts, the film is constructed as a harrowing collection of brutal vignettes of car hijackings, street assassinations and random violence. The film plays like a black *Mean Streets*. Its theme is the cruel fate of its two lead characters, a relatively good though unfocused kid (Tyrin Turner) who is undone by his allegiance to his pathologically unbalanced best friend O-Dog (Larenz Tate). From the opening scene, a brutal Korean grocery store murder, *Menace II Society* is a pessimistic and wholly unsentimental portrait of late 20th-century American life. With Jada Pinkett, Vonte Sweet, MC Eiht, Ryan Williams, Too $hort, Samuel L. Jackson, Charles Dutton and Bill Duke.
VHS: $19937. $19.95.
The Hughes Brothers, USA, 1993, 97 mins.

Messenger
Vittorio De Sica's groundbreaking film *The Bicycle Thief* inspired this contemporary tale about poverty in urban America. Richard Barboza is determined to stay on the straight and narrow until he is faced with a threat to his livelihood and all he has struggled to achieve. This film shows a side of African-American life missing from the more prevalent "gangsta" films made in Hollywood.
VHS: $27009. $79.99.
Norman Loftis, USA, 1995, 80 mins.

Meteor Man
A meteor crashes to earth endowing a man with super powers which he uses for the good of mankind. An upbeat, largely non-violent superhero film starring director Robert Townsend.
VHS: $21409. $19.95.
Robert Townsend, USA, 1993, 99 mins.

Native Son (1986)
Co-production of the PBS American Playhouse features Victor Love as Bigger Thomas in this adaptation of the Richard Wright landmark novel. With Matt Dillon, Elizabeth McGovern and Oprah Winfrey.
VHS: S05330. $29.95.
Jerold Freeman, USA, 1986, 112 mins.

New Jack City
A drug lord is pursued by an interracial police duo in this violent drama. Wesley Snipes portrays the drug dealer and the "Salt and Pepper" team on his trail are Ice-T and Judd Nelson. The plot is simple but the acting top notch. In addition, the supporting cast includes Mario Van Peebles and *Saturday Night Live* alumnus Chris Rock (*CB4*).
VHS: $21405. $19.98.
Laser: LD74739. $29.95.
Mario Van Peebles, USA, 1991, 101 mins.

Nothing But a Man
An impressive collaboration between director Michael Roemer (*The Plot against Harry* and cinematographer and writer Robert Young (*The Ballad of Gregorio Cortez*) about racial attitudes in the 1960s South. Ivan Dixon plays a dignified railroad worker whose desire to lead a normal life with a beautiful schoolteacher (jazz virtuoso Abbey Lincoln) is unhinged by racial politics and discrimination. The Motown soundtrack features Stevie Wonder, Mary Wells and Martha and the Vandellas. With Julius Harris, Gloria Foster, Martin Priest, Leonard Parker, Yaphet Kotto and Stanley Greene.
VHS: $20283. $19.95.
Laser: LD74888. $39.95.
Michael Roemer, USA, 1964, 92 mins.

One False Move
A small masterpiece, this B-movie thriller features wonderful performances by Bill Paxton and Cynda Williams. A trio of criminals stage a grotesque gangland murder and travel to Arkansas, unaware the local sheriff and two L.A. cops await them. The two principal characters confront their pasts. With Michael Beach, Earl Beach, Jim Metzler and Billy Bob Thornton, who co-wrote the screenplay.
VHS: $17057. $19.95.
Laser: LD71541. $34.95.
Carl Franklin, USA, 1991, 103 mins.

Penitentiary III
While still exciting, this third part of the series begins to make the audience yearn for an early release for "Too Sweet". Less a social commentary than a "Rocky in Prison", this film still offers a good deal of action. Leon Isaac Kennedy returns.
VHS: $21466. $14.98.
Jamaa Fanaka, USA, 1987, 91 mins.

A Piece of the Action
Sidney Poitier and Bill Cosby are paired in this film about two con men put to work at a community center. A police officer (James Earl Jones) blackmails the two into becoming more productive citizens. Features Denise Nicholas, Hope Clarke, and Tracy Reed.
VHS: $21434. $19.98.
Sidney Poitier, USA, 1977, 135 mins.

Poetic Justice
John Singleton's follow-up to *Boyz n the Hood* features Janet Jackson as a poet and hairdresser who is trying to cope with the senseless murder of her boyfriend. Jackson reluctantly joins a friend on a trip from South-Central Los Angeles to Oakland in a mail truck. She develops a complicated relationship with an ambitious music producer and postal delivery man (Tupac Shakur). The soundtrack includes numbers by Babyface, Tony! Toni! Tone!, Naughty by Nature and The Dogg Pound. The poetry spoken by Jackson was written by Maya Angelou. With Tyra Ferrell, Regina King and Joe Torry.
VHS: $20221. $19.95.
Laser: LD72331. $34.95.
John Singleton, USA, 1993, 109 mins.

Rage in Harlem
Robin Givens heats up the screen in this action-packed criminal escapade based on a novel by Chester Himes, the author of *Cotton Comes to Harlem*. Givens plays a slick country woman hiding out in the big city with a sizable amount of gold. Actor Bill Duke directs a fine ensemble cast that includes Forest Whitaker, Gregory Hines, Zakes Mokae and Danny Glover as a Harlem gangster known as Easy Money. Bullets fly. Men die. And Givens looks good as the lady in red.
VHS: S15133. $19.98.
Laser: LD71673. $29.95.
Bill Duke, USA, 1991, 90 mins.

River Niger
An adaptation of the Broadway play about the dynamics of an African-American family coping with ghetto life. With James Earl Jones, Louis Gossett Jr. and Cicely Tyson.
VHS: $18830. $29.95.
Krishna Shah, USA, 1976, 105 mins.

Royal Federal Blues— The Black Civil War Soldiers
This award-winning documentary shows the history of African-American soldiers in the Civil War, from their induction into the Union Army all the way to ferocious battlegrounds that marked the divide between freedom and slavery. 45 mins.
VHS: $22048. $19.98.

Sankofa
This remarkable, independently-made film by African-American filmmaker Haile Gerima (*Bush Mama, Harvest: 3000 Years*) has become a quiet boxoffice sensation entirely by word-of-mouth. *Sankofa* is a Ghanaian word that means returning to the past in order to go forward. Gerima uses this concept to transport a fashion model who is possessed by lingering spirits in the Cape Coast Castle to a sugar plantation where she suffers constant abuse as a slave. *Sankofa is an attempt to heal the psychic legacy of slavery and to address those in the African Diaspora who neglect their own history.* "Engrossing and provocative." (*New York Times*).
VHS: $25625. $64.95.
Haile Gerima, USA/Ghana, 1993, 125 mins.

Sky Is Gray
Based on the short story by Ernest Gaines, and starring Olivia Cole, James Bond III and Cleavon Little. From The American Short Story series.
VHS: S01962. $24.95.
Charles Fuller, USA, 52 mins.

Small Time
This prison drama portrays the gritty reality of doing time. If you do "small time" it can make all the difference. Your life could depend on it. Crude and harsh, this film catches the traumatizing environment which over one million Americans call home.
VHS: $20713. $69.95.
Norman Loftis, USA, 1991, 88 mins.

South Central
Oliver Stone executive produced this debut work by Steve Anderson about the Los Angeles neighborhood, overrun by Los Angeles gangs. This film tracks one young man's odyssey from gang member to adopting a life of hope and fulfillment. With Glenn Plummer, Carl Lumbly and Byron Keith Minns. "Uncompromising and authentic" (Roger Ebert).
VHS: $17890. $14.98.
Laser: LD71837. $29.98.
Steve Anderson, USA, 1992, 99 mins.

Stir Crazy
Richard Pryor and Gene Wilder team up again in this comedy about two men convicted of a robbery they didn't commit. They wind up involved with psychotic prisoners, tough guards and an irritable warden. One of the top grossing films of 1980.
VHS: $21440. $14.95.
Sidney Poitier, USA, 1980, 111 mins.

Straight Out of Brooklyn
Dennis Brown has been raised in the projects of Brooklyn—entrapped in a world of desperation, drugs and danger. His parents tell him to study hard, go to college and be patient, but Dennis can't wait any longer. He plans a robbery that'll take them out of Brooklyn forever, only now the neighborhood threatens to close in on him before he can escape. An astonishing tale of struggle and achievement from 19-year-old director Matty Rich. "A strong film...honest and effective...the truth is there and it echoes long after the film is over" (Roger Ebert).
VHS: $15274. $19.98.
Laser: LD75134. $24.98.
Matty Rich, USA, 1991, 83 mins.

Strapped
A gritty urban thriller centering on the character of Diquan. Desperate to free his pregnant girlfriend, who's in jail for dealing drugs, Diquan decides to play the dangerous double game of becoming a police informant and dealing guns at the same time. When the gun dealer finds out Diquan's an informant, he's "strapped". A hard-hitting, compelling film from Forest Whitaker which won the Best First Feature award at the Toronto Film Festival. With Bokeem Woodbine, Kia Joy Goodwin and Michael Biehn.
VHS: $20485. $19.98.
Laser: LD75266. $34.98.
Forest Whitaker, USA, 1993, 102 mins.

Street Wars
Jamaa Fanaka (*Penitentiary*) directs this tale about a violent struggle for power in the inner city. A high school student at an elite military school decides to avenge the murder of his drug lord brother and take over the business. He vows to make the business legitimate—eventually.
VHS: $21392. $89.95.
Jamaa Fanaka, USA, 1994, 90 mins.

Sweet Perfection
The low-budget, debut film of Chicago director Darryl Roberts (*How U Like Me Now?*) was released theatrically as *The Perfect Model*, a shrewd, well-meaning romantic comedy about a black film star who returns to his former neighborhood and falls for the beautiful and fiercely independent sister of a young boy requiring a father figure. With Stoney Jackson, Liza Cruzat and basketball star Reggie Theus.
VHS: $18835. $19.95.
Daryll Roberts, USA, 1989, 90 mins.

Talkin' Dirty After Dark
Martin Lawrence is cast as a struggling stand-up comedian looking for a shot at headlining at Dukies, an inner-city comedy venue. With Darryl Sivad, Renee Jones, Marvin Wright-Bey and Tiny Lister Jr. As the title implies, the on and off-stage material is definitely blue.
VHS: Out of print. For rental only.
Laser: LD72347. $39.99.
Topper Carew, USA, 1991, 89 mins.

To Sleep with Anger
Danny Glover stars as Harry Mention, a mysterious and magnetic visitor from the Deep South who comes to stay with an old friend, named Gideon (Paul Butler), in South-Central Los Angeles. Harry's effect on Gideon and his assimilated black middle-class family is both immediate and profound. He spins tales full of folklore, lucky charms and bad magic that seem exotic and ominous to these urban up-and-comers who have lost touch with the rural tradition.
VHS: $13817. $19.95.
Laser: LD72255. $35.95.
Charles Burnett, USA, 1990, 105 mins.

True Identity
Talented black British comedian Lenny Henry is cast as a struggling American actor who must resort to passing as a white hitman when he learns the secret mob past of a prominent citizen. Frank Langella orders a hit on the New York actor not knowing he has been thoroughly disguised by *Sidewalk Stories* director Charles Lane, his best buddy and a whiz at theatrical make-up. Will Henry stay white and alive long enough for him to audition for *Othello*? With J.T. Walsh, Anne-Marie Johnson, Michael McKean, Peggy Lipton and James Earl Jones as himself.
VHS: $16807. $19.99.
Charles Lane, USA, 1991, 93 mins.

Uptown Saturday Night
Sidney Poitier and Bill Cosby are cheated out of a $50,000 lottery ticket. To get the ticket back they turn to a Black gangster (Harry Belafonte) who bears a striking resemblance to Don Corleone. This comedy's supporting cast includes Lincoln Kirkpatrick, Roscoe Lee Browne, Richard Pryor, Flip Wilson and Calvin Lockhart.
VHS: $21435. $19.95.
Sidney Poitier, USA, 1974, 104 mins.

Waiting to Exhale
Whitney Houston, Angela Bassett, Lela Rochon and Loretta Devine are four African-American women who share their lives and endure a world of romantic ups and downs. Although these are intelligent, educated women, somehow they've all managed to give the best years of their lives to their husbands and boyfriends—to help the men's careers and fulfilling the men's dreams, while putting their own careers and dreams on hold. Now, as another new year approaches, these women are determined to begin this year with a passion for life that no man can take away. Based on Terry McMillan's best-selling novel, *Waiting to Exhale* is a wise, warm and hopeful film about waiting your whole life for that moment when you exhale—when you stop waiting and start actually living your life. With Gregory Hines, Dennis Haysbert, Mykelti Williamson and an uncredited Wesley Snipes.
VHS: $27534. $19.95.
Laser: LD75546. $39.99.
Forest Whitaker, USA, 1995, 124 mins.

Watermelon Man
A great early American independent film, about a bigoted white man who suddenly turns black and sees his life turned upside down. With Godfrey Cambridge, Estelle Parsons.
VHS: S04321. $59.95.
Melvin Van Peebles, USA, 1970, 97 mins.

Zora Is My Name!
A funny yet stirring drama starring Ruby Dee and Louis Gossett Jr. This is the story of Zora Neale Hurston, a Black writer and folklorist best known for her portrayals of life in the rural South of the 30's and 40's. From PBS' American Playhouse. 90 mins.
VHS: Out of print. For rental only.
Laser: LD71400. $39.95.

SPIKE LEE

Clockers
Newcomer Mekhi Phifer stars as Strike, a "clocker" (24-hour drug dealer) who hopes for advancement but finds himself caught between the police and a killer. Harvey Keitel is Rocco, an honest cop searching for the truth, while his partner (John Turturro) is just out for an easy bust. When Strike's law-abiding brother takes the rap for the murder, it's up to Strike to find the real killer and save his selfless brother. Based on Richard Price's book, this violent and suspenseful tale tells another side of the war on drugs. Produced by Martin Scorsese.
VHS: $27305. $99.95.
Laser: LD75478. $39.98.
Spike Lee, USA, 1995, 129 mins.

Crooklyn
Spike Lee's funny, uplifting look at a family in a crowded but cozy Brooklyn neighborhood in the 1970's. It's a slice of life that gets African-American life just right, catching all the humor and joy of that time and place. The great nostalgic soundtrack includes Stevie Wonder, Curtis Mayfield, and Sly and the Family Stone, as well as many others.
VHS: $22377. $19.95.
Laser: LD74603. $34.98.
Spike Lee, USA, 1994, 114 mins.

Do The Right Thing
Spike Lee's powerful, gritty film set in Brooklyn's Bedford Stuyvesant community, called "a great film" by Roger Ebert. Danny Aiello stars as the pizza parlor owner, Spike Lee himself as the delivery boy. Notable for its uncanny depiction of the community, its focus on the moral issues of racism and non-violence—a gripping experience. With Ossie Davis, Ruby Dee, Richard Edson.
VHS: $11445. $19.95.
Laser: LD70023. $39.98.
Spike Lee, USA, 1989, 120 mins.

Jungle Fever
An insightful and provocative drama from Spike Lee that examines urban angst, inter-racial romance and the drug problem in New York City. Wesley Snipes stars as a buppie architect whose physical attraction to Annabella Sciorra, his white temp-secretary, colors all areas of his life. With Ossie Davis, Ruby Dee, John Turturro, Lonette McKee, Anthony Quinn, Spike Lee and Samuel L. Jackson, who won a special award at Cannes for his performance as Snipes' drug addicted brother. Songs by Stevie Wonder.
VHS: $15412. $19.98.
Laser: LD71405. $39.98.
Spike Lee, USA, 1991, 132 mins.

Malcolm X
Spike Lee's controversial biography features an astonishing lead performance from Denzel Washington which captures Malcolm's transformation from Boston street hustler and pimp to his prison conversion and reinvention as devoted Muslim. The narrative covers Malcolm's embrace of Islam and his ascension to brilliant orator and black leader who broke with Elijah Muhammad and underwent a final moral and spiritual recovery on his pilgrimage to the Mecca. Arnold Perl, Lee and an uncredited James Baldwin adapted the screenplay. The cast includes Angela Bassett, Albert Hall, Al Freeman, Jr., Delroy Lindo and Lee. Cinematography by Ernest Dickerson. Music by Terence Blanchard.
VHS: $18855. $24.98.
Laser: Letterboxed. LD71884. $39.98.
Spike Lee, USA, 1992, 201 mins.

Mo' Better Blues
Denzel Washington stars as Bleek Gilliam, a musician who prefers to put his music before his friends and the women in his life. Spike Lee directs and co-stars as an incompetent jazz group manager with a serious gambling problem. A movie with heart and soul that has a real feel for the jazz scene in New York. With Cynda Williams, Joie Lee, Ruben Blades, John Turturro, Wesley Snipes and Robin Harris.
VHS: $13291. $19.95.
Laser: LD74604. $39.98.
Spike Lee, USA, 1990, 129 mins.

School Daze
Spike Lee produced, wrote, directed and stars in this all-black musical comedy about tensions and social divisions at a southern black university, Mission College. The issues raised are as powerful as the dance numbers. With Larry Fishburne, Joe Seneca, Ellen Holly, Ossie Davis and Tisha Campbell. From the maker of *She's Gotta Have It*.
VHS: S07676. $14.95.
Spike Lee, USA, 1988, 114 mins.

She's Gotta Have It
A brazenly comic foray into sexual politics. Tracy Camila Johns stars as Nola Darling—a beautiful, free-spirited artist who simultaneously shares three men for her pleasure, dominance and one-upmanship. Lee's acute comic perception, innovative cutting and hilarious use of montage aesthetics—where Nola's suitors slay her with opening lines and come-ons—are evidence of a stream of consciousness talent and film school sensibility. His father, Bill Lee, composed the music.
VHS: S02777. $14.98.
Laser: LD74463. $49.95.
Spike Lee, USA, 1986, 84 mins.

EARLY BLACK CINEMA

African-American Film Heritage Series I
Facets Video is releasing six historic, artistically important works that trace the origins of an indigenous black American filmmaking network, highlighted by two important films from the pioneering black filmmaker Oscar Micheaux and the brilliant Austrian-born director Edgar G. Ulmer.
Lying Lips. A late film from the gifted Oscar Micheaux examines racial and sexual repression in the story of a charismatic nightclub singer (Edna Mae Harris) unjustly incarcerated for trumped-up murder charges. With Robert Earl Jones, Carmen Newsome, Armanda Randolph and Frances Williams. Directed by Oscar Micheaux, USA, 1939, 60 mins.
VHS: S00786. $24.95.
Moon over Harlem. Edgar G. Ulmer directs this unusual musical about a Harlem widow who falls for a charismatic gangster trapped by his dangerous attraction to the rackets. The cast is augmented by 20 chorus girls, a choir and a 60-piece orchestra conducted by Donald Heywood. With the superb jazz clarinetist Sidney Bechet, his wife, Marieluise, Bud Harris, Cora Green and Izinetta Wilcois. Screenplay by Sherle Castle. Directed by Edgar G. Ulmer, USA, 1939, 67 mins.
VHS: S02163. $24.95.
Black King. Made by an independent white company, *Black King* concerns an amoral con man who fashions a "Back to Africa" movement as a pretext for an elaborate pyramid scheme. Also known as *Harlem Hot Shot*, the film is read by most as a vigorous satire of Marcus Garvey, the Jamaican-born scholar and charismatic leader of a controversial pro-African movement in the 20s and 30s. With A.B. Comathiere, Vivian Baker and Knolly Mitchell. Screenplay by Donald Heywood. Directed by "Bud" Pollard, USA, 1932, 70 mins.
VHS: S07041. $24.95.

Girl from Chicago. Oscar Micheaux's sinister crime melodrama concerns Alonzo Smith (Carl Mahon), a young secret service agent romantically involved with Norma (Starr Calloway), a young Mississippi schoolteacher. The action shifts to New York, where Alonzo, agreeing to intervene for Norma's friend, is accused of murder. With Eunice Brooks, Frank Wilson and Minta Cato. Directed by Oscar Micheaux, USA, 1932, 69 mins.
VHS: S07054. $24.95.

Blood of Jesus. Spencer Williams directed this absorbing work about the scandal that envelops a small rural community when a weak husband accidentally shoots his religious wife, unleashing his own tormented faith and quest for redemption. With Williams, Cathryn Caviness, Heavenly Choir and Juanita Riley. Directed by Spencer Williams, Jr., USA, 1941, 50 mins.
VHS: S07042. $24.95.

Scar of Shame. A powerful silent film about race and class issues. The movie shows the social fissures created by the ill-matched marriage of a black concert pianist who's ashamed of his poor, lower-class wife, whom he conceals from his socially conscious mother. With Harry Henderson, Lucia Lynn Moses, Norman John Stone and Ann Kennedy. The first film produced by the Philadelphia-based Colored Players Film Corp. Directed by Frank Peregini, USA, 1927, 70 mins.
VHS: S15388. $24.95. African-American Film Heritage Series, Complete Set.
All 12 titles.
VHS: S23222. $249.95.
African-American Film Heritage Series I. Complete Set.
VHS: S18845. $129.95.

African-American Film Heritage Series II

Six films which continue to represent the largely unknown, early African-American film tradition.
Song of Freedom. One of Paul Robeson's great roles as an English dockhand who returns to Africa to discover his roots. Features Robeson singing many great songs. England, 1936, 70 mins.
VHS: S01231. $24.95.
Native Son. Richard Wright's landmark novel stars the author himself as Bigger Thomas, the black chauffeur who unintentionally kills a white woman. With Jean Wallace, Gloria Madison. Directed by Pierre Chenal, USA, 1950, 91 mins.
VHS: S03682. $24.95.
Go Down Death. A morality melodrama which puts a minister's reputation in question, bringing him to the brink of Heaven and Hell. With Myra D. Hemmings, Samuel L. Jones. Directed by Spencer Williams, USA, 1944, 50 mins.
VHS: S07043. $24.95.
Duke Is Tops. Lena Horne made one of her earliest film appearances in this all-black musical about a girl who attempts to make it to the big-time while her boyfriend joins a travelling medicine show. With Ralph Cooper, Basin St. Boys, Neck Holmes. Directed by William Nolte, USA, 1938, 80 mins.
VHS: S07047. $24.95.
Harlem Rides the Range. A black-cast western musical with Herb Jeffries struggling to keep the villain (Lucius Brooks) from getting control of a radium mine that belongs to his girl friend's father. USA, 1939.
VHS: S07053. $24.95.
Body and Soul. "An extremely rare film—featuring the first screen appearance by Paul Robeson. Robeson plays the dual role of a preacher who preys on the people and the heroine, and of his brother, a good man. The film, one of the productions of Oscar Micheaux, ran into trouble with the New York censors, and had to change the preacher's role so that he is first a preacher, then detective, and finally an upstanding bourgeois future husband for the heroine, who awakens from her nightmare experience to a happy ending" (Frame By Frame: A Black Filmography). Directed by Oscar Micheaux, USA, 1924.
VHS: S10260. $24.95.
African-American Film Heritage Series II, Set. The complete six-volume series at a special price.
VHS: S20768. $129.95.

The Beulah Show, Vol. 1

This tape contains two episodes of the 50's television series about the lovable "Beulah". Hattie McDaniel, the originator of the role on radio, makes an appearance in the first episode. Ernest Whitman (Green Pastures, Cabin in the Sky) also appears. The second feature features Ethel Waters (Cabin in the Sky, Member of the Wedding) as Beulah. Special guest appearances by Butterfly McQueen and Dooley Wilson. USA, 1951, 60 mins.
VHS: S21389. $24.95.

The Beulah Show, Vol. 2

Louise Beavers appears as the last of the "Beulah"s. She portrays a maid who seems to run the household. The role is an early appearance of African-American film stereotypes on television. Beavers, as well as her predecessors Ethel Waters and Hattie McDaniel, were such solid character actors that the show remains enjoyable today. Ernest Whitman also appears. USA, 1951, 115 mins.
VHS: S21390. $24.95.

Beware

A young man returns to his alma mater, Ware College, to save it from its unscrupulous namesake Benjamin Ware III. In the process he sweeps his old college sweetheart off her feet. The film is a well-made, well-acted musical drama. Features Louis Jordan, Frank Wilson, Emory Richardson and Valerie Black.
VHS: S21419. $24.95.
Bud Pollard, USA, 1946, 60 mins.

The Big Timers

An all-Black cast film featuring "Moms" Mabley and Stepin Fetchit. Bud Pollard, USA.
VHS: S21411. $24.95.

Black Artists Short Subjects, Volume One

These shorts subjects are from the 1940's and are dedicated to important African-Americans in sports, entertainment and industry.
VHS: S21425. $29.95.

Black Artists Short Subjects, Volume Two

Stepin Fetchit, Duke Ellington, Billie Holiday, Cab Calloway, Fester Young and Barney Kessel are all featured in this collection of musical and comedy short films.
VHS: S21426. $29.95.

Black Artists Short Subjects, Volume Three

Spencer Williams, Lena Horne, Teddy Wilson, Fats Waller and Ethel Waters are just some of the important African-American figures who are seen in this collection of comic and musical short subjects.
VHS: S21427. $29.95.

Boardinghouse Blues

Tenant troubles in a show-business boarding house are an excuse for this musical review film notable for its guest appearances by Lucky Millinder's band, Bull Moose Jackson, Una Mae Carlisle and Stump and Stumpy. With Dusty Fletcher, Jackie Moms Mabley.
VHS: S07044. $34.95.
Josh Binney, USA, 1948, 90 mins.

Boy! What a Girl!

All-black cast musical the plot of which revolves around two would-be-producers who are offered half the financing for a show provided they get the other half. With Tim Moore, Elwood Smith, Duke Williams, Al Jackson, Sheila Guyse.
VHS: S07045. $34.95.
Arthur Leonard, USA, 1945, 60 mins.

Broken Strings

A Black cast musical drama concerning a classical violinist who injures his fingers and encourages his son to carry on; however, the son likes swing a lot more than classical music. With Clarence Muse, Cyril Lewis, William Washington, Tommie More.
VHS: S07051. $34.95.
Bernard B. Ray, USA, 1940, 50 mins.

Bronze Buckaroo

Filmed at a Black dude ranch in California, this film is a musical western. "Bob Blake", the hero, and his sidekick, "Dusty", set out to apprehend the men responsible for the death of Blake's father. Features Herbert Jeffries, Lucius Brooks, Artie Young and Flournoy E. Miller.
VHS: S21415. $24.95.
Richard C. Kahn, USA, 1939, 57 mins.

Burlesque in Harlem

The great African-American comedian Pigmeat Markham stars in this dance/musical burlesque. An all-Black cast of dancers, strippers and musicians back him up. 60 mins.
VHS: S21391. $24.95.

Carmen Jones

Dorothy Dandridge plays Carmen, a woman caught between two men and her own unorthodox nature. The men, one a pretty boy and the other a tough sergeant, are portrayed by Harry Belafonte and Brock Peters. Dandridge lures Joe (Belafonte) into deserting from the army and then leaves him for the two-fisted Sgt. Brown (Peters). The supporting cast is every bit as impressive as the main actors and includes Pearl Bailey, Joe Adams and Diahann Carroll in her first film role. Dandridge became the first African-American nominated for a Best Actress Academy Award. The film won a Golden Globe for Best Musical/Comedy in 1955.
VHS: S21385. $19.98.
Otto Preminger, USA, 1954, 105 mins.

Devil's Daughter

A girl returns to take over her late father's Jamaican plantation, where she confronts her jealous half-sister, a crooked overseer and voodoo rituals. Comedy relief from an American servant who believes his soul is embodied in a pig. With Nina Mae McKinney, Jack Carter, Ida James.
VHS: S07046. $34.95.
Laser: CLV. LD71981. $29.98.
Arthur Leonard, USA, 1939, 60 mins.

Dirty Gertie from Harlem

A two-timing showgirl, on the run, takes work at an island hotel, where she wins the heart of the hotel owner, until her vengeful ex-boyfriend catches up with her. With Francine Everett, Don Wilson, Katherine Moore.
VHS: S07048. $34.95.
Spencer Williams, USA, 1946, 60 mins.

Double Deal

An all-Black cast drama with a moralistic message. Two men are rivals for the same girl, and one, a gangster, robs a jewelry store, double-crosses his boss, and implicates the honest rival. With Monte Hawley, Jeni Le Gon, Edward Thompson, Florence O'Brien.
VHS: S07049. $34.95.
Arthur Dreifuss, USA, 1939, 60 mins.

Emperor Jones

Dudley Murphy's adaptation of Eugene O'Neill's play about the personal transformation of Brutus Jones (Paul Robeson), an anonymous man catapulted from a socially insignificant train porter and escaped prisoner to the emperor of a Caribbean island. With Dudley Digges, Frank Wilson and Fredi Washington. On the same program is the documentary short, Paul Robeson: Tribute to an Artist, directed by Scott Turrell.
VHS: S02627. $19.95.
Dudley Murphy, USA, 1933, 72 mins.

Gang War

Two gangs go head to head over a criminal enterprise: the control of a city's juke box business. Ralph Cooper and Lawrence Criner are the competing hoods but the town isn't big enough for both of them. Features Gladys Snyder and Mantan Moreland.
VHS: S21430. $24.95.
Leo Popkin, USA, 1940, 60 mins.

Girl in Room 20

Geraldine Brock and Judy Jones star in this black-cast feature about a talented, small-town singer who discovers that the show business of New York can be no pot of gold.
VHS: S20544. $19.95.
Spencer Williams, USA, 64 mins.

God's Step Children

Oscar Micheaux's film deals with a light-skinned African-American orphan who refuses to acknowledge her race. She winds up in a convent after being disruptive in her all-Black school. Eventually she marries a dark-skinned man. A serious and moving film featuring Alice B. Russell, Carmen Newsome, Jacqueline Lewis and Ethel Moses.
VHS: S21471. $24.95.
Oscar Micheaux, USA, 1937, 65 mins.

Harlem on the Prairie

Herbert Jeffries and Mantan Moreland head the cast of this first all-Black cast western. The plot centers on gold, love and making sure the bad guys get theirs. There are also musical numbers. Features F.E. Miller and Connie Harris.
VHS: S21470. $24.95.
Sam Newfield, USA, 1938, 54 mins.

Hi-De-Ho

Cab Calloway does his song "Hi-De-Ho," with specialty numbers by the dancers and other musical routines. With Ida James and Jeni Le Gon.
VHS: S07058. $34.95.
Josh Binney, USA, 1947, 60 mins.

Jericho

An important film because of the seminal presence of Paul Robeson, who plays a convicted soldier who flees from pre-WWII France to Africa, where he lives as a desert sheik, saving his white comrades, and romancing with Princess Kouka. "How American audiences in the south must have reacted to a Negro hero, who was twice as intelligent, attractive and heroic as the white characters in the film, one can only hazard a guess," wrote Peter Noble in The Negro in Films.
VHS: S02162. $29.95.
Thornton Freeland, Great Britain, 1937, 75 mins.

Juke Joint

Bad News Johnson and July Jones arrive in the West, meet Mama Lou Holiday who takes them in as boarders after they convince her they are actors. With Spencer Williams, July Jones, Inez Newman, Melody Duncan, Katherine Moore.
VHS: S07050. $29.95.
Spencer Williams, USA, 1947, 70 mins.

Junction 88

An early all-Black musical featuring Bob Howard and Pigmeat Markham. USA, 1940, 60 mins.
VHS: S21429. $24.95.

Killer Diller

The story of a magician who does disappearing acts ties together with a variety program of musical numbers including an act by Jackie "Moms" Mabley. With Dusty Fletcher, King Cole Trio, Andy Kirk and Orchestra, and others.
VHS: S07056. $34.95.
Josh Binney, USA, 1948, 80 mins.

Look Out Sister

This film is a musical satire of westerns featuring Louis Jordan and an all-Black cast. Also features Monte Hawley (Tall, Tan and Terrific) and Suzette Harbin.
VHS: S21428. $24.95.
Bud Pollard, USA, 1948, 64 mins.

Marching On

Spencer Williams, Jr., directs this docudrama about the all-Black 25th Infantry. He shows the harsh reality of segregation but also makes it clear that the African-American soldier during World War II was a patriotic and dedicated as his white counterparts. USA.
VHS: S21410. $24.95.

Mark of the Hawk

Sidney Poitier stars as a man put on trial for murder in colonial Africa. In the beginning he sides with the liberation movement but in the end makes a speech that is positive about colonialism as a whole. The cast includes Eartha Kitt who performs "This Man Is Mine". Also featured is Juano Hernandez (Intruder in the Dust).
VHS: S21412. $24.95.
Michael Audley, Great Britain, 1958, 83 mins.

Midnight Ramble

James Avery narrates this exploration of the early black film industry. Over 500 movies were produced between 1910 and World War II that were commonly known as "race movies." Early on they tried to counteract Hollywood stereotypes. Oscar Micheaux is perhaps the best known director who tackled difficult social issues in Black America. His story and the story of late night segregated screenings, the "Midnight Rambles," are the subject of this documentary. 60 mins.
VHS: S24696. $19.95.

Midnight Shadow

John Criner and Frances Redd star in this black-cast feature about a con man who attempts to marry the daughter of a wealthy landowner to secure her dowry.
VHS: S20543. $19.95.
George Randol, USA, 1939, 54 mins.

Miracle in Harlem

A gang tries to take a piece of the action at a Harlem candy shop. The gang leader winds up dead and it appears the shop owner's daughter had a hand in the killing. A landmark all-Black gangster film featuring one of the day's biggest African-American stars, Stepin Fetchit.
VHS: S21417. $19.95.
Jack Kemp, USA, 1948, 69 mins.

Mistaken Identity

A rare look at independent African-American cinema from the 1940's. This mystery musical with an all-black cast is set against the background of a big city nightclub. With Nellie Hill and George Oliver. Includes the production number "I'm a Bangi from Ubangi." Not to be mistaken for True Identity, the recent Charles Lane comedy starring Lenny Henry. USA, 1941, 60 mins.
VHS: S16182. $29.95.

Murder in Harlem

Clarence Brooks (Harlem Rides the Range, Bronze Buckaroo) stars in this story of a night watchman accused of murder. When he finds the body of a white woman in the chemical factory he guards, he must prove his innocence in court. Also stars Laura Bowman, Dorothy Van Engle, Andrew Bishop and Alec Lovejoy. A provocative murder mystery from the director of Girl from Chicago and Lying Lips.
VHS: S21388. $24.95.
Oscar Micheaux, USA, 1935, 102 mins.

Murder on Lennox Ave

An all-Black cast is featured in this gangster film. Mamie Smith appears in one of the musical numbers and is supported by a cast that includes Alec Lovejoy and Edna Mae Harris.
VHS: S21413. $24.95.
Arthur Dreifuss, USA, 1941, 65 mins.

Murder with Music

A musical drama with an all-Black cast. Bob Howard stars as a reporter who goes underground to crack the story of a notorious gangster. Also with Nellie Hill and the music of Noble Sissle.
VHS: S12318. $24.95.
George P. Quigley, USA, 1945, 57 mins.

Paradise in Harlem

Frank Wilson, Mamie Smith, Juanita (Bloody Mary) Hall and Edna Mae Harris star in this all-black musical.
VHS: S08458. $29.95.
Joseph Seiden, USA, 1939, 83 mins.

Rare Black Short Subjects

A collection of rare short-films featuring African-Americans. It includes The Negro in Sports, Entertainment and Industry; The All American Newsreel and Kilroy Was Here.
VHS: S15479. $29.95.

Reet, Petite and Gone

Louis Jourdan and His Tympany Five are featured in this drama about the search for a girl whose measurements fit those prescribed in the will of the hero's uncle. With June Richmond, Lorenzo Tucker, Milton Woods.
VHS: S10059. $29.95.
William Forest Crouch, USA, 1947, 65 mins.

Sanders of the River

Alexander Korda produced this, one of the best films starring the great Paul Robeson, in the story of a British colonialist commissioner who maintains peace with the West African chieftain (Robeson) until a group of white slave traders start trouble.
VHS: S02765. $19.98.
Laser: LD75251. $34.95.
Zoltan Korda, Great Britain, 1935, 85 mins.

Scar of Shame

This early "race movie" depicts turmoil within the black community, around the issues of middle class aspirations and lower class stigma. A composer marries a woman to save her from the dance halls and gunfights of the ghetto. This silent film was filmed in Philadelphia by a mixed race production, a black producer and a white director. The short experimental musical film Sissle and Blake, with Noble Sissle and Eubie Blake, is also included. From the Origins of American Films series, a joint project of the Library of Congress and Smithsonian Video.
VHS: S21266. $34.95.
Frank Peregini, USA, 1927, 90 mins.

Sepia Cinderella

One of the best all-Black cast musicals. The musical romance of a songwriter and singer who, after trials and tribulations, get back together to the tune of his "Cinderella Song." Freddie Bartholomew makes a cameo appearance as himself. Original tinted ending.
VHS: S06913. $29.95.
Arthur Leonard, USA, 1947, 67 mins.

Son of Ingagi

An all-Black cast in one of the rarest of horror films; Zack Williams plays a detective in this "African" style melodrama about hidden gold, murder and theft, with a happy ending. With Laura Bowman, Spencer Williams.
VHS: S06912. $34.95.
Richard C. Kahn, USA, 1940, 70 mins.

Spirit of Youth

Joe Louis plays Joe Thomas, a poor black fighter who climbs to the top of the boxing world. With Mantan Moreland, Clarence Muse, Edna Mae Harris.
VHS: S07059. $34.95.
Harry Fraser, USA, 1937, 70 mins.

Sunday Sinners

A musical feature with lyrics and music by Donald Heywood, writer and composer, who was prominently associated with independent black films from 1932 onwards. With Mamie Smith, Alec Lovejoy, Edna Mae Harris.
VHS: S07055. $34.95.
Arthur Dreifuss, USA, 1941, 65 mins.

Swing

Much of this all-black cast musical directed by Oscar Micheaux is built around the music which is performed from Alabama to Harlem, with the Tyler Twins performing the dance numbers, and also featuring Cora Green, Hazel Diaz, Carmen Newsome, Alec Lovejoy.
VHS: S07057. $34.95.
Oscar Micheaux, USA, 1938, 80 mins.

Tall, Tan and Terrific

Mantan Moreland (Lucky Ghost) portrays a detective out to clear the name of a Harlem club owner, "Handsome Harry", (Monte Hawley) who is accused of murder. Francine Everett stars as "Miss Tall", a waitress at the club and the object of Harry's affections.
VHS: S21416. $24.95.
Bud Pollard, USA, 1946, 60 mins.

Ten Minutes to Live

A film by Oscar Micheaux, a mystery-musical built around a threatening note which gives the heroine only "ten minutes to live." Song and dance numbers, a comedy routine, with Bill Heywood as the nightclub M.C.
VHS: S05293. $39.95.
Oscar Micheaux, USA, 1932, 65 mins.

That's Black Entertainment
The legendary collection of all-black-cast films discovered only recently in Tyler, Texas, "the missing link of American cinema history," presented in a tribute hosted by director William Greaves. This compilation of rare and historic movie footage from the Tyler collection includes appearances by Paul Robeson, Lena Horne (in her first film, *Boogie Woogie Dream*), Sammy Davis Jr., Nat King Cole, Bessie Smith, Cab Calloway, Spencer Williams, Eubie Blake, Ethel Waters, Cicely Tyson, Jeffrey Holder, Stepin Fetchit.
VHS: $11485. $29.95.

Two-Gun Man from Harlem
A bogus preacher from Harlem travels to the old west. As you might suspect from the title, he brings along a couple of guns just in case. Features Herbert Jeffries, Marguerite Whitten and Mantan Moreland.
VHS: $21414. $24.95.
Richard C. Kahn, USA, 1938, 60 mins.

Veiled Aristocrats
Lorenzo Tucker (the "Black Valentino") stars in this story of a lawyer who returns home to find that his light-skinned sister is about to marry a dark-skinned man. His mother has picked a more suitable candidate. Director Oscar Micheaux once again tackles the issue of dark-skinned versus light-skinned African-Americans. Features Laura Bowman.
VHS: $21468. $24.95.
Oscar Micheaux, USA, 1932, 50 mins.

Way Down South
Bobby Breen portrays a young white man who inherits his father's plantation. He battles with a vicious overseer who is appointed caretaker of the land. Clarence Muse stars as "Uncle Caton" in this melodrama which also features musical numbers. The script was co-written by Clarence Muse and Langston Hughes.
VHS: $21431. $24.95.
Bernard Vorhaus, USA, 1939, 62 mins.

Within Our Gates
This is the earliest American feature by an African-American. It tells the story of an African-American woman who seeks a white patron for a school. This film confronts racism directly with depictions of lynching and white on black rape in a plot that may be seen as a response to D.W. Griffith's *Birth of a Nation*. From the *Origins of American Films* series, a joint project of the Library of Congress and Smithsonian Video.
VHS: $21262. $34.95.
Oscar Micheaux, USA, 1919

AFRICAN-AMERICAN ISSUES

African Story Magic
Brock Peters narrates the tale about a young child's odyssey from urban life to discover the power and wonder of ancient African folklore and ritual. 27 mins.
VHS: $17765. $12.98.

Afro-Classic Folk Tales, Vol. I
This collection of Afro-centered folk tales will promote positive self-affirming values among all children. Storyteller Sybil Destu tells two traditional folk tales, about the spider Anansi and about a tiger. The tales are animated. 30 mins.
VHS: $20620. $29.95.

Afro-Classic Folk Tales, Vol. II
This second installment of *Afro-Classic Folk Tales* includes a Brer Rabbit and Woodpecker cartoon, as well as an old African tale told by puppets. 30 mins.
VHS: $20621. $29.95.

Afro-Classic Mother Goose
In this collection the favorite tales of Mother Goose find new expressiveness with an Afro-centric twist. Playtime rhymes are updated in this fresh look at childhood stories. 30 mins.
VHS: $20622. $29.95.

Alice Walker
Pulitzer Prize winner Alice Walker is most famous for novels like *The Color Purple*. In this video she reads passages from that novel, along with *Revolutionary Petunias and Other Poems, Horses Make a Landscape Look More Beautiful* and *The Temple of My Familiar*. It was recorded on January 9, 1989, in Los Angeles, but the interview was conducted by Evelyn White at Walker's Northern California home. From the *Lannan Literary Videos* series. 60 mins.
VHS: $27121. $19.95.

Amiri Baraka
A poet, playwright, novelist, essayist and activist, Amiri Baraka (nee LeRoi Jones) has long championed Black rights. He was instrumental in founding the Congress of African People. On this video he reads works from *Boptrees* and unpublished manuscripts in Los Angeles on February 11, 1991. Baraka then speaks with Lewis MacAdams. From the *Lannan Literary Videos* series. 60 mins.
VHS: $27133. $19.95.

Amos 'n' Andy: Anatomy of a Controversy
This is the first authorized, in-depth look at the landmark, controversial, black comedy team. On top of hilarious clips from the Amos n' Andy TV series and interviews with Redd Foxx, Marla Gibbs and others, find additional footage never before seen on television.
VHS: $15679. $39.95.

Arthur Ashe: Citizen of the World
A moving portrait of a champion in tennis and in life, the late Arthur Ashe. 59 mins.
VHS: $23444. $19.98.

The Assassination of Dr. Martin Luther King, Jr.
This expose considers the clandestine activities of the government, the counterintelligence campaigns of the FBI to discredit King and the civil rights movement, private communications with Lyndon Johnson's top aides, and the final days of King's life. The film uses key FBI files and other government records that have only recently been made public, including the FBI's unsettling request that King take his own life. 90 mins.
VHS: $18512. $59.98.

Autobiography of Miss Jane Pittman
Made for TV tour-de-force for Cicely Tyson, who plays a 110-year-old former slave recalling her life from the Civil War through the civil rights movement. Winner of nine Emmy Awards.
VHS: $00076. $19.95.
John Korty, USA, 1974, 106 mins.

Benjamin E. Mays: Mentor of Martin Luther King, Jr.
This famous author, scholar and philosopher was president of Morehouse College for 27 years. His important influence as an educator and community member was felt by many, including Martin Luther King Jr. and former President Jimmy Carter. In this documentary the lasting legacy of this great role model is finally revealed.
VHS: $20746. $19.95.
Rex Barnett, USA, 20 mins.

Benjamin O. Davis, Jr.: American
A biography of General Davis, the first 20th century African-American graduate from West Point, who founded the legendary Tuskegee Airmen, the elite World War II unit of black aviators who distinguished themselves during combat. 60 mins.
VHS: $18445. $19.95.

Best of Nightline
Louis Farrakhan. 30 mins.
VHS: $14029. $14.98.

Betye and Alison Saar
African-American, mother and daughter artists Betye and Alison Saar are the focus of this tape. Betye is a mixed media artist frequently using "found" objects in her art. Alison is a sculptor whose work is done largely in wood. USA, 30 mins.
VHS: $21456. $49.95.

The Black Americans of Achievement
This collection studies the sacrifices and achievements of 20th century American heroes, including Booker T. Washington, Colin Powell, Martin Luther King Jr., Jackie Robinson, and Malcolm X. "Excellent archival footage and photographs, interviews with historians and family members… paint a lively portrait of the subject and their achievements" (*Video Librarian*).
Booker T. Washington. 30 mins.
VHS: $17383. $39.95.
Colin Powell. 30 mins.
VHS: $17384. $39.95.
Dr. Martin Luther King, Jr. 30 mins.
VHS: $17385. $39.95.
Frederick Douglass. 30 mins.
VHS: $17386. $39.95.
George Washington Carver. 30 mins.
VHS: $17387. $39.95.
Harriet Tubman. 30 mins.
VHS: $17388. $39.95.
Jackie Robinson. 30 mins.
VHS: $17389. $39.95.
Jesse Jackson. 30 mins.
VHS: $17390. $39.95.
Madam C.J. Walker. 30 mins.
VHS: $17391. $39.95.
Malcolm X. 30 mins.
VHS: $17392. $39.95.
Sojourner Truth. 30 mins.
VHS: $17393. $39.95.
Thurgood Marshall. 30 mins.
VHS: $17394. $39.95.
The Black Americans of Achievement: Boxed Set. 360 mins.
VHS: $17395. $479.40.

Black Americans of Achievement Collection #2
Artists, athletes, scholars and explorers are all people who take risks in order to stretch the limits accepted by ordinary folks. Each of these 30-minute tapes features an African-American whose accomplishments are extraordinary.
Muhammad Ali. He boxed his way to an Olympic gold medal and was the first man to win three world championships.
VHS: $24098. $39.95.
Marcus Garvey. This charismatic leader was tremendously influential with his nationalist doctrine supporting racial purity and separatism.
VHS: $24099. $39.95.
James Baldwin. American novelist, essayist and early civil rights leader, Baldwin is acclaimed for his works *Go Tell It on the Mountain, Nobody Knows My Name* and *Another Country*.
VHS: $24100. $39.95.
Matthew Henson. Besides the Eskimos, this man was the only other person of color to accompany Robert E. Peary to the North Pole.
VHS: $24101. $39.95.
Jesse Owens. As a four-time Olympic gold medal winner, Owens' triumph discredited Hitler's fantasy of Aryan superiority during the 1936 Berlin Olympics.
VHS: $24102. $39.95.
Alice Walker. A Pulitzer Prize winner for her novel *The Color Purple*, this prolific author was also a feminist and civil rights activist.
VHS: $24103. $39.95.
W.E.B. Du Bois. Beginning with his role as a founder of the National Association for the Advancement of Colored People, Du Bois remained a key figure in the civil rights movement for over 50 years.
VHS: $24104. $39.95.
Mary McLeod Bethune. A pioneer in education, she helped create the Bethune-Cookman College in 1931.
VHS: $24105. $39.95.

Langston Hughes. This "Poet Laureate of Harlem" was also a noted journalist, dramatist and winner of the Harmon Gold Medal.
VHS: $24106. $39.95.
Elijah Muhammad. During his leadership, the African-American Muslim religious movement thrived and gained national recognition.
VHS: $24107. $39.95.
Black Americans of Achievement Collection # 2, Set of Ten Videos.
VHS: $24108. $399.50.

The Black Athlete
This program chronicles the rise of blacks in professional sports. Features O.J. Simpson, Jesse Owens, Kareem-Abdul Jabbar, Arthur Ashe, Edwin Moses, Lee Elder and many more. With provocative commentary by James A. Michener. 60 mins.
VHS: $16564. $19.95.

Black Brigade
Billy Dee Williams and Richard Pryor star in this World War II film. They are part of an all-Black unit, dropped behind Nazi lines on a sabotage mission, and who are not expected to return. Features Stephen Boyd. USA, 1969, 90 mins.
VHS: $21438. $14.95.

Black History: Lost, Stolen or Strayed
Bill Cosby hosts this examination of the accuracy of the ways in which American historians have traditionally documented significant historical achievements by Black Americans. 60 mins.
VHS: $14604. $19.95.

The Black Military Experience
This interesting collection of shorts about black military life includes *The Negro Soldier, The Navy Steward,* and *The Negro Sailor*.
VHS: $15480. $29.95.

Black Panthers: Huey Newton
A film documentary of the "Free Huey Newton" rally in California, with the speakers including Eldridge Cleaver, James Foreman, Bobby Seale, H. Rap Brown, Stokely Carmichael, and Bob Avakian. Includes the short *Black Panther Newsreel*, featuring interviews with Huey Newton in the Alameda County Jail. 1968, 53 mins.
VHS: $03358. $39.95.

Black Power in America: Myth or Reality?
A survey of some of the changes in American society since the civil rights movement of the 60's, *Black Power in America* opens with a focus on Black Americans like Mayor Tom Bradley of Los Angeles and Franklin Thomas of the Ford Foundation by looking at men who have achieved power and influence difficult to attain in the past, looks at contemporary politics, and at a wide range of events with provocative insights into Black America.
VHS: $10089. $129.95.
William Greaves, USA, 1988

Black Profiles
The lives of famous African-Americans serve as the inspiration for this documentary. Paul Lawrence Dunbar, Booker T. Washington, Dr. George Carver, and Dr. Martin Luther King are all covered in this inspirational and educational work.
VHS: $20625. $29.95.

Black Studies: Then and Now
This examination of African-American culture traces struggles and accomplishments through a vast historical prism, from the end of slavery to the political and social movements led by Dr. Martin Luther King Jr. to the celebrations of Kwanzaa, June tenth and other holidays. Designed for children in grades 4-6.
Black Heritage Holidays. An African-American family honors its cultural heritage by observing Kwanzaa, a holiday involving elaborate table decorations and the dispensing of gifts to award the children's accomplishments. 20 mins.
VHS: $19988. $65.95.
Dr. Martin Luther King, Jr. The life and legacy of Dr. King are examined. The topics explored include the Supreme Court decision outlawing school desegregation, the Montgomery Bus Boycott and the march to Selma. 15 mins.
VHS: $19987. $65.95.
Rebels and Abolitionists. A historical examination of the cruel legacy of slavery and its impact on African-American freedom, this program studies its pre-Civil War roots to the Emancipation Proclamation to the surrender of Confederate troops at Appomattox. 14 mins.
VHS: $19986. $65.95.
Slavery and Plantation Life. This video presents a subjective view of the experiences of being a slave, what it means and feels to be captured, traded and treated as property. The program also studies the origins of slavery. 14 mins.
VHS: $19985. $65.95.
Black Studies: Then and Now, Set.
VHS: $19989. $229.00.

Booker
Levar Burton plays the young Booker T. Washington. He saw the demise of slavery and the degradations of the Civil War. Despite all these hardships, he founded the respected Tuskegee Institute, an institution of higher learning for African-Americans. It's a perfect film for kids as it shows this struggle from the viewpoint of the young Booker. Shelley Duvall and Judge Reinhold are also featured. 58 mins.
VHS: $27620. $29.95.

Booker T. Washington's Tuskegee America
Hugh Downs hosts this look at the fascinating life of a man born a slave. Washington realized the power of education and founded the institute that still bears his name. 24 mins.
VHS: $23558. $49.95.
Laser: LD74786. $99.95.

Booker T. Washington: The Life and the Legacy
A candid, interesting docu-drama on the highly controversial leader of Black America at the turn of the century. His policies of Black economic self-reliance and political accommodation were debated nationwide. With Maurice Woods as Booker T. Washington.
VHS: $03419. $79.95.
William Greaves, USA, 1986, 30 mins.

Charles Drew: Determined to Succeed
This documentary reveals the pioneering work undertaken by African-American research scientist Charles Drew. He formulated the technique of using blood plasma for blood transfusions, saving countless lives in World War II. It's a legacy that changed medicine forever. 30 mins.
VHS: $22416. $19.95.

Charlotte Forten's Mission Half Slave, Half Free Part 2
A compelling story of one woman's determination during the struggle for racial liberation to prove to President Lincoln that the black man is equal to the white man. Starring Melba Moore, Ned Beatty, Moses Gunn and Glynn Turman. 1985, 120 mins.
VHS: $14609. $59.95.

Colin Powell: A Soldier's Campaign
This biographical documentary from A&E tells the story of the highly popular and charismatic general. Born to immigrant parents, he grew up in the Bronx and rose through the ranks in the military to lead the Allied forces in the Gulf War. Includes interviews with his family and friends as well as rare archival footage.
VHS: $27212. $19.95.
Bill Harris, USA, 1995, 50 mins.

Conversation with Gwendolyn Brooks
Pulitzer Prize-winning poet Gwendolyn Brooks, whose works eloquently portrayed scenes of city life and the impact of poverty and neglect in the ghetto, talks about the influences of her family life and her unique contribution to American letters. Produced by the Library of Congress. 28 mins.
VHS: $08130. $49.95.

Conversation with Richard Wilbur
Richard Wilbur, Pulitzer Prize-winning poet, reads some of his favorite poems and reminiscences about his life and work with Grace Cavalieri, poet and host of the national radio series, *The Poet and the Poem*. Produced by the Library of Congress. 28 mins.
VHS: $08131. $29.95.

The Court-Martial of Jackie Robinson
After experiencing racism on his army base, Jackie Robinson wages his own battle against bigotry. He refuses to move to a seat at the back of an Army bus, and because of this he is court-martialed for insubordination. The nightmarish ordeal that followed that action helped to shape the strong and defiant character of a true American hero.
VHS: $13556. $79.98.
Larry Peerce, USA, 1990, 93 mins.

The Cultural Philosophy of Paul Robeson
The open cultural philosophy of Paul Robeson is revealed through writer Sterling Stuckey. Robeson's research into African and world cultures led to his belief that Black Americans suffer from an inferiority complex, nurtured by white oppression. Includes film footage from Robeson's acting and singing career.
VHS: $21905. $19.95.
Rex Barnett, USA, 1994, 30 mins.

Don't Leave Out the Cowboys
An historical overview of the Black Cowboys who seized, settled and developed the Old West from 1865 through the 1880's, through old photographs, prints, slides and a descriptive narrative with much little-known information about the Black Cowboys. 22 mins.
VHS: $10107. $39.99.

Don't Look Back: The Story of Leroy "Satchel" Paige
Satchel Paige was one of the greatest pitchers in the Negro League and possibly the best there ever was. He fought for the day when the Major Leagues would be desegregated. Eventually he would see that day. Stars Louis Gossett, Jr., Beverley Todd, Ossie Davis and Cleavon Little.
VHS: $21387. $19.95.
Richard A. Colla, USA, 1981, 98 mins.

Dr. Martin Luther King, Jr.: A Historical Perspective
A new examination of King's extraordinary life using rare and largely unseen footage and photographs, the program looks at the ideas, thoughts and causes of Dr. King's life. Includes non-profit public performance rights. 90 mins.
VHS: $20542. $59.95.

The Dream Awake
This seven-part video series, told in verse, is a kaleidoscopic portrait of the social, cultural and historical forces that shaped the African-American experience and character. The series looks at Africa, pre-revolutionary and pre-Civil War American life, the rise of the black cowboy and the emergence of the black intellectual. The program studies individualists (Malcolm X, Dr. Martin Luther King) who demanded honor and respect. "Dodson tells the history with pathos and honor, lifting his historic journey to a literary experience" (*Children's House*).
Africa.
VHS: $20004. $39.95.
Resurrection City and the Children.
VHS: $20009. $39.95.
The Amistad, Crispus Attucks, Harriet Tubman, the Emancipation Proclamation.
VHS: $20005. $39.95.
The Black Arts.
VHS: $20010. $39.95.
The Black Cowboy.
VHS: $20006. $39.95.
The Black Quartet.
VHS: $20007. $39.95.
The Martyrs.
VHS: $20008. $39.95.
The Dream Awake, Set.
VHS: $20011. $179.95.

Ebony/Jet Guide to Black Excellence Program 2: The Leaders
Trailblazers L. Douglas Wilder, Governor of Virginia; Marian Wright Edelman, Founder and President of the Children's Defense Fund; and Dr. James P. Comer, Director of Yale University's Child Study Center, explain how they persevered and assumed positions of leadership to open doors for others. 35 mins.
VHS: $16595. $14.95.

Ebony/Jet Guide to Black Excellence Program 3: The Entertainers

TV's No. 1 dad, Bill Cosby; Maya Angelou, author, actress, singer, talk-show host and professor; and Charles Dutton, Broadway, film and TV star, entertain and inspire with their tales of persistence and endurance. 35 mins.
VHS: $16596. $14.95.

Eyes on the Prize

The award-winning PBS series on the Civil Rights movement, covering the years 1954-65, brilliantly interweaves archival footage, news materials, and contemporary interviews with prominent figures who played roles in the incidents, moments and battles for equality and justice.
Eyes on the Prize I: Ain't Scared of Your Jails/No Easy Walk. The Freedom Summer movement is explored in the first episode, looking at the massive number of college students and young activists who poured into the South to test the legal challenges of inequality. The second looks at the charismatic, grass roots origins of Martin Luther King's nonviolent tactics to attack institutional racism in Albany, Georgia, and Birmingham, Alabama, where the city's police chief, Bull Connor, turned attack dogs and fire hoses on demonstrators and captured international attention.
VHS: $16922. $24.95.
Eyes on the Prize I: Awakenings/Fighting Back. The first episode considers the years 1954-56, and the early formation of the protest movement orchestrated by the civil rights organizations, the church, and local leaders to protest Jim Crow laws, the "separate but equal" doctrines, and rampant segregation that existed in the South. The program studies the lynching of Emmett Till and the 1955-56 Montgomery, Alabama boycott, triggered when Rosa Parks refused to give up her seat. *Fighting Back* focuses on the struggle for equal education, studying the historic 1954 Supreme Court ruling, *Brown vs. the Board of Education*, the nine black teenagers who attempted to integrate Central High School in Little Rock, Arkansas in 1957, and James Meredith's risky, life-threatening decision to enter the University of Mississippi in 1962.
VHS: $16920. $24.95.
Eyes on the Prize I: Bridge to Freedom.
VHS: Out of print. For rental only.
Eyes on the Prize I: Fighting Back.
VHS: Out of print. For rental only.
Eyes on the Prize I: Mississippi: Is This America?/Bridge to Freedom. In 1961 Mississippi was the staging ground for the first constitutional struggle and argument, how the civil rights movement would galvanize their energy and forces to empower blacks with the right to vote. *Bridge to Freedom* starts 10 years after the movement began, when, following the private joys, frustrations, landmark victories and eternal struggle, black and white participants converge for history, marching 50 miles for freedom to Selma, Alabama.
VHS: $16924. $24.95.
Eyes on the Prize I: No Easy Walk.
VHS: Out of print. For rental only.
Eyes on the Prize I: Complete Set. All six programs available in a one-volume, boxed set, encased in a beautiful, slipcase edition.
VHS: $16926. $149.98.

Eyes on the Prize II

Eight additional volumes of the award-winning documentary about the Civil Rights Movement covering the years 1964 to 1985.
Eyes on the Prize II: Ain't Gonna Shuffle No More/A Nation of Law? Black pride came to the forefront of the movement with the emergence of Muhammad Ali, the student takeover of Howard University and the first National Black Political Convention in Gary, Indiana. *A Nation of Law?* As the Black Panther Party rises in prominence, the FBI launches hundreds of covert actions against them, resulting in the death of such Panther leaders as Fred Hampton.
VHS: $17215. $24.95.
Eyes on the Prize II: Power!/The Promised Land. Three stories that capture the essence of the movement in the late sixties: The election of Carl Stokes as the first black mayor of a major city, the rise of the Black Panther Party and the uprising in the Ocean Hill-Brownsville section of Brooklyn. *The Promised Land.* The issues of war, poverty and economic justice become intertwined as Vietnam becomes a flashpoint, Martin Luther King, Jr. is assassinated in Memphis and the Poor People's Campaign comes to Washington, D.C.
VHS: $17213. $24.95.
Eyes on the Prize II: The Keys to the Kingdom/Back to the Movement. Court-ordering busing left deep scars in Boston as white parents reacted violently to the enforced change. In Atlanta, affirmative action took center stage with the election of black mayor Maynard Jackson. The Supreme Court sent out mixed signals in the Bakke Decision. *Back to the Movement.* Miami explodes in the worst racial riot in a decade as an all-white jury acquits the white officers accused of murdering a black man during a traffic stop. Harold Washington is elected mayor in Chicago through the grassroots efforts of the black community.
VHS: $17217. $24.95.
Eyes on the Prize II: The Time Has Come/Two Societies. The second generation of the Civil Rights Movement includes such charismatic leaders as Malcolm X and Stokely Carmichael. *Two Societies.* The battle lines are drawn in Watts, Cicero and Detroit as civil unrest shakes the very foundation of the movement.
VHS: $17211. $24.95.

Famous Black Americans

This important series on African-Americans examines their contributions to the country's social, artistic, cultural and political framework. The series covers role models of militant freedom fighters to Civil War heroes, contemporary artists and politicians. Designed for students in grades 4-6.
Black Americans: Artists, Entertainers and More. In recounting the significant artistic accomplishments of painter Henry Tanner, poet Gwendolyn Brooks, opera diva Leontyne Price and actor Sidney Poitier, this program showcases the vast cultural diversity of African-Americans. 20 mins.
VHS: $19996. $65.95.
Black Americans: Political Leaders, Educators, Scientists. The historical legacy of the social, political and civil rights protests is examined through the lives of four figures: Blanche K. Bruce, Thurgood Marshall, Ralph J. Bunche and Shirley Chisholm. 20 mins.
VHS: $19997. $65.95.
Black Heroes: Freedom Fighters, Cowboys & More. This program offers a panoramic study of African-American heroes, from Crispus Attucks, the first patriot to die in the Boston Massacre of 1770, to the seminal contributions of Dr. Martin Luther King Jr., winner of the Nobel Peace Prize. 22 mins.
VHS: $19994. $79.95.
Black Heroes: Builders, Dreamers and More. The historical accomplishments of Dr. Carter Goodwin Woodson, Phyllis Wheatley, Mary McLeod Bethune and Dr. George Washington Carver are highlighted in this special tribute to teachers, preachers and researchers. 23 mins.
VHS: $19995. $65.95.

Famous Black Americans, Set.
VHS: $19998. $229.00.

The Father Clements Story

A touching account of the Chicago priest who works on the city's West Side, and his quest to adopt a troubled young man despite the objections of the Catholic hierarchy. With Louis Gossett Jr., Malcolm-Jamal Warner and Carroll O'Connor.
VHS: $17910. $19.98.
Edwin Sherin, USA, 1987, 100 mins.

FBI War on Black America

Operating under the acronym COINTELPRO (for Counter Intelligence Program), J. Edgar Hoover and the FBI were heavily involved in discrediting and, ultimately, defusing what they saw as a militant threat from Black Americans. This video program rigorously investigates this frightening, government-sanctioned conspiracy. 50 mins.
VHS: $13167. $29.98.

For Us, The Living: The Story of Medgar Evers

In 1958, a civil rights leader emerged in Mississippi who changed the course of black history. Medgar Evers' amazing courage, his lifelong struggle for equal rights and his painfully tragic downfall are recounted here with an extraordinary cast including Howard Rollins Jr., Irene Carra, Margaret Avery and Roscoe Lee Browne. 84 mins.
VHS: $06960. $19.95.

Frederick Douglass: An American Life

A fast-paced, yet intimate portrait of the famous 19th century abolitionist and human rights advocate, Frederick Douglass. The film graphically portrays the people and events which influenced his long and remarkable life, including meetings with such notable figures as Harriet Tubman, John Brown and Abraham Lincoln.
VHS: $03420. $79.95.
William Greaves, USA, 1986, 30 mins.

Frederick Douglass: When the Lion Wrote History

The remarkable history of a truly remarkable man: Frederick Douglass, escaped slave, and brilliant orator who gave a powerful and poignant voice to freedom and the struggle for Civil Rights. 90 mins.
VHS: $23524. $19.98.

Freedom Man

Ossie Davis stars in this dramatization of a true story as Benjamin Banneker, the early American patriot whose achievements rival those of Benjamin Franklin, who worked with the Underground Railroad and saved runaway slaves from bounty hunters. His writings advocated the abolition of slavery and helped educate Thomas Jefferson about the capabilities of Black Americans. A self-taught writer, mathematician, astronomer, clockmaker, as surveyor he helped start the city of Washington, D.C. A forgotten and important part of American history. Recommended by National Education Association. 61 mins.
VHS: $09328. $29.95.

Freedom Road

A made-for-tv movie starring Muhammad Ali as an ex-slave on his way to becoming a U.S. Senator during the Reconstruction Years after the Civil War. Narration by Ossie Davis. Adapted from the Howard Fast novel. With Kris Kristofferson, Ron O'Neal, Barbara O. Jones and Edward Herrmann. Director Jan Kadar's last film.
VHS: $00465. $69.95.
Jan Kadar, USA, 1979, 186 mins.

From These Roots

Using authentic autographs, the film, narrated by Brock Peters and featuring music by Eubie Blake, recreates a vivid portrait of the Harlem Renaissance during the Roaring Twenties. It documents the artistic, social and political re-birth of Afro-America, and includes such well-known individuals as Cab Calloway, Marcus Garvey, Langston Hughes, James Weldon Johnson, Alain Locke, Claude MacKay, Paul Robeson and Ethel Waters.
VHS: $03421. $79.95.
William Greaves, USA, 1986, 28 mins.

Glory

Matthew Broderick stars as Colonel Robert Gould Shaw, the commanding officer of the 54th Massachusetts, one of the first black regiments to form and see combat in the Civil War. Denzel Washington won a Best supporting Oscar for his role as a rebellious soldier who learns what his true duty is. With Morgan Freeman and Cary Elwes. High marks for historical accuracy, Oscars for sound and cinematography.
VHS: $12846. $14.95.
Edward Zwick, USA, 1990, 122 mins.

God's Trombones—A Trilogy

Poems by African-American author/educator James Weldon Johnson are voiced here by James Earl Jones and Dorian Harewood. *The Creation* and *Go Down Death* are visualized by Will Vinton using clay painting, while the *Prodigal Son* is animated in clay by Lindsay Van Blerk. These three, 9-minute short subjects will be an inspiration to everyone.
VHS: $23303. $24.95.

Hale House: Alive with Love

Dr. Lorraine Hale begins by telling the story of one child, born addicted to heroin. From there the story blossoms into the founding of Hale House, a home for children who are born addicted to drugs. 28 mins.
VHS: $21457. $49.95.

Hezekiah Walker and the Love Fellowship Crusade Choir

Recorded during a live performance at Morehouse College, this video combines interviews, worship and music to reveal the beliefs and ideas that motivate this captivating figure. The songs "Christ Did It All", "Make It to That City", "Let the Glory", "I Will Go in Jesus' Name", "Calling My Name" and many more are included. 58 mins.
VHS: $21326. $14.95.

A History of the Civil Rights Movement in America

Lynchings, "Separate but Equal" facilities and Jim Crow laws set the stage for a powerful political transformation. This is an insightful and moving visual history of the Civil Rights movement, featuring interviews with Andrew Young, James Farmer and other leading authorities. 30 mins.
VHS: $24458. $39.95.

A History of the Slavery in America

Slavery in the US was an institution from the 1600's to the early days of Reconstruction. This legacy is reviewed through interviews with leading African-American Studies scholars. 30 mins.
VHS: $24459. $39.95.

Ida B. Wells

This famous African-American woman fought for human rights at a time in American history when these concerns were largely ignored. Her work as a journalist shed important light on the injustices faced by African-Americans in the South after the Civil War. This documentary tells the story of her heroic life.
VHS: $20745. $19.95.
Rex Barnett, USA, 1993, 27 mins.

Ida B. Wells: A Passion for Justice

Toni Morrison reads Ida B. Wells in her own words, while Al Freeman narrates the life story of this famed African-American woman. Archival photographs and lithographs, together with expert scholarly opinion, illustrate Wells' activism as a journalist, a suffragist and an anti-lynching crusader. 53 mins.
VHS: $12313. $125.00.

The Incredible Voyage of Bill Pinkney

Bill Cosby narrates this extraordinary chronicle about the first African-American to navigate his ship alone around the globe. Bill Pinkney turned this opportunity into an inspirational event for his students in the US, who learned important lessons in math, science and geography. This documentary, a winner of the Peabody Award, gives everyone the opportunity to share in his inspirational achievement.
VHS: $23672. $39.98.

The Jackie Robinson Story

Jackie appears as himself in this chronicle of his ascent from an all-black league to become the first Black American to play major league baseball. Ruby Dee appears as his wife.
VHS: $06334. $19.95.
Alfred E. Green, USA, 1950, 76 mins.

Jacob Lawrence

Lawrence is one of the country's most respected artists. This African-American painter grew up in depression-era Harlem and got his schooling in federal workshops. Today his works on African-American themes, particularly history, are widely prized. Interviews and the works of the artist tell this story of artistic excellence. 25 mins.
VHS: $27622. $29.95.

Jacob Lawrence: The Glory of Expression

This documentary is about the life of African-American painter Jacob Lawrence. His work has consisted primarily of epic depictions of the struggles of African-Americans. Considered one of America's greatest modern painters he was the first African-American to have his work exhibited in a major New York gallery. 28 mins.
VHS: $21454. $49.95.

Jesse Owens Story

One of the best TV sports biographies. Dorian Harewood plays the famous black track star who won four Gold medals at the 1936 Olympics in Berlin—which gave Hitler a lot of grief. From his college days to his later exploitation, the life of Owens is profiled. Cast includes George Stanford Brown, LeVar Burton, Debbi Morgan, Tom Bosley, Ronny Cox, George Kennedy and Ben Vereen.
VHS: $10826. $29.95.
Richard Irving, USA, 1984, 174 mins.

The Josephine Baker Story

Outrageous, shocking, sensational Josephine Baker (Lynn Whitfield) was born poor, but achieved fame and fortune through her sizzlingly exotic and erotic dance performances. Her beauty and ambition ensured that she will always be remembered as the first, and possibly most loved, truly international star.
VHS: $14630. $19.98.
Brian Gibson, USA, 1990, 129 mins.

Just Doin' It

A fascinating look at the Black barbershop—which is a lot more than a place to get groomed. It also functions as a community center, a place where gossip and camaraderie mix with philosophy, religion and politics. An engaging view of life in urban black America.
VHS: $03424. $79.95.
William Greaves, USA, 1984, 36 mins.

King

Paul Winfield stars along with Cicely Tyson and Ossie Davis in this five-hour mini-series which recreates the life and struggle of Dr. King in a sensitive and powerful program. With Howard Rollins, William Jordan and Cliff De Young. 3-tape set.
VHS: $20472. $59.98.
Abby Mann, USA, 270 mins.

The Life and Times of Deacon A.L. Wiley

Based on the oratory of a minister born into slavery, this story recounts the drama of a charismatic African-American father. Gregory Alan-Williams created this work based on slave narratives collected under the auspices of the Works Progress Administration of the 1930's. It offers an inspired and key addition to African-American history.
VHS: $21856. $29.95.
Jerry Grady, USA, 1992, 58 mins.

The Long Walk Home

Sissy Spacek and Whoopi Goldberg provide unforgettable performances in this retelling of the Montgomery, Alabama bus boycott in 1955. After Rosa Parks refuses to give up her seat on the bus to a white passenger, the Rev. Martin Luther King calls for a boycott. Goldberg plays the maid who must walk to work until Spacek has her consciousness raised. *Driving Miss Whoopi* it's not.
VHS: $14504. $14.98.
Richard Pearce, USA, 1989, 95 mins.

Looking for Langston

Isaac Julien's biography of black American author Langston Hughes with the poetry of Essex Hemphill and Bruce Nugent with archival footage and period music from the Harlem Renaissance. A film about identity, sexuality, racism, repression, role playing and art.
VHS: $16641. $39.95.
Isaac Julien, Great Britain, 1989, 65 mins.

Malcolm X: El Hajj Malik El Shabazz

This intense documentary examines the life and mysterious death of Malcolm X, considered one of the 20th Century's most charismatic yet controversial civil rights leaders. 60 mins.
VHS: $14605. $19.95.

Malcolm X: His Own Story As It Really Happened

An Oscar-nominated documentary about the turbulent life and times of the legendary black leader, based on his own best-selling autobiography. 92 mins.
VHS: $23442. $19.98.

Malcolm X: Make It Plain

Alfre Woodard narrates this in-depth film portrait of the great leader and religious figure. The story is revealed through the memories of those who knew Malcolm best, including Nation of Islam members and Malcolm's own family. Extensive archival footage of rallies and media interviews is also included. Co-produced by the *American Experience*. 136 mins.
VHS: $24871. $29.95.

Malcolm X: Nationalist or Humanist?

Newsreel footage of this influential thinker, leader and religious figure is compiled on this intriguing video. In addition, there is footage of events leading up to his assassination, and an interview with his wife, Betty Shabazz, filmed just after his death. 14 mins.
VHS: $24589. $95.00.

Martin Luther King Commemorative Collection

Two documentaries on one tape commemorating the late Dr. Martin Luther King: *In Remembrance of Martin* interweaves past and present to take the viewer from the days of the Civil Rights movement to America's first recognition of Martin Luther King National Day; *The Speeches of Martin Luther King* includes some of Dr. King's most famous speeches, including "I Have a Dream" and "I Have Been to the Mountaintop". 115 mins.
VHS: $06540. $29.95.

Martin Luther King, Jr.: I Have a Dream

King's eloquent, passionate speech given August 28, 1963, on the steps of the Lincoln Memorial, before over 200,000 civil rights marchers—a speech that still echoes in our memories. 1986, 25 mins.
VHS: $02361. $14.95.

Martin Luther King, Jr.: Legacy of a Dream

Martin Luther King, Jr. inspired a nation in troubled times. This concise survey, narrated by James Earl Jones, examines the life and times of the civil rights leader, revealing his enduring legacy.
VHS: $15678. $14.98.

Mean to Be Free: John Brown's Black Nation Campaign

A historical documentary about John Brown, who fought to end slavery and gain the rights of citizenship for all black people. Using historical photos and the words of Frederick Douglass and Harriet Tubman, this video is performed and produced by the students and faculty of the Department of Afro-American Studies, University of California, Berkeley. 53 mins.
VHS: $10106. $39.99.

Mrs. Fanny Lou Hamer

This woman was born to sharecroppers, the youngest of 20 children. From these humble beginnings she grew to be one of the most influential voices of the civil rights era. She talks with Gil Noble about her growing political commitment to justice. There is also footage of Civil Rights protests and the 1968 Democratic Convention. 50 mins.
VHS: $24588. $145.00.

Nationtime, Gary

Sidney Poitier and Harry Belafonte narrate the official documentary film record of the First National Black Political Convention held in Gary, Indiana in 1972, which brought together virtually the entire hierarchy of black political power in America. Featured are Reverend Jesse Jackson, Mayor Richard Hatcher, Coretta Scott King, Dick Gregory, Amiri Baraka, Isaac Hayes, Bobby Seale and others. Newly re-edited version. USA, 1974, 58 mins.
VHS: $03423. $99.95.

Negro Soldier

Frank Capra supervised this documentary focusing on black participation in World War II. Langston Hughes hailed it as the most remarkable Negro film ever flashed on the American screen.
VHS: $03347. $19.98.
Frank Capra, USA, 1944, 40 mins.

Nightfighters: The Tuskegee Airmen
In World War II, Lt. Col. Benjamin Davis led an elite black group of bombers, support crew and surgical teams over Italy and North Africa. Though these African-American servicemen valiantly shielded white flyers, the army largely ignored their contribution. This video tells their story. 52 mins.
VHS: S27661. $59.95.

Only the Ball Was White
A superior television documentary on the formation and rise of the baseball Negro Leagues, and the great ballplayers who were denied a chance to play in the racially segregated Major Leagues. The program features interviews with Satchel Paige, Roy Campanella, Buck Leonard, Jimmy Crutchfield, David Malarcher, Effa Manley and Quincy Troupe. Narrated by Paul Winfield. 30 mins.
VHS: S20421. $19.98.

Passin' It On
Dhoruba was one of the best-known leaders from the New York chapter of the Black Panther Party until he was convicted of shooting two NYC police officers. He always denied the charges and fought for 19 years to clear his name. Finally, in 1990, it was proved in court that he was framed. This documentary tells his story. 57 mins.
VHS: S21246. $29.95.

Paul Robeson
This famed performer was known throughout the world not just for his singing and acting ability, but also for his commitment to justice as a socialist and tireless civil rights activist. These beliefs caused him to champion causes unpopular with some Americans, resulting in his eventual blacklisting. A Morehouse College historian helps place Robeson in perspective while footage from throughout his career reveals the extraordinary talents of this extraordinary man. 45 mins.
VHS: S20946. $19.95.

Paul Robeson: On His Shoulders Many Stand
A legendary figure, Robeson was sought after as a Hollywood star and stage actor at a time when African-Americans were often used only for the most stereotypical roles. His groundbreaking performances and commitment to the cause of international human rights led him along a unique path. Ultimately he quit the film industry because he was so ahead of his times. 30 mins.
VHS: S22417. $19.95.

Portraits in Black
Program includes three award-winning films highlighting the Black American experience: Paul Lawrence Dunbar, an early Black poet; Two Centuries of Black American Art; and Gift of the Black Folk, which depicts the lives of Frederick Douglass, Harriet Tubman and Denmark Vesey.
VHS: S01050. $39.95.
Carlton Moss, USA, 60 mins.

The Promised Land
This three-volume documentary, narrated by Morgan Freeman, follows the greatest U.S. migration ever experienced in peacetime. Take Me to Chicago records the large-scale movement of African-Americans from the South to the city of big shoulders. In A Dream Deferred, growing frustration takes its toll on African-American communities in the North. And finally, Strong Men Keep a-Comin' On records the growing success of these communities.
VHS: S24582. $49.95.

Purdy's Station
Based on an historic incident, this drama tells the story of the Underground Railway and the Abolitionist movement as they affect the inhabitants of a small town. Jerusha Moore, a school teacher, discovers that a local black farmer called Purdy is hiding escaped slaves in an abandoned mine. Jerusha must choose between her career and her conscience.
VHS: S21323. $49.95.
Don Coonley, USA, 1990

Race to Freedom: The Story of the Underground Railroad
Tim Reid, Alfre Woodard, Glynn Turman and Courtney B. Vance star in the story of courageous men and women who created America's channel to freedom: the Underground Railroad. 90 mins.
VHS: S23570. $79.95.

Raisin in the Sun
Lorraine Hansberry's famous play is masterfully transformed in a film featuring Sidney Poitier and Ruby Dee. Based on Hansberry's personal life, the film follows the attempts of an impoverished family, blessed with an insurance settlement, to escape their apartment and life.
VHS: S01088. $14.95.
Daniel Petrie, USA, 1971, 128 mins.

The Real Malcolm X
Subtitled An Intimate Portrait of the Man, Dan Rather hosts this documentary. The program details Malcolm's odyssey from street hustler and drug peddler to charismatic leader, orator and spokesman of the Nation of Islam, before his break with Elijah Muhammad. The material features archival footage, excerpts from some of his most interesting speeches and interviews with his contemporaries. 60 mins.
VHS: S17683. $19.98.

Repercussions: A Celebration of African-American Music
A seven-part celebration of the roots of African-American music, shot over a three-year period, documenting the journey that traditional music made across the Atlantic.
Part 1. Born Musicians and On the Battlefield. The first focuses on the professional musicians of West Africa, and particularly the Mandinka Music of the Gambia; the second, on how African musical sensibility came to be integrated into American gospel music, particularly in Alabama, in the form of traditional unaccompanied male gospel quartets. 120 mins.
VHS: S03173. $29.95.

Part 2. Legends of Rhythm and Blues and Sit Down and Listen: The Story of Max Roach. Legends tells the story and records the music of some of the greatest living Blues performers who migrated from Mississippi to the West, generating the way for rock 'n' roll. Legendary performers like Big Mama Thornton, Hound Dog creator Lowell Fulson and Lloyd Glen are featured. Sit Down and Listen concentrates on the Afro-American tradition at its most sophisticated and daring—the art jazz of the post-war East Coast, and on its great leader, drummer Max Roach. 120 mins.
VHS: S03174. $29.95.
Part 3. The Drums of Dagbon and Caribbean Crucible. The first part focuses on the Dagbamba drummers in northern Ghana, and their complex social role; Caribbean Crucible traces the complex and fascinating ties that bind the music of coastal west Africa to the music of Europe, particularly that of England and Spain, in the remote countryside of two Carribean islands. The film explores the sounds of reggae and deejay. 120 mins.
VHS: S03175. $29.95.
Part 4. Africa Comeback: The Popular Music of West Africa. Africa's own popular music industry has grown rapidly over the past two decades, and this final program explores the Highlife of Ghana, the Afro-Beat and Juju of Nigeria. The popular music scene in Ghana is explored through its most famous musicians, including Nana Ampadu and the African Brothers, Koo Nimo, Smart Nkansah and the Sunsum Band and Segun Adewale. 60 mins.
VHS: S03176. $29.95.

The Road to Freedom: The Vernon Johns Story
Vernon Johns was a famous preacher who, after moving to Alabama in 1953, urged his new congregation to stand up for their rights. His story of courage and empowerment is a little known episode that some credit with kicking off the modern civil rights movement.
VHS: S21297. $89.99.
Laser: LD75248. $34.98.

Robert Colescott: The One-Two Punch
This tape is a motivational video dealing with stereotypes from artist Robert Colescott. His work and philosophy are also explored. 28 mins.
VHS: S21455. $49.95.

Rodney King Case: What the Jury Saw in California
This two-hour video is taken from the 150-hour gavel-to-gavel coverage recorded by Court TV in the controversial "police brutality" trial of several Los Angeles police officers earlier this year. Court TV chief anchor and managing editor Fred Graham hosts and interprets the proceedings in an effort to make the legal process understandable to the viewer. USA, 1992, 120 mins.
VHS: S16708. $24.98.

Roots
This monumental six-volume series is presented in a digitally remastered, elaborately designed set. Based on the Pulitzer-prize winning work by author Alex Haley, Roots is a rich, multi-layered portrait that traces the origins of Haley's African-American family, from their pre-Revolutionary war capture and forced resettlement in Africa to the Civil War, Reconstructionism and their demands for equality and justice in the post-war South. Winner of nine Emmy Awards, the program stars LeVar Burton, Louis Gossett Jr., Ed Asner, Olivia Cole, Henry Fonda, Georg Sanford Brown, and Sandy Dennis.
VHS: S17435. $149.92.

Roots: The Gift
A made-for-television work picks up the fortunes of captured African warrior Kunta Kinte (LeVar Burton) and American-born slave Fiddler (Louis Gossett Jr.), their violent rebellion and heroic efforts to organize a slave rebellion and move for freedom through the Underground Railroad. With Alex Haley, Michael Learned, Avery Brooks, Kate Mulgrew and Shaun Cassidy.
VHS: S17434. $59.99.
Kevin Hooks, USA, 1988, 94 mins.

Roots: The Next Generation
The epic continuation of Alex Haley's autobiographical investigation of his family's origins, related through a rich collection of anecdotes, remembrances and personal history, covering the Reconstruction through the 1970's. A 7-volume set digitally remastered and encased in a elaborately designed slipcase. With James Earl Jones (as Haley), Al Freeman Jr., Henry Fonda, Olivia De Havilland, Irene Cara, Dorian Harewood, Ossie Davis, Ruby Dee and Debbie Allen.
VHS: S17436. $149.92.

Separate But Equal
Sidney Poitier, Burt Lancaster and Richard Kiley star in this dramatic re-enactment of an early skirmish in the battle for civil rights. Set in South Carolina in 1950, an NAACP lawyer fights for the use of a single school bus to transport black youngsters to school. He takes his case to the highest court in the land where Chief Justice Earl Warren is faced with a landmark decision.
VHS: S14476. $19.98.
Laser: CLV. LD72029. $39.98.
George Stevens Jr., USA, 1990, 194 mins.

Sitting in Limbo
A bittersweet depiction of inner city ghetto life, its social and personal deprivation reflected in the tender and tough relationship of two black teenagers coping with the despair and poverty of their lives. 96 mins. 1988.
VHS: S18832. $29.95.

Speeches of Martin Luther King
The words of the great leader in a collection of his famous speeches.
VHS: S07027. $19.95.

The Tallest Tree in the Forest
This tape is a look at Paul Robeson, his performances and his political views. From his early days as a performer Robeson refused to be quiet on the issue of race and earned the enmity of many. This along with his views on the Soviet Union (which he regarded in a positive light) led to his blacklisting. USA, 1977, 85 mins.
VHS: S21469. $24.95.

This House of Power
A documentary about the history of the African-American church, from its origins as a separate "invisible institution" among slaves to its present-day role as a major force for social change. Hosted by CBS anchor Hosea Sanders. 60 mins.
VHS: S20545. $29.95.

The Tuskegee Airmen
Laurence Fishburne stars along with John Lithgow and Cuba Gooding, Jr., in this tale of heroic African-American World War II fighter pilots. Four new recruits are given the mission to help defend American troops from the air, but their mission also has another important goal. Their success could prove that the courage and skills of African-Americans are equal to those of their countrymen.
VHS: S27725. $94.99.
Robert Markowitz, USA, 1994, 52 mins.

Wilma
Cicely Tyson and Denzel Washington star in the true story of Wilma Rudolph, who overcame childhood polio to become an Olympic champion, and one of America's greatest athletes.
VHS: S15491. $14.95.
Bud Greenspan, USA, 1977, 100 mins.

A Woman Called Moses
This is the story of Harriet Ross Tubman, founder of the Underground Railroad, who led hundreds of slaves to freedom in the North before the Civil War. To those she helped get to the Promised Land, she became known as Moses. Newsweek called this powerful made-for-TV movie "One of the most moving evocations of the black experience ever." Cicely Tyson is brilliant in the role of Tubman as she matures over a period of eighty years. 200 mins.
VHS: S16561. $89.95.

Women of Brewster Place
Donna Deitch (Desert Hearts) directed this potent drama about a group of women (Oprah Winfrey, Cicely Tyson, Robin Givens, Jackee Kelly, Paula Kelly) who work together to get out of the ghetto in which they live. 2 cassettes.
VHS: S11588. $19.98.
Donna Deitch, USA, 1989, 180 mins.

ASIAN-AMERICAN INDEPENDENTS

Chan Is Missing
A mystery set against the backdrop of San Francisco's Chinatown. The story involves two Chinese taxi drivers who are looking for their business partner, Chan Hung, a middle-aged Taiwan immigrant who has vanished with their money. Their search for clues to Chan's whereabouts leads them to his family, friends and acquaintances, who reveal a great diversity of people and cultural backgrounds that make up life in Chinatown. A great hit on its release.
VHS: S10918. $79.95.
Wayne Wang, USA, 1981, 80 mins.

Combination Platter
This winner of the Best Screenplay at Sundance in 1993 tells the story of an undocumented Chinese waiter in a gritty, remarkably powerful, independent feature by Tony Chan. In the pressure laden world he inhabits, a green card holds the greatest promise for a better life. He finds himself contemplating an American wife, only to reject the chosen woman. But he hadn't counted on a visit from immigration.
VHS: S21747. $89.95.
Tony Chan, USA, 1991, 85 mins.

Coming Out Under Fire
This winner of the Special Jury Award at the 1994 Sundance Film Festival tells the story of nine lesbians and gay male veterans of the U.S. military. Based on Alan Berube's book of the same name, this film fleshes out this often misunderstood case of grave social injustice, using declassified documents, rare archival footage, interviews, photographs and more, and touches on the World War II origins of the current "don't ask, don't tell" policy. B&W.
VHS: S26966. $89.98.
Arthur Dong, USA, 1994, 71 mins.

Eat a Bowl of Tea
Chinese-American filmmaker Wayne Wang spins a tale of returning soldiers in search of brides and old men in need of grandchildren. Set in post-WWII New York, he exposes the shoddy treatment of Chinese immigrants and the notorious exclusion laws that kept families apart for much of this century. An entertaining and invigorating film based on the 1961 novel by Louis Chu. Cast includes Russell Wong, Victor Wong, Eric Tsang Chi Wai and Cora Miao, the director's wife, as the bashful bride from the old country who grows up fast.
VHS: S11484. $89.95.
Wayne Wang, USA, 1988, 102 mins.

Iron & Silk
A martial arts movie with a difference. Mark Salzman stars in an engaging film based on his two years of teaching English in the People's Republic of China in the early 1980's. In his spare time, he takes martial arts classes from a strict but genuine master. This warm and always human drama perfectly captures the people and the political climate. Salzman, in his film debut, makes a favorable impression playing a slightly fictionalized version of himself.
VHS: S15071. $19.98.
Laser: LD75127. $24.98.
Shirley Sun, USA/China, 1990, 94 mins.

The Joy Luck Club
The stories of four women and their mothers are interwoven in this moving tale of exile, loss, and new beginnings. Amy Tan's novel The Joy Luck Club is well realized in this careful adaptation certain to touch everyone.
VHS: S20609. $96.95.
Laser: LD71969. $39.99.
Wayne Wang, USA, 1993, 139 mins.

The Laser Man
From the director of A Great Wall and the producers of The Killer comes this funny merging of science fiction and comedy about an average young man's metamorphosis into a daring and capable super hero. With Tony Leung, Marc Hayashi and Sally Yeh.
VHS: S18161. $39.95.
Peter Wang, USA, 1990, 90 mins.

Pushing Hands
A loving comedy from the director of Eat Drink Man Woman, The Wedding Banquet and Sense and Sensibility. Mr. Chu is a widowed tai-chi master who leaves Beijing to live with his only son in a New York suburb. The result of this incongruous meeting of differing cultures is a warm comedy. Though his daughter-in-law has no use for him and everything seems to change too quickly, Mr. Chu responds the way he knows best, with the traditional tai-chi exercise of Pushing Hands. English and Mandarin with English subtitles.
VHS: S27008. $92.99.
Laser: LD75459. $39.95.
Ang Lee, USA, 1995, 100 mins.

Slam Dance
Director Wayne Wang (Dim Sum, Chan Is Missing) tries something different in this atmospheric contemporary film noir about an amiable professional cartoonist involved in murder. Tom Hulce (Amadeus) is the suspect. With Virginia Madsen, Mary Elizabeth Mastrantonio, Adam Ant and Harry Dean Stanton as a cop.
VHS: S06077. $14.98.
Wayne Wang, USA, 1987, 100 mins.

Smoke
Harvey Keitel, William Hurt, Forest Whitaker, Stockard Channing and Ashley Judd star in this offbeat comedy set in a New York cigar shop. Sparks fly when the manager, played by Keitel, gets involved in the intertwining lives of his colorful customers. A gentle love letter to Brooklyn.
VHS: S26708. $99.99.
Laser: LD75322. $39.98.
Wayne Wang, USA, 1995, 112 mins.

Tokyo Pop
Carrie Hamilton (the daughter of Carol Burnett), visits Japan and finds she strikes a sympathetic chord with a Japanese musician. Yutaka Tadokoro plays the being a rock star. A music-filled rock and roll romantic comedy filmed in the land of the rising sun.
VHS: S07817. $89.95.
Fran Rubel Kuzui, US/Japan, 1988, 99 mins.

The Wedding Banquet
Ang Lee's surprise hit is a poignant and funny story of the gay Taiwanese yuppie (Winston Chao) who lives with his American lover (Mitchell Lichtenstein) and tries to end his family's endless matchmaking attempts by announcing that he's engaged. His parents unexpectedly fly in to see the bride and turn their son's deception into a complicated affair.
VHS: S21895. $94.98.
Laser: LD74593. $39.98.
Ang Lee, USA/Taiwan, 1994, 105 mins.

gay & lesbian CINEMA

The 1993 March on Washington: Prelude to Victory
This moving and entertaining video includes great footage from the event that transformed the nation's capital. Entertainers and events from the entire week leading up to the march are included. Civil rights for lesbians, gays and bisexuals were advanced because of this historic event. 60 mins.
VHS: S19483. $39.95.

27 Pieces of Me
In this bold, independent feature, Tanya (Tina M. Henning), a lesbian sculptor, is forced to confront her sister Ramona (Angelique von Halle) when she arrives on her doorstep unannounced. Both women have been having relationship troubles. Fortunately, Tanya's roommate Bold (Jonathan Harris) helps the two women begin a rapprochement that they desperately need and want.
VHS: S27479. $39.95.
Gerald Donohoe, USA, 1995, 90 mins.

The 28th Instance of June 1914, 10:50 AM
David McDermott and Peter McGough live in another era though contemporary Manhattan surrounds them. The early 20th and late 19th centuries inspire both their art and the way they live. Without electricity or the basics of modern plumbing, they contend with chamber pots and oil lamps. This documentary shows the homoerotic past they create in their work, and the singular lifestyle they pursue together. Quentin Crisp makes an appearance.
VHS: S27082. $29.95.
Barbara Politsch, USA, 1994, 56 mins.

4 Scenes in a Harsh Life
This is a collection of live performances by Ron Athey, one of the most provocative performance artists working today. His rituals make extensive use of S/M and religious sources, combining such disparate elements as leather daddies and evangelism. The result is a mixture of sexual and artistic play. Serious issues of control, consent, illness and even transcendence are joined.
VHS: S22954. $69.95.

A.I.D.S.C.R.E.A.M., Ecce Homo and Final Solutions
Three short experimental films by gay filmmaker Jerry Tartaglia are joined on this video. Along with *A.I.D.S.C.R.E.A.M.*, *Ecco Homo* and *Final Solutions* explore fear, rage, the anti-sex and anti-gay movements and the rise of AIDS consumerism. It's an angry, arrogant and unapologetic collection.
VHS: S27222. $59.95.

Acla's Descent into Floristella
Sold into servitude by his parents, 12-year-old Acla must work underground in sulfur mines. Repeatedly beaten by his owner, the threat of sexual abuse is also ever-present. When he runs away, there are dire consequences for both him and his family. The story is based on the social mores and disturbing sexual practices found in 1930's Sicily. Italian with English subtitles.
VHS: S21544. $69.95.
Aurelio Grimaldi, Italy, 1987, 86 mins.

The Adventures of Priscilla, Queen of the Desert
Terence Stamp returns to the screen in this unlikely farce about three drag queens racing across the Australian outback in order to put on a show. Of course there is more to this film than unbelievably elaborate costumes, campily choreographed lip sync numbers and gay humor. It also tries to say something about love. Great disco numbers from ABBA, Gloria Gaynor, The Village People and Peaches and Herb.
VHS: S24030. $19.95.
Laser: Letterboxed. LD74911. $34.95.
Stephen Elliott, Australia, 1994, 102 mins.

All of Me
Georgette Dee, the famed transvestite cabaret star from Germany, stars as Orlanda. On a concert tour, Orlanda and his/her wife Elisabeth both fall for the same Polish man. This scenario makes for a witty film, and the musical numbers, particularly the title tune, are terrific. German with English subtitles.
VHS: S26867. $39.95.
Bettina Wilhelm, Germany, 1990, 76 mins.

All Out Comedy
Karen Ripley, Marilyn Pittman, Tom Ammiano and Scott Capurro will have you "coming out" of your seats. Filmed live at the San Francisco landmark in the Castro, Josie's Juice Bar. 78 mins.
VHS: S21124. $29.98.

All Women Are Equal & Pentagon Peace March
A pre-operational transsexual explains her values and beliefs in this insightful study of sexual identity by Marguerite Paris. Then Paris offers an impressionistic view of a 1967 anti-war demonstration. The 8mm originals of these works were transformed by optical printing.
VHS: S27223. $69.95.
Marguerite Paris, USA

Amazing Grace
A dramatic story is told in this film about the friendship between 18-year-old Jonathon and 30-year-old Thomas. Jonathon places all his hope for happiness in Thomas, who is HIV positive. Winner of the Wolgin Prize at the 1992 Jerusalem Film Festival and Best Film at Turin's Eighth International Gay-Themed Film Festival. Hebrew with English subtitles.
VHS: S22671. $79.95.
Amos Guttman, Israel, 1992, 95 mins.

And the Band Played On
Based on the influential book of the same name, this star-studded adaptation brings author Randy Shilts's story to the screen. Alan Alda, Richard Gere, Anjelica Huston, Steve Martin, Sir Ian McKellen and Lily Tomlin all appear in prominent roles with Matthew Modine starring as the doctor who would stop an epidemic.
VHS: S20872. $19.98.
Roger Spottiswoode, USA, 1993, 140 mins.

Apart from Hugh
Collin and Hugh have been together for one year. A party commemorating this anniversary forces Collin to reconsider his feelings about their relationship. Commitment, growth and above all, love, are the buzzwords in the air as these two men struggle with their feelings for each other.
VHS: S27613. $39.95.
Jon FitzGerald, USA, 1994, 87 mins.

Armistead Maupin's Tales of the City
The BBC funded this film realization of Maupin's acclaimed series of books. Set in 1970's San Francisco, it captures the heady mix of sexual politics and sheer fun that characterized that time and place. Olympia Dukakis is at the center of an ever more complicated plot that comes to involve a whole group of characters searching for their own Atlantis. Complete Set. Great Britain/USA, 1993, 360 mins.
VHS: S20873. $59.95.

As Is
When a talented writer discovers he has AIDS he turns his anger into a zest for life because of the love and loyalty of his ex-lover and friends. With Robert Carradine, Jonathan Hadary and Colleen Dewhurst.
VHS: S03289. $19.98.
Michael Lindsay-Hogg, USA, 1986, 85 mins.

Ballot Measure 9
This winner of the Special Jury Award at Sundance in 1995 follows the fight around Oregon's Ballot Measure 9. Essentially, the initiative would have denied lesbians and gay men civil rights protection. Though defeated, it was the center of acrimonious debate and tense standoffs. This documentary captures the heroic spirits of the people who stood up against bigotry, even under threat of physical harm.
VHS: S27476. $89.95.
Heather MacDonald, USA, 1995, 72 mins.

Bar Girls
Three women are at the center of a plot about love, desire and the travails of dating in lesbian Los Angeles. The circle grows to include other women, who in turn help and hinder the mating game with advice and miscommunication. It's a fun, honest film about love and romance, for people who understand the importance of relationships. Look for Chastity Bono's cameo on "Scorpio Night."
VHS: S26445. $95.99.
Laser: LD75084. $39.99.
Marita Giovanni, USA, 1995, 95 mins.

The Best Defense, Vol. 1
Every lesbian and gay man could benefit from this demonstration video. It features self-defense that really works. Designed for the average person, it requires no formal training. Nine of the world's best lesbian and gay self-defense instructors show how to protect yourself from hate and ignorance in everyday situations. 50 mins.
VHS: S26817. $29.95.

The Best Way
Marc, the aggressive athletic director at a boys' summer camp, discovers the drama teacher dressed in women's clothes, and is shocked by his attraction to him. Their tense confrontation results in Marc forcing him to confront his suppressed sexuality. French with English subtitles.
VHS: S00120. $49.95.
Claude Miller, France, 1982, 85 mins.

Black Lizard
A hilarious caper movie written originally for the stage by Yukio Mishima; the plot concerns a female jewel thief who kidnaps nubile youths and ferries them to a glitzoid secret island. There she turns them into naked love statues—one of them bizarrely played by Mishima himself. Miss Lizard is portrayed by the transvestite actor Akihiro Miwa, who flounces around in an impossible collection of boas and chokers and turns every flourish of her cigarette holder into an over-the-top arabesque. Called "a tale of love, passion, greed and necrophilia" by the *New York Times*, and "Naughty Japanese noir. Like something from Almodóvar or John Waters" (*Village Voice*). Japanese with English subtitles.
VHS: S16261. $49.95.
Kinji Fukasaku, Japan, 1968, 90 mins.

BloodSisters
San Francisco's dyke leather community bears it all in this in-depth documentary about the pleasures and pains of sadomasochism. Footage from key S/M leather competitions along with images from the 1993 March on Washington and the 25th Anniversary of Stonewall in New York are joined with insightful interviews. This film employs experimental and documentary styles as well as girl punk music.
VHS: S27615. $35.00.
Michelle Handelman, USA, 1995, 77 mins.

Blue Jeans
A young boy is sent to England to improve his English, where he has his first experience with the opposite sex. When his girl friend takes up with a more experienced young man, the young boy confides in one of his supervisors and is taken advantage of. French with English subtitles.
VHS: S00158. $59.95.
Hugues des Roziers, France, 1978, 80 mins.

Boy's Life
A compilation of three short films, *Pool Days*, *A Friend of Dorothy* and *The Disco Years*, offers differing bittersweet and humorous accounts of growing up gay. In each the pain of coming out is tempered by the joys of gay life. 90 mins.
VHS: S26670. $59.95.

Boys in the Band
The first really successful American film to openly deal with homosexuality, Boys in the Band is based on the enormously successful Broadway play by Matt Crowley. An adult, witty and, at times, touching depiction of gay life in the early days of gay liberation. The original nine actors who appeared in the Broadway production take their roles here on film, with exceptional acting by all, but particularly Cliff Gorman being ultra-queeny and Leonard Frey as the birthday boy.
VHS: S00176. $59.98.
William Friedkin, USA, 1975, 119 mins.

Boys' Shorts
This collection of six shorts tackles a variety of issues facing gay communities. AIDS, coming out, relationships, family and, of course, sex, are all explored. *The Dead Boy's Club*, *Relax*, *RSVP*, *Billy Turner's Secret*, *Resonance* and *Marlon Riggs' Anthem* are included in this video.
VHS: S22950. $39.95.
Christopher et al., USA, 1990-1992, 119 mins.

Brother Sun, Sister Moon
Lavish costume epic depicts the story of St. Francis of Assisi, a man so gentle wild animals would eat from his hand, as he rejects the pomp of the Catholic Church. With some interesting characters working on this production, including Alec Guinness as the Pope, Lina Wertmuller in screenwriting capacity and 60's pop star Donovan supplying the music. English dialog.
VHS: S02623. $14.95.
Franco Zeffirelli, Italy/USA, 1973, 121 mins.

California Big Hunks
Sexy young male dancers are featured in this erotic journey of inner fantasy. They have it all: muscle, strength and great bodies, which are soon covered in sweat. They hold nothing back. 60 mins.
VHS: S24846. $14.95.

Can't Stop the Music
A lavish, gay-themed musical that looks at corruption inside the music-publishing industry. The topliners are the 70s act the Village People, each of whom falls madly in love with Valerie Perrine. "It follows that most of the dialogue is gay in-jokes, with the odd music business joke for variety" (*Time Out*). "YMCA" and "Macho Man" are highlights. With Steve Guttenberg, Tammy Grimes, June Havoc and Barbara Rush.
VHS: S20417. $14.98.
Nancy Walker, USA, 1980, 119 mins.

Caught Looking & North of Vortex
These two short films cannily explore issues of homoerotic desire. *Caught Looking* features an interactive computer sex fantasy that samples different styles of erotic experiences. In *North of Vortex* two men and a woman drive across the U.S. in search of adventure.
VHS: S20581. $39.95.
Constantine Giannaris, Great Britain, 93 mins.

Chained Girls
Who and what is a lesbian? Where can they be found? Are they happy with their lives? These are a few of the probing questions asked in this "expose" of New York City lesbians. You'll be fascinated to know that lesbians get married, have cat fights over their femmes, and even initiate young debs into the Daughters of Lesbos. Very rare sleaze from the 60's.
VHS: S23055. $19.98.
Joseph Mawra, USA, 1965, 80 mins.

Changing Face
Twenty-nine is not too young for a mid-life crises for a young, eager, gay man. The only problem is who to turn to. In this sophisticated comedy everyone has problems and advice about love, marriage and friendship. Tom, the central character, has a wide choice of places to look for help, ranging from the complaint department at Bloomingdales to his old high school pal who is still mourning a friend who died of AIDS.
VHS: S22957. $24.95.
Robert Tate/Robert Roznowski, USA, 1993, 103 mins.

Chicken Hawk
This is the much debated documentary about the controversial group known as NAMBLA, the North American Man Boy Love Association. Though they are often seen as victimizers and even criminals, this documentary tries to capture them as they see themselves, as men who have a desire to love boys. Featuring Allen Ginsberg.
VHS: S24526. $34.95.
Adi Sideman, USA, 1994, 60 mins.

Claire of the Moon
Nicole Conn's pioneering lesbian drama. Claire Jobrowski is a carefree, sexually adventurous novelist who shares a cabin with the stern, rigid Doctor Noel Benedict, who specializes in sexual behavior. They're brought together for a writer's workshop in the Pacific Northwest. "An encouraging debut film about love between adults" (*L.A. Weekly*). With Trisha Todd, Karen Trumbo and Caren Graham.
VHS: S19102. $29.98.
Nicole Conn, USA, 1992, 102 mins.

Classic Foreign Shorts—Volume 3: Un Chant d'Amour, Romance Sentimentale
Un Chant d'Amour is Jean Genet's only film, a legendary and long suppressed film masterpiece. "A song of man's love soaring above the sexual ghetto of prison and non-existence" (*Cahiers du Cinema*). 20 mins. *Romance Sentimentale* is usually attributed to Sergei Eisenstein, and although Eisenstein worked on it, it was probably directed by Grigori Alexandrov. Photographed by Tisse and financed by its only player—a wealthy woman who wanted to appear in an Eisenstein film—*Romance Sentimentale* was filmed in Paris during the winter of 1929-30. The film is a somber experimental poem portraying the emotions aroused in a woman (Mara Gitry) by the realization that love is dead. 20 mins.
VHS: S26947. $29.95.

Clay Farmers
A farmhand named Dan forms a close friendship with a handsome young drifter hired by an absentee landowner. Their friendship is tested when they are seen together bathing in the nude at a swimming hole. What exactly do they feel for one another? Also includes *My First Suit*, a hilarious short from New Zealand about a wistful teenager.
VHS: S21321. $69.95.
A.P. Gonzalez, USA, 1989, 90 mins.

Colegas
From the director of *El Diputado*, the story of three friends and their transition into adulthood. A crisis comes about when one of the friends becomes pregnant, and the youths resort to street hustling to raise the funds to solve the problem. Spanish with English subtitles.
VHS: S01562. $89.95.
Eloy de la Iglesia, Spain, 117 mins.

Coming Out Is a Many Splendored Thing
Debbi Daliege's comedy video premieres with clever segmented stories that cover all those "coming out" issues. These bits and pieces are a hilarious exploration of whimsical "coming-out" adventures. Remember and laugh. 35 mins.
VHS: S21123. $24.98.

Coming Out Under Fire
This winner of the Special Jury Award at the 1994 Sundance Film Festival tells the story of nine lesbians and gay male veterans of the U.S. military. Based on Alan Berube's book of the same name, this film fleshes out this often misunderstood case of grave social injustice, using declassified documents, rare archival footage, interviews, photographs and more, and touches on the World War II origins of the current "don't ask, don't tell" policy. B&W.
VHS: S26966. $89.98.
Arthur Dong, USA, 1994, 71 mins.

Common Threads: Stories from the Quilt
Academy Award winner Robert Epstein and Jeffrey Friedman's moving, powerful documentary about five people who died of AIDS and whose names are on panels of the AIDS quilt which now covers over 14 acres. Dustin Hoffman is the narrator. HBO Video will donate all profits from the sale of *Common Threads* to the NAMES Project, which is in charge of the quilt. For more information on the NAMES project, call 415-863-1966.
VHS: S12767. $19.98.
R. Epstein/J. Friedman, USA, 1989, 79 mins.

Creation of Adam
Andrey is a young man who fears his marriage may fall apart because his wife thinks he is gay. A series of events confirm these suspicions as Andrey meets Philip, an enterprising business man who turns his life around. Philip shows Andrey how to love. Russian with English subtitles.
VHS: S26405. $39.95.
Yuri Pavlov, Russia, 1993, 93 mins.

Crocodiles in Amsterdam
Described as a "slapstick female buddy movie," this Dutch feature stars two friends, Gino and Nina. Though thoroughly different, they manage to wrest friendship from the most inauspicious situations. Nina's rebelliousness and Gino's frivolity place them at each other's mercy, and often in hilarious situations. Dutch with English subtitles.
VHS: S26937. $39.95.
Annette Apon, The Netherlands, 1990, 88 mins.

Curse of the Queerwolf
Lawrence Smalbut and Richard Cheese are just average macho guys who court disaster when they pick up two mysterious women. Just as Smalbut realizes that his date is no lady, she/he bites him on the derriere and forever transforms his life. Now when the moon is full, Smalbut finds himself magically transformed into "Queerwolf," a drag queen werewolf. It's a campy horror romp in questionable taste.
VHS: S27659. $14.95.
Mark Pirro, USA, 1994, 90 mins.

Daddy and the Muscle Academy: A Documentary on the Art, Life and Times of Tom of Finland
Tom of Finland was a pioneering gay pornographer whose classic *Ultimate Leather Men* veers between the erotic and the absurd. "A second film will probably be necessary to complete what are here the beginnings of connected discussions concerning the implications of fascistic attractions, fetish-racism, and other generated identity" (David Overbey). English and Finnish with English subtitles.
VHS: S19525. $49.95.
Ilppo Pohjola, Finland, 1991, 55 mins.

Dear Boys
A harsh, stylized and feverish piece about dark sexual fantasies and deep romantic longing, the film concerns the romantic and sexual entanglements of a morose, self-absorbed writer and an uninhibited, carefree young man who recklessly pursues thrills and excitement. This groundbreaking, unapologetically gay work is adapted from Gerard Reve's novel. With Hugo Netsers, Hans Dagelet, Bill Van Dijk, and Albert Mol.
VHS: $17444. $69.95.
Paul de Lussanet, The Netherlands, 1980, 90 mins.

Desert Hearts
Wonderful love story between a repressed English professor who is waiting for a divorce at a dude ranch for women, and a beautiful casino worker in Reno who lives at the ranch with her mother. Adapted from the novel *Desert of the Heart*, by Jane Rule, with a fabulous soundtrack!
VHS: $01919. $29.98.
Donna Deitch, USA, 1985, 96 mins.

Desire
Director Stuart Marshall chronicles the events leading to a crucial chapter in the Gay and Lesbian movement's history: the imprisonment of homosexuals in Nazi concentration camps during World War II. His film examines the "discovery" of homosexuality by the medical and psychoanalytic professions in the 1890s, and the subsequent movements in Germany during the early years of this century demanding recognition of gay and lesbian rights.
VHS: $16632. $39.95.
Stuart Marshall, Great Britain, 1989, 88 mins.

Desire: An Erotic Fantasy Play
Three good-looking, sexy and interesting women form a romantic triangle in this unique lesbian work. It's a skillfully accomplished video where open expressions of sexuality are handled with as much frankness as passion. "A hot lesbian video!" (*Deneuve Magazine*).
VHS: $27234. $49.95.
Janice Kroesen, USA, 1995, 79 mins.

Devotion
This touching and emotional lesbian love story is based on the book of the same name. A comic and her long-term, live-in lover share everything. It's a passionate film filled with humor and warmth.
VHS: $26945. $69.95.
Mindy Kaplan, USA, 1995, 124 mins.

Dominique in "Daughters of Lesbos"
Oversexed women bare it all as they pursue sapphic pleasures in a hothouse of emotion. Their club, known as the New York City Man Haters Society, is not a group to be trifled with. One outrageous peeping tom learns this lesson when he seduces a lesbian's vengeance can be swift like a knife. With Claudia Cheer, Jo Sweet, Sue Akers and Carla Costa.
VHS: $27675. $19.98.
Peter Woodcock, USA, 1967, 65 mins.

The Doom Generation
From the maker of *The Living End* comes another installment of violence and sex cooled by stereotypical generation X elan. Two kids meet up with a bleeding dude and set off to terrorize the motorized world. A stop at a convenience store leaves a talking head without its body and a bizarre family murder/suicide, so the three main characters go on the run and all have sex with each other. Can they evade the gang of skinheads?
VHS: $27521. $94.99.
Gregg Araki, USA, 1995, 83 mins.

Dream Boys Revue
Ruth Buzzi and Lyle Waggoner host a talent and beauty contest where all the good looking women are men. Lip-synched versions of Ann-Margret, Liza, Bette Davis, Marilyn Monroe and Barbra Streisand all compete for a crown at this alternative competition held in Texas. USA, 1985, 74 mins.
VHS: $03950. $19.95.

Dreamers of the Day
Andra, a writer and filmmaker seemingly in charge of her passion for women, is thrown off course by the appearance of Claire. In this romantic comedy, all the careful plans defining Andra's current project vanish amidst a whirlwind of humor and desire.
VHS: $26971. $39.98.
Patricia Spencer, Canada, 1992, 94 mins.

Drifting
Controversial Israeli film called "The best gay film ever made," winner of Israeli Oscars for Best Director, Best Actor and Best Cinematography. Hebrew with English subtitles.
VHS: $00376. $69.95.
Amos Guttman, Israel, 1982, 80 mins.

Dyke TV #1
This innovative cable television show caters to the needs, interests and desires of lesbians. Everything is possible as segments on election results, dyke softball and dyke fashion demonstrate. 47 mins.
VHS: $24578. $24.95.

Dyke TV #2
More information is on offer from the wide ranging world of dykes. This installment includes segments on the Gay Rodeo, rugby, filmmaker Barbara Hammer, breast cancer, Camp Sister Spirit and more. 50 mins.
VHS: $24579. $24.95.

Dyke TV #3
There are endless possibilities for today's enterprising dykes, as this episode amply demonstrates. Lesbian soccer, lesbian life in Mexico and Cuba, domestic partners in Texas and the Lesbian Avenger Awards are all included in this video. 60 mins.
VHS: $24580. $24.95.

Dyke TV #4
This episode includes footage of the International Dyke March and the Gay Games from 1994, along with regular segments like *I Was a Lesbian Child*. 60 mins.
VHS: $24581. $24.95.

Dyke TV #5
This fifth installment of the *Dyke TV* series includes segments on racism and homophobia, Native Americans, Marga Gomez, Jewish music, the Lesbian Herstory Foundation and more.
VHS: $26456. $24.95.

El Diputado
A political thriller about a gay man high in the ranks of the Spanish Socialist Party whose love affair with a 16-year-old boy jeopardizes the fate of the nation. The Advocate said the gay love scenes are among the best ever presented in a commercial film. Spanish with English subtitles.
VHS: $00397. $79.95.
Eloy de la Iglesia, Spain, 1983, 111 mins.

El Sacerdote (The Priest)
An early work by Eloy de la Iglesia, this is the shocking story of a troubled priest fighting for his own soul. Father Miguel fights physical and psychic fantasies of sex and suffers from painful memories of a bizarre childhood. Banned at the time of its original release. Spanish with English subtitles.
VHS: $23576. $79.95.
Eloy de la Iglesia, Spain, 1979, 62 mins.

Empty Bed
John Wylie plays Bill Frayne, a gay man in his sixties who reflects on his younger days, the choices he has made, and the prospect of an empty bed. He lives alone, having been unable to commit himself to a relationship because of a variety of social and personal pressures. Told mostly through flashbacks, this film is a time tapestry where past and present weave together to form a poignant picture of his life.
VHS: $14155. $29.95.
Mark Gasper, USA, 1990, 60 mins.

Ernesto
A lushly mounted, sensitively directed, complex depiction of homosexuality with Martin Halm as the boy who cooly tries anything and Michele Placido as the older, seducing man. "Genuinely erotic…*Ernesto* reconciles the legacies of Pasolini and Fassbinder." Italian with English subtitles.
VHS: $00416. $49.95.
Salvatore Samperi, Italy, 1983, 98 mins.

Erotikus: History of the Gay Movies
Specifically, the history of the male gay film, from early films of posed muscle-boys, through the early films featuring male nudity to the hard-core films of the recent period. Narrated by Fred Halsted. 54 mins.
VHS: $02168. $29.95.

Et L'Amour
This poetic vignette features two women engaged in a sensuous and tasteful erotic interlude. There is no dialog. 24 mins.
VHS: $27449. $24.95.

Even Cowgirls Get the Blues
Uma Thurman, Rain Phoenix, Lorraine Bracco and William Hurt star in this adaptation of Tom Robbins' best-selling novel. Gus Van Sant, director of *Drugstore Cowboy* and *My Own Private Idaho*, brings his remarkable visual style to this high camp road movie set in the early 1970's, about a hitchhiker, free love and lesbian passion. Also features Angie Dickinson, Keanu Reeves, Roseanne Arnold, Crispin Glover, Sean Young and Buck Henry. Music by k.d. lang.
VHS: $22383. $19.95.
Gus Van Sant, USA, 1994, 96 mins.

Extramuros
Carmen Maura, famed for her riveting portrayals in *Women on the Verge of a Nervous Breakdown* and *Law of Desire*, plays a nun who is challenged by her irrepressible lesbian desires. Set in a convent during the Spanish Inquisition, the film is not only a depiction of repressed passion, but a sharply critical look at the relationship between the Church and political power as the convent vies for fame and money through the faked visions and stigmata of the lesbian sisters. Spanish with English subtitles.
VHS: $24033. $39.95.
Miguel Picazo, Spain, 1985, 120 mins.

The Families We Choose
Four lesbian families are shown in this sensitive and informative tape about the families that we choose. These portraits answer key questions about modern life and point to a whole range of inclusive and accommodating family values. 45 mins.
VHS: $25537. $24.95.

Female Misbehavior
Monika Treut's kinky exploration of nonconformist women combines two older short films, *Bondage* (1983), about a sadomasochistic lesbian, and *Annie* (1989), a portrait of former porno star Annie Sprinkle, with two recent documentaries, *Dr. Paglia* and *Max*. The former is a witty send-up of controversial academic Camille Paglia; the latter, a look at a lesbianNative American that shows her transsexual change from woman to man. "Treut is a sexual-political provocateur who in her explorations of the sexual fringe takes us where few filmmakers visit" (*New York Post*).
VHS: $19558. $29.95.
Monika Treut, Germany/USA, 1992, 80 mins.

Fiction and Other Truths: A Film About Jane Rule
Jane Rule has written lesbian fiction that has touched countless women, including the classic *Desert Hearts*. This film explores the author behind the books and features interviews with Helen, her lover of over 40 years. In addition, their political work and their dreams—in short, the essence of their lives—stand revealed in this insightful documentary. Produced by the National Film Board of Canada.
VHS: $27227. $59.95.
Lynne Fernie/Aerlyn Weissman, Canada, 1995, 57 mins.

Films of Barbara Hammer: Lesbian Humor
A collection of six films spanning the career of this exciting filmmaker: *Menses* is a wry comedy on the disagreeable aspects of menstruation; *Superdyke*, a comedy about a troop of shield-bearing Amazons; *Our Trip*, an animated film based on a hiking trip in the Andes; *Sync Touch*, a series of film experiments which propose an aesthetic connection between touch and sight; *Doll House*, a rapid montage of objects arranged in reference to the central prop of a doll house; and *No No Nooky T.V.* confronts the feminist controversy around sexuality with electronic language. "Hammer's satiric use of technology corresponds well with the Eighties repression of sexual expression. If you've ever looked up 'lesbian' in a computer thesaurus, you'll know that it's not listed" (*Independent Media*).
VHS: $08608. $59.95.
Barbara Hammer, 1975-87, USA, 59 mins.

Films of Barbara Hammer: Lesbian Sexuality
A collection of four films by Barbara Hammer, including the landmark *Dyketactics*, the first lesbian lovemaking film to be made by a lesbian. A sensual, evocative montage of 110 images edited to images of touch, an "erotic lesbian commercial." Also includes: *Multiple Orgasm*, a sensual, explicit film; *Double Strength*, a poetic study of a lesbian relationship between two trapeze artists; and *Women I Love*, using the camera as a personal extension of the body.
VHS: $08609. $59.95.
Barbara Hammer, USA, 1974-76, 57 mins.

Films of Barbara Hammer: Optical Nerves
Parisian Blinds and *Tourist*, both films by Barbara Hammer, "investigate the nature of spectator perception in an unfamiliar environment." *The Optic Nerve* is a powerful personal exploration of family and aging; *Place Mattes* explores the space between reaching and touching with animation and optical printing used to create travelling mattes for places. *Endangered*, Hammer's most recent work, has light, life and film as endangered in this exquisite film etched with acid.
VHS: $08611. $59.95.
Barbara Hammer, USA, 1984-88, 44 mins.

Films of Barbara Hammer: Perceptual Landscapes
Four works that explore personal landscapes: *Pools*, made with Barbara Klutinis, is an exploration above and under water of two of the first swimming pools designed by the first woman architect in the U.S.; *Pond and Waterfall* is an exploration of verdant pond growth as well as dynamic light and water reflections; *Stone Circles* is a celebration of ancient pre-patriarchal standing mounds and circles including Stonehenge and Asbury; *Bent Time* is one of Hammer's most ambitious films, in "which she attempts to render visually the scientific theory that time, like rays, curves at the outer edges of the universe" (*L.A. Times*).
VHS: $08610. $59.95.
Barbara Hammer, USA, 1981-83, 54 mins.

Flaming Creatures
Jack Smith's groundbreaking, lyrical queer film is being released in a special limited-edition series to raise funds that will help restore and preserve his other works. This classic may seem tame by current standards, but its great camp style stands the test of time.
VHS: $27242. $195.00.

Flaming Ears
This edgy, sci-fi lesbian fantasy follows the lives of three women: a comic book artist, a performance artist/pyromaniac and and amoral alien who likes lizards. In this cyberdyke movie, love and revenge vie for supremacy amidst violence and ennui in an anti-romantic plea for love of all kinds. German with English subtitles.
VHS: $26936. $39.95.
Angela Hans Sheirl/Ursula Purrer/Dietmar Schipek, Austria, 1991, 84 mins.

The Flavor of Corn
Lorenzo is a handsome, first-year professor with a quiet demeanor. He brings a passion for teaching to his young charges in a small village. As his relationship with his girlfriend deteriorates, he finds himself spending more time with 12-year-old Duilio. Soon Duilio's stepmother is questioning the nature of this amorous friendship. Italian with English subtitles.
VHS: $21545. $69.95.
Gianni Da Campo, Italy, 1994, 89 mins.

Flickers
Theatrical trailers from some of the most intriguing gay-themed films are collected into this feature presentation. *Caligula, Sebastiane, Prick Up Your Ears, My Beautiful Launderette, Cabaret, Nijinsky, The Ritz, The Gay Deceivers* and other classic film previews offer surprising entertainment. 91 mins.
VHS: $27611. $24.95.

For a Lost Soldier
This haunting, true story follows a boy's wartime sexual awakening. It's controversial because this 12-year-old falls in love with a Canadian soldier who is in Holland just at the end of World War II. Ballet star Rudi van Danzig recreates this memory from his childhood to show how a boy falls in love with his handsome liberator. Dutch with English subtitles.
VHS: $21831. $19.98.
Roeland Kerbosch, The Netherlands, 1993, 95 mins.

Forbidden Love: The Unashamed Stories of Lesbian Lives
Tales of lesbian love were luridly exposed in pulp novels of the 1950's. This film mixes documentary footage that shows how important these stories were to lesbians with its own scripted torrid romance. It's a campy homage to the works of fiction that delved into the underworld of 1950's lesbian passion.
VHS: $22054. $69.95.
Aerlyn Weissman, Canada, 1992, 84 mins.

Four Directions: Selections from MIX 94— The NY Lesbian & Gay Film Festival
Four lesbian and gay experimental shorts from the innovative New York-based film festival are joined together on this single video. From desire to politics, these shorts express a wide stylistic and thematic range. Included are *Me and Joe* by Stuart Sherman, *Smoke* by Liz Camps, *Virus* by Stuart Gaffney and *Feeling Anything Being Existing* by Liz Tevaarwerk.
VHS: $27228. $59.95.

Gay for a Day
Three documentaries from Tom Palazzolo dealing with gay issues: *Gay for a Day* is the story of the 1976 Gay Pride Parade; *Costumes on Review* is a hilarious documentary of a gay Halloween party.
VHS: $06112. $39.95.
Tom Palazzolo, USA, 45 mins.

Gay Games IV from A to Q
Highlights include *In the Life* coverage from the Opening Ceremonies as well as *Dyke TV & Network Q* footage showing hunks competing for gold. *Gay Entertainment Television* provides a view of the history and the organization behind the games while *Gay Cable Network* shows the closing ceremonies of this historic event. 60 mins.
VHS: $21702. $24.95.

Go Fish
A beguiling and charming look at the lives and loves of a small group of lesbian women in Chicago. Friends play matchmaker to bring together two very different women: Max, a beautiful, gregarious writer, and Ely, a quiet, thoughtful and almost terminally shy woman. They are, of course, perfect for each other in this gentle and offbeat film.
VHS: $26147. $29.98.
Laser: LD75315. $39.98.
Rose Troche, USA, 1994, 83 mins.

Grief
Alexis Arquette and Craig Chester are featured in this quirky comedy about behind the scenes intrigues set in the offices of an over-the-top soap opera. Camp humor, unfulfilled longing, male homoeroticism and even that standby of television daytime drama, overnight success, are thrown into this crazy mixed-up world of Hollywood's second string producers.
VHS: $22062. $92.95.
Richard Glatzer, USA, 1994, 87 mins.

Growing Up Gay and Lesbian
Brian McNaught, acclaimed author and lecturer, presents "everything you always wanted to know about homosexuality but were afraid to ask" in a sensitive but straightforward question-and-answer session.
VHS: $23430. $39.95.

Harry Weinberg's Notebook
Yariv Kohn's short essay about sexual politics, ethnicity, intolerance and freedom deals with the emotional aftermath when widower Harry enrolls in a creative writing course taught by a lesbian. The writing assignments force Harry to reconsider his bittersweet feelings about his late wife, and to compose a letter to his late friend, gay activist Harvey Milk. With Nate Garnick, Karen Waddell and Irv Hoffman.
VHS: $19532. $54.00.
Yariv Kohn, USA, 1992, 25 mins.

Heaven's a Drag
Mark and Simon, two men in love, are suddenly separated by AIDS and death. Undone by grief, Simon tries to blot out his intense emotions by diving into the swinging life of a gay bachelor. His deceased ex, a former drag artist, is horrified by Simon's actions and refuses to enter Heaven until he is sure that his memory will live on. That means any prospective new paramour of Simon's will have to deal with a queer, territorial ghost.
VHS: $27429. $59.95.
Peter Mackenzie Litten, Great Britain, 1995, 96 mins.

Holy Mary, Remembrance & Vocation
In these three short, experimental films, filmmaker Jerry Tartaglia looks at the Pope in drag, describes memories of Bette Davis from his queer youth, and catches the lyrical existence of The Radical Faeries at their retreat at the Short Mountain Collective in Tennessee.
VHS: $27229. $59.95.
Jerry Tartaglia, USA

Homo Promo
Trailers from dozens of mainstream and major gay or lesbian films have been collected on this video. These coming attractions comprise a serious but ironic look at a difficult past with some great laughs.
VHS: $24835. $39.95.
Jenni Olson, USA, 1991, 62 mins.

Homophobia in the Media and Society 1993 MIT Panel
This panel discussion brings the views of editors, filmmakers and politicians to the sensitive subject of homophobic media institutions. Warren Blumenfeld, Art Cohen, Michael Duffy and A. Victoria Mederos comprise the panel of experts.
VHS: S24717. $29.95.

Homophobia in the Workplace
Brian McNaught, author and lecturer, discusses the issues of homophobia and discrimination in a revealing look at gender roles and the workplace.
VHS: S23431. $24.95.

Homosexual Desire in Minnesota
Originally shot in super 8, this film details gay life in America's heartland during the 1970s. Its 12 parts chart a course from personal development to political action.
VHS: S27230. $59.95.
Jim Hubbard, USA

The Hours and Times
Christopher Munch's feature debut focuses on the circumstances and possible sexual relationship that existed between John Lennon and the Beatles' manager Brian Epstein during a four-day holiday in Barcelona in Spring 1963. A work of delicacy and heartbreak, the film delves into the inner world of each man, depicting Epstein's erotic obsession and Lennon's confusion and pain as an emerging rock and roll icon. With David Angus, Ian Hart and Stephanie Pack.
VHS: S18741. $19.98.
Christopher Munch, USA, 1991, 60 mins.

The Hunger
David Bowie, Catherine Deneuve and Susan Sarandon star in this stylish and moving tale of sophisticated vampires. Deneuve needs new blood in order to keep her 300-year-old lover alive. This film has an erotically charged atmosphere which includes a host of memorable scenes like the lesbian encounters between Deneuve and Sarandon. Ann Magnuson and Willem Dafoe also appear.
VHS: S26970. $19.95.
Tony Scott, USA, 1983, 100 mins.

I Am My Own Woman
The exceptional life of Eastern-bloc transvestite Charlotte von Mahlsdorf is the subject of this film. Her story symbolizes both political resistance and sexual endurance under a repressive regime. It's a documentary with a touch of Brecht that features a true queer free spirit. German with English subtitles.
VHS: S22670. $79.95.
Rosa von Praunheim, Germany, 1993, 91 mins.

I Became a Lesbian and Others Too
Four shorts bring humor and insight to the lesbian experience. Included are: *Heat Wave*, *I Became a Lesbian*, *Cat Nip* and *Le Poisson d'Amour*. From the girl next door to grandma's secret past, even amongst a bunch of cuddly kitties, who knows where lesbian desire can be found lurking? 52 mins.
VHS: S27757. $29.95.

I'll Love You Forever...Tonight
The first American gay feature film to be written and directed by a Latino, *I'll Love You Forever...Tonight* is the story of a group of aimless, young gay men who gather for a weekend by the pool in Palm Springs. It's a simple enough premise but it is brought alive by the emotional conflicts unleashed in their near-accidental couplings. Love and sex don't seem to mesh for these troubled figures. With Paul Marius, Jason Adams, Roger Shank and David Poynter.
VHS: S25563. $49.95.
Edgar Michael Bravo, USA, 1993, 80 mins.

I've Heard the Mermaids Singing
A wonderfully whimsical little comedy about imagination and the rude intrusion of reality in the life of an awkward temp worker with a penchant for photography. Sheila McCarthy is Polly and Paule Baillargeon is her new and surprisingly understanding employer. A reel delight from Canada.
VHS: S06046. $19.98.
Patricia Rozema, Canada, 1987, 81 mins.

Images: A Lesbian Love Story
Claire and Dori have lived together for six years—theirs is a deep bond with an open relationship. Enter Alyx, a dynamic, compelling, sexual, energetic Lesbian who loves life, love, women...and Claire. "At last, a woman-identified and realistic portrayal of women loving women" (Lavender Press).
VHS: S06032. $59.95.
Ruth Barrett/Cynthia Smith, USA, 1987, 54 mins.

Improper Conduct
Controversial, powerful documentary, a series of interviews with fascinating Cuban intellectuals and homosexuals who have been persecuted under the Castro regime. An indictment of Castro, implicating also those who would turn a blind eye toward repression from the left. Spanish with English subtitles.
VHS: S00614. $79.95.
Nestor Almendros, USA, 1984, 112 mins.

In a Glass Cage
A thriller that redefines the horror film. Written and directed by Agustin Villaronga, the story concerns a Nazi concentration camp doctor and his family living in exile in Spain a few years after the war. After a nasty fall leaves him in need of an iron lung, the Nazi finds his new male nurse an indispensable member of the family. With Gunter Meisner, David Sust and Marisa Paredes as Griselda. Spanish with English subtitles.
VHS: S10734. $79.95.
Agustin Villaronga, Spain, 1986, 110 mins.

In the Life: The Funny Tape
Kate Clinton, America's first lesbian stand-up comic, hosts this collection of songs and skits featuring some of the best lesbian and gay talent around. Even the commercials are funny. Lily Tomlin and the late Vito Russo are also featured. 60 mins.
VHS: S21125. $19.98.

The Incredibly True Adventure of Two Girls in Love
Randy is a frolicsome tomboy mechanic who lives with her lesbian aunt and accidentally meets a fellow teen with both a Range Rover and an attitude. Despite their differences, they become the best of friends and eventually realize that there can only be one explanation for their feelings toward one another: They're in love.
VHS: S26816. $19.99.
Laser: LD75406. $39.99.
Maria Maggenti, USA, 1995, 94 mins.

Indigo Girls Watershed
Everything, from the Indigo Girls' biggest hits to their most intimate moments, can be found on this video. Candid and memorable footage from the early years is juxtaposed against clips of them them performing songs like "All Along the Watchtower," "Galileo," "Touch Me Fall," "Least Complicated," "Get Together" and more. 68 mins.
VHS: S26669. $22.98.

An Individual Desires Solution & War Songs
The first of these two experimental films by Lawrence F. Brose confronts AIDS as faced by the artist's HIV-positive lover. In the second work, a poem performance by Paul Schmidt forms the basis for an ode to peace. Together these films manage to create a highly personal view of these important issues.
VHS: S27220. $59.95.
Lawrence F. Brose, USA

Jeffrey
Paul Rudnick's off-Broadway smash comic hit is finally a feature-length film. It stars Steven Weber, Patrick Stewart and Michael T. Weiss, and even includes Sigourney Weaver in a bizarre cameo. It all begins as a young gay man discovers that AIDS makes looking for Mr. Right even more complex and bedeviling. Now, as he finds the ravages of the epidemic coming ever closer, he must decide if he can rise to the challenge and meet what life has to offer with openness and love. Olympia Dukakis, Kathy Najimy, Robert Klein and Nathan Lane are also featured in this delightful comedy.
VHS: S27050. $96.99.
Laser: LD75456. $39.95.
Christopher Ashley, USA, 1995, 92 mins.

Jerker
Hugh Harrison adapts Robert Chesley's play about the relationship between two men, which is revealed entirely through anonymous telephone conversations. "Raw, honest and unapologetic in its portrayal of gay sexuality," the *Philadelphia Gay News* wrote. With Tom Wagner and Joseph Stachura.
VHS: S17118. $19.95.
Hugh Harrison, USA, 1991, 120 mins.

The Jim Bailey Experience
Combining elements of the outrageous and avant-garde, Jim Bailey has been on the cutting edge of drag performers. In this compilation tape, Bailey pulls out all the stops with his dead-on impersonations and photo layouts of Judy Garland, Barbra Streisand, Marilyn Monroe and Madonna.
VHS: S16916. $29.95.

Kamikaze Hearts
Juliet Bashore's dark drama boldly merges documentary and narrative storytelling in a fascinating portrait of the lesbian underground. Sharon ("Mitch") Mitchell, an actress, and Tina ("Tigr") Mennett, a producer, are lovers and junkies. They accentuate the perverse sexual nature of their relationship by making explicit pornographic films. "Only the camera, with verite charm, trembles during kisses here. This dramatic documentary...posits lesbian love as women's place of empowerment within an exaggerated patriarchal world—the real life porn industry" (Alisa Solomon, *The Village Voice*).
VHS: S19104. $59.95.
Juliet Bashore, USA, 1991, 80 mins.

L'Amour Fou
M.M. Serra's film is both a document of a difficult time and a personal exploration of Serra's gay male friends' sexuality. The serenity of the four seasons becomes a metaphor in this beautifully hand-processed work. It shows the fragility and vibrancy of life in a time dominated by AIDS.
VHS: S27231. $59.95.
M.M. Serra, USA

L'Homme Blesse (The Wounded Man)
The sensitive story of a French teenager and his discovery of his own homosexuality, this film directed by Patrice Chereau received the French Cesar. Henri, the teenager, tries to stop an attack on a man in a public toilet, is given a sexy kiss by the attacker, and discovers that he is strongly attracted to men. French with English subtitles.
VHS: S06588. $79.95.
Patrice Chereau, France, 1984, 90 mins.

Last Call at Maud's
A documentary about the closing of San Francisco's oldest-running lesbian bar. The film relates the 23-year history of the bar, related by owner Rikki Streicher, and a larger consideration of empowerment within the gay rights movement. "The documentary makes salient points about lesbians' generally second-league standing to gay men, legalistic problems such as women not being allowed to be bartender, a 70s souring of homosexual pride due to male gay's 'lack of political consciousness,' and the shooting of Harvey Milk" (Derek Elley, *Variety*).
VHS: S19745. $39.95.
Paris Poirier, USA, 1993, 75 mins.

Lesbian Tongues
A discourse on the private battles and personal joy of gender politics and lesbian sex. A wide-range of interview subjects—intellectuals, artists, professionals and dairy farmers—talk about lesbian liberation, life, love and sexual fulfillment. With JoAnn Loulan, Joan Nestle and Barbara Grier.
VHS: S19265. $39.95.

Lesbionage
In this private eye thriller with a sexual twist, two lesbian private detectives are propelled into a complex web of deceit, blackmail, kidnapping and corruption. The demands and pressures to solve the case place a tremendous burden on their personal relationship. With Lou Sullivan, Liz Prescott and Jewelle Gomez. 90 mins.
VHS: S19264. $39.95.

Lesbovision
Ingrid Wilhite's funny and irreverent works have been collected on this video. *L'Ingenue* is about a baby dyke's first cruise bar. In *Lezzie Life* wildly different dykes try to co-exist. Finally, in *Pet Names* lesbian endearments will leave you laughing.
VHS: S25535. $29.95.
Ingrid Wilhite, USA, 1985-1991, 61 mins.

Lessons at the End of Spring
A young boy's loss of innocence within a pre-perestroika Russian prison is the Kafkaesque premise of this harrowing film. The impressive feature debut of writer-director Oleg Kavun, *Lessons at the End of Spring* immediately places him at the forefront of Russia's groundbreaking new wave of angry young filmmakers. A landmark in the evolution of Soviet cinema. Mature themes and extensive male nudity. Russian with English subtitles.
VHS: S15495. $69.95.
Olag Kavun, USSR, 1989, 75 mins.

Lie Down with Dogs
A young gay man, off to enjoy life in Provincetown one summer, lives out the second half of this adage rather too completely. He gets up with fleas but manages to laugh at all the strange romantic and sexual complications which make Provincetown unique. At times clever and sharp, it combines a light comedy with social critique.
VHS: S27075. $99.99.
Laser: LD75444. $39.99.
Wally White, USA, 1995, 84 mins.

Lifetime Commitment: A Portrait of Karen Thompson
After living together as a couple for over four years, Karen Thompson and Sharon Kowalski were hit by a drunk driver. Sharon was disabled, and Karen lost her lover to a legal system that refused to recognize their bond. Sharon's parents did all they could to keep the couple apart, a problem that deepened when Sharon's father, Donald Kowalski, gained full guardianship over his daughter. This video documents the struggle of two women in love, in a system that can't see the value of this bond.
VHS: S19454. $39.95.

Lily Tomlin 3-Pack
The Search for Signs of Intelligent Life in the Universe, *Ernestine: Peak Experiences* and *Appearing Nitely* are the comic standouts joined in this three-tape set. It brings Lily Tomlin's Tony Award-winning performances to video. 120 mins.
VHS: S27478. $59.95.

Lip Gloss
This film exposes the lives of ordinary and extraordinary gender benders. Go shopping with transvestites, drag queens and female impersonators and watch backstage as they transform themselves into an image of glamour and sex.
VHS: S24244. $39.95.
Lois Siegel, Canada, 1992, 75 mins.

Live to Tell
The very first gay and lesbian prom in America is captured on this exciting documentary. It offers a fresh and unique look at growing up lesbian or gay in America. USA, 30 mins.
VHS: S26819. $24.95.

Long Awaited Pleasure
Lois Weaver (*She Must Be Seeing Things*) and Peggy Shaw star in this compelling love story. Made by women for women, it charts an involving romance between two lesbians. It is a realistic portrayal of a theme rarely dealt with as sensitively and openly as is attempted in this film.
VHS: S26972. $39.95.
Giovanna Manana, USA, 1987, 90 mins.

Longtime Companion
The impact of AIDS on the gay community is the subject of this well received and honestly acted drama. Bruce Davison stands out in a distinguished ensemble cast as a man facing the loss of his life partner. With Stephen Caffrey, Patrick Cassidy, Brian Cousins, John Dossett, Mark Lamos, Dermot Mulroney, Mary-Louise Parker.
VHS: S13301. $19.95.
Norman Rene, USA, 1990, 100 mins.

Los Placeres Ocultos
A closeted banker, middle-aged and successful, falls madly in love with a poor but handsome 18-year-old student—with devastating consequences for the young man. Carefully crafted and insightfully scripted, *Los Placeres Ocultos* was the first openly gay film to emerge from Spain following the death of Franco. Virtually unknown to American audiences, this complex updating of *Death in Venice* is among the most powerful affirmations of gay life ever depicted on film. Spanish with English subtitles.
VHS: S11636. $59.95.
Eloy de la Iglesia, Spain, 1977, 97 mins.

The Lost Language of the Cranes
A moody BBC adaptation of David Leavitt's novel about family secrets and sexual identity. The film centers on a young man's sexual declaration and its volatile and revealing consequences on the rest of the family. "Graced with subtle, intense performances" (*Time Magazine*). With Corey Parker, Brian Cox, Eileen Atkins and Angus MacFadyen.
VHS: S18604. $19.98.
Nigel Finch, Great Britain, 1992, 84 mins.

Love Bites
A light-hearted romp about a novice vampire hunter who falls in love with a West Hollywood Count, *Love Bites* stars Kevin Glover in a gay twist on the Dracula theme. When the vampire turns out to be sexier than the vampire stalker had imagined, he soon finds himself falling for the 347-year-old blood-sucker.
VHS: S11640. $29.95.
Marvin Jones, USA, 1988, 60 mins.

Love Game
Tennis star Dana Johnson is caught in the world's oldest indoor sport, the "Love Game." In this romantic comedy, Dana's search for the right woman is both enthralling and funny. This is one of the better lesbian comic features around. USA, 1990, 90 mins.
VHS: S26973. $39.95.

Macho Dancer
From world-renowned director Lino Brocka comes a story of sex, violence and political corruption. Abandoned by his American lover, a handsome teenager from the mountains journeys to Manila in an effort to support his family. With a popular call boy as his mentor, Paul enters the glittering world of the "machodancer"—a world of male strippers, prostitution, drugs, sexual slavery, police corruption and murder. Teeming with sex and erotic Oriental beefcake, *Macho Dancers* is a searing indictment of the hypocrisy and corruption rampant under both the Marcos and Aquino regimes. Uncensored and uncut. Tagalog with English subtitles.
VHS: S14597. $79.95.
Lino Brocka, Philippines, 1988, 136 mins.

Maedchen in Uniform
Legendary film from the German post-Expressionism period, extremely daring for its time in suggesting lesbianism in the story of a young girl whose identity is choked by the authoritarian boarding school she attends. German with English subtitles.
VHS: S02140. $24.95.
Leontine Sagan, Germany, 1931, 87 mins.

The Making of "Bar Girls"
Meet the producer, director and real personalities behind this lesbian romantic comedy. As *Bar Girls* makes its way across the independent circuit, it leaves in its wake curiosity about its origins. Now this documentary will answer all questions.
VHS: S25751. $29.95.
Jennifer Rodes, USA, 1995, 40 mins.

Male Escorts of San Francisco
This documentary tells the story of five male hustlers who advertise in a San Francisco weekly. They have greatly varying interests and experiences. These portraits reveal that commonly held beliefs about the world's oldest profession are often just wrong.
VHS: S22050. $29.95.
Matthew Link, USA, 1992, 42 mins.

Man for Man, Volume I
Four erotic stories feature eight amazing men. They bare all for the camera, in this the first installment of a gay quarterly. There is a costume drama featuring Hercules, a Victorian melodrama, a sculptor and his ideal model, and a luxury evening in a penthouse overlooking London. There are even sections on Ibiza, safer sex, clubs and fashion.
VHS: S22458. $39.95.
Gordon Urquhart, USA, 1993, 59 mins.

Man for Man, Volume II
This sensual all male video is sizzling with a number of exciting scenarios. There is a college boy visiting the steamy South, a Spanish Inquisition dungeon sequence and a gay detective looking for a teenage runaway. Also includes part two of the gay soap opera *Buckingham Place*.
VHS: S24670. $39.95.
Gordon Urquhart, USA, 1993, 55 mins.

Man for Man, Volume III
Stories and travel segments make this third installment of the *Man for Man* series both engaging and erotic. It features stories highlighting Spanish poetry, the epic of Gilgamesh, and Angelo, the sexiest private dick. Visits to Buckingham Palace and Sitges are also included.
VHS: S27174. $39.95.
Gordon Urquhart, USA, 1993, 60 mins.

March in April
Set during the historic march on Washington of 1993, this feature film tells the story of Mark, a man who has never "come out" to his ailing mother. As an assortment of people come to visit him for the big event, he must juggle friends, lovers and family. Keith Meinhold, Barney Frank, Pat Schroeder and Herb Ritts are just some of those who make appearances in this new film.
VHS: S22948. $29.95.
Stephen Kinsella, USA, 1994, 60 mins.

Marching for Freedom: The 1993 March on Washington Video
This video document benefits the National Gay and Lesbian Task Force Policy Institute. Over 700,000 people demonstrated for their rights in Washington D.C. See and hear the joyous sights and sounds of freedom. This country will never be the same again. 78 mins.
VHS: S19453. $29.95.

Massage for Relaxation
Swedish massage, shiatsu, self-massage and reflexology are methods that can help relieve tension anywhere in the body. These techniques are demonstrated to relaxing music by capable men. 45 mins.
VHS: S24847. $14.95.

Meeting Magdalene
Marilyn Freeman's sexy short shows three women trapped in a love triangle overwrought with passion. Sarah is visiting her friend Jean in Olympia, but when Sarah meets Jean's lover, Magdalene, her friendly interests take a dramatic shift. 34 mins.
VHS: S27758. $24.95.

Men in Love
The story of Steven, a young man who has just lost his lover, Victor, to AIDS. Following a moving memorial service in San Francisco, an emotionally drained Steven flies to Hawaii with Victor's ashes—honoring one of his departed lover's last wishes. Struggling with his loneliness and confusion, Steven encounters Peter, a native Hawaiian gardener, and has an affair with him which leads him to a cathartic reawakening of his own sexuality. Starring Doug Self, Joe Tolbe, and Emerald Starr.
VHS: $14086. $39.95.
Marc Huestis, USA, 1990, 87 mins.

Men in Shorts
This collection has something for everyone. Three music videos from John Greyson's feature *Patient Zero* are joined by two juicy Pussy Tourette songs, "Bridgette" and "French Bitch." In addition, *Autobiography* tells of growing up gay in a small Canadian town, while *In View of Her Fatal Inclination, Lilo Wanders Gives Up the Ghost* details a shocking inclination. There is even a bit of history in Pat Rocco's *Kiss*, from 1969.
VHS: $23941. $19.95.

Mitch Gaylord: The Men's Total Body Workout
Mitch Gaylord is fit, and in this video he explains how to work the upper and lower body and the abdominals, with an emphasis on the importance of nutrition.
VHS: $24735. $24.95.

Mom, Dad…I'm Gay
This guide to coming out offers help to both gay youth and their parents. Interviews reveal personal stories of understanding and acceptance. It's a video that helps demystify this often troubling and difficult process. 30 mins.
VHS: $25112. $19.95.

Monaco Forever
Set around the 1956 marriage of Grace Kelly and Prince Rainer, the narrative concerns the confusion set off by an enigmatic American who meets a mysterious French woman as they set off on a string of unusual and madcap romantic adventures. The debut film of Jean Claude Van Damme, who plays the "homosexual."
VHS: $18917. $39.95.
William A. Levey, USA, 1983, 43 mins.

Mondo Rocco (aka It's a Gay World)
This collection of short films by Pat Rocco combines softcore erotica, politics and drag. Rocco was among the first to capture the heady days of Gay Liberation in the late 1960's and 1970's on film. Together these works go some way to preserving that colorful era.
VHS: $25114. $39.95.
Pat Rocco, USA, 1970, 227 mins.

My Father Is Coming
An adventurous German woman receives word from her Bavarian father of his intentions to visit her in New York, where she must pull off an elaborate facade of being married and successful. Her gay roommate poses as her husband but complications ensue when a string of bizarre circumstances result in her father's transformation into an underground sexual icon. With Shelly Kastner, Alfred Edel and Annie Sprinkle.
VHS: $18412. $29.95.
Monika Treut, USA/Germany, 1991, 83 mins.

My Own Private Idaho
In this modern restructuring of the '60s road movie, River Phoenix and Keanu Reeves hustle their way through Seattle, Portland, Idaho and Rome on a quest for River's missing mother. With a meticulous, lyric style, the film combines sprawling landscapes, scenes of passionless sexuality and allusions to Orson Welles' *Chimes at Midnight* as it addresses issues of love, family, politics and homosexuality. A work of great complexity and beauty from the director of *Mala Noche* and *Drugstore Cowboy*.
VHS: $15927. $19.95.
Gus Van Sant, USA, 1991, 102 mins.

Naked Civil Servant
John Hurt delivers a compelling performance in the role of Quentin Crisp, based on Crisp's autobiography as a witty homosexual growing up in England of the 30's and 40's through years of intolerance, ostracism and violence. Hurt's tour-de-force performance brings to life Crisp's unique and often sharp wit at once critical of the society as well as of himself.
VHS: $00914. $19.99.
Jack Gold, Great Britain, 1980, 80 mins.

Night Porter
Controversial film about the perverse relationship between a former SS officer from a Nazi concentration camp and a woman, a former inmate at the camp. From one of Italy's few women directors, with Dirk Bogarde and Charlotte Rampling. English dialogue.
VHS: $00934. $19.98.
Laser: LD72308. $29.99.
Liliana Cavani, Italy, 1973, 117 mins.

Not Angels, But Angels
Young boys in the fast changing world of the Czech Republic find the consumer life is available to them through the sale of their own bodies as prostitutes. This documentary lets them describe their experiences plying the world's oldest trade in a new center for sex tourism. Czech with English subtitles.
VHS: $26404. $39.95.
Wictor Grodecki, Czech Republic, 1994, 80 mins.

Odd Gals Out
Canadian lesbian comedy by Sandra E. Fellner and Sharon Jacobs finds its way to the US in this collection of hilarious skits. Everything from hockey to square dancing is lampooned.
VHS: $25536. $24.95.
Lisa King, USA, 45 mins.

Odd Girl Out
Six vignettes detail the coming out process in Tammy Rae Carland's innovative film. From explaining her sexual orientation to her mother to the vagaries of erotic life, coming out remains a complex but exciting experience.
VHS: $27232. $59.95.
Tammy Rae Carland, USA

Olivia Records 15th Anniversary Concert Highlights
Olivia's first concert video creates a special view of this historic musical event with live performance, interviews, backstage banter and celebration. Features Cris Williamson, Dianna Davidson, Lucie Blue Tremblay, Deidre McCalla, Tret Fure and Nancy Vogl, with special guests Teresa Trull and Robin Flower. 73 mins.
VHS: $16839. $39.95.

On Being Gay
A conversation with Brian McNaught, lecturer, counselor, author of *A Disturbed Peace*, Mayor of Boston's Liaison to the Gay and Lesbian Community, and activist, as he talks about the fallacies, the facts, and the feelings of being gay in a straight world. 86 mins.
VHS: $05994. $39.95.

On Common Ground
An idiosyncratic portrait of the tragedy and triumph of the gay liberation movement, from the political urgency tragedy of the 60s to the extreme alienation and social contradictions of the 90s. Using a neighborhood bar as the communal setting, director and writer Hugh Harrison explores the feelings, passions, energy and excitement of a time and place. Cinematography by Ron Hamill.
VHS: $18245. $14.95.
Hugh Harrison, USA, 1992, 90 mins.

One Adventure
An amusing erotic documentary from the early 1970's, this Pat Rocco film follows eight gay Americans across Europe. Bell bottoms are in full bloom, but there was a serious issue in play. Though it is peppered with short erotic vignettes, this film examines the state of gay rights around the world.
VHS: $22956. $39.95.
Pat Rocco, USA, 1994, 90 mins.

Only the Brave
Two wild teenage girls named Vicki and Alex experiment with everything from drugs and sex to violence and just hanging out. Alex wants to write and finds encouragement, along with a little erotic attention, from her English teacher Kate. Vicki wants to stay like Alex's mother did before she disappeared. Together, these girls explore new boundaries in their friendship until events spiral out of their control. Winner of the Best Feature Film award at the 1994 San Francisco Lesbian and Gay Film Festival.
VHS: $26918. $59.95.
Ana Kokkinos, Australia, 1994, 62 mins.

Orlando
Virginia Woolf's ground-breaking novel about a transsexual from the time of Renaissance England has been transformed into a beautiful film. Tilda Swinton stars with Billy Zane as her romantic American lover while Quentin Crisp reigns as Queen Elizabeth the First.
VHS: $20829. $19.95.
Laser: LD74471. $34.95.
Sally Potter, Great Britain, 1993, 93 mins.

Out for Laughs
An irreverent collection of vignettes on lesbian humor, sensibility and outlaw style in this hilarious send-up of images, stereotypes and media representation. USA, 1992, 30 mins.
VHS: $18916. $29.98.

Out in Suburbia
Eleven lesbians between the ages of 23 and 67 speak frankly about their families, their friends and most importantly, their loves.
VHS: $26820. $39.95.

Out in the Garden & You
Two films from Vincent Grenier are included in this video. The first, *Out in the Garden*, is about the dynamic of being HIV-positive. The second film, *You*, offers a more formal examination of perspective, self reflection and narrative.
VHS: $27233. $59.95.
Vincent Grenier, USA

Out Takes
Gay sensibility, homophobia and gender roles on broadcast television are outlined by juxtaposing scenes from two children's shows, and a prime-time sitcom from Japan. Rex Reed's outrageous critique of Pee Wee highlights the self-perpetuating closet of Hollywood and the perceived subversive threat of the show's gay subtext. Reed's opposition to Pee Wee, and Reuben's (Pee Wee) technique of innuendo, double entendre and gender switching, both appear equally repressed compared to the explicit frankness of the Japanese TV series.
VHS: $11638. $39.95.
John Goss, USA, 1989, 13 mins.

Outcasts
The most controversial film ever released in Taiwan, *Outcasts* is the story of teenage boys abandoned by their families because they are gay, and the efforts of an aging photographer to provide a home and family for these young people. Chinese with English subtitles.
VHS: $05987. $49.95.
Yu Kan-Ping, Taiwan, 1986, 102 mins.

Parting Glances
Authentic gay film centering on the final stages of a love affair, featuring fine performances by Richard Ganoung and John Bolger as the couple, and Steve Buscemi as the artist friend doomed by AIDS. Superb photography by Jacek Laskus.
VHS: $02016. $29.95.
Bill Sherwood, USA, 1986, 90 mins.

Personal Best
Two champion female athletes meet at the 1976 Olympic trials. They start out as friends, wind up as lovers and one day meet again as competitors. Mariel Hemingway stars with Patrice Donnelly.
VHS: $01013. $19.98.
Robert Towne, USA, 1982, 129 mins.

Pink Narcissus
It is a gay classic about obsession, beauty and desire. Bobby Kendall stars as a young man who travels from one erotic fantasy to the next, only reality intrudes in the persons of his Johns and the never-ending fear of aging. In this world of want the young man almost doesn't notice that he may become his own most feared apparition, the faded queen.
VHS: $25888. $39.95.
Anonymous, USA, 1971, 70 mins.

Pink Ulysses
Inspired by the earlier, anonymous *Pink Narcissus*, this film pays homage to all those images of vaguely historical but definitely hunky young men captured in 1950's muscle magazines. Longing for a returning hero is the stuff of which legends are made.
VHS: $26698. $39.95.
Eric DeKuyper, USA, 1993, 98 mins.

Plates
Taylor Mead and Bill Rice, two underground, queer art stars, are featured in this funny and remarkable film from playwright and director Gary Goldberg. Shown at the 1991 Berlin International Film festival, *Plates* harkens to the world of silent film even though it employs non-verbal sound to tell its story.
VHS: $27240. $49.95.
Gary Goldberg, USA, 1991, 11 mins.

Poison
An interwoven trilogy, the film uses three distinct stylistic conventions to explore the writings of Jean Genet, arriving at a profound realization of poison in the human mind, body and soul: A gritty prison drama reveals a homosexual's despair at being constantly confronted by forbidden passions; a campy '50s horror film send-up portrays a scientist's search for the essence of sexuality, and draws a compelling parallel to the HIV crisis when things go awry; and a tabloid mystery criticizes religious sentimentality as it reveals the circumstances surrounding the murder of a wife-beater by his own child, who then flew out the window toward heaven. Winner of the Grand Jury Prize at the Sundance Film Festival.
VHS: $15839. $19.98.
Laser: LD72226. $34.95.
Todd Haynes, USA, 1991, 85 mins.

Pretty Boy
In this unflinching and harshly poetic film, the chronicle of a young runaway boy unfolds on the streets of Copenhagen. There he becomes a street hustler. Before the camera, innocence is plundered and finally lost in this compelling exploration of desire. Danish with English subtitles.
VHS: $23290. $69.95.
Carsten Sonder, Denmark, 1993, 87 mins.

The Queen
Almost forgotten, this documentary charts the pressure-laden world of competition surrounding the drag queen event known as the Miss All-America Camp Beauty Queen Pageant from 1967. At times funny and deadly serious, it offers a truly fascinating glimpse of a queer world that existed prior to Stonewall. Crystal, who also appeared in *Paris Is Burning*, is featured.
VHS: $26294. $59.95.
Frank Simon, USA, 1968, 68 mins.

The Question of Equality
Four documentaries, each one hour long, are collected in this video set about the growth of the lesbian and gay rights movement in the last 25 years. They include *Out Rage 69*, the story of what led to Stonewall and the decade following it; *Culture Wars*, the backlash against gay visibility; *Hollow Liberty*, notable court cases surrounding military discharges and state sodomy statutes and *Generation Q*, which features more than 30 gay and lesbian youths talking about growing up gay.
VHS: $27705. $59.95.

Red Ribbons
Quentin Crisp and Georgina Spelvin star in this story about a group of friends paying tribute to a special person. When Frank succumbs to AIDS, his colleagues and former lovers gather in an impromptu memorial service. Part drama and part video diary, this work reveals the feelings of the loved ones left behind.
VHS: $25722. $39.95.
Neil Ira Needleman, USA, 1994, 90 mins.

Reflections: A Moment in Time
"Bright strong Scorpio looking for friendship." So begins Xaviera's ad in a lesbian correspondence club magazine. She finds a friend, and more, in Megan. together they overcome the pain of racism and the fear of trusting and loving. A lesbian-produced and directed original video. 30 mins.
VHS: $06366. $39.95.

Resident Alien
Quentin Crisp, author and professional pansy, has always led a charming, if not charmed, life. While *The Naked Civil Servant* tells of his early and troubled life in Great Britain, this film shows how celebrity in America suited the grand old dame. Fran Lebowitz, Holly Woodlawn, Michael Musto, and other New York scenesters are featured.
VHS: $25103. $79.95.
Jonathan Nossiter, USA, 1990, 85 mins.

Rich Boy, Poor Boy
A colleague of the late Filipino director Lino Brocka, Piedro de San Paulo's controversial and banned work rips open the Third World taboo. The story concerns an outlawed relationship between a wealthy, Americanized young man and his strong-willed, quiet farmhand. "Brave and brazen, a bittersweet portrait of friendship and desire" (*Bay Area Reporter*). With Victor Viller, Edwyn Casas, Cristina Ocampo. Tagalog with English subtitles. On the same program is *A Boy Named Cocoy*, about a mountain boy's quest to find a better life in Manila.
VHS: $17777. $59.95.
Piedro de San Paulo, Philippines, 1991, 94 mins.

Ritz
Director Richard Lester (*A Hard Day's Night, Three Musketeers*) keeps the pace fast and furious in this crisp farce about Gaetano Proclo hiding out in a men's bathhouse in New York. With Jack Weston, Rita Moreno, Jerry Stiller and F. Murray Abraham.
VHS: $01118. $19.98.
Laser: LD71475. $34.98.
Richard Lester, USA, 1976, 91 mins.

Rock Hudson's Home Movies
With excerpts from some of Rock's most memorable films, this documentary digs into the persona of Hollywood's greatest male sex symbol of the 50's and 60's, whose death from AIDS forever transformed the way America looks at its stars. Mark Rappaport's film was named to multiple Ten Best lists as an original look at an American icon.
VHS: $21090. $39.95.
Mark Rappaport, USA, 1992, 63 mins.

Salmonberries
German director Percy Adlon's political thriller features k.d. lang in her film debut. The story concerns a repressed East German librarian who escapes her oppressive surroundings after her lover is killed trying to scale the Berlin Wall. Devastated and grief stricken, Roswitha (Rosel Zech) travels to Alaska. Trapped in a grim, remote Eskimo outpost, she finds comfort and emotional fulfillment with the sexually ambiguous lang.
VHS: $18844. $29.95.
Percy Adlon, Canada/Germany, 1991, 94 mins.

Salut Victor
This charming tear-jerker follows two older gay men and their budding romance. Victor is gay, and his exuberant spirit inspires Phillipe, a longtime loner, to finally share some of his own unique spirit. French with English subtitles.
VHS: $24834. $39.95.
Anne Claire Poirer, Canada, 1989, 83 mins.

Savage Nights
Cloaked in controversy because its maker and star, Cyril Collard, died of AIDS just days after the film won the coveted Cesar (French Oscar) award, *Savage Nights* is a story of passion and love in the age of HIV. A bisexual photographer finds his life is shared by those he loves in a way that many would find unforgivable. The film provokes and astonishes with its singular perspective; it is all the more incendiary by being rooted in real life. French with English subtitles.
VHS: $22530. $94.99.
Cyril Collard, France, 1993, 126 mins.

Seduction: The Cruel Woman
Pina Bausch dancer Mechtild Grossman plays Wanda, a dominatrix whose troupe services customers and elaborately stages S&M performances in this "stunning" film from German filmmakers Elfi Mikesch and Monika Treut (*Virgin Machine*). Much more important to Mikesch's insinuating camera than the petty tortures are the settings, costumes, and look of each encounter. This is S&M by Avedon, outfits by Dior…By the way, on her off hours, of which there are few, Wanda prefers women. German with English subtitles.
VHS: $12460. $29.95.
E. Mikesch/M. Treut, Germany, 1985, 84 mins.

Sex Is…
This bold documentary charts the growing sexual awareness among a group of men whose personal histories extend from before Stonewall, through the growing AIDS crises and into today's climate of "in-your-face" sexual politics. Its an in-depth look at how these men coped with change and loss inside the sexual revolution.
VHS: $21134. $39.95.
Marc Huestis, USA, 1993, 80 mins.

She Must Be Seeing Things
"A wryly sophisticated comedy…plays like a lesbian homage to *Unfaithfully Yours*," wrote Jay Carr in *The Boston Globe*. Agatha is an international lawyer, Jo a filmmaker. While Jo is on the road with her film, Agatha reads her diary and becomes insanely jealous to the point of dressing up as a man and "shadowing" her. "Groundbreaking in its understated portrayal of sophisticated urban lesbians exploring such dynamics as sex and sexuality, career and commitment, fidelity and companionship. The film gives us characters who are richly realistic and demonstrates that McLaughlin is a complex and refreshingly thoughtful talent…" (*New York Native*).
VHS: $10941. $29.95.
Sheila McLaughlin, USA, 1988, 85 mins.

She's Safe
These hot lesbian short films are also safer sex education. *La Ravissement, Safer Sister, Safe Sex Is Hot Sex, Down on the River, Jill Jacks Off, Current Flow, Cunt Dykula, Girls Will Be Boys, Safe Soap* and excerpts from *Well Sexy Woman* and *Truth or Dare* are joined on this video. 55 mins.
VHS: $24032. $39.95.

Silence=Death
This film serves as an important historical document, exploring the reactions of New York's artistic community to the ravages of AIDS. Responses range from David Wojnorowicz's venomous proclamations and paintings, and painter Rafael Gambas's seething indictment of homophobic bigotry, to Keith Haring's nostalgic longing for the days of care-free sex, and Allen Ginsberg's musing upon his shyer attitude about experimenting sexually. Even with the gentler voices, the film's undercurrent is an angry demand for action and recognition. "Best AIDS film to date…" (*The Guardian*).
VHS: $14148. $29.95.
Rosa von Praunheim/Phil Zwickler, USA, 1990, 60 mins.

Silent Pioneers
Senior members of lesbian and gay communities share their memories of gay life in this documentary. Sometimes tragic, and sometimes funny, their recollections are always personal and poignant. This film offers a unique view of an era less tolerant of sexual minorities.
VHS: $27614. $39.95.
Lucy Winer, USA, 1985, 54 mins.

Silverlake Life: The View from Here

This highly acclaimed documentary was shown on PBS's *Point of View* series. It follows the slow demise of a longtime film and video maker, Tom Joslin, who is dying of AIDS. This unvarnished self-portrait of a man, his lover (Mark Massi), his family and his friends offers an unparalleled look into the heart of the AIDS crises. It won the Sundance Grand Jury Prize.
VHS: S21880. $19.95.
Laser: CLV. LD74626. **$39.95.**
Tom Joslin/Peter Friedman, USA, 1993, 89 mins.

A Simple Matter of Justice

The official video of the 1993 March on Washington shows the diversity of the lesbian, gay and bisexual movement today. It is a powerful look at a key moment which crystallized all the competing interests different aspects of the community bring to this movement. 56 mins.
VHS: S26974. $29.95.

Since Stonewall

Ten great short films from the 70s, 80s and early 90s, reflecting the feelings, fears, humor, artistry, and changing realities of gay America. Featuring a rarely seen work by Gus Van Sant (*Drugstore Cowboy, My Own Private Idaho*) based on a story by William S. Burroughs. Includes *Which Is Scary, Queerdom, A.I.D.S.C.R.E.A.M., Song from an Angel, Triangle, Anton, Bust Up, '976-', Final Solutions* and Van Sant's *Discipline of De*.
USA, 80 mins.
VHS: S15542. $19.95.

Siren

Shot on location in London, this erotic lesbian film has all the makings of a delightful fantasy. Ella is captivated by Jodie, a writer of erotic fiction. At Jodie's lavish estate, titillation and more await this young and sexy couple.
VHS: S27448. $29.95.
Sarah Swords, USA/Great Britain, 1996, 45 mins.

Smashing Ladies

This documentary features some of the best pro women tennis players to ever grace the court. Billie Jean King, Virgina Wade, Margaret Smith Court, Maria Bueno, Margaret Osborne and many more of tennis' most exciting personalities are featured on this video. 60 mins.
VHS: S26975. $19.95.

Split: Portrait of a Drag Queen

International Chrysis was one of Salvador Dali's inner circle. This documentary portrait reveals the person behind the celebrity who appeared as a woman from the waist up, but as a man from the waist down.
VHS: S24245. $39.95.
Ellen Fisher Turk/Andrew Weeks, USA, 1992, 60 mins.

Stiff Sheets

A document of an agitprop/drag fashion show presented by an anonymous collective of gay artists, during a week-long round-the-clock vigil at County/USC Medical Center in Los Angeles. The vigil drew media attention to the lethal lack of public AIDS care and facilities available in L.A.
VHS: S11637. $39.95.
John Goss, USA, 1989, 19 mins.

Stonewall 25:
Global Voices of Pride and Protest!

Past and present join in this celebration that includes political, sporting and entertainment events. Joan Rivers, Pete Seeger, Lee Grant, Charles Busch, Kate Bornstein, Petulia Clark, Chita Rivera, Nathan Lane, Quentin Crisp, David Marshall Grant and Sir Ian McKellen are just some of the celebrities seen. USA, 1994, 90 mins.
VHS: S21703. $24.95.

Stop the Church

Robert Hilferty's controversial documentary takes an irreverent look at the infamous AIDS activist demonstration that invaded Cardinal O'Connor's own parish church, New York City's St. Patrick's Cathedral. ACT-UP NY meetings and preparations help show what the goal was that these activists hoped to accomplish, which was primarily to stop the Church from interfering in the political crisis occasioned by AIDS.
VHS: S27235. $59.95.
Robert Hilferty, USA

Straight from the Heart

This Academy Award-winning documentary explores the experiences of parents learning to love their lesbian and gay children in a world dominated by homophobia. There is a range of stories touching on a variety of experiences, including a religious Mormon family and an African-American family. 30 mins.
VHS: S26030. $24.95.
Dee Mosbacher/Frances Reid, USA, 1994, 30 mins.

The Sum of Us

In this gay romantic comedy a young man finds the search for Mr. Right troubled by his busy-body father. Dad is just concerned for a son who seems unable to find that special someone. Altogether it's a light, amiable tale that is darkened by unexpected misfortune. In sunny Australia, however, things always get bright again. Based on David Stevens' play.
VHS: S26443. $29.98.
Laser: LD75085. **$39.99.**
Kevin Dowling/Geoff Burton, Australia, 1995, 99 mins.

Sunday Bloody Sunday

Nominated for four Academy Awards, *Sunday Bloody Sunday* stars Glenda Jackson, Peter Finch and Murray Head in an unusual love triangle on the rocks. Head plays the enigmatic bisexual involved with both a man and a woman.
VHS: S01283. $19.95.
Laser: LD71182. **$49.95.**
John Schlesinger, Great Britain, 1971, 110 mins.

Super 8½

Bruce La Bruce is back as a tired porn director with a decided lack of lust. With his career in shambles, a documentary about his former glory days offers him the only respite from his currently bleak and empty life. In this campy send-up of art, porn and rip-offs of classic films, queer icons Vaginal Creme Davis and comic Scott Thompson evoke a world grown weary of intimacy. It's rude and funny.
VHS: S26697. $39.95.
Bruce La Bruce, Canada, 1994, 106 mins.

Suzanne Westenhoefer:
HBO Comedy Special

Suzanne Westenhoefer is the first openly gay or lesbian comic to have her own *HBO Comedy Special*. This hysterical lesbian comic skewers everything from the military to performing for less than friendly audiences in this, her first cable TV special. USA, 1994, 28 mins.
VHS: S26940. $19.95.

Swoon

A highly stylized black and white reconsideration of the Leopold and Loeb case, the two University of Chicago students who attempted the perfect crime, the kidnapping of a 12-year-old boy, that resulted in his death. This film provides a historical and sexual context for the crime, finding its roots in homoerotic fixation. With Daniel Schlachet, Craig Chester and Ron Vawter.
VHS: S18518. $19.95.
Tom Kalin, USA, 1991, 92 mins.

Taxi Zum Klo

A smash hit at the Berlin and New York Film Festivals in 1981, *Taxi Zum Klo* is an autobiographical examination of the director's own sexual escapades and fantasies. Frank Ripploh explores every aspect of gay life in Berlin, with hilarious results. German with English subtitles.
VHS: S01304. $79.95.
Frank Ripploh, W. Germany, 1981

Thank You & Goodnight

A highly original film by Jan Oxenberg that uses memory, anecdote and avant-garde representations (such as cardboard cut-outs) to explore the tender, beautiful and emotionally devastating relationship between the filmmaker and her grandmother. "Wildly inventive and unique, it's a cosmic, cerebral comedy of a Woody Allenish sort" (*Toronto Globe*).
VHS: S18269. $19.98.
Jan Oxenberg, USA, 1991, 82 mins.

Third Sex Sinema Volume 1—Vapors

The first volume of the *Third Sex Sinema* series. The notorious short film *Vapors* was banned across America in the 60's and deals with a man's first visit to a New York City gay bathhouse. It was directed by Andy Milligan. Also included is a fun and quirky loop circa early 60's titled *Shoot It Baby*, and the 1960 black and white German import *The Third Sex*, which deals with the sensitive subject of male teacher/male student relations.
VHS: S24737. $19.98.

Third Sex Sinema Volume 2—The Song of the Loon

Richard Armory's novel was realized on film during the height of the sexual revolution. Set in the American West of the 1870's, it follows the growing homoerotic self-awareness and subsequent experiences of a young man. This early gay erotic work is joined by two shorts. *The Coronation* is from the 1960's while *Lot in Sodom* is a silent film from the 1920's.
VHS: S24738. $19.98.
Andrew Herbert, USA, 1970, mins.

Third Sex Sinema Volume 3—The Meatrack

This soft-core relic features a wild plot about a young hustler seemingly lost in a daze of endless cheap sex with men and women until he rescues a young woman. They fall in love and make plans but old habits and traumatic events stand in their way.
VHS: S23060. $19.98.
Michael Thomas, USA, 1970, 71 mins.

The Third Sex

Paula Wesley and Paul Dahlke star in this exploitative look at homosexuality. Parents try to straighten out their son, who is hanging out with a known gay man. It's a shocker. 1959.
VHS: S23187. $24.95.

This Special Friendship

A 16-year-old boy becomes infatuated with a young classmate at a strict Jesuit boarding school. "A masterpiece...shocking in the best sense of the word" (L.A. *Times*). A sensitively directed film with a bravura performance by Didier Haudepin. French with English subtitles.
VHS: S01333. $49.95.
Jean Delannoy, France, 1964, 99 mins.

Three of Hearts

Yurek Bogayevicz's unconventional romantic triangle concerns a beautiful nurse (Kelly Lynch) who hires a handsome male escort (William Baldwin) to seduce the sexually confused English professor (Sherilyn Fenn) who ended their relationship. An interesting investigation into the nature of attraction, gender and sexual role playing. With Joe Pantoliano and Gail Strickland.
VHS: S19476. $19.95.
Yurek Bogayevicz, USA, 1993, 101 mins.

TimePiece

A surprise birthday party is the catalyst for this story about seven gay men in the 1990's. Though fictional, it feels like a documentary as they discuss highly intimate aspects of their lives. From group sex to monogamy and coming out, this film explores experiences shared by many gay men.
VHS: S27241. $29.95.
Kenn Sprenkel/Brian Petraska, USA, 1994, 58 mins.

To Wong Foo, Thanks for Everything! Julie Newmar

Patrick Swayze, Wesley Snipes and John Leguizamo star as beautiful young drag queens out for a jaunt across America. Along the way, they break some hearts, deepen their sense of fashion and even throw a party. This warm comedy is a perfect gender-bending confection. Stockard Channing and Blythe Danner are both featured.
VHS: S27180. $99.99.
Laser: LD75465. **$39.98.**
Beeban Kidron, USA, 1995, 109 mins.

Together Alone

This first feature is a tightly written expose of the feelings and emotions that beset two men just after a casual sexual encounter. Everything from love and commitment to AIDS and unsafe sex come into focus between these intimately acquainted strangers.
VHS: S22949. $39.95.
P.J. Castellaneta, USA, 1991, 87 mins.

Tom Chomont: A Two-Volume Collection

The works of this experimental gay filmmaker are collected on these two videos. *Volume I* contains the short films *Jabbock, The Heavens, Razor Head* and *The Bath*. Volume II features *Spider Jan.16.91, Inner Sanctum, Garden* and *The Mirror*.
Volume I.
VHS: S27237. $69.95.
Volume II.
VHS: S27238. $69.95.
Tom Chomont, USA

Tongues Untied

The late Marlon Riggs was internationally acclaimed for such groundbreaking videos as *Color Adjustment*. Poetry, personal testimony, rap, performance and dance are combined in this singular exploration of the racism and homophobia that black men face daily. Broadcast on the PBS series *P.O.V.*, its beauty and power generated outrage from right-wing politicians. Even so, it remains unmatched for its eloquence.
VHS: S22951. $39.95.
Marlon Riggs, USA, 1989, 55 mins.

The Trials of Oscar Wilde

Peter Finch and John Fraser star in this story based on the loving relationship between Oscar Wilde and Lord Alfred Douglas. John Furnell's *The Stringed Lute* and Montgomery Hyde's *Trials of Oscar Wilde* provide the literary sources for this intriguing film. Also known as *The Man with the Green Carnation*. With Yvonne Mitchell, Lionel Jeffries and Ian Fleming.
VHS: S26878. $24.95.
Ken Hughes, Great Britain, 1960, 123 mins.

Tu Solo

Traditions like bull fighting inevitably depend on venerable institutions. This graceful art is revealed through a true story set in Spain's most prestigious bull fighting school. Students tell their own side of the story, and in a unique tradition, bare all for a nude bullfighting scene.
VHS: S23743. $79.95.
Teo Escamilla, Spain, 1995, 96 mins.

Turnabout: The Story of the Yale Puppeteers

Dan Bessie crafted this documentary about the three gay puppeteers who enchanted Hollywood for 25 years. Their musical extravaganzas, with puppet replicas of celebrities, drew legends like Hitchcock to see their performances. The sophisticated humor of their shows came from a unique camp sensibility, one fostered by these three gay men in a time when being gay was extremely difficult.
VHS: S27492. $39.95.
Dan Bessie, USA, 1992, 55 mins.

Two in Twenty

This lesbian soap opera follows the lives of two households. With humor and suspense, the characters in this soap confront complicated issues such as child custody, lesbian parenting, AIDS, substance abuse, racism, coming out, monogamy, crushes, bisexuality, sex, and of course, therapy. Commercials for fictitious products and services satirize the consumerism at the core of a daytime television experience.
Two in Twenty: Volume 1. 100 mins.
VHS: S16835. $39.95.
Two in Twenty: Volume 2. 100 mins.
VHS: S16836. $39.95.
Two in Twenty: Volume 3. 52 mins.
VHS: S16837. $39.95.
Two in Twenty: Complete Set.
VHS: S16914. $99.95.

Urinal

An innovative first feature, *Urinal* summons seven gay artists from 1937 and gives them an "Impossible Mission": they must research the policing of washroom sex in Ontario, and propose solutions. Each night they convene to present a lecture, with every lecture adopting a different documentary convention. Using interviews with politicians, gay activists and men who have been charged with "gross indecency," hundreds of victims of police entrapment and video surveillance are revealed. A funny and disturbing film that probes into the roots of homosexual discrimination. From Canada's most controversial independent filmmaker.
VHS: S15808. $39.95.
John Greyson, Canada, 1988, 100 mins.

A Valentine for Nelson & Two Marches

New York-based filmmaker Jim Hubbard hand processes his own 16mm film, resulting in intensely personal and moving works. The first is simply a Valentine for his longtime lover. In the second, he contrasts the March on Washington held before AIDS dominated gay life with the later larger gay rights march held in 1993.
VHS: S27221. $59.95.
Jim Hubbard, USA, 1993

Vegas in Space

Drag Queens bring Vegas glamour to an intergalactic battle of outsized proportions. Well, the proportions of the miniature sets are all too obvious, but then so is the drag in this campy, overacted farce. An all-women planet is thrown out of whack by a dastardly crime. Two earth astronauts are sent to help, but there is one condition. They must become women to enter this feminine planet. The rest is showbiz herstory. Features the late Doris Fish.
VHS: S27624. $69.98.
Phillip R. Ford, USA, 1991, 85 mins.

Via Appia

A complex film about gay desire and paranoia. A former German steward travels to Rio to find a mysterious man who left a cryptic message, "Welcome to the AIDS Club," following a sexual encounter. "Via Appia, the nickname of a Rio district where male prostitutes hang out, becomes a grim guided tour of the city's gay subculture, its bars, discos, streets and a beach known as the AIDS farm. The documentary-within-the-film-format justifies this material" (Vincent Canby). With Peter Senner, Guilherme de Padua and Yves Jansen. German and Spanish with English subtitles.
VHS: S18693. $39.95.
Jochen Hick, Germany/Brazil, 1992, 90 mins.

Virgin Machine

Called "steamy" by *The San Francisco Chronicle* and "a lesbian Candide...deliriously obscene" by *The San Francisco Examiner*, *Virgin Machine* is an offbeat black and white comedy about a journalist researching romantic love. The study takes her from German endocrinologists to San Francisco's porn district where she meets Susie Sexpert, a woman who lectures on the relative merits of various strippers and demonstrates dildos the way some women handle tupperware. German with English subtitles.
VHS: S10940. $29.95.
Monika Treut, Germany, 1988, 90 mins.

A Virus Knows No Morals

A black comedy filled with the worst fears, a savagely funny burlesque on the AIDS crisis, irreverent yet deadly serious. Nurses on the night shift roll dice to see which AIDS patient will die next. An epidemic victim is harassed by a reporter on his death bed—he sticks her with a contaminated syringe. The government opens a quarantine called Hell Gay Land. Gay terrorists capture the Minister of Health. An outrageous and yet extremely honest film by von Praunheim, this controversial film shook West Germany. German with English subtitles.
VHS: S09350. $39.95.
Rosa von Praunheim, Germany, 1985, 82 mins.

Viva Eu! & Ex Voto

Tania Cypriano, an experimental Brazilian filmmaker, explores her most poignant life experiences in these two films. In *Viva Eu!*, Cypriano explores her experiences as a woman living with AIDS. In *Ex Voto*, Cypriano takes a look at her ordeal of surviving terrible burns from a horrible fire she was trapped in. Both films show struggle and a commitment to survival.
VHS: S27241. $39.95.
Tania Cypriano, Brazil

Waking Up: A Lesson in Love

The feature debut of documentary filmmaker Greta Schiller (*Before Stonewall*) is a piercing, emotionally honest dissection of a young woman's journey of self-exploration. The film—shot on location in Austin, Texas—is a collection of painful, funny vignettes unfolding in the casual, loose rhythms of the aggressively hip lesbian bar Petticoat Junction.
VHS: S07854. $39.95.
Greta Schiller, USA, 1988, 60 mins.

We Were One Man

A simple French farmer and a wounded, abandoned German soldier are ultimately united in an openly sexual relationship in this award-winning French film. French with English subtitles.
VHS: S01437. $49.95.
Philippe Vallois, France, 1980, 90 mins.

We Were There

In the year of the American Bicentennial, Pat Rocco created this documentary focusing on the Gay Pride Celebrations in San Francisco and L.A. Rocco was instrumental in making and distributing films about visible, open, gay communities. From 1967-78 he produced, wrote, edited, directed and appeared in over 100 shorts and features. This is one of his best documents, a bit of gay history.
VHS: S22955. $19.95.
Pat Rocco, USA, 1976, 30 mins.

The Wedding Banquet

Ang Lee's surprise hit is a poignant and funny story of the gay Taiwanese yuppie (Winston Chao) who lives with his American lover (Mitchell Lichtenstein) and tries to end his family's endless matchmaking attempts by announcing that he's engaged. His parents unexpectedly fly in to see the bride and turn their son's deception into a complicated affair.
VHS: S21895. $94.98.
Laser: LD74593. **$39.98.**
Ang Lee, USA/Taiwan, 1994, 105 mins.

West Coast Crones: A Glimpse into the Lives of Nine Old Lesbians

A touching and revealing documentary which focuses on nine women at crossroads in their lives, as they reflect and candidly discuss how they confront aging. A remarkably honest, heartfelt film which plays against stereotype as it humanly and movingly deals with the issues which pit individuals against society and its mores.
VHS: S16832. $39.95.
Madeline Muir, USA, 1991, 28 mins.

Westler: East of the Wall

Before the wall separating East and West Germany came down it divided not just a nation but thousands of families. This film tells a story about the nearly impossible romance between two gay men on opposite sides of the wall. German with English subtitles.
VHS: S24836. $39.95.
Wieland Speck, Germany, 1986, 94 mins.

When Night Is Falling

Two women find one another in this sensitive love story. Camille is a repressed Catholic professor currently involved with a man. Her whole life changes, however, when she meets Petra, an enigmatic performer from a visiting circus. Before long, the two women embark on a romance that startles everyone, including themselves, with an unforeseen passion.
VHS: S27541. $89.95.
Patricia Rozema, Canada, 1995, 90 mins.

Wigstock: The Movie

It all began with a bunch of New York drag queens who didn't want to stop partying so they put on a show in Tomkins Square Park—in the daytime. Now it has grown into an annual celebration of queer crossdressers from all over. Underground stars The "Lady" Bunny, Jackie Beat, the Mistress Formica, Lypsinka and Joey Arias are joined by RuPaul, Crystal Waters, Alexis Arquette and Deee-Lite on a trip across a landscape of cosmetic wonders.
VHS: S26862. $99.98.
Laser: LD75417. **$39.99.**
Barry Shils, USA, 1995, 82 mins.

Wild Blade

A narcissistic gathering of five people with convulsive sexual desires and unconventional orientation are attracted to a young male prostitute (Stephen Geoffreys) whose married trick dies under mysterious circumstances. The dead man's wife, a deranged pimp and a jealous lover all conspire and negotiate for possession of the hustler. With Sheila Kelley, Carole Scott, Thom Crouch and Geoffrey Paltrowitz.
VHS: S18588. $29.95.
David Geffner, USA, 1992

Wild Life

A video portrait of two 15-year-old gay Latinos, this work by John Goss combines documentary-style interviews with fictional segments in which the young men act out their fantasized day in Los Angeles. As they talk about their lives, we see scenes of them changing into wild style clothes on the street, cruising around "Gay City," meeting their friends at the park, and "throwing attitude." They are questioned about the nature of being gay, relationships with friends and lovers, style and image, and their use of gay language.
VHS: S06509. $49.95.
John Goss, USA, 1985, 40 mins.

Women from Down Under

Australian and New Zealand directors made these lesbian shorts. Italian food, Bulgarian folksinging, truckers and the morning after are just some of the surprising elements that come up in these entertaining works. Included are *Peach, Just Desserts, Excursion to the Bridge of Friendship* and *Jumpin' the Gun.* 52 mins.
VHS: S27609. $29.95.

Word Is Out:
Stories of Some of Our Lives

This is the first major film to explore America's gay culture. Involving a diverse range of people in locales from San Francisco to Boston, the study interviews 26 men and women ranging in age from 18 to 77. Speaking tellingly, funnily and movingly of their experiences, these women and men overturn decades worth of accumulated stereotypes. From the director of *Absolutely Positive.*
VHS: S16077. $79.95.
Mariposa Film Group, USA, 1977, 130 mins.

Wrecked for Life: The Trip and Magic of Trocadero Transfer

Before the arrival of AIDS, the underground gay dance scene in San Francisco generated one of the most exciting nightlife sensations ever known. At the center of this scene was the Trocadero Transfer. In this documentary everything about the all-night parties held there is revealed through interviews with the people who made it happen and those who experienced it.
VHS: S21026. $39.95.
John Goss, USA, 1993, 60 mins.

You Are Not Alone

This Danish film honestly explores the boundaries between friendship and love in a boys' school in a film which is full of nuance, gentleness and humor, reminiscent of the early films of Truffaut. Danish with English subtitles.
VHS: S01491. $79.95.
Nielsen & Johansen, Denmark, 1982, 90 mins.

Young Hearts, Broken Dreams, Episode 1: The Delivery Boy

Eddie Starr and Mark Cannon star in one of the first gay soap operas, the ongoing saga of a troubled gay movie star, his lover, his friends, sex, drugs, Hollywood and life in the fast lane. Adam Harrington, a delivery boy at Paramount Pictures, finds all his romantic longings fulfilled when he meets and moves in with his idol, gay movie star Scottie Edwards. Unfortunately, Scottie is beholden to a ruthless drug lord, and he and Adam decide to skip town together. In the end, however, they must face reality and return to the oversexed world of gay Hollywood.
VHS: S27722. $49.95.
Gerald Gordon, USA, 1990, 45 mins.

Young Hearts, Broken Dreams, Episode 2: The Search

After the disastrous outcome of the first episode, an entirely new cast of characters comes to the foreground in this steamy sequel. Scottie Edwards' brother Matthew and his best friend, Noah, leave Nebraska to come to Hollywood and avenge Scottie's death. Before long, Matt realizes that he's falling for Zech, the handsome detective assigned to Scottie's murder. *The Search* continues the exciting mix of sex, sensuality and emotional ups and downs found in the first episode of this soap opera. Michael Habusch and Robert Spiewak star.
VHS: S27723. $59.95.
Gerald Gordon, USA, 1995, 83 mins.

Zero Patience

An outrageous movie musical, this films depicts an imaginary love story between 19th-century Victorian writer and explorer Sir Richard Francis Burton and "Patient Zero", the Canadian flight attendant accused by the media of being the man who brought AIDS to North America.
VHS: S22669. $79.95.
John Greyson, Canada, 1993, 100 mins.

documentary CINEMA

$8.50/A Barrel! Huit Piastres et Demie and Cajun Visits
Two men, one 82, the other 93, recount what happened in the fishing village of Golden Meadow, Louisiana, during two weeks in the summer of '38. As leaders of opposing sides of the Shrimp War of 1938, each tells the truth, his truth, and each inevitably contradicts the other. Neighbors and relatives don period costumes, drive vintage cars and ride '30s era boats to recreate the shrimp war. Cajun French with English subtitles. Directed by Glen Pitre, 58 mins.
VHS: S06505. $89.95.

The 1993 March on Washington: Prelude to Victory
This moving and entertaining video includes great footage from the event that transformed the nation's capital. Entertainers and events from the entire week leading up to the march are included. Civil rights for lesbians, gays and bisexuals were advanced because of this historic event. 60 mins.
VHS: S19483. $39.95.

27 Pieces of Me
In this bold, independent feature, Tanya (Tina M. Henning), a lesbian sculptor, is forced to confront her sister Ramona (Angelique von Halle) when she arrives on her doorstep unannounced. Both women have been having relationship troubles. Fortunately, Tanya's roommate Bold (Jonathan Harris) helps the two women begin a rapprochement that they desperately need and want.
VHS: S27479. $39.95.
Gerald Donohoe, USA, 1995, 90 mins.

28 Up
Beginning in 1964, director Michael Apted turned his camera on a group of 7-year-old boys and girls from both wealthy and poor families in England, recording their thoughts, hopes and dreams with revealing interviews. He then returned to film these same children every seven years, until the age of 28; all of their most personal moments, from the rapture of discovered love to the despair of dreams long forgotten, are brought vividly to life, played out before the viewer with striking emotional power. A moving and utterly memorable work.
VHS: S14291. $19.98.
Michael Apted, Great Britain, 1984, 136 mins.

Aileen Wuornos: The Selling of a Serial Killer
Wuornos is a 35-year-old lesbian prostitute who murdered seven of her male clients along a Florida interstate. She is "adopted" by Arlene Pralle, a "born-again" woman who sells the story to the highest bidders. This crazy set-up also includes a lawyer with a crazy defense and Wuornos' lover, who dupes the killer into confessing over the phone. It's a documentary about the media frenzy that surrounds sensational criminals and obscures justice.
VHS: S23288. $19.98.
Nick Broomfield, USA, 1992, 87 mins.

Alligator Hunting: A Louisiana Legacy
Lifestyle traditions and the way they have changed around this age-old practice are explored in this fascinating documentary. 60 mins.
VHS: S22393. $49.95.

America in Black & White
A set of three video cassettes featuring five true life video stories by director Scott Jacobs. USA, 89 mins.
Pugs 'N Pols. Featuring three short films by Scott Jacobs: *The Golden Gloves*—a young fighter battles to make his way out of the ghetto through victory in the ring, produced by Scott Jacobs and Tom Weinberg (10 mins.); *Election Night with Jane Byrne*—the historic 1979 triumph of Chicago's first woman mayor over the Democratic machine as seen from inside her private suite, produced by Scott Jacobs, Cynthia Neal and Lilly Ollinger (22 mins.); and *Election Day (Chicago Style)*—vignettes from the key Chicago precincts in Jimmy Carter's 1976 presidential triumph, produced by Scott Jacobs and Valjean McLenighan (7 mins.). USA, 40 mins.
VHS: S13593. $19.95.
The Las Vegas Tapes. Four days and nights on the streets of downtown Las Vegas with Jack the Jam Artist, Toye the Stripper, Angel and The Radio Announcer and Chief Little Fox, the unofficial mayor of Fremont Street. To the tourists, it's glitter gulch; to them, it's home. Directed by Scott Jacobs and Valjean McLenighan. USA, 27 mins.
VHS: S13594. $19.95.
The Real Realness of the Higher Highness. A Bio-Centennial Unity Fair in Golden Gate Park becomes the focal point for this look back at the future past. Greenpeace, Wavy Gravy, Eckankar, Psycho-Acoustics, and Interspecies Communications are featured as old hippies meet the new age in a celebration of the decade to come. Directed by Scott Jacobs. USA, 22 mins.
VHS: S13595. $19.95.
Set of three cassettes.
VHS: S13596. $39.95.

American Dream
The winner of the 1990 Academy award for best documentary, forceful account of the labor strike and political discord in a small, closely knit Minnesota town, at the Hormel Meat Packing plant. Kopple brilliantly covers the issues, background, social and economic context and the key players. The fight literally pitted brother against brother, after some workers crossed the picket line. Kopple strips away the layers of deception and anger to present a startling portrait of Reagan/Bush era greed and the frightening repercussions that breaks up of a community. Kopple worked on the film for more than seven years.
VHS: S17633. $19.98.
Barbara Kopple, USA, 1990, 90 mins.

Amish: Not to Be Modern
Made in cooperation with the Amish community, this is an exclusive portrait of the intensely private Amish. Filmed over a period of one year, we observe the cycles of life in an Amish community, and the important role that every member plays. 57 mins.
VHS: S13169. $29.98.

And Now Miguel
Produced for the U.S. government by Joseph Krumgold, this motion picture depicts a typical Southwestern American family operating as an economic unit. Its members choose to carry on the traditional occupations from father to son.
VHS: S10555. $24.95.
Manuel Cheves, USA, 1953, 62 mins.

And This Is Free
Chicago's Maxwell Street Market is captured in its entirety through cinema verite techniques in this unique film. The filmmaker originally set out to capture blues singers, but he realized that the whole area contained a much fuller picture that could explain the blues. Since Maxwell Street has been transformed by urban renewal, this may be the only way to see the singular mix of people and music that this area once offered. B&W.
VHS: S27154. $19.95.
Mike Shea, USA, 1964, 50 mins.

Anderson Platoon
One of the great films about Vietnam, directed by Pierre Schoendoerffer, the documentary focuses on an integrated combat unit led by Black West Pointer Lt. Joseph B. Anderson, and captures the tension, anger, hopelessness and pathos of armed conflict. Winner of the Academy Award for Best Documentary Feature.
VHS: S02404. $19.95.
Pierre Schoendorffer, France, 1967, 65 mins.

Angelyne
Angelyne is an enigmatic but ubiquitous pin-up model in L.A., her hometown. This documentary finally shows the woman with the amazing figure behind all the hype. She reveals everything from her opinions on men to her thoughts on Barbie. The president of her fan club, her psychotherapist and her lingerie consultant offer their opinions of the fascinating Angelyne. 25 mins.
VHS: S26663. $14.98.

Anima Mundi
This collaboration between director Godfrey Reggio (*Koyaanisqatsi*) and composer Philip Glass (*Einstein on the Beach*) is a naturalistic documentary on the relationship between humans and animals. The film uses a series of close encounters between humans and animals of varying sizes to showcase the diversity of the animal kingdom. "The proud procession of life forms has an incandescence and mystery that neither still photographs nor museum exhibitions can begin to capture" (*New York Times*).
VHS: S19593. $19.98.
Laser: CAV. LD72437. $29.99.
Godfrey Reggio, USA, 1993, 50 mins.

Animals Film
A very powerful, unflinching documentary about the shocking treatment of animals in research and in the food process, this feature-length film is narrated by Julie Christie, and has been banned from television for its graphic footage.
VHS: S05363. $79.95.
Victor Shonfeld, Great Britain, 1985, 120 mins.

Anything I Catch
The rare art and the natural drama of a way of life are shown in this documentary about handfishing. They represent elements of the disappearing Cajun lifestyle and the traditions of this community. 27 mins.
VHS: S22386. $39.95.

Apogee: Life in Motion
Cinematographer Craig McCourry's stunning film, six years in the making, continues the tradition of *Koyaanisqatsi* as he travels the world to capture the visual synergy of man, nature and the built environment. A dazzling collage of music, movement and rhythm from Japan, India, the Seychelles Islands, Hong Kong, Canada and the U.S. 45 mins.
VHS: S21898. $19.98.

Appalachia: No Man's Land
A highly personalized account of the effects of coal mining on several communities on the West Virginia/ Kentucky border. Based on interviews with long-time Appalachians, many of whom have worked for the coal companies, the film is a chronicle of the resilience of a people and their culture in the face of economic and environmental hardships. Produced by Maryknoll Media. 28 mins.
VHS: S04921. $24.95.

Armageddon Express
Two films providing angry protests for peace. In *The Healing of Brian Wilson*, Kris Kristofferson, Joan Baez and the music of Jackson Browne contribute to the profile of Brian Wilson, who had both his legs amputated by a train carrying weapons to the Contras. In *The Arms Race Within*, Bob Dylan adds music to a story about peaceniks who plan to stop a train carrying 180 atomic bombs across America. 90 mins.
VHS: S13168. $19.98.

Arruza
Budd Boetticher's odd homage to the great bullfighter Carlos Arruza, who staged a famous comeback to the ring in the 1960's; a fascinating blend of theater, religion, aesthetics and violence in the Mexican bullring.
VHS: S04702. $39.95.
Budd Boetticher, USA/Mexico, 1967, 91 mins.

Atchafalaya
This video documentary offers a history of the Mississippi River system. Man has changed its course and the basin where it enters the Gulf of Mexico. Wilderness expert C.C. Lockwood presents detailed environmental information about this key ecosystem. 26 mins.
VHS: S22387. $54.95.

The Atomic Cafe
A unique documentary about Cold War paranoia over the Bomb. This chilling documentary by Kevin Rafferty, Jayne Loader and Pierce Rafferty culls newsreel footage and government archives to recreate the hysteria of the Cold War. "A comic horror film, it does more to evoke the what-me-worry social madness of the Cold War than any documentary I've ever seen" (J. Hoberman).
VHS: S00074. $29.95.
Laser: LD75375. $49.98.
Kevin Rafferty, USA, 1982, 88 mins.

Ballot Measure 9
This winner of the Special Jury Award at Sundance in 1995 follows the fight around Oregon's Ballot Measure 9. Essentially, the initiative would have denied lesbians and gay men civil rights protection. Though defeated, it was the center of acrimonious debate and tense standoffs. This documentary captures the heroic spirits of the people who stood up against bigotry, even under threat of physical harm.
VHS: S27476. $89.95.
Heather MacDonald, USA, 1995, 72 mins.

Baraka
Amazing 70mm cinematography tells this global story of human and environmental interdependence. No dialogue is needed in this film that brings the beauty of the earth together with the universal truth of human striving. Music by a number of religious groups and contemporaries like Michael Stearns and Dead Can Dance make this an aural as well as a visual feast. Best Picture, Montreal Film Festival.
VHS: S25539. $29.95.
Laser: LD74951. $39.98.
Ron Fricke, USA, 1992, 96 mins.

The Beer Hunter
Renowned British beer expert Michael Jackson leads this behind-the-scenes tour of breweries in England, Holland, Austria and Germany. It's a three-volume set from the Discovery Channel that is perfect for all beer lovers. 180 mins.
VHS: S25084. $49.95.

Behind the Veil: Nuns
A profoundly stirring record of the turbulent history and remarkable achievements of women in religion from pre-Christian Celtic communities to the radical sisters of the 1980's. Shot on location in Ireland, Italy, Canada and the United States.
VHS: S05800. $29.95.
Margaret Wescott, Canada, 1984, 130 mins.

Belle Case La Follette: 1859-1931
The dramatic life of a charismatic leader and writer in the suffrage movement is revealed in a dramatic first-person perspective in this historical video. It's ideal for women's studies collections. 15 mins. Resource guide available. Video.
VHS: S25758. $95.00.
Resource Guide.
VHS: S25771. $20.00.

Benjamin Britten
Four documentary shorts—landmarks of documentary cinema—produced by the British Documentary Movement, spearheaded by John Grierson. The four documentary shorts are Alberto Cavalcanti's *Coal Face* (1935), Basil Wright and Harry Watt's *Night Mail*, and Muir Mathiesen's *Instruments of the Orchestra* (1947) and Steps of the Ballet (1948).
VHS: S17420. $29.95.

Berkeley in the Sixties
A moving documentary about the 1960's social, political and sexual revolution at the University of California at Berkeley. The documentary traces the anti-war protest movement, the free speech movement, civil rights protests and the formation of the women's movement. Director Mark Kitchell interweaves archival footage with interviews with key leaders of the movement. The soundtrack includes Joan Baez, Mario Savio, Country Joe and the Fish, The Band, Jimi Hendrix and The Grateful Dead. "Probably the best documentary on the sixties to date" (*Village Voice*).
VHS: S18146. $29.95.
Mark Kitchell, USA, 1990, 117 mins.

Best Boy
An intimate and touching documentary, winner of an Academy Award, Ira Wohl's first feature is the story of his cousin Philly, a 52-year old man with the emotional and intellectual age of an eight-year-old, and of his decision to leave home and work on his own. New York Times wrote, "*Best Boy* records Philly's first four days away from home, though it is always in the company of his cousin-the-filmmaker, who carries the camera …*Best Boy* is though more than the story of Philly. It's about a family. Even more affecting than Philly's first days in school are the scenes we see played—sometimes at the side of the screen—between Philly's mother and father…The film is about life, and 'a confusion of love and anguish.' "
VHS: S05283. $29.95.
Laser: CLV. LD70261. $39.95.
Ira Wohl, USA, 1979, 110 mins.

Beyond the Killing Fields
Millions were killed in the Cambodian civil war. This documentary looks at the efforts made by the people and the organizations that have attempted to help survivors rebuild their lives and their country. Shot on location in Cambodia. 28 mins.
VHS: S23132. $19.95.

The Big Bang
How did the universe begin? What is the human spirit? Filmmaker James Toback (*The Pick-Up Artist*) takes his camera into the lives of the acclaimed and the ordinary—from basketball star Darryl Dawkins, gangster-turned-filmmaker Tony Sirico, violinist Eugene Fodor and former boxing-champ Jose Torres to a model, a mother and a restaurateur—and records their answers to the questions we continue to ask ourselves. "Irresistible" (*N.Y. Times*).
VHS: S15000. $19.98.
James Toback, USA, 1990, 81 mins.

Blacks Britannica
One of the most charged and controversial films of recent years, "a relentless, hard-hitting exposure of the racial and economic oppression of Britain's black population, together with their militant resistance" (Clyde Taylor). The scheduled broadcast on PBS was cancelled, and for the next four years, under a federal court injunction, it could not legally be seen by more than 19 persons at one time. It was condemned as a "danger" by officials of the British government, and its premiere run in a London cinema was stopped by court order. An international campaign to defend the film ultimately succeeded in freeing it from all restrictions. *Blacks Britannica* presents an analysis of racism within the context of British history and the post-war crises of British economy. It reflects the resistance of the Black community to escalating attacks on it, both by organized fascist elements on the streets and by successive British governments. "A startling look at the growing politicization of blacks in Britain and an unsettling portrait of an England in transition" (Variety).
Home Video.
VHS: S10841. $49.95.
Institutional with public performance rights.
VHS: S10846. $89.95.
David Koff, Great Britain, 1978, 58 mins.

Blood in the Face
A darkly humorous and frightening closeup view of today's far right movement, *Blood in the Face* uses archival footage and interviews to reveal the workings of the Ku Klux Klan, the American Nazi Party, the Aryan Nations, and David Duke. One of the most controversial and compelling films of 1991. "Riveting… insidiously spooky…full of outrageous details…first rate journalism" (*New York Times*).
VHS: S15462. $29.95.
Bohlen/Rafferty/Ridgeway, USA, 1991

Blue Water: Great Naval Traditions
Naval history overflows with rich legend and lore. These on-going traditions have a direct impact on life aboard warships today. This video offers a tale any old or new "salt" will enjoy. 60 mins.
VHS: S23122. $19.95.

Borneo
A great adventure documentary narrated by Lowell Thomas detailing flying snakes, tree climbing fish and headhunters. USA, 1937, 76 mins.
VHS: S02812. $39.95.

Briefcases and Bomb Shelters
A survival manual published by the West German government for its citizens states that, in the event of nuclear war, you can protect yourself from fallout by covering your head with a briefcase as you beat a hasty retreat to the nearest bomb shelter. This contribution to atomic absurdity provides the inspiration for this satirical documentary on life in the nuclear age. Written, produced and directed by Bob Hercules.
VHS: S15193. $24.95.
Bob Hercules, USA, 1986, 13 mins.

Broken Noses
Photographer Bruce Weber's first directorial effort is the story of professional lightweight boxer Andy Minsker and his small boxing club for boys in Portland, Oregon. This portrait goes far beyond the realm of boxing as we learn that Minsker was raised in a broken home with a stepfather who beat him. Remarkably unaffected, Minsker reveals both a boxer's machismo and a lifetime of unrealized pain. Set to a smoky jazz score by such greats as Chet Baker, Gerry Mulligan and Julie London.
VHS: S16462. $29.95.
Bruce Weber, USA, 1987, 75 mins.

Brother's Keeper
This riveting documentary by Joe Berlinger and Bruce Sinofsky is a reconstruction of the arrest and trial of Delbert Ward in the alleged suffocation and murder of his brother Bill. Set in a small town in upstate New York, Bill, Delbert and their two other brothers lived in a squalid farmhouse with no electricity or running water. *Brother's Keeper* is a powerful work about the nature of justice and community, and the grass-roots campaign to secure Delbert's freedom and exonerate him of the charges.
VHS: S18959. $19.98.
Laser: CLV. LD74472. $39.95.
J. Berlinger/B. Sinofsky, USA, 1992, 105 mins.

Cajun Crossroads
This informed cultural portrait reveals the evolution of the historical roots and expressions of the Cajun people. 59 mins.
VHS: S22385. $49.95.

California Reich
A look at the bizarre yet frightening phenomenon of the Nazi movement in California. These are no Hollywood cartoon characters, but rather ordinary looking folks who could live next door, frustrated and filled with fear and hatred.
VHS: S00206. $49.95.
W. Parkes/Critchlow, USA, 1975, 55 mins.

Carmen Miranda: Bananas Is My Business
Archival footage, film clips, dramatic re-enactments and interviews document the life story and the lasting influence of the Brazilian Bombshell. This fun and interesting film won Best Documentary at the Chicago International Film Festival and the Film Critic's Award at the Brazilian Film Festival. English and Portuguese with English subtitles.
VHS: S27627. $89.98.
Helena Solberg, USA/Great Britain, 1995, 90 mins.

Catwalk
Supermodel Christy Turlington stands revealed in this behind-the-scenes look at fashion. Whether in Milan, Paris or New York, with Kate Moss, Naomi Campbell, Cindy Crawford or Claudia Schiffer, the backstage world of glamour under pressure that she inhabits is eminently watchable. Designers Giorgio Armani, Jean-Paul Gaultier, Karl Lagerfeld and Valentino are also glimpsed in this singular documentary.
VHS: S27650. $49.95.
Robert Leacock, USA, 1995, 95 mins.

Cheniere au Tigre: Island of the Marsh
Dances and stories recall significant events from the 1920's to the 1940's and reveal aspects of Cajun life long forgotten by some, but not everyone. 28 mins.
VHS: S22390. $49.95.

Chicago Maternity Center Story
For more than 75 years, the Chicago Maternity Center provided safe home deliveries for Chicago mothers. But a change in attitude of modern medicine toward home birth and a decline in funding forced its closure. This "powerful and persuasive film" (Roger Ebert) interweaves the story of a young woman about to have her first baby with the history of the center and the fight to keep it open. "A combative, devastatingly researched account of how American medicine has deteriorated since it became a multi-million dollar business" (Sunday London Times).
VHS: S27851. $29.95.
Kartemquin Films, USA, 1976, 60 mins.

Chicago Nazis
From the violent confrontations of the American Nazis led by Frank Collins, these two documentaries on one tape, Marquette Park I and Marquette Park II, offer probing insights into extremism in America. Marquette Park I documents a Nazi rally, Marquette Park II allows rare insights into the preparation for a planned demonstration. What is remarkable about these films is not only the fact that the filmmaker was allowed to film inside the headquarters, but how he has managed to depict the minds of extremists.
VHS: S06473. $39.95.
Tom Palazzolo, USA, 1976-78, 60 mins.

Chicago Politics: A Theatre of Power
Filmmaker Bill Stamets takes us on a startling and often funny tour of the political arena—Chicago style—into the world of politicians and deal makers, including Mayor Harold Washington and Alderman-turned-Republican Eddie Vrdolyak, in the course of the rituals of office, election and the administration of power. A priceless look at the "inside" of the running of a city.
VHS: S05364. $29.95.
Bill Stamets, USA, 1985-87, 87 mins.

Childhood Complete Set
This revealing series examines the difficulties and hardships of growing up, collected from experiments with 12 families on five continents, that features expert opinions on children and families. 360 mins.
VHS: S19381. $149.95.

Christo's Valley Curtain
Nominated for an Academy Award, a documentary about the construction of Christo's Valley Curtain in Rifle Gap, Colorado, in 1972. "It is the finest film I have ever seen about an artist and his work," said The New York Times. "The surprise of the film is the enthusiasm with which this project was greeted by the residents of Rifle and by the construction workers who risked limbs and lives on the stunt."
VHS: S07492. $39.95.
Maysles Brothers, USA, 1974, 28 mins.

Citizen Diplomat
A compelling portrait of Rama Vernon, a tireless traveler for world peace since 1984 (35 trips to the USSR to date). Share in her unique experiences opening up meaningful communication between private citizens and government officials of the US and USSR. Taped at a special lecture near San Francisco, the viewer learns how Vernon became a citizen diplomat, what it means to her, and how citizen diplomacy has affected us all. A woman's inspiring, insightful story of how "one person can make a difference."
VHS: S13719. $29.95.
Paul (Ramana Das) Silbey, USA, 1990, 58 mins.

The City/The Power and the Land
Two rare short films now available on video! The City (44 mins.) and The Power and the Land (39 mins.).
VHS: S14930. $29.95.

Cityscape Compilations
Includes San Francisco by the Golden Gate (10 mins.), Progress: Los Angeles (15 mins.), Long Beach Earthquake (10 mins.), In the Street (13 mins.), Manhattan (11 mins.), Ellis Island (10 mins.) and Century of Progress—Chicago (10 mins.)
VHS: S14931. $29.95.

Classic Documentaries: People and Places
Four classic documentaries from the 1930's are featured. Housing Problems and New Earth, two key works by Joris Ivens, and Basil Wright's two masterpieces, Song of Ceylon and Night Mail.
VHS: S03473. $59.95.
Joris Ivens/B. Wright, Great Britain/Holland, 1930's

Classic Documentaries: The Power and the Land
Three classic documentaries: The Power and the Land was commissioned as a companion film to Pare Lorentz' The River and it was to do for rural electrification what The River did for the TVA. A simple and convincing story of a rural family before and after receiving the benefits of electricity (in 1935 only one farm in ten used electricity), the documentary's extraordinary emphasis on poetry comes from its simple and meticulous closeness to the rhythms of daily life. This tape also contains Lorentz' The River and The Plow That Broke the Plains. (See description elsewhere).
VHS: S04608. $69.95.
Joris Ivens, USA, 1935, 110 mins.

Col. Culpeper's Flying Circus
Deep in the heart of Texas lies the airfield of the Confederate Air Force, where a dedicated group of volunteers have restored and preserved vintage 1939-45 war planes in flying condition. Their skillfully recreated air battles feature Messerschmitts, Spitfires, Mustangs and Flying Fortresses. 50 mins.
VHS: S03418. $19.94.

Colorado Cowboy: The Bruce Ford Story
Bruce Ford is a legend in rodeo. No man has won more championships in the same event. This film explores the roots and horizons of a man pursuing his own dream, a tradition of pride inherited from his father, a legacy of grace. It's a documentary that traces the line between championship and despair in the Western sport of bareback riding.
VHS: S23286. $24.95.
Arthur Elgort, USA, 1993, 78 mins.

Columbus Didn't Discover Us
A politically charged reaction to the events heralding the Columbus quincentennial, this documentary explores the issues discussed in the July 1990 symposium on the cultural, historical and political damage suffered by indigenous cultures and languages through the hemisphere. The historic gathering featured Indian nations from North, South and Central America. "This is an important and valuable testimonial from voices too long suppressed" (Lisa Mitten, American Indian Library Association).
Home Video.
VHS: S17500. $39.95.
Institutional with Public Performance Rights.
VHS: S17686. $59.95.

A Common Destiny:
Walking in Both Worlds—Jewell Praying Wolf James, known as Se-sealth, is an engaging young Lummi tribesman, a hunter and gatherer of the lost and subjugated wisdom of his ancestors. Speaking from a cedar tree-stump in an ancient Northwest forest, he brings to the present the message of his ancestor, chief Seattle, whose name he carries. Directed by Gayil Nalls. The Hopi Prophecy—Thomas Banyacya, now in his 80s, is a spokesman for the Hopi high religious leaders. His words come from the heart as he interprets the potentially apocalyptic message of the petroglyph on Second Mesa. Two parts on one tape. Total length: 60 mins.
VHS: S15436. $24.95.

Common Threads: Stories from the Quilt
Academy Award winner Robert Epstein and Jeffrey Friedman's moving, powerful documentary about five people who died of AIDS and whose names are on panels of the AIDS quilt which now covers over 14 acres. Dustin Hoffman is the narrator. HBO Video will donate all profits from the sale of Common Threads to the NAMES Project, which is in charge of the quilt. For more information on the NAMES project, call 415-863-1966.
VHS: S12767. $19.98.
R. Epstein/J. Friedman, USA, 1989, 79 mins.

Consuming Hunger: Getting the Story
News events from the Third World face a tough fight for Western television air time. Yet images determine the Western World's view of the Third World: the dramatic pictures from Ethiopia launched a major relief effort, yet those pictures almost didn't get aired. Getting the Story shows how the tragedy in Ethiopia went from just another famine to become the most moving news story of the decade, exploring the "rules" of television news and our own attitudes toward the Third World. 28 mins.
VHS: S05844. $24.95.

Consuming Hunger: Selling the Feeling
Selling the Feeling explores the Madison Avenue treatment of problems such as domestic hunger and homelessness, and the conscious decision by the organizers to avoid the political aspects of the problems. The death of thousands in Ethiopia made us aware of the plight of our own poor, hungry and homeless. Yet when the events are over, are we any different as a nation in our treatment of the poor? Produced by Maryknoll Media. 28 mins.
VHS: S05845. $24.95.

Consuming Hunger: Shaping the Image
Shaping the Images raises questions about the impression of Africa created by television coverage of the Ethiopian famine, and, by extension, the images projected of other suffering peoples. What was our response? Was Live Aid an outpouring of generosity or a celebration of Rock and Roll? Are we ready to listen to Africans and our own poor tell their own story? 28 mins.
VHS: S05846. $24.95.

Coverup: Behind the Iran-Contra Affair
A documentary that investigates the Iran-Contra scandal and alleges a web of lies and deceit that "TV could not tell." USA, 1988, 72 mins.
VHS: S07346. $29.95.

Crawfish
This little critter is at the center of an industry key to Cajun traditions. From the economy to gastronomy, crawfish are vital. 27 mins.
VHS: S22388. $59.95.

Crumb
Robert Crumb, the multi-talented underground comic book artist, is profiled in this unique, in-depth documentary portrait. Emerging from a dysfunctional family, it's a wonder that Crumb managed to channel his peculiar take on the world into a relatively socially acceptable form. Part of the great fascination of this film is the revelation that his brothers, both also quite gifted, were not as lucky.
VHS: S27253. $99.98.
Laser: LD75491. $59.95.
Terry Zwigoff, USA, 1995, 119 mins.

Cyberpunk
Cyberpunks are young people who fight technology with technology, idealistic and sometimes romantic figures on the margins of society. They use their wits to outsmart the powers that control information and technology. To some their work has terrifying implications; to others, they are the future hope for individual liberty. With William Gibson, Jaron Lanier, Timothy Leary and Michael Synergy. Directed by Marianne Trench. 60 mins.
VHS: S14714. $29.95.
Laser: LD71452. $49.98.
Bill Viola, USA, 1991, 60 mins.

Daimyo
The unique interaction of the pen and the sword—the civilian and martial arts culture in Japan—is explored in this fascinating program. Feudal landlords, the daimyo owed allegiance to the shogun, defending the land during civil revolution and invasion. As conflicts subsided, the daimyo turned to the peaceful pursuits to provide balance to the practice of martial arts. Life in medieval Japan is explored, including looks at the tea ceremony, No theatre, calligraphy, swordsmanship and archery from horseback. 30 mins.
VHS: S08475. $29.95.

Damned in the USA
Though the Reverend Wildmon tried to have it stopped by the courts, this documentary was not only screened nationwide, it won an International Emmy Award for Best Arts Documentary. This tape looks at the debates fomented by issues like obscenity and free speech, debates that often embroiled artists and politicians in the late 1980s and early 1990s. Jesse Helms, Christie Hefner, 2 Live Crew, Senator Al D'Amato, Andres Serrano, Jesse Helms and Madonna are just some of the public figures voicing their opinions in this riveting film.
VHS: S27259. $49.95.
Paul Yule, Great Britain, 1991, 126 mins.

Dance of Hope
By Oscar-winning director Deborah Shaffer, Dance of Hope features Sting performing his hit song "They Dance Alone" with Peter Gabriel in an Amnesty International concert. This film documents the efforts of relatives of the "disappeared" in Chile to get information on their loved ones from Pinochet's regime. The women involved in the Association for the Relatives of the Detained and Disappeared dance the cueca, Chile's national dance of passion and courtship, alone, to emphasize the loss of their partners. "Haunting in the images of despair, and poignant in a spirit of optimism" (San Francisco Chronicle).
VHS: S14147. $59.95.
Deborah Shaffer, USA, 1989, 75 mins.

Dancing Outlaw
Jesco White is the Dancing Outlaw. His wife says he is three persons: a beautiful man, the Devil himself, and Elvis. Ever since he shot his father he is "the very best mountain dancer in these here parts." Jesco idolized his dad, and keeps his memory alive through Appalachian tap dancing, amid the poverty, ignorance, violence and natural wildness of Boone County. 60 mins.
VHS: S21882. $24.95.

Dark Circle
Multiple award-winning feature documentary portrait of the nuclear age, told through the lives of those who are directly affected by it. Mixing personal stories with recently declassified footage of the secret world where the hydrogen bomb is tested, built and sold. "HHHH —completely riveting," said Roger Ebert in The Chicago Sun-Times.
VHS: S03731. $49.95.
Irving/Beaver/Landy, USA, 1982, 82 mins.

David Holzman's Diary
Jim McBride's seminal underground film is an autocritique about a young filmmaker (screenwriter L.M. Kit Carson) who makes an autobiographical, cinema verite film. It is a film about identity and self-obsession. With Penny Wohl, Louise Levine and Fern McBride. Selected by the National Film Registry as an American Film Classic.
VHS: S18862. $19.98.
Jim McBride, USA, 1967, 74 mins.

Day After Trinity
This haunting examination of the dawn of the nuclear age focuses on the dramatic events surrounding the development of the first atomic bomb. Featuring interviews with scientists and soldiers, and rare, archival footage, it provides a gripping profile of J. Robert Oppenheimer, the bomb's principal architect, and offers a penetrating commentary on the nature of scientific inquiry, the McCarthy era, and nuclear proliferation.
VHS: S00307. $39.95.
Laser: LD75026. $49.95.
Jon Else, USA, 1981, 88 mins.

Deadly Art of Survival
A Bruce Lee-style docu-epic shot in the housing projects of the Lower East Side, the story revolves around the real and imaginary rivals of an idealistic martial arts school led in actual life by the star of the film, Nathan Ingram. This early super-8 feature fuses ghetto kung-fu culture and what was to become hip hop.
VHS: S22605. $39.95.
Charlie Ahearn, USA, 1979, 58 mins.

Deadly Deception
G.E. does more than "bring good things to life." It also is the industry leader in producing nuclear arms components. This challenging video questions the role of corporate responsibility given the deadly influence exerted by this firm's many nuclear installations. Winner of the Academy Award for Best Documentary. 29 mins.
VHS: S21586. $50.00.

Death in the West
One of the most powerful anti-smoking films ever made. Originally produced for British television and vigorously suppressed by tobacco interests, it juxtaposes the healthy, independent image of the Marlboro man, defended in interviews with cigarette company executives, with the stark reality of six smoking cowboys—all dying of smoking-induced illnesses. "A classic film"—C. Everett Koop, former U.S. Surgeon General. 1983, 32 mins.
VHS: S13698. $29.95.

Devil at Your Heels
The late Ken Carter's long-time obsession to be the world's greatest daredevil is the subject of this feature-length documentary. Seen are the five years that are spent in raising $1 million, building a rocket-powered car, and constructing a ten-story take-off ramp for his attempt to jump across a mile-wide stretch of the St. Lawrence River. A portrait of a stunt driver who made his living by risking his life. Produced by the National Film Board of Canada.
VHS: S07672. $79.95.
Robert Fortier, Canada, 103 mins.

Documentary Masterpieces by John Grierson
John Grierson revolutionized the ideas, grammar and shape of the documentary, and this program collects five works he either directed, produced or supervised, from the years 1931 to 1960, beginning with Flaherty's Industrial Britain, Len Lye's Color Box, Granton Trawler, Julien Huxley's The Private Life of the Gannetts, and Hilary Harris's Seawards the Great Ships. 75 minutes.
VHS: S17453. $29.95.

Don't Look Back
One of the best portraits of an artist ever put on film, Don't Look Back is about Bob Dylan and the Sixties. Director Pennebaker, known for Monterey Pop, filmed Dylan during his 1965 English concert tour, capturing both private moments and public performances. With Joan Baez, Alan Price, Donovan.
VHS: S00357. $19.98.
D.A. Pennebaker, USA, 1967, 95 mins.

Down and Out in America
Academy-Award-winning documentary, narrated by Lee Grant, which takes the viewer into the streets and brings the nightmare home. "It's a war. there's no blood, but there will be!" is a quote from this prophetic documentary which examines the plight of America's homeless.
VHS: S04898. $29.95.
Lee Grant, USA, 60 mins.

Dying for a Smoke
This documentary explores the arguments put forward by the two sides engaged in the furious battle over cigarettes. On one side is the multi-billion dollar industry which manufactures cigarettes. On the other is a powerful anti-smoking lobby determined to prevent the deaths of 49,000 Americans each year from cigarette smoke. Chuck Norris, Gregory Hines, Johnny Mathis and Charleston Heston are just some of the stars involved in this struggle.
VHS: S22419. $29.95.

E.M.B. Classics
British documentarian John Grierson (1898-1972) is one of the most important figures in the history of the medium. With Robert Flaherty and the Soviet directors Eisenstein, Kuleshov and Vertov, they essentially founded the ideas, language and texture of the documentary. Grierson specialized making evocative, gripping, and wholly unsentimental documentaries that expressed a real affinity and feeling for the worker. This program, part of the British Documentary Movement, contains three of his best works: Drifters (1929), about turn-of-the-century English workers; Industrial Britain (1933), about the labor process; and Song of Ceylon (1934), produced by Grierson and directed by Basil Wright, about the British colony Sri Lanka from an Orientalist vantage point.
VHS: S17421. $29.95.

Echoes Without Saying
The Coach House is an innovative Toronto-based publishing house. Since 1965 it has produced distinctive and experimental books of fiction, poetry and visual art. Through interviews with editors, writers and staff the work of this unique institution is captured on film. 28 mins.
VHS: S25050. $19.95.

Empire of the Air: The Men Who Made Radio
Jason Robards narrates this two-hour film in which producer Ken Burns uses many of the same production techniques that brought The Civil War to life. The history of the radio from 1906 to 1955 unfolds through archival photographs, newsreels of the period, and interviews with such well-known personalities as Garrison Keillor, Red Barber and radio dramatist Norman Corwin. A rich soundtrack enhances the story of the men who lived and died for control of the empire.
VHS: S16153. $14.98.

England in the Thirties
Three documentary shorts that make up the British Documentary Movement, the brainchild of the brilliant John Grierson, who made films depicting social, political and working conditions in Britain. This volume contains such disparate works as the excellent Grierson-directed Granton Trawler (1934), Alberto Cavalcanti's Pett and Pott (1934), and Harry Watt's North Sea (1938).
VHS: S17417. $29.95.

Epicenter U.

This first-hand account details the story of a multi-cultural group of students at California State University, Northridge, coping with the aftereffects of the Northridge earthquake. Vice President Al Gore and the Honorable Andrew Young appear in this moving document. 28 mins.
VHS: $26178. $24.95.

The Exiles

A documentary portrait of German intellectuals, artists and writers who fled Hitler and resettled in America, where they made seminal contributions to American culture, science, art, nature, film and music.
VHS: $18695. $59.95.
Richard Kaplan, USA, 1990, 116 mins.

Fear Is the Master

This documentary about the Bhagwan Shree Rajneesh, who controlled hundreds of thousands of followers and planned to take over the entire state of Oregon, investigates his techniques as he ruled his empire. 60 mins.
VHS: $09200. $49.95.

Feed

An entertaining documentary about the relationship of politics and image as captured in the New Hampshire primary in January, 1992. With on-camera reports on Bill Clinton, George Bush, Ross Perot, Pat Buchanan and Jerry Brown, the film is a demystification of the election process. Some of its best moments are the illegally captured "backchannel" footage from satellite coverage.
VHS: $18420. $29.95.
Kevin Rafferty/James Ridgeway, USA, 1992, 80 mins.

Festival of Britain

Three documentaries from the British Documentary Movement: Humphrey Jennings's *Family Portrait* (1951) assesses the fallout of the war. *Waverley Steps* (1948) is an essay about city life, and Paul Dickson's *David* deals with coal mining in a discussion of Welsh identity.
VHS: $17419. $29.95.

Fifth, Park & Madison

A document of the New York City 1987 bike messenger strike against Mayor Ed Koch's proposed midtown bike ban—bikes in the air!
VHS: $10200. $39.95.
Dragan Ilic, USA, 1987, 45 mins.

Fingers That Tickle and Delight

Named "Deaf Senior of the Year," teacher, storyteller and comedienne Evelyn Zola is a role model for hearing and deaf people alike. Sent away to boarding school at the age of three to study oral and lip-reading tradition, she eventually found "her people" (the signing community) in Chicago. She now does two stand-up comedy shows a night on an all-deaf cruise of 1100 deaf seniors. Interpreted by Sharon Newmann Solow.
VHS: $21982. $35.00.
Elizabeth Sher, USA, 1993, 32 mins.

Fireworks: The Magic of Pyrotechnics

George Plimpton joins the first family of fireworks, the Gruccis, as they light up the night sky with their awesome pyrotechnical displays. History, ceremony, technology and fun span the globe in this collection of firework events from China, Spain and Disney World.
VHS: $24535. $29.95.

Free at Last

A video celebrating the 25th anniversary of Amnesty International, and its worldwide struggle to protect human rights. A unique look at and inside this Nobel prize-winning organization. 16 mins, 30 mins.
VHS: $06887. $20.00.

Getting Around

Students with disabilities at the University of Oregon explain details of their daily lives at school. Despite a number of differing abilities related to missing limbs, blindness or muscular dystrophy, these individual contribute to the community as they further their education. 28 mins.
VHS: $26005. $40.00.

Girltalk

This remarkable documentary tells the no-frills story of three runaway teenagers living by their wits on the mean streets of Boston. You will meet Pinkie, a 14-year-old dreamer, Mars, an underage stripper in the infamous Combat Zone and Martha, a product of 20 foster homes and institutions who is now facing pregnancy. All these young women have seen too much, too soon, but there is always hope. It may not be pretty, but it's real.
VHS: $15942. $19.98.
Kate Davis, USA, 1987, 85 mins.

Golub

Art, politics and the media intersect in artist Leon Golub's nightmarish images of war, torture, death squads and mercenaries. The documentary follows the creation of one of his monumental canvases, *White Squad X*, detailing his complex and unorthodox techniques. Interweaving scenes of Golub at work, archival footage, interviews with museum-goers and TV news, the film challenges us to question our connection to violence in the modern world and to reassess the relationship between art and society. "*Golub* conveys the exhilarating sense that art is inseparable from both the world that engenders it and the world that receives it" (Jonathan Rosenbaum, *Chicago Reader*).
VHS: $27803. $29.95.
Kartemquin Films, USA, 1988, 56 mins.

The Good Fight

It was one of history's most dramatic expressions of international solidarity when 40,000 volunteers from around the world went to fight the armies of Franco, Hitler and Mussolini in the Spanish Civil War of 1936-39. *The Good Fight* tells the story of 3,200 Americans who volunteered to fight on the side of the Spanish Republic. This vivid series of portraits with 12 of the survivors (half the Americans lost their lives in Spain) brings to life the reasons for joining the foreign conflict, and what it was to be a part of a people's army against fascism in the war that was the rehearsal for World War II. An absorbing and passionate account full of humor, pride and deep sorrow, their interviews are illustrated with rare archival footage of the Lincoln Brigade in Spain as well as Hollywood films, songs and newsreels with such notables as Hemingway himself and Henry Fonda. Narrated by Studs Terkel.
VHS: $12206. $69.95.
Laser: CLV. LD71721. $19.98.
Buckner/Dore/Stills, USA, 1984, 98 mins.

A Great Day in Harlem

Nominated for an Academy Award, this documentary offers a cross-section of jazz greats. In 1958, Art Kane orchestrated a group portrait of jazz musicians. Archival footage of interviews, performances and home movie footage rounds out the feeling of this day when the best jazz performers were gathered together. Art Blakey, Dizzy Gillespie, Charles Mingus, Thelonious Monk, Count Basie and Coleman Hawkins are just some of the musicians who appeared. 60 mins.
VHS: $26699. $19.95.
Laser: LD75324. $39.98.
Jean Bach, USA, 1995, 60 mins.

Great Sadness of Zohara

Nina Menkes combines sound, image and fragments of poetry in this moving film about the journey of a young Jewish woman who is drawn to explore the world of the spirit. Her journey takes her to remote and increasingly desolate regions of the Arab lands—alienating her from the orthodox Jewish community in Israel. This mystical quest culminates in her return to Israel where, indelibly marked, she confronts her loneliness and a devastating sense of exile.
VHS: $07374. $39.95.
Nina Menkes, USA, 1983, 40 mins.

Green Winter

Elda Hartley's documentary won the CINE Golden Eagle. It's an inspiring film about the experience of growing old, that draws on Hartley's experiences as a world traveler and chronicler of cultural, religious and spiritual traditions which present varied perspectives on aging. 30 mins.
VHS: $24724. $19.95.

Gulag Archipelago (Z Archipelagu Gulag)

Two powerful documentaries about gulag life and conditions are included on this videocassette: *Gulag Archipelago* and *Exhumation*. From director Jozef Gebski.
VHS: $15567. $39.95.
Jozef Gebski, Poland, 88 mins.

Gumbo

This innovative and tasty cuisine stretches throughout Acadiana into New Orleans. 30 mins.
VHS: $22391. $39.95.

Guns

Peter Jennings hosts this frightening expose on firearms in America. *Guns* depicts the bloody effect handguns, semiautomatic weapons and other firearms have had on society, including the deaths of some 30,000 people every year. 120 mins.
VHS: $12289. $19.98.

Hands Across America

The moving story of the Hands Across America project, which involved 6½ million Americans forming a 4,124-mile human chain in support of America's hungry and homeless. With musical highlights by Joe Cocker, James Brown, Harry Chapin, John Lennon, The Pointer Sisters, Prince, Lionel Richie and Kenny Rogers.
VHS: $02267. $14.95.

Harlan County U.S.A.

The Academy Award-winning documentary about the efforts of 180 coal-mining families to win a United Mine Workers contract at the Brookside mine in Harlan County, Kentucky, is a fascinating and moving portrait of the valor and courage of the coal-mining families.
VHS: $00542. $29.95.
Barbara Kopple, USA, 1976, 103 mins.

Heaven

Documentary from Woody Allen's former girlfriend and co-star, Diane Keaton. She asks a lot of questions about the Celestial Showplace and gets a lot of odd answers from some strange people filmed at uncomfortable camera angles. Film footage from Hollywood films on the subject are the highlights.
VHS: $05523. $14.95.
Diane Keaton, USA, 1987, 80 mins.

Heavy Petting

From the son of the man who invented white bread, a look back at the sexual attitudes and customs of the 1950's. Director Obie Benz, heir to a Delaware baking fortune, has dug into the film vaults for a compilation documentary that includes sex education films, commercials, popular and not-so-popular vintage movies and other archival footage of the news of the day. He also interviews celebrities like Allen Ginsberg, David Byrne, Sandra Bernhard, William Burroughs, Josh Mostel, Spalding Gray, John Oates and Abbie Hoffman and other people not-as-well-known, on what they remember about puberty.
VHS: Out of print. For rental only.
Laser: LD71036. $19.98.
Obie Benz, USA, 1988, 88 mins.

Helen Keller in Her Story

Though blind, deaf and mute from the age of 19 months, Helen Keller went on to become one of the most celebrated women of two centuries. Made 13 years before her death in 1968, this feature employs newsreels, interviews and rare footage of Ms. Keller at home in Vermont. An Academy Award-winning documentary narrated by Katharine Cornell.
VHS: $16405. $29.95.
Nancy Hamilton, USA, 1955, 50 mins.

The Hemp Video

Did you know: ...the Declaration of Independence and the Constitution were originally written on paper made of hemp? ...Betsy Ross made the first American flag out of hemp? ...before 1937, Levi jeans were made of hemp? It's all here on *The Hemp Video*! With Johnny Marijuanaseed; The Honorable Robert Sweet, U.S. District Court Judge; Don Fiedler, Executive Director of NORML; and many more. "Hemp is the most beautiful and beneficial plant that mankind has ever domesticated on this globe"—Gatewood Galbraith (Candidate for Governor, State of Kentucky).
VHS: $13774. $19.98.

Her Own Words: Pioneer Women's Diaries

The spontaneous observations of pioneer women from the upper Midwest are at the core of this intriguing video. Their experience is brought to life through first-person narration. 15 mins. Resource guide available.
Video.
VHS: $25761. $95.00.
Resource Guide.
VHS: $25774. $20.00.

High Grass Circus

Travel with the acrobats, elephants, lions, jugglers and clowns as they bring the art of the circus to small towns across Canada in this unusual, vivid, and often funny look at the Royal Brothers circus which performs one-night stands in 120 towns each year. Produced by National Film Board of Canada. Canada, 1977, 57 mins.
VHS: $01619. $29.95.

The History of the Condom

A young couple discussing contraception provide the framework for this exploration of the condom. Documentary, dramatization and archival footage, along with the inevitable experts, shed light on these invaluable marital aids. Filmed in six countries, this video provides both a historical understanding and contemporary rationale that explains the usefulness of condoms. The ongoing AIDS crisis is given special emphasis in this respect. 54 mins.
VHS: $26994. $29.95.

Homage to May 19th/Framed

Weather Underground member Kathy Boudin is the subject of a recreated interview in the first film. Photographs, television news footage and written text are used to explore Boudin's transformation. She grew up in middle-class Manhattan but participated in the 1981 Brinks armored vehicle robbery. In *Framed*, dancer/performer Dianne Torr uses material from the French interrogation of Mata Hari.
VHS: $22617. $39.95.
Mary McFerran, USA, 1984-1987, 48 mins.

Hoop Dreams

The groundbreaking documentary about the dream that inspires young men throughout the country, the dream of playing professional basketball for the NBA. Seven years in the making, *Hoop Dreams* is an innovative work that closely focuses on the maze of high school sports, agents and the system as well as on the dreams of escaping the inner city. A remarkable, heartrending piece of history that says a lot about basketball, and about the life we all choose to live. Produced by Kartemquin Films.
VHS: $24386. $19.98.
Laser: Widescreen. LD74943. $49.99.
S. James/F. Marx/P. Gilbert, USA, 1994, 176 mins.

Hotel Terminus: The Life and Times of Klaus Barbie

Marcel Ophuls' award-winning documentary spans 70 years and three continents. Culled from 120 hours of interviews, it traces the 40-year-manhunt for Nazi war criminal Klaus Barbie, the ruthless SS interrogator known as "The Butcher of Lyon." "A shocking, unforgettable film" (Ebert and Siskel). Winner of the Academy Award for Best Documentary and the International Critics Prize at the Cannes Film Festival. Original English-language version (includes French, German and Spanish footage subtitled in English). 2 cassettes.
VHS: $10756. $29.98.
Marcel Ophuls, France/USA, 1988, 267 mins.

House of Un-American Activities

From a maker of "Hoop Dreams"—the riveting story of a filmmaker who looks for the father he never really knew as he draws on a wealth of family archives to uncover his father's persecution by the House Un-American Activities Committee. Also includes *Dream Documentary*, which uses footage from other films to create a surreal and foreboding societal landscape; and *Dreams from China*, a diary-like film essay shot in the wake of Tiananmen Square, presenting a paradox of Chinese politics and society.
VHS: $23209. $29.95.
Frederick Marx, USA, 1989-92, 52 mins.

Houses Are Full of Smoke

Documentary filmmaker Allan Francovich, the award-winning director of *On Company Business*, who investigated the workings of the C.I.A., now turns his cameras on the problems of Central America. Here, from ex-presidents, peasants, and members of the secret police, is what is really going on south of the border. Each of the three volumes focuses on a specific country; Volume I is Guatemala. In Volume 2, Francovich investigates C.I.A. involvement in El Salvador by exposing a cover-up of the death of American citizens as well as of thousands of the local population. Included in this tape is one of the last interviews with Archbishop Oscar Romero before his assassination. Volume 3 centers on Nicaragua.
VHS: $13292. $79.95.
Allan Francovich, USA, 1987, 174 mins.

How to Squash a Squat

This unique documentary chronicles the systematic destruction of a Squatters' building in New York City's East Village by the combined city authorities—Housing and Police—after an arson fire. The squatters fight to save their building, followed by the night and day demolition of their Squat surrounded by the police occupation of three city blocks. A powerful, activist vision of one of the urban nightmares of our time.
VHS: $13349. $39.95.
Franck Goldberg, USA, 1990, 46 mins.

Hoxsey: How Healing Becomes a Crime

In 1924, Harry Hoxsey claimed a cure for cancer—herbal formulas inherited from his great-grandfather. Thousands of patients swore the treatment cured them, and by the 1950's Hoxsey's Texas clinic was the world's largest cancer treatment center, with branches in 17 states. Now Hoxsey's work continues in exile in Mexico and claims a success rate of 80%. Was Hoxsey really a hoax or were "medical experts" trying to suppress alternative therapies? You decide.
VHS: $14578. $29.95.
Ken Ausubel, USA, 1987, 100 mins.

Huit Piastres et Demie!

The shrimp war of 1938 is remembered by two men. The union was pitted against individuals and the drama unfolded in Golden Meadow. 60 mins. In Cajun with English subtitles.
VHS: $22403. $45.95.

The Hutterites

This ethnographic documentary examines the Hutterites, who have survived despite social and religious persecution, forced migration and isolation. The spiritual heirs of Mennonites and Amish, the Hutterites live highly unorthodox lives, outfitted in 16th century dress, cultivate a medieval village pattern and live in collective agrarian societies. Says one minister, "We're in this world, but not of the world." 60 mins.
VHS: $19245. $19.95.

I'm a Civilian Here Myself!

The U.S. Navy hired Robert Benchley to explain how the Navy was making civilians out of sailors. Included are such tidbits on the advantages of civilian life as the right to choose the company of any pretty girl, civil service jobs, insurance. Ava Gardner appears briefly. 25 mins.
VHS: $06931. $19.95.

In Motion: Amiri Baraka

Called "a brilliantly executed documentary" by *The New York Times*, a fascinating exploration of the writer and political activist formerly known as Leroi Jones. Following Baraka from his early days as a poet in New York City's Greenwich Village to his present literary and political activities, *In Motion: Amiri Baraka* is a portrait of a man of singular commitment to social change. Interspersed throughout the film are excerpts from Baraka's powerful play *The Dutchman*, one of the archetypal literary works of the 1960's, as well as scenes from other Baraka plays.
VHS: $10909. $59.95.
St. Clair Bourne, USA, 1985, 60 mins.

In Plain English

Julia Lesage's provocative documentary gathers a group of minority and ethnic activists (African-Americans, Asian-Americans, Hispanics, Pacific Islanders and Native Americans) from the University of Oregon to discuss assimilation, racism, the ways to attack discrimination, ethnic identity and their experiences within a wider college curriculum. 42 mins.
VHS: $17437. $50.00.

In the Blood

A tale of hunter and hunted in the story of two African safaris separated by nearly 80 years. The first, led in 1909 by President Roosevelt, is represented by rare historical footage from the Smithsonian. The President's great-grandson then retraces his ancestor's trail in 1986 and explores the role of the hunter in today's world while pursuing African big game. Brilliant cinematography and a stirring soundtrack depicting the natural magnificence of Africa.
VHS: $12952. $79.95.
George Butler, USA, 1989, 90 mins.

In the Land of the Deaf

A unique and privileged look inside the world of deaf people. A teacher, a woman treated for mental illness because of her deafness, and a newly wed deaf couple offer compelling portraits from a community estimated to comprise 130 million people worldwide in a film which is revealing, moving and often funny. French and French Sign Language with English subtitles.
VHS: $25993. $79.95.
Nicolas Philibert, France, 1994, 99 mins.

In the Shadow of the Stars

Behind the scenes of the San Francisco Opera Company, with chorus singers who aspire to be soloists and who dream of being stars. The film lovingly explores the blurred boundary between private lives and stage spectacles, and creates a rare and privileged look into the grand world of opera. Music by Mozart, Puccini, Rossini, Stravinsky, Verdi, Wagner and others. Winner of the 1992 Academy Award for Best Feature Length Documentary.
VHS: $16640. $24.95.
Irving Saraf, USA, 1992, 93 mins.

Inside the CIA: Assassination

Part Two of a three part series looks at the use of assassination as a tool of U.S. foreign policy.
VHS: $02359. $19.95.
Allan Francovich, USA, 1987, 49 mins.

Inside the CIA: Subversion

Part Three of this series explores the manner in which the CIA has used subversion to destabilize or topple governments whose policies did not match those of the United States. Areas of emphasis are Latin America, Iran and the overthrow of Allende's government in Chile.
VHS: $02358. $19.95.
Allan Francovich, USA, 1987, 67 mins.

Inside the CIA: The History

Part One of a three part series, featuring extensive interviews with David A. Phillips, former head of clandestine operations, and John Stockwell, a 14-year CIA veteran who headed up operations in Angola. The History starts at the end of World War II and examines the CIA's role in the Bay of Pigs invasion and the overthrow of Chile's President Allende.
VHS: $02357. $19.95.
Allan Francovich, USA, 1987, 58 mins.

Inside the Secret Service

At the heart of America's oldest elite law enforcement agency is a tradition of service. Its major job is to protect the President. This inside glimpse of the secretive institution provides a rare view of the attitudes and ideals that shape it. Along with the history of the Secret Service, this video contains the first public statement by the agent who blames himself for the assassination of JFK. 90 mins.
VHS: $25637. $19.95.

Islands

For two brief weeks in 1983, Christo's *Surrounded Islands* blossomed on the waters of Biscayne Bay, Florida: 11 scrub-pine islands surrounded by 6.5 million square feet of bright pink fabric. A three-year struggle, a political drama interwoven with two other Christo projects—the wrapping of the Pont Neuf in Paris, and the Reichstag in Berlin.
VHS: $07494. $59.95.
Maysles Brothers, USA, 1983, 58 mins.

Italy Wins World War III: 1990 Summit

Visionary TV producer and artist Peter Fend leads a strange live cable colloquium on the shape of the world and nation-states as they might look from space after a series of ecological wars.
VHS: $10172. $14.95.
Peter Fend, USA, 1983, 28 mins.

Julian Samuel Trilogy

This is an intelligent, three-part documentary about frontiers in intellectual history, including the Orient and the Middle East. The first volume, *The Raft of the Medusa: Five Voices on Colonies, Nations and Histories* (99 mins.), focuses on issues of emergent nationalism in Asia, with particular attention to the unique cases of Hong Kong and mainland China, Eastern Modernism and Islamic Fundamentalism. In the second installment, *Into the European Mirror* (56 mins.), Julian Samuel explores the concept of frontiers, both real and imaginary. Highlights include Columbus' voyage of 1492 and the Palestinian/ Israeli conquest of today. Issues of "euronationalism" are examined by experts in this thought-provoking video. In the final segment, *City of the Dead and The World Exhibitions* (76 mins.), Samuel takes an in-depth look at modern Islamic culture, including the rise of fundamentalism and the role architecture plays in keeping the sexes separate. Also explored in this video are the way turn-of-the-century World Exhibitions created an international perception of Asia and Asian culture, and the effects of terrorism in modern Egypt. English and French with English subtitles.
VHS: S27357. $99.95.
Julian Samuel, Canada, 1993-1995, 231 mins.

Julie: Old Time Tales of the Blue Ridge

Julie Lyon, the sister of Old Time fiddler Tommy Jarrell, lights this gem of a movie like a flower blooming in the wildwood. Nearing 80, she tells tales of childhood and her first romance. A sweet and enduring film. 11 mins.
VHS: S15302. $19.95.

Just Between Me & God

An environmental love story about a fisherman and his wife; the Mississippi wildlife that they love is threatened by the construction of a drag race track and a raging chemical fire. This moving documentary was filmed on the edge of Memphis' industrial ruins. USA, 8 mins.
VHS: S15006. $29.95.

Kaddish

A riveting profile of a young Jewish activist coming to terms with his father's traumatic past during the Holocaust and the legacy of the struggle passed onto him. Yossi Klein is the young man who brings back the memory of his father Zoltan, a radiant and charming Hungarian Jew who escaped the round-up of Jews, hid out, and was spared the horrors of the Holocaust.
VHS: S09352. $39.95.
Steve Brand, USA, 1985, 92 mins.

Kartemquin Films, Vol. 1: Inquiring Nuns

Set in Chicago in 1967, at the height of the Vietnam War, this disarming, intimate work finds two nuns moving through the city's densely populated streets, asking the question: "Are you happy?" The film pushes beyond the issues of the times and allows its subjects to open their hearts and reveal themselves plainly and simply. "A profound and moving experience for the viewer" (*Chicago Tribune*). USA, 1968, 66 mins.
VHS: S18198. $29.95.

Kartemquin Films, Vol. 2: Winnie Wright, Age 11

Three films by the Kartemquin Films Collective poignantly and honestly deal with personal and social change. In *Winnie Wright, Age 11*, Winnie is the daughter of a steelworker and school teacher watching the dramatic racial and class changes in her neighborhood. She learns valuable and frightening lessons about growing up female, working class and white (1974, 26 mins.). *Now We Live on Clifton*, on the same program, focuses on Pam and Scott Taylor, children who watch their multiracial, working-class neighborhood through an awkward though inevitable gentrification (1974, 26 mins.). *Parents* is an open-ended discussion about a youth group and their feelings about their parents and the "generation gap" (1968, 22 mins.). USA, 1974, 74 mins.
VHS: S18199. $29.95.

Kartemquin Films, Vol. 3: Trick Bag

Three films capture the history and apocalyptic social and personal changes of the Vietnam era. *Trick Bag* (1975, 21 mins.) allows gang members, Vietnam vets and young factory workers to relate their personal experiences of racism. *What the Fuck Are These Red Squares* (1970, 15 mins.) looks at striking students at the School of the Art Institute in the wake of the killing of student protestors at Kent State and Jackson State. *Hum 255* (1969, 28 mins.) traces the activities of two students and their return to the University of Chicago following their expulsion for illegally occupying the Administration building. They confront current students about their attitudes, moral and social values and the meaning of education. USA, 1975, 64 mins.
VHS: S18200. $29.95.

Kartemquin Films: The Complete Set

Volumes 1-3.
VHS: S18201. $74.95.

Koyaanisqatsi

With no dialog, only the music of Phillip Glass, and no characters other than the entire human race and the five elements, this years-in-the-making film is a symphony of sound and image, fast-paced, dazzling, hypnotic.
VHS: S00692. $14.95.
Godfrey Reggio, USA, 1983, 87 mins.

The Lash of the Penitents

A reporter investigates a strange cult in the American Southwest. This film represents his findings. 30 mins.
VHS: S23794. $24.95.

The Last Party

In this guerilla documentary, actor Robert Downey Jr. goes into the streets to examine the 1992 presidential campaign. Captured from a youthful perspective, *The Last Party* presents an unadorned, crazy portrait of the American electoral process, of a campaign more attuned to images and appearance than substance or discussion of issues. "*The Last Party* is frank and frenetic, flippant and frightening" (David Hunter, *The Hollywood Reporter*). With appearances by Mary Stuart Masterson, Oliver Stone, Sean Penn, Spike Lee, Peter Jennings, Oliver North, Jerry Brown and the Rev. Al Sharpton.
VHS: S20198. $89.98.
Mark Benjamin/Marc Levin, USA, 1993, 90 mins.

Last Pullman Car

More than 100 years ago, George Pullman, one of the giants of American industry, built a vast industrial empire. It was supposed to last forever. Yet in 1981, Pullman workers found themselves in the midst of a fight not only for their jobs but the future of the American rail car industry. In this engaging story, 100 years of government, union and corporate policy are traced.
VHS: S27804. $29.95.
Kartemquin Films, USA, 1983, 56 mins.

Legong

A documentary photographed on the island of Bali under the direction of Marquis de la Falaise. "Legong-Dance of the virgins" features an all native cast with authentic native dancing and religious rites. 50 mins.
VHS: S15178. $29.95.

Les Creoles

With interviews of Inez Catalon and Revon Reed among others, and music by Bebe Carriere, Delton Broussard and more great musicians, this tape offers a hearty look at Creole culture and music. The continuing rivalry between devotees of musical traditions La la and Zydeco even get a chance to state their competing claims to greater fame. 28 mins.
VHS: S22395. $49.95.

Let Me Be Brave

Narrated by CBS sportscaster James Brown, this tape chronicles the efforts of 12 mentally handicapped athletes in their courageous attempt to scale Mt. Kilimanjaro in February of 1990. USA, 1991, 45 mins.
VHS: S15472. $14.98.

Life of Adolf Hitler

Paul Rotha's famous documentary uses archival footage to depict the rise of the Nazi party in a powerful study of one of the horrors of history. Much of the footage used by Rotha is rare, including the last films of Hitler before his retreat into the Bunker.
VHS: S00751. $29.95.
Paul Rotha, Great Britain, 1961, 101 mins.

Lifetime Commitment: A Portrait of Karen Thompson

After living together as a couple for over four years, Karen Thompson and Sharon Kowalski were hit by a drunk driver. Sharon was disabled, and Karen lost her lover to a legal system that refused to recognize their bond. Sharon's parents did all they could to keep the couple apart, a problem that deepened when Sharon's father, Donald Kowalski, gained full guardianship over his daughter. This video documents the struggle of two women in love, in a system that can't see the value of this bond.
VHS: S19454. $39.95.

Lines of Fire

In this gritty look at the drug trade, the investigative journalist and documentarian Brian Beker goes into the Golden Triangle, Asia's remote and labyrinthine network of heroin and opium distribution, and relates tales of greed, madness, revenge and destruction. "Made under the sort of conditions even hard-boiled war correspondents would have nightmares about" (*Berlin Journal*). 62 mins.
VHS: S17101. $39.95.

Listen to Britain

Four great poetic documentaries by Humphrey Jennings, all set during World War II by this great English filmmaker: *Listen to Britain, The True Story of Lili Marlene, A Diary for Timothy* and *The Cumberland Story*.
VHS: S02953. $79.95.
Humphrey Jennings, Great Britain, 1942-47, 120 mins.

Listening to America: 20 Years with Bill Moyers

This program joins some of Bill Moyers' most engaging conversations with notable Americans, including Joseph Campbell, Maya Angelou, Ronald Reagan and Joe Namath. Moyers' series *The Power of Myth* and *A World of Ideas* gave him the opportunity to speak with great thinkers, leaders and heroes, resulting in this insightful work.
VHS: S21378. $19.95.

Little Richard: Keep on Rockin'

Catch the original wildman of rock 'n' roll at his onstage finest! Seen through the camera of D.A. Pennebaker, Little Richard tears through "Tutti Frutti", "Lucille" and six more favorites.
VHS: S16092. $14.98.
D.A. Pennebaker, USA, 30 mins.

Lodz Ghetto

This film covers the years 1940-1944 as it chronicles the 200,000 Jews trapped in the Polish ghettos during the German occupation. The film moves from the past and present; the script was developed from the diaries of the survivors and people left behind. Music by Wendy Blackstone. "Your blood turns to ice. To be unmoved by this film is to be made of stone" (*New York Daily News*).
VHS: S17891. $29.95.
Kathryn Taverna/Alan Adelson, USA, 1991

The Long Way Home

Michael Apted took his camera into recording studios and concert venues to follow Russian rock and roll star Boris Grebenshikov, whose recordings were, until recently, only available on the black market in the Soviet Union. With the coming of glasnost, Grebenshikov finds himself free to travel to New York, where he is invited to record his first album with CBS Records. "A superb documentary...rewarding, both musically and dramatically" (*The Dallas Morning News*).
VHS: S14292. $19.98.
Michael Apted, Great Britain, 1989, 82 mins.

Louisiana Story

The last film of the famous father of the documentary, the story of a new oil derrick and its effect upon the Louisiana Bayou country, the boy and his raccoon. With music by Virgil Thompson.
VHS: S00771. $29.95.
Robert Flaherty, USA, 1948, 79 mins.

Madonna: Truth or Dare

The popular musical superstar is the focus, and the executive producer, of this revealing documentary/concert movie that captures the excitement of her 1990 Blonde Ambition world tour. Visit backstage as Madonna chats with Kevin Costner, Sandra Bernhard and Warren Beatty. Come along when she visits her mother's grave. Be there when she leads her dancers and back-up singers in a group prayer. Then sit back and enjoy the sound and fury of blonde ambition in concert.
VHS: S14762. $19.98.
Laser: LD75225. $34.98.
Alek Keshishian, USA, 1991, 118 mins.

Maggie Kuhn: When Biography and History Intersect

Kuhn is the founder of the Gray Panthers, an advocacy group for the aging. At age 87, her boundless intelligence, fierce determination and tremendous courage are a testament to the ageless quality of the human spirit. 56 mins.
VHS: S23199. $29.95.

Mama Florence and Papa Cock

Alan Leder's lyrical, heartwarming documentary is a personal account of an elderly Jamaican couple living amidst the growing tourist trade in Negril, Jamaica. Set to the rhythms of reggae music, the film is a warm and often humorous glimpse of the changing tenor of rural Jamaica reflected in the lives of an old village family. Produced by Alan and Jane Leder.
VHS: S01955. $45.00.
Alan Leder, USA, 1983, 17 mins.

The Man Behind the Muppets: The World of Jim Henson

The late Henson began by fashioning his mother's old coat into the most beloved frog in the world, Kermit. The magical world conjured by this visionary is revealed in this video. It began with *Sesame Street* and led to many feature length films. 85 mins.
VHS: S24928. $19.95.

Man of Aran

One of the masterworks of Robert Flaherty, in which Flaherty's "passionate devotion to the portrayal of human gesture and of a man's fight for his family makes the film an incomparable account of human dignity" (Georges Sadoul). Filmed on the island of Inishmore, it depicts the daily life of people on this isolated island off the coast of Ireland, fishing in their tiny curraghs, the difficulty of their existence, the hunting of a basking shark. A masterpiece.
VHS: S09417. $29.95.
Robert Flaherty, Great Britain, 1934, 76 mins.

Manufacturing Consent: Noam Chomsky and the Media

This remarkable Canadian documentary is a riveting look at the political life and times of the controversial author, linguist and radical philosopher, Noam Chomsky. Chomsky provides shocking examples of media deception as he analyzes the media and democratic societies. A film which has achieved cult status in its remarkable call to Chomsky's charge for viewers to "extricate themselves from this web of deceit by undertaking a course of intellectual self-defense."
VHS: S21851. $39.95.
Mark Achbar/Peter Wintonick, Canada, 1993 180 mins.

Marching for Freedom: The 1993 March on Washington Video

This video document benefits the National Gay and Lesbian Task Force Policy Institute. Over 700,000 people demonstrated for their rights in Washington D.C. See and hear the joyous sights and sounds of freedom. This country will never be the same again. 78 mins.
VHS: S19453. $29.95.

Martha & Ethel

Two invincible, 80-year-old nannies offer a portrait of American life in this documentary. Spanning four decades and crossing the barriers of race, class and sex, this film reveals the heart of the American family. *Martha & Ethel* celebrates the extraordinary legacies of love and discipline these women created, as seen through the eyes of the filmmaker, who herself was brought up by one of the two nannies profiled.
VHS: S26919. $96.99.
Laser: S17402. $39.98.
Jyll Johnstone, USA, 1994, 80 mins.

The Marvelous Toys of Dr. Athelstan Spilhaus

World-famous oceanographer, inventor and toy collector Athelstan Spilhaus shows off more than a hundred of his personal favorite toys. Dating from the 18th and 19th centuries, these one-of-a-kind "automata" spin, waddle, nod and gyrate in hypnotizing detail. 1989, 72 mins.
VHS: S15802. $29.95.

Masters of the Congo Jungle

Produced in 1960 by the Belgian International Scientific Foundation, this is a chronicle of Henri Storck's two-year exploration of the Belgian Congo. Untouched for centuries by outside civilization, the jungle is now disrupted by the invasion of modern man. Storck captures remnants of the ancient African continent, plant and animal life and regional natives co-existing in the simple grandeur and rhythm of the earth.
VHS: S17448. $19.95.

Maxwell Street Blues

A unique historical celebration of the street that was "Chicago's unlikely (and extraordinary) commingling of ancient Jewish merchants, young black musicians, and unspecified patrons, set against a landscape that suggests a war has been recently lost there" (Neil Tesser). In an arresting look at the past and present of Maxwell Street, filmmakers Raul Zaritsky and Linda Williams show the history of the blues on the sidewalks, from the "gospel-styled abstractions of Carrie Robertson, to the quieter religiosity of Jim Brewer, to the voice of experience that is Floyd Jones's and Coot 'Playboy' Venson's, to the hard urban blues of the young players working up their chops." But Zaritsky and Williams are not content with a simple portrait of the blues thriving on this urban strip—they portray Maxwell Street Blues against the background of perpetual social change that makes Maxwell Street both "a hustle and an art." With Arvella Gray.
VHS: S03587. $39.95.
Raul Zaritsky/Linda Williams, USA, 1981, 60 mins.

Miracle of Intervale Avenue

This sensitive exploration searches for the secrets of a once thriving Jewish community in the South Bronx that somehow continues despite the decay that surrounds it. The film shows a remarkable reality of Jews, Blacks and Puerto Ricans interacting and helping each other. What makes this film so moving is the cast of vital, complex and moving characters. 65 mins.
VHS: S06576. $59.95.

Moana, A Romance of the Golden Age

A great film by Robert Flaherty which followed the success of *Nanook of the North*. Flaherty chose the Samoan cultural tradition; he lived for two years on the islands, with the story gradually evolving out of the lives of the native population. Includes the famous sequences of the tattooing of Moana, a part of the initiation into manhood, and dancing the Shiva before a village virgin. An "intensely lyrical poem on the theme of the last paradise" (Herman Weinberg). Silent with music score.
VHS: S07486. $29.95.
Robert Flaherty, USA, 1926, 76 mins.

Monterey Pop

Directed by one of the foremost factual filmmakers in the cinema-verite style, *Monterey Pop* records the events at the immense Monterey International Pop Festival. Featuring Otis Redding, Jimi Hendrix, Janis Joplin, Jefferson Airplane, Ravi Shankar.
VHS: Out of print. For rental only.
Laser: LD70422. $49.95.
D.A. Pennebaker, USA, 1968, 84 mins.

Moving the Mountain

The momentous events surrounding the Tiananmen Square uprisings of May 1989 are at the center of this moving film by Michael (*28 Up, 35 Up*) Apted. Part documentary and part dramatization, it captures the feeling of hope and change that inspired the young demonstrators as they sought democracy and confronted a brutal regime. Newsreel footage and powerful personal testimonies of participants in the Tiananmen Square uprisings make this a powerful and compelling film.
VHS: S26863. $99.98.
Laser: LD75418. $39.99.
Michael Apted, USA, 1995, 83 mins.

Nanook of the North

The classic documentary of the daily life and hardships of an Eskimo family, still considered superb filmmaking and a landmark. Music score by Stanley Silverman, performed by the Tashi Ensemble and conducted by Peter Serkin. Silent.
VHS: S00916. $29.95.
Robert Flaherty, USA, 1922, 55 mins.

Native Land

Narrated by Paul Robeson, this documentary explores the threats to American values contained in the forces unleashed by economic depression. Many of the artists who worked on this project through the collective called Frontier Films were themselves the victims of the HUAC trials in the 1950's. In the debate on American values this film stands as a powerful testament to the enduring traditions of democratic ideals. This collector's version is mastered from the finest print available.
VHS: S20743. $59.95.
Paul Strand, USA, 1942, 88 mins.

Next Step

A new video produced by Amnesty International and narrated by Glenda Jackson examines both the moral and legal implications of state-sanctioned killing on modern society. The video places the death penalty in the international human rights context and presents compelling arguments for its abolition. *Includes graphic footage.* England, 1989, 22 mins.
VHS: S09779. $19.95.

Nowhere to Hide

In dramatic and often graphic scenes, *Nowhere to Hide* shows a far different reality about the Gulf War than what most Americans saw on the nightly news. Although several networks initially expressed strong interest in the footage, all declined to air it, and NBC ended its long affiliation with director Jon Alpert, a seven-time Emmy-winner.
VHS: S15211. $59.95.
Jon Alpert, USA, 1991, 28 mins.

Occupied Palestine

"A complex, sensitive and brutally authentic movie, *Occupied Palestine* delivers its message with unnerving sharpness and accuracy. The simple realities of what it means to live under and to resist occupation have never been so clearly presented to a Western audience," wrote Professor Joel Beinin of Stanford University. *Occupied Palestine* is a film reflecting the Palestinian experience of Zionism and resistance to it. Dramatic, contemporary footage is combined with the testimony of Palestinians as well as Zionist settlers and officials, to develop a fresh perspective on a critical international issue. "Quite simply the best film ever made about the Palestine question" (*Middle East Report*).
Home Video.
VHS: $10842. $49.95.
Institutional with public performance rights.
VHS: $10847. $99.95.
David Koff, USA/Israel, 1987, 88 mins.

Olympia: Festival of Beauty

Part Two of Riefenstahl's extraordinary film about the 1936 Olympics. Engrossingly beautiful, the film provides a glimpse of the Nazi mystique and idealization of the youthful male body. English dialog.
VHS: $00955. $19.95.
Leni Riefenstahl, Germany, 1936, 97 mins.

Olympia: Festival of the People

Leni Riefenstahl was given unlimited resources and full artistic freedom to produce this film of the 1936 Olympic Games in Berlin. *Festival of the People* is Part One. Famous sequences include the men's diving competition, Jesse Owen's sprint races and Riefenstahl's use of telephoto lenses and slow motion. English dialog.
VHS: $00956. $19.95.
Leni Riefenstahl, Germany, 1936, 115 mins.

On the Bowery

An extraordinary, agonizing document, one of the key American documentaries of the last two decades, Lionel Rogosin's film captures the men and women on the Bowery, "who have passed the point of no return, and have reached a hideous sort of happiness achieved at best by gin and whisky, and at worst by a shared squeeze from a can of metal polish" (Basil Wright).
VHS: $03919. $29.95.
Lionel Rogosin, USA, 1956, 65 mins.

One Nation Under God

This documentary exposes the chilling world of right-wing Christian conversion techniques employed against lesbians and gay men. Included in this homophobic arsenal is beauty make-overs for lesbians and tough physical contact sports for gay men, especially football. At the center of this documentary is a couple who embody the failure of this quackery.
VHS: $21027. $29.95.
Teodoro Maniaci/Francine Rzeznik, USA, 1993, 83 mins.

Other Prisoners

A unique documentary looking at prison life from a completely original perspective—that of the guard. Winner of awards as both documentary and as art, *Other Prisoners* observes human character and circumstance with irony and darkly funny humor. "We meet car thieves who learned to hot wire by watching *Adam Twelve* on TV and yard lords who serve the same function in the big house as bankers who charge exorbitant interest to do it in the big world. We watch Cocoa, a gay prisoner who trades sex for cigs (the equivalent of cash inside) and flirts outrageously with a guard, and we hear one of the incarcerated speculate about what would happen to the judges and social workers and police if criminals went on strike…a vivid, haunting work."
VHS: $10931. $59.95.
Stephen Roszell, USA , 1987, 58 mins.

Palazzolo's Chicago

For twenty years Tom Palazzolo has been the purveyor of funny, darkly satirical musings on Chicago, creating low-budget Fellini-esque experimental films on the strange, hypnotic and diverse ethnography of Chicago. This collection of four films is a survey of his best work: *Your Astronauts*, which follows the Apollo 11 parade; *Jerry's*, a classic documentary on a deli owner who prods his customers through blatant terror tactics; *Tattoed Lady of Riverview*, a Diane Arbus-like foray into the freak show carnival as spectacle; and *Enjoy Yourself: It's Later Than You Think*, a panoramic view of a senior citizens' picnic.
VHS: $02655. $39.95.
Tom Palazzolo, USA, 60 mins.

Palazzolo's Chicago Vol. 2

Two priceless gems from filmmaker Tom Palazzolo: *At Maxwell Street* (40 minutes) explores the sounds and textures of the legendary Chicago street on which street peddlers mix with blues musicians; *Labor Day - East Chicago* (25 mins) is a hilarious document of a beauty contest in the neighborhood referred to as East Chicago, Illinois, a steel-town event sponsored by the Lions. A wonderful depiction of hometown rituals.
VHS: $06471. $39.95.
Tom Palazzolo, USA, 65 mins.

The Panama Deception

Barbara Trent's Academy Award-winning documentary explores the ethical and political consequences of George Bush's December 1989 invasion of Panama. Code-named "Operation Just Cause," its strategic intentions were the capture of Panama strongman Manuel Noriega. Trent argues the military offensive masked wide-scale civilian casualties, suppression of the media reports and a pretext for a contemporary Pax Americana. Trent also charges the American media with complicity in refusing to challenge official government reports. Shot on video. Narrated by Elizabeth Montgomery. Music by Sting, Jackson Browne, Jorge Strunz and Ismael Rivera. Banned by the Panamanian government and denied an airing by PBS.
VHS: $18754. $79.95.
Laser: LD72279. $39.99.
Barbara Trent, USA, 1992, 91 mins.

Patchwork: A Kaleidoscope of Quilts

The narrator of this video calls quilts her diaries and albums. Exploring these meaningful and utilitarian folk art objects reveals critical information about the people who make them. 15 mins. Resource guide available.
Video.
VHS: $25763. $95.00.
Resource Guide.
VHS: $25776. $20.00.

The People vs Paul Crump

A powerful documentary—the debut film by William Friedkin (*French Connection*, *To Live and Die in L.A.*)—*The People vs Paul Crump* is an impassioned plea for mercy and justice, based on the true story of Paul Crump—a man who is still in Illinois prison. In 1953, five young black men robbed a food plant in the Chicago Stockyards. Their getaway went awry, one security guard was shot to death, and five employees were severely beaten. Within a week, all five were arrested. The fifth man, Paul Crump, then 22, was sentenced to die in the electric chair. He is sentenced to life in prison, and was at the brink of execution some 15 times between 1953 and 1962. William Friedkin met Paul Crump in jail, believed his innocence, in his record of rehabilitation as a model prisoner, his worth as a human being, that he made this artistic tour-de-force which is an impassioned plea for Crump's return to society.
VHS: $06320. $39.95.
William Friedkin, USA, 1962, 52 mins.

Peyote Road

The United States Supreme Court denied indigenous peoples the right to use peyote in their centuries-old rituals. Religious freedom is at stake. This documentary explores the effects of this decision and its implications for one of the Western Hemisphere's oldest religions. Peter Coyote narrates. USA, 1993, 59 mins.
VHS: $26895. $29.99.

Plow That Broke the Plains/Night Mail

The classic documentary by Pare Lorentz is paired with another documentary classic from England made in 1936. Total running time 49 mins.
VHS: $03364. $29.95.

The Power and the Land: Four Documentary Portraits of the Great Depression

The program begins with two legendary films by Pare Lorentz. *The River* dramatizes the history of the Mississippi River, while *The Plow That Broke the Plains* focuses on the soil of the Great Plains. H.P. McClure's *The New Frontier* offers an enlightening glimpse into an experimental "Rural Community" while Joris Ivens' *Power and the Land* observes the daily activities of a farming family in Ohio. This collector's version has been mastered from the finest source materials available.
VHS: $20744. $59.95.
Joris Ivens, USA, 1938, 38 mins.

Prairie Quilts: A Celebration of the Tall-Grass Prairies

Embroidered and patchwork quilts celebrate Midwestern tallgrass prairie life. It's a dazzling display of a simple native art form. 15 mins. Resource guide available.
Video.
VHS: $25765. $95.00.
Resource Guide.
VHS: $25778. $20.00.

Private Practices: Story of a Sex Surrogate

Documentary study of Maureen Sullivan, a well known sexual surrogate, focusing on professional treatment of two clients over a four month period.
VHS: $07039. $59.98.
Kirby Dick, USA, 1986, 75 mins.

Pumping Iron

An expose of the motivations of men who undergo grueling training in order to transform their bodies into sculpted works of art. Focusing on the competition for the World Bodybuilding Championship, the film stars Arnold Schwarzenegger and Lou Ferrigno.
VHS: $01072. $14.95.
Laser: LD74983. $29.99.
G. Butler/R. Fiore, USA, 1976

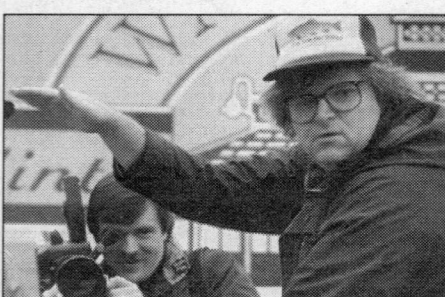

Quiet One

A classic documentary-drama, winner of awards at Venice and Edinburgh, and one of the most penetrating studies of juvenile delinquency ever filmed. The film is the story of a black youth who grows up in Harlem without the love of his parents, and, rejected, falls into delinquency. Sidney Meyers, the director, was apparently influenced by Italian neo-realism and the commentary, written by James Agee, is spoken by Gary Merrill. "A most moving, important and memorable film" (Paul Rotha).
VHS: $06879. $39.95.
Sidney Meyers/Janet Loeb, USA, 1948, 67 mins.

The Race for Mayor

Chicago's 1983 mayoral campaign sparked nationwide interest in the growth of black political awareness. The stunning victory of Harold Washington, a black U.S. congressman, over Chicago's Democratic "machine" heightened the expectations of blacks all over the country. This independent documentary—with Mayor Washington, Jesse Jackson, former mayor Jane Byrne, Richard Daley, and Democratic political boss Edward Vrdolyak—shot in churches, city streets, empty lots, Polish restaurants, political offices and Operation PUSH offices paints a complex picture of the fusing of a new political coalition, and places it in the context of the historic evolution of successive waves of ethnic groups who seek to wrest control from earlier entrenched minorities.
VHS: $02312. $79.95.
H. Gladstone/J. Ylisela, USA, 1983, 29 mins.

The Reluctant Muse

John and Ruth Waddell met at the Art Institute of Chicago over 45 years ago. Their love for the arts and each other brought them together, but at a cost. Ruth channeled her creative energy into their partnership. The concerns of family and finances, and the troubles of infidelity, kept her from fuller artistic expression. This documentary examines what happens when two artists bond. 58 mins.
VHS: $26422. $59.95.
Amy Waddell, USA, 1995, 58 mins.

Ring of Fire

The true story of two brothers, Lawrence and Lorne Blair, who voyaged to the East in search of adventure and found themselves into ten years of danger and mystery, in the last of the lands of real kings and queens, dragons and pirates, cannibals and headhunters, mystics and magicians. Indonesia, the world's largest and most mysterious archipelago was where the Blairs sailed with pirates aboard their black-sailed schooners, struggled through rapids and deep jungles searching for elusive nomadic tribes, witnessed veiled forms of human sacrifice, and gained unique access to the ancient palaces of Java. This remarkable BBC-PBS-Australian television co-production is now available on home video.
Part 1: Spice Island Saga. Filmmaker brothers Lorne and Lawrence Blair encounter gypsy pirates, tropical storms, python hunters and the Greater Bird of Paradise as they sail among the islands of the world's largest and least-explored archipelago. Part one of an extraordinary four-part look at the oceans, islands, peoples of Indonesia. 55 mins.
VHS: $08613. $29.95.
Part 2: Dance of the Warriors. The brothers Blair journey to Indonesia's Komodo Island to film the man-eating Komodo dragon. They also witness virtual warfare on the island of Sumba and journey deep into the swamps of New Guinea to find a tribe of headhunters living 50,000 years in the past. 55 mins.
VHS: $08614. $29.95.
Part 3: East of Krakatoa. In this volume, the brothers travel through Java, Bali and the Celebes Islands to discover an erupting volcano, mystical powers and conscious death. 55 mins.
VHS: $08615. $29.95.
Part 4: Dream Wanderers of Borneo. Explorer brothers Lorne and Lawrence Blair encounter blood-sucking leeches, snakes, quicksand and a week-long tropical storm as they trek 800 miles into the heart of Borneo. They meet with a lost nomadic tribe known as the "dream wanderers". 55 mins.
VHS: $08616. $29.95.
Complete 4-volume set.
VHS: $08617. $89.95.
Laser: (IMAX). LD74935. $39.95.

River and Plow That Broke the Plains

Two important works in the development of the documentary: *The River*, done in 1937, produced by the Farm Security Administration about the Mississippi, and *Plow that Broke the Plains*, from 1936, about the New Deal's efforts to assist farmers hit by the Dust Bowl in Oklahoma.
VHS: $01121. $39.95.
Pare Lorentz, USA, 1937

Road Scholar

The whimsical and offbeat Transylvanian humorist Andrei Codrescu takes off across America in a red convertible. This featured National Public Radio comic has a unique perspective that makes for an engaging and laugh-filled road movie with a twist.
VHS: $25904. $19.98.
Roger Weisberg, USA, 1992, 82 mins.

Robert Coles: Teacher

This documentary addresses the working methods, structure and achievement of renowned child psychiatrist Robert Coles, the Pulitzer Prize winner who interviews children and records their responses to various racial, social, political and economic issues. 57 mins.
VHS: $17103. $39.95.

Roger & Me

The funniest movie you will ever see about thousands of people losing their jobs. Journalist Michael Moore turns a jaundiced eye on the closing of several General Motors plants in his hometown of Flint, Michigan. He also attempts to have a face-to-face confrontation with GM president Roger Smith. This non-fiction film uses humor and creative license to bring attention to a serious display of corporate indifference. With Anita Bryant, Pat Boone, Ronald Reagan and Flint native Bob Eubanks.
VHS: $12231. $19.98.
Laser: LD70667. $24.98.
Michael Moore, USA, 1989, 91 mins.

Roses in December

On December 2, 1980, lay missioner Jean Donovan and three American nuns were brutally murdered by members of El Salvador's security forces. With compassion and sensitivity, this film chronicles Jean's brief life—from her affluent childhood in Connecticut, to her decision to volunteer with the Maryknolls in El Salvador, to her tragic death. This award-winning film is an eloquent memorial to a courageous young woman.
VHS: $09442. $39.95.
A. Carrigan/B. Stone, USA, 1982, 56 mins.

Ross McElwee Films

Two pieces by idiosyncratic American regionalist Ross McElwee (*Sherman's March*), whose "nonfiction is equal parts Samuel Beckett, Jean-Luc Godard and Werner Herzog" (*New York Times*). *Charleen* is a poem to Charleen Watson, a South Carolina writer, mother, teacher, eccentric romantic and the subject of *Sherman's March*. It's "an irresistible force, caught beautifully on the run." On the same program is *Backyard*, a collection of small-town Southern charm, community and off-center humor when McElwee turns the camera on his family and friends.
VHS: $17775. $29.95.
Ross McElwee, USA, 1991, 99 mins.

Running Fence

The film depicts the long struggle by Christo to build a 24-mile fence of white fabric over the hills of California disappearing into the Pacific, at a cost of $3 million. After what seemed to be an insurmountable struggle between the artist and the state bureaucracy, the fence, finally unfurled, brings the community together in celebration of its beauty.
VHS: $07493. $49.95.
Maysles Brothers, USA, 1978, 58 mins.

Salesman

Albert and David Maysles' landmark documentary focuses on a quartet of Bible salesmen and the hopes and frustrations of one man in particular: Paul Brennan. Labeled as "brutally honest," "funny and touching," and "a great insight into America," *Salesman* is a key work of the American documentary cinema.
VHS: $07491. $79.95.
Maysles Brothers, USA, 1968, 85 mins.

The Santa Tapes

His name is Art Baldwin and, according to the *Chicago Tribune*, he was "the only authentic State Street Santa Claus." Warm and compassionate, blunt and irascible, this documentary leads us through his preparations for a day in "The Chair." A fascinating portrait of Santa you've never seen before and will likely never forget.
VHS: $15009. $14.95.
Scott Jacobs, USA, 14 mins.

The Secret Wars of the CIA: John Stockwell

John Stockwell, former CIA case officer in Africa and Vietnam and an advisor to the National Security Council, spells out the story of twisted and secret foreign policy decisions that have presented great threats to global peace. A videotaped presentation that lends an in-depth look at covert actions behind U.S. foreign policy.
VHS: $06603. $45.00.
Gary Meyer, USA, 1987, 94 mins.

Seeds of Destiny

Winner of the Academy Award for best documentary subject of 1946, the film portrays the plight of millions of children who were left at the end of WWII without food, clothing or shelter. Under the sponsorship of the UN Relief fund, a team of Signal Corps cameramen were sent to 14 countries to film children in bombed-out cities and refugee camps. The film raised over $200 million for war relief, ironically earning it the status of one of the top moneymaking films of all time. 21 mins.
VHS: $03349. $39.95.

Seeing Red

A powerful documentary by Julia Reichert and Jim Klein that assesses the cultural, political, social and personal evolution of members of the American Communist Party. The film moves from the idealistic fervor and radical intensity of 30s Depression-era humanism to the harsh persecution of ideas during McCarthy-ism and the onset of the Cold War. The documentary is a deft merging of faces and personalities, from the known to the unknown. It captures their pain, triumph, hurt and redemption. The film also considers the disillusionment following the revelations of Stalin's tyranny and looks at the political exploitation of anti-communist hysteria from J. Edgar Hoover, Richard Nixon and Ronald Reagan. "The film is less about dogma than about American idealism" (Vincent Canby).
VHS: $19234. $39.95.
Julia Reichert/Jim Klein, USA, 1983, 100 mins.

The Shakers

Ben Kingsley narrates this documentary about the New World Shakers. Originating in the French Huguenot community of Manchester, England, these people earned their name because of their violent religious paroxysms. Today their utilitarian way of life continues to fascinate outsiders. 52 mins.
VHS: $24924. $29.95.

Shattered Dreams

A massive, chilling, thoughtful and provocative examination of Israel. Born out of the despair of millions as a utopian haven in the desert, *Shattered Dreams* confronts the realities of Israel today against the background of these utopian beginnings. The film passionately documents what more than 20 years of occupation and expansion have done to the soul of Israel. Provocative and unflinching.
VHS: $12305. $19.98.
Victor Schonfeld, Great Britain, 1988, 173 mins.

Sherman's March

Consistently named on ten best lists all over the country,—"uproarious…it'll put you in a pleased delirium and leave you with a happy daze," (*San Francisco Examiner*); "If Woody Allen made *Gone with the Wind*, it might resemble *Sherman's March!*" (*People Magazine*). The subtitle of the film promises "A Documentary Meditation upon the Possibilities of Romantic Love in the South during an Era of Nuclear Weapons Proliferation," and director Ross McElwee delivers an engaging nonfiction journey through the South in a picaresque tour of contemporary relationships.
VHS: $10929. $29.95.
Ross McElwee, USA, 1985, 155 mins.

Shoah

Claude Lanzmann's landmark, monumental epic of the Holocaust, a 9½ hour assemblage of witnesses—death camp survivors and Nazi functionaries—whose combined testimony amounts to one of the most shattering human documents ever recorded. French with English subtitles.
VHS: $01190. $299.95.
Claude Lanzmann, France, 1985, 570 mins.

Short Subject Potpouri

Three intriguing shorts, including Italian director Roberto Rossellini directing his wife Ingrid Bergman in *The Chicken*. The program also includes two ethnographic documentaries, *A Visit to the Smithsonian* and *A Day with the FBI*.
VHS: $18772. $19.95.

Silent Pioneers

Senior members of lesbian and gay communities share their memories about gay life in this documentary. Sometimes tragic, and sometimes funny, their recollections are always personal and poignant. This film offers a unique view of an era less tolerant of sexual minorities.
VHS: S27614. $39.95.
Lucy Winer, USA, 1985, 54 mins.

Sneakin' and Peekin'

Sneakin' and Peekin' is a funny, revealing trip to a famous nudist camp and its annual Mr. and Mrs. Nude America contest; *I Was a Contestant at Mother's Wet T-Shirt Contest* is a documentary at the Chicago landmark Wet T-Shirt contest at Mother's Bar; *Hot and Nasty* is a very funny look inside the comings and goings of a massage parlor. Americana at its very best (and most hilarious).
VHS: S06111. $39.95.
Tom Palazzolo, USA, 55 mins.

Song of Ceylon

One of the masterworks of the documentary, Basil Wright's lyrical impression of Ceylon in four sections: "The Buddha" deals with the coming of the Buddha to liberate the people from devil-worship, "The Virgin Island" depicts the native Ceylonese culture and economy, "The Voices of Commerce" contrasts traditional methods with new technology, and "The Apparel of a God" reflects the continuity of life and tradition. "Its evocative sensual imagery, its construction, and its skillful, often contrapuntal, use of natural life still have a powerful impact" (Georges Sadoul). With sound by Alberto Cavalcanti, produced by John Grierson.
VHS: S09528. $29.95.
Basil Wright, Great Britain, 1934, 40 mins.

South Sea Adventures

Zane Grey's famous sea yarn: a rare 1932 documentary starring Zane Grey himself, deep-sea fishing and encountering the natives of a south sea island. USA, 60 mins.
VHS: S15176. $29.95.

Spanish Earth

Focusing specifically on the small village of Fuenteduena near Madrid, *Spanish Earth* is a stunning documentary on the Spanish Civil War and the drastic land reform that followed. The beautiful commentary was written and delivered by Ernest Hemingway. Directed and photographed by Joris Ivens. Edited by Helen van Dongen.
VHS: S14648. $29.95.
Joris Ivens, USA, 1937, 54 mins.

Starting Place

Robert Kramer achieved notoriety with his 1969 documentary, *People's War*. After 24 years he returns with a documentary that continues to explore the same subjects and once again reveals the other side of Vietnamese society, rarely seen in this country. It is provocative and elegiac at the same time, reflecting a perspective altered in part by the passing of time and the reasoned expectations of an older, more sober outlook. France/Great Britain/Vietnam, 1993, 80 mins.
VHS: S27649. $39.95.

Stoney Knows How

An extended interview with the late Leonard St. Clair, a paraplegic dwarf, a carnival sword swallower as a child and a tattoo artist since 1928. St. Clair is an ebullient little man with the gift of gab and a fund of bizarre stories about tattooing and other unrelated matters. "Not often does one have the opportunity to meet a man like Stoney," said Vincent Canby in *The New York Times*.
VHS: S09302. $44.95.
Alan Govenar/Bruce Lane, USA, 30 mins.

Straight from the Heart

This Academy Award-winning documentary explores the experiences of parents learning to love their lesbian and gay children in a world dominated by homophobia. There is a range of stories touching on a variety of experiences, including a religious Mormon family and an African-American family. 30 mins.
VHS: S26030. $24.95.
Dee Mosbacher/Frances Reid, USA, 1994, 30 mins.

Streetwise

A powerful, emotionally compelling, sensational documentary about the life of teenagers in Seattle, surviving as pimps, prostitutes, muggers, panhandlers and small-time drug dealers. Critically acclaimed throughout the country, *Streetwise* is a powerful, wrenching film. USA, 1985, 92 mins.
VHS: S01270. $19.98.

Sweetheart

Maury Chaykin stars in this true story of Hal Banks, a convicted felon and Union strongman who is hired to break up left-wing shipping unions. This gripping drama, produced by the National Film Board of Canada, covers 13 years of violence, corruption and political complicity on the docks. 55 mins.
VHS: S07667. $69.95.

Taylor Chain I and II

These two companion films chart a decade of union democracy and collective bargaining. *Taylor Chain I* tells the gritty realities of a seven-week strike at a small Indiana chain factory. Volatile union meetings and tension-filled interactions on the picket line provide an inside view of the tensions and conflicts inherent in typical negotiations, while *Taylor Chain II* returns to the plant nine years later to show how labor and management are working together to save the plant in a faltering economy. "A tiny stick of dynamite!" (*Chicago Tribune*).
VHS: S27802. $29.95.
Kartemquin Films, USA, 1980-84, 63 mins.

Theremin: An Electronic Odyssey

A cross between Albert Einstein and Ed Wood, Leon Theremin pioneered the electronic music revolution four decades before the rise of Electronic Rock. His invention, the Theremin, produced an eerie, warbling sound, and was used on many Hollywood sound tracks, including *Spellbound*, *The Day the Earth Stood Still* and *The Lost Weekend*, and by rock legends Brian Wilson and Todd Rundgren. At the height of his popularity, Theremin was kidnapped by Soviet agents and forced to develop spy technology for Stalin's KGB. Janet Maslin (*The New York Times*) calls it "fascinating," and it is. Winner at the Sundance and San Francisco Film Festivals.
VHS: S27436. $94.98.
Laser: LD75505. $39.99.
Steven M. Martin, USA/Great Britain, 1995, 84 mins.

Through the Wire

Narrated by Susan Sarandon, this documentary is an award-winning and frank portrait of three uncompromising women convicted of politically motivated crimes and an expose of the secretive prison policy that sent them underground. This controversial film was winner of the 1990 Munich Documentary Film Festival.
VHS: S15266. $19.98.
Nina Rosenblum, USA, 1990

Tigrero: A Film That Was Never Made

In 1954, armed with a 16mm camera, film, two cases of vodka and 75 boxes of cigars, director Sam Fuller went to Brazil scouting locations for the action-adventure film *Tigrero*. Although this Darryl F. Zanuck production was cast with John Wayne, Ava Gardner and Tyrone Power, the film was never shot because of insurance problems. All that remains of *Tigrero* is Fuller's intriguing footage of the Karaja tribe and their Amazon Rain Forest home. Forty years later, director Mika Kaurismaki ventures back to this location with Fuller and director Jim Jarmusch to talk with the Karaja about the changing world, talk amongst themselves about Fuller's films and the principles of filmmaking, and tell the story of the film that was never made. This film won the International Critics Award at the 1994 Berlin Film Festival.
VHS: S27618. $89.95.
Mika Kaurismaki, Finland/United Germany/Brazil, 1994, 75 mins.

Time Indefinite

This sequel to the highly acclaimed *Sherman's March* continues the stories of the memorable characters the filmmaker (Ross McElwee) encountered on his leisurely jaunt through his native South.
VHS: S20590. $79.95.
Ross McElwee, USA, 117 mins.

Times of Harvey Milk

Academy Award-winning, powerful documentary about the powerful, charismatic, compassionate, gay San Francisco city official Harvey Milk, who was suddenly assassinated. Winner of numerous awards; a powerful document.
VHS: S01348. $29.95.
Epstein & Schmeichen, USA, 1984, 90 mins.

Tom Palazzolo: Films from the Sixties

Filmmaker Tom Palazzolo uses humor as a weapon in an ironic exploration of the puzzle of the turbulent 1960's. The cultural and political change of this crucial decade is revealed in a collection of short films, ranging from a disturbing account of the 1968 Democratic National Convention to a bitter satire on patriotism during the Vietnam era. The result is a completely original unwrapping of history. The collection includes: *The Bride Stripped Bare*—an ironic film about the ritual which surrounds the unveiling of the large Picasso outdoor sculpture in Chicago called "The Woman;" Palazzolo contrasts real and posed shots of all types of women, in an attempt to make us question whether the sculpture is pornography or a matriarchal symbol (1967, 14 mins.). *Campaign*—a disturbing political account of the events surrounding the 1968 Democratic Convention; the threat of violence is underscored by a relentless backdrop of news flashes and Emergency Broadcast Systems tests (1968, 14 mins.). *Love It, Leave It*—themes of freedom and openness in shots of a southern nudist camp evolve into a visual comparison of militarism and abject poverty; scenes of military formations are tied to male sexuality; the frantic montage closing the film provides real insight into the slogan that defined a generation (1970, 14 mins.). *Venus Adonis*—a sarcastic view of modernism in a black-and-white satire of the bridges, beaches and skyline of Chicago; from this context emerges a narrative starring the *perfect* man and the *perfect* woman; on a city beach they act out a romantic but ultimately tragic story of nuptials and the untimely death of Adonis (1966, 15 mins.). Total program length: 57 mins.
VHS: S13701. $49.95.
Tom Palazzolo, USA, 1991

Tompkins Square Park Police Riot

This controversial video has been the focus of a court battle between city authorities and its maker. Patterson said, "I want to show the tape to the public so that the People would be the Grand Jury." Ultimately this work functions as a basic document of recent urban civil strife in the US.
VHS: S22650. $39.95.
Clayton Patterson, USA, 1988, 90 mins.

Tompkins Square Park, 1989/ Dinkinsville

In the first film a mini-tour of the park reveals squatters being evicted and an impromptu demonstration. Former NYC Mayor Dinkins called the homeless of Tompkins Square Park "worse than hardened criminals." The second work documents the homeless who named their shantytown Dinkinsville, in tribute to the mayor. They had nowhere to go when the police marched on their homes. The result was explosive.
VHS: S22653. $39.95.
Clayton Patterson, USA, 1989, 58 mins.

Treasures of the National Postal Museum/Rarities and Oddities of the National Postal Museum

This package of two documentaries provides highlights into the methodology and working conditions of the world's largest stamp museum, produced in association with the museum and the U.S. Postal Service. Each tape is 40 mins.
VHS: S17183. $19.95.

Triumph of the Will

Enormously controversial film record of a Nazi party solidarity rally at Nuremberg in 1934, crafted by Riefenstahl in her second directorial assignment. A fascinating lesson in the methods used by the Nazis to inspire national support. German with English subtitles.
VHS: S18194. $29.95.
Leni Riefenstahl, Germany, 1936, 80 mins.

The True Story of Lili Marlene

One of the famous documentaries produced by Humphrey Jennings for the British Crown Film Unit is this documentary about the famous World War II song, featuring original historical footage.
VHS: S04478. $29.95.
Humphrey Jennings, Great Britain, 1944, 22 mins.

Turnabout: The Story of the Yale Puppeteers

Dan Bessie crafted this documentary about the three gay puppeteers who enchanted Hollywood for 25 years. Their musical extravaganzas, with puppet replicas of celebrities, drew legends like Hitchcock to see their performances. The sophisticated humor of their shows came from a unique camp sensibility, one fostered by these three gay men in a time when being gay was extremely difficult.
VHS: S27492. $39.95.
Dan Bessie, USA, 1992, 55 mins.

The Unquiet Death of Julius and Ethel Rosenberg

On June 19, 1953, Julius and Ethel Rosenberg, the so-called "atomic spies" of the 1950s, were executed at Sing Sing Prison. Their death only fostered the belief of many Americans that the Rosenbergs were innocent, victims of the anti-Communist paranoia of the 50s, rather than spies who had stolen atomic secrets for the Russians. In his landmark documentary *The Unquiet Death of Julius and Ethel Rosenberg*, Alvin Goldstein looks at the facts and procedures of the Rosenberg case, as well as the climate of the times, interviewing jurors, FBI agents, lawyers for both sides, and the two sons of the Rosenbergs. Using documentary and newsreel footage, Goldstein creates a moving human drama, a "thoroughly researched, solidly developed...superb recreation of history, painting with bold strokes the temper of the times" (*Boston Globe*).
VHS: S04736. $59.95.
Alvin Goldstein, USA, 1974, 83 mins.

Unzipped

Isaac Mizrahi, the New York-based fashion designer, is the central subject of this frothy and humorous documentary. This surprisingly intimate film was directed by Mizrahi's former boyfriend. (They broke up during the editing.) It begins with a depressed Mizrahi contemplating his poorly received Spring 1994 collection and ends with the creation of his Fall collection. Along with supermodels Kate Moss, Cindy Crawford, Linda Evangelista and Naomi Campbell, Mizrahi provides witty insights into the world of fashion and artifice.
VHS: S26999. $99.99.
Laser: LD75453. $39.95.
Douglas Keeve, USA, 1995, 73 mins.

Vali: Witch of Positano

A study in beautiful color of a woman along the Amalfi coast of Italy, living in a hermit's house, dressed like a gypsy, weaving dreams and casting spells. A unique film document.
VHS: S01573. $29.95.
Sheldon Rochlin, USA, 1965, 65 mins.

Vivre pour Manger

The title means "live to eat," but the film is more than about the food of Louisiana; it is a questioning of the language, culture and ecology of Cajun. Cajun French with English subtitles.
VHS: S08154. $79.95.
Stephen Duplantier, USA, 30 mins.

The War Room

Inside the campaign of President Bill Clinton a new telegenic, electoral style was developed that would appeal to a TV-saturated public. D.A. Pennebaker, the acclaimed documentary maker who covered the 1962 campaigns of Kennedy and McGovern, brings his insight to this presidential hopeful, uncovering that most enduring of American traditions, a sophisticated political machine.
VHS: S20840. $14.95.
Chris Hegedus/D.A. Pennebaker, USA, 1993, 96 mins.

Wartime Combat

Two classic documentary works from the British Documentary Movement. The 1943 Oscar-winning *Desert Victory* combines Allied footage and captured Nazi materials to present the full dimension of the punishing Allied victory against Erwin Rommel's forces in the North African campaign. The second program, *Cameraman at War* (1943), is a compilation work of the enormous courage and determination of these professionals to capture the sounds, images and ugliness of the war.
VHS: S17415. $29.95.

Wartime Homefront

The major British documentarian was Humphrey Jennings. This program of the British Documentary Movement contains Jennings's finest works, the brilliant *London Can Take It*, about the individual heroism, valor and sacrifice during the Blitz. The other program is *Fires Were Started*, Jennings's documentary about the Auxiliary Fire Service during 1940/41 German onslaught.
VHS: S17416. $29.95.

Wartime Moments

Three remarkable documentaries from the British Documentary Movement are presented in this volume, highlighting the work of Humphrey Jennings. *Listen to Britain* (1942) chronicles daily life during the war. Harry Watt's *Target for Tonight* (1941) details the precision of a RAF bombing raid on a German depot. Jennings's masterpiece *A Diary for Timothy* (1945), written by E.M. Forster, follows a child's first three months juxtaposed against the massive reconstruction and rebuilding of a physically devastated landscape.
VHS: S17418. $29.95.

What Sex Am I?

Narrated and directed by Lee Grant, this is a journey into the unseen world of transsexuals, transvestites and "she-males." The filmmakers have drawn out revelations from these outcasts, about their tortured childhoods and the surgery that has given them peace of mind. 58 mins.
VHS: S13174. $59.98.

When Abortion Was Illegal: Untold Stories

If anyone wonders why the battle to keep abortion legal goes on, this documentary makes clear exactly what is at stake. Women were often degraded, physically harmed and scarred. Some even became infertile while others died in search of this medical procedure. 28 mins.
VHS: S22053. $29.95.

When Women Kill

Narrated and directed by Lee Grant. A psychological profile of seven trampled women who have been forced to kill. The stories are remarkably similar, their victims most often domineering men. Includes an in-prison confession by Leslie Van Houten, who killed for Charles Manson. 55 mins.
VHS: S13164. $29.98.

Wild Wheels

Harrod Blank directed this excursion into the world of car art. This funky, low-budget film takes the form of a road movie as it examines the car ethos within the textures of Americana. Blank travels the highways to look at the relationship between automobile and its owner, the way a car's styling, design and make-up is connected to freedom and individuality.
VHS: S19742. $29.95.
Harrod Blank, USA, 1992, 64 mins.

Will Eisner

A video portrait of the cartoonist famed for his strip, "The Spirit."
VHS: S10204. $19.95.
Jordi Torrent, USA, 1986, 15 mins.

Women on Cane River

Beginning with Coin Coin, a free woman of color and the founder of Melrose, this documentary explores the lives of interesting women from old Acadia. Cammie Henry was an arts patron at Melrose, while Clementine Hunter was a primitive artist and former slave there. Kate Chopin, a writer ahead of her time, captured Creole and Cajun life at Clouterville. 20 mins.
VHS: S22402. $49.95.

Women with a Past

Brings together four 20th century artists, Christine Choy, Yvonne Rainer, Martha Rosler and Nancy Spero, in videotaped interviews whose shape and editing by Lyn Blumenthal is in itself an examination of the art of documentary. Yvonne Rainer's personal involvement in psychoanalysis manifests itself in scenes such as the one from her film *The Man Who Envied Women*. In *Losing* Martha Rosler explores the ways in which people imagine their lives are separate from, rather than subject to, the world around them. Nancy Spero's political art work found its first real impetus in the Vietnam war. Christine Choy came to the U.S. in the activist 60's. Her personal experience of a mixed ethnic and national background finds expression in the film *Mississippi Triangle*. Produced by the Video Data Bank. 70 mins.
VHS: S06515. $69.95.

Women—For America, for the World

This Academy Award-nominated film celebrates women who have the vision, courage and determination to re-define the meaning of security for the world, as they speak out for our health, educational and economic needs and for the fundamental value in protecting and nurturing our most precious resource—our children. Among the many women appearing in the film are Ellen Goodman, Geraldine Ferraro, Sandra Porter and Joanne Woodward.
VHS: S03792. $45.00.
Vivien Verdon-Roe, USA, 1985, 28 mins.

The Wonderful, Horrible Life of Leni Riefenstahl

An exhaustive, infuriating and unforgettable documentary about Leni Riefenstahl at age 90: actress, filmmaker (*Olympia*, *Triumph of the Will*), propagandist, personal friend of Goebbels and Hitler, photographer, explorer. Filmmaker Ray Mueller confronts Leni as she seeks to remold her image from that of a master propagandist and Nazi to that of a noble and heroic victim of history. Essential viewing. German with English subtitles.
VHS: S23996. $89.95.
Laser: LD75388. $69.99.
Ray Mueller, Germany, 1993, 180 mins.

World Without End

Two world-famous filmmakers, Paul Rotha and Basil Wright, working together at opposite ends of the earth, created a documentary film of hope and progress, which is the story of the work of UNESCO and three other U.N. agencies in Mexico and Thailand. "An important film—the most vibrant and emphatic statement yet made on film about our postwar world" (*Saturday Review*). 50 mins.
VHS: S04963. $49.95.
Rotha/Wright, United Nations, 1953, 50 mins.

Writing in Water and Admiral Bataille & the S.S. Esoterica

Two unique documentaries which challenge the documentary form in their somewhat whimsical approach. Stephen Rozell's *Writing in Water* is a wonderful work about the recollections of a rural Kentucky family, steeped in the southern tradition of storytelling. *Admiral Bataille*, by Jim Newberry, is an experimental documentary about an enigmatic human being, Kris Bataille.
VHS: S05367. $49.95.
Stephen Roszell/Jim Newberry, USA, 43 mins.

LES BLANK

Always for Pleasure

An enjoyable exploration of the mythic quality of New Orleans takes us to a jazz funeral, to a pre-Mardi Gras practice parade, Mardi Gras celebrations, and a St. Patrick's day parade, as well as Mardi Gras celebrations in the black community, including a revival of the black Indian traditions.
VHS: S00040. $49.95.
Les Blank, USA, 1978, 58 mins.

The Best of Blank

Les Blank is one of the true American originals. This program features music arrangements from 15 of his best films, including works from Dizzy Gillespie, Tex Mex, Polish polka, Cajun and zydeco to the American blues (Lightnin' Hopkins).
VHS: S16986. $49.95.

A Blank Buffet

A compilation of the finest scenes of music, people and food selected from thirteen of Les Blank's best films including *The Blues Accordin' to Lightnin' Hopkins*, *Gap-Toothed Women*, *In Heaven There Is No Beer?* and *Burden of Dreams*.
VHS: S16987. $39.95.
Les Blank, USA, 60 mins.

Blues Accordin' to Lightnin' Hopkins

In his own words, and his "own own" music, Lightnin' Hopkins reveals the inspiration for his blues. He sings, he jives, he ponders. He boogies at an outdoor barbecue and a black rodeo. Les Blank has captured Lightnin's blues in their fullest, darkest power.
VHS: S00160. $49.95.
Les Blank, USA, 1975, 31 mins.

Burden of Dreams

Fascinating, chilling account of the making of Werner Herzog's *Fitzcarraldo*, a project beset by a series of disasters while shooting in the jungle. Filmmaker Les Blank has made a compelling film about obsessed genius and the creative process.
VHS: S00190. $59.95.
Les Blank, USA, 1982, 94 mins.

Chicken Real

Les Blank brought all his skill to bear on this documentary for an automated chicken-growing operation that produces 156 million chickens each year. It may be his funniest film—surreal images abound.
VHS: S09303. $44.95.
Les Blank, USA, 23 mins.

Christopher Tree

An early film by Les Blank, on the well-known Tibetan temple gong player. Just rediscovered, the film, with its mystical, mesmerizing music and Asian origins, is an interesting look at Tibetan tradition.
VHS: S12929. $19.95.
Les Blank, USA, 1967, 10 mins.

Chulas Fronteras

Chulas Fronteras provides a magnificent introduction to the most exciting nortena, Southern-Texas musicians, working today: Los Alegres de Teran, Lydia Mendoza, Flaco Jimenez and others. The music and spirit of the people is embodied in their strong family life, and their music.
VHS: S00241. $29.95.
Les Blank, USA, 1975, 58 mins.

Cigarette Blues

A microcosmic Les Blank film in which Oakland bluesman Sonny Rhodes simultaneously addresses three of the filmmaker's long-standing obsessions: death, cigarette smoking and the nature of the blues.
VHS: S09299. $29.95.
Les Blank/Alan Govenar, USA, 6 mins.

Dizzy

Les Blank's earliest music film focuses on the trumpet player himself, who, along with Charlie Parker, Thelonious Monk and others, sparked the change from Jazz into Bop in the 40's. Dizzy talks about his beginnings and music theories, and blows hot music on that famous horn.
VHS: S09298. $44.95.
Les Blank, USA, 20 mins.

Dry Wood

The featured music is that of *Bois Sec* Ardoin and his sons and Canray Fontenot. Theirs is an older, rural style of Cajun music, which, in the film, weaves together incidents in the lives of Fontenot and Ardoin families. The film's highlights include a rollicking country mardi gras, work in the rice fields, a "Mens Only" supper, and a hog-butchering party. Like other Blank films, it expresses respect for living the life.
VHS: S09293. $49.95.
Les Blank/Maureen Gosling, USA, 37 mins.

Gap-Toothed Women

"A love poem to women" (Roger Ebert). An exploration of the self-image of women and pressures to conform to ideals of mass media, concentrating on many unique women who happen to be gap-toothed.
VHS: S02901. $49.95.
Les Blank, USA, 1987, 30 mins.

Garlic Is As Good As Ten Mothers

Blank's gastronomically obsessional film portrait, an exhaustive foray into the history, consumption, cultivation, and culinary and curative powers of garlic, from the kitchens of Chez Panisse and Flint's Bar-B-Que to the international garlic festival.
VHS: S00481. $49.95.
Les Blank, USA, 1977, 51 mins.

God Respects Us When We Work, But Loves Us When We Dance

An original rock music score accentuates this film panorama of the action and more meditative moments occurring at Los Angeles' memorable 1967 Love-In. Earmarks of the alternative abound in this colorful and candid record of a social phenomenon.
VHS: S09297. $44.95.
Les Blank/Skip Gerson, USA, 20 mins.

Hot Pepper

Hot Pepper plunges the viewer deep into the music of Clifton Chenier, and its sources in the surroundings of rural and urban Louisiana. The great French accordionist mixes rock and blues, with his unique version of Zydeco music, a combination of Cajun French and African undertones.
VHS: S00583. $49.95.
Les Blank, USA, 1978, 54 mins.

In Heaven There Is No Beer

A joyous romp through the dance, food, music, friendship, even religion of the polka. Blank takes us through the polka subculture from New London, Connecticut's Polkabration to the International Polka convention—often funny and wry comments on the polka subculture.
VHS: S00616. $49.95.
Les Blank, USA, 1984, 51 mins.

Innocents Abroad

A portrait of the ways American and European cultural, political and social ideas and stereotypes collide. Structured around a group of American tourists, the film observes them moving through London, Amsterdam, Heidelberg, Germany, Venice, Rome, Nice, Avignon and Paris. With music by Bob Dylan and Chuck Berry.
VHS: S16990. $49.95.
Les Blank, USA, 1992, 86 mins.

J'Ai Ete au Bal: I Went to the Dance

The Cajun and Zydeco music of Louisiana is explored by Les Blank, Chris Strachwitz and Maureen Gosling. With rare recordings, stills and footage, interviews and live performances by the greatest names in Cajun and Zydeco music, including Michael Doucet and Beausoleil, Queen Ida and her Bon Temps Zydeco Band, Clifton Chenier, Wayne Toups and many more.
VHS: S12921. $59.95.
Les Blank/M. Gosling & C. Strachwitz, USA, 1989

Marc and Ann

A portrait of Ann and Marc Savoy, the Cajun musical couple: Marc, accordion builder and player, Cajun cook and outspoken defender of his culture, and Ann, an adopted "Cajun" who authored *Cajun Music: A Reflection of a People*. A more personal look at one Cajun family and their appreciation for their culture in the face of encroaching American mall culture.
VHS: S12923. $49.95.
Les Blank, USA, 1990, 30 mins.

Puamana

Les Blank's joyous examination of Irmgard Farden Aluli and her remarkable family of performers and musicians, part of the vibrant musical scene around the Hawaiian island of Lahaina. The film interweaves of concert footage, archival stills and on-screen text to produce "a cinematic translation of the pulse of island life."
VHS: S16991. $49.95.
Les Blank, USA, 1991, 37 mins.

Six Short Films of Les Blank, 1960-1985

From *Running around Like a Chicken with Its Head Cut Off*, Blank's first film, done as an homage to Bergman's *Seventh Seal*, to the 1985 six-minute plea to end smoking entitled *Cigarette Blues*.
VHS: S02904. $59.95.
Les Blank, USA, 83 mins.

Spend It All

The Cajuns of Southwest Louisiana in scenes such as quarter horse racing, accordion building, cooking and the intoxicating music of the Balfa Brothers, Marc Savoy, Nathan Abshire and others. In English.
VHS: S06504. $59.95.
Les Blank, USA, 41 mins.

Sprout Wings and Fly

A compassionate, life-affirming document on the old-time Appalachian fiddler Tommy Jarrell. A fascinating film on the theme that art, music, dance, food and earthly pleasures help human beings live joyously in the face of certain death. "Jarrell is a fabulous fiddler and ballad singer…a fascinating cast of backwoods characters plus a compelling look at one of the central issues facing a civilization" (*Berkeley Monthly*).
VHS: S09301. $44.95.
Les Blank, USA, 30 mins.

A Well Spent Life

With Mance Lipscomb's passing, what was always a strong, beautifully filmed portrait of the man and his music has become a precious document—a love song to beat back the silence of death. This film is a deeply moving tribute to the Texas songster, considered by many to be one of the greatest guitarists of all time. Not discovered until 1960, before then Mance lived by sharecropping, surviving the brutality of a system not much better than slavery. The film captures Mance's music, sets it off with scenes of his hometown of Navasota and combines it all with the miracle of his love.
VHS: S09296. $49.95.
Les Blank/Skip Gerson, USA, 44 mins.

Werner Herzog Eats His Shoe

Blank documents German filmmaker Werner Herzog honoring a vow he made to independent filmmaker Errol Morris that Herzog would eat his shoe if Morris ever finished a film. Morris did (*Gates of Heaven*), and Herzog complies by boiling and consuming his desert boots at the UC Theatre in Berkeley.
VHS: S01443. $39.95.
Les Blank, USA, 1979, 20 mins.

Yum, Yum, Yum!

Les Blank marries his obsession with spicy, down-home food and his fascination for the Cajuns and Creoles of Southern Louisiana, to create this mouth-watering, visceral exploration into the cooking and culture of this region. From the bayous and prairies where this unique cuisine originated to the New Orleans kitchen of celebrity chef Paul Prudhomme, Blank discovers the heart and soul of a people and their cuisine.
VHS: S12922. $49.95.
Les Blank, USA, 1990, 31 mins.

EMILE DE ANTONIO

1968: America Is Hard to See

Veteran documentary filmmaker Emile de Antonio presents a probing analysis of the crucial, kaleidoscopic year 1968, revealing a nation divided: between war and peace, young and old, B&W.
VHS: S07345. $59.95.
Emile de Antonio, USA, 1986, 88 mins.

In the King of Prussia

Emile de Antonio's thought-provoking docu-drama about the Plowshares 8, headed by the Berrigan brothers, who occupied a nuclear weapons plant in Pennsylvania. Martin Sheen stars as the judge presiding over the Berrigans' trial, while Daniel plays himself.
VHS: S00618. $59.98.
Emile de Antonio, USA, 1982, 92 mins.

McCarthy: Death of a Witchhunter

Emile De Antonio's now-classic, rousing film record of the televised 1954 Army-McCarthy hearings dissects the media-clouded history of Cold-War America.
VHS: S01044. $29.95.
Emile de Antonio, USA, 1964, 45 mins.

Millhouse: A White Comedy

Comic and terrifying portrait of Richard Millhouse Nixon. It's all here—Nixon advocating the death penalty for drug dealers, suggesting the use of nuclear weapons in Indochina, photos of Nixon watching go-go dancers in the White House.
VHS: S00857. $39.95.
Emile de Antonio, USA, 1971, 93 mins.

Painters Painting

Warhol, Rauschenberg, Johns and other American key painters are the subject of De Antonio's documentary which captures the visceral personalities at work.
VHS: S00988. $29.98.
Emile de Antonio, USA, 1972, 116 mins.

Plot to Kill JFK: Rush to Judgment

The film explores the theories of Mark Lane, and provides better than any other document a basis for further exploration of the conspiracy-oriented theories surrounding the assassination of John F. Kennedy.
VHS: S01807. $29.95.
Emile de Antonio, USA, 1983, 50 mins.

Vietnam: In the Year of the Pig

One of the most powerful films ever produced about Vietnam, and an Academy Award nominee. "Passionate and committed, yet it impresses by its sobriety… and will be worth seeing after Vietnam for it raises questions" (*Washington Post*).
VHS: S01416. $39.95.
Emile de Antonio, USA, 1968, 103 mins.

DANNY LYON

Born to Film

A complex and moving picture of a child, played by the filmmaker's son, and within it a film of Danny Lyon's childhood, made 35 years earlier by the filmmaker's father. At last, mythology for the middle class. "Lyon's passionate vision has deepened and grown in resonance, and the film is not just family or even social history, but about human continuity, the power of the instinct to survive, the grace that love and play bring to it, the wonder of being alive."
VHS: S05394. $99.00.
Danny Lyon, USA, 1983, 33 mins.

Dear Mark

Made for Mark di Suvero and his sculpture. "The erection of an heroic, skeletal abstract sculpture by Mark di Suvero in France is Dadaistic light comedy, with its Gene Autry soundtrack. The 'heroic' image of the artist at work is ironically undercut by the soundtrack of Gene Autry radio episode in which that cowboy 'hero' smokes out illegal Mexican aliens" (*Films from Pictures*).
VHS: S05393. $99.00.
Danny Lyon, USA/France, 1965/1975-80, 15 mins.

El Mojado

Ironically titled *The Wetback*, *El Mojado* pictures a hero of our times, a Mexican who walks a hundred miles to work in America, tracked by the border patrol. "It's just like hunting animals only it's a lot more fun because you're hunting a live human being. *El Mojado* is about my best friend in New Mexico, an undocumented worker from rural Chihuahua….His name is Eddie and I soon came to regard him as a genius. Eddie could do anything, make anything, fix any car or truck, and usually do it with scraps. We built an adobe house together and every spring I would meet him near the border and smuggle him past the border patrol into the United States. He introduced me to the whole unbelievable world of 'illegal aliens'" (Danny Lyon). English and Spanish with English subtitles.
VHS: S05389. $99.00.
Danny Lyon, USA, 1972, 20 mins.

El Otro Lado (The Other Side)

Made with the rare cooperation of large groups of Mexican campesinos as they walk into this country and live as undocumented workers in citrus groves near Phoenix. Filmed in Queretero and Maripoca County, the campesinos work, sing corredos, and laugh at adversity. "Lyon's images are simple and direct. These men do what they have to do in order to survive. And they do it with remarkable spirit and optimism. Nowhere is this more evident than when the men are making music. They look strong, proud and momentarily free" (Nancy Legge, *The Villager*). Spanish with English subtitles.
VHS: S05392. $99.00.
Danny Lyon, USA/Mexico, 1978, 60 mins.

Little Boy

A radical portrait of New Mexico, with Steve Baer's brilliant diatribe on plutonium ("I think a friend has some in his house"), the Navajo Council for Liberation sit-in at tribal headquarters, Ike de Vargas and Bleak Beauty's own hero, Willie Jaramillo, at war with the police. "Named after the atom bomb that destroyed Hiroshima, *Little Boy* is a king of grand *summa*, Lyon's epic view of America focused through the lens of contemporary New Mexico. The bleak, man-made environment is superimposed uneasily on a harsh, unforgiving landscape, and explosively charged with clashing subcultures…robust, pulsating with energy, but also clouded by a kind of doomed fatality" (*San Francisco Chronicle*).
VHS: S05391. $99.00.
Danny Lyon, USA, 1976, 52 mins.

Llanito

The anglos are a group of retarded boys, Alamo is a pueblo Indian who drinks too much, and Willie Jaramillo makes his film debut as a troubled Chicano child. "*Llanito* deals with people who operate on the fringe of society: Indians, Chicanos, and a group of retarded Anglos. Their collective martyrdom to American society is symbolized by the summary of Christ's passion as recounted by one of the retarded boys, unquestionably one of the most bizarre religious testaments ever recorded" (Pamela Allara, *Pictures from Films/Films from Pictures*).
VHS: S05388. $99.00.
Danny Lyon, USA, 1971, 50 mins.

Los Ninos Abandonados (The Abandoned Children)

A classically realistic film made in the streets of a small Colombian city with a cast of abandoned children, that exhibits the emotions of Chaplin, with music composed and sung by the children. "Unobtrusively, Lyon records the boys' aimless daily lives….*Los Ninos Abandonados* is an angry film with the quietest tones imaginable—and is all the more persuasive for being so" (Kevin Thomas, *Los Angeles Times*). Spanish with English subtitles.
VHS: S05390. $99.00.
Danny Lyon, Colombia, 1974, 63 mins.

Media Man

Danny and Nancy Lyon offer a whimsical, quirky and hilarious look at America. Shot in New York, Mississippi and New Mexico, obsessions like blemish-free tomatoes, tattoo contests, rotten pumpkins and fishing reveal some startling truths about this country—like it's a little strange.
VHS: S21873. $99.00.
Danny and Nancy Lyon, USA, 1994, 60 mins.

Social Sciences 127

A comedy in a Houston tattoo parlour during the Vietnam War. Featuring the hilarious late, great Bill Sanders in his "painless" tattoo shop. Winner, USA Film Festival. "Mr. Lyon's fondness for bizarre images is balanced by a kind of solemn respect for his subjects. This is particularly true in *Social Sciences 127*, about an eccentric, hard-drinking tattoo artist named Bill Sanders who, while he works, rambles on about Vietnam, lesbians, and the art of what he advertises as 'velvety tattoos'" (Vincent Canby, *The New York Times*).
VHS: S05387. $99.00.
Danny Lyon, USA, 1969, 21 mins.

Willie

A realistic film made in Bernalillo, home of Willie Jaramillo and filmmakers Danny and Nancy Weiss Lyon. Defiantly individual and implacable in the face of authority, Willie is repeatedly thrown into jail for relatively minor offenses. The filmmakers gain access to jail cells, day rooms, lunatic wards and the worst cellblock in the penitentiary where Willie is locked up next to his childhood friend and convicted murderer, Michael Guzman. "Lyon deftly blends footage of Jaramillo as an adult with scenes of his more carefree youth. The effect is powerful. One gets the sense of the ravages of time, coupled with a feel for the devastation wrought by a life wasted" (*New Mexican*).
VHS: S05395. $99.00.
Danny & Nancy Weiss Lyon, USA, 1985, 82 mins.

ERROL MORRIS

A Brief History of Time

Errol Morris' documentary about the English physicist Stephen Hawking takes its title from Hawking's best seller. The film explores Hawking's groundbreaking work in quantum physics and the study of the origins of the universe, despite his debilitating physical state, brought about by amyotrophic lateral sclerosis. Morris interweaves anecdotes, family dynamics and Hawking's background into a kaleidoscope of images, movements and sound. Music by Philip Glass.
VHS: S18370. $19.95.
Errol Morris, USA/Great Britain, 1991, 84 mins.

Gates of Heaven

One of the landmarks of American documentary cinema, this funny, inspiring, bizarre look at people and pet cemeteries is really a powerfully revealing statement about Americans' lives and dreams. "Arguably the masterpiece about the American heartland" (J. Hoberman, *Village Voice*); "A masterpiece…One of the top ten films of all time" (Roger Ebert).
VHS: S07307. $19.95.
Errol Morris, USA, 1978, 90 mins.

Vernon, Florida

Errol Morris, the filmmaker who explored pet cemeteries in *Gates of Heaven*, now visits a small town in the Panhandle of Florida to listen to such colorful characters as Snake Reynolds, Henry Snipes, Roscoe Collins and Mr. and Mrs. J.W. Martin and see what they have to say about living in the south and life in general. A funny and unusual documentary.
VHS: S07706. $79.95.
Errol Morris, USA, 1981, 60 mins.

experimental CINEMA

8×8 (A Chess Sonata in 8 Movements)
A masterpiece of experimental film and a projection of the surrealist vision into cinema by its outstanding artists. Described by Richter as "part Freud, part Lewis Carroll," it is a fairy tale for the subconscious based on the game of chess. This chess-sonata is played by a host of artists including Paul Bowles, Jean Cocteau, Julian Levy, Jacqueline Matisse, Jose Sert, Yves Tanguy, Marcel Duchamp, Max Ernst and Alexander Calder. "What interested me is…the poetry of images, the melody and rhythm of forms and colors" (Hans Richter).
VHS: S04359. $59.95.
Hans Richter, USA, 1957, 81 mins.

A.I.D.S.C.R.E.A.M., Ecce Homo and Final Solutions
Three short experimental films by gay filmmaker Jerry Tartaglia are joined on this video. Along with *A.I.D.S.C.R.E.A.M.*, *Ecce Homo* and *Final Solutions* explore fear, rage, the anti-sex and anti-gay movements and the rise of AIDS consumerism. It's an angry, arrogant and unapologetic collection.
VHS: S27222. $59.95.

All Women Are Equal & Pentagon Peace March
A pre-operational transsexual explains her values and beliefs in this insightful study of sexual identity by Marguerite Paris. Then Paris offers an impressionistic view of a 1967 anti-war demonstration. The 8mm originals of these works were transformed by optical printing.
VHS: S27223. $59.95.
Marguerite Paris, USA

American Avant-Garde
Includes three short films from the American avant-garde: *Fall of the House of Usher* (20 mins.), *Lot in Sodom* and *Life and Death of a Hollywood Extra*.
VHS: S14923. $29.95.

American Avant-Garde Films
A collection of five experimental American films spanning 1906-1933; Edwin S. Porter's landmark *Dream of a Rarebit Fiend* (1906, 6 mins., color tints); *Salome*, a bold and stylized version of the Oscar Wilde play starring the dancer Nazimova and based on drawings by Aubrey Beardsley; *The Fall of the House of Usher*, James Watson and Melville Webber's version of Edgar Allan Poe's tale; Watson and Webber's *Lot in Sodom*, an experimental telling of the Old Testament story in terms of homosexuality and the subconscious; and finally Charles Vidor's *The Bridge*, an experimental telling of the Ambrose Bierce story, *Occurrence at Owl Creek Bridge*.
VHS: S09927. $49.95.

Amida/A Mosaic for the Kali Yuga/ Arches/Body Count/Hey Joe
"Throughout all of Reeves's videotapes there is a pervasive sense of feeling of the artist's presence, psyche and spirit, of the artist using the medium as a means of understanding himself…the evolution of his work demonstrates…a refined and spare understanding of the relationship of poetry and image," wrote *Afterimage*. A collection of video work concerned with spiritual ideas, *Amida* explores reincarnation by depicting cycles of existence through images of natural beauty juxtaposed with symbols of death. *A Mosaic for the Kali Yuga* is a meditation on the acceleration, fragmentation and devaluation of truth. *Arches* constructs a poem using text, sound and image in an exploration of language and landscapes in the desert; *Body Count* is an emotionally searing work that ironically presents the fascination of youth with military glory. *Hey Joe* is a psychedelic video set to a Jimi Hendrix song.
VHS: S10417. $59.95.
Daniel Reeves, USA, 32 mins.

Anna Winteler: Der Aufsteig/ Der Abstieg and Horizontal Waltz
Der Aufsteig/Der Abstieg was made in Switzerland in 1988 and is 20 minutes long. *Horizontal Waltz* is from Italy, 1989, and is 7 minutes in length.
VHS: S22585. $90.00.

Antigone: Rites of Passion
Amy Greenfield's daring first feature retells Sophocles' classical tragedy through action, dance and cutting-edge rock music. It transforms the drama of the heroine who defied the State to bury her brother into ceaseless movement and music, haunting sound and words, a mounting outcry against the world's injustices climaxing in an end-of-the-world requiem. A hymn to the extremes of courage, devotion, outrage, eros and death. "Impressive, innovative rock opera film" (*Variety*). With music by Elliott Sharp, Glenn Branca and Diamanda Galas.
VHS: S15437. $29.95.
Amy Greenfield, USA, 1990, 85 mins.

Art Com Video 1: Scandinavia
An indication of the diversity of expression given form through the video medium in Nordic countries—from lyrical abstraction to critique of everyday life to scratch video. Features *Char, en Oversattning* (Karl Druner), *Cricket* (Marikki Hakola), *Elastic Party* (Vibeke Vogel), *The Human Race* (Nicolai Osergard), *Johnny—A Modern Interpretation of Slavology* (Ulrik al Brask), *Menschen* (Ulrik al Brask), *R.E.M.* (Ane Mette Ruge), and other work. 92 mins.
VHS: S13284. $54.95.

Art Com Video 2: Waveforms: Video Japan
A collection of video by artists in Japan that at once represents a diversity of expression, and indicates three themes which underscore Japanese sensibility: Nature, the persistence of cultural traditions, and the embracing of new technology. Features *Mt. Fuji*, Ko Nakajima's electronic interpretation of Hokusai's 19th century woodblock prints; *Flow (3) Part 2*, by Shinsuke Ina, a cascading waterfall rendered and manipulated in video; *Koto Buki*, which documents a ritualistic performance of incantatory music, voice and movement at the tide pools of an inland sea; *Listen the Body*, by Yoshiko Yamaguchi, a body art sound work; *My Gaijin Tengoky*, a humorous view of the idiosyncrasies of Japanese culture; and *Alley o Alley*, an unobtrusive journey through a poor community in Osaka. 57 mins.
VHS: S13285. $49.95.

Art Com Video 3: Max Almy
Max Almy's video investigates contemporary culture, often employing state of the art digital video effects and computer processing. This compilation comprises works from 1979-1989: *Modern Times*, an examination of contemporary romance, communications, politics, sexuality and love; *Deadline*, a fast-paced video about the stress a person experiences in an urban environment; *Leaving the 20th Century*, a trilogy that takes a satiric look at the realities of the 20th century and raises questions about possibilities of the future; *Perfect Leader*, *Drake's Equation* and *Lost in the Pictures*. 52 mins.
VHS: S13286. $49.95.
Max Almy, USA, 1979-89, 52 mins.

Art Com Video 4: Peter Callas
Selected works from Australian video artist Peter Callas, from 1986-1988. His works explore the relationships between commerce, electro-culture, post-industrial environment and time-based art. 28 mins.
VHS: S14905. $49.95.

Art Com Video 5: In Regard of Nature
A collection of recent video from Japan which examines nature—traditional, organic, spiritual and technological. Includes works by Tetsuo Mizuno, Shinsuke Ina, Yo Nakajima and more. 55 mins.
VHS: S14906. $49.95.

Art Com Video 7: Naoko Tosa
A collection of videos by Naoko Tosa, a Japanese video artist whose works employ image processing, computer graphics and digital video effects, music, and, rarely, spoken words to describe mental states. This compilation includes *Trip*, *Pleasure Island*, *Ecstasy* and many more. 60 mins.
VHS: S14908. $49.95.

Art Com Video 8: Maria Vedder
Maria Vedder is considered the mother of German video art in the city of Cologne. Her works de-emphasize narrative in favor of the non-verbal impact of pictures. This compilation features two works: *Der Herzschlag der Anubis (The Heartbeat of Anubis)* and *Silent Language*. Original music by Brian Eno. 10 mins.
VHS: S14909. $49.95.

Art Com Video 9: Women Empowered
Women and their concerns toward the technologies which shape contemporary life are the subject of some of the videos in this collection. Other shorts focus on personal expression, with mythical and psychological aspects given special emphasis. Jeanne Finley's *Which Man Runs…Which Man Sits Still at Home*, Carol Leigh and Dee Russel's *Yes Means Yes and No Means No*, Donna Matorin's *Quickening*, Copper Giloth's *Red Table*, Marjorie Franklin's *Her…Signal*, Jill Scott's *Continental Drift* and Chris Robbins' *Red Channels* are included. 60 mins.
VHS: S21269. $29.95.

Art Com Video 10: Czechoslovakian Selections
A range of artists from this country are represented on this tape, using diverse forms. Works included are *Dogtroep in Prague*, *Bomb*, a political music video by Vidox, Studio Prometheus' animated short *Kantilena* and the springlike *Time of Mirth* by Radek Pilar. 55 mins.
VHS: S21270. $49.95.

Art Com Video 11: Gay and Lesbian Selections
Azian Nururdin's *Wicked Radiance*, Robb Motter's *Lazarus*, Kevin Adam's *Can't Take That Away from Me*, Ylonda Steven's *Down on the River*, Moze Mossanen's *In Which Pier Pasolini Sees His Own Death in the Face of a Boy*, Maureen Bradley's *Hot Sex*, and Cayte Latta's *F2M* comprise this collection of hot, new, hip, gay and lesbian shorts. 59 mins.
VHS: S21271. $49.95.

Art Com Video 12: Creative Insanity
Open as Stephan is the story of a man with an IQ over 160 and a multiple personality disorder, as told by Lee Bridges/Musick. *Tenderloin Blues* is Chuck Haldina's documentary about the people from a notoriously down-and-out district. 71 mins.
VHS: S21272. $49.95.

Art Com Video 14: Rebel Girls
Leslie Singer's *Flipper* is a strangely funny work about football hero worship, while *Handmirror/Brush Set*, by Liz Canning, brings childhood grooming practice alive through a vinyl practice dummy head. *Untitled II* is Monet Clark's seductive/repulsive ritual that attracts voyeurs. *I Love You Mom*, by Madelaine Altman, shows a secretly recorded mother/daughter argument, and *Goldfinger*, by Meg Mack and Steven Cabella, documents a performance of a blonde who laughs at herself and culture. 55 mins.
VHS: S21274. $49.95.

Art of Memory
Experiment with political and religious forms by acclaimed video artist Woody Vasulka. Documentary images of WW II, the Spanish Civil War and the Russian Revolution appear against vistas of Southwestern landscapes.
VHS: S05398. $59.95.
Woody Vasulka, USA, 36 mins.

The Ascent of Man/ In the Absence of Heroes
In *The Ascent of Man*, broadcast video footage and super-8 film are combined in an experimental investigation of patriotism and virtue, while in *In the Absence of Heroes* explores the relationship of warfare to personal trauma and international conflict.
VHS: S21038. $59.95.
Jayce Salloum, USA, 1986/1984, 15 & 40 mins.

Atalanta Strategy
Based on music from the opera *Atalanta* (Acts of God), and using a multi-projector, free-sampling technique to provide video imagery, this is daring video art from Robert Ashley. It is based on the anecdotal material of the second episode of *Willard*. There are three kinds of scenes surrounding the main anecdote, which is sung by Robert Ashley.
VHS: S11644. $49.95.
Robert Ashley, USA, 1984, 27 mins.

Avant Garde & Experimental Film
Five early experimental films: Bunuel and Dali's *Un Chien Andalou*, Joris Ivens and Mannus Franken's *Rain*, Erno Metzner's *Uberfall*, Orson Welles' 1934 *Hearts of Age* and Fernand Leger's *Ballet Mecanique*. Silent, with English subtitles. 74 mins.
VHS: S00079. $29.95.

Avant Garde Program #2
Three early silent German and French experimental works: Eggeling's *Symphonie Diagonale*, Man Ray's *L'Etoile de Mer*, and Rene Clair's *Entr'Acte*, starring Man Ray and Marcel Duchamp. 42 mins.
VHS: S00080. $24.95.

Avant Garde Program #11
Features David Lynch's cult-early-classic *Alphabet* (1970, 4 mins), in which the director of *Eraserhead* uses a stunning combination of media to move at breakneck speed through Lynch's vision of the ABC's; Jean Mitry's *Pacific 231*, a film poem which Mitry photographed and cut to fit a twelve-tone musical divertisement which was written by Arthur Honegger some 14 years earlier when Honegger had been aboard the famous train; Marcel Duchamp's *Anemic Cinema* (1926, 5 mins), a series of verbal and visual puns with nonsense phrases.
VHS: S07696. $39.95.

Avant Garde Program #12
Features Germaine Dulac's *Seashell and the Clergyman*, Chris Marker's famous *La Jetee*—both of these are individually available and separately described in the catalog—and Robert Florey/Slavko Vorkapich's *Life and Death of 9413,—A Hollywood Extra*, made in 1928, the first important American experimental film, influenced by German Expressionistic cinema, a fantasy about an aspiring movie star.
VHS: S07170. $49.95.

Avant Garde Program #14
Three films by the great photographer/artist/filmmaker Man Ray: *Retour a La Raison* (1923, 3 mins) was produced to aggravate audiences at the last great Dada soiree, without the use of a camera, by sprinkling the raw film stock and exposing it light; *Emak Bakia* (1927, 19 mins) is a famous surrealist short in which Man Ray throws the camera into the air; *Les Mysteres du Chateau du De* (1929, 21 mins) features a modern villa designed by Mallet-Stevens as the setting for an unsolved mystery.
VHS: S07169. $39.95.
Man Ray, France, 1921-27, 43 mins.

Avant Garde Shorts/France
Collection of early surreal and avant garde films made between 1914 and 1928: *La Folie du Dr. Tube* (Abel Gance), *Emak Bakia* (Man Ray), *The Smiling Madame Beudet* (Germaine Dulac), *Anemic Cinema* (Marcel Duchamp) and *Charleston* (Jean Renoir). Silent. France, 1914-28.
VHS: S00081. $34.95.

Bachdisc
Music and visuals are beautifully intertwined in this program that combines an accessible and thrilling exploration of J.S. Bach's *Fugue in #4 B minor* and a documentary on the composer's methods and art that captures the full range and excitement of his music.
Laser: LD70102. $49.95.
Juan Downey, USA

Beehive
Film on dance that relates the story of a bumbling drone bee who unwittingly causes the transformation of a worker into a queen. A striking soap opera with dance, animation and high production values.
VHS: S07127. $29.95.
Frank Moore/Jim Self, USA, 1985, 16 mins.

Berks Filmmakers: A Compilation Tape
Works by Gary Adelstein, Jerry Orr, Buddy Kilchesty and Jamie Harrar are combined in this video. Together they offer a view of grassroots filmmaking in Eastern Pennsylvania that is by turns lyrical, psychosexual in focus and critical.
VHS: S27225. $59.95.

Berlin, Symphony of a Great City
Walter Ruttmann's great documentary is a dynamic vision of Berlin, unfolding from dawn until midnight. Ruttmann captured the city's expressive poetry by concealing his camera in vans and suitcases to capture a portrait of the city and its people. Music composed and conducted by Timothy Brock, performed by the Olympia Chamber Orchestra. On the same program is *Opus 1*, a ten-minute essay Ruttman shot in 1922.
VHS: S01931. $24.95.
Walter Ruttmann, Germany, 1927, 62 mins.

The Best of the New York Underground, Year 2
Suicide, intense brutality and steamy sexual situations are found on this extreme video. It includes a number of short independent works, all of which are excessive. *The Operation* is perverse, *Deinstag* is violent, and *Brouhaha* actually features Satan partying. 90 mins.
VHS: S27440. $29.95.

Best of William Wegman
William Wegman is one of the world's most affable subversives. This tape, assembled by Electronic Arts Intermix, is a twenty minute survey of Wegman's vignettes from the years 1970-1978. His dog Man Ray, various props, and the talking stomach are featured in this compilation of Wegman classics which include *Duet*, *Milk Floor Piece*, *Stomach Song*, *Two Lamps*, *Pocket Bookman*, *Massage Chair*, *Deodorant* and *The Spelling Lesson*.
VHS: S06308. $65.00.
William Wegman, USA, 1970-78, 20 mins.

Betaville
Based on Godard's *Alphaville*, this "post-modern nightmare" posits a society governed by fashion.
VHS: S10188. $19.95.
Alyce Wittenstein, USA, 1986, 25 mins.

Bill Viola: I Do Not Know What It Is I Am Like
An epic journey in five chapters, a personal investigation into the inner states and connections to animal consciousness, by one of America's foremost video artists. In a stream of images of striking clarity, depth and beauty, Bill Viola evokes a timeless view of the natural world and our place in it. The five segments are titled *Il Corpu Scuro (The Dark Body)*, *The Language of the Birds*, *The Night of Sense*, *Stunned by the Drum* and *The Living Flame*.
VHS: S03074. $69.95.
Laser: LD70313. $74.95.
Bill Viola, USA, 1986, 89 mins.

Bill Viola: Selected Works
Four works by one of the foremost video artists working today: *Migration* (1976, color, mono, 7:00); *The Reflecting Pool* (1977-79, color, mono, 7:00); *Ancient of Days* (1979-81, color, stereo, 12:21); and *Chott-El-Djerid (A Portrait in Light and Heat)* (1979, color, mono, 28:00). "Compounded of many resonances, each level of meaning interwoven with myriad others, these exquisite 'visual songs' give us the elegant music of the poet's voice" (G. Youngblood).
VHS: S03328. $59.95.
Laser: LD70314. $59.95.
Bill Viola, USA, 1976-79, 54 mins.

Brains by Revlon
A pattern-obsessive, symmetrical work about three extravagantly costumed women discussing three fates, three graces and three fairy tales from *Sleeping Beauty* in this strange, hypnotic exercise in style.
VHS: S17195. $29.95.
Jack Waters, USA, 18 mins.

Cadillac Ranch/Media Burn
A recent re-edit of two Ant Farm projects, *Cadillac Ranch* documents the burying of 10 Cadillacs in Amarillo, Texas as a monument to the Cadillac fin, plus *Media Burn*, a spectacular performance piece.
VHS: S00200. $59.95.
Ant Farm, USA, 1974-75

Cave Girls
A tape by collaborating women artists who develop a pre-thought fantasy of a prehistoric culture of women. Rife with homemade exoticism, this well-received piece verges on the grand themes of female identity. Conceived by Kiki Smith and Ellen Cooper, with music by Bush Tetras and Y Pants.
VHS: S07112. $29.95.
Cara Brownell, USA, 1982, 28 mins.

Chronos
Chronos, meaning the passage of time, is a visual music journey transcending history from the cradle of civilization to modern day Paris. Startling time-lapse images of the Vatican, the Sphinx, the Great Pyramid and nearly 50 other wonders of our world captivate the senses. Photographed in the world's largest film format for IMAX theatres.
VHS: S16731. $19.95.
Ron Fricke, USA, 1991, 40 mins.

CineBLAST! Vol. 1
Eight short, innovative features from independent directors are collected on this video. Included are: *Tough* (Aiyana Elliot), *Fishmind* (Matthias Freier), *Sheep's Meadow* (Brooke Smith), *Hungreed* (Ira Israel), *Watch with Mother* (Sam Serafy), *The Side of the Road* (David Burris), *The Girl from Moush* (Garine Torossian) and *Zinky Boys Go Underground* (Paul Tickell). 111 mins.
VHS: S27619. $79.95.

Cinema of Transgression

Nick Zedd's *Bogus Man & Go to Hell*, John Spencer's *Shithaus*, Lung Leg's *Worm Movie*, Richard Klemann's *A Suicide*, Erotic Psyche's *Mutable Fire*, Tommy Turner's *Simonland*, Richard Kern's *You Killed Me First & King of Sex*, Michael Wolfe's *Niggernight*, and Manuel de Landa's *Judgment Day* and *Ism, Ism*. Extremely graphic scenes of bodily functions, hokey scenes of trumped up ketchup violence, stabbing and severed limbs, some strangely moving and brilliant filmmaking by a wide collection of drug addicts, outlaws, and perennial outsiders.
VHS: $10161. $49.95.

The City Inside Us: Vito Acconci

This video documents the exhibition of the same name held in The Austrian Museum of Applied Arts in Vienna. For this show famed video artist Acconci recreated the existing space with a crucial difference—it was set askew to offer a series of surprising new situations. Interviews with the artist as well as four previous works are highlighted in this tape.
VHS: $22555. $85.00.
Vito Acconci, USA, 30 mins.

Clea Waite: Stella Maris

A stylized examination of the female nude, and the impact of movement and light under water. The filmmaker devises "living sculptures" through a bold black and white interpretation of the triple goddess myths. 15 mins.
VHS: $17206. $19.95.

Commission

Video artist Woody Vasulka's experiment with narrativity through electronic tools is presented in this operatic work that evokes the friendship between composer Berlioz and the violinist Paganini. His ill health, loss of voice and habit of gambling led to his death at an early age.
VHS: $05645. $59.95.
Woody Vasulka, USA, 1987, 45 mins.

Communications Update

An intriguing collection of excerpts from the artists' cable TV series that makes room for broad slapstick, pulp drama, horror stories of the streets, and a wry airy speculation on science and loneliness. Includes work by: Milli Iatrou and Ron Morgan, Eric Mitchell and Squat Theatre, Robert Burden and Dictellio Cepeda, Mark Magill, and Stephen Torton. USA, 1982, 58 mins.
VHS: $07113. $59.95.

Critical Art Ensemble

The Tallahassee-Florida based video performance group of seven lays on the post-modern dog, with a collection of short pieces: *Mirror of Reduction, Misappropriation (after Andy Warhol), Baudrillard's Lasso, Collective Oedipal Revolution, Indefinite Concrete Material, Gift-Wrapped Aporia, Art Film, Mondo Familiae, Limnologic Jargon.* 35 mins.
VHS: $10206. $29.95.

Cupid's Infirmary

Mike Kuchar's new, campy soap opera updates Kuchar's 1960s melodramatic drag extravaganzas. This tape features tattooed torsos of sex-starved "she-men" who are in turn laid bare for analysis and cheap thrills.
VHS: $27226. $59.95.
Mike Kuchar, USA

Dara Birnbaum, Canon: Taking to the Streets 1

Acclaimed internationally as a premier artist, Birnbaum has shown video work in unusual settings like MTV. Her Rio Video Wall has been heralded as the first outdoor video installation. Installation work and tapes critical of broadcast television conventions are just two areas where her influence has been seminal.
VHS: $22557. $90.00.
Dara Birnbaum, USA, 11 mins.

Delphi 1830 & Next Time Everything Will Be Better

In *Delphi 1830*, filmmaker Rick Minnich uses pixilation to document the experience of a filmmaker at the 1993 Berlin Film Festival. In the second work, *Next Time Everything Will Be Better*, he shows a bunch of carefree types banding together to take back post-Wall Berlin.
VHS: $27239. $49.95.
Rick Minnich, Germany

Dennis Day: Oh Nothing

Oh Nothing is a mediated romance, an urban love story created from 1-second "spots", of desire, design, consumerism and distraction. In the city of Toronto, Rebecca (graphics consultant) and Kevin (systems analyst) battle each other, the corporate sponsors, and their own minds in a continual game of distraction. For them, life is a living commercial in which everything is product and nothing is remembered.
VHS: $12753. $65.00.
Dennis Day, Canada, 12 mins.

Dialectics of Romance

This well received piece by video artist and writer Ann Sargent Wooster takes a structuralist though juicy look at formula romance writing, using miniature sets, faceless close-ups and lush dissolves.
VHS: $22645. $29.95.
Ann Sargent Wooster, USA, 1985, 30 mins.

Diane Teramana: The Knitting Factory Show

This is a collection of video works selected personally by this artist from Cincinnati, Ohio. 77 mins.
VHS: $22578. $50.00.

Diderot

Diderot is a serial anthology of artists' works in video. Published by United Media Arts Studies, each issue contains new work specially produced by invited artists to address specific themes or conditions.
Diderot No. 1—The Emperor's New Clothes. Programs commissioned between 1983 and 1986 and produced by artists normally working in other media, including Mark DeGuerre, Lily Eng, Fast Wurms, Brian Scott, Doug Sigurdson and Suzanne Gillies.
VHS: $11646. $69.95.
Diderot No. 2—Television and the Channels of Culture. A special issue addressing the depth and breadth of television, including work by the artists Michael Balser, Sean Cubbitt, Christine Martin, Andrew J. Paterson and Jeanne Randolph.
VHS: $11647. $69.95.

Diderot No. 3— TV Blong Vanuatu John Watt

This title could be translated as, "a day of television from Vanuatu." Watt went to this island to develop an idea. He hoped to simulate a day of community television programming for a television-less society. The resulting tape comes with a booklet which contains an introduction by Rodney Werden.
VHS: $22563. $58.00.

Die Fettecke

Die Fettecke from 235 Media Cologne includes pieces by the masters Joseph Beuys and Nam June Paik, as well as the works of Konig, Naegeli, Staeck, Cladders and others.
VHS: $22556. $70.00.
M. Bielicky/R. Peredo, USA, 40 mins.

Die Todliche Doris

This video documents the performances and concerts put on by this German video art group. Some of their video work is also included. These pieces cover the years 1981-87. 49 mins.
VHS: $22562. $45.00.

Digital Speech and Pressures of the Text

"Rose's terrific sense of humor and genius at timing make him a cross between an intellectual Eddie Murphy and an old-time vaudeville comedian with a Ph.D.," wrote *Afterimage*. *Digital Speech* uses a traveler's anecdote, a perverse variant of a classic Zen parable, as a vehicle for an exploration of language, thought and gesture. *Pressures of the Text* integrates direct address, invented languages, ideographic subtitles, sign language and simultaneous translation to investigate the feel and form of sense, the shifting boundaries between meaning and meaninglessness.
VHS: $09206. $59.95.
Peter Rose, USA, 1984, 30 mins.

Divine Horsemen: The Living Gods of Haiti

Posthumously edited by Teiji and Cherel Ito, a remarkable document of the Rada, Petro and Congo cults of Haiti whose devotees commune with cosmic powers through invocations, voodoo dances and ritual ceremonies. The sound track conveys the power of ritual drumming and singing.
VHS: $00349. $29.95.
Maya Deren, USA, 52 mins.

Dog Star Man

One of the key works of the American avant-garde of the 1960's, Stan Brakhage's *Dog Star Man* is no less than an abstract vision of the creation of the universe, an epic work consisting of a prelude and four parts. Making brilliant use of superimpositions, painting on film, distorting lenses and rhythmic montage, the film is a compelling and truly an eye-opening experience. Silent.
VHS: $04119. $19.95.
Stan Brakhage, USA, 1961-64, 78 mins.

Doug Hall: Storm and Stress

Internationally known and acclaimed video artist Doug Hall creates a visual and aural record of turbulent weather systems and industrial and natural energy. The violence of severe storms is juxtaposed with images of hydroelectric plants, wind tunnels, satellite dishes and other technologies that harness or mimic nature. The general theme: merchandising power. 50 mins.
VHS: $12755. $65.00.

Elisabeth Jappe: Documenta 8— Performance—Action—Ritual

The international art exhibition at Kassel provides the setting for this tape, which includes Allan Kaparow, Charlemagne Palestine, Minus Delta T., Ulrike Rosenbach, Jurgen Klauke and others. 180 mins.
VHS: $22570. $70.00.

Enchanted Landscapes, Volume 2

Visionary nature images set to music by C.H. Deuter, Ray Lynch and Iasos. 40 mins.
VHS: $10227. $29.95.

Ephemeral Films 1931-1960

Join media archaeologist Richard Prelinger as he explores our recent past. What he has discovered will amaze as much as entertain you. Prelinger has perhaps happened upon one of America's greatest surviving time capsules—educational and industrial movies.
To New Horizons: Ephemeral Films 1931-1945. Lets you share the futuristic dreams of pre-World War II America.
VHS: $13599. $39.95.
Laser: LD70321. $39.95.
You Can't Get There from Here: Ephemeral Films 1946-1960. Reviews the golden age of American consumerism.
VHS: $13600. $39.95.
Laser: LD70323. $39.95.

Experimental Avant Garde Series Volume 19 (Very Serious Fun)

Five short films featuring Hitler, Godzilla, Bambi, JFK and the Grim Reaper: *Bambi Meets Godzilla*—Marv Neuland's wry look at what might happen if these two entertainment legends ever got together. *Lambeth Walk Nazi Style*—Len Lye takes newsreel footage of Hitler and his troops and using freeze frames, jump cuts, repeat action and other techniques, pieces it all together and sets it to a popular British jig. *Loves of Franistan*—a funny take-off of big budget film spectaculars. *The Dove*—a wicked takeoff of Ingmar Bergman films; in one scene Death plays badminton instead of chess. *The JFK Workout*—an offbeat training film made in the 60's to promote JFK's physical fitness; includes a discourse on the inferiority of females. This is not necessarily an avant garde work, but it is so weird and silly we just couldn't leave it out. 60 mins.
VHS: $13504. $39.95.

Experimental Avant Garde Series Volume 20 (The Secret Lives of Inanimate Objects)

Four short films: *Ghosts before Breakfast*—Hans Richter's lively absurdist piece featuring juxtapositions of everyday objects taking on new roles in most unusual settings. *Rhythmus 21*—Richter returns to explore the extremely complex form of the simple square. *H2O*—Ralph Steiner's visually delightful study on water. *The Vanished World of Gloves*—Unusual film by Czechoslovakian Jiri Barta that uses live action and animation to tell this story of some gloves that have come to life. 55 mins.
VHS: $13505. $39.95.

Experimental Avant Garde Series Volume 21 (An Attack on Social, Sexual, and Political Order)

Two short films: *Lot in Sodom*—Watson and Webber's famed filming of the Old Testament story complete with homosexual orgies, sensuous sexual dances and a pillar of salt. *L' Historie du Soldat Inconnu*—Henri Storck uses the signing of the Kellogg-Briand pact to launch his hyperbolic attack on everything including, but not limited to, the bourgeoisie, democracy, religion and capitalism. 45 mins.
VHS: $13506. $29.95.

Experimental Avant Garde Series Volume 22

Knights on Bikes, featuring jousting motorcycle drivers, and *Peepshow* are two of famed director Ken Russell's earliest works. *Happy Anniversary*, by Pierre Etaix and Jean-Claude Carriere, stages a number of gags around the celebration of marital bliss. Finally, director Bert Haanstra exposes the nasty truth about the *The Zoo* in this collection of absurd and serious films. 50 mins.
VHS: $22468. $29.95.

Experimental Avant Garde Series Volume 23

CBS' Harry Reasoner travels to San Francisco to report on *The Hippie Temptation*. It's hilarious and features footage of the Grateful Dead. *Dream Flower*, a short film from 1932, shows how poppies grow into the source of mind-altering substances. 60 mins.
VHS: $22469. $29.95.

Figures

Made by rephotographing original footage, frame by frame, to create a painterly image, James Herbert's work features "nudes photographed with such a disquieting ambivalence—a kind of transcendental nostalgia—otherwise unknown in American cinema" (Laurence Kardish). Also included on this tape are *Automan, Soundings, Two Figures, Carnival* and *Limbo District*.
VHS: $14821. $39.95.
James Herbert, USA, 1990, 85 mins.

Films of Charles and Ray Eames

Charles and Ray Eames are among the most influential American designers of this century. Best known for their ground-breaking contributions to architecture, furniture, industrial design and photography, their legacy also includes over 75 innovative short films. The finest of these programs is in a new series, introduced in a narration by Gregory Peck.
Films of Charles and Ray Eames, Volume 1. *Powers of Ten*, the film that revolutionized the way we view our world, takes us on a breathtaking voyage from the interior of an atom to the furthest reaches of the universe. Starting with the closeup of a man's hand, and increasing the distance from the starting point ten times every ten seconds, this startling adventure in magnitudes illustrates as few films ever have the concepts of space and time. 21 mins.
VHS: $13218. $39.95.
Laser: LD70774. $49.95.
Films of Charles and Ray Eames, Volume 2. The second volume in the series consists of seven short films of dazzling impact and variety. From *Toccata for Toy Trains*, a magical look at antique toy trains, to *The Black Ships*, a subtle view of Admiral Perry's opening of Asia as seen through the Japanese art of the time, this collection illustrates the Eames' remarkable warmth, diversity and intelligence. 62 mins.
VHS: $13219. $39.95.
Laser: LD70775. $49.95.
Films of Charles and Ray Eames, Volume 3. The lives of Benjamin Franklin and Thomas Jefferson spanned 120 years and shaped the course of American history. This film, produced and directed by the famous design team of Charles and Ray Eames, is a masterful tribute to the two founding fathers of American independence. Franklin and Jefferson's philosophies and contributions are viewed against the background of the literary, scientific and artistic developments of their time. Using a visual timeline constructed of portraits, documents and other historical artifacts, the interlocking chapters of each man's story are brought to life. Narrated by Orson Welles and Nina Foch, with original music by Elmer Bernstein. USA, 35 mins.
VHS: $15395. $39.95.
Films of Charles and Ray Eames, Volume 4. This design workshop by Charles Eames features *Design Q & A*, one of the most concise and witty statements about design on film. *Goods*, a discussion of the "new convertables" and one of Eames legendary 3-screen slide shows are also included, as well as *IBM Math Peep Shows, SX-70, Polychris Hapus, The Fiberglass Chairs* and *Copernicus.* 59 mins.
VHS: $21522. $39.95.

The Films of Meredith Monk

Two works by dance and performance artist Meredith Monk. *Book of Days* (1986) is a haunting meditation on time and nature, about a perfectly preserved medieval town in Southern France. *Ellis Island* (1981) examines the decaying walls and supernatural presence of the American landmark. 105 mins.
Laser: LD71956. $39.95.

The Films of Scott Bartlett

Visionary—one of America's most celebrated experimental filmmakers. Pioneer—Bartlett's landmark films *Offon* and *Moon 1969* are acknowledged as the earliest expressions of electronic cinema.
Volume 1: The Birth of the Counter Culture. Three landmark films: *Offon*, a classic of experimental film, "a perfect, magical fusion of non-verbal communication and advanced technological filmmaking" (Amos Vogel); *Moon 1969*, "a beautiful, eerie, haunting film, all the more wonderful for the fact that we do not once see the moon—only the manifestations of its powers here on earth" (L.A. Times); *1970*, a dramatic autobiographical film that is a multiplexed portrait of the San Francisco sub-culture of the 1960's, "a lasting testament to a time we will never forget" (L.A. Film Festival). 55 mins.
VHS: $05621. $59.95.
Volume 2: The Future of Human Mythology. The serpent embodies the primal chaotic life force in mythic symbology. *Serpent* uses natural and electronic imagery to convey this elusive force in what is "an outstanding piece of art. Striking, kinetic. A beautiful combination of pure visual poetry and ideas about man and the world" (American Film Festival). Also contains *Medina*, an extraordinary, lucid and lyrical documentary of Morocco, "the richest, boldest, most subtly disciplined evocation of a place that I have ever seen on film" (New York Times). Also included are *Sound of One*, the unique melding of T'ai Chi Ch'uan and filmmaking, and *Heavy Metal*, which employs elaborate optical techniques to create an instant audio-visual trip back to 1929. 52 mins.
VHS: $05644. $59.95.
Volume 3: The Process of Creation. In the summer of 1967, Scott Bartlett's film loops and Glen McKay's light show liquids were mixed through a video effects bank and the results were filmed by Mike McNamee. The finished film was called *Offon*. In 1980, Bartlett recreated the event in a video production class at UCLA. The result is *Making Offon*, a video primer. Wipes, keying and feedback are first illustrated and named, then woven into a sound and picture puzzle of the 60's. In *Making Serpent*, Bartlett narrates and describes the creative process behind *Serpent*, his award-winning film. *Making Serpent* is a step-by-step teaching device that explores film techniques such as how to structure a non-verbal narrative, how to shoot film for special editing techniques, how to isolate universal images in nature, and how to make exciting visuals inexpensively. "Eisenstein's *Film Form* continued on film" (Bruce Baillie). 50 mins.
VHS: $05643. $59.95.
Scott Bartlett, USA, 1968-1980

Fireworks

A collection which includes *Fireworks* (a dissatisfied dreamer awakes, goes out in the night seeking a light...), *Rabbit's Moon* (a fable of the unattainable, combining elements of Commedia dell'Arte with Japanese myth), and *Eaux d'Artifice* (a costumed figure moves through Tivoli gardens...), by perhaps the most important American experimental filmmaker of the post-war years. *Eaux d'Artifice* is included in the National Film Registry.
VHS: $00800. $29.95.
Kenneth Anger, USA, 1947-55, 34 mins.

Flaming Creatures

Jack Smith's groundbreaking, lyrical queer film is being released in a special limited-edition series to raise funds that will help restore and preserve his other works. This classic may seem tame by current standards, but its great camp style stands the test of time.
VHS: $27242. $195.00.

Frank and Koen Theys, Lied Meines Landes II: Die Walkure

This video includes music from *Ring der Nibelungen* by Richard Wagner. Belgium, 1989, 90 mins.
VHS: $22579. $90.00.

Ganapati/A Spirit in the Bush

The artist Daniel Reeves creates a haunting and impressionistic song about the relationship of men and animals, using the poetry of Lorca, Rilke, Kipling and Reeves and location footage of India, Kenya and Thailand matched with archival footage. Reeves's "procession of charged mages involves and implicates the viewer through its silently scrolling text." 45 mins.
VHS: $16736. $59.95.

Germaine Dulac: Smiling Madame Beudet and Seashell and the Clergyman

Two seminal films. *Smiling Madame Beudet* employs some of the techniques of the "theater of silence" and impressionistic camera. The romantic Madame Beudet is married to a dull and insensitive tradesman who irritates her so much that she dreams of other lovers and of killing them. Silent with sparse inter-titles in French. *Seashell and the Clergyman*, scripted by Antonin Artaud, is composed of a series of episodes using Freudian imagery to express the mental anguish of a clergyman who is committed to his calling to celibacy, but is afflicted by sexual torments he cannot resolve. Musical track.
VHS: $05295. $39.95.
Germaine Dulac, France, 1928, 62 mins.

Gerz Jochen Ti Amo
VHS: #22565. $90.00.
Jochen Gerz, France, 1985, 19 mins.

Gorilla Tapes: Death Valley Days/ Lo Pay No Way!
28 mins.
VHS: #22566. $45.00.

Harry Smith's Early Abstraction
Seven abstract animated films described by the filmmaker in such terms as:"optically printed Pythagoreanism in four movements supported on squares, circles, grillwork… hand-drawn animation of dirty shapes… an exposition of Buddhism and the kabala in form of collage."
VHS: #01576. $19.95.
Harry Smith, USA, 1941-57, 24 mins.

Heaven and Earth Magic
"Produced in beatnik obscurity during the late 1950s, this hour-long marvel—a bit like dismembered Victorian valentines enacting a vaudeville version of the Egyptian Book of the Dead—is the real Fantasia—a higher form of hieroglyphics," wrote J. Hoberman in *The Village Voice* of Harry Smith's graphic description of initiation, redemption and spiritual transformation, couched in the language of Qabalah, alchemy and experimental psychology. Applying an extension of surrealist and cut up techniques to animate collages of familiar images, Smith transmutes these elements as an alchemist would, extracting the Philosopher's Stone through patience, cinematic pressure and an intense spirituality.
VHS: #09558. $29.95.
Harry Smith, USA, 1957-62, 66 mins.

Holy Mary, Remembrance & Vocation
In these three short, experimental films, filmmaker Jerry Tartaglia looks at the Pope in drag, describes memories of Bette Davis from his queer youth, and catches the lyrical existence of The Radical Faeries at their retreat at the Short Mountain Collective in Tennessee.
VHS: #27229. $59.95.
Jerry Tartaglia, USA

Home of the Brave
More than a concert film, *Home of the Brave* was originally shown in theatres and presents Laurie Anderson's multi-layered version of life in America with an engaging mix of high-tech wizardry, droll satire and 21st century synthesizer music. Includes *Sharkey's Day*, *Gravity's Angel*, *Language Is a Virus*, *Excellent Birds* and other numbers. 90 mins.
VHS: Out of print. For rental only.
Laser: CLV. LD75394. $39.95.

Hypnotic Places, Exotic Spaces
A 30-minute scenic music visual fantasy which takes the viewer scuba diving into liquid aqua inner space, strolling 35 acres of misty Canadian gardens, to the tropics, and to the English countryside with castle ruins and fallen abbeys. A mixture of art forms ranging from hand-painted cell animation to computer graphics, produced by photographer and visual designer Carol Davis. The music is an eclectic mix of works in this new-age video, designed for relaxation. 30 mins.
VHS: #08788. $19.95.

Illumination
Ken Jenkins' video of beautiful, flowing images, which unfold one out of another in a seemingly endless progression of radiance. Original music by Iasos and Constance Demby. From the creator of special effects for Shirley MacLaine's *Inner Workout*. 30 mins.
VHS: #10239. $29.95.
Laser: LD70239. $29.95.

Inauguration of the Pleasure Dome
"A convocation of magicians assume the identity of gods and goddesses in a Dionysian revel….Dedicated to the few and to Aleister Crowley, and the crowned and conquering child" (Anger). One of the key works of American experimental cinema.
VHS: #00801. $29.95.
Kenneth Anger, USA, 1954, 38 mins.

An Individual Desires Solution & War Songs
The first of these two experimental films by Lawrence F. Brose confronts AIDS as faced by the artist's HIV-positive lover. In the second work, a poem performance by Paul Schmidt forms the basis for an ode to peace. Together these films manage to create a highly personal view of these important issues.
VHS: #27220. $59.95.
Lawrence F. Brose, USA

Introduction to the End of an Argument
Combining Hollywood, European and Israeli film with documentary footage and news coverage, this work critiques representations of Arab culture, the Middle East and the Palestinian people. Mimicry serves as a sly entry point for this audio-visual deconstruction of stereotypes.
VHS: #21037. $59.95.
Jayce Salloum/Elia Suleiman, USA, 1990, 45 mins.

It's Clean—It Just Looks Dirty
A collection of short videos assembled by John Giorno: Cabaret Voltaire in *Truth in the Lord*, Husker Du in *The Girl Who Lives on Heaven Hill*, Powerline, Diamanda Galas in two excerpts from *Eyes without Blood*, Einsturzende Neubauten in *Sand*, Robert Frank/Rudy Wurlitzer/Gary Hill in *Energy and How to Get It* featuring William Burroughs and Doctor John, The John Giorno Band in *Scum and Slime*, David Johansen in *Heard the News*, Robert Wilson and the Civil Wars, excerpts from Howard Brookner's film of Wilson's work with music by Shubert, David Byrne and Philip Glass, Swans' *A Screw*, Psychic TV in *Unclean*, and John Waters' *No Smoking in This Theater*. 60 mins.
VHS: #03945. $29.95.

J.S. Bach
Juan Downey's beautiful documentary on J.S. Bach places the famous composer's career and his powerful music in counterpoint with the gritty reality of his life. Downey's tape reflects on the shifting, symbiotic relations of art and the nature and biography of the individual. An insightful reconstruction of another artist's creative path, as well as of his own.
VHS: #08996. $39.95.
Juan Downey, USA, 1986, 28 mins.

Joan Jonas: Vertical Roll
This classic video by an early pioneer of video art uses one of the primary features of video. The vertical roll that results when two out of sync frequencies meet is interpreted to create perceptual illusions from the rolling image.
VHS: #22587. $65.00.

Juan Downey
Two works by the Chile-born video artist Juan Downey, whose works have been exhibited and collected by countless museums around the world. The first, *Information Withheld*, dramatizes the nature of signs and symbols. From Egypt to Manhattan to Chile, the signs are presented in ascending order of complexity; hieroglyphs to a Michelangelo painting. Also included is *Shifters*, a videotape that aims to "dismantle the narrative mode". Downey distinguishes six recurring themes of imperialism/oppression and uses a subtext concerning class struggle and architecture.
VHS: #12754. $60.00.
Juan Downey, USA, 56 mins.

Just Hold Still
A collection of short films by Jem Cohen, including *Never Change*, a film set to a poem by Blake Nelson, set against the backdrop of rural roads soaked in fog. *Love Teller* is about a carnival side show machine that predicts how passionate a person is. The films are not narrative, but the combination of music, text and imagery create the mood.
VHS: #14820. $34.95.

Klaus Von Bruch: Black Box I
This two-tape package includes Bruch's works *Der Western Lebt* (1984, 4 mins.), *Allierten Band* (1982, 10:30 mins.) and *Verdunstucke* (1990, 60 mins.). Limited edition of 100.
VHS: #22582. $215.00.
Klaus von Bruch, Germany, 1982-90, 14 mins.

La Chute de la Maison Usher
Though directed by Jean Epstein, this French silent version of the Poe classic is also notable for having given apprenticeship to Luis Bunuel. Henri Langlois of the Cinematheque Francaise wrote, "An absolute mastery of editing and rhythm in which slow motion, super-impressions, moving camera shots, and the mobile camera combine to play a totally gratuitous role. The lighting of the sets transforms them and imparts a sense of mystery. The actors were merely objects."
VHS: #06223. $59.95.
Jean Epstein, France, 1928

Love Tapes
Wendy Clarke's spontaneous revelations about love by people of all ages and all walks of life. Some are good, some are bad, all are touching.
VHS: #12675. $29.95.
Wendy Clarke, USA, 1986, 28 mins.

Lucifer Rising
Invocation of My Demon Brother (a conjuration of pagan forces), Anger's most recent, *Lucifer Rising*, "a film about the love generation, the birthday party of the Aquarian Age, showing actual ceremonies to make Lucifer rise."
VHS: #00802. $29.95.
Kenneth Anger, USA, 1969, 39 mins.

Macbeth: The Witches Scenes
Adapting scenes from Shakespeare's *Macbeth*, video artist Miroslaw Rogala projects the action from a mythic, barbaric past to a violent, post-apocalyptic future where order and technology have broken down. Rather than "eyes of newt," the magic possessed by the witches is the computer.
VHS: #16042. $19.95.
Miroslaw Rogala, USA, 1988, 18 mins.

Maek/Muscha/Shafer/Trimpop
Decoder, 87 mins.
VHS: #22571. $45.00.

Magic Eye—The Video, Volume 1
3-D moving images are now possible without special glasses. This video is inspired by the exciting *Magic Eye* book series. Includes original music and sound effects in Dolby Surround. 32 mins.
VHS: #22745. $14.95.

Magic Eye II—The Video, Volume 2
At the next plateau of 3-D viewing pleasure lie these abstract images that seem to move in space and time. Original music and sound effects in Dolby Surround. 30 mins.
VHS: #22746. $14.95.

Man Ray Video
Films by the important experimental filmmaker, photographer and surrealist, Man Ray. *Emak Bakia* was described by Man Ray as a "cine poem", (1927, 18 mins.); *L'Etoile de Mer* (1928, 15 mins.) is based on a poem by Robert Desnos and juxtaposes still lives, masked faces, a woman, a starfish and Paris; *Le Retour a la Raison* (1923) weaves abstract and concrete images; *Les Mysteres du Chateau du De* (1929), filmed at the chateau of the Comte de Noailles, explores the structure and dramatic light effects of the forms of the villa.
VHS: #09050. $24.95.
Man Ray, France, 1927-29

The Man Who Could Not See Far Enough
One of the most exciting, powerful works of independent American experimental cinema, *The Man Who Could Not See Far Enough* uses literary, structural, autobiographical and performance metaphors to construct a series of tableaux that evoke the act of vision, the limits of perception, and the rapture of space. Spectacular, moving multiple images, a physical almost choreographic sense of camera movement, and massive, resonant sound have inspired critics to call it "stunning" and "hallucinatory."
VHS: #09207. $59.95.
Peter Rose, USA, 1981, 33 mins.

Maneaters: A Trilogy
Three mondo trasho vignettes, *Girls Can't Help It!* 1986), *World Peace* (1987), and *Squalid Salad* (1988), centered around female empowerment and sexual liberation. Featuring such underground sensations as Counsualto, Jeep Reis, Randy Rom, Claude Balls, Joey Leatherton and Lucy Poussi.
VHS: #17194. $29.95.

Marcel Odenbach: In the Peripheral Vision of the Witness
Shot on location at Versailles, this videotape examines the conflict between the burden of a heritage of traditions and the desperate attempt to escape from it. West German video artist Marcel Odenbach combines classical and nationalistic images with commercial and media images to illustrate this conflict. A work of tension, comparing individual freedom with the omnipresent mass media.
VHS: #12756. $65.00.
Marcel Odenbach, Germany, 13 mins.

Matta Wagnest and Nicolas Eder: Analog 10001
This combination book and three-tape package is available only within this signed and limited edition of 50 copies.
VHS: #22584. $300.00.

Maurizio Nannucci: Not All at Once
This work comes from the Kasseler Kunstverein in Fridericianum, Kassel, 1993. 15 mins.
VHS: #22572. $30.00.

Maya Deren Experimental Films
A newly re-mastered, top quality reproduction of the leading female experimental filmmaker in cinematic history. Maya Deren's six chamber films included here are: *Meshes of the Afternoon*, *At Land*, *A Study in Choreography for Camera*, *Ritual in Transfigured Time*, *Meditation on Violence* and *The Very Eye of Night*. Silent.
VHS: #00836. $29.95.
Maya Deren, USA, 1943-49, 76 mins.

Menilmontant
An important film made by Dimitri Kirsanov in France, a silent film done without titles which "is not a melodrama but an antecedent to neo-realism, portraying life itself with a sensitive use of natural sets and a feeling for poetry and truth" (Georges Sadoul). In the film, a young girl is seduced by a young man who deserts her when she is pregnant. She contemplates suicide, meets her sister who's since become a prostitute, and is reconciled with her again.
VHS: #07466. $39.95.
Dimitri Kirsanov, France, 1926, 27 mins

Mitch Corber Works
Work by the multi-media performance artist and cable TV pioneer. Includes *Juan in New York*, bike-shot footage mixed with TV soap cuts overlaid with a dense soundtrack of rhetoric and effects; *KGB*, mixed down from a live show on the death of Brezhnev; *Apartheid Aside*, a colorized music video with songs by San Francisco's Toiling Midgets and Morton Subotnick; and *Quiver City*, computer animation and color processing of old people in Brighton Beach.
VHS: #10167. $39.95.
Mitch Corber, USA, 1982-84, 36 mins.

Moving a River
Peter Fend's experimental documentary examines satellite data detailing the ways Iraq's military engineering altered the course of rivers in the Middle East that impacted its physical relationship to Iran.
VHS: #17198. $29.95.
Peter Fend, USA

Music Word Fire and I Would Do It Again: The Lessons
Perfect Lives is an opera commissioned and produced for television by The Kitchen. The Lessons, variations on the theme song from Episode Three of the television opera, introduced the four principal characters in cameo performances. The video and music techniques unique to the seven-episode series are presented in four seven-minute portraits of these four characters.
VHS: #11645. $49.95.
Robert Ashley, USA, 1984, 27 mins.

N. Humbert/W. Penzel: Step Across the Border
90 minutes, 1990.
VHS: #22567. $45.00.

Natural Light: Windance
David Fortney's camera dances of light, motion and substance, that are as sensual and alive as the natural world he photographs, scored to the music of W. Aura, R. Burmer, S. Halpern and Synchestra.
VHS: #10229. $24.95.
Laser: LD70240. $24.95.
David Fortney, USA, 30 mins.

Nature Is Leaving Us
A video opera for prerecorded multi-channel video and sound, live performance and live music, a complex work by video artist Miroslaw Rogala, which addresses the profound subject of man's rupture from nature. This videotape contains both the original program and documentation of the performances and contrasts the immutable rhythms of natural processes with the arhythmia of human urban behavior as reflected in the media.
VHS: #08469. $39.95.
Miroslaw Rogala, USA, 1987, 40 mins.

New Directors: New Short Films
This collection of new works (1993) by young artists includes *Lady Lazarus* by Sandra Lahire, *Weak and Wide Astray* by Tom Paine, *Relax* by Chris Newby and *Floating* by Richard Heslop. In English. Total running time 108 mins.
VHS: #22573. $45.00.

Out in the Garden & You
Two films from Vincent Grenier are included in this video. The first, *Out in the Garden*, is about the dynamic of being HIV-positive. The second film, *You*, offers a more formal examination of perspective, self reflection and narrative.
VHS: #27233. $59.95.
Vincent Grenier, USA

Pascal Aubier Films
Six short films by Pascal Aubier: *Flashback* (1985, 4 mins.), in which a fatally wounded soldier remembers the highlights of his young life in the brief moment before his death; *Les Petits Cons* (1986), in which a young factory worker escapes the boredom of his job by locking himself in the bathroom, where he encounters a strange vision; *Le Cendre* (1985, 4 mins.), an amusing tale of the consequences of intolerance, with an anti-smoking slant; *L'Apparition* (1986, 8 mins.), a darkly humorous exploration of faith and ignorance; *Death of a Rat* (1975, 6 mins.), a serio-comic meditation on the pain and inhumanity of modern technological life; and *Santeuse de L'Ange* (without subtitles), a playful study of eating strawberries and high diving.
VHS: #02905. $49.95.
Pascal Aubier, France, 38 mins.

The Passing
"Art has to be part of one's daily life or it's not honest," explains Bill Viola, perhaps the foremost video artist working today. Viola's *The Passing* is a window into the artist's life, detailing in powerful images the death of Viola's mother and the birth of his son with universal and empathetic themes: birth and death; new and old; beginnings and endings; sadness and joy.
Laser: LD71451. $49.95.
Bill Viola, USA, 1981

Paulette Phillips and Geoffrey Shea: Work
Two Canadian filmmakers/video artists have combined their talents to create a multi-layered piece that examines the concept of work by using various techniques and intertwining several plots. Documentary-style interviews are interspersed with the narrative structure. Employment is presented as a series of pre-packaged lifestyles that suppress the identity of the individual. 35 mins.
VHS: #12757. $65.00.

A Performance by Jack Smith
This is the only known recorded performance piece by the late artist/actor Jack Smith, made from an optically printed 8mm film original. Included are two works shot in Toronto in 1984: *Dance of the Sacred Application* and *Brassieres of Uranus*.
VHS: #27224. $49.95.
Midi Onodera, Canada, 1984

Persistence of Vision
An anthology of artists working in video.
Persistence of Vision, Volume 1: Monitoring the Media. TV's one-way system of selling specific products, commodified lifestyles and homogeneous social values is an extremely limited use of its potential. In this anthology, the video artists use video to undermine and protest the nature of television. Contains: *Why I Got into TV* (Ilene Segalove), *TV Drives People* (Richard Serra), *Three Transitions* (Peter Campbell), *President's World* (Gorilla Tapes), *Excerpts and Euphoria* (Edward Mowbray), *Pastrami Sandwich* and *Dragnet Kiss* (Ilene Segalove), *Composite News Composite* (Nancy Burson), and *Eternal Name* (Ant Farm). 58 mins.
VHS: Out of print. For rental only.
Laser: LD70316. $39.95.
Persistence of Vision, Volume 2: Outside the Lines. This cassette features 11 short works, including *Sun Stone* by Ed Emshwiller; *The Space between the Teeth* by Bill Viola; *Cartas Postales* by Cahen, Huter and Longuet; *Ear to the Ground* by John Sanborn, Kid Fitzgerald and David Van Tieghem; and *Ich Mache Die Schmerz-Probe* by Marcel Odenbach.
VHS: Out of print. For rental only.
Laser: LD70317. $39.95.
Persistence of Vision, Volume 3: New Narrative. An anthology which continues to expand the vocabulary of narrative. Contains: *Actions in the Home* (Graham Young), *Chanayu* (Dalibor Martini and Sonja Ivekovic), *The West Is Alive* (Klaus von Bruch and Keike Melba Fendel), *L.A. Nickel* (Brenda Miller), *Dogs Back and Forth* (William Wegman), *Le Train* (Francois Gerard), *The Woman Who Went Too Far* (Colin Campbell), and *Possibly in Michigan* (Cecilia Condit). 58 mins.
VHS: Out of print. For rental only.
Laser: LD70318. $39.95.

Peter Callas: Night's High Noon: An Anti-Terrain
This Australian artist's work is from 1988 and is 7:30 minutes long.
VHS: #22561. $90.00.
Peter Callas, Australia, 1988, 7 mins.

Peter Russell: The Global Brain
1991, 35 mins.
VHS: #22576. $70.00.

Peter Thompson Films
Three extremely moving documentaries: *Two Portraits*, a diptych film about the filmmaker's father and mother; *Universal Hotel* records the filmmaker's search for historical graphic evidence on medical experiments in deep cold by Nazi doctors; and *Universal Citizen* records an encounter with a former inmate at Dachau, now a smuggler in the Guatemalan jungle.
VHS: #05650. $59.95.
Peter Thompson, USA, 63 mins.

Pier Marton (are we and/or do we) Like Men
An intense expose about male vulnerability from Pier Marton. Filled with subverted and challenging images, as well as a deepness of expression.
VHS: #13302. $69.95.
Pier Marton, 1986, 18 mins.

Pier Marton: Collected Works: 1979-84

Features *Heaven is what I've done (for my fellow beings)* (1984), a PSA to measure our (distr)actions against things that must be done; *Tapes* (1979), the unraveling of personal/collective fears; *Telepathos* (1982), a demystification of the "high-tech" satellite broadcast; *Unity through Strength* (1980-82), revealing fabricated television reality. The subversive art of Pier Marton.
VHS: $13303. $69.95.
Pier Marton, 1979-84, 27 mins.

Pier Marton: Say I'm a Jew

A collage of interviews with Jews who grew up in post war Europe as they experienced. The film progresses from a "memory" of the Holocaust and early self-denial experiences, to a manifesto-like affirmation of Jewish identity. Directed by Pier Marton. 28 mins.
VHS: $13304. $69.95.

Pipilotti Rist

This collection of works by the Swiss performance artist and member of the all-female music-performance group Les Reines Prochaines includes "I'm Not the Girl Who Misses Much", "You Called Me Jacky" and "Pickelporn". Pipilotti has been actively creating art since 1984. 1986-1992, 21 mins.
VHS: $22588. $65.00.

Plates

Taylor Mead and Bill Rice, two underground, queer art stars, are featured in this funny and remarkable film from playwright and director Gary Goldberg. Shown at the 1991 Berlin International Film festival, *Plates* harkens to the world of silent film even though it employs non-verbal sound to tell its story.
VHS: $27240. $49.95.
Gary Goldberg, USA, 1991, 11 mins.

Playboy & Rhonda Goes to Hollywood

Two shorts by the British-born filmmaker Tessa Hughes-Freeland examine sexuality, representation and identity. 35 mins.
VHS: $17197. $39.95.

Prix Ars Electronica

There are 15 selections from computer animation, graphics and computerized music made by the Prix Ars Electronica group on this compilation tape. 45 mins.
VHS: $22574. $45.00.

Rain and Uberfall

Two historically significant films: Joris Ivens' *Rain* is an impressionistic study of a rain shower; Erno Metzner's *Uberfall* brilliantly uses in-camera techniques to depict the hallucinations of a man who is the victim of a street robbery.
VHS: $04361. $44.95.

Raindance: The Experience of Light and Celebration

A sumptuous field of visuals and music reveals the multi-facets of light, and a special luminous quality in all living things, in a celebration of inner wholeness. Composed and narrated by Dorothy Fadiman, with music by Klaus Schulze, Will Ackerman, Alex de Grassi; produced by Michael Wiese. 30 mins.
VHS: $10226. $29.95.

Rare Dutch and Belgian Experimental Program

Includes five short films: *Mystic Lamb* (11 mins.), *Rain* (10 mins.), *New Earth* (23 mins.), *Bridge* (15 mins.) and *Umbrella* (30 mins.)
VHS: $14922. $29.95.

Robert Cahen: L'invitation au Voyage/ Juste le Temps

These two short videos bracket a span of 10 years during which this artist has continued to create work. *L'invitation au Voyage* is from 1973, 9 mins. And *Juste le Temp*, 1983, is 13 minutes long.
VHS: $22560. $90.00.
Robert Cahen, USA, 1973-83, 22 mins.

Rome '78

Felliniesque spectacle and Warhol-like degeneration in an underground cult fest of *Caligula*, shot in color Super-8 and borrowing from the explosive tenets of experimental cinema. With David McDermott, Eric Mitchell and Anya Phillips.
VHS: $17193. $59.95.
James Nares, USA, 1978, 60 mins.

Sabda and Sombra a Sombra

The title *Sabda* refers to the *word*, the original sound of life. Using digital imaging techniques to produce ghostlike, transient figures passing through landscapes, "ancient words and drawn-out beautiful images construct a profound contemplation of human existence." "Reeves' lyrical video poem, a collaboration with some of the great Indian medieval poets. In it Reeves succeeds as few Westerners have in revealing the complex reality that is India" (Deirdre Boyle). *Sombra a Sombra* is an elegy of remembrance and meditation on the architecture of the abandoned as evoked in the writing of the Peruvian poet Cesar Vallejo. Recorded over a period of years in the Alpujanas and Pyrenian mountains of Spain, the tape explores the areas of the heart shaped by the departure of the people and things of this world.
VHS: $06303. $59.95.
Daniel Reeves, USA, 32 mins.

Samadhi and Other Films

Four films by Jordan Belson—"our greatest abstract film poet, he has found how to combine the vision of the outer and the inner eye" (Gene Youngblood). The four films in this volume include *Re-Entry*, an animated metaphor of reincarnation and rebirth; *World*, a dazzling, abstract version of the creation of the world; *Samadhi*, taken from the Sanskrit term meaning "that state of consciousness in which the individual merges with the universal soul"; and *Chakra*, a compelling film re-creating the experience of raising the kundalini through the seven psychic centers in the human being.
VHS: $09557. $19.95.
Jordan Belson, USA, 1964-72, 27 mins.

Sara Hornbacher Early Works

Richly processed and synthesized rapid-cut video by the pioneer video artist. Includes *An American Sequence, Equinox Dance/Polyglot Robot, Raster Relief/ Video Canvas, Writing Degree Z, Dignus Vindice Nodus.*
VHS: $10166. $29.95.
Sara Hornbacher, USA, 30 mins.

Simultaneous

A collection of 10 works by Scott Rankin, video artist on the cutting edge of exploring language, perception, association and metaphor: *Simultaneous* is a self-referential work about consciousness and learning using as a metaphor the controversial theory of hemisphere specialization in the brain. Other works included are: *This and That, Fugue, LA 84* (commissioned for the L.A. Contemporary Exhibitions as a portrait of Los Angeles as a city and as a media center), *Synchronicity, French performance, Swedish Two, Swedish One, Magic*, and *Carousel*. Winner of many awards, the work of Scott Rankin offers daring explorations of the video medium.
VHS: $08612. $59.95.
Scott Rankin, USA, 1980-88, 77 mins.

Smothering Dreams and Thousands Watch

It does in 23 minutes what *Apocalypse Now* and *Deer Hunter* tried to do in 3 hours…One of the most compelling, eloquently visual denunciations of war in any medium," wrote one critic of *Smothering Dreams*. Based on Reeves' own experiences, the tape is an autobiographical reflection on the Vietnam War, "a cathartic recollection, burning anti-war statement and searing analysis of the mass media's role in inculcating violence and aggression from childhood onward" (Deirdre Boyle). With dramatic re-enactments of the ambush of Reeves' platoon in 1969 and of childhood memories, *Smothering Dreams* is a collage of childhood dreams of battle and adult nightmares of the atrocities of war. *Thousands Watch* is an image-processed work that demystifies the suicidal nature of the use of nuclear weapons. Using 1936 newsreel footage cutting between images of war and domestic tranquility, *Thousands Watch* is a uniquely powerful poetic statement.
VHS: $01221. $59.95.
Daniel Reeves, USA, 40 mins.

Stephen Forsyth: Passages

"Passages…urban romanticism reflects an openness to nature and the outside world, while surrendering to the siren song within. A tapestry of lyricism of every kind, from the most secretive to the most expressive…now projecting dreams, now capturing the forces of the elements, now voicing the cries of the heart and its echoes."
VHS: $22564. $65.00.

Susan Rynard

Three works by the Toronto-based video artist Susan Rynard, whose videos have been shown in festivals from Hong Kong to Rio. *Absence* is a fragmented narrative about desire and expectation, leaving the viewer to search for explanations and closure. *Untitled—A Tape about Memory* is a recreation of the sensations of memory through texture, color, mood and movement. And *Within Dialogue (Silence)* portrays a young professional city dweller whose idea of ecology is hewn in concrete, broadloom and nouvelle cuisine. Each shot reverberates in a barren web of table settings and freeways. 15 mins.
VHS: $12758. $65.00.

Takahiko Iimura: Concept Tapes (1975-87)

This collection joins excerpts from nine tapes of this artist's works. "Iimura is a singular and significant filmmaker, but also one of the most important conceptual artists working in any medium" (Malcolm LeGrice).
VHS: $22568. $70.00.
Takahiko Iimura, USA, 1975-87

Takahiko Iimura: John Cage Performs James Joyce

A private performance by composer John Cage is captured on this tape. *Writing for the Fifth Time through Finnegan's Wake* is realized by Cage in three ways—by reading, singing and whispering. 15 mins.
VHS: $22569. $115.00.
Takahiko Iimura, USA, 15 mins.

Tear Jerker

This compilation of works by Joel Baird and Rick Philips reveals the hypocritical attitudes common in the United States. It contains the short films *Tear Jerker, With the Good Witch* and *The Evil Cleric*.
VHS: $27236. $59.95.
Joel Baird/Rick Philips, USA

This Is Not Beirut/ There Was and There Was Not

This personal project finds that the conflicts and complexities that affect a Lebanese person in the West are intimately bound together with the experiences of diverse communities and the jarring perceptions that separate them.
VHS: $21036. $59.95.
Jayce Salloum, USA, 1994, 48 mins.

Tina L'hotsky: Barbie and Snakewoman

Two works by the talented New York writer and Hollywood emigre. *Barbie* is a surreal self-portrait of a young woman cooking and eating a doll. *Snakewoman* chronicles the epic exploits in 1930's Africa of adventurer Patti Astor. Both films were shot by Michael Oblowitz.
VHS: $17204. $39.95.
Tina L'hotsky, USA, 45 mins.

Todd Rutt/Arn McConnell: Shock! Shock! Shock!

A black and white work combining film and video to trace the life of Jim Norman, "a loser so lost only trouble could find him." His story unfolds with a pulp terseness, about a young man trying to escape his past and confront the alien beings intent on colonizing earth. 60 mins.
VHS: $17205. $39.95.

Tom Chomont: A Two-Volume Collection

The works of this experimental gay filmmaker are collected on these two videos. *Volume I* contains the short films *Jabbock, The Heavens, Razor Head* and *The Bath*. *Volume II* features *Spider Jan.16.91, Inner Sanctum, Garden* and *The Mirror.*
Volume I
VHS: $27237. $69.95.
Volume II
VHS: $27238. $69.95.
Tom Chomont, USA

Towers Open Fire

William S. Burroughs and Brion Gysin met Ian Sommerville and Antony Balch during their Beat Hotel days in Paris in 1958-59, an amazingly fertile period that saw the publication and attempted suppression of Burroughs' *Naked Lunch*. These films (Towers Open Fire, The Cut Ups, Bill & Tony and *William Buys a Parrot*) convey the consciousness of the period in the visual language of the artists who defined it.
VHS: $09556. $19.95.
Antony Balch, USA, 1962-72, 35 mins.

Trio

Created by the internationally successful Zone Productions, *Trio* consists of three short musical works. *Suspect No. 1* is a murder mystery where investigation and filmmaking become intermixed. *Zzang Toumb Toumb* is a dance piece with music and movement alluding to the Italian Futurists of the early twentieth century. And *Life and Death of an Architect* portrays the life of one person, with the five stages of their life shot in different styles, each reminiscent of a different popular director. 25 mins.
VHS: $12761. $65.00.

Tripe

Adapted from the play *Ein Mann, Ein Worterbuch* by Franz X. Kroetz (*Hamlet Machine*), this stars Australian director Lindzee Smith as the restless, jobless lover of a lady butcher (Caz Porter), who, much to his discomfiture, keeps a journal.
VHS: $10182. $49.95.
Betsy Sussler, USA, 1980, 58 mins.

TV Party

Writer Glenn O'Brien, a columnist for *Interview* and Artforum, culls vignettes and episodes from his late-night cable talk show in the early 80s, featuring sketches with David Byrne, Debbie Harry, Jean-Michel Basquiat during the outbreak of the Mudd Club's meteoric rise in the downtown art and performance scene. 30 mins.
VHS: $17192. $29.95.

Ulrike Rosenbach: Osho—Samadhi

Germany, 1990, 12 mins.
VHS: $22575. $90.00.

Up to the South

The south of Lebanon is a disputed area where issues like colonialism, terrorism, occupation, resistance, collaboration, experts, spokespeople, leadership, and even the definition of the land itself are hotly disputed. These concerns lead to a critique of documentary traditions and their relationship to a history of representation.
VHS: $21035. $59.95.
Jayce Salloum, USA, 1993, 60 mins.

A Valentine for Nelson & Two Marches

New York-based filmmaker Jim Hubbard hand processes his own 16mm film, resulting in intensely personal and moving works. The first is simply a Valentine for his longtime lover. In the second, he contrasts the March on Washington held before AIDS dominated gay life with the later larger gay rights march held in 1993.
VHS: $27221. $59.95.
Jim Hubbard, USA, 1993

Variety Is the Spice of Life

Program 5 of the *What Does She Want* series, this program imagines a more generous world in which a variety of love and lovers is not just permitted, but welcomed. Jill Kroesen's *Lowell Moves to New York* stars actor Eric Bogosian who made his mark by creating characters like Lowell, a nerd dwelling beneath the facade of one cool guy. Valie Export's *A Perfect Pair* could refer to the handsome couple on display, or to a part of the heroine's anatomy. Max Almy's *Modern Love* is a series of lovers' discourses. Lynn Blumenthal's *Doublecross* traces the journey of a woman through the tricky terrain of sexual exploration. In Linda Look's *Luchare the Flamenco*, usually performed by a man and a woman, takes on new meaning when danced erotically by two women. Finally *Two in Twenty*, a lesbian soap opera, parodies daytime television with a simulation that just might be real. Produced by the Video Data Bank. 75 mins.
VHS: $06514. $59.95.

Video Art: Antonio Muntadas

Three works by Antonio Muntadas, who locates his work in what he calls "the media landscape"—the intersection of art, social sciences and media. *Between the Lines* (1979), focuses on the role of the reporter to deal with the way in which information is selected, scheduled and edited to fit television news programming; *This Is Not an Advertisement* (1985), is a documentation of a 50-second computer-generated message produced by the Public Art Fund's Message to the Public Project, broadcast from the Spectacolor light board in Times Square, and alludes to the fine line between art and advertisement; *Credit* (1984), juxtaposes and edits several TV and film credit sequences together—a rumination on the nature of money and labor.
VHS: $06260. $65.00.
Antonio Muntadas, USA, 1979-85, 55 mins.

Video Art: Ardele Lister

Ardele Lister has produced several award winning tapes, with *Hell*, the work on this tape, winning awards at the Tokyo and other festivals. *Hell* is the modern hell of information storage and retrieval, with "the souls in hell stored on disc and tortured with the latest in digital video effects." Inspired by Dante's *Inferno*, Lister's *Hell* updates the metaphors and locations. Lister employs a full arsenal of gadgetry to make her art stimulating and accessible, using computers that bend, freeze, tilt and spin images.
VHS: $05353. $65.00.
Ardele Lister, Canada, 1985, 17 mins.

Video Art: Blue Moon

Rodney Werden has worked in video art since 1974. His most recent works develop innovative, narrative structures as vehicles for a more complex view of human sexuality, as overt content, issues of gender roles and sexual identity provide the ground for an exploration of the fiction of artistic subjectivity. In Blue Moon the audience observes the parallel events of a prostitute searching for a client intercut with a film producer visiting an old friend and guiltily offering him money for sex. French with English subtitles.
VHS: $05350. $65.00.
Rodney Werden, Canada, 1983, 14 mins.

Video Art: Come on Touch It (Study No. 4 for a Personality Inventory Channel)

A real-time performance by Ian Murray, overlayed on a dense complex of sound and image. Created as a study of a fictional "interactive" 24-hour television station, it displays the artist as being manipulated by a computer. "A balance between seemingly objective and distanced electronic world and the subjective, emotional and philosophical reality of the artist" (*Signal Approach*). Ian Murray's installation, video and audio work is based in the alteration or manipulation of popular forms and mass media products.
VHS: $05351. $65.00.
Ian Murray, Canada, 1983, 34 mins.

Video Art: Damnation of Faust Trilogy

Dara Birnbaum's trilogy renders the Faustian legend contemporary through examining and reflecting upon scenes of the ritualized behavior of Italian youths in New York City playground. Birnbaum's *Faust* urges an examination of the quest for experience and knowledge…her characters describe and define their own stories, and react and respond to their own placement within the narrative. Concluding with a timeline composed of street demonstrations, mass and student activism, *Damnation of Faust* establishes a social framework which can be enlarged from the personal.
VHS: $06301. $65.00.
Dara Birnbaum, USA, 1983-87, 22 mins.

Video Art: Dana Atchley & Eric Metcalfe

Crime Time Comix Presents Steel & Flesh is the work (1980, 12 mins.) in this tape, which is a fast-moving pastiche of poker faces, guns, knives, and suspense, based on the murder mystery comics which Metcalfe drew in his 1950's childhood. Dana Atchley has worked as a designer, publisher, teacher and television producer and artist; Eric Metcalfe is a noted Canadian videotape artist, whose work is noted for fantasy narratives that manipulate the features of comic strips and detective thrillers. Canada, 1980, 12 mins.
VHS: $05348. $65.00.

Video Art: David Askevold

Two works by David Askevold, a prominent Canadian video artist whose work depends on the imposition of arbitrary systems on obscure, psychological and often mystical "information" to arrive at a structural ambiguity: *Rhea* (1982, 6.5 mins.), opens and closes with a wandering spotlight on a dark interior. Faces appear against vague landscapes or without setting to speak the names of others. *Jumped Out* (1984, 12 mins.), is comprised of a sensual drift of images which allude to or trace evidence of psychic energy, a form of energy that surfaces within the image.
VHS: $05352. $65.00.

Video Art: Gary Hill

Four tapes by Gary Hill: *Full Circle*, originally titled "Ring Modulation" sets up a paradoxical circumstance in which a performer attempts to overcome the matter of difference between metal and electronic signals; *Mediations*, an excerpt from a remake of Hill's "Soundings", (1979/1986)—as sand is placed on a loud speaker, it forms patterns which correspond to the frequency of a voice as it is amplified through the speaker; *Around & About* attempts to engage the "positions" of a viewer via a monologue—images are cut to the syllabic rhythm of the spoken word making their content and context susceptible to the utterances of speech.
VHS: $06075. $65.00.
Gary Hill, USA, 1978-86, 12 mins.

Video Art: Helen Doyle

Scars of Memory (Tatouages de la Memoire) is a lyrical, spiritual piece by Helen Doyle dealing with the layers of memory; stripping them away to reveal the core of Sarah, the main character in the tape. Helen Doyle describes the tape as an intimate voyage of discovery verging on the indecent…an invitation to the fantasies of a world outlined in myth and colored in dreams. A co-founder of Video Femmes in Quebec, Helen Doyle is a foremost Canadian video artist concerned with social and political issues. 1984, 33 mins.
VHS: $05340. $65.00.

Video Art: Here in the Southwest

Joyan Saunders' recent work is concerned with alternatives to content and structure of traditional narrative. In *Here in the Southwest*, Saunders deals in a sporting manner with the ideas of biological determinism and sexual difference. Elements of pop wisdom or quasi-scientific pronouncements are subjected to an informal process of deductive reasoning and the ostensibly logical conclusions are diametrically opposed to what is generally held to be true.
VHS: $05349. $65.00.
Joyan Saunders, Canada, 1984, 23 mins.

Video Art: Hygiene

A tape by writer, lyricist, performer and musician by Andy Paterson, whose obsession with history leads him to mythologize about contemporary popular information and video. In *Hygiene*, Paterson weaves stories based on a simple premise and embellishes them with his own unique perspective. *Hygiene* is the story of a woman whose men have done her wrong and who finds a greater sense of self-reliance and self-confidence in her relationship with another woman.
VHS: S05339. $65.00.
Andrew Paterson, Canada, 1985, 41 mins.

Video Art: It Starts at Home

Michael Smith has been hearing about cable TV everywhere. What could be better? Hundreds of channels and guaranteed crystal-clear reception definitely added up to a full day of television. So he thought it over and decided to join the ranks with millions of other cable subscribers. Mike was confident making this "state of the art" improvement to his home entertainment program, but what he ordered and what he got was another story. Through some quirk of technology, Mike's private life and all activity in his home would soon be broadcast to the entire world.
VHS: S06307. $65.00.
Michael Smith, USA, 1982, 25 mins.

Video Art: Jan Peacock

Jan Peacock re-shapes the literary and metaphorical content of situations, building narratives, often from autobiographical sources, which expose and question the values and methods by which we construct and share reality. In *Wallace + Theresa*, the work on this tape, the propensity to read and interpret it as a given condition is construed as a layering of images, sounds, printed and written words and voice—all and each of which reciprocally narrate each other.
VHS: S05343. $75.00.
Jan Peacock, Canada, 1985, 14 mins.

Video Art: Leaving the 20th Century and Perfect Leader

Leaving the 20th Century is a trilogy of experimental videotapes by Max Almy which call attention to the fact that we are approaching a point of departure in history. The tape takes a pointedly satirical look at the realities of this century and raises serious questions about the possibilities of the future. *Perfect Leader* is a short experimental tape which utilizes a combination of live action, audio and video special effects, an original score, and computer animation to probe the questions of political image-making and the marketing of a candidate. "Max Almy's work exploits a narrow gap between quotation and parody....Her high-tech razzle-dazzle videotapes are laden with futuristic special effects and have the breathtaking rhythmic speed of commercials" (*Afterimage*).
VHS: S06300. $65.00.
Max Almy, USA, 1982/83, 15 mins.

Video Art: Les Levine

Levine uses the techniques, tactics and even the sites of popular media—advertising, fashion design and television—and the information they purvey as the target of his work. *Diamond Mind* is a performance tape in which the artist is seen talking about previous experiences in life and showing some of the objects he designed at the time. The performance is concerned with the idea that people are programmed by the images they make for themselves. *Diamond Mind* is in the collection of the Museum of Modern Art and the Centre Georges Pompidou.
VHS: S05341. $65.00.
Les Levine, Canada, 1977, 30 mins.

Video Art: Noel Harding

A retrospective tape of the work of Noel Harding, whose video, film and sculptural installations center around the interaction of props and settings. Through this interaction, he explores very personal notions of illusion and reality, subjective understanding and public perceptions. The works included on the tape are: *Birth's Child*, a mother and child portrait which takes on sculptural qualities; *Simplified Confusions*, a conversational counterpoint and quick cuts which examine the interchange between a woman and a man; *A Serene Composition Suggestive of Pastoral Repose*, a study of combinations of the sensual; *Yellow, M* a fantasy play which reflects the interior landscape; *Out of Control*, a fast-paced, hard-boiled tale of sex, power and intrigue in high places inspired by the story of G. Gordon Liddy; *Houses Belong to Those Who Live in Them*, an examination of the complexities of modern life; and *Elephants*, inspired by the shooting down of the Korean jetliner, composed of image after image to construct an enigmatic work. Total length: 53 mins.
VHS: S05342. $65.00.

Video Art: Not Dead Yet

Edward Mowbray directed this fast-paced documentary about a second generation of punk rockers living in Toronto, offering insight into this segment of culture by videotaping in the streets, bars and homes of punks. Conversations are intercut with the music of the punk bands at the Core of the scene. "The best in-depth look at Canadian punk scene" (*Vancouver Sun*). Mowbray's work in video employs filmic techniques to create a hybrid style of video art and television.
VHS: S05344. $65.00.
Edward Mowbray, Canada, 1984, 56 mins.

Video Art: Prime Cuts

Paul Wong's work in photography, performance and video can be characterized as a visceral personal response to events and conditions of his and his friends' lives. *Prime Cuts* sets to motion the fantasy world of eternal beauty and glamor as portrayed in the fashion tear-sheet. Wong's puppet-like fashion model characters never stop having fun in their endless pursuit of happiness. Non-narrative in structure, the tape considers notions of style.
VHS: S05345. $65.00.
Paul Wong, Canada, 1981, 20 mins.

Video Art: Red Tapes

A classic work from the poet of the 60's New York school, Vito Acconci, an epic of storytelling. Most of the tape takes place while viewing a blank screen; other segments involve props, voice-overs, appropriated images, sound collages, and most importantly, Vito Acconci himself.
VHS: S06299. $65.00.
Vito Acconci, USA, 1976, 142 mins.

Video Art: Rober Racine

Rober Racine's *J'aurais Dit Glenn Gould* is half document, half fiction, based on the style of Glenn Gould's little-known CBC radio documentaries. The tape is a sound collage utilizing both English and French and is interspersed with radio interviews with John Jessop, Glenn Gould's radio documentary assistant editor. The video concerns itself with the issues of radio, music, and video as it creates "a song to listening." "Racine's work is a vast undertaking aimed at decoding cultural forms" (Aurora Borealis).
VHS: S06302. $65.00.
Rober Racine, Canada, 1984, 28 mins.

Video Art: Shut the Fuck Up

Produced by General Idea, *Shut the Fuck Up* was selected at Documenta 8, and exhibited internationally. The tape examines the relationship between mass media and the artist. They incorporate segments from television and film, along with their own commentary, to humorously point out the media's insistence that gossip and spectacle make art and artists interesting to the public. Canada, 1985, 14 mins.
VHS: S05346. $65.00.

Video Art: Telling Motions

"*Telling Motions* is presented in the musical form of variations on a theme. The work utilizes a musical score and poetic texts to explore meanings which are outside the realm of conventional language. The tape explores repetition and change based on the context and treatment of imagery...Memory and learning are explored as the viewer becomes actively engaged in the process of decoding pluralistic "readings."
VHS: S06306. $65.00.
Bill Seaman, USA, 1985/86, 20 mins.

Video Art: Test Tube

General Idea produced this tape at De Appel, Holland, and the tape incorporates television formats and video special effects in a witty and visually sophisticated production. General Idea uses the media to create a complex visual portrait of the artist in the 80's. The tape represented Canada at the Venice Biennale, 1980. Canada, 1979, 28 mins.
VHS: S05347. $65.00.

Video Art: Tomiyo Sasaki

Two works by Tomiyo Sasaki, a Canadian-born artist who lives and works in New York: *Creatures of the Enchanted Isles* is a study for a five-channel, 20-monitor installation work which utilizes images taped on the Galapagos Islands. "The combination of the bizarre and barren volcanic landscape with the strange and unique creatures which inhabit the land makes one ponder basic aspects of nature as Darwin obviously did." *The Dreams of Christopher Columbus* is a mosaic of images, videotaped in India, a study for a much longer and larger work by the same title consisting of 11 channels and 50-300 monitors arranged in the shape of a mandala.
VHS: S06305. $65.00.
Tomiyo Sasaki, USA, 1984-87, 53 mins.

Video Art: Vital Statistics of a Citizen, Simply Obtained

Martha Rosler's *Vital Statistics* acts out the duality of women's consciousness. In the primary scene, a woman's body is measured in a clinical setting and compared with standard measurement. Voice-overs, symbolic scenes, and photographs suggest the implications of enforcing social standards of measurement—whether by the state through its police functions or, more informally, by "common sense."
VHS: S06304. $65.00.
Martha Rosler, USA, 1977, 40 mins.

Video Congress No. 8

Works by the artists Claude Torey, Der Plan, KAOS, John Cage, Jonathon X Jackson, Tony Allard, Etant Donnes, and others who participated in this congress are included in this two-tape package. 120 mins.
VHS: S22580. $90.00.

Video Congress No. 9

Artists who participated in this second congress have works included on this tape. Didier Bay, Kain Karawahn, Mike Hentz, Viebeke Vogel, Pyrolator, Tony Allard, Yvonne Oerlemans and others are represented. 82 mins.
VHS: S22581. $70.00.

Video Works: Miroslaw Rogala (1980-86)

Four video works by the important video artist Miroslaw Rogala: *Love among Machines* departs from the writings of Carlos Drummond de Andrade to explore the relations of modern technology to manners, movements and motivations of earlier eras; *Polish Dance '80* is a short video dance dedicated to the Workers' movement in Poland; *Questions to Another Nation* is a complex work that reflects on the effort to understand and be understood in a foreign culture; *Remote Faces: Outerpretation* is a 7-channel video installation with 8 channel sound by Lucien Czyzewski and live performance, with both video and audio digitally processed, playfully challenging our concepts of language, communication and meaning.
VHS: S08470. $39.95.
Miroslaw Rogala, USA, 1980-86, 39 mins.

Videotape for a Woman and a Man

Amy Greenfield uses human motion, camera lens, editing and optical techniques to "see into, with and through the body." Shot over a period of six months and edited over four years, *Videotape for a Woman and a Man* is "an absorbing and disturbing inquiry into male-female relationships. Photographed in black and white and color, and performed in the nude by Greenfield and dancer Ben Dolphin, it relentlessly examines the possible physical and emotional encounters between a man and a woman....We marvel at and are moved by the poignant spectacle of the human body as an instrument capable of transcending its own reality" (John Guen, *Dance Magazine*).
VHS: S01415. $19.98.
Amy Greenfield, USA, 1979, 34 mins.

Viva Eu! & Ex Voto

Tania Cypriano, an experimental Brazilian filmmaker, explores her most poignant life experiences in these two films. In *Viva Eu!*, Cypriano explores her experiences as a woman living with AIDS. In *Ex Voto*, Cypriano takes a look at her ordeal of surviving terrible burns from a horrible fire she was trapped in. Both films show struggle and a commitment to survival.
VHS: S27241. $49.95.
Tania Cypriano, Brazil

Whoregasm

The title says it all, a blending of film and video art that stars Susan Manson, Rick Strange and director Nick Zedd. On the same program is *I Shit on God*, a five-minute short. 11 mins.
VHS: S17196. $24.95.

William S. Burroughs: Three Films, 1950-1960's

The American author, best known for his wildly imaginative fiction, also made a series of short films. These include *William Buys a Parrot*, *Towers Open Fire*, *The Cut Ups*, *Bill and Tony* and *Ghost at No. 9*.
VHS: S22558. $92.00.
William S. Burroughs, USA, 120 mins.

William Wegman Reel 1

This compilation of early video works by Wegman includes *Microphone*, *Pocketbook Man*, *Abet and Abtu*, *The Ring*, *Randy's Sick*, *Milk/Floor*, *Stomach Song*, *Happy Song*, *The Door*, *William Wegman in Chinese*, *Elbows*, *Dress Curtain*, *Hot Sake*, *Casper*, *Handy*, *Cut and In*, *Plunger Series*, *Nosy*, *Firechief*, *Come In*, *Hidden Utensil*, *Contract*, *Puppet*, *Shadows*, *Ventriloquism*, *Light Trails* and *Cape On*.
VHS: S22589. $65.00.
William Wegman, USA, 1969-70, 30 mins.

William Wegman Reel 2

Wegman videos compiled on this tape include *The Kiss*, *Sanforized*, *Coin Toss*, *Monkey Business*, *Same Shirt*, *Diving Board*, *Straw and String*, *Product*, *In the Cup* and *Treat Bottle*.
VHS: S22590. $65.00.
William Wegman, USA, 1972, 19 mins.

William Wegman Reel 3

This is a collection of Wegman tapes from 1973. It includes *Stich and Tooth*, *Emporer and Dish*, *Lucky T-shirt*, *Rage and Depression*, *Speed Reading*, *Born with No Mouth*, *Dual Function*, *Massage Chair*, *Raise Treat*, *Many Ray*, *Do You Want To?*, *Crooked Finger*, *Crooked Stick*, *Deodorant*, *Bubblebath* and *47 Seconds*.
VHS: S22591. $65.00.
William Wegman, USA, 1973, 18 mins.

William Wegman Reel 4

From 1973-74 comes this compilation of Wegman videos: *Wake Up*, *Trip across Country*, *Down Time*, *Laundromat*, *Saw Movies*, *Cocktail Waiter*, *Nail Business*, *Calling Man Ray*, *New and Used Car Salesman*, *On the Ball*, *Tails*, *Radar Screen*, *Air Travel*, *Criticize*, *Pyramids*, *Symbolize*, *The Letter*, *Snowflakes*, *Growl* and *Spelling Lesson*.
VHS: S22592. $65.00.
William Wegman, USA, 1973-74, 21 mins.

William Wegman Reel 5

Wegman's works from 1977 have been compiled on this tape: *Stalking*, *Nocturne*, *Audio Tape and Video Tape*, *Dancing Tape*, *Hobo on Train*, *Drinking Milk*, *Copyright*, *Buying a House*, *Lerch Hairpiece*, *Tammy and Can of Plums*, *Loves Water*, *Average Guy*, *Over the Drink*, *Marbles*, *Ball Drop* and *Treat Table*.
VHS: S22593. $65.00.
William Wegman, USA, 1977, 27 mins.

William Wegman Reel 6

This is a compilation of William Wegman videos from 1977. *Ball and Can*, *The Reel*, *Eyes of Ray*, *Dog Duet*, *tube talk*, *Stereo Systems*, *Video*, *Joke* and *Furniture* are all included. 19 mins.
VHS: S22594. $65.00.
William Wegman, USA, 1977, 19 mins.

William Wegman Reel 7

Due to popular demand, Wegman has created another video about his dogs. These are the last works made with the now famous, on late Man Ray. Shot in color, this tape features several comic vignettes by the artist and his talented pet Weimeraner, including *Doctor Joke*, *Alarm Clock A and B*, *Smoking*, *Drop It* and *Piano Hands*. 18 mins.
VHS: S12760. $65.00.

Willoughby Sharp's Downtown New York

Distilled from 13 hours of cable TV, this show is hosted by the noted video pioneer and publisher. Artists profiled in on-location clips include: Kathy Acker, Laurie Anderson, Kipper Kids, Gracie Mansion, Michael Smith, Cookie Mueller, Spada and more. Called "a guide for the curious through the dense sub-culture of Downtown New York," Sharp appears with his hilarious sidekick Boris Policeband.
VHS: S07124. $49.95.
Willoughby Sharp, USA, 1986, 58 mins.

The Works of Ken Feingold— Distance of the Outsider

India Time (1987, 46 mins.) was recorded between 1985 and 1988, during which time video artist Ken Feingold lived mostly in India and traveled extensively throughout other parts of Asia. The document shows the people of India in their daily work, and often in response to the fact that they are being recorded by the camera. It is as much about the meeting of cultures, and the imposition of Feingold's own perspective on Indian culture, as it is about Indian culture itself. One might consider it a fascinating ethnography of an American in India.
VHS: S15648. $59.95.
Ken Feingold, 1987, 46 mins.

The Works of Ken Feingold—Fictions

A collection of four wide-ranging video shorts from director Ken Feingold, whose intelligent, disjointed and confrontational style has invited favorable comparisons to radical mainstream directors like Nagisa Oshima and Sergei Eisenstein. Includes *The Smallest Particle* (1987, 8 mins.), *In Shadow City* (a collaboration with Constance De Jong, 1988, 13 mins.), *Irony (The Abyss of Speech)* (1985, 29 mins.), and *Un Chien Delicieux* (1991, 19 mins.). Total length: 69 mins.
VHS: S15650. $59.95.
Ken Feingold, USA, 1985-91, 69 mins.

The Works of Ken Feingold— Life in Exile

Life in Exile is Ken Feingold's ambitious two-part video examining the philosophy and political predicament of the Tibetan refugee community in India. This thoughtful, moving document reveals the turmoil of a disenfranchised and much-abused people, while at the same time presenting a clear view of the spiritual and cultural beliefs which have managed to nurture and sustain them through these painful times. It was created in consultation with the Tibetan Government-In-Exile and the Private Office of the Dalai Lama.
VHS: S15649. $59.95.
Ken Feingold, USA, 1988, 90 mins.

The Works of Ken Feingold— Names in Search of a Body

A kaleidoscopic pair of videos from director Ken Feingold: *5 dim/MIND* (1983, 29 mins.) and *The Double* (1984, 29 mins.). These collected images are from around the world, culled from various films and broadcasts, as well as original footage by the artist. The surreal suppression of conventional continuity, achieved through Feingold's freewheeling, associative editing style, creates a series of signs and symbols which appeal directly to the intellect—personally involving viewers in its philosophical meditations on the world as we know it or, rather, should know it. Produced, directed and edited by Ken Feingold. Total length: 58 mins.
VHS: S15647. $59.95.
Ken Feingold, USA, 1983-1984, 58 mins.

The Works of Ken Feingold—Water Falling from One World to Another

A moody and suggestive pair of short works from highly acclaimed video artist Ken Feingold. This collection, which includes *Water Falling from One World to Another* (1980, 34 mins.) and *Purely Human Sleep* (1980, 28 mins.), contemplates the endless, human pursuit of the invisible, especially as it confronts the limits of the body; limitations which often manage to imprison us, reining in our perceptions of the world around us.
VHS: S15646. $59.95.
Ken Feingold, USA, 1980, 62 mins.

The Works of Ken Feingold: The Complete Set

Includes ten films made between 1980 and 1991, ranging from 8 to 90 minutes.
VHS: S18808. $249.95.

Zbigniew Rybczynski

The cutting-edge director of videos for Mick Jagger, the Art of Noise and the Pet Shop Boys, Rybczynski is an artist and filmmaker who is interested in the experimental and avant-garde, the use of pixilation, compositing and optical printing. This compilation showcases his best works, including *Tango*, which won an Academy Award, and his work with High Definition Television (HDTV).
Laser: LD71959. $99.95.

The Films of James Broughton

Spanning an artistic career of forty years, the collected films of James Broughton represent a remarkable body of work by a leading avant-garde American filmmaker— an undisputed master of the fusion of spoken poetry with moving images. A poet and dramatist as well as a filmmaker, Broughton has transformed all three of these forms into what Stan Brakhage calls "an art of lifelong montage."
Volume 1: Erotic Celebrations. Contains Broughton's 1968 masterpiece *The Bed*—a lyrically erotic celebration of just about everything that could happen on a bed—with an all-nude cast, among them some of San Francisco's best-known artists, and *Erogeny* (1976), an intimate exploration of the landscape of the human body. *Hermes Bird* (1979) and *Song of the Godbody* (1977) continue Broughton's sly attacks on sexual taboos and celebrate the ecstasy of physical awareness with close-up camerawork that caresses the body parts it explores. 47 mins.
VHS: S07284. $29.95.
Volume 2: Rituals of Play. Three important black and white films by Broughton, including the classic *Mother's Day* (1948)—an ironic recollection of childhood games in the nostalgic style of a cluttered family album, enacted by adults, and *Four in the Afternoon* (1951) with four poetic variations on the search for love from a girl of ten to a man of forty. It ends with the comedy *Loony Tom* (1951), picturing the amorous progress of an amiable tramp who makes love to every woman he meets. 48 mins.
VHS: S07285. $29.95.
Volume 3: The Pleasure Garden. A comic fantasy with songs that celebrate the triumph of love and liberty over the forces of restriction. Filmed in the ruined gardens of the Crystal Palace in London with a professional cast, this satiric fairy tale won a prize for poetic fantasy at the Cannes Film Festival of 1954. 38 mins.
VHS: S07286. $29.95.

Volume 4: Autobiographical Mysteries. Both *Testament*
(1974)—an exquisite self-portrait in which the poet-filmmaker
views his life and work with wit and charm in a rich pageantry
of personal imagery, songs, anecdotes and dreams, and
Devotions (1983)—a work made with collaborator Joel Singer
which envisions a world where men have abandoned rivalries
in favor of comradely devotion, featuring 45 different couples
who reveal the many pleasures that men can enjoy together.
Scattered Remains (1988) is a cinematic performance piece in
which Joel Singer creates a multi-faceted portrait of Broughton
acting out his verses in unlikely situations and surprising
camera inventions. 57 mins.
  VHS: S07287. $29.95.
Volume 5: Parables of Wonder. Five important works by
Broughton from the decade of the 70's. *High Kukus* (1973) is a
visualization of a Zen teaching accompanied by fourteen of
Broughton's cuckoo haikus, while *Golden Positions* (1978) is a
series of tableaux vivants that follow the form of a liturgical
service and glorify the naked human body. *This Is It* (1971) is a
playful pseudo-Zen creation myth shot in a home-movie style
with a two-year old Adam in a backyard Eden. *The Gardener of
Eden* (1981) is an intense poetic work that celebrates the
sexual dance of all creation, set in Sri Lanka. The tape
concludes with *Water Circle* (1975), an homage to Lao-Tzu in a
joyful poem read by the filmmaker and set to music by Corelli.
56 mins.
  VHS: S07288. $29.95.
Volume 6: Dreamwood. A spiritual odyssey into the
landscape of the dream in which its poet hero set forth to
rescue the bride of his soul and bring about his own rebirth.
1972, 45 mins.
  VHS: S01575. $29.95.
Complete Set.
  VHS: S07289. $149.75.

BARBARA HAMMER

Lesbian Humor
A collection of six films spanning the career of this exciting
filmmaker: *Menses* is a wry comedy on the disagreeable aspects
of menstruation; *Superdyke*, a comedy about a troop of shield-
bearing Amazons; *Our Trip*, an animated film based on a hiking
trip in the Andes; *Sync Touch*, a series of film experiments
which propose an aesthetic connection between touch and
sight; *Doll House*, a rapid montage of objects arranged in
reference to the central prop of a doll house; and *No No
Nooky T.V.* confronts the feminist controversy around sexuality
with electronic language. "Hammer's satiric use of technology
corresponds well with the Eighties repression of sexual
expression. If you've ever looked up 'lesbian' in a computer
thesaurus, you'll know that it's not listed" (*Independent
Media*).
  VHS: S08608. $59.95.
Barbara Hammer, 1975-87, USA, 59 mins.

Lesbian Sexuality
A collection of four films by Barbara Hammer, including the
landmark *Dyketactics*, the first lesbian lovemaking film to be
made by a lesbian. A sensual, evocative montage of 110 images
edited to images of touch, an "erotic lesbian commercial." Also
includes: *Multiple Orgasm*, a sensual, explicit film; *Double
Strength*, a poetic study of a lesbian relationship between two
trapeze artists; and *Women I Love*, using the camera as a
personal extension of the body.
  VHS: S08609. $59.95.
Barbara Hammer, USA, 1974-76, 57 mins.

Nitrate Kisses
Unlike any other documentary, this work combines Barbara
Hammer's unique experimental film style with archival footage
to yield a unique view of overlooked lesbian and gay history.
From the era of Nazism to today's AIDS epidemic, this work
forces everyone to remember the importance of queer lives
without evading any aspect of love, from the physical to the
sublime.
  VHS: S24031. $39.95.
Barbara Hammer, USA, 1992, 67 mins.

Optical Nerves
Parisian Blinds and *Tourist*, both films by Barbara Hammer,
"investigate the nature of spectator perception in an unfamiliar
environment." *The Optic Nerve* is a powerful personal
exploration of family and aging; *Place Mattes* explores the
space between reaching and touching with animation and
optical printing used to create travelling mattes for places.
Endangered, Hammer's most recent work, has light, life and
film as endangered in this exquisite film etched with acid.
  VHS: S08611. $59.95.
Barbara Hammer, USA, 1984-88, 44 mins.

Perceptual Landscapes
Four works that explore personal landscapes: *Pools*, made with
Barbara Klutinis, is an exploration above and under water of
two of the first swimming pools designed by the first woman
architect in the U.S.; *Pond and Waterfall* is an exploration of
verdant pond growth as well as dynamic light and water
reflections; *Stone Circles* is a celebration of ancient pre-
patriarchal standing mounds and circles including Stonehenge
and Asbury; *Bent Time* is one of Hammer's most ambitious
films, in "which she attempts to render visually the scientific
theory that time, like rays, curves at the outer edges of the
universe" (*L.A. Times*).
  VHS: S08610. $59.95.
Barbara Hammer, USA, 1981-83, 54 mins.

GUILTY PLEASURES

sci-fi
ON VIDEO

20 Million Miles to Earth
Ray Harryhausen is the original master of monster movie special effects. In this sci-fi thriller he manages to animate a gelatinous mass which escaped from a returning American rocketship.
VHS: S24134. $19.95.
Nathan Juran, USA, 1957, 82 mins.

Alien
Space explorers on a routine mission bring an extremely adaptable life form on board that attaches itself on crew members and reproduces itself. Most of the crew pay for the mistake with their lives. Notable special effects and relentless suspense from the director of *Blade Runner*. Screenplay by Dan O'Bannon.
VHS: S02337. $19.98.
Laser: LD72430. $49.98.
Ridley Scott, USA, 1979, 116 mins.

Alien Terror
Boris Karloff plays a deranged scientist who discovers a destructive form of energy that threatens the planet Earth and other solar systems. A galactic visitor seeks to destroy this energy and a violent battle is waged to possess the Alien Terror. 90 mins.
VHS: S09256. $9.98.

Alien Trilogy
All three of the *Alien* films are collected in this gift pack, including Ridley Scott's *Alien* (1979), about an alien presence on an expeditionary force; James Cameron's *Aliens* (1986); and David Fincher's *Alien³*, which finds Ripley (Sigourney Weaver) trapped on a penal colony with an interplanetary monster.
VHS: S19094. $49.98.
R. Scott/J. Cameron/D. Fincher, USA, 1979-92, 389 mins.

Alien³
The third entry of the baroque horror/science fiction series finds Lt. Ripley (Sigourney Weaver) the sole survivor of the previous mission, marooned on a lice-ridden, deep-space penal colony inhabited entirely by men, and acutely aware of a regenerated alien's presence.
VHS: S17770. $94.98.
David Fincher, USA, 1992, 115 mins.

Aliens
An above-average sequel to the Ridley Scott film, this time featuring more thrills than chills. As if one alien weren't bad enough, a return to the infested planet provides the background for a violent confrontation between settlers and the large, futuristic cockroaches.
VHS: S12586. $19.98.
Laser: LD72431. $59.98.
James Cameron, USA, 1986, 138 mins.

Aliens, Dragons, Monsters & Me
Gary Owens and Eric Boardman host this program that features scenes from 13 of the screen's best loved fantasy films, including *King Kong*, *The 7th Voyage of Sinbad*, *Mysterious Island* and *Clash of the Titans*. Ray Harryhausen discusses his career and reveals trade secrets.
Laser: CLV. LD71491. $34.95.
Richard Jones, USA, 1991, 48 mins.

Andromeda Strain
A mysterious virus has wiped out a small town with the exception of one infant and an old drunk. Scientists want to know why as they race against time in a underground high security lab for the answers. With Arthur Hill, David Wayne, Kate Reid and James Olson. From the novel by Michael Crichton.
VHS: S07798. $59.95.
Robert Wise, USA, 1971, 130 mins.

Assignment Outer Space
Rick Von Nutter and Archie Savage star in this beautifully filmed sci-fi feature. The earth is threatened by an addled space ship's massive but haywire force field. Scientists try to save the earth, but Gabriella Farinon manages to distract them from their task just enough to generate suspense.
VHS: S23491. $29.95.
Antonio Margheriti, Italy, 1961, 79 mins.

Atlantis, The Lost Continent
A camp science fiction classic from George Pal (*The Time Machine*) set on the mythical island that sank during a volcanic eruption. The story follows the heroic efforts of a fisherman to aid a beautiful young maiden. Adapted from Sir Gerald Hargreaves' play. Cinematography by Harold E. Wellman. With Anthony Hall, Joyce Taylor, John Dall and Edward Platt.
VHS: S19036. $19.98.
George Pal, USA, 1961, 91 mins.

The Atomic Man
Gene Nelson and Faith Domergue are featured in this sci-fi thriller about a living atomic bomb. A man is hauled to safety from the Thames and recognized by a reporter as a well-regarded nuclear physicist. There is only one problem however: the scientist appears to have a double in good health who is hard at work. Even stranger revelations ensue, and the fate of the planet is at risk.
VHS: S24019. $14.95.
Ken Hughes, Great Britain, 1955, 79 mins.

Attack of the 50 Foot Woman
A neurotic woman with a philandering husband is lured into a spaceship and as, a result of her radioactive encounter, grows to enormous proportions. Of course she then proceeds to wreak havoc on everything around her.
VHS: S14789. $14.98.
Nathan Juran, USA, 1958, 72 mins.

Bamboo Saucer (Collision Course)
Dan Duryea stars in his last film as the leader of a scientific expedition trying to locate a crashed alien spacecraft in Tibet. Lois Nettleton is part of the Soviet search team. The Chinese, however, know the secret of the UFO. With Bob Hastings.
VHS: S04264. $19.95.
Frank Telford, USA, 1967, 103 mins.

The Beast from 20,000 Fathoms
Disturbed by A-bomb testing, a rhedosaurus from the North Pole wakes up from its sleep of ages and lets loose its full fury on New York. Based on a story by Ray Bradbury, this sci-fi film features masterful special effects by the legendary Ray Harryhausen (*Jason and the Argonauts*).
VHS: S14286. $19.98.
Eugene Lourie, USA, 1953, 80 mins.

Beyond the Time Barrier
A jet pilot from the 20th century breaks through a time barrier in the sky and suddenly finds himself lost in an apocalyptic future. After a disastrous third world war, the Earth is menaced by mutants and a deadly virus. Robert Clarke and Darlene Thompkins star.
VHS: S23157. $29.95.
Edgar G. Ulmer, USA, 1959, 75 mins.

Blade Runner
A visually expressive adaptation of Philip K. Dick's futurist novel about Deckard (Harrison Ford), a cynical detective assigned to terminate a group of genetically devolved replicants set loose in Los Angeles, circa 2019. In this special director's cut, Deckard's voice-over narration is eliminated and the original ending is restored. With Rutger Hauer, Sean Young, Edward James Olmos and Daryl Hannah.
VHS: S18596. $19.98.
Laser: LD71873. $39.99.
Ridley Scott, USA, 1982, 117 mins.

Borrower
A twisted tale of an outer space alien who enjoys collecting the heads of foolish earthlings and wearing them in public. His first victim is Tom Towles, Henry's accomplice in murder. With Antonio Fargas, Don Gordon and Rae Dawn Chong as the disbelieving police detective on the track of this most unusual mass murderer. The very juicy special effects are not for the squeamish.
VHS: S14991. $89.95.
John McNaughton, USA, 1991, 97 mins.

A Boy and His Dog
This is a kinky sci-fi tale about a young man, Don Johnson, and his telepathic dog. While searching for food and sex in a destroyed world they happen upon an impotent group of survivors. This group drafts Johnson to father a new generation, but there is little pleasure to be found in their method. Also features Jason Robards and Tiger, the former *Brady Bunch* dog.
VHS: S25715. $29.95.
Laser: Widescreen. LD75446. $49.95.
L.Q. Jones, USA, 1975, 87 mins.

The Brain Eaters
Ed Nelson produced and stars in this AIP science fiction thriller based on Robert A. Heinlein's *The Puppet Masters*. Citizens of a small mid-west town are being taken over by hairy parasites that come from beneath the Earth. Ed is out to stop them. Watch for Leonard Nimoy as a bearded old man. B&W.
VHS: S04094. $9.95.
Bruno VeSota, USA, 1958, 60 mins.

Brain from Planet Arous
John Agar stars in this freaky flick about a floating brain named Gor that invades his body and sets out to conquer Earth. Vol, a rival alien brain, borrows the body of Agar's dog to battle Gor and save the planet. Hosted by Elvira, Mistress of the Dark.
VHS: S13514. $19.95.
Nathan Juran, USA, 1958, 70 mins.

Cat Women of the Moon
3D thrills and chills as Moon Rocket 4 and its crew dodge menacing meteors before touching down on the moon's barren surface. In an underground cavern filled with giant, carnivorous spiders the crew discovers some subterranean sweeties dressed in black tights.
VHS: S14683. $12.95.
Arthur Hilton, USA, 1953, 64 mins.

Classic Sci-Fi Trailers Vol. 1
Movie trailers from some of the infamous sci-fi films from the 50's, including *Tarantula*, *Attack of the 50 Foot Women*, *Man from Planet X*, and *Enemy from Space*. Great camp fun!
VHS: S04097. $29.95.

Cosmic Monsters
Giant killer insects from another dimension invade the Earth when a scientist (Forrest Tucker) accidentally makes a hole in the ionosphere. Helpless humans battle the bugs until an intrepid alien (Martin Benson) arrives in a flying saucer and saves the world. From the makers of the classic *The Crawling Eye*.
VHS: S12383. $14.95.
Gilbert Gunn, USA, 1958, 75 mins.

Crawling Eye
A hideous alien creature descends on the Earth in a cloud of radioactive fog, emerging to wreak havoc and terror as it mutilates and then possesses its helpless victims. Forrest Tucker and Janet Munro star.
VHS: S05672. $19.95.
Quentin Lawrence, Great Britain, 1958, 85 mins.

Dagora, the Space Monster
Dagora, an immense, pulsating cell from outer space, visits Japan in search of carbon, which it uses for energy. Rocket attacks cause multiplication. Real estate and diamond thieves are upset. Trucks, bridges and actors' careers are also damaged. Dubbed in English.
VHS: S05485. $29.95.
Inoshiro Honda, Japan, 1965, 80 mins.

Daredevils of the Red Circle
One of the finest serials of all time, the story of three circus stunt men pursuing a ruthless madman known as 39-0-13. Bent on destroying the wealth of millionaire Horace Granville, 39-0-13 imprisons him and assumes his identity in order to accomplish his evil deeds of destruction. 12-episode serial on two cassettes.
VHS: S11570. $29.95.
John English/William Witney, USA, 1938, 195 mins.

Dark Star
A cult classic that began as a $6,000 project of a group of California students, *Dark Star* is an earth spaceship on a mission to find and destroy any planets likely to cause a supernova. Among the hilarious scenes is the ship's captain, dead, but preserved in cold storage, who talks baseball through electrodes in his head, while bombs which have intelligence threaten to end it all by exploding prematurely.
Laser: LD72210. $39.95.
John Carpenter, USA, 1974, 91 mins.

Day of the Triffids
While much of the earth's population is blinded by a brilliant meteor shower, small plants called triffids undergo horrifying mutations causing them to grow, acquire mobility, and feed on humans. From John Wyndham's famed sci-fi/horror novel.
VHS: S00310. $19.95.
Steve Sekely, Great Britain, 1963, 94 mins.

Day the Earth Froze
Nina Anderson, Jon Powers and Peter Sorenson are superb in this Finnish/Soviet fantasy epic. An evil witch steals the sun and causes nearly everything on the Earth to freeze. There are magic harps, fields of snakes, a wizard and even a magic mill in this singular film.
VHS: S23195. $29.95.
Gregg Sebelious, Finland/Russia, 1959, 67 mins.

The Day the Earth Stood Still
One of the first films to portray aliens from space as advanced saviors rather than menacing monsters. Michael Rennie stars as Klaatu. Intense, high production values and excellent casting with Patricia Neal and Sam Jaffe.
VHS: S02521. $14.98.
Robert Wise, USA, 1951, 92 mins.

The Deadly Mantis
A huge, freakish killer mantis with stunning capabilities to walk, run and fly is unleashed from a million-year deep freeze and terrorizes New York City.
VHS: S18703. $14.98.
Nathan Juran, USA, 1957, 78 mins.

Demolition Man
This sci-fi and action adventure features Sylvester Stallone and Wesley Snipes. When a dangerous 20th century man is reanimated in the not-too distant future, the stage is set for a classic struggle between two men. They square off amidst a treasure trove of special effects and over-the-top, futuristic scenery.
VHS: S20682. $19.98.
Laser: LD72378. $34.98.
Marco Brambilla, USA, 1993, 115 mins.

Devil Girl from Mars
A female Martian lands in England to recruit Earth males for the purposes of intergalactic breeding. She is accompanied by a robot companion that resembles a thin white toaster with a police-car light on top, only taller. With Hazel Court, Andrienne Corri and Hugh McDermott. B&W.
VHS: S18643. $14.95.
David MacDonald, Great Britain, 1954

Dr. Cyclops
Set in the Peruvian jungle, this 1940 landmark science-fiction adventure follows four explorers as they search for legendary physicist Dr. Cyclops. When they discover their missing colleague, they find his brilliant mind warped by radiation. But the half-blind, half-mad scientist uses an experimental body-altering device to reduce his former friends to one-fifth their normal size. Just terrific.
VHS: S10110. $14.98.
Ernest B. Schoedsack, USA, 1940, 76 mins.

Earth vs. the Flying Saucers
Aliens land at a U.S. Army base seeking help for their dying planet, but are greeted with gunfire and armed forces. The aliens are forced to retaliate, which pits earthlings vs. humanoids in a fight for earth's survival. With great early special effects by Ray Harryhausen.
Laser: Includes interview with Ray Harryhausen. LD75042. $34.95.
Fred F. Sears, USA, 1956, 83 mins.

Earth vs. the Spider
A monster spider attacks and traps two teenagers in a large cave web. With June Kenney, Edward Kramer, Gene Roth and Mickey Finn.
VHS: S16411. $29.95.
Bert I. Gordon, USA, 1958, 75 mins.

The Empire Strikes Back
The sequel to *Star Wars* finds our heroes under attack by the Evil Empire. From frozen ice fields to tropical swamps to cities floating in the sky, there is danger to Luke, Han, Chewey and Princess Leia. New characters include Yoda the Wise and Lando Carigissian the good-looking (Billy Dee Williams). May the box office be with you.
VHS: S03477. $19.98.
Irvin Kershner, USA, 1980, 124 mins.

Escape from New York (Director's Cut)
This science fiction film casts a new spin on getting out of the Big Apple. New York is a giant prison where ruthless gangs rule. It's an apocalyptic vision that at times comes close to the violent reality that exists in big cities today. Starring Kurt Russel and Adrienne Barbieau, with Ernest Borgnine, Isaac Hayes and Donald Pleasance.
VHS: S20926. $19.98.
Laser: Letterboxed, special edition includes interview with John Carpenter, trailer and never-before-seen footage. LD74465. $49.99.
John Carpenter, USA, 1981, 106 mins.

F.P. 1 Doesn't Answer
One of the earliest science fiction films. F.P. 1 is a gigantic, floating platform used as a mid-Atlantic airfield to allow planes to refuel on their long, Euro-American flights. When the platform cannot be reached by either telephone or cable, sabotage is suspected. Help arrives to find the crew gassed and the platform in immediate danger of being destroyed. English version. With Conrad Veidt, Jill Esmond.
VHS: S10000. $29.95.
Karl Hartl, Germany, 1932, 74 mins.

The Fantastic Voyage
The cult science fiction thriller in which a team of doctors are miniaturized and set inside the body to operate on the blood clot of a scientist. With Stephen Boyd, Raquel Welch, Donald Pleasance and Arthur Kennedy.
Laser: LD70975. $49.98.
Richard Fleischer, USA, 1966, 100 mins.

First Men in the Moon
A flamboyant adaptation of H.G. Wells's novel about the first settlers in space and their battles with giant warrior ants for control of the moon. Ray Harryhausen did the special visual effects. With Edward Judd, Martha Hyer, Lionel Jeffries, and Erik Chitty.
VHS: S16681. $14.95.
Laser: Widescreen. LD74632. $34.95.
Nathan Juran, Great Britain, 1964, 103 mins.

Flying Saucer
The first movie about UFOs, this classic sci-fi thriller allegedly had to be viewed by the FBI prior to its release. Mikel Conrad stars in his own story as a special agent sent to Alaska, where he finds a flying saucer and diabolical Communist scientists. Denver Pyle gets mixed up in the extraterrestrial adventure on the frozen frontier.
VHS: S12385. $14.95.
Mikel Conrad, USA, 1950, 70 mins.

Forbidden Planet
Nervy, funny and very clever science fiction adaptation of Shakespeare's final play, *The Tempest*, set in the year 2200, about a group of space explorers investigating a previous space flight who encounter an embittered expatriate creating his own society on the abandoned planet with his beautiful daughter and trustworthy robot. Beautiful widescreen photography by George Folsey. With Walter Pidgeon, Anne Francis, Leslie Nielsen and Warren Stevens. Available in two versions, a widescreen from Criterion and letterbox from MGM.
VHS: S00458. $14.98.
Laser: CAV, widescreen, Criterion. LD70989. $99.95.
Laser: CLV, deluxe widescreen, MGM. LD70186. $34.95.
Fred M. Wilcox, USA, 1956, 98 mins.

Gamera
The creature is a jet-powered superturtle reawakened by a nuclear explosion; the turtle wreaks havoc and forces the Army to unleash 'Plan Z.' 79 mins.
VHS: S17540. $9.99.

Gamera vs. Barugon
The jet-powered superturtle Gamera must confront Barugon, a gigantic horned dinosaur hatched from a huge opal, whose horns spew a devastating "rainbow ray."
VHS: S17541. $9.99.
Shigeo Tanaka/Noriaki Yuasa, Japan, 1966, 101 mins.

Gamera vs. Gaos
Gaos, a huge, prehistoric vampire bat, is conjured from an explosion and battles the jet-powered, superturtle Gamera.
VHS: S17542. $9.99.
Noriaki Yuasa, Japan, 1967, 87 mins.

Gamera vs. Guiron
The jet-powered, superturtle Gamera is summoned to outer space when a team of aliens, led by the gigantic, knife-nosed Guiron, abducts a pair of Earth children.
VHS: S17544. $9.99.
Noriaki Yuasa, Japan, 1969, 82 mins.

Gamera vs. Zigra
A giant, alien shark monster descends on the Earth with the intention of conquering the world, though he didn't count on the appearance of the jet-powered, superturtle Gamera.
VHS: S17543. $9.99.
Noriaki Yuasa, Japan, 1971, 90 mins.

Geisha Girl
William Andrews, Martha Hyer and Archer MacDonald are featured in this nearly forgotten sci-fi gem. A mad scientist invents small explosive pills. When he and his Japanese cohorts utterly destroy a small Pacific isle, their dreams of world domination seem assured. That is, until two wacky American G.I.'s find themselves burdened with the pills. Soon mentalists and spies are trying to help them, but they are happily hiding out in a geisha house.
VHS: S23154. $29.95.
George Breakston, USA, 1952, 67 mins.

Ghidrah the 3-Headed Monster
The all-time great Japanese monster rally: bad monster Ghidrah is pitted against three popular creatures: Godzilla, the fire-breathing reptile; Mothra, the B-52 scaled moth; and Rodan, the mega-pterodactyl. English dialog.
VHS: S00496. $19.95.
Inoshiro Honda, Japan, 1965, 85 mins.

The Gifted
This sci-fi thriller follows a black southern family with a special gift. Their supernatural abilities were transported from Africa but possess otherworldly sources. Now they have been discovered by an enemy alien force. A West African king is determined to join his family in America so that The Gifted will not be destroyed.
VHS: S24530. $69.95.
Audrey King Lewis, USA, 1993, 101 mins.

Girl in His Pocket
Jean Marais, Genevieve Page and Jean Claude Brialy star in this unique, French sci-fi adventure. An eccentric scientist discovers a method for shrinking people. He uses his girlfriend as a guinea pig with somewhat comical results.
VHS: S23156. $29.95.
Pierre Kast, France, 1957, 82 mins.

Glen or Randa
A desperate odyssey by the last survivors of an atomic holocaust through the wreckage of a vanished civilization, called "one of the best and most original American films of the year" (Time).
VHS: S00504. $59.95.
Jim McBride, USA, 1971, 94 mins.

Godzilla King of the Monsters
Raymond Burr stars in this remake of the original Japanese classic. Godzilla is awakened by an atomic blast and all of Tokyo watches his antics in terror. Burr acts as narrator, intercut with the hysterically primitive special effects.
VHS: S25030. $19.95.
Inoshiro Honda, Japan/USA, 1956, 79 mins.

Godzilla vs. Biollante
A return of the monster who's been reawakened and threatens world peace and stability. The larger community responds with Biollante, a genetically engineered plant form who feeds off Godzilla. English dubbed.
VHS: S17709. $19.98.
Laser: LD75199. $34.98.
Kazuki Omori, Japan, 1989, 104 mins.

Godzilla vs. Monster Zero
A ferocious monster called Ghidra is menacing Planet X. Godzilla and Rodan are recruited to combat this terror. In return they expect help back home on Earth, but suspicious acting aliens may well have other unforeseen plans. Dubbed in English.
VHS: S25028. $19.95.
Inoshiro Honda, Japan, 1970, 93 mins.

Godzilla vs. Mothra
Radiation is once again wreaking havoc in the natural environment. A radioactive egg leads to a mammoth caterpillar and only Godzilla is big enough to do battle with the segmented worm. It's a race against time because as everyone knows caterpillars turn into big mean moths. Dubbed in English.
VHS: S25027. $19.95.
Laser: LD75200. $34.98.
Inoshiro Honda, Japan, 1964, 88 mins.

Godzilla's Revenge
Director Inoshiro Honda's continuation of the Godzilla saga takes on an aggressive psychological subtext, tapping into a lonely child's dream patterns and associations built around Godzilla's own child and other monsters. "Good juvenile science fiction" (Leonard Maltin).
VHS: S16894. $9.95.
Laser: LD75201. $34.98.
Inoshiro Honda, Japan, 1971, 70 mins.

H.G. Wells' First Men in the Moon
Academy-Award winner Ray Harryhausen created the special effects for this sci-fi adventure starring Edward Judd and Martha Hyer. The terrible creatures of Wells' imagination come to life in this widescreen, deluxe presentation. Peter Finch makes a cameo appearance.
Laser: LD74546. $34.95.
Nathan Juran, USA, 1964, 103 mins.

Heavy Metal
John Candy and Harold Ramis provide the voices for this spellbinding, animated, Heavy Metal-scored feature. Black Sabbath, Blue Oyster Cult, Cheap Trick, DEVO and Stevie Nicks are some of the many performers featured in this fantasy, sci/fi adventure.
VHS: S27756. $22.99.
Laser: LD75579. $39.95.
Gerald Potterton, USA, 1981, 90 mins.

I Married a Monster from Outer Space
Monster-like aliens from another planet inhabit the bodies of people in a small town in hopes of having children with Earth women. Tom Tyron stars as one of these very monsters married to Gloria Talbott.
VHS: S00598. $49.95.
Gene Fowler Jr., USA, 1958, 78 mins.

Idaho Transfer
Peter Fonda (The Hired Hand) directed this little seen environmental futuristic drama set in the year 2044. A team of young scientists from the present day arrive and discover an ecological nightmare. A chilling study of survival and responsibility. With Keith Carradine, Kelley Bohanan, Kevin Hearst and Caroline Hildebrand.
VHS: S09849. $29.98.
Peter Fonda, USA, 1973, 90 mins.

The Illustrated Man
Based on the Ray Bradbury story, Rod Steiger stars as a man whose body paints pictures of horrors to come. With Claire Bloom.
VHS: S00609. $19.98.
Jack Smight, USA, 1969, 103 mins.

In the Mouth of Madness
A masterful tale of terror starring Sam Neill, this film is an homage to the great sci-fi/horror writer H.P. Lovecraft. It begins in an asylum where a madman awaits the end of mankind at the hands of monstrous demons. He thought it was just a story, but that was only what it appeared to be. Charlton Heston has a cameo.
VHS: S25659. $97.98.
Laser: LD75017. $39.99.
John Carpenter, USA, 1995, 95 mins.

The Incredible Melting Man
The sole surviving member of a doomed space mission returns to Earth, only to find that he has been transformed into "The Incredible Melting Man". This horror classic is unforgettable, with gory make-up supplied by Rick Baker.
VHS: S20928. $14.95.
William Sachs, USA, 1978, 86 mind.

The Incredible Petrified World
John Carradine, Robert Clarke and Phyllis Coates star in this underwater sci-fi adventure. Placed in a special diving bell, a crew is off to explore the ocean floor. Unexpectedly, the cable snaps and they are left to fend for themselves amid a strange series of caves that no one ever imagined possible.
VHS: S24068. $14.95.
Jerry Warren, USA, 1957, 67 mins.

Incredible Shrinking Man
One of the best American science fiction films of the 1950's. Grant Williams and Randy Stuart star in the story of an ordinary businessman who encounters a radioactive mist during a boating trip, and finds his growth process suddenly reversed; in two weeks, he's two inches tall. Terrifying.
VHS: S06556. $14.98.
Jack Arnold, USA, 1957, 81 mins.

Invaders from Mars (1953)
One of the definitive "Cold War" sci-fi films, laced with paranoia, in which no one believes a little boy that aliens have landed until the invaders begin to control the town's inhabitants. A surrealistic nightmare.
VHS: Out of print. For rental only.
Laser: LD72257. $39.95.
William Cameron, USA, 1953, 78 mins.

Invaders from Mars (1986)
Remake of the classic 1953 McCarthy era sci-fi film, this from the director of Poltergeist and Texas Chainsaw Massacre. With Timothy Bottoms, Laraine Newman, Louise Fletcher and Karen Black. Special effects by John Dykstra (Star Wars).
VHS: S02000. $19.95.
Tobe Hooper, USA, 1986, 102 mins.

Invasion of the Body Snatchers (1956)
The great Cold War classic. A small American town is taken over by an alien force which turns everyone into a zombie. Kevin McCarthy and Dana Wynter star.
VHS: S00633. $19.95.
Laser: CAV, widescreen. LD70384. $79.95.
Laser: CLV, widescreen. LD70385. $49.95.
Don Siegel, USA, 1956, 80 mins.

Invasion of the Body Snatchers (1978)
Intriguing remake of the Don Siegel classic stars Donald Sutherland and Brooke Adams, with cameos by Siegal and original star Kevin McCarthy.
VHS: S02355. $14.95.
Philip Kaufman, USA, 1978, 115 mins.

Invasion of the Saucer Men
A witty science fiction thriller about a teenager who inadvertently kills an alien. Framed by the extraterrestrials for the murder, he's trapped in the government's secret campaign against the aliens. With Steve Terrell, Gloria Castillo and Frank Gorshin.
VHS: S18416. $24.95.
Edward L. Cahn, USA, 1957, 69 mins.

The Invisible Boy
The robot from Forbidden Planet, Robby falls under the control of an alien superhuman computer intent on world domination. A scientist enlists his ten-year-old son with a mysterious potion that renders him invisible to regain the robot's independence. With Richard Eyer and Philip Abbott.
VHS: S19134. $19.98.
Hermann Hoffman, USA, 1957, 89 mins.

Invisible Dr. Mabuse (The Invisible Horror)
Lex Barker, Karin Dor and Wolfgang Preiss star in this stellar example from the sci-fi series featuring the maniacal German Doctor. Barker is an American detective who has a serious problem. He must find the fiend even though he has concocted a formula for invisibility.
VHS: S23159. $29.95.
Harald Reinl, Germany, 1962, 89 mins.

Invisible Invaders
John Carradine and John Agar are featured in this horror film about space creatures. Aliens find human corpses the perfect vessels for their invasion of earth. Before long a beleaguered group of scientists are the world's only hope against their onslaught.
VHS: S27752. $14.95.
Edward L. Cahn, USA, 1959, 67 mins.

It Came from Beneath the Sea/ 20 Million Miles to Earth
A giant octopus vents its wrath on the city of San Francisco. Kenneth Tobey and Faith Domergue star in the first horror film of this double feature. Ray Harryhausen, the famed special effects animator, joined Charles H. Schneer for their first of many joint efforts. The second feature depicts the rampages of a Venusian monster in the streets of Rome. William Hopper and Joan Taylor star and Ray Harryhausen did the special effects.
Laser: LD74588. $59.95.
Jack Arnold/Nathan Juran, USA, 1953-1957, 79-82 mins.

It Came from Outer Space
Originally shown in 3-D, this classic science fiction adventure was based on a short story by Ray Bradbury. Richard Carlson stars as an astronomer who thinks there is more to the meteor that fell in the desert than meets the eye. With Barbara Rush, Morey Amsterdam and Russell Johnson. B&W.
VHS: S05525. $14.98.
Jack Arnold, USA, 1953, 81 mins.

It! The Terror from Beyond Space
The tension steadily mounts as a space crew tries everything in their power to destroy an alien monster. The climactic scene was described by the Citizen News as "fraught with suspense and excitement."
VHS: S14959. $14.95.
Edward L. Cahn, USA, 1958, 70 mins.

Journey Beneath the Desert (L'Atlantide)
George Riviere and Jean-Louis Trintignant are featured in this sci-fi fantasy. Three lost aviators discover the entrance to Atlantis at a nuclear blast site in the desert. They face countless perils and are forced to confront an evil Queen.
VHS: S23158. $29.95.
Edgar G. Ulmer, France, 1961, 105 mins.

Journey to the Center of the Earth
James Mason and dreamy Pat Boone star in this fantasy/ adventure based on Jules Verne's classic story of a daring expedition into the caverns below the surface of the earth.
VHS: S22554. $14.98.
Henry Levin, USA, 1959, 132 mins.

Journey to the Center of Time
This science fiction adventure weaves back and forth in time, forcing the protagonists to confront age-old enemies and unheard of and unimagined atrocities from the future. It's a roller coaster of terror through time.
VHS: S21559. $24.95.
David L. Hewitt, USA, 1967, 80 mins.

Journey to the Far Side of the Sun
When scientists a hundred years into the future discover a duplicate Earth on the far side of the sun, the stage is set for science fiction and suspense in an entertaining science fiction film which stars Roy Thinnes and Ian Hendry.
VHS: S06923. $19.98.
Robert Parrish, Great Britain, 1969, 99 mins.

King Kong vs. Godzilla
Before Tyson met Spinks, before Rocky met Apollo, these two heavyweights were using Japan as their own private arena. Watch for the battle royale atop Mt. Fuji. See Kong warm up on a giant octopus. Witness Godzilla, in color for the first time, break out of a frozen iceberg and tackle a nuclear sub. With Mie Hama, James Jagi and Michael Keith as the UN reporter.
VHS: S10378. $19.95.
Inoshiro Honda, Japan/USA, 1962, 90 mins.

Krull
This widescreen, deluxe Dolby presentation reveals the epic fantasy of the original film. A young prince tries to rescue his bride from the evil Beast in this sci-fi action adventure. With Ken Marshall and Lysette Anthony.
Laser: LD74544. $39.95.
Peter Yates, USA, 1983, 122 mins.

The Land Unknown
Underneath the tundra of Antarctica there lies a surprise landscape untouched since prehistoric times. Jock Mahoney and Shawn Smith are part of a naval expedition that is marooned in this place where dinosaurs still prevail.
VHS: S20891. $14.98.
Virgil W. Vogel, USA, 1957, 79 mins.

Last Days of Planet Earth
Doomsday is at hand. There are radioactive clouds and mutant bats overhead while on the ground giant slugs leave trails of slime behind them. Dubbed in English. 88 mins.
VHS: S25031. $19.95.
Laser: LD75218. $34.98.

Lost Continent
While searching for a lost atomic-powered rocket, Cesar Romero encounters a cast of prehistoric nightmares. This world of weird greenish hue is inhabited by dinosaurs and prehistoric beasts in this sci-fi classic.
VHS: S13061. $19.95.
Sam Newfield, USA, 1951, 86 mins.

Marooned
Three astronauts are stranded in space and a rescue mission goes under way in this 60's sci-fi thriller. "It has all the zip, zest and zing of a moon walk, and I suspect a computer-fed dictionary could come up with better dialogue," said Judith Crist.
VHS: S00828. $19.95.
Laser: Widescreen. LD75045. $39.95.
John Sturges, USA, 1969, 130 mins.

Mars Needs Women
It's a blunt and horrifying idea: Mars needs women. Five Martians invade the Earth to find mates for their dying planet. They are not planning long and thoughtful courtships for their prospective brides. A science fiction classic.
VHS: S20930. $14.98.
Larry Buchanan, USA, 1968, 80 mins.

Martian Chronicles Series
Contains the complete three-volume set of Martian Chronicles.
Laser: LD71130. $99.95.

Martian Chronicles, Volumes 1-3
Based on Ray Bradbury's famous novel. Rock Hudson, Bernie Casey and Gayle Hunnicutt star. In Martian Chronicles, Volume 1, a clash develops between the Earth colonists and the highly evolved, telepathic Martian natives. Then, in Martian Chronicles, Volume 2, the peaceful but powerful race of Martians try to protect their planet from the invading Earth colonists. Finally, in Martian Chronicles, Volume 3, the powerful conclusion of Bradbury's epic, the Earth colonists discover the essence of the Martians' power. USA, 1979, 360 mins.
VHS: S04411. $14.95.

Master of the World
Richard Matheson wrote the screenplay by adapting two Jules Verne stories, giving Vincent Price, Charles Bronson and Henry Hull a science fiction film worthy of their talents. Bronson must stop the ingenious scientist, played by Price, from becoming master of the world.
VHS: S20933. $14.98.
William Witney, USA, 1961, 104 mins.

Mesa of Lost Women
Allan Nixon and Jackie Coogan find themselves cast in this strange feature about the terrors of a new race of vicious women. A group of people crash land on a desert mesa where a mad scientist is crossing women with giant spiders.
VHS: S23155. $29.95.
Ron Ormond, USA, 1952, 70 mins.

Missile to the Moon
Elvira hosts this hair-raising adventure into the unknown in a camp remake of the classic Cat Women on the Moon.
VHS: S12858. $19.95.
Richard Cunha, USA, 1959, 78 mins.

The Mole People
During an expedition in Asia, three archaeologists discover a subterranean group of albino Sumerians who avoid light and enslave mutant mole men. With John Agar, Cynthia Patric and Hugh Beaumont.
VHS: S18701. $14.98.
Virgil W. Vogel, USA, 1956, 78 mins.

The Monolith Monsters
In this science fiction classic, meteor fragments strewn across the desert grow when they come into contact with water. Geologist Grant Williams and professor Trevor Bardette must stop this stone-cold terror before it envelops the planet.
VHS: S20895. $14.98.
John Sherwood, USA, 1957, 78 mins.

Monster from a Prehistoric Planet
Do you have a yen for large destructive monsters that invade Japan? This time prepare yourself for Gappa the Tripibian, a big reptile bird on display in Tokyo. The trouble really starts when the big bird is found out to be the baby in the family and boy, are his parents steamed!
VHS: S10995. $19.98.
Haruyasu Noguchi, Japan, 1967

The Monster That Challenged the World
In the aftermath of an earthquake, a giant caterpillar awakens and spawns one murderous offspring. The massive creature terrorizes coastal California communities and the Navy must find the means to prevent their spread. With Tim Holt, Audrey Dalton, Hans Conried and Milton Parsons.
VHS: S19135. $14.95.
Laser: Three-disk boxed set. LD74589. $99.98.
Arnold Laven, USA, 1957, 83 mins.

Morons from Outer Space
An engaging satire that explodes the myth of higher life forms. A group of stupid aliens with British accents crash land on Earth; the physical comedy is well played by Mel Smith, Griff Rhys Jones and Dinsdale Landen.
VHS: S00883. $14.95.
Mike Hodges, Great Britain, 1985, 87 mins.

Multiple Futures
Taylor Mead and Holly Adams are featured in this trio of sci-fi spoofs. Whether poking fun at consumer fashion madness, overpopulation, or even AIDS hysteria, these three worst-case-future scenarios finally put sci-fi seriousness to the ultimate test of satire. 108 mins.
VHS: S26089. $59.95.

Mysterians
One of the great Japanese (though dubbed) monster pictures; hilarious camp as a race of super intellects are determined to take over the Earth, mate with the women and enslave the men. English dialog.
VHS: S00912. $29.95.
Inoshiro Honda, Japan, 1958, 85 mins.

Nightfall
Based on the Isaac Asimov story about a civilization dealing with the loss of light and heat from all its suns. David Birney stars as a leader trying to hold his people together using science and logic. Blind shaman Alexis Kanner encourages religious solutions. Minimalist science fiction filmed in a futuristic community in the American southwest.
VHS: S08317. $79.95.
Paul Mayersberg, USA, 1988

The Orbitrons
A cult classic about the political and sexual dynamics on a planet where women control and dominate society, placing men in a subservient position. Music by I Love You, The Drills, Azalea Snail and Alexander Ross. With Diva Haase, Dave Lancet and Lawrence Talbot. Directed by Christopher Frieri.
VHS: S17539. $16.95.

Outland
Sean Connery discovers corruption in mining operations on the moons of Jupiter in this futuristic retelling of High Noon.
VHS: S03536. $14.95.
Laser: LD70736. $34.98.
Peter Hyams, USA, 1981, 109 mins.

Panic in Year Zero
Year Zero refers to a post apocalyptic Los Angeles that has been devastated by a nuclear attack. Ray Milland and Frankie Avalon star in this science fiction thriller, where the placid everyday world of the early 60s has been replaced by a brutal environment devastated by unimaginable cataclysm.
VHS: S20927. $14.98.
Ray Milland, USA, 1962, 92 mins.

Perils of the Planet Mongo
Buster Crabbe stars as Flash Gordon. A feature derived from the serial Flash Gordon Conquers the Universe. USA, 75 mins.
VHS: S15180. $29.95.

Phantasm III: Lord of the Dead
This sequel to the cult classic Phantasm is as murderous and horrifying as the original. Once again, the tall cadaverous mortician is armed with his mysterious and inexplicable shiny spheres. The difference is that this film finally explains the powers contained by these balls.
VHS: S00007. $94.98.
Laser: LD74631. $34.98.
Don A. Coscarelli, USA, 1994, 91 mins.

Phantom from Space
Billy Wilder's brother directed this little sci-fi adventure about an invisible alien (Dick Sands) who crash lands on Earth and then begins killing picnickers.
VHS: S08435. $29.95.
W. Lee Wilder, USA, 1953, 72 mins.

The Philadelphia Experiment— Special Edition
Two sailors are caught in a time-travel experiment gone awry which sends them from 1943 to 1984. Michael Pare stars along with Nancy Allen in this enjoyable yarn. The disk includes a 30-minute "making of" documentary along with the original theatrical preview.
Laser: LD75011. $59.95.
Stewart Raffill, USA, 1984, 135 mins.

Planet of Blood (Queen of Blood)
Roger Corman bought a bad Russian movie with very good special effects and had an entirely new movie made using the space footage of the original. Basil Rathbone heads a crew that includes John Saxon, Dennis Hopper and Forrest J. Ackerman (Famous Monsters Magazine) which finds a female space vampire willing to be rescued.
VHS: S04096. $29.95.
Curtis Harrington, USA, 1966, 81 mins.

Planet of the Vampires
Barry Sullivan and Norma Bengell star in this sci-fi horror flick of intergalactic dimensions. A spaceship is stranded on a mysterious planet where the inhabitants appear to be interested only in sucking the blood of strangers. Dubbed in English.
VHS: S25692. $19.95.
Mario Bava, Italy, 1965, 86 mins.

Planeta Burg
A foreign sci-fi masterpiece! Cosmonauts land on Venus to find themselves in peril by various alien monstrosities. This appears to be the actual print that Roger Corman used to make parts of the negative for Voyage to the Prehistoric Planet (the film cans are addressed to Roger). Visually stunning. Based on a story by Stanislav Lem. Russian with English subtitles.
VHS: S15370. $29.95.
Pavel Klushantsev, USSR, 1962, 73 mins.

Purple Death from Outer Space
Buster Crabbe stars as Flash Gordon. A feature derived from the serial Flash Gordon Conquers the Universe. USA, 75 mins.
VHS: S15179. $29.95.

Purple Monster Strikes
The Purple Monster, sinister vanguard for a Martian invasion of our planet, possesses the body of noted scientist Dr. Cyrus Layton in order to build futuristic weapons of war to assist in the invasion. Only two people, Layton's niece Sheila, and noted criminologist Craig Foster, can stop the Purple Monster and his diabolical plan. 15 episode serial on 2 cassettes.
VHS: S11569. $29.95.

The Quatermass Experiment
A single man is found alone on a returning spaceship. Tension grows as he mysteriously changes into an alien creature. The result is a hideous monster with unimagined powers and the will to see his horrible desires through at any cost.
VHS: S27751. $14.95.
Val Guest, Great Britain, 1956, 79 mins.

Quatermass II
The second (subtitled Enemy From Space) and best of the three notable Quatermass films written by Nigel Kneale. This frightening tale of alien invasion and political paranoia is comparable to 1984 and Invasion of the Body Snatchers. With Brian Donlevy as Quatermass.
VHS: S01077. $49.95.
Val Guest, Great Britain, 1957, 85 mins.

Quatermass Conclusion
The World has begun the countdown to complete destruction, anarchy reigns in Britain's streets, and behind it all is a force of senseless, relentless evil—Professor Quatermass is forced to meet head on. With John Mills, Barbara Kellerman.
VHS: S01078. $59.95.
Piers Haggard, Great Britain, 1979, 105 mins.

Radar Men from the Moon
Republic serial that introduced Commando Cody, with George Wallace and Clayton Moore. All 12 episodes included on this double tape.
VHS: S07018. $29.95.
Fred Brannon, USA, 1952, 152 mins.

Red Planet Mars
A notorious Cold War parable about American and Russian scientists establishing radio contact with Mars. The radio emissions first elicit panic, leading to a religious revivalism and finally to a personal declaration between the countries to peacefully coexist. With Herbert Berghof, Peter Graves and Andrea King.
VHS: S19136. $14.95.
Harry Horner, USA, 1952, 87 mins.

Reptilicus
When scientists unexpectedly uncover the frozen tail of a dinosaur, they prematurely congratulate themselves on their good fortune. Soon the tail begins to grow and before long the entire horrific creature is complete and ready to roam the world once again.
VHS: S20929. $14.98.
Sidney Pink, Denmark, 1962, 90 mins.

Return of the Fly
Sadly, the son of the original fly-man meets the same fate as his tragic scientist father, with Vincent Price reprising his role from The Fly as the understanding family friend. The sins of the fathers are the sins of the sons.
VHS: S14790. $14.98.
Edward Bernds, USA, 1959, 80 mins.

The Return of the Jedi
The last chapter in this popular trilogy delivers more thrills and adventure as the forces of good and evil battle on the forest planet of Endor, inhabited by feisty teddy bears called Ewoks. Also, Jabba the Hut in action. Be there when the victory dance begins. With Mark Hamill, Carrie Fisher, Harrison Ford and the voice of James Earl Jones.
VHS: S03478. $19.95.
Laser: LD71300. $69.98.
Richard Marquand, USA, 1983, 133 mins.

Robocop
The action/science fiction movie of 1987 stars Peter Weller as a Detroit cop gunned down and used as a guinea pig to create a cyborg police officer. All goes well until Robocop starts remembering his past life and enemies. With Nancy Allen, Ronny Cox, Kurtwood Smith and Miguel Ferrer.
VHS: S05637. $19.98.
Laser: CAV/CLV. LD72101. $99.95.
Paul Verhoeven, USA, 1987, 103 mins.

Robot Monster
Ro-man, an ape-like intergalactic exterminator wearing a plastic diving helmet, attempts to vaporize the entire "hu-man" population with his calcinator death ray. When this movie made its debut in 1953 the reviews were so bad its director committed suicide.
VHS: S14682. $12.95.
Phil Tucker, USA, 1953, 62 mins.

Rodan
Rodan! Disturbed from his prehistoric slumber by H-Bomb testing in the Pacific. Foolish humans! Rodan comes to wreak havoc on civilization! A classic thriller. English dialog.
VHS: S01127. $9.95.
Inoshiro Honda, Japan, 1956, 72 mins.

Silent Running
Bruce Dern stars in this sci-fi classic as a botanist preserving the only botanical specimens left on Earth, under huge geodesic domes, whose rebellion takes him on the loneliest adventure of all. Co-scripted by Michael Cimino, with original songs sung by Joan Baez.
VHS: S01200. $19.95.
Laser: LD70079. $34.95.
Douglas Trumbull, USA, 1977, 90 mins.

Soylent Green
Veteran action director Fleischer invents a science fiction fantasy of the distant future, where an absurdly overpopulated New York City forces its citizens to survive on a wafer-like food plant known as Soylent. Charlton Heston is a laconic detective assigned to uncover the details of a murdered industrialist. The film features a final performance from Edward G. Robinson.
VHS: S02362. $19.98.
Laser: Letterboxed. Includes original theatrical trailer. LD71509. $34.98.
Richard Fleischer, USA, 1973, 97 mins.

Space Patrol
Stand by for exciting out-of-this-world action as you blast into the future with Commander Buzz Corry, Cadet Happy and the intrepid crew of the space cruiser Terra. Travel to the farthest reaches of the galaxy on daring missions as the Space Patrol battles mad scientists, zombie-like robots, evil androids and other diabolical 30th century villains in the name of interplanetary justice. Contains not only full episodes but also original commercials in each volume.
Space Patrol Volume 1. 3 episodes. 90 mins.
VHS: S12181. $19.95.
Space Patrol Volume 2. 3 episodes. 90 mins.
VHS: S12182. $19.95.
Space Patrol Volume 3. 2 episodes. 60 mins.
VHS: S12183. $19.95.

Star Trek Generations
Finally the two captains of the Starship Enterprise, John Luc Picard (Patrick Stewart) and Kirk (William Shatner) are joined in an intergalactic quest. They must join forces to save millions. This film includes the cast of the Next Generation crew and both Whoopi Goldberg and Malcolm McDowell.
VHS: S25541. $19.95.
David Carson, USA, 1994, 117 mins.

Star Trek I: The Motion Picture
Most of the television cast was back, with the addition of Persis Khambatta, and director Wise (Sound of Music) just does not have the right feel for the material. Widescreen.
VHS: S01582. $19.95.
Robert Wise, USA, 1979, 132 mins.

Star Trek II: Wrath of Khan
Ricardo Montalban plays Khan, who had been banished to a barren planet in a television episode in 1967 and seeks revenge against Captain Kirk. Fast-paced and highly entertaining, starring the entire crew of the Enterprise. Widescreen.
VHS: S01583. $19.95.
Nicholas Meyer, USA, 1982, 113 mins.

Star Trek III: Search for Spock
Leonard Nimoy is given an opportunity to direct and turns out a very credible film in which Kirk and the crew disobey Starfleet Command in order to save the soul of Mr. Spock. Widescreen.
VHS: S01584. $19.95.
Leonard Nimoy, USA, 1984, 105 mins.

Star Trek IV: The Voyage Home
The Enterprise travels back to the 20th century in this entertaining feature and tries to save the Earth with the help of humpback whales. Widescreen.
VHS: S09568. $14.95.
Leonard Nimoy, USA, 1986, 119 mins.

Star Trek IV: The Voyage Home (Director's Cut)
Director Leonard Nimoy leads you through the special-effects magic of the fourth film in the Star Trek filmography. In a letter-boxed format, this uninterrupted science-fiction epic takes on glorious new meaning. With an environmentally sound message, the Enterprise travels back to the 20th Century and enlists the help of the humpback whales in an effort to save the Earth. With all the familiar faces from the original series.
VHS: S15710. $29.95.
Leonard Nimoy, USA, 1986, 119 mins.

Star Trek V: The Final Frontier
The crew of the Enterprise is hijacked to the center of the universe. A mad Vulcan set this kidnapping plan in motion and it holds surprisingly deep emotional—even spiritual—effects in store for the intrepid crew. William Shatner and Leonard Nimoy are both along for the mystic ride. Widescreen.
VHS: S26352. $19.95.
William Shatner, USA, 1989, 107 mins.

Star Trek VI: The Undiscovered Country
The Federation and the Klingon Empire are set on a wide-ranging peace summit. Captain Kirk the old warrior has his doubts about the impending peace. These fears are realized when an act of sabotage implicates the crew of the Enterprise as renegade terrorists set on destroying the peace summit. The finale is an effective culmination to a long-building, suspense-laden plot. Widescreen.
VHS: S26353. $19.95.
Nicholas Meyer, USA, 1991, 110 mins.

Star Trek: The Cage
The part color, part black and white, never-televised original Star Trek debut television series, one of the most sought-after titles. This special edition includes the long-lost color footage, believed to have been destroyed, from Gene Roddenberry's pilot episode of the Star Trek television series. On the first voyage of the Starship Enterprise, Captain Kirk tries to rescue an earth crew that disappeared 18 years ago but that's now imprisoned in a zoo-like cage, studied by a mysterious life form. 64 mins.
VHS: S09327. $24.95.

Star Wars
Already a classic, a blend of pulp magazine sci-fi, comic book action, and old fashioned cliff-hanger story starring Mark Hamill, Harrison Ford and Carrie Fisher.
VHS: S02866. $19.98.
Laser: CAV. LD71338. $64.98.
George Lucas, USA, 1977, 121 mins.

Star Wars Trilogy (Widescreen THX)
A special collector's edition of the phenomenal science fiction trilogy, George Lucas' Star Wars, Irvin Kershner's The Empire Strikes Back and Richard Marquand's Return of the Jedi, available for the first time in a widescreen THX format that preserves the original aspect ratio of their theatrical releases.
Laser: Letterboxed collector's edition, CAV, additional behind-the-scenes footage. LD72429. $249.98.

Star Wars Trilogy Giftpack
A collector's package of all three of the Star Wars trilogy movies, at a special price.
VHS: S12931. $49.98.

Stargate
Kurt Russell and James Spader star in this sci-fi epic about a gateway to another world. Spader is a professor asked to decode an ancient Egyptian artifact. Before long he and Russell, an Air Force colonel, are on the other side of the universe battling the evil and oppressive Sun god Ra (Jaye Davidson). Great sets and effects.
VHS: S24085. $19.98.
Roland Emmerich, USA, 1994, 119 mins.

Starman
Jeff Bridges and Karen Allen star in this love story about an alien and a human woman. When the alien appears, he takes the form of the woman's recently deceased husband, forcing her to confront a remarkable resurrection. A widescreen, deluxe Dolby presentation.
Laser: LD74545. $34.95.
John Carpenter, USA, 1984, 115 mins.

Strange Invaders
A fun, talented debut film spoof of science fiction invader films which stars Diana Scarwid, Nancy Allen and Louise Fletcher. A UFO lands in a remote area of the midwest during the 1950's, and aliens obliterate the residents of the small town before they assume their human form.
VHS: S05965. $79.95.
Michael Laughlin, USA, 1983, 99 mins.

Tarantula
Scientist Leo G. Carrol's experiment to create the world's largest food supply mutates into a gigantic spider that wreaks havoc on the pastoral countryside. "One of the best giant-insect films, with fast pacing and convincing special effects" (Leonard Maltin). With John Agar, Mara Corday and in a small role, Clint Eastwood.
VHS: S18700. $14.98.
Jack Arnold, USA, 1955, 80 mins.

Teenagers from Outer Space
A teenager from outer space tries to alert the planet Earth about his alien race and their diabolical scheme of destruction. He is pursued by a killer because of this plan, but that does not prevent him from becoming infatuated with a teenage girl. This is a camp classic made on a tiny budget that could only have been produced in the 1950's.
VHS: S24069. $14.95.
Tom Graeff, USA, 1959, 86 mins.

Terror of Mechagodzilla
Outer space fiends use a prehistoric sea creature, the Titanosaurus, and Mechagodzilla in their intergalactic plans to destroy Tokyo. Only Godzilla can battle the two titans and save the Japanese capital. Dubbed in English.
VHS: S25029. $19.95.
Laser: LD75271. $34.98.
Inoshiro Honda, Japan, 1978, 89 mins.

Them!
A 50's masterpiece of the cinema of the fantastic. With atmospheric shadow and light photography, memorable performances by James Whitmore and James Arness (pre-Gunsmoke), and assists from 12 foot long ants.
VHS: S01319. $19.95.
Laser: LD74719. $34.98.
Gordon Douglas, USA, 1954, 93 mins.

They Live
John Carpenter's sci-fi thriller about one man's battle against aliens who are systematically gaining control of the earth. Pro-wrestler Roddy Piper stars as the loner who stumbles upon ghoulish creatures masquerading as humans while they lull the public into submission through subliminal advertising messages! Only specially made sunglasses make the deadly truth visible.
VHS: S10111. $89.95.
John Carpenter, USA, 1988, 95 mins.

The Thing
A chilling morality tale about the responsibility of scientists toward humanity, The Thing was produced by Howard Hawks and stars James Arness as the extraterrestrial. It concludes with the hysterical admonition: "Keep on looking! Watch the skies!"
VHS: S01325. $14.95.
Laser: LD70087. $34.95.
Christian Nyby, USA, 1951, 80 mins.

Things to Come
A sci-fi classic, based on the novel by H.G. Wells. World civilization is on the brink of collapse, in the grasp of evil dictatorship. Raymond Massey plays John Cabal, who hopes to restore peace and save civilization through technology. A humanistic film, and one of the all-time science fiction greats.
VHS: S01326. $19.95.
William C. Menzies, Great Britain, 1936, 87 mins.

This Island Earth
Joseph Newman's science fiction film contains all the classic archetypes: death rays, mutant bugs and, according the the press release, "college sweethearts turned nuclear fission experts." Faith Domergue and Rex Reason star as the lovers/scientists sinister to the planet Metaluna to save it from destruction. A 1955 special effects classic.
VHS: S02613. $19.95.
Laser: LD70088. $34.95.
Joseph M. Newman, USA, 1955, 86 mins.

Threads
The story of the aftermath of a global thermonuclear war, shockingly realistic with graphic effectiveness. Set in Sheffield, England, and told from the vantage points of a working class family and a middle class family.
English Version.
VHS: Out of print. For rental only.
Spanish Version.
VHS: S07291. $64.95.
Mick Jackson, Australia/Great Britain, 1985, 110 mins.

The Three Avengers
Alan Steele stars as Ursus. He must defeat not only a tyrant but an imposter Ursus as well. In the end this hero of mythic proportions manages to defeat all his enemies and save the rightful heir to a powerful kingdom. Dubbed in English.
VHS: S25691. $19.95.
Gianfranco Parolini, Italy, 1964, 97 mins.

THX 1138
Robert Duvall is the androgynous worker who, with his partner, passes up their daily drug requirement in the futuristic society, and begins to feel sexual awakening. George Lucas' first film is a classic science fiction vision of a nightmare future.
VHS: S01340. $19.95.
Laser: Letterboxed. LD74720. $34.98.
George Lucas, USA, 1971, 90 mins.

Time Machine
H.G. Wells' classic novel is adapted in a now-classic film directed by George Pal. Rod Taylor is the time traveler who guns his machine into the distant future only to find a civilization devitalized by endless wars.
VHS: S01346. $19.95.
Laser: Widescreen. LD71156. $34.98.
George Pal, USA, 1960, 103 mins.

Tobor the Great
Tobor is robot spelled backwards. It is also gifted with telepathic powers which help out a lot when enemy agents threaten the lives of its inventor and his grandson. The science fiction thriller is aimed at kids. With Billy Chapin, Lyle Talbot and William Schallert. B&W.
VHS: S04263. $19.95.
Laser: CLV. LD72038. $34.98.
Lee Sholem, USA, 1954, 77 mins.

Unknown World
Using a gigantic drilling machine, a group of scientists are off on an adventure to the interior of the earth in order to escape the perils of the atomic era. An intelligent script and colorful cast make this a worthwhile sci-fi yarn.
VHS: S23152. $29.95.
Terry Morse, USA, 1951, 73 mins.

Valley of the Gwangi
Adventurers in Mexico stumble upon a hidden valley and decide to bring back one of the prehistoric creatures they find, hoping to profit off the venture by displaying him in captivity in a sort of travelling circus. Excellent special effects by Ray Harryhausen (The Seventh Voyage of Sinbad).
VHS: S14287. $19.98.
Laser: LD74724. $34.98.
James O'Connolly, USA, 1969, 95 mins.

Village of the Damned/ Children of the Damned (1960)
Two chilling psychological shockers. Wolf Rilla's 1960 British thriller Village of the Damned is a perverse adaptation of John Wyndham's novel about a group of strange, detached children created by alien visitors plotting to destroy an English village. Anton Leader's 1964 follow-up, Children of the Damned concerns six immensely gifted young children and their ruthless attempt to take over the world. Includes the theatrical trailer for both works.
Laser: LD71653. $39.98.

Village of the Damned
Classic sci-fi thriller about twelve children all born on the same day in a peaceful English village, who terrorize their community with telepathic powers. With George Sanders.
VHS: S02364. $19.98.
Wolf Rilla, Great Britain, 1960, 78 mins.

Village of the Damned (1994)
This remake of the earlier 1960's sci-fi classic captures all the brooding menace of that previous film. Terror is brought to a small town by an unlikely generation of perfect children. They are blond, efficient and alien. As their powers grow, the townspeople realize that no one, not their parents or their teachers, will be able to control them.
VHS: S26369. $19.95.
Laser: LD75293. $34.98.
John Carpenter, USA, 1994, 99 mins.

Voyage to a Prehistoric Planet
Basil Rathbone stars in this sci-fi film about a voyage to Venus in the year 2020. A number of interesting and surprising adventures await the crew of this ship, including dinosaurs, monsters, and most intriguingly of all, invisible Venusians.
VHS: S21557. $24.95.
Jonathon Sebastian, USA, 1965, 80 mins.

Voyage to the Bottom of the Sea
A top cast, thrilling underwater photography, and superb special effects fuel this science fiction classic about an enormous sub trying to save the earth from destruction. Written and directed by the master of the natural disaster genre, Irwin Allen (The Towering Inferno). Starring Walter Pidgeon, Joan Fontaine and Peter Lorre.
VHS: S07815. $14.98.
Irwin Allen, USA, 1961, 105 mins.

Voyage to the Prehistoric Planet
Basil Rathbone co-stars with footage taken from Soviet film Planet of Storms (Planeta Burg) for the second time. See Planet of Blood. An expedition to Venus is the focus of this sci-fi which features Faith Domergue and a pterodactyl. One of Rathbone's last films.
VHS: S04095. $29.95.
Curtis Harrington/John Sebastian, USA, 1965

War of the Gargantuas
A Japanese monster film about the outbreak of war between nasty, green giants called gargantuas and their brown-colored adversaries trying to restore peace. "You're in for a monster extravaganza," says one prominent science fiction magazine.
VHS: S16899. $9.95.
Laser: LD75280. $34.98.
Inoshiro Honda, Japan, 1970, 92 mins.

War of the Worlds
Based on the H.G. Wells novel, this film is everybody's SF classic. Winner of an Oscar for special effects, starring Gene Barry.
VHS: S01430. $14.95.
Byron Haskin, USA, 1952, 88 mins.

Westworld
Author and anthropologist Michael Crichton (The Andromeda Strain) wrote and directed this study of a regressive futureworld gone awry by the horrors of misdirected technology. A futuristic theme park called Westworld becomes a killing ground when robots begin killing the participants. James Brolin and Richard Benjamin star.
VHS: S02363. $24.95.
Michael Crichton, USA, 1973, 90 mins.

When Dinosaurs Ruled the Earth
A pair of Stone-Age lovers defy rampaging dinosaurs, murderous tribesmen and a tidal wave to be together. A fast-paced, enjoyable prehistoric adventure film with fine special effects. Featuring former Playmate of the Year Victoria Vetri.
VHS: S14288. $19.98.
Laser: LD74725. $34.98.
Val Guest, Great Britain, 1970, 96 mins.

When Worlds Collide
A pioneering classic of science-fiction films, When Worlds Collide won the Oscar for its special effects. The potential pulverizing impact of the collision makes a chilling panorama of disaster. The balance between human and planetary drama is excellently maintained as the film builds to its fascinating, unforgettable climax.
VHS: S01446. $14.95.
Laser: LD75366. $44.98.
Rudolph Mate, USA, 1951, 81 mins.

X from Outer Space
Another Japanese giant monster movie. The land of the rising sun is under attack from an outer space organism that mutates into a lizard-like chicken. Expect Tokyo to be severely damaged. Watch for hundreds of extras to flee screaming. This is the movie that set back the Japanese space program for decades.
VHS: S10996. $19.98.
Dazui Nihomatsu, Japan, 1967

The Yesterday Machine
This is a Texas-produced original starring Tim Holt, James Britton and Jack Herman. A fugitive Nazi scientist is plotting from his hideout in the Texas prairie. He invents a time machine so they can go back and save Hitler from suicide. A truly bizzare oddity.
VHS: S23160. $29.95.
Russ Marker, USA, 1963, 85 mins.

Yongary Monster from the Deep
A Japanese-Korean co-production giant monster movie. The title character, who looks like Godzilla's second cousin, emerges to terrorize Asia after an earthquake in China sets it free. Yongary enjoys drinking gasoline, crushing buildings in Seoul and dancing to rock and roll music. Script by Yungsung Suh.
VHS: S10997. $14.98.
Kidduck Kim, S. Korea/Japan, 1967, 100 mins.

Zardoz
Sean Connery delivers a powerful performance in the fantastic vision of a future world divided into two societies, the Eternals and the Brutals. Connery is a superior Brutal who finds his way into the world of the Eternals, setting that society on an entirely new course. The special effects and imaginative vision make for high adventure.
VHS: S01498. $19.98.
Laser: LD71227. $59.98.
John Boorman, Great Britain, 1974, 105 mins.

Zeram
An extravagant science fiction work about a female bounty hunter tracking Zeram, a massive renegade space alien who's drawn to Earth to kidnap humans for the planet Mays. In order to defeat the alien, she must use her smarts, cunning and a warp machine, space bazooka, electric shield and a computer called Bob in this off-center, clever futuristic thriller. English dubbed. Japan, 1992, 92 mins.
VHS: S19326. $19.98.
Laser: Widescreen. LD74963. $39.99.

THE OUTER LIMITS

100 Days of the Dragon
Popular American President conceives of a plan to take over the United States. 52 mins.
VHS: S03319. $12.98.

Architects of Fear
An idealistic scientist is surgically transformed into a bizarre and frightening alien creature in the hope that fear of annihilation at the hands of this creature will bring the warring people of the world together. 52 mins.
VHS: S08059. $12.98.

Behold, Eck!
Peter Lind Hayes stars in a spine-tingling tale of a 2-dimensional alien trapped in our 3-dimensional world.
VHS: S12441. $12.98.

The Bellero Shield
An alien accidentally brought to earth by a scientist's malfunctioning invention confronts Martin Landau and Sally Kellerman.
VHS: S11241. $12.98.

The Borderland
Wealthy industrialist Barry Jones funds his own experiments to reach his dead son.
VHS: S12439. $12.98.

The Brain of Colonel Barham
A disembodied brain floating in a three gallon tank is the pivotal character in this keenly written episode. 52 mins.
VHS: S13984. $12.99.

The Chameleon
With Robert Duvall as a CIA hired assassin.
VHS: S13980. $12.99.
Gerd Oswald, USA, 1964, 52 mins.

The Children of Spider County
A sensitive young man is wrongly accused of murder. 52 mins.
VHS: S13981. $12.99.

Cold Hands, Warm Heart
William Shatner stars as an astronaut who's gone where no man's gone before. 52 mins.
VHS: S13982. $12.99.

Controlled Experiment
Barry Morse plays Martian Inspector Phobos, whose friendship with his fieldman, Carroll O'Connor, leads him to interfere in a forthcoming murder.
VHS: S12434. $12.98.

Corpus Earthling
Robert Culp stars as a man with a metal plate in his head, which allows him to hear aliens plotting to take over the world.
VHS: S11242. $12.98.

Counterweight
Something goes wrong when six astronauts embark on a simulated training mission. 52 mins.
VHS: S13988. $12.99.

Cry of Silence
Eddie Albert and June Havoc portray a farm couple who encounter a nightmare of alien creatures. 52 mins.
VHS: S13985. $12.99.

Demon with a Glass Hand
Robert Culp is a mysterious visitor from Earth's future being pursued by a team of aliens called the Kyben in the Bradbury Building in present day (1964) Los Angeles. He holds the secret of human survival in the prosthetic computer that serves as his hand. Script by Harlan Ellison.
VHS: S06054. $12.98.
Byron Haskin, USA, 1964, 60 mins.

Don't Open till Doomsday
Miriam Hopkins gives a show-stopping performance as an overly-ripe flapper who will stop at nothing to complete her long overdue wedding night scenario.
VHS: S11243. $12.98.

The Duplicate Man
A man clones himself in order to hunt down a "megasoid." 52 mins.
VHS: S13989. $12.99.

Expanding Human
James Doohan ("Scotty") stars as a scientist in this Jekyll-and-Hyde story tinged with Outer Limits touches. 52 mins.
VHS: S13983. $12.99.

A Feasibility Study
A six-block section of Beverly Hills is transported to an alien planet in a grotesque experiment.
VHS: S11244. $12.98.

Forms of Things Unknown
A stormy night, a secluded mansion, a mysterious inventor, two frightened women and a murdered blackmailer who won't stay dead in one of the classic Outer Limits programs.
VHS: S04948. $12.98.

Fun and Games
Nick Adams (The Rebel) stars as an ex-boxer and small-time criminal who is transported with a divorced woman to a distant planet to participate in planetary survival games. If the Earth team loses, the rest of the human race is doomed. Go, Nick, Go. With Nancy Malone, the voice of Robert Johnson and Bill Hart as the alien with the saw-toothed boomerang.
VHS: S08343. $12.98.
Gerd Oswald, USA, 1964, 60 mins.

Galaxy Being
Cliff Robertson in a story about a visitor from outer space. 53 mins.
VHS: S03318. $12.98.

The Guests
A man wanders into an ominous-looking mansion looking for help following a roadside accident and confronts a pulsating brain in the attic.
VHS: S12431. $12.98.

The Human Factor
Sally Kellerman, Harry Guardino and Gary Merrill star in this chilling tale of a psychiatrist's efforts to help a twisted mental patient.
VHS: S12440. $12.98.

I, Robot
Leonard Nimoy stars in this tale that finds a robot on trial for murdering his creator. 52 mins.
VHS: S13987. $12.99.

The Inheritors
Academy Award-winner Robert Duvall challenges four men controlled by one alien mind.
VHS: S04949. $12.98.

The Invisible Enemy
Two astronauts travel to Mars but never return home. A second expedition follows to find out why, and two crew members mysteriously disappear after arrival. Only the Mission Commander and his Captain are left, and realize their enemy are man-eating sand sharks. 52 mins.
VHS: S07315. $12.98.

The Invisibles
Alien parasites are gaining control of high-ranking individuals in government and industry. Don Gordon is an undercover agent for the Government Intelligence Agency sent to stop the Invisibles, which actually look like football-sized crab lice.
VHS: S08344. $12.98.
Gerd Oswald, USA, 1964, 60 mins.

It Crawled Out of the Woodwork
With Ed Asner.
VHS: S11245. $12.98.

Keeper of the Purple Twilight
A distraught scientist is willing to swap his emotions with an alien creature in order to receive the missing equations that will make his antimagnetic disintegrator a reality. This leads to a possible invasion of Earth. With Warren Stevens, Robert Webber and Mike Lane as Ikar in his alien form.
VHS: S06055. $12.98.
Charles Haas, USA, 1964, 60 mins.

Man Who Was Never Born
An astronaut travels through time far into the future where a bacteria invented by a crazed scientist has turned humans into mutants. The astronaut travels back in time to kill the scientist. 52 mins.
VHS: S07316. $12.98.

Man with the Power
Timid college professor invents a device giving him mental control over cosmic energy. 52 mins.
VHS: S03320. $12.98.

The Mice
Henry Silva has a choice: life in prison or be a guinea pig for a scientific "inhabitant exchange" with the planet Chromo.
VHS: S12437. $12.98.

Moonstone
Ruth Roman stars in this story of mysterious anemone-like aliens found buried on the moon in a spheroid space ship.
VHS: S12435. $12.98.

The Mutant
Larry Pennell investigates an earth colony on "Annex One", where a hairless, bug-eyed human mutant (Warren Oates) dominates the colony.
VHS: S12432. $12.98.

Nightmare
A six-man multi-national task force is captured on the planet Ebon and must be killed. But who? 52 mins.
VHS: S07317. $12.98.

O.B.I.T.
U.S. military security forces keep a special eye on the scientists at a Defense Department research center by using a secret electronic surveillance machine called OBIT. The Outer Band Individual Teletracer also allows one-eyed monsters from another world a free trip to Earth. With Peter Breck, Jeff Corey and Joanne Gilbert.
VHS: S08342. $12.98.
Gerd Oswald, USA, 1963, 60 mins.

The Outer Limits
A compendium of eight of the finest episodes of this eerie and provocative science fiction television program that captured '50s paranoia and hysteria, featuring the work of young actors Martin Sheen, Vera Miles, Ed Asner, Martin Landau, Sally Kellerman and Joanne Gilbert. "The best program of its type ever to run on network TV" (Harlan Ellison).
Volume 1.
Laser: LD71841. $99.98.
Volume 2.
Laser: LD71164. $99.98.

The Premonition
A husband and wife are hurled into a limbo state at the moment of their deaths. 52 mins.
VHS: S13991. $12.99.

The Probe
A cargo plane en route to Japan lands on a strange land mass in the uncharted Pacific. 52 mins.
VHS: S13990. $12.99.

The Production and Decay of Strange Particles
Workers at a nuclear power plant are being turned into "force creatures", whose purpose is to create an atomic explosion that will blow a doorway into their dimension. 52 mins.
VHS: S12442. $12.98.

Second Chance
Seven people aboard a space ship ride are transported to another planet to participate in a desperate attempt to prevent a galactic catastrophe.
VHS: S12438. $12.98.

The Sixth Finger
A bitter young coal miner (David McCallum) is transformed into the all-knowing man of the future.
VHS: S04950. $12.98.

Soldier
A crossfire of death beams flings an alien foot soldier from the future back into our present. A man born and bred of violence, he refuses to pacify his warrior instincts in the face of our peaceful world. 52 mins.
VHS: S08061. $12.98.

The Special One
The parents are pleased to find that their son qualifies for a special tutor, but reconsider when they learn of the instructor's strange interest in alien invasions.
VHS: S12433. $12.98.

Specimen: Unknown
A young scientist discovers spores clinging to the walls of his space lab and incubates them. When they mature, he is sprayed with a deadly poison and before anyone realizes it the deadly plants are on a shuttle bound for earth. 52 mins.
VHS: S08060. $12.98.

Tourist Attraction
Ralph Meeker wants to take back to America an enormous, prehistoric, amphibious monster discovered in a Central American country, but is thwarted by the country's dictator (Henry Silva).
VHS: S12446. $12.98.

Wolf 359
Dabney Coleman and Patrick O'Neal are scientists who are faced with the impressive task of cloning an entire planet. 52 mins.
VHS: S13986. $12.98.

The Zanti Misfits
When the Earth is selected by the planet Zanti to serve as a penal colony for the unwanted members of their society, no one expected Bruce Dern to violate the restricted and heavily guarded area of a California ghost town. Leave it to Dern and his wild girlfriend (Olive Deering) to stir up intergalactic trouble.
VHS: S06056. $12.98.
Leonard Horn, USA, 1963, 60 mins.

ZZZZ
A queen bee (Joanna Frank) evolves into a beautiful, red-haired woman and sets her sights on an entomologist (Philip Abbott).
VHS: S12436. $12.98.

cult FILMS

200 Motels
Frank Zappa and the Mothers of Invention get inventive in this free-for-all film that features Ringo Starr as Frank's twin. Theodore Bikel wears an impressive uniform, and an animated featurette on proper dental hygiene is presented along with lots of music and bizarre humor. Made for those who haven't got the money for drugs but can afford to rent a tape.
VHS: S06227. $19.95.
Frank Zappa/Tony Palmer, USA, 1971, 98 mins.

2000 Maniacs
A classic shocker about six tourists who stumble upon a small town called Pleasant Valley that is in the midst of a Centennial celebration—honoring a Civil War massacre! The innocent tourists become unwilling "guests of horror" at the bloody bash. Directed by Herschell Gordon Lewis in gushing blood color.
VHS: S15142. $19.98.
Herschell Gordon Lewis, USA, 1964, 87 mins.

3-D Video Visions: Vol. 1, Deep Space Videoscapes
This cosmic journey goes beyond our solar system to an unseen universe that lies somewhere between the viewer and the screen. From the creators of *Stereograms* and *Superstereograms*. 25 mins.
VHS: S22900. $9.95.

3-D Video Visions: Vol. 2, Stereogram Videoscapes
Amazing 3-D videoscapes challenge the mind, startle the senses and dazzle the eye in this second volume of animated fantasy. 25 mins.
VHS: S22901. $9.95.

Air Force Training Films
Two films featuring Lieutenant Ronald Reagan and Lieutenant Burgess Meredith: *The Rear Gunner* and *Snoopers and How to Blast Them.*
VHS: S10586. $19.95.

Alice in Acidland
This Z-grade, '60s cult work has virtually no relationship to Lewis Carroll, instead using the psychedelic, surreal episodes of a young woman under the influence of LSD as a cautionary moral tale of abuse and degradation.
VHS: S16961. $24.95.

Aliens Cut My Hair
An extravagantly campy video by Michael McIntosh based on the surreal comic strip *Fabulous Space Stories*, by Gentry Johnson. The story unfolds in an outerspace populated by hairdressers, alien transvestites, a vibrator-shaped space ship, and glitter to convey the transporter sequences. When a young ensign shows insufficient compliments for a haircut, the hairdresser announces eternal revenge. "Every bit as campy as it sounds" (Steven Miller, *Seattle Gay News*).
VHS: S18918. $39.95.

Alley Tramp
"She went for anything in pants!" screamed the ads of this notorious, long-thought-lost cult film produced by Herschell Gordon Lewis. The subject is the sexual freedom of 16-year-old Marie. She voyeuristically watches her parents in erotic thrall, an act which unleashes her emerging sexual impulses and she is transformed into a "sex machine." With Annette Courset and Jean Lamee.
VHS: S20096. $24.95.
Armand Pays, USA, 1966

America's Deadliest Home Video
An impressive formal exercise by Jack Perez that's a cross between *They Live by Night* and *Henry: Portrait of a Serial Killer*. A home video enthusiast (former child actor and camp performer Danny Bonaduce) abandons his wife after learning of her affair and is taken hostage by the brutal Clint Dryer gang. He is forced by his captors to film their increasingly bizarre, fiendish and sadomasochistic crime spree. "The most original independent film since *Slacker*" (Christian Gore, *Film Threat*). With Mick Wynhoff, Mollena Williams and Melora alters.
VHS: S18977. $29.95.
Jack Perez, USA, 1992

Anatomy of a Psycho
A quintessential B-movie experience about the outlaw relationship of a young psychopath (Darrell Howe) and his strung-out girlfriend (Judy Howard) who go on a rampage to avenge his brother's state-ordered death. With Pamela Lincoln, Russ Bender and Ronnie Burns.
VHS: S18919. $14.95.
Brooke L. Peters, USA, 1961

Around the World with Fanny Hill
Diana Kjaer stars as Fanny Hill in this loose sequel which chronicles a scandal in Stockholm, casting couches in Hollywood, erotic films in Hong Kong, romance in Venice and a strange resolution in Munich.
VHS: S16976. $29.95.
Mac Ahlberg, Sweden, 1974, 102 mins.

As Nature Intended
Considered by many to be the British Russ Meyer, Harrison Marks caused a storm in England when he released this film in 1961. Three young women on holiday innocently meet up with two other women on the road, and soon their exhibitionist nature is revealed. Skinny dipping leads to nudist camping, where even more women are found without their clothes. Pinup stars Pamela Green, Jackie Salt and Bridget Leonard are featured, with narration by cartoon voice-man Dawes Butler.
VHS: S15914. $29.95.
Harrison Marks, Great Britain, 1961, 65 mins.

Assassin of Youth
Luanna Gardner stars in this exploitation film where one puff of a controlled substance turns kids into fiends. Wild parties and the terrors of marijuana use follow a girl's introduction to this drug. Terrifyingly funny.
VHS: S23180. $24.95.
Elmer Clifton, USA, 1937, 70 mins.

Atrocities of the Orient
The Japanese invasion and occupation of the Philippines is the subject of this exploitation drama that combines combat bloodthirstiness with a strange love story. A Filipino kills his girlfriend so that the Japanese will not defile her. Looting, torturing, bombing and bayonetting are also featured. USA, 1959, 80 mins.
VHS: S05437. $29.95.

Babette in "The Return of the Secret Society"
Babette is a hip, young sex kitten who has travelled the world and is now settling down in New York City. In need of employment, she returns to her former career in "the secret society," a world of mail-order porn and prostitution. She quickly befriends Ramon, a kinky photographer, and finds herself drawn to Carla, one of his favorite models. Together, Carla and Babette pose for Ramon and his camera, initiate a new member into the secret society via a far out candlelight orgy, and join a group of horny young housewives called the Daughters of Lesbos. Very rare sleaze from the 60's. With Claudia Cheer, Jo Sweet, Carla Costa and Sue Akers.
VHS: S27628. $19.98.
Peter Woodcock, USA, 1968, 80 mins.

Back Street Jane
When a pair of beautiful young thieves try to extort drugs from an evil femme fatale, their plan backfires and ends in multiple murder. This modern film noir is stylishly shot and superbly acted, with "non-stop double-crosses and plot surprises in the tradition of (Stanley Kubrick's) *The Killing* and (John Huston's) *The Asphalt Jungle*" (Michael Weldon, *Psychotronic Video*). For mature audiences.
VHS: S16677. $14.95.
Ronnie Cramer, USA, 1989, 95 mins.

Back to the Beach
Frankie Avalon and Annette Funicello revisit the beaches of their youth, this time as the parents of two teenagers. A nostalgic romp with lots of guest stars like Bob Denver, Don Adams, Connie Stevens, The Cleaver Family minus Ward, and Pee Wee Herman, who sings "Surfin' Bird." Fun for the sand set.
VHS: S05528. $19.95.
Laser: LD75152. $34.98.
Lyndall Hobbs, USA, 1987, 92 mins.

Bad Girls Go to Hell
Innocent, naive airheads in high heels are forced into a life of sin by sleazeballs and lesbians—this, believe it or not, was the formula for a whole series of movies called "roughies", made between 1964 and 1967. This 1965 morality tale about a penniless, talentless, brainless woman, lost in New York City, is one of the best of the group. Written, directed and produced by Doris Wishman, the only woman making exploitation movies in the 60s.
VHS: S15143. $19.98.
Doris Wishman, USA, 1965, 98 mins.

Batman
The caped crusader and his sidekick Robin in this first, full-length feature film starring Adam West and Burt Ward, as they battle the Fearsome Foursome: the Riddler (Frank Gorshin), the Penguin (Burgess Meredith), the Catwoman (Lee Meriwether), and the Joker (Cesar Romero). Exciting bat-chases and clever traps as the United Nations delegates face the prospect of being turned into small piles of dust.
VHS: S10794. $19.98.
Leslie Martinson, USA, 1966, 105 mins.

Battle for the Planet of the Apes
The fourth and final sequel, so far, to the famous talking ape series. Roddy McDowall returns as Caesar, the leader of the Simian revolution. He is all in favor of living in peace with the remaining humans, but apes like Claude Akins, John Huston, Paul Williams and Lew Ayres don't quite trust human mutants like Severn Darden.
VHS: S12175. $19.98.
J. Lee Thompson, USA, 1973, 86 mins.

Battle of the Bombs
The best scenes from the worst movies ever made, including *Orgy of the Dead*, *Terror of Tiny Town*, *I Changed My Sex*, and *Hell Is a Place Called Hollywood*. Total length, 60 mins.
VHS: S05200. $39.95.

Beneath the Planet of the Apes
James Franciscus heads up a rescue ship to find out what happened to Charlton Heston and friends. He gets a similar shock and shoddy treatment by talking gorillas and orangutans and a little help from chimpanzees like Kim Hunter. The journey leads to the ruins of the New York subway system, where mutant humans worship the last nuclear weapon. With Linda Harrison, Victor Buono and Maurice Evans.
VHS: S12172. $19.98.
Ted Post, USA, 1970, 100 mins.

Beyond Belief
This film documents actual experiments in ESP, reincarnation, faith healing and other spiritual and psychic phenomena. A frighteningly real expose of unexplainable mysteries that will keep you on the edge of your seat. 94 mins.
VHS: S16575. $19.95.

Big Breakdowns
Hollywood bloopers of the 1930's featuring many of the greatest stars: Humphrey Bogart, Bette Davis, Errol Flynn and the legendary scene of Porky Pig hitting his thumb with a hammer. USA, 27 mins.
VHS: S02233. $19.95.

Bimbos B.C.
While hunting, a barbarian woman accidentally stumbles on the fortress of prehistoric bimbos. They are engaged in a desperate race against time. Their queen was bitten by a radioactive beast and now they must venture into the world in search of an antidote.
VHS: S24759. $9.95.
Todd Sheets, USA, 1992, 85 mins.

Bizarre Sports and Incredible Feats
A collection of bizarre sports in the far corners of the world: soccer-playing elephants, knuckle-racing Eskimos, and cockroach racing! 36 mins.
VHS: S05380. $9.95.

Blast-Off Girls
Herschell Gordon Lewis' cult item about a corrupt talent agent who discovers a grungy bar band known as the Big Blast and ruthlessly exploits them by signing a one-sided contract. He invents their success with the aid of attractive young women who disrupt their stage shows.
VHS: S20101. $24.95.
Herschell Gordon Lewis, USA, 1967, 83 mins.

Blood Feast
The story of Fuad Ramses, maniac Egyptian caterer, was the most tasteless film ever made when it was released in 1963, and was the first movie to use explicit gore. The only thing more appalling than the bloody special effects is the acting. Directed by the "Godfather of Gore", Herschell Gordon Lewis.
VHS: S15137. $19.98.
Herschell Gordon Lewis, USA, 1963, 78 mins.

Blood Orgy of the Leather Girls
A violent feminist revenge movie far more serious than its mock title implies, this feature by the late Meredith Lucas focuses on the efforts of four radically different women to avenge the terrorist tactics waged on them by the school's fascist bullies. With Robin Gingold, Jo Ann Wyman, Melissa Lawrence and David Nudleman. Special appearance by the Wild Breed.
VHS: S18600. $19.95.
Meredith Lucas, USA, 1988

Blood Shack (Director's Cut)
Ray Dennis Steckler's ghoulish work is about an actress (Carolyn Brandt) who inherits a ranch that many believe is demonized by an ancient Indian devil god called "The Chopper," who is responsible for a string of grisly crimes. With Ron Haydock, Jason Wayne, Laurel Spring and John Bates.
VHS: S20144. $24.95.
Ray Dennis Steckler, USA, 1971, 60 mins.

Bloodsucking Pharaohs in Pittsburgh
A group of cannibalistic crazies looking for eternal life try to turn Pittsburgh into blood soup, in this "hilarious" and "campy" feature-length horror film in the tradition of *The Rocky Horror Picture Show* and *Pink Flamingos*.
VHS: S13714. $79.95.
Alan Smithee, USA, 1990, 89 mins.

Body Fever
A grim detective saga set in a bleak, corrosive world of drug trafficking and prostitution. The story follows a criminal genius who declares war on a woman he believes ripped her off. Charlie Smith (Ray Dennis Steckler), who worships Humphrey Bogart, is trying to track the woman down before the gangster finds her. Alternate titles: *The Last Original "B" Movie* and *Super Cool*. With Carolyn Brandt, Bernard Fein and Gary Kent.
VHS: S20145. $24.95.
Ray Dennis Steckler, USA, 1971, 80 mins.

Boinng
Herschell Gordon Lewis' hilarious send-up of the film industry about two amateur pornography fanatics who try their hand at making adult movies and discover the business is fraught with terrifying figures and unforseen complications.
VHS: S20107. $24.95.
Herschell Gordon Lewis, USA, 1963, 70 mins.

Born in East L.A.
Cheech Marin finds himself accidentally deported to Mexico without any identification to prove his citizenship, providing a basis for multiple hijinks.
VHS: S08306. $19.95.
Cheech Martin, USA, 1987, 85 mins.

Bowery at Midnight
Bela Lugosi plays Professor Brenner, a Manhattan psychology prof who secretly runs a Bowery mission to front his criminal activities. His victims, through the aid of a drug crazed medico, are revived and are eager to seek revenge for their shoddy treatment. B&W.
VHS: S04008. $29.95.
Wallace Fox, USA, 1942, 61 mins.

Boys from Brooklyn
Bela Lugosi stars with Ramona the Chimp in this jungle comedy about a mad scientist. USA, 1952, 65 mins.
VHS: S05462. $29.95.

Bring Me the Head of Geraldo Rivera
A cult classic, heralded as "One of the best underground films of the decade" (*Film Threat Video Guide*).
VHS: S25714. $19.98.
Jim Sikora, USA, 1989, 30 mins.

Bushwacked
Hosted by comedian and impressionist Jim Morris, this is 30 minutes of jokes, bloopers and twisted syntax taken from ten years of George Bush's speeches, press conferences and public appearances. Witness some of George's best speaking performances—as he forgets the words to the Pledge of Allegiance, or describes the Communist system as an "Economic Rubic's Cone." This tape "kicks ass." 30 mins.
VHS: S15739. $14.95.

A Certain Sacrifice
Shot like a rock video, this portrait of hustlers and losers stars an unknown Madonna as a 20-year-old woman whose brutal assault occasions an outrageous call of revenge.
VHS: S17690. $14.95.
Stephen Jon Lewicki, USA, 1985, 60 mins.

Chained for Life
The Hilton sisters, Daisy and Violet, are literally joined in this exploitation film about a marriage involving a pair of Siamese twins. One finally murders the hapless husband, thereby setting in motion a dilemma. Who should be prosecuted?
VHS: S23183. $24.95.
Harry Fraser, USA, 1951, 81 mins.

Child Bride
Shirley Miles and Bob Bolinger star in this film about a severe social problem. A school teacher tries to create a public movement against the practice of older, horny country men taking teenage and even preteen brides. A camp classic, its skinny-dipping scenes are not to be missed. This longer version was transferred from a 35mm nitrate print, and offers the only uncut version available.
VHS: S23181. $24.95.
Harry Revier, USA, 1941

Class of Nuke 'em High
Genetic insanity overtakes the local high school when radioactive sludge from the nearby nuclear power plant seeps into the water supply. Wonderful madness!
VHS: S02912. $9.95.
Richard Haines/Sam Weill, USA, 1986, 84 mins.

Cocaine Fiends
An innocent young girl is lured to the glamour of the big city, where she falls into the grasp of a smooth dope peddler. On the pretense of curing her headache he gives her some soothing powder. Before long she is hopelessly trapped in the throes of addiction. Camp has long since overtaken this once serious melodrama.
VHS: S23177. $24.95.
W.A. O'Connor, USA, 1936, 68 mins.

Cold Turkey
The lure of 25 million dollars for any community that can quit smoking causes havoc in this small-town satiric comedy directed by Norman Lear. Dick Van Dyke is the local minister at the forefront of a campaign created by adman Bob Newhart, who never dreamed that anyone could actually win the money.
VHS: S12234. $19.95.
Laser: LD72171. $34.98.
Norman Lear, USA, 1971, 99 mins.

Commies Are Coming, Commies Are Coming!
From the 1950's, this is the definitive anti-Communist documentary, hosted by Jack Webb. Total paranoia reigns. 60 mins.
VHS: S09969. $39.95.

Common Law Wife
Anne MacAddams, Max Anderson, George Edgely and Lucy Kelly are featured in this film about an uncontrollably lustful woman. She preys on everyone from old men to young studs. It has moments of unintentional hilarity followed quickly with intensely dramatic moments. The climax is gritty and shocking.
VHS: S23190. $24.95.
Eric Sayers, USA, 1963, 81 mins.

Confessions of a Vice Baron
Willy Castello stars in this story of a thug gone bad, played to the hilt by a real-life gangster. Through drugs and pimping our hero makes it big, only to lose it all for love. Awful acting and a ludicrous script add up to a rip-roaring good laugh.
VHS: S23178. $24.95.
Harvey Thew, USA, 1942, 70 mins.

Conquest of the Planet of the Apes
The year is 1990. The intelligent chimp baby of Kim Hunter and Roddy McDowall grows up to look and sound just like his dad. When he feels his fellow primates are being mistreated, he leads an armed revolt against the human masters. With Don Murray, Ricardo Montalban, Nathalie Trundy and Severn Darden.
VHS: S12174. $19.98.
J. Lee Thompson, USA, 1972, 88 mins.

Corpse Fucking Art
Nekromantik's director, Jorg Buttgereit, reveals his gore-effect secrets in this revealing behind-the-scenes look at his work. Includes stills, unreleased scenes and the early shocker *Hot Love*. 90 mins.
VHS: S26008. $29.95.

Daddy-O
Also known as *Out on Probation*, this low-rent, grade Z work about teenage rebellion and alienation concerns the pressures placed on a young man to drive the getaway car during a heist. With Dick Contino, Sandra Giles, Bruno VeSota, and Gloria Victor.
VHS: S16972. $9.95.
Lou Place, USA, 1959, 74 mins.

Deadly Weapons
This historic film stars the amazing 73" bust line of Chesty Morgan. Chesty uses "the only two weapons I've used" to fight the Mob and, of course, she wins. Featuring the famous "droopy-pantyhose" gross-out scene and Chesty's famous ten-inch platform heels. Directed by Doris Wishman; many critics consider the two films she made with Chesty Morgan to be the apex of her career. Well, maybe one critic.
VHS: S15141. $19.98.
Doris Wishman, USA, 1970, 90 mins.

Death: The Ultimate Mystery
From painstaking hospital surgery to the ghoulish mummies of ancient Mexico, this program scans the common denominator facing all mankind: death. Narrated by Cameron Mitchell. 97 mins.
VHS: S16573. $29.95.

Deep Throat
Not a documentary about Watergate. Linda Lovelace has disavowed this movie, but it remains the most recognized porno title of all time.
VHS: S00319. $29.95.
Jerry Gerard, USA, 1972, 73 mins.

Deranged
A chilling work inspired by the depraved psycho Ed Gein, a loathsome serial killer whose acts inspired *Psycho* and *The Texas Chainsaw Massacre*. This film features an anonymous, cruel killer (Roberts Blossom) who preserves his mother's corpse and then randomly pursues other women. The film has been remastered and digitally restored. On the same program is the notorious, underground documentary *Ed Gein: American Maniac*. With Alan Ormsby, Cosette Lee and Leslie Carlson.
VHS: S18839. $39.95.
Jeff Gillen, USA, 1974, 110 mins.

Desperate Teenage Love Dolls
This underground thriller is about the rise and fall of a female road crew cum rock group, who record a smash single ("Come On Up to Me"). The band must also content with a sleazy manager and a rival group, the She Devils.
VHS: S16933. $39.95.

Dino
Sal Mineo stars in this "youth with a chip on his shoulder" drama. He's a juvenile delinquent who must choose between the love of a "good" girl or the streets of crime that tempt him into action. With Susan Kohner and Brian Keith, as the social worker.
VHS: S04229. $39.95.
Thomas Carr, USA, 1957, 96 mins.

Double Agent 73
This film stars the 73" bust line of Chesty Morgan. Chesty is special agent 73; her mission is to expose a gang of drug smugglers by photographing them with the camera implanted in her left bazoom. Of course, to use the camera she must constantly "drop her cover." Chesty has to work fast—the camera is programmed to explode. Directed by Doris Wishman.
VHS: S15147. $19.98.
Doris Wishman, USA, 1971, 72 mins.

Dr. Alien!
The sexy new biology instructor Ms. Xenobia is actually a blue-skinned bug-eyed alien scientist. She may look like blonde and bouncy Judy Landers but she is after sexual data on reproduction on the planet Earth. College freshman Billy Jacoby is her nerd guinea pig. With Troy Donahue, Arlene Golonka and Edy Williams as the comic relief.
VHS: S08274. $79.95.
Laser: LD75183. $34.98.
Dave DeCoteau, USA, 1988, 90 mins.

Dr. Caligari
From the director of *Cafe Flesh* comes another adult excursion into the bizarre and surreal. Inspired by the 1919 German classic, the title character is the sadistic granddaughter of the infamous doctor, who has controlling interests in her own asylum. Madaline Reynel stars as the mad doctor who likes to mix up the minds of the mentally maladjusted. With David Perry, Laura Albert, John Durbin and Fox Harris.
VHS: S14004. $89.98.
Stephen Sayadian, USA, 1989, 80 mins.

Dr. Goldfoot and the Bikini Machine
Vincent Price has a diabolical plot to control the world through an army of beautiful, bikini-clad spy machines. These robots will seduce and then embarrass the world into doing his bidding. Frankie Avalon is also featured looking for the beach.
VHS: S25893. $14.98.
Norman Taurog, USA, 1965, 84 mins.

Dr. Goldfoot's the Girl Bombs
Vincent Price is back with yet another diabolical plot to control the world. This time his weapon of choice is a group of even more deadly bikini-clad lovelies. They explode on impact.
VHS: S25894. $14.98.
Mario Bava, USA/Italy, 1966, 79 mins.

Drug Propaganda and Satire Compilation
This hilarious collection includes *Mystery of the Leaping Fish* (1916) with Douglas Fairbanks, *Sinister Harvest* (circa 1930s), *Death Weed* (circa 1920s), and *The Pusher* (circa 1955).
VHS: S15486. $29.95.

Edge of Sanity
So you say you've seen every version of Robert Louis Stevenson's classic tale of dual personalities, *Dr. Jekyll and Mr. Hyde*. Well think again. Anthony Perkins as the good doctor hasn't been himself lately since his experiments with cocaine. This suspense thriller was called "ghoulish fun and games" by Vincent Canby. Cast includes Glynis Barber, David Lodge, Ben Cole and Lisa Davis.
VHS: S10352. $89.95.
Gerard Kikione, 1989, 86 mins.

Erotic Adventures of Pinocchio
A funny takeoff on Pinocchio made in Italy (dubbed in English), as Pinocchio is wakened into life by an oversexed fairy godmother and blunders through a forest of women without losing a splinter.
VHS: S11473. $49.95.
Corey Allen, USA, 1970, 79 mins.

Erotic Touch of Hot Skin
A psychotic fantasy—"hot skin" arouses the animal passion in man. In southern France, Irene and Mark, husband and wife with hot skin, have a shared secret. Florence, the cousin not seen in 10 years, a cool blond, and Julian, the nephew just up with everyone else, while the body of a man lies rotting under ground. Terrific exploitation. With Fabienne Dali, Sophie Hardy, Jean Valmont.
VHS: S04845. $34.95.
Max Pecas, USA/France, 1964, 77 mins.

Escape from the Planet of the Apes
Chimpanzee scientists Kim Hunter, Roddy McDowall and Sal Mineo use Charlton Heston's spaceship to return to the year 1973. When the human military brass considers them a threat to national security, they find refuge in Ricardo Montalban's circus. With Bradford Dillman, Jason Evers, Eric Braeden and William Windom. Mineo's last movie before he was murdered.
VHS: S12173. $19.98.
J. Lee Thompson, USA, 1972, 88 mins.

Even Hitler Had a Girlfriend
Meet Marcus Templeton, a thirty-year-old bachelor who works the graveyard shift as a security guard. He has no friends and no interests—until one day he discovers that beautiful women are willing to come to his house and have sex with him. Joe Bob Briggs called *Even Hitler Had a Girlfriend* the "best drive-in movie of 1992." For mature audiences.
VHS: S16676. $14.95.
Ronnie Cramer, USA, 1992, 98 mins.

Fanny Hill
An English-language update of John Cleland's 18th century novel about a young woman's sexual awakening. Fanny (Diana Kjaer) leaves the countryside for the big city and discovers sex through closed circuit television.
VHS: S16975. $29.95.
Mac Ahlberg, Sweden, 1968, 92 mins.

Feeding Frenzy
With intimations of Orwell's *1984* and Terry Gilliam's *Brazil*, this is a ferocious, dark work about the cold, impersonal reality of day-to-day life and its negative imprint on the individual, "and how it feeds into the industrial machine." Some surreal, stunning video effects.
VHS: S17157. $29.95.

The Female Bunch
Director Al Adamson decided to shoot this at the Charles Manson ranch so he could get just the right atmosphere. Exploitation sleaze about a gang of man-hating women. Lon Chaney plays a drug pusher in his last released film.
VHS: S15371. $29.95.
Al Adamson, USA, 1972, 86 mins.

First Nudie Musical
One of the zaniest movies, which one-ups Mel Brooks and goes beyond. This double spoof of Hollywood musicals and porno pictures was directed by Bruce Kimmel, and involves an aging Hollywood studio on its last legs of decline. Now known for producing only cheap porno flicks like "Stewardesses in Chains," it is in danger of being turned into a supermarket when it's saved by Kimmel, who convinces the studio to make *The First Nudie Musical*. With Cindy Williams.
VHS: S07780. $29.95.
Bruce Kimmel, USA, 1975, 95 mins.

Flesh Gordon
An outrageous parody! The ads read, "Not to be confused with the original *Flash Gordon*." Flesh Gordon and his companion Dale Ardor save the Earth from the clutches of Emperor Wang, who has created chaos with a mysterious sex ray.
VHS: S00450. $29.95.
Howard Ziehm, USA, 1981, 70 mins.

The Flesh Merchant
Joy Reynolds, Guy Manford and Geri Moffat are featured in this exploitation movie about young girls living in shame. They find themselves organized into prostitution by vice lords. From Dan Sonney. 1955.
VHS: S23185. $24.95.

Forbidden Photographs
Charles Gatewood's *The Video* is the primary work of this documentary, with excursions into Manhattan's sexual underground, the Hellfire Club, Forbidden Tattoos, pierced genitals, Naked City and Mardi Gras Madness, with special appearances by Annie Sprinkle, Spider Webb, and Fakir Musafar. B&W and color. 100 mins.
VHS: S17075. $59.95.

Francis Goes to the Races
Francis the talking mule and Peter, played by Donald O'Connor, visit a breeding ranch where love and the good life are found for both these heros. But the ranch is terribly in debt, and only Francis and Peter can raise the money. Fortunately Francis has the inside scoop at the local racetrack.
VHS: S20943. $14.98.
Arthur Lubin, USA, 1951, 91 mins.

Francis in the Navy
This is Donald O'Connor's last appearance as the sidekick of a talking mule and he makes the best of it, appearing in two roles. The problem occurs when he tries to save Francis from being sold off as surplus. Also features a young Clint Eastwood.
VHS: S20945. $14.98.
Arthur Lubin, USA, 1955, 80 mins.

Francis Joins the WACS
Donald O'Connor (Peter) and Francis the talking mule find themselves transferred to a WAC base. This mix-up leads to all kinds of mayhem when the women of the WAC suspect this mistake is actually part of a plot. Oddly enough though, these two turn out to be good for morale in a funny sort of way.
VHS: S20944. $14.98.
Arthur Lubin, USA, 1954, 95 mins.

Francis the Talking Mule
This is the original movie, featuring Hollywood's first talking pack animal—sorry Mr. Ed. In this comedy Francis rescues his buddy, a private in the army, from behind enemy lines, proving that heroics are not the sole preserve of the two-legged species.
VHS: S20942. $14.98.
Arthur Lubin, USA, 1949, 91 mins.

Freaked
At the center of this wacky comedy is a child with unusually large ears. Branded a freak, he manages to get the best of all the kids and adults who would make fun of his unfortunate looks. With a face like his, laughing proves to be the only option.
VHS: S20714. $96.98.
Laser: LD74453. $39.98.
Tom Stern/Alex Winter, USA, 1993, 90 mins.

French Peek-a-Boo
A detective sniffs around a girlie theater and sees more than he ever hoped for in a three-ring circus of can-can girls, show girls, gangster scenarios and some of the most bizarre ballet dances ever filmed. France, 1959. French with English subtitles.
VHS: S23061. $19.98.

From Hollywood to Deadwood
Spine-tingling suspense as two down and out detectives look for a missing sultry starlet. With Scott Paulin and Jim Haynie.
VHS: S14700. $19.98.
Frank Strayer, USA, 1934, 63 mins.

Fugitive Road and Crime of Dr. Crespi
Two "B" movies starring Erich von Stroheim. *Fugitive Road* enabled von Stroheim to recreate his role in *Grand Illusion* in which he played a World War I Austrian officer. In *Crime of Dr. Crespi* he plays a mad scientist in a story loosely based on writings by Edgar Allan Poe.
VHS: S02321. $29.95.
John Auer, USA, 1935, 66 mins.

Gay Deceivers
Spoof in which two hunks try to avoid the draft by claiming to be homosexuals. They move into a gay apartment complex and the fun begins.
VHS: S02221. $59.95.
Bruce Kessler, USA, 1968, 97 mins.

Gentlemen Prefer Nature Girls
Gentlemen love the outdoors, and here we get to see them enjoying themselves in their natural habitat. Join them as they forage for wild berries in some of the most exotic bushes the world has to offer.
VHS: S15155. $19.98.

Ghosts on the Loose (East End Kids Meet Bela Lugosi)
Bela Lugosi plays the leader of a Nazi spy ring in this second meeting with the East End Kids. Huntz Hall and Leo Gorcey and their pals find plenty of slapstick, hidden passageways in a NYC mystery mansion filled with Nazi agents. Ava Gardner plays a newlywed. B&W.
VHS: S04009. $29.95.
William Beaudine, USA, 1943, 64 mins.

Girl Hunters
Mickey Spillane as Mike Hammer! Spillane, in his own creation, gleefully nails that hand of a killer to the floor in this story about a plot involving communist assassins. There's also a bit of booze and lots of beautiful dames. With Lloyd Nolan, Shirley Eaton, Scott Peters.
VHS: S09999. $29.95.
Roy Rowland, USA, 1963, 103 mins.

The Girl, the Body and the Pill
A beautiful, free-spirited health education instructor wants to enlighten her students on the joy of sexual responsibility. The loud objections of the parents and the community forces her instructions underground. The students naturally gravitate to her class in droves.
VHS: S20105. $24.95.
Herschell Gordon Lewis, USA, 1967, 80 mins.

Glitter Goddess of the Sunset Strip
Llana Lloyd's autobiographical, camp melodrama is an impressionistic assembly of Super 8mm home movie footage and period recreations. Lloyd tries to assess the emotional repercussions of her domineering mother's militant lesbian stance. "Mentally intense and satirical, this psycho shocker is shaped to emphasize the fascinating and fragile imperfections of human kind" (*Film Threat Magazine*). With Lloyd and Diane Nelson.
VHS: S18744. $69.99.
Dick Campbell, USA, 1992, 120 mins.

Go, Go, Go, Go World!
A sensational tour of the odd sights and wicked practices around the world in the tradition of *Mondo Cane*, including an Italian chastity belt store, baby exchanges, strippers, mud wrestlers, snake charmers and much more. For mature audiences only. English narration.
VHS: S13499. $24.95.
Marco Vicario/Anthony Dawson, Italy, 1964, 89 mins.

The Gorilla
Bela Lugosi replaced Peter Lorre in the role of Peters the sinister butler, in this Ritz Brothers comedy about a trio of klutzy private detectives out to capture a killer gorilla who escaped from a circus. Cast includes Patsy Kelly, Anita Louise and Lionel Atwill. B&W.
VHS: S04005. $29.95.
Allan Dwan, USA, 1939, 65 mins.

The Gruesome Twosome
Charming Mrs. Pringle and her sick son Rodney have a blossoming business—selling human hair wigs. In order to replenish their hair supply, they put up a "Room for Rent" sign. Just like at the Bates Motel, young women check in, but they never check out.
VHS: S15145. $19.98.
Herschell Gordon Lewis, USA, 1967, 72 mins.

Gun Is Loaded
Lydia Lunch delivers her brutally frank address of the true state of the union. This video super-realization trails her through New York City as she fires her spoken word manifesto. Identifying herself as "the all-American girl-next-door gone bad," Lydia excavates her own sustained damage as a product of this emotionally ravaging environment.
VHS: S12673. $29.95.

Hardcore: The Films of Richard Kern, Vol. 1
A compilation work of underground shorts including *You Killed Me First*, *Submit to Me* and *The Right Side of My Brain*, which features Lydia Lunch, Lung Lee, Henry Rollins and music by Foetus, Inc. 90 mins.
VHS: S17158. $29.95.

Hardcore: The Films of Richard Kern, Vol. 2
This collection of underground shorts will offend and provoke in equal measure, as cult filmmaker Richard Kern offers up his classic collaboration with Lydia Lunch, *Fingered*, *Evil Cameraman* and the short *Moneylove*. 90 mins.
VHS: S17159. $29.95.

Head
One of the cult films of the 60's, with the Monkees in a kaleidoscope of surreal vignettes, full of 60's psychedelia. Written and produced by Rafaelson (*Five Easy Pieces*) and Jack Nicholson.
VHS: S02531. $19.95.
Bob Rafelson, USA, 1968, 86 mins.

Hey Vern! It's My Family Album
Television commercial star Jim Varney in his persona of Ernest P. Worrell finds a family album in the attic and rushes over to share it with good neighbor Vern. The Worrell family flashbacks are preceded by ten memorable Ernest 'n Vern commercials. USA, 1986, 57 mins.
VHS: S00565. $19.95.

High School Caesar
John Ashley has the title role in this absurd slice of Americana, as a wealthy teenager with a burning passion to be the vicious overlord of an on-campus protection plan. Al preys on the lunch money and weekly allowances of the unwitting students.
VHS: S05187. $24.95.
O'Dale Ireland, USA, 1956, 75 mins.

High School Confidential
The incomparable Mamie van Doren stars in one of the truly great camp American films of the 1950's in which a tough-talking gang leader comes in contact with a drug ring and its leader—all in the surroundings of the all-American high school. A great rock musical score.
VHS: S00568. $14.98.
Laser: CLV LD71989. $29.98.
Jack Arnold, USA, 1958, 85 mins.

History of Pornography
The title says it all. Beginning with the erotic literature and drawings of China, Japan and India, the film moves through the first nude photos, comic books and stag films, to the hard-core films of the modern market. The photos, drawings and films are explicit.
VHS: S00574. $29.95.
Hons Wegmunsen, 64 mins.

The Hitler Tapes
This continuation of the compelling, voyeuristic fantasy *Even Hitler Had a Girlfriend* brings more beautiful women to the screen in a variety of kinky, exciting scenarios. From voyeurism to domination to a slow striptease, it's all here and it's all new. 60 mins.
VHS: S26206. $14.95.

Hollywood Dinosaur Chronicles
Doug McClure hosts this historical look back on Hollywood's fascination with the prehistoric. Clips include scenes from *King Kong*, *Godzilla*, *The Lost World*, *Baby* and *Gertie the Dinosaur*. Hear fascinating insights from paleontologists, special effects artists and folks like Charlie Chaplin and Arthur Conan Doyle. 42 mins.
VHS: S13287. $19.95.

The Hollywood Erotic Film Festival

Subtitled *Sexy Shorts of Another Kind*, this adult-oriented program showcases the stimulating works of some of the more daring young filmmakers. This tape does contain explicit animation and erotic special effects. Claims to be as much fun as people can have with their clothes on, so for a real thrill, watch it naked at home. 1987, 75 mins.
VHS: S03755. $59.95.

Hollywood Outtakes

Cinematic bloopers! A visit with Joan (*Mommie Dearest*) Includes Crawford at home with the kids, Bela Lugosi meeting Betty Boop, and W.C. Fields shooting a film during an earthquake.
VHS: S02100. $59.95.
Bruce Goldstein, USA, 1983, 84 mins.

The Hollywood Strangler Meets the Skid Row Slasher

Two perverse killers strike fear and malaise in the sleazy underside of Hollywood. A deranged loner tracks down models, under the pretense of photographing them, and summarily executes them. Ray Dennis Steckler's feature uses voice-over narration and eerie music. Also known as the *The Model Killer*. With Pierre Agostino and Carolyn Brandt.
VHS: S20146. $24.95.
Ray Dennis Steckler, USA, 1979, 72 mins.

Honky Tonk Girl (Highway Hell)

Mary Chauning is featured in this hilarious exploitation film, in the tradition of *Reefer Madness*. The story is about a hitch-hiking prostitution ring. Catching a lift has never been so much fun. 1937.
VHS: S23179. $24.95.

How to Make a Doll

Herschell Gordon Lewis' science-fiction sex comedy about a computer that creates beautiful women. A professor (Robert Wood) grows impatient after a series of orgies with computer-generated women and longs for the real thing. With his sight impaired, he falls for an unattractive woman whom the computer turns into a rabbit when he tells the computer she is his "dreamy bunny."
VHS: S20102. $24.95.
Herschell Gordon Lewis, USA, 1968

I Was a Teenage Serial Killer

Mary is a serial killer who will gladly kill off any annoying man. The result—she may be America's most popular serial killer. 30 mins.
VHS: S26013. $14.95.

The Immoral Three

A tempting trio of illegitimate sisters must avenge their mother's murder within one year to collect a million bucks each. But, as usual, where there's big money, there's big trouble. Double-crossing, triple-crossing and plenty of undressing ensues in Doris Wishman's action-packed "guns 'n' hooters" classic. I won't give away the ending, but…everybody gets killed. Sorry.
VHS: S15148. $19.98.
Doris Wishman, USA, 1965, 82 mins.

The Incredible Mr. Limpet

Don Knotts is just as patriotic as the next guy in this World War II comedy, but they won't let him aid the war effort until he magically turns into a talking fish and becomes a valuable secret weapon. The underwater sequences are animated and allow Knotts to win the heart of a very cute little female with fins. With Jack Weston, Carole Cook and Andrew Duggan.
VHS: S11662. $19.98.
Arthur Lubin, USA, 1964, 99 mins.

The Incredible Shrinking Woman

Lily Tomlin stars in this spoof of the original 50's film *The Incredible Shrinking Man*. She shrinks as a result of chemical pollution in the home and becomes an instant celebrity, only to find herself the target of a large corporation. Also features Charles Grodin and Ned Beatty.
VHS: S21765. $14.98.
Joel Schumacher, USA, 1981, 88 mins.

The Incredibly Strange Creatures Who Stopped Living and Became Mixed Up Zombies

A funky horror movie set in a sleazy roadside carnival about a deranged fortune teller who creates a series of grotesque monsters and imprisons them in the back of her tent. Problems ensue when a string of unsolved murders plague the carny. "Truly bizarre film features gorgeously saturated color, awful acting, hideous dialogue, haunting atmosphere and little plot" (Leonard Maltin). With Cash Flagg, Brett O'Hara, Atlas King, Sharon Walsh and Madison Clarke.
VHS: S20140. $24.95.
Ray Dennis Steckler, USA, 1963, 82 mins.

Iron Thunder

World championship fighter Anthony "Amp" Elmore stars in this thriller about an ambitious young street fighter trying to ascend to the top of the nefarious, corrupt, kickboxing world. 1989, 90 mins.
VHS: S18825. $19.95.

Jimmy, the Boy Wonder

A wickedly subversive "children's film" by cult specialist Herschell Gordon Lewis about a young boy whose soul becomes a battle ground for two magicians. One wants to control him by halting time, and the other tries to reverse the evil deed. The irreverent Lewis enlivens the material with some musical numbers and a half-hour of Italian cartoons blended into the narrative.
VHS: S20100. $24.95.
Herschell Gordon Lewis, USA, 1966

Jive Junction

Unpretentious, occasionally bizarre, World War II era "B" movie about a group of teens who play jitterbug music for the troops. Directed by the master of the "B" movies, screenplay by novelist Irving Wallace.
VHS: S02242. $24.95.
Edgar G. Ulmer, USA, 1943, 62 mins.

Just for the Hell of It

This is the ultimate teenage rebellion film. These kids are really mad—although it's hard to tell exactly why. Maybe it's because they're stoked up on grass, free sex and all that rock music. Roving gangs of teenagers head out onto the streets terrorizing everyone in their way: the old, the crippled, the blind, even infants can't escape their brutality. One question though: Didn't this town have any cops?
VHS: S15152. $19.98.
Herschell Gordon Lewis, USA, 1968, 88 mins.

King Kung Fu

A very funny take-off on King Kong in which Jungle Jumper, a gorilla raised as a lifelong house pet of a Chinese Karate Master, one day uses Kung Fu to attack and defeat him during a lesson. Embarrassed, the Master gets rid of the gorilla, who ends up in Wichita, Kansas, where Rae Fey, who sympathizes with the gorilla's fate, becomes his love interest.
VHS: S11475. $29.95.
Bill Hayes, USA, 1987, 78 mins.

Koroshi

The Secret Agent Movie, shot in color. Patrick McGoohan is Secret Agent John Drake, lured to the Orient by the revival of an ancient Japanese cult of death. Exciting martial arts adventure. 100 mins.
VHS: S09250. $59.95.

Las Vegas Serial Killer

A dark, ferocious urban thriller about a masochistic killer who is released from prison early and is set loose in Las Vegas, where he preys on showgirls and prostitutes. With Pierre Agostino, Ron Jason, Tara MacGowan and Kathryn Downey.
VHS: S20147. $24.95.
Ray Dennis Steckler, USA, 1985, 90 mins.

The Lemon Grove Kids

A surreal satire of the protective innocence of the Bowery Boys, by cult director Ray Dennis Steckler (aka Cash Flagg). Some demented, gross-out humor is the order of the day in this compilation work of three shorts: *The Lemon Grove Kids, Lemon Grove Kids Meet the Green Grasshopper* and *Lemon Grove Kids Go Hollywood*. Ray's dead-on impression of Huntz Hall is reportedly eerie. With Mike Cannon, Carolyn Brandt and Coleman Francis.
VHS: S20142. $24.95.
Ray Dennis Steckler, USA, 1966, 80 mins.

Living Venus

This is one nudie film that no one should miss, simply because it's Harvey Korman's first feature role. The tale of *Pagan Magazine*'s rise and fall, *Living Venus* stars Korman as the staff photographer. He and the magazine's obnoxious publisher are both after the cute cover girl. Who will she go for? Good, kind-hearted Harvey or the sleazebucket? Watch and see.
VHS: S15150. $19.98.
Herschell Gordon Lewis, USA, 1960, 87 mins.

Love Dolls Superstars

This bizarre sequel to *Desperate Teenage Love Dolls* considers the group's transformation and re-emergence in the alternative music scene. The plot includes elements of the supernatural, prostitution, assassination, religious overkill, genocide and space travel.
VHS: S16935. $39.95.

Lucky Pierre

This true cult-film classic stars Chicago vaudeville comedian Billy Falbo and hosts of naked women in five vignettes probably written before electricity. With such clever titles as "Drive-in Me Crazy" and "The Plumber's Friend," you can't help but love it. Plus you get the bonus short film "A Hot Night at the Go-Go Lounge." What a deal.
VHS: S15151. $19.98.
Herschell Gordon Lewis, USA, 1963, 73 mins.

Malamondo

This is another of the films made in the 60's that show the seamier sides of our planet. The Malamondo revealed—literally the bad world—is a strange place never before seen on video.
VHS: S23320. $24.95.
Paolo Cavara, Italy, 1963, 100 mins.

Maniac and Protect Your Daughter

Two cult films from the 1930's. *Maniac* begins like a horror film and then takes off in several directions around a plot in which a lunatic murders a scientist and takes his place experimenting on other psychotics. *Protect Your Daughter* presents a look at the flapper era under the guise of social consciousness.
VHS: S02319. $29.95.
Dwain Esper, USA, 1934, 115 mins.

Microwave Massacre

Jackie Vernon, a frugal GORE-met who likes his flesh done in a flash, loves women, especially between two slices of rye with lettuce and tomatoes. You'll develop a taste for this cannibalistic comedy as Jackie slices sensual sweeties into microwaveable morsels and seasons them with his own brand of horrific humor.
VHS: S14255. $59.95.
Wayne Berwick, USA, 1983, 76 mins.

Miss Melody Jones

A beautiful and talented young woman is exploited and thrown into the seedier underside of Hollywood in this chilling melodrama.
VHS: S18826. $19.95.
Bill Brame, USA, 197386 mins.

Mondo Africana (Original: Africana)

No, this is not just any mondo-sleazo film; this is historically important cinematic sleaze. Although supposedly a "serious" documentary, the filmmakers did go out of their way to film the weird and disgusting—safari hunts, initiation ceremonies, hot-coal walkers, people passing spears through their cheeks—and the narrator hams it up as much as possible. Narrated by Quentin Reynolds. For mature audiences only. USA, 80 mins.
VHS: S13501. $24.95.

Mondo Balardo

Boris Karloff narrates this superbly anachronistic addition to the Mondo movie genre. There is a midget rock and roll star, Japanese bondage, an Asian opium den, children coke addicts in Ecuador, a transvestite bar, and other customs that some consider bizarre. It's the film that is truly weird.
VHS: S23191. $24.95.
Robert Montero, USA, 1964, 86 mins.

Mondo Cane

Fascinating and repulsive! *Mondo Cane* was called the "most argued about film" when released in 1963, featured scenes of the bizarre, such as flagellation, nude painting, primitive rituals. French with English subtitles.
VHS: S00871. $29.98.
Gualtiero Jacopetti, Italy, 1963, 107 mins.

Mondo Cane 2

The controversial sequel to *Mondo Cane*, investigating the horrifying, weird, hideous and bizarre.
VHS: S08523. $59.95.
Gualtiero Jacopetti, Italy, 1964, 94 mins.

Mondo Sleazo (The World of Sleaze)

It's unbelievable, but true. Here are 50 trailers to some of the sleaziest movies ever made. Everything is here—drugs, racism, the supernatural, monsters, bikers…you name it. From the 30's to the 80's, this tape will take you on a guided tour of exploitation. Included are: *Love Life of a Gorilla, Maniac, Cocaine Fiends, The Smut Peddler, The Nine Ages of Nakedness, Violated Love, Werewolves on Wheels, Superchick* and literally dozens more. These movies are so slimy, you'll have to wash your hands after viewing this tape. 100 mins.
VHS: S13668. $29.95.

Moonshine Mountain

Herschell Gordon Lewis' baroque hillbilly cult film concerns a once-prominent country singer who returns home and gets caught up in the surreal intrigue of the community's two outlaw families and a corrupt sheriff, who own and operate the world's largest still. With Chuck Scott, Adam Sorg, Jeffrey Allen and Bonnie Hinson.
VHS: S20097. $24.95.
Herschell Gordon Lewis, USA, 1964, 90 mins.

More Moron Movies

An amusing, low-brow, satirical compilation of grade Z works dusted off for home video browsing. Produced by Len Cella, the titles include *Superman at the Psychiatrist, How to Get Fatter, The Bra Unhooking Champion* and *Broccoli Abuse*.
VHS: S02346. $19.95.
Len Cella, USA, 1986, 60 mins.

Moron Movies

Len Cella has brought over 100 comic short films together for this side-splitting compilation tape. *Animals Should Wear Underwear, Dreaded Wheat, Another Use for Dead Meat, How to Aggravate, The Advantage of Having Warts, Schitt for President, How to Exercise if You're Ugly, Exercise for Fat Ears, How to Clean the Toilet Without Gagging, The Truck Wrestler, A Turd Is a Man's Best Friend, King Dong* and *Another Use for Bad Presidents* are all included. 60 mins.
VHS: S23357. $19.95.
Len Cella, USA, 60 mins.

Movie in Your Face!

Described by its makers as "tasteless, sophomoric and hilarious," it's a frantic comedy in the mode of Woody Allen's *What's Up, Tiger Lily?* that combines and recombines several genres, blissfully speeding up the movies with a series of cameos and star turns. 1990, 85 mins.
VHS: S18160. $39.95.

Mr. Flathead

Rock and roll discord, mayhem and transformation are the quirky ideas and themes of this cult work about Howard, an unemployed, desperate and lonely man whose life is fundamentally altered when "rock and roll lightning strikes." 1992, 85 mins.
VHS: S18058. $19.95.

Murder by Television

Bela Lugosi plays two parts in this murder mystery, one of them being the investigator of the crime. A greedy businessman's attempt to corner the market on the secrets of a television machine are thwarted by a gadget that turns harmless electronic waves into death rays. B&W.
VHS: S03999. $29.95.
Clifford Sanforth, USA, 1935, 60 mins.

Mutant on the Bounty

It was a routine voyage for the spaceship USS Bounty until they beamed aboard a stranded musician named Max. This terrifically titled science fiction comedy explores the dangers of traveling standby in outer space. With Deborah Benson, John Furey, Victoria Catlin. Highly praised by Joe Bob Briggs, the drive-in movie critic.
VHS: S11580. $14.95.
Robert Torrance, USA, 1989, 93 mins.

The Muthers

Set in a desolate South American jungle, Jayne Kennedy is the mistress of a corrupt warden, who orchestrates a daring liberation of women prisoners to escape the harsh living conditions.
VHS: S18827. $29.95.
Cirio H. Santiago, USA, 1976, 101 mins.

My Sweet Satan

Cult director Jim Van Bebber concocts a tale of violence, drugs and heavy metal in this story of Satan worship run amok. A remastered version of *Roadkill: The Last Days of John Martin* and the druggie documentary *Doper* are also included on this video. 60 mins.
VHS: S26012. $24.95.

Naked Venus

A boy and a girl torn apart just because she's a nudist? Can they sweep aside the barriers of prejudice and find true happiness in the buff? With Patricia Conelle.
VHS: S12315. $24.95.
Edgar G. Ulmer, USA, 1958, 80 mins.

Naked Youth

A great exploitation film in which Mamie Van Doren hosts this classic featuring psycho-teens who escape from juvenile prison, flee to Mexico for a head-on collision with deadly drugs and dangerous dolls.
VHS: S05198. $24.95.
John F. Schreyer, USA, 1959, 80 mins.

The Narcotic Story

Art Gilmore narrates this lurid expose about the evils of heroin addiction. Originally intended for police seminars only, it was then released to the general public with a sensational ad campaign. The images of burned-out heroin addicts are campily overdone.
VHS: S23186. $24.95.
Robert W. Larsen, USA, 1958, 75 mins.

Nation Aflame and Probation

Two rare films from the 1930's. *Nation Aflame* (Victor Halperin, USA, 1937, 78 mins.) is an indictment against the Ku Klux Klan and Naziism, and remains relevant today. *Probation* (Richard Thorpe, USA, 1932, 70 mins.) features the first screen appearance of Betty Grable, and is a blend of 30's exploitation and social commentary.
VHS: S02320. $29.95.

National Lampoon's Class of '86

Satiric musical comedy revue.
VHS: S03467. $29.95.
Jerry Adler, USA, 1986, 86 mins.

National Lampoon's European Vacation

The sequel to *Vacation* also stars Chevy Chase as the head of the Griswald family, which wreaks havoc wherever it goes. With Eric Idle.
VHS: S10051. $19.98.
Laser: LD74711. $34.98.
Amy Heckerling, USA, 1985, 94 mins.

Naughty Nostalgia #1

Presented as a historical curiosity are two stag films from the 1920's. More amusing than arousing. Nobody takes off their shoes. Ask your grandfather if he remembers the titles *Mixed Relations* or *Bob's Hot Story*. These silent films are for adults only. USA, 1923, 38 mins.
VHS: S05512. $24.95.

Naughty Nostalgia #2

More stag films from the past. These three titles are from the late 1930's. *The Babysitter, The Opium Den* and *A Day in the Country* all provide nostalgia and nudity. Includes "Nightmare," the ugliest woman ever to appear in a porno movie. These are silent films with a musical score. Adults only. ID's will be required. USA, late 1930's, 42 mins.
VHS: S05513. $24.95.

Night of the Day of the…

Influenced by Woody Allen's *What's Up Tiger Lilly?*, director Lowell Mason has reimagined George Romero's horror masterpiece *Night of the Living Dead* as a burlesque comedy, reshaping the original soundtrack and mixing in new voices and dialogue to alter everyone's perception of the original. "Hilarious, the new cult hit of the 90s is recast with a new soundtrack" (*Mortal Remains*).
VHS: S18241. $34.95.
Lowell Mason, USA, 1992, 90 mins.

Nude on the Moon

Two rocket scientists use Uncle Ted's inheritance to fly to the moon, where they discover a population of nudist "moon dolls" with pipe-cleaner antennae growing out of their bouffant hairdos. Features the classic romantic ballad, "I'm Mooning over You, My Little Moon Doll," and some of the strangest see-through, dirt-brown panties ever witnessed on any creature in the known universe. Written, directed and produced by Doris Wishman. This is one of Ms. Wishman's least favorite films, "because the people are so ugly."
VHS: S15138. $19.98.
Doris Wishman, USA, 1961, 78 mins.

Olga's House of Shame

Olga, the ultimate sadist, moves her headquarters from Chinatown to upstate New York, where she controls a crime syndicate involving narcotics, prostitution and jewel smuggling. An infamous work of sleaze. USA, 1964.
VHS: S23062. $19.98.

One Body Too Many

Bela Lugosi plays a sinister servant in this murder mystery with comedic trimmings. Plot concerns an insurance salesman (Jack Haley) hired to guard the body of an eccentric millionaire overnight. With Lyle Talbot, Jean Parker and Blanche Yurka. B&W.
VHS: S04010. $29.95.
Frank McDonald, USA, 1944, 76 mins.

One Plus One

Leo G. Carroll and Hilda Brauner are featured in this dramatization of the *Kinsey Report*. After participating interviewees talk about it, they go on to do it. Five tales are shown tackling such issues as premarital sex, divorce, affairs and child-bearing.
VHS: S23188. $24.95.
Arch Oboler, USA, 1961, 114 mins.

Palm Springs Weekend

Guys with crew cuts, girls with flips, cars with fins, and fun, fun, fun, as eager young holidaymakers mix and mingle. Starring Troy Donahue, Stefanie Powers, Robert Conrad and Connie Stevens in tight gold lame.
VHS: S12581. $19.98.
Norman Taurog, USA, 1959, 101 mins.

Phantom of Paradise

Outrageous horror-rock comedy featuring pop musician Paul Williams as a notorious record tycoon who sells his soul to the devil for success. William Finley stars as a rock composer victim of an accident that leaves him disfigured and blaming Williams. Macabre and a bit bizarre.
VHS: S01018. $14.98.
Brian DePalma, USA, 1974, 92 mins.

Planet of the Apes
Astronaut Charlton Heston crash lands on a distant world where he finds that human beings are not the dominant species. The novel by Pierre Boulle was adapted for the screen by Rod Serling and Michael Wilson and won a Special Oscar for its outstanding achievement in make-up. Kim Hunter, Roddy McDowall, Maurice Evans, and James Whitmore are some of the stars in simian suits. Followed by four sequels and a couple of TV shows.
VHS: S12171. $19.98.
Franklin J. Schaffner, USA, 1968, 112 mins.

Please Don't Eat My Mother
A sexy remake of the cult classic *Little Shop of Horrors*. This time around, our nerdy hero winds up feeding his plant the bodies of dead lovers. Starring Rene Bond and Buck Kartalian.
VHS: S12314. $24.95.
Carl Monson, USA, 1971, 95 mins.

Pope Must Diet
The original release title did not include the letter "t" in the last word. Robbie Coltrane, a former "Nun on the Run," now upsets the religious community by becoming pope by mistake. With Beverly D'Angelo, Herbert Lom, Paul Bartel, and Alex Rocco as Cardinal Rocco. A good hearted satire with a very controversial title. Watch for *Cinema Paradiso* star Salvatore Cascio as an adorable urchin.
VHS: S15508. $92.98.
Peter Richardson, Great Britain, 1991, 87 mins.

Portrait of a White Marriage
Martin Mull is back in another acerbic satire made for cable TV. As the host of a small town talk show he becomes involved with a local married housewife and is asked to participate in the Founder's Day Parade. With longtime sidekick Fred Willard and "Mary Hartman" co-star Mary Kay Place. Also Jack Riley, Michael McKean, Harry Shearer and Conchata Ferrell. Co-written and co-produced by Mull.
VHS: S08324. $39.95.
Harry Shearer, USA, 1988, 101 mins.

Prehistoric Bimbos in Armageddon City
Old Chicago City is the last outpost of civilization but it is ruled by the evil Nemesis. The prehistoric bimbos, led by Trianna, are the only threat to his evil rule. This wacky film is filled with great action and beautiful but tough women.
VHS: S24593. $19.95.
Todd Sheets, USA, 1993, 70 mins.

Prehistoric Women
The original stone age sex kittens epic that started it all. Filmed in "sin-scope" and "gorgeous cine-color."
VHS: S10057. $9.95.
Greg Tallas, USA, 1950, 74 mins.

The Prime Time
A beautiful, street-smart woman finds herself caught in a sleazy adult world she can't fully handle and seeks out the help of a grim detective she meets at the house of a beatnik artist to save her soul.
VHS: S20104. $24.95.
Herschell Gordon Lewis, USA, 1960, 76 mins.

The Psychic
James F. Hurley's critique of celebrity. After an accident, Dan Thomas learns he has psychic capabilities. The power turns him into a sexual predator, as he uses his skills to coerce and manipulate people. He has a series of affairs, leaves his wife and daughter and becomes famous performing a psychic nightclub act. He goes on television and defames a well-known movie star who doubts his powers by declaring she is a lesbian. With Dick Genoa, Robin Guest and Carol Saenz.
VHS: S20103. $24.95.
James F. Hurley, USA, 1968

Puss Bucket
A controversial reconsideration of a biblical tale, framed as a musical comedy, about two dimwitted brothers who are enlisted to "kill for Jesus," and the mayhem that ensues. Billed as "from the Broadway musical." With Terrence Fleming, Eric Hammer, Brian Sullivan and Gina Cammarotta. Directed and photographed by Lisa Houle.
VHS: S18108. $14.95.

Puzzle Channel, Vol. 1
A series of brain teasers that include picture puzzles, wordies, logic problems, number problems and other useless and unconventional tests. 60 mins.
VHS: S13094. $19.98.

Puzzle Channel, Vol. 2
A series of brain teasers that include murder mysteries, picture puzzles, wordies, logic problems, number problems and more. 60 mins.
VHS: S13095. $19.98.

Rat Fink a Boo-Boo
A stylized parody of the kitsch 60s television series *Batman* features an inept superhero and his sidekick thrust into a series of perilous situations and life-saving adventures. With Vin Saxon, Carolyn Brandt, Titus Moede and Mike Kannon.
VHS: S20143. $24.95.
Ray Dennis Steckler, USA, 1966, 72 mins.

Red
The visual equivalent of the red tape, this perverse work stars the legendary B-actor Lawrence Tierney in a piece about the damaging repercussion of phone hoaxes. 30 mins.
VHS: S17164. $19.95.

Red Nightmare
The now-famous anti-communist propaganda film, produced for the Defense Department by Warner Brothers, as a small-town American finds his community taken over by communists. Narrated by Jack Webb.
VHS: S04717. $29.95.
George Waggner, USA, 1962, 25 mins.

Reefer Madness
This anti-marijuana propaganda film has become a cult classic. Dave O'Brien plays a twitchy, eye-rolling lunatic who sits around talking to himself as he chain smokes the dreaded weed.
VHS: S01102. $19.95.
Louis Gasnier, USA, 1939, 65 mins.

Reform School Girl
A lurid tale about a confused though essentially warm young woman and her self-destructive descent into prison following a hit-and-run murder. With Gloria Castillo, Ross Ford, Edward Byrnes and Sally Kellerman.
VHS: S18362. $9.95.
Edward Bernds, USA, 1957, 71 mins.

Ride the Wild Surf
One of the quintessential early 60s beach movies about young men in Hawaii in search of women and fun. Jan and Dean sing the title cut. With Fabian, Tab Hunter, Barbara Eden and James Mitchum.
VHS: S18361. $14.95.
Don Taylor, USA, 1964, 101 mins.

Robert Ripley: Believe It or Not
Ripley was a cartoonist, a collector, an explorer, an adventurer, a millionaire and a decided eccentric. This is the first in-depth look at the man who brought oddities to a world-wide audience. In this portrait amazing facts like his morbid fear of the telephone (he thought he would be electrocuted) come to light.
VHS: S21746. $14.98.

Rock 'n' Roll Mobster Girls
A fledgling all-girl band (performed and played by the notorious Doll Squad) is led into a Faustian pact with Bruno Multrock, a psychotic promoter who will stop at nothing to be the group's sole promoter. 110 mins.
VHS: S16934. $79.95.

Rock, Baby, Rock It
A rare 50's rock 'n' roll teenage film, hosted by Mamie Van Doren, and featuring 17 songs by obscure early rock legends like Kay Wheeler and rockabilly wildman Johnny Carroll.
VHS: S05199. $9.95.
Murray Douglas Sporup, USA, 1957, 84 mins.

Rockin' Ronnie
America's leading man and our most colorful president to date is the subject of this hilarious, tongue-in-cheek scrapbook, prepared by the creators of the Nightflight program. The off-the-wall comic collection includes such bits as *The Pilot*, *The Detergent Salesmen*, *The Conductor*, *The Gangster*, *The Ballroom Dancer*, *The Actor*. 45 mins.
VHS: S06590. $29.95.

Rocky Horror Picture Show
Now you can do the Time Warp in the privacy of your own home. The cult movie of cult movies is finally available in the U.S. on video. When Brad and Janet are forced to spend the night at the foreboding castle of the sexually ambitious Dr. Frank;+xFurter, they had no idea so many people would stay up late to watch them squirm. With Tim Curry, Barry Bostwick, Susan Sarandon, Richard O'Brien, Meatloaf and Little Nell.
VHS: S14008. $19.98.
Jim Sharman, USA, 1975, 105 mins.

Samurai
A hilarious spy-exploitation film about a Japanese orphan, raised in America, who turns traitor and helps plot the invasion of California. With Paul Fung and Luke Chan.
VHS: S15361. $29.95.
Raymond Cannon, USA, 1946, 62 mins.

Satan in High Heels
Meg Myles and Sabrina Grayson Hall star in this melodrama that exploits the femme fatale image. Meg is a full-figured stripper who ditches her drug-dependent husband and steals $900 from him on the way out. With her booty, she is off to New York, where an older man, and then his son, fall victim to her charms. Eventually she tries to get her forsaken husband to knock off the old codger.
VHS: S23189. $24.95.
Jerald Intrator, USA, 1962, 90 mins.

Schramm
Nekromantik's director Jorg Buttgereit depicts the world of a serial killer in this hypnotizing orgy of sex and violence. It's all seen through the eyes of the killer, Lothar Schramm (Florian Koemer von Gustorf). He is fascinated by a prostitute (Monika M.) and obsessed with death. The result is a well-crafted, surreal vision of love and desire.
VHS: S27510. $29.95.
Jorg Buttgereit, Germany, 90 mins.

Scum of the Earth
An innocent woman is tricked into posing nude for a brutal gang of rednecks. After she is ruthlessly exploited to increase sales of the magazine, she is sexually harassed by one of its members and saved by another of the group.
VHS: S20106. $24.95.
Herschell Gordon Lewis, USA, 1963, 71 mins.

Secrets of Love, Classics of Erotic Literature: Vol. 1
This series of erotic stories is based on works by some of the greatest authors of all time. *The Greenhouse*, by Guy de Maupassant, is a tale of voyeurism. An older couple find their lost passion by watching a younger pair. In *A Country Villa*, adapted from Anton Chekhov's story, a man and wife are captivated by the women of a Turkish-style brothel. 58 mins.
VHS: S23292. $19.95.

Secrets of Love, Classics of Erotic Literature: Vol. 2
The Marquis de Sade's *Augustine* begins this volume of arousing stories. The title character is reputed to be a lesbian until one night when she seduces a man at a ball. In *At the Rose Leaf*, by Guy de Maupassant, a man and his wife find themselves charmed by the same delights. 57 mins.
VHS: S23293. $19.95.

Secrets of Love, Classics of Erotic Literature: Vol. 3
Mandragora, by Niccolo Machiavelli, and *The Contest*, by Geoffrey Chaucer, are adapted in this volume of sexy tales. In the first story a young medical student gets his way with a chaste and virtuous wife through a powerful drug. Then students try to take advantage of an old man with a beautiful wife, leading to surprising consequences. 57 mins.
VHS: S23294. $19.95.

Secrets of Love, Classics of Erotic Literature: Vol. 4
This erotic series brings a unique level of sophistication to romance and sex through well-produced stories written by famous authors. This volume features *The Spanking* by Marguerite de la Navarre and *The Pupil* by Nicolas de la Bretonne. In *The Spanking*, a pretty weaver girl plots revenge against someone who humiliated her. In *The Pupil*, a rich uncle finds that his chambermaids can give his nephew a much needed education.
VHS: S27085. $19.95.
Pierre Grimblat, France, 56 mins.

Secrets of Love, Classics of Erotic Literature: Vol. 5
In Guiseppe Celentano's *The Test of Love*, an heir to the Duke of Mantua must prove his manhood before he can wed a Medici woman. This man must demonstrate his virility with a virgin before several witnesses. In *A Well Deserved Punishment* by Giovanni Boccaccio, a rich merchant tries to control his overly amorous wife.
VHS: S27086. $19.95.
Pierre Grimblat, France, 56 mins.

Secrets of Love, Classics of Erotic Literature: Vol. 6
Jean de la Fontaine's *The Wager of Three Wives* follows three women who engage in adulterous love. *Lady Roxanne*, from Daniel Defoe, concerns a beautiful but poor Lady who must consider the use of her most cherished asset quite carefully. Ingenuity and compromise ensure that contentment is achieved by all concerned, even the Lady's landlord.
VHS: S27087. $19.95.
Pierre Grimblat, France, 56 mins.

Sex and the College Girl
Charles Grodin stars in this campy tale of free love and manipulation set on the sands of Puerto Rico. Two college girls head off on a vacation with definite plans—one wants to get married, and one wants to get lucky. Both are in for a big surprise in this tale of sex, sleaziness, lost virginity and lacking morals.
VHS: S15146. $19.98.
Joseph Adler, USA, 1964, 90 mins.

Sex Education Films of the 40's
Five short films include *Dating Do's and Don'ts*, *USS-VD: The Ship of Shame*, and *Know for Sure*.
VHS: S02586. $34.95.

Sex in the Comics
Live characters re-create all the flamboyant, erotic comics from the 1930's and 1940's.
VHS: S01186. $24.95.
Eric von Letch, USA, 1982, 70 mins.

Sex Madness
Duncey Taylor. Wild dancing and heavy duty makeout sessions lead young ones to pregnancy, social diseases, drugs and even death. Syphilitic madness is the ultimate evil depicted here. This film has all the hallmarks of an enduring exploitation classic. 1937, 50 mins.
VHS: S23176. $24.95.

The Shadow Strikes
Rod La Rocque stars as the famous radio crime fighter who knows what evil lurks in the hearts of men. As a sleuthing lawyer with a secret identity, he stalks a mysterious killer and a gangster chief. All the while the police are trying to pin the crimes on his alter-ego. With Lynn Anders and Walter McGrail. B&W.
VHS: S03338. $39.95.
Lynn Shores, USA, 1937, 61 mins.

She Shoulda Said No
Lila Leeds, Lyle Talbot, Alan Baxter and Jack Elam are the best cast ever assembled in exploitation film history. There are still more horrors caused by marijuana that have not been fully explored elsewhere. Leeds made this film to atone for a real-life marijuana incident. 1949.
VHS: S23182. $24.95.

She-Devils on Wheels
This cult classic was the first feminist biker movie; the story of the "Man Eaters" gang proves that women can slap men around and use them for sexual meat too. Portrayed by real lady bikers from an organization out of Miami called the "Cut-Throats." Watch for the famous "stud line" scene, and always remember the Man-Eaters' motto: "Sex, Guts, Blood, and all men are Mothers!" Directed by Herschell Gordon Lewis, who fashioned a career out of exploiting the forbidden, the tasteless, and the bizarre.
VHS: S15140. $19.98.
Herschell Gordon Lewis, USA, 1968, 90 mins.

Slave Trade in the World Today
Allen Swift narrates this mondo movie, which documents slavery in the contemporary world. Whole tribes sold into bondage, an auction for a rich shiek's harem, and a variety of brutal practices are revealed in this shocking film.
VHS: S23318. $24.95.
Roberto Malenotti, USA, 1964, 87 mins.

Slaves in Bondage
Lona Andre, Donald Reed, Wheeler Oakman and Florence Dudley are featured in this exploitation classic about the perils of prostitution. Young, innocent, country girls are lured into the big city and recruited into a life of ill repute. Spankings, catfights, alcohol abuse and other unsavory goings-on make this a must-see. 1937.
VHS: S23175. $24.95.

Sleazemania
This compilation tape features highlights and previews from some of the sleaziest and sickest movies of all time. It includes only the very best from classics like *Jailbait Babysitters*, *The Flesh Merchants*, *The Young Seducers* and more. 60 mins.
VHS: S26328. $19.95.

Sleazemania Strikes Back
More outrageous highlights and previews have been combined on this over-the-top compilation videotape. Includes footage from *College Girls Confidential*, *Suburban Roulette*, *Beach Blanket Bloodbath* and more. 60 mins.
VHS: S26330. $19.95.

Sleazemania: The Good, the Bad and the Sleazy
There are more clips and previews from schlocky classics on this third *Sleazemania* video. Lenny Bruce in *Dance Hall Racket*, *Striporama*, *Teenage Zombies* and exploitative delights are represented. 60 mins.
VHS: S26329. $19.95.

Something Weird
A disfigured man with psychic abilities meets a witch who will give him back his beautiful face in exchange for a little action. The next thing you know, we're in Wisconsin trying to solve a serial murder case and tripping on LSD. A must-see if only for the possessed, killer bed sheets scene.
VHS: S15149. $19.98.
Herschell Gordon Lewis, USA, 1967, 87 mins.

Sorority Babes in the Dance-a-thon of Death
Sorority women conjure a demon from an ancient crystal ball. Now two nerdy but randy boys are their only hope in fighting this evil. A great shlocky film with a finale set in a disco.
VHS: S24592. $19.95.
Todd Sheets, USA, 1994, 75 mins.

Spooks Run Wild
Bela Lugosi meets the East End Kids during a holiday in the country. Leo Gorcey, Huntz Hall and Co. believe the creepy guy in the cape and evening clothes is the notorious Monster, and boy, are they scared. Lugosi's midget assistant is played by Angelo Rossitto (*Mad Max beyond Thunderdome*). B&W.
VHS: S04006. $29.95.
Phil Rosen, USA, 1941, 69 mins.

Squeal of Death
Cast somewhere between Monty Python and MAD, from the criminally funny minds of young filmmakers Tom Stern and Alex Winter, this program contains three short comedies, including *Aisles of Doom* and *Cherub*.
VHS: S17165. $14.95.

Star Shorts
A six-part dose of comedy vignettes starring Bill Murray, his brother Brian Doyle-Murray, Bobcat Goldthwait, Griffin Dunne and Dom DeLuise. 60 mins.
VHS: S13096. $59.98.

Stewardess School
The *Police Academy* of the skies, with the wild parties, coed showers and the usual mishaps.
VHS: S04692. $79.95.
Ken Blancato, USA, 1986, 84 mins.

Stick It in Your Ear
David awakens in a gothic building and can't remember how he got there. He wanders through the delirious freedom of the counterculture, consuming drugs and free love in vast quantities. David's absence of an identity leads to his transformation to a cold-hearted assassin. A shadow group hires him to kill a woman, but he would rather have sex with her. With Guido Conte, Lance Revson and Michelle Most.
VHS: S20098. $24.95.
Charles Morgan, USA, 1970

Story of O
The adaptation of the famous novel describing the process of love through discipline and obedience, from the director of *Emmanuelle*. English dubbed.
VHS: S01515. $49.95.
Just Jaeckin, France, 1975, 96 mins.

The Strange Hostel of Naked Pleasures
In a haunted hostel the perverse and unnatural desires of its guests leap out of the dream world to haunt their waking hours. Bizarre scenarios characterize this horror film of surrealistic terror. Portuguese with English subtitles.
VHS: S20750. $24.95.
Marcello Motta, Brazil, 1975

Striporama

The greats of Burlesque, including Sally Rand doing her classic *Bubble Dance*, Betty Rowland *The Ball of Fire*, Virginia Bell, Tempest Storm, Scarlett Knight, Helene Renee, in a classic review of the great days of Burlesque. USA, 50 mins.
VHS: S04846. $29.95.
Jerald Intrator, USA, 1953, 65 mins.

Suburban Roulette

In 1967 wife-swapping was a taboo subject, even in the movies. So this morality tale about the steamy underside of suburban living was considered lurid and shocking—especially in its depiction of two housewives who are addicted to sex. Made on an extremely low budget, it's so rough around the edges that, in a fight scene, one of the punches misses entirely, but the intended target falls down anyway. Produced and directed by Herschell Gordon Lewis, a Chicago advertising man turned exploitation filmmaker.
VHS: S15139. $19.98.
Herschell Gordon Lewis, USA, 1967, 91 mins.

Superman & the Mole Men

In his first Superman full-length feature, the Man of Steel investigates when curious creatures from the bowels of the Earth surface through an oil-well shaft. Starring George Reeves.
VHS: S06245. $14.95.
Lee Sholem, USA, 1951, 58 mins.

Surf Nazis Must Die

A camp film with a great title in which, in the wake of a killer earthquake, the beaches of California have been taken over by neo-Nazi punks. Their reign of terror comes to a halt when a retired, fat black woman with a .38 stops them dead!
VHS: S05894. $79.95.
Peter George, USA, 1987, 83 mins.

A Taste of Blood

American cult filmmaker Herschell Gordon Lewis directed this off-center *Dracula* variation about an American who is transformed into a night prowler after swallowing a strange potion. The action shifts from the American Southwest to London, where the stalker goes on a diabolical killing spree. He is pursued by the avenging Dr. Helsing. Screenplay by Donald Stanford. With Bill Rogers, Elizabeth Wilkinson, Thomas Wood and Otto Schlesinger.
VHS: S20095. $24.95.
Herschell Gordon Lewis, USA, 1967, 120 mins.

Teaserama: David Friedman's Roadshow Rarities, Vol. 1

A fascinating underground history on the origins of the exploitation film, showcasing the extraordinary Betty Page in a collection of erotic vignettes and burlesque madness, opposite the self-named Tempest Storm, Cherry Knight, Honey Baer, Trudy Wayne and Chris La Chris.
VHS: S18439. $24.95.

Teenage Confidential

Wild youth set free with violent passions. They were too young to know any better. Highlights from the greatest and greasiest teen flicks ever made are merged with previews and an in-depth interview on teenage delinquency taken from newsreels and government scare films of the 40s and 50s. 60 mins.
VHS: S05185. $24.95.

Teenage Devil Dolls

Mamie Van Doren hosts this "tough" teen film, with the Devil Dolls. Young Cassandra joins a crazy gang where she starts on reefer, graduates to goofballs, and is soon found groveling in garbage, looking for a fix. Naturally, this lands her in the psycho ward, and eventually back on the streets.
VHS: S05204. $24.95.
B. Lawrence Price, USA, 1953, 70 mins.

Teenage Strangler

Bill Posner's funky variation of the juvenile delinquent angst drama follows the deranged activities of a lipstick killer who is suffocating schoolgirls with stockings in Huntington, West Virginia. A member of a local gang called the Fastdogs, Jimmy is a prime suspect. The film weaves in the social protest and outlaw behavior of the 60s B-movie (including drag races, rumbles and rock and roll) within the trappings of the serial killer movie. With Bill A. Bloom, Jo Canterbury and John Ensign.
VHS: S20108. $24.95.
Bill Posner, USA, 1964, 64 mins.

Terror of Tiny Town

One of the classic camp films: a musical Western enacted entirely by midgets. One of the wonders of Hollywood. With Billy Curtis, Yvonne Moray, Little Billy, John Bambury.
VHS: S03056. $19.95.
Sam Newfield, USA, 1963, 63 mins.

They Saved Hitler's Brain

One of the great cult classics: a scientist is kidnapped; his daughter traces him to the mysterious island of Mandoras where a cult of Nazi worshippers is manipulated by the severed head of Adolf. 74 mins.
VHS: S05381. $29.95.

They Wear No Clothes

Where this film is lacking under its pretense as a sociological study, *They Wear No Clothes* makes up in bravado. Not too long on commentary, the film examines those who—by choice or profession—choose to undress. Includes the bonus short, *How to Hold a Husband*. 1941, 55 mins.
VHS: S15913. $19.95.

The Third Sex

Paula Wesley and Paul Dahlke star in this exploitative look at homosexuality. Parents try to straighten out their son, who is hanging out with a known gay man. It's a shocker. 1959.
VHS: S23187. $24.95.

This Nude World

The film that puts the "camp" into Nudist Camp. Travel on a world tour from Camp Olympia in New York (home of the weekend volleyball enthusiasts) to France, Germany and other fun spots on the naked globe. 55 mins.
VHS: S12316. $24.95.

This Stuff'll Kill You

A Herschell Gordon Lewis epic with religious overtones follows the anarchic adventures of some mountain rednecks who set in motion a violent chain of events under the influence of some white lightning.
VHS: S20099. $24.95.
Herschell Gordon Lewis, USA, 1971, 100 mins.

The Thrill Killers

Director Ray Dennis Steckler (aka Cash Flagg) made this grubby shocker about a band of marauders who randomly terrorize wealthy Los Angeles suburbs and kill indiscriminately. With Cash Flagg, Liz Renay, Brick Bardo, Carolyn Brandt and Atlas King.
VHS: S20141. $24.95.
Ray Dennis Steckler, USA, 1965, 82 mins.

Ticket of Leave Man

Tod Slaughter, the horror man of Europe, enacts the role of Tiger Dalton. By day, a respected benefactor for an organization dedicated to help ex-convicts. By night, the head of a criminal syndicate. When the police find out, he is chased through a cemetery. Watch out for open graves. With Marjorie Edwards, John Warwick and Jenny Lynn.
VHS: S04044. $29.95.
George King, Great Britain, 1937, 71 mins.

Tokyo Decadence

Japanese novelist and filmmaker Ryu Murakami adapts his novel *Topaz*, about a prostitute's (Miho Nikaido) search for redemption. Ai falls under the spell of a charismatic dominatrix and tries desperately to reverse her slide into cocaine dependency and sexual slavery. "Murakami adeptly throws us off balance, with deadpan black humor and a complex politic involving the notion of 'wealth without price'" (Toronto Film Festival). With Sayoko Amano, Tenmei Kanou and Masahiko Shimada. Japanese with English subtitles.
VHS: S19176. $29.95.
Ryu Murakami, Japan, 1991, 112 mins.

Too Much, Too Often

A gritty sexual parable from master director Doris Wishman. Women driven to the depths of degradation by the insistent burning of their outsized sexual pangs. The flavor of this film is every bit as enjoyable as its considerable stench.
VHS: S15157. $19.98.
Doris Wishman, USA, 1965

Tower of the Screaming Virgins

The notorious Countess Marguerite stages orgies in her castle and then brutally murders her lovers in this lavish French horror tale featuring equal doses of blood and nudity. USA, 1968, 90 mins.
VHS: S01652. $24.95.

Trader Hornee

A bawdy sex and jungle romp written by David F. Friedman that turns into a hilarious parody of the genre, about a sexy young detective hired to track down the missing heir of the late African explorer and help settle the family estate. What she discovers is everyone is consumed by sex and greed.
VHS: S17038. $29.95.
Tsanusdi, USA, 1970, 72 mins.

Trip to Where?

This outrageous discourse on the evils of LSD was produced by the United States Navy. A group of innocent, upstanding sailors are led astray and experience acid trips that inevitably turn bad (but not quite as bad as the film itself). Highlights include some nice photographic special effects and sexy, young Vic Tayback in a gripping cameo performance as a drug kingpin (before he went legit, opened Mel's Diner and hired Linda Lavin). USA, 56 mins.
VHS: S15386. $24.95.

Truly Tasteless Jokes: The Video

Based on the best-selling books compiled by Blanche Knott.
VHS: S04503. $9.98.

Uptown Angel

A stern moral fable with a taut, realistic texture about a promising young actress unable to realize her dreams, who falls into a deadly cycle of prostitution, drugs and violence.
VHS: S18838. $19.95.
Jay Shannon, USA, 1990, 90 mins.

Vampire Vixens from Venus

Hideous in their original form, three alien drug smugglers transform into beautiful women on Earth. Their drug is derived from the life essence of men and they're on a mission to drain every last drop. A funny sexy sci-fi thriller.
VHS: S23048. $69.95.
Ted A. Bohus, USA, 1994, 90 mins.

Varietease: David Friedman's Roadshow Rarities, Vol. 2

A color exercise in the art and beauty of the striptease act, with world champion Betty Page taking on all rivals, including Lili St. Cyr, Chris La Chris and Vicki Lynn in the title for Anatomy Award of 1955.
VHS: S18440. $24.95.

Vegas in Space

Drag Queens bring Vegas glamour to an intergalactic battle of outsized proportions. Well, the proportions of the miniature sets are all too obvious, but then so is the drag in this campy, overacted farce. An all-women planet is thrown out of whack by a dastardly crime. Two earth astronauts are sent to help, but there is one condition. They must become women to enter this feminine planet. The rest is showbiz herstory. Features the late Doris Fish.
VHS: S27624. $69.98.
Phillip R. Ford, USA, 1991, 85 mins.

Video from Hell

A sneak preview of upcoming Frank Zappa video releases. Including "Uncle Meat," a project started in 1967 with Haskell Wexler as the cinematographer. Clay animation by Bruce Bickford. The videos "G-Spot Tornado", "You Are What You Is", "St. Etienne". Also the true story of *200 Motels* and *Baby Snakes*.
VHS: S04970. $29.95.
Frank Zappa, USA, 1987, 60 mins.

Village of the Giants

A cult classic loosely adapted from H.G. Wells' story about a group of teenagers who experiment with chemical substances. They develop a mysterious food which severely alters their appearance. The teenagers are transformed into walking giants, and proceed to terrorize their community. With Tommy Kirk, Johnny Crawford, Beau Bridges and Ron Howard.
VHS: S19349. $19.95.
Bert I. Gordon, USA, 1965, 80 mins.

Violated

A baffling set of murders is at the center of this strange exploitation extravaganza. The killer slays his victims and then gives them a haircut. A psychopathologist is brought in to give the police advice on hair fetishes, in an erie echo of *Glen and Glenda*. Among the suspects are a paunchy old man who lusts after young girls and a sleazy photographer. With Mitchell Kowal, Wim Hollard, Lili Dawn and Vicki Carlson.
VHS: S23184. $24.95.
Walter Strate, USA, 1953, 78 mins.

Weird America

Charles Gatewood's work documents the "Beyond-the-Fringe never-never land of sexual fetishists," according to *Penthouse* magazine. The work explores such unconventional sexual playgrounds as San Francisco's sadomasochistic underground, New York's nude centers, erotic tattooing and body piercing, with forays into mud wrestling bikers, wet T-shirt contests, and coverage of Mardi Gras breakouts. 85 mins.
VHS: S17089. $59.95.

Weird World of LSD

Terry Tessem, Ann Lindsay and Yolanda Morino star in this expose of countercultural drug use. The effects of LSD have never been so bizarrely portrayed as in this schlocky camp classic. 1967.
VHS: S23192. $24.95.

What's the Matter with Helen?

A lurid thriller about two aging film stars (Shelley Winters and Debbie Reynolds) attempting to conceal their pasts, who open a dance school for child stars. With Dennis Weaver, Agnes Moorehead and Michael MacLiammoir.
VHS: S17535. $14.95.
Curtis Harrington, USA, 1971, 101 mins.

Whore 2

This sequel builds on the controversial themes originally explored in the original Ken Russell production of *Whore*. It too offers a powerful, stark and compelling look at the world's oldest profession. Nightlife will never have quite the same meaning ever again. 85 mins.
VHS: S22531. $94.99.
Laser: LD75284. $34.98.

Wild Guitar

The curiosity film from the early 60s, capturing the pre-Beatles scene in America. Arch Hall Jr. stars as a young, naive, pompadoured pixie who motorcycles into Hollywood with nothing more than a "git-tar" and the clothes on his back, and within minutes of his arrival, appears on TV, becomes a superstar, and falls into the clutches of an unscrupulous, cigar-chomping manager.
VHS: S05188. $9.95.
Ray Dennis Steckler, USA, 1962, 92 mins.

The Wild Women of Wongo

The world of Wongo is filled with hungry alligators, wild women, and sexually unsatisfied tribesmen. It seems the boys are not pleased with their shapeless prehistoric wives, and turn to the gyrating Wongo-ettes for down and dirty tribal dancing. This film must be seen to be believed. Stars Jean Hawkshaw, Johnny Walsh, Mary Ann Webb, Cande Gerrard and Ed Fury.
VHS: S16111. $29.95.
James L. Wolcott, USA, 1959, 80 mins.

The Wild World of Batwoman

The super-heroine battles diabolical evil to save the world in this rare 60's camp feature which pits Bat Woman Katherine Victor and her bevy of beautiful Bat Girls against the evil Ratfink and the scheming Dr. Neon. Racing against their nasty nemesis to find the prototype of a new hearing aid (actually an atomic listening device/nuclear bomb), these sexy super-heroines still have time for their rock'n'rolling bikini beach parties. USA, 1966, 80 mins.
VHS: S10840. $29.95.
Jerry Warren, USA, 1966, 70 mins.

Wild, Wild World of Jayne Mansfield

Jayne Mansfield hosts a tacky tour of Europe's sleaze spots, including topless clubs and nudist camps, providing a droll commentary the whole time. The low point of bad taste is the finale in which gruesome shots of her fatal car accident are followed by a tearful tour of her Purple Palace, hosted by her hubby, Mickey Hargitay.
VHS: S07479. $29.95.
Arthur Knight, USA, 1968, 90 mins.

Witch Doctor in Tails

This one is in the true tradition of Mondo sleazo with visits to a slaughterhouse, firewalkers and a very disgusting look at the sundry rites and mutilations witch doctors perform. For mature audiences only. Narrated, in English, by George Sanders. Italy, 1966, 96 mins.
VHS: S13500. $24.95.

The Wizard of Gore

This mind twister pits unsuspecting women against the gruesome illusions of an evil magician. The beautiful volunteers are magically sawed in half, impaled through the head and gored through the stomach—and then walk away seemingly unharmed. Hours later they are found dead of the same wounds.
VHS: S15144. $19.98.
Herschell Gordon Lewis, USA, 1970, 96 mins

World's Greatest Movie Challenge

A lot of fun—a VCR game which features film clips from some of the greatest motion pictures, offering a dazzling array of stars including John Wayne, Gary Cooper, Bill Crosby, Bette Davis, Helen Hayes, Abbott and Costello—and a challenge in trivia knowledge to the serious as well as casual devotees of Hollywood, the movies, and the stars of yesterday. Comes complete with a formatted answer pad, an instruction book, and a full-size movie poster from "It's a Wonderful Life." Four gamesin one, graduated by degree of difficulty. 88 mins.
VHS: S06322. $39.95.

RUSS MEYER

Beneath the Valley of the Ultravixens

Russ Meyer's self-described "all-out assault on today's sexual mores" with Lavonia, Eufaula Roop, Junk Yard Sal, and others.
VHS: S03539. $79.95.
Russ Meyer, USA, 1979, 90 mins.

Beyond the Valley of the Dolls

Russ Meyer's excursion into studio filmmaking resulted in this melodrama written by film critic Roger Ebert about an all-girl rock group, their relationship with a transsexual manager and their rise and introduction to the Hollywood netherworld of exploitation and flagrant hedonism. "A delirious comedy soused in self-parody but spiked with dope, sex and thrills" (*Time Out*). With Dolly Read, Cynthia Myers, Marcia McBroom and John La Zar.
VHS: S18599. $19.98.
Russ Meyer, USA, 1970, 109 mins.

Blacksnake!

On the Caribbean Isle of San Cristobal, the legendary and sadistic Lady Susan presides over a plantation worked by slaves. When her most recent husband, Jonathan, disappears, his brother Charles arrives to infiltrate the island and search for the missing man. In this strange and violent place he uncovers "ton-ton macoute", brutal white overseers, horribly overused slaves, and a host of unusually obsessed sexual beings. It's a campy and sleazy vision of a historical time, deformed through the singular eye of Russ Meyer.
VHS: S27370. $79.95.
Russ Meyer, USA, 1973, 83 mins.

Cherry, Harry and Raquel

A menage a trois, loosely translated by Russ Meyer: "a trio is not necessarily a crowd."
VHS: S03649. $79.95.

Common-Law Cabin

A busted-out tourist trap under Arizona's hot desert sun, a way out, raunchy dude ranch…"a slow, simmering look at three fast-boiling women at the mercy of themselves." Directed by Russ Meyer.
VHS: S03620. $79.95.

Eve and the Handyman

The King of the Nudies brings his wife to the screen in this, his second film. Like the *Immoral Mr. Teas* before it, Meyer uses narration and music to connect wild imagery as a whirlwind of sex, pinball and modern art sends a handyman mired by conformity into the arms of the voluptuous Eve.
VHS: S16024. $79.95.
Russ Meyer, USA, 1961, 65 mins.

Faster Pussycat! Kill! Kill!

"The story of a new breed of superwomen emerging out of the ruthlessness of our times…." Directed by Russ Meyer.
VHS: S03665. $79.95.
Russ Meyer, USA, 1966, 83 mins.

Finders, Keepers, Lovers, Weepers

"Get a good grip on your popcorn," says Russ Meyer, as this film "socks it to you…the flesh, fantasy and action…unencumbered by parlour analysis or suburban sociology."
VHS: S01527. $79.95.
Russ Meyer, USA, 72 mins.

Good Morning...And Goodbye

"Without compromise, without apology, and without question, Russ Meyer has made an honest motion picture which explores the deepest complexities of contemporary life, as applied to love and marriage in these United States."
VHS: S03648. $79.95.

Immoral Mr. Teas

An early Russ Meyer film, "America's first classic skin-flick…Here was a film which dared to laugh at all the pretentiousness of its predecessors, and for the first time depicted the living pin-up."
VHS: S03644. $79.95.
Russ Meyer, USA, 63 mins.

Lorna

"Without artistic surrender, without compromise, without question or apology, an incredible sensual picture was made. *Lorna*. The story of a woman." Starring Lorna Maitland, "the new standard of beauty by which all women shall be judged."
VHS: S03650. $79.95.
Russ Meyer, USA, 78 mins.

Mondo Topless

Mondo Topless, says Russ Meyer, "captures the basic essence of the (topless) movement…with MOVEMENT! Way out, wild undulatory movement!" Subtitled *Thanks for the Mammaries*.
VHS: S03072. $79.95.
Russ Meyer, USA, 60 mins.

Motor Psycho

Three motorcycle riding hoodlums ravage a small town with their brutal taste for violence. Only they step over the line when they beat and rape Cory's wife, Gail. Teaming up with the licentious Ruby, Cory stalks the killers in this classic blend of gore and sensuality from the Master of Camp.
VHS: S16022. $79.95.
Russ Meyer, USA, 1965, 74 mins.

Mudhoney

A Russ Meyer classic. With Lorna Maitland, Rena Horten, and Lee Ballard as country harlots who have too much fun for one town.
VHS: S03666. $79.95.
Russ Meyer, USA, 92 mins.

Russ Meyer's Up!

"Two-timers, cops, robbers, joints, and mind-boggling, bra-busting women."
VHS: S03315. $79.95.
Russ Meyer, USA, 80 mins.

Supervixens

Meyer calls this film his "epitome of twenty years of gut-tearing film making, a rural Fellini geared for the young and old alike, the sophisticate and the blue-collar. ...A cinematic smorgasbord of erotic fantasy...SIX of the world's most bountiful women...served up from the lusty table of Russ Meyer."
VHS: S03540. $79.95.
Russ Meyer, USA, 1975, 105 mins.

Vixen

Meyer's critical and popular success, as Roger Ebert described it, "a merciless put-on...Erica Gavin is electrifying!"
VHS: S03585. $79.95.

Wild Gals of the Naked West

Into this riotous parody of the Hollywood Old West rides our hero, a five-foot shrimp of a man riding a burro! With his powder-blue ten-gallon hat, rhinestone-studded purple cowboy boots and a pistol of obscene dimensions, he cleans up the town, vanquishing the villainous Snake Wolf and stealing away the vivacious Goldie Nuggets.
VHS: S16023. $79.95.
Russ Meyer, USA, 1962, 65 mins.

ROGER CORMAN

Apache Woman

This Roger Corman work stars Lloyd Bridges as a government affairs specialist hired to quell ethnic tensions between Apaches and white settlers, and falls for the beautiful halfbreed played by Joan Taylor. With Lance Fuller, Morgan Jones and Paul Birch.
VHS: S17029. $14.95.
Roger Corman, USA, 1955, 83 mins.

Atlas

In this mini-epic, Olympic champion Atlas battles Praximedes over the earthly favors of Candia. The most remarkable thing about this film is its shoestring budget. Actually traveling to Greece for the project, Corman clad a handful of extras (himself included) in cardboard costumes to represent massive armies. Stars Michael Forrest, Frank Wolff, Barboura Morris and Walter Maslow.
VHS: S16105. $29.95.
Roger Corman, USA, 1960, 84 mins.

Bucket of Blood

Roger Corman's first vision of Little Shop of Horrors, with Dick Miller getting that life-like quality to his clay sculptures by building them around life-like dead people.
VHS: S08428. $19.95.
Roger Corman, USA, 1959, 66 mins.

Carnival Rock

A rare rock film of the 50s, which features thrill-crazed kids, grimy gangsters and psycho-teens who all clash together in a seedy carnival nightclub, set to the blistering beat of rockabilly, r&b, and classic rock 'n' roll. Featuring music by The Platters, The Blockbusters, David Houston and Bob Luman and His Shadows.
VHS: S05184. $9.95.
Roger Corman, USA, 1957, 80 mins.

Creature from the Haunted Sea

Roger Corman created this and even appears in a cameo in the story of a gangster who tries to cover his tracks by inventing the story of a sea monster.
VHS: S08431. $29.95.
Roger Corman/Monte Hellman, USA, 1960, 76 mins.

Day the World Ended

Set in a postnuclear environment, the story concerns the interplay of a group of survivors, including a geologist, gangster, stripper, gold prospector and retired sea captain. With Richard Denning, Lori Nelson and Adele Jergens.
VHS: S18414. $24.95.
Roger Corman, USA, 1955, 80 mins.

Little Shop of Horrors

Jack Nicholson is the masochist who thrives on dental pain in this very funny cult classic from Roger Corman. The preposterous plot revolves around a young do-nothing who murders people to feed his carnivorous plant.
VHS: S00762. $19.95.
Roger Corman, USA, 1960, 70 mins.

The Masque of the Red Death

Vincent Price stars in this classic screen adaptation of the Edgar Allan Poe tale. It's a lavishly produced effort featuring amazing sets of the horrific castle of Prince Prospero. There, an indifferent nobility pursues their debauched past-times while the countryside endures the scourge of the red death.
VHS: S01719. $14.98.
Roger Corman, USA, 1964, 86 mins.

Shame (The Intruder)

A rare departure from Roger Corman's usual work, The Intruder is a personal statement on race relations in the South, starring William Shatner as a social reformer in a small town.
VHS: S01187. $34.95.
Roger Corman, USA, 1962, 84 mins.

St. Valentine's Day Massacre

A vividly bloody recounting of the infamous Chicago gangland slaying in the mob war between Al Capone and Bugs Moran. This was Roger Corman's first big studio film. Starring Jason Robards, George Segal, Ralph Meeker and, if you look closely, a young Jack Nicholson.
VHS: S13617. $19.98.
Roger Corman, USA, 1967, 100 mins.

Swamp Women

Marie Windsor, Beverly Garland and Michael Connors star in this complicated but campy thriller about a group of women criminals in search of riches and freedom in the Louisiana Bayou. These bad women are guided by two things only: greed and lust.
VHS: S23778. $24.95.
Roger Corman, USA, 1955, 73 mins.

Tales of Terror

Peter Lorre and Basil Rathbone join Vincent Price in these four tales of terror adapted from Edgar Allan Poe stories. It's a classic horror film in which Price has the chance to camp it up.
VHS: S04192. $14.98.
Roger Corman, USA, 1962, 90 mins.

The Terror

Boris Karloff and Jack Nicholson square off in this gothic tale set in the Napoleonic Wars. The young officer is determined to save a beautiful, tormented young woman from the spooky old Baron. Karloff's scenes took two days to shoot. Made on the sets of The Raven.
VHS: S04026. $19.95.
Roger Corman, USA, 1963, 81 mins.

Tomb of Ligeia

A Roger Corman production based on Edgar Allan Poe's work of the same name, starring Vincent Price. Strange events occur when Price marries after burying his first wife.
VHS: S01357. $14.98.
Roger Corman, USA, 1964, 82 mins.

Tower of London

Roger Corman's gothic translation of Shakespeare's Richard III stars Vincent Price as the disfigured warrior Richard Crookback, who's aided by the brutally efficient executioner Mord (Michael Pate). With Joan Freeman, Robert Brown, Justice Eatson and Sara Salby.
VHS: S11286. $14.95.
Roger Corman, USA, 1962, 79 mins.

The Undead

In this camp classic a scientist fixes his gaze on the past and finds a way to magically transport himself into the Dark Ages. Once there he encounters many surprises, including the wholly unexpected Undead.
VHS: S23817. $24.95.
Roger Corman, USA, 1957, 75 mins.

Wasp Woman

A Roger Corman sociological study of White Anglo-Saxon Protestant women who turn into demented killers by using an untested beauty cream. Susan Cabot stars as a cosmetics executive who uses, too late, about the side effects of the latest beauty aid. With Anthony Eiseley, Michael Mark, Bruno VeSota and Barboura Morris. Written by Leo Gordon (Giant Leeches). B&W.
VHS: S09133. $29.95.
Roger Corman, USA, 1959, 73 mins.

X—The Man with the X-Ray Eyes

Ray Milland stars in this classic science fiction film as a scientist who invents a serum that enhances his vision, giving him X-ray eyes. Ultimately it turns out to be a curse. Don Rickles is also featured.
VHS: S06110. $14.98.
Roger Corman, USA, 1963, 79 mins.

JOHN WATERS

Cry Baby

With a decree to "bring back the juvenile delinquent", director John Waters creates a takeoff on 1950's bad kid, teenage hoodlum movies. Johnny Depp is the cry baby: doll, dream boat and delinquent. The seasoned Traci Lords and Hairspray star Ricki Lake star as his admirers. Cast includes Susan Tyrrell, Iggy Pop, Amy Locane and a cameo by Patty Hearst. Great soundtrack, as usual.
VHS: S12775. $19.95.
Laser: LD70020. $34.98.
John Waters, USA, 1990, 85 mins.

Desperate Living

A perverse and demented film from the outcast priest of sleaze, John Waters, dealing with his usually upsetting themes of self-expression, violence, alienation, mental anguish, sexual hijinks and political corruption, done in a fragmented, hyper absurd comic style. With Liz Renay, Mink Stole, Susan Lowe and Edith Massey.
VHS: S00324. $19.98.
John Waters, USA, 1977, 90 mins.

Divine

A special tribute to the most beautiful babe in the world. First up, a short, The Diane Linkletter Story, starring a very young Divine as a naughty girl who wants to: "get high," "get laid," "...and do my thing, momma...." Thankfully there's a moral lesson here, as Diane kills herself. Following that, the only existing performance of the infamous The Neon Woman show. Divine plays the owner of a sleazy strip joint with a lot of problems, including the District Attorney (who doesn't know he's her son) trying to shut the place down, the horny bible-thumping Senator who's just fallen in love with her, and her virginal daughter who has just returned from boarding school and after spending a few minutes in the club has become an alcoholic, heroin-addicted whore who has just married the black janitor. Now that's high comedy.
VHS: S13498. $39.95.
John Waters, USA, 1990, 110 mins.

Hairspray

John Waters' breakthrough commercial work is a funny, witty and extremely well-made piece of mock nostalgia, about the efforts of a politically conscious white girl to integrate a local television bandstand in 1962 Baltimore. Memorable as Divine's final collaboration with Waters, the casting is superb and Waters has grown tremendously as a stylist, with a particularly shrewd use of color and a shock cutting style reminiscent of early Russ Meyer. With Ricki Lake, Sonny Bono, Debbie Harry, Pia Zadora and Ric Ocasek.
VHS: S07303. $14.98.
John Waters, USA, 1988, 96 mins.

The John Waters Collection, No. 1

American satirist John Waters, whose films deal with politics, sex, style, fashion and class, offers three of his works in a specially bound edition: Desperate Living (1977), Polyester (1981) and Hairspray (1988).
VHS: S18167. $49.98.

Polyester

John Waters' lurid satire of middle-class America cast his collaborator Divine as an abused housewife and mother liberated by handsome, campy, drive-in entrepreneur Tab Hunter. The movie is notable for Waters' witty sympathy for outsiders and the exploited. With Edith Massey, Mary Garlington, Ken King, David Samson and Mink Stole.
VHS: S01046. $19.98.
Laser: CLV. LD72109. $49.95.
John Waters, USA, 1981, 86 mins.

Serial Mom

Kathleen Turner is the overly perfect wife and mother of a normal family. When things get just a little too out of hand Mom makes everything all right again with the help of a little murder. Then it becomes a habit, just another of her many ways that make the world a better place for everyone. Sam Waterston and Ricki Lake also star.
VHS: S21505. $19.98.
John Waters, USA, 1994, 93 mins.

PAUL MORRISSEY

Beethoven's Nephew

Paul Morrissey directs this made-in-Europe investigation of Ludwig van Beethoven's obsession with his nephew Karl. The nephew, the sole heir to the Beethoven estate, is not eager for the composer's personal advances. A study in madness that is both touching and humorous.
VHS: S08089. $19.95.
Laser: LD70868. $39.95.
Paul Morrissey, France/Germany, 1985, 103 mins.

Dracula

Warhol's version of the Dracula story finds the Count touring Italy for a marriageable virgin, and there are few to be found. With Joe Dallesandro as a class-conscious estate hand.
VHS: S02301. $79.95.
Paul Morrissey, USA, 1973, 106 mins.

Frankenstein

"Severed limbs, gobs of livid human entrails, a hideously efficient decapitating gadget...are among the treats that slither off the screen...The most outrageously gruesome epic ever unleashed" (Playboy). With Joe Dallesandro, Monique Van Vooren and Udo Kier.
VHS: S02302. $79.95.
Paul Morrissey, Italy/France, 1973, 95 mins.

ED WOOD, JR.

Bride of the Monster

Winner of the Golden Turkey Award, this is another classic from the director of Glen or Glenda and Plan 9 from Outer Space. Starring Bela Lugosi as a mad scientist trying to create a race of giants. Great mad fun!
VHS: S00180. $29.95.
Ed Wood, Jr., USA, 1956, 70 mins.

Crossroad Avenger/Trick Shooting with Kenne Duncan

Tom Keene, Lyle Talbot and Tom Tyler are featured in this half-hour, Western, TV pilot and short feature combination. The first is solid shoot 'em up fare. Then Kenne Duncan displays his amazing sharp-shooting and trick shooter abilities.
VHS: S23171. $29.95.
Ed Wood, Jr., USA, 1954

Ed Wood

Johnny Depp portrays the nearly inconceivable cult film director/cross-dresser Ed Wood in this imaginative biographical film that won an Academy Award for Martin Landau in the role of actor Bela Lugosi, who (in real life) died during the making of one of Wood's notorious films. A truly singular Hollywood achievement about a stranger-than-fiction filmmaker whose atrocious films, like Plan 9 from Outer Space and Glen or Glenda, have become cult classics. With Patricia Arquette and Bill Murray.
VHS: S24321. $19.98.
Laser: Letterboxed. LD74914. $39.99.
Tim Burton, USA, 1994, 127 mins.

The Ed Wood Collection

Now the films of this Hollywood original—Jail Bait: The Director's Cut, Plan Nine from Outer Space and The Night of the Ghouls—are available together. Steve Reeves made his debut for Ed Wood. Despite this flirtation with success, Wood's final film was held by the lab that developed it because he could not pay for its processing. Trailers and commentary about Wood are also included. 224 mins.
Laser: LD74620. $79.95.

The Ed Wood Collection, Vol. 2

Two of Wood's outrageous films starring the immortal Bela Lugosi are joined on this laser disc. Glen or Glenda (1953), Wood's first film, is an homage to transvestite men everywhere, and Wood plays himself, the man who bravely must face his wife with his closely held secret. In Bride of the Monster (1956), Lugosi is a mad scientist bent on the creation of a race of giants. This film contains the sequence of Lugosi desperately battling an inert rubber octopus that was recreated in Tim Burton's Ed Wood. Includes original theatrical trailers.
Laser: LD74937. $69.98.

The Ed Wood Story: The Plan 9 Companion

The career of this strange director is revealed through interviews with cast members Vampira, Gregory Wolcott, Paul Kelton "the cop" Marco and Conrad Brooks. Footage and photos show another side of Wood and there is even a tour of the studio where Plan 9 was shot. 111 mins.
VHS: S24872. $19.98.

Ed Wood: Look Back in Angora

Conrad Brooks hosts this biographical look at Hollywood's perhaps most inept filmmaker, Ed Wood. Infamous for his camp classics Plan 9 from Outer Space and Jail Bait, Wood's passion for film was clearly his undoing. Yet his films are unlike anything ever produced before; he was a true original. 50 mins.
VHS: S22334. $19.95.

Elvira's Midnight Madness: Night of the Ghouls

Triple threat (writer/producer/director) Ed Wood Jr.'s amazing follow-up to Bride of the Monster, featuring the immortal Criswell—possibly the finest actor the cinema has ever known. The living dead walk again when a phony spiritualist accidentally succeeds in reviving a pack of corpses that bury him alive in a blood curdling climax.
VHS: S14471. $9.95.
Ed Wood, Jr., USA, 1959, 69 mins.

Glen or Glenda

One of the funniest exploitation films ever made—starring Bela Lugosi as he tells the story of Glen—or Glenda—who is undergoing a sex change operation, and tells the horror story about fetishism. Not to be missed!
VHS: S00505. $19.95.
Ed Wood, Jr., USA, 1953, 64 mins.

Jail Bait

Lyle Talbot (first screen Lex Luthor) stars in this first effort of Ed Wood, Jr. While many filmmakers improve during the course of their careers, Wood got worse and created the infamous Plan 9 from Outer Space. In this genuine Wood effort, Timothy Farrell leads young Clancey Malone into a life of crime so that when the law closes in, he forces Malone's father to change his face with plastic surgery.
VHS: S06332. $14.95.
Ed Wood, Jr., USA, 1954, 70 mins.

Married Too Young

Ed Wood was brought in to finish the last quarter of the script for this exploitive melodrama, though he was never credited. A pair of high school sweethearts get married on the sly but find the burdens of life too tough. Trouble comes when they get mixed up with a hot car racket. The film climaxes with a crash. Harold Lloyd, Jr., Anthony Dexter and Jana Lund star.
VHS: S23172. $29.95.
Ed Wood, Jr., USA, 1962

Necromania

This low-budget, soft-core horror flick, from master of cult films Ed Wood Jr., was lost until recently. Now this tale about a young couple who happen upon a supernatural sex clinic is available once again. It's a camp classic featuring outrageous dialog, a strange collection of music tracks and offbeat humor.
VHS: S21348. $24.95.
Ed Wood, Jr., USA, 1971, 43 mins.

On the Trail of Ed Wood

A personal documentary about the legendary Hollywood director Edward D. Wood Jr., whose grade Z horror movies earned him the unfortunate nickname of the "world's worst filmmaker." Hosted by Conrad Brooks, a friend of the director, the program studies Wood's perennially campy works, including Plan 9 from Outer Space, Glen or Glenda, Bride of the Monster and Orgy of the Dead.
VHS: S18242. $19.95.

Orgy of the Dead

Ed Wood Jr's masterpiece of erotic horror, winner of the Golden Turkey award.
VHS: S05193. $14.95.
Ed Wood, Jr., USA, 1965, 90 mins.

Plan 9 from Outer Space

Aliens invade earth and revive corpses from a San Fernando Valley cemetery to aide them in their dreams of conquest. Bela Lugosi is featured in this camp classic, but he died shortly after production began. Fortunately he was replaced by a taller man with a cape over his face. Possibly the worst film ever made.
VHS: S01036. $14.95.
Ed Wood, Jr., USA, 1959, 79 mins.

Sinister Urge

One of Ed Wood's least-known films, dedicated to the idea that overweight women in their underwear are the principal cause of juvenile delinquency. Two zealous cops are out to smash the "smut picture racket" and stop a "sex maniac killer" who is motivated by the dirty pictures as the "psycho killer strikes terror in every woman's heart." Originally titled Sinister Sex, the title was too risque for the 1960's and had to be changed.
VHS: S22912. $19.95.
Ed Wood, Jr., USA, 1960, 75 mins.

Take It Out in Trade—The Outtakes

Slates, flubs, unused sex scenes and Ed Wood himself in a screwball sexploitation comedy that marked his return to the director's chair for the first time since Sinister Urge. Three cans of silent Take It Out in Trade outtakes, found in a Santa Monica cutting room, feature an androgynous couple making out in a kitchen, posters of foreign countries, and Ed Wood in a lovely lime green dress, blonde wig, and white go-go boots playing a drag queen named "Alecia."
VHS: S23037. $19.98.
Ed Wood, Jr., USA, 1970

The Violent Years

This recently re-discovered classic by Ed Wood, Jr. (Plan 9) features filthy rich teenage sex kittens who form gangs, rob gas stations, rape rich guys, and strip gown "goody" girls. A cheap thrills masterpiece.
VHS: S05186. $14.95.
Ed Wood, Jr., USA, 1956, 60 mins.

horror FLICKS

The Abominable Dr. Phibes
The disfigured physician, played by Vincent Price, wreaks havoc on a world that he feels wronged him. His revenge is both terrible and imaginative. You can never guess exactly how Dr. Phibes' enemies will meet their deaths, but rest assured, each one is grisly. Also features Joseph Cotten.
VHS: S20931. $14.98.
Robert Fuest, Great Britain, 1971, 94 mins.

Amazing Transparent Man
A great B movie by the incomparable Edgar G. Ulmer. Shot at a Texas state fair because some of the exhibits had a futuristic look, the plot concerns a mad scientist who invents a formula for invisibility in order to make an invisible man his accomplice in bank robberies.
VHS: S06903. $29.95.
Edgar G. Ulmer, USA, 1960, 58 mins.

And Now the Screaming Starts
A pre-"Colbys" Stephanie Beacham weds Ian Ogilvy only to find that the happy couple has moved into a haunted house. A honeymoon of horror results in a gothic tale with Peter Cushing, Herbert Lom and Patrick Magee also in the cast.
VHS: S03765. $79.95.
Roy Ward Baker, Great Britain, 1973, 87 mins.

An Angel for Satan
Barbara Steele has a dual role in this excellent horror film about a woman possessed by the spirit of a statue. This was Barbara's last major Italian horror film. The best video copy available. Italian with NO subtitles.
VHS: S15367. $29.95.
Camillo Mastrocinque, Italy, 1966, 93 mins.

The Ape
Boris Karloff plays an evil doctor obsessed with producing a cure for a dreaded disease by injecting the afflicted with human spinal fluid.
VHS: S13854. $19.95.
William Nigh, USA, 1940, 62 mins.

Apeman
Bela Lugosi literally makes a monkey of himself as a scientist who experiments with a new serum. Also known as *Lock Your Doors.*
VHS: S00065. $19.95.
William Beaudine, USA, 1943, 64 mins.

Army of Darkness
Sam Raimi's film is the third installment of his *Evil Dead III* trilogy. The handsome, appliance store salesman Nash (Bruce Campbell) is sucked through a vortex into the 13th century. While trying to retrieve a text that will return him to the present, Nash inadvertently unleashes a squadron of the walking dead, skeleton figures who lay siege to the village. With Embeth Davidtz.
VHS: S19329. $19.98.
Laser: Letterboxed. LD71886. $34.98.
Sam Raimi, USA, 1992, 81 mins.

Asylum
British chiller contains four tales of madness and murder that are told to the new doctor assigned to a mental institution. Cast includes Peter Cushing, Britt Ekland, Robert Powell, Herbert Lom, Barbara Parkins and Patrick Magee. Script by Robert "Psycho" Bloch. Ghoulish good fun.
VHS: S03766. $29.95.
Roy Ward Baker, Great Britain, 1972, 92 mins.

At Midnight I'll Take Your Soul
A psycho-sexual gothic thriller from Brazil's horror auteur Jose Mojica Marins represents the debut appearance of the evil protagonist Coffin Joe (played by the director). He's a gravedigger whose specter haunts a small town. Coffin Joe is looking for a woman who will bear his child and preserve his demonic reign. Spanish with English subtitles.
VHS: S18982. $24.95.
Jose Mojica Marins, Brazil, 1963

Attack of the Giant Leeches
White trash finds itself on the menu of some oversized swamp pests in this AIP Cheapie executive produced by Roger Corman. When a backwoods bartender finds his trampy wife violating the marital vows, he institutes a shotgun divorce and forces the lovers into the deadly wetlands to meet man-sized monsters in very cheap costumes. With Bruno Ve Sota, Yvette Vickers, Ken Clark and Gene Roth. B&W.
VHS: S09125. $29.95.
Bernard L. Kowalski, USA, 1959, 62 mins.

Awakenings of the Beast
Banned for 18 years by the Brazilian military dictatorship, this grotesque film is a stylish essay about the dangers of drug experimentation. The title refers to LSD, as a drug addict relies on the psychedelic rush to compensate for his tormented visions of loss and terror. Spanish with English subtitles.
VHS: S18984. $24.95.
Jose Mojica Marins, Brazil, 1968

The Bat
One of the great silent horror films. A maniacal killer dressed in a weird bat-like costume terrorizes a group of people in a shuddery, spooky old house riddled with secret passageways. The use of miniatures and the overall cinematography is stunning for its day.
VHS: S15365. $29.95.
Roland West, USA, 1926, 81 mins.

The Bat People
When a biologist is bitten by a winged mammal, he turns from a modern, rational man into a blood-craving, shape-altered beast. He finds this puts a severe damper on his honeymoon. The makeup is said to be convincing in this low-budget shocker. With John Richardson and Ivo Garrani. B&W.
VHS: S05103. $19.99.
Jerry Jameson, USA, 1974, 95 mins.

The Bat Whispers
One of the early great sound films, this remake of the silent 1926 classic *The Bat* is also a great horror film. A group of people gather in an old dark house where they are menaced by a maniacal, yet brilliant, hooded criminal. Hidden in a secret room in the mansion is a fortune in stolen money. Chester Morris and Una Merkel star.
VHS: S23161. $29.95.
Roland West, USA, 1930, 84 mins.

The Beast with Five Fingers
A cult horror movie about a once brilliant pianist now consumed by doubt and self-loathing. Features his classic encounter with the disembodied hand. With Robert Alda, Peter Lorre and Andrea King.
VHS: S17532. $19.98.
Robert Florey, USA, 1946, 88 mins.

Bedlam
Boris Karloff stars as a sadist in charge of an insane asylum during the 18th century, who torments an innocent, sane young girl imprisoned by her evil relative.
VHS: S00113. $19.98.
Mark Robson, USA, 1945, 79 mins.

The Bela Lugosi Collection: Devil Bat/ Scared to Death
Two Bela Lugosi pictures told with unnerving skill. In Jean Yarbrough's *The Devil Bat* (1941), Lugosi experiments with bats and trains them to destroy his enemies. The second feature, Christy Cabanne's *Scared to Death* (1947), was Lugosi's only color film, which chronicles a young woman's death, eerily told from her point of view.
Laser: LD71952. $49.95.
Jean Yarborough/Walt Mattox, USA, 1941-47, 137 mins.

Bela Lugosi Meets a Brooklyn Gorilla
In this spoof of jungle horror movies Bela, as Dr. Zabor, turns one half of a stranded comedy team into a gorilla. The comedy team of Duke Mitchell and Sammy Petrillo are said to be look-alikes of Dean Martin and Jerry Lewis. Screenplay by Irene Ryan's husband Tim.
VHS: S04013. $29.95.
William Beaudine, USA, 1952, 74 mins.

Big Calibre
Bob Steele must battle a mad scientist on the lone prairie who uses corrosive gas against his foes. Lots of action out west in an unusual match-up. With Peggy Campbell and Forest Taylor. B&W.
VHS: S04080. $29.95.
Robert North Bradbury, USA, 1935, 59 mins.

Billy the Kid versus Dracula
Mixed genres meet a low budget with a sixty-year-old John Carradine as the Transylvanian bloodsucker and Chuck Courtney as the infamous western backshooter. This horror western was filmed in Shockorama. With Roy Barcroft, Harry Carey Jr. and Melinda Plowman as Betty.
VHS: S05483. $29.95.
William Beaudine, USA, 1966, 73 mins.

The Black Cat
Edgar G. Ulmer (*Detour*) directs Boris Karloff and Bela Lugosi in this stylish horror work. Ulmer pulled out all the stops in this movie about a young American couple trapped in the house of a demented scientist. With David Manners, Jacqueline Wells, Lucille Lund, and Egon Brecher. From a story by Edgar Allan Poe.
VHS: S17270. $14.98.
Edgar G. Ulmer, USA, 1934, 65 mins.

Black Cat
The short story by Edgar Allan Poe is the inspiration for this Italian-made horror film in which the residents of a small English town find themselves at the mercy of a fiendish feline. Nine lives are more than enough for the revengeful purposes of the cat's owner, an out-of-control clairvoyant. With Patrick Magee, Mimsy Farmer, David Warbec and Al Cliver. Not to be confused with the 1934 and 1941 Bela Lugosi horror films of the same title.
VHS: S15826. $14.98.
Lucio Fulci, Italy/Great Britain, 1986, 93 mins.

The Black Raven
They lived by blood, this motley crew! And squared their debts with murder! So say the ads for this George Zucco thriller. He runs an inn crowded with strangers on a dark and stormy night. With Wanda McKay and Glenn Strange as the comic relief. B&W.
VHS: S04038. $29.95.
Sam Newfield, USA, 1943, 64 mins.

Black Sabbath
Boris Karloff in this tale of "wurdalaks," a variety of vampires that drink only the blood of loved ones. Filmed in Italy, this is an English language version.
VHS: S00139. $24.95.
Mario Bava, Italy, 1963, 99 mins.

Black Sunday
This Barbara Steele Italian horror movie has nothing to do with Middle Eastern Terrorists or hijacked blimps. In her first horror film she plays a dual role: Asa, a reincarnated vampire-witch, and Katia, her innocent great-granddaughter. Heavy on the atmosphere. With John Richardson and Ivo Garrani. B&W.
VHS: S09126. $24.95.
Mario Bava, Italy, 1961, 83 mins.

The Blob
The 1950's gooiest monster is back in a special 30th anniversary remake of *The Blob*, starring Kevin Dillon as a young outcast who must save the town of Arborville from the gelatin.
Laser: LD70350. $49.95.
Chuck Russell, USA, 1988, 92 mins.

Blood Beast Terror
Peter Cushing stars in this well-crafted British horror film in which Wanda Ventham is the beautiful vampire who tears her lovers to death.
VHS: S04786. $39.95.
Vernon Sewell, Great Britain, 1967, 81 mins.

Blood Fiend (aka Theatre of Death)
Are there vampires on the loose in Paris? The local police are stymied by a series of "blood" related murders. The mystery seems to center around a Grand Guignol stage sensation, a beautiful young actress who seems to be in a hypnotic trance. Unquestionably one of Christopher Lee's better low budget shockers. With Julian Glover and Jenny Till.
VHS: S15368. $29.95.
Samuel Gallu, Great Britain, 1966, 91 mins.

Blood Hook
Local jail bait becomes live bait in this horror movie where water sports take on a new and frightening aspect. Teens are hooked and hacked to bits in the backwoods of Wisconsin. Even though it's clear something fishy is going on, the sheriff won't make any waves. Is it any wonder kids keep disappearing as fish food?
VHS: S22675. $14.95.
James Nallon, USA, 1983, 98 mins.

Blood of Dracula
This AIP production stars Sandra Harrison as a student at a private girl's school who is hypnotized into becoming a vampire by the evil headmistress. The ads proclaimed "In her eyes…DESIRE. In her veins…the Blood of a MONSTER!" With Louise Lewis, Gail Ganley, Thomas B. Henry and Jerry Blaine.
VHS: S16409. $9.95.
Herbert L. Strock, USA, 1957, 68 mins.

Blood of Ghastly Terror
John Carradine stars as a doctor with dubious credentials who needs a human subject to test his artificial brain implant. But the doctor's orders don't work when his victim turns into a psychopathic killer. The film has gone under various other titles, including *The Fiend with the Atomic Brain, Psycho a Go Go!, The Love Maniac,* and *The Man with the Synthetic Brain.*
VHS: S08041. $19.98.
Al Adamson, USA, 1972, 87 mins.

The Blood on Satan's Claw
A highly original thriller. The story unfolds in a 17th century English village, where a group of children are stalked by a devil's claw. Also known as *Satin's Skin.* With Patrick Wymark, Linda Hayden, Barry Andrews and Avice Landon.
VHS: S19131. $14.95.
Piers Haggard, Great Britain, 1970, 93 mins.

The Bloody Exorcism of Coffin Joe
Jose Mojica Marins is on a Christmas break with a seemingly normal family when strange occurrences disturb the festive mood, in this Brazilian-made camp horror classic. It seems there was a pact made with the devil for the hand of the family's eldest daughter. Threatening to renege on this deal leads to mounting terrors, culminating in a perverse, ritualistic ceremony that includes naked devil worshippers and cannibalism. Portuguese with English subtitles.
VHS: S21346. $24.95.
Jose Mojica Marins, Brazil, 1972

The Bloody Pit of Horror
Mickey Hargitay, the husband of sexpot Jayne Mansfield, stars in this Italian horror film based on the writings of the Marquis de Sade. He becomes possessed by the spirit of a sadistic castle owner who enjoys making his guests feel uncomfortable. Five sexy models, among others, are shown that torture chambers can be functional as well as decorative.
VHS: S09138. $29.95.
Max Hunter (Massimo Pupillo), Italy, 1965, 87 mins.

The Body Snatcher
A ghoulish tale of murder and mayhem. Val Lewton teamed the duo of Boris Karloff and Bela Lugosi in this tale of an Edinburgh cab driver who supplies the city's medical inspectors with corpses. Based on a story by Robert Louis Stevenson.
VHS: S03253. $19.95.
Robert Wise, USA, 1945, 77 mins.

Brainscan
Frank Langella and Edward Furlong star in this horrific tale about high school kids who encounter the deadliest interactive video game ever. A lonely kid thought his obsession was just a game, but soon deception, desire and death are more than state of the art software.
VHS: S22913. $19.95.
John Flynn, USA, 1994, 96 mins.

Bride of Frankenstein
A superior sequel, mixes wit with chills. Boris Karloff is the Monster, Elsa Lanchester plays the created mate as well as Mary Shelley in the prologue. Marvelous score by Franz Waxman. A classic!
VHS: S06386. $14.98.
Laser: LD70019. $34.98.
James Whale, USA, 1935, 75 mins.

Bride of the Gorilla
Raymond Burr lusts after the mistress of a jungle plantation and is willing to murder all those that stand in his way. Intimidation will only go so far when it is matched with a voodoo curse that causes a drastic change in Burr's appearance. With Lon Chaney Jr., Barbara Payton and Tom Conway. B&W.
VHS: S04033. $29.95.
Curt Siodmak, USA, 1951, 76 mins.

The Brides of Dracula
A Hammer Studio film about a beautiful, naive, young French woman who liberates an imprisoned baron. The baron wakes the undead to carry out his perverse agenda, and now the young woman and the indefatigable Dr. Helsing (Peter Cushing) must restore order.
VHS: S17018. $14.98.
Terence Fisher, Great Britain, 1960, 86 mins.

Buried Alive
Once, Ravenscroft Hall was an asylum for the incurably insane. Now, the isolated mansion is a school for troubled teenaged girls run by charismatic psychiatrist Robert Vaughn. Captivated by his charm, a young woman (Karen Witter) joins his staff. She is soon tormented by nightmare visions of the long-dead victims of a nameless killer. When the students begin to disappear, she realizes he still lives…John Carradine and Donald Pleasance star in this classic tale of terror based on an Edgar Allan Poe story.
VHS: S13005. $39.95.
Gerard Kikione, USA, 1989, 97 mins.

Candyman
British director Bernard Rose's American debut transposes Clive Barker's short story *The Forbidden* from Liverpool to Chicago, with Virginia Madsen as a doctoral candidate who inadvertently unleashes the spirit of "Candyman," a mythological 19th-century black serial killer with a hook for his left hand who was brutally murdered by white racists. With Tony Todd, Xander Berkeley and Kasi Lemmons.
VHS: S18323. $19.95.
Bernard Rose, USA, 1992, 108 mins.

Captive Wild Woman
A doctor, played by John Carradine, steals a killer orangutan and then, through the wizardry of chemical injections and plastic surgery, transforms the beast into a beautiful woman, played by Paula Dupree. Despite her make-over she remains a beast at heart, and when jilted goes on a maddened rampage.
VHS: S21729. $14.98.
Edward Dmytryk, USA, 1943, 61 mins.

Carnival of Souls
The best horror movie ever made in Lawrence, Kansas. Candace Hilligoss plays the only survivor of a traffic accident where a car load of young women goes off a bridge. Shaken by the experience, she leaves town to play the pipe organ in Lawrence where she is haunted by very disturbing spectres. Truly eerie despite its low budget. B&W.
VHS: S04077. $29.95.
Herk Harvey, USA, 1962, 80 mins.

Carrie
Director Brian de Palma breathes life into the Steven King novel about a repressed teenager who uses her telekinetic powers to take revenge on her tormenting school peers. Sissy Spacek stars as the sympathetic Carrie; Piper Laurie plays her pious, crazy mother.
VHS: S12742. $14.95.
Laser: LD70743. $89.95.
Brian DePalma, USA, 1977, 101 mins.

Cast a Deadly Spell
The setting is Los Angeles in 1948, home to a bevy of witches and voodoo. This sci-fi horror whodunit centers on Harry P. Lovecraft (Fred Ward), a gumshoe who must rely on street smarts to find the fabled Necronomicon. Fantastic elements coupled with good effects and a driving plot make for a highly watchable yarn. With David Warner, Julianne Moore, Clancy Brown and Alexandra Powers.
VHS: S25872. $89.99.
Laser: LD75123. $24.98.
Martin Campbell, USA, 1991, 93 mins.

Castle of Blood
Barbara Steele is the bait for a daring reporter who bets he can stay the night in a haunted castle. It seems on "The Night of the Dead" everyone who has died violently in the place returns seeking human blood. The moral of this story is, never trust a woman without a heartbeat. With George Riviere and Margaret Robsham. B&W. Based on E.A. Poe's *Dance Macabre.*
VHS: S09131. $29.95.
Anthony Dawson (Antonio Margheriti), Italy, 1964, 85 mins.

Castle of Evil
The faithful robot of a deceased mad scientist has orders to kill all those that show up on this Caribbean island for the reading of the will. Starring Scott Brady, Virginia Mayo and David Brian. A free funeral was promised if you dropped dead watching this film. Be careful—the offer may no longer be valid.
VHS: S04262. $14.98.
Francis D. Lyon, USA, 1966, 81 mins.

Castle of Fu Manchu
Christopher Lee stars as the evil Oriental magnate who experiments with more deadly potions in his castle near Istanbul, pitted against his nemesis, Nayland Smith of Britain's Home Office.
VHS: S03066. $19.95.
Jess (Jesus) Franco, Germany/Italy/Spain/Great Britain, 1968, 92 mins.

Castle of the Living Dead
Christopher Lee is Count Drago, the sinister host who often changes his unfortunate guests into living statues. This allows him to have lots of company and still save on expenses. Donald Sutherland plays a witch and a sergeant of the guard in his film debut.
VHS: S04053. $29.95.
H. Wise/L. Ricci, Italy/France, 1964, 90 mins.

Cat and the Canary
Honor Blackman, Michael Callen and Edward Fox are featured in this atmospheric thriller. A group gathers in a gloomy mansion to hear the last will and testament of a rich man. The proviso "if something should happen to the initial beneficiary" sets off a murderous night of intrigue.
VHS: S25694. $19.95.
Radley Metzger, Great Britain, 1979, 90 mins.

Cat Girl
A fierce, edgy, horror thriller about a beautiful young woman possessing a long-held family curse, a strange relationship to a ferocious leopard, and the shocking crimes that ensue. Barbara Shelley, Robert Ayres and Paddy Webster.
VHS: S17520. $9.95.
Alfred Shaughnessy, Great Britain, 1957, 69 mins.

Cat People (1942)
A revolutionary horror picture, in which the horror grows by suggestion rather than being depicted. Val Lewton made his name as producer of Cat People. The scare at the swimming pool is a true classic.
VHS: S00220. $19.95.
Laser: LD75377. $49.98.
Jacques Tourneur, USA, 1942, 73 mins.

Cat People (1982)
Paul Schrader's remake of Jacques Tourneur's 1942 classic about an innocent young woman (Nastassia Kinski) whose incestuous relationship with her brother (Malcolm McDowell) results in a terrifying transformation. With John Heard, Annette O'Toole, Ed Begley, Jr., and John Larroquette.
VHS: S06126. $14.98.
Laser: LD72191. $34.98.
Paul Schrader, USA, 1982, 118 mins.

Cat's Eye
A trilogy of horror tales based on some of Stephen King's most successful short stories. An all-star cast is featured in these three thrilling narratives about a radical way to stop smoking, a man forced to walk along a skyscraper ledge, and a stray cat that comes to a little girl's rescue against an evil troll. Starring James Woods, Robert Hays, Drew Barrymore and Alan King.
VHS: S13972. $19.99.
Lewis Teague, USA, 1985, 93 mins.

Cauldron of Blood
Boris Karloff, at the end of his career, plays a blind sculptor in a Spanish art colony. His wife, Viveca Lindfors, is trying to kill him. She rehearses by murdering other people while Karloff unknowingly uses their skeletons in his work. Made in 1967 but not released until 1971.
VHS: S04257. $14.98.
E. Mann (S. Alcocer), Spain/USA, 1967, 95 mins.

Chamber of Horrors
(The Door with Seven Locks)
Leslie Banks plays a villainous host who keeps his dungeon adequately supplied with victims. Based on an Edgar Wallace story, a madman terrorizes the lovely Lilli Palmer to learn her secret. With Cathleen Nesbitt and Richard Bird. Low budget terror. B&W.
VHS: S04060. $29.95.
Norman Lee, Great Britain, 1940, 80 mins.

Circle of Deceit
Dennis Waterman stars as an agent called back into service as a recently killed IRA soldier. He must convince his assumed family in order to complete his mission, but he has inadvertently fallen in love with the widowed daughter of his primary target. 103 mins.
VHS: S24781. $19.98.

Circus of Horrors
Anton Diffring and Erika Remberg star in this frightening horror film, in which an unethical plastic surgeon and a nurse join a bizarre circus in order to escape a deformed patient threatening their lives.
VHS: S04562. $19.95.
Sidney Hayers, Great Britain, 1960, 89 mins.

Clive Barker's "Salome" & "The Forbidden"
Clive Barker made these two shorts in the early 1970's and even appeared in them. They are powerful precursors to his later works. A puzzle book sequence and a skinning segment hint at the gruesome preoccupations that would later bring him infamy. 18 and 36 mins.
VHS: S26726. $24.95.
Clive Barker, Great Britain, 1973-1978, 54 mins.

Coffin Joe's Visions of Terror
This collection of 14 trailers from the films of Brazil's prolific purveyor of gore will show you the very worst that he has to offer. Macabre Nightmare, a short excerpt from Trilogy of Terror, about a man who dreams of being buried alive, is also included. Portuguese with English subtitles.
VHS: S20747. $24.95.
Jose Mojica Marins, Brazil, 1963-1986

The Comedy of Terrors
Vincent Price stars as an enterprising undertaker who decides to supply his own customers when business gets bad. Peter Lorre, Boris Karloff and Basil Rathbone join in this terrifying farce. A full-service undertaker is a great idea and this cast manages to get every laugh and groan imaginable from the campy plot.
VHS: S25892. $14.98.
Jacques Tourneur, USA, 1963, 84 mins.

Condemned to Live
A married couple escape from Savage Africa and head for New England in the days of the Puritans. The catch is that the wife was pregnant and had been bitten by a vampire bat. Son grows up with a taste for blood and murder. With Ralph Morgan, Maxine Doyle and Mischa Auer. B&W.
VHS: S04057. $29.95.
Frank Strayer, USA, 1935, 67 mins.

The Conqueror Worm
Vincent Price is Matthew Hopkins, a dedicated witch hunter in the days of Cromwell. He uses his power of life and death for his own profit and pleasure and eventually ticks off the local populace. This AIP release had Price read E.A. Poe's poem over credits to justify the name change.
VHS: S05104. $14.98.
Michael Reeves, Great Britain, 1968, 95 mins.

The Corpse Vanishes
Bela Lugosi stars as an orchid loving doctor who kidnaps brides at their weddings and drains their blood in order to preserve his aging wife's beauty. A plucky female reporter tracks him to his secret laboratory which comes complete with a dwarf, an oaf and a sinister old woman. B&W.
VHS: S03067. $19.95.
Wallace Fox, USA, 1942, 64 mins.

Corridors of Blood
Boris Karloff stars as a doctor working on an anesthesia, who becomes obsessed and falls outside the law, with Christopher Lee. Originally titled Doctor from Seven Dials.
VHS: S03546. $39.95.
Robert Day, Great Britain, 1958, 90 mins.

Count Dracula
After five Hammer films playing Transylvanian royalty, Christopher Lee left England to try a new approach to the character. This version stars Herbert Lom as Van Helsing and Klaus Kinski as the insect-eating Renfield. Closely based on the Bram Stoker novel.
VHS: S04265. $14.98.
Jess (Jesus) Franco, Spain/Ger./Italy, 1971, 90 mins.

Crawling Hand
When a handsome pre-med student is given the hand of a dead astronaut, Peter Breck rockets off into a frenzy of murder. The teen remake of The Beast with Five Fingers features the music of the Livingstons, including the classic "Papa Oom Mow Mow." With Alan Hale Jr., Richard Arlen, Allison Hayes and Sissy Steffen.
VHS: S10967. $19.95.
Herbert L. Strock, USA, 1962, 89 mins.

Creature from the Black Lagoon
The classic love story of a girl and a gill-man who meet on a moonlit night in the backwaters of the Amazon. Originally in 3-D. Truly one of the better monster movies. With Richard Carlson, Julie Adams and Ricou Browning as the gill-man when he is swimming. B&W.
VHS: S05524. $14.95.
Jack Arnold, USA, 1954, 79 mins.

The Creature Walks Among Us
The second follow-up to The Creature from the Black Lagoon, about the mysterious gill-man who violently reacts against the scientists trying to control him and soften his appearance through plastic surgery. He longs to return to the freedom of the ocean in this strange parable about the dangers of conformity. With Jeff Morrow, Rex Reason and Leigh Snowden.
VHS: S19015. $14.98.
John Sherwood, USA, 1956, 78 mins.

Creepshow
George A. Romero directed a screenplay by Stephen King that is a ghoulish comic tribute to EC Comics. Five tales of the macabre are offered. E.G. Marshall's battle with cockroaches is a standout. King himself acts as a hick farmer who finds something he shouldn't.
VHS: S04184. $19.98.
George A. Romero, USA, 1982, 120 mins.

Crime of Dr. Crespi
Low-budget but fascinating version of Poe's "Premature Burial" with Erich von Stroheim in great form—the entire film was shot in the old Biograph Studios in less than two weeks.
VHS: S06008. $29.95.
John H. Auer, USA, 1935, 60 mins.

Crimes at the Dark House
Tod Slaughter adapts Wilkie Collins' classic The Woman in White for one of the best of his staged melodramas to be filmed. As Sir Percival Glyde, he kills his rich wife and replaces her with an escaped lunatic lookalike. With Hilary Eaves, Sylvia Marriott and Hay Petrie as Dr. Fosco. B&W.
VHS: S04046. $29.95.
George King, Great Britain, 1940, 69 mins.

Crucible of Horror
A gothic thriller with a social edge about an abused wife who poisons her destructive husband and goes slowly mad when his corpse mysteriously appears. With Michael Gough, Sharon Gurney and Yvonne Mitchell.
VHS: S19132. $14.95.
Viktors Ritelis, Great Britain, 1971, 91 mins.

Cry of the Banshee
Witches summon Satan to avenge the many deaths caused by the witch-hunting campaign of Vincent Price.
VHS: S06472. $14.98.
Gordon Hessler, Great Britain, 1970, 87 mins.

Cult of the Cobra
When six servicemen unwittingly disturb a secret and ancient ceremony, powerful and evil forces are unleashed that threaten to destroy them. The cobra goddess can deceive and kill. This camp horror classic stars Richard Long, Marshall Thompson and Faith Domergue.
VHS: S20892. $14.98.
Francis D. Lyon, USA, 1955, 82 mins.

Cult of the Dead
Dr. van Molder (Boris Karloff) studies the unique behavior of an island population practicing sexual ceremonies and offering human sacrifices to a demonic spirit. Investigations lead to a horrifying confrontation with the cult's diabolical high priestess. 90 mins.
VHS: S09257. $19.98.

Curse of King Tut's Tomb
Based on the book Behind the Mask of Tutankhamen, by Barry Wynne. As you might expect with a title like that the word Egypt will be mentioned more than once in the course of this film, which will include both a curse and the burial place of an internationally known member of royalty. Cast includes Robin Ellis, Wendy Hiller, Raymond Burr and Eva Marie Saint. See it if you dare.
VHS: S10386. $19.95.
Philip Leacock, Great Britain, 1980, 96 mins.

Curse of the Werewolf
A Hammer Film Production, starring Oliver Reed as the blood-thirsty man-beast who is gentle and loving by day and kills by night.
VHS: S02722. $14.98.
Laser: LD71440. $34.98.
Terence Fisher, Great Britain, 1961, 91 mins.

Curse of the Yellow Snake
Atmospheric German adaptation of an Edgar Wallace mystery. An ancient Chinese artifact carries a vicious curse: whoever possesses it will win any war they initiate. The film's hero follows the snake's path from Hong Kong to London, up against Chinese imperialist Fighting Hand and a host of other creepy types. Complete with odd camera angles and eerie lighting effects. Dubbed in English.
VHS: S00289. $29.95.
Franz Gottlieb, Germany, 1963, 98 mins.

Dance of Death
Mathias Morteval (Boris Karloff) calls a reunion of his relatives to determine who inherited the family curse of insanity. One by one the heirs are murdered, suddenly and violently. Who would be next to dance with death?
VHS: S09260. $59.95.
Juan Ibanez, Mexico, 1968, 89 mins.

Danger: Diabolik
In reaction to the suave, sophisticated superspy thrillers that ruled their day, this action piece centers on something far darker and unsettling, the presence of "a psychedelic-era outlaw" named Diabolik, a brilliant, cold and impulsive thief. In English.
VHS: S16890. $19.95.
Mario Bava, Italy, 1968, 99 mins.

The Dark Angel
A psychological horror movie about treachery and deception set against the last vestiges of a decaying Victorian sensibility, Peter O'Toole plays a repressed, depraved old man in line to receive the inheritance of his beautiful, virginal niece, who's come to live with him. With Jane Lapotaire, Beatie Edney and Tim Woodward.
VHS: S17769. $19.98.
Peter Hammond, Great Britain, 1991, 148 mins.

Daughter of Horror
Adrienne Barrett, Bruno VeSota and Angelo Rossitto star in this horrific feature narrated by Ed McMahon. A girl wanders through a series of strange events that culminates in her sawing off the hand of the man she murders. There is hardly any dialog in this odd, dream-like film. Originally banned by the New York Board of Censors.
VHS: S23162. $29.95.
John Parker, USA, 1955, 60 mins.

Dawn of the Dead (Director's Cut)
George A. Romero's sequel to Night of the Living Dead is a bleak satire of American consumerism. Three men and a woman escape the ravenous walking dead and gain refuge in a sterile, abandoned shopping mall. Romero charts a series of complicated sexual, racial and political relationships as the flesh-devouring zombies lay siege to their "fortress." With David Emge, Ken Foree, Scott H. Reininger and Gaylen Ross.
VHS: S04563. $14.98.
George A. Romero, USA, 1978, 131 mins.

Dead Eyes of London
A German re-make of the Bela Lugosi chiller Dark Eyes of London, which was based on an Edgar Wallace short story. Once again the director of a home for the blind will use the place as a front for his criminal activities. With Klaus Kinski and Karin Baal.
VHS: S04076. $29.95.
Alfred Vohrer, W. Germany, 1961, 104 mins.

Dead Is Dead
A man is dismembered by a mutant creature and left for dead. Fortunately a woman administers a miraculous drug that saves him. When he pays off a debt with this drug he doesn't realize that it was a bad batch. Now he must get it back somehow.
VHS: S24744. $19.95.
Mike Stanley, USA, 1993, 75 mins.

Dead Men Walk
The reason they walk is that they can't afford to take a bus. But seriously, horror fans, George Zucco plays a double role of brothers with decidedly opposing viewpoints on life and death. There are vampires and mad scientists and Dwight Frye as a maniacal assistant. All in glorious black and white. What more do you want?
VHS: S04037. $29.95.
Sam Newfield, USA, 1943, 67 mins.

Cry of the Banshee

The Dead Next Door
A scientist has invented a virus that takes over a corpse's cells. Then the reanimated flesh is trapped in a cycle of feeding. The virus needs more dead human flesh. In response, the government fights back with the Zombie Squad. They must kill the undead to save humankind.
VHS: S24763. $59.95.
J.R. Bookwalter, USA, 1989, 84 mins.

Dear, Dead Delilah
This grisly thriller deals with the quest to locate $600,000 in cash which belongs to a decrepit old lady (Agnes Moorehead) with a penchant for beheading her relatives. "For axe-murder aficionados only" (Leonard Maltin). With Will Geer, Michael Ansara, Patricia Carmichael and Dennis Patrick.
VHS: S19354. $19.95.
John Farris, USA, 1972, 90 mins.

Deep Red
Dario Argento's account of a man drawn into a sadistic killer's lair when he witnesses a murder and initiates an investigation with the help of a beautiful journalist. Also known as The Hatchet Murders. With David Hemmings, Daria Nicolodi and Macha Meril. English dubbed.
VHS: S17537. $19.98.
Dario Argento, Italy, 1975, 98 mins.

The Demon Barber of Fleet Street
Tod Slaughter, "the horror man of Europe", stars as Sweeney Todd, the industrious barber who turns potential customers into meat pies that are sold at the bake shop next door. All you need is a sharp razor and a trap door under the barber chair. With Eve Lister. B&W.
VHS: S04041. $29.95.
George King, Great Britain, 1936, 68 mins.

Demons 2
Sally Day's 16th birthday starts with promise but ends with demonic possession and gore. An uninvited guest is lurking in her room with an insatiable appetite. It takes over the innocent girl and transforms her party into a macabre dance with death. Music by the Smiths and Dead Can Dance.
VHS: S24954. $14.99.
Lamberto Bava, Italy, 1986, 88 mins.

Devil Bat
Bela Lugosi as a mad scientist who trains bats to suck the blood of selected victims. With Dave (Captain Midnight) O'Brien.
VHS: S03777. $19.95.
Jean Yarbrough, USA, 1941, 69 mins.

The Devil Doll
Lionel Barrymore, disguised as a sweet old granny, shrinks people down to 12 inches using a serum he found while a prisoner on Devil's Island. He uses the little people to gain revenge on his crooked ex-business partners. Great special effects. With Maureen O'Sullivan. B&W.
VHS: S04705. $59.95.
Tod Browning, USA, 1936, 79 mins.

The Devil's Daughter
Herbert Lom (The Dead Zone) and Kelly Curtis (Trading Places) plunge headfirst into a malevolent whirlpool of murder, madness and unholy mayhem in this terrifying supernatural tale of a legion of evil and the woman who uncovers their deadly secret. A supernatural suspense-thriller produced by world-renowned master of shock cinema, Dario Argento.
VHS: S15391. $89.98.
Michele Soavi, USA, 1991, 112 mins.

Devil's Nightmare
Story of possession made in the wake of The Exorcist, only this time the devil wins.
VHS: S03569. $69.95.
Jean Brismee, Italy, 1971, 88 mins.

The Devil's Partner
A stranger shows up in a small desert town to claim an inheritance. He brings his satanic beliefs and soon the townsfolk begin to notice changes in their dusty little burg. With Edgar Buchanan, Jean Allison, Ed Nelson and Richard Crane.
VHS: S04070. $29.95.
Charles R. Rondeau, USA, 1961, 75 mins.

The Diary of a Madman
In this eerie adaptation of Maupassant's short story, Vincent Price is Simon Cordier, an apparently simple man who tells a 19th century magistrate that a sinister evil spirit called Horla induces him to murder. With Nancy Kovack, Chris Warfield and Stephen Roberts.
VHS: S11285. $14.95.
Reginald LeBorg, USA, 1963, 96 mins.

Diary of a Nudist
This brilliant expose gets inside the head, and various other body parts, of a proud and practicing American nudist. Witness the purpled mountains' majesty as they hover effortlessly above the fruited plain. God, I love this country.
VHS: S15154. $19.95.

Doctor X
Lionel Atwill is suspected of performing cannibalistic murders by the police. This brings unwanted suspicion on his Long Island research lab. Beware of the one-armed man. Also keep an ear out for Fay Wray, who screams alot in this movie, originally made in Technicolor.
VHS: S04707. $59.95.
Laser: LD70132. $39.98.
Michael Curtiz, USA, 1932, 80 mins.

Dominion
The Dominion is a group of children vampires who give new meaning to the concept of juvenile delinquent. Aside from the usual feasting on human blood, these pint-sized creatures stage a rock concert that actually will conjure their demonic legion.
VHS: S24747. $19.95.
Todd Sheets, USA, 1994, 70 mins.

Donovan's Brain
Curt Siodmak's story of a scientist turned into a controlled killer under the power of the brain of a dead but very determined industrialist had made before it in 1944, but that cast didn't include a future First Lady. Nancy Davis (Reagan) tries to assist a man whose mind is not his own. Practice makes perfect. B&W.
VHS: S04710. $14.95.
Felix E. Feist, USA, 1953, 83 mins.

Dorian Gray
Helmut Berger, fresh from *The Damned*, stars as the title character in this trash update of the Oscar Wilde story of a hedonist who stays young while his portrait ages. Lots of sex in trendy places like horse stables and steam baths. With Herbert Lom, Marie Liljedahl and Beryl Cunningham.
VHS: S04258. $14.98.
Massimo Dallamano, Italy/Germany/Lichtenstein, 1970, 92 mins.

Dr. Jekyll and Mr. Hyde (Barrymore)
Recognized as the first great American horror film, this classic tale provided matinee idol John Barrymore with a wonderfully grotesque role as an aristocratic physician who is transformed into a brutal murderer. His zestful rendition of the title character has a grand guignol quality that the later versions of this classic cannot match.
VHS: S05382. $29.95.
John S. Robertson, USA, 1920, 96 mins.

Dr. Jekyll and Mr. Hyde (March)
The uncensored version of the 1932 interpretation of the Robert Louis Stevenson classic that won Fredric March an Oscar. The ten minutes that were cut for its re-release have been restored in its home video debut. Wally Westmore created the transformation make-up for this taut and exciting story of the battle of good and evil in the single body of a man of science. With Miriam Hopkins as Ivy, the prostitute, and Holmes Herbert and Rose Hobart.
VHS: S11217. $19.95.
Rouben Mamoulian, USA, 1932, 98 mins.

Dr. Jekyll and Mr. Hyde (Tracy)
The third screen version of Robert Louis Stevenson's novel is the most popular due to Spencer Tracy's performance as Dr. Harry Jekyll, whose experiments bring out the sexually frustrated Mr. Hyde. With Lana Turner, Ingrid Bergman.
VHS: Out of print. For rental only.
Laser: LD70559. $34.98.
Victor Fleming, USA, 1941, 113 mins.

Dr. Phibes Rises Again
Vincent Price reprises his role as Dr. Phibes in this sequel. He travels to Egypt hoping to find an elixir that will revive his lovely wife. She remains perfectly preserved for just this purpose. Once again those who threaten this near-sacred quest suffer unimaginable torments. With Peter Cushing and Robert Quarry.
VHS: S20932. $14.98.
Robert Fuest, Great Britain, 1972, 89 mins.

Dr. Terror's House of Horrors
Five strangers have their fortunes told by tarot cards dealt by the deadly Peter Cushing. One of the better horror anthology films. Werewolves. Vampires. Voodoo. Killer Plants. And a Crawling Hand. With Christopher Lee, Donald Sutherland and Bernard Lee.
VHS: S04260. $19.95.
Freddie Francis, Great Britain, 1965, 98 mins.

Dracula (Lugosi)
Bela Lugosi stars in his most famous role as the debonair Count in this classic version of Bram Stoker's tale of the bloodsucking fiend. Lots to recommend it, including atmosphere galore and the wonderful Lugosi.
VHS: S00371. $19.95.
Tod Browning, USA, 1931, 75 mins.

Dracula (Palance)
This version recasts the count as a misunderstood genius. Richard Matheson's screenplay is faithful to the original novel. With Simon Ward, Nigel Davenport, Fiona Lewis and Jack Palance as Dracula.
VHS: S17913. $59.98.
Laser: LD71838. $29.98.
Dan Curtis, USA, 1973, 100 mins.

Dracula (Spanish Version)
Filmed simultaneously with Tod Browning's celebrated 1931 English language version, this evocative, atmospheric Spanish translation of Bram Stoker's novel is based on the play by Hamilton Deane and John Balderston, adapted in Spanish by B. Fernandez Cue, shot on the same expressionistic sets. With Carlos Villarias, Lupita Tovar and Pablo Alvarez Rubio.
VHS: S17271. $14.98.
George Melford, Spain, 1931, 104 mins.

Dracula's Daughter
This sequel stars Gloria Holden as Countess Marya Zaleska, who turns up in London to investigate a series of disappearances where the bodies of beautiful women are found with their blood drained. With Otto Kruger, Marguerite Churchill, and Nan Grey.
VHS: S17272. $14.98.
Lambert Hillyer, USA, 1936, 70 mins.

Dracula's Last Rites
A mortician creates vampires from the recently dead and terrorizes a family that hampers his scheme when they demand a relative's body for a private wake. With Patricia Lee Hammond, Gerald Fielding, Victor Jorge and Michael Lally.
VHS: S19133. $14.95.
Domonic Paris, USA, 1979, 88 mins.

Dracula—A Cinematic Scrapbook
A fabulously fiendish collection of film trailers and trivia about Dracula. Includes clips from classics like *Nosferatu, Son of Dracula* and *Plan 9 from Outer Space*. With Bela Lugosi and Christopher Lee. 60 mins.
VHS: S14461. $9.95.

Drums of Jeopardy
Warner Oland, in a pre-Charlie Chan phase, as a mad doctor out for revenge. He holds a certain family responsible for the death of his daughter. Torture and poison gas are but two of his methods to eliminate his victims. With June Collyer and Mischa Auer. B&W.
VHS: S04055. $29.95.
George B. Seitz, USA, 1931

Elvira's Midnight Madness: EEGAH!
Featuring two of the biggest attractions in horror and sci-fi: Richard "Jaws" Kiel and Arch Hall Jr. Dick plays a caveman who schleps around the desert looking for grub and girls, while Arch and the Archers spend their time rocking out.
VHS: S14466. $9.95.
Nicholas Merriwether, USA, 1957

Elvira's Midnight Madness: Frankenstein's Daughter
This frightening feature stars Dr. Frankenstein's female creation. It's classic teenage monster movie mayhem, as the Frankenstein femme fatale follows family tradition and delivers plenty of horror.
VHS: S14468. $9.95.
Richard Cunha, USA, 1958, 85 mins.

Elvira's Midnight Madness: Giant Gila Monster
An over-sized lizard satisfies its appetite for town folk until our crooning hero, Don Sullivan, turns it into a crispy critter. Scary!
VHS: S14465. $9.95.
Ray Kellogg, USA, 1959, 84 mins.

Elvira's Midnight Madness: I Eat Your Skin
Voodoo Island becomes even creepier than its name when a mad scientist starts messing with the gene pool. What happen's next is not a pretty sight.
VHS: S14463. $9.95.
Del Tenney, USA, 1964, 82 mins.

Elvira's Midnight Madness: She Demons
A thriller about a crazed Nazi scientist who holds an uncharted island in the grip of terror as he performs unnatural human experiments that turn vivacious beauties into voluptuous monstrosities.
VHS: S14470. $9.95.
Richard Cunha, USA, 1958, 80 mins.

Elvira's Midnight Madness: The Brain That Wouldn't Die
A surgeon saves his girlfriend's head after she is decapitated in a gruesome car accident. He then preserves her head in his lab while he looks for a fresh body to hook her up with.
VHS: S14473. $9.95.
Joseph Green, USA, 1960, 92 mins.

Elvira's Midnight Madness: The Hideous Sun Demon
A toxic tale about a scientist who is accidentally exposed to radiation and turns into a lizard-like lunatic every time he's in the sunshine.
VHS: S14472. $9.95.
Robert Clarke, USA, 1959, 75 mins.

The End of Man
In this more serious horror film, a preacher named Finis Hominis has supernatural powers that aid him as he explores the psychedelic world of hippies and the mysteries of death. By day he cures paraplegics but by night he raises the dead. Portuguese with English subtitles.
VHS: S20749. $24.95.
Jose Mojica Marins, Brazil, 1971

Evil Mind
Claude Rains and Fay Wray in a weird story of the supernatural: a vaudeville mind reader becomes aware that he actually has the power to predict the future.
VHS: S03335. $29.95.
Maurice Elvey, USA, 1935, 70 mins.

Evil of Frankenstein
Peter Cushing stars as Baron Frankenstein in this Hammer Films presentation. The Baron teams up with Zoltan the Hypnotist to explore new methods of making the monster a more productive citizen. Once again the townfolk fail to see the scientific value of the project and break out the torches and farm implements. With Peter Woodthorpe, Katy Wild, Duncan Lamont and Kiwi Kingston as the Creature.
VHS: S12254. $19.95.
Freddie Francis, Great Britain, 1964, 84 mins.

The Exorcist
Intense supernatural thriller about the possession of a 12-year-old girl by a demonic spirit. The highlight of Linda Blair's film career. First to Mercedes McCambridge taunt priests. See green pea soup in a whole new way. Be terrified by the ring of a telephone. With Jason Miller, Ellen Burstyn and Max von Sydow as the exorcist.
VHS: S01818. $19.98.
William Friedkin, USA, 1973, 121 mins.

Eyes Without a Face
A classic horror film from French filmmaker Georges Franju. A guilt-ridden plastic surgeon attempts to rebuild his daughter's face using the skin from unwilling volunteers. A poetic, artistically made study of madness and guilt. With Pierre Brasseur, Alida Valli, and Edith Scob as the faceless daughter. French with English subtitles. B&W.
VHS: S04481. $59.95.
Georges Franju, France, 1959, 84 mins.

The Face at the Window
A horror movie about the efforts to capture "The Wolf," the killer stalking 1880s Paris. With Tod Slaughter, Marjorie Taylor and John Warwick. On the same program is a stylish Ub Iwerks' cartoon, *Spooks*.
VHS: S04045. $24.95.
George King, Great Britain, 1939, 64 mins.

Fall of the House of Usher
Kay Tendeter is Lord Roderick Usher. His sister is dead but he really isn't so sure. This causes great anxiety and a steep decline in property values. With Gwendoline Watford, Irving Steen, Gavin Lee and Lucy Pavey as the Hag. Source material is Edgar Allan Poe.
VHS: S04067. $19.95.
Ivan Barnett, Great Britain, 1952, 70 mins.

Fiend Without a Face
A rocket base in Canada is under attack by a horde of free-moving killer brains with spinal cords that choke their screaming victims. These mutant brains are very fond of human grey matter. For a while they are also invisible. With Marshall Thompson. B&W.
VHS: S04255. $39.96.
Laser: CAV. LD71983. $29.98.
Arthur Crabtree, Great Britain, 1958, 78 mins.

The Fiendish Plot of Dr. Fu Manchu
Peter Sellers' final film is full of villainous fun. He plays two roles: a diabolical criminal mastermind *and* his own Scotland Yard nemesis.
VHS: S14568. $19.98.
Laser: LD71473. $34.98.
Piers Haggard, Great Britain, 1980, 100 mins.

Flesh and the Fiends (Mania)
Peter Cushing stars in this gory tale of body-snatching as the dedicated Dr. Knox. He needs fresh corpses for his medical experiments and studies. Donald Pleasance and George Rose are in the cast and seem likely to be able to provide the Dr. with what he needs.
VHS: S04073. $29.95.
John Gilling, Great Britain, 1960, 87 mins.

The Flesh Eaters
One of the greatest low-budget black and white shockers of all time. A mad, ex-Nazi scientist breeds a strain of flesh-devouring bacteria on a desert island, using victims of a shipwreck as his guinea pigs. Some of the gruesome special effects are amazing. This is not one to show to your young children, yet not really a gore film. And the astonishing climax still packs a jolt.
VHS: S00449. $29.95.
Jack Curtis, USA, 1964, 87 mins.

The Fly
Vincent Price is the mad scientist who experiments with his disintegration machine and has his atomic pattern traded with that of a fly in the original version of this now classic sci-fi theme.
VHS: S03366. $14.98.
Kurt Neumann, USA, 1958, 94 mins.

The Fly II
A new generation of terror in this follow-up to *The Fly*, starring Eric Stoltz and Daphne Zuniga.
VHS: S09791. $19.98.
Chris Valas, USA, 1988, 105 mins.

Fog
A contemporary tale of supernatural horror from the director of *Halloween*, featuring a cast that includes Jamie Lee Curtis, Janet Leigh, Adrienne Barbeau, Hal Holbrook and John Houseman.
VHS: S01317. $19.95.
Laser: LD72301. $29.99.
John Carpenter, USA, 1979, 94 mins.

Frankenstein (Bergin/Quaid)
David Wickes' stylish adaptation of Mary Shelley's baroque classic about a brilliant doctor (Patrick Bergin) who experiments to build the perfect human. His plans go hideously awry and in the process the doctor creates a beast (Randy Quaid)—which responds by trying to avenge his disfigured state. Cinematography by Jack Conroy (*My Left Foot*). With John Mills, Lambert Wilson and Fiona Gillies.
VHS: S19535. $92.98.
David Wickes, USA, 1993, 117 mins.

Frankenstein (Gielgud)
Carrie Fisher, Sir John Gielgud, Robert Powell and David Warner star in this modern version of Mary Shelley's classic. Robert Powell is Dr. Frankenstein, Carrie Fisher his fiancee.
VHS: S02658. $69.95.
James Ormerod, Great Britain, 1984, 81 mins.

Frankenstein and the Monster from Hell
The final effort from Hammer Films' *Frankenstein* cycle is a tongue-in-cheek piece about the weird coincidences and strange developments at a hospital for the criminally insane, under the supervision of our neurotic monster/hero, inevitably played by Peter Cushing. With Shane Briant, Madeline Smith and Dave Prowse.
VHS: S16893. $19.95.
Terence Fisher, Great Britain, 1974, 93 mins.

Frankenstein Meets the Wolfman
This Universal horror film provides a sequel that combines two of their most popular monsters. Lawrence Talbot seeks out the help of a certain notorious mad scientist only to find the doctor dead and his creations quite alive. The townspeople are not pleased to find monsters in their neighborhood. With Lon Chaney Jr., Ilona Massey, Patric Knowles, Dwight Frye and Bela Lugosi as Frankenstein's monster.
VHS: S12253. $14.98.
Roy William Neill, USA, 1943, 72 mins.

Frankenstein—A Cinematic Scrapbook
A diabolically delicious collection of movie trailers and terrifying trivia about the immortal Frankenstein. Includes clips from the original horror classic and such hilarious spoofs as *Abbot and Costello Meet Frankenstein* and Mel Brooks' modern day masterpiece, *Young Frankenstein*. 60 mins.
VHS: S14460. $9.95.
Ted Newsom, USA, 1991, 60 mins.

Frankenstein—The Restored Version
A restored version (containing footage not seen since censors cut the film at the time of its original release) of one of the great Hollywood horror films, with Boris Karloff in this famous adaptation of Mary Shelley's masterpiece.
VHS: S00462. $14.98.
James Whale, USA, 1931, 71 mins.

Freaks
Tod Browning's classic horror film, with a cast of real side-show "freaks"—dwarfs, midgets, Siamese twins— dominated and exploited by the circus strong man and a beautiful aerialist, who eventually band together in a horrifying revenge.
VHS: S01560. $19.95.
Laser: LD70578. $34.98.
Tod Browning, USA, 1932, 66 mins.

From Beyond
From Stuart Gordon, the director of *Re-Animator*, a grisly, ghoulish take based on a story by H.P. Lovecraft. The Resonator is a gruesome machine that activates a special sixth sense—one that makes its victims crave human brains.
VHS: S02938. $19.98.
Stuart Gordon, USA, 1986, 85 mins.

The Fury of the Wolfman
A chiller about a gifted scientist who is transformed into a diabolical wolfman and wreaks havoc on the unsuspecting. With Paul Naschy and Mark Stevens. English dubbed.
VHS: S19352. $19.95.
Jose Maria Zabalza, Spain, 1970, 80 mins.

Galaxy of the Dinosaurs
The rather dimwitted Zyrox, a human-like people with simple desires, stop for lunch on a pleasant looking planet. They never expected a whirlwind of chaotic prehistoric terror, just a nice picnic spot. This is a good, terror-filled film with some great laughs.
VHS: S24754. $9.95.
Lance Randas, USA, 1992, 85 mins.

The Ghost
Barbara Steele stars in this Italian semi-sequel to *The Horrible Dr. Hichcock* as a greedy, scheming, unfaithful wife to the crippled Dr. Hitchcock, a physician with a strong interest in the occult. There was no "t" in the man's name in the first film, but both films have Steele doing what she does best. With Harriet White, Elio Jotta and Peter Baldwin as Dr. Livingstone.
VHS: S09139. $29.95.
Riccardo (Robert Hampton) Freda, Italy, 1963, 96 mins.

The Ghost of Frankenstein
An eerie sequel to *Son of Frankenstein*. Ygor (Bela Lugosi) tries desperately to foil a fiendish plot to switch the monster's brain with the brain tissue of an educated human. With Cedrick Hardwicke, Lon Chaney Jr., Lionel Atwill and Ralph Bellamy.
VHS: S19009. $14.98.
Erle C. Kenton, USA, 1942, 68 mins.

Ghoul
For years a lost cult classic of British horror films, this stars Boris Karloff, with Cedric Hardwicke and Ralph Richardson. Very effective Gothic mood sustained by atmospheric camera work.
VHS: S02931. $29.95.
T. Hayes Hunter, Great Britain, 1933, 68 mins.

Girls School Screamer
There are seven beautiful coeds at this exclusive finishing school, where they ultimately find themselves finished off. It all begins when they are locked in a dark mansion for a night of unspeakable horrors. Suddenly graduation does not seem so terribly important. Getting out alive does.
VHS: S22676. $14.95.
John P. Finegan, USA, 1985, 85 mins.

Goblin
A newlywed couple move into their own home, but there is an unknown previous inhabitant still in residence. He was accidentally conjured from the depths of hell and is in no mood to move back, because he enjoys spreading terror.
VHS: S24745. $19.95.
Todd Sheets, USA, 1993 75 mins.

Graveyard Shift
Another terror-filled tale from Stephen King. This one is based on one of his short stories about a monstrous, primordial rat living in the tunnels underneath a previously abandoned textile mill. When the mill is re-opened one night, the horror begins.
VHS: S13715. $14.95.
Laser: LD75203. $34.98.
Ralph S. Singleton, USA, 1990, 89 mins.

The Greed of William Hart
Tod Slaughter lends himself to recreating the story of Burke and Hare, the Scottish graverobbers. When the supply of cadavers runs low for the medical schools in Edinburgh, Slaughter and Henry Oscar create access to a fresher product, much to the annoyance of the local populace. With Arnold Bell as Doctor Cox.
VHS: S04047. $24.95.
Oswald Mitchell, Great Britain, 1948, 78 mins.

The Green Slime
This campy, stylish tribute to the sci-fi classics of the 50s stars Robert Horton as a hot-headed commander enlisted to save Earth. Filmed entirely in Japan at Toei Studios in Tokyo with a Japanese director and crew—despite its all-Caucasian cast.
VHS: S14958. $19.98.
Kinji Kukasaku, USA/Japan, 1968, 90 mins.

Half Human
Half man, half beast, but all monster! Low budget Japanese chiller from the director of *Godzilla*. With Inoshiro Honda, John Carradine and Kenneth Crane.
VHS: S12779. $14.95.
Inoshiro Honda, Japan, 1958, 78 mins.

Halloween
Considered one of the scariest films ever made, as well as one of the most successful independent films. The godfather of the sub-genre of the high school horror film, with the boogie man who just won't die. With Jamie Lee Curtis and P.J. Soles.
VHS: Out of print. For rental only.
Laser: Letterboxed, special edition. LD74592. $99.98.
John Carpenter, USA, 1978, 90 mins.

Hallucinations of a Deranged Mind
An anti-government assembly of outlawed footage that's a radical critique of censorship and authoritarianism. Brazil horror auteur Jose Mojica Marins assembled sequences from 10 different films that were altered by the military junta. The scenes include a young man ravaged by images of a Coffin Joe. Portuguese with English subtitles.
VHS: S18985. $24.95.
Jose Mojica Marins, Brazil, 1970

Hands of a Stranger
A variation of *Hands of Orlac*, about a gifted pianist who receives a hand transplant from a demented killer and begins acting out violent rages. With Paul Lukather, Joan Harvey and Irish McCalla.
VHS: S18936. $19.95.
Newton Arnold, USA, 1962, 86 mins.

Hands of Orlac
With Christopher Lee, Mel Ferrer, Donald Wolff. A well-done remake of *Mad Love* has Ferrer as the pianist with the transplanted criminal hands and Lee as the man who torments him. Ferrer does a fine performance as the tormented Orlac, who is obsessed by the hands grafted to his wrists after an accident, that he believes belonged to a psychotic stranger.
VHS: S12328. $29.95.
Edmond T. Greville, Great Britain/France, 1960, 95 mins.

The Harvest
Miguel Ferrer stars in this tense psycho-thriller as a screenwriter who uncovers a black market in human parts, or to be more precise, these crooks discover him and steal one of his kidneys. Not satisfied with that, they want to take its mate.
VHS: S21004. $94.95.
David Marconi, USA, 1992, 97 mins.

Hatchet for a Honeymoon
Mario Bava's baroque chiller about a despondent man, haunted by recurring memories of his dead wife, who abducts and kills young brides. English dubbed.
VHS: S19347. $19.95.
Mario Bava, Italy/Spain, 1971, 93 mins.

Haunting Fear
Based on the E.A. Poe short story *The Premature Burial*. Jan-Michael Vincent stars as an unfaithful husband with a surefire plan to scare his wife to death. He and girlfriend Brinke Stevens hadn't counted on Karen Black's troubled spirit being interested in seeking revenge. With Robert Quarry, Delia Sheppard and Michael Berryman, the spookiest looking actor since Rondo Hatton. Scary stuff.
VHS: S15494. $79.95.
Fred Olen Ray, USA, 1991, 88 mins.

The Head
This German horror film is not to be confused with the Monkees psychedelic comic of 1968. French actor Michel Simon invents serum Z, which keeps a dog's detached noggin alive. Horst Frank as Dr. Ood experiments using human subjects like his boss's head. He also transplants the head of a crippled nurse onto the body of a stripper just for fun. B&W.
VHS: S09135. $29.95.
Victor Trivas, W. Germany, 1959, 92 mins.

Hellish Flesh
George Medeiros, played by Jose Mojica Marins, is a scientist obsessed with devising an acid that can dissolve an entire human body. Tragically disfigured by his scheming wife and her gigolo boyfriend, his plans are sidetracked. Ultimately, however, he manages to make his mark in the world of science and on his conniving spouse as well. Made in Brazil. Portuguese with English subtitles.
VHS: S21347. $24.95.

Horror Chamber of Dr. Faustus
The American version of Georges Franju's classic *Eyes without a Face*—a spine-tingling chiller in which the demented physician seeks facial transplants for his disfigured daughter.
VHS: S04074. $29.95.
Georges Franju, France, 1960, 84 mins.

Horror Express
There is a monster defrosting in the baggage car that wants to eat its way through the entire train. Christopher Lee, Peter Cushing and Telly Savalas are determined not to be on the menu when the formerly frozen diner finds it likes to travel by train. Good for its genre.
VHS: S04054. $19.99.
Eugenio Martin, Spain, 1972, 88 mins.

Horror Hotel
A very scary film which concerns witchcraft in New England as a 17th century witch, who is now an innkeeper, lures her victims for their blood and sacrifice to the devil.
VHS: S08432. $29.95.
John Llewellyn Moxey, Great Britain, 1960, 76 mins.

Horror of Dracula
This Hammer film is said to be one of the best vampire movies ever made. Based on the Bram Stoker classic novel, it stars Christopher Lee as the Count and Peter Cushing as his arch foe, Von Helsing. It spawned seven sequels. Sink your teeth in something good.
VHS: S04187. $14.95.
Laser: LD74703. $34.98.
Terence Fisher, Great Britain, 1958, 82 mins.

Horror of It All
Narrated by Jose Ferrer, a look at the dark side of the imagination and movies and some of horror's most popular stars—Boris Karloff, Lon Chaney, Bela Lugosi, John Barrymore, Lionel Atwill, John Carradine and Vincent Price—and a behind-the-scenes examination of how some of horror's most memorable moments were created. 58 mins.
VHS: S05323. $19.98.

Horror of the Blood Monsters
More camp: a scientist traces the wave of vampire killings that's sweeping the earth; John Carradine is the vampire-like inhabitant of a planet whose natives invade earth to feed on human flesh. Also known as *Vampire Men of the Lost Planet, Horror of the Blood Monster, Creatures of the Prehistoric Planet, Horror Creatures of the Prehistoric Planet, Space Mission of the Lost Planet.*
VHS: S08042. $19.98.
Al Adamson, USA, 1970, 85 mins.

Horror Rises from the Tomb
In the 15th century, a knight and his sidekick are beheaded on charges of practicing witchcraft. Revived more than 500 years later, they disrupt a group of vacationers. With Paul Naschy, Vic Winner, Emma Cohen and Helga Line. English dubbed.
VHS: S19351. $19.95.
Carlos Aured, Spain, 1972, 89 mins.

House of Dracula
A gothic sequel to *House of Frankenstein*. The story concerns a doctor who is shocked to watch his personality being turned into that of a destructive monster. With Onslow Stevens, Lon Chaney Jr., John Carradine and Lionel Atwill.
VHS: S19010. $14.98.
Erle C. Kenton, USA, 1945, 67 mins.

House of Frankenstein
Boris Karloff and J. Carrol Naish star in this peculiar horror movie about a twisted scientist and his hunchback assistant who escape from prison, impersonate traveling show performers, and conjure up Dracula, Frankenstein, and Wolfman to carry out their evil intentions. With Lon Chaney, John Carradine, Anne Gwynne, Peter Coe, and Glenn Strange's first appearance as Frankenstein.
VHS: S17275. $14.98.
Erle C. Kenton, USA, 1944, 71 mins.

House of Horrors
Marcel De Lang plays an insane sculptor who befriends an escaped psychopath. It's a rewarding friendship that gives De Lang the opportunity to wreak revenge on all those art critics who have belittled his art works.
VHS: S21728. $14.98.
Jean Yarbrough, USA, 1946, 65 mins.

House of Wax
Vincent Price stars as a demented sculptor who must use human bodies in his wax museum after a fire destroys his hands and his optimistic outlook on life. With Carolyn Jones, Phyllis Kirk and Charles Bronson as the mute assistant. Originally shown in 3-D. Watch for the paddleball man.
VHS: S04188. $59.95.
Laser: LD71809. $34.98.
Andre de Toth, USA, 1953, 88 mins.

The House on Haunted Hill
Vincent Price stars in this classic William Castle film about a group of people who, in order to win a bet with the wealthy Price, try to spend one night in a spooky old mansion with lots of skeletons in its closets.
VHS: S14791. $14.98.
William Castle, USA, 1958, 75 mins.

Human Monster (Dark Eyes of London)
Bela Lugosi in one of the most macabre horror films, as the brilliant but unbalanced Dr. Orloff, who owns an insurance company, works with indigent blind men in his spare time, but is no philanthropist: he is a fiendish killer. Crack Scotland Yard inspector Holt is brought on Orloff's case with hair-raising results.
VHS: S02991. $29.95.
Walter Summers, Great Britain, 1939, 73 mins.

Hush, Hush, Sweet Charlotte
There are strange goings on at Hollis House, where feeble-minded Bette Davis lives protected by her peculiar housekeeper, Agnes Moorehead. Then cousin Olivia de Havilland comes for a visit, and now Bette will have more than headless ex-boyfriends to worry about. With Bruce Dern and Joseph Cotten. B&W.
VHS: S03912. $19.98.
Robert Aldrich, USA, 1965, 133 mins.

I Bury the Living
At a cemetery, the caretaker has a map of plots and uses white pins for vacant plots and black pins for plots with occupants. When the honorary chairman of the cemetery switches the pins around, live plot owners die and buried tenants revive. Tension builds while waiting to see the consequences of the pin switcharoonie. Does the Chairman of the Morgue have supernatural powers? Very spooky and creepy cult favorite. With Richard Boone, Theodore Bikel.
VHS: S12326. $29.95.
Albert Band, USA, 1957, 77 mins.

I Walked with a Zombie
A subtle, atmospheric film loosely based on *Jane Eyre*, from the producer-director team of *Cat People*. The film takes place on the voodoo-ridden island of Haiti, and shows a world in which all that is spiritual has physical extensions. A classic!
VHS: S00602. $19.98.
Jacques Tourneur, USA, 1943, 69 mins.

I Was a Teenage Mummy (1962)
This classic horror flick is introduced by monster movie maven Forrest J. Ackerman. A professor unearths a mummy that becomes obsessed with revenge. Back in Bridgeport, Connecticut, the entire entourage find themselves plagued by the murderous, overwrapped fiend. Includes an interview with the director.
VHS: S25657. $39.95.
Ralph C. Bluemke, USA, 1962, 73 mins.

I Was a Teenage Mummy (1992)
A low-budget thriller, shot in New Jersey, about a beautiful young girl's transformation into a crazed and unearthly monster. The film stars Chris Tsakis, Ahmed Ben "Leo" Kalib and Mark Fucile, and features the original music of A-Bones.
VHS: S17538. $19.95.

The Incredible Doktor Markesan
Boris Karloff is Doktor Markesan, the inventor of a serum that wakes the dead. Actually they are living zombies. The Doktor's nephew and his wife, Dick York and Carolyn Kearney, come to live with him, and their insatiable curiosity sets the stage for terror.
VHS: S21496. $12.98.
Robert Florey, USA, 1962, 50 mins.

The Indestructible Man
No, it's not Arnold Schwarzenegger. But if you guessed Lon Chaney Jr. you may want to see this science fiction tale of a man who returns from the dead to get even with the gang of criminals that did him wrong. With Ross Elliott, Marian Carr and Casey Adams. B&W.
VHS: S04034. $29.95.
Jack Pollexfen, USA, 1956, 70 mins.

Invasion of the Vampires
Carlos Agosti and Bertha Moss star in this extremely atmospheric "vampire in a castle tale." There is a misty cave chock full of coffins where the troops will be marshalled for the invasion. Could this be an arty Mexican horror film?
VHS: S23164. $29.95.
Miguel Morayta, Mexico, 1961, 78 mins.

Invisible Agent
An irresistible boy's fantasy film about a brave and resourceful young kid who fights the Nazis through his skills to render himself invisible. With Ilona Massey, Jon Hall and Peter Lorre.
VHS: S19016. $14.98.
Edwin L. Martin, USA, 1942, 81 mins.

The Invisible Ghost
One of Bela Lugosi's best films. The story concerns a husband who, when hypnotized by his insane wife, commits many blood-thirsty murders.
VHS: S03333. $29.95.
Joseph H. Lewis, USA, 1941, 64 mins.

Invisible Man
A super version of H.G. Wells' fantasy, with Claude Rains playing the scientist who experiments with a drug which, while it makes him invisible, also turns him into a megalomaniac murderer. Terrific special effects, with Gloria Stuart playing the sexy heroine.
VHS: S02943. $14.98.
Laser: LD70041. $34.98.
James Whale, USA, 1933, 72, mins.

The Invisible Man Returns
Vincent Price stars in this sequel as a brilliant scientist who renders himself invisible. Price is falsely accused of killing his brother and turns invisible to pursue his own investigation. With Sir Cedric Hardwicke, Nan Grey, John Sutton and Cecil Kellaway.
VHS: S17273. $14.98.
Joe May, USA, 1940, 81 mins.

The Invisible Man's Revenge
John Hall is an unstable man who wants to claim an estate. A crazed scientist gives him a serum that makes him invisible, thereby allowing him to realize his plans. Things go awry when they disagree and the invisible man cannot regain his appearance.
VHS: S21731. $14.98.
Ford Beebe, USA, 1944, 77 mins.

Invisible Ray
Bela Lugosi and Boris Karloff are teamed in this classic thriller about a scientist who receives the power to kill with a touch of the hand, from a meteorite found during an expedition in Africa.
VHS: S02721. $14.98.
Lambert Hillyer, USA, 1936, 90 mins.

The Invisible Woman
A genius professor renders a beautiful model invisible. In the confusion, a corrupt industrialist who funded the experiment and a savvy gangster fight for control of the formula. With John Barrymore, Virginia Bruce, John Howard and Charlie Ruggles.
VHS: S19011. $14.98.
A. Edward Sutherland, USA, 1941, 72 mins.

Island of Lost Souls
A terrifying adaptation of H.G. Wells' story about a vivisectionist trapped on a desolate island who alters the biological genetics of jungle animals and changes them into pathological man/animal hybrids. With Charles Laughton, Bela Lugosi, Richard Arlen and Stanley Fields.
VHS: S19013. $14.98.
Erle C. Kenton, USA, 1933, 70 mins.

Island Terror
Mutant monsters resulting from bizarre radiation research terrorize a peaceful island. Now two doctors, Peter Cushing and Edward Judd, must combat the creatures who are rapidly reproducing themselves and could conceivably threaten the whole world.
VHS: S20890. $14.98.
Terence Fisher, Great Britain, 1966, 87 mins.

Isle of the Dead
Another Val Lewton production with Boris Karloff in this eerie thriller, set in the Greek islands, about demons, premature burial, and evil possession of the resurrected body.
VHS: S00640. $14.98.
Mark Robson, USA, 1945, 72 mins.

It Lives Again
The sequel to *It's Alive* features more than one killer baby with an organized government program to isolate and eliminate these freaks of nature. Frederic Forrest and Kathleen Lloyd are the new parents warned by John Ryan that their precious little gift needs special care.
VHS: S04186. $14.95.
Larry Cohen, USA, 1978, 91 mins.

It's Alive
Cult director Larry Cohen delivers the ultimate parental nightmare. John Ryan and Sharon Farrell find that not only is their newborn a physical monstrosity, it is also capable of catching and killing its own lunch. With Michael Ansara, Andrew Duggan, and Guy Stockwell. This one is creepy.
VHS: S04185. $14.95.
Larry Cohen, USA, 1974, 91 mins.

Jack the Ripper
This trilogy of terror blends the familiar with the supernatural, depicting the master of menace, Boris Karloff, as the highlight of each story. Includes *The Murder that Never Happened, Where There's a Will* and a shocking interpretation of the grisly *Jack the Ripper* murders, told from the killer's point of view. 70 mins.
VHS: S15915. $29.95.

Jack the Ripper: The Final Solution
A killer stalked late 19th century London. His frenzy of murder remains an unsolved mystery to this day. Using new evidence, this video reveals Jack the Ripper's identity and the conspiracy that kept it a secret for so long. 90 mins.
VHS: S25638. $19.95.

Jack's Back
One hundred years later Jack the Ripper returns to plague Southern California with a duplication of his famous crimes. Is the copy-cat killer the mild mannered medical doctor or his criminal twin brother (both played by James Spader)? Co-worker Cynthia Gibb isn't sure. A creepy and calculating murder mystery and thriller with more red herrings than a fish market in Moscow.
VHS: S07582. $89.95.
Laser: LD75290. $34.98.
Rowdy Herrington, USA, 1988, 97 mins.

Jesse James Meets Frankenstein's Daughter
A strange mix of horror and western genres that imagines a strange meeting between an Old West outlaw and a baroque 18th-century villain. With John Lupton, Estelita, Cal Bolder and Steven Geray.
VHS: S19355. $19.95.
William Beaudine, USA, 1966, 88 mins.

Kill, Baby, Kill
Erica Blanc, Max Lawrence and Fabienne Dall star in this atmospheric horror movie driven by vengeance. A young girl's ghost haunts those who caused her death. The only one who understands this deftly woven scenario is ignored until it is too late. All the required horror movie elements are here, including swirling mists, cobwebbed rooms and even a black cat.
VHS: S23169. $29.95.
Mario Bava, Italy, 1966, 83 mins.

Killer Bats (aka The Devil Bats)
Bela Lugosi (starring as a crazed scientist, of course) seeks revenge against his employer—a cosmetics manufacturer who deprives him of his share of the profits. The bats do the dirty work! One of Lugosi's most notorious pictures.
VHS: S13855. $19.95.
Jean Yarbrough, USA, 1941, 67 mins.

Killer Shrews
They may look like dogs dressed up for Halloween but they still can bite, in this low budget horror movie made in Texas. Produced by and starring Ken Curtis (Festus on *Gunsmoke*) as a mad scientist. With James Best and Miss Universe 1957, Ingrid Goude, as people who know that even giant shrews can't bite through a barrel. B&W.
VHS: S09127. $14.95.
Ray Kellogg, USA, 1959, 70 mins.

Killers from Space
Peter Graves plays a scientist raised from the dead by some monsters with bulging eyes who plan to use him as a spy. Will Peter save the earth from these alien creatures?
VHS: S14464. $9.95.
W. Lee Wilder, USA, 1954, 80 mins.

King Kong (60th Anniversary Edition)
The classic 1933 shocker by Ernest B. Schoedsack in a 60th anniversary edition. The film's daring special effects still astonish and are preserved in this archival print and digitally remastered soundtrack struck from the original optical master track. With Fay Wray, Robert Armstrong, Bruce Cabot, Frank Reicher, Sam Hardy and Noble Johnson. B&W.
VHS: S17035. $16.98.
Laser: CAV. LD70389. $74.95.
Ernest B. Schoedsack, USA, 1933, 103 mins.

King Kong (60th Anniversary Edition/Gift Set)
The classic 1933 monster movie by Ernest B. Schoedsack is presented in a 60th anniversary edition, including a documentary on the making of the film, a theatrical size poster and certificate of authenticity mailed directly to the consumer.
VHS: S17634. $59.98.
Ernest B. Schoedsack, USA, 1933, 103 mins.

King of the Zombies
Another ambitious scientist has come up with the perfect soldier for WWII, the zombie corps. Developed in the laboratory of a castle on a jungle island, the undead train to hit the beach. The cast includes Dick Purcell, Joan Woodbury, Henry Victor and Mantan Moreland as the comic relief. B&W.
VHS: S04061. $29.95.
Jean Yarbrough, USA, 1941, 67 mins.

Kingdom of the Vampires
Jeff is a liquor store clerk who hides his secret rather well. In actuality he is a vampire with a ghoulish mother at home who snacks on the neighborhood kids. Jeff's troubles are compounded when he falls in love, because mother is just a trifle jealous.
VHS: S24760. $9.95.
J.R. Bookwalter, USA, 1991, 90 mins.

Kiss of the Tarantula
Great camp. In the tradition of *Ben*, Susan, the unusual daughter of a mortuary owner, collects tarantula spiders. Shunned by her schoolmates and friends, she uses her deadly pets in acts of hideous revenge. With Eric Mason, Susan Ling. Color, 85 mins.
VHS: S13232. $19.95.
Chris Munger, USA, 1975, 85 mins.

Kiss of the Vampire
In search of a honeymoon destination, a young couple loses their way in the Bavarian forest. Luckily, a distinguished lord invites them to his castle. A nightmare unfolds there featuring a family of vampires. Only Professor Zimmer and his ancient ritual offer them any hope of leaving this Hammer Horror Collection nightmare behind. With Clifford Evans, Noel Willman, Edward De Souza, Jennifer Daniel and Barry Warren.
VHS: S25569. $14.98.
Don Sharp, Great Britain, 1962, 88 mins.

The Leech Woman
A doctor and his wife, played by Phillip Terry and Colleen Gray, venture to Africa together even though age has dampened the doctor's interest in his wife. There they uncover a secret to eternal youth that extracts a terrible price, the blood of young men.
VHS: S20894. $14.98.
Edward Dein, USA, 1960, 77 mins.

The Leopard Man
Something is stalking the young women of a small New Mexico village. Are they the victims of a man who can transform into a leopard? An intriguing, atmospheric thriller from the Val Lewton/Jacques Tourneur production team that brought us Cat People. Based on the novel Black Alibi by Cornell Woolrich. With Dennis O'Keefe and Jean Brooks.
VHS: S00745. $19.98.
Jacques Tourneur, USA, 1943, 66 mins.

The Long Hair of Death
Barbara Steele is back as another vengeful ghost in this Italian horror film. In another life she was the sister of an accused witch who was burned at the stake, while she was hurled to her death by an overreacting Count. Those who deserve punishment are dealt with severely. With Jean Rafferty, Giorgio Ardisson and Halina Zalewska.
VHS: S09132. $29.95.
Anthony Dawson (Antonio Margheriti), Italy, 1964

Lord of Illusions
Scott Bakula stars in this horrifying tale spawned by the dark imagination of Clive Barker. Bakula plays Harry D'Amour, a detective who stumbles upon a mystery. Phillip Swan, a world famous magician, and his wife involve Harry in a murder. If only that were the extent of the troubles. Before long, Harry learns the terrifying truth that illusion is trickery, but magic is real.
VHS: S26859. $96.99.
Laser: Letterboxed. LD75515. $34.98.
Clive Barker, USA, 1995, 109 mins.

The Lugosi Files
A salute to the master of menace, who was buried in his Dracula cloak in 1956 but lives on in the hearts of horror film fans forever. Scenes cover his career from 1931-1955 and include the rare trailer narrated by Bela, Mark of the Vampire, and his tv appearance on "You Asked for It."
VHS: S04014. $29.95.

The Mad Death
Horror reaches an epidemic scale when family pets become rabid killers. With wild beasts attacking and people going mad, one man is given the powers of a dictator. He unleashes the army on a countryside where the most dangerous animals are humans. Great Britain, 120 mins.
VHS: S14330. $49.95.

The Mad Executioners
A mad scientist decapitates his victims and tries to keep their heads alive. Meanwhile, a group of strange vigilantes are capturing and murdering criminals without benefit of a public trial. Scotland Yard investigates to see if there is any connection. Wolfgang Preiss and Chris Howland star.
VHS: S23197. $29.95.
Edwin Zbonek, Germany, 1963, 94 mins.

The Mad Ghoul
A chemistry professor's research into Ancient Egyptian gases pays off when he uncovers one that induces a strange mental state. The victims of this gas experience a paralysis that robs them of their wills and turns them into zombies.
VHS: S21727. $14.98.
James P. Hogan, USA, 1943, 65 mins.

Mad Love
A brilliant but creepy surgeon (Peter Lorre, in his first American role) falls in love with a beautiful actress who shuns him. When her famous pianist husband loses his hands in an accident, the wife turns to the doctor for help. Lorre agrees to operate and grafts on the hands of a murderer, which would rather choke than play piano. This stylish American remake of The Hands of Orlac is directed by famous German cameraman Karl Freund and shot by Gregg Toland (Citizen Kane) with an eerie, expressionistic beauty. With Colin Clive and Frances Drake.
VHS: S16181. $19.98.
Karl Freund, USA, 1935, 83 mins.

The Mad Monster
George Zucco steals the show as a crazed doctor who changes a man into a werewolf for the purposes of revenge. No wonder the monster is cranky. With Johnny Downs, Anne Nagel and the ever popular Glenn Strange. Low budget and lots of unintended laughs.
VHS: S04036. $29.95.
Sam Newfield, USA, 1942, 72 mins.

Madame Satan
Please don't confuse this selection with the 1930 Cecil B. De Mille film of the same name. While that film had a wild party on a zeppelin, this video features a seance of sexuality, as a slave of the devil conjures up the Prince of Darkness and it's time for an unholy orgy with whips and chains and naked people. FOR ADULTS ONLY. 60 mins.
VHS: S03660. $29.95.

The Majorettes
Someone is killing all the beautiful majorettes at a seemingly normal high school. While suspicions abound, no one is able to stop the murderous rampage. Beauty and gore have never been mixed into a more terrifying plot.
VHS: S24752. $9.95.
Bill Hinzman, USA, 1986, 92 mins.

The Man and the Monster
A pianist can't help himself from becoming a hideous monster whenever a certain tune is played. An affliction of this sort is without doubt going to cut down on one's social life and employment possibilities. With Abel Salazar, Marta Roth, and Enrique Rambol.
VHS: S04072. $29.95.
Rafael Baladon, Mexico, 1958, 78 mins.

The Man Who Lived Again
Boris Karloff plays a mad scientist with the ability to transfer minds from one living person to another. He sees his work as a short cut to immortality but unfortunately for him, not everyone wants to swap. With Anna Lee and John Loder. B&W.
VHS: S04016. $29.95.
Robert Stevenson, Great Britain, 1936, 66 mins.

Man-Made Monster
Lon Chaney, Jr., stars as a circus man who has built up an immunity to electricity through his circus performances. This unusual ability gives him the power to harm simply with his touch. It's a useful skill, particularly when he is framed by the unscrupulous scientist who originally helped him.
VHS: S21726. $14.98.
George Waggner, USA, 1941, 59 mins.

The Manster
Not a typo but a Japanese/U.S. co-production about a mad scientist named Dr. Suzuki who injects an American reporter with a diabolical serum that causes him to grow another head. That's just for starters, for the evil head grows another body. Unholy population explosion. This is what happens when you keep your mutant wife in a cage. B&W.
VHS: S09136. $29.95.
K.D. Crane/G.P. Breakston, U.S./Japan, 1959

Mark of the Devil
Herbert Lom is a long way from The Pink Panther in this story of witch hunts and sadism in the 18th century. With Udo Kier of Andy Warhol's Frankenstein fame.
VHS: S05856. $29.95.
Michael Armstrong, Great Britain, 1969, 96 mins.

Mark of the Devil, Part II
The sequel to the most revolting movie of the decade finds the evil Count Balthasar (slayer of hundreds of innocent women) on a witch hunt and after the lovely Countess Von Solmaneau. With Anton Diffring, Erica Blanc and the incredible Reggie Nalder.
VHS: S04848. $29.95.
Adrian Hoven, USA, 1972, 87 mins.

Mark of the Vampire
Most folks would agree that the mark of the vampire is two small holes over the jugular vein. This Tod Browning sound re-make of London after Midnight stars Bela Lugosi as Count Mora and Carroll Borland as his eerie daughter, Luna. With Lionel Atwill, Lionel Barrymore and a special surprise ending. B&W.
VHS: S04706. $59.95.
Tod Browning, USA, 1935, 60 mins.

Mary Shelley's Frankenstein
An all star cast, including Robert De Niro, Kenneth Branagh, Tom Hulce, Helena Bonham Carter, Aidan Quinn and John Cleese, is featured in this lavish but monstrous film. This adaptation follows Shelley's seminal gothic text more closely than past screen incarnations have.
VHS: S24385. $19.95.
Laser: LD74901. $39.95.
Kenneth Branagh, USA, 1994, 123 mins.

The Mask
Elvira, Mistress of the Dark, hosts this camp horror classic also known as Eyes of Hell. The discovery of an ancient mask poses unforseen threats to those around it. This 3-D presentation will make the terrors posed by The Mask seem uncomfortably close and real.
VHS: S00030. $12.95.
Julian Roffman, USA, 1961, 85 mins.

The Mask of Fu Manchu
An adaptation of the Sax Rohmer novel about a deranged Chinese killer (Boris Karloff) squaring off with an expedition studying the relics of Ghengis Khan's tomb. With Lewis Stone, Karen Morley and a campy, exaggerated Myrna Loy as Fu's mischievous and darkly vicious daughter.
VHS: S17533. $19.98.
Charles J. Brabin, USA, 1932, 72 mins.

Midnight at Madame Tussaud's
A financier finds his life is in danger when he bets he can spend the night in the Chamber of Horrors in a popular London tourist attraction. Filmed on location at Madame Tussaud's. With James Carew as Sir Clive, the intended victim, Lucille Lisle and Kim Peacock.
VHS: S04058. $29.95.
George Pearson, Great Britain, 1936, 63 mins.

Mondo Lugosi—A Vampire's Scrapbook
Bela Lugosi, the world's most beloved blood sucker, is profiled in this collection of rare interviews and highlights from his greatest (and sometimes ghastliest) screen appearances. 60 mins.
VHS: S05189. $19.95.

The Monster and the Girl
Ellen Drew plays a character dragged into a life of prostitution by the mob. The plot gets especially strange when her brother is wrongly executed and his brain is transplanted into the body of a gorilla. Now he seeks revenge for the wrongs done to both him and his sister.
VHS: S21730. $14.98.
Stuart Heisler, USA, 1941, 65 mins.

Monster from Green Hell
Man tampers with the unknown when a rocket carrying test animals crashes in Africa's Green Hell. As the local animal population begins to flee, scientists put the blame on ancient legend, but the real problem may be....giant wasps! With Dallas' Jim Davis, Barbara Turner.
VHS: S04849. $29.95.
Kenneth Crane, USA, 1957, 70 mins.

Monster Maker
Half-crazed scientist puts a fantastic discovery to use: an injection of serum turns men into monsters. With J. Carrol Naish and Ralph Morgan.
VHS: S03336. $39.95.
Sam Newfield, USA, 1944, 66 mins.

Monster of Piedras Blancas
When a seven foot tall sea creature removes the heads of two local fisherman, some of the surviving members of a small community decide there may be some truth to the local legends after all. This low-budget monster movie was chosen as the winner of "The Shock Award" by Monster Magazine. Producer Jack Keven designed and wore the killer crustacean suit. Cast includes Lee Tremayne, Forrest Lewis, Don Sullivan, Jeanne Carmen and John Harmon as the superstitious lighthouse keeper. The title translates as the monster from the white rocks.
VHS: S12547. $19.95.
Irvin Berwick, USA, 1959, 72 mins.

Monster of the Island (Island Monster)
Boris Karloff plays Don Gaetano, an elderly philanthropist, who heads a smuggling ring on the island of Ischia. The monster of the title is a human drug importer and a kidnapper of children. Made in Italy, it is said to be Karloff's worst film. For the curious.
VHS: S04024. $29.95.
Robert Montero, Italy, 1953, 87 mins.

Monster on the Campus
When a prehistoric fish is discovered, a rather ordinary academic is accidentally contaminated with its blood, turning him into a rampaging beast. Tranquil Dunsfield University will never be the same. Starring Arthur Franz and Joanna Moore.
VHS: S20893. $14.98.
Jack Arnold, USA, 1958, 76 mins.

The Monster Walks
An eerie movie with some black humor set in a decaying Earlton Manor, a holding pen for the grotesque, a lumbering manservant, a vicious ape, a German maid, a recent corpse and a wheelchair bound relative. The plot concerns the attempted murder of a shrieking heiress. With Rex Lease, Sheldon Lewis and Vera Lewis. On the same program is the Ub Iwerks 1932 horror cartoon, The Cuckoo Murder Case.
VHS: S18682. $24.95.
Frank Strayer, USA, 1932, 59 mins.

Monsters Crash the Pajama Party
In this rare film a combination live act was presented at screenings. Teenage girls invade a haunted house only to find a mad scientist at work conducting odd experiments. When the scientist sends for new victims, his henchmen run toward the camera. The screen goes dark. Real people would run through the theater and grab a woman. Magically she would appear on screen. This video also includes a number of trailers for similar live spook shows that once toured movie theaters.
VHS: S23168. $29.95.
David L. Hewitt, USA, 1965

Monsters on the March
Trailers from 14 of your favorite movie monster attractions. Program includes Isle of the Dead (Karloff), The Return of the Fly (Price), The Thing (From Another World), The Mummy (Karloff), I Walked with a Zombie, The Return of Captain Marvel, and The Wolfman (Chaney Jr.). USA, 1932-60, 25 mins.
VHS: S05486. $19.95.

The Mummy
Boris Karloff in a landmark role as the mummy, accidentally revived by British archeologists after being entombed for 3,700 years. A brooding, dream-like masterpiece of the horror genre.
VHS: S00895. $14.98.
Laser: LD70060. $34.95.
Karl Freund, USA, 1932, 72 mins.

The Mummy's Curse
The final effort of a series which chronicles the adventures of the archeologist Kharis and his assistant Ananka. They're in the Louisiana bayou searching for artifacts though they're inadvertently caught up in the death and mayhem of local characters. With Lon Chaney Jr., Peter Coe and Virginia Christine.
VHS: S19014. $14.98.
Leslie Goodwins, USA, 1944, 62 mins.

The Mummy's Ghost
This sequel to The Mummy's Tomb is a quickly paced affair about a professor and his protege tracking a woman who's the reincarnation of Princess Ananka. With Lon Chaney Jr., John Carradine, Ramsay Ames and Robert Lowery.
VHS: S19012. $14.98.
Reginald LeBorg, USA, 1944, 60 mins.

The Mummy's Hand
The first in the celebrated Kharis series is not a sequel to Karl Freund's The Mummy, but an eerie and effective shocker about a group of archaeologists who search for Egyptian Princess Ananka. The cast includes Dick Foran, Wallace Ford, Peggy Moran, Cecil Kellaway and Charles Trowbridge.
VHS: S17276. $14.98.
Christy Cabanne, USA, 1940, 67 mins.

The Mummy's Tomb
The sequel to The Mummy's Hand balances humor and chills. Famed archeologist Kharis (Lon Chaney Jr.) returns stateside to exterminate the surviving members of an expedition force. With Elyse Knox, John Hubbard and Turhan Bey.
VHS: S19018. $14.98.
Harold Young, USA, 1942, 61 mins.

Murder Mansion
A young couple traveling through an eerie landscape are stranded in a castle full of mysterious noises and unexplained phenomena. With Analia Gade, Evelyn Steward and Andres Resino. English dubbed.
VHS: S19350. $19.95.
Francisco Lara Polop, Spain, 1970, 90 mins.

The Murders in the Rue Morgue (1932)
An expressive horror translation of Edgar Allan Poe's short story. Set in Paris, the film stars Bela Lugosi as the brilliant Dr. Mirakle, who prowls the streets to find an experimental companion for his pet gorilla. Famed director John Huston worked on the screenplay. With Sidney Fox, Leon Waycoff, Brandon Hurst and Noble Johnson.
VHS: S17274. $14.98.
Robert Florey, USA, 1932, 75 mins.

The Murders in the Rue Morgue (1971)
Jason Robards and Lilli Palmer star in this film based upon the Edgar Allan Poe's masterpiece of terror about a horror theater whose staged murders become all too real.
VHS: S00899. $59.95.
Laser: LD75231. $34.98.
Gordon Hessler, Great Britain, 1971, 87 mins.

The Murders in the Rue Morgue (1986)
George C. Scott, Rebecca De Mornay and Val Kilmer star in this adaptation of Edgar Allan Poe's mystery thriller set in 19th-century Paris. Police are baffled by the murder of a woman and her child, especially since the room where it happened is locked from inside. Dupin (Scott) must solve this riddle before anyone will feel safe again.
VHS: S21706. $14.99.
Jeannot Szwarc, USA, 1986, 92 mins.

Mystery of the Wax Museum
Before there was Vincent Price and House of Wax, there was Lionel Atwill, as a semi-crazed sculptor who uses human victims to populate his historical recreations. Fay Wray is a potential and unwilling Marie Antoinette. Filmed in early Technicolor. With Glenda Farrell.
VHS: S04708. $59.95.
Michael Curtiz, USA, 1933, 77 mins.

The Naked Witch
An ancient witch returns to life when a student pulls the stake from her evil heart. She seeks bloody revenge against the local village. Some hilarious shots of her running around naked while someone holds their finger over the camera lens to shield her privates offer priceless cinematic moments.
VHS: S23166. $29.95.
Andy Milligan, USA, 1963, 60 mins.

Needful Things
Based on the novel of the same name by the most famous horror writer of our time, Stephen King, this film is set in a small town that makes a terrible promise. Starring Ed Harris, Max Von Sydow and Bonnie Bedelia.
VHS: S20610. $19.95.
Laser: LD72426. $39.99.
Fraser C. Heston, USA, 1993, 120 mins.

Night of Terror
Bela Lugosi stars as a Hindu servant working at the estate of a wealthy family. Soon the grounds are plagued by a strange, murderous lunatic, who sends chills through the inhabitants of this house. Sally Bane and Wallace Ford also star in this macabre thriller with a twisted ending.
VHS: S22884. $19.95.
Ben Stoloff, USA, 1933, 64 mins.

Night of the Living Dead
George A. Romero's brilliant debut film boldly re-imagines horror conventions in this nihilistic thriller about a group of survivors seeking sanctuary in a farmhouse under siege from the walking dead, flesh-eating zombies that patrol the ravaged landscape. With Judith O'Dea, Duane Jones and Karl Hardman.
VHS: S18644. $16.98.
Laser: CLV. LD72009. $29.98.
George A. Romero, USA, 1968, 96 mins.

Night of the Living Dead 25th Anniversary Documentary
George A. Romero, director of Night of the Living Dead, is joined by John Landis, Wes Craven, Sam Raimi and other creative filmmakers to discuss the impact of this seminal horror flick.
VHS: S24743. $19.95.
Thomas Brown, USA, 1993, 83 mins.

The Night They Killed Rasputin
An atmospheric retelling of the rise and fall of Rasputin, whose seemingly supernatural powers made the czarina into a hypnotic slave. John Drew Barrymore reprises the role his father played in Rasputin and the Empress. A bizarre film. With Edmund Purdon and Gianna Canale. USA, 1962.
VHS: S15369. $29.95.

The Night Walker
William Castle's film about a woman besieged by recurring images and dreams of her dead husband and a handsome, charismatic stranger. With Barbara Stanwyck, Robert Taylor, Lloyd Bochner and Judi Meredith. Screenplay by Robert Bloch.
VHS: S18702. $14.98.
William Castle, USA, 1964, 86 mins.

Nightmare Castle
Barbara Steele plays two sisters tormented by the same husband, the horrible Dr. Arrowsmith. When he finds Barbara #1 fooling around with the gardener he kills them and later marries Barbara #2 to cash in on an inheritance. Grizzly goings on in Italy.
VHS: S04049. $29.95.
Allan Grunewald/Mario Caiano, Italy, 1966, 90 mins.

The Oblong Box
Edgar Allan Poe's classic tale about two brothers and the evil dead; Vincent Price is the British aristocrat tormented by his disfigured brother who's kept in a tower room. With Christopher Lee.
VHS: S04564. $59.99.
Gordon Hessler, Great Britain, 1969, 91 mins.

The Old Dark House
A melodrama with a tongue-in-cheek sense of humor gathers stranded travelers in a mysterious household, where a brutish butler is one of many strange characters. The film stars Boris Karloff, Melvyn Douglas, Charles Laughton, Gloria Stuart, Raymond Massey, and Eva Moore.
VHS: S16180. $24.95.
James Whale, USA, 1932, 71 mins.

Outlaw Drive-In Vol. 1: Horror Comedy Double Feature
Humanoids from Atlantis and *Reanimator* are two over-the-top, grisly films that combine camp humor with terror. In the first, mutated underwater creatures rise to terrorize a small east coast town. It's a graphic opportunity to see seafood gone really bad. Then in *Reanimator* a serum which revives the dead only manages to bring back the worst of human behavior from the great beyond.
VHS: S26467. $14.98.

Ozone
Great effects lift this horror film above the rest. A new drug is accidentally injected into a cop. Suddenly his search for an evil drug lord is transformed into a sinister underworld journey where mutants abound. This drug transforms simple drug users into pawns of a plot for world domination.
VHS: S24590. $29.95.
J.R. Bookwalter, USA, 1994, 83 mins.

Pale Blood
A series of vampire-like murders in Los Angeles attracts the attention of a veteran bloodsucker played by Oscar winner George Chakiris. B-movie action icon Wings Hauser is the cop assigned to investigate in this erotic thriller. With Pamela Ludwig, Diane Frank and Darcy DeMoss as potential blood banks. Highly praised by the Academy of Science Fiction, Fantasy and Horror.
VHS: S15619. $79.95.
Dachin Hsu, USA, 1991, 94 mins.

Pattern for Plunder (Curse of San Michel)
Keenan Wynn, Mai Zetterling and Ronald Howard star in this intriguing British thriller. Some WWII vets decide to find lost Nazi loot. Their search brings them to an ancient castle. Below lies a beach riddled with quicksand where the curse of the tidal wave of San Michel has taken many lives. Mystery and horror are combined in this great B-movie.
VHS: S23193. $24.95.
John Ainsworth, Great Britain, 1962, 73 mins.

The People Under the Stairs
A young African-American becomes entangled in an attempt to rob a bizarre couple. His accomplices are murdered and he is left in the house alone. Eventually he finds the house is peopled by the crazed, almost zombified offspring of the couple. As the plot moves along we find that the evil couple are also the ones responsible for the deplorable conditions of his neighborhood.
VHS: S21393. $19.98.
Wes Craven, USA, 1991, 102 mins.

Perversion
A sick millionaire with unusually unhealthy sexual tastes is at the center of this bizarre film. In one instance he bites off a piece of one of his numerous sexual conquests in order to show it to his friends as a trophy. Portuguese with English subtitles.
VHS: S20748. $24.95.
Jose Mojica Marins, Brazil, 1978

Phantasm II: The Ball Is Back
A horror classic like *Phantasm* screams out for a murderous sequel. Once again the psychic teen calls forth the tall mysterious mortician armed with orbs of death. If there was any confusion about the reality of the terrifying world watched over by this tall man it is dissipated in this film forever.
VHS: S21791. $14.98.
Don A. Coscarelli, USA, 1988, 97 mins.

The Phantom Creeps
Evil reigns as the fiendish Dr. Zorka extracts a mysterious substance from a fallen meteor and uses it to create a robot and a mechanical spider. Starring Bela Lugosi.
VHS: S13856. $19.95.
Ford Beebe, USA, 1939, 75 mins.

The Phantom of the Opera (1943)
The burnished color photography of decorated cinematographer Hal Mohr gives a surrealistic glitter to this remake of the classic Gaston Leroux horror tale. Claude Rains is a crazed, masked phantom terrorizing a Paris Opera House, whom he believes has stolen his music. Rains focuses his obsession on a beautiful soprano (Suzanna Foster) which forces a confrontation with Nelson Eddy. With Hume Cronyn.
VHS: S02720. $14.98.
Laser: LD70221. $39.95.
Arthur Lubin, USA, 1943, 93 mins.

The Phantom of the Opera (1962)
A series of mysterious mishaps, culminating in a terrible opening night incident at a London opera house, are not the work of providence. They are deliberate acts of sabotage perpetrated by a madman. A young, new singing star attracts this dangerous, disfigured man, a once brilliant composer betrayed into oblivion. A Hammer Films classic, featuring Herbert Lom, Heather Sears, Thorley Walters and Michael Gough.
VHS: S25568. $14.98.
Terence Fisher, Great Britain, 1962, 85 mins.

The Phantom of the Opera (1989)
Robert Englund, the actor underneath the macabre makeup of Freddy Krueger, is well cast as Erik Destler, a 19th century composer who makes a bad bargain with the Devil. This insures that he spend most of his spare time in a grotto apartment located beneath a big city opera house. For this remake of the Gaston Leroux novel, the locale has been switched from Paris to London. With Jill Schoelen, Alex Hyde-White, and Stephanie Lawrence as the ill-fated diva.
VHS: S11689. $19.98.
Dwight H. Little, USA, 1989, 93 mins.

Pharaoh's Curse
A fanatical Egyptian is out to stop the unearthing of ancient tombs by killing each member of an archeological expedition. As he completes his task he ages until he himself becomes a mummy.
VHS: S08436. $29.95.
Lee Sholem, USA, 1956, 63 mins.

Poltergeist
When you build a community over a graveyard and don't move the bodies, expect the kind of problems that plague this typically American suburban family. Moving furniture and floating toys lead to alternative dimensions and the lowering of real estate values. With Craig T. Nelson, JoBeth Williams and Heather O'Rourke. Great special effects. Co-written and produced by Steven Spielberg.
VHS: S04502. $19.95.
Laser: CAV, special collector's edition. LD74490. $74.98.
Tobe Hooper, USA, 1982, 114 mins.

Poltergeist II
A satire about middle class normalcy and desire as the white bred Freeling family is subjected to strange attacks, mysterious beings, and supernatural forces. The cast includes JoBeth Williams, Craig T. Nelson, the late Heather O'Rourke, Geraldine Fitzgerald and theater director Julian Beck.
Laser: LD70171. $34.98.
Brian Gibson, USA, 1986, 91 mins.

Prince of Darkness
There is something evil in the basement of an abandoned church that fascinates a small group of scientists and grad students and terrifies members of the clergy. With Donald Pleasence, Victor Wong, Lisa Blount, Jameson Parker and Alice Cooper as the leader of a group of street zombies. Chilling and thoughtful.
VHS: S06921. $14.98.
John Carpenter, USA, 1987, 102 mins.

The Raven
Boris Karloff and Bela Lugosi appear in this horror film based on the works of Edgar Allan Poe, including the title story and *The Pit and the Pendulum*. Lugosi is the doctor with the Poe-obsession, Karloff his innocent victim, about a doctor who blackmails a killer into killing the woman who rejected him.
VHS: S17269. $14.98.
Louis Friedlander, USA, 1935, 62 mins.

Re-Animator
Chicago's very own Stuart Gordon of the Organic Theater, creator of *WARP*, directs this adaptation of an H.P. Lovecraft story. A medical student brings the dead back to life. Done with lots of gusto and humor, which turned this one into a cult classic.
VHS: S01093. $79.98.
Stuart Gordon, USA, 1985, 86 mins.

Red House
Suspense melodrama about a moody farmer's guilty obsession with an old house in the woods where he murdered his parents. With Edward G. Robinson, Rory Calhoun.
VHS: S04065. $19.95.
Delmer Daves, USA, 1947, 100 mins.

The Return of Chandu (Abridged)
Bela Lugosi stars in this feature version of the serial of the same name which incorporates the first six chapters of this occult thriller about a secret death cult and a mysterious princess they wish to sacrifice. With Maria Alba, Lucien Prival and Dean Benton. B&W.
VHS: S08437. $24.95.
Ray Taylor, USA, 1934, 61 mins.

The Return of Dracula
In this horror movie the Count (Francis Lederer) assumes the identity of a murdered Czech painter and infiltrates an idyllic small American town, wreaking havoc and discord among the unsuspecting. With Norman Eberhardt, Ray Stricklyn and Jimmie Baird.
VHS: S19137. $14.95.
Paul Landres, USA, 1958, 77 mins.

Return of the Vampire
Bela Lugosi rises from the crypt in this blood-curdling horror classic. Lugosi is one of a kind as a 200-year-old Hungarian vampire that prowls the English countryside feeding on the jugular of innocent villagers. Roland Varno, Frieda Inescort and Matt Willis also star. 1943.
VHS: S13003. $9.95.
Lew Landers, USA, 1943, 69 mins.

Return to Salem's Lot
Larry Cohen invades Stephen King territory with a terrifying tale of a whole town of vampires in New England. Michael Moriarty is an inquisitive anthropologist aided by director Sam Fuller as a fearless vampire hunter. With Andrew Duggan, June Havoc and Evelyn Keyes.
VHS: S07342. $14.95.
Larry Cohen, USA, 1987, 101 mins.

Revenge of the Creature
This sequel to the horror classic *The Creature from the Black Lagoon* shifts the action from the Amazon to a Florida aquarium theme park as the scientists and citizenry try to fathom the motives and nature of the mysterious gill-man. With John Agar, Lori Nelson, John Bromfield and in a minor role, Clint Eastwood. The movie was originally shown in 3D.
VHS: S19017. $14.98.
Jack Arnold, USA, 1955, 82 mins.

Revenge of the Creature/ The Creature Walks Among Us
Two sequels to the *The Creature from the Black Lagoon* tap into the fears of the outsider. Jack Arnold's 1955 *Revenge of the Creature* finds the mysterious gill-man transferred from the Amazon to a Florida aquarium. In John Sherwood's 1958 sequel, *The Creature Walks among Us*, a group of scientists turn to radical forms of plastic surgery to alter his deformity.
Laser: LD72182. $59.98.

Revolt of the Zombies
Dean Jagger returns dead Cambodian soldiers to a semblance of life and then exploits them for his evil purposes. No wonder they revolt. Stock footage from *White Zombie* featuring Bela Lugosi's eyes is re-used to spice up this tale of voodoo in the Far East. B&W.
VHS: S04059. $29.95.
Victor Halperin, USA, 1936, 65 mins.

Sabaka (The Hindu)
Boris Karloff stars in a tale of an evil cult of fire-worshippers in India. Made on location. His part is small and made to capitalize on a US tv series about an elephant boy. June Foray (the voice of Rocky the Flying Squirrel) is featured as the high priestess of the cult.
VHS: S04025. $29.95.
Frank Ferrin, USA, 1953, 81 mins.

The Sadist
In this phenomenal, low-budget, psycho horror movie, three people encounter disaster on the way to a Dodgers game. They become trapped in an old wrecking yard when their car stalls. A psycho and his girlfriend put these three captives through pure hell.
VHS: S23165. $29.95.
James Landis, USA, 1963, 95 mins.

Samson vs. the Vampire Women
Santo and Lorena Valesquez star in this blood-sucking gore fest. Santo, the masked hero, battles voluptuous vampire women led by Lorena, who employs a number of muscle-bound, caped henchmen. This shlocky classic ends with an hysterical wrestling scene.
VHS: S23163. $29.95.
Alfonso Corona Blake, Mexico, 1961, 89 mins.

The Scare Game
This double feature begins with a love story gone wrong. A young woman thinks she has found her match but the man she loves may not be all he appears to be. Then a game becomes subject to a demon's caprice for sadistic ritualistic scenes.
VHS: S24762. $29.95.
Eric Stanze, USA, 1994, 120 mins.

Scared Stiff
Not to be confused with Jerry Lewis/Dean Martin comedy remake of *Ghostbreakers*. This is a serious tale of a psychiatrist and a female rock star staying in a haunted Charleston mansion where they are not the only ones to go bump in the night. With Andrew Stevens, Mary Page Keller, Josh Segal and David Ramsey. Called "too explicit for the squeamish" by *Variety*.
VHS: S12546. $19.95.
Laser: CLV. LD72027. $29.98.
Richard Friedman, USA, 1986, 85 mins.

Scared to Death
Bela Lugosi plays a mysterious stage magician who wears a Dracula cape and tries to appear ominous most of the time. Filmed in Cinecolor, the plot concerns the plight of Laura, a mental patient in a disturbing sanitarium run by George Zucco. Watch for the green floating masks.
VHS: S04011. $19.98.
Christy Cabanne, USA, 1947, 65 mins.

Schreck
A young horror fan discovers that a murderous Nazi once lived in his home. On the anniversary of the fiend's death they raise his spirit and unleash the ghoul. Now the ghoul is once again free to engage in his deadly rites. 75 mins.
VHS: S24746. $19.95.

Scream and Scream Again
Vincent Price stars as a mad scientist driven to create his own race of beings. Only he needs to do a number of experiments on human samples first. This is one of his later horror films and also features Christopher Lee and Peter Cushing.
VHS: S20934. $14.98.
Gordon Hessler, Great Britain, 1970, 95 mins.

The Screaming Skull
Alex Nicol stars in and directed this shocking supernatural thriller about a man trying to make his wife crazy. The ad for this film promised movie patrons a free burial if they died of fright while watching this picture. I don't know if the offer is still valid, so be careful. With Peggy Webber and John Hudson.
VHS: S04071. $29.95.
Alex Nichol, USA, 1958, 68 mins.

Serpent and the Rainbow
Who do that voodoo that you do so well? Horror filmmaker Wes Craven gets serious with a dramatic tale of an anthropologist's visit to Haiti. Based on the true-life adventures of Wade Davis. With Bill Pullman, Cathy Tyson, Zakes Mokae and Paul Winfield. Expect the unexpected.
VHS: S12252. $19.95.
Laser: LD70076. $34.95.
Wes Craven, USA, 1988, 98 mins.

Seventh Victim
Psychological terror in the form of Satan-worship makes this Val Lewton production appealing. Neophyte Kim Hunter inadvertently stumbles across a devil cult while searching for her lost sister somewhere in Greenwich Village.
VHS: S03252. $19.95.
Mark Robson, USA, 1943, 70 mins.

Shake Hands with the Devil
Set against the brutal Irish 1921 rebellion, James Cagney stars as a Dublin surgeon who commands an IRA faction and believes violence is the only means to achieve political and social liberation from English tyranny. With Glynis Johns, Don Murray, Dana Wyner and Michael Redgrave.
VHS: S19042. $19.98.
Michael Anderson, USA, 1959, 110 mins.

Shatter Dead
In this violent film, religious fervor is seen in all its unmitigated horror. A young woman simply tries to go home but undead creatures confront her at every turn. These zombies are transfixed by a higher power with blood and gore on its mind. This is one low budget film sure to shock the religious but please all gore fans.
VHS: S24761. $29.95.
Scooter McCrae, USA, 1994, 84 mins.

She Beast (Revenge of the Blood Beast)
Barbara Steele plays a modern English tourist possessed by the spirit of a vengeful witch burned to death in Transylvania two hundred years earlier. Against her will she terrorizes a Carpathian mountain village and decreases its population. Talk about a bad vacation. May be first horror movie with Iron Curtain in-jokes.
VHS: S04051. $29.95.
Michael Reeves, Italy/Yugoslavia, 1966, 74 mins.

Shock Cinema Volumes 1-4
Brinke Stevens hosts this introduction to the masters of schlock horror. He interviews directors, writers, FX artists, actors and actresses. It's a behind-the-scenes look at how to make it in the gory world of Hollywood. 60 mins. each.
Shock Cinema Volume 1. Interviews with Charles Band, Fred Olen, Jeff Burr, Scott Spiegel and more.
VHS: S24755. $9.95.
Shock Cinema Volume 2. Forrest J. Ackerman, Robert Quarry, Steve Neill, Deanna Lund, Melissa Moore and others are interviewed in this volume.
VHS: S24756. $9.95.
Shock Cinema Volume 3. This is the volume filled with bloopers, babes and blood.
VHS: S24757. $9.95.
Shock Cinema Volume 4. B-movie make-up effects are explained in this fascinating look at movie magic.
VHS: S24758. $9.95.

Sin You Sinners
June Colbourne, Dian Lloyd and Derek Murcott star in this supernatural tale. A has-been exotic dancer gets her hands on an ancient amulet that enables her to project youthfulness. Through its magic she's able to control those around her as though they were zombies. Watch for the abrupt and twisted ending. 1964.
VHS: S23167. $29.95.

The Skull
Taken from a story by Robert Bloch: Peter Cushing comes into possession of the Marquis de Sade's coveted skull, and its mysterious powers.
VHS: S16898. $19.95.
Freddie Francis, Great Britain, 1965, 83 mins.

Slime People
From the sewers of Los Angeles come subterranean, lizard-like humanoids who take over the town by releasing a deadly wall of fog. Not a documentary but a low-budget and very small-cast monster movie. Can a brave scientist and his two shapely daughters save the human race before it is too late? With Les Tremayne, Susan Hart, Tom Laughlin, and Robert Hutton, who also directed.
VHS: S10968. $19.95.
Robert Hutton, USA, 1962, 76 mins.

The Snake People (Isle of the Snake People)
Boris Karloff made four Mexican horror movies back to back before he died in 1969. This is one of the two to have been released. It concerns a snake cult which turns its victims into zombies. Karloff is the secret leader of the cult. His scenes were all shot in L.A.
VHS: S04027. $29.95.
J. Hill/J. Ibanez, USA/Mexico, 1971, 90 mins.

The Snow Creature
Paula Langston and Leslie Denison are cast in this outrageous horror film about an escaped Yeti. Brought back by a botanist, the creature is held by customs officers. Of course this makes the monster furious and he rampages through Los Angeles. A camp classic.
VHS: S24018. $14.95.
W. Lee Wilder, USA, 1954, 71 mins.

Son of Dracula
Lon Chaney Jr. stars as Count Alucard, a mysterious visitor to the swamp lands of Louisiana. The Count is not the son of Dracula but the authentic bloodsucker himself. Lots of atmosphere in this mis-titled and neglected horror film. With Evelyn Ankers, Louise Allbritton and Robert Paige.
VHS: S06868. $14.98.
Robert Siodmak, USA, 1943, 80 mins.

Son of Frankenstein
The great cast of Basil Rathbone, Boris Karloff and Bela Lugosi star as the son of Dr. Frankenstein returns to the castle some 25 years after the infamous monster's "death." There he meets Ygor (Bela Lugosi), a mad shepherd hiding the lifeless body of the creature, and the son of Frankenstein can't resist re-awakening the creature.
VHS: S10113. $14.98.
Laser: LD70081. $34.95.
Rowland V. Lee, USA, 1939, 99 mins.

Son of Kong
Sequel to the classic. Adventurer Carl Denham returns to Skull Island and finds Kong's offspring: a 30-foot albino gorilla. Once again, full of first-rate special effects.
VHS: S10665. $19.98.
Ernest B. Schoedsack, USA, 1933, 69 mins.

Son of Monsters on the March
More monster movie trailers from ten cult favorites. Titles include *The Vampire Killers* (Sharon Tate), *Dark Star* (John Carpenter), *One Million Years B.C.* (Raquel Welch), *This Island Earth*, *The Damned*, *I Was a Teenage Frankenstein* and *The Rocky Horror Picture Show*. USA/Great Britain/Italy/West Germany, 1955-77, 27 mins.
VHS: S05487. $19.95.

Spider Baby
Lon Chaney Jr. heads a household of inbred cannibals in this bizarre and many-titled horror cheapie. As if that weren't enough, he also sings the theme song. Included in the cast of wackos are Sid Haig, Carol Ohmart and the ever-popular Mantan Moreland. B&W. It's weird.
VHS: S04035. $29.95.
Jack Hill, USA, 1964, 86 mins.

Strait-Jacket
This later, terror-filled Joan Crawford film was written by Robert Bloch, who also penned *Psycho*. Crawford is not to be missed as the insane woman with an axe. After doing time for attacking her husband and his lover, she is finally set free to terrorize once again. Also features George Kennedy and Lee Majors in his screen debut. Includes original insert.
Laser: LD74975. $34.95.
William Castle, USA, 1964, 93 mins.

Strange World of Coffin Joe
Three atmospheric episodes of horror shape this chilling triptych: a perverse dollmaker whose creators take on human form, the allure and dread of necrophilia, and Coffin Joe (Mojica) disguised as a doctor who tortures two unsuspecting travelers who doubt his power. Portuguese with English subtitles.
VHS: S18983. $24.95.
Jose Mojica Marins, Brazil, 1968

A Study in Terror
Jack the Ripper is terrorizing London and there is only one man who can stop him from carving up more English prostitutes. Elementary, dear viewer, it's Sherlock Holmes. John Neville is Holmes and Donald Houston is Watson and the game is soon afoot. A tidy thriller.
VHS: S04384. $69.95.
James Hill, Great Britain, 1965, 94 mins.

Suspiria
Considered by many to be one of the most terrifying and stylized horror films of recent years, *Suspiria* stars Jessica Harper as Susy Banyon, an American student who has enrolled in a German dance academy. On the very night she arrives, two of the students are brutally murdered. It soon becomes apparent that this is only the beginning of a terrifying nightmare. "The most eagerly awaited horror film of the decade...the most stylish and simply one of the best horror films ever made" (Fangoria).
VHS: S10717. $19.98.
Laser: LD71349. $39.95.
Dario Argento, Italy, 1984, 97 mins.

Tales from the Crypt
An HBO horror anthology that unearths the stories that gave comic books a code of values to follow. From the mind of William M. Gaines (*Mad Magazine*) and the pages of E.C. Comics, three top directors try their hand at horror—segments directed by Walter Hill, Robert Zemeckis and Richard Donner include electric chairs, killer Santas and a man who hates cats. 1989, 81 mins.
VHS: S10981. $19.95.

Tales from the Darkside: The Movie
Four ghoulish tales of horror. Watch it if you dare and witness the cat from Hell, the return of the mummy, an artist with a secret terror and a housewife who supplements her food dollar by planning dinner parties around missing children. With Deborah Harry, Christian Slater, David Johansen, William Hickey and Rae Dawn Chong. Based on the works of Stephen King and Arthur Conan Doyle among others.
VHS: S12855. $19.95.
Laser: LD75269. $34.98.
John Harrison, USA, 1990, 93 mins.

Tales of Frankenstein
The classic story, featuring a sharp performance from Anton Diffring. On the same program is Alfred Hitchcock's diabolically witty and entertaining *The Sorcerer's Apprentice*, featuring Diana Dors and Brandon de Wilde.
VHS: S18957. $19.95.

Teenage Zombies
Cult favorite Katherine Victor plays a mysterious woman doctor working on a nerve gas that turns anyone into a mindless slave. When she is interrupted by a group of waterskiing teenagers, they prove to be almost as good a subject as her pet gorilla. With Don Sullivan, Bri Murphy and Mitzi Albertson. B&W.
VHS: S05484. $29.95.
Jerry Warren, USA, 1957, 71 mins.

The Tell-Tale Heart (1963)
Edgar Allan Poe's classic story elaborated into a story of a jealous love murder. With Laurence Payne, Adrienne Cori, Dermot Walsh.
VHS: S05053. $34.95.
Ernest Morris, Great Britain, 1963, 81 mins.

The Tell-Tale Heart (1973)
This classic, based on the famous short story by Edgar Allan Poe, is hauntingly filmed in stark black and white to accentuate the good versus evil theme. The viewer cannot help but be captured this carefully woven web of murder, investigation, and the dreadful reality of betrayal from within. Starring Sam Jaffe.
VHS: S14260. $24.95.
Steve Carver, USA, 1973, 26 mins.

Terror Creatures from the Grave (Cemetery of the Living Dead)
Barbara Steele plays a treacherous wife who will feel the wrath of her murdered husband from beyond the grave. In a small village in Central Europe circa 1900, plague ridden corpses from the twelfth century return to do the bidding of a ghost. English dubbed.
VHS: S04050. $29.95.
R. Zucker/M. Pupillo, Italy, 1965, 85 mins.

Terror in the Haunted House
Classic horror noir about a man returning with his young bride to the house of her nightmare. Filmed in psychorama—a visual process so devastating that it was banned by the Federal Government 25 years ago.
VHS: S05195. $19.95.
Harold Daniels, USA, 1958, 90 mins.

The Texas Chainsaw Massacre
Tobe Hooper's restored cult film is a frightening piece of Americana. This strange subversion of the slasher movie concerns five friends traveling through a flat, nondescript Texas wasteland who encounter a bizarre family and are forced to struggle for their lives. With Marilyn Burns, Allen Danzinger, Paul A. Partain and William Vail.
VHS: S19463. $19.98.
Laser: LD71919. $29.98.
Tobe Hooper, USA, 1974, 81 mins.

The Texas Chainsaw Massacre: A Family Portrait
A curious documentary on the making of Tobe Hooper's 1974 cult classic about five hippies caught in a brutal chase and stalking game with a deranged killer loosely inspired by Ed Gein. The documentary combines interviews with the film's stars and provides previously unseen production photos. 70 mins.
VHS: S19743. $29.95.

Theater of Blood
Vincent Price plays Edward Lionheart, a demented Shakespearean actor who adds murder to his repertoire when he takes gruesome revenge on the eight critics who slighted him. With Diana Rigg, Ian Hendry, Jack Hawkins, Robert Morley and Milo O'Shea.
VHS: S01559. $14.95.
Douglas Bell, Great Britain, 1973, 105 mins.

There's Nothing Out There
A campy horror film about seven teenagers isolated in a mountain cabin and subjected to a series of supernatural encounters. The estimable Joe Bob Briggs says it's already a cult classic. "Fast and funny, it never lets up, like setting off a string of firecrackers" (*Los Angeles Times*).
VHS: S17648. $49.95.
Rolfe Kanefsky, USA, 1990, 91 mins.

This Night I Will Possess Your Corpse
Coffin Joe seeks the perfect woman so that she might bear him a perfect child. Along the way he tortures innumerable innocent women by crushing heads and even employing 50 real tarantulas to terrorize his victims. Finally he is dragged off to hell for a taste of his own medicine. Portuguese with English subtitles.
VHS: S20751. $24.95.

Thriller
Boris Karloff hosts this collection of the best episodes from the classic 1960's television series, *Thriller*. Some of these creepy stories even include Karloff as an actor. Grim tales like these have an unnatural life all their own, which keeps this series entertaining and frightening.
Masquerade. Tom Poston and Elizabeth Montgomery are a newly wed couple who accept the hospitality of a fiendish family. But the honeymooners prove more than a match for their hapless hosts. Co-stars John Carradine. 50 mins.
VHS: S21491. $12.98.
The Grim Reaper. William Shatner is a greedy young man who discovers the truth behind the legend of the Grim Reaper. This fiend exacts a terrible revenge on the murderous young man. 50 mins.
VHS: S21493. $12.98.
The Prediction. Boris Karloff hosts and stars in this episode of *Thriller*. Karloff is a mentalist who can predict the deaths of people around him. Those who ignore his predictions must face the dire consequences. 50 mins.
VHS: S21494. $12.98.
The Premature Burial. In this episode a wealthy old man is accidentally buried alive. Karloff is the friend that saves him from this grisly fate. When the old man marries again, his new young wife plans to put him back just where Karloff found him. 51 mins.
VHS: S21495. $12.98.
The Terror in Teakwood. In this episode a wife faces a mortal terror when her musician husband desecrates the grave of his arch rival. Revenge and rivalry know no bounds between life and death. 49 mins.
VHS: S21492. $12.98.

The Tingler
Finally available on laser disc, the cult classic thriller stars Vincent Price as a mad and maddening scientist. Gimmicky director William Castle had theater seats wired with low-voltage electric charges to shock audiences as the "tingler" appeared on screen. Originally presented in PERCEPTO and highly recommended by John Waters, the king of bad taste. Wire your couch!
VHS: S27552. $14.95.
Laser: LD74846. $34.95.
William Castle, USA, 1959, 82 mins.

Torture Zone
Boris Karloff plays Dr. Mantell, a madman who discovers a lifeform that must be fed human blood to stay alive. Dr. Mantell traps beautiful women, and their blood becomes the life form's nourishment. Who will put an end to the Torture Zone? Also known as *The Fear Chamber (La Camara del Terror)*.
VHS: S09261. $19.98.
Juan Ibanez, USA/Mexico, 1968, 90 mins.

Tower of Evil
What is the ancient secret of the deserted lighthouse on Snape Island? Who is the crazed woman the authorities discover living there? And who is behind the series of brutal psychosexual murders that suddenly start to plague the town?
VHS: S09259. $59.95.
James O'Connolly, USA, 1972, 90 mins.

Tower of Terror
A half-mad lighthouse keeper (Wilfrid Lawson) keeps an eye on the water off the coast of Germany during World War II. Complications arise when a British spy (Michael Rennie) and a female escapee from a concentration camp (Movita) drop by. Much of this movie is said to take place in the dark.
VHS: S04062. $29.95.
Lawrence Huntington, Great Britain, 1941, 80 mins.

Trauma
A runaway teenage girl, befriended by an artist, sets off to discover the secret behind a series of grisly decapitations by a psychotic killer known as the-headhunter. A tense, grisly film.
VHS: S20651. $89.95.
Dario Argento, Italy, 1992, 106 mins.

Treasure of Fear (aka Scared Stiff)
In this madcap murder mystery, Jack Haley plays a newspaper reporter who can never get a story straight. Good fare for fans of *The Tin Man*.
VHS: S13861. $19.95.
Frank McDonald, USA, 1945, 66 mins.

The True Story of Frankenstein
Kenneth Branagh, Mel Brooks, Robert De Niro, Gene Wilder, Peter Bogdanovich, Helena Bonham Carter, John Cleese, Roger Corman, Aidan Quinn, Margaret Atwood and more share insights about their work on various versions of Mary Shelley's gothic classic. Roger Moore hosts this documentary and Eli Wallach narrates. Includes clips of all the best Frankenstein films. 100 mins.
VHS: S25098. $19.95.

Twice Told Tales
Vincent Price heads a fine cast in this trilogy of horrific tales from the pen of Nathaniel Hawthorne. Segments include "Rappaccini's Daughter", "Dr. Heidegger's Experiment" and the ever-popular "The House of the Seven Gables", none of which were named Clark.
VHS: S04709. $14.95.
Sidney Salkow, USA, 1963, 119 mins.

The Unearthly
The *Citizen Kane* of mad scientist epics, featuring John Carradine, Alison (*Attack of the 50 Foot Woman*) Hayes and Tor Johnson. A mad scientist tries to do right but ends up with a lab full of mutant beings. When his two pending experiments fall in love, Dr. Carradine has trouble.
VHS: S05182. $19.95.
Brooke L. Peters, USA, 1957, 76 mins.

The Uninvited
Lewis Allen's elegant ghost tale about a music critic and his sister attempting to solve the questions of unnatural occurrences and supernatural disturbances at a beautiful old house they've just purchased. Gail Russell stars as a beautiful young woman haunted by the past. With Ray Milland, Ruth Hussey, Donald Crisp and Cornelia Otis Skinner.
VHS: S17017. $14.98.
Lewis Allen, USA, 1944, 99 mins.

Unnatural
Erich Von Stroheim, Hildegard Knef and Karl Boehm star in this beautifully shot, Gothic fantasy. Mixing the genes of a murderer and a prostitute, a scientist creates a femme fatale monster. Neff is beautiful, seductive and souless because she has no real parents, only genetic material donors.
VHS: S23153. $19.95.
Arthur Maria Rabenalt, USA, 1952, 90 mins.

The Val Lewton Collection
Lewton produced nine classic horror films in the 40's. All of them are collected on this compilation disc, including *The Ghost Ship, Cat People, I Walked with a Zombie, The Leopard Man, The Seventh Victim, The Curse of the Cat People, Isle of the Dead, Bedlam* and *The Body Snatcher*. 1942-1946, 639 mins.
Laser: LD75000. $179.99.

The Vampire
The granddaddy of Mexican vampire films. German Robles is Count Lavud and producer Abel Salazar is the hero, who gets top billing. With Ariadne Welter and Carmen Montejo as possible blood donors. Salazar and Robles were featured in a sequel, *The Vampire's Coffin*. B&W.
VHS: S04069. $29.95.
Fernando Mendez, Mexico, 1957, 95 mins.

The Vampire Bat
Lionel Atwill stars as a doctor with a need to murder in order to find a blood substitute. Needless to say he doesn't find many volunteers for his radical approach to health care. With Fay Wray, Dwight Frye and Melvyn Douglas. B&W.
VHS: S04031. $9.95.
Frank Strayer, USA, 1933, 63 mins.

Vampire over London
Bela Lugosi plays a mad scientist working on a robot that will aid him in his conquering the world. He also sleeps in a coffin and has a desire for human blood. Mother Riley (Arthur Lucan in drag) is hired to tidy up the scientist's living quarters and soon finds the secret lab, with comic results. Lots of slapstick.
VHS: S04012. $29.95.
John Gilling, Great Britain, 1952, 72 mins.

Vampire People
Also known as *The Blood Drinkers*, this gothic horror work with a B-movie delirium concerns a mad nobleman and his vampire disciples, who terrorize a small town, setting up a mythic showdown with the town's frightened citizens. With Ronald Remy and Ed Fernandez.
VHS: S18326. $29.95.
Gerardo De Leon, Philippines, 1966, 79 mins.

Voodoo Woman
A horror thriller about a deranged scientist who transforms a beautiful, unsuspecting woman into a monster. With Maria English, Tom Conway, Michael Connors and Lance Fuller.
VHS: S17521. $9.95.
Edward L. Cahn, USA, 1957, 77 mins.

The War of the Colossal Beast
The sequel to *The Amazing Colossal Man* finds the anti-hero attempting to deal with his deteriorating face, and his siege of Los Angeles. With Sally Fraser, Roger Pace and Dean Parkin.
VHS: S17904. $9.95.
Bert I. Gordon, USA, 1958, 68 mins.

Werewolf of London
The first recorded film about werewolves concerns a young botanist's efforts to locate a Tibetan flower who's inadvertently transformed into a diabolical killer who's terrorizing London. With Henry Hull, Warner Oland, Valerie Hobson, and Lester Matthews.
VHS: S17277. $14.98.
Stuart Walker, USA, 1935, 75 mins.

Werewolf vs. the Vampire Woman
When the moon is full different monsters compete for victims in the dead of night. It's all out competition and every monster for him/herself in this deadly race for fresh blood and gore between the blood-sucking women of the night and the demonically inspired werewolf.
VHS: S21558. $24.95.
Leon Klimovsky, Spain, 1970, 82 mins.

Wes Craven's New Nightmare
Robert Englund and Heather Langenkamp reprise their role from the original *Nightmare on Elm Street*. This time, however, they're featured in a plot as the Hollywood insiders who cannot get away from the fame their gory blockbuster spun around them. Something was set in motion by the *Nightmare* movies and it is larger and more deadly than any one movie.
VHS: S24061. $19.98.
Laser: LD74941. $39.99.
Wes Craven, USA, 1994, 111 mins.

What Ever Happened to Baby Jane?
An unforgettable performance by Bette Davis as the former child star who torments her bed-ridden sister (Joan Crawford) in one of the great Hollywood horror films.
VHS: S04410. $19.98.
Laser: LD70703. $39.98.
Robert Aldrich, USA, 1962, 132 mins.

What Ever Happened to...
Vanessa and Lynn Redgrave reprise the roles of Blanche and Jane Hudson, characters immortalized by Bette Davis and Joan Crawford in *Whatever Happened to Baby Jane?*. It's the story of two former child stars whose careers were ended by the combination of age and a terrible accident. Now, facing the double hardships of old age and mental illness, sibling rivalry unleashes dark, unforseen terrors.
VHS: S26231. $19.95.
Hank Hines, USA, 1993, 94 mins.

What!
Mario Bava directed this haunting tale. Christopher Lee stars as a sadistic nobleman who whips his brother's wife. Lee turns up dead, but his ghost returns to haunt the castle in this top-notch Italian thriller. This is the uncut, R-rated, theatrically released version.
VHS: S23321. $24.95.
Mario Bava, Italy/France, 1963, 90 mins.

White Zombie
Bela Lugosi followed up his great success in *Dracula* with this disquieting, poetic horror film about Haiti's cult of the "walking dead." Lugosi plays a magician and zombie-master who raises the dead in this film of haunting psycho-sexual imagery.
VHS: S01454. $19.98.
Victor Halperin, USA, 1932, 73 mins.

The Wicker Man
A British police officer goes to a small island off Scotland to find a missing girl, only to discover that the islanders practice a Celtic religion which worships the phallic symbol, and practices human sacrifice. This film quickly became a cult film, and is considered one of the most intelligent horror films ever made.
VHS: S01457. $19.98.
Robin Hardy, Great Britain, 1973, 102 mins.

Winterbeast
A Native American burial ground lies perilously near a winter resort. Before long there is a strange creature terrorizing this settlement. A park ranger and his bumbling sidekick must discover the secret of the Winterbeast.
VHS: S24751. $9.95.
Christopher Thies, USA, 1992, 80 mins.

The Witch's Mirror
A man disfigures his wife's face and then has the bright idea to use the skin from (hopefully) recently dead people to make amends. This Mexican film sounds suspiciously like Franju's *Eyes without a Face* which opened a year earlier. With Rosita Arenas and Armando Calvo.
VHS: S04075. $29.95.
Chano Urueto, Mexico, 1960, 75 mins.

The Witching

Two 17-year-old guys think they are forced into another boring Friday night watching grandma. But the house and the family harbor a secret past that places these teenagers in a battle with evil witches from another dimension.
VHS: S24748. $19.95.
Eric Black, USA, 1994, 70 mins.

Wolf Man

One of the great horror films, with a terrific cast: Bela Lugosi, Claude Rains, Ralph Bellamy, and Lon Chaney as the man cursed by lycanthropy and Rains his unknowing father.
VHS: S04519. $14.98.
Laser: LD70095. $34.98.
George Waggner, USA, 1941, 71 mins.

Wolfen

Albert Finney, Gregory Hines, Tommy Noonan and Diane Venora are featured in this chilling adaptation of Whitley Striber's terror-filled novel. Good effects and superior suspense make this tale of intelligent werewolves a compelling film. It even has an interesting take on environmental and Native American issues.
VHS: S26335. $19.98.
Michael Wadleigh, USA, 1981, 115 mins.

Wolfman: A Cinematic Scrapbook

A compilation documentary featuring Lon Chaney Jr. and his weird assortment of friends with their garish appetites in *Frankenstein Meets the Wolfman, Werewolf in London* and *I Was a Teenage Werewolf*. A behind-closed-doors look at the personalities who worked on the films. With a look at Chaney's final screen performance in a 1962 Halloween special.
VHS: S17536. $9.95.

The World of Vampires

A cranky vampire is determined to bring some grief to a family whose ancestors made life inconvenient for him centuries before. Talk about holding a grudge. With Silvia Fournier and Mauricio Garces. 1960.
VHS: S03768. $29.95.

Zoltan: Hound of Dracula

An inventive *Dracula* tale about a Transylvanian servant and his voracious dog who travel to contemporary Los Angeles to locate the count's last living descendent. "The style varies between spoof and rather nasty horror" (Leslie Halliwell). With Jose Ferrer, Reggie Nalder, Michael Pataki and Jan Shutan. The film's alternate title is *Dracula's Dog*.
VHS: S19242. $9.98.
Albert Band, USA, 1977, 88 mins.

Zombie

Tisa Farrow, Ian McCulloch and Tom Conway star in this monstrous adventure film. When a man is missing, and only his boat, laden down with zombies, surfaces, his daughter decides to investigate. Soon she finds herself surrounded by zombies on an otherwise idyllic island. Dubbed in English.
VHS: S25693. $19.95.
Lucio Fulci, Italy, 1980, 91 mins.

Zombie '90: Extreme Pestilence

A military machine crashes into a forest, unleashing chemicals that propagate a population of undead. Only two doctors know this secret. They are forced into a desperate, gory struggle with these zombies. Directed by Andreas Schnass, dubbed, 80 mins.
VHS: S24750. $29.95.

The Zombie Army

Set in an insane asylum, this horror film brings the terrors of war and the undead together. Two deranged inmates create an army of zombies. Only the elite Lethal Ladies combat troop can stop them from escaping into the outside world.
VHS: S24749. $19.95.
Betty Stapleford, USA, 1991, 82 mins.

Zombie Cop

A routine drug bust takes on a horrific, ghoulish cast when the suspect turns out to be a voodoo priest. Both the cop and the suspect die but return to continue their struggle as members of the undead.
VHS: S24753. $9.95.
J.R. Bookwalter, USA, 1991, 90 mins.

Zombie Island Massacre

The bus breaks down. The driver disappears. Surely everyone should realize something terrible is going to happen. Soon frightened tourists are succumbing to Native charm. In this Caribbean vacation, death makes an unwelcome appearance. Playboy covergirl Rita Jenrette is featured.
VHS: S22677. $14.95.
John Carter, USA, 1984, 85 mins.

Zombie Rampage

A young man sets off to meet his friends at the train station and instead finds himself lost in a world of underworld terror. These inner-city gangs are not just sadistic; they are bloodthirsty zombies.
VHS: S24591. $9.95.
Todd Sheets, USA, 1992, 85 mins.

Zombies on Broadway

Hare-brained press agents Allen Carney and Wally Brown must find a real zombie for a loony nightclub stunt—a quest that leads them to mad scientist Bela Lugosi.
VHS: S13998. $19.98.
Gordon Douglas, USA, 1944, 68 mins.

BLAXPLOITATION FILMS

Black Belt Jones
From the makers of Bruce Lee's breakthrough *Enter the Dragon*, this film combines the energy of blaxploitation films, the anger of social protest movies and baroque flourishes of a gangster melodrama. Karate virtuoso Jim Kelly must prevail against the strong-arm tactics of the Mafia, which is trying to destroy his Watts-based self-defense school. With Gloria Hendry, Scatman Crothers, Alan Weeks and Nate Esformes.
VHS: S18928. $19.98.
Robert Clouse, USA, 1974, 87 mins.

Black Caesar
The talented B-moviemaker Larry Cohen wrote and directed this aggressive inner-city gangster drama that chronicles the spectacular rise of its ambitious hero (former pro football star Fred Williamson). With Art Lund, Julius W. Harris, Gloria Hendry and D'Urville Martin.
VHS: S18929. $19.98.
Larry Cohen, USA, 1973, 96 mins.

Black Gestapo
A Black army takes over the ghetto. In the beginning their aim is to help the citizens but they wind up as the oppressors. The film is a violent, crazed morality tale in which power corrupts absolutely. Features Rod Perry, Charles P. Robinson (*Night Court*), Phil Hoover and Ed Gross.
VHS: S21462. $19.95.
Lee Frost, USA, 1975, 88 mins.

The Black Godfather
In this blaxploitation work of the early 70s, two brothers join a black revolutionary vanguard to prevent the white mob from infiltrating their community and destroying their inner sanctum through a deadly flow of narcotics.
VHS: S18813. $29.95.
John Evans, USA, 1974, 96 mins.

Black Sister's Revenge
A melodramatic revenge from the 70s blaxploitation cycle concerns a naive Mississippi farm girl making the trek to Los Angeles and falling for a street hustler, whose arrest prompts her to make a series of hard decisions.
VHS: S18814. $19.95.
Jamaa Fanaka, USA, 1976, 100 mins.

Black Vengeance
Leslie Uggams is a charismatic singer caught in a strange love triangle with the owners of an isolated motel. With Ted Cassidy, Slim Pickens and Dub Taylor.
VHS: S18815. $29.95.
Richard Robinson, USA, 1989, 90 mins.

Bucktown
Fred Williamson and Pam Grier star in this story of a man returning to his hometown to find that all is not well. He arrives to bury his brother and winds up burying a number of others as well. Grier plays "Aretha", the woman who helps him put the screws to the gang that has terrorized the town.
VHS: S21397. $59.98.
Arthur Marks, USA, 1975, 95 mins.

Cleopatra Jones
A curious blaxploitation work with Tamara Dobson as the title character, a statuesque, beautiful CIA agent who uses her training and martial arts skills to wipe out a nefarious gang of drug dealers. With Shelley Winters, Bernie Casey, Brenda Sykes and Antonio Fargas.
VHS: S18927. $19.98.
Jack Starrett, USA, 1973, 89 mins.

Cleopatra Jones and the Casino of Gold
This film combines the revenge hysteria of a blaxploitation drama (antiauthoritarian political messages) with a high-camp revelry (personified by the outlandish antics of Stella Stevens, a character known as "Dragon Lady"). Coming at the end of the blaxploitation cycle, when the films turned to self-parody, this is a wild, stylized melodrama with cool, suave blacks pitted against hysterical, rampaging whites (including Norman Fell). Ostensibly a sequel to Jack Starrett's 1973 original, the film stars Tamara Dobson as a beautiful CIA agent locked in a mortal duel with drug-empress Stevens. With Tanny, Albert Popwell, Caro Kenyatta and Christopher Hunt.
VHS: S18926. $19.98.
Chuck Bail, USA, 1975, 96 mins.

Coffy
Pam Grier's biggest hit finds her battling the drug dealers who made a junkie out of her young sister. Lots of violent retribution as Nurse Grier becomes a one-woman army against criminal scum. With Allan Arbus, Sid Haig, Bob Minor, Booker Bradshaw and Robert Do Qui as King George.
VHS: S07451. $19.98.
Jack Hill, USA, 1973, 91 mins.

Deadly Drifter
Danny Glover plays a disaffected urban revolutionary whose specialized talents for destruction and death lead to his exploitation and corruption. Also known as *Out*. With Peter Coyote.
VHS: S18817. $29.95.
Eli Hollander, USA, 1982, 85 mins.

Detroit 9000
Set against the urban squalor of Detroit, rogue cops and petty criminals seek a valuable collection of jewels. With Alex Rocco, Hari Rhodes and Vonetta McGee.
VHS: S18818. $19.95.
Arthur Marks, USA, 1973, 106 mins.

Disco Godfather
Rudy Ray Moore mixes martial arts, rap and of course, disco in this action film. Moore portrays the owner of a disco out to topple the nation's largest producer of angel dust. USA, 93 mins.
VHS: S21461. $29.95.

Dolemite
A pastiche of gangster and karate movies set in a stand-up nightclub and centered around Rudy Ray Moore's loose and comic turn as the dark avenger. With Jerry Jones and Lady Reed.
VHS: S18810. $19.95.
D'Urville Martin, USA, 1987, 91 mins.

Dolemite 2: Human Tornado
Brash sequel to Rudy Ray Moore's earlier *Dolemite*, about the criminal activity in the seedy nightclub circuit. With Lady Reed.
VHS: S18823. $19.95.
Cliff Raquemore, USA, 1976, 98 mins.

Fass Black
Black gangsters face down the mob over the control of Hollywood's hottest disco. Music by soul artist Johnnie Taylor.
VHS: S18819. $14.95.
D'Urville Martin, USA, 1977, 105 mins.

Foxtrap
Fred Williamson stars as a tough, unstoppable private eye hired by a wealthy family. They want him to track down a beautiful woman, and after treks through the south of France and Rome, he succeeds. Back in L.A. he finds that he was mislead. Murder and betrayal force him to seek revenge.
VHS: S26344. $14.98.
Fred Williamson, USA, 1985, 88 mins.

Foxy Brown
Pam Grier goes into action when her undercover cop boyfriend is murdered by drug dealers on her own front porch. She isn't happy at all to find that her drug-dealing brother, Antonio Fargas, dropped the dime on her lover. A violent blaxploitation film with Terry Carter, Juanita Brown, Sid Haig, Bob Minor and Peter Brown, who loses more than his heart to foxy Pam Grier.
VHS: S07449. $19.98.
Jack Hill, USA, 1974, 91 mins.

Friday Foster
Pam Grier stars in the title role as a newspaper photographer who uncovers a plot to assassinate black politicians. Based on the syndicated comic strip, the cast includes Yaphet Kotto, Thalmus Rasulala, Eartha Kitt, Godfrey Cambridge, Scatman Crothers, Ted Lange and Jim Backus as Enos Griffith, the evil mobster pulling the strings of death.
VHS: S07447. $59.98.
Arthur Marks, USA, 1975, 89 mins.

Get Christie Love
The protagonist of novelist Dorothy Uhnak's colorful and vibrant street detective, Christie Love (Teresa Graves), goes undercover to destroy powerful drug barons. With Harry Guardino, Louise Sorel and Paul Stevens.
VHS: S18811. $19.95.
William A. Graham, USA, 1974, 100 mins.

The Guy from Harlem
Harlem's seamy underside and the atmospheric streets and dangerous environment form the setting of this vigorous and chilling work about a black private investigator.
VHS: S18821. $14.95.
Rene Martinez, Jr., USA, 1977, 86 mins.

Hit!
A revenge action movie which stars Richard Pryor, Billy Dee Williams and Paul Hampton. Williams is the federal agent who springs into action after his daughter overdoses. He puts together his own revenge squad in order to get nine heroin dealers in Marseilles.
VHS: S21484. $19.95.
Sidney J. Furie, USA, 1973, 134 mins.

I'm Gonna Git You Sucka
A smart and very funny parody of the blaxploitation films of the 1970's. Keenan Ivory Wayans stars with Bernie Casey, Jim Brown, Isaac Hayes and Antonio Fargas. When the brother of the hero O.D.'s from wearing too many gold chains, he assembles an over-the-hill group of public avengers to get the dreaded Mr. Big. With John Vernon, Damon Wayans and Steve James.
VHS: S09397. $19.95.
Laser: LD72137. $34.98.
Keenen Ivory Wayans, USA, 1988, 85 mins.

In Your Face
Little-known blaxploitation feature about a black family who are being harassed by their white suburban neighbors. They are helped by a black motorcycle gang. Also known as *Abar, the First Black Superman*.
VHS: S18824. $19.95.
Frank Packard, USA, 1977, 90 mins.

J.D.'s Revenge
Glyn Turman, Joan Pringle and Lou Gossett star in this well-made black horror film about the evil J.D. Walker, whose vengeful spirit returns from beyond the grave to possess an innocent young man.
VHS: S13768. $14.98.
Arthur Marks, USA, 1976, 95 mins.

Joshua
Originally known as *The Black Rider*, this last wave of the blaxploitation works and nominal western stars former football star Fred Williamson as a peaceful man who tracks down the band of killers who viciously murdered his mother. With Isela Vega, Benda Venus and Stacy Newton.
VHS: S18139. $19.95.
Larry Spangler, USA, 1976, 75 mins.

The Legend of Dolemite: Rudy Ray Moore
A living legend from the world of Black comedy, Moore has been hailed as the Godfather of Rap. For over 30 years he has blended a number of styles without shying away from X-rated material. He has influenced all the biggest stars, from Richard Pryor to Whoopi Goldberg. This video is pure Rudy Ray Moore. Features Snoop Doggy Dogg.
VHS: S22460. $24.95.
Rudy Ray Moore, USA, 1994, 75 mins.

The Mack
One of the most popular (and one of the most violent) blaxploitation films made, *Mack* is the story of a Black pimp in Oakland. With Max Julien, Don Gordon, Richard Pryor, Carol Speed, Roger E. Mosley.
VHS: S21485. $9.98.
Michael Campus, USA, 1973, 110 mins.

The Messenger
After doing time in an Italian prison, Jake Turner (Fred Williamson) is free. That night he sees his beloved wife once again but the next day she is brutally murdered. In an orgy of violent revenge he begins killing off the drug suppliers who first hooked his wife on drugs and then killed her. He then meets a strange rich man who encourages him to seek revenge but ultimately betrays him.
VHS: S26343. $14.98.
Fred Williamson, USA, 1986, 95 mins.

Monkey Hustle
An appealing cast, including Yaphet Kotto and Rudy Ray Moore, bolsters this action comedy shot in Chicago. It is the story of a ghetto neighborhood earmarked for leveling in order to make way for a new expressway coming through.
VHS: S13766. $59.98.
Arthur Marks, USA, 1977, 90 mins.

Mr. Mean
Fred Williamson stars as an amoral, ruthless killer and mercenary who reluctantly enters into a contract with the Mafia, setting off a chain of violent and explosive events. Williamson also wrote the screenplay. With Crippy Yocard.
VHS: S18140. $14.95.
Fred Williamson, USA, 1992, 81 mins.

Petey Wheatstraw
An African-American folktale is retold by "Dolemite" himself, Rudy Ray Moore. The story is that of a man so useless that he cuts a deal with Satan himself—he has to marry the devil's ugly daughter.
VHS: S21460. $29.95.
Cliff Roquemore, USA, 1978, 93 mins.

The Return of Superfly
Curtis Mayfield and Ice-T provide the music for this third sequel to *Superfly*. The plot revolves around "Superfly" and his Harlem exploits—hassling drug dealers and avoiding the cops. Features Margaret Avery, Nathan Purdee and Sam Jackson.
VHS: S21464. $14.95.
Sig Shore, USA, 1990, 94 mins.

Scream, Blacula, Scream
Pam Grier is Lisa, the voodoo princess who must persuade the ferocious black vampire Manuwalde (William Marshall) from draining the life's blood from any more of the black community in Los Angeles. This sequel to *Blacula* features Richard Lawson, Don Mitchell, Lynn Moody and Michael Conrad as the Sheriff. Set in L.A. and Africa.
VHS: S07450. $59.98.
Bob Kelljan, USA, 1973, 95 mins.

Shaft
Richard Roundtree is the title character, a black private detective in New York City who dresses sharp, pleases the ladies and knows just when to crash through a window. Isaac Hayes's theme song won an Oscar. With Moses Gunn, Charles Cioffi, Gwenn Mitchell and Drew Bundini Brown. The action packed script by Ernest Tidyman is based on his own novel.
VHS: S09159. $19.95.
Gordon Parks, USA, 1971, 100 mins.

Shaft in Africa
Richard Roundtree goes to Africa in this action-filled 1970's thriller. Naturally, this lawman brings style and justice to the struggle of black people wherever he goes. In this film he must confront one of mankind's most horrific legacies: that of slavery.
VHS: S26872. $14.95.
John Guillermin, USA, 1973, 112 mins.

Shaft's Big Score
A continuation of the predicaments of the hip and stylish black private eye trying to break up a deadly numbers and racketeering syndicate responsible for the killing of a friend. Features Isaac Hayes' title song, director Gordon Parks' music and a startling climax with Shaft chased by a helicopter. With Richard Roundtree, Moses Gunn and Drew Bundini Brown.
VHS: S18480. $19.98.
Gordon Parks, USA, 1972, 104 mins.

Sheba, Baby
Pam Grier is Sheba Shayne, Private Eye. Her father was murdered by a wealthy white businessman who framed him for some racial riots, and she wants to clear his name. With D'Urville Martin, Austin Stoker, Rudy Challenger, Dick Merrifield as Shark and Charles Broaddus as Hammerhead.
VHS: S07448. $59.98.
William Girdler, USA, 1975, 90 mins.

Soul Vengeance
Savagely beaten and convicted on false charges, Charlie is released from prison and pursues the men responsible, wielding an alarming weapon. 91 mins.
VHS: S18833. $14.95.
Jamaa Fanaka, USA, 1975, 91 mins.

Super Soul Brother
An exuberant social and political comedy about a classic underachiever who ingests a strange potion that endows one with supernatural gifts. With Wildman Steve. 80 mins.
VHS: S18834. $14.95.

Superfly
Ron O'Neal plays a rather curious hero in Gordon Parks, Jr.'s *Superfly*. He is a pimp and a drug dealer who defies the system and manages to leave his life of vice with a hefty retirement fund. Features Carl Lee, Julius Harris, Sheila Frazier and Charles McGregor. Curtis Mayfield provides the music.
VHS: S21465. $19.98.
Gordon Parks, Jr., USA, 1972, 98 mins.

Superfly TNT
This sequel finds "Superfly" in Europe fighting for the independence of Africa. An arms dealer, the suave Roscoe Lee Browne, enlists the ex-hustler to overthrow a brutal dictatorship. This film is the very definition of blaxploitation. Features Sheila Frazier from *Superfly* and Robert Guillaume.
VHS: S21475. $14.95.
Ron O'Neal, USA, 1973, 87 mins.

Truck Turner
The incomparable Isaac Hayes stars in this incredibly violent "blaxploitation" film about a bounty hunter out to capture bail jumpers. With Yaphet Kotto and a musical score from Hayes himself.
VHS: S13767. $14.98.
Jonathan Kaplan, USA, 1974, 91 mins.

Urban Jungle
Part of the new wave of films resembling 70s blaxploitation pictures, it tells the story of a ruthless Housing Commisssioner who forces the poor out into the streets in order to make a quick buck. Somehow this all relates to S & M and drug dealing priests. The heroes of this picture are a couple of two-bit drug merchants who decide to help the community instead of poison it. Their help however, is brutal violence.
VHS: S21467. $79.95.
Daniel Matmor, USA, 1994, 90 mins.

The Wilby Conspiracy
Sidney Poitier is Shack Twala, a Bantu revolutionary in South Africa who has to get out of the country with a cache of diamonds to be used to further the cause. He relies on the reluctant Michael Caine to assist him. An anti-apartheid action thriller with Persis Khambatta, Rutger Hauer, Prunella Gee and Nicol Williamson as the determined pursuer, Major Horn.
VHS: S06064. $14.95.
Ralph Nelson, USA, 1975, 105 mins.

COMEDY ACTS

All Out Comedy
Karen Ripley, Marilyn Pittman, Tom Ammiano and Scott Capurro will have you "coming out" of your seats. Filmed live at the San Francisco landmark in the Castro, Josie's Juice Bar. 78 mins.
VHS: S21124. $29.98.

All-Star Toast to the Improv
Hosted by Robert Klein, with Billy Crystal, Richard Lewis, Martin Mull, Paul Rodriguez and Robin Williams, a celebration of 15 years of outrageous comedy at Los Angeles' Improv Club in an evening of stand-up comedy. 60 mins.
VHS: S08144. $39.95.

America's Favorite Jokes
A collection of jokes ranging from the inane to the ridiculous, usually based on such questions as "How do you circumcise a whale?", "What do wide mouth frogs eat?" and "What's the difference between a Porsche and a porcupine?" 30 mins.
VHS: S07443. $16.95.

Ann Magnuson's Vandemonium Plus
Performance artist, comedian, and star of Susan Seidelman's *Making Mr. Right*, Ann Magnuson combines two comedy specials into one video presentation. The first guest stars Meat Loaf and comedian Eric Bogosian. The second features Magnuson in 30 different characterizations in only 15 minutes. USA, 45 mins.
VHS: S05299. $19.95.

Best of Eddie Murphy— Saturday Night Live
A compilation of the television roles that launched a movie career. More than 30 of Eddie Murphy's most popular sketches are included. See Eddie as Buckwheat, James Brown, Stevie Wonder and Little Richard Simmons as well as the host of "Mr. Robinson's Neighborhood". Relive those great Saturday Nights with Eddie when the show was actually funny. 78 mins.
VHS: S08717. $19.95.
Laser: LD75119. $24.98.

The Best of Minnie Pearl: Let Minnie Steal Your Joke
The first lady of country comedy brings you classic American humor packed with unforgettable laughs and precious moments from her popular segment with Ralph Emery on the *Nashville Now* TV show. 60 mins.
VHS: S23146. $19.95.

The Best of The Kids in the Hall
A collection of sketches that mix the political, social and scatological—in other words, a non-stop revelry for camp, the Queen and her country. In this hip work by the Canadian ensemble, their exuberant humor takes no prisoners. "It's *Monty Python* with a migraine, anxiety made antic, frantic and hilarious" (*USA Today*). With David Foley, Mark McKinney, Scott Thompson, Bruce McCulloch and Kevin McDonald.
VHS: S19880. $59.95.

Best of the Not Necessarily the News
A hysterical tape in the Comedy Club's new series. 60 mins.
VHS: S09807. $39.99.

Bette Midler's Mondo Beyond
Bette Midler stars in a nutty performance at The Comedy Club. 60 mins.
VHS: S09808. $19.98.

Blackstone on Tour
The world's foremost illusionist presents a fast-paced demonstration of his remarkable talents—including the mysterious appearance on stage of a live elephant. A masterful demonstration of the art of illusion. USA, 1981, 60 mins.
VHS: S03239. $39.95.

g u i l t y   p l e a s u r e s   271

Bob Goldthwait: Is He Like That All the Time?
Hilarious stand-up comedy live from the star of Police Academy.
60 mins.
VHS: S11003. $19.95.

Brett Butler: The Child Ain't Right
This hysterical comic finally is available on video. Her stand-up routine will amply demonstrate that this "child ain't right." Contains adult material. 26 mins.
VHS: S24797. $12.95.

But...Seriously
Comic greats Whoopi Goldberg, Richard Pryor, Lenny Bruce, Lily Tomlin, Eric Bogosian, Jack Paar, Billy Crystal and others are joined in this collection of political comedy. These comedians satirize everything, from the civil rights movement to the L.A. riots. 82 mins.
VHS: S26461. $19.95.

The Classic Schiller's Reel Collection
Finally, 15 of the classic comic shorts by Tom Schiller, that were featured on Saturday Night Live, are now available. Comic greats like Bill Murray, Gilda Radner and John Belushi are featured in some of their best performances, in films like La Dolce Gilda and The Acid Generation—Where Are They Now?. 44 mins.
VHS: S21206. $9.99.

Denis Leary: No Cure for Cancer
He was great on Saturday Night Live, but here he can really let loose and reveal the true extent of his wit. Contains adult material. 63 mins.
VHS: S24801. $12.95.

Eddie Murphy Delirious
Eddie Murphy raps about life, sex, childhood and more in this scathing, scatological, stand-up performance.
VHS: S21679. $14.95.
Laser: LD75186. $34.98.
Bruce Gowers, USA, 1983, 69 mins.

Eddie Murphy: Raw
Eddie Murphy's second stand-up performance film, featuring many of his woman-bashing observations on life.
VHS: S21673. $14.95.
Laser: LD75185. $34.98.
Robert Townsend, USA, 1987, 90 mins.

Elayne Boosler
Live from the Bottom Line in New York City, the comedy of Elayne Boosler. She's been called the funniest woman in America and this is a golden opportunity to find out why. With special appearances by David Letterman, Bill Cosby, Dr. Ruth, Brother Theodore and Larry "Bud" Melman. 60 mins.
VHS: S08706. $59.98.

Elayne Boosler: Broadway Baby
An all-new stand-up special from one of the funniest comedians in the business, in an hour of comedy about mothers, sports, shopping, sports, contacts, condoms, pets, and, of course, sex. 60 mins.
VHS: S11692. $59.95.

Elayne Boosler: Live Nude Girls
Though this tape contains adult material, there really aren't any nude girls. But it got your attention and that is exactly the kind of all out humor Boosler does best. 59 mins.
VHS: S24798. $12.95.

Emo Philips Live!
Concert comedy performance by Emo Philips which "captures Philips at his comically eerie best" (New York Post).
VHS: S07163. $39.99.

Gallagher—Melon Crazy
Happiness to some people is a 30-foot melon and the willingness to destroy a wonderful example of the bounty of the land that could probably feed several needy and deserving individuals. But not if Gallagher is around. Rumor has it he started as a contestant on "The Gong Show." Kids, don't try this kind of stuff at home. 58 mins.
VHS: S10816. $19.95.

Gallagher—Over Your Head
The subtitle is probably referring to some sticky and gooey concoction and not the level of the jokes. In this video concert Gallagher speaks his mind on politicians, ancient history and methods of child-rearing. Be prepared to take notes. Familiar items will be destroyed in the Sledge-O-Matic demonstration. 1984. 58 mins.
VHS: S10817. $19.95.

Gallagher—Stuck in the Sixties
Said to be his most inventive collection of props on display to date in this continuing series of childish mayhem. Gallagher pulls out all the stops in still another high energy comic concert that will feature the infamous Sledge-O-Matic in action. 1984. 58 mins.
VHS: S10818. $19.95.

Gallagher—The Bookkeeper
The messiest comic in the business takes on the IRS in this live video concert. The self-proclaimed king of prop comedy—What, did Rip Taylor die?—assaults his audience with a barrage of one-liners and unusual objects. As usual, the Sledge-O-Matic will conclude the act. 58 mins.
VHS: S10814. $19.95.

Gallagher—The Maddest
In the mood for a concert of comedy featuring mutant sofas and assaults on 7-11's? How about freaky guys who wear striped shirts and suspenders? Gallagher is the one name comedian who goes through props the way Warren Beatty goes through girlfriends. Be prepared for a particularly goopy Sledge-O-Matic finale. 60 mins.
VHS: S10815. $19.95.

George Carlin—Live! What Am I Doing in New Jersey?
"This is a country where tobacco kills 400,000 people per year...so they ban artificial sweeteners because a rat died!" Who else but George Carlin, ruthless, reckless and let loose on an unsuspecting New Jersey audience for an hour of unpredictable, caustic, no-holds barred humor. 60 mins.
VHS: S08145. $39.99.

Gilda Radner
Saturday Night Live's Gilda Radner created memorable characters that live on. Roseanne Roseanadanna, Baba Wawa and Lisa Loopner are just some of them. This special memoir uses Radner's own recording of her autobiography, It's Always Something, to showcase some of her delightful humor. 50 mins.
VHS: S25870. $19.95.

The Groove Tube
Now seventies nostalgia, a wild lampoon series of skits that spoof television which gave Chevy Chase his first big break. 75 mins.
VHS: S04622. $39.95.

Hollywood Party
It's party time in Tinsel Town and look who's invited! Laurel and Hardy, The Three Stooges, Jimmy Durante, Mickey Mouse, plus a host of Hollywood's top stars of the '30s and a bevy of beautiful dancing girls! Filled with gags, popular songs, and lavish production numbers. USA, 1934, 69 mins.
VHS: S15420. $19.98.

The Hungry I Reunion
The world-famous nightclub in San Francisco is host to a comedy salute by some of the stars who performed there. Performers include Mort Sahl, Bill Cosby, Jonathan Winters, The Limelighters, Phyllis Diller and Lenny Bruce. Lenny's contribution is presumably pre-recorded. USA, 1980, 90 mins.
VHS: S06165. $29.98.

In the Life: The Funny Tape
Kate Clinton, America's first lesbian stand-up comic, hosts this collection of songs and skits featuring some of the best lesbian and gay talent around. Even the commercials are twisted. Lily Tomlin and the late Vito Russo are also featured. 60 mins.
VHS: S21125. $19.98.

Jackie Mason
A definitive biography of the equal opportunity offender, this tape is also a hilarious compilation of Mason's best schtick. It includes early appearances on The Steve Allen Show and routines from Mason's many Broadway shows. 52 mins.
VHS: S26216. $19.95.

Jay Leno: The American Dream
Jay Leno delves as only he can into the comedic implications of what keeps America a vibrant and hopeful place to be. From Paramount Home video come words and ideas of the man Johnny Carson trusts to host the Tonight Show in his absence. Among the subjects for jest are big cars, flashy clothes and Italian beef sandwiches. In color. USA, 1986, 49 mins.
VHS: S06170. $19.95.

Joan Rivers: Abroad in London
Does "ugly American abroad" mean anything to you? Rivers holds nothing back in this terrific stand-up routine. Contains adult material. 57 mins.
VHS: S24802. $12.95.

Joe Piscopo Live!
One of the sharpest comic impersonators to break out of the comedy circuit in 60 minutes of raucous, rockin' comedy. A panorama of impressions from Phil Donahue and Robert De Niro to Frank Sinatra and David Lee Roth. 60 mins.
VHS: S07572. $39.99.

Judy Toll: Lips Only
Extensive hands-on studies have led Judy Toll to the conclusion, "All men are scum." Brace yourself for this rude, uncensored and downright shocking comedienne. A relentless, hilariously raw video short, men will squirm with laughter, while women relish in the ultimate revenge. 12 mins.
VHS: S15902. $9.95.

Kovacs & Keaton
Two rare television appearances by master comedians—Kovacs is silent in Eugene (1960) as he mimes his way through life, while Keaton is Wrestling with Trouble as he and his buddy get tangled with two real-life wrestlers (1953). USA, 60 mins.
VHS: S01651. $24.95.

Lenny Bruce
Filmed exactly one year before his death in August of 1965, this is the only full-length, unedited recording of America's most brilliant comic. This is not a documentary, but a raw account of Lenny Bruce in performance at a steamy San Francisco nightclub. Includes the animated short Thank You Mask Man. 68 mins.
VHS: S16334. $19.95.

Lenny Bruce Without Tears
Fred Baker's personal, off-beat documentary about his friend Lenny Bruce. The film interweaves memoirs and anecdotes from friends and colleagues, including Steve Allen, Paul Krassner, Kenneth Tynan, Nat Hentoff and Malcolm Muggeridge. "With anger, biting humor and sorrow the film shows the demise of the iconoclastic comic...so plagued by personal demons" (Linda Gross, L.A. Times).
VHS: S18517. $19.98.
Fred Baker, USA, 1992, 75 mins.

Lily Tomlin 3-Pack
The Search for Signs of Intelligent Life in the Universe, Ernestine: Peak Experiences and Appearing Nitely are the comic standouts joined in this three-tape set. It brings Lily Tomlin's Tony Award-winning performances to video. 120 mins.
VHS: S27478. $59.95.

Mambo Mouth
This funny program captures the essence of writer-comedian John Leguizamo's off-Broadway hit. Performing six monologues that illustrate Latin stereotypes, Leguizamo transforms from Loco Louie, a sex crazed 14-year-old, to Manny the Fanny, a female prostitute, to Angel, the epitome of angry Latin machismo, to other poignant characters. The play won both an Obie and an Outer Critics Circle Award.
VHS: S16157. $19.95.
Thomas Schlamme, USA, 1991, 60 mins.

Martin Mull Live from North Ridgeville, Ohio
A classic comedy performance—"an impressive catch of comedy talent."
VHS: S07162. $39.95.

Milton Berle Invites You to a Night at La Cage
Uncle Miltie has been known to put on a dress for laughs now and again, so he is a perfect host for an evening of female impersonation and comedy. With Gypsy, the master/mistress of ceremonies at the La Cage Revue. Filmed in Las Vegas. Watch for Berle as Dolly Parton.
VHS: S04215. $29.95.
Milton Berle/Jim Gates, USA, 1986, 75 mins.

The Mr. Bill Collection
This program highlights the postmodern humor of Mr. Bill, Saturday Night Live's disembodied man of clay. 50 mins.
VHS: S19407. $14.95.

National Expose
A scathing send-up of Hollywood, international celebrities and British royalty from the Spitting Image Team, the merry pranksters who specialize in latex celebrity doubles. On sight are the disastrous repercussion of Cher's plastic surgery, the assassination attempt of Dan Quayle, the Royal family, Elvis, Rod Stewart and the Pope. Breezy, entertaining fun and scandalous.
VHS: S17619. $14.98.

Niall Tobin Live
Master Irish comedian and cabaret performer—Irish, earthy, open and uproarious, in his first video program after his leading role in the award-winning Broadway plays "Borstal Boy" and "Fearless Frank." 82 mins.
VHS: S09164. $29.95.

Paramount Comedy Theater: Volumes 1-3
Howie Mandel hosts a show featuring four young comics: Bruce Mahler, Judy Carter, Philip Wellford and Bob Saget.
VHS: S01913. $19.95.
Joe Hostettler, USA, 1986, 71 mins.

Paramount Comedy Theater: Volume 4
Howie Mandel hosts Delivery Men, featuring five of America's hot new comics: Jimmy Aleck, Maurice LaMarche, Rick Overton, Lou Dinos, Pat Hazell. Jimmy Aleck tells you how not to talk to an auto mechanic. Maurice does uncanny impressions of everyone from Wilma Flintstone to Alan Alda. 71 mins.
VHS: S10053. $29.95.

Paramount Comedy Theater: Volume 5
Cutting Up, again hosted by Mandel, features Dale Gonyea, Lois Bromfield, Teddy Bergeron and Louise Duart. Gonyea presents a musical salute to single sex and famous parents, Bergeron tells how he hooked his VCR to his microwave. 60 mins.
VHS: S10054. $29.95.

Paul Reiser: 3½ Blocks from Home
Paul Reiser, of the hit TV comedy show Mad About You, is at his stand-up best in this great video. Contains adult material. 58 mins.
VHS: S24799. $12.95.

Rap Master Ronnie: A Report Card
Jim Morris stars as the President in this comedy created by Garry Trudeau and Elizabeth Swados and performed at The Comedy Club. 60 mins.
VHS: S09809. $39.99.

Rich Little's Christmas Carol
Snow is falling, shoppers are scurrying about, bells are ringing...Christmas time is here...this time with a twist from the comic genius of master impressionist Rich Little. Here, Little plays the whole gang! W.C. Fields is the sourest scrooge you'll ever see. Paul Lynde is poor Bob Cratchit; Richard Nixon is Marley's Ghost.
VHS: S12476. $14.95.

Rich Little—One's a Crowd
One can certainly be a crowd when that one person is Rich Little, the leading impersonator of the famous people. Now available on home video, Mr. Little performs a cavalcade of movie stars, celebrities and political figures. Included in this parade of impressions are John Wayne, Groucho Marx, Jack Nicholson, Jimmy Stewart, Jack Benny and Ronald Reagan.
VHS: S07787. $19.98.

Richard Lewis—I'm Exhausted
The star of TV's "Anything But Love" as he "whines about life with the rhythm, body language and material of a Woody Allen, the posture of a Groucho Marx and the speed of a Mario Andretti." (People Magazine). 60 mins.
VHS: S11253. $19.98.

Richard Pryor Live! In Concert
The incomparable Richard Pryor brings "truth to humor and humor to truth" in this 1979 concert video which showcases Pryor's greatest moments. "The comedian, uncensored, is at his raunchy best" (Leonard Maltin, Movie and Video Guide). Richard Pryor raps on subjects ranging from race to death to sex to machismo, and tells such famous stories as the time he shot his car and the time his children thought he was joking when he nearly drowned.
VHS: S27199. $19.98.
Jeff Margolis, USA, 1979, 78 mins.

Robert Klein
Multi-talented comic Robert Klein gives a hilarious stand-up and musical performance in this live recording from the campus of New York University. 60 mins.
VHS: S07698. $29.95.

Robin Williams: Comedy Faster Than a Speeding Bullet!
Robin Williams in a live performance. What more needs to be said?
VHS: S04508. $19.98.

Ron Reagan Is the President's Son/The New Homeowner's Guide to Happiness
The shockingly true and hilariously not-so-true story of Ron Reagan, dancer, journalist, writer, interviewer, TV host and all around President's son, and, in a hilarious second piece, when the peace and prosperity promised by the purchase of an American Dream House is disturbed by the incessant din of barking dogs, our unhappy-go-lucky married couple will try anything for a wholly silent night; but can valium laced raw steaks be anything but a recipe for disaster? 60 mins.
VHS: S08146. $39.99.

Rude: Rudy Ray Moore
A live concert performance of comic and actor Rudy Ray Moore in his best known impersonation, Dolemite, taken from the film character. 86 mins.
VHS: S18831. $19.95.

Sam Kinison: Family Entertainment Hour
An irreverent performance by the late shock comedian Sam Kinison, who luxuriates in his scatological mixture of sex, death, religion and intolerance. With the Randy Hansen Band. 50 mins.
VHS: S18719. $19.95.

Saturday Night Entertainment
4 volumes of the best (and funniest selections) from comedians who have made Saturday night famous.
The Best of Gilda Radner.
VHS: S09413. $19.98.
The Best of Dan Aykroyd.
VHS: S09414. $14.95.
The Best of John Belushi.
VHS: Out of print. For rental only.
Laser: LD72211. $34.98.
The Best of Chevy Chase.
VHS: S09416. $19.98.

Scrambled Feet
Jeffrey Hadow, John Driver and Roger Neil, the three original award-winning New York cast members, are joined by Madeline Kahn in blackout sketches, comedy routines and jokes. USA, 1982, 100 mins.
VHS: S03238. $39.98.

Spalding Gray: Terrors of Pleasure
The master storyteller, actor and performance artist (Swimming to Cambodia) recounts one man's obsession for a piece of land to call his own—a simple enough dream that turned into a nightmare of beetle-filled beams and de-centralized heating in a house that was simply sinking into clay. 60 mins.
VHS: S07574. $39.95.

Steve Allen's Golden Age of Comedy
The best from Steve Allen's early TV shows, featuring a bevy of stars associated with his funny show. The outrageous comedy skits and music includes appearances by Bob Hope, Johnny Carson, Abbott and Costello, Mel Brooks and Jimmy Durante. 49 mins.
VHS: S03309. $59.95.

Tim Allen: Men Are Pigs
Home Improvement is not the only skill that Tim Allen possesses. Here he shows the comic side of himself that is perfect for a stand-up format. Contains adult material. 30 mins.
VHS: S24800. $12.95.

Toast to Lenny
Bill Cosby, Steve Allen, George Carlin and Mort Sahl (to name a few) gather at Hollywood's Troubadour to pay tribute to the trailblazing comedy of Lenny Bruce. Includes anecdotes, rare film clips and reflections by those who knew him best. 60 mins. 1984.
VHS: S04500. $59.95.

Uptown Comedy Express
Arsenio Hall, Chris Rock, Robert Townsend, Barry Sobel, Marcia Warfield are featured in this presentation of a wild and funny showcase from Los Angeles' Ebony Theatre that strikes back at Jesse Jackson, preachers, alcohol, sexual relationships and more.
VHS: S11252. $19.95.

Victor Borge: On Stage with Audience Favorites
Two video cassettes with some of his funniest—and classic—performances, released on two separate tapes. At 75 Borge is "still one of the funniest people in the world" (L.A. Times). Volume 1 includes: Introducing Mozart, My Favorite Barber, Early American Folksong, Introducing Marylyn Mulvey, Croatian Folksong, Aria from "Rigor Mortis" by Joe Green, Viennese Dance No. 1 by Friedman-Gaertner, The Timid Page Turner, and Complete Piano Selections. Volume 2 includes: Birthday Improvisations, Sahan Arzruni with the 2nd Rhapsody by Liszt, Salieri Opera, Inflationary Language, Phonetic Punctuation, Viennese Dance No. 2 by Friedman-Gaertner, Danish Lullaby, Improvisation, Complete Piano Selections.
Volume 1.
VHS: S05847. $29.95.
Volume 2
VHS: S05848. $29.95.

Whoopi Goldberg: Fontaine...Why Am I Straight?
The comic operation on the moral backbone of America from Jim and Tammy Faye Bakker and Jerry Falwell to Jesse Jackson and the Reverend Al Sharpton, with Whoopi Goldberg in a live performance. In the character of Fontaine, she's out of the Betty Ford clinic, and taking on the real world. 51 mins.
VHS: S11004. $59.99.

Without You I'm Nothing
Sandra Bernhard's adaptation of her off-Broadway show is a documentary-like examination of the nature of performance, identity and the culture of celebrity. In a brilliant dialectic on the relationship of performer and audience, Bernhard inhabits various roles and personalities to make hilarious comments about music, art, fashion, politics and sex. With John Doe, Steve Antin and Cynthia Bailey, a beautiful black woman who's Bernhard's alter ego.
VHS: S13266. $19.98.
Laser: C.L.V. LD72096. $29.98.
John Boskovich, USA, 1990, 90 mins.

The Young at Heart Comedians
Comic talk-show host David Brenner introduces seven senior members of a profession that tells jokes for a living. Filmed in front of a live audience and backstage, veteran stand-up comics Henny Youngman, Norm Crosby, Jackie Gayle, George Gobel, Jackie Vernon, Shelly Berman and Carl Ballantine do their stuff. They have over 300 years of experience in the business. USA, 1984, 77 mins.
VHS: S07442. $29.95.

ELVIS PRESLEY

Clambake
Elvis Presley plays a millionaire's son who trades places with a poor water ski instructor (Will Hutchins) to see if he's got the right stuff to make it on his own on the beach in Florida. He sings seven songs, romances Shelley Fabares and tangles with playboy Bill Bixby.
VHS: S03929. $19.95.
Arthur Nadel, USA, 1967, 99 mins.

Double Trouble
Elvis Presley gets involved with jewel smuggling, teenaged heiresses, and rock and roll in swinging London and Brussels, Belgium. He sings nine songs including "Long-Legged Girls with Short Dresses On" and "Old McDonald". With Annette Day, John Williams and the Wiiere Brothers.
VHS: S03930. $19.95.
Norman Taurog, USA, 1967, 90 mins.

Elvis on Tour
The King of Rock and Roll is the focus of this concert-documentary that features numerous songs sung in a number of cities. It also examines Elvis the man and takes a private peek at his personal life. Colonel Tom Parker serves as technical advisor.
VHS: S03931. $19.95.
Pierre Adige/Robert Abel, USA, 1972, 93 mins.

Elvis Stories
Titled "hysterical video tabloid and cure for Bambi fever," this fun video features John Cusack as the amazing burger king whose patties transmit messages from Elvis in "Corkey's Elvis Patties." Then "Elvis Lennon" proposes that Elvis and John Lennon were the same person, as Rick Saucedo, Ben Stiller, Joel Murray and others act in this hilarious collection of strange Elvis stories. 30 mins.
VHS: S11258. $14.95.

Elvis—That's the Way It Is
An entertaining and engaging documentary of Elvis, live on stage at the International Hotel in Las Vegas. Photographed by Lucien Ballard. Twenty-seven songs are presented, including "Blue Suede Shoes", "Heartbreak Hotel", "Crying Time" and "That's All Right Mama".
VHS: S03932. $24.95.
Laser: LD71151. $34.98.
Denis Sanders, USA, 1970, 107 mins.

Elvis: The Echo Will Never Die
Tom Jones, B.B. King, Sammy Davis Jr., Ursula Andress and David Marsh join Casey Kasem in this personal tribute to Elvis Presley, recounting his musical roots and rise to fame to his final days. USA, 1983, 50 mins.
VHS: S01806. $29.95.

Follow That Dream
Elvis Presley and his family move to Florida where they try to homestead a prime piece of real estate. Naturally there is serious opposition. With Arthur O'Donnell, Joanna Moore, Simon Oakland, and Jack Kruschen. Elvis sings the title tune and three others.
VHS: S03927. $19.95.
Laser: Letterboxed. LD72334. $34.98.
Gordon Douglas, USA, 1962, 111 mins.

Frankie and Johnny
Elvis Presley and Donna Douglas (The Beverly Hillbillies) play riverboat entertainers and lovers who like to fight because they make up so well. A popular folk ballad becomes an excuse for Elvis to sing twelve more lesser-known songs. With Nancy Kovack.
VHS: S03928. $19.95.
Fred De Cordova, USA, 1966, 88 mins.

Harum Scarum
Elvis Presley plays a motion picture-recording star kidnapped

---

on a tour of the Middle East. He must escape, stop a royal assassination, romance a princess and still find the energy to sing nine songs, including "Harem Holiday" and "Hey Little Girl". With Mary Ann Mobley.
VHS: S03936. $19.95.
Gene Nelson, USA, 1965, 95 mins.

Heartbreak Hotel
A fictional fable about the King of Rock and Roll. Elvis Presley (David Keith) finds himself kidnapped by an ambitious teenager who wants to cheer up his mother. Tuesday Weld is the big Elvis fan who snaps out of her depression when he decides to stay awhile in her run-down hotel and help with the chores. With Charlie Schlatter and a whole lot of shaking going on.
VHS: S09574. $89.95.
Chris Columbus, USA, 1988, 101 mins.

Jailhouse Rock
Elvis Presley goes to prison for accidentally killing a man in a bar fight, and is signed to a musical contract following his performance on a tv show in prison. He follows a strange road to success and learns what's really important. Seven songs. With Mickey Shaughnessy, Judy Tyler and Dean Jones as the disc jockey who gives him a "break."
VHS: S00648. $19.95.
Laser: LD71157. $34.98.
Richard Thorpe, USA, 1957, 96 mins.

Kid Galahad
Elvis Presley put on boxing gloves before Sylvester Stallone was out of high school. He even had Charles Bronson as his corner-cut man as ol' swivel hips tries to more than go the distance to win the big fight and his trainer's sister. With Gig Young, Joan Blackman.
VHS: S03933. $19.95.
Phil Karlson, USA, 1962, 95 mins.

Live a Little, Love a Little
Elvis Presley is an ambitious photographer working for two different bosses, one of whom wouldn't approve of the job at the girlie magazine. Somehow he finds the time to sing four songs, romance Michele Carey, and see what develops with bosses Don Porter and Rudy Vallee. With Sterling Holloway as the milkman. Based on the novel Kiss My Firm and Pliant Lips by Dan Greenburg.
VHS: S08085. $19.95.
Norman Taurog, USA, 1968, 89 mins.

Speedway
Elvis Presley plays a winning stock car driver who gets in trouble with the IRS when his manager, Bill Bixby, puts too much of his client's money on slow horses, who race at a different sort of track. The government sends Nancy Sinatra to investigate. With Gale Gordon.
VHS: S03934. $19.95.
Norman Taurog, USA, 1968, 90 mins.

Spinout
Elvis Presley races fast cars and leads a rock and roll band with a girl drummer, as he is pursued by four women. Shelley Fabares, Diane McBain, Dodie Marshall and Deborah Walley as the drummer limit the King to only five songs. What lucky girl will Elvis meet at the altar? Place your bets. The technical advisor for this film was Colonel Tom Parker.
VHS: S08086. $19.95.
Norman Taurog, USA, 196, 95 mins.

Stay Away Joe
Elvis Presley is a Navajo Indian rodeo star with a plan to better the life of his family on the reservation by raising cattle. When he barbecues the bill the government gets upset. With Burgess Meredith and Katy Jurado as his parents and L.Q. Jones as Navajo pal. Elvis sings only two songs and romances Susan Trustman and Quentin Dean.
VHS: S08087. $19.95.
Peter Tewkesbury, USA, 1968, 102 mins.

This Is Elvis
Unusual and quite good documentary combines historical footage with actors playing Elvis at various parts of his life. 144 mins.
VHS: S01329. $19.98.
Malcolm Leo/Andrew Solt, USA, 1981, 144 mins.

Trouble with Girls (a.k.a. How to Get into It)
Elvis Presley manages a traveling Chautauqua show, sings two songs and tries to prevent trouble between the locals and the members of the troupe. With Marlyn Mason, Sheree North, Edward Andrews, John Carradine, Anissa Jones and Dabney Coleman. From the novel by Day Keene and Dwight Babcock.
VHS: S08088. $19.95.
Peter Tewkesbury, USA, 1969, 105 mins.

Viva Las Vegas
One of the King's best films. He co-stars with Ann-Margret as a Grand Prix driver who wants to sing, dance and operate expensive motor vehicles at high speed while in the company of a vivacious redheaded swimming instructor. With Cesare Danova and William Demarest.
VHS: S03935. $19.95.
Laser: LD70701. $34.98.
George Sidney, USA, 1964, 86 mins.

SERIALS

Ace Drummond
The Universal serial in 13 chapters, of Captain Eddie Rickenbacker's exploits in the sky, directed by Ford Beebe and Cliff Smith. Featuring aerial stunts and action with John Kind, Jean Rogers, Noah Beery Jr., Lon Chaney Jr. and Ed Cobb. From a very good quality print.
VHS: S13212. $29.95.
Ford Beebe, USA, 1936, 260 mins.

The Adventures of Captain Marvel
A very popular serial from Republic wherein young Billy Batson has only to say the magic word Shazam and he turns into Captain Marvel, an adult and very tough crime fighter. The villain of record is the evil Scorpion, who needs five ancient

---

lenses to rule the world. Tom Tyler is the Captain. Frank Coghlan, Jr. is Billy. B&W.
VHS: S06051. $29.95.
Laser: LD71967. $39.98.
William Witney/John English, USA, 1941, 12 chapters

The Adventures of Frank and Jesse James
The archetypal bad boys of the West undertake a program for restitution to the community they plundered by their search for gold and profit in a silver mine in thrilling serial. 180 mins.
VHS: S18375. $29.98.

The Adventures of Rex & Rinty
A stolen prize horse teams up with a wandering dog to help oust various villains. 12 chapters. USA, 1935, 234 mins.
VHS: S15604. $29.95.

Black Widow (Cliffhanger Serials #5)
An Asian king sends his daughter to America to steal an atomic rocket engine in this lively serial from Republic studios. With Bruce Edwards, Virginia Lindley, Carol Forman. 13 deadly episodes on two videocassettes.
VHS: S15087. $29.98.
Spencer Bennet/Fred Brannon, USA, 1947

Burn 'em Up Barnes
Our hero, "Burn 'em Up", battles gangsters and must endure fiery crashes, explosions and other perils, but still finds time to race everything from cars to speedboats like a bat out of ….! 12 episodes. USA, 1934, 240 mins.
VHS: S15600. $29.95.

Cliffhangers: Adventures from the Thrill Factory
Film historian Leonard Maltin considers the world of the Republic Cliffhanger serials, reflecting on the heroes, stunts, gimmicks and actors. 46 mins.
VHS: S18376. $14.98.

The Clutching Hand
Our hero, Craig Kennedy, faces a myriad of fiendish pitfalls, ruthless gunmen and diabolical devices before he unmasks the sinister master criminal—Clutching Hand. 15 chapters. USA, 1936, 308 mins.
VHS: S15599. $29.95.

The Crimson Ghost
A Republic serial about the efforts of the title character to capture and control a machine that can short circuit electricity. Behind the grinning skull mask and the black shroud lurks Bud Geary using the voice of I. Stanford Jolley. Also in the cast is Clayton Moore (The Lone Ranger) as a villainous thug. With serial queen Linda Stirling and Charles Quigley. B&W.
VHS: S06048. $29.95.
William Witney/F. Brannon, USA, 1946, 12 chapters

Cyclone of the Saddle
A western serial about the loneliness and solitude of the American frontier and a violent range war. With Rex Lease, Bobby Nelson, William Desmond and Yakima Canutt.
VHS: S18902. $19.95.
Elmer Clifton, USA, 1935, 53 mins.

Darkest Africa
Fifteen episodes of a cliffhanger series following the adventures of animal trainer Clyde Beatty in the wild landscapes of Africa. Laser disk contains original theatrical trailer. 270 mins.
VHS: S17410. $29.98.
Laser: LD71703. $49.98.

Dick Tracy
Ralph Byrd stars in this complete 15-episode compilation as Dick Tracy battles the sinister Spide Gang. 255 mins.
VHS: S12857. $24.95.

Don Daredevil Rides Again
In this serial, 12 adventures center around Don Daredevil, a mysterious presence in a border town hired to protect ranchers and their legally gained land from a ruthless baron. 167 mins.
VHS: S18372. $29.98.

Federal Agents vs. Underworld Inc. (Cliffhanger Serials #5)
An archeologist disappears after discovering the legendary Golden Hands of Kurigal, in this adventure serial from the Republic studios. With Kirk Alyn, Rosemary La Planche and Roy Barcroft. 12 episodes on two videocassettes.
VHS: S15085. $29.98.
Fred Brannon, USA, 1949

Fighting Devil Dogs (The Tornado of Doom)
A Republic serial that featured "the Lightning," a popular master of menace who could destroy ships, dirigibles and cities and town with his awesome electronic thunderbolt. Out to stop him are those brave and daring "fighting devil dogs" led by U.S. Marine hero Lee Powell. With Bruce Bennett, Eleanor Steward and Montagu Love. B&W.
VHS: S06050. $29.95.
William Witney/John English, USA, 1938, 12 chapters

The Fighting Marines
The U.S. Marines must battle the "Tiger Shark", a modern day pirate who has thwarted their every effort to build an airstrip on a Pacific island. 12 episodes. USA, 1935, 214 mins.
VHS: S15597. $29.95.

Flash Gordon (Rocket Ship)
Larry "Buster" Crabbe is Flash. Charles Middleton is Ming the Merciless. Jean Rogers and Frank Shannon are Dale and Dr. Zarkov. This is the feature made from the first 13-part serial. Great fun for kids of all ages. With Hawkmen, Lionmen, Monkeymen and a horned gorilla. B&W.
VHS: S05492. $29.95.
Frederick Stephani, USA, 1936, 69 mins.

Flash Gordon Conquers the Universe
The third serial adventure starring Buster Crabbe as Alex Raymond's creation Flash Gordon. Carol Hughes is the new Dale. They must battle Ming on the planet of Frigia, meet rock men and borrow costumes from Robin Hood. Charles Middleton plays Ming, as usual, for every drop of villainy he can muster. B&W.
VHS: S05543. $29.95.
Ford Beebe/Ray Taylor, USA, 1940, 235 mins.

Flying Disc Men from Mars (Cliffhanger Serials #5)
A young aviator uncovers a plot by evil Martians to conquer Earth in this science fiction serial from the Republic studios. Starring Walter Reed, Lois Collier, Gregory Gay and James Craven. 12 episodes on two videocassettes.
VHS: S15083. $29.98.
Fred Brannon, USA, 1951, 167 mins.

G-Men vs. the Black Dragon
This thrill-packed 1942 serial exposes the infamous Black Dragon Society, pitting special agent Rex Bennett against the Axis spy ring intent on crippling the U.S. war effort. Expect crackling non-stop action loaded with futuristic robot planes, Oriental torture chambers, and even a deadly raven with a poison-tipped beak. 15 episode serial on 2 cassettes.
VHS: S11566. $29.95.

Great Moments from Serials
Clips from rare silent serials, including Plunder (1920), with Pearl White; The Fatal Ring (1917); The Lightning Raider (1919); Hazards of Helen with Helen Holmes; Leap from the Water Tower—The Iron Claw (1916), with Sheldon Lewis; Shielding Shadow (1917); Steel Trail (1923) with William Duncan and Edith Johnson; Captain Kidd (1922, with Eddie Polo); The Third Eye with Eileen Percy; White Eagle, The Tiger's Trail and The Timber Queen with Ruth Roland; and A Woman in Grey with Arline Pretty. 64 mins.
VHS: S08864. $24.95.

The Green Hornet
A crusading publisher in disguise fights various organized rackets with the help of his loyal sidekick who happens to be a judo expert. 13 episodes. USA, 1940, 265 mins.
VHS: S15602. $29.95.

The Invisible Monster (Cliffhanger Serials #5)
A scientist and criminal mastermind called The Phantom Ruler implements a new plan for smuggling in dastardly aliens in this thrilling serial from Republic. With Richard Webb, Aline Towne, Lane Bradford and John Crawford. 12 episodes on two videocassettes.
VHS: S15086. $29.98.
Fred Brannon, USA, 1950

Jesse James Rides Again
In this rousing, pistol-packing cliffhanger, Jesse flees the law after being wrongly accused of leading the historic 1876 Northfield, Minnesota bank robbery—only to clash with hooded raiders pillaging farmers in his name. A frontier adventure at its gun-slinging best. 13 episode serial on 2 cassettes.
VHS: S11565. $29.95.
Laser: C.L.V. LD71998. $39.98.

Jungle Drums of Africa (Cliffhanger Serials #5)
A mining engineer puts an end to a villainous hunter on the trail of uranium deposits in this adventure serial loaded with stock wildlife shots. Produced by the Republic studios. With Clayton Moore, Phyllis Coates, Johnny Spencer and Roy Glenn.
VHS: S15088. $29.98.
Fred Brannon, USA, 1953

Junior G-Men
The Dead End Kids and The Little Tough Guys join forces with the FBI to foil international terrorists and save the free world in this timeless, action-packed serial. 2-tape set, 250 mins.
VHS: S09211. $24.95.

King of the Rocketmen (Lost Planet Airmen)
Tristram Coffin is Jeff King, alias Rocket Man, who must do his darndest to stop the diabolical Dr. Vulcan from destroying any more of New York City with his decimator. The suit was re-used for the Commando Cody serials and the scenes of destruction are from Deluge. With Mae Clarke. B&W. A Republic serial.
VHS: S06053. $29.95.
Laser: C.L.V. LD72000. $39.98.
Fred Brannon, USA, 1949, 12 dha chapters

King of the Texas Rangers
This Republic serial boasts to be "the all time ace of action". It stars "Slingin' Sammy" Baugh—a popular football hero—as a modern Texas Ranger aided by the pre-Cisco Kid Duncan Reynolds. They must deal with such villainous types as Ray Barcroft, Neil Hamilton, Bud Geary, Jack Ingram and Kenne Duncan, a very tough group of hombres. 12 episodes.
VHS: S08328. $29.95.
Laser: C.L.V. LD72001. $39.98.
William Witney, USA, 1941, 195 mins.

The Last of the Mohicans
All the excitement and memorable characters of James Fenimore Cooper's classic novel come to life in this gripping adventure starring Harry Carey. 12 chapters. USA, 1932, 214 mins.
VHS: S15601. $29.95.

The Little Rascals Collection
This group of children is responsible for some of the funniest films from the 1930's and 1940's. These beautifully restored and mastered prints are introduced by Leonard Maltin, expert and co-author of the definitive book, The Little Rascals—The Life and Times of Our Gang. Each volume is 70 mins.
The Little Rascals, Volume 1. Fly My Kite, Honkey Donkey, Beginner's Luck and Reunion in Rhythm.
VHS: S21777. $14.95.
The Little Rascals, Volume 2. Hook and Ladder, The First Round-up, Teacher's Beau and Hearts and Thumps.
VHS: S21778. $14.95.
Laser: LD74823. $124.99.
The Little Rascals, Volume 3. Teacher's Pet, School's Out, Love Business and Spooky Hooky.
VHS: S21779. $14.95.

The Little Rascals Volume 4. *Readin and Writin, The Kid from Borneo, Sprucin Up* and *Pay as You Exit.*
VHS: S21780. $14.95.

The Little Rascals, Volume 5. *Bouncing Babies, Pups Is Pups, Dogs Is Dogs* and *Glove Taps.*
VHS: S21781. $14.95.

The Little Rascals, Volume 6. *Free Wheeling, Mike Fright, Washee Ironee* and *Fishy Tales.*
VHS: S21782. $14.95.

The Little Rascals, Volume 7. *Helping Grandma, Spanky, Little Papa* and *Two Too Young.*
VHS: S21783. $14.95.

The Little Rascals, Volume 8. *Shiver My Timbers, Choo-Choo!, Divot Diggers* and *Bored of Education.*
VHS: S21784. $14.95.

The Little Rascals, Volume 9. *When the Wind Blows, The Pooch, Mush and Milk* and *Framing Youth.*
VHS: S21785. $14.95.

The Little Rascals, Volume 10. *Birthday Blues, For Pete's Sake!, The Lucky Corner* and *Arbor Day.*
VHS: S21786. $14.95.

The Little Rascals, Volume 11. *The First Seven Years, Hi-Neighbor!, The Pinch Singer* and *Rushin' Ballet.*
VHS: S21787. $14.95.

The Little Rascals, Volume 12. *Boxing Gloves, Mama's Little Pirate, Our Gang Follies of 1938* and *Hide and Shriek.*
VHS: S21788. $14.95.

Gift Set. All twelve volumes.
VHS: S21789. $149.95.

Little Rascals: Divot's Diggers and Mama's Little Pirate
Tee up for outrageous antics as the Rascals take to the fairway; Spanky and his daring gang go hunting for a treasure in a deep, mysterious cave.
VHS: S09242. $9.95.

Little Rascals: Our Gang: Don't Lie
Spanky, Alfalfa, Buckwheat, Froggy and Darla will keep you laughing in five of their most hilarious adventures from the original "Our Gang" series. Includes: *Don't Lie, Bubbling Troubles* and *The Big Premiere.* 54 mins.
VHS: S16853. $12.95.

Little Rascals: Pinch Singer and Framing Youth
When a radio station runs an amateur contest with a $50 prize, the enterprising gang holds a goon-show audition. In <FT1231Framing Youth, comical crooner Alfalfa rehearses for a radio talent contest with the all-too-expert guidance of Spanky.
VHS: S09239. $9.95.

Lost City
The complete 12-chapter series, starring Kane Richmond and George "Gabby" Hayes.
VHS: S10607. $69.95.

Manhunt in the African Jungle
This Republic Serial, the forerunner to the hit film *Raiders of the Lost Ark*, chronicles the action-packed adventures of Secret Service agent Rex Bennett and his quest to obtain a sacred Arab religious artifact. His mission: to thwart the Nazis from obtaining the artifact, who want to use it to turn the Arabs against the Allied forces. 15 episode serial on 2 cassettes.
VHS: S11568. $29.95.
Laser: LD71706. $39.98.

Manhunt of Mystery Island
A brilliant scientist who's discovered a possible solution to the energy crisis has been kidnapped, occasioning a frenzied race to solve the crime or face eternal dependence on oil, in these 15 episodes of the Republic Pictures cliffhanger series. Laser disc contains the original theatrical trailer. 219 mins.
VHS: S17411. $29.95.
Laser: LD71704. $39.98.

Masked Marvel
Twelve exciting episodes in this Republic serial about a heroic masked insurance investigator who must defend this nation of ours against foreign peril. The time is World War II and spies from the land of the rising sun find that some Americans are ready for them. With Tom Steele, William Forrest, Louise Currie and Rod Bacon. USA, 1943.
VHS: S08329. $29.95.

Master Key
Directors Ray Taylor and Lewis D. Collins fashioned this 13-chapter mystery serial about a secret Nazi plan dubbed "The Master Key" to create panic and hysteria in war-time America. With Milburn Stone, Jan Wiley, Dennis Moore and Alfred LaRue. 240 mins.
VHS: S17493. $24.95.

Miracle Rider
The legendary Tom Mix plays a Texas Ranger who vows to save the "Ravenhead" Indian tribe from the ruthless villain "Zaroff." 15 chapters. USA, 1935, 300 mins.
VHS: S15598. $29.95.

The Mysterious Dr. Satan
The title character in this Republic serial wants to, surprise, take over the world. He has a robot to back him up. Only the heroic Copperhead can possibly stop him and protect society. With Eduardo Ciannelli as the Doctor and Robert Wilcox as the hero with the copper mask. B&W.
VHS: S06049. $29.95.
William Witney/John English, USA, 1940, 15 chapters

The New Adventures of Tarzan—Collector's Edition
This 12-chapter adventure serial was made by Edgar Rice Burroughs' own production company, and represents the Tarzan true to Burroughs' original vision from his famous novel. The story follows a brilliant archeologist who discovers an earth shattering secret, and enlists Tarzan to help him on his desperate quest. 244 mins.
VHS: S16631. $24.95.

Nyoka and the Tigermen
An action-packed cliffhanger classic that chronicles the efforts of an African expedition to locate the fabled Lost Tablets of Hippocrates, golden artifacts that contain a cure for cancer. But beautiful Arab ruler Vultura and her band of cutthroats seek the tablets for their own use. 15 episode serial on 2 cassettes.
VHS: S11567. $29.95.
Laser: LD71707. $59.98.

The Original Flash Gordon
A box set of the original Flash Gordon movie serials by King Features—starring the young Buster Crabbe. Action-packed adventure! Includes *The Deadly Ray from Mars, The Peril from Planet Mongo, Spaceship to the Unknown* and *The Purple Death from Outer Space.* Four videocassettes. Total time: 6 hrs.
VHS: S13887. $79.95.

Painted Stallion
An original Republic Cliffhanger serial in twelve chapters. Indians are on the warpath but are subdued by a mysterious masked rider who helps the U.S. government lead the first wagon train safely through the Santa Fe Trail. With Ray "Crash" Corrigan. 212 mins.
VHS: S13229. $29.98.
Laser: CLV. LD72014. $39.98.

Panther Girl of the Kongo
In this Republic Pictures cliffhanger series, 12 episodes of terror and shocks are presented when a demented scientist constructs giant, deadly animals out of ordinary species, unleashing a wave of death and destruction. 167 mins.
VHS: S17412. $29.98.
Laser: LD71705. $39.98.

The Perils of Pauline
Starring Pearl White, this is a ten-chapter serial made in 1914.
VHS: S07490. $39.95.

Perils of the Darkest Jungle
Linda Stirling, the queen of the serials, stars as the appropriately-clad Tiger Woman in the first of her six starring serials for Republic. Rumor has it the jungle is missing as this jungle serial as the villainous LeRoy Mason tries to steal Linda's oil lands. With Allan Lane as the good guy. 12 episodes.
VHS: S08327. $29.95.
Laser: LD71708. $39.98.
Spencer Gordon Bennett, USA, 1944, 196 mins.

Phantom Empire
The most unusual serial of the 1930's and perhaps the entire sound era features the original singing cowboy (Gene Autry) in his premier starring role. From Radio Ranch to the subterranean empire of Murania, Autry battles evil robots, mad scientists and unearthly terrors. 2-tape set, 250 mins.
VHS: S09210. $24.95.

Phantom of the West
An interesting serial containing ten episodes about a Phantom hovering over a western community, where one of its inhabitants is a killer. Ross Lederman directed Tom Tyler, Dorothy Gulliver, Tom Santschi, Kermit Maynard, Joe Bonomo and Tom Dugan.
VHS: S17492. $24.95.
David Ross Lederman, USA, 1931, 185 mins.

The Phantom Rider
A mysterious avenging spirit, known as the Phantom Rider, patrols the countryside, challenging the marauders and bandits and bringing peace to the indigenous tribes in this serial. 167 mins.
VHS: S18374. $29.98.

Radar Patrol vs. Spy King (Cliffhanger Serials #5)
International saboteurs threaten America's defense system. Who will come to the rescue? A lively and suspenseful serial from Republic Studios. Starring Kirk Alyn, Jean Dean, Anthony Warde and George J. Lewis. 12 episodes on two videocassettes.
VHS: S15084. $29.95.
Fred Brannon, USA, 1950

The Return of Chandu (The Magician)
As the immortal villain Count Dracula, Bela Lugosi sucked the neck of many a fair maiden. In a rare performance as the romantic Chandu the Magician, he's out to save the neck of an exotic Egyptian Princess who's to be sacrificed on a South Sea island. The hand is quicker than the eye in this suspenseful tropical adventure with plenty of tricks and plot twists. Complete serial. 206 mins.
VHS: S11262. $24.95.

Riders of Death Valley
During the California gold rush, vigilantes protect the mines of decent folk against the evil advances of enemy raiders. 15 chapters. USA, 1941, 285 mins.
VHS: S15603. $29.95.

Robinson Crusoe of Clipper Island
An original Republic Cliffhanger serial in fourteen chapters. An airlines tropical island base is mysteriously destroyed and investigator Ray Mala journeys to Clipper Island to uncover the identity of the saboteurs. Is it a newly arrived passenger or the is it the natives' High Priest? Fourteen segments set in the South Seas. 256 mins.
VHS: S13230. $29.98.
Laser: CLV. LD72024. $39.98.

S.O.S. Coastguard
An original Republic Cliffhanger serial presented in twelve chapters. Bela Lugosi is Boroff, a diabolical scientist who has created a deadly disintegrating gas. It's up to Ralph Byrd and the U.S. Coastguard to prevent Boroff from delivering his lethal invention to menacing foreign powers. Good special effects. 224 mins.
VHS: S13231. $29.98.
Laser: CLV. LD72032. $39.98.

Shadow of Chinatown (The Yellow Phantom)
Bela Lugosi stars in this fifteen-chapter serial as Victor Poten, a mad scientist hired to drive Chinese merchants out of business on the West Coast. More money was said to be spent on the salaries of Lugosi and co-star Bruce Bennett than on the production values. B&W.
VHS: S04001. $24.95.
Bob Hill, USA, 1936, 70 mins.

Son of Zorro
Son of Zorro chronicles the efforts of a returning Cavalry officer to battle the forces of outlawry that have left his home in a state of disorder. To combat his foes he dons the garb of his famous ancestor, Zorro, and becomes an avenging masked rider. Told in 13 episodes. USA, 1947, 164 mins.
VHS: S08326. $29.95.
Laser: CLV. LD72031. $39.98.

Spy Smasher
Republic's second favorite serial hero after Captain Marvel was also a comic book hero. For the movies Kane Richmond was aided by a newly added twin brother in his fight against the Nazi menace. With Sam Flint, Marguerite Chapman, Hans Schumm and Tristram Coffin. 12 action-packed episodes. USA, 1942.
VHS: S08330. $29.95.

Tarzan and His Mate
Johnny Weissmuller and Maureen O'Sullivan star in this epic story of jungle romance. In this one Tarzan pounces on lions, wrestles crocodiles and defeats a charging rhino to protect his precious mate.
VHS: S14309. $19.98.
Jack Conway, USA, 1934, 93 mins.

Tarzan Escapes
One of the all-time best of the classic MGM *Tarzan* series, *Tarzan Escapes* begins when a safari leader snares Tarzan in a steel cage, planning to exhibit him in a freak show. But as long as they're in the jungle, they're on Tarzan's turf. Johnny Weissmuller and Maureen O'Sullivan star.
VHS: S14310. $19.98.
Richard Thorpe, USA, 1936, 95 mins.

Tarzan Finds a Son
Tarzan (Johnny Weissmuller) and Jane (Maureen O'Sullivan) adopt "Boy," the lone survivor of a plane crash, and fight off the young man's various relatives. With Johnny Sheffield and Ian Hunter.
VHS: S17905. $19.98.
Richard Thorpe, USA, 1939, 90 mins.

Tarzan the Tiger
A complete, early version of Tarzan, directed by Henry MacRae, with Frank Merrill, Natalie Kingston and Al Ferguson. Produced as a serial, this is the complete, 15-chapter version.
VHS: S08863. $49.95.
Henry MacRae, USA, 1929

Tarzan's New York Adventure
Tarzan (Johnny Weissmuller) and Jane (Maureen O'Sullivan) go on a cross-Atlantic journey to rescue "Boy," who's been kidnapped by evil circus promoters. With Johnny Sheffield, Virginia Grey and Charles Bickford.
VHS: S17906. $19.98.
Richard Thorpe, USA, 1942, 72 mins.

Tarzan's Secret Treasure
Tarzan (Johnny Weissmuller) enlists the aid of a skillful photographer when Jane (Maureen O'Sullivan) and "Boy" (Johnny Sheffield) are kidnapped by three greedy gold seekers. With Reginald Owen, Barry Fitzgerald and Tom Conway.
VHS: S17907. $19.98.
Richard Thorpe, USA, 1941, 81 mins.

Tim Tyler's Luck
This rare Universal 12-chapter serial is now available from an excellent original print. Directed by Ford Beebe and starring Frankie Thomas, Frances Robinson, Al Shean, Norman Willis. 235 mins.
VHS: S13276. $29.95.

Trader Tom and the China Seas
Set against a backdrop of romance, danger and espionage, this serial focuses on two undercover agents, an island trader and a shipwrecked woman, who join forces to help the UN safeguard the strategically important Asian corridor. 167 mins.
VHS: S18373. $29.98.

Undersea Kingdom
An original Republic Cliffhanger serial in twelve chapters. When mysterious man-made earthquakes threaten the world, navy lieutenant Ray "Crash" Corrigan leads a submarine expedition to the undersea kingdom of Atlantis. There, naturally, he finds the Atlantians at war with the fiendish Unga Khan, and must use his super-human strength to save the world. 226 mins.
VHS: S13228. $29.98.
Laser: CLV. LD72041. $39.98.

The Whispering Shadow
Bela Lugosi plays Professor Adam Strang, the proprietor of the House of Mystery Waxworks. Is he the mysterious madman seeking world domination in this 12-part serial, who kills with a radio death ray and speaks to his followers over a television monitor? Rent this tape and find out. B&W.
VHS: S10103. $29.95.
Al Herman/Colbert Clark, USA, 1933, 228 mins.

Zombies of the Stratosphere (Satan's Satellites)
Judd Holdren (*Commander Cody*) is Larry Martin, a caped rocketeer who goes to Mars to alter an evil plot that could destroy the Earth with Atomic weapons. Leonard Nimoy is featured as an evil Martian henchman named Narab. Much of the footage is borrowed from earlier Republic serials. B&W.
VHS: S06052. $29.95.
Laser: CLV. LD72042. $39.98.
Fred Brannon, USA, 1952, 12 chapters

Zorro's Black Whip
An original Republic Cliffhanger serial in twelve chapters. This Zorro's a woman! Glamorous Linda Sterling dons leather, lace and a black mask to avenge the murder of her brother by a gang of outlaws. She vows to protect the innocent, but first must survive avalanches, explosions and a gun fight a minute. 182 mins.
VHS: S13226. $29.98.
Laser: CLV. LD72043. $39.98.

Zorro's Fighting Legion
An original Republic Cliffhanger serial in twelve chapters. When the evil Don Del Oro stirs up the Indians and steals government gold shipments, Diego Vega (Reed Hadley) assumes a black cape and sword to become the legendary swashbuckler. Zorro upholds justice, here accompanied by his gang of "Avengers".
VHS: S13227. $29.98.
Laser: CLV. LD72044. $39.98.

TRAILERS & COMMERCIALS

Baby Boomer Television
Relive television's Golden Years by a look at the promos for dozens of shows, including the NBC Peacock, Mickey Mouse Club, Howdy Doody Show, Flintstones, Honeymooners, Amos 'n Andy, Bewitched, The Lone Ranger and dozens more. 60 mins.
VHS: S26081. $29.95.

Beer Commercials
A collection of dozens of beer commercials from around the country, including Ballantine Ale, Budweiser, Gunther, Miller Party Time, Schlitz, Falstaff, Duquesne, Hamms (featuring Stan and Ollie) and National Bohemian. 60 mins.
VHS: S26077. $29.95.

Best Classic Commercials from the 50's and 60's, Vol. 1
From the Golden Age of Television come messages that urge you to grease your hair with Brylcreem or to drink Bosco Chocolate Drink. There are hilarious promos for Bonomo's Turkish Taffy, Old Gold Dancing Cigarettes and Double Mint with the Double Mint Twins as well. 30 mins.
VHS: S21339. $14.95.

Best Classic Commercials from the 50's and 60's, Vol. 2
Some of TV's early celebrities can be seen making pitches for the products of yesteryear in this great collection of early commercials. George Reeves, the TV Superman, spots Sugar Smacks using his X-ray vision, while Lucy and Desi do their bit for Phillip Morris. Nancy Reagan and Sandra Dee are just some of the other stars that can be seen selling something in this collection. 60 mins.
VHS: S21340. $14.95.

Car Commercials
A 60-minute compilation of 1940's, 50's and 60's commercials for cars, including the Lark, DeSoto, King Kong for Volkswagen and the 1964 Stingray.
VHS: S26071. $29.95.

Cartoons Celing Commercials: Vol. 1
A video collection of highly entertaining commercials featuring cartoon characters as the product pitchmen. Loads of fun. 60 mins.
VHS: S13799. $19.95.

Cartoons Celing Commercials: Vol. 2
The second volume in this collection of amusing commercials hosted by some of our favorite cartoon characters. 60 mins.
VHS: S13800. $19.95.

Cast Commercials
Hollywood stars and characters push their favorite (and most lucrative) stuff. Includes the Beverly Hillbillies for Kellogg's Corn Flakes and Winston, Mr. Ed for Studebaker, Leave It to Beaver for Purina Dog Chow and the Monkees for Kellogg's Rice Krispies. 60 mins.
VHS: S26073. $29.95.

Celebrity Commercials
Louis Armstrong (Suzy Cute), Harpo Marx (Pepsi), Cybil Shepherd (Cover Girl), Willie Mays (Gillette), John Wayne (Camel), Ronald Reagan (Boraxo), Marilyn Monroe (Union Oil Company) and Groucho Marx (De Soto) are among the dozens of stars in this compilation of Americana. 60 mins.
VHS: S26076. $29.95.

Cereal Commercial Tapes
A collection of zany commercials that constitute pure Americana.
Cereal Commercial Tapes Volume 1: Soggy Celebrities. Over 70 commercials that pour milk over Superman, Space Patrol, Tom Corbett-Space Cadet, The Lone Ranger, Lost in Space (intro), Captain Midnight, The Monkees, Jimmy Durante, Danny Thomas and a full bowl of others. Color and B&W. 60 mins.
VHS: S09704. $24.95.
Cereal Commercial Tapes Volume 2: Famous Animated Flakies. Bullwinkle in over his head in milk, Bugs Bunny, Elmer Fudd, Yogi Bear and Boo-Boo, Daffy Duck, Snaggle-Puss, Top Cat, Cheerios Kid, Rocky and more of these fine cartoon actors in over 60 commercials. 60 mins.
VHS: S09705. $24.95.
Cereal Commercial Tapes Volume 3: Snap, Crackle, Poppourri. The rarest, obscurest, weirdest, oddest, looniest, and most eccentric cereal commercials to be made. This is the widest variety pack containing 60 different commercials all celebrating what America eats for breakfast. 60 mins.
VHS: S09706. $24.95.

Cereal Commercials
Over four dozen commercials for breakfast cereals, including Kellogg's Raisin Bran, Corn Flakes, Super Sugar Crisp, Coco Krispies, Corn Kix, OK's, Cheerios, Cocoa Puffs and more. 60 mins.
VHS: S26078. $29.95.

Cigarette Commercials
Muriel Cigars, the Flintstones for Winston, Lark, Bel Air, Pall Mall 100's, Kool, Camel, L&M (with Nick Adams), Parliament, Philip Morris, Chesterfield (Men of America) and more than three dozen other commercials are featured in this compilation of tobacco's most memorable ads. 60 mins.
VHS: $26079. $29.95.

Classic Animation Commercials from the 50's and 60's, Vol. 1
Many animators found their way into television when producers realized that animation provided a quicker and easier medium than live talent. Fred Flintstone and Barney Rubble as well as Bugs and Daffy are some of the animated celebrities that are joined by the Gillette Razor Blade Parrot, the Hamms Beer Bear and the Cheerios Kid in this nostalgic collection. 60 mins.
VHS: $21335. $19.95.

Classic Car Commercials from the 50's and 60's, Vol. 1
Campy road trips are the order of the day in this collection of chrome- and finned-filled commercials from the golden era of American cars. Fords, Edsels, Buicks, Chevys and a Volkswagen make the most of their small screen appearances. 60 mins.
VHS: $21338. $19.95.

Classic Cereal Commercials from the 50's and 60's, Vol. 1
Snap, Crackle and Pop along with this fantastic collection of vintage commercials. Lucky Charms, Sugar Smacks and Twinkles the Flying Elephant are all great ads, as Tony the Tiger would say. Even if Trix are for kids, these ad spots are great entertainment for everyone. 60 mins.
VHS: $21334. $19.95.

Classic Cigarette Commercials from the 50's and 60's, Vol. 1
Before the Surgeon General put an end to it, television and its greatest stars were in the business of selling cigarettes. To name just a few, Dick Van Dyke, Joey Bishop and Steve McQueen all make appearances in favor of puffing away. All the well-known brands are here, including some that no longer exist. 60 mins.
VHS: $21336. $19.95.

Classic Commercials Volume 1
Classic commercials of the 50's, including Old Gold's dancing cigarettes, Muriel cigars, Garry Moore selling S.O.S., Arthur Godfrey selling Lipton Soup and Dinah Shore selling Chevy, to mention a few.
VHS: $07060. $34.95.

Classic Commercials Volume 2
See King Kong selling Volkswagens, The Lone Ranger selling Pizza rolls, Lucy and Desi selling Philip Morris, Jack Benny for Texaco, Boris Karloff for A-1 steak sauce, Dustin Hoffman selling Toyotas, and more.
VHS: $07061. $34.95.

Classic Commercials Volume 3
Commercials for Hula-Hoop and Frisbee, Billy de Wolfe for Ban, Bob Hope and Dinah Shore for Chevrolet, Edsel, Barbie Doll, Ozzie Nelson for Kodak, Bing Crosby for Ducks Unlimited, 5th Dimension for Jello, and much more.
VHS: $07062. $34.95.

Classic Doll Commercials of the 50's and 60's
Baby boomers will suddenly remember all those dolls they once longed to possess, including Betsy Wetsy, Chatty Cathy, Tuesday Taylor, Tiny Tears, Revlon Dolls, the Playtex Baby and of course Barbie. These are just some of the doll commercials included from the Golden Age of Television.
VHS: $21333. $19.95.

Commercial Best
Some of the best commercials of the 50's and the 60's, including Coppertone, K-Tel Stars, Alka Seltzer (Cave Man), Charlie the Tuna for Star-Kist, Pan Am and the Houston Astros for Desenex. 60 mins.
VHS: $26074. $29.95.

Commercial Best—2
A second volume of some of the most memorable commercials of the past 30 years, including Morris for 9-Lives, O Cedar, Goober for Country Pop, John Lennon for *TV Guide* and Louise Lasser for Toyota. 60 mins.
VHS: $26075. $29.95.

Commercial Jingles
Some of the unforgettable commercial jingles from America's past, including Coca-Cola's "Zing! What a Feeling," "Make Friends with Kool Aid," Pepsi's "Taste That Beats the Others Cold" and "From the Valley" of—naturally, the Green Giant. 60 mins.
VHS: $26072. $29.95.

Commercial Mania
An hour of the most incredible, insidious, and entertaining commercials from the 50s and 60s. 60 mins.
VHS: $05202. $29.95.

Commercials from Around the World
An international mixture of amusing and creative commercials. 60 mins.
VHS: $13098. $9.98.

Good Old Days
Arthur Godfrey, Jimmy Durante, Championship Wrestling, Brenda Lee, Connie Francis, Fats Domino, Barbara Stanwyck, Ford Theater, Loretta Young, Lloyd Bridges, Jane Wyman, Pat Boone and Our Miss Brooks are among the dozens of commercials featured from the golden days of television. 105 mins.
VHS: $26082. $29.95.

Kid-A-Vision
Children are the object of the messages for Wheaties, Funny Face, Time Bomb, Twinkies, Fruit Loops and dozens of other sugar-laden cereals and candies as well as toys, chewing gum, stencils and, naturally, Welch's Grape Juice. 60 mins.
VHS: $26080. $29.95.

Next Week Promos
Dozens of advance promotional TV announcements for television shows, including *77 Sunset Strip, Route 66, Green Hornet, Untouchables, Racket Squad, Gunsmoke, Wild, Wild West, Cheyenne* and *Walt Disney Presents.* 60 mins.
VHS: $26088. $29.95.

Pop Culture Classics from the 50's and 60's
Rootie Kazootie, Howdy Doody, Andy's Gang and Bobby Darin are among the TV stars who appear in this collection of rare and early footage. In addition, there are bloopers from *Gunsmoke, The Red Skeleton Show* and *Twilight Zone.* 60 mins.
VHS: $21337. $19.95.

The President Fights the Japs... And Dirt
Ronald Reagan's career as an actor led to some ironic film roles, considering that he later became President of the U.S. *Recognition of the Japanese Zero Fighter* shows him as a young pilot who is learning to recognize the enemy. In *Borax Spots,* Reagan's turn as pitchman for Borax laundry detergent shows exactly how talented he is at selling soap. 23 mins.
VHS: $24073. $9.95.

The Return of Video Yesterbloop
Warner Brother Studio performers blow lines, get mad and say words that cannot be repeated in church. Among the hotheads are Edward G. Robinson, John Garfield, Bette Davis, James Cagney, Claude Rains and Ronald Reagan. Also Bogart and Bacall, Errol Flynn and Eve Arden. USA, 1941-47, 27 mins.
VHS: $05446. $19.95.

Show Promos
Television commercials for dozens of television's best-remembered shows, including *Love American Style, Bewitched, The Flintstones, FBI, Rifleman, Lawrence Welk Show, Avengers, Outer Limits* and *Lost in Space.* 60 mins.
VHS: $26086. $29.95.

Show Promos 2
Dozens more promotional TV announcements of shows, including *The Brady Bunch, Rifleman, ABC Wide World of Sports, Bullwinkle, Disneyland, My Friend Flicka* and *The Lone Ranger.* 60 mins.
VHS: $26087. $29.95.

Silent Era Trailers
This set includes footage of some of the rarest films of the silent era. Trailers with Greta Garbo, John Gilbert, Victor McLaglen. Included are *Barclays the Magnificent, The Rookies* and many others. 43 mins.
VHS: $13211. $19.95.

Son of Video Yesterbloop
A three-part collection of some of your favorite stars missing lines, messing up, getting mad or making off-color remarks. See Jackie Cooper, William Powell, Lou Costello and Carole Lombard cuss. Witness a cow taking a dump in front of Red Skelton. Also outtakes from *Gunsmoke, The Twilight Zone* and the world of sports. For mature viewers. USA, 1930-70, 54 mins.
VHS: $05458. $24.95.

Teenage-A-Go-Go
Teenagers are at the center of dozens of television commercials for Cheer, Twister, Clark's Teaberry Gum, Clearasil, *Shindig, The Patty Duke Show, Soul Train* and *The Ed Sullivan Show.* 100 mins.
VHS: $26085. $29.95.

Television Toys Vol. 1
A special collection of television commercials honoring marketing gimmicks from the '50s, '60s and '70s. With a focus on favorite shows and serials, toys featured include the Dick Tracy 2-way radio, the Man from U.N.C.L.E. secret bracelet, the Captain Midnight decoder, and Mr. Potato Head. 60 mins.
VHS: $16546. $24.95.

Television Toys Vol. 2
More familiar toy commercials from the '50s, '60s and '70s. Includes Colorforms, Fanner Fifty guns, Twister, Etch a Sketch, the Steve Canyon helmet, Duncan Yo Yo's, G.I. Joe and more! 60 mins.
VHS: $16547. $24.95.

Theatrical Trailers
Twenty-five horror and exploitation trailers from the 1930's through the 1960's, including such great coming attractions as *Killing from Space, Things to Come, Head for the Hills, Weird Woman, Cuban Rebel Girls,* and 20 others.
VHS: $05058. $34.95.

Toon-A-Vision
Animation in the service of commerce in over 50 commercials, including Woody Woodpecker for Kellogg's, *The Road Runner Show, Speed Racer, Rocky and His Friends, Felix the Cat, Beanies, Green Lantern* and *Mighty Mouse Playhouse.* 90 mins.
VHS: $26084. $29.95.

COMICS & THEIR CREATORS

Batmania: From Comics to Screen
The story of Batman from an obscure bat image in the Mary Roberts Rinehart novel, *The Bat,* to the comic book creation of writer/illustrator Bob Kane, to the 15-chapter serial. This is the first story of the career of Batman, from comics to screen. 45 mins.
VHS: $10947. $14.99.

Comic Book Confidential
From Spiderman to Zippy the Pinhead, from the scariness of *Tales from the Crypt* to the sophisticated commentary of *Maus, Comic Book Confidential* brings you into the world of comics. Includes interviews with Stan Lee, William M. Gaines, Lynda Barry and more.
VHS: Out of print. For rental only.
Laser: CLV/CAV. LD70103. $49.95.
Ron Mann, Canada, 1990, 85 mins.

The Comic Book Greats: Overkill
This volume looks at the personalities and work of illustrators Rob Liefeld and Todd McFarlane in their comic book creation, *Overkill.*
VHS: $16960. $15.95.

The Comic Book Greats: Rob Liefeld
This volume considers the career of the gifted 23-year-old illustrator and his new work, *Die Hard.* Liefeld discusses his working methods and provides insights and lessons on illustration, layout and design.
VHS: $16959. $19.95.

The Comic Book Greats: Sergio Aragones
This work traces the fantastical career of Sergio Aragones, the illustrator whose gift for mining humor in the commonplace begins with his revolutionary work in *Mad Magazine,* animation work in television's *New Laugh In, Speak Up America* and *Dick Clark's Bloopers & Practical Jokes.*
VHS: $16958. $19.95.

The Comic Book Greats: Todd McFarlane
A behind-the-scenes look at Todd McFarlane, whose early assignments with *Batman* and *Coyote* led to comic history with his *Spiderman #1.* Talking candidly about his work with host Stan Lee, Todd reveals his plans for the future and some of his new characters.
VHS: $16419. $19.95.

Crumb
Robert Crumb, the multi-talented underground comic book artist, is profiled in this unique, in-depth documentary portrait. Emerging from a dysfunctional family, it's a wonder that Crumb managed to channel his peculiar take on the world into a relatively socially acceptable form. Part of the great fascination of this film is the revelation that his brothers, both also quite gifted, were not as lucky.
VHS: $27253. $99.98.
Laser: LD75491. $39.95.
Terry Zwigoff, USA, 1995, 119 mins.

The History of the Comics
This complete chronicle of comic book and comic serial history begins in 1900. Complete with colorful examples of familiar and rare characters, and interviews with the artists who created them.
The History of the Comics Volume 1. The growth of the press into a mass medium at the turn of the century provided a framework within which cartoons and illustrations became known as "the comics." Among the characters popularized during this period are Little Nemo, Krazy Kat, Betty Boop, Dick Tracy, The Phantom, Little Orphan Annie, Popeye, Flash Gordon and Tarzan. 90 mins.
VHS: $16800. $19.95.
The History of the Comics Volume 2. Superheroes were born shortly before WWII, and saw active duty on the Allied side. This period featured many incredible characters with a variety of superhuman powers. In the '50s and '60s, events created a whole new cast of comic characters for the "baby boom" generation: *Superman, Batman, Captain Marvel, Steve Canyon, Peanuts, Beetle Bailey, Barbarella.* 90 mins.
VHS: $16801. $19.95.
The History of the Comics Volume 3. The underground movement of the sixties produced an alternative tradition using line-art. Many of these comics appeared in the form of "prozines" and "fanzines." Included in this era: *Vampirella, Conan, Furry Freak, Spiderman, Little Annie Fanny, "Creepy"* and *"Eerie"* magazines, and more. 90 mins.
VHS: $16802. $19.95.
The History of the Comics Volume 4. Comic superheroes have now become more human, and face contemporary concerns like ecological disaster and drugs. Meanwhile, the independent comics carry on, faithful to the spirit of the underground in publications like *"Heavy Metal"* and *"Epic."* The weekly Japanese comic phenomenon *"Manga, Manga"* is often over 300 pages long, and provides a glimpse of what's ahead for comics in the 21st century. 90 mins.
VHS: $16803. $19.95.
The History of the Comics. All four volumes in one pre-pack.
VHS: $16804. $79.80.

Hooked on Comix
Finally a documentary explores the often misunderstood phenomenon of underground comic books. Nineteen of the most famous comics are covered, including *Hate, Yummy Fur, Naughty Bits, Yahoo, Bad Boys, Slutburger, Love and Rockets* and *Cereal Killings.* Music by bands like Beat Happening and Bikini Kill are featured on the soundtrack. 60 mins.
VHS: $23857. $29.95.

Masters of Comic Book Art
Award-winning author Harlan Elison hosts this fascinating look at the new generation of innovative comic book artists, including "maus" creator Art Spiegelman. Each artist is interviewed and their work examined in the context of the comic book art genre. 61 mins.
VHS: $08462. $19.95.

Fine Arts

ARTS

on video

art
ON VIDEO

15th Century: Renaissance in Full Bloom

The flowering of the Renaissance in 15th Century Italy. Included are Botticelli's *Birth of Venus*, Fra Angelico's beautiful paintings, Venetian architects Codussi and Lombardo, the Bellini's Carpaccio, Andrea del Castagno and many others, as the camera moves from Florence to Rome, Ferrara, Urbino, Mantua and Venice. Produced by Rizzoli. 59 mins.
VHS: S13254. $39.95.
Laser: LD70789. $99.95.

20th Century American Art: Whitney Museum of American Art

Three Whitney Museum of American Art releases.
American Art '85: A View from the Whitney. Documents the 1985 Whitney exhibit with lively commentary from the artists, critics and the curators; featured artists are Dara Birnbaum, Robert Breer, Eric Fischl, Donald Judd, Elizabeth Murray, Susan Rothenberg, David Salle, Kenny Scharf, and Ned Smith. Critics interviewed are Arthur Danto and Carter Ratcliff. 28 mins.
VHS: S07080. $29.95.
American Art Today: A View from the Whitney. An informative and entertaining overview of the Whitney Museum's 1987 biennial exhibition of new American art. Artists Ross Bleckner, Peter Halley, Annette Lemieux, Robert Lobe, Nam June Paik, Tzhar Patkin, Judy Pfaff, Richard Prince talk about their work, and art historian Robert Pincus-Whitten discusses the artists' concepts within the framework of post-modernism. 28 mins.
VHS: S07081. $29.95.
20th Century American Art: Highlights of the Permanent Collection. Presents the dramatic story of American art in the 20th century, offering an enticing look at the Museum's collection of art including such noted artists as O'Keefe, Stella, Warhol, Pollock, Rothko, Hopper, Lichtenstein and de Kooning, exploring Abstract Expressionism, Pop and Minimalism. 28 mins.
VHS: S07079. $29.95.
Gift Pack.
VHS: S07078. $79.95.

20th Century Art at the Metropolitan Museum

Philippe de Montebello, director of New York's Metropolitan Museum of Art, is the host of this tour of the inaugural installation in the museum's new Lila Acheson Wallace wing, which displays selections from more than 8,000 paintings, sculptures, works on paper, and objects of design and architecture created by American and European artists in this century. Featured in this video are works by Klee, O'Keefe, Bonnard, Kandinsky, Picasso, Matisse, Pollack, de Kooning, Rauschenberg and many others. The Metropolitan Museum of Art. 60 mins.
VHS: S05234. $39.95.

Academia Museum of Venice

The Academia, Venice's most important museum, holds more than six centuries of art. This program ventures into original locations to highlight the works of Titian, Veronese, Giorgione, the Bellinis, Veniziano, Tiepolo and Canaletto. 60 mins.
VHS: S20185. $39.95.

African-American Art: Past and Present

A comprehensive survey of African-American art. With more than 65 artists represented, the program is divided into three programs: African Art, 18th and 19th Century Fine Art Survey, and 20th Century Fine Art Survey: In the Artist's Words. 90 mins.
VHS: S20319. $199.00.

African-American Artists: Affirmation Today

Sculptor Frederick Brown and painters Sam Gilliam, Lois Jones and Keith Morrison discuss their work, their influences and the importance of their heritage. These masters detail not only their technique but also how they overcame prejudice to succeed. 29 mins.
VHS: S24867. $85.00.

Alejandro Obregon Paints a Fresco

Demonstrating the techniques and formulas of fresco painting, Colombian artist Obregon works on a moving or portable wall in front of the camera. Many of the artist's most important stylistic traits are shown in this demonstration: exuberant color, emphasis on the horizontal, and masterly handling of glazes. Directed by Jose Gomez Sicre, 21 mins.
English Narration. William D. Clark.
VHS: S06748. $60.00.
Spanish Narration. Luis Vivas.
VHS: S06749. $60.00.

Alexis Smith: Life in America

Alexis Smith works within received forms of found objects. Her art combines storytelling, conceptual art and collage. This documentary explores the facets of Smith's art, related in her voice, words and actions, as she moves through streets and alleys in search of materials and objects. 27 mins.
VHS: S20312. $49.95.

Altering Discourse: The Works of Helen and Newton Harrison

This program interweaves narrative, text, music and visuals to provide insight into the notions of "conceptual environmental artists" Helen and Newton Harrison. 13 mins.
VHS: S20352. $39.95.

American Art at the Huntington

A walking portait of the Huntington galleries, in which a time machine allows us to move from the early colonial period to contemporary times, studying the works of Copley, Stuart, Sargent, Cassatt, Church and Harnett. 15 mins.
VHS: S19638. $19.95.

American Craft: Clay, Functional Pottery

Finished pottery from 48 American artists is shown in this video, including works by Warren MacKenzie, Cynthia Bringle, John Glick, Don Pilcher and Paula Winokur. A variety of forms, functions and techniques are also shown. 20 mins.
VHS: S22189. $39.95.

American Craft: Clayworks

The late 1960's were a time of great change for ceramic art. A wide range of bodies and styles came into view. Raku, bisque-firing, china paints, lustres, underglazes, decals and acrylic paints were just some of them. Artists David Gilooly, Patti Warashina, Jack Earl and Richard Shaw show some of their work. 20 mins.
VHS: S22190. $39.95.

American Craft: Contemporary Ceramics

This is one of the most comprehensive selections of recent functional and non-functional ceramics available. Eighty-five artists are shown on the occasion of Joseph Wedgewood's birth. 20 mins.
VHS: S22192. $39.95.

American Craft: Contemporary Clay—Diverse Soup Tureen Forms

Seventy-five ceramicists, including David Gilooly, Warren MacKenzie, Patti Warashina and Paula Winokur, are featured in this examination of functional works. A variety of traditional forms and recent pop, sculptural and conceptual trends are showcased. 20 mins.
VHS: S22191. $39.95.

American Impressionist: Richard Earl Thompson

Born in 1914, Richard Earl Thompson has often been compared to Monet. Influenced deeply by the masters of Impressionism, his work is the study of brilliant colors and fleeting seasons, and the emotions they evoke. Find dozens of remarkable paintings in this essay on an often overlooked American treasure. 30 mins.
VHS: S16076. $24.95.

Andrew Wyeth: The Helga Pictures

Charlton Heston narrates this portrait filmed at Chadds Ford where many of Wyeth's famous Helga pictures were painted, and examines 44 of the Helga pictures, including 22 nudes that have created a storm of controversy in the art world, examining the meaning and mystery of Wyeth's work.
VHS: S05639. $39.95.
Gene Fairly, USA, 1987, 36 mins.

Andy Warhol

This is the first major profile made since the death of the American Pop Cult leader and self-styled superstar. Featured are conversations with a dozen of his closest associates—discussing his family, the art world, and those he worked with. 78 mins.
VHS: S07604. $39.95.

Andy Warhol/Keith Haring

Two documentaries about two figures of the pop art movement. *Andy Warhol: Made in China* follows Warhol and his friends on their 1985 expedition of mainland China. *Drawing the Line: A Portrait of Keith Haring* looks at the relationship of Haring's art to its social and political context.
Laser: LD70833. $19.98.

Andy Warhol: The Scope of His Art

Few individual artists have had the impact of Andy Warhol on contemporary society and its art. This insightful program explores the method and message of Andy Warhol's paintings and graphics from the beginning of his career to his last works. 25 mins.
VHS: S09460. $174.00.

Anti-Credo

Rapid montage in Super 8mm film of the Rivington Street Sculpture Garden in New York City, now destroyed, by Swiss performance artist and founder of the Neoist movement.
VHS: S10194. $39.95.
Monty Cantsin, USA, 1988, 30 mins.

Apprentice to the Gods: Ruben Nakian

Produced by the Smithsonian Institution; an intimate portrait of the late sculptor's pioneering spirit through different phases of his career, from his youth at the Art Students League and Beaux Art to his series of monumental works. Includes rare footage of an artist whose career has spanned the most important periods of art in American history and places him with such Abstract Expressionists as Jackson Pollock and David Smith. 28 mins.
VHS: S06558. $39.95.

The Art and Life of Georgia O'Keefe

She is one of the most beloved of American artists. From abstractions to realism, this acclaimed program explores in images and her own words the entire sweep of Georgia O'Keefe's vision. 29 mins.
VHS: S09464. $174.00.

Art and Recreation in Latin America

Games people play and the art and architecture they enjoy are presented. Focus is on the Spanish and Indian influences to be found today. Bilingual English-Spanish narration.
VHS: S07426. $59.95.

The Art of Andrew Wyeth

This video journal of discovery into the art of Andrew Wyeth visits Chadds Ford, Pennsylvania and transports you through the years between Brandywine winters and Maine summers, the beloved places which inspired Wyeth's masterpieces. 29 mins.
VHS: S09463. $89.95.
Laser: LD70779. $59.95.

The Art of Central America and Panama

The most well known artists of the region are shown painting in their native environments, demonstrating techniques and styles that distinguish the artists of this area from other artists around the world. Made several years ago, many of the artists shown have had a profound impact on the development of art in their countries. Directed by Jose Gomez Sicre, 29 mins.
English Narration. William D. Clark.
VHS: S06755. $80.00.
Spanish Narration. Luis Vivas.
VHS: S06756. $80.00.

Art of Folk Art

A general survey of the collection from the museum of American Folk Art discussing the definitions of major styles of folk art in America with museum administrators and curators, plus interviews with Pichio Odio and Malcah Zeldis, two prominent American folk artists currently living in New York City. 11 mins.
VHS: S07456. $59.95.

Art of Haiti

A powerful documentary from Chicago filmmaker Mark Mamalakis on the absorbing art movement that has emerged from the rage, poverty and passion of Third World cultures, specifically Haiti. The film includes interviews with artists Philome Obin and Rigaud Benoit and detailed retrospectives of painters Hector Hyppolite and Andre Pierre. The "program is…exquisitely shot and edited, giving the feeling that some of the paintings could have been made from your film." The works of twelve prominent artists are juxtaposed with voice-over narration, interviews and traditional Haitian folk music.
VHS: S03471. $39.95.
Mark Mamalakis, USA, 1982, 26 mins.

Art of Indonesia: Tales from the Shadow World

Girding the Equator like a string of emeralds, the 13,000 islands of Indonesia are dotted with steaming volcanoes, cascading waterfalls and magnificent temple ruins. This documentary explores Indonesia's ancient treasures and its shadow world—the rituals, myths, and performances by which the harmony of the universe is maintained. Shot on location in Java and Bali, produced by the National Gallery of Art and the Metropolitan Museum. 28 mins.
VHS: S13234. $29.95.

Art of the American West

Three sections: Before the White Man (Albert Bierstadt, Thomas Moran, Charles Wimar, Henry Farny, Thomas Hill, Worthington Whittredge, Frederic Remington), Westward Expansion (Charles Christian Nahl, C.M. Russell, Remington, Frank Schoonover and others), and The Old West Is Dead (the influence of modern art in the works of Thomas Hart Benton, Georgia O'Keefe, Ernest Blumenshein, Victor Higgins). 50 mins.
VHS: S07657. $89.50.

Art of the Dogon

Travel to the steep cliffs and arid plains of Mali in West Africa and discover the art of the Dogon people. Possessing one of the richest art traditions in Africa, the Dogon have for centuries created powerful sculpture to use in various rituals and in their daily life. Through rare film footage from the Metropolitan Museum of Art, witness the beauty of Dogon ritual dances and ceremonial worship. 28 mins.
VHS: S08476. $29.97.

Art of the Fantastic

A review of an exhibition of fantastic and magic realist art at the Indianapolis Museum of Art, including an interview with the curators of the exhibition. Narrated in English by Roger Wilkinson. 30 mins.
VHS: S08310. $30.00.

Art of the Western World

Michael Wood hosts this comprehensive survey of the Western World's seminal paintings, sculptures and architecture. This video series offers unusual historical and visual perspectives in four volumes.
Volume 1: The Classical Ideal. A white garment of churches in the Romanesque and Gothic styles are featured in this video. 100 mins.
VHS: S26880. $29.95.
Volume 2: The Early Renaissance. This volume looks at the high Renaissance realms of light and features of the Baroque. 150 mins.
VHS: S26881. $29.95.
Volume 3: An Age of Reason, An Age of Passion. The Age of Reason flowed into an Age of Passion. This video ends with the fresh view pioneered by Impressionism and Post-Impressionism. 100 mins.
VHS: S26882. $29.95.
Volume 4: Into the Twentieth Century—In Our Own Time. The final volume explores the art of our own time. 100 mins.
VHS: S26883. $29.95.

Art of the Western World

A ten-volume PBS series shot on location in Europe and America. Hosted by historian and journalist Michael Wood, the program studies the evolution of Western art, from its origins through the Reformation and Renaissance, Impressionism, Baroque, Modernism, Realism, and other significant movements. With each segment, Wood is joined by leading art historians who offer historical, social and artistic overviews of each period and its leading figures. The laserdisc version offers exciting opportunities to view hundreds of still pictures contained in each volume.
Vol. 1: Greece and Rome. Moving from the Acropolis to the Colosseum, from Athens' Parthenon to Rome's Pantheon, Wood examines the beauty and form of Greek sculpture and architecture.
Laser: LD72183. $99.95.
Vol. 2: Romanesque and Gothic. Michael Wood discusses art produced during the Middle Ages, placing special emphasis on Gothic cathedrals in Chartres, Notre Dame and St. Denis as well as important Romanesque churches.
Laser: LD72231. $99.95.
Vol. 3: The Early Renaissance. The birth of the Renaissance is the focus of this program, highlighted by Michael Wood's journeys through Florence and Venice, where he examines the works of Giotto, Masaccio, Donatello, Botticelli and Bellini, as well as the major Flemish and German artists, van Eyck and Durer.
Laser: LD72232. $99.95.
Vol. 4: The High Renaissance. The Renaissance reaches its zenith with the work of Leonardo da Vinci, Michelangelo and Raphael. Wood travels to Italy, where he studies Leonardo's *The Last Supper*, Michelangelo's *David*, the Sistine Chapel and St. Peter's and Raphael's *School of Athens*. The program also looks at Venetian artists Titian and Veronese and the architect Palladio.
Laser: LD72233. $99.95.
Vol. 5: The Baroque. Michael Wood studies the aesthetic influences of Baroque art and design, from the fountains of Rome to Madrid's Prado Museum to Rubens' baronial mansion in Flanders. Leading historians provide a social context for the work.
Laser: LD72234. $99.95.
Vol. 6: An Age of Passion. Political upheavals and social turbulence are mirrored in the wit and playfulness of Fragonard, the Romantic Delacroix and the neoclassical Ingres. The program also studies the valuable input of Goya and English artists Constable and Turner.
Laser: LD72235. $99.95.
Vol. 7: Realism and Impressionism. This program moves from the birth of modernism, with the flowering of Realism, signified by Courbet, to the birth of impressionism, including the works of Monet, Degas and Manet and the post-impressionists van Gogh, Cezanne, Seurat and Gauguin. The program also studies Pre-Raphaelites, such as England's Millais and Rosetti and America's Homer, Eakins and Whistler.
Laser: LD72236. $99.95.
Vol. 8: Into the Twentieth Century. In the 20th century, art enters a new phase. Picasso and Braque are the leading practitioners of Cubism in Paris. Klimp, Schiele and Kokoschka are behind Vienna's radical avant-garde. The program also considers modernism between the two World Wars, studying the works of Matisse, Leger, Miro, Calder, Mondrian and Frank Lloyd Wright.
Laser: LD72237. $99.95.
Vol. 9: World War II and Beyond. New York emerges as the center of Western art in the aftermath of World War II. This program examines the outbreak of Minimalism, the Pop Art movement, Abstract Expressionism and the Action Paintings of Jackson Pollock, Jasper Johns and Robert Rauschenberg. The volume studies the principal international movements of the 1970s and 80s.
Laser: LD72238. $99.95.
Art of the Western World: Volumes 1-9.
Laser: LD72241. $875.00.

Art on Film/Film on Art

This five-part series of films on art conceived by various teams of filmmakers and art experts is an anthology of 14 films and videos intended to open up discussion of the way people interpret works of art on film and videotape. The films examine the tensions between art expert and filmmaker, the confusion between the art object and the art being depicted and how to reimagine content and form.
Program 1: Balance: Film/Art. The works include *The Payum Portraits* (1988, 15 mins.), directed by Bob Rosen and Andrea Simon; *Funerary Painting of Roman Egypt* (1990, 14 mins); and *MA: Space and Time in the Garden of Ryoan-JI* (1989, 16 mins), by Taka Iimura.
VHS: S20330. $99.00.
Program 2: Film Sense/Art Sense. The works contained are *Giorgione's Tempest* (1988, 11 mins), by Stephanie Tepper; *The First Romantic Picture* (1988, 17 mins), by Trevl and Richard P. Rogers; and *A Window to Heaven* (1990, 20 mins).
VHS: S20331. $99.00.
Program 3: Film Form/Art Form. The works are Mark Whitney's *Leonardo's Deluge* (1989, 14 mins), Edin Velez's *A Mosque in Time* (1990, 8 mins), and Nadine Descendre's *Sainte-Genevieve, the Pantheon of Domes* (1989, 16 mins.).
VHS: S20332. $99.00.
Program 4: Film Voice/Art Voice. The works are Keith Griffiths' *De Artificial* and *Perspective or Anamorphosis* (1991, 15 mins.), Richard Greenberg's *Architecture of Transcendence* (1988, 9 mins.), and Anita Thatcher's *Painted Earth: The Art of the Mimbres Indians* (1989, 15 mins.).
VHS: S20333. $99.00.
Program 5: Film/Art: Subject and Expert. The works are Philip Haas' *A Day on the Grand Canal with the Emperor of China or Surface Is Illusion but So Is Depth* (1988, 46 mins.) and Judy Marie's *Gombrich Themes* (1989, 46 mins.).
VHS: S20334. $99.00.
Art on Film/Film on Art, Set. A five-tape boxed set.
VHS: S20335. $349.00.

Art Treasures of Spain

This collection of three videos documents the works of three artists dear to Spain. Goya, El Greco and Hieronymous Bosch were all masters of their time. Today their paintings are part of the rich artistic patrimony of the Iberian Penisula.
El Greco. A warm and brilliant examination of the range and glory of the work of El Greco is presented in this video. This artist used his Byzantine Greek heritage to become the symbol of Spanish thought and art. 60 mins.
VHS: S22922. $24.95.
Goya: His Life and Art. This is an introduction to Goya's work and the critical period in Spanish history which he recorded. Goya's paintings show Spain in the period spanning the decline of neo-classicism, the devastation of the Napoleonic Wars, and the rise of Romanticism and Impressionism. 44 mins.
VHS: S22921. $24.95.
Hieronymous Bosch. Though alive at the time of the Renaissance, this painter epitomizes the Middle Ages, particularly its bitter vision of sin. This video displays the works collected by Phillip II, now housed in the Prado. Bosch's visualization of man on Earth relied on extraordinary detail and imagination. 30 mins.
VHS: S22923. $24.95.
Complete Set.
VHS: S22924. $69.95.

Artists Are Special People... Just Like You!

Anyone can learn to draw! This stimulating four-part program helps students develop their powers of observation, introduces viewers to the five basic elements of drawing and encourages them to loosen up their creative muscles as they use these basic elements to construct simple and complex pictures and images. 32 mins.
VHS: S09461. $141.00.

The Artists Talk (Los Artistas Hablan)

Five prominent Latin American artists are interviewed, including Raquel Forner, Enrique Grau, Alejandro Obregon, Ramirez-Villamizar and Fernando de Szyszlo. In Spanish only.
VHS: S21811. $40.00.

Arts 21 Video Magazine

The first edition of this video magazine is an exciting way to learn more about art and keep abreast of what's happening at the center of the contemporary art scene, New York. Featured are the recent, critically acclaimed New York gallery shows of Alex Katz, Susan Rothenberg, Frank Stella, David Salle, Eric Fischl, Robert Morris, Cindy Sherman and Martha Diamond. Actor and video artist Steve Meyer provides the narration.
VHS: S07509. $69.95.
Steve Meyer, USA, 1987, 28 mins.

Arts of Islam

From Spain to India, from Turkey to Morocco, the art of Islam has molded the cultural eye of millions of people over more than a millennium. This program explores Islamic art as one of the great cultural forces in world history and shows how it captivates the eye and engages the imagination. 26 mins.
VHS: S09462. $174.00.

Beatrice Wood: Mama of Dada

Even at the age of 102, Beatrice Wood continues to influence younger artists with her definitive, free-wheeling ways. She was central to the American Dada movement and is the last surviving member of this group. In this video she recalls her friends Man Ray, Picabia and others, and her ex-husband Marcel Duchamp. USA, 1993, 57 mins.
VHS: S27102. $29.95.

Behind the Scenes

Magicians Penn and Teller host this look at the creative process. The program examines the craft and precision of artist David Hockney, photographer Carrie Mae Weems, jazz percussionist Max Roach and composer Allen Toussaint. The program is designed to encourage children to get involved in the arts and expand their intellectual and creative capacities. 180 mins.
Tape 1: With Robert Gil de Montes/Wayne Thiebaud.
VHS: S19358. $14.95.
Tape 2: With David Hockney/Nancy Graves.
VHS: S19359. $14.95.
Tape 3: With Carrie Weems.
VHS: S19360. $14.95.
Tape 4: With Max Roach/Allen Toussaint.
VHS: S19361. $14.95.
Tape 5: With JoAnn Falleta/David Parsons.
VHS: S19362. $14.95.
Tape 6: With Julie Taymor.
VHS: S19363. $14.95.
The Complete Set.
VHS: S19364. $99.95.

Ben Nicholson: Razor Edge

Looks back on the life work of the man who jolted 1930's British art out of its doldrums with his uncompromising abstract style. 60 minutes.
VHS: S01780. $39.95.

Berthe Morisot: The Forgotten Impressionist

This painter was the only woman among the famed Impressionist practitioners, and she was influential with the better-known men of this movement. Obscured by their fame, she has recently become recognized again for her work. This video is based on the 1987 exhibit which rescued her masterworks from undeserved obscurity. With Teri J. Edelstein.
VHS: S22944. $49.95.

Beyond Tradition: Contemporary Indian Art and Its Evolution

Based on the award-winning book of the same title, this video gives a sensitive overview of American Indian Art and its development through the centuries. Emphasizing southwest cultures and tribes, over 300 examples of prehistoric, historic and contemporary artworks are shown to promote a comprehensive understanding and appreciation of the subject. 45 mins.
VHS: S15763. $29.95.

Bigger Splash

An innovative blend of fact and fiction reflecting the world of David Hockney, arguably the most important and celebrated artist of our time. This feature incorporates Hockney's art and unabashed lifestyle in bold and daring ways and parallels his brilliant work in painting, design and photography. "Moving, gossipy and just a little bit shocking. Constructed in the studios, the swimming pools, the beds and baths of Hockney and friends who orbit around him" (*Newsday*).
VHS: S08116. $69.95.
Jack Hazan, Great Britain, 1985, 102 mins.

Birth of the Renaissance: Giotto to Masaccio

In this program, the camera travels to Florence, Siena, Pisa, Mantua and Padua to discover early Renaissance masterworks in these cities. Included are the art and architecture of Alberti, Brunelleschi, Luca della Robbia, Donatello, Michelozza, Giotto, Martini, Lorenzetti and Masaccio. Produced by Rizzoli. 58 mins.
VHS: S13255. $39.95.
Laser: LD70788. $99.95.

Blizzard's Wonderful Wooden Toys

Richard Blizzard has assembled this special video of seven of his most popular wooden toys and models to make. Here are projects carefully designed to suit all abilities, ranging from an easy-to-make sand pit to his tour-de-force, a 1907 Rolls Royce Silver Ghost, nearly three feet long, which will challenge the most skilled woodworker. 108 mins.
VHS: S07610. $19.95.

Breakthrough: A Portrait of Aristides Demetrios

This Cine-Golden Eagle winner profiles San Francisco sculptor Aristides Demetrios, who creates abstract metal monuments of monolithic process, and is an intriguing portrait of an artist's dream as it gets transformed into a massive sculpture—on camera. 45 mins.
VHS: S04646. $39.95.

Brice Marden

In this film, shot over a period of nine years in the artist's studio, Marden paints large monochromatic panel works, diptychs and triptychs, and emerges as an articulate and provocative spokesman for his own work. 22 mins.
VHS: S08275. $39.95.

Burchfield at the Met

John I.H. Baur guides the viewer through a visual presentation of the works of the Charles E. Burchfield which are on display at New York's Metropolitan Museum of Art. Viewers learn visual style, techniques and the various stages of his three major works. 23 mins.
VHS: S20307. $39.95.

Burchfield's Vision

Burchfield's Vision examines the peculiar range and power of artist Charles E. Burchfield, who died in 1967 after producing more than 4,000 pieces of work. The program allows glimpses of Burchfield's journals, which offer an inside view of his feelings, philosophy and spiritual growth. 60 mins.
VHS: S20308. $49.95.

Caravaggio and the Baroque

Caravaggio, Correggio, Lotto, Parmigianino, Tintoretto. New masters find deeply emotional directions in art as the High Renaissance gives way to the Baroque. In Venice, we see Sansovino's plans for St. Marks Square, while Palladio invents the country villa. In Rome, architects Bernini and Borromini define the city with graceful fountains and St. Peter's Cathedral. Produced by Rizzoli. 53 mins.
VHS: S13252. $39.95.
Laser: CAV. LD70791. $99.95.

Caravaggio Conspiracy

Reconstructs the true story of an artful sleuthing operation: journalist Peter Watson disguises himself as a shady art dealer, and with the cooperation of Sotheby's, Christie's, and the law, recovers some of the world's most lamented stolen masterpieces. 60 minutes.
VHS: S05126. $59.95.

Case Study House Program 1945-1966: An Anecdotal History & Commentary

The Case Study House program, initiated by John Entenza of *Arts & Architecture* magazine in 1945, is one of Southern California's most important contributions to architecture. The program featured designs for 36 experimental modern housing prototypes by some of the most important architects of the region at that time. Of these, 25 were built. Produced in conjunction with an exhibition of the work at the Museum of Contemporary Art, Los Angeles. 58 mins.
VHS: S14588. $39.95.

Caspar David Friedrich: The Borders of Time

Peter Schamoni's award-winning film on Caspar David Friedrich, one of the greatest of the Romantic artists, uses his paintings, alongside dramatic film of the landscapes which inspired him, to bring the viewer close to his work. Dramatized scenes construct a picture of his life, and put his work in an historical and intellectual context. Heading the cast of fine actors, Helmut Griem takes the role of Friederich's friend and pupil, Carl Gustav Carus, who after his death published *In Memory of the Landscape Painter Friederich*, together with fragments from the artist's own writings. Carus defends his mentor and acts as narrator of his story. Caspar David Friederich himself only appears, like one of the figures in his paintings, with his back to the camera—a small, silent observer of the natural world, in which he saw reflected his inner vision. 39 mins.
VHS: S13750. $39.95.

Centre Georges Pompidou

The Centre Georges Pompidou, which opened in January 1977, is now the world's most-visited center of the arts. This documentary reviews the daily activities of this highly successful cultural center matching the revolutionary concepts of the institution with an imaginative use of video effects. 60 mins.
VHS: S07608. $39.95.

Cezanne: The Riddle of the Bathers

Paul Cezanne is one of Modernity's undisputed founders. Among his paintings, a special preoccupation with a specific theme stands out: that of "the bathers." This film traces the riddle of the bathers, a curious fixation that resonates across Cezanne's entire career as a painter. 57 mins.
VHS: S27566. $19.95.

Chagall

Explores Marc Chagall's life and work and documents the history of the artist who began his life as a poor Russian Jew, yet, before his death, became the grand old man of French Art. 55 minutes.
VHS: S02391. $39.95.
Laser: LD70782. $75.00.

Chancay, The Forgotten Art

The Chancay culture predates the Inca, and is documented in this fascinating film made on location in Chancay, on the Pacific coast line of central Peru. The textiles and pottery shown demonstrate the influences of other cultures on the Chancay as well as giving us a feel for the expressive, imaginative works of art created by this very early civilization. Directed by Jose Gomez Sicre, 17 mins.
English Narration. Paul A. Ritacco.
VHS: S06753. $50.00.
Spanish Narration. Luis Vivas.
VHS: S06754. $50.00.

Chilean Indian Legends

"Susana Guevara Mueller, sister of Chilean artist Alvaro Guevara, friend of Picasso, and an artist whose works have been exhibited in the U.S. and overseas, has captured the charm and drama of ancient Indian legends in a series of excitingly colorful, imaginative paintings depicting the creation of the world, mythical monsters, sea sagas and the tale of a sacred tree high in the icy Andes." 12 mins.
VHS: S07537. $39.95.

Chinese Brush Painting

This ancient technique continues to hold great expressive promise for artists of all types. Part one introduces the basic equipment and techniques needed to practice this art, while part two progresses to more complex and challenging projects. 90 mins.
VHS: S24366. $19.95.

Chris Burden: A Video Portrait

During the early 70's, Chris Burden's shockingly simple, unforgettable performances took the jaded art world by surprise. In this documentary, Chris Burden talks about his works of the past 20 years: from the performances of the 70's to the sculpture and installations of the 80's. 28 mins.
VHS: S14582. $39.95.

Christo's Valley Curtain

Nominated for an Academy Award, a documentary about the construction of Christo's Valley curtain in Rifle Gap, Colorado, in 1972. "It is the finest film I have ever seen about an artist and his work," said *The New York Times*. "The surprise of the film is the enthusiasm with which this project was greeted by the residents of Rifle and by the construction workers who risked limbs and lives on the stunt."
VHS: S07492. $39.95.
Maysles Brothers, USA, 1974, 28 mins.

Chromosome XL

Six painters work on a single canvas, sharing and changing each other's images, in this fascinating time lapse view of the artistic process. 1986, 14 mins.
VHS: S10191. $19.95.

Citizen Barnes: An American Dream

A portrait of the eccentric life and behavior of Dr. Albert C. Barnes (1872-1951), who amassed a huge collection of art. The Barnes Foundation, which opened in 1925 outside Philadelphia, features an amazing number of French works, including 180 Renoirs, 69 Cezannes, 60 Matisses and works by Manet, Monet, Degas, Van Gogh, Rousseau, Picasso and Modigliani.
VHS: S19357. $29.95.
Jaubert/Pilard, France/USA, 1992, 52 mins.

City Louvre (La Ville Louvre)

This documentary goes behind the scenes for the first time at the Louvre. It was shot during the ongoing renovations that culminated with the opening of the pyramid. Now the public will see hidden aspects of this incomparable museum that have never been seen before. French with English subtitles.
VHS: S25106. $59.95.
Nicolas Philibert, France, 1990, 80 mins.

City Wildlife: Mice, Rats & Roaches

Sculptor Christy Rupp produced this TV show of science-oriented information about vermin, then the subject of her art. An interview with a cockroach expert (who dissects one), curious set-ups, includes the classic shot of a rat eating a Big Mac Hamburger.
VHS: S10202. $29.95.
Christy Rupp, USA, 1980, 28 mins.

Clementine Hunter

Mrs. Clementine Hunter is one of the most widely acclaimed African-American folk painters. When she died at the age of 101, she left over 4,000 images behind. Her legacy recreates a past that stretches back to her life on Melrose plantation in Louisiana during the era of Reconstruction. Despite the hardships of that time, Mrs. Hunter's work captures a joy in living that few artists can match.
VHS: S27100. $24.95.
Katina Simmons, USA, 1994, 22 mins.

Climate of New York

During the 30's and 40's, Rudy Burckhardt's photographs inspired Edwin Denby to write a series of poems on the city. This unique collaboration has been reproduced with Denby reciting his poetry against a background of Burckhardt's photographs. 8 mins.
VHS: S02758. $39.95.

Cloisters: The Grandeur of Medieval Art

The Cloisters are a branch of the Metropolitan Museum in New York that is dedicated to medieval art. Phillipe de Montebello, the museum director, escorts viewers through these galleries featuring manuscripts, stained glass, precious objects and the well-known Unicorn Tapestries. 27 mins.
VHS: S24273. $49.95.

Collecting America: Folk Art and the Shelburne Museum

A stunning exploration of the thousands of American folk objects housed in Vermont's Shelburne museum. Narrated by Ann Sothern and hosted by John Wilmerding, the film plays homage to the craftsmanship of folk art. More than 100,000 art objects are housed in this unique museum dedicated to preserving American folk art history. 28 mins.
VHS: S06606. $29.95.

Connecting—Grades K-8

An interdisciplinary approach to visual learning for young students. Connecting draws its content from all subjects, stimulating visual, experimental learning. Themes are "webbed" to extend meaning and find relationships, expand understanding and make connections. Covers rhythms and patterns, change and transformation, grids. A 200-page manual accompanies.
VHS: S09087. $239.00.

The Conquest of Form: The Art of William Latham

View the fantastic works of William Latham—the computer artist whose computer sculptures have been created by a process of technological evolution. Using this medium, he has explored a multidimensional space of millions of sculptural forms. 60 mins.
VHS: S13901. $29.95.

Conversation with Roy Lichtenstein and The New German Art

First there is a look at the Whitney exhibition of Lichtenstein works with an interview of the artist in his Southampton studio. In the second short feature, Donald Kuspit and Benjamin Buchloh discuss the neo-expressionist work of Keifer, Penck, *et al.*
VHS: S22655. $29.95.
Ross Skoggard, USA, 1980-1982, 40 mins.

Cowboy Art

Explores this uniquely American genre which helped transform the cowboys and Indians legends into a mythology. Explores the revival of interest in this genre, and shows "cowboy artists" at work at a Pueblo village in New Mexico and at a round-up ranch in Texas. 55 minutes.
VHS: S03584. $39.95.

The Creative Act: Paths to Realization

A nine-part series summarizing the reasons, goals and philosophy regarding the creative work of contemporary artists, including how each of the artists feels as an artist in today's society. Each artist recounts important early experiences which helped shape his or her motivations and ideas regarding creative activity. Illustrations from childhood and adolescence, student days and early works are included. The emphasis is on conscious aspects of the development of concepts and style. The series is based on *The Creative Act: Paths to Realization*, by Franz Geierhaas, associate professor of psychology at Trenton State College and a writer on art. Geierhaas introduces the series, interviews the artists, and summarizes the visits to the artists' studios. Each part is 30 mins.
Clarence Carter: Paintings and Printmaking.
VHS: S07542. $29.95.
Werner Drewes: Paintings and Printmaking.
VHS: S07543. $29.95.
John Goodyear: Kinetic Paintings and Sculptures.
VHS: S07544. $29.95.
Richard Kemble: Woodcuts and Sculptures.
VHS: S07545. $29.95.
Jacob Landau: Paintings and Printmaking.
VHS: S07546. $29.95.
Naoko Matsubara: Woodcuts.
VHS: S07547. $29.95.
Clare Romano: Paintings and Collagraphs.
VHS: S07548. $29.95.
John Ross: Paintings and Collagraphs.
VHS: S07549. $29.95.
Burton Wasserman: Serigraphs and Constructions.
VHS: S07550. $29.95.

Cubism and Non-Objective Art

The work of Braque and Picasso, Gris, Duchamp and Leger are explored, as well as the work of Kandinsky, Mondrian, Brancusi and others. A second segment covers the surrealists through the work of artists such as Dali, Magritte, Arp, Ernst, Miro and Tanguy.
VHS: S09074. $59.95.

Cuenca, Ecuador

A film about the II International Bienal of Painting held in Cuenca, Ecuador in June of 1989. Spanish, 30 mins.
VHS: S15289. $70.00.

Dancing Hands: Visual Arts of Rita Blitt

Unfolds the development of Blitt's art including painting, minimal pastels, acrylic and monumental sculpture inspired by drawings drawn with both hands simultaneously. 25 mins.
VHS: S07636. $59.95.

David Hockney

In recent years, Hockney's painting has taken a back seat to his work in photography. During the filming of this production, Hockney invited the crew to his London studio, where he applies his photography innovations to motion pictures, and creates an experiment. 55 mins.
VHS: S01624. $39.95.

David Hockney at the Tate
Since he burst onto the art scene in the mid 1960s, David Hockney has become one of the most successful British painters. To mark the artist's 50th birthday, London's Tate Gallery staged a major retrospective of his work. Melvyn Bragg joins Hockney at the Tate for an exclusive, private view of the exhibition in which they discuss works from all stages of Hockney's remarkable career. 55 mins.
VHS: S10266. $39.95.
Laser: LD70115. $39.95.

David Manzur Paints a Picture
A short documentary showing this well known Colombian painter demonstrating the techniques of fresco painting as it is applied to a modern painting. Made during the artist's figurative period. He is a master of chiaroscuro, flashing beams of light with dramatic intensity across spaces murky with a velvety darkness. Directed by Jose Gomez Sicre. Narrated in English by William D. Clark. 21 mins.
VHS: S06747. $40.00.

David: The Passing Show
Celebrates the story of David (1748-1825), artist of the French Revolution and leader of the Neo-classical movement. Twice taken political prisoner and finally exiled, David continued to work, producing two remarkable landscapes from the view outside his jail cell window. Produced by the BBC. 50 minutes.
VHS: S02382. $39.95.

A Day in the Country: Impressionism and the French Landscape (Kirk Douglas)
Camille Pissarro, Claude Monet, Vincent Van Gogh, Paul Cezanne, Alfred Sisley, Edouard Manet and Pierre-August Renoir are all featured in this video hosted by Kirk Douglas. He takes viewers through the homes and landscapes which inspired the Impressionist movement. 55 mins.
VHS: S23504. $99.95.
Laser: LD74763. $159.95.

A Day in the Country: Impressionism and the French Landscape
Forty of the most important landscape works from the Impressionist movement, featuring the works of Monet, Cezanne, Van Gogh, Matisse, Manet, and others, are shown here. The narration presents an overview of the movement and specific commentary on the paintings, set to music by Debussy. 27 mins.
VHS: S05744. $29.95.

A Day on the Grand Canal with the Emperor of China (or surface is illusion but so is depth)
World-famous artist David Hockney invites the viewer to join him on a magical journey down a 72-foot-long, legendary, 17th-century Chinese scroll. As he unrolls the richly detailed painting, Hockney traces the Emperor Kangxi's grand tour of his southern domains. The bustling streets and waterfronts of 300 years ago come alive as Hockney spins a dazzling discourse on eastern and western perspective and their relationship to his own artistic vision. "Splendid!" (Janet Maslin, *The New York Times*); "A fascinating and quietly moving film" (David Bordwell, *University of Wisconsin at Madison*).
VHS: S14902. $39.95.
Laser: CLV. LD74627. $39.95.
Philip Haas, USA, 1990

The Decoy
This film traces the history of the seemingly pedestrian duck decoy. First used by the Native Americans, it later became an intricate test of the woodcarver's skill. Dan Brown, a champion carver, shows how these figures evolved and how they continue to be deployed. 30 mins.
VHS: S24365. $19.95.

Definitive Dali: A Lifetime Retrospective
Archival footage, home film excerpts and interviews with Salvador Dali's friends and colleagues highlight this extraordinary dramatic portrait of Dali's unique life and career in painting, sculpture, writing, fashion and film. 75 mins.
VHS: S08388. $29.95.

Degas, Erte & Chagall
Three of this century's most influential artists are studied in this film. *Degas in New Orleans* portrays the artist's little-known visit here. *Diana Vreeland* tells the story of Erte, his life and works, from Paris to Hollywood. In the third segment, *Marc Chagall* gives us a personal view of some of his greatest works.
VHS: S03968. $69.95.

Degas: The Unquiet Spirit
Explores the life and work of a complex man and an unorthodox artist, controversial especially for his treatment of women as subjects whom he often showed in "earthy" and unglamorous activities. Includes many original paintings, drawings and prints to show Degas' favorite settings—the ballet class, racecourse, railway. 65 mins.
VHS: S02385. $39.95.
Laser: LD70785. $75.00.

Delacroix: The Restless Eye
The film uses the artist's own journal to tell the story of one of France's greatest painters, who was also a passionate lover of music and an accomplished writer. The journal illustrates the places and people Delacroix knew, and treats us to rare glimpses of his childhood drawings as well as a new look at his famous masterpieces. Produced by the BBC. 65 mins.
VHS: S02384. $39.95.

Delta Solar and the Four Seasons
The kinetic sculpture by the Venezuelan artist Alejandro Otero, set in the garden of the Air and Space Museum in Washington, D.C., is the subject of this short film. The sculpture owes its name to the Delta structure and contains dozens of rust-proof, light weight, steel reels that move with the slightest breeze. Highly polished, each reel reflects the ambience that surrounds it. Set to the music of Vivaldi's *Four Seasons*, the camera has recorded an inspiring visit to this monumental structure during each change of the seasons. Directed by Angel Hurtado, 13 mins.
English Narration. Renee Channey.
VHS: S06798. $40.00.
Spanish Narration. Herbert Morales.
VHS: S06799. $40.00.

Documentary Urge: Tom Arndt
Narrated by Garrison Keillor, this documentary shows photographer Tom Arndt in action: stalking his prey at the Minnesota State Fair, and preparing for a retrospective of his work. Arndt follows in the tradition of Walker Evans and Robert Frank, his acknowledged heroes, as a photographer of the American scene. 22 mins.
VHS: S02644. $39.95.

Drawing on Life
A documentary about David Fincham, a gifted artist who ruminates on his work and life since he was diagnosed with AIDS. His exuberant humor counterbalances the conversations about the nature of art, politics, culture and tensions of being Catholic and gay.
VHS: S19641. $39.95.
Richard L. Harrison, USA, 1992, 30 mins.

Drawing the Line: A Portrait of Keith Haring
Keith Haring, successor to Andy Warhol's pop zeitgeist, was an artist whose playful, simplistic drawings made a serious commentary on the 1980's. His work—kinetic iconography whose roots are to be found in primitivism—speaks to our collective subconscious. As evidence of this, his paintings, drawings and sculptures are to be found throughout the spectrum of mass culture, from skateboards to subway walls. This revealing portrait of Haring's work and world views contains interviews with Leo Castelli, Dennis Hopper and many other leaders of the international art scene. 30 mins.
VHS: S12594. $19.95.

Dream Window: Reflections on the Japanese Garden
The Japanese garden is for many a reflection of the inner state. In their intricate design and structure, they were conceived as retreats for people to tap into their natural world. The program contrasts the vibrant, dense milieu of contemporary Japanese life with the contemplative and interior landscape of the traditional garden. 85 mins.
VHS: S20320. $29.95.
Laser: LD72242. $34.95.

East Side Story
The artist's sculptural and philosophical essay on breaking glass and light bulbs.
VHS: S10181. $29.95.
Jim Sutcliffe, USA, 1982, 28 mins.

Edouard Manet
Award-winning director Didier Baussy has created an engrossing, comprehensive portrait of the great Impressionist. Close-up views of the artist's works, filmed at splendid Manet exhibitions in Paris and New York, are highlights of this sweeping biography. 60 mins.
VHS: S10268. $39.95.

Edouard Manet: Painter of Modern Life
Presents the work of the great painter in the context of his 19th century world. Manet believed that a serious painter should explore modern life, and his paintings feature Paris, its fashionable society, and friends, such as Baudelaire and Zola, whose writings provide the narrative background for this program. Cine Golden Eagle Award. Produced by the Metropolitan Museum of Art. 27 minutes.
VHS: S02386. $29.95.
Laser: LD70783. $75.00.

Edouardo Chillida
Spain's finest living sculptor draws inspiration from the culture and landscape of his native Basque country. The program profiles both the man and his work, capturing the power of his abstract sculptures. 60 minutes.
VHS: S02392. $39.95.

Edvard Munch
This biographical dramatization of Norway's most famous artist reveals the tumultuous events of his life as recorded in Munch's own memoirs. With stuffy 19th-century Oslo as the background, the creative process of one of the world's foremost expressionist painters emerges. Norwegian and German with English subtitles.
VHS: S20594. $79.95
VHS: S20594. $79.95
Peter Watkins, Norway/Sweden, 1973, 167 mins.

Edward Hopper: The Silent Witness
The great American realist painter Edward Hopper emerges in this thoughtful docudrama. It traces his steps along the Eastern Seaboard using his works, from museums like the Whitney, the Art Institute of Chicago and MOMA, as clues to his itinerary. 43 mins.
VHS: S25854. $19.95.

El Greco
Recreates the career of this great painter against the scheme of the Counter-Reformation which inspired his work. Filmed on location in Toledo and Venice, the film traces El Greco's beginnings as a Byzantine icon painter in Crete, and explores both the religion of El Greco's times and his personal spiritual quest, explored in his masterpieces from the great churches and museums of Madrid to New York. 60 mins.
VHS: S02379. $39.95.

Embryo
Embryo is a visual and narrative journey through lost wax bronze casting. Katherine Michaels explores the intricate steps of the process and meditates on the symbolism surrounding the origins of metallurgy. With Native American flute music by R. Carlos Nakai. 28 mins.
VHS: S15744. $49.95.

End of the Art World
Andy Warhol, Robert Rauschenberg, Jasper Johns, Michael Snow, Roy Lichtenstein and other prominent artists are the subject of this free-wheeling film by Alexis Krasilovsky. "With a quality of humor possible only with depth of understanding, Alexis Krasilovsky presents a catalogue of interviews with modern artists in which the shooting style as well as the aural material's format rehearses the personal style, the aesthetics, and the assumption of each artist about the nature of his art" (Artforum).
VHS: S07773. $29.95.
Alexis Krasilovsky, USA, 1971, 35 mins.

Esso Salon of Young Artists
A selection of works of prize-winning artists at the Esso Salon of Young Artists. Narrated in Spanish by Luis Vivas. 16 mins.
VHS: S06752. $40.00.

Ethel Kvalheim, Rosemaler
One of America's foremost folk artists, Ethel Kvalheim, talks about her life and work. This beautifully presented video portrait makes a valuable library resource. 18 mins. Resource guide available.
Resource Guide.
VHS: S25772. $20.00.
Video.
VHS: S25759. $95.00.

The Etruscans
Recent art finds are used to depict the daily life of these ancient people, who survived for eight centuries on the Italian peninsula until they were defeated by Rome. 17 mins.
VHS: S15531. $45.00.

European Video Library
A 12-episode series focusing on European artists and art movements.
Caravaggio. Caravaggio was a revolutionary painter whose subject matter and dramatically lit scenes transformed painting throughout Italy and Europe. Despite the success of his work, he had a difficult career and a short life marked by turbulent interludes. 30 mins.
VHS: S26014. $29.95.
The Early Italian Renaissance: Brunelleschi—Donatello—Masaccio. Brunelleschi transformed architecture, Donatello brought new plasticity to sculpture and Masaccio achieved great breakthroughs in the realm of painting. Together these three men forged new ways, without which the Renaissance would be unimaginable. 27 mins.
VHS: S26017. $29.95.
French Gothic Architecture. French Gothic masterpieces from Chartes, Notre Dame, Amiens, Reims and the Saint Chappelle in Paris are the subject of this video. These works tell a history of technical breakthroughs and plastic innovation expressive of a monumental world view. 25 mins.
VHS: S26018. $29.95.
Giorgione. Even though only a small body of this master's work exists, Giorgione's intriguing style, expressive of a mysterious view of nature, haunts viewers to this day. This video helps explains such enigmatic works as the "Dresden Venus" and the "Tempest." 24 mins.
VHS: S26015. $29.95.
The Italian Romanesque. From Sant'Ambrogio in Milan to the Monreale Cathedral in Sicily, this video depicts the greatest achievements of the Italian Romanesque. It is a tradition of varied richness based on a pious world view. 26 mins.
VHS: S26016. $29.95.
Klee. All aspects of Paul Klee's life and career, 1879-1940, are explored in this video. He left a great legacy of work. Special attention is given to the Bauhaus years and his relation to Kandinsky. 25 mins.
VHS: S26019. $29.95.
Leonardo da Vinci. This documentary offers an overview of da Vinci's life, 1452-1519. From his early works in Florence to the later accomplishments of the "Mona Lisa" and the fresco of the "Last Supper," this genius demonstrated amazing versatility. He also left a great many intriguing drawings illustrating amazing and imaginative machines. 30 mins.
VHS: S26020. $29.95.
Munch and Ensor. Edvard Munch and James Ensor pioneered new expressive methods in paint that helped inspire German Expressionism. This video examines the works and the lives of these two innovative and influential artists. 21 mins.
VHS: S26022. $29.95.
Palladio. This master of classical architecture fused Greek and Roman elements and thereby achieved a new Renaissance architecture. The video begins with a tour of the early Town Hall in Vincenza and continues with a detailed look at the many villas Palladio built in the nearby countryside of the Veneto. 28 mins.
VHS: S26021. $29.95.
Rome: Art and Architecture, Part One. This video offers a unique approach to the great monuments of the eternal city. The narrator follows an itinerary made up of the many fountains which water the city. Some were erected in classical times while others date from the late Renaissance. All the most important sites are visited, including the Forum, Castel Sant'Angelo, the basilicas, Saint Peter and the Pantheon. 39 mins.
VHS: S26024. $29.95.
Rome: Art and Architecture, Part Two. Once again the glorious, eternal monuments of Rome are on view, in this second episode of the series. 39 mins.
VHS: S26025. $34.95.
Titian. Titian's great achievements with color are thoroughly explored in this video. All aspects of this painter's work, including his innovations in composition and light, are illustrated. 27 mins.
VHS: S26023. $29.95.

Everlasting France
This outstanding art film shows the building and major works from the Legion of Honor affiliated with the Fine Arts Museums of San Francisco. Hosted by noted art historian Rosamond Bernier. 30 mins.
VHS: S15049. $29.95.

Exit in 3
A short story saga of a metaphorical investigation into the lives of three artists—Jerry Kearns, Elaine Lustig Cohen, and Hunt Slonem. Using interviews and video portraits interwoven with elements of fiction, this tape made by the New York alternative arts space juxtaposes the works of three different artists as a new approach to documentary that deals with the problem of translating the medium of painting into that of TV.
VHS: S07114. $49.95.
Papo Colo, USA, 1985, 23 mins.

Eye of Painter: Judy Rifka and Frank Mann
Bold statements from two modern painters in their studio are recorded on this video. It is shot with an eye for detail. Rifka and Mann are seen at work, which gives a sense of their aesthetic struggles.
VHS: S22662. $19.95.

Faith Ringgold Paints Crown Heights
African-American artist Faith Ringgold illustrates the folk tales of 12 distinct cultures who call Crown Heights home. This inspirational documentary shows how diverse cultures have contributed to the American spirit, using Ringgold's beautiful paintings. 28 mins.
VHS: S26040. $49.95.

Faith Ringgold: The Last Story Quilt
From the day she learned to draw, Faith Ringgold has worked steadily to master her craft and communicate her vision: to present a realistic view of the black female in society. This film is an insider's look at how one woman has fulfilled her dream of becoming an artist. Cine Gold Eagle Award. 28 min.
VHS: S18392. $24.95.

The Fantastic World of M.C. Escher
In this engaging documentary, the person behind the famous, heavily patterned artworks is revealed at last. From the landscapes in Spain and Italy that inspired him, to accounts from his friends, this film will explore many aspects of Escher and his art. 50 mins.
VHS: S21341. $19.95.

Fauvism and Expressionism
The Fauves emerged as a reaction against Impressionism and Post-Impressionism. Early modern art is explored through the work of Matisse, Rouault, Derain and Vlaminck; in *Expressionism* the work of Nolde, Munch, Kokoschka, Beckmann and others are explored.
VHS: S09072. $59.95.

The Feast of the Gods
Using computer graphics and animation, *The Feast of the Gods* shows how the 16th century masterpiece of the same name looked at various stages of its history. A collaborative effort of Giovanni Bellini and Titian, the painting was altered several times during its history. Filmed on location in Ferrara, Venice, Mantua and the National Gallery. 27 mins.
VHS: S11755. $29.95.
Laser: LD70114. $39.95.

Fernando de Szyszlo of Peru Paints a Picture
Fernando de Szyszlo was a pioneer in the field of abstract art in his native Peru. Absorbed with pre-Columbian cultures, the camera finds him in his small, secret studio that faces the sky and the sea. He paints undisturbed to the music of Vivaldi and Bach, taking up to three weeks to complete a painting as he works with transparent colors over opaque colors and must wait for each stage to dry. Directed by Jose Gomez Sicre. Narration in Spanish only, by Luis Vivas. 22 mins.
VHS: S06750. $60.00.

First Modern Sculptor: Donatello, 1386-1466
Donatello was the greatest sculptor of the early Italian Renaissance. A pioneer in the use of linear perspective, he also promoted the revival of Greco-Roman culture and realism in art. Filmed in Florence, Siena, Venice, Padua, and London, this program reveals the astonishing variety of his work. Sequences shot in modern day workshops illustrate the sculptor's amazing range of skills. Three eminent contemporary sculptors—Elisabeth Frink, Peter Rockwell, and the late Henry Moore—describe the inspiration they gained from his work. England, 60 mins.
VHS: S13745. $39.95.

Four Fashion Horses
Colorful, imaginative studio set ups present clothes by artists and innovative designers. Designed as a sales scheme, the tape vividly presents a little-known convergence of art and fashion.
VHS: S10183. $19.95.
Sophie Vielle, USA, 1983, 28 mins.

Frame and Context: Richard Ross
Photographer Richard Ross discusses his art, life and satirical, deadpan style of photography. 16 mins.
VHS: S20353. $39.95.

Francis Bacon
Widely regarded as the greatest British painter of this century, Bacon's work further fetches more on the open market than almost any other living painter. This program follows Bacon from his studio where he starts work every day at dawn, to his favorite club and gambling joint in Soho, and explores how his way of life affects his vision of the world. 55 mins.
VHS: S07607. $39.95.

Francisco Oller
A film on the life and works of this 19th century Puerto Rican master, made in conjunction with the retrospective of this great artist's work in 1986. Oller, though born in Puerto Rico, studied in Spain and lived part of his life in France, working with such well known artists as Monet, Pissarro and Cezanne. Directed by Angel Hurtado, 25 mins.
English Narration. Renee Channey.
VHS: S06808. $70.00.
Spanish Narration. Ivan Silva.
VHS: S06809. $70.00.

Frans Hals of Antwerp
This program presents an extensive montage of Hals' canvases and examines the various stages in his work. 54 mins.
VHS: S16599. $39.95.

Frederic Remington: The Truth of Other Days

Near the turn of the century, Frederic Remington popularized the myths, legends and images of the Old West, and this program traces the career of the brilliant painter, sculptor and author. Hundreds of original artworks are showcased while narration by Gregory Peck, interviews, location footage, archival footage and period photographs create an illuminating frame around the works of one of America's finest artists. The program also explores Remington's direct influence on filmmakers such as John Ford and his continuing influence on today's popular culture. 58 mins.
VHS: S12367. $39.95.

Frescoes of Diego Rivera

Explores the great beauty and political expression in Rivera's most extensive body of work, examining the artist and his techniques, using archival footage filmed during his work on murals created for the Ford Motor Company, and location footage of his most recognized efforts. In addition, the film explores the man and his politics, creating a complex and fascinating portrait of one of the geniuses of the twentieth century. 35 mins.
VHS: S10306. $29.95.

Frida Kahlo

Sada Thompson narrates this fascinating look at Frida Kahlo, the center of the Mexican renaissance of the 20's and 30's, both as an artist, a woman and a tragic figure. A catastrophic accident at the age of 16 left Kahlo with severe injuries. During her recuperation, she began to paint, first portraits and later more complex works with the themes of death and her loss of motherhood. *Frida Kahlo* profiles Frida's work, her increasing interest in politics, and her tempestuous relationship with her husband, Diego Rivera. 62 mins.
VHS: S08477. $39.95.

Gaudi

This program details the methods and contributions of the visionary architect who reshaped our ideas and theories about form through his unique applications of function, reality and art. 25 mins.
VHS: S17223. $29.95.

George Bellows: Portrait of an American Artist

This documentary, produced by the Smithsonian, explores the life and work of George Bellows, one of the major figures of 20th century American art, with commentary by Margaret Christman, research historian at the National Portrait Gallery. 28 mins.
VHS: S02510. $49.95.

Georgia O'Keefe

For the first time in this film, O'Keefe appeared on camera to talk candidly about her work and life, showing how nature and the mountains and desert of New Mexico figure prominently in her work. Produced by WNET. 60 minutes.
VHS: S02349. $39.95.
Laser: LD70118. $39.95.

Gericault: Men and Wild Horses

The program sets the work of this enigmatic French painter against the background of his time. Events of the early 19th century are presented "newsreel" style, including archival footage from silent movies of the period. Called "The Madman" by his contemporaries, Gericault was a man in conflict with his own age. Produced by the BBC. 60 minutes.
VHS: S03583. $39.95.

The Gods of Beauty: A Portrait of the Visionary Artist: Mona Boulware Webb

A delightful portrait of surrealist artist and outsider Mona Boulware Webb. Now in her 70s, Mona Webb was a protege of Aldous Huxley and Krishnamurti during the 1950s. She creates expressionist art on a grand assemblage scale, and her greatest work is the quirky and mystical house she has spent the past four decades transforming. The entire three-story house is painted and sculpted in wild, psychedelic forms.
VHS: S27165. $49.95.
Niels Nielsen, USA, 1990-1995, 29 mins.

Gothic Art

Enter a shimmering Gothic universe and discover the elements that allowed these master artisans to pile stone upon stone—the development of the rib vault and the flying buttress and how stained glass is made. 27 mins.
VHS: S09491. $174.00.

Graffiti/Post-Graffiti

Exhibitions at Sidney Janis, Fashion Moda and Fun Galleries were instrumental in popularizing and promoting the acceptance of graffiti art. This documentary explains the 80's phenomenon and includes interviews with artists Lady Pink, Crash, Keith Haring, John Michel Basquiat, Futura and others. 30 mins.
VHS: S22620. $34.95.
ART/New York, USA, 1984, 30 mins.

Great Tales in Asian Art

Four mythic tales are revealed through masterpieces of Asian art in this video. Indian painting, Indonesian sculpture, Javanese shadow play, Korean masked drama and Japanese paintings on screens and scrolls are all explored here. This beautiful joining of literature and the visual arts was filmed on location in four countries. 82 mins.
VHS: S26927. $19.95.

The Hague School

Documents the 19th century group of Dutch artists who took painting out of the studio and into nature, captured the vanishing rural beauty of the Hague, and had a profound influence on Van Gogh and Mondrian. 45 minutes.
VHS: S01800. $39.95.

Hans Hartung: A German Destiny

Born in Germany 1904, Hans Hartung was one of the most influential figures in the development of 20th-century art. A fascinating program that takes a close look at this experimental modernist and his "spontaneous" style. 55 mins.
VHS: S15294. $29.95.

Harry Callahan, Eleanor and Barbara

Callahan's photographs of his wife and daughter, taken over a period of 25 years, provide an important insight into his creativity. 18 mins.
VHS: S04104. $39.95.

Henry Moore

A moving portrait of the great sculptor of the century, revealing Moore to be a man of humor, compassion and sincerity, with many revealing close-ups of his masterpieces. Moore is interviewed on camera by Sir Hugh Weldon. 52 mins.
VHS: S04350. $49.95.

The Hermitage Museum of St. Petersburg—Series 1

This four-disc, boxed set highlights the masterpieces created between the 16th and 20th centuries, including those of El Greco, Goya, Rubens, Van Dyke, 17th century Flemish painters, Rembrandt, the 17th century Dutch Masters, and the French classical style that shaped the 17th and 18th centuries. The program details the emergence of modernism, impressionism and post-impressionism, the works of Matisse and Picasso, and 20th century art. 240 mins.
Laser: LD71765. $189.95.

The Hermitage Museum of St. Petersburg—Series 2

Researched by the Hermitage Museum of St. Petersburg, Russia, this program traces post-Renaissance art and sculpture from Russia in the early 18th century, its Oriental art collection, and the decorative art of Italy, France and England. The program also looks at ancient Egypt and Greek and Roman classicism, the Middle Ages and early Italian Renaissance, and concludes with the High Italian Renaissance and art of the Netherlands, from the 15th and 16th centuries. 300 mins.
Laser: LD71766. $169.95.

The Hermitage: A Russian Odyssey

St. Petersburg's premier museum houses one of the world's greatest art collections, assembled by the Czars of Russia over centuries of conquest and patronage. Noted commentator, journalist and critic Rod Macleish leads the viewer through 300 years of history and art in an exploration of this storied collection.
Part I, Catherine the Great: A Lust for Art. Peter the Great built St. Petersburg for the glory of his dynasty. In this episode the role of this monarch and the pivotal influence of his successor, Catherine, are examined. The Queen is credited with bringing Western culture into Russia. She amassed a great quantity of artworks by such masters as Rembrandt, Rubens, Breughel and Watteau in less than 40 years, resulting in a collection greater than the Louvre had assembled in over 400 years.
VHS: S21366. $29.95.
Part II, Tyrants and Heroes: The Nineteenth Century Czars. The Napoleonic invasion and a succession of weak Czars left their imprint on the Hermitage. It was during this era, however, that the great collection of Scythian gold from prehistoric Russia was discovered and added to the collection.
VHS: S21367. $29.95.
Part III, From Czars to Commissars: A Museum Survives. Preserving this collection during the Russian Revolution and the horrendous 900-day Nazi siege of the city was a momentous task. Despite these depredations, the collection survived and grew to include 20th-century masters like Picasso, Matisse and Renoir.
VHS: S21368. $29.95.
Complete Set. Three tapes.
VHS: S21369. $79.95.

History of Poland in Painting (Historia Polski w Malarstwie)

A survey of the major historical events of the country through the artistic visions of Poland's top painters: Jan Matejko, Wojciech Kossak, Jacek Malczewski, Piotr Michalowski, Artur Grottger. All the best in the tradition of Polish historical painting.
VHS: S15579. $39.95.
Bozena Walter, Poland, 1988, 109 mins.

Homage to Chagall

A study of the life and works of the great Russian artist, superbly filmed in color, and with narration by James Mason. Included is rare footage of Chagall and Madame Chagall—"an affectionate and visually beautiful celebration of both the man and his art" (*New York Times*). In English.
VHS: S04722. $79.95.
Laser: LD71044. $19.98.
Harry Rasky, Canada, 1977, 90 mins.

Howard Terpning: The Storyteller

Howard Terpning's paintings function as visual stories depicting Native Americans. Along with the works, this video shows the artist at work. His compositions offer a glimpse of a lifestyle rarely seen elsewhere. 30 mins.
VHS: S26806. $49.95.

The Hudson River and Its Painters

The mid-nineteenth century saw the growth of America's first native school of landscape painters, artists inspired by the compelling beauty of the Hudson River Valley, who portrayed this and other romantic wilderness areas with an almost mystical reverence. This video explores the life and work of the major artists of what came to be known as the Hudson River School—Thomas Cole, Asher Durand, Frederic Church, Albert Bierstadt, John Kensett, Jasper Cropsey, Worthington Whittredge, Sanford Gifford, and George Inness. It presents more than 200 paintings, prints and photographs of the period and juxtaposes them with dramatic location photography of the Hudson River area. The Hudson Company in association with The Metropolitan Museum of Art. 57 mins.
VHS: S05233. $39.95.

Hungers of the Soul: Be Gardiner, Stone Carver

Shot on location in Honduras and North Carolina, this documentary shows the creative life of the famed Southern sculptor Be Gardiner. Her work is prized throughout the Southeastern United States.
VHS: S27101. $39.95.
Gorham Kindhem, USA, 1994, 54 mins.

II International Biennial of Painting: Cuenca-Ecuador

A special exhibition of contemporary Latin American art was held in the Museum of Modern Art at Cuenca, Ecuador. Mario Martinez narrates this aesthetic journey, which also includes general information about the historic city of Cuenca. Spanish language with no subtitles. 30 mins.
VHS: S21813. $35.00.

Illustrated Guide to Caricature

The art of making people look ridiculous has influenced politics, society, and the arts for centuries. Luck and Flaw, two contemporary caricaturists, take viewers on an unusual, eye-opening journey through the history of this appealing art form. A survey of works by such early caricaturists as Low, Daumier, Dantan and Cruikshank is enriched by views of contemporary caricature by Gerard Scarfe, Ralph Steadman, Steve Bell and Ralph Sallon.
VHS: S10269. $29.95.

Impressionism and Post Impressionism

Developed by Gale Murray, Ph.D. Shows the brilliance of Monet, Renoir, Degas, Manet and others, and then the harmony of work and color in the work of Cezanne, order and permanence of Seurat, dynamism of Van Gogh, Toulouse-Lautrec. 44 mins.
VHS: S07656. $59.95.

Impressionism Boxed Set

Three artists, Monet, Degas and Van Gogh, are revealed in separate tapes devoted to each artist. Their legacy to painting is revealed through careful analysis of their works. 153 mins.
VHS: S24795. $79.95.

Impressionism: A Visual Revolution

Winner of the Gold Medal at the National Educational Film Festival, this colorful history is of the revolutionary Impressionist movement. Viewers observe how principles of color, light, shade, line and form were used by artists that radically introduced a new way of seeing. 40 mins.
VHS: S09468. $174.00.

In a Brilliant Light: Van Gogh in Arles

A portrait of Van Gogh's climactic 444 days in the south of France, the film focuses on the artist's work rather than on his life, and dispels many of the myths surrounding this legendary painter. Produced by the Metropolitan Museum of Art. 57 minutes.
VHS: S02718. $39.95.

In the Studio with Ibram Lassaw

An overview of the art and life of Ibram Lassaw, one of the country's preeminent abstract sculptors. Lassaw's innovative efforts to imagine the world of three-dimensional expression are examined from his diverse range of works. Lassaw also discusses his artistic philosophy and working methods. 12 mins.
VHS: S20310. $39.95.

Ingres: Slaves of Fashion

Investigates the life and work of Ingres (1780-1867), who was in his own day admired by many, but loved by few. The program studies another paradox: how Ingres, known as a revolutionary artist, could have inspired the new Romantic movement. Produced by the BBC. 50 minutes.
VHS: S02383. $39.95.

Interviews with Artists, Program 4: Three Installation Artists

Three installation artists are interviewed. Susan Leibovitz Steinman, an environmental activist/sculptor, discusses the motivation behind her work in site-specific public installation using recycled materials. Jeanne O'Connor combines photography, painting, drawing and sculptural elements to create a sense of memory of places. And M. Luise Stanley talks about her narrative work, her sketchbooks and her building of her own private Pompeii Villa for an exhibition in San Francisco.
VHS: S21981. $35.00.
Elizabeth Sher, USA, 1993, 35 mins.

Isabel Bishop: Portrait of an Artist

The master of romantic realism who captured on canvas the world of New York—the hobos, shop girls, the weary day-to-day existence of life in the city, all painted from the perspective of her studio in Union Square. This program brings to light one of America's true masters in a unique pairing of the artist at work and scenes recreating her most important paintings. 26 mins.
VHS: S10310. $29.95.

Isamu Noguchi

Born of an American mother and a Japanese father, sculptor Isamu Noguchi transcended two worlds to become an artist of international renown, "at once the purest of sculptors and one of the most socially oriented, exulting in large public projects" (Hilton Kramer, *New York Times*). This unique video probes the psyche of a creative genius, exploring the effects of an unusual childhood and the artist's reconciliation with his heritage. Apprenticed to Brancusi, Noguchi embraced the arts of furniture design, calligraphic brush drawings, set design, and took the humble Japanese lantern and developed it into its trademark Akari lamp. 52 mins.
VHS: S10305. $39.95.

Islands

For two brief weeks in 1983, Christo's *Surrounded Islands* blossomed on the waters of Biscayne Bay, Florida: 11 scrub-pine islands surrounded by 6.5 million square feet of bright pink fabric. A three-year struggle, a political drama interwoven with two other Christo projects—the wrapping of the Pont Neuf in Paris, and the Reichstag in Berlin.
VHS: S07494. $59.95.
Maysles Brothers, USA, 1983, 58 mins.

Jack Levine: Feast of Pure Reason

Shows America's foremost Social Realist painter, as he stands before an empty canvas, and with breathtaking virtuosity, creates a painting on-camera. Directed by David Sutherland. 58 minutes.
VHS: S02747. $39.95.

Jackson Pollock

This biography of Jackson Pollock looks at his work, his concept of "action painting" and his part in the abstract expressionist movement. 52 mins.
VHS: S17725. $39.95.

Jacob Lawrence

Lawrence is one of America's most respected artists. This African-American painter grew up in depression-era Harlem and got his schooling in federal workshops. Today his works on African-American themes, particularly history, are widely prized. Interviews and the works of the artist tell this story of artistic excellence. 25 mins.
VHS: S27622. $29.95.

Jacob Lawrence: The Glory of Expression

This documentary is about the life of African-American painter Jacob Lawrence. His work has consisted primarily of epic depictions of the struggles of African-Americans. Considered one of America's greatest modern painters he was the first African-American to have his work exhibited in a major New York gallery. 28 mins.
VHS: S21454. $49.95.

Jacques Lipchitz

A fascinating glimpse of a serious artist and the artistic process, this program allows Lipchitz to tell his own story, recalling his early life in Lithuania, the height of the Cubist movement, and his post WW2 years in New York and Italy. With a handful of artists, he helped forge a new direction in art with his friends and co-workers Picasso, Diego Rivera, Juan Gris, Gertrude Stein, Soutine and Modigliani. Filmed working at the height of his creative powers, the program also demonstrates his warm talent as a storyteller. 58 mins.
VHS: S10304. $39.95.

James C. Christensen: The Art of Imagination

James C. Christensen is a unique artist who changes the rules of reality in his highly imaginative and complex art. Rich symbolism hidden in his work is explained in this video. The result is an invitation to participate in a world of fantasy. 31 mins.
VHS: S26807. $49.95.

Jasper Johns: Ideas in Paint

A revealing portrait of Jasper Johns which covers his remarkable work that helped usher in Pop Art and Minimalism. The documentary includes intimate conversations and footage of Johns working, with commentary by his colleagues Leo Castelli, the late composer John Cage, choreographer Merce Cunningham and other noted artists and art critics. 56 mins.
VHS: S17728. $39.95.

Jewish Museum

The story behind the thousands of paintings, sculptures, and photographs in the collection of the Jewish Museum in New York City. 18 mins.
VHS: S03888. $29.95.

Joan Miro: Constellations— The Color of Poetry

A retrospective filmed at the Miro Museum in Barcelona, this video offers a unique insight into the visual world of Miro, which fuses passion, sexuality, philosophy and flights of fancy into an ecstatic carnival of symbols. With historic newsreel footage, a tour of Miro's studio and a performance by the La Claca Theater in Miro-designed costumes. 52 mins.
VHS: S21904. $29.98.

Joe Coleman

On a rainy night a visit to Joe's 20th century bizarre memorabilia museum on New York's Lower East Side offers the perfect art experience. Coleman is a painter and performance artist who was banned in Boston and censored by Bob Barker from *The Price Is Right*. His exploding performances may have something to do with his outre reputation.
VHS: S22651. $39.95.
Clayton Patterson, USA, 1989, 59 mins.

John Baldessari: Some Stories

Presented without commentary, this film reveals the thinking behind his work and provides clues to the understanding of the artist's paintings, photographic work and books. What emerges is a portrait of a thoughtful, quietly rebellious artist who has influenced a large number of younger artists over the last 20 years. 28 mins.
VHS: S14581. $39.95.

John Marin's New York

A video representation of artist John Marin's complex *New York City Series*. Marin's modernist style melded tenets of Impressionism, Cubism and Futurism to create a signature aesthetic. This series examines New York's artistic, social and cultural evolution, from the years 1910-53. With an original jazz score by Derek Smith and Jay Leonhart.
VHS: S19901. $29.98.

John Piper: Piper's Way
Takes a close look at the career of England's foremost neo-Romantic artist. Documents much of Piper's recent work, including his stained glass design for Coventry Cathedral. 55 minutes.
VHS: S01799. $39.95.

Joseph Beuys, Public Dialogues
Famous performance artist Beuys is seen in his first public appearance in the U.S. in this video. He outlines his political and artistic philosophies.
VHS: S22654. $49.95.
Willoughby Sharp, USA, 1974, 120 mins.

Jules Feiffer: Feiffer's Follies
A relaxed visit with one of America's most celebrated political satirists. Filmed at Feiffer's summer home at Martha's Vineyard. Shows Feiffer as he creates a typical Feiffer character on-camera. 55 minutes.
VHS: S03586. $19.95.

Julio Rosado del Valle
A visit to the studio of the prominent Puerto Rican artist, Julio Rosado, in San Juan. Narrated in Spanish by Luis Vivas. 13 mins.
VHS: S06759. $40.00.

Junior Museum
By understanding how artists use different media to express their deepest thoughts and feelings, students are able to better appreciate the arts. This program orients elementary students to the basic principles of design and technique used by major artists throughout the ages. 55 mins.
VHS: S09469. $210.00.

Kazimir Malevich: Breaking Free of the Earth
The most inscrutable of the Russian revolutionary artists, Kazimir Malevich had the misfortune to die in official Soviet disfavor, and to remain under that disapproval for decades afterwards. Now political changes have opened the doors to these hidden storerooms, and Malevich's pictures can be publicly viewed once again. This program documents the first major retrospective of his work since his death more than 50 years ago, providing viewers with analyses and commentary on his work that is vivid, precise and personal. 52 mins.
VHS: S13742. $39.95.

Kinetic Sculpture Windcarver
Former architect Merrill Prentice measures the slightest currents of air and designs common materials into delightful, ever-changing sculptures. The wonder of the creative process is revealed along with humorous anecdotes and even a discussion about the philosophy of public and private art. A valuable video for all art students, or even those who simply love great art.
VHS: S14593. $49.95.

Klee
This video biography covers the life and work of Paul Klee (1879-1940), whose vast output coincided with some of the most important developments in modernism. The video highlights Klee's work during the Bauhaus period and focuses on his relationship with Kandinsky. 25 mins.
VHS: S17226. $29.95.

L'Art Vetraria (The Art of Glass)
This program goes inside the craft and discipline of art glass, through the objects of Josh Simpson, who discusses the technical and creative mechanics involved, as well as the personal consequences of sustaining a 3000-year old tradition. 30 mins.
VHS: S20309. $39.95.

L.A.—Suggested by Art of Ruscha
Los Angeles is stylishly rendered in Conklin's sunset-hued homage to painter Edward Ruscha. L.A., the city of heretics, malcontents, messiahs, and "the city of pools, palm trees, and real estate," is both inspiration and obsession for Ruscha.
VHS: S00698. $29.95.
Gary Conklin, USA, 1981, 28 mins.

The Landscapes of Frederic Edwin Church
This program studies the work of Frederic Edwin Church, whose style is described as "magnificent, dramatic, sweeping, fantastic and poetic," tracing his career as a important figure in the Hudson River School, the country's leading 19th-century landscape painters. 29 mins.
VHS: S15300. $29.95.

Lascaux Revisited
Prehistoric paintings in a cave were accidentally discovered by French schoolchildren. The drama of this true story is recreated in this video through animation. Even more exciting is the footage of these remarkable ancient works of art which have been closed to the public since 1963.
VHS: S27099. $29.95.
Jacques Willemart/Norbert Aujolat, USA, 1995, 35 mins.

Left Right
Sculptor and architect Robert Parker, at home in Guelph, Canada, moves among stones and bones dressed in a loincloth. 1984, 20 mins.
VHS: S22659. $29.95.
Robert Parker, USA, 1984, 20 mins.

Legacy of the Mamluks
Based on the first major international exhibition of the art of the Mamluks at the Smithsonian—the art of the Mamluk Dynasty, one of the most formidable regimes of the Middle Ages, ruling most of the parts of Egypt, Palestine and Syria. An amazing retrospective of work in metalwork, glasswork, illustrated manuscripts, ceramics and woodwork. 30 mins.
VHS: S06561. $39.95.

Lempad of Bali
From the co-director of the acclaimed series Ring of Fire comes this remarkable portrait. Lempad was a great Balinese artist who died a fully conscious death (he invited his whole family to attend) at the age of 116. He had become an oracular source for every variation of Balinese mythology, and was known throughout Europe in the 1920s for his extraordinary religious and erotic art.
VHS: S16622. $19.95.
Lorne Blair, USA, 1979, 60 mins.

Leonardo, Michelangelo, Raphael and Titian
Pinnacle of Renaissance artistic achievement. Journey from Florence to the Vatican, Rome and Venice to view masterworks, including Leonardo's Mona Lisa, The Last Supper and Adoration of the Magi; Michelangelo's David and newly restored Sistine Chapel; Giorgione's Tempest; Titian's dramatic portraits and more. Produced by Rizzoli. 56 mins.
VHS: S13253. $39.95.
Laser: LD70790. $99.95.

Leonor Fini
Noted for her surreal fantasy paintings, the Italian-Argentine painter Leonor Fini has a life deeply rooted in her immediate surroundings and in the people and places she treasures. In this program the Belgian film director Chris Vermorcken has created a loving portrait that places what Fini loves side by side with what she paints. The film takes us into Fini's home, where we meet the 19 cats who share her life and who constantly turn up in her paintings. We also view a number of her canvases, which together offer a tribute to the exotic and the erotic. 86 mins.
VHS: S13744. $39.95.

Life of Leonardo da Vinci
A brilliant, massive portrait of Leonardo da Vinci in five parts, produced by Italian State Television and directed by acclaimed Italian filmmaker Renato Castellani. This man who painted the Mona Lisa and the Last Supper, one of the great geniuses of history, comes alive in an exhaustive study of da Vinci and his period. Part I: 1452-1482, covers the first 30 years of da Vinci's life, the circumstances of his birth and childhood, as well as his influences. Part II: 1482-1500, covers da Vinci leaving Florence for Milan to work for Duke Ludovico Sforza, his scientific studies as well as The Last Supper. At age 50, Leonardo returns to his home in Florence. Parts IV & V: 1500-1519. While in Florence, Raphael is introduced to da Vinci, and Leonardo meets and forms a bitter rivalry with Michelangelo. In 1506, he leaves again for Milan. 4½ hours total. 3 cassettes in slipcase.
VHS: S12189. $99.95.

Light of the Gods
This video brings brilliantly to life the world of Homer, Sappho, Herodotus and Sophocles in the engaging story of the evolution of Greek art, narrated by Colleen Dewhurst. The film abounds with examples of Greek representational art, from the stylized stick figures of the Geometric period to the exquisitely carved and painted images of the early classic era, accompanied by quotations from the works of noted thinkers and poets.
VHS: S06712. $29.95.
Suzanne Bauman, USA, 1987, 28 mins.

Living Monuments in Jewish Spain
The Medieval life of Jewish Spain is recreated through illuminated manuscripts from the period. They are a source of amazing information about everyday family life, including the celebration of festivals and clothing styles. 21 mins.
VHS: S23246. $39.95.

Los Angeles Murals
More than 500 murals adorn the walls of Los Angeles, suggesting the vital energy, cultural richness and diversity of the city. This program showcases the city's most talented mural artists and conservators. 11 mins.
VHS: S20356. $39.95.

Louise Nevelson in Process
Nevelson was in her seventies before critics recognized her contribution to sculpture in America. In this documentary, Nevelson creates two new sculptures on camera, providing a rare opportunity to share in the unfolding of her unique process. Produced by WNET. 30 mins.
VHS: S02719. $29.95.

Louvre (Boyer)
NBC-produced documentary about the most famous art museum in the world, France's Louvre. Narrated by Charles Boyer.
VHS: S01712. $24.95.
John Sughrue, USA, 1978, 53 mins.

Louvre 200
A three-part series exploring the evolution of the museum in European culture.
Part 1, A Museum in Time: Louvre 1793-1993. Founded in 1793, the Louvre is the largest museum in the world, holding more than 360,000 works. The program studies the commemoration of the Bicentennial and the openings of the Richelieu wing and the Great Louvre. 60 mins.
VHS: S18847. $29.95.
Part 2, At the Louvre with the Masters. Drawing on the memoirs and published works of Courbet, Degas and Cezanne, this program reveals the extraordinary influence on these 19th century artists in their art and work. The program suggests the multifaceted functions the Louvre served to the leading artists— part school, studio, salon, laboratory and collection of technique and accomplishment. The program also considers the inspiration of Delacroix, Zola, Durantt, Monet, Renoir, Manet and Picasso. 60 mins.
VHS: S18849. $29.95.
Part 3, Selected Places. This program considers the splendor and wonder of the Louvre, highlighted by the old Louvre, the Winged Victory of Samothrace, the Venus de Milo, the Mona Lisa, the great sculpture courts, the installation of Taureax of Khorsabad and the apartments of the Duke de Mornay, among others. 60 mins.
VHS: S18848. $29.95.
Complete Set. Parts 1, 2 and 3.
VHS: S18850. $79.95.

The Louvre
The most famous treasure-house of art in the world. Pause and admire such masterpieces as the "Winged Victory", "Venus de Milo" and of course, the "Mona Lisa". Exquisite works beautifully presented. 55 mins. English narration.
VHS: S05280. $69.95.

The Louvre: Thousands of Masterpieces
Produced under the aegis of the museum's curators, each videodisc volume is stored with multiple images recreated in color and beautiful detail, with an indexed guide book, on screen catalog information, and motion sequences with a French and English soundtrack that walks you through the museum's greatest works.
Louvre Vol. 1: Paintings and Drawings. More than 2,400 works showcasing 18,000 still frames and 29 motion sequences (with narration) covers the Louvre's groundbreaking Western art section, covering the 13th to mid-19th centuries.
Laser: LD70299. $99.95.
Louvre Vol. 2: Sculptures and Objets d'Art. Some 5,000 still frames and 21 narrated motion sequences capture the extraordinary range and beauty of multiple examples of sculpture, furniture, jewelry and other three dimensional works.
Laser: LD70300. $99.95.
Louvre Vol. 3: Antiquities. With 23 narrated motion sequences and 6,000 still frames, this fascinating program considers the 1,200 ornaments, monuments, textiles, vessels and status borne from the civilizations of Greece, Rome and Egypt.
Laser: LD70301. $99.95.

Magic Work-Shop of Reveron
The fantastic life of the Venezuelan painter as revealed in the objects and dolls at his studios. Co-produced with the National Gallery of Venezuela. 23 mins.
English Narration. Roger Wilkison.
VHS: S06796. $60.00.
Spanish Narration. Hector Myerston.
VHS: S06797. $60.00.

Magicians of the Earth
Philip Haas is the acclaimed director of many films, including the recent Angels and Insects. This video collection of four of his documentaries (The Giant Woman & The Lightning War, Young Man's Dream & A Woman's Secret, Seni's Children and Kings of the Water) shows native artists working in traditional forms. The highly original films are scored by David Byrne.
Laser: LD75012. $89.95.
Philip Haas, USA, 1989-1990, 224 mins.

Malagan Art of New Ireland
In the South Pacific of Papua, New Guinea, the New Irelanders honor their ancestors by staging elaborate ceremonies known as malagans. Days of dancing, feasting, singing and speechmaking culminate in the dramatic unveiling of large wooden sculptures, which are hidden in the secret enclosures near the clan's burial grounds. This film documents a contemporary malagan in vivid detail, from the roasting of the pigs to the carving of intricate masks and poles used during this complex cycle of festivities. 28 mins.
VHS: S02631. $39.95.

Manabu Mabe Paints a Picture
This documentary shows the renowned Japanese-Brazilian artist creating an abstract painting in his studio. His phantasmal images of reality are akin to those executed by his ancestors in old Japan with foliage and clouds and glimmerings of water, more suggestive of environment in Brazil. On large canvases he abstracts and combines the legacy of his ancestors with the vibrancy and music of the world he lives in today. Directed by Jose Gomez Sicre. Narrated in English by William D. Clark. 13 mins.
VHS: S06746. $40.00.

Marcel Duchamp: A Game of Chess
A driving force behind many modern movements—Dada, surrealism, futurism and kinetic/conceptual art—Marcel Duchamp did more than any artist in his century to change the concept of art. 56 mins.
VHS: S15295. $29.95.

Marisol
Discussions with Sydney Janis, art dealer, and Dale McConathy, New York University, on Venezuelan artist Marisol's sculptures and the acquisition of "Madonna, Nino, Santa Ana and San Juan." A detailed visual examination of the wood sculpture is enhanced by the process of packing the sculpture for shipment. 13 mins.
VHS: S07455. $39.95.

Mary Cassatt: Impressionist from Philadelphia
The first film to celebrate Mary Cassatt's remarkable career—her years in Paris, her relationship with Degas, the influence of her socially prominent Philadelphia family, told with on-location footage and stills. The best examples of her work reveal the quality, variety and originality of her work. Produced by WNET/Channel Thirteen. 30 minutes.
VHS: S02389. $29.95.

Masaccio: A View of Mankind
Lawrence Gowing's documentary chronicles the life and times of Masaccio and highlights his frescoes at the Santa Maria Novella and the Church of the Camines' Brancacci Chapel in Florence. 40 mins.
VHS: S18761. $39.95.

Masterpieces of British Art
The Yale Center for British art is home to the most comprehensive collection of British art outside Great Britain. Among its outstanding paintings, the collection includes 15 Turners, 21 Gainsboroughs, 7 Reynolds and 44 Constables. This program highlights major works from this collection. Also included is an interview with Paul Mellon, revealing how his marvelous collection was created. 30 mins.
VHS: S13251. $29.95.

Masterpieces of Italian Art: Greek to Gothic
Beginning with the glorious Greek temples in Sicily's Valley of Temples, the camera lovingly reveals Italy's early artistic masterpieces. Includes Greek sculpture, Etruscan tombs, Roman architecture, the Catacombs, early Christian mosaics in Ravenna, Romanesque churches and the great Gothic cathedrals. Produced by Rizzoli. 58 mins.
VHS: S13256. $39.95.
Laser: LD70787. $99.95.

Masterpieces of the Met
A superb introduction to one of the world's finest art institutions, hosted by museum director Philippe de Montebello, as he leads the viewer on this tour of 5,000 years of world civilization. Included are such noted works as Van Gogh's Cypresses, Degas' The Dance Class, Vermeer's Young Woman With a Water Jug, artifacts from the Egyptian tombs, African sculpture, Oriental painted screens, and art objects from around the world. 55 mins.
VHS: S06349. $29.95.
Laser: LD71133. $29.95.

Masters of Illusion
This program studies the artistic and scientific discoveries of the Renaissance period, studying the theories of light, texture and form through the works of Brunelleschi, Michelangelo, Leonardo da Vinci, Botticelli and Raphael, and their relation to evolving technology and visual innovation. 30 mins.
VHS: S15297. $29.95.

Masterworks of Painting
There is a difference between looking at a painting and seeing a painting. What makes a great painting great? This video museum of the world's great paintings is a private course in art appreciation, illuminating the principles of art: color, line, shape, light, composition and design. 51 mins.
VHS: S09471. $198.00.

Matisse Voyages
Traces the development of the artist's brilliantly colored work, from his early canvasses, images of dance and music, and odalisques, to his cut-out pieces and his decorations for the Chapel of the Rosary at Venice. Filmmaker Didier Baussy draws on a wealth of paintings, archival footage, photographs, and extracts from his Notes of a Painter to capture the richness of the artist's legacy and the splendors of his achievements. 58 mins.
VHS: S10267. $39.95.

Max Ernst
This retrospective celebrates the 100th anniversary of the birth of Max Ernst, one of the most influential artists of this century. Revealing what Ernst called "the private brittle places of refuge," this program considers Ernst's involvement with the Surrealist movement, his retreat to Provence, his flight to New York and life in America, and his eventual return to Europe. 90 mins.
VHS: S15994. $39.95.

Max Ernst/Marcel Duchamp
Two documentaries on one tape about two pivotal artists; the first is a 40-minute documentary on the life and work of Max Ernst, the second a 10-minute interview conducted with Marcel Duchamp in the late 1960's.
VHS: S04360. $29.95.

Memories of Monet
This American Film Festival Blue Ribbon Winner blends superb views of Monet's gardens at Giverny with his paintings. Narration from Claire Bloom is drawn from the memoirs of American Impressionist Lilla Cabot Perry who was a student and friend of the French Impressionist master. 29 mins.
VHS: S16202. $39.95.

Metropolitan Museum Boxed Set
This three-part video collection includes Masterpieces of the Met, showcasing some of the Met's many masterpieces; Merchants and Masterpieces, a discussion of the people and the art that shaped the history of the Met; and Cloisters: The Glories of Medieval Art, about The Cloisters, the branch of the Met devoted to religious and Medieval art. Philippe deMontebello, the director of the Met, narrates. USA, 175 mins.
VHS: S24794. $79.95.

Mexican Arts
This program turns to the crafts of Mexico, revealing the unique style of the natives as a reflection of their Indian and Spanish heritage. Spanish narration with no subtitles. 10 mins.
VHS: S16368. $29.95.

Michael Todd: Jazz
Artist Michael Todd's work has a connection to the rhythms and texture of jazz improvisation. This work studies his art, and the technique and motivation his working methods comprise. 6 mins.
VHS: S20357. $39.95.

Michelangelo: Self Portrait
A two-disc set that contains two feature length works about the art and life of Michelangelo, including The Titan, Richard Lyford's 1950 documentary narrated by Fredric March, that won an Academy Award. On the second soundtrack are two hours of readings from Michelangelo's memoirs and diaries that establishes a social, personal and artistic context within the larger Renaissance period.
Laser: LD70305. $99.95.

Miro: Theatre of Dreams
Profiles one of the major figures of 20th century art, the only surrealist whose work survived in the face of new trends. Miro is shown here at the age of 85, working in his studio and embarking on an entirely new venture: an original theatrical production. Produced by the BBC. 60 minutes.
VHS: S02395. $39.95.
Laser: LD70784. $75.00.

Mirtala
This three-part series offers an unparalleled look into the creative process and artistic accomplishments of the sculptor Mirtala.
Mandalas: Visions of Heaven and Earth. Mirtala's work blends images of circular sculptures with cosmic sounds of Michael Stern's "Planetary Unfolding," conjuring up origins and roots. "Mirtala's bronzes have the magical quality of uniting reality and illusion; she adds poetry to the human condition and forges it into sculpture" (Boston Herald). 22 mins.
VHS: S20313. $39.95.
Poetry in Bronze. This video offers an interview with Mirtala. Her amazing sculptures offer an appreciative audience a path to the self through contemplation of beauty. Introduction by Paul Nagano. 30 mins.
VHS: S24855. $39.95.
The Human Journey. In a series of sculptures by Mirtala, the artist examines freedom and individuality. Beautifully photographed in their natural settings, the sculptures highlight the poetic intensity of Mirtala's work. 25 mins.
VHS: S20314. $39.95.
Mirtala, Complete Set.
VHS: S24856. $110.00.

Mobile: By Alexander Calder

The first work placed in the National Gallery's East Building was the last major work by Alexander Calder, the man who forged an art through mobiles. This is a behind-the-scenes introduction to the architect, engineer and museum officials who met the challenge of building this complex piece. 25 mins.
VHS: S16203. $29.95.

Moire

A look at the kinetic art works of Venezuelan artist Jose Maria Cruxent, who has played a decisive part in the trend in South America. Directed by Angel Hurtado, 8 mins.
English Narration. William D. Clark.
VHS: S06765. $25.00.
Spanish Narration. Amelia Bruce.
VHS: S06766. $25.00.

Mondrian

This program considers the work of Piet Mondrian (1872-1944), whose work was characterized by his search for spiritual enlightenment, order and structure. His paintings of straight perpendicular lines and basic colors represent some of the highest and most mature peaks of abstract art. 30 mins.
VHS: S17225. $29.95.

Mondrian: From Naturalism to Abstraction

Made in collaboration with leading galleries, this impressionistic documentary on the life and formal influences of Dutch painter Piet Mondrian examines his evolution from naturalism to abstraction. 52 mins.
VHS: S19585. $29.95.

Monet Legacy of Light

Monet devoted his life to capturing nature's kaleidoscope of color and light on canvas. Letters, journals, interviews and the painter's own timeless images are used to tell his story. 27 mins.
VHS: S24274. $29.95.

Money Man

Philip Haas' film about J.S.G. Boggs, a gifted artist whose elaborate reproductions of United States currency blur the distinction between the artist and the counterfeiter. Arrested by the Bank of England and jailed in Australia, Boggs goes to Washington where his "art" is confiscated, in the process subverting "icons" and material in a bold, exciting way.
VHS: S19639. $39.95.
Philip Haas, USA, 1992, 60 mins.

Monroe Wheeler and MOMA

For 35 years, Monroe Wheeler was a close advisor to the directors of the Museum of Modern Art; this unique documentary captures Wheeler at the age of 86, talking about the formative years and his close associations with some of the world's most famous artists and writers, including Matisse, Calder, Pavel Tchelitchew, Somerset Maugham and Katherine Anne Porter. Personal photos and art illuminate his stories. 30 mins.
VHS: S07541. $29.95.

Monsieur Rene Magritte

Magritte said it was the subject, rather than artistic technique, which creates a beautiful painting. This presentation takes us to the places that fired Magritte's imagination. Winner of the Paris International Art Film Festival. 60 minutes.
VHS: S02394. $39.95.

Moscow Treasures and Traditions

More than 200 national treasures were part of a unique exhibit that traveled to the U.S. Icons, paintings, engravings, precious metal work, porcelains, costumes and armor were included to show the range and depth of Russian/Soviet traditions. This video also shows how the exhibit was formed by curators in both the US and Russia. 48 mins.
VHS: S24863. $24.95.

Mountain in the Mind

Hong Kong artist Wucius Wong explains the traditional Chinese approach to landscape painting: the need to create both the essence of nature and the emotion of the artist contemplating it. Follow Wong closely as he visits Minnesota landmark Minnehaha Falls, and then paints it from memory in his studio. 28 mins.
VHS: S15762. $39.95.

Mr. Five Percent: Calouste Gulbenkian

Shrewd Armenian businessman Calouste Gulbenkian collected art from all over world. He amassed the largest private collection attributable to one person in this century. Rare antiquities, jewelry, sculpture and paintings by such masters as Rembrandt, Rubens, Degas and Monet are seen in this documentary, against the backdrop of his favorite cities, including Istanbul, Paris and Venice. 59 mins.
VHS: S20855. $39.95.

Musee d'Orsay

The world's most extensive collection of impressionist and post-impressionist art is on display in this program, featuring the masterpieces of Monet, Degas, Gauguin, Renoir and Whistler. The second side has 11,000 images culled for 2,100 of the museum's finest works. With French and English dialog.
Laser: LD70304. $199.95.

The Museum of Modern Art of Latin America

A guided tour of this unique museum specializing in the collection of contemporary Latin American art with the founder and first director of the Museum, Sr. Jose Gomez Sicre. Gomez Sicre points out the important works by Latin American artists and explains the part each of those artists played in the development of art in their own countries. Directed by Julio Delgado, with narration in English by Renee Channey. 14 mins.
VHS: S06800. $40.00.

Museum Without Walls Series

This series of eight tapes has been called "a splendid art course for art majors or just those who would like an introduction to the great world of art." Color.
Crete and Mycenae. Over a hundred years ago, archeologist Heinrich Schliemann unearthed the massive and fabled Lion Gate, leading him to pronounce that he had found the graves of Agammemnon and his companion. His discovery helped add another piece to the most fascinating and mysterious archeological puzzle, Crete. This documentary, filmed on Crete and at Mycenae, unveils the findings of Schliemann and those who went before and after him. Hans Horsfeld, 1970, 54 mins.
VHS: S02281. $24.95.
Cubist Epoch. Based on an exhibition originally shown at the L.A. County Museum of Art and the Metropolitan Museum, this video studies the works of Picasso, Braque, Gris, Leger, Gleized, Villon, Delaunay and their followers. Bruce Seth Green, 1971, 53 mins.
VHS: S02276. $24.95.
Germany-Dada. Filmed with the cooperation of original Dadaists Hans Richter and Richard Hauelsenbeck, this unique video collage of art, music and poetry is an alphabet of German Dadaism, and also a true Dadaist experience in itself. Helmut Herbst, 1968, 55 mins.
VHS: S02634. $24.95.
Giotto and the Pre-Renaissance. Described as a truly artistic experience, this documentary records each of the major cycles of Giotto's frescoes. Included are his masterpieces at the Upper and Lower Church of San Francesco, Assissi, the Arena Chapel in Padua, and St. Croce in Florence. Lionella Torossi, 1969, 47 mins.
VHS: S02277. $24.95.
Goya. Perhaps no other artist in Spanish history so brilliantly documented the time in which he lived, and this documentary captures Goya's most prominent works: the etchings, war scenes, bullfight sequences, tapestries, and portraits of royalty and friends. Jesus Santos, 1971, 54 mins.
VHS: S02278. $24.95.
Le Corbusier. Explores the revolutionary ideas of author, abstract artist, prophet and teacher Le Corbusier, as it travels through architecture and urban renewal, and conducts an in-depth tour of his most important buildings, from the hills of France to the Himalayas. Filmed by one of Le Corbusier's own collaborators, Carlos Vilardebo. Carlos Vilardebo, 1970, 46 mins.
VHS: S02282. $24.95.
Picasso: War, Peace and Love. A sensitive and moving tribute to the single most influential figure in the history of 20th century art, Pablo Picasso. The cassette documents Picasso's major works, as well as many previously unknown and unfamiliar pieces, as it travels through museums, galleries and private collections, including a tour of his studio near Cannes. Lucien Clergue, 1970, 51 mins.
VHS: S02275. $24.95.
The Greek Temple. A fascinating journey through the remains of a sacred city that has stood for over 2,000 years in the forbidding regions of southern Italy. The video also travels through the remains of Acropolis, Delphi, Agrigento and Sounion, as it traces the evolution of temples in Magna Grecia through the Doric, Ionic and Corinthian styles and includes models and animated reconstructions of some of the most magnificent of the ancient shrines. Hans Horsfeld, 1969, 54 mins.
VHS: S02280. $24.95.

National Gallery of Art

One of the best art videos, this extensive tour through Washington's National Gallery features a history told by its director, J. Carter Brown, with an examination of the 1,645 important art works held by the gallery, annotated by both Brown and the curators.
VHS: S05638. $39.95.
Laser: LD70778. $98.00.

Native American Indian Artist Series

A profile of seven contemporary artists representing diverse backgrounds and styles. Available individually, or order the complete set of six tapes at a savings.
Charles Loloma. The world famous Hopi jeweler displays some of his most stunning work, and discusses his heritage. His interests, inside and outside the reservation, are revealed in his art, which uses only materials indigenous to his homeland: iron, wood, ivory, coal, turquoise, lapis lazuli and shell. 29 mins.
VHS: S15755. $49.95.
Fritz Scholder. Fritz Scholder, a California Mission Indian, creates prints and paintings that depict today's Indian caught between ancient tradition and modern society. 29 mins.
VHS: S15756. $49.95.
Helen Hardin. Helen Hardin attempts to integrate two parts of herself, the Indian and the artist, painting sophisticated and colorful geometric patterns and traditional motifs of dancers, deer, the sun and seasons. 29 mins.
VHS: S15757. $49.95.
Medicine Flower and Lonewolf. Two potters from Santa Clara Pueblo in New Mexico have revived and extended the traditional forms and techniques of their pre-Columbian ancestors. 29 mins.
VHS: S15758. $49.95.
R.C. Gorman. R.C. Gorman, a Navajo painter and printmaker, is shown in his Taos, New Mexico studio working on one of a suite of paintings dedicated to the Navajo woman. 29 mins.
VHS: S15759. $49.95.
Allan Houser. A Chiricahua-Apache, Allan Hauser creates stone, wood and bronze homages to the American Indian. As he works, Hauser talks of his personal life and beliefs, and explains how his heritage has contributed to his art. 29 mins.
VHS: S15760. $49.95.
Complete set. 6 tapes.
VHS: S15754. $250.00.

Native Grace: Prints of the New World 1590-1876

After Europeans discovered the New World, a long period of exploration followed. Accompanying these explorers were gifted artists—men like DeBry, Catesby, Audubon, Catlin, Bodmer and Moran, who recorded the grandeur they saw in drawings and paintings. Featured in this unique video is the artistic genius of Audubon's birds and mammals, DeBry's depictions of the Indians of the Southeast, Catesby's 18th century color prints of American plants and wildlife. 31 mins.
VHS: S08136. $29.95.

The Nature of the Artist: Homer Winslow

Hosted by art critic and historian John Wilmerding, this program considers the evolution of Winslow's art, from his Civil War illustrations to the primal, beautiful images of nature appearing throughout his work. 29 mins.
VHS: S15299. $29.95.

Neoclassicism, Romanticism, Realism

Developed by Dr. Gale Murray. Covers first the period of 1750-1850, revealing the Romantics' interest in nature, picturesque, violent, sublime, through the works of David, Delacroix and others. Realism shows the dominance of the movement in 1850 through the works of Courbet, Daumier, Corot and others. 44 mins.
VHS: S07655. $59.95.

New Ways of Seeing: Picasso, Braque and the Cubist Revolution

This program chronicles the landmark exhibition at New York's Museum of Modern Art, hailed by The New York Times as "the greatest exhibition ever devoted to a single phase of 20th century art." Filmed on location at the museum, the program presents a provocative view of Cubism and the extraordinary artistic collaboration of Picasso and Braque. 66 mins.
VHS: S11754. $29.95.
Laser: LD70119. $49.95.

New World Visions: American Art and the Metropolitan Museum

A two-part series that interweaves painting, sculpture, decorative arts and architecture in an exploration of uniquely American art forms. Using the collections of the Museum as a starting point, the programs were shot on location in New York, Pennsylvania, Washington D.C. and New England. A co-production of WNET and the BBC. 58 minutes each.
Part 1: Covers the years 1650-1820.
VHS: S01797. $39.95.
Part 2: Covers the years 1820-1914.
VHS: S01803. $39.95.

Nine Artists of Puerto Rico

A visit to the studios of Puerto Rico's most prominent artists, with actor Jose Ferrer as narrator. This film discusses the artists of his native land who developed in the 1970's: Lorenzo Homar, Julio Rosado del Valle, Olga Albizu, Rafael Villamil, Rafael Ferrer, Julio Micheli, Luis Hernandez Cruz, Edgardo Franceschi and Jose Alicea. Directed by Jose Gomez Sicre, 16 mins.
English Narration.
VHS: S06762. $40.00.
Spanish Narration.
VHS: S06763. $40.00.

Norman Rockwell's World... An American Dream

This Academy Award-winning video details the artistic life of one of America's best loved illustrators. Using the artwork and the commentary of Rockwell himself in combination with old film footage and staged reenactments, the Saturday Evening Post covers once again come alive.
VHS: S03396. $24.95.
Laser: LD70120. $24.95.
Robert Deubel, USA, 1972, 30 mins.

Nudes in Limbo

A documentary that closely observes the employment of the unclothed human form in abstract and artistic dimensions and settings. Both the male and the female body will be presented in this color compilation distributed by the MCA corporation. 1983, 53 mins.
VHS: S06160. $29.95.

NY/New Wave at P.S. 1

This episode from the long running video magazine views the art show that broke Robert Mapplethorpe. New Wave is a look at the seminal art show which marked the convergence of art and music in the late 1970's. Curator Diego Cortez is also featured in a rare interview.
VHS: S22619. $34.95.
Art/New York, USA, 1984, 30 mins.

Of Myths and Men

A lecture on portrait painting as seen through presidential portraits in early America at the Smithsonian's National Portrait Gallery in Washington. 28 mins.
VHS: S02637. $39.95.

On the Rocks

The famed cave paintings of Lascaux and Altamira, in Southwestern Europe, are the focus of this documentary. Douglas Mazonowicz examines the artistic ability of prehistoric man using his expert knowledge on the subject. 25 mins.
VHS: S22109. $119.00.

Other World of Winston Churchill

As a result of early defeats on the political scene, Winston Churchill undertook a voyage of exploration into painting, stating, "And then it was that the muse of painting came to my rescue." This video portrait of Churchill's "second career" as a painter is told in his own words, and through anecdotes by Paul Maze (his painting instructor), Field Marshall Lord Montgomery, Merle Oberon and others. 54 mins.
VHS: S12763. $29.95.

Otto Dix: The Painter Is the Eyes of the World

The first comprehensive study of German artist Otto Dix looks at the life and works of the much maligned artist who was blacklisted by the Nazis for his paintings depicting the horrors of war. 58 mins.
VHS: S15293. $29.95.

Pablita Velarde: An Artist and Her People

Pablita Velarde is a Native American artist who paints the history of her ancient people. Found materials and other materials supply her pigments. Her work ensures future generations will know the vital traditions and legends of her tribe. 20 mins.
VHS: S26805. $49.95.

Painters Painting

Warhol, Rauschenberg, Johns and other American key painters are the subject of De Antonio's documentary which captures the visceral personalities at work.
VHS: S00988. $29.98.
Emile de Antonio, USA, 1972, 116 mins.

Painting That Fools the Eye: Trompe L'Oeil

Trompe l'oeil means—literally—fools the eye. This award-winning program examines how artists create this extraordinary artistic illustration, the set of rules which allow the artists to open up the creative imagination and provide leaps of fantasy within a limited format. 32 mins.
VHS: S09474. $174.00.

Paolo Veronese: Between Art and Inquisition

This film finds the right historical context for Paolo Veronese, his "irreverent" paintings during the Inquisition, and largely religious pieces intended to celebrate Venetian culture and society, the centerpiece of European life. The film examines Veronese's influence on such diverse artists as Eugene Delacroix and Hermann Hesse.
VHS: S18760. $39.95.
Renate Liebenwein, Great Britain, 60 mins.

Paul Cadmus: Enfant Terrible at 80

Cadmus created scandal and controversy in the 30s and 40s with his brash, satirical paintings. In this award-winning production, he recalls those days as he performs on camera the two tasks for which he is best known: drawing the male nude, and painting in the ancient medium of egg yolk tempera. Directed by David Sutherland. 64 minutes.
VHS: S02396. $39.95.

Paul Cezanne: The Man and His Mountain

Focuses on Cezanne's use of a single image—the Mont St. Victoire in Cezanne's native Provence—to define form, color and light. Richly illustrated with his paintings and views of the countryside, the film opens with the artist at the age of 67, at odds with both his peers and critics, and traces Cezanne's career to his final recognition as the father of modern painting. 60 minutes.
VHS: S02388. $39.95.
Laser: LD70781. $75.00.

Paul Gauguin: The Savage Dream

This National Gallery of Art co-production explores the artist's obsessive search for a "savage" alternative to his own culture, which drove him to that far point of the earth and became a critical aspect of Gauguin's art and life. Shot on location in Tahiti and the Marquesas, the film focuses on Gauguin's final years and his monumental artistic achievement during this period. The story is told, to a great extent, in Gauguin's own words. 45 mins.
VHS: S07605. $39.95.

Peru Virreinal

Colonial art from the private collection of Barboza Stern. Exhibited at the Art Museum of the Americas in 1989. Spanish, 20 mins.
VHS: S15288. $50.00.

Picasso

For many, the paintings and sculptures of Pablo Picasso represent the crowning achievements of 20th century art. Over 1,500 works are presented here, creating an unmatched resource that documents the range and creativity of this monumental figure. The work is divided into 57 chapters, each beginning with a biographical sequence on Picasso. Featuring essays by Helene Seckel, Brigitte Leal and Marie-Laure Bernadae, curators at Paris's Musee Picasso. 1992, 30 mins.
Laser: CAV. LD75514. $124.95.

Picasso (Musee Picasso)

Centered around the recent opening of Musee Picasso in Paris, Picasso takes the opportunity to examine the collection created by Picasso, the work he felt would be his personal legacy to the world. The spirit of the artist is echoed in the dramatic theater of corrida, the ring of the bullfight, and the images of regional Spain.
VHS: S08478. $39.95.

Picasso: The Man and His Work

A major, two-part survey of the work of the legendary 20th century artist, which explores more than 600 of his works, many of which have never been seen in public. Director Edward Quinn captures Picasso at work and at play, during the last 22 years of his life. On two cassettes (90 minutes total).
VHS: S02757. $69.95.
Laser: LD72213. $145.00.

Pierre Bonnard

This program explores Bonnard's style through a look at his paintings gathered for a major retrospective at the Paris Centre Pompidou. 55 minutes.
VHS: S02390. $39.95.

Pierre Bonnard and the Impressionist Vision

Using such world class paintings in the collection of the Minneapolis Museum of Art as Bonnard's Dining Room in the Country, Vuillard's Place St. Augustin and Pissarro's Place du Theatre Francais, this program explores Bonnard's relationship with his contemporaries and his desire to depict the poetry of life in his art. 12 mins.
VHS: S04377. $49.95.

Points of Convergence

An extensive panorama of pre-Columbian cultures of Costa Rica: the Choroctega, the Huetar and the Brunca. Also included in this film is the beautiful gold collection of pre-Columbian works from the Central Bank of Costa Rica. Through the pottery, gold work and other artifacts shown in this film, one develops an appreciation for the rich imagination and expressive power of all three cultures. Directed by Angel Hurtado. Narration by John Gavin.
English Narration.
VHS: S06770. $40.00.
Spanish Narration.
VHS: S06771. $40.00.

Poleo and Poetic Figuration

A documentary about the life and work of the world-renowned Venezuelan painter Hector Poleo, who lives in Paris and New York today, but has never escaped the strong attachment for the old Caracas of his childhood. Poleo is considered one of the precursors of the Neo-Realist school of New York. This prolific artist's style is, as he describes it, "a mixture of fusion of abstraction and elements of the dream world…" "The artistic development of Hector Poleo reflects the four attitudes which, in turn, he has assumed toward life: the people-oriented man, the skeptic, the pessimist, and the poet which is so beautifully brought out in this short film. Directed by Angel Hurtado, 28 mins.
English Narration. Roger Wilkison.
VHS: S06781. $80.00.
Spanish Narration. Andres Morales and Hector Myerston.
VHS: S06782. $80.00.

The Popes and Their Art: The Vatican Collection

A work that shows the breadth and historical value of the art hanging within the splendor and spectacle of the Vatican. This program looks at the important works of Michelangelo, da Vinci and Raphael. Narrated by James Mason. 60 mins.
VHS: S19236. $24.95.

Portrait of Civilization

Host Edwin M. Adams relates the history of frescoes beginning with ancient Minoan culture, and draws a line to the High Museum of Art in Atlanta and the Church of the Frescoes in North Carolina, where artist Jeff Mims creates a new fresco step-by-step. An informative study of a unique art form which suggests that the frescoes of today will offer future civilizations a continuing portrait "as long as the wall shall stand." 30 mins.
VHS: S15749. $29.95.

Pre-Real Estate

A document of New York artists setting up the insurgent art exhibition that engendered New York's ABC No Rio.
VHS: S10197. $29.95.
Mitch Corber, USA, 1979/80, 28 mins.

Profile of an Artist: Moriziu Gottlieb

Dead at 23, this artist managed to attain a career summed up in the phrase, "the Jewish Rembrandt". Through a vivid and detailed examination of his work, the life of this artist and his world of 19th-century Eastern Europe is brought to life. 40 mins.
VHS: S23254. $29.95.

Protest Art

A freewheeling documentary on militant guerilla poster artist Robbie Conal, a professional painter whose hilarious political caricatures are found in major cities. The action alternates between grainy, coal black streets and well-lit galleries in San Francisco and New York, as the film dissects Conal's efforts to hammer home political truths and make vital the connection between image, representation and reality. 56 mins.
VHS: S20337. $39.95.

Public Sculpture: America's Legacy

Sculptures are presented and then the audience is taken on a tour to see and understand how each work functions in a public place. In this way both the nature of the work and its role in history is carefully elucidated. 29 mins.
VHS: S24868. $85.00.

Puerto Rican Painting: Between Past and Present

A review of an exhibition of Puerto Rican art, sponsored by the Squibb Corporation. Interviews with the curators and the artists. In English.
VHS: S08311. $40.00.

Raoul Dufy: Painter and Decorator

Perhaps best-known for his colorful paintings of people at play, Dufy was also one of the most adventurous artists of the 20th century, as evidenced by his variety of ceramics, wall hangings, furniture, and fabric designs. Interviews with friends and colleagues, along with close-up views of his work, reveal why many consider Dufy to be one of this century's most influential designers and an innovative painter who ranks alongside Matisse and Leger. 58 mins.
VHS: S10265. $39.95.

Raphael

This biography of Renaissance artist Raphael examines his breakthrough works in Urbino, Perugia and Florence within the context of his late period at the Vatican. 60 mins.
VHS: S20186. $39.95.

Raphael Series

For four centuries "The Divine Raphael" (1483-1520) was unquestioned as the greatest of all painters, and he is undeniably still the artist of the most far-reaching influence. This three-part series presents a challenge to re-appraise his work. David Thomson, former art critic of the London Times, wrote and narrates these three films, which were shot on location in Urbino, Perugia, Florence and Rome—places where Raphael lived and worked. 58 minutes each.
Raphael: Legend and Legacy.
VHS: S02377. $39.95.
Raphael: The Apprentice Years.
VHS: S02375. $39.95.
Raphael: The Prince of Painters.
VHS: S02376. $39.95.

The Real Estate Show

In this archival video footage artists set up the insurgent art exhibition that spawned ABC No Rio.
VHS: S22661. $29.95.
Mitch Corber, USA, 1979-1980, 28 mins.

Reality and Hallucinations

A look at the life and work of the master draftsman and printmaker, Mexican artist Jose Luis Cuevas. Cuevas begins and completes a drawing in the film and needs no model, as he dispenses with reality and relies on imagination, on remembrances of people and things past. Little by little a form takes shape, comes to life before our eyes. Filmed on location in the artist's studio in Mexico and Paris, during the early career of the artist, this film was awarded the prestigious National Prize of Fine Arts of Mexico in 1981. Directed by Angel Hurtado. Narration by Jose Ferrer. 23 mins.
English Narration.
VHS: S06786. $60.00.
Spanish Narration.
VHS: S06787. $60.00.

Rebellion of the Santos

The carved wooden images of saints made in Puerto Rico during the 18th and 19th centuries. The texts are extracted from the book of the same title by Marta Traba. Filmed on location in the museum of Santos, San Juan. 15 mins.
English Narration. Renee Channey.
VHS: S06810. $45.00.
Spanish Narration.
VHS: S06811. $45.00.

Red Grooms Talks about Dali Salad

In his work Dali Salad, Red Grooms used paper, vinyl, aluminum, wood, steel, plastic and even ping pong balls to create a lively and humorous portrait of Salvador Dali. This behind-the-scenes look at the production process shows Grooms' three-dimensional print as it was made. 4 mins.
VHS: S03311. $29.95.

Red Is Green: Jud Fine

The work of Southern California artist Jud Fine documents social drift and the inability of people to communicate. This video looks at the style, textures and thematic preoccupations of his art. 11 mins.
VHS: S20355. $39.95.

Rediscovering a Forgotten Legacy

Traces the fascinating history of a rare collection of plaster casts that originally graced the halls of Metropolitan Museum of Art until 1938. Rediscovered in 1975 by the Queens Museum, the plaster casts were stored in a warehouse under a viaduct in New York; their discovery and restoration is shown in detail. 9 mins.
VHS: S07510. $39.95.

Rembrandt

A two-part documentary on Rembrandt van Rijn covers the 40-year period between his first and last self-portraits. The second part considers the elaborate, painstaking restoration of Rembrandt's masterpiece, "The Night Watch," which was nearly destroyed by vandals in 1975. 56 mins.
VHS: S17310. $29.95.

Rembrandt and Velazquez: Two Faces of the Seventeenth Century

The film takes an in-depth look at two masterpieces from the Metropolitan Museum of Art: Rembrandt's 1660 Self Portrait, and the 1650 Portrait of Juan de Pareja by Velazquez. The Rembrandt work is viewed in context of many other Rembrandt self-portraits, while the Velazquez painting is viewed by itself. Produced by the Metropolitan Museum of Art. 28 minutes.
VHS: S02380. $29.95.

Rembrandt—1669

The final years of the artist's life and varied career, detailing the tension between his egotistical, self-centered celebrity and the contemplation, insight and emotional refinement of his art. An investigation of a man's art and life, the movie reveals the fascinating process and discoveries Rembrandt's art was heir to. "A fascinating life, a near perfect union of form and content" (Variety). With Frans Stelling, Tom de Koff and Aye Fil. Dutch with English subtitles.
VHS: S17766. $39.95.
Jos Stelling, The Netherlands, 1977, 114 mins.

Remington & AVA: American Art

Frederic Remington immortalized the wild west in his paintings and sculptures, capturing for all time the intimate drama of the unbridled American spirit. The spirit of Remington lives on in the contemporary frontiers of American art, here paired on video with AVA, the prestigious Awards in the Visual Arts, narrated by Arthur Godfrey.
VHS: S03969. $69.95.
Laser: LD70116. $39.95.

Return to Glory: Michelangelo Revealed

Hailed as the most significant art event of the century, this is a unique film record of the first phase of the 12-year endeavor to restore Michelangelo's masterpiece, The Sistine Chapel. Superbly produced by Nippon Television, this video is an elegant and accurate account of the remarkable events that have lead to a radical reassessment of Michelangelo—both the artist, and the man. 52 mins.
VHS: S04354. $29.95.

The Roar of the Gods

A fascinating panoramic view of the pre-Hispanic culture found in San Augustin, Colombia. Stray finds of pottery from this area date back in time to the early centuries of the first millennium B.C. Monoliths found here are as tall as four meters—with carvings unique to the area. Directed by Angel Hurtado. 20 mins.
English Narration. Douglas Fairbanks, Jr.
VHS: S06779. $60.00.
Spanish Narration. Gloria Valencia.
VHS: S06780. $60.00.

Robert Colescott: The One-Two Punch

This tape is a motivational video dealing with stereotypes from artist Robert Colescott. His work and philosophy are also explored. 28 mins.
VHS: S21455. $49.95.

Robert Motherwell and the New York School: Storming the Citadel

An investigation of Abstract Expressionism, centered on one of its most important figures, Robert Motherwell (1915-1991). The program considers artists who comprised the movement (Pollock, de Kooning, Mark Rothko, Franz Kline), and the social and political context that deeply influenced their work. 56 mins.
VHS: S17729. $39.95.

Robert Parker

The sculptor, one of the pre-eminent members of the Rivington School, at his forge and on the street scavenging metal. Produced for Japanese Television. 1987, 20 mins.
VHS: S10201. $24.95.

Robert Vickrey: Lyrical Realist

Described as "the world's most proficient artist in egg tempera," Robert Vickrey is observed during the creation of his magic realist paintings. Filmed on location at his studio on Cape Cod and favorite spots in Manhattan, the viewer discovers an enchanted realm of children, nuns and office workers wandering through the labyrinths of contemporary civilization. Cine Golden Eagle. 30 mins.
VHS: S06557. $39.95.

Rodrigue: Acadian Artist

This documentary profiles a well-known Cajun artist. 25 mins.
VHS: S22392. $59.95.

Roland Reiss

Artist Roland Reiss works within extreme forms, from miniatures to large-scale pieces, that are attuned to different emotional and analytical ideas. This program examines his art and ideas, studies his feelings, motivations and thematic concerns. 8 mins.
VHS: S20358. $39.95.

Romanesque Art

This program follows the development of a unique iconography synthesizing the elements found in Roman, Byzantine, Spanish and Islamic as well as Nordic design. 28 mins.
VHS: S09476. $174.00.

Romare Bearden and Charles White: Griots of Imagery

This intriguing documentary explores the work of these famous African-American artists. From paper, canvas and board they managed to create art that reflected the culture and consciousness of black people in America. 27 mins.
VHS: S22932. $99.95.

Ron English

A self-portrait emerges from interviews and paintings by the outlaw neo-pop artist Ron English. His work and promotional gimmicks exude a homespun populist conviction and shameless hucksterism. His upbeat theme song says it all: "I'm going to make it in the 90's."
VHS: S22626. $14.95.
Ron English, USA, 1992, 30 mins.

Rosamond Bernier: The Metropolitan Museum of Art Lecture Series

This collection of lectures brings Bernier's astounding learning and her unique insights to video. Whether discussing modern masters or royal patrons, her lectures offer a fascinating glimpse into the wonder of art.
Taste at the Top: Francois I/Charles I.
VHS: S25642. $19.95.
Taste at the Top: Christina of Sweden/Catherine the Great.
VHS: S25643. $19.95.
The French Impressionists: The Cast of Characters.
VHS: S25645. $19.95.
The French Impressionists: Modern Art and Modern Manners.
VHS: S25645. $19.95.
The French Impressionists: Paris by Day and by Night.
VHS: S25646. $19.95.
The French Impressionists: An Accessible Paradise.
VHS: S25647. $19.95.
The Modern Masters: The Matisse I Knew/The Matisse Nobody Knew.
VHS: S25639. $19.95.
The Modern Masters: The Picasso I Knew/The Picasso Nobody Knew.
VHS: S25640. $19.95.
The Modern Masters: The Miro I Knew.
VHS: S25641. $19.95.

The Rotund World of Botero

This video is both a tribute and an expose of the famed artist. He tells of his early life in Colombia and his growing international fame. There are also segments that show him at work on a fresco and a sculpture, and most importantly, we see him at work in his home just outside Bogota. 56 mins.
VHS: S24364. $29.95.

Roy Lichtenstein

A rare interview with the influential American artist Roy Lichtenstein, one of Pop Art's pioneers. Lichtenstein talks in an interview about his current work, the Pop explosion and the history of Western Art. 55 min.
VHS: S18391. $39.95.

Running Fence

The film depicts the long struggle by Christo to build a 24-mile fence of white fabric over the hills of California disappearing into the Pacific, at a cost of $3 million. After what seemed to be an insurmountable struggle between the artist and the state bureaucracy, the fence, finally unfurled, brings the community together in celebration of its beauty.
VHS: S07493. $49.95.
Maysles Brothers, USA, 1978, 58 mins.

Saint Gaudens: Masque of the Golden Bowl

A lush dramatization of the life and work of Augustus Saint Gaudens, pre-eminent sculptor of the American Renaissance, as seen and recorded in his own words and those of his contemporaries. Shot on Location in Boston, New York and New Hampshire. Produced in association with the Metropolitan Museum of Art. 60 mins.
VHS: S03398. $39.95.

Santa Fe: Artists of New Mexico

Native American artists along with other artists are featured on this video. R.C. Gorman, Allan Houser, Jacqueline Shutiva, Marie Romero, Jemez Pueblo, Bunny Tobias, Charles Greeley, Fred Prescott, Paul Lutonsky and David Dear Silversmith are included. 46 mins.
VHS: S26803. $49.95.

The Secret of Life and Death: Allan Ruppersberg

Ruppersberg's work involves research in the everyday world and the recognition of something authentic, something telling, in the midst of a tidal wave of visual information. In this portrait, the artist leads us on an unusual tour of his exhibition at the Museum of Contemporary Art, in Los Angeles. 29 mins.
VHS: S14583. $39.95.

Secret World of Erotic Art

Enter the world of erotic images created by world-renowned artists but rarely seen in museums or art history classes; erotica by Manet, Calder, Toulouse-Lautrec and many others are included in this video. 51 mins.
VHS: S09973. $59.95.

Seurat: Point Counterpoint

Defines the life and work of Georges Seurat, one of the most influential artists of the Post-Impressionist generation. Highlighted by conversations with artists Henry Moore and Bridget Riley, the program provides a close look at the creator of the pointillist technique. Produced by the BBC. 75 minutes.
VHS: S02387. $49.95.

Shalom of Safed

Shalom lived in Galilee as a watchmaker until his 58th year, when he began to paint. This video explores the vision of Shalom's acclaimed folk art and the spiritual and physical sources that inspired his work. 30 mins.
VHS: S23255. $29.95.

The Shock of Futurism

Italian Futurism was at the forefront of 20th century avant-garde impulses and helped form the basis of modern art. This program concerns the works of Boccioni, Balla, Carra and Severini, and relates how their visions and ideas shaped cubism, Dada and Pop art. 23 mins.
VHS: S17224. $29.95.

Siena: Chronicles of a Medieval Commune

Siena's reputation for a thriving merchant community, as an environment for artists and craftsmen, and for its saints, established the city as one of the major centers of Medieval and Renaissance culture. This film, based on contemporary sources and shot in Tuscany, focuses on the civic and religious institutions of Siena, and captures Sienese life and society during its golden age. 27 mins.
VHS: S08479. $29.95.

Similar Differences: Betye and Alison Saar

Mother and daughter artists, Betye and Alison Saar's work encompasses multi-cultural, racial, generational and religious symbols, elements and concerns. This video offers a glimpse into the similarities and differences of these two unique individuals. 10 mins.
VHS: S14584. $49.95.

The Singing Sculpture

Philip Haas' film was made in honor of the 20-year history of British cabaret performers Gilbert and George's astonishing show, The Singing Sculpture. The comics' crazed, inspired performance carries a manic intensity. 20 mins.
VHS: S19640. $39.95.
Philip Haas, USA, 1991, 20 mins.

Smithsonian World: The Wyeths: A Father and His Family

Both a portrait of the Wyeth family and a tribute to the family's patriarch, N.C. Wyeth, this video shows the unique and troubled relations that bind this creative clan. Home movies and interviews with the various family members, including Andrew, a respected painter in his own right, make this an exhaustive and intimate look at a talented family. 58 mins.
VHS: S27376. $19.98.

Soldner: Thrown and Altered Clay

A new work by the talented avant-garde ceramist Paul Soldner, who revolutionized American-style raku and changed the shape of contemporary ceramics. More than 50 examples of his work are on view in the video. 37 mins.
VHS: S18006. $39.95.

Soto, A New Vision of the Art

A retrospective view of the Venezuelan kinetic artist, Jesus Soto, who is considered one of the major forerunners of the universal kinetic movement. Since his days as a student in Paris, Soto has continued to experiment with the temporal and movement relationships which involve the viewer as an active agent and participant in his work. This film was awarded Cine's Golden Eagle Award. Directed by Angel Hurtado. Narration by Herbert Morales. 45 mins.
English Narration.
VHS: S06772. $120.00.
Spanish Narration.
VHS: S06773. $120.00.

South Americans in Cordoba

A documentary about the Cordoba Biennial in Argentina, a major exhibition of painting and sculpture from South America. Narrated in Spanish by Luis Vivas. 13 mins.
VHS: S06751. $40.00.

The Spirit of Haida Guaii

This program celebrates the craft, dedication and hard work of artist Bill Reid to produce a 20-foot, seven-tone bronze piece, *The Spirit of Haida Guaii*. The program includes a rare look at the first sequence of animated Haida art. The video also explores the mythology of the creatures rowing the canoe. "Bill Reid has brought back northwest native art to the 20th century" (Levi Strauss). 48 mins.
VHS: S20318. $54.95.

Studio Melee Sampler

Schematic computer-animated presentation and documentary of an interactive video installation constructed from old machine parts and painted backdrops.
VHS: S10208. $19.95.
Terry Mohre, USA, 1984, 20 mins.

Suleyman the Magnificent

Explores the political, social and cultural background of the Ottoman Empire, focusing on the reign of Sultan Suleyman (1520-1566), under whose auspices the Empire spread to encompass parts of Africa, Europe and Asia. Art and architecture flourished under the Sultan. Produced by the National Gallery of Art and the Metropolitan Museum of Art. 57 mins.
VHS: S03399. $39.95.

Superstar: The Life and Times of Andy Warhol

This is no ordinary documentary. Its subject is one of the most controversial artists of our time, a man who made celebrity an art form. *Superstar* traces Warhol's career from his beginnings as a commercial artist to his jaw-dropping appearance on *The Love Boat* (a brief clip that is alone worth the price of the video). Was Warhol a great artist or a mere hypester? In all the postures and roles he assumed, which was the real Warhol? An ambitious film that endeavors to answer the myriad of questions surrounding the man and the myth. USA, 1991.
VHS: S15135. $14.98.

Taliesin: The Tradition of Frank Lloyd Wright

Frank Lloyd Wright designed over 1,000 structures in a career that spanned more than half a century. Many of his most enduring architectural triumphs came during the time he immersed himself in the vitality and energy of the Taliesin Fellowship.
VHS: S15301. $29.95.

Theatre of Indifference

A document of David Finn's installation projects in New York's East village, on the Bowery and elsewhere. Video artist Mitsuru Hayashi uses an inset frame of local action, setting up a diptych with images of the sculptor at work.
VHS: S10199. $24.95.
Mitsuru Hayashi, USA, 1987, 24 mins.

Thomas Eakins: A Motion Portrait

Shot on location in Philadelphia, the film combines dramatic sequences in which all dialog has been verified as authentic with archival footage, still photographs, and interviews to create a moving portrait of a man who was not recognized as one of America's greatest painters until many years after his death in 1916. Narrated by Sam Waterston. Produced in association with the Metropolitan Museum of Art. 60 mins.
VHS: S03397. $39.95.

Threads of Survival

Master weaver Nhu Fang Yang and her daughter-in-law apprentice Ia Moua Yang sit at their traditional bamboo loom and describe the life of the Hmong. Brightly colored and intricately textured story cloths portray such events as the Hmong fleeing Laos after the Vietnam War. 25 mins.
VHS: S26808. $49.95.

Tintoretto

The words of Jean-Paul Sartre guide this look at Tintoretto. Sartre was fascinated by the Venetian master's rebellion against 16th century convention and by his visionary style. Filmed in Venice. Winner of the 1984 Montreal Festival of Films on Art. 52 minutes.
VHS: S02378. $39.95.
Laser: LD70780. $75.00.

Titan—Story of Michelangelo

An extraordinary documentary presented by Robert Flaherty which re-creates the work, life and times of Michelangelo without showing a glimpse of a human actor. The film is at once an exciting tribute to the work of the master, and an impressive cinematic tour-de-force. With narration by Frederic March.
VHS: S07297. $79.95.
Robert Flaherty, USA, 1950, 67 mins.

Titian

The greatest painter of the Venetian school is one of the most celebrated names in the history of art. This study by award-winning film director Didier Baussy offers an in-depth appraisal of the master's work. 60 mins.
VHS: S12408. $39.95.

Titian: The Venetian Colorist

Tiziano Vecellio, better known as Titian, brought to full maturity Renaissance painting in Venice. This overview of Titian's work shows how he was both one of the most important artists of the Italian Renaissance and a mentor for some of the latest European masters. 1991, 28 mins.
VHS: S14540. $29.95.

Torres-Garcia and the Universal Constructivism

A documentary about the life and work of the renowned Uruguayan artist Torres-Garcia, who spent many years in Paris and was among the pioneers of the movement known as Universal Constructivism. Working with Mondrian and Van Doesburg, he founded the "Circle in the Square" group and held to his ideas, reacting to the flamboyant Western culture around him by advocating a return to order and stability, which is clearly seen in his art. Directed by Angel Hurtado, 30 mins.
English Narration. Paul Anthony.
VHS: S06777. $90.00.
Spanish Narration. China Zorrilla.
VHS: S06778. $90.00.

Toulouse-Lautrec

Henri de Toulouse-Lautrec (1864-1901), a great artist and devotee of Parisian night life, painted his haunts with a sharp eye that saw beneath the gay surface to the corruption underneath. In the superb lithographic posters he produced for these clubs, Lautrec pioneered a style that shaped the future of graphic art. He created striking images by focusing on simple but dramatic shapes and using flat, pure colors. This program, produced in conjunction with an exhibit of Lautrec's work at London's Royal Academy, follows his colorful life and groundbreaking work through the presentation of historic photographs, location shots of Montmartre, and present-day lithography print works. Prominent artists, critics and scholars add richness to the program with comments on their favorite works from the exhibition. England, 60 mins.
VHS: S13741. $39.95.

Treasures of the British Crown

Sir Huw Wheldon, former managing director of the BBC, takes the viewer on a journey through the incomparable riches of the largest private art collection in the world, as Queen Elizabeth, Prince Philip, the Queen Mother, and other members of the Royal family speak on camera for the first time about the wonders of the collection. Produced by the BBC. 100 mins.
VHS: S03390. $19.94.

The Trecento: Italian Art and Architecture in the Fourteenth Century

Dividing the Middle Ages and the Renaissance, the *Trecento* (the Fourteenth Century) represents a complex and vital age of artistic activity which shared characteristics of both periods it separated. Travel through Florence, Assisi, Padua, Venice and other cities while exploring the works of artists like Giotto and the Pisanos. 26 mins.
VHS: S15809. $29.95.

Turner at the Tate

Joseph Mallord William Turner (1775-1851), considered by many to be England's finest painter, was a man of extraordinary energy and initiative. He was enormously successful in his own time and is recognized today as one of the world's great and truly original artists. In 1987 London's Tate Gallery opened a special gallery, The Clore Wing, to house his massive collection of Turner's works. Produced to coincide with the opening, this program explores Turner's genius from a variety of perspectives: artists, designers, and scholars of note comment on their favorite works from the collection. 55 mins.
VHS: S13743. $39.95.

Uffizi, Florence's Treasure House of Art

The fascinating story of one of the world's oldest and most important museums, the Uffizi in Florence, from the beginning to modern times. The splendor of Renaissance life comes to life through the most well-known masterpieces by such artists as Botticelli, da Vinci, Michelangelo, Piero della Francesca, Paolo Uccello and Rafael. 60 mins.
VHS: S07467. $29.95.

Understanding Contemporary American Realist Painting

This award-winning survey of the contemporary American Realist movement includes key works of such artists as Close, Eddy, Leslie, Beal, Estes, Fish and Pearlstein, and introduces viewers to the concept of visual perception, the key to a clear understanding of art. 40 mins.
VHS: S09478. $174.00.

Understanding Surrealism: Painters of the Dream

From Dali's highly-charged dream scapes and Magritte's subtle icons to Miro's joyous fantasies of color and playful biomorphic forms, this award-winning study of Surrealism shows how these artists used accident as a technique and how free-wheeling experimentation lead can lead to a surprising and unique metamorphosis of one form into another. 36 mins.
VHS: S09479. $174.00.

Understanding the Art of the Renaissance: Ideas and Ideals

The art of the Renaissance comes alive in this illuminating study of the wide range of styles and schools as seen in painting, sculpture and architecture. 27 mins.
VHS: S09477. $164.95.

Unknown Secrets: Art and the Rosenberg Era

This touring exhibition depicted a variety of artists who have responded to the death of Julius and Ethel, the only Americans sentenced to death for espionage by a public jury. Using interviews and documentation of the exhibition, this essay focuses on the peculiarities of the case which give rise to question the fatal verdict. Featuring visual works by Picasso and Sue Coe, and readings of Arthur Miller and Adrienne Rich. 1990, 30 mins.
VHS: S16324. $50.00.

Van Gogh Revisited

A documentary made on the van Gogh centenary; Leonard Nimoy narrates this program about the post-impressionist painter's life and work, with period photographs, a catalog of his finest works and excerpts from his letters.
Laser: LD70311. $69.95.

Van Gogh: A Museum for Vincent

This visually stunning documentary about history's most popular painter features the world-famous collection of the Rijksmuseum Vincent van Gogh in Amsterdam—which is dedicated exclusively to van Gogh's work. 32 mins.
VHS: S15095. $29.95.

Varga Girls: The Esquire Magazine Images of Alberto Vargas

Vargas's paintings defined an entire era's concept of the beautiful pin-up girl. His images were featured in over 60 published *Esquire* issues. This video examines these works and also offers a personal look at Vargas himself. 55 mins.
VHS: S26292. $19.95.

Vassily Kandinsky

A native of Russia, he taught at the Bauhaus, and became a leader of the abstract impressionist movement in Paris. Kandinsky's emotional use of color and forms pulsates through the film, shot during a major retrospective at the Paris Centre de Pompidou. 60 minutes.
VHS: S02393. $39.95.

Velazquez: The Nobleman of Painting

Didier Baussy's film on Velazquez deals with the special relationship between an artist and his king. Passionate about painting, Philip IV was the largest art collector of his time, and Velazquez was the servant of this passion. Baussy was able to take full advantage of the Velazquez exhibition at the Prado in Madrid. 60 mins.
VHS: S16600. $39.95.

Vibrant Mirror

A kinetic visual work by Venezuelan artist Alejandro Otero. Narrated by William D. Clark.
Vibrant Mirror. English version.
VHS: S06775. $30.00.
Vibrant Mirror. Spanish version.
VHS: S06776. $30.00.

Victory over the Sun: A Reconstruction of the 1913 Futurist Performance

One of the first gasps of Russian futurism, this work reconstructs the 1913 opera that featured costumes and sets by Kasimir Malevich, music by Mikhail Matiushin and text by Aleksei Kruchenykh. "As though the Wizard of Oz had met Alice in Wonderland with some help from Doctor Who" (*The London Times*). 39 mins.
VHS: S20316. $250.00.

Vicus

A documentary about pre-Columbian ceramics and jewelry of the Vicus culture of Peru—a nation of hunters who may have reached the agricultural stage of development, who settled in the region of Vicus a century before the birth of Christ. Directed by Jose Gomez Sicre. Narration by Dolores del Rio. 18 mins.
English Narration.
VHS: S06760. $50.00.
Spanish Narration.
VHS: S06761. $50.00.

Videotape with Joseph Beuys

An interview conducted by former *Avalanche* magazine publisher Willoughby Sharp with the important underground German artist Beuys, taken at the height of his career. 30 mins.
VHS: S17202. $29.95.

Vincent van Gogh: His Art and Life

In life, he sold but one minor piece. In death, his works command millions of dollars. This award-winning program chronicles the fascinating career of Vincent van Gogh, who painted the majority of his surviving 800 paintings in the brief span of a decade, with his major masterpieces painted in the last four years of his career. 25 mins.
VHS: S09480. $174.00.

Vincent: A Dutchman

The eyes of the world turned to the works of Vincent van Gogh when two of his paintings established astronomical price records. Actor Christopher Reeve narrates this recounting of Van Gogh's extraordinary life as told through his letters and paintings. Filmed on location in France and the Netherlands, the viewer is treated to an insightful biography, his work and the scenes he painted. 30 mins.
VHS: S08480. $29.95.

Visions of the Arawaks

Over a decade, surreal artist Penny Slinger has realized a body of work inspired by this group, utilizing their images, their authentic instruments and the close symbiotic relationship they share with their environment. Rare, live footage of these people and over 100 paintings by Slinger form the bulk of this rich tapestry. 70 mins.
VHS: S21187. $39.95.

Vizcaya Museum and Gardens

Come discover the magical grandeur and beauty of Vizcaya—a magnificent Italian Renaissance-style villa built by industrialist James Deering and now a renowned museum of European decorative arts. 30 mins.
VHS: S06688. $29.95.

Voices in Celebration

Filmmaker Aviva Slesin explores the multiple functions and possibilities of art, through a penetrating documentary on history, ritual and creative process of the National Gallery. 45 mins.
VHS: S15298. $29.95.

Willem de Kooning: Artist

Paintings by Willem de Kooning are prized the world over as superb examples of the New York school. He worked both abstractly and with the figure. This film shows him at work and in conversation with friends. There are also 31 paintings captured here for home viewing.
VHS: S26718. $29.95.
Robert Snyder, USA, 32 mins.

World Folk Art: A Multicultural Approach

Six new programs which explore the meaning of folk art and how it has been passed down through history within different cultures tied by the thread of common themes. The vast collection of the Museum of International Folk Art has been richly photographed to provide a resource for this excellent series. Includes *An Introductory Overview, The Influence of Tradition, The Influence of Religion and Spirituality, The Influence of Architecture and Natural Designs, A Product of the Community* and *Expression of Cultures.*
VHS: S15492. $185.00.

The World of a Primitive Painter

Film on renowned painter Jose Antonio Velasquez, on location in his village of San Antonio and in Tegucigalpa, Honduras. A barber by trade, Velasquez had a passion to paint, and with no training he created canvas after canvas with intricate detail, painting the cobblestones of the village streets and the tiles of the rooftops. Awarded *Cine's* Golden Eagle in the U.S. Directed by Angel Hurtado, 20 mins.
English Narration. Shirley Temple Black.
VHS: S06767. $60.00.
Spanish Narration. Maria Elena Walsh.
VHS: S06768. $60.00.

World of Light: A Portrait of May Sarton

May Sarton is an American artist. This document shows her life as woman and offers an intriguing glimpse into the workings of a strong creative mind. Her courage is an inspiration.
VHS: S19452. $59.95.

STILL PHOTOGRAPHY

The Art of Erotic Photography

World-famous lensman John Kelly shares his professional secrets. He travels to a lush tropical island to capture four gorgeous amateur models for a calendar promotion. 60 mins.
VHS: S22215. $19.95.

The Art of Nature: Reflections on the Grand Design

Tom Skerritt narrates this meditation on beauty, the language nature uses to communicate with us. Spectacular scenery from all over the world is seen. Time-lapse photography exposes natural processes not otherwise visible to the naked eye. Based on the best-selling photography book of the same title. Featuring the music of Michael Gettel.
VHS: S27313. $19.95.
Gray Warriner, USA, 1995, 50 mins.

The Classroom Collection

This six-part series discusses techniques, mechanics, aesthetics and style in a comprehensive guide to photography.
Vol. 1: Basic Camera Techniques.
VHS: S20339. $24.95.
Vol. 2: Basic Daylight Exposure and Equivalent Exposures.
VHS: S20340. $24.95.
Vol. 3: Metering and Exposure Controls.
VHS: S20341. $24.95.
Vol. 4: Advanced Camera Techniques.
VHS: S20342. $24.95.
Vol. 5: Black and White Techniques.
VHS: S20343. $24.95.
Vol. 6: Careers in Photography.
VHS: S20344. $24.95.
The Classroom Collection, Set. A set of six tapes.
VHS: S20345. $129.00.

A Day in the Life of America

On a single day 200 hundred respected photographers were given the assignment to capture America. This video, produced by ABC News' *20/20*, is the result. 18 mins.
VHS: S23723. $99.95.

A Day in the Life of The Soviet Union

In May 1987, 50 Western- and 50 Eastern-bloc photographers tried to record the essence and spirit of the Soviet Union on a single day. This video, produced by ABC News' *20/20*, reveals a rich cultural landscape. 18 mins.
VHS: S23724. $99.95.

Dorothea Lange: A Visual Life

The great photographer is revealed through examples of her work and interviews with both the artist and her family. Lange was pivotal to the development of documentary photography traditions and her work remains an aesthetic achievement that continues to inspire photographers today.
Home Video.
VHS: S24404. $39.95.
Public Performance Rights/Institutional.
VHS: S24405. $199.00.

Gordon Parks: Visions

Gordon Parks: Best selling author, award-winning photographer, writer and director of *Shaft* and *The Learning Tree.* The varied work of this famed photo-journalist will affect you like no other has. This is the world through his eyes. 60 mins.
VHS: S14608. $19.95.

Helmut Newton: Frames from the Edge

One of the world's leading photographers, whose style has been stamped on the image of many of the world's most beautiful people and has enjoyed amazing success as a Svengali of the glitterati. Newton talks of his life and work, his approach to photography, how he selects the right girl. Charlotte Rampling, Catherine Deneuve, Sigourney Weaver and Karl Lagerfeld comment on the man. 60 mins.
VHS: S12409. $39.95.

Horace Bristol: Photojournalist

This program examines the life and work of photojournalist Horace Bristol, whose innovative work in the 1930s for *Life* and *Fortune* made his reputation. 13 mins.
VHS: S20354. $39.95.

Images 150 Years of Photography

This six-part documentary series traces the technical and aesthetic development of early photographers, the birth of the amateur documentary, the objectifying of images, photographs as a use for exploration and science, for documenting social realism, and explores photography as an artistic expression. The works are culled from 20 collections in museums, archives and private collections in the United States, Canada, Britain and France.
Images 150 Years of Photography: Domestic Memories.
VHS: S17299. $29.95.
Images 150 Years of Photography: The Pencil of Nature.
VHS: S17298. $29.95.
Images 150 Years of Photography: The Best or Nothing.
VHS: S17300. $29.95.
Images 150 Years of Photography: The Eyes of the Empire.
VHS: S17301. $29.95.
Images 150 Years of Photography: The Real Thing.
VHS: S17302. $29.95.
Images 150 Years of Photography: The Magic Mirror.
VHS: S17303. $29.95.

Imogen Cunningham: Never Give Up

In 1901, Imogen Cunningham saved up $15 and sent away for a camera and a correspondence course. Over a span of 70 years, she photographed the famous and the unknown (or infamous as she prefers to call them). *Never Give Up* is a philosophy she lived. Though she was 90 years old at the time this fascinating documentary was produced, she never quit working and she never quit dreaming. Produced by Ann Hershey, 28 mins.
Home Video.
VHS: S16833. $29.95.
Institutional with Public Performance Rights.
VHS: S20961. $125.00.

Masters of Photography: Andre Kertesz

Andre Kertesz claimed he was born for the camera; he reflects on his boyhood in Hungary and his life in Paris. Leading a walking tour of New York City, he photographs a young girl, The Cloisters, and his beloved Washington Square. A heartwarming profile of the man his colleagues call "the father of 35 millimeter photography." 30 mins.
VHS: S16206. $29.95.

Masters of Photography: Diane Arbus

The only film profile of this woman who photographed those living on the fringes of society. This video explores her work through her own words and the images that stunned visitors at her show in the Museum of Modern Art. 30 mins.
VHS: S16205. $29.95.

Masters of Photography: Edward Steichen

Steichen died in 1973 at the age of 95. Drawing images from his whole career which range in subject from celebrities to architecture to advertising to nature, he made this profile when he was 86. "You must establish an intimate relationship between yourself and what you're photographing," he says, "whether it's a can of beans or Greta Garbo." 30 mins.
VHS: S16207. $29.95.

On Assignment

A six-tape series of tapes for learning photography and videography, this series is authored by Brian D. Ratty, nationally known photographer and graduate of the Brooks Institute of Photography.
Photographic Design. Fast-paced and packed with information, this tape is designed for any photographer serious about understanding and using the principles of good photographic design. Includes information on camera and lens choices, framing, selective focus, design elements, design principles, light direction, light quality, control of light and color, psychology of color.
VHS: S06939. $29.95.
Photographic Light. Each half-hour chapter explores and illustrates how light works in photography. This video is designed to help better control and manipulate light in photography. Includes information on direction, form, contrast, color, measuring light, tonal control, film latitude, natural light, available light, electronic flash, artificial light.
VHS: S06938. $29.95.
The Business of Photography. How to make a living as a photographer: interviews with art directors and editors who buy freelance photography and give profitable assignments. Three half-hour chapters including choosing your direction, portfolios, how the business works, editing, the interview, staff photographer opportunities, breaking in and staying in, reps and stock agencies, major markets and freelancing.
VHS: S06941. $29.95.
The Darkroom. Brian D. Ratty, the nationally known photographer, hosts this educational review of darkroom materials and techniques. Included are an overview of darkroom layouts, equipment, developing methods for both black and white and color films, proofing and even special printing methods, as well as many other important techniques. 90 mins.
VHS: S21083. $29.95.
The Studio. Detailed and practical ideas about how to lay out and equip a photographic studio to gain optimum results for product and people photography. Includes three half-hour chapters covering studio layout and design, lighting for the studio, still life photography, classic view camera, loading sheet film, view camera techniques, shifts, swings and tilts, formal portraits and candids.
VHS: S06940. $29.95.
Video Guide to Basic Photography. *The Video Guide to Basic Photography* is the starting point for any person wishing to learn photography. This is a practical, easy-to-follow guide, containing three half-hour chapters. Includes how the camera works, F Stops, shutter speeds, camera lenses, film, available light, flash photography, steady shooting, finding pictures, portraits.
VHS: S06937. $29.95.
Video Guide to Basic Videography. Lights, camera, action...This basic guide to videography takes the mystery out of shooting effective, entertaining videos. This basic tape is the starting point for any person wishing to learn the exciting world of video, presented in three half-hour chapters. Includes video theory, formats, cameras/recorders, using your camera, pre-production, production, post-production, basic maintenance, lighting for video and video markets.
VHS: S06942. $29.95.

Photography

Camera techniques and developing and printing black and white are illustrated by Doug Rinehart, including operation of single lens reflex cameras, shutter speeds, lenses, filters, film, enlarging techniques. 44 mins.
VHS: S07652. $59.95.

Photography Video Series— The Classroom Collection

This six-part video series is a perfect education aid for teaching technique, content and style, with the use of computer generated graphics, charts and examples. Each volume is approximately 15 minutes, and covers daylight exposure, meter, advanced camera techniques, black and white technique and possible careers in photography. 90 mins.
VHS: S17681. $129.00.

Pirelli Calendar

One of the world's most famous annual calendars, the Pirelli Tire Company's calendar features the work of top photographers and designers as they combine the female form and the lure of the road (symbolized by the famous Pirelli Tire Tread mark). Follow the evolution of the calendar from its early days to the growing sophistication of today's calendar, including the most recent issue, as Gillian Lynne, award-winning choreographer of *Cats*, works her magic on the dance elements of the '88 calendar. 39 mins.
VHS: S08488. $19.95.

The Real Weegee

A biography of the talented street photographer Weegee (nee Arthur Fellig), whose photographs captured post-war, urban American life. Weegee's dual themes were alienation and loneliness found in the marginal and powerful—hustlers, gangsters, prostitutes, thieves and presidents. The program features more than 100 of Weegee's photographs. 60 mins.
VHS: S18699. $19.95.

Remembering Edward Weston

Weston's photographic work has defined both the field of photography and the course of art history. His clear images of common objects, vegetables, shells and other natural forms has changed our understanding of the medium. This video offers a view of the artist and the man through interviews with close family members and friends. 30 mins.
VHS: S22802. $29.95.

Stereo Photography: Places and Times Remembered

Philip Brigandi charts the evolution of stereo (3-D) photography between 1850 and 1940. Brigandi was a top stereo photographer with the Keystone View Company. His memories highlight the career of President McKinley, the destruction of the Civil War, the birth of the transcontinental railway, the birth of aviation and the inventions of the Wright Brothers. The photographers' works include Eadweard Muybridge and Matthew Brady. 40 mins.
VHS: S20336. $39.95.

Strand: Under the Dark Cloth

Using samples of his exquisite work and interviews with those who knew him, director John Walker has created a unique portrait of one of the most fascinating figures of contemporary art: photographer Paul Strand.
VHS: S14748. $29.95.
John Walker, Canada, 1990, 81 mins.

W. Eugene Smith

The life and work of this brilliant photographer, whose passion for social justice marked his desire to create photographs that were works of art, are explored in this film. In addition to showcasing over 600 of Smith's stunning photos, the program includes a dramatic recreation in which actor Peter Riegert portrays Smith, with dialog taken from Smith's diaries and letters. 87 min.
VHS: S18390. $39.95.

APPLIED ART

Arno Werner, Master Bookbinder

Arno Werner, born in West Germany, studied with the famous Ignatz Wiemeler, a disciple of the Arts and Crafts movement in England. The video examines the history of bookbinding, Werner's step-by-step techniques, and personal and professional opinions about life and the pursuit of distinguished craftsmanship. 28 mins.
VHS: S06563. $39.95.

Art Ache—Art Is Long, Life Is Short?

This program assesses the role of art in contemporary culture, and the way money and the media have changed people's attitudes and ideas about art. 45 mins.
VHS: S18784. $39.95.

Art Ache—The Game of Art and How to Play It

Drawing on the models of Christie's and Sotheby's in New York and the Cologne Art Fair, this documentary examines the issues facing galleries, dealers, collectors and shifting tastes in the art market, assessing issues of money versus conservation, investment versus art. 45 mins.
VHS: S18782. $39.95.

Art Ache—The Image of an Artist

Drawing from Andy Warhol's exhibition at the Museum Ludwig in West Germany, this program explores the complicated issues of an artist's relationship to his career, celebrity, identity and the media. 45 mins.
VHS: S18783. $39.95.

Art Ache—The Complete Set

Includes *Art Is Long, Life Is Short?, The Game of Art and How to Play It* and *The Image of an Artist.*
VHS: S18785. $99.95.

Art in Its Soul: Provincetown Art Colony

Combines oral histories, archival footage, still photos and works of art to trace Provincetown's evolution into a major art colony. Artists recall the early 1900s, when art students came from around the world to study with Charles Hawthorne and the years of Hans Hoffman, who left his indelible mark on abstract impressionism. Includes Halper, Harmon, Soyer, Gross, Stout, Hensch, Moffet, Hopper, Kanths, Dickenson, Frankenthaler, Pollock, Grooms, Kline, Avery, de Kooning and Motherwell. 34 mins.
VHS: S07511. $40.00.

Art of Navajo Weaving

Explores the traditional art of Navajo weaving and its origins, with visits to a contemporary Navajo weaving family, showing how artists create magnificent pieces of art. 56 mins.
VHS: S08304. $29.95.

Banks' Florilegium: The Flowering of the Pacific

A rich mixture of art, history, science and travel, written and narrated by *Time Magazine* art critic Robert Hughes. Joseph Banks was a botanist who accompanied Captain Cook on his first circumnavigation of the globe. The film visits such places as Madeira, Tierra del Fuego, Tahiti and New Zealand, where Banks recorded over 700 new species of plants. Produced by the BBC. 60 minutes.
VHS: S01848. $39.95.

Before You Visit a Museum

This orientation program gives students insightful background so they will get the most out of their museum visit and take advantage of every opportunity to learn. "...this is a useful introduction for intermediate classes who will visit a museum." 16 mins.
VHS: S09465. $115.00.

Commercial Art: General, Vol. 1

An overview of career possibilities in commercial art fields, including graphic design, computer art and neon design. 30 mins.
VHS: S19926. $39.95.

Commercial Art: Media, Vol. 2

This video offers career insights from three artists who have staked out careers in the following disciplines: cartoonist, scenic designer and photographer. 30 mins.
VHS: S19927. $39.95.

Commercial Art: Design, Vol. 3

This volume shows the careers of a fashion designer, industrial designer and architect. 30 mins.
VHS: S19928. $39.95.

Computer as an Art Tool

Explores the various techniques and programs used to create computer-generated art. The painting, assemblage, collage and videos chosen feature pioneers in the use of computers to create art, including Manfred Mohr, Darcy Gebarg, Mark Wilson, Isaac Victor Kerlow, Jeremy Gardiner, Margot Lovejoy, Haresh Lalvani, Robert Moran, Micha Riis, Eli Lapid, Roy Blomster and Olive Sabato. 12½ mins.
VHS: S06559. $39.95.

Costakis the Collector

George Costakis' private collection of Russian avant-garde art is the most comprehensive record of an art movement ever amassed. This film tells the story of this movement before and after the Revolution and of the man who saved its greatest works from obliteration. 54 mins.
VHS: S13221. $39.95.

Curator's Choice

A 1982 exhibition at the Metropolitan Museum of Art in which no item's price exceeded $5,000 provides a framework for this exploration of the work of a museum's curator. The five department curators who are interviewed discuss their day-to-day work and the long-range value in serving historic preservation. 25 mins.
VHS: S04647. $29.95.

Dream Weaver

Helena Hernmarch creates tapestries that hang in major buildings all over the world. As she and her assistants work on two new pieces, Hernmarch comments on her development of photo-realism on the loom, the discovery of techniques to stimulate three dimensions on a flat surface, and the concepts of applied creativity and design. 28 mins.
VHS: S15747. $49.95.

The Eighteenth Century Woman

Using the Metropolitan Museum's costume collection as a point of departure, this documentary provides an in-depth look at the role of women in the 18th century when "to be direct was to be dull, and dullness was the greatest of sins." Includes interviews with Philippe de Montebello, director of the museum, as well as costume curator Stella Blum and Vogue Magazine editor Diana Vreeland. 60 mins.
VHS: S04648. $39.95.

Fine Art: General, Vol. 1

This program offers an overview of career opportunities that exist in the visual art field. The video illustrates the various fields of study of fine arts—a painter, a pastel artist, an art appraiser and a gallery owner. 30 mins.
VHS: S19923. $39.95.

Fine Art: Production, Vol. 2

This program presents alternate careers in fine art production, including the professions of a sculptor, a printmaker, and a potter, who offer insights and advice on the correct steps toward becoming a financially independent artist. 30 mins.
VHS: S19924. $39.95.

Fine Art: Education, Vol. 3

This program looks at careers in art restoration, art history and high school level art instruction. 30 mins.
VHS: S19925. $39.95.

Flowers and Gardens

The most familiar use of flowers in art is in painted still life, but flowers at the Metropolitan Museum are also used in huge floral displays arranged weekly, and in the gardens and courtyards of the Museum itself. 25 mins.
VHS: S04649. $29.95.

Forms of Artistic Expression: Glass and Sculpture

"Stained Glass: Painting With Light" explores the beauty and art form of stained glass; "Sculpture—Process of Discovery", the molding of sculpture from rock, and the process of discovery. 31 mins.
VHS: S05842. $19.95.

Gifts from the Fire: The Ceramic Art of Brother Thomas

Brother Thomas Bezanson, a Benedictine monk, is a ceramic artist working with porcelain in the Chinese and Japanese traditions. This film weaves the story of the artist, his work and his philosophy with the technical aspects of the making of a single piece of art. 29 min.
VHS: S18393. $19.95.

Glenville School Computer Graphics

Shows animated designs created by fifth and sixth grade students in Greenwich, CT, on an Apple II computer. Includes a 36-page booklet, *An Easy Guide for Creating Computer Graphics in Elementary Schools.* 8½ mins.
VHS: S06560. $39.95.

Hidden Treasures

Jewelry collector and instructor Christie Romero hosts this informative program on antique and vintage jewelry of the last two centuries, defining major characteristics, style and periods and what to look for in assessing value and worth.
VHS: S18262. $24.95.

Inside Tips on Discovering Antiques

This instructive guide provides lessons and insights into finding the best buys on antiques. Frank Farmer Loomis IV is an acknowledged expert and appraiser who wanders from outdoor markets to country stores in search of valuable works. He offers a practical guide in the buying and selling of antiques and collectibles. 40 mins.
VHS: S20350. $29.95.

Knights and Armor

The reality of knighthood is captured in this document based on the actual experiences of Sir William Marshall. This video brings the viewer to battlegrounds and ancient courts where knights fought and lived. Includes a visit to Graz, Austria, the site of a great collection of armor. 100 min.
VHS: S24492. $29.95.

Maria! Indian Pottery of San Ildefonso

Indian pottery maker Maria Martinez demonstrates the traditional Indian ways of making pottery. Beginning with the spreading of sacred corn, you will see gathering and mixing of clay, construction and decorating of pottery and building of the firing mound. 27 mins.
VHS: S06698. $29.95.

Masks from Many Cultures

This video unveils more than 100 masks, representing the various images with sequences of dances and festivals. The program includes masks from Mardi Gras in New Orleans, Dominican Republic, New Guinea, Bali, China, Tibet, Japan, Korea, Mexico, Guatemala, Bolivia, Native Americans and several African nations. 21 mins.
VHS: S18514. $39.95.

Meet the Caldecott Illustrator: Jerry Pinkney

The award-winning illustrator of *The Talking Eggs* invites viewers into his studio to watch him work on his delightful watercolor and pencil drawings. "My satisfaction," he says, "comes from the actual marks on the paper, and when it sings it's magic." 1991, 21 mins. Public Performance Rights.
VHS: S13892. $81.95.

Merchants and Masterpieces

Meet the collectors whose vision and generosity built the Metropolitan Museum of Art. J. Pierpont Morgan, Robert Lehman, Benjamin Altman, the Rockefellers, and the Webbs were passionate collectors pursuing magnificent art. Based on Calvin Tomkins's history of the museum, this program provides a rare opportunity to discover the people who originally collected the Met's masterpieces. 87 mins.
VHS: S12368. $39.95.

Metropolitan Cats

The cat—as expressed in the art of different cultures through history. In an examination of more than 4,000 years of art housed at New York's Metropolitan Museum, this program explores the charm and mystery of the cat as a vehicle for reflecting both the artist and society. 30 mins.
VHS: S04651. $39.95.

Norman Rockwell and the Saturday Evening Post

A charming video biography of America's popular and beloved artist, Norman Rockwell, through rare footage, photographs and intimate interviews with his friends and colleagues. 60 mins.
VHS: S09872. $39.95.

Paper and Silk: The Conservation of Asian Works of Art

This program begins with a brittle 18th century Chinese scroll painting in hundreds of fragments. We are led through the restoration process; from the initial piecing together of the work to its re-backing and in-painting and eventual remounting. 26 mins.
VHS: S02697. $39.95.

Queen Mary's Doll's House

Not only one of England's most beautiful and stately homes, it is also one of the most surprising. This special video celebration lifts the splendid facade and tours the miniature mansion's sumptuous staterooms, luxurious bedrooms and enchanting gardens. From the exquisite Chippendale chairs to the handwritten book of poems by Rudyard Kipling, everything is a miracle of miniature craftsmanship. From the BBC. 50 mins.
VHS: S12390. $19.95.

Quilt on the Wall: Portrait of Jan Myers

Contemporary textile artist Jan Myers weds her utilitarian respect for quiltmaking with her own desire for self-expression. Antique quilts and historical photographs provide the backdrop as we watch Myers make a patchwork quilt from beginning to end. 28 mins.
VHS: S00203. $39.95.

Raggedy Ann and Andy

Collectors will enjoy this documentary that both explores and explains the history of these classic cloth dolls. Dating and distinguishing their origins is a valuable and enjoyable pursuit. In addition, the life of the originator, Johnny Gruelle, is portrayed through interviews and photographs. 90 mins.
VHS: S25744. $49.95.

Shodo, The Path of Writing

Introducing the manifestations of calligraphy in Japan, this program visits advertisers, monks, students and the kabuki theater. Masters demonstrate various techniques, their reverence for special inks and brushes, and the origins of texts and ideograms. 1980, 30 mins.
VHS: S16209. $29.95.

Story of English Furniture: Volume 1

Narrated by Arthur Negus and Hugh Scully, and scripted by noted British antiques expert Bernard Price, this 2-volume video series explores the evolution of English furniture, which proceeded in tandem with architectural innovation and the growth of interior design. The furniture is viewed in the context of some of England's most magnificent architecture. Among other things covered are the points of detail and design which make it easy to date furniture and distinguish an original from a more recent reproduction. Volume 1: From the Middle Ages to the Eighteenth Century. 107 mins.
VHS: S03392. $19.94.

Story of English Furniture: Volume 2
Volume 2 covers the late 18th century through the present day. 105 mins.
VHS: S03393. $19.94.

Story of Fashion Volume 1: Remembrance of Things Past
The fashion of the early 20th century had its roots in the 19th, influenced particularly by the work of Charles Worth. This program traces the fashion of haute couture, from Worth through Coco Chanel, as revealed in the rise and fall of the corset and reflected in the wardrobes of the era's most famous women. 60 minutes.
VHS: S07625. $29.95.

Story of Fashion Volume 2: The Art and Sport of Fashion
Innovations in art, such as cubism and surrealism, greatly influenced the fashions of the '20s, '30s, and '40s, as did the glamorous stars of Hollywood. This film explores fashion's evolution from Coco Chanel to Christian Dior. 64 minutes.
VHS: S07626. $29.95.

Story of Fashion Volume 3: The Age of Dissent
From the '50s to today, from Dior to Dynasty, fashion has evolved into a huge international business with a new breed of superstar designers. The Age of Dissent shows how fashion is not just a business, but is show business—with theatrical fashion shows, extravagant product launches, and lavish photographic sessions that rival the film industry in opulence and cost. 61 minutes.
VHS: S07627. $29.95.

The Tournament
Chivalry may be dead, but many of its beautiful artifacts survive in the armour collection of the Metropolitan Museum, one of the world's greatest armories. Collection curator Dr. Helmut Nickel narrates this fascinating glimpse of medieval society. 30 mins.
VHS: S04656. $29.95.

Tradesmen and Treasures: Gothic and Renaissance Nuremburg
Documents the remarkable flowering of art and culture in Nuremberg during the 14th to 16th centuries, as the city evolved from a trade center of the Holy Roman Empire to a Renaissance city. Works of art by Durer, Veit and Kraft are featured. Produced by the Metropolitan Museum and Bayerische Rundfunk. 55 mins.
VHS: S03402. $39.95.

Vermillion Editions
As one of the country's most distinguished print studios, Vermillion Editions attracts artists from all over the U.S. to Minnesota to work with master printer Steven Andersen. This program opens with a brief overview of modern American printmaking and then goes behind the scenes into the studios to show artists making highly complex prints on paper. 55 mins.
VHS: S04193. $49.95.

Voyages: The Journey of the Magi
The Biblical journey of the Magi has inspired artists for nearly 2,000 years. This program recreates their actual route, setting the event in both its cultural and archeological contexts. As sites in the journey of the Wise Men are seen, artifacts and coins dating from the period offer additional insight into an event which generated a wealth of art. Narrated by art historian and archeologist Karl Katz; filmed in Jerusalem and Bethlehem. 30 mins.
VHS: S04653. $29.95.

Wildlife Decoy Carvers
Carving duck decoys has transcended its early uses in hunting and has become a folk art form of considerable accomplishments. This documentary looks at wildlife decoy carvers and their unique art.
VHS: S03417. $19.95.

Windcarver
Former architect T. Merrill Prentice studies the slightest air currents before handcrafting common materials into delicate, moving sculptures. Captured in the heat of his creative process, Tim discusses his philosophies of public and private art with several humorous anecdotes. Many of his works are featured, photographed in mesmerizing detail. 28 mins.
VHS: S15748. $49.95.

Work in Process: The Furniture of Larry Hendricks
Laurence Hendricks explores his theory of style and function as an outgrowth of Shaker and Bauhaus traditions. With examples of his work, he discusses the value of apprenticeship and the high level of experience, education and information required to become a master craftsperson in the modern world. Close-up photography of his hands in action follow the creation of a new piece from conception to completion. 28 mins.
VHS: S15745. $49.95.

ART TECHNIQUES

Acrylic
The brushes, palettes, paints, painting surfaces of acrylic, use of various mediums, scumbling, drybrush, spattering, impasto and painting with instruments other than brushes. Gail Price. 37 mins.
VHS: S07644. $59.95.

American Craft Council: Fiber-Coiled Basketry
Illustrates the process of making continuous coil baskets with yarn, raffia, beads, feathers and techniques to alter their form and composition. Shows completed pieces incorporating the described stitches as well as historical basketry. 20 mins.
VHS: S07660. $39.95.

American Craft Council: Masks and Face Coverings
Portrays the many ways man has sought to alter, disguise, protect and immortalize his face. Symbolic, ritualistic, historic and contemporary masks are shown created from a wide range of materials. 21 mins.
VHS: S07661. $39.95.

American Craft Council: Papermaking USA and The Handmade Paper Book
Presents the work of 34 artists who approach papermaking from varied perspectives. The Handmade Paper Book highlights examples by 16 artists who go beyond the traditional book to create unique, three-dimensional art objects. 20 mins.
VHS: S07662. $39.95.

Art Smart Videotape Series
This series of 12 videos on pottery, drawing, printing and jewelry provides hands-on instruction laid out in a clear, step-by-step process. Basic skills are presented for different grade levels, and each video concludes with a summary of major steps covered.
Basic Screen Printing.
VHS: S22104. $49.95.
Basic Jewelry.
VHS: S22105. $49.95.
Cast Jewelry.
VHS: S22106. $49.95.
Figure Drawing.
VHS: S22100. $49.95.
Fundamentals of Drawing.
VHS: S22099. $49.95.
Glazing and Firing.
VHS: S22098. $49.95.
Handbuilt Pottery.
VHS: S22095. $49.95.
Handbuilt Clay Sculptures.
VHS: S22096. $49.95.
Photo Screen Printing.
VHS: S22103. $49.95.
Portrait Drawing.
VHS: S22101. $49.95.
Relief Printing.
VHS: S22102. $49.95.
Wheel Thrown Potters.
VHS: S22097. $49.95.

Basic Art by Video I: Painting
I in a series of III tapes introduces drawing, design, and color, the building blocks of painting, right in the instructor's studio. Step-by-step, fine artist Charles Haddock teaches classic technique in the tradition of the masters.
VHS: S03994. $74.95.

Basic Art by Video II: Drawing & Design
II in a series of III tapes demonstrates that drawing and design skills, though intuitive, must consciously be nurtured and developed under professional guidance.
VHS: S03995. $74.95.

Basic Art by Video III: Color
III in a series of III tapes demonstrates the poetic nature-colors from Renaissance through Impressionism to Modern, bypassing the raw beginners' colors.
VHS: S03996. $74.95.

Batik as Fine Art
Cloth dyeing and alternate waxing is a staple of folk art. Professor Helen Carkin examines its transformation from textile art to a more accessible fine art. She shows the use of color and its relation to the color wheel, and takes the viewer on a step-by-step process from making a pinning frame to framing the finished work. 30 mins.
VHS: S17209. $39.95.

Beadmaking
Glass, fire and the imagination are the chief building blocks that go into the manufacture of beads. Michael Max, a glass artist and educator, demonstrates his original techniques in a step-by-step process. Anyone can learn to make and decorate these tiny jewel-like wonders. 60 mins.
VHS: S25737. $39.95.

Ceramics
Ceramics handbuilding, ceramics mixing, wedging, throwing and ceramics decorating, glazing and firing are demonstrated at the Anderson Ranch Arts Center. 35 mins.
VHS: S07649. $39.50.

Ceramics: Handbuilding
Popular ceramist Ro Mead presents this two-part video.
Ceramics: Handbuilding Part 1. The artist, working in her own studio, demonstrates creative ways to make coil and pinch pots and slab forms. She also creates a drape-mold platter decorated with inlaid colored clays. 45 mins.
VHS: S11657. $29.95.
Ceramics: Handbuilding Part 2. In Part 2, Ro Mead expands on her first video and creates slab forms decorated with inlaid colored clay including a cylindrical vase, a drape-mold bowl and tiles decorated with airbrush. 45 mins.
VHS: S11658. $29.95.
Ceramics: Handbuilding (Complete). Both parts of this 2-part series at a special price.
VHS: S11659. $54.95.

Ceramics: Introduction to Throwing on the Potter's Wheel
Virtuoso potter Stephen Jepson offers a comprehensive, easy-to-follow program on the basics of understanding the Potter's wheel. Jepson runs the viewer through the intricate process step-by-step, with special emphasis on mechanics and methodology. 53 mins.
VHS: S19643. $39.95.

Charles Reid: Flowers in Watercolor
From contour drawing to last brush stroke, you watch a beautiful still life with flowers emerge—seeing it from the artist's point of view. A fascinating study of how Reid achieves the freshness for which his paintings are acclaimed.
VHS: S09712. $69.95.

Clay in a Special Way
Shows the process of teaching clay to students of diverse abilities, including handicapped children, resulting in a successful creative experience as well as developing positive human interaction and communication. 15 mins.
VHS: S07640. $49.95.

Collage Methods
Different kinds of paper are put together demonstrating the basic techniques of two-dimensional collage. Colored and stained paper, tissue, letters and pictures are all arranged using collage methods. 20 mins.
VHS: S22077. $24.95.

Color Perceptions
Illustrates basic color theory and practice including the use of primary, secondary and complementary colors. Artist Arthur Turner emphasizes learning by direct perception of color phenomena. 44 mins.
VHS: S07654. $59.95.

Color: The Artist's Inspiration
Lively illustrations and practical demonstrations bring alive the study of color. This comprehensive, two-volume program displays lively modern and classic paintings to show how color theory is applied by real artists in the studio and how color has been used during various eras in the history of art. 42 mins.
VHS: S09466. $359.00.

Contour Drawing
Contour lines free the imagination as it sharpens the viewer's observation. This program helps students understand the power of contour lines and shows them the variation and interest that can be achieved with various materials, including pastel, marker, pencil, crayon and paint. 13 mins.
VHS: S09467. $105.00.

Controlling Watercolor
Tony Couch explains in simple terms the behavior of water, paint and paper in painting and demonstrates control of these elements using brush, water and sponge to create three critical textures. 55 mins.
VHS: S07628. $39.95.

Creating Abstract Art
Abstraction and abstract art are explained using easily understood examples. The simplification of shapes, distortion, emphasis on overlapping shapes and fracturing, contour continuation are explained. Ultimately these examples and techniques reveal how design becomes more important than subject matter in art-making. 20 mins.
VHS: S22076. $24.95.

Creating Nonobjective Paintings
Artist and teacher Gerald F. Brommer shows how to create nonobjective works through a variety of techniques. Texture, color fields, gesture and collage are some of the main issues covered. In addition, noteworthy examples of nonobjective art show students the emotional and creative range of this type of artwork. 26 mins.
VHS: S27639. $24.95.

Creating the Decorative Cloth
A video for highlighting the techniques deployed in creating four different kinds of decorative cloth—tapestry, brocade, embroidery and pile. The expert commentary demonstrates the distinct features that separate the four structures. 45 mins.
VHS: S20351. $39.95.

Creating with Ceramics
Shows a montage of historical ceramic pieces and then illustrates techniques of clay gathering, mixing, wedging, throwing, handbuilding, glazing and firing. Ceramicists demonstrate different techniques and types of pottery. 26 mins.
VHS: S07634. $59.95.

Creating with Watercolor
Cecile Johnson captures the beauty of basic watercolor techniques as she applies them in several demonstration paintings including a barn, a street scene, and a mountain landscape. 20 mins.
VHS: S07633. $39.95.

Crizmac Master Pack
A specially developed art video for students in grades 4-8, this tape explores the life and work of six modern artists, including Monet, van Gogh, Gauguin, Picasso, Kandinsky and Chagall. After introducing the artists, studio activities that relate to the artist's work are demonstrated combining art history and studio skills.
VHS: S09077. $209.00.

Dance of the Wheel
An apprentice and disciple of the legendary potter Michael Cardew, Todd Piker has built one of the few wood-fired tube kilns in the United States. He takes the viewer through the creative and emotional process of the elemental art of pottery: Earth - Water - Fire. For potters at all levels of experience. 28 mins.
VHS: S14595. $49.95.

Drawing and Sketching with Markers
Using step-by-step demonstrations, artist Tony Couch shows the techniques he uses to create fine art with markers—showing that skillful handling of this drawing media can give you exceptional works of art. 60 mins.
VHS: S14133. $39.95.

Drawing I
Drawing with the pencil (basic drawing techniques to render texture, value, shading, negative and positive space), and drawing techniques (use of charcoal, pen and ink, crayon, felt tips and washes on varied textures). Gail Price. 33 mins.
VHS: S07641. $59.95.

Drawing II
Drawing landscapes, seascapes, cityscapes, and drawing people and animals are taught by Gail Price. 39 mins.
VHS: S07642. $59.95.

Drawing III
Includes drawing with charcoal and pastels, drawing with mixed media and drawing with markers. 64 mins.
VHS: S07643. $89.50.

Drawing in the Source: Lita Albuquerque
Extracting the mystical relationship of humankind to earth and earth to the cosmos, Lita Albuquerque has explored a variety of mediums ranging from ephemeral earthworks, stream of consciousness writings and drawings to large scale paintings, sculptures and installations. This profile reveals her thoughts, motivations, inspirations and concerns. 9 mins.
VHS: S15767. $39.95.

Drawing Landscapes with Pencil and Ink
Tony Couch shows you just how easy it is to create professional-looking drawings using basic methods with pencil and ink—and you'll be able to incorporate these techniques into your drawings after viewing this video program. 60 mins.
VHS: S14134. $39.95.

Drawing Methods with Gail Price
A series of nine drawings lead aspiring artists through many methods for enhancing and finishing drawings, including crayon resist. Gail Price employs felt tip markers, ink pens, colored pencils, crayons, and even twigs and a palette knife in this exploration of drawing techniques.
VHS: S20989. $24.95.

Drawing: Learning Professional Techniques
Artist and educator Tony Couch shows the professional drawing techniques he feels are necessary to create a work of art. These include contour drawing, gesture drawing, perspective, cross-hatching and modeling. Then he completes several drawings in pencil, ink, and colored markers using the techniques demonstrated. 55 mins.
VHS: S14132. $39.95.

Elementary Art Appreciation Videos— Understanding Painting Series
Children in grades 3-8 will learn how to view artistic masterpieces by focusing on line, shape and the language of art. Developing a mood in portraiture and the use of color and line to express ideas is thoroughly explained for young audiences.
Abstraction, Light, and Color.
VHS: S26605. $34.95.
Approaching a Painting.
VHS: S26601. $34.95.
Composition and Realism.
VHS: S26602. $34.95.
Landscape, Seascape.
VHS: S26603. $34.95.
Portraits, People.
VHS: S26604. $34.95.
Elementary Art Appreciation: Understanding Painting Video Set.
VHS: S26606. $165.00.

Elements and Principles of Design with Artist Tony Couch
Tony Couch graphically explains how the elements of design, including line, shape, value, color, texture and direction, are used to build a design. He shows how each of the principles of design, balance, harmony, gradation, repetition, contrast, dominance and unity apply to each of the elements. 47 mins.
VHS: S11261. $39.95.

Figure Drawing and Painting with James Kirk
Kirk uses many existing drawings to show the use of dry media (pens, crayons, pencil) in drawing and sketching figures, both human and animals. He defines such concepts as contour line vs. gesture line, value and composition, and then demonstrates the application of the same skills to a watercolor painting of a seated nude. 60 mins.
VHS: S12861. $39.95.

Flat Brush Writing
Flat brush calligraphy is ideal for signs, banners and fabric writing. Fran Strom illustrates the essential brush techniques, the works of water colors and water based points, practiced on the basic Roman Capital letters. 80 mins.
VHS: S17208. $39.95.

Forrest Bales Presents Basic Latex Mold Making
Forrest Bales has been at the forefront of latex molds for more than 15 years. This instructional video considers the craft, technique, materials and tools needed from conception through completion. The video also provides step-by-step instructions on how to arrange and apply the materials. 32 mins.
VHS: S20338. $39.95.

Graphic Arts Training Library
Clip Art: Use and Fundamentals: Using Pre-Prepared Art Creatively. Teaches the fundamentals of designing and producing effective finished art work using limited-budget, camera-ready graphics in a variety of applications, including newsletters, ads, brochures, and T-shirts. 45 mins.
VHS: S10861. $69.95.
Desktop Design 1: Basic Electronic Graphic Techniques. Presents a balanced overview of desktop design techniques and typesetting principles plus basic information on software and hardware and takes a step-by-step approach to simple graphic projects to demonstrate the elements of good design and typography. 30 mins.
VHS: S10852. $49.95.
Desktop Design 2: Creative Design with PostScript Drawing Software. This video highlights several major applications, beginning with the finished project and retracing the designer's steps to completion. Each project uses either Adobe Illustrator 88 or Aldus FreeHand in conjunction with ancillary software and hardware. Projects covered include chart design, type catalog, title page, multicolor magazine and book covers, electronic graphics in a newspaper ad and special segments on graphic tricks and tips. 45 mins.
VHS: S10853. $69.95.

Desktop Design 3: Creative Design with Page-Layout Software. This video highlights several major applications, beginning with the finished project and retracing the designer's steps to completion. Each project uses a current program such as Aldus PageMaker, Ready, Set, Go!, or Quark XPress in conjunction with ancillary software and hardware. Projects include a newsletter, brochure, full-page ad layout and special segments on graphic tips and tricks. 45 mins.
VHS: S10854. $69.95.

Graphic Design 2: The Application of Good Design. Reveals how to create presentations that sell by watching professional designers working on rough layouts, comprehensives, and dummies. Computer aids for preparing effective designs are also demonstrated. 45 mins.
VHS: S10859. $69.95.

How to Draw and Sell the One Minute Caricature, with Jim van der Keyl

This program teaches you all you need to know about drawing quick sketch caricatures. Jim has drawn at major amusement parks including Great America, Universal Studios Tour, and Magic Mountain. He has also worked on Disney animated features. 70 mins.
VHS: S16208. $39.95.

How to Draw Comics the Marvel Way

Stan Lee, the father of Marvel Comics and the creator of Spiderman and the Incredible Hulk shows you how to put your visions of super heroes on paper. 59 mins.
VHS: S08897. $19.95.

The Illustrated Figure

Taken from the program *Techniques for the Professional Illustrator*, and hosted by educator Jana Lyn-Holly, this program shows the processes and work extending from figure drawing to finished illustration, encompassing drawing, quick step-by-step sketches, full color work, black and white line drawing, and water colors. 30 mins.
VHS: S17210. $39.95.

Let's Create Art Activities (For Ages 5-10)

An instructional video supervised by teacher Ann Felice, featuring her students as they engage in various exercises, problem solving and creative endeavors, including creative clay, fold-dyed paper, pasta mosaics and snazzy sunglasses. 45 mins.
VHS: S18645. $29.95.

Life Drawing Video Workshops by Ruth Block

An exhaustive series of eight lessons, each beginning with a brief lecture defining the principles of the exercise and following with the necessary demonstrations of technique. Instruction is succeeded by the model(s)' pose, where "real time" is given to allow for participation in the exercise. Each tape comes with an information booklet. The complete set includes eight tapes, 729 minutes all told.
VHS: S15750. $449.00.

Lifting a Curtain: Conservation of Rubens' Crowning of St. Catherine

Documents the cleaning and restoration of Peter Paul Rubens' magnificent painting The Crowning of St. Catherine, in the collection of the Toledo Museum of Art. The viewer has a rare opportunity to see the care given to the masterpieces as paintings conservator Gabrielle Kopelman engagingly explains and demonstrates the techniques required to clean and restore the painting. 30 mins.
VHS: S03562. $39.95.

Making Stained Glass Windows

Learn the delicate art of making stained glass windows from Tim Yockey, master craftsman working in the Pacific Northwest, including the design, glass cutting, leading, soldering, puttying and finishing. 100 mins.
VHS: S09942. $54.95.

Maskmaker

Jackie Miller's video workshop is a guide to the fabrication and painting of *papier mache* masks. The program demonstrates the basic skills required for the process, distilled from a 10-hour course.
VHS: S19644. $39.95.
Jack Johnson, USA, 1992, 130 mins.

Maskmaking Introduction

Carole Sivin demonstrates techniques for using basic materials to make a variety. An instructional program is enriched by historical examples from different cultures. 35 mins.
VHS: S15549. $39.95.

Maskmaking with Paper

Peggy Flores demonstrates in an articulate and clear way the art of constructing paper masks. Complete techniques and easily accessible materials are shown. 18 mins.
VHS: S20629. $24.95.

Maskmaking Workshop

Carole Sivin expands on the basic maskmaking techniques to produce interesting examples for performance, decoration, and fantasy. 50 mins.
VHS: S15550. $39.95.

Mobiles: Making Art That Moves

Go mobile! From the first mobiles created by Alexander Calder and exhibited in 1932, this program follows the evolution of style and technique and the endless search for creative expression. 22 mins.
VHS: S09472. $93.00.

Oil Painting: Simplifying Outdoor Painting

A video showcasing the simple methods that painter John Stobart has developed during his 35-year career. The video provides an overview of the basic requirements an artist needs in order to paint nature. It includes a lesson on drawing and the nature of perspective, with special emphasis on preparation of canvas and the materials required for a field trip. 60 mins.
VHS: S19645. $24.95.

Oriental Art—Grades 5-12

Students gain new insights into the Chinese and Japanese cultures through calligraphy, paintings and woodblock prints. The philosophy and the art's connection with history is explored.
VHS: S09088. $75.00.

Paint with Strings 'n Things

Julie Abowitt shows how to paint using a ball of string, tempera paint, an old sponge and paper. 30 mins.
VHS: S09888. $9.95.

Paint Without a Brush

Give paintbrushes the brush with this new and create way to paint using just cotton swabs, tempera and construction paper. 30 mins.
VHS: S09887. $29.95.

Paint!

John Fitzmaurice Mills shows some of the basic techniques and materials used by artists, and explores the problems faced by a painter in translating reality onto his canvas. A BBC production.
VHS: S10285. $19.95.

Painting Barns in Watercolor

Tony Couch prepares a detailed drawing of barn buildings on location. The drawing is a lesson in itself as the artist uses line and value to make his reference drawing. In the studio, he draws a value sketch and prepares the watercolor paper for painting. He illustrates how color, shape, texture and value are used in painting barns, trees, grass and sky. 50 mins.
VHS: S11183. $29.95.

Painting Streams, Rocks and Trees in Watercolor

Well-known artist Tony Couch shows how to paint a mountain stream as he shares his painting skills in lessons on painting trees, mountains, rocks and water. The camera shows step-by-step painting skills with close-up views of his brush and palette. 55 mins.
VHS: S11182. $29.95.

Painting with Stephen Quiller

Crystal Productions presents five new art instruction videos with artist and teacher Stephen Quiller. Each tape focuses on a single topic or medium including watercolor, composition, color, visualization and experimental water media.
Color. Color concepts and different color combinations are presented in an exploration of this vital aesthetic component. Among those issues explored are primary, secondary and intermediate colors, after-image, intensity, contrast, value and monochromatic and analogous color. 18 mins.
VHS: S20898. $24.95.
Composition. Students will learn how to develop compositions from different subjects, and the importance of various shapes and values which can trigger ideas for larger scale paintings. Sketches also figure prominently in this instruction toward landscape painting. 18 mins.
VHS: S20897. $24.95.
Experimental Water Media. Combining different media like graphite, charcoal, colored pencils, pastels and even oil pastels can enliven traditional watercolor. Collage also offers greater creative flexibility. All these techniques are ably demonstrated in this final tape. 19 mins.
VHS: S20900. $24.95.
Visualizing What You Paint. More spontaneous and creative work will result when students are motivated to see and visualize their subjects with the techniques employed in this segment. Negative shapes, painting around the subject, even painting from light to dark and vice versa can all lead to more inspired paintings. 19 mins.
VHS: S20899. $24.95.
Watercolor Methods. Different types of papers, brushes and pigments are explored in this demonstration of watercolor techniques. A variety of key approaches, including wet-on-wet, drybrush and other innovative methods, are included in this easy-to-follow tape. 18 mins.
VHS: S20896. $24.95.
Painting with Stephen Quiller, Set.
VHS: S20901. $99.75.

Paper Play

Julie Abowitt demonstrates how tissue paper can be used to make collages and decorate other items such as bottles, jars and cans. 30 mins.
VHS: S09886. $9.95.

Papermaking and Bookbinding

Sandy Kinnee and Mollie Favour show handmade paper, papermaking techniques, and bookbinding using simple equipment. 59 mins.
VHS: S07650. $89.50.

Pencil Drawing with Gail Price

Using graphite and colored pencils, as well as a variety of papers and techniques, artist Gail Price leads the viewer through a series of ten drawings that illustrate the basics of drawing. Includes examples of scumble, smudge, stipple, hatching and cross-hatching. 20 mins.
VHS: S20988. $24.95.

Philip Pearlstein Draws the Artist's Model

A video workshop focusing on the painting and teaching ideas of one of the most important artists of the century; Pearlstein relates important ideas about art history and drawing the human nude figure to demonstrate techniques available to artists. Adapting sophisticated computer systems to this style of art, Pearlstein demonstrates step-by-step process of how to draw the human figure. 90 mins.
VHS: S08280. $69.95.
Laser: LD70306. $99.95.

Pointed Brush Writing

As part of its series on calligraphy, Fran Strom details the history of pointed brush writing, which began with ancient Chinese artists. Strom demonstrates the technique of handling the brush, and applying those skills to the Roman Capital alphabet, and shows its practical and commercial applications. 60 mins.
VHS: S17207. $39.95.

Portraits in Watercolor with James Kirk: Elements of Design

Noted teacher and artist James Kirk covers the elements of design in drawing and painting and demonstrates a series of work-along exercises that lead directly to painting a portrait. 60 mins.
VHS: S09949. $39.95.

Portraits in Watercolor with James Kirk: Magic of Light and Dark

James Kirk guides you through a progression of different approaches to portrait painting. Follow along as Kirk implements and weighs each of the design elements in actual paintings. 60 mins.
VHS: S09950. $39.95.

Potter's Song: The Art and Philosophy of Paul Soldner

Soldner discusses his work and demonstrates the techniques to create his non-functional raku pottery. He also his lifestyle and theories of education for the potter.
VHS: S07635. $39.95.

Printmaking

Sandy Kinnee demonstrates introduction to printmaking and printmaking with basic equipment including relief, intaglio, lithography and serigraphy, and making prints with linoleum blocks, found objects, metal relief plates, plaster relief blocks, stencils, cutout cardboard plates. 38 mins.
VHS: S07651. $59.95.

Raku Ceramics with James Romberg

Raku artist and teacher James Romberg brings a subtle and fascinating form within reach of amateur potters, explaining this serendipitous art rooted in centuries-old Japanese ceremonies which is enjoying a powerful renaissance in the U.S. 75 mins.
VHS: S12865. $39.95.

Sculpture and the Creative Process

Dale Lamphere explores the creative process of the sculptor in his studio starting with initial thumbnail sketches in clay. He then makes the maquette and the armature and sculpts the finished work. 29 mins.
VHS: S16565. $39.95.

Slip Casting

Slip moldmaking and slip casting techniques; demonstrates making an original piece of pottery and then preparing it for multiple reproduction, including the complete process of making pottery from slip cast molds. Wendy Lopez, ceramicist. 37 mins.
VHS: S07648. $59.95.

Stretching the Canvas with Guest Host Peter Sellars

Producer/director Peter Sellars visits a number of California artists in their respective environments. A revealing trip inside the studio that depicts the artists at ease with their work. 59 mins.
VHS: S15768. $39.95.

Tempera

Tempera painting and tempera methods are demonstrated by Gail Price using tempera mixing, color mixing, dry brush techniques. 44 mins.
VHS: S07653. $59.95.

Time Exposure

Portrays the history of photography through the work of William Henry Jackson, who made 40,000 glass negatives. Reenactments demonstrate wet-plate photography, developing, solar printing. Includes dramatic on-location filming of the scenes of many of his photographs. 28 mins.
VHS: S09071. $29.95.

Traditional Basketmaking with John McGuire

This high-level professional instructional tape, suitable for both beginning and advanced basketmakers, presents traditional New England basketmaking with nationally acclaimed historian, author and basketmaker, John McGuire. 90 mins.
VHS: S08242. $69.95.

Water Media Techniques: Acrylic and Casein

Stephen Quiller demonstrates the special properties and handling characteristics of acrylic and casein and then shows how they can be used to create both transparent and opaque washes, impasto textures, and special effects. 60 mins.
VHS: S13297. $39.95.

Water Media Techniques: Watercolor and Gouache

Stephen Quiller works with various media and often combines them to create mixed media paintings. In this program, he shows the use of watercolor and gouache through small demonstration studies and then demonstrates landscape painting. 60 mins.
VHS: S13296. $39.95.

Watercolor I

Basic equipment and principles of watercolor, watercolor composition, techniques and watercolor demonstrations. Cecile Johnson. 40 mins.
VHS: S07645. $89.50.

Watercolor II

Mastering watercolor techniques through demonstration and learning watercolor skills through bold, positive, colorful brushwork as well as the construction of objects. Irving Shapiro. 45 mins.
VHS: S07646. $59.95.

Watercolor III

Design and composition in watercolor painting, and watercolor techniques in landscapes and seascapes. Tony Couch. 47 mins.
VHS: S07647. $59.95.

Watercolor Painting Pt. 1: Wet and Spontaneous

Watercolor artist Judy Howard demonstrates the art and techniques of watercolor, introducing color theory and exercises to help understand the behavior of water color paint. 60 mins.
VHS: S09947. $39.95.

Watercolor Painting Pt. 2: Taming the Wet Medium

In this program Judy Howard helps the student gain more control to achieve more harmonious colors and looseness, and to understand the step-by-step development of a painting. 60 mins.
VHS: S09948. $39.95.

Watercolor Symbols: Rocks, Puddles and Weeds

Demonstrates painting symbols for rocks, puddles, weeds and grasses, as well as the "spatter" technique. 55 mins.
VHS: S07630. $39.95.

Watercolor Symbols: Trees and Water

Demonstrates painting symbols for trees and water. 55 mins.
VHS: S07629. $39.95.

The Way Pots Pour

Potter and teacher Marvin Bartel shows the common problems which afflict many teapots. This video includes basic physics demonstrations about the way liquids pour, as well as advice on how potters can design effective spouts.
VHS: S21990. $35.00.

Winter's Soft Mantle

Tony Couch demonstrates step-by-step how to complete a painting of farm buildings in the snow with special instruction on how to paint rough wood, soft snow and cast shadows. 115 mins.
VHS: S07631. $49.95.

Workshop in Oils with William Palluth

60 minutes each.
Autumn Landscape. William Palluth illustrates step-by-step through the painting of this colorful and detailed autumn landscape. Sketch and color print included.
VHS: S08928. $29.95.
Oil Painting Technique. A must for the serious artist or art teacher, revealing secrets including wood textures, shadows and reflections, soft edges, wet-on-wet, and glazes.
VHS: S08933. $29.95.
Starting to Paint. *For the beginning artist, William Palluth shows the basic brushes, brush strokes and paints to show how to apply oil paints to canvas while keeping colors clean and rich.*
VHS: S08935. $29.95.
Winter Landscape. A nostalgic snow scene featuring a magnificent bare tree in a step-by-step oil painting instruction. Includes a sketch and print.
VHS: S08936. $29.95.
Workshop in Oils: Mountain Landscape. William Palluth instructs how to paint this dramatic scene depicting the Mount of the Holy Cross in Colorado. Follow Bill as he mixes and supplies each color with depth, one of the most sought after effects in landscape painting. Sketch included. 60 mins.
VHS: S15751. $29.95.
Workshop in Oils: Sunset. You'll enjoy painting this nostalgic summer scene with warm light from an evening sky reflecting off a quiet stream. In this workshop, artist William Palluth shows how mixing large pools of color can make painting so much easier, as well as promote harmony in blending. Perfect for beginners. Sketch included. 60 mins.
VHS: S15752. $29.95.

WorldScape

The distinguished American naturalist and maritime artist John Stobart hosts this massive 13-part series. 390 mins.
WorldScape: Beer.
VHS: S19658. $19.95.
WorldScape: Greenwich.
VHS: S19653. $19.95.
WorldScape: Hilton Head.
VHS: S19656. $19.95.
WorldScape: Honfleur.
VHS: S19652. $19.95.
WorldScape: Jersey.
VHS: S19655. $19.95.
WorldScape: Laguna Beach.
VHS: S19650. $19.95.
WorldScape: Lyme Regis.
VHS: S19648. $19.95.
WorldScape: Martha's Vineyard.
VHS: S19654. $19.95.
WorldScape: Maui.
VHS: S19647. $19.95.
WorldScape: Montserrat.
VHS: S19649. $19.95.
WorldScape: Savannah.
VHS: S19651. $19.95.
WorldScape: St. Barthelemy.
VHS: S19646. $19.95.
WorldScape: Westport Point.
VHS: S19657. $19.95.
WorldScape: The Complete Series.
VHS: S19659. $19.95.

Yvonne Jacquette: Autumn Expansion

Yvonne Jacquette discusses the process of painting her 27 foot, three-panel work "Autumn Expansion" during its 1981 exhibition at the Brooke Alexander Gallery. 13 mins.
VHS: S08254. $39.95.

ARCHITECTURE

1071 5th Avenue: Frank Lloyd Wright and the Guggenheim Museum
Although this museum opened in 1959, it did not fulfill all of Wright's original intentions. Sir Richard Rogers explores the disputes, money problems and personality clashes that plagued this building. F. Murray Abraham and Claire Bloom are featured reading Wright's letters, offering still more insights into the drama surrounding the erection of this masterwork.
VHS: S22150. $29.95.

The Architecture of Doom
A brilliant documentary which explores the inner workings of the Third Reich and illuminates the Nazi aesthetic in art, architecture and popular culture. Director Peter Cohen uses this analysis of Nazi art and architecture to shed new light on German popular culture, which made Hitler possible. Music by Richard Wagner, footage of Hitler and his Nazi party and rare films and memorabilia are combined to show how a civilized country supported a frustrated artist who became a maniacal despot.
VHS: S26346. $59.95.
Peter Cohen, USA, 1995, 119 mins.

Chicago's Riverfront: Where the Present Meets the Past
The Chicago River was the link between the Mississippi River and the Great Lakes, fostering the growth of the city of Chicago during the 19th Century. Today it is a showcase of striking modern architecture and historical buildings adapted to new uses. 30 mins.
VHS: S14590. $29.95.

Frank Lloyd Wright: The Office for Edgar J. Kaufmann
A documentary about the artistry and architectural innovation of Frank Lloyd Wright in designing the office for Edgar J. Kaufmann in 1935-37. The period coincides with Wright's historic Fallingwater House. 28 mins.
VHS: S19637. $29.95.

Frederick Law Olmsted and the Public Park in America
Olmsted's first major work was the composition of New York's Central Park in 1858. The project was fraught with obstacles—political, financial and topographical—yet the completed park serves as a testament to Olmsted's unique and pioneering vision. With a dramatic rhetoric depicting this exceptional undertaking, the film blends documentary elements and dramatizations of actual events. 58 mins.
VHS: S16000. $39.95.

The Lakefront: Parks and Plans
"City in a Garden" is the slogan that inspired the Burnham 1909 plan for Chicago. In this video, the development of the Lakefront and Grant Park are detailed as they affected the face of the contemporary Midwestern metropolis. Includes a companion guidebook.
VHS: S27496. $34.95.

The Loop: Where the Skyscraper Began
A unique confluence of forces and events led to the development of this key modern architectural form. Technology and circumstances surrounding the genesis of the skyscraper are at the center of this video. Includes a companion guidebook.
VHS: S27494. $34.95.

Michigan Avenue: From Museums to the Magnificent Mile
At one end it is heavy with retail giants. At the other, this world renowned boulevard is home to key cultural institutions. The growth of Chicago's most fashionable and prestigious Avenue is revealed in this video. Includes a companion guidebook.
VHS: S27495. $34.95.

Modern Marvels Series
A series of tapes which explore major accomplishments of modern engineering and building.
Empire State Building. This is the miraculous story behind the building of the world's most famous skyscraper. It was the world's tallest for over a generation and it remains a monument for the ages. 50 mins.
VHS: S22091. $19.95.
Grand Coulee Dam. This mammoth dam is the result of both engineering bravado and a colossal vision. Many said it couldn't be done because of the obstacles that stood in the way. And yet here it is, a man-made wonder.
VHS: S22090. $19.95.
Las Vegas. Only in the contemporary era of jet travel and publicity could a city emerge that seems to be based on the ephemeral image of a mirage. This unique tourist site's origin is on view in this video. 50 mins.
VHS: S26235. $19.95.
Mount Rushmore. It took over 15 years to create the largest sculpture the world has ever seen. Carved from the raw stone of a living cliff, this memorial to four of America's greatest presidents is a testament to the bold character of the nation. 50 mins.
VHS: S22092. $19.95.
Panama Canal. A story of drama, history and action emerges in this documentary about the building of this ever-vital canal. Its union of the two oceans through the heart of the Western Hemisphere changed the modern face of the Americas. 50 mins.
VHS: S22093. $19.95.
The Eiffel Tower. Originally ridiculed as ugly, Gustave Eiffel's tower came to be regarded as a masterpiece of engineering. Today it is recognized the world over as an icon for Paris, the City of Light. This is the story of an inspired vision. USA/France, 1994, 50 mins.
VHS: S26232. $19.95.
The Golden Gate Bridge. It was originally believed that no bridge could span the San Francisco Bay. Then the longest suspension bridge on Earth opened to the public. A story of an engineering wonder is revealed in this video. 50 mins.
VHS: S26233. $19.95.
The Statue of Liberty. A design emerged in France for a colossal statue. The site in New York harbor required that an entire country, the United States, be convinced that it was possible.
VHS: S26234. $19.95.

Once There Was a Ballpark
Martin Sheen hosts this informative and entertaining look at the history of baseball stadiums. From the humble beginnings in the streets through the original wooden bleachers, and on to more modern concrete structures, it's all here, including a look at some of the most beloved structures still standing, like Wrigley Field. 108 mins.
VHS: S21707. $19.98.

Places We Live: Complete Set
All three volumes of this "Weird and Wonderful Houses" series at a special price.
VHS: S20541. $75.00.

Places We Live: Dream Houses
A person's house is his self image, his autobiography as ghostwritten by the architect. Mark Twain's house suited him so well that he became convinced he himself designed it. Other houses visited are Fenway Court in Boston, recreating a Venetian palazzo; the house at Vizcaya; Frank Lloyd Wright's Hollyhock House; Saarinen's Cranbook House and Henry Davis Sleeper's Beauport. 58 mins.
VHS: S20539. $29.95.

Places We Live: Houses for Individualists
A look at some fantastic houses built by individualists—houses built by people with creative dreams, original needs or compulsions and the ability to design and erect the unconventional. The program shows a guest house in the shape of a yellow dragon with slides for stairs, a spherical house, a house shaped like a snail, and many more. 28 mins.
VHS: S20540. $29.95.

Places We Live: Way Out Architecture
Some of the more unusual places Americans have designed as habitats and the kinds of people who design them and live in them are examined in this freewheeling look at modern architecture. Among them are an underwater house, a $3-million concrete tent, space ships and Noah's ark. The program also looks at the unorthodox architects who create the structures. 44 mins.
VHS: S20538. $29.95.

Pyramid
Based on his popular book, David Macaulay brings the mysteries of ancient Egypt to vivid life in this unique documentary. Combining location photography and animation, Pyramid describes the planning, construction and cultural significance of the Great Pyramid of Giza, the world's largest pyramid. 57 mins.
VHS: S15761. $69.95.

Soleri's Cities: Architecture for Planet Earth and Beyond
A portrait of architect Paolo Soleri, a student of Frank Lloyd Wright, who believes the massive population centers have created vast social and environmental threats to daily life. Soleri has proposed rebuilding the American city, which he calls the Arcology, integrating ecological principles within innovative architectural designs, to alleviate stress, overcrowding, urban despair and tumult. 30 mins.
VHS: S20023. $19.95.

The World of Buckminster Fuller
Buckminster Fuller, the visionary creator of the geodesic dome, was influential across a range of fields. He coined the concept of the "Spaceship Earth," and gave voice to ecological concern in a time of unshakable faith in progress. This film from Robert Snyder offers a thorough biography of this unique genius.
VHS: S12220. $29.98.
Robert Snyder, USA, 85 mins.

PERFORMANCE ART

4 Scenes in a Harsh Life
This is a collection of live performances by Ron Athey, one of the most provocative performance artists working today. His rituals make extensive use of S/M and religious sources, combining such disparate elements as leather daddies and evangelism. The result is a mixture of sexual and artistic play. Serious issues of control, consent, illness and even transcendence are joined.
VHS: S22954. $69.95.

Antigone: Rites of Passion
Amy Greenfield's daring first feature retells Sophocles' classical tragedy through action, dance and cutting-edge rock music. It transforms the drama of the heroine who defied the State to bury her brother into ceaseless movement and music, haunting sound and words, a mounting outcry against the world's injustices climaxing in an end-of-the-world requiem. A hymn to the extremes of courage, devotion, outrage, eros and death. "Impressive, innovative rock opera film" (Variety). With music by Elliott Sharp, Glenn Branca and Diamanda Galas.
VHS: S15437. $29.95.
Amy Greenfield, USA, 1990, 85 mins.

Best of Radio Thin Air
Highlights from the best of the long running cable TV poetry/music show are joined in this video. Taylor Mead, John Zorn, Elliot Sharp, Lydia Lunch, Pete Seeger, numerous "New Beat" poets, East Village performance art, poetry and music videos are all included.
VHS: S22663. $29.95.
Mitch Corber, USA, 1990-93, 105 mins.

A Bitter Message of Hopeless Grief
Living in a fictional world all their own, Survival Research Labs' machines act out scenarios of perpetual torment, exasperating consumption, and tragic recognition.
VHS: S26470. $25.00.
Jon Reiss/Fictional Worlds/Mark Pauline/Matt Heckert, USA, 1988, 13 mins.

Cabaret Voltaire Presents...
A comprehensive video guide to Cabaret Voltaire and their radical incorporation of musique concrete, tribal, tape collage, industrial noise and techno. The 14 tracks include "Diskono," "Trash (Part 1)," "Badge of Evil," "Landslide," and "Seconds Too Late." 90 mins.
VHS: S19614. $19.95.

Carmen
Bizet's tale of temptation, desire, obsessive love and death is placed in the nightclubs and graffiti-laced streets of contemporary New York. Dance images, the sex life of a penguin, and scientific writings on volcanoes and glaciers also play a part in this updated opera.
VHS: S22644. $29.95.
Ann Sargent Wooster, USA, 1990, 20 mins.

Cirque du Soleil: We Reinvent the Circus
This video captures the original tour of the highly innovative and rightfully famous circus troupe from Canada. Experience the daring feats, the fantastic costumes, and the wonderful music which has captivated audiences the world over. An Emmy Award winning program. 55 mins.
VHS: S15623. $19.95.

Dream Man
An adaptation of James Carroll Pickett's one-man performance stars Michael Kearns as a harsh, Lenny Bruce-like commentator who conjures up elaborate, witty and profane sexual fantasies over the phone lines. "Straight forward, poetically insightful," wrote Daily Variety. Includes an interview with the playwright.
VHS: S17117. $19.95.
Hugh Harrison, USA, 1991, 90 mins.

Eric Bogosian: Confessions of a Porn Star
Eric Bogosian performs a variety of routines that cross the line between stand up comedy and performance art. This tape brings together some of his best bits, including selections from Our Gang, The Pacer, Porno, Beat Poet and more.
VHS: S26706. $24.95.
Rob Klug, USA, 1995, 60 mins.

The Films of Meredith Monk
Two works by dance and performance artist Meredith Monk. Book of Days (1986) is a haunting meditation on time and nature, about a perfectly preserved medieval town in Southern France. Ellis Island (1981) examines the decaying walls and supernatural presence of the American landmark. 105 mins.
Laser: LD71956. $39.95.

Gary Goldberg—Four Films: Plates, Mesmer, Usher and TV Head
These shorts feature two icons of the downtown New York underground film/performance scene, Taylor Mead and Bill Rice. Their stage-show-based vignettes reveal quietly seething emotions that boil over into explosive climaxes.
VHS: S22506. $39.95.
Gary Goldberg, USA, 1992, 40 mins.

Halber Mensch
Electric performances, industrial set design, performance art and superb production values highlight this long-form video, directed by Sohgo Ishii, of Einsturzende Neubauten's classics Drawings of Patient O.T. and Halber Mensch. The numbers include "Armenia," "Sehnsucht," "Abfackeln," "Z.N.S." and "Schaben." 60 mins.
VHS: S19609. $19.95.

Homage to Hermann Nitsch (Apologies to Don Garlits)
A wild night at No Se No featuring performance artist, poet, critic and curator Michael Carter is captured in this video. Carter indicts modern car culture.
VHS: S22623. $19.95.
Michael Carter, USA, 1987, 20 mins.

Impact Addict Videos
Described as "the Evel Knievel of performance art" (The Village Voice), performance artist/stunt man David Leslie performs four harrowing assignments, including being wired with firecrackers, boding the heavyweight amateur champion, and simultaneously dueling with six New York City dojo masters. 30 mins.
VHS: S17199. $39.95.

In a Storm Even Dinosaurs Trip & Invasion of the Amazons
Swiss performance artist Penelope Wehrli creates dreamy films with strong images of female courage. Between heroes and heroines there is often a desert that could be characterized as a place of entrapment. 29 mins.
VHS: S22646. $29.95.
Penelope Wehrli, USA, 29 mins.

Judgment Day
A long-form video of Diamanda Galas' incendiary concert performances, shot by H-Gun Corp in Chicago, during her 1992 Plague Mass tour. Judgement Day distills her best works from the Saint of the Pit, Divine Punishment, Red Death and Plague Mass albums. The tracks include "There Are No More Tickets to the Funeral," "Let My People Go," "Blind Man's Day" and "Gloomy Sunday." 60 mins.
VHS: S19610. $19.95.

Love Lion
San Francisco poet and playwright Michael McClure joins Ray Manzarek, keyboardist for legendary group The Doors, in a performance of words and music. 70 mins.
VHS: S14715. $29.95.

Nouvelle Experience: Cirque du Soleil
The French Canadian troupe Cirque du Soleil has transformed the circus into an exciting, novel performance experience. This video reveals the magic of their innovative techniques, where lions and tigers have been replaced with wit and fantasy. 82 mins.
VHS: S25921. $19.95.

A Performance by Jack Smith
This is the only known recorded performance piece by the late artist/actor Jack Smith, made from an optically printed 8mm film original. Included are two works shot in Toronto in 1984: Dance of the Sacred Application and Brassieres of Uranus.
VHS: S27224. $59.95.
Midi Onodera, Canada, 1984

Performing at the San Francisco Museum of Modern Art Groundbreaking Ceremony
On April 8, 1992, this short and to the point show by Survival Research Labs stopped traffic in downtown San Francisco for 15 minutes. The staging of this event represents a sincere effort by a major art institution to align itself with more edgy, defiant work. 10 mins.
VHS: S26468. $15.00.

The Pleasures of the Uninhibited Excess
Three fast-moving Survival Research Labs performances from 1989-1990 are well documented in this video. It includes Illusions of Shameless Abundance, ArtSpace Computer-Controlled Installation and A Carnival of Misplaced Devotion.
VHS: S26469. $25.00.
Leslie Asako Gladsjo, USA, 1991, 45 mins.

Return of the Goddess for the New Millennium
This unique video performance blends environmental, sociological, and metaphysical/archetypal imagery with compelling interpretive dance movement and music. Experience archetypal Goddess energy in a vibrant dancer's expression of sensuality, openness and empowerment. Dance concept, choreography and performance by Jamie Miller; music composed and performed by Paul (Ramana Das) Silbey. "Ms. Miller dances with such passion that I kept waiting for smoke to pour out of the VCR…the wildest, most intense, incredibly powerful Goddess invocations that I have ever experienced" (Harvest Magazine). "Powerful, controversial, deeply moving" (Lawrence Ferlinghetti). Note: This video contains scenes of partial nudity and erotic dance movement. 1989, 32 mins.
VHS: S13720. $29.95.

The Rocket Movie
A re-enactment of performance artist/stuntman David Leslie's gonzo attempt to scale a mountain of watermelons before a large, adoring crowd. 32 mins.
VHS: S17200. $39.95.

Seven Machine Performances 1979-1982
This tape contains a selection of early Survival Research Labs performances. It is vital for anyone curious about how these events grew and developed.
VHS: S26471. $20.00.
Joe Rees, USA, 1983, 50 mins.

Sphinxes Without Secrets
Feminism, activism and women's performance art are explored in this engaging video. Annie Sprinkle, Rachel Rosenthal, Diamanda Galas and Holly Hughes are just some of the artists who discuss their work, as well as the motives and inspirations that drive them. 90 mins.
VHS: S25113. $39.95.

Stunt: A Musical Motion Picture
In this collage of images, representation and meta-reality, the performance artist and stunt man David Leslie orchestrates a spectacular pageant that pays homage to the respective spirits of James Brown, Evel Knievel, Bruce Lee and Julie Andrews. 35 mins.
VHS: S17201. $39.95.

Survival Research Laboratories
Founded in 1979 by Mark Pauline, this organization of artists and technicians is dedicated to exploring the potential for redirecting the techniques, tools and tenets of industry and science by staging mechanized presentations in the U.S. and Europe. Each performance consists of a unique set of ritualized interactions between machines, robots and special effects devices with humans present only as operators or audience.
Baited Trap: A Tale of Meat, Torment and Murder. "A wonderfully simple noir-ish romp through brutality and revenge inside a family that runs a meat packing plant. SRL's horrifying machines figure prominently" (Forced Exposure). 1986, 12 mins.
VHS: S10953. $14.95.
Bitter Message of Hopeless Grief. Living in a fictional world all their own, SRL's machines act out scenarios of perpetual torment, exasperating consumption and tragic recognition. 1988, 13 mins.
VHS: S10952. $18.00.
Scenic Harvest from the Kingdom of Pain. Three machine performances from 1983-1984. "Disturbing, fascinating, recommended" (Richard Gere, L.A. Reader). 1984, 45 mins.
VHS: S10951. $20.00.
Will to Provoke: An Account of Fantastic Schemes for Initiating Social Improvement. A documentation of SRL's 1988 European tour with shows in Amsterdam and Copenhagen. SRL ferrets out and satirizes assorted icons of cultural pride in two of Europe's more libertarian social democracies. 1988, 48 mins.
VHS: S10950. $19.98.

Videotape for a Woman and a Man
Amy Greenfield uses human motion, camera lens, editing and optical techniques to "see into, with and through the body." Shot over a period of six months and edited over four years, Videotape for a Woman and a Man is "an absorbing and disturbing inquiry into male-female relationships. Photographed in black and white and color, and performed in the nude by Greenfield and dancer Ben Dolphin, it relentlessly examines the possible physical and emotional encounters between a man and a woman….We marvel at and are moved by the poignant spectacle of the human body as an instrument capable of transcending its own reality" (John Guen, Dance Magazine).
VHS: S01415. $19.98.
Amy Greenfield, USA, 1979, 34 mins.

Virtues of Negative Fascination
This videotape documents the five most recent performance spectacles by the Survival Research Laboratories. Power and intricate, radio-controlled machines clash in parking lots and nightclubs of San Francisco, horrific photo images rotate on stands, bombs explode, fires start. SRL spectacles, frequently covered by national print and TV media, are a cross between mechanized warfare and demolition derbies.
VHS: S10203. $29.95.
Survival Research Labs, USA, 1986, 80 mins.

dance
ON VIDEO

3 by Martha Graham
Features three original dances choreographed by and starring Martha Graham. One of the giants of American dance, Graham is the subject of a new biography and the inspiration to her company's triumphant return to Broadway. Originally aired on television, this program has been remastered for home video. "Extraordinary" (*New York Times*). USA, 87 mins.
VHS: S15397. $59.95.

Ailey Dances
The Alvin Ailey Dance Theater, recorded live at New York's Center Theater, performs "Night Creatures", set to a Duke Ellington Concerto; "Cry", created by Ailey as a birthday present to his mother; "Lark Ascending", influenced by Ailey's trip to Scotland; and "Revelations", the Company's signature piece, created in 1960. USA, 1982, 85 mins.
VHS: S03638. $39.95.

Alice in Wonderland: A Dance Fantasy
A multimedia interpretation of Lewis Carroll's work full of colorful costumes and sets. The performance interweaves dance, music, art, mime, theater and acrobatics. The music is composed by Viktor Kalabis and played by the Czech Philharmonic Orchestra. With the Prague Chamber Ballet. 27 mins.
VHS: S19175. $19.98.

Alicia
Cuban by birth, Alicia Alonso is perhaps the most venerated "American" dancer in the history of ballet. This is a portrait of the still active ballerina, including excerpts from the "Black Swan Pas de Deux" from *Swan Lake* and the complete *Carmen Ballet*. 70 mins.
VHS: S07095. $19.95.

All the Best from Russia
The best in ballet, the best in folk-dancing, the best in all-round entertainment from inside Russia. Here are the Bolshoi Ballet and the Don Cossack dancers, the Armenian Folk Ensemble and the incomparable treasures in the fabulous Hermitage Museum, a variety of colorful, exciting entertainment. 52 mins.
VHS: S03965. $64.95.

Anna Karenina
Maya Plisetskaya and Alexander Godunov star in this ballet choreographed by Plisetskaya to music by Rodion Schedrin and based on Tolstoy's famous novel. A very cinematic rendering of the famous Bolshoi company production never before seen in the U.S. 81 mins.
VHS: S08531. $29.95.

Anna Sokolow
This notable modern dance choreographer speaks about her career with the aid of film clips and demonstrations of her choreographic process. Rehearsals of *Rooms* are particularly illuminating. 20 mins.
VHS: S25972. $39.95.

Anyuta
Brimming with sly humor and graceful balalaika melodies, *Anyuta* captures deftly the delicate color and flavor of Chekhov's Russia. Ekaterina Maximova of the Bolshoi dances in the title role, with the production choreographed by Vladimir Vasiliev and featuring the cream of the Bolshoi, Kirov and Maly ballet companies. 68 mins.
VHS: S03155. $39.95.

The Art of the 20th Century Ballet
This program presents three ballets, introduced by their choreographer, Maurice Bejart. Includes *Bolero*, *Adagietto* and *Ce qui l'amour me dit*. A pioneering new style of dance combining the traditional with modern techniques. 75 mins.
VHS: S15627. $34.95.
Laser: LD70276. $34.95.

The Arthur Murray Dance Lesson Series
Hosted by Terry Leone, this series of easy-to-follow dance lessons runs the gamut of dancing styles. Complete with a brief history of each dance and informative notes on timing and measures, this series features top dance couples from around the globe.
Cha Cha.
VHS: S16780. $19.95.
Dancin' Dirty.
VHS: S16781. $19.95.
Fox Trot.
VHS: S16782. $19.95.
Mambo.
VHS: S16783. $19.95.
Merengue.
VHS: S16784. $19.95.
Nightclub.
VHS: S16785. $19.95.
Rumba.
VHS: S16786. $19.95.
Salsa.
VHS: S16787. $19.95.
Samba.
VHS: S16788. $19.95.
Swing.
VHS: S16789. $19.95.
Tango.
VHS: S16790. $19.95.
Waltz.
VHS: S16791. $19.95.

Backstage at the Kirov
A remarkable portrait of the great company which has given the world Balanchine, Nureyev, Baryshnikov and Makarova. 1983, color, 83 mins.
VHS: S02430. $14.95.

The Balanchine Celebration: Part One
Darci Kistler, Nilas Martins and Kyra Nichols are featured in this video, along with Paris Opera Ballet prima ballerina Isabelle Guerin and Kirov ballet star Zhanna Ayupova. Selections from *Apollo*, *Vienna Waltzes*, *Union Jack*, *Theme and Variations*, and other Balanchine works, along with the complete *Scherzo a la Russe*, reveal Balanchine's Russian and European roots.
VHS: S27060. $29.98.
Matthew Diamond, USA, 1993, 86 mins.

The Balanchine Celebration: Part Two
Darcey Bussell and Lindsay Fischer dance a *pas de deux* from *Agon*. Then, American Ballet Theater prima ballerina Susan Jaffe stars with Nikolaj Hubbe in *Western Symphony*, while Damian Woetzel and Margaret Tracey lead in the patriotic *Stars and Stripes*. Finally, *Who Cares?*, featuring Jeremy Collins and Viviana Durante, brings the era of Gershwin alive.
VHS: S27059. $29.98.
Matthew Diamond, USA, 1993, 86 mins.

The Balanchine Essays: Arabesque
Now the inimitable Balanchine style and technique are available on video. Merrill Ashley, of the New York City Ballet, and Suki Schorer, of the School of American Ballet, demonstrate the principles and steps employed by the great choreographer. 45 mins.
VHS: S24683. $29.97.

The Balanchine Essays: Passe and Attitude
The incomparable technique of choreographer George Balanchine is clearly presented in this video. New York Ballet principals Suki Schorer and Merrill Ashley demonstrate Balanchine's interpretation and teaching of passe and attitude. Excerpts from *Agon*, *Diamonds*, *La Source*, *Swan Lake*, *The Nutcracker* and more are included.
VHS: S27058. $29.98.
Merrill Brockway, USA, 1994, 45 mins.

The Balanchine Essays: Port de Bras and Epaulement
George Balanchine's technique is presented by New York Ballet principals Suki Schorer and Merrill Ashley in this video. It demonstrates Balanchine's interpretation and teaching of port de bras and epaulement and features excerpts from *Divertimento No. 15* and *Symphony in C*.
VHS: S27061. $29.98.
Merrill Brockway, USA, 1994, 43 mins.

Balanchine, Dancing for Mr. B: Six Balanchine Ballerinas
Anne Belle made this documentary featuring interviews with six Balanchine prodigies who danced for the New York City Ballet. Maria Tallchief, Melissa Hayden, Allegra Kent, Merrill Ashley and Darci Kistler are featured and excerpts from some of Balanchine's most acclaimed ballets are included. 86 mins.
VHS: S24681. $29.97.

Balanchine, Robert Schumann's Davidsbundlertanze
Ib Anderson, Karin von Aroldingen, Jaques D'Amboise, Suzanne Farrell and Peter Martins are just part of an all-star cast called upon to perform Balanchine's final masterpiece. 43 mins.
VHS: S24682. $29.97.

Balanchine: Prodigal Son/Chaconne
Mikhail Baryshnikov, the greatest male dancer of modern times, stars with Karin von Aroldingen in the Balanchine/Prokofiev classic from the 1920's, *Prodigal Son*. Suzanne Farrell and Peter Martins, principal dancers from the New York City Ballet, then perform *Chaconne*. 57 mins.
VHS: S24679. $29.97.

Balanchine: The Four Temperaments, Andante from Divertimento No. 15, Tzigane
The first of these ballets, *The Four Temperaments*, is perhaps Balanchine's greatest achievement. *Tzigane* features the incomparable Suzanne Farrell, and Mozart's *Andante from Divertimento No. 15* features the New York City Ballet and their incomparable, flawless technique. 54 mins.
VHS: S24680. $29.97.

Ballerina: Karen Kain
Rudolph Nureyev has said of this dancer that "in her, the star quality is unmistakable." The first ballerina from North America to perform with Bolshoi Ballet, Miss Kain performs with Roland Petit's corps de ballet in Carmen, Coppelia and Romeo and Juliet. Included also are her insights on dance. 54 mins.
VHS: S03963. $64.95.

Ballerina: Lynn Seymour
Rudolph Nureyev is one of the many male stars performing here with Miss Seymour in performances of Kenneth MacMillan's Romeo & Juliet, Sir Fredrick Ashton's Two Pigeons, and Intimate Letters with Galina Samsova. Here also is recorded the world premiere performance of Mac and Polly. 56 mins.
VHS: S03964. $64.95.

Ballerinas
Carla Fracci is featured in a lavish recreation of the golden days of ballet in Paris, portraying dance stars of the 19th century, 10 ballerinas whose art and fame are legendary. Ms. Fracci dances excerpts from such classics as *Giselle*, *Coppelia*, *La Sylphide*, *Sleeping Beauty* and others, and is partnered by such great male dancers as Vladimir Vasiliev, Michael Denard, Richard Cragun and Peter Schaufuss. USA, 1985, 108 mins.
VHS: S04688. $39.95.

Ballet Class for Beginners
David Howard's ballet class for beginners is an excellent learning and teaching tool designed by America's foremost ballet master, introducing the beginning ballet student to the technique and vocabulary of classical ballet. Featuring Allison Potter with music by Whit Kellog.
VHS: S04689. $39.95.

Ballet Class—Intermediate-Advanced
Specially designed by David Howard to expand the classical vocabulary, movement potential, and kinetic awareness of the student. Dancers and teachers alike are given the possibility to participate in this unique class which features Cynthia Harvey and Peter Fonseca of the American Ballet Theatre.
VHS: S05851. $39.95.

Ballet Favorites
Beloved solos, pas de deux and ensembles including Mikhail Baryshnikov and Cynthia Harvey in *Don Quixote*, Natalia Makarova in *Swan Lake*, and Lesley Collier and Anthony Dowell in *The Nutcracker*. Other excerpts from *Romeo and Juliet*, *Sleeping Beauty*, *Giselle*. 59 mins.
VHS: S07922. $19.99.

Ballet Folklorico Nacional de Mexico
The richness of Mexican culture, its myths and traditions, comes alive through the artistry of the Ballet Folklorico in a production unequaled in pageantry and color. 110 mins.
Spanish Narration.
VHS: S05273. $59.95.
English Narration.
VHS: S05732. $59.95.

Ballet for Children and Adults
Kathryn Anderson, former soloist with the Boston Ballet, hosts this valuable instructional tape. Ballet attire, training methods, equipment and etiquette are all covered by this great ballerina. French terms are explained and there is even a Q & A section for some of the most commonly asked questions about this dance form. 48 mins.
VHS: S22441. $29.95.
Karl Brown, USA, 1932, 63 mins.

Ballet Russe
From choreographer Peter Anastos comes this hilarious Emmy Award-winning production of a dance parody. New Jersey's Garden State Ballet performs *Yes Virginia*, *Another Piano Ballet* and *Forgotten Memories*, which takes dead aim at prime time soap operas.
VHS: S12660. $19.95.

Ballet Workout
An elegant way to achieve a lithe, supple body, improve your carriage and attain the look and grace of a professional dancer. Melissa Lowe, a former soloist and principal dancer with several ballet companies, guides this body re-shaping series of exercises. 83 mins.
VHS: S11446. $19.95.

The Ballet Workout II
Melissa Lowe's instructional program looks at ways to hone and shape up your body, using the rigorous techniques and stretching exercises of the ballet dancer. 70 mins.
VHS: S19688. $19.95.

Ballroom Dancing Advanced
Instructor Theresa Mason showcases six popular social dances, including the Fox Trot, Waltz, Tango, Rumba, Cha-Cha and Swing. She also reviews beginner and intermediate steps. 60 mins.
VHS: S19005. $29.95.

Ballroom Dancing for Beginners
The basic techniques of ballroom dancing, including elements, dance position, understanding music and patterns for the fox trot, waltz, tango, rumba, cha cha and swing, taught by Teresa Mason and Susan Major. 57 mins.
VHS: S09935. $29.95.

Ballroom Dancing: Intermediate
This tape is designed for those who want to increase their ballroom dancing skills beyond the beginner's level. Master techniques for the most popular dances like the fox trot, the tango, the waltz and more. 48 mins.
VHS: S15094. $29.95.

Baryshnikov at Wolf Trap
This performance from 1975 shows the incredible Mikhail Baryshnikov at the peak of his artistic talents. Recorded at the Wolf Trap Farm Park for the Performing Arts in Virginia, the video features Baryshnikov in a series of solos and *pas de deux* with a variety of partners, including Gelsey Kirkland. Hosted by Beverly Sills. 50 mins.
VHS: S14751. $29.95.

Baryshnikov Dances Carmen
Ballet superstar Mikhail Baryshnikov stars in this sexy dance version of the Bizet classic, co-starring the legendary Zizi Jeanmaire as Carmen, and choreographed by Roland Petit.
VHS: S13059. $29.95.

Baryshnikov Dances Sinatra
Mikhail Baryshnikov dances three classy ballets featuring the choreography of Twyla Tharp: *Sinatra Suite*, a duet for Baryshnikov and Elaine Kudo set to a medley of songs by Sinatra, including "Strangers in the Night"; *Push to Shove*, set to rags by Joseph Lamb and Haydn symphonies; and *The Little Ballet*, featuring Baryshnikov, Deirdre Carberry and three other ABT dancers performing one of Tharp's most balletic works. 60 mins.
VHS: S10876. $19.95.

Baryshnikov: The Dance and the Dancer
A profile of Mikhail Baryshnikov which includes a look at his life and work, with footage of his performances while still dancing in Russia, as well as his work at ABT, including an insider's view of his new ballet, "Configurations." 85 mins.
VHS: S01926. $19.95.

Bill T. Jones: Dancing to the Promised Land
This video is built around the rehearsal and performance of Jones' epic, *Last Supper at Uncle Tom's Cabin/The Promised Land*. In the process, the work and creative processes of one of the most respected powers in American modern dance is revealed. 60 mins.
VHS: S21868. $29.98.

The Birmingham Royal Ballet in Tchaikovsky's The Nutcracker
A favorite at Christmas, this ballet follows the dreams of a young girl as she awaits Christmas morning. In her amazing journey she meets a handsome prince, a sugar plum fairy and the dreaded Rat King. This traditional work continues to enchant both children and adults. 98 mins.
VHS: S26298. $39.95.

Black Tights
Four sparkling ballets by Roland Petit featuring Petit and three great partners: Zizi Jeanmaire as Carmen and The Diamond Cruncher, Moira Shearer as Roxanne in Cyrano de Bergerac, and Cyd Charisse in A Merry Mourning. Maurice Chevalier is the host.
VHS: S03215. $29.95.
Terence Young, France, 1960, 120 mins.

Blue Angel
Renowned French choreographer Roland Petit's highly acclaimed ballet makes its North American debut in video in a superb stage production featuring the Ballet National de Marseilles. This is the ballet rendition of Heinrich Mann's dramatic story of the alluring Rosa Frohlich, the dancer at the famous Blue Angel Cabaret.
VHS: S10713. $29.95.

Bolshoi at the Bolshoi
Full-length ballet performances featuring the Bolshoi Ballet at the historic Bolshoi Theatre, under the direction of Yuri Grigorovich, newly recorded and mastered in digital stereo sound and digital D-2 video.
Sleeping Beauty. Original choreography by Marius Petipa, featuring Nina Semizorova and Alexi Fadeyevich.
VHS: S10419. $39.95.
The Nutcracker. Original choreography by Lev Ivanov, featuring Irek Mukhamedov and Natalya Archipova.
VHS: S10418. $39.95.

The Bolshoi Ballet
Paul Czinner's highly acclaimed film of the Bolshoi Ballet in performance stars Galina Ulanova in a complete *Giselle* (with Nikolai Fadeyechev) and *The Dying Swan*; plus five shorter ballets including such Bolshoi signature works as the "Walpurgisnacht" from *Faust* (with Struchkova) and *Spring Water* (set to a score by Rachmaninoff). Color, 95 mins.
VHS: S13683. $49.95.

Bolshoi Prokofiev Gala
To celebrate the 100th birthday of Russian composer Sergei Prokofiev in November, 1991, a gala benefit concert was staged at the Bolshoi Theater in Moscow. Yuri Grigorovich directs the dance greats Ludmila Semenyaka, Alexander Vetrov, Yuri Vasyuchenko, Nina Semizorova, Natalya Archipova and many other top performers. Includes excerpts from *Romeo & Juliet*, *Ivan the Terrible* and *Stone Flower*, as well as profiles of the Bolshoi Ballet and the life of Prokofiev. 170 mins.
VHS: S16507. $29.95.

Bolshoi Soloists
A loving tribute to the Bolshoi Ballet, featuring the Bolshoi with music of Tchaikovsky, Albinoni, Adam and Gershwin, in many treasured favorites, and featuring soloists Nina Timofeyeva and Michail Lavroski. 40 mins.
VHS: S06847. $39.95.

Bolshoi: Les Sylphides
With music by Frederic Chopin and the Bolshoi Ballet, choreographed by Mikhail Fokine, featuring Natalia Bessmertnova, Alexandre Beofatyriov and Galina Koslova. 34 minutes.
VHS: S02687. $49.95.

Book of Shadows
This ground-breaking video ballet employs experimental techniques in sound, performance, video and choreography to create a new and moving work. This winner of numerous awards explores the many incarnations of the goddess in a mythic landscape.
VHS: S21065. $29.95.
Janis Mattox, USA, 1993, 25 mins.

Bryony Brind's Ballet—The First Steps
Bryony Brind, Senior Principal Dancer with the Royal Ballet Convent Garden, has created this unique new ballet video which for the first time teaches the viewer the basic principles and movements of ballet. The program has been specifically designed so that it can be used by individuals, groups of friends, or by teachers in a class.
VHS: S10716. $29.95.

Bujones in Class
Fernando Bujones demonstrates his personal ballet technique that has made him one of the most sought-after guest artists in the world. A unique learning and teaching tool, the video was specifically designed by Bujones to teach the techniques of classical ballet. 31 mins.
VHS: S10021. $39.95.

Bujones: In His Image
Considered one of the leading male ballet dancers in the world, this program is a compilation of his greatest performances, with excerpts from "Le Corsair," "Raymonda," "Don Quixote," "7-Greek Dances," "Swan Lake," "Giselle" and "La Bayadere." There are also revealing discussions with Bujones about his life. 62 mins.
VHS: S03613. $39.95.

Carmen
The Carmen Suite presents ballerina Maya Plisetskaya in one of her critically most acclaimed and popular roles. The music, by Rodion Schedrin, is based on Bizet's score, and the ballet is choreographed by Alberto Alonso. Other works on the tape include Prelude, pairing Plisetskaya with Vladimir Vasiliev; Raymonda, originally choreographed by Marius Petipa and performed to a score by Glazunov; and The Dying Swan, to music by Saint-Saens. 1973, color, 73 mins.
VHS: S02432. $29.95.

The Catherine Wheel
A collaboration between choreographer Twyla Tharp and Talking Heads lead singer David Byrne merges classical dance with non-traditional movement in the story of the 4th century martyr, St. Catherine. "A major event in our theater, (with) dancing of astonishing beauty and power" (The New Yorker). 88 mins.
VHS: S02962. $29.97.
Laser: LD71632. $39.97.

Celebration—Royal Ballet
This exuberant program commemorates the 50th anniversary of Britain's Royal Ballet. The company's luminaries, including Sir Frederick Ashton, Dame Alicia Markova, Kenneth Macmillan and Sir Robert Helpman, are featured in a program that combines performances, rehearsals, interviews and archival film to provide a fitting celebration. Glimpses of rare performances including the very young Margot Fonteyn in Polonia, Giselle, La Fille Mal Gardee. 50 mins.
VHS: S10307. $39.95.

Charles Weidman: On His Own
The career of modern dance pioneer Charles Weidman (1901-1975) is traced from his roots in Lincoln, Nebraska, to the last work he choreographed in 1974. Includes rare footage. USA, 1990, 59 mins.
VHS: S15334. $49.95.

Checkmate
From the series Masterpieces of British Ballet comes this ballet in one act with prologue choreographed by Ninette de Valois and with music composed by Sir Arthur Bliss. Performed by dancers from Sadler's Wells Royal Ballet and Royal Ballet Orchestra. A game of love and death, played according to the rules of chess. 45 mins.
VHS: S13243. $29.95.

Children of Theatre Street
Provides an unprecedented glimpse inside the Kirov Ballet School where Nijinsky, Baryshnikov, Makarova and Nureyev were taught the tricks of their elegant trade. Presented by the late Princess Grace of Monaco and shot on location in Leningrad.
VHS: S02422. $39.95.
Robert Dornheim/Earle Mack, USA, 1977, 92 mins.

Choreography by Balanchine: Selections from Jewels/ Stravinsky Violin Concerto
Great dancers are featured in these excerpts from Balanchine works. Suzanne Farrell and Peter Martins dance in Diamonds. Merrill Ashley, Bonita Borne, Gerard Ebitz, Karin von Aroldingen, Heather Watts, Daniel Duell and Sean Lavery perform the ensemble piece Emeralds. Then, Peter Martins, Bart Cook, Karin von Aroldingen and Kay Mazzo perform Stravinsky Violin Concerto, along with members of the New York City Ballet.
VHS: S27062. $29.98.
Merrill Brockway, USA, 1977, 56 mins.

Cinderella (Berlin)
Grimm's wonderful fairy tale becomes even more magical with Prokofiev's music, here recreated by the Berlin Comic Opera with Hannelore Bey as Cinderella and Roland Gawlick as the Prince. 75 minutes.
VHS: S03379. $24.95.

Cinderella (Bolshoi)
The great 1961 color motion picture featuring the Bolshoi Ballet performing the timeless fairy tale. This unique mixture of film, dance and music stars Raisa Struchkova in the title role and a score by Sergei Prokofiev.
VHS: S01927. $55.00.

Cinderella (Maguy Marin/Lyon Opera Ballet)
Choreographer Maguy Marin's highly sophisticated, highly imaginative version of the Cinderella story, conceived of and performed by the Lyon Opera Ballet. Marin evokes childlike wonder by envisioning her characters as live dolls, with human feelings projected onto them by the children identify with their playthings. Prokofiev's wistful score, edited and restructured for this presentation, captures the familiar feelings of childhood and the happy endings all fairy tales promise. 87 mins.
VHS: S12217. $39.95.
Laser: LD71424. $34.95.

Classic Kirov Performances
A rare compendium recreates some of the legendary Kirov Theatre performances, including Anna Pavlova's work as The Dying Swan. The program features Natalia Dudinskaya, Galina Ulanova, Vakhtang Chabukiani, Konstantin Sergeyev, Altynai Asylmuratova and Tatyana Terekhova, in performances from Romeo and Juliet, The Nutcracker, Sleeping Beauty and Don Quixote. 110 mins.
VHS: S18568. $29.95.

Coppelia
Features Fernando Bujones, one of the most acclaimed dancers of the American Ballet Theatre, in a 1980 performance with the Ballets de San Juan, Puerto Rico. 110 mins.
VHS: S02417. $39.95.

Course in Rumba
The sensuality of the Flamenco-Rumba comes alive in this video. Famed dancer Pilar Perez de Guzman joins Carmelo Greco and Adrian El Chino to elucidate the character and intensity of this art form. Recommended for the intermediate/advanced level. 50 mins.
VHS: S21057. $40.00.

Creole Giselle (Dance Theatre of Harlem)
Using the story and original classical choreography of this repertory staple, Dance Theatre of Harlem founder Arthur Mitchell has set the ballet in 1841 Louisiana. Giselle is danced by Virginia Johnson, and Eddie J. Shellman co-stars as Albert. This remains one of the Dance Theatre of Harlem's most popular works. 88 mins.
VHS: S13931. $29.95.

Dance and Myth, The World of Jean Erdman Part 1: The Early Dances
Jean Erdman worked with Martha Graham but broke away to pursue her own vision. This video includes her works The Transformations of Medusa (1942), Creature on a Journey (1943), Passage (1946), Ophelia (1946), Hamadryad (1948) and Daughters of the Lonesome Isle (1945). 60 mins.
VHS: S26742. $29.95.

Dance and Myth, The World of Jean Erdman Part 2: The Group Dances
The Perilous Chapel (1949) and Solstice (1950) show the evolving work of Jean Erdman. 60 mins.
VHS: S26743. $29.95.

Dance and Myth, The World of Jean Erdman Part 3: The Later Solos
These works represent the culmination of a life dedicated to dance. Included are Pierrot, The Moon (1954), Changing Woman (1951) and Fearful Symmetry (1957). 60 mins.
VHS: S26744. $29.95.

Dance Black America
Narrated by Jeffrey Holder, this four-day festival held at the Brooklyn Academy of Music is a celebration of African-American dance. Includes performances by the Alvin Ailey American Dance Theater and the Charles Moore Dance Theater. 1983, 87 mins.
VHS: S15335. $49.95.

Dance of Darkness
Edin Velez's provocative documentary studies the intricate and obscure butoh, Japan's avant-garde dance form.
Laser: LD70105. $49.95.

Dance Theater of Harlem
The New York Times has hailed this program as "a triumph, a sheer utter triumph." Now the energy, creativity and classical perfection of the Dance Theater of Harlem has been captured in dazzling performances of four signature pieces. The American classic Fall River Legend, choreographed by Agnes de Mille, tells the notorious story of Lizzie Borden. Troy Game, by Robert North, is a dynamic satire of the machismo attitudes inherent in sports. The Beloved, a ballet for two dancers by Lester Horton, confronts the themes of violence and fanaticism. John Henry, choreographed by Arthur Mitchell, is a celebration of the strength of the human will. 117 mins.
VHS: S12215. $39.95.

Dancers
Mikhail Baryshnikov stars in this drama about the backstage romantic intrigues, travails and triumphs of a world-class ballet company as they prepare to perform the ballet "Giselle."
VHS: S06368. $19.98.
Herbert Ross, USA, 1987, 99 mins.

Dances of the World—France
A colorful kaleidoscope in dances from the central regions of France featuring groups from Morvan. You'll experience the bourree, the polka, rondes and other dances as they are kept alive by some of the region's most outstanding folk groups. Featuring La Sabotee Sancerroise, Les Enfants du Morvan and Le Groupe de La Soyotte. 60 mins.
VHS: S10400. $39.95.

Dancing
This 8-part series probes the traditions of dance in communities around the world—from the often misunderstood waltz to the eloquent gestures of an Asante court dance in Ghana, and from the latest hip-hop in Morocco to a ballet class in Russia and a modern dance rehearsal in New York. Filmed on location on five continents, it explores the oldest and most compelling of languages: the art of communication called dance.
Vol. 1: The Power of Dance. In its great diversity, dance is the thread which connects all people—from the great classics of England's Royal Ballet and Japanese Kabuki to Broadway's rich jazz and tap heritage; from the hundreds of children in Jacques d'Amboise's National Dance Institute learning dances from around the world to the latest video art choreography and the Hip Hop dances of New York City streets. 58 mins.
VHS: S18394. $29.95.

Vol. 2: The Lord of the Dance. Dancers and dances have been worshipped as divine and feared as manifestations of the devil. Here we trace the cultural belief that shaped the great traditions of sacred and secular dance. Christianity has had an ambivalent view of dance in worship; Hinduism throughout India and the Yoruban religion of Nigeria combined worship and dance to create great dance/theater traditions. 58 mins.
VHS: S18395. $29.95.
Vol. 3: Sex and Social Dance. Social dance can be as refined as the waltz or as sexy as the tango. Dance of one community may shock another whose social values and gender roles differ. We all dance, but what social values and ideals are told through the dances we do? 58 mins.
VHS: S18397. $29.95.
Vol. 4: Dance at Court. In royal courts of the world, dance not only reached a pinnacle of elegance but played a role in the preservation of power and the maintenance of order and control. This function lives on in European ballet, the imposing dance of Asante kings in Africa, the refinement of Japan's Bugaku and the otherworldliness of the Javanese Bedoyo. 58 min.
VHS: S18396. $29.95.
Vol. 5: New Worlds, New Forms. In the Americas, dance became a medium for cultural fusion among African and European peoples. Here their steps and styles combined, creating dances that can be read as cultural maps. From the Samba in Bahia and Candomble in Salvador, Brazil, to the Lindy Hop in the Catskills, New York State, and Rock and Roll in Baltimore, Maryland, cultural fusion has shaped the great popular dances of the 20th century. 58 min.
VHS: S18398. $29.95.
Vol. 6: Dance Center Stage. The demands of a growing middle class created a new relationship between dancer and audience. Illustrated are the dazzling theatrical traditions of Japan's Kabuki and Russia's Kirov Ballet, both adapted over generations to entertain wider, changing audiences. 58 min.
VHS: S18400. $29.95.
Vol. 7: The Individual and Tradition. This segment features extraordinary individuals who revolutionized dance: Isadora Duncan, Martha Graham, Katherine Dunham, George Balanchine, Twyla Tharp, Eiko and Koma, Sardono Kusumo and Garth Fagin. 58 min.
VHS: S18400. $29.95.
Vol. 8: Dancing in One World. Less than 100 years ago, people from one part of the globe might have had no idea what people from other places looked and sounded like or how they moved. Today, television and satellite bring Rock and Roll to Bali, for example, and Yoruba ritual dances appear in rock videos. Are the traditional dances dying out? The new pan-culturalism is exciting, but will it change the face of dance forever? Are we racing toward a single global culture or will ancient traditions continue into the 21st century? 58 min.
VHS: S18401. $29.95.
Dancing, Complete Set.
VHS: S18402. $199.95.

Danza Flamenco de Hoy
Three of Spain's finest young dancers—Beatriz Martin, Esther Ponce and Adrian—perform a variety of traditional dance styles including Martinete, Tientos, Algrias and Tango. With singers La Tobala, Rafael Fajardo and Pedro Montoya. 60 mins.
VHS: S16513. $40.00.

Daphnis and Chloe
This Sydney Dance Company production features choreography by Graeme Murphy and music by Maurice Ravel. Starring Carl Morrow as Daphnis and Victoria Taylor as Chloe, this sensual ballet tells the story of two young lovers brought together by Cupid who learn the meaning of love and desire. 60 mins.
VHS: S07601. $39.95.

Denishawn: The Birth of Modern Dance
This unique video tells the story of one of the least publicized, yet most influential modern dance companies in America, founded by Ruth St. Denis and her husband Ted Shawn at the turn of the century. 40 mins.
VHS: S15093. $29.95.

Don Quixote (Ananiashvili)
Prima ballerina Nina Ananiashvili exhibits her technical command in this Russian State Perm Ballet production of composer Leon Minkus' work. Ananiashvili and Aleksei Fadeyetchev dance the lovers Kitri and Basilio. Aleksandr Astafiev is the knight; Evgeny Katusov is his comic squire Sancho Panza. 120 mins.
VHS: S19898. $24.95.

Don Quixote (Kirov Ballet)
The tremendous resources of the Kirov Ballet flash and dash through the four acts of joyous Petipa and Gorsky choreography, making Don Quixote a visual treat. The action centers around Don Quixote's quest to perform chivalrous deeds. Tatyana Terekhova and Farukh Ruzimatov are featured as the lovers Kitri and Basilio. Hailed as one of the greatest large cast ballet productions ever recorded on film. 120 mins.
VHS: S08795. $39.95.

Don Quixote (Nureyev)
Rudolf Nureyev stars and co-directs this film version of the famous ballet, with Lucette Aldous and Sir Robert Helpmann in the title roles, with the dancers of the Australian Ballet and choreography by Marius Petipa. 110 mins.
VHS: S06896. $39.95.

Early Dance Part 1: From the Greeks to the Renaissance
A concise history of dance unfolds in this first section of a two-part series. Demonstrations detail the works of early Greek theater and English masques. Music, narration, costumes and performances tell the story of dance. 24 mins.
VHS: S25973. $39.95.

Early Dance Part 2: The Baroque Era
Beginning with the burlesque entertainments of the Louis XIII era, this video traces the evolution of dance through a theatrical tradition that culminates in ballet. Even Louis XIV performed in these ballet spectacles. 30 mins.
VHS: S25974. $39.95.

Erich Hawkins' America
Hawkins' choreography on American themes is evident in the works Plains Daybreak, Hurrah, Ahab and God's Angry Man. This video also includes portions of his other works Classic Kite Tails and Black Lake. 57 mins.
VHS: S25874. $49.95.

Erik Bruhn Gala: World Ballet Competition
This gala, presented in honor of the first Erik Bruhn prize, features dancers from four of the companies with which he is most closely associated. Breathtaking performances of pas de deux and variations include choreography by Bruhn, Glen Tetley, Kenneth Macmillan and Antony Tudor. Natalia Makarova makes a special appearance. 90 mins.
VHS: S10270. $39.95.

Essential Ballet
A unique collection featuring the greatest stars of the Russian ballet, in performances in Moscow and London. Part I includes the Kirov Ballet in highlights from Swan Lake (with Mikhalina and Liepa), The Nutcracker (with the Vaganova Ballet Academy) and Drigo's Diana and Actaeon. Part II is a special outdoor performance in Red Square with Maya Plisetskaya in her final performance as the Dying Swan, Nina Ananiashvili in Sleeping Beauty and Don Quixote, and Le Corsaire, Giselle and The Firebird.
Laser: LD72366. $34.95.

An Evening with Ballet Rambert
Three short ballets from one of dance's most innovative companies. Included are "Sergeant Early's Dream," choreographed by Christopher Bruce to British, Irish and American folk tunes; "Intimate Pages," using Janacek's Second String Quartet; and Robert North's "Lonely Town, Lonely Street," a jazz ballet.
VHS: S03738. $39.95.

An Evening with Nederlands Dans Theater
Jiri Kylian's Nederlands Dans theater in "Svadebka," choreographed to one of Stravinsky's most challenging works; "La Cathedrale Engloutie," a ballet to Debussy's composition; "Torso," a ballet choreographed to all in exile to music by Japanese composer Toru Takemitsu; and "Sinfonietta."
VHS: S03739. $39.95.

An Evening with Royal Ballet
Rudolf Nureyev and Dame Margot Fonteyn head a cast of legendary artists performing excerpts from "The Sleeping Beauty," "Les Sylphides" and "Le Corsaire." 87 mins.
VHS: S04424. $39.95.

An Evening with the Alvin Ailey American Dance Theater
Four rhythmic pieces from Alvin Ailey, including Divining, Revelations, The Stack-Up and Cry.
VHS: S19332. $39.95.

An Evening with the Bolshoi Ballet
Excerpts from eight ballets made famous by the Bolshoi, permitting viewers to see the Corps de Ballet and soloists, including "Paganini" and music by Rachmaninoff, Ravel's "Bolero" and "Waltz," and Prokofiev's "Stone Flower." 90 mins.
VHS: S03147. $39.95.

A Feast of Irish Set Dances
Set dancing has been very much a part of the living tradition in Ireland, especially in rural areas, for at least four centuries. In this vibrant video, you will see young and old keeping the set dancing tradition alive. 56 mins.
VHS: S11999. $29.95.

Fiesta Gitana!
Pilar Perez de Guzman continues his series of Flamenco videos with the help of the incomparable Angelita Vargas, a dancer renowned for her passionate and elegant abilities. They are joined by some of the greatest practicing flamenco dancers, singers and guitar players in this bravado display of Spanish soul. 32 mins.
VHS: S21059. $34.00.

Firebird
American choreographer Glen Tetley gives a new look to Stravinsky's The Firebird, stylishly performed in this new release by the Royal Danish Ballet. 55 mins.
VHS: S08481. $39.95.

Firestone Dances
These rare performances from The Voice of Firestone television series show superstars at the top of their careers. Rudolf Nureyev, Jacques D'Amboise, Melissa Hayden, Maria Tallchief, Carla Fracci, Henning Kronstam, Kirsten Simone and Oleg Tupine dance on this video. 50 mins.
VHS: S26703. $24.95.

Flamenco
A rare treat for Flamenco lovers, this video provides a magnificent portrayal of Flamenco and its performers. The rhythms and lyrics are inherited folklore and part of daily life, but the techniques are arduously studied, and each of the four distinct schools of flamenco in Spain is represented.
VHS: S05588. $39.95.

Folkloric Ballet of Mexico
Created by choreographer Amalia Hernandez in 1952, the Folkloric Ballet combines modern creativity with a thorough research of history. These dances reveal the cultural values of pre-Hispanic Mexico, and its evolution through the centuries. 113 mins.
VHS: S16371. $49.95.

Folkmoot USA
Relive the first-ever North Carolina International Folk Festival through this entertaining program. In addition to dances and music, the program shows what goes on at the festival between performances. 60 mins.
VHS: S10404. $39.95.

Fonteyn & Nureyev: The Perfect Partnership
A collector's item that traces the famous pair of ballet dancers from their first ballet in 1962, to their grand finale 17 years later. 90 mins.
VHS: S04686. $39.95.

Fred Astaire Dance Series
The Fred Astaire Dance Studios developed this series of six programs, presenting the newest steps and old favorites.
Fred Astaire Ballroom Dancing.
VHS: S09102. $19.99.
Fred Astaire Latin Dancing.
VHS: S09103. $19.99.
Fred Astaire Western Dance.
VHS: S09104. $19.99.

French Folk Dances
Learn three exciting French dances performed by students: Le Branle a Six from Brittany, La Boulangere from Alsace-Lorraine, and La Contra-Danse from Haiti. Also includes audio-cassette, directions and guide with cultural and costume information. 45 mins. English narration.
VHS: S05285. $59.95.

French Folk Dancing Video, Volume 2
More folk dancing in the French language high school classroom, with authentic folk dances performed by high school students. This volume contains Le Branle du Quercy, Saint Ferreol from Catalogne and La Bastringue from Quebec. 35 mins.
VHS: S09058. $49.95.

Gaite Parisienne
Victor Jessen followed the Ballet Russe de Monte Carlo around America for several years filming bits and pieces of Gaite Parisienne, hoping to put together a complete performance. The finished film is a triumphant and loving tribute to the company and its principles, including Alexandra Danilova, Frederic Franklin and Leon Danielian. 38 mins.
VHS: S07094. $39.95.

Garth Fagin's Griot New York
Choreographer Garth Fagin, jazz master Wynton Marsalis and sculptor Martin Puryear collaborated on this acclaimed dance piece. Griot, the West African term for storyteller, inspired this testament to the diverse stories of New York City. Features the Wynton Marsalis Septet. 87 mins.
VHS: S24726. $24.98.
Laser: LD74903. $29.98.

George Balanchine's The Nutcracker
Macaulay Culkin stars in this ballet masterpiece, composed by Tchaikovsky. The cast includes former NYC Ballet dancers with narration by Kevin Kline. This unforgettable story of a dreamy young girl and her nutcracker soldier unfolds at night when a battle breaks out between a dashing prince and the evil king of the rats. 93 mins.
VHS: S22420. $19.99.

German Folk Dances
Authentic folk dances performed by students include: Siebenschritt and S'Trommt Em Babeli from Switzerland and Das Fenster, danced throughout Germany. Also includes audio-cassette, directions and guide with cultural and costume information. 42 mins. English narration.
VHS: S06838. $59.95.

German Folk Dancing Video, Volume 2
Volume 2 of folk dancing in the German language classroom, with folk dances performed by high school students, contains D'Hammerschmedsgselln from Bavaria, Brandiswalzer from Switzerland and Zillertaler Laendler from Austria. 35 mins.
VHS: S09054. $59.95.

Ghost Dances
Choreographer Christopher Bruce created this contemporary ballet in response to a letter from the widow of Chilean folk singer/writer Victor Jara, murdered during the military junta that brought Pinochet to power, which described the plight of the South American people. Performed to a selection of Jara's work and traditional folk music, Ghost Dances evoke the natural gaiety and courage of the South American people. 40 mins.
VHS: S08482. $39.95.

Giselle (Alonso)
Thousands watched transfixed during the MET Opera Centennial Gala as Alicia Alonso danced an excerpt from Giselle, the role of her first major triumph. This film, made almost twenty years earlier, offers her complete portrayal of the part, capturing Alonso as one of the most virtuosic and touching Giselles of all time. 99 mins.
VHS: S07096. $19.95.

Giselle (Baryshnikov)
Live from Lincoln Center, Mikhail Baryshnikov and Natalia Makarova in a brilliant American Ballet Theatre production taped live at Lincoln Center. 95 mins.
VHS: S09895. $22.95.

Giselle (Bolshoi)
A classic production of the Bolshoi's staging of Giselle. "I've never seen so sharp and clear a live performance ballet tape. And the stereo sound track is a knock out" (Roy Hemming, Video Review).
VHS: S19521. $39.95.

Giselle (Bujones)
Ballet virtuoso Fernando Bujones stars in this brilliant production of Giselle with the Ballet Teatro Municipal of Rio de Janeiro. Supreme among the romantic ballets, Giselle has never before been delivered with such intensity as in this performance by Bujones, "the finest male classical dancer this country has ever produced" (NY Post). 104 mins.
VHS: S13665. $29.95.

Giselle (Nureyev)
Rudolf Nureyev and Lynn Seymour are the principal dancers in this recording choreographed by Jules Perrot and Jean Coralli. With Monica Mason and Gerd Larsen. 78 mins.
VHS: S18191. $29.95.

Giselle...The Making of
Marcia Haydee recreates both the choreography of her adaptation of Giselle and the creative process of rehearsal and directing that makes this performance possible. The Corps de Ballet of the Stuttgart Ballet Company is featured in this video. 29 mins.
VHS: S27005. $19.98.

Godunov: The World to Dance In
A provocative portrait of a man whose personal odyssey has led from a fatherless childhood and his 1979 defection from the Kirov Ballet to superstardom in the United States. Included are dazzling performances with Cynthia Gregory and Maya Plisetskaya. 60 mins.
VHS: S02421. $39.95.

Green Fire and Ice
The Trinity Irish Dancers are among America's foremost ethnic dance troupes. They have won numerous Gold Medals at the annual World Championships of Irish Dancing in Ireland. This documentary shows the ins and outs of this troupe from rehearsal to performance and international competition. 30 mins.
VHS: S22056. $19.95.

Hanya: Portrait of a Pioneer
This video traces the career of dancer/choreographer Hanya Holm—from her early days in Germany in the 1920s, through her work on the Broadway stage, to being regarded as one of the famous "four pioneers" of modern dance. USA, 1985, 60 mins.
VHS: S15338. $49.95.

Holiday of Ballet
In 1981, Amanda McKerrow of Washington D.C. became the first American ever to win the gold medal in the International Competition of Ballet Artists in Moscow. This behind-the-scenes look at the competition captures both the heartbreak and the joy of this annual event.
VHS: S13057. $29.95.

Horton Dance Method
This instructional video demonstrates the modern dance training method created by Lester Horton and used by Alvin Ailey and other noted companies. From warm-up exercises through fortifications, this comprehensive program is both a great workout and a solid foundation for the serious dancer.
VHS: S13054. $29.95.

I Am a Dancer
A portrait of the great Rudolf Nureyev, from his homely beginnings in 1938 to one of the century's great dancers and superstars. Includes excerpts from many of Nureyev's greatest moments, including Sleeping Beauty, Marguerite and Armond, La Sylphide. 1970, color, 90 mins.
VHS: S01928. $19.98.

Il Ballarino: The Art of Renaissance Dance
Learn authentic Renaissance court dances—and the gestures and step vocabulary associated with them—from Il Ballarino, the first instructional video of its kind. USA, 1990, 33 mins.
VHS: S15339. $44.95.

Ilona Vera's Ballet Class: Developing a Personal Style
Provides instruction in how to get the most out of taking class. Primarily developed for dancers who have reached an intermediate level and aspire for professionalism in their work. Based on the famed Vaganova (Kirov) method, considered one of the most definitive methods of exercising the body. 73 mins.
VHS: S08693. $29.95.

Introduction to Ballroom Dancing
Learn to swing, rumba, cha cha, waltz and fox trot on video in this unique tape featuring instructor Margot Scholz, a member of the Imperial Society of the Teachers of Dance. For those with little or no previous dance experience or a refresher for those with prior experience. 68 mins.
VHS: S10877. $19.95.

Invitation to the Dance
Gene Kelly wrote, directed, choreographed and performed in this three-part tribute to his fascination with movies and movement. "Circus", "Ring around the Rosy" and "Sinbad the Sailor" each incorporate Kelly's love of dance. "Sinbad" is partially animated by the Hanna-Barbera studios. With Claire Sombert, Carol Haney, Tamara Toumanova and Igor Youskevitch.
VHS: S06169. $19.98.
Gene Kelly, USA, 1956, 93 mins.

Isadora Duncan Dance
The technique and repertory perfected by Duncan are demonstrated by the Isadora Duncan Ensemble in this video. It contains the complete works: Under the Scarf, Slow Mazurka, Dance of the Blessed Spirit and Dubinushka, as well as a number of excerpts from other works. 60 mins.
VHS: S25873. $49.95.

Israel in Dance: Shalom in Action
The Shalom Dance Company tries to bring all the traditions of the inhabitants of modern Israel together in their unique works. During rehearsal, backstage and in performance this troupe never forgets the importance of its mission. 53 mins.
VHS: S23256. $29.95.

Israel's Folk Dance Festival
A rare and exciting collection of the best Hebrew folk dance groups performing in Israel, filmed at the picturesque Zemach, on the beautiful shores of the Sea of Galilee. 60 mins.
VHS: S05757. $59.95.

Ivan the Terrible Ballet
The original cast stars in one of the most dazzling of all Bolshoi Ballet productions, based on Sergei Eisenstein's classic film of murder and intrigue. With Yuri Vladimirov, Natalia Bessmertnova. USSR, 1977, 91 mins.
VHS: S09226. $29.95.

Jazz Dance Class with Gus Giordano
Covers the warmup, basic jazz techniques, jazz walks, centre barre, and the professional dancer in a teaching tape of elements of jazz dancing. 63 mins.
VHS: S09936. $39.95.

Jazz Workout
An exercise tape which is also designed as an introduction to jazz dancing. It includes a warm-up, floor progressions and dance combinations. Ann Coombes, a dance instructor for over 10 years, leads a class that helps beginners develop a routine and paces accomplished dancers through their workouts. The warm-up sessions include stretches, flexes, stomach and thigh strengthening exercises. 55 mins.
VHS: S10878. $19.95.

Jesus, The Son of Man
An interesting ballet featuring Ivan Marko and other distinguished Hungarian dancers in a modern recreation of the teachings of Jesus that are relevant today—with music by Liszt, Shostakovich, and Xenakis. 72 mins.
VHS: S09629. $29.95.

Jose Greco in Performance
A 1959 performance of Jose Greco that captures the famous dancer at the peak of his career, accompanied by a hand-picked troupe of singers and musicians. Selections include "Pastoral Romance", "Castellana", "Cordoba", "Granada" and "Wedding Dance". 26 mins.
VHS: S13246. $24.95.

Khovanschina
This Bolshoi opera tells the story of the violent and turbulent era of Peter the Great's regency. Shostakovich orchestrated this work by Mussorgsky, who died before he could finish it. The incomparable ballerina Maya Plisetskaya is featured. Russian with English subtitles. USSR, 1959, color, 131 mins.
VHS: S02253. $69.95.

Kirov Ballet in London
A thrilling program that captures the excitement and visual grandeur of a Kirov Ballet performance on stage in London during 1988, with a special guest appearance by Natalia Makarova, who is reunited with her former company after an absence of 17 years. Includes many favorites, including Kingdom of the Shades from La Bayadere, selections from Swan Lake, Don Quixote, Le Corsaire, Le Papillon. 128 mins.
VHS: S12591. $39.95.

The Kirov Ballet in Tchaikovsky's Sleeping Beauty
Natalia Dudinskaya, Natalia Makarova, Valeri Panov, Alla Sizova and Yuri Soloviev are featured in this classic film version of the ballet as choreographed by Marius Petipa. This Cinemascope masterpiece is presented in letterbox format to preserve the unmatched beauty and integrity of the performance.
VHS: S24889. $29.95.
A. Dudko/K. Sergeyev, Russia, 1964, 84 mins.

Kirov Ballet: Classical Ballet Night
Live performances by the world-renowned Kirov Ballet, featuring some of the famous Pas De Deux of the Classic repertory, including Diana and Actheon, Esmeralda, Flower Festival in Genzano, the Canteen Keeper, Venice Carnival and Pas de Quatre. Dancers include Irina Kolpakova, Gabriela Konleva, Elena Evteeva. 95 minutes.
VHS: S02688. $39.95.

Kirov Classics
This first-ever studio recording of the world-famous Kirov Ballet was made by the award-winning director Thomas Grimm at the Danmarks Radio Arhus Dance Studio, the most advanced facility of its kind. It showcases highlights from their repertoire, both classic and contemporary: Chopiniana, Petrushka, Barber's Adagio and many more. 174 min.
VHS: S18403. $39.95.

Kirov Soloists
Irina Kolpakova, the prima ballerina of the Kirov, dances and presents this film dedicated to the work of the principal dancers of the Kirov, including behind-the-scenes looks at rehearsals, and full-fledged performances, giving a glimpse into how the Kirov Ballet tradition is carried from one generation to another. With Sergei Berezhnoi, Olga Tcheytchikova, Tatiana Terekhova, and music by Pugni, Villa-Lobos and Offenbach. 55 mins.
VHS: S06848. $39.95.

Kylian Collection
Jiri Kylian and the Nederlands Dans Theater perform works by Debussy, Schoenberg and Chavez, and Haydn's Silent Cries, which won the first International Video Dance Grand Prix in 1988.
Laser: LD71449. $34.95.

Isadora Duncan Dance
(see above)

La Bayadere (Kirov)
Choreographed by Petipa to music by Minkus, and first performed by the Kirov Ballet in 1877, this production was filmed at the Kirov Ballet in Leningrad. 126 mins.
VHS: S02416. $39.95.

La Bayadere (Royal Ballet)
Natalia Makarova choreographed and designed the Royal Ballet's production of La Bayadere, using elaborate stage effects, spectacular sets and a brilliant cast headed by Irek Noukhamedov and Darcey Bussell. This Covent Garden production is considered the definitive production. 124 mins.
VHS: S17308. $29.95.

La Sylphide
Winner of the VIRA Award, a reconstitution of the Taglioni ballet, achieved by Pierre Lacotte. The recreation includes original costume and set designs, and features Michel Denard, Ghislaine Thesmar and the Paris Opera Ballet Company. 81 mins.
VHS: S03162. $39.95.

Lady of the Camellias
John Neumeier directs this Hamburg Ballet production. 125 mins.
VHS: S09359. $39.95.

The Land of Sweet Taps
This is a fun-filled adventure for children ages 4-8 who want to learn tap dancing. In addition to the fundamental sounds, rhythms and steps there are shuffles and digs. The lyrics are fun and memorable, helping children remember the timing of the music. 57 mins.
VHS: S21701. $19.95.

Learn the Art of Flamenco (Videos Flamencos de la Luz)
The esteemed instructional series produced by Pilar Perez de Guzman of Madrid, Spain. An invaluable teaching tool that helps you perfect your technique.
Course in Sevillanas. The most popular dance in Spain. 60 mins.
VHS: S15322. $40.00.
Course in Castanets. Develop speed, precision and ease. 54 mins.
VHS: S15323. $40.00.
Course in Rumba. Enjoy the sensuality of Flamenco-Rumba. 45 mins.
VHS: S15324. $40.00.
Flamenco Show. Fandangos, Alegrias, Soleares and more. 40 mins.
VHS: S15326. $28.00.
The Bases of Flamenco Dance. For the aficionado or intermediate student. 45 mins.
VHS: S15325. $40.00.

Legend of Love
Part of the Bolshoi at the Bolshoi series, Legend of Love ballet is a colorful story set in an opulent, oriental palace in ancient Turkey. Featuring Maria Bilova. 1990, 111 mins.
VHS: S14551. $39.95.

The Leningrad Legend
Natalia Makarova is the narrator for this behind-the-scenes look at today's Kirov Ballet. The company's great past is recalled in film clips, but the focus of the program is on future developments. 71 mins.
VHS: S14749. $29.95.

The Little Humpbacked Horse
Vladimir Vasiliev and Maya Plisetskaya bring to life this 19th century Russian fairytale in one of the Bolshoi's most popular ballets. USSR, 1961, color, 85 mins.
VHS: S02441. $29.95.

Lovers of Teruel
The talents of Lyudmila Tcherina, one of the greatest dance tragediennes, and Raymond Rouleau, one of France's outstanding directors, combine to make a ballet film of exceptional beauty. With cinematography by the great Claude Renoir, and music by Mikis Theodorakis. 90 mins.
VHS: S03152. $39.95.

Ludmila Semenyaka Bolshoi Ballerina
A selection of jewel-like performances by the legendary prima ballerina, performing excerpts from many of her famous roles, including the Rose Adagio from Sleeping Beauty, and selections from Swan Lake, Spartacus, The Talisman, The Nutcracker. 60 mins.
VHS: S12592. $29.95.

Macbeth
The Shakespeare masterpiece in a stunning production by the Bolshoi Ballet taped live at Moscow's historic Bolshoi theatre. Choreographed by Vladimir Vasiliev and featuring Alexei Fadeyechev and Nina Timofeyeva. 105 mins.
VHS: S03154. $39.95.

Mademoiselle Fifi
This Canadian Broadcasting Corporation production is the only existing document of ballet's beloved star Alexandra Danilova in a complete performance. Along with her partners from the Ballet Russe de Monte Carlo, Michael Maule and Roman Jasinski, this ballet legend helped popularize the art in North America. 20 mins.
VHS: S19401. $29.95.

Magic of the Bolshoi Ballet
This video is a rare collection of the most historic performances by the leading dancers of the famed Bolshoi Ballet Company. Archival films from the past 50 years feature Soviet dance legends such as Ulanova, Plisetskaya, Vasiliev, Fadeyechev and many others in scenes from The Sleeping Beauty, Romeo and Juliet, Don Quixote, and other ballets rarely seen in the West. 60 mins.
VHS: S10714. $29.95.

Magic of the Kirov Ballet
This extraordinary program contains an outstanding selection of highlights from the Kirov's extensive classical repertoire, including dazzling sequences from choreographer Marius Petipa's interpretations of La Bayadere, Le Corsaire, The Sleeping Beauty, Raymonda, Swan Lake, Paquita and Don Quixote. Current members Farukh Ruzimatov, Tatyana Terekhova and Olga Chenchikova are featured. 60 mins.
VHS: S08794. $29.95.

Makarova Returns
In this emotionally charged program, ballerina Natalia Makarova returns to the Kirov Ballet nearly 20 years after her defection from the USSR. 60 mins.
VHS: S14750. $29.95.

Margot Fonteyn Story
In a career spanning more than four decades, Margot Fonteyn achieved perfection in the most demanding of the arts and thrilled audiences worldwide. On the eve of her 70th birthday, Dame Fonteyn finally agreed to tell her life story in this landmark video. Her candid revelations are augmented by archival film and interviews with mentors, partners and proteges such as Ninette de Valois, Frederick Ashton, Robert Helpmann and Rudolf Nureyev. 90 mins.
VHS: S10271. $39.95.

Martha Graham:
An American Original in Performance
A true pioneer in the American dance, Martha Graham has become a legend, and this film contains three of her historic performances: *A Dancer's World*, *Night Journey*, *Appalachian Spring*. 93 mins.
VHS: S07694. $39.95.
Laser: LD72346. $99.95.

Martha Graham: The Dancer Revealed
This famed choreographer has shaped modern dance. She died in 1991 at the age of 97 leaving behind a legacy of achievement that will certainly endure. In this documentary, seven decades of her life and work are chronicled, revealing the person behind the legend. Interviews with Agnes de Mille, Erick Hawkins, Ron Profas and many others are included. 60 mins.
VHS: S21814. $24.95.

Mary Wigman 1886-1973
Here is a vivid film portrait that captures Mary Wigman's enduring historical significance as one of the founders of German expressionist dance. Narrated by Wigman herself, with an accompanying voice-over in English. USA, 1991, 47 mins.
VHS: S15340. $44.95.

The Maryinsky Ballet
The former Kirov Ballet has been transformed into the Maryinsky, and this compilation studies the company's works, including *Chopiniana*, *Petrushka*, *Barber's Adagio*, *Le Corsaire*, *The Fairy Doll* and *Paquita*. The program highlights its three greatest performers, Altynai Asylmuratova, Larissa Lezhnina and Farukh Ruzimatov. 147 mins.
VHS: S18890. $39.95.

Masters of Tap
This exuberant documentary introduces viewers to the lively history of tap dance with three acknowledged masters, Charles "Honi" Coles, Chuck Green and Will Gaines, serving as a guide and teacher. Coles, often called the greatest living exponent of tap dancing, entertains the audience with his experiences in show business during the 20's and 30's, and demonstrates his mastery with the audience. 61 mins.
VHS: S08483. $39.95.

Mayerling
Kenneth MacMillan's ballet, danced to Franz Liszt's music, is a powerful dramatic work concerning the tragic love affair of Crown Prince Rudolph and 17-year-old Mary Vestera. It captures the elegance of the Austro-Hungarian Empire in its twilight. Performed by the Royal Ballet and the Orchestra of the Royal Opera House. 135 mins.
VHS: S21052. $39.95.

Mazowsze:
The Polish Song and Dance Ensemble
Made for Polish television, this is a rare 1971 performance of the Polish ensemble Mazowsze, one of the world's most interesting and popular folk collectives. 40 mins.
VHS: S18551. $29.95.

Medea
Filmed in the Soviet Union and never seen by Western audiences, this extraordinary one-act ballet freely interprets the classic drama by Euripides. With Marina Goderdzishvilli and Vladimir Julukhadze. 70 mins.
VHS: S03153. $39.95.

The Men Who Danced: The Story of Ted Shawn's Male Dancers 1933-1940
The Men Who Danced presents the story of the first all-male dance company in the U.S. It includes historic footage of the company performing in the 1930's, capturing the beauty and rigor of Ted Shawn's brilliant choreography. USA, 1986, 30 mins.
VHS: S15342. $44.95.

Merry Widow Ballet
Choreographed by Ruth Page, this beguiling, romantic ballet features Patricia McBride and Peter Martins in a memorable performance based on the Franz Lehar opera. 60 mins.
VHS: S11767. $39.95.

Mid-Eastern Dance: An Introduction
An award-winning two-hour course, beginning and intermediate levels, in the art of the belly dance, taught by Kathryn Ferguson, internationally recognized performer and teacher of Oriental dance. Includes preparation, understanding of Oriental rhythms, music, finger cymbals, and much more. 122 mins.
VHS: S09799. $39.95.

Moiseyev Ballet
Igor Moiseyev is world-renowned both for his choreography and for the dance company that he founded. This video shows a number of his key works, including *Partisans*, *Polyanka*, *Two Boys in a Fight*, *The Cunning Makanu* and other dances that make clear the source of this troupe's fame. 120 mins.
VHS: S24363. $39.95.

Moiseyev Dance Company: Gala Evening
The non-stop excitement and acrobatic dancing of this world-famous dance ensemble introduces the viewer to the many faces of folk dancing in the Soviet Union. Performed as a part of the cultural spectacle of the 1980 Moscow Olympics, choreographed by Moiseyev, and featuring working the bar and the floor, the Moldavian folk dance, the soccer match, Tajik's Dance of Happiness, Azerbaijan Shepard dance, and Ukrainian Gepak dance. 70 minutes.
VHS: S02615. $39.95.

Murray Louis in Concert Volume 1: Dance Solos
This videotape documents Murray Louis' extraordinary career as a dance soloist, drawing on choreography from his first concert in 1953 to today. None of this live performance footage has been previously released on film or video. USA, 1989, 52 mins.
VHS: S15341. $49.95.

Natasha
Natalia Makarova, universally acknowledged as one of the greatest ballerinas of our age, dances from "On Your Toes," "Romeo and Juliet," "Manon," "A Month in the Country," "Carmen," "Proust Remembered" and "Bach Sonata," as well as solos in "Dying Swan" and "Les Sylphide." Winnner of the British Television's Best Art Program of the Year. 70 mins.
VHS: S03614. $39.95.

Nijinsky
Herbert Ross directs this portrayal of the most celebrated dancer of the early 20th century caught in a love triangle between the ballerina he married and the domineering mentor he loved, Diaghilev. With brilliant dance sequences.
Herbert Ross, USA, 1986, 125 mins.
VHS: S09897. $14.95.

Nina Ananiashvili and International Stars, Vol. 1
This magnificent Russian ballerina, currently with the American Ballet Theater, dances *Le Spectre de la Rose* with Farukh Ruzimatov and *The Sleeping Beauty* with Aleksei Fadeechev. Artists from the Bolshoi, The Royal Danish Ballet and the Kirov are also included. Aleksandr Sotnikov directs the 21st Century Orchestra.
VHS: S21760. $24.95.

Nina Ananiashvili and International Stars, Vol. 2
Ananiashvili dances with Aleksei Fadeechev in *The Dying Swan* and *Moods*. In *Don Quixote* she appears with Farukh Ruzimatov, Irma Nioradze and Rose Gad. Other selections feature artists from the Bolshoi, the Royal Danish Ballet and the Kirov. Aleksandr Sotnikov directs the 21st Century Orchestra.
VHS: S21761. $24.95.

Nina Ananiashvili and International Stars, Vol. 3
Ananiashvili dances with Aleksei Fadeechev in *Ramonda* and with Rose Gad and Tatyana Terekhova in *Pas de Quatre*. This 1993 gala, taped in Japan, also features artists from the New York City Ballet, the Dusseldorf Ballet, the Paris Opera Ballet, the Bolshoi, the Royal Danish Ballet and the Kirov in scenes from still more works. Aleksandr Sotnikov directs the Shinsei Nihon Symphony Orchestra.
VHS: S21762. $24.95.

Nina Ananiashvili and International Stars, Vol. 4
Ananiashvili dances "Grand Pas" from *Don Quixote* with Aleksei Fadeechev. This 1993 gala features premier artists from the New York City Ballet, the Bolshoi, the Royal Danish Ballet and the Kirov in scenes from *Bayaderka*, *The Talisman* and *Giselle*. Aleksandr Sotnikov directs the Shinsei Nihon Symphony Orchestra.
VHS: S21763. $24.95.

The Nutcracker (Baryshnikov)
Baryshnikov and Kirkland star in the ballet extravaganza with the ever-popular music of Tchaikovsky. USA, 1984.
VHS: S01813. $19.98.

The Nutcracker (Bolshoi)
The entire corps of the Bolshoi join in this live recording with Vladimir Vasiliev and Ekaterina Maximova in the lead as well as Vjacheslav Gordeyev and Nadia Pavlova. Recorded in 1978, color, 87 mins.
VHS: S08219. $16.95.

The Nutcracker (Royal Ballet)
Leslie Collier and Anthony Dowell appear as the leads in this Royal Ballet production. 1983, color, 120 mins.
VHS: S02448. $19.95.

Nutcracker: Fantasy on Ice
Dorothy Hammill and Robin Cousins star in this version of Tchaikovsky's ballet—on ice. 85 mins.
VHS: S03862. $19.95.

The Nutcracker: Kirov Ballet
The Kirov Ballet perform this holiday classic at St. Petersburg's renowned Mariinsky Theater. It's a tale of romance, bravery and honor told through a little girl's fantastic dream. Her Christmas gift, the nutcracker comes alive in a burst of music and dance that every child and adult will enjoy. 95 mins.
VHS: S22885. $29.95.
Laser: LD74621. $34.95.

On Your Toes...The Making of
George Balanchine made history in 1936 with his brilliant choreographic fusion of ballet and Broadway traditions known as *On Your Toes*. Prima ballerina Marcia Haydee is at the forefront of this 1990 recreation featuring the work of choreographer Larry Fuller. The creative process of rehearsal and directing are included in this video. The Corps de Ballet of the Stuttgart Ballet Company performs. 30 mins.
VHS: S27007. $19.98.

Onegin
The National Ballet of Canada in a delightful production of Tchaikovsky's story ballet, based on a tragic poem by Pushkin. Sabina Alleman dances the young girl who becomes involved with a handsome stranger (Frank Augustyn). Choreographed by John Cranko.
VHS: S03691. $39.95.

Paris Dances Diaghilev
The Ballets Russes perform four works which highlight the revolutionary technique and form of impresario Serge Diaghilev. The works are reproduced in their original sets, costumes and choreography, and filmed at the Paris Opera House in 1990. The four dances are Fokine's *Petrouchka* and *Le Spectre de la Rose*, and Nijinsky's *L'Apres-midi d'un Faune* and *Noces*. 84 mins.
VHS: S17278. $29.97.
Laser: LD71634. $39.97.

Paris Opera Ballet: Seven Ballets
Seven ballets by the Paris Opera, including their famous performance of *The White Ballet*, featuring soloists Patrick Dupond, Sylvie Guillem, Noella Pontois and Manuel Le Gris. 66 mins.
VHS: S06849. $39.95.

Paris Opera Ballet: Six Ballets
Norbert Schmucki choreographed a collection of Pas De Deux ensembles to the music of Shostakovich, Meyerbeer and Tchaikovsky, including The Black Swan from *Swan Lake*. Featuring the Corps de Ballet of the Paris Opera, and Patrick Dupond, Noella Pontois and Sylvie Guillem. 58 mins.
VHS: S02686. $39.95.

Pas de Deux
A collection of sixteen stars taped at the 1984 Los Angeles International Ballet Festival, including Patricia McBride of New York City Ballet, Michel Denard of Paris Opera Ballet and Yoko Morishita of Matsuyama Ballet. Program narrated by John Clifford.
VHS: S02949. $29.95.

Pavlova
International film star Leslie Caron hosts this magnificently staged video tribute to the legendary ballerina Anna Pavlova. This newly choreographed program features many of the world's greatest performing sequences from Pavlova's most famous ballets, including rare performance footage of the late Patrick Bissell in scenes from *Don Quixote* and *Sleeping Beauty* with former Bolshoi Ballet star Valentina Kozlova. Marianna Tcherkassky of ABT is partnered by Frank Augustine in *Giselle* and former ABT soloist Jolinda Menendes recreates Pavlova's most famous role, *The Dying Swan*. 81 mins.
VHS: S03833. $29.95.

Peter Martins: A Dancer
A behind-the-scenes look at one of the world's foremost male dancers, featuring three full pas-de-deux with Suzanne Farrell, Heather Watts and Daniel Duell. 54 mins.
VHS: S03157. $39.95.

Plisetskaya Dances
A rare documentary about the legendary Soviet ballerina, capturing her in some of her most famous roles, including scenes in *Romeo and Juliet*, *Swan Lake*, *Sleeping Beauty*, *Spartacus*, and *Don Quixote*. USSR, 1964, B&W, 70 mins.
VHS: S02450. $29.95.

Pointe by Point
The definitive ballet teaching aid based on Barbara Fewster's years of experience in overseeing the training of many of Britain's most talented dancers. An invaluable companion to teachers throughout the world, guiding the dancer's first tentative steps on pointe. The program embraces two levels of training: the course for beginners, and the course at a Pre-Elementary to Elementary level, a logical progression from Part I, designed to increase technique and encourage confidence. 45 mins.
VHS: S11542. $39.95.

Points in Space
The critically acclaimed collaboration for the screen by choreographer Merce Cunningham, composer John Cage and filmmaker Elliott Caplan. The first half features BBC's documentary interviews with Cunningham, Cage and members of the company as well as scenes from rehearsals in New York and London. The second half features *Points in Space*, performed by Cunningham and the Dance Company. 55 mins.
VHS: S11769. $39.95.

Portrait of Giselle
Features Sir Anton Dolin in conversation with eight of the greatest Giselles of this century, illustrating their comments on the role with rare film footage of their performances dating from as early as 1932. With Alicia Alonso, Natalia Makarova, Galina Ulanova. 98 mins.
VHS: S04687. $39.95.

Puss in Boots
Featuring the National Ballet of Marseilles, a fanciful ballet adaptation of the famous fairytale to the music of Tchaikovsky, with dancer Patrick Dupond in the role of Puss, and recorded before a live audience. A wonderful introduction to the world of ballet, and a delight for audiences of all ages. 90 mins.
VHS: S06350. $29.95.

Raymonda (Bolshoi/Bessmertnova)
A sumptuously staged production of the Bolshoi's *Raymonda*, with music by Aleksandr Glazunov and choreography by Yuri Grigorovich. The performance features Natalia Bessmertnova and Yuri Vasyuchenko.
VHS: S19520. $39.95.

Raymonda (Bolshoi/Semenyaka)
A glorious ballet that boasts a magical score by Alexander Glazunov, filled with melody, color, dazzling costumes, grand scenery and effects. This 1986 production was filmed at the Bolshoi, features choreography by Yuri Grigorovich, and superstars Ludmila Semenyaka and Irek Mukhamedov. 146 mins.
VHS: S05993. $39.95.

Red Shoes
Presentation by the Children's Theatre of Minneapolis of the ballet based upon Hans Christian Andersen's story.
VHS: S02209. $9.95.

Riverdance—The Show
American dancers Michael Flatley and Jean Butler are at the center of this thrilling dance experience. It joins traditional Irish dance and music with the passion of more recent American styles. It is as if a mixture of *Dirty Dancing* with the chemistry of Torvill and Dean were added to Irish folk ways.
VHS: S27643. $24.95.

Road to the Stamping Ground
Stamping is an important element in aboriginal dance. In 1980, on a remote island off the Australian coast, there occurred the largest gathering of tribal dancers ever held. One of the few outsiders allowed to witness the event was choreographer Jiri Kylian, who subsequently inspired a ballet by what he had seen. 60 mins.
VHS: S02423. $39.95.

The Romantic Era
Four of the world's prima ballerinas in performances and conversations illustrating the romantic style as evident in the ballet. The legendary ballerinas are Alicia Alonso of the Ballet Nacional de Cuba, Carla Fracci of La Scala, Ghislaine Thesmar of the Paris Opera Ballet, and Eva Evdomikova of the Berlin Opera. Each ballerina stars in her own production, as well as a collaboration with all four dancers at the completion of the program, called "Le Grand Pas de Quatre," choreographed by Sir Anton Dolin. 89 mins.
VHS: S04659. $39.95.

Romeo and Juliet (Bolshoi Ballet)
A dazzling production of the Bolshoi Ballet's *Romeo and Juliet*, with music by Sergei Prokofiev, choreography by Yuri Grigorovich. The performance is danced by Irek Mukhamedov and Natalia Bessmertnova.
VHS: S19519. $39.95.

Romeo and Juliet (Bolshoi Ballet 1975)
The Bolshoi's two most dynamic soloists, Natalia Bessmertnova and Mikhail Lavrovsky, give a stunning performance as the ill-fated lovers. This vivid performance was filmed at the Bolshoi Theatre's Bicentennial Anniversary gala. 1975, 108 mins.
VHS: S06895. $29.95.
Laser: LD71310. $49.95.

Romeo and Juliet (Macmillan)
Wayne Eagling and Alessandra Ferri star as the ill-starred lovers, in a production choreographed by Kenneth Macmillan. Produced by the BBC. 140 mins.
VHS: S02419. $39.95.

Romeo and Juliet (Nureyev)
Margot Fonteyn and Rudolf Nureyev team with the Royal Ballet in the classic of tragic love.
Paul Czinner, Great Britain, 1966, 124 mins.
VHS: S01889. $19.95.

Romeo and Juliet (Preljocaj)
Angelin Preljocaj's new choreography of Sergi Prokofiev's ballet is performed by the Lyon Opera Ballet. With Pascale Doye and Nicolas Dufloux. 90 min.
VHS: S18404. $39.95.

Romeo and Juliet (Ulanova)
Ballerina Galina Ulanova created the role of Juliet when Prokofiev originally wrote his most famous ballet, and here is her historic interpretation preserved for posterity.
VHS: S02746. $29.95.

The Royal Ballet in Tchaikovsky's The Sleeping Beauty
This performance from the Royal Opera House of Covent Garden is a superb realization of the acclaimed ballet. It is based on the age-old tale of a princess forced to slumber for 100 years until a prince comes to her aid. The timeless quality and deepfelt romance of this story appeals to audiences of all ages. 132 mins.
VHS: S26299. $39.95.

Rudolf Nureyev
This startling biography tells Rudolf Nureyev's story in his own words. Drawing from a variety of sources, the program includes news clips, revealing footage of the infamous ballet dancer reflecting on his past, and of course, breathtaking segments of Nureyev in performance. Includes interviews with Ninette de Valois, Margot Fonteyn, Roland Petit and Nureyev's sister, Rosa. 90 mins.
VHS: S15993. $39.95.

Russian Ballet: The Glorious Tradition, Vol. 1
An historical preservation of ground-breaking Russian ballet, including *Don Quixote*, featuring Mikhail Baryshnikov and Lyudmila Semenyaka; *Corsaire*, with Nina Ananiashvili and Andris Liepa; *La Bayadere*; *The Nutcracker* and *Swan Lake*.
VHS: S18721. $39.95.

Russian Ballet: The Glorious Tradition, Vol. 2
A valuable inner view of the historical and aesthetic shifts in Russian ballet, captured through rare archival materials and films never shown in the West. This two-volume retrospective showcases the form's dominant figures, from Vera Karalli's sublime interpretation of *The Dying Swan* in 1914, through 40s footage of Marina Semenova and Natalia Dudinskaya, to more recent footage of Galina Ulanova, Maya Plisetskaya and Michail Gabovich. The concluding footage is the amazing *Quixote Act Three grand pas de deux*, with Ekaterina Maximova and Vladimir Vasiliev. 71 mins.
VHS: S18994. $39.95.

Russian Ballet: The Glorious Tradition, Vol. 3

As the third installment of this all-encompassing history of Russian Ballet, *The Glorious Tradition* brings more footage of the brilliant stars of the dance world. Galina Ulanova, Maya Plisetskaya, Mikhail Baryshnikov, and Yuri Soloviev are included. 67 mins.
VHS: S20693. $39.95.

Russian Folk and Dance

Tony Randall narrates the performances of these four great Russian troupes. Dance from the Ukraine, song, dance and instrumentalists from Siberia, dance from Samarkand, melodies and dance from northwestern Russia. 70 mins.
VHS: S03149. $59.95.

Sacred Trances in Bali and Java

Invisible spirits are brought down to enter the bodies of trance dancers who perform super feats in Bali and Java. 30 mins.
VHS: S06487. $49.95.

Shape Up

A complete exercise program including warm-up, beginner, intermediate, advanced and aerobic routines, specially designed for dancers and non-dancers alike by America's ballet master, David Howard.
VHS: S10064. $39.95.

Sleeping Beauty (Bujones)

Fernando Bujones performs "Sleeping Beauty" as a guest artist of the Ballet del Teatro Municipal in Santiago, Chile, in this 1982 performance. 120 mins.
VHS: S03159. $39.95.

Sleeping Beauty (Kirov/Fedotov)

Featuring Victor Fedotov, this rendition of Tchaikovsky's Sleeping Beauty is presented by the Kirov Ballet with choreography by Marius Petipa and Oleg Vinogradov.
VHS: S15734. $34.95.
Laser: LD71872. $59.95.

Sleeping Beauty (Kirov/HBO)

The Kirov Ballet, joined by the Orchestra of the Leningrad Theatre, with Irina Kolpakova as Princess Aurora, and with Sergei Berezhnoi, Lubov Kunakova and Vladimir Lopukhov. England, 1983.
VHS: Out of print. For rental only.
Laser: LD70288. $59.95.

Sleeping Beauty (Kirov/Homevision)

A live recording of the romantic ballet whose spiritual core is preserved in the outstanding and unique, classical traditions of the Kirov Ballet. Choreographed by the visionary Oleg Vinogradov, this version features Farukh Ruzimatov as Prince Desire and the extraordinary 19-year old Larissa Lezhina in the title role.
VHS: S12405. $39.95.

Sleeping Beauty on Ice

Adapted from Charles Perrault's original French fairy tale of the sleeping princess, with choreography by Lar Lubovitch and featuring ice skating of Olympic skaters Robin Cousins and Rosalynn Somners.
VHS: S05929. $29.95.
Tom Gutteridge, USA, 1987, 62 mins.

Soviet Army Chorus, Band and Dance Ensemble

A special opportunity to see and hear this internationally popular group, filmed in various locations all over Russia, as they sing, dance and play. 70 mins.
VHS: S03148. $59.95.

Spanish Folk Dances

Learn three authentic dances including the Huaino from Peru, Jesucita en Chichuahua from Mexico and Rado Blanquita from Spain. Also includes audio-cassette, directions and guide with cultural and costume notes. 40 mins. English narration.
VHS: S05254. $59.95.

Spartacus (Bolshoi/Mukhamedov)

A muscular and sumptuous staging of the lyrical ballet that combines exuberant athleticism and compact grace. Irek Mukhamedov dances the title role with a score by Aram Khachaturian. "First class" (*Chicago Sun-Times*). 132 mins.
VHS: S19524. $39.95.
Laser: LD72258. $59.95.

Spartacus (Bolshoi/Vasiliev)

A very important film, performed by the Bolshoi Ballet, interpreting a contemporary work about the Roman slave who sparks a rebellion. Stars Vladimir Vasiliev and Natalia Bessmertnova. Color.
VHS: S02068. $29.95.
Laser: LD71334. $49.95.
Preben Montell, USSR, 1977, 95 mins.

Speaking in Tongues

A breathtaking and imaginative collaboration with the Paul Taylor Dance Company, designer Santo Loquasto (who works with Woody Allen), and musical theorist Matthew Diamond, interlocking dance and music, told in the expressive vernacular of the Company. "A masterwork" (*New York Times*). 54 mins.
VHS: S17279. $24.97.
Laser: LD71635. $34.97.

Stars of the Russian Ballet

Short works exemplify some of the Russian ballet's great works—scenes from *Swan Lake* feature Galina Ulanova, and a rare record of Ulanova and Plisetskaya dancing together in Boris Asafiev's *The Fountain of the Bakhchisarai*. The performers are from both the Bolshoi and the Kirov ballets. 1953, color, 80 mins.
VHS: S02456. $59.95.

Step into Ballet

Former Royal Ballet star Wayne Sleep presents this easy-to-follow and entertaining guide to the art of ballet. Even choosing the correct shoes and costume—those first important steps—are thoughtfully explained. All the early stages of ballet training are shown, including basic positions like the arabesque, pirouettes and many other important techniques. 50 mins.
VHS: S21700. $19.95.

The Stone Flower

Part of the *Bolshoi at the Bolshoi* series, *The Stone Flower* ballet was inspired by the rich heritage of Russian culture and folk dance. With music by Sergei Prokofiev. 1990, 107 mins.
VHS: S14550. $39.95.

Stuttgart Ballet

"Superb tribute to one of the genuine treasures of the ballet world" (*Dance Magazine*). Included on the program are excerpts from two ballets by founder John Cranko.
VHS: S01887. $29.95.
Rolf Zimmermann, Germany, 1983, 60 mins.

Swan Lake (ABT/Makarova)

This triumphant performance of Swan Lake is both an historic and artistic achievement as the first-ever live telecast of a full ballet, and an Emmy Award winner. Natalia Makarova plays the dual roles of Odile and Odette, bringing breathtaking eloquence to Tchaikovsky's ballet. Ivan Nagy heads the supporting cast. 122 mins.
VHS: S08713. $22.95.

Swan Lake (Ananiashvili)

Tchaikovsky's ballet is performed by the Russian State Perm Ballet, with Nina Ananiashvili dancing the part of Odette. With Aleksei Fadeyetchev. 132 mins.
VHS: S19739. $24.95.

Swan Lake (Bolshoi/Mikhalchenko)

A century after its creation, Tchaikovsky's lyrical ballet remains the most popular piece in the Bolshoi's repertory. Yuri Grigorovich, the company's current artistic director, has adapted the traditional choreography in order to showcase the special talents of today's Bolshoi dancers. Featuring Alla Mikhalchenko, Yuri Vasyuchenko. USSR, 1989, 128 mins.
VHS: S12823. $39.95.

Swan Lake (Bolshoi/Plisetskaya)

Maya Plisetskaya, the legendary ballerina, stars in this famous version of the ballet. USSR, 1957, color, 81 mins.
VHS: S02458. $29.95.

Swan Lake (Kirov/Ivanov)

Filmed in St. Petersburg's Kirov Theater, this production of the Kirov dancing the quintessential Romantic ballet links Tchaikovsky's music with the legendary Ivanov/Petipa staging. Igor Zelensky dances the role of the Prince. "Show-stopping athletic exuberance and proper bravura form" (*The New York Times*). 116 mins.
VHS: S03146. $39.95.
Laser: LD71633. $39.97.

Swan Lake (London Fest/Makarova)

A landmark interpretation of the classical masterpiece in the London Festival Ballet production, with Natalia Makarova realizing her vision born of 20 years experience of dancing the classical ballet. With innovative sets evoking the perfect atmosphere of magic and mystery. 116 mins.
VHS: S12216. $39.95.

Swan Lake (Nureyev)

Rudolf Nureyev choreographed and dances in this historic production of Tchaikovsky's timeless ballet. John Lanchbery leads the Vienna Symphony.
VHS: S12654. $24.95.
Laser: LD71358. $34.95.

Sylvie Guillem

At only 24 years of age, Sylvie Guillem has already enjoyed a most brilliant career dancing all over the world and as a choreographer in her own right. During this one-hour portrait, we discover a young woman whose personality has remained unaffected by this meteoric rise to fame. 54 mins.
VHS: S11753. $49.95.

Tales of Beatrix Potter

The Royal Ballet, in association with the Royal Opera House in Covent Garden, presents a program based on the children's stories of Beatrix Potter. Many of her favorite characters are here, including the two Town Mice, Mrs. Tiggy-Winkle, Squirrel Nutkin and Jeremiah Puddleduck. Music by John Lanchbery.
VHS: S01992. $19.98.
Reginald Mills, Great Britain, 1971, 86 mins.

Tango

The Ballet Ensemble of the Grand Theatre Company of Geneva performs a series of pieces to the vibrant and throbbing rhythms of the tango. Choreographed with great originality by the talented and famous Oscar Araiz and performed by some of the finest dancers in Europe. 57 minutes.
VHS: S03380. $39.95.

Tap Dancing for Beginners

One of the best ways to start dancing life, introduced by Henry le Tang. Coordination, agility, timing and rhythm are stressed.
VHS: S04746. $39.95.

A Tribute to Alvin Ailey

This two-part program celebrates this dance world legend with performances of four of his works: *For Bird with Love, Witness, Memoria* and *Episodes*. Each dance is introduced by Judith Jamison, the dancer and choreographer whose career was nurtured to stardom by Ailey and who has succeeded him as director of their company. 120 mins.
VHS: S15992. $39.95.

Troy Game

Created for the London Contemporary Dance Theatre by Robert North in 1974, *Troy Game* is a steady fixture in repertoires of both the LCD and the Dance Theater of Harlem. Choreographed to Brazilian folk music, Bob Downes, and drum instrumental pieces, the ballet begins with the London company in warm-up class, led by Artistic Director Robert Cohan, intercut with his commentary on the ballet, and a complete performance. 39 mins.
VHS: S08485. $39.95.

The Tsar's Bride

The Bolshoi performs a quintessential example of the work of Nikolai Rimsky-Korsakov, celebrating the extravagance and pageantry of Tsarist Russia. Russian with English subtitles. USSR, 1966, B&W.
VHS: S02461. $59.95.

Twist

Canadian independent filmmaker Ron Mann, who specializes in cultural documentaries (*Comic Book Confidential*), made this entertaining work about the history of the 50s dance craze. Mann interweaves archival footage and interviews with Chubby Checker, Hank Ballard, Joey Dee and various dancers to comment on the racial, social and artistic implications of the Twist. Mann argues the movement was the catalyst for American rock and roll. Cinematography by Bob Fresco.
VHS: S19732. $9.98.
Laser: LD72280. $49.95.
Ron Mann, Canada, 1992, 78 mins.

The Ultimate Swan Lake

Opulent interpretation is exquisitely danced by the Bolshoi, featuring Natalia Bessmertnova, Boris Akimov and Alexander Bogatyrev. Choreographed by Yuri Grigorovich with the Moscow Symphony Orchestra, narrated by Gene Kelly. 126 mins.
VHS: S03781. $39.95.

Video Dictionary of Classical Ballet

An innovative tool for learning and studying the movements of ballet over and over again, this four-cassette, 270-minute program provides the viewer with an index to over 800 steps, all of them numbered and correspondingly indicated in the accompanying booklet. Produced in association with the Metropolitan Opera Guild and Capezio, the dictionary features Merrill Ashley, Denise Jackson, Kevin McKenzie and Georgina Parkinson. 4 cassettes. 270 mins.
VHS: S03143. $99.95.

White Night of Dance in Leningrad

Two great dance troupes, the Soviet Kirov Ballet and the French Ballet of the 20th century, join together in this rare and extraordinary dance program. Filmed in Leningrad. 83 mins.
VHS: S15092. $29.95.

With My Red Fires/New Dance: Dance Works by Doris Humphrey

Includes two masterpieces of modern choreography by world-renowned choreographer Doris Humphrey. "With My Red Fires" (1936) and "New Dance" (1935) are parts of a dance trilogy, the general theme of which is human relationships. Exciting and evocative work. USA, 1978, 65 mins.
VHS: S15336. $49.95.

World's Young Ballet

This fascinating look at the world of international ballet competitions features a young, pre-defection Mikhail Baryshnikov competing in Moscow in 1969. Ballet legends Maya Plisetskaya and Alicia Alonso are among the judges in this tense and thrilling documentary.
VHS: S13053. $29.95.

Yuri Grigorovich: Master of the Bolshoi

A revealing profile of one of the greatest choreographers of our time, featuring excerpts from great Bolshoi Ballet productions, including *Spartacus, Swan Lake, Ivan the Terrible, The Golden Age, Romeo and Juliet, The Legend of Love*. 67 mins.
VHS: S12593. $29.95.

music
ON VIDEO

OPERA

Abduction from the Seraglio (Dresden)
Mozart's merry song-play is performed by the Dresden State Opera conducted by Harry Kupfer and starring Carolyn Smith-Meyer and Barbara Sternberger. Love and faith overcome power and egotism in this timeless masterpiece. 130 mins.
VHS: S03372. $79.95.

Abduction from the Seraglio (Glyndebourne)
This early Mozart opera is both exotic (set in a harem) and humorous, and stars Ryland Davies and Valerie Masterson. This new Glyndebourne Festival release marks the completion of the VAI series from the Festival.
VHS: S02424. $49.95.

Adriadne auf Naxos (Strauss)
This Metropolitan Opera production features the dramatic soprano Jessye Norman in the title role and Kathleen Battle as Zerbinetta. James Levine conducts the Metropolitan Opera Orchestra with soloists Tatiana Troyanos and James King. In Hi-Fi stereo, 148 mins.
VHS: S16401. $34.95.

Adriana Lecouvreur
This La Scala production of the Francesco Cilea opera dramatizes the story of the celebrated 18th century rivalry of the actress with the Princess of Bouillon for the Count of Saxony's love. The difficult role requires a great soprano, and Mirella Freni sings at the height of her vocal maturity. With Peter Dvorsky, Fiorenza Cossotto and Ivo Vinco. Directed by Lamberto Puggelli. Italian with English subtitles. 157 mins.
VHS: S13188. $39.95.

Agrippina
The rare opera by Handel, telling of the insidious tricks of power-hungry Empress Agrippina, in a remarkable new production by Michael Hampe at the Schwetzingen Palace, featuring Barbara Daniels, David Kuebler, and Gunter von Kannen. Arnold Ostman conducts the Cologne Opera and the London Baroque Players. Performed in Italian with English subtitles. 160 mins.
VHS: S04640. $49.95.

Aida (Downes)
Doomed but fated to be beautifully sung, the romance between Radames the Egyptian prince and Aida, an Ethiopian princess, is a standard of opera repertory the world over. Edward Downes conducts a strong cast which includes Cheryl Studer, Luciana d'Intino and Dennis O'Neill. Sung in Italian with English subtitles. 150 mins.
VHS: S26296. $39.95.

Aida (Gencer, Cossotto, Bergonzi)
The singing is superb. This is the only video that captures these legendary greats together in Verdi's opera. In Italian, 150 mins.
VHS: S24560. $34.95.

Aida (La Scala)
Luca Ronconi's production of Verdi's much-loved masterpiece conducted by Loren Maazel; Luciano Pavarotti heads an exceptional cast including Ghena Dimitrova, Maria Chiara, Nicolai Ghiaurov. Italian with English subtitles.
VHS: S03685. $39.95.

Aida (Metropolitan Opera)
This very special performance of Verdi's *Aida* won an Emmy. James Levine conducts the Metropolitan Opera Chorus and Orchestra. Performers include Aprile Millo, Placido Domingo, Dolora Zajick, Sherrill Milnes and Dimitri Kavrakos. A treat.
VHS: S15448. $34.95.
Laser: LD70177. $59.95.

Aida File
Luciano Pavarotti, Carlo Bergonzi, Grace Bumbry, Dame Eva Turner and Renata Tebaldi delve into the making of one of the most popular operatic works in a rare backstage glimpse featuring excerpts from the famous La Scala production starring Pavarotti and many other well-known performances. 77 mins.
VHS: S11752. $39.95.

Albert Herring
Benjamin Britten's comic opera, adapted from a short story by Guy de Maupassant, tells the story of how the title character becomes the May Queen. Bernard Haitink conducts the London Philharmonic at Glyndebourne Festival. 150 mins.
VHS: S03410. $29.95.

Amahl and the Night Visitors
The most-often performed opera in America, and a Christmas tradition, Giancarlo Menotti's wonderful work stars Teresa Stratas, and other Metropolitan Opera stars Giorgio Tozzi, Willard White and Nico Castel. USA, 1985.
VHS: S01957. $19.95.

Andrea Chenier
Placido Domingo stars in the title role of this production from Royal Opera House Covent Garden, with Anna Tomowa-Sintow, Giorgio Zancanaro, and Julius Rudel conducting the Royal Opera House. 118 mins.
VHS: S02411. $29.95.

Arabella
Sir Georg Solti directs the Vienna Philharmonic Orchestra in Richard Strauss' opera. Gundula Janowitz stars in the title role, and is joined by Rene Kollo, Bernd Weikl, Margarita Lilowa and Martha Modl. In Hi-Fi stereo, 150 mins.
VHS: S17680. $34.95.
Laser: LD71422. $59.95.

Aria
Ten different directors select a different aria and have free rein to do anything that they want. The world of opera meets the medium of film with an eclectic mix of music and imagery. Robert Altman, Ken Russell, Derek Jarman, Jean-Luc Godard, Nicolas Roeg, Julien Temple, Bill Bryden, Franc Roddam, Charles Sturridge and Bruce Beresford go off in different directions. Cast includes Buck Henry, Theresa Russell, John Hurt, Anita Morris and Peter Fonda's daughter Bridget.
VHS: S07452. $14.98.
Ken Russell, et al., Great Britain, 1988, 90 mins.

As Frozen Music
The story of the remarkable Sydney Opera House, now the famous landmark on Sydney's skyline, home to Luciano Pavarotti, Joan Sutherland, Janet Baker and other stars. 55 mins.
VHS: S06562. $49.95.

Attila
La Scala presents a rare revival of this early Verdi masterpiece. The superstar cast includes Samuel Ramey, Cheryl Studer, Giorgio Zancanaro, Kaludi Kaludov. Conducted by Riccardo Muti and directed by Jerome Savary, this production was received with great acclaim by the Italian public. 118 mins.
VHS: S16003. $39.95.

The Australian Opera Series
SONY presents four classic operas, performed by Dame Joan Sutherland with Richard Bonynge conducting the Elizabethan Sydney Opera. Each volume is in stereo and contains a libretto and a playbill.
Die Fledermaus. 142 minutes.
VHS: S02428. $39.95.
Il Trovatore. 138 minutes.
VHS: S02429. $39.95.

Barber of Seville
Live from Lincoln Center, with Beverly Sills heading a dazzling New York City Opera cast in this witty, sumptuous production of Rossini's comic masterpiece conducted and directed by Sarah Caldwell. 157 mins. Italian with English subtitles.
VHS: S09894. $22.95.

The Beggar's Opera
Roger Daltry, lead singer of The Who, and 1986 Academy Award winning actor Bob Hoskins (of Mona Lisa) had a distinguished cast in this British television production of John Gay's ballad opera. Adapted by Jonathan Miller, the exuberant production brings to life the corruption, lust and greed of low-life London.
VHS: S03741. $39.95.
Laser: LD71431. $59.95.

Billy Budd
Adapted from Melville's great novel, Benjamin Britten's gripping opera of sadism and injustice on board a British man-of-war. Britain's leading baritone, Thomas Allen, displays his superb abilities as a singer and his phenomenal acting skills in this splendid English National Opera production. 151 mins.
VHS: S10262. $39.95.

Bizet's Carmen
The definitive version of this classic opera, shot entirely on location in Andalusian Spain, featuring Placido Domingo and Julia Migenes-Johnson. Soundtrack by the Orchestre National de France, conducted by Lorin Maazel. French with English subtitles.
VHS: S01790. $19.95.
Francesco Rosi, France/Italy, 1984, 151 mins.

Bluebeard's Castle
Sir Georg Solti conducts the London Philharmonic Orchestra, under the direction of Miklos Szinetar, in this recording of Bartok's opera. With Sylvia Sass and Kolos Kovats. 58 mins.
VHS: S17679. $24.95.
Laser: LD71795. $29.95.

Carmen (Bolshoi)
Bizet's famous work was realized in 1959 through the brilliant pairing of Italian tenor Mario del Monaco with the incomparable company of the Bolshoi Opera. Mezzo-soprano Irina Arkipova stars in the title role while the Armenian baritone Pavel Lisitsyan briefly appears as Escamillo. Sung in Italian and Russian. 68 mins.
VHS: S20694. $39.95.

Carmen (Covent Garden)
Carmen, one of the world's favorite operas, celebrates its first new production at Covent Garden in nearly 20 years. The fateful story of jealousy and passion between the gypsy Carmen and her rival lovers is superbly realized in this all-star cast, including Maria Ewing as Carmen and Luis Lima as Don Jose. Zubin Mehta conducts. Two cassettes, 180 mins.
VHS: S16001. $49.95.

Carmen (Met)
The Metropolitan Opera and Chorus, conducted by James Levine, are featured in this complete performance of Bizet's opera with soloists Agnes Baltsa, Jose Carreras, Leona Mitchell and Samuel Ramey. 2 laser disks.
VHS: S18537. $44.95.
Laser: LD70884. $69.95.

Carole Farley in "The Telephone" and "La Voix Humaine"
The talented American soprano Carole Farley stars in this two 20th-century operas about the relationship between love and the telephone. La Voix Humaine is adapted from Jean Cocteau's play. Conducted by Jose Serebrier and the Scottish Chamber Orchestra. 66 mins.
VHS: S17132. $24.95.
Laser: LD71548. $39.95.

Carteri in "La Traviata"
Carteri was 24 when this film of the great opera was made for television in 1954. Her vocal quality is perfect for the role of a woman who was mature in terms of experience but not age. In Italian, 51 mins.
VHS: S24559. $34.95.

Cavalleria Rusticana
American diva Shirley Verret gives a mesmerizing portrayal of Santuzza in Mascagni's masterpiece. Rising tenor star Kristjan Johannsson sings the role of Turiddu with fiery passion and vocal opulence in this live 1990 performance from Siena, staged in honor of the 100th anniversary of the opera's world premiere. 85 mins.
VHS: S13999. $39.95.
Laser: LD70906. $39.95.

Cavalleria Rusticana and I Pagliaci
Herbert von Karajan leads the Orchestra and Chorus of the esteemed La Scala Opera House in moving renditions of these Italian opera favorites.
VHS: S27437. $34.95.
Laser: LD75506. $59.95.

Charles Gounod's Romeo et Juliette
Gounod realized an opera of enduring magic by adapting Shakespeare's tragic romance. Robert Alagna and Leontine Vaduva bring terrific vocal talent to the title roles under the direction of Charles Mackerras. This video does justice to the ideal of unending love. Sung in French with English subtitles. 170 mins.
VHS: S26297. $39.95.

Charm of La Boheme
Jan Kiepura and Maria Eggarth, Europe's popular singing couple of the thirties, are captured in this adaptation of Puccini's opera, sung in German with English subtitles.
VHS: S10591. $29.95.

Cinderella
Famous Glyndebourne production of Rossini's witty and vivacious adaptation of the Cinderella story, featuring American mezzo-soprano Kathleen Kuhlman. 155 mins.
VHS: S02413. $39.95.

Claudio Monteverdi: L'Orfeo
Nikolaus Harnoncourt conducts the Monteverdi Ensemble of the Zurich Opera House in this adaptation of L'Orfeo. Directed and designed by Jean-Pierre Ponnelle.
VHS: S19108. $24.95.

Cosi Fan Tutte (Chatelet Theater)
John Eliot Gardiner's cycle of Mozart operas were the cause of much excitement in Europe. Now Americans can see Gardiner's work in this video recording originally shot on HDTV at the Chatelet Theater in Paris.
VHS: S20644. $44.95.
Laser: LD72375. $69.95.

Cosi Fan Tutte (Glyndebourne)
Mozart's witty look at Romantic foibles is a Glyndebourne Festival production, starring Thomas Allen and Sylvia Linderstrand and conducted by John Pritchard. Italian with English subtitles.
VHS: S02447. $49.95.

Cosi Fan Tutte (La Scala)
Mozart's classic opera and comedy of manners receives lavish treatment in this La Scala production. With Daniela Dessi, Delores Ziegler, Jozef Kundlak, Alessandro Corbelli and Adeline Scarabelli. Directed by Riccardo Muti. Italian with English subtitles. 186 mins.
VHS: S13187. $49.95.

Cosi Fan Tutte (Sellars)
Peter Sellars' interpretation of Mozart is set in a seaside diner frequented by Vietnam veterans. Susan Larson, Janice Felty, Frank Kelly, James Maddalena, Sue Ellen Kuzma and Sanford Sylvan "perform with a degree of naturalness and dramatic commitment that is almost unheard of on the operatic stage" (San Francisco Chronicle). Craig Smith conducts the Vienna Symphonic Orchestra and Arnold Schoenberg Choir. In Hi-Fi Stereo, 199 mins.
VHS: S16517. $44.95.
Laser: LD71463. $69.95.

Cosi Fan Tutte (Vienna)
Mozart's great opera about the vagaries of romantic love is captured as it was presented by the Vienna State Opera. Teresa Stratas, Edita Gruberova, Delores Ziegler, Luis Lima, Ferruccio Furlanetto, Paolo Montarsolo and Nikolaus Harnoncourt join the Vienna Philharmonic for this engaging production. 175 mins.
VHS: S21988. $44.95.
Laser: LD74539. $69.95.

Das Rheingold
Herbert Von Karajan and the Berlin Philharmonic Orchestra staged this extravagant and brilliant film adaptation of Wagner's *Das Rheingold*, in a famous 1974 Salzburg recording. With Thomas Stewart, Brigitte Fassbaender and Peter Schreier. 145 mins.
Laser: LD71755. $59.95.

The Daughter of the Regiment (Sills)
A spirited production of Donizetti's opera, highlighted by Sills' lead performance. "Her supremely confident form, her zest and vivacity prove infections with the other performers and the entire audience." With William McDonald, Spiro Malas and Muriel Costa-Greenspon. Conducted by Charles Wendelken-Wilson. 118 mins.
VHS: S17695. $39.95.

The Daughter of the Regiment (Sutherland)
Joan Sutherland is featured in this wonderful Australian Opera production of Donizetti's opera. Italian with English subtitles.
VHS: S09358. $39.95.

Death in Venice
Death in Venice was the last opera by Benjamin Britten, presented here in a highly acclaimed performance from the Glyndebourne Touring Opera. Robert Tear stars as Aschenbach, with Alan Opie and Michael Chance. Graeme Jenkins conducts the London Sinfonietta. Sung in English. 138 min.
VHS: S18382. $39.95.

Der Ring
James Levine conducts the Metropolitan Opera Orchestra and Chorus with a host of world renowned soloists, in Wagner's complete "Ring" cycle.
Das Rheingold. The first chapter of Wagner's monumental Ring. James Levine conducts the Metropolitan Opera Orchestra with soloists Morris, Ludwig, Jerusalem, Wlaschiha, Zednick, Rootering, Salminen. German lyrics with English subtitles. 162 mins.
VHS: S16048. $34.95.
Laser: LD71194. $59.95.
Die Walküre. Behrens, Norman, Ludwig, Lakes, Morris, Moll are in principal roles. German lyrics with English subtitles. 243 mins.
VHS: S16049. $44.95.
Laser: LD71195. $82.50.
Gotterdammerung. Soloists include Behrens, Saliminen, Ludwig, Raffell, Lisowska and Wlaschiha. German lyrics with English subtitles. 280 mins.
VHS: S16051. $44.95.
Laser: LD71197. $82.50.
Siegfried. Featuring Morris, Zednik, Behrens, Wlaschiha, Svenden, Upshaw and Salminen. German lyrics with English subtitles. 252 mins.
VHS: S16050. $44.95.
Laser: LD71196. $82.50.
Complete Set. Four cassettes, 937 mins.
VHS: S16052. $159.80.
Laser: LD71198. $307.45.

Der Rosenkavalier (Bavarian State)
Carlos Kleiber conducts the Bavarian State Opera and Chorus, with soloists Gwyneth Jones, Brigitte Fassbaender, Lucia Popp, Manfred Jungwirth, Benno Kusche and Francisco Araiza. In Hi-Fi Stereo. German with English subtitles. 182 mins.
VHS: S16520. $44.95.

Der Rosenkavalier (Schwarzkopf)
Herbert von Karajan conducts and Elisabeth Schwarzkopf stars in this memorable film of Richard Strauss' charming comedic opera. Now available in a double-cassette set with English subtitles and a newly remastered soundtrack. 190 mins.
VHS: S02270. $59.95.

Der Rosenkavalier (Vienna)
Carlos Kleiber conducts Felicity Lott, Barbara Bonney, Anne Sofie Otter and Kurt Moll with the backing of the Vienna State Opera Chorus and Orchestra, in this telling devotion of the Strauss opera. Based on a stage production by Otto Schenk. 193 mins.
VHS: S23909. $44.95.
Laser: LD74797. $69.95.

Destination: Mozart—A Night at the Opera with Peter Sellars
Peter Sellars' recent productions of Mozart, set in contemporary America, are probably the most radical and iconoclastic opera stagings of our time. Mr. Sellars is widely regarded as the most exciting director at work on the international theater and opera scene today. This special program gives viewers a revealing look at Sellars' controversial productions of Mozart's *Don Giovanni*, *Marriage of Figaro* and *Cosi Fan Tutte*. His unconventional approach to these musical masterpieces led him to set them in the South Bronx, Trump Tower and a Long Island diner, respectively. All the opera excerpts are subtitled, and interviews with Sellars and his collaborators are included. 60 mins.
VHS: S13664. $29.95.

Die Entfuhrung aus dem Serail (Bohm)
This 1980 performance features Karl Boehm conducting the Bavarian State Opera Orchestra and Chorus. Soloists include Edita Gruberova, Reri Grist, Francisco Araiza, Norbert Orth and Martti Talvela. In Hi-Fi Stereo. German with English subtitles. 146 mins.
VHS: S16521. $34.95.

Die Entführung aus dem Serail (Drottningholm)
Mozart's famous opera, set in a Turkish Sultan's harem, is beautifully realized in this staging at the Royal Palace in Stockholm. The famous 18th century Drottningholm theater is used to great effect, including the original costumes, scenery, and machinery from that time, and featuring the Drottningholm Orchestra and Chorus. 133 mins.
Laser: LD72372. $59.95.

Die Fledermaus (Schenk)
Discover the pure pleasure of opera with Otto Schenk's delightful production of Johann Strauss' classic comedy of ruses, revenge and mistaken identity.
VHS: $12653. $34.95.

Die Fledermaus (Sutherland/Pavarotti)
This most effervescent of all Johann Strauss operettas is a perennial favorite, with its tide of bright Viennese dance music and charmingly nonsensical plot. Bidding farewell in this Covent Garden production that also hosts Luciano Pavarotti and Marilyn Horne. The cast assembles, paying tribute to Sutherland, in the famous party scene. 180 mins.
VHS: $16005. $39.95.

Die Frau ohne Schatten
Sir Georg Solti conducts the Vienna Philharmonic Orchestra. With Cheryl Studer, Thomas Moser, Eva Marton, Robert Hale and Marjana Lipovsek. 203 mins.
VHS: $19753. $44.95.
Laser: LD71962. $69.95.

Die Meistersinger von Nurnberg (Jerusalem/Bayreuth)
Staged and directed by Wolfgang Wagner, this production includes an all-star cast: Siegfried Jerusalem, Bernd Weikl, Hermann Prey, Graham Clark and Marga Schiml.
VHS: $15446. $44.95.
Laser: LD70232. $82.50.

Die Meistersinger von Nurnberg (The Australian Opera)
Wagner's masterpiece is brought to glorious life by the renowned Australian Opera. An enchanting love story, as well as an intriguing exploration of the conflict between tradition and innovation in art, Die Meistersinger is masterfully conducted by Charles Mackerras, who brings absolute sureness of touch to the demanding score. 277 mins., two videocassettes.
VHS: $15168. $49.95.

Die Soldaten
Zimmermann's opera receives a rare staging by the Staatsoper Stuttgart. Bernhard Kontarsky conducts a cast led by Nancy Shade, William Cochran and Mark Munkittrick. German with English subtitles. 111 min.
VHS: $18383. $29.95.

Die Zauberflote (Araiza)
Francisco Araiza, Lucia Popp and Kurt Moll are the featured singers in this magical production of Mozart's charming opera The Magic Flute.
VHS: $12652. $34.95.

Die Zauberflote (Battle)
James Levine conducts the Metropolitan Opera Chorus and Orchestra in this production. With Kathleen Battle, Luciana Serra and Barbara Kilduff. Production design by David Hockney. 169 mins.
VHS: $17674. $34.95.
Laser: LD71790. $59.95.

Don Carlo
Placido Domingo, Grace Bumbry, Mirella Freni, Louis Quilico, Nicolai Ghiaurov in Verdi's opera, conducted at the Met by James Levine. Italian with English subtitles. Stereo, 1983, 214 mins. 2 cassettes.
VHS: $02433. $29.95.

Don Giovanni (Glyndebourne)
Benjamin Luxon stars in Mozart's operatic masterpiece, as the wily and roguish Don. Leo Goeke, Elizabeth Gale, and Rachael Yakar also star in this Glyndebourne Festival production. Bernard Haitink conducts the London Philharmonic in this 1977 performance. Italian with English subtitles. 173 mins.
VHS: $03217. $59.95.

Don Giovanni (Muti)
Mozart's opera is directed by theatrical great Giorgio Strehler, with Thomas Allen in the role of Don Giovanni, in a La Scala production under the direction of Riccardo Muti. 177 min.
VHS: $18385. $49.95.

Don Giovanni (Ruggero Raimondi)
Raimondi discusses the music and performs the title role in selections from Mozart's masterwork. 60 mins.
VHS: $20569. $24.95.

Don Giovanni (Salzburg)
Herbert Von Karajan conducts the Vienna Philharmonic and Samuel Ramey, Kathleen Battle, Ferruccio Furlanetto and Anna Tomowa-Sintow in this performance from the Salzburg Festival. 193 mins.
VHS: $27572. $34.95.
Laser: LD74558. $79.98.

Don Giovanni (Sellars)
In Peter Sellars' interpretation, Mozart's Don Giovanni meets modern-day Harlem. Craig Smith conducts the Vienna Symphonic Orchestra and the Arnold Schoenberg Choir. With soloists Eugene Perry, Herbert Perry, Dominique Labelle, Lorraine Hunt, Carroll Freeman, James Patterson, Ai Lan Zhu and Elmore James. In Hi-Fi Stereo, 190 mins.
VHS: $16515. $44.95.
Laser: LD71461. $69.95.

Don Giovanni (Siepi)
The incomparable Cesare Siepi stars in this legendary Salzburg production of Mozart's masterpiece. Wilhelm Furtwangler conducts a cast which also includes Elisabeth Grummer, Lisa Della Casa, Erna Berger, Anton Dermota and Otto Edelmann. Color, 129 mins. (two cassettes)
VHS: $13682. $59.95.

Don Pasquale
Barbara Hendricks performs in this production of Donizetti's opera at the Aix-en-Provence Festival. As Norina she brings her youthful vitality and incisive intelligence to one of the trickiest tragic-comic roles in the repertoire. This artist is captured at work by Hungarian director Marta Meszaros in one of Europe's most beautiful cities. Another in the series My Favorite Opera. 60 mins.
VHS: $21294. $24.95.

Elektra (Marton)
Elektra, Richard Strauss' gripping musical interpretation of Sophocles' tale of horror and revenge, is given a compelling production by the innovative East German director Harry Kupfer. Brigitte Fassbaender triumphs with her overpowering portrayal of the mad, guilt-ridden Klytemnestra. Cheryl Studer is radiant as the vulnerable Chrysothemis, and Eva Marton gives an exultant performance as the vengeful Elektra. Under Claudio Abbado's baton, the Vienna Philharmonic gives a superlative account of Strauss' eerie and compelling score. 108 mins.
VHS: $13747. $39.95.

Elektra (Nilsson)
Richard Strauss' 20th century operatic masterpiece features the great Birgit Nilsson as Elektra, with a cast including Leonie Rysanek, Mignon Dunn, Robert Nagy, Donald McIntyre. James Levine conducts the Metropolitan Opera Orchestra. 1980. 112 mins. German, English subtitles.
VHS: $05642. $22.95.

Elixir of Love
Donizetti's opera is performed by the Bratislava Radio Symphony Orchestra with a cast including Melanie Holliday, Miroslav Dvorsky, Alfredo Mariotti. Italian with no subtitles.
VHS: $08108. $39.95.
Frank De Quell, Hungary, 1980, 90 mins.

Ernani
Verdi's hot-blooded, romantic opera comes to life with the exemplary performances of Luciano Pavarotti, Leona Mitchell, Sherrill Milnes and Ruggero Raimondi. James Levine conducts the Metropolitan Opera. Sung in Italian with English subtitles. 142 mins.
VHS: $04420. $22.95.

Essential Opera
Twelve selections from Bizet's Carmen and Puccini's Madame Butterfly, performed by such important figures as Luciano Pavarotti, Placido Domingo, Joan Sutherland, Mirella Freni and James Levine. 56 mins.
VHS: $17431. $24.95.
Laser: LD71756. $29.95.

Essential Opera II
This sequel to Essential Opera features Opera's biggest stars singing some of the most popular music in opera, including Pavarotti singing excerpts from Rigoletto and Cecilia Bartoli singing her signature aria from the Barber of Seville. Joan Sutherland, Placido Domingo, Kiri Te Kanawa, Jose Carreras and conductor Sir Georg Solti are also featured.
VHS: $20645. $29.95.
Laser: LD72376. $34.95.

The Essential Sutherland
Thirteen of Joan Sutherland's great roles at the Australian Opera, prefaced by remarks from Sutherland and her husband, conductor Richard Bonynge. Highlights include several duets, from La Traviata with Luciano Pavarotti, and from Semiramide with Marilyn Horne. 116 mins.
VHS: $18310. $29.95.
Laser: LD71846. $34.95.

Eugene Onegin (Bolshoi)
Called "one of the great romantic masterpieces yet achieved within the operatic form," Tchaikovsky's opera is performed by the Bolshoi opera singers with some of Russia's best actors doing the acting. Russian with English subtitles. USSR, 1958, color, 106 mins.
VHS: $02067. $39.95.

Eugene Onegin (Covent Garden)
This film of Tchaikovsky's most "Russian" work combines the resources of Covent Garden, a brilliant international cast conducted by Sir Georg Solti, Decca and a great filmmaker, Peter Weigl. The tragic story, based on Pushkin's "verse novel", is cloaked in some of Tchaikovsky's most beautiful and melodic music. Stars Anna Reynolds, Teresa Kubiak, Julia Hamari, Enid Hartle, Bernd Weikl and Stuart Burrows. In Hi-Fi Stereo. 116 mins.
VHS: $14114. $24.95.
Laser: LD71420. $29.95.

Eugene Onegin (Kirov)
The Kirov Opera and Ballet theatre in a dazzling operatic production of the Tchaikovsky opera with text by Pushkin. Stars Evgenia Gorokhovskaya, Tatiana Novikova and Larissa Dyadkova. Russian language, English subtitles. 155 mins., 2 cassettes.
VHS: $04685. $69.95.

Falstaff (Glyndebourne)
Verdi's final work is a tribute to Falstaff, Shakespeare's roguish hero. Donald Gramm stars and is given strong support by Benjamin Luxon. John Pritchard conducts the London Philharmonic on this Glyndebourne Festival production. English subtitles.
VHS: $02465. $49.95.

Falstaff (Solti)
Sir Georg Solti conducts the Vienna Philharmonic Orchestra in director Gotz Friedrich's staging of Verdi's final opera. With Gabriel Bacquier. 126 mins.
VHS: $18626. $34.95.

Falstaff (Zeffirelli)
James Levine assembled a stellar cast, including Paul Plishka in the title role, Mirella Freni, Marilyn Horne, Barbara Bonney and Frank Lopardo, for this production of Verdi's last opera. Franco Zeffirelli's staging evokes the original Shakespeare play through scenery reminiscent of the theater at Stratford-on-Avon. 126 mins.
VHS: $24874. $34.95.
Laser: LD74908. $59.95.

Fidelio (Covent Garden)
Conducted by Christoph Dohnanyi, Alfred Dresden's production of Fidelio moves at a compelling pace and conveys Beethoven's theme: the triumph of love and freedom over forces of evil and oppression. The impressive cast includes Gabriela Benackova, Josef Protschka, Robert Lloyd and Marie McLaughlin. 150 mins.
VHS: $16006. $39.95.

Fidelio (Glyndebourne)
Elisabeth Soderstrom portrays the courageous Leonore in Peter Hall's stirring production of Fidelio. Bernard Haitink conducts this Glyndebourne Festival opera presentation. This is a top-quality presentation that all Beethoven fans will cherish.
VHS: $02431. $39.95.

The Fiery Angel
Set in medieval Germany, this five-part opera by Sergei Prokofiev follows the tempestuous tale of a young woman named Renata who has a vision of a fiery angel. The explosive content of this striking work resulted in a ban that was not lifted until 1991. Galina Gorchakova, Sergei Leiferkus and The Kirov Opera and Orchestra join the Royal Opera House, Covent Garden, for this singular operatic experience. 123 mins.
VHS: $26482. $34.95.
Laser: LD75094. $39.95.

The Flying Dutchman
Leif Segerstam leads the Orchestra and Chorus of the Savonlinna Festival in this colorful outdoor production of The Flying Dutchman, the first of Wagner's operas to have international success.
VHS: $15453. $39.98.
Laser: LD70208. $49.98.

Francesca da Rimini
The rare Metropolitan Opera production of Riccardo Zandonai's Francesca da Rimini is a legendary production. 1984.
VHS: $10031. $22.95.

Frederick Delius: A Village Romeo and Juliet
Delius' best-known opera, directed by Peter Weigl, with baritone Thomas Hampson, and with Sir Charles Mackerras conducting the ORF Symphony Orchestra and Arnold Schoenberg Choir. Hi-Fi stereo, 113 mins.
VHS: $16776. $24.95.
Laser: LD71516. $49.95.

Fritz Wunderlich—Live
This tape compiles rare kinescope footage of this remarkable tenor which stars The Magic Flute, Die Entfuhrung aus dem Serail, Onegin and other operas reveal the musical virtuosity of this singer. 47 mins.
VHS: $24037. $34.95.

The Ghost of Versailles
John Corigliano's opera is the comic completion of the Beaumarchais trilogy, preceded by The Marriage of Figaro and The Barber of Seville. Conducted by James Levine and performed by the Metropolitan Opera Orchestra and Chorus. With Teresa Stratas, Marilyn Horne, Hakan Hagegard and Gino Quilico. 180 mins.
VHS: $18313. $44.95.
Laser: LD71848. $59.95.

Giovanna d'Arco
Iconoclastic German film director Werner Herzog joins forces with conductor Riccardo Chailly in this stunning new production of Verdi's seventh opera, the story of Joan of Arc, the maid of Orleans. A fascinating production.
VHS: $15452. $39.98.
Laser: LD70207. $49.98.

Giulio Cesare
This production of Handel's opera was designed by Peter Sellars and transposes the action from Egypt under the Roman Empire to contemporary Middle East. With Jeffrey Gall, Susan Larson, Mary Westbrook-Geha, Lorraine Hunt and James Maddalena. 237 mins.
VHS: $17675. $44.95.
Laser: LD71791. $82.50.

Glyndebourne Festival Opera: A Gala Evening
Before closing for reconstruction, Glyndebourne hosted this extraordinary gala evening. Montserrat Caballe, Felicity Lott, Ruggero Raimondi, Benjamin Luxon, Kim Begley, Frederica von Stade and Cynthia Haymon are just some of the performers featured in this singular video event. 120 mins.
VHS: $24308. $29.95.

The Golden Ring
Humphrey Burton's documentary follows Sir Georg Solti's recording of Gotterdammerung with the Vienna Philharmonic, featuring Birgit Nilsson, Wolfgang Windgassen and Dietrich Fischer-Dieskau. 89 mins.
VHS: $17678. $24.95.
Laser: LD71794. $34.95.

Gotterdammerung
Daniel Barenboim conducts Siegfried Jerusalem, Phillip Kang, Bodo Brinkman, Gunter von Kannen, Annie Evans and the Bayreuth Festival Choir and Orchestra in the concluding opera of Wagner's Ring Cycle. 270 mins.
VHS: $22910. $44.97.
Laser: LD74625. $99.97.

Great Opera Gala for Armenia
At the Bolshoi theater in Moscow, a benefit for war-torn Armenia brought the talents of Alfredo Kraus, Yevgeni Nesterenko, Hermann Prey, Carlo Berganzi and Irina Archipova together for a night of great singing, featuring arias from operas by Verdi, Puccini, Mozart, Wagner, Mussogorsky, Leoncavallo and many more. 120 mins.
VHS: $21062. $24.95.

Great Scenes from Der Ring des Nibelungen
The Ring Cycle at Bayreuth, directed by Patrice Chereau, under the musical direction of Pierre Boulez, used a stellar cast of internationally renowned Wagnerians. This condensed version brings the best moments of this production together on one video. 115 mins.
VHS: $25026. $29.95.

The Great Waltz
A 1955 television production of the life and art of "The Waltz King," Johann Strauss Jr., featuring opera performers Patrice Munsel and Jarmila Novotna and an appearance by Bert Lahr. 78 mins.
VHS: $18723. $39.95.

Hansel and Gretel (Met)
Though universally acclaimed for its magical evocation of childhood nostalgia, this production of the Metropolitan Opera was greeted by New York Times critic John Rockwell as "...artwork very much for adults." Suffused with power by the haunting voices of leads Frederica von Stade and Judith Blegen and the perverse hypnotic spell of Rosalind Elias' witch. Filmed on Christmas Day, 1982.
VHS: $02629. $22.95.
Nathaniel Merrill, USA, 1982, 104 mins.

Hansel and Gretel (Vienna)
There's no sweeter introduction to opera than Humperdinck's charming adaptation of the beloved fairy tale. Sir George Solti conducts the Vienna Philharmonic.
VHS: $12648. $24.95.

The House of Magical Sounds
Based on the book by renowned conductor Claudio Abbado, this is the story of a boy mesmerized by the power of opera, who is determined to conduct great music. This charming and compelling story joins animation, live action and performances by great musicians, including Abbado himself. Narration by Raul Julia.
VHS: $23277. $19.95.

I Pagliacci (Gobbi)
A filmed version which stars Tito Gobbi, Gina Lollobrigida (though not her voice), Onella Fineschi, Afro Poli, as filmed in 1948, in a classic Gobbi performance. B&W, 89 minutes.
VHS: $03375. $29.95.

I Pagliacci (Zeffirelli)
Franco Zeffirelli directs this lavish film of Leoncavallo's tragic opera. The incomparable Placido Domingo performs one of his most famous operatic arias, "Vesti la Giubba". Georges Pretre leads the chorus and orchestra of La Scala.
VHS: $12657. $24.95.

I Pagliacci and William Tell
The Rome Opera Chorus and Orchestra accompany Gobbi in this film version of the opera I Pagliacci. Then they join forces again in selected highlights from a 1947 version of William Tell. 68 mins.
VHS: $24038. $34.95.

I Vespri Siciliani
Giuseppe Verdi's I Vespri Siciliani epitomizes the elegant style of the Paris Opera. Under the direction of Riccardo Muti, the La Scala orchestra delivers a blazing tour de force in the large ensemble scenes and a sensitive intimacy to the quieter moments. The excellent cast includes soprano Cheryl Studer and tenor Chris Merritt. 214 mins., two videocassettes.
VHS: $15163. $49.95.

Idomeneo (Drottningholm)
Idomeneo was Mozart's first serious opera. This critically acclaimed production is doubly enhanced by the charming Drottningholm Court Theater in Stockholm, featuring both the Drottningholm Orchestra and Chorus under the direction of Michael Hampe. 143 mins.
Laser: LD72373. $59.95.

Idomeneo (Met)
Metropolitan Opera production features Luciano Pavarotti in Mozart's early masterpiece. With Ileana Cotrubas, Hildegard Behrens, John Alexander; James Levine conducts. 185 mins.
VHS: $04422. $29.95.

Il Barbiere di Siviglia (Glyndebourne)
Maria Ewing is the bewitching Rosina while John Rawnsley plays the role of Figaro the barber in this production from Glyndebourne. Sylvain Cambreling conducts this exciting version of Rossini's most renowned opera. 154 mins.
VHS: $26902. $24.97.

Il Barbiere di Siviglia (La Scala)
Directed by Jean-Pierre Ponnelle, conductor Claudio Abbado and members of the Coro e Orchestra del Teatro alla Scala perform Gioacchino Rossini's comic opera. With Luigi Alva, Enzo Dara and Teresa Berganza. Italian lyrics with English subtitles. 142 mins.
VHS: $17750. $34.95.

Il Barbiere di Siviglia (Met)
Recently recorded live from the stage of the Metropolitan Opera, conducted by Ralf Weikert and sung by some of the greatest voices of our time, including Kathleen Battle and Leo Nucci. 161 mins.
VHS: S14123. $34.95.
Laser: LD71430. $59.95.

Il Matrimonio Segreto
This Cimarosa masterpiece is a gem of the operatic repertoire; the tale of the amorous bumblings of Bolognese gentry masterfully performed by Barbara Daniels, Carlos Feller, Claudio Nicolai and David Kuebler. Cologne Opera production recorded at Schwetzingen Palace's rococco theatre. Performed in Italian with English subtitles. 140 mins.
VHS: S04642. $49.95.

Il Re Pastore
This festive and passionate "serenade", in which action and characters are delineated by the scoring of the arias, is an important step in Mozart's exploration of the operatic medium. Blasi / McNair / Vermillion / Hadley / Ahnsjo. With Sir Neville Marriner and the Academy of St. Martin In the Fields. 116 mins.
VHS: S15733. $29.95.
Laser: LD70286. $39.95.

Il Ritorno d'Ulisse in Patria
Michael Hampe's lavish production of Monteverdi's epic tale of love and steadfastness in a brilliant new realization by Hans Werner Henze has been the triumph of recent Salzburg Festivals. Thomas Allen reveals a gorgeous range of tone as Ulysses, alongside the intensity of Kathleen Kuhlman's performance as the hero's long-abandoned wife, Penelope. 187 mins. 2 cassettes.
VHS: S12407. $49.95.

Il Signor Bruschino
Gelmetti leads the Schwetzingen Festival performance of one Rossini's best loved works.
VHS: S15457. $34.98.
Laser: LD70216. $39.98.

Il Trovatore (Del Monaco)
Musical greats Mario Del Monaco, Gencer, Barbieri and Bastiani star in this 1957 production of the opera directed by Previtali. Together they comprise a production team that knows no equal. 124 mins.
VHS: S24328. $34.95.

Il Trovatore (Marton)
Verdi's heroic composition of 1853 is filled with unforgettable melodies, was an immediate success and always has been one of the most popular of his operas. This Metropolitan Opera performance features superstars Eva Marton and Luciano Pavarotti, conducted by maestro James Levine. 133 mins.
VHS: S15719. $34.95.
Laser: LD70284. $59.95.

Il Trovatore (Pederzini)
Gianna Pederzini, the amazing mezzo soprano, is cast as Azuncena in this classic bel canto work. Verdi's music is sung in the original Italian without subtitles. The burning of Azuncena's mother is realized filmically rather than through the traditional narration.
VHS: S25532. $39.95.
Carmine Gallone, Italy, 1949, 102 mins.

In the Shadow of the Stars
Behind the scenes of the San Francisco Opera Company, with chorus singers who aspire to be soloists and who dream of being stars. The film lovingly explores the blurred boundary between private lives and stage spectacles, and creates a rare and privileged look into the grand world of opera. Music by Mozart, Puccini, Rossini, Stravinsky, Verdi, Wagner and others. Winner of the 1992 Academy Award for Best Feature Length Documentary.
VHS: S16640. $24.95.
Irving Saraf, USA, 1992, 93 mins.

Jenufa
Under the direction of Nikolaus Lehnhoff, the renowned Glyndebourne Festival Opera brings to life Leos Janacek's masterpiece Jenufa. This highly acclaimed 1989 production resurrects the Brno version of the opera, unseen and unheard since its 1904 debut. Featuring the London Philharmonic Orchestra conducted by Andrew Davis, and the brilliant soprano Anja Silja. 119 mins.
VHS: S15164. $39.95.

Julius Caesar
Handel's opera performed in Berlin by the English National Opera Company featuring Janet Baker and Valerie Masterson. 179 minutes.
VHS: S03370. $59.95.

Katya Kabanova
Janacek's incandescent score, played by the London Philharmonic Orchestra, under the baton of Andrew Davis, has seldom achieved such perfect unity with the dramatic action in this landmark production. Tobias Hoheisel's designs—a combination of stark outlines and the flaring colors of Edvard Munch's expressionistic world—provide the setting. Niklaus Lenhoff's intense production achieves a harrowing realism in its depiction of the suffocating and frustrated emotions destroying a straight-laced, middle-class household. 99 mins.
VHS: S13748. $39.95.

Khovanschina (Kirov)
Mussorgsky's unfinished score, completed by Shostakovich, creates a powerful opera drama about 17th-century Russian intrigue. Featuring the Kirov, this production dates from 1953, when the death of Stalin led to a great burst of liberalization. As a result the clash of conservative and progressive forces in this work take on a greater resonance. 205 mins.
VHS: S22220. $49.95.
Laser: LD74596. $49.95.

Khovanschina (St. Petersburg)
St. Petersburg's acclaimed orchestra and opera company present the 1953 production of Mussorgsky's opera about change and progress, set in 17th-century Russia. The struggle between conservative, inward-looking elements and progressives who look to reform in the future is especially relevant in today's world.
VHS: S20975. $44.95.
Laser: LD72404. $69.95.

Khovanschina (Vienna State Opera)
A live recording made in February 1989 of Mussorgsky's Khovanschina in the performing edition by Dmitri Shostakovich. Conducted by Claudio Abbado and featuring the great Bulgarian bass Nicolai Ghiaurov, with Paata Burchuladze as Dossifei, and Ludmila Semtschuk. 182 mins. 2 cassettes.
VHS: S12410. $49.95.

King Priam
Michael Tippet's operatic retelling of the legend of Troy follows the Homeric characters through their loves, loyalties and vengeance. This Kent Opera production is recorded in English and features Rodney McCann in a compelling portrayal.
VHS: S03742. $49.95.

Kiri Te Kanawa: My World of Opera
A compilation video selected by Dame Kiri Te Kanawa that reproduces her favorite scenes and features her opposite Jose Carreras, Placido Domingo, Janet Baker, Barbara Bonney, Thomas Allen, Robert Lloyd, Vladimir Altantov, Ileana Cotrubas, Mirella Freni and Neil Shicoff. Highlights include Strauss' Der Rosenkavalier, Offenbach's The Tales of Hoffmann, Verdi's Otello and Don Carlo, Puccini's La Boheme and Strauss' Die Fledermaus. 59 mins.
VHS: S19933. $24.97.
Laser: CLV. LD72180. $29.97.

L'Africaine
Placido Domingo and Shirley Verret star in this acclaimed San Francisco Opera production of Meyerbeer's masterwork, the story of explorer Vasco da Gama, who falls in love with the beautiful and exotic Selika on the African continent. Two cassettes, 190 mins.
VHS: S10261. $49.95.

L'Elisir d'Amore
Luciano Pavarotti stars as the lovesick Nemorino in Donizetti's beloved opera. With Judith Blegen, Sesto Bruscantini and Nicola Rescigno conducting the Metropolitan Opera Orchestra and chorus. Recorded in 1981. Italian, English subtitles, 132 mins.
VHS: S05641. $22.95.

L'Incoronazione di Poppea (Glyndebourne)
Maria Ewing stars in this Glyndebourne Festival production of Monteverdi's opera, based on the story of the Roman Emperor Nero. Nero falls for the scheming but seductive Poppea as the allegorical figures of Fortune, Virtue and Love look on. A new production from Peter Hall. 120 mins.
VHS: S24362. $29.95.

L'Incoronazione di Poppea (Zurich)
Monteverdi's masterpiece is performed by the Monteverdi Ensemble and Choir of the Zurich Opera House, conducted by Nikolaus Harnoncourt. Solos by Yakar, Tappy, Schmidt, Esswood. In Hi-fi stereo, 162 mins.
VHS: S16044. $34.95.
Laser: LD71193. $69.95.

L'Innocenza ed il Piacer
Recorded live at the beautiful rococo theatre of Schwetzingen Palace, a double bill of operas by Christoph Gluck commemorating the anniversary of his death in 1787. Echo et Narcisse and Le Cinesi are performed in original 18th century costumes, with the acclaimed Concerto Cologne playing authentic Baroque instruments. With Kurt Streit, Sophie Boulin, Christine Hoegnman. French with English subtitles. 130 mins.
VHS: S07084. $49.95.

La Boheme (Gardelli)
Puccini's most renowned opera was staged at The Royal Opera House Covent Garden under Lamberto Gardelli's direction. This production features Ileana Cotrubas and Niel Shicoff as Mimi and Rudolfo, while Marilyn Zschau and Thomas Allen are Musetta and Marcello. 118 mins.
VHS: S26904. $24.97.

La Boheme (Levine)
Lavish Metropolitan Opera production filmed live, with costumes and sets designed by Franco Zeffirelli, and with some of Met's greatest singers: Teresa Stratas, Richard Stilwell, Renata Scotto, Jose Carreras, Allan Monk, James Morris. James Levine conducts. Italian with English subtitles. Stereo, 1982, 141 mins.
VHS: S02180. $22.95.

La Boheme (Omnibus)
Alistair Cook hosts this 1953 presentation of an opera by Pucini. Sponsored by AMF Bowling Pinspotters, the opera is sung in English by members of the Metropolitan Opera Company. Featuring Brian Sullivan, Nadine O'Connor, and Brenda Lewis. USA, 1953, 81 mins.
VHS: S05864. $29.95.

La Boheme (Pavarotti)
Luciano Pavarotti stars in this magnificent stage production of Puccini's most beloved opera, performed by the Genoa Opera Company. Filmed live in Peking while the Company toured the People's Republic of China. Italian with English subtitles.
VHS: S10710. $39.95.

La Boheme (San Francisco Opera)
Luciano Pavarotti and Mirella Freni star in this San Francisco Opera production of Puccini's great love story. 120 mins.
VHS: S11749. $39.95.

La Boheme (The Australian Opera)
Baz Luhrmann, the director of Strictly Ballroom, updated Puccini's classic opera to Paris in 1950. It gives him the chance to capture something of the glamour of the era and bring out the dramatic romance of this compelling operatic work. Features Julian Smith conducting the Australian Opera.
VHS: S26221. $29.95.
Laser: LD75046. $59.95.

La Boheme (Zeffirelli)
Franco Zeffirelli's historic production of Puccini's grand opera features Mirella Freni. Herbert von Karajan conducts the orchestra of La Scala.
VHS: S12649. $24.95.

La Cambiale di Matrimonio
Gelmetti leads this performance of Rossini's rarely performed La Cambiale di Matrimonia at the Schwetzingen Festival.
VHS: S15454. $34.98.
Laser: LD70210. $39.98.

La Cenerentola (Bartoli)
Cecilia Bartoli recreates the young woman who inhabits a fairytale world of utter despair broken by the promise of love. The Houston Symphony and the Houston Grand Opera Chorus, under the direction of Bruno Campanella, render this unforgettable opera into a vital production. Originally part of PBS's Great Performance series.
VHS: S27634. $34.95.
Laser: LD75539. $59.95.

La Cenerentola (Salzburg Festival)
Renowned bel canto specialists Ann Murray and Francisco Araiza, under the masterful baton of Riccardo Chailly, infuse Rossini's Cinderella story with new fire and brilliance. This delightful Salzburg Festival production captures the fairy-tale quality of the opera but also emphasizes Rossini's gentle satire on personal relationships. 160 mins.
VHS: S12369. $39.95.

La Cenerentola (von Stade)
A Dutch adaptation of Cinderella transforms the classic fairy tale into a charming opera, featuring Frederica von Stade in the title role.
VHS: S12650. $34.95.

La Clemenza di Tito (Drottningholm)
A lavish production of Mozart's late opera performed at the Drottningholm Court Theatre, with the Drottningholm Court Theatre Orchestra, featuring Dahlberg, Pulson and Soldh as soloists.
Laser: LD72055. $59.95.

La Clemenza di Tito (Glyndebourne)
A stellar cast, conductor and director combine forces in this Glyndebourne production of Mozart's final opera. Nicholas Hytner (Miss Saigon) directs this production conducted by Andrew Davis. The international cast includes Ashley Putnam, Diane Montague and Philip Langridge in a brilliant interpretation of the title role. 150 mins.
VHS: S16007. $39.95.

La Clemenza di Tito (Vienna Philharmonic)
Mozart's last opera, as performed by the Vienna Philharmonic Orchestra and Vienna State Opera Chorus under the baton of James Levine. Soloists include Tatiana Troyanos, Carol Neblett, Catherine Malfitano and Eric Tappy. Recorded in 1980.
VHS: S15634. $34.95.

La Damnation de Faust
Berlioz' masterpiece hybrid of opera and oratorio, La Damnation de Faust was composed in 1846 and includes some of his finest and most original music. Performed in London's Royal Albert Hall, this is yet another triumph for Georg Solti and the Chicago Symphony Orchestra. 134 mins.
VHS: S15736. $34.95.
Laser: LD71432. $59.95.

La Donna del Lago
Rossini's romantic opera, based on Sir Walter Scott's poem The Lady of the Lake, is staged in a spectacular production at La Scala. June Anderson leads an all-star cast of top bel canto singers under the direction of Riccardo Muti with staging designed by famed German filmmaker Werner Herzog. 167 mins.
VHS: S21364. $49.95.

La Fanciulla del West
Puccini's neglected masterpiece receives new attention in this glittering production from La Scala. Renowned stage director Jonathan Miller assembles a talented cast: Placido Domingo, Juan Pons and Mara Zampieri. Loren Maazel conducts this "original spaghetti western", set during the 1849 California Gold Rush. 145 min.
VHS: S16004. $39.95.

La Favorita
Donizetti's opera sung by Sofia Lazzaro, Franca Tamantini and Paolo Silveri. Opera sung in Italian, narration in English. Sophia Loren appears in an uncredited, small supporting role.
VHS: S02240. $29.95.
Italy, 1952, 89 mins.

La Forza del Destino
A dramatic production of Verdi's great opera featuring Leontyne Price in a performance at the Metropolitan Opera, taped live in 1984. Italian with English subtitles.
VHS: S07010. $29.95.

La Gazza Ladra
This production boasts a star-studded cast in one of Rossini's most brilliant works for the stage. Ileana Cotrubas stars in this story of a servant girl accused of stealing a silver spoon; Bruno Bartoletti conducts the production. 172 mins.
VHS: S11750. $49.95.

La Gioconda
Placido Domingo and Eva Marton star in this sumptuous Vienna State Opera production of Ponchielli's famous melodrama. Set against an historical background of tyranny and intrigue in Venice. 169 mins.
VHS: S10263. $49.95.

La Scala di Seta
Gianluigi Gelmetti conducts the Stuttgart Radio Symphony Orchestra at the Schwetzingen Festival. Set in Paris, this one-act opera by Rossini is a comic farce in which two newlyweds plot to hide their wedded bliss from the bride's father. With Alberto Rinaldi, Luciana Serra and Alessandro Corbelli. In Hi-Fi Stereo, 100 mins.
VHS: S16551. $34.97.
Laser: CLV. LD71484. $39.97.

La Traviata (Covent Garden)
Covent Garden, under the guidance of Sir Georg Solti, staged this new production of the Verdi favorite. Angela Gheorghiu, Frank Lopardo and Leo Nucci are featured.
VHS: S26450. $34.95.
Laser: LD75087. $59.95.

La Traviata (Glyndebourne)
This 1987 production by Glyndebourne was directed by Sir Peter Hall. It stars Marie McLaughlin as Violetta, Walter MacNeil as Alfredo, and Brent Ellis as Germont. The acclaimed production has been set in its own period by designer John Gunter; one of the main features of the set design is a profusion of mirrors in virtually every scene. A moving and emotional experience. 133 mins. Italian with English subtitles.
VHS: S07602. $39.95.

La Traviata (Moffo)
One of the greatest operatic films ever made, featuring a tour-de-force of Verdi's work by the incomparable soprano Anna Moffo, whose interpretations of Violetta were hailed throughout the world. Supporting cast includes Franco Bonisolli, Gino Vechi and the Orchestra of the Rome Opera House. Color, 113 mins. Italian with English subtitles.
VHS: S14817. $39.95.

La Traviata (Sills)
Giuseppe Verdi's La Traviata is conducted by Julius Rudel and performed by the New York City Opera company. Beverly Sills delivers a virtuoso performance as Violetta. With Henry Price and Richard Fredricks. 144 mins.
VHS: S17694. $39.95.

La Traviata (Zeffirelli/Domingo)
Zeffirelli's film of Verdi's La Traviata is an exquisitely designed, opulently mounted production made expressly for the movie medium. Placido Domingo, one of the greatest tenors, and Teresa Stratas, a renowned soprano, star, featuring music performed by the New York Metropolitan Opera Orchestra and Chorus, directed by James Levine. Italian with English subtitles.
VHS: S00713. $29.98.
Laser: LD70043. $34.98.
Franco Zeffirelli, Italy, 1982, 105 mins.

La Vie Parisienne
Offenbach's opera, produced by the Opera de Lyon in a production by Alain Francon, starring Helene Delavault, Claire Wauthion, Jean-Yves Chatelais, Jean-Francois Sivadier. Conducted by Jean-Yves Ossonce. 1991, 158 mins. French with English subtitles.
VHS: S20508. $39.95.

Lakme
Norman Ayrton's 1976 production of Delibes' Lakme is a tour-de-force for soprano Joan Sutherland. With Huguette Tourangeau, Clifford Grant and Henri Wilden. Sung in French with translated libretto. 154 mins.
VHS: S18386. $39.95.

Le Barbier de Seville
Josette Day, Andre Bauge, the great Charpin and Jean Galland appear in Rossini's opera adaptation. Acted and sung in French, without English subtitles. France, 1934, 52 mins.
VHS: S06986. $24.95.

Le Grandi Primadonne
World renowned sopranos Marilyn Horne and Montserrat Caballe perform arias and duets by Handel, Rossini, Offenbach and Puccini in these excerpts from their concert in Philharmonie Hall in Munich, Germany.
VHS: S15581. $19.95.

Le Nozze di Figaro (Gardiner)
John Eliot Gardiner's restaging of Mozart's operas using period instruments reveals a wholly new perspective on this classic work. Taped on HDTV in Paris, this production employs the Welsh baritone Bryn Terfel, the Monteverdi Choir, and the English Baroque Soloists. 170 mins.
VHS: S22457. $44.95.
Laser: LD74607. $59.95.

Le Nozze di Figaro (Sellars)
Set in Trump Tower, this performance of Peter Sellars' inventive pursuit of the Mozart essence is conducted by Craig Smith with the Vienna Symphonic Orchestra and Arnold Schoenberg Choir. With soloists Jeanne Ommerle, Sanford Sylvan, David Evitts, Sue Ellen Kuzma, Susan Larson, James Maddalena and Frank Kelly. In Hi-Fi Stereo, 183 mins.
VHS: S16516. $44.95.
Laser: LD71462. $69.95.

Legend of Tsar Saltan
The Dresden State Opera presentation of Rimsky-Korsakov's sparkling fantasy written to celebrate the centennial of Pushkin's birth. Contains the famous "Flight of the Bumblebee". 98 mins.
VHS: S02827. $39.95.

Leonard Bernstein Conducts West Side Story
You are invited into the recording studio to watch an historic performance: Leonard Bernstein conducting his own West Side Story, performed by Kiri Te Kanawa and Jose Carreras. A beautiful recording of an historic moment: this was a first for Bernstein.
VHS: S12651. $24.95.

Les Brigands
The Lyon Opera production of Offenbach's operetta transposes the hijinks of the Italian mountain bandits to gangland Chicago. With Michel Tremont, Valerie Chevalier, Colette Alliot-Lugaz. Conducted by Claire Gibault. 1989, 122 mins. French with English subtitles.
VHS: S20507. $39.95.

Les Contes d'Hoffmann
Director Louis Erlo's production of Offenbach's fantasy opera transposes it into a realistic 20th-century setting, in this Lyon Opera production conducted by Kent Nagano and featuring Daniel Galvez-Vallejo, Nathalie Dessay, Barbara Hendricks, Isabelle Vernet and Jose Van Dam. 1993, 110 mins. French with English subtitles.
VHS: S20509. $39.95.

Les Huguenots (The Australian Opera)
Dame Joan Sutherland's farewell performance is a gala triumph of spectacle, pageantry, and drama. This grand production captures the horror and tragedy of the St. Bartholomew's Day Massacre, as well as the splendor and romance of 16th-century France. Richard Bonynge conducts this splendid revival of director Lotfi Mansouri's highly praised 1981 production. 200 mins., two videocassettes.
VHS: S15165. $49.95.

Les Troyens
Hector Berlioz' masterpiece, uncut, with Tatiana Troyanos, Jessye Norman, Placido Domingo, Alan Monk and Paul Plishka, with James Levine conducting at the Metropolitan Opera. French with English subtitles. 253 mins.
VHS: S04419. $29.95.

Live from the Met Highlights Volume 1
Selected performances from the Metropolitan Opera include excerpts from the Centennial Gala, including Un Ballo in Maschera, La Boheme, Don Carlo, Tannhauser, and Lucia di Lammermoor. 70 mins.
VHS: S04423. $29.95.

Lo Frate 'nnamorato
Enter the sparkling world of 18th-century commedia musicale! Pergolesi's Lo Frate 'nnamorato is a jewel of an opera, rediscovered and mounted by Riccardo Muti and the forces of La Scala to universal acclaim. This sumptuous production reflects the superb alliance of musical and artistic talent brought together to make this little-known baroque masterpiece a triumph of the stage. 171 mins., two videocassettes.
VHS: S15162. $49.95.

Lohengrin (Bayreuth)
This splendid opera was recorded at the great Wagner Festival held in Bayreuth, Germany—home of the Bayreuth Festival Theatre, designed and built by the composer specifically for the performance of his own operas. 200 mins.
VHS: S14800. $44.95.

Lohengrin (Met)
A Live from the MET performance featuring soprano Eva Marton and Leonie Rysanek, along with Peter Hofman in the title role, in Wagner's masterwork. German with English subtitles.
VHS: S07183. $29.95.

Lohengrin (Vienna State Opera)
The power and radiance of Wagner's score expresses his deeply felt belief that love is essentially mystical. The forces of the Vienna State Opera conducted by Claudio Abbado bring this operatic milestone to magnificent realization. The title role is brilliantly performed by tenor Placido Domingo, ably partnered by soprano Cheryl Studer as Elsa. 180 mins., two videocassettes.
VHS: S15167. $49.95.

Love of Destiny
The creative vision of Czech filmwriter/director Peter Weigl, who creates a powerful dramatic story through the combination of dramatic imagery and operatic aria. Opera star Peter Dvorsky evokes in every chosen aria his emotions toward an unknown woman—a fatal guide—which creates a connection between reality and this woman. Arias from Cavalleria Rusticana, Tosca, Un Ballo in Maschera and others are featured. 60 mins.
VHS: S11768. $19.95.

Lucia di Lammermoor (Moffo)
Anna Moffo stars as Lucia in this entrancing opera. Filmed on location in Scotland by Mario Lanfranchi, this beautiful video highlights Moffo's expressive coloratura soprano. Also starring Giulio Fioravanti and Paolo Washington. 108 minutes.
VHS: S02273. $49.95.

Lucia di Lammermoor (Sutherland)
One of Joan Sutherland's most famous roles, here in a MET production with Alfredo Kraus, Pablo Elvira, and Paul Plishka, with Richard Bonynge conducting.
VHS: S07567. $22.95.

Lucrezia Borgia
Donizetti's dramatic opera is produced by the Australian Opera, conducted by Richard Bonynge. With Joan Sutherland, Ron Stevens, Richard Allman and Margreta Elkins. Italian libretto with English subtitles. 138 mins.
VHS: S18728. $39.95.

Macbeth (Deutsche Opera)
Recorded at the Deutsche Opera Berlin, this new production of Verdi's Macbeth won immediate critical acclaim. Giuseppe Sinopoli conducts with Renato Bruson and Mara Zampieri in leading roles. Italian with English subtitles. 150 mins.
VHS: S07086. $39.95.

Macbeth (Glyndebourne)
Verdi's operatic version of Macbeth is dramatically staged in this Glyndebourne Festival production. Kostas Paskalis and Josephine Barstow star as the doomed Macbeths; John Pritchard conducts the London Philharmonic. English subtitles.
VHS: S02466. $79.95.

Macbeth (Verdi)
Claude d'Anna's acclaimed adaptation of the prestigious Riccardo Chailly recording is shot in a castle in the Ardennes. Featured are Leo Nucci and Shirley Verret. Orchestra is the Teatro Comunale di Bologna. 138 mins.
VHS: S17407. $34.95.
Laser: LD71702. $59.95.

Madama Butterfly (La Scala)
An exquisitely Oriental production of Puccini's great lyrical-tragic opera stars Yasuko Hayashi in the title role, with Hak-Nam Kim, Peter Dvorsky and Giorgio Zancanaro supporting. The production was mounted by Keiuta Asari, with costumes by Hanae Mori and sets by Ichiro Takeda. Italian with English subtitles.
VHS: S03687. $39.95.

The Magic Flute (Gewandhaus Orchestra, Leipzig)
Mozart's opera is performed by the Gewandhaus Orchestra of Leipzig, conducted by Gert Bahner. This lavish production stars Hermann Polster and Magdalena Falewicz. 157 mins.
VHS: S03371. $79.95.

The Magic Flute (Glyndebourne)
Sung in German (with English subtitles), this Glyndebourne Festival production features striking sets by David Hockney. Leo Goeke, Felicity Lott, and Thomas Thomaschke star with Bernard Haitink and the London Philharmonic. 164 mins.
VHS: S02164. $59.95.

The Magic Flute (The Australian Opera)
The Australian opera, renowned for its interpretations of Mozart, reveals its definitive talents in "the most believable and simply beautiful production you are likely to see anywhere." Soprano Yvonne Kenny with Richard Bonynge conducting. Sung in English. 160 mins.
VHS: S08694. $39.95.

Makropulos Case
A powerful production of Janacek's 20th-century operatic masterpiece, performed by the Canadian Opera Company and Stephanie Sundine. Sung in the original Czech, with English subtitles. 123 mins.
VHS: S13244. $49.95.

The Man Who Mistook His Wife for a Hat
Michael Nyman's chamber opera, adapted from the case studies of Dr. Oliver Sacks (Awakenings), examines the difficulties of perception and identity of those suffering from the disease. 75 mins.
VHS: S17287. $39.95.

Manon Lescaut
Puccini's ultimate love story is sung in English in a brilliant performance at the Metropolitan Opera. In the Bel Canto videotape series.
VHS: S02630. $22.95.

The Marriage of Figaro
Kiri Te Kanawa leads a fine cast in this performance of Mozart's story of domestic class struggle. John Pritchard conducts the London Philharmonic. English subtitles. 168 mins.
VHS: S02446. $59.95.

Massenet's Manon
Live from Lincoln Center, the New York City Opera's production of Massenet's story of love won and lost, with Beverly Sills, Henry Price, Richard Fredericks, with the New York City Opera Orchestra conducted by Julius Rudel. French with English subtitles.
VHS: S09160. $22.95.

The Medium
Menotti shows a deft hand as a filmmaker in his own film of his own opera, "The Medium," starring Marie Powers and Anna Maria Albergetti. One of the most important contemporary operas, with the symphony orchestra conducted by Thomas Schippers.
VHS: S00842. $39.95.
Gian-Carlo Menotti, USA, 1950, 80 mins.

Meet the Met
Favorite opera scenes from Aida, Otello, Turandot, Die Fledermaus and other works are staged with the Metropolitan Opera Orchestra and Choir under the direction of James Levine and Ralf Weikert. Kathleen Battle, Jessye Norman and Eva Marton are just some of the great singers included in this unique video. 101 mins.
VHS: S23911. $29.95.
Laser: LD74798. $34.95.

Mefistofele
The San Francisco State Opera brings Boito's opera to magnificent realization under the baton of Maurizio Arena, with bass Samuel Ramey. 159 mins.
VHS: S13223. $39.95.

The Merry Widow (The Australian Opera)
The delightful melodies of Franz Lehar's The Merry Widow, sung by the incomparable soprano Joan Sutherland. This glittering production is directed with elegance and a glorious sense of fun by Lotfi Mansouri. Conductor Richard Bonynge draws out the charm and beauty of the score and leads the Elizabethan Philharmonic Orchestra with great aplomb. 151 mins.
VHS: S15166. $39.95.

The Metropolitan Opera Gala 1991: 25th Anniversary at Lincoln Center
"A grand scaled tribute to a great opera company" is what the New York Times called this "Who's Who" evening of world renowned singers: Pavarotti, Studer, Domingo, Freni, von Otter, Prey, Daniels, Nucci, Ghiaurov, Svenden, Diaz, Hampson, Anderson, Battle, von Stade, Milnes, Ramey, Furlanett, Millo. James Levine conducts the Metropolitan Opera Orchestra and Chorus in Verdi's Rigoletto [Act III] and Otello [Act III], as well as J. Strauss' Die Fledermaus [Act II]. Also includes the first-ever duet by Pavarotti and Domingo. In Hi-Fi stereo, 167 mins.
VHS: S16053. $34.95.
Laser: LD71199. $69.95.

Midsummer Night's Dream
Peter Hall's magical production of Benjamin Britten's opera, in an unforgettable performance at the Glyndebourne Festival. With Ileana Cotrubas, James Bowman and Curt Appelgren. Bernard Haitink conducts the London Philharmonic. 194 mins.
VHS: S03411. $29.95.

The Mikado (D'Oyly Carte)
In Japan, a timid official is appointed Lord High Executioner and finds that his first intended victim is the Emperor's son, travelling incognito. This first film version of Gilbert and Sullivan's comic opera features the D'Oyly Carte Company, the same company that premiered The Mikado in 1885.
VHS: S05357. $39.95.
Stuart Burge, Great Britain, 1939, 93 mins.

The Mikado (Miller)
Jonathan Miller's version of the classic operetta by Gilbert and Sullivan is a wonderfully warm, comic interpretation featuring an art deco set design and top singers and performers. Produced for Thames Television.
VHS: S12550. $39.99.

Mitridate, Re di Ponto (Ponnelle)
Mozart was just 14 when he composed this opera seria, a tragedy set in early Roman times. Director Jean-Pierre Ponnelle uses an 18th-century theater in which to stage this production, with Nikolaus Harnoncourt conducting the Concentus Musicus Wien. With Gosta Winbergh, Yvonne Kenny, Ann Murray, Anne Gjevag and Joan Rodgers. Hi-Fi stereo, 124 mins.
VHS: S16777. $34.95.
Laser: LD71517. $69.95.

Mitridate, Re di Ponto (Vick)
This production of Mozart's early masterpiece, written when he was only 14, was staged by Graham Vick for the Mozart Bicentennial celebrations in 1991. It received the 1992 Olivier Award for The Most Outstanding Achievement of the Year in Opera. This brilliant succession of arias and duets illustrates young Mozart's debt to the great Baroque masters. 170 mins.
VHS: S21365. $49.95.

Mlada
Rimsky-Korsakov's rarely performed four-act opera ballet is finally available on home video. Recorded at the Bolshoi in Moscow, this recording features famed members of the Ballet and Opera troupes which carry the Bolshoi name. Alexander Lazarev conducts. 198 mins.
VHS: S22074. $49.97.
Laser: LD74496. $69.97.

Music from Wagner's Ring
This program features selected orchestral music from Wagner's The Ring of the Nibelungen. Erich Leinsdorf conducts this program, which also includes the Preludes and Interludes from Wagner's final opera, Parsifal. 78 mins.
VHS: S22008. $19.95.

My Favorite Opera: Alfredo Kraus, Werther
Alfredo Kraus returns to the site of his debut, the Teatro San Carlo in Lisbon, to reprise his favorite role. Jules Massenet's Werther gives this tenor the opportunity to portray the ultimate character of the Romantic era, first seen in Goethe's landmark novel. 60 mins.
VHS: S21815. $24.95.

Nobel Jubilee Concert: Kiri Te Kanawa
Mezzo-soprano Dame Kiri Te Kanawa and conductor Sir Georg Solti lend their skills in this concert to celebrate the Nobel Foundation's 90th Jubilee and occasion the 200th anniversary of Mozart's death. Kiri Te Kanawa performs five arias. 86 mins.
VHS: S18468. $24.95.

Norma
Joan Sutherland in her signature bel canto opera role filmed in the 1970s and performed by the Australian Opera, conducted by Richard Bonynge. With Margreta Elkins, Ron Stevens and Clifford Grant. Italian libretto with English subtitles. 153 mins.
VHS: S18727. $39.95.

Oedipus Rex (Norman)
Peter Gelb directed this film of the 1992 Saito Kinen Festival production with Jessye Norman as Jocasta and the orchestra conducted by Seiji Ozawa. Stage direction by Julie Taymor.
VHS: S20552. $29.95.
Laser: LD72365. $29.95.

Oedipus Rex (Palmer)
One of the musical masterpieces of the 20th century, sung in Latin, and recorded at the Carre Theatre, Amsterdam, this production features Felicity Palmer, Neil Rosenhein and Anton Scharinger, with Bernard Haitink conducting. Jean Cocteau's libretto is adapted from Sophocles. Cassette also includes "The Flood," created by Stravinsky for George Balanchine.
VHS: S03744. $49.95.

Opera Favorites by Puccini
An all-star evening of highlights from the most beloved opera composer, including Kiri Te Kanawa in Manon Lescaut, Neil Shicoff in La Boheme, Eva Marton in Tosca, and live from the Arena di Verona, Madama Butterfly, as well as other arias. 59 mins.
VHS: S07924. $19.99.

Opera Favorites by Verdi
Featured in this highlights program is Mirella Freni singing Ernani at La Scala, Kiri Te Kanawa singing "Ave Maria" from Otello, the triumphal march from Aida, Jose Carreras singing I Lombardi, as well as Barbara Hendricks in Falstaff and the patriotic chorus from Nabucco. 55 mins.
VHS: S07923. $19.99.

Opera Imaginaire
Twelve animated opera arias are combined in this unique video. It's an interesting concept for introducing opera to new audiences, even though opera fanatics will enjoy these animated interpretations as well. Works by Mozart, Bizet, Puccini, Rossini, Gounod, Verdi and others are given a whole new perspective in these challenging short films. 50 mins.
VHS: S23751. $19.98.
Laser: LD74931. $29.99.

Opera—Two to Six
A unique gathering of opera's brightest stars explores the fascinating world of ensemble singing. Stars include Joan Sutherland, Jerome Hines, Nicolai Gedda and Mildred Miller. Highlighted is a long segment from the second act of Tosca with Gobbi and Sutherland in a role she never sang on stage. 60 mins.
VHS: S08473. $39.95.

Operafest
A gala concert reopening the Zurich Opera House in December 1984, featuring selections from Donizetti's "Don Pasquale", Wagner's "Tannhauser" and Mozart's "Die Zauberflote" along with many others.
VHS: S03941. $49.95.
Gianni Paggi, Switzerland, 1984, 92 mins.

Orfeo ed Euridice
Originally conceived for the Berlin Komische Oper and directed by Harry Kupfer, this startling, surreal version of Gluck's masterpiece won the Olivier Award for Most Outstanding Achievement in Opera. Kupfer's Orfeo is a young everyman in jeans and leather jacket whose beloved Euridice dies in a car accident. He sets off, guitar in hand, to charm the beasts of an inner-city concrete jungle who may be able to restore Euridice to life. 89 mins.
VHS: S16598. $29.95.

Orlando Furioso
The San Francisco Opera presents Vivaldi's magnificent opera based on a section of one of the greatest poems of the Italian renaissance by Ariosto. Marilyn Horne sings the virtuoso role with Susan Patterson as Angelica and Kathleen Kuhlman as Alcina.
VHS: S12411. $39.95.

Otello (Berlin)
Verdi's magnificent opera is performed by the Berlin "Komische Opera" and stars Hanns Nocker and Christa Noack Van Kamptz. The tragic story of the Moor, Desdemona, and the treacherous Iago is performed with an operatic cast of hundreds. A unique production. 123 mins.
VHS: S04743. $39.95.

Otello (Del Monaco)
The great tenor Del Monaco stars in this version of Verdi's opera based on the Shakespeare play. Filmed in 1958, Del Monaco's performance is considered a classic of the genre. 134 mins.
VHS: S23960. $34.95.

Otello (Domingo/Solti)
This production of Verdi's opera is conducted by Sir Georg Solti. With Placido Domingo, Kiri Te Kanawa and Russian baritone Sergei Leiferkus. Italian with English subtitles. 146 mins.
VHS: S20418. $39.95.

Otello (Vickers)
Jon Vickers' towering performance highlights Herbert von Karajan's masterful production of Verdi's immortal opera. Also featuring Mirella Freni.
VHS: S12656. $34.95.

Parsifal (Bayreuth)
A splendid interpretation of Wagner's last opera, performed at the Bayreuth Festival Theatre.
VHS: S15735. $44.95.
Laser: LD70289. $89.95.

Parsifal (Berlin)
Richard Wagner's opera is conducted by Daniel Barenboim with the Staatskapelle Berlin, John Tomlinson, Falk Struckman and Waltraud Meier. 244 mins.
VHS: S21736. $44.97.
Laser: LD74495. $89.94.

Parsifal (Met)
James Levine conducts this version of Wagner's opera at the Metropolitan in New York. The story of the Knights of the Holy Grail provided this composer with the tragic and mythical basis for one of his most moving works. Waltraud Meier and Siegfried Jerusalem are featured.
VHS: S20913. $44.95.
Laser: LD72400. $82.50.

Parsifal (Syberberg)
Syberberg's (Our Hitler) remarkable homage to Richard Wagner, with Edith Clever. Syberberg explores Wagner's last, mystic opera, with a challenging style, using Wagner's face as a set. The actors perform to a recording expressly made for the film. German lyrics with English subtitles.
VHS: S00995. $79.95.
Hans Jurgen Syberberg, Germany, 1982, 255 mins.

Pavarotti in Central Park
This renowned tenor is joined by members of the New York Philharmonic, the Boys Choir of Harlem and Leone Magiera for an open air concert performance. He sings many great songs, including works by Verdi, Donizetti, Ellington and other great composers.
VHS: S23882. $29.95.
Laser: LD74795. $34.95.

Pelleas et Melisande
Pierre Boulez conducts this staging of Debussy's famed opera with the Welsh National Orchestra. Andrei Serban brought the concerns of the symbolists to the operatic stage, shifting the emphasis of this form to recitative and atmosphere.
VHS: S20909. $34.95.
Laser: LD72399. $59.95.

The Perfumed Handkerchief
The classic comedy of manners presents Western opera lovers with their first opportunity to experience Chinese opera in all of its musical and visual splendor. Steve Allen and Jayne Meadows provide commentary on the performance, with English subtitles for the performance. 70 mins.
VHS: S02826. $39.95.

Peter Grimes
Phillip Landridge stars as Peter Grimes, a proud fisherman who descends into madness. This opera is a bleak tragedy that foregrounds the hypocrisy of a small town. The English National Opera and Chorus perform under the direction of David Atherton.
VHS: S26483. $34.95.
Laser: LD75095. $69.95.

Pique Dame—The Queen of Spades
The Kirov Opera and Orchestra of St. Petersburg are featured in this two-volume collection of recordings of Tchaikovsky's opera.
VHS: S19918. $44.95.
Laser: LD72045. $69.95.

Placido Domingo: Gala De Reyes
Performed with the Symphonic Orchestra of Madrid, at the National Auditorium, Placido Domingo gives a bravura performance. Domingo is joined by Teresa Verdera, Guadalupe Sanchez and Paloma Perez Inigo. 60 mins.
Laser: LD71934. $29.95.

Prince Igor (Haitink)
Alexander Borodin's full-length masterpiece is directed by Andrei Serban, with members of the Royal Ballet performing the *Polovtsian Dances*, and with the Royal Opera Chorus. Performed by Sergei Leiferkus, Anna Tomowa-Sintow and Paata Burchuladze. Conducted by Bernard Haitink. 186 mins.
VHS: S18311. $44.95.
Laser: LD71847. $69.95.

Prince Igor (Kirov)
A rare treat to see this powerful, lush spectacle by Borodin, with the Polovtsian Dance sequences choreographed by Mikhail Fokine. The full opera score is sung by the Kirov Opera. Russian with English subtitles. USSR, 1972, 110 mins.
VHS: S02451. $69.95.

Queen of Spades (Bolshoi)
Directed by Roman Tikhomirov with the Bolshoi Opera bringing a stunning cinematic adaptation of one of Tchaikovsky's most popular operas. Russian with English subtitles. USSR, 1960, color.
VHS: S02999. $69.95.

Queen of Spades (Glyndebourne)
Tchaikovsky's operatic interpretation of Pushkin's ghost story. This Glyndebourne Festival production features Yuri Marusin, Nancy Gustafson and Sergei Leiferkus. Russian with English subtitles. 168 mins.
VHS: S18729. $49.95.

The Rake's Progress
Stravinsky's operatic masterpiece became a glorious success for the Glyndebourne Festival's 1977 season! Starring Felicity Lott, Leo Goeke, Samuel Ramey and Rosalind Elias, and designed by David Hockney, this is a masterful production. 144 mins.
VHS: S02457. $49.95.

The Return of Ulysses
Dame Janet Baker gives a virtuoso performance as Penelope in Monteverdi's majestic opera based on Homer's *Odyssey*. This Glyndebourne Festival performance from 1973 also features Benjamin Luxon and Richard Lewis. Raymond Leppard conducts. Italian with English subtitles. 152 mins.
VHS: S02445. $59.95.

Richard Wagner Edition—Bayreuth Fest
The unprecedented offering of the ten operas produced every year at the theater Wagner had specially built. Each program is a state-of-the-art recording, with such conductors as Pierre Boulez, Woldemar Nelsson and Horst Stein, expert casting and first-rate stagings. The ten operas are *Das Rheingold, Siegfried, Die Walkure, Gotterdammerung, Der Fliegende Hollander, Lohengrin, Tristan und Isolde, Tannhauser, Parsifal* and *Die Meistersinger von Nurnberg*. 35 hours, 30 mins.
VHS: S17404. $489.95.
Laser: LD71698. $789.95.

Rigoletto (Gobbi)
A hunchbacked court jester causes tumult and misfortune in the Court of the Duke of Mantua. Verdi's opera is performed by the Orchestra del Teatro dell'Opera di Roma. With the voices of Tito Gobbi, Mario Del Monaco and Giuseppina Arnaldi. Sung in Italian. Dubbed in English.
VHS: S03374. $49.95.
Laser: LD71303. $59.95.
Giulio Fiaschi, Italy, 1954, 90 mins.

Rigoletto (Miller)
Jonathan Miller's brilliant new interpretation of Verdi's tragic opera shifts the story to mob-controlled Manhattan in the 1950s. This lavish production features inventive staging and memorable performances. Recorded live and sung in English. 140 mins.
VHS: S10911. $39.99.

Rigoletto (Pavarotti)
The legendary Luciano Pavarotti stars in Jean-Pierre Ponnelle's acclaimed production of Verdi's opera of court corruption. Ponnelle's work in stage and television brings a grandly colored vitality to opera interpretations.
VHS: S12658. $24.95.
Laser: LD71302. $59.95.

Rigoletto at Verona
Enjoy Verdi's *Rigoletto*, presented at the ancient Roman amphitheater in Verona, Italy. This beautiful production features top-quality digital hi-fi. 115 mins.
VHS: S02467. $74.95.

Ring Cycle
Wagner's extraordinary *Ring*, from the celebrated staging at the Bayreuth Festspielhaus directed by Patrice Chereau, with the participation of the Bayreuth Festival Orchestra conducted by Pierre Boulez.
Das Rheingold. 144 mins.
VHS: S16772. $34.95.
Laser: LD72289. $59.97.
Die Walkure. 269 mins.
VHS: S16773. $44.95.
Laser: LD72290. $99.97.
Siegfried. 228 mins.
VHS: S16774. $44.95.

Robert Ashley: Perfect Lives
Robert Ashley performs solo voice, and Jill Kroesen and David Van Tieghem sing as the chorus, with "Blue" Gene Tyranny on keyboards and David Van Tieghem providing non-keyboard percussion in this video of Robert Ashley's seven-part opera, originally produced in 1984. The video was produced for television by John Sanborn at New York's The Kitchen. 181 minutes on two cassettes.
VHS: S20866. $95.00.

Roberto Devereux
Donizetti's rarely performed opera features Beverly Sills in her acclaimed portrait of Elizabeth I, supported by John Alexander, Susanne Marsee and Richard Fredericks. Conducted by Julius Rudel. Italian with English subtitles. 145 mins.
VHS: S18344. $39.95.

Rusalka
David Poutney's acclaimed production of Dvorak's fairytale fantasy opera, performed by the English National Opera, and re-set in an Edwardian nursery. This English-language production features Eilene Hannan, Rodney McCann and Ann Howard, with Mark Elder conducting.
VHS: S03745. $49.95.

Sadko
The Kirov Opera and Orchestra bring Rimsky-Korsakov's story of love and sacrifice to a unique video offering. Sadko is a minstrel who falls in love with a sea goddess. Though he leaves everything to join her, tragically he must lose her in the end. 174 mins.
VHS: S23908. $44.95.
Laser: LD74796. $59.95.

Salome (Ewing/Hall)
Peter Hall's production of Strauss' *Salome* features American soprano Maria Ewing, tenor Kenneth Riegel and bass-baritone Michael Devlin. Conducted by Edward Downes. German with English subtitles. 103 mins.
VHS: S20419. $39.95.

Salome (Malfitano/Weigl)
From the Deutsche Oper Berlin comes director Peter Weigl's new production of Richard Strauss' one-act opera *Salome*. Catherine Malfitano stars in the title role, Simon Estes is the unfortunate John the Baptist, and Horst Hiestermann is King Herod. Conducted by Giuseppe Sinopoli. In Hi-Fi Stereo, 109 mins.
VHS: S16552. $34.97.
Laser: CLV. LD71485. $39.97.

Salome (Stratas/Boehm)
Richard Strauss' third opera, performed by Karl Boehm and the Vienna Philharmonic Orchestra, with Teresa Stratas and Bernd Weikl. 102 mins.
VHS: S15633. $24.95.

Samson et Dalila
Placido Domingo, Shirley Verret and Wolfgang Brendel star in a magnificent performance of Saint-Saens' moving work. This San Francisco Opera production was unanimously hailed by the critics as a triumphant, extravagant spectacle. 118 mins.
VHS: S10264. $39.95.

Semiramide
Marilyn Horne, Samuel Ramey and June Anderson are cast in this Metropolitan Opera production of Rossini's elaborate opera. John Copely places this superb cast in a strong and effective production that gives firm ground to their accomplished bel canto singing. 220 mins.
VHS: S25853. $39.95.

The Seven Deadly Sins
Peter Sellars' bold opera production of Kurt Weill's work brings stars Teresa Stratas and Nora Kimball to the Weill fable *The Seven Deadly Sins*. This London production features the Lyon Opera of France.
VHS: S24687. $29.95.

Siegfried
Daniel Barenboim conducts Siegfried Jerusalem, Graham Clark, John Tomlinson, Gunter von Kannen and the Bayreuth Festival Orchestra in this exciting performance of Wagner's opera. 244 mins.
VHS: S22909. $44.97.
Laser: LD74624. $99.97.

Simon Boccanegra (Milnes)
Sherrill Milnes is Simon Boccanegra in Verdi's opera about a passionate Renaissance ruler willing to die in order to unite his warring countrymen. Taped live at the Met in 1984. Italian with English subtitles.
VHS: S07037. $29.95.

Simon Boccanegra (Te Kanawa)
Conducted by Sir Georg Solti and performed by the Royal Opera House, Giuseppi Verdi's opera was hailed for its performances by Kiri Te Kanawa, Alexandra Agache and Roberto Scandiuzzi. 137 mins.
VHS: S17701. $34.95.
Laser: LD71799. $59.95.

Stiffelio (Carreras)
Conductor Edward Downes leads the Orchestra and the Chorus of the Royal Opera House in this staging of Verdi's middle-period work that was banned by the Italian government censors. Jose Carreras is a Protestant minister whose faith is shattered when he discovers his wife is involved with a family friend. With Catherine Malfitano, Gregory Yurisich, Gwynne Howell and Robin Leggate. Italian with English subtitles.
VHS: S20420. $39.95.

Stiffelio (Domingo)
Placido Domingo stars as Stiffelio, a minister trapped in the throes of a troubling divorce. James Levine conducts the Met's thrilling performance of this long-lost opera by Verdi. It was censored in its day for openly confronting the possibility of divorce, and only uncovered in 1968.
VHS: S27431. $29.95.
Laser: LD75504. $39.95.
Brian Large, USA, 1993, 115 mins.

Tannhauser (Bayreuth)
Wagner believed that *Tannhauser* was the most meaningful of all his operas. It certainly contains some of his most unforgettable music. A bravura international cast, led by Dame Gwyneth Jones, tells the dramatic true story in this famous Gotz Friedrich production, conducted by Colin Davis at Bayreuth. 151 mins.
VHS: S14115. $39.95.

Tannhauser (Marton)
Eva Marton is Elisabeth, Tatiana Troyanos is Venus and Richard Cassily is Tannhauser in Richard Wagner's great opera. German with English subtitles. 1982, 176 mins. 2 cassettes.
VHS: S02007. $29.95.

Tosca (Corelli)
Renata Heredia Capnist, Carlo Tagliabue and Antonine Votto join the incomparable Franco Corelli in the Puccini opera. The story revolves around jealousy, love and tragic death.
VHS: S24850. $34.95.
Carmine Gallone, Italy, 1956, 113 mins.

Tosca (Domingo/Behrens)
This 1985 version recorded live at the Metropolitan Opera features Placido Domingo, Hildegard Behrens, Cornell MacNeil, Italo Tajo. The stage director is Franco Zeffirelli. In English subtitles. Stereo, 127 mins.
VHS: S02460. $22.95.

Tosca (Domingo/Milnes)
Puccini's tragic drama about the dedicated painter, the passionately jealous singer and the demonic chief of police is performed by Placido Domingo and Sherrill Milnes.
VHS: S12655. $29.95.
Laser: LD71373. $59.95.

Tosca (Marton)
This Arena di Verona production features Eva Marton, Giacomo Aragall and Ingvar Wixell. In Italian. 1984, 124 mins.
VHS: S10097. $24.95.

Tosca (Tebaldi)
A newly discovered film recording of the incomparable Renata Tebaldi at the peak of her vocal and dramatic powers in a 1961 performance of Puccini's masterpiece, filmed live at the Stuttgart Staatsoper. George London portrays Scarpia and the cast also includes Eugene Tobin. Franco Patane conducts. B&W, 130 mins.
VHS: S19398. $39.95.

Tristan and Isolde
Wagner's great romantic opera, with Daniel Barenboim conducting the Choir and Orchestra of the Bayreuther Festspiele with solos from Schunk, Meier, Schwarz, Becht and Kollo. In Hi-Fi stereo, 245 mins.
VHS: S16046. $44.95.
Laser: LD71189. $89.95.

Trouble in Tahiti
A rare video performance of Leonard Bernstein's 1951 opera. Bernstein conducts the London Symphony Wind Band in a production which incorporates performers singing before an animated set. With Nancy Williams, Julian Patrick, Antonio Burler, Michael Clark and Mark Brown. 46 mins.
VHS: S17312. $29.95.

Turandot (San Francisco)
Eva Marton stars in the San Francisco Opera production of Puccini's popular work. Famed artist David Hockney designed the sets, and Michael Sylvester, Kevin Langan and Lucia Mazzaria are featured. Together they enliven this story of love triumphant over barbaric cruelty. 123 mins.
VHS: S25917. $29.95.

Turandot (New York)
Eva Marton performs Puccini's famous opera. Conducted by James Levine in New York.
Laser: LD71281. $59.95.

The Turn of the Screw
Benjamin Britten's 1954 chamber opera based on the Henry James novel is realized in this film by Petr Weigl. In Hi-Fi stereo, 115 mins.
VHS: S16771. $24.95.

Un Ballo in Maschera (Pavarotti/Millo)
With Luciano Pavarotti as Gustavo III, Leo Nucci and Aprile Millo. Conducted by James Levine and performed by the Metropolitan Opera Orchestra and Chorus. 137 mins.
VHS: S17673. $34.95.
Laser: LD71789. $59.95.

Un Ballo in Maschera (Pavarotti/Ricciarelli)
Luciano Pavarotti, Katia Ricciarelli and Louis Quilico in Verdi's opera of political intrigue. Italian with English subtitles. Stereo, 1980, 130 mins.
VHS: S02464. $22.95.

Under the Arbor
Robert Greenleaf's new opera follows the budding romance of two distant cousins in the South. Religion, guilt, magic and voodoo inflect this seemingly simple tale set on Chattahoochee River in 1943. The music is as beguiling as the singers. 112 mins.
VHS: S26376. $29.95.

Verdi/Donizetti: An Evening with Joan Sutherland & Luciano Pavarotti
A gala filmed at the MET in 1987, this tape features two of the world's biggest opera superstars in scenes from three of the most famous Italian operas. 115 mins.
VHS: S15635. $24.95.
Laser: LD70281. $34.95.

Wagner: Scenes from "The Ring" at the Met
James Levine conducted Jessye Norman, Siegfried Jerusalem, James Morris and other noted singers in his masterful rendition of the entire Ring cycle. Key scenes from this complex work have been collected on this singular video, offering a wonderful introduction to Wagner's masterpiece. Directed by Brian Large. 86 mins.
VHS: S27633. $29.95.

War and Peace
Valery Gergiev leads the Kirov Opera in this astounding performance of Prokofiev's opera. Based on Leo Tolstoy's famed work, Prokofiev captures the epic sweep of his acclaimed novel. Olga Borodina, Aleksandr Gergalov, Yelena Prokina, Gegam Grigorian and more are featured. 248 mins.
VHS: S27072. $44.95.
Laser: LD75443. $82.50.

Werther
The famous stage director Peter Weigl directs this charming version of Jules Massenet's opera based on Goethe's famous novella: the story of young Werther who falls in love with Charlotte who, however, following the wishes of her mother, marries another man. With Peter Dvorsky, Brigitte Fassbaender, Magdalena Vasary. Sung in French with no subtitles.
VHS: S08111. $39.95.
Peter Weigl, Germany, 1986, 107 mins.

Who's Afraid of Opera
World-famous soprano Joan Sutherland and her magical puppet friends present a series of opera highlight programs designed for the whole family. Each program highlights two operas. Joining Sutherland in these unique programs are her funny puppet friends Sir William, en elderly, erudite goat; his nephew, Little Billy; and, Rudy, the boisterous lion. The puppets punctuate storylines with bits of humor which balance the tragic overtones of some of the operas and add great humor and suspense to the lighter, comical ones. Together they relate the stories in English, and the arias are sung in their original language with costumes and sets directly from the opera house. Each of the films is designed to make adults and children who are unfamiliar with opera comfortable with this area of western culture and to appreciate the stories and music of opera. Produced and conceived by Nathan Kroll, and the London Symphony Orchestra is directed by Richard Bonynge, with the puppets created by Larry Berthelson.
Who's Afraid of Opera Vol. 1. Features *Faust* and *Rigoletto*. 60 mins.
VHS: S05249. $29.95.
Who's Afraid of Opera Vol. 2. Features *La Traviata* and *Daughter of the Regiment*. 60 mins.
VHS: S05250. $29.95.
Who's Afraid of Opera Vol. 3. Features *The Barber of Seville* and *Lucia di Lammermoor*. 60 mins.
VHS: S05251. $29.95.
Who's Afraid of Opera Vol. 4. Features *Mignon* and *La Perichole*. 60 mins.
VHS: S05274. $29.95.
Who's Afraid of Opera Complete. The complete, four-volume set at a special discount price.
VHS: S05329. $113.81.

William Tell
Rossini's final opera feature Chris Merritt in the role of Arnold, produced at La Scala under the direction of Riccardo Muti. Two videocassettes. 239 min.
VHS: S18384. $49.95.

Wolfgang Amadeus Mozart
Three productions of Mozart's da Ponte operas, recorded at Stockholm's Royal Palace, are conducted by Arnold Ostman and performed by Drottningholm Court Theatre Orchestra.
Cosi Fan Tutte.
Laser: LD71851. $59.95.
Don Giovanni.
Laser: LD71849. $59.95.
Le Nozze di Figaro.
Laser: LD71850. $69.95.

Wozzeck
Claudio Abbado conducts the Vienna State Opera in this powerful recording of Alban Berg's gripping operating drama *Wozzeck*. Franz Grundheber plays the soldier Wozzeck who, driven mad with jealousy, stabs his mistress Marie (sung by Hildegard Behrens) to death before drowning himself. Philip Langridge stars as Andres in this moving performance of one of the great classics of modern music. 98 mins.
VHS: S11758. $39.95.

Xerxes
London's *Financial Times* called this production "one of the glories of the English National Opera's recent history." Handel's comic opera—revolving around the love intrigues of the great Persian King Xerxes—in a performance conducted by Sir Charles Mackerras. 2 cassettes. 180 mins.
VHS: S11751. $49.95.
Laser: LD71700. $69.95.

CLASSICAL MUSIC

Abbado in Berlin: The First Year
This documentary considers the first year in Berlin of conductor Claudio Abbado, the late Herbert von Karajan's successor. The program includes a concert performance of Mahler's *Symphony No. 1*. 114 mins.
VHS: S17671. $29.95.
Laser: LD71787. $34.95.

Adagio
A music video based on the score of Anton Bruckner's *Adagio*, from his *Symphony No. 9 in D minor*, in which cinematographer Tim Chu provides an emotional and personal visualization. Conducted by Eugen Jochum, the music is in stereo and hi-fi. 30 mins.
VHS: S09115. $19.95.

After the Storm: The American Exile of Bela Bartok
The great Hungarian composer Bela Bartok spent the last five years of his life as a man without a country, a refugee from war-torn Europe. He spent these years, 1940-45, in the United States, where few people understood the greatness of his genius. He struggled with sickness and poverty, yet he composed some of the greatest music of his career, including the *Concerto for Orchestra*, the *Sonata for Solo Violin* and the *Third Piano Concerto*. England/Hungary, 75 mins.
VHS: S13749. $39.96.

Aldo Ciccolini
Pianist Ciccolini performs around the world. In this video he interprets Chopin's *Sonata 3 in B Minor, Op. 58*, Ravel's *Pavane for a Deceased Child* and Schubert's *Sonata 3 in B Flat, Op. 960*. 79 mins.
VHS: S27696. $14.95.

All That Bach
A diverse and brilliant group of musical talents, including jazz pianist Keith Jarrett, the Canadian brass, contralto Maureen Forrester, early-music specialist Christopher Hogwood and the Academy of Ancient Music, join in a celebration of the genius of J.S. Bach. Highlights include excerpts from the Italian Concerto and the French Suite, the Well-Tempered Clavier, and The Art of the Fugue. Canada, 1985, 50 mins.
VHS: S03090. $39.95.
Laser: CLV. LD70771. $34.95.

Andre Watts in Concert
This brilliant concert, taped live at Lincoln Center in 1985, features selections by Beethoven, Liszt, Scarlatti and Gershwin, and amply proves Leonard Bernstein's description of the teenage Andre Watts as "not just another great young pianist…he's one of those special giants." 90 mins.
VHS: S08711. $22.95.

The Art of Conducting
A miraculous look at great conductors of the past: Toscanini, Furtwangler, Walter, Klemperer, Stokowski, Koussevitzky and Reiner. Adapted from the award-winning BBC television program, this program uses rare archival material, and image and audio restoration to present dramatic—and unprecedented—moments like Wilhelm Furtwangler's hair-raising rehearsal of Brahms' *Fourth Symphony* with the Berlin Philharmonic during the first post-war tour of England. "The most fascinating program ever made about classical music." 120 mins.
VHS: S22461. $29.97.
Laser: LD74756. $34.97.

Artur Rubinstein
Two short films of the great pianist: the first part shows Rubinstein at a recording session, playing for his children, and exhibiting his technique with the music of Liszt, Chopin and Mendelssohn; in the second part, Rubinstein performs an all-Chopin program, and together with Heifetz and Piatagorsky interprets the music of Schubert and Mendelssohn. 78 mins.
VHS: S03144. $19.95.

Artur Rubinstein Piano Concerto #3 and Piano Concerto #1
On the tenth anniversary of his death, this video captures the genius of the virtuoso pianist as he performs these two concerts at Amsterdam's Concertgebouw Hall in August 1973, at the age of 86.
VHS: S16907. $24.95.

Ashkenazy Observed
Barenboim, Harrell and Perlman headline this moving tribute with support from the Swedish Radio Symphony Orchestra. A Christopher Nupen documentary.
VHS: S15459. $29.98.
Laser: LD70217. $34.98.

At the Haunted End of the Day… A Profile of Sir William Walton
Over 20 pieces of music of Sir William Walton are featured, including a special piece written for the Coronation of King George VI titled "Crown Imperial," and the music for his good friend, Sir Olivier's Shakespeare roles of "Richard III," "Hamlet," and "Henry V." Contributing artists to this Prix Italia winning film are Julian Bream, Ralph Kirschbaum, Yvonne Kenny, Yehudi Menuhin, Sacheverell Sitwell, Lord Olivier. 120 mins.
VHS: S03698. $59.95.

Bach Goldberg Variations
A complete performance of Bach's *Goldberg Variations* by the pianist Andras Schiff. 81 mins.
VHS: S19631. $29.97.
Laser: LD71927. $34.97.

Bach Violin Concerto No. 2
Herbert Von Karajan conducts the Berlin Philharmonic in Bach's *Violin Concerto No. 2* and *The Magnificat*.
Laser: LD74575. $29.98.

Beethoven Concerti
The complete set of all five Beethoven concerti performed by renowned pianist Murray Perahia at the Royal Festival Hall London. Available as a set, or individual volumes.
Beethoven Concerti Vol. 1: Piano Concertos 1 & 3. Murray Perahia joins the Academy of St. Martin in the Fields conducted by Neville Marriner; an additional segment interviews Perahia about Beethoven the man and the musician. 86 mins.
VHS: S09864. $29.95.

Beethoven Concerti Vol. 2: Piano Concertos 2 & 4.
Piano concerto Number 4 in G Major, written in 1808, and Piano Concerto No. 2. Performed by Murray Perahia at Royal Festival Hall London. 75 mins.
VHS: S09865. $29.95.
Beethoven Concerti Vol. 3: Piano Concerto 5. The last of the composer's concertos, Number Five in E Flat Major, written in 1811, and known as "The Emperor Concerto." Also contains interviews of the pianist, Murray Perahia, on Beethoven, the composer. 49 mins.
VHS: S09866. $29.95.
Set.
VHS: S09867. $79.95.

Beethoven in Berlin: New Year's Eve Concert, 1991
This all-Beethoven concert features the *Egmont Overture; Ah! Perfido; Choral Fantasy* and *Leonore III Overture*. With soprano Cheryl Studer and pianist Yevgeny Kissin. Claudio Abbado conducts the Berlin Philharmonic Orchestra. Includes narration by Bruno Ganz. In Hi-Fi stereo, 90 mins.
VHS: S16045. $29.95.
Laser: LD71191. $34.95.

Beethoven Piano Concerto No. 1 and No. 2
Leonard Bernstein had worked with Krystian Zimmerman and the Vienna Philharmonic on the last three Beethoven Piano Concertos. After Bernstein's death the Philharmonic voted to complete the recording cycle with Zimmerman as both soloist and conductor. This recording is the result. 70 mins.
VHS: S20643. $29.95.
Laser: LD72374. $34.95.

Beethoven Piano Concerto No. 3 and No. 4
Leonard Bernstein conducts the Vienna Philharmonic with soloist Kristian Zimmermann.
Laser: LD71797. $34.95.

Beethoven Piano Concerto No. 3 and Brahms Piano Concerto No. 1
The legendary Arthur Rubinstein is the pianist in two works by Beethoven and Brahms with the Concertgebouw Orchestra conducted by Bernard Haitink.
VHS: S18535. $24.95.

Beethoven Piano Concerto No. 4 and No. 5
The great pianist Claudio Arrau performs with Philadelphia Orchestra and the London Symphony Orchestra under the batons of Riccardo Muti and Sir Colin Davis, respectively.
VHS: S15445. $24.95.
Laser: LD70231. $34.95.

Beethoven Piano Concerto No. 5, "The Emperor"
Pianist Krystian Zimmermann performs Beethoven's fifth piano concerto, *The Emperor*, with conductor Leonard Bernstein leading the Vienna Philharmonic Orchestra.
VHS: S17700. $24.95.
Laser: LD71798. $29.95.

Beethoven Piano Sonata No. 30, No. 31 and No. 32
Rudolf Serkin performs Beethoven's Piano Sonatas No. 30 op. 109, No. 31 op. 110 and No. 32 op. 111.
VHS: S18542. $24.95.
Laser: LD70871. $34.95.

Beethoven Symphony No. 1 and No. 2
Leonard Bernstein conducts the Vienna Philharmonic in this historic recording. 85 mins.
VHS: S17676. $24.95.
Laser: LD71792. $34.95.

Beethoven Symphony No. 1, No. 2, No. 6 ("Pastoral") and No. 8
Herbert von Karajan made these filmed performances of the complete Beethoven symphonies in the '60s and '70s, when he was at the vigorous height of his brilliance. Featuring the Berlin Philharmonic Orchestra. 117 mins.
VHS: S15714. $24.95.

Beethoven Symphony No. 2 and No. 3
Herbert von Karajan conducts the Berlin Philharmonic.
Laser: LD74580. $34.48.

Beethoven Symphony No. 3 ("Eroica") and No. 7 (Bernstein)
Conducted by the legendary Leonard Bernstein, this inspired reading of two of Beethoven's finest symphonies is sure to electrify audiences. The years from 1803 to 1822 were among the most productive of Beethoven's entire life; he composed no fewer than six symphonies—including the two performed here. Witness the epitome of Beethoven's heroic music. 97 mins.
VHS: S13890. $24.95.
Laser: LD70872. $34.95.

Beethoven Symphony No. 3 ("Eroica") and No. 7 (von Karajan)
The Berlin Philharmonic led by Herbert von Karajan is captured in these historic recordings from the '60s and '70s. 84 mins.
VHS: S15716. $24.95.

Beethoven Symphony No. 4 and No. 7
Carlos Kleiber conducts the Concertgebouw Orchestra, Amsterdam, in this recording.
VHS: S18541. $24.95.
Laser: LD70876. $34.95.

Beethoven Symphony No. 4 and No. 8
Leonard Bernstein conducts the Vienna Philharmonic in two Beethoven symphonies and the incidental music to the ballet *The Creatures of Prometheus*. 99 mins.
VHS: S17677. $24.95.
Laser: LD71793. $34.95.

Beethoven Symphony No. 4, No. 5, "Coriolan" Overture and "Egmont" Overture
Herbert von Karajan conducts the Berlin Philharmonic in these definitive recordings from the '60s and '70s. 82 mins.
VHS: S15715. $24.95.

Beethoven Symphony No. 5 (Solti)
Sir Georg Solti conducts the Chicago Symphony Orchestra in Beethoven's *Symphony No. 5* and the *Egmont Overture*.
Laser: LD74574. $34.95.

Beethoven Symphony No. 5 and No. 6
Leonard Bernstein conducts the Vienna Philharmonic in two symphonies by Beethoven and the Leonore Overture No. 3, Opus 72a.
VHS: S18536. $24.95.
Laser: LD70877. $34.95.

Beethoven Symphony No. 6 and No. 7
Herbert von Karajan conducts the Berlin Philharmonic.
Laser: LD74582. $34.95.

Beethoven Symphony No. 9 (Bernstein)
Leonard Bernstein conducts the Vienna Philharmonic in Beethoven's *Ninth Symphony*, performed on the 200th anniversary of the composer's birth. Performers are Placido Domingo, Gwyneth Jones, Shirley Verret and Martti Talvela, as well as the Vienna State Opera Chorus. 78 mins.
VHS: S19003. $29.95.
Laser: LD70869. $34.95.

Beethoven Symphony No. 9 (Karajan)
Herbert von Karajan conducts the Berlin Philharmonic with the Choir of the Deutsche Opera Berlin and soloists Anna Tomowa-Sintow, Agnes Baltsa and Jose van Dam.
VHS: S15717. $24.95.
Laser: LD70873. $34.95.

Beethoven, Schumann, Brahms
Featuring a selection performed by Alexis Weissenberg on piano, Pierre Amoyal on violin, with Brahms' "Lieders" sung by Teresa Berganza. 55 mins.
VHS: S03829. $34.95.

Beethoven—Klassix 13
Anthony Quayle and Balint Vaszonyi lead this expedition into the extraordinary life of Beethoven, including his home in Bonn, his life in Vienna, his turbulent mind, and the agony over his crushing deafness. 60 mins.
VHS: S10895. $24.95.

Beethoven Violin Concerto (Karajan)
Herbert Von Karajan conducts the Berlin Philharmonic.
Laser: LD74587. $34.95.

Beethoven Waldstein and Appassionata
The Sonata No. 21, Opus 53 and Sonata No. 23, Opus 57 are performed here by Daniel Barenboim. In Hi-Fi Stereo.
Laser: CLV. LD70209. $29.98.

Bernstein (Candide)
Filmed live at the Barbican Centre in London in 1989, this was the first and only time Bernstein ever conducted *Candide*, and it was Bernstein's last major recording of his own music.
VHS: S15219. $34.95.
Laser: LD71444. $59.95.

Bernstein Conducts Bernstein
Leonard Bernstein conducts the Israel Philharmonic Orchestra in *Chichester Psalms*, with the Wiener Jeunesse-Chor; his Symphony No. 1, *Jeremiah*, with featured soloist Christa Ludwig; and his Symphony No. 2, *The Age of Anxiety*, with pianist Lukas Foss. 80 mins.
VHS: S18467. $24.95.

Bernstein in Paris: The Ravel Concerts
Bernstein conducts the National Orchestra of France in a program of music by Maurice Ravel, including *La Valse*, *Tzigane* and *Bolero*. Bernstein also performs Piano Concerto No. 1 and mezzo-soprano Marilyn Horne performs *Sheherazade*. 87 mins.
VHS: S18567. $29.95.

Bernstein in Vienna: Beethoven Piano Concerto No. 1 in C Major
Leonard Bernstein conducts the Vienna Philharmonic in Beethoven's *Piano Concerto No. 1 in C Major* in honor of the composer's 200th birthday. 45 mins.
VHS: S18704. $29.95.

Bernstein on Broadway
Though hailed as a masterful conductor, Leonard Bernstein also composed some of Broadway's most innovative theatrical music. Included in this video are songs from his musicals *On the Town*, *West Side Story* and *Candide*. Among the unforgettable tunes collected here are "New York, New York," "Maria," "America," "I Feel Pretty" and more, sung by stars like Tyne Daly, Kiri Te Kanawa and Cleo Laine. USA, 74 mins.
VHS: S27208. $29.95.

Bolero/Pictures at an Exhibition
Dutoit and the Montreal Symphony Orchestra perform these works by Ravel and Mussorgsky with dances choreographed by Lar Lubovitch and interpreted by MOMIX. This work received Grand Prize at the 28th Chicago International Film Festival.
VHS: S20908. $29.95.

Boulez in Salzburg
This concert video captures Pierre Boulez's premier performance leading the Vienna Philharmonic at the 1992 Salzburg Festival. Works by Stravinsky, Debussy, Bartok and a piece by Boulez make up this exciting program. 94 mins.
VHS: S24261. $29.95.
Laser: LD74843. $34.95.

Brahms Piano Concerto No. 1 and No. 2
Leonard Bernstein conducts the Vienna Philharmonic with pianist Krystian Zimmerman.
VHS: S18538. $24.95.
Laser: LD70891. $29.95.

Brahms Piano Concertos
Sergiu Celibidache conducts the Munich Philharmonic in this recording of Brahms' concertos. Daniel Barenboim is featured on the piano. 109 mins.
VHS: S26906. $29.97.

Brahms Quartets
Demonstrates how a record is made and features the Brahms *Piano Quartets op. 25* and *op. 26*.
Laser: LD74567. $29.98.

Brahms Sextets
Features the Brahms Sextets *op. 18* and *op. 36* as it shows how a record is made.
Laser: LD74566. $29.98.

Brahms Symphony No. 1
Seiji Ozawa conducts the Saito Kinen orchestra's recording of Brahms' first symphony. "The performance maintains a sense of lyrical continuity even when most impassioned" (*The New York Times*). 60 mins.
Laser: LD71545. $29.95.

Brahms Symphony No. 1 and No. 2
Herbert Von Karajan conducts the Berlin Philharmonic in Brahms' first two symphonies. 86 mins.
VHS: S17430. $24.95.
Laser: LD71754. $34.95.

Brahms Symphony No. 3 and No. 4
The two Brahms symphonies are conducted by Herbert von Karajan and performed by the Berlin Philharmonic Orchestra. 74 mins.
VHS: S17698. $24.95.
Laser: LD71796. $34.95.

Brahms German Requiem (Ein Deutches Requiem)
Herbert von Karajan conducts the Berlin Philharmonic in this performance of Brahms' German Requiem.
Laser: LD70178. $34.95.

Brahms—Klassix 13
Anthony Quayle and Balint Vaszonyi host this drama about the life of Brahms, from his tavern brawls to the writing of his first symphony, to his hopeless love for Clara Schumann. 60 mins.
VHS: S10896. $24.95.

Brendel on Beethoven
In his London home, Alfred Brendel shares his thoughts on Beethoven's sonatas. Then Brendel performs the *Tempest* sonata. Filmed for the BBC. 59 mins.
VHS: S24688. $29.95.

Bruckner Symphony No. 8
Herbert von Karajan conducts the Vienna Philharmonic in a performance of the Bruckner *Symphony No. 8*. In Hi-fi Stereo, 85 mins.
Laser: LD74564. $34.98.

Bruckner Symphony No. 9 (Berlin)
Herbert von Karajan conducts this work with the Berlin Philharmonic.
Laser: LD74584. $34.98.

Bruckner Symphony No. 9 in D Minor, Te Deum (Vienna)
Herbert von Karajan directed the filming of this 1978 performance in addition to conducting the Vienna Philharmonic Orchestra and chorus with soloists Anna Tomowa-Sintow, Agnes Baltsa, David Kendall and Jose van Dam. In Hi-Fi stereo, 89 mins.
Laser: LD71465. $34.95.

Burning Poles: Cecil Taylor in Performance
"The American aesthetic landscape is full of idiosyncratic marvels: poet Walt Whitman, the composer Charles Ives, filmmaker D.W. Griffith, the painter Jackson Pollock, and the searing, visionary pianist Cecil Taylor. His playing has been said to resemble Niagara Falls, a volcano, a great river, thunderheads, a high wind, a cannonade, a stampede" (*The New Yorker*). 60 mins.
VHS: S14718. $19.95.

Canadian Brass: Home Movies
The popular Canadian Brass in an entertaining retrospective of their home movies, archival footage, live arrangements and musical performances. The show includes "Thus Spake Zarathustra," "Amazing Grace" and "Pachelbel's Canon." 53 mins.
VHS: S19105. $24.95.
Laser: LD71894. $29.95.

Carlos Kleiber: Mozart Symphony No. 36 and Brahms Symphony No. 2
On the occasion of the 150th anniversary of the Vienna Philharmonic, Carlos Kleiber conducted this world-renowned orchestra in these two works.
VHS: S18453. $29.95.
Laser: LD71867. $34.95.

Carnival of the Animals
Glenn Close and Jeremy Irons bring to life the hilarious verses Ogden Nash wrote to accompany Saint-Saens's beloved musical score, here performed in its original chamber orchestra version by a unique ensemble made up of some of New York's best instrumentalists. The perfect way to introduce children to classical music. 30 mins.
VHS: S13240. $19.95.

A Celebration in Vienna
Leonard Bernstein wrote, narrated, performed and conducted this special program on Beethoven's 200th birthday, with excerpts from *Piano Concerto 1 in C Major*, the "Ode to Joy", and rehearsal and scenes from *Fidelio*. Soloists include Placido Domingo, Gwyneth Jones and Shirley Verret, with the Vienna Philharmonic and the Vienna State Opera Chorus. 90 mins.
VHS: S17313. $29.95.

A Century of Russian Music
A glorious concert video starring Maxim Shostakovich and Viktoria Mullova, recorded live with the London Symphony Orchestra. Glinka, Tchaikovsky and Shostakovich, whose music is synonymous with the heritage of Russian composition, are presented, including performances of Glinka's overture to "Russlan and Ludmila," Tchaikovsky's "Violin Concerto", and Shostakovich conducting the orchestra in a brilliant rendition of his father's response to political repression, the "Symphony No. 5". 95 mins.
VHS: S11543. $19.95.

Charles Ives:
Good Dissonance Like a Man
Dramatized biography of the great American composer Charles Ives, which blends words with music and photography to create a moving portrait of the artist. Peabody Award winner. 60 mins.
VHS: S04151. $39.95.

Christmas at Ripon Cathedral
Ripon Cathedral, founded in 664 A.D., is the second oldest Christian place of worship in Great Britain. It is the perfect setting for this inspirational program which features some of Britain's finest musical talents, including Dame Janet Baker, the Huddersfield Choral Society and the Black Dyke Mills Band, performing traditional Christmas music. The cathedral's own choir also sings five beautiful Christmas carols. 60 mins.
VHS: S07600. $29.95.
Laser: LD70328. $34.95.

Christmas from St. Patrick's Cathedral
From the historic church in Dublin, Ireland, a holiday program of music and poetry. Selections include "What Child Is This?", "Go Tell It on the Mountain" and "Adeste Fideles", performed by the West Point Cadet Glee Club and Radio Telefeis Eire Convert Orchestra and Philharmonic Choir. With the poetry of Kavanaugh and Yeats. Soloists include Dennis O'Neill and Bernadette Greevy. 1989, 55 mins.
VHS: S09060. $29.95.

Christmas Goes Baroque
Subtitled *Performed in the Style of Bach, Handel and Vivaldi*, this heartwarming Christmas show alternates scenes from Zurich, Switzerland, with musical selections including "Silent Night," "Alle Jahre Wieder," "God Rest Ye Merry Gentlemen," and "O Tannenbaum." With the CSSR State Philharmonic Orchestra, conducted by Peter Breiner.
Laser: LD72245. $29.95.

Christmas Oratorio
The Dresden Philharmonic performs Bach, sung by the Choir of the Holy Cross. 91 minutes.
VHS: S07498. $39.95.

Classical Christmas
An opulent video presentation with music interpreted through scenes of nature's winter, and classical images from Christmas season, as well as the historic artwork of Currier and Ives. Highlights include "Deck the Halls," "Joy to the World," "Nutcracker Suite," "Silent Night," and "Messiah" selections. 30 mins.
VHS: S05618. $19.95.

Classical Images—A Concert in Nature
Visual interpretations of all-time favorites, including Mozart, Tchaikovsky and Debussy, performed to spectacular visual looks a nature. The New Philharmonic Orchestra performs. 45 mins.
VHS: S04679. $29.95.

Classical Music from Moscow
These programs cater to classical music enthusiasts, celebrating Shostakovich's and Tchaikovsky's artistic achievement and savoring the performances of their compositions. 110 mins.
VHS: S12724. $19.95.

Claudio Arrau—Volumes 1, 2, 3, 4
Widely regarded as one of the great pianists of the century, these historic performances capture Arrau in interpretations of Beethoven's *Emperor Concerto*, and compositions by Liszt, Chopin, Debussy.
Volume 1.
VHS: Out of print. For rental only.
Volume 2.
VHS: S07690. $29.95.
Volume 3.
VHS: S07691. $29.95.
Volume 4.
VHS: S07692. $29.95.

The Cleveland Orchestra:
A Portrait of George Szell
This *Bell Telephone Hour* television episode presents a portrait of conductor George Szell. He brought the Cleveland Orchestra to a high standard recognized the world over. Szell's rehearsal of Beethoven's *Symphony No. 5* is especially indicative of his artistic ability. 60 mins.
VHS: S22439. $24.95.

The Cleveland Quartet
The Cleveland Quartet performs Beethoven's *String Quartet in D dur (Op. 18, no. 3)* and Brahms' *Quintet with Piano (Op. 34)*. As a special feature, the celebrated Cleveland Quartet performs Brahms' *Quintet with Piano (Op. 34)* on Paganini's own treasured and virtually priceless Stradivariuses.
VHS: S27197. $14.95.

Concert Aid
Originally produced by Oxfam, this is a spectacular recording of Beethoven's Symphony No. 5 performed by the BBC Symphony Orchestra with Sir Georg Solti conducting. Since 1942, Oxfam has worked with the poor around the world, and all of the profits from the performances for the cassette were donated. 40 mins.
VHS: S04681. $19.95.

Das Konzert
This powerful musical event captures the triumphant concert of Daniel Barenboim and the Berlin Philharmonic that greeted the fall of the Berlin Wall. *Beethoven's Symphony No. 7* and *Piano Concerto No. 1* are on this program. 112 mins.
Laser: LD74557. $29.98.

David Oistrakh in Performance
Virtuoso violinist David Oistrakh masterfully interprets works by Leclair, Prokofiev, Shostakovich, Kreisler, Debussy and Ravel in this rare filmed performance in 1962. 52 mins.
VHS: S09225. $19.95.

David Oistrakh:
Remembering a Musician
In rare footage from the musical archives of the Soviet Union, Oistrakh plays scintillating and emotional performances of such works as the intermezzo movement from Lalo's "Symphonie Espagole," excerpts from Shostakovich's F minor Sonata and other works. 60 mins.
VHS: S03166. $39.95.

The Debussy Etudes Performed and Discussed by Mitsuko Uchida
Piano virtuoso Mitsuko Uchida performs the etudes and provides commentary. In Hi-Fi stereo, 70 mins.
VHS: S16047. $29.95.
Laser: LD71190. $34.95.

Debussy/Ravel
The legendary Herbert von Karajan, conducting the great Berlin Philharmonic, is the star of this enchanting film containing the music which came to symbolize the Romantic era: *Prelude a l'Apres-Midi d'un Faune* by Debussy, and the *Daphnis and Chloe* suites by Ravel. Debussy and Ravel were the masters of the passionate, emotional music of this era, and this film contains their most accessible works. 53 mins.
VHS: S14119. $24.95.

Discovering the Music of the Middle Ages
All walks of life, from the nobles and the clergy to the peasants, found music an indispensable part of life during the Middle Ages. It was played in church, in the castle and in the village. 20 mins.
VHS: S23517. $49.95.

Dvorak in Prague: A Celebration
Yo-Yo Ma, Itzhak Perlman, Frederica von Stade, Seiji Ozawa and the Boston Symphony Orchestra join forces on the occasion of the 100-year anniversary of Dvorak's *New World Symphony*. A variety of his music is performed in this Sony production set in Prague.
VHS: S21073. $24.98.

Dvorak: Symphony No. 9 in E Minor, From the New World
Sergiu Celibidache conducts the Munich Philharmonic in a performance of Dvorak's most widely known work. In addition, this video includes a wide-ranging portrait of this legendary conductor. It's a rare opportunity to learn about Celibidache, because he has shunned recordings of his performances.
VHS: S26908. $29.97.
Jan Schmidt-Garre, Germany, 113 mins.

Early Musical Instruments
The authentic, complete and fascinating guide to the instruments of Henry the Eighth, Gabrieli, Byrd, Purcell, Bach and Mozart—shawm, bibiou, dulzaina, zampogna, crumhorn, gemhorn, tromba—the whole range of instruments which are ancestors to the modern instruments. The six-part series is narrated by David Munrow, one of the pioneering authorities on early music, and performed by the Early Music Consort of London, with Christopher Hogwood.
Bowed Instruments. In the 11th century, European musicians tried to make their instruments sound like the human voice; instead of plucking the strings, they began drawing a piece of wood or bone across them to sustain the tone. By Elizabethan times, the viol was the aristocrat of bowed instruments.
VHS: S05594. $29.95.
Brass Instruments. The development of brass instruments from the lowly cow horn, with the associations of bone and wooden ancestors of the trumpet associated with pomp and royalty.
VHS: S05595. $29.95.
Flutes and Whistles. The first musical instruments developed when primitive man used tubes of bamboo, bone or wood to produce whistling sounds, later applied to create a wide range of folk and concert instruments.
VHS: S05591. $29.95.
Keyboard and Percussion. A close look at such rarities as the dulcimer and the hurdy-gurdy, as well as better-known instruments like the organ, harpsichord and kettledrums.
VHS: S05593. $29.95.
Plucked Instruments. The roots and foreign branches of the guitar family tree, and a good look at the more important of the many relatives of this instrument.
VHS: S05592. $29.95.

Reed Instruments.
The development of reeds from those played loudly by the Saracens to frighten the horses of the Crusaders, to the 17th century forerunners of today's orchestra.
VHS: S05590. $29.95.
Complete six-volume set.
VHS: S05589. $149.00.

Erick Friedman Plays Fritz Kreisler
Friedman plays the works of the beloved Kreisler, the recital consisting of ten selections, including the ever-popular "The Old Refrain." 90 mins.
VHS: S03150. $39.95.

Evening with Danny Kaye
Danny Kaye conducts the New York Philharmonic with a little help from Zubin Mehta in a concert that soars with the music of Tchaikovsky and Beethoven and sparkles with Kaye's incomparable clowning. 109 mins.
VHS: S09896. $22.95.

Four American Composers
Unique musical profiles, directed by Peter Greenaway (*Drowning by Numbers, The Cook, the Thief, His Wife and Her Lover*), that offer startling and intimate insights into the music and ideas of four very original American composers. Greenaway takes as his starting point performances given by the artists in London and creates an exciting musical experience. Four volumes.
(1) John Cage. 60 mins.
VHS: S14720. $19.95.
(2) Philip Glass. 60 mins.
VHS: S14721. $19.95.
(3) Meredith Monk. 60 mins.
VHS: S14722. $19.95.
(4) Robert Ashley. 60 mins.
VHS: S14723. $19.95.
Complete four-volume set. 240 mins.
VHS: S14719. $69.95.

The Four Seasons
Antonio Vivaldi's *Four Seasons* is combined with the beautiful countryside of Switzerland in this award-winning presentation. Excellent for music appreciation classes. 14 mins.
VHS: S23503. $49.95.

Four Ways to Say Farewell
In an essay illustrated with rehearsal scenes, Leonard Bernstein offers a moving, lucid analysis of Gustav Mahler's *Ninth Symphony*. The Vienna Philharmonic Orchestra is featured. 57 mins.
VHS: S26794. $19.95.

Franz Liszt: Annees de Pelerinage
In this video program, Austrian pianist Alfred Brendel (long renowned for his performances of Liszt) introduces the pieces in the *Anees de Pelerinage* with his own commentary and then performs them with the consummate artistry that has made him one of the pre-eminent pianists of the century. 115 mins.
VHS: S15628. $24.95.

Frederich Gulda/Mozart No End and the Paradise Band
Gulda is a famed classical musician and jazz performer whose unique interpretations are well-regarded. In this video he presents his own treatments of Mozart works, including *The Marriage of Figaro, Coronation Concerto* and *Piano Sonata in C*, together with his own original works. 96 mins.
Laser: LD74556. $29.98.

From Mao to Mozart
This is the document of the visit of Isaac Stern to the People's Republic of China in 1979. Mr. Stern happily exercised his musical passport to share the best of western classical music with the people of China. Featuring the music of Mozart.
Laser: LD70996. $39.95.
Murray Lerner, 1980, 84 mins.

Gala Tribute to Tchaikovsky
Famed opera singers Kiri Te Kanawa and Placido Domingo join a host of ballet stars like Vivian Durante and conductors Sir Edward Downes, Stephen Barlow and Barry Wordsworth to perform selected highlights of music by Tchaikovsky, Rachmaninoff and Rimsky-Korsakov. 135 mins.
VHS: S21053. $39.95.

George Frederick Handel: Honour, Profit and Pleasure
A remarkable portrait of Handel in the cultural and social context of the England in which he created—and which his creations mirror. Portrayed by Simon Callow, Handel emerges as an extraordinary musician with ordinary motivations.
VHS: S05587. $29.95.

Glenn Branca: Symphony No. 4
Documentary of the musician's European tour with performance footage and music.
VHS: S10193. $19.95.
Arleen Schloss, USA, 1984, 10 mins.

The Glenn Gould Collection
A remarkable series of videos charting the unique career of music's idiosyncratic genius.
Program I: Prologue. Features Beethoven's *Piano Sonata No. 31* (Third Movement), an excerpt from Bach's *Partita No. 2*, the announcement of Glenn Gould's death, Gould discussing Russian music and performing Beethoven's *Eroica Variations*, Bach's *Well-Tempered Clavier II: Prelude and Fugue* and Sir William Walton's *Facade: Scotch Rhapsody*.
VHS: S21935. $29.98.
Program II: Sonatas and Dialogues. Gould in conversation with Yehudi Menuhin and then performing Bach's *Violin Sonata No. 4*, Beethoven's *Sonata for Piano and Violin No. 10*, and Schoenberg's *Phantasy for Violin and Piano Accompaniment*.
VHS: S21936. $29.98.
Program III: End of Concerts. Gould talks about concerts and Paul Hindemith, appears as Karl-Heinz Klopweiser, and performs Bach's *Partita No. 5*, Sweelinck's *Fantasia in D*, Beethoven's *Bagatelle op. 126, no. 3*, Krenek's *Wanderlied im Herbst*, Bach's *Well-Tempered Clavier II: Fugue BWV 891*, Beethoven's *Piano Sonata No. 17* and the fourth movement of Hindemith's *Sonata No. 3*.
VHS: S21938. $29.98.

Program IV: So You Want to Write a Fugue?
Gould talks about Beethoven and appears in his "So You Want to Write a Fugue?". He is also shown performing Bach's *Well-Tempered Clavier II: Fugue BWV 876*, Berg's *Piano Sonata op. 1*, Beethoven's *Piano Sonata No. 30*, Bach's *Piano Concerto No. 7* and Bach's *Well-Tempered Clavier II: Prelude and Fugue BWV 878*.
VHS: S21939. $29.98.
Program V: The Conductor. Glenn Gould appears as Sir Nigel Thwitt-Thornwaite, talks about Wava and conducts the Russell Oberlin Orchestra in Bach's *Cantata "Widerstehe doch der Stunde" BWV 43*, excerpts from Beethoven's *Symphony No. 6, Pastorale* and Bach's *Brandenburg Concerto No. 5*.
VHS: S21940. $29.98.
Program VI: The Earliest Decade. Gould is the soloist in Bach's *Piano Concerto No. 1 BWV 1052*, the first movement of Beethoven's *Piano Concerto No. 1* and Beethoven's *32 Variations*.
VHS: S21941. $29.98.
Program VII: A Russian Interlude. Gould performs Prokofiev's *Visions fugitives No. 2* and *Piano Concerto No. 2*, Scriabin's *Preludes op. 33* and *op. 45*, and Shostakovich's *Piano Quintet op. 57*.
VHS: S21942. $29.98.
Program VIII: Interweaving Voices. Gould performs Bach's *Art of the Fugue BWV 1080 Contrapunctus IV*, Beethoven's *Variations op. 34*, Hindemith's *Das Marienleben: Argwohn Josephs*, Webern's *Piano Variations op. 27* and Beethoven's *Sonata for Piano and Cello No. 3* (with cellist Leonard Rose).
VHS: S21943. $29.98.
Program IX: Mostly Strauss. Gould talks about Strauss and Mozart, and is seen performing Strauss's *Cacilie*, Mozart's *Piano Sonata No. 13* and Strauss's *Burleske for Piano and Orchestra*.
VHS: S21944. $29.98.
Program X: Rhapsodic Interludes. Glenn Gould talks about *Elektra*, discusses *La Valse*, and performs the transcription of an excerpt from Schubert's *Symphony No. 5*, the piano transcription of an excerpt from Strauss's *Elektra*, Schoenberg's *Pierrot Lunaire*, Ravel's *La Valse*, Debussy's *Premiere Rhapsodie pour Clarinette* and Strauss's *Violin Sonata op. 18, 1st Movement*.
VHS: S21945. $29.98.
Program XI: Ecstasy and Wit. Glenn Gould appears as Myron Chianti, talks about Richard Strauss and performs Beethoven's *Piano Sonata No. 17, op. 31, no. 2, Der Sturm*, Scriabin's *Prelude op. 49, no. 2*, Strauss's *3 Ophelia-Lieder op. 67*, Bach's *Goldberg Variations BWV 988* and Casella's *Ricercare No. 1 on B-A-C-H*.
VHS: S21946. $29.98.
Program XII: Epilogue. Glenn Gould discusses *The Emperor Concerto* and performs Bach's *The Well-Tempered Clavier II: Prelude and Fugue BWV 872* and *Prelude and Fugue BWV 891*, and Beethoven's *Piano Concerto No. 5, The Emperor*.
VHS: S21947. $29.98.
Program XIII: The Goldberg Variations—Glenn Gould in Conversation with Bruno Monsaingeon. Gould's first recording of the Goldberg Variations in 1951 was a revelation. It displayed something essential about the creative process and made him a legend besides. Now a film shot in 1981 brings this musician's career full circle. 59 mins.
VHS: S23928. $29.98.
Program XIV: The Question of Instrument—Glenn Gould in Conversation with Bruno Monsaingeon. Gould takes up a key question regarding the original instruments movement: should Bach's work be played on a harpsichord or on a piano, an instrument developed only after Bach's time? This great pianist and thinker offers some provocative insights. 57 mins.
VHS: S23929. $29.98.
Program XV: An Art of the Fugue—Glenn Gould in Conversation with Bruno Monsaingeon. Bach perfected the fugue, a compositional technique of interweaving of voices. Master pianist Glenn Gould explores the philosophical underpinnings of the fugue and its importance beyond music. 57 mins.
VHS: S23930. $29.98.
Program XVI: On the Twentieth Century—Glenn Gould Talks About and Plays Music by Sriabin, Schoenberg, Webern, Strauss, and Hindemith. From the romanticism of Strauss to the scientifically inspired tonal system of Schoenberg, Gould performed the music of this century with passion and conviction. This is a fascinating program of contemporary works. 58 mins.
VHS: S23931. $29.98.

Glenn Gould Collection: Laser
Two programs are featured on each laser disc.
Program I and Program II.
Laser: LD74532. $29.98.
Program III and Program IV.
Laser: LD74533. $29.98.
Program V and Program VI.
Laser: LD74534. $29.98.
Program VII and Program VIII.
Laser: LD74535. $29.98.
Program IX and Program X.
Laser: LD74536. $29.98.
Program XI and Program XII.
Laser: LD74537. $29.98.

Glenn Gould Plays Beethoven
After decades of silence, Glenn Gould is suddenly being rediscovered, perhaps because of the wonderful Canadian biopic *32 Short Films About Glenn Gould*. The newest release is *Glenn Gould Plays Beethoven*, a wonderful concert for Beethoven fans and Gould fans alike. Gould plays *The Emperor Concerto, Bagatelle (Op. 26 No. 3)* and the *F-Minor Variations (Op. 34)*. 60 mins.
VHS: S21915. $19.95.

Glenn Gould's Greatest Hits
Highlights from the Glenn Gould Collection include Gould playing Bach's *Goldberg Variations BWV 98*; the *Violin Sonata No. 4*, 2nd movement (with Yehudi Menuhin), Beethoven's *Bagatelle op. 126* and 2nd movement of *Sonata for Piano and Cello No. 3* (with Lenn Rose). Then Gould does "So You Want to Write a Fugue." He appears as Sir Nigel Thwitt-Thornwaite, conducts Mahler's *Ulricht*, and plays Walton's *Facade: Scotch Rhapsody* and Scriabin's *Prelude op. 49*.
VHS: S21948. $29.98.
Laser: LD74538. $29.98.

Glenn Gould: A Portrait
Glenn Gould was one of the most imaginative pianists of our time, and this portrait uncovers many of the creative roles he played as an explorer of sound through interviews with his father, friends, colleagues, combined with radio and television performances that reflect his vast range of music. 107 mins.
VHS: S07693. $29.95.

Glory of Spain
Tribute to the art and music of Spain, shot at the Prado Museum, and featuring performances by soprano Victoria de los Angeles, pianist Alicia de la Rocha, and guitarist Andres Segovia. Composers Falla, Granados, and Albeniz are featured, along with masterpieces by El Greco, Velazquez and Goya.
VHS: S03216. $49.95.

Going on Fifty
A look at the private and professional life of conductor Zubin Mehta and his work as the musical director of the Israeli Philharmonic Orchestra. 60 mins.
VHS: S07768. $39.95.

Grand Duo:
Itzhak Perlman and Pinchas Zukerman
Filmmaker Christopher Nupen captures the 1976 European tour of violinists Itzhak Perlman and Pinchas Zukerman. Filmed at the Royal College of Music in London, selections include Wieniawski's *Etudes Caprices, Opus 18*, Spohr's *Duo Concertante, Opus 67*, Leclair's *Sonata, Opus 3*, Handel/Halvorsen's *Passacaglia in G minor*, Mozart's *Duo No. 1 in G major* and Wieniawski's *Caprice in A minor*. In Hi-Fi Stereo, 90 mins.
VHS: S16512. $29.97.
Laser: LD71460. $34.97.

Great Music from Chicago
Andre Kostelanetz conducts the Chicago Symphony Orchestra. Selections include "Polovetzian Dances" by Borodin, "The Mother Goose Suite" by Ravel, "Rhapsody Espana" by Emanuel Chabrier, and "Intermezzo" by Samuel Barber. Ken Nordine is the program's host. USA, 1957, 55 mins.
VHS: S05519. $24.95.

The Guarneri Quartet
This world-famous quartet plays two works to the accompaniment of pianist Mikhail Rudy, Mozart's *String Quartet in D Dur, K.575* and Brahms's *Quartet No. 1 for Piano and Strings, Op. 25*. The performances captured on this tape testify to the enduring reputation of The Guarneri Quartet. 68 mins.
VHS: S27567. $14.95.

The Guarneri String Quartet
The internationally-renowned string quartet performs the Beethoven Quartets Nos. 9 and 11 as recorded at the Mansion at Old Westbury Gardens, New York, and introduced by Hal Linden. 58 mins.
VHS: S09827. $29.95.

Guitarra
A four-hour series featuring world-renowned classical guitarist Julian Bream, who traces the evolution of the Spanish guitar from 1500 to the present day. Bream plays against a backdrop of the magnificent old buildings and panoramic landscapes of Spain, creating a visual evocation of the culture that spawned this special music. Each volume is 60 mins.
Guitarra: The 20th Century—The Last of the Romantics and the Guitar.
VHS: S02197. $39.95.
Guitarra: The Classical Heritage and the Transition to Romanticism.
VHS: S01843. $39.95.
Guitarra: The Golden Age and the Baroque Guitar.
VHS: S01838. $39.95.
Guitarra: The Poetic Nationalist and the Spirit of Spain.
VHS: S01825. $39.95.

Harnoncourt and Beethoven
Nikolaus Harnoncourt is shown conducting Beethoven's *Symphonies No. 8* and *No. 6, the Pastoral*. Then a behind-the-scenes look is offered by footage of this great conductor rehearsing the Chamber Orchestra of Europe through *Symphonies Nos. 1-8*. 118 mins.
VHS: S22462. $29.95.

Haydn at Esterhaza Hogwood
Includes a brief documentary that outlines Haydn's remarkable career, followed by a collection of superb performances featuring three complete Haydn symphonies brought to life by conductor Christopher Hogwood and The Academy of Ancient Music. 106 mins.
VHS: S15631. $24.95.
Laser: LD70277. $34.95.

Haydn Cello Concertos No. 1 & 2
Mstislav Rostropovich is the soloist and conductor of the Academy of St. Martin in the Fields in this performance.
VHS: S18534. $24.95.
Laser: LD71030. $34.95.

Hector Berlioz
Symphonie Fantastique, Op. 14
Symphonie Fantastique, recorded at the Conservatoire National Superieur d'Art Dramatique, performed by the Orchestre Revolutionnaire et Romantique, and conducted by John Eliot Gardiner. 55 mins.
VHS: S18317. $29.95.
Laser: LD71855. $29.95.

Heifetz
The great violinist performs Bruch's Scottish Fantasy and Bach's Chaconne, plus works by Mozart, Debussy, Rachmaninoff, Kornbgold, Prokofiev and Gershwin.
VHS: S02945. $39.95.

Heifetz Master Classes
Maestro Jascha Heifetz, this century's greatest violinist, becomes Professor Heifetz in these rare, filmed seminars from the early 1960's taken from his legendary workshops at USC. The brilliant musician can be seen coaxing, cajoling, inspiring and occasionally terrifying his pupils as he imparts his unquestioned genius and lifetime of musical experience. Learn the secrets of intonation, phrasing and vibrato from the man whose name has become synonymous with the violin. Part 2 contains never-before-released footage showing Heifetz in a rare, humorous parody of a violin student giving an audition.
Heifetz Master Classes Part I. 120 mins.
VHS: S12772. $49.95.
Heifetz Master Classes Part II. 120 mins.
VHS: S12773. $49.95.
Heifetz Master Classes Pre-Pack. Both volumes (240 mins.) of the Heifetz Master Classes at a special combined price.
VHS: S12774. $79.95.

High Fidelity
From the director of *From Mao to Mozart* comes this fascinating journey with the Guarneri String Quartet on their recent world tour. *High Fidelity* celebrates the 25 years the quite diverse Guarneri members have managed to stay together to become among the most long-lived, most successful and most popular string quartets in the world. "Pure pleasure" (Vincent Canby).
VHS: S12825. $39.95.
Allan Miller, USA, 1989, 85 mins.

Hoffnung Festival Concert
Music lovers everywhere have delighted in the special madcap parody contrived by Gerald Hoffnung in this gala evening of symphonic caricature featuring the Hoffnung Festival Orchestra. 59 mins.
VHS: S09828. $29.95.

Horowitz in Moscow
The drama and excitement of Vladimir Horowitz's extraordinary 1986 concert in Moscow, his first visit back to Russia since he left in 1925. The program includes Scarlatti sonatas, Mozart's "Sonata in C Major" and a selection of Schubert, Liszt, Chopin, Rachmaninoff and Scriabin, in one of the legendary performances of the 20th century. Color. USSR, 1986, 120 mins.
VHS: S01862. $29.95.

Horowitz in Vienna
Witness the musical wizardry of the legendary Vladimir Horowitz in this special 90-minute video capturing one of the last performances he ever gave. Horowitz—the dramatic storyteller, a musical conversationalist who needed no words. 90 mins.
VHS: S13889. $24.95.
Laser: LD71418. $24.95.

Horowitz Plays Mozart
Vladimir Horowitz performs Mozart's Piano Concerto No. 23 K. 488 with the Orchestra del Teatro ala Scala Milano conducted by Carlo Maria Giulini.
VHS: S18540. $24.95.
Laser: LD71047. $29.95.

Horszowski: Live at Carnegie Hall
A rare concert performance by the late pianist Mieczyslaw Horszowski as he plays Bach, Beethoven, Schumann, Chopin and Mendelssohn. 94 mins.
Laser: LD71926. $34.97.

Huberman Festival
This series of stereo programs won the Best Program of the Year Award, and features Isaac Stern, Itzhak Perlman, Pinchas Zuckerman, Shlomo Mintz, Henryk Szeryng, Ivy Gitlis and Ira Haendel, and Zubin Mehta conducting the Israel Philharmonic Orchestra. Each is 45 minutes.
Volume 2: Mozart: Sinfonia Concertante and Handel: Passcaglia.
VHS: S06399. $19.95.
Volume 3: Tchaikovsky: Concerto in D Minor and Vivaldi: Concerto in A Minor.
VHS: S06400. $19.95.
Volume 4: Mendelssohn: Concerto in E Minor and Bach: Concerto in D Minor.
VHS: S06401. $19.95.
Volume 5: Bach: Brandenburg Concerto No. 6 and Vivaldi: Concerto in B Minor.
VHS: S06402. $19.95.

Igor Stravinsky's Symphony of Psalms
Stravinsky found inspiration in sources ranging from Greek Orthodox Liturgy to the 19th century composer Verdi. Now this singular work has been preserved on video, capturing its innovative and abstract sounds. 30 mins.
VHS: S22930. $19.95.

In Celebration of the Piano
An all-star tribute to the Steinway piano taped live at Carnegie Hall, and hosted by Van Cliburn. Performances by Murray Perahia, Alfred Brendel, Rudolf Serkin, Alexis Weissenberg, Lazar Berman and 20 others! 100 mins.
VHS: S13241. $39.95.

In the Steps of Chopin:
Portrait by Byron Janis
Janis takes us through the stations in Chopin's life, demonstrating the pianistic techniques Chopin taught his pupils, examining differences between manuscript and published versions of some of the pieces, and showing both his technical virtuosity and exceptional affinity with Chopin in performances of a broad range of Chopin pieces.
VHS: S05586. $29.95.

Isaac Stern: A Life
This video documents the 70th year of the great violinist Isaac Stern. He was honored in his hometown of San Francisco with an endowed chair and a concert for 30,000 people. But this video also shows the busy season performed by Stern, as it follows him across the world performing his favorite works by Beethoven. Gregory Peck narrates. 122 mins.
VHS: S26003. $34.95.

Israel in Egypt
The Jerusalem Symphony Orchestra, under the direction of John Currie, performs "The Exodus" and "Songs of the Sea" on the shore of the Red Sea directly across from Pharaoh's Island. The Scottish National Choir and the Edinburgh Festival Choir sing. Includes English subtitles of the oratorio text. 90 mins.
VHS: S26107. $29.95.

Israel Philharmonic Welcomes Berlin Philharmonic
Zubin Mehta, music director for life of the Israel Philharmonic, brought these two great musical forces together in Tel Aviv. It was an historic moment, cementing a new era in unity and peace. A Sony Music production. 98 mins.
Laser: LD74553. $29.98.

Itzhak Perlman
Beethoven's violin concerto, with Carlo Maria Giulini conducting the Philharmonia Orchestra. Perlman's brilliant technique and the superlative recording make this a feast of both sight and sound. 45 mins.
VHS: S08239. $19.95.

Ivo Perelman—Live in New York
"One of the most distinctive and imposing tenor sax voices to come along in years" is how *Downbeat Magazine* describes the jazz world's latest sensation, saxophonist Ivo Perelman. In this, his first video, he is joined by guest artists Flora Purim, Geri Allen, Fred Hopkins, Andrew Cyrille, Mino Cinelu and Elson Nascimento for an evening of spectacular music-making, taped live at The Knitting Factory. 58 mins.
VHS: S14065. $29.95.

Ivo Pogorelich in Castello Reale di Racconigi
Ivo Pogorelich performs works by Chopin, Mozart and Haydn.
VHS: S18539. $24.95.
Laser: LD71029. $34.99.

Ivo Pogorelich in Villa Contarini
Pianist Ivo Pogorelich performs music of the 19th century. Includes works by: Scriabin, Chopin (Sonata #2, Polonaise Op. 44) and others. 52 mins.
VHS: S14963. $24.95.

Jacqueline du Pre and the Elgar Cello Concerto
Du Pre performs this lyrical concerto with Daniel Barenboim and the New Philharmonia Orchestra. An intimate portrait of a legendary musician.
VHS: S15460. $29.98.
Laser: LD70218. $34.98.

James Galway Plays Mostly Mozart
The flamboyant maverick James Galway, with his golden flute and flawless technique, completely enthralls the audience in this concert of Handel, Mozart and Vivaldi's "The Four Seasons," arranged for the flute by Mr. Galway, in a live performance at the Mostly Mozart Festival of Lincoln Center.
VHS: S09162. $22.95.

John Cage: Man and Myth
An intimate visit with the sage of conceptual music and collage poetry. At ease and affable, Cage discusses his new pursuits, theories, memories and friends. Includes several compositions. Directed by Mitch Corber. 60 mins.
VHS: S14104. $49.95.

John Kim Bell: A Profile of the First North American Indian Conductor
John Kim Bell tells the story of a talented and passionate young man who broke through social barriers. From his 1981 conducting debut with the Toronto Symphony to associate to Zubin Mehta of the New York Philharmonic, *John Kim Bell* is a cinematic portrait of a vibrant and charismatic conductor. 41 mins.
VHS: S04682. $29.95.

Karajan Conducts
Herbert von Karajan conducts the Berlin Philharmonic in a series of lighter works, including pieces by Verdi, Bizet, Liszt, Weber and Wagner. 78 mins.
VHS: S17127. $24.95.
Laser: LD71543. $34.95.

Karajan in Salzburg
Susan Froemke and Peter Gelb follow the famous conductor in Salzburg; cinematography by Edward Lachmann.
VHS: S18533. $24.95.
Laser: LD71074. $34.95.

Karajan: Early Images, Vol. 1
In collaboration with the talented French filmmaker Henri-Georges Clouzot (*The Wages of Fear*), conductor Herbert von Karajan launched a series of performance films that attempted to achieve a "visual reinterpretation of a performance." Shot in black and white, this video shows von Karajan in preparation for conducting Beethoven's Fifth symphony, Schumann's Fourth symphony and Dvorak's Ninth symphony, "From the New World."
VHS: S16904. $24.95.
Laser: LD71526. $34.95.
Henri-Georges Clouzot, France/Germany, 1968

Karajan: Early Images, Vol. 2 (1965-66)
An anthology of Herbert von Karajan's work with the Vienna Symphony Orchestra. The highlights are Karajan's rehearsal for Schumann's *Symphony No. 4*, and a performance of Mozart's *Concerto for Violin and Orchestra, No. 5*, with Yehudi Menuhin. The film is directed by the important French filmmaker Henri-Georges Clouzot (*The Wages of Fear*).
VHS: S19894. $29.95.
Laser: LD72002. $34.95.
Henri-Georges Clouzot, France, 89 mins.

Krystian Zimmerman Plays Chopin & Schubert
This recital of popular Chopin/Schubert piano repertoire highlights the artistry of one of the most exciting young pianists. Digitally recorded in Hi-Fi stereo, 104 mins.
VHS: S16424. $24.95.

Kyoto Vivaldi: The Four Seasons
Antonio Vivaldi's baroque masterpiece is one of the most popular classical pieces of all time and receives a stunning performance by the Japanese Kyoto Ensemble, with the ancient capital city of Kyoto serving as background for this visual discovery. This unique video interpretation of Vivaldi's timeless classic adds a new dimension to the classic. 45 mins.
VHS: S03821. $19.95.

Lazar Berman in Recital
Pianist Lazar Berman performs a number of Chopin's works, including *The Polonaise, Op. 26, No.1, Op. 40, No.3, Op. 40, No.2, Op. 26, No.2, Op. 44* and *Op 53*. In addition he plays Liszt's *Funerailles*. 62 mins.
VHS: S27697. $14.95.

Leonard Bernstein Place, A Musical in Celebration of Leonard Bernstein's 75th Birthday
Live from Alice Tulley Hall in Lincoln Center, the Bernstein family hosts this concert of songs, chamber music and jazz. Friends like Lauren Bacall, Isaac Stern, Wynton Marsalis, Phyllis Newman and Jerry Hadley contribute to the festivities. 87 mins.
VHS: S22934. $19.95.

Leonard Bernstein: Schumann/Shostakovich
On a Japanese tour, Leonard Bernstein conducts the New York Philharmonic in Robert Schumann's *Symphony No. 1* (Spring) and Dmitri Shostakovich's *Symphony No. 5*. 93 mins.
VHS: S19583. $29.95.

Leonard Bernstein: The Gift of Music
This documentary honors the vision and talents of Leonard Bernstein. It reveals Bernstein as a brash showman who intuitively understood the emotional resonance of music on the public. Highlights include excerpts from his "Young People's Concerts," Bernstein conducting the New York Philharmonic in Moscow in 1959, and his interpretations of Beethoven and Mahler. 90 mins.
VHS: S19754. $29.95.

Leonard Bernstein: The Rite of Spring in Rehearsal
Bernstein inspires a youth orchestra to perform with primal force in this production of Igor Stravinsky's groundbreaking masterpiece. As a result, Bernstein's unique genius as both a musician and a teacher comes through. 60 mins.
VHS: S27695. $19.95.

Leonid Kogan
With piano accompaniment by his daughter Nina, dynamic performances of Tchaikovsky's *Melodie* and *Valse Scherzo*, Glazunov's *Entracte*, Brahms' *Scherzo*, Kreisler's *Liebesfreud*, Bizet's *Carmen*, and a set of Paganini variations. 60 mins.
VHS: S03882. $19.95.

The Life and Loves of Mozart
A critical, uncompromising portrait of the great composer Wolfgang Amadeus Mozart, during the breakdown and disintegration of his final, poverty-stricken years. Oskar Werner plays Mozart. 87 mins. English dubbed.
VHS: S17454. $29.95.

Little Drummer Boy
Leonard Bernstein reveals the inner character of a composer close to his heart—Gustav Mahler. This documentary essay explores the influence of Jewish origins on Mahler's life and compositions. 85 mins.
VHS: S26793. $19.95.

Looking at Music with Adrian Marthaler, Vol. 1
Swiss TV and film director Adrian Marthaler is a creative magician who takes pop music video techniques to create imaginative, exhilarating and often hilarious images of classical music. In Volume 1 are Bach's Brandenburg Concerto No. 2, Gershwin's Rhapsody in Blue, Honegger's Concertino, and Saint-Saens' Danse Macabre. Pianist Ilana Vered and Matthias Bamert conducting the Basel Radio Symphony are featured.
VHS: S05615. $29.95.

The Love of Three Orchestras
Leonard Bernstein's generous and loving spirit inspired this autobiographical essay about his relationship to three orchestras. Performances spanning four decades with the New York, Vienna and Israel Philharmonics serve as demonstrations of this love. 88 mins.
VHS: S26475. $19.95.

The Loves of Emma Bardac
Acclaimed classical piano duo Katia and Marielle Labeque portray the daughters of Emma Bardac, the product of her liaisons with composers Debussy and Faure. This award-winning program features the music of Bizet, Debussy and Faure performed by the Labeques. 1991, 60 mins.
VHS: S15801. $34.95.
Laser: LD71477. $34.98.

Maestro's Company—Volume 1
An inventive introduction to opera for children. Little Johnny and Tina lose a soccer ball but find a subterranean opera community living under an old theatre. The operatic talents are all played by puppets with the voices of Joan Sutherland, Renata Tebaldi, and Placido Domingo. Volume 1 contains *The Barber of Seville* and *La Traviata*. 60 mins.
VHS: S09116. $29.95.

Maestro's Company—Volume 2
Johnny and Tina continue to learn about the wonderful world of opera from the dedicated Maestro who lives underneath a disused opera theatre. The Maestro may look like a puppet but he know his stuff. Famous opera talents like Joan Sutherland and Placido Domingo lend their voices to the bodies of puppets. With selections from *Rigoletto* and *Hansel and Gretel*. In color. 60 mins.
VHS: S09117. $29.95.

Mahler Symphony No. 1 and No. 4
Leonard Bernstein conducts the Vienna Philharmonic.
VHS: S16404. $24.95.
Laser: LD71123. $34.95.

Mahler Symphony No. 2
Soloists Sheila Armstrong, Janet Baker, the Edinburgh Festival Chorus and the London Symphony Orchestra are featured in this performance of Mahler's Resurrection Symphony conducted by Leonard Bernstein.
VHS: S18531. $24.95.
Laser: LD71124. $34.95.

Mahler Symphony No. 3

This program features the composer's Third Symphony, conducted by Leonard Bernstein and performed by Vienna Philharmonic Orchestra. The program also features Mahler's unfinished Tenth Symphony.
VHS: S16905. $34.95.
Laser: LD71527. $59.95.

Mahler Symphony No. 3 and No. 10

Leonard Bernstein conducts the Vienna Philharmonic in this breathtaking fusion of the composer's and conductor's art in performance. Bernstein's Mahler was legendary and this video catches him at the height of his interpretive powers with the most responsive of orchestras. 67 mins.
VHS: S14121. $34.95.

Mahler Symphony No. 3 in D Minor

Bernard Haitink leads the Berlin Philharmonic with Florence Quivar, the women of the Ernst-Senff Choir and the Tolzer Boys Choir in this rendition of Mahler's *Symphony No. 3*. Filmed at the Schauspielhaus in Berlin, it won an Edison award for fine audio recording. 106 mins.
VHS: S20976. $29.95.

Mahler Symphony No. 4 in G

Bernard Haitink conducts this work, considered by some to be among Mahler's most accessible. This was filmed at the Schauspielhaus in Berlin with the Berlin Philharmonic. 60 mins.
VHS: S20642. $29.95.

Mahler Symphony No. 5

Leonard Bernstein's definitive and historic interpretation of Mahler's fifth symphony. Performed by the Vienna Philharmonic Orchestra. 72 mins.
VHS: S15636. $24.95.
Laser: LD70282. $34.95.

Mahler Symphony No. 6

This performance was filmed in 1976 in Vienna at the Musikverein, and features Leonard Bernstein conducting the Vienna Philharmonic Orchestra. In Hi-Fi stereo, 84 mins.
VHS: S16423. $24.95.
Laser: LD71446. $34.95.

Mahler Symphony No. 7

Leonard Bernstein conducts the Vienna Philharmonic. 83 mins.
VHS: S17126. $24.95.
Laser: LD71542. $34.95.

Mahler Symphony No. 8

Edda Moser, Judith Blegen, Hermann Prey and Jose Van Dam are among the soloists in this performance, with Leonard Bernstein conducting the Vienna State Opera Chorus and the Vienna Philharmonic.
Laser: LD71125. $34.95.

Mahler Symphony No. 9

Leonard Bernstein conducts Berlin Philharmonic in this great 1971 performance. Hi-Fi stereo, 83 mins.
VHS: S16779. $24.95.
Laser: LD71518. $34.95.

Majestic Marches

A visual tour of the Soldier Museum and the Plassenburg Castle in Germany is offset by musical selections from Wagner, Meyerbeer, Saint-Saens, Van Suppe, Rimsky-Korsakov, Tchaikovsky and Mendelssohn, including "Wedding March," "Marche Militaire," "Coronation March," "Festive March" and the march from *Sleeping Beauty*. With the Slovak Philharmonic Orchestra, conducted by Richard Hayman.
Laser: LD72247. $34.95.

Making Music: The Emerson String Quartet

A close look, through conversation and performance, at the personal and musical qualities that must combine to make an ensemble of excellence. It gives a sense of involvement with the four articulate young men who are the Quartet, while helping to illuminate chamber music. "This is what making music is all about—a warm, personal, and often humorous interaction between the members of a truly first-rate string quartet" (*Choice*). 28 mins.
Public Performance.
VHS: S09271. $89.95.
Home Video.
VHS: S09272. $29.95.

Mendelssohn Symphonies No. 3 & 4

Mendelssohn's "Italian" and "Scottish" symphonies are performed in concert by the Chicago Symphony Orchestra under the direction of Sir Georg Solti. Korean violinist Kyung-Wha Chung joins the orchestra to perform Mendelssohn's *Violin Concerto*. In Hi-Fi Stereo, 97 mins.
VHS: S17409. $24.95.
Laser: LD71425. $34.95.

Midori Live at Carnegie Hall

Works by Mozart, Strauss, Beethoven, Ernst, Chopin and Ravel are performed by this acclaimed violinist, accompanied by Robert MacDonald on piano.
Laser: LD74573. $24.98.

Moussorgsky/Holst/Debussy: Ormandy and the Philadelphia Orchestra

Eugene Ormandy and the Philadelphia Orchestra, American musical legends, perform "La Mer", "The Planets" and "Pictures at an Exhibition". 108 mins.
VHS: S14966. $29.95.
Laser: LD71423. $34.95.

Mozart (3 Pieces)

Three pieces: two for flute, performed by soloist Alain Marion, and one for piano, performed by Jeremy Menuhin. 55 mins.
VHS: S03822. $19.95.

Mozart (Biography)

History's greatest musical genius is explored in A&E's masterful look at the famous composer, from his beginnings as a child prodigy, which made him the darling of the European courts. Later leading a life of excess, Mozart died alone and poverty-stricken at 35, leaving behind work that would revolutionize nearly every area of music. Featuring musical performances by conductor Zubin Mehta, violinist Isaac Stern and flutist James Galway. 50 minutes.
VHS: S27653. $19.95.

Mozart "Haffner"/Solti

Sir Georg Solti conducts the Chicago Symphony Orchestra in Mozart's *Symphony No. 35* and Gustav Mahler's *Symphony No. 5*.
Laser: LD74571. $29.98.

Mozart Ensemble Salzburg

The acclaimed Mozart Ensemble Salzburg performs two of Mozart's *Divertimenti* as the camera takes us to scenic and historical sites of the great city. Intercut with dancers from La Scala, completing their visual expression of Mozart with traditional costuming. Georg Homosky, violinist and founder of the ensemble, leads the group. 65 mins.
VHS: S16229. $19.95.

Mozart on Tour: Volume 1 (London—The First Journey)

The first part of this documentary/performance series hosted by Andre Previn starts with this childhood visit to the British capital, where Mozart and his family were idolized by the royal court. The London influence was later felt in works like Piano Concerto No. 23, performed here by Vladimir Ashkenazy and the Royal Philharmonic Orchestra. A trip to Paris in 1778 resulted in the Symphony No. 31, performed by Jeffrey Tate and the Salzburg Mozarteum Orchestra. In Hi-Fi stereo, 75 mins.
VHS: S16427. $34.95.
Laser: LD71448. $34.95.

Mozart on Tour: Volume 2

With an introduction by Andre Previn, this documentary/performance investigation into the history of this great artist continues over the Alps in Italy, where Mozart was introduced to the "Manzuoli style" of virtuoso singing, and to the newly developed pianoforte instrument. In Mantua, Heidrun Holtmann performs *Piano Concerto No. 1 in F* and *Piano Concert No. 4 in G*. Marc Andrae conducts the Orchestra Della in Milan through *Piano Concerto No. 5 in D*, with American pianist Malcolm Frager. In Hi-Fi Stereo, 113 mins.
VHS: S16522. $24.95.
Laser: LD71466. $34.95.

Mozart on Tour: Volume 3

The third installment depicts Mozart at his musical and emotional turning point, in Mannheim where he meets soprano Aloysia Weber (and her sister Constanze). Gianluigi Gelmetti conducts the Radio Symphony Orchestra of Stuttgart, with pianist Christian Zacharias performing Piano Concertos No. 6 and No. 8. With an introduction by Andre Previn. Hi-Fi stereo, 109 mins.
VHS: S16770. $24.95.
Laser: LD71515. $34.95.

Mozart on Tour: Volume 4

Set in 1778, this program details Wolfgang Amadeus Mozart's arrival in Paris, the tragic death of his mother, and his return to Salzburg. Over the next two years he works on his important opera, *Idomeneo*, until he's summoned by the Archbishop of Vienna, and commissioned for a new work.
VHS: S16906. $24.95.
Laser: LD71528. $34.95.

Mozart on Tour: Volume 5

This volume of the video biography of Mozart centers on one of his most creative periods, the writing of his two greatest works, *The Marriage of Figaro* and *Don Giovanni*. Hosted by Andre Previn, the conductor and soloist with the European Chamber Orchestra. 100 mins.
VHS: S17133. $24.95.
Laser: LD71549. $34.95.

Mozart on Tour: Volume 6

This installment of the remarkable series on Mozart's life and work details his reconciliation with his father and newfound happiness with his wife, Constanze. This program looks at *Munich: A Staging Post* and *Frankfurt: Coronation*. Includes piano concertos No. 26 in D Major and No. 19 in F Major.
VHS: S17669. $24.95.
Laser: LD71785. $34.95.

Mozart on Tour: Volume 7

The final part considers Mozart's masterpieces, *Vienna: The Best City for My Metier*, Piano concerto No. 20 in D Minor, with pianist Ivan Klansky conducted by Jiri Behlolavek and the Virtuosi di Praga. The program concludes with *Vienna: The Last Year*, piano concerto no. 27 in B flat, with pianist Aleksandar Madzar, Andre Previn and the Royal Philharmonic Orchestra. 115 mins.
VHS: S17670. $24.95.
Laser: LD71786. $34.95.

Mozart Piano Concertos No. 9, K. 271 and Jeunehomme

This program combines images with music, alternating portraits of such important landmarks as Bishops Place, Brixen, Southern Tyrol, the Church of St. Peter and Gratsch in Southern Tyrol with Mozart's piano concertos No. 9, K. 271 and *Jeunehomme* and *No. 27, K. 595*, performed by pianist Wolf Harden.
Laser: LD72243. $29.95.

Mozart Quintets by the Emerson String Quintet

The highly acclaimed chamber music ensemble performs some of Mozart's clarinet and string quintets.
Laser: LD70214. $34.98.

Mozart Serenade K. 361 Gran Partita

Frans Bruggen conducts the Orchestra of the 18th Century in this performance of Mozart's famous serenade.
Laser: LD70287. $29.95.

Mozart Story

Biography of Mozart and his contemporaries Haydn and Beethoven featuring the Vienna Philharmonic. Austria, 1937, 95 mins.
VHS: S02248. $29.95.

Mozart, Smetana, Dvorak, Janacek

Performed by the Czech Philharmonic Orchestra conducted by Vaclav Neuman. 48 mins.
VHS: S03823. $19.95.

Mozart—Klassix 13

Anthony Quayle and Balint Vaszonyi explore Mozart's creative process, his house in Salzburg, the life in Vienna, and the haunting spectre of death which invaded his dreams. 60 mins.
VHS: S10897. $24.95.

Mozart/Barenboim Volume 1

Daniel Barenboim performs Concertos for 2 & 3 Pianos under the direction of Sir Georg Solti and the Berlin Philharmonic Orchestra.
VHS: S15455. $29.95.
Laser: LD70211. $29.98.

Mozart/Barenboim Volume 2

Daniel Barenboim as pianist performs Mozart's Piano Concerto No.21 and his Sonata No. 10.
Laser: LD70212. $29.98.

Mozart/Barenboim Volume 3

Daniel Barenboim as pianist performs Mozart's Piano Concerto No. 20 and his Sonata No. 8.
Laser: LD70213. $29.98.

Mozart: Concert in Tarascon Castle

The Polish Chamber Orchestra conducted by Jerry Maksymiuk performs a glorious all-Mozart concert within the opulent confines of Tarascon Castle in France. The concert includes flutist Alain Marion's interpretation of Mozart's Flute Concerto No. 2, the Piano Concerto No.9 in E Flat Major. 60 mins.
VHS: S12152. $19.95.

Mozart: Divertimento. K. 334/ Strauss: Also Sprach Zarathustra

Herbert Von Karajan conducts the Berlin Philharmonic in this thrilling performance. 81 mins.
Laser: LD74559. $34.95.

Mozart: Serenade Posthorn/ Serenade Notturno

A tour of Italy, highlighted by a visit to the Velthurns Castle, built in the 12th century at the foot of the Dolemites, is accompanied by two major works by Wolfgang Amadeus Mozart. The musicians are post hornist Hans Gansch, flutist Vojtech Samec, oboeist Jozef Cejka and bassoonist Peter Gazenl.
Laser: LD72244. $29.95.

Mozart: Symphonies 39-41

Observing the 200th anniversary of Mozart's death, Nikolaus Harnoncourt conducts the Chamber Orchestra of Europe in a selection of the composer's final symphonies. 116 mins.
VHS: S19632. $29.97.
Laser: LD71928. $34.97.

Mozart: The Dissonant Quartet

In a concert filmed exclusively for Voyager, the Angels Quartet gives a stunning performance of the Quartet in C minor, with music scholar Robert Winter's commentary on the second soundtrack.
Laser: LD70303. $49.95.

Murray Perahia in Performance: The Aldeburgh Recital

This recital, recorded in hi-fi at Aldeburgh, offers riveting performances of repertoire all new to the Perahia discography. Featuring works by Beethoven, Schumann, Liszt and Rachmaninoff.
VHS: S15803. $24.98.
Laser: LD74565. $29.98.

Murray Perahia's Mozart

In this high definition video production, Perahia, the acclaimed pianist, performs Mozart's *Piano Concertos K.467* and *K.595*. 119 mins.
Laser: LD74555. $29.98.

Mussorgsky: Pictures at an Exhibition (Nupen)

A three-part collaboration between filmmaker Christopher Nupen and pianist/conductor Vladimir Ashkenazy. Ashkenazy conducts the Swedish Radio Symphony Orchestra in a 1922 Leo Funtek orchestration, and gives a solo performance filmed in concert at London's Barbican Centre. In Hi-Fi Stereo, 96 mins.
VHS: S16510. $29.97.
Laser: LD71458. $34.97.

Mussorgsky: Pictures at an Exhibition (Solti)

Sir Georg Solti conducts the Chicago Symphony Orchestra.
Laser: LD74568. $24.98.

Nello Santi, Guglielmo Tell

Performance footage and documentary scenes are joined to give an intimate look at this conductor as he contemplates, rehearses and interprets his favorite opera. From the Swiss countryside, where it all happened, to the innermost thoughts of the maestro, this video gives new depth to this operatic work. 60 mins.
VHS: S22931. $24.95.

Neville Marriner Conducts the Academy of St. Martin in the Fields

The historic, stately home of Longleat House provides the ideal setting for the classic music of Bach, Handel, Mozart, Grieg, Pachelbel, Borodin, Gluck and Rossini, performed by the Academy of St. Martin in the Fields. 55 mins.
VHS: S03164. $29.95.

New Sousa Band

Keith Brion conducts this concert of rousing John Philip Sousa music at The Barns of Wolf Trap. Also stars New York City opera star Eric Mills.
VHS: S12424. $29.95.

New Year's Concert 1992

Carlos Kleiber leads the Vienna Philharmonic Orchestra through a recreation of the finest works of Nicolai, J. Strauss I, J. Strauss II, and Josef Strauss. 90 mins.
Laser: LD71701. $34.96.

New Year's Concert 1993

Riccardo Muti and the Vienna Philharmonic Orchestra provide a joyous New Year's performance, with selections from Josef Strauss, Johann Strauss and Joseph Lanner. "Boundless enthusiasm. It was, without a doubt, one of the most joyful New Year's concerts in the history of the event." 100 mins.
VHS: S18315. $29.95.
Laser: LD71853. $34.95.

New Year's Concert 1994—Wagner Gala

Claudio Abbado leads the Berlin Philharmonic Orchestra in this collection of excerpts from four Wagner operas: *Tannhauser*, *Lohengrin*, *Die Meistersinger von Nurnberg* and *Die Walkure*. Cheryl Studer, Waltraud Meier, Siegfried Jerusalem and Bryn Terfel are featured singers.
VHS: S20978. $29.95.
Laser: LD72406. $34.95.

New Year's Eve Concert 1985

Herbert Von Karajan conducts the Berlin Philharmonic in this celebratory concert that features music by Weber, Leoncavallo, Puccini, Liszt and Ravel. 55 mins.
VHS: S26705. $29.95.
Laser: LD74563. $29.98.

New Year's Eve Concert 1987

Herbert Von Karajan conducts the Berlin Philharmonic in this celebratory concert that features the music of Josef and Johann Strauss.
Laser: LD74577. $34.98.

New York Philharmonic

A historic concert of the New York Philharmonic's 139th season in honor of Isaac Stern's 60th birthday. Three great living violinists—Isaac Stern, Itzhak Perlman and Pinchas Zuckerman—join in an evening which is their first joint public performance. Performing music of Bach, Mozart, Vivaldi and Brahms, with the New York Philharmonic conducted by Zubin Mehta, this is one of the treasured moments of Lincoln Center.
VHS: S09161. $29.95.

Of Men and Music

A wide-ranging and innovative program on the relationship of art and performance, with five astonishing talents—pianist Artur Rubinstein, violinist Jascha Heifetz, sopranos Nadine Conner and Jane Pierce, and conductor Dimitri Mitropoulos and the Philharmonic Symphony Orchestra—discussing the nature of their work and art. 85 mins.
VHS: S18028. $29.95.

Once at a Border... Aspects of Stravinsky

A unique historical document, a celebration of the life, passions and music of Igor Stravinsky. Features are documents, photographs and film never before available, including appearances by Marie Rambert, George Balanchine, Nadia Boulanger, as well as "Les Noches," never before seen. 166 mins.
VHS: S03696. $69.95.

Orchestra!

Maestro Sir Georg Solti and Dudley Moore are your guides to the workings of an orchestra. They take the viewer for a look at the many different instruments that are part of a symphony orchestra and trace the music of famous composers from Bach to Stravinsky. Three volumes.
Volume 2: Lower Strings, Brass, Percussion.
VHS: S14798. $24.95.
Volume 3: Piano, The Conductor, The Making of Orchestra!
VHS: S14799. $24.95.

Orient Express Panorama Music

This film follows that fabled train from London to Budapest, capturing the beautiful scenery of Europe with music reflecting each place, performed by the quintet *I Salonisti*. 49 mins.
VHS: S15630. $24.95.
Laser: LD70279. $34.95.

Otto Klemperer's Long Journey Through His Times

A remarkable film about a legendary musician and human being: Otto Klemperer lived and made music through two world wars to become a great interpreter of Brahms, Beethoven, Bach and Wagner. Through rare archival footage and interviews, filmmaker Philo Bregstein takes the viewer on a revealing journey through eight decades and across four continents, as this extraordinary artist battled Hitler, McCarthy and personal tragedy to become one of the supreme artists of our century. German with English subtitles.
VHS: S08220. $59.95.
Philo Bregstein, Germany/Holland, 1984, 96 mins.

Ozawa

Shot on location in Tanglewood, Salzburg, Berlin, Tokyo and Osaka, a portrait of the work and life of Boston Symphony's musical director and conductor Seiji Ozawa by documentary filmmakers Albert and David Maysles. Rare scenes of the maestro as teacher and student are interwoven with discussions, rehearsals and performances featuring Rudolf Serkin, Yo-Yo Ma, Jessye Norman.
VHS: S05606. $29.95.
Maysles Brothers, USA, 1986, 60 mins.

Papal Concert to Commemorate the Holocaust
In St. Peter's Basilica this special concert was held to underscore the Catholic Church's recent recognition of the State of Israel. Richard Dreyfuss hosts this event, with Gilbert Levine conducting the London Royal Philharmonic. Music by Beethoven, Bernstein, Schubert and other famed composers is included. 90 mins.
VHS: S22448. $19.98.

Pinchas Zukerman: Here to Make Music/The Ghost
Through performance and personal recollection, *Here to Make Music* documents the musical developments of the acclaimed violinist over seven years in six different countries. The performances include Mozart's *Symphony No. 29* with the English Chamber Orchestra. In *The Ghost*, Zukerman is joined by Jacqueline du Pre and Daniel Barenboim for a complete performance of Beethoven's *Piano Trio, Opus 70*. In Hi-Fi Stereo, 91 mins.
VHS: S16511. $29.97.
Laser: LD71459. $34.97.

"Play Bach"— The 1989 Munich Concert
Jacques Loussier, the celebrated french jazz pianist, applies his own distinctive style of jazz to the classics of Bach. This video documents the concert his jazz trio played in Munich in 1989. 84 mins.
VHS: S15046. $29.95.
Laser: LD71442. $34.95.

Polish Chamber Orchestra
A brilliant performance of Mozart's "Eine Kleine Nachtmusik," and Haydn's "Symphony No. 45," conducted by Jerzy Maksymiuk. 60 mins.
VHS: S03165. $29.95.

Prokofiev: Classical Symphony
Herbert von Karajan conducts the Berlin Philharmonic in this thrilling performance. Also includes Tchaikovsky's *Piano Concerto No. 1.*
Laser: LD74578. $29.98.

Prokofiev: Romeo and Juliet
Charles Dutoit conducts the Montreal Symphony Orchestra in a performance of Prokofiev's *Romeo and Juliet*, the orchestra is outfitted in 18th-century costumes and interacts with the audience. "Extraordinary" (*Gramophone*). 58 mins.
Laser: LD71547. $29.95.

Prokofiev: Symphonie Classique (Celibidache)
"I do not make the music. I create the circumstances where the music comes to life" (Sergiu Celibidache). The maestro leads the Munich Philharmonic in a rehearsal and complete performance of Prokofiev's *"Classical" Symphony*. In Hi-Fi Stereo, 57 mins.
VHS: S27000. $29.97.
Laser: CLV. LD71483. $29.97.

Quartet
An illustrated performance film of Schubert's "Rosamunde" quartet which, among other things, focuses on the craft of instrument-making as compared to the crafts of the composer and musician. Dutch filmmaker Anton van Munster's film won the top prize at the Chicago International Film Festival. 35 mins.
VHS: S15626. $19.95.

Ralph Kirkpatrick Plays Bach
A rare memento of one of the greatest harpsichordists in a recital of J.S. Bach. The performance features the Toccata in D, Chromatic Fantasy and Fugue and Partita No. 5 in G.
VHS: S05585. $29.95.

Remembering Jacqueline du Pre
Christopher Nupen made this inspiring and revealing film portrait of the musician Jacqueline du Pre. Her miraculous musical talent is an inspiration to her fans. 56 mins.
VHS: S26926. $19.95.

Richard Nanes in Recital in Moscow and Kiev
A brilliant composer and performer, Nanes performs some of his greatest piano works in this video. *Rhapsody and Fugato No. 2*, *The Grand Etude No. 2* and the *Piano Concerto No. 2 A/Solo* are included. 60 mins.
VHS: S24830. $19.95.

Richard Nanes— The Holocaust Symphony No. 3
Taped live at the Kiev Opera House during the Kiev International Music Festival, this video preserves the premier of this important and powerful new work. It is a meditation on the Holocaust. The Kharkiv Festival Orchestra performs. 60 mins.
VHS: S22437. $19.95.

Robert Schumann: Piano Concerto in A Minor, Op. 54; Pyotr Ilyich Tchaikovsky: Piano Concerto No. 1 in B Flat Minor, Op. 23
Sergiu Celibidache conducts and Daniel Barenboim is featured on the piano in this recording with the Munich Philharmonic. 77 mins.
VHS: S26907. $29.97.

Rodrigo: Concierto de Aranjuez Pepe Romero
This film tribute to the composer Pepe Romero contains a documentary about this artist as well as the music he composed. This latter segment combines the actual Palace of Aranjuez, where the composer and his wife are seen touring the grounds with his acclaimed musical composition. Joaquin Rodrigo and the Academy of St. Martin in the Fields, with Sir Neville Marriner, are featured. In Spanish and English with English subtitles. 97 mins.
VHS: S22219. $19.95.

Rosalyn Tureck at the Teatro Colon
Pianist Rosalyn Tureck made her stunning video debut in this recital in Buenos Aires, highlighting works by J.S. Bach, Mendelssohn, Schubert and Brahms, with particular emphasis on Bach's *Chaconne in D Minor*. 90 mins.
VHS: S18345. $29.95.

Rostropovich: Dvorak & Saint-Saens Cello Concerti
Filmed in London and conducted by Carl Maria Giulini, two extraordinary performances by Mstislav Rostropovich, playing Dvorak's Cello Concerto and Saint-Saens' Cello Concerto No. 1. 65 mins.
VHS: S04680. $29.95.

Rubinstein in Concert
The artistry of Artur Rubinstein is preserved in this 1975 concert performance recorded in London's Fairfield Hall. Rubinstein performs Chopin's *Piano Concerto No. 2*, Grieg's *Concerto for Piano and Orchestra* and Saint-Saens' *Second Piano Concerto*. Andre Previn conducts the London Symphony Orchestra.
VHS: S12659. $24.95.

Rubinstein Remembered
1987 marks the 100th anniversary of the birth of the legendary pianist, and this remarkable documentary, hosted by his son, actor-composer-conductor John Rubinstein, traces Artur Rubinstein's career from its beginnings in Lodz, Poland, to its enduring international fame. He performs excerpts from Chopin, his favorite composer, chats and tells his inimitable stories, and is fondly remembered by his family and others. 58 mins.
VHS: S04701. $49.95.

Rudolf Serkin Performs Beethoven
This recital filmed in 1987 at the Konzerthaus, Vienna, features the late American piano virtuoso performing the last three Beethoven sonatas. Digitally recorded in Hi-Fi stereo, 70 mins.
VHS: S16425. $24.95.

Scarlatti, Debussy, Ravel
Scarlatti and Debussy pieces as interpreted by Martha Argerich on piano and Misha Maisky on cello. Ravel pieces feature Argerich and Nelson Freire on pianos. 47 mins.
VHS: S03834. $39.95.

Schubert—Klassix 13
Anthony Quayle and Balint Vaszonyi lead us through the Schubert "garage" where his greatest works were written, to the Viennese night life and a gathering of 19th century students in an intriguing portrait of an intriguing composer. 60 mins.
VHS: S10898. $24.95.

Schubert: Final Three Sonatas
Schubert's final three sonatas, C minor, A and B-flat, are performed by Alfred Brendel, recorded in London in 1988 by director Humphrey Burton. "A monument of the recorded piano repertoire and it embodies a high point in traditional perceptions of Schubert's most popular piano works" (*Washington Post*). 106 mins.
VHS: S17668. $24.95.
Laser: LD71784. $34.95.

Schubert: The Greatest Love and the Greatest Sorrow
Christopher Nupen continues his series of musical portraits with this look at the life of Franz Schubert. Pianist/conductor Vladimir Ashkenazy is featured performing some of Schubert's greatest works and some of those performed much less frequently, such as *Die Stadt*. 84 mins.
VHS: S22908. $24.95.
Laser: LD74623. $34.97.

Schubert: The Trout
The historic 1969 performance. Pianist Daniel Barenboim, Itzhak Perlman, Jacqueline du Pre, and conductor Zubin Mehta are featured in Schubert's classic.
VHS: S15461. $24.95.
Laser: LD70219. $29.98.

Segovia at Los Olivos
Guitarist Andres Segovia looks back on his stunning career and performs some of the music with which he is most closely associated. This film by Christopher Nupen examines one of the longest performing careers of the 20th century and highlights some of the wonderful music by Andres Segovia. 57 mins.
VHS: S27196. $19.95.

The Segovia Legacy
This video tribute to Andres Segovia presents revealing interviews and historic performance footage of the legendary Spanish guitarist whose career spanned nearly a century. Includes performances on television, in concert halls, and at the White House. A treasure for the many devoted lovers of this man, known as the "father" of the classical guitar. 60 mins.
VHS: S13666. $29.95.

Segovia: The Song of the Guitar
More beautiful and passionate music from the "father" of modern classical guitar. This Christopher Nupen documentary will be a treasure for fans of this master.
VHS: S15458. $29.95.
Laser: LD70235. $34.98.

Seiji Ozawa: Boston Symphony Orchestra
Winner of Tanglewood's highest honor, the Koussevitzky Prize, Seiji Ozawa has led the BSO for 17 years. Recorded live in hi-fi at Osaka Festival Hall in Japan, featuring Richard Strauss' *Also sprach Zarathustra*.
VHS: S15805. $24.98.
Laser: LD71481. $29.98.

Serebrier Conducts Prokofiev
Jose Serebrier conducts the Sydney Symphony Orchestra and the Melbourne Symphony Orchestra in these live performances of the works of Prokofiev, Tchaikovsky and Beethoven. 134 mins.
VHS: S03151. $39.95.

Sergei Rachmaninoff: Piano Concerto No. 2
Herbert von Karajan conducts this concert at the Berlin Philharmonic. With pianist Alexis Weissenberg, and Mstislav Rostropovich and violinist Ulrich Koch performing Richard Strauss' *Don Quixote*. In Hi-Fi stereo, 83 mins.
VHS: S16778. $24.95.

Soldiers of Music
Mstislav Rostropovich returned to the Soviet Union after more than a dozen years. Though he lost his citizenship he was welcomed as a hero. This documentary includes interviews and tearful private reunions with close friends. The music is unforgettable. 90 mins.
Laser: LD74554. $29.98.

Solti in Budapest: A Bartok Concert
A truly Hungarian music video program featuring the music of the great Bela Bartok, one of the 20th Century's greatest classical composers. With pianist Alexis Weissenberg and the Chicago Symphony Orchestra, Andras Schiff (piano). Includes *Dance Suite*, *Piano Concerto No. 3*, and *Concerto for Orchestra*. 88 mins.
VHS: S15632. $24.95.

Solti: The Chicago Symphony Orchestra
Sir Georg Solti and the Chicago Symphony perform two staples of the classical repertory: Mozart's *Haffner* and Mahler's *Symphony No. 5*. Hi-fi stereo sound.
VHS: S15807. $24.98.
Laser: LD71480. $54.98.

Song of the Birds: A Biography of Pablo Casals
The program explores Pablo Casals' virtuoso technique and subtle craft. Various musicians and artists such as Yehudi Menuhin, Mstislav Rostropovich, Alexander Schneider and King Juan Carlos comment on Casals' life and work. 66 mins.
VHS: S18566. $24.95.

The Spanish Guitar
Six solo performances by Pedro Sierra, J.L. Morgan and Jose Cortes demonstrate the three basic styles found in this musical tradition—modern, classical and gypsy. A brief explanation follows each solo to explain the technique of flamenco guitar. 45 mins.
VHS: S21058. $40.00.

Stanislav Bunin in Tokyo
Bunin's career was launched after winning first prize in Warsaw's prestigious Chopin competition. Seven of Chopin's most popular compositions form the central part of the recital program which Bunin recorded live in Tokyo. Hi-fi stereo sound.
VHS: S15806. $24.98.
Laser: LD74570. $24.98.

The Story of the Symphony
A remarkable series of programs produced by the BBC, in which Andre Previn conducts the Royal Philharmonic Orchestra in some of the most popular and important works in the concert repertoire. All of the programs are recorded in stereo hi-fi, and the series won the 1984 British Academy Award for Best Television Sound.
Beethoven: Symphony No. 7 and Excerpts from Symphony No. 5.
VHS: S03111. $39.95.
Berlioz: Symphonic Fantastique.
VHS: S03112. $39.95.
Brahms: Symphony No. 4.
VHS: S03114. $39.95.
Haydn and Mozart: Symphony No. 87 and Symphony No. 39. 90 mins.
VHS: S02713. $39.95.
Shostakovich: Symphony No. 5.
VHS: S01830. $39.95.
Tchaikovsky: Symphony No. 6 (Pathetique).
VHS: S03113. $39.95.

Strauss: Death and Transfiguration
Herbert Von Karajan conducts the Berlin Philharmonic in *Death and Transfiguration* and *Metamorphosis*.
Laser: LD74576. $29.98.

Strauss: Don Quixote
Herbert Von Karajan conducts the Berlin Philharmonic. 46 mins.
Laser: LD74560. $29.98.

Strauss: Ein Heldenleben
Herbert Von Karajan conducts the Berlin Philharmonic. 50 mins.
Laser: LD74561. $29.98.

Strauss: Eine Alpensinfonie
Herbert Von Karajan conducts the Berlin Philharmonic. 56 mins.
Laser: LD74562. $29.98.

Tchaikovsky Competition: Violin & Piano
"All the musicality of the event laced with all the tension of a thriller..." *London Times*. "Absolutely spellbinding...technique, virtuosity and style...it is Mullova's presence and performance that are the core of the tape...some of the finest sound engineering for home video..." Rob Baker, *N.Y. Daily News*. Pavel Kogan conducts the Moscow Symphony. (HiFi-Stereo).
VHS: S03966. $74.95.

Tchaikovsky Symphony No. 4 and No. 5
Tchaikovsky's Fourth Symphony in F minor (1876) and Fifth Symphony in E minor (1888) are presented here, conducted by Herbert von Karajan and the Berlin Philharmonic Orchestra.
VHS: S16903. $24.95.
Laser: LD71525. $34.95.

Tchaikovsky Symphony No. 6 ("Pathetique") & Piano Concerto No. 1
In this richly musical performance film, Alexis Weissenberg and the Berlin Philharmonic, under the baton of Herbert von Karajan, give dazzling exhibitions of virtuosity in these much loved, Romantic works. Impassioned, dramatic, sad, and triumphant. 85 mins.
VHS: S14118. $24.95.

Tchaikovsky Violin Concerto Op. 35
Itzhak Perlman is the soloist and Eugene Ormandy leads the Philadelphia Orchestra in this performance of Tchaikovsky's Violin Concerto, Op. 35.
Laser: LD71359. $24.95.

Telemann: Recorded Suite Concerto Violins and Concerto for Horns
This travelogue looks at a glass factory and museum at Frauenau, Germany, and the Palace of Thurin and Taxis at Regensburg. The tour also includes views of St. George and St. Martin Monastery Church of Weltenburg-Kelheim.
Laser: LD72246. $29.95.

A Time There Was... A Profile of Benjamin Britten
Prix Italia winning film biography of one of the foremost composers of the 20th century, including excerpts from several major operas, including *Peter Grimes* and *Death in Venice*, as well as priceless footage of Britten rehearsing and conducting, as well as playing Mozart with Sviatoslav Richter, and his home movies. 120 mins.
VHS: S03697. $69.95.

The Unanswered Question: Six Talks at Harvard by Leonard Bernstein
In this critically acclaimed series, Leonard Bernstein examines all types of music, including folk songs, pop hits and symphonies. Drawing on his insights as a master composer and conductor, he explores works ranging from Mozart and Beethoven, through Wagner and Mahler, to Ravel and Copland in search of a musical grammar. Bernstein also analyzes the crisis of twentieth century music, as expressed in Charles Ives' "The Unanswered Question," with a close analysis of works by Schoenberg and Stravinsky. Containing over 13 hours of material, this deluxe boxed set includes six individual programs: (1) *Musical Phonology*; (2) *Musical Syntax*; (3) *Musical Semantics*; (4) *The Delights and Dangers of Ambiguity*; (5) *The Twentieth Century Crisis*; (6) *The Poetry of the Earth*.
VHS: S16799. $149.95.

Victor Borge: Live from London
The incredible Victor Borge in a London performance of his best-loved classic(al) routines. Beginning with some hilarious variations on Chopin's *Waltz in C-Sharp Minor*, Borge moves on to a series of send-ups of other classical greats. A madcap medley as only Victor Borge could interpret it. USA, 50 mins.
VHS: S14932. $29.95.

Vienna in Music
An impressionistic blending of music and images, Peter Lodyinski's film contrasts the sights and traditions of Viennese locations with various Strauss polkas and waltzes, performed by the Vienna Philharmonica conducted by Willi Boskovsky, backed by the Vienna Boys' Choir. Includes "The Blue Danube," "The Emperor" waltzes, "Pizzicato" Polka and "Radetsky" March. 92 mins.
VHS: S19893. $29.95.

Vienna New Year's Concert 1991
Claudio Abbado conducts the Vienna Philharmonic in the 1991 New Year's Concert of works by Johann and Josef Strauss.
VHS: S16402. $24.95.
Laser: LD71445. $34.95.

Vivaldi: 4 Seasons (Karajan)
Herbert Von Karajan conducts the Berlin Philharmonic, featuring Anne-Sophie Muller.
Laser: LD74583. $29.98.

Vivaldi: Le Quattri Stagioni (The Four Seasons) (Nupen)
Christopher Nupen's 1981 filmed account of Vivaldi's chamber piece, recorded in the Abbey Library in Polling, Germany. Performed by violinist Gidon Kremer, harpsichordist Philip Ledger and the English Chamber Orchestra. 43 mins.
VHS: S17672. $24.95.
Laser: LD71788. $34.95.

Vivaldi: Violin Concerti
All the most memorable sights of Venice are showcased in this tour. The church of Santa Maria della Salute, the Piazetta San Marco, Doges' Palace, the island of San Giorgio Maggiore and the heart of it all, the Piazzo San Marco, are on view, accompanied by the violin compositions of Antonio Vivaldi. 60 mins.
Laser: LD74752. $29.95.

Vladimir Horowitz, Sergei Rachmaninoff Piano Concerto No. 3
Zubin Mehta and the New York Philharmonic played together with Horowitz at New York's Lincoln Center to produce this singular musical achievement. No other concerto was more closely associated with Horowitz and this is the only video featuring him performing his signature work. 44 mins.
VHS: S26222. $29.95.

Vladimir Horowitz: A Reminiscence
Vladimir Horowitz was perhaps the century's most acclaimed and beloved pianist. Wanda Toscanini Horowitz, his widow and the daughter of the great Toscanini, hosts this collection of home movie footage and his concert hall performances, offering the quintessential profile of a great musician.
VHS: S21075. $24.98.

Wagner
Five-hour British dramatization of the life, loves and music of Richard Wagner features the last performance by Richard Burton, with a stellar cast also including Sir Laurence Olivier, Sir John Gielgud, Vanessa Redgrave as Cosima. England, 1984, 300 mins.
VHS: S01425. $29.98.

Wagner Concert in Leipzig
This exciting video presents an all-Wagner concert performed in the new Leipzig Gewandhaus. Internationally acclaimed conductor Kurt Masur leads the Gewandhausorchester in a thrilling and varied program including the overture to *Tannhauser*, Overture and Liebestod from *Tristan and Isolde*, overture and vocal excerpts from *Die Meistersinger von Nurnberg* and *The Wessendock Lieder*. Bass Theo Adam and soprano Karan Armstrong are featured. 90 mins.
VHS: S11770. $29.95.

Wagner: The Complete Epic
This is the complete, 9-hour epic never before available on videocassette. Richard Burton performs as Wagner— scoundrel, joker, philosopher, con-man, poet, refugee, virulent political orator, a legend in his own time and one of the greatest composers who ever lived. Lensed on location and in more than 200 separate locations in six different countries, and co-starring Sir Laurence Olivier, Sir John Gielgud, Sir Ralph Richardson and Vanessa Redgrave as Cosima Wagner. The music is conducted by Sir Georg Solti. 4 cassettes, 540 mins.
VHS: S11721. $124.95.

The Winner's Gala Concert
This video features performances from the Gala Concert for the International Tchaikovsky Competition of 1990. Performers include Berezovsky, Suwanai, Rivinius, Voigt, and Choi. A brilliant collection of talented, young musicians. 114 mins.
VHS: S15451. $29.98.

Yehudi Menuhin
Tony Palmer's intimate profile of the virtuoso violinist Yehudi Menuhin assembles interviews with his contemporaries Stefan Grappelli and Ravi Shankar, intimate discussions with his mother and footage recording with his son Jeremy. 120 mins.
VHS: S18758. $39.95.

Yehudi Menuhin: Brahms Violin Concerto in D
Recorded at the Gewandhaus in Leipzig, East Germany, Menuhin's performance of this major concerto sparkles with outstanding brilliance. The concerto is preceded by a personal introduction by Menuhin, and two pieces of unaccompanied Bach make up the encores. 60 mins.
VHS: S03163. $29.95.

Yehudi Menuhin: Concert for the Pope
A summer concert for Pope John Paul II performed by Yehudi Menuhin, Citizen of the World, in 1983, in beautiful Castelgrandolfo. Includes Vivaldi's Concerto in D, Op.89; Vivaldi's "La Cassia" Concerto in B Flat; Bach's aria "Erbarme Dick, mein Gott" from the St. Matthew Passion sung by Mira Zakai; and Mozart's Adagio K. 261 and Rondo K. 373. With the Polish Chamber Orchestra conducted by Jerzy Maksymiuk. 53 minutes.
VHS: S03377. $39.95.

Yehudi Menuhin: Tribute to J.S. Bach (1675-1750)
All-Bach concert by Menuhin given at the Barbican in London, featuring Bach's Concerto for Violin in A Minor, the Peasant Cantata BWV 212 with Nicolas Rivebq baritone and Alison Hargen soprano, Bach's Partita in E Major for solo violin, the Coffee Cantata BWV 211. With the English Chamber Orchestra, conducted by Menuhin. 90 mins.
VHS: S03378. $39.95.

Yevgeny Kissin in Tokyo
Recorded live in Japan, *Kissin in Tokyo* captures this brilliant artist performing works by Rachmaninoff, Liszt, Chopin and Scriabin. A young artist who "measures up to his already formidable reputation." Hi-fi stereo sound.
VHS: S15804. $24.98.
Laser: LD74569. $24.98.

Yevgeny Kissin Plays
Yevgeny Kissin 1990 recital at Munich's Bavaria Musikstudios, as he performs pieces by Schubert, Brahms, Bach, Liszt and the melody from "Orphee". 92 mins.
VHS: S15755. $29.95.
Laser: LD71963. $34.95.

CLASSICAL, NON-OPERATIC VOCALS

Adventures of Don Quixote
Feodor Chaliapin, the famed bass, left this unforgettable record of his talent on film. Though primarily an actor, in this film he sings four songs by Jaques Ibert. Two versions were cast, one in English and the other in French, both of which are included on this videocassette. 118 mins.
VHS: S20695. 39.95.
VHS: S20695. $39.95.

Anna Moffo in Opera and Song
American soprano Anna Moffo achieved instant stardom with a performance of Puccini's *Madama Butterfly* for Italian television. Her captivating performance on the "Voice of Firestone" includes arias from *La Boheme, Madama Butterfly, Faust*, and *Pagliacci*; plus songs by Richard Rodgers and others. 1958-63, 30 mins.
VHS: S13627. $24.95.

Anna Russell Farewell Concert
The hilarious comedienne in her farewell concert in her famous routines: "The Ring Cycle," "How To Become a Singer," "Wind Instruments I Have Known," "A Gilbert and Sullivan Operetta," "On Pink Chiffon," "Jolly Old Sigmund Freud" and other folk tunes.
VHS: S00058. $59.95.
Phillip Byrd, Great Britain/USA, 1984, 85 mins.

Ariel Ramirez: Misa Criolla
Jose Carreras is featured in this classic by Argentine composer Ariel Ramirez. It combines traditional Argentine folk music with the striking melodies of this contemporary artist. Damien Sanchez conducts.
VHS: S21989. $29.95.
Laser: LD74540. $29.95.

Bach's Christmas Oratorio
A stunning performance of Bach's oratorio with Katharina Beidler, Heidi Riess, Arnim Ude, and the Dresden Philharmonic and Chorus.
VHS: S05581. $39.95.

Barbara Hendricks
Whether performing at the Met, LaScala or the Berlin Opera, Hendrick's captivating voice make her a true diva. This video includes excerpts from *Der Rosenkavalier, The Marriage of Figaro* and *Rigoletto*, along with songs by Schubert and Rachmaninoff. 47 mins.
VHS: S26215. $19.95.

Berlioz: Requiem (Bernstein)
Leonard Bernstein conducts the Orchestre National de France, the Orchestre Philharmonique de France and Les Choeurs de Radio France, with lead tenor Stuart Burrows, in a performance of Hector Berlioz's *Requiem*. 98 mins.
VHS: S19410. $29.95.

Beethoven: Missa Solemnis
Herbert von Karajan conducts the Berlin Philharmonic in Beethoven's intensely moving, sacred work—*Missa Solemnis*. The vocalists include Ruza Baldani and Eric Tappy. 83 mins.
VHS: S14964. $24.95.
Laser: LD70179. $34.95.

Birgit Nilsson: The Bell Telephone Hour
Perhaps the leading interpreter of Richard Wagner's opera heroines in this century, the great Swedish soprano Birgit Nilsson is here seen and heard performing a variety of arias written by Puccini, Verdi, and Wagner. Magnificent. 45 mins.
VHS: S14447. $29.95.

Bizet Concert (Caballe)
This program features Montserrat Caballe in a rare performance of *Clovis and Clotilda*. She is joined in the cantata by tenor Gerard Garino and bass Boris Martinovic. Jean-Claude Casadesus conducts the Orchestra National de Lille. Also includes *L'Arlesienne Suite No. 1* and the *Symphony in C*. 95 mins.
VHS: S16509. $19.95.

Blanche Thebom in Opera and Song
The great Blanche Thebom is featured in this "Voice of Firestone" classic performance. Includes arias from *Il Trovatore, Don Carlo, Samson et Dalila*; plus songs. 1950-59, 30 mins.
VHS: S13690. $24.95.

Boast of Kings
The renowned boys' choir of Chapel of King's College, Cambridge University, in a unique blend of travelogue and music performance, featuring "Ave Maria," "Nunc Dimittis," Allegri's "Miserere" as well as popular favorites by Cole Porter and Randy Newman. 60 mins.
VHS: S05905. $39.95.

Canteloube: Songs of the Auverge
Filmed on location in the Auverge, Kiri Te Kanawa performs selections from her bestselling recording *Songs from the Auverge*. Jeffrey Tate conducts the English Chamber Orchestra.
VHS: S12661. $34.95.

Carmina Burana (Cardiff)
This performance of Carl Orff's choral masterpiece was filmed during the Cardiff Festival of Choirs in Wales. Soloists Thomas Allen, Norma Burrowes and Kenneth Bowen are joined by the Royal Philharmonic Orchestra, along with the Cardiff Polyphonic Choir, the Dyfed Choir and the Llandaff Cathedral Choiristers. Latin with English subtitles. 60 mins.
VHS: S16230. $19.95.

Carmina Burana (Polygram)
This popular and captivating choral work by Carl Orff is instantly recognizable with its insistent rhythms, its tender settings of love poems and its massive orchestral and choral arrangements. 64 mins.
VHS: S14802. $24.95.
Laser: LD71426. $34.95.

Carols for Christmas
Twenty-four popular carols are lavishly illustrated with works of art and images of Christmas from the Metropolitan Museum of Art in New York. Boy soprano Aled Jones sings. 60 mins.
VHS: S26476. $19.95.

Carols from Christchurch, Oxford
Oxford Cathedral is the setting for this rare musical performance. Christchurch choristers sing such carols as "O Little Town of Bethlehem" and "Silent Night." Alec McCowen and Ian Charleson also provide readings. 30 mins.
VHS: S21821. $19.95.

Cecilia Bartoli—A Portrait
An in-depth look at the career of mezzo-soprano Cecilia Bartoli is followed by a recital at the London Savoy Hotel that features Bartoli singing seven Rossini arias, plus works by Mozart, Vivaldi and Pergolesi. In Hi-Fi Stereo, 90 mins.
VHS: S16426. $24.95.
Laser: LD71447. $34.95.

Christmas Carols from England
A joyous, heartwarming program of words and music of the Christmas season at the majestic York Minister Cathedral, featuring King's Singers, Benjamin Luxon and the Northern Sinfonia, conducted by Robin Stapleton. Carols include "Silent Night" and "O Holy Night." 50 mins.
VHS: S19595. $19.95.

Christmas Time in Vienna
Placido Domingo and Dionne Warwick join the Vienna Boys Choir and the Vienna Symphonic Orchestra to perform this concert of Christmas songs. Filmed at the imposing Hofburg Palace, it includes such favorites as "O Holy Night", "Smile", "As Time Goes By", "Ave Maria" and many more. 75 mins.
VHS: S22875. $19.95.
Laser: LD74758. $34.95.

Christmas with Eleanor Steber
Highlights from Steber's Memorable Firestone Christmas telecasts, including "Silent Night," "White Christmas," "The First Noel," Mozart's "Alleluia," and many more Christmas favorites. 1950-57, 30 mins.
VHS: S13626. $24.95.

Christmas with Luciano Pavarotti
A very special program with the great baritone performing Christmas favorites.
VHS: S10722. $19.95.

Dame Kiri Te Kanawa
This biography of Dame Kiri includes footage from some of her best works, including her performance as the Countess in Strauss' *Capriccio*. 106 mins.
VHS: S18757. $39.95.

Del Monaco at His Most Thrilling
In 1969 at age 54, this great tenor performed a concert for television that revealed his talents were wondrously intact. Excerpts from *Norma, Macbeth, Il Trovatore, Otello* and other works are performed by this peerless singer. 37 mins.
VHS: S24329. $34.95.

Easter with Fred Waring
This "Voice of Firestone" telecast of March 23, 1959, features Fred Waring and the Pennsylvanians in an inspiring program of Easter music, including "He Is Risen," "Were You There," "Hallelujah," and others. B&W, 25 mins.
VHS: S13684. $24.95.

Eleanor Steber in Opera and Oratorio
This "Voice of Firestone" telecast, featuring soprano Eleanor Steber, includes arias from *Le Nozze di Figaro, La Boheme, Otello, Lohengrin, Messiah*, and others. 1950-56, 45 mins.
VHS: S13685. $34.95.

Eleanor Steber Sings Love Songs
Eleanor Steber performs songs by Jerome Kern, Rodgers & Hammerstein, Cole Porter, Victor Herbert and others. From the renowned *Voice of Firestone Series*. 55 mins.
VHS: S16083. $34.95.

Ev Viva Belcanto
World renowned sopranos Marilyn Horne and Montserrat Caballe perform works by Vivaldi, Meyerbeer, Mercadante and Rossini in excerpts from their concert in Munich Germany.
VHS: S15580. $19.95.

Eva Marton in Concert
Eva Marton, one of the world's foremost dramatic sopranos, returns to her native Hungary to give a concert of Italian operatic arias. Julius Rudel conducts the Hungarian State Orchestra in this very special concert, which includes selections from some of Marton's most famous roles, including *La Gioconda, Tosca* and *Manon Lescaut* as well as the haunting "Ebben, ne andro lontana" from Catalani's *La Wally*, made famous in the Jean Jacques Beineix film, *Diva*. 90 mins.
VHS: S13746. $39.95.

Evelyn Laye and Conchita Supervia in Evensong
Beverly Nichols wrote the book and play on which this rarely seen film adaptation is based. Beverly's one-time employer, the great Australian soprano Nellie Melba, is at the center of this traumatic story. She was simultaneously adored and exploited. Excerpts from *La Boheme, Cerentola* and *La Traviata* punctuate this amazing tale. 83 mins.
VHS: S24034. $34.95.

Evening with Placido Domingo
This gala benefit was performed on the evening of June 21, 1987 at the Wembly arena in London. It was a memorable event to aid the Save the Children fund. This film of that performance captures Domingo, the artist and humanitarian, in arias of Verdi, Puccini, Lehar and selections from Spanish operas. 55 mins.
VHS: S07684. $19.95.
Laser: LD74969. $29.99.

Faure/Poulenc Concert
Soprano Barbara Hendricks performs Faure's *Requiem* and Poulenc's *Gloria* from the Saint Denis Basilica. 70 mins.
VHS: S17316. $19.95.

Ferruccio Tagliavini in Opera and Song
This "Voice of Firestone" telecast features Ferruccio Tagliavini performing arias from *Tosca, La Boheme, L'Elisir d'Amore, Martha*; plus songs. 1950-54, 45 mins.
VHS: S13689. $34.95.

Final Romance Starring Jose Carreras
The story of the life and music of the 19th century tenor Julian Gayarre, who was considered the greatest tenor of his age. The production stars Jose Carreras as Gayarre in the story of his singing career and love for his childhood sweetheart, Alicia. It is a passionate and tragically tender tale with musical excerpts from the operas of Donizetti, Verdi, Bizet, Wagner and others. 120 mins. Subtitled in English.
VHS: S11639. $39.95.

Franz Schubert: Schwanengesang
Schubert's last great work, published the year after his death in 1828, showcases the German lied as the seminal art form of the 19th century. German with English subtitles. 56 mins.
VHS: S17130. $24.95.
Laser: LD71546. $29.95.

Gala Concert with Luciano Pavarotti
This is the video of the famous concert Luciano Pavarotti gave at the magnificent Olympic Hall in Munich, Germany. Pavarotti performs before a wildly enthusiastic crowd of thousands, singing many of his greatest arias and songs.
VHS: S10711. $19.98.

George London in Opera and Song
This "Voice of Firestone" telecast features bass-baritone George London, and special guest sopranos Dorothy Warenskjold and Nadine Conner. Includes arias from *Boris Godunov* and *Le Nozze di Figaro*; songs by Rodgers & Hammerstein, Kern, Romberg, and others; plus duets with Warenskjold and Conner. 1953-55, 45 mins.
VHS: S13631. $34.95.

Golden Age of Opera
Programs from the *Voice of Firestone* telecasts, which brought the world's greatest opera singers into the homes of music lovers.
Bidu Sayao in Opera and Song. From telecasts in 1951-52, selections from *Manon, Madama Butterfly, Gianni Schicchi*, as well as many popular songs. 45 mins.
VHS: S12912. $34.95.
Eleanor Steber in Opera and Song, Vol. 1. From telecasts in 1949-51, selections from Rodgers and Hammerstein, Charpentier, Victor Herbert, Mozart (*Marriage of Figaro*), and Verdi's *La Forza del Destino*). 50 mins.
VHS: S12911. $34.95.
Eleanor Steber in Opera and Song, Vol. 2. 'One of the most ravishing voices and accomplished singers ever produced in the United States" (J. Ardoin on soprano Eleanor Steber). This "Voice of Firestone" telecast includes arias from *Ernani, Madama Butterfly* and *Die Fledermaus*; ensembles from *Rigoletto, Faust* and *Lucia*; plus songs 1951-54, 45 mins.
VHS: S13625. $29.95.
Jussi Bjoerling in Opera and Song. Bjoerling sings selections from Victor Herbert, Puccini, Gounod, Strauss, Leoncavallo and "Prayer of Thanksgiving." 40 mins.
VHS: S12910. $34.95.
Lauritz Melchior in Opera and Song. From 1951 telecasts, works by Wagner (*Meistersinger, Die Walkure, Flying Dutchman*) and popular songs by Rodgers and Hammerstein and others. 45 mins.
VHS: S12916. $34.95.
Leonard Warren in Opera and Song. The legendary baritone sings "A Little Bit of Heaven" and "None But the Lonely Heart" as well as selections from *Carmen, Faust, Un Ballo in Maschera*. 45 mins.
VHS: S12914. $34.95.
Licia Albanese in Opera and Song. From a 1951 telecast, popular songs and selections from *I Pagliacci*. 26 mins.
VHS: S12913. $29.95.
Presenting Joan Sutherland. Joan Sutherland sings selections from *La Boheme, Semiramide, Les Huguenots*, with Richard Bonynge conducting. 26 mins.
VHS: S12917. $29.95.
Renata Tebaldi and Franco Corelli. Selections from Mascagni's *Cavalleria Rusticana*, Puccini's *Turandot, Tosca, Madama Butterfly*. 35 mins.
VHS: S12909. $34.95.
Richard Tucker in Opera and Song. From 1957, Tucker sings Neapolitan love songs, selections from *Aida, Carmen, The Student Prince, I Pagliacci, Rigoletto*. 45 mins.
VHS: S12918. $34.95.
Riise Stevens in Opera and Song. From 1951 and 1954 telecasts, selections from *Carmen* and popular songs by Rodgers, Berlin, Jerome Kern. 45 mins.
VHS: S12915. $34.95.

The Great Caruso
Mario Lanza is cast as Enrico Caruso, the fabled Italian singer who had a voice that could shatter glass as well as hearts. This musical biography follows Caruso from his formative years in Naples to his triumphs in the great opera house of the world. With Ann Blyth, Dorothy Kirsten and Jarmila Novotna. Story by Dorothy Caruso.
VHS: S06145. $19.98.
Laser: LD72176. $34.98.
Richard Thorpe, USA, 1951, 108 mins.

The Great Sopranos: Voices of Firestone Classic Performances
Leontyne Price, Renata Tebaldi, Joan Sutherland, Bidu Sayao, Birgit Nilsson, Eleanor Steber, Licia Albanese, Patrice Munsel, Jeanette MacDonald, Anna Moffo, Roberta Peters and Helen Traubel can all be seen on this compilation video. 58 mins.
VHS: S26701. $34.95.

The Great Tenors: Voices of Firestone Classic Performances
This stellar collection of performers includes some selections which have never been heard before. Jussi Bjoerling, Franco Corelli, Nicolai Gedda, James McCracken, Lauritz Melchior, Jan Peerce, Ferruccio Tagliavini, Jess Thomas and Richard Tucker all appear on this video. 58 mins.
VHS: S26702. $34.95.

Handel: Messiah (Cardiff)
"This is the way a performance of *The Messiah* is intended to be performed." In this production, the London Baroque Players, the Cardiff Polyphonic Choir and soloists Norma Burrowes, Helen Watts, Robert Tear and Willard White perform *The Messiah* to the original scoring.
VHS: S13362. $19.95.

Handel: Messiah (Marriner)
An all-star performance at the Point Theatre in Dublin, conducted by Sir Neville Marriner and performed by the Orchestra and Chorus of Academy of St. Martin in the Fields. With Sylvia McNair, Anne Sofie von Otter, Michael Chance and Jerry Hadley. 157 mins.
VHS: S18314. $24.95.
Laser: LD71852. $59.95.

Haydn: The Creation (Bernstein)
Soloists Lucia Popp, Judith Blegen, Thomas Moser and Kurt Moll are featured in this performance of Haydn's oratorio with the Choir and Orchestra of the Bayerische Rundfunk conducted by Leonard Bernstein.
VHS: S18530. $24.95.
Laser: LD71031. $59.95.

Haydn: The Creation (Hogwood)
Christopher Hogwood and the Academy of Ancient Music present Haydn's The Creation—sung entirely in English.
VHS: S16403. $34.95.
Laser: LD71871. $34.95.

Haydn: The Creation (Muti)
Riccardo Muti conducts the great oratorio by Haydn.
Laser: LD74572. $29.98.

Helen Traubel in Opera and Song
This "Voice of Firestone" telecast includes two arias from *Die Walkure* plus six songs. 1950, 30 mins.
VHS: S13688. $34.95.

I Capuleti e I Montecchi
The great soprano, Katia Ricciarelli, sings her favorite operatic role from Vincenzo Bellini's version of *Romeo and Juliet*. It's set in the illustrious Teatro la Fenice in Venice, where we see her sing both in rehearsal and in performance. 60 mins.
VHS: S20941. $24.95.

I Live for Art—The Great Toscas
A film featuring fifteen world-renowned sopranos, whom we see both in performances, as Tosca, and in candid interviews. The result is a composite portrait of the prima donna, going beyond the conventional image. With Maria Callas, Montserrat Caballe, Renata Tebaldi, Dame Kiri Te Kanawa, Galina Vishnevskaya and others. 91 mins.
VHS: S04683. $39.95.

Igor Gorin in Opera and Song
Culled from his performances on *The Voice of Firestone* telecasts, this program features Igor Gorin as he performs arias from *La Traviata*, *I Pagliacci*, *Herodiade* and *The Barber of Seville*, as well as some popular songs. 55 mins.
VHS: S17427. $34.95.

Jan Peerce in Opera and Song
The glory of Peerce's singing was in the solidity and power of the tone, the consistency of the timbre throughout the range, and the sheer exuberance of his presentation. This "Voice of Firestone" telecast includes "Vesti la giubba" from *Pagliacci*, plus songs by Rossini, Rodgers & Hammerstein, and Herbert. 1950, 25 mins.
VHS: S13630. $24.95.

Jan Peerce, Marian Anderson & Andres Segovia
This historic film captures performances by three legends in the world of music. Jan Peerce and Nadine Conner perform three arias for which they are famous. Included are vignettes of the life of Marian Anderson, including a program of traditional spiritual favorites, and Andres Segovia permits the audience into the seclusion of his Paris studio as he performs traditional and contemporary numbers. 60 mins.
VHS: S11720. $19.95.

Janet Baker Full Circle
Janet Baker began her career singing in the Glyndebourne Chorus, and now, at the peak of her career, makes her farewell to opera from the same Glyndebourne stage. This profile is an intimate look at one year in the life of an international star— the final year in Dame Janet's operatic career. Included are several performance extracts of this great mezzo soprano from her final performances at the Royal Opera House, Covent Garden, the English National Opera and Glyndebourne. 75 mins.
VHS: S03168. $39.95.

Jessye Norman: A Christmas Concert
A revealing collection of Christmas songs by the remarkable Jessye Norman, featuring spirituals ("Go Tell It on the Mountain"); "He Shall Feed His Flock," from Handel's *Messiah*; and the inspired works of Gounod, Bach, Brahms and Schubert. Conducted by Lawrence Foster and the Orchestre de L'Opera de Lyon. 68 mins.
VHS: S17667. $24.95.
Laser: LD71783. $34.95.

Jessye Norman: Live
Jessye Norman hypnotized the audience at Austria's prestigious Hohenems Festival in 1987. This recital features works by Handel, Schubert, Schumann, Brahms and Strauss, and of course Norman's signature encore "He's Got the Whole World in His Hand". In Hi-Fi Stereo, 60 mins.
VHS: S16274. $24.95.

Joan Sutherland in Concert
A program rich in classical numbers from the dramatic to the light-hearted, displaying the enormous range of Sutherland, whose voice has thrilled music lovers for more than a quarter of a century. 49 mins.
VHS: S03160. $39.95.

Joan Sutherland: Making "Lamke"
Joan Sutherland and Richard Bonynge take you inside their production of Delibes' *Lamke*. Beginning with costume and scenic design, to dance, orchestral, and voice rehearsals, to grand opening night, you'll see the opera bloom under your eyes! 60 mins.
VHS: S02438. $64.95.

Jon Vickers Sings Verdi and Puccini
Rare Canadian Broadcasting Corporation performances by Jon Vickers are collected on this videotape. Act I of *Tosca*, Act II of *Manon Lescaut* and Act IV of *Il Trovatore* are included. Mary Simmons and Louis Quilico are also featured. 80 mins.
VHS: S19400. $39.95.

Jose Carreras
This world-renowned tenor, accompanied by the Vienna State Opera, sings a varied program of works by Puccini, Massenet, Faure and many others. This event has been hailed as the miracle concert, because it was presented just after his recovery from bone marrow treatments for leukemia. 140 mins.
VHS: S20984. $24.95.

Jose Carreras and Friends
The "Royal Gala Evening" held for Their Royal Highnesses Prince and Princess Michael of Kent starred Jose Carreras, Agnes Baltsa, Katia Ricciarelli and Ruggero Raimondi. Accompanied by the London Arts Orchestra conducted by Jacques Delacote, the program includes favorite operatic arias and duets, as well as popular songs. 90 mins.
VHS: S22006. $24.95.

Jose Carreras in Concert
Jose Carreras in a live performance at the Komische Oper in East Berlin, performing arias by Puccini, Leoncavallo, Respighi and others, and in a rousing encore Bernstein's *Tonight*. 90 mins.
VHS: S07685. $19.95.

Jose Carreras in Salzburg
Tenor Jose Carreras performs *Seven Spanish Songs* by Manuel de Falla at the Great Festival House in Salzburg. Of course the enthusiastic audience is rewarded with a number of encores, including Leoncavallo's *Mattinata* and *Granda*. 111 mins.
VHS: S21061. $24.95.

Jose Carreras' Comeback Recital in Spain
The long-awaited video of Jose Carreras' comeback recital at Peralada Castle in Spain. The tenor, who has undergone two bone marrow transplants in his fight against leukemia, performs a wonderfully varied program of songs by Tosti, Puccini, Massenet, Faure and others. This video record of Carreras' emotional comeback is a treasure. 82 mins.
VHS: S10413. $19.95.

Jose Carreras: A Life Story
This biography of the elusive Spanish tenor Jose Carreras traces his work as a prodigy, performing at age seven; his subsequent opera performances; his collaboration on Bernstein's *West Side Story*; and the private anguish of his battle with cancer. With Montserrat Caballe, Placido Domingo and Luciano Pavarotti. 77 mins.
VHS: S18625. $29.95.
Laser: LD71874. $34.95.

Jose Carreras: A Tribute to Mario Lanza
Acclaimed tenor Carreras performs the songs of matinee idol and pop star Mario Lanza. Filmed in London's Albert Hall with a full orchestra, the songs featured in this tribute have never had more rich or heartfelt interpretations.
VHS: S21734. $29.97.
Laser: LD74494. $34.97.

Jose Carreras: Four Days with the Famous Tenor on the Road
A contemplative documentary about the life, art and off-stage personality of tenor Jose Carreras. The film captures four days in his life, during production on the film *Misa Criolla*. The film shows Carreras during rehearsals, interacting with his admirers and conferring with his son. 31 mins.
VHS: S19897. $19.95.

Jose Carreras: Music Festival in Granada
This live concert was filmed in Granada during one of Spain's largest annual music festivals. Carreras gives an electrifying performance of songs by Tosti, Puccini, de Falla and others. In Hi-Fi stereo, 93 mins.
VHS: S16797. $24.95.

Jussi Bjoerling in Opera and Song, Vol. 2
This "Voice of Firestone" telecast features Jussi Bjoerling, a first-class tenor of exquisite refinement and effortless grace. Including the "Flower Song" from *Carmen*, plus songs by Schubert, Leoncavallo, and Herbert. 1950, 26 mins.
VHS: S13624. $24.95.

Kathleen Battle at the Metropolitan Museum
Kathleen Battle performs a solo recital with works from Gershwin, Handel, Mozart, Strauss, Liszt and Puccini.
VHS: S17240. $24.95.
Laser: LD71631. $29.95.

King's College Choir: The Festival of Nine Lessons and Carols
Stephen Cleobury conducts the King's College Choir in Cambridge, in the seasonal concert of carols, including "Silent Night," "Hark! The Herald Angels Sing," "Oh Come, All Ye Faithful" and "O Little Town of Bethlehem." On the same program is a 50-minute BBC documentary that presents an inside view of the King's College Choir. 110 mins.
VHS: S19751. $34.95.
Laser: LD71960. $34.95.

The King's Singers at Wells Cathedral
Amid the medieval splendor of England's Wells Cathedral, the King's Singers perform a feast of Christmas music. Classics like "Noel, Noel" and even modern works like Paul McCartney's "We'll All Stand Together" are included. 30 mins.
VHS: S21820. $19.95.

Kiri Te Kanawa: Royal Gala Concert
Kiri Te Kanawa in her first solo recital at Royal Opera House, presenting songs by Schubert, Schumann, Strauss, Wolf and others. 60 mins.
VHS: S07686. $19.95.

Kiri! Her Greatest Hits Live
On her 50th birthday Kiri Te Kanawa sang arias by her favorite composers, including works by Mozart, Puccini and Richard Strauss. In London's Royal Albert Hall, she was accompanied by the London Symphony Orchestra and Chorus directed by Stephen Barlow. Show tunes by Gershwin, Rogers and Hammerstein, Bernstein and Andrew Lloyd Webber, as well as music from her Native New Zealand, round out this one-of-a-kind program.
VHS: S21776. $29.95.
Laser: LD74497. $34.95.

La Gran Scena Opera Company
"Impressive...virtuosic...outrageous...very funny" (*New York Times*). A videotaped performance in Munich by New York's very original company.
VHS: S02947. $49.95.

La Grande Notte a Verona
In celebration of the 75th anniversary of the Festival of the Arena di Verona, this concert brought together singers Jose Carreras, Ruggero Raimondi, Montserrat Caballe, Eva Marton, Samuel Ramey, Ileana Cotrubas and many others to benefit the Jose Carreras International Leukemia Foundation. A contribution by Placido Domingo is also included. 122 mins.
VHS: S20985. $24.95.

La Stupenda: A Profile of Dame Joan Sutherland
At the Sydney Opera House on October 2, 1990, Dame Joan Sutherland bade farewell to opera. This tape looks back on her marvelous singing career, which spanned 42 years and brought joy to millions. Includes her final performances as well as interviews with her and some of her closest friends. 90 mins.
VHS: S15629. $24.95.
Laser: LD70280. $34.95.

Last Night of the Proms: The 100th Season
Welsh baritone Bryn Terfel and percussionist Evelyn Glennie are at the center of this riotous night of glorious music. *Last Night of the Proms* is traditionally an unbridled celebration. The BBC Orchestra, under the direction of Andrew Davis, performs music by Bach, Walton, Wood, Elgar, Massenet and others. 112 mins.
VHS: S24971. $29.97.

Lauritz Melchior in Opera and Song, Vol. 2
This "Voice of Firestone" telecast includes arias from *Lohengrin*, *I Pagliacci*, *The Student Prince*; plus songs. 1950-52, 40 mins.
VHS: S13687. $34.95.

Leonard Warren in Opera and Song, Vol. 2
This "Voice of Firestone" telecast features the dramatic baritone Leonard Warren. Also featuring a special guest appearance by soprano Eleanor Steber. Includes arias from *Barber of Seville* (Warren) and *Tosca* (Steber); duet from *Maytime* (Romberg); plus songs by Speaks, Huhn, and Herbert. 1949, 27 mins.
VHS: S13623. $24.95.

The Life of Verdi
This is a collector's edition of an epic drama based on the life of Giuseppe Verdi. Filmed in Italy, Leningrad, Paris, and London, it features a stereo score of Verdi's great works sung by Renata Tebaldi, Maria Callas, Luciano Pavarotti, Birgit Nilsson, and others. 600 minutes.
VHS: S03161. $124.95.

Lisa Della Casa in Opera
The incomparable soprano in a program of arias and duets from *La Boheme* and *Tosca*. With Nicolai Gedda, Richard Tucker and Giuseppe Campora. From the *Voice of Firestone* series. 30 mins.
VHS: S16081. $24.95.

Luciano Pavarotti—The Event
The world's favorite tenor gives a gala concert in Milan to celebrate the World Cup heroes. A must for every music buff's collection, as Pavarotti performs the best-loved operatic arias and songs from the works of composers such as Donizetti, Mozart, Verdi, and Puccini. This engaging performance features no less than six encores! Don't miss it. 88 mins.
VHS: S13654. $29.98.

The Maestro and the Diva
Dame Kiri Te Kanawa and Sir Georg Solti join forces in this collection of Richard Strauss songs, including the famed "Four Last Songs." Recorded by Sony Music in Manchester with the BBC Orchestra. 118 mins.
Laser: LD74552. $29.98.

Magnificat for Solo, Chorus and Orchestra
Bach composed this Magnificat for the Christmas Vesper Service in 1723. In keeping with the tradition, Christmas carols, sung by an additional choir in the choir loft, are added to the Magnificat in this performance filmed in the 800-year-old Church of St. Nicholas in Leipzig. With Peter Schreier, Heidi Riess, Gothart Stier, and the New Bach Collegium Maximum.
VHS: S05584. $29.95.

The Magnificent Victoria de los Angeles
From the BBC archives comes de los Angeles in this live 1968 recital, accompanied by the great pianist Gerald Moore. The performance includes songs by Granados, Faure, Ravel and others. 50 mins.
VHS: S16469. $29.95.

Margaret Price: Ruckert Lieder
Margaret Price's clear voice perfectly accentuates the drama of Friedrich Rukert's poems, which have been orchestrated by Gustav Mahler for this production. 30 mins.
VHS: S26925. $19.95.

Maria
Maria Callas, in a moving, honest and vital portrait told through her filmed appearances, newsreel footage, interviews with her and her colleagues, directed by Tony Palmer (Wagner). Winner of the Gold Medal, New York Film and TV Fest. 90 mins.
VHS: S07093. $39.95.

Maria Callas Concert: 1959 Hamburg
A terrific portrait of the legendary diva as she performs in Hamburg from Spontini's *La Vestale* and Bellini's *Il Pirata*, as well as favorites from *The Barber of Seville* and Verdi's *Don Carlo*. Filmed during the 1959 Callas Hamburg concerts. 65 mins.
VHS: S03878. $39.95.

Maria Callas Concert: 1962 Hamburg
The second, triumphant return of Maria Callas to Hamburg, in a memorable performance which includes Berlioz' *Carnival Romain*, *Le Cid*, selections from *Carmen*, *Ernani*, *La Cenerentola* and *Don Carlo*. 65 mins.
VHS: S03521. $39.95.

Maria Callas: Life and Art
A celebration of the singing and dramatic skills of the great diva, with an exploration of the woman behind the public persona. the film features excerpts from Callas' performances in *Tosca*, *La Traviata*, *Norma*, and others, as well as interviews with some of the people who knew her best, including Franco Zeffirelli, Giuseppe Di Stefano, S.A. Gorlinsky and Carlo Maria Giulini. 78 mins.
VHS: S04911. $19.95.

Mario Lanza: The American Caruso
Mario Lanza did more to bring classical music and opera to the masses through the popular art of movies than anyone before or since. Through clips from his most popular films and recordings and through interviews with co-workers like Zsa Zsa Gabor and Anna Moffo, Lanza's turbulent life is frankly presented. The program is guest-hosted by Placido Domingo. 68 mins.
VHS: S14446. $29.95.

Messe Solennelle
Berlioz' composition was lost in the 19th century, only to be rediscovered in an Antwerp organ loft in 1991. This world premiere is performed by the Monteverdi Choir and the Orchestre Revolutionnaire et Romantique and conducted by John Eliot Gardiner. Shot on location in Westminster Cathedral in October 1993. 59 mins.
VHS: S20977. $29.95.
Laser: LD72405. $29.95.

MET Centennial Gala
Grace Bumbry, Montserrat Caballe, Eva Marton, Placido Domingo, Jose Carreras and nearly 100 other singers celebrate the centennial of the Metropolitan Opera with Leonard Bernstein and James Levine conducting. Stereo, 1983, color, 231 mins. 2 cassettes.
VHS: S02444. $29.95.

Montserrat Caballe and Jose Carreras in Moscow
Live from the Bolshoi Theatre, a performance of favorite arias and duets by Puccini, Verdi, Rossini, Bellini and others, and a selection of popular Catalan songs. 120 mins.
VHS: S20567. $24.95.

Montserrat Caballe: The Woman, the Diva
A portrait one of this century's great operatic sopranos, one who feels a deep sense of identification with the roles she portrays. Caballe performs arias from ten selections around the world, and offers a deep insight into her life as an opera star. 62 mins.
VHS: S03167. $39.95.

More Songs of Placido Domingo in Mexico, Vol. 2
The beautiful songs of this Latin American country are featured, as sung by this great tenor accompanied by his musical friends. 70 mins.
VHS: S22041. $19.98.

The Moscow Virtuosi
One of the world's greatest chamber ensembles, formed by Vladimir Spivakov, *The Moscow Virtuosi* interprets works by Bach and Mozart, in a concert taped at the Municipal Theater in Torrejon de Ardoz, Spain. 68 mins.
Laser: LD71935. $34.95.

Mozart Coronation Mass
Herbert Von Karajan conducts the Berlin Philharmonic.
Laser: LD74585. $29.98.

Mozart Great Mass in C Minor
Leonard Bernstein conducts the Bavarian Radio Symphony Orchestra with soloists Arlene Auger, Frederica von Stade and Frank Lopardo in this April 1990 concert which was organized to celebrate the opening of borders between East and West Germany. In Hi-Fi stereo, 81 mins.
VHS: S16518. $24.95.
Laser: LD71464. $34.95.

Mozart Mass in C Minor, K.427
Helmuth Rilling is seen both in rehearsal and in a full production of this grand piece in the Knight's Hall, Wolfegg. 60 mins.
VHS: S22007. $24.95.

Mozart Requiem (Bernstein)
A joyous performance film of Mozart's final gift to the world. The Bavarian Radio Chorus and Symphony Orchestra is conducted by Leonard Bernstein, with an all-star cast including Maria Ewing and Jerry Hadley. Filmed in the beautiful Abbey Church, Diessen (Ammersee), Upper Bavaria, July 1988. 65 mins.
VHS: S14116. $24.95.

Mozart Requiem (Davis)
Mozart's last work is shrouded in mystery and legend. It was commissioned by an enigmatic stranger and never finished. Mozart wrote presciently that he believed that the requiem was for himself. In this unforgettable performance, Colin Davis conducts the Bavarian Radio Symphony Orchestra and Chorus, with internationally renowned soloists Edith Mathis, Trudeliese Schmidt, Peter Schreier and Gwynne Howell. 57 mins.
VHS: S10274. $29.95.

Mozart Requiem (Karajan)
Herbert Von Karajan conducts the Berlin Philharmonic in this Sony Music performance.
Laser: LD74586. $29.98.

Mozart Requiem K and Mass in C Minor
Virtuoso conductor John Eliot Gardiner leads the Monteverdi Choir and English Baroque Soloists in a performance of Mozart's final two unfinished masses, filmed in Barcelona on the 200th anniversary of the composer's death. With Barbara Bonney, Anne-Sofie von Otter, Anthony Rolfe Johnson and Alastair Miles. 100 mins.
VHS: S19106. $24.95.
Laser: LD71895. $34.95.

Mozart: The Requiem from Sarajevo
Jose Carreras, Zubin Mehta and Ruggero Raimondi join forces to perform this musical masterpiece in war-torn Sarajevo. The Choir of the Cathedral of Sarajevo and the Orchestra of Sarjevo also took part in this remembrance for all those who have died in this city under seige. 50 mins.
VHS: S25635. $19.95.

Music of the Night
Jose Carreras, under the musical direction of George Martin, sings the music of Andrew Lloyd Webber. With Marti Webb, Jane Harrison, and the Choir of St. Paul's Cathedral.
VHS: S15456. $24.98.
Laser: LD70215. $29.98.

Musical Masterpiece at Masada
Stars Zubin Mehta and the Israel Philharmonic. Mehta and company perform Mahler's Second Symphony at the historic mountain of Masada as the grand finale of Israel's 40th Anniversary Celebrations last year.
VHS: S10712. $29.95.

My Heart's Delight
Luciano Pavarotti sang this concert of songs by Puccini and his contemporaries, including Franz Lehar's "You Are My Heart's Delight", in his hometown, Modena, Italy. On this occasion, born of his gratitude to his compatriots, Pavarotti was accompanied by soprano Nuccia Focile. 86 mins.
VHS: S20974. $29.95.
Laser: LD72403. $34.95.

Nicolai Ghiaurov
A tribute to the world-renowned basso Ghiaurov, he is shown performing in his greatest operatic roles. They include Don Giovanni, Don Quixote, Boris Godunov, and Mephistopheles. 120 mins.
VHS: S03373. $59.95.

Ode to Freedom
This program documents the historic live recording of Beethoven's Ninth Symphony in East Berlin's Schauspielhaus on Christmas Day 1989, just after the collapse of the Berlin Wall. The concert features members of three choruses and six orchestras. Hi-Fi stereo, 92 mins.
VHS: S16815. $24.95.
Laser: LD71519. $34.95.

Opera Favorites Sung by Placido Domingo and Kiri Te Kanawa
Two of opera's best known and most exciting performers in magnificent moments from some of the world's greatest operas, recorded live, with English subtitles. Includes highlights from Die Fledermaus performed at the Royal Opera House at Covent Garden, Otello from Arena di Verona, Ernani from La Scala, and selections from Les Contes d'Hoffman, La Fanciulla del West. 59 mins.
VHS: S10910. $39.99.

Opera Stars in Concert, Volume 1
Filmed live in Spain, international opera greats Alfredo Kraus, Katia Ricciarelli, Paolo Coni, Lucia Valentini-Terrani and Ruggero Raimondi perform favorite arias and duets. The Symphonic Orchestra of Madrid is conducted by Gian Paolo Sanzogno, opening with Verdi's I Vespri Siciliani, and then quoting the beloved works of La Traviata, Tosca, I Puritani, Semiramide, Lucrezia Borgia, Don Carlos, Faust and Tales of Hoffman. 60 mins.
VHS: S16506. $24.95.

Opera Stars in Concert, Volume 2
In this compendium of the world's finest performers, filmed live in Madrid, Alfredo Kraus, Katia Ricciarelli and Ruggero Raimondi perform a series of thrilling arias, from Verdi, Puccini, Rossini, Donizetti, including Rigoletto, Elisir d'Amore, and The Barber of Seville. The program also features Paolo Coni and Lucia Valentini-Terrani. 60 mins.
VHS: S17309. $24.95.

Opera Stars in Concert, Volume 3
Performed live in Barcelona, this program of features Alfredo Kraus, Paolo Coni, Renata Scotto, Mellanie Holiday, Ramon Vargas and Gail Gilmore performing sections from Macbeth, Don Carlos, Elisir D'Amore and Rigoletto. 80 mins.
VHS: S17315. $24.95.

P.D.Q. Bach's "The Abduction of Figaro"
The infamous P.D.Q. Bach's only full-length opera is presented here by Professor Peter Schickele. It features the "corpse de ballet," the "Dance of the Seven Pails," and more!
VHS: S02191. $49.95.

Patrice Munsel in Opera and Song
Lyric soprano Patrice Munsel became the youngest singer to debut with the Metropolitan Opera in 1943. Her performances on the Voice of Firestone programs are recollected, as she performs arias from The Daughter of the Regiment, Die Fledermaus, La Boheme, Louise and Madama Butterfly. 55 mins.
VHS: S17428. $34.95.

Pavarotti & Friends
On September 27, 1992, Italian tenor Luciano Pavarotti returned to his hometown and gathered an international cast of pop and classical stars for a gallery charity concert to help fund local disease research, performing popular and classical music. With Sting, Suzanne Vega, The Neville Brothers, Bob Geldof, Brian May, Zucchero, Lucia Dalla and Patricia Kaas. 70 mins.
VHS: S18312. $29.95.

Pavarotti & Friends 2
Bryan Adams, Michael Kamen and Andreas Vollenweider join Pavarotti for this collection of songs performed in concert. Featuring a variety of operatic and popular music, including "All for Love," "Please Forgive Me," "Night Fire Dance," "Ave Maria" and "O Sole Mio."
VHS: S25922. $29.95.
Laser: LD75033. $34.95.

Pavarotti & Friends Together for the Children of Bosnia
Luciano Pavarotti joined Bono, the Edge, Brian Eno, Michael Bolton, Meat Loaf, Simon le Bon, Zucchero, Dolores O'Riordan, The Chieftains, Italian rap sensation Jovanotti and conductor Michael Kamen for a special benefit concert on behalf of the children of Bosnia. This video captures the event, staged in Modena, Italy, in September of 1995. Ultimately, Pavarotti's efforts will help build a music center in the Bosnian town of Mostar.
VHS: S27625. $29.95.
Laser: LD75535. $34.95.

Pavarotti and Levine in Recital
Join Luciano Pavarotti and James Levine on the stage of the Metropolitan Opera in New York, in a recital of operatic arias and popular art songs, including works by Rossini, Bellini and Puccini's "Nessun Dorma" from Turandot. In Hi-Fi stereo, 72 mins.
VHS: S14113. $24.95.
Laser: LD71419. $24.95.

Pavarotti and the Italian Tenor
Over the course of this hour-long documentary Pavarotti makes clear in both interview segments and musical performances the importance of the Italian tenor tradition to his own career. He comments frankly on his influences, including Caruso and Gaggle. This video also features songs and arias never released on video before.
VHS: S26484. $29.95.
Laser: LD75096. $34.95.

Pavarotti in Concert in China
The great tenor in recital in Beijing, China, from his historic 1986 tour. From Verdi and Puccini arias to Italian classics like O Sole Mio, Pavarotti proves once again why he is the world's most beloved opera singer.
VHS: S13058. $29.95.

Pavarotti in Confidence with Peter Ustinov
Pavarotti is the tenor acclaimed for his great voice and ability to bring opera to new audiences throughout the world, from Central Park to the World Cup. Peter Ustinov goes behind the public persona of this singer to uncover the man and the ideas and passions that drive him. Excerpts from folk songs and arias are included. 50 mins.
VHS: S22933. $19.95.

Pavarotti in Hyde Park
An all-new video production that was taken from this summer's concert in London's Hyde Park by the world's favorite tenor Luciano Pavarotti.
VHS: S15218. $24.95.
Laser: LD71443. $34.95.

A Pavarotti Valentine
Pavarotti sings 19 of his greatest hits, including "Nessun Dorma" from Turandot, selections from L'Elisir d'Amore,, "O Sole Mio," and others, as recorded at a recital from the Teatro Petruzzelli in 1984. 77 mins.
VHS: S14816. $29.95.

Pavarotti—Master Class at Juilliard
Incomparable tenor Luciano Pavarotti sings and coaches top young singers at the Juilliard School of Music. Using arias by Puccini, Mozart and Verdi, Pavarotti guides students through the elements of breath control, phrasing and interpretation. The subtle discipline of opera singing is revealed. 60 mins.
VHS: S12762. $29.95.

Placido Domingo & Rostropovich
Placido Domingo is at his versatile best in a concert from the Roman Theater in Merida, Spain. He not only sings some of his favorite arias, but also conducts the orchestra for Mstislav Rostropovich's performance of a Haydn Cello concerto. Domingo also sings and plays piano to Rostropovich's cello in Massenet's Elegy, plus Tchaikovsky's 1812 Overture and a Carmen duet with soprano Olga Borodina. 60 mins.
VHS: S15939. $24.95.
Laser: CLV. LD74628. $34.95.

Placido Domingo: A Musical Life
At last there is a documentary that explores the man behind the opera superstar. This video shows Domingo in private moments with his wife Marta and his three sons at their spectacular Acapulco home. It also shows him at work as he flies to Madrid to record a zarzuela song and conduct an opera by Bellini. 90 mins.
VHS: S24307. $29.95.

Placido Domingo: His 25th Anniversary Concert at the Roman Amphitheater of Verona
Placido Domingo returns to Verona to commemorate his earlier smashing success in the city's ancient outdoor amphitheater. Cecilia Gasdia joins Placido, who sings his favorites from Verdi and Puccini, including Act 1 of Othello, Act 3 of Aida and Act 3 of La Boheme.
VHS: S27173. $19.95.
Drazen Siriscevic/Armando Tasso, Italy, 1995, 100 mins.

Placido Domingo: Hommage a Sevilla
Placido Domingo honors the cultural diversity and historical importance of Seville, the setting for many great operas and the site for Expo '92. With scenes from Don Giovanni, The Barber of Seville, Carmen and Fidelio, conducted by James Levine of the Vienna Symphony Orchestra.
VHS: S17128. $24.95.
Laser: LD71544. $29.95.

Placido Domingo: Live from Miami
Superstar tenor Placido Domingo performs at the Miami Arena to a standing-room-only crowd. Joined by the talented American soprano Ana Panagulias, Domingo presents a bounty of favorite arias, duets and songs by Puccini, Donizetti, Meyerbeer and others. 60 mins.
VHS: S15938. $24.95.
Laser: CLV. LD71488. $29.95.

Placido Domingo—Zarzuela
Live from the National Auditorium of Madrid, tenor Placido Domingo performs an "all-zarzuela" concert to an enthusiastic crowd which includes Spain's King Juan Carlos and the royal family. Domingo is joined by some of Spain's leading zarzuela performers, including Guadalupe Sanchez, Teresa Verdera and Paloma Perez Inigo. Also featured is the colorful dancing of the Ballet Espanol. 69 mins.
VHS: S16227. $24.95.

Placido Grandisimo
Officially opening the Seville World Expo, Placido Domingo gives a thrilling live concert performance to a capacity crown at the Seville Stadium. He performs favorite arias by Puccini and Bizet, as well as a selection of popular Spanish songs and zarzuelas. Soprano Julia Migenes joins Domingo in a duet from Carmen, and also performs solos from Puccini and Gershwin. As the exciting concert reaches its climax, the crowd demands an encore from Domingo, the moving "El Grito de America." 60 mins.
VHS: S16228. $24.95.

Placido in Prague
Placido Domingo performed a concert in the Prague Concert Hall, where he was joined by Angela Gheorghiu. Works by Puccini, Donizetti, Mozart, Verdi and other great composers make this memorable musical evening an incomparable event. 94 mins.
VHS: S24361. $19.95.

Placido: A Year in the Life of Placido Domingo
Travel around the world with Placido Domingo and enjoy his matchless performances in Tosca, Tales of Hoffmann, Otello, Ernani, and other great operas. Offstage, you'll get an intimate portrait of the man Opera News called "the King of the opera," seeing his methods of training, rehearsal, and everyday life. 105 mins.
VHS: S02453. $19.95.

Puccini
The composer of some of the world's most popular operas, Madama Butterfly, La Boheme and Tosca, Puccini became involved in an appalling scandal which nearly ruined his career. His tragic story unfolds in this dramatic program which features Robert Stephens, Judith Horwath and Virginia McKenna. The inclusion of a present-day production of his unfinished Turandot shows parallels between the composer's life and work. Stereo hi-fi. 135 mins.
VHS: S02749. $59.95.

Renata Scotto in Concert
This live 1991 concert from Budapest offers the complete Les Nuits d'Ete of Berlioz, plus arias by Handel, Mozart and Puccini. In Stereo. 68 mins.
VHS: S16080. $29.95.

Renata Scotto: Prima Donna in Recital
Diva Renata Scotto performs in Tokyo, accompanied by pianist Thomas Fulton on this 1984 video. She performs the music of Puccini, Verdi, Liszt, Rossini, and others.
VHS: S02452. $39.95.

Renata Tebaldi Live!
Tebaldi may well have been the leading non-coloratura Italian soprano of the century. Despite a vocal crisis in the 1960's, she recovered to become a viable verismo soprano. This video shows her in all her early greatness and also captures the more glamorized era of her later career. 25 mins.
VHS: S24558. $34.95.

Requiem (Webber)
Andrew Lloyd Webber's Requiem was first performed in February, 1985, at St. Thomas' in New York. Captured live, this production stars Placido Domingo and Sarah Brightman, the choirs of Winchester Cathedral and St. Thomas', and the orchestra of St. Luke's conducted by Lorin Maazel. 60 mins.
VHS: S02454. $19.95.

A Requiem for Mozart
The bicentennial performance of Mozart's Requiem, presented in the same church where the requiem mass for his memorial service was held. Sir Georg Solti conducts the Vienna Philharmonic Orchestra and the Vienna State Opera Choir. With Cecilia Bartoli, Arlene Auger, Vinson Cole and Rene Pape. In Hi-Fi Stereo, 100 mins.
VHS: S16043. $24.95.
Laser: LD71192. $34.95.

Riise Stevens in Opera and Song, Vol. 2
This "Voice of Firestone" telecast includes arias from Samson et Dalila, Carmen, Orfeo ed Euridice; plus songs. 1951-59, 45 mins.
VHS: S13686. $34.95.

Robert Merrill in Opera and Song
This "Voice of Firestone" telecast features the pure, mellow baritone of Robert Merrill. Includes arias from Carmen, The Barber of Seville, Pagliacci, Hamlet, and Trovatore; songs by Weill, Leoncavallo, and others. 1955-59, 50 mins.
VHS: S13629. $34.95.

Robert Merrill in Opera and Song, Vol. 2
The Voice of Firestone brings more songs and arias from America's most beloved baritone. Music by Massenet, Verdi, Gounod, Romberg, Jerome Kern, Rodgers and Hammerstein and others. 55 mins.
VHS: S16084. $34.95.

Roberta Peters in Opera and Song
Her appearances on the "Voice of Firestone" telecasts amply display the brilliant vocalism and delightful personality which made Roberta Peters one of the most famous and beloved sopranos of our time. Includes arias from The Magic Flute, Lucia, La Traviata, and Lakme; plus songs by Arditi, Friml, and others. 1952-57, 50 mins.
VHS: S13628. $34.95.

Roberta Peters in Opera and Song, Vol. 2
In this second volume of her work from the Voice of Firestone efforts, Peters performs arias from Don Giovanni, The Tales of Hofmann, Rigoletto, and a string of popular songs and music. 55 mins.
VHS: S17429. $34.95.

Ruggero Raimondi
In this revealing documentary, Raimondi's life amidst the international world of opera is highlighted by his performances of great male roles. Rossini's Moses in Egypt, Massenet's Don Quichotte and Mussorgsky's Boris Godunov are stellar showcases for Raimondi, but he is especially renowned for Don Giovanni, which he conducts himself in this video. 50 mins.
VHS: S26214. $19.95.

Schmidt: My Song Goes Round the World (Ein Lied Geht Um die Welt)
Schmidt plays a man consumed by love, in this film filled with beautiful music. His rendition of "Mal d'amore" is reason enough to see and hear the film. German with English subtitles. 79 mins.
VHS: S24036. $34.95.

Sherrill Milnes at Juilliard: An Opera Master Class
Six advanced students perform and are then critiqued and instructed by renowned baritone Sherrill Milnes at Juilliard. 75 mins.
VHS: S04152. $39.95.

Sherrill Milnes' Homage to Verdi
Renowned operatic baritone Sherrill Milnes presents this look at the work of Verdi, including a description of his life and the operas he composed. Milnes performs arias from La Traviata, Rigoletto, Macbeth, Nabucco, and others, proving once again that he is America's premiere baritone. 56 mins.
VHS: S03156. $39.95.

Sherrill Milnes: An All-Star Gala
This exciting musical portrait of the great American baritone also features performances by Placido Domingo, Mirella Freni, Julia Migenes and Peter Schreier. Produced by the Italian television network RAI. 60 mins.
VHS: S26430. $24.95.

Shirley Verret
A film biography of the great black diva, following her professional and private life during the course of a year. Performance extracts show her in many of the dramatic opera roles which she made her own: Iphigenie at the Paris Opera, Tosca at the Arena di Verona, Dalila at the Royal Opera House Covent Garden, and Carmen at La Scala. 60 mins.
VHS: S04684. $39.95.

Silent Night with Jose Carreras
A special Christmas journey to Austria, where he sings such favorites as White Christmas, O Come All Ye Faithful, and, of course, Silent Night. 40 mins.
VHS: S07687. $19.95.

The Soldier's Tale (L'Histoire du Soldat)/Symphony of Psalms
The Nederlands Dans Theater appears in The Soldier's Tale, conducted by David Porceljin; Symphony of Psalms is conducted Leonard Bernstein and performed by the London Symphony Orchestra and English Bach Festival Chorus.
Laser: LD70408. $34.95.

Songs of a Wayfarer/Songs on the Death of Children—Mahler
Leonard Bernstein's final Mahler recording (recorded in Vienna) in collaboration with American baritone Thomas Hampson, who performs three song cycles. "Hampson darkens or lightens his tone in accordance with the sense of the text and responds alertly to Bernstein's subtleties of phrasing" (Gramophone). With the Vienna Philharmonic Orchestra. 76 mins.
VHS: S17432. $24.95.
Laser: LD71757. $34.95.

Songs of Mexico: Placido Domingo: Volume 1
The opera superstar sings an exceptional collection of traditional Mexican songs. 75 mins.
VHS: S22040. $19.98.

The Sorceress
This film of seduction, starring Opera's most alluring soprano, Kiri Te Kanawa, features the greatest love songs by Handel. She is accompanied by the Academy of Ancient Music under the direction of Christopher Hogwood. Dressed in elaborate and sumptuous costumes, this enchantress will delight viewers with her famed voice. 50 mins.
VHS: S21328. $29.95.

Spirituals in Concert
Two of the great divas of the opera stage, Kathleen Battle and Jessye Norman, join forces in this unique performance video to sing a collection of well-known and lesser-known Spirituals. James Levine conducts. Including: "Swing Low, Sweet Chariot" and "He's Got the Whole World in His Hands." 91 mins.
VHS: S14120. $24.95.
Laser: LD71421. $34.95.

St. John Passion
Filmed at St. Thomas Church, Leipzig, where Bach conducted the first performance. Performed by Peter Schreier, Venceslava Hruba-Freiberger, Alain Zaepffel, Hermann-Christian Polster, and the Choir of the St. Thomas Church, Leipzig.
VHS: S05583. $39.95.

St. Matthew Passion
Filmed at the St. Thomas Church in Leipzig where Bach himself was the organist for 25 years. With Peter Schreier, Regina Werner, Rosemarie Lang, Siegfried Lorenz, Theo Adam, and the Choir of the St. Thomas Church, Leipzig.
VHS: S05582. $39.95.

The Story of Carol
Christmas carols originated in dances dating back to the seventh century. This documentary traces the pagan roots of these songs. The first printed carol appeared in 1521. Later they were condemned by the Puritans, only to be revived in the Victorian era. 52 mins.
VHS: S21822. $19.95.

Stratasphere
An emotion-packed, intimate film portrait of Teresa Stratas, one of the greatest voices of the present day. In a mixture of revealing interviews and stirring performance footage, Ms. Stratas tells the story of her childhood as the daughter of poor Greek immigrants in Toronto, and her rise to fame on stage of the Metropolitan Opera in New York, as well as her relationships with the famous, including Lotte Lenya and Mother Teresa, to whom Ms. Stratas dedicates a portion of her income. The opera star is seen in rehearsal for Puccini's La Boheme with Franco Zeffirelli. 87 mins.
VHS: S12278. $29.95.

Symphony for the Spire
A spectacle of music and theater in a concert to support the Prince of Wales' Salisbury Cathedral Spire Appeal. The program features Placido Domingo, Jessye Norman, Ofra Harnoy, Kenneth Branagh, Charlton Heston and the English Chamber Orchestra. The highlights include Harnoy's rendition of The Flight of the Bumble Bee, Norman's Morgen Op. 27 No. 4 and Domingo's Be My Love. Conducted by Richard Armstrong. 65 mins.
VHS: S19420. $19.95.

Ten Tenors
Bergonzi, Corelli, Gigli, Keipura, Lauri, Volpi, Martini, McCormack, Piccaver, Schipa and Tagliavini are the great tenors seen in this compilation video. These excerpts are taken from various Bel Canto videos.
VHS: S24852. $34.95.

Thomas L. Thomas in Opera and Song
The vocal talents of the great Welsh baritone is the focus of this Voice of Firestone presentation. Featuring arias from Hamlet and Un Ballo in Maschera, as well as songs by Rudolf Friml, Jerome Kern, Rodgers & Hammerstein and others. Also highlighted are traditional folksongs. 55 mins.
VHS: S16082. $34.95.

The Three Sopranos
This memorable recital presents three of the world's greatest sopranos together on the same stage. Ileana Cotrubas, Elena Obraztsova and Renata Scotto created magic in front of a sold-out crowd at the Roman Amphiteater of Siracuse, Italy, performing selections from favorite operas such as Carmen, Tales of Hoffmann, Aida, Pagliacci and more. 67 mins.
VHS: S15940. $24.95.
Laser: C.I.V. LD71489. $29.95.

The Three Tenors in Concert: Carreras, Domingo, Pavarotti
The three greatest tenors in the world side by side on the same stage in Rome during the World Cup soccer finals in 1990. Conducted by Zubin Mehta. Don't miss this once-in-a-lifetime musical treasure! 89 mins.
VHS: S14107. $24.95.
Laser: LD70905. $34.95.

The Three Tenors
Jose Carreras, Placido Domingo and Luciano Pavarotti join conductor Zubin Mehta for this singular musical event. On the occasion of soccer's World Cup in 1994, they performed together in Los Angeles. Operatic arias, popular music and even a salute to the music of Hollywood make this an unforgettable collaborative effort.
VHS: S21991. $29.98.
Laser: LD74542. $39.98.

Three Tenors: Encore
Tenors Jose Carreras, Placido Domingo and Luciano Pavarotti, under the direction of conductor Zubin Mehta, are captured in this fascinating, backstage documentary culled from hours of video and performance footage of their In Concert video that sold a phenomenal 10 million recordings. Narrated by Derek Jacobi. Features Nessun dorma, A mare chiaro, Rondine al nido, and Mattinata. 1992, 57 mins.
VHS: S17365. $19.95.
Laser: LD72299. $29.95.

Verdi: Requiem (La Scala/von Karajan)
Of the hundreds of recordings of the great Verdi Requiem there is one which could be described as definitive. Leontyne Price, Fiorenza Cossotto, Luciano Pavarotti—together with the chorus and orchestra of La Scala, Milan—are conducted by Herbert von Karajan in a performance for the ages. 85 mins.
VHS: S14117. $24.95.

Verdi: Requiem (London/Abbado)
Recorded live from Edinburgh's Usher Hall, Verdi's brilliant choral piece is conducted by Claudio Abbado and performed by the London Symphony Orchestra, the Edinburgh Festival Chorus and four distinguished soloists, Margaret Price, Jessye Norman, Jose Carreras and Ruggero Raimondi. 97 mins.
VHS: S18759. $29.95.

Vespers of the Blessed Virgin
Filmed in the extraordinary setting of St. Mark's Basilica in Venice, where Monteverdi himself served as maestro di capella from 1613 to 1643, this is a 1989 performance of Monteverdi's masterpiece. 111 mins.
VHS: S14803. $29.95.
Laser: LD71441. $34.95.

Victoria de los Angeles in Recital
The first complete recital by the beloved soprano to be released on video, taped at the 1989 Palacio de la Musica in Barcelona, on the 45th anniversary of her recital career. Among the selections are songs by Granados, de Falla, Mompou, Albeniz, and a seductive rendition from Carmen.
VHS: S12919. $39.95.

A Victorian Christmas in Songs
In this modern dress classic, Dennis O'Neill, one of Britain's greatest tenors, performs a series of traditional Welsh Christmas classics. Shot at the medieval Penhow Castle. 52 mins.
VHS: S17983. $29.95.

Vienna Boys' Choir Sings Mozart at the Chapel of the Hofburg, Vienna
A thrilling program of Mozart's choral masterpieces, from the early "Waisenhaus-Messe" to the late period "Ave verum corpus", performed by the world-renowned Vienna Boys' Choir, conducted by Uwe Christian Harrer. 72 mins.
VHS: S18316. $29.95.
Laser: LD71854. $34.95.

Visions of Gregorian Chants
The Benedictine Monks of St. Wandrille perform their timeless and traditional meditations to soothe the soul. This music has brought millions solace. Now combined with visuals that awaken the senses and release anxiety, this spiritual experience is available on video. 45 mins.
VHS: S21293. $9.99.

Wagner in Bayreuth
This two-part program interweaves a 25-minute documentary narrated by Wagner's grandson Wolfgang that describes the birth of the Salzburg festival, a behind-the-scenes look at the Festspielhaus, and the second part that features excerpts of Tannhauser, Lohengrin, Der fliegende Hollander, Rheingold, and Die Walkure. 70 mins.
VHS: S17405. $9.95.
Laser: LD71699. $19.95.

War Requiem
Benjamin Britten's requiem features Anthony Rolfe Johnson, Luba Orgonasova and Boje Skovhus as soloists with the Monteverdi Choir, the NDR Choir, and the Tolzer Boys Choir, and the NDR Symphony Orchestra conducted by John Eliot Gardiner in this live performance at the Church of St. Mary in Lubeck, Germany, as part of the Schleswig-Holstein Festival. 87 mins. Hi-Fi Stereo.
VHS: S20555. $29.95.
Laser: LD72367. $34.95.

Young Caruso
Musical biography of Enrico Caruso starring Ermanno Randi but featuring the singing of Mario del Monaco of the New York Met. With an early performance by Gina Lollobrigida.
VHS: S02238. $29.95.
Italy, 1951, 77 mins.

Zubin Mehta and Leontyne Price
The magnificent lyric-dramatic soprano Leontyne Price joins the New York Philharmonic's Zubin Mehta for a glorious concert of Mozart, Verdi, and Strauss. Opening with Mozart's Jupiter Symphony, this is a magical concert. 94 mins.
VHS: S08712. $22.95.

WORLD MUSIC

African Dance and Drumming
Culturally and artistically rich African music directly inspires dance, song, language and even clothing. Renowned choreographer Margo Blake and master drummer Dr. David Closson present this interactive program suitable for children from elementary school to the high school level.
VHS: S22479. $99.95.

African Drumming
Baba Olatunji is a master of African drumming. He presents essential techniques, rhythmic patterns and concepts for drummers at all levels. The spiritual power of drumming and drums are the focus of this informative video. 60 mins.
VHS: S22707. $39.95.

African Guitar
Anthropologist Gerhard Kubrik's personal field recordings from 1966-1993 are collected on this video. Kubrik is a widely recognized expert who has written several books and countless articles on the music of sub-Saharan Africa. Now the rich textures of African fingerstyle guitar music can be seen and heard in an accessible format.
VHS: S25057. $24.95.

Afrika Bambaata and Family: Electric Dance Hop
This collection features the very first rap music videos. Bambaata is often called the godfather of hip hop music because of his innovative and enduring style. 60 mins.
VHS: S24022. $9.98.

Alan Stivell
With his Celtic harp and other exotic instruments, Alan Stivell weaves a mystical spell that transforms his traditional music into modern form. Considered one of Europe's major musical exports, Stivell captivates his audience and carries them through a concert of Celtic magic. 60 mins.
VHS: S15728. $24.95.

Alle Brider: The Flying Bulgar Klezmer Band
Dance and sing along to this music video featuring klezmer music, including a Yiddish folk tune that has a "hidden merengue." 5 mins.
VHS: S23250. $16.95.

Antonio Carlos Jobim: An All Star Tribute
Jobim is world famous as the co-founder and leading composer behind the distinctive Brazilian music known as Bossa Nova. His runaway hit "The Girl from Inpanema" is just a fraction of his output. This video features jazz giants, Herbie Hancock, Shirley Horn, Joe Henderson and Jobim himself performing some of Jobim's greatest works. 60 mins.
VHS: S24666. $19.98.

The Art of Fingerstyle Guitar
Folk, blues and ragtime have expanded the range of fingerstyle guitar. This video joins different artists like John Renbourn, Stefan Grossman, Martin Carthy, Bob Brozman and more to show the range of possibilities with this instrument, from the Celtic to the Hawaiian to jazz.
VHS: S25058. $24.95.

Ashkenaz: Eastern European Jewry
This video offers a nostalgic look at the music of Eastern European Jewry. Yiddish folk songs, liturgical music, Klezmer melodies and even Yiddish theater tunes are all here. The origins of Ashkenazic music are traced with the help of vintage archival footage taken before World War II. 28 mins.
VHS: S21710. $39.95.

Aswad "Live"
After a long and fruitful career, Britain's premiere rock/reggae band topped the charts with the infectious "Don't Turn Around" followed by "Give a Little Love". These titles plus twelve more songs from a sell-out concert filmed at Hammersmith Odeon in December 1988 are included. Recorded in Hi-Fi stereo, 70 mins.
VHS: S16159. $19.95.

Batouka: The First International Festival of Percussion
Sacred drums from Haiti, Kora from West Africa, Brazilian Birimbau, Ingouma from Burundi—pulsating rhythms from the skin and wood of drums keeping alive the unwritten history of life. The percussion instruments speak the language of rhythm in this unique record of the festival in Guadeloupe which brings together the musical traditions of the great cultures of West Africa, Peruhl, Bambara, Senonfo, Malimko.
VHS: S07745. $24.95.
M. Huraux/F. Migeat, France, 1986, 52 mins.

The Best of Shabba Ranks
One of Jamaica's most famous and successful artists, Shabba is the first dance hall singer to win a Grammy. This compilation of his songs was created from a number of concerts staged in Jamaica. Songs like "Wicked in My Bed", "Them Bow", "Gal You Good" and "Golden Touch" are featured.
VHS: S22201. $29.95.

Bob Marley Legend
A personal, musical compilation of Marley's most popular concert appearances and video clips, combined with rare interview footage and video clips. 55 mins.
VHS: S03901. $29.95.

The Bob Marley Story: Caribbean Nights
This award-winning documentary traces the life of Bob Marley, from interviews with his friends and family to rare archive footage of interviews with Marley himself. We remember the brilliant and evocative music he gave the world, music that stretched back over nearly two decades. This program captures the feel and timelessness of that music and the man himself. 100 mins.
VHS: S14108. $19.95.

Brian Eno: Imaginary Landscapes
A visual profile of a modern artist at the cutting edge of technological change and popular taste. This video brings together Brian Eno's work in sound, vision and light. It explains the development of his music in visual terms, based on landscapes and images that have shaped his life as an artist. Directed by Duncan Ward and Gabriella Cardazzo. 40 mins.
VHS: S14713. $19.95.

Brother with Perfect Timing
When he left South Africa in the 60's, Abdullah Ibrahim took the unique mixture of Arabic, African, Oriental and European cultures with him. In this film, Ibrahim reveals himself as a casually charismatic storyteller, in an articulate, self-told portrait echoed in music from Ekaya, his band of saxophones, brass and rhythm section.
VHS: S07741. $29.95.
Chris Austin, USA, 1987, 90 mins.

Cajun Visits
A portrait of the diverse language and ethnicity of traditional Cajun music. Features six of the finest players—Dennis McGee, Wallace "Cheese" Read, Canray Fontenot, Leopold Francois, Robert Jardell and Dewey Balfa—discussing their art. Includes nine songs on the fiddle, Acadian accordion and guitar. In Cajun French with English subtitles.
VHS: S06507. $44.95.
Yasha Aginsky, USA, 29 mins.

Canadian Brass Live
The famous Canadian brass Ensemble featured in what the Washington Post called "an atmosphere of total enjoyment in which laughter freely mingles with gasps of amazement." The program includes "Carnival of Venice," Fats Waller's "Handful of Keys," "Canonza No. 4" by Gabrieli and Bach's "Little Fugue in G Minor." 50 mins.
VHS: S08929. $24.95.

Canadian Reggae Music Awards
The 6th annual Canadian Reggae Music Awards show. Includes appearances by Foxy Brown, John Holt, Leroy Gibbon, Frankie Paul and many, many more.
VHS: S15329. $29.95.

Caribbean Music and Dance
The folk music and dance of Honduras, Grenada, Jamaica and Haiti, filmed on location. Narrated in English by Von Martin. 25 mins.
VHS: S06804. $70.00.

Chase the Devil
Nationally-aired PBS documentary gives a street-level perspective of the religious music of the Appalachians, with a behind-the-scenes tour of the provocative culture. From Beats of the Heart series.
VHS: S12608. $19.95.

The Chieftains in China
This video presents the Irish group on their tour of China in performance with accomplished Chinese musicians.
VHS: S15706. $24.95.

Chopi Music of Mozambique and Banguza Timbila
A unique look at the Chopi People and their expressive xylophone music and rituals. This most complex of African music has endured despite oppression and war.
Ron & Ophera Hallis, Canada, 1989, 60 mins.

Clifton Chenier: The King of Zydeco
Clifton Chenier and his Red Hot Louisiana Band perform "Black Gal", "Clifton's Zydeco", "Cher Catin", "J'aime pain de mais", "Every Now and Then", "Let the Good Times Roll" and "I'm a Hog for You".
VHS: S10357. $49.95.

Cobra Live
Cobra is wild, mad as shad, dynamic and comical as he performs live in concert at Roy Wilkins Park, Queens, New York City. This young man from St. Mary, Jamaica, is another reggae great who is bringing the world hits like "Flex, Time to Have Sex".
VHS: S22198. $29.95.

Cool Runnings: The Reggae Movie
All the sounds and sights of the 1983 Sun Splash Festival held in Jamaica are available on home video. Directed by Robert Mugge. Artists include Ziggy Marley and the Melody Makers, Gil Scott-Heron, Musical Youth and more.
VHS: S13248. $19.95.
Robert Mugge, Jamaica, 1983, 105 mins.

Country Stars: A New Tradition
Live from the chapel of Fisk University, a county music jamboree. Includes "Ain't Livin' Long Like This", "Don't Be Cruel", "Blues Stay Away from Me", "Blue Moon of Kentucky", "Chill Factor", "You Ain't Woman Enough". 60 mins.
VHS: S11700. $19.95.

Crowning of the Browning
This reggae splash at Roy Wilkins Park features J.D. Smooth, Blacka Ranks, Penny Irie and Little Vicious. Songs like "Man Fi Dead", "Love Black Woman", "Love Mi Browning" and "Stamina Daddy" are included.
VHS: S22207. $29.95.

Dennis Brown: The Living Legend
This collection features over 18 reggae songs by this great singer, including "How Could I Live", "Should I", "So Long" and "Sorry".
VHS: S22202. $29.95.

Discovering the Music of Africa
African music is demonstrated by a Ghanaian drummer with several of his associates. This demonstration clarifies how drums are used both for music and communication in Africa today. 22 mins.
VHS: S23511. $49.95.

Discovering the Music of India
This sophisticated musical tradition can trace back its origins without interruption nearly 4000 years. The instruments of both northern and southern India are demonstrated in this video, along with the hand gestures and facial expressions of Indian dance. 22 mins.
VHS: S23513. $49.95.

Djembefola
This master of percussion is steeped in the traditions of his native Guinea, West Africa. From his early career with the National Djoliba Ballet to the development of his current unique style, this musician has combined the best of his musical heritage with his own definitive sensibility. French, English and African dialects with English subtitles.
VHS: S20914. $39.95.

Downbeat vs. Addies
This KG Reggae Video production features artists Ackie and Saltfish from Japan, Duggie Fresh, Half Pint and Mac Daddy.
VHS: S22214. $29.95.

Esoteric Nature of Music
Explores views in ancient cultures regarding music and its effect on consciousness. 47 mins.
VHS: S06486. $49.95.

Evelyn Glennie in Rio/Fiesta
A unique portrait of Evelyn Glennie, one of the most remarkable young musicians of our time. Though profoundly deaf from an early age, this young Scottish musician triumphed over seemingly impossible odds to become one of the world's finest percussion players. It introduces her early life and career, then follows her visit to the famous Carnival in Rio de Janeiro—a musical voyage of discovery at the world's most colorful and vibrant festival. Includes performances of Bizet's Carmen Suite and Rosauro's Concerto for Marimba and Strings. With the London Symphony Orchestra. 93 mins.
VHS: S15737. $24.95.
Laser: LD71433. $34.95.

Everyone Sings/Cantemos Todos!
Records Carlos Meija Godo's Misa Campesina at St. John the Divine Church in New York City. A spectacle of poetry and dance recounting the Central American experience.
VHS: S10198. $29.95.
Doug Eisenstark, USA, 1986, 30 mins.

Fela in Concert
Fela Anikulapo Kuti is perhaps the most celebrated Black African musician today, a revolutionary cultural symbol to the people of Nigeria and the world over. A taped concert in Paris in June 1981 captures the charisma Fela exerts on stage. 1981, 57 mins.
VHS: S02111. $29.95.

Fela Live
This tape captures all the excitement of Fela Anikulapo Kuti and his Egypt 80 Band at their peak. Perhaps Africa's most celebrated performing artist, Fela's spectacular stage show extends his musical epics unlike any other performance.
VHS: S15516. $29.95.

Frank Yankovic: America's Polka King
Yankovic extended the polka into popular culture during the 1940's and 1950's. This documentary explores the success of this unique performer and explains how he has sold millions of records with tunes like "The Blue Skirt Waltz" and "Just Because". 58 mins.
VHS: S24306. $29.95.

Fresh, Vol. III
Another KG Reggae Video production, this one features reggae artists Freddie McGregor, Tinga Stewart, Ken Booth, China Man, Quata, Lady P., Johnny Nice and Richie Stevens.
VHS: S22206. $29.95.

Hassidut: Hassidic Music
Music is central for the Hassidic community. Famed Rabbi Nahman of Bratslav taught his students that one can pray not only through word but also through song. Filmed in the Hassidic community, beautiful melodies from prayers, celebrations and other significant events are included. 28 mins.
VHS: S21709. $39.95.

Hawaiian Rainbow: The Magic and the Music of the Islands
A unique examination of the music and culture of the island paradise by award-winning filmmaker Robert Mugge. "Mugge clearly felt some of the magic and the mystery—the mana—that gives Hawaiian music its spine, and this rubs off on the viewers in little jolts" (Honolulu Star-Bulletin). Mugge's musical portrait combines the sounds of the Hawaiian slack-guitar, the strumming of the ukelele and the a capella and falsetto singing of native Hawaiian musicians to illustrate the intriguing history of traditional Hawaiian music.
VHS: S08699. $29.95.
Robert Mugge, USA, 1989, 90 mins.

Hot Shot
This reggae music video features performances by Papa Beto, Wild Apache, Clement Irie, Chinna Man, Leroy Smart, Papa Skull, Frankie Paul and more.
VHS: S15330. $29.95.

In South Louisiana/ Dedans le Sud de la Louisiane
By featuring an extraordinarily wide variety of Cajun and Creole musicians, this video uses the music to explore the culture it represents. Included are funny interviews with legendary accordionists Nathan Abshire and Bec Fontenot. In Cajun French with English subtitles.
VHS: S06508. $49.95.
Jean Pierre Bruneau, USA, 43 mins.

John Renbourn & Stefan Grossman
Two of the world's premier acoustic guitarists join forces to define and explore the parameters of European and American styles. From traditional folk standards to modern jazz, this program highlights the differences and similarities of these two fine musicians. 60 mins.
VHS: S15725. $24.95.

John Renbourn Group
The John Renbourn Group embraces musical elements as diverse as Renaissance, British folk, modern jazz, classical and blues. Renbourn, one of Britain's preeminent guitarists, leads the group which features the pristine voice of Jacqui McShee. Her vocal rendering of English and Irish ballads woven with flute, bagpipe, dulcimer and guitar can only be described as hypnotic. 60 mins.
VHS: S15730. $24.95.

Johnny McEvoy in Concert
Without a doubt one of the most successful recording stars in the history of Irish music, John McEvoy sings such favorites as Grandma's Feather Bed, Botany Bay, Town I Loved So Well, Eileen Is Waiting, The West Awake. 53 mins.
VHS: S06651. $29.95.

Juju Music: King Sunny Ade
King Sunny Ade and Ebenezer Obey perform the urban tribal music of Nigeria, known as juju, which blends lively traditional songs and instruments with Western musical influences. 1988, 51 mins.
VHS: S14741. $19.95.

Kevin Burke and Michael O'Domhnaill
Two former members of the Irish group Bothy Band, Kevin Burke and Michael O'Domhnaill, present a concert of traditional Irish folk music. 60 mins.
VHS: S19214. $24.95.

Konkome—Nigerian Music
West Africa's thriving pop music scene comes alive in this vibrant program featuring Sunny Ade, Sonny Okosun, Fela and the Ljadu Sisters. Captures the stunning cultures that shape African pop, Highlife, Juju to Afro-rock and reggae.
VHS: S08892. $19.95.

Kumu Hula: Keepers of a Culture
A colorful, expertly lensed and edited documentary by a master documentarian that is a serious look at the history and ancient traditions represented in the dances of the Hawaiian people. The hulas feature various troupes of dancers attired in vibrantly colored costumes performing against the backdrop of some of Hawaii's most scenic panoramas.
VHS: S12331. $29.95.
Robert Mugge, USA, 1989, 85 mins.

Laibach: A Film from Slovenia
Laibach's Eastern block renditions of The Beatles and Rolling Stones classics give their work a distinctive sound and poetic edge. The 17 tracks include "Kinderreich," "Fiat," "Cariamici," "The Great Seal," "Sympathy for the Devil," and "Across the Universe."
VHS: S19612. $19.95.

Land of the Look Behind
Land of the Look Behind started as a documentary on the funeral of Bob Marley. Somewhere along the line it became a spiritual poem/drama about the strange and beautiful lives of the Jamaican people. It is a life of poverty and oppression in the land of paradise, capturing the cries of a people struggling painfully to survive. The film becomes an exploration of man's search for dignity and joy.
VHS: S08937. $19.95.
Alan Greenberg, USA, 1982, 88 mins.

Le Mystere des Voix Bulgares: A Bird Is Singing
This amazing Bulgarian women's ensemble was recorded live during their 1993 tour of Bulgaria, Poland and Norway. Their traditional Bulgarian choral music was nominated for two Grammy awards in 1994. 80 mins.
VHS: S22228. $19.98.

Les Blues de Balfa
The Balfa Brothers are the most renowned Cajun musicians of southwest Louisiana, the first Cajun group to take their music outside of Louisiana. Tragically, Rodney and Will Balfa were killed in an auto accident in 1979. In this film, surviving member Dewey Balfa traces the development of his musical family and its contribution to Cajun music. Music includes the Balfa Brothers, Allie Young, Rockin' Dopsie, and the Cajun Playboys.
VHS: S09292. $44.95.
Yasha Aginsky, USA, 28 mins.

Manu Dibango: King Makossa
Filmed concert in Belgium, December 1981, featuring saxophonist Manu Dibango from Cameroon. Known as Africa's Hippest Hopper, Dibango is influenced by the legacy of Charlie Parker.
VHS: S02112. $29.98.
Philippe Antoine, 1981, 55 mins.

Master Blaster, Vol. I
Admiral Bailey, Junior Reid, Leroy Smart, Jack Raddics, Little Kirk, Professor Nuts and Wayne Wonder are presented, singing their acclaimed songs "Fight over My Body", "Bad Boys", "Bonafide", "All My Love" and many others. From KG Reggae Video Productions.
VHS: S22196. $29.95.

Master Blaster, Vol. II
In this video, Ken Booth, Tony Rebel, Buju Banton, Simpleton and Capleton are presented singing their acclaimed songs. "Freedom Street", "Wagonist", "Woman No Fret" and "Coco Cola Shape", as well as many other songs, are included.
VHS: S22199. $29.95.

Missa Luba
Featuring music of the African Mass, Missa Luba achieved instant fame when it appeared in the acclaimed 1968 film If. These haunting folk songs from Kenya pulsate with the colorful and seductive musical experiences of a powerful land and its people, brimming with all the necessary ingredients to become the cult music of the nineties. 51 mins.
VHS: S13888. $24.95.
Laser: LD71232. $29.95.

Mizike Mama
Zap Mama is the acclaimed Zairian-Belgian five-woman a cappella group which has made world music into a truly international phenomenon. They sing in many languages, including Spanish, Creole, Swahili, French, Arabic, Pygmy and even English. This documentary explores the roots of their music and its novel, sophisticated blend of various cultural influences. French, English and African dialects.
VHS: S20915. $39.95.

Moon Drum (Twelve dream song evocations by John Whitney)
An impressionistic evocation of the mood, color, and feel of Native American art, created with computer graphics. Art of the Pueblo, Hopi, Ogala Sioux; iconography, images of animal deities and pictographs, plus much more. Includes 12 short films. 60 mins.
VHS: S14717. $19.95.

Music of the Spirits
A unique look at Zimbabwe's famed mbira master, Stella Madamombe, by Canadian filmmaking team Ron and Ophera Hallis, providing insight into the roots of African music.
VHS: S12930. $49.95.
Ron & Ophera Hallis, Canada, 1988, 30 mins.

Musica Para Hot Sundays
Documentary of the summer musical series in New York city parks, this colorful tape shows the sweet side of the city as both kids and grown-ups swirl in a salsa-like beat. Produced by Yomoma Arts. 1985, 27 mins.
VHS: S10160. $19.95.

The Ninja Man Rides Again
Junie Ranks, Richie Stevens, Ghost and Culture and I Papa Beto are showcased in this KG Reggae Video production.
VHS: S22200. $29.95.

One Hand Don't Clap
This film takes you deep into the Caribbean for an exploration of the vibrant rhythms of Calypso/Soca Music, as performed by two dynamic artists, Lord Kitchener and Calypso Rose. 1988, 92 mins.
VHS: S14742. $19.95.

Our Musical Heritage Series
American Folk Music. The indebtedness of American folk music to British and Irish ballads, the development of American folk music through European and African influences. 21 mins.
VHS: S05831. $19.95.
Country and Western Music. The growth of country music from dance parties, casual events, to the formalization of country and western through the advent of western musical instruments. 23 mins.
VHS: S05832. $19.95.
Electronic Music. An exploration of the technology that makes music and sound synthesizing possible, and the complexities achievable through the use of a digital synthesizer. 21 mins.
VHS: S05833. $19.95.
Music of Africa. Focuses on the music of western Africa, with special attention to the music of Ghana, and the rattles, bells and drums of Ghanaian music blended with voice to create a distinctive musical style. 22 mins.
VHS: S05835. $19.95.
Music of India. The coordination of string, wind and percussion instruments which creates a provocative and sensuous style, which, when integrated with movement and voice, provides a primal level of communication. 22 mins.
VHS: S05836. $19.95.
Music of Japan. The five-tone system of Japanese music, reflecting the beauty of nature, and integration with movement and dance. 22 mins.
VHS: S05837. $19.95.
Music of Latin America. Starting with the roots of Indian music, the foundations of Latin music in the co-mingling of wind and percussion and string instruments, the Spanish and Portuguese influences. 20 mins.
VHS: S05838. $19.95.
Music of the Middle Ages. The roots of medieval music in religious or secular pursuits, the solemn rituals, romantic ballads and social tunes of the age of chivalry. 20 mins.
VHS: S05839. $19.95.
Music of the Middle East. An exploration of the diverse instruments and styles of middle-eastern music, its relationship to dance, and its emotional base. 21 mins.
VHS: S05840. $19.95.
Russian Folk Music. The religious and folk foundations of Russian music, its humorous songs and dances, and the robust rhythms characteristic of Russian dances. 22 mins.
VHS: S05841. $19.95.

Rags & Tangos (Rifkin)
Pianist Joshua Rifkin plays a sensational collection of tangos by the Brazilian "King of Pop Music", Ernesto Nazareth, and ragtime from composer Scott Joplin.
Laser: LD70233. $34.95.

Rainbow: Live Between the Eyes
Ritchie Blackmore and his group Rainbow live in concert. 77 mins.
VHS: S07020. $29.95.

Reggae Beach Rock, Vol. II
Thriller U, Jack Raddics, Shacka Shamba, Ghost and Culture, Pinchers and Ninja Manew are all included in this KG Reggae Video production.
VHS: S22204. $29.95.

Reggae Go-Go Style Dirty Dancing, Vol. III
This video features erotic, X-rated and kinky dancing, all to the music and beat of sensational hard or soft reggae.
VHS: S21891. $24.95.

Rhythm of Resistance
Nationally-aired PBS documentary gives a street-level perspective of Black South African music, with a behind-the-scenes tour of the provocative culture. From Beats of the Heart series.
VHS: S12605. $24.95.

Rhythms of the World Anthology
Both Peter Gabriel and Bobby McFerrin, longtime ardent supporters of World Beat music, offer insight into the musical styles of this collection of world bands. Includes performances by Buckwheat Zydeco, Fela Kuti, King Sunny Ade, and many more. 57 mins.
VHS: S15624. $19.95.

Rockers—It's Dangerous
Set within a world of poor Jamaican Rastafarians, this reggae film offers a variation of the legend of Robin Hood. Leroy "Horsemouth" Wallace and Richard "Dirty Harry" Hall star, with a soundtrack that includes reggae greats Burning Spear, Bunny Wailer, Third World, Peter Tosh and many more.
VHS: S23027. $24.95.

The Romany Trail, Part I
Subtitled Gypsy Music into Africa, the first part investigates the lost gypsy tribe inside Egypt, as a group travels up the Nile, through the ancient town of Luxor, around the location of pharaoh's tombs. The journey moves from Cairo to Karnak, introducing us to gypsy dancing performers, magicians, acrobats, musicians, fortune tellers and mystics. 60 mins.
VHS: S16967. $24.95.

The Romany Trail, Part II
The second part opens in India, tracing the origins of the initial gypsy forms, providing an insider's portrait of this enclosed world, one of bear trainers, puppeteers, actors and musicians. The action shifts to Eastern Europe, with communism on its last legs, and goes inside the workers' hotels, homes and street theater where the gypsies develop their craft and methods. 60 mins.
VHS: S16968. $24.95.

Roots, Rock, Reggae
A street-level tour of the vital music scene in Kingston, with rehearsal and concert footage that captures vintage performances by Toots and the Maytals, Jimmy Cliff, the Heptones and Ras Michael.
VHS: S08893. $19.95.

RSW In Video
RSW's 1989 Soundclash album reverberated through the United Kingdom and America with its distinctive merging of house, reggae, funk and postpunk sound. The six tracks of this video include "Kray Twins", "Cocaine Sex", "Biting My Nails" and "Probably a Robbery". 30 mins.
VHS: S19613. $19.95.

Sepharad: Judeo-Spanish Music
Five hundred years after the expulsion of Spanish Jewry, the musical heritage of the Sephardim is alive and well. The film focuses on music first sung by Spanish singers in the Middle Ages, lullabies, wedding tunes, synagogue melodies and songs of mourning, performed in the rich traditional style of the Sephardim. 27 mins.
VHS: S21711. $39.95.

Shock Out with Metro Media
100% dance hall, this video features reggae artists Sky Juice, Peter Metro, Danny Dread, Dicky Ranking, Nicodemus and Blacka Ranking.
VHS: S22195. $29.95.

"Still Life" at the Penguin Cafe
Britain's brightest young choreographer, David Bintley, joins forces with alternative musicians The Penguin Cafe Orchestra. This program includes the complete performance, as well as a short documentary about the Penguin Cafe Orchestra. In Hi-Fi stereo, 89 mins.
VHS: S16258. $24.95.
Laser: LD71427. $34.95.

Structures from Silence
A dream flight through soft liquid universes on waves of Steve Roach's almost transparent music. Marianne Dolan's motion paintings offer celestial navigation for the imagination. 30 mins.
VHS: S10228. $24.95.

Super Clash Round I
Featuring Shabba Ranks vs. Ninja Man live in Saint Mary. A devastating reggae performance highlighted by rapid fire gun salute.
VHS: S15328. $29.95.

Talk of the Town: Shabba Ranks
Shabba's reggae hits "Wicked in Bed", "Twice My Age", "Idle Jubbie", "Pay Down Pon It", "Hard and Stiff", "Best Baby Father" and many more are included in this video recorded live at Dinasty.
VHS: S22197. $29.95.

Teiman: Music of Yemenite Jewry
Yemenite Jews have perfected singing and rhythm, drumming and dancing over centuries. World-renowned vocalists Ofra Haza and Noa (Acinoam Nini) are just some of the talented performers who illustrate the Yemeni rhythms that have conquered the world stage. 27 mins.
VHS: S21712. $39.95.

Tex-Mex
Nationally-aired PBS documentary gives a street-level perspective of the music of the Texas-Mexican borderlands, with a behind-the-scenes tour of the provocative culture. From Beats of the Heart series.
VHS: S12609. $19.95.

There'll Always Be Stars in the Sky
An entry from the 14-part series Beats of the Heart, this volume explores the Indian film industry. The staple of the country's astonishing output is its lavish, melodramatic, highly stylized musicals. This is an insider's viewpoint, interweaving interviews and behind-the-scenes footage with actors, directors and location shooting. 60 mins.
VHS: S16966. $24.95.

Time Will Tell: Bob Marley
An engaging documentary about Bob Marley and his band The Whalers, his collaboration with Peter Tosh, and the roots of his music, steeped in Third World ethnography, poverty and social protest. Produced by Rocky Oldham and directed by Declan Lowney, with Marley performing his classics, "One Love," "Stir It Up," "No Woman No Cry," "Get Up Stand Up," "I Shot the Sheriff," and "Redemption Song."
VHS: S17433. $19.95.
Declan Lowney, Great Britain, 1991, 85 mins.

Transformation Is Our Secret
A video featuring the music of avant-garde composer Elliott Sharp. The composer slinks through desolate urban landscapes as his ear-rattling, atonal scores set the pace.
VHS: S10165. $19.95.
Mitsuru Hayashi, USA, 1987, 20 mins.

Various Artists Featuring Raymond Kane Ki Ho'alu: That's Slack Key Guitar
Slack Key Guitar is a unique Hawaiian tradition. This unique finger-picking style developed after Spanish cowboys introduced the guitar to Hawaii in the early 1800's. Raymond Kane's story reveals the unique trajectory of this music.
VHS: S25912. $29.95.

Ziveli! Medicine for the Heart
The culture and music of the Serbian-American communities of Chicago and California. Made in association with Serbian-American anthropologist Andrei Simic and the University of Southern California's Visual Anthropology program, the film focuses on the vital culture strengths of these immigrants from Yugoslavia, who helped form the backbone of industrial America. Music, dancing, the Orthodox church, and featuring the Popovich Brothers, the Kapugi Brothers, and Dunav. 1987, 50 mins.
VHS: S02902. $49.95.

Zydeco
Exploration of Louisiana creole culture and the fast-paced music that mixes Cajun, Rhythm and Blues and Afro-Caribbean music into that unique sound called Zydeco.
VHS: S02907. $49.95.
Nicholas Spitzer, USA, 1984, 57 mins.

Zydeco Gumbo
Clifton Chenier and John Delafose, Boo Zoo Chavis, Terence Semian and Willis Prudhomme star in this spicy gumbo of zydeco. From the old dance halls—like Richard's in Lawtell and Slim's-Y-Ki-Ki in Opelousas—to the Zydeco Festival in Plaisance, this tape features the hottest Zydeco performers in Southwestern Louisiana.
VHS: S12344. $19.95.
Dan Hildenbrandt, USA, 1988, 28 mins.

Zydeco: Nite 'n' Day
This colorful documentary takes the viewer to the bayous of the deep south and into the musical world of Zydeco. It focuses on the heritage of Zydeco music while explaining the distinctions between Zydeco, Cajun and Creole music. Featuring Buckwheat Zydeco and Rockin' Dopsie & the Zydeco Twisters. 56 mins.
VHS: S14521. $19.95.

FOLK MUSIC

America's Music: Folk 1
Theodore Bikel hosts this review of American folk music, including many of its best-known performers: Glenn Yarbrough, Buffy Ste. Marie, The New Christy Minstrels, Odetta, Hoyt Axton, Theodore Bikel, the Blue Flame String Band, and film clips of The Limeliters, Leadbelly and Burl Ives. 60 mins.
VHS: S05036. $19.95.

America's Music: Folk 2
The Limeliters, Josh White, Jr., Jean Richie, Doc Watson, Dave Van Ronk, Mary McCaslin and Jim Ringer, and John McEuen are featured in the second part of this folk series. 60 mins.
VHS: S05037. $19.95.

An American Songster
A musical portrait of John Jackson, singer/guitarist and banjo player from Virginia. Jackson's career is traced from discovery in a gas station by folklorist Chuck Perdue to international recognition.
VHS: S04167. $19.95.
Renato Tonelli, USA, 1985, 30 mins.

Bert Jansch Conundrum
A dominant force in British folk music, Bert Jansch's work as a singer and guitarist has influenced the musical scene on both sides of the Atlantic. Along with violinist/mando-cellist Martin Jenkins and bassist Nigel Smith they formed the Bert Jansch Conundrum. Jansch's intricate guitar style is the focal point of the trio, while Jenkins and Smith add a mixture of traditional acoustic and electric settings that contribute to the group's unusual and arousing sound. 60 mins.
VHS: S15731. $24.95.

Cooler Than Country— The Bluegrass Mountaineers
Formed in the early 60s, the Bluegrass Mountaineers represent the honest, hardworking, traditional music loved across America. Outstanding vocals and inspiring banjo, fiddle, bass, mandolin and guitar accompaniment make this video a musical delight. 43 mins.
VHS: S26505. $19.95.

Cooler Than Country—The Lewis Family
The first family of bluegrass Gospel music, the Lewis Family, are a wellspring of family entertainment. Though they are professional entertainers of the highest order, they remain friendly and sincere upholders of the values of Gospel music. 38 mins.
VHS: S26504. $19.95.

Dave Van Ronk
A legend in his own time, Dave Van Ronk was one of the central figures in the folk movement that flourished in the late fifties and early sixties, nurturing such performers as Bob Dylan and Phil Ochs. His tough, gravelly voice and intricate guitar style complement his colorful, bawdy personality. 60 mins.
VHS: S15726. $24.95.

Discovering American Folk Music
Both the British Isles and the traditions of Africa have shaped the sounds of American folk music. The transformations of British ballads and lyric songs are traced as they evolved in the US, while the impact of African music is followed through the growth of spirituals and the blues. 21 mins.
VHS: S23519. $49.95.

Doc and Merle Watson
Doc Watson, probably America's greatest flat-picking guitarist, joins his son Merle and Michael Coleman on bass for a concert recorded in 1980. This performance is a showcase of native folk traditions. A visit at home with the Watsons in North Carolina is also included.
VHS: S25911. $29.95.

Doc Watson: Doc's Guitar Jam Featuring Doc Watson, Tony Rice, Dan Crary, Steve Kaufman & Jack Lawrence
Recorded at the 1992 Merle Watson Festival in Wilkesboro, North Carolina, this jam session showcases the talents of five master flatpicking guitarists. They harmonize, improvise and play up a storm. Two bonus tracks feature Doc Watson and his friends David Grisman, Bela Fleck, Mark O'Conner and Jerry Douglas.
VHS: S27317. $29.95.

Doc Watson: Rare Performances 1963-1981
This North Carolina native enriched the 1960's folk music boom with his distinctive music. In fact, he was a major inspiration for the whole movement. This collection of his appearances shows why he has been such an inspiration to countless other folk musicians.
VHS: S24220. $19.95.

Doc Watson: Rare Performances 1982-1993
By the 1980's Doc Watson had redefined the acoustic guitar's role in American folk music. In these later performances he is joined by duet partners Jack Williams, Merle Watson (Doc's son) and Rickey Skaggs, as well as string band performers Mark O'Conner, Tony Rice, Bela Fleck, David Grisman and Jerry Douglas.
VHS: S24221. $19.95.

Elizabeth Cotten
Born in 1893, Cotten inspired every fledgling fingerpicker of the folk boom era with her classic *Freight Train*. A North Carolina native, she is revealed in this video as more than a one song legend. This performance/interview was taped when she was 85. In it, she displays her ease with a variety of musical styles. 59 mins.
VHS: S22492. $19.95.

An Evening with the Kingston Trio
A 1989 live performance by the Kingston Trio recorded at Rockefellers in Houston, Texas. The show features original members Bob Shane and Nick Reynolds backed by some of the hottest musicians in the business. USA, 1990, 70 mins.
VHS: S15091. $19.95.

Folk City 25th Anniversary Concert
Recorded live at the legendary Greenwich Village club. The silver anniversary show includes the artistry of Richie Havens ("Freedom"), Arlo Guthrie ("Inch by Inch"), Joan Baez ("Improv Blues"), Tom Paxton ("Yuppies in the Sky"), The Roches ("Face Down at Folk City"), Suzanne Vega ("Crackin' "), Peter Yarrow ("Puff the Magic Dragon") and many more songs and performers. 83 mins.
VHS: S13288. $19.95.

Jim McCann & The Morrisseys
Two concerts, filmed in Ireland, featuring Jim McCann, formerly of the Dubliners, and the Morrisseys, one of Ireland's most popular folk groups. 55 mins.
VHS: S06653. $29.95.

John Fahey/Elizabeth Cotten: Rare Interviews and Performances from 1969
These seminal role models were presented on Laura Weber's 1960's TV series, *Guitar, Guitar*. As exponents of American primitive guitar, they make a perfect combination. Fahey is like the father of the style, while Cotten is like its Grandma Moses. Their comments and their performances are captured in this rediscovered episode.
VHS: S22489. $19.95.

Kingston Trio & Friends Reunion
The original members of the Trio (Nick Reynolds, Bob Shane and Dave Guard) perform their greatest hits as they are joined by Tommy Smothers and Mary Travers, and by Lindsey Buckingham, John Stewart and George Grove and Roger Gambill. Includes "Tom Dooley", "Scotch and Soda", "A Worried Man" and "M.T.A." 50 mins.
VHS: S20565. $19.95.

Mike Seeger: Fret and Fiddle
Seeger is a master of Oldtime music, the basis of hillbilly, bluegrass and country and western music. Before radio and recorded music it was played everywhere on special occasions. Like its musical descendants, Oldtime spoke about a variety of topics, from hunting to love. 55 mins.
VHS: S22487. $19.95.

Norman Blake & The Rising Fawn Ensemble
Norman Blake is one of the leading exponents of flatpicking guitar. He performed with such diverse artists as Bob Dylan, Johnny Cash and Kris Kristofferson before forming the Rising Fawn Ensemble. Blending guitar, cello and mandolin, they create dense, evocative music. 60 mins.
VHS: S15727. $24.95.

Peter, Paul and Mary: 25th Anniversary Concert
A moving concert by the timeless troubadours of folk music, with classic hits from their eight gold and five platinum albums, including "Blowin' in the Wind", "Puff, The Magic Dragon", "Leaving on a Jet Plane", "If I Had a Hammer", "This Land Is Your Land". 88 mins.
VHS: S12477. $19.95.

Pure Pete Seeger
Bill Moyers visits the singer, storyteller and activist on his 75th birthday at home in the New York Hudson Valley. This warm, funny video reveals the humane and witty man who fused folk music and political change into a way of life. 60 mins.
VHS: S24926. $29.95.

Steeleye Span: A 20th Anniversary Celebration
Formed in 1969, Steeleye Span became the preeminent folk/ rock band of the 70s. By the end of the 80s they had recorded over a dozen albums and sold millions. This exciting concert was recorded on their 20th Anniversary tour and features all their greatest hits. Celtic Rock at its best. 60 mins.
VHS: S15705. $24.95.

Talking Feet
A video by Mike Seeger, the renowned Old Time folk musician and instructor. *Feet*, the first documentary in this genre, showcases Southern-style solo mountain dancing, including flatfoot, buck, hoedown, and rural tap dancing.
VHS: S12925. $49.95.
Mike Seeger, USA, 1989, 90 mins.

Tony Rice: The Video Collection
Tony Rice practices flatpicking guitar styles that are praised in both bluegrass and innovative acoustic guitar circles. This tape features three different settings: an all-star jam session with Sam Bush and Bela Fleck, a set with Ricky Skaggs and David Grisman and a performance by the Tony Rice Unit at the 1992 Merle Watson Festival.
VHS: S27318. $29.95.

Troubadours of Folk Music
Great folk artists participated in a two-day concert series at the UCLA campus in Westwood in 1993. This video brings the best of their work to new audiences. Jefferson Starship, Arlo Guthrie, Janis Ian and John Prine are just a few of the artists featured. 54 mins.
VHS: S22463. $19.98.

A Vision Shared: A Tribute to Woody Guthrie & Leadbelly
Special performances of Guthrie and Leadbelly songs performed by John Mellencamp, Pete Seeger, Arlo Guthrie, Bruce Springsteen, Taj Mahal, Little Richard, U2 and more. USA, 72 mins.
VHS: S15312. $14.98.

The Weavers: Wasn't That a Time
Joyful, Academy Award-winning documentary about the legendary folksingers, The Weavers, who won the hearts of America in the 1950's with such songs as "Goodnight Irene" and "This Land Is Mine." With Pete Seeger, Lee Hays, Ronnie Gilbert, Fred Hellerman, Arlo Guthrie, Holly Near, Don McLean, Peter, Paul and Mary.
VHS: S01439. $19.98.
Jim Brown, USA, 1982, 78 mins.

Woody Guthrie: Hard Travelin'
The life and music of Woody Guthrie as traced through the eyes of his son Arlo, from the director of *The Weavers: Wasn't That a Time*. Woody's music is sung by Arlo as well as Pete Seeger, Judy Collins, Joan Baez and others.
VHS: S01481. $59.95.
Jim Brown, USA, 1984, 74 mins.

GOSPEL MUSIC

Al Green... Everything's Gonna Be Alright
Al Green Live at the Celebrity Theater in Anaheim, California. 60 mins.
VHS: S21611. $29.95.

Al Green: On Fire in Tokyo
Legendary soul singer Al Green has become one of gospel music's shining lights. This stirring concert performance features Green at his best, singing such inspiring songs as "Everything's Gonna Be Alright," "You Brought the Sunshine into My Life" and "None But the Righteous". 1988, 60 mins.
VHS: S14547. $29.95.

All-Star Gospel Show
Paul Simon, Andrae Crouch, the Edwin Hawkins Singers, Jennifer Holliday, The Mighty Clouds of Joy, The Oak Ridge Boys and Luther Vandross are featured in this soul-stirring hour of gospel filmed at the First Presbyterian Church in Hollywood. Includes *His Eye Is on the Sparrow*, *Oh Happy Day* and the stunning medley *Still Waters Run Deep*, *Bridge over Troubled Water*. 60 mins.
VHS: S00032. $19.99.

Allen & Allen: Live in Florida
This piano sax duo won national acclaim for their hit song "A-Blazing Grace." Now their versions of standard religious songs like "Silent Night" and "Jesus Is Love" are joined together with original notes on this video. In all their music they bring a fresh feel to Gospel music.
VHS: S26909. $14.95.

Allen T.D. Wiggin
The Gospel performer and Epic recording artist performs live in New York City. 60 mins.
VHS: S21612. $29.95.

Amazing Grace with Bill Moyers
With help from Judy Collins, Johnny Cash, Jessye Norman, Marion Williams and the Boys Choir of Harlem, host Bill Moyers presents a study of the most popular and enduring hymn of the English language. 87 mins.
VHS: S12936. $24.95.

America's Music: Gospel 1
Gospel music, hosted by Levar Burton, with Andrae Crouch, The Winans, The Archers, Marion Williams, Doug Miller, Walter Hawkins Family, and a rare film clip of Mahalia Jackson singing "When the Saints Go Marching In." 60 mins.
VHS: S05042. $19.95.

America's Music: Gospel 2
Sandra Crouch and Friends, Wently Phipps, The Chambers Family, Linda Hopkins, Reba Rambo and Donny McGuire, Mel Carter are featured, together with a film clip of Mahalia Jackson singing "Bless This House." Hosted by Levar Burton. 60 mins.
VHS: S05043. $19.95.

Angelic Gospel Singers
"Sweet Home", "Touch Me Jesus" and "Somebody's Praying for Me" are the featured songs.
VHS: S21613. $29.95.

Arvis Strickling Jones: From the Inside Out
A live performance featuring Dorothy Norwood and the First Union Choir. 60 mins.
VHS: S21614. $29.95.

Bishop Jeff Banks/Revival Mass Choir
Recorded live at A.M.E. Church in Newark, New Jersey. "Didn't I Tell You", "Let Me Talk in the Spirit" and "You Can Make It If You Try" are featured. 60 mins.
VHS: S21615. $29.95.

Bobby Jones Gospel
Ten volumes.
Volume 1. Bobby Jones, New Life Singers, Rejoice, Lloyd Lindroth, Second Coming and Rythem, David Len Jones and a special salute to Coretta Scott King.
VHS: S05529. $29.95.
Volume 2. Bobby Jones, New Life Singers, Williams Brothers and the Savannah Community Choir.
VHS: S05530. $29.95.
Volume 3. Bobby Jones, New Life Singers, The Impressions, Mary Harris and the Jud Edmonds Gospel Troup.
VHS: S05531. $29.95.
Volume 4. Bobby Jones, New Life Singers, The Ray Manning Singers and Rev. Al Green.
VHS: S05532. $29.95.
Volume 5. Bobby Jones, New Life Singers, Betty Griffin and the Spear Family Singers.
VHS: S05533. $29.95.
Volume 6. Bobby Jones, New Life Singers, Margaret Spence, The Futch Brothers and Susie Nelson (Willie's daughter).
VHS: S05534. $29.95.
Volume 7. Bobby Jones, New Life Singers, Myrna Summers, Darnell Hickman, Robin Junson and Jeff Lavalle.
VHS: S05535. $29.95.
Volume 8. Bobby Jones, New Life Singers, Rev. James Moore, Michael Charles and Evelyn Cosby.
VHS: S05537. $29.95.
Volume 9. Bobby Jones, New Life Singers, Stephene Stone Frierson, Milton Biggham and a special salute to Oprah Winfrey.
VHS: S05538. $29.95.

Volume 10: Special Christmas Show. Bobby Jones, New Life Singers, Jimmy Hill, Shirley Ceasar, Rejoice and Dorothy Norwood.
VHS: S05539. $29.95.

Breathe on Me: Rev. James Cleveland
A live performance with the Northern and Southern Community choirs of the G.M.W.A. 60 mins.
VHS: S21616. $29.95.

Clark Sisters
A live concert by the Clark sisters recorded at the World of Faith Christian Center in Detroit. 85 mins.
VHS: S21617. $29.95.

Clouds of Joy
A live concert by the Mighty Clouds of Joy. 60 mins.
VHS: S21618. $24.95.

Commissioned in Concert
A concert at the State Theatre in Detroit. With a special appearance by Derrick Brinkley. 90 mins.
VHS: S21619. $29.95.

D.F.W. Mass: "I Will Let Nothing Separate Me"
Includes "I Will Say Yes to The Lord", "Don't Give Up" and other songs.
VHS: S21620. $29.95.

Douglas Miller Live in Houston
Shirley Caesar, Dr. Bobby Jones and Sarah Jordan Powell, as well as many other gospel singers, join Miller for this inspiring concert. Miller is backed by a choir featuring Houston's best singers in songs like "We Are the Ones", "Hold On", "Power", "My Strength" and many more.
VHS: S26223. $14.95.

Down Memory Lane: Rev. James Cleveland
Recorded live at the Mount Pigsah Baptist Church in Chicago. Also features Inez Andrews, Albertina Walker and the Barnet Sisters. 60 mins.
VHS: S21621. $29.95.

Dr. Charles G. Hayes and the Cosmopolitan Church of Prayer
Includes "I'll Never Forget", "My Soul Cries Out" and "Step Back Let God Do It".
VHS: S21622. $29.95.

Florida Mass Choir: "Higher Hope"
Recorded live in Lakeland, Florida. Features the songs "Higher Hope", "Waymaker" and "I Found the Answer." USA, 1990.
VHS: S21623. $29.95.

Florida Mass Choir: "Now I Can See"
Recorded live in Lakeland, Florida, with Rev. Arthur T. Jones. 60 mins.
VHS: S21624. $29.95.

Georgia Mass Choir: "I Sing Because I'm Happy"
Recorded live at the Greater Rising Star Baptist Church. USA, 1993.
VHS: S21625. $29.95.

Glory of Gospel, Vol. 1
Talented young Gospel performers from choirs and colleges across the U.S. perform. 60 mins.
VHS: S21626. $29.95.

Glory of Gospel, Vol. 2
Revival themes and the rhythm of African song are explored. 60 mins.
VHS: S21627. $29.95.

Glory of Gospel, Vol. 3
Part 3 continues with performances by a new generation of Gospel singers. 60 mins.
VHS: S21628. $29.95.

Glory of Gospel, Vol. 4
The U.S. Airforce Choir, Rutgers University Choir and others perform. 60 mins.
VHS: S21629. $29.95.

Gospel
"There is great energy, joy, and faith in this movie... The performers' singing gives glory to the Lord and what we get is very unselfconscious, unrestrained, joyous music" (Roger Ebert). With Edwin Hawkins, The Mighty Clouds of Joy, and Rev. James Cleveland.
VHS: S00519. $39.95.
Leivick/Ritzenberg, USA, 1982, 92 mins.

Gospel Keynotes Live
Filmed at Jackson State University.
VHS: S21630. $29.95.

Gospel's Best from Saturday Night Sing
Culled from the syndicated TV show, these clips offer some of gospel's greatest performers singing their best-known works. The Williams Brothers' "Lord How I Depend on You", Ricky Dillard's "Lift Up Jesus", Daniebelle Hall's "O Se Baba", Daryl Coley's "I'll Be with You", The Fairfield Four's "Swing Down, Chariot", Albertina Walker's "I Can Go to God in Prayer" and other famous Gospel songs are joined on this tape. 45 mins.
VHS: S21327. $14.95.

Greatest Week in Gospel
Marvin and Rickie Johns, Soul Stirrers, Nicholas, The Five Blind Boys, Commissioned, Pop Staples, Higher Dimensions and Deleon all appear.
Part 1. 80 mins.
VHS: S21631. $29.95.
Part 2. 80 mins.
VHS: S21632. $29.95.
Part 3. 80 mins.
VHS: S21633. $29.95.
Part 4. 80 mins.
VHS: S21634. $29.95.

Hallelujah: A Gospel Celebration
The original Five Blind Boys, Inez Andrews and Bishop Kelsey star in this piece of gospel music history. Filmed in 1965 in a cathedral in Germany, this was the first black gospel performance in Europe. 60 mins.
VHS: S14610. $19.95.

Heavenly Host and The Sons of Calvary
Celebration, spectacle and spiritual enlightenment are the themes of this program, with live concert footage of the two Georgia-based gospel acts moving through the South, spreading their words and music.
VHS: S17498. $39.95.

Homecoming
Willie Neal Johnson, the Gospel Keynotes, Robert Blair and the Fantastic Violinaires, the Jackson Southernaires and the Williams Brothers all appear. 55 mins.
VHS: S21635. $29.95.

How Great Thou Art
This program celebrates the wonder of God's country through a unique combination of visual grandeur and favorite hymns. The highlights are a magnificent Haleakala Volcano represented by "How Great Thou Art"; white water rapids and waterfalls viewed to the strains of "Deep River"; a beautiful shot of a full moon overlooking Zion National Park contrasted with "Nearer, My God, to Thee"; the snow-capped landscapes of Yosemite National Park giving way to a haunting rendition of "Ave Maria"; and the surf cascading against the rocks of California's Big Sur to "Ode to Joy". 57 mins.
Laser: LD72249. $34.95.

Jackson Southernaires
Recorded live at Jackson State University in Mississippi. Features the songs "What Shall I Render" and "What a Friend We Have in Jesus." USA, 1987.
VHS: S21637. $29.95.

Jesus Paid It All
Recorded live in Atlanta, GA, this tape features Rev. Donald Vails and Rev. R.L. White. USA, 120 mins.
VHS: S21638. $29.95.

L. Barnes & Red Budd Choir: So Satisfied
Recorded at the Center Stage Theater in Atlanta. 55 mins.
VHS: S21639. $24.95.

L.A. Mass Choir
The L.A. Mass Choir is captured live in Anaheim with a guest appearance by Higher Dimension. USA, 60 mins.
VHS: S21640. $29.95.

Mahalia Jackson
Mahalia Jackson and *Elizabeth Cotten* are paired here in a duo of filmed biographies of these remarkable ladies. Returning to her origins in New Orleans, Mahalia sings such favorites as "Down by the Riverside" and "A Close Walk with Thee," while the over-80, incomparable Miss Cotten presents her original version of "Freight Train."
VHS: S03967. $64.95.

Mahalia Jackson: "Give God the Glory"
Mahalia Jackson's final tour of Europe is the setting for this documentary which studies the singer's life and music. 88 mins.
VHS: S21636. $29.95.

Matters of the Heart
Commissioned is a fresh gospel group that brings new vigor to their message with help from pop greats like Run D.M.C. In this video they perform their acclaimed songs "Work on Me", "Stand", "Love Is the Way" and "Dare to Believe", as well as many others.
VHS: S22094. $14.95.

McDonald's Gospelfest
Marilyn McCoo and Glynn Turman host this gospel celebration. Featuring Edwin Hawkins, Daryl Coley, and The Conquerors.
Part 1. 60 mins.
VHS: S21641. $24.95.
Part 2. 60 mins.
VHS: S21642. $24.95.

Mississippi Mass Choir
Recorded live at the Mississippi State Coliseum. USA, 120 mins.
VHS: S21643. $29.95.

Mississippi Mass Choir: God Gets the Glory
USA.
VHS: S21644. $29.95.

New Jersey Mass Choir
The New Jersey Mass Choir is filmed live at the Aaron Davis Hall in New York City. With Donnie Harper and the New Jersey Mass Choir. USA, 1992, 60 mins.
VHS: S21645. $29.95.

New York Restoration Choir: Thank You Jesus
Includes "We Worship You", "Lamb of God" and "Ain't That Love".
VHS: S21646. $29.95.

Oh Happy Day
A foot stampin', hand clappin' reach for the heavens in these live performances of gospel music superstars, including Shirley Caesar, The Mighty Clouds of Joy, Walter Hawkins and the Hawkins Family, Rev. James Cleveland and The Clark Sisters. 60 mins.
VHS: S07175. $29.95.

Parade of Stars
A four part series featuring the work of Gospel's greatest.
Vol. 1. 60 mins.
VHS: S21648. $29.95.
Vol. 2. 1989, 60 mins.
VHS: S21649. $29.95.
Vol. 3. 1990, 60 mins.
VHS: S21650. $29.95.
Vol. 4: Live Gospel. 1990, 60 mins.
VHS: S21651. $29.95.

Pentecostal Community Choir with Minister Keith Pringle
Includes "No Greater Love", "Help Him Lift Me Up" and others.
VHS: S21652. $29.95.

Pilgrim Jubilees
Recorded live in Jackson, Mississippi. Includes "We're the People" and "Feel the World".
VHS: S21653. $29.95.

Rev. Clay Evans: I'm Going Through
Recorded live at the Fellowship Baptist Church in Chicago.
VHS: S21658. $29.95.

Rev. Ernest Davis, Jr., and the Wilmington Chester Mass Choir: "He's Preparing Me"
Recorded live at the Church of Atlanta Lighthouse. 80 mins.
VHS: S21656. $29.95.

Rev. F.C. Barnes and Co.
A live performance from Atlanta.
VHS: S21654. $24.95.

Rev. James Cleveland and the L.A. Gospel Messengers
Includes "We're on Business for The King", "Great Things" and others.
VHS: S21655. $29.95.

Rev. James Moore: Live with The Mississippi Mass Choir
Includes "We Worship Christ The Lord", "God Don't Need No Matches" and "God Will Take Care of You". 80 mins.
VHS: S21657. $29.95.

Rick Grundy Chorale
Video performances by Gospels recent stars include "I'm Standin' Here" and "Just Say the Word". 60 mins.
VHS: S21659. $24.95.

Roots of Gospel
The New World Gospel Choir performs in Biblical locations.
Part 1. 60 mins.
VHS: S21660. $24.95.
Part 2. 45 mins.
VHS: S21661. $24.95.

Say Amen, Somebody
A joy filled celebration of gospel music! "It's one of the happiest movies in a long, long time. There is no way that I can recommend it any more highly," said Roger Ebert.
VHS: S01162. $29.95.
George Nierenberg, USA, 1983, 100 mins.

The Sensational Nightingales: Ministry in Song
Includes "Nichodemus", "It's Gonna Rain" and "Ain't That Love".
VHS: S21662. $29.95.

Songs Are Free
A new Bill Moyers special on the power of song, with guest Bernice Johnson Reagon—the founder and artistic director of the a cappella vocal group Sweet Honey in the Rock. Performer, activist, songwriter and scholar, Reagon demonstrates for Moyers her belief that "When we sing, we announce our existence. Singing is running this sound through your body. You cannot sing a song and not change your condition." Singing is everywhere in the documentary—in performances, educational workshops, and archival film clips of a young Reagon and "women warriors" like Fannie Lou Hamer and Ella Baker who led the Civil Rights movement. Reagon sings several old favorites and recounts the role they have played in her own remarkable life. 60 mins.
VHS: S13651. $19.95.

T'ain't Nothin' Changed
A musical look back at the history of Gospel. Features Dr. Mattie Moss Clark. 60 mins.
VHS: S21663. $29.95.

Tramaine Hawkins
Feature "I'll Give It to You", "Praise the Name of Jesus" and other songs. 90 mins.
VHS: S21664. $24.95.

Walter Hawkins and Love Alive IV
Includes "Solid Rock", "I Can't Bear It", "He Knows" and other songs. 1990, 60 mins.
VHS: S21665. $29.95.

Wanda Nero Butler: New Born Soul
The award-winning gospel singer is captured live in San Francisco. Special guest appearance by Arvis Strickling Jones. 60 mins.
VHS: S21666. $29.95.

Williams Brothers: "I'm Just a Nobody"
Recorded live at Jackson State University, Mississippi. Includes "I'm Just a Nobody", "He'll Understand" and "Jesus Made a Way".
VHS: S21667. $29.95.

Willie Banks and the Messengers
"For the Wrong I've Done", "Hear Me When I Call" and "God Is Still in Charge" are performed along with other songs. 60 mins.
VHS: S21668. $29.95.

Willie Neal Johnson and the New Keynotes: "The Country Boy Goes Home"
Recorded with the Tyler Chapter Choir in Tyler, Texas. Includes "With God I'm Satisfied" and "Hold On".
VHS: S21669. $29.95.

The Winans: Live in Concert
A live performance featuring Vanessa Bell Armstrong. 120 mins.
VHS: S21670. $29.95.

The Winans: Return
Grammy winners The Winans sing selections from their Gospel hit album *Return*. Includes "It's Time" and "Friend of Mine". 81 mins.
VHS: S21671. $24.95.

JAZZ, BLUES AND R&B

40 Years of MJQ
The Modern Jazz Quartet got their start in a seemingly unlikely place. They met while working for the bebop big band of Dizzy Gillespie. Since their formation, this quartet has continued to pursue a unique and dignified style influenced by both classical and jazz greats. "Sketch," "Alexander's Fugue," "Adagio from Concierto de Aranjuez" and "A Day in Dubrovnik" are among the selections included on this video. 58 mins.
VHS: S24066. $19.98.

Abbey Lincoln: You Gotta Pay the Band
In its 5-star review of Abbey Lincoln's album of the same name, *Down Beat* stated, "Lady Day and Pres must have revisited Earth the day this record was made." The video edition features live and studio versions of the songs on the album, as well as clips of the 1950s and 1960s movies in which Abbey starred. Also includes interviews with Stan Getz, Tony Bennett, Ruth Brown and Spike Lee. 58 mins.
VHS: S15713. $24.95.
Laser: LD70283. $19.95.

Accent on the Offbeat
Jazz original Wynton Marsalis and choreographer Peter Martins joined forces to produce this unusual dance performance. Both the intimate collaborative process and the final performance employing the New York City Ballet on the stage of Lincoln Center are included in this amazing chronicle.
VHS: S21074. $24.98.

After Hours
Coleman Hawkins, Roy Eldridge, Cozy Cole. 27 mins.
VHS: S03192. $24.95.

Airto & Flora Purim: The Latin Jazz All Stars
The infectious sounds and rhythms of Brazilian jazz are showcased in this 1985 Queen Mary Jazz Festival. The highlight is the virtuoso percussionist Airto Moreira and the six-octave vocalist Flora Purim backed by an 11-piece group, including saxophonist Joe Farrel and the Batucaje Dance Troupe. 60 mins.
VHS: S04341. $29.95.

Albert King
Albert King's musical influences are seen and heard in the classic numbers "Blues Riff", "The Grass Ain't No Greener", "Born under a Bad Sign", "They Call It Stormy Monday" and "Let the Good Times Roll".
VHS: S19681. $19.95.

Alberta Hunter (Smithsonian Jazz Series)
The Grand Lady of the Blues, the late Alberta Hunter, is featured in this toe-tapping concert taped at the Smithsonian Institute. Alberta's down-and-dirty blues and tender ballads are performed with her trademark sass and sensitivity.
VHS: S05421. $29.95.

Alberta Hunter: My Castle's Rocking
An impressionistic portrait of the legendary singer and songwriter, including "Downhearted Blues", "Handy Man", the music of Armstrong and her final interview. "Exhilarating and moving" (*L.A. Times*). 59 mins.
VHS: S17611. $19.98.

America's Music: Blues 1
Utilizes interviews with the artists, stills, film clips of Bessie Smith and others, and rousing performances from Linda Hopkins (St. Louis Blues), B.B. King, Leata Galloway, Eddie Cleanhead Vinson, Erne Andrews, Vi Redd, "Pee Wee" Crayton. 60 mins.
VHS: S05032. $19.95.

America's Music: Blues 2
Brock Peters narrates the second volume of the birth of the blues, featuring such blues greats as Joe Williams, Paula Kelly, Esther Phillips, Bobby McGee, Buddy Guy and Junior Wells, Dorothy Donigan, Joe Williams and Addie, with film clips of Mamie Smith, Count Basie and Big Joe Turner. 60 mins.
VHS: S05033. $19.95.

America's Music: Jazz Then Dixieland 1
Al Hirt hosts this look at Dixieland, with film clips and stills, and performances by Woody Herman, Clora Bryant, Scotty Plummer, Della Reese, Al Hirt, Johnny Guarnieri. 60 mins.
VHS: S05038. $19.95.

America's Music: Jazz Then Dixieland 2
Al Hirt continues with music by Bob Crosby, The Hessions, Scatman Crothers, Al Hirt, Teddy Buckner, Judy Carmichael, Irma Thomas. 60 mins.
VHS: S05039. $19.95.

America's Music: Rhythm and Blues 1
Billy Eckstine hosts this look at rhythm and blues, with featured artists including Eckstine, Ruth Brown, Billy Preston, Gloria Lynne, Sheer Delight, and film clips of Amos Milburn, Louis Mordan and Scatman Crothers. 60 mins.
VHS: S05034. $19.95.

America's Music: Rhythm and Blues 2
Brock Peters hosts the second volume of the rhythm and blues series which features Brook Benton, Scatman Crothers, Mary Wells, O.C. Smith, Sam Moore, and film clips of Slim Gaillard. 60 mins.
VHS: S05035. $19.95.

America's Music: Soul 1
Host Leon Kennedy documents the evolution of soul from rhythm and blues through the music of James Brown. With Brown's "Rap Payback," "Jam," Ben E. King's "Spanish Harlem," "I Who Have Nothing," May Bond Davis' "This Is It," Tyrone Davis' "Turn Back the Hands of Time" and "Turning Point," Maxine Nightingale's "Lead Me On," "I Don't Miss You At All" and "Right Back Where We Started From," Tyrone Davis' "In the Mood," and James Brown's "The Man Understand." 60 mins.
VHS: S05040. $19.95.

America's Music: Soul 2
Leon Kennedy continues his documentation of soul music with Gladys Knight and the Pips "I Will Fight," "Best Thing That Ever Happened," "Midnight Train to Georgia," Rufus Thomas' "Do the Push and Pull," "Walking the Dog," Carla Thomas' "I Like What You Do To Me," Jerry Butler's "Hey Western Union Man," Freda Payne's "Band of Gold," "Bring the Boys Home," Percy Sledge's "You Had to Be There," Gladys Knight and the Pips' "Save the Overtime," "Neither One of Us." 60 mins.,
VHS: S05041. $19.95.

And This Is Free
Chicago's Maxwell Street Market is captured in its entirety through cinema verite techniques in this unique film. The filmmaker originally set out to capture blues singers, but he realized that the whole area contained a much fuller picture that could explain the blues. Since Maxwell Street has been transformed by urban renewal, this may be the only way to see the singular mix of people and music that this area once offered. B&W.
VHS: S27154. $19.95.
Mike Shea, USA, 1964, 50 mins.

Anything for Jazz
A portrait of Jaki Bayrd, pianist, composer and band leader. 25 mins.
VHS: S03184. $19.95.

Archie Shepp: I Am Jazz...It's My Life
One of the most controversial figures on the jazz scene is captured pontificating on his favorite subjects—the African origins and revolutionary purpose of jazz, the social invisibility and isolation of blacks—but in the film's club sequences Shepp, whether on tenor or soprano sax or shouting his poems of protest, swings like bad and expertly builds his solos to an exciting climax. With Siegfried Kessler piano, Wilbur Little bass, Don Mumford and Clifford Jarvis drums and Cheikh Tidiane Fall percussion.
VHS: S12332. $19.95.
Frank Cassenti, France/USA, 1984, 52 mins.

Aretha Franklin: Live at Park West
From the PBS Series *Soundstage*, Aretha Franklin performs many of her soul gold hits, including "Think", "Respect" and "Rock Steady". 60 mins.
VHS: S20491. $19.98.
Laser: LD74840. $29.99.

Arhoolie Records' 25th Anniversary Party
27 songs in thrilling live performance fill this anniversary concert celebrating Arhoolie Records' first quarter century of recording great down-home American music. Features J.C. Burris, Los Campesinos de Michoacan, Dick Oxtot's Golden Age Jazz Band, Charlie Misselwhite Blues Band, Rose Maddox, Michael Doucet, Ann Savoy, Danny Poullard and Cajun All Stars, Katie Webster with Juke Joint Johnny and the Hot Links. 120 mins.
VHS: S10358. $39.98.

Art and Jazz in America
A four volume series by Faith and John Hubley.
Art and Jazz in America: John and Faith Hubley's Of Men and Demons. Quincy Jones composed the masterful score for this striking animated film about a simple farmer. This farmer confronts nature with a barrage of technical measures. Also included: *Of Stars and Men*, a short film about man and the universe set to music from Bach, Beethoven, Handel, Mozart and Vivaldi. 65 mins.
VHS: S24277. $19.95.
Art and Jazz in America: John and Faith Hubley's The Hole. The title film won an Academy Award. It is about two construction workers debating the fate of the world. Dizzy Gillespie and George Matthews provide the voices for these animated characters. *The Hat* is a similar short animated film featuring Gillespie and Dudley Moore as soldiers patrolling a border. In *Dig* Quincy Jones provides the score while Maureen Stapleton and Jack Warden provide the voices for a fantasy about a boy, his dog and their unique adventure. 58 mins.
VHS: S24278. $19.95.
Art and Jazz in America: John and Faith Hubley's Voyage to Next. The title animated film was nominated for an Academy Award. It features the voices of Maureen Stapleton and Dizzy Gillespie as Mother Earth and Father Time. Gillespie also supplies the music. Five other short films are included: *Tender Game*, *Eggs*, *Urbanissmo*, *Harlem Wednesday* and *Adventures of an* *. Music by Benny Carter, Ella Fitzgerald, Lionel Hampton and others. 51 mins.
VHS: S24279. $19.95.

fine arts on video

Art and Jazz in America: The Cosmic Eye. Faith Hubley devised this amazing animated tale about alien musicians who bring a message of peace to the earth. The observations of these creatures yield a variety of perspectives about the nature of our planet. Music by Benny Carter and others. 72 mins.
VHS: S24276. $19.95.

Art Blakey (Smithsonian Jazz Series)
Superstar siblings Wynton and Branford Marsalis join the amazing drummer Art Blakey in this hard bop concert at the Smithsonian. Grammy-winner Wynton solos in Kurt Weill's "My Ship," demonstrating the trumpet virtuosity that has made him one of the best-selling jazz artists of all time.
VHS: S05425. $29.95.

Art Blakey and the Jazz Messengers: The Jazz Life
Fuller Love, Little Man, My Ship, New York, Gypsy Folktales, The Theme. Recorded live at Seventh Avenue South, and featuring Wynton Marsalis. 55 mins.
VHS: S07742. $29.95.

Art Ensemble of Chicago: Live from the Jazz Showcase
Members of the quintet perform in quasi-African costumes, masks and face paint, surrounded by two tons of instruments, all the while sharing musical and visual jokes as they go caroming through the history of jazz. The show touches on be-bop, New Orleans jazz, 1960's funk and a ballad, amid percussion interludes. 50 mins.
VHS: S12333. $19.95.

Art Farmer (Smithsonian Jazz Series)
Few trumpeters have ever made their instrument sound as tender as Art Farmer, as this concert video clearly proves. Pianist Fred Hersch, bassist Dennis Irwin and drummer Billy Hart accompany Farmer as he spins his wistful magic around a group of classic ballads.
VHS: S05429. $29.95.

At the Jazz Band Ball
Some of the greatest music, song and dance from the jazz age is captured on sound film between 1925-1933. Duke Ellington's Cotton Club Orchestra, Louis Armstrong, Bill "Bojangles" Robinson, Bessie Smith and the Dorsey Brothers are included in this collection of music legends. Bix Beiderbecke's only appearance on sound film has been found and added to this tape. 60 mins.
VHS: S23059. $19.95.

B.B. King Live at Nick's
From the beginning there has always been just one king of the Blues, B.B. King. This legendary singer is taped live at Nick's in Dallas, proving, as if it needed proving, that the thrill is not gone. 50 mins.
VHS: S21063. $14.95.

B.B. King Live in Africa
B.B. King performs a classic hour of Blues in a legendary performance in Africa, including "Ain't Nobody Home," "The Thrill Is Gone," and "Sweet Sixteen." 52 mins.
VHS: S11701. $19.95.

Barney Kessel 1962-1991
Kessel's legendary guitar music is one of the most original voices produced by jazz. This video captures 30 years of his performances with a number of jazz greats. In the span of his career he played with Lester Young, Charlie Parker, Billie Holiday, Art Tatum and other famed jazz greats.
VHS: S24219. $19.95.

Barry Harris: Passing It On
A musical portrait of Barry Harris, pianist and teacher. 23 mins.
VHS: S03190. $29.95.

Beale Street
Beale Street is where W.C. Handy wrote the blues, where Boss Crump abused his power, and where Martin Luther King marched days before his death in 1968. Beale Street has been the victim of urban renewal, and this film is a unique oral history of the street. Among the Beale Streeters featured are B.B. King, the Hooks Brothers, Bobby Blue Bland, Prince Gabe, Maurice "Fess" Hulbert, and Rufus Thomas.
VHS: S07770. $39.95.
Krasilovsky/Rickey/Baldwin, USA, 1981, 28 mins.

Ben Webster: The Brute and the Beautiful
A fascinating look at the legendary jazz saxophonist Ben Webster. The film traces his origins in Kansas City in the 1920s, his collaborations with Duke Ellington, Benny Carter, Teddy Wilson, Gerry Mulligan and Jimmy Witherspoon, and his European exile and final performance in Holland, in September, 1973. 60 mins.
VHS: S17964. $24.95.

Benny Carter (Smithsonian Jazz Series)
The legendary composer/arranger/trumpeter/saxophonist performs jazz standards like "Misty" and "Take the A Train." Carter, 74 years young at the time, performs with a quintet that also features Kenny Barron on piano and George Duvivier on bass.
VHS: S05426. $29.95.

Benny Carter: Symphony in Riffs
Winner of the Grammy Lifetime Achievement Award, Benny Carter is known as a principal architect of the Big Band sound. Lena Horne, Dizzy Gillespie, Andre Previn, Ella Fitzgerald, David Sanborn and Quincy Jones are just some of the personalities who contribute to this loving portrait of Carter.
VHS: S26787. $24.95.
Harrison Engle, USA, 1989, 58 mins.

Benny Goodman: At the Tivoli
A filmed concert from the Tivoli Gardens in Copenhagen, where Benny Goodman performs "Lady Be Good," "I Should Care," "Send in the Clowns," "Airmail Special Delivery," "The World Is Waiting" and "For the Sunrise." Goodman is accompanied by violinist Sven Osmussen, drummer Charly Antolini, pianist Don Haas, trumpet player Jimmy Maxwell, guitarist Harry Pepe and bassist Peter Witte. 50 mins.
VHS: S19004. $29.95.

Big Ben: Ben Webster in Europe
A world of heart, tenderness and terror is the world of Big Ben Webster in this picture of the extraordinary musician who played tenor sax in nearly every great band of the thirties and forties, including the Kansas City bands of Andy Kirk and Benny Moten and his long association with Duke Ellington. Music includes "My Romance", "Perdido", "You'd Be So Nice to Come Home To".
VHS: S12334. $19.95.
Johan van der Keuken, Holland, 1967, 31 mins.

The Bill Evans Trio
Bill Evans is joined by Marc Johnson and Joe La Barbera in this video of outstanding jazz performances.
VHS: S26788. $19.95.
John Beyer, USA, 1979, 58 mins.

Bix
This famed trumpeter revolutionized jazz. In this first-rate musical biography his life and times are recreated based on the known facts. He is seen playing in some of the original locations including spots throughout the Midwest where Bix began. Hoagey Carmichael and Pee Wee Russel are just some of the figures seen accompanying him, performing songs like "Dardenella" and "Stardust." In English.
VHS: S20939. $29.95.
Pupi Avati, Italy/USA, 1990, 100 mins.

Black Jazz and Blues
Three short films: The St. Louis Blues featuring Bessie Smith (1929), Duke Ellington and Billie Holiday in Symphony in Black, and Louis Jordan with the Fletcher Henderson Orchestra in Caldonia. USA, 44 mins.
VHS: S02237. $24.95.

Black Moses of Soul
Isaac Hayes and The Movement serve up a heaping order of Hot Buttered Soul in this live performance which includes such classic songs as "I Stand Accused", The Jackson 5's "Never Can Say Goodbye" and a soulful rendition of The Doors' "Light My Fire." 80 mins.
VHS: S14941. $19.95.

Blues Legends: Son House & Bukka White
Filmed in the 60s, these performances communicate the power and eloquence of legendary blues masters. Introduced by Taj Mahal.
VHS: S15515. $29.95.

Blues Like Shower of Rain
Country blues through historic photographs and field recordings, featuring Paul Oliver. 30 mins.
VHS: S03185. $24.95.

Blues Masters, Vol. 1
An encyclopedic account of the history, personalities and evolution of the American blues masters, including Son House, Leadbelly, Bessie Smith, Mamie Smith, Roy Milton and His Orchestra, Jimmy Rushing, Ethel Waters and Big Bill Broonzy. The documentary merges archival recording footage and photographs. The highlight is a raucous version of "St. Louis Blues" by Leadbelly and Bessie Smith. 51 mins.
VHS: S19163. $19.98.

Blues Masters, Vol. 2
A compendium of vintage performers is a highlight reel of the greatest blues musicians of their era. This program explores the gifts and personal drive that contributed to their distinctive sounds and charismatic voices. Blending archival performance footage and rare photographs, the show spotlights Ida Cox, Billie Holiday, Big Mama Thornton, Muddy Waters, Joe Turner, Joe Williams, Buddy Guy, Jimmy Witherspoon and B.B. King. 51 mins.
VHS: S19164. $19.98.

Blues Up the Country
Diverse country traditions from the Mississippi Delta to the Piedmont region are captured on this collection of country blues. Taped between 1962 and 1970, it reveals a musical landscape which nurtured artists like John Jackson, Pink Anderson, Jesse Fuller and Ethel & George McCoy.
VHS: S26428. $24.95.

Bluesland: A Portrait in American Music
This complete visual history of the blues is hosted by Keith David and includes appearances by Robert Palmer and Albert Murray. Musical footage of legendary greats Bessie Smith, B.B. King, Muddy Waters, Dinah Washington and many more is included. 90 mins.
VHS: S23324. $29.98.
Laser: LD74753. $39.98.

Bob James Live
The gifted pianist and composer Bob James fronts an eclectic septet showcasing Kirk Whalum, performing "Taxi", "Zebra Man", "Unicorn" and "Ruby" at the 1985 Queen Mary Jazz Festival. 56 mins.
VHS: S19227. $19.98.

Bobby Short at the Cafe Carlyle
The darling of cafe society singer/pianist with his lively interpretations of Tin Pan Alley songs. 65 mins.
VHS: S03384. $29.95.

Boogie in Blue
An ebullient, lively and colorful documentary biography of Harry "the Hipster" Gibson, called "the mad boogie woogie genius" of his era. The film interweaves performance material, archival photography and interviews with Gibson and his family to present a textured portrait of the man and his music. Directed by Gibson's daughter Arlena Gibson and granddaughter Flavyn Feller. 40 mins.
VHS: S17914. $24.95.

Born to Swing
Count Basie alumni Buddy Tate, Jo Jones and Gene Krupa. 50 mins.
VHS: S03193. $19.95.

Branford Marsalis: Steep
Powerful live performances and insightful interviews with soprano/tenor player Branford Marsalis, a rising star in the jazz world. Performances include "Swingin' at the Haven", "Crescent City", "Lament", "Giant Steps" and many more. USA, 89 mins.
VHS: S15309. $14.98.

Buddy Barnes
I've Been to Town, Don't Fight It, It's Chemistry, Color of My Life, My Ship, Pick Yourself Up, Long Before I Knew You, Guess I'll Hang My Tears Out to Dry, and Penny by Penny. 30 mins.
VHS: S05424. $19.95.

Built by Hand String Trio
Three musicians from New York want to "take the audience on a trip." Charles Burnham on violin, James Emery on guitar and John Lindberg on bass make up the String Trio of New York, and with this tape you can experience their unique, frantic, acoustic psychedelia. Songs include "Wise Old Owl Blues", "Texas Koto Blues", "Multiple Reasons" and "Seven Vice". 30 mins.
VHS: S12335. $24.95.

Carla Bley and Steve Swallow: Very, Very Simple
This duo play the bass and piano in their own inimical way. Their long working relationship and friendship ensure the audience a captivating experience. They play as one without the help of a conductor, which means that together they achieve a special, intimate stage of rapport with their listeners. "Soon I Will Be Done with the Troubles of the World," "Lawns," and "Very, Very Simple" are included in this video. 32 mins.
VHS: S24065. $19.98.

Carmen McRae Live
Jazz's legendary lady gives a supreme vocal performance of 21 standards, including "That Old Black Magic", "I Get Along without You Very Well," "Thou Swell", "But Not for Me" and "What a Little Moonlight Can Do". 82 mins.
VHS: S12011. $39.95.
Laser: LD70332. $39.95.

Carnegie Hall Salutes the Jazz Masters
Betty Carter, Al Foster, Pat Metheny, Herbie Hancock, Roy Hargrove, Bruce Hornsby and Yosuke Yamashita are just some of the artists who performed during this historic concert. 120 mins.
VHS: S21298. $24.95.
Laser: LD72423. $34.94.

Celebrating Bird: The Triumph of Charlie Parker
The only authorized documentary on the late, great Charlie Parker, tracing his beginnings in Kansas City to his final years in New York, featuring interviews with friends, family, colleagues, as well as archival clips and historic performances of "Confirmation," "Ballade," "A Night in Tunisia," "Just Friends," and more. 58 mins.
VHS: S05401. $29.95.

Chester Zardis: The Spirit of New Orleans
A colorful documentary on the life and art of the revolutionary African-American bassist Chester Zardis, who is seen playing in concert with Danny Barker, Louis Nelsom, Jeanette Kimball, Wendell Brunious and Dr. Michael White. Leading jazz authorities Alan Lomax and William Russell contribute their insights and assessments of Zardis's work.
VHS: S19124. $29.95.
Preston McClanahan, USA, 1989, 88 mins.

Chicago Blues
A fascinating study of Chicago Blues, including Johnnie Lewis, Muddy Waters, Buddy Guy, Junior Wells and H.B. Hutto, with narration and comments by Dick Gregory.
VHS: S00232. $19.95.
Harley Cokliss, Great Britain, 1972, 50 mins.

Chick Corea Keyboard Workshop
A private lesson with Chick Corea. From Bach's "Goldberg Variations" to his own "Yellow Nimbus", musicians learn methods of composition, improvisation and practice. 60 mins.
VHS: S11523. $39.95.

Chick Corea: Electric Workshop
Chick Corea, Grammy Award-winning keyboardist, guides viewers through the entire composition process, from conception to the finished composition. 60 mins.
VHS: S11522. $39.95.

Chico Hamilton: The Jazz Life
The Theme, Encore, Sweet Dreams Too Soon, The Baron, Space for Stacy, First Light, Clinton Avenue, Erika. 53 mins.
VHS: S05417. $29.95.

Cobham Meets Bellson
All-star drummers Billy Cobham and Louie Bellson face off and alternate in virtuosity. 36 mins.
VHS: S03382. $19.98.

Coltrane Legacy
An hour-long compilation of precious jazz clips that show the reasons for the enormous impact John Coltrane continues to have on the world of jazz.
VHS: S04619. $39.95.

Curtis Mayfield: Live at Ronnie Scott's
One of Curtis Mayfield's last performances before a paralyzing accident, the founding member of the legendary Impressions performs "Little Child Running Wild", "It's Alright", "People Get Ready" and "We Gotta Have Peace". 58 mins.
VHS: S20492. $19.98.

Dave Holland Quartet: Vortex
Dave Holland and his crew—Steve Coleman, Smitty Smith, Kenny Wheeler and Robin Eubanks—join forces for this unique jazz experience. "Vortex", "Homecoming" and "Wiguts Waits for Watts" are three tunes that give these musicians a chance to demonstrate their amazing virtuosity. 62 mins.
VHS: S26039. $19.98.

David, Moffet, Ornette
In the spring of 1966 Ornette Coleman wrote and recorded the soundtrack for a Living Theatre project called Who's Crazy?. This film is a record of the three days Ornette spent in the studio making music with virtuoso bass-player David Izenzon and drummer Charles Moffet. The film explores the strength and clarity which three individuals working together can bring to the search for freedom in jazz.
VHS: S07749. $19.95.
Dick Fontaine, USA, 1966, 26 mins.

The Dexter Gordon Quartet
Dexter Gordon, the star of 'Round Midnight, plays alongside his companions George Cables, Rufus Reid and Eddie Gladden. Together they create an unforgettable jazz performance on this videotape.
VHS: S26790. $19.95.
John Beyer, USA, 1979, 58 mins.

Diana Ross Live
Diana Ross reinterprets the works of Billie Holiday, Rodgers and Hart, George Gershwin and Count Basie. Includes "God Bless the Child," "My Man", "Good Morning Heartache" and "The Man I Love" in a 1992 New York concert.
VHS: S18319. $19.95.
Laser: LD71856. $34.95.
Steve Binder, USA, 1992, 90 mins.

Different Drummer: Elvin Jones
A portrait of Elvin Jones with rare footage of John Coltrane. 30 mins.
VHS: S03189. $24.95.

Discovering Jazz
Black American 19th-century traditions are the source of jazz. Rhythmic and melodic innovations transformed European music into an exciting new form. From Dixieland and the blues to swing and bop, jazz is the music of the 20th century. 21 mins.
VHS: S23509. $49.95.

Dizzy Gillespie: A Night in Chicago
In this 90-minute concert, Dizzy plays "Swing Low, Sweet Cadillac," "Embraceable You," " 'Round Midnight" and "A Night in Tunisia". 53 mins.
VHS: S19173. $19.98.

Dizzy Gillespie: A Night in Tunisia
This dazzling concert performance is followed by Dizzy discussing how Afro-Cuban rhythms altered the form of mainstream American jazz. 28 mins.
VHS: S19224. $19.98.

Dizzy Gillespie: Jazz in America
Dizzy Gillespie assisted by Ray Brown on bass and Paquito Rivera on alto sax, recorded live in Redondo Beach, California, in February 1981.
VHS: S00350. $19.95.
Stanley Dorfman, USA, 1981, 60 mins.

Dizzy Gillespie: Live in London
A concert recorded at London's Royal Festival Hall features "Manteca","A Night in Tunisia" and "Moody's Mood for Love". 91 mins.
VHS: S19002. $29.95.

Django, A Jazz Tribute
Bireli Langrene, the groundbreaking young guitarist, performs this musical tribute in honor of Django, accompanied by Django's son Babik Reinhardt. Together they negotiate the complex melodies of the jazz innovator. Django, the leader of the Hot Club of France, composed memorable songs that live on 50 years after they were first recorded. 26 mins.
VHS: S24064. $19.98.

Don Cherry's Multikulti
Together with Ornette Coleman, Cherry assumed a leading position in the jazz vanguard of the 1960's. His interpretations of centuries-old vocal traditions continue to glow. This video documents Cherry's work at the prestigious Days of Jazz in Stuttgart, Germany, and includes "Walk to the Mountain," "Bemsha Swing" and "Trans Love Airways," among others. 57 mins.
VHS: S24067. $19.98.

Dr. John Teaches New Orleans Piano
A complete two-tape series taught by Mac (Dr. John) Rebennack.
Dr. John Teaches New Orleans Piano—Part One. This great video lesson is jammed full of powerful playing, slowed-down instruction, and the wonderful personality of one of the premier artists of our time. Covered are the styles of Professor Longhair, Pine Top Smith, Fats Domino, James Booker and others. 60 mins.
VHS: S09691. $49.95.
Dr. John Teaches New Orleans Piano—Part Two. Continuing his fascinating tour through the dynamic world of New Orleans piano, Dr. John teaches the styles of Huey Piano Smith, Tuts Washington, Allen Toussaint and Mac (Dr. John) Rebennack himself. 60 mins.
VHS: S09692. $49.95.

Dr. John: New Orleans Swamp
New Orleans renegade Dr. John incorporates rhythm and blues, zydeco, Cajun, soul and voodoo refrains as he performs "Walk Right In/Shake, Rattle and Roll", "Whole Lotta Loving", "Every Day I Have the Blues", "Call a Doctor" and "Such a Night". 60 mins.
VHS: S18717. $19.98.

Duke Ellington
With his Orchestra, Duke Ellington plays "Take the A Train," "Satin Doll," "Things Aren't What They Used to Be" and other numbers. 24 mins.
VHS: S19888. $29.95.

Dukes of Dixieland and Friends
In this 75-minute video, The Dukes of Dixieland join the New Orleans Pops Orchestra in an exciting dose of New Orleans Symphonic jazz. The Dukes' program draws on a variety of New Orleans music in the intense, brassy Dixieland style.
VHS: S10150. $29.95.

Eartha Kitt: The Most Exciting Woman in the World
In a live concert performance Eartha Kitt lives up to the sobriquet coined by Orson Welles to describe her musical and performative abilities: the most exciting woman in the world. She sings "C'est Si Bon", " Here's to Life" and many other favorites, proving that she is indeed an undisputed jazz and blues legend. 60 mins.
VHS: S20940. $24.95.

Eddie Jefferson Live from Jazz Showcase
Filmed in Chicago two nights before Jefferson was shot and killed, he is accompanied here by Richie Cole's Quartet. Songs include "Moody's Mood for Love", "I Cover the Waterfront", "Night in Tunisia", "How High the Moon" and a lot more. 50 mins.
VHS: S12336. $19.39.

Elvin Jones Jazz Machine
Elvin Jones is recognized as a master drummer of jazz. Since the mid-1960's, when he played with Coltrane's groundbreaking quartet, this drummer has been looked to as a leader within this musical tradition. Sonny Fortune, Chip Jackson, Willie Pickens and Ravi Coltrane accompany Jones in this collection of unmatched musical performances. 58 mins.
VHS: S24063. $19.98.

Ernie Andrews: Blues for Central Avenue
Ernie Andrews, the blues singer, tells his own story from L.A. of the 30's and 40's, as he reminiscences about big bands, after-hours clubs, gambling, bathtub gin and the segregation that was a fact of life. As he talks about his life, he sings the blues in recent performances. With Buddy Collette and Harry (Sweets) Edison.
VHS: S07744. $39.95.
Lois Shelton, USA, 1986, 50 mins.

An Evening with Lena Horne
The legendary Lena Horne was recorded live in a spectacular birthday celebration, backed by the Count Basie orchestra, featuring her signature show stoppers "Come Runnin'", "Squeeze Me", "I've Got the World on a String" and "The Lady Is a Tramp." 72 mins.
VHS: S23569. $19.95.

The Fingerpicking Blues of John Jackson
John Jackson details the finer points of the Piedmont style of blues. Turnarounds, slide technique, runs and other elements of his own unique two-finger style are captured on this video. He also teaches several songs and provides some fascinating historical reminiscences. 60 mins.
VHS: S24870. $39.95.

Freddie King in Concert
King's expressive vocals, guitar playing, and bluesy melodic hooks give his work a powerful and individual sound. Footage from concerts given between 1970-75 is collected here to show him at his peak. This tape starts with an interview of the man who performed such hits as "Sweet Home Chicago", "Whole Lotta Love", "Ghetto Woman", "Woke Up This Morning" and many more. 58 mins.
VHS: S22485. $19.95.

Freddie King: Free Stage
On January 20, 1973, Freddie King and a quartet funked up the studio of KERA-TV in Dallas while performing for the *Free Stage* series. This performance is featured along with King describing his career. A singular portrait of King and his music is achieved through this union.
VHS: S23306. $24.98.

Freddie King: The!!!!Beat—1966
Dead at the age 42 in 1976, King still managed to create a body of unforgettable music. This collection of concert performances shows his unique blend of Southern R&B and mid-60's mod. The video concludes with three tunes performed in Sweden in 1973. 60 mins.
VHS: S22491. $19.95.

The Gadd Gang Live
Afficonados will revel in this dynamic performance of R&B-based jazz from the Gadd Gang: Steve Gadd, Eddie Gomez, Ronnie Cuber, Cornell Dupree and Richard Tee. 60 mins.
VHS: S12008. $29.95.
Laser: LD70329. $29.95.

George Shearing: Lullaby of Birdland
The only known live concert of the virtuoso jazz pianist, filmed in 1991 at the Paul Masson Winery. 56 mins.
VHS: S17610. $19.98.

Gil Evans and His Orchestra
Featuring the Brecker Brothers, Lew Soloff, Mike Mainieri and Billy Cobham, with Gil Evans and his 20-piece orchestra interpreting tunes from Gershwin, Mingus, Monk and Hendrix. 57 mins.
VHS: S03369. $29.95.

Gil Scott-Heron: Black Wax
Storm Music, Washington, D.C., Paint It Black, Waiting for the Axe to Fall, Billy Green Is Dead, Angel Dust, Fun, Winter in America, Whitey on the Moon, Alien, Black History Johannesburg, B Movie. 80 mins.
VHS: S05419. $29.95.

Good Mornin' Blues
A documentary about the evolution of country blues. Featuring the work of Bukka White, Big Joe Williams, Furry Lewis, Johnny Shines, Sam Chatmon and Gus Cannon. Recordings by Son House, Charlie Patton and Willie Brown.
VHS: S17998. $24.95.

Gospel According to Al Green
Though acclaimed for such 1970's standards as "Can't Get Next to You" and "Let's Stay Together," today Al Green is committed to Gospel music. This film shows how one of the best loved pop stars of an earlier era found a new home in the traditions of gospel music.
VHS: S26786. $24.95.
Robert Mugge, USA, 1984, 94 mins.

A Great Day in Harlem
Nominated for an Academy Award, this documentary offers a cross-section of jazz greats. In 1958, Art Kane orchestrated a group portrait of jazz musicians. Archival footage of interviews, performances and home movie footage rounds out the feeling of this day when the best jazz performers were gathered together. Art Blakey, Dizzy Gillespie, Charles Mingus, Thelonious Monk, Count Basie and Coleman Hawkins are just some of the musicians who appeared. 60 mins.
VHS: S26699. $19.95.
Laser: LD75324. $39.98.
Jean Bach, USA, 1995, 60 mins.

Great Guitarists
Charlie Byrd, Barney Kessel and Herb Ellis are the featured performers in this video on history's greatest jazz guitarists. Also featuring Joe Byrd and Wayne Phillips.
VHS: S26789. $19.95.
John Beyer, USA, 1979, 58 mins.

Great Guitars
The jazz guitar supergroup featuring Herb Ellis, Barney Kessel and Charlie Byrd displays each of these masters in a concert of inspired jazz guitar. "Outer Drive", "Favela", "Alfie", "Agua de Beber" and "Flying Home" are just some of the songs performed by these legendary musicians. 59 mins.
VHS: S22415. $19.95.

Grover Washington, Jr. in Concert
Leading jazz/pop enthusiast Grover Washington, Jr. performs "Just the Two of Us", "Winelight" and his band membersRichard Tee, Steve Gadd and Eric Gale. "Perhaps the finest audio of any home video to date" (*Billboard*). 60 mins.
VHS: S19228. $19.98.

The Guitar of Rory Block
A master interpreter of the Mississippi blues, Rory Block shows how to play some of her most requested numbers. This two-tape set is a treasure trove of guitar techniques enlivened by a great performer and her best works.
VHS: S24869. $79.95.

Gypsy Guitar: The Legacy of Django Reinhardt
This program about the gifted jazz guitarist looks at his influences in a Parisian guitar shop, a Liverpool pub, gypsy sites in Holland, and Samois-Sur-Seine, the remote French village where Reinhardt spent the final years of his life. Featured musicians include his son Babik Reinhardt, Bireli Lagrene, Gary Potter and the Gypsy Kids.
VHS: S17963. $24.95.

Hampton Hawes All Stars
Hampton Hawes, piano, Leroy Vinnegar, bass, Bobby Thompson, bass, Joe Turner, vocals, Bobby Thompson, drums, Sweets Edison, trumpet, Sonny Criss, saxophone, and Teddy Edwards, saxophone, drive through "Memory Lane Blues," "Feeling Happy", "Shake, Rattle and Roll," and "Teddy's Blues." 28 mins.
VHS: S07469. $29.95.

Harlem Hotshots
A compilation of the best rhythm and blues and jazz stars of music's golden age. Featured are Lionel Hampton in *Airmail Special*, *Love You Like Mad*, Dizzy Gillespie in *Dizzy Atmosphere*, *Boogie in C*, Ruth Brown (*Have a Good Time*), Big Joe Turner, Bill Bailey and others. 50 mins.
VHS: S04852. $24.95.

Harlem Swings Volume 1
This collection of swing greats contains performances by Eubie Blake, Don Redman, Cab Calloway, Louis Armstrong, Duke Ellington, Les Hite and other jazz bands of the 1930's.
VHS: S21420. $29.95.

Harlem Swings Volume 2
Swing greats Nat King Cole, Lionel Hampton, Sarah Vaughan, Nipsy Russel, Count Basie, Dinah Washington and more perform their classic hits. Also included are *The Nat King Cole Story*, which charts the rise of this singular entertainer, and *Basin Street Review*.
VHS: S21421. $29.95.

Harlem Swings Volume 3
In this collection, swing greats Dusty Fletcher, Ethel Waters, Louis Jordan and comedian Stepin Fetchit perform in all black cast musical comedy short subjects.
VHS: S21422. $29.95.

Harlem Swings Volume 4
This collection of Harlem greats has the Harlem Hotshots, Louis Armstrong, The Ebony Trio, Lena Horne, Lionel Hampton, Ruth Brown and others.
VHS: S21423. $29.95.

Harlem Swings Volume 5
The "Rock and Roll Review" in this volume features Duke Ellington, Larry Darnell, Coles and Atkins, The Clovers, Nat "King" Cole, Lionel Hampton, Martha Davis and others.
VHS: S21424. $29.95.

Herbie Hancock Trio: Hurricane!
One of modern jazz's brightest stars appears in this electric performance.
VHS: S16727. $19.98.

Hugh Shannon: Saloon Singer
Billie Holiday was one of his biggest fans, and here Shannon performs during a live set at David K's in New York. 55 mins.
VHS: S03386. $29.95.

Imagine the Sound
Enjoy the sounds and performances of Cecil Taylor, Archie Shepp, Paul Bley and Bill Dixon, in this exuberant profile of four legendary figures from the Free-Form Jazz world.
VHS: S13597. $39.95.
Laser: LD70315. $39.95.

Implosions
Cutting-edge work by Stanley Clarke, Randy Brecker, McCoy Tyner, Peter Erskine and more. 50 mins.
VHS: S14967. $19.95.

It's a Mean Old World & Born in the Blues
Rev. Pearly Brown and Arthur "Big Boy" Crudup are revealed in this pair of insightful portraits. Brown is a bottleneck guitarist and gospel singer, while Crudup is a blues artist. Both musicians share a musical eloquence that succeeds in touching others. 65 mins.
VHS: S26357. $19.95.

Jack Sheldon and New Orleans
Jack Sheldon and New Orleans—a portrait of one of the most original and distinctive trumpet voices in jazz. A rollicking performance shot on Bourbon Street at Lulu White's Mahogany Hall joins Jack with West Coast compatriots Dave Stone, John Pisano, Frank Capp. 60 mins.
VHS: S10153. $29.95.

Jackie McLean on Mars
Conversation and music with J. McLean. 31 mins.
VHS: S03186. $24.95.

Jammin' with the Blues Greats
English Blues met Chicago Blues and Memphis Blues at New Jersey's Capitol Theater in June of 1982. The result was a magical concert where famed blues legends from these three traditions jammed together. John Mayall's Bluesbreakers, Mick Taylor (Rolling Stones), John McVie (Fleetwood Mac), Colin Allen (Rod Stewart's Band), Albert King, Etta James, Buddy Guy, Junior Wells, and the 83 year old Sippie Wallace are all on this video. 90 mins.
VHS: S21985. $19.98.

Jazz
Earl Hines, piano and vocal, with Coleman Hawkins. 28 mins.
VHS: S05834. $19.95.

Jazz Africa: Herbie Hancock/Foday Musa Suso
Part of the *Jazzvisions* series, this program features Jazz superstar Herbie Hancock leading an ensemble of top African musicians and a few special guests. 54 mins.
VHS: S14968. $24.95.

The Jazz Age
Fred Allen narrates this look at American life between the end of the First World War and the beginning of the Depression. Morals, manners, and even the way Americans thought of themselves were profoundly altered during the Jazz Age. 60 mins.
VHS: S23056. $19.95.

Jazz Hoofer: Baby Laurence
Laurence's only filmed dancing performance. 30 mins.
VHS: S03179. $19.95.

Jazz in America: Gerry Mulligan
Gerry Mulligan is the featured artist in this great series of jazz performance tapes. 60 mins.
VHS: S03140. $19.95.

Jazz in Exile
Some of the finest American jazz musicians have been drawn to Europe, and this classic jazz documentary captures many of them: Richard Davis, Phil Woods, Dexter Gordon, Randy Weston, Johnny Griffin, and many others.
VHS: S00653. $29.95.
Chuck France, USA, 1978, 58 mins.

Jazz Is My Native Language
Vibrant, fast paced documentary gives an in-depth look at the music and life of Toshiko Akiyoshi. "No artist has yet emerged to surpass Toshiko Akiyoshi as a creative composer; her position is comparable to that of Duke Ellington or Stan Kenton in earlier years" (Leonard Feather, *Jazz Critic*).
VHS: S02647. $29.95.
Renee Cho, USA, 60 mins.

Jazz Is Our Religion
Looks at the lifestyles and attitudes of jazz musicians through the photographs and works of the British jazz journalist Valerie Wilmer. The technique is quick-cut stills, with a wave of voices—musicians Jo Jones, Dizzy Gillespie, Sunny Murray, the poet Ted Joans and others—providing a personal and often wryly knowing commentary, with music by drummer Art Blakey, saxophonist Johnny Griffin, and a group of celebrated jazz drummers.
VHS: S04168. $19.95.
Val Wilmer, Great Britain, 1985, 50 mins.

Jazz Masters: Vintage Getz
The work of Stan Getz is showcased in this program, in collaboration with virtuoso bassist Marc Johnson and drummer Victor Lewis. Volume 1 features "Over the Edge", "From the Heart", "Answer without Question", "Sippin' at Bell's" and "Tempus Fugit". Volume 2 was recorded in Paul Masson's California vineyard and contains the works "Lush Life", "Desafinado", "Alone Together" and "It's You or No One".
Vol. 1.
VHS: S18515. $19.98.
Vol. 2.
VHS: S18516. $19.98.

Jazz Odyssey: Beyond El Rocco
This film noir style docudrama unveils the legendary players and historic venues that defined Australia's Modern Jazz scene for over five decades. The history of bebop, fusion and its crossover inrock and funk make for an engaging story. Shot on location in Australia. A two-volume set, 102 mins.
VHS: S25630. $29.98.

Jazz on a Summer's Day
The concert movie that came first—before *Woodstock*, *Monterey Pop*, *The Last Waltz* and *Gimme Shelter*—is still among the best. On a hot summer's day in Newport, Rhode Island in 1958, jazz greats Louis Armstrong, Thelonious Monk, and Ania O'Day get together with Chuck Berry, Mahalia Jackson, and Diane Washington among others to make this glorious gem of a movie.
VHS: S12198. $59.95.
Bert Stern, USA, 1958, 85 mins.

Jazz Shorts
Four shorts include: *Honky Tonk Bud*, featuring the music of Edward Wilderson Jr. and the rap poetry of John Toles-Bey; *Bird Lives*, an animation piece directed by Peter Bodge; *Daybreak Express*, which features a ride on a New York subway set to the music of Duke Ellington and directed by D.A. Pennebaker (*Don't Look Back*, *Monterey Pop*); and *Is That Jazz?*, a performance piece by Gil Scott-Heron directed by Robert Mugge. 30 mins.
VHS: S02995. $19.95.

Jazz: Earle Hines and Coleman Hawkins
Hines sings and plays piano while Hawkins adds saxophone. Includes "Crazy Rhythm" and "But Not for Me". 28 mins.
VHS: S21676. $24.95.

Jazzball
A musical compilation features the talents of such artists as Duke Ellington, Cab Calloway, Louis Armstrong, Gene Krupa and the song stylings of Miss Peggy Lee. A full hour of jazz so hot it's cool. USA, 1958, 60 mins.
VHS: S07436. $19.95.

Joe Cool Live
New York City's first call players display their incredible abilities with special guest Sadao Watanabe. Jams include "Trans Himalayan", "Dr. Potato Head", "Borderland" and "Sometimes Bubba Gets Down". 90 mins.
VHS: S12007. $34.95.
Laser: LD70330. $34.95.

Joe Pass in Concert
This consumate jazz improvisor was likened to Art Tatum for his ability to combine virtuosity, taste and harmonic invention. Though he accompanied great singers like Ella Fitzgerald and Frank Sinatra, his genius shone brightest as a soloist. Shot at Christ College, Brecon, Wales in 1991, it captures his transformation of a range of styles and standards.
VHS: S23305. $24.98.

Joe Williams (Smithsonian Jazz Series)
He's become famous once in a lifetime, as Count Basie's star vocalist and as Bill Cosby's father-in-law on *The Cosby Show*. He's Joe Williams, the King of the Blues, performing in concert with Kirk Stuart on piano, Keeter Betts on bass and Steve Williams on drums.
VHS: S03828. $29.95.

Joe Williams: A Song Is Born
In collaboration with pianist George Shearing, this live concert of the redoubtable Joe Williams, voted best male vocalist in the 1992 Down Beat Critics' poll, provides an intimate and up-close portrait of his singing prowess. Filmed in 1991 at the Paul Masson Winery. 58 mins.
VHS: S17609. $19.98.

John Hartford
John Hartford plays music loaded with references to blue grass and old-time traditionalism in this eclectic video collection of his best work. 60 mins.
VHS: S19213. $24.95.

John Lee Hooker & Friends
John Lee Hooker performs with Albert Collins, Ry Cooder, Robert Cray, John Hammond, Charlie Musselwhite, Bonnie Raitt and other musicians on this video. Performances collected here range from 1984 to 1992 and show why Hooker is a serious musician who can still manage to perform on MTV.
VHS: S27491. $19.95.

John Lee Hooker: Rare Performances, 1960-1984
John Lee Hooker is one of the foremost blues performers of the postwar period. Over five decades his music has entertained the world with a sound firmly grounded in the traditions of his home state, Mississippi. This compilation of his performances shows how his music stretched a rich tradition into contemporary times.
VHS: S27490. $19.95.

Johnny Taylor Live in Dallas
Rhythm and blues great Johnny Taylor performs live in Dallas, Texas. Includes "Who's Makin' Love to Your Old Lady", "Just Because" and "I Don't Want to Lose Your Love". 60 mins.
VHS: S21680. $24.95.

Journey Through Jazz
The Dan Jordan Trio guides students through the many facets of jazz. Students will enjoy improvisation as they move through the blues to ragtime, swing, be-bop, cool jazz, fusion and the avant garde.
VHS: S22478. $99.95.

Kenny Drew Live
Kenny Drew, one of the most interesting jazz pianists, performs "Hushabye" and "Saint Thomas" with his frequent collaborators Niels-Hennigh Orsted Pedersen and Alvin Queen. 55 mins.
VHS: S18380. $19.95.

Koko Taylor: Queen of the Blues
This profile of Koko Taylor recalls the highlights of her career to date, and captures live performances. An inside look at one of the most visible female blues artists. 60 mins.
VHS: S15877. $19.98.

Konitz: Portrait of Artist
Through conversations with the musician and a fair sampling of his work, this film gives a portrait of Lee Konitz, jazz saxophone great from the 1940s. Songs include "Stella by Starlight", "Subconscious Lee", "She's Wild as Springtime" and more. 83 mins.
VHS: S12339. $19.95.

L.A. All Stars: Hampton Hawes
With Big Joe Turner, Sweets Edison and Hampton Hawes doing "Memory Lane Blues", "Feeling Happy", "Shake, Rattle and Roll" and "Teddy's Blues". 28 mins.
VHS: S05634. $24.95.

Ladies Sing the Blues
This program combines concert and archival footage in a bold essay on the evolution of blues and jazz and looks at the personalities who made the music. With Bessie Smith, Lena Horne, Billie Holiday, Dinah Washington and Sarah Vaughn. 60 mins.
VHS: S19223. $29.95.

Lady Day:
The Many Faces of Billie Holiday
Considered by many to be the greatest jazz singer of all time, Billie was also the victim of vicious racism, personal tragedy and drug addiction. Yet she remained a fighter, as this video portrait proves in remembrances by fellow jazz stars Carmen McRae, Harry "Sweets" Edison, Milt Gabler and Mal Waldron. And there's plenty of Lady Day herself, from her own words (as read by actress Ruby Dee) to generous film clips featuring her singing her best-loved songs. 60 mins.
VHS: S13929. $19.95.

Last Date: Eric Dolphy
A film about saxophonist Eric Dolphy shot during his final recording session in Hilversum in June, 1964. Dolphy's contemporaries Buddy Collette, trumpeter Ted Curson, pianist Jaki Byard and Richard Davis comment on his art and life.
VHS: S19123. $29.95.
Hans Hylkema, USA, 1991, 92 mins.

Last of the Blue Devils
This great jazz documentary feature documents the world of Kansas City Jazz, with Count Basie and His Orchestra, Big Joe Turner and Jay McShann. "This beautiful film is about life and jazz and how they interact" (Newsweek). USA, 1979, 90 mins.
VHS: S00726. $19.95.

The Leaders: Jazz in Paris 1988
The group of Arthur Blythe, Lester Bowie, Cecil McBee, Kirk Lightsey, Chico Freeman and Don Moye make up The Leaders, a jazz band which defines itself as "schizo music". Seven songs are performed here by these singularly great, collectively unique artists. 54 mins.
VHS: S12340. $19.95.

Lee Ritenour and Friends, Vol. 1
In a concert performance at the Coconut Grove, Lee Ritenour is joined by Joao Bosco, Steve Lukather, Ernie Watts, Phil Perry, Bob James, Harvey Mason and Brian Bromberg, in "Night Rhythms," "Harlequin," "Malibu," "Up-Town," "Odile, Odila," "Etude" and "Asa." 58 mins.
VHS: S19660. $19.95.

Lee Ritenour and Friends, Vol. 2
From the Coconut Grove, Lee Ritenour collaborates with Bob James, Tuck and Patti, Ernie Watts, Paulinho da Costa, Brian Bromberg and Alan Broadbent in some virtuoso recordings of "24th Street Blues," "Stolen Moments," "Love Is the Key," "Better Than Anything," "Everything's Gonna Be All Right," "Westchester Lady" and "Bahia Frank." 58 mins.
VHS: S19661. $19.95.

Legends of Bottleneck Blues Guitar
Rare recordings from 1965-70 are joined in this work, resulting in a collection of the best examples of bottleneck guitar styles. Popular in the Deep South, this sound reflects the Hawaiian lap slide technique. Among the great practitioners of the bottleneck blues included here are Son House, Fred McDowell, Mance Lipscomb, Johnny Shine, Furry Lewis and Jesse Fuller. 58 mins.
VHS: S22481. $19.95.

Legends of Country Blues Guitar
Blues was born at the beginning of the 20th century among black rural musicians. Fortunately, the blues was kept alive by a number of fluid and improvisational performers who inspired the blues revival of the 1960's. From the legendary artists Mississippi John Hurt, Son House, Gary Davis, Big Bill Broonzy, Robert Pete Williams and others, this video offers a collection of the best blues. 58 mins.
VHS: S22482. $19.95.

Legends of Country Blues Guitar: Volume 2
The Blues rediscovery of the sixties brought new acclaim to many veteran artists from the "Golden Age" of country blues. Bukka White, Big Joe Williams, Son House, Houston Stackhouse, Rev. Gary Davis, Lead Belly and Sam Chatmon are just some of the legendary performers from that earlier time gathered in this video. 58 mins.
VHS: S22490. $19.95.

Legends of Jazz Guitar, Volume III
Jim Hall, Barney Kessel, Herb Ellis, Charlie Byrd and Tal Farlow are just some of the musicians featured on this third installment of the series. Their performances cover a range of styles, from Cole Porter to the Bossa Nova.
VHS: S25913. $29.95.

Legends of the Delta Blues
The Mississippi Delta is the home of the blues. Musical legends Sun House, John Lee Hooker, Johnny Shines and Bukka White are shown on this tape as they performed in the 1960's and 1970's. Earthy and vital, their music has inspired many musicians, including the famed Muddy Waters.
VHS: S26429. $24.95.

Les McCann Trio
Les McCann, piano and vocals, Jimmy Rowser, bass, and Donald Dean, drums, perform "Right On," "Sunny," "With These Hands," and "Compared to What" at Shelly's Manne Hole Club in Los Angeles. 28 mins.
VHS: S04170. $19.95.

Let the Good Times Roll
Let the Good Times Roll embraces over 40 performances demonstrating the history, heritage and influence of the New Orleans scene on American music. Featured musicians include the Dirty Dozen Brass Band, John Lee Hooker, Wynton Marsalis and Band, Robert Cray, Queen Ida, and the Neville Brothers. 86 mins.
VHS: S16038. $19.95.

Lightnin' Hopkins:
Rare Performances 1960-79
Hopkins is the embodiment of Texas country blues. He inspired a host of artists, especially fellow musicians. This video traces his development subsequent to his rediscovery in 1959. It offers a fresh reflection of one of the most creative blues musicians ever heard.
VHS: S23304. $24.98.

Lionel Hampton
Air Mail Special, Smooth Sailing, Hamp's Boogie Woogie. 24 mins.
VHS: S05418. $19.95.

Live at the Village Vanguard Vol. 1
The hottest sounds from the coolest cats. Freddie Hubbard on trumpet. Ron Carter on bass. Cedar Walton tickles the ivories and Lenny White is on drums. Tunes include "Happy Times", "Guernica", "Little Waltz" and "Fantasy in D". Recorded live at the Village Vanguard.
VHS: S09118. $29.95.
Bruce Buschel, USA, 1982, 59 mins.

Live at the Village Vanguard Vol. 2
The Michael Petrucciani Trio performs jazz just the way you like it in this second volume in the Village Vanguard series. With Palle Danielsson on bass; Eliot Zigmund on drums and guest star Jin Hall on guitar. For your viewing and listening pleasure they play "Gitgo", "All Alone", "Firewaltz" and "Left Alone". In color and stereo. HiFi.
VHS: S09119. $29.95.
Bruce Buschel, USA, 1982, 57 mins.

Live at the Village Vanguard Vol. 3
More hot jazz sounds recorded live at the Village Vanguard. Guitarist John Abercrombie is backed up by Michael Brecker on tenor sax, Peter Erskine on drums and Marc Johnson on bass. They perform "Dreamstepper", "Blues for Sarha", "Tavia's Tune", "Max", "Juicey Brucey" and "Subconscious Lee".
VHS: S09120. $29.95.
Bruce Buschel, USA, 1986, 58 mins.

Live at the Village Vanguard Vol. 4
The Mal Waldron Quartet, featuring Mal Waldron, Woody Shaw, Charles Rouse, Reggie Workman and Ed Blackwell, performs "Git-Go," "All Alone," and other numbers. 56 mins.
VHS: S12192. $29.95.

Live at the Village Vanguard Vol. 5
Lee Konitz and Friends perform "Max", "Dreamstepper", "A Story Often Told," and other numbers. 62 mins.
VHS: S12193. $29.95.

Live at the Village Vanguard Vol. 6
The Dave Murray Quartet performs "Off Season," "Lovers," "Morning Song," and other numbers. 56 mins.
VHS: S12194. $29.65.

Lou Rawls Show with Duke Ellington
Rawls sings "Oh Happy Day" and other gospel and blues standards while Ellington adds his classics including "Satin Doll" and "Sophisticated Ladies". 48 mins.
VHS: S21677. $19.95.

Louie Bellson and His Big Band
Featuring the Brecker Brothers, Lew Soloff, Tom Malone, Herb Geller and Howard Johnson, in an all-star live concert. 55 mins.
VHS: S03383. $29.95.

Louis Armstrong
Backed by his band members Tommy Young, Billy Kyle and vocalist Jewel Brown, Armstrong performs numbers such as "When It's Sleepy Time Down South," "C'est Si Bon" and "When the Saints Go Marching In." 24 mins.
VHS: S19887. $29.95.

Louis Armstrong:
The Gentle Giant of Jazz
Satchmo worked his way up from the Dixieland music of New Orleans to Chicago and the world of Jazz, ultimately conquering the whole world with his music. Hugh Downs hosts. 24 mins.
VHS: S23557. $49.95.

Lowell Fulson and Percy Mayfield
Lowell Fulson was one of the greatest blues guitarists to emerge from the California Blues scene. Here is a collection of his greatest songs, including "Every Day I Have the Blues", "Reconsider Baby", "Tramp". Approx. 30 mins.
VHS: S12338. $19.95.

Mabel Mercer: A Singer's Singer
A 17-song set that captures the artistry of the grand dame of popular song. 42 mins.
VHS: S03385. $29.95.

Mabel Mercer:
Cabaret Artist "Forever and Always"
The last performance of the incomparable grand dame of popular song. Live from Cleo's in New York, Mabel performs her unique and timeless renditions of 20 songs from The Great American Songbook. A touching evening of entertainment from the lady who inspired Frank Sinatra. 58 mins.
VHS: S10792. $24.95.

Mance Lipscomb in Concert
This tenant farmer began life as a slave. Despite these hardships, he sang and played the blues all his life. Discovered in 1960, he was soon in demand at festivals, concerts and clubs around the country. This tape presents a rare TV concert recorded in Texas that captures the genius of Mance's music. 58 mins.
VHS: S22488. $19.95.

Mark Naftalin's Blue Monday
Starring John Lee Hooker and Charlie Musselwhite. Hooker's Mississippi origins are combined here in spontaneous performances with the California harmonica sound of Charlie Musselwhite. 30 mins.
VHS: S12337. $24.95.

Marty Robbins/Ernest Tubb
Marty Robbins and Ernest Tubb perform 26 songs. Robbins' include "Singin' the Blues", "Times Goes By", "I Can't Quit" and "Pretty Words". Ernest Tubb performs "Walkin' the Floor over You", "So Many Times", "Tomorrow Never Comes" and "They'll Do It Every Time". 60 mins.
VHS: S19211. $24.95.

Masters of Comic Blues:
Mance Lipscomb and Lightnin' Hopkins
Rare archival footage of these Blues greats, shot in the '60s, which vividly captures the eloquence of their visionary music. Hosted by Taj Mahal. 60 mins.
VHS: S15702. $24.95.

Masters of Comic Blues:
Rev. Gary Davis and Sonny Terry
Shot in the 60s, this intimate video captures these great Blues artists at their best—communicating the power and brilliance of the American Blues as played by its masters. Hosted by Taj Mahal. 60 mins.
VHS: S15704. $24.95.

Max Roach: Jazz in America
An hour of jazz with Max Roach on drums, Calvin Hill on bass, Cecil Bridgewater on trumpet and Odean Pope on tenor sax, recorded live at the Blues Alley in Washington, DC, on March 2, 1981.
VHS: S00834. $19.95.
Stanley Dorfman, USA, 1981, 60 mins.

Mel Lewis (Smithsonian Jazz Series)
The late drummer fronts the big band that has performed every Monday night for more than a decade at New York's legendary Village Vanguard. This young, 17-piece ensemble rips through three pieces by Herbie Hancock and one by Bob Brookmeyer, proving that the jazz orchestra is alive and well.
VHS: S03831. $29.95.

Mel Lewis and His Big Band
Swinging big-band jazz with Mel Lewis and his 19-piece jazz band. 38 mins.
VHS: S03381. $19.98.

Mel Torme
New York State of Mind, Here's That Rainy Day, Born to Be Blue, Blues in the Night, Oh Lady Be Good, When Sunny Gets Blue, Down for Double. 52 mins.
VHS: S05407. $29.95.

The Memories:
Music from The Yank Years, Volume 1
Johnny Desmond, Maxine Sullivan, the Debonaires and friends and the Parke Frankenfield Orchestra join forces to bring back the music of the Swing era. "Sentimental Journey" and "Stardust" are just some of the sentimental oldies performed in this video. 45 mins.
VHS: S23669. $14.95.

The Memories:
Music from The Yank Years, Volume 2
Fran Warren, Bobby Burnett, the Debonaires and friends sing along with the Frankenfield Orchestra in this second volume to bring back still more music from the Swing era. "You've Changed", "I'll Get By" and "C'est Si Bon" are only a few of the great tunes that will charm listeners. 45 mins.
VHS: S23670. $14.95.

Messin' with the Blues
Chicago blues legends Muddy Waters, Buddy Guy and Junior Wells perform the music born of bad luck, cheap booze, torrid love and centuries of oppression. Their musical style strongly influenced a generation of rock 'n' roll artists. Recorded June 28, 1974, at the Montreux Jazz Festival, Switzerland, this gritty performance includes such classics as "Messin' with the Kid," and "Got My Mojo Workin'." 1974, 54 mins.
VHS: S13676. $19.95.

Michael Feinstein & Friends
Michael Feinstein performs favorites by George and Ira Gershwin, Irving Berlin, Harold Arlen and Duke Ellington. Rosemary Clooney joins Feinstein for several solo numbers and duets. In Hi-Fi stereo, 60 mins.
VHS: S16798. $24.95.

Mike Mainieri: The Jazz Life
Crossed Wires, Flying Colors, Sara's Touch, Bamboo, Song for Seth, Bullet Train, T-Bag. 60 mins.
VHS: S05410. $29.95.

Mingus
A cinema-verite portrait of this great bassist/composer and some of the hard times that came his way. There is superb Mingus in action at a nightclub near Boston, scenes of him conducting his big band, composing, singing and reciting his own poetry. Most of the film, though, takes place in his cluttered New York loft as he awaits eviction in the wake of a legal tangle with New York City.
VHS: S07743. $19.95.
Thomas Reichmann, USA, 1968, 58 mins.

Minnie the Moocher
A rollicking, nostalgic tour of the Harlem clubs of the 30's and 40's. Rare footage shines the spotlight on the great entertainers like Cab Calloway, performing the title song. 55 mins.
VHS: S09245. $19.98.

Mississippi Blues
Tavernier and Parrish approach the Mississippi Delta through its townspeople and its music—Delta Blues and gospel. They explore their own knowledge of this world—Tavernier's from reading Faulkner and Mark Twain, Parrish's from his intimate knowledge of the South. And they skillfully link the drama with such questions as the relationship of the church to politics, and the relationship of music to the life in the Mississippi Delta.
VHS: S09244. $29.95.
Parrish/Tavernier, USA/France, 1983, 101 mins.

Modern Jazz Quartet
The grand old gentlemen of jazz (John Lewis on piano, Milt Jackson on vibraphone, Percy Heath on bass and Connie Kay on drums) celebrate their 35th anniversary in a performance at the Arts Festival in Freiburg, Germany. 60 mins.
VHS: S20568. $19.95.

Monk in Oslo
A documentary about the art and music of jazz virtuoso Thelonious Monk. The film has a vivid sense for Monk's gestures and rhythms, as it quietly celebrates the art and dynamic interplay within the quartet as they perform "Lulu's Back in Town", "Blue Monk" and " 'Round Midnight". Produced for the Norwegian Broadcasting Corporation.
VHS: S19120. $19.95.
Harald Heide Steen Jr., 1966, 33 mins.

Moscow Sax Quintet: The Jazznost Tour
Russia's singular jazz group finds a distinctive sound for American classics as the five virtuoso saxophone players and a rhythm section play riffs on the Beatles, Gershwin, Fats Waller and Charlie Parker. "You hear the breathtaking virtuosity of ensemble work when they take Bird's improvised solos and play them in five-part harmony at breakneck speed, as if there were one single player" (Jazziz). 62 mins.
VHS: S19225. $19.95.

Mr. Boogie Woogie
A documentary profile of Moses Vinton, Beale Street's outstanding blues pianist, who was at the center of the Memphis rhythm and blues explosion. The documentary takes up Vinson's life at the present moment, exploring through the recollections of employers, his sister, friends who "made it", and with Vinson himself, the complex causes of his current obscurity. In the process, we discover Vinson as a personality and as a symbol of the minority artist, or, indeed, any artist who finds himself in an inhospitable environment.
VHS: S07769. $39.95.
Alexis Krasilovsky, USA, 1978, 30 mins.

Muddy Waters
A program about the extraordinary Chicago blues artist Muddy Waters. Born on a plantation near Clarksdale, Mississippi, Waters moved to Chicago and developed music which combined the idiom of the Mississippi Delta with the harsh poetry of the Chicago streets. The numbers include "Hoochie Coochie Man," "My Home Is in the Delta," "Baby You Don't Have to Go" and "I'm a King Bee."
VHS: S19679. $19.95.

Music and Comedy Masters (Volume 1)
Includes "Blues and Boogie" with Maxine Sullivan & Nat King Cole, "Murder in Swingtime" with Les Hite & Orchestra, "Ain't Misbehavin' " with Fats Waller & Louis Armstrong, "Bubbling Over" with Ethel Waters, "Boogie Woogie Dream" with Lena Horne, and "Caledonia" with Louis Jordan.
VHS: S15473. $29.95.

Music and Comedy Masters (Volume 2)
Includes: "Minnie the Moocher" (Cab Calloway), "Jittering Jitterbugs" (Hamtree Harrington), "Heavenly Choir" and "St. Louis Blues" (Bessie Smith), "Showtime at the Apollo" (Mantan Moreland, Lionel Hampton & Nat King Cole), and "Hi De Ho" with Cab Calloway.
VHS: S15474. $29.95.

Music and Comedy Masters (Volume 3)
Includes performances by Marian Anderson, Sarah Vaughn, Duke Ellington ("Symphony in Black"), and the Basin Street Review with Lionel Hampton, Nat King Cole, Nipsey Russell and Dinah Washington.
VHS: S15475. $29.95.

Music and Comedy Masters (Volume 4)
Includes: "Come to Baby Do" by the Nat King Cole Trio, "Bundle of Blues" by Duke Ellington, Cab Calloway's "Jitterbug Party", Count Basie & Orchestra, Louis Armstrong, Harlem Hotshots, Sugar Chili, and "Black and Tan" by Duke Ellington.
VHS: S15476. $29.95.

Music and Comedy Masters (Volume 5)
Includes "Sepian Swing" with Cab Calloway and The Nat King Cole Trio, "Sepia Stars on Parade" with Herb Jeffries, Fats Waller, Bill Robinson, Dorothy Dandridge, The Mills Brothers, Louis Armstrong, Nat King Cole and Louis Jordan, and "Rhapsody in Black and Blue" by Louis Armstrong & Orchestra.
VHS: S15477. $29.95.

Music and Comedy Masters (Volume 6)
Includes "Dry Bones" by the Delta Rhythm Boys, "Open the Door Richard" by Dusty Fletcher, "Slow Poke" by Stepin Fetchit, and "Spying the Spy"—a rare 1915 Black short subject on private eye stories.
VHS: S15478. $29.95.

Music Classics, Vol. 1
Includes hit songs by Charlie Barnet, Duke Ellington, Billy Burt, Bill "Bojangles" Robinson, Fats Waller, Cyd Charisse and Stan Kenton, Artie Shaw and Harry "Hipster" Gibson. All accompanied by orchestra. 60 mins.
VHS: S15871. $19.98.

Music Classics, Vol. 2
Includes hit songs by Tex Beneke, Victor Young, Duke Ellington, Artie Shaw, Eubie Blake, Stan Kenton and Gene Krupa. All accompanied by orchestra. 60 mins.
VHS: S15872. $19.98.

Music Classics, Vol. 3
Includes hit songs by Stan Kenton, Ina Ray Hutton, Count Basie, Tommy and Jimmy Dorsey, Harry James, the Dinning Sisters and Dizzy Gillespie. All accompanied by orchestra. 60 mins.
VHS: S15873. $19.98.

Musicians in Exile
Some of the innovators of world music must now live outside their home countries for political reasons. This film presents their stories and music, uniquely shaped by their living circumstances. Featuring Paquito Riviera and Daniel Ponce. 1990, 75 mins.
VHS: S14739. $19.95.

Mystery, Mr. Ra
Despite the epic scope of Sun Ra's 35-year career, *Mystery, Mr. Ra* is only the second document of the career of this remarkable musician, band leader, philosopher, shaman, commune leader and cosmic messenger. Acclaimed French filmmaker Frank Cassenti comes up with an entertaining, informative, deeplyfelt report that contains rare footage of the orchestra tuning up and rehearsing, plus a rewarding spectrum of excerpts from Ra's Afro-psychedelic circus of a show. 51 mins.
VHS: S12341. $19.95.

Nancy Wilson at Carnegie Hall
The Grammy Award winning song stylist gives her all in a memorable concert with full-string orchestra…a highlight of the JVC Jazz Festival in New York's Carnegie Hall. 52 mins.
VHS: S10793. $19.98.

The Nat King Cole Story
An exquisite video portrait of singer and jazz pianist Nat King Cole. A moving tribute to this peerless music legend. 30 mins.
VHS: S13882. $29.95.

Nat King Cole: The Unforgettable
A documentary that examines the life and career of Cole, from his beginnings as a jazz pianist to his success as a vocalist and songwriter. 90 mins.
VHS: S09209. $24.95.

The New Music
John Carter and Bobby Bradford. 29 mins.
VHS: S03180. $19.95.

New Orleans: Til the Butcher Cuts Him Down
A superb study of the history and men who played New Orleans jazz, through the eyes of one of its greatest trumpet players, Punch Miller. Kid Punch played with all the greats including King Oliver, Kid Ory, Jelly Roll, Morton, Louis Armstrong. This film is about his life and the changes New Orleans music went through in his lifetime.
VHS: S03191. $29.95.
Philip Spalding, USA, 1971, 53 mins.

Newport Jazz Festival
The 1962 Newport Jazz Festival is preserved on this video, including performances by acclaimed musicians The Oscar Peterson Trio, Lambert Hendricks and Bavan, Roland Kirk, The Clara Ward Singers, Ruby Braff, Pee Wee Russel, Duke Ellington and his Orchestra and many others.
VHS: S21565. $29.95.

One Night Stand: Lionel Hampton and an All-Star Jazz Ensemble
Hampton plays vibes, piano and drums in this program hosted by Mel Torme. Buddy Rich, Gene Krupa, Teddy Wilson, Zoot Sims and B.B. King are some of the artists who also appear in this tape. Johnny Mercer even sings a medley of his unforgettable hits.
VHS: S21759. $29.95.

One Night with Blue Note, Part 1
Bouquet, Canteloupe Island, When You Wish upon a Star, Jumpin' Jack, Moanin', Broadside, Little B's Poem. 55 mins.
VHS: S05411. $29.95.

Oregon
One of the most original improvisational jazz bands around, with Ralph Tower, Trilok Gurtu, Glenn Moore and Paul McCandles in their unique combinations of sounds rooted in traditional American jazz. 60 mins.
VHS: S09825. $24.95.

Oscar Peterson: Music in the Key of Oscar
A 40-year musical history of jazz pianist Oscar Peterson is detailed in this documentary. It begins with his early days as a Montreal boogie-woogie sensation and continues into the present. Peterson himself narrates. Quincy Jones, Ella Fitzgerald, Dizzy Gillespie and more jazz greats are also featured. A two-volume set, 106 mins.
VHS: S25631. $29.98.

Out of the Blacks Into the Blues
An interesting two-part work about the political, social and artistic impulses of the American blues.
Part One: Along the Old Man River. Features Bukka White, Furry Lewis, Roosevelt Sykes, Robert Pete Williams, Brownie McGhee and Sonny Terry.
VHS: S17999. $24.95.
Part Two: A Way to Escape the Ghetto. This program looks at self-expression and the pure joy of playing, considering the works of B.B. King, Willie Dixon, Mance Lipscomb, Brownie McGhee, Junior Wells, Buddy Guy, Sonny Terry and Arthur "Big Boy" Crudup.
VHS: S18000. $24.95.

Outside in Sight: Music of the United Front
Portrait of the San Francisco jazz group United Front featuring percussionist Anthony Brown, bassist Mark Izu, Lewis Jordan on sax and George Sims on trumpet.
VHS: S03920. $40.00.
G.Chapnick/S.Wood, USA, 1986, 60 mins.

Paris Reunion Band
From the mid 50's to the late 60's Paris was the jazz capital of the world. Its guru was Kenny Clarke and to his memory the Paris Reunion Band was constituted for this live taping at Stuttgart of some of the greats of this era: Woody Shaw and Nat Aderley, Joe Henderson and Nathan Davis, Curtis Fuller, Idris Muhammad, Walter Bishop Jr. and Jimmy Woode. 57 mins.
VHS: S09824. $24.95.

Percy Mayfield: Poet Laureate of the Blues
When Percy Mayfield died in 1984, the day before his 64th birthday, the blues lost one of its truly unique personages. In this mixture of performance and reminiscence with pianist Mark Naftalin, the film captures Mayfield at the height.
VHS: S07748. $29.95.
S. Sutherland/M. Prussian, USA 1986, 30 mins.

Phil Woods in Concert: With Joe Sudler's Swing Machine
A collaboration between bop altoist Phil Woods and Joe Sudler's Swing Machine, a sinuous collective of great soloists, performing the emotionally charged, exuberant numbers "Groovin' High", "Body and Soul" and "Blues in Ecstasy". 67 mins.
VHS: S19229. $29.98.

The Phil Woods Quartet
Mike Melillo, Steve Gilmore and Bill Goodwin round out the Phil Woods Quartet. They make some of the best jazz to be heard anywhere.
VHS: S26791. $19.95.
John Beyer, USA, 1979, 58 mins.

Piano Legends
Chick Corea narrates a look at the great piano jazz performers, from Fats Waller and Jelly Roll Morton to Oscar Peterson and Thelonious Monk. 60 mins.
VHS: S03213. $39.95.

Quincy Jones: A Celebration
Ray Charles and James Ingram are among the stars performing in this musical tribute to the great Quincy Jones. 60 mins.
VHS: S21672. $14.95.

Reed Royalty
This documentary traces the uses and development of jazz reed playing. Narrated by Branford Marsalis, who also performs two soprano saxophone numbers, the work includes archival footage of Omer Simeon, Artie Shaw, Woody Herman, Benny Goodman, John Coltrane, Ornette Coleman and others. 60 mins.
VHS: S17425. $29.95.

Ron Carter & Art Farmer: Live at Sweet Basil
The musicianship of Ron Carter and Art Farmer has brought them each renown in their separate ventures.
VHS: S16728. $19.98.

Ron Carter Live: Double Bass
The jazz great is captured live at NHK 101 Studio in New York, recorded in digital sound and thoughtfully shot on high definition video. Among his many mind-blowing selections are "Double Bass", "Waltz", "Blues for D.P.", "The Third Plane" and "Eight—Sometimes I Feel Like a Motherless Child". 55 mins.
VHS: S16002. $19.95.

Roots: Salute to the Saxophone
This program looks at the stylistic and musical contributions of the saxophone in the evolution of American jazz. The program highlights four virtuosos—Arthur Blythe, Chico Freeman, Nathan Davis and Sam Rivers—altering compositions and arrangements on works such as "After Dark" and "Parker's Mood". 52 mins.
VHS: S18378. $19.95.

Roy Ayers Live
Roy Ayers' melding of disparate jazz styles has made him one of most intriguing figures since the 60s. In this performance, Ayers is accompanied by Rex Rideout, Dennis Davis, Donald Nicks and Zachary Breaux and performs such classics as "Hot", "Mystic Voyage" and "Night in Tunisia". 52 mins.
VHS: S18381. $19.95.

Sarah Vaughan: The Divine One
Friends, family and fellow musicians including Billy Eckstine, Roy Haynes, Joe Williams and others talk about this unmatched songstress. Her performances of "Misty", "Someone to Watch over Me", "I've Got a Crush on You" and "Send in the Clowns" are among her legendary standards included here.
VHS: S26857. $34.95.
Matthew Seig, USA, 1991, 60 mins.

Saxophone Colossus
Robert Mugge's stirring tribute to American musical genius Sonny Rollins, an electrifying record of a supreme jazz artist at work, featuring his *G-Man, The Bridge, Concerto for Tenor Saxophone and Orchestra,* and *Don't Stop the Carnival.*
VHS: S05651. $29.95.
Laser: LD71333. $39.95.
Robert Mugge, USA, 1986, 101 mins.

The Search for Robert Johnson
A documentary about the visionary rhythm and blues performer Robert Johnson. His life and art are reproduced through documentary footage and interviews with his contemporaries (John Hammond, David "Honeyboy" Edwards, Johnny Shines) and the musicians whose work he influenced (Keith Richards, Eric Clapton).
VHS: S16882. $19.98.

Sentimental Journey
Pearl Bailey hosts a trio of special programs dedicated to some of the greatest moments in musical television. Discover the roots of today's contemporary sound with appearances by Sammy Davis Jr., Mel Torme, Patti Page, Maurice Chevalier, Duke Ellington, Lionel Hampton, Eartha Kitt, Stevie Wonder and Sara Vaughan. 147 mins.
VHS: S16587. $29.95.

Shelly Manne Quartet
Shelley Manne, drums, Ray Brown, bass, Hampton Hawes, piano, and Bob Cooper, saxophone, perform "Blues in the Basement," "Stella by Starlight," and milestones at Shelly's Manne Hole Club in Los Angeles. 28 mins.
VHS: S04169. $19.95.

Shirley Horn: Here's to Life
Shirley Horn quietly takes up the mantle of great song stylists like Nat "King" Cole, Sara Vaughan and Tony Bennett. This program also includes other performances by Horn and her trio, and interviews with people who helped her career, including Quincy Jones and Carmen McRae.
VHS: S16524. $19.95.

Sippie
A portrait of blues singer, songwriter Sippie Wallace. 23 mins.
VHS: S03195. $24.95.

Solo Tribute: Keith Jarrett
The magician of the keyboard casts his spell with "The Night We Called it a Day", "Sweet and Lovely", "I Got It Bad", "That Ain't Good", "Summertime" and 10 more classics. 102 mins.
Laser: LD70777. $39.95.

Sonny Rollins Live at Loren
37 mins.
VHS: S03182. $24.95.

Sound??
John Cage's enigmatic questions about sound are intercut with some of the most ambitious experiments of Rahsaan Roland Kirk. While Kirk plays three saxes at once, switches to flute, incorporates tapes of birds played backwards, and finally hands out whistles to the audience and encourages them to accompany him, Cage is preparing a piece for musical bicycle with David Tudor and Merce Cunningham.
VHS: S07747. $24.95.
Dick Fontaine, USA, 1967, 27 mins.

Space Is the Place
This unclassifiable work combines the crude energy and militant outrage of the blaxploitation film with footage of Ra's Intergalactic Arkestra performing their classics "Watusi", "Outer Spaceways Inc." and "The Satellites Are Spinning". "Sun Ra's *Close Encounter* with *Sweet Sweetback* is somewhere between *The Seventh Seal* and *El Topo*" (Michael Shore, *MTV News*).
VHS: S19121. $24.95.
John Coney, USA, 1974, 63 mins.

Stan Getz: A Musical Odyssey
In 1977, Getz went "home" to Israel and jammed with Israeli musicians for three weeks. It was a moving experience which also allowed Getz to showcase his improvisational talents as he worked with an Arab quartet, a Yemenite dance troupe, the Piamenti Brothers Band, and renowned Klezmer clarinetist Giora Feldman.
VHS: S24304. $36.00.
Herbert Dorfman, USA, 1978, 60 mins.

Standards II: With Keith Jarrett
"With a Song in My Heart", "When You Wish upon a Star", "On Green Dolphin Street", "Waltz", "Blame It on My Youth" and "Georgia on My Mind" lead a dazzling jazz showcase performed by three of the greats: Keith Jarrett, Gary Peacock and Jack DeJohnette. 91 mins.
Laser: LD70334. $39.95.

Stanley Jordan: Magic Touch
When You Wish upon a Star, Touch of Blue, Jumpin' Jack, Lady in My Life. 19 mins.
VHS: S05409. $16.95.

Stanley Turrentine: In Concert
This video concert stars one of the best-selling jazz musicians of all time, Stanley Turrentine. Turrentine's warm, masculine tenor sax sound has made him a favorite with both jazz fans and the general public for decades. Now, in this concert recorded at New York's Village Gate, Stanley talks about his career and plays the songs he's known for all around the world. 60 mins.
VHS: S13930. $29.95.

Stefan Grossman
Stefan Grossman's solo concert performances reflect a panorama of fingerstyle techniques and styles ranging from country blues to ragtime to Celtic melodies to jazz-based compositions. Beginning his studies with guitar legend Rev. Gary Davis at age 15, he became an integral part of the infamous "blues mafia". 60 mins.
VHS: S15729. $24.95.

Stephane Grappelli in New Orleans
A front row seat in a terrific French Quarter Club performance of the great jazz violinist at work. 60 mins.
VHS: S10151. $29.95.

Stephane Grappelli— Live in San Francisco—1985
Excellent coverage of the 78-year-old jazz violinist in two early 1980's Bay Area performances—at the Paul Masson Vineyards in Saratoga and at the Great American Music Hall in San Francisco. Grappelli and his trio of accompanists romp through an eclectic set of tunes. 60 mins.
VHS: S12343. $19.95.
C. Broullon/R. Poirer, USA, 1985, 60 mins.

Steve Lacy: Lift the Bandstand
A portrait of Steve Lacy, with his music. 50 mins.
VHS: S03181. $19.95.

The Story of Jazz
In this impressive array of jazz performance clips over 30 artists can be seen, including Louis Armstrong, Count Basie, John Coltrane, Miles Davis, Ella Fitzgerald, Dizzy Gillespie, Benny Goodman, Billie Holiday, Thelonious Monk, Charlie Parker, Sarah Vaughn, Lester Young and more. 90 mins.
VHS: S23325. $29.98.
Laser: LD74754. $39.98.

Straight No Chaser: Thelonious Monk
A revealing portrait of the great Monk, featuring more than 25 Monk songs, including "Round Midnight", "Ask Me Now" and "Ruby, My Dear", and featuring an amazing insight into the personal life of the troubled but extraordinary musician.
VHS: S13023. $19.98.
Charlotte Zwerin, USA, 1989, 89 mins.

Sun Ra: A Joyful Noise
Sun Ra and his Arkestra into the space age by way of Ancient Egyptian mythology. 60 mins.
VHS: S03177. $19.95.

Super Drumming
A who's who of the world of drums and drummers: Louie Bellson, Ian Paice, Gerry Brown, Simon Phillips, Nippy Noya, Cozy Powell and Pete York. Highlights include Bellson's "Deep Skin" and "The Laid Back Heart Attack Tango". 53 mins.
VHS: S09823. $19.95.

Swing: Best of the Big Bands Vol. 1
Contains 18 complete performances including Tommy Dorsey (Opus One); Rosemary Clooney and Tony Pastor (Movie Tonight); Billie Holiday (God Bless the Child); Duke Ellington (Frankie & Johnny) and also featuring Hi-Los, Ray Anthony, Benny Carter, Harry James, Charlie Barnet and Gene Krupa. 50 mins.
VHS: S07529. $24.95.

Swing: Best of the Big Bands Vol. 2
20 complete performances including The Dorsey Brothers (Yes, Indeed), Nat King Cole (Route 66); Woody Herman (Caldonia); Sarah Vaughn (Don't Blame Me); and also Charlie Barnet, Lionel Hampton, Ralph Marterie, Gene Krupa, Stan Kenton, Tex Benecke and Glenn Miller Orchestra. 50 mins.
VHS: S07530. $24.95.

Swing: Best of the Big Bands Vol. 3
19 performances including Count Basie (Red Bank Boogie); Gene Krupa (Stompin' at the Savoy); The Ink Spots (If I Didn't Care); Harry James (Brave Bulls) and also featuring Jimmy Dorsey, Les Brown, Duke Ellington, Teresa Brewer and Charlie Barnet. 50 mins.
VHS: S07531. $24.95.

Swing: Best of the Big Bands Vol. 4
18 complete performances including Tex Beneke and the Glenn Miller Orchestra (Little Brown Jug); The Mills Brothers (Paper Doll); Louis Prima (That Old Black Magic); Buddy Rich (Burn) and also featuring Count Basie, Ray Anthony, Jimmy Dorsey, The Skylarks and Ray Kenton. 50 mins.
VHS: S07532. $24.95.

Swingin' the Blues: Count Basie
The legendary Count Basie led the most enduring Swing band ever. This video documentary follows the musical growth of a phenomenal musician. Interviews from band members, and with Basie himself, are just part of the story. The music, songs like "One O'Clock Jump", "Air Mail Special", "I Left My Baby" and "Blues in Hoss Flat", among others, show how Swing gave its name to an entire era.
VHS: S26855. $34.95.
Matthew Seig, USA, 1992, 60 mins.

Taj Mahal
The self-taught Taj Mahal plays more than 12 instruments, including guitar, piano, harmonica, banjo and mandolin. His music alternates between funk and sophisticated charm, in "Cakewalk into Town," "Fishin' Blues," "Sweet Home Chicago," "Going up the Country Paint My Mailbox Blue" "My Little Sugar Mama."
VHS: S19682. $19.95.

Talmage Farlow
A portrait of Tal Farlow with Tommy Flanagan. 58 mins.
VHS: S03178. $29.95.

Tenor Legends: Coleman Hawkins in Brussels, 1962
Hawkins' performances in the 1920's with Fletcher Henderson's Band established the tenor sax as a major instrument for jazz solos. At the Adolphe Sax festival this innovator was recognized for his accomplishments. Over two days backed by George Arvanitas, Mickey Baker, Jimmy Woode and Kansas Fields, Hawkins' magic was captured on film. 57 mins.
VHS: S22414. $19.95.

Tenor Titans
This documentary explores the early pioneers, in particular the radical contributions and innovations of Coleman Hawkins, with commentary from Branford Marsalis. This invaluable program showcases Hawkins, Bud Freeman, Lester Young, Stan Getz, and performances by Sal Nistico, Eric Dion, Frank Foster and Eddie "Lockjaw" Davis, Dexter Gordon, Charlie Rouse, to the rhythm and blues influence of Sam Taylor and Illinois Jacquet, to the modern era of John Coltrane, Sonny Rollins and David Murray. 60 mins.
VHS: S17426. $29.95.

Texas Tenor: The Illinois Jacquet Story
The life, art and music of Illinois Jacquet, who developed a revolutionary, highly improvised sound that established the tenets of rhythm and blues while performing with Lionel Hampton's band. The documentary reproduces the shiny, ecstatic moments of orchestral jazz as well as any film made, its beauty and rounded shapes and sharp punctuations, the delirium and sensuality of performance, the congregational ecstasy" (Peter Watrous, *New York Times*).
VHS: S19119. $24.95.
Arthur Elgort, USA, 1991, 81 mins.

Thelonious Monk: American Composer
The music of Thelonious Monk tells a tale of groundbreaking innovation. Tunes like "'Round Midnight," "Blue Monk," "Criss Cross," "Just a Gigolo" and others are included in this portrait of the musical genius. His followers Randy Weston, Barry Harris, Ben Riley, Billy Taylor and family members share their insights.
VHS: **S26858. $19.98.**
Matthew Seig, USA, 1991, 60 mins.

Time Groove
Original compositions by Harold Farberman performed by an all-star percussion ensemble made up of renowned jazz artists Alex Acuna, Louie Bellson, Vic Firth, Steve Gadd, Harvey Mason, and Dave Samuels. 70 mins.
VHS: **S13632. $29.95.**

Toots Thielmans in New Orleans
The great jazz harmonica player surrounds himself with a young surging rhythm section featuring Fred Hersch and Harvie Swartz, in a stirring live performance. 60 mins.
VHS: **S10152. $29.95.**

The Toshiko Akiyoshi Jazz Orchestra: Strive for Jive
Composer and pianist Toshiko Akiyoshi's band grafts the bebop of the Western big band with the music of the East. The program is a live performance of the 16-piece band, performing "Yellow Is Mellow", "Strive for Jive", "Autumn Sea" and "Warning, Success May Be Hazardous to Your Health". 48 mins.
VHS: **S19172. $19.98.**

Tribute to John Coltrane
Wayne Shorter, Eddie Gomez, Jack DeJohnette, Dave Liebman and Richie Beirach pay tribute to the master jazzman in this once-in-a-lifetime session. 57 mins.
Laser: **LD71379. $29.95.**

Tribute to Sidney Bechet
Saxophonist Bob Wilber and the Smithsonian Jazz Repertory Ensemble salute the master of the soprano sax, Sidney Bechet. The great New Orleans traditional jazz musician is remembered in songs he helped popularize, such as "Summertime" and "Daydreams."
VHS: **S13055. $29.95.**

Trumpet Kings
Wynton Marsalis hosts this look at the great trumpet players of jazz, from Louis Armstrong to Miles Davis and Lester Bowie. 72 mins.
VHS: **S03212. $39.95.**

The Universal Mind of Bill Evans
Legendary composer and pianist Bill Evans teaches the viewer the meaning of jazz, through live performance and engaging discussion. Hosted by Steve Allen. 1966, 45 mins.
VHS: **S14740. $19.95.**

Vassar Clements
This concert highlights the virtuoso fiddler Vassar Clements, whose music is steeped in country, modern jazz, swing and blue grass. 60 mins.
VHS: **S19215. $24.95.**

We Like the Blues: Vol. 1
Featuring blues-influenced contemporary performers such as Dr. John, The Fabulous Thunderbirds, Steve Marriott, Ten Years After, and more. 51 mins.
VHS: **S03825. $19.95.**

We Like the Blues: Vol. 2
Featuring John Martyn, Dr. John with Chris Barber's New Orleans Jazz Band, Climax Blues Band and more. 51 mins.
VHS: **S03826. $19.95.**

Willie Dixon
Chicago blues artist Willie Dixon interweaves traditional elements of black folklore and storytelling with the pessimism and soulful intensity of country blues. The numbers include "29 Ways," "I Think I Got the Blues," "It Don't Make Sense," "Gonna Rock This House Tonight" and "T'ain't Nobody's Business."
VHS: **S19680. $19.95.**

The World According to John Coltrane
Extensive performance footage of songs like "My Favorite Things" and "Naima" capture this musician in unexpected moments of musical intimacy. Made in full cooperation with Alice Coltrane, this documentary offers the definitive version of Coltrane's life.
VHS: **S26856. $19.98.**
Robert Palmer/Toby Byron, USA, 1991, 60 mins.

Wynton Marsalis: Blues and Swing
Live performances, interviews and master classes with jazz trumpeter Wynton Marsalis. Selections include "Knozz Moe King", "Caravan", "Big Butter and Egg Man", "Cherokee" and many more. USA, 79 mins.
VHS: **S15310. $14.98.**

Zoot Sims Quartet
Zoot Sims, saxophone, Roger Kellaway, piano, Larry Bunker, drums, Chuck Berghofer, bass, sparkle in "Zoots Piece," "My Old Flame," "On the Trail," and "Motoring Along" at Dontes Jazz Club in Los Angeles. 28 mins.
VHS: **S04171. $24.95.**

OTHER MUSIC

!Male! (In Excelsis Corruptus Deluxe)
The Foetus Inc. line-up, comprised of Clint Ruin, Norman Westberg (Swans), Al Kizys (Of Cabbage and Kings) and David Ouimet (Cop Shoot Cop), gathered for this live performance of their recent American tour. The numbers include "Free James Brown," "Fin," "Honey I'm Home," "Butterfly Potion" and "Death Rape 2000." 75 mins.
VHS: **S19616. $19.95.**

11th and B: East Village Summer of Love
A French group made this music video featuring the music of Alan Vega, Marty Rev (both of Suicide) and the False Prophets. Each song is bracketed by a verite documentary of Scott Borofsky spray-painting a mural on a tenement wall. Together these elements capture the feeling of this art-filled New York neighborhood.
VHS: **S22649. $19.95.**
Marie Martine, USA, 1985, 20 mins.

America's Music: Country & Western 1
Gene Weed hosts a Country Jamboree with everything from Cajun to Country Rock, and featuring performers including Sylvia, Razzy Bailey, Eddie Dean, Doug Kershaw, and Patti Page. 60 mins.
VHS: **S05030. $19.95.**

America's Music: Country & Western 2
Gene Weed continues with presentations by Moe Bandy, Jerry Lee Lewis, Terry Gregory, Ricky Skaggs and Terry Gregory. 60 mins.
VHS: **S05031. $19.95.**

Andy Williams in Concert at Branson
This phenomenal pop star sings some of his most memorable hits at the theater named for him in Branson, Missouri. "Born Free", "Days of Wine and Roses" and even the theme from *The Godfather* are included in this exciting program, along with many other great songs. 85 mins.
VHS: **S22004. $14.95.**

Angel Chants
Beautiful chant music is paired in this video with some of history's most celebrated artists. Van Gogh, Botticelli, Raphael and Rubens are just some of the painters represented in this singular video experience.
VHS: **S22744. $9.95.**

Barbra Streisand: A Happening in Central Park
Includes the songs "People", "Second Hand Rose", "Cry Me a River" and "Silent Night". 60 mins.
VHS: **S22023. $19.98.**

Barbra Streisand: Color Me Barbra
In Streisand's second TV special she sings "Yesterdays", "The Minute Waltz" and "Where Am I Going", as well as other songs, in various settings within an art museum. 60 mins.
VHS: **S22026. $19.98.**

Barbra Streisand: Putting It Together— The Making of the Broadway Album
This is a behind-the-scenes look at recording sessions from Barbra's popular *Broadway Album*. Includes several tracks recorded for this album as well as music videos.
VHS: **S22025. $19.98.**

The Beatles Story: Days of Beatlemania 1962-1970
Rare footage recreates the mania which surrounded this pop group from their earliest Liverpool days. The phenomenon quickly spread from England to America. This video includes interviews with band members at critical points in their careers, as well as interviews with members of the Beatles' inner circle. 60 mins.
VHS: **S27698. $14.95.**

Beethoven Lives Upstairs
It is 1820s Vienna, and Ludwig Van Beethoven is desperately trying to compose his Ninth Symphony. As he struggles to balance his musical obsession with the reality of his increasing deafness, Beethoven rents the upstairs flat in the depressed household of ten-year-old Christoph. He watches and listens as Beethoven swiftly turns his house into chaos.
VHS: **S16706. $19.98.**
David Devine, USA, 1990, 51 mins.

Bill Monroe: Father of Bluegrass Music
In this documentary the fiery radical and originator of this true American musical form emerges to contradict the stereotypes of gentle country grandfather who peaceably strums his guitar on the front porch. Ultimately he will be remembered as a true innovator and consummate performer.
VHS: **S20755. $19.95.**
Steve Gebhardt, USA, 1993, 91 mins.

Bizet's Dream
Young Michelle is inspired by the newest operatic work written by her piano teacher, Georges Bizet. The plot of *Carmen* leads her to imagine a scenario involving her parents in a love scandal. This delightful story mixes fact and fiction to offer an intriguing portrait of the great composer Bizet. 53 mins.
VHS: **S26213. $19.98.**

Black Easter
A collection from Flaming Lips, including "2001 Intro," "Ode to C.C. (Part Two)," "Dream Sequence for Lou Reed," "Can't Stop the Spring," "Unplugged," "With You," "Prescription Love," "Maximum Dream for Evil Knievel" and "Staring at the Sound." 55 mins.
VHS: **S19627. $19.95.**

Border Clash Volume 1
This reggae dance extravaganza features Skull Man, Tonto Metro, Bean Man & Ghost, Bounty Killer & Anthony Red Nose, Lady Saw and Terry Ganzie.
VHS: **S21888. $24.95.**

Border Clash Volume 2
Ninja Kid, General B, Round Head, Louie Culture, Captain Barkly, Wicker Man, Little Chris, Professor Nut and Daddy Screw are featured in this reggae video.
VHS: **S21889. $24.95.**

Brian Wilson: "I just wasn't made for these times"
Brian Wilson, the musical visionary behind the Beach Boys, stands revealed in this feature length documentary. Made by record producer Don Was, it manages to get inside Wilson's life, his eccentricities, his troubled childhood and the strange home life he himself led as a distant father. Though some delicate points are not investigated, including the death of Wilson's brother, Beach Boy drummer Dennis Wilson, this film is good at explaining the source and achievements of Brian Wilson's pop innovations.
VHS: **S26949. $19.99.**
Don Was, USA, 1995, 69 mins.

Buju on Top
Little Major, Little Flipper, Lady P., Junior Cat, Little Ray, Super Sass, Itchy Ranks, Rony Rebel, Alton Black, Wayne Wonder and Buju Banton are featured in this reggae video.
VHS: **S21890. $24.95.**

Cage/Cunningham
For 45 years, composer John Cage and choreographer Merce Cunningham have collaborated. On this video, the importance of their association and their interaction with other leading figures in art, literature, dance and music are explored. 95 mins.
VHS: **S26792. $19.95.**

Carole King in Concert
Filmed live at Hartford's Bushnell Hall during Carole's 1993 *Color of Your Dreams* tour, this program shows the range of this famed vocalist/song writer. 82 mins.
VHS: **S22005. $19.95.**

The Changer: A Record of Times
Cris Williamson's landmark album, *The Changer and the Changed*, marked the start of women's music. Interviews with the most important singers of this vital musical tradition are featured. Along with Williamson, Meg Christian, Bonnie Raitt, June Millington, Vicki Randall, Holly Near, Margie Adams and many others recall this album on the occasion of Williamson's 1990 concert in Berkeley. Musical clips from 1975 are also featured.
VHS: **S19450. $39.95.**

Chantmania
It all began when Father Connif was excommunicated for teaching his choral ensemble "99 Bottles of Grog on the Wall". This classic is joined by a number of other soulful but mindless ditties, like "Losing My Religion", "We Will Rock You", "Smells Like Teen Spirit" and "Do Ya Think I'm Sexy", for a hilarious but religious experience.
VHS: **S22536. $12.98.**

Chet Atkins & Friends
The Everly Brothers, Emmylou Harris, Waylon Jennings, Mark Knopfler, Michael McDonald, Willie Nelson in a super session filmed in Nashville brings together the best artists in a tribute to the man and the music. From his moving solo performance of *I Just Can't Say Goodbye* to the rousing, all-on-stage *Corinna, Corinna*, it was music from the heart. 60 mins.
VHS: **S05125. $19.99.**

Chet Atkins 1955-1975
"Mr. Guitar", Chet Atkins, is featured playing all over the world on this video. From Nashville to Norway, his singular style and virtuosity set a standard which other guitarists can only hope to emulate.
VHS: **S27314. $29.95.**

Chet Atkins 1975-1995
For over 40 years, Chet Atkins has been associated with the finest Nashville-based fingerstyle guitar sounds. In the second half of his career, the span covered in this video, his continued growth as a musician is amply illustrated.
VHS: **S27315. $29.95.**

COMM3TV Vol. 1
An overview of the hard rock and distinctive sounds putout by the Brooklyn-based label, including Brenda Kahn, Poopshovel, Arson Garden, Zuzu's Petals, Big Trouble House and Cattle Prod. 50 mins.
VHS: **S19618. $19.95.**

Dancehall Vibes
A raunchy reggae dance video which features Glammor Wayne, Sugar Minott, Alton Black and Mr. Big Wood.
VHS: **S21892. $24.95.**

Dead Can Dance: Toward the Within
This film provides an in-depth look at the music of Dead Can Dance. It features excerpts from a mesmerizing performance at the Mayfair Theater in Santa Monica and revealing interview footage. Together these elements provide a glimpse into the workings of this singular musical partnership. 75 mins.
VHS: **S22508. $19.98.**
Laser: **LD74609. $34.98.**

Devo: The Complete Truth About De-Evolution
A look at Devo, whose distinctive voice, enigmatic lyrics and heady stage shows secured their reputation. The numbers include "Whip It," "Beautiful World" and "Satisfaction."
Laser: **LD71931. $49.95.**

Dewey Balfa—The Tribute Concert
On May 17, 1992, musicians gathered to honor the great Cajun fiddler. 60 minutes of incredible music by this master are featured.
VHS: **S22384. $44.95.**

Disarmament: Savage Republic
A performance video of the group's 1986 concert for the participants of the Great Peace March for Nuclear Disarmament. "Muted color ghosts images of the republic float over and under all around one another, breaking down, dissolving, changing, reassembling, repeating. [It is] somewhat psychedelic" (Jon Killough). 55 mins.
VHS: **S19629. $19.95.**

Discovering Country and Western Music
Country and Western has enjoyed explosive popularity the world over. This program traces the development of this popular style, measuring the impact of mass media and growing urbanization on this enduring music. 23 mins.
VHS: **S23510. $49.95.**

Discovering Electronic Music
Electronics are now used to alter music through scientific understanding of the physical basis of music. The sound synthesizer can create, envelop and even filter sound, resulting in new and more precise aural compositions. 23 mins.
VHS: **S23516. $49.95.**

Dope, Guns and Fucking Up Your Videodeck, Vol. I
A raucous collection of cutting edge video clips by Dr. Sphincter ("Your Guest Host with the Most"), Helmet ("Bad Mood"), Helios Creed ("The Rant"), Cows ("Cartoon Corral"), King Snake Roost ("Top End Killer") and Tar ("Les Paul Worries"). 50 mins.
VHS: **S19623. $19.95.**

Dope, Guns and Fucking Up Your Videodeck, Vol. II
A radical collection of exuberant videos, most of them shot on high quality 16mm, features the distinctive lyrics and hard-edged soul of Helmet, Cows, Helios Creed, Surgery, Vertigo, Boss Hog, Tar, Godbullies, Cosmic Psychos, The Crows and With Your Host. 50 mins.
VHS: **S19619. $19.95.**

Eddie Fisher: A Singing Legend
The 50s' most popular singer had a string of hits that made him a household name. In this collection of his best performances are renditions of "Wish You Were Here," "You Oughta Be in Pictures," "Thinking of You," "In Old New York," "May I Sing to You" and many more. 40 mins.
VHS: **S21219. $19.98.**

Endless Summer: Donna Summer's Greatest Hits
In celebration of the Disco Diva's 20th anniversary, this collection of her hits is available on video. Her classic tunes "I Feel Love", "Last Dance", "MacArthur Park", "She Works Hard for the Money", "Unconditional Love" and many more are included. 60 mins.
VHS: **S23433. $19.95.**

Fingerstyle Guitar
The performances in this video series present two generations of artists who advanced the acoustic guitars cause. Folk, blues and country roots offer a springboard into personal harmonic and melodic pathways. Artists who bridged the gap between folk styles and the innovations of folk, baroque, American primitive guitar, New Age, and even new acoustic are all included in this thorough collection.
Volume 1: New Dimensions and Explorations. Peter Finger, Loe Kottke, Brad Jones, Adrian Legg, John Fahey, Bert Jansch, Jorma Kaukonen, Preston Reed and Woody Mann perform on this volume.
VHS: **S22494. $19.95.**
Volume 2: New Dimensions and Explorations. Dave Evans, John Renbourn, Stefan Grossman, John Knowles, Pat Donahue, Marcel Dadi, Duck Baker, Chris Procter, El McMeen and Joe Miller play on this video collection of acoustic guitar greats.
VHS: **S22495. $19.95.**
Volume 3: New Dimensions and Explorations. Steve Howe, Larry Coryell, Pepino D'Agostino, Martin Carthy, Martin Taylor, Bob Brozman, Martin Simpson and Tim Sparks are all featured in this last volume.
VHS: **S22496. $19.95.**

Flashbacks: Easy Lovin'
Tom Jones, Linda Ronstadt, The Carpenters, Kenny Rogers and Bobby Darin are all included, singing some of the most beautiful ballads of yesteryear. 30 mins.
VHS: **S24669. $14.98.**

Flashbacks: Pop Parade
Dionne Warwick, Jim Croce, Raquel Welch, The 5th Dimension, Sonny & Cher and many other superstar pop singers are included in this blast from the past. 30 mins.
VHS: **S24668. $14.98.**

Flashbacks: Soul Sensations
Ike & Tina Turner, Gladys Knight and the Pips, Lou Rawls and more soul icons from the 1960's are included on this amazing look back at a great time in music. 30 mins.
VHS: **S24667. $14.98.**

Follies in Concert
From the Avery Fisher Hall at Lincoln Center, 18 stars of the performing arts salute the music and talent of Stephen Sondheim. With Carol Burnett, Barbara Cook, Andre Gregory, George Hearn, Phyllis Newman, Mandy Patinkin, Lee Remick, Elaine Stritch and the New York Philharmonic. USA, 1987, 90 mins.
VHS: **S06997. $14.95.**

Gentlemen Jim Reeves: The Story of a Legend
This famed country singer was tragically killed at the height of his powers in an airplane crash on July 31, 1964. In this absorbing video his story is finally told. A number of his hit songs, including "Bimbo", "Four Walls", "He'll Have to Go" and "Adios Amigo", reveal the extent of Jim Reeves' monumental talent.
VHS: **S18705. $19.95.**

George Crumb: The Voice of the Whale
A unique portrait of Pulitzer Prize-winning American composer George Crumb; his life, his art, and the connections between the two. Included in this film are performances from Crumb's "Vox Balaenae for Three Masked Players," samples of the rural gospel music which has influenced Crumb of the exotic instruments and unusual effects which figure in his compositions.
VHS: **S07746. $24.95.**
Robert Mugge, USA, 1976, 54 mins.

George Jones: Golden Hits
Along with rare interview footage, this video features film clips of Jones performing his hit songs from the times when they were at the top of the charts, from 1959 up until today. "The Door," "Golden Ring," "Near You" and "The Race Is On" are just some of the songs included. 50 mins.
VHS: S21698. $19.95.

Grokgazer
Todd Rundgren's music is paired with fantastic computer-generated art reminiscent of pop/psychedelic imagery from the 1960's. This visual concert hall for the mind showcases intricate and evolving forms, colors and shapes. 45 mins.
VHS: S26091. $14.95.

Hated: GG Allin and the Murder Junkies
A portrait of GG Allin, the punk artist who was found dead from a drug overdose on the Lower East Side in June, 1993. Allin's sado-masochistic act resulted in more than 50 arrests. The songs include "Die When You Die," "Snakeman's Dance," "I Wanna Kill You" and "Bite It You Scum." *Hated* lies somewhere between the satiric world of *Spinal Tap* and the tragic world of *Dream Deceivers* (*The Village Voice*).
Todd Philipps, USA, 1993, 60 mins.

Heartworn Highways
James Szalpski's documentary about the rebirth of country music around Austin and Nashville in the mid-70s. The film looks at the artists, music, and maverick performers who rebelled against the Nashville establishment to form a new American idiom. "Superbly conceived and executed, it's by far the best musical documentary I've seen since *Woodstock*" (Austin American-Statesman). With Guy Clark, Townes Van Zandt, David Allan Coe, Barefoot Jerry, Steve Young, Steve Earl and the Charlie Daniels Band.
VHS: S19122. $29.95.
James Szalpski, USA, 1981, 92 mins.

High Lonesome
Mac Wiseman narrates the story of Bluegrass music. It's all here, from the origins of Bluegrass in the Kentucky foothills to the innovations of modern times. Bill Monroe and other seminal figures are featured. Only the music itself could tell a tale that begins with the upheavals of the Great Depression and follows through into our own era. 95 mins.
VHS: S23041. $19.95.

The Highwaymen: On the Road Again
Johnny Cash, Willie Nelson, Kris Kristofferson and Waylon Jennings combine their talents in this concert filmed during a European tour. The highlights are Cash's "Folsom Prison Blues," Nelson's "Always on My Mind" and "Crazy," Kristofferson's "Help Me Make It through the Night" and Jennings' "Luckenbach, Texas." 60 mins.
VHS: S19582. $14.95.

Hot Tuna: 25 Years and Runnin'— Live at Sweetwater
Jefferson Airplane guitarist Jeff Kaukonen and bassist Jack Casady decided to play some old blues tunes. The result is *Hot Tuna*. Now, 25 years later, they still play the blues. This concert performance was taped at the Sweetwater, a Bay Area landmark. Interview footage and appearances by guests like Bob Weir of the Grateful Dead make this video a terrific musical experience. 60 mins.
VHS: S22493. $19.95.

House of Usher—Malice in Wonderland
This music video provides insight into the musical development and parallel evolution of 3-D computer animation that defines Formaldehyde, the record label from Berlin, Germany. It offers a collaborative format, where composers and computer animators were free to fuse these different art forms. 30 mins.
VHS: S22227. $14.98.

In Love with These Times
The program features numbers by Verlaines, Gordons, Tall Dwarfs, The Chills, Snapper, Headless Chickens and Straightjacket Fits. 60 mins.
VHS: S19626. $19.95.

It's Hullabaloo!
Shows of the popular music show from 1965-66 are collected in this set of four volumes. Famous guest hosts like Frankie Avalon, Annette, Soupy Sales and Petula Clark will inspire uncontrollable outbreaks of nostalgia. But it's music from The Shangri-Las, Marianne Faithfull, Brenda Lee, The Rolling Stones, The Supremes, Lola Falana, The Everly Brothers and more that make this collection so worthwhile. Each video is approximately 60 mins.
VHS: S27638. $79.98.

Jeanette MacDonald in Performance
A 1950 performance that stands as a testament to the artistry of Jeanette MacDonald, with selections including "If I Could Tell You," "California Here I Come", "Will You Remember", "Italian Street Song", "In My Garden" and more. 23 mins.
VHS: S13245. $24.95.

Jim Reeves/Ray Price (with Ernest Tubb)
The spirited and classic country entertainers Jim Reeves and Ray Price are highlighted in this video collection, with some additional performances from Ernest Tubb. Jim Reeves' output includes "I've Lived a Lot in My Time", "Then I'll Stop Loving You" and "Down in the Caribbean". Ray Price sings "Crazy Arms", "One Broken Heart Don't Mean a Thing" and "You Done Me Wrong". Ernest Tubb concludes the video with seven songs, including "If I Never Have Anything Else", "Dear Judge" and "I'm with a Crowd". 60 mins.
VHS: S19212. $24.95.

John Cage: I Have Nothing to Say and I Am Saying It
The visionary avant-garde composer John Cage reflects on his art and music as he discusses his philosophy, creative habits and the chance element of composing. In addition artist Robert Rauschenberg and choreographer Merce Cunningham discuss *Minutiae*, their collaboration with Cage. The late composer's *4'33"* is also performed. With Laurie Anderson, Yoko Ono, Joel Jacobs and David Tudor. 56 mins.
VHS: S18731. $39.95.

John Cage: Mushrooms et Variations
This modernist American composer has brought Zen and the values of silence to the traditions of serious music. His influence has been felt across many artistic traditions, including the development of Fluxus and the concerns of the mass media arts. 75 mins.
VHS: S22559. $113.00.

Karen Akers: On Stage at Wolf Trap
Cabaret singer Karen Akers interprets the work of Steven Sondheim, Jacques Brel, Peter Allen and Andrew Lloyd Webber in this live performance. "The quintessential cabaret singer" (*The New York Times*). 59 mins.
VHS: S19230. $29.98.

Legendary Theatre Organists
Rare footage from American films of the 1930's is combined with solo presentations, pictorials and sing-alongs celebrating the legendary organ accompanists to silent film. Featuring Jesse Crawford, Ann Leaf, Reginald Foort, Lew White, Dick Liebert and Don Baker. The program is hosted by organist Gaylord Carter.
VHS: S01659. $39.95.

Legends of Old Time Music
Though widely acknowledged as the source of bluegrass and country, Old Time music is an exciting genre in its own right. This video explores Old Time music's many varieties and demonstrates its blend of Celtic, African and American influences.
VHS: S24372. $29.95.

Legends of Traditional Fingerstyle Guitar
Artists of the fingerstyle guitar, whether using two- or three-finger picking, with or without picks, have fashioned a truly influential body of music. Their innovations inspire musicians to this day. Merle Travis, Elizabeth Cotten, Mance Lipscomb, Brownie McGhee and Josh White demonstrate their virtuosity on this video. 58 mins.
VHS: S22483. $19.95.

Liberace
A comprehensive collection of this audacious performer's vast output. All the diamonds, dazzle and dashing that make his music so popular are showcased in this three-volume set.
Volume 1. 75 mins.
VHS: S15874. $19.98.
Volume 2. 75 mins.
VHS: S15875. $19.98.
Volume 3. 75 mins.
VHS: S15876. $19.98.

Light Dance
Santana's music will lead you through this visual exploration of the natural world. The patterns of light and color found in a variety of mystical landscapes are revealed in this inspired video. From the outermost vistas of the universe to fields of wildflowers, this tape offers a visual feast. 40 mins.
VHS: S26092. $19.95.

Listen Up: The Lives of Quincy Jones
A feature-film portrait of legendary composer and arranger Quincy Jones. Tracing his illustrious career from a chart-busting pioneer of pop music's early years to composing scores for over 40 movies and producing/ arranging the top selling album of all time—Michael Jackson's *Thriller*. Featuring appearances by Ray Charles, Frank Sinatra, >Rev. Jesse Jackson, Ice-T, Barbra Streisand and dozens more.
VHS: S14105. $19.98.
Laser: LD70614. $29.98.
Ellen Weissbrod, USA, 1990

Live at the Bradford
Powerful performances from the Mission of Burma's *Vs.* and *Calls and Marches* albums, including some breathtaking versions of "That's How I Escaped My Certain Fate," "Mica," "Outlaw," "Peking Spring," "He Is, She Is," "Fun World," "Max Ernst" and "Academy Fight Song." 35 mins.
VHS: S19624. $19.95.

Lyrics by Tim Rice
Britain's most famous lyricist is the object of this special musical tribute. Marti Webb, Elaine Paige and David Essex join to perform a selection of Tim Rice's most popular songs, including hits co-written with Andrew Lloyd Webber, such as "Jesus Christ Superstar" and "Don't Cry for Me, Argentina." 52 mins.
VHS: S21699. $14.95.

Marvin Gaye
This video is a a look at the life and music of the late Marvin Gaye. Hosted by Smokey Robinson, the tape also features Ashford and Simpson and Motown founder Berry Gordy, Jr. 60 mins.
VHS: S21675. $19.95.

Merle Travis: Rare Performances 1946-1981
The great American musician Merle Travis is captured in all his versatility in this collection of film footage spanning over 35 years. His fingerstyle technique is widely influential—after all, he wrote over 900 songs. 60 mins.
VHS: S22484. $19.95.

Michael Crawford: A Touch of Music in the Night
Talented vocalist Michael Crawford is seen performing in the studio, singing classics like "When You Wish upon a Star" and "If You Could See Me Now". His newer hits "The Power of Love" and "She Used to Be Mine" are also included, along with many more favorites. 40 mins.
VHS: S20689. $19.95.
Laser: LD72319. $29.98.

The Mills Brothers Story
This nostalgic documentary about one of the most beloved vocal groups spans more than 50 years of their show business history. Through film clips dating back to 1932, you'll hear many timeless Mills Brothers songs, including "Paper Doll," "You Always Hurt (The One You Love)", "Till Then" and "Yellow Bird". 56 mins.
VHS: S15856. $29.95.

Music for the Movies: Bernard Herrmann
This documentary was nominated for an Academy Award because it so successfully illustrates the importance of music to the movies. Herrmann worked on over 50 films during his career, including the legendary *Citizen Kane*. Though most widely known for his work with Hitchcock on films like *The Man Who Knew Too Much* and *Psycho*, he also collaborated with other great directors, such as Martin Scorsese on *Taxi Driver*. Includes clips from these and other films.
VHS: S26668. $24.98.
Laser: LD75108. $24.98.
Josh Waletzky, USA, 1992, 58 mins.

Music for the Movies: The Hollywood Sound
During the golden age of Hollywood, from the 1930's to the 1950's, musical accompaniment in American film reached a high point. Based on the achievements of 19th century masters, these scores transformed films into overwhelming sensory experiences. This BBC documentary explains their evolution. Under the direction of John Mauceri, the BBC National Orchestra of Wales performs this tribute to Hollywood films like *Laura* and *Casablanca*.
VHS: S26917. $24.98.
Laser: LD75401. $29.98.
J. Waletzky/M. Smilow, Great Britain, 86 mins.

Music with Roots in the Aether
Performances by and interviews with David Behrman, Philip Glass, Alvin Lucier, Gordon Mumma, Pauline Oliveros, Terry Riley and Robert Ashley, in this 14-hour (seven 2-hour cassettes) overview of the contemporary American composing scene. Produced in 1976.
VHS: S20867. $450.00.

Natural Selections
A merging of visuals and progressive instrumental music offers selections from Tangerine Dream, Jan Hammer, David Lanz & Paul Speer, Michael Stearns and James Reynolds. "A feast of sight of sound" (*Los Angeles Times*). 50 mins.
VHS: S19594. $14.95.

Nature of Music
What is music? Why has every society throughout the world—and throughout history—regarded it as so important? To answer these questions, award-winning producer/director Jeremy Marre travels the globe examining everything from the throat songs of Inuit Eskimos to Wagner's *Ring* at Bayreuth. 135 mins.
VHS: S11756. $49.95.

New Wave Hits of the '80's, Volume 1
This is the most comprehensive series of 80's music ever. "Video Killed the Radio," "Star," "Love Plus One," "Come on Eileen", "Girls on Film," "I Eat Cannibals", "I Want Candy" and "Twilight Zone" are just some of the tunes included in this video. 35 mins.
VHS: S22446. $14.98.

New Wave Hits of the '80's, Volume 2: Just Can't Get Enough
This is the continuation of the most comprehensive series of 80's music ever. Included are "Pop Muzik", "I Ran (So Far Away)", "Mickey", "In a Big Country", "True", "Stand By", "One Thing Leads to Another", "Metro" and many more. 35 mins.
VHS: S22447. $14.98.

No Alternative
Alternative rock bands like Soul Asylum, Smashing Pumpkins and Soundgarden join directors Tamra Davis (*Guncrazy*), Derek Jarman (*War Requiem*), Nick Gomez (*Laws of Gravity*), Jennie Livingston (*Paris Is Burning*) and Hal Hartley (*Simple Men*) in a compilation of short films and music videos that serve as a massive public education campaign for HIV/AIDS prevention among millions of teenage and twenty-something music fans worldwide. 65 mins.
VHS: S21040. $14.95.

Ozric Tentacles—Live at the Fridge
This stereo video by the Ozric Tentacles was recorded live in Brixton, U.K. The tracks "Space Jam," "OG-HA-BE", "Erpland", "Sunscape", "The Throb", "Sniffing Dog" and many other songs are included.
VHS: S22229. $19.95.

Papa John Creach: Setting the Record Straight
Legendary 71-year-old Papa John jams with Eddie "Cleanhead" Vinson, Jorma Kaukonen, Red Callender and George Winston in this unique documentary. Through interviews, rehearsals and major concert appearances over a five-year period, Papa John is revealed as a violinist capable of an unprecedented variety of musical styles. 60 mins.
VHS: S23302. $29.95.

Paul Anka '62
An insightful documentary filmed in 1962, when Anka was at the crest of his popularity, featuring excerpts of many of his greatest hits, including "Lonely Boy", "Diana", "Put Your Head on My Shoulder" and others. 34 mins.
VHS: S20566. $14.95.

Perfect Harmony
A celebration of Tanglewood's 50 years of music is featured in this concert hosted by Marvin Hamlisch. Seiji Ozawa, John Williams and a host of Tanglewood fellows from around the world are also featured. Includes musical selections from Beethoven's *Leonora Overture #3*, John William's *E.T.* and Tchaikovsky's *1812*. 48 mins.
VHS: S26219. $19.95.

Peter Gabriel: Secret World Live
This pop star's exciting show combines spectacle and music. Filmed live at Modena, Italy, it captures the performance of Gabriel's many hits, including "Steam", "Digging in the Dirt", "Red Rain", "Kiss That Frog", "Don't Give Up" and many more.
VHS: S22534. $24.95.
Laser: LD74815. $39.99.

Psychedelic High
It's a collection of psychedelic hits hosted by VH-1's Peter Noone, including The Byrds, The Moody Blues, The Who, Blue Cheer, Small Faces, The Rice, Thunder Clap Newman, and even The Crazy World of Arthur Brown. 32 mins.
VHS: S20980. $14.98.

Pussy Galore: Maximum Penetration
An ode to the honesty and power of Pussy Galore, the New York band fronted by lead singer Jon Spencer. "They're the blood and guts of New York City. Homeless bums in subway stations, the Tompkins Square Riot, dirt, the Hudson river, smut and drug addicts all somehow get wrapped up, dropped in the meat grinder, and squeezed into the grooves of every…album" (Rich Shupe, *Reflex Magazine*). 50 mins.
VHS: S19628. $19.95.

The Real Patsy Cline
Patsy Cline's amazing story, from her humble beginnings through her meteoric rise to her tragic end, add up to a gripping documentary. Rare and classic performances of her hits make this an unforgettable tribute to the legendary country music singer. 48 mins.
VHS: S27568. $14.95.

Red Hot + Country
The Red Hot organization organized this concert featuring great country singers and musicians. Clint Black, Billy Ray Cyrus, Sammy Kershaw, Kathy Mattea, Levon Helm (The Band), Carl Perkins, Earl Skruggs and other greats participated in this AIDS awareness musical special. 70 mins.
VHS: S24725. $19.95.

The Road to God Knows Where
Cinema verite that follows the experiences of Nick Cave and the Bad Seeds during a recent road tour. Bracketed by five video clips, the film offers memorable covers of John Lee Hooker's "Mini Skirts," "I'm Gonna Killa That Woman" and Johnny Cash's "The Singer." The 24 tracks include "Sorrow's Child," "Getting to Phoenix," "Saint Huck" and "Wade in the Water." 113 mins.
VHS: S19611. $19.95.

Rock in the UK
The Hollies, The Spencer Davis Group with Stevie Winwood, The Kinks, Jethro Tull and even The Bee Gees are just some of the recording artists singing their most popular hits in this collection hosted by Peter Noone of VH-1. 32 mins.
VHS: S20979. $14.98.

Rockroots
This educational musical journey traces the roots and rhythms of American pop music from its rural beginnings to the latest technology. The Rockroots Band takes a live audience through all the trends, including folk, blues, swing, R&B, country, rockabilly, Motown, British invasion, rap and more.
VHS: S22477. $99.95.

Shindig! The Righteous Brothers
The Righteous Brothers perform their hits "Unchained Melodies," "You've Lost that Lovin' Feeling," "Little Latin Lupe Lu," "Justine" and "Night Time Is the Right Time." 30 mins.
VHS: S19634. $9.98.

Sinatra
This five-hour authorized biography of Frank Sinatra, produced by his daughter Tina, traces his extravagant life, his rise as the premier singer to Hollywood matinee idol, turbulent personal life, highly publicized marriages, alleged mob connections and complicated relationships with the Kennedys. With Olympia Dukakis, Rod Steiger, Philip Kasnov as Sinatra, Nina Siezmaszko, Marcia Gay Harden and Gina Gershon.
VHS: S17708. $29.98.
Laser: LD71801. $69.98.
James Sadwith, USA, 1992, 245 mins.

Sound: Rahsaan Roland Kirk and John Cage
Two experimental musicians of the first rank here team up in a mesmerizing work. Recorded in 1967, 27 mins.
VHS: S21678. $24.95.

The Spike Jones Story
The first documentary made about this innovative musical humorist. Discover Spike Jones' personal and professional history, including some of his most popular recordings: "Cocktails for Two," "Der Fuehrer's Face," "All I Want for Christmas Is My Two Front Teeth", as well as rarely seen 1950's rock & roll parodies. Meet personal friends, family members, and the zaniest of his collaborators, The City Slickers. 60 mins.
VHS: S15857. $29.95.

Symphony of Wonders
Locations such as the Taj Mahal, the Colosseum, St. Peter's Basilica, the Eiffel Tower, the Great Pyramids, the Amazon, Ayers Rock, Machu Picchu, Mt. Rushmore, the Statue of Liberty and the Grand Canyon are set to musical scores composed specifically for the program. 52 mins.
Laser: LD72248. $34.95.

The Tahitian Choir Volume II
On Rapati Iti, an isolated South Sea island, the chants and dances remains pure, recalling an earlier time. This second volume contains music from this place that once again beguiles listeners with its haunting simplicity and undeniable strength.
VHS: S22413. $19.95.

Times Ain't Like They Used to Be
Subtitled *Early Rural and Popular American Music 1928-1935*, this documentary provides insight into American popular music. The program features the only known footage of pioneer Jimmy Rodgers, who originated country music. The video features archival footage of Whistler's Jug Band, Bob Wills, Jack Johnson's Jazz Band, Otto Gray's Cowboys and Bascom Lamar Lunceford. 70 mins.
VHS: S19209. $24.95.

Tony Bennett: The Art of the Singer
Joseph Mantegna narrates this retrospective look at Tony Bennett's life and music. Despite his incredible run of hits in the 1950's, Bennett ran into trouble with changes in musical taste in the late 1960's. Now he may be enjoying his greatest popularity ever. 60 mins.
VHS: S26916. $19.98.

Twelve O'Clock High, Vol. 1
A vivid collection of the hippest sound in alternative music, with works by Pussy Galore, Savage Republic, Crime and the City, Thin White Rope, Live Skull, Mudhoney, Tall Dwarfs, American Music Club and Soul Asylum. 58 mins.
VHS: S19625. $19.95.

Twelve O'Clock High, Vol. 2
A collection of leading video clips, including vital works from The Flaming Lips, Bad Brains, Babes in Toyland, Foetus, Inc., David Atherton, Thin White Rope, Afghan Whigs and Buffalo Tom. 50 mins.
VHS: S19622. $19.95.

Ute Lemper Sings Kurt Weill
Twenty-one Weill songs are included in this performance based on Lemper's show at the Paris cabaret Les Bouffes du Nord. This songstress brings her own compelling interpretation to standards like "The Ballad of Mack the Knife," "September Song," "Trouble Man," "Die Rote Rosa" and more.
VHS: S23910. $29.95.

Video Network Program One
An eclectic collection of videos from leading Pacific Northwest indy bands, including Nirvana, Mudhoney, Mark Lanegan, The Fluid, Thee Headcoats, Dwarves, Tad, Afghan Whigs, Seaweed, Beat Happening and Walkabouts. 50 mins.
VHS: S19621. $19.95.

Video Network Program Two
A provocative collection of 21 music videos by leading alternative music groups. With cover art by Peter Bagge. The numbers include Sub Pop's "It," Fastbacks' "Gone to the Moon," Big Chief's "Drive It Off," Pond's "Agatha" and Codeine's "Realize." 70 mins.
VHS: S19615. $19.95.

A Visit with Alan Jay Lerner
This lyricist wrote words to songs in many hit musicals. "My Fair Lady," "Camelot," "Brigadoon," "Paint Your Wagon" and the smash "Gigi" are his creations. Of course, there are even more, and they are also included in this video collection.
VHS: S25787. $24.95.

A Visit with Arthur Schwartz
Schwartz is the famed songwriter who collaborated with many lyricists, but he is especially well-known for his work with Howard Dietz. "Dancing in the Dark," "Alone Together," "Make the Man Love Me" and "That's Entertainment" are just some of the songs included on this video, that give an idea of his range.
VHS: S25789. $24.95.

A Visit with Burton Lane
This great songwriter not only discovered Judy Garland and worked with the biggest stars, including Astaire, Crawford and Gable, he also composed the tunes "Old Devil Moon," "Everything I Have Is Yours," "Too Late Now," "How About You," "On a Clear Day" and more.
VHS: S25788. $24.95.

A Visit with Charles Strouse
Master songwriter Strouse produced a number of great songs. Hits like "Tommorrow," "One Boy," "Bye Bye Birdie," "Applause," "Easy Street," "One Last Kiss" and other unforgettable tunes are featured on this video.
VHS: S25786. $24.95.

A Visit with E.Y. "Yip" Harburg
The great songwriter is featured on this musical video. Songs like "Over the Rainbow," "It's Only a Paper Moon," "April in Paris," "Brother, Can You Spare a Dime?," "Old Devil Moon" and more are included.
VHS: S25785. $24.95.

A Visit with Kander and Ebb
Liza Minnelli worked with this songwriting duo so much that it is only fitting she introduce this video. "Maybe This Time," "All That Jazz," "New York, New York" and "Cabaret" offer just some indication of the intense but humorous demeanor behind this great team.
VHS: S25790. $24.95.

A Visit with Mitchell Parish
An amazing Tin Pan Alley songwriter, Parish wrote songs that are still popular. On this video, "Stairway to the Stars," "Volare," "Sweet Lorraine" and "Stardust" reveal the magic of his lyrics.
VHS: S25791. $24.95.

A Visit with Sheldon Harnick
Harnick's songs are distinctively witty, complex and often dark. This video includes his signature works "Sunrise, Sunset," "If I Were a Rich Man," "Matchmaker, Matchmaker" and many more.
VHS: S25792. $24.95.

We've Come for Your Daughters
A compilation work of the emerging acts on the vibrant Seattle label, including Treepeople, Icky Joey, Deadspot, Tonedogs, Vexed, Hammerbox and Coffin Break. 40 mins.
VHS: S19617. $19.95.

Weathered and Torn
A documentary on the final tour of The Dream Syndicate offers live and unreleased versions from their albums *Medicine Show*, *Ghost Stories* and *Out of the Grey*, including "Now I Ride Alone," "Weathered and Torn," "Drinking Problem," "Still Holding On to You," "The Side I'll Never Show" and "Boston." 65 mins.
VHS: S19620. $19.95.

Webb Pierce/Chet Atkins
Two country masters are captured in this video assembly of their greatest works. Webb Pierce performs "I'm Walkin' the Dog," "More and More," "I'm Gonna See My Baby Tonight" and "He's in the Jailhouse Now." Chet Atkins does spirited renditions of "Pickin' the Blues," "Georgia Camp Meeting" and "Arkansas Traveller." 60 mins.
VHS: S19210. $24.95.

Webb Pierce: Greatest Hits
A compilation distilled from filmed performances of the unique voice of Webb Pierce, the country star who enjoyed popularity. He once had 69 hit songs in a row. This program contains 17 of his best known works, including "Wondering," "There Stands the Glass," "In the Jailhouse Now" and "More and More." 52 mins.
VHS: S19896. $14.95.

Wildlife Fantasia
A video that matches music to images of wildlife in search of freedom, joy and spontaneity. In Borneo's rain forest, orangutans slumber under the green canopy through the haunting strains of Roger's "The Virgin Slumber Song"; dolphins and sea lions frolic to the swirl of Debussy's "Reflections on the Water"; Antarctic penguins are captured to Bizet's "Jeux d'Enfants"; and a bald eagle sweeps across the Yellowstone National Park to the strains of a Brahms symphony. 48 mins.
Laser: LD72250. $34.95.

Woodstock 94
This recreation of the original Woodstock concert brought a whole new generation to the ideals of peace, love and music, through a collection of legendary and new performers. Aerosmith, Melissa Etheridge, Peter Gabriel, Metallica, Red Hot Chili Peppers, Salt N' Pepa and more played in the greatest musical weekend since the original concert took place over 25 years ago. 165 mins.
VHS: S22877. $24.95.
Laser: LD74944. $49.99.

Words for the Dying
An examination of the musical collaboration between John Cale, a member of the 60s band Velvet Underground, and avant-garde theorist and producer Brian Eno. Filmmaker Ron Nilsson shows the process of recording a new album, *Words for the Dying*, based on four Dylan Thomas poems. 80 mins.
VHS: S18642. $19.95.

ROCK PORTRAITS & SUPERSTARS

The Band: The Authorized Video Biography
Some of The Band's best music is featured in this video, along with clips of their appearances from *American Bandstand*, *The Ed Sullivan Show* and *The Last Waltz*. Musical giants Eric Clapton, Emmylou Harris, Van Morrison, Todd Rundgren, George Harrison and others testify to the lasting influence of The Band's down-to-earth rock style.
VHS: S26518. $19.95.
Laser: LD75325. $39.98.

Barnes and Barnes Zabagabee
A star-studded retrospective of the world's popular music video artists, featuring Rae Dawn Chong, Mark Hamill, Jose Ferrer, Shaun Cassidy, Stephen Stills, Rosemary Clooney, Weird Al Yankovic, Dr. Demento and featuring the "Original Fish Heads." 40 mins.
VHS: S05197. $19.95.

The Beatles
This tribute to the Fab Four covers their career from the early days in Liverpool to the tragic murder of John Lennon in New York City. A concise history complete with highlights of their performances. 60 mins.
VHS: S16556. $19.95.

Beatles Collection
A priceless collection of video history with *The Beatles: The First U.S. Visit*, and complete versions of *A Hard Day's Night*, *Help!* and *Magical Mystery Tour*. Four cassettes in slipcase collector set.
VHS: S20547. $79.98.

The Beatles' First U.S. Visit
A day-to-day audio-visual diary of the Beatles' first American visit in 1964. Includes rare news, concert and television footage as you go behind the scenes with the Beatles at their hotels and on the road. Also featuring numerous live performances of some of their greatest early hits. England, 85 mins.
VHS: S15172. $24.98.

The Best of 120 Minutes
For six years and still counting, MTV's *120 Minutes* program has offered a weekly showcase of music videos from the best and brightest in cutting edge rock. Includes videos by such artists as: Sonic Youth, Love and Rockets, Violent Femmes and more. 40 mins.
VHS: S14943. $14.95.

The Best of New Wave Theatre, Vol. 1
Highlights from this award-winning cable show, featuring 45 Grave, Suburban Lawns, The Unknowns, Fear, The Blasters, Surf Punks, The Plugz and more, hosted by Peter Ivers. 60 mins.
VHS: S05191. $29.95.

The Best of New Wave Theatre, Vol. 2
Featuring Legal Weapon, Killer Pussy, The Circle Jerks, Fear, The Angry Samoans, Top Jimmy and the Rhythm Pigs and more. 60 mins.
VHS: S05192. $29.95.

Beyond the Doors
An investigation of three cult figures of the music scene of the 60's—Jimi Hendrix, Janis Joplin and Jim Morrison—with the theory that all three were assassinated. Gregory Allen Chatman plays Jimi Hendrix, Riba Meryl is Janis Joplin, and Bryan Wolf plays Jim Morrison. 117 mins.
VHS: S11598. $79.95.

Big Black "Live"
Chicago's powerhouse band rips their way through the detritus to perform startling numbers from their albums *Atomizer* and *Bulldozer and Lungs*. The numbers include "Dead Billy," "Jordan MN," "Kerosene" and "Steelworker." 50 mins.
VHS: S20249. $19.95.

Bizarre Music Television
A collection of the most insane, bizarre and outrageous music videos ever made, including Julie Brown's "Home Coming Queen's Got a Gun," Barnes and Barnes' "Fish Heads," and more. 60 mins.
VHS: S05201. $19.95.

Bo Diddley and the All Star Jam Show
Celebrate with Bo Diddley and friends during this rock 'n' roll All Star Jam Show filmed live at the Irvine Meadows Amphitheatre on October 25, 1985. With Ron Wood, Carl Wilson, Mick Fleetwood, John Mayall and more. USA, 55 mins.
VHS: S15741. $19.95.

Buried Treasures: Volume 1— Breakthrough Directors
A collection of music videos by some of the most innovative video directors to date. This compilation includes samples from Jean-Baptiste Mondino, Jean Paul Goude, David Fincher, Zbigniew, Terence Donovan, Bernard Rose and Russell Mulcahy. Music by The Buggles, Art of Noise, Tom Waits, Grace Jones and more. In Hi-Fi stereo, 30 mins.
VHS: S16160. $14.95.

Buried Treasures: Volume 2— Reggae Classics
This compilation has a reggae theme and has been carefully compiled from nearly two decades worth of videos. Includes performances by Black Uhuru, Bob Marley and the Wailers, and more. 30 mins.
VHS: S15625. $14.95.

Buried Treasures: Volume 3— Rap Source
Captures the unique genesis of the rap movement in music video. Highlights of the program include the earliest works by Eric B. & Rakim and the rare 1992 live version of "Bring the Noise," a collaboration between Anthrax and Public Enemy. With Def Jeff, Isis and Professor X. 35 mins.
VHS: S16684. $14.95.

California Rock
A greatest hits anthology of early 60s California rock, extolling freedom and youth. The titles include Canned Heat's "Let's Work Together," Santana's "Jingo," The Byrds' "So You Want to Be a Rock and Roll Star" and The Grateful Dead's "One More Saturday Night." 33 mins.
VHS: S19314. $14.98.

Carpenters—Yesterday Once More
This retrospective of the music of Karen and Richard Carpenter offers a rare look at a legendary career. For more than a decade, the camera's eye tracked the entertainment phenomenon of the Carpenters—giving this classic collection a wonderful variety. Including performances of some of their greatest hits, including: "We've Only Just Begun" and "Top of the World." 55 mins.
VHS: S14109. $19.95.

Casey Kasem's Rock and Roll Goldmine: The British Invasion
Casey Kasem hosts a nostalgic musical trip back to the city with flowers in its hair. The Summer of Love and all those cool sounds from groups like The Grateful Dead, Santana, Country Joe and Fish, Big Brother and The Holding Company with Janis Joplin, and Van Morrison. Heavy. 39 mins.
VHS: S08035. $19.95.

Chuck Berry: Hail! Hail! Rock and Roll
A documentary-concert film about one of the founding fathers of rock and roll made on the occasion of his sixtieth birthday bash at the Opera House in St. Louis. Chuck doesn't say anything he doesn't want to, but lets the music do all the talking he needs. With Keith Richards, Julia Lennon, Etta James, Robert Cray and many others.
VHS: S06076. $79.95.
Taylor Hackford, USA, 1987, 120 mins.

Chuck Berry: Live at the Roxy
Chuck Berry performs with his trademark abandon in this exuberant rock and roll concert. Displaying his showmanship, Berry performs "Move Over Beethoven," "Hail, Hail Rock and Roll," "Reelin' and Rockin' " and "Johnny B. Goode," among others. Berry is joined in a special appearance by Tina Turner. 60 mins.
VHS: S19895. $14.95.

Chuck Berry: Rock and Roll Music
The founding father of Rock and Roll is featured live in this 1969 performance. Filmmaker D.A. Pennebaker of *Don't Look Back* fame captures his best-known songs, including *Johnny B. Goode*, *Maybelline*, and *Sweet Little Sixteen*. 45 mins.
VHS: S16089. $14.98.

The Clash: Rude Boy
This award-winning semi-documentary captures the social hurricane that swept through the decaying failure of England through the eyes of an unemployed anarchist named Ray Gange. At the eye of that storm was the rock band, the Clash. An interesting film about one of the most important bands in the recent history of popular music.
VHS: S15470. $19.98.
Jack Hazan, Great Britain, 1980, 130 mins.

Compleat Beatles
Everything the Beatles did best, from the early days at the Cavern Club through eight incredible years to the rooftop goodbye concert during the recording of "Let It Be." The Beatles in concert, in films and in rare footage. Narrated by Malcolm McDowell. England, 1982, 119 mins.
VHS: S00261. $19.95.
Laser: Re-mastered. LD74484. $34.98.

The Concert for Bangladesh
This groundbreaking concert documentary brought together some of the rock and roll world's greatest figures. The highlights include a collaboration of Ringo Starr and George Harrison, Bob Dylan's return to live performing after a two-year absence, and a virtuoso turn by guitarist Eric Clapton. With Billy Preston, Leon Russell, Ravi Shankar and Klaus Voormann. "One of the proudest and most remarkable moments in the colorful history of rock and roll" (Robert Hilburn, *Los Angeles Times*).
VHS: S00262. $19.95.
Laser: LD75306. $39.98.
Saul Swimmer, USA, 1972, 95 mins.

The Creation of the Woodstock 1969 Music Festival: Birth of a Generation
Archival photographs, rare film footage and interviews with the producers, planners and performers from this event recall some of the magic of the fabled gathering. 500,000 young people claimed a place and a time for their music and inadvertently named a generation, the Woodstock generation. 60 mins.
VHS: S24313. $19.99.

Crosby, Stills and Nash: Acoustic
Crosby, Stills and Nash perform their greatest hits live at San Francisco's Warfield Theater in November, 1991, with these favorites: *Deja Vu*, *Helplessly Hoping*, *Guinnevere*, *Marrakesh Express*, *Suite: Judy Blue Eyes*, *Wooden Ships*, and many more! 80 mins.
Laser: LD72295. $29.95.

Cure—Staring at the Sea
A collection of videos featuring the nihilistic British band The Cure. Songs include "Killing an Arab," "Boys Don't Cry," "Play for Today," "Close to Me" and more. 82 mins.
VHS: S04583. $24.98.

The Cutting Edge
A two-volume collection of the best of The Cutting Edge. Features the highlights from the MTV program featuring The Fleshtones. With Dale Alvin, REM, Willie Dixon, Tom Waits, Jonathan Richman and the Modern Lovers, The Blasters, The Alarm, Red Hot Chili Peppers, Benjamin Weisman, Stan Ridgeway, and Husker Du. Each volume 60 mins.
Volume 1.
VHS: S05205. $24.95.
Volume 2.
VHS: S05206. $24.95.

David Bowie—The Glass Spider Tour
A live two hour concert featuring the vocal talents of entertainer and musician David Bowie. An uncut performance to be released after a 44 minute version is shown on tv on ABC. Musical guests include Peter Frampton.
VHS: S06608. $29.95.
David Mallet, 1988, 120 mins.

Direct Art, Good Lovin' Guitar Man and Other Works
Includes music videos of the Jickets. With Chett Grant, Larry Lame. Includes *Good Lovin' Guitar Man*, *Heterosexual Love*, *Bloody Stump*.
VHS: S10207. $29.95.

Dominoes: Portrait of a Decade
Called "one of the few pieces to authoritatively capture the view from inside the counterculture" by *Video Review*, *Dominoes* is a unique audio-visual portrait of the 60s, conveying the director's view that in the turbulent decade "one thing led to another like dominoes." Composed of footage from both TV news and independent filmmakers, juxtaposed with a soundtrack including B.B. King's "The Thrill Is Gone" and the Rolling Stones' "Gimme Shelter".
Laser: CAV. LD70106. $49.95.
John Lawrence Re, USA, 1989, 59 mins.

Don't Look Back
One of the best portraits of an artist ever put on film, *Don't Look Back* is about Bob Dylan and the Sixties. Director Pennebaker, known for *Monterey Pop*, filmed Dylan during his 1965 English concert tour, capturing both private moments and public performances. With Joan Baez, Alan Price, Donovan.
VHS: S00357. $19.98.
D.A. Pennebaker, USA, 1967, 95 mins.

The Doors
Oliver Stone investigates the life of poet-musician Jim Morrison and discovers the rock idol couldn't handle drugs, women or success. Val Kilmer does a reasonable job impersonating the lead singer of *The Doors*, but as wild as the film concerts get, the albums are better. With Meg Ryan, Kyle MacLachlan and Crispin Glover as Andy Warhol. This is the end, my friend.
VHS: S14534. $14.98.
Oliver Stone, USA, 1991, 138 mins.

The Doors: A Tribute to Jim Morrison
This rock document includes exciting live concert footage of The Doors in their prime, and revealing interviews with the individual band members and other music greats. Excerpted numbers include "Light My Fire," "L.A. Woman," "The End" and "Back Door Man." USA, 60 mins.
VHS: S13804. $14.98.

Dr. Demento's 20th Anniversary Collection
For the first time ever, over a dozen classic twisted tunes have been captured on this spectacular video put together by the doctor himself. Featuring madcap artists such as Spike Jones and Weird Al Yankovic, as well as jazz giants Cab Calloway and Fats Waller. Celebrate two decades of musical lunacy. 45 mins.
VHS: S13794. $19.95.

Edie in Ciao! Manhattan
The real-life story of Edie Sedgwick, Warhol superstar, *Vogue* fashion model, heiress to a fortune and a blitzed-out druggie. *Vogue* dubbed her a youthquaker, and *Life* photographed her as a baby-faced mannequin dressed up in Momma's castoff clothes. "This is Sunset Boulevard for real, an Acid Aged Snake Pit," wrote Richard Corliss in *Time*.
Laser: LD70917. $39.95.
John Palmer/David Weisman, USA, 1972, 92 mins.

Enrico Macias Live at the Olympia
Experience the many moods of Enrico Macias in this 1985 performance in front of a sellout audience in Paris. 1985, 105 mins.
VHS: S16191. $69.95.

Freedom Beat: The Video
UK artists against apartheid freedom concert, recorded live on January 5, 1988, including performances by Peter Gabriel, Sade, Elvis Costello, The Style Council, Princess, Maxi Priest and others. 70 mins.
VHS: Out of print. For rental only.
Laser: LD70993. $39.95.

Gimme Shelter
In 1969, the Maysles Brothers followed the Rolling Stones on their North American tour, the climax of which was a free concert for 300,000 fans in Altamont, California. Featuring some of the Stones' most beloved songs, as well as appearances by Tina Turner, Jefferson Airplane and The Flying Burrito Bros., *Gimme Shelter* remains much more than a performance film.
Laser: LD71467. $34.95.
Maysles Brothers/Charlotte Zwerin, USA, 1970

Girls Bite Back
A collection of live recordings from leading alternative groups of the 80s, including Siouxsie & the Banshees, The Slits, Nina Hagen and Girlschool a.m., supplemented by interviews and footage of backstage rehearsals.
VHS: S18257. $19.95.
Wolfgang Buld, USA, 1992, 45 mins.

Go Go Big Beat
This rare rock film presents many of the top 60's British Beat groups in a concert setting, including The Hollies, The Animals, Lulu, The Mersey-Beats and many more.
Kenneth Hume, Great Britain, 1964, 25 mins.
VHS: S05203. $29.95.

Graffiti Bridge
Prince returns as "The Kid" to face his old nemesis from *Purple Rain*, Morris Day. Once again the two battle over a woman. The focus of the film is the music.
VHS: S21437. $14.95.
Prince, USA, 1990, 90 mins.

Grateful Dead Movie
Both concert footage, and behind-the-scenes backstage mechanics, with Jerry Garcia and Leon Gast—and The Grateful Dead in their original, full-length feature.
VHS: S04787. $39.95.
Jerry Garcia, USA, 1976, 131 mins.

The Great Rock and Roll Swindle (The Sex Pistols)
Julien Temple's strange and brilliant essay about the decadence of the extraordinary British punk act, the Sex Pistols. The film intersperses early footage with late period set pieces, including Sid Vicious' elegant and dark cover of *My Way*. "It adds up to the most innovative comic strip fantasy since Tashlin" (*Time Out*). With Malcolm McLaren, Sid Vicious and Johnny Rotten.
VHS: S18405. $24.98.
Julien Temple, Great Britain, 1979, 104 mins.

Guitar Legends
This program looks at the techniques of acoustic and electric guitar players and considers their musical roots and influences. The works include Jeff Beck's "Definitely Maybe", Johnny Winter's "Johnny B. Goode", B.B. King's "Heartbreaker", Jimi Hendrix's "Hey Joe" and Eric Clapton's (with Delaney and Bonnie) "Tribute to Robert Johnson". 33 mins.
VHS: S19315. $14.98.

Hard Day's Night
Richard Lester meets John, Paul, George and Ringo in this exuberant film following an average day in the life of the Beatles as they take under their wing Paul's grandfather while they prepare for a television special in London. Along the way there are 15 now classic songs and a non-stop barrage of verbal and visual gags. Special Edition contains over 15 minutes of bonus footage.
VHS: S04500. $19.98.
Laser: CAV. LD70374. $79.95.
Laser: CLV. LD70375. $49.97.
Richard Lester, Great Britain, 1969, 108 mins.

Heart and Soul
The official Monkee videography, featuring music videos from their album *Pool It*, as well as interviews. 40 mins.
VHS: S05877. $16.95.

The Hours and Times
Christopher Munch's feature debut focuses on the circumstances and possible sexual relationship that existed between John Lennon and the Beatles' manager Brian Epstein during a four-day holiday in Barcelona in Spring 1963. A work of delicacy and heartbreak, the film delves into the inner world of each man, depicting Epstein's erotic obsession and Lennon's confusion and pain as an emerging rock and roll icon. With David Angus, Ian Hart and Stephanie Pack.
VHS: S18741. $19.98.
Christopher Munch, USA, 1991, 60 mins.

Hullabaloo
This four-volume boxed set brings back all the best 60's music from the hit television show *Hullabaloo*. Sonny and Cher, Petula Clark, The Yardbirds, Sammy Davis, Jr., The Everly Brothers, Trini Lopez, The Mamas and the Papas, and Chuck Berry are just a few of the legendary performers featured on this collection. Even the Hullabaloo dancers are back again. Each volume is 60 minutes long.
VHS: S24086. $79.98.

I Wanna Hold Your Hand
Exhilarating comedy on Beatlemania from Robert Zemeckis. Seven teenagers will do anything to see the Fab Four on the Ed Sullivan Show. Will Jordan accurately impersonates Sullivan. With Nancy Allen, Bobby DiCicco, Marc McClure, Susan Kendall Newman, Theresa Saldana, Wendie Jo Sperber and the undefinable Eddie Deezen as the crazy kids. Featuring 17 songs by John, Paul, George and Ringo.
VHS: S08499. $19.95.
Robert Zemeckis, USA, 1978, 104 mins.

Imagine: John Lennon
Subtitled the definitive film portrait. Lennon himself eerily narrates his life story, taken from the tapes he made previous to his murder. Culled from over 200 hours of material supplied by his widow, Yoko Ono. 36 songs are featured.
VHS: S08498. $24.98.
Laser: LD70598. $24.98.
Andrew Solt, USA, 1988, 100 mins.

James Brown & Guest B.B. King
James Brown, the "Godfather of Soul," in a taped concert at the Beverly Theater, where he performs "It's a Man's World", "Papa's Got a Brand New Bag", "Hot Pants" and "Sex Machine." Also featured are B.B. King—who performs his legendary "Thrill Is Gone"—and Michael Jackson, who does a song and dance number. 66 mins.
VHS: S19581. $14.95.

James Brown: The Lost James Brown Tapes
Discovered in the archives of producer Alan Douglas, this is a previously unseen 1979 performance of "Mr. Dynamite" himself. Highlights include a heart-stopping 20-minute rendition of *Sex Machine*. 60 mins.
VHS: S16090. $14.98.

Janis
Rock immortal Janis Joplin in the best cinematic portrait of her stellar but troubled career. Through interviews and concert footage, the documentary traces the gritty-voiced rocker from her childhood to superstardom.
VHS: S03310. $19.95.
Howard Alk/Seaton Findlay, Canada, 1974, 97 mins.

Jerry Lee Lewis: I Am What I Am
The real-life story of "The Killer" as told by Lewis himself and a host of celebrities, including Kris Kristofferson, Roy Orbison, Johnny Cash, Chuck Berry, Dick Clark and Mickey Gilley. Loaded with live performances of Lewis' great hits, including "Great Balls of Fire", "Whole Lotta Shakin' Goin' On", "Breathless" and "Crazy Arms".
VHS: S09608. $19.95.

The Jimi Hendrix Story
A documentary on Jimi Hendrix, perhaps the most innovative player in history. The filmmakers interweave concert footage and interviews with the enigmatic figure and his confidantes and collaborators. The songs include "Purple Haze," "Wild Thing" and "Johnny B. Goode", directed by Joe Boyd, John Head and Gary Weis.
VHS: S02818. $19.98.
Boyd/Head/Weis, USA, 1973, 102 mins.

Jimi Hendrix: Experience
Narrated by British blues master Alexis Korner, *Experience* features Hendrix on- and off-stage in 1967. The program also includes a rare acoustic performance.
VHS: S16091. $14.98.
Peter Neal, 33 mins.

Jimi Hendrix: Woodstock
This legendary rock star was perhaps the finest guitarist and vocalist of his generation. Now on the occasion of the 25th anniversary of the amazing event that was Woodstock, his performance from this concert has been transferred to laserdisc. 57 mins.
Laser: LD74498. $24.98.

Jimi Plays Berkeley
Classic Hendrix live at the 1970 Berkeley Memorial Day Concert with Mitch Mitchell on drums and Billy Cox on bass.
VHS: S00655. $19.98.
Peter Pilafian, USA, 1971, 55 mins.

Joe Cocker: Mad Dogs & Englishmen
This neglected work is considered by many to be one of the classic rock films of the 1970s, along with *The Last Waltz* and *Woodstock*. This outrageous rock tour comes complete with traveling groupies, psychedelic drugs, families and their dogs—a fantastic, loving portrait of an excessive musical era which will likely never be repeated again. Presented in letterbox format.
VHS: S15742. $19.95.
Pierre Adidge, USA, 1971, 119 mins.

John Lennon and the Plastic Ono Band—Live Peace in Toronto, 1969
Lennon's first performance before a live audience in three years—his first with the Plastic Ono Band and Eric Clapton on the guitar. A turning point in his career and a milestone in the history of Rock 'n Roll. Includes "Money", "Cold Turkey", "Give Peace a Chance", "Blue Suede Shoes", "You Make Me Dizzy, Miss Lizzy". 56 mins.
VHS: S09035. $19.99.

John Lennon Live in New York City
This blockbuster video pays tribute to the dream and features John and Yoko's last concert together, and ends with an angry, defiant "Give Peace A Chance". 55 mins.
VHS: S04947. $19.95.

John Lennon: The Bed-In
On May 26, 1969, John Lennon and Yoko Ono moved into Room 1742 of the Queen Elizabeth Hotel in Montreal, and for seven days, from their bed, talked about peace to anyone who would listen. This program features 74 minutes of conversations with Timothy Leary, Tommy Smothers and Al Capp among others. Also includes the classic live bedroom recording of "Give Peace a Chance", "Instant Karma", "Remember Love", John's acoustic version of "Because" and many more.
VHS: S18223. $24.95.

Killdozer "Li'l Baby Huntin'" Live
This hard-edged trio from Madison perform some dazzling works from their *Burl and Snakeboy* album. The highlights are covers of Neil Diamond and Neil Young, as well as "Hamburger Martyr" and "King of Sex." 50 mins.
VHS: S20247. $19.95.

Latino Session
Latin artists combine their distinct sounds for a powerful anthology. The major works include Carlos Santana's versions of "America the Beautiful" and "Mandela", Ruben Blades' "Ojos De Perro Azul" and "Muevete", and collaborations with Celia Cruz, Tito Puente and Poncho Sanchez. 60 mins.
VHS: S19317. $19.98.

Led Zeppelin: Song Remains the Same
The midnight cult favorite on video! Led Zeppelin's legendary 1973 concert appearance at Madison Square Garden, featuring 13 of the band's best songs. USA, 1976, 137 mins.

Lifestyles of the Ramones
This program looks at the evolution of the music of the Ramones, with interviews with the members of the band they influenced, Talking Heads, and Debbie Harry. 58 mins.
Laser: LD70263. $29.95.

Little Richard: Keep on Rockin'
Catch the original wildman of rock 'n' roll at his onstage finest! Seen through the camera of D.A. Pennebaker, Little Richard tears through "Tutti Frutti", "Lucille" and six more favorites.
VHS: S16092. $14.98.
D.A. Pennebaker, USA, 30 mins.

Live Skull "Skullf*ck"
This mercurial, brooding act is captured live during a 1987 *Cloud One* tour, with additional works from their albums *Bringing Home the Bait* and *Pusherman*. The numbers include "Fort Belvedere," "Sparky" and "Wallow in It." 45 mins.
VHS: S20248. $19.95.

Lou Reed
Legendary Lou Reed performs all of his best-known hits, including songs from The Velvet Underground. 60 mins.
VHS: S06551. $19.95.

Madonna: Truth or Dare
The popular musical superstar is the focus, and the executive producer, of this revealing documentary/concert movie that captures the excitement of her 1990 Blonde Ambition world tour. Visit backstage as Madonna chats with Kevin Costner, Sandra Bernhard and Warren Beatty. Come along when she visits her mother's grave. Be there when she leads her dancers and back-up singers in a group prayer. Then sit back and enjoy the sound and fury of blonde ambition in concert.
VHS: S14762. $19.98.
Laser: LD75225. $34.98.
Alek Keshishian, USA, 1991, 118 mins.

Magical Mystery Tour
One of the Beatles' last appearances together, this musical fantasy features such songs as "I Am the Walrus" and "Fool on the Hill." 60 mins.
VHS: S04691. $19.95.
Laser: CLV. LD72095. $29.95.

Mamas & The Papas: Straight Shooter
The life, loves and music of John Phillips, "Mama" Cass Elliott, Michelle Phillips and Denny Doherty in one of the archetypal 60's recreations. 80 mins.
VHS: S09793. $19.95.

Metal Roots
This heavy metal sampler includes Black Sabbath's "Iron Man" and "Black Sabbath", Alice Cooper's "Eighteen", Steppenwolf's "Rock Me" and Deep Purple's "Highway Star". 38 mins.
VHS: S19316. $14.98.

Ministry: In Case You Didn't Feel Like Showing Up
A documentary on Ministry's last tour, combining visuals and music and the crazed attention and energy of its audience. "This live concert is an unmitigated classic" (*Video Review*).
Laser: LD70257. $29.95.

Monterey Pop
Directed by one of the foremost factual filmmakers in the cinema-verite style, *Monterey Pop* records the events at the immense Monterey International Pop Festival. Featuring Otis Redding, Jimi Hendrix, Janis Joplin, Jefferson Airplane, Ravi Shankar.
VHS: Out of print. For rental only.
Laser: LD70422. $49.95.
D.A. Pennebaker, USA, 1968, 84 mins.

Moscow Peace Festival Volume One
On August 12, 1989, seven American heavy metal bands rocked the Lenin Stadium in Moscow. 200,000 Soviet fans listened to Bon Jovi play "Wild in the Streets", "Blood on Blood" and "Wanted Dead or Alive". Also appearing on Volume One are Skid Row, doing "Makin' a Mess", "Youth Gone Wild" and "Holidays in the Sun", plus Cinderella performing "Coming Home", "Nobody's Fool" and "Shake Me". 120 mins.
VHS: S13267. $19.98.

Moscow Peace Festival Volume Two
The beat goes on with the heavy metal stylings of Ozzy Osbourne, Motley Crue, Gorky Park and the Scorpions. This two-day Woodstock in Moscow was dedicated to the motto that rock 'n' roll can make a difference. Songs include "My Generation", "In the Name of Rock 'n' Roll", "Wild Side", "Suicide Solution", "Paranoid", "Big City Nights", "Long Tall Sally", "Still Loving You". 120 mins.
VHS: S13283. $19.98.

Orchestral Tribute to the Beatles
Joan Collins hosts this program which features the Royal Philharmonic Orchestra in classic renditions of famous Beatles songs, performed for the Queen of England. 52 mins.
VHS: S04945. $14.95.

Paul McCartney Special
This complete retrospective of McCartney's career, explored through interviews, previously unreleased film and video clips plus footage of the Beatles at work at Abbey Road studios is punctuated by such hits as "I'm Amazed", "I Saw Her Standing There", "Take It Away". 60 mins.
VHS: S04944. $14.95.

Pink Floyd: The Wall
Bob Geldof stars as Pink, the burned-out rock star slowly going out of control. Conceived and written by Pink Floyd's Roger Waters, with animation by Gerald Scarfe and songs off the album.
VHS: S01030. $19.98.
Laser: LD70654. $34.98.
Alan Parker, Great Britain, 1983, 95 mins.

Pointer Sisters Live in Africa
The dazzling Pointers team up with a native African band in a sizzling hour of swing and standards. Includes "Ring Ding Do," "Salt Peanuts" and "Steam Heat." 45 mins.
VHS: S11702. $19.95.

Prince: Sign "O" the Times
Prince's new, critically-acclaimed concert film, which intersperses dramatic vignettes with Prince's top singles.
VHS: S06618. $19.95.

Pump Up the Volume
An alienated and politically disaffected teenager (Christian Slater) in an Arizona suburb makes pirate radio broadcasts venting his spleen and his libido. He eventually finds himself heading a student revolution in this exciting and affecting comedy-drama with a genuine lift. Written and directed by Canadian independent filmmaker Allan Moyle (*Montreal Main*, *The Rubber Gun*). "*Pump Up the Volume* qualifies as a generational statement in the same way *Rebel without a Cause* did 35 years ago, but without any of the defeatism or masochism of that earlier picture. Don't miss it (Jonathan Rosenbaum)."
VHS: S13554. $19.95.
Allan Moyle, USA, 1990, 105 mins.

Punk and Its After Shocks
In this absorbing documentary, filmmaker Wolfgang Buld shot live recordings by The Clash, The Police, Sex Pistols, Madness, Jam and other seminal acts from December 1979 to January 1980, crosscut with interviews that establish the political, social and artistic flowering of the movement.
VHS: S18256. $19.95.
Wolfgang Buld, USA, 1992, 85 mins.

The Punk Rock Movie
Vulgar, chaotic, noisy and rude, *The Punk Rock Movie* captures the era's great bands and safety-pinned fans in all their raw glory. Candid on- and offstage footage provides a rare look at young rock 'n' rollers who uncompromisingly dared to believe in themselves and their music. With Siouxsie and the Banshees, The Sex Pistols, The Clash, Generation X with Billy Idol and more. 80 mins.
VHS: S12180. $39.95.

Purple Rain
Prince's film debut is a semi-autobiographical account of an up-and-coming musician. Tormented by family problems, he takes his frustrations out on those around him, risking his career and relationships. One of these relationships is with a young woman (Apollonia Kotero) who has her own musical ambitions. A subplot involves a bitter rivalry with another musician played humorously by Morris Day. Also features Olga Karlatos, Clarence Williams III and Jerome Benton.
VHS: S21473. $19.95.
Laser: LD70660. $24.98.
Albert Magnoli, USA, 1984, 111 mins.

Quadrophenia
A compelling adaptation of the Who's classic rock opera featuring Sting. Inspired soundtrack by the Who, and startling images of the street fighting between Mods and Rockers in 1964 England.
VHS: S01076. $19.95.
Franc Roddam, Great Britain, 1979

The Residents: Twenty Twisted Questions
This "alternative music" group began breaking the boundaries and corrupting notions of pop in 1971. Self-made pioneers of the music video, they became—and remain—the definitive audiovisual concept band. *Twenty Twisted Questions* documents two decades of musical innovation, bold experimentation and independent vision. 60 mins.
Laser: CAV. LD71486. $49.95.

Ringo Starr and His All-Starr Band
The legendary drummer of The Beatles is joined by musicians Joe Walsh, Burton Cummings, Todd Rundgren, Nils Logfren, Dave Edmunds and Zak Starkey as they perform versions of "Yellow Submarine," "I Can't Tell You Why," "Bang on the Drum," "American Woman," "In the City," With a Little Help from My Friends," "You're Sixteen," "Rocky Mountain Way," "No Time," "I Hear You Knocking" and many others. 120 mins.
VHS: S19914. $19.98.

Rock, Rock, Rock
The film debut of Tuesday Weld. She plays a teenager with a problem. She needs to raise money for a strapless formal for the prom after father took away her charge card. Made in the Bronx in nine days. Great bands include Frankie Lymon and the teenagers, LaVern Baker, Chuck Berry, The Moonglows and rock promoter Alan Freed. Connie Francis supplies the singing voice for the 13-year-old Weld. B&W.
VHS: S10389. $19.95.
Will Price, USA, 1956, 85 mins.

Rolling Stones—25 x 5: The Continuing Adventures of the Rolling Stones
The definitive history of the Rolling Stones, told for the first time ever by the band themselves. Rocking with a soundtrack of nearly 40 songs, this video-document takes you inside the Stones' personal archives. 129 mins.
VHS: S15311. $19.98.

Rrrecords "Testament" Vol. II
This work penetrates an obscure though growing phenomenon, the emerging international industrial underground that highlights clips from Japanese act Merzbow and Americans Arcane Device, Chop Shop, Generator, Monty Cantsin and works from Naram Sin, Takell-Kizimecca and Pile of Cows. 55 mins.
VHS: S20246. $19.95.

Running out of Luck
Mick Jagger's feature-length film, the story of a rock and roll superstar (Mick) who's isolated from the real world by the beautiful-people hangers-on, features nine songs from Mick's *She's the Boss* solo album.
VHS: S01522. $79.98.
Julien Temple, USA, 1985, 88 mins.

San Francisco Sound
Casey Kasem showcases the sounds of Haight-Ashbury and the "Summer of Love" in this video flashback to one of rock's most experimental periods. Van Morrison, Carlos Santana, Janis Joplin and The Grateful Dead are featured. 39 mins.
VHS: S08036. $19.98.

Sgt. Pepper's Lonely Heart's Club Band
The Brothers Gibb invade the sacred territory of Beatlemania for this all star musical romp. When the Bee Gees are not singing, guest performers include George Burns, Steve Martin, Billy Preston and Peter Frampton. Comedy provided by Frankie Howerd and Donald Pleasance.
VHS: S07811. $19.98.
Michael Schultz, USA, 1978, 111 mins.

Shindig! British Invasion, Vol. 1
A collection works from the best English groups of the 60s, including Gerry and the Pacemakers ("Don't Let the Sun Catch You Crying"), Manfred Mann ("Doo Wah Diddy"), Searchers ("Needles and Pins"), The Honeycombs ("Have I the Right") and Freddy and the Dreamers ("I'm Telling You Now"). 30 mins.
VHS: S19635. $9.98.

Shindig! British Invasion, Vol. 2
One of the most important developments in rock and roll is recounted in this program of musical acts who changed the shape and texture of American music, featuring Freddy & the Dreamers, Manfred Mann, The Zombies, The Animals, Gerry & the Pacemakers, The Yardbirds, and The Searchers. 30 mins.
VHS: S17403. $14.95.

Shindig! Frat Party
Presenting an all-star lineup of talent, this fast-stepping music and dance program is guaranteed to get you onto the dance floor. Featuring The Kingsmen, The Isley Brothers, and the sensational Little Richard. 1965, 30 mins.
VHS: S13927. $14.95.

Shindig! Groovy Gals
Screaming teens dance to songs of first love, heartache and undying devotion performed live by the legendary ladies of pop music. Includes Aretha Franklin, Tina Turner and Petula Clark. 30 mins.
VHS: S14688. $12.95.

Shindig! Jackie Wilson
This volume of the popular series features electrifying performances by Jackie Wilson—lighting up the stage like only he could, with acrobatic moves, an illustrious voice, and a raw sexuality that helped turn him into a legend. 1965, 30 mins.
VHS: S13928. $14.95.

Shindig! Jerry Lee Lewis
It's "The Killer" setting the stage ablaze with his fancy licks and rip-roaring voice. Includes "Great Balls of Fire" and "Whole Lotta Shakin' ". 30 mins.
VHS: S15642. $14.95.

Shindig! Legends of Rock 'n' Roll
A compendium of classic rock and roll performances culled from the '60s music series, featuring The Righteous Brothers, Jerry Lee Lewis, Aretha Franklin, Tina Turner, Bo Diddley, Little Anthony and the Imperials, Johnny Cash, the Everly Brothers, Chuck Berry, and the Godfather of Soul, James Brown. 30 mins.
VHS: S17402. $14.95.

Shindig! Motor City Magic
This episode of the classic prime-time pop music show features performances from The Four Tops, The Supremes, Smokey Robinson and the Miracles, The Temptations, and Marvin Gaye. 1964, 30 mins.
VHS: S13926. $14.95.

Shindig! Sixties Superstars
Get an eye- and earful of the hottest rock acts of the '60s. Includes performances by The Byrds and The Mamas & Papas. 30 mins.
VHS: S15643. $14.95.

Shindig! Soul
Your heart will ache and feet will fly as the sensual and soothing sounds of sweet soul music are performed live by some of the all-time greats. Includes Booker T and the MGs, James Brown and Aretha Franklin. 30 mins.
VHS: S14687. $12.95.

Shindig! The Kinks
This great 60s group is captured in the numbers, "You Really Got Me," "Set Me Free," "See My Friends," "All Day and All of the Night" and "I'm a Lover Not a Fighter." 30 mins.
VHS: S19636. $9.98.

Simon and Garfunkel: The Concert in Central Park
On September 19, 1981, Paul Simon and Art Garfunkel set foot on a stage in front of half a million adoring fans who were gathered in Central Park in New York City to witness musical history—the reunion, after 11 long years, of two of the most talented performers to make music during the turbulent 60's. USA, 1982, 87 mins.
VHS: S15345. $14.98.

Stone Temple Pilots: Live
The energy of today's hottest band, winner of a Grammy for Best Hard Rock Performance with Vocal, is captured in this video that features footage from their breakthrough tour. "Vasoline", "Silvergun Superman", "Crackerman", "Meatplow", "Still Remains", "Creep", "Andy Warhol" and "Plush" are among the songs included. 80 mins.
Laser: LD74644. $29.98.

Storytelling Giant: The Talking Heads Retrospective
Ten music videos featuring The Talking Heads plus original segments made especially for this collection. Includes *Crosseyed and Painless, Once in a Lifetime, Wild Wild Life, Love for Sale, This Must be the Place, Burning Down the House, And She Was, Stay Up Late, Road to Nowhere, The Lady Don't Mind*. 60 mins.
VHS: S06638. $19.98.

Thin White Rope: The Axis Calls
A documentary of The Rope's final tour was shot on location in Europe. A fascinating companion piece to their recent *One That Got Away*, the film contrasts the difficulties of the road with their exuberant stage shows at huge festival gigs. The musical highlights are live versions of "Ruby Sea," "Hunter's Moon," "Red Sun" and "The Fish Song." 75 mins.
VHS: S20250. $19.95.

Time Warner Presents the History of Rock 'n' Roll
Over 10,000 hours of concert and archival footage have been culled to compile this complete history of Rock 'n' Roll. Ten volumes, each covering a specific aspect of this cultural phenomenon, show everything from Elvis to the MTV revolution.
Volume 1: Rock 'n' Roll Explodes. Blues, gospel and jazz are fused into a new musical sound. This volume features Elvis Presley, Chuck Berry, Fats Domino, The Beatles and more.
VHS: S24087. $19.98.
Volume 2: Good Rockin' Tonight. Buddy Holly, Dick Clark, Bono, The Ronettes, and even The King were all caught up in the 50's teen idol craze. *American Bandstand* made idols overnight and set alight a new dance fad every week.
VHS: S24088. $19.98.
Volume 3: Britain Invades, America Fights Back. The Beatles and The Stones vied for influence against Motown and the California sound.
VHS: S24089. $19.98.
Volume 4: Plugging In. Dylan, The Byrds, Jimi Hendrix, The Who and The Beatles all participated in the musical experimentation of the 1960's.
VHS: S24090. $19.98.
Volume 5: The Sounds of Soul. Motown transformed popular music with stars like Sam Cooke, Sam and Dave, Ray Charles, The Jackson 5, Whitney Houston and so many more.
VHS: S24092. $19.98.
Volume 6: My Generation. A full-fledged counterculture emerged and rock played a major role shaping this new cultural force. The Jefferson Airplane, Janis Joplin, The Doors, Neil Young, The Grateful Dead and a host of other performers made the music that transformed a generation.
VHS: S24092. $19.98.
Volume 7: Guitar Heroes. Hendrix, Van Halen, Duane Allman, Clapton, Townsend, Slash, U2 and other guitar heroes set new standards for rock and roll.
VHS: S24093. $19.98.
Volume 8: The 70's: Have a Nice Decade. Metal, glam, disco, reggae and funk were innovations from new stars like Elton John, Steely Dan, Pink Floyd, Frampton and Springsteen.
VHS: S24094. $19.98.
Volume 9: Punk. Before Nirvana and Green Day there were The Sex Pistols, Iggy Pop, The Ramones, Elvis Costello, The Talking Heads and other musical icons.
VHS: S24095. $19.98.
Volume 10: Up from the Underground. Rap and alternative conquered musical worlds through MTV. R.E.M., U2, Smashing Pumpkins, Salt'n'Pepa, and even Michael Jackson made it big through music videos.
VHS: S24096. $19.98.
Time Warner Presents the History of Rock 'n' Roll, Complete Set.
VHS: S24097. $159.92.
Laser: LD74966. $199.99.

Todd Rundgren: 2nd Wind Live Recording Sessions
Not a concert, but a live recording session taped in San Francisco at the Palace of Fine Arts, July 1990. Includes interviews with the band and Todd's introductions to each song. Presented in a four-camera, split-screen format to capture the entire orchestra's performance. 1990, 37 mins.
VHS: S14686. $12.95.

True Story of 200 Motels
A one-hour documentary on the making of Frank Zappa's bizarre 1971 comic musical. Vintage private footage from Frank's personal archives plus behind-the-scenes of the actual shooting and recording. With Ringo Starr, Theodore Bikel, Keith Moon and such songs as "Sleeping in a Jar," and "Strictly Genteel." The inside history of the first feature-length film to be shot on video in 6 days. 60 mins.
VHS: S08348. $29.95.
Laser: LD70196. $39.98.

U2: Rattle and Hum
A concert film from the hot Irish group of musicians as they tour the United States and visit places like Elvis Presley's Graceland and a church in Harlem. Songs include "Where the Streets Have No Name", "With or Without You" and "Pride (In the Name of Love)". With the musical talents of Larry Mullen Jr., Adam Clayton, Bono and The Edge.
VHS: S09924. $19.95.
Laser: LD75279. $34.98.
Phil Joanou, USA, 1988, 90 mins.

Under the Cherry Moon
Prince stars as Christopher Tracy, an American musician on the French Riviera, living off the bank accounts of rich, bored divorcees. But he didn't count either on confronting the heiress' enraged father, or on falling in love.
VHS: S01816. $19.98.
Laser: LD74723. $34.98.
Prince, USA, 1986, 80 mins.

Video Band War Dance
A collection of music video art from the San Francisco-based War Dance. Includes *War Dance, Reagan Commercials, California Zones*, and other pieces. 30 mins.
VHS: S10210. $29.95.

Video Void VIII
A collection of rock, jazz music and poetry recorded at Neither/Nor, the now-closed East village bookstore and performance space. This tape is fresh and lively.
VHS: S10192. $29.95.
Rick van Valkenburg, USA, 1987, 30 mins.

Virge Piersol Short Pieces
A fixed camera black-and-white documentary of musical performances at Jeffrey Lohn's loft. A good portrait of the NYC "art band" aesthetic, featuring solo performances by Laurie Anderson, Rhys Chatham, Glenn Branca.
VHS: S10190. $49.95.
Virge Piersol, USA, 1978, 58 mins.

Welcome to My Nightmare
Alice Cooper's original nail-raising rock 'n' roll spectacular is now available on video. For the uninitiated, Alice is only a stage name for an energetic guy with a fondness for large snakes and the Grand Guignol. Songs include "Eighteen", "School's Out" "Only Women Bleed" and "The Awakening". An elaborate rock theatre production from 1975. USA, 1975, 84 mins.
VHS: S09853. $19.95.

What's Love Got to Do with It
Based on the autobiography of pop diva Tina Turner, this film follows her rise to stardom. It includes the controversial realization of her tempestuous marriage to abusive Ike Turner, and her remarkable comeback.
VHS: S20607. $96.95.
Laser: LD74456. $39.99.
Brian Gibson, USA, 1993, 118 mins.

Women in Rock
A collage of rare historical footage, music videos, and interviews featuring Brenda Lee, Carole King, Tina Turner, Janis Joplin, Bangles, Madonna, Grace Slick in Jefferson Airplane, and many more.
VHS: S01993. $29.95.
Stephanie Bennett, USA, 1986, 57 mins.

Woodstock
Never-before-seen performances by rock legends Canned Heat, Janis Joplin, Crosby Stills and Nash, Jefferson Airplane, Jimmy Hendrix and many others bring alive the spirit of the event that defined a generation. This newly available director's cut of the highly acclaimed documentary, winner of the Academy Award in 1970, shows how three days of peace and music changed the world. Widescreen.
VHS: S06044. $29.98.
Laser: LD70712. $49.98.
Michael Wadleigh, USA, 1970, 225 mins.

Yessongs
The musical rock group Yes is featured in this concert film that follows their 1973 World Tour. Songs include "Roundabout" and "All Good People". Musical fans of this major rock group will not be disappointed. With the video you can have all the encores you want. 70 mins.
VHS: S02252. $14.98.
Laser: LD75023. $39.99.

You Can't Do That: The Making of A Hard Day's Night
When the early Beatles film *A Hard Day's Night* started shooting in Chicago in 1964, few expected that either the film or its subjects would be so wildly successful. Now, over 30 years later, the story behind this film is available on video. Phil Collins appeared as an extra in the film and he appropriately hosts this documentary. 65 mins.
VHS: S24382. $19.98.

Zachariah
The first rock Western stars Country Joe and the Fish, The James Gang, the New York Rock Ensemble, John Rubinstein, Dick Van Patten, Pat Quinn, and a very young Don Johnson. The script is by members of The Fire Sign Theatre. Bizarre and offbeat. Get down and boogie, little dogies. Yee haw meets right on.
VHS: S07155. $19.98.
George H. Englund, USA, 1971, 93 mins.

MUSIC INSTRUCTION

Acoustic Guitar Musicianship
Russ Barenberg teaches this intensive course to help the acoustic guitarist add style and musicality to his or her playing. Russ shows how to achieve good tone, keep solid time, understand accenting and articulation, compose solos, and improvise freely using hammers and pulls, melodic ornamentation, slides, variations, vibrato, damping and syncopation; a variety of great tunes are taught, including "For J.L.", "Old Joe Clark", and others.
VHS: S09702. $49.95.

Banjo Picking Styles
Learn a variety of techniques as played by the hottest young player, Bela Fleck. Bela shows the stylistic innovations that will add sparkle, interest and new repertoire to your playing. 60 mins.
VHS: S09688. $49.95.

Basic Guitar Set-Up and Repair
Harvey Citron guides this clear step-by-step instruction on how to take care of the minor repairs and set-up that will have your instruments playing perfectly. 90 mins.
VHS: S09678. $49.95.

Beginning Bluegrass Piano
Perfect for those who want to play banjo in the style of Earl Scruggs and other bluegrass pickers—from scratch. Learn basic rolls, left-hand fingerpicking and nine all-time favorite bluegrass songs. With Pete Wernick. 120 mins.
VHS: S09686. $49.95.
Laser: LD71273. $24.95.

Beginning Blues Piano
The only requirement for taking this video course is to want to play blues, boogie woogie or rock and roll piano. With no written music to learn and David Cohen's easy-to-follow instructions, even a beginner will be improvising blues riffs, and sound great doing it. 60 mins.
VHS: S09689. $49.95.

Beginning Electric Bass
A two-tape series taught by Roly Salley.
Beginning Electric Bass—Part One. Here is the easiest way to learn the electric bass. Within five minutes the student is getting hands-on experience from a professional, learning the fundamentals of bass playing. This video teaches left and right-hand techniques, scales, theory and a number of great bass lines in country, blues, rock and R&B styles. 60 mins.
VHS: S09684. $49.95.
Beginning Electric Bass—Part Two. On his second one-hour video lesson, bassist Roly Salley moves on to more complex bass lines and patterns. He teaches left-hand exercises, 12-bar blues, inversions, turn-arounds and a wide range of helpful tips on performing, playing with a rhythm section, and equipment. 60 mins.
VHS: S09685. $49.95.

Bluegrass Mandolin
Sam Bush details the dominant mandolin styles, from Bill Monroe to Newgrass. You'll see, up close, Sam's amazing right-hand picking techniques and left-hand fingering as he teaches ten great tunes. 90 mins.
VHS: S09694. $49.95.

Choreography of the Hands: The Work of Dorothy Taubman
Taubman is well-known among pianists for her summer institute at Amherst College, where she helps ailing musicians. Through the study of physiological principals she locates the movements which lead to chronic pain and then sets about correcting these dangerous repetitive motions. Now this video brings her theories and techniques to a wider audience.
VHS: S22943. $79.95.

Contest Fiddling Championship Style
Mark O'Conner, a true champion, takes apart three of his award-winning tunes, showing up close the fine points of his playing to help you improve yours. In addition, Mark is shown in performance with a band as he would play in a Texas-style fiddle contest. 60 mins.
VHS: S09682. $49.95.

Drum Course for Beginners with Louie Bellson
Drummer Louie Bellson shows how to play drums at its most basic level. Bellson illustrates hand positions, note and rest values, time signatures, staff and dynamics. 53 mins.
VHS: S12153. $29.95.

Elementary Guitar Practice and Theory with Barney Kessel
The grand master of the guitar introduces students to the guitar parts, strings, tuning, tone production and music theory, and then follows guides for sight reading, chords and songs to play. 77 mins.
VHS: S12154. $29.95.

Frank Gambale: Monster Licks and Speed Picking
Innovative guitarist Frank Gambale demonstrates his speed/sweep picking technique and presents a method for developing Monster Licks. Playing each example slowly twice through, Gambale demonstrates his picking technique in the context of scales, pentatonics, arpeggios and triad examples.
VHS: S11524. $39.95.

The Hammer Dulcimer
This easy to follow, comprehensive beginner's course on video makes it easy to see the way the hammers are held, where the notes are found, and how to make exciting music almost immediately. Taught by John McCutcheon. 90 mins.
VHS: S09696. $49.95.

How to Play Flutes of the Andes
Learn to play the haunting and powerful music of the Andes mountains. The members of Sukay teach two of the most popular wind instruments: the zampona (pan pipes) and the recorder-like kena. Quentin Howard and Carlos Crespo demonstrate the songs and techniques, and the entire quartet plays them as they would in performance. 45 mins.
VHS: S09698. $49.95.

An Intimate Lesson with Tony Rice
Here is the fabulous Tony Rise picking style, slowed down and brought up close so you can clearly see what he is doing and how he's doing it. Tony demonstrates a variety of techniques through six songs and instrumentals taken from his most recent albums. 60 mins.
VHS: S09677. $49.95.

Jazz Class for Kids
Jazz choreographer Bob Rizzo is a jazz dance instructor for kids 9-16. Joined by the Riz-Biz Kidz, the program offers training in beginning, intermediate and advanced levels. The class floor stretches and progressions feature turns, jumps and step-by-step combinations. 55 mins.
VHS: S19411. $29.95.

Jerry Douglas' Dobro Techniques
One of the world's top Dobro players shares years of experience as he teaches the dynamic techniques and musical skills that make his Dobro playing so powerful. Jerry demonstrates the left and right hand positions, bar pull-offs and hammer-ons, forward and reverse bar slants, string pulls and picking sequences, as well as invaluable tips on musicianship and equipment. Note-by-note breakdowns of great tunes like "Fireball Mail" and "Cincinnati Rag" are also included.
VHS: S09700. $49.95.

Learn to Play Autoharp
A wonderful one-hour video lesson in which John Sebastian provides a step-by-step learning guide to the autoharp, one of our most beautiful—and easiest—traditional instruments. Includes the use of fingerpicking techniques and how to pick out melodies and play instrumentals in the styles of the great traditional players. 60 mins.
VHS: S09695. $49.95.

Learning Blues Piano— Intermediate Level
This lesson is for those who have some background in blues piano. Taught in a clear and easy style, David Cohen covers theory, blues scales and improvisation techniques, shuffle and straight rhythms, endings, intros, turnarounds, and more. 60 mins.
VHS: S09690. $49.95.

Learning the Bluegrass Fiddle
Kenny Kosek shows how to hold the instrument, proper use of the bow and other techniques that will make starting or continuing fiddle playing easy and fun. You'll learn riffs, double-stops and exciting solos to numerous hot fiddle tunes. 90 mins.
VHS: S09681. $49.95.

Learning to Fingerpick— Intermediate Level
A perfect follow-up to *Learning to Fingerpick*, this is a challenging and exciting step into blues and country fingerpicking with more complex instrumentals and new left- and right-hand techniques. Taught by Harry Traum. 60 mins.
VHS: S09674. $49.95.

Learning to Fingerpick—Level 1/2
An elementary knowledge of guitar chords is all you'll need to get started picking out syncopated melodies while maintaining a steady bass accompaniment in the styles of Merle Travis, Mississippi John Hurt and others. 60 mins.
VHS: S09670. $49.95.

Learning to Flatpick

Harry Traum guides this beginner's video to the joys of country and bluegrass flatpicking. You'll see how to hold the pick and play scales, bass runs, hammer-ons, and melodies to some of America's favorite songs. 60 mins.
VHS: S09676. $49.95.

Learning to Play Blues Guitar—Part 1

Harry Traum teaches the right- and left-hand techniques of traditional finger-style blues. Chord progressions, turnarounds, walking basses, picking techniques, blues riffs, and several complete songs and instrumentals are taught, along with the elements of blues improvisation. 60 mins.
VHS: S09675. $49.95.

Learning to Play Blues Guitar—Part 2

Delves into the many possibilities and intricacies of blues in the key of A, as played by Brownie McGhee, Big Bill Broonzy and other blues masters. Happy Traum teaches new chord positions, bass runs, turnarounds, licks and solos, and the tape includes several wonderful songs with which to practice.
VHS: S09699. $49.95.

Legends of Flatpicking Guitar

In the 1960's Doc Watson proved that fiddle tunes could flow as well under an acoustic guitar pick as under a fiddle's bow. His work inspired a number of other American folk musicians including Norman Blake, Dan Crary and Tony Rice. 90 mins.
VHS: S24369. $29.95.

Legends of Jazz Guitar, Volume I

Since the 1920's jazz has been enlivened by the sounds of the acoustic guitar. Wes Montgomery, Joe Pass, Barney Kessel and Herb Ellis are just some of the musicians featured on this video.
VHS: S24370. $29.95.

Legends of Jazz Guitar, Volume II

More jazz greats are on offer in this video. For example, Wes Montgomery is featured on a pair of 1965 BBC performances while Barney Kessel can be seen playing the BBC Blues. Joe Pass also contributes two pieces and Charlie Bird shows how a classical guitar can swing.
VHS: S24371. $29.95.

Let's Play the Piano and All Those Keyboards

This revolutionary video teaching technique will have the student reading music and playing a popular tune with chord accompaniment after only two half-hour lessons. It prepares students to play any form of music—classical, jazz, pop, country. The video course contains the equivalent of over one year of private keyboard instruction.
VHS: S10715. $39.95.

Listening for Clues: Wynton on Form

Structure and form, Wynton Marsalis maintains, are the key to following music, like a good story. In this episode from the BBC series, he shows listeners how to discern a number of forms using music from Prokofiev, Gershwin, Ellington and Ives. 54 mins.
VHS: S25685. $19.98.

Mastery of the Flamenco Guitar

Guillermo Rios studied for 17 years in Spain with the masters of flamenco guitar. Now this video and the enclosed 28-page booklet condense the bulk of his experiences. Its 16 exercises are useful for beginners and advanced students alike. 95 mins.
VHS: S21060. $49.95.

Play Bluegrass Banjo by Ear

Bill Keith conveys an understanding of basic music theory for the banjo that opens vast possibilities for all players. Includes details of right-hand rolls, harmonized scales, pentatonic runs and licks, and more. 60 mins.
VHS: S09687. $49.95.

Rick Danko's Electric Bass Techniques

For the first time, the dynamic bassist of The Band details some of the exercises, picking techniques and musical ideas that have formed his style through the years. Rick teaches scales, exercises, and great bass lines to get you really rocking. 60 mins.
VHS: S09683. $49.95.

Rock and Roll Rhythm Guitar

A complete two-tape series taught by Amos Garrett.
Rock and Roll Rhythm Guitar Part One. A master of rhythm guitar styles and techniques teaches the chops of the great rock and soul rhythm players. Covered in this lesson are the styles of Chuck Berry, Bo Diddley, Wilson Pickett and James Nolin. Also taught are damping techniques, alternate chord shapes, two-guitar drills. 90 mins.
VHS: S09679. $49.95.
Rock and Roll Rhythm Guitar Part Two. This video documents and teaches the styles of Steve Cropper and the Memphis Sound, Al Green, Albert King, and others. Included are drills and exercises plus tips on holding the pick, getting the best tone, keeping time and other invaluable information. 73 mins.
VHS: S09680. $49.95.

Singing for Tin Ears

This tape is an encouraging and enjoyable lesson that will turn listeners into singers. It will help break down inhibitions, teach pitch perception and basic music theory, and get anyone started making wonderful vocal music. Taught by Penny Nichols. 60 mins.
VHS: S09697. $49.95.

Snare Drum Rudiments with Pat Petrillo

Renowned New York studio drummer Pat Petrillo explains and demonstrates snare drum rudiments, including the roll, diddle, flam and drag. Each rudiment is demonstrated at slow, medium and fast speeds. 30 mins.
VHS: S11527. $34.95.

Sousa to Satchmo: Wynton on the Jazz Band

The transformation of European symphonic music in the American marching band and Ragtime traditions led to jazz. Wynton Marsalis traces this history into New Orleans. Music from Sousa, Joplin and Armstrong are featured in this BBC episode. 55 mins.
VHS: S25686. $19.98.

Steve Smith, Part 1

Named Best Instructional Music Video by the American Video Conference, this definitive drumming clinic with former Journey drummer Steve Smith details jazz and rock styles, concepts and practicing methods. 55 mins.
VHS: S11525. $39.95.

Steve Smith, Part 2

A demonstration of more advanced styles and concepts of drumming. Smith covers fusion drumming, soloing, creativity, double bass drumming and creating a drum part. Concert and performance footage features Smith's groups Steps Ahead and Vital Information. 52 mins.
VHS: S11526. $39.95.

Tackling the Monster: Wynton on Practice

In this video both Yo-Yo Ma and Wynton Marsalis discuss their strong negative reactions to the necessity of practice. Fortunately, Marsalis has a 12-point plan to combat this challenge. Marsalis and Yo-Yo Ma work through Ellington's "Mood Indigo." 54 mins.
VHS: S25687. $19.98.

Trumpet Course Beginner-Intermediate with Clark Terry

The jazz trumpet player and teacher introduces the trumpet, its accessories and the usage of mutes, and provides music theory in relation to actual performance. Then Clark Terry presents warm-up exercises utilizing simple intervals, harmonics and scales. 52 mins.
VHS: S12155. $29.95.

Why Toes Tap: Wynton on Rhythm

Wynton Marsalis focuses on rhythm in this educational video from the BBC. Using two renditions of the Nutcracker, he shows how composers use rhythm to create distinctive sounds and evoke a variety of emotions. 53 mins.
VHS: S25684. $19.98.

You Can Play Guitar

Happy Traum teaches this three-part course.
Chords and Chord Progressions. Shows the beginner, close up, the proper way to play chords on the guitar and how they fit together in creating music. Includes songs, exercises, playing ideas and advice. 60 mins.
VHS: S09671. $49.95.
Right-Hand Techniques. Strumming and picking techniques, and how they can be used to enhance songs and make them more exciting. Includes rhythmic variations, left and right-hand damping, alternating bass notes, hammering-on, classical-style arpeggios and the basics of traditional fingerpicking.
VHS: S09672. $49.95.
Understanding the Guitar. An exploration of the fingerboard to provide a solid understanding of the relationships of notes, frets and strings. Guitarists at all levels will benefit from this lesson, gaining a more complete understanding of the instrument. 60 mins.
VHS: S09673. $49.95.

You Can Play Jazz Piano

You will see as well as hear how to play jazz and pop piano, learning chord progressions, scales and modes, proper fingering and improvising, on both blues and standard tunes. Clear and concise, with no music to read, especially created for beginning/intermediate jazz players. Three-tape set.
VHS: S09693. $119.95.

children's video

25 Classic Cartoons
Three full hours of color cartoons in each volume, featuring Bugs Bunny, Mighty Mouse, the Three Stooges, Superman and many more. USA, 180 mins. each.
25 Classic Cartoons: Vol. I.
VHS: S15034. $19.95.
25 Classic Cartoons: Vol. II.
VHS: S15035. $19.95.
25 Classic Cartoons: Vol. III.
VHS: S15036. $19.95.
25 Classic Cartoons: Vol. IV.
VHS: S15037. $19.95.

50 Below Zero (plus Thomas' Snowsuit)
Follow the antics of Jason's sleepwalking father. The video includes the story *Thomas' Snowsuit*, in which Thomas is forced to wear his plain, ugly, brown snowsuit. Animated stories by acclaimed author Robert Munsch. Ages 2-6. 25 minutes.
VHS: S24984. $12.95.

Abuela's Weave
Esperanza's *abuela*, her grandmother, is unmatched in her weaving skills. She shares the gift of traditional Mayan tapestry with her granddaughter. Together they decide to sell their wares in the market, but Abuela's birthmark may frighten away customers. Esperanza must sell their works alone.
VHS: S21884. $44.95.

Adventures in Dinosaur City
When three totally hip teens get accidentally zapped into the prehistoric stomping grounds of freaked-out dinosaurs, they find themselves in a stone age fantasy. Joining forces with a crime-fighting tyrannosaurus named Rex and his right-claw reptile Tops, they embark on a fossil-fueled mission to retrieve a stolen power cell and save Saur City from melting down into a big Jurassic jacuzzi.
VHS: S16814. $89.98.
Laser: CLV. LD71966. $29.98.
Brett Thompson, USA, 1992, 88 mins.

The Adventures of a Two-Minute Werewolf
In this comic adventure, Walt has two major concerns. One is a bully, the other is a werewolf. Walt finds that he can't stop himself from transforming into a werewolf. Before long, however, he discovers that there are some advantages to this problem. 29 mins.
VHS: S23475. $49.95.

Adventures of Babar
Babar, King of the Elephants and hero of the classic children's story, is brought to life in these volumes, each 60 minutes in length.
Volume 1. Eleven episodes, including Babar's arithmetic lesson, Babar's car, a meal at the old lady's house, Babar and the flower vendor and more. USA, 1985.
VHS: S00017. $19.95.
Volume 2. Eleven episodes, in which Babar takes a fishing trip, learns to read music, goes on a picnic, makes pastry and more. USA, 1985.
VHS: S00018. $19.95.
Volume 3.
VHS: S04861. $19.95.
Volume 4.
VHS: S04862. $19.95.
Volume 5.
VHS: S04863. $19.95.
Volume 6.
VHS: S04864. $19.95.
Volume 7.
VHS: S04865. $19.95.

The Adventures of Blinky Bill: Blinky Bill's Zoo/Magician
In *Blinky Bill's Zoo* the animated Koala bear Blinky gets together with his "mates" to build a zoo for a human girl that they have discovered. In *Magician* a magic show leads to disaster for Blinky. 48 mins.
VHS: S24247. $12.99.

The Adventures of Blinky Bill: Blinky's Fire Brigade/Fund Run
Blinky Bill, the animated koala bear from down under, decides to set up the town's first fire brigade. Then in *Blinky Bill's Fund Run*, Blinky turns to fundraising for charity. Greedy dingos threaten his plans however. 48 mins.
VHS: S24248. $12.99.

The Adventures of Chico
Young Chico describes his escapades with wild animals—including a pet bird who saves him from a snake—in this heartwarming, live-action film set in Mexico. B&W, 54 mins.
VHS: S10577. $24.95.

The Adventures of Jay Jay the Jet Plane
Model airplanes come to life in the storybook land of Tarrytown. This is the setting for stories filled with heart, humor and humanity. Joyful lessons about life, family and friends—those things that really matter—are on this delightful children's tape. Ages 2-8, 25 mins.
VHS: S22941. $12.95.

The Adventures of Pete and Pete: Farewell My Little Viking
An adult conspiracy from Wellville targets Little Pete's idol, Artie. Though Artie is the strongest man in the town—a snake—in this movie, he may actually find himself driven from the town because his foes have a powerful ally, Pete's dad. 50 mins.
VHS: S24719. $9.98.

The Adventures of Tintin: Cigars of the Pharaoh
Since the '30s the adventures of this ordinary man have been recognized throughout the world for both charm and suspense. In this story, Tintin's vacation to Egypt is detoured by a tombful of ancient mummies and a case of international diamond smuggling. 45 mins.
VHS: S23933. $12.98.

The Adventures of Tintin: The Secret of the Unicorn
Once again this seemingly ordinary fellow is caught in a story of mystery and suspense. Tintin and his loyal dog Snowy are involved in a swashbuckling quest for sunken treasure. It all begins innocently enough, with an ancient map. 45 mins.
VHS: S23934. $12.98.

African Story Magic
Brock Peters narrates the tale about a young child's odyssey from urban life to discover the power and wonder of ancient African folklore and ritual. 27 mins.
VHS: S17765. $12.98.

Afro-Classic Folk Tales, Vol. I
This collection of Afro-centered folk tales will promote positive self-affirming values among all children. Storyteller Sybil Destu tells two traditional folk tales, about the spider Anansi and about a tiger. The tales are animated. 30 mins.
VHS: S20620. $29.95.

Afro-Classic Folk Tales, Vol. II
This second installment of *Afro-Classic Folk Tales* includes a Brer Rabbit and Woodpecker cartoon, as well as an old African tale told by puppets. 30 mins.
VHS: S20621. $29.95.

Afro-Classic Mother Goose
In this collection the favorite tales of Mother Goose find new expressiveness with an Afro-centric twist. Playtime rhymes are updated in this fresh look at childhood stories. 30 mins.
VHS: S20622. $29.95.

Alejandro's Gift
Alejandro plants a garden in the desert that attracts a number of animals. When he digs a well even more animals show up, rewarding him for his thoughtfulness with their company. It's a delightful read-along video that kids will love. 7:28 mins.
VHS: S22345. $39.95.

Alexander and the Terrible, Horrible, No Good, Very Bad Day
Everything goes wrong for Alexander in this animated version of Judith Viorst's delightful book. From gum in his hair to bullies in the yard, the world seems to conspire against Alexander until he decides to move to Australia. 30 mins.
VHS: S23276. $12.95.

Alexander, Who Used to Be Rich Last Sunday
Based on the book by Judith Viorst. Alexander's grandparents gave him five dollars making him rich on Sunday. After a spending spree his fortune is lost. This video will teach students the value of saving. 14 mins.
VHS: S23445. $69.95.
Laser: LD74760. $99.95.

All About ABC's
Children have fun visiting Alphabet Land with Letter Lizard and Magic Man. Ages 2-6.
VHS: S24359. $6.99.

All I See
Cynthia Rylant's story about friendship between a young boy and a painter is strikingly brought to life by Peter Catalanotto's illustrations in this iconographic video presentation. 8 mins.
Public Performance Rights.
VHS: S13891. $104.00.

All the Money in the World
Quentin saves a leprechaun from a well and is granted three wishes. He wastes two but on his third try he asks for all the money in the world. The world economy is brought to a standstill, turning his money into a worthless commodity. This gives him a new appreciation of that which money cannot buy. Based on the book by Judith Viorst. 23 mins.
VHS: S22372. $49.95.

All the Troubles in the World
Isaac Asimov wrote this story about a civilization run by an all-powerful computer called the Multivac. A boy's father tries to sabotage the machine, and his son is drawn into the plot. Despite this scheme the Multivac has a far more powerful but unforseen enemy. 22 mins.
VHS: S23450. $49.95.

Alphabet Soup
Artist William Wegman's dog Fay and her offspring, Batty, Chundo and Crooky, teach kids the about the alphabet. They do everything to make these lessons memorable, from balancing a boat on Fay's head to make alphabet soup. Don't forget the apples and zucchini! Ages 3 and up.
VHS: S26141. $12.95.
William Wegman, USA, 1995, 30 mins.

Alvin and the Chipmunks: Love Potion #9
In *Love Potion #9*, Valentine's Day finds the Chipmunks at the mercy of Cupid. But that is only the first of four shorts collected on this video. *Theodore and Juliet, Dear Diary* and *Dr. Simon and Mr. Heartthrob* continue the theme of comic romance featuring the antics of the lovable rodents. 25 mins.
VHS: S27363. $12.99.

The Amazing Bone and Other Stories
The adventures of various humans and animals are shown in this collection of four award-winning animated films taken from favorite children's literature. The title piece, narrated by John Lithgow, is about a young pig who spends her time with a talking bone. 30 mins.
VHS: S11226. $14.95.

The American Dream Contest
Kids between the ages of nine and seventeen were asked to create a concept for a short film on something that's special about our country. Host Michael Landon, in one of his last projects, presents the twelve winners: refreshing and inspiring views of America, filled with humor and heart, imagination and surprises. USA, 47 mins.
VHS: S15003. $29.95.

Amos Fortune, Free Man
Haunting spirituals furnish the background for this sensitive adaptation of the Newbery Award-winning story of Prince At-mun, who was captured, sold at auction, and freed as Amos Fortune. 46 mins.
VHS: S08401. $119.00.

Anansi and the Talking Melon
Eric Kimmel's book is brought to life in this delightful children's video. Anansi is trapped inside a melon. Elephant thinks he has grown a talking fruit and sets off to present this treasure to the king. 11 mins.
VHS: S24720. $37.95.

Angela's Airplane (plus The Fire Station)
Angela wanders onto a huge, empty plane, pushes some buttons and winds up flying it. Also includes a short story, *The Fire Station*. Animated stories by Robert Munsch. Ages 2-5. 25 minutes.
VHS: S24985. $12.95.

Animal Antics
Professor Iris goes on a safari looking for elephants. Kids will love this delightful puppet series episode that is rich in both educational possibilities and simple, plain fun. 40 mins.
VHS: S26057. $12.95.

Animals Are Beautiful People
A program which looks at the creatures living in Africa. This documentary will fascinate and educate children with its magnificent footage. *The Gods Must Be Crazy* filmmaker Jamie Uys spent four years filming African animals.
VHS: S03886. $19.98.

Animals of the Bible
Ostriches, lions, lambs, camels, donkeys and more are all included in this video for children ages 6-10. For each animal listed in the video a story from the *Bible* is related. 30 mins.
VHS: S23123. $14.95.

Animation for Kids: Vol. 1, Cartoon Critters— The National Film Board of Canada
An inventive collection of leading children's animation, produced under the auspices of the National Film Board of Canada. The works include *Dingles, Every Dog's Guide to Home Safety, The Tender Tale of Cinderella Penguin, Every Dog's Guide to the Playground* and *The Sound Collector*. 60 mins.
Laser: LD71939. $39.95.

Anna Marie's Blanket
In this read-along video, Anna must explain to her favorite blanket that she must go alone to nursery school. Of course the blanket is sad to be left behind. This is the story of how Anna helps her blanket overcome its loneliness. 10:15 mins.
VHS: S22358. $39.95.

Archer's Adventure
A wonderful family film from Australia about a daring young boy who takes a prize-winning racehorse across the wild outback in order to compete in the big race in Melbourne.
VHS: S04952. $19.95.
Denny Lawrence, Australia, 1985, 120 mins.

Are You Afraid of the Dark? "Ghostly Tales"
In this pair of spooky episodes, *Tale of the Frozen Ghost* and *Tale of the Shiny Red Bicycle*, there are enough chills for the whole family. Melissa Joan Hart makes a surprise appearance. A new music video compiled from horror story highlights is also included. 50 mins.
VHS: S20661. $14.98.

Are You My Mother?
P.D. Eastman's appealing children's stories *Are You My Mother?, Go, Dog Go* and *The Best Nest* are transformed into charming animated shorts that kids will love. 30 mins.
English Narration
VHS: S22016. $14.95.
Spanish Narration
VHS: S22015. $14.95.

Art Party
Professor Iris is at it once again with her amusing antics. Now this puppet professor sets to work painting a masterpiece. 40 mins.
VHS: S26058. $12.95.

Arthur's Birthday
Marc Brown's lively watercolors are enhanced through touches of animation. John Guth's musical score delightfully complements this story about Arthur and his friend Muffy who plan birthday parties for the same day. 10 mins.
VHS: S12257. $62.00.

Arthur's Pet Business
Marc Brown's popular storybook character returns in this iconographic video. Arthur learns about patience and responsibility when he starts his own pet business. 10 mins.
VHS: S12258. $62.00.

Astronomy 101: A Family Adventure
Subtitled *A Beginner's Guide to the Night Sky*. Join Michelle and her mother as they show you how they explore the night sky together. Astronomy proves to be a fascinating family activity. This video really helps kids get started. It is most refreshing to see the mother/daughter team as the focus of the activity. Filmed on location at the Chicago's Adler Planetarium, this video combines science and fun. 25 minutes.
VHS: S24358. $19.95.

At Home in the Coral Reef
A living coral reef is the subject of this read-along video. In this tropical underwater tour children will see all kinds of unique and colorful wildlife. It's informative and beautiful to see. 11:15 mins.
English Version
VHS: S22362. $39.95.
Spanish Version
VHS: S22363. $39.95.

At the Zoo
Join the other kids on the visit to the zoo. With charming songs. Monkeys, elephants, giraffes, zebras, meerkats, aardvarks, sea lions, exotic birds, polar bears and dolphins star in this entertaining children's video. Toe-tapping, hand-clapping original music make this an unforgettable and educational visit to the zoo. Ages 2-8.
VHS: S24595. $14.95.

Attic-in-the-Blue
An imaginative animated work about an ancient whaler who embarks on a dangerous mission to the Attic-in-the-Blue to find his lost love. He is helped by his octopus-like companion. Winner of 1992 Best Animated Film, Chicago International Children's Film Festival and New Orleans International Film and Video Festival. 27 mins.
Home Video.
VHS: S18930. $14.95.
Public Performance Rights.
VHS: S18406. $39.95.

Babar Comes to America
Join Babar the Elephant when he, his Queen Celeste and cousin Artur are invited to America to make a movie. Getting to Hollywood proves to be quite a struggle when they are sidetracked several times along the way. USA, 1984, 23 mins.
VHS: S00084. $14.95.

Babar the Movie
A feature-length, animated adventure. The kingdom is threatened by an invasion of very mean rhinos and it is up to young Babar to save the day. With the help of his friends in the animal kingdom, he attempts to use a positive mental attitude and a little cunning to beat the evil rhino horde.
VHS: S11696. $24.95.
Alan Bunce, USA, 1988, 79 mins.

Babar: Babar Returns
This charming episode finds Babar and his daughter Flora in the kitchen whipping up some midnight snacks, when Babar begins to tell Flora and the audience an enchanting tale with an important lesson about concentrating on our strengths rather than our weaknesses. 1989, 49 min.
VHS: S13443. $14.95.

Babar's First Step
In this story, Babar the elephant tells his son Alexander about a incident from his childhood. A hunter terrorizes the herd, causing the death of a loved one. Babar's anger gives him the strength to confront the hunter while the rest of the herd escapes. An animated fable of growing up and responsibility. 49 mins.
VHS: S12813. $14.95.

Baby Animal Fun
Live footage of baby animals interacting with kids. All ages. 1989, 30 mins.
VHS: S24596. $29.95.

Baby Animals Just Want to Have Fun
Peter Puppy, Raindance the Pony and other favorite baby animals romp around in five humorous adventure stories. Enchanting songs and live photography in this video will make children adore baby animals even more.
VHS: S02996. $14.95.

Baby Songs Series
A very good series of live action music videos for preschoolers, ages 1-5. 30 minutes each.
Baby Songs 2: More Baby Songs. Hap Palmer is back! Good for babies; relates at their level: tickling, playing, walking—fun! This video combines live action and animation for the very young, ages infant to 8. 30 mins.
VHS: S24337. $12.98.

Baby Songs Christmas. Interesting, singable, multicultural, fun. 1991.
VHS: S24597. $14.95.

Baby Songs Presents: Baby Rock. Ten songs by original artists are presented in this live action/animation video for the very young, ages infant to 8. 30 mins.
VHS: S24339. $12.98.

Baby Songs Presents: Follow Along Songs with Hap Palmer. Songs designed for children to enact the lyrics, including "The Mice Go Marching," "Parade of Sticks," and "Homemade Band."
VHS: S24772. $12.98.

Baby Songs Presents: John Lithgow's Kid-Size Concert. Acoustic guitar, a wonderful actor and a chance to sing along. With "I Can Put My Clothes on By Myself," "Getting Up Time," and "What a Miracle I Am." Songbook included. 1990.
VHS: S24341. $12.98.

Baby Songs: Even More Baby Songs. Ten charming songs by Hap Palmer that reach into a child's everyday life for their subject matter. More catchy tunes are featured in this video which combines live action and animation for the very young, ages infant to 8. 30 mins.
VHS: S24338. $12.98.

Baby Songs: Sing Together. Nine sing-alongs. 1992.
VHS: S24598. $14.95.

Baby Songs: Super Baby Songs. More great sing-along tunes for tykes with Hap Palmer. This video combines live action and animation for the very young, ages infant to 8. 30 mins.
VHS: S24340. $12.98.

Baby Vision
Fascinating films made for children from 9 to 36 months of age! From New Zealand. For infant to age 3. 45 minutes each tape.
Baby Vision Volume 1. *Volume 1* centers on soft images, a bit of narration and music related to toys and animals.
VHS: S24342. $14.95.
Baby Vision Volume 2. More magnificent images. *Volume 2* centers on soft images, a bit of narration and music related to motion, plants and liquids, such as waterfalls and juice being poured.
VHS: S24343. $14.95.

Baby's Morningtime
Greet the day with a song and a smile as Judy Collins sings the works of Robert Browning, Emily Dickinson, Gertrude Stein and others. Enhanced by Ernest Troost's winsome score and Sesame Street's Daniel Ivanick's animation. 25 minutes, infant to age 6.
Home Video.
VHS: S17136. $12.98.
Public Performance Rights.
VHS: S17149. $50.00.

Baby's Nursery Rhymes
Mother Goose gets a refreshing update in this animated version of Kay Chorao's "The Baby's Lap Book", sung by Phylicia Rashad, star of The Cosby Show. Set to the sparkling contemporary music of Jason Miles. California Book & Video Award, Parents' Choice Award, TV Guide Top 10 List for Children's Home Video, Oppenheim Toy Portfolio Award. 26 minutes, ages 1-6.
Home Video.
VHS: S17137. $12.98.
Public Performance Rights.
VHS: S17150. $50.00.

Baby-Sitter's Club Videos
The popular Scholastic Book series is every bit as popular on video. Seven diverse girls start a business, and together they can solve any problem. Live action. USA. Ages 6-12. 30 minutes each.
The Baby-Sitters' Club: Christmas Special (1991). A very moving Christmas story, with the girls at a hospital Christmas party, when diabetic Stacey lands in the hospital herself after too many cookies.
VHS: S24356. $14.95.
The Baby-Sitters' Club: Claudia and the Missing Jewels. The mystery unfolds when Claudia launches a jewelry-making business, and a pair of earrings is stolen.
VHS: S24354. $14.95.
The Baby-Sitters' Club: Claudia and the Mystery of the Secret Passage. Claudia follows a note found in a secret passage, as the Baby-Sitters hope to settle an ancient feud.
VHS: S24344. $14.95.
The Baby-Sitters' Club: Dawn and the Dream Boy. Concerns the rivalry between two sisters thinking of going to a teen dance with the same boy. Note: the subject is dating.
VHS: S24355. $14.95.
The Baby-Sitters' Club: Dawn and the Haunted House. Dawn thinks Claudia is spending too much time with the neighborhood "witch," in this story about appreciating differences.
VHS: S24351. $14.95.
The Baby-Sitters' Club: Dawn Saves the Trees. When the city plans to build a road through the local park, Dawn leads the Baby-Sitters in a fight to save the trees. Deals with recycling and conservation.
VHS: S24346. $14.95.
The Baby-Sitters' Club: Jessi and The Mystery of the Stolen Secrets. The Baby-Sitters go undercover to find out who is stealing club secrets.
VHS: S24347. $14.95.
The Baby-Sitters' Club: Kristy and the Great Campaign. A third-grader's bid for class president yields a look at self-concept and gender stereotypes.
VHS: S24353. $14.95.
The Baby-Sitters' Club: Mary Ann and the Brunettes (1990). Two girls' clubs find a rational way to work out their differences. Note: the subject concerns teenage girls and conflict over two girls who want to date the same boy.
VHS: S24350. $14.95.
The Baby-Sitters' Club: Stacey Takes a Stand. The Baby-Sitters help Stacey figure out what to do when she is torn between her divorced mom and dad.
VHS: S24348. $14.95.
The Baby-Sitters' Club: Stacey's Big Break. Stacey has a chance at fashion modelling. A dialogue ensues concerning priorities and anorexia.
VHS: S24352. $14.95.
The Baby-Sitters' Club: The Baby-Sitters Remember. A very nice review of the best and funniest adventures.
VHS: S24349. $14.95.
The Baby-Sitters' Club: The Baby-Sitters and The Boy Sitters. The boys start their own baby-sitting club!
VHS: S24345. $14.95.

Bach's Fight for Freedom
Produced for HBO, this involving children's story concerns a young boy who reluctantly becomes an assistant to the great German composer Johann Sebastian Bach. At first they don't work well together. In the end, however, they do find an understanding between them. This is a tale about the positive power of ambition. From *The Composers' Specials* series. 53 mins.
VHS: S26745. $19.98.

Back to the Forest
When tree-chopping townspeople invade their forest home, the heroic birds and animals outwit them with sheer ingenuity. Masterminded by Peter's elfin magic, the animals' escapades will have children on the edge of their seats. Fully animated and full of Mother Nature's wisdom.
VHS: S12583. $24.95.

Ballet Shoes
Refusing to let a money crunch hinder their ballet career, three young girls decide to pursue their dreams. The possibilities and realities of fame and fortune are creatively displayed in this live-action film based on the Noel Streatfield children's novel of the same name. 120 mins.
VHS: S12636. $29.95.

Bananas in Pajamas: Birthday Special
B1 and B2 go all out to prepare for birthday fun. Preschoolers will love the fun, music and humor of these festive goings-on. USA, 1995, 25 mins.
VHS: S27194. $9.95.

Bananas in Pajamas: Cuddles Avenue
B1 and B2 teach preschoolers important and fun lessons using music and humor. In this engaging story they play a trick on their friends. It all ends well however, once the mischief is revealed and they sit down to a treat of honey cakes and yellow jelly. USA, 1995, 25 mins.
VHS: S27193. $9.95.

The Banshee
In this nighttime fantasy, a mysterious Banshee comes to a village in search of someone to share her loneliness. But among the village folk there is a special kind of strength and security that is far more powerful than the compelling song of the lonely Banshee. An enchanting tale by award-winning author Karen Ackerman, with illustrations by David Ray.
VHS: S16337. $44.95.

Barney and the Backyard Gang
A series with a strong quality focus, combining favorite, traditional songs and rhymes, live action and animation. Each show features Sandy Duncan as "Mom" to kids Michael and Amy. The children and their neighborhood friends have a special pal, Barney the dinosaur, who magically comes to life to lead the Backyard Gang through the shows. Aimed at children 2-8.
A Day at the Beach. Contains video, storybook and audio cassette.
VHS: S09787. $24.95.
Barney Goes to School. Barney and pals enjoy finger painting, creative learning and the search for Zippity the hamster. 1990.
VHS: S24599. $14.95.
Barney in Concert. Barney and the two-year-old Baby Bop perform fun songs which encourage interaction. 1991.
VHS: S24600. $14.95.
Barney's Best Manners. A picnic, with songs and games which teach manners, including "Does Your Chewing Gum Lose Its Flavor," "Please and Thank You," and "Snackin' on Healthy Food."
VHS: S24601. $14.95.
Barney's Birthday. Birthday songs and birthday customs from around the world. 1993.
VHS: S24602. $14.95.
Barney's Campfire Sing-Along. Fun with camping, animals, stars and forest safety.
VHS: S24603. $14.95.
Barney's Home Sweet Homes. Discover the variety of homes—homes for animals and homes for people—around the world and under the sea.
VHS: S24604. $14.95.
Barney's Magical Musical Adventure. When the Backyard Gang builds a sand castle, Barney takes them to a real castle. 1992.
VHS: S24605. $14.95.
Rock with Barney. Barney sings some of his favorite songs.
VHS: S24606. $14.95.
Waiting for Santa. Barney and the Gang travel to the North Pole to learn the true meaning of Christmas. 1991.
VHS: S24607. $14.95.

Barney's Imagination Island
Fun with songs, rhymes and problem solving. Barney helps his friends go sailing and they discover a toy inventor who learns about sharing from the visitors. 1994. 48 minutes.
VHS: S24940. $19.99.

Barney's Safety Video
Kids join B.J., Barney and firefighter Frank to learn about important safety issues such as crossing the street and safety at home. 48 minutes.
VHS: S24942. $14.95.

Barry's Scrapbook: A Window into Art
Join Barry Louis, a singer and writer of children's songs, as he visits an art museum and meets a collage artist, an illustrator and a sculptor. He sings about art and recyclables.
VHS: S22130. $26.95.

Bartholomew and the Oobleck
A jazz-loving boy's dreams come true when he plays a real musician's trumpet in this adaptation of Rachel Isadora's book. 11 mins.
VHS: S08403. $62.00.

Basil Hears a Noise
A vigorous and heartwarming Muppets musical tale with Basil and his friends trapped inside an enchanted forest where they must find the inner courage to overcome their fear and conquer their personal demons. Special appearance by Elmo, the furry red monster. 28 mins.
VHS: S19159. $12.98.

BBC Children's Favorites
This BBC video of the animated pieces "Ivor the Engine," "Bagpuss" and "Clangers" promises to be delightful time after time. 55 mins.
VHS: S12638. $19.95.

Beady Bear
Based on the book by Don Freeman, a stuffed bear realizes he needs more than just a cave—he needs love! Ages 3-8. 8 minutes.
VHS: S24508. $37.95.

Beanstalk
This great kid's movie follows young Jack Taylor as he schemes to make it big. His chance comes when a wacky scientist (Margot Kidder) unloads her recently discovered seed pods on him. Soon an enormous beanstalk leads him on the path to riches and adventure. He never expected a family of giants, however.
VHS: S22902. $92.95.
Michael Paul Davis, USA, 1994, 80 mins.

The Bear
In this story by William Faulkner, a boy discovers the value of wilderness as he confronts a bear. Nicknamed Old Ben, this bear has guided the boy's father and his friends for years. Tension mounts as the boy grows up until he finally must confront this legendary creature himself. 24 mins.
VHS: S23471. $79.95.

The Bear Who Slept Through Christmas
Little Ted E. Bear wants to discover the meaning of Christmas, while the rest of the town sleeps. Ages 1-8.
VHS: S24360. $12.98.

Beauty and the Beast
A beautifully animated version of the famous story, featured on PBS's Long Ago and Far Away. CINE Golden Eagle, Chicago International Children's Film Festival, TV Guide 10 Best Videos. Recommended by American Library Association, Parents' Choice Award. 30 minutes, ages 5-12.
Home Video.
VHS: S11416. $12.98.
Public Performance Rights.
VHS: S17143. $50.00.

Bebe's Kids
The late Robin Harris' (*Mo' Better Blues, House Party*) nightmare children are brought to life in this animated feature. The lead character is out for a day of romance but winds up stuck with Bebe's Kids. Features Faizon Love, Vanessa Bell Calloway, Wayne Collins, Jonell Green, Marques Houston, Tone-Loc and Nell Carter.
VHS: S21453. $92.95.
Laser: LD75118. $24.98.
Bruce Smith, USA, 1992, 74 mins.

Beebtots
Four animated films which are BBC Children's Favorites. In this collection, the King of the Nogs may have an unwelcome party guest, Clangers are visited by a Gladstone bag, Bagpuss receives a gift and Ivor the Engine is slowed by falling snow. 52 mins.
VHS: S12637. $19.95.

Beethoven Lives Upstairs
It is 1820s Vienna, and Ludwig Van Beethoven is desperately trying to compose his Ninth Symphony. As he struggles to balance his musical obsession with the reality of his increasing deafness, Beethoven rents the upstairs flat in the depressed household of ten-year-old Christoph. He watches and listens as Beethoven swiftly turns his house into chaos.
VHS: S16706. $19.98.
David Devine, USA, 1990, 51 mins.

Beezbo
A lesson in manners for the neighborhood kids takes place when a furry alien, Beezbo, crashes his spaceship on earth and he transforms himself to look human. While looking human is easy, behaving so is not. Recommended for ages up to 10 years old.
VHS: S03484. $14.95.
R.C. Bailey, USA, 1985, 48 mins.

Berenstain Bears and the Messy Room
Brother and Sister's room is a mess. Mama is about to toss everything out when Papa Bear offers a neat solution. Animated, 30 mins.
VHS: S07716. $14.95.

Berenstain Bears and the Missing Dinosaur Bone
Also includes "Bears in the Night" and "The Bear Detectives." 30 mins.
VHS: S12771. $9.95.

Berenstain Bears and the Trouble with Friends
The new girl cub in the neighborhood is the same age as Sister Bear—and just as bossy. Mama Bear helps both cubs learn that you can't always have your own way if you want to be friends. 30 mins.
VHS: S09230. $14.95.

Berenstain Bears and the Truth
Brother and Sister bear learn that breaking Mama Bear's trust in them is worse than breaking her lamp. Animated, 30 mins.
VHS: S07715. $14.95.

Berenstain Bears and Too Much Birthday
Is there such a thing as too much birthday? Sister doesn't think so, but she learns the hard way when she coaxes Mama and Papa to throw a big bash for her sixth birthday.
VHS: S09229. $14.95.

Berenstain Bears Forget Their Manners
Mama Bear is determined to teach Papa Bear and her kids the necessity of patience and politeness, with hilarious results. In *Berenstain Bears and the Wicked Weasel Spell*, the evil Archweasel McGreed orchestrates a dastardly plan to rule Bear County.
VHS: S18615. $14.95.

Berenstain Bears Get in a Fight
Brother and Sister Bear turn a minor disagreement into a major war, and it is up to Mama Bear to call a truce. Animated. 30 mins.
VHS: S07713. $14.95.

Berenstain Bears Get Stage Fright
Sibling rivalry comes in the form of the stage play *Grizzlystiltskin*, in which Brother and Sister Bear have leading roles. In *Berenstain Bears Go Bonkers over Honkers*, Bigpaw's four small pet geese wreak havoc on the idyllic Bear County.
VHS: S18616. $14.95.

Berenstain Bears in the Dark
When Brother reads Sister a scary story, she can't fall asleep in the dark. Papa Bears helps sister conquer her fear. 30 mins.
VHS: S09231. $14.95.

Berenstain Bears Learn about Strangers
When Papa Bear tells the cubs they should never talk to strangers, Sister thinks all strangers are ominous. It's up to Mama to bring some common sense to the problem. Animated, 30 mins.
VHS: S07714. $14.95.

Berenstain Bears Videos
Based on the best-selling books by Jan and Stan Berenstain, the videos are of high quality, featuring a charming bear family which works out problems in a thoughtful and entertaining manner. Animated. Ages 3-8. 20-30 minutes each.
Berenstain Bears Christmas Tree. Papa Bear realizes that Christmas trees are also animals' homes.
VHS: S24509. $9.98.

Berenstain Bears: No Girls Allowed
Brother Bear and his friends create a mysterious clubhouse strictly off limits to Sister Bear and her friends. In *Berenstain Bears and the Missing Dinosaur Bone*, the Bear Detectives pursue the trail of a rare dinosaur bone stolen from Actual Factual's Museum.
VHS: S18614. $14.95.

Berenstain Bears: The Bears' Christmas
Also contains "Inside Outside Upside Down" and "The Bike Lesson." 30 mins.
VHS: S12770. $9.95.

Bernard and the Genie
Lenny Henry (*True Identity*) showcases his gift for mimicry in this comedy which transfers the Aladdin legend to a contemporary London context, with the genie (Henry) helping a shy young London man overcome his fears about a dazzling young woman. With Rowan Atkinson and musician Bob Geldof.
VHS: S19095. $19.98.

Best Christmas Pageant
Loretta Swit stars in this heartwarming adaptation about what happens when the nastiest bunch of kids in town decide they want to participate in this year's Christmas pageant. 60 mins.
VHS: S08405. $19.95.

Best Friends Part I
A video for children with or without pets, this series of animated stories demonstrates how to act responsibly toward our animal friends and our environment in general. A mouse, dog, turtle, rabbit and frog tell what they want to receive from a human friend in the first part of a two-program series. 25 mins.
VHS: S14990. $14.95.

Best Friends Part II
A fish, cat, guinea pig, pony and bird take their turns in telling entertaining animated stories informing children how to respect and care for our best pet friends. 25 mins.
VHS: S15240. $19.95.

Best of Babar, Vol. 1
Six complete episodes of new adventures with the King of the Elephants, Babar. Included are *Babar Gets Sunstroke, Babar and the Bicycle, Babar and the Cheese Fondue* and more. USA, 1986, 30 mins.
VHS: S02620. $14.95.

Best of Babar, Vol. 2
The King of Elephants and his friends have more fun in this laugh-filled collection of six episodes about a billiard game, a masked ball, a postman, astronomy, sewing and theater. 30 mins.
VHS: S02621. $14.95.

Best of the Fests: For Kids
Eight great short films for kids, all of which have won major film festival awards. Featuring hilarious house cats, roosters, dancers, rope-jumpers, flying pumpkins, talking money, and even metal dogs of India....Includes *Pumpkin Madness, Metal Dogs of India, The Rooster, Skip It, Housecats, Fanaround, Charlie's Boogie Woogie* and *Travels of a Dollar Bill*. 40 mins.
VHS: S13834. $14.95.

The Best Valentine in the World
Getting a head start early in November, Ferdinand Fox gathers sticks, flowers, ribbon and lace to make something different for Florette: a purple valentine. He works long and hard until it's all finished. But when Valentine's Day comes, things don't turn out the way he expects. At least not at first...
VHS: S16338. $44.95.

Beyond Blame: Challenging Violence in the Media
This comprehensive series offers a number of well-reasoned steps that can help children understand and counteract the overwhelming media fascination with violence. Children are directly addressed, but caregivers of all type are also catered to. Finally this vital issue can be dealt with through concrete, positive means developed by media literacy experts and violence prevention specialists. The set contains five videos, handouts, lesson plans and outlines.
VHS: S26326. $249.95.

The Big Fat Fabulous Bear
The Big Fat Fabulous Bear is already a well known character in children's books by Janosch. Now he is featured in this collection of animated films surrounded by a host of lovable animal characters. Together they experience a number of adventures that also impart important lessons to kids.
VHS: S23993. $24.95.

Big Red
Real firefighters offer kids a unique view of the preparation, tools and large trucks that go into fighting big fires. Kids will even learn valuable safety lessons in this enjoyable and educational tape. Ages 2-8, 25 mins.
VHS: S23087. $19.95.

Big Rigs: Close Up and Very Personal
This episode from the *Close Up* series shows preschoolers the intricacy and power of these great machines. The big rigs are seen inside and out, in order to explain how they work and how they function as transportation for goods. 30 mins.
VHS: S24216. $14.95.

Biggest and the Best
Three short discussion starter films on topics facing teenagers: *Heartburn* challenges teens to examine some common misconceptions about love, *Eagle Beak* helps teens see that self-image is often founded on wrong input, and *Face Value*, winner of five international awards, is a provocative look at peer pressure. 26 mins.
VHS: S09796. $59.95.

The Biggest Bears
All kinds of bears in their wild habitat are shown in this exciting documentary narrated by a five-year-old Alaskan boy. The makers travelled across Alaska, Canada and Russia in order to create this unparalleled musical adventure.
VHS: S22160. $14.95.

Bill Cosby's Picture Pages
Bill Cosby is joined by his pen pal Mortimer Ichabod in these interactive videos. Together they help pre-schoolers understand basic learning skills, including shapes, sounds and numbers. 30 mins.
What Goes Where? Among the activities on this tape are a counting class, super shapes, making a match and identifying letters.
VHS: S22132. $9.95.
What's Different? Among the segments in this program are ship shapes, adding games, fill in the letter, counting class and a connect-the-dots game to make a birdhouse.
VHS: S22133. $9.95.
What's Missing? Name that sound, count the bounces, make a match, connect the dots, put words together and enjoy some really fun rhymes in this video.
VHS: S22134. $9.95.

The Birthday Dragon
The magic continues in this animated film about Emily and the Railway Dragon. They play and fly together as they celebrate a very special day. Ages 3 and up. 30 mins.
VHS: S24513. $9.98.

Bizet's Dream
Young Michelle is inspired by the newest operatic work written by her piano teacher, Georges Bizet. The plot of *Carmen* leads her to imagine a scenario involving her parents in a love scandal. This delightful story mixes fact and fiction to offer an intriguing portrait of the great composer Bizet. 53 mins.
VHS: S26213. $19.98.

Blue Ribbon Stories Vol. 1
Two stories, *The Three Billy Goats Gruff* and *The Little Red Hen*, are featured in this animated video from Scholastic Productions, including activity segments featuring two puppets who encourage young viewers to participate.
VHS: S04136. $14.95.

Blue Ribbon Stories Vol. 2
Two more stories from Scholastic's Blue Ribbon Storybook Video: *Harold and the Purple Crayon* and *The Bremen Town Musicians*. 30 mins.
VHS: S04155. $14.95.

Bluetoes the Christmas Elf
It's Christmas Eve at the North Pole and all of Santa's helpers are busy packing the sleigh for takeoff...all except for one sad, unnamed elf, who is too young and entirely too clumsy to help. Then in a dream come true, the little elf is airborne with Santa, delivering toys to all the girls and the boys of the world. On this wondrous journey through the winter night, the tiny elf makes a heartwarming sacrifice that helps Santa and ultimately earns him the name Bluetoes. 27 mins.
VHS: S12480. $14.95.

Bobby's World
Comedian Howie Mandel devised this ultra cool cartoon about a boy who lives in a typical suburban neighborhood. Step inside *Bobby's World* however, and it's a totally different story. From his pint-sized perspective there are adventures and laughs galore.
VHS: S25623. $9.98.

The Bollo Caper
Art Buchwald's book about a magnificent golden leopard called Bollo is adapted in this animated show. Bollo escapes fur hunters and manages to get to Washington D.C., where he saves his life by being listed on the endangered species list. 23 mins.
VHS: S23451. $49.95.

The Box
Three award-winning shorts from the National Film Board of Canada. *The Box* explores alternate realities of fantasy, animation and live action about an artist's creation that comes to life. *The Story of Cinderella* reinterprets the classic tale with charming illustration executed by fifth grade students. *Mary of Mile 18* is a warm and simple animated work about a young woman whose life is transformed when she finds an abandoned puppy. 30 mins.
VHS: S18560. $14.98.

The Boy Who Cried Wolf
Jack Otis Moore has reinterpreted Aesop's fable in an illustrated children's book. This video is directly photographed from this charming book. 6 mins.
VHS: S24910. $42.95.

The Brave Frog
An all-animated adventure about a poor tree frog named Jonathan who moves to the woodland community of Rainbow Pond, where he's forced to battle vicious cats, giant sea monsters and sneaky snakes, and, worst of all, the selfish ruler of Rainbow Pond, King Leopold. 1995, 91 mins.
VHS: S23330. $14.95.
Laser: LD74839. $34.95.

Brum: The Big Adventures of a Little Car
Motoring in from England, Brum is a spunky, miniature, 1920's-style car. He is always ready to roll to the rescue. Each volume in this series contains three live-action Brum misadventures. From Random House Home Videos, 30 minutes each.
Volume 1: Brum and the Baby Carriage.
VHS: S22975. $9.95.
Volume 2: Brum and the Bank Robbers.
VHS: S22976. $9.95.
Volume 3: Brum and the Little Girl Lost.
VHS: S22977. $9.95.
Volume 4: Brum to the Rescue.
VHS: S22978. $9.95.

Bugs Bunny's Looney Christmas Tales
The Warner Brothers cartoon gang celebrates with funny reworkings of *A Christmas Carol* and *'Twas the Night before Christmas*. 25 mins.
VHS: S13035. $12.95.

Bugs Don't Bug Us
Insects, spiders and other invertebrates interact with children in this tape. Some of the most common of these creatures are revealed in a friendly and casual way. Detailed views of motion and eating habits as well as the complete transformation of a caterpillar to a butterfly make this an exceptional viewing experience. 35 mins.
VHS: S22381. $19.95.

Bump—My First Video
An evocative adaptation of six stories narrated by Simon Cadell detailing the whimsical adventures of the precocious elephant Bump and his peculiar friend Birdie. 30 mins.
VHS: S19423. $12.98.

Buron B. Blackbear and Beyond the Stars
From Mother Earth to the outer reaches of our Universe, this delightful duo of animated stories will fill a child with wonder, awe, laughter and joy. USA, 1985, 30 mins.
VHS: S04767. $14.95.

The Busy World of Richard Scarry: A Trip to the Moon
Lowly Worm is an animated worm who inhabits a world filled with warm animal friends. Two stories are included on this video in addition to the story which shows Lowly Worm, Huckle Cat and their friends visiting the moon. Based on Richard Scarry's popular characters. Perfect for preschoolers. 25 mins.
VHS: S27421. $9.95.

The Busy World of Richard Scarry: Mr. Frumble's New Car
Three episodes from the popular cartoon series seen on *Nick Jr.* and *Showtime* are joined on this video. 25 mins.
VHS: S26625. $9.95.

The Busy World of Richard Scarry: The Busiest Firefighters Ever
Three episodes from the delightful animated television series are included on this video. Kids love it on *Nick Jr.* and *Showtime*. Now these cartoons, with their animated animal characters, are available at any time to delight children. 25 mins.
VHS: S26624. $9.95.

The Busy World of Richard Scarry: The Snowstorm
Snow storms are the stuff of childhood dreams. The world is covered in white, and if it's an especially snowy day, school might even be cancelled. This story and two others featuring Lowly Worm, Huckle Cat and their friends in Busytown are joined on this videotape based on Richard Scarry's popular books. 25 mins.
VHS: S27422. $9.95.

By Way of the Stars
This wild west adventure tale will delight kids and parents. A courageous boy embarks on a voyage of excitement and daring. Along the way he learns not only about the wide open spaces of America, but also about his own capabilities.
VHS: S25849. $19.95.

Caddie Woodlawn
The hardships and pleasures of the pioneer life is the life of Caddie Woodlawn in this compelling adaptation of Carol Ryrie Brink's Newbery Medal-winning book. 38 mins.
VHS: S07689. $119.00.

Cadillacs and Dinosaurs: "Rogue" and "Dino Drive"
Two episodes from the dinosaur-laden animated series are joined on this video. In the first episode, *Rogue*, a rampaging Tyrannosaurus Rex threatens to turn humans against the dinosaurs. Then, in *Dino Drive*, Jack and Hannah try to round up a herd of triceratops that they can be harmed by Governor Scharnhorst and her dinosaur-poaching pals. USA, 1993, 46 mins.
VHS: S27553. $9.99.

Cadillacs and Dinosaurs: "Wild Child" and "Pursuit"
In *Wild Child*, Jack and Hannah find a boy with mysterious powers that control dinosaurs. Poachers immediately hope to kidnap this boy in order to trap the unsuspecting giant creatures. In *Pursuit*, Jack is wrongfully accused of a crime. He must clear his name and retrieve a powerful weapon that could spell disaster for dinosaurs. USA, 1993, 46 mins.
VHS: S27554. $9.99.

Call It Courage
This video presentation of Armstrong Sperry's book tells the story of a Polynesian chief's son called "The Boy Who Was Afraid," who has to overcome his fear of the sea. 50 mins.
VHS: S08406. $119.00.

Can I Be Good?
Children see themselves as a golden retriever sees them in this enjoyable read-along video. A puppy tries to be good, but he can't help being just a puppy. Finally he becomes an indispensable member of the family that loves him just as he is. 11 mins.
VHS: S22359. $39.95.

Candles, Snow and Mistletoe
This original music fantasy unfolds as Sharon, Lois and Bram take a trip home for the holidays. On the way, they meet an assortment of eccentric fellow passengers, including an adorable elephant. Together they take the ride of their lives and rediscover the true meaning of the holiday season. 50 mins.
VHS: S22224. $9.98.

Caribbean Kids
Stories about real kids of Hispanic backgrounds who live and learn in today's world. Original entertaining musical backgrounds. 55 mins.
English Version.
VHS: S06729. $29.95.
Spanish Version.
VHS: S06730. $29.95.

Carnival of Animals
Carnival of Animals is the tale of Camille, a young boy who writes a magical musical story of an imaginary carnival. Before your eyes a tea set floats away, and dancing turtles and chickens turn into clowns. 30 mins.
VHS: S16755. $19.95.

The Cat and the Fiddler
This story about a traveling fiddler and his cat is adapted from Jackey Jeter's book, illustrated by Lionel Kalish. Produced by Thomas Sand. 11 mins.
VHS: S23493. $39.95.

Catch Me If You Can
An entertaining and educational way for younger children to learn about animal behavior and its importance for animal survival. Includes two complete programs: *The Predators* and *The Grazers*. Each is 26 minutes.
VHS: S23359. $39.95.

A Caterpillar's Wish
Written and illustrated by first graders in Washington, D.C., this inventive tale follows Chad Caterpillar, who longs for wings like the kind his friend Janet Ladybug sprouts. Fortunately, Chad is eventually transformed into a yellow butterfly. 6 mins.
VHS: S19603. $39.00.

Chanuka at Bubbe's
Delightful Muppet-like characters create an irresistible cast in this program explaining the traditions and significance of Chanuka. Great family entertainment. USA.
VHS: S14949. $19.95.

Charles the Clown
Watch Charles Kraus become a clown right before your eyes. A fascinating look at the fine art of clowning. Live action. Ages 3-8. 30 minutes.
VHS: S24515. $9.98.

The Charlie Brown and Snoopy Show, Volume 6
Snoopy's Football Career shows how lean and mean a beagle can be. Then, in *Chaos in the Classroom*, pandemonium breaks out among the Peanuts characters. Both episodes are included in this video. 46 mins.
VHS: S25548. $9.95.

The Charlie Brown and Snoopy Show, Volume 7
Two cartoons featuring the Peanuts gang are joined on this video. In *It's That Team Spirit, Charlie Brown*, the gang tries to rouse the positive energy that will help the Peanuts emerge victorious on the baseball diamond. *Snoopy and the Giant* is a humorous retelling of *Jack and the Beanstalk* starring Snoopy and Woodstock. 46 mins.
VHS: S25549. $9.95.

The Charlie Brown and Snoopy Show, Volume 8
In *Snoopy's Brother Spike*, the well-travelled Beagle comes to visit. Then, *Snoopy's Robot* tells the story of a labor-saving device with a difference, making sure someone does all the work. 46 mins.
VHS: S26164. $9.95.

The Charlie Brown and Snoopy Show, Volume 9
In *Peppermint Patty's School Days*, Patty takes on the education system, while in *Sally's Sweet Babboo*, the troubled romance of Charlie Brown's little sister and Linus faces a significant crisis: Linus' indifference. 46 mins.
VHS: S26165. $9.95.

Charlie Brown Christmas
The Peanuts gang discovers the true meaning of Christmas in this modern holiday classic. Animated. 30 mins.
VHS: S09513. $12.95.

A Charlie Brown Thanksgiving
Charlie Brown is host to more friends than he could have possibly expected in this cartoon about Thanksgiving. All the Peanuts characters are reason enough to give thanks. 24 mins.
VHS: S26162. $12.95.

Cherries and Cherry Pits
Bidemmi is a child with a rich imagination who loves to draw with her colored markers, and tell stories. One day Bidemmi draws pictures of herself as she buys a bag of cherries. One by one, she eats the cherries, but she saves the pits for her own special purpose.
VHS: S16339. $44.95.

Chicken Minute (Not Just for Kids)
This children's comedy charts the relations of Mama Chicken, blues enthusiast and virtuoso cook, and Minute, a charming vegetarian fox. The colorful cast includes Anatole Bonbon the alligator and Mudbelly, the local monster. English and French with English subtitles. 120 mins.
Laser: LD71940. $39.95.

Chicken Sunday
A story by Patricia Polacco about loss, acceptance and assimilation. A young Russian-American girl is initiated into a neighbor's family following the death of her grandmother. She must stake out a series of new relationships and friendships and learns about trust, love and family bonds.
VHS: S19999. $44.95.

A Child's Garden of Verses
This animated interpretation of Robert Louis Stevenson's collection of poems for children is beautifully interpreted. 26 mins.
VHS: S19545. $12.98.

Chingis Khan
This is the story of a great leader and military strategist who learned to survive the hard lessons of the Mongolian steppe as a young boy. Children will be fascinated by the story of this genius who conquered China and Persia and established the greatest contiguous land empire in the world.
VHS: S16340. $44.95.

Choo Choo Trains: Close Up and Very Personal
In this episode from the *Close Up* series, preschoolers learn about the mystery and importance of these amazing machines. Along with the close-ups, there are plenty of panoramic views of Colorado and New Mexico where trains transport both people and goods. 30 mins.
VHS: S24218. $14.95.

A Christmas Carol
Charles Dickens' perennial holiday classic is presented in unique, spellbinding animation. Featuring narration by Michael Redgrave, this film will delight children with the tale of a rich old man transformed by the promise of Christmas. Alastair Sim is the voice of Scrooge. 30 mins.
VHS: S22515. $14.98.

Christmas Carousel
Four heartwarming cartoon tales certain to become a part of everyone's holiday traditions are featured on this video. They include *The Little Brown Burro, The Christmas Racoons, Tukiki and his Search for a Merry Christmas* and *Santa's Pocket Watch*. Two-volume set, 120 mins.
VHS: S23145. $24.95.

The Christmas Collection
This program celebrates the cheer of Christmas. The highlight of the collection is the story of Good King Wenceslas. The program features sacred and secular musical pieces that honor popular Christmas traditions. Designed for children from kindergarten through 3rd grade.
Christmas Celebrated in Song, Vol. 1. This program answers long-standing questions about the history of Christmas hymns, their origins and the people who created them. The program uses pictures and music to illustrate eight different hymns. 17 mins.
VHS: S19982. $37.95.
Christmas Celebrated in Song, Vol. 2. Highlighted by music, this special program explores the traditions of gift giving, caroling, Christmas trees and St. Nicholas. 11 mins.
VHS: S19983. $37.95.
The Story of Good King Wenceslas. A faithfully researched history of the ancient legend charges this tale of the avuncular and lovable king. 15 mins.
VHS: S19981. $37.95.
The Christmas Collection, Set. A set of three tapes.
VHS: S19984. $99.00.

Christmas Cracker
In this animation from the National Film Board of Canada, a man builds a spaceship to gather a star for the top of his Christmas tree. *The Story of Christmas* uses cut-out historical figures to narrate the joy and pleasures of Christmas. *The Great Toy Robbery* recasts Santa as a western cartoon ambushed by a deranged trio, awaiting rescue from an actual hero. *The Energy Carol* reworks Dickens' classic about a miserly energy company autocrat who learns a valuable lesson in trust and giving. 30 mins.
VHS: S18563. $14.98.

Christmas Reunion
A classic children's story stars James Coburn and Edward Woodward as they travel back in time 50 years to discover a wholesome past.
VHS: S23478. $69.95.

Christmas Star
A recreation of the journey of the Magi and the Nativity while studying ancient Babylonian and Roman astronomical statistics and modern scientific principles to legitimize the authenticity of the Star of Bethlehem. 60 mins.
VHS: S19547. $14.95.

Christmas Stories
Four favorite stories suitable particularly for children ages 3-10, including *The Twelve Days of Christmas; Little Drummer Boy; Morris's Disappearing Bag*, about a magical gift to the youngest child in a family; and *The Clown of God*, about a juggler who performs in a church on Christmas Eve.
VHS: S01685. $14.95.
Freitag/Sporn, USA

The Christmas That Almost Wasn't
Wonderful songs and characters make this an enchanting live-action film about children who save Christmas when Santa Claus is unable to pay the rent. 95 mins.
VHS: S05309. $19.99.

Cinder-Elly
Fairy tale magic and fast-paced rhyming make this read-along video a delight for children. A modern day Cinderella tries to win the affections of a Prince Charming, a local basketball player. Only her fairy godmother, a shopping cart lady, can give her the help and confidence she needs.
VHS: S22347. $39.95.

Circus: 200 Years of Circus in America
Jack Perkins hosts this look at the history of the Big Top and its many attractions. Clowns, acrobats, magicians and animal trainers have delighted audiences for generations. This definitive work explores the past, present and future of this enduring entertainment. 60 mins.
VHS: S24209. $19.95.

Clarissa Explains Dating
From Nickelodeon's top-rated show, the precocious star of *Clarissa Explains It All* offers teenagers advice and smart ideas about the etiquette of dating.
VHS: S20287. $14.98.

Clarissa Explains It All: "Take My Brother, Please"
From the popular *Nickelodeon* serial of the same name come these two episodes: *Darling Wars* and *Brain Drain* show Clarissa and her obnoxious brother Ferguson at their combative best. The brother you can do without is always easy to annoy. 55 mins.
VHS: S20662. $14.98.

Clarissa Explains It All: Ferguson Explains It All
Ferguson is Clarissa's obnoxious little brother, the infamous character from the popular *Nickelodeon* series. In the title episode Ferguson is bent on controlling the minds of those around him. In the second episode he reaches new lows while campaigning for school president. 60 mins.
VHS: S24721. $14.98.

Classic Jonny Quest: Bandit in "Adventures Best Friend"
Bandit is surely Jonny Quest's best friend and he is featured in the episodes on this video. Included are *Adventures Best Friend, Attack of the Tree People, Terror Island* and two bonus cartoons, *Classic Space Ghost* and *Two Stupid Dogs*.
VHS: S27520. $12.98.
Hanna-Barbera Productions, USA, 1964, 60 mins.

Classic Jonny Quest: Dr. Zin in "Master of Evil"
Master of Evil, Riddle of the Gold and *The Robot Spy*, together with two bonus cartoons, *Classic Space Ghost* and the world premiere of *Cow and Chicken*, are compiled on this video. The villainous Dr. Zin is a fiend who keeps Jonny Quest and his friends under constant threat.
VHS: S27519. $12.98.
Hanna-Barbera Productions, USA, 1964, 60 mins.

Classic Jonny Quest: Hadji in "Mysteries of the East"
Hadji is Jonny Quest's childhood friend, and he takes center stage in these episodes. *Mysteries of the East* is joined by *Calcutta Adventure* and *Pirates from Below*, along with two bonus cartoons, *Classic Space Ghost* and the world premiere of *Johnny Bravo*.
VHS: S27518. $12.98.
Hanna-Barbera Productions, USA, 1964, 60 mins.

Classic Jonny Quest: Jonny Quest vs. the Cyber Insects
Dr. Zin's most diabolical plan forces Jonny and all his family and friends into their most exciting adventure. This is the final group of episodes and all the Quest characters, including Hadji, Race, Dr. Quest, Jessie and Bandit are featured.
VHS: S27516. $14.98.
Hanna-Barbera Productions, USA, 1964, 90 mins.

Classic Jonny Quest: Race Bannon in "An Army of One"
These classic '60s animated cartoons combine suspense and heroism in a manner unlike anything visible on television today. This video features the episodes *An Army of One, Mystery of the Lizard Men* and *Double Danger*, plus two bonus cartoons, *Classic Space Ghost* and the world premiere of *Dexter's Laboratory*.
VHS: S27517. $12.98.
Hanna-Barbera Productions, USA, 1964, 60 mins.

Classic Stories for Children
Beautifully designed and dressed puppets tell four classic children's stories using voice-over narration, dramatic action (puppets) and musical numbers. Includes *Rapunzel, The Frog Prince, Rumpelstiltskin* and *Jack and the Beanstalk*.
VHS: S15134. $24.95.
Peter Babakitis, USA, 1990, 37 mins.

Classroom Holidays
A continuation of the stories about Jim and his first-grade classmates. Created by Miriam Cohen and illustrated by Lillian Hoban, the stories highlight issues of trust, warmth, independence, humor and compassion. Intended for children from kindergarten through 3rd grade.
Bee My Valentine: A Valentine's Day Story. Little George is hurt when he receives fewer valentines than his peers. He hides out in a coatroom until Jim devises a music fest that uplifts George's spirits. 8 mins.
VHS: S20060. $44.95.
Don't Eat Too Much Turkey: A Thanksgiving Story. When Anna Maria writes a Thanksgiving play, she believes that entitles her to cast and direct the work, which upsets her classmates. The teacher intervenes and settles the dispute by getting the entire class involved in the production. 8 mins.
VHS: S20058. $44.95.
Liar, Liar, Pants on Fire: A Christmas/Chanukah Story. Alex has difficulties adjusting to his new environment and starts telling a string of lies to cover up his discomfort. At the Christmas party, he summons up enough strength to tell the truth. 7 mins.
VHS: S20059. $44.95.
Starring First Grade: An Anytime Celebration. Jim is upset when he is forced to play a tree rather than a troll in the school play. The kids have to deal with adjustments and problem solving in arguing over roles. 8 mins.
VHS: S20061. $44.95.
Classroom Holidays, Set. A collection of four programs on the joys and confusion of first grade. 31 mins.
VHS: S20062. $159.95.

Clementine's Enchanted Journey
With a lot of hope, endless determination and the help of a very special guardian angel, this 10-year-old adventurer trades in his wheel chair for a magic flying bubble, and embarks on travel through time to meet Leonardo da Vinci and Pinocchio. Animated. 95 mins.
VHS: S09624. $39.95.

Clifford's Fun With...Series
Clifford the Big Red Dog and his owner Emily Elizabeth are the stars of these Scholastic Learning Library videos developed by early childhood specialists, geared toward ages 3-8. (The books have sold millions of copies.) 30 minutes each.
Clifford's Fun with Opposites. Clifford shows kids about things that are different. The big red dog will delight kids as he instructs them about the concept of opposites in this animated short.
VHS: S24517. $12.95.
Clifford's Fun with Rhymes. Clifford and Emily Elizabeth want to join the Rhyme Cats, but must solve these rhyming riddles. Engaging.
VHS: S24516. $12.95.
Clifford's Fun with Shapes and Colors. In this short animation, the big red dog teaches kids about shapes. Join the scavenger hunt searching for shapes and colors. Full of songs and fun.
VHS: S24518. $12.95.
Clifford's Fun with Sounds. In this short animation, the big red dog shows kids how to have fun with sounds.
VHS: S24519. $12.95.

Cloudy with a Chance of Meatballs
Adaptation of Judy Barrett's fantasy about the land of Chewandswallow and the day the skies stopped raining their sensible, square meals three times a day. 15 mins.
VHS: S08408. $44.95.

A Colt Called Lucky
This is the story of a wild mustang living in the desert mountains of the Southwest. 14 mins.
VHS: S23459. $49.95.

Construction Ahead
This new *How We Work 2 Pack* includes "Road Construction" and "Building Construction." Foreman Scott will show kids how everyone works together with cranes, bulldozers and trucks to build massive buildings. Then he will show how demolition works. In the consecutive piece road building on site is featured. 70 mins.
VHS: S21311. $14.98.

A Conversation with Magic
Nickelodeon produced this show with Linda Ellerbee to explain to kids the exact differences between the HIV virus and AIDS, as well as how this disorder is transmitted, and how to interact with people with AIDS. This is a frank look at an important subject, geared toward children.
VHS: S21257. $29.95.

Cookie Monster's Best Bites
Annette Benning drops by to help Cookie Monster, one of Sesame Street's most beloved muppets, sort out the difference between a "Cookie Here and There." A large assortment of treats awaits kids in this song-filled, cookie-crunching delight. 30 mins.
VHS: S26659. $12.98.

Corduroy Bear
Three bear stories! *Corduroy* is a loveable stuffed bear who goes searching for a missing button; *Blueberries for Sal* is about an adventure of a little girl and a baby bear; *Panama* is about the search for a wonderful smell, with Little Bear and Little Tiger.
VHS: S00270. $14.95.
Gary Templeton, USA, 1986, 38 mins.

Corletto and Son
Young Mike Corletto wants to follow in his father's footsteps as an ironworker, but his father has big college plans for him. Against the advice of parents and teachers, Mike sees no reason to prepare for college, and a day in health class provides him with life-saving instruction that helps him save his father's life and re-evaluate his goals. 27 mins.
VHS: S09875. $14.95.

Cougar
In this Mississippi River adventure two children find themselves trapped in a house with a wild cougar. Though they escape from this animal, one of the children is kidnapped. Now they must rely on the wild animal they once feared. 28 mins.
VHS: S23497. $49.95.

Courage of Sarah Noble
During pioneer times, eight-year-old Sarah Noble and her father journey into the wilderness to build a new home. Adapted from Alice Daigliesh's Newbery Award-winning book. 49 mins.
VHS: S08409. $119.00.

Cranberry Birthday
The birthday of that cantankerous yet loveable old salt, Mr. Whiskers, seems to be everyone's favorite holiday except for Mr. Whiskers himself! A potluck supper birthday party and surprise present from Maggie help change his mind.
VHS: S14187. $44.95.

Cranberry Easter
With Easter approaching, the town of Cranberryport anticipates the fun and celebration of the Easter Egg hunt, until Seth spoils everybody's mood with the shocking announcement that he's moving.
VHS: S20013. $44.95.

Cranberry Holidays: Christmas
Mr. Whiskers is caught in a double dilemma: his fussy sister is coming to take him out of his messy house, and nasty neighbor Mr. Grape claims his ice skating pond. A last-minute house cleaning saves the day.
VHS: S14184. $44.95.

Cranberry Holidays: Halloween
Mysterious pirates try to capture Maggie and Mr. Whiskers on their way to the Halloween party with money for the new dock.
VHS: S14182. $44.95.

Cranberry Holidays: Thanksgiving
Who is trying to steal Grandma's bread recipe? Is it the slick gentleman who "smells of lavender" or the rough and tumble, "fishy" Mr. Whiskers?
VHS: S14183. $44.95.

Cranberry Holidays: The Complete Set
Includes *Halloween, Thanksgiving, Christmas* and *Valentine*. Four titles on one videocassette.
VHS: S14186. $159.95.

Cranberry Holidays: Valentine
In the continuing adventures of Maggie and charming Captain Whiskers, we visit Cranberryport to discover who is secretly sending the old seafarer sweet valentines.
VHS: S14185. $44.95.

Cranberry Mystery
Mr. Whiskers and Maggie pursue a group of nefarious thieves who are stealing valuable antiques and relics from Cranberryport. 11 mins.
VHS: S20014. $44.95.

Cranberry Summer
In this animated series, Mr. Whiskey and Maggie experience a host of complications from attending to a sick donkey in Cranberryport. The donkey's demands for food and shelter force them to stage an unforgettable Fourth of July fundraiser.
VHS: S20012. $44.95.

Cri-Cri: El Grillito Cantor
This tribute to the most important composer and singer of Latin American children's music, Francisco Gabilondo Soler. Featured are the songs that three generations have enjoyed, animated by Walt Disney: *La patita, El chorrito, El rey Bombon, El ropero* and *Los cochinitos Dormilones*. This is your ticket to the fantastic world of Cri-Cri, the Singing Cricket. In Spanish. 90 mins.
VHS: S16366. $39.95.

Cricket in Times Square
Chester the musical cricket and his friends Tucker the Mouse and Harry the Cat are the stars in Chuck Jones' animated adaptation of George Selden's Newbery Award-winning bok. 30 mins.
VHS: S07763. $14.95.

Critter Songs
This upbeat video captures a mixture of live action visuals and children's art work in a celebration of our connection with the animal world. The video shows children how they can be a part of nature. Ages 3 to 12.
VHS: S23358. $39.95.

Cro
The Children's Television Workshop produced this animated series that spins entertaining and informative problem-solving stories from the perspective of a hip woolly mammoth named Phil. Normally these creatures are extinct, but Phil was thawed out by Dr. C and her lab assistant Mike. Phil often fondly recalls the old days when he and Cro, a Cro-Magnon boy, used to solve problems together. 45 mins. each.
Adventures in Woolyville.
VHS: S22979. $9.98.
Have Mammoths Will Travel.
VHS: S22980. $9.98.
It's a Wooly Wooly World.
VHS: S22981. $9.98.

Curious George
Based on the books by Margaret and H.A. Rey featuring the adventures of the mischievous little monkey George. Ages 2-6.
Curious George Goes to Town. Join George at the airport, at the library, at a wedding and in an ice cream shop. 20 mins.
VHS: S24610. $9.98.
Curious George: Fun in the Sun. In this short animated film, monkey shines in the sunshine as our affable ape visits a mini-marathon, plays with a runaway pachyderm, paints a billboard, and goes to the amusement park. 20 mins.
VHS: S24609. $19.95.
The Adventures of Curious George. A puppet animation version. 1986.
VHS: S24771. $12.95.

A Currier & Ives Christmas
The lithographs of the Currier & Ives collection as well as other classic traditional scenes of Christmas form a visual backdrop for a tune-filled musical for home viewing. Lyrics are provided on many of the songs so that everyone can join in. USA, 90 mins.
VHS: S04267. $29.95.

d'Aulaire's: Abraham Lincoln
This d'Aulaire book on Abraham Lincoln won a Caldecott Medal for its comprehensive look at an American hero from his humble beginnings to his mighty accomplishments. Part of the children's *Holidays* series.
VHS: S14180. $44.95.

d'Aulaire's: Benjamin Franklin
As a writer, printer, inventor, politician, diplomat and statesman, Benjamin Franklin helped shape the country and change the world. Part of the children's *Holidays* series.
VHS: S14179. $44.95.

d'Aulaire's: Christopher Columbus
Beginning when Columbus was a young boy in Genoa, Italy, this video follows him through shipwreck and war, to the New World and back again. Part of the children's *Holidays* series.
VHS: S14177. $44.95.

d'Aulaire's: George Washington
When George was born the country was little more than wilderness, but he was instrumental in mapping its future. Part of the children's *Holidays* series.
VHS: S14178. $44.95.

d'Aulaire's Holiday Biographies: Complete Set
Includes *Christopher Columbus, Abraham Lincoln, Benjamin Franklin* and *George Washington*. Four titles on one video cassette.
VHS: S14181. $159.95.

Daddy Can't Read
In this ABC Afterschool Special a girl joins an adult literacy program and discovers that her father can't read. This enjoyable show explores the stigma attached to illiteracy and treats it as a social problem that can be solved through patience and effort. This film is part of the Project Literacy U.S. (PLUS) Campaign. 28 mins.
VHS: S23470. $49.95.

Daisy-Head Mayzie
No longer lost after many a year—*Daisy-Head Mayzie* is finally here! This animated version of Dr. Seuss' last book also includes footage of *The Making of Daisy-Head Mayzie*. Ages 3+. 40 minutes.
VHS: S24805. $9.98.

Dan Crow's Oops!
Crow, respected as an educator as well as a songwriter/performer, stars in this concert video guaranteed to keep his fans happy. He's also the voice performing the title song for *The Adventures of Milo and Otis*. 30 mins.
VHS: S15307. $14.98.

Dancing with the Indians
Based on the book by Angela Shelf Medearis, this award-winning video tells the story of a young Black girl and her family's annual visit to and participation in the ceremonies of the Seminole tribe that during the Civil War, some 70 years earlier, had given sanctuary to her grandfather, an escaped slave. Ages 6-12. 8 minutes.
VHS: S24521. $37.95.

Danger Mouse Matinee #1
England's top-rated non-violent animated show. In this episode Baron Greenback, a scheming tadpole, threatens to destroy the world until the world is saved by the suave, dashing rodent—Danger Mouse. Animated.
VHS: S00295. $14.95.
Brian Cosgrove, USA, 1983, 60 mins.

Danger Mouse Matinee #2
Four zany adventures of Danger Mouse and his sidekick, Penfold. In *Who Stole the Bagpipes?* Danger Mouse retrieves stolen bagpipes from the clutches of a mechanical monster; in *The Odd-Ball Run-A-Round*, our heroes find secrets in a rugby ball; *The Return of Count Duckula* has Danger Mouse fighting the evil Count, and in *Public Enemy*, the evil Baron Greenback causes Danger Mouse to lose his memory.
VHS: S00296. $14.95.
Brian Cosgrove, Great Britain, 1984, 60 mins.

Danger Mouse Matinee #3
Dashing Danger Mouse and his faithful companion Penfold are back in an all new adventure: *The Dream Machine, The Chicken, The Four Tasks of Danger Mouse*, and *The Planet of the Cats*.
VHS: S00297. $14.95.
Brian Cosgrove, Great Britain, 1984, 60 mins.

Danger Mouse Matinee #4
Further adventures of the greatest secret agent in the world! Four new episodes: *Die Laughing, Day of the Suds, 150 Million Years Lost* and *Rogue Robots*. With the valuable assistance of Penfold.
VHS: S00298. $14.95.
Brian Cosgrove, Great Britain, 1984, 60 mins.

Danger Mouse Matinee #5
More adventures from the irrepressible (and lovable) English mouse.
VHS: S04345. $12.95.

Daniel and the Towers
Streetwise 10-year-old Daniel Guerra forms an unlikely friendship with Italian immigrant Sam Rodia, who spent over 30 years building the Watts Towers in Los Angeles. Through Rodia, Daniel gains hope and a new set of values, and he crusades to save Rodia's lifework when the county slates it for demolition. With Alan Arbus, Carmen Zapata, Michael McKean and Miguael Alamo. 58 mins.
VHS: S16013. $29.95.

Danny and the Dinosaur and Other Stories
Danny's friend for the day is the very Dinosaur that he had just been admiring in the Museum. What child wouldn't want to ride, go for a swim and play hide-and-seek with a real, live dinosaur? Also includes *The Camel Who Took a Walk, The Happy Lion* and *The Island of Song*. For ages 3-8. 35 mins.
VHS: S14494. $14.95.

Daredevil Ducks
The adventurous trio of Huey, Dewey and Louie challenges the villainous Beagle Boys in *The Money Vanishes*, and in *Home Sweet Homer*, Huey, Dewey and Louie take an unexpected trip back in time. 44 mins.
VHS: S06595. $14.95.

David and the Magic Pearl
Beautifully illustrated with large, distinct illustrations, *David and the Magic Pearl* bursts with original characters and humor as David makes a lot of friends and frees the animals. 75 mins.
VHS: S12381. $19.95.

David the Gnome—Volume 1
Based on the best-selling Dutch children's books, *Gnomes* and *The Secret of the Gnomes*, the story of Gnome-Doctor David, who has magical powers and cures the mentally and physically sick and wounded creatures. Forever on the run all over the world, he is often in danger by the troublesome Trolls, sneaky Snotgurgles, fires and floods. 45 mins.
VHS: S03292. $19.95.

Davy Crockett and the River Pirates
Davy Crockett, King of the Wild Frontier, meets Mike Fink, King of the River, in this classic Disney adventure. This film launched the Crockett-mania of the mid-1950's. 81 mins.
VHS: S22982. $19.99.

A Day at the Zoo
Desi Arnaz, Jr. hosts this fascinating look at animals from around the world. Action footage and interesting facts about the creatures found at the zoo make for an enjoyable children's video. 30 mins.
VHS: S22760. $14.98.

Day Dreamer
An imaginative, animated retelling of Hans Christian Andersen's tale about a young dreamer. With voices of Ray Bolger, Boris Karloff, Burl Ives, Tallulah Bankhead and Patty Duke. 80 mins.
VHS: S17369. $19.95.

The Day Jimmy's Boa Ate the Wash
This collection of four animated shorts is perfect for kids. In addition to the story of the title, there is a story about *Monty*, an alligator taxi; *The Great White Man-Eating Shark*, a cautionary tale; and *Fourteen Rats and a Rat Catcher*. 35 mins.
VHS: S22168. $14.95.

A Day with Horses
Casey introduces kids to one of their best animal friends, the horse. We'll see how horses take baths and even get to kiss a wobbly baby horse. Sing-alongs included, ages 3-8. 30 mins.
VHS: S24494. $10.95.

A Day with Lions and Other Cats
Casey introduces kids to some fascinating facts about felines. For example, tigers love to swim and lions live in families just like people. Sing-alongs included, ages 3-8. 30 mins.
VHS: S24495. $10.95.

A Day with Monkeys
This volume from the highly entertaining children's series *Real Animals* introduces kids to lovable monkeys using sing-alongs, important facts and just plain fun. Ages 3-8, 30 mins.
VHS: S24820. $10.95.

A Day with Whales
Another of the children's series *Real Animals*, this video introduces kids to intriguing whales using sing-alongs, important facts and just plain fun. Ages 3-8, 30 mins.
VHS: S24819. $10.95.

Dear Mr. Henshaw
Adaptation of Beverly Cleary's book about a young boy who becomes author Boyd Henshaw's number one fan and begins a series of personal letters that help him find his own place in the world.
VHS: S08410. $119.00.

Diamonds on Wheels
Three English teenagers looking forward to entering a 24-hour road rally find a second-hand driver's seat in an old junkyard. Little do they know that it is filled with stolen gemstones and villainous mobsters are eager for their return. With Peter Firth (*Equus*). From Disney. Great Britain, 1973, 84 mins.
VHS: S06901. $69.95.

Dig Hole, Build House
Joe is a builder and Susan is an architect. They join forces in order to show how concrete is poured into a hole in order to form the foundation of a house. It's perfect for truck crazy kids ages 3-10, 30 mins.
VHS: S25531. $14.95.

The Dingles
From the National Film Board of Canada, *Dingles* is the outlandish adventures of a grandmother and her three energetic cats. Other shows on the tape include *Little Red Riding Hood* (cell animation conjures up a world of children, wolves, grandmothers and wood choppers), *The Boy and the Snow Goose* (special relationship between a shy young boy and the goose he encounters), and *The Lion and the Mouse* (a delightful reworking of the Aesop fable). 30 mins.
VHS: S18562. $14.98.

The Discovery of the Americas
The discovery of the Americas is told with clear language and panoramic illustrations. Long before Columbus, many other movements and migrations took place in the Americas over thousands of years. There were Stone Age explorers, the Mayan civilization, the voyages of the Vikings as well as Columbus, Magellan and Balboa. Told by Betsy and Giulio Maestro.
VHS: S16342. $44.95.

Discovery Stories
Imaginative situations are presented through beautifully illustrated stories to make children aware of the world in which they live, and the need to protect it and find positive ways in which to live. 25 mins.
VHS: S10316. $29.95.

Disney Presents Bill Nye the Science Guy: Dinosaurs, Those Big Boneheads
What large ferocious creatures are loved by every kid on the planet? Dinosaurs of course, and Bill Nye is just the guy to explain to kids the science behind these prehistoric creatures. In-home experiments and special guests help make this another kid-pleasing science adventure. 47 mins.
VHS: S22337. $12.99.

Disney Presents Bill Nye the Science Guy: Outer Space Way Out There
Kids love the puns, jokes and cool science facts that Bill Nye tells. This video is so way out, it's stratospheric. It presents the hard science on outer space in an MTV like format with in-home experiments and special guests. 47 mins.
VHS: S22336. $12.99.

Disney Presents Bill Nye the Science Guy: The Human Body
Bill will take kids on a journey to the inner most parts of the human body. There is no more fun way to explore the cardiovascular system or the nervous system. 47 mins.
VHS: S22338. $12.99.

Divorce Can Happen to the Nicest People
A video specially designed for kids who ask the toughest questions. In a half hour of video animation, the video employs love, honesty and a sense of humor to explain some of life's toughest questions...helping to take the mystery and pain out of this difficult time. USA, 1987, 30 mins.
VHS: S04762. $19.95.

Doctor De Soto and Other Stories
Doctor De Soto is the Academy-Award short film about a dentist who finds a way to treat a crafty fox with a sore tooth. Other films on the tape include *Curious George Rides a Bike, The Hat* and *Patrick*.
VHS: S00353. $14.98.

The Dog Days of Arthur Cane
Arthur Cane is a spoiled child who scoffs at the magic powers of an amulet worn by James, an exchange student from Africa. Magically transformed, Arthur becomes a guide dog for a blind man and learns about love, kindness and friendship. Based on T. Ernesto Bethancourt's book. 29 mins.
VHS: S23452. $49.95.

The Dog Who Had Kittens
Based on the book by Polly M. Robertus. Baxter the Basset Hound adopts Eloise the cat's kittens. Ages 5-8. 14 minutes.
VHS: S24522. $37.95.

Dogsong
A 14-year old Eskimo, uncomfortable with the modern ways adopted by his people, embarks on a grueling 1,400 mile journey by dog sled across mountains, tundras and ice fields in this adaptation of Gary Paulsen's Newbery Award-winning book. 40 mins.
VHS: S08155. $119.00.

Doing Things: Eating, Washing, In Motion
This Bo Peep video compares children engaged in everyday activities like eating, washing and playing. Some animals like the same foods as kids and everyone likes a mud bath. This non-narrated tape has musical accompaniment that makes it suitable for a variety of situations. 27 mins.
VHS: S22378. $19.95.

Don Cooper: Mother Nature's Songs
Entertainer Don Cooper encourages imaginations to blossom as children see, hear and imitate nature in this delightful sing-along video featuring "The Not Ready for Bedtime Players." USA, 30 mins.
VHS: S15321. $19.95.

Don Cooper: Songs of the Wild West
This sing-along video with guitarist Don Cooper takes the kids back to the time of Cowboys and Indians, when buffalos roamed and eagles soared. Featuring "The Not Ready for Bedtime Players." USA, 30 mins.
VHS: S15320. $19.95.

The Donkey's Dream
The little donkey is drowsy. He and his master approach Bethlehem...This poetic re-telling of the Christmas story from the point of view of the patient donkey is a perfect first introduction for small children. By Barbara Helen Berger.
VHS: S16343. $44.95.

Dot and Dash, Volume 1
These two puppets inhabit a world where dots, lines, shapes, and colors come together in fun and whimsical ways. From these simple means they bring forth a rich and imaginative understanding of the world.
VHS: S26153. $12.99.
Nikki Tilroe, USA, 1993, 30 mins.

Doug, Vol. 1: How Did I Get into This Mess?
This popular children's program uses innovative animation to show the loneliness of 11-year-old Doug Funnie. He develops secret crushes, imagines himself as a superhero and often feels awkward and painfully square. The stories follow the comic adventures of his friend Skeeter Valentine, Doug's obnoxious neighbor Mr. Dink and his painful infatuation with the beautiful and amazing Patti Mayonnaise. 40 mins.
VHS: S19088. $9.98.

Doug, Vol. 2: Patti, You're the Mayonnaise for Me
Three programs detail Doug's infatuation with Patti Mayonnaise: *Doug's Out in Left Field, Doug's Dinner Date* and *Doug's Fair Lady*. The program contains two music videos, highlighted by the Beets' *Killer Tofu*. 40 mins.
VHS: S19089. $9.98.

Down Buttermilk Lane
This read-along video is beautifully illustrated by John Sanford's paintings, which depict the Pennsylvania Dutch Country. It tells the story of an Amish family and includes scenes from their everyday life. Images of horse-drawn carriages, traditional cooking and socializing make this vivid video an ideal introduction to another culture. 7:25 mins.
VHS: S22349. $19.95.

A Dozen Dizzy Dogs
Count up to twelve and back again with a lively, entertaining crew. Checkered dogs, dogs with stripes, dogs with spots, dogs with funny hats...all these dogs and more populate this funny, zany counting adventure. From the *Bank Street Read-Along Story Video* series. The story is told twice—once to familiarize children with the characters and story; the second time with words printed onscreen so children can easily follow along. For ages 3-8. 30 mins.
VHS: S13528. $14.99.

Dr. Seuss
These videos, based on the books by Dr. Seuss, receive a special mention. They are loved by adults and kids alike, who often find in them a special life-affirming message important today. The stories are wildly imaginative, usually focusing on a positive theme in a positive manner, usually presenting males and females in multi-dimensional ways. The videos are also noted for stimulating an interest in reading the books they are based upon.
Dr. Seuss' ABC. ABC fun plus two other stories: *I Can Read with My Eyes Shut* (featuring the Cat in the Hat) and *Mr. Brown Can Moo—Can You?*, full of interactive fun. Animation/book based. Ages 2-6. 30 minutes.
VHS: S24523. $14.95.
Dr. Seuss' Sleep Book. An epic poem recreates the classic book with narration by Madeline Kahn. Follow these crazy creatures as they prepare to sleep. Ages 2-7. 30 minutes.
VHS: S24813. $9.95.
Dr. Seuss: Hop on Pop. Three Dr. Seuss stories for the youngest readers. *Hop on Pop* is simple rhyming fun. *Oh Say Can You Say?* tells a story in tongue twisters kids love. And *Marvin K. Mooney, Will You Please Go Now!* completes the set of three wonderful word worlds whirling, whew! Ages 3-6. 30 minutes.
VHS: S24525. $14.98.
Dr. Seuss: Horton Hatches the Egg. Horton the Elephant helps out Mayzie the lazy bird by sitting on her egg while she goes on vacation. Ages 3-8.
VHS: S24811. $9.95.
Dr. Seuss: Horton Hears a Who. Dr. Seuss teams up with the wonderful Chuck Jones to bring Horton, the lovable elephant, and his wild and woolly friends to life. Filled with songs and tongue-twisting verse. "A person's a person. No matter how small." Also includes *Thidwick the Big-Hearted Moose*. Ages 3+. Chuck Jones, 1970, 26 mins.
VHS: S24810. $9.95.
Dr. Seuss: I Am NOT Going to Get Up Today! A little boy claims that he will not get out of bed today. Other stories: *The Shape of Me and Other Stuff, Great Day for Up* and *In a People House*. Interesting animation. Nice for the under 6 year olds. Animation/book based. Ages 2-6. 25 minutes. 1991.
VHS: S24812. $9.95.

Dr. Seuss: The Cat in The Hat Comes Back.
With three Dr. Seuss stories: *The Cat in the Hat Comes Back*, this time with bunches of little cats, *Fox in Socks*, the amazing rhyming tongue twister and *There's a Wocket in My Pocket*. Ages 3+. 30 minutes.
VHS: S24524. $14.98.

Dr. Seuss Video Festival
Two Dr. Seuss favorites: *Horton Hears a Who* and *How the Grinch Stole Christmas*. 48 mins.
VHS: S01700. $29.95.

Dr. Seuss: Green Eggs and Ham & Other Stories
The classic children's book is now available in a fully animated video cassette. Brilliantly whimsical and highly entertaining, this collection of Dr. Seuss stories will charm children. Kids everywhere will love *Green Eggs and Ham*. Approximately 30 mins.
VHS: S21536. $14.98.

Dr. Seuss: Grinch Grinches the Cat in the Hat
Two of the Doctor's favorite characters cross paths and it's up to the Cat in the Hat to "ungrinch" the Grinch.
VHS: S10096. $14.98.

Dr. Seuss: Hoober-Bloob Highway
An exotic story about a ribbon of light that leads to a floating island.
VHS: S10093. $14.98.

Dr. Seuss: How the Grinch Stole Christmas
A timeless Dr. Seuss classic featuring the crotchety Grinch who tries to eliminate Christmas for the Whos down in Whoville, only to discover the true meaning of Christmas. Narrated by the great Boris Karloff. 26 mins.
VHS: S03534. $14.95.

Dr. Seuss: Pontoffel Pock
After the timid Pock gets a piano that magically takes him anywhere, the young man understands how to appreciate himself. Adapted by Dr. Seuss, this radiantly animated film contains the confidence-building lessons and simple fun found in the beloved books. 30 mins.
VHS: S10094. $14.98.

Dr. Seuss: The Butter Battle Book
On the last day of summer, ten hours before fall, representatives from the Yooks and Zooks wonder about destroying the world for once and for all. Charles Durning narrates this allegorical children's tale about a common people foolishly divided over whether to consume their bread butter side up or butter side down. 30 mins.
VHS: S12843. $9.95.

Dr. Seuss: The Lorax
The well-known Dr. Seuss book that warns against uncontrolled progress is adapted by the author into an equally poignant animated film. The loveable Lorax speaks for the trees when they are threatened with the profit-greedy Once-ler and tells a contemporary message about concern for ecology. 30 mins.
VHS: S10092. $14.98.

Dr. Zoology: The Tamarin Mystery
Dr. Zoo leads an undercover operation called the Eco-Adventures Travel Agency. Together with his assistant Nabe and a computer, The Magic Ring, a virtual rain forest, and Kidspower, Dr. Zoo is able to save Tammie, one of the mysterious and endangered Golden Lion Tamarins, from the evil PolyMorfus. In fact, his efforts save the globe from ecological disaster will teach kids that they too have the power to save the planet. Ages 5-10.
VHS: S27694. $19.95.
Ron Hankison, USA, 1995, 25 mins.

Dragonfly's Tale
When the Ashiwi tribe celebrates abundant food with a joyous food fight the Corn maidens are disappointed and show their disdain with a poor harvest and famine. The villagers leave to find a better life and leave two small children behind. They fashion the first firefly from a withered cornstalk, which flies to the Corn maidens. Soon the plentiful harvest returns, as do the villagers, who are wiser and kinder.
VHS: S21883. $44.95.

Droopy and Company
Droopy is back, and he's brought some of his canine crazies with him! Watch as he takes on Butch Bulldog in a series of ill-fated contests. Includes: *Mutts about Racing, One Droopy Knight, Grin and Share It, Sheep Wrecked, The Hungry Wolf*, and *Officer Pooch*.
VHS: S15664. $12.95.

Drug Free Kids
This instructional program is designed to aid parents in recognizing and dealing with childhood drug abuse. Familiar faces who are advising that kids say no to drugs include Ken Howard, Jane Alexander, Ned Beatty, Marla Gibbs and Melissa Gilbert. USA, 1987, 70 mins.
VHS: S03641. $19.95.

Earth Daze
Professor Iris takes kids on an exploration of the amazing world we inhabit. Of course there is plenty of fun to lighten this fascinating video. 40 mins.
VHS: S26060. $12.95.

Earthworm Jim: Assault and Battery/Trout!
Peter Puppy is Earthworm Jim's faithful and devoted sidekick. Together with Snott, Earthworm Jim's slurping, mucus-oozing friend, they do battle against Queen Slug-For-A-Butt, whose proper title is actually *Queen Pulsating, Bloated, Festering, Sweaty, Puss-Filled, Malformed Slug-For-A-Butt*). This tape also includes interviews with some of the creators and animators of the *Earthworm Jim* series. USA, 1995, 40 mins.
VHS: S27425. $9.98.

Earthworm Jim: Bring Me the Head of Earthworm Jim/Sword of Righteousness

In this first installment of the *Earthworm Jim* series, Jim does battle with Professor Monkey-For-A-Head, the mad scientist with a chimpanzee grafted to his forehead, and with Psy-Crow, the bounty hunter hired by the evil Queen Slug-For-A-Butt to capture Earthworm Jim. Includes interviews with the creators and animators of *Earthworm Jim*. USA, 1995, 40 mins.
VHS: S27423. $9.98.

Earthworm Jim: Conqueror Worm/Day of the Fish

Peter Puppy, Earthworm Jim's faithful and devoted sidekick, appears in *Conqueror Worm* as Monster Dog. Then, in *Day of the Fish*, Jim must do battle against Bob, the world's most cruel and spiteful goldfish, and #4, Bob's "legs". This tape features interviews with the creators and animators of the *Earthworm Jim* series. USA, 1995, 40 mins.
VHS: S27424. $9.98.

Earthworm Jim: The Book of Doom/The Egg Beater

Don't be fooled! While Evil the Cat may look like an innocent, purring Tabby, this scheming feline is really the demon Overlord of the fiery prison colony of a planet known as Heck. No sooner has Jim defeated the felonious kitten, than he must defend the world against Henchrat, a villainous rodent whose only goals in life are to defeat Earthworm Jim and to open his own macrame shop. Yeech. Includes bonus interviews with the creators and animators of *Earthworm Jim*. USA, 1995, 40 mins.
VHS: S27426. $9.98.

The Easter Bunny

The secretive Easter Bunny fools foxes, enters houses without a sound, leaves his Easter eggs and silently slips away. A charming story by Winifred Wolf.
VHS: S16344. $44.95.

Eco, You, and Simon, Too!

A music video that uses computer graphics to teach young children lessons about friendship, nutrition and the preservation of the environment. Eco is a smart, energetic sea otter puppet and Simon is his intuitive, curious human friend. 40 mins.
VHS: S17110. $14.95.

Ed & Chester Bible Stories

Selected Bible stories come to life with these puppet plays by talented African-American puppeteer Ed Winters. 30 mins.
VHS: S20624. $29.95.

Ed & Chester Show

Puppet plays and skits by Ed Winters illustrate delightful tales that instruct and teach African-American values. 55 mins.
VHS: S20623. $29.95.

Eek! Stravaganza

America's favorite animated cat, Eek, is the most helpful, friendly and courteous soul imaginable. Though he claims it never hurts to help, Sharky the psychotic sharkdog, Elmo the elk and Amy girlfriend constantly prove Eek wrong. Eek is the Kid's Network's most banged up character.
VHS: S25622. $9.98.

Eight Super Stories from Sesame Street

A video twin-pack featuring Oscar the Grouch, Big Bird, Cookie Monster, Grover and the rest of the gang. Ages 2-6. 30 minutes.
VHS: S24993. $12.95.

Elm-Chanted Forest

Fantasy Forest is in an uproar in this children's animated feature when it faces the wrath of the evil Cactus King. The woodland creatures band together to fight this menace using lavish production values and a first rate story. Oscar winning producer Doro Vlado Hrelijanovic invites you to listen carefully to the wind. You may just hear the all-animal marching band. USA, 1986.
VHS: S08227. $39.95.

Elroy's Toy

Elroy wants to work on his computer, but a couple of zany characters lure him away to a magic world of computer animation. A rainbow train travelling through a dream land and a bee in sneakers flying to outer space are just two of the amazing images found in this fantasy video. 30 mins.
VHS: S24130. $14.98.
Laser: LD75421. $29.99.

Emerald City of Oz

Margot Kidder narrates this animated adaptation of Frank Baum's continuing adventures of Dorothy. USA, 1988.
VHS: S08412. $19.98.

The Empty Pot

Based on a tale by Demi, *The Empty Pot* focuses on the efforts of Ping, an excellent gardener, to win the Emperor's unusual test in selecting an heir, the one who is able to raise flowers from a seed furnished by the emperor. Ping is frustrated when his seed won't sprout. "Demi's story is gracefully and sparely told, accompanied by delicately detailed artwork filled with plants, animals, and traditions that clearly place the story in ancient China" (*The Horn Book*).
VHS: S20000. $44.95.

The Enchanting Travels of Benjamin of Tudela

In this animated short Benjamin is seen travelling to the communities he described in his *Book of Travels*. Barcelona, Constantinople, Jerusalem, Baghdad and Cairo are just a few of the places he visited. 9 mins.
VHS: S23260. $24.95.

Encyclopedia Brown: The Boy Detective— The Case of the Missing Time Capsule

Idaville's favorite pint-sized sleuth does some tricky detective work and saves the town's centennial celebration from disaster. Live action. 50 mins.
VHS: S11236. $14.95.

End of the Game

Julio Cortazar wrote a short story about a teenage girl named Jen who goes to visit her cousins Julie and Samantha. Through adventure and fantasy they learn about rivalry and change. 17 mins.
VHS: S23454. $79.95.

Ernst

Elisa Kleven's charming story about a young crocodile who loved to think "what if?" is an entertaining story lyrically narrated and set against sprightly music. 1991, 10 mins. Public Performance Rights.
VHS: S13895. $62.00.

Esteban and the Ghost

A merry tinker decides to investigate the mournful howl that echoes through Grey Castle and finds a strange figure unlike anything he ever imagined. A presentation of Sibly Hancock's story.
VHS: S08411. $62.00.

Every Child

1979 Academy Award winner *Every Child* is the story of a baby who appears mysteriously on the doorstep of a busy executive, and is subsequently moved from household to household. With four other fine animated shorts: *Catour*, *The Magic Flute*, *Log Driver's Waltz* and *The Town Mouse and the Country Mouse*. 30 mins.
VHS: S15794. $14.95.

Ewok Adventure

The impish, furry creatures from *Return of the Jedi* are now in their own film. After a crash landing on the planet of Endor, two Earthling youngsters befriend the magical Ewoks and embark on a thrilling quest to find their captive parents. USA, 1984, 96 mins.
VHS: S14558. $14.95.

Ewoks: The Battle for Endor

The lovable, furry Ewoks in their second special-effects filled adventure. 98 mins.
VHS: S14557. $14.95.

The Ezra Jack Keats Library

This animated children's video includes the Ezra Jack Keats stories *The Snowy Day*, *Whistle for Willie*, *Peter's Chair*, *A Letter to Amy*, *Pet Show* and *The Trip*. 45 mins.
VHS: S22161. $14.95.

The Fall of Freddie the Leaf

Freddie the Leaf began as a small healthy sprout on a tree top. With the first frost he shivers with cold and fear. Fortunately his wise friend Daniel helps him prepare for change and the mystery of death. Based on the book by Leo Buscaglia. 16 mins.
VHS: S22367. $79.95.
Laser: LD74597. $99.95.

A Family Concert Featuring the Roches

Live concert footage, mime segments and animation enliven this video. It features music from the 1994 Parent's Choice Award winning album, *Will You Be My Friend?* Undoubtedly the Roches won this award because their music appeals to children and adults alike. 60 mins.
VHS: S26623. $14.95.

Family Dog: Doggone Girl Is Mine and Family Dog Goes Homeless

Family Dog in puppy love and Family Dog befriends a homeless woman. Two animated comedies. 47 mins.
VHS: S20550. $12.98.

Family Dog: Enemy Dog and Show Dog

Family Dog and the Binfords keep up with the neighbors. Family Dog shows off his ability for cat-astrophe. Two animated programs of this canine comedy from Steven Spielberg and Tim Burton. 47 mins.
VHS: S20549. $12.98.

Family Dog: Hot Dog at the Zoo and Eye on the Sparrow

Family Dog gets a little too close at the zoo. Family Dog turns bird dog. Two animated adventures. 47 mins.
VHS: S20551. $12.98.

The Family Farm: Thomas Locker

A brother and sister design a plan using pumpkins and flowers to save their family's farm in this animated film showing contemporary farming. Fun, toe-tapping bluegrass music encourages children to follow the story. 12 mins.
VHS: S14197. $44.95.

Farm Animals: Close Up and Very Personal

Close-ups of cows, pigs, sheep, donkeys, goats, ducks, chickens, turkeys and horses make this episode from the *Close Up* series particularly appealing to preschoolers. They can see all these animals without any fear, and it's allergy free. 30 mins.
VHS: S24151. $14.95.

The Farmer's Huge Carrot

Written and illustrated by kindergarten children in West Columbia, Texas, this engaging story details the efforts of a farmer and his wife to grow a vegetable garden in the midst of a summer drought. 4 mins.
VHS: S19602. $39.00.

Fat Albert Christmas Special

Bill Cosby's famous cartoon character Fat Albert in a special Christmas tribute.
VHS: S10723. $19.95.

Fat Charlie's Circus

Fat Charlie loves the circus. He tries to duplicate a circus act by jumping from a tree into a glass of water. Fortunately Charlie learns an important lesson from his Grandmother, who saves him. This read-along video is an inspiring moral tale. 10:30 mins.
VHS: S22361. $39.95.

Fay's 12 Days of Christmas

Renowned artist William Wegman celebrates the joy of Christmas with his dog Fay and her offspring, Batty, Chundo and Crooky. Kids will love watching these dogs decorate and prepare for the season. There is even a dream sequence of Santa's workshop as the dogs dream of Christmas morning. Ages 3 and up.
VHS: S26142. $12.95.
William Wegman, USA, 1995, 30 mins.

Felix the Cat

Fun-filled action for kids of all ages with *Felix the Cat*, one of the most popular cartoon characters! Felix was created in 1914 by Pat Sullivan, and the episodes here feature the evil Professor, absent-minded Poindexter, and Rock Bottom. In color. USA, 1959, 56 mins.
VHS: S00438. $19.95.

Ferdy

Based on the ever-popular series of Czech children's books by Ondrej Sekora, a cartoon adventure in bugville. Ferdy the ant and his friends set out on a comic expedition to spy on the camp of red ants, and everything goes wrong....
VHS: S03293. $19.95.

Fine White Dust

Cynthia Rylant's Newbery honor book is adapted in this presentation of her story about a 13-year-old boy who learns that appearances can be deceiving, when he falls under the spell of a charismatic stranger.
VHS: S08413. $69.95.

Fingermouse, Yoffy and Friends

Children will be intrigued by the stories of discovery as told by Yoffy, Fingermouse and other finger-puppet friends in this 3-tape series that includes music and sound effects. With educational lessons accompanying each story, the American Library Association calls the series a "combination of imaginative play and substantive story." 180 mins.
VHS: S15539. $100.00.

Fire and Rescue

Fact-filled and exciting, this video takes kids into a fire station, and shares the facts of the job of firefighting. The video shows men and women of diverse backgrounds. Ages 4+. 30 minutes.
VHS: S25040. $29.95.

First and Second Grade Feelings

Adolescence is evoked in these prize-winning tales by Miriam Cohen, illustrated by Lilliam Hoban, that deal with fraternity, independence, self-realization and honesty. "A multi-ethnic classroom, a loving teacher...amusing antics of Jim and the other children, natural sounding dialogue: who could ask for anything more?" (*Bulletin of the Center for Children's Books*). Intended for children in kindergarten through third grade.
Jim's Dog, Muffins. Following the death of his dog, Jim is withdrawn and pensive and refuses to speak to his first-grade classmates. As his friends try to understand Jim's reaction to death, Paul helps him deal with his sorrow and loss. "Numerous books have dealt with the effect of a pet's death on a child, but few are as true to a child's feelings" (*The Horn Book*). 7 mins.
VHS: S20041. $44.95.
So What? Jim feels ostracized because he is smaller than everybody else in the first grade. He tries to start a club and people abandon him. But a sympathetic girl from Chicago helps him overcome his insecurity and teaches him valuable lessons in independence. 8 mins.
VHS: S20042. $44.95.
See You in Second Grade! Jim, Paul, Danny, George and Anna Maria celebrate at the end-of-the-year picnic on the beach. The teacher helps them recall the fantastic experiences of First Grade and they eagerly await the forthcoming year in Second Grade. 7 mins.
VHS: S20044. $44.95.
The Real-Skin Rubber Monster Mask. Jim is excited about wearing his real-skin rubber monster mask until he seeks his reflection on Halloween and fears that he's being transformed into a monster. Willy comes to his aid. 11 mins.
VHS: S20043. $44.95.
First and Second Grade Feelings, Set. A collection four titles. 33 mins.
VHS: S18696. $159.95.

First Christmas

An orphaned shepherd boy experiences firsthand the joy of the Nativity. Animated, with the voices of Angela Lansbury and Cyril Ritchard. 23 mins.
VHS: S13038. $12.95.

Five Lionni Classics

The power of imagination is the theme of these five animated pieces based upon Leo Lionni's popular animal fables. Frederick, Cornelius and Swimmy are featured in animation by Lionni and Giulio Gianini.
VHS: S02846. $19.95.
Giulio Gianini, Italy, 1986, 30 mins.

Five Sesame Street Stories

Included in this collection are five exciting adventures, including *Super-Grover* and *Big Bird Brings Spring to Sesame Street*. Ages 2-6. 30 minutes.
VHS: S24992. $5.95.

Five Stories for the Very Young

The five stories are *Changes*, about the adventures of two wooden dolls; *Harold's Fairy Tale* reveals how the title character employs purple crayons to create stories; *Whistle for Willie* teaches Peter how to whistle. The other tales are *Drummer Hoff* and the famous story, *Caps for Sale*. Animated.
VHS: S00447. $14.95.
Gene Deitch, USA, 1986

Fledgling

An adaptation of Jane Langton's Newbery Honor fantasy tells the story of eight-year-old Georgie, who longs to fly. Her dream comes true after she meets a mysterious Canadian goose. 38 mins.
VHS: S09902. $110.00.

A Flight to the Finish

A race is being held in Odyssey, and Dylan and Sherman are in the thick of it. Taunted by their new neighbors, Holly and her mischievous cat Jasper, Dylan and Sherman are determined to beat them to the finish line. But when Holly's car careens out of control, Dylan must choose to either follow his conscience and help her or continue on and win the race. His dilemma provides an exciting lesson in caring for others. USA, animated, 30 mins.
VHS: S15054. $14.98.

The Flyaway Pantaloons

After they're blown off a clothesline, a pair of women's pantaloons undertake a colorful odyssey through the streets, markets, corners and textures of a Renaissance city. 9 mins.
VHS: S20001. $36.95.

Follow My Leader

Jimmy must undergo rehabilitation after an accident involving a firecracker. He was blinded and is naturally angry at the friend responsible for the accident. As Jimmy learns to forget his anger, his guide dog emerges as a vital link in his effort to enjoy life once more. Based on James B. Garfield's book. 29 mins.
VHS: S23472. $79.95.
Laser: LD74762. $99.95.

Follow That Bunny!

This "hoppin'" claymation musical shows the adventures of some energetic bunnies when Spring almost never came one year. 27 mins.
VHS: S18023. $12.98.

Follow That Fish

Take a ride on a turtle's back and swim past eels, octopi, glowing fish—even a shark! From the *Bank Street Read-Along Story Video* series. The story is told twice—once to familiarize children with the characters and story; the second time with words printed onscreen so children can easily follow along. For ages 3-8. 30 mins.
VHS: S13529. $14.99.

Follow the Drinking Gourd

Ron Richardson narrates this iconographic video presentation of Jeannette Winters' moving story about Peg Leg Joe and a brave group of runaway slaves who follow the Drinking Gourd north to freedom on the Underground Railroad. 12 mins.
VHS: S12259. $62.00.

Four for Thrills, Edgar Allan Poe, Etc.

Here is a quartet of exciting and colorful animated shorts containing Edgar Allan Poe's classic *Masque of the Red Death*, Harry Belafonte's presentation of *The Hand* and the immortal *Casey at the Bat*, and the story of *The Hangman* as told by Herschel Bernardi.
VHS: S03957. $64.95.

The Fourth King

An original, animated Christmas story featuring sing-along songs, loveable animals and an important lesson about friendship and humility. USA, 30 mins.
VHS: S15221. $14.95.

Freddie the Frog

Ben Kingsley, James Earl Jones and Nigel Hawthorne provide the voices for this animated feature starring *Freddie the Frog*. Freddie is actually a cursed prince, but he makes the best of his situation by becoming a secret agent. Before long he discovers that the mastermind behind a diabolical plot is the same relative that turned him into a little green superhero. This action-filled adventure features music by George Benson, Patti Austin and Grace Jones.
VHS: S25741. $19.98.

Fright Fest

Three of Nickelodeon's top animated series are represented in this collection of creepy cartoons: *Doug*, the painfully average kid, *Ren and Stimpy*, the nauseating Chihuahua/house cat pair, and toddlers from *Rugrats*. Each have a scary contribution to make. Kids will love it.
VHS: S21733. $12.98.

Frog

Arlo Anderson adds a magic frog who is really a prince to his reptile collection, and the web-footed wizard turns his life upside down with wacky results. Shelley Duvall, Elliott Gould, Paul Williams star.
VHS: S06365. $29.95.
Laser: LD71063. $29.98.
David Grossman, USA, 1987, 95 mins.

Frog and Toad Are Friends

Five short stories by Arnold Lobel of the two best friends, including *Spring*, *The Story*, *A Lost Button*, *A Swim*, and *The Letter*. Amazing animation. Ages 4-8. 18 mins.
VHS: S24765. $12.95.

Frog and Toad Together

Easy-going Frog and excitable Toad share several amusing adventures and make some important discoveries. The *Dragons and Giants* story could be a bit frightening. This multiple award-winner, directed by John Matthews, is presented in stop-action animation. Ages 4-8. 30 mins.
VHS: S24988. $12.95.

Frosty the Snowman
Featuring the voices of Billy DeWolfe and Jackie Vernon; narrated by Jimmy Durante. When he's brought to life, Frosty tries to thwart the plans of an evil magician. 30 mins.
VHS: S10797. $12.98.

Gallavants
Ganterville is home to a colony of evolutionary ants with a can-do attitude. The characters are delightful, particularly Shando, who learns that it doesn't pay to cut corners on the way to adulthood. This original animated feature is full of laughter and song. 100 mins.
VHS: S25111. $19.95.

Garden of Abdul Gasazi
A boy lets his dog wander into a magician's forbidden garden in this award-winning tale of Chris Van Allsburg's cautionary tale. 8 mins.
VHS: S08157. $114.00.

Garfield Goes Hollywood
Jon, Odie and the irrepressibly languorous Garfield find excitement through a Tinseltown talent contest. While Garfield is busy auditioning for the TV show "Pet Search," "Johnny Bop and the Two-Steps" make their bid to be the world's next singing sensation. Only one of this trio, however, is actually convinced that fame and fortune through stardom await them. This animated special is perfect for the whole family. Voices by Lorenzo Music. USA, 1987, 30 mins.
VHS: S12785. $12.95.

Gateway to the Mind
A wonderful, animated excursion through the world of the senses—touch, smell, taste, sight and sound—with Dr. Frank Baxter. Discover that grasshoppers can hear with their stomachs, fish can taste with their bodies, and sometimes the things we see aren't what they appear to be. Written and directed by master animator Chuck Jones. 58 mins.
VHS: S14226. $19.98.

Gentle Giant
The feature film that launched the tv series Gentle Ben. A gentle, orphaned bear cub grows very large and causes some problems in public relations for Dennis Weaver and Vera Miles.
VHS: S04237. $39.95.
James Neilson, USA, 1967, 93 mins.

Gerald McBoing Boing
Four hilarious stories about a small boy who can only produce such sound effects as "boing boing!" The first of the four sequences was an early creation of Dr. Seuss, produced in 1950. Featuring Marvin Miller as the voice of Gerald McBoing Boing.
VHS: S00490. $19.95.
Robert Cannon, USA, 1955, 29 mins.

Gerald McBoing Boing Collection
From the famous UPA cartoon show, this character was created by Dr. Seuss.
Dusty of the Circus. Color, animated, 31 mins.
VHS: S13437. $9.95.
Favorite Animals. Color, animated, 31 mins.
VHS: S13435. $9.95.
Favorite Painters. Color, animated, 30 mins.
VHS: S13436. $9.95.
Favorite Sing-a-Long Songs. Color, animated, 20 mins.
VHS: S13434. $9.95.
Favorite Stories and Tales. Color, animated, 28 mins.
VHS: S13433. $9.95.
The Silly Twirliger Twins and Their Funny Friends. Color, animated, 18 mins.
VHS: S13438. $9.95.

Gerbert Is Ben Franklin
This delightful video will entrance kids with an historic look at the life of Ben Franklin as played by Gerbert. One of America's founding fathers, Franklin was not just a gifted leader, but a man of charm and wit.
VHS: S26289. $14.95.
Richard Tiffany, USA, 1992, 30 mins.

Gerbert Is Marco Polo
Gerbert and his pal Roary are off to China as Gerbert imagines himself to be the Italian explorer Marco Polo. This puppet's tale will intrigue children with the historic achievements of this intrepid figure from the past.
VHS: S26291. $14.95.
Richard Tiffany, USA, 1992, 30 mins.

Gerbert Is Mozart
The 18th-century musical genius will come alive for kids in this historic recreation of Mozart's life starring the puppet Gerbert. Gerbert starts by fantasizing about being the composer, but soon realizes that it takes talent, hard work and practice to reach any goal.
VHS: S26290. $14.95.
Richard Tiffany, USA, 1992, 30 mins.

Gerbert Is Tom Sawyer
Kids will love this historically inspired cartoon featuring Gerbert Sawyer. He travels down the Mississippi with America's most original humorist, Mark Twain.
VHS: S26151. $12.99.
Richard Tiffany, USA, 1992, 30 mins.

Get Ready for School
Based on Richard Scarry's popular characters. Young Brewster's first day of nursery school finds him overcoming his fears and having a great time learning things and making friends. Ages 3-7. 30 minutes.
VHS: S25034. $9.95.

Ghost Writer: Into the Comics
The Children's Television Workshop has created another hip, fresh, comic mystery adventure. This one features a contest and a surprise appearance by Spike Lee. 99 mins.
VHS: S22194. $14.98.

Ghost Writer: Who Burned Mr. Brinker's Store
From the creators at Children's Television Workshop comes this hip, fresh and funny series. In this video a mystery adventure is set in motion to find the culprit who burned Mr. Brinker's store. The truth will either set Jamal free or get him burned. 95 mins.
VHS: S22193. $14.98.

Glass Slipper
This sentimental, musical version of the classic Cinderella story alternates between dramatic setpieces and rich, romantic fantasy sequences filled with song and dance. Stars Leslie Caron and Keenan Wynn.
VHS: S13643. $19.98.
Charles Walters, USA, 1955, 94 mins.

A Golden Treasury of Nursery Rhymes
A mosaic of children's classic nursery rhymes is visualized in this fully animated video collection. 40 mins.
VHS: S19430. $14.99.

Golden Voyage of Sinbad
A spectacular adventure set in mysterious ancient lands inhabited by incredible creatures. Sinbad (John Philip Law) finds an intriguing map and sets sail for the uncharted island of Lemuria. His companions: a mysterious and intriguing slave girl and Prince Koura.
VHS: S12999. $14.95.
Gordon Hessler, USA, 1973, 105 mins.

Good King Wenceslas
Illustrator Jamichael Henterly's rich medieval details and deep warm colors convey the warmth of this beloved holiday story about a kindly king who is moved by the unfortunate plight of a peasant. 6 mins.
VHS: S12260. $57.00.

Good Morning Miss Toliver
Acclaimed teacher Kay Toliver takes us to her New York City school, where we glimpse her incredible combination of math, art, acting and fun. First seen on PBS. Ages 8+. 26 minutes.
VHS: S24981. $24.95.

Good Morning Sunshine
"Songs For a Day Full of Wonder," by Patti Dallas and Laura Baron. Fascinating instrumentation with dulcimers and recorders. Real kids dance and play. Ages 2-6. 30 minutes.
VHS: S24895. $14.95.

Good Morning, Good Night: A Day on the Farm
Wake up with a little child and then watch as all the farm animals start a new day. First there's a little breakfast and then a romp, even some chores. Finally the day is done and everyone, a little tired, goes to sleep once again. Folk songs accompany this delightful video, perfect for sing-alongs. 17 mins.
VHS: S22379. $19.95.

Good Morning, Granny Rose!
Children will love this romp in the Ozarks with Granny Rose and her old dog, Henry. "Don't just lay there like a sack of potatoes, Henry!," Granny Rose says as they hurry off after breakfast to watch the sunrise. From the story by Warren Ludwig.
VHS: S16346. $44.95.

A Good Thing About Spots
A shy leopard cub learns to appreciate his spots. 14 mins.
VHS: S23458. $49.95.

Goosebumps: The Haunted Mask
This is the pilot from the current hit on the Fox Kids Network. It all began innocently enough when a girl, tired of being teased by boys, put on a frightening mask. It worked, but she soon discovered she couldn't take off the mask.
VHS: S27192. $14.98.
R.L. Stine, USA, 1995, 44 mins.

Granpa
This beautifully animated video about exploring the imaginary worlds of each other's future and past is based on John Burningham's prize winning book and was created by the same team responsible for the perennial best-seller The Snowman. Narrated by Peter Ustinov. 30 mins.
VHS: S15305. $14.98.

Great Bible Stories
Narrated and animated bible stories for children, with two complete stories on each video. Each tape is 30 minutes.
Abraham/Naaman and the Slave Girl.
VHS: S07411. $14.99.
Apostle Paul/Prodigal Son.
VHS: S07419. $14.99.
David and Goliath/Gideon.
VHS: S07409. $14.99.
Moses/Samuel and Saul.
VHS: S07410. $14.99.
Noah's Ark/Joshua.
VHS: S07408. $14.99.
Story of Peter/Phillipian Jailer.
VHS: S07417. $14.99.

Greg & Steve Live! In Concert
Greg & Steve perform "ABC Rock", "The World Is a Rainbow", "Friends" and other popular children's favorites. 60 mins.
VHS: S20468. $19.95.

Greg & Steve Musical Adventures
Greg & Steve sing their way through six different musical adventures, including "The Three Little Pigs", "Heavenly Music", "We've Got the Whole World", "Down by the Bay" and more. 30 mins.
VHS: S20469. $14.95.

Greyling
Jane Yolen based this original story on Scottish fishermen's tales of "selchies," the magical creatures who are human on land and seals in the water. A sad, childless couple live on one of the islands off the coast of Scotland. Their lives change one day when the fishermen bring home an orphaned seal pup (who turns out to be a selchie) and whom the fisherman and his wife view as their own beloved son.
VHS: S16347. $44.95.

Gulliver's Travels
Gulliver has been trapped by the tiny Lilliputians. After he wins their trust, he learns they are engaged in a war with the nearby island of LaFuscoe. His adept handling of the situation averts disaster. His gigantic size can stave off disaster in this miniature animated kingdom. From the Enchanted Tales series.
VHS: S27371. $14.98.
Diane Eskenazi, USA, 1996, 48 mins.

Halloween
This iconographic presentation of Gail Gibbon's book explores the history, meanings and trappings of one of childhood's most favorite and colorful holidays. 6 mins.
VHS: S24914. $37.95.

Happy Birdy
In this birthday video, a bird hosts the party. Combining animation and puppetry, the words to songs are spelled out on the screen, encouraging viewers to sing along. Ages 4-7. 30 minutes.
VHS: S25033. $9.98.

Happy New Year, Charlie Brown
Even though it's a new year, some things never seem to change. In this cartoon, the Peanuts gang celebrates the coming year, but then it's back to homework for Charlie Brown. 25 mins.
VHS: S26163. $12.95.

Harbor Tugs at Work
This video follows in the traditions of the children's video I Love Toy Trains. It shows how harbor tugs work for an audience ages two and up. Captain Evans and his crew are helpful and informative guides to the modern world of harbors and their cargo. 30 mins.
VHS: S24357. $14.95.

Harold and the Purple Crayon and Other Harold Stories
Gene Deitch, the world's foremost animator of classic children's books, explains how he learned from Crockett Johnson. Harold and the Purple Crayon, Harold's Fairy Tale and A Picture for Harold's Room are animated shorts that make this video a delight for children. 30 mins.
VHS: S22166. $14.95.

Hawk, I'm Your Brother
Will Rogers Jr. narrates this story of Native American culture based on the book by Byrd Baylor. Young Rudy Soto wants to fly without the expense of taking an airplane into the wild blue yonder. He seeks advice from a captured red-tailed hawk for natural flying tips. This children's story was winner of a Peace Pipe Award. USA, 25 mins.
VHS: S13294. $14.99.

Henry and Mudge in Puddle Trouble
It's spring and Henry and his 180-pound dog Mudge encounter the first spring flower, a gigantic puddle and a box full of kittens.
VHS: S08464. $71.95.

Henry and Mudge in the Green Time
Summer, the perfect time for a boy and his dog to picnic in the park—based on Cynthia Rylant's story of two best friends—Henry and his dog, Mudge.
VHS: S08414. $71.95.

Henry and Mudge Under the Yellow Moon
Henry and his dog Mudge never do things the same way, and falling leaves, scary Halloween tales and a Thanksgiving visitor provide fun for the two friends.
VHS: S08395. $71.95.

Henry Hamilton: Graduate Ghost
Former Civil War soldier Hamilton is having a hard time as a ghost because he's too nice. The Specter Inspector is not convinced Henry can haunt a great mansion so he is assigned to the Landry family as a test of his spooking abilities. Henry loses no time and teaches the Landrys a host of self-affirming ideals. 29 mins.
VHS: S23448. $49.95.

Henry's Cat: The Birthday Caper
Henry's Cat is the enormously popular British cartoon, created for children 3 and up. This tape contains two episodes: The Birthday Caper and The Great Adventure. 32 mins.
VHS: S09001. $9.95.

Here Comes a Roller Coaster
Dave and his son Taylor will show kids some of the most daunting roller coasters at Six Flags Theme Park. Also includes a look at the Batman ride and the Log Jammer. Ages 3-8, 35 mins.
VHS: S24488. $12.95.

Here Comes Peter Cottontail
When Peter Cottontail tries to become chief Easter Bunny, he's suddenly challenged to a contest by his arch rival, Evil Irontail, and instantly finds himself up to his ears in trouble. Peter and his magical friend, Seymour S. Sassafrass, race to distribute the most eggs on Easter Sunday. Animated, with the original recording sung by Danny Kaye, and narrated by Vincent Price. 53 mins.
VHS: S11600. $14.95.

Here Comes the Cat and Other Cat Stories
Animated features The Cat and the Collector, Cat and Canary and Millions of Cats are joined with the title story for a collection sure to please cat lovers of all ages. 30 mins.
VHS: S22167. $14.95.

Here We Go—Vol. 1
An informative show that captures children's fascinations with some of the most exciting vehicles ever made, including zeppelins. Narrated by Lynn Redgrave, Parents' Choice award. 33 mins.
VHS: S04996. $12.95.

Here We Go Again
Featuring 14 thrilling sequences from around the world, Here We Go Again continues the educational series on transportation. Lynn Redgrave provides valuable information and excitement at each intriguing location. Among other vehicles, kids will get to ride on a San Francisco cable car, farm tractor, police car, and propeller airplane. 60 mins.
VHS: S16759. $12.95.

Herman & Marguerite
A tale of an insecure worm and a frightened caterpillar (later a butterfly) who learn to look at themselves and each other with love and respect as they help bring spring to the earth. A discussion guide which suggests ways of using storytelling accompanies. Told by master storyteller Jay O'Callahan. Public performance rights included.
VHS: S09268. $19.95.

Hey, What About Me?
A warm, straight-forward attempt to talk to Pre-Schoolers about adjusting to new siblings. Teaches games, lullabies and bouncing rhymes. American Film Institute Video Award, American Academy of Pediatrics suggested media list. 25 minutes, ages 2-6.
Home Video.
VHS: S10149. $14.95.
Public Performance Rights.
VHS: S17154. $14.95.

Hills of Home
Lassie and a lonely Scottish highlands country doctor confront the elements, local superstition and abject poverty. The doctor receives Lassie as payment for services and the two develop a deep bond.
VHS: S19138. $19.98.
Fred M. Wilcox, USA, 1948, 97 mins.

The Holiday Collection
In this series, children discover the foundations and traditions of our national holidays. They learn how April 1st evolved into a day of pranks and the strange tradition behind the groundhog's search for his shadow on February 2nd. The series also looks at the origins of St. Patrick's Day, Thanksgiving and Christmas. Designed for children from kindergarten through 3rd grade.
Special Spring Days. Children learn the background of three spring holidays: the origins of Groundhog Day; the story of St. Patrick; and how the first day of April became a day for trickery. 19 mins.
VHS: S19991. $37.95.
Thanksgiving Tales. Two versions of the Thanksgiving holiday, the familiar telling of the pilgrims and the First Thanksgiving, and the story of an Indian who befriends a group of strangers and helps bring spring to the rugged frontier life. 20 mins.
VHS: S19990. $37.95.
The Twelve Days of Christmas. Children are taught the private joys and special pleasures behind an enduring season classic, the popular carol that discusses the epiphanies of the 12 days. 13 mins.
VHS: S19992. $37.95.
The Holiday Collection, Set.
VHS: S19993. $99.00.

Holidays for Children Video Series
This 12-volume set offers an interactive children's video experience. It explores the customs, rituals and folklore underlying some of the major traditional American holidays. Traditional music, animation and live-action sequences hosted by Michael Keck make this series an entertaining but educational resource for children. Each volume is 30 mins.
Arbor Day.
VHS: S24460. $29.95.
Chinese New Year.
VHS: S24461. $29.95.
Christmas.
VHS: S24462. $29.95.
Cinco de Mayo.
VHS: S24463. $29.95.
Easter.
VHS: S24464. $29.95.
Halloween.
VHS: S24465. $29.95.
Hanukkah/Passover.
VHS: S24466. $29.95.
Independence Day.
VHS: S24467. $29.95.
Kwanzaa.
VHS: S24468. $29.95.
Rosh Hashana/Yom Kippur.
VHS: S24469. $29.95.
Thanksgiving.
VHS: S24470. $29.95.
Valentine's Day.
VHS: S24471. $29.95.
Holidays for Children Video Series. 12-volume set.
VHS: S24472. $359.40.

Homer Price Stories
Two Homer Price stories, based on Robert McCloskey's now classic stories, set in fictional town of Centerburg, with Homer, the 10-year-old boy, growing up in the world of the 50's. 40 mins.
VHS: S03519. $14.95.

Horses: Close Up and Very Personal
This episode from the Close Up series emphasizes the physical attributes of these magnificent animals so that preschoolers will understand their power. Horses are seen in a variety of environments, from the workaday world of the farm to the world of sports. 30 mins.
VHS: S24214. $14.95.

Horton Hears a Who
Dr. Seuss teams up with the wonderful Chuck Jones to bring Horton, the lovable elephant, and his wild and woolly friends to life. Filled with songs and tongue-twisting verse. "A person's a person. No matter how small."
VHS: S00582. $14.95.
Chuck Jones, USA, 1970, 26 mins.

How a Car Is Built
Kids will travel down a Ford assembly line nine miles long. They will see how the Ford Mustang is built. Everything from precision robots to powerful metal presses to the arduous painting process is fully detailed. 30 mins.
VHS: S26004. $14.95.

How Beaver Stole Fire
In this sand animation short, a Native American tale about the origin of fire is beautifully realized. 12 mins.
VHS: S23507. $39.95.

How It's Done: From Baseball Bats to Potato Chips
This fascinating behind the scenes look at the production of everyday objects will fascinate kids. Detective Howie Dunn leads kids on a tour that explains how bats, orange juice, cherries, and even potato chips are made. 34 mins.
VHS: S23964. $9.99.

How It's Done: From Roller Coasters to Ice Cream
Howie Dunne does it again. This time his tour shows how roller coasters, ice cream, softballs, TV news broadcasts and more are prepared and made available to consumers. 32 mins.
VHS: S23965. $9.99.

How to Hide Stories
Ruth Heller has composed six beautiful tales involving birds, amphibians and reptiles engaged in clever games of hide-and-seek with Mother Nature. The stories deal with transformation and how animals camouflage in nature, realized through striking illustrations and a rhyming text. Designed for children in kindergarten through 3rd grade.
How to Hide a Butterfly and Other Insects.
VHS: S20020. $44.95.
How to Hide a Crocodile and Other Reptiles.
VHS: S20015. $44.95.
How to Hide a Gray Treefrog and Other Amphibians.
VHS: S20019. $44.95.
How to Hide a Polar Bear and Other Mammals.
VHS: S20016. $44.95.
How to Hide a Whip-Poor-Will and Other Birds.
VHS: S20017. $44.95.
How to Hide an Octopus and Other Sea Creatures.
VHS: S20018. $44.95.
How to Hide Stories, Set.
VHS: S20021. $239.95.

Howdy Doody Time: A 40-Year Celebration
Buffalo Bob Smith, Howdy Doody and the gang from Doodyville are joined by Clarabell The Clown, Phineas T. Bluster, Princess Summer-Fall-Winter-Spring, the Flubadub and the rest of the Doodyville regulars from the pioneering children's series.
VHS: S05220. $9.95.

The Hubley Collection: Volume 3
Moonbird, Tall Time Tales, Windy City and *Cloudland* are included in this volume of animation by Faith and John Hubley. It combines two classics with two recent releases, to explore wondrous worlds, magical themes, native art and mythology. 36 mins.
VHS: S21523. $39.95.

Hullabaloo
Preschoolers will learn about numbers, colors, time and more in a fun and exciting way. Games, animation, and the lovable Ted Bear use repetition and reinforcement to build a secure relationship with kids that makes these lessons highly effective and entertaining. Each episode is 30 mins.
All About Opposites!
VHS: S24976. $12.95.
All About Shapes!
VHS: S24977. $12.95.
Colors!
VHS: S24972. $12.95.
Count with Me!
VHS: S24973. $12.95.
Everything Grows!
VHS: S24974. $12.95.
Making Fun!
VHS: S24978. $12.95.
Nature Friends!
VHS: S24975. $12.95.
Time!
VHS: S24979. $12.95.

Human Race Club: A Story About Fights Between Brothers and Sisters
Sibling rivalry and handling uncomfortable feelings are the topics dealt with in this volume of the animated children's series created by Joy Berry. The stories include *Casey's Revenge* and *The Lean Mean Machine*. 60 mins.
VHS: S10990. $29.95.

Human Race Club: A Story About Making Friends, a Story About Prejudice and Discrimination
Children learn about discrimination, prejudice and friendship in the animated stories *The Fair Weather Friend* and *Unforgettable Pen Pal*. From Joy Berry, the founder of the Human Race Club. 60 mins.
VHS: S10989. $29.95.

Human Race Club: A Story About Self-Esteem, a Story About Earning Money
A fully animated children's series that emphasizes proper values and valuable tips on growing up. This volume deals with self-esteem and earning money in the stories *The Letter on Light Blue Stationery* and *A High Price to Pay*. Created by Joy Berry, the best-selling author of over 250 self-help books for children. 60 mins.
VHS: S10988. $29.95.

The Hunchback of Notre Dame
Victor Hugo's touching and dramatic love story is transformed in this animated musical. Quasimodo plays the bells for his only friends, the bats at the top of the Notre Dame belfry. Then one day he happens to see the beautiful gypsy girl, Melody, walking by. His desire for her leads him down to the streets of Paris, where he must protect her from the dastardly Captain of the Guard. USA, 1996, 48 mins.
VHS: S27418. $14.98.

Hundred Dresses
Based on Eleanor Estes' Newbery Award-winning book about Wanda Petronski, who wears the same faded blue dress every day. When she tells two classmates that she has a hundred dresses at home, she becomes the target of a daily game of tease. 36 mins.
VHS: S08159. $119.00.

Huxley Pig
The creation of children's storyteller and illustrator Rodney Peppe, *Huxley Pig* has a magical personality given to flights of fancy and dreams. He hates Horace the Rodent, heights, water, but he compensates through his favorite activities, eating, performing, dressing up or day dreaming. Each film contains five 10-minute adventures.
Huxley Pig and the Sea Monster.
VHS: S17173. $14.98.
Huxley Pig at the Beach.
VHS: S17172. $14.98.
Huxley Pig Makes a Movie.
VHS: S17174. $14.98.

I Can Build
A family works together to build a two-story playhouse. The family cooperation of big sister, younger brother, mom and dad is nice. The step-by-step process is shown, from shopping to sawing to hammering. Combining live action and 3-D animation, this video shows youngsters how a house is constructed from the ground up. Ages 2-8. 25 mins.
VHS: S24547. $14.95.

I Have a Friend
A small boy tells of his very special friend, who keeps his dreams secret and safe. At night his friend disappears, but will be waiting for him with the sun. The friend is the small boy's shadow. 7 mins.
VHS: S12261. $62.00.

I Love Big Machines
Big machines of every type are shown and explained to kids in fun but informative ways. Trains, airplanes, excavators, steam tractors, bull dozers and giant cranes are featured in this fascinating children's video. 30 mins.
VHS: S24213. $14.95.

I Love Toy Trains 3-Video Set
Toy trains of all sorts are shown on some of the most intricate set-ups in this fascinating video series. Kids will love this snappy and funny program that informs without ever becoming preachy or boring. It's perfect for toy trains lovers of all ages. Each tape is 30 mins.
VHS: S24212. $39.95.

I Need a Hug!
In this rhyme, composed and illustrated by first-grade students at Clara Barton Elementary in Bordertown, New Jersey, a sad, lonely bug who longs for love and acceptance wants a hug, except the other bugs are too busy to notice his pain. Finally he finds a soulmate. 6 mins.
VHS: S19600. $39.00.

I Want to Be an Artist When I Grow Up
This video, designed for children in grades K-5, provides an overview of the various careers the art field offers. 15 mins.
VHS: S19929. $28.99.

I'll Fix Anthony
Anthony can read, but he won't read to his younger brother Nicholas. Nicholas dreams of revenge when he turns six years old. This is a charming story of sibling rivalry sure to delight viewers. Based on the book by Bill Britain. 14 mins.
VHS: S22371. $69.95.
Laser: LD74600. $99.95.

I'm Not Oscar's Friend Anymore and Other Stories
Four book-based stories centered on friendship, including: *Creole*, with a bird whose appearance frightens the other animals; *Hug Me*, with a porcupine desperate for a hug; and *Birds of a Feather*, about differences. Ages 4-9. 30 minutes.
VHS: S24533. $9.95.

Imaginaria
A state-of-the-art computer animation for children. It will take your kids to 13 fantastic worlds. There are sing-alongs, stories, and dance numbers to startle the imagination.
VHS: S20649. $14.98.

Imagine That!
Nice video about a young boy adjusting to preschool. Would be helpful to either kids in preschool or children preparing to go to preschool. Ages 3-6. 30 minutes.
VHS: S24534. $9.95.

In Coal Country
This iconographic video presentation evokes the flavor of Judith Hendershot's award-winning story about the life of a miner's family in the 1930's, seen through the eyes of a young girl. 11 mins.
VHS: S12262. $62.00.

In My Own Backyard
In this read-along video children will learn about all the things that used to live in their backyard. From agrarian America all the way back to the time of the dinosaurs, it's a fascinating look at history, geology and more. 11:17 mins.
English Version.
VHS: S22364. $39.95.
Spanish Version.
VHS: S22365. $39.95.

In Search of Dr. Seuss
This animated and live-action adventure feature will take the whole family on a journey to find Dr. Seuss. Kathy Najimy, Christopher Lloyd, Eileen Brennan, Andrea Martin, Patrick Stewart and other stars, as well as the voices of Billy Crystal and Howie Mandel, are showcased in this enchanting film. All new musical productions make this video even more engaging. 90 mins.
VHS: S24804. $14.98.
Laser: LD75486. $49.99.

In the Tall, Tall Grass
If you were a fuzzy caterpillar crawling through the tall, tall grass on a sunny afternoon, what would you see? You'd see ants and bees and birds—hip-hopping bunnies too. This backyard tour, created with bold, colorful paintings and large simple words, is one no child will want to miss.
VHS: S16348. $44.95.

Ira Says Goodbye
Based on Bernard Waber's story, Ira is upset when his best friend Reggie has to move away. Ages 5-9. 1989, 18 mins.
VHS: S24532. $37.95.

Ira Sleeps Over
Michael Sporn's whimsical animation is based on Bruce Weber's children's story about the trepidation and fears experienced by Ira on his first night away from home, when he sleeps over at Reggie's house. Adapted from Weber's musical *Lyle, Lyle Crocodile*. 27 mins.
VHS: S19546. $12.98.

It Could Always Be Worse
A poor man learns to count his blessings when he asks his rabbi for advice on how to cope with his crowded household. A charming adaptation of Margot Zemach's award-winning Yiddish tale. 9 mins.
VHS: S08160. $65.00.

It Zwibble: Earthday Birthday
This animated film features a clan of dinosaur babies that will delight children even as they remind kids about the importance of the environment. Join a dinosaur family that wants to protect the earth. After a journey seeing the beauty as well as the destruction of the Earth, we see that even small gestures can help our Earth. Ages 3-8.
VHS: S24514. $9.98.
Michael Sporn, USA, 30 mins.

It's in Every One of Us
Enchanting to both adults and children, this video blends Wernher Krutein's heart-warming images of the global family with David Pomeranz's music and lyrics as a celebration of the human spirit. 5 mins.
VHS: S10230. $17.95.

It's Like This, Cat
A delightfully-illustrated adaptation of Emily Neville's Newbery Award-winning book tells the story of 14-year-old David, who is launched into a series of neighborhood adventures after he acquires a cat. 34 mins.
VHS: S08161. $119.00.

It's Not Always Easy Being a Kid
The puppets at The Judy Theatre help children acquire skills for living. In this video, young Charlie comes to grips with his failure at school by working with a tutor. Then a fable and song examine the temptation to smoke cigarettes and help find an alternative for feeling good about oneself. Ages 7-10.
VHS: S24713. $19.95.

It's Not Easy Being Green
The Muppets sing 13 crowd-pleasers, with Kermit on his ukulele. Includes "Bein' Green," "Somewhere over the Rainbow" and "In a Cabin in the Woods." Ages 2-7. 37 minutes.
VHS: S24941. $12.99.

It's the Great Pumpkin, Charlie Brown
All the Peanuts characters are here in this cartoon about friendship, dreams and Halloween. Linus believes in the Great Pumpkin and convinces his pal Charlie Brown to lay in wait for the mythical figure, which results in disappointment, but is hilarious nonetheless. 25 mins.
VHS: S26161. $12.95.

It's the Muppets!
The acclaimed *Muppet Show*, now in a video series, presents highlights. Hear Kermit's "It's Not Easy Being Green," Pig-Latin musicals, episodes of *Pigs in Space*, and more! Ages 4-7. 38 minutes each tape.
Meet the Muppets!
VHS: S24711. $12.99.
More Muppets!
VHS: S24712. $12.99.

Ivor the Engine
Ivor the Engine contends with elephants on the line and fire-breathing Welsh dragons in these charming stories. Two volumes set in the gentle landscape of the Valley of Wales.
Ivor the Engine and the Dragons. 59 mins.
VHS: S16146. $14.98.
Ivor the Engine and the Elephants. 60 mins.
VHS: S16145. $14.98.

Jacob Have I Loved
Amanda Plummer plays Louise in this adaptation of Katherine Paterson's Newbery Award-winning novel about a young girl growing up on a tiny, isolated Chesapeake island and her relationship with her twin sister. 55 mins.
VHS: S07697. $119.00.

The James Marshall Library
A Tale of Two Chickens, Goldilocks and the Three Bears, The Three Little Pigs and Red Riding Hood are all told by the witty James Marshall. These delightful children's animated tales are complemented by a brief documentary about Marshall himself. 43 mins.
VHS: S22684. $14.95.

Jane Hissey's Old Bear Stories: Friends, Friends, Friends
Once again these charming "Old Bear" books delight viewers with their toy room antics. Whether escaping from a musty old attic in *Old Bear* or taking a midnight ride with a baby owl in *Hoot*, Old Bear turns imaginative play into beguiling children's entertainment.
VHS: S27415. $9.98.
Kevin Griffiths, Great Britain, 1996, 30 mins.

Jane Hissey's Old Bear Stories: Happy Birthday Old Bear
The characters from the "Old Bear" storybooks come alive in the three stop-motion episodes collected on this video. First, in *Ruff*, Ruff the dog's friends realize that Ruff has never had a birthday. They soon set things right, and the fun grows in the stories *The Birthday Band* and *Fancy Dress Parade*.
VHS: S27416. $9.98.
Kevin Griffiths, Great Britain, 1996, 30 mins.

Janey Junkfood's Fresh Adventure
Emmy award-winning TV special, wildly fun, which aims to excite and educate children (and families) about healthy food. Ages 5-13.
VHS: S24768. $99.00.

Janosch
The unusual storytelling bear presents a collection of stories in which objects have regained their magic, stories of lasting friendship, fables about being strong, being weak, about dreams and daydreams. Based on the acclaimed children's stories by Janosch, whose books have won innumerable international awards. Fully animated. 116 mins.
VHS: S10332. $39.95.

Jay O'Callahan: A Master Class in Storytelling
Storytelling sparks imagination. In *Master Class*, O'Callahan shows what makes a story work and how characters can be brought to life. "Jay O'Callahan is a one-man cultural renaissance. These tapes should be required viewing for all between the ages of five and ninety-five" (*Video Librarian*). 33 mins. color, with workshop guide. Public performance rights included.
VHS: S09265. $59.95.

Jazz Time Tale
A sensitive work about a young girl's social and personal transformation following her encounter with the legendary piano player Fats Waller. Narrated by Ruby Dee. Directed by Michael Sporn. 29 mins.
VHS: S17764. $9.98.

Jeremy Around the World
The adventures of Jeremy and his pal Raven as they search for Cousin Hector, who has been captured by the greedy Wolf. Jeremy's amazing suitcase turns into an auto, a helicopter, a jeep or any other vehicle. 90 mins.
VHS: S03845. $29.95.

Jessi Sings Songs from Around the World
Jessi Colter sings 25 international children's songs, including such favorites as "La Cucaracha", "This Land Is Your Land", "Funiculi, Funicula", "London Bridge", "Too Ra Loo Ra Loo Ral", and even "Aloha Oe". 57 mins.
VHS: S21875. $14.98.

Jimbo and the Jet-Set
Here's the lovable little junior jet with big ideas. Follow the world-wide adventures of Jimbo to fun and excitement in far-off lands. Two precious volumes.
Jimbo and the Jet-Set, Volume 1. 50 mins.
VHS: S16143. $14.98.
Jimbo and the Jet-Set, Volume 2. 54 mins.
VHS: S16144. $14.98.

Jing, A Chinese Girl
Jing is an 11-year-old girl at the center of this chronicle. Over two days her experiences reveal intriguing aspects of life among those living in the world's most populous country. This video explores a number of issues affecting the quality of life for the Chinese people, including population control and competition. 18 mins.
VHS: S23720. $99.95.

Jingle Bell Rap!
Members of the all-dog band, the K9 Four, are all tuned up for a special hometown Christmas concert and gala tree lighting ceremony. Then their town's search for the proper pooch to play the part of Santa Claws runs into some heavy sledding. 25 mins.
VHS: S13031. $9.98.

Joe Scruggs First Video
A blend of animation, live action and enchanting songs for ages 3-8. Recommended by the American Library Association, Video Librarian, Parents' Choice Award. 30 minutes.
VHS: S17139. $14.95.

Joe Scruggs in Concert
Children's music videos for the whole family. Includes Joe, his guitar, puppets and giant props. The audience is fascinating as they sing along, clap along and sign along. Ages 3-8. 51 minutes.
VHS: S24536. $14.95.

Joey Runs Away and Other Stories
When Joey the kangaroo tires of hearing his mother's complaints about his messy room (her pouch), he tries out other accommodations, like a pelican's bill and finally a mail pouch, before deciding that there really is no place like home. Also includes *The Cow Who Fell in the Canal, The Bear and the Fly* and *The Most Wonderful Egg in the World*. For ages 3-8. 28 mins.
VHS: S14490. $14.95.

Johnny the Giant Killer
In this fantastic animated feature a young boy must rescue his friends from an evil ogre. Only with the help of bees can he hope to come to their rescue. Dubbed in English.
VHS: S25704. $19.95.
Jean Image, France, 1967, 68 mins.

Josephine's Imagination
Based on the story by Arnold Dobrin, the video features his illustrations. The story is about a young Black Haitian girl and her mother, who earns a living selling at the colorful market. Josephine makes little dolls from the throw-away bits of things from the market. Soon she has a good little business going. Even the boys like her dolls. Told with a simple, lovely French/Haitian Creole dialect, this is a very warm, gentle film which shows Haitian culture at its best. 14 minutes.
VHS: S24537. $69.95.

Jumanji
Fantasy and reality combine in this adaptation of Chris Van Allsburg's Caldecott Medal winning story about two bored children who find a mysterious game which startlingly comes to life. 13 mins.
VHS: S08163. $65.00.

The Jungle Books, Set I
This dramatic presentation of the all-time children's classic features sound effects ingeniously recorded at the London Zoo. Includes *Mowgli's Brothers, Rikki-Tikki-Tavi, Tiger! Tiger!* and *Toomai of the Elephants*. For Grades 2-6.
VHS: S14208. $139.95.

A Jungle for Joey
A baby orangutan gets himself a new home. 14 mins.
VHS: S23461. $49.95.
Laser: LD74761. $99.95.

Jungle King
Being king of the jungle is not just a privilege, it's a responsibility. In this funny, animated feature a lion has his paws full learning how to rule over the wild animals of hisdomain. Overcoming his easy-going nature and discovering the majesty within himself is a recipe for good-natured humor.
VHS: S21363. $14.98.

Junglies: First Day at School
A vivid collection of vignettes which dramatize individual situations of young children caught up in the awe and wonder of adolescence. 30 mins.
VHS: S19433. $14.99.

Just Grandma and Me
One of Mercer Mayer's best-loved stories comes to life in this 1995 release. Ages 4-9. 30 minutes.
VHS: S25000. $12.95.

Just Me and My Dad
Mercer Mayer's ever-popular "Little Critter" is off to the woods for his first camp-out with Dad. Based on the book of the same title. Ages 4-8. 30 minutes.
VHS: S24999. $12.95.

Just So Stories, Set I
Kipling's tales have been entertaining children since the turn of the century. This valuable and imaginative edition is no exception. Includes four tales: *How the Whale Got His Throat, How the Camel Got His Hump, How the Rhinoceros Got His Skin* and *The Sing-Song of Old Man Kangaroo*. Grades P-3.
VHS: S14209. $139.95.

A Kid's Eye View of Ecology
Kids will want to sing along with children's entertainer Michael Mish's lively introduction to environmental preservation for young people. Mish and three children present a fast-paced overview of a wide range of topical environmental issues. USA, 1991, 28 mins.
VHS: S15200. $59.95.

Kids Love the Circus
The second in the *Kids Love...* series, this video takes kids into the world of the circus. Beyond that, it encourages them to explore the power of their own imaginations, a realm where high-wire acts and clowns rule supreme. 30 mins.
VHS: S23120. $14.95.

Kino's Story Time, Vol. 1
Stories read by Tom Selleck, John Ritter, Valerie Bertinelli and Kim Karnsrithong are featured in this first volume hosted by the lovable puppet Kino. These well crafted stories were first available on Public Television. Kids will love hearing them and seeing some of their favorite TV personalities at the same time.
VHS: S21983. $12.98.

Kino's Story Time, Vol. 2
John Goodman, Mark Ritts, Tatyana Ali, Shari Belafonte and Zachary Bryan read stories along with Public Television's puppet star Kino in this collected volume. These favorite children's tales are newly rendered by famous personalities. Kids will certainly enjoy these classics.
VHS: S21984. $12.98.

Kino's Story Time, Vol. 3
Ellen DeGeneres (*Ellen*), Patricia Richardson (*Home Improvement*), Elena Epps and Kelly Williams (*Family Matters*) and Meshach Taylor (*Designing Women*) are featured on this video, reading stories to the puppet Kino and his children friends. Kids will learn about the exciting world of books from this video. 60 mins.
VHS: S26392. $12.98.

Kitten Companions
This program examines the friendships between children and kittens, as children see the actions and behavior of kittens and learn how to respond to them. 30 mins.
VHS: S18225. $14.95.

The Knight Travellers
Dylan Taylor discovers the important parts of life when he and his dog, Sherman, become involved with the rescue of a time transport machine from a diabolical villain. This animated video is based on the radio program *Adventures in Odyssey*. 30 mins.
VHS: S15053. $14.98.

Knots on a Counting Rope
In this poignant story of love, hope and courage, the counting rope is a metaphor for the passage of time and the boy's emerging confidence in facing his greatest challenge—his blindness. Grades P-3.
VHS: S14198. $44.95.

Lamb Chop in the Land of No Numbers
Puppeteer Shari Lewis and her beloved sidekick Lamb Chop are featured in this wonderful children's video that is sure to please all kids. 48 mins.
VHS: S24249. $12.95.

The Land of Pleasant Dreams
This is a series of animated videos in which children fall off to sleep and enter a lovely dreamland where their experience helps them know what to do in real life. 1987. Ages 2-6. 30 minutes each video.
A Fence Too High. Lacey, the quilted lamb, is convinced she can't win the fence-jumping contest. Peter helps her realize that she'll never succeed if she doesn't try. Includes *A Tailor-Made Friendship.*
VHS: S24543. $14.95.
Bearly There At All. Threads, the bear, wants to be special like his other animal friends. He simply needs a friend to remind him that he too has something special. Also includes *A Girl with the Pop-Up Garden* 30 mins.
VHS: S24545. $14.95.
Is It Soup Yet? RicRac, the rabbit, is brewing a pot of luscious soup, but when his friends ask to add their favorite ingredients, they learn that too many cooks can spoil the soup. 30 mins.
VHS: S24544. $14.95.

Lassie: Martians at the Martins
Two episodes from the classic TV show, *Man from Mars* and *Timmy vs. the Martians*, reveal this canine's otherworldly interests. This video from Nickelodeon also includes the rarely screened *Pup Files.* 55 mins.
VHS: S25525. $9.98.

Lassie: Mother Knows Best
Only Mom can rival Lassie for intelligence, resourcefulness and loyalty. In these two episodes June Lockheart shares center stage with the famed canine. First *The Wrong Gift* surprises Mom, then *The New Refrigerator* leaves Lassie out in the cold. 55 mins.
VHS: S25517. $9.98.

Lassie: To Fetch a Thief
Two episodes show Lassie sleuthing her way through mystery. Only a fearless young boy called Timmy and his trusty collie can save two people wrongly accused of crime. 55 mins.
VHS: S25519. $9.98.

Lassie: To the Rescue
The two episodes on this video show Lassie at her heroic best. Both are literally cliffhangers. In the first, a precarious cliff road gives way, while in the second little Timmy gets too close to the edge of the Grand Canyon. Includes Nickelodean's Lassie Camping Quiz. 55 mins.
VHS: S25518. $9.98.

Lassie's Great Adventure
Taken from the long-running television series and not the collection of MGM series, this enchanting children's work charts the episodes of the determined, eager dog and her amazing tales. With June Lockhart and Jon Provost.
VHS: S18897. $19.95.

Leader of the People
John Steinbeck wrote this widely anthologized story about the Tiflins, a ranching family who figure in the *The Red Pony* cycle of stories. Valuable as literature, this work also reveals much about the American frontier. 23 mins.
VHS: S23447. $79.95.

Legend of Manxmouse
Based on the popular Manxmouse book by Paul Gallico, filled with songs and bright, vivid animation, this is the legend of Manxmouse and Manxcat, the long-eared mouse who looks like a rabbit. When it comes to mice, Manx has no equal. 85 mins.
VHS: S12380. $39.95.

Les Miserables
Victor Hugo's classic novel is translated in an easy-to-follow animated production, spanning 40 years of French history. 60 mins.
VHS: S09189. $29.95.

Let's Get a Move On!
Millions of families move each year. Learn how to survive the impact of changing places, saying goodbye, adjusting to new people, new situations and new spaces. American Film Festival Award, Parents' Choice Award. 25 minutes, ages 4-10.
Home Video.
VHS: S17140. $14.95.
Public Performance Rights.
VHS: S17155. $34.90.

Let's Make a Map
First a street and its buildings are rendered as cardboard models, then as wooden blocks, and then as pieces of cloth. From these last elements a two-dimensional world emerges that reflects the real world of three dimensions. 11 mins.
VHS: S23726. $49.95.

Life and Adventures of Santa Claus
How St. Nick became associated with Christmas, in this animated film based on the book by L. Frank Baum (*Wizard of Oz*). 49 mins.
VHS: S13037. $12.95.

Lights: The Miracle of Chanukah
Judd Hirsch narrates this animated feature about the origins and meaning of the candles that are lit over the eight days of Chanukah. Kids will be fascinated by the significance of this vital story. The voices of Leonard Nimoy and Paul Michael Glaser are featured.
VHS: S22071. $16.95.

Linnea in Monet's Garden
The delightful best-selling children's book is now an animated feature. Linnea and her friend Bloom travel from Sweden to Monet's garden. While they are enjoying this magical and inspirational place, it comes to life.
VHS: S22181. $19.95.
Lena Anderson/Christina Bjork, Sweden, 1993, 30 mins.

The Lilith Summer
Based on the book by Hadley Irwin. Ellen, 11 years old, and Lilith, 77, are tricked into taking care of each other. They overcome their initial resentment of having to "sit" one another and develop a sincere affection. 28 mins.
VHS: S22369. $99.95.
Laser: LD74599. $119.95.

Liszt's Rhapsody
Franz Liszt craved the creative outlet of musical composition and was acclaimed for his skills as a pianist. In this story, a young Gypsy violinist appears who helps him achieve his greatest success. This film is perfect for children. It is the third episode from the Emmy Award-winning *The Composer's Specials* series.
VHS: S27417. $19.98.
David Devine, USA, 1995, 53 mins.

The Little Ant
Professional storyteller David Novak offers a unique perspective on the traditional folktale in this read-along video. The Little Ant sets off a chain reaction of accusation when he accuses a snowflake of making him trip. Perfect for children.
VHS: S22351. $39.95.

The Little Crooked Christmas Tree
Christopher Plummer narrates this animated version of the classic children's book. This is a warm tale about a Christmas tree farm and the little misshapen tree that grew crooked to protect a dove and her nest. The Appleby Boys Choir perform Christmas carols. 30 mins.
VHS: S22514. $14.98.

Little Drummer Boy
Featuring the voice of Jose Ferrer and the Vienna Boys Choir, narrated by Greer Garson. Animagic version of the tale of a lonely boy whose only gift for the Christ child was his drumming. 30 mins.
VHS: S10796. $12.98.

Little Drummer Boy Book II
The continuing story of the little hero of the beloved holiday song. Animated, with the voices of Greer Garson and Zero Mostel. 23 mins.
VHS: S13036. $12.98.

A Little Duck Tale
This tender, heart-warming story portrays the true life adventures of "Chibi" and his duckling brothers and sisters as they struggle for survival in downtown Tokyo. Children and parents alike will find joy in this tale of determination and triumph. 55 mins.
VHS: S17012. $19.95.

The Little Engine That Could
The classic tale of imagination, perseverance and hope to overcome existing hurdles and obstacles is boldly re-imagined in this warm, animated adaptation. 30 mins.
VHS: S18252. $12.98.

The Little Fox
This animated feature follows the story of an orphaned fox who is raised by his wise, good-hearted uncle. He learns how to hunt and survive in the forest. It's based on the book of the same name which has been delighting children for years. 80 mins.
VHS: S22440. $14.90.

A Little Girl and Gunny Wolf
Wilhemina Harper's story is adapted for this video by an actual inner-city kindergarten class. It tells the story of a little girl who is captured by a Gunny Wolf but escapes by singing the wolf a song. 6 mins.
VHS: S23492. $39.95.

Little Lou and His Strange Little Zoo
The adventures of a young black boy who lives in the city. Author/illustrator Mark Rubin offers children an interesting way to become involved in learning activities in language arts, social studies and guidance, with a special emphasis on brotherhood, human relations and cooperation.
VHS: S06726. $29.95.

Little Nemo, Adventures in Slumberland
This delightful animated feature will enchant children who follow the fantastic trip of a young boy through the sleeping world. Aside from the wonders of dreams there are the forbidding dangers of nightmares. Based on Winsor McCay's early 20th century comic strip classic. Featuring the voice of Mickey Rooney.
VHS: S22945. $14.95.
Misami Hata, Japan, 1990, 85 mins.

Little Nezha Fights Great Dragon Kings
Animation brings traditional Chinese mythology to life in the story of Nezha, the boy who challenges the mighty Dragon King of the Eastern Sea. 59 mins.
VHS: S16149. $14.98.

Little People Videos
Based on the Fisher-Price toy characters, these fun videos have high production quality and also promote positive values, such as friendship. Ages 2-6. 30 minutes each.
Little People: Christmas Fun.
VHS: S24806. $14.95.
Little People: Favorite Songs.
VHS: S24807. $14.95.
Little People: Fun with Words.
VHS: S24808. $14.95.
Little People: Three Favorite Stories.
VHS: S24809. $14.95.

The Little Prince
Antoine de Saint-Exupery's classic book has been adapted for this claymation film. Children will love this story of a young boy who goes off in search of matters of consequence and realizes, with the help of a fox, that trivia often obscures the most important things. Narrated by Cliff Robertson, 27 mins.
VHS: S26616. $14.95.

Little Sister Rabbit
A witty portrait of the activities and movements of Big Brother Rabbit and his fiercely individualistic and stubborn younger sister. 25 mins.
VHS: S18022. $12.98.

Little Toot
The brave tug boat Little Toot sets off on the adventure of his life carrying three motherless puppy-dog children in search of their father.
VHS: S16750. $12.98.
Don Spencer, USA, 1992, 52 mins.

Living and Working In Space: The Countdown Has Begun
Interviews with space professionals. Famous calculus teacher Jaime Escalante and a former student look at outer space activities. Ages 8+. 60 minutes.
VHS: S24982. $19.95.

Living in the World Around Us Series
Commercialization. "Drugs: A Primary Film" shows the benefits and dangers inherent in the drugs in a common medicine cabinet; "Seeing through Commercials" is an explorations of how commercials are structured to influence our daily lives. 24 mins.
VHS: S05827. $19.95.
Cooperation. "I Want...You Want" teaches how a boy who only said "I Want" learns cooperation and sharing; "Pulling Together" are the further cartoon adventures which emphasize cooperation; and "A Time And Place" teaches that there is a time and place for everything. 25 mins.
VHS: S05828. $19.95.
May We See Ourselves. "All about Bobby" teaches how to understand others; "Old Eyemo Sees the Truth", how to see oneself through understanding others. 28 mins.
VHS: S05829. $19.95.
Perception. "Use Your Ears" explores the nature of sounds—warnings, sharing, identification, happiness; "Use Your Eyes", how to see the real image; "Light Is Many Things", the life, knowledge, energy that comes from light. 31 mins.
VHS: S05830. $19.95.

A Look Around Endangered Animals
Did you know that rhinos don't see very well? Elephants like to have a lot of company? The cuddly panda isn't a bear at all? *A Look around Endangered Animals* includes segments on the Siberian tiger, the manatee and the gray wolf, among others.
VHS: S16345. $44.95.

Look What Happens at the Car Wash
From soap to wax, this kid's video shows exactly how both an automated and a hand car wash work. Kids will learn important skills and ten new words along the way. This lively and entertaining tape uses great videography, animation and music. 30 mins.
VHS: S26218. $12.95.

Lyle, Lyle Crocodile: The House on East 88th Street
He cooks! He cleans! But he's a crocodile...and he's living in the bathtub of the Primm's new house. Narrated by Tony Randall. Fully animated. 25 mins.
VHS: S11237. $14.95.

M.C. Higgins, The Great
Sarah Mountain is threatened by strip mining and 13-year-old M.C. Higgins dreams of escape for himself and his impoverished family. Based on Virginia Hamilton's Newbery Award-winning book. 42 mins.
VHS: S08164. $119.00.

Ma's Motors
A handicapped Taiwanese boy struggles successfully for a career in auto mechanics. His family, the church and a boy he does not know get involved. They demonstrate how, through love and concern, the handicapped can flourish and fulfill their potential. Produced by Maryknoll Media. 28 mins.
VHS: S04931. $24.95.

Madeline
Her heart was big, her size was small, and Madeline was loved by all! Christopher Plummer narrates this best-loved children's classic. Fully animated. 30 mins.
VHS: S11235. $14.95.

Madeline Collection
The tales of Madeline's adventures at boarding school.
Madeline and The Dog Show. Madeline and the rest of the boarding school arrive to register Genevieve, the dog (who saved Madeline in *Madeline's Rescue*) for a dog show. Unfortunately, Genevieve is rejected for lack of a pedigree. Find out how she wins anyway! Ages 3-12.
VHS: S24764. $12.95.
Madeline in Cooking School. Madeline makes a very important choice. Recommended.
VHS: S24888. $12.95.
Madeline in London. Madeline and the rest of the boarding school visit a friend in London. Madeline gets caught up in adventures and even receives a medal from the queen. Ages 3-12. 30 minutes.
VHS: S24548. $12.95.
Madeline's Christmas. Everyone at the boarding school is sick, so Madeline changes her holiday plans to help them. The show ends with a rhyme about love. 24 mins. Ages 3-12.
VHS: S24549. $12.95.

Madeline and the Easter Bonnet
Madeline and the girls become the hit of the fashion show when their horse's tattered hat is transformed into a wonderful Easter bonnet. Narrated by Christopher Plummer. Ages 3-12. 30 minutes.
VHS: S24997. $12.95.

Madeline and The Toy Factory
The girls go on a tour of a toy factory. Madeline poses as a doll herself and becomes the prized possession of a sad and lonely little girl. Narrated by Christopher Plummer. Ages 3-12. 30 minutes.
VHS: S24998. $12.95.

Madeline's Rescue and Other Stories About Madeline

These three animated shorts are based on the outstanding children's books by Ludwig Bemelmans: *Madeline's Rescue, Madeline and the Bad Hat,* and *Madeline and the Gypsies.* 23 mins.
VHS: S13334. $14.95.

Madre Tierra

From The Multi-Coloured Workshop in Uruguay, this nine-part series of animated films is the product of a unique collaborative experience between Danish and Uruguayan animators and South American artists. Nine of the Uruguayan artists each then made one four-minute animated film. Also included are film clips of the production studio and the artists at work. Ages 8-12. 57 minutes. Includes Public Performance Rights.
VHS: S24742. $39.95.

Magic Eye—The Video for Kids

This video is aimed at children and seeks to educate them about the possibilities of 3-D images that seem to move in both space and time. Includes original music and sound effects in Dolby Surround. 30 mins.
VHS: S22747. $14.95.

The Magic Flute

This animated adventure is based on the Mozart opera. It tells the story of a prince who rescues a beautiful princess from dire peril. Mark Hamill, Michael York and Samantha Eggar provide the voices for this delightful feature, one sure to appeal to children. 44 mins.
VHS: S24021. $14.95.
Laser: LD74982. $29.99.

The Magic of Discovery

A collection of seven films for pre-schoolers by the National Film Board of Canada. *Body Talking* is a musical journey in body language, showing how you can "not say a word and still be heard." *The Animal Movie* shows a boy discovering each animal's specialization, and his own! *Adventures* is about a little raccoon who strays too far from home. *The Sky Is Blue* follows a little boy who explores the sky and outer space…on the tail of a kite. *A Sense of Touch* goes from bath water to bubble gum, from bananas to beards, with a nice musical score. *Matrioska* brings to life nesting Russian dolls, who perform a Russian folk dance. *Dimensions* looks at proportions, starting with a girl and boy who don't fit in furniture. Ages 3-6. 60 minutes.
VHS: S24556. $99.00.

The Magic of Lionel Trains 3-Video Set

Lionel toy trains are world renowned. Tom McComas shows the viewer some of the largest and most elaborate set-ups ever devised for Lionel trains. There are charming anecdotes, great train accessory action, and tips that explain to kids how they can build their own layouts. 30 mins.
VHS: S24215. $49.95.

The Magic School Bus For Lunch

Lily Tomlin is the voice of Ms. Frizzle in this animated science series. Her adventures on the magic bus bring a host of scientific problems and principles to life. Other stars, such as Malcolm Jamal-Warner, Little Richard and Ed Begley, Jr., are also featured. 30 mins.
VHS: S23296. $12.95.

The Magic School Bus Gets Eaten

Lily Tomlin is host for this undersea adventure featuring The Magic School Bus. It's a tough but enjoyable underwater lesson in the law of the jungle. 30 mins.
VHS: S25109. $12.95.

The Magic School Bus Gets Lost in Space

Lily Tomlin plays Ms. Frizzle, the go-getting heroine of this animated science series. On the magic bus, a host of other stars, such as Robby Benson, Carol Channing, Tyne Daly and Dom Deluise, join Tomlin to explore the wonders of science. 30 mins.
VHS: S23297. $12.95.

The Magic School Bus Hops Home

Lily Tomlin is the voice of Miss Frizzle on these animated educational adventures. Kids will love this trip to inland waterways. 30 mins.
VHS: S25108. $12.95.

The Magic School Bus Inside Ralphie

This time The Magic School Bus takes an interior journey to see what makes Ralphie tick. Kids will love this educational look at the human body. 30 mins.
VHS: S25110. $12.95.

The Magic School Bus Inside the Haunted House

Lily Tomlin is the voice of Ms. Frizzle, the school teacher who leads her students on the magic bus into yet another exciting adventure. This time the class is thrilled about a trip to the sound museum until they realize it is in a spooky mansion. 30 mins.
VHS: S26176. $12.95.

The Magic Thinking Cap

A family is on their way to the Judy Theater for their usual puppet workshop, but a crisis sours the mood and Dad gets abusive. Fortunately the Magic Thinking Cap, a contraption that examines underlying thoughts and emotions, helps them get a grip on what the family really thinks and feels. 30 mins.
VHS: S21275. $19.95.

The Magic Voyage

History is turned into animated fun in this version of Christopher Columbus' famous voyage to the new world. It's a little known fact that Chris was helped by his friend the talking woodworm named Pico, and that together they saved the magical firefly Marilyn from the evil swarm lord.
VHS: S20754. $19.95.

A Magical Field Trip to the Denver Mint

Rosie O'Flanigan takes a group of children along for an inside look at the way money is made. The people and machines that make coins are explained in this educational video. 14 mins.
VHS: S23728. $79.95.

A Magical Field Trip to the Post Office

Rosie O'Flanigan shows a young girl the many activities that take place in a post office. In addition to the importance of various jobs and machines, this video clarifies the role of stamps, showing how they are made and used. 15 mins.
VHS: S23729. $79.95.

Make Way for Ducklings and Other Classic Stories by Robert McCloskey

These stories are now wonderful animated shorts that children will enjoy. *Lentil, Blueberries for Sal, Time of Wonder* and *Burt Dow: Deep Water Man* are included with the favorite, *Make Way for Ducklings.* 60 mins.
VHS: S22162. $14.95.

The Man in the Santa Claus Suit

Fred Astaire is unforgettable as a guardian angel who helps three troubled men rediscover their own holiday spirit in this tender, live-action Christmas fantasy.
VHS: S10724. $19.95.
Corey Allen, USA, 1979, 96 mins.

Maps: Symbols and Terms

Reading maps requires simple skills that this video explains. With these skills youngsters will have the whole world at their fingertips. 13 mins.
VHS: S23725. $49.95.

Maps: Where Am I? (3rd Edition)

A helicopter ride gives children the opportunity to see a neighborhood as it might appear from a map. It's a process that helps them relate the world of solid objects to the abstract markings of two-dimensional maps. 11 mins.
VHS: S23727. $49.95.

Marc Brown's Play Rhymes

From the author and illustrator of *Arthur's Eyes,* this captivating program invites young viewers to explore language and rhymes.
VHS: S08397. $89.00.

The Marvelous Land of Oz

At the center of this cartoon is Tip, a young boy who escapes to Oz in order to evade his evil guardian, the witch Mombi. There Tip encounters all the familiar characters, the Scarecrow, Glinda and Dorothy, as well as other new friends. A plot threatens the Emerald City but a forgotten heir to the throne of this fabled land may just save the day. 90 mins.
VHS: S24229. $19.98.

The Mask of the Dancing Princess

In an imaginary kingdom of the 17th century, 10-year-old Princess Rosamond demands a birthday present she should not have: a child identical to herself. In this tale of mistaken identity, she is carried away by a group of gypsy actors and begins a hard new life in a strange land before she develops into a gracious and worthy ruler.
VHS: S16349. $44.95.

Master of the World

An animated adventure of a mad scientist and his attempt to rule the civilized world from the deck of his deadly flying machine, the Albatross. Robur the Conqueror is the brainchild of Jules Verne, and is part of the Classics for Kids Collection. 1976, approx. 50 mins.
VHS: S03633. $19.95.
Laser: Widescreen. LD74980. $39.99.

Mathnet: The Case of The Unnatural

In the *Mathnet* series by Children's Television Workshop, a young detective team investigates answers while learning concepts related to math. Lefty Cobbs is a washed up pitcher, but something strange is happening to him. Suddenly he is hitting one-handed homers, pitching faster than anyone in history and sending crazy code messages to his pal Babs. This is a case for Mathnet. Ages 8-12.
VHS: S24550. $9.95.

The Maurice Sendak Library

Three great stories by Maurice Sendak. First, four little poems set to music from Sendak's *The Nutshell Library: Alligators All Around, Pierre, One Was Johnny* and *Chicken Soup with Rice.* Then, *Where the Wild Things Are,* one of Sendak's classics. Finally, *In the Night Kitchen,* a little boy dreams of a special time in the kitchen where bakers bake cake, dough airplanes fly, and everyone dances to the deliciously syncopated music. Includes *Getting to Know Maurice Sendak,* a personal talk with the author/illustrator. 35 mins.
VHS: S11229. $14.95.

Max's Chocolate Chicken

This collection of popular children's stories makes a wonderful animated video. *Max's Chocolate Chicken* by Rosemary Wells, is joined by Janet and Allan Ahlberg's *Each Peach Pear Plum,* Emily Arnolds McCully's *Picnic,* and Maud and Miska Petersham's *The Circus Baby.* 36 mins.
VHS: S22163. $14.95.

Meet Your Animal Friends

Lynn Redgrave hosts this visit with baby animals, to the delight of infants and toddlers, who giggle with glee at the funny antics of sheep, deer, horses, dogs and other species. 60 minutes, ages 1-6.
VHS: S17013. $12.95.

Mega Man: 20,000 Leaks Under the Sea

In the first episode on this video, Mega Man and his sidekick Roll and Rush, the robo dog, find themselves lured into an underwater trap. The adventure continues in *The Strange Island of Dr. Wily.* This time, Dr. Wily has a plan involving a remote island that spells disaster for Mega Man. Suitable for ages 8 and up. 45 mins.
VHS: S27557. $9.99.

Mega Man: Robosaur Park

Mega Man and his sidekick Roll and Rush, the robo dog, blast into action in this fully animated series. In the title episode, Mega Man leads the Robo Commandos into action against robotic dinosaurs which have been programmed to attack. In *The Ice Age,* the second episode included on this tape, Ice Man and Dr. Wily hope to start a new ice age. Mega Man is set to foil their evil plan. Great for kids ages 8 and up. 45 mins.
VHS: S27556. $9.99.

Mega Man: The Beginning

Mega Man and his robo dog, Roll and Rush, confront the good-bots pressed into service by the diabolical Dr. Wily. This opening episode of the action-packed children's series could be both the beginning and the end if Mega Man fails. Next, in *Electric Nightmares,* Dr. Wily devises an intriguing plot to turn ordinary appliances against his nemesis, Mega Man. For ages 8 and up. 45 mins.
VHS: S27555. $9.99.

Merlin and the Dragons

Old Merlin the Magician tells young Arthur stories that inspire him to become the magnificent King Arthur. Narrated by Kevin Kline. Children's Video Report Top 15 Kidvids. 27 minutes, ages 5-12.
Home Video.
VHS: S17007. $12.98.
Public Performance Rights.
VHS: S17144. $50.00.

Merry Christmas Space Case

The Goober twins swagger toward Buddy McGee in their red sweat shirts with the big G's on the front. Are they from outer visiting Buddy for Christmas? James Marshall has once again created hilarious characters that will have children roaring with laughter.
VHS: S16354. $44.95.

The Mighty River

This animated film recreates the grace, beauty and tragedy of nature, presenting a passionate lesson about human impact on our fragile natural resources. Academy Award nominee. Ages 11 to adult. 24 mins.
VHS: S23361. $89.00.

Mike Mulligan and His Steam Shovel

Three treasured children's books are adapted into three animated video pieces in which a whale rescues Burt Dow, the Moon Man visits Earth and the collection's title duo are helped by a little boy. 30 mins.
VHS: S00854. $14.95.
Morton Schindel, USA, 1986, 30 mins.

Milk Cow. Eat Cheese.

A multicultural group of kids learns the relationship between cows and dairy products in this video. Kids will love seeing how everyday things are made. There's even a visit to an ice cream factory. Ages 3-10.
VHS: S26094. $14.95.
Bonnie Scott, USA, 1995, 30 mins.

Mine and Yours

Live-action and animated stories and songs in this colorful, well-produced video which carries a message about sharing and cooperation. Katie wants to keep Renee's birthday present. Ages 3-6. 25 minutes.
VHS: S24554. $9.95.

Mister Magoo's Christmas Carol

Animated favorite Mister Magoo doesn't have a ghost of a chance as Scrooge when he learns the true meaning of Christmas in this fun musical version of Charles Dickens' holiday classic. 1962, 52 mins.
VHS: S13042. $12.95.

Mister Rogers' Neighborhood: Circus Fun

Joining the circus with the acclaimed PBS children's show virtually guarantees that children will be entranced by this episode. The emphasis is on fun.
VHS: S23024. $9.98.

Mister Rogers' Neighborhood: Going to School

This PBS television series won countless awards for excellence and was popular with an entire generation of kids. In this episode the issue of going to school is calmly dealt with in a way that will reassure nervous youngsters. USA, 28 mins.
VHS: S27155. $9.98.

Mister Rogers' Neighborhood: Kindness

Tommy Tune joins Mr. Rogers in this episode from the long running PBS children's show. This series has been a staple of pre-schooler television viewing for a generation. Parents have long relied on the simple charms and humor of the acclaimed show.
VHS: S23023. $9.98.

Mister Rogers' Neighborhood: Learning Is Everywhere!

Mr. Rogers shows children how they can turn any experience into a learning experience. It's perfect for children who might think that learning can't be fun. USA, 28 mins.
VHS: S27156. $9.98.

Mister Rogers' Neighborhood: Love

Who could explain the complexities of this central emotion better than Mr. Rogers on his long-running PBS children's show? Of course, he gets some help from his teddy bear.
VHS: S23026. $9.98.

Mister Rogers' Neighborhood: Making Music

From the long-running PBS children's show comes this episode, enlivened by a visit from the acclaimed cellist Yo-Yo Ma. Kids will love this easy-going introduction to the world of classical music.
VHS: S23025. $9.98.

Mister Rogers' Neighborhood: Our Earth: Clean and Green

Important lessons about the relationship between humans and the environment are at the center of this episode from the classic PBS series. USA, 28 mins.
VHS: S27157. $9.98.

Mister Rogers' Neighborhood: The Doctor, Your Friend

Visiting a physician, while important, can be a frightening experience for children. In this video, Mister Rogers explains why doctors are to be trusted. After all, they really are trying to help. USA, 28 mins.
VHS: S27158. $9.98.

Mister Rogers: Dinosaurs & Monsters

Mister Rogers helps young people understand what scary monsters are and are not about. Mister Rogers visits a museum to show dinosaurs, and with the help of Lady Aberlin and Handyman Negri, he clears up confusion about what is real and what is fantasy. USA, 1986, 64 mins.
VHS: S00893. $19.98.

Mister Rogers: Music and Feelings

Mister Rogers, aided by Ella Jenkins, explores the many moods of music along with cellist Yo-Yo Ma and the entire gang from the Neighborhood of Make-Believe. 65 mins.
VHS: S05012. $19.98.

Mister Rogers: Musical Stories

Mister Rogers invites children into a land of musical make-believe with two musical stories for children: *Potato Bugs and Cows* and *A Granddad for Daniel.* 59 mins.
VHS: S05897. $19.98.

Mister Rogers: What About Love

A trolley will take you to the enchanting Neighborhood of Make Believe in this reassuring program about the value of love and the confusing feelings that can come along with it. 51 mins.
VHS: S05011. $19.98.

Mister Rogers: When Parents Are Away

Mister Rogers advises parents and their children on how to handle the times of separation. It covers babysitters and day-care and contains songs, outings and a special visit to the "neighborhood of make believe" with King Friday and Queen Sara Saturday. Can you say, "We'll be back soon?" USA, 1987, 66 mins.
VHS: S04380. $19.98.

Moira's Birthday (plus Blackberry Subway Jam)

Moira's birthday is coming and she wants a big party! The video also includes *Blackberry Subway Jam,* about a subway that pulls into Jonathan's house, where all the passengers pile out. Animated stories by Robert Munsch. Ages 2-6. 25 minutes.
VHS: S24996. $12.95.

Mole's Christmas

On Christmas Eve, Mole and his friend, the Rat, find themselves stranded in the snow. Soon they are thinking of home and in a flash they are there, warming themselves against a fire. The joy of this scene is completed when a group of carolling mice happen by. With the voices of Richard Briers, Peter Davison and Imelda Staunton. From *The Wind in the Willows* Collection.
VHS: S26673. $12.98.
Martin Gates, Great Britain, 1995, 28 mins.

Mommy's Office

Watercolor illustrations make this story of a little girl visiting mom at work especially charming. She realizes that mommy's office work is similar to her own school day activities. Just the right message for working mothers to impart to their own children through this read-along children's video. 6:19 mins.
VHS: S22348. $39.95.

Monster in My Pocket with The Schnozzes

This video joins two delightful animated adventures. *Monster in My Pocket* is the story of a whole cast of good and bad monsters struggling against each other after they have been rendered tiny in an escape attempt. *The Schnozzes* are animals with big noses who try to make the most of their prominent schnozzes. Great for kids. 30 mins.
VHS: S26097. $12.99.

Monsters of the Greek Myths

Based on the Wonder-Book and Tanglewood Tales of Nathaniel Hawthorne, these ancient stories tell of the confrontations of great heroes with the horrific monsters that populated the mythical Greek landscape. Includes *The Chimaera, The Gorgon's Head, The Minotaur* and *The Dragon's Teeth.* For Grades 4-9.
VHS: S14203. $159.95.

Mop Top

Based on the story by Don Freeman. Moppy finally sees himself as others do. (His head is literally mistaken for a mop.) He begins to appreciate a neat-looking appearance. Ages 4-8. 10 minutes.
VHS: S24555. $37.95.

More Stories for the Very Young

The Little Red Hen, Petunia, Not So Fast Songololo, The Napping House and *Max's Christmas* are cartoons small children will enjoy. 38 mins.
VHS: S22686. $14.95.

Morris the Moose

Two stories from Bernard Wiseman's beginning reading books are realized through stop motion animation in this video. *Morris the Moose Goes to School* introduces Morris to the alphabet and numbers. Then in *Morris Has a Cold,* Boris the Bear tries to nurse his friend back to health. 28 mins.
VHS: S23875. $12.95.

The Mouse and the Motorcycle

On vacation, a lonely boy meets a talkative little mouse named Ralph. When the boy shares his fancy toy motorcycle with Ralph, our very tiny hero embarks on a very big adventure. Based on the book by Beverly Cleary. 41 mins.
VHS: S16579. $9.98.

Mouse on the Mayflower
From the creators of *Here Comes Peter Cottontail*, this enchanting children's tale illustrates the country's formation and social emergence. With the voices of Tennessee Ernie Ford, Eddie Albert, June Foray and Paul Frees. 48 mins.
VHS: S18863. $12.98.

Mouse Soup
John Matthews' stop animation is used to tell the story of a mouse who manages to save himself from becoming dinner. The weasel who captures him is so taken by the mouse's stories that he forgets his hunger pangs. Buddy Hackett provides the mouse's voice.
VHS: S21260. $12.98.

Move Like the Animals
This exercise-movement tape helps children develop balance, coordination and motor sequencing skills while moving to original songs and music. Moshe Feldenkrais' movement awareness lessons are captured in this lively musical exercise video for children. As kids learn to walk like a bear, roll like a cat and crawl like an alligator they will develop coordination and motor sequencing skills. Ages 3-8, 24 mins.
VHS: S24551. $19.95.

A Movie Star's Daughter
A young adult drama about fitting in and following your heart. Dena is the new kid in school but it helps that her dad is a Hollywood heartthrob. Still, she wonders how much of the attention is due to her dad and who her real friends will turn out to be. With Frank Converse as the famous father. 1979, 46 mins.
VHS: S10984. $14.95.

Moving Machines
In this tape children experience the excitement of big machines. A bulldozer, a cement truck, a crane and many others are included. Children play with toy machines that will help other kids to identify with the use of these powerful machines. Fun percussion musical accompaniment. 25 mins.
VHS: S22380. $19.95.

Mowgli's Brothers
"…Haunting, sensitive and beautiful" raved *Variety* magazine about this animated version of Rudyard Kipling's *The Jungle Book*, which introduced Mowgli, a human child raised by a wolf and befriended by Baloo the bear. Lessons about love, justice and loyalty will captivate children in this Chuck Jones film narrated by Roddy McDowall. 30 mins.
VHS: S03015. $14.95.

Mr. Bubble Gum
Having a little brother can be a big pain! Eli's older brother calls him Mr. Bubble Gum, because he sticks to him like gum. Follow along as he and his brother pal Roberta invent a new soft drink, go trick-or-treating, and find out that having a little brother may not be so bad after all. From the *Bank Street Read-Along Story Video* series. The story is told twice—once to familiarize children with the characters and story; the second time with words printed onscreen so children can easily follow along. For ages 3-8. 30 mins.
VHS: S13527. $14.99.

Mr. Magoo Show
Five Mr. Magoo cartoons per volume.
Volume 1. Color, 1960, 25 mins.
VHS: S13412. $9.95.
Volume 2. Color, 1960, 25 mins.
VHS: S13413. $9.95.
Volume 3. Color, 1960, 25 mins.
VHS: S13414. $9.95.
Volume 4. Color, 1960, 25 mins.
VHS: S13415. $9.95.

A Mr. Magoo Special: Uncle Sam Magoo
Color, 1970, 53 mins.
VHS: S13419. $12.95.

Mr. Magoo's Literary Classics
Our near-sighted hero stumbles through some of the greatest stories ever told.
Cyrano de Bergerac/A Midsummer Night's Dream. Color, 1964, 50 mins.
VHS: S13424. $12.95.
Don Quixote De La Mancha. Color, 1964, 50 mins.
VHS: S13422. $12.95.
King Arthur/The Count of Monte Cristo. Color, 1964, 50 mins.
VHS: S13423. $12.95.
Man of Mystery. An animated quartet of the most suspenseful stories of all time. Magoo plays Sherlock's assistant Dr. Watson, the mad scientist Dr. Frankenstein, the Count of Monte Cristo and famous detective Dick Tracy. Color, 1964, 50 mins.
VHS: S13425. $12.95.
The Three Musketeers. Color, 1964, 50 mins.
VHS: S13421. $12.95.

Mr. Monster
Five-year-old Eli's monster collection is taking over the whole bedroom! Everybody thinks Eli's monster phase is cute—everybody but his big brother, that is. Find out what happens when Eli's brother and his friend Roberta hatch a plot to get rid of the monsters forever. From the *Bank Street Read-Along Story Video* series. The story is told twice—once to familiarize children with the characters and story; the second time with words printed onscreen so children can easily follow along. For ages 3-8. 30 mins.
VHS: S13530. $14.99.

Mr. Popper's Penguins
The fun begins when mild-mannered Mr. Popper unexpectedly receives an Antarctic penguin and decides to keep it as a pet. Jim Backus narrates this adaptation of Richard and Florence Atwater's classic story. 42 mins.
VHS: S10050. $119.00.

Mrs. Frisby and the Rats of Nimh
Mrs. Frisby, a widow-mouse, needs to find a new home before her family is uprooted by the gift of a farmer's plow. She receives unexpected help from a secret society of super-intelligent rats. An award-winning adaptation of Robert O'Brien's Newbery Award-winning book. 82 mins.
VHS: S08165. $119.00.

Mrs. Piggle-Wiggle
Shelley Duvall presents this new series for kids of all ages. Jean Stapleton stars as the lovable lady with a knack for helping kids—and their parents—out of the stickiest situations. From the top of her piled-up red hair to the tips of her funky platform shoes, she's a genius when it comes to finding uncommon solutions to common, everyday challenges.
Mrs. Piggle-Wiggle: The Answer-Backer Cure and The Chores Cure.
VHS: S22874. $12.98.
Mrs. Piggle-Wiggle: The Not-Truthful Cure and The Radish Cure.
VHS: S22872. $12.98.
Mrs. Piggle-Wiggle: The Pet Forgetters Cure and The Never-Want-To-Go-To-Bedders Cure.
VHS: S22873. $12.98.

Muppet Treasure Island Sing-Alongs
Kermit the Frog and his Muppet buccaneers storm the high seas with comic fervor and pirate songs in this charming video. Sing-alongs with new characters, including Pirate Girl and her pirate friends, Monty, Polly and Clueless, make this great entertainment for kids and parents alike. Featuring two songs from the Muppet feature film *Muppet Treasure Island.*
VHS: S27434. $12.99.
Brian Henson, USA, 1996, 30 mins.

Muppets on Wheels
Kermit hosts this show featuring a new Muppet character called Lindy. She is precocious, and together with Kermit she indulges a passion for cars, trains and trucks. Soon they happen upon a group of kids and other Muppets who share their fascination. Perfect for preschoolers. 30 mins.
VHS: S25914. $12.99.

Muppets Take Manhattan
The Big Apple will never be the same as the Muppets head for the Great White Way, and Miss Piggy and Kermit finally head for the altar. 94 mins.
VHS: S08256. $14.98.

The Murky Water Caper
Follow the adventures of Billie Beaver, Molly Duck, Devin the Dolphin, Toots the Trout and a host of other characters as they seek the help of Detective Trout to discover who's been polluting the local stream. Written by children's playwright Deborah Rodney Pex. Ages 6-10. 30 mins.
VHS: S23360. $59.95.

Murmel, Murmel, Murmel (plus The Boy in the Drawer)
The story of a little girl who discovers a real, live baby in her sandbox. The tape includes the story *The Boy in The Drawer*, about a boy the size of a sock who lives in Shelly's dresser drawer. Animated stories by Robert Munsch. Ages 2-6. 30 minutes.
VHS: S24986. $12.95.

Mushfest: Nickelodeon
A collection of Nickelodeon's most inspired romantic moments are preserved in hilarious vignettes from *Rugrats, Hey Dude* and *Doug.*
VHS: S20288. $14.98.

Music and Magic
"Positive Music Videos for Today's Kids." These MTV-style videos promote positive values. Ages 5-11.
VHS: S24714. $9.98.

Music Box
Winner of the Cine Golden Eagle; a parable about a dreary man whose life is suddenly changed by the gift of a magical music box from a group of gospel-singing angels. 28 mins.
VHS: S09797. $14.98.

Musical Tales
Introduce children to the beauty and enchantment of the classics with these beautifully animated puppet films of fairy stories set to the music of Tchaikovsky, Stravinsky and Delibes.
Volume 1: *The Nutcracker* and *Petrushka.* 35 mins.
VHS: S16147. $12.98.
Volume 2: *Coppelia* and *The Sleeping Beauty.* 32 mins.
VHS: S16148. $12.98.

Mutzmag
A live action adaptation of the Appalachian folktale, set around 1920, about a young woman named Mutzmag, and her adventures with her half-sisters, gullible young women Mutzmag saves from two backwoods ogres. The tale unfolds in the vernacular and idiom of the Appalachians.
VHS: S17413. $59.00.
Tom Davenport, USA, 1993, 53 mins.

My Body Me
Professor Iris will make kids laugh even as they learn about their bodies and themselves. 40 mins.
VHS: S26059. $12.95.

My Brother Sam Is Dead
Winner of the Newbery Honor Book, James Lincoln Collier and Christopher Collier's historical story focuses on the Meekers, a nonpartisan family which is affected by the Revolutionary War. 26 mins.
VHS: S08166. $119.00.

My Family and Other Animals
A charming program about one boy's experience on a strange and beautiful island where he encounters many bugs and other small animals. 23 mins.
VHS: S13207. $14.98.

My Principal Lives Next Door
Ben Johnson thought life was a breeze until Mrs. Strictly, the school's principal, moved in next door, setting off a panic. After experiencing trouble with his math papers, he discovers that the principal is a nice person to turn to. Written and illustrated by third-grade students of Sanibel, Florida Elementary School. 8 mins.
VHS: S19599. $39.00.

My Sesame Street Home Video
Featuring the Jim Henson cast of *Sesame Street Muppets* and the *Sesame Street Live* cast. Ages 2-6.
A New Baby in My House. Mrs. Snuffleupagus helps older brother Snuffy understand his feelings about his new baby sister. Snuffy's little sister makes him upset when she breaks his toy. Mrs. Snuffleupagus then tells her two children a story about a prince who feels neglected because of his new baby sister. With a story-within-a-story and six little musical numbers. From the acclaimed Children's Television Workshop. Ages 2-6.
VHS: S24557. $9.98.
Bedtime Stories & Songs. Big Bird, Kermit the Frog and the Cookie Monster tell stories and sing lullabies that children will ask for night after night.
VHS: S02836. $9.98.
Big Bird's Favorite Party Games. Big Bird's having a party and everyone's invited. There's music, participation games, and even a game of "Oscar says."
VHS: S07710. $9.98.
Big Bird's Story Time.
VHS: S24630. $9.98.
Count It Higher: Great Music Videos from Sesame Street. A collection of Sesame Street music videos. Enjoy the Doo Wop Hop and others!
VHS: S07712. $9.98.
Getting Ready to Read. Big Bird and Bert and Ernie present songs, stories and rhymes designed to show children how some words look and sound, and how letters can be blended to become words.
VHS: S02830. $9.98.
Getting Ready for School. The crowd shares basic skills for getting along in school.
VHS: S24631. $9.98.
I'm Glad I'm Me. Bert and Ernie encourage children to identify parts of their own bodies and to develop a sense of pride and self-esteem.
VHS: S02835. $9.98.
Learning About Letters. Big Bird and his friend Alphabet Day introduce the entire alphabet, with help from the rest of the Muppets. Cookie Monster's favorite letter is "C", of course, because it stands for "cookie."
VHS: S02833. $9.98.
Learning About Numbers. Children will learn to count from 1 to 20 with the help of the Count and Big Bird.
VHS: S02834. $9.98.
Learning to Add and Subtract.
VHS: S24632. $9.98.
Play Along Games & Songs. Big Bird and his friends present some of the most popular games from the television show, games that will familiarize children with counting, reading and reasoning skills.
VHS: S02837. $9.98.
The Alphabet Game. Sunny Friendly is the host of a new game show, Alphabet Treasure Hunt. There are prizes and surprises, and children can play along.
VHS: S08172. $9.98.
The Best of Ernie and Bert. When Sesame's Big Bird turns the pages of Ernie's scrapbook, each picture comes to life and everyone relives the adventures of Bert and Ernie.
VHS: S07711. $9.98.
The Best of Elmo. From the acclaimed Children's Television Workshop comes the furry Elmo and some charming songs for preschoolers.
VHS: S24511. $9.98.

My Side of the Mountain
Ted Eccles and Theodore Bikel star in this adaptation of Jean Craighead George's novel. It features a 13-year-old who sets out on an adventure in the wilderness. 38 mins.
VHS: S23457. $49.95.

The Mysterious Island
Jules Verne's science fiction masterpiece is told in this Classics for Kids series as a young boy and his friends face amazing perils when they are shipwrecked on a strange, exotic island.
VHS: S03018. $16.95.
Laser: Includes interview with Ray Harryhausen. LD75044. $34.95.
Leif Gram, USA, 1987, 49 mins.

The Mysterious Tadpole and Other Stories
Based on a story by Steven Kellogg, *The Mysterious Tadpole* concerns a birthday gift from Uncle McAllister that appears to be a tadpole—but turns out to be much more! Louis' affection for his pet, and his determination to keep it, make this story heartwarming and lots of fun. Other stories included are: *The Five Chinese Brothers*, by Claire Bishop; *Jonah and the Great Fish*, retold and illustrated by Warwick Hutton; and *The Wizard*, by Jack Kent. Animation. 30 mins.
VHS: S11225. $19.95.

Mystery of Harris Burdick
In the introduction, Chris Van Allsburg relates how a man named Harris Burdick illustrated and wrote 14 stories. Now, years later, all that remain are the illustrations with their titles and brief captions. A wonderful creative experience for children.
VHS: S14190. $44.95.

National Geographic Geo Kids: Bear Cubs, Baby Ducks, and Kooky Kookaburras
Sunny Honeypossum, Bobby Bushbaby and Balzac de Chameleon tell how different wild animals grow from infancy to young adulthood. The footage of a mother monkey caring for her baby is unforgettable.
VHS: S21961. $12.95.

National Geographic Geo Kids: Camouflage, Cuttlefish, and Chameleons Changing Color
Once again the animated characters Bobby Bushbaby, Uncle Balzac and Honeypossum introduce animal wonders to children five and under. The camouflage of these various creatures will fascinate viewers. 35 mins.
VHS: S23947. $12.95.

National Geographic Geo Kids: Chomping on Bugs, Swimming Sea Slugs, and Stuff that Makes Animals Special
In this combination of animation and live footage children will be introduced to the wonders of nature through Bobby Bushbaby and Honeypossum. The sticky tongue chameleon is sure to be a hit, especially with children five and under. 35 mins.
VHS: S23948. $12.95.

National Geographic Geo Kids: Cool Cats, Raindrops, and Things That Live in Holes
While playing hide-and-seek, Sunny Honeypossum and Bobby Bushbaby discover a tree hole. Balzac de Chameleon then explains to them the variety of animals that make their home in these natural crevices.
VHS: S21962. $12.95.

National Geographic Geo Kids: Flying Trying and Honking Around
The delightful characters Sunny Honeypossum, Bobby Bushbaby and Balzac de Chameleon host this fascinating look at birds. These characters are all created by the maker of the Muppet Babies. Together they help kids explore the world of flight.
VHS: S21960. $12.95.

National Geographic Geo Kids: Tadpoles, Dragonflies and the Caterpillar's Big Change
Animated characters Bobby Bushbaby, Uncle Balzac and Honeypossum explore live action footage of amazing wildlife for children five and under. These characters experiment with transformations, but their fooling around cannot compete with the butterfly that emerges from a cocoon. 35 mins.
VHS: S23946. $12.95.

National Geographic Really Wild Animals
This series of documentaries will take kids to exotic locations to see how the animals they love really live. An animated globe called Spin narrates, with the voice by Dudley Moore.
Swinging Safari. This safari through the Serengeti Plain and on to the Kalahari Desert will reveal the wild life of Africa. Cheetahs, crocodiles, rhinos, lions, and chimpanzees are all seen in their actual environments. 44 mins.
VHS: S20611. $14.95.
Wonders Down Under. Weird creatures from the unique eco-systems down under star, including kangaroos, platypuses, and koala bears. Australia's unusual animals arise from this continent's comparative isolation from the rest of the world. This video will change all that for your family. 45 mins.
VHS: S20612. $14.95.
Deep Sea Dive. The earth's last great frontier is also home to some of the world's most fascinating creatures. Whales, dolphins and sharks share this wild life refuge. Underwater photography lets you see these animals in action.
VHS: S20613. $14.95.
Adventures in Asia. Spin leads children on a whirlwind tour of the largest continent. There are huge manta rays in the Red Sea, rare panda bears in China, reclusive orangutans in the swamps of Borneo and even elephants on the Indian subcontinent. 40 mins.
VHS: S21212. $14.95.
Totally Tropical Rainforest. The rainforest is home to a greater variety of living things than any other eco-system on earth. From this abundance a variety of curious creatures stand out. Spin reveals tarantulas, aggressive piranha fish and the strange, slow-moving sloths that are just some of the animals unique to these forests.
VHS: S21213. $14.95.
Amazing North America. In the frozen north there are white wolves and polar bears, but in the swamps near the Gulf of Mexico alligators lie in wait submerged beneath murky, warm waters. This great diversity includes some of the most commonplace of animals, like the ground squirrel. Spin shows how each one fits into his own ecological niche.
VHS: S21214. $14.95.

Native Indian Folklore
Five stories from the National Film Board of Canada. *Christmas at Moose Factory* shows Christmas in the Native American Cree settlement presented through children's drawings; *Salmon People* is a West Coast Legend of the Salmon Princess, contrasted with today's native-owned fishing boats and canneries (25 mins.); *The Man, the Snake and the Fox* presents a puppet enactment of an Ojibwa tale; *Medoonak the Stormmaker* presents an exciting stage performance of an ancient Micmac legend about taming the weather; and *Summer Legends* an animated version of the Micmac legend that explains the cycle of the seasons. Ages 6-12. 71 minutes.
VHS: S24775. $99.00.

Nature Stories
Four stories deal with various subjects, including eggs, mammals, flowers and plants. Designed for children in grades 1-4. 75 mins.
VHS: S20026. $159.95.

Nestor the Long-Eared Christmas Donkey
A kind-hearted burro, mocked for his ears, takes a special journey to Bethlehem. With the voices of Roger Miller, Brenda Vaccaro and Paul Frees. 23 mins.
VHS: S13034. $12.95.

The New Adventures of Peter Rabbit
An all new version of Beatrix Potter's delightful character is featured in this animated video. Peter and his friends journey through the countryside and discover new adventures and thrills. Along the way they sing memorable songs and generate big laughs. 48 mins.
VHS: S23932. $14.98.

New Coat for Anna
Anita Lobel's illustrations bring to life Harriet Ziefert's book, set in post-World War II, as Anna and her mother decide to use their most cherished possessions in order to get the coat Anna has dreamed about.
VHS: S08398. $59.00.

Nick Jr.: Allegra's Window: Storytime Sing-Along
Allegra and her friends introduce kids to ten irresistible songs. The result is a popular sing-along video that kids will be able to watch and participate with. USA, 1995, 35 mins.
VHS: S27311. $12.95.

Nick Jr.: Eureeka's Castle: Wide Awake at Eureeka's Castle
Eureeka is a wizard in the making. In this video she and her entire castle full of friends take kids on a special tour of all their favorite sleepless nights. USA, 1995, 35 mins.
VHS: S27312. $12.95.

Nick Jr.: Gullah Gullah Island: Play Along with Binyah and Friends
Kids will enjoy this video that encourages them to play along with their Gullah Gullah Island friends. They will dance and clap as they learn one game after another. This video offers a unique opportunity to experience one of the oldest African-American traditions surviving in the United States. USA, 1995, 30 mins.
VHS: S27310. $12.95.

The Night Before Christmas
Jerry Styner provides the narration and original music for this adaptation of the holiday classic. Children will love this version of Clement C. Moore's enduring poem. 10 mins.
VHS: S23474. $49.95.

Nina's Strange Adventure
A young river otter uses special magic to travel to the land of her dreams. 14 mins.
VHS: S23460. $49.95.

No Greater Gift
Based on a real-life account, the poignant drama of Nick Santana and Keith Williams, two 12-year olds from different backgrounds who are drawn together by their illnesses, but torn by the realization that they will soon be separated. When Nick accepts the fact that his disease is fatal, he must make a decision that could save his new friend's life. USA, 1986, 45 mins.
VHS: S04764. $19.95.

Noah's Ark
Embark on one of the greatest adventures of all time as Academy Award-nominee James Earl Jones narrates this beautifully animated adaptation of Peter Spiers' acclaimed children's book, complemented by a dynamic, evocative score from Grammy-winner Stewart Copeland. Winner of the Action for Children's Television Award and CINE Golden Eagle. Recommended by American Library Association and Video Librarian. Ages 5-12. 27 minutes.
VHS: S11415. $12.98.

Noel
The story of a magical Christmas tree ornament that comes to life as it is passed down from one generation to the next. Ages 4+.
VHS: S24612. $12.95.

A Norman Rockwell Christmas
Eddie Albert hosts this nostalgic, heartwarming look at Christmas scenes based on the illustrious world created by Norman Rockwell. Music accompaniment by the world famous Pacific Chorale augments the perfect works created by this famous American painter and illustrator. 50 minutes.
VHS: S21810. $19.98.

Norman the Doorman and Other Stories
Although Norman's job is to stand guard at the mouse entrance to the Museum of Art, his ambition is to become an artist, in the adaptation of the story by Don Freeman. Other stories include Brave Irene, by William Steig, and Lentil, by Robert McCloskey. Animated. 30 mins.
VHS: S11228. $14.95.

"Not Now!" Said the Cow
Crow asks for help planting corn. "Not Now!" answers Cow. "I'm asleep," baas Sheep. "Nix, Nix!" peep the Chicks. Find out what Crow really wants—and what he does when turned down by all the other animals. From the Bank Street Read-Along Story Video series. The story is told twice—once to familiarize children with the characters and story; the second time with words printed onscreen so children can easily follow along. For ages 3-8. 30 mins.
VHS: S13531. $14.99.

Not Now, Bernard
Five charming Anytime Tales stories by David McKee which are inventive tales about personal self-expression. 35 mins.
VHS: S19431. $14.99.

The Nutcracker
Dudley Moore narrates and the Moscow State Orchestra performs music by Tchaikovsky in this delightful animated version of the classic childhood romance. A host of lovable characters, including a charming prince, a plum fairy and a young girl, Marie, will delight all kinds of audiences. It is especially useful for introducing youngsters to classical music. From the Storyteller's Classics series, animated. 27 mins.
VHS: S26342. $9.98.

Nuzzling with Nozzles: A Magical Adventure
Starring in their first animated feature, Blinky, Pinky and Sandy go from one delightful adventure to another in a splendid mix of reality and fantasy. 110 mins.
VHS: S10333. $39.95.

Off on a Comet
Jules Verne's story of Captain Sevadec, who finds that he has been swept off the earth with a small group of others and is hurtling out into space. An animated classic.
VHS: S04425. $19.95.
R. Slapczynski, USA, 1979, 52 mins.

The Old Curiosity Shop
An animated version of the Charles Dickens story about Little Nell and her grandfather and their many adventures in 18th century England. When they are evicted from the Old Curiosity Shop these two brave and optimistic souls must fend for themselves. 1984, 72 mins.
VHS: S06161. $59.98.

Old Man of Lochnagar
From the BBC, a children's story written and narrated by the Prince of Wales. It's about ticklish eagles, tame grouse, sea haggis and the Gorms—tiny people who live in the Scottish hillsides. 20 mins.
VHS: S12640. $19.95.

On Christmas Eve
Peter Collington's award-winning tale is an imaginative rumination on the mysteries of Christmas, as a young girl becomes concerned about the physical obstacles which surround Father Christmas on his hazardous journey. 25 mins.
VHS: S19434. $14.99.

On Our Way to School
Shari Lewis, Lamb Chop and friends lead kids in a romp through activities which help prepare pre-schoolers. Ages 2-6.
VHS: S24613. $9.95.

Once Upon a Forest
A chemical spill forces the young "furlings" to leave their forest home in order to help one of their friends, who inhaled the toxic fumes. This charming, animated feature raises key environmental issues in a way that will involve young viewers without scaring them. Features the voice of Ben Vereen.
VHS: S19346. $24.98.

Once When I Was Scared
The drama and power of Ted Rand's imaginative paintings bring to life Helena Clare Pittman's heartening story of the conquest of a young boy's fear of the cold, dark wood. 11 mins.
VHS: S12263. $57.00.

One Fish Two Fish Red Fish Blue Fish
Three classic Dr. Seuss stories—One Fish Two Fish Red Fish Blue Fish; Oh, The Thanks You Can Think and The Foot Book—are now animated shorts. Kids will enjoy the offbeat humor of these cartoons.
Spanish Narration.
VHS: S22017. $14.95.
English Narration.
VHS: S22018. $14.95.

One Terrific Thanksgiving
Irving Morris Bear asks his friends to hide his Thanksgiving food so he doesn't eat it before the feast. When he tries to locate it anyway, he learns that there's more to Thanksgiving than food. From the storybook by Marjorie Weinman Sharmat.
VHS: S16350. $44.95.

One, Two, Buckle My Shoe
A heartwarming and engaging collection of more than 35 traditional nursery rhymes. 35 mins.
VHS: S19432. $14.99.

One-Minute Bible Stories (New Testament)
Shari Lewis and Lamb Chop are joined by Florence Henderson to recreate these charming stories from the New Testament. 26 different tales are animated and narrated, bringing these enduring stories to young audiences. 30 mins.
VHS: S21380. $14.99.

One-Minute Bible Stories (Old Testament)
Five-time Emmy Award-winner Shari Lewis brings 26 stories from the Hebrew Bible to life with the help of her hand puppet, Lamb Chop. In under one minute's time, these two use their unique comic style and animation to tell these delightful tales in a new and refreshing way that preserves their essential values. 30 mins.
VHS: S21379. $14.99.

Orange Cheeks
A hilarious tape of a young boy's visit with his wise grandmother, from whom he learns about love, told by master storyteller Jay O'Calllahan. Complements Jay O'Calllahan: A Master Class in Storytelling. 8 mins. Public performance rights included.
VHS: S09266. $39.95.

Orca Whales and Mermaid Tales
Meet the huge Orca whales and the mysterious manatees, once thought to be mermaids! Watch a baby manatee and find out about the Orca's blowhole. Nature. Ages 4-12.
VHS: S24614. $14.95.

Original Tales and Tunes
Little K.J. is the guide for a song-filled journey combining live action and puppetry. Ages 2-8.
VHS: S24615. $14.95.

The Other Way to Listen
This second volume in the stories of American Indian culture explores the wonders of the natural world. Have you ever heard corn sing? Or heard what a rock has to say to a lizard? A wise old man takes a young boy on an informative hike through the desert to learn its secrets. Narrated by Will Rogers Jr. USA, 1990, 20 mins.
VHS: S13295. $14.99.

Owl Moon and Other Stories
Five short animated films based upon popular children's literature charmingly tell the stories of people and animals learning about themselves. The title piece shows a child who looks for the great Horned Owl with his father. 35 mins.
VHS: S13969. $14.95.

Ozma of Oz
Dorothy's return to Oz sets off a series of adventures as she tries to save the Royal Family of Ev. Her old friends the Tin man, the Lion and the Scarecrow brave harrowing travails with her, including the evil but magical Nome King. This joyful, animated film will delight children. 90 mins.
VHS: S24230. $19.98.

Paper Bag Princess
Hits the question of sex-role stereotyping head-on. After rescuing the prince from a dragon, when the prince is not only unappreciative but downright rude, the princess leaves him to fend for himself. Turns traditional princess stories, fairy tales and dragons on their heads. All ages. Animation/Fairy Tales. Canada, 1993. 25 minutes.
VHS: S24616. $12.95.

Paws, Claws, Feathers and Fins
Dogs, cats, gerbils, hamsters...even a pony! An award-winning video to help families consider the ups and down of taking a pet into their home. Ages 4-12. 30 minutes.
VHS: S24617. $14.95.

Peep and the Big Wide World
Three simple, amusing and fresh episodes on the adventures of Peep, a newly hatched chick. Chirp, an excitable robin, accompany Peep on her thrilling travels. Sure to enrich the imaginations of the very young. Smart animation, with the voice of Peter Ustinov. 30 mins.
VHS: S15790. $14.95.

Peeping Beauty by Mary Jane Auch
Poulette the Hen is starstruck and dreams of becoming a famous ballerina. A slick talent scout, a fox, offers her the lead in his production of "Peeping Beauty." Now she must stay on her toes to avoid debuting as dinner. 10 mins.
VHS: S24911. $37.95.

Pegasus
Mia Farrow tells the enchanting life of Pegasus, the winged horse in Greek myths that was transformed into a dazzling star constellation. Parents Magazine selected this animated adventure for its Best of the Year List, Parent's Choice Award. 25 mins.
Home Video.
VHS: S16162. $12.98.
Public Performance Rights.
VHS: S17145. $50.00.

People
Cara and her grandfather embark on an animated journey across a wide cultural array of peoples and traditions. Various styles of animation and 11 original songs make this video highly entertaining as well as educational. Music by Heavy D, Al Jarreau, Chaka Khan, Vanessa Williams and others is featured. 60 mins.
VHS: S26485. $12.95.

Pepito's Dream
An adaptation of the Pepito trilogy, three books by John and Margaret Travers-Moore, this heartwarming tale chronicles a young boy's determination to quell the violence and discord in his neighborhood, and his long-held dream to deliver a speech before the United Nations. 27 mins.
VHS: S17280. $14.95.

Peppe the Lamplighter
Turn-of-the-century New York is hard for an Italian immigrant. Peppe lights lamps, a job his father finds disappointing. But when Peppe's sister disappears, Peppe's job proves essential in finding her. This tale of pride is a beautifully illustrated read-along video.
VHS: S22346. $39.95.

Peppermint Rose
From the creators of Care Bears and Strawberry Shortcake comes a 12-year old girl transported into the fantasy world of the Land of Peppermint Rose, where she's sent to locate a stolen flower that's the source of the land's magic. 25 mins.
VHS: S18321. $14.95.

Pete Seeger's Family Concert
Join the live outdoor concert. A mix of folk songs, favorite kids songs and originals from the folk master. Ages 4-6. 45 minutes.
VHS: S24620. $14.95.

Peter and the Wolf (Animation)
Dudley Moore and the Moscow State Orchestra join forces to bring this classic fairy tale into a contemporary animated form. The woods are brimming with humorous characters that all fear the wolf. This cartoon has a surprise ending that emphasizes living together in harmony. It also makes a good introduction to the music of Sergei Prokofiev. From the Storyteller's Classics series, animated. 28 mins.
VHS: S26341. $9.98.

Peter and the Wolf (Live Action & Animation)
Chuck Jones provides the animation for this live-action/animated feature. It's inspired by Sergei Prokofiev's musical tale, which in turn drew on older Russian folktales. Kirstie Alley and Lloyd Bridges are among the cast featured in this beguiling family film. 60 mins.
VHS: S27527. $14.98.

Peter & the Wolf (Live Action & Puppetry)
Sting provides all the voices, live actors play Peter, the Grandfather and the Hunters wearing Marx Brothers masks, and puppets from the cutting-edge U.K. puppeteers Spitting Image are featured. This new production of Prokofiev's fantasy is accompanied by the Chamber Orchestra of Europe conducted by Claudio Abbado. 50 mins. Hi-Fi stereo.
VHS: S20556. $29.95.
Laser: LD72368. $29.95.

Peter and the Wolf (Puppetry)
People, animals and personified instruments accompany a full symphony orchestra to tell the favorite story of Sergei Prokofiev. Narrated by a Prokofiev puppet himself, Peter and the Wolf tells how a composer writes music using a special musical alphabet called notes. A perfect introduction to the sights and sounds of the orchestra, thanks to the magic of master puppeteer Jim Gamble. 30 mins.
VHS: S16753. $19.95.

Peter and the Wolf: Moscow Musical Theatre for Children
Natalia Sats, who collaborated with Sergei Prokofiev to create Peter and the Wolf, narrates this musical classic in English for the first time. This video is a souvenir of Sat's 50th anniversary performance with the Moscow Musical Theatre for Children. 1986, 58 mins.
VHS: S13893. $19.95.

Peter Cottontail
Join in the fun of this seasonable romp as Peter Cottontail, Jimmy Skunk, Buster Bear, Johnny Woodchuck and the rest of the gang hop, skip and jump through the enthralling Green Forest. Each change of season provides a new mystery and challenge. 50 mins. each.
Peter Cottontail: Autumn Fun.
VHS: S17918. $9.95.
Peter Cottontail: Spring Fun.
VHS: S17916. $9.95.
Peter Cottontail: Summer Fun.
VHS: S17917. $9.95.
Peter Cottontail: Winter Fun.
VHS: S17915. $9.95.

Peter Ustinov: The Orchestra
This award-winning program features 28 excerpts from the classical repertoire, all carefully selected to be appealing to the young listener. Each excerpt is used to illustrate musical concepts of the sound of a particular instrument.
VHS: S13409. $19.98.

Peter-No-Tail
Not to be confused with Peter Cottontail. This animated children's story concerns the adventures of a country kitten who travels to the big city. Such familiar voices as Ken Berry, Dom DeLuise, Larry Storch, June Lockhart and Tina Louise are to be heard in the tale of a cat who is missing an important appendage.
VHS: S06164. $59.95.
Stig Lasseby/Jan Gissberg, USA, 1983, 22 mins.

Philip Hall Likes Me, I Reckon
Ruby Dee narrates this adaptation of Bette Greene's Newbery Award-winning book about a bright, 11-year-old black girl who has a crush on the smartest boy in her class. 29 mins.
VHS: S08167. $119.00.

A Picture Book of Martin Luther King, Jr.
Based on the book by David A. Adler. A straightforward, fact-filled text joins with warm, realistic illustrations to capture the life and times of Dr. King, fostering an appreciation and understanding of his efforts to secure equal rights for all people. Deals with historical events in a positive manner. Ages 6-10. 9 minutes.
VHS: S24618. $37.95.

Picturebook Classics: Adam's Smile
Adam's grandmother says his smile could light the world. When he is taken to a dark, hidden world, Adam finds that only he can save the world from the creatures of darkness—through the power of his smile. For Grades 1-3.
VHS: S14192. $44.95.

Picturebook Classics: Five Secrets in a Box
Virginia, the younger daughter of Galileo, opens her father's gold box to find five objects that reveal the world to her—and us—in new and wonderful ways. For Grades 1-6.
VHS: S14195. $44.95.

Picturebook Classics: The Porcelain Cat
When the old sorcerer decides to turn a porcelain cat into a real one that will catch the rats that are gnawing on his books, he sends his apprentice, Nickon, on a quest to find the charm needed for the enchantment. For Grades 1-3.
VHS: S14193. $44.95.

Picturebook Classics: Complete Set
Includes Adam's Smile, The Porcelain Cat, The Beast in the Bathtub and Five Secrets in a Box. Four video cassettes.
VHS: S14196. $139.95.

Piggy Banks to Money Markets
A group of kids share the facts about money: saving, investing, spending, earning...in an exciting manner. Produced with consultation from the American Banking Association, National Council on Economic Education and Inc. Magazine. Includes original songs, computer graphics and a fun group of kids. Ages 5-12. 30 minutes.
VHS: S24619. $14.95.

Pigs and David's Father
Join the chase when Megan lets the pigs out. Then join Julie when she meets her neighbor's unusual dad. Ages 3-12.
VHS: S24766. $12.95.

The Pigs' Wedding and Other Stories
Porker and Curlytail are two pigs in love. When they invite all of their favorite friends to their wedding, everyone comes—including the rain. The lovely music and animation will capture your heart. Also includes The Selkie Girl, The Happy Owls, A Letter to Amy and The Owl and the Pussy-Cat. All ages. 39 mins.
VHS: S14492. $14.95.

Pink Christmas
The Pink Panther is cold and hungry in Central Park until his search for food uncovers the true spirit of Christmas in this touching classic from Blake Edwards.
VHS: S13065. **$14.98.**

Pocahontas (Animation)
The Indian princess Pocahontas falls in love Captain John Smith from the Old World. She saves his life, but is separated from him and travels to England, accompanied by her animal friends, to find him. This charming animated film follows her adventures as she struggles to find true love. From the *Enchanted Tales* series. 48 mins.
VHS: S25887. **$14.98.**

Pocahontas (Stop-Motion Animation)
The story of legendary Native American woman Pocahontas is told in this well-crafted, stop-motion animation. As the savior of Jamestown settlers (including John Rolfe, her future husband), her story has fascinated Americans for over 300 years.
VHS: S27433. **$9.95.**
John Matthews, USA, 31 mins.

Pocahontas: Her True Story
At age 12, this Native American princess saved the life of Captain John Smith and changed forever the course of history of the British American colonies. This documentary charts her achievements as an ambassador, stateswoman, peacemaker and visionary. 50 mins.
VHS: S25837. **$19.95.**

Poky Little Puppy's First Christmas
Sweet little Poky is now on video. While the family searches for the perfect Christmas tree, Poky wanders off, falls into a deep hole and meets his rescuer, a little skunk named Herman. Narrated by Donald Sutherland. Ages 2-5. 30 minutes.
VHS: S25001. **$9.95.**

Poky's Favorite Stories
These Golden Book favorites are now on video. Parents probably read them as kids. This compilation features the animated stories *The Poky Little Puppy and The Patchwork Blanket, The Sailor Dog* and *Little Toad to the Rescue.* Ages 2-5. 30 mins.
VHS: S24990. **$5.95.**

Pollyanna
Elizabeth Archand stars as the orphaned Pollyanna Whittier, who comes to a small English town to live with her stern Aunt Polly and ends up spreading happiness wherever she goes, in this BBC version of the classic story.
VHS: S19093. **$24.98.**
Jayne Wyndham-Davis, Great Britain, 1973, 155 mins.

The Portrait
Julie is a promising young art student recovering from a suicide attempt. While recuperating she is inspired by a young girl named Sarah who is terminally ill with cancer. Sarah's enthusiasm helps Julie realize the preciousness of life. 30 mins.
VHS: S22373. **$149.95.**
Laser: LD74601. **$169.95.**

Prince Cinders
This prince is stuck at home doing housework while his three brothers live it up around town. Suddenly everything changes when a magical fairy godmother appears. She makes Prince Cinders into a he-man, but that is the beginning of his troubles, as he encounters the problems of masculinity. 30 mins.
VHS: S24211. **$19.95.**

The Princess and the Goblin
In this animated feature an enchanting princess and an outrageous goblin inhabit a world of magic and adventure. Can beauty succeed where cunning and deception are rife? Children will be enthralled by this tale of imagination gone wild. 82 mins.
VHS: S22946. **$24.95.**

Puff the Magic Dragon
Puff, the magic dragon made famous by Peter, Paul and Mary, comes alive in this animated version with the voice of Burgess Meredith as Puff. USA, 1984, 45 mins.
VHS: S01071. **$14.98.**

Puppy Pals
A program about the joy and spirit of puppies, especially their attraction to children, which encourages a friendship between youngsters and animals. With a sing-along soundtrack. 30 mins.
VHS: S18264. **$14.95.**

The Puzzle Place: Rock Dreams
Kids will learn about themselves in these charming episodes from the popular Puzzle Place kids. They visit a recording studio and laugh about their own experiences with musical fortune and fame. Includes performances by The Boys Choir of Harlem and a Native American rock band called Red Thunder. 55 mins.
VHS: S24685. **$14.98.**

The Puzzle Place: Tuned In
Children learn that there is more to life than what they see on television in this video featuring the Puzzle Place kids. Lessons like these are invaluable. 55 mins.
VHS: S24686. **$14.98.**

Quarterback Princess
Can a girl find happiness and popularity as a star quarterback? Helen Hunt stars as the daring heroine of this movie based on a true story.
VHS: S05898. **$59.98.**

Raffi:
Young People's Concert with Raffi
A concert video of singable songs by the internationally acclaimed children's entertainer Raffi. Songs include "Down by the Bay," "He's Got the Whole World," and many more.
VHS: S01524. **$19.95.**
David Devine, USA, 1984, 50 mins.

A Rainbow of My Own
Based on the book by Don Freeman. After a rainy afternoon of playing imaginary games with a rainbow, a boy goes home to find a real rainbow waiting in his room. Ages 4-8. 5 mins.
VHS: S24621. **$37.95.**

Ramona
Here's Ramona, the star of Beverly Cleary's best-selling children's classics, as the star of her own true-to-life videos. Meet Sarah Polley as the spunky and lovable Ramona. Based on stories from Cleary favorites, your whole family will cheer as Ramona, Beezus and the Quimbys come to life! Each video contains two stories. 60 minutes each.
Ramona: Goodbye, Hello.
VHS: S10969. **$14.95.**
Ramona: Great Hair Argument.
VHS: Out of print. For rental only.
Ramona: New Pajamas.
VHS: S10972. **$14.95.**
Ramona: Perfect Day and Bad Day.
VHS: S06863. **$29.95.**
Ramona: Rainy Sunday and Mystery Meal.
VHS: Out of print. For rental only.
Ramona: Ramona's Bad Day.
VHS: Out of print. For rental only.
Ramona: Siblingitis.
VHS: S10975. **$14.95.**
Ramona: Squeakerfoot and Goodbye, Hello.
VHS: S06861. **$29.95.**
Ramona: The Patient.
VHS: S10974. **$14.95.**

Reach for the Sky
A realistic look at a young girl's sacrifice in training to become a champion gymnast. Ages 4+.
VHS: S24622. **$19.95.**

The Real Story Videos Series
Well known celebrities are the voices for the leading characters in this series of reinvestigations of well-known children's stories, songs and rhymes. While the actual story may be short, the videos imagine an entire life surrounding the material. Contemporary, upbeat, imaginative and surprising. Ages 4-8. Each video is approximately 25 minutes.
The Real Story of Baa Baa Black Sheep.
VHS: S25047. **$12.95.**
The Real Story of Happy Birthday to You.
VHS: S25045. **$12.95.**
The Real Story of I'm A Little Teapot.
VHS: S25042. **$12.95.**
The Real Story of Itsy Bitsy Spider. Recommended. With Cosby show star Malcolm Jamal-Warner and singer Patti LaBelle. Very engaging.
VHS: S25041. **$12.95.**
The Real Story of Rain, Rain Go Away.
VHS: S25044. **$12.95.**
The Real Story of Three Little Kittens.
VHS: S25043. **$12.95.**
The Real Story of Twinkle Twinkle Little Star.
VHS: S25046. **$12.95.**

Really Rosie
Maurice Sendak's *Really Rosie* tells the story of Rosie and her neighborhood friends the Nutshell Kids. All the kids perform in Rosie's poems and songs. Featuring music composed and sung by Carole King.
VHS: S01094. **$19.95.**
Sheldon Ross, USA, 1985

ReBoot: Talent Night
Bob, Dot and Dot's brother Enzo are three characters who live in a mainframe computer. This computer-animated series follows their adventures battling the evil computer viruses Megabyte and Hexadecimal. In this episode, Dot prepares a surprise birthday event for her younger brother. USA, 25 mins.
VHS: S27152. **$12.95.**

ReBoot: The Great Brain Robbery
Megabyte takes over Enzo's brain. Only a miniaturized Bob can save the day. Once he is small enough, he is sent into Enzo's head to battle Megabyte on the terrain that is Enzo's mind. USA, 25 mins.
VHS: S27153. **$12.95.**

Rechenka's Eggs
Old Babushka is preparing her famous eggs for the Ukrainian Easter Festival when she takes in an injured goose whom she names Rechenka. They live happily together until one terrible day when Rechenka accidentally breaks all of Babushka's lovingly crafted eggs. From the award-winning book by Patricia Polacco.
VHS: S16351. **$44.95.**

Red Balloon
A classic childhood fantasy with appeal for viewers of every age. This is a story of Pascal, a French boy who befriends a red balloon which follows him everywhere. A touching allegory of the magic powers of love and friendship. No dialog.
VHS: S01098. **$14.95.**
Albert Lamorisse, France, 1956, 34 mins.

Red Balloon/White Mane
Albert Lamorisse's *Red Balloon* is a priceless classic about a young boy's friendship with a red balloon. 1956, 38 mins. His *White Mane* explores man's relationship to nature; it chronicles the efforts of bandits to capture a wild white stallion, and a young boy who rescues him. Winner of the International Grand Prize, Best Short Film, Cannes Film Festival. 1952, 38 mins.
VHS: S18762. **$24.95.**
Laser: LD70443. **$29.95.**

Rembrandt's Beret
It is rumored that a secret hall spans the Arno River in Florence linking two great museums, the Uffizi Gallery and the Pitti Palace. Tiberius finds more than a rumor as he discovers the Hall of the Old Masters. When some of the paintings come to life, Tiberius gets to talk with Rembrandt, and receives the master painter's beret and brushes as a first step to becoming a great artist himself.
VHS: S16352. **$44.95.**

Ren & Stimpy: Nothing But Shorts: The Unwashed Collection
Twenty-two outrageous cartoon shorts featuring MTV's bizarrely lovable duo Ren & Stimpy are collected on this video, including the classics *Log, Dr. Stupid* and *Powdered Toastman.* Sometimes they're hard to swallow, but they're always tasteless. Incidentally, 11 of these shorts have never been broadcast. 40 mins.
VHS: S27081. **$14.98.**

Rescue Party
Arthur C. Clarke's story is adapted in this thought-provoking film. A surveying spaceship is diverted to Earth in order to save its population. Students join this ship as the planet is doomed. The outcome of this story will leave the audience pondering the significance of these aliens' actions. 20 mins.
VHS: S23473. **$79.95.**

Richard Scarry Series
The videos are as enjoyable as the well-liked books. Join the fun in Busytown with Huckle Cat, Lowly Worm and friends. Great for the ages 2-6 set.
Richard Scarry's Best Busy People Video. A fun look at jobs and occupations in Busytown.
VHS: S24623. **$9.95.**
Richard Scarry's Best Counting Video. The friends are back all over town—count down! 20 mins.
VHS: S24625. **$9.95.**
Richard Scarry's Best Ever ABC Video. This time, the fun is centered at the Busytown School. 20 mins.
VHS: S24624. **$9.95.**
Richard Scarry's Best Learning Songs Ever. Join the Busytown crowd singing about letters, numbers, shapes and other fun things.
VHS: S24626. **$9.95.**

Richard Scarry's Sergeant Murphy's Day Off and Two Other Stories
There are three stories from the popular Nick Jr. cable television children's s show on this video. It contains more imaginative and colorful characters. 25 mins.
VHS: S25920. **$9.95.**

Richard Scarry's The Best Birthday Present Ever and Two Other Stories
In addition to the title story, this video of the popular Nick Jr. cable network cartoon show includes two other stories. Kids love these tales featuring a variety of talking animals. 25 mins.
VHS: S25919. **$9.95.**

Rights from the Heart
This moving collection of short, animated films, produced by the film board of Canada, illustrates the United Nations Declaration the Rights of a Child. International in outlook, these films bring out the values that should govern everyone. Peace, dignity, tolerance, freedom, equality, and solidarity are not just words, but the eternal guarantee of humanity. Public performance rights for institutions are included. 40 mins.
VHS: S18966. **$39.95.**

Rikki-Tikki-Tavi
To protect his human family, pet mongoose Rikki-Tikki-Tavi must battle two evil cobra snakes. Adapted from a Rudyard Kipling story, this animated piece is narrated by Orson Welles. 30 mins.
VHS: S03017. **$14.95.**

Rings Around the World
Don Ameche hosts a lively program of circus acts from around the world. For the entertainment of the entire family come spectacular performers from Sweden, Germany, Switzerland and the US, as well as other parts of the globe. The big top is now on video, where every seat is at center ring. 1967, 79 mins.
VHS: S06830. **$69.95.**

Rip Van Winkle
Washington Irving's classic tale of man who fell asleep in one era and wakes up in another is adapted for this new video. This character tried to escape his wife, but found that he got far more than he bargained for. 18 mins.
VHS: S23495. **$79.95.**

Road Construction Ahead
George the friendly construction worker takes kids for an inside look at the trucks used while building a road. From the initial surveying to the final laying of the asphalt, they are all there. It's a fascinating exploration of the men and machines that make it all happen. 30 mins.
VHS: S21325. **$19.95.**

Roald Dahl's Dirty Beast
With illustrations by Quentin Blake, this program conjures up a fantastic universe of frightening animals who perform crazy antics in comic verse. Voiced by Prunella Scales and Timothy West. 30 mins.
VHS: S19425. **$12.98.**

Roald Dahl's Revolting Rhymes
Roald Dahl's wacky humor is fully rendered through the illustrations of Quentin Blake in this collection of six children's stories that surprise with their wit, style and originality. 30 mins.
VHS: S19424. **$12.98.**

Robert McCloskey Library
Six short films, all of which are adaptations of the popular children's books by Robert McCloskey: *Lentil, Make Way for Ducklings, Blueberries for Sal, Time of Wonder, Burt Dow: Deep-Water Man* and a short documentary about Robert McCloskey at work. 55 mins.
VHS: S13335. **$19.95.**

Roll of the Thunder
Original watercolor and pastel illustrations highlight this award-winning adaptation of Mildred Taylor's Newbery Award-winning book based on her experiences growing up with her close-knit black family during Depression-era Mississippi. 46 mins.
VHS: S07703. **$119.00.**

Romper Room: Ask Miss Molly
Where do bananas come from? How do you count money? Where does Shamu the Killer Whale live? A fascinating introduction for children about the wonders of nature. 40 mins.
VHS: S06361. **$14.98.**

Romper Room: Kimble's Birthday
Miss Molly and friends give Kimble the Bear a birthday celebration complete with magic tricks, a pinata, and of course, a cake. A birthday present any pre-schooler will love. 30 mins.
VHS: S06362. **$14.98.**

Romper Room: Outta Space
The Romper Room gang investigates the stars, visits a spaceship, and interviews a real-life astronaut. An entertaining introduction to out-of-this-world wonders. 30 mins.
VHS: S06363. **$14.98.**

The Rory Story
Rory (*Kidrock*) stars in this funny, fictitious story about how she broke into the recording business. Her adorable puppet, and back-up singers, The Incredible Piglets, are also along for the ride in this entertaining children's film. 60 mins.
VHS: S15306. **$14.98.**

Rosenschontz:
The Teddy Bears' Jamboree
These children's music pioneers perform 15 of their greatest hits on this video compilation. Kids will love the sing-alongs accompanied by ample teddy bear hugging, dancing and tossing. In fact, it's an interactive experience for the whole family. 62 mins.
VHS: S24207. **$12.98.**

Rosie's Walk and other stories
An over-eager fox stalks an innocent hen to a catchy barnyard tune. Winner of the CINE Golden Eagle award. Also includes *Charlie Needs a Cloak*, *The Story about Ping* and *The Beast of Monsieur Racine.* Ages 2-8. 32 mins.
VHS: S14493. **$14.95.**

Roxaboxen
Alice McLerran's treasured *Roxaboxen* is a hill of sand and rocks and old wooden boxes. But Marion and her sisters, neighbors and friends all remember it as a special place: a sparkling world of jeweled homes, streets edged with the whitest stone, and two ice cream shops.
VHS: S16353. **$44.95.**

Rudolph the Red Nosed Reindeer
Burl Ives narrates this musical tale, presented in Animagic, of how Rudolph overcame the other reindeers' ridicule to save Christmas. 53 mins.
VHS: S10795. **$12.98.**

Rugrats, Vol. 1: Tales from the Crib
A revealing examination of childhood adolescence, captured from the unique vantage point of its one-year-old hero Tommy Pickles, a brave child when he's left to his own devices. With his comrade in arms, Chuckie, the two devise a means to liberate their pet sea monkeys in the three episodes, *Toy Palace, Real or Robots* and *Beach Blanket Babies.* The program also features two claymation vignettes about the young super hero Inside Out Boy. 40 mins.
VHS: S19086. **$14.98.**

Rugrats, Vol. 2: A Baby's Gotta Do What a Baby's Gotta Do
Tommy Pickles and his gang of Rugrats venture on a metaphysical quest to find the answers to such riddles as where the light goes in the dark, in three terrific tales: *Monster in the Garage, Touchdown Tommy* and *Let There Be Light.* The program also contains two claymation episodes of the Inside Out Boy, a young superhero who protects children. 40 mins.
VHS: S19087. **$14.98.**

Rugrats: A Rugrats Passover
The Rugrats babies are the key characters in this telling of the story of Passover. The Rugrats babies (and even some of the adults) don't seem to understand the importance of celebrating Passover, "a holiday without presents", and participating in a Passover Seder. When Grandpa tells them the story of Moses leading the Hebrews away from the Pharaoh and slavery, everyone finds something to believe in. Animated, 25 mins.
VHS: S27080. **$9.98.**

Runaway Ralph
In this sequel to The Mouse and the Motorcycle, Fred Savage plays a kid at summer camp who has no friends till he meets the rambunctious mouse, Ralph. Based on the book by Beverly Cleary. 42 mins.
VHS: S16580. **$9.98.**

Rupert
The animated adventures of Rupert the Bear and his friends Bill Badger, Tiger-Lilly and Jack Frost in a faraway land of dragons and sea-serpents, reached only by the animal underground railway. Narration by Ray Brooks. 57 mins.
VHS: S13204. **$14.98.**

Rupert and the Runaway Dragon
More stories about Rupert the Bear, in a world where dragons run away, robbins turn yellow, eggs hatch fire birds and trees house goblins. 37 mins.
VHS: S13205. **$14.98.**

Ruth Heller's Nature Stories
Questions about plants and animals are asked and answered in meaningful and amusing stories that young children will love. Includes four programs: *Animals Born Alive and Well, Chickens Aren't the Only Ones, Plants That Never Ever Bloom* and *The Reason for a Flower.* For Grades 1-4.
VHS: S14175. **$139.95.**

Sadako
Eleanor Coerr's story of an ill Japanese adolescent girl is narrated by Liv Ullmann with music by George Winston. Sadako has leukemia because of the residual radiation left by the bombing of Hiroshima. She is beset by the threat of despair when a friend reminds her of the belief that a thousand paper cranes may cause the gods to grant her a wish. Ages 8 and up. 30 mins.
VHS: S24930. **$195.00.**

Sammy and Other Songs from Getting to Know Myself
Singer/songwriter Hap Palmer is back, encouraging the audience to join in this exploration of body movement and feelings. This movement participation video gets kids to stretch, jump, and just enjoy the feeling of moving about. It also covers body image, the position of the body in space, identifying body parts, as well as moods and feelings. Ages 3-9.
VHS: S24627. **$19.95.**

The Sand Castle
1977 Academy Award winner *The Sand Castle* is a fable of great humor and appeal from director Co Hoedemann. The Sandman sculpts magical creatures who build a castle and then celebrate their new home. But an uninvited guest arrives to start the wind blowing. With the delightful animated shorts *The North Wind and the Sun*, *Alphabet* and *The Owl and the Lemming*. 30 mins.
VHS: S15795. $19.98.
Co Hoedemann, Canada, 1977, 30 mins.

Santa Claus Is Coming to Town
Featuring the voices of Mickey Rooney, Keenan Wynn and the Westminster Children's Choir; narrated by Fred Astaire. Animagic. Sombertown is a dull place until Kris Kringle imports the spirit of Christmas. 53 mins.
VHS: S10798. $12.98.

Sarah, Plain and Tall
Set on the Midwestern prairie, this video presentation of Patricia MacLachlan's book tells the story of Sarah, who answers a pioneer's ad for a wife, but misses her home in Maine, the ocean and her family.
VHS: S08400. $119.00.

Savannah Smiles
A touching children's film about Savannah, a six-year old runaway, who is thrown together with two escaped convicts in a crazy comedy of errors.
VHS: S04298. $19.95.
Pierre de Moro, 104 mins.

Scholastic Productions
Series of pre-teen videos combining entertainment with insights into the world around them. 60 minutes each.
The Almost Royal Family. Combines comedy and adventure as the Hendersons inherit an island that turns out to be a separate country. They enjoy their royal status until complications begin.
VHS: S04163. $19.95.
The Great Love Experiment. This is the Emmy-Award-winning story of a "love experiment"—four seniors try to change a nerd's luck, through friendship.
VHS: S04165. $19.95.

Schoolhouse Rock: America Rock
The Preamble, *I'm Just a Bill*, *No More Kings* and other historical ditties from the Emmy Award-winning television series teach kids about the U.S. 30 mins.
VHS: S26414. $12.95.

Schoolhouse Rock: Grammar Rock
This video contains cartoons from the Emmy Award-winning television series. It teaches kids basic grammar with the short films *Conjunction Junction*; *Lolly, Lolly, Lolly, Get Your Adverbs Here*; *Interjections* and more cartoons. Great animation and upbeat singable songs make this tape a must for kids. 30 mins.
VHS: S26412. $12.95.

Schoolhouse Rock: Multiplication Rock
The Emmy Award-winning television series taught math to kids with short films like *My Hero, Zero*; *Three Is a Magic Number*; *Figure Eight* and other easy-to-sing songs. Kids love these cartoons. 30 mins.
VHS: S26415. $12.95.

Schoolhouse Rock: Science Rock
These episodes from the animated Emmy Award-winning television series focus on science. Great sing-along videos like *Electricity, Electricity*; *Them-Not-So-Dry-Bones*; *Interplanet Janet* and more make this tape perfect for kids. 30 mins.
VHS: S26413. $12.95.

Scuffy the Tugboat and Friends
Remember the Golden Books you read as a kid? *Scuffy the Tugboat* is now in video format. Also included are other Golden Book titles: *What Was That!* and *Theodore Mouse Goes to Sea*. Ages 2-6. 30 minutes.
VHS: S24989. $5.95.

Sea Dream
A lively animated film about a girl who escapes into an underwater fantasy after having a bad day. She "dives" through her quilt into the sea where she joins a friendly octopus for tea. After a wonderful day together, the little girl swims back to her bed, refreshed by a trip into fantasy. With the hallucinatory *Nebule* and *The Sound Collector*. 30 mins.
VHS: S15793. $19.98.

Seabert: Good Guys Wear White
A fun-filled adventure with Seabert, who is out to make a better world for all by fighting poachers, hunters and other evil forces that threaten wildlife. Animated.
VHS: S09188. $39.95.

Seal Morning
Along the desolate Norfolk coast of England, an orphaned girl is sent to live with her reclusive aunt. The girl, Rowena, adjusts to her new surroundings by exploring the wild countryside of the region. Her discovery of a baby seal helps her aunt break out of her seclusion toward a new family life. 103 mins.
VHS: S25060. $19.95.

Season on the Water
Heather and Billy's father is reluctant to take them out on the water because he was scared at sea for two days. Heather's determination changes his mind however, providing valuable insights about family relationships. 26 mins.
VHS: S23453. $79.95.

Seasons and Holidays Around the World
These are colorful, dramatic stories that tell how real people in Mexico, China, Britain and Sweden celebrate the holidays most meaningful to them. Many diverse cultures and societies are explored in holiday gatherings around the world. In England, they celebrate with a party that originated in the Druid religion. The Swedes have a special Christmas tale about Jultomenten arriving in his sleigh. Explore!
Halloween in Britain.
VHS: S16362. $34.95.
Christmas in Mexico.
VHS: S16363. $34.95.
Chinese New Year.
VHS: S16364. $34.95.
Christmas in Sweden.
VHS: S16365. $34.95.

A Second Chance
Starring Richard Mulligan. Friendship, loyalty, guilt and regret come under scrutiny as events lead up to the accidental shooting of a boy's best friend. 27 mins.
VHS: S23446. $79.95.

The Secret World of Alex Mack: In the Nick of Time
Alex was accidentally drenched with strange chemicals from the Paradise Valley Chemical Plant. In these two episodes she manages to outwit the company employees who try to track her down and even cope with the usual teenage troubles. It's all made possible by her special and amazing powers. USA, 1996, 55 mins.
VHS: S26915. $9.98.

Sesame Street Home Video Visits
Pre-schoolers love Sesame Street's "get-acquainted" approach to making places like the firehouse and the hospital less frightening. 30 minutes each.
Sesame Street Visits the Firehouse. After Oscar's trash can catches on fire, the crew visits the firehouse.
VHS: S24634. $9.98.
Sesame Street Visits the Hospital. Big Bird is afraid when he has to go to the hospital; but after he finds out more, he feels better.
VHS: S24635. $9.98.

Sesame Street Kids' Guide to Life: Learning to Share
Elmo has trouble with learning to share. Fortunately, Big Bird, the Cookie Monster, Oscar, Elmo's best friend Zoe and special guest Katie Couric can teach him how. This video is a great way for kids to learn key values. It also includes a number of delightful songs.
VHS: S26913. $12.98.
Lisa Simon, USA, 1996, 45 mins.

Sesame Street Presents: Follow That Bird!
Big Bird is lost—trying to get home to Sesame Street. With the help of his Muppet friends, he'll find his way, but not before he runs into meanies like Chevy Chase, John Candy, Joe Flaherty, and other special stars.
VHS: S04388. $19.98.
Laser: LD74702. $34.98.

Sesame Street Specials
Travel with Big Bird and the Sesame Street gang to exciting and often faraway places such as China, Japan and the Metropolitan Museum of Art in these award-winning Sesame Street specials.
Big Bird in China. Big Bird's desire to find the legendary Chinese phoenix bird leads him and Barkley, the dog, to an exciting adventure in China. Along the way, they visit with Chinese schoolchildren and learn some Chinese words and songs. 75 mins.
VHS: S05373. $12.98.
Big Bird in Japan. Join Big Bird and Barkley the Dog on their visit to Japan. Meet with Japanese people as well. 75 mins.
VHS: S24633. $12.98.
Christmas Eve on Sesame Street. Holiday skits and songs, with Big Bird figuring out "How does Santa Claus, who is 'built like a dump truck', get down all those skinny little chimneys?" The whole gang is involved in this charming story which uncovers the true Christmas spirit. 60 mins.
VHS: S05379. $12.98.
Don't Eat the Pictures: Sesame Street at the Met. This one-hour musical follows the adventures of Big Bird, Snuffy, Cookie Monster, and the rest of the Sesame Street gang as they find themselves accidentally locked in the Metropolitan Museum overnight. 60 mins.
VHS: S05374. $12.98.
Put Down the Duckie. Sesame Street's Ernie learns to play the saxophone. Originally aired as a PBS special in 1988, this all-star musical combines Gladys Knight and the Pips, Danny DeVito, Patti LaBelle, Barbara Walters, James Taylor, Paul Simon and many other celebrities. 45 mins.
VHS: S23130. $12.98.
Sesame Street Celebrates Around the World. Join the party as the Sesame Street crowd celebrates New Year's Eve around the world: Mexico, Japan, Portugal, Israel, Norway and Germany. Shot on location, this video features a global New Year's Eve party filled with culturally diverse music and customs. Originally broadcast on New Year's Eve 1993, it features an appearance by Lily Tomlin. 60 mins.
VHS: S23129. $12.95.
Sesame Street's 25th Birthday: A Musical Celebration. A musical birthday party featuring an hour of musical favorites. Twenty musical numbers, including favorites like Ernie's "Rubber Duckie." Also includes new magic, like a finale with the South African *a capella* singing group Ladysmith Black Mambazo. Ages 4-7. 60 mins.
VHS: S24636. $12.98.

Sesame Street: Big Bird Sings!
Big Bird invites his pal Snuffy to look through his precious scrapbook. Snuffy is amazed at the array of memories recalled by photos, souvenirs and handmade trinkets. Kids will join right in the fun, especially the 11 sing-along songs. 30 mins.
VHS: S26621. $12.98.

Sesame Street: Do the Alphabet
Baby Bear cannot remember all his letters. Big Bird has an amazing method including games, songs and special surprises that make learning the ABC's easy and fun. Kids learn best with the help of friends like Big Bird.
VHS: S26912. $12.98.
John Ferraro, USA, 1996, 45 mins.

Shakespeare: The Animated Tales
A series of fully-animated, close-captioned videos, each of which abridges one of the Shakespeare plays to 30 minutes. For ages 10 and up.
A Midsummer Night's Dream.
VHS: S21932. $14.95.
Hamlet.
VHS: S21930. $14.95.
Macbeth.
VHS: S21931. $14.95.
Romeo and Juliet.
VHS: S21933. $14.95.
The Tempest.
VHS: S21934. $14.95.
The Twelfth Night.
VHS: S21935. $14.95.

Shamu & You
Featuring live kids, animation, wild-life footage and songs. Ages 4-10. 30 minutes each video.
Shamu & You: Exploring the World of Birds.
VHS: S24637. $14.98.
Shamu & You: Exploring the World of Fish.
VHS: S24638. $14.98.
Shamu & You: Exploring the World of Mammals.
VHS: S24639. $14.98.
Shamu & You: Exploring the World of Reptiles.
VHS: S24640. $14.98.

Shari Lewis: Kooky Classics
Join Shari and friends as they tour the world of classical music, from Brahms to Mozart. 55 mins.
VHS: S24641. $19.95.

Shari Lewis: Lamb Chop in the Haunted Studio
Shari Lewis and Lamb Chop are determined to film their show in a studio bedeviled by the hilarious antics of Count Dracula, Frankenstein and the Phantom. These monsters create an atmosphere of levity and make-believe scariness that is just right for children. 60 mins.
VHS: S26454. $12.95.

Shari Lewis: Lamb Chop in the Land of No Manners
Shari Lewis, with her sassy sidekick, the adorable puppet Lamb Chop, takes youngsters on a magical journey to a place where they don't have to follow any rules or take turns. 44 mins.
VHS: S14519. $19.95.

Shari's Christmas Concert
Miss Shari Lewis and her cuddly and often very shy friend Lamb Chop ring in the holiday season in this video for children of all ages. Shari conducts a symphony orchestra, sings, dances and provides the Merry in Merry Christmas. 50 mins.
VHS: S07718. $9.95.

Sharon, Lois & Bram's Elephant Show
Featuring the veteran children's entertainers and a life-sized puppet elephant, this multiple award-winning series was designed to impart social skills, to strengthen preschool-age developmental abilities and to provide pre-reading and language experiences in a fun manner. Uses music, sing-along, games, live action, visits with real people, and on-location visits to interesting places. Ages 3-6. Each video is 30 minutes each.
Sleepover. 12 songs, including *Where's My Pajamas, Ham 'n Eggs* and *Ten in the Bed*. 30 mins.
VHS: S16491. $14.95.
Live in Your Living Room. 10 songs, including *Little Rabbit Foo Foo, Pufferbellies* and *Canadian Jig Medley*. 30 mins.
VHS: S16492. $14.95.
Back by Popular Demand...Live. 10 songs, including *Jelly, Jelly in My belly, Keep on the Sunny Side* and *Chugga-Chugga*. 30 mins.
VHS: S16493. $14.95.
Treasure Island. 9 songs, including *Lot's of Worms, Going over the Sea* and the *The Shanty Medley*. 30 mins.
VHS: S16494. $14.95.
Who Stole the Cookies? 10 songs, including *Cookie Jar, My Little Rooster* and *Apple Pickers Red*. 30 mins.
VHS: S16495. $14.95.
Soap Box Derby. 10 songs, including *Get Out and Get Under, Going to Kentucky* and *I'm a Little Piece of Tin*. 30 mins.
VHS: S16496. $14.95.
Pet Fair.
VHS: S24645. $14.95.
Radio Show.
VHS: S24646. $14.95.

Shelley Duvall's Bedtime Stories (Collection)
Seven of the best of these children's stories are joined in this special collection. Included are *Elbert's Bad Word*, *Weird Parents*, *Patrick's Dinosaurs*, *What Happened to Patrick's Dinosaurs*, *There's a Nightmare in My Closet*, *There's an Alligator Under my Bed* and *There's Something in My Attic*. 78 mins.
VHS: S23223. $39.98.

Shelley Duvall's Bedtime Stories: Aunt Ippy's Museum of Junk
Jodi and Jimi love visiting Aunt Ippy's shop, a hotbed of recycling and rebuilding. One day they explore the entire fascinating kingdom in search of a special object. Narrated by Kathy Bates. *Uncle Wizmo's New Car*, the story of Jodi and Jimi in a used car lot, is also included. Ed Begley, Jr., narrates. 26 mins.
VHS: S21806. $12.98.

Shelley Duvall's Bedtime Stories: Bootsie Barker Bites
Lisa has trouble playing with the beastly Bootsie. But one day, she turns the table on her for biting friend. Narrated by Rhea Perlman. Then Shelley Long narrates *Ruby the Copycat*. Ruby copies the prettiest girl in class and learns an important lesson; it's better to be yourself. 26 mins.
VHS: S21805. $12.98.

Shelley Duvall's Bedtime Stories: Elbert's Bad Word and Weird Parents
Elbert's Bad Word: At a very proper party, little Elbert overhears a most improper word; then the word pops out of Elbert's mouth at the worst possible moment. Narrated by Ringo Starr. *Weird Parents*: Once there was a boy whose parents were so weird and kooky he was embarrassed to be seen with them, until he realized they were very special. Narrated by Bette Midler.
VHS: S16992. $12.98.

Shelley Duvall's Bedtime Stories: Elizabeth and Larry and Bill and Pete
Elizabeth and Larry: For years, Elizabeth and her pet alligator Larry were the best of friends. But when Larry discovers he doesn't look anything like Elizabeth, it causes an alligator identity crisis. Narrated by Jean Stapleton. *Bill and Pete*: On the banks of the river Nile, Bill the alligator and his pal Pete the Toothbrush Bird work together to keep Bill from being made into a suitcase. Narrated by Dudley Moore.
VHS: S16993. $12.98.

Shelley Duvall's Bedtime Stories: Little Toot and the Loch Ness Monster and Choo Choo
Little Toot and the Loch Ness Monster: Full of curiosity about creatures of the deep, the tugboat little Toot sails to Scotland to search for the Loch Ness Monster. Narrated by Rick Moranis. *Choo Choo*: Deciding to see the wide world for herself, a little steam engine runs away from the train yard. Narrated by Bonnie Raitt.
VHS: S16994. $12.98.

Shelley Duvall's Bedtime Stories: Moe the Dog in Tropical Paradise
Moe, the family dog, works at an ice cream factory in the frozen north. He and a friend dream of an expensive tropical holiday until Moe resourcefully finds a unique solution. Narrated by Richard Dreyfuss. Then Morgan Freeman narrates *Amos, The Story of an Old Dog and His Couch*. 26 mins.
VHS: S21771. $12.98.

Shelley Duvall's Bedtime Stories: My New Neighbors
Billy Crystal narrates this story about a young boy who meets his neighbors and discovers that they are very strange indeed. Also included is *Rotten Island*, a place where monsters and mayhem rule, narrated by Charles Grodin. 26 mins.
VHS: S21770. $12.98.

Shelley Duvall's Bedtime Stories: The Christmas Witch
Angela Lansbury narrates and Shelley Duvall hosts this animated tale about a witch who was no good at being bad. Instead, the witch decides to spread the spirit of Christmas. This delightful children's tale features three original holiday songs. 27 mins.
VHS: S26437. $12.98.

Shelley Duvall's Bedtime Stories: The Little Rabbit Who Wanted Red Wings
Shelley Duvall narrates this story of an imaginative rabbit who gets his wish for wings, only to discover that being yourself is really the best thing. *Katy No-Pocket* has a problem. She's a mother kangaroo with no pouch for her baby, until she finds the perfect all-purpose pocket. Narrated by Mary Steenburgen. 26 mins.
VHS: S21804. $12.98.

Shelley Duvall's Bedtime Stories: Tugford Wanted to be Bad
This animated feature follows Tugford the mouse in his adventures to be like the bad guys in the movies. But his outlaw scheme backfires and he almost foils his own birthday party. Narrated by Steve Martin. *Little Penguin's Tale*, narrated by Candice Bergen, is also included. It's the story of a penguin who almost meets disaster. 26 mins.
VHS: S21769. $12.98.

Shelley Duvall's Tall Tales and Legends
This hour-long program from the creator of the beloved *Faerie Tale Theatre* features celebrities such as Elliot Gould, Beverly D'Angelo, Jamie Lee Curtis, Brian Dennehy, Carol Kane, Steve Guttenberg, Martin Mull, Martin Short, Randy Newman, Ed Asner and Molly Ringwald in stories ranging from *Johnny Appleseed* and *Casey at the Bat* to *Annie Oakley* and *The Legend of Sleepy Hollow*.
VHS: S25784. $54.98.

Sherlock Holmes Cliffhangers
Students led through these gripping and dramatic puzzles practice observation, organization, sequencing and reasoning as they uncover the evidence from the clues presented. At a key point, the students must match wits with the master sleuth by answering focus question. Includes four tales: *The Musgrave Ritual*, *The Adventures of the Priory School*, *The Adventure of the Norwood Builder* and *A Case of Identity*. For Grades 5-12.
VHS: S14204. $159.95.

Sherlock Holmes Spellbinders
These four tales show the master at his best. Holmes inspires viewers to follow his methods of scholarly research, careful observation and acute deduction. Includes *The Adventure of the Three Students*, *The Adventure of the Reigate Puzzle*, *The Adventure of the Solitary Cyclist* and *The Adventure of the Lion's Mane*. For Grades 5-12.
VHS: S14176. $159.95.

Sherlock Holmes' Greatest Cases
The sleuth of sleuths is called upon to render assistance where simple mortals are totally perplexed. Each case challenges the viewer to think like the detective and come up with the solution. Includes four classic mysteries: *A Scandal in Bohemia, Silver Blaze, The Adventure of the Dancing Man* and *The Red-Headed League.* For Grades 5-12.
VHS: S14205. $159.95.

Showdown at Lonesome Pellet
Wild and furry days with the coney people on the frontier is the subject of this read-along children's video. The notorious Pointy Brothers are the meanest outlaws in the West. They have come to terrorize the quiet coney town of Lonesome Pellet. But a stranger promises to clean up the town in three days. Is he coney enough to do the job?
VHS: S22352. $39.95.

Sign Songs: Fun Songs to Sign and Sing
Sign language can enhance the learning of all children. This is a great tape for kids, who can learn new songs/new signs and sign-along. Eleven delightful songs by Ken Longquist, who sings and plays guitar, are signed by John Kinstler. Ages 3-8. 29 minutes.
VHS: S24983. $49.95.

Silas Marner
Alison de Vere's animated adaptation of George Eliot's masterly Victorian novel about the fall and redemption of the weaver Silas Marner, a man who loses everything, but regains his strength and identity through a beautiful baby girl. 28 mins.
VHS: S16995. $59.99.

Silent Mouse
The story of the famous carol "Silent Night" starts in a little town in Austria where a chain of strange events happened on Christmas eve 1887. In *Silent Mouse,* Lynn Redgrave reveals a curious and charming story of mice and men. 1990, color, 60 mins.
VHS: S14989. $19.95.

Simon the Lamb
Simon the lamb turns bright blue. The rest of the flock reject him because he's different. Find out how they come to accept him. Ages 3-9.
VHS: S24936. $12.95.

Simply Magic: Episode 2
Joanie Bartell is an substitute teacher who leads students on journeys to different places, times and planets. Ages 3-10.
VHS: S24648. $14.98.

A Singing Stream: A Black Family Chronicle
This film charts the living tradition of black gospel music in the lives of an ordinary family, the Creedmoors from North Carolina. Shape note singing, backyard harmonizing, quartet programs and church services are just part of the way this music inspires and preserves family life. 60 mins.
VHS: S26356. $19.95.

Six Stories About Little Heroes
Jay O'Callahan's original tales on the universal themes of courage, friendship and truth are examples of how all of us can draw upon the power of the imagination to create our own stories. In *Six Stories,* the subjects include O'Callahan's creations of a king, various children and assorted frogs and bees. 38 mins. Public performance rights included.
VHS: S09267. $19.95.

Sleeping Beauty
Dudley Moore narrates this tale of triumphant young love while the Moscow State Orchestra performs music by Tchaikovsky in this wonderful animated version of the universally loved fairy tale. Together these elements offer a compelling introduction to the music of the great Russian composer. From the *Storyteller's Classics* series, animated. 27 mins.
VHS: S26339. $9.98.

Smile for Auntie and Other Stories
Smile for Auntie is the hilarious tale of silly Auntie who sings, dances, does anything to make a baby smile. Other films are *Make Way for Ducklings, The Snowy Day,* and *Wynken, Blynken and Nod.*
VHS: S01218. $19.95.

SNICK Vol. 1: Nick Snicks the Family
Saturday Night Nickelodeon interweaves four separate shows framed by the charming *The Adventures of Pete and Pete,* about two brothers. *Clarissa Explains It All* blends live action and animation, as Clarissa is horrified when her father volunteers to speak at her school function; in *The Ren & Stimpy Show,* Ren takes in a seven-year-old, 400-lb. delinquent jailbird; the teenage variety show *Roundhouse* uses comedy, dance and music to explore the rhythms and difficulties of teenage life; and the eerie anthology series *Are You Afraid of the Dark?* presents the frightening tale of the Hungry Hounds. 85 mins.
VHS: S19084. $14.98.

SNICK Vol. 2: Nick Snicks Friendship
In this inspired volume of four different works, each playing off personalities, individuals and personal habits, Saturday Night Nickelodeon presents an anthology show: how will Clarissa respond to her best friend moving with roller derby mom? Will Stimpy's newfound persona as a Giant isolate him from his friends? How will a new Roundhouse kid adjust to a new community and a different social setting? The final program considers the lonely existence of ghosts. 85 mins.
VHS: S19085. $14.98.

Snoopy Double Feature: Play It Again, Charlie Brown, and She's a Good Skate, Charlie Brown
Lucy has it all arranged for Schroeder to debut as a rock musician. Then Snoopy coaches Peppermint Patty toward a career in figure skating. Snoopy may be firm, but he says it's for Patty's own good. 50 mins.
VHS: S26167. $12.95.

Snoopy Double Feature: What a Nightmare, Charlie Brown, and It's Magic, Charlie Brown
At first Snoopy doesn't realize that he's dreaming (after all, he's never been a hardworking sled dog). Then Snoopy inadvertently becomes a magician. If only he could reverse the trick and get Charlie Brown to reappear. 49 mins.
VHS: S26166. $12.95.

Snowman
An Academy Award Nominee, this delightful animation weaves a spell of magic enchantment as a young boy's snowman comes to life and escorts the boy on a fantasy dream visit to the North Pole.
VHS: S01222. $14.95.
Diane Jackson, USA, 1982, 26 mins.

Something Good (plus Mortimer)
This is the tale of Tyya, a little girl whose dad refuses to buy her any "good stuff"—like cookies and candy—at the market. Plus Mortimer, who's unwilling to be quiet and go to bed. Animated stories by Robert Munsch. Ages 2-7. 30 minutes.
VHS: S24987. $12.95.

Sometimes I Wonder
A brother and sister run away from home to Grandma's ranch, where their favorite mare is beginning to foal. The children gain insights about the special gifts family life brings. 45 minutes, ages 5-12.
VHS: S17141. $14.95.

Sound Around
This tape explores the sounds made by toys, household objects and appliances, as well as those sounds made by animals and people. It's a great tool for understanding human sameness and differences as children are seen listening to, generating and imitating these sounds. 27 mins.
VHS: S22382. $19.95.

Soviet Bedtime Stories— Films for Children
Included on this tape are *A Monkey Leads the Band, The Wolf and the Tailor, The Miracle Frost, Little Cucumbers Adventures* and more. Each film is a fable, with a wide range of animation techniques rendered. 60 mins.
VHS: S12725. $19.98.

Space Case
A fun Halloween story in which a thing from outer space comes to earth to visit Buddy McGee. "A terrific comedy, crisply told, and illustrated by James Marshall's inimitable caricatures." From the storybook by Edward Marshall.
VHS: S16361. $44.95.

Spirits of the Rainforest
Children boat down an actual river, sharing myths, magic and legends of the Michiguenga Indians, who still live in the rainforest. Ages 8+.
VHS: S24767. $19.95.

Spooky Stories
A collection of strange and eerie stories about wild animals, old hunters, small women, monsters, tailors and a greedy old fat man, created by Paul Galdone. Intended for children from kindergarten through 4th grade.
The Greedy Old Fat Man. A greedy fat man devours his breakfast and in succession, a boy, a girl, a dog, a cat, a fox and several rabbits. A squirrel challenges him, declaring, "You can't catch me, old man!" 7 mins.
VHS: S20066. $44.95.
The Monster and the Tailor. The Grand Duke hires a tailor to design a pair of trousers, but he insists the craftsman make them in a ghoulish graveyard populated by a wild and spooky monster. 9 mins.
VHS: S20065. $44.95.
The Tailypo. An old hunter detaches the tail of a wild varmint, and the animal responds by stalking him each night, calling for his "Tailypo." 11 mins.
VHS: S20063. $44.95.
The Teeny-Tiny Woman. A small woman discovers a teeny-tiny bone and encounters strange noises emanating from a teeny-tiny cupboard. 7 mins.
VHS: S20064. $44.95.
Spooky Stories, Set. A collection of four programs. 34 mins.
VHS: S20067. $159.95.

Spoonbill Swamp
On a typical day in the swamp, an alligator mother and a spoonbill mother tend to their young. Children will be fascinated by the similarities and differences between these two animals as they read along with this video. 9:30 mins.
VHS: S22354. $39.95.

Spot Goes to School
The pages of Eric Hill's best-selling pop-up books come to life in this charming program. In the first of five stories, new student Spot learns just how much fun going to school can be. 30 minutes, from Walt Disney Home Video.
VHS: S22974. $9.95.

Starstruck
An Emmy award winning short about a talented 16-year-old girl who doesn't know how best to use her musical ability. Young Alice is torn between listening to her mother or pursuing her dreams. With Rini Alvarado and Lee Curreri from *Fame.* 1981, 32 mins.
VHS: S08692. $14.95.

Stingiest Man in Town
Charles Dickens' *A Christmas Carol* is slyly retold with the voices of Walter Matthau, Tom Bosley, Theodore Bikel and Robert Morse. 50 mins. Animated.
VHS: S13039. $12.95.

The Stolen Necklace
Anne Rockwell's book about a princess who loses her necklace is adapted by William Claiborne in this video. Apparently, mischievous monkeys are to blame for this theft. 9 mins.
VHS: S23494. $39.95.

Stories from the Black Tradition
A Story—A Story, Mufaro's Beautiful Daughters, Why Mosquitoes Buzz in People's Ears, The Village of Round and Square Houses and *Goggles* are now enjoyable children's animated shorts. These cartoons will instill children with pride. 52 mins.
VHS: S22685. $14.95.

Stories to Remember: Bedtime
Judy Collins sings 17 lullabies to music by Ernest Troost. This fully animated video is just right for those before-bedtime moments, especially for preschoolers.
VHS: S27401. $9.95.

Stories to Remember: Rhymin' Time!
Phylicia Rashad (*The Cosby Show*), accompanied by the music of Jason Miles, sings 36 nursery rhymes on this video. Animated shorts, adapted from the books of Kay Chorao, accompany this episode of the *Stories to Remember* series.
VHS: S27399. $9.95.

Stories to Remember: Singing Time!
Judy Collins sings 18 poems to beautifully animated films. The soothing imagery is perfect for children ages five and under. This series has won seven Parent's Choice Awards and is widely known through the Disney Channel. Music by Ernest Troost.
VHS: S27398. $9.95.

Stories to Remember: Storytime!
Arlo Guthrie sings and tells 11 charming children's stories. This fully animated video is a terrific source of entertainment for preschoolers.
VHS: S27400. $9.95.

Story of a Silent Night
Featuring the Vienna Boys Choir, this video uncovers the story of this popular Christmas carol as it was written in 1818 by Father Joseph Mohr. Now translated into over 120 languages, this beautiful carol has become a timeless Christmas favorite. 55 mins.
VHS: S23143. $29.95.

The Story of Christmas
In this animated feature the miraculous birth of Jesus is experienced from the kindly perspective of a wise old donkey, a humorous ox and a feisty young donkey. When the evil King Herod schemes against the Christ child, these resourceful barnyard animals must find a way to spread the alarm.
VHS: S22958. $14.95.

The Story of Lassie
Lassie touched Americans in her feature films, over the radio and on television. Interviews with famous stars featured in Lassie stories, like Roddy McDowall and Janet Leigh, are interspersed with clips from some of the most memorable moments of Lassie's long career. Hosted by June Lockhart. 60 mins.
VHS: S25996. $24.95.

Storybook
Eight-year-old Brandon finds himself inside a magical storybook world where he must believe in himself in order to survive. Fortunately his dog Leo and a host of new and outlandish friends are there to help him battle the dark rule of Queen Evilia. Milton Berle is featured in a surprise cameo.
VHS: S26041. $92.98.
Lorenzo Doumani, USA, 1995, 88 mins.

The Storytellers Collection
With its entertaining blend of regional and ethnic sources, this unique collection of stories told by four of America's most accomplished storytellers offers an enchanting look at a tradition as old as the spoken word. Four volumes.
Animal Stories. A cast of lovable creatures with lessons. 30 mins.
VHS: S14775. $14.95.
Magic Tales. Enter a world of fantasy and moonlight. 30 mins.
VHS: S14773. $14.95.
Scary Stories. Creepy creatures and slithery slimies. 30 mins.
VHS: S14774. $14.95.
Tall Tales, Yarns and Whoppers. Featuring giant animals and superhuman feats. 30 mins.
VHS: S14772. $14.95.
Complete four-volume set.
VHS: S14776. $59.80.

Storytelling with Sandy Jenkins: Learning and Sharing
Jenkins reveals how to tell children wonderful stories that are not only entertaining but also educational and enriching. This advice can help anyone at any level of ability. 45 mins.
VHS: S25968. $24.98.

Strange Case of the Cosmic Rays
The mysteries of the universe are revealed in this fun and fact-filled galactic thriller. Elements of the atom, powerful particles and radiation research are presented in a simple and easily understood format. Animation by Shamus Culhane (*Betty Boop, Snow White*); produced, written and directed by Frank Capra. 55 mins.
VHS: S14227. $19.98.

The Stranger in Time
Heather Kottek and Amy Seely are at the center of this wild, whimsical rollercoaster ride through time. Magically, a twist in the fabric of time throws a pioneer girl into the present-day world of an average American teenage girl named Andi. It's a funny, warm story perfect for kids and adults alike.
VHS: S25848. $19.95.

The Sun the Wind and the Rain
This is the story of two mountains. The earth made one. Elizabeth in her yellow sun hat made the other. Lisa Westbrung Peters describes the creation and evolution of mountains by comparing the centuries-long geological process to Elizabeth's sand sculptures. Ted Rand's spectacular paintings illuminate the basic concepts of the story. The result is an unusually evocative first lesson in geology.
VHS: S16355. $44.95.

Swan Lake
Music by the great Russian composer, Tchaikovsky, is featured in this animated film. Narration by Dudley Moore and a musical performance by the Moscow State Orchestra make this new version of the classic story a must for children, which will help them grow to appreciate serious music. From the *Storyteller's Classics* series, animated. 27 mins.
VHS: S26340. $9.98.

The Sweater
A heartwarming tale of mail order mix-up and the trauma of a small boy passionate for hockey. Award winning animation in a style reminiscent of the 1940's, this funny yet poignant film conveys the universal fears and joys of childhood. With the charming shorts *The Ride* and *Getting Started.* 30 mins.
VHS: S15791. $14.95.

Swiss Family Robinson
Based on the story by Johann Wyss, this is an animated adaptation of the classic story. A family shipwrecked on an island faces adventure and mystery as they try to build a new life.
VHS: S03019. $19.95.

Tail of the Tiger
The story of a boy's fascination with airplanes and his friendship with a crusty old war veteran who owns a real Tiger aircraft.
VHS: S02683. $59.95.

Tales of Beatrix Potter
These animated cartoons bring the delightful antics of Peter Rabbit across to kids. They will love his adventures in the beautiful English countryside, modeled on the illustrations of Beatrix Potter. 43 min.
VHS: S24496. $12.98.

Tales of Beatrix Potter: Vol II
This is a delightful, animated collection of stories featuring the tiny creatures of the English countryside as only Beatrix Potter can imagine them. Peter Rabbit is always up to some mischief in the garden. 46 mins.
VHS: S24497. $12.98.

Tales of Washington Irving
An animated look at one of the world's least animated men, Rip Van Winkle. The literary creation of 19th Century American author Washington Irving, that old sleepy head has his story told along with that of the Headless Horseman in *The Legend of Sleepy Hollow.* 1970, approx. 48 mins.
VHS: S03632. $19.95.

The Talking Eggs
Written by Robert San Souci and illustrated by Jerry Pinkney, this video presentation of the 1990 Caldecott Honor book tells the magical folktale of sweet Blanche, her spoiled sister and her greedy mother. Blanche's kindness is rewarded by an old witch who transports her to a miraculous world where talking eggs dramatize that the plainest of objects may conceal wondrous treasures. 1990, 21 mins. Public Performance Rights.
VHS: S13894. $65.00.

The Talking Reference Library
This introductory program employs claymation and live-action to teach children how to utilize a library's resources, including the use of encyclopedias, dictionaries, atlas and almanac. Offers valuable, easy lessons in understanding key terms, indexes, maps, graphs and cross-referencing. "[The] claymation techniques bring books to life. This series is an excellent teaching resource for all elementary/middle school learning centers and libraries" (*School Library Journal*). Designed for children in grades 4-6.
The Animated Dictionary. The dictionaries on the library shelf boldly come alive and help a student, struggling with his creative writing assignment, in the correct spelling of a word. 22 mins.
VHS: S19950. $65.95.
The Animated Atlas. A young student enchanted by the story of Amelia Earhart and her historic flight across the Atlantic Ocean visits the reference shelf, and voices from the books aid her in learning about maps and atlases. 20 mins.
VHS: S19951. $65.95.
The Animated Encyclopedia. Through claymation effects, an entire shelf of reference books assumes three-dimensional shape and life. The video helps students understand the contents of the encyclopedia. 17 mins.
VHS: S19952. $65.95.
The Animated Almanac. Claymation is used to demonstrate how almanacs are indexed and organized. 15 mins.
VHS: S19953. $65.95.
The Talking Reference Library, Set. A set of four programs on how to use reference books. 60 mins.
VHS: S19954. $229.00.

Tara the Stonecutter
When Tara is granted his wish for wealth and power, he learns that he is actually more powerful simply being himself. 8 mins.
VHS: S23505. $39.95.

Tawny Scrawny Lion's Jungle Tales
These Golden Book favorites are back, now on video. This tape includes the classics *The Saggy Baggy Elephant, The Tawny Scrawny Lion* and *Rupert the Rhinoceros.* Ages 2-5. 30 minutes.
VHS: S25002. $5.95.

Teddy Bears' Jamboree
Gary Rosen and Bill Shontz present 15 of their greatest hits live in concert. Great humor and smart songs entertain the live concert audience of kids, parents and bears. Ages 1-10. 60 minutes.
VHS: S24653. $12.98.

The Teddy Bears' Picnic
The teddy bears come alive to a party in the forest for one day each year. This time a real girl, Amanda, gets to attend. Ages 4-8. 30 minutes.
VHS: S24652. $9.95.

Telephone Tips for Kids, Volume 1
This video shows what can happen when a telephone message is mishandled. Auntie Bella and her life-sized puppet house guests are at the center of this funny story. The Telephone Doctor then shows kids how to take messages and how to dial an emergency phone number. Produced by Telephone "Doctor," ages 3 and up. 21 mins.
VHS: $25891. $9.95.

Tell Me Why:
This series of encyclopedias is based on the book and newspaper series by Arkady Leokum. Each volume presents and answers over 50 questions with colorful graphics and film footage, guaranteed to capture any child's imagination.
A Healthy Body. 30 mins.
VHS: $12807. $19.95.
Americana. 30 mins.
VHS: $12800. $19.95.
Anatomy and Genetics. 30 mins.
VHS: $12808. $19.95.
Animals and Arachnids. 30 mins.
VHS: $12804. $19.95.
Beginnings: Civilization and Gov't. 30 mins.
VHS: $12812. $19.95.
Birds and Rodents. 30 mins.
VHS: $12802. $19.95.
Tell Me Why: Customs and Superstitions.
VHS: $26309. $19.95.
Tell Me Why: Electricity and Electric Safety.
VHS: $26310. $19.95.
Fish, Shellfish and Underwater Life. 30 mins.
VHS: $12805. $19.95.
Tell Me Why: Flight.
VHS: $26307. $19.95.
Flowers, Plants and Trees. 30 mins.
VHS: $12797. $14.95.
Gems, Metals and Minerals. 30 mins.
VHS: $12798. $19.95.
Tell Me Why: Geography.
VHS: $26312. $19.95.
Tell Me Why: How Things Work.
VHS: $26308. $19.95.
Insects. 30 mins.
VHS: $12799. $19.95.
Life Forms and Animal Oddities. 30 mins.
VHS: $12801. $19.95.
Mammals. 30 mins.
VHS: $12803. $19.95.
Medicine. 30 mins.
VHS: $12809. $19.95.
Prehistoric Animals and Reptiles. 30 mins.
VHS: $12806. $19.95.
Science, Sound and Energy. 30 mins.
VHS: $12811. $19.95.
Space, Earth and Atmosphere. 30 mins.
VHS: $12795. $19.95.
Sports and Games. 30 mins.
VHS: $12810. $19.95.
Tell Me Why: Time, Money, and Measurement.
VHS: $26311. $19.95.
Water and Weather. 30 mins.
VHS: $12796. $19.95.
Tell Me Why: 24-Volume Set.
VHS: $26407. $478.80.

Ten Tall Soldiers
There is a Royal Reward to any citizen or soldier for the positive identification of the nasty and naughty monster that has been prowling the castle with the express purpose of disrupting the Royal Routine and badly scaring the Royal Personage. A witty text full of alliteration to rhyme with Hilary Knight's childlike humor and imaginative drawings.
VHS: $16356. $44.95.

The Tenth Good Thing About Barney
When Barney the cat died his family gave him a funeral in the backyard. To help her son through his grief, his mother suggests he think of ten good things about Barney. Based on the book by Judith Viorst. 13 mins.
VHS: $22368. $49.95.
Laser: LD74598. $99.95.

Thanksgiving Day by Gail Gibbons
This adaptation of Gibbons' book details the rich history, traditions and customs surrounding the celebration of Thanksgiving. Graphic illustrations and clear text are used throughout. 6 mins.
VHS: $24912. $37.95.

There Goes a Boat
Come with Captains Becky and Dave into the wonderful world of big ships in this fascinating voyage of discovery for children about tankers, freighters, passenger ships and submarines.
VHS: $23006. $10.95.

There Goes a Bulldozer
A children's video which features a live action introduction to heavy construction. Foreman Dave guides youngsters around the heavy earth-moving machinery that shapes our environment. 30 mins.
VHS: $20605. $10.95.

There Goes a Fire Truck
Fireman Dave indulges children's fascination with all the trappings of fire fighting, including fire department trucks, boats, and even helicopters. 30 mins.
VHS: $20606. $10.95.

There Goes a Helicopter
Becky and Dave take kids on an adventure to the world of whirly gigs. Helicopters can rise straight up in the air and fly at fantastic speeds. This makes choppers ideal for the military, and is vital to saving lives. Ages 3-8, 35 mins.
VHS: $24487. $12.95.

There Goes a Monster Truck
Becky and Dave take kids on the wildest ride imaginable. These monster trucks are powerful; they can even crush cars. And yet this video is completely safe. Ages 3-8, 35 mins.
VHS: $24489. $12.95.

There Goes a Motorcycle
Kids will get a front row seat along with Becky and Dave as they explore these two-wheeled motorized machines. It's all here from stunt bikes to racing. Ages 3-8, 35 mins.
VHS: $24486. $12.95.

There Goes a Police Car
Officers Becky and Dave lead children through the paces that these hard-working cars endure everyday. Kids will be thrilled to see the inside of these vehicles that serve the nation's lawmakers as they do their duty. 35 mins.
VHS: $21253. $10.95.

There Goes a Race Car
The green flag goes down and the action never stops as drivers Becky and Dave learn about race cars and the people who make them go.
VHS: $23007. $10.95.

There Goes a Spaceship
Astronauts Becky and Dave visit the Kennedy Space Center and Space Camp, experience the challenges of living in space and find out what it takes to be a NASA astronaut.
VHS: $23008. $10.95.

There Goes a Train
Engineer Dave stars in this videotape aimed at children. Kids will learn in this fun but educational tape about the ways trains work, how they travel and how they are powered, as well as the ins and outs of the job. 35 mins.
VHS: $21251. $10.95.

There Goes a Truck
Dave is joined by Becky in this jaunt aboard a large truck, capable of traveling many miles with a heavy load. These machines carry nearly everything we use. Kids will be fascinated by their power and the ingenuity of their design as well as the romance of the road. 35 mins.
VHS: $21254. $10.95.

There Goes an Airplane
Flying with Pilot Dave is fun and kids will learn things too, including how these wonders of the modern age achieve the miracle of flight. Jet fighters are among the most exciting aircraft available today. 35 mins.
VHS: $21252. $10.95.

There's a Cricket in the Library
Written by fifth-grade students of McKee School in Oakdale, Pennsylvania, this charming tale follows the adventures of a cricket caught in the library, who displays no manners or good library behavior and has to be reminded by the children of about the need to obey rules. Illustrated by Morgan Windsheimer. 4 mins.
VHS: $19601. $39.00.

There's a Witch Under the Stairs
Anyone who has ever worried about witches (or ghost or monsters or other scary creatures) will know exactly how Frances feels. She knows there's a witch under the stairs to the basement. She has tried lots of tricks to get rid of that witch but so far nothing has worked. She makes her own special witch's brew but that doesn't make the witch disappear.
VHS: $16357. $44.95.

Things That Fly Sing-Alongs
Everything from hot air balloons to hang gliders to rockets are explored by Kermit the Frog and his friends in this video. All "song barriers" are broken as Kermit and his friends sing seven delightful and original Muppet sing-alongs.
VHS: $27435. $12.99.
Brian Henson, USA, 1996, 30 mins.

Thirteen Moons on Turtle's Back
Subtitled A Native American Year of Moons, Abenaki Indian Joseph Bruchac and poet Jonathan London discuss the history of Native American legend and mythology, focused on the belief of the thirteen moons of the year. The writers contrast legends within different Native American tribes to show how the cultures identified the cycles of the moon with the seasons.
VHS: $20002. $44.95.

This Is America, Charlie Brown: The Music and Heroes of America
Schroeder shows how tunes known by nearly every kid in the country are actually related to an important event in American history. It's both fun and educational. 25 mins.
VHS: $25550. $9.95.

This Is America, Charlie Brown: The Smithsonian and the Presidency
When the Peanuts visit the Smithsonian, it inspires an imaginary visit to the life and times of Abraham Lincoln, Theodore Roosevelt and Franklin Roosevelt. 25 mins.
VHS: $25551. $9.95.

Thomas the Tank Engine & Friends
From Shining Time Station, the award-winning PBS children's show that is heralded for presenting a fascinating learning environment, filled with positive values. Very young kids everywhere have fallen in love with Thomas the Tank Engine, whose character was popularized in The Railway Series written by Rev. W. Awdry. Ages 3-7.
Trust Thomas & Other Stories. 40 mins.
VHS: $16485. $12.98.
Thomas Gets Tricked & Other Stories. 40 mins.
VHS: $16486. $12.98.
James Learns a Lesson & Other Stories. 40 mins.
VHS: $16487. $12.98.
Tenders & Turntable & Other Stories.
VHS: Out of print. For rental only.
Thomas Breaks the Rules & Other Stories.
VHS: Out of print. For rental only.
Better Late than Never & Other Stories. 40 mins.
VHS: $16490. $12.98. Perry's Ghostly Trick & Other Thomas Stories. This wonderful children's video is from the wildly successful series featuring Thomas the Tank Engine.
VHS: $21986. $12.98.
Thomas' Christmas Party & Other Favorite Stories. George Carlin is the storyteller for this special animated video. It joins eight stories featuring the charming train engine Thomas. Two are for Christmas while the other six are sturdy favorites.
VHS: $21987. $12.98.
Rusty to the Rescue. This collection of stories features Thomas the Tank Engine and assorted friends as they engage in a variety of live-action animation adventures. Perfect for kids. 37 mins.
VHS: $23966. $12.98.

The Special Letter and Other Stories. These new, animated adventures featuring the charming locomotive Thomas the Tank have never been shown on TV. Kids will love visiting the Island of Sodor to see Thomas and the gang, including Rusty, Sir Handel, Daisy and all the rest. Features a host of great songs. 37 mins.
VHS: $26212. $12.98.

Thomas the Tank Engine & Friends: Thomas & His Friends Help Out
This special hour-long collection features the best stories in which Thomas and his pals turn to help others. George Carlin tells the stories in which the pack of train friends help a group of villagers stranded in a snowstorm, Percy brings Annie and Clarabel safely through a thunderstorm, and James pulls his own when he helps out a very long train that's in trouble. From Thomas' Helping Collection.
VHS: $27309. $12.98.
David Mitton, USA, 1993, 60 mins.

Three Robbers and Other Stories
Three fierce robbers terrify the countryside until they meet a little girl named Tiffany whose charm turns their gold to good. Other films on the program are Leopold the See-Through Crumbpicker, The Island of the Skog and Fourteen Rats & A Rat-Catcher.
VHS: $01336. $14.95.

Three Sesame Street Stories
Included in this collection are three tales, starring Big Bird, Oscar the Grouch and the Cookie Monster. Ages 2-5. 30 minutes.
VHS: $24991. $5.95.

Thumpkin and the Easter Bunnies
The lovable and charismatic Bumbling Thumpkin is the centerpiece of this warmhearted and endearing family classic about the heroic quest for the original Easter egg hunt. 26 mins.
VHS: $18021. $12.98.

Thunder Cake
A loud clap of thunder booms and rattles the windows of Grandma's old farmhouse. "This is Thunder Cake baking weather," calls Grandma, as she and her granddaughter scurry around the farm gathering the necessary ingredients. A real Thunder Cake must reach the oven before the storm arrives—but the list is long, not easy to follow and the storm is coming closer every minute. From the award-winning story by Patricia Polacco.
VHS: $16358. $44.95.

Thunderbird 6
The Tracy brothers, leaders of an International Rescue team, are back and this time are faced with a plot to steal their fabulous fleet of rescue planes. 1968, 90 mins.
VHS: $16856. $19.98.

Thunderbirds Are Go
Streak through uncharted worlds of adventure with the incredible Tracy team! Earth's favorite electronic puppets launch a dangerous rescue in space. 1966, 94 mins.
VHS: $16855. $19.98.

The Tick
He is seven feet tall, blue, and he possesses powers and abilities that no ordinary mortal can match. He is The Tick, the Fox network animated superhero. Together with his sidekick Arthur he jumps into action in a valiant effort to rid the city of villains forever. This volume includes the episodes The Tick vs. The Idea Man and The Tick vs. Chairface Chippendale.
VHS: $25617. $9.98.

Tickle Tune Typhoon: Let's Be Friends
This live concert outing by the Tickle Tune Typhoon entourage features a "typhoon" of award-winning songs with messages ranging from racial tolerance to an understanding of differently abled persons; "Skin" reveals a harmony in our multiracial society; "Everyone Is Differently Abled" focuses on what people can do, not what they can't; "Pearly White Waltz" stresses the importance of brushing one's teeth. 60 mins.
VHS: $16758. $14.98.

Timmy's Special Delivery
Timmy the Angel is touched when a brother and sister make their Christmas wish—that the other will receive a gift. Ages 2-7. 30 minutes.
VHS: $25003. $12.95.

Tinka's Planet
An entertaining introduction for elementary-school children to the need for recycling. When Tinka discovers that not all trash needs to be thrown away, she begins to collect her family's cans, bottles and newspapers. On her first visit to the local recycling center she learns how recycling can help preserve the environment. Inspired to do something more for the environment, she convinces other kids in the neighborhood to join her in a recycling campaign.
VHS: $12321. $24.95.
Ben Swets/Donna Worden, USA, 1990, 12 mins.

Tiny Toon Adventures: The Best of Buster & Babs
Steven Spielberg presents two short stories. Buster Bunny asks the beautiful young woman Babs to the dance in Prom-Ish Her Anything. Babs is a contestant on an important game show in thirteensomething. 30 mins.
VHS: $18489. $12.95.

Tiny Toon Adventures: Tiny Toon Music Television
A satire about the empty, soulless exercises on MTV, as guest video jockeys Babs and Buster do a fantastic spin on "The Name Game", "Particle Man", "Nothing Compares to You" and "Yakkity-Yak". 30 mins.
VHS: $18490. $12.95.

Tiny Toon Adventures: Tiny Toons in Two-Tone Town
A spoof of two film staples, the pessimistic social comedy about 30s depression-era toonsters, Two-Tone Town, and the solemn, feel-good hit of the 80s, Fields of Honey. "If you watch it, you will love it." 30 mins.
VHS: $18491. $12.95.

Tiny Toon Big Adventures
Buster and Babs quake, rattle and roll in Journey to the Center of Acme Acres. And time-traveling Plucky must rush back to the present to finish his homework in A Ditch in Time. 42 mins.
VHS: $20493. $12.95.

Tiny Toon: Fiendishly Funny
Plucky's imagination gets the best of him in Duck in the Dark. Hampton's diet puts him cheek-to-crumb with the Little Cake of Horrors. In The Night of the Living, Pets closes in on Elmyra. And Babs and Buster get really mad at a mad scientist in Hare-Raising Night. 38 mins.
VHS: $20494. $12.95.

Tiny Toon: Island Adventures
Where will the treasure map lead? The Tiny Tooners find out in No Toon Is an Island. Next, Buster and Babs Go Hawaiian for some wicky-wacky fun. 42 mins.
VHS: $20495. $12.95.

To Bathe a Boa
A clever boa tries all kinds of evasive techniques in order to avoid a bath. Children may very well recognize someone very familiar as they read along to this fun, rhyming video. 8 mins.
VHS: $22355. $39.95.

Today Was a Terrible Day
Based on the book by Patricia Reilly Giff. On a day with one mishap after another, young Ronald finally has a reason to smile, when he discovers he can read by himself. Ages 4-8. 8 minutes.
VHS: $24655. $37.95.

Treasure Island
Robert Louis Stevenson's classic epic of the high seas will delight children in this animated version. Charming animated characters (including a talking parrot and a wisecracking cat and mouse duo) make this cartoon even more appealing to kids. From the Enchanted Tales series. USA, 1996, 48 mins.
VHS: $26914. $12.98.

Treasury of Animal Stories, Set I
Delightful video versions of Beatrix Potter's perennial classics. Includes four stories: The Tale of Peter Rabbit, The Tale of Benjamin Bunny, The Tale of Squirrel Nutkin and The Tale of Jeremy Fisher. For Grades 3-4.
VHS: $14210. $19.95.

Treasury of Children's Stories: Stories to Help Us Grow
Beginning with an alligator who learns not to be scared of the dark, this collection of three delightfully illustrated stories shows how other friendly animals deal with common problems of insecurity. 25 mins.
VHS: $10315. $29.95.

Tribal Design Grades 4-12
A multicultural program introduces tribal art from different cultures, including Africa, New Guinea, pre-Columbian Mexico, Alaska and Pacific Northwest Coast Indian. Demonstration of studio activities are also illustrated.
VHS: $09076. $249.00.

Trolls and the Christmas Express
Children will be charmed by this wonderful animated video in which mischievous trolls bring some humbug into Santa's workshop. 1981, 25 mins.
VHS: $13043. $12.95.

Truck Song
Diane Siebert celebrates trucks and truckers with rhymed verse that evokes the driving rhythm of a transcontinental truck journey. 13 mins.
VHS: $22370. $49.95.

Tubby the Tuba
Dick Van Dyke and Pearl Bailey provide the voices for this charming animated feature. It's based on the popular children's album about a tuba who performs in the Great Orchestra. He is frustrated with playing only "oompahs," so he sets off into the world and strikes it big in the circus.
VHS: $25889. $12.98.
Alexander Schure, USA, 1977, 81 mins.

'Twas the Night Before Christmas (1982)
Clement Moore's classic poem comes to charming new life in this animated film, with voices of Joel Grey, Tammy Grimes, John McGiver and George Gobel. 24 mins.
VHS: $13033. $12.95.

'Twas the Night Before Christmas (1991)
It's that old favorite Christmas poem in a wonderful, animated presentation. Ages 2-6. 27 mins.
VHS: S24944. $14.98.

Unchained Goddess
The Goddess of Weather, along with the characters of Wind, Rain and Clouds, helps explain what weather really is. Animated by Shamus Culhane, most famous for his Betty Boop, and directed by Frank Capra. From the Bell Science Collection. 54 mins.
VHS: S16333. $9.95.

The Veldt
In this Ray Bradbury story the house of a family does all the housework. It cooks, cleans, and even reads to and comforts the children. In the playroom it brings the children's fantasies to life. Soon ominous images of the African Veldt bring this sci-fi story to a traumatic conclusion. 24 mins.
VHS: S22374. $79.95.

Video Storybreak
Bob Keeshan, "Captain Kangaroo," hosts this animated series of four books that children themselves have put on the best-seller lists.
Arnold of the Ducks. A young boy, lost in the wild, is rescued and reared as their own by ducks. When he is found and returned to his human parents, they must learn to adapt to a son who goes "quack." 25 mins.
VHS: S08250. $14.98.
C.L.U.T.Z. This story is set in the very near future, when servants are robots. The Pentax family, which can't afford the latest mechanical butler, settles for an older model, a good-hearted robot whose comical imperfections earn him his name. 25 mins.
VHS: S08252. $14.98.
Chocolate Fever. When chocolate-lover Henry Green breaks out in "measles," made of pure chocolate, he learns too much of anything can make for disastrous results. 25 mins.
VHS: S08253. $14.98.
How to Eat Fried Worms. Having bet he can eat a worm a day for 15 days, Billy is in for some unusual meals. His friends try to sabotage the bet but Billy devises a clever plan that will allow him to keep his honor and still win. 25 mins.
VHS: S08251. $14.98.

The Visitor
State-of-the-art special effects and an original musical score highlight this powerful science fiction story about human greed and treachery. Based on the Ray Bradbury story. 22 mins.
VHS: S22375. $79.95.
Laser: LD74602. $99.95.

Waiting for Grandma
This claymation film features Allegra, who is so excited about Grandma's visit that she can hardly sit still. Fortunately, Allegra learns to make time fly until Grandma arrives with stories, songs and special surprises. Features the song "Holiday with Grandma." 30 mins.
VHS: S26635. $12.95.

Waldo Kitty
The adventures of a Walter Mitty Kitty, who has only to imagine himself in the role of super hero. USA, 1975, 48 mins.
VHS: S05631. $19.95.

A Walk in the Wild
Youngsters will learn about ecology and the environment through this read-along video. The illustrations are based on an actual visit to the Arkansas National Wildlife Refuge in Texas. 9:30 mins.
VHS: S22357. $39.95.

Waltzing Matilda
Animated clay animals sing this famous Australian folk song. Kangaroos, koalas, emus and many other bush inhabitants sing along. 8 mins.
VHS: S23455. $49.95.

Wanted: The Perfect Guy
A young boy concerned about his mother devises a wacky scheme to find her Mr. Right. He places a personal ad which leads to a series of Mr. Wrongs, until the right one turns up. An ABC afterschool special. 28 mins.
VHS: S23449. $49.95.

Water Is Wet
A very special children's film produced by the Erikson Institute for Early Childhood Education which was made to engage the imaginations and learning spirit of urban and rural pre-schoolers who weren't pre-disposed to "learn" in the classroom. Water Is Wet is a visual and auditory exploration of simple elements, always striving to engage the child's imagination and sense of discovery in learning more about them. The film's unique accomplishment is to do so in a fun, fast-paced way, engaging the child on his/her own level.
VHS: S03490. $39.95.
Gordon Weisenborn, USA, 1968, 65 mins.

The Way to Start a Day
Based on the book by Byrd Baylor, this animated children's film looks at how people in various countries all over the world get up in the morning. I understand kicking and screaming is quite popular in Finland. Peter Parnall is responsible for the computer graphics. Winner of the CINE 1989 Golden Eagle Award. USA, 1990, 12 mins.
VHS: S13293. $14.99.

We Learn About the World
Available in both an English and a Spanish version, this tape introduces young viewers into the world of shapes, colors, feelings, and concepts of big and little numbers.
English Version.
VHS: S06727. $29.95.
Spanish Version.
VHS: S06728. $29.95.

We're Back! A Dinosaur's Story
This is the Spielberg story of dinosaurs who escape extinction and come to New York, delighting the children who love these mammoth creatures. Voices from John Goodman, Martin Short, Julia Child, Jay Leno, and Walter Cronkite are featured in this animated film.
VHS: S20627. $24.98.
Laser: Letterboxed. LD72370. $24.98.
Steven Spielberg, USA, 1992

A Week in the Life of a Chinese Student
Young students from Beijing are the subjects of this documentary about life in the People's Republic of China. 20 mins.
VHS: S23722. $99.95.

Welcome Back Wil Cwac Cwac
Everyone's favorite little duckling is back with a waddle and a quack as Wil Cwac Cwac and his barnyard buddies share delightful lessons about love, friendship and growing up. For ages 2-5. Animated. 40 mins.
VHS: S11601. $14.95.

What Do You Want to Be When You Grow Up? Heavy Equipment Operator
Kids learn all about the big machines that go into heavy construction, including bulldozers, scrapers, excavators, backhoes and more. It's all here, from moving mountains of earth to transporting tons of steel overhead. 30 mins.
VHS: S23980. $15.95.

What Do You Want to Be When You Grow Up? Railroaders
Three kids, Allison, Armondo and Jacob, go for a train ride and learn all about engines, boxcars, flatcars, hoppers, tankers and more. They talk with engineers, brakemen, switchmen and even tie gangs. Perfect for kids fascinated with trains. 30 mins.
VHS: S23981. $15.95.

What's New Mr. Magoo
Four Mr. Magoo cartoons per volume.
Volume 1. Color, 1978, 42 mins.
VHS: S13416. $12.95.
Volume 2. Color, 1978, 42 mins.
VHS: S13417. $12.95.
Volume 3. Color, 1978, 42 mins.
VHS: S13418. $12.95.

What's Under My Bed and Other Creepy Stories
Four animated films, all of which are scary adaptations of children's books: What's under My Bed by James Stevenson, narrated by Barnard Hughes; The Three Robbers by Tomi Ungerer; Georgie, by Robert Bright; and Teeny-Tiny and the Witch-Woman, by Barbara Walker, illustrated by Michael Foreman. 35 mins.
VHS: S13332. $19.95.

Whatever Happened to Dinosaurs
Will Vinton's claymation accurately animates the past world of the mighty dinosaurs. When a young boy decides to report on these creatures for school, he goes to a museum and finds important facts and more that explain what might have happened to these prehistoric animals. 30 mins.
VHS: S23274. $9.95.

When the Wind Stops
Charlotte Zolotow's book about an inquisitive child is adapted in this charming short. Questions about wind, ocean waves, ships, airplanes and much more reveal the interconnectedness of life. 11 mins.
VHS: S23456. $49.95.

Where Did I Come From?
Based on the best-selling book, this animated film proves, among other things, that sex education is quite possibly fun. This film tells the story of conception through birth and takes the chance of laughing along with its subject. It answers questions parents may have chosen to avoid. An informative, educational tool to sex education.
VHS: S02459. $19.95.
Steve Walsh, 1985, 27 mins.

Where in the World/Kids Explore
With a pen pal and a secret clubhouse, viewers join the live-action journey to some interesting spots around the world. Using a combination of colorful graphics, animation and dance, we see real kids finding out about the culture, geography, geology, ecology and history of their destination. Ages 5-11. Each video is 30 minutes.
Where in the World Volume 1. Kids Explore Mexico. Investigate the mysteries of the Aztec and Mayan ruins, have dinner with a fun-loving Mexican family, join guitar players and flamenco dancers, see festivals, visit Mexico City, have fun!
VHS: S24945. $9.95.
Where in the World Volume 2. Kids Explore Alaska. Pan for gold, join "Gold Rush Days," race with a sled dog team, share a little Eskimo life, meet the Coastal Indians and visit a wilderness bush family.
VHS: S24946. $9.95.
Where in the World Volume 3. Kids Explore Kenya. Meet nomadic herders; unearth ancient skulls in the Great Rift Valley; find out about tribal family life; enjoy music, dance and a visit to Nairobi.
VHS: S24947. $9.95.
Where in the World Volume 4. Kids Explore America's National Parks. Explore the rain forests and seashore of Olympic; see the granite walls and giant Sequoia trees of Yosemite and look at pioneer life at Fort Vancouver. Yellowstone, Grand Canyon, Grand Teton and more—walks, wildlife, waterfalls...whew!
VHS: S24948. $9.95.

Where on Earth Is Carmen Sandiego?
Turner network's animated series features the world's greatest thief, Carmen Sandiego, and the teenage private eyes Zack and Ivy. Together these daring sleuths track Carmen across the globe, learning all about the world along the way.
Where on Earth Is Carmen Sandiego? Vol. 1. A Date with Carmen, Parts 1 and 2.
VHS: S25618. $9.98.
Where on Earth Is Carmen Sandiego? Vol. 2. By a Whisker and Dinosaur Delirium.
VHS: S25620. $9.98.
Where on Earth Is Carmen Sandiego? Vol. 3. The Good Old Bad Old Days and The Stolen Smile.
VHS: S25619. $9.98.
Where on Earth Is Carmen Sandiego? Vol. 4. Split Up and Moondreams.
VHS: S25621. $9.98.

Where the Forest Meets the Sea
Jeannie Baker's story and illustrations take the reader on an extraordinary visual journey to an exotic, primeval wilderness, which is threatened by civilization. Grades P-3.
VHS: S14199. $44.95.

Where the Lilies Bloom
Based on the Newbery Award-winning book by Vera and Bill Cleaver, Where the Lilies Bloom tells the story of four children who are left orphaned by the death of their father. Determined to stay together despite all odds, the children hide their father's death from the state and learn to fend for themselves.
VHS: S16848. $14.95.
William A. Graham, USA, 1973, 97 mins.

Where the Wild Things Are/ Higglety Pigglety Pop!
Two delightful one-act operas taped live at Glyndebourne Festival Opera are joined in this title. Both feature the stories and designs of Maurice Sendak, acclaimed children's book author. The first introduces Max the lovable monster, while the second features the adventures of Sendak's own pet terrier. 105 mins.
VHS: S22947. $29.97.
Laser: LD74645. $34.97.

Where's Spot
This is a well-regarded set of stories featuring a puppy who has entertaining adventures. Based on the books by Eric Hill, the six stories on the tape include Spot Goes Splash and Spot Finds a Key. Ages 2-4. 30 minutes.
VHS: S24657. $14.99.

Which Way, Weather?
One of the award-winning Bo Peep Productions. This video is made with the developmental needs of the youngest viewers in mind. The tape features the weather, and demonstrates ways for young children to enjoy various weather conditions. See multicultural children swimming, sailing, flying kites, ice skating, sledding, pumpkin picking, puddle stomping and more. Ages 18 months to 6 years. 30 minutes.
VHS: S24658. $19.95.

Whiffle Squeek
Ted Rand's swashbuckling illustrations have been partially animated in this iconographic video presentation of Caron Lee Cohen's story of Whiffle Squeek, the sea-sailing cat. 10 mins.
VHS: S12266. $62.00.

The Whipping Boy
In this Newbery Award-winning tale, Jemmy, an orphaned rat-catcher, and the arrogant Prince Bat exchange identities to confuse kidnappers and learn valuable lessons in compassion, loyalty and friendship. 38 mins.
VHS: S20040. $59.00.

Whistlepunks & Sliverpickers: A Fun Look at Forestry
Children will love this video field trip through the logging industry. Full of fun, games, and plenty of noise, this tape shows everything there is to know about logging and milling jobs. The scenery is breathtaking.
VHS: S25542. $19.98.
Ibex Communications, USA, 1994, 30 mins.

The White Seal
Another animated version from The Jungle Book stories, this delightful video shows the adventures of a special baby seal who prevents the slaughter of his tribe. Roddy McDowall narrates this Chuck Jones production of the Rudyard Kipling tale. 30 mins.
VHS: S03016. $14.95.

Who Will Be My Friend?
A film which helps kids deal with starting school. Molly brings her toy dinosaur to school. Conflict resolution, full of songs and stories. Ages 3-6. 25 minutes.
VHS: S24659. $9.95.

Why, Charlie Brown, Why?
When one of Charlie Brown's classmates is ill, he learns that it's in times of trouble that friends need each other most of all. This is a lesson about life for all the Peanuts kids. 25 mins.
VHS: S25547. $9.95.

The Wild Christmas Reindeer
A marvelously original Christmas story in which Santa asks Teeka to get his reindeer ready to fly on Christmas Eve. Teeka is both excited and worried because she has never worked with the reindeer before, and they've been running wild and free on the tundra. Can she catch them, and groom them? Once she finds the reindeer, Teeka's strong hand does more harm than good, and soon the reindeer are wilder than ever. How will she get them ready to pull Santa's sleigh on time?
VHS: S16359. $44.95.

Wildlife Symphony
Combines symphony music with animals at play in their native habitats. Ages 2+.
VHS: S24814. $9.95.

Will Vinton's Claymation Easter
From the creator of the California Raisins, the forms and shape of claymation are centered around Easter tales and myths. 27 mins.
VHS: S18020. $12.98.

Will We Miss Them? Endangered Species
The bald eagle, the mountain lion, the rhinoceros and the giant panda are just some of the creatures examined in this carefully illustrated read-along video. Over a dozen species are discussed. 9:30 mins.
VHS: S22356. $39.95.

Willie McBean and His Magic Machine
The claymation wizards Rankin & Bass conjure up an extraordinary world from Christopher Columbus to King Arthur, as the brilliant young kid Willie McBean travels from the Stone Age to the mythological wild West to battle his nemesis, Rasputin Von Rotten. 94 mins.
VHS: S17370. $19.95.

Wind and Water
For all ages. Bustling Hong Kong is background for this story of an aged widow and an aging missioner. He helps her find shelter and she helps him discover a deeper meaning in life. A dramatic story of person-to-person caring. Produced by Maryknoll Media. 28 mins.
VHS: S04938. $24.95.

Wind in the Willows, Volume #1
A beautiful, full-length animated version of the classic children's book with extraordinary animation and voices supplied by some of England's leading stage and film actors.
VHS: S01465. $14.95.
Mark Hall, Great Britain, 1984, 78 mins.

Wind in the Willows, Volume #2
Three animated adventures based on the popular children's story Wind in the Willows, with the characters of Badger, Mole, Ratty and the flamboyant Toad of Toad Hall.
VHS: S01466. $14.95.
Mark Hall, Great Britain, 1983, 60 mins.

Wind in the Willows, Volume #3
Three adventures featuring characters from Kenneth Grahame's stories: Great Steamer, Buried Treasure and Mole's Cousin.
VHS: S00716. $14.99.
Mark Hall, Great Britain, 60 mins.

Wind in the Willows, Volume #4
Three adventures based on Kenneth Grahame's classic: Grand Annual Show, Open Road Again and Wayfarers All. Populated by Badger, Mole, Ratty, and the Toad of Toad Hall.
VHS: S01467. $14.99.
Mark Hall, Great Britain, 1983, 60 mins.

Wings: A Tale of Two Chickens and Other Stories by James Marshall
Finally Marshall's stories appear in charming animated versions. Wings: A Tale of Two Chickens, Goldilocks and the Three Bears, The Three Little Pigs and Red Riding Hood are all included. 43 mins.
VHS: S22165. $14.95.

Winnie the Pooh
Using the original illustrations of E.H. Shepard, this video includes four stories from the classic A.A. Milne books. 60 mins.
VHS: S13206. $14.98.

Winnie the Pooh: Un-Valentine's Day
Winnie the Pooh and his pals are set on celebrating Valentine's Day by giving each other cards, but Rabbit insists they cancel the holiday. Last year too much litter was generated by these notes of affection. This video also has a version of The Three Little Piglets. 30 mins.
VHS: S27365. $14.99.

Wisdom of the Gnomes: The Gold Diggers & Mystery in the Forest
It's a quest for buried treasure in this exciting adventure starring David the Gnome and helpful animal friends. 50 mins.
VHS: S16584. $9.98.

A Wish for Wings That Work
Berkeley Breathed's (Bloom County) comic piece about Opus, the flight-obsessed penguin, and Bill, his brain-addled feline companion, who are enlisted into service when Father Christmas is unable to answer the bell. 30 mins.
VHS: S19592. $12.98.
Laser: LD71925. $24.98.

The Wish That Changed Christmas
An enchanting animated adaptation of The Story of Holly and Ivy. Ivy, a disillusioned orphan, boards a train on Christmas Eve and entertains no thoughts of happiness until she receives a mysterious message that catapults her on a magical odyssey to find the grandmother she's always longed for. Voices by Paul Winfield and Jonathan Winters. 23 mins.
VHS: S19178. $12.98.

Wishbone: Homer Sweet Homer
Wishbone imagines himself in another scenario sure to inspire kids to read. In this episode he is transported back to ancient Greece as Odysseus, the hero of Homer's The Odyssey. The goddess Calypso would ensnare Wishbone, but he thinks of his sweet Emily and somehow finds his way back home. 30 mins.
VHS: S27068. $12.95.

Wishbone: The Prince and the Pooch
Mark Twain's The Prince and the Pauper is cleverly reinterpreted for today's kids in this charming episode. While Joe merely wants to be a coach, Wishbone ends up as both the Prince of Wales and a lowly pauper in this tale of role switching and big trouble. 30 mins.
VHS: S27070. $12.95.

Wishbone: The Slobbery Hound
Wishbone is the sleuthing dog who inspires kids to read. In this episode based on Sir Arthur Conan Doyle's The Hound of the Baskervilles, Wishbone dons a cape and demeanor reminiscent of Sherlock Holmes. It's up to him to track down the mystery curse of the Baskerville family. 30 mins.
VHS: S27067. $12.95.

Wishbone: Twisted Tail
Kids will want to read Charles Dickens' *Oliver Twist* after watching Wishbone in *Twisted Tail*. Joe's house is burglarized and fingers start pointing to the new kid, Max. Meanwhile, Wishbone is trapped by a gang of colorful criminals on the streets of London. 30 mins.
VHS: $27069. $12.95.

The Witch Who Turned Pink
Spooky witches, pet werewolves, singing pumpkins and a clairvoyant owl come together to create this animated tale of Halloween. USA, 24 mins.
VHS: $15220. $14.95.

The Witch's Hat
A witch's magical brew turns out to be a mischief maker. What is the witch to do when the pot plays tricks on her? A delightful story by Tony Johnston thoughtfully illustrated by Margot Tomes.
VHS: $16360. $44.95.

The Wombles
Developed by the creators of Paddington Bear, *The Wombles* are fury creatures obsessed with the care and preservation of the environment. They live in an expansive park in London in the area around Wimbledon. These works use technology and puppet animation and vivid storytelling to convey their message of hope and inspiration.
The Wombles: Orinoco & the Ghost. 50 mins.
VHS: $17176. $14.98.
The Wombles: Sticky End. 50 mins.
VHS: $17175. $14.98.

The Wonderful Wizard of Oz
L. Frank Baum's delightful children's book has been faithfully adapted in this feature-length animated film. As a result it contains many scenes not found in the MGM musical. Narrated by Margot Kidder. 90 mins.
VHS: $24228. $19.98.

Wonders of Aladdin
Donald O'Connor is the lucky Aladdin who finds a magic lamp that contains a magic genie who must grant him three wishes. Vittoria de Sica is the genie in this children's adventure made in Europe. With Noelle Adam, Milton Reid and Terrence Hill (Mario Girotti).
VHS: $06206. $14.95.
Henry Levin, France/Italy, 1961, 93 mins.

A World Alive
Spectacular wildlife footage encourages children to appreciate the diverse lives and beauty of this planet's creatures. Narrated by James Earl Jones, this video received the National Educational Film Festival Award and includes a dramatic musical score by Kit Walker. 25 mins.
Home Video.
VHS: $13839. $14.95.
Public Performance Rights.
VHS: $17146. $34.95.

The World of Baby Animals
This two-volume set contains videos about a variety of young creatures. Every kind of animal is shown, from bobcats and kangaroos to elephant seals, bison and horned owls. Six award-winning cinematographers made it possible. 100 mins.
VHS: $25062. $29.95.

World of David the Gnome: Rabbits, Rabbits Everywhere
From the pages of Will Huygen's best-selling book, an enchanting, magical adventure with Tom Bosley as the voice of David the Gnome, the world's smallest doctor. 45 mins.
VHS: $09893. $14.95.

The Worlds Below
Sweeping sea lions...snowstorms of plankton...starfish in motion...forests as majestic as any on land. Swim with a newborn seal and slide into a wondrous journey of wave-swept rocks, vast submerged plains, and the mysterious depths of the ocean. 50 minutes, family.
Home Video.
VHS: $17135. $19.95.
Public Performance Rights.
VHS: $17147. $34.95.

Xuxa Celebration with Cheech Marin
The fun starts with a cheery tune-filled tale about a kooky school bus ride courtesy of Cheech Marin. Then Xuxa's own games begin. Watch out for the gooey Gloop. Learn how to build a monster with Xuxa or do the Xuxa Cha-cha. In addition kids will learn about the planets, the moon, hawks and owls and much more.
VHS: $20665. $14.98.

Xuxa: Fantastic Birthday Party
Xuxa is the world's most famous children's entertainer, from Brazilian television. Her kinetic energy inspires peppy song and dance numbers which will entertain everyone, especially kids. This blond dynamo will make any birthday memorable. 40 mins.
VHS: $20664. $14.98.

Yes, I Can Help
Kermit helps his nephew Robin learn all about the world and how to fit in. It all began when Kermit was a Muppet Baby. These reminiscences offer perfect, insightful lessons for preschoolers. 30 mins.
VHS: $25915. $12.99.

Yes, I Can Share
Kermit shares more memories of his Muppet Baby days with his young nephew Robin. 30 mins.
VHS: $25916. $12.99.

Yes, Virginia, There Is a Santa Claus
The Emmy Award-winning special.
VHS: $13040. $12.95.

Yonder
Using one and two-part harmony, this icononographic video presentation transforms Tony Johnston and Lloyd Bloom's narrative poem into a beautiful song. One family's history is illuminated through the planting of a plum tree. 11 mins.
VHS: $12267. $57.00.

You Can Choose
A ten-volume series.
Volume 1: Cooperation. Part of a series which imparts positive social values in a fun manner. Moose learns how to cooperate. Ages 6-11.
VHS: $24701. $59.95.
Volume 2: Being Responsible. Rhonda Bird must choose between having a good time and her responsibilities. This video reminds us that positive social values can be imparted through media. This is best when done in a fun, engaging, dramatic manner, as this video does. Ages 5-8.
VHS: $24702. $59.95.
Volume 3: Dealing with Feelings. When Tuggy Turtle tries to hide his fears about going on a weekend camp out, his friendship with Moose is almost ruined. Together they discover the importance of accepting feelings and expressing them honestly and positively.
VHS: $24703. $59.95.
Volume 4: Saying No. Missie Mouse has to choose whether to say no to a friend or do something she knows is wrong. When Missie's best friend Rhonda tries to pressure her into smoking cigarettes, Missie agonizes over her options before discovering that there are many ways to say no.
VHS: $24704. $59.95.
Volume 5: Doing the Right Thing. Two girls struggle over a money-filled wallet, which they find on the playground. A good effort at imparting good values. Ages 6-11.
VHS: $24705. $59.95.
Volume 6: Dealing with Disappointment. Missie Mouse must learn to handle disappointments in a positive way when her baseball team falls into last place.
VHS: $24706. $59.95.
Volume 7: Appreciating Yourself. Tuggy learns that being himself is better than pretending to be something he's not. When Tuggy becomes troubled by feelings of inadequacy, his friends help him to recognize and appreciate his positive inner qualities.
VHS: $24707. $59.95.
Volume 8: Asking for Help. Moose learns not to let pride or embarrassment get in the way of asking for help. After ruining a group science project, Moose finds that the only good way to cope with his secret reading problem is to get the help he needs to overcome it.
VHS: $24708. $59.95.
Volume 9: Being Friends. Rhonda, Missie and Fiona learn about the complex nature of friendship. When Missie is not invited to the "in" party, the three girls are forced to deal with differences in their relationships with each other.
VHS: $24709. $59.95.
Volume 10: Resolving Conflicts. Tuggy and Rhonda learn that there are ways to resolve disagreements without fighting. When a dispute between them puts their class art project in jeopardy, Tuggy and Rhonda learn to work out interpersonal conflicts in a peaceful and positive way.
VHS: $24710. $59.95.
Complete Set. The ten-volume set.
VHS: $24829. $549.50.

You Can Do It
Shari Lewis uses her delightful puppets, Lamb Chop, Hush Puppy and Charley Horse, to help her teach kids how to make their own puppet shows and magic tricks. USA, 1984, 60 mins.
VHS: $04441. $19.95.

You're a Good Man, Charlie Brown
Based in part on the popular stage play, this animated feature is a cartoon tribute to the man of the hour, featuring the entire Peanuts cast of characters. Together they celebrate the sometimes wishy-washy but always honest Charlie Brown. 49 mins.
VHS: $25546. $9.95.

The Z Was Zapped
Chris Van Allsburg presents a trip through the alphabet with the help of vivid verbal descriptions and three-dimensional drawings. Whimsical and sophisticated, this is an educational program that will keep children on their toes.
VHS: $14191. $44.95.

Zeezel the Zowie Zoon in the Color Chase
Kids will love following Zeezel on his imaginative, fun-filled chase to recapture his missing colors. This exciting live action short contains live singing and dancing, as well as vivid animation. Ages 1½ and up. 30 mins.
VHS: $24859. $12.98.

Zero Hour
Based on the Ray Bradbury story. Mink plays a strange game with her friends called "Invasion." At first Mink's mother discounts the precision and zeal of the children, but after a barrage of explosions the parents lock themselves in the attic. Now Mink has a surprise end for her special game. 20 mins.
VHS: $22376. $79.95.

Ziggy's Gift
Ziggy, one of the most popular children's characters, comes to home video in a stocking-stuffer price.
VHS: $01580. $19.98.

Zoobilee Zoo
This Emmy Award-winning series hosted by Ben Vereen uses stories to encourage and educate children about their own self-worth. Endorsed by the American Federation of Teachers and recommended by the National Education Association each tape contains three full episodes.
Blue Ribbon Zooble and Other Stories. Learning that honesty is its own reward or discovering that even when it's difficult, doing the right thing is worth the effort, are just some of the lessons brought up by the Blue Ribbon Zooble. Children will see that accepting friends means accepting their similarities and differences. 70 mins.
VHS: $20676. $9.95.

Land of Rhymes & Other Stories. Favorite childhood singalongs like "Old MacDonald Had a Farm," and "Three Blind Mice" can teach youngsters about rhymes. Most importantly they will learn the value of listening to friends. 70 mins.
VHS: $20672. $9.95.
Laughland and Other Stories. "The Alphabet Song", "I'm a Little Teapot" and "Twinkle Twinkle Little Star" are sung by the Zoobles, encouraging children everywhere to sing along. While these songs will entertain kids, they will also realize that sometimes its more fun to give than to receive, and it never pays to jump to conclusions. 70 mins.
VHS: $20673. $9.95.
A Sticky Situation and Other Stories. Making mistakes is a normal part of learning, a lesson easily garnered from the Zoobles when they accidentally get glued together. Children will also love Backwardville, where everything is done backwards. 70 mins.
VHS: $20675. $9.95.
Zooble Hop and Other Stories. Children will be keen to get up and dance the Zooble dance steps, but they will also understand that even those who can't dance should be treated nicely. Doing something for yourself and not having someone do it for you is another lesson found in this interactive tape.
VHS: $20674. $9.95.

FAIRY TALES

The Adventures of Peer Gynt
Based on the classic story, Peer Gynt travels through an exciting world of witches, trolls and wild animals. Green Hilda, the powerful Mountain King and Peer Gynt vividly come to life in this production designed by master puppeteer Jim Gamble. 30 mins.
VHS: $16754. $19.95.

Aesop & His Friends
A delightful cartoon film festival of family entertainment which includes most of Aesop's best-loved stories, from *The Fox and the Crow* to *The Boy Who Called Wolf*.
VHS: $03956. $64.95.

Aladdin and His Magic Lamp
An early adaptation of one of the stories from *One Thousand and One Nights*, about an impoverished boy whose possession of a magic lamp endows him with superior powers and imagination. With Patricia Medina, Richard Erdman and John Sands.
VHS: $18024. $9.95.
Lew Landers, USA, 1952, 68 mins.

Ashpet: An American Cinderella
Set in the rural South in the early years of World War II, *Ashpet* is a humorously touching version of Cinderella, the world's most popular fairy tale. From the Brothers Grimm Series. Includes Public Performance Rights.
VHS: $12251. $35.00.
Tom Davenport, USA, 1988, 45 mins.

Bearskin (Or the Man Who Didn't Wash for Seven Years)
A young man triumphs over the Devil through endurance and force of character. Based on the Grimm Brothers' fairy tale, the setting is transposed to the South just after the Civil War. All ages.
VHS: $04370. $30.00.
Tom Davenport

Bill Cosby: Aesop's Fables
Bill Cosby stars as Aesop the master storyteller in a program that combines live action and animation. Featured story is *The Tortoise and the Hare*. USA, 1986, 30 mins.
VHS: $02514. $14.95.

Brer Rabbit and the Wonderful Tar Baby
The comic adventures of that original American troublemaker, Brer Rabbit—Bugs Bunny's great grandfather—are among the funniest and most cherished stories of our culture. The classic and hilarious tale of how he outsmarts his wily nemesis, Brer Fox, with a clever contraption he calls a "tar baby", in the story read by Danny Glover.
VHS: $12475. $9.95.

Bristlelip
An American version of Grimm's "King Thrushbeard," in which a haughty young woman learns how to treat other people. Recommended for all ages. 20 minutes.
VHS: $04373. $30.00.

Cinderella
The timeless story of the cinder girl who becomes a princess comes alive in this Rankin/Bass Studio animation. 30 mins.
VHS: $03595. $11.95.

Classic Christmas Stories
A collection of children's Christmas favorites, including *Rudolph the Red-Nosed Reindeer*, *Silent Night*, *Jingle Bells* and *The Story of the Nutcracker*. Designed for children from kindergarten through 3rd grade.
Rudolph the Red-Nosed Reindeer Stories. In these holiday programs, the fabled reindeer Rudolph not only saves Christmas but helps some rabbits who are missing. 25 mins.
VHS: $19977. $34.95.
Silent Night/Jingle Bells. Two separate programs about the wonder of Christmas. *Silent Night* tells the history of a carol which was used for a Christmas service in 1854. *Jingle Bells* is an adventure set to the heart-warming music. 20 mins.
VHS: $19978. $34.95.
The Nutcracker. This program introduces children to the classic ballet. 16 mins.
VHS: $19979. $34.95.
Classic Christmas Stories, Set.
VHS: $19980. $89.00.

Dreadlocks and the Three Bears
Draws on the works of collage artists Leo Lionni, Romare Bearden and Varnette Honeywood to tell the story of Dreadlocks, who finds herself in the home of the Three Bears, in Teddy Bear Forest, while visiting her aunt. Written and illustrated by Alile Sharon Larkin.
VHS: $18327. $14.95.

Elephant's Child
From Rudyard Kipling's *Just So Stories*, the story of how the elephant got his trunk. Narrated by Jack Nicholson, music by Bobby McFerrin.
VHS: $02843. $14.95.
Mark Sottnick, USA, 1986, 30 mins.

The Emperor's New Clothes and Other Folktales
The emperor leads a parade of his loyal subjects against a background of lively jazz music; wait until you see the emperor's new clothes! Based on the famous story by Hans Christian Andersen. Also includes *Why Mosquitoes Buzz in People's Ears* and *Suho and the White Horse*. For ages 4-9. 30 mins.
VHS: $14489. $19.95.

European Folk Tales
This collection has been assembled from the work of the world's most talented animators. *European Folk Tales* will delight both children and adults. Produced by British animator John Halas.
Volume One. *The Lovelorn Giant*, *The Trumpeter* and *The Tower of Mice*. 34 mins.
VHS: $23485. $49.95.
Volume Two. *The Vixen and the Hare*, *The Lady and the Apple* and *The Unlucky Boy*. 38 mins.
VHS: $23486. $49.95.
Volume Three. *The Christmas Feast*, *The Ass and the Stick* and *The Green Mountain*. 35 mins.
VHS: $23487. $49.95.
Volume Four. *The Cinderella Barber*, *The Pear Tree* and *The Chameleon Cat*. 34 mins.
VHS: $23488. $49.95.
Volume Five. *The Princess and the Goat Boy*, *Enormous Lies* and *The Bag of Winds*. 35 mins.
VHS: $23489. $49.95.
Volume Six. *The Laughing Mirror*, *Katalina and Katalin* and *The Seven Flames*. 34 mins.
VHS: $23490. $49.95.

Fables and Fairy Tales
This collection of fables and fairy tales features stories with a moral which engage the mind with playful wit. "These fables have been teaching stories for centuries. Their simple problems and morals illustrate basic, universal values; their characters and situations have become part of our language" (*Landers Film Reviews*). Designed for children in kindergarten through 3rd grade.
Aesop's Fables. A delightful collection of animal tales, myths and legends that is humorous and entertaining. 30 mins.
VHS: $19968. $37.95.
Fairy Tale Masterpieces. A collection of stories—including *The Tortoise and the Hare*, *The Wolf in Sheep's Clothing* and *Rumpelstiltskin*—are dramatized to help children develop language and listening skills. 24 mins.
VHS: $19970. $37.95.
The Art of Storytelling: Tall Tales. The precise craft and daring rhythm of a gifted storyteller are involved through two familiar folk tales about Pecos Bill and Annie Christmas. 20 mins.
VHS: $19969. $37.95.
Fables and Fairy Tales, Set.
VHS: $19971. $99.00.

Faerie Tale Theatre
The fairy tale series produced by Shelley Duvall features well-known actors and top directors in live-action realizations of the tales. All of the tapes run 60 minutes, are closed captioned, with many in hi-fi stereo.
Beauty and the Beast.
VHS: Out of print. For rental only.
Cinderella. With Jennifer Beals, Matthew Broderick and Jean Stapleton. 1984.
VHS: $02879. $14.98.
Dancing Princesses. With Lesley Ann Warren, Peter Weller and Roy Dotrice. Directed by Peter Medak, USA, 1984, 60 mins.
VHS: $02880. $14.98.
Emperor's New Clothes.
VHS: Out of print. For rental only.
Frog Prince.
VHS: Out of print. For rental only.
Little Mermaid.
VHS: Out of print. For rental only.
Little Red Riding Hood.
VHS: Out of print. For rental only.
Pinocchio.
VHS: Out of print. For rental only.
Princess and the Pea. With Tom Conti, Liza Minnelli and Beatrice Straight. 1983.
VHS: $02890. $14.98.
Puss in Boots.
VHS: Out of print. For rental only.
Rapunzel.
VHS: Out of print. For rental only.
Sleeping Beauty.
VHS: Out of print. For rental only.
Snow Queen.
VHS: Out of print. For rental only.
Three Little Pigs. Billy Crystal, Jeff Goldblum, Valerie Perrine. 1984.
VHS: $03597. $14.98.
Thumbelina.
VHS: Out of print. For rental only.

Fairy Tale Classics
A fresh version of familiar fairy tales in full color and complete sound production to motivate reading and stimulate interest in reading as a source of pleasure for young learners.
Volume 1: The Ugly Duckling, The Shoemaker and The Elves.
VHS: $06716. $29.95.
Volume 2: Puss in Boots, The Fisherman and His Wife.
VHS: $06717. $29.95.
Volume 3: Tom Thumb, The Three Pigs.
VHS: $06718. $29.95.
Volume 4: King Midas and the Golden Touch, The Three Bears.
VHS: $06719. $29.95.
Volume 5: Snow White and Rose Red, Jack and the Beanstalk.
VHS: $06720. $29.95.
Volume 6: Little Red Riding Hood, The Happy Prince.
VHS: $06721. $29.95.
Volume 7: Paul Bunyan, The Story of Pecos Bill.
VHS: $06722. $29.95.
Volume 8: Cinderella, Peter and the Magic Goose.
VHS: $06723. $29.95.
Volume 9: Johnny Appleseed, The Golden Blackbird.
VHS: $06724. $29.95.
Volume 10: Rip Van Winkle, Old Stormalong.
VHS: $06725. $29.95.

Fairy Tales from Exotic Lands
Treasures from children's literature which reflect the ancient tradition of storytelling that is the heritage of children the world over. These tapes reveal insights into different cultures and traditions. Each tape is 30 mins.
Tales from Europe: The Ugly Duckling, The Good Woman (Norway), The Glass Ax (Hungary), The Hobyahs (England).
VHS: S06731. $29.95.
Tales from Africa (Central): Old Man and Deer, The Origin of the Animals, The Law of Mapaki, Musar and His Parents.
VHS: S06732. $29.95.
Tales from Asia: Hok Lee and the Dwarf (China), The Rajah's Son and the Princess (India), The Jellyfish and the Monkey (Japan).
VHS: S06733. $29.95.
Tales from the North American Indians: Hiawatha and the Magic Arrows, The Monster of Niagara, The Green Mouse and the Buffalo, Nanook—The Eskimo Boy.
VHS: S06734. $29.95.

Flower Storm
Two boys prevent their countries from going to war with one another in this charming Iranian folk tale. This animated short evokes the style of Persian miniatures. 9 mins.
VHS: S23506. $39.95.

The Frog King
A wonderful adaptation of the famous fairy tale about the importance of valuing others as well as the awkwardness of growing up. When a young princess breaks her promise of friendship to a frog, the frog follows her home, and is ultimately transformed into a handsome prince. Notable Children's Film, American Library Association, Blue Ribbon Winner, American Film Festival.
VHS: S04376. $30.00.
Tom Davenport, USA, 1983, 15 mins.

The Gingerbread Man
Eric Kimmel's retelling of the classic tale is brought directly to video. A fast runner is no match for a sly fox and it's a very important lesson if you are a delicious gingerbread man. 6 mins.
VHS: S24913. $37.95.

Golden Tales and Legends, Vol. 1
Delightful, live-action stories for bedtime. Includes The Fir Tree, The Great Fish of Maui and Billy Goat's Gruff. 60 mins.
VHS: S13067. $39.98.

Golden Tales and Legends, Vol. 2
More bedtime stories for children. Includes The Juggler, The Golden Apple and The Iron Mountain. 60 mins.
VHS: S13068. $24.98.

The Goose Girl
An ancient folktale about endurance and the ultimate triumph of virtue through honorable means. As the story opens, a widow sends her daughter on a journey to be married. Along the way, the daughter's maid takes advantage of the girl's vulnerability and forces her to exchange places, with the real bride forced to tend geese. Cine Golden Eagle.
VHS: S04372. $30.00.
Tom Davenport, USA, 1983, 18 mins.

Hallo Spencer Presents Robin Hood and Sleeping Beauty
The Spencerville Players, puppeteers, present rich and funny interpretations of two classic tales. 45 mins.
VHS: S19663. $9.99.

Hansel and Gretel, An Appalachian Version
A wonderful adaptation of the famous fairy tale, set in an Appalachian setting, with all the actors cast local townspeople. "With this film, [Davenport] has translated a European folk story into the American idiom, making it part of our common heritage" (Previews). Winner of the Cine Golden Eagle.
VHS: S04375. $30.00.
Tom Davenport, USA, 17 mins.

Happily Ever After
The classic legend of Snow White and the Seven Dwarfs is updated in this witty animation, using the voices of today's best-loved celebrities. Dom DeLuise, Phyllis Diller, Zsa Zsa Gabor, Edward Asner, Carol Channing and Tracey Ullman are featured.
VHS: S23028. $24.95.
Laser: LD72288. $29.95.

Happily Ever After Fairy Tales
This series of animated videos gives a new, multicultural look to classic fairy tales. Harry Belafonte, Danny Glover, Cheech Marin, Rosie Perez, Denzel Washington, B.D. Wong, the series narrator, Robert Guillaume, are featured.
Cinderella.
VHS: S25875. $9.98.
Hansel and Gretel.
VHS: S25879. $9.98.
Jack and the Beanstalk.
VHS: S25880. $9.98.
Little Red Riding Hood.
VHS: S25881. $9.98.
Rapunzel.
VHS: S25878. $9.98.
Rumpelstiltskin.
VHS: S25882. $9.98.
The Emperor's New Clothes.
VHS: S25876. $9.98.
The Frog Prince.
VHS: S25877. $9.98.

Happy Birthday Moon and Other Stories
Frank Asch's Happy Birthday Moon, about the Bear misreading the echoes of his own voice as the moon's response to his invitation, is the centerpiece of the five tales. The others are: Ezra Jack Keats' Peter's Chair, Audrey Wood's The Napping House, Eric Blegvad's retelling of Three Little Pigs, and Edward Lear's The Owl and the Pussy Cat.
VHS: S11224. $14.95.

Jack and the Dentist's Daughter
Based on Grimm's The Master Thief, and set in small-town America in the 1930's, this wonderful adaptation of the fairy tale is the comical story about a clever hero who wins his true love by using his head. Jack, a poor farmer's son, wants to marry the daughter of the town dentist, can't come up with the money, and has to resort to being a Robin Hood to win his love. Cine Golden Eagle.
VHS: S04371. $30.00.
Tom Davenport, USA, 1984, 38 mins.

Katharine Hepburn: World of Stories
Katharine Hepburn recalls her grandfather's storytelling prowess in this vivid, finely crafted collection of six short stories for young children. The stories are Jack and the Beanstalk, The Nightingale, The Musicians of Bremen, Beauty and the Beast, The Emperor's New Clothes and Tattercoats. 78 mins.
VHS: S19737. $19.95.

Light Princess
A classic story of love and hope based on George McDonald's inventive fairy tale about an evil witch who curses a Princess with total levity, as a result of which the girl can never take anything seriously. A deft mix of live action and dazzling animation highlights this wonderful BBC production.
VHS: S07180. $19.98.
Andrew Gosling, Great Britain, 1985, 56 mins.

The Little Match Girl
New Year's Eve 1999 finds homeless little Angela selling matches on the streets of Times Square in this updated adaptation of a Hans Christian Andersen story from animator Michael Sporn. Narrated by F. Murray Abraham. For ages 5 and up. 30 mins.
VHS: S13904. $14.95.

The Magic Pony
This enchanting animated tale follows a boy who catches a flying horse. Together they overcome the greedy emperor and live happily ever after with a beautiful princess. With voices by Jim Backus.
VHS: S02547. $39.95.
Ivan Ivanov-Vano, Russia, 1977, 80 mins.

The Magic Voyage of Sinbad (Sadko)
The colorful Russian fantasy is about a bearded hero from Novgorod who is on a quest to find the bird of happiness. He apparently isn't particular about the exact color. He also isn't Sinbad. A neat ploy to recruit an American audience for '61 release with anglicized cast names.
VHS: S04087. $29.95.
Alexander Ptushko, USSR, 1952

Martin the Cobbler
This claymation adaptation of Leo Tolstoy's engaging short story is narrated by his daughter, Alexandra Tolstoy. A cobbler who has lost his family is all alone and angry at God. When a holy man leaves him a bible he finds new inspiration by reading the tale of a rich merchant who invited the lord to be his guest. 27 mins.
VHS: S26615. $14.95.

The Marzipan Pig
Narrated by Tim Curry, this is the touching tale of a marzipan pig whose sweetness is enchanting. A beautiful film from animator Michael Sporn. For ages 5 and up. 30 mins.
VHS: S13905. $14.95.

Mr. Magoo's Literary Classics: Little Snow White
Our near-sighted hero stumbles through one of the greatest stories ever told. Color, 1964, 50 mins.
VHS: S13420. $12.95.

The Nutcracker
Based on the classical music tale by Peter Tchaikovsky and performed with a full symphony orchestra, this adaptation features wonderful puppet performances from Jim Gamble, master puppeteer for the Los Angeles Music Center. Watch as the Sugar Plum Fairy guides Clara through a fantasy world of Toy Soldiers, Cossack Acrobats, Arabian Dancers, Chinese Dragons and a Christmas tree that comes to life. 30 mins.
VHS: S16752. $19.95.

Nutcracker Prince
The classic E.T.A. Hoffman tale, The Nutcracker and the Mouseking, is presented in animated form and backed up the music of Peter Ilyich Tchaikovsky. Megan Follows (Anne of Green Gables) supplies the voice for young Clara, who discovers adventure and romance one magical night just before Christmas. With Keifer Sutherland as the gallant wooden prince, Phyllis Diller as the evil Mouse Queen and Peter O'Toole as a very old soldier named Pantaloon. The music is performed by the London Symphony Orchestra.
VHS: S15098. $19.98.
Paul Schibli, USA, 1990, 74 mins.

Once Upon a Brothers Grimm
An enchanted forest provides the setting when Jacob and Wilhelm Grimm meet the fairy-tale characters from their most famous stories: Hansel and Gretel, Little Red Riding Hood, Sleeping Beauty and others. With Dean Jones, Paul Sand, Teri Garr, Arte Johnson and Ruth Buzzi. 102 mins.
VHS: S16570. $39.95.

The Pied Piper/Cinderella
Wonderful British puppet animation of two classic tales. 70 mins.
VHS: S04552. $14.95.

Pinocchio
Sandy Duncan stars in this musical version of the classic tale about a puppet called Pinocchio who becomes an irrepressible little boy. Danny Kaye plays Gepetto, the wood carver. 76 mins.
VHS: S16571. $39.95.

Princess and the Swineherd
A charming adaptation of the fairy tale by Hans Christian Andersen, as the Prince sends the Princess he wants to marry precious gifts—a rose and a nightingale. But the Princess only wants things artificial, and so the Prince dons the clothing of a swineherd to be near his beloved, and charms the cool Princess. In English. Germany, 1960, 82 mins.
VHS: S07507. $29.95.

The Rabbit Ears Collection
The universal traditions of storytelling and music are charmingly celebrated in the animated programs of the Rabbit Ears We All Have Tales series. Each narrated by famous actors like Kathleen Turner and Denzel Washington, these entertaining programs showcase the folklores of peoples around the world and are set to the sounds of various musicians. Grammy and Parents' Choice awards have been given to Rabbit Ears.
A Gingerbread Christmas. Susan Saint James narrates this effervescent tale about the Prince and Princess of Gingerbread, called into action to save the town of Gloomsbury, where Christmas has been cancelled. Music by Van Dyke Parks. 30 mins.
VHS: S17773. $9.95.
Aladdin and the Magic Lamp. Distinguished British actor John Hurt displays his virtuosity as he tells this engaging story from The Tales from 1001 Arabian Nights. Mickey Hart supplies the music for this animated film.
VHS: S24048. $9.98.
Anansi. Reggae hit-makers UB40 and Oscar-winner Denzel Washington unite to recount the Jamaican tale of Anansi the spider, who outwits a prideful snake and wins all stories for himself. In the end, Anansi gets caught in his own web of lies—losing his hair in the process. 30 mins.
VHS: S14454. $9.95.
Annie Oakley. Keith Carradine reprises his prize-winning stage role of American humorist Will Rogers to narrate this spirited, wonderfully textured tale of Annie Oakley, the sharpshooter whose extraordinary skills demythologized the American West and made her the international star of Buffalo Bill's Famous Wild West Show. 30 mins.
VHS: S17025. $9.95.
Brer Rabbit and Boss Lion. Actor Danny Glover narrates this lively installment in the Rabbit Ears "American Heroes & Legends" series. When the peaceful folk of Brer Village are threatened by mean old Boss Lion, it is up to Brer Rabbit to teach the troublemaker a powerful lesson in how to properly behave. Blues legend Dr. John supplies a down-home score full of gritty Bayou blues. For ages 5 and up. USA, 1992, 30 mins.
VHS: S16811. $9.95.
David and Goliath. Branford Marsalis' jazz score finds the proper mood and tempo in Mel Gibson's retelling of the story of the preordained shepherd boy chosen to be the king of the Israelites. Illustrated by Douglas Fraser.
VHS: S18004. $12.98.
Davy Crockett. Nicholas Cage narrates the story of the legendary American woodsman, known to some as "The King of the Wild Frontier." He claimed to be half-alligator, half-snapping turtle with a touch of earthquake thrown in. This bodacious entry in the Rabbit Ears series of "American Heroes & Legends," includes the knee-slapping music of David Bromberg. For ages 5 and up. USA, 1992, 30 mins.
VHS: S16812. $9.95.
East of the Sun, West of the Moon. Internationally renowned actor Max von Sydow and award-winning composer Lyle Mays dramatically retell this Scandinavian tale of a young girl who, in order to reclaim her lost love, enlists the help of the four winds.
VHS: S14103. $9.95.
Emperor and Nightingale. Glenn Close narrates the famous Hans Christian Andersen story about the Emperor who is given a gift of a mechanical singing bird only to learn that the genuine song of the real nightingale is truly the best of all. With music by Mark Isham and illustrations by Robert Van Nutt. 40 mins.
VHS: S04904. $14.95.
Emperor's New Clothes. When two swindlers cleverly announce that the magical garments they are weaving for the Emperor are invisible to anyone lacking intelligence, who has the courage to speak the truth? Sir John Gielgud tells the Hans Christian Andersen fairytale.
VHS: S12474. $14.95.
Finn McCoul. Hero Finn McCoul and his clever wife work together to defeat a brutish giant in this modern re-telling of an Irish folk tale. Narrated by comedienne Catherine O'Hara, this animated video contains music performed by the Irish quintet Boys of the Lough. 30 mins.
VHS: S16996. $9.95.
Five Chinese Brothers. John Lone narrates this tale about five brothers. Music by Bill Douglas and David Austin.
VHS: S24047. $9.95.
Follow the Drinking Gourd. Subtitled A Story of the Underground Railroad, Morgan Freeman narrates this tale, adapted from the folksong, about one family's bid for freedom, achieved through the Underground Railroad. The gritty blues score is by Taj Mahal. 30 mins.
VHS: S17888. $9.95.
How the Leopard Got His Spots. Narrated by Danny Glover.
VHS: S09506. $14.95.
How the Rhinoceros Got His Skin and How the Camel Got His Hump. Jack Nicholson narrates, Bobby McFerrin performs and Tim Raglin draws in this animated video showing the moral sources of the rhino's skin and the camel's hump according to Rudyard Kipling's Just So Stories. 30 mins.
VHS: S04903. $14.95.
Jack and the Beanstalk. Monty Python's own Michael Palin returns this classic tale about Jack and a dimwitted ogre to its decidedly English origins as only he can. Music by Dave Stewart of the Eurythmics.
VHS: S14102. $9.95.
John Henry. Denzel Washington narrates a poetic, dreamy and mythic tale about the physically imposing, tireless nation builder who singlehandedly defeated the steam drill in a steel driving competition. Legendary blues performer B.B. King provides a gritty, textured score. 30 mins.
VHS: S17887. $9.95.
Johnny Appleseed. This cartoon is narrated by Garrison Keillor, author and radio personality. It tells the tall tale that explains how apples came to be so prevalent in the young United States. Music by Mark O'Conner.
VHS: S24040. $9.98.
Jonah and the Whale. Jason Robards recounts the fantastic and amazing tale of the man who must summon up all his creativity, will and imagination to save the people of Nineveh when he's swallowed by a whale. Illustrated by Jeffrey Smith; music by George Mgrdichian.
VHS: S18005. $12.98.
King Midas and the Golden Touch. Narrator Michael Caine adds a regal touch to the classic Greek tale of King Midas, in which a misguided monarch learns that there are some things that are more precious than gold. Music by Ellis Marsalis and Yo-Yo Ma. For ages 5 and up. 30 mins.
VHS: S14681. $9.95.

Koi and the Kola Nuts. Oscar-winner Whoopi Goldberg humorously tells this African folktale about the proud son of a chief who sets out to find his rightful place in the world. Grammy and Oscar-winning composer Herbie Hancock provides the inimitable score. 30 mins.
VHS: S16549. $9.95.
Legend of Sleepy Hollow. Glenn Close narrates Washington Irving's classic tale about timid schoolmaster Ichabod Crane and his encounter with the legendary Headless Horseman. Illustrated by Robert Van Nutt. 40 mins.
VHS: S08128. $14.95.
Mose the Fireman. Michael Keaton tells the story of this legendary fireman. His bravery was without equal. An animated short with music by John Beasley and Walter Becker. Perfect for kids.
VHS: S24039. $9.98.
The Night Before Christmas. Meryl Streep narrates this traditional retelling of the holiday classic. The program also includes some of the best loved yuletide carols sung by the Edwin Hawkins Singers, the Christ Church Cathedral Choir and the Oscar-winning Miss Streep. For ages 5 and up. USA, 1992, 30 mins.
VHS: S16813. $9.95.
Noah and the Ark. Kelly McGillis narrates the poetic and heroic tale of Noah. Illustrated by Lori Lohstoeter; music by Paul Winter Consort.
VHS: S18003. $12.98.
Paul Bunyan. Jonathan Winters reads the story that captures the spirit of early America. The hilariously exaggerated exploits of Paul's logging adventures in the northern United States represent the best in the proud tradition of American storytelling.
VHS: S12473. $14.95.
Laser: LD71820. $24.95.
Peachboy. The story of a peasant couple who discover a boy inside a giant peach; they take him in and he grows up to become a great warrior who sets off to vanquish a band of ogres. Sigourney Weaver's tender reading and Ryuichi Sakamoto's (Oscar winner—The Last Emperor) rich score combine to tell Japan's most revered children's story. For ages 4 and up. 30 mins.
VHS: S13779. $9.95.
Pecos Bill. One of the most popular tall tales of the old American Wild West—the legend of Pecos Bill, raised by coyotes from an early age until he discovered cowboys and became king of the range. Narrated by Robin Williams, with illustrations by Tim Raglin. 30 mins.
VHS: S07166. $14.95.
Pinocchio. Danny Aiello narrates this animated version of the novel written by Italian author Carlo Collodi about a lonely, frustrated toymaker named Gepeto and his astonishing creation, a wooden marionette who comes to life. Music by the Les Miserables Brass Band.
VHS: S18132. $9.95.
Princess Scargo and the Birthday Pumpkin. Geena Davis recounts this Native American myth about the selfless act of a young girl who refuses her priceless birthday gift in order to help her village. With music by Michael Hedges. 30 mins.
VHS: S18131. $9.95.
Puss in Boots. Tracey Ullman's comedic genius and veteran jazz violinist Jean Luc Ponty's spirited score animate this hilarious version of the beloved French story. 30 mins.
VHS: S15640. $9.95.
Red Riding Hood and Goldilocks. Meg Ryan reads the classic story of Little Red Riding Hood and the much-beloved tale of Goldilocks and the Three Bears.
VHS: S12472. $14.95.
Rip Van Winkle. Academy Award-winning actress Anjelica Huston tells the amusing tale of a man who somehow managed to sleep so long that he woke up in a new era. A great animated film sure to be enjoyed by everyone, kids and grown-ups alike. Jay Unger and Molly Mason provide the music.
VHS: S24042. $9.98.
Rumpelstiltskin. Kathleen Turner retells this popular Grimm's fairytale about a young woman who is forced to promise her firstborn child to a mysterious little man in return for the ability to spin straw into gold. Tangerine Dream provides the haunting musical score. In Hi-Fi Stereo. 30 mins.
VHS: S16548. $9.95.
Squanto. The very first Thanksgiving, when the pilgrims learned to share and celebrate the bounty of the New World, emerges from the past in this animated short. Graham Greene, Native American actor, narrates. Music by Paul McCandles.
VHS: S24041. $9.98.
Stormalong. John Candy relates the fantastic and hilarious adventures of the rude, brutish captain and his magnificent times on the seven seas. 30 mins.
VHS: S17774. $9.95.
Tailor of Gloucester. The poor tailor of Gloucester is worn to a ravelling, for he has no more twisted silk for his buttonholes thanks to his naughty cat Simpkin, but with the help of special friends, finds that a kind favor is returned. Narrated by Meryl Streep; illustrations by David Jorgensen. 30 mins.
VHS: S07167. $14.95.
The Boy Who Drew Cats. A touching story in which a Japanese boy, whose only talent is in drawing cats, sets out alone into a countryside haunted by a mysterious demon. Narrated by William Hurt; music by Mark Isham. For ages 5 and up. 30 mins.
VHS: S14680. $9.95.
The Bremen Town Musicians. Bob Hoskins tells the story of a group of mesmerizing musicians. Eugene Friesen supplies the music.
VHS: S24052. $9.98.
The Firebird. Hollywood great Susan Sarandon narrates this classic Eastern European folk tale about a prince, a beautiful girl and the magical firebird. Music by Mark Isham.
VHS: S24049. $9.98.
The Fisherman and His Wife. Narrated by Jodie Foster.
VHS: S09499. $14.95.
The Fool and the Flying Ship. A Russian folktale about a country man who tries to marry a Tsar's daughter is hilariously presented thanks to the comic genius of Robin Williams, who provides the voices. Music by the Klezmer Conservatory Band adds to this video's wackiness. 30 mins.
VHS: S13778. $9.95.
The Gingham Dog and the Calico Cat. The Gingham Dog and the Calico Cat are two Christmas presents who just don't get along—until Christmas Eve when they fall out of Santa's sleigh and get lost in a great forest. Narrated by Amy Grant; music by Chet Atkins. For ages 5 and up. 30 mins.
VHS: S14679. $9.95.
The Monkey People. Raul Julia brilliantly narrates this fantastical fable from the Amazon rainforest about a village of people whose extreme laziness has hilarious and devastating consequences. Music by Lee Ritenour. 30 mins.
VHS: S15641. $9.95.
The Savior Is Born. Actor Morgan Freeman gives a resonant reading of the first Christmas, from the gospels of Matthew and Luke. Beautifully illustrated by Robert Van Nutt. Music by the Christ Church Cathedral Choir of Oxford, England.
VHS: S18002. $12.98.
The Song of Sacajawea. Hollywood star Laura Dern recounts this haunting tale from the time when Native Americans and European immigrants worked together. Music by David Lindley.
VHS: S24043. $9.98.

The Tale of Jeremy Fisher and the Tale of Peter Rabbit.
Two famous English stories, animated, about the disobedient bunny Peter Rabbit and the angler frog, Mr. Jeremy Fisher. Based on Beatrix Potter's tales, with a narration by Meryl Streep, music by Lyle Mays, and illustrations by David Jorgensen. 30 mins.
VHS: S04902. $14.95.

The Talking Eggs. Sissy Spacek tells this engaging parable about mysterious talking eggs. Michael Doucet together with Beau Soleil provide the music.

The Tiger and the Brahmin. Ben Kingsley and Ravi Shankar, master of the sitar, weave a colorful retelling of this traditional Indian tale about a Brahmin who makes the deadly mistake of freeing a hungry tiger from its cage. 30 mins.
VHS: S14455. $9.95.

The White Cat. Emma Thompson, famed British actress, tells the story of a charming creature. Joe Jackson provides the music.
VHS: S24050. $9.98.

Three Little Billy Goats Gruff/The Three Little Pigs. Narrated by Holly Hunter.
VHS: S09498. $14.95.

Thumbelina. Narrated by Kelly McGillis.
VHS: S09497. $14.95.

Tom Thumb. John Cleese, the comedic actor who achieved fame in the Monty Python Show, brings his gift for humor to this tale of the wee man no bigger than his father's thumb. Elvis Costello supplies the music for this animated short.
VHS: S24046. $9.98.

Rapunzel, Rapunzel
Suspense—with a happy ending— with 19th century Shaker songs played by a flute and cello, in the American setting of Grimm's tale about Rapunzel, who lets down her hair, and is finally rescued and her sight restored by the handsome prince.
VHS: S04374. $30.00.
Tom Davenport, USA, 16 mins.

Ray Harryhausen Compilation: Five Classic Fairytales
Before perfecting the magic that appears in favorites Seventh Voyage of Sinbad and Jason and the Argonauts, Ray Harryhausen made his mark with a series of short animated subjects based on the Mother Goose nursery rhymes. Includes: Hansel and Gretel, Little Miss Muffet, The Story of King Midas, Rapunzel and Little Red Riding Hood. 60 mins.
VHS: S16264. $29.95.

Reader's Digest Children's Classics
Animated series of the best loved children's stories. Each tape is in color, 26 minutes in length.
Remarkable Rocket. David Niven narrates this Oscar Wilde story of a conceited rocket who learns a lesson in humility.
VHS: S02838. $14.95.
Little Mermaid. The Hans Christian Andersen tale about the beautiful mermaid who exchanges her voice for human form. Narrated by Richard Chamberlain.
VHS: S02840. $14.95.

Red Riding Hood
Isabella Rossellini and Craig T. Nelson star as the faithful little girl who must brave the forest and the big, bad wolf in order to bring her grandmother a basket of goodies.
VHS: S09815. $14.95.
Laser: CAV. LD70337. $99.95.
Laser: CLV. LD70338. $49.97.
Adam Brooks, USA, 1988, 84 mins.

Red Shoes
The story The Red Shoes, by Hans Christian Andersen, is a charming favorite that receives a hip and delightful updating by animator Michael Sporn with music by reggae star Jimmy Cliff. As today's story goes, Lisa and Jennie are best friends. They share everything until Lisa's parents win the lottery and the now jealous and selfish Lisa steals a pair of magical red shoes from Jennie. With the shoes on her feet, she is caught in an energetic dance which she can not stop only when she realizes that friendship is the most precious gift of all.
VHS: S12353. $9.98.
Michael Sporn, USA, 1990, 30 mins.

Rip Van Winkle
Washington Irving's haunting tale is brought to life in this claymation adaptation. It follows the story of a farmer who inadvertently manages to doze for 20 years. When he wakes, he has great difficulty explaining his absence and adjusting to another era. Narrated by Will Geer. 27 mins.
VHS: S26619. $14.95.

Rumpelstiltskin
Paul Zelinsky's Caldecott Honor book spins the magic of the Grimm Brothers fairy tale.
VHS: S08399. $29.95.

The Selfish Giant
In this animated version of Oscar Wilde's enduring fable, a lonely ogre keeps his gates locked and forbids the town children from playing in his beautiful garden. With the joyful voices of the children gone, the garden is frozen until a little boy shows the giant the rewards of sharing. 25 mins.
VHS: S02841. $12.98.

Singing Princess
A snake charmer, his beautiful sweetheart, a wicked prince and a magic genie. Winner of the Grand Prize at the International Children's Film Festival, this enchanting animated musical fantasy features the voice of Julie Andrews as the singing princess. 66 mins.
VHS: S08127. $19.99.

The Snow Queen
Gerda is a little girl who sets out to rescue a friend under the spell of the evil Snow Queen in this Hans Christian Andersen fantasy. The tale is magically told with actors, animated characters and beautiful illustrations. 54 mins.
VHS: S16150. $19.98.

The Snow Queen
Sigourney Weaver narrates this expressive adaptation of Hans Christian Andersen's moving tale about a young girl's fantastic efforts to rescue her playmate from the ice prison of the Snow Queen. Animated by a group of Russian artists whose work is on view for the first time, The Snow Queen is taken from the picture book by Susan Jeffers and Amy Ehrlich. Music by Jason Miles. 30 mins.
VHS: S17970. $12.98.

The Star Child
Oscar Wilde's childlike tale will delight children with its intriguing storyline. Two woodcutters find a small child at the site where a shooting star lands. One of them takes him home, where he raises the boy together with his wife. The result is a willful and mischievous youngster, until one day a beggar woman appears and transforms the "Star Child." This claymation adaptation is 27 mins.
VHS: S26618. $14.95.

Steadfast Tin Soldier
The Hans Christian Andersen story narrated by Jeremy Irons featuring captivating illustrations by David Jorgensen and an original score by Mark Isham.
VHS: S02845. $14.95.
Mark Sottnick, USA, 1986, 30 mins.

Story of the Dancing Frog
Renowned animator Michael Sporn directed this charming story about George, who is no ordinary frog. He is a multi-talented entertainer whose leaps and bounds bring him to fame and fortune. George and his devoted friend Gertrude set out to dance their way around the world in this adventure based on the story by Quentin Blake, narrated by Amanda Plummer.
VHS: S12003. $14.95.
Michael Sporn, USA, 1986, 30 mins.

Strega Nonna and Other Stories
Big Anthony finds himself ankles deep in trouble (and pasta) when he tries to use Strega Nonna's magic pasta pot without her permission. Blue Ribbon winner at the American Film Festival. Also includes Tikki Tikki Tembo, The Foolish Frog and A Story—A Story. Ages 4-9. 35 mins.
VHS: S14491. $14.95.

Tall Tales: Annie Oakley
Jamie Lee Curtis gives a spirited performance as "Little Sure Shot" Annie Oakley in this colorful biography of the master sharpshooter. Co-starring Brian Dennehy as Buffalo Bill and featuring actual footage of Annie filmed in 1903 by Thomas Edison. 53 mins.
VHS: S10751. $9.98.

Tall Tales: Casey at the Bat
Elliott Gould brings joy to Mudville and gives America its national pastime in this tongue-in-cheek version of Ernest Lawrence Thayer's immortal poem. With Carol Kane and Howard Cosell. 53 mins.
VHS: S10752. $9.98.

Tall Tales: Darlin' Clementine
Shelley Duvall is the darling of the gold camps in this lively version of the story behind a legendary American folk song. With Ed Asner, David Dukes, John Matuszak and Gordon Jump, narrated (and title song performed) by Randy Newman, this whimsically clever tale makes the West come alive. 49 mins.
VHS: S10749. $9.98.

Tall Tales: Johnny Appleseed
Martin Short travels the frontier as Johnny Appleseed, the American legend in a burlap sack who taught the importance of individuality, self-sufficiency and eating an apple a day. With Anne Jackson, Rob Reiner, and Molly Ringwald. 52 mins.
VHS: S10747. $9.98.

Tall Tales: Legend of Sleepy Hollow
Ed Begley Jr. is Ichabod Crane in Washington Irving's American classic about a timid teacher who encounters a headless ghost one dark Halloween night. Featuring Charles Durning, Tim Thomerson, and Beverly D'Angelo, this fun-filled tale is galloping fun. 51 mins.
VHS: S10748. $9.98.

Tall Tales: Pecos Bill
Steve Guttenberg gives Texas its unique style as Pecos Bill, the King of the cowboys, in this high-flying tall tale about one of the most colorful legends in American history. With Martin Mull, Rebecca De Mornay and Claude Akins. 50 mins.
VHS: S10750. $9.98.

Tell Me a Story: Aladdin
Three classic fairy tales, Aladdin, The Pied Piper of Hamelin and Jack and the Beanstalk, are boldly realized in this enchanting children's collection. Narrated by Jan Francis. 30 mins.
VHS: S19428. $12.98.

The Tender Tale of Cinderella Penguin
Here's a new twist on an old favorite! Academy Award nominated, this whimsical version casts Cinderella as a penguin who loses her magic flipper. A kingdom-wide search has Prince Charming uncovering the right webbed foot. With four more animated shorts: Metamorphoses, Mr. Frog Went A-Courting, The Sky Is Blue and The Owl and the Raven. 30 mins.
VHS: S15792. $14.95.

The Tin Soldier (Plummer)
A heartwarming adaptation of the Hans Christian Andersen tale about the comic adventures of two lonely mice who inadvertently place the Tin Soldier in danger and then set out to rescue him. Narrated by Christopher Plummer. 30 mins.
VHS: S08727. $9.95.

The Tin Soldier (Struthers)
Children will enjoy this engaging ballet story narrated by Sally Struthers. It's about a toy soldier given to a little boy. When the toy soldier falls in love with a beautiful paper doll ballerina, an unexpected confrontation with a jealous and evil Jack-in-the-Box sends him on a dangerous adventure. Only his love for the ballerina can help him overcome insurmountable odds. 63 mins.
VHS: S22107. $19.95.

Tom Thumb
Tom is a little boy—a very little boy. Just about the size of his father's thumb. Tom's curiosity gets him into some difficult situations—he is baked in a cake, gulped by a cow, carried away by a raven, and swallowed by a fish! Though very small, his courage and wit, along with the help of some animal friends, saves King Arthur's Court from the wrath of an angry giant. Narrated by Dom DeLuise from the storybook by Richard Jesse Watson. 30 mins.
VHS: S16484. $9.95.

Ugly Duckling (Cher)
The unforgettable fairy tale by Hans Christian Andersen narrated by Cher and illustrated by the striking paintings of Patrick Ball.
VHS: S02844. $14.95.
Mark Sottnick, USA, 1986, 30 mins.

Ugly Duckling (Children's Circle)
Three fairy tales: Hans Christian Andersen's Ugly Duckling; The Stonecutter, a Japanese fable about a stonecutter who seeks great riches; and The Swineherd, another Hans Christian Andersen classic about a princess who scorns the love of an honorable prince.
VHS: S01392. $14.98.
Gene Deitch, USA, 1986

The Velveteen Rabbit (Plummer)
Christopher Plummer narrates this charming, animated adaptation of Margery Williams' timeless story. 25 mins.
VHS: S09891. $14.95.

The Velveteen Rabbit (Streep)
Meryl Streep narrates this children's classic, first published in 1922. George Winston provides the music, David Jorgensen the illustrations.
VHS: S05108. $14.95.
Mark Sottnick, USA, 1985

The Velveteen Rabbit (Claymation)
Margery Williams wrote the well-loved tale on which this claymation short was based. A toy rabbit learns that love can transform life. After the rabbit receives lavish attention from a little boy, this toy eventually becomes real to his young friend. This tape also includes the claymation version of The Twelve Months, the Czech equivalent of the Cinderella story. 27 mins.
VHS: S26617. $14.95.

Victor Borge Tells Hans Christian Andersen Stories
Hans Christian Andersen's children's tales, including The Princess and the Pea, The Emperor's New Clothes and The Ugly Duckling, are brought to life by master storyteller Victor Borge. Illustrations by Rob Gilbert and Cecilia Laureys.
VHS: S19696. $24.95.

Wisdom of the Gnomes: Klaus the Judge & The Stolen Mirror
Dany must help Klaus the Judge solve all kinds of problems for their fellow Gnomes and animal friends in these delightful adventures. 50 mins.
VHS: S16583. $9.98.

Wonderful World of the Brothers Grimm
A top notch adaptation of fairy tales by the Brothers Grimm woven together with a depiction of the lives of the Brothers. Laurence Harvey, Claire Bloom, Oscar Homolka, Barbara Eden, Buddy Hackett and others star, and one of the highlights is the animated sequence created by George Pal in which Hackett battles a fire-breathing dragon.
VHS: S11156. $19.95.
Laser: LD70135. $39.98.
Henry Levin, USA, 1962, 129 mins.

WALT DISNEY FILMS

The Adventures of Huck Finn
Stephen Sommers wrote and directed this Disney adaptation of Mark Twain's classic novel about the shifting friendship between Huck Finn (Elijah Wood), an energetic, go-for-broke kid, and Jim (Courtney B. Vance), a runaway slave who is desperately trying to secure his freedom. With Robbie Coltrane, Jason Robards, Ron Perlman and Dana Ivey.
VHS: S19726. $96.95.
Laser: Letterboxed. LD72340. $39.99.
Stephen Sommers, USA, 1993, 108 mins.

Aladdin
A highly entertaining, Disney animated feature about the epic struggle between Aladdin, an impoverished young boy, and the cruel Jafar, both in love with the Sultan's daughter Princess Jasmine and desperate to gain control of the magic lamp. The fun is provided by Robin Williams' manic and brilliantly inventive turn as the genie inside the lamp. Academy award-winning score by Alan Menken, with prize winning songs by Tim Rice and Howard Ashman.
VHS: S18747. $24.99.
Musker/Clements, USA, 1992, 90 mins.

Aladdin & Jasmine's Moonlight Magic
Disney characters Aladdin, Jasmine and Genie find new adventures in these romantic, magic-laced cartoons. In Moonlight Madness, Aladdin entices Jasmine to join him on a date but he gets distracted by the promise of treasure. Then, in Some Enchanted Genie, Genie falls in love. 45 mins.
VHS: S27358. $12.99.

Alice in Wonderland
Disney animation based on the Lewis Carroll favorite, wonderfully entertaining! Memory of the Cheshire Cat will remain even after its smile disappears.
VHS: S05322. $26.99.
Laser: CAV. LD74998. $49.99.
Walt Disney, USA, 1951, 75 mins.

Anne of Green Gables
Canadian actress Megan Follows, Tony Award winner Coleen Dewhurst and Richard Farnsworth are featured in this award-winning epic that follows the provocative life drama of Anne Shirley, an endearing orphan, from her struggles as an adolescent to her triumphs as a young woman.
VHS: S05376. $59.95.
Kevin Sullivan, Canada, 1985, 197 mins.

Ariel's Undersea Adventures: Whale of a Tale
Two short, animated films, Whale of a Tale and Urchin, show the enchanted underwater realm first seen in The Little Mermaid. Ariel is joined by Sebastian and Flounder as well as other new, lovable characters in these cartoons. 44 mins.
VHS: S27364. $12.99.

The Aristocats
An animated comedy from Disney, this film has engaging characters, humor and a suspense-laden plot. An heiress leaves her fortune to her cat, Duchess, and her kittens. If only they were out of the way, a certain butler would be a lot wealthier. That's when Thomas O'Malley Cat, a streetwise alley cat, Roquefort, The Detective Mouse, and The Siamese Cat come to the rescue. With the voices of Eva Gabor, Phil Harris, Sterling Holloway, Scatman Crothers, Paul Winchell, Nancy Kulp and others.
VHS: S27539. $26.99.
Wolfgang Reitherman, USA, 1970, 78 mins.

The Big Green
Disney is behind this inspiring tale, featuring Olivia d'Abo and Steve Guttenberg. D'Abo is a new teacher at the local school who decides to use soccer in order to energize her students. With the help of a local sheriff (Guttenberg), the kids discover the pride and purpose of preparing for a match against a team from a neighboring town.
VHS: S27366. $19.99.
Holly Goldberg Sloan, USA, 1995, 99 mins.

Blue Yonder
Peter Coyote and Art Carney star in this tale of a boy who travels back in time in order to experience his grandfather's adventures as a pioneer aviator. A Walt Disney release.
VHS: S07767. $69.95.
Mark Rosman, USA, 1986, 89 mins.

Cartoons Go to War
Walt Disney and directors Chuck Jones and Frank Capra provided some of the diverse Hollywood talent enlisted by the United States war effort during World War II. Their amazing creations, ranging from characters like Private Snafu and Mr. Hook to the Academy Award winning Der Fuehrer's Face are joined on this video.
VHS: S27623. $19.95.
Sharon K. Baker, USA, 1995, 50 mins.

Cinderella
Walt Disney's animated classic feature based on the Charles Perrault fairy tale tells the magical tale of an abused young woman with the only foot in the kingdom to fit a certain glass slipper. With the help of her fairy godmother and a few small animals she dazzles the prince on her night off from household drudgery. With the voices of Ilene Woods, Eleanor Audley, William Phipps and Verna Felton as the magic wand waver.
VHS: S07785. $26.99.
Wilfred Jackson/Clyde Geronimi/Hamilton Luske, USA, 1950, 74 min.

Disney Animation
Your child will delight to these videos of their favorite Disney characters.
Canine Commando Starring Pluto.
VHS: S03046. $14.95.
Here's Donald!
VHS: S03033. $14.95.
Here's Goofy!
VHS: S03034. $14.95.
Here's Mickey!
VHS: S03032. $14.95.
Here's Pluto!
VHS: S03035. $14.95.
Importance of Being Donald.
VHS: S03045. $14.95.
Silly Symphonies.
VHS: S03036. $14.95.
Tale of Two Chipmunks.
VHS: S03048. $14.95.
Winnie the Pooh and a Day for Eeyore.
VHS: S03039. $14.95.
Winnie the Pooh and the Honey Tree.
VHS: S03041. $14.95.
Winnie the Pooh and the Blustery Day.
VHS: S03042. $14.95.
Winnie the Pooh and Tigger Too.
VHS: S03043. $14.95.

Disney Love Tales
The cartoons Mickey's Delayed Date, Pluto's Heart Trob and Mr. Duck Steps Out show Mickey Mouse, Pluto and Donald Duck experiencing all the joy and humor that love can bring. 25 mins.
VHS: S27361. $12.99.

The Disney Primitive Collection: Alice
Between 1925 and 1927, Disney released a series of silent shorts with the adorable character, Alice. Includes Alice in the Jungle, Alice Jailbird, Alice Orphan, Alice Rattled by Rats, Alice the Toreador, Alice's Tin Pony, Alice Solves a Puzzle, Alice Chop Suey and Alice's Eggplant. 70 mins.
VHS: S16263. $29.95.

Disney Sing-Alongs
Sing along to classic Disney tunes with these captioned clips from famous Disney cartoons.
Disney's Sing-Along.
VHS: S03038. $14.95.
Disney's Sing-Along Songs: Zip-A-Dee-Doo-Dah.
VHS: S03049. $14.95.
Disney's Sing-Along Songs: The Lion King: Circle of Life.
This collection of animated musical numbers contains songs from such mega-blockbusters as The Lion King, and the upcoming feature, Pocahontas. Kids will treasure this chance to sing songs along with their favorite Disney characters. 30 mins.
VHS: S22984. $14.95.

Disney Sweetheart Stories
Mickey and Minnie Mouse reminisce about the most cherished moments from their animated romance. Donald Duck and Pluto join in the fun. Included are *Mickey's Rival*, *In Dutch* and *Nifty Nineties*. 23 mins.
VHS: S27360. $12.99.

Disney's Beginnings
Eight early Disney efforts, some from his days in Kansas City from his first company, called Laugh-O-Grams, the remainder done in Hollywood from the series known as Alice in Cartoonland. Includes *Mechanical Cow*, *Alice Rattled by Rats* and *Great Guns*.
VHS: S00347. $24.95.
Walt Disney, USA, 1920-27, 55 mins.

Donald in Mathmagic Land
In this highly acclaimed film, a curious Donald Duck ventures into a wonderful world of fantasy, discovering that you can have fun with math, fun with fractions and laughs with logic. 27 mins.
VHS: S06593. $14.95.

Dumbo
The animated Disney classic about a baby elephant born with oversize ears. Assisted by his only friend, a mouse named Timothy, Dumbo learns to use his large ears to become the world's only flying elephant.
VHS: Out of print. For rental only.
Laser: LD70959. $49.99.
Walt Disney, USA, 1951, 63 mins.

Fantasia
The magic of Disney animation is gloriously blended with the music of eight classical pieces conducted by Leopold Stokowski. Relive those memorable moments with dancing mushrooms and hippos, dinosaurs, demons, abstract shapes, centaurs, and a certain sorcerer's apprentice who Walt felt needed a career boost.
VHS: S14755. $24.95.
Walt Disney Productions, USA, 1940, 116 mins.

Great Expectations
For the first time, Disney tackles Dickens. Bound to have family appeal, this is an award-winning adaptation of Dickens' masterpiece with a strong cast, including Jean Simmons, Anthony Hopkins and John Rhys-Davies.
VHS: S13016. $49.95.

Heavyweights
Camp Hope is place for overweight kids to get lean and mean. Disney finds in this comic situation a story that gets to the lighter side of feeling left out as a kid. The out-of-shape youngsters manage to change their hard-edged fitness guru (Ben Stiller) and even have fun at summer camp.
VHS: S27537. $14.99.
Steven Brill, USA, 1994, 97 mins.

Heidi
Johanna Spyri's beloved novel about a young girl in the Alps is beautifully realized in this Disney adaptation. Jason Robards, Jane Seymour, Patricia Neal and Noley Thornton are all featured in this new version, shot in Austria, of the children's classic.
VHS: S21867. $19.99.
Michael Rhodes, USA, 1993, 167 mins.

High-Flying Hero
Disney's heroic new adventurer—Launchpad McQuack—finds his courage put to the test in *Hero for Hire* in which the Beagle Boys trick him into performing good deeds that turn out to be crimes, and in *Launchpad's Civil War*, his participation in an annual Civil War pageant explodes into pandemonium. 44 mins.
VHS: S06596. $14.95.

The Incredible Journey
Accidentally left behind when a family moves away, three pets find themselves stranded and alone. This Disney classic charts the perilous journey faced by these animals as they make their way across the Canadian wilderness to their new home.
VHS: S21864. $19.95.
Fletcher Markle, USA, 1963, 80 mins.

The Jungle Book
Jason Scott Lee, Sam Neil, Cary Elwes and John Cleese are featured in this Disney live-action remake of Rudyard Kipling's adventure. A youngster lives in the jungle with wild animals as his best friends until the presence of civilization and his own human nature challenge this idyllic life.
VHS: S24773. $22.99.
Laser: Widescreen. LD74956. $39.99.
Stephen Sommers, USA, 1994, 111 mins.

The Lion King
Disney's animated feature tells the heart-warming tale of a young lion cub who nearly loses his birthright as king of all that he surveys. Matthew Broderick, Jeremy Irons, James Earl Jones, Robert Guillaume, Richard "Cheech" Marin and Whoopi Goldberg are some of the stars who supply the voices.
VHS: S23053. $26.99.
Laser: Letterboxed, CLV, THX. LD74930. $29.99.
Rob Minkoff/Roger Allers, USA, 1994, 88 mins.

Man of the House
In this Disney comedy, 12-year-old Ben (Jonathan Taylor Thomas) rebels when his mother (Farrah Fawcett) falls for a new man (Chevy Chase). Even though the boy was abandoned by his real father six years before, he is determined to thwart his mother's romance. Comic anarchy reigns as his plan to drive away his mother's suitor misfires.
VHS: S27536. $14.99.
James Orr, USA, 1995, 96 mins.

The Many Adventures of Winnie the Pooh
Only Walt Disney could manage so delightful a screen adaptation of the classic children's book by A.A. Milne. Pooh and his friends Christopher Robin, Tigger, Eeyore, Piglet and others are all here. This original production includes a special "making of" bonus program.
VHS: S27480. $24.99.
Laser: LD75513. $29.99.
Walt Disney, USA, 1977, 83 mins.

Mary Poppins
This beloved Disney film combines brilliant, animated sequences with a delightful story about Julie Andrews as a magical nanny who transforms the lives of the children in her care. With Dick Van Dyke, Glynis Johns, Ed Wynn.
VHS: S01589. $26.99.
Laser: LD71132. $44.99.
Robert Stevenson, USA, 1964, 140 mins.

Mickey and the Beanstalk
Mickey, Donald and Goofy are the hilarious giants destined to confront Willie the Giant in this vivid version of the timeless childhood story. 29 mins.
VHS: S06592. $14.95.

Mickey Loves Minnie
Disney's Mickey and Minnie Mouse join Donald and Daisy Duck, Pluto and Fifi for love, laughter and romance. *Society Dog Show*, *Donald's Double Trouble* and *The Brave Little Tailor* are included. 25 mins.
VHS: S27359. $12.99.

Muppet Babies: Be My Valentine
Jim Henson's award-winning Muppet Babies lead kids through lessons for making Valentines as the Muppet Babies make some Valentines themselves. Meanwhile, Baby Gonzo is playing Cupid to win Baby Piggy's heart. This animated short is both informative and fun to watch. 25 mins.
VHS: S27362. $12.99.

Pete's Dragon
Another Disney favorite that combines animation with live action, this time featuring Helen Reddy, Mickey Rooney and Red Buttons, in the heartwarming story of a lonely boy who is befriended by a klutzy dragon.
VHS: S01590. $24.99.
Don Chaffey, USA, 1977, 134 mins.

Pocahontas
Mel Gibson's voice is featured as John Smith in this Disney animated blockbuster. The story of the Native American princess who rescued and married an English colonist has long captivated North Americans. Now this story is updated to highlight some of the less savory aspects of the American conquest, although these themes are handled gently. Featuring the voices of Irene Bedard, Linda Hunt, David Ogden Stiers and the hit song "Colors of the Wind."
VHS: S26928. $26.99.
Mike Gabriel/Eric Goldberg, USA, 1995, 81 mins.

Reluctant Dragon
One of Disney's best—the story of the undragonlike dragon who'd rather sip tea and sing slaphappy songs until two pals decide to teach him the fine art of ferociousness. Also includes the bonus cartoon *Morris the Midget Moose*. 28 mins.
VHS: S03040. $14.95.

Robin Hood
Walt Disney's feature-length animated cartoon, which tells what really happened in Sherwood Forest, from the point of view of the animals. This great story includes a brilliant collection of endearing characters and songs.
VHS: S02183. $24.99.
Wolfgang Reitherman, USA, 1973, 83 mins.

Snow White and the Seven Dwarfs
Walt Disney's masterpiece tells the unforgettable story of a young woman who dreams of meeting Prince Charming but is foiled by a jealous woman. Of course she is helped in her struggle with this evil witch by those charming little people, the seven dwarfs.
VHS: S21316. $26.99.
Walt Disney, USA, 1937, 83 mins.

Squanto: A Warrior's Tale
Based on the true story of Squanto, the Native American who was kidnapped by 17th-century English settlers. Transported back to Plymouth, he escaped and found refuge in a monastery. Eventually he returned home and fostered peace between the English and his tribe, culminating in the first Thanksgiving.
VHS: S27538. $14.99.
Xavier Koller, USA, 1993, 101 mins.

Sword in the Stone
The animated version of the King Arthur legend from the studios of Walt Disney, as based on the book by Theodore H. White. "A thorough delight…the songs are bright and singable, the artwork lovely and the plot charming in its twists and turns" (Judith Crist).
VHS: S02182. $26.99.
Laser: CAV. LD74999. $49.99.
Wolfgang Reitherman, USA, 1963, 79 mins.

Three Caballeros
Donald Duck, Joe Carioca and Panchito are the title characters in this Latin American comedy travelogue that combines animation and live action. Donald goes on a fantasy filled trip to Brazil, Mexico and a special visit with Pablo the Penguin and Little Gauchito and his flying donkey. With Auroir Miranda, Carmen Molina and the voice of Clarence Nash as Donald. 70 mins.
VHS: S07527. $26.99.
Norman Ferguson, USA, 1945, 70 mins.

Tom and Huck
Disney is behind this updated film version of Mark Twain's classic novel *The Adventures of Tom Sawyer*. After witnessing a murder Tom and Huck must leave town to evade the perpetrator. Fortunately, there is a map for buried treasure in this tale, giving the boys a perfect entree to adventure.
VHS: S27640. $19.99.
Laser: LD75573. $29.99.
Peter Hewitt, USA, 1995, 91 mins.

Willie the Operatic Whale
Walt Disney's beloved animated featurette tells the tale of Willie, a singing whale who dreams of performing at the Met. Also included are the Oscar-winning *Ferdinand the Bull* and *Lambert, the Sheepish Lion*. 29 mins.
VHS: S14549. $12.99.

Wind in the Willows
J. Thaddeus Toad's mad mania for motorcars drives his dear friends Moley, Rat and MacBadger into a frenzy. Disney animation brings this Kenneth Grahame classic to life. Also included are two Disney cartoons, *Motor Mania* starring Goofy and *Trailer Horn* starring Donald Duck and Chip 'n' Dale.
VHS: S01464. $14.95.
Walt Disney, USA, 1982, 47 mins.

Winnie the Pooh: Making Friends, Learning
Three stories with Pooh, Piglet and Tigger. About "sharing, caring and growing up." Animated. Ages 1-5.
VHS: S24660. $12.99.
Disney Productions, USA, 27 mins.

WONDERWORKS FILMS

African Journey
In this fast-paced adventure, Luke, a high school student from Canada, and Themba, an African youth, forge a lasting friendship despite their vastly different cultures. With Jason Blicker, Alan Jordon, Pedzisai Sithole and Eldinah Tshatedi. 174 mins.
VHS: S15785. $79.95.

Almost Partners
Teenager Molly McCue finds herself enmeshed in New York City's biggest mystery when she joins forces with a reluctant police detective. Their unlikely partnership develops into a special friendship. With Paul Sorvino and Royana Black. 58 mins.
VHS: S14480. $29.95.

And the Children Shall Lead
In this compelling story taken from our recent history, a young black girl is profoundly moved by the coming of the civil rights movement to her sleepy Mississippi town. Starring Danny Glover, Levar Burton and Denise Nicholas. From the Rainbow Television Workshop. 60 mins.
VHS: S12404. $14.95.

The Boy Who Loved Trolls
More than anything, 12-year-old Paul wishes that all the wonderful stories he reads about trolls and mermaids and far away kingdoms could be real. Imagine his amazement when one day a loveable old troll named Ofoeti appears and transports him to a fabulous fantasy world. Starring Sam Waterston and Susan Anton. 58 mins.
VHS: S14481. $29.95.

Bridge to Terabithia
Katherine Paterson's powerful story about a poor boy and an imaginative girl who share a secret hiding place they call Terabithia. But their friendship is severed when she is accidentally killed. 33 mins.
VHS: S13235. $29.95.

Brother Future
A slick, inner-city kid from Detroit named T.J. is knocked unconscious while fleeing the police. He wakes up in 1822 Charleston, South Carolina, where he is taken captive as a slave. Before he can get home, T.J. must learn some hard lessons about life and what it takes to keep the dream of freedom alive. USA, 1991, 110 mins.
VHS: S15786. $29.95.

Caddie Woodlawn
This fanciful story is based on the Newbery Award-winning book by Carol Ryrie Brink. A high-spirited frontier girl actively opposes warlike frontiersmen who try to ambush a Native American tribe. Ages 8 and up, 120 mins.
VHS: S24275. $29.95.

The Canterville Ghost
Strange, unexplained occurrences in an old English manor are turning the Otis family's dream vacation into a nightmare. One night they meet the long-dead Sir Simon de Canterville—and discover just how cowardly a ghost can be. Starring Richard Kiley. 58 mins.
VHS: S14483. $14.95.

The Chronicles of Narnia
This video collection features the magical land of Narnia, with its mythical creatures, menacing villains and marvelous heroes. Based on the wonderful series of books by C.S. Lewis.
Prince Caspian and the Voyage of the Dawn Treader. The magical land of Narnia is ruled by the corrupt King Miraz. His nephew Prince Caspian calls on Lucy, Peter, Susan and Edmund to help him defeat Miraz and restore Narnia to its former glory. Their adventure leads them to a golden lake, a giant sea serpent, a fierce dragon, and finally the edge of the world. A WonderWorks/BBC co-production starring Richard Dempsey, Sophie Cook, and Jonathon Scott. Great Britain, 174 mins.
VHS: S14158. $29.95.
The Lion, the Witch, and the Wardrobe. In a strange castle in the English countryside, four children open the door of an old wardrobe—and find themselves transported to the magical kingdom of Narnia. The children discover that the evil White Witch has turned all of her enemies to stone, and they are the only ones capable of defeating her. A WonderWorks/ BBC co-production starring Barbara Kellerman, Richard Dempsey, and Sophie Cook. Great Britain, 174 mins.
VHS: S14157. $29.95.
The Silver Chair. In this best-selling adaptation of the C.S. Lewis classic novel, two school friends enter the land of Narnia, where they meet the lion-king Aisan, who has a special, risky request. *The Chicago Tribune* calls this BBC production "first-rate entertainment." 174 mins.
VHS: S14159. $29.95.
The Chronicles of Narnia, Complete Set. Set of three 2-tape volumes.
VHS: S19403. $79.95.

City Boy
Adapted from Gene Stratton Porter's novel *Freckles*, this children's work is about a young man who leaves Chicago and unexpectedly finds romance in the majestic forests of the Pacific Northwest. Set at the turn of the century, the film explores the relevant issues involved in the heated conflict between loggers and conservationists. With Christian Campbell, James Brolin and Christopher Bolton.
VHS: S19508. $29.95.
John Kent Harrison, Great Britain/Canada, 1993, 120 mins.

Clowning Around
14-year-old Sim has grown up in a series of foster and welfare homes. Although life was tough, his dream of becoming a world-class clown survived. Despite various odds and his new foster parents' objections, he is determined to make his dream a reality. Filmed on location in Australia and Paris, and featuring Clayton Williamson, Jean-Michel Dagory, Ernie Dingo and a special appearance by Van Johnson. 174 mins.
VHS: S16012. $29.95.

Clowning Around 2
This charming children's film continues the story of 16-year-old Sim, who isn't content to be just a traditional clown. The film is an emotional journey from Paris to Montreal and Australia, where Sim finally has the chance to own a circus and control his own destiny. With Clayton Williamson, Frederique Fouche, Jean-Michel Dagory and Ernie Dingo. 180 mins.
VHS: S19510. $29.95.

The Fig Tree
Upset by the mysterious passing of her mother, a nine-year-old girl lives unhappily with the fear of death. This live-action adaption of the Pulitzer Prize-winning short story by Katherine Anne Porter has been praised by *The New York Times* as "a memorable little gem." 58 mins.
VHS: S13524. $14.95.

Frogs!
In this whimsical sequel to the 1987 award-winning *Frog*, Gus, a would-be singer who was turned into a frog then restored to human form, once again disrupts the life of his friend Arlo. Now Arlo must deal with a wicked witch and a polluted city pond in addition to his own teenage trials and tribulations. Starring Shelley Duvall, Elliott Gould, Scott Grimes, Judith Ivey and Paul Williams. 116 mins.
VHS: S16009. $29.95.

A Girl of the Limberlost
A poetic adaptation of Gene Stratton Porter's sensitive study about a young girl's maturity in the rural countryside of the Midwest at the turn of the century. With Joanna Cassidy and Annette O'Toole. 111 mins.
VHS: S13239. $29.95.

Gryphon
With a little bit of magic, a substitute teacher in an inner-city school changes the life of a Hispanic boy. This film is based on a Charles Baxter short story with the message about "not dismissing people who care for you" (*Variety* magazine).
VHS: S13525. $14.95.

The Haunting of Barney Palmer
In this suspenseful tale of the supernatural, young Barney Palmer fears he has inherited the Scholar family curse when he is haunted by the spirit of his dead great uncle. But there is more here than meets the eye. His older sister Tabitha is guarding a shocking secret! Alexis Banas, Ned Beatty, Eleanor Gibson, Meridith Braun and Michelle Leuthart star. 58 mins.
VHS: S16014. $29.95.

Hector's Bunyip
When mistakenly placed in an orphanage, young Hector relies upon a giant imaginary best friend to return him to his family, in this PBS live-action movie. 58 mins.
VHS: S13526. $14.95.

Hiroshima Maiden
Susan Blakely and Richard Masur star in this moving drama inspired by a true story. After World War II, a group of young Japanese women called the Hiroshima Maidens were brought to live with American families while undergoing plastic surgery for scarring caused by the bomb. This is the gripping story of one such woman and the impact she has on her American family, particularly the young son. Winner of many international film and television awards. 60 mins.
VHS: S12398. $29.95.

Hoboken Chicken Controversy
When the Bobowicz family asked their son Arthur to pick up a turkey for Thanksgiving, they weren't expecting him to bring home a 266-pound live chicken named Henrietta. It's set in Hoboken, in this wild comedy from the multiple Emmy-award-winning production team. With Gabe Kaplan, Dick Van Patten and Peter Billingsley. 60 mins.
VHS: S12403. $14.95.

Home at Last
Billy, a streetwise kid from New York City, is sent to a Nebraska farm to live with a Swedish immigrant family. At first fearful and resentful, he rejects the Andersons until a crisis threatens them all, and Billy must find his inner strength to realize that he truly belongs. Based on the Orphan Trains which resettled children in the Midwest at the turn of the century. 58 mins.
VHS: S15789. $29.95.

The House of Dies Drear
The Small family discovers too late that their new home hides some dark and frightening secrets. Wait until Walter Small and his son Thomas uncover the murderous mysteries that still haunt the old house. Starring Howard Rollins, Gloria Foster and Moses Gunn. 116 mins.
VHS: S14484. $29.95.

How to Be a Perfect Person in Just Three Days
Based on Stephen Manes' hilarious book, this shrewd comedy studies the monumental fall and rise of a bright, gifted 12-year-old outsider who seeks help from the notorious Dr. K. Pinkerton. With Wallace Shawn and Ilan Mitchell-Smith.
VHS: S13236. $29.95.

Jacob Have I Loved
Based on the popular novel by Katherine Paterson. Bridget Fonda stars in this thoughtful study in sibling rivalry. Louise (Fonda) has always felt that her sister was the favored child and so sets out to find her own special place in her small world. Produced by KCET-TV. 60 mins.
VHS: S12396. $29.95.

Konrad
In this hilarious, heartwarming story, factory-made "instant child" Konrad is perfect in every way, and mistakenly delivered to the eccentric Mrs. Bartolotti. When the factory realizes its mistake, it demands Konrad's return, but his new mom has other ideas! With Max Wright, Polly Holliday, Huckleberry Fox and Ned Beatty. 116 mins.
VHS: S16010. $29.95.

The Little Princess
Based on the classic by Francis Hodgson Burnett, this is the story of Sara Crewe, the little rich girl forced into a life of poverty when her father dies penniless. Once the prize pupil at her boarding school, Sara becomes a servant for the cold-hearted school mistress and her heretofore jealous classmates. Three parts. Produced by London Weekend Television. 180 minutes total.
VHS: S12401. $29.95.

The Lone Star Kid
11-year-old Brian Zimmerman lives in Crabb, Texas—population 400. To obtain adequate police and emergency services, and to keep Houston from swallowing up the tiny burg, Brian decides to modernize his town. With the help of his parents and friends, young Brian makes history when he is elected mayor. Starring Chad Sheets, James Earl Jones and Charlie Daniels. 58 mins.
VHS: S16008. $29.95.

Maricela
A young girl struggles to find her place in American culture when her mother, who was a schoolteacher in El Salvador, must now work as a live-in housekeeper to an affluent family. Can Maricela fit in at her new home and school and still remain true to her old values? 58 mins.
VHS: S15787. $29.95.

The Mighty Pawns
An impassioned work about the efforts of an idealistic young teacher who offers valuable alternatives to inner city kids, the intricate, fascinating world of chess. Winner of the Silver Plaque at the 1987 Chicago International Film Festival. 60 mins.
VHS: S13238. $14.95.

Miracle at Moreaux
Loretta Swit stars in this compelling drama based on a true story. In World War II occupied France, a nun and her young charges risk their lives to harbor a group of Jewish children escaping from the Nazis. 60 mins.
VHS: S12402. $29.95.

My Friend Walter
While visiting the Tower of London, Bess encounters the ghost of her ancestor—Sir Walter Raleigh. Bess enlists Raleigh's help to save her family's farm. With Ronald Pickup, Prunella Scales and Polly Grant. 93 mins.
VHS: S19509. $29.95.

Necessary Parties
A fundamentally loving family is jeopardized when the parents decide to divorce. Fifteen-year-old Chris Mills is unable to accept his parents' decision and is determined to fight the divorce by legal means. He has learned in school that young people have rights too and he dares to claim those rights for himself with his six-year-old sister. With the help of an eccentric part-time lawyer/mechanic and the support of some good friends, Chris pleads to the court for the right to intervene in the divorce action as a "necessary party", thus forcing a situation that changes the course of all their lives. Alan Arkin, Barbara Dana and Adam Arkin star. 120 mins.
VHS: S12399. $29.95.

Runaway
Based on Felice Holman's novel *Slake's Limbo*, this film concerns the plight of a boy who retreats from society, living underground in the subway ducts underneath New York City's massive subway system for believing he caused the accidental death of a friend. With Charles S. Dutton, Jasmine Guy and Gavin Allen. 59 mins.
VHS: S13237. $14.95.

Spirit Rider
Adapted from Mary-Ellen Lang Collure's novel *Winners*, this quiet children's story focuses on the social dislocation experienced by Native American Jesse Threebears. Growing up in a series of foster homes, Jesse is reluctantly repatriated to the reservation where he was born. Both resisting change and struggling to fit in, Jesse travels the rocky road to forgiveness and acceptance. His journey climaxes in a thrilling horse race that will decide his future. With Herbie Barnes, Gordon Tootossis, Michelle St. John, Graham Greene and Adam Beach. 115 mins.
VHS: S19511. $29.95.

Sweet 15
Marta Delacruz is a typical American teenager who can't wait to wear makeup, date boys and be treated like an adult. In the Mexican tradition, when a girl turns 15, she is symbolically ushered into adulthood by a Mass and a party known as a Quinceanera. Samuel Delacruz (Tony Plana), Marta's hard-working, traditional father, is having a difficult time letting his little girl become a woman. But Marta is forced to grow up quickly when she accidentally discovers that her father has never become an American citizen. It is then that she realizes that becoming an adult means more than a festive Quinceanera. 120 mins.
VHS: S12400. $29.95.

Taking Care of Terrific
An imaginative teenager, her boyfriend, and a sheltered little boy team up with a street musician to plan a joyous evening for several bag ladies living in the local park. However, their well-intentioned efforts get them in trouble. Featuring Melvin Van Peebles as the street musician. 58 mins.
VHS: S15788. $29.95.

Walking on Air
Confined to a wheelchair, young Danny's greatest dream is to be able to fly. During a physical therapy class he discovers the wonderful feeling of weightlessness that swimming can bring. Taking his dream one more step, Danny fights friends, family and NASA so that he and his handicapped friends can become part of the space program. Starring Lynn Redgrave, this futuristic drama is based on a story by Ray Bradbury and won the Red Ribbon at the American Film Festival. 60 mins.
VHS: S12397. $14.95.

Waltzing Through the Hills
Andy and his little sister Sammy live in a small town in western Australia. When their mother dies, Andy fears he and Sammy might be separated. He resolves to take Sammy to their grandparents in England but in order to get to the boatyards in Perth, they must make a dangerous, secret journey through the wilds of the Australian outback. Winner of many international awards. 60 mins.
VHS: S12395. $29.95.

Words by Heart
In the early 1900's, Lena Sills and her parents are the only black people living in Bethel Springs, Missouri. When Lena wins a Bible recitation contest at school, the commandment "love thy neighbor" clashes with the townspeople's prejudice. Charlotte Rae and Robert Hooks star. 116 mins.
VHS: S14482. $29.95.

You Must Remember This
A budding basketball star discovers that her beloved great-uncle, now a barber, was one of the early great black film directors in the late '40s. She helps him to accept his past and, in the process, unearths a rich cultural legacy. Starring Robert Guillaume, Tim Reid, Vonetta McGee, Tyra Ferrell, Vonte Sweet. 90 mins.
VHS: S16011. $29.95.

FEATURE FILMS FOR KIDS

The Adventures of Matt the Gooseboy
In this heartwarming, animated feature, a simple peasant boy makes a stand against injustice and tyranny by leading the evil Lord Blackheart on a wild goose chase. It's a story packed with hilarious adventure, where good triumphs over evil. 80 mins.
VHS: S23874. $24.90.

Adventures of Milo and Otis
A live action children's adventure story about the exploits of Milo the dog and Otis the cat, narrated by Dudley Moore. Called "delightfully pure and fresh" by the *L.A. Times*. See for yourself how much mischief one canine and one feline can get into in the Land of the Rising Sun.
VHS: S11483. $19.95.
Masanori Hata, Japan/USA, 1989, 89 mins.

The Adventures of Oliver Twist
An animated version of Charles Dickens' novel about an opportunistic young boy who is trying to survive on London's mean streets. By circumstance, Oliver is forced into the evil employ of Fagin, a master thief and pickpocket who exploits children for his own gain. 91 mins.
VHS: S19429. $14.99.

Alakazam the Great!
Alakazam the monkey is the new king of the animal world. Unfortunately, he is as arrogant as he is powerful. The lessons of Merlin only make him more difficult. Only an adventurous journey with a close human friend can help this monkey learn the value of virtue. It's a perfect animated feature for kids. Featuring the voices of Frankie Avalon and Jonathan Winters.
VHS: S27074. $14.98.
Laser: LD75487. $39.99.
James H. Nicholson/Samuel Z. Arkoff, USA, 1967, 84 mins.

Alice in Wonderland
An enchanting children's version of Lewis Carroll's story is remade as a vibrant musical by the Children's Theatre Company and School, under the direction of John Clark Donahue. Music by Hiram Titus.
VHS: S18990. $39.98.
John Driver, USA, 1982, 81 mins.

The Amazing Panda Adventure
Ryan Slater, brother of Christian Slater, stars opposite one of the world's most lovable creatures, the endangered Panda. This feature-length adventure film was shot on location in the wilds of mainland China. It tells how one boy struggles to save this miraculous creature from destruction.
VHS: S26931. $19.98.
Laser: LD75405. $34.98.
Christopher Cain, USA, 1995, 85 mins.

Andre
This film is based on the book *A Seal Called Andre*, by Harry Goodridge and Lew Dietz. It tells the true story of a seal who befriends a harbor master and his family. Starring Tina Majorino, Keith Carradine and Chelsea Field.
VHS: S23435. $14.95.
Laser: Widescreen. LD75148. $34.98.
George Miller, USA, 1994, 94 mins.

Anne of Avonlea
The critically-acclaimed sequel to the award-winning *Anne of Green Gables*, with Colleen Dewhurst, Wendy Hiller and Megan Follows as Anne Shirley. "Destined to tug at hearts, young and old, for decades to come" (*San Francisco Chronicle*).
VHS: S11443. $29.95.
Laser: LD70838. $39.99.
Kevin Sullivan, Canada, 1987, 224 mins.

Anne of Green Gables
A tender and humorous coming-of-age tale starring Anne Shirley and Tom Brown.
VHS: S03256. $39.98.
Laser: LD70839. $39.99.
George Nicholls, USA, 1934, 79 mins.

Any Friend of Nicholas Nickleby Is a Friend of Mine
Humorous tale of friendship based on a story by Ray Bradbury and set in a small Illinois town. Stars Fred Gwynne.
VHS: S02671. $59.95.
Ralph Rosenblum, USA, 1981, 55 mins.

Babe
Wonderful special effects make this film a magical and captivating experience that kids and adults can both enjoy. Babe, a pig, arrives on a farm where all the animals have a purpose. Through his ambitions, he makes friends among all the animals and changes forever the utilitarian view that would have destined him for the dinner table. George Miller (*Mad Max*) co-produced this wonderful barnyard fable.
VHS: S27088. $22.98.
Laser: LD75448. $34.98.
Chris Noonan, USA, 1995, 92 mins.

Bach and Broccoli
A truly wonderful film for children—and family—from Andre Melancon, the director of *The Dog Who Stopped the War*, winner of the Best Film prize at the 1987 Chicago International Festival of Children's Films. In *Bach and Broccoli*, 11-year-old Fanny meets her uncle Jonathan for the first time. They are strong-willed, independent people who are worlds apart. Fanny's best friend, Broccoli, her pet skunk, adds to the hilarity in this humorous tale of the odd couple as they learn to love and need each other. Produced by Rock Demers.
VHS: S06616. $14.95.
Andre Melancon, Canada, 1987, 96 mins.

Baker's Hawk
Clint Walker and Burl Ives star in this family film that captures the essence of father-son relationships. Filmed in the mountains of Utah, the story is told through the eyes of a boy in the year 1876.
VHS: S00087. $39.95.
Lyman Dayton, USA, 98 mins.

Balto
Balto is a part husky and part wolf and, as a result, an outcast among canines. Fortunately, his other animal friends cherish him for his noble spirit. This side of Balto comes to the foreground when a blizzard cuts off his village and the local children desperately need medicine. This animated feature stars the voices of Kevin Bacon, Bridget Fonda, Bob Hoskins and Phil Collins.
VHS: S27430. $19.98.
Laser: LD75503. $34.98.
Simon Wells, USA, 1995, 78 mins.

Beethoven's 2nd
Charles Grodin stars in this story of dog family life. Beethoven the St. Bernard meets Missy, and the result is a houseful of puppies. Sadly Missy is the pawn in a human divorce. Debi Mazar plays the cruel kidnapper who jeopardizes this young canine family. It's a perfect film for kids.
VHS: S21865. $24.98.
Laser: Letterboxed. LD74933. $24.98.
Rod Daniel, USA, 1993, 88 mins.

Benji
America's most lovable mutt, in his first feature film. Benji saves two kids from kidnappers and wins a home and a place in everyone's heart.
VHS: S04866. $19.99.
Joe Camp, USA, 1974, 86 mins.

Benji Takes a Dive at Marineland
America's huggable hero takes on Marineland, and comes up swimming.
VHS: S06342. $19.98.
Joe Camp, USA, 60 mins.

Benji the Hunted
The canine superstar is separated from his trainer Frank Inn and must survive by his wits in a wilderness section of the Pacific Northwest. In addition to looking out for his own well being, he becomes the guardian of an orphaned litter of cougar pups and annoys a local woodsman.
VHS: S06831. $89.95.
Joe Camp, USA, 1987, 89 mins.

Benji's Very Own Christmas Story
Benji and his friends journey to a magical kingdom to meet Kris Kringle and learn how Christmas is celebrated all over the world.
VHS: S04452. $14.95.
Joe Camp, USA, 1983, 60 mins.

The Big Friendly Giant
A young orphan named Sophie is at the center of this fascinating animated adventure. Sophie and her friend the Big Friendly Giant go on a worldwide crusade to rid the world of frightening, bone-crunching giants. Based on the story by Roald Dahl.
VHS: S27481. $24.98.
Brian Cosgrove, USA, 1990, 95 mins.

Bingo
Chuckie is a little boy separated from the dog he loves when his family moves from Denver to Green Bay. Fear not, Bingo is a most resourceful pooch and should be able to catch up, if he can only escape from the pound. With Robert J. Steinmiller, David Rasche and Cindy Williams.
VHS: S15667. $14.95.
Matthew Robbins, USA, 1991, 87 mins.

Black Beauty (1933)
Esther Ralston, Alex Kirkland and Hale Hamilton star in this film adaptation of Anna Sewell's delightful novel. A young girl comes to the rescue of an injured race horse. This noble beast touches all who come to know and respect his pristine character. A delight for children and adults alike.
VHS: S22601. $19.95.
Phil Rosen, USA, 1933, 70 mins.

Black Beauty (1971)
Based on the classic novel by Anna Sewell, *Black Beauty* is the story of a friendship between Mark Lester and his horse. Outstanding family entertainment.
VHS: S00136. $14.95.
James Hill, Great Britain, 1971, 105 mins.

Black Beauty (1994)
A superb British cast, including Sean Bean, David Thewlis and Andrew Knott, is featured in this most faithful film version of Anna Sewell's delightful novel. Children have always loved this story of an indomitable black horse who personifies freedom. Everyone who came into contact with this magnificent animal was touched by his spirit.
VHS: S22412. $19.98.
Laser: LD74605. $34.98.
Caroline Thompson, USA, 1994, 88 mins.

Black Stallion Returns
A sequel to the popular *Black Stallion* in which Kelly Reno loses his horse in Morocco and only gets him back after a series of hair-raising adventures.
VHS: S12428. $19.98.
Robert Dalva, USA, 1983, 93 mins.

The Black Stallion
An exciting viewing experience for all ages, *The Black Stallion* follows the adventures of a young boy and his magnificent Arabian horse. With Teri Garr, Hoyt Axton and Mickey Rooney, presented by Francis F. Coppola.
VHS: Out of print. For rental only.
Laser: LD70527. $34.98.
Carroll Ballard, USA, 1979, 118 mins.

Born Free
This wonderful story is based on the best-selling novel about a lioness raised in captivity. On the beautiful open savannah, a game warden is forced to kill a dangerous lioness. He and his wife adopt and raise one of her cubs until they realize this young lion must adapt to the wild.
VHS: S26177. $12.95.
James Hill, USA, 1965, 94 mins.

The Borrowers
Based on the best selling classic by Mary Norton, this wonderful children's film follows the adventures of a wee family who live under the floorboards of an English house until they decide to leave for the great outdoors. Starring Ian Holm and Sian Phillips, and hosted by Richard Lewis.
VHS: S21055. $19.98.
Laser: LD74461. $49.99.
John Henderson, Great Britain, 1993, 199 mins.

Boy Named Charlie Brown
The first full length animated feature film based on the beloved characters created by Charles Schultz. With the voices of Peter Robbins, Pamelyn Ferdin, Glenn Gilger and Andy Pforsich. The original songs are by Rod McKuen and acclaimed jazz artist Vince Gauraldi.
VHS: S07813. $14.98.
Bill Melendez, USA, 1969, 85 mins.

The Brave Little Toaster
Five electrical appliances in a country cottage suddenly feel dumped when their young owner mysteriously disappears. Together they set off for the big city in search of their beloved master, their quest becoming an unforgettable journey. "A family film in the truest sense of the term: one that adults can enjoy as well as children!" (LA Times)
VHS: S14257. $19.99.
Jerry Rees, USA, 1984, 90 mins.

Camel Boy
From the creator of *Dot and the Kangaroo*, an animated adventure story about the unique friendship between Ali, an Arabian boy, and his camel during a journey across the Great Victoria Desert in Western Australia.
VHS: S02703. $69.95.
Yoram Gross, Australia, 1984, 78 mins.

Care Bears Movie
The cuddly characters in the feature-length movie that became a boxoffice sensation.
VHS: S01609. $14.98.
Arna Selznick, USA, 1984, 75 mins.

Casper
Amazing special effects render this tale of a friendly ghost more real and exciting than previous tales of good-humored haunting. Bill Pullman is a ghost therapist hired by a pair of greedy crooks, Eric Idle and Cathy Moriarty, to help rid a manor of spooks.
VHS: S26372. $22.98.
Laser: LD75078. $34.98.
Brad Silberling, USA, 1995, 101 mins.

The Challengers
After the death of her father, 11-year-old Mackie Daniels moves to a small town. Even if life has not been fair to her, she has a plan for the future, and before long she has made new friends, joined a band and become a Challenger. Everything seems fine, or is it?
VHS: S21156. $89.95.
Eric Till, USA, 1989, 97 mins.

Charlotte's Web
One of the enduring children's films, this is a story of friendship and salvation, with Charlotte the spider trying to save her friend Wilbur the pig from the bacon factory. Wonderful animation, and with the voices of Debbie Reynolds, Paul Lunde and Agnes Moorehead.
VHS: S00230. $14.95.
Charles A. Nichols, USA, 1979, 94 mins.

A Child's Christmas in Wales
A wonderful adaptation of Dylan Thomas' memories of Christmas in Wales, reliving the child's youth in one magical evening.
VHS: S07446. $9.98.
Don McBrearty, Canada, 1988, 55 mins.

Chitty Chitty Bang Bang
Dick Van Dyke is a slightly offbeat inventor in this modern fairy tale about a magical car. Charming songs, whimsical humor, wonderful special effects and enough suspense to make this a treat for the whole family.
VHS: S00236. $19.98.
Laser: Letterboxed, chapter search. Includes original theatrical trailer. LD71647. $39.98.
Ken Hughes, USA, 1968, 143 mins.

Christmas Story
Based on a novel by best-selling author Jean Shepherd, this slightly twisted tribute to the original, one-hundred-percent, red-blooded, two-fister American Christmas is set in Indiana during the 1940s and follows the adventures of Ralphie (Peter Billingsley) as he pursues the gift of his dreams. Roger Ebert called it "Norman Rockwell crossed with Mad Magazine."
VHS: S01832. $19.95.
Bob Clark, USA, 1983, 90 mins.

Clarence the Cross-Eyed Lion
Solid, old-fashioned family entertainment. This alternately comic and dramatic adventure story takes place in the jungles of Africa. Starring Betsy Drake, Richard Haydn, and Marshall Thompson.
VHS: S13642. $19.98.
Andrew Marton, USA, 1965, 98 mins.

Courage Mountain
Johanna Spyri's beloved storybook character is all grown up in this daring adventure set in World War II. Juliette Caton stars as Heidi, a lovely teenager who leads a daring escape from an orphanage across the war-torn countryside and over the Swiss Alps. Charlie Sheen co-stars as Peter, her best friend, who races against time to save her.
VHS: S14548. $14.95.
Christopher Leitch, USA, 1989, 92 mins.

Courage of Lassie
The lovable animal hero Lassie stars as a young pup who is rescued by a teenager (Elizabeth Taylor) and nursed back to health after being accidentally shot.
VHS: S16845. $19.98.
Fred M. Wilcox, USA, 1946, 93 mins.

Curly Top
Shirley Temple is the mop-topped charmer adopted by a millionaire in love with her beautiful sister. Shirley sings "Animal Crackers in My Soup."
VHS: S05899. $19.98.
Irving Cummings, USA, 1935, 74 mins.

The Deerslayer
The James Fennimore Cooper novel from his Leatherstocking Tales is presented as a family drama about two men from different cultures who rescue a Mohican princess. With Steve Forrest as Hawkeye and Ned Romero as Chingachgook.
VHS: S06866. $19.95.
Richard Friedenberg, USA, 1978, 98 mins.

A Dog of Flanders
A heartwarming children's story based on the novel by Ouida about a young child's desire to be a painter; the young boy and his grandfather find their lives changed significantly upon the arrival of a stray dog. Upon his grandfather's death, the boy calls upon the dog to help realize his potential.
VHS: S02523. $19.95.
James B. Clark, Great Britain, 1959, 96 mins.

Dot and the Bunny
Funnybunny is a floppy-eared rabbit with a silly grin whose one goal in life is to be a hopping kangaroo. In this delightful, full-length animated feature from Australia, he just about gets his wish as Dot, the young heroine, tries to find a lost baby kangaroo named Joey in order to return him to his home in Kangaroo Valley.
VHS: S00361. $29.98.
Yoram Gross, Australia, 1982, 79 mins.

Dot and the Santa Claus
A sensitive Christmas tale of a little girl who discovers the true meaning of Christmas while looking for a lost kangaroo. Feature-length animation.
VHS: S10742. $14.98.
Yoram Gross, Australia, 1979, 73 mins.

The Dragon That Wasn't (Or Was He?)
Baby dragons have their own special appeal but when they start to mature and grow larger and larger, one must consider returning them to their own special place. This is the problem facing Ollie B. Bear in this animated feature about Dexter, the growing baby dragon. Ollie must journey beyond the Misty Mountains and quickly.
VHS: S06132. $19.95.
Bjorn F. Jensen/Bob Maxfield, 1983, 96 mins.

Dreaming of Paradise
A fully animated feature film set in a future where humans have polluted the earth so much that they must now live underground. Spike and her small band of friends gain hope from the popular myth that one day man will return to a paradise of blue skies and green meadows, and their subsequent search for this Paradise is both funny and exciting. This delightful feature was winner of the Best Animated Film Award at the 1988 Chicago International Children's Film Festival.
VHS: S15007. $24.99.
J. Hastrup, USA, 1987, 75 mins.

Ele, My Friend
A heartwarming children's tale about the unbreakable bond created when a small, shy boy must summon enough strength and courage to rescue his best friend, an endangered baby elephant known as Ele.
VHS: S19917. $89.95.
Dharan Mandrayar, India, 1993, 104 mins.

Far from Home:
The Adventures of Yellow Dog
After a storm a teenage boy is washed ashore in the Pacific Northwest with only his dog. Together they make do in the wilderness even as the boy's family desperately tries to locate him. This is an entertaining, heartwarming film perfect for any age group.
VHS: S24853. $19.98.
Laser: Widescreen. LD74979. $39.99.
Phillip Borsos, USA, 1994, 81 mins.

Fearless Frida and the Secret Spies
Frida (Annette Brandt) is a curious little girl who always leads her friends into mischief. Armed with a camcorder, Frida and her friends accidentally discover truly illicit activity. Once they have the tape to prove it, these kids are under the gun to outwit the criminals. If they succeed they could become heroes. Dubbed in English.
VHS: S27166. $59.95.
Soren Ole Christensen, Denmark, 1995, 71 mins.

Felix the Cat: The Movie
One of the world's most popular cartoon characters is back to delight kids in his first feature-length movie! This thrill-a-minute fantasy displays sensational animation, outrageous adventure, and is loaded with brand-new songs.
VHS: S14531. $19.99.
Tibor Hernadi, USA, 1991, 83 mins.

Five Weeks in a Balloon
An unlikely crew sets off on a daring balloon expedition across uncharted Africa, in this lighthearted version of a Jules Verne fantasy. Starring Cedric Hardwicke, Red Buttons, Fabian, and Peter Lorre.
VHS: S04602. $19.98.
Irwin Allen, USA, 1962, 101 mins.

Flight of the Dragon
The time of King Arthur and his court is the centerpiece of this tale of a 20th century young man thrown into a time warp and locked into a battle of good and evil, knights, flying dragons and magic wizards. Animated.
VHS: S17371. $19.95.
Arthur Rankin, Jr., USA, 1982, 98 mins.

For the Love of Benji
The sequel to the original, with Benji pitted against an international espionage ring.
VHS: S04451. $19.99.
Joe Camp, USA, 1977, 85 mins.

Free Willy
Willy is a three-ton Orca whale who was captured and put on display at a Pacific Northwest aquatic park. He's befriended by a troubled 12-year-old boy (Jason James Richter), who orchestrates a daring and dangerous plan to set him free. "The most rousing family adventure since E.T." (Bob Campbell, Newhouse News).
VHS: S19727. $19.98.
Laser: LD71933. $39.98.
Simon Wincer, USA, 1993, 98 mins.

From the Mixed-Up Files
of Mrs. Basil E. Frankweiler
This light-hearted adventure starring Lauren Bacall is perfect for the whole family. Claudia is a young girl who decides to run away from home as part of her Claudia Appreciation plan. Together with her brother she takes up residence in New York's Metropolitan Museum. As the children dodge guards they become entranced by a mysterious statue. They resolve to discover something of its origins, and that's when they meet the odd and reclusive Mrs. Frankweiler, played by the legendary Lauren Bacall.
VHS: S26695. $89.95.
Laser: LD75416. $39.99.
Marcus Cole, USA, 1995, 92 mins.

Gay Purr-ee
The voice of the great Judy Garland highlights this colorful, feature-length cartoon about a country cat who finds amour—and danger—in turn-of-the-century Paris. Other celebrity voices include: Robert Goulet, Red Buttons, Hermione Gingold (Gigi) and the late Mel Blanc. Co-written by animation great Chuck Jones.
VHS: S13441. $14.95.
Laser: LD70580. $34.98.
Abe Levitow, USA, 1962, 85 mins.

George's Island
When a spineless social worker and a meddling schoolteacher show concern for a "troubled" child, ten-year-old George is forced into an evil foster home away from the eccentric grandfather he loves. The boy, his grandfather and friend Bonnie make a wild escape attempt and end up stranded on George's Island. Top prize at the 1990 Chicago International Children's Film Festival. With Sheila McCarthy, Maury Chaykin and Nathaniel Moreau.
VHS: S16040. $19.95.
Laser: LD72298. $34.95.
Paul Donovan, Canada, 1990, 90 mins.

Gold Diggers:
The Secret of Bear Mountain
Two girls, Christina Ricci and Anna Chlumsky, join forces to uncover a legendary treasure in gold. Friendship and loyalty give them the courage to brave the treacherous caverns of Bear Mountain, a locale shrouded in mystery and superstition.
VHS: S27654. $99.99.
Laser: LD75560. $39.99.
Kevin James Dobson, USA, 1995, 94 mins.

Goldy, The Last of the Golden Bears
Gold prospector Ned Rivers teaches two young orphans how to survive in the wilds of the California Sierra Mountains. Jesse is an 11-year-old tom girl and her friend Goldy is the last of the Golden Bears. This peaceable trio is interrupted when a circus steals Goldy away. But Jesse won't give up her best friend without a fight.
VHS: S20981. $14.98.
John Quinn/Trevor Black, USA, 1984, 91 mins.

Goldy II: Saga of the Golden Bear
Once again Jesse, a young girl who dreams of becoming a cowboy, and her friend, the last Golden Bear, find their friendship endangered by interfering adults. This time Jesse turns to the whole gamut of circus animals to save Goldy from a lifetime of confinement.
VHS: S20982. $14.98.
Trevor Black, USA, 1986, 92 mins.

Goldy III
This is a tender story about the friendship that develops between a young girl and a bear. A sly magician played by Cheech Marin wants to buy Goldy the bear, but Jesse rescues the animal and runs away with him. While hiding in the forest she meets Freedom (Mr. T), who has mysterious powers. This adventure is a wonderful story for kids and parents alike. 104 mins.
VHS: S22128. $92.98.
Laser: LD75202. $34.98.

The Great Land of Small
A magical family film, set in a maple forest. Only the wise fool Mimmick can see the entrance of Fritz, the hobbit-like creature from the enchanted Land of Small. So begins the magical tale of two youngsters old enough to explore but still young enough to dream. Smart, capable Jenny, 12, and the mischievous David, 7, are about to be treated to the most harrowing, mystical and wonderful adventures imaginable.
VHS: S05311. $14.95.
Vojtech Jasny, Canada, 1987, 94 mins.

Gulliver's Travels
Max Fleischer's evocation of Jonathan Swift's classic fantasy of the sailor Gulliver, shipwrecked on the shores of Lilliput, is one of the high achievements of Hollywood animation. The Lilliputians are only thumb-high, but they're as cantankerous and perhaps more determined than humans. A delight.
VHS: S18185. $19.95.
Max Fleischer, USA, 1939, 71 mins.

Gumby the Movie
Gumby, the popular children's toy from the 1960's, is back in a claymation, feature-length film. He has his own band and his own dog. The dog is important because when he hears the band perform he cries tears that turn into pearls. As a result Gumby's dog is kidnapped and the entire gang is propelled into a series of zany adventures.
VHS: S26692. $19.95.
Art Clokey, USA, 1990

Gypsy Colt
An inspirational story about a spirited horse. After the parents of a girl are forced to sell the horse to a racing stable, the horse escapes and travels 500 miles to be reunited with her. With Donna Corcoran, Ward Bond, Frances Dee and Larry Keating.
VHS: S19035. $19.98.
Andrew Marton, USA, 1954, 72 mins.

Heidi (1937)
A family classic that should be part of every childhood, featuring curly-haired Shirley Temple as the orphaned girl who goes to live with her grandfather on a Swiss mountaintop.
VHS: S00560. $19.98.
Allan Dwan, USA, 1937, 88 mins.

Heidi (1953)
Winner of the Grand Prize at the Venice Film Festival, this adaptation of the Johanna Spyri book was especially made for a children's audience. With Elsbeth Sigmund as Heidi. English version.
VHS: S03790. $29.95.
Luigi Comencini, Switzerland, 1953, 98 mins.

Hideaways
Based on the popular Newbery Award-winning book From the Mixed-Up Files of Mrs. Basil E. Frankweiler. The legendary Ingrid Bergman headlines this wondrous tale of two children who run away to a secret hideout brimming with intrigue and excitement: New York's Metropolitan Museum of Art. Also starring Richard Mulligan and Madeline Kahn.
VHS: S02715. $19.98.
Fiedler Cook, USA, 1973, 105 mins.

The Indian in the Cupboard
A young boy experiences a series of unexpected adventures when one of his toys, an Indian figure, miraculously comes alive. There is also a diminutive cowboy action figure that shares the toe. Together they experience conflicts and humorous situations in a plot that is sure to delight kids.
VHS: S26661. $22.95.
Frank Oz, USA, 1995, 97 mins.

Iron Will
This feature film is based on a true-life story about a young man and his team of sled dogs. Together they race across the snow-covered fields of the frozen North to secure a $10,000 prize that can save the family farm. It's a Disney classic.
VHS: S21105. $96.98.
Charles Haid, USA, 1993, 105 mins.

Island of the Blue Dolphins
Based on Scott O'Dell's award-winning children's classic, the heart-warming adventure of a 19th century Indian girl who becomes stranded on a remote island off the California coast.
VHS: S05331. $59.95.
James B. Clark, USA, 1964, 99 mins.

Island of the Lost
Anthropologist Richard Greene gets shipwrecked on an uncharted South Sea isle with Luke Halpin (Flipper) and Robin Mattson (Santa Barbara).
VHS: S04261. $19.95.
J. Florea/R. Browning, USA, 1968, 92 mins.

Jack Frost
This live-action film showcases the folktales of Russian poet Alexander Pushkin, whose stories have been compared to Cinderella and The Ugly Duckling. The myths and folklores recorded in the 17th century by the poet are regarded as the beginnings of modern Russian literature.
VHS: S03594. $19.95.
Aleksandr Rov, USSR, 1965, 81 mins.

Jack the Giant Killer
Dazzling special effects and adventures transform the original Jack and the Beanstalk legend into an exciting film with Jack the farmer saving the beautiful Princess from numerous monsters.
VHS: S13644. $14.95.
Laser: LD72138. $34.98.
Nathan Juran, USA, 1961, 94 mins.

Josh Kirby...Time Warrior!
Journey to the Magic Cavern
In this adventure, Josh Kirby travels underground to the lair of the Mushroom People. There he must confront the powers of the mind-melding metalhead, Dr. Zoetrope. He must succeed and rescue the lovely Princess Azabeth. With Corbin Allred, Jennifer Burns, Derek Webster and Matt Winston.
VHS: S27419. $89.95.
Ernest Farino, USA, 1995, 93 mins.

Journey Through Fairyland
Brilliant animation accompanied by original music as well as orchestral masterpieces such as Flight of the Bumblebees and The Nutcracker. This is intended as an introduction to classical music for both children and adults. Full-length animated feature. 95 mins.
VHS: S09168. $19.98.

Jumanji
Robin Williams stars as man who was unwittingly trapped inside a mysterious board game. Two modern-day kids inadvertently activate the game and bring both him and a host of computer generated safari animals out of a world of fantasy and into the everyday world of their small-town home. With Kirsten Dunst, Bonnie Hunt, David Alan Grier and Bebe Neuwirth.
VHS: S27652. $19.98.
Laser: LD75559. $39.99.
Joe Johnston, USA, 1995, 104 mins.

A Kid in King Arthur's Court
Thomas Ian Nicholas plays 14-year-old Calvin Fuller, a bright, typical Little Leaguer. When an earthquake rumbles his California hometown, he is magically transported to 12th-century Camelot and the Court of King Arthur. Before long, he is fighting the good fight against the villainous Lord Belasco.
VHS: S27367. $19.98.
Michael Gottlieb, USA, 1995, 90 mins.

Kidnapped
David Balfour is the orphan who sets out to find his only living relative, Ebenezer Balfour, but his scheming uncle has stolen his inheritance and arranged to have his young nephew kidnapped and sold into slavery. 49 mins.
VHS: S03020. $19.95.

Land Before Time
An animated feature directed by Don Bluth (An American Tail) about cute and cuddly baby dinosaurs. Presented by George Lucas and Steven Spielberg, five young dinos take a perilous journey to find their parents and a legendary valley with lots of food. A tiny brontosaurus named Little Foot is the hero. A cranky tyrannosaurus is the relentless villain.
VHS: S09598. $19.95.
Laser: CAV. LD74945. $49.98.
Don Bluth, USA, 1988, 70 mins.

Land of Faraway
(Mio in the Land of Faraway)
Based on the story by Swedish author Astrid Lindgren (Pippi Longstocking), this is an adventure tale about young boy with an important mission to perform. He must battle the evil knight Kato for control of the land of Faraway. With Timothy Bottoms, Christopher Lee, Susannah York, Christian Bale and Nicholas Pickard as Mio. Available only in EP mode.
VHS: S07973. $9.99.
Vladimir Grammatikov, Norway/Sweden/USSR, 1987, 95 mins.

Lantern Hill
Colleen Dewhurst won an ACE award in this story of Jane Stewart, a young girl who has been sent to live with her wealthy grandmother after her mother is stricken with polio. Cut off from her former friends and enrolled in a private school, Jane has a great deal of trouble adjusting. But she is soon distracted from these everyday trials when she finds out that her missing father (Sam Waterston) is still alive. Based on the book by Lucy Maude Montgomery.
VHS: S13546. $29.95.
Kevin Sullivan, USA, 1990, 112 mins.

Lassie
The canine hero of all times is back in this full-length adventure film. When the Turner family moves to Virginia, they encounter a number of problems, both financial and domestic. Fortunately the relationship between a boy and his dog can weather even the most insurmountable troubles.
VHS: S22889. $95.95.
Daniel Petrie, USA, 1994, 95 mins.

Lassie Come Home
The first and the best of the Lassie films: the story of a poor family that's forced to sell its dog, but she makes a remarkable journey to return to them. One of the all-time great tearjerkers, with Roddy McDowall, Elizabeth Taylor, Donald Crisp.
VHS: S12429. $19.98.
Fred M. Wilcox, USA, 1943, 88 mins.

The Last Unicorn
This animated tale features the voices of Alan Arkin, Tammy Grimes and Angela Lansbury as the Last Unicorn searches for her roots and the secret of all the unicorns.
VHS: S04605. $14.98.
Jules Bass, USA, 1982, 95 mins.

Leapin' Leprechauns
An American hopes to build a theme park at a beautiful location in Ireland. Unfortunately, there is a group of leprechauns whom he must displace. The tiny creatures fight back, using all their mischievous powers to thwart his greedy plans. This antic film is a great family comedy, chock full of magical humor.
VHS: S25739. $92.95.
Ted Nicolaou, USA, 1995, 84 mins.

Legend of Sea Wolf
Adaptation of the Jack London tale starring Chuck Connors as Captain Wol Larson, with Barbara Bach and Joseph Palmer.
VHS: S02701. $24.95.
Joseph Green, USA, 92 mins.

Legend of the White Horse

Jim Martin is a geologist with the unfortunate habit of standing up for his principles. Now it's gotten him fired—again. Eager for work, he accepts a surveying job in a distant country, and sets off with his young son. Arriving in the remote land, they move into the mountain home of a reputed witch and her beautiful, blind ward, Jewel (Allison Balson). But there is another inhabitant in the wild mountain wilderness—a magical white horse.
VHS: S15068. $59.98.
Domaradzki/Morgenstern, USA, 1985, 91 mins.

The Lion, The Witch and the Wardrobe

An adaptation of C.S. Lewis' *The Chronicles of Narnia*, about four children hurled from a strange wardrobe closet into an expressive land of mythical creatures and talking animals. Winner of the Emmy for Best Animated Special. 95 mins.
VHS: S19158. $12.98.

Little Lord Fauntleroy

Alec Guiness and Ricky Schroder star in this adventure of a poor boy taken from the squalor of a New York slum to the splendor of aristocratic England.
Jack Gold, USA, 1980, 98 mins.
VHS: S00760. $19.95.

The Little Princess

Young Sara Crewe has the perfect life with her father in fabled India. All that ends with the onset of war. Sara is sent to a New York boarding school, where she clashes with a strict headmistress. Somehow she overcomes the hardships of this fate and manages to change both her own life and the fortunes of those around her.
VHS: S26210. $24.94.
Laser: LD75041. $34.98.
Alfonso Cuaron, USA, 1995, 97 mins.

Long John Silver

Robert Newton (Disney's *Treasure Island*) once again stars as the swashbuckling pirate in this delightful color film based on the Robert Louis Stevenson children's classic. In this film, Long John Silver seeks hidden treasure, rescues the governor's daughter and battles his arch-enemy on Treasure Island. Featuring Rod Taylor as Israel Hand.
VHS: S27335. $19.95.
Byron Haskin, Australia, 1954, 106 mins.

Looking for Miracles

Based on the novel by A.E. Hotchner. A coming-of-age tale, set in Depression-era Canada, about two long-separated brothers with almost nothing in common who renew their relationship over the course of one long summer.
VHS: S13547. $29.95.
Kevin Sullivan, Canada, 1989, 90 mins.

Man and Boy

A family film which stars Bill Cosby as a Civil War veteran who, together with his son, takes off after the thief who stole their horse. With Gloria Foster, Leif Erickson.
VHS: S21486. $59.98.
E.W. Swackhamer, USA, 1972, 98 mins.

Maya

A natural wildlife story built around the relationship between a father and son. A young boy (Jay North) estranged from his father, a wildlife hunter whom he blames for losing his nerve, befriends a young native boy. The two undertake a perilous journey in the bush, putting their lives in danger and forcing the young man to reevaluate his father. With Clint Walker, I.S. Johar, Sajid Kahn and Jairag.
VHS: S19033. $19.98.
John Berry, USA, 1966, 91 mins.

Misty

The creators of *A Dog of Flanders* work their magic again in this warmhearted tale of two lonely children and a beautiful, wild pony. Based on Marguerite Henry's award-winning children's novel *Misty of Chincoteague*. Great family entertainment. With David Ladd and Pam Smith.
VHS: S14282. $19.98.
Laser: LD75230. $34.98.
James B. Clark, USA, 1961, 92 mins.

Moon Stallion

A mystical tale from the BBC, enchanting for both adults and children. A professor researches the legend of King Arthur and a strange apparition of a wild, white horse is seen. These mysteries lead the man's blind daughter into adventures far removed from the 20th century. 90 mins.
VHS: S12635. $29.95.

My Dog Shep

Silent star William Farnum heads the cast in this family entertainment about an old man who teams up with a young runaway boy and his German shepherd, Shep. Together they foil kidnappers and greedy relatives. With Tom Neal, Grady Sutton, Al St. John and Flame.
VHS: S05706. $29.95.
Ford Beebe, USA, 1946, 70 mins.

My Family Treasure

A magical children's tale about a woman's search for a family treasure bequeathed by the Czar to her family before the Russian Revolution. The complex story unfolds over decades, and charts the heroism of a young woman to restore her eccentric family's wounded pride. With Theodore Bikel, Dee Wallace Stone, Bitty Schram and Alex Vincent.
VHS: S19734. $79.95.
Rolfe Kanefsky/Edward Staroselsky, USA, 1992

My Friend Flicka

Roddy McDowall stars as a young boy determined to tame and befriend a wild horse in this screen version of Mary O'Hara's acclaimed novel. This poignant story of trust, love and hope was one of the most popular family films of the forties. With Preston Foster.
VHS: S14211. $14.98.
Harold Schuster, USA, 1943, 89 mins.

My Neighbor Totoro

This charming animation features the lovable, over-sized creatures called Totoros, who possess qualities that make them children's best friends. In this enchanting fantasy they will warm your heart and delight you with their magical antics.
VHS: S21354. $19.98.
Laser: LD74635. $29.98.
Hayao Miyazaki, Japan, 1993, 76 mins.

Namu, The Killer Whale

An adventure story about a dedicated marine biologist (Robert Lansing) who captures a massive killer whale, begins to study its nature and manner and eventually develops a relationship with the whale. With Lee Meriwether, John Anderson and Richard Erdman.
VHS: S19032. $14.95.
Laslo Benedek, USA, 1966, 88 mins.

National Velvet

Classic family film starring Elizabeth Taylor at her loveliest as the spunky young girl who hopes to enter and win Britain's Grand National Steeplechase race. With the help of a rascal stableboy (Mickey Rooney), she may just achieve her dreams. Great family entertainment.
VHS: S01789. $19.98.
Laser: LD70636. $69.98.
Clarence Brown, USA, 1944, 125 mins.

Never Cry Wolf

From the director of *Black Stallion*, a spectacular film about the odyssey of a young biologist sent to study the habits of wolves in the Arctic. With Charles Martin Smith and Brian Dennehy, based on the book by Farley Mowat.
VHS: Out of print. For rental only.
Laser: LD71254. $34.95.
Carroll Ballard, USA, 1983, 105 mins.

Neverending Story

Wolfgang Petersen immerses the audience in a classical fairytale, the story of a young boy for whom the tale of *The Neverending Story* is so real, he becomes the hero in a mythical empire populated by magical beings. His task is, of course, to save this magical world from destruction.
VHS: S00926. $14.95.
Laser: Letterboxed. LD70639. $34.98.
Wolfgang Petersen, Germany/USA, 1984, 94 mins.

Neverending Story II: The Next Chapter

A continuation of Wolfgang Petersen's 1984 surprise about a young boy struggling to come to terms with his mother's death and his father's detachment, who escapes to a magical world called Fantasia, where he's pressed to save the life of a beautiful young girl.
Laser: LD70640. $29.98.
George Miller, USA/Germany, 1990, 89 mins.

The New Adventures of Black Beauty

This two-volume set follows the continuing saga of that childhood favorite, the horse Black Beauty. It begins when 12-year-old Vicky is introduced to a horse and then finds herself involved in adventure. Despite her growing attachment to Black Beauty she may have to leave for New Zealand. 120 mins.
VHS: S25061. $29.95.

New Adventures of Pippi Longstocking

A brand new film based on the classic children's books by Astrid Lindgren, with Pippi back for fun, laughter and a lot of mischief in brand new adventures.
VHS: S08062. $14.95.
Ken Annakin, USA, 1988, 100 mins.

Our Little Girl

Shirley Temple runs away from home in this sentimental tale about a little girl who comes to believe her parents don't love her. Joel McCrea co-stars.
VHS: S09994. $19.98.
John S. Robertson, USA, 1935, 65 mins.

The Painted Hills

A Lassie adventure story set against an 1870 California gold backdrop, in the High Sierras. Lassie must avenge the death of a kindly prospector murdered by his greedy partner after the old man struck a rich gold vein. Adapted from Alexander Hull's novel *Shep of the Painted Hills*. With Paul Kelly, Bruce Cowling, Gary Gray and Art Smith.
VHS: S19140. $19.98.
Harold F. Kress, USA, 1951, 70 mins.

Panda and the Magic Serpent

An animated feature from Japan narrated in English by Marvin Miller, the man who distributed the checks on *The Millionaire*. Panda and Mimi the raccoon travel with Hsu Hsien, a young man, through the Chinese countryside and meet wizards, magic snakes and fish, and the all-powerful dragon god.
VHS: S05473. $29.95.
Kazuhiko Okabe, Japan, 1961, 74 mins.

The Peanut Butter Solution

Winner at the 1986 Children's International Festival of Children's Films, the story of Michael, an average boy living in Montreal, with a vivid imagination. When he concocts a peanut butter solution which makes his hair grow forever, he becomes the object of a kidnapping.
VHS: S02600. $19.95.
Michael Rubbo, Canada, 1985, 96 mins.

Phantom Tollbooth

Milo drives into animated fantasyland through the phantom tollbooth into the Kingdom of Wisdom. Rescued from danger by a ticking watch dog named Tock, Milo embarks on a mission to end the terrible feud between numbers and words by rescuing Rhyme and Reason from the Castle in the Air.
VHS: S01020. $19.95.
Chuck Jones, USA, 1967, 90 mins.

The Phoenix and the Magic Carpet

Mrs. Wilson travels to England from the U.S. with her three children because she must settle the affairs of her late father. To their surprise the three children discover an egg which hatches into the mythical Phoenix. Soon they set off together on a magic carpet adventure. Sir Peter Ustinov has a cameo appearance.
VHS: S26524. $92.99.
Zoran Perisic, USA, 1994, 80 mins.

The Pied Piper of Hamelin

Van Johnson and Claude Rains are featured in this delightful retelling of the famous children's tale. The rats disappear, but in the end they don't go alone, as the children of the village find themselves mesmerized by the Pied Piper.
VHS: S23799. $24.95.
Bretaigne Windust, USA, 1957, 87 mins.

Pippi in the South Seas

Further adventures of Pippi Longstocking, the character created by Astrid Lindgren.
VHS: S01726. $19.95.
Olle Hellbron, Sweden, 1974, 99 mins.

Pippi Longstocking

The famous children's book by Astrid Lindgren is transformed into a film. Set in a small town in Sweden, Pippi, the red-haired girl, beguiles the local children with her stories and antics, accompanied by her monkey and her horse. In this story, Pippi is brought into conflict with tramps who are after her gold, and with Miss Prusselius, the school mistress, who wants to put her into a home.
VHS: S01032. $19.95.
Olle Hellbron, Sweden, 1973, 99 mins.

Pippi on the Run

Further adventures of Pippi Longstocking, based on the book by Astrid Lindgren. Here Pippi must watch over Tommy and Annika as they try to assert their independence from their parents. Featuring Inger Nilsson as Pippi. Sweden, 1974, 99 mins.
VHS: S01727. $19.95.

Pippi's Holiday Vacation (Pippi Goes on Board)

This screen adaptation of the book by Astrid Lindgren follows the adventures of the outrageous little girl Pippi Longstocking. When Pippi finds that she must attend school in order to earn a summer vacation, everyone enjoys her fun antics, except for her school teacher.
VHS: S21999. $19.95.
Olle Hellbron, Sweden, 1974, 83 mins.

The Point

This amusing and touching feature-length animation tells of the troubles encountered by a round-headed little boy born into a world of pointy-headed people. It all begins when a father lures his son away from the television to tell him a story about the Pointed Village. Excellent musical score by the late Harry Nilsson.
VHS: S25004. $14.98.
Fred Wolf, USA, 1970, 74 mins.

The Polar Bear King

The young king of Summerland refuses to marry an evil witch. In spite she turns him into a fearsome polar bear. He seeks refuge in Winterland, the home of a beautiful young princess who sees beyond his accursed appearance. Now she must find a way to help this exiled king.
VHS: S20859. $19.95.
Ola Solum, USA, 1993, 87 mins.

Pound Puppies and the Legend of Big Paw

Every dog has his day as Cooler and the gang make their feature film debut with this musical full-length animated adventure. 76 mins. 1988.
VHS: S09892. $79.95.

Prancer

This heart-warming holiday fantasy stars Rebecca Harrell as a nine-year-old girl who discovers a wounded deer and becomes convinced that it is Santa's own Prancer. Her attempts to heal the wounded animal and return it to Santa Claus before Christmas unite her troubled family and touch the residents of the small town. With Sam Elliott, Rebecca Harrell and Cloris Leachman.
VHS: S13351. $19.95.
John Hancock, USA, 1989, 102 mins.

Prince Brat and the Whipping Boy

George C. Scott stars in this enchanting children's fairy tale about a princely brat who gets mixed up with a young orphan. It's a case where mistaken identity creates the chance for both a little comeuppance and a lot of fun. Based on Sid Fleischmann's novel *The Whipping Boy*.
VHS: S26948. $95.99.
Laser: LD75428. $34.95.
Syd Macartney, USA, 1995, 96 mins.

Raggedy Ann and Andy: A Musical Adventure

The beloved patchwork dolls come alive in this animated adventure as they venture into the deep woods of fantasy to rescue a kidnapped friend. With the voices of Didi Conn, Mark Baker, Fred Stuthman, Joe Silver and 16 songs by *Sesame Street*'s Joe Raposo. Highlights include Camel with Wrinkled Knees singing "Song Blue."
VHS: S04601. $14.98.
Richard Williams, USA, 1977, 85 mins.

Rescuers Down Under

The animated adventures of Bernard and Miss Bianca, the world's bravest mice, continue as they travel to Australia to assist a small boy in protecting a giant golden eagle from a ruthless poacher.
VHS: S14981. $24.99.
H. Butoy/M. Gabriel, USA, 1991, 110 mins.

The Return of the Sand Fairy

Based on the book by Edith (*Railway Children*) Nesbit, this is a British adventure about a fantastic, furry gremlin who can make wishes come true and the four children he befriends. Great Britain, 1993, 139 mins.
VHS: S21973. $89.98.

The Return of Tommy Tricker

From the wilds of the Northern Tundra to the beaches of the South Seas, adventure follows in Tommy Tricker's wake. He has a special method for getting around: he goes via postage stamps. This simple and effective mode of travel plunges him into a series of exciting troubles.
VHS: S25852. $19.95.
Michael Rubbo, Canada, 1994, 97 mins.

The Road Home

Kris Kristofferson, Danny Aiello and Charles Martin Smith star in this tale of two orphaned brothers. They face poverty and a dreary orphanage that wants to separate them in the East. Only the promise of Father Flannagan's Boys' Town in Nebraska seems to guarantee them some measure of respite from the Great Depression, so they set off across the country. Ultimately their journey inspires a nation. Mickey Rooney makes a cameo appearance as Father Flannagan. Winner at the Chicago International Children's Film Festival.
VHS: S27410. $95.99.
Dean Hamilton, USA, 1995, 90 mins.

The Runaways

Johnnie Thomas is a lonely and unhappy boy on the run from his foster home. He befriends Yama, an escaped leopard from an animal park, and the tender and hopeful story of *The Runaways* unfolds. With Dorothy McGuire and Joseph Albee.
VHS: S01611. $49.95.
Harry Harris, USA, 1975, 76 mins.

Samson and Sally: The Song of the Whales

A wonderful Norwegian children's film adapted from the book *The Song of the Whale* by Bent Haller, a warm, funny and gripping adventure of two young whales who set off for an exciting journey through the beautiful but sometimes dangerous world of the ocean in search of the legendary Moby Dick. First-rate animation. In English.
VHS: S10966. $14.95.
Jannik Hastrup, Denmark, 1984, 70 mins.

The Sand Fairy

A BBC adaptation of Edith Nesbith's novel about a strange and wondrous creature who is a canny combination of E.T. and Yoda. He befriends a group of outcast children and dazzles them with magic and hope, sending them through time and history to help them realize their enchanting dreams. 139 mins.
VHS: S19067. $89.98.

The Sandlot

Baseball, the American sports obsession, is the central part of this charming family entertainment. A shy young boy joins a funny ragtag team and learns that how you play the game is the best route to acceptance and belonging.
VHS: S20668. $19.98.
David Mickey Evans, USA, 1993, 100 mins.

Santa Claus: The Movie

Enchanting, heartwarming tale of a master toy maker who discovers a magical kingdom of elves at the north pole. Featuring Dudley Moore as Patch, an eager-to-please elf who becomes mixed up with a toy tycoon's plan to take over Christmas.
VHS: S04800. $19.95.
Jeannot Szwarc, USA, 1985, 104 mins.

Sarah and the Squirrel

Mia Farrow plays a young girl separated from her family who learns to survive the wilds with the help of animals in this story which mixes live action with animation. USA, 1983, 73 mins.
VHS: S04604. $29.98.

Sarah Plain and Tall

Glenn Close and Christopher Walken star in this acclaimed Hallmark Hall of Fame production about an opinionated Maine schoolteacher who travels to Kansas in 1910 to look after the children of a widowed farmer. With Lexi Randall, Margaret Sophie Stein, Jon de Vries and Christopher Bell. Based on the Newbery Medal winning children's novel by Patricia MacLachlan. Nominated for nine Emmys.
VHS: S15617. $14.98.
Laser: CLV. LD72026. $29.98.
Glenn Jordan, USA, 1991, 98 mins.

The Secret Garden (1949)

A well-made adaptation of Frances Hodgson Burnett's classic children's novel about the transcendent powers of a young girl to change and influence the dark and foreboding residents of a depressed Victorian estate. With Margaret O'Brien, Herbert Marshall, Dean Stockwell and Gladys Cooper.
VHS: S18564. $19.98.
Fred M. Wilcox, USA, 1949, 92 mins.

The Secret Garden (1984)

Frances Hodgson Burnett's world-famous tale about a lonely orphan who finds new strength and saves her reclusive young cousin from a life of solitude with the help of a very special secret place. A BBC production starring Sarah Hollis Andrews, David Patterson.
VHS: S07181. $14.98.
Katrina Murray, Great Britain, 1984, 107 mins.

The Secret Garden (1987)

This Hallmark adaptation of Frances Hodgson Burnett's story about an isolated, abandoned young orphan who discovers a magical garden and unlocks its hidden power and beauty. Shot in the baroque Highclere Castle in England. With Gennie James, Barret Oliver, Jadrien Steele, Derek Jacobi and Billie Whitelaw. "Very handsome and engrossing" (*Washington Post*).
VHS: S17033. $14.98.
Laser: LD71540. $29.98.
Alan Grint, USA, 1987, 100 mins.

The Secret Garden (Animated)

Frances Hodgson Burnett's unforgettable children's book is now a feature-length animated film featuring the voices of Derek Jacobi and Glynis Johns. It's the story of an orphaned girl who finds solace in the unkempt garden that sits just outside her brooding ancestral home. Five original songs are included. 72 mins.
VHS: S22519. $16.95.
Laser: LD74919. $39.99.

Secret of Nimh
A modern-day classic based on the award-winning book by Robert O'Brien. A distinguished cast including Elizabeth Hartman, Dom DeLuise and John Carradine provides the voices in the story of the widowed farm mouse whose home is threatened by oncoming plows. Seeking help, she discovers a society of super-intelligent rats.
VHS: S07966. $19.95.
Don Bluth, USA, 1982, 84 mins.

The Secret of the Seal
This enchanting tale charts the friendship of Tottoi, an isolated young boy, and a Mediterranean seal that many considered extinct. Set on a beautiful Italian island, *The Secret of the Seal* follows Tottoi as he feverishly tries to save the seal and his mother from poachers.
VHS: S19419. $24.95.
USA, 1992, 90 mins.

Serendipity, The Pink Dragon
This animated feature tells the story of a little boy stranded on a tropical island who meets a pink dragon named Serendipity. The dragon's wisdom and kindness fills their adventures with wonder and excitement. Based on the book by Stephen Cosgrove.
VHS: S12776. $24.95.
Jim Terry, USA, 1989, 90 mins.

Sherlock the Undercover Dog
Two courageous kids team up with a fast-talking police dog to collar a gang of bumbling smugglers in this hilarious comedy.
VHS: S22893. $19.95.
Richard Harding Gardner, USA, 1995, 80 mins.

Shipwreck Island
Share an exciting live-action adventure with eight boys whose sailing yacht is shipwrecked on a deserted island. A two-week vacation soon becomes a two-year adventure when one boy accidentally sets their boat adrift. Floating aimlessly, the boat eventually runs aground on an island inhabited only by wild animals. Here the boys must learn to hunt and survive the challenges of nature without the help of grown-ups. Don't miss the excitement when a band of renegade sailors arrive and try to take Shipwreck Island for themselves! Color.
VHS: S13884. $19.95.
USA, 1961, 85 mins.

Sinbad and the Eye of the Tiger
A sequel to the rousing children's adventure story *Golden Voyage of Sinbad* has the title hero (Patrick Wayne) dueling monsters to break the spell of an evil sorceress. Special visual effects by Ray Harryhausen. With Jane Seymour, Taryn Power, and Margaret Whiting.
VHS: S16682. $14.95.
Sam Wanamaker, Great Britain, 1977, 113 mins.

Skylark
A lyrical sequel to *Sarah, Plain and Tall*, Patricia MacLachlan's evocative children's book about a Maine school teacher (Glenn Close) drawn to a widowed Midwestern farmer (Christopher Walken) and his family. With Lexi Randall, Christopher Bell and Margaret Sophie.
VHS: S18750. $14.98.
Joseph Sargent, USA, 1992, 98 mins.

Smoke
Before there was "Eat My Dust," there was this Disney drama starring Ron Howard. The title refers to the name of an ailing dog that teenaged Ronny and his stepfather (Earl Holliman) nurse back to health, only to have the dog's true owner show up.
VHS: S10068. $69.95.
Vincent McEveety, USA, 1970, 89 mins.

The Smurfs and the Magic Flute
The first animated film featuring the delightful Smurfs. Set during the Middle Ages, a travelling peddler leaves a magic flute behind at the King's castle. Now the King and his knight must prevent young William from capturing the flute.
VHS: S01608. $14.95.
Jose Dutillieu, Belgium/France, 1975, 74 mins.

Snoopy, Come Home
This charming animated feature centers on Snoopy and Woodstock as they run off to the big city...with Charlie Brown in hot pursuit.
VHS: S07814. $14.98.
Bill Melendez, USA, 1972, 70 mins.

Snow White
The famous Grimm fairy tale is brought to life in this German version. There is a lovely young woman, seven dwarves and a prince to charm everyone, except, of course, the evil witch.
VHS: S25705. $19.95.
Erich Kobler, Germany, 1955, 76 mins.

Snowy River, The McGregor Saga: The Race
Based on the ballad *The Man from Snow River*. Australia, 1993, 87 mins.
VHS: S22014. $14.98.

Son of Lassie
Now grown to manhood, Joe Carraclough has gone off to the RAF training school, leaving behind his beloved Lassie and her pup Laddie. Ever faithful Laddie follows Joe to the academy and stows away aboard Joe's plane as it embarks on a dangerous mission.
VHS: S16847. $19.98.
S. Sylvan Simon, USA, 1945, 100 mins.

Song Spinner
Patti LuPone and John Neville are opposing characters in this mythical story about a young girl named Aurora who receives a magical gift. In the tiny world where she lives, noise of any kind is illegal, as decreed by King Frilo (Neville). When the mysterious Zantalalia (LuPone) arrives, she brings with her a "song-spinner," a glistening gift for Aurora that makes music. Now Aurora's gift for song promises to change the kingdom of Shandrilan from a silent and gloomy place to a joyful, music-laden paradise.
VHS: S27420. $89.98.
Laser: LD75511. $39.99.
Randy Bradshaw, USA, 1995, 95 mins.

Sounder
Paul Winfield stars as a Black sharecropper in Louisiana who steals food in a desperate attempt to feed his family. Cicely Tyson portrays his wife, providing love and strength to keep the family together.
VHS: S01235. $14.95.
Laser: LD75336. $29.98.
Martin Ritt, USA, 1972, 105 mins.

Stone Boy
A family drama starring Glenn Close and Robert Duvall as parents of a 12 year old who inadvertently kills his older brother while hunting. Wilford Brimley is featured as the understanding grandfather.
VHS: S02026. $59.98.
Christopher Cain, USA, 1984, 93 mins.

The Story of 15 Boys
This fully animated feature film is based on the Jules Verne novel, *Two Years Vacation*. The story—about 15 boys who become shipwrecked on a deserted island—shows how we must work together if we are to survive. Animated.
VHS: S16757. $14.99.
Yoshio Kuroda, USA, 1987, 80 mins.

The Story of Seabiscuit
Shirley Temple stars as Margaret O'Hara. Haunted by her jockey brother's death, she agrees to marry Ted Knowles only if he gives up riding. But when her meddling uncle convinces her that a horse named Seabiscuit will triumph only with Ted in the saddle, the clever Irishman must convince his niece that she'll come out a winner, too!
VHS: S16849. $19.98.
David Butler, USA, 1950, 93 mins.

Stowaways on the Ark
A beautifully animated children's adventure bringing to life Noah and the Ark with an extra special twist... the Ark has a surprise visitor, Willie the Woodworm. Musical score composed by Frank Pleter, with special effects by John Japl. In English.
VHS: S11695. $39.95.
Wolfgang Urchs, Germany, 1987, 90 mins.

Summer of the Colt
Two exuberant boys discover laughter and adventure in this hit from the Chicago International Children's Film Festival. Daniel is visiting his grandfather in the Argentine countryside when he encounters a mysterious colt. This beautiful animal seems to embody the very spirit of freedom.
VHS: S25850. $19.95.
Andre Melancon, Canada, 1989, 96 mins.

Summer with Selik
This spectacular film shows the developing bond between a teenage girl and a baby seal that she finds on the Norwegian coast. Sadly, the girl grows to love her new friend Selik but as he grows he must be returned to the sea. It's a touching film about a key right of passage to adulthood for this teenager. 60 mins.
VHS: S25995. $29.95.

The Sun Comes Up
A lonely widow (Jeanette MacDonald) blames her son's dog Lassie for her husband's death but eventually learns about Lassie's friendship and loyalty through a young orphan's (Claude Jarman Jr.) love for the dog. MacDonald's last film; she performs five songs. With Lloyd Nolan, Dwayne Hickman, Percy Kilbride and Margaret Hamilton. Music by Andre Previn.
VHS: S19139. $19.98.
Richard Thorpe, USA, 1948, 93 mins.

Susannah of the Mounties
Shirley Temple helps tame the West as the lone survivor of an Indian raid who's taken in a by a kindly Mountie. When all-out war threatens, it's Shirley who saves the day and shows the adults how to live in peace. Co-stars Randolph Scott.
VHS: S09997. $19.98.
William A. Seiter, USA, 1939, 79 mins.

Swallows and Amazons Forever!: Coot Club
This BBC adaptation of a series of books written by Arthur Ransome set on English waterways and lakes in the 1930's continues with the adventures of children in the Coot Club. They are dedicated to protecting nesting sites and let loose a ship they fear will damage one. Now they may well find trouble from the sabotaged crew.
VHS: S24827. $29.95.
Andrew Morgan, Great Britain, 1995, 90 mins.

Swallows and Amazons Forever!: The Big Six
Originally a series of books written by Arthur Ransome set on English waterways and lakes in the 1930's, two of these stories have now been made into captivating films by the BBC. This first film introduces the six children who make up the central characters. They explore a world of skill, nature and friendship.
VHS: S24828. $29.95.
Andrew Morgan, Great Britain, 1995, 90 mins.

The Swan Princess
A handsome hero and a beautiful young princess make this feature-length animation a must for children and grown-ups alike. Jack Palance, John Cleese, Steven Wright and Sandy Duncan provide the voices for this charming, legendary fairy tale.
VHS: S25610. $24.98.
Laser: LD75029. $29.99.
Richard Rich, USA, 1995, 90 mins.

Swiss Family Robinson
Jonathon Wyss' book of the same name is adapted for the screen in this early version of the much admired tale. A man decides to move his family to Australia, but the ship is destroyed, forcing them to make do on a deserted island. There the harshness and beauty of the landscape challenge and inspire this family to be better than they thought they could be.
VHS: S21560. $24.95.
Edward Ludwig, USA, 1940, 92 mins.

Tadpole and the Whale
The story of a 12-year-old girl and her relationship with some of the world's most spectacular undersea creatures, including Elvar the dolphin, her best friend. Academy of Canadian Television and Cinema Award, London Film Festival Award, International Ecological Film Festival Award. Family.
VHS: S17134. $29.95.
Dominique Ricard, Canada, 1987, 91 mins.

Tall Tale
Patrick Swayze, Scott Glenn and Oliver Platt star in this imaginative recombination of legendary tall tales. Pecos Bill, Paul Bunyan and John Henry come to the aid of a young boy who must go head-to-head with a greedy land-grabber in this epic from Disney.
VHS: S26150. $99.98.
Jeremiah Chechik, USA, 1994, 97 mins.

Third Stone from the Sun
A strange sailing ship that speaks (Linda Hunt is the voice) guides a young boy on a mysterious but important journey. He must retrieve a lost treasure. Along the way he discovers the importance of the natural world and his place in it.
VHS: S24741. $19.98.
Jan C. Nickman, USA, 1994, 85 mins.

The Three Worlds of Gulliver
The special effects wizardry of Ray Harryhausen highlight this tale of Gulliver (Kerwin Matthews) and his voyages to the lands of Liliput and Brobdignag. Filmed in Superdynamation. The classic satire of Jonathan Swift comes in three sizes. With Jo Morrow, June Thorburn and Peter Bull. Also giant alligators and squirrels in this live-action fantasy.
VHS: S06829. $14.95.
Laser: Includes interview with Ray Harryhausen. LD75043. $34.95.
Jack Sher, Great Britain, 1960, 98 mins.

Thumbelina
Hans Christian Andersen's story of a wee person who follows her heart will delight children with its cheerful message. Adversity need not overpower even the smallest among us because there is someone to love for everyone. This animated feature includes music by Barry Manilow.
VHS: S21255. $19.98.
Laser: CAV, letterboxed. LD72421. $34.98.
Don Bluth/Gary Goldman, USA, 1994

Toby and the Koala Bear
A young boy and his pet koala bear and a friendly aborigine are pitted against the challenging Australian bush in this tale of companionship and courage that uses animation set against live backgrounds. Australia, 1981, 76 mins.
VHS: S04603. $19.98.

Tommy Tricker and the Stamp Traveller
From the producer of *Bach and Broccoli*, *The Dog Who Stopped the War*, a fast-paced family delight in which stamp collecting becomes anything but a passive hobby for the smooth-talking Tommy Tricker as he snatches a valuable stamp. The theft unveils the secret of travelling on the head of a postage stamp and sends Tommy and his pal on a whirlwind adventure around the globe.
VHS: S07816. $14.95.
Michael Rubbo, Canada, 1987, 101 mins.

Trailing the Killer
Very much like a Disney true-life nature series, this is the story of a sheep dog, part wolf, accused of killing sheep. Cast: Ceasar, the wolf dog, Frances MacDonald, Heinie Conklin, Tom London.
VHS: S10372. $19.95.
Herman C. Raymaker, USA, 1932, 63 mins.

Travels of Marco Polo
The brave Marco Polo fights for peace and justice in the exotic Far East in this classic tale of wondrous adventure.
VHS: S03021. $19.95.
William Novik, France, 1953, 48 mins.

A Troll in Central Park
Warner Brothers brings the voices of Dom DeLuise, Cloris Leachman, Hayley Mills and Charles Nelson Reilly to this fantastic animated tale. Dismissed from the kingdom, a troll finds that his only refuge is New York's Central Park. There he befriends a little girl and her skeptical brother.
VHS: S23113. $19.99.
Laser: Widescreen. LD74837. $34.98.
Don Bluth, USA, 1994, 76 mins.

Tuck Everlasting
This endearing children's film follows a young girl called Whynnie, who, while daydreaming in the woods one day, discovers the tiny Tuck family. Together they share a special secret. But this secret has the power to drive the Tuck family from their home and separate them from their beloved friend Whynnie forever.
VHS: S20983. $14.98.
Frederick King Keller, USA, 1981, 90 mins.

Twice upon a Time
An animated adventure from executive producer George Lucas (the *Star Wars* and *Indiana Jones* trilogies). A dog and his man are unlikely heroes in this crazy-quilt story involving the mysterious theft of the Cosmic Clock!
VHS: S13442. $14.95.
John Korty/Charles Swenson, USA, 1983, 75 mins.

Vincent and Me
This Emmy Award-winning children's film is highly imaginative. Jo is a spirited young artist with a miraculous gift—she paints just like the acclaimed 19th-century painter Vincent Van Gogh. The result is a colorful, comical and slightly crackpot story.
VHS: S25851. $19.95.
Michael Rubbo, Canada, 1990, 100 mins.

Where the Red Fern Grows
A young boy yearns for two Red-bone coon hounds amidst the splendor of the Ozarks. But life is hard in Depression-era Oklahoma. Facing adventure and tragedy with his new canine friends, Billy ultimately learns of love and hope. With James Whitmore, Beverly Garland and Stewart Peterson.
VHS: S01447. $19.98.
Norman Tokar, USA, 1974, 108 mins.

Where the Red Fern Grows, Part II
A continuation of Wilson Rawls' classic about a young boy's coming of age, helped along by his special relationship with two Redbone hound puppies. With Wilford Brimley, Doug McKeon, Lisa Whelchel and Chad McQueen.
VHS: S17875. $89.95.
Jim McCullough, USA, 1992, 105 mins.

White Fang and the Hunter
Another screen version of the Jack London novel about a boy and his dog in the great white north. Starring Robert Wood and Pedro Sanchez and featuring lots of snow and scenic vistas.
VHS: S03640. $19.98.
Laser: LD71208. $39.99.
Alfonso Brescia, Italy, 1985, 87 mins.

Willie Wonka and the Chocolate Factory
Amusing and unconventional story based on the children's book by Roald Dahl features Gene Wilder as a madcap candy man. With Jack Albertson.
VHS: S01604. $19.98.
Laser: LD70707. $34.98.
Mel Stuart, US, 1971, 94 mins.

The Yearling (1946)
Twelve-year-old Jody confronts the joys and pains of growing up when the needs of his beloved pet fawn compete with those of his struggling family. Marjorie Kinnan Rawlings' novel is touchingly brought to the screen by Gregory Peck, Jane Wyman and Claude Jarman, Jr., who received an Academy Award for portraying a child enduring harsh pioneer life.
VHS: S01488. $19.95.
Laser: LD70716. $39.98.
Clarence Brown, USA, 1946, 129 mins.

The Yearling (1994)
In the aftermath of the Civil War, a family experiences the poverty and turmoil that beset the South. In this setting, a boy finds a young orphaned deer that soon becomes the object of his affections. This heartwarming story is perfect family entertainment, based on Marjorie Kinnan Rawlings' classic novel. Peter Strauss and Jean Smart star.
VHS: S22442. $19.95.
Rod Hardy, USA, 1994, 98 mins.

Young Magician
A wonderful children's film from producer Rock Demers. Peter's got magical power, but no practical control...and this spells trouble for his family, his friends, and the whole city. He ends up on the run until another boy genius teaches him the real, not-so-magical, power of practice and discipline.
VHS: S07034. $14.95.
Waldemar Dziki, Canada/Poland, 1987, 99 mins.

Young People
Shirley Temple gets to reprise some of her best moments in this stirring melodrama. Older footage reveals why this young girl needs a normal home in a normal town. Though her parents take her to an ideal place, the town residents are suspicious and treat them rather coldly, until disaster strikes.
VHS: S25910. $14.98.
Allan Dwan, USA, 1940, 79 mins.

Zebra in the Kitchen
When twelve-year-old animal lover Chris is hired at the city zoo, he is less than happy about the run-down facilities. So naturally, the mischievous assistant unlocks all the cages, creating mass hysteria as the mild mannered creatures wander into toy stores, butcher shops and bedrooms. Stars Jay "Dennis the Menace" North.
VHS: S16844. $19.98.
Ivan Tors, USA, 1965, 92 mins.

CHILDREN'S ACTIVITIES

All About Kids' Safety
How safe is your child when he rides his bicycle or walks down the street? If there was a fire in your home, what would your child do? This animated program effortlessly teaches children basic rules about bicycle, pedestrian, and fire safety. Produced by Fred Calvert in cooperation with the National Safety Council. 40 mins.
VHS: S13220. $19.95.

Alphabet Library
A child's home and world become a library where things familiar to children are presented in an alphabetical review. Each volume of this series is 30 mins.
Alphabet City
VHS: S10319. $29.95.
Alphabet House
VHS: S10321. $29.95.
Alphabet Zoo
VHS: S10322. $29.95.

Amazing Things, Vol. 1
Dr. Misterio is a magician and a prankster. He also encourages children to participate in the creative process by turning basic household objects into toys and performing simple feats of magic. 56 mins.
VHS: S13070. $9.98.

Amazing Things, Vol. 2
More interactive, make-it-yourself magic from Dr. Misterio. Perfect for parties and rainy afternoons. 55 mins.
VHS: S13071. $9.98.

Animal Alphabet
This unique program lets kids and their parents travel the globe with live action animal photography and colorful animated letters.
VHS: S04134. $14.95.

Art Lessons for Children
Art teacher Donna Hugh demonstrates how easy it is to produce beautiful art projects using simple, inexpensive materials. Each volume several complete lessons.
Volume 1: Easy Watercolor Techniques. All you need is a box of watercolor paints, a brush, construction paper, a black crayon and a black felt-tipped pen for these four lessons:(1) Watercolor Flowers; (2) Watercolor Discovery; (3) Desert Scene; (4) Opaque Watercolors.
VHS: S16155. $29.95.
Volume 2: Easy Art Projects. These three lessons each use a limited number of readily available materials to open the creative minds of children everywhere: (1) Working with Oil Pastels; (2) Foil Art; (3) Printmaking.
VHS: S16156. $29.95.
Volume 3: More Fun with Watercolors. Watercolors, using simple, commonplace materials. Four lessons. 53 mins.
VHS: S17843. $29.95.
Volume 4: Felt Pen Fun. Four more lessons from art teacher Donna Hugh. 58 mins.
VHS: S17844. $29.95.
Volume 5: Animals of the Rain Forest. Beginning with oil pastels, white tempera paint, a brush and black crayon, this video will take children on an art-making expedition through the rain forest. Three animals—a toucan, a baby iguana and an anteater—are not only used as models, but each is carefully described emphasizing their relationship to the environment in which they live.
VHS: S22089. $29.95.
Volume 6: Plants of the Rain Forest. In this tape children can see how plants grow in the rain forest, one of the earth's most fascinating climates. Then art teacher Donna Hugh demonstrates techniques used to make beautiful artworks depicting this interesting and unusual plants. 48 mins.
VHS: S21250. $29.95.

Baby Goes...Songs for the Season
Original sing-alongs that bring toddlers and Christmas together are featured on this video. Kids will learn about baking cookies and enjoy sledding, skating and even shopping. Finally it's time to wrap the presents and wait for Santa. For ages 1-6. 30 mins.
VHS: S25967. $9.95.

Baby Goes...Songs to Take Along
Children ages six and under will enjoy these songs that help them learn by doing. This video goes everywhere, from the market to the beach, and shows how a number of different tasks are accomplished, like counting, dressing and getting ready for bed. 30 mins.
VHS: S23943. $12.95.

Baby Songs
Live action music video for young kids from singer/songwriter Hap Palmer. Ten songs include "Piggy Toes" and "Security". USA, 1987, 30 mins.
VHS: S03520. $12.98.

Baby's Bedtime
Judy Collins invites young viewers on a gentle journey into dreamland with this new collection of best-loved lullabies. Tuck your child in to the beautiful animation and memorable melodies of "Hush Little Baby", "The Land of Nod", "Lullaby and Good Night" and other classics. Parents' Choice Award. 26 minutes, infant to age 6.
Home Video.
VHS: S11417. $12.98.
Public Performance Rights.
VHS: S17148. $50.00.

Baby's Storytime
Singer-songwriter Arlo Guthrie brings his whimsical wit and music to this warm, lighthearted re-telling of such children's classics as "The Three Pigs", "Henny Penny" and "Little Red Riding Hood". A delightful adaptation of Kay Chorao's children's book animated by Oscar nominee Michael Sporn. 26 minutes, infant to age 6.
Home Video.
VHS: S11418. $12.98.
Public Performance Rights.
VHS: S17151. $50.00.

The Best of Beakman's World
The quirky scientist Beakman takes his viewers on an intellectual odyssey as he provokes children into asking important and fundamental questions about life, art, science, nature and their existence. Beakman finds an accessible means of conveying scientific information, using wit, visual shocks and surprise to issue challenges, offer facts, solve problems and demonstrate experiments that can be accomplished at home. 60 mins.
VHS: S19160. $14.95.

Bethie's Really Silly Clubhouse
Silly songstress Bethie is the perfect host who always enjoys a good knock-knock joke. This video features a good story that will teach kids about animals even as it entertains them. Ages 2-8.
VHS: S24512. $14.98.

Bill Cosby's Picture Pages:
What's That Shape and More Fun
Bill Cosby is one of the world's great entertainers and he has always had a special appeal for children. This video brings his unique talents to an engrossing educational experience suitable for children ages 4 to 7. 30 mins.
VHS: S22952. $9.95.

Bill Cosby's Picture Pages:
Who's Counting and More Fun
Bill Cosby once again shares his charm and wit with children through this educational video, suitable for children ages 4 to 7. It's fun and interactive. 30 mins.
VHS: S22131. $9.95.

Boy Scout Advancement Program:
First Class
An instructional video designed to assist the Scout in obtaining the next level of Scouting achievement. Map-making and tracking techniques are covered as well as cooking, camping and conservation skills. The rules of safe swimming are reviewed in this supplemental tape to the Official Boy Scout handbook. 45 mins.
VHS: S07518. $24.95.

Boy Scout Advancement Program:
Second Class
This video using real Scouts continues the Scouting program on the second rank. Demonstrations in first aid, life saving techniques, and tips on hiking, camping and communicating are all covered. Be prepared to learn how the Scout Law applies to everyday life. 51 mins.
VHS: S07517. $24.95.

Boy Scout Advancement Program:
Tenderfoot
Based on the number two best seller of all time, *The Official Boy Scout Handbook.* Featuring real Scouts in real situations demonstrating the skills needed to obtain the rank of Tenderfoot. Program includes pitching a tent, basic wilderness training and how to make a safe campfire. 63 mins.
VHS: S07516. $24.95.

Child of Mine: The Lullaby Video
Thirteen different female artists perform an eclectic and touching collection of lullabies that acknowledge the special bonds between mother and child. The artists include Mary-Chapin Carpenter, Rosanne Cash, Gloria Estefan, Dionne Warwick and Carole King.
VHS: S20300. $19.98.

Children's Chants and Games
Playground chants and games are illustrated in this video. Some of these games reflect ancient origins while others mirror contemporary tensions and conflicts. 15 mins.
VHS: S23520. $49.95.

Christmas Sing-Along Video Album
A collection of Christmas favorites, including "We Wish You a Merry Christmas", "Silent Night", "Jingle Bells" and others, in a special sing-along program.
VHS: S10726. $19.95.

Clean Your Room, Harvey Moon!
Harvey Moon's room is a mess! Socks, marbles, trains and even a map of the brain are crowding on his rug and hiding under his bed, and his mother won't let him watch cartoons until his room is spotless. This Saturday morning cleaning spree is told in upbeat verse with a true-to-life humor. Pat Cummings won the Coretta Scott King Award for illustration.
VHS: S16341. $44.95.

Clifford's Fun with Letters
Clifford, the big red dog, is the star of over 17 million Scholastic books. Join him and his friends as they learn and play with the alphabet. For ages 3-8. 30 mins.
VHS: S13733. $12.95.

Clifford's Fun with Numbers
Clifford and his friends are led children through fun and games with numbers in this fully animated learning adventure. For ages 3-8. 30 mins.
VHS: S13732. $12.95.

Clifford's Sing-Along Adventure
Clifford and his friends lead children at home in a musical adventure that gets them to sing, dance, clap and compose their own songs. Features old and new music classics, live action and video animation. For ages 3-8. 30 mins.
VHS: S04154. $14.95.

Creative Dance for Preschoolers
Imparts the fun of movement together with important basic principles. Ages 3-6. 60 minutes.
VHS: S24608. $42.95.

Creative Movement:
A Step Towards Intelligence
Melissa Lowe's instruction is designed to help children develop self-awareness and confidence and develop their expressive capabilities. The program shows children having fun singing, clapping and moving to music, learning motor skills and coordination. 80 mins.
VHS: S19687. $19.95.

Decline of Western Civilization—
Part II—The Metal Years
Penelope Spheeris follows up her high-decibel look at the punk rock scene with another loud and outrageous concert documentary interview show. Groups include Megadeth, Lizzie Borden, Odin, Seduce and Poison in concert. The truth about backstage and on-the-road revelations from Ozzy Osbourne, Kiss, Aerosmith and Motorhead. Sex, groupies, Satan and make-up tips are discussed.
VHS: S08345. $19.95.
Penelope Spheeris, USA, 1988, 90 mins.

E-Z Bread Dough Sculpture
Young viewers will be rolling in dough after they learn how to create twists, animals and braids with ordinary bread dough. 30 mins.
VHS: S09885. $29.95.

Ella Jenkins Live at the Smithsonian
Legendary folksinger Ella Jenkins performs with the children of the Smithsonian Institute's Early Enrichment Center. Lots of fun, playful songs for children. 1991.
VHS: S15497. $14.95.

Ella Jenkins: For the Family
Ella Jenkins, a recognized national treasure, sings eleven favorite children's songs. Ages 3-7. 30 minutes.
VHS: S25036. $14.95.

The Flying Fruit Fly Circus
A documentary on the Flying Fruit Fly Circus, an Australian-based, youth performing arts company that was founded in 1979. The program offers thrilling spectacle, as the 40-member troupe—entirely made up of children—perform various tumbling acts. 50 mins.
VHS: S19642. $24.95.

Fun in a Box
These award-winning animated and live-action films promote positive values and offer ideas for fun and games.
Fun in a Box #
1: *Ben's Dream.* From acclaimed author Chris Van Allsburg. Also includes *Fish* and *The Red Ball Express.* 30 mins.
VHS: S16309. $14.95.
Fun in a Box #
2: *New Friends.* Howard, by James Stevenson, is the highlight of this program that also includes *Metal Dogs of India* and *Why Cats Eat First.* 30 mins.
VHS: S16308. $14.95.
Fun in a Box #
3: *The Birthday Movie.* This interactive video is hosted by the birthday spirit who knows all about fun and games. 30 mins.
VHS: S16307. $14.95.

Fun with Clay
Young viewers learn the basics of clay, including the pinch, coil and slab method of clay, working with household objects. 30 mins.
VHS: S09881. $9.95.

Ghostwriter
A blend of expressive graphics, innovative effects and celebrity guest stars highlight this children's game about a team of youthful sleuths who are befriended by the ghostwriter. He's a secret friend who communicates clues and signals through reading and writing. 105 mins.
VHS: S19157. $14.98.
Laser: LD72189. $34.98.

Great Ape Activity Tape
Three activity experts demonstrate 15 activities to chase away boredom or rainy day blues for children 3-8 as they learn a variety of crafts, tricks and games. 30 mins.
VHS: S04156. $14.95.

A Great Day for Singing
James Durst performs 25 traditional songs and nursery rhymes for children ages 3-7 years old. Any child will find this treasury of sing-alongs simply irresistible. "Old MacDonald" and "Row, Row, Row Your Boat" are just some of the favorites included. 30 mins.
VHS: S24217. $14.95.

Helping Your Baby
Sleep Through the Night
This practical guide to parenting provides insights, suggestions and effective ways for helping a child sleep uninterrupted. "The information is presented in a way that educates, informs and encourages the new parent" (*Journal of the American Medical Association*).
VHS: S19577. $9.95.

Hip Hop Animal Rock Workout
A 30-minute workout tape featuring a zany cast of kids and cartoon animals work out together in the enchanted forest. Featuring the hottest tunes and dance steps, this video is great fun for all kids ages 6-9. 30 mins.
VHS: S24531. $9.98.

Holiday Sing-Along with Mitch
Mitch Miller invites you to sing along with his gang of talented music makers in this video collection of some of the all-time favorite Christmas tunes.
VHS: S04981. $19.95.

How Come?
From the *Learn About Living Series* designed to help children sort out the challenges of growing up. Through the use of live action and animation, Windjammer Way becomes a fantasy playground for imaginative minds to explore. Other titles in the series include *Mine and Yours, Never Talk to Strangers* and *Who Will Be My Friend?* Ages 3-6. 30 mins.
VHS: S24995. $9.95.

How to Fold a Paper Crane
A pair of speaking, that is signing, hands, are accompanied by voice-over to explain *How to Fold a Paper Crane.* The paper crane is a symbol of peace and this video makes this simple but delicate craft available to everyone. Perfect for the classroom. 30 mins.
VHS: S27340. $125.00.

The Huggabug Club: I'm One of a Kind
This live-action children's show is full of songs and dance numbers that can brighten a kid's day. All the lovable flowers and bugs of the Huggabug Club join in the fun for an uplifting message that will make kids glad to be themselves. 27 mins.
VHS: S27501. $12.98.

The Huggabug Club: School Days
Kids can be worried about the inevitable first day of school. This video shows the Huggabug Club members singing their way through this anxious moment in a young person's life. It has lessons that can turn school into an exciting new part of a child's experience. 27 mins.
VHS: S27502. $12.98.

The Huggabug Club:
You Can't Win 'em All
Sometimes children have trouble with losing at games or even just waiting their turn. Songs from the Huggabug Club gang teach vital lessons that can show kids winning isn't everything. Playing by the rules and staying focused on fun is more important. 27 mins.
VHS: S27503. $12.98.

I Can Dance
An insightful introduction to ballet, specially designed for children. Professional dancer Debra Maxwell has developed a program for girls and boys aged seven years and older. The program familiarizes children with plies, center work and the five basic positions. 30 mins.
VHS: S17314. $19.95.

I'm a Ballerina Now
This video was designed to aid and inspire hopeful children. Dance exercises are shown and illustrated with lyrics that help children remember the proper steps. Then a true adult ballerina is seen performing the same steps. 40 mins.
VHS: S24831. $14.95.

In Search of the Missing Numbers
Presents basic addition and subtraction concepts in a fun format as Brad and Melissa go into Blasteria in the search of missing numbers. For ages 6-9. 60 mins.
VHS: S09964. $19.95.

Joshua's Masai Mask
With a jazzy text and splashy illustrations, this read-along video is a special experience for all children. Joshua loves playing his kalimba, a traditional African musical instrument, even though his friends all like rap. His uncle gives him a magical mask that helps Joshua overcome this problem. 11:30 mins.
VHS: S22353. $39.95.

The Joy of Life
In this charming interactive tape, children can be guided through the mysteries of human sexuality with the help of their parents. Five-minute segments slowly build to cover a wide range of topics. The story concerns two cousins who ask their grandmother about the facts of life. Everything crucial is covered, from sexual attraction to safe sex and AIDS. 72 mins.
VHS: S22867. $39.95.

Juggle Time
Learn confidence while learning to juggle in this fun-filled program designed to teach juggling in slow motion by using scarves. Three colorful scarves included in package. Questar/Mercom Gold Award, National Educational Film and Video Festival Award. 30 minutes, ages 5-12.
VHS: S17138. $14.95.

Kids Get Cooking: The Egg
This celebration of food and cooking will thrill kids as they learn recipes, experiments, crafts and more. Puppets Herb and Bea add to the comedy, cooking and songs. Endorsed by the National Education Association. 30 minutes, ages 4-10.
Home Video.
VHS: S10148. $14.95.
Public Performance Rights.
VHS: S17152. $34.90.

Kids Kitchen:
Making Good Eating Great Fun for Kids!
Join the juggling nutrition magician and her diverse group of kids as they learn to create delicious, nutritious snacks without cooking. Ages 5-10.
VHS: S24769. $99.00.

Kids Learning Through Fun
These 13 tapes offer both valuable skills and important values to children through an engaging cast of puppets. Music and guests round out the charming elements that make each episode in the series come alive. These tapes are not just fun, but upbeat and positive. 30 mins. each.
A Good Education.
VHS: S26255. $14.95.
A Good Attitude.
VHS: S26264. $14.95.
A Good Sense of Humor.
VHS: S26265. $14.95.
A Helping Hand.
VHS: S26262. $14.95.
Being Conscientious.
VHS: S26266. $14.95.
Completing a Task.
VHS: S26256. $14.95.
Enthusiasm.
VHS: S26261. $14.95.
Good Manners.
VHS: S26257. $14.95.
Planning Your Time.
VHS: S26258. $14.95.
Positive Thinking.
VHS: S26260. $14.95.
Responsibility.
VHS: S26263. $14.95.
Special Friends.
VHS: S26267. $14.95.
Training and Practice.
VHS: S26259. $14.95.

Kids Love Trains
The sights and sounds of all different kinds of trains are available on this video. Red Wagon Music turns traditional train songs into snappy rap and reggae jingles. Their own original train songs are also included. 30 mins.
VHS: S21697. $14.95.

Kidsongs Music Video Stories
A series of sing-a-long music videos, which are designed for children from pre-school to ten years old, featuring performances by the Kidsongs Kids, multi-racial, multi-ethnic, multi-talented boys and girls. Based on the PBS series, the videos also include themes and concepts which are developmentally important. The content is geared toward 2-6 year olds, but also interests older kids, as the subplot involves the older children who produce the show. We see children doing interviews, kids using cameras, kids in the control rooms. Ages 2-10. 25 minutes each tape.
A Day at Old MacDonald's Farm.
VHS: S06639. $14.98.
A Day with the Animals.
VHS: S06640. $14.98.
A Day at the Circus.
VHS: S06647. $14.98.
A Day at Camp.
VHS: S24538. $14.98.
Boppin' with Biggles.
VHS: S24722. $14.98.
Cars, Boats, Trains and Planes.
VHS: S06641. $14.98.
Country Sing-Along.
VHS: S24723. $14.98.
Good Night, Sleep Tight.
VHS: S06642. $14.98.

I'd Like to Teach the World to Sing.
VHS: S06643. $14.98.
If We Could Talk to the Animals.
VHS: S24539. $14.95.
Let's Play Ball!
VHS: S24540. $14.95.
Ride the Roller Coaster.
VHS: S24541. $14.95.
Sing Out, America!
VHS: S06644. $14.98.
The Wonderful World of Sports.
VHS: S06645. $14.98.
Very Silly Songs.
VHS: S24542. $12.95.
We Wish You a Merry Christmas.
VHS: S24784. $12.95.
What I Want to Be!
VHS: S06646. $14.98.

Lamb Chop's Sing-Along, Play-Along
Lamb Chop, the adorable hand puppet, gets top billing over her friend and creator Shari Lewis in this children's video that combine songs and games for the audience at home to join in. You too can interact with Shari and her talented Lamb Chop. 45 mins.
VHS: S07704. $9.95.

The Land of Sweet Taps
This is a fun-filled adventure for children ages 4-8 who want to learn tap dancing. In addition to the fundamental sounds, rhythms and steps there are shuffles and digs. The lyrics are fun and memorable, helping children remember the timing of the music. 57 mins.
VHS: S21701. $19.95.

Landmark
A three-volume set of imaginative, interactive programs that instruct children on the important lessons of problem solving, analysis, questions, play games, learn valuable skills and how to have fun. With audio, video and visual guidelines and 45 minutes of historic newsreel footage.
Fun and Games.
Laser: LD70297. $39.95.
The First National Kidisc: Vol. 1.
Laser: LD70296. $39.95.
The History DisQuiz.
Laser: LD70298. $39.95.

Language Primer
A blend of animation, music and sound effects is used to relate wordless stories about Max, a mouse. The program is designed to encourage children to take an active role in the learning process. The video instructs children on basic language skills: sequencing, recognizing a main idea, recalling details, storywriting and storytelling. The programming is "very effective, providing appealing contrast while learning writing skills" (Video Rating Guide for Libraries). Designed for children in kindergarten through 3rd grade.
Adventuresome Max: Discovering the World. In eight vignettes, Max establishes friendships with an army of ants, an outcast snail and an alien from another world, in the process learning valuable information about himself and the outside world. 18 mins.
VHS: S19960. $49.95.
Max in Motion: Developing Language Skills. Eight stories are expressed without words, each focusing of Max, an eccentric mouse with an innovative flair for problem solving. 18 mins.
VHS: S19959. $49.95.
Max's Library: Beginning to Write. With the aid of puppets and animation, children learn how to create a short story—from conception through execution. They develop storytelling by learning to define a beginning, a middle and an end. 16 mins.
VHS: S19961. $49.95.
Language Primer, Set. A set of three programs. 48 mins.
VHS: S19962. $129.00.

Let's Create a Better World
This how-to video shows kids environmentally safe projects. In addition, it increases awareness of nature and underscores the importance of environmentalism. Ages 6-12. 70 mins.
VHS: S25612. $29.95.

Let's Create for Halloween
Just right for the holidays, this tape shows how to make six art projects with a Halloween theme. Music and special surprises will not only delight kids, but also help motivate them. This video offers a safe way for children to participate in Halloween. USA, 1995, 60 mins.
VHS: S25613. $29.95.

Let's Create for Pre-Schoolers
Six exciting projects are featured in this video that will lead children through concepts dealing with color and shape. It's educational, informative, and certain to keep young minds engaged. Kids learn about colors and shapes in these six art projects accompanied by music. Ages 2-5.
VHS: S24546. $24.95.

Let's Create for Thanksgiving
In this video kids will see the family holiday of Thanksgiving through an artistic lens. The art projects included here both inform children about Thanksgiving and celebrate the best of this holiday. There is even a demonstration that can transform turkey. USA, 1995; 60 mins.
VHS: S25614. $29.95.

Let's Create Fun Jewelry for Boys and Girls
The art club creates jewelry from everyday items. Children will be amazed at the rings, medallions, pins and other accessories they can make. Many make great gifts. 60 mins.
VHS: S25611. $29.95.

Let's Sing Along
Interactive music and sounds provide the inspiration for kids to play along with the child hosts on the video. Ages 2-6. 25 minutes.
VHS: S25038. $14.95.

Look and Learn
Lessons in letters, numbers and words for kids 3-6.
Alphabet Soup. Sing-Along, Flying Pictures, Flipping Words and Jaunty Rhymes, animated.
VHS: S06449. $19.95.
Barefoot Bear. Features read-along word recognition and story words that change color at a read-along pace.
VHS: S06451. $19.95.
Bear Dreams. Teaches word recognition games and road-to-reading with lessons of friendship.
VHS: S06452. $19.95.
Hello Numbers. Features a one-to-one numbers games and songs with count-along to ten and by tens to 100.
VHS: S06450. $19.95.

Macmillan Video Almanac for Kids
Indoor Fun. Contains four individual chapters on one 30-minute cassette, each of them an informative and interactive segment meant to be viewed while using simple household materials: body talk, making faces, a close look at volcanoes and a short journey into space. "A real milestone in children's video." 30 mins.
VHS: S08105. $26.95.
Rainy Day Games. Includes Soap Bubble Magic, A Secret Language, Kite Flying, String Figures. Each of the segments is viewed while using simple household materials. 30 mins.
VHS: S08106. $26.95.

Make a Puppet, Make a Friend
Learn how an ordinary paper bag can be transformed into a playful puppet. 30 mins.
VHS: S09882. $29.95.

Making Music in the Classroom, Program 3, Ages 3-7
The third in the series contains more of John Langstaff's enjoyable musical educational method. Step-by-step techniques prove especially effective with children ages 3-7. Both classroom tapes include an instructional guide for teachers.
VHS: S23683. $24.95.

Making Music in the Classroom, Program 4, Ages 7-11
Absorbing, fun and instructive, this final installment of John Langstaff's musical video series is as much fun as the first.
VHS: S23684. $24.95.

Making Music with Children, Program 1, Ages 3-7
In this introductory video, John Langstaff demonstrates, easily and effectively, basic musical principals for children ages 3-7. Rhythm games, movement activities, simple percussion accompaniments and singing games help children learn in a fun way. Booklets with words and music are included with all these tapes.
VHS: S23681. $24.95.

Making Music with Children, Program 2, Ages 7-11
Langstaff's inspirational teaching method will captivate children in this second video, aimed at children ages 7-11. It contains still more story songs, street cries, sea chanties, folk songs and rounds. Even musical elements like pitch are covered, and the value of music from different cultures is emphasized.
VHS: S23682. $24.95.

Math Rock Countdown
Concentrates on building basic multiplication and division skills and developing strategies for solving problems in the format of a music show as Treva Sue and the Bleaters use math facts to tell their country rock music story. For ages 6-9. 60 mins.
VHS: S09965. $19.95.

Monkey Moves
Based on the acclaimed movement and learning methods of Dr. Moshe Feldenkrais, this marvelous musical exercise-movement tape helps children develop balance, coordination and motor sequencing skills while moving to original songs and music. Put together by Dr. Stephen Rosenholtz, a well qualified educator, known also for his Feldenkrais movement videos for adults. Ages 3-8, 26 mins.
VHS: S24552. $19.95.

More Preschool Power
Pre-School age "teachers" show how to tie shoes, brush teeth, make fruit salad and play with shadow puppets. Packed with songs, music, jokes and tongue-twisters. Recommended by Parents Magazine, Parents' Choice Award, California Children's Video Award. 30 minutes, pre-school.
VHS: S17008. $14.95.

Mr. Men: In the Great Alphabet Hunt
Mr. Men is an inventive brand of cartoon figures which aid children in understanding the alphabet and language. 30 mins.
VHS: S19426. $12.98.

Mr. Wizard's World of Air and Water Wizardry
Don Herbert, TV's Mr. Wizard, hosts a tour through the world of air and water with a series of fascinating demonstrations that you can do at home. 44 mins.
VHS: S05107. $19.98.

Muppet Babies: Be My Valentine
Jim Henson's award-winning Muppet Babies lead kids through lessons for making Valentines as the Muppet Babies make some Valentines themselves. Meanwhile, Baby Gonzo is playing Cupid to win Baby Piggy's heart. This animated short is both informative and fun to watch. 25 mins.
VHS: S27362. $12.99.

My First Activity Series
A fun, intellectually stimulating series of videos adapted from the My First Book Series, providing instructional, easy-to-follow guidelines to a series of activities, including the construction of musical instruments, awareness of ecology and environmental issues, unlocking creativity, understanding nature, conducting science experiments and learning how to make interesting and fun things to eat. Backed by lively musical accompaniment. "The production is excellent, with carefully spoken narration and clear, simple cinematography" (Video Review).
My First Music Video.
VHS: S20293. $14.98.
My First Green Video.
VHS: S20294. $14.98.
My First Activity Video.
VHS: S20295. $14.98.
My First Nature Video.
VHS: S20296. $14.98.
My First Science Video.
VHS: S20297. $14.98.
My First Cooking Video.
VHS: S20298. $14.98.
My First Magic Video. This video explains how to stage a magic show at home using simple but captivating illusions. Step-by-step instructions are provided by a professional magician. 45 mins.
VHS: S25520. $14.95.
My First Party Video. Chock full of creative ideas, this video will help make any party more enjoyable. Crazy hats, crocodile invitations, birthday cake, masks and more are all explained in clear, colorful demonstrations. 45 mins.
VHS: S25521. $14.95.

My New York
Premier folk artists reveal vibrant New York City's through vivid and detailed illustrations in this read-along video. Central Park Zoo, Chinatown, the ferry to Ellis Island and the Empire State Building are depicted. Children will love it.
VHS: S22350. $39.95.

Never Talk to Strangers
From the Learn About Living Series, designed to help children sort out the challenges of growing up. Teaches caution when children are approached by strangers. Uses animals as the "strangers," which helps to make the subject less frightening. Other segments are I Had a Bad Dream, about the scary subject of nightmares, and The House That Had Enough, about a messy girl. Ages 5-8. 30 mins.
VHS: S24994. $9.95.

Nickelodeon Presents How to Throw a Double Dare Party
The Double Dare award-winning action game show on video stars Marc Summers as host, with each game demonstrated with a list of required props and ingredients, with some classics such as Whip Cream and Cherry Pie Wheelbarrow included. 60 mins.
VHS: S11196. $14.98.

Nonsense and Lullabyes: Nursery Rhymes
A collection of eighteen nursery rhymes updated with new twists and beautifully animated by renowned filmmaker Michael Sporn. Original music and songs are by Caleb Sampson and the all-star roster of narrators includes Karen Allen, Eli Wallach, Linda Hunt, Courtney Vance, Heidi Stallings and Phillip Schopper.
VHS: S16466. $9.98.
Michael Sporn, USA, 27 mins.

Nonsense and Lullabyes: Poems for Children
Classic poems like Edward Lear's "The Owl and the Pussycat" and Robert Louis Stevenson's "Autumn Fires" are featured with new children's poems like Russel Hoban's "Homework" to make up this collection. With the voices of Karen Allen, Eli Wallach, and Linda Hunt.
VHS: S16467. $9.98.
Michael Sporn, USA, 27 mins.

Pat-A-Cake, Pat-A-Cake
Sixteen favorite children's rhymes and songs are clearly illustrated in this delightful video. Easy to follow, this tape will allow children to learn age-old favorites at their own pace and have fun doing it. 30 mins.
VHS: S21531. $14.95.

Pictures and Letters: A Video Picture Dictionary
The real world of children is presented in alphabetical order to provide an interesting review of the letters of the alphabet, and an interesting vocabulary-building activity for parents and teachers. 30 mins.
VHS: S10318. $29.95.

Postman Pat's 123 Story
Postman Pat teaches young children the basics of counting in this humorous, simple tale. 30 mins.
VHS: S19422. $12.98.

Postman Pat's ABC Story
A delightful, educational program about the charming postman who teaches children about language, thought and action. 30 mins.
VHS: S19421. $12.98.

Preschool Power #3
Pre-Schoolers learn to do things for themselves—things like putting on gloves, making a paper fan, sweeping up spills, making French bread, making giant bubbles, setting up dominoes. Recommended by the American Library Association. 30 minutes, pre-school.
VHS: S17010. $14.95.

Preschool Power: Jacket Flips & Other Tips
How to button, buckle, zip, wash hands, put on jackets, tidy rooms, make snacks and pour without spilling a drop. Featuring the proven methods of Maria Montessori, Pre-Schoolers will learn the lasting gift of self-reliance. New York Film Festival Award. Recommended by American Library Association. 30 minutes, pre-school.
VHS: S17009. $14.95.

Printmaking Gadgets
With just some paper, old toys and tempera paint, children can create their own pictures, greeting cards, pen holders and wrapping paper. 30 mins.
VHS: S09883. $9.95.

Problems for Young Consumers
Presenting real consumer problems for children to face and solve—problems they are likely to meet in their everyday lives—such as an advertisement that misleads and leaves a child disappointed and unhappy. Includes What Do You Pay? (unit pricing), The Big Sale (comparable value), Buy Now—Pay Later (Credit), and The Street Vendor (guaranteed quality). 25 mins.
VHS: S10313. $29.95.

Professor Iris
The series that makes education fun, as originally aired on The Learning Channel.
Birthday Party. In this video kids will learn how to organize and cooperate as they party with Professor Iris and her friends at the Learning Channel.
VHS: S23018. $19.95.
Creepy Critters. Professor Iris is back, this time introducing kids to snakes, bats, bugs and bees, in this entertaining and educational pre-science lesson. First aired on The Learning Channel. Ages 2-6. 40 minutes.
VHS: S24520. $12.95.
Let's Do It. From the Learning Channel comes this creative and fun video featuring Professor Iris. Kids will learn about sports, dancing and games as they discover new ways to play.
VHS: S23017. $19.95.
Music Mania. Kids learn about musical instruments as they sing and play with Professor Iris in this video from the Learning Channel. Professor Iris is the perfect puppet companion to take kids on a musical, educational journey.
VHS: S23016. $19.95.
Space Cadets. Professor Iris is back helping young kids understand science. This time, a rocket ship is the classroom. First aired on The Learning Channel. Ages 2-6. 40 minutes.
VHS: S24650. $12.95.

Raffi in Concert with the Rise and Shine Band
A young children's concert with the incomparable Raffi and his Rise and Shine Band. Songs feature: "Time to Sing," "Bathtime," "Apples and Bananas" and "Everything Grows." Great Fun! 50 mins.
VHS: S14110. $19.95.
Laser: LD71290. $29.98.

Rainy Day Magic Show
Magician Mark Mazzarella instills a sense of wonder while demonstrating how to turn everyday things into an entire magic show. For ages 6 and up. USA.
VHS: S14952. $19.95.

See How They Grow
This collection of four tapes takes children inside the mysteries of animal behavior—charting from infancy to adulthood the growth of pets, farm animals, wild animals and insects and spiders. Each video contains four different animals, and is set off by musical accompaniment. "This timeless video collection will bring kids and parents back again and again" (The Playground).
See How They Grow: Farm Animals.
VHS: S20290. $14.98.
See How They Grow: Insects and Spiders.
VHS: S20291. $14.98.
See How They Grow: Pets.
VHS: S20289. $14.98.
See How They Grow: Wild Animals.
VHS: S20292. $14.98.

Sesame Songs
Stories, games, songs and the wonderful Sesame Street crowd. 30 minutes each. Ages 2-6.
Sesame Songs: Dance Along! The Muppets and other Sesame Street characters demonstrate such dances as The Count's "Batty Bat" and Bert's favorite, Doin' the Pigeon.
VHS: S12769. $9.98.
Sesame Songs: Elmo's Sing-Along Guessing Game. Kids sing along the clues as they try to guess the answers to Elmo's questions in this TV game show take-off. 1991.
VHS: S24628. $9.98.
Sesame Songs: Monster Hits! Ten Sesame Street hit songs performed by the loveable and furry monsters. Sing along with "C is for Cookie," "That Furry Blue Mommy of Mine" and "Fuzzy and Blue."
VHS: S12264. $9.98.
Sesame Songs: Rock & Roll! Sesame Street characters call in their requests to DJ Jackman Wolf. Songs include "Count up to Nine," and "The Word Is No."
VHS: S12768. $9.98.
Sesame Songs: Sing Yourself Silly! James Taylor is the musical guest for this potpourri of Sesame Street's silliest songs, including the "Honker Duckie Dinger Jamboree," "The Everything Is in the Wrong Place Ball," "Jellyman Kelly" and the ever popular "Lady Bug Picnic." Also includes visits from Pete Seeger, Paul Simon and Rhea Perlman.
VHS: S12265. $9.98.
Sesame Songs: Sing, Hoot and Howl. Big Bird hosts such sing-along favorites as "Proud to Be a Cow," "The Insects in Your Neighborhood," and "Cluck Around the Clock."
VHS: S24629. $9.98.
Sesame Songs: Sing-Along Earth Songs. Join Sesame Street's Grover to find out about the importance of protecting the earth.
VHS: S24649. $9.98.
Sesame Songs: We All Sing Together. The Sesame Street crowd is back! This time, Herry the anchor monster discovers the variety of shapes, colors and sizes of different kids. Full of songs, fun and favorite Sesame Street characters.
VHS: S24656. $9.98.

Sesame Street Start to Read Books

These videos are based on the popular "Start to Read Books" series. Large print permits children to read along with Big Bird, the well known Sesame Street character. Suitable for ages three and up. Each tape features three stories and is 30 minutes long.
Don't Cry Big Bird and Other Stories.
VHS: S21949. $14.95.
Ernie's Big Mess and Other Stories.
VHS: S21950. $14.95.
Ernie's Little Lie and Other Stories.
VHS: S21951. $14.95.
I Want to Go Home and Other Stories.
VHS: S21952. $14.95.

Shari Lewis: 101 Things for Kids to Do

A fun activity tape, including arts & crafts, games, magic tricks and more. 60 minutes.
VHS: S24642. $9.95.

Shari Lewis: Don't Wake Your Mom

This innovative program gives kids something to do for 45 minutes while a parent takes that needed break. With characteristic charm, Shari Lewis makes magic out of the classic question, "Is it time yet?" 45 mins.
VHS: S16158. $14.95.

The Sign for Friends

Follow the signs for music, laughter and happy faces. This video teaches kids how to sign as they sing and count along. Host David Parker shows his young friend how it's done. Perfect for kids ages 4-8. 30 min.
VHS: S24490. $14.95.

Sign-Me-A-Story

Any child, hearing-impaired or hearing, would enjoy these two tales told in American Sign Language. Sesame Street's Linda Bove, deaf herself, is a wonderful narrator and role model. Along the way, we learn a couple of signs ourselves! Ages 3-12.
VHS: S24643. $14.95.

Silly Tales and Tunes

Disc jockey K.J. is back, hosting comical stories and sing-along songs. Ages 2-8.
VHS: S24644. $12.95.

Simply Magic: The Rainy Day Adventure

Joanie Bartell leads a sing-along program about a poolside party and a magical car. 1993. Ages 3-10. 45 minutes.
VHS: S24647. $14.98.

Skating Safe for Kids

This hip video uses a fun story to instruct kids ages six and up how to skate safely. Gail Shrawder is a recognized instructor who will explain "10 Rules of the Road." She also instructs kids on basics like how to balance themselves, stop, and turn. 30 mins.
VHS: S23858. $24.95.

Something Special

Develops awareness of the importance of the arts for a balanced education. Children are shown in classes in the visual arts, music, dance and theatre, illustrating the value of art for children. 28 mins.
VHS: S07638. $39.95.

Spinning Tops and Tickle Bops

This animated children's collection features three different stories: *The Animal's Picnic Day*, *Spinning Tops* and *The Planet of the Tickle Bops*. For those viewers who are wondering what a tickle bop is, and why they rate an entire planet, the answer can only be found by watching this tape. USA, 30 mins.
VHS: S03642. $14.95.

Squiggles, Dots and Lines

Ed Emberly presents his drawing alphabet, a tool for kids to unlock their creativity. Fourteen kids share their fun-telling stories and create a giant mural. Parents' Choice Award. 30 minutes, ages 5-12.
Home Video.
VHS: S10147. $14.95.
Public Performance Rights.
VHS: S17153. $34.90.

Stop, Look and Cook!

Set in a dairy farm, an apple orchard and a nice kitchen, this video teaches kids how to make some nutritious recipes along with a side of sign language. Host David Parker is effective and appealing, perfect for kids ages 4-8. 20 min.
VHS: S24491. $19.95.

Table Manners for Kids: Tots to Teens

A series of vignettes designed to instruct children and young adults on proper etiquette and how to apply those rules in an actual restaurant setting.
VHS: S19662. $14.95.

This Pretty Planet

This collection features 13 folk songs by Tom Chapin, who is joined with special guests Jon Cobert and Michael Mark. The songs include "Alphabet Soup" and "Sing a Whale Song." "These songs are wittier and catchier than most in kiddom, and Chapin may be the most charming performer on earth" (*Forbes Newspapers*).
VHS: S20299. $14.98.

Twinkle Twinkle Little Star

Seventeen songs and rhymes that have always been popular with children are showcased in this charming video. Children will learn to sing along to all their favorites in this simple and straightforward illustration of childhood songs. 40 mins.
VHS: S21532. $14.95.

Vegetable Print Shop

Children use fruits and vegetables to create pictures, including using sliced artichokes, apples and pears as printmaking tools. 30 mins.
VHS: S09884. $29.95.

Wee Sing Series

This series of videos continues the positive tradition of the popular book/audio cassette series which has brought song to so many. Aimed for ages 2-8.
Wee Sing: Grandpa's Magical Toys. Peter and his friends visit the world's most wonderful Grandpa. In turn, Grandpa shows them the importance of remaining young at heart. Grandpa leads the children into a special world where toys come alive and songs are fun to sing. 1988. 60 minutes. Ages 2-8.
VHS: S24843. $12.95.
Wee Sing: King Cole's Party. Jack and Jill, Little Boy Blue and Mary and her Little Lamb voyage to King Cole's Castle to celebrate 100 years of peace. This charming live-action children's video includes over 20 favorite nursery rhymes engagingly performed. 54 mins.
VHS: S26360. $12.95.
Wee Sing: The Best Christmas Ever. Twenty holiday songs and a variety of fingerplays will enchant kids in this video trip to the North Pole. Four kids set off to help Santa save the holiday. Together these friends learn how to overcome personal challenges with help from each other. 56 mins.
VHS: S26362. $12.95.
Wee Sing: The Big Rock Candy Mountains. Lisa and her friends the Snoodle Doodles travel together to a fantasyland of candy. Along the way they learn about the importance of friendship, kindness, recycling and the joys of healthy food. 61 mins.
VHS: S26359. $12.98.
Wee Sing: The Marvelous Musical Mansion. A great cast of characters performs over 20 songs, in every room of this mansion. Oddly, however, there is a mystery afoot. Who stole the missing musical treasures? Kids will love the music and intrigue, and will enjoy an important lesson about self-esteem and consideration for others. 61 mins.
VHS: S26361. $12.98.
Wee Sing in Sillyville. This video features a girl and a boy who bring harmony to the land of Yellow Spurtlegurgles and Green Jingleheimers. 20 nonsense songs. Parents will remember some of these classics. 1990. 30 minutes.
VHS: S24842. $12.95.
Wee Sing Together. Encourages kids to sing along in this mixture of live action and special effects. 1985. 60 minutes.
VHS: S24841. $12.95.
Wee Sing Train. Kids ride along, making exciting stops along the way, singing, dancing and learning. Ages 2-8.
VHS: S24844. $12.95.
Wee Sing Under the Sea. When Granny painted an underwater seascape, she never expected it to come alive. Now she and her grandson Devin can explore a new world where they meet amazing creatures. This delightful children's video is full of songs and information about environmentalism. 60 mins.
VHS: S23273. $14.95.

Wizkids: Careers in Science

This award-winning show encourages girls and children of color to pursue careers in science. An African-American agronomist and a Native American geneticist explain the gratifications of science. 25 mins.
VHS: S23275. $165.00.

Workout with Daddy & Me

Combining physical activities with games and songs to enhance learning, coordination and socialization, *Workout with Daddy and Me* provides a fun and easy way to exercise with your child. Complete with an activity book. 30 mins.
VHS: S16483. $12.98.

Workout with Mommy & Me

Millions of parents have attended *Mommy and Me* classes for more than 15 years. Now you and your child can take the class at home. Complete with an activity book, this fun-filled exercise program is led by award-winning gymnast and dance instructor Barbara Peterson Davis. 30 mins.
VHS: S16482. $12.98.

"You Can" Videos

A series of unique, reality-based family and educational programs targeting kids ages 2-6 which aims at empowerment through positive, nurturing messages. Non-violent and aiming to show girls and boys equally. 30 minutes each video. Ages 2-6.
You Can Be an Artist.
VHS: S24938. $12.95.
You Can Fly a Kite.
VHS: S24939. $12.95.
You Can Ride a Horse. Come along with the You Can Kids as they visit a stable, watch a blacksmith at work, learn about horseback riding and more. Full of fascinating facts about horses, with catchy sing-alongs and nice musical backdrop. Perfect for children ages 2-8, this video demonstrates basic horseback riding skills together with catchy original songs performed by kids and the chorus Peaceful Generation. In addition there are grooming demonstrations and exciting stunts. 30 mins.
VHS: S24770. $12.95.

You on Kazoo!

The video comes with a kazoo. Seven kids have a blast inviting the viewers to join the kazoo fun as they mimic animals and machines. Ages 3-8. 30 minutes.
VHS: S25037. $14.95.

Zillions TV: A Kid's Guide to Toys and Games

Zillions TV warns children about the foolish linkage of money and quality. This program teaches kids how to use science, math and problem-solving capabilities in order to assess the quality of video games, walkie-talkies, food, movie tickets, boom boxes and mountain bikes, among other products. The work features two songs, "Check It Out," a rap music video, and "Shop Around," a cover of the classic song that promotes comparison shopping. 30 mins.
VHS: S20024. $19.95.

FOREIGN LANGUAGES FOR CHILDREN

Aladdin and the Magical Lamp (Aladino y La Lampara Maravillosa)

This is a charming film adaptation of the delightful tale concerning the discovery of a magical lamp. Clavillazo, Ana Bertha Lepe and Oscar Pulido star. Spanish with NO subtitles. 89 mins.
VHS: S23921. $24.95.

Asterix

This inventive program charts the amazing tales of Asterix. In French. 220 mins.
Asterix et Cleopatre.
VHS: S19807. $39.95.
Asterix le Gaulois.
VHS: S19809. $39.95.
Douze Travaux d'Asterix.
VHS: S19808. $39.95.

Asterix in Britain

Based on the book by Goscinny and Uderzo, *Asterix in Britain* continues the adventurous antics of the little Gaulish hero as the little guy takes on one big empire.
VHS: S12527. $39.95.
Pino van Lamsweerde, Belgium, 1985, 85 mins.

Asterix vs. Caesar

Asterix returns to battle Caesar and his Roman legions in this fun-filled adventure famous the world over. With his giant friend Obelix at his side, the little Gaulish warrior turns friends, Romans and countrymen on their ears when he decides to save the beautiful Falbala and her prince from some very hungry lions. The results are hilarious. Fully animated.
VHS: S12526. $39.95.
Paul & Gaetan Brizi, France, 1985, 85 mins.

Babar et le Pere Noel

This French adaptation of de Brunhoff's classic has won the 1987 Gemini Best Animated Program. Babar is on a journey to find Father Christmas. Threatening his search is Babar's arch enemy, Rataxas the Rhinoceros. Throughout, the animation is lively and colorful. French without subtitles. 24 mins.
VHS: S09053. $39.95.

Babar le Film

A wonderfully touching, animated treatment of de Brunhoff's classic stories about the king of elephants. *Babar le film* relates the story of how he saved Celesteville. French with *no* subtitles. 77 mins.
VHS: S19804. $49.95.

Bonjour les Amis!

Moustache is France's most beloved animated character. Now this charming cat helps introduce the French language to children in a collection of three tapes which combine animation and live action. 50 mins each.
Bonjour les Amis! Volume 1.
VHS: S23608. $19.95.
Bonjour les Amis! Volume 2.
VHS: S23609. $19.95.
Bonjour les Amis! Volume 3.
VHS: S23610. $19.95.
Bonjour les Amis! Set of 3 Volumes.
VHS: S23611. $54.95.

Carlitos, Dani y Luis Alfredo

Three puppets and their human companion use song, movement and dialogue to teach basic language and social skills. Four different segments cover colors, shapes, health, conservation and healthy eating. The program is accompanied by a parent/teacher guide with vocabulary, language exercises and followup tasks. Spanish and English. 30 mins.
VHS: S19775. $39.95.

Classic Stories in Spanish

Children will delight in seeing these familiar favorites in Spanish. The colorful animation will hold the attention of young students as they listen to the story unfold. Perfect for those just learning Spanish. *Don Quixote* and *The Three Little Pigs* are the stories included. 23 mins.
VHS: S06833. $39.95.

Cri-Cri: El Grillito Cantor

This a tribute to the most important composer and singer of Latin American children's music, Francisco Gabilondo Soler. Featured are the songs that three generations have enjoyed, animated by Walt Disney: *La patita*, *El chorrito*, *El rey Bombon*, *El ropero* and *Los cochinitos Dormilones*. This is your ticket to the fantastic world of Cri-Cri, the Singing Cricket. In Spanish. 90 mins.
VHS: S16366. $39.95.

Disney Canta con Nosotros

Jiminy Cricket hosts this series of memorable Disney movie songs with on-screen lyric titles in Spanish. Students will be able to confidently sing along and reinforce their listening, reading and speaking skills. *Snow White*, *Peter Pan*, *The Little Mermaid* and *Beauty and the Beast* are covered in four volumes. Spanish narration, 30 mins.
VHS: S24785. $72.00.

El Pequeno Tren (The Little Train)

A trip to fantasyland offers the perfect opportunity to meet Little Red Riding Hood, the Little Soldier and other characters from famous children's stories. Animated. Spanish with NO subtitles. 1985, 89 mins.
VHS: S23914. $24.95.

An Elephant Named Illusion (Un Elefante Color Illusion)

Pablo Luis Codevilla and Ubaldo Martinez star in this whimsical adventure story. A young boy decides to steal a young and friendly elephant. Spanish with NO subtitles.
VHS: S23920. $24.95.
Derlis Maria Beccaglia, Argentina, 1970, 85 mins.

Erase Una Vez

A prince and a princess are separated by war in this animated adventure/romance. Windaria is the magical world they call home. Spanish with NO subtitles. 1987, 92 mins.
VHS: S23915. $24.95.

French Fairy Tales—Blanche Neige

Fully animated stories selected from the classics in children's literature. Includes: Blanche Neige and Les Troit Petits Cochons. French with no subtitles.
VHS: S06884. $39.95.

French Fairy Tales—Le Petit Chaperon

Fully animated stories in French with no subtitles. Includes two stories: Le Petit Chaperon Rouge and La Belle et La Bete.
VHS: S06885. $39.95.

Heidi

This is an animated version of the classic tale of a young girl who frolics amidst the alpine landscape and brings happiness to her grandfather and a crippled girl. Spanish with NO subtitles. 1975, 93 mins.
VHS: S23913. $34.95.

In My Own Backyard

In this read-along video children will learn about all the things that used to live in their backyard. From agrarian America all the way back to the time of the dinosaurs, it's a fascinating look at history, geology and more. 11:17 mins.
English Version.
VHS: S22364. $39.95.
Spanish Version.
VHS: S22365. $39.95.

Jay Jay the Jet Plane and His Flying Friends

Model planes come to life in the storybook land where not even the sky is the limit. (Yes, some of the planes are female.) With joyful lessons about life, family, friends and things that really matter. Ages 2-8. 30 minutes.
Volume 1. Tito Turbinitas y Sus Amigos Voladores/El Primer Vuelo de Tito Turbinitas y Otros Tres Cuentos. This collection of four stories features Tito Turbinitas and his other airplane friends in four animated shorts. Children will enjoy these non-violent and educational stories. Spanish language, ages 2-8, 30 mins.
Volume 2. Old Oscar Leads the Parade and Three Other Stories. This collection features Old Oscar and his other airplane friends in four animated shorts. Children will enjoy these non-violent and educational stories. Ages 2-8, 30 mins.
VHS: S24575. $12.95.

Kaliman, El Hombre Incredible (Kaliman, the Incredible Man)

Jeff Cooper, Nino del Arco, Susana Dosamantes and Adriana del Arco star in this film based on the adventures of the well-known comic book character. Children treasure his heroic exploits. Spanish with NO subtitles.
VHS: S23923. $24.95.

L'homme a la Dague

In this episode from the French television series *Les Enquetes de Sans Atout*, a 14-year-old detective follows a mysterious stranger. "The speech is colloquial, the settings contemporary, the characters believably French" (*Video Rating Guide for Libraries*). 26 mins.
VHS: S19796. $39.95.

La Musique Folklorique

This video contains 11 of the best known French songs, performed in evocative settings such as a castle and a horse-drawn carriage. Each song contains a short note on its origins. The songs include "Au Clair de la Lune," "Frere Jacques" and "Chevaliers de la Table Ronde." 48 mins.
VHS: S19801. $39.95.

La Publicite en France—Volume 1

A fascinating look into the world of French TV commercials. See how the French advertise a variety of products. Explore the similarities and differences with our own TV ads. Includes script. 35 mins.
VHS: S05743. $49.95.

La Publicite en France—Volume 2

A new volume of commercials from France, with the subjects including clothing, cosmetics, perfumes, automobiles, supermarkets, and more. 26 mins.
VHS: S11200. $49.95.

La Rana Valiente (The Brave Frog)

In this touching animated film two frogs team up against the cruel King of Rainbow Pond. If only they can get him to change his ways so that their home becomes a peaceful place to inhabit, then it might be the best kind of home imaginable. In Spanish with no English subtitles. 91 mins.
VHS: S23917. $24.95.

Las Aventuras de Pinocchio

This animated version of the Pinocchio story will delight children. A lonely old puppet maker carves a puppet who magically becomes the son he always hoped for. Spanish with NO subtitles. 1986, 95 mins.
VHS: S23924. $24.95.

Le Noel de Mickey

This program reimagines Mickey Mouse as a French-speaking Bob Cratchit in the wonderful Disney adaptation of Dickens' immortal *A Christmas Carol*. French with no subtitles. 25 mins.
VHS: S19811. $24.95.

The Little Engine that Could

The enchanting children's tale about desire, hope, courage and optimism is beautifully animated within a French and Spanish context. 30 mins.
French Narration.
VHS: S19812. $19.95.
Spanish Narration.
VHS: S19813. $19.95.

Magical Coqui—Puerto Rico—Mi Tierra!

Aimed at younger viewers, this cassette contains a delightful original story about a small boy and his pet Coqui (tree frog) in Puerto Rico. Also, there is a presentation of music and beautiful pictures about life in Puerto Rico designed to present the viewers with an appreciation for the island and a taste of its culture. The program is presented first in English, and then repeated in Spanish. 40 mins.
  VHS: S10789. $59.95.

Posada Navidena

Pepe Serna is Scrooge in this Spanish-language version of the Charles Dickens classic *A Christmas Carol*. As the ghosts of Christmas visit the old, greedy businessman Scrooge, he has a change of heart and learns the true meaning of the holiday season.
  VHS: S23345. $19.95.

Ravioli

The daily life, activities, incidents and drama of a German family called the Duewels are explored in this prize-winning series, personalizing their struggles and pain, and the often difficult intergenerational relationships. German *without* subtitles.
Ravioli I. 75 mins.
  VHS: S17231. $39.95.
Ravioli II. 75 mins.
  VHS: S17232. $49.95.
Ravioli III. 75 mins.
  VHS: S17233. $39.95.
Ravioli IV. 97 mins.
  VHS: S17234. $39.95.

Sesame Street: Plaza Sesamo

Sesame Street is finally available in Spanish! For use in teaching Spanish, the videos can work for ages 2-12. Each video is 30 minutes.
De Campamento Con Montoya: Big Bird Goes Camping. Camping with the crew from Sesame Street is an opportunity to experience the wonders of nature. At the same time, this camping trip gives kids a chance to learn about the many things one encounters in the wild. In Spanish.
  VHS: S19757. $25.00.
El Alfabeto de Montoya: Learn the Alphabet with Bert and Ernie. Sesame Street characters, including Big Bird, help kids learn the alphabet by talking about animals. Actual footage of these creatures will fascinate kids even as it helps them remember their ABC's. In Spanish.
  VHS: S19760. $25.00.
Plaza Sesamo Canta: Favorite Songs from Past Shows. Stories, games, songs and the wonderful Sesame Street crowd make this video a trip to the imagination. In Spanish.
  VHS: S19758. $25.00.
Vamos a Imaginar: Learn About Sounds and Shapes. It's great fun to take a trip using only your imagination. Sesame Street characters employ just a few shapes and sounds to bring kids a world of diversion, fun and possibility. In Spanish.
  VHS: S19759. $25.00.
Viaja Con Nosotros: Big Bird and Oscar Go to Venezuela and Mexico. This special tour of Latin America voyages to Machu Pichu, Buenos Aires and the Amazon. Kids will be entertained and amazed; and they will learn something about the world. In Spanish.
  VHS: S19756. $25.00.
Plaza Sesamo Complete Set. The children's program *Sesame Street* is finally available in Spanish. 150 mins.
  VHS: S19761. $110.00.

Shalom Sesame

It's a long way from Sesame Street to Israel. Violinist Itzhak Perlman and Broadway and television star Bonnie Franklin team up with the Muppet and Israeli casts of "Rechov Sumsum", the Israeli version of Sesame street, to introduce American children to the people, places, cultures and languages of Israel. Each program is 30 mins.
Aleph-Bet Telethon. Subtitled *Discovering the Hebrew Letters*, Kippi ben Kippod and Jerry Stiller are called to action when the Hebrew alphabet mysterious vanishes, so the two respond by holding a special telethon to track down the mysterious letters.
  VHS: S17122. $22.95.
Chanukah. *Shalom Sesame* celebrates the Festival of Lights as Jeremy Miller goes on an exploration through memory and time in the ancient village of Modi'in in the land of the Maccabees.
  VHS: S17119. $22.95.
Jerusalem. Experience the golden beauty of Israel's City of Peace as Itzhak Perlman, Bonnie Franklin and their young Israeli friends take you on a tour of Jerusalem from the Old City to the holy places of the Christian, Moslem, Armenian and Jewish Quarters.
  VHS: S08386. $22.95.
Journey to Secret Places. Jeremy Miller and Kippi ben Kippod move through a strange tunnel that transports them into the unsettling, vibrant cultures of Israel's exotic, mysterious regions.
  VHS: S17121. $22.95.
Kibbutz. Bonnie Franklin travels to Kibbutz Ein Gedi on the shore of the Dead Sea and shares with the kibbutz kids their unique way of life.
  VHS: S08384. $22.95.
Kids Sing Israel. In this glorious finale, Kippi, Sarah Jessica Parker and the children of Israel host a rousing mixture of traditional Israeli and Hebrew songs with the best loved *Sesame Street* tunes.
  VHS: S17124. $22.95.
Land of Israel. Meet your new Israeli friends from "Rechov Sumsum," including an oversized porcupine, Kippy ben Kipod; Moishe Oofnick, the neighborhood grouch; Bentz and Arik. Mary Tyler Moore joins Bonnie Franklin and Itzhak Perlman in this tour of Israel.
  VHS: S08382. $22.95.
Passover. In this film subtitled *Jerusalem Jones and the Lost Afikomann*, the talented young actor Sarah Jessica Parker (*L.A. Story*) stars as Jerusalem Jones. Parker must find the lost afikomann and determine whether Miriam's bread will rise.
  VHS: S17123. $22.95.
People of Israel. They came from Sweden, Russia, Ethiopia, Egypt, India and America. Now they're Israeli kids. Join them and Itzhak Perlman as they explore the colorful mix that makes up Israel's people.
  VHS: S08385. $22.95.
Sing Around the Seasons. In this educational program about the landscape, people and culture of Israel, the *Sesame Street* gang orchestrate a sing-along, celebrate the country's changing seasons, and explore holidays and festivals and its flair for celebration and ritual.
  VHS: S17120. $22.95.
Tel Aviv. Itzhak Perlman introduces his hometown, including the colorful, bustling Carmel Market, the Tel Aviv boardwalk and beach, and the ancient city of Jaffa.
  VHS: S08383. $22.95.

Singing French Songs for Children (Les Petits Chanteurs de Paris)

Enjoy the musical mastery of the world famous National Boys Choir of Paris as they sing numerous traditional French songs. Includes "Au Clair de la lune", "Le pont d'Avignon" and "Il pleut bergere".
  VHS: S14206. $49.95.

Spanish Cartoon Classics

Three cartoon heroes, Bugs Bunny, Woody Woodpecker and Porky Pig, are available in Spanish. Each video is 30 mins.
El Cerdito Porky.
  VHS: S19834. $9.95.
El Conejo Bugs.
  VHS: S19835. $9.95.
Woody El Pajaro Loco.
  VHS: S19836. $9.95.

Spanish Club: Fiesta!

A live-action video featuring Senora Reyes and her Spanish language club as they explore the meaning of fiesta. The program uses traditional Hispanic songs and stories to teach culture as well as language. For children ages 2-8.
  VHS: S21923. $19.95.

Spanish Club: Los Animales!

Senora Reyes and the Spanish Club Kids explore the world of animals in Volume 2 of this series, which uses traditional Hispanic songs and stories for children ages 2-8.
  VHS: S21924. $19.95.

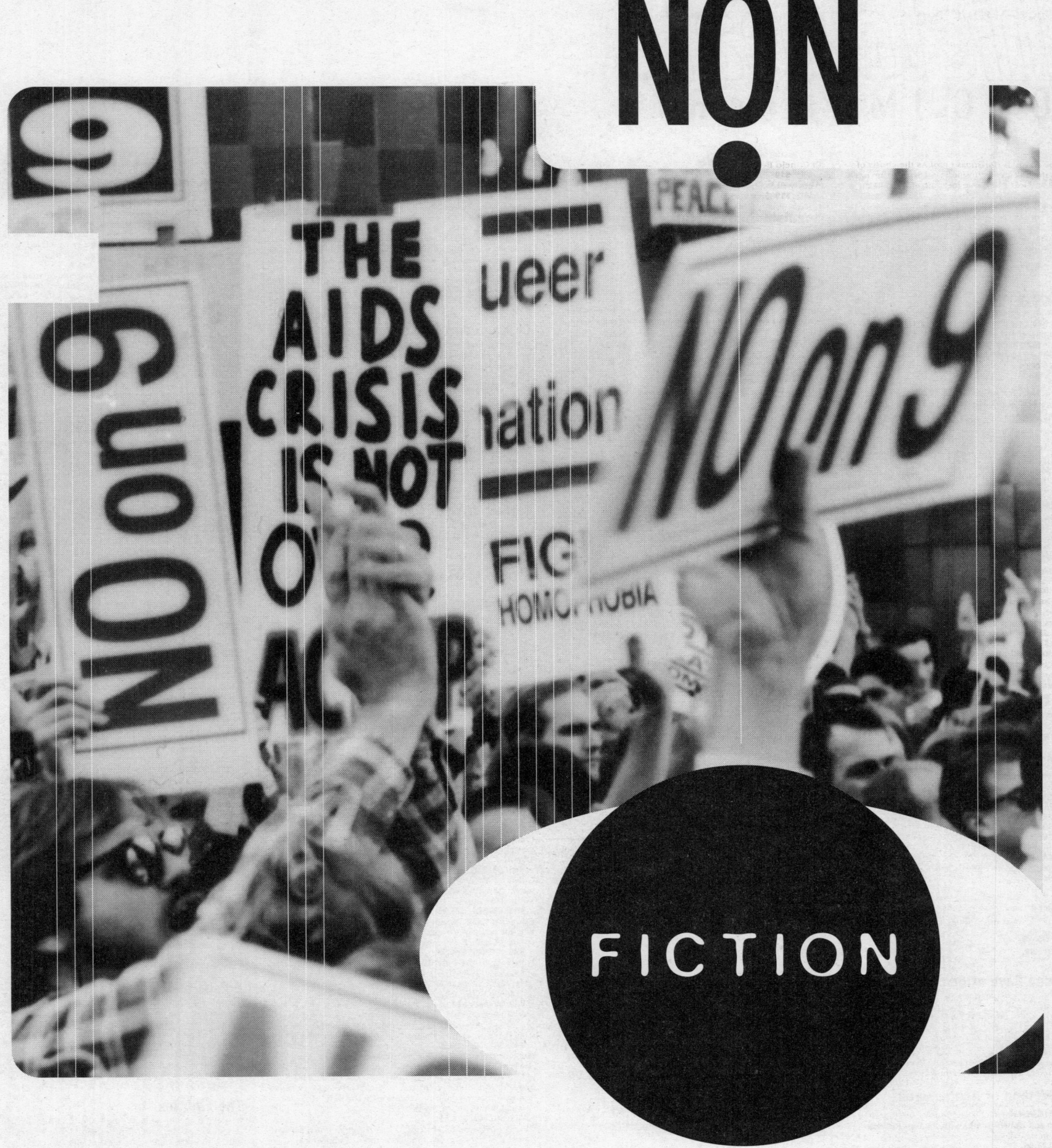

NON

FICTION

video

historical
DOCUMENTARY

60 Minutes: 25 Years
This special celebration of America's longest-lasting and most watched news program provides an in-depth look at this vital newsmagazine. There are reprises and updates of some of the most memorable feature stories by the famed correspondents. Profiles of George Burns, Ray Charles, Barbra Streisand, Jackie Gleason, Oprah Winfrey and Lena Horne are also included. Hosted by Charles Kuralt. 95 min.
VHS: S21715. $19.98.

Age of Anxiety (1952-1958)
During Eisenhower's presidency, the first Republican president in 20 years, the world took on an ominous cast. Though the Korean War ended, and Stalin's death brought a smiling Khrushchev to power, many troubles remained, particularly the arms race. And the end of the decade witnessed the birth of Castro's Cuba. 24 mins.
VHS: S23597. $99.95.

Agriculture Hall of Fame
This official shrine honors and preserves the history of U.S. agricultural achievement which is now presented on this video. There is an 1854 train station, a 1917 schoolhouse, a blacksmith shop and a vast array of agricultural antiques from across the country. 32 mins.
VHS: S23427. $24.95.

America Fever
The title refers to the wave of emigration that swept 19th-century Norway. This is the story of one woman who, after careful preparations, made the long trek to a new land. Includes public performance rights.
VHS: S22149. $126.50.

America's Castles
Visit the homes of seven of America's most powerful turn-of-the-century industrialists and entrepreneurs. Their "castles" brought a scale of grandeur and opulence hitherto unknown to this side of the Atlantic. In this documentary it's all visible, from the imposing grounds to the majestic interiors. 100 mins.
VHS: S21066. $29.95.

American History
Birth of a Nation Series
Critical moments in the transformation that brought America from colonial status to independence are documented in this insightful series of seven videos.
Colonial America in the 1760's. 17 mins.
VHS: S23526. $49.95.
Taxation Without Representation. 16 mins.
VHS: S23527. $49.95.
Prelude to Revolution. 16 mins.
VHS: S23528. $49.95.
Lexington, Concord, and Independence. 17 mins.
VHS: S23529. $49.95.
Fighting for Freedom. 18 mins.
VHS: S23530. $49.95.
A Nation in Crisis. 16 mins.
VHS: S23531. $49.95.
The Living Constitution. 16 mins.
VHS: S23532. $49.95.

American Pie
A video about the regions, communities, people and institutions that make the divergent cross sections and fabrics of "America."
VHS: S16874. $14.98.

The American Revolution
A&E presents this super-documentary about the birth of the nation, in six volumes. Kelsey Grammar, Bill Daniels and Cliff Robertson narrate events, posing as the founding fathers. Dramatic re-enactments employ on-site locations and period detail to bring this epic struggle to the screen. The battles are incredible. Each episode is 50 mins. Available only as a 6-volume set.
VHS: S23612. $99.95.

American Women of Achievement
Video Collection
This series provides in-depth biographies of notable historic women. As a group they overcame the barriers placed in their way, to transform not only their own time but also our current legacy as Americans. Each 30-minute-long volume relies on archival resources and expert opinion.
Abigail Adams. (1744-1818) Women's rights advocate.
VHS: S24436. $39.95.
Jane Addams. (1860-1935) Social worker.
VHS: S24437. $39.95.
Marian Anderson. (1902-1993) Singer.
VHS: S24438. $39.95.
Susan B. Anthony. (1820-1912) Woman suffragist.
VHS: S24439. $39.95.
Clara Barton. (1821-1912) Founder, American Red Cross.
VHS: S24440. $39.95.
Emily Dickinson. (1830-1890) Poet.
VHS: S24441. $39.95.
Amelia Earhart. (1897-1937?) Aviator.
VHS: S24442. $39.95.
Helen Keller. (1880-1968) Humanitarian.
VHS: S24443. $39.95.
Sandra Day O'Connor. (1930 - Present) Supreme Court Justice.
VHS: S24444. $39.95.
Wilma Rudolph. (1940 - Present) Champion Athlete.
VHS: S24445. $39.95.
American Women of Achievement Video Collection. 10-volume set.
VHS: S24446. $399.50.

Anarchy U.S.A.
Made in 1966, this shameful propaganda piece maintains that the Civil Rights movement is part of a worldwide communist plot to destroy America. Its description of an untenable conspiracy for a "Soviet Negro Republic" might be humorous were it not so vile. 78 mins.
VHS: S24080. $24.95.

Anatomy of a Riot
This video looks at the roots of the Los Angeles riots in the aftermath of the first Rodney King trial. The program offers video accounts and eyewitness interviews with people who witnessed the violence. 47 mins.
VHS: S20422. $19.98.

Battle of Washington/
Monocacy/Bill Shore
This re-enactment traces the battles of Jubal Early's army up to and including the threat posed to the U.S. Capitol. Civil War buffs will be riveted by this unique view of the war between the states. Narrated by Bill Shore. 59 mins.
VHS: S22046. $14.98.

The Best of Times (1920-1924)
E.G. Marshall hosts this look at a nation enamored by motion picture stars. Chaplin, Keaton, Will Rogers and Fatty Arbuckle are just some of the celebrities that emerge on film and radio. Harding maintains his popularity despite a number of scandals. 25 mins.
VHS: S23584. $99.95.

Between the Wars (1918-1939)
Eric Sevareid narrates this look at the tumultuous era between the wars. Prosperity and peace gave way to bust and international tension. In the public eye, sports heroes, film stars and daredevils took people's minds off the troubles of the times. 25 mins.
VHS: S23589. $99.95.

Bloody Korea: The Real Story
The role of the United States Marines in the battle for South Korea is not well known despite the vital participation of this branch of the armed forces in the Korean War. Rare archival footage, interviews with Congressional Medal of Honor recipients and interviews with the Marines who served in Korea are combined in this documentary about the forgotten heroes of "The Forgotten War."
VHS: S27245. $29.95.
Paul Hansen, USA, 1994, 60 mins.

The Brave New Age (1903-1912)
E.G. Marshall narrates this documentary. The introduction of the Model T, a beginning crusade for prohibition, and even the San Francisco earthquake give some indication of the momentous changes ahead. Roosevelt's presidency ushered in this era, but even his energy could not keep him at the nation's helm. 25 mins.
VHS: S23578. $99.95.

Camelot
Kathleen Turner narrates this documentary about the fabled court of King Arthur. Eminent scholars venture through England and Wales searching for clues to the fate of this kingdom. Tintangel Castle and Arthur's alleged burial mound at Glastonbury are just two sites visited on this video. From the A&E Ancient Mysteries: New Investigations of the Unsolved series. 50 mins.
VHS: S27001. $19.95.

Cavaliers & Craftsmen—
Colonial Williamsburg and Jamestown
Explores two of America's earliest and most important colonies. Panoramic vistas provide the timeless backdrop for the rich details of colonial life—the clothes, the crafts and the artifacts. 30 mins.
VHS: S11122. $19.95.

A Century of Women
Jane Fonda narrates this series, which documents and celebrates the women of the 20th century. An incredible group of performers have been collected for this task, including Sally Field, Meryl Streep, Glenn Close, Erica Jong, Gloria Steinem, Joan Baez, Twyla Tharp, Chris Evert and Maya Angelou.
A Century of Women: Image and Popular Culture. A fascinating exploration of the changing concepts of "ideal beauty" illuminates the discrepancy between the way women are supposed to appear and their own self image. Clips of fashions reveal how this ideal repeatedly denied the physical reality of a woman's body.
VHS: S21744. $19.98.
A Century of Women: Sexuality and Social Justice. This comprehensive look at women's efforts to shape their own destinies and establish a system of justice shows that they fought not only for themselves, but for all Americans.
VHS: S21743. $19.98.
A Century of Women: Work and Family. The balancing act of labor and family love is not an invention of the 1990's. For many women in the early years of the century, it was a matter of life or death.
VHS: S21742. $19.98.
Complete Set.
VHS: S21745. $49.98.

Charlemagne
The life and times of medieval Europe's most heroic figure are brilliantly portrayed in an epic telling of intense passions, bloody betrayals and the political intrigues that surround this extraordinary leader. It is also the compelling story of one man, Charles, whose great loves and private sorrows must be set aside for the public good. Faced with the overwhelming task of bringing Christianity and political order to a world racked by ignorance and corruption, Charlemagne traces the rise of a prince to his place in history as the first Emperor of The Holy Roman Empire. With Christian Brendel. 5-tape set, 300 mins.
VHS: S27396. $89.95.

Chicago and Its Gangsters
Dubbed a "travelogue with a difference," this program debunks the myths and media-driven association of Chicago gangsters by detailing the characters, figures and deeds of the leading underground figures.
VHS: S16974. $19.95.

Cipango
A video concerning the dramatic interplay between Christopher Columbus, Queen Isabella and Martin Pinzon. The author compresses the events of four different voyages and concentrates on the shifting relationship between Columbus and Queen Isabella. 48 mins.
VHS: S20244. $39.95.

Clouds of War (1916-1917)
A number of key political events occurred in this year. America entered World War I, while Pancho Villa provoked the American military along the border. The A.F. of L. was founded as women and African Americans fought for their rights, and President Wilson was re-elected. Narrated by E.G. Marshall. 24 mins.
VHS: S23580. $99.95.

CNN 1994: The Year in Review
O.J. Simpson, the U.S. military in Haiti, the L.A. earthquake, and peacemaking in Israel and Northern Ireland are just some of the groundbreaking events covered in this look back at the top news stories of 1994, by the top news channel—CNN. Hosted by Bernard Shaw.
VHS: S25742. $14.98.

Colonial Williamsburg
Filmed entirely on location, these programs provide a portrait of what life was like in Colonial America.
Basket Making in Colonial Virginia. The crafting and many uses of the basket are explored in this film. 28 mins.
VHS: S07824. $24.95.
Chelsea Porcelain from the Williamsburg Collection. Narrated by Graham Hood, curator and director of the Colonial Williamsburg Department of Collections, this video explains the history of Chelsea porcelain, and how it came to America. 22 mins.
VHS: S07835. $24.95.
Colonial Clothing. The early Virginia colonists surrounded themselves with elegant, often extravagant fashions and furnishings. This program shows the fashions of 200 years ago. 17 mins.
VHS: S07836. $24.95.
Colonial Naturalist. Based on the life and work of English naturalist Mark Catesby, an exploration of 18th century Virginia. 55 mins.
VHS: S07825. $24.95.
Cooper's Craft. Master Cooper George Petengell demonstrates why the resident Cooper was an indispensable craftsman in colonial Virginia. 28 mins.
VHS: S07826. $24.95.
Doorway to the Past. Like a modern detective manual, this video shows how archaeologists skillfully uncovered and interpreted a host of artifacts to re-create the life and lifestyles of colonial Williamsburg. 28 mins.
VHS: S07840. $24.95.
Flower Arrangements of Williamsburg. Flowers were a year-round pleasure in colonial Williamsburg, and this video demonstrates how the colonists brightened their lives. 30 mins.
VHS: S07839. $24.95.
Forged in Wood, Building Anderson's Blacksmith Shop. James Anderson was a blacksmith and entrepreneur who played an essential role in the American revolution. This film tells the story of the re-creation of Anderson's shop, a project that was undertaken for, and often with the help of, visitors to colonial Williamsburg. 32 mins.
VHS: S07841. $24.95.
Glorious System of Things. A dramatization which shows how the early American colonists learned of important scientific discoveries through "circuit lecturers." 58 mins.
VHS: S07837. $24.95.
Gunsmith of Williamsburg. The gun was a vital part of life and this docu-drama demonstrates the loving care that went into the making of each firearm. 59 mins.
VHS: S07828. $24.95.
Hammerman in Williamsburg. Details the work and involvement in the community of the local blacksmith at a modest Williamsburg forge of the 1770 period. 37 mins.
VHS: S07827. $24.95.
Music of Williamsburg. Virginia's 18th century capital provides the background for this exploration of the music and instruments of colonial America. 40 mins.
VHS: S07834. $24.95.
Musical Instrument Maker of Williamsburg. The results of the instrument maker's craft is a tribute to one of our country's most specialized groups of artisans. 53 mins.
VHS: S07838. $24.95.
Search for a Century. Covers the excavation and interpretation of the early 17th century settlement of Martin's Hundred, lying within Carter's Grove Plantation along the James River in Virginia. 58 mins.
VHS: S07833. $24.95.
Silversmith of Williamsburg. A visual essay on the art of silversmithing as it was practiced in 18th-century Virginia. 4 mins.
VHS: S07829. $24.95.

Williamsburg Sampler. Details the architecture, gardens, textiles, furniture, and other facets of the colonial heritage in a snapshot of 18th-century American life. 28 mins.
VHS: S07830. $24.95.
Williamsburg—Story of a Patriot. A reenactment of the crucial years when every colonist faced the issue of taxation without representation and the forces which led to the commitment for total independence. 36 mins.
VHS: S07831. $24.95.
Williamsburg File. The story of the role of archeology in recreating the original capital of Virginia. From old forgotten maps to the diaries and letters of Thomas Jefferson, each discovery played a part. 45 mins.
VHS: S07832. $24.95.

Columbus: Man and Myth
Part of an extraordinary series produced to commemorate the anniversary of Columbus' arrival in America, this volume covers the origins, the power and the personalities involved with Columbus' travels, with the fact separated from the fiction. Public performance rights included. 35 mins.
VHS: S12641. $125.00.

Coming of Age (1924-1928)
E.G. Marshall narrates this documentary about the flapper era. Despite peace, prosperity and prohibition, the nation was influenced by momentous events and personalities. Footage of Lon Chaney in The Phantom of the Opera, Al Capone in Federal Court and Lindbergh's transatlantic flight are included in this video. 25 mins.
VHS: S23585. $99.95.

Crime Inc.
A series of seven documentaries produced by Thames Television on the American gangster underworld.
All in the Family. What the Mafia is really like—as told by the insiders who tell all. 50 mins.
VHS: S09019. $14.99.
Birthright of the Gangsters. The link between organized crime and gambling. 52 mins.
VHS: S09025. $14.99.
Make It Legitimate. How the Mob takes over legitimate businesses for their own use. 51 mins.
VHS: S09024. $14.99.
Making of the Mob. A history of mob activity in Chicago—America's Crime Capital. 50 mins.
VHS: S09020. $14.99.
Mob at Work. A revealing portrait of the Mob's stranglehold on organized labor. 51 mins.
VHS: S09023. $14.99.
Old Mob and the New. A shocking portrait of the drug abuse explosion in America and the criminals who fuel it. 51 mins.
VHS: S09022. $14.99.
Racket Busters. How today's Strike Force is fighting organized crime. 51 mins.
VHS: S09021. $14.99.

Crusades
Terry Jones from Monty Python is featured in this historical series that presents an overview of the great crusades. They represent one of Europe's largest mass migrations. This series is shot on location in Europe and the Middle East to show the facts behind the mythology of knights and their chivalric codes. Features animated mosaics and statues along with computer graphics. Four videos are included, each 50 mins.
VHS: S24956. $59.95.

Dealers in Death
This is it! All the true stories of America's most notorious mobsters and murderers from the bloody Twenties and Thirties. Authentic footage of Al Capone, John Dillinger, Bruno Hauptmann, Bonnie & Clyde, and more. Narrated by Broderick Crawford. 60 minutes.
VHS: S02473. $19.95.

Edison's Miracle of Light
Though many greeted his prediction that his new invention, the electric light, would make oil lamps and gas light obsolete with profound skepticism, Thomas Alva Edison proved to be more than right. Despite his foresight, Edison lost control of the very industry he founded. Peter Coyote narrates this look at how "the wizard of Menlo Park" lost control of his greatest invention in a maze of patents, corporations and industry. From PBS' The American Experience series. USA, 60 mins.
VHS: S27341. $19.95.

The Eighties
Respected anchor persons Jane Pauley and Tom Brokaw host this startling collection of stories and events that rocked the '80s, marking a decade of radical changes. A revealing encapsulation drawing interviews and images from the extensive press coverage of the NBC News Team. 90 mins.
VHS: S15898. $14.95.

The Entrepreneurs:
An American Adventure
Hosted by Robert Mitchum, this six-part series focuses on a variety of self-made executives.
(1) The Entrepreneurs. A focus on inventors who created and marketed their own products. 50 mins.
VHS: S16194. $19.98.
(2) The Land and Its People. Featuring entrepreneurs who developed the land's resources. 50 mins.
VHS: S16195. $19.98.
(3) Expanding America. Depicting those behind our ever-expanding network of transportation systems. 50 mins.
VHS: S16196. $19.98.
(4) Made in America. People who refined mass production factories are the focus of this episode. 50 mins.
VHS: S16197. $19.98.
(5) Giving 'Em What They Want. Profiles entrepreneurs who identified consumers' appetites. 50 mins.
VHS: S16198. $19.98.
(6) Instant America. Represents professionals who built communications and information systems. 50 mins.
VHS: S16199. $19.98.

Epic Voyages of History

Tim Severin retraces five of the epochal voyages of the past in this series. Using the best available evidence, he tries to capture the feeling of these early travelers, through an examination of their means of travel and a close look at their itinerary. In the process he brings the past alive.
In Search of Genghis Khan. This episode explores both the legend and traces left behind by this military giant, as well as the people descended from the legendary Mongol hordes. Their lives are largely unchanged from the 13th century, when Khan first burst forth onto the world stage. 54 mins.
VHS: $22919. $29.95.
The Brendan Voyage. In the 6th century, the Irish monk Brendan is said to have sailed a leather boat across the Atlantic to Newfoundland. The crew of this episode recreate the "Stepping Stone Route," enduring gales and ice floes as they travel through the Hebrides and the Faroes, then on to Iceland, and finally, along the coast of Greenland. 54 mins.
VHS: $22915. $29.95.
The First Crusade. The 2500-mile route from Northern Europe to Jerusalem comprises the greatest land journey of the Middle Ages. Starting at the castle of Duke Godfrey de Boulion, a hero of the First Crusade, they plodded along with a one-ton medieval battle charger toward the Holy Land. 54 mins.
VHS: $22918. $29.95.
The Jason Voyage: The Quest for the Golden Fleece. The exciting legend of Jason and the Argonauts is relived by the crew of a new ship based on a 20-oar replica of a Bronze Age galley. Along the 1500-mile route of legend they discovered many of the same hardships endured by Jason, as well as plausible explanations for some of the fantastic experiences retold by legend. 54 mins.
VHS: $22917. $29.95.
The Sinbad Voyage. Was Sinbad simply a fictional character, or were his travels based on the real experiences of Arab sailors along the silk and spice route to China? A crew of 20 sailed a ship, held together with 400 miles of coconut rope, over 6000 miles. They traveled from the Arabian Sea to India and China living as a real life Sinbad might have. 54 mins.
VHS: $22916. $29.95.
Epic Voyages of History, Set.
VHS: $22920. $125.00.

Equality: A History of the Women's Movement in America

Comprehensive coverage of the U.S. women's movement from the 18th century onward is found in this important video. It details the compelling story of the challenges and triumphs encountered by women seeking equality. USA, 30 mins.
VHS: $26746. $39.95.

Fires of Kuwait

One of the most harrowing visual memories during the Gulf War was the destruction of Kuwait's oil fields, and the raging fires unleashed as the routed Iraqi troops set fire to more than 600 oil wells. "A mesmerizing spectacle of something unique and unspeakable" (Los Angeles Times). 36 mins.
Laser: LD71946. $39.95.

Forty Days of Musa Dagh

An international production about the genocidal policies of the Turks against the Armenians in the early part of the 20th century, the story follows the life of one man who leads Armenian fighters from the top of Mount Musa Dagh for 40 days.
VHS: $02185. $69.95.
Sarky Mouradian, USA, 105 mins.

Freedom's Heritage— The Miracle of America

This program examines the political and social framing of America, how the key concepts of liberty, equality and individuality—shaped out of the Spirit of 1776—evolved into a national platform. The program outlines key phrases and important early writings that defined American patriotism. 26 mins.
VHS: $20272. $29.95.

From Stump to Ship: A 1930 Logging Film

More than a documentary about logging, this is an essential American document—a film about the last surviving long log drive on the Machias River in Maine. Not only are the techniques, danger and excitement captured in this unique and only film record, but the 1930 film, which was newly reconstructed by scholars and filmmakers, represents a remarkable look at a vanished way of American life.
VHS: $08259. $39.95.
Alfred Ames, USA, 1930-88, 28 mins.

Frontline: Waco

Behind the scenes of the momentous incident in Waco, Texas, lies a web of conflicting evidence. This Frontline episode explores what the government knew, or should have known, before approving a plan that led to the death of David Koresh and 80 of his followers.
VHS: $27379. $19.95.

Great American Monuments: The Presidential Memorials

A number of intriguing questions are answered in this informative video. For example, it discloses who stole stones from the Washington Monument and reveals the identity of President Nixon's secret four a.m. rendezvous at the Lincoln Memorial. Many of these stories are told for the first time. USA, 50 mins.
VHS: $26932. $19.95.

Great American Monuments: The War Memorials

This touching examination of America's heroic tributes covers a number of unforgettable sights. From Arlington's endless white crosses to the stirring Vietnam Memorial, these monuments inspire both sadness and pride. USA, 50 mins.
VHS: $26933. $19.95.

Great American Monuments: The White House

An historical tour of the "People's House" is featured on this video. Built with slave labor, it saw happier times, such as the occasion of Trisha Nixon's wedding. Modern day operations are also explained. USA, 1994, 50 mins.
VHS: $26934. $19.95.

Great American Speech Series: Lincoln's Gettysburg Address

Charlton Heston reads this important American speech, which is illustrated by original art, archival photographs, graphics and historical re-enactments. The historical events are effectively recalled in this video. 15 mins.
VHS: $23523. $49.95.

Great American Speech Series: Patrick Henry's "Liberty or Death"

Barry Sullivan reads this important American speech. The historic events leading to Henry's call for independence are evoked through original art, archival photographs, graphics and historical re-enactments. 15 mins.
VHS: $23521. $49.95.

Great American Speech Series: Washington's Farewell

This great American speech is read by William Shatner. Original art, archival photographs, graphics and historical re-enactments help illustrate the political and personal context in which this address was originally presented. 15 mins.
VHS: $23522. $49.95.

The Great Campaign (1917-1918)

E.G. Marshall narrates this look at the year when America fought to make the world safe for democracy. Chaplin, Fairbanks and Mary Pickford did their bit to keep the nation's morale high. 25 mins.
VHS: $23581. $99.95.

Great Crimes of the Century

Five of the most devastating and the most talked about crimes of the century are the subject of this tape. Using rare archival footage shot during the original investigations, this is the story of Charles Manson, Clifford Irving, Leopold and Loeb, D.B. Cooper and the Boston Strangler. 60 mins.
VHS: $13166. $39.98.

The Guns of August

An absorbing portrait of warfare during World War I, adapted from Barbara Tuchman's Pulitzer prize-winning book. The film combines archival footage, photographs, narrative and graphics to reveal the horrors of the great war. Narration by Fritz Weaver.
VHS: $18253. $19.98.
Laser: LD71845. $34.98.
Nathan Kroll, USA, 1964, 99 mins.

Headline Stories

Four volumes of headlines and newsreel footage from 20th-century American history and culture.
Headline Stories: America in Sports. A collection of newsreel footage on the most important American sporting events from the late 19th century to the modern era, following the exploits and personalities of Bobby Jones, Knute Rockne, Babe Ruth, Babe Didrikson, Jesse Owens, Joe Louis, Joe DiMaggio, Arnold Palmer and the birth of the Super Bowl. 95 mins.
VHS: $18797. $29.95.
Headline Stories: America in the News. Subtitled 87 Fascinating Events that Shaped America, 1901-65, this compendium culls newsreel footage from the Hearst News library for a panoramic vision: the Wright brothers, the First World War, the Scopes Monkey trial, Sacco and Vanzetti, the Depression, the Hindenburg, Kennedy and Nixon debates, Vietnam and Kennedy's assassination. 105 mins.
VHS: $18796. $29.95.
Headline Stories: American Nostalgia. This program explores the social and cultural fabric of the country by focusing on its entertainers, including Rudolph Valentino, Mickey Mouse, Clark Gable, Howard Hughes, the FBI and gangsters, Hope and Crosby, Rita Hayworth, Marilyn Monroe and Elvis. 108 mins.
VHS: $18798. $29.95.
Headline Stories: World War II. This compilation deals with the Second World War, documenting the rise of fascism in Italy, Germany and Japan, the Blitz, the Vichy government, Pearl Harbor, the Battle of Guadalcanal, the North African campaign, D-Day, Iwo Jima, the Manhattan Project, Hiroshima and Nagasaki, the Japanese surrender and the Nuremberg trials. 98 mins.
VHS: $18799. $29.95.
Headline Stories: The Complete Set.
VHS: $18800. $79.95.

The Heartbeat of America

A probing investigative look at the mega-giant automobile manufacturer General Motors. A combination of historical footage and personal interviews portray the rise and fall of the corporation and look at one of the most important issues facing the future: the mass production of "clean cars." 87 mins.
VHS: $23386. $89.95.

History's Turning Points

This series of six videos, first screened by the Learning Channel, presents 13 key historical moments from the last 2000 years, including history of the Black Death, the Great Wall of China, the siege of Constantinople, the conquest of the Incas and the marriage of Pocahontas. Exciting events that span the globe, from Ancient Greece to the detonation of the atom bomb, are included.
VHS: $25835. $149.95.

Hooray for Abbie!

This video tribute to Abbie Hoffman features the Abbie memorials from the Summer of 1989—The Palladium New York—plus the picnic at Washington's Crossing. There are fond remembrances by many friends, including Peter Yarrow, Paul Krassner, Allen Ginsberg, Norman Mailer, Jerry Rubin, The Fugs, Bobby Seale, Dave Dellinger, David Amram, Richie Havens and William Kunstler. Also features brother Jack Hoffman and his wife, Anita. 76 mins.
VHS: $21846. $29.95.

In Service to America

The most comprehensive documentary on women in the military ever produced, In Service to America interviews a wide range of knowledgeable sources, from military experts to the women in uniform themselves. It covers the entire history of women in the United States military from the Revolutionary War to Operation Desert Storm. USA, 60 mins.
VHS: $27243. $29.95.

Journey to Freedom: The Immigrant Experience

Over the last century, mass immigration has shaped this country. Newsreel footage, artwork and vintage photos capture this fascinating story. 13 mins.
VHS: $23742. $89.95.
Laser: LD74787. $109.95.

Kent State

Fine dramatization of the killings of four students at Kent State by Ohio National Guardsmen in Spring 1970. Originally made for television, co-written by Emmy winner Gerald Green.
VHS: $02156. $39.95.
James Goldstone, USA, 1981, 120 mins.

The Korean War

An authoritative, ten-hour video series on the Korean War, produced by Korean Television Network. The program welds archival footage with interviews. The five-volume set details the origins of conflict, the strategies and battles, the armistice and uneasy truce that still exists today. Narrated by James Whitmore.
Volume 1: The Division & North and South. 120 mins.
VHS: $17319. $19.95.
Volume 2: The Omens of War & Tempest. 120 mins.
VHS: $17320. $19.95.
Volume 3: To the North & A Different War. 120 mins.
VHS: $17321. $19.95.
Volume 4: Stalemate of Truce & War on the Homefront. 120 mins.
VHS: $17322. $19.95.
Volume 5: Truce & Epilogue-Reflections. 120 mins.
VHS: $17323. $19.95.
Complete Five-Volume Set. 600 mins.
VHS: $17324. $99.75.

Life in a California Mission in 1790

Within the Spanish-speaking missions of Colonial California, self-sufficient communities took shape. 14 mins.
VHS: $23534. $49.95.
Laser: LD74765. $99.95.

Life in a Gold-Mining Camp 1850

The thrill of the gold rush is relived in this video about life in a mining town. 18 mins.
VHS: $23536. $49.95.
Laser: LD74767. $99.95.

Life in a Midwestern Small Town 1910

Inventions and cultural changes transformed American rural life just after the turn of the century. This program documents these key changes. 18 mins.
VHS: $23538. $49.95.
Laser: LD74769. $99.95.

Life in America 1800

This is an in-depth look at a farming family in central New York State at the dawn of the 19th century. 16 mins.
VHS: $23535. $49.95.
Laser: LD74766. $99.95.

Life in an Eastern Seaport Town 1870

Shipbuilding, sailmaking and ropemaking are unique skills that were at the center of town life in the late 19th century. This video explains the historical importance of these techniques. 17 mins.
VHS: $23537. $49.95.
Laser: LD74768. $99.95.

Life in the 30's

Despite the ravages of the depression, this decade spanned a surprisingly multi-faceted time in American culture. Alexander Scourby narrates this look at an era famous for Benny Goodman and the birth of Swing, even as millions were desperate for a better life. 60 mins.
VHS: $23057. $19.95.

The Lincoln Assassination

Although revered today as one of America's greatest presidents, in his time many hated Lincoln because of his policies and strong convictions. This video explores the various plots hatched by assassin John Wilkes Booth and his cohorts in their efforts to destabilize the union. They even planned to kill all the members of Lincoln's cabinet. 50 mins.
VHS: $26662. $19.95.

Louisiana Boys: Raised on Politics

The history of politics in Louisiana, a state which has been historically ruled by notorious figures who governed by a combination of smarts and terror. With its free-spending and high-rolling elections, Louisiana's political campaigns resemble a charged, carnival atmosphere. The documentary traces the disparate political fortunes of Huey "The Kingfish" Long, his brother Earl, Jimmie Davis, Edwin Edwards and David Duke. 52 mins.
VHS: $19412. $19.95.

Mafia: The History of the Mob in America

This documentary series is a cold-blooded examination of organized crime in the 20th century. Beginning with the imposition of Prohibition, the origins of these gangs are traced up through the Second World War. By this time, they had emerged as permanent features on the American scene in the shape of enduring family enterprises. In the first volume, The Prohibition Years, Birth of the American Mafia, Congress' move to outlaw alcohol in 1919 spawned an unforseen side effect—the growth of an underground market that could never be wiped out. Jewish and Irish gangs were among the first to emerge. Then the Mafia is seen coming from Sicily to take over this business, with murderous methods (100 mins.) The second volume is The Kennedys and the Mob. Between the imposition of prohibition and the emergence of Camelot, Joe Kennedy, the father of a powerful clan, kept up his dealings with underworld figures. But his sons had a different opinion of these men and persecuted them from Washington (50 mins.) In Unions and the Mob, the third volume, we see how traditional union strength was muscled over into a new and potent force, mob-controlled trade unions. They fought ruthlessly with the communists for sympathy and won. Even the Ford Company was not safe from the influence of these teamsters (50 mins.) And in the fourth volume, Empire of Crime, World War II and the Allied invasion offer great growth opportunities to the mob. From Sicily they expanded throughout Italy to cover the country with their influence in the blackmarket, while they also used the years of occupation to expand their legitimate business interests in the U.S. (50 mins.) Narrated and hosted by Bill Kurtis.
VHS: $21247. $59.95.

Man and the State: Hamilton and Jefferson on Democracy

Conflicting intellectual currents helped shape the growth of American democracy. Hamilton and Jefferson debate their views on significant crises experienced in the development of the nation. 26 mins.
VHS: $23701. $79.95.

Man and the State: Roosevelt and Hoover on the Economy

Hoover and Roosevelt are forced to debate their opposing views on the role of government in the face of the Great Depression. The open-ended nature of this film leaves the viewer free to decide who is right regarding the welfare of the general public. 25 mins.
VHS: $23700. $79.95.

The Man Who Saw Tomorrow

Nostradamus, the 16th century physician and philosopher, predicted many of the events that have transpired in modern times. Orson Welles narrates this tantalizing documentary on the man and his accurate forecasts. 96 minutes.
VHS: $02487. $19.98.

March of Time: American Lifestyles

Originally produced as a newsreel by Time Magazine, The March of Time was seen monthly for sixteen years by more than 20 million people in more than 50,000 theatres around the world. This unique documentary provides a fascinating look at the American world in the first half of the 20th century. Narrated by Westbrook Van Voorhis, produced by Louis de Rochemont.
Show Business: The War Years 1939-1945. American lifestyles are documented through a 40-year history of filmmaking, including features on Charlie Chaplin and Al Jolson, Bob Hope on one of his first USO tours, the British challenge to Hollywood with Stewart Granger, Ann Todd, Ronald Colman, Ida Lupino. 73 mins.
VHS: $03025. $19.95.
Show Business: The Post-War Years 1946-1950. The Nightclub Boom shows pleasure-hungry Americans heading for nightclubs with scenes featuring Jimmy Dorsey, Eddie Condon, Ed Wynn, Bert Lahr, the heyday of radio and the ever-popular soap opera, the glamour of New York theatre with Rex Harrison, Charles Boyer, Maxwell Anderson, Robert Sherwood, Maggie Garland, the development of the LP record, and Beauty At Work—the look at the "glamour" life of a top model. 92 mins.
VHS: $03026. $19.95.
American Family: The War Years 1941-1945. The role of ethnic groups in building industrialized America, the contribution of men and women to the war effort, America's food supply and its role in the War, and why the U.S. can't provide enough meat during the war. 89 mins.
VHS: $03027. $19.95.
American Family: The Post-War Years 1946-1948. Child development coupled with the oftentimes hilarious outcome of the "scientific study of babies," the booming black market in babies, and the explosive circumstances of adoption, the effect of the war, radio, comics and the Atomic Age on children, the growing segment of an aging population, and the increasing problems of divorce. 89 mins.
VHS: $03028. $19.95.
America's Youth 1940-1950. Case histories of debutante daughters and the depression-ridden children of the poor, the effect of war on children, the role models for teenage girls, the fight for more modern schools, and educational techniques and facilities in the 40s. 90 mins.
VHS: $03029. $19.95.
American Fashion and Leisure 1945-1950. The role of being beautiful, from Fifth Avenue's most exclusive salons of mysterious beauty concoctions, Americans traveling in Mexico, the story of the fashion industry, the popularity of boxing, a funny look at Americans vacationing, and men fighting baldness, exercising at a health club and trying to stay slim. 105 mins.
VHS: $03030. $19.95.
March of Time: American Lifestyles, Giftpack. The complete set.
VHS: $05336. $99.95.

Merrily We Go Along

Subtitled The Early Days of the Automobile, this documentary examines the evolution of the automobile in American society. The role is captured through a succession of transitions, from horse and buggy to horseless carriages. 60 mins.
VHS: $19249. $19.95.

The Mob

From Lucky Luciano to the Teflon Don, American mob bosses have always written their own rules. Today the Feds are breaking down their walls of silence with new technology and tougher laws. Mob insiders, Federal officers, Mafia experts and other figures from both sides of the war are featured in this expose from A&E. 250 mins.
VHS: $26691. $59.95.

A More Perfect Union: The Story of the U.S. Constitution

Combining illustrations and text, this program details the events in Philadelphia during the framing of the United States Constitution. Intended for children in grades 2-5. 15 mins.
VHS: $20056. $44.95.

Motion Picture History of the Korean War

From the hip anarchy of Robert Altman to the personal anti-war heroics of war vets Sam Fuller and Robert Aldrich, the Korean War has been served well in fictional film. Now a short documentary with newsreel footage provides an unsettling period piece of a nearly forgotten, tragic war.
VHS: S02581. $34.95.

Mount Vernon— Home of George Washington

This sensitive and artfully filmed program marks the first time that Mount Vernon has been filmed in its entirety, including its architecture and furnishings, its gardens and the surrounding plantation. Tells about George Washington the man, his personal interests, and life in 18th century Virginia. 30 mins.
VHS: S11476. $29.95.

Multicultural Peoples of North America Series

These videos celebrate the heritage of 15 diverse cultural groups of North America, blending folklore, customs, traditions and family dynamics to illustrate immigration history. "[A] noteworthy series especially valuable as a North American resource" (*Booklist*). 30 minutes each.
African Americans.
VHS: S20359. $39.95.
The Amish.
VHS: S20360. $39.95.
Arab Americans.
VHS: S20361. $39.95.
Central Americans.
VHS: S20362. $39.95.
Chinese Americans.
VHS: S20363. $39.95.
German Americans.
VHS: S20364. $39.95.
Greek Americans.
VHS: S20365. $39.95.
Irish Americans.
VHS: S20366. $39.95.
Italian Americans.
VHS: S20367. $39.95.
Japanese Americans.
VHS: S20368. $39.95.
Jewish Americans.
VHS: S20369. $39.95.
Korean Americans.
VHS: S20370. $39.95.
Mexican Americans.
VHS: S20371. $39.95.
Polish Americans.
VHS: S20372. $39.95.
Puerto Rican Americans.
VHS: S20373. $39.95.
Multicultural Peoples of North America. The complete 15-volume set.
VHS: S24408. $599.25.

Murder of the Century

Harry K. Thaw shot and killed Stanford White, New York's leading turn-of-the-century architect. Behind this cold-blooded murder was a steamy tale of intrigue, jealousy and passion. Both men were involved in an unlikely love triangle with model and showgirl Evelyn Nesbit and each man wanted her for himself alone. David Ogden Stiers narrates this fascinating documentary about the so-called "Murder of the Century." From PBS' *The American Experience* series. USA, 60 mins.
VHS: S27340. $19.95.

National Geographic Video: Search for Battleship Bismarck

This video relives the final days of the ill-fated battleship, interviews the survivors of the 1941 battle, and explores the haunting underwater remains discovered in June 1989 by Dr. Robert Ballard, who led the exploration of the R.M.S. *Titanic*. 60 mins.
VHS: S11656. $19.95.

New Beginnings (1895-1904)

During these key years President McKinley was assassinated and Theodore Roosevelt became President. Technological wonders also left their mark on the era. Footage of the first flight at Kitty Hawk and the opening of the New York subway show the importance of innovation during this time. E.G. Marshall narrates. 25 mins.
VHS: S23577. $99.95.

The New Europeans

This program demonstrates the repercussions of European unification. The works point out the inevitable tensions between extreme nationalism and the fear of cultural imperialism, the loss of ethnic identity and the difficulties in resolving the issue of a common currency. The series offers a historical view of unification, of past successes and failures. "To understand what's happening in Europe, and the impact of unification on the United States, this series is a must" (*New York Daily News*). 180 mins.
Program 1: Road to Unity.
VHS: S19366. $29.95.
Program 2: Global Agendas.
VHS: S19367. $29.95.
Program 3: Regional Dreams.
VHS: S19368. $29.95.
The New Europeans, Set.
VHS: S19369. $79.95.

New York the Way It Was

58 minutes each.
New York the Way It Was. This is a nostalgic look at Coney Island and other quintessentially New York traditions, from egg creams to the Giants and the Dodgers. Everything that made New York the most exciting place to be in the 30's, 40's and 50's is lovingly recreated for one last look.
VHS: S23118. $19.95.
New York the Way It Was: The Old Neighborhood. A sentimental tour of old time New York neighborhoods is featured on this video. Famous New Yorkers Tito Puente and former mayor Ed Koch are just some of the celebrities who help recall those homey but exciting sections found throughout the five boroughs.
VHS: S26676. $19.95.
New York the Way It Was: Wish You Were Here. Coney Island, the Catskill Mountains, the Rockaway beaches and many other sites were fun places dear to New Yorkers. In this nostalgic video journey memories of these places are brought back for one more special visit. 58 mins.
VHS: S26675. $19.95.
New York the Way It Was: The Series. Includes all three titles.
VHS: S26674. $59.85.

Nova—Disguises of War

The many sides of military deception are examined—from simple camouflage to the ultra-sophisticated Stealth Bomber. 60 mins.
VHS: S14501. $14.98.

Number 10 Downing Street: A Unique Film History

An unprecedented peek behind the front door of one of the world's most famous addresses, this production marks the first time cameras were permitted to roam freely through the public and private rooms of the Prime Minister's domain. Includes interviews with former Prime Ministers, their families and staff, as well as with Prime Minister Margaret Thatcher. Produced by the BBC. 110 mins.
VHS: S03389. $19.94.

The Oldest Living Confederate Widow Tells All

Diane Lane, Donald Sutherland, Cicely Tyson and Anne Bancroft star in this humorous and irreverent look at the history of the Civil War. Great performances explain why this film was nominated for nine Emmy Awards. Also features Blythe Danner, E.G. Marshall and Gwen Verdon. 180 mins.
VHS: S26449. $92.95.

Over There, 1914-1918

An excellent documentary compiled in France from newsreel footage and government film of the period. The result is an examination of World War I, but with a difference; this time the point of view is that of a lowly foot soldier. 90 mins.
VHS: S16262. $29.95.

The Passing Storm (1931-1933)

In America entertainers like Jack Benny, Mae West, Gable and Garbo provided some relief from the world's troubles. Europe, however, turned to despots like Hitler and Mussolini for help. E.G. Marshall hosts this account of the tense 1930's. 24 mins.
VHS: S23588. $99.95.

Paul Revere: The Messenger of Liberty

Cliff Robertson narrates this look at Paul Revere, the patriot who was instrumental in alerting the colonists of the advancing British troops and much more. 24 mins.
VHS: S23556. $49.95.
Laser: LD74785. $99.95.

Policing the Peace (1948-1951)

After the war, a series of events demanded vigilance and commitment from the great powers. Gandhi was assassinated and North Korean troops crossed into South Korea, while in the Middle East, Egypt took control of the Suez Canal and Israel invaded Sinai. 24 mins.
VHS: S23596. $99.95.

Power and Prejudice (1926-1928)

Hosted by E.G. Marshall, this documentary reveals an era of controversy. Bootlegging, mobsters, Sacco and Vanzetti, the KKK and communism all offered cause for anxiety to the American public. Footage of Babe Ruth's sixtieth home run and Hoover's election are also included in this video. 24 mins.
VHS: S23586. $99.95.

Prairie Cabin: A Norwegian Pioneer Woman's Story

An immigrant pioneer woman learns to love the American prairie, which becomes her new home. 15 mins. Resource guide available.
Video.
VHS: S25764. $95.00.
Resource Guide.
VHS: S25777. $20.00.

The Price of Peace (1917-1918)

Though America has won the war, prisons are full of conscientious objectors. E.G. Marshall narrates this look at a country of startling contrasts. 24 mins.
VHS: S23582. $99.95.

Ramparts We Watch

The first feature-length film produced by the staff of March of Time, the film was begun in 1939 as an account of the forces which drew the country into World War I, but what emerged was a propagandistic document urging people to prepare for defense as World War II approached. The movie re-creates the 1914-18 era as reflected in the lives of several people in a small New England town; interwoven with dramatic incidents is actual newsreel footage, including clips from the Nazi film *Feuertaufe*, an account of the German invasion of Poland.
VHS: S06878. $39.95.
Louis De Rochemont, USA, 1940, 90 mins.

The Real Richard Nixon

Historian Frank Gannon hosts this exhaustive, three-volume look at the real Richard Nixon. Exclusive, newly released interview footage, photographs and rare home movies reveal an amiable man who destroyed the prestige of the office he served. Everything is covered, from his Quaker upbringing to his work in California and Washington. Gannon also describes his feelings for his wife and the trauma of his resignation. This 3-volume set includes *The Real Richard Nixon: Early Life*, *The Real Richard Nixon: Pat* and *The Real Richard Nixon: Twenty Eight Days*. USA, 1995, 202 mins.
VHS: S26967. $49.99.

Rediscovering America

Finally, the secrets and myths of a forgotten culture are revealed. It's our American culture that needs de-mystifying. Roger Kennedy, Director of the Smithsonian Institution's National Museum of American History, offers a fascinating, fresh perspective on the legends and legacies found in our own backyard. 60-100 minutes each.
Vol. 1: The Real American Cowboy.
VHS: S21797. $19.95.
Vol. 2: Indians Among Us.
VHS: S21798. $19.95.
Vol. 3: Railroads, Robbers and Rebels.
VHS: S21799. $19.95.
Rediscovering America, Set.
VHS: S21800. $49.95.

The Rights of Passage (1919-1920)

Even as President Wilson proposes his ill-fated League of Nations, Bolsheviks are coming to power in Russia. At home, Americans are preoccupied with peace-time activities like making money and going to the flicks. Hosted by E.G. Marshall. 24 mins.
VHS: S23583. $99.95.

The Schwartzkopf Four-Pack

Four programs on the nature of war and battle, hosted by Gen. Norman H. Schwartzkopf (Ret.), the former general commander of American ground forces in the Gulf War. The works are *Hitler and Stalin*, about the unholy alliance between two authoritarians; *The Year of the General*, stories about the men who altered the complexity of World War II; *Remember Pearl Harbor* which reconstructs the activities of Dec. 7, 1941 through Japanese footage and previously unveiled readings of letters, diaries and personal documents; and *Schwartzkopf in Vietnam: A Soldier Returns*, a personal essay as the general returns to Vietnam for the first time since 1970, and openly discusses his feelings. 300 mins.
VHS: S19541. $99.98.

The Secret Service

The history and techniques of the most celebrated bodyguards of modern times are revealed in this four-volume boxed set. Assassinations and high tech innovations have shaped the elite force. Interviews, commentary and behind-the-scenes footage reveal the true story behind the Secret Service.
VHS: S26095. $59.95.
Benjamin Magliano, USA, 1995, 200 mins.

Secrets of the Rock: Return to Alcatraz

Documentary footage and the actual narratives of former prisoners recreate the horrific legacy of "the Rock," America's most notorious prison. Legendary escape attempts, infamous prisoners, the "Battle of Alcatraz," and the brutal facts of solitary confinement are all detailed. USA, 60 mins.
VHS: S27391. $19.95.

Sex and Justice

This document explores the complicated issues of class, race, sex and male sexual aggression within the context of the gripping Anita Hill/Clarence Thomas hearings. With commentary by Gloria Steinem.
VHS: S18986. $24.95.
Julian Schlossberg, USA, 1993, 76 mins.

Smithsonian World

A broad intellectual journey into history, science, nature and travel, following the aims and principles of the Smithsonian Institute. The series is a kaleidoscopic and impressionistic account of scientific and technological accomplishment which examines different relations—man to society, the individual to art, and social and cultural movements and their historical context.
Smithsonian World: A Usable Past. An impressionistic and vibrant travelogue that moves through time and across continents to explore different cultures, landscapes and people. 56 mins.
VHS: S19200. $14.98.
Smithsonian World: Heroes and the Test of Time. A vivid look at two radically different men: the military general George A. Custer and the painter Thomas Eakins. 58 mins.
VHS: S19196. $14.98.

Speeches of Franklin D. Roosevelt

The speeches of America's great President.
VHS: S07028. $19.95.

Speeches of Winston Churchill

Some of the most memorable speeches of the great British leader.
VHS: S07035. $19.95.

Stalking the President

Subtitled *A History of American Assassins*, this revealing documentary examines the various assassination attempts in the history of the American presidency. The film also considers issues of motivation and conspiracy in the attempted assassinations of Presidents Lincoln, Garfield, McKinley, Roosevelt, FDR, Truman, Kennedy, Nixon, Ford and Reagan. 50 mins.
VHS: S18136. $19.95.

The Story of the Statue of Liberty

Examines the assembling of the statue, built and designed by French architect Frederic Bartholdi, that was bequeathed to the United States as an enduring symbol of liberty, equality and freedom. Intended for children in grades 2-5. 7 mins.
VHS: S20057. $44.95.

Studs Terkel's Chicago

Studs Terkel is Chicago's self-appointed chronicler. During the course of a career that began in the Great Depression, Studs has been a radio soap opera gangster, host of his own television show, disc jockey, jazz critic, and Prix Italia-winning broadcaster. He is most famous for his books of oral history, recording America's past and present in the words of the ordinary people he interviews so sympathetically. This program presents a history of Chicago in the words of its people and the music of its incomparable blues players, all filtered through the unique lens of Studs' viewpoint. 60 mins.
VHS: S13751. $19.95.

The Tarnished Dream (1929-1931)

E.G. Marshall tells the story of a country devastated by the crash of 1929. Vivid images of a population out of work bring home the gravity of this time, when one in four Americans could not find a job. 25 mins.
VHS: S23587. $99.95.

Thomas Jefferson: A View from the Mountain

Though renowned as a champion of freedom, former President Thomas Jefferson also owned slaves. Famed documentarian Martin Doblmeier, with the help of narrators Sissy Spacek, Danny Glover and others, examines this seemingly contradictory figure. He even explores the most salacious aspect of Jefferson's life: his purported liaison with his Monticello slave, Sally Hemmings.
VHS: S27509. $29.98.
Martin Doblmeier, USA, 1995, 114 mins.

Treating the Casualties of the Gulf War

A unique look at the human aftermath of the war. While American casualties were light, some American soldiers suffered disabling injuries or severe stress. The video also examines the fact that our intense bombing virtually wiped out Iraq's ability to treat its victims, a high percentage of whom were children. USA, 1991, 29 mins.
VHS: S15213. $25.00.

Trial of the Avco Ploughshares

A real life political trial is dramatically recorded in this unique video—the only time cameras have been permitted in a courtroom to film a trial of political activists. Seven men and women, including a mother of 13, were charged with trespass and malicious damage for hammering on computer systems and office equipment in AVCO Systems Division, a manufacturer of nuclear weapons components in Massachusetts. This program captures the emotionally charged struggle between prosecution, judge and defendants over "defense of justification."
VHS: S11495. $45.00.
Julie Gustafson/John Reilly, USA, 1987, 60 mins.

United States Naval Academy: 150 Years in Annapolis

Beginning with the legendary John Paul Jones, this unique American institution has forged the men who run the nation's Navy. Everything is here, including painful memories of the time when graduates fought each other during the Civil War.
VHS: S26935. $19.95.
Don Horan, USA, 1995, 50 mins.

The Unquiet Death of Julius and Ethel Rosenberg

On June 19, 1953, Julius and Ethel Rosenberg, the so-called "atomic spies" of the 1950s, were executed at Sing Sing Prison. Their death only fostered the belief of many Americans that the Rosenbergs were innocent, victims of the anti-Communist paranoia of the 50s, rather than spies who had stolen atomic secrets for the Russians. In his landmark documentary *The Unquiet Death of Julius and Ethel Rosenberg*, Alvin Goldstein looks at the facts and procedures of the Rosenberg case, as well as the climate of the times, interviewing jurors, FBI agents, lawyers for both sides, and the two sons of the Rosenbergs. Using documentary and newsreel footage, Goldstein creates a moving human drama, a "thoroughly researched, solidly developed…superb recreation of history, painting with bold strokes the temper of the times" (*Boston Globe*).
VHS: S04736. $59.95.
Alvin Goldstein, USA, 1974, 83 mins.

Valley Forge

The Pennsylvania Association of the Sons of the Revolution filmed this program at the actual historic site of a battle waged in the winter of 1777. There, the Continental Army defended the cause of liberty despite crushing hardship. 24 mins.
VHS: S23731. $49.95.

Virtual 60's

Dr. Timothy Leary is the perfect host for this 1990's look at the decade of expanded consciousness, the 1960's. The concept of virtual reality makes this series not only different but completely unique. Some of the biggest rock stars of the era are shown, including Canned Heat, Iron Butterfly, Humble Pie and Blood, Sweat and Tears, as well as many others. It's almost as if a 60's-style rock festival were available on video. Each tape is 50 mins.
The Consciousness Tape.
VHS: S21818. $14.95.
The Love Tape.
VHS: S21817. $14.95.
The Peace Tape.
VHS: S21816. $14.95.
Virtual 60's, Pre-Pack Special.
VHS: S21819. $39.95.

Votes for Women?! 1913 U.S. Senate Testimony

Kate Douglas Wiggin, the author of *Rebecca of Sunnybrook Farm*, argues against the vote for women. Progressive writer Belle Case La Follette offers an opposing view and testifies in favor. 15 mins. Resource guide available.
Video.
VHS: S25767. $95.00.
Resource Guide.
VHS: S25780. $20.00.

Wars in Peace
This series looks at battles waged across the frontiers of a number of countries. Many of these wars involved the great powers, as they struggled with issues of politics, religion and economics.
Wars in Peace: 6-Tape Brick. 468 mins.
VHS: $25990. $149.95.
Wars in Peace: Iran/Iraq—Afghanistan. Iran and Iraq consumed vast quantities of resources fighting to control that incredibly valuable resource—oil. The former USSR sought to destroy the growing Islamic fundamentalist fervor emerging in Afghanistan. 80 mins.
VHS: $25987. $29.95.
Wars in Peace: Korea—Vietnam. Though it began as a border dispute, the war in Korea escalated into a red-hot war that engaged the principal protagonists of the Cold War. It was also the United Nations' first war. Vietnam was the first war waged nightly on television, and it marked the growing importance of helicopters in warfare. 80 mins.
VHS: $25984. $29.95.
Wars in Peace: Terrorism—Lebanon. Terrorism relies on random, extreme violence that forces the world to acknowledge intractable conflicts. In Lebanon, the Israelis attack the PLO in order to stop its forays into Israel and the occupied territories. 80 mins.
VHS: $25986. $29.95.
Wars in Peace: The Falklands—Special Forces. Argentina's push to gain territory in the South Atlantic underestimated the force of the British response. Special Forces are specially trained troops sent to areas where regular forces dare not venture. 80 mins.
VHS: $25988. $29.95.
Wars in Peace: The Gulf War. Sadam Hussein plunged into Kuwait, but his forces were ultimately repelled and the tiny kingdom was regained. Nevertheless, Iraqi forces left a considerable amount of destruction behind. 68 mins.
VHS: $25989. $29.95.
Wars in Peace: The Six Day War—Yom Kippur. Israel defeated the combined forces of three Arab countries in just six days. Unfortunately, the Israelis did not anticipate the Arab reprisal, launched on the holiest day of the Jewish year. 80 mins.
VHS: $25985. $29.95.

Watergate Scandal and Resignation of President Nixon
The complete story of the Watergate maelstrom, Nixon's near impeachment, and his final dark days prior to his sudden resignation. From ABC News. 60 mins.
VHS: $12681. $24.98.

Watergate—The Deluxe Boxed Set
This series of three videos reveals the truth behind the government scandal that shocked the nation and destroyed the presidency of Richard Nixon. Interviews with actual participants and never-before-seen interviews with Nixon himself make this Discovery Channel presentation a unique historic document.
VHS: $23870. $49.95.

Watergate: The Secret Story
Mike Wallace attempts to shed new light on the political circumstances and events behind Nixon's motives that led to Watergate and his humiliating resignation from the Presidency. 60 mins.
VHS: $17684. $19.98.

The Wild West
This ten-hour miniseries is a mosaic of two-bit hustlers and visionary dreamers, of vicious outlaws and true believers. "Scholarly and lively, *The Wild West* tells a big story by telling a lot of little stories" (Bob Wisehart, *The Sacramento Bee*). Narrated by Jack Lemmon. Parts voiced by more than 40 actors, including Joe Don Baker, Lloyd Bridges, Tim Curry, Dana Delaney, Larry Fishburne, Lee Grant, Graham Greene, Christine Lahti, Lyle Lovett and Wes Studi. Directed by Academy Award-winning documentarian Keith W. Merrill (*The Great American Cowboy*).
Volume 1: Cowboys/Settlers. In this two-episode program, *Cowboys* documents the rugged individualism of the mythic American figure. *Settlers* examines the stress and personal toll of wagon trains and the determination of the men and women who survived. 90 mins.
VHS: $19125. $19.98.
Volume 2: Gunfighters/Townspeople. In this two part program, *Gunfighters* extols the legends, actions and circumstances behind the notorious gunslingers, including Bat Masterson, Wyatt Earp and the Daltons. *Townspeople* looks at the determination of the anonymous shopkeepers, professionals and people who forged communities. 90 mins.
VHS: $19126. $19.98.
Volume 3: Indians/Soldiers. In *Indians*, Native American tribes fight for their land, property and right to exist, as Sitting Bull, Geronimo and Red Cloud adopt desperate measures to ensure their survival. In *Soldiers*, Civil War veterans, emancipated slaves and resettled immigrants secure the vastly expanding American outposts. 90 mins.
VHS: $19127. $19.98.
Volume 4: Dreamers and Wayfarers/Chroniclers. *Dreamers and Wayfarers* celebrates the craft, skills and effort of the innovative thinkers and eccentric technicians who developed the transcontinental railroad. *Chroniclers* charts an emerging social and aesthetic evolution, the number of artists, writers, journalists and photographers who left to capture the West's voice, physical representation and mythic nature. 90 mins.
VHS: $19128. $19.98.
Volume 5: Searchers/Mythmakers. *Searchers* examines the efforts of explorers to assess the full dimension of the West and preserve its legacy and vast riches for future generations. *Mythmakers* is a kaleidoscopic investigation of the characters and outsized figures of the New West, as dime novelists transform Annie Oakley, Wild Bill Hickok and Sitting Bull into larger-than-life characters. 90 mins.
VHS: $19129. $19.98.
The Wild West, Complete Set.
VHS: $19130. $75.92.

Winds of Change (1912-1916)
Chaplin, Keaton, Will Rogers, Fatty Arbuckle and Sarah Bernhardt left their indelible impression on this era as the first international stars. Their fame is juxtaposed with the disaster of the age, the sinking of the *Lusitania*. E.G. Marshall narrates. 25 mins.
VHS: $23579. $99.95.

A Woman's Place
Julie Harris narrates this tribute to "Remarkable American Women," highlighting achievements by women in the arts, science, business, athletics, and more. Rare footage and photographs highlight this uplifting celebration of the women who dared to be the best. 25 mins.
VHS: $05745. $39.95.

Women and the American Family
The struggle of women for equal rights has led to some of the most controversial problems of our times. This program examines the issue from a historical perspective, looking at the role of women in the next century, and the related problem of the changes that will occur with respect to the American family and its place in American society. 28 mins.
VHS: $10784. $29.95.

Women First & Foremost: Volume One: "Remember the Ladies"
Rita Moreno and Dee Wallace Stone host this video about inspiring women who pioneered new paths in a variety of professions. Journalism, education, and medicine are all areas that were once off limits to women. Through determination and talent, the women detailed in this volume changed all of that.
VHS: $27046. $24.95.
Scott Mansfield, USA, 1995, 60 mins.

Women First & Foremost: Volume Two: "Touching the Clouds with Pen and Plane"
Few have heard of the bravery which characterized women soldiers like Revolutionary War hero Deborah Gannet. That may be because she was forced to assume a man's identity and fight under the name Robert Shurtleff. Rita Moreno and Dee Wallace Stone host this second volume about women who trailblazed new areas in a number of professions.
VHS: $27047. $24.95.
Scott Mansfield, USA, 1995, 60 mins.

Women First & Foremost: Volume Three: "A Lady in the Spotlight"
Though women movie stars are very well known, the women who work behind the scenes in the entertainment industry are often overshadowed by their male colleagues. Rita Moreno and Dee Wallace Stone host this volume which details the work of many women, including the first woman film director, a leading Broadway lyricist and the first woman network co-anchor.
VHS: $27048. $24.95.
Scott Mansfield, USA, 1995, 60 mins.

World War I Complete Set
CBS News produced this historic overview of the issues, events and dominant personalities of the First World War, painstakingly rendered through the use of vivid archival and combat footage. The five-volume program examines the causes of the war, the rise of nationalism, the assassination of Archduke Ferdinand and the German sinking of the Lusitania, the expansion of the war and America's belated involvement. The program maps the major strategic campaigns in Europe and Asia, the barbaric nature of trench warfare at Verdun, the massive destruction and casualties suffered on all sides, the emergence of air power and the long-term consequences of the war. The program concludes with a complex reading of the political issues that led to the peaceful negotiation of the armistice that brokered a precarious peace. 530 mins.
VHS: $19536. $139.98.

The Year of the Generals
From CBS News Videos, General Norman H. Schwarzkopf and Charles Kuralt consider the greatest commanders and strategically important battles of World War II, interweaving combat footage, memoirs and readings by the actors Mel Gibson and Anthony Hopkins. 94 mins.
VHS: $17776. $19.98.

WORLD WAR II

Aces
This program traces the evolution of fearless aerial warrior pilots from World War I to Vietnam. Includes high-tech dogfight footage. 60 mins.
VHS: $13114. $19.98.

Adolph Hitler's Home Movies
Eva Braun, mistress of Hitler, filmed these silent home movies which show top Nazi officials relaxing in Hitler's mountaintop estate. It is incredibly eerie to watch men like Albert Speer, Martin Borman, Joseph Goebbels and Heinrich Himmler in this domestic setting. Musical score provided. 53 mins.
VHS: $24070. $14.95.

After Mein Kampf?
Produced in war-time England, the first actual documentary footage and dramatic reconstruction of the rape of Poland, the seizure of the low countries, and the attacks on Great Britain. Probably the first non-German production about Hitler, obviously meant as war-time propaganda, but remarkable. England, 1940, 43 mins.
VHS: $01620. $24.95.

Allied Fighting Machines of World War II
A look at the evolution of Allied fighting units during World War II captured in historical footage and subgrouped into three one-hour sections. *Allied Fighters*, detailing the Mustangs, Spitfires, the Lightnings and Corsairs; *Allied Bombers*, about American and British bomber offenses, the Flying Fortresses, the Lancasters and Liberators; and *Allied Armor*, about the fierce fighting on the eastern and western fronts, as the Sherman, Churchill and T-34 divisions changed the course of the war. 180 mins.
VHS: $18791. $59.95.

America at War
This wide-ranging program looks at the military and political campaigns of the American military, beginning with Pearl Harbor and moving through the Persian Gulf, with specific attention to Korea, the Bay of Pigs, Vietnam, Grenada, Panama and Operation Desert Storm.
VHS: $17954. $29.95.

American Caesar Vol. 1
John Huston hosts this portrait of one of the all-time military legends: General Douglas MacArthur. Volume 1 follows MacArthur from his days as a forgotten hero, soldiering in the Philippines, to the eve of Pearl Harbor, to his becoming the last shogun of the new Japan.
VHS: $03138. $24.95.

Appointment in Tokyo
A documentary compiled from archive footage taken from the vaults of various government agencies. This World War II video emphasizes the Pacific theatre of operations as told from the perspective of the war fought in the air. Expect dogfights, bombing runs, aircraft carriers and kamikazes. B&W, 56 mins.
VHS: $09521. $19.95.

The Architecture of Doom
A brilliant documentary which explores the inner workings of the Third Reich and illuminates the Nazi aesthetic in art, architecture and popular culture. Director Peter Cohen uses this analysis of Nazi art and architecture to shed new light on German popular culture, which made Hitler possible. Music by Richard Wagner, footage of Hitler and his Nazi party and rare films and memorabilia are combined to show how a civilized country supported a frustrated artist who became a maniacal despot.
VHS: $26346. $59.95.
Peter Cohen, USA, 1995, 119 mins.

Attack in the Pacific
Armed Forces Information Film #3 details the fight against the Japanese during World War II in the Pacific.
VHS: $02588. $19.95.

Axis Fighting Machines of World War II
A documentary about Axis power military weaponry and forces of World War II, captured in historical footage subdivided into three one-hour sections. *Axis Fighters* shows German and Japanese bombers such as the ME-109, FW-190 and Zero; *Axis Bombers* looks at the German and Japanese blitzkriegs, the Stukas, HG-111s and ground attack aircraft; and *Axis Armor* focuses on the Panzers and Tigers of the Nazi blitzkrieg, as well as sections on Japanese and Italian armor. 180 mins.
VHS: $18792. $59.95.

The Battle of Arnhem
Drawing on British, German and Dutch photo and sound archives, this program looks at Field Marshall Montgomery's ambitious though problematic "Market Garden" strategy, the campaign to capture the river crossings in Holland during the final push on Berlin.
VHS: $17955. $29.95.

Battle of London
Actual war footage of the first serial attacks on London are featured in this documentary. Though bombers devastated the city, Londoners persevered. 1941, 16 mins.
VHS: $26677. $19.95.

The Battle of Midway
Roosevelt insisted that this documentary about the decisive World War II Pacific Battle be made for the mothers of America. John Ford directed this terrific film that was edited in secret and released just days after its completion. Henry Fonda narrates. 20 mins.
VHS: $21993. $19.95.

Battle of San Pietro/Marines Have Landed
The U.S. War Department presents two documentaries of Marine action during World War II. Music by the Mormon Tabernacle Choir.
VHS: $02587. $19.95.

The Battle of the Bulge
By mid-1944 it seemed that Allied victories were irreversible, until this battle broke any hint of complacency. Eisenhower threw 250,000 men into the struggle, hoping to end the war. The grueling experiences of the fighting men who endured freezing cold and terrible carnage is finally told in this documentary. 90 mins.
VHS: $24697. $19.95.

Best of Nightline
Austrian President Kurt Waldheim. 30 mins.
VHS: $14050. $14.98.
Klaus Barbie and His Connections. 30 mins.
VHS: $14028. $14.98.

Blitzkrieg, The Lightning War
Be there as Nazis storm the democracies of Western Europe with venomous tank warfare. From the series *The Nazis*. 50 mins.
VHS: $12729. $24.98.

Bob Hope Remembers World War II
Bob Hope offers a nostalgic tribute to the G.I. generation in this look at the European Theatre and D-Day. Contains a full-length video, a souvenir book, and two audio cassettes.
VHS: $23047. $49.95.

Bombardier: The Real Story
Rare footage from the National Archives and interviews with famous bombardiers reveal the importance of bombardiers to the Allies' winning of World War II. 50 mins.
VHS: $27249. $24.95.

Bombers
The plane and bomb have formed a pact that has changed the way wars are fought and won. See how balloons and zeppelins are used to drop bombs, how the first bombers were utilized in 1921, and how they have become increasingly complicated. 60 mins.
VHS: $13123. $19.98.

Breakthrough
D-Day, the infamous day marking the beginning of the end of World War II in Europe, was a success because of the dedication of thousands of young men. This film shows the courageous warriors who made it happen, including actual footage of the battle.
VHS: $21028. $19.98.
Lewis Seiler, USA, 1950, 91 mins.

Cameramen at War
The story of the British Film Unit newsreel cameramen during both world wars, produced by the British Ministry of Information and compiled by Len Lye. Special highlights include sensational footage from campaigns in France, Norway, and North Africa, as well as over the skies of England. 26 mins.
VHS: $03346. $29.95.

Combat America
American propaganda financed by the Army Air Corps concerns the heroism, skill and courage of the 351st Air Bombardment Group, stationed in England. Narrated by Clark Gable, an Air Force captain.
VHS: $18953. $19.95.

Crusade in Europe
A series on the American campaign in Europe, based on General Dwight D. Eisenhower's memoirs. The series employs war footage taken from the U.S. Army, Navy and Coast Guard, the British War Office, the National Film Board of Canada and captured Nazi materials. The program highlights strategic sessions with Allied and Axis power leaders and generals. Narrated by Westbrook Van Voorhis and Hugh James. 520 mins.
Vol. 1: War Declared. Subtitled *America Joins the Fight*, the program considers Hitler's rise, the Japanese attack on Pearl Harbor, the first draft, Churchill's visit to America and Eisenhower's appointment as head of military operations in the European theater. 60 mins.
VHS: $18707. $19.95.
Vol. 2: The First Offensive. The program considers the North African campaigns and the assaults on Algiers, Oran and Casablanca, and portrays Eisenhower's strategies and his showdowns with German Field Marshal Erwin Rommel, the "Desert Fox." 77 mins.
VHS: $18708. $19.95.
Vol. 3: Assault on Italy. As Allied forces gain strategic control of North Africa, Eisenhower settles on Mussolini's fractured Fascist base in Italy. This program looks at the psychological implications of war and reconstructs Mussolini's rise and bloody fall from power.
VHS: $18709. $19.95.
Vol. 4: D-Day. Subtitled *The Turning Point*, this program considers the accumulation of power and material as Allied forces invade Normandy, the Battle of the Beachhead, the Nazi surrender of Paris to de Gaulle and the continued pursuit of Nazi forces through France. 101 mins.
VHS: $18710. $19.95.
Vol. 5: Hitler's Last Stand. This program examines the final German offensive, the Battle of the Bulge, the Battle of Walcheren Island and the Allies' last major offensive against the Nazis. The show also looks at Churchill's crossing of the Rhine, the Battle of Berlin and the Allies' crushing victory. 101 mins.
VHS: $18711. $19.95.
Vol. 6: Victory. In *The Forging of Peace*, the ramifications of the war and the tense and uneasy peace that exists are explored through the Four-Power Pact, the Nuremberg trials, the Yalta Conference and the formation of the United Nations. The program also provides a series overview. 81 mins.
VHS: $18712. $19.95.
Vols. 1-6: Collector's Edition.
VHS: $18713. $99.95.

Crusade in the Pacific
Six volume collection exploring the land and sea battles that ravaged the Pacific during World War II.
Volume 1. The Pacific in Eruption, Awakening in the Pacific, The Rise of the Japanese Empire, America Goes To War in the Pacific. 115 mins.
VHS: $03131. $19.95.
Volume 2. The U.S. and the Philippines, The Navy Holds—1942, Guadalcanal: America's First Offensive, War in the North—The Aleutians, and The Road Back—New Guinea. 130 mins.
VHS: $03132. $19.95.
Volume 3. Up the Solomons Ladder: Bougainville; Attack in the Central Pacific: Makin and Tarawa; The War at Sea; Speeding Up the Attack—the Marshalls. 115 mins.
VHS: $03133. $19.95.
Volume 4. Stepping Stones to the Philippines; Battle for the Marianas; The War in the China-Burma-India Theatre; Palau: The Fight for Bloody Nose Ridge; MacArthur Returns to the Philippines. 115 mins.
VHS: $03134. $19.95.
Volume 5. Bloody Iwo: The Capture of Iwo Jima; At Japan's Doorstep: Okinawa; The Air War on Japan; The Surrender and Occupation of Japan. 115 mins.
VHS: $03135. $19.95.
Volume 6. Shifting Tides in the Orient; War in Korea; The Problem of Asia and the Pacific. 115 mins.
VHS: $03136. $19.95.

D-Day: The Great Crusade
The storming of the Normandy beaches on D-Day, June 6, 1944, began the final chapter of World War II. This historic video is a unique and detailed record of the events of D-Day. The planning and preparation of Operation Overlord, its code name, was one of the greatest military maneuvers of all time. 112 mins.
VHS: $04900. $39.95.

The Darkest Hour (1939-1941)
In this video the effects of war throughout Europe are shown. Though FDR pledges to keep the U.S. out of war, Pearl Harbor changes everything. Before long war has broken out all over the world. Eric Sevareid narrates. 25 mins.
VHS: $23592. $99.95.

Day of Freedom—Our Fighting Forces (Tag Der Freiheit)
Leni Riefenstahl (*Triumph of the Will*) directs this propaganda documentary on the armed forces of Nazi Germany. Military parades, lots of flags and leaders. Planes fly in a swastika formation. This short film was thought to have been lost. No dialog or narration. Original music score.
VHS: $05504. $19.95.
Leni Riefenstahl, Germany, 1935, 17 mins.

December 7th, Midway, Bougainville
This award-winning film focuses on three crucial episodes in the Pacific Theatre, including the infamous sneak attack on Pearl Harbor, and the Battle of the Midway. 60 mins.
VHS: $10026. $19.95.

Desert Victory

The longest chase in military history, the British Eighth Army's pursuit of Rommel's Afrika Korps from El Alamein to Tripoli, is shown via authentic footage. Of the 26 cameramen who filmed *Desert Victory*, four were killed, six wounded and seven captured. Tobruk was actually taken by the film unit, which arrived several hours before the fighting forces. Directed by Colonel David MacDonald of the Army Photographic Unit, *Desert Victory* was important as a propaganda film, bringing home to English audiences the first evidence of a turning point in the North Africa war. 60 mins.
VHS: S04479. $39.95.

Die Deutsche Wochenschau #1 (The German Weekly Newsreel)

Four newsreels from Nazi Germany are presented in this collection now available on video. Combat footage of the Luftwaffe over Greece and Crete. Winter fighting in Finland and Russia. U-Boats in the North Atlantic. Also fabric being made from waste paper. German with no subtitles. WWII as seen from another viewpoint. Germany, 1941, 50 mins.
VHS: S05500. $24.95.

The Eagle Has Landed

The fully-restored adaptation of Jack Higgins's World War II adventure novel about a Nazi plot to kidnap Winston Churchill. With Robert Duvall, Michael Caine, Jenny Agutter, Donald Pleasance and Donald Sutherland.
VHS: S17281. $9.98.
John Sturges, Great Britain, 1976, 134 mins.

The Eagle's Nest: Hitler's Secret Center of Power

A fascinating documentary series which chronicles the rise and fall of the Third Reich. You'll see rare color footage of the inner circle of Nazi fanatics, unique contemporary interviews with Albert Speer and other survivors, and much more.

Vol. I: The Early Years. As Germany struggles with the aftermath of WW I, the unstable Weimar Republic finds itself unable to control the splinter parties of both Left and Right. Failed artist Adolf Hitler discovers his true calling, politics, and becomes a member of the rising National Socialist party. Eventually, Hitler takes command of Germany, stirring it to a frenzy of nationalism and racism. German economic strength and military might increases, and Hitler hosts the '36 Olympic games. 60 mins.
VHS: S13660. $29.95.
Vol. II: Europe Falls before the Reich. A now fascist Germany annexes Austria. Hitler meets with Mussolini at the Berghof, while plans are laid to march into Czechoslovakia. Hitler's bold plan begins with the seizure of the Sudetenland, followed by the cynical non-aggression pact with Stalin. 60 mins.
VHS: S13661. $29.95.
Vol. III: A World War. In the summer of 1939 Europe realizes the awesome power of the Reich, but it is already too late. German armor rolls over most of the continent. The mask is removed, and the face of Germany's "New Order" becomes terrifyingly clear to the world. This program ends with the Swastika flying over Red Square in Moscow and, for a brief moment, it appears that the "master plan" has succeeded. 60 mins.
VHS: S13662. $29.95.
Vol. IV: The End of the Reich. The tide turns, as Hitler's forces, spread too thin and short of supplies, must assume the defensive. The prolonged war on the Eastern Front has drained Germany, and defeat becomes inevitable, though Germans continue to fight frantically to keep their hold. The U.S. has entered the war and the allies deliver the "coup de grace." A postscript shows a defeated Germany immediately after the war. 60 mins.
VHS: S13663. $29.95.

End of the Ordeal (1943-1945)

After D-Day the Yalta conference sets the stage for a divided Europe. The U.S. ends the war in the Pacific by bombing Hiroshima and Nagasaki. Eric Sevareid hosts this look at the final days of a terrible era. 24 mins.
VHS: S23594. $99.95.

Enola Gay and the Atomic Bombing of Japan

A&E crafted this video which shows every step of the military action that ended the war. From the development of the bomb to the devastation wrought on Japanese cities, dramatic footage shows the methodical process that changed the face of warfare. 75 mins.
VHS: S26690. $19.95.

Entertaining the Troops: American Entertainers in World War II

"As bad a time as that was," says Dorothy Lamour, "there was a happy atmosphere around Hollywood. It was like everybody was trying to hold up everybody else's morale." This unique documentary tells how Hollywood pitched in on the war effort, through film clips, reminiscences and newsreel footage, as American entertainment marshaled its forces to raise not only money but the spirits of the country's fighting men. With Abbott and Costello, Jack Benny, Bob Hope, Andrews Sisters, Lucille Ball, Dorothy Lamour, Mel Blanc, Bill Crosby, Lena Horne and many others.
VHS: S10945. $14.95.
Robert Mugge, USA, 1989, 90 mins.

Fahnen Junker

From bayonet fighting to blasting bunkers, glacier climbing to sniper fire, here is the tough training that molded the leaders of Nazi armies. This original 1943 Nazi film depicts the life at German schools for infantry officers. 17 mins. German with English subtitles.
VHS: S08313. $24.95.

Fight for the Sky

This British series utilizes rare footage, much of it obtained from archives in Eastern Europe, to document the air war during WWII. Available as a pre-pack (four tapes) at a discount, or individually.
Battle of Britain. With the surrender of France in 1940, the threat of invasion hung heavily over Britain and the British strategy to meet the German threat was due to one man—Sir Hugh Dowding. This documentary, using much newly discovered footage, gives full justice to the exceptional commander and to all the men and women who, during the dark summer of 1940, inflicted the first defeat on German arms. 60 mins.
VHS: S12455. $29.95.

Elite Forces.

The paratroopers played a crucial role in WWII, providing some of the war's greatest heroes. The supposedly impregnable Belgian fortress of Eban-Emael, designed to stop an army, was eliminated by a handful of airborne attackers; the capture of Crete in 1941 by a purely airborne assault remains the great classic of its kind. This is their unique story. 60 mins.
VHS: S12453. $29.95.
Fighter Aces. The story of Air Aces charts the history of aerial combat from the Great War to the dawn of the jet age, using archive footage, much of which has been unavailable in the West since World War II, and documenting such aces as Baron von Richtofen, Oswald Boelcke, Billy Bishop, Herman Goering, Joseph Frantisek, Erich Hartman and others. 60 mins.
VHS: S12457. $29.95.
History of the Luftwaffe. The Luftwaffe became the handmaiden of Hitler's dream of conquest and a vital component of the blitzkrieg. But the fuhrer's continual demands upon his air force as he fanatically pursued his grand design forced the Luftwaffe into the role of a workhorse. 60 mins.
VHS: S12454. $29.95.
Pre-pack.
VHS: S12458. $113.81.

Fight of the Sky

Explores the lifestyle and heroism of the American Fighter Pilots who flew missions over Germany in World War II, illustrating the various types of fighters used to escort the bombers deep into enemy territory. 54 mins.
VHS: S10029. $29.95.

Franklin D. Roosevelt: The New Deal

The early years of this presidential giant are illuminated through photographs and newsreel appearances. 23 mins.
VHS: S23559. $49.95.

Franklin D. Roosevelt: The War Years

From 1941 to 1945, crucial events, anxieties and hard work kept this American President occupied with weighty matters that impacted the whole world. 20 mins.
VHS: S23561. $49.95.

Franklin D. Roosevelt: War Comes to America

The growing threat of European and Asian dictators is explored in this look at America before the Second World War. 20 mins.
VHS: S23560. $49.95.

Fuhrer: Rise of a Madman

Adolph Hitler's rise to power is plotted, from the many unsuccessful attempts to gain German leadership, to the horror of WWII and finally his suicide in the bunker. 108 mins.
VHS: S09253. $39.95.

George Stevens: A Filmmaker's Journey

An intimate documentary about the Hollywood director, the film weaves interviews, remembrances, on-camera interviews with his collaborators and colleagues, footage from his films and footage he shot during World War II. The interviews include Warren Beatty, Katharine Hepburn, Fred Astaire, Frank Capra and John Huston. "A wonderfully informative tribute, lit together with love, intelligence, wit and, most important of all, a knowledge of film history" (Vincent Canby).
VHS: S18971. $29.95.
Laser: LD71556. $49.95.
George Stevens Jr., USA, 1984, 111 mins.

George Stevens: D-Day to Berlin

Director George Stevens shot this documentary footage which depicts American efforts in Europe during World War II. It includes some of the most extensive color footage available of both the Normandy invasion and the fall of Berlin. This film won 3 Emmy Awards and was originally commissioned by Dwight D. Eisenhower. George Stevens, Jr. narrates. With William Saroyan, Irwin Shaw and Ivan Moffat.
VHS: S26760. $19.98.
Laser: LD75408. $29.99.
George Stevens, USA, 50 mins.

Good Morning Mr. Hitler

Six weeks before the outbreak of World War II, a three-day festival in Munich celebrated "2,000 Years of German Culture." An amateur cameraman wangled permission to film the event. The result is this unique look at Hitler and the German people celebrating Nazi ideals. The contemporary filmmakers who retrieved this long-lost footage frame the material by showing an audience of elderly Germans watching this extraordinary home movie. Included is the production of the man who published *Mein Kampf*. It was she who had always said, "Good morning, Mr. Hitler," at Hitler's request.
VHS: S26995. $29.95.
Luke Holland/Paul Yule, Germany, 1994, 52 mins.

Great Days of History

A new series which culls rare footage of world archives to provide a comprehensive history of major events of the 20th century.
D-Day: 6 June 1944. This program relives the landings in Normandy in June, 1944. It shows the planning, the assembly of air, sea and land forces by Allied command, the embarkation from England across the Channel, the attack and landings, and the fierce German defense. 52 mins.
VHS: S09432. $29.95.
Mediterranean Front. This unique visual record shows the efforts of the Free French to gather and train in North Africa for the landing and reconquest of France from the south. The campaign that followed the Mediterranean landings is documented to its end in Marshall Keitel's final surrender. 26 mins.
VHS: S09431. $29.95.
World War II: Part I—Munich to the Battle of Britain. The signposts of the war: Mussolini's adventure in Ethiopia, Franco's brutal insurrection in Spain, Hitler's annexation of the Sudetenland. This program begins with the Anschluss of Austria and the Munich nonaggression pact. Includes rare footage from German War archives, including the destruction of Warsaw, the phony war, Dunkirk, the invasion of France, the Battle of Britain. 60 mins.
VHS: S09428. $29.95.

Guadalcanal & The Shores of Iwo Jima

The Japanese depended heavily on two Pacific islands from which to launch their aggressive air attacks: Guadalcanal and Iwo Jima. The Marines were called on to wrest these islands from the Japanese, and both times were successful. This program examines these battles. 60 mins.
VHS: S13137. $19.98.

Guilty Men

This short film shows a variety of guilty men. Included are scenes depicting the Nuremberg trials, executions of war criminals, the organization of Hitler Youth Camps, the Versailles Peace Treaty, Trotsky's storming of the Winter Palace in St. Petersburg, Trotsky's speech against Stalin, the progression of anti-Jewish propaganda and Gestapo terrorist acts. 1946, 40 mins.
VHS: S26683. $19.95.

Here Is Germany

Considered one of the most impressive documentaries made by the U.S. government during WWII, this film took over two years to produce. It draws heavily on hundreds of German motion-picture sources, tracing the development of Germany as a military power from the time of Frederick the Great to the end of the Third Reich. 52 mins.
VHS: S03348. $29.95.

Hidden Army

The 18,000,000 women who worked in American industry during World War II were the "hidden army" whose efforts helped the US and its allies vanquish their enemies. Produced by the U.S. Army Signal Corps to bolster sagging morale and lagging production, this film features hard-to-find footage of women performing "men's" jobs, from electronics assembly to fork-lift operation, providing valuable insight into this vital but underrated aspect of the war effort. 17 mins.
VHS: S06255. $59.95.

The History of World War II: Battle of Midway

John Ford's documentary on the Battle of Midway, the large-scale naval engagement that irrevocably changed the course of the war, giving the momentum to the American forces. Ford was hurt during the shooting.
VHS: S19677. $19.95.
John Ford, USA, 1943, 18 mins.

The History of World War II: December 7th

John Ford re-staged the Japanese attack on Pearl Harbor by using Hollywood sound stages to approximate the confusion, panic and disorder. Winner of the Academy Award for Best Documentary Production in 1943.
VHS: S19676. $19.95.
John Ford, USA, 1943, 34 mins.

The History of World War II: Desert Victory

This British-made documentary chronicles the battles of the American Army and German Nazi units under the command of Field Marshall Rommel, the Desert Fox. During the making of the film, four British cameramen were killed, seven wounded and six captured. Winner of the 1943 Academy Award for Best Documentary Feature. 54 mins.
VHS: S19678. $19.95.

Hitler

Learn how a sexually-confused nobody rose to power and turned his sick beliefs into a national ideology. From the series *The Nazis*. 50 mins.
VHS: S12733. $24.98.

Hitler Youth Quex

This Nazi propaganda film tells the story of a boy at odds with his abusive and unemployed communist father. At a communist camp, the boy is disturbed by his comrades and joins the Nazis instead. Ultimately a group of Left-wing radicals hunts him down. Based on K.A. Schenzinger's novel. German with English subtitles.
VHS: S23801. $24.95.
Hans Steinhoff, Germany, 1933, 100 mins.

Hitler's Henchmen (MPI)

Made by the United States government, this film was pulled from circulation in 1946 because of its attack on the German people. Originally titled *Here Is Germany*, this is a classic propaganda documentary on the "Germanic War Spirit". 58 mins.
VHS: S13112. $39.98.

Hitler: The Final Chapter

This video documentary puts to rest the myths about Adolf Hitler's final days. Many wondered if he lived, but this tape offers the facts about the madman's demise. 51 mins.
VHS: S25991. $29.95.

Hitler: The Whole Story

This is the story behind the madman who oversaw the cataclysmic destruction of World War II, Adolph Hitler. The ruthless would-be ruler of all Europe is revealed in this documentary, using detailed biographical materials and historic research.
VHS: S20938. $49.95.

How Hitler Lost the War

A provocative account that challenges a lot of conventional theories about the Germans' defeat in World War II, suggesting Allied victory was due to Hitler's strategic mistakes. The film is told from the perspective of high-ranking Third Reich military officers and uses animated maps, documentary footage and interviews. 67 mins.
VHS: S18135. $29.95.

Hymn for a Nation

Arturo Toscanini conducts the NBC Orchestra in this World War II tribute to the fight against Fascism and Nazism. Music by Verdi. USA, 1944.
VHS: S02592. $34.95.

Kamikaze

Extraordinary newsreel footage is deployed in this documentary about the conflict between the U.S. and Japan during World War II. Kamikaze pilots were a tactic used by the Japanese when they sensed that the tide had turned against them. The US response was a controversial measure. Atomic war was seen as a final solution that would lead to the surrender of Japan.
VHS: S24083. $14.95.
Perry Wolf, USA/France, 1961, 85 mins.

Kamikaze: Death from the Sky

The Allied forces were utterly confounded by the emergence of the Kamikaze fighter pilots from Japan during the end of World War II—soldiers on a suicide mission who would crash their bomb-laden aircraft onto the decks of U.S. naval carriers in the Pacific. This is the remarkable story of the doomed Kamikaze. 60 mins.
VHS: S13139. $29.98.

Life of Adolf Hitler

Paul Rotha's famous documentary uses archival footage to depict the rise of the Nazi party in a powerful study of one of the horrors of history. Much of the footage used by Rotha is rare, including the last films of Hitler before his retreat into the Bunker.
VHS: S00751. $29.95.
Paul Rotha, Great Britain, 1961, 101 mins.

Listen to Britain

Four great poetic documentaries by Humphrey Jennings, all set during World War II by this great English filmmaker: *Listen to Britain, The True Story of Lili Marlene, A Diary for Timothy* and *The Cumberland Story*.
VHS: S02953. $79.95.
Humphrey Jennings, Great Britain, 1942-47, 120 mins.

The Lonely Struggle: Marek Edelman, Last Hero of the Warsaw Ghetto Uprising

This cardiologist from Lodz is the last surviving member of the leadership that marshalled the heroic forces of resistance which fought the Nazis under hopeless circumstances. This insider's account vividly recreates a moment of unparalleled courage. 60 mins.
VHS: S23236. $39.95.

March of Time: America at War

A six-volume series.
American Defense, Part 1. America's New Army; Men of the Fleet; Prelude to Victory; We Are the Marines. 112 mins.
VHS: S05090. $19.95.
American Defense, Part 2. The Navy and the Nation; Invasion!; Airways to Peace; Naval Log of Victory; Back Door to Tokyo; Uncle Sam, Mariner? The Unknown Battle. 126 mins.
VHS: S05091. $19.95.
Friend and Foe, Part 1. Battlefields of the Pacific, Far East Command, The Argentine Question, India in Crisis, India at War, the Fighting French, One Day of War—Russia, 1943. 116 mins.
VHS: S05086. $19.95.
Friend and Foe, Part 2. The New Canada; Inside Fascist Spain, Then Japan, Portugal—Europe's Crossroads; Sweden's Middle Road; South American Front— 1944. 87 mins.
VHS: S05087. $19.95.
Friend and Foe, Part 3. The Irish Question, Underground Report; British Imperialism—1944; What To Do with Germany; Inside China Today; Report of Italy; Memo from Britain. 113 mins.
VHS: S05088. $19.95.
On the Homefront. Our America at War; Then Air Raids Strike; Men in Washington—1942; The FBI Front; Bill Jack vs. Adolf Hitler; The West Coast Question; Spotlight on Congress. 114 mins.
VHS: S05089. $19.95.
March of Time: America at War, Gift-Pack. All six volumes of the March of Time America at War series, with a special collector's edition gift-pack.
VHS: S06406. $99.95.

March of Time: Post War Problems and Solutions

A new series of March of Time compilations, winner of the Special Academy Award in 1936, hosted by Westbrook Van Voorhis.
America's Post-War Problems, Part 1. Post-war jobs? Post-war farms. The returning veteran wanted: more homes. Problem drinkers. Is everyone happy? The American cop. 125 mins.
VHS: S06454. $19.95.
America's Post-War Problems, Part 2. The teachers' crisis. Your doctors—1947. New trains for old. T-men in action. The presidential year. Stop—Heavy Traffic. The nation's mental health. 119 mins.
VHS: S06455. $19.95.
Post-War Problems Beyond, Part 1. The new U.S. frontier. Palestine problem. 18 million orphans. Justice comes to Germany. Report on Greece. The new France. 107 mins.
VHS: S06456. $19.95.
Post-War Problems Beyond, Part 2. World Food problem. The Soviet's neighbor, Czechoslovakia. Germany—handle with care. Storm over Britain XIII/13. Turkey's 100 million. End of an Empire? Policeman's holiday. 125 mins.
VHS: S06457. $19.95.
Modern Main Street U.S.A. Public relations….This means you. White collar girls. Farming pays off. Mid century: half-way to where? Where's the fire? 120 mins.
VHS: S06458. $19.95.
Post-War Problems and Solutions Gift-Pack. All five volumes of this March of Time series, at a special price.
VHS: S06453. $89.95.

March of Time: Trouble Abroad

A continued look at the world during the first half of the 20th century.
Germany and Other Problems. Inside Nazi Germany, Russians in Exile, Old Dixie's New Look, One Million Mission, Arms and the League, Brain Trust Island, Nazi Conquest — No. 1, Crime and Prison. 93 mins.
VHS: S08052. $19.95.
Spotlight on War. Men of Medicine, G-Men of the Sea, Threat to Gibraltar, Man at the Wheel, Prelude to Conquest, Father Divine's Deal, The British Dilemma, U.S. Fire Fighters. 91 mins.
VHS: S08053. $19.95.

Tensions Increase. Junk and War, England's DORA, Fiorello La Guardia, Crisis in Algeria, U.S. Secret Service, Alaska's Salmon War, Britain's Gambling Fever. 76 mins.
VHS: S08051. $19.95.

Uncle Sam: The Observer. Inside the Maginot Line, Uncle Sam: The Good Neighbor, The Refugee — Today and Tomorrow, State of the Nation, Mexico's New Crisis, Young America. 75 mins.
VHS: S08054. $19.95.

War Abroad: Depression at Home. Poland and War, The Dust Bowl, Goods for Sale, The 49th State, Babies Wanted, Rockefeller Millions, Rehearsal for War, The Spoils System, Youth in Camps. 71 mins.
VHS: S08050. $19.95.

War, Peace and America. The Mediterranean — Background for War, Japan — Master of the Orient, Dixie — U.S.A., War, Peace and Propaganda, Metropolis — 1939. 91 mins.
VHS: S08055. $19.95.

Complete Set.
VHS: S08049. $119.70.

March of Time: War Breaks Out

A six-volume series.

Americans Prepare, Part 1. Uncle Sam, the Farmer (with war raging in Europe, the farmer's task of feeding Americans at home and abroad is enormously increased) and The Ramparts We Watch (controversial feature which explores the effect war has on citizens of an average American town). 118 mins.
VHS: S05080. $19.95.

Americans Prepare, Part 2. Labor and Defense; Uncle Sam: The Non-Belligerent; Men of the FBI (The FBI combats espionage); New England's Eight Million Yankees (New England prepares for war); Thumbs Up, Texas! and Main Street, U.S.A. 113 mins.
VHS: S05081. $19.95.

Praying for Peace. The Vatican of Pius XII (Pope Pius XII tries to bring about peace) and The Story of the Vatican. 71 mins.
VHS: S05085. $19.95.

The Military Prepares. Soldiers with Wings; Crisis in the Pacific, the U.S. Navy: 1940; Gateways to Panama; Arms and the Men; Crisis in the Atlantic; Sailors with Wings. 124 mins.
VHS: S05082. $19.95.

The Battle Beyond, Part 1. Battle Fleets of England; Newsfronts of War: 1940; The Republic of Finland; Canada at War; The Philippines: 1898-1946; Spoils of Conquest. 107 mins.
VHS: S05083. $19.95.

The Battle Beyond, Part 2. On Foreign Newsfronts; Britain's Royal Air Force; Mexico: Good Neighbor's Dilemma; Australia at War; China Fights Back; Peace: By Adolf Hitler; Norway in Revolt. 112 mins.
VHS: S05084. $19.95.

March of Time: War Breaks Out, Gift-Pack. All six volumes of the March of Time War Breaks Out series in a special gift-pack.
VHS: S03031. $99.95.

March to the Fuhrer

A propaganda classic produced during Hitler's reign in Germany—a showcase for Hitler's means of building mass hysteria. German with NO subtitles.
VHS: S10592. $29.95.

The Marines Are Coming

Conrad Nagel and William Hayes are featured in this melodramatic short film. A marine lieutenant is confronted with a beautiful Latin dancer who will simply not leave him alone. 1934. 71 mins.
VHS: S26684. $19.95.

The Marines at Tarawa/ To the Shores of Iwo Jima

These two documentaries bring the terrifying reality of Pacific World War II battlefields to the screen. To the Shores of Iwo Jima even won an Oscar for Best Documentary. Few works show the details of war with this kind of graphic intensity. 20 mins each.
VHS: S21992. $19.95.

Marines Have Landed

This program tells the story of the U.S. Marines, unmatched in their fight against the Axis during World War II. Their most celebrated battles are recounted here, using dramatic footage. 60 mins.
VHS: S13136. $19.98.

Mein Kampf

The most credible and accurate depiction of the actual steps taken by Adolf Hitler to conquer the world. In this specially remastered and re-released original length version, the mind-numbing truth of these events is laid bare. Every shot in this film is authentic, including never-before-seen footage from the secret archives of the Nazi SS Elite Guard.
VHS: S02548. $39.95.
Erwin Leiser, USA, 1960, 120 mins.

Mein Krieg (My Private War)

An eerie compilation of home movies and oral histories of six Wehrmacht soldiers who were involved in the Nazi invasion of the former Soviet Union. The images of the war (soldiers swimming in the Black Sea, bombed out landscapes and literally thousands of dead bodies) are contrasted with the soldiers' memories and reminiscences of their experiences. "Mein Krieg is annotated only by the veterans themselves as they explicate the material they produced nearly a half-century before" (J. Hoberman, The Village Voice).
VHS: J19859. $69.95.
Harriet Eder/Thomas Kufus, Germany, 1990, 90 mins.

Men Against Tanks/ Engineers to the Front

A Nazi-produced documentary, as German soldiers re-enact combat exploits for this elaborate and frightening film showing how infantrymen battle Soviet armored attacks. In Engineers to the Front, German engineer/soldiers—the men who paved the way for the blitzkrieg—lift mines, build bridges and force river crossings under fire. 58 mins. German with English subtitles.
VHS: S08312. $39.95.

Mig Alley

Mig Alley was a combat zone in Northwest Korea where formations of up to 200 jets would dogfight at speeds up to 1200 m.p.h. This program is a recording of this fantastic period. 60 mins.
VHS: S13119. $19.98.

Mine Eyes Have Seen the Glory: The Women's Army Corps

Mariette Hartley, award-winning actress and the author of the best-selling autobiography Breaking the Silence, narrates this look at the Women's Army Corps. Known as WAC, the Corps was founded during World War II, paving the way for today's gender-integrated armed forces. Includes interviews with former directors, officers and enlisted women of the WAC.
VHS: S27301. $29.95.
Dane Hansen, USA, 1996

More Than Broken Glass: Memories of Kristallnacht

The night of November 9, 1938 is forever etched in the minds of the Jewish people. Through archival footage, photographs and interviews with witnesses, a sharp portrait is created of the time and place. 57 mins.
VHS: S12904. $39.95.

Mussolini: Rise and Fall of a Dictator

New facts revealed about Italy's controversial figure, from his sexual relationship with his mistress to his love/hate relationship with his father. 105 mins.
VHS: S09252. $39.95.

National Geographic Video: Last Voyage of the Lusitania

When the Lusitania was sunk by a German U-boat, few thought that anyone would ever look upon this magnificent ship ever again. Now underwater photography grants us a close look at the remains of a disaster that claimed 1200 innocent lives in 18 minutes.
VHS: S21150. $19.95.

National Geographic Video: The Lost Fleet of Guadalcanal

Dr. Robert Ballard leads a joint expedition with the U.S. Navy in the South Pacific to unearth the ships, planes, materials and wreckage from the fierce World War II battles. The program blends archival footage of the battles with stories and anecdotes related by survivors and participants. 60 mins.
VHS: S18991. $19.95.
Laser: LD71889. $29.95.

Nazi War Crime Trials

This collection contains five newsreels, one theatrical trailer and a short documentary from the Soviet Union on the Nuremberg Trials. Includes footage of executions by firing squad and by hanging of Nazi war criminals. Also the trial of Yamashita, the Tiger of Malaya, is covered, even though he was not a Nazi. USSR film in English. USA/USSR, 1945, 67 mins.
VHS: S05506. $29.95.

Nazi War Crimes

Witness the Nazis' shocking slaughter of over 200,000 innocent civilians at the Ukrainian Babi-Yar ravine. From the series The Nazis. 50 mins.
VHS: S12731. $24.98.

Nazi War Crimes: Babi-Yar

Babi-Yar, a pastoral Ukrainian ravine outside Kiev, was occupied by the Nazis in 1941 and used for human extermination experiments. Testimonies of victims who escaped complete a portrait of an incident in history never to be forgotten. 50 mins.
VHS: S12711. $19.95.

Nazis Strike

The Nazis move through Europe, taking over Czechoslovakia and Poland. Using rare documentary footage, this film looks at the Nazi conquest of Europe. 40 mins.
VHS: S03059. $19.95.

Nazis...Lest We Forget!

The first film on this tape, Nuremberg und Sein Lehre (Nuremberg and Its Lesson), was created to show the German people the full extent of Nazi atrocities. Footage from camps makes it quite unnerving. Narrated in English. Then, to the strains of Luftwaffe songs, Flieger am Feind (A Nazi Newsreel), shows how the Nazis used air power to terrorize urban populations and fight the allies. 35 mins.
VHS: S24077. $19.95.

The Newsreel Library of World War II

While the war raged in distant European lands, the newsreel brought pictures of battles to the local theater screen. This was the only opportunity the country had to search for familiar faces fighting overseas. Emotional images that united the nation included the rise of Hitler, France's surrender, the battles of Normandy, Patton's amazing offensive, and the dramatic end of the war.
VHS: S15949. $29.95.

Nightfighters: The Tuskegee Airmen

In World War II, Lt. Col. Benjamin Davis led an elite black group of bombers, support crew and surgical teams over Italy and North Africa. Though these African-American servicemen valiantly shielded white flyers, the army largely ignored their contribution. This video tells their story. 52 mins.
VHS: S27661. $59.95.

Normandy Invasion

The largest sea invasion ever attempted is chronicled in this detailed account of the June 6, 1944 assault on the beaches of Normandy, using rare documentary footage.
VHS: S02580. $19.95.

Normandy: the Great Crusade

Normandy was the site where the great reclamation of the European continent began ending the iron grip of the Third Reich. This documentary tells the history of that famous battle with expert documentation based on genuine archival and biographical sources.
VHS: S20937. $19.95.

Nostalgia World War II Video Library #1

Produced by the U.S. War Department, these three short films made in 1944-45 let the folks on the homefront know we were winning but it wasn't over just yet. Battle Wreckage shows the need for more steel. The Wars Speed Up, narrated by Jose Ferrer, with Robert Mitchum in a brief role, reminds us "that the war begins every day." It Can't Last expresses the hope of all involved. USA, 1944-45, 46 mins.
VHS: S05502. $24.95.

Nostalgia World War II Video Library #2

The early days of the war on the American homefront. The building of the Alcan highway. Veronica Lake cuts her hair to benefit work safety in war factories. Unnecessary personal travel tips. The biography of a ball bearing. Plus much more. Camouflage in New Guinea. USA, 1942-43, 51 mins.
VHS: S05505. $24.95.

Nostalgia World War II Video Library #3

U.S. combat footage from the land, the sea and the air courtesy of the Signal Corps and the U.S. Coast Guard. Beach landings in the Mediterranean. Dogfights over England. Bombing missions in the Pacific. The building and launching of a new transport ship, from luxury liner to troop transport. And much more. USA, 1944, 61 mins.
VHS: S05496. $24.95.

Nostalgia World War II Video Library #4

An unusual collection of Hollywood and U.S. Government film shorts which included nine dramatic episodes. Performers include Ronald Reagan, Burgess Meredith, Susan Hayward and Richard Arlen. Songs include "Keep 'Em Rolling," and "We've Got Another Bond to Buy," sung by Bing Crosby. USA, 1943-45, 61 mins.
VHS: S05494. $24.95.

Nostalgia World War II Video Library #5

The aftermath of the war is dealt with in two short subjects. Diary of a Sergeant is a dramatized documentary of the life of Harold Russell, who lost both hands in the war and later won an Oscar for his role in The Best Years of Our Lives. The second short, The Atom Strikes, traces the development of the A-Bomb and visits Nagasaki and Hiroshima for the dramatic results of science at war. USA, 1945, 53 mins.
VHS: S05510. $24.95.

Nostalgia World War II Video Library #6

The fight against Japanese imperialism is documented in this three-part collection. Inside Fighting China (1944), Target Japan (1944), and The Fleet That Came to Stay (1946), which is directed by Budd Boetticher, each reflect the feelings of the time. See America fight back.
VHS: S05497. $24.95.
Budd Boetticher, USA, 1942-46, 52 mins.

Nostalgia World War II Video Library #7

Combat footage from Tarawa beach. Hawaiian Jungle Training. P-47's in action over England. A hill in Italy that took $2 million to take. Also Elisha Cook Jr. as a scared GI in Baptism of Fire (1943), a short film so realistic it was nominated for an Oscar for Best Documentary. USA, 1943-44, 57 mins.
VHS: S05498. $24.95.

Nostalgia World War II Video Library #8

Selected footage of the Big One as seen by the Signal Corps. See "dead Japanese, stinking in the sun." Witness "American soldiers with war in their faces." From New Guinea to Anzio beach to Burma and Britain. Also a "Private Snafu" cartoon with the voice of Mel Blanc. American propaganda at its finest. USA, 1944, 59 mins.
VHS: S05495. $24.95.

Nostalgia World War II Video Library #9

Ronald Reagan narrates The Fight for the Sky. Vice President Henry A. Wallace explains The Price of Victory. And the Signal Corps documents our men in uniform and bombing raids over Germany and in the Pacific. Highlights of the Army and Air Force in action. USA, 1942-44, 61 mins.
VHS: S05499. $24.95.

Nostalgia World War II Video Library #10

San Pietro is the unforgettable documentary by John Huston that shows in detail a key World War II battle over an Italian farming valley. Story of a Transport is also a documentary about war produced by the American armed forces. It shows how troops were transported by ship overseas. 59 mins.
VHS: S24079. $14.95.

Nostalgia World War II Video Library #11

This collection of short documentaries tells the story of the US at war. It includes What Makes a Battle, The Fifth Army Report from the Beachhead, Freedom Comes High, The 957th Day and We Said We'd Come Back. 60 mins.
VHS: S24072. $19.95.

Nostalgia World War II Video Library #12

These seven short films detail a number of specific issues about the US effort in the Second World War. Objective...Security, The Army Nurse (includes footage of Gary Cooper), Photography Fights, Lt. General Holland M. Smith, Sixth War Loan Appeal, RAF and 8th Air Force Report from Britain and Target Invisible are all included in this compilation. 67 mins.
VHS: S24084. $24.95.

Nova—Echoes of War

At the beginning of World War II, radar was a crude warning device. By 1945, it was a sophisticated electronic eye that could pinpoint and track aircraft and guide bombing missions at night. This program explores the unprecedented collaboration between civilian scientists and military that turned the war into a technological chess match. 60 mins.
VHS: S11650. $14.98.

Nuremburg

This captured footage of Nazi concentration camps is quite disturbing and not for those who are easily upset. 1945, 23 mins.
VHS: S26681. $19.95.

The Nuremburg Trials

Russian-made documentary of the trial of Nazi war criminals includes historical footage of the Soviet Union before the German invasion. English dialog.
VHS: S02617. $19.95.
S. Sviliv, USSR, 50 mins.

Of Pure Blood

The secret details of Hitler's plan to transform Germany into a pure Aryan nation are uncovered. From the series The Nazis. 50 mins.
VHS: S12734. $19.98.

Our Job in Japan

A U.S. propaganda film like this shows how much attitudes have changed since the war. It describes how the defeated Japanese should be regarded once they were no longer a clear military threat. 1943, 18 mins.
VHS: S26682. $19.95.

Our Soviet Allies, World War II

Four historical programs combine authentic WWII footage with recollections of misty-eyed veterans to document the great Soviet victories of World War II. From the Inside the Soviet Union series. 80 mins.
VHS: S12710. $19.95.

Out of the Ashes (1945-1949)

As the trials at Nuremberg and the military tribunal in Tokyo condemn Nazis and war criminals to death, the Cold War begins and communism is established in China. 24 mins.
VHS: S23595. $99.95.

P.O.W.—Americans in Enemy Hands: World War II, Korea and Vietnam

This inspiring documentary tells the stories of nine different men who were captured in three wars. With amazing candor they describe the imprisonment and torture that they survived. Their stories provide a glimpse into the resiliency of the human spirit. Directed by Carol L. Fleischer. 93 mins.
VHS: S21248. $19.95.

Patton: Old Blood and Guts

Ronald Reagan narrates Patton's warrior legacy in this program about the American commander who led his men farther, faster and harder. 25 mins.
VHS: S09251. $19.95.

Payoff in the Pacific

This World War II documentary focuses on the land war in the Pacific. Produced by the U.S. government, archive footage follows the Marines and the Army as they fight island to island against a well entrenched enemy. Authentic combat footage is presented in black and white. 59 mins.
VHS: S09523. $19.95.

Pearl Harbor: 50 Years After

From the people at CNN comes a powerful new look at the events of Pearl Harbor. Host Bob Cain takes you behind the scenes and onto the battlefield, examining America's involvement in the biggest war the world has ever known. USA, 60 mins.
VHS: S15303. $19.98.

Pearl Harbor: Two Hours That Shook the World

ABC News joined forces with Japan's oldest and largest network to produce this retrospective of the attack on Pearl Harbor. 100 mins.
VHS: S15879. $19.98.

Piece of Cake: Complete Set

During World War II, an RAF Hornet Squadron must undergo the rites of passage that will make them seasoned fighter pilots. Their aristocratic CO is arrogant and overconfident. Eventually the concerns of his squadron overtake his attitude as adventure and heartache build toward the climactic battle.
VHS: S21689. $129.96.
Ian Toynton, Great Britain, 1994, 650 mins.

Prelude to War (1935-1939)

Eric Sevareid hosts this documentary about the years just before the outbreak of World War II. As the Axis powers align for war, Japan conquers one third of China. When Stalin suddenly signs a peace pact with Hitler, the U.S. prepares for war. 22 mins.
VHS: S23591. $99.95.

Private Film Collection of Eva Braun

Life at Hitler's mountain refuge—the Berghof—filmed by his mistress, Eva Braun. Spectacular Alpine panoramas highlight scenes of Nazi leaders, foreign diplomats, and local visitors, with candid views of Hitler in war and peacetime chatting with children, conferring with subordinates, relaxing after victories, and recovering after Stalingrad offer a unique picture of the Fuehrer's private life. English commentary. Color. 60 mins. Germany 1936-43.
VHS: S08314. $29.95.

PT 109

Oscar-winner Cliff Robertson is the war hero (and subsequent president) John F. Kennedy in this somewhat routine WW II drama about the U.S. patrol boats that tried to cut off Japanese supply lines in the Solomon Islands. When the craft is nearly sliced in half by a Japanese destroyer, a young Jack Kennedy struggles to save the crew. Also on tap are several shorts and "trailers" to upcoming releases on this two-cassette package.
VHS: S02562. $19.98.
Laser: Letterboxed. LD70737. $39.98.
Robert McKimson, USA, 1963, 159 mins.

Raid on Rommel

In North Africa during World War II, a British officer releases his prisoners of war and leads them on an assault on Tobruk. Stars Richard Burton, John Calicos, Clinton Greyn and Wolfgang Preiss.
VHS: S16301. $14.95.
Henry Hathaway, USA, 1971, 99 mins.

Remember Pearl Harbor

This deeply moving 50th anniversary commemoration of the attack on Pearl Harbor is presented in a style similar to the highly acclaimed Civil War series. It features exclusive interviews and commentary, as well as never-before-seen Japanese footage. USA.
VHS: S15352. $14.98.

Report from the Aleutians
American forces live under tough conditions from which they raid Japanese bases. Written and directed for the U.S. Armed Forces by John Huston, and narrated by John Huston with additional narration by Walter Huston. 45 mins.
VHS: S02589. $34.95.

Return to Iwo Jima
Hosted by Ed McMahon, a documentary about four American and two Japanese veterans as they return to Iwo Jima. Produced by PBS for the February 19, 1985 anniversary commemorating the 40 years since the famous island battle.
VHS: S02405. $29.95.

The Rise and Fall of Adolf Hitler
This exhaustive biography covers the tumultuous career of the failed Austrian artist who nearly conquered the world: a series of events and people, a chemistry of history and current happenings, a confluence of economic, psychological, and political forces that turned a thousand minor, innocuous events into a huge and murderous whole. There had been wars before, and slave labor and genocide, and treaties made to be broken and propagandists who came to believe their own propaganda; what made this feature different is documented in this program: its vast scope, its documentation on film, and its central character, Adolf Hitler. 150 mins.
VHS: S13361. $39.94.

Road to Rome/Thunderbolt
The film focuses on World War II and the crucial air war over Italy as the 12th Air Force and the 57th Fighter Group took control of the skies over Italy. 57 mins.
VHS: S10061. $29.95.

Rolling Thunder
Rolling Thunder was a bravado U.S. operation against North Vietnam in the first years of the war. Aerial bombing helped immobilize the enemy, and Vietnam provided the biggest airlift in history. 60 mins.
VHS: S13116. $19.98.

Rommel—The Desert Fox
The complete story of the Nazi Field Marshal who masterminded the Blitzkrieg in Europe and North Africa. From the series The Nazis. 50 mins.
VHS: S12730. $24.98.

Secret Life of Adolf Hitler
The rise and fall of the Third Reich told with actual footage, interviews with Hitler's sister, a fellow prisoner with Hitler before he came to power, and others. Unusual and seldom-seen footage, including Eva Braun's home movies; narrated by Westbrook van Voorhis. USA, 1958, 53 mins.
VHS: S01621. $24.95.

Seeds of Discord (1933-1936)
As Hitler and Mussolini eye world domination, Gandhi dreams of freeing India from the British. Batista seizes power in Cuba, Japan invades Manchuria, and King Alexander of Yugoslavia is assassinated in France. FDR allies the U.S. with the Soviet Union. Eric Sevareid hosts this look at the political turmoil of the 1930's. 24 mins.
VHS: S23590. $99.95.

Silent Victory
Few people realize that U.S. submarines sank over five million tons of Japanese shipping during World War II, accounting for more than half the shipping sunk during World War II. This accomplishment stands as one of the all-time greatest achievements of naval history. USA, 50 mins.
VHS: S27250. $24.95.

The Silver Fleet
Ralph Richardson, Esmond Knight and Googie Withers star in this World War II drama. Though he appears to collaborate with the Nazis, a Dutch shipbuilder is actually leading a double life. In fact, he heads a group of anti-Nazi resistors.
VHS: S23811. $24.95.
Gordon Wellesley, Great Britain, 1943, 87 mins.

Sinai Commandos
This thriller deals with a suicide squad during the Six-Day War, which is responsible for a mission vital to the survival of Israel. 99 mins.
VHS: S03061. $29.95.

The Smashing of the Reich
A documentary on the last days of the German war machine. Archive footage includes the landing at Normandy, Bastogne, the Elbe River crossing, concentration camp survivors, and the liberation of Paris. Told without hysterics. See how to win a war in 84 minutes. USA, 1962, 84 mins.
VHS: S10067. $29.95.

Song of Survival
They survived 3½ years of Japanese prison camp in World War II. These courageous Dutch, Australian and British women were helped by the music of Beethoven, Schubert and Chopin, which they created without instruments in a unique choir. Using rare archival footage and recreation of the music, this tape tells the stirring story of brave women in a remote prison camp in Sumatra. 57 mins.
VHS: S05806. $29.95.

Soviet War Stories from World War II
Four short programs that explore mixed memories of World War II, from a variety of Soviet perspectives. Included are The Great Exploit, Classmates, Heroic Exploit and Celebration on Victory Day. 115 mins.
VHS: S12709. $24.95.

Speeches of Adolf Hitler
Utilizing English subtitles, this starting video presents Adolf Hitler's most dramatic speeches: revealing the demonic phases the evil Fuhrer used to hypnotize the German people. 50 mins.
VHS: S12308. $19.98.

Stillwell Road
A study of the building of the Burma road, an important supply route carved out of the mountains. Narrated by Ronald Reagan, produced by the U.S. Army. 1945, 51 mins.
VHS: S03062. $19.95.

Submarine Warfare
Gene Kelly narrates this documentary which was produced by the U.S. Department of Defense. Rare footage includes looks at the USS Guadalcanal, the Naval Task Force in pursuit of a 1944 German submarine. 53 mins.
VHS: S03065. $29.95.

Target for Tonight
This British documentary on a bombing raid on Germany won an Oscar in 1941. Filmed with the cooperation of the Royal Air Force, it uses everyone from the Commander-in-Chief to the air mechanic doing their jobs for the camera. "A direct hit," says Walter Winchell. England, 1941, 50 mins.
VHS: S05508. $24.95.

Terror of the Third Reich
This video follows the rise of Hitler's Nazi Germany in three parts: Terror of the Third Reich, Hitler Youth Movement and Day of Freedom. The first segment focuses on Hitler and the second describes the indoctrination of young people. The last segment is directed by the uniquely gifted but controversial director Leni Riefenstahl. It records the training procedures of the German army. 62 mins.
VHS: S26556. $19.95.

Through Hell and High Water
This video details the little-known role of the Merchant Marine during the Second World War. Their valor and dedication is the stuff of legend. 30 mins.
VHS: S27248. $24.95.

Time Capsule: War in Europe
Europe was in flames. Great Britain was on the verge of being conquered. The Russian border had been crossed by Nazi troops. From across the ocean, the fighting forces of the US came to join the French, British and Russian soldiers to forge the winning alliance that changed the course of the war. 30 mins.
VHS: S22716. $19.95.

Time Capsule: War in the Pacific
It began in Hawaii. The blue skies over this tropical paradise turned black with smoke from the surprise Japanese attack. Unprepared but undaunted, America rose up to build a formidable array of forces. The war in the Pacific stands as a testimony to the will of the American people. 30 mins.
VHS: S22717. $19.95.

To the Shores of Iwo Jima
A rousing film about the assault of the Marines on Iwo Jima and the 25-day siege, as well as a history of the battle of Guadalcanal, one of the bloodiest battles of World War II. 41 mins.
VHS: S03064. $29.95.

Town Meetings: Pearl Harbor
Ted Koppel links viewpoints around the nation as he looks back at the historical issues of the attack on Pearl Harbor 50 years ago. 50 mins.
VHS: S15884. $19.98.

True Glory (Gen. Dwight D. Eisenhower)
Garson Kanin and Carol Reed directed this testimonial to the men who fought in Europe from D-Day to VE Day. Stars Peter Ustinov and Frank Harvey.
VHS: S10578. $19.95.

Tunisian Victory
Produced jointly by the U.S. and British governments, this wartime documentary looks at the struggle for North Africa, from the initial landings to the ultimate victory. 74 mins.
VHS: S03063. $29.95.

The Turning Point (1941-1944)
Hitler faces a crushing loss on the Russian front, while MacArthur leads the U.S. forces in the Pacific. Finally Eisenhower leads the Allies to their first decisive victory in Europe. As Germany prepares for a forceful attack, Italy surrenders and the Japanese are stopped at the Battle of Midway. Eric Sevareid hosts. 23 mins.
VHS: S23593. $99.95.

The Twisted Cross
Using Allied military footage, Nazi propaganda films, newsreels of the period and reconstructed dramatic sequences simulating key events in Hitler's career, The Twisted Cross presents a vivid panorama of events leading up to WWII. Among the more disturbing moments captured from pre-Third Reich history is Hitler's "Beer Hall Putsch of 1923", and his dictation of Mein Kampf to confidant Rudolf Hess. USA, 1956, 53 mins.
VHS: S04446. $29.95.

Tyranny of Adolf Hitler
From the creators of the acclaimed series The World at War comes this special 3-part documentary about life in Hitler's Germany. Using archive footage and interviews, The Third Reich follows Hitler's rise to power, his mobilization against Europe, and Germany's crippling defeat in World War II. Told in the compelling words of ordinary people who survived an extraordinary time. Available individually, or as a three-part set.
A Nation Falls.
VHS: S10253. $19.99.
Hitler's Master Plan.
VHS: S10252. $19.99.
New Regime.
VHS: S10251. $19.99.
Third Reich 3-Pack.
VHS: S10254. $39.99.

U.S.S. Arizona: The Life and Death of a Lady
Beginning with her launch in 1915, this journal follows the U.S.S. Arizona through her history of service to the Navy, which ended abruptly with the bombing of Pearl Harbor. Including never-before-seen photographs and interviews with still living crew members, the documentary goes underwater for a look at the ship today as she lies entombed with nearly 1000 seamen. 47 mins.
VHS: S16326. $19.95.

The Unknown Soldier
Hosted by World War II Navy Veteran Jason Robards, this originally-aired PBS documentary presents the life stories of six American servicemen who died in action during World War II and whose bodies were never recovered or identified. The personal profiles are told through combat footage of the battles they fought, mementoes, letters, and interviews with family members. 60 mins.
VHS: S02406. $29.95.

V for Victory
The Second World War is explored in this documentary series that recounts the battles, campaigns, strategies, political fortunes and global importance from the Japanese bombing of Pearl Harbor to the emergence of atomic warfare. Hosted by veteran journalists Eric Sevareid and Edwin Newman. It "lets you see the face of war in gritty detail" (Philadelphia Inquirer).
Vol. I: Pearl Harbor to Midway. Japan's daring predawn raid plunges America into the global war. 45 mins.
VHS: S18287. $14.95.
Vol. II: Guadalcanal and the Pacific Counterattack. This program looks at the American assault on Japan's strategic dominance in the Pacific theater. 45 mins.
VHS: S18288. $14.95.
Vol. III: North Africa and the Global War. This episode considers the deployment of American troops, airmen and sailors to various parts of the world, from North Africa to Burma, the Atlantic Ocean and the European airfields. 45 mins.
VHS: S18289. $14.95.
Vol. IV: Anzio and the Italian Campaign. The difficult and harsh American offensive in Italy. 45 mins.
VHS: S18290. $14.95.
Vol. V: D-Day and the Battle for France. This episode studies the Normandy Invasion and the largest amphibious assault in history, codenamed Operation Overload. 45 mins.
VHS: S18291. $14.95.
Vol. VI: Tarawa and the Island War. This program studies the painful and tragic repercussions of the island war in the Pacific. 45 mins.
VHS: S18292. $14.95.
Vol. VII: Women at War—From the Home Front to the Front Lines. From the factories to the battlefield, this program considers the contributions, pain and sacrifice of the American women. 45 mins.
VHS: S18293. $14.95.
Vol. VIII: The Battle of the Bulge and the Drive to the Rhine. The Third Reich's last major offensive and counterattack of the Allies' penetration into Germany is chronicled in this episode. 45 mins.
VHS: S18294. $14.95.
Vol. IX: Iwo Jima, Okinawa and the Push on Japan. Two of the war's seminal battles are recounted in this portrait of American and Japanese encounters in the Pacific theater. 45 mins.
VHS: S18295. $14.95.
Vol. X: The Eagle Triumphant. The final installment looks at the hard-fought victories in Europe and Asia. 45 mins.
VHS: S18296. $14.95.
V for Victory, Boxed Set.
VHS: S18297. $149.50.

Victory at Sea, Volumes 1 to 6
Now Victory at Sea is available in a new format—six volumes in a Collector's Edition Gift Set. Each volume contains compilations of the individual episodes listed above and runs 120 minutes.
Volume 1: Episodes 1-4.
VHS: S02210. $19.98.
Volume 2: Episodes 5-8.
VHS: S02211. $19.98.
Volume 3: Episodes 9-12.
VHS: S02212. $19.98.
Volume 4: Episodes 13-16.
VHS: S02213. $19.98.
Volume 5: Episodes 17-21.
VHS: S08900. $19.98.
Volume 6: Episodes 22-26.
VHS: S08901. $19.98.
Boxed Set (6 Volumes; 26 Episodes).
VHS: S02215. $99.00.

Visions of War
A multi-volume series covering the history of modern warfare, using archival footage and interviews in color.
Cassino. One of the most harrowing battles of the war, involving soldiers from 16 countries. 50 mins.
VHS: S10087. $19.95.
Memorial Flight. The historical Battle of Britain Memorial Flight showcases British aviation's most revered aircraft, the Lancaster, Spitfire, and Hurricane. 50 mins.
VHS: S10049. $19.95.
The Bulge. The largest single pitched battle of the Western Front, involving over one million troops. 50 mins.
VHS: S10086. $19.95.
Warsaw. The tragic story of the 1944 Warsaw Uprising, one of the most controversial epics of the war. 50 mins.
VHS: S10085. $19.95.
Complete Set.
VHS: S08084. $259.95.

Waldheim: Commission of Inquiry
A video tribunal searches out the "real" story in the conflicting reports about the past of Austria's President Waldheim, who was also the former secretary of the United Nations. USA, 1988.
VHS: S07305. $79.99.

War Chronicles Volume 1— The Greatest Conflict
Presents a breathtaking overview of World War II, from 1939 to 1945. 35 mins.
VHS: S02119. $14.95.

War Chronicles Volume 6— Bomber Offensive: Air War in Europe
Graphically depicts the most disastrous air encounters of the War. 35 mins.
VHS: S02124. $14.95.

War Chronicles Volume 7— The Battle of the Bulge
A close-up look at the largest pitched battle in the history of American arms. 35 mins.
VHS: S01960. $14.95.

War Chronicles Volume 8— The Battle of Germany
Shows the American forces breaking through at Saint-Lo and entering Nazi concentration camps. 35 mins.
VHS: S06411. $14.95.

War Chronicles Volume 10— Jungle Warfare: New Guinea to Burma
In addition to the Japanese troops, American soldiers fought disease, heat and millions of things that crawled and slithered. The video series continues in its efforts to provide compelling documentary footage of the hard fought war in the Pacific. In black and white and color, with host Patrick O'Neal. When these GI's say it's a jungle out there, they mean it. 35 mins.
VHS: S09857. $14.95.

War Chronicles Volume 12— The Bloody Ridges of Peleliu
Veterans and history buffs will find something of value in this video home library of World War II. This installment, hosted as usual by Patrick O'Neal, shows intense footage of the U.S. Marines under fire, about 600 miles east of the Philippines. For five months they battled the Japanese who retreated to fight from caves on this volcanic island in the West Caroline Islands group. 35 mins.
VHS: S09859. $14.95.

War Chronicles Volume 13— Return to the Philippines
General Douglas MacArthur promised he would return to the Philippines when he was evacuated on March 16, 1942 to the safety of Australia. He kept that promise when he returned on October 20, 1944 and landed on Leyte. This installment of the video history of that great conflict details the bombardments and frontal assaults that freed the Philippines from the Japanese invaders. 35 mins.
VHS: S09860. $14.95.

War Chronicles Volumes 1-8—Pre-Pack
The first eight volumes of The War Chronicles in a bonus edition library collector's case.
VHS: S06412. $119.60.

War on Land and Sea
This British-produced series documents key elements of WWII, using rare, previously unavailable footage. Available in individual volumes, or as a 4-pack.
Churchill's War. This video takes us through Churchill's war, using much newly discovered footage and featuring, where possible, original recordings of the great speeches, in a look at Churchill the statesman and Churchill the Commander. 60 mins.
VHS: S12450. $29.95.
D-Day-Assault on Fortress Europe. Four years in the planning, two in the organizing, and one day in execution, the landing in Normandy was easily the largest and most extraordinary combined military operation ever attempted, and a crucial one. Using rare footage, this documentary examines this historic day which turned the tide in the war. 60 mins.
VHS: S12452. $29.95.
Dunkirk: The Battle for France. Dunkirk, the brilliantly-executed withdrawal of land forces minus all their equipment across the Channel which came to be regarded as almost a major victory, became a bitter symbol of British betrayal for the French. The visions conjured up of a ragged fleet of fishing boats, yachts and dinghies sailing the channel, their pilots risking life and limb to save soldiers from certain defeat or captivity, is vividly realized using very rare footage. 60 mins.
VHS: S12451. $29.95.
Waffen SS. The SS had its beginnings in the turbulent street politics of the Weimar Republic. It became Heinrich Himmler's personal power base, and under him the SS grew into a vast private army and state-within-the-state. After the war, the Waffen SS were burdened with the near-exclusive blame for the most hideous crimes of the Nazi regime. 60 mins.
VHS: S12456. $29.95.
4-pack.
VHS: S12459. $113.81.

War Stories
Combining the recollections of combat veterans, personal photographs and archival footage, War Stories captures the history of World War II as never before. A gripping tribute to all the men and women who lived and fought in the second World War. Five volumes.
Airmen of World War II. 50 mins.
VHS: S14778. $19.95.
D-Day. 50 mins.
VHS: S14781. $19.95.
Remembering Pearl Harbor. 50 mins.
VHS: S14777. $19.95.
The Fighting Marine: 1942-45. 50 mins.
VHS: S14779. $19.95.
The Merchant Marines. 50 mins.
VHS: S14780. $19.95.
Complete five-volume set.
VHS: S14782. $99.75.

The War Years: Britain in World War II
An anthology of familiar men and famous battles that set the tone of British involvement in the Second World War. The program considers the human scale and dimension—the people who remained behind the lines to endure the Blitz, enlisted in the Home Guard and prepared for a possible invasion.
Vol. 1: The Phoney War. In the aftermath of the Hitler/Chamberlain agreement for "peace in our time," Britain declares war following the Nazi invasion of Poland and Czechoslovakia. The program looks at the early stages of the war, the Navy campaigns, Dunkirk and the political ascension of Winston Churchill.
VHS: S17949. $29.95.
Vol. 2: The Battle of Britain. Britain sustains heavy casualties as western Europe falls under German occupation, and Hitler initiates his massive bombing campaigns on British civilian and military targets. Air raid shelters are part of everyday texture. The Blitz is on.
VHS: S17950. $29.95.
Vol. 3: The Blitz. Despite massive bombing raids, Hitler can't achieve air superiority, though major sections of London are in ruin. German U-boats intercept Atlantic convoys and more than 40,000 are killed.
VHS: S17951. $29.95.

Vol. 4: The Tide Turns. Despite a series of military setbacks that lead to chronic food and supply shortages, women take an active presence in the factories, armed forces and civil defense. Britain's military fortunes change with the American intervention and the German debacle on the Russian front.
VHS: $17952. $29.95.

Vol. 5: The Final Chapter. German forces are crushed in Russia, and following D-day, 300,000 Allied soldiers are waging battle in the French countryside. Despite its last gasp technological offensive, the V-1 and V-2 rocket launchers, Berlin is surrounded by enemy forces and Hitler commits suicide.
VHS: $17953. $29.95.

Warlords
A series of seven videos capturing the heroes and tyrants of Word War II, narrated by Hal Holbrook.
Churchill: The Private War. A monumental leader, Churchill defied Hitler's onslaught to the very end. The story of a man who found himself through war. 30 mins.
VHS: $09031. $14.99.
Hitler's Master Race: The Mad Dream of the S.S. They swore to fulfill Hitler's dream of German Supermen. New archival footage exposes the madness that almost succeeded. 30 mins.
VHS: $09030. $14.99.
Hitler: Portrait of a Tyrant. Even in his early days, the sadistic side of Adolf Hitler reigned unsuppressed. 30 mins.
VHS: $09028. $14.99.
Kamikaze: Mission of Death. Their lives were a rehearsal for death. Rare footage exposes the training and preparation for their deadly missions. 30 mins.
VHS: $09032. $14.99.
MacArthur: The Defiant General. American superhero and military genius. Defiance was his badge of courage and his downfall. 30 mins.
VHS: $09027. $14.99.
Patton: The Man Behind the Myth. Uncovered: Patton's merciless approach to war, his lust for glory. 30 mins.
VHS: $09026. $14.99.
Rommel: The Strange Death of the Desert Fox. He crushed Europe and Africa beneath his iron fist. New evidence uncovers Hitler's fear of the man known as "the desert fox." 309 mins.
VHS: $09029. $14.99.

Warsaw Uprising Chronicle (Kroniki Powstania Warszawskiego)
A unique documentary from 1944 Poland about the Warsaw Uprising against Nazi occupation. The film was confiscated and badly mutilated by communist censors; here it is restored to its best available form. Moving footage from a turbulent time.
VHS: $15562. $39.95.

Why We Fight
A seven-part series produced for the U.S. War Department, designed to convince the American public that WWII deserved their support.
No. 1: Prelude to War. Produced by Frank Capra, this film skillfully combines newsreel footage of the Japanese invasion into Manchuria, the Italian incursion into Ethiopia, and the German blitz of Eastern Europe. Directed by Ernst Lubitsch, USA, 1942, 53 mins.
VHS: $01052. $19.95.
No. 2: The Nazis Strike. Directed by Frank Capra and Anatole Litvak, this documentary uses newsreel footage and scenes from *Triumph of the Will* to prove that Nazis are not nice people. Also a British comic short, *Schichlegruber Doing the Lambeth Walk.* USA, 1942, 44 mins.
VHS: $05503. $24.95.
No. 3: Divide and Conquer. The German war machine continues its march through Europe, Denmark and Norway fall, the Maginot Line in France crumbles and the country surrenders. The British Army is defeated on the continent and crosses the Channel from Dunkirk. 1943, 60 mins.
VHS: $03057. $19.95.
No. 4: Battle of Russia. The battle of Stalingrad climaxes this account of the Nazi invasion of the Soviet Union. 1943, 83 mins.
VHS: $00104. $19.95.
No. 5: Battle of Britain. An account of the unbreakable spirit of London residents during the six week bombing blitz by the German Luftwaffe. Narration by Walter Huston. Directed by Frank Capra, USA, 1943, 52 mins.
VHS: $00102. $19.95.
Laser: LD70862. $59.95.
No. 6: Battle of China. This look at China focuses on the way in which the people harnessed all the country's resources to oppose the Japanese invasion. 1944, 67 mins.
VHS: $00103. $19.95.
No. 7: War Comes to America. Documents the gradual shift of opinion from isolationism to support for the US entry into World War II. Narration by Walter Huston. Directed by Frank Capra, USA, 1945, 66 mins.
VHS: $01428. $19.95.

Wings of the Luftwaffe Fighter Attack
The Discovery Channel produced this video which reveals the superior aircraft of the Luftwaffe. For example, the FW 190 was a deadly success, while the ME 262 was the only true successful jet fighter bomber. These were among the greatest aircraft of the era. 60 mins.
VHS: $25093. $9.95.

Wings over Europe
Stukas, Yaks, Spitfires and the Flying Fortress are just some of the planes that soared into history during the Second World War. This *Discovery Channel* documentary explores the evolution of these aircraft as fighting machines. 60 mins.
VHS: $26049. $19.95.

World at War
This massive, 26-volume series covers virtually all of World War II.
World at War Vol. 1: A New Germany.
VHS: $09363. $19.98.
World at War Vol. 2: Distant War.
VHS: $09364. $19.98.
World at War Vol. 3: France Falls.
VHS: $09365. $19.98.
World at War Vol. 4: Alone—Britain.
VHS: $09366. $19.98.
World at War Vol. 5: Barbarossa.
VHS: $09367. $19.98.
World at War Vol. 6: Banzai—Japan Strikes.
VHS: $09368. $19.98.
World at War Vol. 7: On Our Way—America Enters the War.
VHS: $09369. $19.98.
World at War Vol. 8: Desert—The War in North Africa.
VHS: $09370. $19.98.
World at War Vol. 9: Stalingrad.
VHS: $09371. $19.98.

World at War Vol. 10: Wolfpack.
VHS: $09372. $19.98.
World at War Vol. 11: Red Star.
VHS: $09373. $19.98.
World at War Vol. 12: Whirlwind.
VHS: $09374. $19.98.
World at War Vol. 13: Tough Old Gut.
VHS: $09375. $19.98.
World at War Vol. 14: It's a Lovely Day Tomorrow.
VHS: $09376. $19.98.
World at War Vol. 15: Home Fires.
VHS: $09377. $19.98.
World at War Vol. 16: Inside the Reich.
VHS: $09378. $19.98.
World at War Vol. 17: Morning.
VHS: $09379. $19.98.
World at War Vol. 18: Occupation.
VHS: $09380. $19.98.
World at War Vol. 19: Pincers.
VHS: $09381. $19.98.
World at War Vol. 20: Genocide.
VHS: $09382. $19.98.
World at War Vol. 21: Nemesis.
VHS: $09383. $19.98.
World at War Vol. 22: Japan.
VHS: $09384. $19.98.
World at War Vol. 23: Pacific—The Island to Island War.
VHS: $09385. $19.98.
World at War Vol. 24: The Bomb.
VHS: $09386. $19.98.
World at War Vol. 25: Reckoning.
VHS: $09387. $19.98.
World at War Vol. 26: Remember.
VHS: $09388. $19.98.

The World at War
This documentary recounts the international unrest that led to America's involvement in World War II. Narrated by Paul Stewart, all footage is authentic. B&W, 44 minutes.
VHS: $02926. $19.95.

World War II with Walter Cronkite: The War in Europe
This five-volume set, which was produced by CBS News, examines the major developments of the Second World War. The program studies the European Campaign, the Nazis' seizure of power; the rise of Hitler; the strategies of German's war machine and its leaders Goebbels, Goering and Hess; the early German naval dominance; the German occupation of Paris; the rise of the French Resistance; and the irrepressible American military genius, General George S. Patton. The program concludes with the defeat of the German army, the homefront and the Nuremberg trials. 450 mins.
VHS: $19539. $129.98.

World War II with Walter Cronkite: The War in the Pacific
CBS News produced this comprehensive four-volume study on the fight for control of the Pacific theater. The program opens with the Japanese attack on Pearl Harbor and considers its immediate aftermath. It then studies the technological developments in aircraft that shifted the balance of power, and concludes with an examination of the military campaigns in Burma, Tarawa, Okinawa and Hiroshima. 360 mins.
VHS: $19538. $99.98.

World War II—Hearst Metronome News
From the archives of the Hearst Metronome News Library, actual newsreel footage that documents World War II. Each volume is 51 mins.
World War II—Volume 1.
VHS: $08139. $19.95.
World War II—Volume 2.
VHS: $08140. $19.95.
World War II—Volume 3.
VHS: $08141. $19.95.
World War II—Volume 4.
VHS: $08142. $19.95.

World War II: From Breadlines to Boomtimes
This three-volume documentary set describes how America responded to the global conflict. Still afflicted by the historic depression, on December 7, 1941, the nation was irrevocably drawn into war. Men and women mobilized to convert the economy into a war machine, a process that transformed the US so that it emerged as the most powerful country in the world. 170 mins.
World War II: From Breadlines to Boomtimes Volume 1.
VHS: $22713. $24.95.
World War II: From Breadlines to Boomtimes Volume 2.
VHS: $22714. $24.95.
World War II: From Breadlines to Boomtimes Volume 3.
VHS: $22715. $24.95.
World War II: From Breadlines to Boomtimes, Complete Set.
VHS: $22712. $69.95.

World War II: The Eastern Front
Goya paintings and Russian poems are combined with historic footage of the Second World War to expose the inhumanity of war. The Soviet Union suffered terrible ravages and tribulations during this tragic conflagration. 30 mins.
VHS: $23739. $69.95.

World War II: The War Chronicles
This seven-volume series documents the whole tragic unfolding of the global conflict whose effects dominated our century. North Africa, Normandy, Anzio, the Battle of the Bulge and the war in the Pacific, including Okinawa, are all places which live on in memory. Now combat footage and expert commentary explain the strategies and forces that behind these battles. Each volume is 70 mins.
VHS: $24388. $99.95.

Yankee Samurai: The Little Iron Men
This program highlights the accomplishments of the 100-442nd regiment during World War II, 4,800 Japanese-American soldiers who formed the most decorated American unit in the war. While 120,000 other Asians were being held in "internment camps" in western states, these Americans were intent on proving their loyalty to the States and fought with incredible valor and sacrifice. 50 mins.
VHS: $13138. $29.98.

The 81st Blow
An historical document made up of footage and stills shot by the Nazis. A compilation of testimony from witnesses who appeared at the Eichmann trial provides a telling narrative. The film's title refers to the story of a Jewish boy in one of the ghettoes, who was struck with 80 blows. He survived and immigrated to Israel, where he found that no one believed his story—which for him was the 81st blow. Academy Award nominee.
VHS: $06570. $79.95.
Jacquot Ehrlich/David Bergman/Haim Gouri, Israel, 1974, 115 mins.

America and the Holocaust: Deceit & Indifference
Hal Linden narrates this troubling look at the US. Beset by anti-Semitism and a government determined to keep critical information suppressed, the chance to rescue hundreds of thousands from the Nazis was lost. B&W, 60 mins.
VHS: $23051. $19.95.

Bound for Nowhere: The St. Louis Episode
Witness the dramatic voyage of over 900 Jews, among them 200 children, who fled Nazi Germany. Turned away from their expected Cuban refuge, they are forced back to European countries. This document stands as testimony to the indifference of other nations to assist the Jews. 1939, 9 mins.
VHS: $16310. $60.00.

Camp of Hope and Despair: Westerbork Concentration Camp, 1939-45
From this camp in Eastern Holland more than 100,000 Dutch Jews were deported at the hands of the Nazis. Despite the terror that awaited them, Jewish classes, celebrations, religious services and weddings continued at Westerbork on a regular basis. Eyewitness accounts from survivors, photographs and films are joined to tell this story of strained normalcy in the face of doom. 70 mins.
VHS: $23237. $39.95.

Chasing Shadows
Filmmaker Naomi Gryn accompanies her father to his Carpathian hometown, Berehovo. Evoking the world of his childhood when half the town was Jewish, Hugo provides his daughter with beautiful memories that all lead to one bitter end: the Jews being shipped to the crematorium at Birkenau. A deeply personal film augmented by rare footage showing Carpathian Jewish farmers and newsreels of the Hungarian troops "liberating" Berehovo.
VHS: $16320. $54.00.
Naomi Gryn, Great Britain, 1990, 52 mins.

Child in Two Worlds
To save their lives, many Jewish parents gave their children over to Christian foster parents. These babies, now in their 50's and 60's, tell their amazing stories of survival and how they returned to their parents' way of life. Consider Halinka, who as a baby was thrown, wrapped in a pillow, over the Warsaw ghetto wall into the hands of a Polish policeman. Winner of the Golden Calf Award for Best Documentary, 1993. Dutch with English subtitles. 90 mins.
VHS: $22335. $39.95.

Choosing One's Way: Resistance in Auschwitz/Birkenau
Crematorium #4 was destroyed by inmates who succeeded in smuggling gun powder past Nazi guards. This act of heroism uses archival footage to tell a story nearly forgotten. Ellyn Burstyn narrates. Winner of the Hugo, 1994 Chicago Film Festival. 30 mins.
VHS: $23244. $39.95.

The Cross and the Star
Subtitled *Jews, Christians and the Holocaust,* John Michalczyk's documentary interweaves archival footage of Nazi Germany, propaganda films, television shows, and contemporary interviews to make a connection between the death camps, Nazi Nuremberg laws and the possible complicity and collaboration of the institutional churches and orders of the Catholic and Protestant leaders. A former Jesuit priest, Michalczyk considers the Gospel of St. John, the sermons of St. Augustine, and the writings of Martin Luther to trace the evolution of anti-Semitism. 55 mins.
VHS: $17102. $29.95.

Dark Lullabies
A very moving film: they are the children of survivors and of the perpetrators of the Holocaust. Polarized as their heritage is, many of this generation share a legacy of silence. Filmmaker Irene Angelico, herself a child of survivors of concentration camps, takes a deeply personal journey: she asks, what happened, and why? Through interviews with survivors and their children, she searches for comprehension in this powerful and emotional quest. Produced by the National Film Board of Canada.
VHS: $07663. $69.95.
Irene Angelico/Abbey Jack Neidik, Canada, 1982, 82 mins.

Demjanjuk Trial: The State of Israel vs. John Demjanjuk
This is the trial of the Cleveland auto mechanic accused of being "Ivan the Terrible", the man who supervised the gas chambers at Treblinka. Israel won extradition, but the case became entangled in legal issues larger than the man's guilt or innocence. In this video, the courtroom drama and surrounding issues are unveiled. 50 mins.
VHS: $12905. $49.95.

The Double Crossing: The Voyage of the St. Louis
A film about the May 1939 voyage from Hamburg to Havana of some 900 Jewish refugees, that was aborted when Cuban authorities reneged on their promise and refused them admittance. The documentary includes archival footage and contemporary interviews with survivors of the journey. 29 mins.
VHS: $17942. $39.95.

Escape to the Rising Sun
The story of 20,000 Jews who fled Nazi persecution in Europe and took refuge in Shanghai throughout WWII. Using archival footage of the Japanese occupation, as well as first-hand accounts from fifteen Jewish survivors, the film examines living conditions before the liberation of Shanghai. English narration and subtitles.
VHS: $16323. $90.00.
Diane Perelsztejn, Belgium, 1990, 95 mins.

Exile
A remarkable attempt by a filmmaker to come to terms with her family's past—Alexis Krasilovsky, the filmmaker, travels to Czechoslovakia, Austria and Florida to discover the reason for her family's secrecy through talks with relatives who suffered persecution during Hitler's time. "Remarkable" (*Los Angeles Times*).
VHS: $07771. $39.95.
Alexis Krasilovsky, USA, 1984, 28 mins.

Flames in Ashes
Using testimony of eyewitnesses and recently discovered film footage, this video explores how Jews in innumerable ways resisted the Nazis. The voices of those who survived the horrors of the Holocaust, both murderers and resistance fighters, tell the story that defines the differing dimensions of Jewish resistance in Europe before and during the war. 90 mins.
VHS: $06572. $79.95.

For the Living: The Story of the U.S. Holocaust Memorial Museum
Ed Asner narrates this in-depth view of the nation's premier museum devoted to the Holocaust. The Museum's architect, designers and curators are all seen exploring the complexity of this historical event from Auschwitz and Treblinka to the Warsaw Ghetto and the forests of Poland. 50 mins.
VHS: $20903. $19.95.

Force of Evil
Interviews with a Danish Jew rescued from a concentration camp, a Jehovah's Witness, a German emigre in Shanghai, a Dutch woman who risked her life to rescue Jewish children and a former Hitler youth combine with archival footage to trace the career of Nazi war criminal Adolph Eichmann. Narrated by Lindsay Crouse.
VHS: $16312. $100.00.
Steven Schlow, USA, 1989, 60 mins.

Hanna's War
The heroic resistance of Hanna Senesh, a Hungarian Jew who was trained as a commando and a spy by the British in Palestine and sent back into Nazi-controlled Europe. Maruschka Detmers is cast as Hanna with Ellen Burstyn as her courageous mother. An epic war movie written and directed by Canon Films' Menahem Golan. With Anthony Andrews, David Warner, and Donald Pleasance as the police interrogator. Based on a true story.
VHS: $09842. $19.98.
Menahem Golan, Hungary/Iceland/USA, 1988, 149 mins.

Holocaust (Chomsky)
Meryl Streep stars in this fictional account of two families in Hitler's Germany between 1935-1945. Inge (Streep) watches as her family is torn apart and strewn across a war-torn land, while the Dorf family joins the war effort, with Erik Dorf (Michael Moriarty) penetrating to the heart of the despised SS. This dramatic series won eight Emmy Awards. Also features James Woods.
VHS: $20936. $39.98.
Marvin J. Chomsky, USA, 1978, 390 mins.

Holocaust (Sontag)
In *Dark Places,* writer and social critic Susan Sontag, with a group of present day students, explores the meaning of Hitler's genocide. This powerful documentary is complemented by *How Came Israel?, The Good Omen,* and Herschel Bernardi's narrating *The Hangman,* three gripping shorts which probe and elaborate on the same theme.
VHS: $03984. $69.95.

The Holocaust and Yad Vashem: Displaced Persons
These two films are co-produced by Yad Vashem and the Israel Film Service. The first traces the rise of Nazism from its beginning in 1918 through to its terrifying results. Not only are events like Kristallnacht documented, there are important segments devoted to Jewish partisans and the Warsaw Ghetto uprising. *Displaced Persons* tells the story of the SS *Fearless,* an illegal immigrant ship that brought many survivors of Nazism to Palestine.
VHS: $24250. $14.98.

The Holocaust as Seen Through the Eyes of a Survivor
Through documentary footage and artwork, David Bergman, a survivor of the Holocaust, personalizes his experience for viewers. 30 mins.
VHS: $23741. $69.95.

The Holocaust in Memory of Millions
Walter Cronkite leads this tour of the United States Holocaust Memorial Museum. Bone-chilling re-creations, searing photographs and the poignant testimony of survivors are all found in this monument to the human spirit. From the Discovery series.
VHS: $23015. $19.95.

Holocaust, Polish Jews (Holocoust, Zydzi Polscy)
Moving documents of the miserable life Polish Jews suffered through while living in the Warsaw Ghetto during World War II. These are among the most significant postwar Eastern European documentaries made. Three short films are included: *Requiem for 500 Thousand* (directed by Jerzy Bossak—one of the founders of modern Polish cinema—the teacher of Wajda and Polanski), *An Ordinary Day of SS-man Schmidt* and *Silence.* 50 mins.
VHS: $15566. $39.95.

The Janovska Camp at Lvov
Between 1941 and 1944, 200,000 Jews (around one third of the Jews in Galicia) were taken to Janovska, just outside Lvov, Ukraine. Only 300 survived. In 1990, some of the survivors returned to reconstruct a memory of that place. Simon Wiesenthal and Rabbi David Kahane, former Chief Rabbi of the Israeli Air Force, are among those who offer their testimony. English and Hebrew with English subtitles. 52 mins.
VHS: S23241. $39.95.

The Journey of Butterfly
Charles Davidson's choral work *I Never Saw Another Butterfly* was at the center of commemorative proceedings marking the 50th anniversary of the establishment of the Ghetto Theresienstadt in Czechoslovakia. This ghetto was part of the Nazi final solution. Interviews with survivors and the musical performers round out this documentary about a painful memory. 60 mins.
VHS: S27637. $19.95.

Last Sea
When survivors of the Holocaust realized that they had neither a home to return to nor families to welcome them, thousands set out on the perilous journey to the Land of Israel. They travelled by truck or by train, many went by foot over the Alps; they had to cross the sea aboard dangerously overcrowded ships. The faces of the witnesses are never shown; only their voices are heard, as they retell stories of survival and redemption. "A film should not explain but show…The film recounts an extraordinary epic, astounding in truth, gigantic in scope" (Elie Wiesel). 90 mins.
VHS: S06571. $79.95.

The Last Seven Months of Anne Frank
This international Emmy Award-winning documentary picks up where Anne Frank's diary left off. Eight women who knew the Frank family recount the travails of the Franks in the concentration camps of Westerbork, Auschwitz, Birkenau and Bergen-Belsen. 75 mins.
VHS: S23251. $49.95.

Liberation
Ben Kingsley, Whoopi Goldberg and Patrick Stewart all narrate this documentary about the liberation of Europe from the Nazis. As Allied forces gathered their strength, Jews across the continent faced a continued onslaught of terror. Newsreel footage, radio broadcasts and stories from European Jews make this a compelling look at a disastrous era. 100 mins.
VHS: S26513. $14.98.

Married with a Star
Wax Werkendam wed Clara de Vries in the heart of Amsterdam's Old Jewish Quarter during the Nazi occupation. The film of this wedding bears silent witness to a forgotten place. It is now the focus of the story of this couple and their guests, most of whom did not survive. 33 mins.
VHS: S23238. $39.95.

Max and Helen: A True Story
Martin Landau stars as Nazi hunter Simon Wiesenthal in this tense tale of survival and love about Max, his fiancée Helen and her sister Miriam, who are sent from Poland to a Nazi work camp. Max begs Helen to join him in escaping the brutal conditions of the camp, but her sister is too ill. Max flees to Russia but is arrested and exiled to Siberia. It is 20 years before he is free to search for Helen, whose memory has become his only reason for living. With Treat Williams, Alice Krige. Based on the book by Simon Wiesenthal.
VHS: S12312. $14.98.
Great Britain, 1990, 94 mins.

Murderers Among Us: The Simon Wiesenthal Story
Ben Kingsley is cast as the famous Holocaust survivor who became the premiere Nazi hunter. *Variety* praised this made-for-cable epic film for its "enormous power and suspense." With Renee Soutendijk, Craig T. Nelson, Jack Shepherd and Paul Freeman. Script co-written by Abby Mann.
VHS: S14006. $89.99.
Brian Gibson, USA/GB/Hungary, 1989, 157 mins.

Not Like Sheep to the Slaughter: The Story of the Bialystok Ghetto
A historically important work about the heroic Jewish resistance during the Holocaust, set during the summer of 1943, centering on the underground activities of Mordechai Tenenbaum, who led the fight against the Nazi program to liquidate the Bialystok ghetto. The program uncovers new evidence and archival materials. English language version. 150 mins.
VHS: S17940. $79.95.

Opening the Gates of Hell: American Liberators of the Nazi Concentration Camps
A harrowing documentary that interviews a number of American servicemen who liberated the Nazi concentration camps, recalling their shock and dread at what they experienced. The innocent Jews re-imagine the bravery, generosity and humanity of the troops. "Most of all, they remember with great clarity the day they opened the gates of hell." 45 mins.
VHS: S17943. $39.95.

Preserving the Past to Ensure the Future
Ray Errol Fox's film deals with the one and a half million children who were murdered under Nazi persecution. He talks with people from all walks of life as they express their profound shock at the incomprehensible realities which are confronted upon visiting the children's memorial in the Yad Vashem museum in Jerusalem. Current news footage of racist violence around the world is juxtaposed with images from the children's museum to make a powerful experience for the viewer. 15 mins.
VHS: S12903. $29.95.

The Rails to Hell…and Back
David Bergman survived the Holocaust. In this film he recounts the suffering experienced by his family and millions of others because of Nazi persecution. 66 mins.
VHS: S23740. $89.95.

Raoul Wallenberg: Between the Lines
Through interviews with colleagues, Holocaust survivors, newsreels and rare footage shot by Nazi camera crews and others, this controversial story of Raoul Wallenberg's heroic campaign to save thousands of Jews from Budapest is relived. With diplomatic maneuvers and ingenious tactics, this Swedish diplomat stood fast against Nazi leader Adolph Eichmann's scheme of mass extermination. When the Russians invaded Budapest, Wallenberg was imprisoned and Soviet officials claim to this day that he died in July of 1947, disputing evidence of sightings, as late as 1979, which appear to prove otherwise. 1984, 90 mins.
VHS: S13677. $29.95.

The Righteous Enemy
Beginning with the story of his father who was interned by Italians occupying Yugoslavia's Adriatic coast during WWII, Rochlitz enlarges his account to show how Italian officials prevented the deportation of some 40,000 Jews in Italian-occupied zones of France, Greece and Yugoslavia. English commentary and subtitles.
VHS: S16318. $90.00.

The Road to Wannsee: Eleven Million Sentenced to Death
On January 20, 1942, 11 million Jews were sentenced to death at Wannsee. The trajectory that led to this death sentence—Hitler's political rise to power, the neutralizing of his opponents, and his obsession with eliminating the Jews—is the subject of this documentary. Archival footage and interviews with respected historians are featured. Dutch with English subtitles. 50 mins.
VHS: S23233. $39.95.

Schindler
The black marketeer, womanizer, gambler and Nazi spy who saved over 1000 Jews from Hitler's death camps is revealed, in this documentary, through interviews with witnesses of his deeds and the survivors of his efforts. Schindler's widow, his driver Richard Rechen (who drove Schindler to safety at the war's close), and the mistress of Amon Goeth (the "Butcher of Plaszow"), speaking just hours before her suicide, are included in this fascinating, British-produced portrait of Oskar Schindler.
VHS: S21096. $49.95.

Schindler (The True Story)
Amidst the tragedies of the Third Reich, Oskar Schindler emerged as a hero who saved many of his Jewish employees despite the risk it posed to his own safety. This documentary records the enormity of his achievement. 52 mins.
VHS: S26600. $19.95.

Shoah
Claude Lanzmann's landmark, monumental epic of the Holocaust, a 9½ hour assemblage of witnesses—death camp survivors and Nazi functionaries—whose combined testimony amounts to one of the most shattering human documents ever recorded. French with English subtitles.
VHS: S01190. $299.95.
Claude Lanzmann, France, 1985, 570 mins.

Simon Wiesenthal: Freedom Is Not a Gift from Heaven
This is the life story of the world's greatest Nazi hunter, from his childhood in Ukraine, to his wartime experiences in various concentration camps, through his liberation by Americans in 1945, all told on the occasion of his 85th birthday. 60 mins.
VHS: S23234. $39.95.

So Many Miracles
A haunting memory piece about two Holocaust survivors, Israel and Frania Rubinek, who, joined by their actor son Saul, return to the small Polish village of Pinczow for an emotional reunion with Zofia and Ludwig Banya. Along with their son Maniek, the Banyas sheltered the Rubineks from the Nazis for 28 months.
VHS: S19533. $36.00.
Smalley/Sarin, Canada, 1987/93, 58 mins.

Sorrow: The Nazi Legacy
Six Swedish teenagers, two of whom are Jewish, travel to Auschwitz. Beginning in Wannsee, they embark on an emotional journey that cannot help them comprehend the full weight of that terrible time. They meet a survivor who inspires them with hope, and the son of Hans Frank, the Nazi governor General of Poland, upon their return. 33 mins.
VHS: S23240. $39.95.

Sosua
In 1938, 32 nations met at the Evian Conference to find new homes for endangered European Jews. Only the Dominican Republic offered sanctuary. In 1940, a group of Jews escaping Nazi persecution found a haven on this beautiful Caribbean island of Sosua. This is their courageous story. 30 mins.
VHS: S12891. $34.95.

Survivors of the Holocaust
Steven Spielberg, in association with the Survivors of the Shoah Visual History Foundation, brings this intimate collection of survivor testimonials to video. In addition, there is archival footage and extra material hosted by Ben Kingsley. "A superlative chronicle of the Holocaust…heartrending yet uplifting…an outstanding living history lesson" (*TV Guide*).
VHS: S27402. $19.98.

Theresienstadt: Gateway to Auschwitz
More than 140,000 Jews were interned at the Czech fortress town of Terezin. This model ghetto was a transit camp for Auschwitz. Of the 15,000 in Theresienstadt who were under 15, less than 100 survived. Now the story of hope that was nourished by these children through a variety of cultural activities stands revealed in this prize-winning documentary. 57 mins.
VHS: S23242. $39.95.

They Risked Their Lives: Rescuers of the Holocaust
From 1986-1988 Gay Block and Malka Drucker interviewed and photographed more than 100 Gentile Holocaust rescuers who defied the Nazis to shield Jews during the war. Block's video chronicles the passionate and heroic acts of these brave men and women, their selfless courage and manifest honor. 54 mins.
VHS: S17941. $39.95.

Together at Last
Aaron Zeigelman thought that he, his mother and his sisters were the only Zeigelmans to survive the Holocaust. A genealogist discovered that in fact a large branch of the family had survived. In celebration, Aaron invited the entire family to New York. 58 mins.
VHS: S23248. $39.95.

Tsvi Nussbaum: Boy from Warsaw
For many the defining icon of the wide-scale Jewish suffering and oppression was the young boy, his arms held up, as the Nazis held their guns at his back. This provocative, revealing documentary considers the intervening life of that young man, Dr. Tvsi C. Nussbaum, as "well as a moving testimony of that era." 50 mins.
VHS: S17944. $39.95.

The Visas That Saved Lives
Chiune Sugihara awoke one summer morning in 1940 to discover that 200 people were awaiting his help. He was the Japanese consul in Lithuania, and he took it upon himself to write 1600 visas that saved an estimated 2000-6000 lives. This is the story of a man who sacrificed his own career to help those no one else would. Japanese with English subtitles. 115 mins.
VHS: S23252. $49.95.

The Warsaw Ghetto
Taken in part from the photo albums and cinefilms of Nazi Heinrich Himmler, this film augments those images with an extremely rare collection of newsreel footage depicting the Warsaw ghetto during the Nazi occupation of Poland. From its inception to its fiery demolition in 1943, this film documents the lives of the over 500,000 Jews who were crowded into the one-square-mile area that was the Warsaw Ghetto, put to work by the Third Reich in Nazi factories, and given only fractions of the rations allotted to "Aryan" Germans and Poles.
VHS: S05179. $29.95.
Poland, 1969, 52 mins.

We Were So Beloved
More than 20,000 German Jewish refugees settled in Washington Heights in Upper Manhattan during the 30's and created a solid, secure middle-class enclave dubbed "Frankfurt-on-Hudson." Director Manfred Kirchheimer, one of the refugees, unravels the complexities of the people who were his friends, neighbors and parents, all of them powerfully shaped by the Nazi experience. "Though *We Were So Beloved* is mostly about those who escaped the immediate effects of the Holocaust," wrote Vincent Canby in *The New York Times*, "it is a no less harrowing examination of conscience than *Shoah* and Marcel Ophuls' *Sorrow and the Pity*. In this limited, quite commonplace landscape of Washington Heights, Mr. Kirchheimer finds ghosts not always visible to the naked eye."
VHS: S09443. $65.00.
Manfred Kirchheimer, USA, 1986, 145 mins.

We Were There: Jewish Liberators of the Nazi Concentration Camps
Among the liberators of the Nazi Concentration Camps were numerous Jewish G.I.s. This video chronicles the moving accounts of the Jewish American soldiers who were present at the liberation of the camps, the unforgettable atrocities they witnessed, and the victims of the Holocaust that they liberated. Many of the G.I.s developed lifelong friendships with the Holocaust survivors they rescued. Ultimately, this film tells a story of love and renewal that grew out of horrific circumstances.
VHS: S27251. $24.95.
Paul Hansen, USA, 1994, 40 mins.

Who Shall Live and Who Shall Die?
Laurence Jarvik's searing documentary on the role of American Jewry in World War II as the U.S. government and American Jewish community fail to respond to the atrocities across the Atlantic.
VHS: S04723. $29.95.
Laurence Jarvik, USA, 1978, 90 mins.

Witness to Genocide
A brutal exposé about Hitler's twisted plan to eliminate an entire race through torture and execution. From the series *The Nazis*. 50 mins.
VHS: S12732. $24.98.

Witness to the Holocaust: Trial of Adolf Eichmann
This record presents the extensive testimony and evidence which revealed the scope of Eichmann's responsibility, including numerous eye-witness accounts. The first comprehensive examination of Eichmann. 90 mins.
VHS: S06633. $39.95.

The World of Anne Frank
This docudrama highlights selected moments of Anne Frank's important diary. Rare film footage, photographs, and interviews with Anne's father and those who risked their lives hiding her, bring important background information to the story of this young girl. 28 mins.
VHS: S23243. $39.95.

THE VIETNAM WAR

The 317th Platoon
A brilliant evocation of the senselessness of war during the last days of the French occupation of Indochina, based on the director's own experiences of being taken prisoner at Dien Buen Phu. The film tells of the platoon's retreat, focusing on a career soldier and the commanding young lieutenant as they make their way through ambushes, betrayals, rain, jungle, villages, pain, disease and inexorable fatigue to inevitable annihilation. With awesome cinematography by Raoul Coutard. With Jacques Perrin, Bruno Cremer, Pierre Fabre and Manuel Zarzo. French with English subtitles.
VHS: S13224. $59.95.
Pierre Schoendoerffer, France, 1965, 100 mins.

Anderson Platoon
One of the great films about Vietnam, directed by Pierre Schoendoerffer, the documentary focuses on an integrated combat unit led by Black West Pointer Lt. Joseph B. Anderson, and captures the tension, anger, hopelessness and pathos of armed conflict. Winner of the Academy Award for Best Documentary Feature.
VHS: S02404. $19.95.
Pierre Schoendoerffer, France, 1967, 65 mins.

Dear America: Letters Home from Vietnam
More than 30 celebrities read the actual letters of Vietnam veterans accompanied by striking visual footage and nostalgic music of the times. A touching salute to those who fought and to those who died. Readers include Robin Williams, Martin Sheen, Matt Dillon, Willem Dafoe, Tom Berenger, Howard Rollins Jr., Michael J. Fox, Sean Penn and Kathleen Turner. Based on the book by the same name.
VHS: S09921. $19.98.
Bill Couturie, USA, 1988, 87 mins.

The Fall of Saigon
For three days panic reigned in Saigon, the former capital of South Vietnam. As crowds filled the streets, helicopters filled the skies offering hope of a way out. Those who left and those who stayed behind offer chilling testimony to that troubled critical moment in time that marked the end of the war in Vietnam in this *Discovery Channel* production. 90 mins.
VHS: S26043. $19.95.

Great Days of History: Prelude to Vietnam
The rise and fall of French imperial ambitions in Indochina from the 18th century to the battle of Dien Bien Phu are detailed here using rare footage from the French Army Archives. 56 mins.
VHS: S09437. $29.95.

Kindred Men of a Dark War
Beyond the politics and controversy which surrounded the Vietnam War were the men who served on the battle lines. This video is the simple testimony of three decorated Vietnam War heroes. The candid and often emotional video examines the human bond among those who find themselves in great danger. Each of the men has a unique story to tell about fear, uncommon valor and an unbreakable love for their brothers in combat. 28 mins.
VHS: S10136. $24.95.

No Time for Tears— Vietnam: The Women Who Served
Seven oral histories from former nurses, Red Cross volunteers and intelligence officers are intricately woven into a moving documentary. The entire story is here, from their having to adjust to horrific conditions to their troubling homecomings. Includes period music from The Beach Boys and Credence Clearwater Revival.
VHS: S26453. $75.00.
Elizabeth Bouiss, USA, 1993, 60 mins.

Of Heroes & Helicopters
A fascinating account of the role played by helicopter pilots during the Vietnam War is offered on this video. Powerful stories from these men, including two Congressional Medal of Honor Winners, describe how they helped "save the day" for thousands of soldiers. USA, 60 mins.
VHS: S27246. $29.95.

Program for Vietnam Veterans
Charles Haid ("Hill Street Blues") hosts an evening of speeches and entertainment aimed at Vietnam era vets.
VHS: S02743. $19.95.

Television's Vietnam
Produced by the conservative group "Accuracy In Media," narrated by Charlton Heston and praised by Reagan, this was produced to counter the PBS series *Vietnam: A Television History*.
VHS: S02745. $14.95.
Peter Rollins, USA, 1984, 116 mins.

Turbulent End to a Tragic War: America's Final Hours in Vietnam
The story of the fall of Saigon, America's last desperate bastion in the Vietnam War, of the soldiers and civilians who fled on the final day, as well as those left behind. From ABC News. 60 mins.
VHS: S12690. $24.98.

Vietnam
This seven-volume series, produced by CBS News, studies the roots of the conflict, the American involvement during the French Indochina war, the partitioning of the country, the American military "advisors" dispatched to Saigon, the Gulf of Tonkin episode, the escalation of the war, the Tet Offensive, Richard Nixon's political victory, the invasion of Cambodia and the restricted role of American support troops. With the conclusion of the war, the fall of Saigon, the program studies the personal and social implications, the countercultural protests to end the war and the psychologically scarred veterans who returned, victims of post-traumatic stress disorder (PTSD). With reporting by Dan Rather, Ed Bradley and Charles Kuralt. Hosted by Walter Cronkite. 750 mins.
VHS: S19540. $139.98.

Vietnam Experience
Images of the Vietnam War are combined with the music and lyrics of Country Joe McDonald. 30 mins.
VHS: S04527. $19.95.

Vietnam Home Movies
Powerful personal documentaries of the Vietnam War featuring the amateur footage shot in 8mm by soldiers during their tour of duty. Each veteran narrates his own segment of the tape.
Vietnam Home Movies Vol. 1. 30 mins.
VHS: S11915. $19.99.
Vietnam Home Movies Vol. 2. 30 mins.
VHS: S11916. $19.99.

Vietnam War Story III
Three new, award-winning, true-to-life stories based on the Vietnamese experience. *Malone* is the story of a flippant soldier who is lost in the jungle; *Dusk to Dawn*, the story of a young marine's self-doubts; and *The Promise*, the story of Mary, a young nurse who arrives for her tour of duty, facing the agony of wounded and dying men. 90 mins.
VHS: S11008. $79.99.

Vietnam—The Hot Red War
This is the first film released in the United States that gives enthusiastic, partisan voice to our enemies in Vietnam, the communists of the North, the "patriots of Nam". A powerful film that will fuel explosive emotions. 55 mins.
VHS: S12714. $24.95.

Vietnam: Chronicle of War
CBS News produced this documentary which traces the steps of U.S. involvement in Vietnam, narrated by Walter Cronkite. 89 mins.
VHS: S02642. $19.98.

Vietnam: In the Year of the Pig
One of the most powerful films ever produced about Vietnam, and an Academy Award nominee. "Passionate and committed, yet it impresses by its sobriety… and will be worth seeing after Vietnam for it raises questions" (Washington Post).
VHS: S01416. $39.95.
Emile de Antonio, USA, 1968, 103 mins.

Vietnam: Remember
Documentary footage traces the pivotal battle of Khe Sanh and how the American G.I.'s survived the fierce jungle fighting. Also: on patrol on a deadly search for Vietcong. 60 minutes.
VHS: S02314. $39.95.

Vietnam: The Secret Agent
The first comprehensive look at the history, effects and implications of the deadly contaminant used in the defoliant called Agent Orange. The film exposes the climate of fear and frustration among veterans exposed to Agent Orange while in Vietnam.
VHS: S01998. $29.95.
Jacki Ochs, USA, 1983, 56 mins.

Vietnam: Time of the Locust
A collection of short films addressing several sides of the Vietnam War: Time of the Locust, funded by the American Friends Service Committee, containing suppressed footage shot by Japanese television; A Day in Vietnam, narrated by Jack Webb; and The Battle, another government-sponsored film in which Marines are shown driving Vietnamese out from caves. USA, 55 mins.
VHS: S01997. $29.95.

Vietnam: Two Decades and a Wake Up
This documentary follows eight battle-scarred veterans as they return to the land of their nightmares in order to free their wounded psyches and make peace with the past. 60 mins.
VHS: S13886. $19.98.

War at Home
A major film about the anti-war movement in America, concentrating on the growth of the anti-war movement in Madison, Wisconsin. The film emerges as a compelling story of how this movement grew as a genuine revolt against government policy, and documents how both policy and values were challenged and changed.
VHS: S01999. $29.95.
Glenn Silber, USA, 1976, 100 mins.

We Can Keep You Forever
A dramatic documentary that examines the possibility that many of America's M.I.A.'s are still alive and being held captive in Vietnam and Laos. Called "compelling" by The New York Times, and endorsed by former POW senator John McClain. Based on a year-long investigation by British TV journalists. 75 mins.
VHS: S07678. $59.95.

The Wild Ones: The Air Cavalry in Vietnam
The Air Cavalry was perhaps the most effective flying force ever conceived. These hunter-killer helicopter teams were relentless in their Vietnam War search-and-destroy missions. Given the difficulty of their task, these forces developed bonds with one another that would last a lifetime. USA, 50 mins.
VHS: S27247. $29.95.

THE CIVIL WAR

Abe Lincoln in Illinois
Raymond Massey reprised his stage role in this historical drama, based on Robert Sherwood's Pulitzer prize-winning play, following Lincoln's life from his backwoods beginnings to his election as President.
VHS: S03225. $19.95.
John Cromwell, USA, 1940, 110 mins.

American History: The Civil War
Famous events from the Civil War are recounted and analyzed, including Lincoln's campaign for President, John Brown's Abolitionist movement, the battles of the Merrimac and the Monitor, Bull Run and Gettysburg. 30 minutes.
VHS: S02136. $29.95.

Atlanta Cyclorama— The Battle of Atlanta
Relive the Battle of Atlanta with a visit to the world-famous Atlanta Cyclorama. See the entire Cyclorama show, learn the complete story of this key Civil War battle, the events that led up to it and the story behind the restoration of the Cyclorama. 30 mins.
VHS: S11478. $29.95.

Battle of Antietam
Focusing on the battle of Antietam, the single bloodiest day in American history, and what many consider the turning point in the War between the States, this battlefield tour is led by historian William K. Brown as he points out crucial spots in the fight, and with the aid of photographs, sketches and maps, describes the various strategies of the Confederate and Union armies. 56 mins.
VHS: S08019. $29.95.

Blue and the Gray
The Civil War is refought with an impressive grouping of big stars and a cast of thousands. This TV mini-series includes the talents of Stacy Keach, Lloyd Bridges, Colleen Dewhurst, Warren Oates, Rory Calhoun, John Hammond, Rip Torn, Geraldine Page, Paul Winfield and Gregory Peck as Abraham Lincoln. Great battle scenes. Story by John Leekly and Bruce Catton.
VHS: S12845. $29.95.
Andrew V. McLaglen, USA, 1988

The Civil War (Ken Burns/PBS)
Ken Burns' brilliant nine-part documentary about the American Civil War from PBS chronicles the Civil War from its causes in 1861 through the assassination of Lincoln in 1865. Five years in the making, this staggering achievement should be required viewing for anyone interested in American history. Complete set.
VHS: S14823. $149.98.
Ken Burns, USA, 1990, 680 mins.

The Civil War (Parade Video)
Experience the greatest battles of the Civil War with this series of five collector's editions. (This series is not to be confused with the PBS series directed by Ken Burns.)
Antietam: The Bloodiest Day in American History. Narrated by Dr. Jay Luvass, co-editor of the U.S. Army War College Guide.
VHS: S13543. $14.95.
Chickamauga: River of Death. Narrated by John Cissell, Chief Interpreter, National Park Service.
VHS: S13545. $14.95.
Gettysburg: July 1st-3rd, 1863. The Civil War's greatest battle. Narrated by Bruce Catton and Stacy Keach.
VHS: S13542. $14.95.
New Market: Field of Honor. Narrated by Joseph W.A. Whitehorne, U.S. Army Historian.
VHS: S13544. $14.95.
The Civil War Photographers. Featuring the photographs of Matthew B. Brady, Alexander Gardner, George N. Barnard, George S. Cook, Timothy H. O'Sullivan, James Gibson and many others. Narrated by Gary Merrill.
VHS: S13541. $14.95.

Civil War Diary
Based on the award-winning novel Across Five Aprils, this is the story of a courageous young man struggling to save his family from the devastation brought on by the Civil War. Winner of the coveted International Heritage Award 1990. USA, 82 mins.
VHS: S15276. $79.95.

Civil War Journal
In 13 episodes this thorough documentary sifts through diaries and historical photographs for a glimpse of our nation's most traumatic historic crises. It combines little known facts with personal observations and factual re-enactments. From the opening canon blast at Fort Sumter Danny Glover will lead you through this highly entertaining look at America's Civil War.
VHS: S20597. $119.95.

Civil War Journal, Set II
This six-volume collection continues the story of the war between the states. It includes Robert E. Lee, Fredericksburg, The War Reporters, Lincoln and Gettysburg and many more. Altogether there are 13 50-minute episodes detailing every aspect of this wrenching historic event.
VHS: S25867. $119.95.

The Civil War
The story of America's Civil War is told through original black-and-white illustrations, created during the war by artists at the scene of the battles. See Manassas, Gettysburg, Shiloh, Vicksburg, and other moments come alive in this vivid program. 30 minutes.
VHS: S02470. $29.95.
Laser: LD72292. $229.95.

The Civil War: 125th Anniversary Series (Classic Images)
A series of exciting and informative videotapes, for sale on an individual basis only, dramatizing the greatest battles of the Civil War.
1st Manassas.
VHS: S14886. $29.95.
Shiloh.
VHS: S14887. $29.95.
Antietam.
VHS: S14888. $39.95.
Chancellorsville.
VHS: S14889. $29.95.
Gettysburg.
VHS: S14890. $39.95.
Vicksburg.
VHS: S14891. $29.95.
Spotsylvania.
VHS: S14892. $29.95.
Atlanta.
VHS: S14893. $39.95.
Franklin.
VHS: S14894. $29.95.
Appomattox.
VHS: S14895. $39.95.

Civil War: The Fiery Trial
Recounts the enduring drama of America's bloodiest conflict. On site photography, archival photographs, period art and music tell the story of the war's major campaigns, battles and leaders. Narrated by Edwin Newman.
VHS: S08461. $19.95.

The Divided Union
An extraordinary series of six 1-hour tapes on the Civil War—perhaps the most ambitious project ever undertaken to document the history, feelings, and contradictions of America divided. The set, featuring hundreds of rare photographs, documents, and interviews with the top experts on the Civil War, comes complete with an annotated index which refers to numbered sections within each tape, with a facsimile of the Gettysburg Address, and other supplementary informative material, and has been issued in a very limited designer edition which is available for a limited time only. Complete 6-tape set.
VHS: S06108. $499.95.

Faces of Battle Series
Exciting dramatizations of famous Civil War conflicts. Filmed on the privately-owned battle sites. Three videocassettes for sale on an individual basis only.
Bentonville. The Appomattox of the West.
VHS: S14898. $29.95.
Cedar Mountain. Led by Stonewall Jackson.
VHS: S14896. $29.95.
Petersburg. Excellent re-creation of African-American troops in action.
VHS: S14897. $29.95.

Gettysburg (Documentary)
The Battle of Gettyusburg, fought from July 1-3, 1863, is authentically recreated on location by a cast of thousands in this thrilling video history of one of America's fiercest conflicts. 40 mins.
VHS: S09946. $29.95.

Gettysburg (Martin Sheen)
The Civil War's most famous battle, at Gettysburg, is the center of this epic featuring stars Tom Berenger and Martin Sheen. It combines costume drama detail and riveting war scene footage to bring that troubled event to life.
VHS: S20616. $24.98.
Ronald F. Maxwell, USA, 1993, 254 mins.

Gettysburg Battlefield Tour
This inspiring video tour of the Gettysburg National Military Park takes the viewer chronologically through the decisive battles of the Civil War, and concludes with a stirring rendition of Lincoln's Gettysburg Address. 35 mins.
VHS: S09945. $29.95.

Grant and Lee
Grant and Lee experienced the Civil War from opposite sides. Here they both discuss their decisions and personal views. If Grant experienced his fight as a battle for justice, Lee saw in his utter defeat the end of a way of life. 33 mins.
VHS: S23734. $79.95.

Great Campaigns of the Civil War: Touring Civil War Battlefields, Volumes I and II
Great battles from the West, including Shiloh, Vicksburg, Chickamauga, Ft. Donelson and New Orleans, are portrayed in this documentary. Two-volume set, 120 mins.
VHS: S23133. $49.95.

Great Union Presidents
A documentary that probes the personal and public lives of two complicated, fascinating presidents, Abraham Lincoln and Ulysses S. Grant. 60 mins.
VHS: S19664. $9.99.

Guns of the Civil War
This documentary series of three tapes examines the weapons which fought the war between the States.
Vol. 1: A Greater Moral Force.
VHS: S20601. $24.95.
Vol. 2: Measure for Measure.
VHS: S20602. $24.95.
Vol. 3: Against the Thunderstorm.
VHS: S20603. $24.95.
Complete set.
VHS: S20600. $69.95.

Ironclads: The Monitor and the Merrimac
Tells the story of the two astonishing vessels that fought the most memorable naval battles of the Civil War, and forever revolutionized maritime warfare. Noted experts discuss how the distinctive ships came to be built, how they influenced later fighting craft. Period prints, etchings, photographs and paintings re-create the first battle between iron ships, with dramatic undersea images of the Monitor now resting on the floor of the Atlantic Ocean. Narrated by Edwin Newman. 30 mins.
VHS: S11125. $19.95.

Lincoln
This four-hour program is a biography of the 16th President which interweaves the personal and political with background materials and commentary provided by actors playing Lincoln's important contemporaries. The program utilizes rare archival materials and Lincoln-era memorabilia. With the voices of Arnold Schwarznegger, Oprah Winfrey, Jason Robards, James Earl Jones, Glenn Close, Eli Wallach, Ossie Davis, Olympia Dukakis, Maureen Stapleton and Richard Thomas.
Vol. 1: The Making of the President. An accumulation of personal details, images of his home, books and personal effects, that reveal roots and origins.
VHS: S18111. $14.98.
Vol. 2: The Pivotal Year: 1863. At the height of the Civil War, Lincoln led the Union in the formation of the Emancipation Proclamation and the freeing of the slaves. The program focuses on the events and stories behind the president's Gettysburg Address.
VHS: S18112. $14.98.
Vol. 3: "I Want to Finish this Job": 1864. The fractured political and social order of the Civil War was the dominant issue of Lincoln's 1864 re-election campaign. He was determined to maintain his promise to preserve the Union.
VHS: S18113. $14.98.
Vol. 4: "Now He Belongs to the Ages": 1865. The filmmakers move beyond the fanaticism of John Wilkes Booth to explore the collective guilt and rage of those who felt the president turned back their heritage and traditions.
VHS: S18114. $14.98.
Lincoln, Complete Set.
VHS: S18110. $49.98.

Mr. Lincoln's Springfield
Return to President Lincoln's cherished hometown and the only home he ever owned. Through historic photographs, this program conveys a vivid impression of Mr. Lincoln's relationship with his family and fellow townspeople. 30 minutes.
VHS: S02488. $29.95.

A Nation Asunder
Imagine that the spectacle of the American Civil War was unfolding right before you. A Nation Asunder is the first program on the Civil War to interweave photographs, documents and footage of war veterans with early filmed dramatizations. The result is a frighteningly real landscape of battle and emotional testimony taken from actual Civil War transcriptions. A stunning, two-volume (each sold separately) re-creation of the Civil War.
Part I: Brother Against Brother (1861-1863). 55 mins.
VHS: S15686. $19.98.
Part II: The Tide Turns (1863-1865). 55 mins.
VHS: S15688. $19.98.

Robert E. Lee
History comes alive in this video biography of Robert E. Lee, from his birth in the Virginia aristocracy to the fiery battlefields of the Civil War and his presidency of an emerging Southern University. Original music by Grammy-winner Jon Carroll complements footage of the landmarks of his life, historic photographs, paintings and images. 30 mins.
VHS: S09489. $19.95.

Royal Federal Blues— The Black Civil War Soldiers
This award-winning documentary shows the history of African-American soldiers in the Civil War, from their induction into the Union Army all the way to ferocious battlegrounds that marked the divide between freedom and slavery. 45 mins.
VHS: S22048. $19.98.

Smithsonian's Great Battles of the Civil War
In this comprehensive seven-volume history, the battles and strategic importance of the Civil War's seminal conflicts are played out within their vast social, military and political implications. The episodes mix re-enactments of the various campaigns, eyewitness accounts, period reconstruction and photographs, paintings and artifacts, original illustrations, period music and interviews with important scholars and historians. The series was written and directed by filmmaker Jay Wertz. Each episode is 60 mins.
Volume I.
VHS: S17094. $29.95.
Volume II.
VHS: S17095. $29.95.
Volume III.
VHS: S17096. $29.95.
Volume IV.
VHS: S17097. $29.95.
Volume V.
VHS: S17098. $29.95.
Volume VI.
VHS: S17099. $29.95.
Volume VII.
VHS: S23230. $29.95.

Songs of the Civil War
Featuring 25 popular songs from the Civil War era—folk, country, bluegrass, gospel—some standards, others rare. And each is introduced with insightful narrative and performed just as they were 130 years ago. Co-produced by Ken Burns, director of the Award-winning PBS series The Civil War. 60 mins.
VHS: S14603. $19.98.

The Speeches of Abraham Lincoln
An historic presentation of Lincoln's immortal words authentically illustrated with visual records of America's past. Includes rare photographs of Lincoln's life and times, original newspaper clippings, and texts of the actual speeches. All of Lincoln's most famous speeches are presented here, including, of course, The Gettysburg Address. 45 mins.
VHS: S15689. $19.98.

Stones River National Battlefield
This National Park Service program explores the history, tactics and strategies of the Battle of Stones River, the Civil War's single bloodiest day of fighting in Tennessee. It also features fascinating living history demonstrations of firing artillery, the key arm in deciding battle's outcome. 35 mins.
VHS: S09182. $29.95.

Stonewall Jackson
Tells the remarkable life story of the legendary Confederate General from his orphaned youth in Appalachia to his daring exploits on Civil War battlefields. Historians discuss Jackson's idiosyncratic personality and his great campaigns, from his boyhood in western Virginia to his early combat success in the Mexican War to his bold feats and tragic death in the War between the States. Contemporary photography, archival photographs and rare manuscripts and art work highlight this biography. 309 mins.
VHS: S11117. $19.95.

Touring Civil War Battlefields
A unique journey to the actual battlefields as they were and as they are today, where the heroic encounters of the Civil War actually happened. Thousands of authentically-trained volunteers re-enact the battles of Appomattox, the first and second Bull Run, Antietam, Fredericksburg, Gettysburg, and the final surrender at Appomattox. USA, 1986, 60 mins.
VHS: S04697. $39.95.

Ulysses S. Grant
Tells the extraordinary story of the one-time shop clerk who became commander of the Civil War's victorious union armies, and the 18th President. Traces Grant's life from his upbringing in rural Ohio to his troubled tenure as president. Historians unlock Grant's distinctive temperament, his military ingenuity, his peacetime woes through archival photographs and rare documents, as well as contemporary photography of the major sites of Grant's life. 30 mins.
VHS: S11118. $19.95.

War Between the States (1800s)
Negro slavery and divided sentiments among the states of the North and South are the subjects vividly portrayed here, conflicts of interest which led inevitably to the bloodiest conflict in American history and which are still of grave concern even today.
VHS: S03973. $64.95.

Women and the Civil War
This program looks at the heroism and struggles of women in the Union and Confederate armies during the Civil War. The program profiles the achievements of two women, Belle Reynolds and Kady Brownell, who marched alongside and fought with their husbands in battle. 30 mins.
VHS: S20271. $29.95.

Yankee Thunder, Rebel Lightning!
Two comprehensive, one-hour videos tell the story of the Civil War from beginning to end, covering the major campaigns of both Eastern and Western theaters, political considerations, African-American troops, the Nurses' Corps and more.
VHS: S14899. $59.95.

cultural DOCUMENTARY

America's Castles II
During the Age of Invention (1913-1929) the wealthy built sumptuous residences that served as fantasyland homes to America's dreamers. Homes from the Rockefellers, the Fords and others are featured. Perhaps Donald Trump's Palm Beach residence, Mar-a-Lago, outdoes them all. 100 mins.
VHS: S25926. $29.95.

The Amish Folk
An overview of the Amish of southeastern Pennsylvania, including their origins, church meetings, crafts, homes, farms, and schools. With Amish songs and hymns on the soundtrack. 32 mins.
VHS: S15535. $45.00.

Art Meets Science
Five groups of speakers who are experts from different disciplines share their ideas. 58 minutes each.
Crisis of Perception. Four radically different speakers—artist Jacques van der Heyden, scientist Francisco Varela, Carmelite nun Mother Tessa Bielecki and economist J.M. Pinheiro Neto—contrast Buddhist theories of knowledge with modern science. They debate the conflict between the "unknown" nature of reality and what we perceive, examining the relationship between the subject and object of what they're seeing. "The fundamental act of perception is precisely that drawing out into the visible something that wasn't there previously" (Francisco Varela).
VHS: S18631. $29.95.
From Fragmentation to Wholeness. A symposium on creativity, featuring four speakers—artist Robert Rauschenberg, physicist David Bohm, the Dalai Lama and Russian economist Stanislav Menshikov—articulating concepts about science, nature, art and biology. The speakers talk about the ways of implementing these ideas and theories and creating a compassionate and caring society.
VHS: S18629. $29.95.
The Chaotic Universe. Five renowned speakers—composer John Cage, artist John Chamberlain, physicist Ilya Prigogine, philosopher Huston Smith and bank executive F. Wilhelm Christians—examine order and breakdown. They discuss the nature and organization of living systems, the creativity and wonder found in chaos and an unconventional world that makes up multiple perspectives.
VHS: S18630. $29.95.
The Shifting Paradigm. A group of experts, including artist Marina Abramovic, physicist Fritjof Capra, priest and Hindu scholar Raimon Panikkar and former IMF director H.J. Witteveen, discuss the primary ecological threat to the planet, why people dread change and the place of creativity in altering perceptions of reality.
VHS: S18632. $29.95.
The Transforming World. Artist Lawrence Weiner, biologist Rupert Sheldrake, Tibetan Buddhist teacher Sogyal Rinpoche and Credit Lyonnais director J.M. Leveque discuss art and the breakdown of science, reincarnation and the morphogenetic field. They examine shifting trends in biology and physics, a closer study of the living earth and a particular emphasis on the contributions and insights of Third World societies and culture.
VHS: S18633. $29.95.
Art Meets Science, Complete Set.
VHS: S18846. $129.95.

Civilization
Historian Kenneth Clark explores the civilization of mankind from the Dark Ages to the 20th century, in 13 programs.
Programs 1 & 2. In *The Skin of Our Teeth*, Clark undergoes a spiritual quest of the Dark Ages, exploring the Byzantine Ravenna, the Celtic Hebrides, Norwegian Vikings and Charlemagne's chapel at Aachen. In *The Great Thaw*, the program studies the rebirth of European civilization in the 12th century.
VHS: S18733. $29.95.
Program 3 & 4. Clark assesses the accomplishments and evolution of late Middle Ages architecture and culture in France and Italy in *Romance and Beauty*. In *Man—The Measure of All Things*, Clark examines the revitalization of classicism, exploring the Renaissance centers of Urbino and Mantua.
VHS: S18734. $29.95.
Programs 5 & 6. In the first program, *The Hero as Artist*, Clark examines the Papal Room in the 16th century and its influence on the art of Michelangelo, Raphael and da Vinci. In *Protest and Communication*, Clark considers the impact of Reformation and the various artists influenced in Germany, France and England.
VHS: S18735. $29.95.
Programs 7 & 8. In *Grandeur and Obedience*, Clark looks at Rome and the Counter-Reformation, the place of Michelangelo and Bernini, the impact and extensive influence of the Catholic Church, and the dreamy splendor of St. Peter's. In the second program, *The Light of Experience*, technological innovations such as the telescope and microscope allow for greater information and detailed interpretation.
VHS: S18736. $29.95.
Programs 9 & 10. Clark notes how rococo architecture is mirrored in the musical flow and complex symmetry of 18th century composers Bach, Handel, Haydn and Mozart in *The Pursuit of Happiness*. In the follow-up program, *The Smile of Reason*, dissention and uproar in 18th century Paris suggests the pre-revolutionary dissatisfaction with the ancien regime. Clark also studies the expansive European palaces and Jefferson's Monticello.
VHS: S18737. $29.95.
Programs 11 & 12. In *The Worship of Nature*, the belief that divinity guides nature undermined Christianity's authority and unleashed the Romantic Movement. In *The Fallacies of Hope*, Clark explores the dissolution of the French aristocracy and how the Revolution led to Napoleon and a collection of authoritarian bureaucracies. The Romantic artists reveal their disillusionment.
VHS: S18738. $29.95.
Program 13. In *Heroic Materialism*, Clark concludes the series by assessing the materialism and humanitarianism of 20th century ideas and thought, from Britain's industrial landscape to the functional skyscrapers of contemporary New York City.
VHS: S18739. $29.95.

Civilization, Complete Set.
VHS: S18740. $149.95.

Connections
James Burke is back making connections between the discoveries and inventions that criss-cross history, joining disparate places, people and events. The odd and surprising chain of happenstance occurrences that result in objects and processes which are integral to modern life will continue to surprise any viewer.
Deja Vu. We have all been there before and James Burke can prove it: history repeats itself. Pizarro beat the Incas, German philosophy went to South America, environmentalism bored Napoleon and Hitler's plans misfired. Believe it or not, it is all connected.
VHS: S20972. $19.95.
Echoes of the Past. In this episode James Burke starts mulling over the secret of the universe, which not surprisingly takes him on a long journey across a variety of temporal and spatial boundaries. Buddhist tea ceremonies, Florentine architecture, Roman ruins and even radio telephones on luxury liners all emerge from his contemplation of the big question.
VHS: S20968. $19.95.
Getting It Together. Swat teams are not just collections of dedicated and sophisticated crime fighters. Their work represents a variety of technologies ranging from artillery to air rescue to anaesthesia and beyond. Burke looks at the history of these developments, finding they are related not just in the present but historically as well.
VHS: S20965. $19.95.
High Times. When James Burke unwraps a sandwich it's hardly a surprise that this mundane action should lead to a discussion that involves World War II defense radar, French neo-Impressionist painters, tapestries and Versailles, 16th century traders in Asia and the most famous clock in the world.
VHS: S20971. $19.95.
Photo Finish. The Le Mans 24-hour race leads Burke to his own excursion through the relationship between photography and bullets, relativity and Hollywood movies, railroads and gaslights, raincoats and blimps, telegraphs and solar power, which, in turn, are all related to speed racing.
VHS: S20969. $19.95.
Revolutions. James Watt may be indelibly connected to the steam engine in the minds of schoolchildren, but it is his secret life that's up for consideration here. Modern office work, fertilizers, Italian cemeteries, safety matches, landing on the moon, X-rays, imitation diamonds, even the revolution in genetics are related to his more private pursuits.
VHS: S20963. $19.95.
Sentimental Journeys. India holds the key to many of the puzzles investigated by James Burke in this travelogue of unexpected connections. Prison reform and blue dye, shock treatment and the Bunsen burner, disease and the Russian Orthodox church, a perfect glass and surveying, even the Himalayas and the inside of a star—all these things are connected in Burke's universe.
VHS: S20964. $19.95.
Separate Ways. In the 18th century the debate over slavery divided many nations, political parties and even families. From these disparate camps, separate lines of development grew that only rejoined in our time, resulting in the greatest threat to peace we know.
VHS: S20970. $19.95.
Something for Nothing. In this chain of exploration, something impossible happened 400 years ago that would one day lead to outer space. Along the way pigeon lovers, the Pope, Black Sea hurricanes, 18th century experimental vicars and even Victorian lavatories become intricately enmeshed in the dream of space travel.
VHS: S20967. $19.95.
Whodunit? Here's a clue. In 1902 someone stole a set of billiard balls and became the most famous crook in history. If you need more information consider these other clues: money from the Dominican Republic, rock samples from Mont Blanc, Emperor Charles V's debts, the island of Hispaniola, French mirrors, charts of the U.S. East Coast in 1775, Charles Darwin's cousin and even the FBI are involved.
VHS: S20966. $19.95.
Complete Set.
VHS: S20973. $179.95.

Connections: The Journey Continues
This series, featuring James Burke, presents a history of technology and culture that reveals the present-day world in a wholly new light. The 10 half-hour episodes were created especially for the Learning Channel.
New Harmony. The discovery of cobalt, a blue dye used in Ming vases, has proved crucial to the development of computer chips. In addition, microscopic bugs inspired the novel *Frankenstein*, which in turn inspired the ideology of socialism.
VHS: S25855. $19.95.
Hot Pickle. There is a strong connection between tea, Chinese opium dens, the jungle adventurer who founded the London zoo, and a switch that releases bombs.
VHS: S25856. $19.95.
The Big Spin. A medical accident begins a chain of events that leads through a search for Helen of Troy, police blotters, 17th century flower power, soda pop, the discovery of oil, microfossils and earthquake detection.
VHS: S25857. $19.95.
Bright Ideas. The inventor of the bottle cap could never have forseen the effects of his discovery. It led to razors and clock springs which enable the Hubbell telescope to measure the universe.
VHS: S25858. $19.95.
Making Waves. Hairdressers, Gold Rush miners, English parliamentarians, Scotsmen, Irish potato farmers, Revolutionary War loyalists and innovative printers are all connected in this episode.
VHS: S25859. $19.95.
Routes. A sick lawyer changes farming and thereby triggers the French Revolution. This cataclysmic event is only one effect of the ailing man's actions. His work also led to the invention of radio.
VHS: S25860. $19.95.

One Word. One medieval word triggers a trip to Istanbul. From there it's back to England, where the effects of this word help foment the Industrial Revolution. Then a Swedish connection links these events to the invention of cultural anthropology.
VHS: S25861. $19.95.
Sign Here. Dutch piracy inspires the establishment of international law and French probability math. But this story continues through phonetics, Victorian seances and, ultimately, the invention of mechanical flight.
VHS: S25862. $19.95.
Better Than the Real Thing. Jefferson uncovered some technology in Paris that led to the zipper. But this chain of events had far more momentous implications. It led to the discovery that vitamins are essential to human health.
VHS: S25863. $19.95.
Flexible Response. Robin Hood stands at the beginning of this adventure that threads through medieval showbiz, Dutch swamp draining, decimals, the US currency and ends with the Tornado Fighterbomber.
VHS: S25864. $19.95. Connections: The Journey Continues Series.
VHS: S25865. $149.95.

Cousteau: Calypso's Search for Atlantis
Legend has it that thousands of years ago, the island of Atlantis once housed an advanced civilization, which then vanished completely in a violent cataclysm. Cousteau examines the roots of Plato's account of Atlantis in an exploration of the Minoan civilization that flourished on Crete during the Bronze Age.
VHS: S08363. $24.95.

The Cousteau Odyssey: Blind Prophets of Easter Island
An exploration of the riddles of the colossal, 1000-year-old stone heads on Easter Island, and the puzzling history of the islands' inhabitants. 58 mins.
VHS: S08359. $24.95.

Disappearing World: Ongka's Big Moka, The Kawelka of Papua, New Guinea
Ongka, an endearing and charismatic tribal leader of the Kawelka tribe of New Guinea, has spent five years as an orator and negotiator to amass the 600 pigs and assorted valuables which he will give away in a festive ceremony, a moka. Unforeseen events threaten his largesse, stirring up rumors of sorcery and a threat of war. 60 mins.
VHS: S23043. $19.95.

Disappearing World: The Herders of Mongun-Taiga, The Tuvans of Mongolia
Along the Siberian-Mongolian border in the Sacred Wilderness, the descendents of the aboriginal Siberian people continue to live in yurts, movable felt tents. These nomads herd yaks, sheep, horses and goats. Farming is impossible. Under these harsh conditions, they must produce all their basic necessities on the spot. 60 mins.
VHS: S23046. $19.95.

Disappearing World: The Island of Malaita, The Lau of the Solomon Islands
The extraordinary Lau people live on man-made coral islands in a South Sea lagoon. Their traditional culture, the "Life of Custom," is threatened by the imminent demise of their two, aged spiritual leaders. Though islands neighboring their home show modern influences, they continue to sing their choral music without any traces of encroaching Christian traditions. 60 mins.
VHS: S23044. $19.95.

Disappearing World: The Kayapo, Indians of the Brazilian Rainforest
Life changed dramatically for the fiercely independent Kayapo when gold was discovered on their land in 1982. The Amazon was opened up for prospecting and thousands of Brazilians invaded their homeland, creating one of the world's largest gold mines. The Kayapo were forced to adapt to a life of business or see their traditions destroyed. 60 mins.
VHS: S23045. $19.95.

Disappearing World: The Masai Women, The Masai of Kenya
The Masai herd animals in the East African Rift Valley of Kenya and Tanzania. They are proud of their cattle, but only the men have rights to the herds. Women are wholly dependent. With a Masai elder as a guide, this video explains what it means to be a woman in this male dominated society. 60 mins.
VHS: S23042. $19.95.

Dreamworlds: Desire/Sex/Power in Rock Video
Editing together excerpts from 165 different rock videos, Sut Jhally demonstrates the negative and dangerous representations of women contained in popular television images. The program recontextualizes pop culture to reveal the role videos play in how young people think and behave. 55 mins.
VHS: S16420. $195.00.
Sut Jhally, USA, 1990, 55 mins.

Easter Island
A documentary filmed on location on Easter Island, exploring the mysterious monolithic stone monuments. 25 mins.
English Narration. Joan Crawford.
VHS: S06757. $70.00.
Spanish Narration. Felicia Montealegre.
VHS: S06758. $70.00.

Easter Island: A Vanished Culture
Its inhabitants once called it "Te Pito o te Hanua," or the Navel of the World. The gigantic stone statues, artistic temple platforms and mysterious writings have puzzled explorers and anthropologists. This program examines theories that attempt to uncover exactly who created these artifacts and what then happened to them. Information from the recently deciphered "rongo runes" is highlighted. 44 mins.
VHS: S22926. $29.95.

Essential Alan Watts: Man in Nature and Work as Play
Alan Watts gives two lectures. The first examines the differences between nature and man, the confusion of symbols with reality, and the oversimplification of language. In the second program, Watts talks about the extreme divisions between work and play. 58 mins.
VHS: S20423. $29.95.

Explore!
New Age explorer Douchan Gersi and his camera travel to the world's most remote regions in search of primitive peoples, exotic animals and adventure. Hosted by James Coburn and Douchan Gersi. 60 minutes each.
And the Gods Moved to Aiwan/Between Gods and Men.
VHS: S24288. $19.95.
Blue Men of the Sahara/From Timbuktu to the Stars.
VHS: S24285. $19.95.
Dancers of Evil/The Tooth of Buddha.
VHS: S24291. $19.95.
Headhunters of Borneo/Jungles of Borneo.
VHS: S24281. $19.95.
In the Footsteps of Genghis Khan/Once Upon a Time, Afghanistan.
VHS: S24292. $19.95.
Journal from India/The Wheel of Karma.
VHS: S24289. $19.95.
Kaaba, Center of the Universe/Bandits, Pirates and Flying Carpets.
VHS: S24286. $19.95.
Land of Living Gods/Kingdom Beneath the Sky.
VHS: S24293. $19.95.
Land of Sheba/Sanctuaries of Stone.
VHS: S24283. $19.95.
Lost Road to Nubia/Bodies of Art, Bodies of Pain.
VHS: S24282. $19.95.
Orphans of the Sun/Magic Healing, Magic Death.
VHS: S24284. $19.95.
The Last Empire of Sailing Ships/Festival of Tears.
VHS: S24290. $19.95.
Wolves of Freedom/Puppets of God.
VHS: S24287. $19.95.
Complete 13-Volume Gift Set. 780 mins.
VHS: S24294. $239.00.

A Glorious Accident
In this series eminent scientists expound on the place of man in the cosmic puzzle, first in individual interviews, and then as a group at a fascinating round table discussion. It's an exhaustive and comprehensive attempt to address the most puzzling questions of our secular age. Eminent biologist Stephen Jay Gould looks at the puzzle which life presents. In *Disturbing the Universe*, physicist Freeman Dyson discusses his theories on the nature of an all-encompassing concept. In *Wittgenstein's Vienna*, scientific historian Stephen Toulmin charts the key influence of the 20th-century philosopher who first examined the significance of language in the shaping of human perception. In *Consciousness Explained*, philosopher Daniel C. Dennet argues that consciousness not just a matter of awareness. *New Science of Life* features biochemist Rupert Sheldrake. *Awakenings* offers a glimpse of how the human mind actually works, by neuroscientist Oliver Sacks. And *A Clash of Minds, Parts 1 & 2*, is a roundtable discussion at which these six recognized leaders of their respective fields bring their disparate perspectives together. This fascinating meeting of minds reconfigures the perceptions that govern our world. Only available as a set.
VHS: S21377. $179.95.

The History of Santa Claus
Everyone recognizes Santa yet few actually know who he really is or where he comes from. This fascinating docudrama recreates the history of this figure, tracing his origins back through history and even pre-history across the globe. Ancient Shamanic cave paintings, pagan Germanic gods, St. Nicholas and even the home of reindeer are shown. 54 mins.
VHS: S21823. $19.95.

John Edgar Wideman
The evolving role of the black man in today's society is one of the themes James Edgar Wideman incorporates in his writing. Wideman read from *The Stories of John Edgar Wideman* and unpublished works in progress in Los Angeles on April 6, 1993. In addition, he discussed his work with Michael Silverblatt. From the *Lannan Literary Videos* series. 60 mins.
VHS: S27141. $19.95.

La Belle Epoque
Douglas Fairbanks Jr. narrates how the elite of London, Paris and New York society lived in that carefree age when the pursuit of beauty and romance was a way of life, aided by newsreel clips, paintings, photographs, period costumes and re-enactments. Interviews with La Belle Epoque greats Erte, Jacques-Henri Lartigue and suffragist leader Enid Goulden-Bach provide individual and often idiosyncratic memories of the age. 105 mins.
VHS: S04650. $39.95.

Language and Consciousness
Professor Stephen Pinker guides the viewer through four half-hour segments about language and consciousness. His studies at the Center for Cognitive Neuroscience make him eminently qualified to lead this amazing video series. 120 mins.
VHS: S23632. $44.95.

Legacy

Author Michael Wood (*Search for Trojan War*) traces the rise and fall of the Asian and Western civilizations that flourished and altered our cultural perspective.
Central America: The Burden of Time. Despite racist attacks from Europe and their cultural isolation, the Mayans and Aztecs created sophisticated societies with their cities, pyramids and kings. 60 mins.
VHS: S18229. $29.95.
China: The Mandate of Heaven. This program considers the valuable resources discovered in China and introduced to the west, particularly iron-casting, gunpowder and printing. 60 mins.
VHS: S18230. $29.95.
Egypt: The Habit of Civilization. As the first great nation, Egypt remains a powerful player in world politics and culture. 60 mins.
VHS: S18231. $29.95.
India: The Empire of the Spirit. Ancient India is preserved through Hindu traditionalism, the culture that was born 5,000 years ago. 60 mins.
VHS: S18226. $29.95.
Iraq: The Cradle of Civilization. The centerpiece of the first cities built 5,000 years ago on the banks of Euphrates in southern Iraq, where it commands a terse hold on the fragile social order. 60 mins.
VHS: S18227. $29.95.
The Barbarian West. As the world enters the 21st century, this program considers the violent histories of western civilization and its exploitation of other cultures. 60 mins.
VHS: S18228. $29.95.
Legacy, Complete Set. The complete set at a special price.
VHS: S19377. $149.95.

Marija Gimbutas: The World of the Goddess

An absorbing view of the culture, religious beliefs, symbolism and mythology of the prehistoric, pre-patriarchal cultures of Old Europe, who revered and celebrated the Great Goddess of Life, Death and Regeneration in all her many forms: of plants, of stone, of animals and humans. By the scholar who has made the exploration of these cultures her life work. Marija Gimbutas, Ph.D., is professor of archaeology at UCLA and the author of *The Language of the Goddess*. Directed by Ralph Metzner. A video presentation of the *Green Earth Foundation*. USA, 1990, 103 mins.
VHS: S14933. $29.95.

Men and Women: Talking Together

A no-holds-barred discussion by two provocative voices on issues relative to the men's and women's movements, author Deborah Tannen (*You Just Don't Understand*) and poet Robert Bly (*Iron John*). "Together they examine how gender dialect works and reveal disturbing truths about the male power elite" (*Publishers Weekly*). 58 mins.
VHS: S20213. $29.95.

Nomads of the Wind

This five-part mini-series details the arduous process of colonization and cultural development that is the history of Polynesia. The people who settled these islands developed a sturdy sea-faring way of life. In the process they have had a lasting impact on the land and the sea. Each episode is 60 mins.
Episode 1: The Faraway Heaven. Two thousand years ago the first Polynesian peoples voyaged to the Pacific islands currently known as Tahiti and the Marquesas. They brought plants, animals, fishing skills and horticulture to volcano-dominated landscapes containing blue lagoons and bountiful reefs.
VHS: S23974. $19.95.
Episode 2: Crossroads of the Pacific. The west Pacific islands of Fiji, Tonga and Samoa are the cradle of Polynesia. From these beautiful islands these unique people spread their influence ever further eastward.
VHS: S23975. $19.95.
Episode 3: Burning Their Boats. The story of the mutinous seamen from the HMS *Bounty* echoes the story of the people and wildlife of Polynesia. As these English sailors burned their boat and resolved to live indefinitely on Pitcairn Island, Polynesians living nearby worshiped giants who had made a similar commitment to Easter Island.
VHS: S23976. $19.95.
Episode 4: Distant Horizons. The final great migrations of the Polynesians were their most ambitious. To the North lay Hawaii's tropical splendor while to the Southwest lay New Zealand and its unique but challenging ecosystems.
VHS: S23977. $19.95.
Episode 5: The Pierced Sky. Captain Cook and other European explorers changed Polynesia forever. The characterization of their influence continues to veer between an ideal of discovery and simple exploitation.
VHS: S23978. $19.95.
Nomads of the Wind, Set.
VHS: S23979. $89.95.

Old-Fashioned Christmas

A nostalgic look at the tradition of Christmas as celebrated in America and Europe over the years. Starring Jane Morgan, John Raitt, The Lennon Sisters, Florence Henderson, Earl Wrightson, Mildred Miller, Rosemary Clooney, Thomas Mitchell, Howard Keel, and Phyllis Curtin. 55 mins.
VHS: S08472. $19.95.

The Presence of the Goddess

The development and history of the Goddess in western civilization is finally uncovered and documented in this intriguing video. Her influence has had a humanizing effect throughout successive ages. Her inspiring ways connect all people with the earth we live on. 46 mins.
VHS: S21599. $39.95.

The Shakers in America

This tape examines the history and major contributions of the influential Shaker movement, which began in America in 1774. With interviews, songs, and a look at the art and architecture of the people. 29 mins.
VHS: S15533. $50.00.

Smithsonian World: The Living Smithsonian

The vast range of world-wide activities which this institution supports are explored and explained in this video. It offers a behind-the-scenes look at the people who create the exhibits which document America's ambitions and accomplishments. 58 mins.
VHS: S27377. $19.98.

The Spirit of the Mask

Harvard professor and author Wade Davis (*The Serpent and the Rainbow*) hosts this documentary about the cultural and social origins of Canada's Northwest Coast native people. The program describes their secret and elaborate uses of masks, myths, gestures and rituals and explores relations between the natural and the spiritual. 50 mins.
VHS: S19114. $19.95.

The Story of Carol

Christmas carols originated in dances dating back to the seventh century. This documentary traces the pagan roots of these songs. The first printed carol appeared in 1521. Later they were condemned by the Puritans, only to be revived in the Victorian era. 52 mins.
VHS: S21822. $19.95.

The Story of Inanna, Queen of Heaven and Earth

Through voice, gesture and song, acclaimed storyteller Diane Wolkstein recreates the legend of the ancient Sumerian goddess Inanna. This epic tale was lost for 4,000 years and only recently translated from long-buried clay tablets. Includes images of Sumerian art and the landscape of Sumer.
VHS: S25918. $65.00.
Diane Wolkstein, USA, 1988, 50 mins.

Treehouse People: Cannibal Justice

The Korowai are an elusive people who have maintained their unique way of life for thousands of years in the rain forest. On this Smithsonian Expedition, this isolated group of people is revealed in all their mystery. They may even practice ritual cannibalism. 50 mins.
VHS: S25869. $24.95.

The Wedding of Palo

Dr. Knud Rasmussen, the famed explorer, was filming a documentary about Greenland when he passed away in 1933. This film is what remains. It shows telling details about the native peoples of this frozen region and includes hunting sequences and courting traditions. 72 mins.
VHS: S24081. $24.95.
F. Dalsheim/K. Rasmussen, Denmark, 1935, 72 mins.

ANCIENT CIVILIZATIONS

Alexander the Great

The exploits of this historic figure transformed the world, leaving a lasting impact on both eastern and western civilization. This documentary traces his accomplishments from the Adriatic to the Himalayas. English dialog.
VHS: S22049. $29.95.

Ancient Greece Volume 1

Filmed on location, these two programs, *Art in Ancient Greece* and *Mining in Ancient Greece*, give the modern viewer a fresh perspective on two key cultural and technological achievements. 120 mins.
VHS: S25648. $29.95.

Ancient Greece Volume 2

Bacchus, the God of Wine and *Fire Walking in Greece* present important insights into the religious and philosophical beliefs of Ancient Greece. The attitudes and concepts forged there continue to influence the modern world. 120 mins.
VHS: S25649. $29.95.

Ancient Mysteries

Using modern technology, scientific analysis, high-tech evidence and recent archaeological developments, the films in the *Ancient Mysteries* series are on the cutting edge of discovery.
The Great Pyramid. Archaeologists and other scientists investigate the secrets of this enigmatic monument. Their results make this video a fascinating journey through time. They even use a robot mini-cam to penetrate the heart of the edifice. USA, 1995, 100 mins.
VHS: S26102. $19.95.
The Odyssey of Troy. For 3000 years, the legend of Troy has inspired human imagination. Now this video exposes new evidence about the fabled Trojan Horse and the illustrious figures of Helen and Achilles. Narrated by Kathleen Turner. USA, 1995, 50 mins.
VHS: S26101. $19.95.

The Ancient Romans: An Urban Lifestyle

This film traces the influence of Rome's urban society on contemporary Western ways. 12 mins.
VHS: S23705. $99.95.

The Ancient Romans: Builders of an Empire

The structures erected by this civilization reflect the political, commercial and artistic life of its people. 14 mins.
VHS: S23703. $99.95.

The Ancient Romans: People of Leisure

Great theater and sporting events filled the many Roman amphitheaters, to delight the population of this mighty civilization. 13 mins.
VHS: S23704. $99.95.

Ancient Warriors

The Discovery Channel produced this three-volume documentary about warlike societies that shaped the face of history. *Barbarian Forces* shows how warring hordes impacted peaceful peoples. Then the clash between religion and war is explored in *Soldiers of the East*. *Classical Warriors* reveals that the success of Western civilization was often won by the sword.
VHS: S24583. $49.95.

Athens and the Greek Spirit

Explore this vibrant city with this colorful tour, featuring the history, customs, food, and fun of the Greek culture. 30 mins.
VHS: S05784. $24.95.

Dawn of the Greek Gods

Here are the ultimate symbols of the heroic gods of Greek mythology—a time before light and darkness, when chaos was the only force in the universe. Includes four programs: *From Chaos to Chronos*, *Titans vs. Olympians*, *The Powers of the Olympians* and *The Reign of Zeus*. For Grades 5-10.
VHS: S14200. $159.95.

Greek Fire

A provocative, visually startling documentary series that explores the pervasive influence of ancient Greece to our lives today. Features the classicists and writers Oliver Taplin, George Steiner, Kenneth Dover and Bernard Knox. Five volumes.
(1) **Source and Myth.** 56 mins.
VHS: S14708. $24.95.
(2) **Politics and Sex.** 56 mins.
VHS: S14709. $24.95.
(3) **Tragedy and Architecture.** 56 mins.
VHS: S14710. $24.95.
(4) **Science and Art.** 56 mins.
VHS: S14711. $24.95.
(5) **Ideas and War.** 56 mins.
VHS: S14712. $24.95.
Complete five-volume set. 280 mins.
VHS: S14707. $99.95.

Heroes of the Greek Myths

Four superb dramatizations of classic Greek myths. Includes *Hercules and the Golden Apples*, *The Golden Fleece*, *Hector and Achilles* and *The Cyclops Cave*. For Grades 7-9.
VHS: S14201. $159.95.

Heroines and Goddesses of the Greek Myths

The four myths presented in this series are told to Arete, an imaginary young lady of ancient Athens. And each can be appreciated on several levels for its insights into life and its moral teaching. Includes *Atalanta*, *Athene and Arachne*, *Demeter and Persephone* and *Pandora*. For Grades 5-10.
VHS: S14202. $159.95.

The Hidden City of Petra

The long vanished Nabateans carved this rose-colored city from solid rock in the Jordanian mountains. Kathleen Turner narrates this video exploration of the haunting site which is the chief remnant of this vanished creators. From the A&E *Ancient Mysteries: New Investigations of the Unsolved* series. 50 mins.
VHS: S27003. $19.95.

King Tut: The Face of Tutankhamen

A four-part series about King Tut. The series begins in Egypt, 1922, when archeologist Howard Carter discovers the vast treasure of the boy pharaoh Tutankhamen. Host and author Christopher Frayling reveals the disruptions and misfortune that followed Carter, including the strange "curse," the death of Carter's benefactor, and the cultural influence of Tut on music, film, art, fashion and architecture. 200 mins.
VHS: S19062. $59.95.
Laser: CLV. LD72218. $69.95.

King Tut: Tomb of Treasure

This program describes archeologist Howard Carter's obsessive, eight-year search for the sacred burial chamber of King Tutankhamen, who was buried with a king's ransom upon his death when he was 18 years old. The program also looks at the ancient shrine, and goes inside the Cairo Museum and the New Orleans Museum of Art for a view of the amazing artifacts. 25 mins.
VHS: S17693. $29.95.

Macedonia, The Land of a God, Vol. 1: Aina, Aiges, Dion and Pella

This first part of the definitive series begins an in-depth look at the land north of Greece. Its powerful rulers spread Hellenic culture to the frontiers of ancient civilization. Dimitri Pandermalis, the noted Greek scholar of classical archeology, supervised this video. 90 mins.
VHS: S25650. $29.95.

Macedonia, The Land of a God, Vol. 2: Aina, Aiges, Dion and Pella

The second part of this series continues to examine both the influence and the achievements of Macedonia. Once again Dimitri Pandermalis, the noted Greek scholar of classical archeology, supervised this scholarly video. 90 mins.
VHS: S25651. $29.95.

The Mysteries and Splendors of Ancient Egypt

Travel 1,000 miles through Egypt, from the Pyramids of Giza to the Sudan border and discover the wonder of the ancient civilization that prospered there. See Giza, Luxor, Karnak, Abu Simbel, and the Egyptian Museum.
VHS: S05773. $24.95.

Mystery of the Sphinx

Charlton Heston hosts this fascinating exploration of the world's most imposing monumental sculptures. Some researchers date this work at 8,000-10,000 years old. The murky origins of the Sphinx inspire a range of theories and speculation, including the startling prediction by famed American psychic Edgar Cayce that there would be a hidden room inside this stone sentinel. 95 mins.
VHS: S21190. $29.95.

Myths of the Pharaohs

The myths found in Egyptian tomb paintings are the source for this animated short film. Through these myths the ways of ancient Egyptians are brought alive for contemporary audiences. 12 mins.
VHS: S23715. $49.95.

National Geographic Video: Egypt: Quest for Eternity

This video offers a relatively low cost guided tour of the world of ancient Egypt. It comes complete with pyramids, temples, sand and the River Nile. You bring the snacks. 60 mins.
VHS: S03675. $19.95.

National Geographic Video: In the Shadow of Vesuvius

Discover the secrets of Herculaneum and Pompeii, buried in the violent volcanic eruption of A.D. 79. 60 mins.
VHS: S09931. $19.95.

Nile: River of Gods

The Nile's ancient course has inspired mankind from time immemorial. This documentary from the *Discovery Channel* reveals the unique relationship of this river to God, man and nature through 5000 years of recorded history. 100 mins.
VHS: S26042. $19.95.

Nova—Ancient Treasures from the Deep

Amazing discoveries from a centuries-old underwater wreck and its golden cargo. 60 mins.
VHS: S14502. $14.98.

Pompeii: Buried Alive

Kathleen Turner guides viewers through the mysterious sites of a an ancient Roman city buried alive. Pompeii acts as a time capsule that preserved Roman customs and the personal traumas of the people who actually died there. From the A&E *Ancient Mysteries: New Investigations of the Unsolved* series. 50 mins.
VHS: S27002. $19.95.

The Pyramids and the Cities of the Pharaohs

Egyptologists and video artists recreate the era of Ancient Egypt. This splendid civilization created imposing monuments using simple tools that are still awe-inspiring. Both the pyramids and the Lighthouse at Alexandria are covered. 65 mins.
VHS: S24368. $29.95.

Sacred Sites: Prehistoric Monuments of Europe

Sites included in this documentary are the avenues of Megaliths at Carnac in Brittany; the nearby royal tomb at Gavrinis; the temple under the sea on the isle of Er-Lanic, in Corsica; the oldest sculptures in Europe, the Nuraghens in Sardinia; and more. 43 mins.
VHS: S22929. $29.95.

Secrets of the Mummy

A long-dead Egyptian grudgingly yields ancient secrets to a multitalented team of scientists through the first filmed autopsy of an actual mummy.
VHS: S22542. $19.95.

Seven Wonders of the Ancient World

Philo of Byzantium, approximately 2,000 years ago, compiled a list consisting of two statues, a temple, a roof-top garden, two tombs, and a lighthouse. Ancient Romans considered these to be the seven wonders of the world. Only the Great Pyramid of Giza still stands in its original form, and is the oldest wonder, built around 2560 B.C. This fascinating video reveals the story behind each wonder, and the people responsible for the construction and function of each. 60 mins.
VHS: S12292. $29.95.

The Story of Rome and Pompeii

This program uses computer technology to conjure up the spectacle and grandeur of Rome and Pompeii. The program covers the social and political atmosphere of Rome, such as the Circus Maximus and Colosseum. 60 mins.
VHS: S20189. $29.95.

Time Life's Lost Civilizations

Sam Waterston hosts this *Time Life* ten-volume series about earlier civilizations. Gripping reenactments and stunning photography help reanimate long-dead cultures from four continents. Each volume is 60 mins.
Aegean: Legacy of Atlantis. The fabled lost city of Atlantis has inspired explorers and adventurers for centuries. This volume shows how the search for the city of Troy led to discoveries confirming the existence of an Aegean civilization that dates back 6000 years. USA, 1995.
VHS: S26885. $19.99.
Africa: A History Denied. Europeans maintained that sub-Saharan Africa held no significant advanced civilizations. Now archeologists and scholars have confirmed that African empires organized trade which enriched Europe with gold and ivory. This volume explores the legacy of these forgotten people. USA, 1995.
VHS: S26886. $19.99.
China: Dynasties of Power. Imperial China began with the ancient Shang people over 4000 years ago. Often attributed to legend, contemporary scientists have now uncovered evidence of their shadowy existence. Lucky accidents involving construction crews were instrumental to this scholarly breakthrough. USA, 1995.
VHS: S26887. $19.99.
Egypt: The Quest for Immortality. This volume opens with a recreation of the 70-day embalming ceremony performed for Ramses the Great, Egypt's mightiest pharaoh. It spans 3½ millennia to show both the glory of Ancient Egypt and the blunders performed by primitive archeologists. USA, 1995.
VHS: S26888. $19.99.

Greece: A Moment of Excellence. In a brief historical period, Greece, led by Athens, gave the world trial by jury, the Symposium, the Olympic Games, and most importantly, democracy. Even the Acropolis stands as a testament to this enduring innovative spirit. USA, 1995.
VHS: S26889. $19.99.

Inca: Secrets of the Ancestors. The Incas ruled the mountainous spine of South America prior to the Spanish conquest. Their culture was only the latest of many South American civilizations dating back thousands of years. USA, 1995.
VHS: S26890. $19.99.

Maya: The Blood of Kings. Scientifically advanced, the Maya have confounded archaeologists for decades because of their mysterious disappearance. After building elaborate cities and road networks they simply abandoned these works for the jungles of Central America.
VHS: S26891. $19.99.

Mesopotamia: Return to Eden. *Time Life* was granted special access to the site on Ancient Sumer in Iraq for this volume. The Sumerians established the world's first civilization 4000 years ago. USA, 1995.
VHS: S26892. $19.99.

Rome: The Ultimate Empire. Almost 2000 years ago Ancient Rome established a transportation system with nearly a quarter of a million miles of road. This network bound an empire that stretched from Scotland to the Holy Land. Within this region, language, technology and culture shaped a world in the image of Rome itself. USA, 1995.
VHS: S26893. $19.99.

Tibet: The End of Time. Tibetan civilization faces dissolution through the ravages of the 20th century. The current Dalai Lama, Tibet's god-King, may well be the last sovereign crowned in his native land. Fortunately, his ascension to the throne in 1940 has been preserved on film. USA, 1995.
VHS: S26894. $19.99.

Tut: The Boy King

An eyewitness account of the traveling exhibit; in Egypt, 1922, archeologist Howard Carter discovered the vast riches and astonishing treasures within the tomb of the boy pharaoh Tutankhamen, known as King Tut. This work reveals the fullness of the splendor and excitement. Narrated by Orson Welles. 55 mins.
VHS: S04447. $24.95.

Tutankhamen: The Immortal Pharaoh

The University of Houston produced this singular view of the wonderfully preserved contents of this young king's tomb. 12 mins.
VHS: S23716. $49.95.

IDEAS & PHILOSOPHY

Bill Moyers' World of Ideas

Bill Moyers crosses the American landscape talking with scientists, writers, artists, philosophers and historians. This series of three tapes, adapted from the award-winning PBS series, includes conversations with novelist E.L. Doctorow, historian Barbara Tuchman, philosopher Noam Chomsky, physicist Chen Ning Yang.
Bill Moyers' World of Ideas, Volume 1: The National Soul. Bill Moyers discusses myth, morality and ethics in the American consciousness with E.L. Doctorow, Barbara Tuchman, psychiatrist Willard Gaylin, professor of religion Elaine Pagels, poet and novelist Louise Erdrich, playwright August Wilson and author Terry Brazelton. 90 mins.
VHS: S11517. $19.95.
Bill Moyers' World of Ideas, Volume 2: Crisis of Democracy. Do we have a democracy? Political philosopher Sheldon Wolin, novelist Joseph Heller, historian Henry Steele Commager, journalist and novelist Tom Wolfe, and linguist and philosopher Noam Chomsky challenge our economic and political assumptions. 90 mins.
VHS: S11518. $19.95.
Bill Moyers' World of Ideas, Volume 3: Dissolving Boundaries. Bill Moyers explores a new global reality with sociologist Robert Bellah, environmental scientist Jessica Tuchman Mathews, Nigerian novelist Chinua Achebe, science fiction writer Isaac Asimov, novelist Carlos Fuentes and anthropologist Mary Catherine Bateson. 90 mins.
VHS: S11519. $19.95.
Bill Moyers' World of Ideas, Giftpack. Contains all three volumes of the series.
VHS: S11520. $49.95.

Bill Moyers: Your Mythic Journey

Bill Moyers and Sam Keen, former editor of *Psychology Today*, show us how we can explore our lives and make sense of where we are today. Keen encourages us to discover the stories we've been living out without ever knowing it, and to ask anew the vital questions: "Who am I, where am I going, and who will go with me?" 58 mins.
VHS: S13877. $19.95.

Focus for the Future

Willis Harman, president of the Institute of Noetic Sciences and author of the book *Global Mind Change*, presents an overview of today's rapidly changing world as an era of great evolutionary opportunity. He contrasts industrial-age views with entirely new perspectives. 97 mins.
VHS: S10142. $39.95.

Greatest Thinkers Series

A series of 30-minute videotapes developed by the International Center for Creative Thinkers. Hosted by Dr. Edward de Bono of Cambridge University, the series explores the philosophy of major thinkers. In-studio demonstrations highlight various principles which are further illustrated in dramatized sequences.
Aristotle.
VHS: S11502. $49.50.
Clausewitz.
VHS: S11503. $49.50.
Columbus.
VHS: S11504. $49.95.
Descartes.
VHS: S11505. $49.50.
Freud.
VHS: S11506. $49.95.
Jesus.
VHS: S11507. $49.50.
Machiavelli.
VHS: S11508. $49.50.
Marx.
VHS: S11509. $49.50.
Moses.
VHS: S11510. $49.50.
Nietzsche.
VHS: S11511. $49.50.

Pavlov.
VHS: S11512. $49.50.
Rousseau.
VHS: S11513. $49.50.
Wiener.
VHS: S11514. $49.50.

Hero's Journey

Explore the worlds of mythology and religion, as they affect modern man, and how they shaped the life of Joseph Campbell. Campbell, famous scholar and teacher, was best known for his compelling interpretations of myth, and how the images and symbols of those myths bring logic and meaning to our lives. *Hero's Journey* portrays the development of Campbell's personal philosophies as they evolve and how they were influenced by the events of his life. Drawing on rare footage of Campbell's lectures and workshops, the film is a remarkable look at an equally remarkable man. 51 mins.
VHS: S08487. $39.95.

Jacques Lacan's Psychoanalysis Part One

A priceless document for anyone interested in contemporary thought and analysis. In interviews with Jacques-Alain Miller, Jacques Lacan, the famous French psychoanalyst called by many the French Freud, exposes with unexpected simplicity his most complex theories of the unconscious; the cure, the difference between psychoanalysis and psychotherapy, love and women. "For anyone hoping to understand the institutionalization of Freudian thought and the challenge Lacan represents, this is an essential work." French with English subtitles.
VHS: S18142. $69.95.
Benoit Jacquot, France, 1974, 60 mins.

Jung on Film

Share a special viewing experience! This compelling film interview with Carl Gustav Jung represents a rare record of an original genius. In *Jung on Film* the pioneering psychologist tells us about his collaboration with Sigmund Freud, the insights he gained from listening to his patients' dreams, and the fascinating turns taken by his own life. Dr. Richard I. Evans, a 1989 Presidential Medal of Freedom nominee, interviews Jung, giving us a rare glimpse into the life and career of this important historical figure. 77 mins.
VHS: S13738. $29.95.

Love, Death and Eros

Controversial psychiatrist and author R.D. Laing, one of the pioneers of radical psychotherapy, explores the topics of sex and love. 58 mins.
VHS: S12207. $29.95.

Man and the State: The Trial of Socrates

Sentenced to death for his ideas, Socrates' trial and sentence represents a momentous event of great significance for Western civilization. Can a society repress ideas it feels are dangerous? Does a man have a moral obligation to ignore unjust laws? 29 mins.
VHS: S23698. $79.95.

Matter of Heart: The Extraordinary Journey of C.G. Jung into the Soul of Man

An affectionate but probing documentary of the enormous contribution of Carl Gustav Jung to modern psychology, this remarkable film has become not only a boxoffice hit, but a must-see film for anyone even remotely interested in the foundations of psychoanalytic thought. USA, 90 mins.
VHS: S04719. $79.95.

Power of Myth (Joseph Campbell)

The brilliant historian/mythologist/thinker Joseph Campbell, in a dialogue with Bill Moyers, explores the foundations of culture and our being in this incredible six-part series.
First Storytellers. On myths and the environment—In this program, Campbell discusses the importance of accepting death as rebirth (as in the myth of the buffalo and the story of Christ), the rite of passage (in primitive societies), the role of mystical Shamans, and the decline of ritual in today's society. 60 mins.
VHS: S07387. $24.95.
Hero's Adventure. Long before medieval knights charged off to slay dragons, tales of heroic adventures were an integral part of all world cultures. Heroic stories are still being told. In fact, Joseph Campbell says modern technology is reflected in works such as George Lucas' *Star Wars Trilogy.* Campbell discusses how the hero's journey is possible today in everyday life, and challenges everyone to see the presence of a heroic journey in his or her own life.
VHS: S07385. $24.95.
Love and the Goddess. On women in mythology—In addition to love of God, Campbell talks about romantic love, beginning with the 12th century troubadours. According to Campbell, the troubadours were "the first ones in the West who really considered love in the same sense we think of it now, as a person-to-person relationship." Then Campbell addresses questions about the image of women—as goddess, virgin, Mother Earth. 60 mins.
VHS: S07389. $24.95.
Message of the Myth. On the relevance of myths—Campbell begins this hour comparing the creation story in genesis with creation stories form around the world. His discussion with Bill Moyers includes the question, why do we need myths? Myths, Campbell believes, are clues to the spiritual potentialities of human life. Because the world changes, religion has to be transformed and new mythologies created. Unfortunately, Campbell says, people today are stuck with old metaphors and myths that don't fit their needs. 60 mins.
VHS: S07386. $24.95.
Masks of Eternity. On divinity—In the culminating hour of the series, Campbell provides challenging insights into the concepts of God, religion and eternity, as revealed in the Christian teachings and the beliefs of Buddhists, Navajo Indians, psychologist Carl Jung, and others. 60 mins.
VHS: S07390. $24.95.
Sacrifice and Bliss. On the meaning of sacrifice and following your bliss—Campbell begins this program stressing the need for every one of us to find our sacred place—"a place of creative incubation." In the midst of today's fast-paced, technological world, we all need a sacred place, he says, to sense a true feeling for life. Campbell also discusses the role of sacrifice in myth, which he says symbolizes the necessity for rebirth. He also talks about the significance of sacrifice—in particular, a mother's sacrifice for her child, and the sacrifice in the relationship in marriage.
VHS: S07388. $24.95.
Complete Set.
VHS: S07590. $124.95.

The Simple and the Complex

Nobel Laureate Dr. Murnay Gell-Mann addresses the relationship between everyday experience and the sub-atomic realm. Chaos theory reveals that initial conditions are critical to the unfolding of large-scale events. 60 mins.
VHS: S23626. $34.95.

Soul

A complex documentary that investigates the relationship of science and religion and notes how the theoretical breakthroughs in thinking and science have opened up discussion on the origins of the universe and the inner workings of the mind. Originally produced by the BBC, this three-volume series charts the spiritual repercussions of innovative scientific reasoning, with commentary from noted physicist Stephen Hawking (*A Brief History of Time*), theoretical physicist Paul Davies and the science writer and philosopher Danah Zohar. 210 mins.
Soul 1: Soul of the Universe.
VHS: S18306. $19.95.
Soul 2: The Evolving Soul.
VHS: S18307. $19.95.
Soul 3: Silicon Soul.
VHS: S18308. $19.95.
Soul: The Complete Set.
VHS: S18309. $59.85.

Spirit and Nature (Bill Moyers)

Bill Moyers hosts this PBS special on religion and the environment. Six representatives of various spiritual backgrounds gather at Middlebury College in Vermont to exchange ideas. The speakers include his Holiness Tenzin Gyatso, the 14th Dalai Lama of Tibet, a Native American elder of the Onondaga Nation, and many more. With music by the Paul Winter Consort.
VHS: S14488. $29.95.
Gail Pellet, USA, 1991, 58 mins.

Wisdom of the Dream: C.G. Jung and His Work in the World

This three-part series traces Jung's work and message throughout his life—his split with Freud, the major works published on dreams and the psychology of religion, his travels, in particular to New Mexico, and his discovery of the collective conscious. The director uses authentic visual references of Jung's home and consulting room and the film contains previously undiscovered home movies shot during Jung's travels to Africa, plus an interview recorded in 1956.
Wisdom of the Dream Vol. 1.
VHS: S10303. $29.95.
Wisdom of the Dream Vol. 2.
VHS: S10311. $29.95.
Wisdom of the Dream Vol. 3.
VHS: S10312. $29.95.

With a Silent Mind

A richly detailed biographical portrait of Krishnamurti's life and teachings produced by Evelyne Blay. The film blends Krishnamurti's own deep insights with the impressions of scientists, authors, educators, teachers, artists and friends, and with extraordinary archival footage from India, England and America in the 20's and 30's. 60 mins.
VHS: S12482. $29.95.

The World Within

A new and enlightening film focusing on Jung's Red Book, in which he recorded images from his unconscious. These are creations, Jung comments, "which have carried me out of time into seclusion; out of the present into timelessness." A fascinating glimpse into the philosophy and personal life of C.G. Jung.
VHS: S14747. $79.95.
Suzanne Wagner, USA, 1990, 80 mins.

The World's Philosophies

Dr. Huston Smith, emeritus professor of philosophy at Syracuse, points out the three essential relationships of existence: the relationship to nature, other people and ourselves. This understanding helps him synthesize various world philosophies. 60 mins.
VHS: S23631. $34.95.

NATIVE AMERICAN CULTURE

500 Nations

Kevin Costner hosts and produced this extraordinary eight-volume series about the many peoples who lived in North and Central America long before the arrival of Europeans. This series was filmed on location from Central American jungles to the Canadian Arctic. Computer animation also is deployed to recreate the actual history of this land. Each volume is 47 mins.
VHS: S24383. $139.98.
Laser: LD74900. $139.92.

Ancient America: Indians of the Northwest

Wes Studi, the famed Native American Cherokee who played in *Last of the Mohicans, Geronimo: An American Legend* and *Dances with Wolves*, narrates this in-depth look at the original inhabitants of the Northwest. 60 mins.
VHS: S21601. $59.95.

Ancient America: Indians of the Southwest

In America's beautiful Southwestern lands Native Americans have left traces of their culture dating back thousands of years. Join Wes Studi, the "scene stealer" from a number of recent successful Hollywood Westerns including *Dances with Wolves*, for a fascinating look at the peoples who shaped this unique landscape. 60 mins.
VHS: S21602. $59.95.

Ancient Indian Cultures of Northern Arizona

Explore the ruins of ancient Indian cultures as you wander the mesas and deserts of Arizona. Visit five national monuments: Montezuma Castle, Wupatki, Tuzigoot, Walnut Canyon, and Sunset Crater, and discover the Sinagua and Anasazi civilizations. 30 minutes.
VHS: S02469. $29.95.

Art of Navajo Weaving

Explores the traditional art of Navajo weaving and its origins, with visits to a contemporary Navajo weaving family, showing how artists create magnificent pieces of art. 56 mins.
VHS: S08304. $29.95.

Bear Tribe Storytelling

A fresh collection of Native American folktales and legends, related by Moriah Vecchia, a renowned storyteller and songstress. 60 mins.
VHS: S18094. $34.95.

Brooke Medicine Eagle: Dancing Awake the Drum

Brooke will lead the viewer through the transforming effects of the Sacred Circle. Dancing, singing and drumming are just some of the necessary preparations needed to begin this spiritual journey. Brooke will explain how to prepare for the changing earth. 60 mins.
VHS: S21231. $29.95.

Contemporary and Native American Readings

Richard Chamberlain's gentle creative spirit shines as he recites some consciousness raising excerpts from a work by Joseph Campbell. He also includes an address to the President of the United States by Native Americans reminding us of our obligation as protectors and wardens of the earth. 82 mins.
VHS: S10219. $29.95.

The Dakota Conflict

The personalities, events and conflicts that were a part of the war for America's Great Plains are depicted in this program narrated by Garrison Keillor and Floyd Red Crow Westerman. 60 mins.
VHS: S19630. $19.95.

Dancing Awake the Drum

Brooke Medicine Eagle takes part in the transformation that occurs in dancing and drumming the Sacred Circle. 60 mins.
VHS: S20159. $29.95.

Daughters of the Anasazi

The traditional pottery of the Southwest is enjoying a new popularity, and now viewers can see how it is made. Filmed in New Mexico in 1990, this unique program presents a detailed examination of ancient techniques—explaining each step of the fascinating processes. 28 mins.
VHS: S14591. $24.95.

Discovering American Indian Music

The songs and dances of Native Americans comprise a rich musical tradition. Ceremonial functions and the social significance of these musical works are discussed. The pieces are presented by performers in authentic costumes. 24 mins.
VHS: S23508. $49.95.

The Divided Trail/Walk in Balance

Three Chippewa tribe members who were lured away from their home to the big city are the subjects of this moving documentary. They struggle with the historic grievances that have hurt their people as well as the modern injustices of alcoholism, mental illness, and systematic discrimination that continue to plague the first Americans.
VHS: S20734. $89.95.
Jerry Aronson, USA, 1978, 33 mins.

Dragonfly's Tale

When the Ashiwi tribe celebrates abundant food with a joyous food fight the Corn maidens are disappointed and show their disdain with a poor harvest and famine. The villagers leave to find a better life and leave two small children behind. They fashion the first firefly from a withered cornstalk, which flies to the Corn maidens. Soon the plentiful harvest returns, as do the villagers, who are wiser and kinder.
VHS: S21883. $44.95.

End of the Trail

During the great Westward migration, Native Americans were continuously and rapaciously displaced for a greedy, young nation. This is a sobering if honest account of a tragic time in the history of the US. 60 mins.
VHS: S23058. $19.95.

The Faithkeeper

Bill Moyers and Oren Lyons, chief of the Turtle Clan of the Onondaga Nation, discuss ancient Native American prophecies of the ecological disasters we now face, recount how democracy was modelled on Indian confederations, and reveal the legends of the Turtle Clan. 1991, 58 mins.
VHS: S14576. $19.95.

Feminine— Ancient Vision, Modern Wisdom

Wabun Wind of the Bear Tribe draws on her own life experiences as well as years of research to discuss matriarchy and the beginning of patriarchy to elucidate not only the origin of anger between men and women, but also shed new light upon the subjects of women's power, the moon cycles and menstrual cycles, stereotyping of women, sexuality, relationships and raising children. 77 mins.
VHS: S07725. $34.95.

Four Corners of Earth

The roles and culture of Seminole women are documented in this unique portrait of vanishing Seminole life. Traditional values and changes brought about by the 20th century are seen through the eyes of women living on the Seminole reservations in South Florida.
VHS: S06959. $59.95.

From the Heart of the World: The Elder Brother's Warning

Deep in the mountains of Colombia, the descendants of an ancient Tairona priesthood still rule. In cities more than a thousand years old, the ascetic Kogi tribe has preserved the culture and concepts of an advanced civilization wiped out by the conquistadors. This is the original, uncut, feature-length version of the edited *Nature* program shown on PBS. USA, 88 mins.
VHS: S15435. $29.95.

Fulfilling the Vision
The Lakota generation of the 70's and 80's has its own story, related to the continuity of Lakota spirituality. Beginning in 1990, this video examines the social and political reality of this people today. It goes on to relate the lessons contained in the Vision Quest and the Sun Dance, lessons that could benefit anyone. 30 mins.
VHS: S21595. $29.95.

Geronimo
A true story which tells how a Native American brave becomes the most feared Apache war chief. He was legendary for the ferocious battles he fought on behalf of his people and his amazing ability to dodge capture by the US army. Originally shown on the Turner Home Entertainment channel. 102 mins.
VHS: S20637. $92.98.

Geronimo and the Apache Resistance
In 1886, the United States government mobilized 5,000 men to capture one man: the legendary Apache, Geronimo. In this moving testament to the human spirit, we follow Geronimo through decades of injustices. This is a missing piece of American history that tells the truth about the settling of the frontier. 60 mins.
VHS: S13807. $19.95.

Geronimo: The Last Renegade
In this two-tape set, the story of competing legendary frontiersmen is told in detail. Geronimo avoided capture by the U.S. Cavalry after inspiring his people to fight for their lands. *Custer and the 7th Cavalry* tells the story of this flamboyant and eccentric military man who met his fate at Wounded Knee. Both videos are 50 mins.
VHS: S21548. $19.95.

Hawk, I'm Your Brother
Will Rogers Jr. narrates this story of Native American culture based on the book by Byrd Baylor. Young Rudy Soto wants to fly without the expense of taking an airplane into the wild blue yonder. He seeks advice from a captured red-tailed hawk for natural flying tips. This children's story was winner of a Peace Pipe Award. USA, 25 mins.
VHS: S13294. $14.99.

Her Mother Before Her: Winnebago Women's Stories of Their Mothers & Grandmothers
Contemporary Native American women talk about their childhoods and their families. Despite cultural differences, the experiences of these women are profoundly universal. 22 mins. Resource guide available.
Video.
VHS: S25760. $95.00.
Resource Guide.
VHS: S25773. $20.00.

Hopi Prayer for Peace
This video contains the latest efforts by the elders of Hotevilla, of the Hopi Nation, to reach out to the world community in an attempt for universal peace. The Hopi, whose very name means "peace", have been attempting since the conclusion of World War II to address the nations of the world and deliver their message, which is also a warning. 27 mins.
VHS: S07728. $39.95.

How Beaver Stole Fire
In this sand animation short, a Native American tale about the origin of fire is beautifully realized. 12 mins.
VHS: S23507. $39.95.

Howard Terpning: The Storyteller
Howard Terpning's paintings function as visual stories depicting Native Americans. Along with the works, this video shows the artist at work. His compositions offer a glimpse of a lifestyle rarely seen elsewhere. 30 mins.
VHS: S26806. $49.95.

I Will Fight No More Forever
In the 19th century, the United States government made 1,000 treaties with Indian tribes throughout the country. They honored less than 100. *I Will Fight No More Forever* is the tragic story from this time, about the Nez Perce and their 1,700-mile, 108-day fighting retreat, led by the courageous Chief Joseph. Highly recommended, this docu-drama is a rare and accurate portrayal of the plight of the 19th century American Indian. With James Whitmore, Sam Elliott and Ned Romero.
VHS: S12764. $29.95.
David Wolper, USA, 109 mins.

In the Land of the War Canoes
Edward S. Curtis devoted his life to documenting the world of dwindling Native American cultures. In this film, Curtis told a story of love and revenge among the Kwakiutl Indians of Vancouver Island. Curtis spent three years with the Kwakiutl to meticulously recreate their way of life before the white man came. In addition to the magnificent painted war canoes, the film pictures authentic costumes, ceremonial dances and religious rituals. Silent with soundtrack from 1972 restoration.
VHS: S16431. $39.95.
Laser: LD71816. $29.95.
Edward S. Curtis, USA/Canada, 1914, 47 mins.

Incident at Oglala
Michael Apted's documentary about Leonard Peltier, the Native American activist who's served more than 15 years in federal prison for the murder of two FBI agents, despite evidence suggesting prosecutorial misconduct, perjury and other testimony contradicting the government's case. Narrated and produced by Robert Redford, with much of its research derived from Peter Matthiessen's *In the Spirit of Crazy Horse.*
VHS: S17442. $19.98.
Michael Apted, USA, 1991, 92 mins.

The Indian & His Homeland: American Images, 1590-1876
This video features the art of noted explorer artists such as Catlin, Bodmer, Audubon and Catesby, providing a 300-year survey of the impact of European civilization on the New World—in particular, its devastating effect on the lives and cultures of the American Indians and native wildlife. USA, 30 mins.
VHS: S15080. $29.95.

Indians of North America, Collection I
Based on the book by Chelsea House, this ten-volume series describes the histories and cultures of America's native peoples through examinations of their music, crafts and ceremonies. Archival footage and photographs help uncover the truth behind the myths and stereotypes that obscure the original inhabitants of this land. 30 minutes each.
The Apache.
VHS: S20990. $39.95.
The Aztec.
VHS: S20991. $39.95.
The Cherokee.
VHS: S20992. $39.95.
The Cheyenne.
VHS: S20993. $39.95.
The Comanche.
VHS: S20994. $39.95.
The Iroquois.
VHS: S20995. $39.95.
The Maya.
VHS: S20996. $39.95.
The Navajo.
VHS: S20997. $39.95.
The Seminole.
VHS: S20998. $39.95.
The Yankton Sioux.
VHS: S20999. $39.95.
Indians of North America, Collection I, Set. Includes *The Cherokee, The Cheyenne, The Comanche, The Iroquois, The Maya, The Navajo, The Seminole, The Yankton Sioux, The Apache* and *The Aztec.*
VHS: S23649. $399.50.

Indians of North America, Collection II
The well-regarded book from Chelsea House Publishers inspired this video series about Native Americans. Both historical and contemporary struggles are examined by consulting historians and living tribe members. This series tackles the myths and misconceptions that have long obscured the truth about the first Americans. Each episode is 30 minutes long.
The Chinook.
VHS: S23638. $39.95.
The Creek.
VHS: S23639. $39.95.
The Crow.
VHS: S23640. $39.95.
A History of Native Americans.
VHS: S23641. $39.95.
The Huron.
VHS: S23642. $39.95.
The Lenape.
VHS: S23643. $39.95.
The Menominee.
VHS: S23645. $39.95.
The Narragansett (Enishkeetompauog).
VHS: S23645. $39.95.
The Potawatomi (Bode wad mi).
VHS: S23646. $39.95.
The Pueblo.
VHS: S23647. $39.95.
The Ten-Volume Set.
VHS: S23648. $399.50.

Ishi, The Last Yahi
In this chronicle, narrated by Linda Hunt, the story of Ishi unfolds. He was the sole surviving member of the Yahis of California, a Native American tribe exterminated by the U.S. After 40 years alone and near starvation, he left the land and entered the world of the white man. Photos, archival footage, recordings and commentary are used in this indictment of "manifest destiny". B&W, 60 mins.
VHS: S23052. $19.95.

Joy Haro
As a member of the Muscogee (Creek) nation, the poet Joy Haro draws on the experience of her people. This winner of the American Book Award read from *She Had Some Horses* and *In Mad Love and War* in Laguna Beach on February 18, 1989. Lewis MacAdams conducted the interview. From the *Lannan Literary Videos* series. 60 mins.
VHS: S27118. $19.95.

Lakota Woman
Irene Bedard makes her screen debut in this drama about the actual Native American protest at Wounded Knee in 1973. A Native American cast gives this film great passion, enabling it to depict the struggle against silence waged by a united group of 2000 who vowed never to be silenced again.
VHS: S23942. $79.98.
Laser: LD74917. $39.99.
Frank Pierson, USA, 1994, 113 mins.

Life in the Woodlands Before the White Man Came
Through re-enactments the day-to-day life of Native Americans is demonstrated in this video. 12 mins.
VHS: S23533. $49.95.
Laser: LD74764. $99.95.

Live and Remember
The Lakota world view is detailed in four sections, entitled *Song & Dance, Oral Tradition, Living Today* and *Medicine & Spirit World.* Superb performances along with photos and archival drawings are interspersed with information about this Native American people. Shot entirely on location at the Rosebud Reservation, South Dakota. 30 mins.
VHS: S21596. $29.95.

Maria! Indian Pottery of San Ildefonso
Indian pottery maker Maria Martinez demonstrates the traditional Indian ways of making pottery. Beginning with the spreading of sacred corn, you will see gathering and mixing of clay, construction and decorating of pottery and building of the firing mound. 27 mins.
VHS: S06698. $29.95.

Mesa Verde
Visit the world-famous cliff dwellings of Mesa Verde to study the ruins of an ancient Indian civilization that flourished for 1,000 years and then vanished forever. 23 mins.
VHS: S06489. $29.95.

Monument Valley: Navajo Homeland
Discover the majestic beauty of Monument Valley and the mystical bond between the Navajo and their ancient homeland. This is a spectacular land shaped over eons of time, a land of vast open spaces and towering buttes, of natural arches and prehistoric ruins. The culture and craft of the Navajo men and women is also examined. USA, 30 mins.
VHS: S15081. $29.95.

The Moon's Prayer: Wisdom of the Ages
Native Americans preserved the beauty and utility of the American Northwest for centuries. Then settlers invaded these lands and transformed them through deforestation and the proliferation of dams. Today Native Americans are again fighting to preserve and in some cases restore the vitality of this region, using age-old techniques and modern methods. 51 mins.
VHS: S21574. $85.00.

More Than Bows and Arrows
Finally, a documentary that charts how the achievements of Native Americans have contributed to the shape of modern North America. From religion to science, and even architecture, the ingenuity of ancient ways have informed and built the contemporary world. 60 mins.
VHS: S20732. $29.95.

Mountain Wolf Woman: 1884-1960
A Winnebago woman's own words are used to tell the story of her life. Her granddaughter, Naomi Russell, narrates. This video is based on the book by anthropologist Nancy Oestreich Lurie. 17 mins. Resource guide available.
Resource Guide.
VHS: S25775. $20.00.
Video.
VHS: S25762. $95.00.

Native American Herbology for Beginners
Holistic health educator Kay Moon Dreamer offers some advice for the gathering and use of various native herbs. 55 mins.
VHS: S20155. $24.95.

Native American Indian Artist Series
A profile of seven contemporary artists representing diverse backgrounds and styles. Available individually, or order the complete set of six tapes at a savings.
Charles Loloma. The world famous Hopi jeweler displays some of his most stunning work, and discusses his heritage. His interests, inside and outside the reservation, are revealed in his art, which uses only materials indigenous to his homeland: iron, wood, ivory, coal, turquoise, lapis lazuli and shell. 29 mins.
VHS: S15755. $49.95.
Fritz Scholder. Fritz Scholder, a California Mission Indian, creates prints and paintings that depict today's Indian caught between ancient tradition and modern society. 29 mins.
VHS: S15756. $49.95.
Helen Hardin. Helen Hardin attempts to integrate two parts of herself, the Indian and the artist, painting sophisticated and colorful geometric patterns and traditional motifs of dancers, deer, the sun and seasons. 29 mins.
VHS: S15757. $49.95.
Medicine Flower and Lonewolf. Two potters from Santa Clara Pueblo in New Mexico have revived and extended the traditional forms and techniques of their pre-Columbian ancestors. 29 mins.
VHS: S15758. $49.95.
R.C. Gorman. R.C. Gorman, a Navajo painter and printmaker, is shown in his Taos, New Mexico studio working on one of a suite of paintings dedicated to the Navajo woman. 29 mins.
VHS: S15759. $49.95.
Allan Houser. A Chiricahua-Apache, Allan Hauser creates stone, wood and bronze homages to the American Indian. As he works, Hauser talks of his personal life and beliefs, and explains how his heritage has contributed to his art. 29 mins.
VHS: S15760. $49.95.
Complete set. 6 tapes.
VHS: S15754. $250.00.

Native American Prophecy & Ceremony
Gain insight into the Native American sacraments of the peace pipe, sweat lodge, and ritual dancing. Honored medicine men present challenging prophecies regarding how our civilization must return to a way of life in harmony with nature and the Great Spirit or face destruction. 25 mins.
VHS: S10394. $24.95.

Native American Ritual: Healing Crystals
Oh Shinnah Fastwolf explains the use of healing crystals such as amethyst, garnet, and quartz in Native American Ritual. The force fields such gems set up can protect one's psychic center from inharmonious vibrations in the environment and draw out negative energies. Concludes with her song about the need to maintain the ancient ways of her people. 24 mins.
VHS: S06924. $29.95.

Native American Ritual: Healing Way Song
Oh Shinnah Fastwolf, a healer and entertainer of Mohawk and Apache ancestry, shows the methods of sensitizing the hands to the field of psychic energy that flows between them. She teaches an ancient song, which includes a healing rite never before permitted to be recorded. 24 mins.
VHS: S06925. $29.95.

Native American Sweat Lodge Ceremony
Experience the sacred Native American sweat lodge ceremony from beginning to end. Learn about the health and spiritual benefits that Native Americans have known for centuries. 90 mins.
VHS: S10392. $39.95.

The Native Americans
This six-part series of 40-minute long videos tells the story of America's original inhabitants. Native Americans are themselves the writers and the directors, as well as the featured subjects, of this series. Set against a backdrop of majestic lands, five distinct geographic regions (the Northeast, tribal peoples of Northwest, tribes of the Southeast, the Great Plains and natives of the Southwest) emerge, each with its own distinctive beauty and traditions. Robbie Robertson wrote the original score.
VHS: S25752. $59.98.

Native Americans—An Overview
American Indian traditions are explored through the rituals of a contemporary powwow. Through dance and the elaborate design of costumes, Native Americans reenact the daily life of their ancestors. 30 mins.
VHS: S20270. $49.95.

Native Indian Folklore
Five stories from the National Film Board of Canada. *Christmas at Moose Factory* shows Christmas in the Native American Cree settlement presented through children's drawings; *Salmon People* is a West Coast Legend of the Salmon Princess, contrasted with today's native-owned fishing boats and canneries (25 mins.); *The Man, the Snake and the Fox* presents a puppet enactment of an Ojibwa tale; *Medoonak the Stormmaker* presents an exciting stage performance of an ancient Micmac legend about taming the weather; and *Summer Legend* is an animated version of the Micmac legend that explains the cycle of the seasons. Ages 6-12. 71 minutes.
VHS: S24775. $99.00.

Native Land: Nomads of the Dawn
The highly regarded Native American author Jamake Highwater traces the steps of the nomads who discovered the Americas. These peoples created complex social structures where nature, the animal world and the cosmos were intimately entwined in widely held moral beliefs and ideals. 57 mins.
VHS: S27529. $19.98.

Navajo Code Talkers
Shortly after the onset of World War II, Phillip Johnson, the son of Navajo reservation missionaries, realized that a code in Navajo would be impenetrable to the Japanese. Twenty-nine Navajos were recruited to work as radio operators, thereby providing the US war effort with a top-secret communications link. This film tells their story of service and heroism. 27 mins.
VHS: S22801. $29.95.

Nomadic Indians of the West
Across the majestic wilds of the West, Native Americans have lived, hunted and traveled for centuries. In this documentary Wes Studi hosts the concluding episode. 60 mins.
VHS: S22880. $59.95.

On the Pow Wow Trail
On the Pow Wow Trail is an entertaining and informative focus on the preservation of Native American customs, traditional dress and dance. Follow young Chad Killscrow and friend Mike Roberts as they travel from pow wow to pow wow on the majestic plains of Oklahoma, New Mexico, Colorado and Montana, and recreate ceremonies established centuries before them. 45 mins.
VHS: S15850. $14.95.

Pablita Velarde: An Artist and Her People
Pablita Velarde is a Native American artist who paints the history of her ancient people. Found materials and other materials supply her pigments. Her work ensures future generations will know the vital traditions and legends of her tribe. 20 mins.
VHS: S26805. $49.95.

Paha Sapa: The Struggle for the Black Hills
The story of the Lakota Sioux Indians' past and present struggle for the Black Hills of South Dakota is movingly portrayed in this documentary, which was nominated for an Emmy Award as Best Documentary of the year. 60 mins. 1994.
VHS: S23331. $29.95.

People of the 7th Fire
Native American oral traditions, teachings and prophecies reveal overlooked ways to care for our selves and our environment. This is a collaborative message from many North American native nations that emphasizes co-existence with the earth. A fascinating and comprehensive look at Native Americans in today's society. 55 mins.
VHS: S27657. $24.95.

Peyote Road
The United States Supreme Court denied indigenous peoples the right to use peyote in their centuries-old rituals. Religious freedom is at stake. This documentary explores the effects of this decision and its implications for one of the Western Hemisphere's oldest religions. Peter Coyote narrates. USA, 1993, 59 mins.
VHS: S26895. $29.99.

Picuris Indians
This visually stunning production examines the unrehearsed moments of the Picuris Indians at the location of their ancient pueblo, nestled in a "shangri-la" set in the rock formations of the Picuris mountains of north central New Mexico. 60 mins.
VHS: S20317. $150.00.

The Primal Mind
Jamake Highwater's book of the same name caused a sensation for its insights regarding the different perceptions experienced by Native Americans and Americans of European descent. This documentary shows how Native American techniques and customs influenced and transformed the work of famous artists like Jackson Pollock, Martha Graham, Pablo Picasso and others. 57 mins.
VHS: S27528. $19.98.

Quest for Wisdom
Bear Heart, a traditional elder, medicine man and spiritual and tribal leader, discusses the philosophy of Native people, detailing their relationship and intimate connection to nature and the interconnection between ceremony and daily life. 50 mins.
VHS: S18035. $24.95.

Return to the Sacred Hoop
Native American grandfather Wallace Black Elk, a Lakota healer, teacher and leader of the new generation of Earth Warriors, offers insights and messages about achieving harmony and balance. 45 mins.
VHS: S20160. $29.95.

Rolling Thunder: Healer of Meta Tantay
Rolling Thunder is the controversial medicine man and prophetic Cherokee healer who worked with the Grateful Dead as a spiritual leader. Broadcasted on a book with this rock group that brought him widespread notoriety in the 1970's. Now his spiritual ways, including his shocking prophecies for the future, have been updated for the 90's in this fascinating video. 58 mins.
VHS: S21598. $19.95.

Santa Fe: Artists of New Mexico
Native American artists along with other artists are featured on this video. R.C. Gorman, Allan Houser, Jacqueline Shutiva, Marie Romero, Jemez Pueblo, Bunny Tobias, Charles Greeley, Fred Prescott, Paul Lutonsky and David Dear Silversmith are included. 46 mins.
VHS: S26803. $49.95.

The Search for Ancient Americans
A revealing documentary about the long-term archeological finds of five separate discoveries that have helped scientists to unlock the mysteries of ancient civilizations.
VHS: S17730. $14.98.

The Shadow Catcher: Edward S. Curtis and the North American Indian
Photographer, anthropologist and filmmaker Edward S. Curtis forged a tradition among American eccentric genius that worked its way out of the frontier and into the mainstream of the 20th century. Spending over three decades with Native Americans (1896-1930), Curtis completed the most intensive anthropological study ever taken with over 40,000 photographs, 20 volumes of text and some of the earliest motion pictures capturing Native American religious ceremonies.
VHS: S16619. $29.95.
Teri McLuhan, USA, 1976, 88 mins.

Sioux Legends
Native Sioux act out the legends of their philosophy and religion against the backdrop of the Black Hills and the Badlands of South Dakota. The forces of nature are central to their world view. 20 mins.
VHS: S23733. $49.95.

Sisters & Friends: Winnebago Women's Stories
Contemporary Native American women share their stories with each other and, through video, with the viewer. This video is filled with love and laughter. 15 mins. Resource guide available.
Video.
VHS: S25766. $95.00.
Resource Guide.
VHS: S25779. $20.00.

Sun Bear on Power
During this time of earth changes, Sun Bear emerges as a powerful figure who has successfully guided many people who are in search of fuller and happier lives. Sun Bear is a man of Ojibwa descent who has studied with medicine people from many tribes and traditions. In this video, he teaches gentleness as a source of great strength. "In past generations, people knew how to find and follow their path to power. Today we have been taught to give our power away to a society that often misuses it." Produced by the Bear Tribe. 65 mins.
VHS: S06258. $49.95.

Sun Bear: Earth Changes
"The Earth Changes prophesied by many Native traditions have already begun. People need look no further than the daily news to see proof of this. These times of great change are a time of cleansing, and of moving forward. The people who are going to survive the changes are people who can walk in a sacred manner, who live in harmony with each other and the earth. This is what we are being prepared for by the changes." (Sun Bear). Sun Bear is a man of Ojibwa descent who has studied with medicine people, whose life forms a bridge between Native and non-Native cultures. Produced by the Bear Tribe. 65 mins.
VHS: S06259. $49.95.

The Sun Dagger
A fascinating documentary about the discovery of the celestial calendar of New Mexico's ancient Anasazi tribe. With commentary written by Joseph Campbell, the show examines the ethnographic evidence of this vibrant culture that thrived in the desolate desert environment more than 1000 years ago. Narrated by Robert Redford. 60 mins.
VHS: S19113. $19.95.

Tahtonka
Buffalo represented a key element of life for the Native Americans who lived on the Great Plains. In this historical re-enactment, the culture of these original Americans is examined, beginning before the European invasion and continuing up until the Wounded Knee massacre. 30 mins.
VHS: S23732. $49.95.

They Lied to You in School
Mohawk elder Ray Fadden, director of the Six Nations Indian Museum in New York State, sets the record straight about the valuable contributions made to civilization by indigenous people. His vivid talk covers agriculture, medicine and the origins of democracy—facts literally "written out" of history. 30 mins.
VHS: S18095. $24.95.

Thirteen Moons on Turtle's Back
Subtitled *A Native American Year of Moons*, Abenaki Indian Joseph Bruchac and poet Jonathan London discuss the history of Native American legend and mythology, focused on the belief of the thirteen moons of the year. The writers contrast legends within different Native American tribes to show how the cultures identified the cycles of the moon with the seasons.
VHS: S20002. $44.95.

Thunderheart
Michael Apted's documentary-like feature was inspired from actual events in the mid '70s. This work stars Val Kilmer as a half-Sioux FBI agent assigned to investigate the murder of a militant Native American in the South Dakota, Oglala nation. He uncovers a possible government conspiracy, appalling social conditions, and tribal and ethnic warfare between pro-government Indians and the progressive, traditionalists. With Sam Shepard, Fred Ward, and Graham Greene as a reservation police officer.
VHS: S17220. $19.95.
Laser: LD71578. $34.95.
Michael Apted, USA, 1992, 119 mins.

Tribal Legacies: Last Stand at Little Big Horn
A historical corrective to the events and circumstances behind one of the most famous and inaccurately reported battles in history. The program invokes the views of the Lakota Sioux, Cheyenne and Crow, developed through oral histories and drawings. 60 mins.
VHS: S18358. $19.95.

Vision of the Medicine Wheel (with Sun Bear)
Experience the Medicine Wheel Gathering with an understanding of the true essence of Sun Bear's vision. Inspired by his insight into the Earth Change prophecies and desire to create personal and planetary healing, this program is filled with interviews on ceremony, healing and Earth Changes, along with a dedication to the seventh generation. Features the ceremonies, drums and songs of Brooke Medicine Eagle, Wallace Black Elk, Brant Secunda and major Native and Earth Teachers from around the world. 60 mins.
VHS: S18096. $29.95.

Vision of the Sacred Pipe (with Wallace Black Elk)
This Lakota/Scottish Elder from South Dakota began his reign as a hero of the New Earth Warrior during Wounded Knee in the 1970's. In this program, he takes the viewer into the most sacred of ceremonies of the Cannupa (Sacred Pipe) and into the Inipi (sweat lodge). 60 mins.
VHS: S18090. $24.95.

Walk in Balance
Sun Bear, a Chippewa medicine man, writer, teacher and philosopher, adopts his teachings and practices in developing a vital, well-balanced, stress-free life through traditional and contemporary healing techniques. 60 mins.
VHS: S18091. $34.95.

Winnebago Women: Songs & Stories
Contemporary Native American women share their traditions in art and music through this video. The result is a moving tape, perfect for all types of libraries. 19 mins. Resource guide available.
Video.
VHS: S25768. $95.00.
Resource Guide.
VHS: S25781. $20.00.

Wiping the Tears of Seven Generations
This video relates the story of how the Lakota Nation mourned the loss of its loved ones for 100 years until the mid-80's, when, inspired by dreams and visions of unity and spiritual awakening, a group of 300 Lakota horseback riders began to bring their people out of mourning through a traditional ceremony they called "Wiping the Tears". Winner of the 1991 American Indian Film Festival "Best Video" Award. 50 mins.
VHS: S18092. $29.95.

Wolf Nation
The Northern Arapaho Wolf Society performs their native "Wolf Dance" in celebration of the historic reintroduction of the wolf to Yellowstone National Park. Called one of the greatest triumphs of this decade, it was filmed by world-renowned wildlife photographer Jim Brandenburg. 30 mins.
VHS: S27656. $19.95.

Yanomami
Considered the last intact indigenous culture in the Americas, the Yanomami are now threatened by the encroachment of gold mining, development and disease. This documentary provides an in depth look at the Yanomami with the help of a group of anthropologists, doctors and journalists. 58 mins.
VHS: S21572. $95.00.

RELIGION

According to Kossoff
David Kossoff, master storyteller and Biblical scholar, magically recounts some of the best-loved stories of the Old Testament—simply, earnestly. Phenomenally successful on British television, this series is the antithesis of overblown Biblical epics.
Story of Adam and Eve.
VHS: S05570. $19.95.
Story of David.
VHS: S05573. $19.95.
Story of Elijah.
VHS: S05579. $19.95.
Story of Gideon.
VHS: S05575. $19.95.
Story of Jacob.
VHS: S05571. $19.95.
Story of Jonah.
VHS: S05572. $19.95.
Story of Joshua.
VHS: S05577. $19.95.
Story of Ruth.
VHS: S05574. $19.95.
Story of Samson.
VHS: S05576. $19.95.
Story of Samuel.
VHS: S05578. $19.95.
Story of Tobias.
VHS: S05580. $19.95.

Ancient Mysteries
Using modern technology, scientific analysis, high-tech evidence and recent archaeological developments, the films in the *Ancient Mysteries* series are on the cutting edge of discovery.
Ark of the Covenant. This real-life search for the Ark of the Covenant is based on new interpretations of the Bible. The possible whereabouts of this ancient artifact remain a mystery that must still be solved. This tape offers new answers to the age-old question: whatever became of this sacred repository? 50 mins.
VHS: S21687. $19.95.
Enigma of the Dead Sea Scrolls. In 1947, a shepherd boy found the Dead Sea Scrolls. Originally hailed as a window to the origins of Christianity, they were soon removed from public scrutiny. This is the story of the discovery, authenticity and cover-up that make these artifacts so intriguing. 50 mins.
VHS: S23106. $19.95.
Shroud of Turin. This artifact is held by many to be the burial shroud of Jesus Christ. Investigations into the history and the composition of this shroud are documented on this video. Conflicting results may well ensure that the true nature of this cloth remains a mystery. USA, 1995, 50 mins.
VHS: S26100. $19.95.
Who Wrote the Bible?: Probing the Eternal Mysteries Behind the Origins of the Holy Scriptures. Richard Kiley and Jean Simmons host this serious documentary filmed on location in the Holy Land. Leading Biblical scholars discuss the latest scientific research on the world's most widely read book and tackle questions regarding Moses, the Torah, the Dead Sea Scrolls and more. The theological insights and scientific facts on the Holy Scriptures will leave the faithful inspired and the scholarly fascinated. Two-volume set. 1994-1995, 150 mins.
VHS: S27203. $29.95.

Ancient Tales from a Promised Land
In this adaptation of 14 Old Testament stories, shot on location in the Holy Land, the gifted British actor Tony Robinson brings a storyteller's flair and passion to each staged telling.
Vol. I: Joshua Smashes Jericho/Joshua in Trouble Valley. In the first story, the Israelites, led by Joshua, emerge from the desert after 40 years to assume control of the land of Canaan. Joshua's strike against Canaanite towns is interrupted by his difficulties with a dishonest soldier and a corrupt mayor. 30 mins.
VHS: S18298. $19.95.
Vol. II: Deborah and the Headbanger/Gideon Gets His Wolly Wet. The Israelites turn to Deborh to repel the Canaanite offensive. In the second story, Gideon destroys the Canaanites' Corn Goddess. 30 mins.
VHS: S18299. $19.95.
Vol. III: Gideon's Exploding Pickle Pots/Samson Gets Knotted. Under the direction of Gideon, the disadvantaged Israelite army routs the Canaanites, awaiting the landing of the Philistines. In the second program, the able bodied though weak minded Samson must deal with the repercussions of marrying a Philistine woman. 30 mins.
VHS: S18300. $19.95.
Vol. IV: Samson Gets a Haircut/Samuel and the Spooky Goxbox. Delilah betrays Samson by revealing the nature of his superhuman strength. In the second story, Samuel is crowned the leader of the Israelites, and the Ark of the Covenant is stolen by the Philistines. 30 mins.
VHS: S18301. $19.95.
Vol. V: Saul Rips Up His Camel/David Gets a Good Gig. After elected to find a proper Israeli kingdom, Saul is disowned by the prophet Samuel for his delusions of grandeur. Greatness is expected from the harp-playing shepherd David. 30 mins.
VHS: S18302. $19.95.
Vol. VI: David and the Hairy Man Mountain/Saul Goes Bonkers. David is immortalized following his stunning defeat of the Philistine giant, Goliath, which enrages Saul. In the second story, Saul is humiliated by David's influence and orchestrates his removal from power. 30 mins.
VHS: S18303. $19.95.
Vol. VII: Saul Bumps into a Witch/David Gets to Number One. Saul seeks answers from the Witch of Endor but is unnerved by what he finds. In the second story, David's ascendancy is complete and the Israelites settle in Jerusalem, though their comfort is short-lived. 30 mins.
VHS: S18304. $19.95.
Ancient Tales from a Promised Land. Boxed Set.
VHS: S18305. $119.70.

Archaeology: Mysteries of the Holy Land
Scientists and historians take their cue from the Hebrew Bible to see if they can unlock some of the Holy Land's most confounding secrets. This fascinating excursion is from the Discovery Channel. 80 mins.
VHS: S25085. $24.95.

Ave Maria
Though revered by millions, little is actually known about the Virgin Mary. This documentary explores the history of this religious figure and her continuing influence, particularly among women. 51 mins.
VHS: S24925. $29.95.

The Bible on Video: The Book of Genesis
A dramatic collection of vignettes dramatizing the biblical history and poetic storytelling of the *Book of Genesis*. The program reimagines the days of creation, Adam and Eve's removal from the Garden of Eden, the haunting tale of Cain and Abel and the steadfast heroism of Noah. It is available in two versions, the King James (KJV) and Revised Standard (RSV), and in two languages, English and Spanish.
RSV—English.
VHS: S19705. $79.95.
RSV—Spanish.
VHS: S19706. $79.95.
KJV—English.
VHS: S19707. $79.95.
KJV—Spanish.
VHS: S19708. $79.95.

The Bible on Video: The Gospel of Luke
The Genesis Project's daunting attempt to reconstruct the *Gospel of Luke* using authentic details, including a word-for-word biblical text created in the original languages—Hebrew, Greek and Aramaic—narrated by Orson Welles, Alexander Scourby and Jose Ferrer. The film recreates the Easter story, from the birth of Jesus to his crucifixion at Golgotha. The program is available in two versions, the King James (KJV) and Revised Standard (RSV), and in two languages, English and Spanish.
RSV—English.
VHS: S19701. $79.95.
RSV—Spanish.
VHS: S19702. $79.95.
KJV—English.
VHS: S19703. $79.95.
KJV—Spanish.
VHS: S19704. $79.95.

Blood and Honey
The British actor and author Tony Robinson (*The Black Adder*) is in the Holy Land to narrate a series of gripping, stylized retellings of Old Testament stories.
Volume 1. 30 mins.
VHS: S17184. $14.95.
Volume 2. 30 mins.
VHS: S17185. $14.95.
Volume 3. 30 mins.
VHS: S17186. $14.95.
Volume 4. 30 mins.
VHS: S17187. $14.95.
Volume 5. 30 mins.
VHS: S17188. $14.95.
Volume 6. 30 mins.
VHS: S17189. $14.95.
Volume 7. 30 mins.
VHS: S17190. $14.95.
Complete Set. 210 mins.
VHS: S17191. $99.65.

Brides of Christ
Brenda Fricker (*My Left Foot*) stars in a searing, award-winning, British drama that captures the restless desperation of a reclusive society and its encounters with the outside world. From student Rosemary's rejection of rigid sexual moral codes to Sister Paul's decision to leave the convent for a radical priest, this is a critically-acclaimed, riveting production. Three tapes in a boxed set. Total length: 300 mins.
VHS: S21903. $59.95.

The Crucifixion/How Jesus Died: The Final 18 Hours
Medical experts Dr. John Bonica and Dr. Frederick T. Zugibe join Yale historian Ramsay MacMullen for this in-depth look at the final 18 hours in the life of Jesus Christ. The forensic and historic facts provide the basis for this accurate glimpse of that historic event. Directed by John Dauer, USA.
VHS: S27724. $29.95.

Discovering the Feminine
In 1990, two years before his death, Father Bede Griffiths suffered a stroke. This personal crisis allowed him to understand the importance of the feminine in all aspects of life. Through his humor and with great humility, he explains his insight in this lecture. 32 mins.
VHS: S21853. $29.95.

Emmanuel Swedenborg— The Man Who Had to Know
A documentary on the romantic philosopher who inspired poets and religious thinkers of his time. 30 mins.
VHS: S06485. $29.95.

The History and Interpretation of the Bible
Father Bede Griffiths explores methods by which the Bible was recorded, and how changes in Christian thinking affect its interpretation. 40 mins.
VHS: S21854. $29.95.

The Holy Koran
The Holy Koran is a penetrating study of the holy book of Islam which explains for the western mind why this religion is such a force in the world today. *Islamic Science* shows in detail how the people of the Moslem world have contributed to today's civilization and culture. *The Religious Experience* compares the world's religions.
VHS: S03982. $64.95.

Holy Land & Holy City
The Holy Land at Christmas offers a heart-warming look at the holy land during the holy season when many Christian sects gather to share a common legacy. *The World of the Vatican II* gives us an artist's chronicle of the activities in the Holy City of Rome during the reign of Pope John XXIII.
VHS: S03983. $64.95.

A Human Search: The Life of Father Bede Griffiths
Benedictine monk Father Bede, a great mystic and visionary, is revealed in this intimate portrait. His profound union of Eastern mysticism, Western religions and modern science offers a unique and inspired perspective. Through his exceptional learning and deep spirituality he speaks directly to the human spirit. 60 mins.
VHS: S21852. $29.95.

In Search of Angels
Debra Winger narrates this exploration of the myths, meanings and allure of these otherworldly creatures. Shot on locations around the world, images of angels from all eras are used to elucidate their enduring powers. Interviews with celebrities, including playwright Tony Kushner and singer Rickie Lee Jones, make this a fascinating documentary. 60 mins.
VHS: S22960. $29.98.

In Search of Historic Jesus
A controversial adaptation of the best-selling Sunn Classic book about the quest to find Jesus and the Shroud of Turin. With John Rubinstein, John Anderson and Andrew Bloch. Narrated by Brad Crandall.
VHS: S17909. $19.98.
Henning Schellerup, USA, 1976, 95 mins.

In Search of Noah's Ark

Recreation of the biblical tale leads into an account of the search for the historical Ark, featuring photos, personal accounts and archaeological information. USA, 1976, 95 mins.
VHS: S02829. $19.98.

In the Company of Angels: Biblical Truths About God's Glorious Creatures

Ten respected scholars spanning the Catholic, Evangelical, Orthodox and Jewish faiths are joined here to investigate the nature of these spiritual figures. Angels are spoken of in the Bible, and this documentary begins with Biblical times in order to answer basic questions about the nature and significance of angels. The result is a moving and informative video. Produced and written by Janet Russo and Sue Kiner. 60 mins.
VHS: S27487. $19.95.

Inside the Vatican, with Sir Peter Ustinov

From inside Vatican City and across Europe, Ustinov leads this four-volume video history of one of the world's most wealthy, powerful and art-laden institutions. Each volume is 50 mins.
VHS: S23937. $59.95.

Jesus and His Times

A three-sided laser disk that vividly portrays the dusty roads, people, villages and ancient cities of the Holy Land as they appeared during the time of Jesus. On-site footage was specifically filmed to depict the feeling of Jesus' life and message. Produced by Reader's Digest. 180 mins.
Laser: CLV. LD72360. $59.95.

Jesus from the Gospel (KJV)

This collection of films based on the King James Version of the Bible is narrated by Alexander Scourby. These are word-for-word re-enactments of the Scripture. Nothing has been added or subtracted. It's as if Jesus were reliving the events and teachings that form the core of His Gospels.
Jesus from the Gospel: The Birth.
VHS: S21721. $14.95.
Jesus from the Gospel: The Parables.
VHS: S21722. $14.95.
Jesus from the Gospel: The Passion.
VHS: S21723. $14.95.
Jesus from the Gospel: The Set.
VHS: S21724. $39.95.

Jesus from the Gospel (RSV)

This collection of films based on the Revised Standard Version Bible is narrated by Orson Welles. These are word-for-word re-enactments of the Scripture. Nothing has been added or subtracted. It's as if Jesus were reliving the events and teachings that form the core of the Gospels.
Jesus from the Gospel: The Birth.
VHS: S21717. $14.95.
Jesus from the Gospel: The Parables.
VHS: S21718. $14.95.
Jesus from the Gospel: The Passion.
VHS: S21719. $14.95.
Jesus from the Gospel: The Set.
VHS: S21720. $39.95.

Jesus—His Life

A&E's Biography series captures the essence of the life of Jesus. The mysteries and myths surrounding his life are examined by leading scholars and historians. In the Holy Land, new archeological explorations yield fresh insights that round out this thoroughly fresh approach to an enduring story. 100 mins.
VHS: S27642. $19.95.

Journey Through the Bible Lands

Watch the Bible come to life in this video tour of the Holy Land. Follow the path of Moses and the Israelites through the desert of Sinai. Continue into Negev, past the ancient walls of Hebron, to Bethlehem, the birthplace of Jesus. Retrace the Stations of the Cross along the via Dolorossa to the Church of the Holy Sepulchre. 45 mins.
VHS: S10775. $24.95.

The Life and Times of Jesus

Armand Assante narrates this series; Betty Buckley provides readings from the Gospel for this unique production.
VHS: S22550. $19.98.
The Last Days of Jesus. The tragic fate of Jesus remains one of the most moving accounts of human suffering and redemption. His example in life and death remains a testament to love and forgiveness.
VHS: S22552. $19.98.
Who Was Jesus? Through an examination of the teachings and the events that made up Jesus' life, the nature of this extraordinary historical figure is thoroughly explored. His unique philosophy offers solace to millions.
VHS: S22551. $19.98.
The Life and Times of Jesus, Gift Pack.
VHS: S22553. $49.98.

Living Islam

A tour around the history, the faith(s) and the cultures of Islam with focus on what it means to be a Muslim today. The programs capture the excitement and ecstasy of great Muslim festivals, and the beautiful and evocative places of the Islamic world.
Islam and Modernity. This program looks at the tensions within Islamic states as they attempt to make their laws and practices compatible with the 21st century while remaining true to the spirit of the faith. 50 mins.
VHS: S20465. $29.95.
Islam in the Minority. Over 40% of the world's Muslims live as minorities, but is it possible to live a true Muslim life outside the Islamic world? This program asks whether Muslims suffer particular discrimination and whether life in a secular society compromises their faith. 50 mins.
VHS: S20463. $29.95.
The Challenge of the Past. The three empires' greatness and subsequent decline explain many differences in Muslim thinking as the Ottoman empire confronted Europe and Christianity, as the Mughals achieved a synthesis with Hinduism, while the Saffavid dynasty was characterized by the shi'a/sunni split. 50 mins.
VHS: S20462. $29.95.
The Last Crusade. As many nations both East and West, from Algeria to Malaysia, face an Islamic revival, this program looks at the revolutionary and reforming spirit of Muslims. Why is a need for change sweeping through Muslim societies? What kind of change do the radicals want? And do they wish to achieve it by peace or violent means? 50 mins.
VHS: S20466. $29.95.

The Muslim Family. Explores the position of women under shari'a law in Egypt and Iran and asks how much is laid down by the faith and how much is added by the confines of local or tribal custom. In Indonesia, Muslim women are seen in jeans and short skirts working alongside those in the jilbab. Is this Islam or a heresy? 50 mins.
VHS: S20464. $29.95.
The Prophet, the Book and the Desert. An introduction to the essentials of Islam, which is deeply woven around the life of Muhammad, the Prophet of Allah. The program finds a living saint in the dunes of Timbuktu converting villagers to Islam. 50 mins.
VHS: S20461. $29.95.
Living Islam, Complete. All six volumes in one set.
VHS: S20467. $149.95.

Lost Years of Jesus

There are 18 years missing in the Biblical account of the life of Jesus. These years are explored in this acclaimed documentary, originally produced for television.
VHS: S06249. $29.95.
Richard Bock, USA, 1986, 93 mins.

The Making of a Modern Mystic

This is an in-depth look at Andrew Harvey, the youngest ever Fellow of All Souls Oxford. He is a best-selling novelist, poet and mystic, who was recently profiled in the New York Times Magazine. 59 mins.
VHS: S21847. $29.95.

Man of Peace: A Video Portrait of Pope John Paul II

A sensitive biography of the humble man who has great influence over the lives all who see and hear him, the "Jet-Age Pope" who reaffirms the message of Jesus Christ. This video takes the viewer inside the Vatican and to private audiences with Prince Charles and Princess Diana, opera star Pavarotti and Father Martin Jenco, as well as on the Pope's visit to Mother Teresa in India, and the face-to-face meeting with his assailant in which he forgives him. USA, 1986, 58 mins.
VHS: S04747. $29.95.

Martin Luther

Nial MacGinnis of the Old Vic stars as one of the prominent leaders of the Protestant Reformation. Unlike most of the early church reformers, Martin Luther was not burned at the stake and lived to see his work spread and prosper. The compelling dramatization covers most of the major developments.
VHS: S03947. $29.95.
Irving Pichel, Great Britain, 1953, 105 mins.

Martin Luther, His Life and Time

Produced by the Lutheran Film Division, this film traces the birth, youth and great reformation within the Church. Silent with music score. USA, 1924, 101 mins.
VHS: S04367. $29.95.

Mary Magdalene: An Intimate Portrait

Penelope Ann Miller hosts this examination of the mysterious woman follower of Jesus. She was there even at his death, and yet is not thought of as one of his close disciples. Instead, she is remembered as the bad girl, the prostitute of the New Testament. This video explores her story and the important role sexuality and power play in shaping her reputation. USA, 1995, 43 mins.
VHS: S27006. $19.98.

Merton: A Film Biography

The first film biography of Thomas Merton—writer, religious philosopher, and Trappist monk—in this acclaimed examination of his life and work. Contains interviews with those who knew him, including the Dalai Lama, Lawrence Ferlinghetti, Ernesto Cardenal, and Joan Baez. "A brilliant and creative masterpiece."
VHS: S09441. $29.95.
Paul Wilkes, USA, 1984, 57 mins.

Mysteries from the Bible

This film explores the biblical wonders and powers of God as described through the miracles of Moses and Jesus. Many of their works are convincingly recreated for the screen. 96 mins.
VHS: S16574. $19.95.

Mysteries of the Ancient World Gift Set

Darrin McGavin, Dennis Weaver and William Devane host this series, which explores a number of age-old mysteries. Science has been baffled by the religious and spiritual mysteries examined in these four volumes: Mysteries of the Ancient World (Shroud of Turin, Pyramids, Nostradamus), The Incredible Discovery of Noah's Ark, Ancient Secrets of the Bible and Ancient Secrets of the Bible, Part 2. Four-volume set.
VHS: S23750. $54.98.

The Mysteries of the Bible: The Story Continues

A journey of discovery into the origins, enigmas and contradictions of the scriptures continues in the second installment of A&E's video series on the Bible. The latest scientific findings and archeological discoveries shed new light on enduring mysteries. Shot throughout the Holy Land, this series explores both prophets and stories from the old testament as well as the very last days of Jesus as recorded in the New Testament. 50 mins each.
Volume 1: Queen Esther.
VHS: S26580. $14.95.
Volume 2: The Apocalypse.
VHS: S26581. $14.95.
Volume 3: Execution of Jesus.
VHS: S26582. $14.95.
Volume 4: The Philistines.
VHS: S26583. $14.95.

Volume 5: Abraham.
VHS: S26584. $14.95.
Volume 6: Prophets.
VHS: S26585. $14.95.
Volume 7: Joseph.
VHS: S26586. $14.95.
The Greatest Mysteries of the Bible: The Story Continues Set.
VHS: S26587. $99.95.

Mystery of the Sacred Shroud

The ancient cloth imprinted with an image of Christ—is it a medieval hoax or proof of Jesus' crucifixion? Richard Burton narrates this investigation into the Shroud of Turin. 86 mins.
VHS: S16572. $29.98.

The Naked Truth

Jordan Maxwell, Derek Partridge and Bill Jenkins destroy the wall of lies engineered by organized religion, to obscure the truth about early spiritual wisdom. Judaism, Christianity and Islam have all participated in this deception to consolidate their own power in this world.
VHS: S21232. $34.95.

Opiates of the Masses: Religion in the USSR

The battle between church and state was never more profound than in the Soviet block. This film, made just before the Gorbachev reforms, seems to indicate that the church was winning the battle. 105 mins.
VHS: S12716. $24.98.

The Pope in America

Covers Pope John Paul II's historic visit to Denver in 1993. Produced by CNN. 60 mins.
VHS: S20510. $14.98.

Pope John II: Statesman of Faith

Before he inhabited the Vatican, this religious leader kept the Catholic faith alive behind the iron curtain. This video biography from A&E tells his whole story, beginning in a Polish village and leading to his succession as Pope. 50 mins.
VHS: S23935. $19.95.

Pope John Paul II

The full-length feature about the life of Pope John Paul II, covering a span of 40 years to his election to the Papacy in 1978 as the first non-Italian Pope in over four centuries. Albert Finney stars as the Pope.
VHS: S04497. $79.95.
Herbert Wise, USA, 1984, 147 mins.

Pope John Paul II: Seven Days of Eternity

A lavish keepsake of the celebration of Holy Week in Rome hosted by Joseph Campanella. Includes the pomp and pageantry of everything from Palm Sunday to the somber rite of Good Friday, to glorious Easter Sunday. 48 mins.
VHS: S13172. $19.98.

Priests of Passion

This documentary focuses on the vow of celibacy taken by a number of Catholic priests who had to confront their commitment to the church when they fell in love. David Rice, himself a former priest, went from Germany to Brazil to New Jersey as he traced these troubled men.
VHS: S20589. $29.95.
Nick Gray, USA, 51 mins.

The Rabbit Ears Collection

The universal traditions of storytelling and music are charmingly celebrated in the animated programs of the Rabbit Ears We All Have Tales series. Each narrated by famous actors like Kathleen Turner and Denzel Washington, these entertaining programs showcase the folklores of peoples around the world and are set to the sounds of various musicians. Grammy and Parents' Choice awards have been given to Rabbit Ears.
Joseph and His Brothers. Musician and actor Ruben Blades tells the inspiring story of a brother betrayed. Though mistreated by his family, Joseph overcomes their treachery and forgives them. Music by Strunz and Farah.
VHS: S21258. $14.98.
Moses in Egypt. Danny Glover narrates this animated version of the delivery of the Israelites from slavery. Grammy Award-winning Gospel musicians Sounds of Blackness perform the musical score in this episode from The Greatest Stories Ever Told series.
VHS: S21258. $12.98.
Moses the Lawgiver. Another episode in the The Greatest Stories Ever Told series, this cartoon continues the story of the Israelites and their new found freedom. Moses received the Ten Commandments and after 40 years led his people to the Promised Land. Narrated by Ben Kingsley.
VHS: S21259. $12.98.
Parables That Jesus Told. Acclaimed author and radio star Garrison Keillor relates parables from the New Testament. They offer important insights in Jesus' own words. David Lindley wrote the music.
VHS: S24053. $14.98.
The Creation. Amy Grant tells the story of the creation of the world by God in seven days. Children will enjoy this adaptation from the first pages of the Bible. Bela Fleck and The Flecktones provide the music.
VHS: S24054. $14.98.
The Lion and the Lamb. The animated Christmas story of a fierce lion who escapes from the circus and finds refuge with a meek lamb in a stable. Narrated by Hollywood legends Christopher Reeve and Amy Grant. Music by Lyle Mays. 23 minutes.
VHS: S24056. $9.98.

Rapture of Being: Pir Vilayat Inayat Khan

The Sufi path, says Pir Vilayat, is one of merging our individual existence with the divine reality. The dancing of Sufis is an expression of the dynamic shifting equilibriums of life, striving from moment to moment toward the higher states of being. In Part II of this program, Pir Vilayat focuses on details of Sufi meditation practices. 90 mins.
VHS: S13321. $49.95.

The Riddle of the Dead Sea Scrolls

This feature-length documentary probes the mysteries of the Bible. It offers startling new perspectives on the most miraculous stories. Unfathomable exploits, such as the turning of water into wine or the very nature of Jesus and Mary, have emerged in the scrolls in more rational terms that are accesible to everyone. 80 mins.
VHS: S22966. $19.95.

Roots and Wings: A Jewish Congregation

Too few Christians understand the Jewish Faith. This video introduces the living community of Judaism, a religion with thousands of years of history and tradition, that has managed to survive in predominantly Christian societies. 28 mins.
VHS: S22476. $19.95.

Seeking God: The Way of the Monk at the Monastery of Christ in the Desert

The simple patterns of the monastic existence are interwoven with candid interviews with the monks themselves. The result is a fascinating expose of this hidden way of life dominated by a fervent belief in God. 58 mins.
VHS: S26813. $24.95.

Silent Witness

Documentary based on the book The Shroud of Turin. Medical examiners, theologians, physicists and historians trace the probable history of this burial cloth and attempt to reconstruct the events of the last days of Jesus Christ.
VHS: S01201. $69.95.
D.W. Rolfe, USA, 55 mins.

Six Little Angels

Angels are everywhere, but they are especially visible in this video. Six children explain, through both action and song, the hidden aspects of everyday life as apprehended by angels. 30 mins.
VHS: S26814. $9.95.

Song of the Holy Land

Inspired footage, favorite Christian hymns and Hebrew songs of praise capture the spirit, beauty and sacred heritage of Israel. The timeless grandeur and majesty of the Holy Land comes alive in this musical celebration. 65 mins.
VHS: S23137. $29.95.

The Story of David

Rivalry between the enterprising David and his daunting foe, Goliath, sets in motion one of the Bible's best remembered stories. Timothy Bottoms stars as King David, the most famous underdog of recorded history. Released on two videocassettes, 191 mins.
VHS: S20681. $29.95.

Story of Islam

Over three years in the making, this is a brilliant journey through Islam's history. We are introduced to the culture, philosophy and staples of this way of life, a religion that is gathering tremendous momentum in the west: today they have over one billion devotees. 120 mins.
VHS: S13170. $24.98.

The Story of Jacob and Joseph

Set in the land of the Bible, this famous tale of two brothers is brought to life. Jealousy and envy are poisonous traits, but forgiveness holds out hope even between the most divided of siblings. Featuring Colleen Dewhurst and Keith Mitchell. 96 mins.
VHS: S20680. $19.95.

Testament

Writer and archeologist John Romer hosts this fascinating series that explores the cultural and historical origins and authorship of the most influential book ever written, the Bible. Each volume is 52 mins.
As It Was in the Beginning. Explores the development of ideas about God and holiness from the East to the God of Moses and the Exodus, and addresses historical fact in Old Testament stories.
VHS: S09481. $29.95.
Chronicles and Kings. The rise and fall of ancient Israel and the role of Jehovah in the development of the Jewish nation. The period between the establishment of the kingdom in the Promised Land and the exile of the Jews in Babylon.
VHS: S09482. $29.95.
Gospel Truth. The historical remains of the time, place and perhaps the life of Jesus and how the Christian Bible came into being.
VHS: S09484. $29.95.
Mightier than the Sword. The historical context into which Jesus was born, the background against which the New Testament was written, the period in which the Old Testament achieved its final shape.
VHS: S09483. $29.95.
Paradise Lost. The evolution of the Bible from unquestioned sacred book to object for study, and the historical and cultural influences that generated this changing point of view. Beginning with the 14th century Renaissance poet Petrarch, proceeding to Martin Luther, and concluding with the impact of scientific knowledge in the 19th century.
VHS: S09487. $29.95.

Power and the Glory. The sole source of learning during the Dark Ages, the Bible was used to justify social order. The artistry lavished on it made these stories and characters central to medieval culture. This program concludes in 1453, when Constantinople fell and Gutenberg printed his first Bible.
VHS: S09486. $29.95.
Thine Is the Kingdom. The story of Christianity from the transformation of the Roman Empire into a Christian one; the conversion of Constantine, the correspondence between Sts. Jerome and Augustine; how Bible stories came to be used.
VHS: S09485. $29.95.

Thomas Berry: Dreamer of the Universe
Ecotheologian Berry is a highly regarded American monk whose writings have inspired a whole generation of environmentalists. This controversial figure is revealed in an intimate conversation. He is perhaps one of the greatest spiritual thinkers of our time. 57 mins.
VHS: S21848. $29.95.

Video Outlines of Asian Religions
An in-depth series which looks at the principal beliefs of Hindu and Buddhist countries. Produced by scholars Nancy Moore Gettleman and Richard Sherburne.
Volume 1: Absorption in Brahman. The story of Hinduism—ancient India, Aryans—from polytheism to monist God. Karma-Rebirth-Caste. Religions: Liberation vs. Salvation. Three Paths: Action-Devotion-Knowledge. Four stages of life: Student-householder-forest dweller-sannyasin. 30 mins.
VHS: S23350. $69.95.
Volume 2: The Great Awakening. The rise of Buddhism in India. Siddhartha Hautama Four Truths No Soul. Monastic life. Theravada and Mahayana: Arhats & Bodhisattvas. Yoga Meditation and Emptiness. Decline in India. 45 mins.
VHS: S23351. $69.95.
Volume 3: Diamond Path. Hinduism and Buddhism intermingle in Nepal. Early history; later: Newars-Malla and Shah dynasties. Rana control-restoration. Tantric Buddhism, the Swift path, Mandala-Mantra-Mudra. Visualization and Thankas ritual objects. 45 mins.
VHS: S23352. $69.95.
Volume 4: Dalai Lama's and Tulku's Living Bodhisattvas. Mahayana Buddhism in Tibet. Early history and shamanist religion (Bon). Conversion of early kings and growth of Buddhist monastic orders. Tibetan translation of Buddhist scriptures. Kanjur and Tengyur. Mongol influence and Buddhocracy by Dalai and Panchen lamas. Jesuit missionaries: first Westerners in the Forbidden Kingdom. 45 mins.
VHS: S23353. $69.95.
Volume 5: Incarnate Buddha—Kings of the Dragon. Buddhism in Bhutan. Early history: the outpost of Tibetan monastic sects; 17th-century beginnings of new nation; Shabdrung, the monk-tulku-king founder; Dharma-rajas and Deb-rajas; division of secular and religious powers; Dzons: the monastery-fortress governance; unification and first modern education. 45 mins.
VHS: S23354. $69.95.
Companion Text: Himalayan Journey of Buddhism. This provides an effective written reference to reinforce the Video Outline of Asian Religions video series.
VHS: S23355. $69.95.

Voyages: The Journey of the Magi
The Biblical journey of the Magi has inspired artists for nearly 2,000 years. This program recreates their actual route, setting the event in both its cultural and archeological contexts. As sites in the journey of the Wise Men are seen, artifacts and coins dating from the period offer additional insight into an event which generated a wealth of art. Narrated by art historian and archeologist Karl Katz; filmed in Jerusalem and Bethlehem. 30 mins.
VHS: S04653. $29.95.

Walk in Crusader Jerusalem
A prominent archeologist and a Dominican abbot retrace the steps of a pilgrim to Crusader Jerusalem. Their explorations uncover both an important period of the city's history as well as the place of Jerusalem in the mind of twelfth century Christendom. 34 mins.
VHS: S10465. $29.95.

Where Jesus Walked
A video journey through Nazareth, Jericho, Capernaum and Jerusalem, capturing the beauty of the Holy Land, as it follows the footsteps of Jesus, his baptism at the Jordan River, Baptism on the Mount, and his final walk through the streets of Jerusalem. USA, 60 mins.
VHS: S04695. $29.95.

The Wisdom of a Prophet (2 Lectures)
"A New Vision of Reality in the Light of Modern Science" is an exploration of the relationship between science and spirituality. "A New Vision of Reality in the Light of Christian Mysticism and Hindu Advait" goes beyond the dogma of religions and scientific rationalism to an unexpected essence.
VHS: S21855. $29.95.

The Wisdom of Faith with Huston Smith
Hinduism, Buddhism, Confucianism, Christianity, Judaism and Islam, six of the world's great religions, are all examined and compared in this five-video set. It's A Bill Moyers Special that uses art, architecture, music and poetry to illustrate the common heart of religious experience.
VHS: S27605. $119.95.

Within Thy Gates, O Jerusalem: The City and the Temple
Following Jewish pilgrims to Jerusalem, at the time of the birth of Christianity, the film unfolds the Holy City with its many sites. The description of the sites and events is based on Joseph Flavius, the rich archeological findings and a mini model of Jerusalem. 32 mins.
VHS: S10466. $29.95.

Worship the King
Stunning visuals, passages from Scripture and classic hymns create an inspirational experience. This video includes excerpts from the 21st Psalm, the Sermon on the Mount, and hymns, including "Amazing Grace", "A Mighty Fortress Is Our God" and "O Worship the King". 55 mins.
VHS: S23136. $29.95.

BIOGRAPHIES & MEMOIRS

Abraham Lincoln
James McPherson, Princeton University historian and Pulitzer Prize winner for his Battle Cry of Freedom, hosts this fascinating story of Abraham Lincoln from his boyhood to the White House. 35 mins.
VHS: S12190. $19.95.

Albert Einstein: How I See the World
William Hurt narrates this program which chronicles the ways in which the world's most famous Nobel Prize winner became its most eloquent advocate for peace. Much of it is told in Einstein's own words, excerpted from his diaries, personal letters and writings. PBS, 60 mins.
VHS: S15637. $19.98.

Albert Einstein: The Education of a Genius
Einstein failed exams, cut classes—and set the world of modern physics on its ear! Here is his story, filled with vivid images of the ordinary occurrences that led him to his theories. 44 mins.
VHS: S05739. $39.95.

Amazing Howard Hughes
Millionaire, flyer, playboy, film mogul—Howard Hughes had it all. The story of the legendary eccentric comes alive with all the mystery that made him an American hero. 119 mins.
VHS: S04541. $19.95.

Amelia Earhart
Diane Keaton and Rutger Hauer star in this biography of America's most famed woman aviator. Her disappearance left the nation stunned. Even so the legend of a strong woman who dared to do exactly what she dreamed of lives on. Her story is more fascinating than fiction and more inspiring than fantasy because she really did make history. 95 mins.
VHS: S21825. $92.98.

Amelia Earhart: The Price of Courage
Kathy Bates narrates the story of America's most highly acclaimed woman hero. Earhart was the first woman to fly across the Atlantic solo. Combining a taste for daredevil antics with her charismatic presence, she became a national hero. Her untimely and mysterious demise makes her story an enduring and fascinating tale. B&W, 60 mins.
VHS: S23050. $19.95.

American Lifestyle Series: Inventors
This series offers a view of truly great Americans. These lives stand as testament to the virtues and values of individuality, creativity, and leadership. Creative explorers on the technological frontier have shaped not only this country but the world. This series offers three great examples of this inventive spirit.
Benjamin Franklin: Citizen-Sage of a New Age. Hugh Downs explores the genius of Franklin, one of the most important scientists, inventors and writers of his day. 24 mins.
VHS: S23551. $49.95.
Laser: LD74780. $99.95.
Alexander Graham Bell. Biographical detail abounds in this program about the American legend. Hugh Downs narrates a look at this teacher of the deaf, inventor, scientist and poet. 24 mins.
VHS: S23552. $49.95.
Laser: LD74781. $99.95.
Thomas Edison's Glenmount. Edison called his magnificent Victorian mansion his workbench. Here he perfected the phonograph, the motion picture camera, and incandescent and florescent lighting. 23 mins.
VHS: S23553. $49.95.
Laser: LD74782. $99.95.

American Lifestyle Series: Military Leaders
This series offers a view of truly great Americans. These lives stand as testament to the virtues and values of individuality, creativity, and leadership. E.G. Marshall hosts these two video biographies of great American leaders.
Sam Houston and Texas: A Giant Man for a Giant Land. Rich in intriguing personal and political facts, this program presents Houston, the first president of the Republic of Texas. 24 mins.
VHS: S23545. $49.95.
Laser: LD74775. $99.95.
Stratford Lee and Robert E. Lee. This video offers a profile of Lee, a general many considered to be the greatest military mind ever produced by the American armed forces. A tour of his family home is also included. 24 mins.
VHS: S23546. $49.95.
Laser: LD74776. $99.95.

American Lifestyle Series: U.S. Presidents
This series offers a view of truly great Americans. These lives stand as testament to the virtues and values of individuality, creativity, and leadership. This collection of six biographical tapes about the great presidents of the US is hosted by E.G. Marshall.
Love, Liberty, and the Pursuit of Conscience: John Adams and Massachusetts America. The story of the first Vice President and the second President is intertwined with the founding of the U.S. 24 mins.
VHS: S23539. $49.95.
Thomas Jefferson's Monticello. Jefferson's home in Charlottesville, Virginia, is presented as a setting where he exercised his many skills and interests. 24 mins.
VHS: S23540. $49.95.
Laser: LD74770. $99.95.
Theodore Roosevelt's Sagamore Hill. This rambling, informal house on Long Island's northern shore reflects the many aspects of the 26th president, Theodore Roosevelt. 23 mins.
VHS: S23541. $49.95.
Laser: LD74771. $99.95.
Woodrow Wilson: Peace and War and the Professor President. This program presents the career and loves of the scholar president. 23 mins.
VHS: S23542. $49.95.
Laser: LD74772. $99.95.
Andrew Jackson's Hermitage. This program visits the home President Andrew Jackson planned, developed and lived in with his beloved Rachel. 23 mins.
VHS: S23543. $49.95.
Laser: LD74773. $99.95.

Franklin D. Roosevelt's Hyde Park. FDR's home near the Hudson River is featured on this video. There are reminders of his childhood, his early career, his struggle with polio and his years as President. 24 mins.
VHS: S23544. $49.95.
Laser: LD74774. $99.95.

Andrew Carnegie: The Original Man of Steel
Hugh Downs hosts this version of Carnegie's life story. This industrialist's legacy still influences the country through his many philanthropic enterprises, including libraries, universities, institutes and more. 24 mins.
VHS: S23554. $49.95.
Laser: LD74783. $99.95.

The Beauty Queens
The cosmetic, beauty and treatment industry affects nearly everyone's life. This series portrays three exceptional women of the 20th century, all of whom founded vast empires by cooking up formulas on their kitchen stoves.
Volume 1: Helena Rubinstein. Born in 1870 into an impoverished Polish family, Helena Rubinstein became a shrewd business woman, married a Russian prince and lived to the age of 95. Glamorous, tempestuous and exotic, Rubinstein had a unique sense of personal style and she triumphed over extreme odds to be successful. 60 mins.
VHS: S10300. $29.95.
Volume 2: Elizabeth Arden. Elizabeth Arden's fundamental belief was that beauty was an intelligent cooperation between nature and science, a partnership to develop a woman's natural assets. She was the first person to really develop the beauty salon and health farm business. This portrait traces Arden's success and reveals her as a woman whose fame and temper hid an insecure and fragile personality—one who loved horses more than she did people. 60 mins.
VHS: S10301. $29.95.
Volume 3: Estee Lauder. The richest self-made woman in the world, now in her eighties, Estee Lauder is still the inspiration behind the business. She is a promotional genius and a living legend—the last of the old style, grand slam beauty queens whose lives were beauty and who made fortunes from pots of cream. This film looks at the career and style of this remarkable woman whose company now earns an estimated $1.3 billion a year.
VHS: S10302. $29.95.

Biography
Programs first broadcast on Arts and Entertainment, which uses interviews, archival footage and photographs to trace the lives of modern legends.
Elizabeth Taylor.
VHS: S20437. $19.95.
Elvis: Story of a Legend.
VHS: S20438. $19.95.
George Bush: His WWII Years.
VHS: S20443. $19.95.
Jackie Robinson.
VHS: S20442. $19.95.
Jacqueline Kennedy Onassis.
VHS: S20439. $19.95.
Joe DiMaggio.
VHS: S20440. $19.95.
John Gotti: A Mafia Story.
VHS: S20441. $19.95.
Ronald Reagan: The Many Lives.
VHS: S20444. $19.95.

Buckminster Fuller: Grandfather of the Future
A last interview with the great inventor, architect and visionary. Fuller discusses the "invisible" new reality, which has recently made it possible to maintain the planet's entire population at a higher standard of living than anyone has ever known. 25 mins.
VHS: S08305. $29.95.

Colin Powell: A General's General
Produced by CNN, the life story of Colin Powell, the first African-American to become Chairman of the Joint Chiefs of Staff. 60 mins.
VHS: S20512. $14.98.

Colin Powell: A Soldier's Campaign
This biographical documentary from A&E tells the story of the highly popular and charismatic general. Born to immigrant parents, he grew up in the Bronx and rose through the ranks in the military to lead the Allied forces in the Gulf War. Includes interviews with his family and friends as well as rare archival footage.
VHS: S27212. $19.95.
Bill Harris, USA, 1995, 50 mins.

The Complete Churchill
The definitive four-part profile of the English statesman, politician and military leader, in a special collector's edition boxed set. Written and narrated by Martin Gilbert, Churchill's official biographer, the program covers the amazing spectrum of his life, mixing interviews, commentary, research and archival footage. Directed by Maris Appugliese. 200 mins. "Historically comprehensive and fact-packed" (The Wall Street Journal).
VHS: S17073. $59.95.
Laser: CLV. LD72075. $69.95.

Conquest of Everest
A beautifully filmed documentary about the Sir Edmund Hillary expedition to Mt. Everest. The film also chronicles the history of the mountain, its discovery and naming and previous attempts to reach the summit, as well as Hillary's elaborate preparations for the climb, and the final, triumphant reach to the summit. Academy Award nominee. England, 1953, 78 mins.
VHS: S05601. $19.95.

Don't Call Me Bugsy
This movie shows the rise and fall of Benjamin Siegel, arguably the flashiest gangster in American history and the man who built Las Vegas. Interviews, archival footage and contemporary photographs reveal the man "with a face for the movies and a nose for crime." 70 mins.
VHS: S17026. $19.98.

Double Exposure: The Story of Margaret Bourke-White
Farrah Fawcett is cast as pioneering photojournalist Margaret Bourke-White in this theatrical release that contains additional footage not included in the made-for-cable tv version. Frederic Forrest plays the man she loved, when she was not globetrotting and shooting famous people like Gandhi with her camera for Life Magazine. With David Huddleston, Ken Marshall and Mitchell Ryan. Based on the biography by Vicki Goldberg.
VHS: S09781. $79.98.
Lawrence Shiller, USA, 1989, 94 mins.

Dwight D. Eisenhower: From Soldier to President
This video reveals the life of this statesman's early life and shows how it prepared him for the highest elected office in the land. 19 mins.
VHS: S23564. $49.95.

Dwight D. Eisenhower: Library and Museum
From documents, pictures, special displays and exhibitions throughout the library, this video tells a story about President Eisenhower's personal life and how his presidency affected the history of the U.S. 58 mins.
VHS: S23425. $24.95.

Dwight D. Eisenhower: The Presidential Years
In addition to trouble overseas there was trouble at home. This president faced the challenge of enforcing school desegregation. 19 mins.
VHS: S23565. $49.95.

Eisenhower—A Place in History
Before Dwight David Eisenhower served as president of the United States, he was better known for his military career as a Five Star General during World War II. This U.S. government documentary tells the story of that life in color and black and white footage. Filmed at the Eisenhower Library in Abilene, Kansas. 52 mins.
VHS: S09522. $19.95.

Eisenhower: Soldier/Statesman
David MacCullough narrates this two-tape set about one of America's most highly regarded military heroes and presidents. In Part One, Soldier, Ike's early years in Kansas include, his education, early career and participation in WW II are all here. Part Two traces his career as a statesman, from McCarthy through the beginnings of the Cold War. B&W, 150 mins.
VHS: S23049. $39.95.

Eleanor Roosevelt Story
This award-winning documentary traces Eleanor Roosevelt's overcoming of personal obstacles to shape a humanitarian agenda. Narrated by Archibald Macleish, Francis Cole and Eric Sevareid.
VHS: S17646. $19.95.
Richard Kaplan, USA, 1965, 91 mins.

Eleanor, First Lady of the World
Jean Stapleton stars in this biography of Eleanor Roosevelt. With E.G. Marshall, Coral Browne, Joyce Van Patten and Gail Strickland.
VHS: S17487. $19.98.
John Erman, USA, 1982, 100 mins.

Famous Americans of the 20th Century: The Story of Babe Ruth
No sports hero in American history has thrilled fans as "The Babe" did. He was the greatest baseball player who ever played. Part of the acclaimed documentary series. USA, 55 mins.
VHS: S14916. $29.95.

Famous Americans of the 20th Century: The Story of Charles Lindbergh
In 1927, Charles Lindbergh made the first non-stop, solo, trans-Atlantic flight to Paris in 33.5 hours. This insightful documentary examines the ups and downs of his dramatic life. USA, 55 mins.
VHS: S14911. $29.95.

Famous Americans of the 20th Century: The Story of Douglas MacArthur
In WWII, Douglas MacArthur commanded the U.S. Forces in the Far East and accepted the Japanese surrender aboard the U.S.S. Missouri. Includes actual footage of events, and interviews. USA, 55 mins.
VHS: S14910. $29.95.

Famous Americans of the 20th Century: The Story of Dwight D. Eisenhower
This is the story of victory in WWII and the "Eisenhower years" (1952-60), a period that shaped the second half of the 20th century. A fascinating historical documentary. USA, 55 mins.
VHS: S14915. $29.95.

Famous Americans of the 20th Century: The Story of Franklin Delano Roosevelt
This president's tough-minded attitude and relief programs altered the conduct of American life throughout the 20th century. A powerful documentary of the man and his incredible influence. USA, 100 mins.
VHS: S14918. $29.95.

Famous Americans of the 20th Century: The Story of G.I. Joe
The story of young men who learned how to fight and were dying for freedom in lands across the Atlantic and Pacific oceans. Part of the renowned documentary series. USA, 55 mins.
VHS: S14914. $29.95.

Famous Americans of the 20th Century: The Story of Harry S Truman

President Truman is the man who approved the dropping of two atomic bombs on Japan, in August 1945; he felt it was the only way to save the lives of 300,000 American G.I.s. Learn more about that decision from this special documentary. USA, 55 mins.
VHS: $14919. $29.95.

Famous Americans of the 20th Century: The Story of Helen Keller

A story of courage and faith; Helen Keller, shut off from the world of sight and sound, grew into a highly intelligent and sensitive woman who wrote, spoke and labored incessantly for the betterment of others. A documentary portrait. USA, 55 mins.
VHS: $14917. $29.95.

Famous Americans of the 20th Century: The Story of Henry Ford

Henry Ford introduced mass ownership of automobiles and sparked the 20th century industrial revolution in America. A fascinating video documentary. USA, 55 mins.
VHS: $14913. $29.95.

Famous Americans of the 20th Century: The Story of Knute Rockne

From the sandlots of Chicago, Knute Rockne became the most well-known college coach in American football history. A documentary portrait. USA, 55 mins.
VHS: $14920. $29.95.

Famous Americans of the 20th Century: The Story of Thomas Edison

Eager to release man from toil and tedium, Edison would patent over 1,000 inventions during his lifetime. A compelling video documentary of the man and world-shaking work. USA, 55 mins.
VHS: $14912. $29.95.

FDR

Emmy Award-winning producer David Grubin wrote and produced this collection of four 30-minute videos about America's great president, Franklin Delano Roosevelt, which offers a fresh, incisive and at times surprising view of this key historical figure. Originally produced for PBS' The American Experience. Historian David McCullough narrates.
Fear Itself. Begins with Roosevelt's paralysis from polio at the age of 39 and follows his relentless struggle to rehabilitate himself. The segment ends with Roosevelt achieving the highest office in the land in a landslide victory.
VHS: $24838. $19.95.
The Center of the World. Explores Roosevelt's family background, looking for clues as to how the coddled child of rich parents confounded those who dismissed him as an ambitious lightweight.
VHS: $24839. $19.95.
The Grandest Job in the World. Focuses on the first two terms of Roosevelt's presidency and documents how his programs and personal style restored hope to Americans who were gripped by despair.
VHS: $24837. $19.95.
The Juggler. This segment is devoted to the wartime years, making use of FDR's remarkable correspondence with Winston Churchill to chart the cunning way FDR maneuvered support for England before leading his country through the greatest war in history.
VHS: $24698. $19.95.
FDR, The Boxed Set. Includes all four titles.
VHS: $24840. $69.95.

First Ladies

Produced by ABC News, this humorous and historical program examines the public and private lives of 45 first ladies. From the tender love story of John and Abigail Adams to Betty Ford's candid discussions about her alcoholism, First Ladies studies the women behind the presidents. 60 mins.
VHS: $12269. $19.98.
Laser: LD70229. $34.95.

First Ladies

From Martha Washington to Barbara Bush, this program introduces you to some of the most distinguished women who have been the nation's highest unofficial officials. Visit the Smithsonian's unique collection of First Ladies' gowns, accessories and furnishings and learn how they are being preserved. 1989, 60 mins.
VHS: $14542. $29.95.

Ford: The Man and the Machine

Cliff Robertson stars in this critical biography of auto magnate Henry Ford. Hope Lange stars as Ford's wife and Heather Thomas as his mistress.
VHS: $17711. $49.95.
Allan Eastman, USA, 1987, 200 mins.

Frontline: Hillary's Class

Six of Hillary Rodham Clinton's classmates from the Wellesley College Class of 1969 talk about coming into their own at a key moment in the trajectory of women's progress. They explain significant turning points, the paths they chose and the price exacted from them for their decisions.
VHS: $24886. $19.95.

The Gangsters: Bugsy, Dutch and Al

Bugsy Siegel, Dutch Shultz and Al Capone controlled and corrupted the American dream with their syndicated crime organizations. Running bootleg liquor, brothels, and extortion and gambling houses, they infiltrated the government and police force, drawing their iron grip even tighter around the throats of a terrorized nation. Included in this bloody expose is rare and explicit footage revealing their ruthless rampages, as well as Bonnie and Clyde's, John Dillinger's and others. 58 mins.
VHS: $15923. $19.95.

Harry S. Truman: Library and Museum

This video tour of the library's artifacts and exhibitions will impart the feeling of a personally narrated tour. Often it offers a more detailed view of the exhibits than could be gained from an actual visit to the site itself. 57 mins.
VHS: $23426. $24.95.

Harry S. Truman: Suddenly, Mr. President

Though his presidency held the promise of continuing policies, it ushered in a new age. Truman became the first man to use a nuclear bomb. 20 mins.
VHS: $23562. $49.95.

Harry S. Truman: The Challenges of Office

Between 1948 and 1952, Truman faced down the challenge of a new aggressor and shaped the policies of a new and bitter cold war. 20 mins.
VHS: $23563. $49.95.

Helen Keller: Separate Views

The Helen Keller story is a colorful dramatization of the life of that remarkable woman and her teacher, Annie Sullivan. Part two has Katharine Cornell, Martha Graham, and President Dwight Eisenhower narrating her fascinating biography.
VHS: $02063. $69.95.

Hillary Rodham Clinton: Changing the Rules

This First Lady stirs public opinion as few other political figures can. She is one of Washington's most intriguing and controversial players, who has welded her largely ceremonial position into one of unrivaled influence. This biography looks at the unique personality behind the politician. 50 mins.
VHS: $21684. $19.95.

Hoffa: The True Story

A documentary portrait of James R. Hoffa. The program chronicles Hoffa's rise from obscure union official to president of the International Brotherhood of Teamsters, his war with Attorney General Robert Kennedy, questions of mob influence and infiltration, his prison stay for racketeering and jury fraud, and the events surrounding his disappearance in July 1975. 50 mins.
VHS: $18109. $19.95.

Houdini, The Life of the World's Greatest Escapologist

Houdini's career as a magician, illusionist and spiritualist is revealed in this film exploration of his life. He flirted with death so often that many of his fans still believe he will come back. This film begins with a seance at Niagara Falls. Then through photos, dramatizations and interviews it traces the career of this charismatic dreamer. 60 mins.
VHS: $26217. $19.95.

Hugh Hefner: Once Upon a Time

An entertaining portrait of Hugh Hefner, the controversial founder and publisher of Playboy magazine. The filmmakers use the occasion of Hefner's recent wedding to a former Playmate to assess his life and work. Produced by the team of David Lynch and Mark Frost. Narrated by James Coburn.
VHS: $18322. $89.95.
Robert Heath, USA, 1992, 90 mins.

Indomitable Teddy Roosevelt

Remarkable documentary footage combined with dramatization, with narration by George C. Scott, music by John Philip Sousa. "History with a wallop and a heart" (Tom Shales, Washington Post).
VHS: $01888. $79.95.
Harrison Engle, USA, 1983, 94 mins.

Jim Thorpe—All American

Also known as Man of Bronze, this touching biography stars Burt Lancaster as the multi-talented Native American athlete who became an Olympic champion and who almost single-handedly put pro football on the map. A film about triumph and tragedy, as Thorpe eventually succumbs to drink.
VHS: $15988. $19.98.
Laser: LD74706. $34.98.
Michael Curtiz, USA, 1951, 107 mins.

LBJ: The Early Years

Randy Quaid does an exceptionally fine job impersonating Lyndon Baines Johnson in the made-for-tv biography of the 36th President of the United States. Patti Lupone is equally fine as Lady Bird. The years 1934-1963 are covered in this inside look at a politician's rise to power. With Pat Hingle, Kevin McCarthy, Morgan Brittany, Barry Corbin and Charles Frank as J.F.K.
VHS: $07918. $19.95.
Peter Werner, USA, 1987, 144 mins.

Lord of the Universe

The Alfred I. Dupont award-winning documentary on the Guru Maharij Ji's attempt to levitate the Houston Astrodome. USA.
VHS: $15195. $24.95.

MacArthur

A large scale biography of the strategist and general that traces his life and work from World War II to the Korean War, when he was dismissed by Harry Truman for insubordination and defying direct orders. With Gregory Peck as the eponymous general, Ed Flanders, Ed O'Herlihy, Sandy Kenyon and Art Fleming.
Laser: LD70052. $39.98.
Joseph Sargent, USA, 1977, 130 mins.

Milton Hershey: The Chocolate King

In this A&E biography, the origins of one of America's most successful business empires are revealed in the story of a man from a humble background. He was born on a farm and quit school at the fourth grade. Despite the odds, he built a business that sold confections to the ordinary person. Hershey differed from his contemporaries in that he treated his workers with respect. From the A&E Biography series.
VHS: $27170. $19.98.
Don Horan, USA, 1995, 50 mins.

The Model T Man from Michigan, America: Henry Ford and His Horseless Carriage

Ford's motor car and assembly line methods transformed manufacturing and modern life. This video explores the complex personality behind these innovations and shows the interiors of his many homes. Hosted by E.G. Marshall. 24 mins.
VHS: $23555. $49.95.
Laser: LD74784. $99.95.

The Nixon Interviews with David Frost

A five-volume collection of David Frost's famous, controversial interviews with former president Richard Nixon. The programs look at the wide-scale domestic, international and personal repercussions of the Nixon administration, including Vietnam, the war at home, the Silent Majority, Nixon's foreign policy in China, Russia, the Middle East, Central America, the implications of Watergate and the cover-up, Spiro Agnew's resignation, Nixon's relationship with Henry Kissinger, the missing footage of the Watergate tapes, John and Martha Mitchell and the ideological composition and makeup of the Supreme Court.
Volume 1: Watergate.
VHS: $17248. $19.98.
Volume 2: The World.
VHS: $17249. $19.98.
Volume 3: War at Home and Abroad.
VHS: $17250. $19.98.
Volume 4: The Final Days.
VHS: $17251. $19.98.
Volume 5: The Missing 18½ Minutes and More.
VHS: $17252. $19.98.

Nova—Albert Einstein

This enlightening television science series examines the life of one of the most influential men of science in this century, Albert Einstein. The encyclopedia says he was born in Ulm, Germany on March 14, 1879, and advanced the theory of relativity at the age of 26. This program from Nova can tell you a lot more about this genius. USA, 60 mins.
VHS: $06027. $19.95.

Patton: A Genius for War

A&E's Biography series reveals the life of this controversial World War II General. His brilliant military maneuvers broke Hitler's Thousand Year Reich, but his unorthodox ways disturbed his own Allied colleagues. 100 mins.
VHS: $27601. $19.95.

Paul Harvey's The Rest of the Story

Popular radio host Paul Harvey relates anecdotes, stories and personal accounts from his true life radio series, The Rest of the Story. 60 mins.
VHS: $17848. $19.95.

Paul Revere: The Midnight Rider

Not only did Paul Revere announce the coming of the British in his famed midnight ride, he actually led the Sons of Liberty and helped organize the Boston Tea Party. In addition to his civic work, he crafted fine silver, which led him into a career as a successful industrialist. This A&E biography shows all sides of this amazing historic figure. From the A&E Biography series. USA, 1995, 50 mins.
VHS: $27172. $19.98.

Portraits of American Presidents

Beginning with the first man to occupy the office, to the current president, this documentary presents the men who filled the office of President of the United States. This exceptional three video collection places all the presidents in the context of their times, gives a brief assessment of their character, the events leading up to their election, their families, and the conflicting social and political influences at work on them. Volume 1: The Presidents of a New Nation—1789-1829. Volume 2: The Presidents of a National Struggle—1829-1901. Volume 3: The Presidents of a World Power—1901-1992.
VHS: $17263. $59.95.

Profiles of Power

A series of tapes on 20th Century leaders—men who had immeasurable impact on history.
Profiles of Power: Franklin D. Roosevelt. A fascinating account of FDR's legacy from the Depression to the terrifying World War II. 40 mins.
VHS: $11142. $19.95.
Profiles of Power: Gandhi. Utilizing rare footage, the life of this century's eloquent spokesman for nonviolence brilliantly comes alive. 45 mins.
VHS: $11147. $19.95.
Profiles of Power: Hitler. This highly collectable video chronicles the fascinating rise and fall of one of history's most controversial leaders. 45 mins.
VHS: $11146. $19.95.
Profiles of Power: Lenin. Utilizing rare footage, Lenin's life unfolds against the backdrop of Russia's Revolution. 45 mins.
VHS: $11145. $19.95.
Profiles of Power: Mussolini. Il Duce was the second most hated villain of the century; from his humble origins to his rise to ultimate power in Italy. 45 mins.
VHS: $11143. $19.95.
Profiles of Power: Winston Churchill. Learn how Churchill alone stood firm when all the world seemed to cower before Hitler. 45 mins.
VHS: $11144. $19.95.

The Real Stories of Capone, Dillinger and Bonnie & Clyde

From New York to Chicago, these accounts bring to life three uniquely American stories and the infamous personalities behind them, captured in rare footage and newsreel accounts of the gangster era of the roaring 20s and the restless 30s. 75 mins.
VHS: $23138. $29.95.

Richard M. Nixon Remembered

After the hype and confused facts surrounding Oliver Stone's epic drama Nixon, a documentary with the actual historical facts is a vital antidote to the growing pressures of infotainment. This CNN documentary shows Richard M. Nixon as a flawed and intriguing individual. Featuring insights from such political figures as President Bill Clinton and Henry Kissinger.
VHS: $27513. $14.98.

Richard Nixon Reflects

Like a phoenix rising from the ashes, former President Richard Nixon returns again to center stage in this candid and revealing 90-minute video memoir. Utilizing never before seen footage from his own personal archives, and extensive interviews conducted by Morton Kondracke, Richard Nixon Reflects provides enlightening and often entertaining anecdotes from his rather colorful political life. Includes his personal thoughts on Kennedy, Reagan, Bush and Gorbachev, as well as his opinions on his own handling of Watergate. 90 mins.
VHS: $13605. $24.98.

Richard Nixon— Checkers, Old Glory, Resignation

A brief look at the former president as seen in three media events. Checkers is a 30-minute paid political announcement aired during the 1952 Presidential campaign. For those who don't remember, Checkers was a pet cocker spaniel. The other segments cover a short Flag Day speech in 1957 and his resignation speech in 1974. USA, 1952-74, 45 mins.
VHS: $05509. $24.95.

Richard Nixon: Man and President

A&E's Biography series looks at the life of one of America's most controversial presidents. Born on a modest California ranch, Nixon rose to prominence despite a number of overwhelming setbacks. In retrospect, his lifetime achievements balance brilliant political successes with nearly unimaginable disaster. 100 mins.
VHS: $27602. $19.95.

Silent Victory—The Kitty O'Neil Story

Stockard Channing stars in this true story of the world's greatest stunt woman who also happens to be deaf. With Colleen Dewhurst, James Farentino, Brian Dennehy.
VHS: $06429. $29.98.
Lou Antonio, USA, 1979, 100 mins.

Sir Terence Conran

Terence Conran, the man who has changed the face of home and style and created a business empire in the process, talks about his life and career. Head of a retail empire including Habitat, Mothercase, BHS and Richard Shops, this documentary examines the man behind this astounding design revolution and the widespread influence of Conran's ideas on modern living. 55 mins.
VHS: $07606. $39.95.

The Speeches of Famous Women: From Suffragette to Senator

Elizabeth Stanton, Eleanor Roosevelt, Betty Ford, Betty Friedan, Carol Mosely Braun and Barbara Boxer have all courageously fought for the rights of women. They are just a few of the women featured in this singular collection of inspiring oratory. From The Speeches Collection. USA, 1995, 56 mins.
VHS: $27279. $19.98.

The Speeches of General Douglas MacArthur

Heroic General Douglas MacArthur was the most dynamic military speaker of the 20th century. Relive his bold "I shall return" speech, his reflections on the arms race and more. 55 mins.
VHS: $12311. $19.95.

The Speeches of Gerald Ford

Chosen to succeed Spiro Agnew as Vice President, he eventually replaced Richard Nixon as President as well. Speeches from Ford's presidential career show his acceding to office, the pardoning of Nixon, his honoring of Queen Elizabeth during her visit to the U.S., his acceptance of the Republican nomination for President and, finally, his farewell to Congress and the nation. From The Speeches Collection. USA, 1995, 55 mins.
VHS: $27277. $19.98.

The Speeches of Harry S. Truman

He "gave 'em hell" when he led the American people through the Korean war and crusaded against communism without compromise. This fascinating cassette documents the speeches at the beginning of the Cold War era of Harry S. Truman. 55 mins.
VHS: $12310. $19.98.

The Speeches of Jimmy Carter

Jimmy Carter was the 39th President of the United States. This collection of speeches features his views on a variety of issues, ranging from support for human rights and international peace to the troubling energy crisis of the late 1970s. From The Speeches Collection. USA, 1995, 55 mins.
VHS: $27276. $19.98.

The Speeches of Lyndon B. Johnson

Lyndon B. Johnson's term as President is documented on this video through a series of speeches he gave while holding the highest office of this country. Much is included, from his continuation of the Kennedy legacy of supporting civil rights to his decision not to run for reelection as President. From The Speeches Collection. USA, 1995, 57 mins.
VHS: $27275. $19.98.

The Speeches of Richard M. Nixon

The tumultuous Nixon era is recreated through Nixon's speeches in Communist China to his sad resignation press conference. 55 mins.
VHS: $12306. $19.98.

The Speeches of Ronald Reagan

"The Great Communicator" inspired many with his oratorical ease. This video showcases highlights of his speaking career, beginning with a 1964 speech lauding Barry Goldwater for President and continuing through to such gems as his debate with former CIA director George Bush. The "Evil Empire" and "Star Wars" speeches, as well as his final words as President, are also included. From The Speeches Collection. USA, 1995, 69 mins.
VHS: $27274. $19.98.

The Story of Will Rogers
A biography of the irreverent political humorist. This program traces Rogers' idiosyncratic life from the rugged individualist whose self-deprecating humor concealed a harsh critique of American society to his death in an Alaskan plane crash. Narrated by Bob Hope. "An altogether superior biography" (*New York Times*). 60 mins.
VHS: S19246. $19.95.

Thomas Jefferson: In Pursuit of Liberty
This is a fascinating portrait of Jefferson and his legacy. As one of the U.S.' founding statesmen he had a profound impact on the young nation. Period paintings, documents and archival footage are combined with images of Monticello and other sites to explain his legacy. President Jimmy Carter, Supreme Court Justice Sandra Day O'Conner and George F. Will all lend their perspectives on this political visionary.
VHS: S24406. $29.95.

Thomas Jefferson: Philosopher of Freedom
This biography tells the amazing history behind one of the country's most intriguing founding fathers. He drafted the Declaration of Independence, fought tirelessly for free speech and U.S. expansion, and even excelled in science and architecture. This video examines whether he really sired many children with his slave and engaged in a troubling affair while working for the U.S. in Paris. From the A&E *Biography* series.
VHS: S27171. $19.98.
Adam Friedman/Monte Markham, USA, 1995, 50 mins.

Truman
Gary Sinise is superb as one of the United States' most pivotal presidents. The rise to prominence of this simple farmer, shopkeeper and county politician coincided with the growing influence of America. He made key decisions and stood by them, including his decision to open the nuclear age with the bombing of Hiroshima and Nagasaki. USA, 1995, 130 mins.
VHS: S26998. $94.99.

Will Rogers
A wise and wistful look at America's favorite son, who for 25 years endeared himself to the nation with his sense of humor. 23 mins.
VHS: S06423. $19.98.

Will Rogers: Champion of the People
Honesty, wry humor and a down-to-earth philosophy endeared this American to the entire nation. Starring Robert Hays. 54 mins.
VHS: S06426. $12.98.

World Without Walls—Beryl Markham's African Memoir
A remarkable documentary about an equally remarkable woman, Beryl Markham—aviatrix, race horse trainer, elephant tracker, irresistible woman—who led a life of unparalleled romance and adventure as the "other" woman in the love triangle between Dennis Finshatten and Karen Blixen (*Out of Africa*). This documentary captures the spectacular scenery of Africa, and offers a unique insight into the English society of Kenya in the 1920's. Winner of the special jury prize at the San Francisco International Film Festival. 60 mins.
VHS: S04368. $29.95.

You May Call Her Madam Secretary
Frances Perkins, the first woman to hold high public office in the nation, is almost unknown today. Yet she was a leading social reformer, a driving force behind protective laws on which our lives depend, an inspiring figure in American and women's history. The film traces the rise of social conscience in this country: from the outrage that followed the Triangle Shirtwaist Fire in 1911 to the revolutionary legislation of the New Deal. In this moving and often witty documentary, actress Frances Sternhagen presents Perkins' complex character on camera, using the words from her oral history and papers. Includes Public Performance Rights. 57 mins.
VHS: S09263. $49.95.

Zona Gale: 1874-1938
The first woman to win a Pulitzer Prize in drama is the subject of this fascinating video. This author's success can be a source of inspiration to all writers. 15 mins. Resource guide available.
Resource Guide.
VHS: S25783. $20.00.
Video.
VHS: S25770. $95.00.

THE KENNEDYS

The Assassination of JFK (Dennis Mueller)
This intriguing film reveals how rogue elements of the CIA and FBI may have allied themselves with organized crime and Texas oil money in a plot to kill the president. Utilizes rare archival footage and original documents.
VHS: S16792. $79.98.
Dennis Mueller, USA, 1992, 78 mins.

Best Evidence: Disguise and Deception in the Assassination of John F. Kennedy
Author David S. Lifton hosts this "research video" into the JFK assassination, focusing on the autopsy and the critical 12 hours following the shooting. Lifton claims that the President's body was secretly intercepted, the wounds altered, autopsy findings faked, and that the assassination conspiracy reached the highest levels of the U.S. government. 30 mins.
VHS: S12162. $14.95.

Beyond JFK: The Question of Conspiracy
A provocative documentary by award-winning filmmaker Barbara Kopple (*Harlan County, U.S.A.; American Dream*) investigates the issues and background materials introduced in Oliver Stone's film *JFK*, offering new research and interviews with the main participants. Narrated by CBS journalist Ike Pappas.
VHS: S17878. $19.98.
Barbara Kopple, USA, 1991, 90 mins.

Four Days in November
A tribute to John F. Kennedy, drawn from more than 8 million feet of newsreel, amateur footage, tapes and photos, this tape vividly chronicles the events surrounding his death and the gunning down of his assassin. 123 mins.
VHS: S07476. $29.95.

Grey Gardens
An eccentric mother and daughter are hidden away in a decaying East Hampton mansion; the mother is Edith Bouvier Beale, the daughter, Edie—aunt and cousin of Jacqueline Bouvier Kennedy. Called "hilarious, horrifying and tragic," and "as compelling a drama as Tennessee Williams might hope to achieve," *Grey Gardens* is a funny, moving descent into American classic decay.
VHS: S07438. $79.95.
Maysles Brothers, USA, 1976, 94 mins.

He Must Have Something
This is the real story of Jim Garrison, the New Orleans law man who investigated the assassination of JFK on his own time. 88 mins.
VHS: S22396. $49.95.

J.F.K. (Documentary)
Watch the rise of John Fitzgerald Kennedy from his early years through WWII, including his family life and his secret side, as well as his final tragic day in 1963. 60 mins.
VHS: S16554. $19.95.

Jack: The Last Kennedy Film
John Kennedy narrates this personal portrait of one of the century's most beloved and charismatic figures. Rare family and historic archival footage tell the story of the milestones that marked the progress of his personal and public lives.
VHS: S21351. $14.98.

Jacqueline Kennedy Onassis Remembered
This charming women continued to transform herself throughout a lifetime shaped by some of the most momentous events of our time. Beginning as a reporter, she quickly adapted to the role of a politician's wife and ultimately first lady. Part One offers an autobiographical overview while parts Two and Three are original early broadcasts consisting of a White House tour conducted by the First Lady herself, and an interview with the Kennedy family just before Jack entered the White House.
VHS: S21352. $14.98.

The JFK Assassination: The Jim Garrison Tapes
Jim Garrison faces the camera to tell the suppressed story surrounding the fateful day of November 22, 1963. Includes actual footage of the crime, recordings of the plotters, new witnesses, new evidence and a complete examination of the record. "If you thought *JFK* was important and you want the factual background to the maligned Garrison investigation, see this film" (Oliver Stone). 1991, 90 mins.
VHS: S16751. $19.98.

The JFK Conspiracy
Hosted by James Earl Jones, *The JFK Conspiracy* exams the events of the day. The program teams the shared opinions of government officials, eye witnesses and director Oliver Stone with expert testimony, photographs, documents and evidence. Includes the complete Zapruder film and six minutes of footage from the House Select Committee on Assassination. 98 mins.
VHS: S16713. $24.98.

JFK Gift Set
A beautifully packaged, three-cassette collection contains the director's cut of Oliver Stone's *JFK*, with 17 minutes of additional footage, and Barbara Kopple's video documentary, *Beyond JFK: The Question of Conspiracy*, a further probing of the issues and connections introduced by the film.
VHS: S17879. $19.98.
Laser: *JFK*—CAV; *Beyond JFK*—CLV. LD71836. $149.98.

JFK: The Day the Nation Cried—November 22, 1963
James Earl Jones reviews the brief life of John F. Kennedy—his triumphs, failures, contribution to history. The moving documentary combines the tragic events of Kennedy's assassination with the remembrances of those who knew him best. 52 mins.
VHS: S10790. $19.95.

JFK: The End of Camelot
In this dramatic and historic documentary from the Discovery Channel, witnesses of JFK's fateful end speak about the experience of this momentous event. The result is a moving document of memory and loss. 90 mins.
VHS: S25076. $19.95.

John F. Kennedy and the Nazi Spy
Much has been learned about JFK's sexual conduct, most of it inconsequential. This tape examines the possibility of leaks that could have occurred due to his infidelities. The subject of the JFK affair had her own agenda. Was she successful? 50 mins.
VHS: S13101. $24.98.

John F. Kennedy's Lost Pathway to Peace
Narrated by Robert Vaughn, a moving portrait of the Kennedy presidential legacy, with Kennedy's emphasis on the strategy of world peace, with rare and historical film clips bringing alive the Kennedy message.
VHS: S07141. $29.95.
Dr. Joseph A. Bagnall, USA, 1985, 30 mins.

John F. Kennedy—The Commemorative Album
A three-part presentation on the life and times of JFK put together by CBS News. Walter Cronkite, Dan Rather and others review the life and death of the man and talk to his mother, Rose Kennedy, for insight into the earlier years. Twenty-five years after the motorcade in Dallas, Kennedy comes alive again on video. USA, 1982, 110 mins.
VHS: S07682. $19.98.
Laser: LD70254. $59.95.

John F. Kennedy: Challenges and Tragedy
Despite his tragically short time in the White House, President Kennedy managed to achieve a great deal, as this video shows. 18 mins.
VHS: S23567. $49.95.

John F. Kennedy: The New Generation
The unique personality of this charismatic president is evoked, and the issues he faced as a leader are examined. 23 mins.
VHS: S23566. $49.95.

Kennedy's Ireland
Part of the great immigrant wave of the 1800's during the Irish potato famine, the Kennedy family moved to America in search of a better life. This tape is an examination of one great family's ethnic heritage. 71 mins.
VHS: S13100. $29.98.

Kennedys
This is the definitive look at America's most powerful and controversial family. Using rare footage, the history of the family is traced to the present with the emergence of a new generation of Kennedys. 100 mins.
VHS: S13099. $19.98.

The Kennedys (American Experience)
A no-holds-barred investigation into the Kennedys, the political dynasty whose charismatic, provocative and firm hold on our political, social and economic institutions is arguably untouched by any rival American family. Produced in association with WGBH/Boston and London's Thames Television.
The Kennedys #1 (American Experience). 120 mins.
VHS: S17344. $19.95.
The Kennedys #2 (American Experience). 120 mins.
VHS: S17345. $19.95.
The Kennedys (American Experience), Complete Set. 240 mins.
VHS: S17346. $39.95.

Kennedys Don't Cry
A definitive look at America's first family, this biography traces their rise to prominence from the days of Joe Kennedy's empire building to the political rise of Jack, Bobby and Teddy. Narrated by Cliff Robertson. 100 mins.
VHS: S02313. $59.95.

The Kennedys of Massachusetts
William Peterson, Annette O'Toole, Charles Durning, Steven Weber and Tracy Pollan star in this film adaptation of Doris Kearn Goodwin's best-selling novel, *The Fitzgeralds and The Kennedys*. This epic film recounts major events in the life of the Kennedy family, from Joe Kennedy's courtship of Rose to the inauguration of J.F.K. 278 mins.
VHS: S26393. $39.98.

The Killing of President Kennedy
A penetrating examination of one of the most devastating events of our time, with rare dramatic film footage and never-before-seen interviews. Based on a two-year House of Representatives investigation, the film reveals startling new theories as to who was really responsible for Kennedy's death and why government agencies tried to conceal vital facts. 80 minutes.
VHS: S02305. $14.98.

Life in Camelot: The Kennedy Years
This is the first and only telling of the JFK story through the President's own words. Utilizing original audio tapes from his private library collection, never-before-published photographs and re-discovered film footage from the '50s and '60s, this essay defines the life and times of one great man and his era. 55 mins.
VHS: S16531. $9.95.

The Men Who Killed Kennedy
A new theory about JFK's murder is at the center of this A&E documentary. It posits that Robert Kennedy knew something of the assassination plot because it was modeled on his own plot to kill Castro. Interviews, including one with a colonel who admits to being trained for eliminating witnesses, and image technology that reveals how autopsy photos were faked, make this a must-see video. 50 mins.
VHS: S27600. $19.95.

Plot to Kill Robert Kennedy
On the anniversary of Robert Kennedy's assassination, this film contradicts the single-assassin theory, alleging that investigators ignored conflicting eyewitness accounts, disregarded testimony and destroyed evidence. USA, 1988, 95 mins.
VHS: S07347. $59.95.

Reasonable Doubt
Rare film and interview footage fill this documentary on the assassination of President John F. Kennedy, giving credibility to the theory that there was more than a single gunman involved in the tragedy that shook the nation. 60 mins.
VHS: S12950. $29.95.

Robert Kennedy and His Times
This well acted biography stars Brad Davis, as the young Bobby Kennedy, alongside Ned Beatty, Veronica Cartwright and Jack Warden, in this terrific look at the Kennedy clan. The double-cassette dramatic biography is based on the best-selling book by Pulitzer-Prize winner and Kennedy confidante Arthur M. Schlessinger, Jr. 309 mins.
VHS: S25753. $24.95.

Second Gun
A documentary which explores who really killed Robert F. Kennedy, exploring an alleged coverup of the assassination and questions who really killed Robert Kennedy.
VHS: S07364. $19.95.

The Speeches of John F. Kennedy
President Kennedy's greatest speeches in a unique video collection.
VHS: S07030. $19.95.

The Speeches of Robert F. Kennedy
The Senator from New York was one of the most charismatic speakers of our time. Now you can hear his eulogy at his brother John's funeral, his ironic reflections on Vietnam, and more. 55 mins.
VHS: S12307. $19.98.

Thank You, Mr. President
John F. Kennedy was a master of the press conference; this program highlights the best moments from his bi-weekly meetings. His wit, charm, and intelligence shine through, as he discusses U.S.-Soviet relations, nuclear war, women's rights, and more. 45 mins.
VHS: S02125. $19.95.

A Tour of the White House
Jacqueline Kennedy is seen at that unique time in her life when she was at the center of the mystique that was Camelot. Here she shows viewers her home, The White House. 60 mins.
VHS: S23795. $24.95.

The Two Kennedys
A look at the Kennedy assassinations—were they separate incidents, or part of a larger conspiracy? This video explores the evidence. B&W, 115 minutes.
VHS: S02311. $59.95.

Two Men in Dallas
In this 1987 documentary, author and leading Kennedy assassination theorist Mark Lane (*Rush to Judgment, Plausible Denial*) interviews Roger Craig, the Dallas deputy sheriff, who recounts his eyewitness version of the events on November 22, 1963, and Craig's subsequent charges that his testimony (which contradicts large portions of the Warren Commission) were suppressed.
VHS: S17006. $29.95.

POLITICAL & CONTEMPORARY EVENTS

1993: A Year in Review
A look back at the tumultuous events that made history in 1993. Produced by CNN. 60 mins.
VHS: S20513. $14.98.

Are We Scaring Ourselves to Death?
John Stoessel originally made this documentary for ABC news. Now this examination of public hysteria around a number of issues is available for home viewing. From crime to cancer to consumer reporting, this journalist examines the scary statistics that litter the airwaves. 50 mins.
VHS: S24324. $19.98.

Arming Dictators
Throughout the 1980's, while the U.S. government opposed dictatorships in the Soviet Bloc, it also supplied over $80 million to ruthless dictators elsewhere. Indonesia, Zaire, Saudi Arabia and El Salvador are just some of the places examined in this documentary, where U.S. tax dollars were used to brutally repress innocent people. 28 mins.
VHS: S21590. $25.00.

Best of Nightline
Assassination Attempt Against President Reagan. 60 mins.
VHS: S14020. $14.98.
Assassination Attempt Against Pope John Paul II. 85 mins.
VHS: S14021. $14.98.
Challenger Disaster. 60 mins.
VHS: S14040. $14.98.
Freeing of the Hostages. 150 mins.
VHS: S14019. $14.98.
Highlights. Celebrate a decade of memorable moments from the ground-breaking, late-night news forum. Experts, politicians, the most controversial interviews conducted by the irrepressible Ted Koppel are the focus of this special. 50 mins.
VHS: S12680. $19.98.
Judge O'Conner Nominated for Supreme Court. 30 mins.
VHS: S14022. $14.98.
Oliver North. 30 mins.
VHS: S14047. $14.98.
President Reagan's Farewell Address. 30 mins.
VHS: S14016. $14.98.
Ronald Reagan Elected President. 120 mins.
VHS: S14015. $14.98.
The First Nightline. 30 mins.
VHS: S14015. $14.98.
U.S. Invades Panama. 60 mins.
VHS: S14062. $14.98.

Beyond Goodwill
Teenagers from the two super powers join forces to combat problems neglected during the Cold War. Restoring forests in Costa Rica, helping survivors of the Armenian earthquake, even providing relief for the homeless of Washington State are just some of the ways these young people hope to overcome distrust through joint action. 58 mins.
VHS: S21587. $85.00.

Beyond Hate
This series of three titles offers an intriguing examination of racial hatred in a number of settings. Experts, politicians, the perpetrators of hate crimes and their victims are all heard in this fascinating series.
Beyond Hate. From Los Angeles to Northern Ireland, both age-old and newly minted prejudices mar the political and social landscape of the contemporary world. This first in the series an overview gives some indication of the scope of the problem. Nelson Mandela, Jimmy Carter, Elie Wiesel and Vaclav Havel are just some of the people who grapple with the lasting legacy of hate. With Bill Moyers. 88 mins.
VHS: S14285. $29.95.
Facing Hate with Elie Wiesel. At 15 Wiesel saw his family destroyed by the Nazi death camps. Ever since he has struggled to understand hatred and its role in world affairs. A prolific writer, human rights leader and even a Nobel Prize winner, his insights, garnered over a lifetime of work for social justice, are an invaluable contribution to this subject. With Bill Moyers. 58 mins.
VHS: S15738. $19.95.
Hate on Trial: The Trial of Tom & John Metzger. In 1990, these two leaders of the White Aryan Resistance were charged with inciting the murder of a young Ethiopian man in Portland Oregon. Three skinheads, all serving long prison terms, were the actual killers. Exclusive courtroom footage follows the case of the Metzgers, tried as advocates for hate. With Bill Moyers. 146 mins.
VHS: S15869. $39.95.
Beyond Hate. Three-title boxed set.
VHS: S19336. $99.95.

The Bill of Rights in Action:
Capital Punishment
The case of a convicted murderer provokes a number of questions about capital punishment. Does it deter crime? Is it cruel and unusual punishment? When is it appropriate to the crime? 23 mins.
VHS: $23690. $79.95.

The Bill of Rights in Action:
De Facto Segregation
School busing is a contentious issue. This film shows how problems arise when the law tries to counteract the effects of de facto segregation. 22 mins.
VHS: $23692. $79.95.

The Bill of Rights in Action:
Due Process of Law
The case of a student who is summarily suspended illustrates the problems of eliminating due process in order to avoid violence and anarchy. The student participated in a campus demonstration. Now viewers must decide if he was denied his rights through immediate suspension. Or was the safety of others more important? 23 mins.
VHS: $23687. $79.95.

The Bill of Rights in Action:
Equal Opportunity
An arbitrator is presented with a case where a black worker is promoted over a white worker even though the white worker has greater seniority. This program is left open-ended for the viewer to decide. 22 mins.
VHS: $23689. $79.95.

The Bill of Rights in Action:
Freedom of Religion
A woman refuses a blood transfusion for religious reasons, even though it may save her life and preserve the health of her developing fetus. Lawyers debate the free exercise of religious practice in the face of this dangerous situation. 23 mins.
VHS: $23694. $79.95.

The Bill of Rights in Action:
Freedom of Speech
Viewers can decide who is right in this case about an unpopular speaker. Lawyers argue the constitutional issues before a court of appeals by weighing the rights of the individual against the community's need for law and order. 18 mins.
VHS: $23685. $79.95.

The Bill of Rights in Action:
Freedom of the Press
No law can abridge the freedom of the press. Does this grant reporters the right to refuse information to criminal investigations? This video explores these issues through a case about just such a reporter. 23 mins.
VHS: $23691. $79.95.

The Bill of Rights in Action:
Juvenile Law
Two brothers, ages 15 and 18, are treated dramatically differently upon arrest. This scenario demonstrates the way adult and juvenile law vary. Should juveniles be treated as adults under the law? Viewers confront this question in this film. 23 mins.
VHS: $23688. $79.95.

The Bill of Rights in Action:
The Privilege Against Self-Incrimination
Accused criminals are protected from forced or coerced confessions by the 5th amendment. Now advanced technologies challenge the importance of this constitutional right. Lawyers present opposing sides around this contentious issue in this dramatic, open-ended program. 22 mins.
VHS: $23696. $79.95.

The Bill of Rights in Action:
The Right to Privacy
Does electronic police surveillance violate the constitutional right to privacy? Law enforcement has always had to weigh the importance of the right to privacy against their ability to protect the public good. 23 mins.
VHS: $23695. $79.95.

The Bill of Rights in Action:
The Story of a Trial
Two young men are accused of a misdemeanor offense. Following their progress through arrest, arraignment and trial, the importance of due process and constitutional safeguards is revealed. 21 mins.
VHS: $23686. $79.95.

The Bill of Rights in Action:
Women's Rights
A high school girl is prohibited by a state law from swimming on a boy's team. Between the 14th amendment and its promise of equal protection, and the physical differences between men and women, there is a contentious area explored by lawyers who argue this case. 22 mins.
VHS: $23693. $79.95.

Biting the Bullet
A moving profile of workers and community and industrial leaders in areas hard hit by military cutbacks, from a former ammunition plant on the Gulf Coast of Mississippi to the empty naval shipyards of Southern California. A timely and provocative program. USA, 1991, 28 mins.
VHS: $15207. $75.00.

The Blame Game:
Are We a Country of Victims?
John Stossel, a journalist with ABC news, examines what he calls the victim movement. He probes the failures of social security, the limits of lawsuits and the diminishment of self-reliance and individual responsibility. 50 mins.
VHS: $24325. $19.98.

The Bottom Line
This program looks at the daily life and difficulties faced by the elderly. Two stories are intertwined, both posing a series of moral and ethical dilemmas on the distinction between life and the quality of life. 30 mins.
VHS: $17932. $49.95.

Campaign Against the Death Penalty
Amnesty International produced this documentary examining the issues surrounding the death penalty and the campaign by human rights organizations to repeal it.
VHS: $07764. $20.00.

Changing the Law
American life is governed by the law. This program examines complex legal issues confronting our contemporary society. Are laws inflexible or does interpretation of the law offer society's changing needs room to grow? 23 mins.
VHS: $23735. $79.95.

Childhood in America
"Educators, bureaucrats and advocates heatedly discuss the roles of family, government and community in reversing the problems of teen pregnancies, dropouts and child care in America" (Booklist). The program also covers five experimental programs in the United States. 90 mins.
VHS: $19384. $29.95.

CIA: The Secret Files
This four-part, collector's boxed set is a behind-the-scenes portrait of the Central Intelligence Agency and its intriguing cast of characters. The show chronicles covert missions, unsanctioned wars, diabolical coups and illegal assassinations. With unprecedented access into the inner workings of the CIA, this program reveals the nature of the work of the "organization dedicated to secrecy and survival." Narrated by Jack Perkins. 200 mins.
VHS: $17902. $59.95.

CNN Video:
Arms Race on America's Streets
In this riveting documentary, produced by America's number one all news network, the violence caused by the arms race on America's streets is examined in depth. It is an invaluable contribution to the ongoing debate around the role of guns in our society. 50 mins.
VHS: $21107. $14.98.

CNN Video: Work in Progress
America's workplace is being transformed by evolving technology and the new global interdependency. The result is greater stress as workers strive to compete under threat of losing their livelihood. This documentary explores these factors as they impact the workaday world. 45 mins.
VHS: $21109. $14.98.

Cocaine…
The Source and the Consequences
This film chillingly portrays narco terrorism: how cocaine is grown by the mountainous native tribes in Colombia, sold through huge drug cartels that control entire governments, and ultimately finances third world unrest. 45 mins.
VHS: $09201. $39.95.

Conversation with Ross Perot
This 75-minute interview shows where Ross Perot stands on a variety of issues as an American, a Texas businessman and a potential world leader. His faith in common sense and traditional values are expressed, as are his efforts to free MIA's in Southeast Asia.
VHS: $16707. $19.98.
Sue Ann Taylor, USA, 1992, 75 mins.

The Cosmic Joke
A compelling documentary on the consequences of the global population explosion. Experts predict the population will double in the next 100 years. This two-part program looks at the issues and solutions. The first program looks at innovative efforts in Mexico and Indonesia to control birth rates. The second program examines women's roles and education and their relation to overpopulation. 120 mins.
VHS: $19375. $49.95.

The Cost of Caring
Addressing the financial and emotional impact of long term care for the elderly, the stories of three married couples and their families reveal limitations in our national health care system. A dramatically important study to individuals coping with current policies affecting health care. 30 mins.
VHS: $16386. $39.95.

Culture of Aging
Attitudes toward aging and the aged vary from culture to culture. This program looks at how older people remain determined to lead active and productive lives in a world that seems to place a greater value on the pleasures of youth than on the wisdom and experience of age. Produced by Maryknoll Media. 28 mins.
VHS: $09068. $24.95.

The Election
The concluding video polls a wide range of voters and leads a discussion about social, political and economic difficulties of the country.
VHS: $16885. $19.95.

Enemy Mine
Gil Rossellini presents images of six modern European countries in conflict in this series which "give[s] voice to ordinary people whose lives are forever altered by ethnic violence."
Albania: White Faces. This film was the first Western film shot in Albania. It shows the horrors of family feuding which has been a constant problem in the Balkans for centuries. One man acts to stop the violence. 55 mins.
VHS: $26725. $29.95.
Cyprus: The Moment Time Stood Still. The memories and nightmares of the Greek Cypriots who have been separated from their homeland by the Turkish invasion of 1974 inspired this sensitive and provocative film. 55 mins.
VHS: $26722. $29.95.
Germany: Cracks in the Land. This film explores the psychological aftermath of the falling of the Berlin wall. Two people who now share the same city have an ironic and sad affinity. 55 mins.
VHS: $26724. $29.95.
Hungary: Where the Water Is Deep. A murder outlines the hatred between Hungarians and their Gypsy neighbors. Mistrust and anger divide this beautiful land. 55 mins.
VHS: $26723. $29.95.
Italy: South of Italy. Giuseppe's bank once offered hope to small local farmers, but mobsters have forced his hand. Now Giuseppe must face the specter of a takeover from a Northern institution certain to be less sympathetic to local needs. 55 mins.
VHS: $26720. $29.95.
Northern Ireland: The Kickhams. An unusual football team is at the heart of this controversial story. The Kickhams are at the heart of Belfast, and as a result, have no playing field of their own. 55 mins.
VHS: $26721. $29.95.

The Expanding Nuclear Club
Though the arms race between the U.S. and the USSR appears to be over, 15 other nations are possible new members of this exclusive club. The proliferation of these deadly weapons may actually be encouraged by the spread of nuclear power plants throughout the world, a process supported by the U.S. government. This documentary illuminates the dimensions of this growing problem with the help of key advisors, including former arms control negotiator Paul Warnecke. 28 mins.
VHS: $21583. $25.00.

Family of Women
Women's peace encampments are vital sources of power in today's feminist movement. Meet the women who follow this dream in the 90's. USA, 36 mins.
VHS: $26821. $29.95.

Fragile Balance (1955-1961)
The Cold War and arms race spur technological innovation that keeps the world on edge. Sputnik, the Soviet satellite, brings a new dimension to this competition. Soon a newly elected President Kennedy will redefine American military policy in order to pursue a goal in outer space. 24 mins.
VHS: $23598. $99.95.

Kids in the Crossfire:
Violence in America:
Answering Children's Questions
Peter Jennings moderates this live special which examines violence in our society through the eyes of America's youth. 70 mins.
VHS: $22990. $19.98.

Life Remembers 1993
Life magazine's retrospective of the personalities and events that made the year 1993 a memorable year: Audrey Hepburn, Arthur Ashe, Thurgood Marshall, Rudolph Nureyev, Dizzy Gillespie, Lillian Gish, and many more. 60 mins.
VHS: $20532. $14.98.

Man and the State:
Burke and Paine on Revolution
Locked in debate, Burke and Paine state their conflicting views on man, political change, and liberty. Events from the French Revolution are dramatically re-enacted in front of them, underscoring the importance of their concerns. 28 mins.
VHS: $23699. $79.95.

Man and the State:
Machiavelli on Political Power
Niccolo Machiavelli debates his influential ideas on political power. The resulting film will stimulate discussion on contemporary problems in government, history and literature. 28 mins.
VHS: $23697. $79.95.

Man and the State:
Marx and Rockefeller on Capitalism
Pushed into the 20th century, these 19th-century figures debate the evolution of their opposing philosophies, communism and capitalism. 26 mins.
VHS: $23702. $79.95.

Manufacturing Consent:
Noam Chomsky and the Media
This remarkable Canadian documentary is a riveting look at the political life and times of the controversial author, linguist and radical philosopher, Noam Chomsky. Chomsky provides shocking examples of media deception as he analyzes the media and democratic societies. A film which has achieved cult status in its remarkable call to Chomsky's charge for viewers to "extricate themselves from this web of deceit by undertaking a course of intellectual self-defense."
VHS: $21851. $39.95.
Mark Achbar/Peter Wintonick, Canada, 1993 180 mins.

May Day—May Day
Filmed in seven countries on International Labour Day, 1987, this video is about the abuse of trade unionists' human rights and their struggle to make their voices heard and achieve official recognition. The video places special emphasis on Guatemala. Produced by Amnesty International. 1987, 30 mins.
VHS: $09780. $19.95.

The Military on Campus
Nearly 300 universities receive millions in research funds from the military, with some 60 campuses getting over 3 million dollars each year. Seventy percent of computer science research money from the federal government also comes from the military. What role should the military play in the intellectual life of America's colleges and universities now that the cold war is over? 28 mins.
VHS: $21589. $25.00.

New Immigrants
Immigration is a continuing American story, and each period brings different faces and different elements to a growing America. Who the newest immigrants are, and how they join American society in the last decade of the 20th century is the focus of this program. 28 mins.
VHS: $10783. $29.95.

New US-USSR Relationship
Barbara Marx Hubbard, leading futurist speaker, currently serves as host for those who travel to the USSR to establish groups fostering the concept of the Global Family. In this forum she explores US and USSR relations and their impact on the Global Family. 75 mins.
VHS: $10224. $29.95.

The Nomination
This program re-examines the fortunes and failures of the winning candidates from both parties, and considers the prospect of an independent challenger and its impact on the selection of the president.
VHS: $16884. $19.95.

Oliver North: Memo to History
No doubt, one of the memos not shredded. Actually, this is a compilation of excerpts of the testimony at the Congressional Iran-Contra hearings. USA, 1987, 90 mins.
VHS: $04501. $19.95.

Out of the Silence:
Fighting for Human Rights
In 1948, the Declaration of Human Rights ushered in a new era in human rights awareness. This documentary chronicles the global struggle waged on behalf of all people everywhere. 55 mins.
VHS: $23650. $69.95.

Peter Jennings Reporting:
Men, Sex and Rape
Peter Jennings and ABC News travel to Palm Beach, Florida, site of the highly publicized William Kennedy Smith rape trial, to raise questions about men and rape for which no easy answers exist. 75 mins.
VHS: $16795. $29.98.

The Powers of the Presidency:
Armed Intervention
Military intervention is a course of action often chosen by the President despite conflicting and continually changing intelligence information. How can the President respond swiftly to complex international situations? This question is posed for the viewer, who must decide when intervention is appropriate. 23 mins.
VHS: $23738. $79.95.

The Powers of the Presidency:
Economic Controls
In this open-ended program the powers of the President are examined in regard to the imposition of wage and price controls. The scenario goes like this: there is runaway inflation and the Congress does nothing. Can the President set limits on the economy and what will the effects of this control be? 23 mins.
VHS: $23737. $79.95.

President Clinton:
Answering Children's Questions, 1993
In a special town meeting, live from the White House with Peter Jennings, children in the audience and from all over the country have the opportunity to ask questions and voice their concerns to President Bill Clinton. 105 mins.
VHS: $22988. $19.98.

President Clinton: Answering Children's Questions, 1994

One year later, children have another chance to express their opinions and concerns to President Clinton, with Peter Jennings as the moderator. 90 mins.
VHS: S22989. $19.98.

The Primary

Three documentaries from the innovative program *The 90's* that provide a kaleidoscopic view of the inner dynamics of the American political process. *The Primary* considers the events, activities and strategic importance of Arkansas governor Bill Clinton's primary victory in Illinois opposite Carol Mosely Braun's stunning, historically unprecedented contest for the Democratic nomination in the U.S. Senate. "A video tour de force," wrote the *Chicago Tribune's* Rick Kogan.
VHS: S16883. $19.95.

The Prize

An eight-part documentary based on Daniel Yergin's book on the relationship between oil, money and politics. The documentary opens with the initial well drilled in 1859 Pennsylvania, and traces the western democracies' increasing dependence on oil, the foundation of "oil economies," and the various global and regional wars fought over its control, including the Iraqi's invasion of Kuwait and the aftermath of the Gulf War. Narrated by Donald Sutherland, the program interweaves first-person accounts, interviews, letters and personal memoirs to create a dazzling and provocative vision. Two programs per tape. Each tape is approximately 60 mins.
The Prize, Vol. 1: The Trust Busters/The Oil Wars.
VHS: S17720. $49.95.
The Prize, Vol. 2: The Black Giant/Oil, War and Strategy.
VHS: S17721. $49.95.
The Prize, Vol. 3: Fill'er Up/A New Center of Gravity.
VHS: S17722. $49.95.
The Prize, Vol. 4: The Oil Weapon/Oil's New World Order.
VHS: S17723. $49.95.
The Prize, Complete Set.
VHS: S17724. $149.95.

Proudly We Hail

This patriotic video takes viewers through all of this country's wars, from the Revolutionary War to Vietnam, to answer why most Americans hold the flag so dear. Narrated by Robert Stack.
VHS: S14901. $29.95.

Talks by Michael Parenti

Michael Parenti is the brilliant observer of press and media and its manipulation of contemporary politics, reality and values, and the author of books including *Inventing Reality, Democracy for the Few, Power and the Powerless, The Sword and the Dollar* and *Make Believe Media: The Politics of Entertainment.* In this series of videotapes, he discusses some of the dominant issues of our time.
Crimes of Empire: Bush's War in the Middle East. Takes a close look at the excuses given for intervention in the Gulf and the real, underlying reasons (updated version).
VHS: S15595. $19.95.
Democracy and U.S. Intervention. Looks at the differences between a Marxist and liberal analysis of political life, and the myth of "national security."
VHS: S15589. $19.95.
Human Nature and Politics. Looks at the political dimensions of "What is Human Nature?" A critique of the conservative concepts.
VHS: S15592. $19.95.
Imperialism and the Bush Hypocrisy. A critique of Bush's foreign and domestic policies, including the invasion of Panama.
VHS: S15593. $19.95.
Imperialism, Drugs and Social Control. Parenti discusses the link between US intervention and the CIA's use of drugs abroad and at home.
VHS: S15594. $19.95.
Inventing Reality. Parenti discusses the monopoly ownership of the media, news distortions and ideological control.
VHS: S15586. $19.95.
Michael Parenti Interview. Includes discussions of Corporatism and the US political scene, as well as media distortion of the Gulf War.
VHS: S15596. $19.95.
Monopoly Culture and Academic Freedom. The class basis of our "independent" cultural, legal and educational institutions.
VHS: S15587. $19.95.
Rambo and the Swarthy Hordes. A talk Michael Parenti gave in Hollywood on the political images of the entertainment media. Treats actual movies that propagate imperialistic and racist themes.
VHS: S15591. $19.95.
The Political Uses of Religion. Parenti examines the ways in which the Right use religion to manipulate people; contains kind words about liberation theology.
VHS: S15588. $19.95.
The Sword and the Dollar. The history of imperialism and the forced mal-development of the Third World are examined.
VHS: S15590. $19.95.

Terrorism: The New World War

Beirut, London, Paris: these are the battlegrounds of the modern world. Their goals may be political or religious, but the brutal reality of terrorist activities has spread through the world in epidemic proportions. From ABC News. 60 mins.
VHS: S12683. $24.98.

Torture in the Eighties

An overview of the use of torture by governments around the world, produced as a part of Amnesty International's Campaign to end the use of torture of prisoners and detainees around the world. 1985, 14 mins.
VHS: S06889. $15.00.

TVTV: Four More Years

A documentary on the anarchic events surrounding the 1972 Republican National Convention in Miami, framed through the guerrilla tactics of the outlaw television activists at TVTV, who trained their cameras on the pure spectacle of the absurd. B&W, 60 mins.
VHS: S15557. $24.95.

United States Elections: How We Vote

All elements of the voting process, including registration, voting, tabulation, and procedures that protect the rights of voters and candidate are explored in this film. 14 mins.
VHS: S23736. $79.95.

Walk with the People

Why would people leave their own country, their families and even profitable careers to serve the poor in Asia, Africa, and Latin America? In this film, a Maryknoll priest, Sister, Brother and lay missioner speak of what motivates them, and of the joys and heartaches of giving themselves to those in need. Produced by Maryknoll Media. 28 mins.
VHS: S04936. $24.95.

Wall Street Journal Video: Emerging Powers

Four one-hour guides to the emerging economic powerhouses of China, Mexico, Brazil and India are joined in this informative video set. It offers insider information to these fast-growing markets with detailed analysis of the risks, from political instability and roller-coaster currency to a lack of current and reliable information. Investors will get a unique view on these tempting but unknown developing economies.
VHS: S27658. $79.95.
David Royle, USA, 1996

What Is the Third World?

Does the term "third world" still have any meaning? What are the obligations of developed nations toward developing countries? What does faith demand of us as individuals with respect to our brothers and sisters in the "Third World" nations? And what are the real needs of these countries? Produced by Maryknoll Media. 28 mins.
VHS: S09069. $24.95.

Women in Construction

Five women, a carpenter, an architect, a sheetmetalworker and plumbing and electrical apprentices, discuss the challenges they face in the traditionally male world of construction. 15 mins.
VHS: S22155. $126.50.

Women in Policing

Six police officers with differing specialties and varying levels of experience present their views on this unique career. It's definitely a job with a future; one of these women has been at it for over 20 years. 15 mins. Resource guide available.
Resource Guide.
VHS: S25782. $20.00.
Video.
VHS: S25769. $95.00.

ENVIRONMENTAL & GLOBAL ISSUES

Acid Rain

This program explains clearly how acid rain is created and what is being done to better understand its effects on the environment. Winner of Gold Medal at the International Film and TV Festival in New York. 36 mins.
VHS: S12268. $104.00.

After the Warming

James Burke moderates this series on the aftermath of the Greenhouse Effect. "Fast-paced production, visually interesting and full of ideas to mull over and to act on" (*Washington Post*).
After the Warming: Tape One. Burke suggests the ecological impact of what various warming scenarios beginning in the year 2050 will contain. Burke shows "how life on earth has often altered by changing weather patterns." 60 mins.
VHS: S18059. $29.95.
After the Warming: Tape Two. Burke studies the means that could be employed to respond to the environmental crisis, particularly the impact of global warming on food supplies and the effects of increased rainfall and deforestation. 60 mins.
VHS: S18060. $29.95.
After the Warming: Complete Set.
VHS: S18061. $49.95.

America's Defense Monitor: Bringing the Troops Home

A major portion of our military budget goes to support 500,000 American troops stationed abroad at over 300 foreign military bases. Bush administration supporters advocate keeping sizeable forces overseas, while other experts believe, in light of recent world events, that it is time to dramatically reduce the U.S. military presence around the world. 1990, 29 mins.
VHS: S13962. $29.95.

America's Defense Monitor: National Security in the 90's

With the Cold War officially over, what constitutes our national security? This provocative, forward-thinking episode asks the experts how we can secure a strong America—economically, socially, and militarily. 1990, 29 mins.
VHS: S13958. $29.95.

America's Defense Monitor: The Great Arms Debate

What should the size, role, and cost of our armed forces be now in the post-Cold War era? Is there any hope for a "peace dividend?" Some call for a smaller military and restraint in the weapons programs. Former Defense Secretary Cheney makes the case for staying the course. 1990, 29 mins.
VHS: S13961. $29.95.

America's Defense Monitor: The Language of War

"Pre-Dawn Vertical Insertion." "Violence Processing." "Permanent Pre-hostility." Does the military use language to clarify or camouflage the reality of war and the preparations for war? Though sometimes humorous, this program raises very serious questions about the critical impact of language on public debate and public policy. 1990, 29 mins.
VHS: S13960. $29.95.

America's Defense Monitor: The UN's Blue Helmets

The United Nation's peacekeeping forces have played a quiet but important role in many parts of the world, helping to monitor and prevent conflicts between warring countries or factions. As the Cold War ends, what will be the world role for the UN? 1990, 29 mins.
VHS: S13959. $29.95.

Atomic Memories

Before the United States and the Soviet Union learned to live together in peace and harmony, there was a time when mutually assured destruction was a major concern. This nostalgic documentary looks back on an era when the U.S. government felt it was necessary to produce films like *Duck and Cover, The Effects of Atomic Bomb Explosions* and *Survival under Atomic Attack.* Also featured is footage of the A-bomb test at the Bikini Atoll.
VHS: S13314. $19.95.

Battle for the Trees

A multiple award winner, this is a highly effective look at the impact of clearcutting, the potential for alternatives that balance economic needs with forest preservation, and the role of multi-national corporations which are increasingly logging old growth forests. 57 mins.
VHS: S23372. $95.00.

Bound by the Wind

This video document presents the dramatic, international impact of nuclear testing on the people who live downwind from the U.S., Soviet and French test sites—people who have suffered extremely high rates of cancer. Includes interviews with Andrei Sakharov and others. USA, 1991, 40 mins.
VHS: S15205. $75.00.

Building Bombs

A rich, personal look at the social and environmental impact of the Savannah River Plant in South Carolina, where weapons-grade plutonium and tritium are manufactured. This is a thoughtful film on an important topic that has proven to be an effective catalyst with a wide-range of audiences. 1989, 54 mins.
VHS: S13957. $95.00.

The Business of Hunger

In many Third World countries, cash crops are exported while the poor go hungry. This phenomenon, one of the major causes of world hunger, is examined in Latin America, Africa, Asia, and the U.S.A. Winner of American Film Festival. 28 mins. Produced by Maryknoll Media.
VHS: S04922. $24.95.

Buster and Me

Robin Goodrow stars as Robin in this award-winning program. Today's children are increasingly aware of the prospect of nuclear war and this awareness affects their lives. *Buster and Me* uses puppets to address these feelings, bring them out in the open, give children the sense that they are not alone and give them a feeling of hope and power.
VHS: S03811. $45.00.
Christina Mercalf, USA, 1983, 28 mins.

Call for Peace: The Military Budget and You

Based on a moving speech by Congressman Ronald V. Dellums, with narration by Harry Belafonte, the film asks, "Do we (the American people) want to live or do we want to die? If we want to live, we must make our every act a furtherance of world peace." Alice Walker, author of *The Color Purple* said, "If we wish to die, all that is required is a continuation of ourselves as we are. Ponder the message of this film and choose to act. Choose to live."
VHS: S03804. $45.00.
Steve Rauh, USA, 1983, 28 mins.

Centerpiece for Peace

In this talk, former astronaut Brian O'Leary explores the possibilities of future space programs. Here he expands on his statement, "we are experiencing a quantum leap in our awareness of ourselves as citizens of the universe, and as leaders of a new society whose exploits hover at the edge of our imagination." 52 mins.
VHS: S10223. $29.95.

Changing Tides Along the Mediterranean

One of the world's most historic seas is dying. This moving documentary follows a group of young people from 14 nations as they come together to learn about these environmental problems and seek solutions. An inspiring example to youth. 23 mins.
VHS: S10890. $45.00.

Chernobyl

The graphic and otherwise unavailable facts about the after-effects of Chernobyl—the blast site, the people and areas affected, and the questions: What are the statistical risks? Who will develop cancer? Whose children will be mutants? The Chernobyl accident is expected to cause an additional 20,000 to 200,000 deaths in Western Europe.
VHS: S05281. $29.95.

Choice or Chance II

The Pentagon spends over $1.5 billion a year for advertising aimed at filling the ranks of the military with young recruits. But for many, the military may be the wrong choice. This colorful, factual presentation explores such questions as: What are a recruiter's promises really worth? Does military training help in civilian life? What are the potential problem areas recruiters ignore? 20 mins.
VHS: S10891. $75.00.

Choices for the Future

John Denver hosts this inspiring new look at options for a peaceful, sustainable future. Featured are perspectives offered by Ted Turner, Ram Dass, astronaut Rust Schweickart, Jean-Michel Cousteau, Robert Muller, Dr. Robert Bourne and others. From the first Choices for the Future Symposium held at Snowmass, Colorado in 1986. Produced by he Windstar Foundation. 45 mins.
VHS: S04313. $29.95.

Civilized Defense Plan

A thought-provoking program which illustrates an important proposal for using international economic pressure to help eliminate weapons of mass destruction and reduce armed aggression. Graphic techniques and interviews with experts including Lloyd J. Dumas, Professor of Political Economy at the University of Texas, and Benjamin Ferencz, former chief prosecutor at the Nuremberg War crimes trials. 30 mins.
VHS: S10883. $29.95.

Cleaning Up Toxics at Home

This program gives simple and practical advice on how we can reduce pollution from households and protect our families from the toxic hazards found in our homes. An important, hands-on program for anyone concerned about the potential hazards posed by the chemicals we all use daily. 1990, 30 mins.
VHS: S13945. $59.95.

Cleaning Up Toxics in Business

Small businesses of all kinds are making remarkable changes to protect our environment. This program shows businessmen and women a variety of innovative solutions to comply with increasingly strict environmental regulations. 1990, 30 mins.
VHS: S13946. $59.95.

Common Table

Focus on a new understanding of indigenous cultures and practices in the Philippines and Africa. 28 mins.
VHS: S04923. $24.95.

Conserving America: Champions of Wildlife

Ospreys in Massachusetts, turtles in Texas, baby bears in Oregon—wherever species are endangered, concerned conservationists are working to restore lost habitat and provide sanctuary for injured birds and animals. 1988, 58 mins.
VHS: S13948. $29.95.

Conserving America: The Challenge on the Coast

Nearly 75% of Americans live within 50 miles of the coast. Yet nearly half of the country's coastal wetlands have disappeared. It's clear today that we all must do our part to protect these invaluable resources. 1989, 58 mins.
VHS: S13950. $29.95.

Conserving America: The Rivers

Only 1% of America's rivers are protected by the Federal Wild and Scenic Rivers Act. Some concerned citizens are lobbying governments to pass protective legislation to keep our rivers safe from pollution, contamination, dams, channelization, and industrial development. 1988, 58 mins.
VHS: S13949. $29.95.

Conserving America: The Wetlands

America's swamps and marshes are our richest and least understood landscapes. 300,000 acres of wetlands disappear each year—filled in to build airports, industrial plants, and housing. But attitudes are changing, and people are beginning to work together to protect these unique habitats. 1990, 58 mins.
VHS: S13951. $29.95.

Coyoteland

Jay April used a hand-held camera to document this story about the competition between wildlife and urbanization. A coyote carries away a pet dog, leading residents to call on a trapper. His view of wild life is contrasted with an elderly woman who articulates a defense in favor of the coyote. The result is a humorous and provocative film about the conflicts of contemporary life. 17 mins.
VHS: S21582. $59.95.

Danger at the Beach

Ted Danson explores the 10,000 miles of coastline under siege by rot, decay, dead animals and medical waste. The film documents the destruction of marine life.
VHS: S16879. $14.98.

Dash McTrash and the Pollution Solution

Designed for primary grades, *Dash McTrash* is an excellent course in ecological awareness and action. This collection features five episodes, including his adventures with the Bogs, Anna Mae, Uncle Don, the Big Cleanup, and "E for Ecology."
VHS: S14173. $59.95.

Day After Trinity

This haunting examination of the dawn of the nuclear age focuses on the dramatic events surrounding the development of the first atomic bomb. Featuring interviews with scientists and soldiers, and rare, archival footage, it provides a gripping profile of J. Robert Oppenheimer, the bomb's principal architect, and offers a penetrating commentary on the nature of scientific inquiry, the McCarthy era, and nuclear proliferation.
VHS: S00307. $39.95.
Laser: LD75026. $49.95.
Jon Else, USA, 1981, 88 mins.

Deadly Deception

G.E. does more than "bring good things to life." It also is the industry leader in producing nuclear arms components. This challenging video questions the role of corporate responsibility given the deadly influence exerted by this firm's many nuclear installations. Winner of the Academy Award for Best Documentary. 29 mins.
VHS: S21586. $50.00.

Deafsmith, A Nuclear Folktale

One day Texas farmer John Smith returned home to find a mysterious crew of people placing seismographic cables on his land. That was the start of Deafsmith County's struggle to prevent all of the nation's high-level nuclear waste from being buried beneath their farms. 1990, 43 mins.
VHS: S13953. $85.00.

Defending America: The Price We Pay

A thorough, timely examination of the causes, costs and consequences of military spending. This film takes a close look at a variety of issues, including military waste, procurement policies, the effects on research, contribution to the national debt, impact on jobs, and the trade-offs with social programs. An insightful study. 1989, 58 mins.
VHS: S13964. $75.00.

Direct Connection

Fifteen teenagers from Sierra Mounain High School, California, videotape a message of hope for peace and mutual understanding to an equal number of Soviet students. Produced by Michael Killigrew, 30 mins.
VHS: S04311. $29.95.

Disarmament: A Public Opinion Poll

In June, 1982, there were rallies held throughout the world in support of the U.N. Conference on Disarmament. Video artist Skip Blumberg and hundreds of crew members collaborated on the most expansive video project to date. They recorded more than 3,000 interviews in 60 locations around the world. This tape features the most interesting, most humorous and most eccentric of these interviews with individuals of all races, colors, professions, offering a panorama of characters expressing their hopes, fears and concerns about the nuclear issue. 1982, 30 mins.

VHS: S08527. $29.95.

Does the U.S. Need Nuclear Weapons?

A thought-provoking assessment of our nuclear stockpile of 17,000 weapons at an annual cost of $30 billion. A wide range of political experts and military personnel provides a compelling argument for ridding ourselves of these weapons of mass destruction. 25 mins.

VHS: S23391. $35.00.

A Dream of Peace

In 1987 the entire country of New Zealand became a nuclear free zone, banning nuclear ships from the country's ports. *A Dream of Peace* is a closer look at the motivations and historical developments that led to New Zealand's nuclear-free declaration. Through archival news footage and interviews with key leaders, including former Prime Minister David Lange, the video describes the events surrounding the declaration and its significance for other countries. Produced by the New Zealand Foundation for Peace Studies. 12 mins.

VHS: S11486. $29.95.

The Earth at Risk Environmental Video Series

Former MTV host Kevin Seal presents this fascinating and fun, 10-volume set which examines important environment issues of our time. Science is both important and enjoyable. Each volume is 30 mins.
Acid Rain.
VHS: S24425. $39.95.
Clean Air.
VHS: S24426. $39.95.
Clean Water.
VHS: S24427. $39.95.
Degradation of the Land.
VHS: S24428. $39.95.
Extinction.
VHS: S24429. $39.95.
Global Warming.
VHS: S24430. $39.95.
Nuclear Energy/Nuclear Waste.
VHS: S24431. $39.95.
The Ozone Layer.
VHS: S24432. $39.95.
The Rainforest.
VHS: S24433. $39.95.
Recycling.
VHS: S24434. $39.95.
The Earth at Risk Environmental Video Series. 10-volume set.
VHS: S24435. $349.50.

Earth First! The Struggle for the Australian Rainforest

Highlights the plight of our oldest living link with the past, the majestic rain forests. Set in Australia, the program looks at a 70 square kilometer stand of rainforest, which is all that remains from an age when Australia was the center of a mighty supercontinent called Gondwanaland, covered by a magnificent emerald rainforest. It is also the story of people who went to the most extraordinary lengths to save these rain forests—who stirred the conscience of a nation through their dramatic, risk-taking actions. 58 mins.

VHS: S11489. $39.95.

The Earth Is the Lord's: Ecology as a Religious Concern

Ecologists David Ehrenfeld and Wes Jackson of the Land Institute talk about ways to control environmental damage. Rabbi Ismar Schorsch then explains how Judaism can preserve creation and not abuse it. 60 mins.

VHS: S24501. $29.95.

Eclipse of the Man-Made Sun

The imagery and language used to describe nuclear energy and nuclear weapons are redolent with metaphysical and divinely derived metaphors. This documentary explores how these technologies were presented in ways that continue to impact contemporary society. Animation, archival footage, special effects and commentary from assorted experts illuminate this fascinating idea. 50 mins.

VHS: S21585. $95.00.

Ecology of the Urban Environment

This program discusses concepts of ecology in relation to improving daily urban life, including issues of sanitation, water supply, air pollution, population, housing patterns and urban wildlife. 28 mins.

VHS: S20282. $29.95.

The Edge of History

Twelve distinguished men and women, including Admiral Noel Gayler, former commander of the Pacific fleet, stress the crucial need for cooperation in international affairs, both in arms controls talks and in citizen diplomacy. Filmed at the Stanford Symposium on the Prevention of Nuclear War. Winner at many film festivals.

VHS: S03795. $45.00.
Thiermann/Verdon-Roe, USA, 1984, 28 mins.

Experimental Animals

Some 300,000 military personnel were deliberately exposed to nuclear blasts during WWII in an effort to determine whether soldiers could fight and survive the blast. Now coping with serious health problems, these individuals are not receiving the aid they need from the government that used them as human guinea pigs. A compelling story combining archival footage of soldiers and sailors during exposure tests and personal interviews. 35 mins.

VHS: S23389. $79.00.

Exploring Ecology

This program instructs children on the need to preserve the environment. Students are asked to process information and organize solutions to problems pertaining to natural resources, endangered species, ecosystems, non-renewable energy sources and alternative energy resources. For children in grades 4-6.
Air, Water & Soil Resources. An examination of our vital resources—air, water and soil—that explains their importance. The program also shows solutions to pollution and depletion of these resources. 15 mins.
VHS: S19963. $36.95.
Energy Resources. This program studies the importance of nonrenewable energy resources—including fossil fuels. The program examines how the fuels are formed, measured and processed. 13 mins.
VHS: S19965. $36.95.
Future Resources. Emerging technology and valuable energy resources developed for future use, including solar, hydroelectric, wind and geothermal, are contrasted through the advantages and disadvantages they pose to the environment. 13 mins.
VHS: S19966. $36.95.
Wildlife Resources. This program studies wildlife and plant resources, including endangered species. The concepts of ecosystems and habitats and niches are examined. 13 mins.
VHS: S19964. $36.95.
Exploring Ecology, Set.
VHS: S19967. $129.00.

Final Chapter

Christopher Plummer narrates this award-wining documentary that explores what would happen if a nuclear war were to take place, which presents evidence gathered by over 100 international scientists who have faced the fateful realities. An alarming, scientific exploration, *The Final Chapter* compels one to think about the unthinkable. 75 mins.

VHS: S06553. $59.95.

First Strike: Portrait of an Activist

Early one Sunday morning, 28-year-old Susan Komisaruk entered Vandenburg Air Base and spent two uninterrupted hours damaging military computer equipment linked to first-strike missile guidance systems. *First Strike* is a compelling portrait of individual commitment, tracing Komisaruk's evolution from a 22-year-old MBA student at the University of California to her arrest, trial and imprisonment. Produced by Doug Dibble. 38 mins.

VHS: S10885. $39.95.

Fueling the Future

Originally produced for PBS, this comprehensive series looks at energy use in four major areas: transportation, farming, housing and disposable products. Along the way viewers will realize how our values and dreams are shaped by current energy usage, often without regard for the future. Each episode is 58 mins. In *Running on Empty*, lively archival footage recreates the dramatic rise of the automobile as a primary means of transportation within this century. Viable alternative fuels are then examined along with the prospects for revitalizing public transportation. *Hot Wiring America's Farms* relates how heavy fossil fuel use has allowed American farms to become among the most productive on the planet. Yet this very success may ultimately destroy the lands upon which we depend for survival. This episode examines the impact of energy intensive agriculture and presents more energy-efficient alternatives. *No Deposit, No Return* demonstrates how America's throw-away lifestyle provides many conveniences, but how much energy are we simply throwing out with the trash? This video reveals the enormous costs of this wastefulness and shows how we can get to the core of the waste problem. And *No Place Like Home* discusses how today's suburban communities force residents to be continually on the go, consuming large quantities of fuel and human energy in the process. This episode shows how these communities evolved in the era of cheap energy and what some designers are doing to counteract this trend.

VHS: S21567. $299.00.

Genetic Time Bomb

Because of a dramatic decline in crop diversity, the world may be facing a serious shortage in the food supply. A look at the agricultural changes that could lead to catastrophe, and the importance of maintaining biodiversity and the increase in "seed savers"—those individuals who are cultivating thousands of rare and threatened species of fruits and vegetables. 50 mins.

VHS: S23378. $150.00.

Get It Together

A positive, fast-paced look at the contributions of young people of all races to transform their communities and protect the environment. Produced by Youth for Youth, the video profiles several organizations, including Detroit Summer, youth working to improve America's inner cities; YouthBuild in New York, which builds low-income housing; and young Mexican-American women in California speaking out against pollution. 28 mins.

VHS: S23363. $59.95.

Ghosts Along the Freeway

The building of the freeway system displaces thousands of homeowners. This is a concise, highly effective look at the impact on two neighborhoods of the arrival of a superhighway. Historic photographs and personal interviews with former residents merge to create a memorable, prize-winning video on the environment, transportation and urban development. 10 mins.

VHS: S23385. $79.00.

Global Brain

World-renowned philosopher, scientist and humanitarian Peter Russell presents an empowering and optimistic vision of humanity's potential. This captivating program is used by U.S. diplomats, English and Swedish television, and multinational corporations in management development programs. Based on Peter Russell's best-selling book.

VHS: S03810. $39.00.
Chris Hall, Great Britain, 1985, 35 mins.

Global Dumping Ground: The International Traffic in Hazardous Waste

Few Americans realize that the hazardous waste we generate here is one of our country's leading exports to third world nations. This PBS Frontline special report reveals how toxic exports have become big business—and a serious health hazard to the citizens of foreign nations. 1990, 60 mins.

VHS: S13947. $99.95.

The Global Gardener

Bill Mollison is a practical visionary who believes sustainable agriculture can transform the way we live through "permaculture", or permanent agriculture. His methods are demonstrated in this series for four distinct climactic regions: *In the Tropics, Arid Lands, Cool Climates* and *Urban*. 30 mins. each.

VHS: S21576. $49.95.

Gods of Metal

Nominee for the Oscar for Best Documentary, this powerful documentary is about the nuclear arms race and people of faith who are trying to stop it. The arms race is analyzed from a Christian perspective, showing the economic and social effects on people in the United States and the Third World, especially the poor.

VHS: S03799. $24.95.
Maryknoll Films, USA, 1983, 27 mins.

Greenbucks: The Challenge of Sustainable Development

Major corporations have responded to environmental regulations with concrete steps that recognize the limits of development. Volkswagen and ABB are two firms who are developing cleaner, renewable technologies compatible with both the environment and profitability. This tape will help inspire other business people to understand the relationship of the environment to the future of economic development. 55 mins.

VHS: S21577. $195.00.

Greenhouse Crisis: The American Response

Based on research by the Union of Concerned Scientists, this video details the potential consequences of global warming, and stresses the need for energy efficiency and renewable forms of energy. Specific ways individuals can help to resolve this critical environmental problem are highlighted. Produced by the Union of Concerned Scientists. 11 mins.

VHS: S12320. $20.00.

Greenpeace's Greatest Hits

Featuring the daring true-life adventures of the dedicated Greenpeace volunteers who risk arrest, assault, and even their lives to stop pollution, slow the nuclear arms race and save wildlife. There are no special effects here—just real men and women putting themselves through some of the most hair-raising exploits ever seen. 60 mins.

VHS: S14095. $29.95.

Growing Like a Weed

Green, weed-free lawns are a North American obsession at odds with the environment that are only sustainable through extreme chemical dependence. This program encourages alternative methods by revealing how damaging lawn maintenance can be and by showcasing different, easier to maintain ground-covering plants. 29 mins.

VHS: S21579. $59.95.

Heroes of the Earth

An inspiring testimony to the power of individual action, this story profiles people who are fighting to protect the environment, often at great personal risk. Hosted by Ed Begley, Jr. 45 mins.

VHS: S23374. $59.95.

How Then Shall We Live?

This is a unique, independently-produced television series nationally broadcast on PBS, focused on the issues of consciousness and human survival.
America's Secret Nuclear Policy. Daniel Ellsberg, whose release of *The Pentagon Papers* helped to end the Vietnam War, reconstructs a hidden history of American nuclear diplomacy. "The United States has used its nuclear weapons about a dozen times...secretly. Used them the way a gun is used when you point it at somebody's head in a confrontation, whether you pull the trigger or not. The American people didn't know much of what was happening. We were lied to throughout that process." 56 mins.
VHS: S04758. $49.95.
Caring for an Endangered Planet. Dr. Helen Caldicott, M.D., founder of Physicians for Social Responsibility, proposes options for protecting and preserving life on earth: "The diagnosis is that we have a terminally ill planet. When terminally ill patients come into the emergency room, we work on them, we put them in intensive care, and very occasionally, one survives with absolutely dedicated work and a total commitment to their salvation. But there's no short cut. You've got to really make a total commitment. And the commitment is to save the planet." 50 mins.
VHS: S04757. $49.95.

Dialogue for Human Survival.

Ram Dass and Daniel Ellsberg explore the interrelationships of their spiritual and political paths toward peace. Ellsberg: "I take as my preoccupation the postponing and avoiding of a nuclear war." Dass: "I also would like to have my actions reduce the probability of some kind of holocaust." 58 mins.

VHS: S04759. $49.95.

Hunger and Land at Home and Overseas

Third World farmers have long faced the problem of being forced off their land by expanding agribusiness corporations. Today many American farmers are losing their land to high debts, high interest, high costs. The family farm is being replaced by the corporate farm. What are the relationships between this trend here and the situation of farmers in Asia, Africa and Latin America? Produced by Maryknoll Media. 28 mins.

VHS: S06267. $24.95.

The Infinite Voyage: Crisis in the Atmosphere

Learn about this fragile planet and what can be done to save it in this absorbing and timely program. 58 mins.

VHS: S16463. $14.98.

The Infinite Voyage: Fires of the Mind

This exciting voyage takes you on a trip into the complex universe of the human brain. Find out how we think, learn and create. 58 mins.

VHS: S16464. $14.98.

The Infinite Voyage: Sail On, Voyager

Share the joy of discovery as the "Voyager" spacecraft travels over four billion miles, gathering previously unknown facts about the solar system. 58 mins.

VHS: S16465. $14.98.

The Keepers of Eden

An environmentally aware video that provides a guided tour of the innovative efforts by important zoo and park administrators and scientists to fight off the rapid decline of various species of wildlife.

VHS: S17731. $14.98.

Kimbark: Focus on Environmental Education

Parents, teachers and administrators interested in how environmental education can be incorporated into all aspects of the primary school curriculum will find this program which examines the system set up at the Kimbark Elementary School in San Bernadino, California both stimulating and inspiring. 1988, 30 mins.

VHS: S13940. $45.00.

Large Dams, False Promises

The direct result of building dams worldwide is the major destruction of vast ecosystems and uprooting of ancient cultures who live along those areas being dammed. Are large dams a wise way to manage waterways or could smaller scale alternatives be explored in order to maintain existing cultures that are being so drastically affected? 36 mins.

VHS: S23384. $89.00.

Last Epidemic

Called "overwhelming," "harrowing," and "devastating" by newspapers including the *San Francisco Chronicle*, *Washington Post* and *Video Review*, this powerful film conveys in plain language the effects of one or more nuclear weapons on a civilian population, while using visuals which actually show the effects of a nuclear explosion. It describes the drastic damage to the environment and the long-range devastation to the planet.

VHS: S03780. $45.00.
Eric & Ian Thiermann, USA, 1981, 28 mins.

Life on Earth Perhaps

At times whimsical, at times terrifyingly blunt, this film looks at the unthinkable—Nuclear War—in a way that brings the issues into sharp focus. Cleverly put together mixing animated and documentary footage, this British production confronts the history of war.

VHS: S04309. $45.00.
Oliver Postgate, 29 mins.

Lifepulse

The habitat is planet Earth. From primeval chaos to the rise of the primates and man, this film reveals the close relationship between all the world's wild places. It's a spectacular journey from the dark coldness of the ocean depths. A journey through the furnace of volcanoes where the incandescent glow of molten lava builds the land, to frozen glaciers and the dripping wet canopy of humid rainforests. With access to the unique and internationally famous archive of the BBC's Natural History Unit, the film reflects the continuity and interdependence of all the planet's life. 90 mins.

VHS: S14112. $19.95.

Living with Disaster

A documentary that considers the groundbreaking methods scientists are developing to more accurately gauge natural catastrophes such as earthquakes, volcanoes and hurricanes.

VHS: S17732. $14.98.

Logging Siberia

One of the world's most important environmental battles is taking place in the largest remaining ancient forest on earth. A portrait of the beauty of the Siberian forest, the dangers it faces, and forest policy alternatives that could help preserve the Taiga. 28 mins.

VHS: S23371. $45.00.

Losing Control?

Bill Kurtis hosts this program, which questions whether a nuclear war could begin by accident, even with warmer relations between the U.S. and the Soviet Union. The heart of the film is a frightening, plausible scenario that starts in the Middle East and escalates to an unintended confrontation between the two superpowers. Among the experts featured are former Defense Secretary Robert McNamara, Senator Sam Nunn, former Assistant Secretary of Defense Richard Perle and MIT computer scientist Joseph Weizenbaum. 58 mins.

VHS: S11487. $45.00.

Many Faces of Homelessness
Homelessness is a worldwide and growing phenomenon. The problems of homeless people are poorly understood and are challenging societies and individuals in new ways. Being homeless can mean a lot more than being houseless. It is also a symptom of value breakdowns in society. Special insights from those involved with homeless people bring to life video features from Hong Kong and Bolivia. Produced by Maryknoll Media. 28 mins.
VHS: S06266. $24.95.

March for Disarmament
A documentary that captures the spirit and essence of the historic June 12, 1982, March for Disarmament. From extensive coverage of the event, the tape features Joan Baez, Theodore Bikel, Dr. Helen Caldicott, Dick Gregory, Abbie Hoffman, Coretta Scott King, Holly Near, Susan Sarandon, and a crowd of nearly a million. Produced by Willow Mixed Media. USA, 1982, 28 mins.
VHS: S07413. $34.95.

The Media and the Image of War
A look at how America's image is perceived in terms of war and violence. Is the portrayal of war on film and TV creating a false sense of history and values? Leading experts discuss the media and its creation of contemporary myths of American warmongers as heroes. 26 mins.
VHS: S23394. $35.00.

Mile Zero: The Sage Hour
A remarkable story of four Canadian high school students who decided they had to do something to promote nuclear disarmament. So they rounded up a used station wagon and organized a cross-country speaking tour. Their goal was to reach one out of every 20 high school students. The film follows their nine-month adventure as they travel and speak coast-to-coast to 120,000 students in 362 schools, ending with a celebration at "Mile Zero" on the Pacific Coast. Co-produced by the National Film Board of Canada. 48 mins.
VHS: S10887. $75.00.

The Military and the Environment
Is the Pentagon protecting us or poisoning us? The military uses and disposes of huge quantities of the most deadly substances known: nuclear wastes, nerve gas, and hundreds of toxic chemicals. Yet the handling of these substances is often done secretly and without any civilian regulation or oversight. State representatives and journalists shed light on the military's soiled record in this area. A remarkable study. 1990, 29 mins.
VHS: S13944. $25.00.

Need for Christian Peacemaking
Father George Zabelka, chaplain for the men who dropped atomic bombs on Hiroshima and Nagasaki, is featured in this moving statement about his conversion to peacemaking, the basis for Christian peacemaking, and his personal testimony against nuclear madness.
VHS: S03807. $45.00.
A. Nelson/E. Thiermann, USA, 1986, 28 mins.

The Non-Proliferation Treaty: Dead at 25?
This highly informative video examines the Nuclear Non-Proliferation Treaty on the eve of its expiration date, 1995. The treaty has helped stem the spread of nuclear weapons and is looked at in ways in which it may be improved. 26 mins.
VHS: S23393. $35.00.

Nova—Chernobyl
History's worst nuclear power plant disaster occurred on April 26, 1986 in Chernobyl, USSR. Includes actual footage of the disaster and its aftermath, including Chernobyl as it stands today, as well as opposing views on the long-term health effects of the disaster. 60 mins.
VHS: S11249. $29.98.

Nuclear Bombs in Our Future
An investigation into the world's nuclear weapon supply, what should be done about further acquisition of weapons, and what role the U.S. would play in preventing their spread. Interviews with a range of experts with opposing views on these important issues. 28 mins.
VHS: S23392. $35.00.

The Nuclear Threat at Home
A comprehensive look at the dangers generated by bomb factories, waste created by them, atmospheric nuclear testing, and intentional radiation releases. The need to clean up these sites is imperative, the cost staggering at $300 million. 26 mins.
VHS: S23390. $35.00.

Nuclear Winter: Changing Our Way of Thinking
The most important study of our time by leading scientists reveals that the use of a small fraction of the world's nuclear arsenal would have such devastating climactic consequences that civilization as we know it would be destroyed and the human species would probably become extinct. Dr. Carl Sagan discusses the results of the research into the global consequences of nuclear war.
VHS: S03801. $65.00.

Nuclear Winter: Growing...
A mini-documentary including a six-minute segment incorporating computer graphics and scientific information on the consequences of nuclear war. Designed for workshops, classrooms, or TV as a brief introduction to the subject. 20 mins.
VHS: S03802. $45.00.

Our Biosphere: The Earth in Our Hands
Robert Redford takes you on a tour of the Smithsonian's National Museum of Natural History and looks at models which scientists have created to help unlock the mysteries of our planet and its fragile ecology. 1991, 55 mins.
VHS: S14546. $29.95.
Laser: CAV. LD72179. $34.95.

Our Fragile Earth: Energy Efficiency and Renewables
First there is a brief history of energy use and the limits of fossil fuel. Then this documentary explores renewable energy resources, including solar energy, wind power, geothermal power, hydropower and biomass. This award-winning work also tells students how to make a difference right now, through sensible conservation techniques. 22 mins.
VHS: S21566. $65.00.

Our Threatened Heritage
Every minute more than 50 acres of tropical forest are destroyed or seriously degraded. Several species a day are lost to extinction as a result. This tape, produced by The National Wildlife Federation, provides a concise overview of the destruction of rain forests and what can be done to stop it. Images of the fascinating wildlife and towering trees are vividly presented along with comments from global experts about the causes and potential solutions to the destruction. 19 mins.
VHS: S10889. $29.95.

Ozone and the Politics of Medicine
A documentary on the harmful effects of the depletion of the ozone layer and the controversial therapies employed in Europe but banned in the United States and Canada. 30 mins.
VHS: S20153. $29.95.

Ozone: Cancer of the Sky
The destruction of the Earth's ozone layer is one of the most critical environmental issues of our time. What is causing depletion of this fragile layer? How serious a threat does it pose to life on the planet? What can be done to reverse this threat? 40 mins.
VHS: S23367. $79.95.

Peace Please: Children and War
Peace Please is a multidimensional montage crossing 14 cultures addressing the psychology of war and its effects on children and all humanity. In addition to showing the horrors of war, this program presents positive examples of organizations and people who make a difference. Can we create a better world? Yes, with compassion, understanding and motivation for change. Written and narrated by Wendy Schofield and Jake Whiteley. Produced by Wendy Schofield. 29 mins.
VHS: S14537. $48.00.

The Peace Tapes
This chronicle follows the peace movement from the '50s to the present. Featuring a myriad of controversial personalities, the program showcases the infamous Smothers Brothers' Draft Dodgers Rag. 60 mins.
VHS: S16200. $19.98.

People of Faith and the Arms Race
Produced by the Presbyterian Peacemaking Program, a unique, self-directing video workshop designed to help people of differing perspectives engage in dialog about the arms race. Six different sessions are included on the tape: Peace in the Bible, Telling Personal Nuclear Age Stories, Biblical-Theological Perspectives, What Do We Know About the Arms Race?, What Is the Church's Role? and Doing Peacemaking. 105 mins.
VHS: S10884. $39.95.

People to People
The story of "Target Seattle" and its citizens, who decide to talk and visit with the citizens of their sister city of Tashkent in the Soviet Union. Captured through the eyes of a young photographer, the pilgrimage for peace proceeds across the seas to Moscow, Leningrad, Samarkand and eventually to Tashkent.
VHS: S03806. $45.00.
Marlow Boyer, USA, 1985, 28 mins.

Planting Seeds for Peace
A timely documentary promoting intercultural dialog and understanding in the Middle East. The program focuses on the relationships among four Arab, Jewish and Palestinian teenagers who come together in the United States to share their cultures, break down stereotypes, and present their perspectives on the Middle East conflict to American young people. Along the way, they develop close friendships and a better understanding of each other's cultures. 23 mins.
VHS: S10892. $75.00.

Poligon
Thousands of residents living near the Soviet nuclear test site of Semipalatinsk were harmed by ambitious Soviet nuclear arms tests. This extraordinary film, shot just before the fall of USSR, reveals the extent of the damage inflicted on this region as well as the rationale behind the development of ever more deadly arms. The last interview given by Andrei Sakharov is also included. 58 mins.
VHS: S21584. $125.00.

Prophets and Loss
This documentary features a range of the world's most informed and profound thinkers on the environmental crisis and the path to a viable future: Carl Sagan, Paul Ehrlich, Bill Hare, Kenyan Professor Richard Oding, Soviet Physicist Ronald Sagdeev and many more. A tough examination of global issues and a clear agenda for what needs to be done. Introduction by actor-environmentalist Robert Redford. USA, 1991, 49 mins.
VHS: S15198. $95.00.

Protectors and Polluters
A horrifying look at the unregulated disposal of toxic waste at military bases across the country. Experts tour the worst offenders, including an air force base, munitions plants, a chemical weapons facility and other sites. 28 mins.
VHS: S23382. $35.00.

Question of Power
A moving and definitive media history of the nuclear power controversy, with inspirational portraits of successful grassroots opposition to the "peaceful atom."
VHS: S03813. $95.00.
David L. Brown, USA, 1986, 60 mins.

Regard for the Planet
A portrait of the global village, captured through more than 50,000 photographs by the photojournalist Marc Granger, from the Grand Canyon to Pakistan and the Far East.
Laser: LD70307. $99.95.

Reliability and Risk: Computers and Nuclear War
Produced by an organization of computer professionals, this short documentary explores our increasing dependence upon computers to make crucial military decisions. The unreliability inherent in complex systems is examined and chilling examples of typical failures are chronicled. Produced by Jonathan Schwarz for Computer Professionals for Social Responsibility. 20 mins.
VHS: S04310. $35.00.

Rhonda Abrams: Lament of the Sugar Bush Man
Acid rain destroys both the forest ecosystem and sugar maples. This documentary chronicles the woes of a maple sugar farmer who together with his family is seeing a way of life destroyed. The destruction they face bodes ill for other environments and other people who are not directly tied to the land. 1987, 12 mins.
VHS: S22586. $65.00.

Right Human Relations
A thought-provoking look at the development of "human rights" from the time of Moses through the 20th Century. With a special focus on the creation of the United Nations in 1945 and the subsequent adoption of the "Universal Declaration of Human Rights." 1990, 28 mins.
VHS: S13963. $29.95.

Rights & Wrongs: Human Rights in the World Today
Charlayne Hunter-Gault narrates this five-volume series that provides an in-depth look at human rights issues in the world today.
The Power of Human Rights. An introduction to human rights issues. Includes segments on the history of human rights, peace solutions and a human rights high school in a Brooklyn 9th grade class. 20 mins.
VHS: S23395. $49.95.
The World's Children. The human rights of children are explored in this insightful video featuring the stories of a 13-year-old African American boy in Washington, D.C., a 15-year-old girl from India and the seven million street children of Brazil. 26 mins.
VHS: S23396. $49.95.
Women Under Attack. Two of the most terrifying human rights issues facing women in several countries are explored. Featured are an investigation into how rape is systematically used as a weapon of war, the forced mutilation of female genitals for cultural and religious reasons and the emerging women's movement. 30 mins.
VHS: S23397. $49.95.
U.S. & Canada. Concerns of human rights abuses within the U.S. and Canada are revealed. Highlighted are civil rights of the 60's, tribal lands of James Bay, a taxpayer-funded military training school in Georgia and native Hawaiians—victims of history who are fighting for the right to live on their native lands. 32 mins.
VHS: S23398. $49.95.
Around the World. Records of the major human rights hot spots around the world and the ongoing debate over how to support human rights most effectively. China, Sarajevo and Somalia are examined. 30 mins.
VHS: S23399. $49.95.
Five-tape set.
VHS: S23400. $199.00.

River That Harms
Documents the largest radioactive waste spill in U.S. history—a national tragedy that has received little media attention. With the sound of a thunderclap, 94 million gallons of water contaminated with uranium mining waste broke through a United Nuclear Corporation storage dam in 1979 and poured into the Puerco River in New Mexico. This film tells the story of this tragedy and the toll that it continues to take on the Navajos, who have lost the use of their water and witnessed the sickness and death of their animals.
VHS: S12323. $95.00.
Colleen Keane, USA, 1987, 45 mins.

The Rotten Truth
This winner of the Media and Methods Awards Portfolio explores ways to reduce solid waste. A tour of the world's largest landfill reveals fascinating details about the problems posed by garbage, and the promise of recycling.
VHS: S23270. $34.95.

The Rush to Burn
This film examines whether the practice of waste incineration is safe, whether the government is adequately regulating this process, and the alternatives to toxic burning. 1989, 35 mins.
VHS: S13943. $55.00.

Save Our Planet
A young student receives elemental lessons in what needs to be done to preserve and sustain the environment. Armed with this knowledge, the young man sets about informing his classmates, friends and family about their own involvement and responsibilities. 30 mins.
VHS: S20281. $39.95.

Save the Earth: A How-To Video
A lively hour-long look at the practical, everyday things individuals can do to help restore the environment. With cameo appearances by celebrities such as Chevy Chase and Charlton Heston. 1990, 60 mins.
VHS: S13938. $19.95.

Scrapping Chemical Weapons
This documentary looks at ways the U.S. and the Soviet Union can destroy their highly toxic chemical weapons arsenals now that the Cold War is over. USA, 1991, 28 mins.
VHS: S15201. $25.00.

Secret World of the CIA
A distinguished CIA agent reveals the chilling secrets of a career in international espionage. The Secret World of the CIA presents the explosive personal story of former agent John Stockwell, winner of the CIA's Medal of Merit and the National Security Council coordinator of the covert war in Angola under Henry Kissinger. Stockwell provides a rare inside look at the life on the front lines of covert operations and ultimately makes a plea for radically altering how our government conducts clandestine operations around the world. 35 mins.
VHS: S11493. $49.95.

Solid Solutions: Rural Waste Confronts the Waste Crisis
No longer strictly a big city problem, mounting solid waste has become a major problem in our country's rural areas. This film presents a positive look at how four rural communities have arrived at creative solutions to the growing problems of waste management. 30 mins.
VHS: S23381. $79.00.

Spaceship Earth: Our Global Environment
This unique program demonstrates the amazing interdependence of human, natural, an technological systems. Hosted entirely by young people, it is an excellent discussion starter: fast-paced, factual, educational, and entertaining. Good for teenage and adult audiences. 1990, 25 mins.
VHS: S13936. $39.95.

Star Wars: A Search for Security
A critical look at the proposed Strategic Defense initiative, featuring leading supporters and critics of the Star Wars defense system. In a fast moving, visually exciting and informative presentation, the film explores the key questions about the Star Wars plan. Narrated by Ed Begley Jr.
VHS: S03793. $35.00.
Ian Thiermann, USA, 1986, 28 mins.

Starving for Sugar
For centuries peasant workers have sweated in tropical heat to satisfy the world's sweet tooth. Now even the impoverished existence of sugarcane workers is being reduced to a greater state of misery as scientists and large corporations turn out a cheaper sweetener in the form of high fructose corn sugar. Starving for Sugar probes the brave new world of biotechnology and looks at the human and social price of this scientific progress in a call for a new sense of social responsibility to accompany scientific advances. Produced by Maryknoll Media. 60 mins.
VHS: S07720. $49.95.

A Step Away from War
Paul Newman leads the audience through a video on ending all nuclear explosions by discussing the role of nuclear weapons explosions in fueling the arms buildup, why a U.S./Soviet test ban would avert possible nuclear war; among those featured are Admiral Gene La Rocque; Congressman James Leach; Dr. Glenn Seaborg, former chairman of the Atomic Energy Commission; and Robert Stuart, chairman emeritus of National Can Company.
VHS: S03794. $35.00.
Cntr. for Defense Inf'n., USA, 1986, 28 mins.

Strategic Cooperation Initiative
Retired Air Force General Jack Kidd draws on his over 48 years of military perspective to develop a constructive platform for world peace. He offers a six-part strategy for radical change in the way world powers interact that eschews SDI and nuclear arms in favor of international cooperation in space exploration. 90 mins.
VHS: S10222. $29.95.

Survival of Spaceship Earth
Commissioned by the United Nations Conference on the Human Environment, Spaceship Earth was nominated for ten Emmy awards and has been the #1 environmental film in the nation. Narrated by Raymond Burr, hosted by Hugh Downs, and introduced by Rue McClanahan. "The finest ecological film we have seen" (BBC, London). Kit Parker Video is donating a portion of the sales proceeds from this tape to the UN Environment Program. 63 mins.
VHS: S13731. $24.95.
Laser: LD71767. $34.95.

Survivors
An eloquent and powerful study of the devastating effects of nuclear war, this is the first English language film of Japanese-American survivors caught in the atomic bombings of Hiroshima and Nagasaki. Personal testimonials and archival footage are meshed to present a remarkable story of the physical, social and psychological problems faced by the survivors. 35 mins.
VHS: S23388. $89.00.

Three Mile Island Revisited
An exploration of the devastating outcome of America's worst nuclear disaster, the incidence of rising cancer deaths and birth defects are documented. As the owners of the nuclear power plant quietly reach monetary settlements with ex-residents, they publicly claim that no one was harmed. Award winner. 30 mins.
VHS: S23387. $59.95.

Through the Eyes of the Forest
From the unique perspective gained by a successful preservation movement, this documentary shows the intrinsic value of old-growth forests. Bowen Gulch is an old-growth forest in the Colorado Rockies that was saved through a variety of tactics, including demonstrations, letter-writing and economic boycotts. This story illustrates the controversy that has grown up around these invaluable resources. 59 mins.
VHS: S21573. $75.00.

Times Beach, Missouri
The first town condemned by the federal government for toxic waste contamination, this film recounts the town's story through interviews with former residents and government officials. Significant segments focus on the relationship between government officials and the chemical industry, as well as the media's part in downplaying the dangers of dioxin. Multiple award winner. 57 mins.
VHS: S23379. $89.95.

To What End?
This timely analysis, narrated by Marvin Kalb, explores the four major long-term policy options our nation could pursue in an attempt to reduce the risk of nuclear war while maintaining national security. Interviews with 15 leading experts, policy makers, government officials and scientists, as well as the Soviet government perspective by a top arms control adviser to Mikhail Gorbachev. Among those featured are Robert McNamara, former Secretary of Defense, Randall Forsberg, Institute for Defense and Disarmament Studies and others. 58 mins.
VHS: S10882. $99.95.

Toxic Racism
Poor and minority populations suffer most from industrial and toxic pollution, yet benefit least from clean-up programs, according to a variety of studies. This devastating look at discrimination profiles three communities fighting for their health, safety and human rights. 56 mins.
VHS: S23380. $149.00.

U.S. Campaign Against the Death Penalty
A look at the historical background and current uses of the death penalty in the U.S., an arbitrary and racially discriminatory practice which violates human rights. Produced by Amnesty International. 1987, 28 mins.
VHS: S06888. $20.00.

Water and Hunger
A mini-course in world awareness for all ages, an examination of water—beautiful and serene or raging and destructive—nourisher of life of cause of death. A powerful film about the world's hungry, revealing the conditions, causes and effects of poverty and starvation in several countries. 24 mins. Produced by Maryknoll Media.
VHS: S04937. $24.95.

The Water Cycle
A portrait of the continuing battle over water, history of water wars, and the underlying issues of resource use, development, and individual action. Provokes questions into the issues of the proper use of this treasured natural resource. 28 mins.
VHS: S23375. $79.00.

We All Live Downstream
America's most historic river, the Mississippi, has become a 2300-mile toxic waterway. This documentary explores the problems and the stories of people who live along the river, many of whom are now fighting to save the Mighty Mississippi. USA, 1990, 30 mins.
VHS: S15202. $39.95.

We Can Make a Difference
Concerned about the environmental crisis, 12 high school students decided to make a video that would inspire other young people to save their planet. The students worked on the project for an entire school year, interviewing hundreds of children ages 4-18. A testimony to the power of young people. 1989, 16 mins.
VHS: S13941. $55.00.

Weapons Bazaar
An eye-opening look at how weapons makers actually sell guns, tanks, aircraft and bombs to the Pentagon and Congress. Admiral La Rocque, Director of Center for Defense Information, leads the tour of a trade show with a difference. Among the amazing facts revealed are why the Falklands War was a "good opportunity" for the British Aerospace Corporation, and how razzle-dazzle games and displays promote cruise missiles, Pershing II and Trident submarines.
VHS: S03798. $35.00.
Cntr. for Defense Inf'n., USA, 1985, 28 mins.

Weapons in Space
A thoughtful analysis of the feasibility and consequences of space-based defenses. Four distinguished Americans—Dr. Henry Kendall, physicist; Dr. Carl Sagan, astronomer; Dr. Richard Garwin, physicist and National Defense Consultant; and Admiral Noel Gayler, former commander-in-chief of the Pacific Fleet—comment on these questions based on a televised tele-conference on space weapons.
VHS: S03800. $45.00.
Union Concerned Scientists, USA, 1984, 28 min.

What Soviet Children Are Saying About Nuclear War
A group of American psychiatrists led by Eric Chivian, M.D., and John Mack, M.D., visited two Soviet Pioneer camps and interviewed Soviet girls and boys aged 10-15. The result is an extraordinary documentary which is informative, refreshing and inspiring.
VHS: S03796. $45.00.
Int'l. Phys. for Prev. Nuc. War, 1983, 22 mins.

When Governments Kill
Produced by Amnesty International with college students in mind, this video examines the death penalty both internationally and in the United States. It answers the tough questions and lets students know how they can participate in the struggle for abolition. 1989, 24 mins.
VHS: S12783. $20.00.

When the People Lead
Twenty-three Americans from Northern California—doctors, lawyers, a city planner, homemakers, firefighters, school teachers, nurses, business men and women —decide to visit the Soviet Union and make friends. Their adventures, confrontations, and human encounters give the viewer a deeper understanding of modern-day Soviet life. Produced by Sharon Tennison, 40 mins.
VHS: S04312. $35.00.

When the Salmon Runs Dry
Salmon were once abundant in the Columbia river of the Pacific Northwest. Today competing interests, Native Americans, farmers, fishers and power managers must all find a way to balance their demands on this mighty river in order to ensure that the salmon survive. 51 mins.
VHS: S21581. $85.00.

When the Spill Hit Homer
Homer is a quiet fishing community that was devastated by the Exxon Valdez oil spill. This community, and other nearby Alaskan Native villages, are still trying to recover from this event and the inadequate clean-up efforts that followed. Dramatic home video footage and angry interviews offer a searing indictment of development in pristine environmental areas. 27 mins.
VHS: S21575. $85.00.

Where Have All the Dolphins Gone?
In the last 30 years, the dolphin world has been devastated by the tuna industry, which continues to use the deadly "purse seine" nets that needlessly entrap dolphins. Over 6 million spinner, spotted, and common dolphins have been killed by U.S. and foreign fishing fleets. Relentless, widespread destruction is pushing some dolphin communities to the brink of extinction. *Where Have All the Dolphins Gone?* documents the confrontation between major multi-national companies and environmental groups, which see the plight of the dolphins as symbolic of the crisis facing many species today. Narrated by George C. Scott. Produced by the Marine Mammal Fund. 58 mins.
VHS: S12322. $59.95.

Where There Is Hatred
Recent events in the world have shown that nonviolence means much more than turning the other cheek. From Chile to the Philippines, from Palestine to Eastern Europe, people have forced major changes using the tactics of nonviolence. This video is a dramatic witness to the power of people who use nonviolence as an effective strategy for peacemaking. *Where There Is Hatred* looks at both the moral and practical aspects of this strategy and suggests its application to turn societies around. Produced by Maryknoll Media. 56 mins.
VHS: S11714. $39.95.

Wilderness: The Last Stand
Narrated by Susan Sarandon, this is a powerful look at the status of America's last remaining virgin forests. It examines the impact of Forest Service policies, documenting the devastating harm caused by clearcutting. 53 mins.
VHS: S23373. $95.00.

Will Our Children Thank Us?
Dr. Benjamin Spock, active in the anti-nuclear movement, narrates this documentary about three New Englanders and how the controversy over the build-up of nuclear armaments has affected their lives. Produced by The Documentary Guild. USA, 1984, 58 mins.
VHS: S07412. $44.95.

Wind: Energy for the 90's and Beyond
How can we harness the power of the wind? In California we already are. Wind power provides enough energy for a city the size of San Francisco for one full year. Combining graphics, animation and interviews with leading experts, this documentary explores the nationwide potential for wind energy and the obstacles holding back this renewable resource. 24 mins.
VHS: S21570. $59.95.

Working for Peace: The Nuclear Issue
The U.S. Catholic bishops defined the nuclear arms race as more than a political issue and said that the questions surrounding it are moral ones. This documentary discusses how the nuclear race involves more than the U.S and U.S.S.R.; that it destroys people as it filters down to the poorest of the Third World. Produced by Maryknoll Media. 28 mins.
VHS: S06261. $24.95.

World of Refugees
Millions of people across the world live exiled as refugees, while most of the world remains unaware of their situation. The causes may differ, but their plight and their problems are similar. Concerned leaders examine what people of faith and good will can and are doing to aid these people. Visual segments include refugee camps in Mexico and Macao. Produced by Maryknoll Media. 28 mins.
VHS: S06268. $24.95.

The Yes! Tour: Working for Change
Youth for Environmental Safety (Yes!) is a concerned group of teenage environmentalists who crisscross the country in a cramped old station wagon delivering their message to 200,000 students a year. Their goal is to inform young people about environmental issues. 29 mins.
VHS: S23364. $59.95.

You Can Beat the A-Bomb
You Can Beat the A-Bomb is just the first of four films from the 1950's collected on this video. If this film is strangely funny, *One Plane, One Bomb* with Edward R. Murrow is simply chilling. *Warning Red* and *The House in the Middle* round out this collection, made in a time when many believed it was possible to survive nuclear attack. 60 mins.
VHS: S24075. $19.95.

You Can't Grow Home Again
This Emmy Award-winning documentary explores the richness and diversity of Costa Rica's rain forests. Their destruction impoverishes the biodiversity of the planet and poses a threat to human survival.
VHS: S23272. $49.95.

EDUCATION & HISTORY

1970: Year of Protest
Nixon bombs Cambodia, Kent State, the Equal Rights Amendment, the Chicago 7, Chappaquiddick. 48 mins.
VHS: S13146. $19.98.

1971: Year of Disillusionment
Pentagon Papers are printed in the Washington Post, riots wage at Attica, hunger wars in Bangladesh, expose on the My Lai massacre. 48 mins.
VHS: S13145. $19.98.

1972: Year of Summits
Nixon beats McGovern, Olympians are held hostage, SALT talks begin, George Wallace is shot, Bobby Fischer is the American chess champion. 48 mins.
VHS: S13144. $19.98.

1973: Year of Watergate
U.S. troops withdraw from Vietnam, Yom Kippur War wages, Watergate grand jury proceedings are televised, Agnew resigns. 48 mins.
VHS: S13143. $19.98.

1974: Year of Resignation
Nixon resigns and Ford pardons him, anti-busing demonstrations in Boston, Gay rights demonstrations in New York, streaking and Hank Aaron. 48 mins.
VHS: S13142. $19.98.

1975: Year after the Fall
New York City talks bankruptcy, Saigon falls to Communism, Thatcher becomes Prime Minister, Suez canal re-opens, Patty Hearst is arrested, UN equates Zionism with racism. 48 mins.
VHS: S13141. $19.98.

1976: Year of the Bicentennial
Carter is elected president, Viking spacecraft lands on Mars, Legionnaire's disease, mud wrestling, Idi Amin. 48 mins.
VHS: S13140. $19.98.

1977: Year of the Southern President
Sadat and Begin start peace talks, New York has a blackout, Gary Gilmore is executed, punk rock, *Rocky* wins an Academy Award, CNN is launched, Elvis dies. 48 mins.
VHS: S13182. $19.98.

1978: Year of Moral Dilemmas
Proposition 13 wins in California, Nazis march in Skokie, Camp David accords are drawn, Jonestown, jogging, disco and roller skating, Rev. Sun Myung Moon. 48 mins.
VHS: S13183. $19.98.

1979: Year of Overthrow
Chinese invade Vietnam, Amin is overthrown, Sandinistas oust Somoza, the Shah flees, Skylab falls, Thurman Munson dies, Three Mile Island almost explodes. 48 mins.
VHS: S13184. $19.98.

Above and Beyond the Call of Duty
The history of the Congressional Medal of Honor. Combining rare combat footage and interviews with recipients, this documentary provides an intriguing account of America's greatest heroes and the extraordinary actions for which they received the Medal of Honor. 120 mins.
VHS: S09199. $49.95.

Alcatraz: America's Toughest Prison
The toughest prison in American history in this documentary tracing the island's infamous career through Al Capone, Machine Gun Kelly, the Birdman of Alcatraz and others. Interviews with ex-cons are interwoven against the backdrop of the violence which marked the prison. Narrated by William Conrad. 54 mins.
VHS: S05174. $29.95.

America Grows Up (1850-1900s)
An Industrial Nation and *A World Power* trace America's course from a nation of farms and villages to status of one of the leading industrial nations of the world in a matter of decades. The American system of manufacturing is analyzed here along with a developing and new foreign policy.
VHS: S03976. $64.95.

American Foundation Series
A series of 30 minute tapes specifically designed for junior and senior high school students, which explores the political and philosophical foundations of American society. 30 mins each.
American Ideas in the Twentieth Century.
VHS: S06745. $29.95.
Birth of a Nation: The Thirteen Colonies.
VHS: S06742. $29.95.
Colonists Become Citizens: The Evolution of Freedom.
VHS: S06743. $29.95.
Technology and Environment: The Economic Development of America.
VHS: S06744. $29.95.

American Heroes Series
30 minutes each.
18th Century—The Age of Revolution. Includes George Washington, Benjamin Franklin, Patrick Henry and Thomas Jefferson.
VHS: S06735. $29.95.
19th Century—Growth of America. Includes Lewis and Clark, Daniel Boone, Andrew Jackson and Abraham Lincoln.
VHS: S06736. $29.95.
20th Century—Recent Times. Includes Woodrow Wilson, Franklin D. Roosevelt, John F. Kennedy and Martin Luther King.
VHS: S06737. $29.95.

American History for Children
Children's education experts have developed this series about major issues in American history. These lively videos incorporate music, animation, stories and dramatization in order to make history come alive. Diverse viewpoints are included to convey the various elements that make up American society. Each episode of this 12-volume set is 25 minutes long.
American History for Children: African-American Life. African-American life from slavery to the Emancipation Proclamation, and the legacy of Dr. Martin Luther King, Jr., are joined in this video.
VHS: S26751. $29.95.
American History for Children: American Independence. Everything from the Declaration of Independence to a biography of Thomas Jefferson is shown in this episode. Trips to Liberty Hall and the Liberty Bell are also included, and it shows how a child's day might have been under British rule.
VHS: S26749. $29.95.
American History for Children: Early Settlers. This video concentrates on the settling of New England with a discussion of the Mayflower and the Mayflower Compact. It then explains the origin of the Thanksgiving holiday. A child's view of colonial Williamsburg rounds out this look at the early settlers.
VHS: S26748. $29.95.
American History for Children: Equal Rights for All. The Bill of Rights, the Abolitionist movement, the woman's suffrage movement and biographies of Abraham Lincoln and Susan B. Anthony provide vital background for this enduring American concern.
VHS: S26752. $29.95.

American History for Children: Immigration to the U.S. Beginning with an exposition of immigrant desires, this video goes on to explain the drama of the Atlantic passage from Europe. It includes a story of an immigrant child's experience. Diversity is addressed with a discussion of early Chinese immigration and newer immigrants.
VHS: S26755. $29.95.
American History for Children: Native American Life. This video begins with life in North America before European contact. It continues on to detail an overview of Native American history that includes seminal events like the Trail of Tears. It concludes with a look at contemporary Native American life.
VHS: S26747. $29.95.
American History for Children: National Observances. National holidays from Veteran's Day to Labor Day are fully discussed in this video. Election Day and the history of American elections receive special attention.
VHS: S26757. $29.95.
American History for Children: U.S. Songs and Poems. Patriotic songs like "The Star Spangled Banner," "America the Beautiful," "My Country 'Tis of Thee," "Yankee Doodle" and more are explained in this final episode.
VHS: S26758. $29.95.
American History for Children: United States Constitution. Along with the story of the Constitution, biographies of George Washington and Ben Franklin, as well as the history of the great Seal, illuminate this key moment in American history.
VHS: S26750. $29.95.
American History for Children: United States Flag. From the origins of the flag to the current code of proper flag handling, everything about this vital American symbol is discussed in this video. Betsy Ross' role in the flag's creation, the National Anthem and the Pledge of Allegiance are also explained.
VHS: S26753. $29.95.
American History for Children: United States Expansion. Pioneer life and the experiences of a child pioneer make this volume particularly exciting to devotees of the Western frontier. The achievements of Lewis and Clark as well as the forced relocations of Native Americans and other vital issues are also addressed in this video.
VHS: S26754. $29.95.
American History for Children: Washington D.C. Important structures in Washington illustrate the story of this capitol city's development. The White House, The Capitol, the Lincoln, Jefferson and Vietnam Memorials and the Supreme Court building are included.
VHS: S26756. $29.95.
American History for Children. The complete 12-volume set.
VHS: S26759. $359.40.

American History: A Bilingual Study
A special series of tapes, available in two versions: Spanish and English. These unique programs were adapted from film strips or slide presentations, and cover the development of the American continent.
Becoming a Modern Nation. The Spanish-American War and World War I. English narration.
VHS: S06374. $29.95.
Becoming a Modern Nation. The Spanish-American War and World War I. Spanish narration.
VHS: S06375. $29.95.
Discovery and Exploration. Columbus and the Spanish explorers. John Cabot and the English explorers. The French in New France. Henry Hudson and New Amsterdam. Spanish narration.
VHS: S06380. $29.95.
Discovery and Exploration. Columbus and the Spanish explorers. John Cabot and the English explorers. The French in New France. Henry Hudson and New Amsterdam. English narration.
VHS: S06381. $29.95.
Divided House—The Second American Revolution. Historical background, the events of the Civil War, Civil War personalities, the legacy and aftermath of the Second American revolution. English narration.
VHS: S08930. $29.95.
Divided House—The Second American Revolution. Historical background, the events of the Civil War, Civil War personalities, the legacy and aftermath of the Second American revolution. Spanish narration.
VHS: S08931. $29.95.
Expansion and Growth: 19th Century America. West to the Mississippi, The Louisiana Territory, Conquest of New Spain, Manifest Destiny—To The Pacific. English narration.
VHS: S06370. $29.95.
Expansion and Growth: 19th Century America. West to the Mississippi, The Louisiana Territory, Conquest of New Spain, Manifest Destiny—To The Pacific. Spanish narration.
VHS: S06371. $29.95.
First American Revolution: 1750-1789. Background. Causes of the 1776 revolt. Revolutionary War events. Results of the first American revolution—the Constitution. English narration.
VHS: S06382. $29.95.
First American Revolution: 1750-1789. Background. Causes of the 1776 revolt. Revolutionary War events. Results of the first American revolution—the Constitution. Spanish narration.
VHS: S06383. $29.95.
Industrial America—The Third American Revolution. Early industry in America. The American industrial revolution. Labor unions and an industrialized society, modern technology and its impact on the world. English narration.
VHS: S06372. $29.95.
Industrial America—The Third American Revolution. Early industry in America. The American industrial revolution. Labor unions and an industrialized society, modern technology and its impact on the world. Spanish narration.
VHS: S06373. $29.95.
Transformation of American Society. Changing life styles. Rise of the cities. Civil rights. Communications for people and industry. English narration.
VHS: S06378. $29.95.

Transformation of American Society. Changing life styles. Rise of the cities. Civil rights. Communications for people and industry. Spanish narration.
VHS: **S06379. $29.95.**

Twentieth Century America. The Great Depression. World War II. Emergence of the United States in the world community. The future in science and space. English narration.
VHS: **S06376. $29.95.**

Twentieth Century America. The Great Depression. World War II. Emergence of the United States in the world community. The future in science and space. Spanish narration.
VHS: **S06377. $29.95.**

Americans Courageous (1600-1950s)

The Gloucesterman is a celebration of the people of this historic Massachusetts town over a 400-year period, a rousing story told in song and dance and heroic action at sea. Paired with *Not for Ourselves Alone*, a record of victory in four U.S. military crises, here is a great tribute to American courage and resourcefulness.
VHS: **S03970. $64.95.**

Americans on Everest

A spectacular documentary of the first American ascent up the world's tallest mountain. Shot by the mountaineers themselves and including the first motion pictures ever taken from Everest's summit, the film is a stirring record of one of the greatest adventures of our time. Originally presented as a National Geographic special, *Americans on Everest* is narrated by Orson Welles. USA, 50 mins.
VHS: **S15001. $39.95.**

Ancient Egypt

Explores the art and architecture of ancient Egypt through paintings and sculpture of kings, queens and noble persons and temples, tombs and pyramids. Available in three versions.
Ancient Egypt—Elementary School.
VHS: **S09078. $89.00.**
Ancient Egypt—High School.
VHS: **S09080. $199.00.**
Ancient Egypt—Middle School.
VHS: **S09079. $119.00.**

Ancient Greece

Basic concepts of Greek architecture are discussed and related to Stonehenge, Crete and archaic Greek temples. The temples on the Acropolis and sculpture show achievements during the Golden Age of Greece. Available in three versions.
Ancient Greece—Elementary School.
VHS: **S09081. $89.00.**
Ancient Greece—High School.
VHS: **S09083. $189.00.**
Ancient Greece—Middle School.
VHS: **S09082. $109.00.**

Ancient Rome

Art and architecture are explored and students see how the arch, vault, and dome relate to the aqueduct, Coliseum, Baths and Pantheon. Sculptures and mosaics trace Roman history. Available in three versions.
Ancient Rome—Elementary School.
VHS: **S09084. $89.00.**
Ancient Rome—High School.
VHS: **S09086. $189.00.**
Ancient Rome—Middle School.
VHS: **S09085. $109.00.**

Attack: Battle of New Britain

Created by the U.S. Army Signal Corps, this unique documentary covers the exceptionally bloody Marine Assault on New Britain in the Pacific. 56 mins.
VHS: **S05626. $19.95.**

Before the Industrial Revolution

Video sequences of numerous hand crafts and trades, including soap making, bread making, sheep shearing, wheel wrighting, horseshoeing and more. 18 mins.
VHS: **S15532. $45.00.**

Best of Nightline

Achille Lauro Hijacked. 30 mins.
VHS: **S14038. $14.98.**
Artificial Heart. 30 mins.
VHS: **S14026. $14.98.**
Baby Fae. 30 mins.
VHS: **S14033. $14.98.**
General Manuel Noriega Indicted. 30 mins.
VHS: **S14049. $14.98.**
Geraldine Ferraro. 30 mins.
VHS: **S14031. $14.98.**
Jackie Robinson. 70 mins.
VHS: **S14045. $14.98.**
Jim & Tammy Faye Bakker. 80 mins.
VHS: **S14046. $14.98.**
Jimmy Swaggart. 55 mins.
VHS: **S14051. $14.98.**
John Belushi's Career. 30 mins.
VHS: **S14024. $14.98.**
John Lennon Murdered. 30 mins.
VHS: **S14018. $14.98.**
Ku Klux Klan. 30 mins.
VHS: **S14017. $14.98.**
T.V. Evangelists. 75 mins.
VHS: **S14044. $14.98.**
The Titanic. 30 mins.
VHS: **S14043. $19.98.**

Between the Wars, 1918-1941

A unique, eight-volume series about the world between the two World Wars, hosted by Eric Sevareid.
Between the Wars, 1918-1941, Vol. 1. Versailles: The Lost Peace/Return to Isolationism. 60 mins.
VHS: **S11914. $19.99.**

Between the Wars, 1918-1941, Vol. 2. The First Salt Talks/America in the Pacific. 60 mins.
VHS: **S11906. $19.99.**
Between the Wars, 1918-1941, Vol. 3. Radio, Racism and Foreign Power/The Great Depression. 60 mins.
VHS: **S11907. $19.99.**
Between the Wars, 1918-1941, Vol. 4. FDR and Hitler: Rise to Power/The Dynamics of Power. 60 mins.
VHS: **S11908. $19.99.**
Between the Wars, 1918-1941, Vol. 5. Recognition of Russia/Latin America: Intervention in Our Backyard. 60 mins.
VHS: **S11909. $19.99.**
Between the Wars, 1918-1941, Vol. 6. Italian-Ethiopian War/The Spanish Civil War. 60 mins.
VHS: **S11910. $19.99.**
Between the Wars, 1918-1941, Vol. 7. The Phony War/FDR and Churchill: The Human Partnership. 60 mins.
VHS: **S11911. $19.99.**
Between the Wars, 1918-1941, Vol. 8. Japan Invades China/War Comes to Pearl Harbor. 60 mins.
VHS: **S11912. $19.99.**
The entire 8-volume series.
VHS: **S11913. $169.99.**

Brute Force: The Definitive History of War Technology

George C. Scott presents the evolution of military hardware honed from primitive inception to high-tech perfection. From the Arts & Entertainment Network's highly acclaimed series, this collection is compiled in two deluxe boxed sets.
Air Weapons. *Fighters, Bombers, Helicopters.* The first armed aircraft were little more than glorified barnstormers. Today's sophisticated flying machines require highly trained top 26 guns, who must be fearless amidst the flak. Three cassettes, 50 minutes each.
VHS: **S15837. $44.95.**
Ground Weapons. *Tanks, Artillery, Infantry.* Watch the turrets turn through 70 years of battle. Learn the history of the only weapon systems impervious to weather or electronic interference. Speak with foot soldiers having fought as far back as WWII. Three cassettes, 50 minutes each.
VHS: **S15838. $44.95.**

Capitol to Capitol

This dramatic news special provides coverage of a unique live event: discussions held between the White House and the Kremlin, the United States and Soviet Union via the news media, broadcasts shown simultaneously in both countries. An essential program in understanding the goals and lifestyles of our world counterpart. 55 mins.
VHS: **S13180. $19.98.**

City out of Wilderness: Washington

A definitive history of Washington, D.C., utilizing the prints, documents, daguerrotypes and Matthew Arnold photographs as well as spectacular aerial photography to evoke the spirit of the capital city. Produced by the U.S. Capitol Historical society. 28 mins.
VHS: **S03737. $19.95.**

Colonial America (1500-1600)

Recalled here are *The Beginnings* and *The Way of Life* in America's earliest days, when France, Spain and Great Britain were fighting for the riches of the virgin continent. Illustrated here are customs and traditions which set patterns for life as we live it in the United States today.
VHS: **S03971. $64.95.**

Columbus

This extraordinary series, produced to commemorate the anniversary of Columbus' arrival in America, covers the man and the history of his travels in seven separate volumes. Public performance rights included.
First Voyage. The ships, the crews, the means of navigation and the first landings in the New World are featured on this tape. 35 mins.
VHS: **S12642. $125.00.**
God and Gold. The business side of discovery and the relentless missionary zeal of Columbus and his followers are the focus of this tape. 35 mins.
VHS: **S12645. $125.00.**
La Genovesita Di Columbo. Leading scholars and experts of the greater Genoa area discuss, *in Italian*, the Genoese ancestry, birth and citizenship of Columbus.
VHS: **S12647. $175.00.**
Later Voyages. The lands and cultures Columbus encountered after the Americas. Also investigated are his fall from power, his later years and the summary of his lasting contributions. 35 mins.
VHS: **S12646. $125.00.**
New World. Historians, linguists, and modern explorers re-create the pre-Columbian Indians of the Caribbean; their cultures, conflicts, languages, and the colonies Columbus established in their midst. 35 mins.
VHS: **S12644. $125.00.**
Search for La Navidad. Long a mystery, the location for Columbus' ill-fated first settlement is actively investigated by scientists, technicians and others. 35 mins.
VHS: **S12643. $125.00.**

Construction of Hoover Dam

In this classic documentary (vintage 1936, B&W) you will witness Hoover Dam's construction and re-live the almost insurmountable problems faced by its engineers and builders. 35 mins.
VHS: **S06690. $29.95.**

The Fabulous 60's

The ten volumes of this series trace the epic 1960's, year by year. Narrated by Peter Jennings. 60 minutes each.
Volume 1: 1960. Kennedy vs. Nixon, Princess Margaret marries, the U-2 incident, Voerward assassination attempt, Elvis goes into the army.
VHS: **S02963. $19.95.**
Volume 2: 1961. The Bay of Pigs, Roger Maris' 61st home run, Kennedy Inauguration, Eichmann Trial, the pill, the twist, romance between Burton and Taylor.
VHS: **S02964. $19.95.**
Volume 3: 1962. James Merideth of the University of Mississippi, Thalidomide tragedy, the Cuban missile crisis, John Glenn, the China-India border war, the death of Marilyn Monroe.
VHS: **S02965. $19.95.**
Volume 4: 1963. Smoking scare, Peace Corps, the assassination of President Kennedy, the Playboy Magazine phenomenon, the March on Washington, the Great Train Robbery.
VHS: **S02966. $19.95.**
Volume 5: 1964. The Gulf of Tonkin, Beatles invade the U.S., New York World's Fair, Teddy Kennedy's plane crash, the murder of three civil rights workers in Mississippi.
VHS: **S02967. $19.95.**

Volume 6: 1965. Selma March, Watts, murder of Malcolm X, Sinatra-Farrow courtship, miniskirts, Bob Dylan and the Rolling Stones, the blackout in the Northeast.
VHS: **S02968. $19.95.**
Volume 7: 1966. Warren report controversy, Indira Gandhi in India, Aberfan disaster, Reagan in California, Maddox and Bond in Georgia, Batman, bomb lost in Spain.
VHS: **S02969. $19.95.**
Volume 8: 1967. Hippies in Haight-Asbury, Expo '67, Queen Mary's last voyage, Cassius Clay refuses to be drafted, riots in Detroit, Che Guevara assassinated in Bolivia, Bonnie and Clyde.
VHS: **S02970. $19.95.**
Volume 9: 1968. Tiny Tim, the first heart transplants, Jackie and Ari, Martin Luther King assassination, Robert Kennedy's death, Chicago Democratic convention, Nixon elected.
VHS: **S02971. $19.95.**
Volume 10: 1969. Woodstock, Apollo moon landing, Tricia Nixon profile, World Series—Mets win; Prince Charles' investiture, Nixon's inauguration.
VHS: **S02972. $19.95.**

Fields of Armor

The Discovery Channel's series reveals the history of armed machines that transformed the nature of warfare in the 20th century. From the soldiers who were there and fought in the great tank battles you will experience what these machines meant for the most savage land battles in living memory.
Volume I: Desert Attack. The sands of North Africa and the Middle East were the setting for two decisive tank battles: the battle of El Alamein in World War I, and the fight for the Golan Heights in the October War. See how these machines increased the efficiency of man's most deadly enterprise, war. 90 mins.
VHS: **S20696. $14.95.**
Volume II: Birth of Blitzkrieg. In this episode the growth of tank technology from 1916-1942 is seen as a development that preceded the know-how needed to deploy these machines most effectively. That is, until Hitler's feared Wehrmacht perfected the strategy. 90 mins.
VHS: **S20697. $14.95.**
Volume III: Battle of Armor. With the advent of nuclear arms at the close of World War II, many thought tanks had become obsolete. In *Battle of Armor* these war machines prove their enduring capacity in the Korean War. Even today tanks line both sides of the border that separates these countries, a testament to the usefulness of this technology. 90 mins.
VHS: **S20698. $14.95.**
Volume IV: Cold War to Gulf War. Armored strategy continues to evolve in different situations around the globe. Vietnam, Afghanistan, and the Gulf War all hold painful lessons about the advancement of armored vehicle warfare. 90 mins.
VHS: **S20699. $14.95.**
Deluxe Boxed Set. Over six hours in length, this collection contains all four volumes of the series *Fields of Armor*. Taken together, these insightful documentaries offer the war buff an unparalleled look at the history of tanks and the effects they had on war.
VHS: **S20700. $54.95.**

Footloose in History—Grades 5-12

A fast-moving, entertaining view of history combines art, architecture, fads and fashions, dealing with art as a consequence of historical, economic, social and political thinking of various periods.
VHS: **S09089. $149.00.**

The Game of Monopoly (1870-1914)

Industrial Giants and *Trust Busters* examine the rise to wealth and power of the industrial titans like Carnegie, Rockefeller, and Vanderbilt. Here is the story of how President Theodore Roosevelt fought the monopolists and enforced the principle that corporations are no more above the law than the humblest citizen.
VHS: **S03977. $64.95.**

Gathering Strength (1840-1914)

Immigration and *The Pacific Northwest* explore the differences between the "old" immigrants from northern Europe and the "new" immigrants, the waves of settlers from eastern and southern Europe. In rich detail here is the story of how the new manpower was found for the needs of the nation's burgeoning industries.
VHS: **S03975. $64.95.**

Great Commanders

Filmed on locations throughout the world, a look at six individuals who were military greats. Leading experts talk about their achievements, with 3D computer animation used to illustrate each commander's particular skills.
Alexander the Great—The Battle of Issus. At the time of his death, at age 32, Alexander had conquered more of the known world than anyone before or since, and had established himself as a great commander and conqueror. 45 mins.
VHS: **S20454. $24.95.**
Georgi Zhukov—The Battle of Berlin. The Battle of Berlin, which finally destroyed the Nazi regime, was a difficult military objective and Zhukov's ultimate triumph, which led to him being called the greatest commander of the Second World War. 45 mins.
VHS: **S20459. $24.95.**
Horatio Nelson—Battle of Trafalgar. At Trafalgar, Nelson secured a mastery of the seas that brought the expansion of the British Empire. 45 mins.
VHS: **S20456. $24.95.**
Julius Caesar—The Battle of Alesia. At the Battle of Alesia, Caesar used technological superiority and tactical cunning against a force which outnumbered him more than five to one in his quest for Gaul. 45 mins.
VHS: **S20458. $24.95.**
Napoleon Bonaparte—The Battle of Austerlitz. At Austerlitz, Napoleon won a spectacular victory against Austria and Russia which justifies his reputation as the greatest modern commander. 45 mins.
VHS: **S20457. $24.95.**
Ulysses S. Grant—The Battle of the Wilderness. At the beginning of the Civil War, Ulysses S. Grant worked in a store, but within four years he commanded the Union Armies, and in The Battle of the Wilderness established his military genius in an indecisive tangle in a dense forest which became a vital strategic victory. 45 mins.
VHS: **S20455. $24.95.**
Great Commanders, Complete. The six-volume set of the *Great Commanders* series.
VHS: **S20460. $119.95.**

Great Days of History

A new series which culls rare footage of world archives to provide a comprehensive history of major events of the 20th century.
The Battle of Verdun. This program retraces the battle that became synonymous with trench warfare in World War I. Archival footage makes clear the enormous sacrifice in lives by the French defenders and German attackers. 26 mins.
VHS: **S09426. $29.95.**

Great Debates: JFK vs. Richard Nixon

The 1960 Presidential debates—two of history's greatest figures square off in a series of debates that are as fresh and exciting today as they were when they were broadcast. 60 mins.
VHS: **S12693. $24.98.**

Historical Heritage Series

The Missions. Told in the form of a diary, the daily life of old California missions, their construction and daily life, and an exploration of the missions of the southwest. 35 mins.
VHS: **S05816. $19.95.**
The Trappers. The major thrust west of the fur trappers, beaver and buffalo hunts, and the westward push to California. 31 mins.
VHS: **S05817. $19.95.**

History of the Twentieth Century, Volume 1

1900-1909. The newest technological fad is the moving picture. McKinley is assassinated. Teddy Roosevelt becomes President. An earthquake destroys San Francisco. This is a chronicle of the first decade of our century. 60 mins.
VHS: **S12699. $19.98.**

History of the Twentieth Century, Volume 2

1910-1919. Roosevelt organizes the "Bull Moose" party. The Lusitania is torpedoed off the Irish coast, 1200 people are killed. World War I begins. 60 mins.
VHS: **S12700. $19.98.**

History of the Twentieth Century, Volume 3

1920-1929. World War I ends, America's veterans try to resume their lives. Prohibition is established. Al Capone wreaks havoc in Chicago. The stock market crashes, and Babe Ruth hits 61 home runs. 60 mins.
VHS: **S12701. $19.98.**

History of the Twentieth Century, Volume 4

1930-1939. Fifteen million American are out of work due to the depression. Prohibition is repealed. Hitler is elected Prime Minister of Germany. DiMaggio plays for the Yankees, who win four World Series in a row. 60 mins.
VHS: **S12702. $19.98.**

History of the Twentieth Century, Volume 5

1940-1949. Pearl Harbor is bombed by the Japanese. World War II rages. The Nazis institutionalize death camps like Auschwitz. FDR dies. An atomic bomb is detonated over Japan in 1945. 60 mins.
VHS: **S12703. $19.98.**

History of the Twentieth Century, Volume 6

1950-1959. A cold war wages between the US and the USSR. Hungarian liberals are crushed by Russians in a 10-day revolution. Castro rules Cuba. Television comes to town. Eisenhower and Nixon team up. 60 mins.
VHS: **S12704. $19.98.**

History of the Twentieth Century, Volume 7

1960-1964. Kennedy and Nixon square off on TV. Bay of Pigs and the Berlin Wall is built. Roger Maris hits 61 home runs. JFK tours Dallas in an open convertible. 60 mins.
VHS: **S12705. $19.98.**

History of the Twentieth Century, Volume 8

1965-1969. Protesters fight the war at home. Violence rocks the '68 Democratic Convention. Martin Luther King is shot and killed. Apollo 11 lands on the moon. 60 mins.
VHS: **S12706. $19.98.**

History of the Twentieth Century, Volume 9

1970-1979. The National Guard kills four students at Kent State. America invades Cambodia. Nixon resigns. Iranians storm the embassy in Tehran and take Americans hostage. 60 mins.
VHS: **S12707. $19.98.**

Images of the '80s

The Reagan years…the Space Shuttle…Jim and Tammy…AIDS…the Berlin Wall. Join host Peter Jennings for a dramatic and comprehensive replay of the people, places and happenings that shaped a decade. From ABC News. 55 mins.
VHS: **S12678. $19.98.**

Independence: Texas Gains Its Freedom

1836, Washington, Texas. In this dramatic reenactment, Sam Houston and other heroes of Texan history meet to declare Texas a free nation from Mexico. Official State Film of the Texas Sesqui-centennial. 30 mins.
VHS: **S06674. $19.95.**

Independence: Birth of a Free Nation

Narrated by E.G. Marshall, this award-winning program recreates the dramatic events that led to the Declaration of Independence and the establishment of the Constitution. Ben Franklin, Thomas Jefferson, John Adams and George Washington tell the historic events that took place in Philadelphia during the late 70's. 28 mins.
VHS: **S09181. $29.95.**

Inside the White House

President George Bush and Barbara Bush are your guides for this intimate insider's tour of the White House's historical hallways. This private video tour will also take you inside Lincoln's "haunted" bedroom and the private second floor and into rooms never seen by most Americans. 50 mins.
VHS: **S12270. $19.98.**

Korea: MacArthur's War

Described as "the sour little war," over 2,033,000 people lost their lives in a war that ended in a stalemate. Perhaps the most fierce battle of the war was the one fought between General MacArthur and President Truman, this is the story of both battle of wills and battle for blood. 60 mins.
VHS: **S13135. $24.98.**

Life Looks Back
Relive the most memorable events of the shocking 60's, soul-searching 70's and soaring 80's in this *Life* magazine compilation of photographs and film footage. Quotations, faces and events that capture the heart of our times. 30 mins.
VHS: S15901. $14.95.

March of Time: Great Depression
Multiple Academy Award series on the Great Depression.
March of Time: Economy Blues. Army, Father Coughlin, Croix de Feu, Ethiopia, Bootleg Coal, CCC, Palestine, Neutrality, G.O.P. 81 mins.
VHS: S07553. $19.95.
March of Time: Prosperity Ahead? The Lunatic Fringe, U.S. Milky Way, Labor vs. Labor, The Football Business, The Presidency, New Schools for Old. 103 mins.
VHS: S07556. $19.95.
March of Time: Reality and America's Dreams. Conquering Cancer, Mormonism—1937, Midwinter Vacations, Birth of Swing, Enemies of Alcohol, Child Labor. 98 mins.
VHS: S07557. $19.95.
March of Time: Time Marches In. Sainoji, Speakeasy Street, Belisha Beacons, Buchsbaum, Fred Perkins, Metropolitan Opera, Germany, Huey Long. 85 mins.
VHS: S07552. $19.95.
March of Time: Trouble Beyond Our Shores. Japan-China, Narcotics, Townsend Plan, Pacific Islands, TVA, Diebler, Moscow, Hartman Discovery, Father Divine. 80 mins.
VHS: S07554. $19.95.
March of Time: War and Labor Woes. Veterans of Future Wars, Arson Squads in Action, Jockey Club, Field Trails, League of Nations Union, Railroads, Relief. 107 mins.
VHS: S07555. $19.95.
Complete Set.
VHS: S07551. $99.95.

March of Time: The Cold War
A four-volume set by March of Time chronicling the Cold War, winner of four Academy Awards as well as 48 national and international awards.
March of Time—Changing Attitudes. This volume deals with the Cold War and its beginnings. Reports on atomic power, political crises in Italy, revolutions in Greece, and a special section on "the Russia that nobody knows." 88 mins.
VHS: S09836. $19.95.
March of Time—Hostility Grows. The perilous times following World War II are chronicled, including America's new air power, an answer to Stalin, the battle for Germany, and a report on the atom, as well as new voices in Asia. 90 mins.
VHS: S09837. $19.95.
March of Time—Peace or War? The third in the Cold War series looks at Japan under General MacArthur, changing views in Russia, and the future of Sweden. Tensions rise in this newsreel series as the super powers jockey for position. 83 mins.
VHS: S09838. $19.95.
March of Time—Time Marches On. The world in turmoil as March of Time covers Formosa, Morocco and Iran, as well as a report on Yugoslavia's General Tito. Is he a new ally in securing world peace? 105 mins.
VHS: S09839. $19.95.
Gift Pack of 4 Volumes.
VHS: S09835. $69.95.

Mercenary Game
This film explores the private rites and rituals of a mercenary training camp. Filmed at a "merc" camp in Georgia, this frightening and fascinating documentary features rare footage of an actual mercenary raid. 60 mins.
VHS: S13177. $39.98.

Music, Memories & Milestones
Rare, archival, British newsreel footage captures four decades that changed the world.
1930's. The era of the Big Band, rise of Fascism in Europe, terrible worldwide depression, Edward and Mrs. Simpson, Jesse Owens makes history, Amelia Earhart, Adolf Hitler, and Woody Herman's "At the Woodchopper's Ball" is in every dance hall. 60 mins.
VHS: S12412. $19.95.
1940's. The fighting, bravely optimistic days of WWII, the politicians of the time—Churchill, Hitler, Roosevelt, Stalin—the days of rebuilding and hope after the war, the proclamation of the state of Israel. 60 mins.
VHS: S12413. $19.95.
1950's. Elvis, the 4-minute mile, Sputnik. Symbols of a world recovered from war, its energy restored as prosperity returned. Suez, Korean War, Hungarian Revolution. 60 mins.
VHS: S12414. $19.95.
1960's. The era of sexual liberation, flower power, the Cuban missile crisis, the Berlin Wall erected, Vietnam, the Mid-East 6-day war. 60 mins.
VHS: S12415. $19.95.
Music, Memories & Milestones 4-Pack. The 1930's, 40's, 50's, and 60's (4 cassettes) at a special price.
VHS: S12416. $75.81.

Mutiny on the Western Front (WWI)
Here for the first time is the untold story of *World War I* filmed on locations in France, Germany and "down under." This is a startling portrait of the 300,000 Australian Anzac volunteers, suffering the largest share of casualties of the war, who mutiny against their incompetent and callous French and British commanders.
VHS: S03980. $69.95.

A Newsreel Library of America in Sports
Except for the World War II reports, sports highlights were the most popular moments of the theatrical newsreel. Among the 79 stories featured in this collection, find Knute Rockne's "Go-Go" speech, Babe Ruth's special game in Wrigley Field, Jesse Owens in Hitler's Berlin, the Jack Dempsey story, Lou Gehrig's farewell and the first Super Bowl. 90 mins.
VHS: S15947. $29.95.

A Newsreel Library of America in the News
Newsreels were shown regularly in the nation's movie theaters from the early 1900s to the late 1960s when television preempted their role. Audiences depended on the newsreel to bring life to events around the nation and the world. This collection of 87 segments includes the Wright brothers' first flight, the Stock Market crash of 1929, the Hindenburg disaster, the Scopes trial and Sinatra and the Bobby Soxers. 90 mins.
VHS: S15946. $29.95.

A Newsreel Library of American Nostalgia
After reporting national disasters, wars, politics and social upheavals, the newsreel usually ended with an odd story or personality reflecting the comic side of life. Find 107 examples of lighthearted trivia in this program, including the premiere of Mickey Mouse, Elvis in the Army, the "It" Girl of the '20s, the Bikini Sensation, when 1937 Miss America said "No" and Clark Gable, Rita Hayworth and Marilyn Monroe taking Hollywood by storm. 90 mins.
VHS: S15948. $29.95.

Portraits from the Past
Original archive film documentaries on the life and times of two outstanding historical personalities: *Ace of Aces* is a presentation of the Eddie Rickenbacker story, from World War I air race to 20th century hero; *FDR* is the Franklin D. Roosevelt story told through the newsreels of the day. 28 mins.
VHS: S10781. $29.95.

Presidents
Historical footage from the ABC News archives reveals the profoundly different styles and personalities of America's presidents. From George Washington to George Bush, from Andrew Jackson's rambunctious inauguration to the Reagan years, this program reveals little-known facts about the men who led and shaped the destiny of the country. 60 mins.
VHS: S12272. $19.98.

Reagan Years
A history of the life and times of Ronald Reagan, tracing his life from college football player to charismatic politician, including an examination of the two terms of his presidency, and his legacy. 75 mins.
VHS: S07717. $29.95.

Reagan's Way
Steal from the poor and give to the rich? No, this is a loving and respectful tribute to Ronald Reagan; family man, managerial wizard. For those who still have a color portrait of the president on your walls, this tape is for you. 52 mins.
VHS: S13102. $39.98.

Red Baron
An informative and engaging look at the legendary personality of aviation, Manfred von Richthofen, the Ace of Aces, nemesis of Allied flyers, and the greatest aerial tactician of World War I. Through interviews with the last surviving pilots, rare World War I footage, dogfights, crashes, and the Red Baron's last flight and controversial death are explored. 60 mins.
VHS: S09915. $29.95.

The Roots of Democracy (1700s)
The dynamic forces which shaped America are revealed in studies of *The Economy* and the beliefs of the foresighted men who drafted *The Constitution*, and gave us the *Bill of Rights* and the amendments guaranteeing our rights to religious freedom, freedom of speech, of the press, of assembly and of equal justice under the law.
VHS: S03972. $64.95.

San Francisco Earthquake
A complete account of the 15 seconds when the San Francisco Bay Area stood on the brink of annihilation, and the deadly aftermath of the 7.1 quake. This tape features dramatic footage of the heroes and victims of this natural disaster. From ABC News. 60 mins.
VHS: S12679. $14.98.

Secret War: Volume 1
The highly acclaimed BBC series about World War II. In Volume 1, *The Battle of the Beams* covers the mysterious radio signals from Germany which could guide enemy night bombers to a pin-point target anywhere in the British Isles. Professor R.V. Jones of the R.A.F. Scientific Intelligence recounts how the "Beams" were first discovered and then countered. *To See for a Hundred Miles* is the story of wartime radar, and the struggle to keep one step ahead of the enemy. 101 mins.
VHS: S07594. $19.94.

Secret War: Volume 2
Two more episodes: *Terror Weapons*—in the early hours of June 13, 1944, a small German aircraft crashed and exploded in Bethnal Green, killing six civilians. Rescue workers could find no German crew. That was because there were none. The VI had arrived, and with it, a new, terrifying era in warfare. This account traces the grim, fascinating detective work which finally uncovered the existence of Hitler's revenge weapon. *If....* is the story of weapons which might have been; weapons as diverse as the incredible Giant Panjandrum and the equally extraordinary Gigant, a glider almost as large as a jumbo jet. The famous German woman test pilot, Hanna Reitsch, recounts her testing of the Gigant as well as the rocket powered Komet fighter. 100 mins.
VHS: S07595. $19.94.

Secret War: Volume 3
The Deadly Waves—Although the magnetic mine had been invented by the British in 1917, interest had languished in Britain between the wars, and it was the Germans who developed the device to deadly effectiveness. This is the story of how two naval officers fearlessly dismantled the first German magnetic mine. *Still Secret* is the story of how British intelligence penetrated the German codes known as Enigma. To this day, the entire story has yet to be told—but is recounted here by the men and women involved. 102 mins.
VHS: S07596. $19.94.

Sixties Headlines
Emphasizing the incredible amount of headline from the 1960's, this tape includes everything from Martin Luther King to Vietnam, Neil Armstrong to the Beatles, JFK to Woodstock. 30 mins.
VHS: S13150. $14.98.

The Statue of Liberty
This tribute to Lady Liberty follows her from her creation in Paris to her arrival in New York, and features her embodiment in film, fine art, and popular music. Contributors include Mario Cuomo, Milos Forman, Ray Charles, and others. 60 minutes.
VHS: S02294. $24.98.

This Is America
A history of America from 1917 to 1932, including the Big Crash and the Depression, a history of the first World War, as well as American presidents, through rare footage. Also on the same program is the film *The American Road*, a history of the automobile, reportedly directed by John Ford, and narrated by Raymond Massey. USA, 1932.
VHS: S09525. $29.95.

Time Warp: 1954
Ike and Mamie, The Honeymooners, Liberace, The Reagans, Marlon Brando, Betty Furness, Speedy Alka Seltzer, Creature from the Black Lagoon, the McCarthy Hearings, the Eniwetok Atoll, H-Bomb blast and more. 79 mins.
VHS: S13147. $19.98.

Time Warp: 1960
The Kennedys, Castro, Khrushchev, Elvis, Marilyn, Mickey Mantle, Nixon, Hitchcock, Jerry Lewis, Princess Margaret, the Debates, the Twist, the U-2 incident, Crisis in Algeria, South Africa and more. 83 mins.
VHS: S13148. $19.98.

Time Warp: 1964
The Johnsons, Roy Orbison, the Beatles, Malcolm X, Barry Goldwater, Cassius Clay, GI Joe, Carol Doda, Lester Maddox, Martin Luther King, Dick Van Dyke, Gulf of Tonkin, the Long Hot Summer, surfing and more. 85 mins.
VHS: S13149. $19.98.

Two Great Crusades (1935-1945)
The New Deal and *World War II* are the subject here, the two greatest crises to confront the nation since the Civil War. Emerging from the paralyzing depression of the 30's, America in the 40's enters a war on two fronts, against the Japanese and Nazi Germany, and highlights the unheralded efforts of Americans on the home front.
VHS: S03979. $64.95.

War of 1812
From the English attack on the U.S. frigate Chesapeake through the battle of Lake Erie and the creation of The Star Spangled Banner, this video history covers all of the crucial naval battles that were fought for control of the Atlantic coast and the supremacy of the Great Lakes. 21 mins.
VHS: S09490. $29.95.

Warring & Roaring (1914-1929)
World War I and *The 1920's*, with startling realism and boldness, reveal how the United States vacillated between isolationism and involvement and finally for the first time plunged into a European conflict which was followed by a decade of paradoxes called both "The Age of Normalcy" and "The Era of Wonderful Nonsense."
VHS: S03978. $64.95.

Where America Began: Jamestown, Colonial Williamsburg and Yorktown
Historic sites and life in Colonial America of 250 years ago—militia musters, fifes and drums, skilled craftsmen, authentic buildings, and the dramatic events of the important chapters of American history. 30 mins.
VHS: S10102. $29.95.

Within These Walls
An intimate program on the personal and political significance of the White House, its symbolism, its architectural history, and the various men and women who lived there, providing an important human scale and dimension. With an introduction by the First Lady and a closing speech by the president. 33 mins.
VHS: S17719. $19.95.

nature VIDEOS

Adventure

Six tapes of exciting adventures from around the world. 60 minutes each.
Fishing the Himalayas. Angler John Bailey travels from the high lakes of Kashmir to the wild rivers of the upper Ganges in search of the mighty *mahseer*, one of the world's great sporting freshwater fish.
VHS: **S14728. $19.95.**
Return to the Jade Sea. Archeologist Andrew Hartley explores Kenya's Lake Turkana, one of the least known regions on the African continent and a rich hunting ground for traces of an advanced Stone Age culture.
VHS: **S14729. $19.95.**
The Black Pearls of Polynesia. Christina Dodwell journeys by sailing vessel through Polynesia along the ancient route of the Pearl Passage, diving with fisherman in Fiji, Tonga and Tahiti.
VHS: **S14725. $19.95.**
The Logan Challenge. Following in the footsteps of the first expedition up Mount Logan in 1925, an extraordinary achievement which was filmed, three adventurers set out to take their husky dog team to the summit.
VHS: **S14727. $19.95.**
The Wildman of China. An American anthropologist and a British crypto-zoologist search for the *yeren*, a huge ape-like creature said to prowl the remote regions of central China.
VHS: **S14726. $24.95.**
To the Island of the Aye-Aye. A search and rescue expedition into the remote interior of northeastern Madagascar with Gerald Durrell, the world's foremost animal conservationist.
VHS: **S14724. $19.95.**
Adventure: Complete Set. The complete set at a special price.
VHS: **S19337. $124.95.**

African Shark Safari

In treacherous waters, the great white shark lies in wait for a tasty morsel. This video documentary shows photographers studying the great whites who congregate to feed on young penguins and seals. 60 mins.
VHS: **S26044. $19.95.**

Alaska's Three Bears and the Alaska Mother Goose

Shelly Gill and Shannon Cartwright are Alaska's most popular children's book creators. These clever stories join charming illustrations with actual live footage of Alaska's abundant wildlife and breathtaking scenery. 45 mins.
VHS: **S23083. $24.95.**

Alaska's Whales and Wildlife

Alaska's southeast coast contains a treasure trove of unmatched natural wonders, including the world's largest temperate rainforest and massive glaciers. Naturalists guide the viewer through these ecosystems, revealing the unique plant and animal life contained in these areas. Brown bears, bald eagles and humpback whales are just some of the wildlife shown. 46 mins.
VHS: **S21580. $59.95.**

Alaska's Wildlife

On this Alaskan safari there is an abundance of unique wildlife. Brown bears gorge themselves on salmon; caribou wander the tundra, and the Dall sheep engage in heated mating ritual. Whistling swans, bald eagles, puffins and walruses are seen in this exciting wildlife documentary. 30 mins.
VHS: **S23968. $14.95.**

Alaskan Safari

Fascinating adventure film travels through the North Country by airplane and dogsled to track moose and grizzly bear as well as seals, sea lions and walrus.
VHS: **S02264. $19.95.**
R. & B. Hayes, USA, 1986, 93 mins.

Alien Empire: We Are Not Alone

They surround you every day, and yet if you look closely you realize that they are utterly different and completely alien to everything you know. This video brings the secret world of insects to life with state-of-the-art macrophotography and digital effects. Three-tape set. Each tape is approximately 60 mins.
VHS: **S27414. $49.99.**

America's Western National Parks

From the Sierra Nevada of California to the Badlands of South Dakota, from the depths of the Grand Canyon to the peaks of the Olympic Mountains, you'll explore the very best of more than 40 national parks and monuments in a way you never imagined. USA, 60 mins.
VHS: **S15078. $29.95.**

The American West: Land of Beautiful Places

In this journey of images and harmonies some of the most beautiful scenery from the Western United States is joined with moving music for a unique video experience. Yosemite, Yellowstone, the Grand Canyon, Monument Valley and many other famous sites are included in this breathtaking work. 40 mins.
VHS: **S21064. $19.95.**

Among the Wild Chimpanzees

In 1960, Jane Goodall set out for Tanzania's remote Gombe Stream Game Reserve to study the behavior of man's closest living relative, the chimpanzee. With dedication and perseverance, she earned the trust of a wild chimp community, and has now spent two landmark decades observing their varied personalities and rich life. National Geographic. 59 mins.
VHS: **S04887. $19.95.**

Ancient Sea Turtles: The Last Voyage?

With fascinating footage, this documentary provides an overview of the extraordinary natural history of sea turtles, including their mysterious migrations and primeval egg-laying habits. Informative and entertaining. USA, 1991, 25 mins.
VHS: **S15203. $59.95.**

Animal Babies in the Wild

An entrancing look at baby animals from Africa to the Arctic, captured on this video which uses live photography, stories and songs, that capture the hearts of children 2-8.
VHS: **S04135. $14.95.**

Animal Wonders from Down Under

A new series exploring the unique wildlife of Australia issued as a six-volume set.
Tiny Carnivores/Wombat. Many of the Australian marsupials are carnivores, small but fierce predators of insects, spiders. Looks at the native cats, the Tasmanian Devil, and Wombats—pig-like marsupials as endearing as the koala. 50 mins.
VHS: **S07356. $14.95.**
Complete Set.
VHS: Out of print. For rental only.

Animals of Africa: From the Sky to the Sea

The gregarious pink throated, web-footed cormorants as they breed and gather nesting materials; baby sea pups as they are born and cared for in a communal nursery; and the antics of the rare black-footed African penguins that live underground in burrows.
VHS: **S09563. $29.95.**

Animals of Africa: Hippos, Baboons and the African Elephant

Joan Embery hosts this look at baboons, hippos, and African elephants.
VHS: **S01684. $29.95.**

Animals of Africa: The Land of the Elephants

Experience a highly ritualized form of combat as two sables conduct a dance of dominance; watch hippos nibble on fragile hyacinths and frolic in the world's largest bathtub; and see playful elephants who only weigh a ton.
VHS: **S09564. $29.95.**

Antarctica

Representing the last great wilderness on Earth, Antarctica conceals a treasure trove of wildlife and rugged, beautiful terrain. From unlocking the secrets of ancient glacial ice to watching the underwater ballet of penguins swimming, this documentary captures the raw feel and power of nature. Filmed in IMAX. 40 mins.
VHS: **S23972. $29.95.**
Laser: **LD75007. $39.95.**

Ape Man: The Story of Human Evolution

Walter Cronkite hosts a riveting four-volume set tracing the story of mankind's ascent. Filmed on location in Africa and featuring the latest scientific evidence. The four volumes are: *The Human Puzzle, Giant Strides, All in the Mind* and *Science and Fiction.* Boxed set, 200 mins.
VHS: **S21901. $79.95.**
Laser: CLV. **LD74748. $79.95.**

Arctic Refuge: A Vanishing Wilderness

The concerns of the oil and gas industry, who want to drill across this 100-mile stretch of land, threaten the annual migrations of animals who gather every spring at the coastal plain of the Arctic National Wildlife Refuge. Narrated by Meryl Streep.
VHS: **S16876. $14.98.**

Ascent of the Chimps

A chimpanzee enclosure which mimics the conditions of the wild was built at the Arnhem Zoo in the Netherlands in 1971. Lorne Greene explores the life of the thriving chimpanzee community at the Zoo which, surprisingly, reflects many human social elements. USA, 22 mins.
VHS: **S03095. $14.95.**

Audubon Society Videoguides to the Birds of North America

Combines bird sights and sounds for simple and accurate identification of 505 North American species. Moving and still pictures show each bird's distinctive markings and behavior, with computer-animated range maps showing breeding and wintering areas for each species. Bird calls and sounds from the Cornell Laboratory of Ornithology complement the narration and visuals.
Volume 3: 77 species of pigeons and doves, cuckoos, owls, nighthawks, hummingbirds, swifts, trogons, kingfishers and woodpeckers. 75 mins.
VHS: **S01672. $29.95.**
Laser: **LD72224. $35.95.**
Volume 5: Part 2 of songbirds: 109 species of warblers, orioles and blackbirds, tanagers, grosbeaks, finches, buntings and sparrows. 80 mins.
VHS: **S02959. $29.95.**
Volume 2: 105 species of water birds, including herons and egrets, cranes, shorebirds, gulls, terns and alcids. 78 mins.
VHS: **S03123. $29.95.**
Laser: **LD72223. $35.95.**
Volume 1: 116 species of loons, grebes, pelicans and their allies, swans, geese and ducks, hawks, vultures and falcons, and the chicken-like birds (pheasants, grouse, quails, ptarmigans). 94 mins.
VHS: **S03211. $29.95.**
Laser: **LD70847. $39.95.**

Volume 4

98 species of songbirds: flycatchers, larks, swallows, crows and jays, titmice and chickadees, nuthatches, creepers, wrens, thrushes, waxwings, shrikes, thrashers and vireos. 75 mins.
VHS: **S05966. $29.95.**
Laser: **LD72225. $35.95.**

Audubon: Greed and Wildlife: Poaching in America

Richard Chamberlain narrates the story of grizzlies, bald eagles, alligators and thousands of other threatened or endangered species that are killed in senseless slaughter each year. In shocking and horrifying footage, witness the tragic waste of our wildlife and discover what is being done to stop illegal hunting. 60 mins.
VHS: **S12133. $14.98.**

Audubon: Sharks

Peter Benchley narrates the story of the shark—reviled, feared and destroyed through the ages, and now finally earning the respect and appreciation it deserves. Discover the emerging truths of this misunderstood species, including remarkable applications in cancer treatment and human skin grafting. 60 mins.
VHS: **S12132. $14.98.**

Australian Ark Documentary Series

A look at the fascinating land of Australia and the unique animal world that inhabits that land.
Amazing Marsupials. Astonishing footage of Tasmanian devils, kangaroos, koalas and wombats, the numbat, which is shown feasting on termites, as well as rare footage of the now-extinct marsupial wolf. 79 mins.
VHS: **S03815. $19.95.**
Changing Face of Australia. A geological history told through the rock formations found there. Some of the land is inconceivably old, such as the vast Western Shield which rose from the sea three billion years ago and contains fossils dating from the dawn of life. Spectacular scenery and vivid contrasts highlight this program. 54 mins.
VHS: **S03816. $19.95.**
Coming of Man. A program which examines man's 50,000 year stay in Australia, with particular attention to carved symbols which inexplicably resemble carvings in Siberia and South America. 67 mins.
VHS: **S03817. $19.95.**
Farthest West. An examination of the eerie windswept scrubland in Western Australia and the life that thrives in this almost alien area. The plump bottle-trunked monsters called baobabs, technicolor parrots and cockateels, lizards and elusive numbats make for an interesting program. 50 mins.
VHS: **S03818. $19.95.**
Green World. A look at the Australian rain forest and the unique plant and animal life that call it home. View the world's tallest hardwood trees soaring over 300 feet into the air, bats the size of a small fox that travel in flocks of 25,000, and giant flightless birds. 52 mins.
VHS: **S03819. $19.95.**

Avalanche Awareness

Snow avalanches are the single greatest hazard to the unwary back-country traveller. Combining spectacular live footage with practical safety tips, this film clearly presents the fundamentals of avalanche safety in a simple and straightforward way. Endorsed by the National Mountain Rescue Association and the U.S. Forest Service. 1988, 28 mins.
VHS: **S13699. $29.95.**

BBC Wildlife Special Volume 1

Meerkats United: Perched upright on a termite mound in the Kalahari Desert, a furry brigand, only 12 inches tall, gazes with beady eyes across the arid wilderness. He's a meerkat, and he's on sentry duty. He is a kind of mongoose, creatures who live in gangs and use brilliant teamwork to survive the hostile environment. Co-operation within each gang is remarkable. They share everything. This delightful film follows the lives of one band of the Meerkats for whom survival means one for all and all for one! *The Impossible Bird:* The ostrich. The world's largest bird, who can't fly but can run at 40 mph! It lays an egg equal to twenty hen's eggs, and can kick a man to death. This unique study of the ostrich, filmed in Kenya, probes the world of this remarkable bird. 55 minutes.
VHS: **S07592. $24.95.**

BBC Wildlife Special Volume 2

Tidbits: The blue tit is a welcome guest in every garden; no bird table or nest box is complete without one. This beautiful film examines the private life of this familiar bird. It shows how the male feeds and cares for its mate, how their first tiny nestling is born, and how they avoid such hazards as a cat and a sparrow hawk. It is an affectionate look at the blue tit, everybody's favorite bird. *Nightlife:* In the dead of night is the time we sleep but for many animals nighttime is far from dead. It's the hour when the barn owl pounces on the luckless vole, the fox stalks his prey, beetles mate and the nightingale sings. Through the eyes and ears of these nocturnal animals this fascinating film unfolds and tells the story of one night in the English countryside. 55 minutes.
VHS: **S07593. $24.95.**

BBC Wildlife Specials: Aliens from Inner Space/The Fastest Claw in the West

Cuttlefish, squid and octopus—do these unusual ocean creatures "talk" to each other? Are they perhaps trying to contact us? *Aliens from Inner Space* allows us to judge for ourselves. *The Fastest Claw in the West* shows us pugnacious, belligerent and apparently fearless Mantis shrimp audacious enough to engage in battle with octopus twice their size and 20 times their weight. Special camera techniques and exceptionally high speed photography examine the behavior of this remarkable underwater creature. Narrated by David Attenborough. 48 mins.
VHS: **S11765. $19.94.**

BBC Wildlife Specials: Birds of a Sun God/In-Flight Movie

David Attenborough narrates these two programs. The first focuses on the birds that can hover motionless, fly backwards and even upside down—hummingbirds. They lay the smallest eggs, have the fastest wingbeats, and the most dazzling plumage. *In-Flight Movie* is the story of how birds fly. Using a remarkable new filming technique, the camera takes to the air for the experience of a lifetime. This unique film enables you to fly in the clouds with a flock of geese. 58 mins.
VHS: **S10289. $24.95.**

BBC Wildlife Specials: On the Tracks of the Wild Otter/The Mouse's Tale

The story of a rare man searching for a rare animal. The animal is the otter; the scene is the Shetlands. The stars of the film are the wild otters themselves, living their free and natural lives in these remote and beautiful islands. *The Mouse's Tale* follows the adventures of four species of mice in and around a country cottage in Wiltshire, England. Narrated by David Attenborough. 83 mins.
VHS: **S11763. $19.94.**

The Big Wet

Australian monsoons unleash dynamic changes on the environment. This video details the effects of cyclones and electrical storms, which are inevitably followed by dry spells and fire. Together this pattern of wet and dry sets the tone for a unique ecosystem. 60 mins. From the Discovery Channel.
VHS: **S25070. $19.95.**

The Biggest Bears

All kinds of bears in their wild habitat are shown in this exciting documentary narrated by a five-year-old Alaskan boy. The makers travelled across Alaska, Canada and Russia in order to create this unparalleled musical adventure.
VHS: **S22160. $14.95.**

Binocular Vision

A wonderfully entertaining look at the National Audubon Society's Christmas Bird Count. A documentary about bird watchers and birding, a lighthearted yet intimate look at the people who share the passion. *Binocular Vision* looks at the Annual Christmas Bird Count, in which some 40,000 people throughout the U.S. and Canada watch and count birds.
VHS: **S09438. $24.95.**
Robert Machover, USA, 1988, 26 mins.

Birds

This ten-part series is a fascinating portrait of various birds of prey. The series includes programs on bird watching, the variety of birds, seabirds, migration, basket weaving and nest building, eagles, storks, swans and owls.
Birds: A Little Owl's Story.
VHS: **S17297. $29.95.**
Birds: Concerning Swans.
VHS: **S17295. $29.95.**
Birds: Eagles International/Eagles: The Majestic Hunters/Where Eagles Fly.
VHS: **S17294. $29.95.**
Birds: Getting to Know Birds.
VHS: **S17288. $29.95.**
Birds: Seabirds.
VHS: **S17291. $29.95.**
Birds: Talons, Beaks and Nests.
VHS: **S17289. $29.95.**
Birds: The Feathered Athletes.
VHS: **S17293. $29.95.**
Birds: The Masterbuilders.
VHS: **S17292. $29.95.**
Birds: The Migration of Birds—Fight for Survival.
VHS: **S17290. $29.95.**
Birds: The Year of the Stork.
VHS: **S17296. $29.95.**

Birds (Pet Care)

Dr. Michael Fox hosts this instructional video, with pointers on choosing the bird, bird song meanings, displaying affection, bird training, bird diets, exercise and more. 30 mins.
VHS: **S09622. $14.95.**

Bo-Ru the Ape Boy

This fascinating documentary delves into the relationships that grow between humans and animals. Major C. Court produced and directed this unique effort. 35 mins.
VHS: **S23792. $24.95.**

Bride of the Beast

Osa and Martin Johnson created this unusual documentary that was shot on location in Africa. 57 mins.
VHS: **S23793. $24.95.**

Canyon Dreams

The majestic Grand Canyon captured by director Jan Nickman with rare perception and sensitivity. Original music by Tangerine Dream. 45 mins.
VHS: **S10960. $29.95.**

Carlsbad Caverns & Guadalupe Mountains National Parks

An entirely new video program featuring the Carlsbad Caverns, New Cave and nearby Guadalupe Mountains National Park, exploring how caverns are formed, with detailed closeups of formations, bat flight.
VHS: **S06665. $29.95.**

Christian the Lion
Ten years after the making of *Born Free*, this docudrama finds Bill Travers and Virginia McKenna once again involved with the welfare of a member of the lion family. They help a London Zoo-born animal back to the wilds of Kenya. A sequel of sorts to *Lion at World's End*.
VHS: S12840. $29.95.
Bill Travers, Great Britain, 1976, 89 mins.

Coastal Habitat Set
Castaways of Galapagos, Orca Whales and Mermaid Tales and *Penguins in Paradise* are all part of this three-volume set from the Discovery Channel's *Mother Nature: Tales of Discovery* series. Together these videos document unique coastal landscapes in varying climates.
VHS: S25088. $39.95.

Commune with the Dolphins
This film takes the viewer into the deep and up in the air with Nature's most lyrical and magnificent creatures. Filmed by Emmy award-winning cinematographer Rober Riger and underscored musically by composer/ arranger Carlos Alornar, this footage brings the power, compassion, energy and serenity of dolphins. 25 mins.
VHS: S07729. $29.95.

Cousteau: Alaska: Outrage at Valdez
In a Cousteau Society special report, Jean-Michel Cousteau takes us on a voyage to investigate first-hand the devastating impact of the 1989 Exxon Valdez oil spill in Alaska. 57 mins.
VHS: S13025. $19.98.

Cousteau: Amazon: Snowstorm in the Jungle and Rigging for the Amazon
Penetrate the dark mysteries of the Amazon basin and confront the awesome power of the source of cocaine. Then see how the Cousteaus prepared for their most challenging expedition. 90 mins.
VHS: S13028. $19.98.

Cousteau: Journey to a Thousand Rivers
Join Cousteau on a monumental expedition into the vast and mysterious realm of the Amazon River system. 98 mins.
VHS: S14736. $19.98.

Cousteau: Lilliput in Antarctica
Cousteau is accompanied by six children from around the world on a spectacular odyssey to Antarctica, where they are greeted by huge glaciers, humpback whales, penguins and elephant seals. 48 mins.
VHS: S13026. $19.98.

Cousteau: Papua New Guinea: The Center of Fire
In Papua New Guinea Cousteau divers explore the remains of violent World War II battles: a 500-foot Japanese freighter and a famous B-17 Flying Fortress, still remarkably intact. 60 mins.
VHS: S13027. $19.98.

Cousteau: Pioneers of the Sea
A special biographical film salute to Captain Cousteau upon his 75th birthday, featuring rare photographs and remarkable footage from some of his greatest expeditions. 60 mins.
VHS: S13024. $19.98.

Cousteau: River of the Future
How man is adversely influencing the Amazon's delicate and vitally important ecosystem, and how, perhaps, he can save it. 98 mins.
VHS: S14738. $19.98.

Cousteau: Tahiti Fire Waters
Cousteau pilots the *Calypso* to the beautiful islands surrounding Tahiti in the South Pacific. With stunning photography, his team examines the effects upon nature and the economies of local cultures of continued testing of nuclear weapons. 60 mins.
VHS: S13029. $19.98.

Cousteau: The Great White Shark
Jean-Michel Cousteau and his team of divers and scientists embark on an ambitious expedition to track and film the great white shark.
VHS: S17738. $19.98.

Cousteau: The New Eldorado— Invaders and Exiles
A fascinating examination of the Amazon's inhabitants and their struggle with the ever-invading modern world. 98 mins.
VHS: S14737. $19.98.

Cousteau 2—Bering Sea: Twilight of the Alaskan Hunter
Jacques and Jean-Michel Cousteau study the hunting traditions of an ancient people colliding with the modern ways of life and the struggle to preserve the different species unique to this ice-encrusted region. 48 mins.
VHS: S13558. $19.98.
Laser: LD71566. $29.95.

Cousteau 2—Borneo II: Forests Without Land
Jacques and Jean-Michel Cousteau investigate the incomparable beauty and fragility of the third largest island in the world. The abundant mangrove thickets that comprise the island hold a wealth of fish and other underwater life. 48 mins.
VHS: S13560. $19.98.

Cousteau 2—Haiti: Waters of Sorrow
Jacques and Jean-Michel Cousteau investigate Haiti. It was once a lush island, abundant in natural resources. Today it is dying a slow death caused by massive overpopulation, and its predicament reveals trends forthcoming to Third World countries the world over. 48 mins.
VHS: S13557. $19.98.
Laser: LD71565. $29.95.

Cousteau 2—Riders of the Wind
The turbo-sail system developed by Jacques Cousteau, Lucien Malavard and Bertrand Charrier operates much like conventional sailing, but with heightened efficiency and the hope of revolutionizing the shipping industry of the future. 48 mins.
VHS: S13562. $19.98.
Laser: LD71567. $29.95.

Cousteau 2—Thailand: Convicts of the Sea
Jacques and Jean-Michel Cousteau explore the effects of undersea tin-ore mining, including vast canyons on the ocean floor and clouds of sliding mud, creating regions uninhabitable by any marine life, including seaweed. 48 mins.
VHS: S13559. $19.98.

Cousteau 2—Western Australia: Out West Down Under
Jacques and Jean-Michel Cousteau study the encroachment of humanity on the fragile western coastline of Australia threatening ocean communities of tremendous vitality and untold wealth. 48 mins.
VHS: S13561. $19.98.

Cousteau 2—Series Gift Pack
Contains all six titles listed above plus a "Save the Planet" computer disk which includes graphic illustrations, a global-warming scenario game, resources for environmental action, energy-saving tips and shopping guidelines. Available for either IBM or Apple Macintosh computers and their compatibles. 388 mins.
VHS: S13563. $119.98.

The Cousteau Odyssey
Clipperton: The Island Time Forgot. Six hundred miles off the coast of Mexico, the now-barren island of Clipperton has a startling history of human survival and depravity. Captain Cousteau and a survivor re-visit its horrifying past. 58 mins.
VHS: S08360. $24.95.
Mediterranean: Cradle or Coffin? Calypso studies the impact of industry, urbanization, tourism and fishing on the fragile beauty and bounty of the virtually landlocked Mediterranean region. 58 mins.
VHS: S10943. $24.98.
Time Bomb at Fifty Fathoms.
VHS: S10944. $24.98.

Creatures Great and Small
James Whitmore and James Earl Jones narrate this fascinating look into the past and present of dinosaurs, which ruled the world for 140 million years, and insects, which predate the dinosaurs by at least 100 million years. 1989, 60 mins.
VHS: S14541. $29.95.

Death on the Wing
Lorne Greene hosts this program about the migration of the majestic Golden Eagle from summer in Idaho to winter in Texas, as the devoted Golden Eagle parents, mated for life, strive to feed and protect their offspring.
VHS: S06328. $14.95.
Charles Greene/Stephen W. Dewar, USA, 1984, 30 mins.

Demons of the Deep
From the Bahamas comes this gripping firsthand account of spectacular physical action photography. Shark and barracuda feeding frenzies are revealed in close camera work, made possible by free-swimming divers, unhindered by safety cages. The basics of shark and barracuda biology are also made clear in this video, thereby separating fact from fiction. 60 mins.
VHS: S21796. $19.95.

Desert Under Siege
A beautifully shot production that provides a concise overview of desert ecology and an examination of the human endeavors that threaten this fragile ecosystem. USA, 1991, 28 mins.
VHS: S15204. $85.00.

Desert Vision
The magical Southwest captured in breathtaking imagery with original music by David Lanz and Paul Speer. 50 mins.
VHS: S10958. $29.95.

Devil Island
Travel to the deserted island of Mona, off the coast of Puerto Rico, the home of one of the largest lizards in the Western Hempisphere, the Mona iguana. Lorne Greene hosts. 30 mins.
VHS: S06323. $14.95.

Dinosaurs
The Smithsonian Institution's own collection of artifacts is key to this documentary about the new controversies surrounding the mammoth beasts from the past. The lives of these creatures as well as their extinction and the way information is uncovered about them is all shown in this fascinating video.
VHS: S21268. $29.95.

The Dinosaurs
This fascinating four-part set follows the story of dinosaurs, those mammoth creatures who are known to us only through fossils. Fortunately scientists the world over have painstakingly recreated their stories. Dr. John Ostrun, the paleontologist who inspired the character Alan Grant in *Jurassic Park*, is featured.
Flesh on the Bones. The mysteries start to unravel. Where did dinosaurs live, how fast did they move, and were they hot- or cold-blooded? Find out some astonishing answers to questions about a 200-million-year-old mystery.
VHS: S21750. $14.98.
The Death of the Dinosaur. The most fascinating and puzzling question of all is, "Why did the dinosaurs disappear?" Share in the theories of the cause of their demise, which range from massive meteors to violent volcanoes to disease.
VHS: S21752. $14.98.
The Monsters Emerge. A fascinating look at how a skeptical world first reacted to the proposed existence of dinosaurs. Join lively bone-hunts and an expedition with a real-life Indiana Jones in this exciting video.
VHS: S21749. $14.98.

The Nature of the Beast.
Travel around the world with scientists in their quest to find answers to how dinosaurs originated, and how these animals came to dominate the entire planet for over 140 million years. From Argentina to Nova Scotia to the Western U.S., learn about recent discoveries, such as the existence of "good lizard mothers."
VHS: S21751. $14.98.
The Complete Set.
VHS: S21753. $39.98.

The Discoverers
Reverberating with the passion to discover our world, this video charts the earliest voyages that mapped the earth. It continues up into the present day by examining contemporary space launches. The challenges, lessons and exhilaration of mankind's unending quests are charted in *The Discoverers*. 38 mins. Filmed in IMAX.
Laser: LD74733. $39.95.

Discovering Gardens
An entertaining series on England's most beautiful and elaborate gardens, the series shows the care and skill brought to each house and garden. Hosted by Gyles Brandrell and Michele Brown.
Vol. 1: Trelissick, Cornwall/East Lambrook, Somerset. At the foot of Trelissick house and garden, we're introduced to the famous Cornish garden, its effervescent spring glory richly planted with summer favorites.
VHS: S17956. $29.95.
Vol. 2: Cotehele, Cornwall/Docton Mill, Devon. A contemporary study of the Cotehele House, which overlooks the River Tamar, with its medieval history and glory. The second part looks at the efforts of Stephen and Irish Pugh and their garden crafted in the hills of the coastal North Devon.
VHS: S17957. $29.95.
Vol. 3: Bicton Park, Devon/Mapperton, Dorset. A visually spectacular view of the contemporary oriental garden, the Palm House, created by Bill Hearne, and an 18th century Italianate renaissance garden. The second part looks at an exquisite Italianate garden, a 17th-century water garden and Victor Montague's wild valley garden.
VHS: S17958. $29.95.
Vol. 4: Stourhead, Wiltshire/Glendurgan, Cornwall. This stunning landscape epitomizes the 18th-century English idea. The second part looks at the components of the wild areas of a beautiful hidden valley, and the mazes at Glendurgan.
VHS: S17959. $29.95.
Vol. 5: Tresco, Isles of Scilly/Mount Edgcumbe, Cornwall. Brandell and Brown study the amazing Abbey Gardens, the world's sole garden-heliport. In the second piece they interact with Gods in the Italian Garden and a geyser in the New Zealand garden.
VHS: S17960. $29.95.
Vol. 6: St. Michael's Mount, Cornwall/Trewithen, Cornwall. Follow Lord St. Leven on the perilous, storm-lashed garden in the first part, and then move to England's finest spring garden, a setting overladen with rhododendrons, camellias and magnolias.
VHS: S17961. $29.95.

Dolphin Adventure
In this fascinating underwater adventure, dolphins are captured on film in the open ocean for the first time. These intelligent creatures are revealed as never before in this film, winner of the "Cup of the Prime Minister of Italy Award" at the Milan Film Festival. Special appearance by Buckminster Fuller.
VHS: S23671. $19.95.
Michael Wiese, USA, 1994, 60 mins.

Dolphins
Commune with the dolphins. Enjoy graceful acrobatics and sensuous swimming in the ocean at the Dolphin Research Center, Grassy Key, Florida. Lush music by Private Music Artist Carlos Alomar to the filmed images by Robert Riger. 25 mins.
VHS: S10242. $29.95.

Dolphins, Close Encounters
George Page narrates this exploration of the research focused on the abilities of these large sea mammals. Study shows that they are highly intelligent and aware creatures who are also capable of great affection. 60 mins.
VHS: S24376. $19.95.

Drought
A highly evocative film which examines the dry seasons and their place in the rhythm of the Australian climate. The cycle of drought, fire and flood is part of the natural order rather than a series of unpredictable catastrophies. The film explores the Australian aborigine's attitude to drought and examines the theories of its causes—sunspots, volcanic eruptions, eccentricities of our planet's orbit. 58 mins.
VHS: S10292. $24.95.

Ducks Under Siege (National Audubon)
Narrated by John Heard. With over half the duck population in North America already gone, can we be certain that future generations of children will ever behold the breathtaking sight of migrating ducks racing across the sky? 60 mins.
VHS: S09004. $14.98.

Ducks Unlimited's Videoguide to Waterfowl and Game Birds
For the hunter and naturalist, bird identification is a must. *Ducks Unlimited's Videoguide to Waterfowl and Game Birds* gives a comprehensive system of sight and sound identification for our 43 species of waterfowl and 21 upland game birds of North America. Breath-taking footage, still photographs and computer-animated video graphics simulating the birds' appearance under low-light conditions with wingbeats calibrated to actual speed for each species focus today's technology on identifying birds in flight.
VHS: S03998. $74.95.
Laser: LD70958. $39.95.

Earth Bridge
The Earth Bridge Project is an innovative, nature-based leadership development program that brings together high school students of different cultures and helps them develop a deepened respect for nature, for their own cultural heritage and for the culture of others. 28 mins.
VHS: S23366. $59.95.

Earth Dance
David Fortney's visual poem about nature and beauty, "tall grasses dancing in the wind, water cascading wildly and clouds moving across the sky in silent majesty." 30 mins.
Laser: LD70244. $24.95.

Earth Day Special
This is the celebrity-strewn television special that celebrated the 20th anniversary of Earth Day. Everyone from Candice Bergen to Carl Sagan partakes, profits go to the People of the Earth Foundation. 95 mins.
VHS: S12751. $9.95.

Earth Dreaming
Georgianne Cowan's mythological journey reveals the texture, rhythm and shape of the earth, punctuated by Steve Roach's haunting, ethereal score. 23 mins.
Laser: LD70241. $24.95.

Earthquake! Disaster in L.A.
Experience the first-hand devastation of a major quake, including actual footage taken during the 1987 Whittier Quake. A Cal Tech seismologist discusses the effects of a larger future quake in Southern California. 53 mins.
VHS: S10028. $19.95.

Echo of the Elephants
Echo is the matriarch of a family of African elephants. Her calf Ely was born unable to walk. This nature documentary reveals the lives of these great animals in startling detail, allowing each creature to appear as a complete individual.
VHS: S24373. $19.95.

Eco-Rap: Voices from the Hood
A multi-ethnic group of young men and women learn about local environmental hazards and express their concerns using the urban poetry of rap music. The video features the best of Eco-Rap music with contemporary graphics. 38 mins.
VHS: S23362. $59.95.

Endangered
Largely because of human activity, our planet loses 100 species each day. This video provides a clear introduction to how human activities are endangering thousands of species, why protecting nature's diversity is critical to us all and how the Endangered Species Act works to help us do that. 30 mins.
VHS: S23365. $29.95.

The Ends of the Earth
Western Australia is home to spellbinding creatures who inhabit a dry and foreboding landscape. The thorny devil, the frilled lizard, the banjo ray and the sinister saltwater crocodile are just some of the more intriguing animals featured in this video. 60 mins. From the Discovery Channel.
VHS: S25073. $19.95.

Eruption of Mt. St. Helens
Witness the explosive eruption of Mt. St. Helens and its devastating aftermath as photographed by men who narrowly escaped the Mountain's wrath. Enter the devastated area only hours after the eruption and witness the incredible destruction. 30 mins.
VHS: S05736. $29.95.

Explorers: A Century of Discovery
Produced to commemorate the Centennial anniversary of the National Geographic Society, this tribute to the pioneers covers their contributions that have made the wonders of the world accessible. 60 mins.
VHS: S07394. $19.95.

Eyewitness
This fascinating PBS nature series is unlike any other available. It combines state of the art computer animation to explore how each animal evolved and how it actually works. In addition it includes wildlife segments that reveal each creature's relationship to its environment. Perhaps the most interesting segments are those which explain how man uses animals to express some of the most noble concepts. Each episode is 30 mins.
Eyewitness Amphibian.
VHS: S24962. $12.95.
Eyewitness Bird.
VHS: S24958. $12.95.
Eyewitness Cat.
VHS: S24959. $12.95.
Eyewitness Dinosaur.
VHS: S24964. $12.95.
Eyewitness Dog.
VHS: S24960. $12.95.
Eyewitness Elephant.
VHS: S24965. $12.95.
Eyewitness Fish.
VHS: S24963. $12.95.
Eyewitness Horse.
VHS: S24966. $12.95.
Eyewitness Insect.
VHS: S24968. $12.95.
Eyewitness Jungle.
VHS: S24969. $12.95.
Eyewitness Reptile.
VHS: S24961. $12.95.
Eyewitness Shark.
VHS: S24967. $12.95.
Eyewitness Skeleton.
VHS: S24970. $12.95.

Finite Oceans
This Discovery Channel video about environmental risk to the world oceans was made in conjunction with the Smithsonian Institution/Times Mirror exhibit. Dr. Roger Payne explores political, economic and environmental aspects of this pressing concern.
VHS: S25097. $19.95.

The Fire Below Us
May 18, 1980, was the day that the Mount St. Helens volcano exploded without any warning. This documentary combines dramatic eyewitness accounts, spectacular footage of the devastation, and clear scientific explanations of this natural event. 68 mins.
VHS: S25738. $24.95.

First Time Garden
For millions of new home owners and enthusiastic gardeners, this video is an essential aid to creating a beautiful and practical garden. The information-packed video traces the complete development of a bare and muddy building site into a flourishing garden. A BBC production. 90 mins.
VHS: S10282. $19.94.

Fish (Pet Care)
Dr. Michael Fox hosts this video featuring Joe Yaiullo, senior aquarist at the New York Aquarium, with tips on setting up a fresh water aquarium, tank size, filtration assembly, conditioning the tank, choosing the fish, maintaining good water, feeding, and more. 30 mins.
VHS: S09627. $14.95.

The Floating World
A portrait of undersea life and visuals choreographed to the works of Bach, Debussy, Elgar, Franck, Handel, Harvey, Offenbach and Tchaikovsky. 45 mins.
Laser: LD70247. $29.95.

Following the Tundra Wolf
Robert Redford narrates this award-winning account of the feral tundra wolf. The filmmakers document the animal's rituals and behavioral patterns. 48 mins.
VHS: S12158. $14.98.

Forest Habitat Set
This three-volume set from the Discovery Channel's *Mother Nature: Tales of Discovery* series features *When Bears Go Fishing*, *The Business of Beavers* and *Antlers Big and Small*. Together these tapes offer an exhaustive look at the life of the forest.
VHS: S25086. $39.95.

The Forest Through the Trees
Northern California's majestic redwood forests are an irreplaceable national treasure. While the world's attention is on the devastation of rainforests, here in the U.S. the last remaining stands of virgin redwoods are being destroyed at a much faster rate. This a thoughtful, visually spectacular film on a complex issue of national importance. 1990, 58 mins.
VHS: S13935. $85.00.

Friendly Gray Whales
A journey to Mexico's lagoons for an encounter with these friendly whales and for a study of their behavior, including underwater. 30 mins.
VHS: S10921. $29.95.

Frozen Eden
The vast journeys of the caribou in the vast Ungava Peninsula where the last giant caribou herds thunder across frozen Eden on their annual thousand-mile migration. Narrated by Lorne Greene. USA, 22 mins.
VHS: S03094. $14.95.

Galapagos: My Fragile World (National Audubon)
Narrated by Cliff Robertson. An extraordinary journey to the magical, almost prehistoric world of the Gapalagos Islands through the eyes and photographic lens of lifetime resident and world-renowned photographer Tui De Roy. 60 mins.
VHS: S09002. $14.98.

Gardens of the World
Audrey Hepburn hosts this six-part series that looks at more than 50 gardens for their historical, cultural and aesthetic principals, with narration by Hepburn and Michael York.
Country Gardens. This program studies the pleasures of country gardens, with their pungent sense of smell, taste and touch. Audrey Hepburn looks at imposing gardens such as the Giardino del Ninfa, cottage gardens in England and farmhouse gardens connected to Chilcombe House in Dorset (UK). Commentary by garden designers John Brookes and Ryan Gainey. 27 mins.
VHS: S20325. $24.95.
Flower Gardens. Claude Monet's garden at Giverny showcases the proper display of flowers. The color schemes beautifully contrast with the grace and elegance of the borders specific to the Tintinhull House in Somerset, England. The program also includes the native flora of America's Southwest. With special commentary by Penelope Hobhouse. 27 mins.
VHS: S20324. $24.95.
Formal Gardens. Audrey Hepburn shows the evolution of formal design, visiting the luscious gardens of Renaissance-period Italy, the luminous 17th-century gardens of France, and England's elaborate 20th-century gardens. With guest commentary by garden authority Penelope Hobhouse. 27 mins.
VHS: S20323. $24.95.
Public Gardens and Trees. Audrey Hepburn travels to the elegantly restored gardens at Mt. Vernon, formerly owned by George Washington. Hepburn also discusses the diversity and vast number of public gardens in Paris, including the "pocket parks," the grand royal gardens. 27 mins.
VHS: S20326. $24.95.
Roses and Rose Gardens. Audrey Hepburn studies the historical importance of the rose, which has a deep symbolic meaning relevant to legend, romance and beauty. With a lecture by author Graham Stuart Thomas. 27 mins.
VHS: S20321. $24.95.
Tulips and Spring Bulbs. Audrey Hepburn reveals the vast history of bulbs and their connection to the history of Holland. The program shows the bulb's transformation from sleeping bulb to full bloom. 27 mins.
VHS: S20322. $24.95.
Gardens of the World, Set. The complete set of six programs is a collector's edition preserved in a beautiful box set.
VHS: S20327. $139.95.

Gems and Minerals
This program explores the Smithsonian's vaults, containing some of the rarest gems in the world, including a 4.6-billion-year-old meteorite and the legendary 45½ carat Hope diamond. 1989, 45 mins.
VHS: S14544. $29.95.
Laser: LD70228. $34.95.

Giant Sequoias
Largest of all living things! Learn about these amazing trees and their relationships with other forest inhabitants. Experience the splendor of the Giant Sequoia groves found in Sequoia and Yosemite National Parks. 30 mins.
VHS: S06669. $29.95.

Gift of the Whales
The fascinating story of a young, Native American boy's rediscovery of life. The arrival of the whales was a gift…just for him, with the video capturing spectacular, never before seen photography of the largest creatures to grace the earth, in a blend of entertainment and education. 30 mins.
VHS: S10961. $29.95.
Laser: LD71004. $24.95.

The Great Barrier Reef
This highly acclaimed production is a spellbinding glimpse under the sea, off the coast of Australia on the Great Barrier Reef. Prince Philip narrates the story of the undersea life and ecological balance of this beautiful reef. 57 minutes.
VHS: S03291. $69.95.

The Great Bears of Alaska
Intimate behavior of the Great Bear is shown on this video with startling clarity. It's like coming face to face with one of these magnificent creatures in the wild, only much safer. 60 mins. From the Discovery Channel.
VHS: S25071. $19.95.

Great Dinosaurs Set
A collection of four programs about the massive beasts who roamed in prehistoric times, including profiles of the Brontosaurus, Stegosaurus, Triceratops and Tyrannosaurus. 35 mins.
VHS: S20055. $159.95.

Great White
This video brings the great white shark closer than ever before. Renowned as the most fearsome killing machine on earth, this animal's awesome force is a wonder of nature. A Discovery Channel production. 90 mins.
VHS: S25082. $19.95.

Grizzly & Man: Uneasy Truce (National Audubon)
Can grizzlies and man live peacefully together? This is the question explored in this award-winning Audubon special about the uneasy coexistence of man and bear, narrated by Robert Redford.
VHS: S09561. $14.98.

Help Save Planet Earth
Ted Danson hosts this guide full of everyday tips on how to protect and save the environment (and often save money at the same time). How to conserve water, heat and electricity, preserve trees and conserve energy are among the hundreds of suggestions. Features Beau Bridges, Lloyd Bridges, Jamie Lee Curtis, Cheech Marin and many others.
VHS: S13052. $14.98.

Hunters of Chubut
Lorne Greene travels to the rugged Atlantic Coast of Argentina where sea lions and penguins battle and breed in a packed, frenzied colony. In this beautiful, violent world, even these large hunters fall prey to the biggest, most powerful predators on earth—the Killer Whale. USA, 22 mins.
VHS: S03091. $14.95.

Huntress
Lorne Greene narrates this tape about a young cougar's odyssey for independence.
VHS: S10039. $14.95.

I Dig Fossils
A father and his son go exploring in the Mazon Creek region of Illinois. There they uncover fossils of leaves that were probably chewed on by prehistoric reptiles. This video offers clear information about the search for fossils and explains how these imprints of the past are made. 25 mins.
VHS: S23856. $19.95.

If Dolphins Could Talk
Dolphins have survived natural calamities, but now they're confronted by their greatest threat—man. This program looks at the efforts by scientists and biologists to "protect the closest relative of man in the seas." Narrated by Michael Douglas.
VHS: S16877. $14.98.

In a Time of Headlong Progress
Over 90% of the lush rainforests in Brazil's Bahia have been destroyed. This destruction now threatens the economic well-being of the region as well as the habitat of the golden-headed lion tamarin. This is a lively, comprehensive look at the complex economic and social issues behind deforestation and the hopeful, innovative work of pioneering Brazilian conservationist Cristina Alves. 45 mins.
VHS: S23369. $125.00.

In Celebration of Trees
Trees are the world's oldest living things. Their majesty and grandeur make this video from the Discovery Channel a true delight to watch. Somehow the serenity of towering trees seems to defy time itself. 60 mins.
VHS: S25081. $19.95.

In Good Hands: Culture and Agriculture in the Lacandon Rainforest
While inefficient agricultural methods are destroying many of the world's rainforests, the Lacandon Maya of Chiapas in Southern Mexico have been practicing a sustainable form of rainforest farming for centuries. Dr. James Nations, an ecological anthropologist, shows how the Lacandon farm in the forest, and how culture, mythology and religion influence their agricultural methods. 27 mins.
VHS: S23368. $125.00.

In the Company of Whales
Come travel in the company of the largest animals to ever live on earth…powerful creatures of extraordinary grace and intelligence…masters of the watery realm where they have existed for over 30 million years. Featured on The Discovery Channel. 90 mins.
VHS: S17011. $24.95.

In the Kingdom of the Dolphins
A fascinating look at the dolphin, filmed in the clear waters of a remote corner of the Carribean, as journalist Hardy Jones and marine biologist Julia Whitty spend seven summers filming these magical creatures in their natural habitat. Spectacular underwater photography. 50 mins.
VHS: S03427. $24.95.

In the Wild: Dolphins with Robin Williams
Robin Williams hosts this intimate portrait of creatures many believe to be highly intelligent and affectionate. Plenty of information about dolphins is provided by experts, but the most intriguing aspect of this video is the personal rapport Williams cultivates with them. 60 mins.
VHS: S27775. $19.98.

In the Wild: Grey Whales with Christopher Reeves
Grey whales were once nearly extinct. Fortunately, their numbers have increased from a low of a few hundred to approximately 22,000. Reeve took the trip of a lifetime just before his accident, following these animals along their difficult migration from Siberia to Baja. 60 mins.
VHS: S27776. $19.98.

In the Wild: Pandas with Debra Winger
Pandas were shrouded in mystery until very recently. Even today, as they come close to extinction, little is known about these reclusive animals. Winger and her son travel the route used by the first Western woman to find pandas. After a long journey, they discover that Professor Pan Wenshi has successfully protected a panda and her young cub from danger. 60 mins.
VHS: S27777. $19.98.

The Incredible Story of Dogs
This three-tape series follows the story of dogs from ancient times all the way to the present. All kinds of breeds and their origins are showcased, including Labradors, Maltese, and German Shepherds. *Vol. I, Fatal Attraction* traces the evolution of dogs into domesticity. *Vol. II, Matters of Life and Death: Gods and Gladiators* celebrates the many roles of dogs today. Then *Vol. III, A Question of Breeding: What Price Friendship?* examines people's obsession with man's best friend.
VHS: S21535. $59.95.

The Infinite Voyage: Great Dinosaur Hunt
The Infinite Voyage series takes viewers on a fascinating trip to unlock the mysteries of how the dinosaur lived—*not how it perished*. 60 mins.
VHS: S12186. $14.98.

The Infinite Voyage: The Future of the Past
Artist and scientists pool their resources to develops ways to preserve civilization's heritage for future generations. 58 mins.
VHS: S19201. $14.98.

The Infinite Voyage: The Living Clock
This exciting blend of science and technology studies the intricate biology of time and detail. 58 mins.
VHS: S19202. $14.98.

The Infinite Voyage: Unseen Worlds
Some of the Unseen Worlds in this *Infinite Voyage* program are a black hole in the Milky Way galaxy, the interior of a human heart, and an atomic accelerator. 60 mins.
VHS: S12188. $14.98.

Inky, Dinky Spider
Lorne Greene narrates this tape about the *Bola* spider as she begins her "weapon"—a long strand of sticky silk weighted every few inches with a unique, pear-like drop of silk. When the bola is completed, the spider sends out an odor to attract males, who will be caught in her web. 30 mins.
VHS: S05001. $14.95.

Insects
Insects make up over 80% percent of all animal life on earth. Learn how they have evolved and adapted to survive for eons.
Laser: LD70227. $34.95.

Inside Hawaiian Volcanoes
Backed up by awesome graphics and stunning live action footage, this video is a colorful, devastating portrait of the volcanic activity on a tropical island. Narrated by Roger Mudd. 25 mins.
VHS: S18430. $19.95.
Laser: CAV. LD72263. $29.95.

Invasion of the Dinosaurs
A program that attempts to consider unresolved questions about the activities, patterns and mental processes of the dinosaurs, covering their dominance and extinction. The scientists employ the technological aid of Dinamation—lifelike robots—to interpret the animals' movements. 30 mins.
VHS: S18715. $9.95.

Island of the Dragons
Komodo Dragons are direct descendants of dinosaurs. These formidable, man-eating monsters are one of the most incredible inhabitants found on the Indonesian Archipelago. Some of the animals' most surprising secrets are revealed in this video. 60 mins. From the Discovery Channel.
VHS: S25072. $19.95.

Island of Whales
Experts brave perilous waterways to pursue the gray, humpback killer whales on Vancouver Island. Narrated by Gregory Peck. 55 mins.
VHS: S18240. $19.95.

It's a Male's World
The unusual sexual dynamics of the Hamadryas, a species of baboon whose social hierarchy operates as a male tyranny, is explored in this nature documentary hosted by Lorne Greene. 30 mins.
VHS: S06325. $14.95.

Journey into Life
An Academy Award nominee in 1990, this powerfully moving film captures the most amazing moments of creation on the remarkable journey that ends with the miracle of birth. 30 mins.
VHS: S23144. $14.95.

Just Call Me Kitty
A charming video which is all about cats—dubbed the "Everything you ever wanted to know about cats guide for the home viewer." With Persians, calicoes, and hundreds of loveable cats. 60 mins.
VHS: S11114. $14.95.

Kangaroos Under Fire
Three million kangaroos are slaughtered annually and the video investigates the uncertain future of Australia's national symbol. 25 mins.
VHS: S06496. $49.95.

Kuiseb the Vanishing River/ Kalahari Bigfoot (BBC Wildlife Special)
For many months of the year, all that can be seen of the modern Kuiseb river is the dry bed snaking its empty way from Southwest Africa to the Atlantic Ocean. Only with flash flooding or other special rainfall conditions does the surface riverbed become a waterway. It has to wait for the life-giving waters as do all the animals that depend on it. Nearby in the grasslands which fringe the Kalahari desert lives an animal which looks as if it could be a cross between a rabbit and a kangaroo. In fact, it's the spring hare, a rodent, and for its size it has just about the biggest feet around. 55 mins.
VHS: S12393. $19.94.

Land of the Birds
Unique and beautifully feathered, the cassowary, lyrebird and bowerbird take flight in one's imagination, as well as in the wide blue sky in this look at nature's first aeronautical pilots.
VHS: S05236. $29.95.

Land of the Leopard
John Varty, born and raised in Africa, and his trusted friend Elmon Mhlongo develop a unique relationship with a family of wild leopards. Gripping and compelling sequences filmed over five years describe the territorial behavior of the female leopard, her mothering of cubs, and the stalking skills the cubs must learn in order to survive. 60 mins.
VHS: S04696. $29.95.

Last Wilderness
Frazier Island, a magical fairy-tale landscape, is made up entirely of sand, woven together by the protective roots of the trees that populate its soil. An exploration of this unique, fragile island off Australia's coast.
VHS: S05237. $19.95.

Life and Death in the Great Barrier Reef
The manta ray seems dangerous, the great white shark is a killer. A fascinating look at this underwater wilderness, the Great Barrier Reef, the mighty edifice, covered with coral polyps.
VHS: S05238. $19.95.

Life in the Desert
Nothing moves under the infernal mid-day sun of Australia's desert outback. At dusk, however, the desert blossoms with mammals, birds and reptiles. A desperate struggle for survival among the heartiest of creatures is about to begin.
VHS: S05239. $19.95.

Life in the Southern Seas
Come face to face with a curious pack of sea lions or find out that a hole in the ground is really a snug little home to a mutton bird and a tiger snake. A fascinating look at Australia's wilderness.
VHS: S05240. $19.95.

Loch Ness Discovered
This video seeks to answer the question, "Is there a prehistoric creature hiding in the murky depths of Loch Ness?" Scientists brave ridicule in the first serious investigation of the underwater lair of this mysterious beast. From the Discovery Channel.
VHS: S22540. $19.95.

Lost Worlds/Vanished Lives
David Attenborough uses fossils to boldly recapture the daily activity of dinosaurs, providing a valuable look at the evolution of the earth. "Attenborough is affable and often amazing" (*New York Post*). 240 mins.
VHS: S19382. $99.95.

A Love Story: The Canada Goose
The wetlands of North America, the breeding grounds for one of the largest, most intelligent and adaptable birds on earth, this is the powerful story of love and devotion as the birds raise their young in the face of constant danger from racoons, minks and man. Narrated by Lorne Greene. 30 mins.
VHS: S04999. $14.95.

Luray Caverns
The largest and most popular caverns in eastern America; explores how the Luray caverns in Virginia were formed, and includes an autumn excursion to Luray's neighboring attraction, Shenandoah National Park. 30 mins.
VHS: S09183. $29.95.

The Magnificent Whales
In this video, more than 20 different species of whales and dolphins are showcased. Shot around North America and Hawaii. 60 mins.
VHS: S18428. $29.95.

Mammoth Cave National Park, Kentucky
The mysterious world of Mammoth cave, the longest cave on Earth, including its unique formations such as helicites, gypsum flowers, soda straws and flowstone. 30 mins.
VHS: S10044. $29.95.

Man of the Trees

Moved by his great love of life, Richard St. Barbe Baker dedicated most of his 92 years to preserving the world's forests. *Man of the Trees* presents the remarkable life of this vibrant New Zealander who travelled the world in defense of trees—a cause he saw as essential to planetary survival. St. Barbe Baker is shown at work spreading his love of trees to New Zealand, North America and African tribes, whom he inspired to create a ceremonial dance for tree planting. Through his efforts, billions of trees were planted, and his life serves as an inspiration for anyone concerned about the impact of deforestation on the ecosphere. 26 mins.
VHS: S11488. $29.95.

The Man Who Loves Sharks

Stan Waterman is one of the world's finest underwater cinematographers. Some of the most memorable adventures and exotic creatures of his career are captured in this journey through dangerous waters. 90 mins.
VHS: S21795. $19.95.

Man-Eaters of India

Not the latest diet craze in the sub-continent but another National Geographic video. This stunningly photographed exploration is devoted to the deadly big cats of the Kumaon region of that diverse country. It pays special tribute to Jim Corbett, the man who saved the tigers from extinction. 60 mins.
VHS: S03676. $19.95.

Marmot Mountain/Yellowstone Below Zero (BBC Wildlife Special)

The Austrian Tyrol in spring is an idyllic land of flower-filled meadows and glistening peaks. The hills are alive with the sound of marmots. For in the brief season ahead, these playful rodents, who are likened to overweight squirrels, struggle to gain the nourishment that will enable them to survive another eight harsh months under the snow. *Yellowstone Below Zero* explores the incredible beauty and dramatic change in lifestyle that takes place within the park during the first few weeks of winter.
VHS: S12394. $19.94.

Master Hunter of the Night

The fabled night predator—the great horned owl—is examined in this documentary led by Kay Mc Keever, a pioneer in the rehabilitation of owls. As Kay helps an injured owl. Narrated by Lorne Greene. USA, 22 mins.
VHS: S03092. $14.95.

Monster Forces of Nature

Tornadoes, hurricanes, erupting volcanos, earthquakes and floods are shown in all their awe-inspiring force by this collection of scientific films. High tech equipment on planes, boats and satellites were used by NASA to gather this educational material. 90 mins.
VHS: S24692. $39.95.

Mountain Habitat Set

Mountains harbor a variety of creatures. This three-volume set from the Discovery Channel's *Mother Nature: Tales of Discovery* series features videos that show some of the fascinating inhabitants of these upper climes. *Good Neighbor Ground Squirrel, When Goats Go Climbing* and *Curious Cougar Kittens* are included.
VHS: S25089. $39.95.

Mutual of Omaha's Spirit of Adventure Series

Wildlife expert Jim Fowler hosts this series, produced by Emmy Award winner John Wilcox, which displays incredible, rare footage of endangered species in their own habitats, allowing the viewer to be a part of these exotic and sometimes dangerous expeditions. Guest hosts include Peggy Fleming, Christopher Cross, Peter Benchley, and Diana Nyad.
Mount Everest American Firsts. 50 mins.
VHS: S14070. $19.98.
Struggle to Survive—China's Giant Panda. 50 mins.
VHS: S14071. $19.98.
Challenging China's Yangtze, Part I & II. 90 mins.
VHS: S14072. $19.98.
Beneath the Sea—The Galapagos. 50 mins.
VHS: S14073. $19.98.
Uncovering China's Hidden Wildlife. 50 mins.
VHS: S14074. $19.98.
Twilight of the Gorilla. 50 mins.
VHS: S14075. $19.98.
Headhunter's Legacy. 50 mins.
VHS: S14076. $19.98.
Africa's Poaching Wars. 60 mins.
VHS: S14077. $19.98.
Antarctic Odyssey. 50 mins.
VHS: S14078. $19.98.
Voices in the Wild. 50 mins.
VHS: S14079. $19.98.
Rafting into Siberia. 50 mins.
VHS: S14080. $19.98.
Whales and Dolphins. 50 mins.
VHS: S14081. $19.98.

Mysterious Black-Footed Ferret (National Audubon Video)

Wyoming's scarce and endangered resident who fights man, disease and inbreeding, yet defies extinction with the help of man's intervention. Narrated by Loretta Swit. 60 mins.
VHS: S08289. $14.98.

Mystery of the Full Moon

In this award-winning, entertaining and absorbing film, the filmmakers examine the mystery that the moon holds for us as the center of many of our oldest myths and legends, and its effect upon the planet: how it raises tides in the oceans, the atmosphere, and the very core of Earth itself. 50 mins.
VHS: S10293. $24.95.

National Geographic Geo Kids: Bear Cubs, Baby Ducks, and Kooky Kookaburras

Sunny Honeypossum, Bobby Bushbaby and Balzac de Chameleon tell how different wild animals grow from infancy to young adulthood. The footage of a mother monkey caring for her baby is unforgettable.
VHS: S21961. $12.95.

National Geographic Geo Kids: Cool Cats, Raindrops, and Things That Live in Holes

While playing hide-and-seek, Sunny Honeypossum and Bobby Bushbaby discover a tree hole. Balzac de Chameleon then explains to them the variety of animals that make their home in these natural crevices.
VHS: S21962. $12.95.

National Geographic Geo Kids: Flying Trying and Honking Around

The delightful characters Sunny Honeypossum, Bobby Bushbaby and Balzac de Chameleon host this fascinating look at birds. These characters are all created by the maker of the Muppet Babies. Together they help kids explore the world of flight.
VHS: S21960. $12.95.

National Geographic Video

The National Geographic Society has always been renowned for their award-winning television specials; now these great programs are available on home video! 60 minutes each.
African Wildlife. Filmed in Etosha National Park in Namibia over a two-year period, *African Wildlife* captures animal behavior in extraordinarily close range.
VHS: S02061. $19.95.
Atocha: Quest for Treasure. The exciting tale of Mel Fisher's 16-year search for sunken treasure that went down with the Spanish galleon *Atocha* in 1622.
VHS: S02060. $14.95.
Creatures of the Namib Desert. Burgess Meredith narrates this look at Africa's Namib desert, a vast wilderness of sand, sun and open spaces where nature has learned to adapt and flourish.
VHS: S03053. $19.95.
Iceland River Challenge. Follow 12 adventurers as they run a wild Icelandic river through glacial caverns, violent gales, and crashing rapids, and see breathtaking footage of man against nature.
VHS: S02055. $19.95.
Land of the Tiger. Enter the mysterious world of the tiger, one of earth's most feared predators. Experience their beauty and strength as you visit their jungle home.
VHS: S02056. $19.95.
Polar Bear Alert. Jason Robards narrates a journey to Churchill, Manitoba, where the residents have learned to live with a unique wildlife problem. Each fall, the largest, most deadly carnivore in the Arctic migrates through this isolated Canadian village on an annual northwest trek.
VHS: S03055. $19.95.
Save the Panda. Join scientists as they track these rare creatures through bamboo-forested mountain ranges in central China. Narrated by Richard Basehart.
VHS: S02062. $19.95.
The Gorilla. Meet Koko, the world's most famous gorilla, in this engaging look at the mountain gorilla of central Africa. She's able to communicate by American sign language, telling everyone exactly what she'd like!
VHS: S02058. $19.95.
The Sharks. This famous *Geographic* film takes you underwater into the fascinating world of sharks—350 different species, of which only 20 are dangerous to humans. Learn the truth about these terrifying big fish!
VHS: S02057. $19.95.
Yukon Passage. Embark on a danger-filled journey through the Alaskan Yukon, as four adventurers face the Arctic circle as they travel 1,800 miles on foot, skis, raft, and dogsled. Jimmy Stewart narrates.
VHS: S02059. $19.95.

National Geographic Video: Africa's Stolen River

In the Savuti region of Botswana, one of nature's unfathomable mysteries plays itself out when a river slowly begins to disappear. Thought once to have been a lake, the channel appeared in 1957 and vanished again in 1982, creating a struggle for the animals whose lives depend upon the channel. 60 mins.
VHS: S09275. $19.95.

National Geographic Video: African Animal Oasis

A precarious excursion into the depths of Africa's wild animal kingdom, to Tanzania's Ngorongoro Crater, where the abundant supply of water alters an extinct volcanic crater into a spectacular wildlife oasis. 60 mins.
VHS: S19342. $19.95.

National Geographic Video: Amazon: Land of the Flooded Forest

A documentary about the exotic and fragile creatures and wildlife of the Amazon. 60 mins.
VHS: S18893. $19.95.

National Geographic Video: Antarctic Wildlife Adventure

The 50-foot schooner *Damien II* sets off to the most remote continent, Antarctica. Its rocky coasts and azure seas are home to fascinating wildlife, including penguins, humpback whales, elephant seals and more. 60 mins.
VHS: S25899. $19.95.

National Geographic Video: Australia's Improbable Animals

A land forgotten by time—an island where strange and fascinating creatures evolved in isolation from the rest of the world. This National Geographic special investigates the mysterious world of animals "down under." 60 mins.
VHS: S06610. $19.95.

National Geographic Video: Braving Alaska

Martin Sheen narrates this documentary about the pioneers in America's largest state. They hunt for survival. Groceries and mail are delivered by plane. Warmth is precious as the temperature drops to 60 degrees below zero during the hard winter. Within this harsh environment however, there is an unmatched beauty. 60 mins.
VHS: S22039. $19.95.

National Geographic Video: Cats: Caressing the Tiger

Though house cats are beloved pets, their behavior is not so far removed from their ferocious cousins in the wild. This video explores the mystery of the ordinary housecat to uncover basic facts. Once and for all it is clearly explained how cats always manage to land on their feet. 60 mins.
VHS: S23949. $19.95.

National Geographic Video: Creatures of the Mangrove

Explores the unique wildlife community on the lush coast of Borneo. Produced by National Geographic. 60 mins.
VHS: S07393. $19.95.

National Geographic Video: Crocodiles: Here Be Dragons

This program ventures into the treacherous Grumeti River in Africa to capture footage of the ferocious crocodiles. 60 mins.
VHS: S18892. $19.95.

National Geographic Video: Cyclone!

Tornadoes from the Midwest's "Tornado Alley," Hurricane Andrew in Florida, and powerful typhoons in the Pacific are all shown in this fascinating exploration of cyclone storms. Scientists are still struggling with how to track and predict these powerful, killer weather systems.
VHS: S27662. $19.95.
Richard J. Wells, USA, 1995, 60 mins.

National Geographic Video: Elephant

The largest, strongest and among the most intelligent animals to walk this planet, the elephant is examined in this in-depth look at a truly magnificent creature. 60 mins.
VHS: S11653. $19.95.

National Geographic Video: Eternal Enemies: Lions and Hyenas

This documentary about the battle between lions and spotted hyenas, as they fight for territory in northern Botswana, is remarkable for the eerie, nighttime footage. 60 mins.
VHS: S19343. $19.95.

National Geographic Video: Giant Bears of Kodiak Island

This is a documentary about the largest carnivores on Earth. They hunt for salmon in the rich rivers in order to gorge themselves for the hard winter. In this harsh environment they raise their cubs with surprising tenderness. 60 mins.
VHS: S22038. $19.95.

National Geographic Video: Great Explorers Gift Box

A compelling ethnographic study collects four works: Al Reinert's documentary about the Apollo space missions, *For All Mankind*; the historic climb of the world's highest summit, *Return to Everest*; a documentary about the 100-year travel expedition, *The Explorers: A Century of Discovery*; and the fearless, brilliant cinematographers who risked their lives to create their art, *Cameramen Who Dared*.
VHS: S18843. $79.95.

National Geographic Video: Great Whales

Slaughtered by man to near extinction, these benign undersea creatures are beautifully documented in this National Geographic exploration.
VHS: S06297. $19.95.

National Geographic Video: Hawaii: Strangers in Paradise

Documents the painstaking efforts of conservationists to preserve the natural and wildlife habitats of the ancient green turtle, the monk seal or Hawaiian honeycreeper threatened in the Hawaiian Islands.
VHS: S18842. $19.95.

National Geographic Video: Himalayan River Run

A death-defying ride down a wild Mt. Everest river as the National Geographic explores the daredevils who take a thrilling adventure.
VHS: S05886. $19.95.

National Geographic Video: Hunt for the Great White Shark

Great white sharks are featured in this video in all their fury and grandeur. They are seen in their natural surroundings and the experience of a shark attack victim makes clear the awesome force these creatures possess. 55 mins.
VHS: S24677. $19.95.

National Geographic Video: Invisible World

Each moment events take place that the eye cannot perceive because these occurrences are too small, too fast, too slow, or beyond the spectrum of visible light. Some of the captivating sights that will forever alter our perception and knowledge of our world are in this National Geographic documentary. 60 mins.
VHS: S06611. $19.95.

National Geographic Video: Jewels of the Caribbean

Coral reefs shelter a world of incredible but hidden beauty. There are schools of brightly colored fish amid the sandy plains and sea grasses of these unique underwater ecosystems. Special attention is given to dolphins, manatees and other rare creatures. 55 mins.
VHS: S24678. $19.95.

National Geographic Video: Killer Whales: Wolves of the Sea

This documentary looks at how killer whales pursue their prey for food gathering. The program includes some stunning underwater documentary footage of whales on the attack. 60 mins.
VHS: S19915. $19.95.
Laser: LD72019. $29.95.

National Geographic Video: Lions of Darkness

Renowned filmmakers Dereck and Beverly Joubert filmed this story of a growing lion pride in Botswana. It begins as three young, aggressive outsiders invade and depose the pride's aged leader. Soon there are new cubs attesting to the vigor of this change. One cub's struggle to survive was especially harrowing and yet allowing nature to take its own course proves especially rewarding.
VHS: S21807. $19.95.
Laser: LD74633. $34.95.

National Geographic Video: Lions of the African Night

A startling look at 30 African lions as they stalk their prey at night, fending off their constant enemy—hunger—in this National Geographic look at wildlife in Africa. 60 mins.
VHS: S06609. $19.95.

National Geographic Video: Mysteries of Mankind

The subject: the human race. The questions: who are we, and where did we come from? Controversies about how we evolved still abound. Explored here is the mystery, taking the viewers around the world and back in time millions of years in search for answers. 60 mins.
VHS: S09276. $19.95.

National Geographic Video: Nature's Fury!

Earthquakes, hurricanes and floods are powerful natural occurrences that have a drastic impact on human lives. This video features heroic individuals fighting everything from earthquakes in San Francisco to floods in France and China to tornadoes in the American Midwest to hurricanes in Bangladesh and Florida.
VHS: S27663. $19.95.
Jaime Bernanke, USA, 1994, 60 mins.

National Geographic Video: Ocean Drifters

The powerful currents of the open ocean carry a surfeit of unusual animals that can travel up to 100 miles a day. Loggerhead turtles, Portuguese men-of-war, seahorses and other remarkable drifters are featured in this wildlife video. 55 mins.
VHS: S24676. $19.95.

National Geographic Video: Rain Forest

An exploration of a Central American rain forest, highlighting the delicate balance of some of the world's most unusual flora and fauna.
VHS: S03856. $19.95.

National Geographic Video: Reptiles and Amphibians

National Geographic searches for exotic reptiles such as the komodo dragon, the largest of all lizards; encounters the crocodile, which has remained relatively unchanged since the era of the dinosaur; and tracks the evolutionary link to our past by examining the creatures that have long inspired fascination and fear. 60 mins.
VHS: S11655. $19.95.

National Geographic Video: Rhino War

This National Geographic special program explores the desperate fight to save the rhino, an endangered species, from extinction. 60 mins.
VHS: S07391. $19.95.

National Geographic Video: Rocky Mountain Beaver Pond

Tireless worker, exceptional parent, and highly skilled builder, the beaver has earned its reputation as nature's great architect and engineer. 60 mins.
VHS: S08056. $19.95.

National Geographic Video: Search for the Great Apes

Dian Fossey is featured in this documentary on her pioneering fieldwork with Africa's mountain gorillas. 60 mins.
VHS: S09930. $19.95.

National Geographic Video: Season of the Cheetah

On the great open plains of the Serengeti, one of nature's fastest animals, the cheetah, hunts its prey in a never-ending quest for survival. This National Geographic documentary follows three cheetah brothers as they work together on the hunt.
VHS: S20822. $19.95.

National Geographic Video: Secret Leopard

Enter the private world of the wild leopard. In this intimate profile, you will observe the stealth of this elusive big cat amidst other predators such as the lion, hyena and cheetah—and discover the leopard's survival instinct. 60 mins.
VHS: S08058. $19.95.

National Geographic Video: Secrets of the Wild Panda

In central China a research team has spent ten years studying the panda in the wild. Their work is critical to the survival of this unique creature. Among their crucial findings is a body of research tracking the nurturing of a newborn panda. 60 mins.
VHS: S25897. $19.95.

National Geographic Video: Shark Encounters

Underwater filmmaker Mike deGruy reenacts the sequences of a vicious shark attack he suffered in his efforts to capture the world of sharks. The program also blends in new material to provide an eerie context for the sharks' aggression. 60 mins.
VHS: S19916. $19.95.

National Geographic Video: Strange Creatures of the Night

Astonishing nocturnal scenes of the eerie vampire bat, the great horned owl and wild hyena, in the world of darkness. 60 mins.
VHS: S10243. $19.95.

National Geographic Video: Survivors of the Skeleton Coast

Southwestern Africa's Namib desert offers one of the Earth's harshest climates. Despite scorching temperatures and flash floods, nature's creatures adapt and survive. National Geographic shows how in new footage shot on location in this inhospitable landscape.
VHS: S20823. $19.95.

National Geographic Video: The Grizzlies

This National Geographic documentary explores the fascinating world of the feared monarch of the wild, following their life cycle.
VHS: S05885. $19.95.

National Geographic Video: The Predators Collection

A four-program collection of National Geographic Videos, including *African Animal Oasis; Eternal Enemies: Lions and Hyenas; Crocodiles;* and *Grizzlies.*
VHS: S19344. $79.95.

National Geographic Video: Those Wonderful Dogs

These beloved pets are also tireless helpers to their human masters. They help uncover earthquake victims, star in movies, and even act as messengers in time of war. All these feats are included in this tribute to "man's best friend." 60 mins.
VHS: S23950. $19.95.

National Geographic Video: Volcano

A heartbreaking piece about the death-defying pursuits of filmmakers and naturalists Maurice and Katia Krafft, who actively pursued volcanic activity and were killed during an eruption. 60 mins.
VHS: S18891. $19.95.

National Geographic Video: White Wolf

Follow a pack of wild arctic wolves through their remote and unforgiving wilderness in this National Geographic program about the fascinating creature. 60 mins.
VHS: S09932. $19.95.

National Geographic Video: Wild Survivors

Wild animals from Africa to the Caribbean deploy clever methods to hide their presence. Some blend into the background while others masquerade as other less harmful things. In this wildlife documentary from National Geographic, learn the secrets of these crafty, often invisible creatures.
VHS: S20821. $19.95.

National Geographic Video: Zebra: Patterns in the Grass

A program about the spectacle of the great zebra migration in Botswana: a 300-mile journey studded with glorious scenery. The film also traces the evolution of the foal into a full grown zebra. 60 mins.
VHS: S18841. $19.95.

The National Zoo

Take a private tour of the Smithsonian's living animals collection. Join seven-year-old Jenny and her friend Max as they meet the most famous and unusual residents of the National Zoo. 1989, 50 mins.
VHS: S14545. $29.95.
Laser: LD70225. $34.95.

Natural States

The lush Pacific Northwest in a blend of scenic cinematography and original music by David Lanz and Paul Speer. 45 mins.
VHS: S10959. $29.95.

The Nature Connection

Part of the prize-winning series in which Dr. David Suzuki takes children on an enchanting adventure with invaluable lessons and first-hand perspectives of how science and nature are related to human behavior and what everyone can do to protect the environment. 360 mins.
The Nature Connection, Vol. 1. In *Buying a Rainforest* Dr. Suzuki and a group of children buy private tracts of the rainforest and discover how their investment has preserved its beauty. In *Urban Ecology* Dr. Suzuki and the children from a Toronto suburb intermix with city kids to examine nature within an urban setting. 60 mins.
VHS: S19665. $19.95.
The Nature Connection, Vol. 2. In the first part, *Fishing the Ocean* Dr. Suzuki and the children examine the life and work of a Newfoundland fisherman. In the second part, *Where Our Food Comes From,* the group receives lessons in farm life, including milking, weeding and harvesting. 60 mins.
VHS: S19666. $19.95.
The Nature Connection, Vol. 3. In *Merv's Forest* the group visits a 150-acre farm to learn how careful selective logging and forest management preserve forest creatures without ecological damage. In *Water Works* Dr. Suzuki and his group examine the Great Lakes basin to study the role of water in the biosphere. 60 mins.
VHS: S19667. $19.95.

The Nature Connection, Vol. 4. In *The Badlands* the group explores fossil evidence in Dinosaur Provincial Park. In *A Winter Walk* the children take a dazzling walk to imagine how animals preserve their winter homes in hostile or threatening areas. 60 mins.
VHS: S19668. $19.95.
The Nature Connection, Vol. 5. In *Carmanah* the group explores the temperate rainforest in Carmanah Valley on Vancouver Island. In *Grasslands* the group discovers a vast 900-acre research ranch in the Albertan foothills. 60 mins.
VHS: S19669. $19.95.
The Nature Connection, Vol. 6. In *Tide Pools* Dr. Suzuki and his daughters bring a group of children to visit their cottage, where they study tide pools which teem with marine life. In *Cattail Country,* set in a marsh within a large industrial space, the group finds a wide variety of plants and animals. 60 mins.
VHS: S19670. $19.95.

Nature of Sex

This six-part series developed by the television series *Nature* tours the realm of animal and human sexuality as it travels the globe filming courtship displays and fights for dominance, mating, birthing, and caring for young. 60 minutes each.
A Time and a Place. Explores how the sun, moon and seasons of nature profoundly influence courtship, mating and birth.
VHS: S20431. $19.95.
A Miracle in the Making. Graphically shows the ingenious ways in which animals mate, prepare for birth and deliver their young.
VHS: S20434. $19.95.
Sex and the Human Animal. The origins of human sexuality are investigated by looking at other social animals and the various ways in which different cultures define sexual roles.
VHS: S20433. $19.95.
The Primal Instinct. Looks at the remarkable variety of ways the sexual urge is expressed among the Earth's countless species.
VHS: S20430. $19.95.
The Sex Contract. Focuses on how animals select partners and explores the duration of that contract, which might last a moment or a lifetime.
VHS: S20432. $19.95.
The Young Ones. Takes a look at life after sex, exploring the bond between parent and offspring.
VHS: S20435. $19.95.
Nature of Sex, Complete Set. The six-volume set.
VHS: S20436. $99.95.

Nature Perfected: The Story of the Garden

This enlightening documentary series is devoted to the art of gardening throughout history. From the ancient gardens of Pompeii to contemporary New York, it promises to open new vistas for all those engaged in perfecting nature.
Tape I. Program One: Paradise on Earth. Program Two: Ancient Spirits: China and Japan.
VHS: S25665. $29.95.
Tape II. Program Three: The Heritage of Rome. Program Four: Garlands of Repose.
VHS: S25666. $29.95.
Tape III. Program Five: Gardens of Conquest. Program Six: New Perspectives.
VHS: S25667. $29.95.
Tape IV. Program Seven: The Landscaping of England. Program Eight: Moving On.
VHS: S25668. $29.95.
Tape V. Program Nine: Glory and Grandeur. Program Ten: The Machine and the Garden.
VHS: S25669. $29.95.
Tape VI. Program Eleven: Grounds for Change. Program Twelve: The Genius of the Place.
VHS: S25670. $29.95.
Nature Perfected: The Story of the Garden, Set.
VHS: S25671. $119.95.

Nature Series

Tapes from the critically-acclaimed and most-watched series on public television, exploring the mysteries of the natural world.
Darkness in the Grass.
VHS: S04138. $29.95.

Nature's Fury: A Decade of Disasters

From ABC News comes this stunning spectacle of nature's more destructive impulses. Witness the earthquakes, tornadoes, floods, raging fires and bitter cold that have tested man's endurance in the past decade. 60 mins.
VHS: S12682. $24.98.

Nature's Great African Moments

This beautifully photographed documentary displays the wildlife riches of Africa. Lions on the hunt, wildebeest migrating, flamingos in flight and prowling crocodiles are seen as they exist in the wild. Narrated by Avery Brooks. 60 mins.
VHS: S24374. $19.95.

Nature's Symphony

A program that interweaves beautiful, poetic images of nature scored to the works of Tchaikovsky, Strauss, Mozart and Puccini. 60 mins.
Laser: LD70237. $34.95.

North of Capricorn

Home to two of the world's highest waterfalls, incredibly long snakes, fat toads and giant butterflies, this is a fascinating look at the unique wilderness of Australia's northern territories, a land barely explored.
VHS: S05241. $19.95.

Nova—All American Bear

What enables the American black bear to go without food and water for six months? Looks at the bear's hibernation, habitat, eating and mating patterns. 60 mins.
VHS: S09404. $14.98.

Nova—Animal Olympics

Actress Lee Remick hosts this fascinating presentation of animal athletes doing what they do best. See a cheetah do a 65-mile-an-hour dash. Observe a lizard actually walking on water. Witness a sperm whale hold its breath for 82 minutes—well, maybe not all 82 minutes, as this is only an hour-long tape. 60 mins.
VHS: S07579. $29.98.

Nova—Can Elephants Be Saved?

An investigation of the epic struggle involved in the survival of elephants in Africa. The program warns that unless immediate intervention by wildlife authorities and scientists takes place and anti-poaching laws are enacted, the animals could become extinct. 60 mins.
VHS: S19117. $14.98.

Nova—Cities of Coral

The Caribbean coral reef is a beautiful and chaotic metropolis teeming with life, where hundreds of different species of fish vie for survival. This program uses spectacular photography to unravel the mysteries of the underwater world. 60 mins.
VHS: S11247. $14.98.

Nova—In the Land of the Polar Bears

Take a wondrous look at a unique Arctic landscape and its diverse population in this Nova Series program. 60 mins.
VHS: S09818. $14.98.

Nova—Killer Quake!

Even though L.A. is still recovering, newly discovered faults could lead to more devastating natural disasters. This documentary explores the science that seeks to explain earthquakes.
VHS: S24875. $19.95.

Nova—Little Creatures Who Run the World

Through amazing close-up photography, Howard University's Edward Wilson reveals the hidden world of ants. It's a world governed by violent predation; tactical warfare and intimate partnerships.
VHS: S24878. $19.95.

Nova—Predictable Disaster

Explains how, where and why earthquakes occur, if they can be accurately predicted, and why they are so devastating. 60 mins.
VHS: S09403. $14.98.

Nova—Signs of the Apes, Songs of the Whales

Do animals understand us? Or do they learn required responses to get rewards? This special *Nova* program explores language in the animal world and their awe-inspiring ability to communicate with themselves, and with man. 60 mins.
VHS: S06968. $29.98.

Nova—The Bermuda Triangle

Nova takes a hard look at this watery graveyard which has claimed so many lives and caused so much immense fascination, as this program explores the mystery of the strange occurrences which have resulted in thousands of mysterious disappearances. 60 mins.
VHS: S06967. $29.98.

Nova—The Case of the Flying Dinosaur

This exploration reveals scientific findings whose theories lead to the belief that birds are descendants of dinosaurs. 1991, 60 mins.
VHS: S16816. $14.98.

Nova—The Shape of Things

A dazzling look at the world of nature up close and personal. Using time-lapse photography, computer animation and microphotography, Nova examines a drop of water, the construction of snowflakes and how crystals are formed. Also an inside look at a beehive in action. 60 mins.
VHS: S07578. $19.95.

Nova—Visions of the Deep

The popular television science series goes below sea level to explore the fascinating world of underwater photography and moviemaking. *Nova* explores the world of Al Giddings and his work on such films as *The Deep* and *For Your Eyes Only.* Find out the hazards of asking a shark to do retakes. USA, 60 mins.
VHS: S06026. $29.98.

Nova—Yellowstone's Burning Question

Nova uncovers the astounding story of the fires that affected over a million acres of Yellowstone National Park in 1988, examines the controversy that surrounded the park's "let burn" policy, and reveals nature's miraculous process of rebirth. 60 mins.
VHS: S11652. $14.98.

Nursery Habitat Set

The Discovery Channel presents this three-volume set from their *Mother Nature: Tales of Discovery* series which explore young animals. The *Nursery Habitat Set* includes *Springtime Toddler Tales, Babes in the Woods* and *Bringing Up Baby.* Kids will love this look at a variety of cuddly animals.
VHS: S25087. $39.95.

The Ocean Blue: Man's Relationship to the Sea

This four-part series looks at the different ways that the sea affects humankind today. The imagination, weather, war and even health are broad areas where the sea continues to offer important input into the modern world.
The Sea of Imagination. The sea has always held a strong fascination for mankind. This program explores the realm of imagination between Melville's *Moby Dick* and Jules Verne's *20,000 Leagues Under the Sea,* that is between fear, superstition and reality. 53 mins.
VHS: S24916. $29.95.
Water and Weather. El Nino is a weather system that grows every year beginning around Christmas time. This video explores its physical underpinnings and its effects on man and culture. All the best efforts to curb this weather system's strength have failed. 53 mins.
VHS: S24917. $29.95.

Struggle for the Seas. Today modern navies have technology that appears to dwarf the human capacities of their staff. This video traces a history of important naval battles from ancient times into the present, when the US cruiser Vincennes downed a civilian Iranian airliner. 53 mins.
VHS: S24918. $29.95.
The Healing Sea. The sea is the source of life on the planet. Now scientists explore its depths and uncover important answers to some of life's mysteries. From Alzheimer's disease to cancer and chemical warfare, the sea holds many surprising possibilities that will affect how we live. 53 mins.
VHS: S24919. $29.95.
Four-Part Set.
VHS: S24920. $99.95.

Ocean Symphony

An original musical score is combined with breathtaking underwater photography. From the icy Antarctic to the warm waters of the Caribbean the viewer is invited to marvel at the wonders of the deep. Eleven segments include jelly fish, sharks and a variety of whales.
VHS: S03923. $29.95.
Al Giddings, USA, 1987, 47 mins.

Oceans of Air

Earth's four dominant climate types are revealed in this Discovery Channel documentary—the Olympic Peninsula of Washington, a lush rainforest, alpine glaciers and arid deserts of the prairies serve as examples. 60 mins.
VHS: S25079. $19.95.

Olympic National Park: Wilderness Heritage

Experience the essence of Olympic National Park: glacier-carved mountains, rugged Pacific coastline and lush rain forest. You'll also discover, close-up, the native plant and animal life which resides in this beautiful region—known to many as the jewel of the Northwest. USA, 30 mins.
VHS: S15079. $29.95.

On the Edge of Extinction: Panthers and Cheetahs

Loretta Swit narrates this entertaining and fascinating view of two imperiled animals and what is being done to protect them from extinction. 60 mins.
VHS: S08290. $14.98.

Orca: Killer Whale or Gentle Giant

Orcas—called killer whales—are more feared than understood. This film gives us an unusual window into the world of these magnificent marine mammals and challenges popular misconceptions about so-called "killer whales." An outstanding program for all ages. 1990, 26 mins.
VHS: S13952. $59.95.

Our Natural Heritage Series

Baby Animals. "Moose Baby," which follows a baby moose from infancy to adulthood; "Tembo—The Baby Elephant", the story of a baby elephant, and "Now I Am Bigger," the exploration of the growth of a baby chick. 42 mins.
VHS: S05818. $19.95.
Environments. "A Stream Environment" explores the beginnings and substance of streams, and "Ark", the exploration of environments corrupted by pollution and destruction, and how we might prevent a bleak environmental future. 29 mins.
VHS: S05819. $19.95.
Living Together. "Birds in Your Backyard," shows how to attract birds with a feeding tray, bath and nesting structure; "A Park Community" explores the building of parks as a defense against the concrete nature of cities, and "Communities of Living Things" explores the relationship between growing things and their surroundings. 36 mins.
VHS: S05820. $19.95.
Pretty Insects. "Butterflies Are" teaches the principles of collecting and studying butterflies; "The Aphid Eaters" follows Eve as she finds a cluster of yellow insect eggs that she collects and hatches, and watches eat aphids. 30 mins.
VHS: S05824. $19.95.
Seashores. "The Atlantic Coast" follows the Coast from the Bay of Fundy with gigantic tides, to the rockbound New England shores, the marshes of the Chesapeake to the Florida Keys; "The Pacific Coast" explores the diversity of the Coast's sandy beaches, shoreline flowers. 25 mins.
VHS: S05822. $19.95.
Survival of the Fittest. In "Greenhouse," a young boy discovers the beauty of flowers and the pain that the destruction of beauty causes; in "The Last Pigeon," a young boy participates in racing with homing pigeons. 26 mins.
VHS: S05825. $19.95.
The Mountains. "The Rocky Mountains" discovers the open fields, forests, meadows and rivers of the Rockies; "The Mountains" is a celebration of the diverse geological formations of mountains. 31 mins.
VHS: S05821. $19.95.
The Plains. "The Desert" explores the flora and fauna of the extreme climates; "The Prairie," the animals, insect and plant life in this ecologically precious environment; "The Meadow" the ecosystem of the spring and summer's inhabitants. 43 mins.
VHS: S05823. $19.95.
Western Birds and Flowers. "Waterbirds of the Western Flyways" follows the feeding, nesting of rare western waterbirds; "Wildflowers of the West" is a panorama of floral gems of the West. 27 mins.
VHS: S05826. $19.95.

Paleo World

This three-volume series from Discovery brings the largest and smallest creatures from prehistory to life. Dinosaurs and other creatures are examined using the latest theories, with cutting-edge 3-D graphics, and robotic models from the Dinamation International Society.
Paleo World, Volume 1: Rise of the Predators. This video has it all, from the tiny creatures who discovered that survival was just a swallow away, to the huge flesh-eating dinosaurs: the snake-quick velociraptor, poison-spitting dilophosaurus and that king of the jungle, *T. rex.*
VHS: S23019. $14.95.
Paleo World, Volume 2: Sea Monsters. Early mammals swam among giant squid and enormous sharks in the primordial seas. Some established themselves on land and prospered. Others made the return trip to becomes today's whales and dolphins.
VHS: S23020. $14.95.
Paleo World, Volume 3: Mysteries of Evolution. Is evolution more complex than we believe? Was *Homo sapiens* the only human species? Just what did kill the dinosaurs? In this volume these exciting questions are thoroughly explored.
VHS: S23021. $14.95.
Paleo World Deluxe Boxed Set.
VHS: S23022. $39.95.

Penguin World

From the storm-driven isles of the southern coastal oceans to the frozen tundra of Antarctica, this video provides a rare glimpse into various penguin habitats, from the four-pound and smaller Fairies to the 90-pound Emperors. 45 mins.
VHS: S18429. $29.95.
Laser: CAV. LD74460. $34.95.

People of the Forest

Follow 20 years of love and rivalry within a tribe of chimpanzees from the forests surrounding Lake Tanganyika. Based on the research of naturalist Jane Goodall, this rich tapestry of emotion and drama, narrated by Donald Sutherland, is captured by wildlife photographer Hugo van Lawick. 90 mins.
VHS: S17014. $24.95.

A Pipeline and Animals

This is a whimsical look at the wildlife along the route of the trans-Alaska pipeline. Mel Blanc narrates as footage depicts bears, beavers, moose, musk oxen, foxes, ducks, geese and more against the breath-taking Alaskan landscape. 28 mins.
VHS: S23971. $19.95.

Pity the Pilot Whale

The pilot whale is unprotected by international whaling regulations. This powerful video examines their nature and fate and how two countries treat these intelligent creatures differently. Narrated by James Coburn. 50 mins.
VHS: S23377. $59.95.

Predators of the Wild

A look at nature's most dangerous animals. These realistic documentaries were shot on location. 312 mins.
Predators of the Wild: African Survival. A waterhole in Africa is like Piccadilly Circus in London or Times Square in New York. Sooner or later, all creatures show up. Some come to drink or bathe. Others come to hunt. Giraffes and elephants are fearsome but lions are crafty predators. 52 mins.
VHS: S22339. $19.95.
Predators of the Wild: Bats. In some areas these swarming creatures of the dark consume up to 30,000 pounds of insects nightly. Nearly 25% percent of all mammals are bats. And yet only three bat species are true vampires, that require blood for sustenance. 51 mins.
VHS: S22342. $19.95.
Predators of the Wild: Cheetah and Leopard.
VHS: S19220. $19.95.
Laser: LD71902. $24.98.
Predators of the Wild: Crocodiles and Alligators. Perhaps a primal memory gives these scaly creatures—virtually unchanged since Earth was dominated by dinosaurs—their fierce savagery. From the water's edge to its murky depths these animals await their prey with endless patience. 49 mins.
VHS: S22340. $19.95.
Predators of the Wild: Giant Tarantula. Soft, even pleasant to the touch, but at what price? The giant tarantula is the largest and one of the most venomous spiders in the world. While waiting near its three-foot burrow, it conserves its energy and then pounces on insects, frogs, snakes, birds and rodents. 51 mins.
VHS: S22343. $19.95.
Predators of the Wild: Grizzly Bear.
VHS: S19221. $19.95.
Laser: LD71903. $24.98.
Predators of the Wild: Hunters and the Hunted.
VHS: S19218. $19.95.
Laser: LD71900. $24.98.
Predators of the Wild: Killer Whale.
VHS: S19219. $19.95.
Laser: LD71901. $24.98.
Predators of the Wild: Lion.
VHS: S19216. $19.95.
Laser: LD71898. $24.98.
Predators of the Wild: Shark.
VHS: S19217. $19.95.
Laser: LD71899. $24.98.
Predators of the Wild: Snake. Fearsome and fascinating, these creatures are responsible for the deaths of 40,000 people each year. Some 2000 species, 85% percent of them harmless to man, slither across the land or swim in the ocean deep. See how an anaconda can smother a much larger animal—in this instance an alligator! 52 mins.
VHS: S22341. $19.95.
Predators of the Wild: Wolf. Bone numbing howls sear the night sky. The eerie cries, slightly out of tune, drift from one to the other, keeping these animals in touch over a wide area. It's time for the hunt and the pack must be called together. Deer and livestock alike are not safe from these clever predators.
VHS: S22344. $19.95.
Predators of the Wild: Gift Pack. Includes Cheetah and Leopard, Grizzly Bear, Hunters and the Hunted, Killer Whale, Lion and Shark.
VHS: S19222. $119.93.
Laser: LD71904. $99.98.

Prehistoric Beasts

Four videos delve into the myth and power of prehistoric animals that ruled the Earth more than 65 million years ago. With their massive size and astonishing physical skills, they altered the ecological balance. Intended for children in grades 1-6.
Archaeopteryx. What was the exact nature of this beast, bird or dinosaur? This tree climber could float from tree branches to escape danger or catch prey but its vast wings were used to trap insects. 10 mins.
VHS: S20046. $44.95.
Plesiosaurus. This air-breathing marine reptile is believed to be the first giant reptile. Its bones were discovered and studied after lying dormant beneath the sea for millions of years. 10 mins.
VHS: S20047. $44.95.
Pteranodon. Scientists have been fascinated by this amazing beast, which descended from reptiles, had an amazing wing span of 23 feet and could fly. 12 mins.
VHS: S20048. $44.95.
Woolly Mammoth. A plant-eating, tusked creature of the Ice Age, this mammal had an elaborate, two-layer coat of hair for keeping warm. 11 mins.
VHS: S20049. $44.95.
Prehistoric Beasts, Set. This set contains four titles: Archaeopteryx, Plesiosaurus, Pteranodon and Woolly Mammoth. 43 mins.
VHS: S20050. $159.95.

The Private Life of Plants

Sir Richard Attenborough hosts this BBC production. It looks at plants all over the world, from Borneo to Tasmania, in order to reveal some intriguing secrets. Plants have unique methods that help them perceive and respond to their surroundings.
Volume 1: Branching Out. Plants can see and count and even communicate with one another. That's how they manage to live in harmony with each other. Their function goes well beyond producing oxygen and food for other organisms.
VHS: S26980. $19.98.
Volume 2: Putting Down Roots. In this volume, the intricate security systems which ensure plant development and growth are examined. Deadly poisons, sharp barbs and menacing spikes are just some of the weapons used by plants to protect their leaves from mutilation.
VHS: S26981. $19.98.
Volume 3: The Birds and the Bees. Flowers direct insects and animals to their pollen centers. Some plants attract their partners to the pollen with appealing blooms which actually point out their prize and simultaneously ensure pollination.
VHS: S26982. $19.98.
Volume 4: Plant Politics. Plant interactions mirror those of animals and people. Since there is always a limited supply of energy, water, oxygen and minerals, each plant's positioning is critical for its survival.
VHS: S26983. $19.98.
Volume 5: Living Together. Plants do compete for survival. In some instances however, plants actually develop symbiotic relations that generate a necessary co-dependence.
VHS: S26984. $19.98.
Volume 6: It's a Jungle Out There. Plants survive in places where humans have not found ways to exist. These sturdy plants maintain a ferocious appetite for survival that allows them to thrive in brutally harsh environments.
VHS: S26985. $19.98.
The Private Life of Plants: Collector's Edition. The complete six-volume set.
VHS: S26986. $79.98.

Procreation in the Wild

From Antarctica to Africa and Asia, this video reveals exactly how a number of animals, including hippos, giraffes, elephants, tigers, monkeys and more, procreate. This is the wildlife video that actually shows the wild thing. 90 mins.
VHS: S24693. $39.95.

Queen of the Elephants

Author Mark Shand undergoes a 300-mile odyssey tracing the migratory route of the endangered Indian elephant. These mammoth creatures are capable of both great affection and unmatched destruction. Of course their greatest challenge lies not in their natural environment but in the ever-encroaching reach of man. 90 mins.
VHS: S20902. $19.95.

Quest for the Dolphin Spirit

A first-person account from producers Liz and Steve Weiss, who, with their one-year-old daughter in tow, travel the world's beaches and ocean communities to learn about the peculiar and fascinating relations between dolphins and humans. 46 mins.
VHS: S17608. $24.95.

Rain Forests: Proving Their Worth

With stunning visuals, rare archival footage, first-person accounts, and an original soundtrack, this documentary provides a provocative look at a crucial effort to save the rain forests and the people who inhabit them. Forceful work creatively presented. 1990, 31 mins.
VHS: S13934. $85.00.

Realm of the Alligator

The mysterious wilderness of Okefenokee, 700 miles of swampland on the Georgia-Florida border, eerie, forbidden, darkly beautiful, and brilliantly explored in this National Geographic documentary, which follows scientists as they study the behavior of the giant and powerful alligator. 59 mins.
VHS: S04885. $19.95.

Return of the Great Whale

Filmed in the "national park of ocean," this documentary is an environmental success story about the re-emergence of humpback and blue whales into the coastal waters of northern California, where fishing and whaling industries once hunted these magnificent mammals to the brink of extinction. 50 mins.
VHS: S04150. $39.95.

Roadrunner Clown of the Desert/ Punk Puffins and Hard Rock (BBC Wildlife Special)

The Road Runner, that lovable cartoon character, actually exists. A real bird that cannot fly, but can zip around the desert at speeds of up to 30 miles per hour in hot pursuit of insects, mice and reptiles. Punk Puffins ventures off to the island of St. Lararia off the coast of Alaska where more than a half million birds make their summer home. The most spectacular are the tufted puffins—dumpy, clown-like birds with white faces, orange beaks and wild plumes on their heads. 55 mins.
VHS: S12392. $19.94.

Savage and Beautiful

A breathtaking look at the animal kingdom, narrated by Donald Sutherland, with a compelling soundtrack by Vangelis.
VHS: S06552. $14.95.

Saviors of the Forest

Tired of filming TV commercials, two Los Angeles "camera guys" decide to do their part for the environment by exposing the villains responsible for destroying the rain forests. Along the way they meet a range of paradoxical characters, including poor people who cut down forests to survive, environmentalists trying to import an "ecological" sawmill, timber companies campaigning for reforestation and Hollywood producers who use rain forest plywood to build their sets. 90 mins.
VHS: S23370. $95.00.

A Sea Otter Story: Warm Hearts and Cold Water

The heartwarming tale of orphaned sea otters is at the center of this insightful documentary. The Monterey Bay Aquarium rears these animals and trains them so that they can be released into the wild. George Page narrates. 60 mins.
VHS: S24375. $19.95.

Sea Turtles: Ancient Nomads (National Audubon)

Jane Alexander narrates this program featuring stunning wildlife and underwater photography which constitutes an intimate look at the behavior of wild sea turtles and their perilous fight for survival. 60 mins.
VHS: S09559. $14.98.

Secrets of the Desert Sea

The story of how life is sustained in the Sea of Cortez. Through unique photography, viewers see the interconnectedness of life in this sea and see how each creature fits into the larger ecosystem. Produced by the award-winning team of Hardy Jones and Julia Whitty. 50 mins.
VHS: S07591. $14.98.

Shark Attack Files

Shark attack victims who survived speak about their experiences in this surprising video. Also the stories of those who weren't so lucky are told. This video attempts to discover if these attacks are deliberate and malicious or just a case of mistaken identity. 60 mins.
VHS: S26047. $19.95.

Shark Bait

Shark attacks are on the rise world-wide. A leader in shark research is struggling to find a safe, practical chemical repellant that can save both divers and sharks from harm. 60 mins.
VHS: S26045. $19.95.

Shark Hunter

This dramatic video demonstrates how Vic Hislop tracks and catches sharks—whalers, hammerheads, tiger sharks, the Great Whites. Vic reveals the truth about sharks, through spectacular underwater shark segments. 60 mins.
VHS: S09917. $29.95.

Sharks: Predators or Prey?

A fascinating look at shark behavior, revealing the serious threat to some shark populations through overfishing. Mixing humor with hard facts, Sharks dispels some of the common myths about these complex creatures of the deep. 20 mins.
VHS: S23376. $79.95.

Slaves of the Harvest

Documentary on the hunting of fur seals on the Priboff Islands off the coast of Alaska. Produced by Greenpeace. 25 mins.
VHS: S06497. $49.95.

Small World

Insects seem alien to man at first glance, yet on closer inspection they share many human traits. This examination of the habitat of the miniature, filled with industrious, sociable and sexually active creatures is a remarkable wildlife documentary.
VHS: S05243. $19.95.

Smithsonian World: Zoo

The National Zoological Park has been a vital institution for 100 years. This video celebrates Washington D.C.'s link to the larger natural world. It also allows Zoo Director Michael Robertson to share his vision of a futuristic biopark. 58 mins.
VHS: S27375. $19.98.

Splendors of the Sea

The sea contains many bizarre creatures. A number of the most exotic are captured in this video featuring stunning underwater photography. 60 mins. From the Discovery Channel.
VHS: S25074. $19.95.

The Story of America's Great Volcanoes

From deep within the earth, the most violent natural act manifests itself in Alaska, Washington, Oregon, Idaho, Hawaii, Arizona and California. Learn the exciting histories of these geologic wonders through spectacular photography and a concise, entertaining narrative. 56 mins.
VHS: S16636. $29.95.

Super Shark Collection

This three-volume set from the Discovery Channel explores the underwater world where sharks rule supreme as the most feared predators. Great White, Demons of the Deep and The Man Who Loves Sharks capture these brutal animals in all their ferocity. 180 mins.
VHS: S25083. $54.95.

Survival in the Wild

The widely respected British Broadcasting Company is well known for its commitment to the production of excellent documentaries. Now for the first time a series of BBC wild life films are available. A wide range of the earth's creatures are featured in this series as they struggle to survive.
Deadly Illusions. Not all deadly hunters use speed or brute strength to find their quarry. Some use cunning, stealth, or even disguise. Chameleons meld into their background while a snapping turtle lures victims with false offers of food. This documentary uncovers the secret weapons of the world's wild life.
VHS: S20703. $14.95.
Pack Hunters. Many of the world's most ferocious animals hunt in packs, including grizzly bears, vampire bats, and white wolves. In this film the social and communication skills are revealed that allow these powerful animals to join their abilities for the common good of survival.
VHS: S20701. $14.95.
Predators and Prey. Solitary hunters have an intricate relationship with those animals that they feed upon, their prey. In this episode tigers, sharks, cheetahs and leopards are all seen honing their unique skills as they seek sustenance in a cruel war of survival.
VHS: S20702. $14.95.

Symphony to America the Beautiful

This musical journey across America captures the beauty of the changing seasons set to the music of Brahms, Vivaldi, Mozart and other classical composers. Two-volume set, 120 mins.
VHS: S23135. $39.95.

Tales of the Snow Monkey

Follows four groups of Snow Monkeys, from those relatively untouched in the far North to the coddled and celebrated darlings of the South, each with its inventive way of surviving. Narrated by Lorne Greene. 30 mins.
VHS: S05000. $14.95.

Tales of Wood and Water

Sailing in a windjammer and gliding in a graceful schooner are just some of the experiences detailed in this video. The Discovery Channel shows the pride and crafting which goes into superb craft like these. 60 mins.
VHS: S25080. $19.95.

Tornado Chasers

Most people flee these awesome natural phenomena. With winds that rage up to 300 miles an hour, tornadoes can reduce entire towns to mere kindling. This video shows a group of people who risk their lives and cruise "Tornado Alley" in Oklahoma to capture images of twisters close-up. Narrated by Bill Kurtis.
VHS: S26096. $19.95.

Trials of Life

Sir David Attenborough, the renowned naturalist, leads an exploration of the mysteries of animal behavior in this acclaimed, 12-part documentary series. The winner of two Ace Awards, this series is often more fantastic than any invention of the imagination.
Arriving.
VHS: S15609. $19.98.
Continuing the Line.
VHS: S17749. $19.98.
Courting.
VHS: S17748. $19.98.
Fighting.
VHS: S17745. $19.98.
Finding Food.
VHS: S15611. $19.98.
Finding the Way.
VHS: S15613. $19.98.
Friends & Rivals.
VHS: S17746. $19.98.
Growing Up.
VHS: S15610. $19.98.
Home Making.
VHS: S15614. $19.98.
Hunting/Escaping.
VHS: S15612. $19.98.
Living Together.
VHS: S17744. $19.98.
Talking to Strangers.
VHS: S17747. $19.98.
Trials of Life, Collector's Gift Set.
VHS: S15615. $199.98.
Laser: LD74965. $199.99.

Tropical Kingdom of Belize

This National Geographic Video takes the armchair traveler to the Central American nation of Belize. Formerly British Honduras, this tiny nation is said to feature one of the most diverse natural environments in the world. See for yourself. 60 mins.
VHS: S03677. $19.95.

Tropical Rainforest

This IMAX documentary film explores the incredible diversity of life found in the world's rain forests, as well as the problems faced by these fragile ecosystems. 90% of the world's species are found here and yet many of these may become extinct before they are even discovered. Filmed in Australia, Central and South America, and Asia. 40 mins.
VHS: S22666. $29.95.
Laser: LD74550. $39.95.

Tropical Sweets

Bill Patterson's fresh mosaic of music, the sounds and rhythms of nature and a cascading symphony of tropical images and quixotic delights. 40 mins.
Laser: LD70245. $29.95.

The Undersea World of Jacques Cousteau

Twelve fascinating programs from Jacques Cousteau's award-winning series are now available on video. These exciting adventures are unparalleled in their cinematography and visual beauty. 60 minutes each.
The Smile of the Walrus.
VHS: Out of print. For rental only.
The Unsinkable Otter.
VHS: Out of print. For rental only.
Octopus-Octopus.
VHS: Out of print. For rental only.
Dragons of Galapagos.
VHS: Out of print. For rental only.
Forgotten Mermaids.
VHS: Out of print. For rental only.
Whales.
VHS: Out of print. For rental only.
Flight of Penguins.
VHS: Out of print. For rental only.
Desert Whales.
VHS: Out of print. For rental only.
The Singing Whale.
VHS: Out of print. For rental only.
A Sound of Dolphins.
VHS: Out of print. For rental only.
Diving for Roman Plunder. Jacques Cousteau and the crew of the Calypso attempt to retrieve the art objects and golden plunder from an ancient Roman galley that sank centuries ago.
VHS: S08357. $24.95.

Unseen World of Chiricahua

Explores the scenic beauty and natural history of Chiricahua National Monument in Arizona. Learn how the plants and animals have learned to adapt to this evolving geological fantasyland and depend on each other to survive. 30 mins.
VHS: S09184. $29.95.

Volcano
See a volcanic eruption in progress, photographed at close range, and experience the force, heat, lava flow, and fire that is created. 29 mins.
VHS: S05734. $29.95.

Volcanoes of Hawaii
Spectacular eruption footage, including the recent eruption which overran Kalapana Village and entered the sea, highlights this fascinating program that shows the many moods of Hawaii's Mauna Loa and Kilauea volcanoes. 30 mins.
VHS: S08459. $29.95.

Voyage of the Great Southern Ark
Australia's unique geological forms and exotic animals and plants have intrigued generations. This program takes audiences on a sweeping journey through the history of the Australian continent and its inhabitants, from 4.2 billion years ago to modern times. Gleaning information from the latest technology and the most respected experts in the field, this enthralling video presents a panoramic survey of our planet's development. Everywhere in Australia the primeval and the modern co-exist, forming a dramatic visual history of the earth's evolution. 138 mins.
VHS: S10288. $39.95.

Voyage to Save the Whales
An award-winning documentary of Greenpeace's early campaign to save the whale in 1975 and 1976. 30 mins.
VHS: S06498. $49.95.

Walk in the Forest
Journey into the heart of America's rain forests, the old-growth forests of the Pacific Northwest. See the remarkable diversity of life hidden there. Feel the warmth of summer, the terror of fire, the blessing of rain. This beautiful portrait details the delicate balance of plants and animals that make this region a living whole. "Outstanding" (*Booklist*). First Prize winner, Chicago Film Festival. 1976, 28 mins.
VHS: S13697. $24.95.

Water Journey
Jon Child's aquatic journey from thunder storm through forest, marsh, pond, lake, and river. Winner of Film as Environment award. Natural sounds of water, birds and insects. An ambient escapade. 60 mins.
VHS: S10241. $29.95.

Whale for the Killing
Strong performances by Peter Strauss and Richard Widmark plus a poignant lesson in ecology distinguish this story about one man's attempt to save a stranded whale. 145 mins.
VHS: S10100. $59.98.

Whales! (National Audubon)
Johnny Carson narrates this moving look at whales—after years of senseless slaughter, the whale is not the focus of international preservation efforts. Audubon investigates this change in attitude and features some spectacular whale-watching, with unique underwater photography. 60 mins.
VHS: S09560. $14.98.

Whalesong: Whales and Dolphins of the Pacific
Narrated by Lloyd Bridges, this documentary explores underworld sea life. 40 mins.
VHS: S17221. $24.95.

Wild Alaska
Dale Johnson leads this rare wildlife video shot in the Alpine tundra in the shadow of Mt. McKinley, following the migrating caribou, musk ox, and a dramatic life struggle between a caribou and grizzly. 60 mins.
VHS: S05968. $29.95.

Wild Australia on Video
A wildlife adventure down under: the world of the koala, kangaroo, platypus, echidna, numbat and crocodile, as well as a rare segment of the Tasmanian tiger, now extinct. 60 mins.
VHS: S09908. $29.95.

Wild India
The safari of a lifetime is featured on this video from the Discovery Channel. In the teaming jungles of the Himalayas lurk a variety of rare and fascinating creatures. The camera crew goes all out to stalk these animals. 90 mins.
VHS: S25077. $19.95.

The Wild World Series: Daisy Discovers the World
A young sea lion is simply curious. In this beautifully photographed wildlife film, curiosity is all it takes for this young animal to start an exciting adventure. 15 mins.
VHS: S23462. $49.95.

Wildflowers of the Cajun Prairies
Prairie grasses and flowers once reached to shoulder height. Now the remnants of this ecosystem must be rescued in southwest Louisiana. 28 mins.
VHS: S22394. $44.95.

Wilds of Madagascar
The island of Madagascar was separated from the mainland of Africa more than 165 million years ago; its flora and fauna have evolved in near isolation. This trek to remote sunken forests discovers the crowned lemur, the leaf-tailed geeko and the souimanga sunbird. 60 mins.
VHS: S10245. $19.95.

The WIPP Trail
The acronym for the Waste Isolation Pilot Project, this video, narrated by Robert Redford, explores the current nuclear waste controversy. As a massive backlog of close to 300 million cubic feet of nuclear waste piles up at U.S. defense facilities, pressure is mounting to open the Waste Isolation Pilot Plant in southeastern New Mexico. Technical review of WIPP, waste transportation, emergency response, public information and democratic process are the issues addressed in this citizen-produced, engaging dialog which focuses on one of the dominant political, ecological and safety issues of our time. 60 mins.
VHS: S08790. $24.95.

Wolves
Wolves examines the ecological contributions of these animals. Narrated by Robert Redford.
VHS: S16875. $14.98.

Wonders of God's Creation
This documentary series of three videos looks at the mysteries and beauty of the creation of the universe. The programs are *Planet Earth: Sanctuary of Life*, a panoramic view of the ecological, environmental and physical beauty of the earth; *The Animal Kingdom: Great Are Thy Works*, an observation of animals and species; *Human Life: The Crown of Creation*, a piece about the interlocking human mysteries, the brain, the hand and skeletal system and the components of the heart. Available in two editions, the Deluxe Edition with a gold-embossed slipcase with Creation booklet, and Standard Edition, with Creation booklet.
Wonders of God's Creation. Deluxe Edition.
VHS: S17267. $79.95.
Wonders of God's Creation. Standard Edition.
VHS: S17268. $59.95.

Wood Stork: Barometer of the Everglades (National Audubon)
Narrated by Richard Crenna. The wood stork, a fragile figure whose delicate existence mirrors that of all the wildlife in Florida's Everglades, is now an endangered species. 60 mins.
VHS: S09003. $14.98.

World of Discovery: Beautiful Killers
Naturalist filmmaker Nicolas Noxon presents a kaleidoscopic work about the habits and lifestyle of the killer whales moored off the coast of British Columbia. The program studies the controversial confinement and commercialization of theme parks and aquariums. 50 mins.
VHS: S19309. $19.98.

World of Discovery: Cougar: Ghost of the Rockies
Wildlife filmmaker Jim Dutcher and mountain lion specialist Dr. Morris Hornocker undertake a rugged two-year expedition to track a mountain lion and her kittens. 50 mins.
VHS: S19307. $19.98.

World of Discovery: Realm of the Serpent
This exotic video examines the daily rituals of the snake. The program features Burmese cobra charmers, the emergence of the green tree python in the rain forest, a Texas rattle snake round up and the identification of a fer-de-lance in Central America. 50 mins.
VHS: S19310. $19.98.

World of Discovery: Shark Chronicles
Naturalist filmmaker Al Giddings deploys underwater photography to document the ferocious nature and predatory instincts of the shark. 50 mins.
VHS: S19305. $19.98.

World of Discovery: The Secret Life of 118 Green Street
Billions of uninvited houseguests invade the average home every day. This universe swarming with life is not visible to the naked eye, but it can be revealed through the wonder of microscopic photography. 50 mins.
VHS: S22518. $19.98.

World of Discovery: Wildebeest: Race for Life
These stately creatures run a gauntlet of life, birth and death. The African plain they inhabit is plagued by predators from crocodiles to lions. 50 mins.
VHS: S22517. $19.98.

World of Discovery: Wolf: Return of a Legend
Wildlife photographer and wolf expert Jim Dutcher captures the camera-shy wolf up close. These intriguing creatures are shown in their natural habitat for the first time. 50 mins.
VHS: S22516. $19.98.

World of Herbs
A five-part, three volume program studies the origins, history and multiple uses of herbs, based on the book by Lesley Bremness. "An excellent series, and a surefire circulator in public libraries" (*Video Librarian*). 200 mins.
VHS: S17382. $79.95.

Yellowstone-Teton Wildlife
Set amidst the breathtaking scenery of Yellowstone and Grand Teton National Parks, this program follows the wildlife through the changing seasons, including grizzly and black bears, owls, elk, moose, coyotes, bald eagle, porcupine and others. 45 mins.
VHS: S10924. $29.95.

Yesterday's Heroes
Venture to scenic Australia and experience the harsh and fatal reality of horses, donkeys and camels whose strong backs helped build the island continent. Yesterday's heroes are today's courageous warriors fighting for life against a civilization bent on their destruction. Lorne Greene hosts. 30 mins.
VHS: S06324. $14.95.

---

100 Years of Olympic Glory
The wondrous feats of the modern Olympics have been compiled on this two-tape, three-hour-long set. Contemporary figures such as Nadia Comaneci, Mark Spitz and Mary Lou Retton, as well Olympians from long ago like Jesse Owens, have brought the world together through triumphant athletic feats. Now the story of their efforts is compellingly told in this documentary through priceless archival footage. 180 mins.
VHS: S27505. $29.98.

1986 Tour de France: LeMond and Hinault Challenge
This British produced documentary captures the grueling and historic challenge between Bernard Hinault and Greg LeMond. This is the race that placed an American rider in the forefront of the cycling world. Commentary by Phil Liggett. 53 mins.
VHS: S16215. $29.95.

1987 Tour of Ireland: Nissan Classic
Running three hours in length, this video gives the viewer a complete look at one of pro cycling's best races. The action is fast paced, and the in-depth interviews with Sean Kelly, Stephen Roche and Greg LeMond are enlightening. 180 mins.
VHS: S08926. $59.95.

1988 Iditabike Race: Bicycling on Snow
This race pushes the sport to its outer limits. Conditions can range from slush and 40 degrees to a blizzard at 40 below, riding over snow covered lakes and dog-sled paths both day and night. This exciting race is gaining in popularity and now you can experience it first hand. 25 mins.
VHS: S09222. $24.95.

1989 World Championship: LeMond's Victory
Balancing pure action and great sports drama, this video showcases footage from previous LeMond victories in both amateur and professional cycling. In the recent World Championship, Fignon makes a desperate bid for victory, but LeMond provides the brilliant counter. Directed by Kent Gordis. 48 mins.
VHS: S16221. $29.95.

1990 Paris-Roubaix: A Photo Finish!
Motorcycle and helicopter cameras reveal the critical action of this truly thrilling race. Phil Liggett offers a steady stream of fascinating anecdotes and insights, as well as an encyclopedic knowledge of the riders. 98 mins.
VHS: S16217. $39.95.

1990 Tour de France: Greg LeMond—The Best Yet!
This no-nonsense, insightful portrait relives the moments that led to LeMond's third Tour victory. "Virtually every major break is covered…some of the best high-speed descent shots we've ever seen" (*Bicycling*). With commentary from Paul Liggett. 102 mins.
VHS: S16213. $39.95.

1990 World Cycling Championships: The Complete Story!
Previously unseen highlights from this remarkable two week event consists of road races, time trials, and velodrome action. Includes moments of glory for Connie Young and Michael Hubner, and an interview with World Champion Rudy Dhaenens. With commentary by Paul Liggett. 60 mins.
VHS: S16220. $29.95.

1991 Liege-Bastogne-Liege: Cycling's Oldest Classic
The oldest bike race is fought in the Belgian Ardennes among the world's top riders. This account of the 1991 Liege-Bastogne-Liege captures Moreno Argentin's fourth win at this famous classic. Written by commentator Phil Liggett. 90 mins.
VHS: S16218. $39.95.

1991 Paris-Roubaix: A Fight to the Finish!
After losing the toughest classic race of all by a millimeter the previous year, Canadian Steve Bauer returns to the Hell of Northern France to try again for victory. This grueling course follows over 267 kilometers, including 22 sections on ancient cobblestones. Introduced and narrated by Phil Liggett. 90 mins.
VHS: S16216. $39.95.

1991 Tour de France: Miguel Indurian—The New Tour Champion!
The 1991 Tour introduced Spaniard Miguel Indurian as the newest, and most surprising, winner since Laurent Fignon in 1983. Witness the agony of Greg LeMond as he battles against illness and exhaustion in his attempt to defend his crown. See all the decisive moves made in the Pyrenees as three men—Indurian, Chiapucci and Bugno—set the Tour afire with their strength and determination. Commentary by Paul Liggett. 90 mins.
VHS: S16212. $39.95.

1991 World Cycling Championships: One of Cycling's Greatest Prizes
See Italian Gianni Bugno win an exciting sprint finish to capture the men's professional road race at the World Cycling Championships in Stuttgart, Germany. Commentary by Phil Liggett. 60 mins.
VHS: S16219. $29.95.

1992 Paris-Roubaix
Cyclists Kelly, Van Hooydonck, LeMond, Argentin, Sorensen, Bugno and others compete on a trail that stretches more than 250 km over ancient cobblestone. 90 mins.
VHS: S16558. $39.95.

1992 Tour of Flanders
One of the greatest single-day cycling races covers 272 km over bone-crushing cobblestones though the winding hills of Belgium. Legendary star Sean Kelly battles Van Hooydonck, LeMond, Argentin, Sorensen, Bugno and other greats. 90 mins.
VHS: S16557. $39.95.

1994 Winter Olympic Highlights
The very best of winter sports will be available on this collection of highlights from the 1994 Olympic Games set in Lillehammer, Norway. Everything from the opening and closing ceremonies to all the most-watched competitions in skating, skiing, hockey, and more will be included in this timely video. 60 mins.
VHS: S20669. $19.98.

1994 Winter Olympics Figure Skating Competition and Figure Skating Exhibition Gift Set
Figure skating fans will be engrossed by this two-tape collection containing the gold medal-winning performances of all the Olympic Champions. America's greatest hopefuls, like 1988 gold medalist Brian Boitano, are sure to inspire with their unmatched talents.
VHS: S20670. $39.98.

23 Days in July: Tour de France
The film follows Australian star Phil Anderson in his attempt to win the 1983 Tour de France. Anderson, riding for the Peugeot Team, discusses his training and strategy for winning cycling's most famous race. Cycling journalist John Wilcoxson provides analysis, day-to-day coverage of the race and its leading riders.
VHS: S04467. $34.95.
Tim Sullivan, 50 mins.

America Screams
Vincent Price has found a new way to make people scream: roller coasters. Hold on for plenty of laughs, chills and thrills as the master of horror presents the ultimate scream machines: the 13-story Loch Ness Monster, upside-down backwards King Kobra, double-track Rebel Yell and triple-loop Mindbender. Plus the highest, longest and fastest coaster in the world, Colossus. From Coney Island to Disneyland, the bone-rattling best in amusement parks. 30 mins.
VHS: S12382. $14.95.

America's Greatest Olympians
Edwin Moses, Jackie Joyner-Kersee, Jesse Owens, Mark Spitz, Greg Louganis, Bruce Jenner and Muhammad Ali are just some of the athletic superstars who have made the United States a super-competitor at all Olympic competitions. The history of the games is inextricably entwined with the success of these Americans. That history is recreated on this video. 120 mins.
VHS: S27506. $19.98.

American Challenge: In the Observer Singlehanded TransAtlantic Race
The intimate on-board story of seven solo sailors facing an ultimate challenge: The Observer Singlehanded TransAtlantic Race. Automatic cameras installed on their boats recorded unique close-up views of men and women facing constant danger. 3,000 miles of pounding to windward strips away the veneer to reveal the human spirit alone against the inexorable power of the sea. "The most exciting sea documentary I have ever seen" (William F. Buckley Jr.). 57 mins.
VHS: S06345. $49.95.

Arc Across the Atlantic
An international view of sailing; 204 boats converge in Las Palmas to start the first Atlantic Rally for Cruisers. 3700 miles later, the boats finish in Barbados. This is the spirited tape of the sailors, families, and amateur crews in the tense race. 52 mins.
VHS: S05946. $29.95.

Around Alone
53-year old businessman Dodge Morgan decides to sail around the world without stopping, alone. This inspiring adventure story shows how he realized that dream aboard the *American Promise*. Morgan confronts his fears, copes with loneliness and gear problems, fierce gales and mountainous seas of the southern Ocean, and finally comes home after 150 days at sea, having shattered the old record and becoming the first American to sail around the world solo. 58 mins.,
VHS: S06344. $59.95.

Around Cape Horn
In 1929, the last great days of commercial sail were passing. During that year, Captain Irving Johnson sailed aboard the massive bark *Peking*. He narrates this program filming the crew's daily activities, as well as spectacular scenes during a wild storm as the ship rounded the feared Cape Horn. 37 mins.
VHS: S05942. $29.95.

Artistry on Ice
American Olympic silver medalist Nancy Kerrigan and Olympic gold medalist Brian Boitano are just two of the international figure skating stars featured in this collection of beautiful performances. This video offers a unique opportunity to see the world's greatest skaters doing routines never seen on TV.
VHS: S24818. $19.98.

Baseball
Ken Burns (*Civil War*) turns his attention to the American national pastime in this 18-hour epic which spans 150 years of the game that is America. Released on nine tapes in a collector's boxed set.
VHS: S21896. $179.98.
Laser: LD74841. $299.99.
Ken Burns, USA, 1994, 1080 mins.

Baseball Card Collector
Millions of baseball card hobbyists will love this program narrated by Mel Allen, the voice of the New York Yankees, with much information on new and classic cards, including buying, trading, rating and collecting. 40 mins.
VHS: S09101. $19.99.

Baseball in the News
Newsreels from 1951 to 1967 are the source for this nostalgic look at baseball. America's favorite pastime remains the stuff of lore. Now some of the most talked about sporting incidents from the past are available for viewing once again, in this boxed set.
VHS: S21683. $44.95.

Baseball in the News Series

Some of baseball's greatest moments in the World Series, All Star games, spring training and off-diamond highlights in three volumes tracing the recent history of baseball. Each program is approx. 60 mins.
Baseball in the News Volume 1: 1951-1955. Giants' Thomson fires the shot heard round the world; Joltin' Joe Di Maggio strokes the last home run; Bye Bye Beantown: Braves move to Milwaukee; and the Dodgers take the series from the Yankees.
VHS: S11119. $29.95.
Baseball in the News Volume 2: 1956-1960. Don Larsen hurls the perfect game in title contest; Dodgers play the last game at Brooklyn's Ebbets Field; White Sox win the first pennant in 40 years; Bobby Richardson smashes series slam for Yankees; and Mazeroski's blast brings Pirates world championship.
VHS: S11120. $29.95.
Baseball in the News Volume 3: 1961-1967. Willie Mays blasts four homers in a single game; Casey Stengel takes Mets to the first spring training; Cards trump Yanks in Series; Orioles sweep Dodgers for World Championship.
VHS: S11121. $29.95.

Baseball's Greatest Hits

An all-star collection of music videos celebrating America's great national pastime, with the all-star lineup featuring *I Love Mickey* with Mickey Mantle and Teresa Brewer; Dave Frishberg's *Van Lingle Mungo*; Terry Cashman's *Willie, Mickey and the Duke*; Bruce Springstone's *Take Me Out to the Ball Game*; rare, vintage TV commercials featuring baseball's greatest stars and footage from the vaults of major baseball. 30 mins.
VHS: S12184. $14.95.

Born to Run

The story of Sebastian Coe, his training program, racing strategy and motivation, the isolation and constant pain that are an intrinsic part of his mental and physical preparation for every race.
VHS: S05545. $39.95.

The Boys of Summer

An affectionate and informative documentary on the Brooklyn Dodgers. Recall the memories made in Ebbets Field. See once again the exploits of Duke Snider, Roy Campanella, Carl Erskine and Preacher Roe. Flatbush was never the same after they let the Bums leave; now the good old days are available on tape. 1983, 90 mins.
VHS: S02619. $19.98.

Budo Sai: The Spirit of the Samurai

A program about various martial arts styles and techniques that have emerged in the 20th century. Shot at the Budo Sai Festival, the program features 12 masters demonstrating Kendo, Karate, Aikido and Capoeira, a form of Brazilian street fighting. 70 mins.
VHS: S19733. $29.95.

Champion Acrobats of China

Performances by the women acrobats of China, who have dedicated years to mastering the most dangerous routines.
Champion Acrobats of China: Flying Lotus.
VHS: S16729. $19.98.
Champion Acrobats of China: Steel Silk.
VHS: S16730. $19.98.

Comeback

A documentary on the life of German boxer Max Schmeling, following his career from the early years of boxing to his later match for the World Championship against America's Joe Louis. German silent and sound.
VHS: S07502. $29.95.

The Cycling Experience

A documentary of spectacular California location photography and New Age music that takes the form of a travelogue, told from the cyclists' perspective. 52 mins.
Laser: LD70255. $29.95.

David Carradine's Kung Fu and Tai Chi Workouts

This class for beginners uses the principles of Kung Fu and Tai Chi workouts to strengthen the connection between mental and body awareness. 116 mins.
Laser: LD71950. $39.95.

Double Exposure

John and Dan Egan join Rob and Eric DesLauriers for this ski extravaganza. Together they outrun avalanches in Wyoming, tackle 14,000' peaks in Russia and explore the most difficult terrain in Romania, Turkey, Yugoslavia and North America.
VHS: S22052. $19.95.

Endless Summer

Join Robert August and Mike Hynson as they follow the summer season to Senegal, Ghana, Nigeria, South Africa, Australia, New Zealand, Tahiti, Hawaii and California in search of the perfect wave. Still the ultimate surf film!
VHS: S14250. $19.96.
Bruce Brown, USA, 1964, 90 mins.

Eurocycling—Motorola Team

For two weeks, Paul Liggett went behind the usually closed doors of one of the world's top teams to see how they prepare for the season's two most important classics: Paris-Roubaix and Liege-Bastogne-Liege. "Packed with documentary comments and full of information on tactics and training, this is a must for every cycling fan" (*Velo News*). 90 mins.
VHS: S16222. $34.95.

The Falcon Gentle

A video survey of the history and practice of falconry. The training of the Peregrine falcon, using dogs and falcons for hunting grouse, the relationship between falcon and falconer, etc. 33 mins.
VHS: S15538. $35.00.

Fitness Fables: #1

The Cat Who Had to Be Best. Narrated by Tony Randall, these fables include simple exercises designed by the Directors of Conditioning, U.S. Olympic Ski Team. Music by Phil Baron. For ages 3-8. USA.
VHS: S14953. $19.95.

Fitness Fables: #2

Detective Squirrel/Missing Tree. Narrated by Tony Randall, these fables include simple exercises designed by the Directors of Conditioning, U.S. Olympic Ski Team. Music by Phil Baron. For ages 3-8. USA.
VHS: S14954. $19.95.

Fitness Fables: #3

Monkey Who Only Watched T.V. Narrated by Tony Randall, these fables include simple exercises designed by the Directors of Conditioning, U.S. Olympic Ski Team. Music by Phil Baron. For ages 3-8. USA.
VHS: S14955. $19.95.

Friendship Sloop: A Heritage Retained

Two Maine boat builders are dedicated to preserving the Friendship sloop—a graceful, classic, able and rugged boat first built in the 1800's as a sturdy fishing vessel. One builder uses the old craft of shaping wood by hand, the other uses modern materials of fiberglass and epoxy. The annual homecoming of sloop owners is a slice of Americana in their bonding of love for the Friendship sloop and keeping alive the heritage. Winner of many awards. 28 mins.
VHS: S06348. $39.95.

Full Cycle: A World Odyssey

Cyclists travel nine countries in this mammoth trek with an environmental twist. Mark Schulze and Patty Mooney lead the tour through the U.S.A., Canada, Costa Rica, Greece, Switzerland, Great Britain, Tahiti, Australia and India. Along the way cultural, historical and geographical information is revealed, along with glimpses of natural scenery. 108 mins.
VHS: S25624. $39.95.

Gay Games II: Highlights

This program features outstanding scenes from this nine-day event. Includes the parade of 3500 athletes, the inspirational keynote address by the late Dr. Tom Waddell and San Francisco Mayor Diane Feinstein. There are highlights of all 18 sports events with interviews of both men and women athletes. 60 mins.
VHS: S16841. $39.95.

Gay Games III & Cultural Festival Opening and Closing Ceremonies

Opening Ceremonies: Stars the Parade of Athletes, International Festival Chorus, Joelle Rabu, Carol Pope, Lorraine Segato and an array of eloquent speakers. *Closing Ceremonies:* Highlights the Gay/Lesbian Bands of America, Awarding of the Dr. Tom Waddell trophy, passing of the flag, and performing finale that includes the Nylons. Lesbian activist/comic Robin Tyler emcees the 1990 celebration. 192 mins.
VHS: S16834. $49.98.

Gay Games IV from A to Q

Highlights include *In the Life* coverage from the Opening Ceremonies as well as *Dyke TV & Network Q* footage showing hunks competing for gold. *Gay Entertainment Television* provides a view of the history and the organization behind the games while *Gay Cable Network* shows the closing ceremonies of this historic event. 60 mins.
VHS: S21702. $24.95.

Glory of Their Times

The story of the early days of baseball, from the very beginning of the sports, covering the period 1896-1916. 60 mins.
VHS: S05235. $14.98.

Golden Decade of Baseball 1947-1957

Brent Mussberger narrates two programs covering the unforgettable era of baseball.
Golden Decade of Baseball Part 1. Covers Jackie Robinson's arrival, Di Maggio's comeback, the shot heard round the world, and Bill Bevan's no hitter. 30 mins.
VHS: S12159. $14.95.
Golden Decade of Baseball Part 2. Covers Willie Mays, Mickey Mantle's greatest catch ever made, and the Dodgers and Giants leaving New York. 30 mins.
VHS: S12160. $14.95.

Great Moments at the Winter Games

An overview of the most outstanding performances at the Winter Olympics, featuring such great athletes as Sonja Henie, Jean-Claude Killy and Dorothy Hammill. 47 mins.
VHS: S05889. $14.95.

Greatest Goals World Cup USA '94

This video features a stunning 56 goals from the World Cup matches in the U.S. Team members from many countries are seen at their best, including Houghton (Ireland), Dahlin (Sweden), Romario (Brazil), Salenko (Russia), Wynalda (U.S.A.), Batistuta (Argentina) and many more. 45 mins.
VHS: S23434. $14.95.

Greatest Sports Follies

Crammed full of accidents and mistakes just waiting to happen in football, basketball, baseball, tennis and ice-skating with Football's Hall-of-Fame Fumbles, College Basketball's Outrageous Coaches, Bloopers on Ice, Tennis in Turmoil and Baseball Gone Bats. 45 mins.
VHS: S12350. $14.98.

Hank Aaron: Chasing the Dream

Hanks Aaron's stats make this one of the greatest players of all time. He battled racism and hatred but still managed to overtake Babe Ruth's homerun record. Now his amazing story is available on video. 95 mins.
VHS: S25039. $14.98.

Highlights of Famous Fights

Joe Louis, Sugar Ray Robinson, Gene Tunney, Max Baer, Cassius Clay, Johnson, Willard, Carnara and others are featured in this full-length compilation of famous scenes in the history of boxing.
VHS: S09529. $29.95.

Holst: The Planets, Featuring the Duchesnays

Olympic sensations Paul and Isabelle Duchesnays perform their figure skating artistry to the symphonic music of Gustav Holst, as choreographed by Lar Lubovitch. Solo, ensemble ice dance and precision group skating are all incorporated in this video. Also features figure-skating champion Brian Orser. 55 mins.
VHS: S23867. $19.95.

Idols of the Game

Three videos track the evolution and contributions of key American sports heroes. Through their stories across a range of different sports, the fascinating development of the modern super athlete comes into view. Each video is 95 mins.
Babes in Boyland. Women have slowly won respect in the male-dominated world of American sports. The unlevel playing fields and the obstacles faced by pivotal female sports superstars are recounted in this video.
VHS: S27765. $19.98.
Inventing the All-American. Formerly amateurs who rose on skill and luck alone dominated American sports. The current American athlete, however, relies on a level of professionalism once unimagined. This transformation is outlined in the first video of the series.
VHS: S27764. $19.98.
Love and Money. Big business and the promise of big money have captured the soul of sports. Once players were loyal to fans and their hometown; now marketing is a vital indicator of how careers and teams will develop.
VHS: S27766. $19.98.
Idols of the Game: Three-Pack.
VHS: S27767. $39.98.

Idols of the Ring

Bill Stern narrates this compilation film showing boxing greats from the first half of the 20th century. In addition to famous boxers like Jack Dempsey and Joe Louis, there is footage depicting bouts from as far back as 1906. This film offers a singular opportunity to see the history of this sport and the men who made it great. 76 mins.
VHS: S24071. $14.95.

The Immortals

The performances of Sonja Henie of Norway, Uhlrich Wehling of East Germany, Burger Ruud of Norway, Toni Sailer of Austria and Billy Fiske of the U.S. have assured them sports immortality. This is the story of these great athletes. 47 mins.
VHS: S05890. $14.95.

The Impossible Hour: Ole Ritter & Eddie Merckx

The Impossible Hour follows Danish racing star Ole Ritter as he tries to regain his record for the hour ride. He had set the record in 1968, only to have it shattered by Eddie Merckx in 1972. A film about human limits and the quest for the heroic.
VHS: S04468. $29.95.
Jorgen Leth, Denmark, 48 mins.

Jack Dempsey

A knockout view of the heavyweight champ who led the world into the Golden Age of Sports when he defeated Jess Willard in the first major sporting event to occur after WWI. 22 mins.
VHS: S06420. $14.98.

Joe Louis

A challenging glimpse of the "Brown Bomber" who became the youngest heavyweight champ at the age of 23, including Louis' KO of Max Schmeling. 24 mins.
VHS: S06422. $14.98.

Joe Louis—For All Time

A documentary with plenty of punch that doesn't duck and weave when it comes to the less attractive parts of the life of The Brown Bomber. The legendary heavyweight boxing champ, who was born Joseph Louis Barrow, successfully defended his title 25 times. He was also the victim of cocaine, racism and the I.R.S. Color and B&W.
VHS: S08118. $29.95.
Peter Tatum, USA, 1985, 89 mins.

King of the Hill

A look at big league baseball from the inside, from the experience of Ferguson Jenkins, one of the few Canadian-born players to make the major leagues. Filmed over the last two years Fergie played for the Chicago Cubs before being traded to the Texas Rangers, this story captures the frustrations, the satisfaction and much of the humorous side of baseball. Produced by the National Film Board of Canada.
VHS: S04365. $29.95.
W. Canning/D. Brittain, Canada, 57 mins.

Knute Rockne and the Fighting Irish

The latest from the American Sports Heroes series chronicles the life of the winningest coach in collegiate football. Rockne coached the Fighting Irish of Notre Dame from 1919 until his death in 1931. Join host Paul Hornung, former Green Bay and Notre Dame star, as he chats with special guest moose Krause, the legendary athletic director and Rockne recruit. 45 mins.
VHS: S11572. $9.95.

L.L. Bean Guides

Several excellent guides to activities in the outdoors, produced by the famous house of L.L. Bean.
L.L. Bean Guide to Fly Fishing.
VHS: S05302. $29.95.
L.L. Bean Guide to Outdoor Photography.
VHS: S05303. $29.95.

La Course en Tete: The Eddie Merckx Story

This outstanding film follows star Eddie Merckx at the peak of his career through the challenge of Europe's best races from the World Championships to the Tour de France. A rare portrait of "The Babe Ruth of Cycling," and an extraordinary document of human endurance and courage.
VHS: S04466. $59.95.
Joel Santoni, 110 mins.

Little League's Official How-to-Play-Baseball Video

The definitive video look at baseball—"a four-bagger!" 70 mins.
VHS: S12161. $19.95.

A Man Named Lombardi

Vince Lombardi gave to the game of football and to the men he led a philosophy of life that became a legend. Filled with interview, this tape is narrated by George C. Scott. 55 mins.
VHS: S13072. $29.98.

Mike Tyson: The Inside Story

Forty-one wins, one loss and thirty-five knockouts are the facts behind this star boxer's rise to fame. Before his troubled relationship with Robin Givens took him out of the ring, his promoter, Don King, had managed to place Tyson firmly in the spotlight. This is his story.
VHS: S25629. $19.98.

National Geographic Video: Return to Everest

In May, 1953, Sir Edmund Hillary and Tenzing Norgay became the first men to conquer the world's highest peak. Now, more than 30 years later, they return to Mount Everest to celebrate their historic ascent. 60 mins.
VHS: S10244. $19.95.

National Pastime: A History of Major League Baseball

A five-video set celebrates baseball from its beginnings to the present, showcasing the greatest players, moments and records. 345-minute boxed set.
VHS: S21971. $69.98.

Not So Great Moments in Sports, Take Three

More of the most memorable mishaps, madness and mayhem sports has ever seen. Host: Tim McCarver. 45 mins.
VHS: S12560. $14.99.

Official History of Baseball

This two-tape set is a comprehensive review of baseball's history, with rare footage, new and exclusive interviews, tracing baseball from 1869 to the present. 155 mins.
VHS: S21970. $24.95.

Olympiad Series

Jesse Owens Returns to Berlin. Using actual film highlights of the fateful 1936 Olympics and Owens' personal, on-camera recollections, Bud Greenspan, the host, retells the story of one of sports' greatest triumphs—in which the 22-year old Owens defeated Hitler's showcase for the "master race." Emmy Awards. USA, 1964, 46 mins.
VHS: S06635. $14.95.
The Marathon. The thrilling history of Olympics' most grueling competition. Highlights include the event's ancient origins, Abebe Bikila striding barefoot to victory in Rome, and Joan Benoit's historic win in the first-ever Women's Olympic marathon. USA, 1974, 46 mins.
VHS: S06636. $14.95.
They Didn't Have a Chance. Inspiring stories including the survivor of a near-fatal plane crash who returned to Olympic greatness…the marathon champion who ran for Japan but claimed history for his occupied Korean homeland…the gold-medal comeback of the sprinter labeled "an old man." USA, 1979, 46 mins.
VHS: S06637. $14.95.

Once There Was a Ballpark

Martin Sheen hosts this informative and entertaining look at the history of baseball stadiums. From the humble beginnings in the streets through the original wooden bleachers, and on to more modern concrete structures, it's all here, including a look at some of the most beloved structures still standing, like Wrigley Field. 108 mins.
VHS: S21707. $19.98.

Only the Ball Was White

A superior television documentary on the formation and rise of the baseball Negro Leagues, and the great ballplayers who were denied a chance to play in the racially segregated Major Leagues. The program features interviews with Satchel Paige, Roy Campanella, Buck Leonard, Jimmy Crutchfield, David Malarcher, Effa Manley and Quincy Troupe. Narrated by Paul Winfield. 30 mins.
VHS: S20421. $19.98.

The Other Side of the Mountain

Jill Kinmont was an Olympic hopeful until she suffered a skiing accident that left her paralyzed. Marilyn Hassett stars in this true life story of courage and recovery. With Beau Bridges, Dabney Coleman and Belinda J. Montgomery.
VHS: S07806. $19.95.
Larry Peerce, USA, 1975, 101 mins.

The Other Side of the Mountain, Part 2

Jill Kinmont was a shoo-in for the Olympics in downhill skiing until a skiing accident occurred. In Part 2 of her true-life story, she must overcome depression and the death of the man who helped her recover. Features Marilyn Hasset and Timothy Bottoms.
VHS: S21766. $19.98.
Larry Peerce, USA, 1978, 99 mins.

Play Chess! The United States Chess Federation Guide

Learn how to play and how to improve your game plan with expert tips and tricks from the U.S. Chess Federation. 60 mins.
VHS: S07424. $19.99.

Play Soccer, Jack Charlton's Way: The Collection Set

All three volumes feature instruction by the famed English soccer star, Jack Charlton. He played for the winning English team at the World Cup event in 1966 and coached the Irish team in 1994. Now his expertise is available for everyone. 170 mins.
VHS: S24783. $59.98.

Power Moves

Emmy Award-winning director Jan C. Nickman explores the human form and its spectacular achievements in the world of sports. Greg Louganis is just one of the athletes whose movements yield their intricate beauty to this powerful cinematographic work. A rock climber, a skier and a snowboarder are also featured. 40 mins.
VHS: S24131. $19.98.
Laser: LD75420. $29.99.

Return to the Snow Zone

The new James Angrove/Jon Long ski film takes the viewer to the edge of his/her seat and back again. From the high alpine reaches of Kashmir, India, to the menacing north wall of Mount Currie in the Coastal Range of British Columbia, Canada, their new action-packed documentary covers three continents. Soundtrack includes music by Yello and Midnight Oil.
VHS: S15327. $39.95.
Angrove/Long, Canada, 1990, 65 mins.

River of the Red Ape

This classic whitewater river journey took place in Sumatra, as a crack team of wilderness explorers from Sobek made the first attempt to navigate the wild Alas River. William Devane narrates this exciting trip into the world's largest orangutan rain forest wilderness. 57 minutes.
VHS: S03531. $39.95.

Sails and Sailors: J Boats '37

Three short films: in Sails and Sailors, a period newsreel film in color has been preserved and improved to show a glimpse of the famous race of 1937; in Weetamoe, a fantastic sail aboard the Clinton Crane designed Weetamoe, and Yachting in the Thirties shows famous boats and races of the 30's. 46 mins.
VHS: S05941. $24.95.

Seaflight/Windflight

Champion surfers from Hawaii and Southern California challenge Waimea Bay's 20' waves, shoot the Banzai Pipeline and perform 360° flips on their sailboards in two spectacular films on the sports of surfing and windsurfing. 1985, 26 mins.
VHS: S14450. $19.95.

Soviet Athletes—Summer Sports

The United States boycotted the Summer Olympics of 1980, but the games went on nonetheless. These are Soviet films about the famous games. 70 mins.
VHS: S12721. $19.95.

Soviet Athletes—The Gymnasts

The extraordinary performances of many Soviet super-gymnasts at Olympic competitions have inspired international youth to adopt an unhindered devotion to training and competition. 65 mins.
VHS: S12720. $19.98.

Soviet Athletes—Winter Sports

The rigid, vigorous coaching techniques that make Soviet athletes champions are documented thoroughly. This tape also introduces strange regional games, including a polo-like game where teams fight over a dead goat. 60 mins.
VHS: S12722. $19.95.

Sports Illustrated 25th Anniversary Swimsuit Video

A winner all the way, a behind-the-scenes look at the making of the 25th anniversary swimsuit issue.
VHS: S09307. $19.99.

Stars and Water Carriers

A concise, colorful chronicle of the Giro d'Italia. This extraordinary film by the world's foremost bicycle-race filmmaker recreates the magic of the moment, and brings the Giro's thrills and disappointments home to every viewer.
VHS: S04465. $49.95.
Jorgen Leth, Denmark, 90 mins.

Steeper and Deeper

More than beautiful scenery and great skiers, this film follows men on downhill trajectories that take your breath away. It truly captures stunts that are steeper and deeper than anything ever done before.
VHS: S22051. $19.95.

Story of Great Black Baseball Players

From the first black player to today's superstars, this compilation of baseball greats is hosted by Ernie "Mr. Cub" Banks and includes everyone from Jackie Robinson to Hank Aaron to Ozzie Smith. Once forbidden in the "major" leagues, this is a look at some of history's and today's most dominant players.
VHS: S12664. $19.95.

A Sunday in Hell

Probably the finest cycling film ever made, A Sunday in Hell follows the Paris-Roubaix road race, an event which taxes the energies of Europe's finest riders.
VHS: S02009. $59.95.
Jorgan Leth, France, 110 mins.

Super Duper Baseball Bloopers 2

A two-tape set that includes on-the-field antics, off-the-wall wackiness and baseball's clubhouse clowns. Each video is 40 minutes and includes such moments as Comedian Bill Murray explaining baseball to a foreigner.
VHS: S21972. $14.95.

Those Who Endured

About a rare group of Winter Games athletes who, unable to accept defeat, persisted in competing at the Olympics until the elusive gold medal was won. Among the athletes in this program are Eugenio Monti of Italy, the bobsledder who won two gold medals in 1968, skiers Andrea Mead Lawrence of the United States and Rosi Mittermaier of West Germany. 47 mins.
VHS: S05891. $14.95.

To Win at All Costs: The Story of the America's Cup

A lively, informative, and often amusing look at the yacht race which has found clubs, men, and countries challenging for the most prestigious trophy in yachting. Beginning with the re-enactment of the first race in 1851, it follows through the lifting of the Cup from American grasp in 1983; with much archival footage. 56 mins.
VHS: S05934. $29.95.

Torvill & Dean with the Russian All-Stars

Jayne Torvill and Christopher Dean have thrilled audiences world-wide since their unparalleled triumphs in the Olympic ice-skating championships. In this breathtaking extravaganza from the tour that broke box office records, Torvill and Dean join forces with Russia's top professional skaters. 78 mins.
VHS: S16136. $24.98.

The Tour du Pont: Hammer and Hell

Highlights from America's premiere competition pits Americans against top Europeans on familiar ground, providing high-powered action and drama over the course of this eleven day stage race. 90 mins.
VHS: S16223. $29.95.

The Trial of Red Riding Hood: A Fantasy on Ice

A charming musical fairy tale on ice, this video blends the skating artistry of Canadian Olympic Silver Medalist Elizabeth Manley, as Red Riding Hood, and the comic talents of Alan Thicke, as Phineas T. Wolf. 50 mins.
VHS: S23140. $19.95.

TVTV Goes to the Super Bowl

Bill Murray and Christopher Guest are the irreverent hosts of this hilarious program that deconstructs the hypocrisy and greed of sport's most famous game, centered around the 1976 game between the Dallas Cowboys and Pittsburgh Steelers, focusing on the players, their wives, coaches, owners and the media. 60 mins.
VHS: S15194. $24.95.

Ultimate Challenge: Around the World Alone

Seventeen sailors set out from Newport at the start of the First solo race around the world that would take eight months to complete. Each man must look within himself to find the will and the courage to continue. Ten of the 17 starters cross the finish line—for each it is a victory. 58 mins.
VHS: S06346. $49.95.

Ways at Wallace and Sons and The Bank Dory

The ill-fated coasting schooner John F. Levitt went down on her maiden voyage; the story here is of the New England shipbuilders taking us from the laying of the keel through the launching; The Bank Dory documents the building of one of the famous Bank dories. 58 mins.
VHS: S05943. $39.95.

Yachting in the Thirties

Four programs using rare archival footage to detail the adventure, spirit and energy of this peculiar sport, including pieces on racing strategy and the various transatlantic courses, boats and personalities that define the sport's allure and prestige. 45 mins.
VHS: S05945. $24.95.

TRAVEL

Acadia National Park & Cape Cod National Seashore

Explore glacier carved Acadia, where forest-draped mountains descend to the sea. Travel to charming Cape Cod, a special blend of natural and historical heritage. 30 mins.
VHS: S06667. $29.95.
Laser: LD70251. $29.95.

Alaska Stories

W.C. Thompson wrote and narrated this fascinating travelogue about his trip to the largest state. There are three stories that offer the perfect excuse to leave the road and explore sights that few tourists ever see, such as glacial calving and sites of the historic Gold Rush. 47 mins.
VHS: S24915. $24.95.

America's Great National Parks

A lavishly produced, three-volume, slipcased set of four videos documenting the great parks in the National Park System: The Story of Yellowstone, The Story of Yosemite, The Story of Grand Canyon, and a special Hidden Treasures of America's National Parks. 270 minutes total.
VHS: S13347. $89.95.
Laser: LD70236. $59.95.

Around the World in 80 Days, Volume One: Outward Bound

Complete with visas, running shoes, and an inflatable globe, Michael Palin sets off to circumnavigate the world in 80 days using only the forms of transport available to the fictional Phineas Fogg. From London to Alexandria and Bombay to Madras, Outward Bound, the first volume of Palin's Around the World in 80 Days, charts the first 28 days of his 80 day adventure. England, 164 mins. on two cassettes.
VHS: S13739. $29.95.

Around the World in 80 Days, Volume Two: Homeward Bound

From Madras to Singapore and back to London via Hong Kong, Shanghai and Calcutta, Palin uses a balloon, dog sled and container ship on his deadline dash back to the Reform Club in London. England, 172 mins. on two cassettes.
VHS: S13740. $29.95.

Audubon Zoo

This walking tour of the New Orleans zoo is great for kids. 30 mins.
VHS: S22401. $35.95.

Bali—Impressions of Paradise

Hindu ceremonies, central to Balinese culture, music, dance and drama, infused with rich symbolism, Balinese batik, shadow plays, painting, maskmaking, carving and jewelry and a majestic landscape define this paradise. 32 mins.
VHS: S12864. $24.95.

Barbados, A Culture in Progress

A panoramic and personal view of Barbados, narrated by Claudette Colbert. Ms. Colbert has a home on the island and through her eyes you feel and see the beauty of the island's natural environment, the work of the native artists and relaxed life style of the inhabitants. Directed by Angel Hurtado. Narrated in English. 15 mins.
VHS: S06774. $40.00.

Belgrade Ancient and New

This insightful film reveals the history of this key city, that sits at the confluence of two great rivers. As a result of this fortuitous site, the metropolis is also the place where two great civilizations meet.
VHS: S24594. $19.95.

Bent's Old Fort N.H.S. & Great Sand Dunes National Monument

Bent's Fort, a Castle on the Plain, and the Great Sand Dunes in Colorado—geology in motion. 46 mins.
VHS: S06671. $29.95.

Big Bend National Park, Texas

Discover the tremendous variety of wildlife and plant communities, the park's spectacular hiking trails and its incredible geology. 30 mins.
VHS: S06675. $29.95.

The Big Dig

A comprehensive view of a major public works project is on view in this video. The depression of the central artery and the building of the third tunnel under Boston Harbor is a fascinating enterprise.
VHS: S25009. $19.95.

Bourbon Street

This is a fun look at the historic neon strip in New Orleans known as Bourbon Street. Fascinating archival footage reveals the story behind the most famous collection of bars, nightclubs and honkytonks in the nation. 60 mins.
VHS: S22397. $41.95.

Bryce, Zion & Grand Canyon's North Rim

This program lets you visit the most popular features of these three treasured national parks, with the emphasis on Bryce and Zion in Utah. 25 mins.
VHS: S06660. $29.95.

California Big Sur Coastline

Explores the coast from San Simeon to Monterey along the coast highway, including the ocean, cliffs, Big Sur, wildflowers.
VHS: S06016. $29.95.

Canal Street: Great Wide Way

The culture and history of this New Orleans thoroughfare is the subject of this interesting documentary. It's a memorable trip aided by photographs from the past. 30 mins.
VHS: S22399. $41.95.

Canyon de Chelly & Hubell Trading Post

Explore deep red-rock canyons, ancient Anasazi cliff dwellings and age-old Navajo tradition with visits to two national park areas in an exploration of the geology of the canyon, and visits to Antelope House, White House, and Navajo craftsmen at work. 30 mins.
VHS: S10928. $29.95.

Cape Cod: The Sands of Time

Tells about the formation of Cape Cod by ice, wind and waves, accounts for the forces of erosion, and looks at the wooden ships, the men of iron, the story of Henry David Thoreau and his writings of Cape Cod, and a fascinating look at why the Italian inventor Marconi chose Cape Cod to be the site of the first wireless radio station to transmit a message between the U.S. and Europe. 43 mins.
VHS: S10923. $29.95.

The Chronicle Travel Library

Alaska. This surprising state boasts Grizzly bears, caribous, moose, glaciers, humpback whales, salmon, and trees worth $10,000. Visit Anchorage, Ketchikan, Sitka, Juneau, and Fairbanks; see the Waterfall Resort, a sports fisherman's paradise. It's a state you won't forget. 55 mins.
VHS: S05726. $29.95.
America's Secret Places. Here's a video for you explorers who want to escape civilization, to find your own fairylands and lands of Oz; places where the nearest road is 40 miles away. You'll find your secret refuge in places smooth and rough, dry and wet, high and low, barren and abundant; from Maine to Florida, up through the Heartland to the Northern Coast of California. 54 mins.
VHS: S05719. $29.95.
Australia. The former home of the America's cup, Australia is the oldest, flattest, and driest continent. Yet it boasts more snow than Switzerland. This travel adventure takes you to see the world's supply of opals, to wild camel country, a Koala bear sanctuary and the mystical Olga mountains in an absolute paradise. 60 mins.
VHS: S05713. $29.95.
California's North Coast. This haunting production captures the Gold Coast, visits the Sonoma Valley, Cape Mendocino, and the giant redwoods. 60 mins.
VHS: S05720. $29.95.
England. The color, pomp, and circumstance of Royal London blend with the timeless and pastoral beauty of old England on this magnificent program. 53 mins.
VHS: S05540. $29.95.
Family Outings: Northern California. This video explores the range of places to go and things to do for adventurous families in Northern California's water wonderlands, forest adventures, worlds of natural wonders, airborne thrills, and more. 60 mins.
VHS: S05546. $29.95.
Hong Kong. This crisp, quick-paced video hustles through the heart of the Orient—Hong Kong. See the three principal areas—Hong Kong Island, Kowloon, and the New Territories—that combine the mystique of ancient China, the elegance of Colonial Britain, and the energy of the New World. 48 mins.
VHS: S05718. $29.95.
New Zealand. See placid lakes, Alpine peaks, totem poles, tomatoes that grow on trees, the famous flightless Kiwi bird, and much more. This colorful tape surveys beautiful New Zealand, and does not forget the scenic North and South Islands. 56 mins.
VHS: S05721. $29.95.

Paris and the Seine.

Take this elegant and enchanting 500-mile journey down the Seine River from its source near Dijon. The river meanders through some of the most beautiful landscapes of France until it reaches Paris, where you'll see the city's famous sights and go on some off-beat excursions, finally arriving at Le Havre. 58 mins.
VHS: S05722. $29.95.
Rome. Visit famed Roman attractions such as the Colosseum, Trevi Fountain, Piazza Di Spagna, and the Vatican. This video is a virtual catalog of Rome and its people, an excellent preview of what you'll see there—and what you will never forget. 57 mins.
VHS: S05723. $29.95.
Scotland. Ride—by motor home—through a country of unhurried people, and stop for awhile to appreciate gurgling little rivulets, startling rock formations, razor-sharp mountain ranges and, believe it or not, palm trees! See the cities of Melrose, Kirkcudbright, Dunfermline, Edinburgh, Glasgow, Inverness, and other ancient sites. 55 mins.
VHS: S05268. $29.95.
Spain. Roman, Islamic, and Arabic influences are apparent in the mixture of Spain's people and its architecture. The land of such legends as Don Juan, Don Quixote, and Carmen is all part of this video filled with enlightening information and entertaining historical facts. 55 mins.
VHS: S05724. $29.95.
The Orient Express. Take a five-day, 1500-mile trip from Paris to Istanbul aboard the elegant blue train that was once the transportation of aristocracy. Enjoy the Old World elegance of Reims, Salzburg, and Vienna, then take a surprise side excursion into the Transylvanian countryside. This trip of excitement and historical intrigue will be embedded in your mind forever! 62 mins.
VHS: S05265. $29.95.

Colorado's Narrow Gauge Railroads

On the late 1800s, daring engineers carved railroads through the Rockies to link the mountain boomtowns of Colorado. The colorful past is relived along the four remaining narrow gauge railroads still operating. 55 mins.
VHS: S09943. $29.95.

Complete Yellowstone

This video tour of Yellowstone through all the seasons captures all of the magnificent park's scenic, thermal and wildlife attractions, including spectacular geyser eruptions, bubbling hot pools, roaring rivers and waterfalls. 60 mins.
VHS: S09944. $29.95.

Cruising the Chesapeake Bay and Potomac River

Designed for recreational boaters, a visual introduction to two of the most popular waterways anywhere, with a rich sampling of the best known sights and destinations of these scenic and historic waters. 30 mins.
VHS: S11123. $29.95.

Death Valley

Learn of Death Valley's geological treasures and of man's struggle to survive here. 26 mins.
VHS: S06664. $29.95.

Denali Wilderness, Alaska

Set amidst the pristine wilderness of Denali National Park, this award-winning program lets you join moose, wolves, grizzly bears and caribou in a four-season struggle for survival. 30 mins.
VHS: S06661. $29.95.

Discover California

From the fabulous coastline to the towering Sierra, from the sun-drenched cities and deserts to the inspiring scenery of Yosemite, Sequoia, Kings Canyon and the Redwoods. 60 mins.
VHS: S06692. $29.95.

Discover Portugal!

A comprehensive look at the hustle and bustle of Lisbon, and the violent volcanic landscape of the Azores, in a joyous look at Portugal today. 60 mins.
VHS: S23348. $29.95.

Egyptian Adventures

The mysteries and exotic beauty of Egypt in an exploration of the pyramids of Giza, Cairo, Alexandria, and Esmailia; a visit to the Sinai Peninsula with its vast deserts and beaches; and Mount Sinai, where Moses is said to have received the Ten Commandments. This adventure also includes a river boat down the Nile from Aswan to Luxor and Thebes, as well as a visit to the ancient temples at Abu Simbel, Philae, Luxor and Kamak. 20 mins.
VHS: S05872. $24.95.

European Balloon Adventures

Ten years ago, Buddy Bombard created a new concept in travel: the balloon vacation. These aerial nature walks tour over fortified castles, private chateaux and architectural wonders of medieval villages, often at altitudes that allow the traveler to speak with people on the farms and villages below. Delight in the lolling scenery as pleasure seekers of all ages roam the clouds above and explore the sights below in this enchanting jaunt across Europe.
VHS: S15844. $19.95.

Everglades: Big Cypress, Biscayne, Fort Jefferson

A tour of four national park areas, with a look at the variety of plant and animal life. 56 mins.
VHS: S10920. $29.95.

Explore Colorado

Capture the breath-taking scenery and pioneer spirit of Colorado, including her natural wonders, mining towns, scenic railroads and historic sites. 60 mins.
VHS: S06683. $29.95.

Exploring Antarctica

Now you can visit the frozen continent that holds 90 percent of the world's fresh water without worrying about frostbite or runaway dog teams. Questar Home Video presents a detailed geographic and historical tour of a land mass where the ice can be three miles deep. See killer whales at play and penguins at home, as well as some very unusual marine life. 60 mins.
VHS: S13264. $29.95.

Florida! America's Vacationland

Enjoy Florida's natural splendor, unique wildlife, rich history and many exciting attractions. 60 mins.
VHS: S06685. $29.95.

Fodor's Video Guides

Each of these guides, from the creators of the best-selling travel guides, is 75 minutes.

Fodor's Bangkok.
VHS: S10341. $29.95.
Fodor's Hawaii.
VHS: S10030. $29.95.
Fodor's Hungary.
VHS: S10340. $29.95.
Fodor's London.
VHS: S05018. $29.95.
Fodor's Mexico.
VHS: S04958. $29.95.
Fodor's Singapore.
VHS: S10342. $29.95.

Glacier Bay

Glacier Bay National Park is the site of amazing scenery and abundant wildlife. Towering ice pinnacles and natural ice sculptures lay behind cavorting whales and flying seabirds. 35 mins.
VHS: S24225. $14.95.

Glacier National Park, Montana

This is a land of majestic mountains and deep, blue lakes; a land of sweeping panoramas and glacier-carved valleys. This is where the grizzly bear roams and bald eagles soar. 30 mins.
VHS: S06701. $29.95.

Grand Canyon & Petrified Forest

Capture the Grand Canyon experience. Spectacular vistas, summer thunderstorms, raft and mule expeditions, plus Petrified Forest National Park—Arizona's prehistoric wonder. 45 mins.
VHS: S06663. $29.95.

Grand Canyon National Park

One of Nature's spectacular sights showing the Canyon's South Rim from season to season, at sunrise and sunset, including a helicopter trip to out-of-the-way waterfalls and monuments.
VHS: S06017. $29.95.

Great Castles of Europe

Return to a time when a man's castle was his home, his livelihood and maybe even his only safe refuge. Some of the structures examined in this fascinating series were built as fortifications, while other were intended as private, sumptuous retreats.
Vol. 1: France and Spain. The castles of Spain date from early medieval times. Some were built to resist the Moors while others were strengthened and beautified by these Islamic invaders. The French castle Chambord, built for a king's brief encounter with a countess, and the fortress at Chenocceau, a massive keep built on a man-made island, are included in this tour. 90 mins.
VHS: S21152. $19.95.
Vol. 2: Germany and Romania. Along the Rhine some of Europe's most spectacular scenery can be found, including a range of castles built on these shores to keep watch over the river. In Bavaria, the late 19th-century fantasy, "mad" King Ludwig's Neuschwanstein, is a fairybook wonder that inspired Walt Disney's magic kingdom. Finally, Brancastle, the home of Dracula, offers an authentic gothic setting filled with evocative shadows. 90 mins.
VHS: S21153. $19.95.
Vol. 3: British Isles. From England's Warwick castle to the Scottish Isle of Skye, and all the way to Ireland's Bunratty castle, this volume shows the famed strongholds of these seafaring Islands where the bloody past is never fully lost as long as these magnificent structures still stand. 90 mins.
VHS: S21154. $19.95.
Three-Volume Deluxe Boxed Set.
VHS: S21155. $54.95.

Great Cities of Europe

This grand tour of Europe's most renowned cities includes glimpses of London, Dublin, Amsterdam, Munich, Vienna, Salzburg, Madrid, Paris, Athens and Rome. Viewers see romantic castles, picturesque canals, lively piazzas, splendid parks. 60 mins.
VHS: S10780. $24.95.

Great Smoky Mountains

Discover the natural wonders and pioneer spirit of three national park areas with this tour of the Great Smokies, The Blue Ridge Parkway, and the mountain beauty of Shenandoah. Includes visits to many historical sites and Appalachian folk centers. 60 mins.
VHS: S10927. $29.95.
Laser: LD70250. $29.95.

Guardians of the Night

A documentary which studies the evolution of the Lighthouse. Shot on location in the United States, France, Britain and Canada, the program laments the replacement of lighthouses with more sophisticated technology. 52 mins.
VHS: S19671. $24.95.

Hawaii: The Pacific Paradise

This two-tape set includes *Hawaii: Paradise Sought* and *Hawaii: Paradise Found.* 1000 years of history and drama make up the traditions of these idyllic islands, from the original Polynesian settlers to today's climate of tourism and travel, based on an amalgam of Eastern and Western cultures. 120 mins.
VHS: S21068. $39.95.

Hawaiian Paradise

A picturesque journey to six of the islands, interconnected with images, sounds and music, "as vibrant as the island itself."
92 mins.
Laser: LD70238. $34.95.

Historic San Simeon Castle

A home movie that weaves together footage of famous Hollywood stars and personalities at this palatial California estate.
VHS: S18899. $19.95.

Home Waters

Rob Perkins reveals an aspect of New England rarely seen. This travelogue video follows him in a canoe over 100 miles along the Connecticut River from Canada to Long Island Sound.
VHS: S24887. $19.95.

If These Walls Could Speak

Vincent Price hosts this entertaining series of the mysteries and secrets of some of the world's great castles, palaces and historical sites. Each tape is 30 minutes.
Edinburgh Castle.
VHS: S05110. $19.95.
Fushimi Castle.
VHS: S05111. $19.95.
Kilmainham Jail.
VHS: S05114. $19.95.
Kronborg Castle.
VHS: S05115. $19.95.
Mt. Vernon.
VHS: S05116. $19.95.
Palace of Versailles.
VHS: S05118. $19.95.
Virginia City.
VHS: S05123. $19.95.

Knott's Berry Farm, California

This is where the Old West meets the 20th century—head on! Ride a steam locomotive, a stage coach, or a thrill ride like the Corkscrew. Great family fun. 38 mins.
VHS: S06684. $29.95.

Kodak Travel Series

Olympic Range. From snow-covered peaks to peaceful streams, immerse yourself in the beauty of Washington state's famous rain forest, with firs and cedars as tall as skyscrapers.
Laser: LD70252. $29.95.

L.A. Journal, Vol. 1

An impressionistic tapestry of Los Angeles that is conveyed through a collection of photographs that document the pleasures and diversity in daily city life. The program captures the glamorous hot spots and urban blight. On three digital soundtracks are an original score by Carl Stone, a selection of early California music and poetry readings by Angelenos.
Laser: LD71930. $24.95.

Lakewold: Where the Blue Poppy Grows

A tour of Washington State's renowned Lakewold Gardens, which were finely crafted by landscape architects Thomas Church and the Olmsted brothers. 58 mins.
VHS: S19672. $29.95.

Las Vegas & the Enchanted Desert

The most up-to-date video available on the hottest and fastest-growing travel destination in the country—an exciting oasis of extravagance, entertainment and fun. Stereo. USA, 45 mins.
VHS: S15082. $29.95.

Las Vegas and Hoover Dam

Experience fabulous Las Vegas—including gambling, hotels, the Strip, showgirls. Marvel at the incredible design and grandeur of mighty Hoover Dam. Plus, witness the Great Colorado River Flood of 1983. 25 mins.
VHS: S06691. $29.95.

Laura McKenzie's Travel Tips

A video guide hosted by Laura McKenzie, a noted travel expert, which answers the questions where to go, what hotel to stay at, how to pack, where to find the night life, and much more.
Alaska.
VHS: S04614. $24.95.
Arizona.
VHS: S04612. $24.95.
Athens.
VHS: S02037. $24.95.
Austria. Vienna's Lippizan stallions, Salzburg, the city of Mozart, Innsbruck's Olympic village, ski resorts and Austria's famous castles.
VHS: S04992. $24.95.
Australia.
VHS: S07361. $24.95.
Boston.
VHS: S04615. $24.95.
Eastern Canada.
VHS: S11207. $19.95.
Egypt.
VHS: S02038. $24.95.
English Countryside and Scotland.
VHS: S11209. $19.95.
Florida.
VHS: S07324. $24.95.
Hawaii.
VHS: S02039. $24.95.
Hong Kong. Kowloon, Wan Chai, Causeway Bay, Aberdeen, Repulse Bay, Macao.
VHS: S04995. $24.95.
Ireland. Includes information on Dublin, Blarney, Cork, Limerick, Shannon.
VHS: S02040. $24.95.
Las Vegas. Surrounding day trips to casinos, revues, calico, Hoover Dam.
VHS: S04993. $24.95.
London. Devoted to all the spots both within London and also within a day's journey, such as Windsor Castle, Stratford-on-Avon and Warwick Castle.
VHS: S02041. $24.95.
Los Angeles. Includes the Hollywod celebrity home tours, Palm Springs, the Southern California beaches and more.
VHS: S02042. $24.95.
Mainland China.
VHS: S11210. $19.95.
Mexican Beaches.
VHS: S04613. $24.95.
Morocco. Information about Casablanca, Rabat, Marrakesh, and day trips to Agadir and Taroudannt.
VHS: S02043. $24.95.
Munich and Bavaria. An introduction to King Ludwig's castle, the Salt Mines of Berchresgaden, Bavarian beer halls, medieval towns.
VHS: S04990. $24.95.
Netherlands.
VHS: S11205. $19.95.
New York City.
VHS: S04616. $24.95.
New Orleans. The French quarter, Bourbon Street jazz, creole cuisine, the Mississippi River ferries, plantations.
VHS: S04991. $24.95.
New Zealand.
VHS: S07325. $24.95.
Paris.
VHS: S02044. $24.95.
Queensland, Australia.
VHS: S11208. $19.95.
Rome. The guide to the Eternal City includes information on Vatican City, Pompeii, and the Amalfi Coast.
VHS: S02045. $24.95.
San Francisco. Learn about the famous sights such as the Golden Gate Bridge, Ghirardelli Square, Fisherman's Wharf and surrounding points of interest.
VHS: S02046. $24.95.
Spain. Includes information on Madrid, Granada and Toledo, as well as Tangiers, Morocco and Costa del Sol.
VHS: S02047. $24.95.
Switzerland.
VHS: S02048. $24.95.
Tahiti and French Polynesia.
VHS: S11206. $19.95.
The Caribbean.
VHS: S07323. $24.95.
The French Riviera.
VHS: S11211. $19.95.
Venice. St. Mark's square, the Doge's palace, the famed canals and gondolas, Venetial glassworks.
VHS: S04994. $24.95.
Washington, D.C.
VHS: S04617. $24.95.
Western Canada.
VHS: S07326. $24.95.

Mount Rainier

Washington state's Mt. Rainier National Park is the crown jewel of the Cascade peaks. Lush forests of cedar, hemlock and fir flourish on its volcano-born slopes. 28 mins.
VHS: S06668. $29.95.

Mt. Rushmore and The Black Hills of South Dakota

Explore Mt. Rushmore and the surrounding Black Hills with all its unique natural wonders and Old West heritage. See the Badlands, Custer State Park, Wind Cave and more. 30 mins.
VHS: S06700. $29.95.

Mt. Rushmore— Four Faces on a Mountain

In this inspiring National Park Service film, you will see the faces of Presidents Washington, Jefferson, Lincoln and Roosevelt being carved from Mt. Rushmore in rare black and white film. 30 mins.
VHS: S06666. $29.95.

Mush, You Malamutes!

Father Bernard R. Hubbard compiled this ethnographic film about his journey in search of a fabled tropical valley allegedly located in the heart of Alaska. It contains unique footage of this harsh landscape and the people who live there. 68 mins.
VHS: S24082. $24.95.

National Monuments of Southern Arizona

Explore the splendid scenery and fascinating natural and cultural history of eight National Park Service locations in Southern Arizona, including Saguaro, Organ Pipe Cactus, Tonto and Tumacacori. 30 mins.
VHS: S06672. $29.95.

A New England Clambake

This regional culinary tradition can be prepared on the beach, on the back yard barbecue, on the stove, and even in the microwave. It's all explained in this video.
VHS: S25008. $14.95.

Over America

Aerial photography spanning the entire US is joined with an original Hi-Fi stereo musical score. The result is this unique video experience. High definition cameras show amazing detail of the coasts, mountains and great expanses of wilderness that are the unique heritage of this land. 80 mins.
VHS: S25736. $24.95.

Over New England

A vivid travelogue of the beauty, splendor, grace and tradition of New England, examining its unique history, geography and landscape. 60 mins.
VHS: S19393. $19.95.

Over Washington

This video studies the beauty and history of Washington State. The program is "backed by a lush musical score" (*Booklist*). 60 mins.
VHS: S19390. $19.95.

Pikes Peak Country, with Colorado Springs

Explore the area's scenic wonders and visit over 40 of its finest attractions, including museums, historic sites and rustic towns. 50 mins.
VHS: S06697. $29.95.

Polynesian Cultural Center

This CINE Golden Eagle award winner is a colorful portrait of one of Hawaii's most popular tourist attractions. The arts, crafts and game demonstrations highlight the nighttime extravaganza of the Pageant of the Long Canoes and Maori greeting ceremony. 38 mins.
VHS: S09951. $29.95.

Rocky Mountain National Park

Discover the Crown Jewel of Colorado—a land of towering peaks, where fully one-third of the park is above the tree line. See some of North America's most splendid mountain lakes and drive spectacular Trail Ridge Road—the highest continuous highway in the U.S. 30 mins.
VHS: S06673. $29.95.

San Simeon: Hearst's Castle

Ken Murray tours the magnificent castle that was once the playground of the wealthy—including the furniture, sculpture and art. 28 mins.
VHS: S09972. $12.95.

Scenic Seattle

Tour Seattle's scenic, historical and cultural attractions, as well as the beautiful surrounding area. 30 mins.
VHS: S06682. $29.95.

Scenic Wonders of America

Three programs, *Atlantic Vistas, Pacific Frontiers* and *American West*, offer a naturalist portrait of the landscape, mountains and water. 180 mins.
Laser: LD70230. $49.95.

Seasons of the Heart

This is a journey through Fairbanks and Alaska's untamed interior. Every season in the "Golden Heart" of this state is magical. Summer festivals, wildlife, the Northern Lights, dog sleds and more are on view. 28 mins.
VHS: S24223. $14.95.

Shenandoah Valley of the Virginias

Discover why Shenandoah Valley is known as the crowning glory of the Virginias; explore the Blue Ridge Mountains, the countryside of George Washington, Stonewall Jackson, Robert E. Lee and Woodrow Wilson, and visit the battlefields and museums of the Civil War. 30 mins.
VHS: S10925. $29.95.

Shenandoah—The Gift

Shenandoah National Park is a symbol of renewal, hidden away in the sleepy hollows of Virginia's mountains. Through black and white footage, see Shenandoah as it was developed in the 1920's and 30's. 20 mins.
VHS: S06670. $29.95.

Southern California

From San Diego to Santa Barbara, including L.A. and Hollywood, this stimulating film whisks you to the most exciting scenic, cultural and tourist attractions in the Southland. 30 mins.
VHS: S06693. $29.95.

St. Charles Avenue: Mansions and Monarchs

The history and beauty of America's grandest boulevard is revealed in this documentary about New Orleans' most fashionable area. 30 mins.
VHS: S22398. $41.95.

St. Charles Streetcar

Peter Fountain narrates this lively historical look at the world's oldest street railway along New Orleans' most history-laden boulevard. 30 mins.
VHS: S22400. $49.95.

The Story of America's Canyon Country

This program concerns the landscape carved out by the Colorado River, the "Grand Circle," the breathtaking scenery and 11 national parks around Utah, Arizona, Colorado and New Mexico that comprise the mythology and history of the American west. The areas covered include Monument Valley, Bryce Canyon, Cedar Breaks, Capitol Reef and the Grand Canyon. 60 mins.
VHS: S17264. $29.95.

The Story of America's Great Northwest

Spanning its entire history, dating back 200 million years, this program considers the beauty of this area and its formation from nature, fire, glaciers and water. The work also features episodes about the conflicts between Native Americans and the settlers, gold seekers, entrepreneurs, and travelers. 60 mins.
VHS: S17266. $29.95.

The Story of America's Historic Inns

A travelogue of Americana which visits the inns, taverns and various stagecoaches and offers telling anecdotes about local history, architectural wonder and scenic high points. The program features visits to St. Francis Inn, Stillman's Inn, St. James Hotel, San Ysidro Ranch, Robert Morris Inn, Monmouth Plantation, and Wolf Creek Tavern. 60 mins.
VHS: S20188. $29.95.

The Story of America's Last Frontier: Alaska

This program chronicles the history and emergence of Alaska, from prehistoric to the post-atomic and its status as the last frontier, a cultural gateway, with its national parks, preserves and monuments. The epic work includes sections on the caribou crossing at Kobuk, the Eskimo and Indian battles, Mt. McKinley, North America's tallest peak, the "forgotten war" during World War II, the Gold Rush, and its U.S. purchase in 1863. 60 mins.
VHS: S17265. $29.95.

SuperCities

SuperCities is a series of beautifully photographed, professionally produced short films which bring the world's favorite cities to life in your living room. All titles are available in hi-fi stereo.
Amsterdam. This canal-lined city is known both for its beauty and its traditionally liberal outlook. It attracts young people from the world over by offering all the pleasures of modern life in a civilized and understanding setting. 30 mins.
VHS: S26111. $9.95.

Bangkok. A vast, modern city has sprung up between the temples of old Bangkok. This video shows a place marked by vivid contrasts and vibrant energy. 30 mins.
VHS: S26112. $9.95.

Barcelona. The Catalonian capital maintains a strong sense of identity and history balanced with a contemporary flair. As host to the 1992 Olympics, this city took the opportunity to prove both its attractiveness and openness to foreign visitors. 30 mins.
VHS: S26113. $9.95.

Berlin. A turbulent and central role in the 20th century has defined the face of this unique historic city. Today Berlin joins a multiplicity of styles at the heart of a newly unified Europe. 30 mins.
VHS: S26125. $9.95.

Berne & Lucerne. These two Swiss cities combine a medieval legacy with vibrant, contemporary urban life. Berne is both a perfectly preserved medieval town and the capital of Switzerland, and Lucerne has the best preserved city walls still standing in Europe. 30 mins.
VHS: S26126. $9.95.

Budapest. The Hungarian capital betrays a zest for life unbowed by the passage of centuries. Much has been preserved and restored in this Central European city on the Danube. 30 mins.
VHS: S26127. $9.95.

Cairo. Africa's largest city is home to Pharonic treasures, Muslim edifices of unmatched grandeur and a busy, modern way of life. The Nile and the Pyramids appear eternal amid the bustle. 30 mins.
VHS: S26128. $9.95.

Florence. The city of the Renaissance lures visitors with architectural and artistic treasures. It's all on view in this video, from Michelangelo to Vasari, Donatello and Giotto. 30 mins.
VHS: S26114. $9.95.

Hong Kong. The gateway to China is a vast, modern metropolis, noted for its density. Amidst the crowds lie a variety of attractions, including some of the best shopping available. 30 mins.
VHS: S26115. $9.95.

Istanbul. The fabled Constantinople combines the best of East and West. This former capital of the Roman Empire maintains a unique historical legacy. 30 mins.
VHS: S26116. $9.95.

Johannesburg. South Africa's commercial capital is a lively setting for museums, galleries, theaters and markets. The city's diversity is key to its vibrancy. 30 mins.
VHS: S26129. $9.95.

Lisbon. Once the richest city in Europe, Lisbon still offers an air of relaxed elegance. Though destroyed by an earthquake in the mid-18th century, it remains a favorite destination for travelers. 30 mins.
VHS: S26117. $9.95.

London. The capital of the once mighty British Empire combines a rich legacy with an unmatched cosmopolitan style. London's monuments are beautifully displayed in this video. 30 mins.
VHS: S26118. $9.95.

Madrid. From the Prado, one of the world's greatest art museums, to the nightlife around the Puenta del Sol, Madrid offers something for every visitor. 30 mins.
VHS: S26130. $9.95.

Marrakesh & Fez. Both of these cities have spanned centuries to emerge as vibrant, lively places that still offer much to the contemporary world. 30 mins.
VHS: S26131. $9.95.

Mexico City. The largest city on Earth proudly preserves a heritage that combines an Aztec legacy, Spanish colonial influence, and the contemporary verve of modern Mexico. 30 mins.
VHS: S26132. $9.95.

Munich. Beerhalls are not the only sites offered by the Bavarian capital. There are palaces, baroque churches and peerless museums in this city of riches. 30 mins.
VHS: S26133. $9.95.

New York. The "city that never sleeps" is the perfect place for a whirlwind video tour. Skyscrapers cram together in this dynamic, American, "can-do" setting. 30 mins.
VHS: S26119. $9.95.

Paris. With boulevards and monuments unmatched the world over, the "City of Light" is the ideal European metropolis, and is wonderfully documented on this video. 30 mins.
VHS: S26120. $9.95.

Prague. The city of a thousand spires survived the terrors of World War II and the depredations of a moribund communist government. As a result, it offers treasures from another era. 30 mins.
VHS: S26134. $9.95.

Rio de Janeiro. Rio's Carnival and the Copacabana beach have fixed this city in the popular imagination as an exotic and vibrant destination. This video shows the uninhibited spirit of the city which invented the Bossa Nova. 30 mins.
VHS: S26121. $9.95.

Rome. From ancient times to the present, Rome has played a vital role in world history. The video shows Rome's treasures from the ancient world, the medieval era, the Renaissance and more. 30 mins.
VHS: S26122. $9.95.

St. Petersburg. Founded by Tsar Peter the Great to orient Russia toward Europe, this city offers a lovely melange of European influences, with sumptuous palaces and majestic canals which still stand despite a turbulent history. 30 mins.
VHS: S26123. $9.95.

Stockholm. Built on 14 islands, this Nordic city seems to float on water. Despite its ethereal appearance, it contains a host of solid and elegant sites both old and new. 30 mins.
VHS: S26135. $9.95.

Venice. Along ancient canals, gondolas float by magnificent sites such as the Basilica of San Marco, the Doge's Palace and the Campanile. 30 mins.
VHS: S26124. $9.95.

Vienna. Architectural majesty is evident in a variety of buildings at the heart of the old Hapsburg Empire. The Ringstrasse Boulevard circles one of the most beautiful cities in Europe. 30 mins.
VHS: S26136. $9.95.

Surprising Amsterdam

Capture the essence of one of the world's great cities. Some of the major sights include Dam Square, the Jordaan, and Vondel Park. Visit Anne Frank's house, then take a leisurely cruise down the quaint canals. 30 mins.
VHS: S10767. $24.95.

Switzerland's Glacier Express

All aboard for the famous "Glacier Express" rail trip through the Swiss Alps. Travel by train from St. Moritz to Zermatt, stopping for breathtaking views and scenic villages. It's a trip to remember! 52 mins.
VHS: S05762. $29.95.

Switzerland, the Alpine Wonderland

Journey to Switzerland, famous for clocks, rich chocolate and breathtaking scenery. Explore the Jungfrau mountain area and hear yodelers in Grindelwald. Visit Neuchatel, one of the country's watchmaking centers, then shop in elegant Lausanne. Shiver in the dungeon of the Chateau de Chillon. Visit the international city of Geneva and marvel at Zermatt's magnificent neighbor—the Matterhorn. 55 mins.
VHS: S10770. $24.95.

Tales from the Map Room

Even if X doesn't always mark the spot, maps can illuminate both the past and the present. This series explores the enormous variety of maps both ancient and modern, and includes the related history and politics that shaped mapmaking. Each of the six half-hour programs focuses on a single theme.
Metropolis. Every aspect of city life requires maps. Tourism, transportation, emergency services, planning and of course politics depend on them. London is the model for this look at the relationship between history, the growth of a great city and the art of mapmaking.
VHS: S21528. $69.95.
On the Road. From medieval pilgrims to today's car atlases, maps chart the explosion of human travel. This program traces the evolution of maps from the time of Charles II to contemporary atlases. Map reading skills and unconventional tactile maps are also covered.
VHS: S21527. $69.95.
On the Rocks. For centuries navies lost more ships on the rocks offshore than they did to enemies. In Normandy before D-Day there was a plot to chart the beaches of this vital coastline. Maritime maps are still vital as the sea continually shifts its beds and shorelines.
VHS: S21529. $69.95.
Paths of Glory (Fog of War). From the Battle of Culloden to the Gulf War, maps can spell the difference between victory and defeat. The private collection of the Duke of Cumberland, the fortifications designed for Louis XIV at Mauberge and even the maps used in World War I, make this abundantly clear.
VHS: S21526. $69.95.
Plumb Pudding in Danger. Forty percent of Third World boundaries are said to be the work of Britain and France. Early maps were used to settle local property disputes. Then it was realized maps could enhance the power of the state. Collecting taxes, establishing borders, and even defining areas of colonization are important functions made easier by maps.
VHS: S21525. $69.95.
A Tissue of Lies. All map design is a compromise, because the Earth is not flat. A designer must know what to include and what to omit. The confines, conventions, imagination and politics employed in mapmaking are the theme of this episode.
VHS: S21524. $69.95.
Tales from the Map Room. The complete six-volume set.
VHS: S21530. $375.00.

Teton Country

Set in Wyoming's Grand Teton National Park. No roads, no cars—just the fantastic wilderness and wildlife for which the park is noted. 30 mins.
VHS: S06699. $29.95.

Touring Alaska

Fascinating view of the uniqueness of Alaska from the wilderness of the great parks to the life of the people in the cities and countryside. Includes cruise information and coastal fjords and glaciers. USA, 56 mins.
VHS: S03325. $29.95.

Touring America's Ghost Towns

This video brings alive 11 of America's deserted ghost towns. It's all here—a collection of anecdotes and history of America's past, gone but never to be forgotten. Ghost towns include Buckskin Joe, CO; Coloma, CA; Virginia City, NV and eight more. USA, 1991, 60 mins.
VHS: S15517. $29.95.

Touring America's Historic Inns

A one-of-a-kind video that features nine very special historic inns that are still in operation in the United States; it also explores the exciting history of each longstanding venue, including the famous people who have visited there. Includes the Beekman Arms in New York and the St. James Hotel in New Mexico. USA, 1992, 60 mins.
VHS: S15518. $29.95.

Touring America's National Parks

A journey through 17 of the nation's greatest natural treasures, including Yellowstone, the Everglades, Mesa Verde, and the Great Smokies. USA, 56 mins.
VHS: S03290. $29.95.

Touring Hawaii

An unusual video that goes beyond the most popular sights to areas seldom seen, such as Waimea Canyon, Wailua River, coral reef diving and Volcanoes National Park. USA, 32 mins.
VHS: S03326. $29.95.

Virginia Plantations—
Mount Vernon, Monticello and
Other Great Houses of Old Virginia

Explores the world of colonial Virginia's great estates, focusing on two of America's most famous homes, George Washington's Mount Vernon, located on the banks of the Potomac, and Thomas Jefferson's mountaintop Monticello. A handful of other historic plantations in Tidewater, Virginia, including Stratford Hall, birthplace of Robert E. Lee, and Sherwood Forest Plantation, are also glimpsed. 30 mins.
VHS: S11124. $19.95.

Virginia's Civil War Parks

From the war's first major battle at Bull Run to the final surrender at Appomattox, Virginia was the arena where North and South fought many of their bloodiest battles. This program gives a full account of the events and visits the battlefields at Manassas, Richmond, Fredericksburg, Chancellorsville, Wilderness, Spotsylvania, Petersburg and Appomattox. 55 mins.
VHS: S10926. $29.95.

Voices from the Ice, Alaska

This is a land still dominated by active glaciers, where you will hear the roar of crashing ice and see the exquisite beauty of a timeless yet constantly changing land. 20 mins.
VHS: S06677. $29.95.

Washington Monuments

Robert Prosky narrates this informative and picturesque tour of our capital's major landmarks, including the White House, the Vietnam War Memorial, the Supreme Court and Library of Congress. 30 mins.
VHS: S08460. $19.95.

Washington, D.C.

Explore Washington's rich heritage, magnificent architecture, historical treasures, and honored memorials and monuments. Tour inside the Smithsonian Museums and the Library of Congress. Visit the White House, the Capitol, the Lincoln and Vietnam Memorials, and much more. 30 mins.
VHS: S06695. $29.95.

Washington, D.C.: An Inspiring Tour

A complete guide to Washington's rich historical heritage, magnificent buildings, national museums, memorials and monuments. 55 mins.
VHS: S10922. $29.95.

Whitewater Adventures

Orange Torpedo Trips. The company that pioneered commercial use of inflatable kayaks on whitewater rivers invites you to command your own kayak on a wild taste of river recreation. *California Whitewater.* Whitewater Voyages handles day trips in California and extended expeditions on other continents. If you're looking for free-reined adventure or a relaxing dream ride, a whitewater vacation is the sure find.
VHS: S15848. $19.95.

Yellowstone & Grand Teton

Discover the wonders and wildlife in two of America's most inspiring parks. Yellowstone, a geological showcase, features the most spectacular geyser field in the world, Old Faithful, and emerald hot pools. 42 mins.
VHS: S06659. $29.95.

Yosemite National Park

60-minute tape shows the parks' popular valley area from a rafting trip down the Merced River to the mighty waterfalls, in spring, fall, and winter. Classical music and natural sounds accompany the scenery.
VHS: S06015. $29.95.

Yosemite—Seasons & Splendor

Finally, a video program equal to the splendor of Yosemite! See unsurpassed scenic beauty and learn of Yosemite's fascinating geological and natural wonders. 40 mins.
VHS: S06662. $29.95.

Yosemite: The Fate of Heaven

Robert Redford narrates this breathtaking look at "the most beautiful valley in the world" on the occasion of Yosemite's 100th anniversary. The amazing natural wonder is seen through the eyes of whose who struggle to preserve it—the rangers, trail builders, fire-fighters and naturalists.
VHS: S12005. $14.98.
Laser: LD71221. $29.95.
Jon Else/John Korty, USA, 1989, 61 mins.

Zion Canyon—Treasure of the Gods

IMAX technology, coupled with Dolby Surround audio, captures the splendor of Zion Canyon and the Southwest. A bird's eye view of this landscape enlivens the tales and myths which were inspired by this majestic scenery. USA, 38 mins.
Laser: LD75008. $39.95.

AIDS

AIDS 101: Tammy Talks with Teenagers
Tammy Boccomino explains exactly how one can and cannot contract HIV. She has been asymptomatic for over 10 years. In this video she is accompanied by Dr. James Jarvis in a discussion format that helps reassure kids even as it informs them how to combat this serious disease. 44 mins.
VHS: S25806. $169.95.

AIDS—What You Need to Know
The Surgeon General's report to the world on AIDS attempts to separate myths from reality in covering the devastating disease. 30 mins.
VHS: S09202. $39.95.

AIDS: A Test of the Nation
AIDS impacts on many of the problems facing women, children and families in America today. This videotape addresses the larger issues of reproductive rights, access to quality health care and the standard of living for many women and children in our society. Produced by Gay Men Health Crisis. 28 mins.
VHS: S11422. $19.95.

AIDS: Allie's Story
Allie Gertz claims she was exposed to HIV from spending one night with a friend. She is a young, heterosexual, who died and who belies all stereotypes about people with AIDS. Before Allie died she urged people to learn from her example. Now her family continues her mission. This ABC 20/20 presentation includes a discussion of the risk faced by college students. 14 mins.
VHS: S25811. $129.95.

AIDS: Alternative Therapies and the Struggle for Legalization
This program examines legalized treatments and alternative therapies and drugs—contrasting their effectiveness—and the government regulation of their use. 76 mins.
VHS: S20152. $29.95.

AIDS: Bleach, Teach and Outreach
The issue of needle exchange in New York City has long been a contentious one. This videotape documents New York City's needle exchange program in its first year. Interviews with representatives of groups such as the Association of Drug Abuse, Prevention and Treatment discuss the issues involved in trying to stem the spread of HIV among intravenous drug users in New York City. Produced by Gay Men Health Crisis. 24 mins.
VHS: S11423. $19.95.

AIDS: Doctors, Liars and Women: AIDS Activists Say "No" to Cosmo
In January 1988, a group of women from the AIDS Coalition to Unleash Power organized a protest against Cosmopolitan magazine for publishing an article that gave seriously misleading information to women about AIDS. Doctors, Liars and Women documents the process of organizing AIDS activists around issues pertinent to women. Produced by Gay Men Health Crisis. 23 mins.
VHS: S11424. $19.95.

AIDS: Everything You Should Know
Whoopi Goldberg joins Dr. Alexander Levine to present the facts about how one can and cannot contract HIV. They also explain how AIDS destroys the body's immune system. 28 mins.
VHS: S25802. $149.95.
Laser: LD75002. $169.95.

AIDS: Prostitutes, Risk and AIDS
Prostitutes are frequently scapegoated as the vectors of HIV transmission. This fallacy is often based upon prejudice that evolves out of stereotypical representations we see in the media. This videotape provides an analysis of these images in the context of sex workers and health care professionals who are actively educating the public about safer sex and IV drug use. Produced by Gay Men Health Crisis. 28 mins.
VHS: S11425. $19.95.

AIDS: PWA Power
A diverse group of people with AIDS/ARC talk about their experiences, giving valuable insight to those recently diagnosed with AIDS. First-person accounts about the birth of the PWA self-empowerment movement are included. Produced by Gay Men Health Crisis.
VHS: S11426. $19.95.

AIDS: Safer Sex Shorts
You can have hot sex without placing yourself at risk for AIDS or other STD's!). A series of erotic and explicit "shorts" combine the driving rhythm of music videos with slick, rapidly edited images, like safer sex advertisements. Scenarios include Something Fierce, a condom demonstration, Midnight Snack featuring oral sex, Car Service, making it in the back seat, Current Flow, safer sex for women who have sex with women, and Law and Order, with some serious S/M. Approximately 25 mins. Produced by Gay Men Health Crisis.
VHS: S11427. $19.95.

AIDS: Seize Control of the FDA
On October 11, 1988 at 7:00 a.m., hundreds of AIDS activists from around the U.S. seized control of the Food and Drug Administration in Rockville, Maryland. This tape documents the action and addresses the issues that motivated this non-violent direct action. Produced by Gay Men Health Crisis. 28 mins.
VHS: S11428. $19.95.

AIDS: What Are the Risks
This program provides a clear explanation of Acquired Immuno-Deficiency Syndrome and various methods of transmission. Social and psychological aspects of this disease are also explored from the perspective of the family and friends of people with AIDS, as well as from the perspectives of PWA's themselves. 30 mins.
VHS: S25814. $144.95.

AIDS: Women and AIDS
"Women take care of everyone, who takes care of women?" Although women have been dying of AIDS since 1981, little attention has been paid to their particular situation. Women and AIDS explores the underlying issues of how AIDS highlights problems such as racism, sexism, child care and lack of adequate health care for women. Produced by Gay Men Health Crisis. 28 mins.
VHS: S11430. $19.95.

AIDS: Work Your Body
The purpose of this video is to help those who are HIV positive, asymptomatic or otherwise, to develop strategies for living with HIV infection. By aggressively pursuing prophylactic treatments and diligently maintaining one's health, an HIV positive person can take steps to prevent the development of AIDS and actively pursue a healthy existence. Produced by Gay Men Health Crisis. 28 mins.
VHS: S11431. $19.95.

Beginnings: You Won't Get AIDS
Animation, live action sequences, songs and the Surgeon General's guidelines about HIV and AIDS are joined in this video, to reassure kids about this serious disease. Nothing that they do on any normal day exposes them to the dangers of this disease. 14 mins.
VHS: S25805. $79.95.
Laser: LD75001. $99.95.

Best of Nightline
AIDS. 30 mins.
VHS: S14027. $14.98.
Rock Hudson Suffers from AIDS. 30 mins.
VHS: S14036. $14.98.
Ryan White. 60 mins.
VHS: S14052. $14.98.

Clean Needles Save Lives
This video documents the illegal efforts of militant activists with ACT-UP and their needle exchange program in New York. The program combines interviews with recovering drug users discussing how to reduce risk and incorporate safer sex practices. 28 mins.
VHS: S18775. $20.00.

Come Sit by Me: AIDS Education
This story by Dr. Margaret Merrifield explores the fears and emotions of young children who learn about AIDS and HIV when a young boy is shunned by his peers. 8 mins.
VHS: S25803. $69.95.

Come Sit by Me: AIDS Education and Thumbs Up for Kids: AIDS Education
This first story is by Dr. Margaret Merrifield. It explores the fears and emotions of young children who learn about AIDS and HIV when a young boy is shunned by his peers. 8 mins. Then former Romper Room teacher Ruby Petersen Unger leads a children's discussion about HIV, AIDS and the transmission of the virus. She introduces an HIV-positive youngster with whom the kids can enjoy playing and whom they can also touch. 23 mins.
Laser: LD75003. $129.95.

Facts About AIDS
This program dispels persistent myths about AIDS. It also stresses the belief that limiting sexual partners can be helpful in avoiding contact. Condoms, spermicides and government findings about AZT therapy and the danger of HIV infection for pregnant women are also discussed. 11 mins.
VHS: S25813. $129.95.

Fear of Disclosure
Phil Zwickler and David Wojnarowicz explore the psychological and social implications of informing a potential lover you are HIV-positive. 5 minutes.
VHS: S18777. $10.00.

Fit!
A landmark exercise video launched by and for gay men, this rigorous exercise program studies the relationship of aerobics and stress reduction movements on the immune system. The program combines a cardiovascular workout with the tenets of yoga and relaxation. 50 mins.
VHS: S18261. $29.95.

Growing Up in the Age of AIDS
This ABC News Special is hosted by Peter Jennings and features leading experts in health and medicine and questions by a studio audience. 75 mins.
VHS: S16088. $19.98.

Hope for the Future: Confronting HIV in Children and Adolescents
Four families recall the pain they felt upon learning their children were HIV-positive. Information about advances in pediatric AIDS and the comfort these stories provide may prove helpful to others. 15 mins.
VHS: S25812. $129.95.

An Informed Approach to HIV Antibody Testing
An informative and sensitive video that considers the personal and social consequences of testing. From the GMHC's Living with AIDS cable program. 22 mins.
VHS: S18774. $20.00.

"It Is What It Is"
An important educational video that discusses teen sexuality, HIV prevention and social isolation, the program is split into three 20-minute segments. The program is accompanied by a discussion guide. "This is the first AIDS education video I've seen that realistically addresses the complex issue of teen sexuality, coming out and AIDS" (Rev. Margaret A. Reinfeld, American Foundation for AIDS Research).
VHS: S18781. $50.00.

Just Say kNOw to AIDS: Abstinence
Teens will learn about HIV and AIDS from doctors and health care experts. Facts are provided by these experts while HIV-positive individuals describe their experiences with the virus. 47 mins.
VHS: S25807. $169.95.

Just Say kNOw to AIDS: Safer Sex
Teens will learn about HIV and AIDS from doctors and health care experts. Facts are provided by these experts while HIV-positive individuals describe their experiences with the virus. 47 mins.
VHS: S25808. $169.95.

Listen Up!
This video provides teenagers with clear information about AIDS. They learn about the difference between HIV and AIDS, methods of transmission, and popular myths spread about the virus. Rap music is provided by Hard Corps. 11 mins.
VHS: S25810. $129.95.

Living Proof
A group of lesbians and gay men dealing with the aftermath of their alcohol and drug addictions speak about the issues related to their communities regarding substance abuse and HIV status in the context of recovery. 28 mins.
VHS: S18779. $20.00.

Living Proof: HIV and the Pursuit of Happiness
Based on Carolyn Jones' photo project of the same name, this documentary follows the lives of subjects seen in that landmark exhibit and book, Living Proof. It will change the way people perceive Persons Living with AIDS, that is, PWAs. Men, women and children show that they have not given up but continue to fight and live.
VHS: S22454. $29.95.
Kermit Cole, USA, 1993, 72 mins.

The Plan (Addictions—HIV)
Robert and Eileen have addictive personalities which make their experiences with HIV helpful for those struggling with both chemical dependency and the HIV virus. This video charts their progress from dependency and denial to recovery, and the struggle with this chronic syndrome caused by HIV. 38 mins.
VHS: S25809. $169.95.

Positive
The New York City gay community's response to the AIDS crisis is powerfully documented in Positive. Rosa von Praunheim has captured the spirit of activism generated by playwright Larry Kramer, musician and co-founder of People With AIDS Coalition (PWA) Michael Callen, and New York filmmaker and journalist Phil Zwickler. They have chosen to act and speak out, refusing to be "AIDS victims." Having neither the time nor the patience to mince words, their groups, like ACT-UP and Queer Nation, demand a response to the epidemic that has threatened to annihilate them. An immensely important historical document.
VHS: S14152. $29.95.
Rosa von Praunheim/Phil Zwickler, USA, 1990, 80 mins.

Positive 20s
Poignant but often humorous, this documentary focuses on a support group for young people dealing with HIV infection. Young people are very much at risk for infection. This documentary offers vital information for everyone. USA, 30 mins.
VHS: S26818. $24.95.

Positive Faith
This documentary tells the story of four avowed Christians who have the HIV virus. One explains how his church reacted to his status. Another relates how a Navy-administered HIV test led to his discharge. One is a survivor since 1979, and the final story belongs to a woman who was infected at age 13. 28 mins.
VHS: S22055. $29.95.

Safer Encounter (Encuentro sin Riesgo)
This is an erotic and explicit video specifically targeted to Latino gay men. It all begins when two sexy men meet at a bar. A variety of techniques are shown that will maker safer sex easier to understand, and just as importantly, a hot time. From New York's Gay Men's Health Crises. 15 mins.
VHS: S19484. $20.00.

Thinking About Death
This program reflects on death, mortality, isolation and loss from multiple perspectives in dealing with the specter of AIDS/HIV and the effects on companions, family and friends. 28 mins.
VHS: S18780. $20.00.

Thumbs Up for Kids: AIDS Education
Former Romper Room teacher Ruby Petersen Unger leads this children's discussion about HIV, AIDS and the transmission of the virus. She introduces an HIV-positive youngster with whom the kids can enjoy playing and whom they can also touch. 23 mins.
VHS: S25804. $79.95.

Time Out— The Truth About HIV, AIDS and You
This educational film about AIDS awareness, prevention, and responsibility stars legendary basketball player Magic Johnson and actor and talk show host Arsenio Hall and was directed by Malcolm-Jamal Warner. Features guest appearances by Paula Abdul, Luke Perry, Jasmine Guy, Tom Cruise, Kirstie Alley and others. 42 mins.
VHS: S17105. $19.95.

Video Against AIDS, Volumes 1, 2 & 3
This series of three programs brings together the response of independent film and video makers to the AIDS crisis. Video against AIDS #1: PWA Power contains Survival of the Delirious by Michael Balser and Andy Fabo, which invokes metaphors from Native American mythology and weaves them into a narrative concerned with the often hallucinatory effect the epidemic has on people living with AIDS (14 mins.) and Work Your Body, produced by the New York City Gay Men's Health Crisis, offering a variety of life-affirming testimonies from HIV antibody positive people. The second section is concerned with discrimination and contains Amber Hollibaugh and Alisa Lebow's Second Epidemic, an informative documentary on discrimination cases negotiated by New York City's Human Rights Commission through the lives of two people living with AIDS. AIDS and Women contains several works: Safe Sex Slut, a pro-safe sex education reminder from Carol Leigh, a member of the activist prostitutes group, COYOTE; Cori: A Struggle for Life (18 mins.), which recounts the heroic battle of one woman to care for her baby daughter who has been infected with AIDS from a blood transfusion; and Jean Carlomusto and Maria Maggenti's Doctors, Liars and Women: AIDS Activists Say No to Cosmo (23 mins.), which documents the angry protest made against Cosmopolitan magazine by women from AIDS Coalition to Unleash Power, a protest against the magazine for publishing dangerously misleading information concerning the risk of AIDS to women. Video against AIDS #2: The three sections of this program are titled Resistance, Mourning and Community Education. Canadian producer John Greyson's The AIDS Epidemic adopts a music-video format to preach against "ADS"—acquired dread of sex. Barbara Hammer's Snow Job—The Media Hysteria of AIDS (8 mins.) critiques the representation of AIDS in the popular press, where the distortions amount to a "snow job" that justifies the continuation of society's practices of homophobia and sexual discrimination. In We are NOT Republicans Adam Hassuk and Robert Huff document the disruption of the 1988 Republican presidential convention by AIDS activists; Stiff Sheets, produced by John Goss, similarly indicts public officials and politicians for lack of adequate and humane care of AIDS patients in Los Angeles by documenting a mock fashion show staged by ACT UP activists. Mildred Pearson: When You Love a Person recounts a mother's dedication to her son when she learns he is gay and gravely ill from AIDS; The Inaugural Display of the Names Project Quilt commemorates the unparalleled public memorial when the Quilt's first 1,920 panels (one for each person dead from AIDS) were unfolded in Washington, D.C. Danny (20 mins.), is a heartfelt and complex commemoration of a young man: the stages of Danny's illness are visualized as he discusses his life, his family, and the disease. Set Met Ko, by Patricia Benoit, is a model fictional analysis of attitudes and misconceptions about AIDS within a Haitian-American neighborhood. Video against AIDS #3: The three sections of this program deal with Loss, Analysis and Activism. Emjay Wilson's A Plague Has Swept My City is an associate evocation of the fear and confusion generated by the epidemic. Ann Akiko Moriyasu's Gab focuses on a dear friend who died of AIDS; Andre Burke's A intricately weaves layers of sound and image to question the threat to sexual desire and identity posed by AIDS. British producer Isaac Julien's This Is Not an AIDS Advertisement offers a lyrical and meditative celebration of life and sexuality. Tom Kalin's They Are Lost to Vision Altogether is a poetic retaliation against right-wing homophobia and anti-AIDS hysteria; Pratibha Parmar's Reframing AIDS offers a wide-ranging global analysis of the AIDS epidemic. Youth Against Monsterz' Another Man is a short retort to the Jerry Falwells of the world; Testing the Limits, produced by the collective of the same name, documents the range of activist responses to the AIDS crisis. Set of three tapes, produced by the Video Data Bank.
VHS: S16265. $150.00.

What Ramon Did
Esai Morales leads an all-star cast in this drama about a Latino and former IV drug user who returns home. The film begins at a wedding and goes on to explore the feelings of fear and pain that are caused by the lead character's HIV status within his community. Also features an information segment featuring former U.S. Surgeon General C. Everett Koop. 30 mins.
VHS: S25815. $149.95.

SCIENCE

Bell Science: About Time
Dr. Frank Baxter talks about the importance of time. Did you know ships couldn't find their way around without an accurate timepiece and that our clocks are set to the Earth's rotation? These and other amazing facts are revealed in this Technicolor animated short written and directed by Frank Capra and Jack Warner. USA, 53 mins.
VHS: S14940. $19.95.

Bell Science: Hemo the Magnificent
Peabody Award-winning professor Dr. Frank Baxter, with the help of a few animated characters and some microscopic photography, takes us on a tour of the body's amazing plumbing system, featuring the most powerful and mysterious muscle, your heart. Animation by Shamus Culhane. Filmed in Technicolor. Directed by Frank Capra and Jack Warner. USA, 54 mins.
VHS: S14939. $19.95.

Bell Science: Our Mr. Sun
This educational film, written and directed by Frank Capra, explores the mysteries of the most important star in the universe—detailing the significance the sun has played throughout history. Enlightening entertainment. 1959, 60 mins.
VHS: S13925. $19.95.

Bell Science: The Alphabet Conspiracy
Along with Doctor Frank C. Baxter and the animation of Friz Freleng, you'll explore the roots of language, how sounds are made, and even how animals communicate. An enjoyable look at the basics of communication. 1956, 60 mins.
VHS: S13924. $19.95.

Bell Science: Thread of Life
Peabody Award-winning professor Dr. Frank Baxter helps unravel how heredity and environment help shape our looks, in this mixture of animation and microscope time-lapse photography. Produced by Jack Warner. USA, 52 mins.
VHS: S15090. $19.95.

Birth of the Lamaze Method
Lamaze, a French physician, developed his method after observing the breathing techniques used by Soviet women preparing for delivery. This amazing film goes right to the source, providing insight into the same birthing techniques that so impressed Dr. Lamaze. 50 mins.
VHS: S12726. $19.98.

Body Atlas Boxed Set

New techniques reveal the interior of the body and all its amazing abilities. Everything is visible, including muscle, bone, skin, the respiratory system, glands and hormones, the senses, the brain, the heart and the reproductive system. This series of six videos was first screened by the Learning Channel.
VHS: S25836. $149.95.

Brain Sex

Are men and women really different? Provocative new research offers intriguing evidence that gender differences may actually result from physical differences at the level of the mind. This documentary explores some of the latest research in this area and its weighty implications. Three-volume set, 135 mins.
VHS: S26052. $39.95.

The Brain

Amazing images of the human brain at work and investigations of the brain's mysterious powers in a unique, 3-volume set.
Vol. 1: Evolution & Perception. Travel to the dawn of time and explore the texture of thought of our remote ancestors.
VHS: S23011. $19.95.
Vol. 2: Memory/Miraculous Mind. True tales of damaged brains reveal the intricacies of memory and the remarkable ability of the brain to recover and function.
VHS: S23012. $19.95.
Vol. 3: Matter over Mind. Consciousness, creativity, the emotions, our sense of self—are these all products of biochemistry? Science explores the role of the neurotransmitter serotonin.
VHS: S23013. $19.95.
The Brain, Complete Set. Deluxe boxed set of three volumes.
VHS: S23014. $49.95.

The Building Blocks of Life

Clones and genetic engineering, biogenic industries as growth stocks: clearly the age of the computer is giving way to the age of genetics. As a result, *Cell Structure I* and *II* offer an exciting package, anticipating tomorrow's headlines as they examine the basic unit of all life, the cell, of which there are 60 trillion in a single human body.
VHS: S03988. $64.95.

Cellular Automata

A video demonstration, with award-winning science writer Rudy Rucker, of the popular CA Lab cellular automata software. Rapidfire images of hallucinatory beauty. 30 mins.
VHS: S13896. $29.95.

Death: The Trip of a Lifetime

The original PBS series is an odyssey in search of life's profound mystery. Greg Palmer hosts this look at how human cultures respond to the universal experience of death. A unique and compelling aspect of *Death: The Trip of a Lifetime* is Palmer's use of humor interspersed with pathos. Four one-hour programs make up the series.
Going for Glory.
VHS: S20478. $29.95.
Letting Go.
VHS: S20477. $29.95.
The Chasm.
VHS: S20475. $29.95.
The Good Death.
VHS: S20476. $29.95.
Death: The Trip of a Lifetime, Set. The four-volume set.
VHS: S20479. $99.95.

Dinosaur!

Walter Cronkite hosts this four-part series that's part travelogue, part detective story, interweaving state-of-the-art graphics, animation and astonishing special visual effects to explore the dinosaurs.
Birth of a Legend—Tale of an Egg.
VHS: S18769. $19.95.
Giant Birds of the Air—Tale of a Feather.
VHS: S18770. $19.95.
The First Clue—Tale of a Tooth.
VHS: S18767. $19.95.
The Fossil Rush—Tale of a Bone.
VHS: S18768. $19.95.
Dinosaur! Boxed set of four tapes, or one laser disc. 200 mins.
VHS: S18771. $69.95.
Laser: LD70226. $69.95.

Disney Presents Bill Nye the Science Guy: Dinosaurs, Those Big Boneheads

What large ferocious creatures are loved by every kid on the planet? Dinosaurs of course, and Bill Nye is just the guy to explain to kids the science behind these prehistoric creatures. In-home experiments and special guests help make this another kid-pleasing science adventure. 47 mins.
VHS: S22337. $12.99.

Disney Presents Bill Nye the Science Guy: Outer Space Way Out There

Kids love the puns, jokes and cool science facts that Bill Nye tells. This video is so way out, it's stratospheric. Bill presents the hard science on outer space in an MTV like format with in-home experiments and special guests. 47 mins.
VHS: S22336. $12.99.

Disney Presents Bill Nye the Science Guy: The Human Body

Bill will take kids on a journey to the inner most parts of the human body. There is no more fun way to explore the cardiovascular system or the nervous system. 47 mins.
VHS: S22338. $12.99.

Emergency: Health Care in America— A National Town Meeting

Host Ted Koppel travels to Chicago to discuss the growing problems pointing to the lack of a nationwide comprehensive health care plan. A panel of experts field questions raised by members of a studio audience. 120 mins.
VHS: S16796. $29.98.

Expansion of Life

Discover the chain of life with this look at the evolutionary spiral. Begin with single-cell life and progress to invertebrates, fish, amphibians, reptiles then finally explore primates and modern man. 59 mins.
VHS: S03987. $64.95.

Forces of Life

Here is a four-part study of the essential properties which make up our physical universe. Considered in turn are the *Origin of the Elements, Chemical Change,* the *Origin of Rocks and Mountains* and the dynamics of *Magnetism and Electricity.* This group of films represents a primer for physical science studies.
VHS: S03989. $64.95.

The Great Quake of '89

Produced by ABC News Interactive and hosted by anchor Diane Sawyer, this program investigates the phenomenal destructive capacities of earthquakes, studying the 1989 Loma Prieta earthquake that hit Northern California and the 1906 San Francisco quake.
Laser: LD70112. $49.95.

The Greatest Adventure

NASA footage helps reconstruct the history of space exploration that culminated in the 1969 landing on the moon. From the invention of liquid fuel and Werner Von Braun's experiments with rockets all the way to Neil Armstrong's big step for mankind, the history of scientific discovery is revealed. Narrated by Orson Welles. 54 mins.
VHS: S21098. $14.98.

Heart to Heart: The Truth About Heart Disease

Heart disease is the number one killer of both men and women. This video reveals the facts and disproves the fictions about this silent killer.
VHS: S25007. $14.95.

The Infinite Voyage: Life in Balance

Part of the acclaimed science series. Would you indiscriminately destroy your own home? Undoubtedly, the answer is no. But that is precisely what mankind is doing to Earth. The long-term effects of our disturbances to the ecosystem are unknown, but some researchers say they could be deadly. This program explores the many ways humans of the 20th century are altering evolution. 58 mins.
VHS: S14993. $14.98.

The Infinite Voyage: Miracles by Design

This program studies the personal repercussions of how breakthroughs in science impact our daily lives. 58 mins.
VHS: S19203. $14.98.

The Infinite Voyage: The Champion Within

Part of the acclaimed science series. Explore exercise and physiology to discover the reasons some bodies gain or lose abilities, the mysteries of performance levels, and the impact of aging. Using athletes as living laboratories, scientists are making important discoveries that may affect your life in some unexpected ways. 58 mins.
VHS: S14992. $14.98.

The Infinite Voyage: To the Edge of the Earth

Part of the acclaimed science series. Go with scientists to five far-flung locations where they are using the latest tools to answer some of the planet's oldest questions. Their discoveries could impact how we treat fragile ecosystems in years to come. 58 mins.
VHS: S14994. $14.98.

An Interview with David Bohm: Quantum Physics and Philosophy

David Bohm is a brilliant physicist who blends physics with philosophy. He sees the universe as an undivided wholeness which can only be comprehended with capabilities beyond rational thought. Intuition, insight and intelligence are the human faculties which can grant one experience of this wholeness. 52 mins.
VHS: S26717. $29.95.

Life on Earth

A natural history written and hosted by David Attenborough—a four hour program on two cassettes. This video encyclopedia spans in detail the complete story of evolution, was filmed in over 100 locations in more than 30 countries, and features amazing wildlife photography. Produced by the BBC. 225 mins.
VHS: S03285. $39.95.

Lifesense

The actual perception of animal senses is beautifully transposed in this award-winning documentary from the BBC. Now people can understand how a host of animals, from the average dog to microscopic parasites, view the world and human beings. 175 mins.
VHS: S26033. $39.98.

Machine Dreams

This wide-ranging film explores mankind's love affair with the machine. From a Marilyn Monroe robot to artificial intelligence, this film traces the enduring fascination and obsession that drives innovation in robotics, cybertechnology and supercomputers.
VHS: S14150. $59.95.
Peter Krieg, Germany, 1989, 87 mins.

Metamorphosis

Rupert Sheldrake, the originator of theory on morphogenetic fields; Ralph Abraham, a mathematics expert on chaos, and Terence McKenna, a shamanologist and ethno-pharmacologist, debate the relationship between chaos, creativity and imagination in this expansive video seminar. 88 mins.
VHS: S26180. $29.95.

Michael Idvorsky Pupin

Pupin became one of the most widely respected mathematicians of his time. His inventions in the field of X-rays continue to shape this enduring technology. Born in a village near Belgrade, the story of his emigration to the U.S. and his education both here and in Europe became the subject of his Pulitzer-Prize winning autobiography. This documentary traces the trajectory of this amazing individual.
VHS: S21538. $24.95.

Miracle of Life

An incredible voyage through the human body as a new life begins. With magnification of up to half a million times, the video actually documents what happens at the moment of conception, and follows the development of the embryo, fetus, and finally, birth. 60 mins.
VHS: S04355. $19.95.
Laser: LD70302. $75.00.

The Miracle Planet

A six-part series on the mysteries and beauty of the planet. "Serious science delivered like jewels of knowledge amid images and music that create an epic experience" (*Seattle Post Intelligence*). Narrated by Bill Kurtis.
Life from the Sea. This episode looks at the beauty, depth and size of the blue oceans that cover two thirds of the planet. 60 mins.
VHS: S18235. $29.95.
Patterns in the Air. This program considers the formation of the ozone layer, the emergence of plants and wildlife and the impact of the atmosphere on the life and nature of the planet. 60 mins.
VHS: S18236. $29.95.
Riddles of Sand and Ice. This video looks at the extreme changes in climate. It notes how tropical plants once grew at the South Pole and considers whether these vast changes in temperature and climate might strike again. 60 mins.
VHS: S18237. $29.95.
The Heat Within. This program explores the heat the earth releases from its interior, responsible for breaking continents and the vast mineral deposits. 60 mins.
VHS: S18234. $29.95.
The Home Planet. This program considers the value systems and efforts of humans to safeguard and protect the resources of the planet. 60 mins.
VHS: S18238. $29.95.
The Third Planet. Craters represent the unknown clues about collisions with meteorites. Can we unlock the mystery about the disappearance of the dinosaurs? 60 mins.
VHS: S18233. $29.95.
The Miracle Planet, Set. "A stellar series" (*Booklist*). 360 mins.
VHS: S19379. $149.95.

National Geographic Video

The National Geographic Society has always been renowned for their award-winning television specials; now these great programs are available on home video! 60 minutes each.
Miniature Miracle: The Computer Chip. With the help of computers and robots, medical science, aviation and the arts have made tremendous breakthroughs. This fascinating National Geographic special takes a look at what has made it possible: the tiny computer chip.
VHS: S03054. $19.95.
The Incredible Human Machine. Go on a fantastic journey through the inner world of the human body and see, through sophisticated microcamera techniques, the microscopic world inside us.
VHS: S02008. $14.95.

Nikola Tesla: The Genius Who Lit the World

Tesla was the amazing Serbian inventor who emigrated from the Balkans to the US just before the turn of the century. His inventions include fluorescent light, the laser beam, wireless communication, wireless transmission of electricity and—perhaps his greatest achievement—alternating current. This biography is a tribute to his ingenuity.
VHS: S21537. $24.95.

Nova—Adventures in Science: Hurricane!

Follow scientists into the eye of the world's most deadly storms in this amazing documentary. Between walls of hurling clouds ten miles high lies a valley of clear blue sky. First-hand accounts of Hurricane Camille, the most destructive storm to ever strike the United States, and of Hurricane Gilbert, one of the worst hurricanes ever, round out his absorbing look at these powerful weather systems.
VHS: S26910. $19.95.
Larry Engel/Thomas Lucas, USA, 1989, 60 mins.

Nova—Adventures in Science: In Search of Human Origins

Three episodes (*The Story of Lucy, Surviving in Africa* and *The Creative Revolution*) from *Nova* tell the story of the evolutionary past of humanity. From the growth of sexual politics to the birth of technology, all purportedly had a significant impact on the growth of human beings. Three-tape set. Each episode is 60 mins.
VHS: S27325. $59.85.

Nova—Adventures in Science: Making of a Doctor

Beneath the skin of every person is a miraculous world, one explored in this three-part series. *Miracle of Life* starts the series, exploring conception and continuing to follow the progress of a fetus through its wondrous development. In *Universe Within,* a tour of the human body via micro-photography is on offer, while the final installment, *What's New About Menopause,* explores the possibilities and controversies surrounding technological developments that can postpone or even reverse the effects of menopause.
VHS: S27098. $19.95.

Nova—Adventures in Science: Mystery of the Senses

This five-part series explores the five senses through a variety of intriguing segments. From the quietest place on earth, to one of the most fragrant, the five senses shape our perceptions of the world around us. This video shows the richness of the sensual environment.
VHS: S27327. $69.95.

Nova—Adventures in Science: Tornado!

Over one thousand tornadoes, some travelling as fast as 70 miles an hour, occur in the United States every year. The inside of these dynamos can reach 300 miles an hour. *Nova* follows a "chase team": scientists who track these storms.
VHS: S26911. $19.95.
Larry Engel/Thomas Lucas, USA, 1985, 60 mins.

Nova—Earthquake

"Only fools, charlatans and liars predict earthquakes..." This exciting analysis challenges an age-old expression in in-depth accounts of possible future predictions of the world's most frightening natural disaster. 1991, 60 mins.
VHS: S16818. $14.98.

Nova—The Science of Murder

Statistics say there will be two murders in this country in the next hour. NOVA attempts to find out why we kill ten times more often in the United States than in any other so-called civilized nation in the world. America's medical detectives take on a disturbing case and tell who done it and who will become another statistic. 60 mins.
VHS: S07580. $29.98.

Nova—The Universe Within

This video takes viewers on a journey through the human body. Microscopic photography and stunning graphics make this invisible realm visible.
VHS: S24879. $19.95.

Nova—What's New About Menopause?

New research has transformed our understanding of this stage in the aging process. Now controversy brews as scientists enable women to postpone menopause or even to bear children long after its onset.
VHS: S24876. $19.95.

Nova—Wonders of Plastic Surgery

The techniques of medicine's miracle workers are examined in this fascinating Nova series program. 60 mins.
VHS: S09819. $14.98.

Origin of Life (& Scopes Footage)

Evolution and *Beginnings of Life* start with Darwinian Theory and go on to illustrate the different stages of animal and human development from the beginnings of fossil history. As an update for the contemporary controversy, actual footage of the Scopes Trial with Clarence Darrow and William Jennings Bryan from the Rohauer Collection is included.
VHS: S03773. $64.95.

Origins of Man: Complete Set

Both *Retracing Man's Steps* and *The Big Bang and Beyond* at a special discount.
VHS: S20536. $49.95.

Origins of Man: Retracing Man's Steps

From fossils and bones, paleontologists have pieced together a family tree of man's ancestors. This program follows the rise of symbolic thinking and the development of speech from gestural language in an attempt to trace man's efforts to adapt in the journey of *Homo sapiens.* 33 mins.
VHS: S20534. $29.95.

Origins of Man: The Big Bang and Beyond

An examination of how life began, this program looks at five billion years of evolution in an attempt to understand the structure of the universe. The key to its survival may lie in avoiding the threat from man's own cultural evolution—tool-making, symbolic thought and adaptability. 30 mins.
VHS: S20535. $29.95.

Planet Earth: 7-Volume Boxed Set

Various aspects of the wondrous planet we call home are explored in this inventive and fascinating Emmy Award-winning series. Everything from the conundrums of climate to the Earth's position in the cosmos to the fate of this blue planet are discussed in depth in these videos. Each tape is approximately one hour. Narrated by Richard Kiley. 403 mins.
VHS: S27326. $99.98.

Reproduction of Life

Reproduction of Life tastefully and scientifically presents the entire process of human reproduction from conception through prenatal development to birth itself. With *Kittens Are Born,* younger viewers learn first-hand about birth and are helped to develop an enlightened and positive attitude toward the natural phenomenon.
VHS: S03993. $64.95.

Science Primer

These special science programs help children understand the five senses, the animal world and the four elements that compose matter. Designed for children from kindergarten through 3rd grade.
Earth, Air, Water, Fire. From ancient civilization, the four basic elements make up matter. This video helps children understand the elements of the world they inhabit. 19 mins.
VHS: S19955. $49.95.
The Five Senses. The five senses are called the "windows of the world," which process signals to the brain and keep us attuned to our environment. This program helps children understand the feelings and information their senses convey. 27 mins.
VHS: S19956. $49.95.
Habitats. Children are introduced to the habitat of plants and animals. The program studies plants and animals in their natural environments, above and below ground, in the sea and in the air. 35 mins.
VHS: S19957. $49.95.
Science Primer, Set. A collection of three programs. 110 mins.
VHS: S19958. $129.00.

Secrets of the Code
The magic of the genetic code is explained through animated graphics. This video explains how different codes make each species and each individual different.
VHS: S23271. $34.95.

Shape of the World Set
A six-tape educational set about cartography, or mapping, from ancient civilization to contemporary times. These "sophisticated, well-edited programs combine exploration, science, religion [and] math" (*Booklist*). 360 mins.
VHS: S19380. $149.95.

Smithsonian World
A broad intellectual journey into history, science, nature and travel, following the aims and principles of the Smithsonian Institute. The series is a kaleidoscopic and impressionistic account of scientific and technological accomplishment which examines different relations—man to society, the individual to art, and social and cultural movements and their historical context.
Smithsonian World: A Desk in the Jungle. A sympathetic and thrilling document about scientists who specialize in idiosyncratic and quirky subject matter, going beyond traditional science. 60 mins.
VHS: S19194. $14.98.
Smithsonian World: Crossing the Distance. This program studies compelling achievements in science, art and technology and the determination and will of the people responsible. 54 mins.
VHS: S19197. $14.98.
Smithsonian World: Designs for Living. This work looks at man's resourcefulness and valor and his ability to adapt to wildly disparate events, situations and demands. 52 mins.
VHS: S19199. $14.98.
Smithsonian World: On the Shoulders of Giants. This program traces the practices and methods of a scientific sleuth. 58 mins.
VHS: S19193. $14.98.
Smithsonian World: Speaking without Words. A new means of expression and communication are created through universal sounds, signs and languages. 58 mins.
VHS: S19195. $14.98.
Smithsonian World: The Last Flower. This documentary examines the painstaking efforts of scientists and activists to devise measures to save vanishing or extinct treasures. 55 mins.
VHS: S19198. $14.98.

Surviving the Big One: How to Prepare for a Major Earthquake
Host Henry Johnson provides a detailed guide to preparing for a major earthquake. The program also provides coping strategies for the difficult weeks after the first major shockwaves.
VHS: S16395. $19.95.

Understanding Science
This series explains basic scientific principles using clear diagrams and easy-to-follow instructions. Children will be led through fascinating demonstrations that demystify the wonders of science.
Understanding Science, Vol. 1: Scientific Problem Solving. This video explains the correct procedures for solving a quandary the scientific way. A simple experiment is demonstrated that can be easily recreated in the classroom. Lab safety procedures are also presented. 17 mins.
VHS: S22142. $39.95.
Understanding Science, Vol. 2: Matter. Matter's physical and general properties are defined and described in this video. Phase transformations, including gas laws, are included. 22 mins.
VHS: S22143. $39.95.
Understanding Science, Vol. 3: Energy. Dr. Science explains heat energy, how it moves, what substances conduct it, and its relationship to temperature. The wave model is also discussed. 22 mins.
VHS: S22144. $39.95.
Understanding Science, Vol. 4: Ecosystems. Six biomes are compared, with explanations of how plants and animals disperse and interact. The cycles and rhythms of all living things are the focus of this volume.
VHS: S22145. $39.95.
Understanding Science, Vol. 5: Classification of Living Things. The kingdoms which define living organisms are discussed, including the evolutionary adaptations that affect Monera, Protista and Fungi.
VHS: S22146. $39.95.
Understanding Science, Vol. 6: Weather Systems. Weather patterns, atmospheric factors, heat transfers and global wind patterns are all explained in this episode. A historical overview presents the evolution of weather over the course of global climactic change.
VHS: S22147. $39.95.
The Series of Six Volumes.
VHS: S22148. $239.70.

The Video Encyclopedia of Psychoactive Drugs
Scientists, law enforcement agents, counselors, drug historians and professors are brought together in this comprehensive 10-volume set. It provides the most up-to-date information on drug education available. Each volume is 30 mins.
Alcohol and Alcoholism.
VHS: S24473. $39.95.
Alcohol: Teenage Drinking.
VHS: S24474. $39.95.
Amphetamines: Danger in the Fast Lane.
VHS: S24475. $39.95.
Barbiturates: Sleeping Potion or Intoxicant?
VHS: S24476. $39.95.
Cocaine and Crack: The New Epidemic.
VHS: S24477. $39.95.
Heroin: The Street Narcotic.
VHS: S24478. $39.95.
Marijuana: Its Effects on Mind and Body.
VHS: S24479. $39.95.
Nicotine: An Old-Fashioned Addiction.
VHS: S24480. $39.95.
Prescription Narcotics: The Addictive Painkillers.
VHS: S24481. $39.95.
Teenage Depression and Suicide.
VHS: S24482. $39.95.
The Video Encyclopedia of Psychoactive Drugs. The complete 10-volume set.
VHS: S24483. $399.50.

Viruses and Bacteria: The Story of the Warm Wet Spots
Educator and TV personality Ruby Peterson explains how germs cause disease. She shows how the body's interior can nurture and fight off disease. Humor, popular music, demonstrations and computer graphics makes this educational video easy to understand. 21 mins.
VHS: S25801. $149.95.

World Population
This program is a striking depiction of actual population growth from 1 A.D. to the present and of projected future growth to the year 2020. The visual presentation makes the statistical information exciting and easily understood. 1990, 7 mins.
VHS: S13939. $29.95.

Your Family's Health
This series examines some broad, important areas of health, in easy-to-understand language, through six steps. It explores relations between doctors and patients, over-the-counter medicine, headaches, stress, sports injuries and preventative medicine.
Tape 1. This program includes *How to Talk to Your Doctor* and *Over-the-Counter Medicines.* The first segment talks the viewer through appropriate use of the medical system, while the second segment clarifies the many medications available to non-professionals. 53 mins.
VHS: S24921. $29.95.
Tape 2. *Dealing with Headaches* offers practical advice on these common and paralyzing maladies. *Stress* is about a widespread condition that can be alleviated with a variety of techniques. 54 mins.
VHS: S24922. $29.95.
Tape 3. *Kids, Parents, and Sports* addresses the pros and cons of youth sports with expertise provided by coaches and professional athletes. *Preventing Injuries* talks about common sense and risk-taking before outlining preventative measures in five areas. 52 mins.
VHS: S24923. $29.95.
Three-Tape Set.
VHS: S24929. $75.00.

MATHEMATICS

Child's Play Video Flash Cards—Math
An innovative new series of video programs designed to help students learn mathematics, combining basic instructional methods with high tech. The programs are designed to enable students to master the fundamentals of addition, subtraction, multiplication and division. Each program is divided into a training, reinforcement and drill segment. The programs were specifically developed for elementary school students, grades 2-6, and all four programs are available in English and Spanish versions.
Addition (English).
VHS: S06282. $11.95.
Addition (Spanish).
VHS: S06283. $11.95.
Multiplication (English).
VHS: S06284. $11.95.
Multiplication (Spanish).
VHS: S06285. $11.95.
Subtraction (English).
VHS: S06286. $11.95.
Subtraction (Spanish).
VHS: S06287. $11.95.
Division (English).
VHS: S06288. $11.95.
Division (Spanish).
VHS: S06289. $11.95.

Consumer Math
A program for understanding math and its practical applications, including Decimals, Fractions and Percents in the home and business, banking, budgeting, insurance, taxes, profits, discounts, commissions and investments. Study guide included. 120 mins.
VHS: S17478. $39.95.

Expecting Miracles
Four couples candidly explore their problems with infertility over a three year period. A look at the medical processes and techniques doctors use to help increase the chances of having a child. 60 mins.
VHS: S16392. $39.95.

Intermediate Algebra
These videos instruct students in rational numbers, rational expressions, real numbers and radicals, relations and functions, exponential functions, logarithmic functions and quadratic equations. Three-tape set, 360 mins.
VHS: S17479. $119.95.

Math Primer
Lollipop Dragon and Box teach kids important lessons and theories about math and numbers, offering practical instruction on the numbers 0-9, including the concept of a number line, how to understand coins and bills and how to read and set different clocks and watches. Designed for kindergarten through 3rd grade.
Box Introduces Numbers. Students learn how numbers represent a specific quantity, and are given illustrated examples of numerals 0-9 for practical usage and better understanding. 27 mins.
VHS: S19948. $60.95.
Money and Time Adventures of the Lollipop Dragon—I. This important video instructs children about money-counting skills and techniques, explaining the value of dollars and cents. 34 mins.
VHS: S19946. $60.95.
Money and Time Adventures of the Lollipop Dragon—II. Time-skills lessons and exercises show young viewers how to correctly tell time in hours, half-hours and minutes. The program also discusses the proper ways to use time. 34 mins.
VHS: S19947. $60.95.
Math Primer, Set. A set of three programs about number systems and practical applications. 85 mins.
VHS: S19949. $159.00.

Math...Who Needs It?
Meet the famous calculus teacher Jaime Escalante (who inspired the film *Stand and Deliver*), some of his students, plus Bill Cosby, Dizzy Gillespie and other guest celebrities, in this TV special. Ages 8<FT130>+. 60 minutes.
VHS: S24980. $19.95.

Mathematics Series
Instructors guide these comprehensive video review courses, which can be used either in the classroom or studied independently.
Arithmetic Review. 120 mins.
VHS: S08755. $39.95.
Calculus I. 2 tape set, 240 mins.
VHS: S08760. $79.95.
Calculus II. 2 tape set, 240 mins.
VHS: S08761. $79.95.
Decimals. 120 mins.
VHS: S08757. $39.95.
Elementary Algebra. Ten comprehensive lessons, in a 3 tape, 360-minute set.
VHS: S08759. $159.95.
Fractions. 2 tape set, 240 mins.
VHS: S08756. $79.95.
Percents. 120 mins.
VHS: S08758. $39.95.
Probability. 2 tape set, 240 mins.
VHS: S08762. $79.95.
Statistics. 2 tape set, 240 mins.
VHS: S08763. $119.95.

Pre-Calculus
A preparation video on the prerequisites of the more difficult calculus courses. Topics considered are theory of equations, transcendental functions, polar coordinates, conics, sequences, series, matrix algebra and determinants. Study guide included. Four-tape set, 480 mins.
VHS: S17481. $159.95.

Trigonometry
This program details problems and examples of trigonometric functions, graphs, applications, equations and identities. Two-tape set, 240 mins.
VHS: S17480. $79.95.

SPACE EXPLORATION

1st Flight of the Space Shuttle—STS-1
This documentary lets you re-live the historic maiden voyage of Shuttle Columbia. Includes a comprehensive overview of the shuttle program and its technology. 30 mins.
VHS: S06702. $29.95.

America in Space: The First 25 Years
This is NASA's best. 25 years of history-making space exploration compressed into one dynamic program. From the 1958 Explorer 1 launch to the Shuttle Challenger STS-7 flight—and everything in-between—it's all here for you to enjoy. 50 mins.
VHS: S06708. $29.95.

Apollo 13—The Untold Story
Genuine footage of the disastrous Apollo 13 space mission gives this video documentary an incredibly immediate feeling. Interviews with the astronauts who were aboard the completely sealed spacecraft and the engineers on the ground convey not just the facts, but the feelings of those involved. Billy Mumy, from *Lost In Space*, hosts. 50 mins.
VHS: S26374. $19.95.

The Apollo Legacy
Beginning with the Apollo space missions, this video explores where that legacy of space exploration will lead. Japan, Russia and the United States all have the commitment to continue exploring our solar system. Inhabited space stations and even peopled missions to Mars lie in the not too distant future. 45 mins.
VHS: S26762. $14.98.

The Astronomers: Collector's Set
We have learned more about the universe in the last ten years than we have in the last several centuries combined; this series imparts that recently discovered knowledge. Narrated by acclaimed actor Richard Chamberlain, *The Astronomers* was produced with the largest grant ever for a single identical TV series, and it took over five years to complete. This collector's edition includes all six of the fascinating programs in the popular PBS series. 360 mins. Six videocassettes.
VHS: Out of print. For rental only.
Laser: LD70845. $124.95.

The Billion Dollar Image
The Viking Spacecraft has landed on Mars. Capture the joy and excitement of those who watched as the space craft sent back its first revealing photographs of the Martian landscape. Includes interviews with famous visionaries, including Ray Bradbury, Carl Sagan and others. 30 mins.
VHS: S06678. $19.95.

Blue Planet
Using photographic evidence collected by astronauts on five space shuttle missions, *Blue Planet* is a breathtaking view of Earth from deep space. The program also examines the ecological issues that shape the Earth's future. "A stunning look at our planet as a living being—beautiful, volatile and extremely vulnerable" (*The Washington Post*). 42 mins.
VHS: S19741. $39.95.
Laser: LD71942. $39.95.

Blueprint for Space
This program charts the evolution of spaceflight, focusing on the visionaries and dreamers who designed, developed and paved the way for space travel. The film merges paintings, archival footage and computer animation to examine the earliest conceptions, such as ancient Chinese rockets and today's scientific breakthroughs. Narrated by astronaut Alan Shepard. 58 mins.
VHS: S19740. $24.95.

Conquest
A thrilling look at man's shining achievements in space. See how the dream of traveling to the moon was realized by scientists as we trace back to World War II planning and progress, to modern day technology. 180 mins.
VHS: S12735. $59.98.

Contact UFO: Alien Abductions
First in a series dedicated to evidence regarding UFOs, *Alien Abductions* reveals theories from a number of leading experts, including Boston Planetarium astronomer Walter Webb, *Intruders and Missing Time* author Budd Hopkins, Center for UFO Studies President Mark Rodeghier and Betty Hill, a UFO abductee. 90 mins.
VHS: S16201. $19.95.
Laser: CLV. LD74642. $29.98.

Cosmos 1: The Shores of the Cosmic Ocean
On the first leg of this awe-inspiring cosmic journey, *Cosmos* host Dr. Carl Sagan takes viewers to the edge of the universe aboard the spaceship of the Imagination. Through beautiful (and accurate) special effects, we witness quasars, exploding galaxies, star clusters, super novas, and pulsars, and returning to the Solar System, enter an astonishing recreation of the Alexandrian Library, the seat of learning on earth 2000 years ago.
VHS: S10691. $19.98.

Cosmos 2: One Voice in the Cosmic Fugue
Dr. Sagan's Cosmic Calendar makes the 15-billion-year history of the universe understandable and frames the origin of earth and the evolution of life, from microbes to humans. Our understanding of how life developed on earth enables us to venture to other worlds for imaginative speculations on what forms life might take elsewhere.
VHS: S10692. $19.98.

Cosmos 3: The Harmony of the Worlds
Historical re-creation of the life and times of Johannes Kepler, the last scientific astrologer, the first modern astronomer, and the author of the first science fiction novel. Kepler provided the insight into how the moon and the planets move in their orbits and ultimately how to journey to them.
VHS: S10693. $19.98.

Cosmos 4: Heaven and Hell
A descent through the hellish atmosphere of Venus to explore the broiling surface serves as a warning for our world about the possible consequences of the greenhouse effect. Then Dr. Sagan leads viewers on a tour of the Solar System to see how other heavenly bodies have suffered from various cosmic catastrophes.
VHS: S10694. $19.98.

Cosmos 5: Blues for a Red Planet
Is there life on Mars? Dr. Sagan takes viewers on a never-before-seen look at the red planet through the eyes of science fiction authors and then through the unblinking eyes of two Viking spacecraft that have sent thousands of pictures of the stunning Martian landscape back to Earth since 1976.
VHS: S10695. $19.98.

Cosmos 6: Traveller's Tales
An inside view of the excitement of Voyager's expeditions to Jupiter and Saturn is then compared with the exhilaration of 17th century Dutch explorers who ventured in sailing ships halfway around our own planet in their quest for wealth and knowledge. The newly acquired treasures of our present golden age of exploration are the focus of this episode.
VHS: S10696. $19.98.

Cosmos 7: The Backbone of the Night
Humans once thought the stars were campfires in the sky and the Milky Way "the backbone of the night." In this fascinating segment, Carl Sagan takes viewers back to ancient Greece, when the right answer to such a basic question as "What are the stars?" was first glimpsed. He visits the Brooklyn elementary school of his childhood where this same question is being asked.
VHS: S10697. $19.98.

Cosmos 8: Travels in Space and Time
A startling voyage to see how star patterns change over millions of years is followed by a journey to the planets of other stars, and a look at the possibility of time travel—which takes us to Italy, where the youthful Albert Einstein first wondered what it would be like to ride on a beam of light.
VHS: S10698. $19.98.

Cosmos 9: The Lives of the Stars
Using computer animation and amazing astronomical art, astronomer and Cosmos host Dr. Carl Sagan shows how stars are born, live, die and sometimes collapse to form neutron stars and black holes. Viewers then journey to the future to witness the last perfect day on Earth, 5 billion years from now, after which the Sun will engulf our planet in its fires.
VHS: S10699. $19.98.

Cosmos 10: The Edge of Forever
Dr. Sagan leads viewers on an awesome trip to a time when galaxies were beginning to form, journeys to India to explore the infinite cycles of Hindu cosmology, then shows how humans of this century discovered the expanding universe and its origin: The Big Bang. He disappears down a black hole and reappears in New Mexico to show viewers an array of 27 telescopes probing the furthest reaches of space.
VHS: S10700. $19.98.

Cosmos 11: The Persistence of Memory
The brain is the focus of this fascinating portion of our journey as Dr. Sagan examines one of the other intelligent creatures with which we share the planet Earth— the whale. Then we wind through the maze of the human brain to witness the architecture of thought. We see how genes, brains and books store the information necessary to human survival.
VHS: S10701. $19.98.

Cosmos 12: Encyclopedia Galactica
Are there alien intelligences? How could we communicate with them? What about UFO's? The answers to these questions take us to Egypt to decode ancient hieroglyphics, then to the largest radio telescope on Earth, and in the Spaceship of the Imagination, to visit other civilizations in space. What is the lifespan of a planetary civilization? Will we one day hook up with a network of civilizations in the Milky Way Galaxy?
VHS: S10702. $19.98.

Cosmos 13: Who Speaks for Earth?
Through the use of startling special effects we retrace the 15-billion-year journey from the Big Bang to the present. The tragic story of the martyrdom of Hypatia, the woman scientist of ancient Alexandria, is told. This is the famous Cosmos episode on nuclear war in which Dr. Sagan argues that our responsibility for survival is owed not just to ourselves but also to the Cosmos, ancient and vast, from which we spring.
VHS: S10703. $19.98.

Cosmos 14: Ted Turner Interviews Dr. Carl Sagan: An Update
The preceding 13 episodes of Cosmos show how the fragility and vulnerability of our planet is best appreciated when viewed from a global perspective. Here in this newly recorded episode, Ted Turner talks with Dr. Sagan about ways to preserve the planet Earth and the people on it.
VHS: S10704. $19.98.

Cosmos Gift Pack A
Episodes 1-4 plus episode 5 of Cosmos for free.
VHS: S10705. $79.98.

Cosmos Gift Pack B
Episodes 6-9 of Cosmos plus the Cosmos paperback for free.
VHS: S10706. $79.98.

Cosmos Gift Pack C
Includes episodes 10-13 plus the Ted Turner/Carl Sagan episode (14) for free.
VHS: S10707. $79.98.

Cosmos: The Complete
Includes all 14 episodes on 7 videocassettes, (2 episodes per tape), plus a free Cosmos paperback book.
VHS: S10708. $199.98.

Creation of the Universe
Award-winning science journalist Timothy Ferris hosts this widely acclaimed exploration of some of the most challenging theories in contemporary science. Dazzling special effects, music by Brian Eno, and an interview with Dr. Stephen Hawking. Science magazine hails it as "...nothing short of a masterpiece." 90 mins.
VHS: S12940. $19.98.
Laser: CLV. LD70104. $49.95.

Destination: Universe
Tackles America's involvement in space exploration from the past, present and future. 44 mins.
Laser: LD70248. $29.95.

The Dream Is Alive
Narrated by Walter Cronkite, this is arguably the best space documentary ever made. Over 25 million viewers have enjoyed this film in the giant IMAX theatres countrywide—an experience the astronauts say is "the closest to being there." Take a window seat on the space shuttle and experience man's dream of living and working in space. Hi-Fi Surround Stereo. USA, 40 mins.
VHS: S15076. $29.95.
Laser: LD70274. $39.95.

Earth to Space for Peace
Dr. Carol Rosin, president of the Institute for Security and Cooperation in space, actively works with others to bring about a joint space program with the Soviets to stop the Strategic Defense Initiative. Here she explains how space programs help to unite the world in contrast to the way military programs divide it. 90 mins.
VHS: S10221. $29.95.

Exploration: Space
Four films—Mysteries of the Universe, Astro Smiles, Mercury Exploration and Challenger Explosion—show the achievements of NASA. This collection reveals the mysteries of space. 120 mins.
VHS: S24691. $39.95.

Filling in the Blanks
This documentary takes its viewers behind the frenzied efforts to restore the Smithsonian's Air and Space Museum, the site's most popular tourist attraction.
VHS: S16872. $14.98.

Flight of Apollo 11
Complete coverage of the entire flight: launch, moon orbit, walking on the moon, recovery and more. Breathtaking scenes. 30 mins.
VHS: S06703. $29.95.

Flight of the Dream Team
An exhilarating portrait of the world's finest skydivers performing their ballet of movement and "aerobatics" to R.J. Miller's musical score.
Laser: LD70249. $34.95.

Flyers
Flyers has earned a permanent place in film history for its unforgettable stunt flying sequences. A stuntman climbs from the wing of one airplane and is rescued in mid-air by a companion plane, a Corsair crashes on the deck of a carrier, and an F-15 test flight clocks in at 2½ times the speed of sound. From the IMAX Motion Picture, in Surround Sound. 34 mins.
Laser: CAV. LD71493. $39.95.

For All Mankind
From 1968 to 1972, 24 astronauts traveled to the moon. This is their story, told in their words, in their voices, using the images of their experiences. Winner of the Grand Prize at Utah's Sundance Film Festival in 1989.
Laser: CLV. LD70986. $39.95.
Laser: CAV. LD70987. $99.95.

From Disaster to Discovery: The Challenger Explosion
The story of the Challenger explosion and the seven who died, as well as the investigation into the fiasco. Finally, the rebirth of the shuttle system is highlighted and America's return to space. From ABC News. 60 mins.
VHS: S12689. $24.98.

From Here to Infinity
Patrick Stewart hosts this video exploration that travels to the known ends of the universe and beyond. State-of-the-art computer graphics and never-before-seen spacescapes make this documentary a must for sci-fi fans and trekkers. 43 mins.
VHS: S25833. $14.95.

Hail Columbia!
From its opening shots of the Kennedy Center launch, this documentary examines the 1981 maiden voyage of Columbia, the first space shuttle. 40 mins.
Laser: LD71945. $39.95.

History of Flight and The Golden Days of Flight
Two NASA programs in one. The first examines man's quest to fly farther, faster and higher as well as the technology that enabled him to do so; the second takes us back to the first days of powered flight as aviation pioneer Paul Garver relates his experiences with Orville Wright, Charles Lindbergh, Glenn Curtis, Amelia Earhart and Howard Hughes. 56 mins.
VHS: S06705. $29.95.

History of the Apollo Program
From the early test flights to the historic manned landings on the moon, this documentary recounts each of the Apollo flights. The best footage from all of the flights. 30 mins.
VHS: S06704. $29.95.

Hoagland's Mars, Vol. I, The NASA/Cydonia Briefings
Richard Hoagland presents new theories of the tetrahedral geometries of the Cydonian structures—which he believes are evidence that intelligent life existed on Mars. 83 mins.
VHS: S20162. $34.95.

Hoagland's Mars, Vol. II, The U.N. Briefing, the Terrestrial Connection
Drawing on computer-enhanced photos from NASA's 1976 Viking mission, Richard Hoagland explores the relationship between the "face," a pyramid-like structure surrounding Mar's Cydonia region, and some ancient Earth monuments, including the Sphinx. 80 mins.
VHS: S18037. $44.95.

Hoagland's Mars, Vol, III, The Moon/Mars Connection
Are there ancient alien bases on the moon? Richard Hoagland presents evidence of extraterrestrial intelligence in this comprehensive three-hour video. He links moon bases to those bases he discovered on mars.
VHS: S24694. $49.95.

Hubble Space Telescope: Rescue in Space
Follow the astronauts of NASA during one their most daring and important space flights ever, the retrieval and repair of the Hubble space telescope. Images from this complex machine offer dramatically improved views deep into outer space. This documentary follows the mission from pre-flight preparation all the way through to the successful completion of this historic task. 50 mins.
VHS: S21774. $24.95.

The Infinity Series: Part 1— The Solar System
Using moving images and photographs captured from NASA and other leading observatories, this program considers the solar system from the perspective of alien guides, looking at the sun and its relationship to the planets and their moons, the asteroids and comets and their working systems. The program also looks at the formation of the solar system and the planets. 60 mins.
VHS: S18469. $19.95.

The Infinity Series: Part 2—Deep Space
This program looks at the formation of the universe, its growth and development, the evolution and death of various types of stars, and the status, destination and eventual death of the universe. 60 mins.
VHS: S18470. $19.95.

The Infinity Series: Part 3— The Light Beyond Light and Life
Part 3 examines the dark edges of the universe, the probability of extraterrestrial existence and what their life might entail. 60 mins.
VHS: S18471. $19.95.

The Infinity Series: Part 4— The Crystal Space/Time Ship
The final segment considers the metaphysical "soul" of the universe and everything that falls under its realm. With music by the Celestial Mechanics. 45 mins.
VHS: S18472. $19.95.

Journey into Space
Highlights from the first 24 Space Shuttle missions are set against an exciting musical score composed by Craig Jackson. Rarely-seen, spectacular footage of NASA astronauts doing what they do best in outer space. Also liftoff, reentry and thrilling views of our planet. USA, 1986, 28 mins.
VHS: S03922. $29.95.

Jupiter, Saturn and Uranus
The Voyager Missions in this film produced by the Jet Propulsion Laboratory for NASA, taking the viewer on a billion-mile journey to the giant planets, exploring the planets, moons, magnetic fields, geology and weather through the eyes of Voyager 1 and 2. 58 mins.
VHS: S06710. $29.95.

Jupiter, Saturn, Uranus & Neptune
An all-new video program featuring the very latest images, information and computer animation from the missions to the outer planets, including Voyager's last stop in our Solar System—Neptune. USA, 30 mins.
VHS: S15077. $29.95.

Kennedy Space Center: Window to the Universe
Tour NASA's awesome launch facilities and exhibits and re-live many of the history-making missions which blasted off here. 30 mins.
VHS: S06687. $29.95.

Lift Off to Space
This program gives a complete history of the rivalry between the U.S. and the Soviet Union to be the first on the moon, using spectacular footage of Glenn's first orbit and Armstrong's first steps. 60 mins.
VHS: S13115. $19.98.

Liftoff
Patrick Stewart narrates this exciting behind-the-scenes documentary, which follows the crew of the spacecraft Columbia on a successful mission. These astronauts repair a satellite and retrieve the stranded Long Duration Facility from a dangerously low orbit. From their dramatic perspective, forest fires in the Amazon and even their nighttime landing provide a dazzling new experience. 50 mins.
VHS: S21874. $19.98.

Man on the Moon
Culled from 32 hours of CBS footage of the mission to the moon, this program includes a retrospective interview with Walter Cronkite and all of the three astronauts, as well as a look back at President Kennedy's historic 1960's speech that set the stage for that decade's space exploration program.
VHS: S09604. $19.95.

Mercury Spacecraft Missions and Legacy of Gemini
The drama of the first years of America's space programs with two historical NASA programs. The Mercury and Gemini missions gave us many firsts in space, and the videos explore space veterans in action—John Glenn, Ed White, Virgil Grissom, and many others. 56 mins.
VHS: S06707. $29.95.

Meteorites
Tens of hundreds of small meteorites strike the earth every year. These messengers from the heavens could tell us the secrets to the formation of the solar system. Or one large one could destroy the world as we know it. These objects, worshipped by the Anasazi, are thoroughly explored in this fascinating documentary package, with computer graphics and images from Voyager II. 84 mins.
VHS: S22455. $29.95.

Moon Shot
In this documentary, new footage never seen before shows the behind the scenes story of this historic challenge that changed forever man's relationship to outer space. It was not just a race between nations, but a race between the men who flew, the astronauts themselves. 189 mins.
VHS: S21209. $19.98.

National Geographic Video: For All Mankind
Al Reinert's documentary uses the footage of the Apollo flights as found art, from John Kennedy's bold proclamation of the New Frontier to a stylized rumination on the vast expansiveness, infinity and peculiar serenity of space.
VHS: S18840. $19.95.
Al Reinert, USA, 1989, 80 mins.

The New Solar System
The space age has revealed hitherto unsuspected secrets about our own corner of the universe. This documentary brings those discoveries together. The inner planets, gas giants, a comet crashing into Jupiter, asteroids, volcanoes and more are explored in this fascinating video. 60 mins.
VHS: S23973. $24.95.

Nova— Countdown to the Invisible Universe
The entire universe is revealed in a whole new way. A spacecraft called IRAS explores the infrared wavelength beyond the rainbow and maps this previously hidden region of the sky.
VHS: S24883. $19.95.

Nova—Death of a Star
On February 23, 1987, one of the most violent events since the creation of the universe was observed by a Canadian astronomer, and then by scientists worldwide. It was the first supernova visible at close range in nearly 400 years.
VHS: S24884. $19.95.

Nova—Eclipse of the Century
During the total solar eclipse of July 11, 1991, scientists struggled to pack all the experiments and measurements possible into a brief span. The eclipse lasted just four minutes and luckily it was visible from the advanced observatories of Mauna Kea.
VHS: S24885. $19.95.

Nova—One Small Step
How did America win the Space Race? A look at the first orbit around the Earth, the Mercury and Apollo missions, and the Russian and American space race. 60 mins.
VHS: S09405. $14.98.

Nova—Rescue Mission in Space
This video follows the astronauts of the Space Shuttle mission to repair the Hubble Space Telescope. In addition, this video shows the stunning work performed by the telescope since its repair.
VHS: S24877. $19.95.

Nova—Russian Right Stuff: The Mission
This episode chronicles the arduous training of cosmonauts involved in the Soviet Space Station MIR. 1991, 60 mins.
VHS: S16817. $14.98.

On Robot Wings: A Flight Through the Solar System
Features footage from Jet Propulsion Laboratory; you'll fly On Robot Wings over planets and moons as if aboard a high-speed, low-flying spacecraft and explore—close-up—the features of Earth, Venus, Mars and Uranus' moon Miranda. 30 mins.
VHS: S16627. $24.95.

One Giant Leap
The untold, inside story of the Apollo 11 moon mission is revealed in this documentary from the Discovery Channel. Young, brazen scientists entered into one of the greatest calculated risks in history in order to conquer the trip to the moon.
VHS: S23225. $19.95.

One Small Step for Man
A captivating look at the story of the Apollo missions, culminating with Armstrong's historic walk on the moon. 60 minutes.
VHS: S02293. $39.95.

Out of This World: The Apollo Moon Landings
A program about the history of the manned space flights, the origins of the Apollo project, and the events and personalities responsible for the groundbreaking journey of Apollo 11. In addition to Apollo 11, the documentary also looks at the accomplishments of Apollos 12 through 17. 60 mins.
VHS: S18484. $24.95.

Planet Mars and Mercury
Two NASA programs tracing man's sometimes imaginative theories of Mars, from its discovery in 1669 to the historic Viking landing on its surface. The second program explores the planet Mercury in startling detail, with photographs and findings from the Mariner 10 mission. 52 mins.
VHS: S06706. $29.95.

The Planets Deluxe Collector's Edition
A special collector's edition of the space program The Planets, with some supplementary materials, including four color posters by Geoffrey Chandler, a facts booklet, Peterson First Guides Astronomy, and the U.S. Space Camp catalog. 56 mins.
VHS: S17629. $34.95.

The Planets
A wonderful depiction of the planets from the perspective of photographs taken from the U.S. and Soviet space flights, computer animation and digital special effects. The program is scored by Isao Tomita and heavily influenced by Gustav Holst's musical suite, "The Planets." "Factual, fascinating, beautiful and just plain fun" (The Planets). 56 mins.
VHS: S17628. $19.98.
Laser: CAV. LD72222. $29.95.

Racing for the Moon: America's Glory Days in Space
The story of America's race for space; from the shock of Sputnik to John Glenn's first orbit to Armstrong's first steps on the moon. From ABC News.
VHS: S12685. $24.98.

Satellite Imaging: The Jet Propulsion Laboratory
These four movies demonstrate a variety of remarkable data visualization techniques. They include a startling aerial ride over a three-dimensional Southern California landscape and a simulated flight over the towering mountains and steep canyons of Miranda, a moon of Uranus. 20 mins.
VHS: S13897. $19.95.

Satellite Rescue in Space: Shuttle Flights 41C & 51A
Join the shuttle crew as they narrate the most interesting and spectacular scenes to date depicting life aboard the space shuttle. 42 mins.
VHS: S06686. $29.95.

Smithsonian Air and Space, Dreams of Flight: Beyond the Moon
It all began with man's first steps on the lunar surface during the Apollo 11 mission. Now dreams of exploring worlds beyond our solar system fire the imagination. This video discovers the reality within the dream. 50 mins.
Laser: LD74751. $34.95.

Smithsonian Air and Space, Dreams of Flight: To the Moon...
This video is another chapter in the never-ending saga of mankind's dreams of flight. Visionaries like H.G. Wells made the way for man's adventures in space. In this story, science fiction becomes science fact. 50 mins.
Laser: LD74750. $34.95.

Space Age Program

A six-part documentary series on space exploration. Narrated by Patrick Stewart, the program considers the quest for Mars, celestial sentinels, satellites, the moon and the origins of the universe, as well as a philosophical and scientific inquiry into the nature of heaven.
Space Age Program 1: Quest for Planet Mars.
VHS: S17712. $24.95.
Space Age Program 2: Celestial Sentinels.
VHS: S17713. $24.95.
Space Age Program 3: The Unexpected Universe.
VHS: S17714. $24.95.
Space Age Program 4: To the Moon and Beyond.
VHS: S17715. $24.95.
Space Age Program 5: Mission to Planet Earth.
VHS: S17716. $24.95.
Space Age Program 6: What's a Heaven For?
VHS: S17717. $24.95.
Space Age Program: Deluxe 6-Tape Boxed Set.
VHS: S17718. $99.95.

Space Dreaming

Marianne Dolan's expressive, sensual and quite beautiful celestial ballet of images, movement, sound, dance and the origins of creation, in collaboration with composer Steve Roach. 30 mins.
Laser: LD70242. $24.95.

Space Race

From the Soviet point of view. When the USSR put a rocket named Sputnik in the air, the United States came to attention. This program portrays the enthusiasm for space exploration, and the movie-star-like celebrity of Yuri Gagarin, the astronaut who captured the attention of the nation and the world. 100 mins.
VHS: S12712. $24.95.

The Space Shuttle

From Mission Control in Houston, the Discovery Channel brings the story of America's premier spacecraft. The technicians and scientists that keep the shuttle working and flying have an immense and complicated task. They must not only get it off the ground but they must bring it back intact.
VHS: S23224. $19.95.

Space Shuttle:
Flights STS-1 Through STS-8

Enjoy the triumphs of the first eight shuttle flights. Features two NASA films—Opening New Frontiers and We Deliver—summarizing the accomplishments of flights 1 through 8. Includes spectacular views from space, satellite deployments, experiments and more. 60 mins.
VHS: S06709. $29.95.

Symphony to the Planets

Leonard Nimoy narrates this double video set which examines the history of our galaxy and man's exploration of space. Two episodes, Part One: A Star to Call Home and Part Two: Mysteries Beyond Our Reach, combine footage and resources from NASA and the National Air and Space Museum in Washington, D.C. Classical music comprises the score. Two-tape set, 120 mins.
VHS: S26366. $29.95.

Time and Light

Part of the PBS series drawing on the resources of the Smithsonian Institution, Time and Light explores time as measured by man, plants and animals, peering into the vast stretches of space to the origins of time as reflected in Earth's most distant stars.
VHS: S16871. $14.98.

To Be an Astronaut

From the archives of ABC News, this overview of America's space program starts with the preparation for the seven original Mercury astronauts, through the daring odysseys of Apollo, to today's Shuttle experience. 45 mins.
VHS: S10851. $14.95.

To Fly

This non-stop trip through the history of flight begins in the 1800s and travels up through the present. The natural beauty of the United States, the wonder of human ingenuity and the rewards of persistence are wrapped up in one emotional, historical, exhilarating event. From the IMAX Motion Picture, in Surround Sound. 27 mins.
Laser: CAV. LD71492. $34.95.

Universe (Mastervision)

A comprehensive look at what mankind knows today about our sun and solar system as well as the seemingly infinite number of other stars and galaxies in all universal space and time. An awe inspiring look at the heavens in all their majesty and mystery.
VHS: S03985. $64.95.

Universe (Shatner)

Journey through our solar system and beyond to the Milky Way with William Shatner as he takes you on an information-packed tour of the Universe. Learn the theories behind black holes, pulsars, and other space phenomena. 30 minutes.
VHS: S03774. $29.95.

Uranus: I Will See Such Things

Ancient moons with 16-mile-high cliffs and surface temperatures 300 degrees below zero. The geology, the weather, the moons, the magnetic fields—even the operation of Voyager 2—all are explored. 29 mins.
VHS: S06679. $29.95.

Voyage to the Outer Planets and Beyond

Isaac Asimov presents this musical video voyage in outer space—in a classical music video which features rare NASA and JPL footage set to the music of Gustav Holst's The Planets. This musical video voyage through space includes a NASA-prepared brochure, "A Look at the Planets", "Space Almanac", and a list of astronomical events between now and the year 2001. 54 mins.
VHS: S06321. $39.95.

The Voyager Odyssey

A journey through infinity, to the outer reaches of the solar system, captured in this documentary combining space photography, computer animation, and special digital effects, in the four-billion-mile trip from Jupiter to Neptune. "A gorgeous, inspirational experience that's stunning in its audio quality and video excellence" (Entertainment Weekly). 44 mins.
Laser: LD70246. $34.95.

A Walk Through History

This exhaustive look at the Apollo 11 space mission documents the first human space walk. Spectacular photography of the Earth and the landscape features of the Moon add to the excitement. It all culminates with the planting of the American flag on lunar soil. 22 mins.
VHS: S26761. $9.98.

We Remember:
The Space Shuttle Pioneers 1981-1986

The first and only complete documentary on the landmark adventures of America's Space Shuttle during the first five years, from Columbia's first launch to Challenger's final mission. A unique historic document. 58 mins.
VHS: S08137. $29.95.

Where None Has Gone Before

A subjective view of the Voyager's around the world flight, and the development of the space telescope and its extraordinary capacity to see seven times greater into space and examine previously hidden underwater caves.
VHS: S16873. $14.98.

TRANSPORTATION

The 10 Greatest American Cars

A look at the evolution of the design, styling and engineering of the best American cars. The program assembles a group of experts, automotive writers, collectors and critics to debate and discuss the craftsmanship, speed and muscle of the greatest machines. Photographed by Bill Anwelier. Narrated by Jack Perkins. 50 mins.
VHS: S19345. $19.95.

21st Century Jet

Boeing's 777 represents a $5 billion undertaking in technological, organizational and marketing terms. This documentary shows the first critical year of progress in the manufacturing of this flying marvel. 58 mins.
VHS: S25734. $19.95.

777: First Flight

The Boeing 777 is the largest, most complex aircraft ever built. It is the first to be designed electronically. This video exposes the drama of its test period. All aspects of the process, from the top corporate level to the workers who build and maintain it, are on view. This reflects a new corporate attitude of no secrets and no rivalry. 57 mins.
VHS: S25735. $19.95.

The Air Mail Story

Produced in collaboration with the Smithsonian Institutions' National Postal Museum and the U.S. Postal Service, this program looks at the pioneering efforts in air mail postage and its contribution to modern aviation. 40 mins.
VHS: S17178. $19.95.

Always Ready:
The U.S. Coast Guard Story

Founded in 1789 to end smuggling, this is the story of the invaluable arm of the U.S. Navy. 45 mins.
VHS: S13133. $29.98.

Amtrak's X2000 Demonstration

The need for development and refining new equipment to serve the Northeast Corridor paved the way for the sleek, high-speed X2000, a cutting-edge Amtrak train that astounded people with its futuristic design, speed and comfort. 30 mins.
VHS: S20085. $19.95.

Anchors Away: The U.S. Navy Story

From its birth more than two centuries ago to its accomplishments in Vietnam, this is an historical account of the Navy and its missions. 45 mins.
VHS: S13132. $29.98.

Bicycle: A Celebration of the Invention

This new video from the BBC celebrates every aspect of the evolution of the bike, from its earliest form to the achievements of Eddie Merckx and Greg LeMond at the Tour de France. 115 mins.
VHS: S16559. $34.95.

Blue Angels

Dennis Quaid narrates as the Blue Angels, a top-notch flight team, demonstrate precision flying using the most advanced military jets. The F-18 Hornet offers an unforgettable ride. Music by Queen, Billy Joel and Los Lobos is included. 100 mins.
VHS: S22088. $29.95.

Blue Angels:
Around the World at the Speed of Sound

The thrill, precision and aerial artistry of the Navy's Blue Angels. Host Dennis Quaid opens the cockpit on this legendary squadron as they take off on their first European tour in 20 years. Footage includes the Angels over Russia, where they encounter MIG fighters, and the team's illustrious history, revealed through archival footage. 100 mins.
VHS: S21902. $29.95.

Branchline Railway

The late Sir John Betjeman presents this little known film which captures the atmosphere of the 24-mile stretch of the now vanished Somerset and Dorset railway. It celebrates a working, living railway complete with dirty locomotives, clean stations with flowers, and austere gas-lit waiting rooms, in a return to a vanished age. 47 mins.
VHS: S07612. $19.94.

British Rail Journeys

Four volumes covering the British Isles from the unique vantage point of British Rail are included in this set. Within each region a wide-ranging itinerary shows the alternating dramatic and gentle landscapes which are famous the world over. Included are Northern England: Settle to Carlisle, North Wales: Chester to Aberystwyth, Central Highlands: Edinburgh to the Isle of Skye and South West: Exeter to Penzance. Each video is 55 mins.
VHS: S27641. $79.80.

Carrier: Fortress at Sea

The Discovery Channel brings a month aboard an actual aircraft carrier to light in this illuminating video. On multiple stories, 5800 men and women work day and night to keep a deadly arsenal of conventional and nuclear weapons ready for use. 100 mins.
VHS: S26051. $24.95.

Choppers

This program follows the colorful evolution of the helicopter, from initial conception to today's complex machines. Includes information on how choppers were used in times of war. 60 mins.
VHS: S13124. $19.98.

Citizen Soldiers: The U.S. Army Story

Using rare, restored footage and photographs, the triumphs over the British through the present are interwoven into a comprehensive history of America's armed victories. 45 mins.
VHS: S13134. $29.98.

Cleared for Takeoff

Fred Levine leads kids through the nation's busiest airport, Chicago's O'Hare. An actual United Airlines pilot takes kids into the control tower, the luggage sorting area and the front row seat of a jet.
VHS: S25688. $19.95.

Dawn of the Jet Age: The First 25 Years

This program traces the first 25 years of the jet plane, beginning with pilots and designers of the 30's, to the first breaking of the sound barrier, to wartime jet use. 60 mins.
VHS: S13121. $19.98.

Early Birds

An interesting, informative look into the world of automotive nostalgia, highlighting the 1955, 1956 and 1957 models of the Thunderbird—a product of the Ford Motor Company. Burt Reynolds and Glen Campbell are out for a quick spin while Ronald Hughes narrates an interview with Thunderbird restoration expert Jim Weatherly. 41 mins.
VHS: S11115. $14.95.

Flying Machines

Meet the Smithsonian staff dedicated to preserving the history of aviation. This exhilarating look at the National Air and Space Museum presents cockpit-views of the Wright Flyer, the Spirit of St. Louis and the Enola Gay. 1989, 60 mins.
VHS: S14543. $29.95.
Laser: LD70224. $34.95.

Formula 1 Saga

An exciting series that takes us into the world of circuits, champions and their cars from the beginning of Formula 1 racing until today. Rare footage features the legends of Formula 1 racing, including Stirling Moss, Alain Prost, Jackie Stewart, Ayrton Senna, Niki Lauda, Nigel Mansell and others. Great cars in action: Renault, BMW, Mercedes, Ferrari, Fiat, Alfa Romeo and more.
Volume 1: The Cars. Parts 1 and 2 of "The Legendary Cars" looks at their specialists and manufacturers. 90 mins.
VHS: S21918. $19.98.
Volume 2: The Drivers. A look at the great drivers and their rivalries. 90 mins.
VHS: S21919. $19.98.
Volume 3: The Thrill of Formula 1. The dangers and art of Formula 1 racing and its economics. 90 mins.
VHS: S21920. $19.98.
Volume 4: The Grand Prix. The Grand Prix weekend, the Monaco Grand Prix and the turbo era of Formula 1 racing. 90 mins.
VHS: S21921. $19.98.
Formula 1 Saga, Complete Set. A pre-packed, 4-volume set.
VHS: S21922. $79.80.

From the Wake of the Bow

Our maritime heritage, from pirogues and skiffs to tankers. Hosted by Louisiana Governor Edwards. 59 mins.
VHS: S22389. $42.50.

Ghost Trains of the Old West Volume 1

The first volume in this series introduces the breathtaking beauty of the landscape dominated by early steam locomotives. The iron horse was responsible for the development of the wilderness. 60 mins.
VHS: S24484. $19.95.

Ghost Trains of the Old West Volume 2

The second volume in this series picks up where Volume 1 left off. 60 mins.
VHS: S24485. $19.95.

The Golden Age of the Automobile

See many autos from past years and discover the reasons for the demise of marques such as La Salle, Auburn, and Pierce Arrows, and learn about the development of many of today's engineering advances. 55 minutes.
VHS: S02250. $29.95.

Great American Eastern Train Rides

Two volumes reveal the itineraries of classic and historic train routes in key Eastern states. From Blue Mountain, Pennsylvania, to Cumberland, Maryland, some of the most scenic countryside and quaint train technology is shown in this comprehensive video set. 120 mins.
VHS: S26367. $29.95.

Great American Train Rides

Vintage steam and diesel locomotives, cabooses, electric trolleys and interurbans bring unforgettable experiences to this video. Sixteen truly American adventures are shown from the Colorado Rockies to California's Redwood coast. Two-volume set, 120 mins.
VHS: S23134. $29.95.

Great Railway Journeys

This series travels along some of the world's most spectacular rail systems. Each program visits a different country, including Ireland, Pakistan, Russia, Brazil, South Africa and China. Great feats of engineering, romantic landscapes and the charm of trains are joined in this collection. 50 minutes each.
Capetown to the Lost City. Hosted by author Rian Malan.
VHS: S23216. $19.95.
Derry to Kerry. Hosted by Michael Palin.
VHS: S23212. $19.95.
Hong Kong to Ulaanbaatar. Hosted by Clive Anderson.
VHS: S23217. $19.95.
Karachi to Kyber Pass. Hosted by Mark Tully.
VHS: S23215. $19.95.
Santos to Santa Cruz. Hosted by poet and novelist Lisa St. Aubin de Teran.
VHS: S23214. $19.95.
St. Petersburg to Tashkent. Hosted by prima ballerina Natalia Makarova.
VHS: S23213. $19.95.
Six-Volume Set.
VHS: S23218. $99.95.

Great Railway Journeys of the World:
Confessions of a Train Spotter

A tribute to the unique way in which long train journeys allow the traveller time for observation. Comedian Michael Palin fulfills his dream as a childhood train spotter and travels the length of Britain by train—from Euston to the Kyle of Lochalsh—on a fascinating journey of history and rediscovery. There are diversions to lesser-used lines including the Flying Scotsman, the York Railway Museum, to Edinburgh at Festival time, and across the breathtaking Forth Railway Bridge. A BBC production. 59 mins.
VHS: S10297. $19.94.

Great Railway Journeys of the World:
Flying Scotsman

O.S. Nick, railway expert, is the guide to this video survey of today's steam railway scene. This video focuses on two locomotive personalities from the history of steam: the 4472 Flying Scotsman on its last non-stop London to Edinburgh run, and an impressive 1/8 scale model of the largest steam locomotive ever built, the Union Pacific Big Boy. A BBC production. 98 mins.
VHS: S10296. $19.94.

Great Railway Journeys of the World:
India

Brian Thompson is the guide armed with a 30 pound rail pass and only a hazy notion of destination as he boards the '85 Down Madras Mail and heads south. On his leisurely five-day journey from the noise and heat of Bombay to the calm of Cochin he passes through four states, crosses the dusty Deccan plain and visits Ooctamund, a cool hill retreat built by the British in the days of the Empire. Produced by the BBC. 60 mins.
VHS: S10298. $19.94.

Heritage to Glory:
The U.S. Marine Corps Story

Real footage describes the action and events the Marines have seen in the two World Wars. This is the history of brave marines. 45 mins.
VHS: S13130. $29.98.

History of Naval Aviation

Fifty years of Naval Aviation is covered in this program. Includes interviews with pilots, footage of the Wright brothers' first public test flights and rare filmed accounts of World War I and II air battles fought over the Atlantic and South Pacific. 84 mins.
VHS: S13128. $29.98.

The History of the Volkswagen

Though a popular culture icon, the bug was actually designed with the political aims of National Socialism in mind. Hitler opened the Volkswagen factory personally in 1938. This video shows how, despite this inauspicious start, the beetle was transformed into the beloved bug. 30 mins.
VHS: S24833. $14.95.

Iron Road

From the PBS program The American Experience series, this program examines the construction of the transcontinental railroad. 60 mins.
VHS: S17177. $19.95.

Irving Johnson High Seas Adventurer

Highlights Johnson's exciting life beginning with his introduction to the sea aboard the Peking in 1929. Seven of Johnson's round-the-world voyages aboard the brigantine Yankee are charted, illustrated with National Geographic's striking footage of stops in South Pacific Islands. 43 mins.
VHS: S05944. $34.95.

Jets: The New Generation

War in Vietnam required a new generation of fighter planes. From the Voodoo Reconnaissance to the deadly napalm bombers, this program studies these aircraft and the role they played. 60 mins.
VHS: S13120. $19.98.

Kitty Hawk

This program examines the competition that took place prior to the Wright brothers' historic flight at Kitty Hawk, the flight itself, and the evolution of engine-powered planes. 60 mins.
VHS: S13125. $19.98.

Last of the Giants: Vol. 1:
Union Pacific's Big Boys

A 1959 documentary that traces the social and industrial development of the biggest locomotive ever designed, the aptly-named "Big Boy," which pioneered the development of Union Pacific steam power. 25 mins.
VHS: S20082. $19.95.

Last of the Giants: Vol. 2: The Cheyenne Shops

A follow-up to *Last of the Giants*, incorporating much of the unused footage that was shot by Union Pacific cameramen over a three-year period in the 50s. The film features interviews with contemporary Union Pacific workers who discuss their experiences on the famous locomotives. 60 mins.
VHS: $20083. $39.95.

Last Train Across Canada

Murray Sayles, the veteran war correspondent, travels across the Canadian Dream, 7000 miles of transcontinental railways. Along the way he encounters a vast array of Canadians, including Native Americans, mounties, fishermen from the maritime provinces and cowboys in the prairie. The wildlife is breathtaking. 110 mins.
VHS: $23119. $29.95.

Locomotion: The Amazing World of Trains

This set of four tapes includes: *Vol. 1, Engines of Enterprise*, the story of America's first big business; *Vol. 2, Taming the Iron Monster*, a history of how early railway construction literally moved mountains; *Vol. 3, The War Machines*, a chronicle of trains from the Civil War to the Second World War; and *Vol. 4, Magic Machines and Mobile People*, which shows how trains change society, including a look at the fastest trains running today.
VHS: $21249. $79.95.

The Lost Ships Collection

Three National Geographic videos are collected in this package which celebrates the determination, courage and skills of explorer Dr. Robert Ballard. The films are *Secrets of the Titanic*, *Search for the Battleship Bismarck* and *The Lost Fleet of Guadalcanal*. 180 mins.
VHS: $18992. $59.95.

Marathon of Steam

This four-volume series will appeal to all train fans. The series criss-crosses the country in search of the most exciting, nostalgic and historic trains. 120 mins.
Volume 1. Two documentaries, *Narrow Rails Still Shine* and *Rotary Snowplow through the Rockies*, are included in this volume. They take the viewer through Colorado and New Mexico.
VHS: $22151. $19.95.
Volume 2. These three short films show the Illinois Railway Museum and follow a train ride up to the top of Bear Mountain. The 4-6-2 Pacific is also featured.
VHS: $22152. $19.95.
Volume 3. Spectacular scenery and classic railroads are showcased in this collection of three films: *BCR Steam, NKP Autumn Spectacular* and *819 Arkansas Steam*.
VHS: $22153. $19.95.
Volume 4. The 90-minute film *Steam in St. Louis* captures the excitement of four steam locomotives which operate for the St. Louis NRHS convention. Then *Sierra Railways* tours the historic facilities of this well-known railroad.
VHS: $22154. $19.95.

Mighty Steam Series

This collection examines the steam-powered locomotives that defined the building of the American frontier. The series includes the Norfolk Western, the Canadian Steam, Cotton Belt and Union Pacific. 180 mins.
Canadian Steam.
VHS: $20089. $19.95.
Cotton Belt 819.
VHS: $20090. $19.95.
Norfolk Western 1218.
VHS: $20088. $19.95.
S.P. Daylight 4449.
VHS: $20091. $19.95.
Union Pacific 844.
VHS: $20092. $19.95.
Union Pacific 3985.
VHS: $20093. $19.95.
Mighty Steam Series, Set. A collection of six tapes.
VHS: $20094. $239.00.

Modern Warplanes

The most sophisticated fighter jets plan their attack strategies with the aid of radar, sonar and satellites. This program shows how the modern war plane evolved with each war to become powerful, high-tech machines. 60 mins.
VHS: $13122. $19.98.

Moving Beyond Auto America

Seventeen of the nation's foremost transportation experts critically analyze our love affair with the car and ask how much longer we can rely on this energy-intensive method of transportation. Alternatives like electric cars, magnetic trains, light rail systems and low-tech as well as highly futuristic approaches are all explored in this video. 28 mins.
VHS: $21569. $59.95.

National Geographic Video: Love Those Trains

Celebrate a slice of history and ride the rails of the world in this look at the romance, majesty and adventure of trains, from steam engines to sleek diesels. 60 mins.
VHS: $11408. $19.95.

National Geographic Video: Superliners: Twilight of an Era

Experience life aboard the magnificent and luxurious *Queen Elizabeth II* in a nostalgic look at the great vessels of a time gone by. 60 mins.
VHS: $08057. $19.95.

National Geographic Video: The Great Indian Railway

Steam engines have been transforming the Indian landscape since 1853. Now endangered by progress, the massive and powerful engines are on view in this video. For over a century they have performed myriad tasks, like climbing into the Himalayas or bringing commuters into central Bombay. 111 mins.
VHS: $25898. $19.95.

The New Ford

Originally shot in the late 1920's, this footage demonstrates how the Model A Ford was assembled and tested. All the major components are covered and the car's many abilities are revealed through grueling road circuits. New music has been added to this originally silent film.
VHS: $22108. $29.95.

Nova—Aircraft Carrier!

Round-the-clock life aboard the aircraft carrier Independence is captured on this video. A wealth of technology and know how makes flying at sea possible.
VHS: $24880. $19.95.

Nova—Daredevils of the Sky

Preparing to compete in the 1992 World Aerobatic Championship, the members of the US team practice snap rolls, loops, humpty bumps and hammerheads. Stunning in-air photography captures these skill-sharpening escapades.
VHS: $24881. $19.95.

Nova—Mysterious Crash of Flight 201

Flight 201 crashes in a remote Panamanian jungle. This video charts the investigation waged by federal authorities to determine the cause of the accident. The case offers a daunting puzzle that requires close scrutiny of twisted and charred remains.
VHS: $24882. $19.95.

Nova—The Blimp Is Back

This documentary examines the evolution of the modern dirigible, and the scientific and mathematic principles required to sustain lift, flight and movement, from the famous Goodyear blimp to the strange and bizarre Cyclocrane. 60 mins.
VHS: $19119. $14.98.

Nova—War from the Air

Nova takes an in-depth look at the creation and destruction of bombs. Includes authentic war footage, films of actual bombings, and the bombing strategy. 60 mins.
VHS: $11248. $14.98.

Railway Adventures Across Europe: Volume 1

Bernie Kopell ("Doc" from television's *The Love Boat*) hosts these three enchanting railway trips. The Scottish Highlands are on view in *Bagpipes, Trains and Highland Games*, while *Next Stop—The English Riviera* heads South. Finally *The William Tell Express* gives an Alpine view of Switzerland. 66 mins.
VHS: $27488. $19.98.

Railway Adventures Across Europe: Volume 2

Bernie Kopell takes viewers on two tours of Great Britain in *Adventures Across Time* and *Wild, Wild Wales*. Then, in *Mainline to the Matterhorn*, a view of the stateliest Swiss mountain is the chief attraction. 66 mins.
VHS: $27489. $19.98.

Return of the Scorcher

This spirited celebration of the bicycle asks why this cheap, clean, quiet and healthy method of transportation isn't more widely used in America. Filmed in China, Europe and the U.S., this documentary explores the reasons behind the varying popularity of the bicycle in these different areas. It just might inspire a redefinition of the very idea of progress.
VHS: $21568. $85.00.

Romancing the Classics

Over 125 classic cars, custom models and hot rods are showcased in this video. Music from the 50's and 60's accompanies these cars, resulting in a great music video for classic car enthusiasts. 40 mins.
VHS: $24832. $14.95.

S.O.S. Titanic

On April 10, 1912, the world's most luxurious liner set on her maiden voyage. *S.O.S. Titanic* tells her story from leaving Southampton until her tragic and sudden end four days later. This docu-drama features a mix of archival footage and artifacts with a cast including David Janssen, Cloris Leachman, Susan St. James, David Warner, Ian Holm and Beverly Ross.
VHS: $13046. $29.95.
Billy Hale, USA, 1990, 109 mins.

Sea Power: A Global Journey

Six episodes center around the voyage of a vessel that represents one of the various aspects of man's relationship with the sea: trade, defense, ownership of resources, the quest for knowledge and passenger travel. A U.S.-Japanese-British-Portuguese-Dutch co-production.
Program 1: Lifeblood. Oceans are the arteries of the world and oil is today's lifeblood. Centuries ago it was grain, gold or copper. This program defines how this lifeblood affects the rise and fall of empires.
VHS: $21963. $29.95.
Program 2: Ruling the Waves. Navies are the means by which nations control their coasts and interests. This program examines the evolution of naval force and demonstrates how navies fit into the present geopolitical environment.
VHS: $21964. $29.95.
Program 3: Trade Winds, Trade Wars. Commerce and competition, trade wars and tariffs. Consumer goods glow easily from Asia to the West via the efficiency, speed and low cost of container freight. This is a look at the innovation and economics of sea power.
VHS: $21965. $29.95.
Program 4: Passage to Paradise. Since the earliest voyages of discovery, man has braved the seas in pursuit of dreams of pleasure, adventure and freedom. Yet while some escape the realities of life aboard luxurious pleasure cruises, others risk the perils of the open sea in a desperate bid to fulfill their dreams.
VHS: $21966. $29.95.
Program 5: Who Owns the Oceans? Over 70% of the planet's surface is covered by ocean, and below it lie untold resources. Yet unchecked exploitation can create environmental catastrophe.
VHS: $21967. $29.95.
Program 6: A Depth of Knowledge. Those who know best how to use the seas have the greatest power over them. Today, power lies in the ability to protect and preserve as well as to use and control the seas. This program examines the new information and technology that allow man to monitor and map the global ocean.
VHS: $21968. $29.95.
Sea Power: A Global Journey, Complete Set. The six-volume, boxed set.
VHS: $21969. $149.95.

Seapower

A history of the modern navy, this documentary vividly recreates the excitement and danger of the struggle for control of the seas using unique archival footage as well as new material of British and U.S. naval vessels at sea. Produced by the BBC. 109 mins.
VHS: $03395. $19.94.

SeaWings

The fastest and deadliest planes ever launched from an aircraft carrier are featured in this *Discovery Channel* documentary series. These aircraft make use of any stretch of open sea, turning it into a staging area for sophisticated air power. Three-volume set: each 60 mins.
VHS: $26050. $29.95.

Secrets of the Titanic

National Geographic covers the spectacular underwater discovery of the "unsinkable" *Titanic* on the floor of the Atlantic Ocean. 60 mins.
VHS: $02014. $19.95.

Spruce Goose and RMS Queen Mary

A must for aviation and maritime buffs! Experience a complete tour of these two marvels of engineering and learn of their fascinating history. 53 mins.
VHS: $06689. $19.95.

Steam Across America: Vol. I: The East

A view of Norfolk and Western, the last major type of steam powered locomotives that dominated railway transportation through the first half of the 20th century. 35 mins.
VHS: $20086. $39.95.

Steam Across America: Vol. II: The West

A glimpse at the vanishing moments of steam-driven locomotives, in particular the Union Pacific "Challengers" and "Big Boys". 35 mins.
VHS: $20087. $39.95.

Steam Days 2

Railroad enthusiasts should relish this BBC production that is, not surprisingly, a sequel to *Steam Days*. Travel once more on the Great Western Railway, a distinguished line that still transports thousands of holiday goers to the Cornish Riviera. Spend an hour with freight trains that belch smoke and recall simpler times. England, 60 mins.
VHS: $09863. $19.94.

Steam Days: Travels with a Duchess and the Fishing Line

Railroad enthusiast Miles Kington relives the boyhood pleasures in this celebration of the steam age, encountering some of the great engines, famous lines and wonderfully eccentric people who keep steam alive in Britain. *Travels with a Duchess* examines The Duchess of Hamilton, one of the most famous passenger trains built in the 30's. *The Fishing Line* is the West Highland Fishing line built to transport herring at the end of the 19th century. 60 mins.
VHS: $07611. $19.94.

Steam Kings and Iron Horses

Historical railroad footage is at the center of this video, where you can enjoy a trip on the fabled Coast Daylight. The famous steamers *Tom Thumb, The Atlantic, Memnon, Royal Blue 1310, Britannia, DeWitt Clinton, Camelback* and more are all seen on this tape. B&W. Silent with musical score.
VHS: $27483. $19.95.

Story of Naval Air Power

Through the years, the U.S. Navy has excelled in making their planes faster, higher and able to go farther than ever before. This program traces the innovations that were made in design, radar, and landing gear. 60 mins.
VHS: $13117. $19.98.

Strange Planes

A six-hour series on the history and evolution of unusual aircraft, studying aeronautical engineering, off-beat innovation and cutting edge technology. A "sometimes amusing, sometimes bizarre and at times astonishing, yet always interesting series" (*Washington Post*).
Drones, Mutants and Midgets. A behind-the-scenes look at the personalities and stories behind the conception and planning of bizarre aviation designs. 60 mins.
VHS: $18285. $14.95.
Eyes in the Skies. An appreciation of the history of spy planes, such as the U2 and its use in clandestine aviation. 60 mins.
VHS: $18282. $14.95.
Giants. The breakthroughs in mammoth aviation, from the dirigible to the Spruce Goose to large passenger jets. 60 mins.
VHS: $18283. $14.95.
Parasites. A look at craft that "piggyback" on a larger, mother ship, from the early Curtis fighters stored in dirigibles to the Space Shuttle. 60 mins.
VHS: $18283. $14.95.
Strange Shapes. This program studies the various and often remarkable shapes launched by humans, including the Flying Wing, the precursor of the Stealth Bomber. 60 mins.
VHS: $18281. $14.95.
Vertical Take-Off. This program considers the planes capable of leaping into the sky without advantage of a runway, and other models that were designed to but failed. 60 mins.
VHS: $18284. $14.95.
Six-Tape Set.
VHS: $18286. $89.70.

Submarine: Steel Boats, Iron Men

The challenges and interactions faced by 130 officers and personnel confined in the restricted spaces of a submarine. The program features interviews with submarine commanders, provides an overview of the strategic uses of the craft and contains a special interview with author and naval authority Tom Clancy. 59 mins.
VHS: $18569. $19.95.

Subway: The Empire Beneath New York's Streets

Beneath the fierce commotion on the streets of the Big Apple lies an astonishing network of tunnels, turnstiles and technology. This video explores the subterranean labyrinth of New York, including the finances of this system and the mysterious money train. Experimental rail cars and even the legendary disasters of this, the world's largest subway system, are also shown. 50 mins.
VHS: $21546. $19.95.

Supercharged: The Grand Prix Car

In 1924, a British Sunbeam defeated the speed restrictions set by Grand Prix regulations by super-charging the engine. This was the beginning of one of the greatest eras in the history of motor racing. Bugatti, Alfa Romeo, Maserati and Mercedes Benz all appeared in a series of dramatic and sometimes dangerous races. Using unique film and lovingly restored cars, this program recreates the Golden Age of motor racing. A BBC production. 50 mins.
VHS: $10299. $19.94.

Swiss Rail Journeys

From the vantage points afforded by Swiss rail lines these videos explore the history and sights of the land at the heart of Europe. From beautiful lakes and valleys to some of the most breathtaking alpine scenery anywhere, there is unmatched adventure along these routes.
The Albula Line, Chur to St. Moritz. 50 mins.
VHS: $20916. $19.95.
The Appenzell Railway, Gossau to St. Gallen. 50 mins.
VHS: $20924. $19.95.
The Arosa Line. 50 mins.
VHS: $20919. $19.95.
The Bodensee-Toggenburg Railway, Lake Zurich to Lake Constance. 50 mins.
VHS: $20925. $19.95.
The Breunig Line, Part 1, Interlaken to Meiringen. 50 mins.
VHS: $20920. $19.95.
The Breunig Line, Part 2, Meiringen to Luzerne. 50 mins.
VHS: $20921. $19.95.
The Davos Line, Landquart to Davos and Filisur. 50 mins.
VHS: $20917. $19.95.
The Emmental Railways, Montier to Thun. 50 mins.
VHS: $20923. $19.95.
The MOB, Montreaux to Zweisimmen. 50 mins.
VHS: $20918. $19.95.
Six-Volume Boxed Set. Contains the Albula, Davos, MOB, Arosa and Breunig Line tapes.
VHS: $20922. $99.95.

Tanks: Monsters in Motion

This program is a complete history of tank warfare, from their first appearance as armored tractors to their heyday in World War II, where they were instrumental in the Invasion of Poland, North Africa, and the Battle of Kursk. 50 mins.
VHS: $13127. $29.98.

Those Magnificent Men in Their Flying Machines

A rousing documentary history of the daredevils and pioneers of airplanes, from the Wright Brothers to the pilots of World War II. 60 mins.
VHS: $02983. $39.95.

Titanic

This four-volume set is the most complete chronicle of that fated ocean liner, the *Titanic*. From its construction and christening to the gala maiden voyage, and on to the terror of its final night, the entire tale of this doomed vessel is told. The series concludes with the dramatic discovery of the wreck in deep seas.
VHS: $22182. $59.95.
Laser: CLV. LD74749. $79.95.

Titanic: A Question of Murder

This tragic event, the sinking of an unsinkable oceanliner, is finally the subject of a TV inquiry. Journalist Peter Williams examines some key issues, including the lack of life boats and a boat drill, and missing government files. 52 mins.
VHS: $25844. $19.95.

Titanic: The Nightmare and the Dream

Dr. Robert Ballard led the expedition to locate and film the watery grave that contains the wreckage of the *Titanic*. Discovered on September 1, 1985, under 2½ miles of ocean, this documentary offers breathtaking footage from the sea floor. 52 mins.
VHS: $25845. $19.95.

Titanica

A look at the events and circumstances behind the most notorious shipwreck in naval history, the *Titanic*, which, on its maiden voyage, struck an iceberg and sank, April 15, 1912. Naturalist director Stephen Low shot the film during the expedition of the Akademik Keldysh to the site of the Titanic's sinking in the North Atlantic. 94 mins.
Laser: LD71947. $69.95.

Top Flight

William Shatner hosts this celebration of the 40th anniversary of the United States Air Force. From the Wright Brothers to "The Right Stuff," it takes us into the cockpit to witness some of this nation's most historic and heroic moments. With thrilling aerial footage and personal stories of the men and women behind the achievements. USA, 47 mins.
VHS: $15398. $29.95.

Train Now Departing

When the steam locomotive was abandoned in the 60's, a piece of history disappeared, but nothing could dampen the fire of the steam enthusiast. About a thousand trains survived the scrap heap; some are in museums, others are back on the lines in pristine condition—a breath of the past and a noisy reminder that the spirit of the steam age lives on. Produced by the BBC.
Train Now Departing Part One. 87 mins.
VHS: $12388. $19.94.
Train Now Departing Part Two. 86 mins.
VHS: $12389. $19.94.

Treasures of a Lost Voyage

A rich, historic shipwreck gives up its long lost treasure to a group of high tech adventurers and a submersible robot. Gold worth millions draws them in, resulting in this entertaining documentary. 60 mins. From the Discovery Channel.
VHS: $25075. $19.95.

Trolley

This program is a nostalgic, sentimental tribute to the ingenuity and perseverance in the construction and deployment of America's street cars. 60 mins.
VHS: $17179. $19.95.

Union Pacific's 40th Anniversary Steam Excursion

On the 40th anniversary of the debut steam excursion on the Union Pacific Railroad, the Rocky Mountain Railroad Club sponsored a historic retracing of the original route. The trip originated in Denver and ended in Laramie, Wyoming. 60 mins.
VHS: $20084. $29.95.

Visual History of Cars

A three-volume extensive history of cars with facts, rare car footage from yesterday and today.
Visual History of Cars—Volume 1. Covers Jeep, Volkswagen, Firebird and Thunderbird. 115 mins.
VHS: $11254. $59.95.
Visual History of Cars—Volume 2. Covers Lincoln, Cadillac, Mercedes Benz and Jaguar. 115 mins.
VHS: $11255. $59.95.
Visual History of Cars—Volume 3. Covers Aston Martin, Corvette, BMW and Mustang. 115 mins.
VHS: $11256. $59.95.

Wheels a' Rolling

This pageant play was produced for the 1934 Chicago Railroad Fair. It is a unique stage production, preserved on film, that tries to capture the epic sweep of America's railroads and their progress across the continent. 30 mins.
VHS: $24078. $14.95.

Wild Blue Yonder: The U.S. Air Force Story

From the "flyboys" of the first warplanes (1909), to dogfights of the World Wars, to precision bombing, Enola Gay and the jet age, this is the history of American aviation warfare. 45 mins.
VHS: $13131. $29.95.

Wings of the Red Star

Now that the Cold War is over, Russian MIG's can be documented in this three-volume set from the Discovery Channel. *Vol. 1: Duel over Korea, Vol. 2: The Phantom's Foe* and *Vol. 3: The Foxbat* show precisely why these brutal fighters were so feared. 180 mins.
VHS: $25091. $39.95.

Wings over the Gulf, Vol. 1: First Strike: F-15 Eagle, F-117A, Nighthawk

The Discovery Channel obtained recently declassified footage which shows the F-15 Eagle, the F-117A and the Nighthawk in action during the Gulf War. This is a look at the real strategy deployed by these fighters. 60 mins.
VHS: $25094. $9.95.

Wings over the Gulf, Vol. 2: In Harm's Way: Tornado, A-6 Intruder

The Tornado and A-6 Intruder were two of the aircraft that made military history in the Gulf War. Now the Discovery Channel can show the effective technology that defeated Saddam Hussein. 60 mins.
VHS: $25095. $9.95.

Wings over the Gulf, Vol. 3: The Final Assault: F-16 Falcon, A-10 Thunderbolt

In Operation Desert Storm, both the F-16 Falcon and the A-10 Thunderbolt II were indispensable fighting machines. The Discovery Channel shows the role played by these amazing aircraft, using actual footage from the war. 60 mins.
VHS: $25096. $9.95.

Wings over the Gulf: Complete Set

This three volume set includes *First Strike: F-15 Eagle, F-117A, Nighthawk, In Harm's Way: Tornado, A-6 Intruder* and *The Final Assault: F-16 Falcon, A-10 Thunderbolt.* 180 mins.
VHS: $26152. $24.95.

Wings over the World

From the Wright Brothers' wobbly take-off to beyond the sound barrier, this 13-part series tells the stories of the great aircraft—commercial aircraft, war planes, helicopters, supersonic jets—and of their inventors, combining interviews with the aircraft pioneers, stories of struggle, heart-stopping success and heart-breaking failure, and spectacular aerial photography of both yesterday and today. Narrated by Richard Todd.
A Tale of Two German Giants. The story of Claude Dornier and Willy Messerschmidt from the days of Count Zeppelin through the fighter aircraft of World War II to their success in postwar European aviation. 49 mins.
VHS: $13371. $24.95.
Boeing: The Red Barn. From William Boeing's first seaplane to World War Two to Boeing Aircraft's post-war emergence as a leader in passenger transport. 49 mins.
VHS: $13370. $24.95.
Fokker: A Dream Fulfilled. From Anthony Fokker's first company in Germany to its move to Holland during World War I to Fokker Aircraft's role in World War II—on both sides. 49 mins.
VHS: $13373. $24.95.
Higher, Further and Faster. The race to build and beat the Concorde. 49 mins.
VHS: $13377. $24.95.
Igor Sikorsky: A Man and His Dream. From the beginnings of Russian aviation to modern helicopters. 49 mins.
VHS: $13369. $24.95.
In Defense of Neutrality. The history of Swedish aviation and how Sweden became a combat-ready country with no military runways. 49 mins.
VHS: $13374. $24.95.
Legacy of a Legend Builder. Roy Chadwick's accomplishments, from his early work with Alliot Verden Roe to the Avro Lancaster bombers. 49 mins.
VHS: $13375. $24.95.
McDonnell-Douglas: A Tale of Two Giants. The early years of this giant of aviation. 49 mins.
VHS: $13368. $24.95.
Project Cancelled. Projects both tragic and hilarious that never got off the ground. 49 mins.
VHS: $13380. $24.95.
The Dassault Dream. From the earliest days of French aviation to the present. 49 mins.
VHS: $13378. $24.95.
The Dream Becomes the Disaster. Great Britain's early passenger aircraft from the de Havilland Comet to the Nimrod. 49 mins.
VHS: $13376. $24.95.
The Lockheed Legend. From the Lockheed brothers' start in a garage in 1910 to spy planes. 49 mins.
VHS: $13372. $24.95.

Wings over Water: History of American Naval Aviation

Subtitled *The Complete Video History of American Naval Aviation*, this program considers the historical, strategic and personal role of naval aviation in America's emergence as a world power. The program covers the vast historical arc, from Teddy Roosevelt's Rough Riders through the present, dealing with technological development, foreign relations, international tension and wartime experiences. 59 mins.
VHS: $18570. $29.95.

Woodsmen and River Drivers

Archival footage is extensively used to document a vanished work life, together with oral histories in the story of the men who drove wood down Maine's Machias River. A project of the Northeast Archives of Folklore, this look at life in Maine in the early years of the century is both fascinating and moving.
VHS: $14818. $29.95.

World of Discovery: Red Express: The Trans-Siberian Railroad

An ethnographic travelogue captured through Russia's Trans-Siberian Express. This work follows 6000 miles and seven time zones, capturing a history, time and place that has remained closed. 50 mins.
VHS: $19308. $19.98.

World of Discovery: Tall Ship: High Sea Adventure

An adventure aboard *The Danmark*, a tall ship. Set in the raging North Atlantic, the program examines the technical responsibilities of sailing, joining the 80 cadets dealing with 13-story masts and 12,000 feet of rope and wires. 50 mins.
VHS: $19306. $19.98.

X-Planes

This is a program about experimental planes and the men who flew them. Includes daring feats by test pilots, the Wright brothers, Chuck Yeager and NASA pilots. 60 mins.
VHS: $13118. $19.98.

COMPUTERS

Bits & Bytes

An up-to-date look at personal computers which uses animated sequences and step-by-step instruction to look at the two principal "platforms"—PC-compatibles and Macintoshes.
Basics. Looks at simple DOS and Windows commands for PCs, function keys, the workings of a hard disk, the binary system, computer safety, "booting," saving, retrieving and printing text, ROM and RAM, and measuring the speed of the CPU. 29 mins.
VHS: $20447. $19.95.
Files. Introduction to databases: files, record fields, freeform, flat-file and relational databases, mail-merge, database applications in a video store and an airline reservation system, hypercard for the Mac, encyclopedias on CD-ROM, cache memory. 29 mins.
VHS: $20450. $19.95.
Messages. Simple file-transfer programs, parallel and serial ports, local area networks, file-servers, e-mail, analog vs. digital, modems, baud rate and communication protocol, uploading and downloading, electronic bulletin boards and on-line information services. 29 mins.
VHS: $20451. $19.95.
Numbers. Spreadsheet applications, including Lotus, Excel, playing "what-if" games, macros and templates for spreadsheets, displaying numbers in chart form, multi-tasking, the concept of computer speed. 29 mins.
VHS: $20449. $19.95.
Pictures. Paint and draw programs and bit-mapped vs. vector graphics, scalable fonts and the PostScript language, business presentation programs, screen resolution and VGA or Super VGA cards, scanning and retouching photos, desktop video and multi-media. 29 mins.
VHS: $20452. $19.95.
Words. Word processing principles: wrap-around text, insert, delete, cut and paste, change the appearance of text, WYSIWYG, macros, CRTs and pixels, formatting disks, combining text and graphics, desk top publishing, and a look at the Mac and IBM's OS/2 and WordPerfect and Word for Windows. 29 mins.
VHS: $20448. $19.95.
Bits & Bytes, Complete Set. The six volumes of the *Bits & Bytes* modern computer series.
VHS: $20453. $99.95.

Bits and Bytes Set

A comprehensive series designed to demystify the computer and other technology and make their functions and capabilities more accessible and easier to learn. Designed by computer training experts, the series looks at emerging technologies, the principles behind computer use and introductions to basic programming. 180 mins.
VHS: $19376. $149.95.

Chaos: A Video Demonstration

In this video, Rudy Rucker shows a wide range of chaotic graphics produced by CHAOS: The Software. A wonderful introduction to chaos theory. 30 mins.
VHS: $13903. $29.95.

The Creative Spirit Complete Set

This engaging work attempts to examine the relationship of creativity and output. Produced by IBM, the provocative series examines creativity in a number of disparate fields, and how to further it for your own potential. 240 mins.
VHS: $19378. $99.95.

D-Base for D-Base III, An Introduction

Conquer the world of computer software. Learn how to set up files, enter information, add, edit and delete data from your data base, as well as retrieve and display your data. For the first time user, little or no experience is required. 30 mins.
VHS: $12576. $14.95.

DOS—Disc Operating System, An Introduction

The heart of your computer, learn how to use your computer faster and more efficiently via the DOS. Learn how to log in, set time and date, use directory commands, format, copy and erase discs, copy and delete files. Professional instructors give practical examples. 30 mins.
VHS: $12574. $14.95.

The Dream Machine

This popular series is a look at high-tech computer graphics, surveying state-of-the-art developments in hardware and software.
Volume 1: Visual Computer.
 Laser: LD70107. $49.95.
Volume 2: Computer Dreams.
 Laser: LD70108. $49.95.
Volume 3: Computer Visions.
 Laser: LD70122. $49.95.

Fractal Lumination

Beau Lee is an artist explorer of hyper-dimensional realities who combines computer-generated designs based on fractal mathematics with music from diverse sources. William Aura, Craig Chaquico, The Soto Band and EKO are just some of the musical contributors heard on this unique video. 50 mins.
VHS: $23865. $19.95.

How to Produce a CD-ROM

An introduction to the steps involved in producing a CD-ROM, from concept to development to production. Several examples of CD-ROM productions are included. 20 mins.
VHS: $22790. $149.00.

Lotus 123, An Introduction

How to use the world's most popular spread sheet program. Learn how to set up spread, enter text and numerical information, use formulas and ranges. Also provided is instruction on cell format and cell edit entries, as well as erasing cells and saving spreadsheets. 30 mins.
VHS: $12575. $19.95.

Lotus 123, Database

Will teach you to understand database concepts such as entering information into your database; add, edit and delete data; retrieve and display data. Work through all database features with easy, step-by-step examples.
VHS: $12580. $14.95.

Lotus 123, Graphs

We will show you how to use graph features of Lotus 123. You will define data ranges, create pie charts, bar charts and stacked bar charts. The power of graphs explained with easy, step-by-step examples.
VHS: $12579. $14.95.

National Center for Baseball in the News Series

Some of baseball's greatest moments in the World Series, All Star games, spring training and off-diamond highlights in three volumes tracing the recent history of baseball. Each program is approx. 60 mins.

Supercomputing Applications

Animated visualizations which represent the state-of-the-art in scientific computing. Includes a computer simulation of the global climactic effects of increased greenhouse gases and a study of the landscape dynamics of Yellowstone National Park. 60 mins.
VHS: $13898. $25.00.

Spacetime Visualization

These 3D visual effects allow the viewer to "see" objects moving at near light speed velocities through computer simulation techniques. 20 mins.
VHS: $13899. $20.00.

Staking a Claim in Cyberspace

Converging technologies in computers, telephones and interactive TV offer a new challenge for community organizers. They are working to ensure that the Information Superhighway will be accessible for all people, leaving no one left out of the information revolution. 30 mins.
VHS: $23105. $19.95.

Supercomputing Review, Vol. 1

An outstanding collection of the latest visualizations from three leading supercomputer centers: San Diego, Pittsburgh, and Ohio. 30 mins.
VHS: $13900. $25.00.

The Video Guide to the Internet

This informative visual overview of the internet features graphics and demonstrations of key tools such as e-mail, World Wide Web and Mosaic. The history and more importantly the future of this growing technology is explained and demystified for the home viewer. 45 mins.
VHS: $24311. $19.95.

Virtual Reality

A compendium presenting an overview of the exciting field of virtual reality. This tape features demonstrations from research laboratories that are at the forefront of this exciting new technology. Discover what the future has in store. 60 mins.
VHS: $13902. $29.95.

Wordperfect Quickstart

Thirty minutes to introduce novices to the wonders of WordPerfect, including practical examples, help menus, keyboard functions, and how to edit, delete and insert text. 30 mins.
VHS: $11521. $14.95.

Wordperfect, An Introduction

The most popular, easy to use, professional word processing package today is WordPerfect 5.0. Learn the most often used WordPerfect functions and special keyboard functions: creating and saving a document, deleting and inserting text into your documents. 30 mins.
VHS: $12577. $19.95.

Wordstar, An Introduction

If you need to get up and running on Wordstar, then this is the instruction program for you. Learn Wordstar's special functions: creating and saving a document, editing, inserting and deleting text, reformatting your document. 30 mins.
VHS: $12578. $19.95.

Your First Computer: A Consumer's Guide to Buying and Using

Experienced instructors reveal step-by-step methods and easy-to-follow examples that will help you use your computer right away. Explained are how computers store and retrieve information, the different types of software available and which type of computer to purchase for your needs. 30 mins.
VHS: $12573. $14.95.

personal GROWTH

The 12 Steps
A video collection of five tapes and workbook of the process developed by Alcoholics Anonymous and used in other recovery programs. Recovering addicts explain each step, stressing the benefits of recovery.
VHS: $18654. $149.95.

Abbey Semel, M.S., R.D., Lic. A, and Stephen Rechtschaffen, M.D.: Nutrition for Life
We are what we eat. This video is an informative guide for achieving wellness through food. The effects of various foods are discussed as they affect both the mind and the body. Suggestions are made that can be followed at home or even in restaurants. 110 mins.
VHS: $23211. $39.95.

Addiction and Responsibility
Francis Seeburger is the respected chair of the Philosophy Department at the University of Denver. He has written about the spiritual craving that underlies all addictions. Like the Saint, the addict has devoted him or herself completely to one thing, and these longings can lead to spiritual redemption. 60 mins.
VHS: $23620. $34.95.

Addiction, Attachment, and Spiritual Crisis
Christina Grof describes her struggle with alcoholism, which led to her unique spiritual insights. Addiction results from a yearning for spiritual union. The crises associated with this yearning can lead to higher states of personality integration. Grof is the author of The Thirst for Wholeness. 60 mins.
VHS: $23629. $34.95.

Adoption: Your Guide to Success
Explores various adoption methods as well as the emotional ups and downs experienced by adoptive parents and birth mothers. Host Jobeth Williams dispels many of the myths surrounding adoption. Features interviews with attorneys, agency officials, counselors and psychologists. 75 mins.
VHS: $16391. $34.95.

The Adventure of Self-Discovery
With Stanislav Grof, MD. The innovative psychotherapist and author of Beyond the Brain and Realms of the Human Unconscious describes the stages of the birth process and how they relate to attitudes we develop later in life. 90 mins.
VHS: $08623. $49.95.

Adventure of the Spirit
Richard Bach has written such important books as Jonathan Livingston Seagull. In this video he shares his insights about the relationship between fact and fiction. Reality is ultimately much deeper than the physical world apprehended by the senses. 60 mins.
VHS: $23618. $34.95.

Affirmations for Living Beyond Cancer
Dr. Bernie Siegel is the well-recognized author and lecturer whose practice offers hope to those living with cancer. Inner balance can lead to greater strength and a state of wellness. This video combines the latest techniques, supported by medical research, to regaining wellness with natural sounds and positive affirmations.
VHS: $27475. $24.95.
Jan C. Nickman, USA, 1995, 30 mins.

Alan Watts: The Art of Meditation
Filmmaker Elda Hartley made a number of films with Alan Watts from 1965 until his death in 1973. This video brings the best of those works together. Watts demonstrates meditative disciplines, including posture, breathing and concentration. Also included is Hartley's film Meditation: The Inward Journey.
VHS: $26138. $19.95.
Elda Hartley, USA, 1965-1973, 50 mins.

Alternative Medicine Natural Home Remedies
This video will help you learn how to treat more than 50 common health conditions using inexpensive, natural methods. Dr. Jay Gordon shows how to use ordinary ingredients such as garlic, honey and ginger root for relief from conditions like acne, allergies, anxiety, toothaches and warts. 52 mins.
VHS: $22687. $29.95.

Angel Stories, Volume 1
Angels have emerged as legitimate harbingers of messages from another reality. Interviews reveal actual encounters between people and these mythic figures that some thought existed only in scripture. 60 mins.
VHS: $22748. $19.95.

Angel Stories, Volume 2
Angels seem to proliferate as more and more people come forward to claim direct contact with these spiritual entities. This volume continues to explore the reality of angels in our midst. 60 mins.
VHS: $22749. $19.95.

Arising from Flames: Overcoming Anger Through Patience
The Dalai Lama speaks about positive and negative desire. Through training we can reduce anger and hatred and increase love and forgiveness. His Holiness also speaks of transforming society by changing the individual. He explains how to calm the mind and relates his own difficult circumstances. 60 mins.
VHS: $22709. $29.95.

Art and Science of Human Transformation
Jean Houston, the author of The Possible Human, The Search for the Beloved and Godseed, presents three new tapes on human potential.
Walking the Life Journey. The vision of sacred stewardship, the discovery of "The Possible Society," with a vivid recollection of Jean Houston's mentor, Margaret Mead, discussion of the legend of the Grail, and a vision of humanity as "the beings who live for all life." 90 mins.
VHS: $10144. $39.95.
Creating a World That Works. Jean Houston sets the perspective of what it's like to be here now—at this critical point in human history. Using processes—the crossing of the Crystal Bridge and its empowerment, heart-to-heart linking, and the ancient dance of Enos Mythos—participants discover ingredients they need to fulfill themselves as planetary stewards. 102 mins.
VHS: $10146. $39.95.

The Art of Aikido
This harmonious system of defense blends the movement of an attacker into his own downfall. Dr. Lee, Ah Loi and 7th Dan articulate Shikko (knee walking), techniques from a kneeling position, bowing etiquette, parrying, hitting, blocking, throwing and breakfalling training. 45 mins.
VHS: $26847. $24.95.

Awakening Your Body's Energies
With George Leonard. This aikido trainer and author of The Silent Pulse demonstrates several awareness exercises in which the viewer can participate, including balancing, centering and transforming pain to energy. 90 mins.
VHS: $08628. $49.95.

Balance and Coordination for Seniors
Using movements from T'ai-Chi, Master Bob Klein and Jean Goulet demonstrate how to be more flexible and avoid falls. This instruction will help seniors prevent strains and accidents. 70 mins.
VHS: $23667. $19.95.

Becoming Orgasmic
Nineteen out of twenty women are said to be helped by the techniques revealed in this video. Increasing desire and comfort can open up new pathways to orgasm and greater fulfillment. 83 mins.
VHS: $25055. $29.95.

Benefits of Long-Term Meditation
With Shinzen Young. Meditation practices can lead to permanent changes in the awareness of the self and the transcendence of the ego, says an ordained Buddhist Monk and scholar of Buddhism. 30 mins.
VHS: $08644. $29.95.

Bernie Siegel, M.D.: How to Never Grow Old and Die Young at Heart
Drawing upon his unique approach with people facing chronic or catastrophic illness, Dr. Siegel shares new information about living healthy and dying young at heart. He is the author of the best-selling book, Love, Medicine, and Miracles. 65 mins.
VHS: $23202. $39.95.

Bioenergy: A Healing Art
An intelligent, mind-stretching video, this tape explores the unique ability of bioenergy to facilitate healing and our own bioelectric being. Poignant stories from clients and interviews with Polish healer Mietek Wirkus, as well as researchers Dr. Robert Becker, Elmer Green, PhD., and Steve Fahrion, give a complete picture of this amazing phenomenon. 46 mins.
VHS: $22688. $29.95.

Body and Soul: The Complete Workout
Handsome David Torres is joined by a group of sexy workout partners as he guides the viewer through a day of complete fitness. This attractive trainer from Los Angeles explains the importance of body-building techniques, aerobic exercise, good nutrition and a positive outlook. 60 mins.
VHS: $23128. $29.95.

Boundaries of the Soul: Explorations in Jungian Analysis
With June Singer, Ph.D. Jungian analysis focuses on unconscious archetypes that operate beneath cultural conditioning, says this analyst and author of Boundaries of the Soul. Transformation, she says, must emerge from within this dynamic interplay of images. 90 mins.
VHS: $08621. $49.95.

A Call to Greatness
Isana Mada believes that many people are experiencing an awakening but that the isolation of the ego keeps us from full awareness. In this video she describes the essential process of surrender that leads to spiritual alignment with the higher Self. 60 mins.
VHS: $23627. $34.95.

Callanetics
Callan Pinkney, author of the best-selling book, demonstrates her innovative deep-muscle exercise technique that "sheds years off your figure in hours without putting pressure on your back." 60 mins.
VHS: $10956. $24.95.

Caroline Myss: Energy Anatomy and Self Diagnosis
A pioneer in the study of energy medicine and the relation to human consciousness, Caroline Myss discusses her research into the power centers of the body. The program also examines why people are unable to heal and the reasons people fall into patterns of behavior. 170 mins.
VHS: $20224. $59.95.

Chen Style T'ai-chi-Ch'uan
Step-by-step instructions of the "cannon fist" form, where the soft exterior disguises great power, are found in this video. Many camera angles are used to ease the learning experience and self-defense applications are shown for each movement. Features Master Tseng and Yun Xiang. 90 mins.
VHS: $26826. $19.95.

Chinese Chi-Gung Health
This ancient Chinese health exercise combines slow movements, special breathing techniques and concentration to bring vitality and health to the body. Movements based on the snake and tiger, as well as the philosophy behind this healing method, are explored. 60 mins.
VHS: $22701. $24.95.

Chinese Herbs for Health
This video explains the cooking of medicinal Chinese herbs and teas, even the creation of an herbal health kit. It is designed for newcomers. Acupuncturists Harriet Beinfeld and Efrem Korngold, authors of the definitive text on Chinese herbs, Between Heaven and Earth, and Chef/Zen master Ed Brown are featured. 59 mins.
VHS: $22697. $24.95.

Chinese Kickboxing
Complete instructions for the full contact T'ai-chi-Ch'uan system of kickboxing are included in this video. Punching, kicking, grappling, ground fighting and the use of animal styles, such as the snake, tiger, monkey, crane and drunken movements are all explained by Master Bob Klein. 2-tape set, 230 mins.
VHS: $26825. $19.95.

Chinese Kung-fu
Master Tseng is certified by the Taiwanese government. He demonstrates step-by-step instructions which explain the snake, tiger, monkey, crane, drunken and mantis styles. With Yun Xiang. 50 mins.
VHS: $26832. $19.95.

Circle of Recovery
Bill Moyers' moving PBS special on recovering from drug and alcohol addiction. Moyers focuses on a group of seven African-American men in northern California, who are overcoming addiction to become mirrors of hope in their community. USA.
VHS: $15268. $19.95.

Colin Wilson: The High and the Low
In this moving program Colin Wilson shares with us his personal struggle in dealing with states of panic and depression; in Part II he elaborates on his Laurel and Hardy theory of consciousness as a model for attaining optimal mental functioning. 90 mins.
VHS: $13322. $49.95.

Coming Down from the Mountain: The Men's Movement
New from bestselling author John Lee is a groundbreaking video which explores the essence of the Men's Movement today and shows how men can break destructive cycles and begin living fuller lives. Joining John are Shepard Bliss, Jed Diamond and Dan Jones. 54 mins.
VHS: $18088. $24.95.

Compassion in Action
With Ram Dass. Ram Dass probes the nature of helping relationships. He suggests that when we look deeply into human beings, no matter how desperate the situation, we are able to honor and learn from them. 90 mins.
VHS: $08630. $49.95.

The Conference Faculty: Aging Conference Highlights
A compilation of key moments from the Omega's Culture in Transition Conference is found on this video. It provides an overview and panel discussion that ties many issues together. Ram Dass, Marion Woodman, Rabbi Zalman Schachter, Mary Catherine Bateson, gerontologist Harry Moody, and Sufi Master and Omega cofounder Pir Vilayat Khanmins all offer their views. 117 mins.
VHS: $23204. $29.95.

Conscious Living/Conscious Dying
With Stephen Levine. Genuine healing occurs when we take ourselves mercifully into our own hearts and accept the totality of our lives. A poet and meditation teacher, Levine is the author of Healing into Life and Death and Who Dies?. 90 mins.
VHS: $08631. $49.95.

A Conversation with Thomas Moore
Thomas Moore, author of the bestsellers Care of the Soul and Soul Mates, offers inspiration in the last place anyone would think to look; within the self. His lectures help people to accept themselves rather than to improve themselves. 60 mins.
VHS: $26137. $19.95.

The Couple's Guide to Great Sex over 40, Volume 1
This informative and erotic series explores sex in mid-life and beyond. Four real couples discuss the pros and cons of sex in their 40's, 50's and 60's. Techniques to facilitate communication and experimentation, the use of toys, and positions that accommodate back problems are included. Even erection difficulties and oral sex are addressed. 60 mins.
VHS: $26418. $34.95.

The Couple's Guide to Great Sex over 40, Volume 2
In this video, health topics like exercise and diet are discussed as they affect sex. Interviews with couples also reveal the changes brought on by aging, including menopause. In addition, penile injections, vacuum devices for erections and positions that facilitate deep penetration are shown, all in an explicit and erotic manner. 60 mins.
VHS: $26419. $34.95.

Covert Bailey's Smart Exercise: Burning Fat, Getting Fit
Bailey is the author of the book The New Fit or Fat. Now this prolific author shares his tips for healthful toning and exercise in this video. He can help you achieve your right to a healthy body. 82 mins.
VHS: $23944. $14.98.

Crystal Vista
Visual effects and space music combine to create a fantasy otherworldly experience. Music track.
VHS: Out of print. For rental only.
Laser: LD70243. $24.95.
Iasos, USA, 1982, 30 mins.

Cultivating Mindfulness
With Charles T. Tart. The underlying cause of most social and personal problems is lack of mindfulness. The author of Waking Up discusses how difficult it is to translate meditative awareness to daily life. 30 mins.
VHS: $08645. $29.95.

The Da Vinci Body Series: Vol. 1
Subtitled A Workout for the Renaissance Man of the 90s, this program takes the viewer through rigorous movements, exercises and routines to explore the best means to achieve maximum strength and conditioning for the upper body. With a step-by-step narration.
VHS: $18260. $24.95.

Deepak Chopra: Body, Mind and Soul
Chopra's view on the nexus between these three vital elements of human existence has been read by nearly six million readers in his five best sellers. This two-tape set brings his unique teachings to an easy-to-follow video format. 120 mins.
VHS: $27759. $39.98.

Designed Brain
Bob Samples, director of Solstice Seminars and author of seven books, mixes humor with content in covering natural and cultural approaches to reality, and the different qualities of apprehending and comprehending mind. He illustrates the important roles played by intuition, intelligence and creativity. 102 mins.
VHS: $10143. $39.95.

Diet for a New America: Your Health, Your Planet
Host John Robbins takes us on a journey into the great American food machine, drawing ideas from his Pulitzer Prize nominated book. In simple, startling pictures, he reveals the dramatic impact of our daily food choices on the health of both our bodies and the environment. 60 mins.
VHS: $16388. $19.95.

Discovering Everyday Spirituality
Thomas Moore, author of the best sellers Care of the Soul and Soulmates, hosts this four-video set. Interviews with five individuals reveal how one can garner greater satisfaction in everyday life through a deeper knowledge of humanity. 180 mins.
VHS: $27760. $79.98.

Discovering the Mystical Yucatan: Activating the Energy of the Heart
Psychotherapist, channeller and past-life facilitator Susan Drew visits the sacred sites of Chichen Itza, the Loltun Caves, Uxmal, Kabah, Sayil, Cabo and Tulum. The journey takes place during the acceleration of the Time Shift energy. 60 mins.
VHS: $20157. $24.95.

Discovering Your Expressive Body
Basic concepts in dance training utilizing Bartenieff fundamentals, with Peggy Hackney and Irmgard Bartenieff. This comprehensive demonstration provides a basis for expanded knowledge of movement principles that lead to an articulate, more expressive body. USA, 1981, 60 mins.
VHS: $15337. $49.95.

Dr. Bernie Siegel
Dr. Siegel, a surgeon and teacher at Yale New Haven Hospital and prominent author of two best selling books, Love, Medicine and Miracles and Peace, Love and Healing, outlines the way patients can respond to the crisis of illness. He helps them to assume more control over their lives, resolve conflicts in their relationships, and then focus more energy toward healing. USA, 75 mins.
VHS: $15606. $29.95.

Dr. Devious: More Dance in Cyberspace
Virtual reality offers new possibilities in this surreal inner landscape of the subconscious. This program welcomes you to relax, enjoy and contemplate the "alpha state where your subconscious mind resides."
VHS: S18924. $19.95.

Dr. Ji Liang Chen: Ba Duan Jin Qi Gong (Eight Pieces of Brocade)
Qi Gong is the ancient Chinese system of mind, breath and body that develops and refines the Qi, the vital force. Dr. Chen is a Shaolin master from the Beijing Traditional Chinese Medical Hospital. Eight exercises are explained by Dr. Chen in this video, that build strength and wisdom by harnessing Qi. 78 mins.
VHS: S23206. $36.00.

Dr. Sandra Scantling's Ordinary Couples, Extraordinary Sex
Ordinary Couples, Extraordinary Sex goes beyond self-imposed limits to explore new vistas in sexuality, giving couples the tools to transform ordinary sex into extraordinary sex.
Discovering Extraordinary Sex. Dr. Scantling is a licensed clinical psychologist and certified sex therapist. She shares her research in this video with the help of three couples. They go beyond self-imposed limits to reach new vistas in sexuality. 60 mins.
VHS: S23938. $29.95.
Getting Creative with Sex. Beyond the routine which often characterizes sex for many long-term couples, there lies a realm of creative sex. This video presents advanced exercises and suggestions to help couples have more fun with each other. 60 mins.
VHS: S23939. $29.95.
Keeping Sex Extraordinary. Dr. Scantling engages in one-on-one sessions with her patients. This permits viewers to see how her suggestions lead to dramatic, real-life improvements in sexual intimacy. 60 mins.
VHS: S23940. $29.95.

Drugs and the Law
Steven B. Duke, a distinguished law professor, points out that the many problems associated with drugs actually result from the prohibition of drugs. Death by violence and overdose, theft, health risks and law enforcement expenditures are just some of the problems that result from current drug policies. 60 mins.
VHS: S23628. $34.95.

Eagle Claw Kung-fu
This extremely vigorous Kung-fu style is demonstrated by Master Tseng and Yun Xiang. Step-by-step instructions explain the defense application of each movement. 56 mins.
VHS: S26824. $19.95.

Ebony/Jet Guide to Black Excellence Program 1: The Entrepreneurs
In this charismatic, revealing series about African-American achievement and empowerment, this program profiles the will and determination of three successful entrepreneurs: publisher John H. Johnson; Maxima Corporation CEO Joshua I. Smith; and actress and television commentator Oprah Winfrey. 35 mins.
VHS: S17100. $14.95.

Edible and Medicinal Herbs Vol. I
Dr. Sharol Tilgner introduces a variety of wild edible and medicinal herbs. Identifying and collecting these plants for food and medicine are a vital technique amply illustrated by this video. Perfect for beginners or the seasoned herbalist. 60 mins.
VHS: S22698. $29.95.

Edible and Medicinal Herbs Vol. II
In Volume II, Dr. Sharol Tilgner covers 20 new plants. From the woods to an herb garden, there are detailed instructions on gathering and preparing these edible and medicinal plants. 60 mins.
VHS: S22699. $29.95.

Emotionally Free
Based on the book by Dr. David Viscott, this how-to video presents a program for self-actualization based on letting go of the past to live in the moment. 60 mins.
VHS: S20470. $19.95.

Emotions of Life
Here three critical mental crises are examined: *Aggression* deals with our fears and frustrations in commonplace situations; *Depression* is a study of abnormal behavior; *Addiction* deals with alcoholism as a model of drug dependence with its attendant impact on the family and society.
VHS: S03992. $64.95.

Essentials of Karate with Chris Thompson
In addition to a brief history of Karate, basic step-by-step instruction emphasizes the power of this martial art. Punching, blocking, sparring, stance training, free fighting and the five basic Kata are shown at various film speeds. 45 mins.
VHS: S26850. $24.95.

The Euro Guide to Sexual Fitness: Sexercise
Exercises are demonstrated in this video which promise to enhance sexual capability and sexual desire. Actual couples show caresses and massage methods that sensitize the body. Renewed interest, greater energy and responsiveness along with new and less inhibited communication should result. 65 mins.
VHS: S26417. $29.95.

An Evening with Dr. Bernie Siegel
"It can be a lifesaver," says Ann Landers. Dr. Siegel is a surgeon who wrote the best-selling book *Love, Medicine and Miracles.* His basic themes are the healing qualities of love and peace of mind. His techniques utilizing dreams, drawings, music, patient participation and responsibility are helping to change the way medicine is taught and practiced. The tape includes stories of hope, discussion of the role of the subconscious, and a guided imagery exercise with music. "If you or someone you care about has a life-threatening illness, this video will give you hope." 108 mins.
VHS: S10138. $39.95.

Everybody Rides the Carousel
Based on the theories of Erik Erikson's influential psychoanalytic teachings, this animated feature presents a profound and joyous excursion through life. All the stages of life, with the accompanying inner feelings and conflicting emotions, are beautifully rendered. 72 mins.
VHS: S22869. $39.95.

Evolution of the Magical Child
A three-session video by Joseph Chilton Pearce, a leading expert and spokesman on the development of human intelligence from infancy to adulthood. Pearce re-examines concepts of childbirth, rearing and schooling, stresses the critical issue of bonding and early imprinting. He looks at trends and practices in Western society which damage our creative potential, and follows the maturity of the magical child into adolescence and the challenges of adult life.
Evolution of the Magical Child—Volume 1. *The New Physics* and *Intelligence and Intellect.* 86 mins.
VHS: S10139. $39.95.
Evolution of the Magical Child—Volume 2. *Emotions and Relationships* and *Stages in Human Development.* 88 mins.
VHS: S10140. $39.95.
Evolution of the Magical Child—Volume 3. *Bonding and Integration* and *Imagery, Symbol and Metaphor.* 99 mins.
VHS: S10141. $39.95.

Explorations into Consciousness
Deepak Chopra has brought alternative medicine into the mainstream. His meditation therapies combine the forces of the mind and the body into a single wellspring of health. This best-selling author shows how the spiritual and the physical are linked. 35 mins.
VHS: S26801. $14.95.

Eye-Tripping Psychedelics
A three-volume series that approximates, through computer color-generated images, the sensation of psychedelic experiences. Each video is equipped with a pair of neon laser light disrupting glasses. 40 mins. each.
Vol. 1: Mesmerize.
VHS: S18050. $19.95.
Vol. 2: Brain Bliss.
VHS: S18051. $19.95.
Vol. 3: Hue Heaven.
VHS: S18052. $19.95.

Fat City
Host Roger Bingham explains several theories on why some people gain weight and others do not, and gives pointers on how to trigger weight loss. 30 mins.
VHS: S16389. $19.95.

Fit or Fat for the 90s
The video version of Covert Bailey's best-selling books, *Fit or Fat* and *The New Fit or Fat.* Bailey explains the relationship between good eating and body mechanics, and tells you how to get fit and stay fit.
VHS: S15622. $14.98.

Food for Thought
This program examines the environmental impact of America's love for beef: how it affects water resources, top soil, grain supplies, global warming and the fate of the rainforests. Hosted by Roger Bingham. 30 mins.
VHS: S16390. $19.95.

From Here to Alternity: Adventures of a Scientist
With John C. Lilly, MD. The author of *Center of the Cyclone* and *The Mind of the Dolphin* reveals a life of deep inner exploration, suggesting that within the province of the mind every limit is a belief system to be tested and transcended. 90 mins.
VHS: S08624. $49.95.

From Light to Enlightenment
In the sequel to his book *Light: Medicine of the Future*, Dr. Jacob Liberman challenges assertions that diseases are cured only through medicine. He sets up the guidelines for a new science that re-imagines the way personal experience impacts our ability to heal ourselves. 114 mins.
VHS: S20161. $29.95.

Fun with Herbs
Beverly Fennell shares her lifetime experience, previously available only to Hyssop Hill students. Planning and planting a garden, harvesting, drying, preserving and using herbs for gourmet meals are all covered in this video. Wreath making, potpourri and herbal cosmetics are also demonstrated. 60 mins.
VHS: S22700. $29.95.

Future of Humanity
A dialog between Krishnamurti and David Bohm which took place in England in 1983. Starting with the questions "Are psychologists really concerned with the future of man? Are they concerned with the human being conforming to the present society or going beyond that?", the conversation embarks on the incredible journey of the unconditioned mind and asks if the consciousness of mankind can be changed through time. 60 mins.
VHS: S12481. $29.95.

Gabrielle Roth: The Wave
The Wave imagines rhythms as the key to seeing life as energy, motion and movement. 40 mins.
VHS: S20222. $24.95.

Geomancy: Consciousness and Sacred Sites
Based on a 12-year study of sacred sites, John Steele describes how the heart is a "living organism." He describes sacred geometry, the levels of consciousness, forgetting who we are and how to remember. 59 mins.
VHS: S10393. $39.95.

Get Off the Karmic Wheel
Aileen Nobles presents a workshop in this video which illustrates the techniques put forward in her best-selling book, *Get Off the Karmic Wheel.* These spiritual journeys will clear the emotional body and release limiting belief systems, allowing a merger with a higher self. 120 mins.
VHS: S22703. $33.00.

Gifts from the Healing Earth, Volume I
Ellen Hopman leads this magical walk through a New England forest in spring, gathering ingredients. Then she prepares these elements in her kitchen. Finally, Hopman reveals how she found her way to the healing powers of herbalism. 70 mins.
VHS: S22942. $29.95.

Go for It!
A presentation by Oscar-winning filmmaker Vivienne Verdon-Roe at John Denver's "Choices for the Future" Conference. An inspiring story of how one person can overcome inhibitions and succeed in making a difference. Relating her own personal experiences, Vivienne encourages people to get involved in ending the arms race and other issues of importance. 42 mins.
VHS: S11494. $24.95.

The Good Sex Guide—Series No. 1
Margi Clarke hosts this television series compiled on three videos that is unafraid of asking questions about that most intimate of human activities: sex. The series combines factual information with the advice of health experts and the sexual experiences of ordinary people, all in a fun and engaging format. Sexual habits, size, sexual confidence and sexual etiquette are just some of the issues covered in these tapes.
VHS: S27348. $59.98.
Mike Adams/Richard Trayler-Smith/Martin Head, Great Britain, 1995, 175 mins.

The Good Sex Guide—Series No. 2
Margi Clarke is back for this second compilation of the unabashed series, once again available in a three-tape set. The importance of sex, mismatched sex drives, finding the perfect mate, love triangles, hidden triggers of sexual attraction, sexual fidelity, monogamy and more are discussed on these tapes.
VHS: S27349. $59.98.
Mike Adams/Richard Trayler-Smith/Martin Head, Great Britain, 1995, 175 mins.

The Guide to Advanced Sexual Positions
Explicit demonstrations using a variety of positions and even furniture make this video a surefire way to expand a sexual repertoire. Specific erogenous zones respond to positions that also permit deeper penetration. Overall intense sexual excitement and heightened intimacy are possible with the techniques shown here. 30 mins.
VHS: S26420. $19.95.

Guide to Getting Girls
How to project sex appeal, opening lines, how to make a woman eager to be with you are explained. 55 mins.
VHS: S10079. $29.95.

A Guide to Rational Living: The Principles of Rational-Motive Therapy
With Albert Ellis, Ph.D. Working to change your personal philosophy is a valid therapeutic technique which can lead to genuine growth. Albert Ellis, author of more than 50 books, is one of the most influential figures in modern psychology. 90 mins.
VHS: S08625. $49.95.

Healing and the Mind, Set
A five-tape boxed set of Bill Moyers' important series that reimagines different means of considering the mind and body.
VHS: S18639. $129.95.

Healing and the Mind: Healing from Within
Bill Moyers studies the controversial methodology of Jon Kabat-Zinn, who teaches Buddhist meditation techniques to alleviate pain. Moyers also examines the work of David Spiegel, a therapist who believes group psychotherapy prolongs the lives of women suffering from advanced cases of breast cancer. 58 mins.
VHS: S18636. $29.95.

Healing and the Mind: The Art of Healing
Bill Moyers visits Boston, Dallas and rural Oregon to study whether emotional stability lessens patients' vulnerability to disease and improves their chances of recovery. Moyers looks at a counseling program for an open-heart patient and her family, an intensive care unit for premature babies where nurses help mothers connect with their children, and a hospital that has radically changed its physical settings and services to aid patients in their physical and emotional healing. 58 mins.
VHS: S18637. $29.95.

Healing and the Mind: The Mind Body Connection
In a series of interviews with prominent specialists, Bill Moyers studies the mysterious connections between the mind and body. Psychologist Margaret Kemeny talks about how state of mind influences the immune system. Neuroscientist David Felten talks about how a patient's response to his condition affects how the body responds. Neuroscientist Candace Pert, who discovered the opiate receptor, relates how chemicals travel between the mind and body. 58 mins.
VHS: S18635. $29.95.

Healing and the Mind: The Mystery of Chi
Journalist Bill Moyers travels to China to examine the relationship of the mind and body, from the perspective of an ancient civilization. Chinese culture is dominated by Taoism, a philosophy governed by the yin-yang, two interdependent though opposite forces of nature that influence life. The traditional, unconventional nature of Chinese medicine—the use of herbs, acupuncture, massage and meditation—is to balance the flow of the chi, a mysterious energy that rages through the body. 58 mins.
VHS: S18634. $29.95.

Healing and the Mind: Wounded Healers
At a cancer retreat in Bolinas, California, Bill Moyers looks at the center's philosophy of helping patients cope with and accept their condition. Moyers follows the individual acts of a group of people who relate their individual stories and engage in a variety of activities, including yoga, meditation, relaxation and prayer, to overcome their fear, rage, hopelessness and despair. 58 mins.
VHS: S18638. $29.95.

Healing and the Unconscious
Dr Brugh Joy says the unconscious is composed of multiple, autonomous personalities. These personalities affect the state of our health. Esoteric rites and initiations were designed to call forth particular personalities from the unconscious at appropriate stages of development. 90 mins.
VHS: S13328. $49.95.

Healing from Within
Lani and Jama Smith heal through the principle that the mind, body and spirit are one. Many physical ailments are outward manifestations of suppressed emotions and negative programming. These healers use their own special energy and intuition to help others break free of disease. 60 mins.
VHS: S22691. $19.95.

A Healing Journey
Sree Chakravarti was a sickly housewife who became a spiritual healer. She claims that the pace of modern life does not allow us time to appreciate one another and that this in turn leads to illness. 60 mins.
VHS: S23616. $34.95.

The Healing Mind
Dr. Chopra grew up in India where he watched his physician father work. From this early exposure to the art of healing he developed a keen interest and a unique approach. He diagnoses diseases by touching the pulse. From his own healing center, Dr. Chopra instructs patients how meditation, yoga, music and purification therapies can help the body regain control. 60 mins.
VHS: S22689. $29.95.

Healing Sexual Abuse: The Recovery Process
This is an empowering journey through the recovery and healing process of sexual abuse victims. Meet survivors who remember painful events from their childhood, acknowledge what happened and put the experience behind them. Hosted by Dr. Eliana Gil. Also includes a resource guide. 60 mins.
VHS: S16383. $39.95.

Healing with Ancient Sound
A panel discussion held at the 4th National Unity in Yoga conference with panelists David Frowley, Cathryn Wersen and Eleanor Leatham discussing the history and uses of sound, the relationship of sound to the cosmos, and use of sound in meditations. 90 mins.
VHS: S10216. $29.95.

Healing with Shaolin Acupressure
Migraines, sinus tension headaches, ear infections, back pains, menstrual cramps and more can be healed through acupressure techniques. Master Robert Lyons, along with a minor student, shows how to find these pressure points and apply the appropriate pressure. 110 mins.
VHS: S26836. $19.95.

Healing Yourself with Mental Imagery
With Martin Rossman, MD. Mental imagery can provide a valuable adjunct to traditional medicine. The author of *Healing Yourself* shows how to dialog with one's symptoms and to interact with an "inner advisor" who can provide personal health guidance. 90 mins.
VHS: S08632. $49.95.

Health and Your Whole Being
With Kenneth R. Pelletier, Ph.D. What constitutes a balanced lifestyle? How can diet, exercise and stress management combine to produce optimal states of health? One of the world's foremost health authorities focuses on the details of developing a personal holistic health program. 90 mins.
VHS: S08619. $49.95.

Health Power
Health Power is a practical guide for feeling and looking better. Body composition, flexibility, strength, endurance and cardiovascular efficiency can be evaluated in your own home. Then a special fitness program can be designed just for you. Marc Sorenson, Ed.D., of the National Institute of Fitness and Neal Barnard, M.D., President of the Physician's Committee for Responsible Medicine are both featured. 45 mins.
VHS: S22692. $19.95.

Healthy Aging
Healthy Aging shows you how you can have more control over your longevity than you might think. Offering simple ways to prolong good health, the program outlines methods of diet, exercise, and stress control that contribute to a sounder lifestyle. Hosted by Ken Pelletier. Also includes a resource guide. 60 mins.
VHS: S16387. $39.95.

Herbal Preparations for Home Remedies
Holistic health educator Kay Moon Dreamer demonstrates the effective use of herbs in the preparation of folk remedies. 55 mins.
VHS: S20156. $24.95.

Homeopathic Care for Infants and Children

Nationally known pediatrician Dr. Lendon Smith discusses the most commonly used homeopathic remedies for bedwetting, colds, chicken pox, measles, ear infections, flu, teething, constipation, sore throats, diarrhea, etc. A remedy chart for easy diagnosis is included. 45 mins.
VHS: S22694. $24.95.

Homeopathic Care for Pets

Narrated by the nationally recognized consultant and lecturer on veterinary homeopathy Dr. Christine Chambreau, this video explains the most-used homeopathic veterinary methods. All five remedies discussed are found to be highly effective for feline acne and other skin ailments, arthritis, nervousness and digestive disorders. 45 mins.
VHS: S22695. $24.95.

Homeopathic Care for the Family

David E. Karp explains the 14 most commonly used homeopathic remedies. These are good for such routine ailments as bruises, cuts, scrapes, burns, shock, food-poisoning, motion sickness and more. 45 mins.
VHS: S22693. $24.95.

How Then Shall We Live?

This is a unique, independently-produced television series nationally broadcast on PBS, focused on the issues of consciousness and human survival, available for the first time on home video.
Awakening to Life Through Truthful Relationship and **On Pain, Perfection and the Work to Relieve Suffering.** Ram Dass, the author of *Miracle of Love* and *How Can I Help?* discusses social action, personal relationship, and the cultivation of a compassionate heart: "One dies as one lives…Once that starts to fall into place, then the question is how you use the moment to moment experiences of your life as a vehicle for awakening." 58 mins.
VHS: S04755. $49.95.
Finding a Path to an Open Heart and **Wisdom Has No Fear of Death.** Ram Dass explores the awakening of a higher consciousness: "There is a way of shifting consciousness so that you can see what we are is a collection of souls. And you can look further than that and see that we are all one in the form of the many. You see that a starving person or a dying person or a frightened person is you. You dive into service. The whole trip of "What's good for me? What do I want? What do I need? just becomes less interesting. And that's where the power is that changes the universe." 58 mins.
VHS: S04754. $49.95.
From Tragedy to Grace: Stages in the Process of Dying and **The Experience of Dying: A Guided Meditation.** Stephen Levine offers a transformational experience of the dying process: "The stages of dying are states of mind that occur during the process of letting go, during the process of acknowledging loss. It has a lot to do with ego death, the death of those things that block the heart." 51 mins.
VHS: S04754. $49.95.
No Other Generation: Twelve Voices from the 37th Year of the Nuclear Age. Ram Dass, Daniel Ellsberg, Dr. Helen Caldicott and nine other leading teachers and activists illuminate a mode of consciousness that combines spiritual wisdom, political awareness and psychological understanding. Appearing are Phillip Deere, Patricia Ellsberg, Chellis Glendinning, Ken Keyes Jr., Joanna Macy, Theodore Roszak, Swami Satchidananda, John Steiner and Diane Thomas. 54 mins.
VHS: S04760. $49.95.
Opening to Grief: The Threshold Task and **Purification by Fire: The Passage through Pain.** Stephen Levine, author of *A Gradual Awakening*, examines the healing nature of grief and the art of living with loss and impermanence. "What we've come together to do, all of us, is to stop postponing death. To come into the very presence of death. To confront death so profoundly that we take it within us, and therefore can go beyond it. As long as we're postponing death, we're postponing life" (Stephen Levine). 54 mins.
VHS: S04753. $49.95.

How to Conduct a Dream Workshop: A Practical Introduction

With Jeremy Taylor. Dream workshops are based on the premise that all dreams are in the service of health and wholeness. Jeremy Taylor, author of *Dreamwork*, is a leading advocate of leaderless dream workshops. 90 mins.
VHS: S08626. $49.95.

How to Live Between Office Visits, with Dr. Bernie Siegel

Dr. Siegel teaches how to embrace life, NOW, teaching how to overcome disease, emotional wounds and negative self-images to achieve peace. 80 mins.
VHS: S23332. $29.95.

How to Reawaken Your Sexual Powers

Becoming a better partner and lover or gaining a more rewarding relationship are possible through focusing on the fundamental powers of nature. Five attractive couples demonstrate techniques for increasing physical strength and enhancing emotional, mental and sexual energy. Better communication and trust will result from these techniques. 53 mins.
VHS: S22710. $39.95.

How to Spar Against Karate

Master Robert Lyons details exactly how to spar against Karate in tournaments. Blocking punches and kicks while delivering devastating attacks is vital. One-on-one instruction makes it all easy to follow. 80 mins.
VHS: S26840. $19.95.

How to Spar Against Tae Kwon Do

Master Robert Lyons spars with a Black Belt Tae Kwon Do expert. Detailed instruction on theory, footwork, punches, kicks and combinations is included. 80 mins.
VHS: S26841. $19.95.

How to Stop the One You Love from Drinking and Using Drugs

Hosted by Mariette Hartley, an insightful program that shows how to stop tragedy and start the healing by bringing together selected family, friends and the substance abuser in a situation called Intervention. 56 mins.
VHS: S09899. $24.95.

Hsing-I

Basic and intermediate training methods of this internal martial art are shown in this video. In addition, the philosophy of the five elements, the circulation of energy and the basic techniques and short form are included. 45 mins.
VHS: S26848. $24.95.

Human Dilemma: Explorations in Existential Psychotherapy

With Rollo May, Ph.D. The renowned author of *Love and Will* proposes that genuine growth comes from confronting the pain of existence rather than escaping into banal pleasures. Genuine joy emerges from appreciation of life's dilemmas. 90 mins.
VHS: S08618. $49.95.

I Love You, Let's Work It Out

A self-help video from Dr. David Viscott about overcoming obstacles to intimacy in the personal quest for love, commitment and emotional security.
VHS: S20471. $19.95.

Interconnectedness and Social Policy

Stephen Schwartz, author of *The Secret Vaults of Time*, founded the Society for the Anthropology of Consciousness. His understanding of prayer can help people fit into the fabric of nature. 60 mins.
VHS: S23630. $34.95.

Internal Power ("Chi") in the Martial Arts

Internal energy training has been shrouded in secrecy. Generating and channeling this force is demonstrated in this video for practical self-defense applications. Master Bob Klein covers such topics as neutralizing the opponent's force, penetrating the defense and how to achieve maximum power and speed with the minimum effort. 60 mins.
VHS: S26835. $29.95.

An Interview with Stephen Levine: Healing and Dying

As the author of *Healing into Life and Death*, *Meetings at the Edge* and *Who Dies*, Levine has been acclaimed as the most inspirational teacher on death, dying and healing of our time. He gives forthright advice on how to deal with this tragic but fundamental aspect of human life.
VHS: S22968. $39.95.

Intimacy and Sexual Ecstasy

This highly acclaimed video presents the finest methods known for creating deep feelings of love and sexual fulfillment in an intimate relationship. "Attractive" couples tastefully demonstrate ways to create more fun and romance in your Love Life. "…presents the keys to great sex….The tone is light and supportive, the information practical" (*Self Magazine*).
VHS: S15291. $39.95.

Introduction to Aromatherapy

A perfect visual introduction to the world of scent, this video is helpful for home or business use. Live classroom excerpts plus selections on history, distillation and plant identification, as well as actual consultations and massage demonstrations, reveal the tried and true techniques of effective oil application. 95 mins.
VHS: S22696. $29.95.

Japanese Shiatsu Massage Made Simple

This detailed instructional video includes stretching exercises for the masseur and techniques for massaging every part of the body. These techniques offer a tried and true method for achieving inner peace. 120 mins.
VHS: S23651. $19.95.

Jazzercise

Judy Sheppard Missett hosts a complete, physiologically sound sequence of 18 routines that include a warm-up, stretching and special cardio-vascular and muscle toning exercises.
VHS: S10965. $19.95.

Joan Halifax: Elder as Healer

Anthropologist, Buddhist and shaman Joan Halifax has lived in communities with elder teachers in remote areas of the world. In this workshop at the Omega Conference on Aging, she discusses how to develop and understand the potential elders in all of us. 105 mins.
VHS: S20223. $39.95.

The Journey Back: Professionals Recovering from Addiction

Much of the attention given to drug addiction is centered around the underemployed and criminal; the problem of drug and alcohol abuse in professional life is easily overlooked. These are the personal stories of a doctor, lawyer, policeman and pilot who have broken the shackles of addiction and successfully fought their way back to a happier, more fulfilling life. 60 mins.
VHS: S16384. $39.95.

Ju Jutsu—Traditional Japanese Unarmed Combat with James Shortt

Originally this art was used to disarm Samurai. Traditional fighting techniques of the respected Ryoi Shinto Ryu School are used on this video. Technique and instruction for defense against weapons are displayed through many examples. 45 mins.
VHS: S26849. $24.95.

Kung-fu Exercise Workouts

Two vigorous Kung-fu workouts and warm-ups are included on this videotape. Flexibility, fluidity, speed and stamina, as well as self defense ability, can all be enhanced by these regimens. Snake, tiger, monkey, crane and drunken Kung-fu movements are all clearly demonstrated by Master Bob Klein. 120 mins.
VHS: S26823. $19.95.

Leadership from Within

What is the difference between management and leadership? James M. Kouzes, president of Tom Peters Group Learning Systems, suggests that in order to live in a manner which exemplifies their values, leaders must become clear about their own priorities. He offers several exercises for values clarification and self-understanding. 90 mins.
VHS: S13325. $49.95.

Leo Buscaglia: Give Love

This uplifting talk with 8,000 delighted fans features dozens of Leo's humorous stories, penetrating insights and his inspiring joy of life.
VHS: S09597. $29.98.

Letters to a Dying Friend

Anton Grosz explains how the death of a friend prompted him to compile evidence concerning what happens when we die. He skillfully guides us through the stages presented in the classic Buddhist text *The Tibetan Book of the Dead*. 60 mins.
VHS: S18089. $29.95.

Life After Life: Understanding Near-Death Experience

With Raymond A. Moody, MD. Do near-death experiences represent an authentic encounter with a world beyond? Best-selling author Raymond Moody explores the nature and significance of these profound experiences for both those whose lives brush against death and their loved ones. 90 mins.
VHS: S08620. $49.95.

Living as a Peaceful Warrior

With Dan Millman. The author of *Way of the Peaceful Warrior* shows that the focused attention of the athlete can be applied to all facets of daily life—from eating and walking to working and relating to others. 90 mins.
VHS: S08627. $49.95.

Living with High Blood Pressure

Hosted by tennis legend and heart attack victim Arthur Ashe, this highly acclaimed video presents vital information about how to control high blood pressure, using clever animation, realistically reenacted vignettes, case histories and a knowledgeable commentary. 59 mins.
VHS: S10137. $34.95.

Louise L. Hay: Receiving Prosperity

Taken from a provocative session with her audience, author and teacher Louise L. Hay explores issues of identity, fulfillment, relationships and recognition, and how to achieve them.
VHS: S17607. $19.95.

Love Skills

A guide to the pleasures of sex introduced by Dr. Joshua Golden, demonstrated by five couples. Explicit sexual activity. 56 mins.
VHS: S07371. $29.98.

The Lover's Guide to Sexual Creativity

The five senses can and do function as aphrodisiacs in this explicit video. Two couples demonstrate foreplay enhanced by erotic scents and flavors, as well as seductive sights and sounds. This video can spark the erotic imagination. 30 mins.
VHS: S26421. $19.95.

Lucid Dreaming

Lucid dreams are dreams in which you are aware of the dreaming state. Dr. Stephen LaBerge is a researcher at Stanford who has written extensively on this subject. In this video he explains techniques that can lead to reduced stress, problem solving and anxiety reduction. 60 mins.
VHS: S23613. $34.95.

Lucky Vanous: The Ultimate Fat-Burning System

Work out with the Lucky Vanous, the Diet Coke poster boy who is infamous for the television commercial in which he bared his chest to the delight of the women working in the office next door.
VHS: S23866. $14.98.

A Magical Journey

With Terrence McKenna. Three complete half-hour programs featuring a leading thinker in the area of alternative realities, including *Hallucinogens and Culture*, *Time and the I Ching* and *The Human Future*. 90 mins.
VHS: S08633. $49.95.

Mantra Meditation for Beginners with Wolfgang Arndt

In the Yoga of the mind, the goal is to focus on the highest and attain a state of joy and bliss. This non-sectarian video displays the methods and mantras of this simple but transforming practice in an easy-to-follow manner. 90 mins.
VHS: S22959. $24.98.

Marion Woodman: King Lear As an Image in Eldering

Shakespeare's *King Lear* faces the storms of fate and powerlessness associated with old age. He is initiated into the soul values that lead to his inner Queen. This Jungian analysis deploys this model for a new understanding of aging that honors femininity, nature and soul. 43 mins.
VHS: S23203. $39.95.

The Meaning of Health

Bill Moyers leads this invigorating round table discussion about the very definition of health. A number of doctors debate the purpose and form that healing should take, emphasizing the long-forgotten, sacred objectives that have inspired healers for centuries. 35 mins.
VHS: S21189. $19.95.

Memory Skills

Greg Proops sets out to find amazing facts about memory and to try out different memory techniques in a unique BBC series about how memory works.
Memory Skills, Vol. 1: Associations. Total recall, the secrets of memory improvement, a look at hypnosis as a tool to recovering childhood memories, the thoughts of Roger Cooper (who spent five years in an Iranian jail), and the strange world of 1950's American neurosurgeon Wilder Penfield.
VHS: S21974. $13.95.
Memory Skills, Vol. 2: Sequences. Using a traditional memory technique of creating images in the mind, Greg Proops tries to remember the sequence of jokes for his stand-up comedy act.
VHS: S21976. $13.95.
Memory Skills, Vol. 3: Names/Faces. Proops forces a group of trainee security guards to employ police technology to try to reproduce his face from their memories. Learn how to remember faces and names.
VHS: S21978. $13.95.
Memory Skills, Vol. 4: Numbers. The program explains how to remember numbers and factual information based on association, and features advice from memory champion Dominic O'Brien.
VHS: S21975. $13.95.
Memory Skills, Vol. 5: Places. Proops takes us on a lightning tour of the main theories of forgetting. Learn how to make good use of external memory aids. Hear why the cast of a long-running play are still forgetting their lines and see vacationers helped to locate their cars at the airport after a long vacation in the sun.
VHS: S21977. $13.95.
Memory Skills, Vol. 6: Creating Lasting Impressions. Proops meets with advertising creative directors to discuss how they would advertise a TV series about memory in a way that would make people remember to watch it. Why we stand a better chance of getting people to remember what we are saying if we can amuse them.
VHS: S21979. $13.95.
Memory Skills: Complete Set. The six-tape set.
VHS: S21980. $59.95.

Memory, Suggestion and Abuse

Dr. Michael Apko explains how memory reconstructs the past. Through this understanding Dr. Apko shows that the trauma of past sexual abuse can be created through the reconstructive possibilities of memory. 60 mins.
VHS: S23617. $34.95.

Metaphoria

An award-winning documentary that examines processes of the brain during dreams and conditions altered by virtual reality and other artificial intelligence. The hosts who grapple with ideas and concepts behind computer animation and scientific inquiry are Dr. John C. Lilly (who invented the isolation tank), MIT professor Marvin Minsky, Native American Sam Sapiel and computer poet Michael Newman.
VHS: S18232. $19.95.

Metaphysics and Modern Science

Willis Harman is president of the Institute of Noetic Sciences. Dr. Harman believes that the integration of human consciousness into the body of human knowledge will lead to new directions in the study of life and death. 60 mins.
VHS: S23614. $34.95.

Mind as a Myth

With U.G. Krishnamurti. This disquieting Indian skeptic and author of *The Mystique of Enlightenment* asks whether the mind exists as a distinct entity apart from our thoughts about it? 30 mins.
VHS: S08638. $29.95.

Mind Power

With Bernie Zilbergeld. You can transform and improve your life by harnessing the power of your mind, according to the author of *Mind Power*. He suggests a number of powerful techniques for self actualizations. 30 mins.
VHS: S08653. $29.95.

Mind-Body Problem

With Julian Isaacs. This experimental psychologist doubts we will ever explain the mind in terms of neurological functioning. This view, he says, is inconsistent with the valid evidence of parasychology. 30 mins.
VHS: S08639. $29.95.

Minds, Brains and Science

With John Searle. The author of *Intentionality* challenges the notion that the human mind operates like a computer, pointing out that many human faculties are not achievable through artificial intelligence. 30 mins.
VHS: S08640. $29.95.

The Montauk Project: Experiments in Time

In 1943 the Philadelphia Project was begun, a 40-year research endeavor that involved invisibility, psychotronics (mind control) and the actual manipulation of time itself. Three researchers give first-hand accounts, and show the abandoned site on Long Island where this extraordinary series of experiments occurred. 95 mins.
VHS: S22705. $29.95.

Myrna Lewis, M.S.W.: Love and Sex After 60

This video offers a frank and open discussion on the physical, emotional and social issues that can enhance or interfere with later life sexuality. Lewis is a psychotherapist and gerontologist at New York's Mount Sinai School of Medicine. 105 mins.
VHS: S23201. $29.95.

Mystery of Incarnation

With Richard Grossinger. To understand our spiritual origins we must look to nature—for our most intimate relationship is with our own biology. The author of *Planet Medicine* discusses the biology of consciousness. 30 mins.
VHS: S08649. $29.95.

Natural Healing with Crystals

Dr. Richman, a chiropractor and expert on nutrition and herbs, uses crystals for balancing and healing the body. 60 mins.
VHS: S10212. $29.95.

Near Death Experience

Death is feared but near death experience teaches us that this need not be so. Extraordinary personal accounts from four people and top researchers like Kenneth Ring and Melvin Morse clarify this amazing phenomenon. 105 mins.
VHS: S22704. $29.95.

The Next Epoch

The Next Epoch presents hopeful evidence that we are at a critical point in our evolution and suggests that if we are to move into the next epoch, we must consciously nurture new values and attitudes that emphasize cooperation to solve our global problems. Featuring interviews with Dr. Jonas Salk and others. USA, 1991, 28 mins.
VHS: S15206. $39.95.

Nothing to Lose: Fat Lip Reader's Theatre

Fat and feisty women speak, act and sing about being fat in '80s America. Dramatic vignettes, snappy answers to street taunts, poetry, song and comedy will provoke laughter, tears and anger. The message is fat positive and challenges the diet-obsessed, fat-hating culture we live in. 30 mins.
VHS: S16838. $29.95.

Nude Yoga

Four beautiful women demonstrate the ancient exercises of Yoga completely nude. These techniques develop strength and flexibility, increase circulation and align the spinal column. This tape makes it easy to learn this enjoyable and relaxing health regimen.
VHS: S26523. $19.98.

Number and Meaning

With Arthur M. Young. The author of *Geometry of Meaning* has developed a "theory of process" which integrates science with ancient teachings. Numbers, says Young, are more than abstract representations of quantity. 30 mins.
VHS: S08648. $29.95.

Of Sound Mind and Body

A group of experts, including Deepak Chopra, Bernie Siegel, Don Campbell, Ray Lynch, Steven Halpern and Jill Purce, investigate the way sound enforces or establishes healing. 70 mins.
VHS: S20164. $39.95.

On the Nature of Love

Eastern philosopher and wise man Krishnamurti explains his wise philosophy of love and loving in this thought-provoking program. 58 mins.
VHS: S12208. $29.95.

On the Wild Side... Meeting with Remarkable Women

Wild women are living their lives by reclaiming a creative spirit. Once unfettered by society, they become freer and more open. In this video, inspiring women share their wisdom. They are real live models of a new way of being, women who encourage other women to step out from under limiting ideas. 30 mins.
VHS: S22972. $24.98.

Opening Doors Within

Subtitled *A Guided Journey with Eileen Caddy*, this provocative and spiritually uplifting program about New Age ideas and philosophy focuses on the Findhorn Community and its ruminations on love, healing and finding an "inner voice." "This is one of those videos that will be lovingly shared with small groups of friends for a long time" (Carol Wright, *NAPRA Trade Journal*).
VHS: S17605. $29.95.

Opening to Angels

The angelic realm is open to those individuals who can attune themselves to the higher spiritual realm where these creatures hover. Inspirational advice from a number of respected new age spiritual teachers and healers will show the way to finding this positive influence in everyday life. 60 mins.
VHS: S21229. $29.95.

Pakua Chang

Master Ji, a direct descendant of Sun Lu-t'ang, demonstrates this internal martial art. This video includes the basic stepping and walking circle, eight palm techniques, direction changes and the full Swimming Dragon form. 55 mins.
VHS: S26846. $24.95.

Pattern and Transformation

With Jill Purce. The author of *The Mystic Spiral* traces her investigations into patterning in nature and form. The program contains a demonstration of an ancient Mongolian "polyphonic" chanting technique. 30 mins.
VHS: S08647. $29.95.

The Philosophy of Tantric Yoga

Swami Chetanananda shows that tantric yoga is not about sex but about focusing on life energy (kundalini). The ultimate goal remains a unity of consciousness. This teacher has written extensively on the subject and shares his knowledge in this enlightening video. 60 mins.
VHS: S23615. $34.95.

Planetary Birth

Barbara Marx Hubbard sees a positive future involving a quantum change in consciousness. Humans will achieve this higher state through a fuller awareness of the larger planetary being. She sees great religious figures as templates that can aid this evolution. 60 mins.
VHS: S23624. $34.95.

Politics of Love

Leo Buscaglia's inspirational guide to help one create more joy in life through self-actualized, mature love. Produced by WTTW. USA, 1983, 50 mins.
VHS: S03664. $29.95.

The Power of Dreams

A journey into the world of dreaming. 60 minutes each.
The Power of Dreams: Sacred Sleep. This spiritual journey explores the meaning of dreams within Native American, Australian Aboriginal, Tibetan, Jewish, Islamic and Christian religious cultures. Dreams have always been considered messages from the gods. Perhaps dreams still hold vital information today.
VHS: S22963. $29.95.

The Power of Dreams: Search for Meaning. After 90 minutes of sleep, we enter the world of dreams. The latest scientific methods are joined with an artist's dreamscapes to uncover insights about the hows and whys of the chemical cocktail that transports us each night into a place of fantastic wonder or utter horror.
VHS: S22962. $29.95.
The Power of Dreams: The Creative Spark. How do dreams mold us? From Ancient Greece to modern times doctors have used dreams to heal. Look inside the world of dreams using the latest 3-D holograms and brain mapping available. Dreams hold the key to progress and beauty.
VHS: S22964. $29.95.
The Power of Dreams: 3-Volume Set.
VHS: S22965. $69.95.

Practical Self Defense

Master Bob Klein shows that even average people can defend themselves. Muscles are not vital if you can use your opponent's force against him. Klein reveals how to control the attacker's attention and then balance and neutralize his force. It's perfect for women and children. 90 mins.
VHS: S26831. $29.95.

Praying Mantis Kung-fu

The Northern Mayflower mantis form is show from two angles in natural surroundings. Master Bob Klein demonstrates step-by-step instructions which explain the defense applications of the mantis stance. 94 mins.
VHS: S26830. $19.95.

Prejudice: Answering Children's Questions

Host Peter Jennings leads a studio audience of children on an exploration of prejudice—or what he calls "the child of ignorance." 75 mins.
VHS: S16794. $19.98.

Presence of the Past

With Rubert Sheldrake. Were there any "laws of the universe" at the time of the "big bang"? This Oxford trained biologist and author of *A New Science of Life* says that all laws developed as "habits" over time. 30 mins.
VHS: S08646. $29.95.

Primordial Tradition

With Huston Smith. The profound author of *Religions of Man* delineates common threads in all spiritual traditions. Modern western society, he says, is deviating from an understanding of the soul and spirit. 30 mins.
VHS: S08636. $29.95.

The Psychodynamics of Liberation

With Kathleen Speeth, Ph.D. True liberation involves attaining an awareness of our unity and interconnectedness, says this clinical psychologist and author of *The Gurdjieff Work and Gurdjieff: Seeker after Truth*. 90 mins.
VHS: S08622. $49.95.

Push Hands (Kung-fu's Greatest Training Secret)

A unique Chinese two person exercise which develops fluidity, internal energy (chi), concentration and the ability to neutralize aggression is clearly demonstrated by Master Bob Klein in this video. Complete instructions for defense applications are included. 120 mins.
VHS: S26829. $19.95.

Pushed to the Edge

A *20/20* special edition focusing on the growing numbers of women who are fighting back against abusive partners and rapists. 50 mins.
VHS: S15880. $19.98.

Qualities of High Performance

With Lee Pulos. This innovative psychologist describes work with outstanding achievers in athletics and business, pointing out that qualities of success can be developed in all individuals. 30 mins.
VHS: S08651. $29.95.

A Question of Authority

A host of moral, ethic, religious and personal decisions are weighed when a mother, in an advanced state of pregnancy, is declared "brain dead" from the complications of a fall. The hospital wants to deliver her child, though her husband, fearing irreversible brain damage, refuses. 25 mins.
VHS: S17931. $49.95.

Quiet Garden

Visits to a quiet garden for relaxation, for active visualization through the Neuro-Linguistic Programming method, and for tranquil sights and sounds for enjoyment. Created by Yvan Miron. 60 mins.
VHS: S10232. $29.95.

Rabbi Zalman Schachter, Life Harvest: The Missing Piece to Wholeness

All must pass from simply aging to sage-ing. Ordained in the Lubavitcher community, but knowledgeable about many faiths, Schachter explains the integration of life experience into a wholeness of being. 35 mins.
VHS: S23200. $29.95.

Ram Dass: Aging and Awakening the Potential of Change

Change is the most constant aspect of life, and yet everyone resists change, especially aging. Ram Dass maps the path of conscious aging, showing how to substitute joy for fear and wonderment for dismay. His teaching offers those of any age a transforming vision of the years to come. 63 mins.
VHS: S23198. $29.95.

Ram Dass: Facing Death

The certainty of dying affects everyone. Ram Dass illuminates the journey toward death and beyond with gentle understanding, knowledge, insight and humor. This video documents a workshop from the Omega's Culture in Transition Conference. It's a valuable guide for those facing death, particularly those who see death as an enemy. 105 mins.
VHS: S23205. $39.95.

Recovering the Soul: A Scientific and Spiritual Search

Dr. Larry Dossey examines the relationship between healing and consciousness in a penetrating exploration at the crossroads of medicine and mysticism, religion and physics. Dossey's synthesis of ideas leads him to the threshold of a new era in medicine and uses information from many quarters—from the Spindrift experiment's documented effects of directed and non-directed prayer on growth and healing to the findings of Candace Pert, former director of the National Institutes of Health. 60 mins.
VHS: S12483. $29.95.

Reflections in a Forest

Three moments in a forest for relaxation: the first guides to relaxation, the second offers access to inner resources, the third provides a soothing ambience without dialog. 60 mins.
VHS: S10231. $29.95.

Relax

A program on the techniques of stress management, introducing fresh visuals and sounds. 60 mins.
Laser: LD70253. $29.95.

Revitalize Your Body

Master Bob Klein describes a program of exercises appropriate to recovering from injury. All levels are catered to in this video. 90 mins.
VHS: S23661. $29.95.

Riane Eisler: Reclaiming Our Past, Recreating our Future: Reflections on The Chalice and the Blade

At the dawn of modern civilization, says Riane Eisler, humanity shifted from a partnership model of social interaction to a dominator model. In this lucid discussion, she discusses many of the ideas behind her ground-breaking book, *The Chalice and the Blade*. 90 mins.
VHS: S13323. $49.95.

Rolling Thunder: The Unity of Man and Nature

Intertribal medicine man Rolling Thunder contrasts the notion of life in harmony with nature with the idea of mankind as dominator over nature. He describes the natural powers of native peoples, describes his role as a healer using shamanistic methods, and also describes his journeys to the other world of spirits. 90 mins.
VHS: S13324. $49.95.

Sacred Passions

Set in the beautiful area around Maui, this erotic travelogue is a spiritual journey into the mind, following Gavin Dillard and a group of young men who believe in Tantric rituals and the redemptive and fulfilling nature of erotic technique. It's "a sensual guide to the erotic that invites us to leave guilt and fear behind, and celebrate the sacred passions within."
VHS: S17794. $39.95.
Scott Craig, USA, 1990, 60 mins.

Sacred Sex: A Guide to Intimacy and Loving

In the ancient tantric beliefs, the hidden potency of sexual loving is the seed of all creativity and transcendence. Six couples demonstrate the key to sacred sex. It allows for greater intimacy and pleasure. Through tantric principles love-making becomes a transcendent ritual. 70 mins.
VHS: S22969. $29.98.

Saki Santorelli, Ed.D.: Responding to Stress

Dr. Santorelli is Associate Director of the Stress Reduction Center at the University of Massachusetts Medical Center. His proven techniques for stress management include meditation, relaxation, sensory awareness, centering and creative problem solving. 115 mins.
VHS: S23207. $39.95.

Satori

Satori, the sudden flash of enlightenment sought by Zen Buddhists, is only attainable through an intuitive, non-rational way of thinking. This video shows the effects of this belief at a Zen monastery, a business school, a street festival, and a Shinto ceremony inside a factory. 30 mins.
VHS: S26139. $19.95.

Secrets of EuroMassage

Provocative, sensual massage techniques from the continent of romance, Europe. This informative and authoritative video tape was developed in consultation with leading massage experts.
VHS: S14003. $29.99.

Self and Society

With Jane Rubin. How can we live a meaningful life in a social milieu that lacks clear values? One response, says philosopher Rubin, is to define oneself by accepting as a role model one who is truly committed. 30 mins.
VHS: S08637. $29.95.

Self and Universe

With Arthur M. Young. How can there be separate things in a universe that is interconnected? The author of *The Reflexive Universe* suggests that we can be separate beings in a universe created by God. 30 mins.
VHS: S08635. $29.95.

Self Defense with Pressure Points

For anyone who wants to learn self-defense against larger opponents, this video demonstrates exactly how it is done. Reaching pressure points in actual fighting and grappling situations can be integrated with other fighting techniques. Master Robert Lyons is featured. 70 mins.
VHS: S26827. $19.95.

Self-Defense for Children

Breaking holds from stronger attackers, attacking out of headlocks, groundfighting, footwork, kicks, punches, blocks and combinations are all included in this video. Master Robert Lyons can give your child the skills needed to feel more confident and unafraid. 75 mins.
VHS: S26838. $39.95.

Self-Help Stress Reduction

Michael Reed Gach, founder of the Accupressure Institute's international professional training program, shares specific explanations and demonstrations for accupressure and trigger points to relieve tension and headaches, and to increase concentration and memory. 58 mins.
VHS: S10214. $29.95.

The Seth Phenomena

The energy personality essence, Seth, spoke through author Jane Roberts for over 20 years. In an exclusive interview with Jane's husband Robert Butts, this story is finally revealed. 40 photos and paintings by Rob and Jane and the only known footage of Jane speaking as Seth are featured. 70 mins.
VHS: S22706. $29.95.

The Seven Spiritual Laws of Success: A Practical Guide to the Fulfillment of Our Dreams

A companion to his best-selling book *The Seven Spiritual Laws of Success*, this video expounds on Dr. Deepak Chopra's concept that success is the universal desire to achieve a "progressive expansion of the state of happiness." Dr. Chopra talks about the state of happiness and the elements of his philosophy through his seven easy-to-comprehend principles for "success."
VHS: S27188. $19.98.

Sex and the Sacred: A Conversation with Sam Keen

Best-selling author Sam Keen discusses his views on sex, religion, taboos and erotic life. He finds that the great religious thinkers shattered conventional wisdom, laying the groundwork for a new kind of intimacy. It is one based on commitment to the individual. Ultimately, there are no surefire techniques but simply methods to cherish another person. 90 mins.
VHS: S26716. $29.95.

Sexual Positions for Lovers

Four typical couples illustrate a full catalog of lovemaking positions in explicit detail. G-spot and clitoral stimulation, along with instructions for deeper penetration, are all clearly shown. Other positions for those facing arthritis, back problems, pregnancy, or obesity are also included. 53 mins.
VHS: S25056. $29.95.

Shaolin Chun Hop Kuen

This system is a common link between all the martial arts. It uses moves from Kung-fu, Karate and Tae Kwon Do. Master Robert Lyons demonstrates moves that will help any martial arts student. 80 mins.
VHS: S26839. $19.95.

Shaolin Fighting Crane Kung-fu

Step-by-step instructions with Master Robert Lyons show footwork, weight distribution and sources of power key to this style. This comprehensive video features applications shown at slow and full speed. 120 mins.
VHS: S26844. $19.95.

Shaolin Northern Tiger Kung-fu

This comprehensive video features Master Robert Lyons describing step-by-step instructions. Footwork, weight distribution and sources of power are explained. Applications are shown at slow and full speed. 120 mins.
VHS: S26843. $19.95.

Shaolin Sabre

The beautiful, swashbuckling Mayflower Sabre form, complete with leaps, whirlwind slashes and piercing strikes, is demonstrated in this video by Master Bob Klein. This inertial form is both fluid and explosive. Complete instructions and self defense applications are included. 60 mins.
VHS: S26834. $19.95.

Sharing the Joy of Nature

Designed by leading naturalist Joseph Cornell, *Sharing the Joy of Nature* is a video workshop on the awareness and appreciation of outdoor wilderness. Children and adults alike will cultivate enthusiasm and respect for our environment using his eight-step method. Through a process called "flow learning," you will find a method of awakening others to the techniques and games Cornell has developed. The Sierra Nevada mountains provide an inspired backdrop for this perfect introduction to nature activities. 40 mins.
VHS: S15685. $22.95.

Shiatsu Massage—Advanced

Accupressure and meridians are integral to Asian medical theory and diagnosis. These detailed demonstrations reveal the value of Shiatsu techniques. 120 mins.
VHS: S23663. $19.95.

Snake Style Kung-fu

Master Tseng and Yun Xiang demonstrate step-by-step instructions which explain the form and defense applications of this style. This unusually beautiful style uses vibrations from the body to generate power. 90 mins.
VHS: S26833. $19.95.

Speaking of Sex: It's More Than Just Talk

This video contains the most current and reliable information about sex. Typical couples show how to deepen intimacy, with explicit instructions and demonstrations. There is also expert guidance from five top sex educators. 60 mins.
VHS: S25054. $29.95.

Spirituality and the Intellect
With Jacob Needleman. The essential tension between our material and spiritual natures is often forgotten as we pursue contemporary concerns, says the author of *The Heart of Philosophy* and *The New Religions*. 30 mins.
VHS: S08634. $29.95.

Stephan Rechtschaffen, M.D.: Holistic Health—A Guide for Living
This program was developed during a Wellness Weekend on the Omega campus. It offers a view of holistic health and suggests ways to achieve it. Diet, exercise, lifestyle, attitude and evolving principles of longevity are all featured. 95 mins.
VHS: S23208. $39.95.

A Still, Small Voice
Chicago news anchor and journalist Bill Kurtis hosts this program about mystical experiences and transcendent moments. 60 mins.
VHS: S17182. $19.95.

Stress Management
With Janelle M. Barlow. This human development consultant and author of *The Stress Manager* offers suggestions for both becoming aware of how stress influences our bodies and for discharging its effects. 30 mins.
VHS: S08650. $29.95.

Stress Reduction Exercises
Stress leads to many ailments, some of which are life-threatening. Master Bob Klein outlines a basic stress reduction program in this video. 74 mins.
VHS: S23659. $24.95.

Stretching Your Whole Body
Jean Goulet explains how to relax the body in order to eliminate aches and prevent injury. 75 mins.
VHS: S23660. $19.95.

Super Abdomens Workout
This video is designed to emphasize exercises concentrating on the abdomen. It is useful for anyone involved in sports, dance or martial arts. 45 mins.
VHS: S23665. $19.95.

Surviving Divorce
John Bradshaw lays the emotional groundwork for helping people move on with their lives after a divorce. In his familiar style, Bradshaw, divorced himself, walks his viewers through the emotional trauma and self-denials of divorce. 60 mins.
VHS: S18087. $24.95.

T'ai-Chi Chuan: Chinese Moving Meditation
Master Bob Klein demonstrates the movements of the Yang short form from two angles, in a natural setting, with beginning level instructions. 48 mins.
VHS: S23657. $19.95.

T'ai-Chi Chuan: Movements of Power and Health
Master Bob Klein demonstrates the movements of the Yang short form, emphasizing basic coordination, the flow of energy (chi) and concentration exercises, all leading to stress reduction. 120 mins.
VHS: S23658. $29.95.

T'ai-Chi for Inner Beauty, with Jean Goulet
Jean Goulet demonstrates the 20-movement Yang short form. Along the way she explains the spiritual and physical ideals behind each movement. It will help the viewer move with greater grace and natural beauty. 60 mins.
VHS: S23656. $19.95.

T'ai-Chi for Seniors
Master Xue Dejun demonstrates the movements of the Yang long form for seniors. These techniques can rejuvenate seniors by revitalizing the body. 45 mins.
VHS: S23666. $24.95.

T'ai-Chi Massage
Learn how to give a pleasurable and relaxing massage based on the movements of T'ai-Chi. Accupressure, stretching, face massage, breathing techniques and even foot massage are covered. 60 mins.
VHS: S23662. $19.95.

T'ai-Chi Sword Forms
Master Bob Klein reveals the art of graceful sword movements from the Yang sword form to the intermediate fighting form in this video. Step-by-step instructions, defense applications, sword applications and free style sword fighting practice are all included. 120 mins.
VHS: S26828. $19.95.

T'ai-Chi-Ch'uan (Chen Man-Ching's Short Form)
This video includes preparatory exercises, basic training methods, a discussion of posture variations in the different styles, a demonstration of form and detailed training in the individual movements. 55 mins.
VHS: S26851. $24.95.

T'ai-Chi-Ch'uan Kung-fu
Master Bob Klein shows step-by-step instructions of the ancient Chinese movements that are the basis of Kung-fu. Self-defense applications for each movement, weight distribution, breathing, the use of chi (internal energy) and the beginning "push hands" exercise are all explained. 120 mins.
VHS: S26822. $19.95.

T'ai-Chi: The Inner Teachings, with Master Bob Klein: Body Awareness
In-depth training of the Yang short form, a slow, relaxing exercise, is featured in this video. These movements are practiced throughout China to stimulate energy and promote health. Master Bob Klein also explains the principals behind this form of exercise. 97 mins.
VHS: S23652. $19.95.

T'ai-Chi: The Inner Teachings, with Master Bob Klein: Chinese Chi-Gung Health Exercises
These enjoyable exercises combine relaxing, flowing movements with breathing and concentration techniques. Stress reduction strengthens the immune system, enhances the senses and promotes clearer thinking. 56 mins.
VHS: S23655. $19.95.

T'ai-Chi: The Inner Teachings, with Master Bob Klein: Harmonious Relationships
Enjoyable two-person exercises can help people open up to one another. Ultimately this can relieve stress and eliminate deep-seated fears. 45 mins.
VHS: S23654. $19.95.

T'ai-Chi: The Inner Teachings, with Master Bob Klein: Harmony of Mind and Body
This video explores the relationship between the mind and internal energy. The Yang form can be used to achieve a complete harmony of the mind. 52 mins.
VHS: S23653. $19.95.

Tai Chi for Health
Innovative exercises to tone muscles, improve flexibility and reduce stress. An excitingly different workout. 60 mins.
VHS: S08722. $9.98.

Tantra Love: Eastern Secrets of Intimacy and Ecstasy for Western Lovers
This professional, non-explicit (no nudity), instructional video explains in simple language and dramatic visuals how to make sexual energy and romantic love positive, even spiritual. "Excellent introduction to the Tantric Way" (*Better World* magazine). 60 mins.
VHS: S15290. $29.95.

Teachings of the Masters
Jonette Crowley channels White Eagle to expound on the four states of the Master: Truth, Love, Invisibility and Compassion. Through these words of wisdom and guided meditation, you can touch the Master within yourself. 70 mins.
VHS: S22961. $24.95.

Thai Kickboxing
Thai kickboxing at its best is demonstrated by Master Robert Lyons on this video. Learn theory, stances, footwork, kicks, punches and elbow, leg and arm blocks through one-on-one instruction. Great for street self-defense. 110 mins.
VHS: S26837. $19.95.

Thinking Allowed
An extraordinary series of conversations with leading thinkers on the cutting edge of knowledge and discovery. Each tape is 30 minutes, and is hosted by Dr. Jeffrey Mishlove, psychotherapist and television and radio interviewer.
Approaches to Growth: East and West. There are striking parallels between western psychotherapeutic methods such as gestalt therapy and the approaches of Sufism and Buddhism. In this discussion, Claudio Naranjo, psychiatrist and author of *The One Quest*, describes his personal experiences with the Arica training system. 30 mins.
VHS: S07902. $29.95.
Becoming More Fully Human. The problems of society result less from an intrinsic evil in human nature than from our failure to stop repeating behavior patterns from the past. Change, says Virginia Satir, begins with learning to accept and understand the many parts of yourself. Ms. Satir, one of the most influential psychologists today, is the author of *Conjoint Family Therapy*, *Peoplemaking*, *Self Esteem* and other books. 30 mins.
VHS: S07846. $29.95.
Beyond the Post-Modern Mind. The modern western world view is dominated by the materialist values of science. According to Huston Smith, this withdrawal of emphasis from human values—and from essential elements such as meaning, quality and purpose—has led to widespread alienation and social discontent. Dr. Smith is former professor of religion at MIT, and author of *The Religions of Man* and *Beyond the Post-Modern Mind*. 30 mins.
VHS: S07908. $29.95.
Challenging Assumptions. Donald Michael, Ph.D., former policy analyst for the National Science Foundation and the Joint Chiefs of Staff and the author of *The Next Generation* and *The Uncertain Society*, suggests that we are frequently misled by the certainties offered by politicians and social reformers, adding that by admitting our uncertainties we can begin to learn. 30 mins.
VHS: S07861. $29.95.
Common Threads in Mysticism. Robert Frager, founder of the California Institute for Transpersonal Psychology, shares his wide experience as a student and participant in diverse spiritual traditions, including Sufism, aikido. 30 mins.
VHS: S07903. $29.95.
Communication and Congruence. Virginia Satir, influential psychologist and founder of family therapy, describes how internalized "rules" for social behavior limit our communication. Ms. Satir demonstrates various communication styles—deprecation, blaming, intellectualizing and irrelevance—and how they are used to cover up feelings of low self-esteem. 30 mins.
VHS: S07859. $29.95.

Communication as Healing. All healing comes from a non-verbal "knowingness" within each of us, says Patricia Sun, spiritual teacher. Ms. Sun explores the nature of the healing process and demonstrates her use of sound as a method of focusing on her own healing consciousness. 30 mins.
VHS: S07863. $29.95.
Consciousness and Hyperspace. Nineteenth century theologians developed the idea of multiple dimensions to explain the idea of God in scientific language. Physicist Saul-Paul Sirag discusses recent theories of multiple dimensions, which have been fabricated to account for sub-atomic interactions, and the implications of these theories for the psychology and technology of the 21st century. 30 mins.
VHS: S07868. $29.95.
Consciousness and Quantum Reality. The mysteries of sub-atomic physics offers startling new perspectives on the human mind. Nick Herbert, author of *Quantum Reality*, points out that no matter how one interprets the equations of quantum physics the results lead to amazing and paradoxical concepts. Perhaps time runs backward as well as forward. Perhaps multiple independent universes are created each second. 30 mins.
VHS: S07869. $29.95.
Consciousness and Computers. William Whitson is currently involved in creating computer databases containing the world's great ethical and humanitarian teachings. Foreign affairs specialist and former Rand Corporation executive, he describes the role of computers in the democratization of knowledge claiming that "gaming" capabilities once limited to the military and industrial elite are now available to those of us seeking world peace. 30 mins.
VHS: S07877. $29.95.
Consciousness and the Martial Arts. One of the goals of martial artists is to cultivate an awareness both of their own subtle physiological rhythms and those of others. George Leonard, an aikido instructor and one of the founders of the consciousness movement, is the author of *The Ultimate Athlete*. 30 mins.
VHS: S07878. $29.95.
Course in Miracles. A home study system to unlearn the attitudes that separate the individual from his/her potential for spiritual unity, lead by Judith Skutch Whitson, president of the Foundation for Inner Peace. 30 mins.
VHS: S07899. $29.95.
Creativity in Business. In today's competitive environment, humanistic values are essential at every level of the corporation, according to Stanford professor Michael Ray. Dr. Ray, author of *Advertising and Communication Management*, describes how to apply principles of consciousness expansion, intuition and creativity in the business world. 30 mins.
VHS: S07872. $29.95.
Cult of Information. One of America's foremost social critics, Theodore Roszak, the author of *The Making of the Counter-Culture*, delivers a scathing indictment of the over-selling of computer and high-tech ideology to the American public under the argument that we are in the danger of becoming lost in the erroneous fascination with the information processing model of the mind. 30 mins.
VHS: S07874. $29.95.
Dark Side of Excellence. Business training techniques often focus mindlessly on "positive thinking", glossing over the need for executives to engage in soul-searching and self-renewal. John O'Neil, president of the California School of Professional Psychology, discusses the unfortunate trend in business to treat success as an all-consuming end in itself. 30 mins.
VHS: S07871. $29.95.
Developing and Applying Psychic Abilities. Kevin Riverson, psychic trance medium, gained attention as the focus of Shirley MacLaine's *Dancing in the Light*. In this program, Kevin predicts that the use of psychic intuitives for solving scientific and social problems will become an integral part of our culture. 30 mins.
VHS: S07898. $29.95.
Emerging New Culture. Dr. Fritjof Capra, the best-selling author of *The Tao of Physics* and *The Turning Point*, discusses the new holistic culture that has emerged in the late 20th century, arguing that the biological sciences, quantum physics and systems theory will provide a theoretical foundation which will supersede the decaying culture based on a linear, mechanistic world view. 30 mins.
VHS: S07886. $29.95.
Evolution: The Great Chain of Being. Philosopher Arthur M. Young, inventor of the Bell helicopter, describes three different types of evolution: physical evolution of the form of the body, evolution of the group soul of a species, and personal evolution. 30 mins.
VHS: S07897. $29.95.
Explanations of the Supernatural. Michael Scriven, Ph.D., calls to task those who maintain that all psychic claims must be either fraud or error. Dr. Scriven is a multi-disciplinary scholar who has made significant contributions to mathematics, logic, philosophy of science, ethics, education, psychology and parapsychology. 30 mins.
VHS: S07883. $29.95.
Global Mind-Changes. There is increasing global emphasis on the inner life of the mind. Futurist Willis Harman suggests that a new set of values, emerging spontaneously in many social strata and in different parts of the world, is having an impact in the world of business and corporate training. 30 mins.
VHS: S07887. $29.95.
Governance, Uncertainty and Compassion. Donald Michael, emeritus professor of University of Michigan, says that when we can acknowledge the existential realities of our uncertainty, our need for community and our isolation in the face of death, we are led to a position of compassion from which genuine long-range planning may proceed. 30 mins.
VHS: S07889. $29.95.
Health in the Workplace. Many businesses are beginning to appreciate the importance of optimal psychological and physical health within the workforce. Kenneth Pelletier, author of *Mind as Healer/Mind as Slayer* and other books, suggests that workers are no longer viewed as replaceable, but as the company's greatest asset. 30 mins.
VHS: S07870. $29.95.
Holographic Brain. With a better understanding of neurological functioning, says Dr. Harl Pribram, we may find the groundwork for a new approach to understanding spiritual and mystical experiences. Dr. Pribram, professor of neuropsychology at Stanford, is the author of *Languages of the Brain*. 30 mins.
VHS: S07895. $29.95.
Incorporating Creativity. Innovation, at every level of the corporation structure, is possible, argues William Miller, management consultant and author of *The Creative Edge*. Every individual, says Miller, has the capacity to overcome creative blocks by looking for answers which satisfy the desires and values of the heart. 30 mins.
VHS: S07873. $29.95.
Inner Mechanisms of Healing. Important breakthroughs in the field of neuroimmunology suggest that the human nervous system and the immune system are intimately linked. Brendan O'Regan, vice-president of research for the Institute of Noetic Sciences, notes the shift of emphasis in healing research from documenting the role of mind in healing to searching for an understanding of how and why healing occurs. 30 mins.
VHS: S07865. $29.95.

Learning to Use ESP. If you've read *Psychic Discoveries behind the Iron Curtain*, you are aware of the pioneering work of Czechoslovakian parapsychologist Dr. Milan Rzyl. Here he shares his personal experiences as a hypnotist and researcher, describing his training methods and their practical applications. 30 mins.
VHS: S07884. $29.95.
Metaphors of Transformation. Ralph Metzner is well known as a consciousness explorer. Here he stresses the importance of metaphor in guiding and understanding personal development. He focuses on the many forms of the metaphor of death and rebirth and of the journey. Dr. Metzner is author of *Opening to Inner Light*, *Maps of Consciousness*, and co-author of *The Psychedelic Experience*. 30 mins.
VHS: S07849. $29.95.
Mind over Machine. Human intuition and perception are basic and essential phenomena of consciousness, so such, they will never be replicated by computers. This is the challenging notion of Hubert Dreyfus, architect of the artificial intelligence establishment, and professor at University of California/ Berkeley. 30 mins.
VHS: S07876. $29.95.
Mind-Body Connection. Eleanor Criswell, psychologist and managing editor of *Somatics*, points out that the mind-body connection can be approached through many disciplines, suggesting enormous possibilities for controlling mind and body. 30 mins.
VHS: S07881. $29.95.
New Science of Life. Biologist Rupert Sheldrake, author of *A New Science of Life* and *The Presence of the Past*, has stimulated and even startled the scientific world by challenging the mechanistic thinking in the life sciences. Dr. Sheldrake proposes a bold alternative to the idea that genetic programming is solely responsible for diversity of form, development of behavior and the development of mind in living creatures. 30 mins.
VHS: S07867. $29.95.
On Dreams and Dreaming. Patricia Garfield, Ph.D., author of *Creative Dreaming* and *Women's Bodies, Women's Dreams*, offers various methods of working with dreams to make them a source of positive value and growth. 30 mins.
VHS: S07851. $29.95.
Past Life Regression and Spirit Depossession. Edith Fiore, fascinating author of *You Have Been Here Before* and *The Unquiet Dead*, discusses her transformation from a conventional behavior therapist to a specialist in the application of spiritual principles of reincarnation and spirit possession to psychotherapy. 30 mins.
VHS: S07892. $29.95.
Personality Development and the Psyche. Helen Palmer, Ph.D., founder of the Center for the Investigation and Training of Intuition, shows how to open your mind to a range of intuitive and psychic experiences. 30 mins.
VHS: S07856. $29.95.
Physics and Consciousness. Witty and profound, physicist Fred Alan Wolf is the author of the National Book Award-winning *Taking the Quantum Leap* as well as *Starwave* and *Body Quantum*. Dr. Wolf's far-ranging thinking extends the understanding of quantum physics as it applies to your body and mind, suggesting that you are inextricably connected with all that exists in the physical universe. 30 mins.
VHS: S07866. $29.95.
Power of Ritual. Anna Halprin, director of the Tamalpa Institute, draws on her own experience battling cancer to discuss the psychological value of body movement and symbolic action in recognizing inner negativity and transforming its power into a healing experience. 30 mins.
VHS: S07852. $29.95.
Practice of Meditation. Buddhist teacher of Vipasana (mindfulness) meditation and author of *Living Masters of Buddhism* Jack Kornfield, Ph.D., shows how to quiet the mind so we become aware of our unconscious tensions and how to heal those tensions. 30 mins.
VHS: S07855. $29.95.
Psychic and Spiritual Healing. Can the methods and ideas of native spiritual healers be incorporated into modern psychological and medical practice? Psychologist Stanley Kripper tells of his experiences with native shamans and healers in the Americas and Asia. Dr. Krippner is the author of *Human Possibilities* and *Realms of Healing*. 30 mins.
VHS: S07862. $29.95.
Psychokinesis, or Mind over Matter. Dr. Julian Isaacs, professor of parapsychology at John F. Kennedy University, shows how to learn psychokinesis through the attainment of zen-like concentration, and both focus on and indifference to the experimental task. 30 mins.
VHS: S07885. $29.95.
Psychological and Spiritual Blindspots. Patricia Sun, spiritual teacher and expert in conflict resolution, suggests that through a return to innocence you can rediscover your connection with the world in a healing manner. 30 mins.
VHS: S07858. $29.95.
Psychology of Religious Experience. One of the most widely read writers in the field of philosophy and religion, Huston Smith's classic book, *The Religions of Man*, has sold over two million copies. In this program, Dr. Smith discusses the relation between psychedelic experience and religious practice, the god within and the cultivation of psychic experiences within religious and shamanic traditions. 30 mins.
VHS: S07843. $29.95.
Psychotherapy and Spiritual Paths. Dr. Seymour Boorstein, the editor of *Transpersonal Psychotherapy*, discusses his transformation from a conventional and atheistic psychiatrist to a student of spirituality. 30 mins.
VHS: S07891. $29.95.
Science and Religion. While conventional religion and science are often in conflict, there is a growing convergence between non-reductionistic science and internally oriented religious traditions. Willis Harman points out that this movement reflects an important new area of public interest. 30 mins.
VHS: S07906. $29.95.
Science and Spiritual Traditions. Western science and traditional spiritual practice are both dedicated to the search for truth. Charles Tart, professor of psychology at the University of California, suggests that we may someday be able to specify which types of spiritual discipline would be most beneficial for difference people. 30 mins.
VHS: S07905. $29.95.
Self-Observation. Countless factors can mitigate against self-observation in Western society. Charles Tart, noted psychologist and author of *Waking Up*, suggests you begin by learning to focus on seemingly trivial details such as bodily sensations. 30 mins.
VHS: S07847. $29.95.
Sound and Healing. The use of sound in healing is based on the principle that the entire universe is created of vibrations and can be influenced through these vibrations. Jill Purce, the author of *The Mystic Spiral*, discusses the role of sound in traditional cultures as a means of harmonizing and healing the human body. 30 mins.
VHS: S07864. $29.95.
Spirit and Soma. The human organism and biosphere are part of one system, says Stanley Keleman, a leading pioneer of psychotherapy from a somatic perspective. The author of numerous books including *Emotional Anatomy*, he discusses the unity of spirit and soma (the body). 30 mins.
VHS: S07880. $29.95.

Spiritual Channeling. Alan Vaughan, one of America's best-known and most tested psychic intuitives, describes the channeling process. 30 mins.
VHS: S07900. $29.95.

Spiritual Training. Irina Tweedie, author of *Daughter of Fire*, a diary of her intensive spiritual training in India with a Sufi master, describes the bliss, peace and love—and the despair, hatred and loneliness—of her years of training in the Sufi tradition. 30 mins.
VHS: S07857. $29.95.

Spirituality and Psychology. True psychology is incomplete without an understanding of the spiritual yearnings of human beings. Frances Vaughan, a transpersonal psychotherapist, stresses that all spiritual traditions ultimately offer a means toward transcendence of the limited self.
VHS: S07890. $29.95.

Staying Alive: Psychology of Human Survival. We cannot live authentic lives without feeling touched by the major problems of the planet. Roger Walsh, professor of psychiatry at U.C. Irvine urges that by becoming aware of the roots of these problems in ourselves, we can begin to heal our culture of its dangerously insane condition. 30 mins.
VHS: S07888. $29.95.

Sufi Path. The Sufis are inheritors of a tradition which has influenced many world religions. Mrs. Irina Tweedle, a Sufi teacher, describes the teachings and devotional practice of the Sufis. 30 mins.
VHS: S07904. $29.95.

Thinking About Thinking. Michael Scriven, Ph.D., is a philosopher and multi-disciplinary scholar whose specialty is the process of thinking itself. He describes how individuals and organizations can examine the logic of their own decisions. Dr. Scriven is the author of *The Logic of Evaluation* and other books. 30 mins.
VHS: S07860. $29.95.

Time and Destiny. The qualitative and cyclical nature of time is the subject of this discussion with mathematician, physicist and philosopher Charles Muses, author of *Destiny and Control in Human Systems*. 30 mins.
VHS: S07896. $29.95.

Tools for Thought. Howard Theingold, author of *Tools for Thought: The History and Future of Mind-Expanding Technology*, says that the revolution in personal computers is yet to occur. In the next ten years personal computers will be sufficiently powerful to realize the dreams of many innovators who write about "fantasy amplifiers," and "computerized villages." 30 mins.
VHS: S07875. $29.95.

Toward a New Paradigm of the Unconscious. In extraordinary circumstances your mind is capable of accessing information from anywhere in time or space, according to evidence provided by Stanislav Grof. Author of *The Realms of the Human Unconscious*, Dr. Grof is an innovative psychotherapist who has attempted to integrate the divergent schools of Freud, Jung, and Reich with insights from the leading edge of contemporary physics and biology. 30 mins.
VHS: S07845. $29.95.

Transcending Limitations. James Fadiman, author of *Be All That You Are* offers several techniques to help individuals recognize and discard attachments to old attitudes and outworn ideas. A distinguished psychotherapist, Dr. Fadiman is the past president of the Association for Transpersonal Psychology. 30 mins.
VHS: S07848. $29.95.

Transforming the Human Body. Michael Murphy has spent years cataloging the ways in which human abilities can be transcended and the human body transformed. Founder of the Esalen Institute and the author of *Psychic Side of Sports*, he describes how to consciously control physical evolution through religious and athletic disciplines, biofeedback and medicine. 30 mins.
VHS: S07879. $29.95.

Understanding Extra-Sensory Perception. One of America's foremost parapsychology researchers, Dr. Charles Tart, discusses factors that facilitate ESP performance in the laboratory and in the world. 30 mins.
VHS: S07882. $29.95.

Understanding Mythology. Joseph Campbell, one of the world's foremost mythologists and interpreters of myth, in a provocative discussion as he argues against literal interpretation of ancient myth, claiming that modern science provides the raw material for future myths which can serve to unite all humankind as one biological and spiritual unit. 30 mins.
VHS: S07842. $29.95.

Universal Organism. The so-called laws of nature may actually be more like habits and instincts than immutable and inviolable principles, says Rupert Sheldrake Ph.D., biologist and author of the controversial *A New Science of Life*. From his perspective, all of creation may be viewed as a living organism. 30 mins.
VHS: S07894. $29.95.

Value and Purpose in Science. Consciousness, rather than being a property which emerges at higher orders of complexity, is a basic principle intrinsic to every level of creation, according to this program with philosopher Arthur M. Young. 30 mins.
VHS: S07907. $29.95.

Visionary Experience or Psychosis? The psychiatric community errs in treating visionary experience as a form of mental illness, says Jungian psychotherapist John Weir Perry, the author of many books, including *The Heart of History* and *The Far Side of Madness*. 30 mins.
VHS: S07893. $29.95.

Waking Up. Charles Tart, Ph.D., author of *Altered States of Consciousness*, suggests how to begin to wake up by allowing awareness to become conscious of itself. 30 mins.
VHS: S27049. $29.95.

What Is Chaneling? Arthur Hastings, Ph.D., explores the phenomenon known variously as spirit communication, trance mediumship or chaneling. 30 mins.
VHS: S07901. $29.95.

Working with Creative Energy. Shakti Gawan, author of the best-selling *Creative Visualization*, explains how to use visualized images as blueprints for events that manifest in our lives, providing instructions for a basic visualization technique. 30 mins.
VHS: S07850. $29.95.

Working with Dreams. Jeremy Taylor, founder of the movement for leaderless dream work groups and the author of *Dream Work*, points out that dreams are held in disrepute by mainstream institutions because they challenge closed systems of thought. He suggests that techniques such as lucid dreaming be used for purposes of healing and overcoming addictions. 30 mins.
VHS: S07853. $29.95.

The Thirteen Stones of the Universal Wheel

Maria Heller guides newcomers to the Universal Wheel, a movement that recognizes the interconnectedness of all things. This movement does not take the place of any culture or religion. Instead it teaches one how to realize the self without the separations between species, races, genders or ideologies. 60 mins.
VHS: S22967. $29.98.

Time & The More It Changes

Alan Watts is a charismatic philosopher and Zen mystic. This series of informal video talks finds him musing on the meaning of time and change, causality, ambition and the effect of the present on the past. 50 mins.
VHS: S26181. $29.95.

Time and Transformation

Peter Russell is a visionary writer and filmmaker who maintains that humans are part of a continual progression toward greater self-awareness. However, only a shift in consciousness will avert disaster. He believes we must create universal spiritual wisdom. 60 mins.
VHS: S23622. $34.95.

The Total Self

Hal Stone, Ph.D., author of *Embracing Heaven and Earth*, discusses what is the nature of the self. He proposes that we are not unitary beings, but consist of many autonomous sub-personalities and energy complexes. 90 mins.
VHS: S13327. $49.95.

Touch of Love...The Massage

A simple and beautiful way to learn the techniques of full body massage. Couples demonstrate how to stroke and relax each area of the body as the program invites you to experience the art of sensual massage.
VHS: S10955. $29.95.

Training Techniques of the Shaolin

A candid interview with Master Robert Lyons describes life behind the mysterious walls of the Shaolin Temple. Daily routines and constant physical and mental training are required. Chi-gung power and fighting techniques are explained. 70 mins.
VHS: S26842. $19.95.

Tranquility Through Tai Chi

Baiqing Li and Mei H. Li teach the 24-movement, simplified version of this healing martial art. A brief history of Tai Chi, together with careful, simple and repeated instruction, guarantee the viewer easy facility with these techniques. From stress reduction to lower blood pressure, the health effects of this exercise are invaluable. 50 mins.
VHS: S22230. $29.95.

The Transformation of Man

J. Krishnamurti, physicist David Bohm and psychiatrist David Shainberg debate the future of mankind's evolving consciousness in this video. They brilliantly expound on the possibility of a radical transformation of human beings and the way they see the world. 240 mins.
VHS: S26182. $39.95.

Unlocking Your Body: Regaining Youth Through Somatic Awareness

According to Thomas Hanna, founder of the discipline of somatics, many of the effects of aging—aching muscles and joints, stooped postures, stiffness and weakness—are unnecessary and reversible. He explains how to establish body awareness and release contracted muscles through simple exercises. 90 mins.
VHS: S13326. $49.95.

Unlocking Your Subconscious Wisdom

Dr. Marcia Emory is an author and teacher who outlines steps that help unlock the intuitive mind. This series of exercises will eliminate obstacles that lead to distortions. 60 mins.
VHS: S23621. $34.95.

The Unquiet Dead: An Introduction to Spirit Depossession Therapy

With Edith Fiore, Ph.D. What connection do we have with the souls of the departed? Psychologist Edith Fiore describes diagnosis and treatment of apparent spirit depossession and leads us through an actual depossession technique. 90 mins.
VHS: S08629. $49.95.

Virtual Reality

Dr. Timothy Leary lectures on the multiple possibilities of how to operate, teleport the brain and interconnect with other tele-persons and virtual reality, the technology capable of producing the impression of alternate worlds or experiences. 95 mins.
VHS: S18034. $29.95.

Waking Up the Power Within: The Freedom to Heal

Deepak Chopra takes viewers from modern quantum physics to ancient Vedic philosophy in search of perfect physical health and spiritual health and happiness. Unbounded freedom, relinquishing the known and stepping into the unknown is key. 60 mins.
VHS: S22690. $29.95.

The Way of the Wizard

This video from Deepak Chopra holds the key to love, personal fulfillment and spiritual growth. The road to magic begins with the pure potential that lies in everyone's hearts and minds. Based on the best-selling book *The Way of the Wizard*. 80 mins.
VHS: S27319. $19.95.

Wellness Series: Positive Imagery

This self-improvement series is based on the important concept of Imagery, the bridge between mind and body. Recent research has shown that mental images are involved in whether we stay well or become ill. The series combines the research of Dr. Jeanne Achterberg and Dr. G. Frank Lawlis with the creative skills of visual music artist Jon Mark.
Success Achievement.
VHS: S10233. $29.95.
Depression Manager.
VHS: S10234. $29.95.
Pain Manager.
VHS: S10235. $29.95.
Stop Smoking.
VHS: S10236. $29.95.
Stress Manager.
VHS: S10237. $29.95.
Weight Manager.
VHS: S10238. $29.95.

What Is Kundalini?

With Lee Sannella. This medical doctor and author of *Kundalini: Psychosis or Transcendence?* describes the changes in the nervous system that can result from intensive spiritual disciplines. 30 mins.
VHS: S08643. $29.95.

What Makes Work Meaningful?

With Dennis T. Jaffe. Workers today are demanding a sense of self-actualization on the job. The author of *Take This Job and Love It* suggests how we can find meaning, commitment and passion in our work. 30 mins.
VHS: S08652. $29.95.

When Bad Things Happen to Good People

Harold Kushner provides this video presentation of the cornerstone ideas and philosophy of his theories and teachings. 60 mins.
VHS: S17180. $14.95.

White Crane Kung-fu

This ancient, spectacular style is demonstrated by expert Bob Stannells. The "Siu Hok Kune" basic set is seen at various speeds including a helpful slow motion analysis of every aspect. History, fist forms, kicking techniques, stance exercises and a two-man sparring set are also featured in this video. 45 mins.
VHS: S26845. $24.95.

Women's Health Series

An informative eight-volume series on women's bodies and women's health.
Women's Health Series: After Pregnancy: A New Start. In the first few weeks after giving birth there are some important facts all young parents should know. This video explains the facts clearly and without inspiring fear. 34 mins.
VHS: S24253. $19.98.
Women's Health Series: Breast Cancer: Replacing Fear with Facts. In addition to explaining the risks caused by breast cancer, this video demonstrates the proper way to conduct your own examination. 37 mins.
VHS: S24255. $19.98.
Women's Health Series: Contraception: Know Your Options. This is a clear review of contraceptive methods for both men and women. 39 mins.
VHS: S24256. $19.98.
Women's Health Series: Infertility: The New Solutions. After explaining some of the causes of infertility in men and women, this video explores some of the treatment options currently available to treat this condition. 30 mins.
VHS: S24252. $19.98.
Women's Health Series: Menopause: Guidelines to a Healthy Life. This informative video explains the effects of menopause, including its symptoms and the physical changes endured by a maturing body. 31 mins.
VHS: S24251. $19.98.
Women's Health Series: Menstruation: Understanding Your Body. This video covers menarche, the menstrual cycle—including what is considered normal and abnormal—and PMS. 28 mins.
VHS: S24258. $19.98.
Women's Health Series: Pregnancy: Nine Special Months. The nine months of pregnancy require some basic health methods that can help insure both the health of the woman and her baby. 40 mins.
VHS: S24257. $19.98.
Women's Health Series: Sexually Transmitted Diseases: The Keys to Prevention. Understanding the transmission, prevention and recognition of these infectious diseases can help combat these maladies, which often inspire considerable anxiety. 39 mins.
VHS: S24254. $19.98.

Yang Long Form of T'ai-Chi Chuan

Master Bob Klein demonstrates the movements of the Yang long form from two different angles. Instructions are given for weight distribution, breathing and the names of movements. 75 mins.
VHS: S23664. $19.95.

You Can Heal Your Life

Based on the principles and ideas formulated by author, teacher and metaphysical counselor Louis L. Hay, this video deals with acquiring self-worth, self-esteem and self-definition.
VHS: S17606. $24.95.

PARENTING & THE HOME

The Art of Dining: The Business Lunch

Manners expert Marjabelle Young Stewart offers insights and proper strategies for pulling off the politically important business lunch. Mrs. Stewart offers advice on choosing the restaurant, ordering the meal, managing difficult foods and the correct etiquette of tipping. 27 mins.
VHS: S20191. $14.95.

The Art of Dining: The Formal Dinner

Marjabelle Young Stewart shows how to plan, prepare and orchestrate a formal dinner: writing the invitations, handling the proper seating arrangements, using utensils, making toasts and making a refined exit. 36 mins.
VHS: S20192. $14.95.

A Baby's World

This three-volume set explores the growth of babies from infants into walking, talking and thinking human beings. It offers compelling insights into the growth process, which remains a miraculous transformation. Each volume is 45 mins.
Vol. 1: A Whole New World.
VHS: S26053. $14.95.
Vol. 2: The Language of Being.
VHS: S26054. $14.95.
Vol. 3: Reason and Relationships.
VHS: S26055. $14.95.
Three-Volume Set.
VHS: S26056. $39.95.

Child Development: The First Two Years

A comprehensive guide to your children's emotional, spiritual and physical development. This program is designed to impart confidence and valuable teaching tools to young parents. The development is broken into four parts: 0-3 months, 3-6 months, 6-12 months and 12-24 months. The topics covered include physical growth, touching, diapering, language development, sounds and communications, mobility and motor skills and playing with other children. 47 mins.
VHS: S19174. $19.98.

Creative Parenting: The First Twelve Months

This program distills a series of expert opinions on the proper methods and instructions in the raising of babies during their vital first year. Hosted by Beau Bridges.
VHS: S19578. $9.95.

The Discovery Year

This program, hosted by Christopher Reeve, shows how babies learn to focus their senses, roll over, grasp objects, crawl, explore and finally stand up and walk unaided. Three sets of parents respond to the different personalities of their infant. 46 mins.
VHS: S20537. $29.95.

Far Eastern Cookery

A celebration of the myriad of distinctive flavors of the Far East, this video presents 16 of Madhur Jaffrey's own favorite dishes from Thailand, Japan, Korea, Hong Kong, the Philippines, Malaysia, Vietnam and Indonesia. 60 mins. A BBC Production.
VHS: S10280. $29.95.

Four Seasons in Polish Cooking

How to prepare the most delicious Polish dishes; includes a booklet full of recipes. The program is hosted by Katarzyna Pospieszynska. 110 mins. Narration in English.
VHS: S11382. $29.95.

The Gifts of Fathering

Dr. Ron Klinger, President of the Center for Successful Fathering, hosts this video about parenting for kids up to the age of 10. He details the importance of an active father role and explains how it can be achieved and maintained. 32 mins.
VHS: S26026. $19.98.

Great Chefs of the West

Visit the kitchens of some of the hottest chefs west of the Mississippi and their secrets to an array of culinary masterpieces as well as down home favorites.
VHS: S10159. $15.95.

Great Chefs: A Holiday Table

A Great Chefs video sampler of traditional Christmas and holiday dishes with a companion recipe booklet. Includes Christmas Pudding from England, a French Yule Log, a German Roast Goose and a whole suckling pig prepared Cajun style. 10 recipes.
VHS: S10156. $19.95.

Great Chefs: Appetizers

Eleven of the finest chefs in America reveal their techniques preparing appetizers ranging from Pepper Oysters to Empress Mushrooms.
VHS: S10157. $19.95.

Great Chefs: Desserts

Twelve spectacular desserts from twelve of the finest chefs in America—from New Orleans' Bananas Foster to Chicago's rich chocolate and Bourbon Pecan Cake. 12 recipes.
VHS: S10158. $19.95.

Great Chefs: Great BBQ

A definitive video survey of the famous restaurants from the hotbeds of American barbecue: Teas brisket, Cajun pork roast, the famous Rendezvous, Leonard's and Willingham's in Memphis, the K.C. Masterpiece Restaurant in Kansas City, and a number of mouth-watering side dishes and nontraditional sauces. 90 mins.
VHS: S10154. $19.95.

Great Chefs: New Orleans Jazz Brunch

Features historical footage of early creole cooking, a section on coffee and its relationship to New Orleans. Then you enjoy the famous version of a Japanese tea ceremony. Then you enjoy the famous Breakfast at Brennan's, and a companion recipe booklet. 60 mins.
VHS: S10155. $19.95.

Jewish Mothers Video Cookbook

Now, for the first time, the secrets of traditional Jewish cooking, previously passed only from mother to daughter, are revealed for all to enjoy. This cassette leads you step by step through 16 delicious kosher recipes including appetizers, side dishes, main courses and desserts. Comes complete with a recipe booklet. 90 mins.
VHS: S06573. $34.95.

Ken Hom's Chinese Cookery

Ken Hom takes the lid off Chinese cookery and reveals the secrets of popular Chinese dishes, showing how they can be prepared without special equipment or unusual ingredients. A BBC production. 60 mins.
VHS: S10278. $19.94.

A Kid's Guide to Divorce

More than half of the children under the age of 18 are affected by divorce. This program helps children deal with the emotional and psychological repercussions associated with the strain and trauma of divorce.
VHS: S20027. $125.00.

A Kid's Guide to Drug, Alcohol and Smoking Awareness
Prepared for children from kindergarten through third grade, this program points out the aspects of drug, alcohol and tobacco abuse among children. The program examines substance abuse in factual, clear presentations.
VHS: S20028. $145.00.

Kids for Safety
This award-winning program is hosted by five energetic kids who explore the basic and necessary rules of personal safety. For ages 3-10. USA.
VHS: S14951. $19.95.

Kids, Sex, and Choices
An in-depth look at the highly controversial issue of sex education in our schools. Should abstinence or birth control be taught, and are these subjects appropriate for students at all? This award-winning documentary lets you "sit-in" on classes and hear what educators, parents and kids have to say. 60 mins.
VHS: S16394. $39.95.

Madhur Jaffrey's Indian Cookery
Fabulous, foolproof recipes for anyone who loves the exotic taste of good Indian food, in this practical, step-by-step video. Madhur Jaffrey, using ingredients which are readily available, shows how to cook eight wonderfully authentic Indian dishes, including Tandoori Style Chicken. A BBC production. 60 mins.
VHS: S10279. $19.94.

Mediterranean Cookery
The cuisine of intense flavors, brilliant colors and simple, clean tastes which evoke images of the sun and the sea, in two volumes produced by the BBC.
Volume 1: France, Italy and Spain. Top chefs and talented home cooks demonstrate authentic dishes from each country, using widely available ingredients. 90 mins.
VHS: S10308. $19.94.
Volume 2: Egypt, Turkey, Morocco and Greece. The culinary diversity of the region is indicated by the wide range of traditional specialties demonstrated by top chefs and in the home. 90 mins.
VHS: S10309. $19.94.

Mr. Baby Proofer
Danny "Mr. Baby Proofer" McNeill leads a room-by-room guide to providing a child-safe environment. McNeill is recognized nationwide as the foremost authority on child safety. 30 mins.
VHS: S16585. $14.95.

New and Improved Kids
Host Loni Anderson takes us to the heart of what it means to raise loving, responsible children. 1989, 47 mins.
VHS: S14452. $29.95.

Newborn Care
A reassuring program that guides parents through the basic skills they need to care for their infants. Includes a 20-page booklet that explains many subjects new parents will encounter during the first months of their child's life. 1989, 43 mins.
VHS: S14448. $24.95.

Nova—Baby Talk
The remarkable journey of the life of language—from infant cries to adult speech. 60 mins.
VHS: S14500. $14.98.

On Fire: A Family Guide to Fire Safety
Host Henry Johnson demonstrates simple, easy-to-remember techniques on how to fight, control, or escape from fires. Includes home safeguards, travel precautions, tips on use of fire safety equipment and a resource guide.
VHS: S16396. $19.95.

On the House: Restoring a Victorian House
Welcome to Number 50, once a dirty, neglected Victorian house, but under the loving care of "On the House," Britain's equivalent of PBS's "This Old House," it is restored to all its former glory. A BBC production. 98 mins.
VHS: S10283. $29.95.

Pat Paulsen on Wine
Legendary comedian, presidential candidate and winemaker Pat Paulsen in a funny—and very informative—video on wine in his three cheers for the red, white and rose! "Pat clearly demonstrates he knows as much about wine as he does about the Presidency," says Tommy Smothers.
VHS: S08120. $19.95.

Perfect Baby
An in-depth examination of state-of-the-art genetic engineering, a science which could cure genetically-transmitted disease, but could also signal a frightening future where genes are tested and manipulated at whim. This outstanding program prepares us for the ethical choices of the not-too-distant future: just how perfect do we want our children to be? 59 mins.
VHS: S13181. $19.98.

T. Berry Brazelton: The Changing Family and Its Implications
Brazelton's books on child-rearing are found in American homes across the country. Now he expounds on the dangers posed to families by the challenge of working parents. This is an important topic where Brazelton's insights are particularly troubling. 50 mins.
VHS: S24927. $29.95.

Vintage: A History of Wine by Hugh Johnson
One of the world's great wine experts presents this definitive, four-volume history of wine.
Vintage: A History of Wine Volume 1. Hugh Johnson explores the wines of today's Middle East, tracing the history of wine from its prized status in ancient Egypt to its prohibition in Islam. In northern Spain, Johnson discusses the history of Bacchanalian rites as Catholic parishioners douse themselves with wine in Dionysian frenzy. Then Johnson scrutinizes the grape-growing regions and marvels of the ancient houses of Greece, and finally discusses the debate in Germany between beer and wine by analyzing German wines. 116 mins.
VHS: S11185. $29.95.
Vintage: A History of Wine Volume 2. Wines of the torch-lit catacombs of Saint Emilion and the great sherry houses of Spain that are directly descended from Medieval tradition. On the golden slopes of Cote d'Or, Johnson tastes the region's savory wines, explaining how heat, rain and air mold a wine's character. Finally, the story of champagne, from its "invention" by Dom Perignon to celebrations at Maxim's. 116 mins.
VHS: S11186. $29.95.
Vintage: A History of Wine Volume 3. Wine and War: Madeira and Port—how war and politics have shaped the destiny of many of the wines now considered classics; Power of the Purse: Bordeaux Wines—how can a single region produce such diverse wines? The Devastator: Phylloxera—the insatiable parasite that destroyed Europe's vineyards in the late 19th century; Johnson reveals why today almost all European wines are grafted onto American stems. 116 mins.
VHS: S11187. $29.95.
Vintage: A History of Wine Volume 4. Migrating Vine: Wine in Australia; The Grape Goes West: California Wines—the evolution of some now great wines; and Vin Nouveau: Today and Tomorrow—the technology that will improve the future of wine making, why vineyards will thrive in the monsoon-drenched areas of Japan and how a winery in Tuscany was completely automated. 116 mins.
VHS: S11188. $29.95.

What's a Parent to Do?
John Stossel explores the trials and tribulations of parenting in this compilation of his *20/20* reports. 50 mins.
VHS: S15882. $19.98.

When Mom and Dad Break Up
Hosted by Alan Thicke and developed in conjunction with family experts, a reassuring and entertaining program that tackles the questions children of divorced parents frequently ask, with kid-to-kid straight talk, music and animation. 32 mins.
VHS: S09898. $24.95.

TEST PREPARATION

GED Math Review
A video instruction to prepare for the General Educational Development test, including Arithmetic, Charts and Graphs, Probability and Statistics, Algebra and Geometry. Study guide included. 120 mins.
VHS: S17476. $39.95.

GMAT Math Review
A comprehensive video review course on the Graduate Management Admission Test includes sections on Arithmetic, Algebra, Geometry, Word Problems and Data Sufficiency. Study guide included. 120 mins.
VHS: S17473. $39.95.

GMAT Verbal Review
A video review of the GMAT verbal section details Analytical Reasoning, Reading Comprehension, and Sentence Correction. Study guide included. 135 mins.
VHS: S17474. $39.95.

LSAT
An in-depth video review that analyzes the Law School Admission Test entrance exam, with special emphasis on Reading Comprehension, Reasoning Analytically, Logical Analysis and Writing Sample Techniques. Study guide included. Two-tape set, 240 mins.
VHS: S17475. $79.95.

SAT/Analogies
An in-depth review of how analogy questions are deployed in standardized testing and the means to achieve a high score. The program details the logic behind analogy questions and how to recognize and attack relationships and patterns. Study guide included. 120 mins.
VHS: S17470. $39.95.

SAT/Reading Comprehension
A review of the skills and strategies students should master for reading comprehension on the SAT, PSAT, ACT and other standardized testing. Study guide included. 120 mins.
VHS: S17469. $39.95.

Secrets of Writing the College Admission Essay
A written essay is an important part of the college admission process. 60 mins.
VHS: S08764. $39.95.

Test Preparation Series
Experienced teachers, working at the chalkboard, guide students through intensive review courses crammed with important tips, insider test-taking strategies, and confidence building hints. The comprehensive reviews stress problem solving and are designed to prepare for even the most difficult and challenging questions.
ACT Math Review. High school seniors take the American College Testing Assessment for college admission. 120 mins.
VHS: S08737. $39.95.
ACT Verbal Review. 120 mins.
VHS: S08738. $39.95.
ASVAB Review. The Armed Services Voluntary Aptitude Battery tests. 120 mins.
VHS: S08749. $39.95.
Basic English/ESL. 120 mins.
VHS: S08753. $79.95.
Firefighter Exams Review. 120 mins.
VHS: S08751. $39.95.
GRE Math Review. Review for the Graduate Record Exam for admission to graduate school. 120 mins.
VHS: S08741. $39.95.
GRE Verbal Review. 120 mins.
VHS: S08742. $39.95.

MAT Review. College graduates take the Miller Analogies Test for admission to graduate school. 73 mins.
VHS: S08740. $39.95.
Math and Verbal Review for Civil Service Exams. For federal, state and city jobs. 120 mins.
VHS: S08748. $39.95.
NTE Review. Prospective teachers take the National Teacher Examination Core Battery in order to attain a license. 110 mins.
VHS: S08745. $39.95.
Police Officer Exams Review. 120 mins.
VHS: S08750. $39.95.
Post Office Exams Review. 120 mins.
VHS: S08752. $39.95.
Rapid Review for the SAT. This time-saving study tool gives the viewer a quick brush up in math and verbal areas tested on the SAT. 90 mins.
VHS: S08736. $39.95.
SAT-PSAT Math Review. High school juniors and seniors take the Scholastic and Preliminary Scholastic Aptitude Test for college admission. 120 mins.
VHS: S08733. $39.95.
SAT-PSAT Verbal Review. 120 mins.
VHS: S08734. $39.95.

TOEFL Review
A comprehensive study of the Test of English as a Foreign Language with emphasis on comprehension, structure, written expression, vocabulary and reading. Study guide included. Three-tape set, 360 mins.
VHS: S17472. $119.95.

LANGUAGE ARTS

Basic Grammar Series
The three films in this series feature a robot, humans, and an assortment of whimsical objects that teach lessons in grammar. Each is 8 mins.
Modifiers (Adjectives and Adverbs).
VHS: S23465. $49.95.
Nouns.
VHS: S23463. $49.95.
Verbs.
VHS: S23464. $49.95.

Beginning American Sign Language Video Course
Join the Bravos, an upbeat modern family with a deaf father, hearing impaired mother and two fun-loving children. American Sign Language instructor Billy Seago guides the adventure, highlighting the grammatical and cultural aspects of ASL. Each lesson includes introduction to new vocabulary, visits with the Bravo family, cultural notes, grammatical notes, vocabulary review sessions and practice sessions. Produced by Sign Enhancers.
Lesson 1: Meet the Bravo Family.
VHS: S23409. $69.95.
Lesson 2: Breakfast with the Bravos. Breakfast and dining.
VHS: S23410. $69.95.
Lesson 3: Where's the TV Remote?
VHS: S23411. $69.95.
Lesson 4: Let's Go Food Shopping!
VHS: S23412. $69.95.
Lesson 5: Review Tape.
VHS: S23413. $69.95.
Lesson 6: Read Any Good Fingers Lately?
VHS: S23414. $69.95.
Lesson 7: A School Daze.
VHS: S23415. $69.95.
Lesson 8: A School Daze—The Sequel.
VHS: S23416. $69.95.
Lesson 9: Dollar Signs.
VHS: S23417. $69.95.
Lesson 10: Review Tape.
VHS: S23418. $69.95.
Lesson 11: Playing in the Park.
VHS: S23419. $69.95.
Lesson 12: The Doctor Is In!
VHS: S23420. $69.95.
Lesson 13: Business as Usual.
VHS: S23421. $69.95.
Lesson 14: Let's Go Clothes Shopping.
VHS: S23422. $69.95.
Lesson 15: Review Tape.
VHS: S23423. $69.95.
Lesson 16: The People Behind the Bravo Family.
VHS: S23424. $69.95.

Child's Play Video Flash Cards—Spell Well
An innovative new series of video programs designed to help students learn spelling, combining basic instructional methods with high tech. The programs develop competency in correct spelling of words that do not fit the phonic rules. The programs were developed by Harold Weitzberg and Dr. Richard Zweig, who is an experienced language remediation expert who has developed numerous diagnostic remediation programs over the last 20 years. The programs provide a multi-modality approach for input and reinforcement that include listening, seeing, and writing tasks. Each program is 30 minutes, and the programs are geared toward individuals of all age groups.
Spell Well 1.
VHS: S06290. $11.95.
Spell Well 2.
VHS: S06291. $11.95.
Spell Well 3.
VHS: S06292. $11.95.
Spell Well 4.
VHS: S06293. $11.95.

Functional Reading—I Can Read Signs
For beginning readers who will recognize many familiar signs, this program generates that all-important first feeling of success leading toward positive learning attitudes overall. Simple stills of common street and commercial signs can be a boon, especially in urban elementary and foreign language classrooms. They can be used to develop functional reading skills, build vocabulary, and reinforce motor skills in primary and intermediate reading. 30 mins.
VHS: S10317. $29.95.

Intermediate English/ESL
An important and valuable 25-lesson, interactive course that allows the viewer to listen to, speak, read and write English, finding a grammatical approach in the details and events of everyday life. Study guide included. Two-tape set, 240 mins.
VHS: S17486. $79.95.

Language Stories
A collection of educational videos about language, thought and action. The works concentrate on sentence structure and proper usage.
A Cache of Jewels and Other Collective Nouns. The text is created from collective nouns and enlivened by bright, beautifully colored drawings. 11 mins.
VHS: S20068. $44.95.
Kites Sail High. This video breaks down verbs in ebullient, musical verses. "The verses are accompanied by bold, gaily colored graphics that are especially striking for their skillful use of pattern and design" (*Publisher's Weekly*). 11 mins.
VHS: S20070. $44.95.
Many Luscious Lollipops. Subtitled *A Book about Adjectives,* this work points out, "adjectives [are] terrific when you want to be specific…" 8 mins.
VHS: S20069. $44.95.
Merry-Go-Round. This book about nouns highlights the different functions nouns serve. 16 mins.
VHS: S20071. $44.95.
Language Stories, Set. A collection of four programs. 46 mins.
VHS: S20072. $159.95.

Learning About Me
In this educational series, an eccentric witch and a giant green dragon join forces to instruct children on the need for honesty, forgiveness, responsibility, developing self-worth and respect and having the capacity to listen and communicate with their peers. "A lively, up-to-date program for the primary grades, designed to help children explore their own individuality in ways that will develop their capacity for making responsible choices" (*Booklist*). Designed for kindergarten through 3rd grade.
A Is for Autonomy. Children learn how to unlock the mysteries of their own identities by solving intricate riddles. A special game called "Hidden Treasure" enables them to discover what is unique and special about their lives. 16 mins.
VHS: S19943. $37.95.
B Is for Belonging. By telling frightening stories around a campfire, children learn to bond, share personal experiences and make friendships. 18 mins.
VHS: S19944. $37.95.
Ipsilwhich Adventures. Inability to communicate almost destroys an important cookout, until Lollipop Dragon and Apple Blossom intervene and teach the children how to get along. 23 mins.
VHS: S19942. $37.95.
Learning About Me, Set. A set of three programs. 55 mins.
VHS: S19945. $99.00.

Library Skills
Designed for middle school, high school and college students, this video program instructs on preparing and writing a research paper, from inception to completion, enhanced by colorful video graphics.
Finding Sources of Information.
VHS: S17483. $39.95.
Selecting and Defining a Topic.
VHS: S17482. $39.95.
Taking Notes and Organizing Your Ideas.
VHS: S17484. $39.95.
Writing the Paper.
VHS: S17485. $39.95.

The Power of the Word
This PBS-sponsored series from the Bill Moyers Collection includes readings by some the most internationally acclaimed poets living and working today. They are featured in a number of settings and given the opportunity to discuss not just their work, but the importance and vitality of this immortal artform.
Ancestral Voices. Garret Kaoru Hongo reflects on his Japanese-American heritage in much of his work, while Native American poets Joy Harjo and Mary Tallmountain draw on the strengths of their traditions. Together these three bring out the importance of diverse traditions in the realm of poetry. 60 mins.
VHS: S21224. $29.95.
Dancing on the Edge of the Road. Stanley Kunitz is one of America's leading poets. His work is tempered by advice learned over a lifetime of composing. This profile offers a close look at the man and his work, including his strong belief in reading aloud. 60 mins.
VHS: S21226. $29.95.
The Living Language. The living tradition of oral poetry is accentuated by two poets, James Autrey and Quincy Troupe. Autrey writes about the business world and the South of his youth. He often brings his work to places like business meetings and even church. Troupe is a professor of Third World literature who reads to all kinds of audiences, even prisoners. 60 mins.
VHS: S21223. $29.95.
The Simple Acts of Life. This program was filmed at the Geraldine R. Dodge Poetry Festival. Every other year, poets gather there to discuss and read their work to each other and students. Robert Bly, Galway Kinnel, Sharon Olds, Octavio Paz and William Stafford are included. 60 mins.
VHS: S21222. $29.95.
Voices of Memory. Li-Young is a famed poet whose work explores the ties he maintains with Chinese culture, even though he has never lived in China. For Gerald Stern, memory offers a path to his Jewish heritage, which he then reconstructs in his work. Poetry readings and extensive interviews with both men are included. 60 mins.
VHS: S21225. $29.95.
Where the Souls Live. Robert Bly, Lucille Clifton and W.S. Merwin are all featured reading and discussing their work. Bly's emphasis on the spiritual nature of poetry makes him a vital voice on the state of the human soul. Clifton draws on her experiences as a black woman to craft her art, while Merwin examines human relationships and our ties to nature. 60 mins.
VHS: S21227. $29.95.
Complete Six-Volume Set.
VHS: S22595. $119.95.

Quickwick: Your Library Guide
Quickwick, a very special lightning bug, teaches young children how to use their local library. Includes the use of puppets, colorful drawings, and live-action photography in an actual library setting. Five instructional episodes.
VHS: S14207. $179.95.

Story of English

The highly acclaimed televisions series hosted by award-winning reporter Robert MacNeil, in a remarkable journey through the history of the English language. Mounted in a five-cassette series. Program 1: *An English Speaking World*—More than 320 million people speak it as their first language. How has it risen to such prominence? Program 2: *Mother Tongue*—Follows the origin of English from its Anglo-Saxon roots. Program 3: *A Muse of Fire*—Shakespeare's words and the King James Bible represent the full flowering of English. Program 4: *The Guid Scots Tongue*—Traces the remarkable effect the Scots have had on the spread and sound of English. Program 5: *Black on White*—Examines the beginnings of Black English. Program 6: *Pioneers! O Pioneers!*—Walt Whitman's phrase evokes the spirit behind the evolution of early American English. Program 7: *The Muvver Tongue*—19th century British colonialism played an important role in the spread of English throughout the world. Program 8: *The Loaded Weapon*—Investigates the Irish influence on the language. Program 9: *Next Year's Words: A Look into the Future*—Latin, now considered "dead", was once a universal language. Does a similar fate await English? Available only as a complete set.
VHS: S08492. $139.95.

Strunk & White: The Elements of Style

Finally on video—the classic guide to clear, effective writing. Now you can learn the fundamentals of precise writing in under two hours, just by watching and listening. Plus, a free copy of the *Elements of Style* book is included as a handy reference guide. Featuring Charles Osgood. 112 mins.
VHS: S13879. $29.99.

Teacher Training Series

This teacher-to-teacher series features master teachers giving new or experienced teachers a creative and focused approach to the teaching of great classics in the classroom. Each video includes complete lesson plans with aims, motivations, objectives, discussion questions, and homework assignments.
Teaching Hamlet. 30 mins.
VHS: S08766. $39.95.
Teaching Macbeth. 50 mins.
VHS: S08767. $39.95.
Teaching Romeo and Juliet. 30 mins.
VHS: S08768. $39.95.
Teaching Julius Caesar. 30 mins.
VHS: S08769. $39.95.
Teaching Othello. 30 mins.
VHS: S08770. $39.95.
Teaching The Great Gatsby. 25 mins.
VHS: S08775. $39.95.

OTHER EDUCATIONAL VIDEOS

The Geography Tutor

This series by Tell Me Why video contains six volumes that cover various elements of geography. It explains all those different principles that define the face of the Earth. Nationally acclaimed geography instructors make this series a helpful tool for any teacher or student.
Volume 1: Map and Globe Terms. 18 mins.
VHS: S22135. $49.95.
Volume 2: Types of Maps and Map Projections. 18 mins.
VHS: S22136. $49.95.
Volume 3: Map Skills. 18 mins.
VHS: S22137. $49.95.
Volume 4: Earth's Physical Features. 18 mins.
VHS: S22138. $49.95.
Volume 5: Weather and Climate. 18 mins.
VHS: S22139. $49.95.
Volume 6: Global Problems and Issues. 18 mins.
VHS: S22140. $49.95.
Complete Set.
VHS: S22141. $299.70.

The Schlessinger Teen Health Video Series

Sex, abortion, homosexuality, date rape and abuse are all sensitive issues dealt with in this unique guide to health and education for teens. Experts from the University of Pennsylvania, the Children's Hospital of Philadelphia and Temple University School of Medicine emphasize prevention and coping in a non-judgmental manner. Each volume is 30 mins.
Abusive Relationships. Interviews with abused individuals, an abuser and a therapist reveal the natural cycle of emotion which constitutes abusive behavior. Grades 8-12.
VHS: S24409. $39.95.
AIDS. People living with AIDS share their experiences with this syndrome and their views on sex, condoms and life. Grades 7-12.
VHS: S24410. $39.95.
Birth Control. All varieties of birth control are examined, including abstinence and sex without intercourse. Grades 7-12.
VHS: S24411. $39.95.
Cancer. Interviews with experts and cancer patients reveal the many types, causes and treatments for cancer. Grades 7-12.
VHS: S24412. $39.95.
Child Abuse. Recognizing child abuse and what to do about it are covered in this volume. In addition, the potential damage caused to innocent adults accused of abuse is examined. Grades 7-12.
VHS: S24413. $39.95.
Eating Disorders. Interviews with youngsters who experienced anorexia nervosa and bulimia are balanced with therapists discussing these dangerous disorders. Grades 7-12.
VHS: S24414. $39.95.
Nutrition/Diet. Expert advice on nutrition is loaded with important tips and key do's and don'ts. Grades 5-9.
VHS: S24415. $39.95.
Peer Pressure. Kids will benefit from these useful tools that help them resist pressure by reinforcing their own individuality. Grades 5-9.
VHS: S24416. $39.95.
Puberty. Emotional and physical changes that occur during puberty are explained in this volume. Grades 5-9.
VHS: S24417. $39.95.
Self-Esteem. The difference between high and low self-esteem is explained, along with methods to improve one's own self-image. Grades 7-12.
VHS: S24418. $39.95.
Sexual Harassment. Distinctions between harassment and appropriate behavior are explained so that concepts like date rape and healthy affection are rendered more understandable. Grades 7-12.
VHS: S24419. $39.95.
Sports Medicine. Two expert doctors provide tips on how to avoid and recognize injury. Grades 7-12.
VHS: S24420. $39.95.

STDs (Sexually Transmitted Diseases). The prevention and identification of STDs is explained, together with the option of abstinence. Grades 8-12.
VHS: S24421. $39.95.
Teen Pregnancy. Teen mothers discuss pregnancy and motherhood. Adoption and abortion are also explained. Grades 7-12.
VHS: S24422. $39.95.
Teen Sexuality. This is an open and frank look at teen sexuality. Sexual intercourse, abstinence, homosexuality, sex without intercourse, birth control, disease prevention and more topics are included. Grades 7-12.
VHS: S24423. $39.95.
The Schlessinger Teen Health Video Series. 15-volume set.
VHS: S24424. $599.25.

OCCULT/NEW AGE

Alien Dreamtime

A visual chronicle of Terence McKenna's techno-shamanic visions and rave culture, this video captures a rare moment in psychedelic history. McKenna's rap ambient musings from Space Time Continuum and digeridoo master Stephen Kent enter new sensory territory. 60 mins.
VHS: S22708. $19.98.

Ancient Mysteries

Using modern technology, scientific analysis, high-tech evidence and recent archaeological developments, the films in the *Ancient Mysteries* series are on the cutting edge of discovery.
Bigfoot. Does Yeti exist? Is Sasquatch only an imaginary creature? This investigation is set on finding the answers to the questions posed by the riddle of this elusive creature, seen only at the most outer reaches of untamed wilderness. 50 mins.
VHS: S21685. $19.95.
Vampires. The world of the undead, from corpses with pulses to graves where no vegetation will grow, is the focus of this fascinating video. Unraveling the mystery of these legendary creatures is not a task for the faint-hearted. 50 mins.
VHS: S21686. $19.95.
Witchcraft in America. From the witchcraft of Salem, Massachusetts, to 19th-century Caribbean voodoo and even modern-day ritual ceremony, all these practices offer evidence of the power mustered by the dark arts. In this video, filmed live, the secrets of witchcraft are unveiled as never before. 50 mins.
VHS: S21688. $19.95.

Aroma Massage

Beautifully filmed, this video teaches the techniques and benefits of massage with essential oils. It explains the correct and safe way to give or receive a massage. This video demonstrates effleurage, kneading, vibration and percussion strokes. 60 mins.
VHS: S22702. $24.95.

Arthur C. Clarke: World of Strange Powers

Two episodes, *Warnings from the Future* and *Have We Lived Before?* make this video an exciting foray into the mysteries of the human mind. Clarke, author of *2001*, looks at startling instances of clairvoyance, prophecy and memories of past lives. 56 mins.
VHS: S26368. $19.95.

Telegrams from the Dead

In 1848, two young girls heard strange rapping noises in their otherwise quiet upstate New York hometown. This simple incident started the spiritualism craze that spread throughout the US. Ellen Burstyn narrates this documentary, which uses re-enactments and archival resources to chart the growth of the spiritualism phenomenon. 60 mins.
VHS: S24695. $19.95.

UNIDENTIFIED FLYING OBJECTS

Chariots of the Gods

Controversial and revealing film adapted from Erich Von Daeniken's best-selling book, dealing with the theory that many ancient civilizations developed advanced knowledge brought to earth by extra-terrestrial visitors. A cult hit. 90 mins.
Laser: LD70915. $39.95.

Countdown to Alien Nation

Investigative journalist Michael Lindemann reports on the various phases of the government's UFO cover-up since 1947, and discusses the serious consequences of alien-human interaction, and "how you can prepare for the unprecedented changes ahead." 115 mins.
VHS: S18043. $29.95.

Crop Circle Update

The British founder of the Circle Phenomenon Research, Colin Andrews, presents additional evidence to support his claims on the historical developments of the evolving "crop circles." 120 mins.
VHS: S18038. $29.95.

The Extraterrestrial Influence

A channeled workshop develops theories on the way early human beliefs were influenced and evolved by their extraterrestrial ancestors. 90 mins.
VHS: S20170. $39.95.

Farewell Good Brothers

The Discovery Channel has collected these tales from people who claim to have been aboard UFO's. This is an offbeat and hilarious look at extraterrestrial contactees—a cult for our own times.
VHS: S22541. $19.95.

The Flying Saucer Mystery

The mysteries of UFO's are investigated in this early sci-fi documentary. Completely camp and sensationalistic in its approach, it has an appealing sense of fun that has been lost ever since the invention of ET. There are also 30 minutes of sci-fi trailers added to round out the feeling of the era.
VHS: S23151. $29.95.

Flying Saucers

This program argues the government has extensive knowledge of the existence of UFOs, and charges they're suppressing it from the public. 90 mins.
VHS: S18041. $29.95.

Geosophy

Why did the ancients build sacred sites around our planet-circles, pyramids, henges, standing stones? Why did they make massive use of crystals? construct leys? develop geomancy and use sacred geometry all over the world? The world-renowned researchers and philosophers carrying on pioneer work in Earth Mysteries in Britain are developing a new science—geosophy—rediscovering knowledge from the remote past. 95 mins.
VHS: S08530. $29.95.

The Grand Deception of 1995

The director of the Civilian Intelligence Network argues that a secret international government will orchestrate an extraterrestrial event in 1995 to initiate an oppressive New World Order. 100 mins.
VHS: S18039. $29.95.

Hidden Memories: Are You a UFO Abductee?

One of the foremost authorities on UFO abduction, Budd Hopkins, examines the symptoms adults and children report experiencing in cases of abduction. 90 mins.
VHS: S20165. $29.95.

Human Encounters with Aliens

John Mack is a professor of psychiatry at Harvard. He argues that physical evidence makes memories of alien encounters fundamentally different from other similar recollections. Dr. Mack is the author of *Abduction: Human Encounters with Aliens*. 60 mins.
VHS: S23619. $34.95.

The Mystery of Crop Circles: Messages from Another World?

Michael Hesemann, the publisher of Germany's leading UFO magazine, produced this documentary that investigates the unsolved enigmas of England's Crop Circle phenomena. The work features interviews with authorities Colin Andrews, Pat Delgado, John Michell and George Winfield. 120 mins.
VHS: S20171. $39.95.

Nova—UFOs: Are We Alone?

From the most popular and enlightening television science series comes the home video version you can play any time you like. This cassette explores the fascinating world of unidentified flying objects. *Nova* claims to have an answer to this puzzling phenomenon. What do they know that you don't? Rent this tape and find out. USA, 60 mins.
VHS: S06025. $29.98.

One on One on UFOs

A three-volume video interview series that explores the possibilities of UFOs, the existence of an alien presence, government complicity, the psychological consequences of people who maintain they were abducted, and Colin Andrews discussing the phenomenon of "crop circles" (pictograms). 190 mins.
One on One on UFOs: Vol. 1.
VHS: S18045. $29.95.
One on One on UFOs: Vol. 2.
VHS: S18046. $29.95.
One on One on UFOs: Vol. 3.
VHS: S18047. $29.95.

The Pleiadian Connection

Swiss farmer Eduard "Billy" Meier's collection of personal encounters with cosmonauts from *The Pleiades*. The program discusses Pleiadian messages "about Earth's history, man's spiritual development and laws of creation." 60 mins.
VHS: S18044. $39.95.

Preparing for Contact

Lecturer Lyssa Channeling Germane believes contact between Earth and alien beings is an inevitable occurrence, and offers insights into how society might relate to different extraterrestrial civilizations. 50 mins.
VHS: S20169. $24.95.

Roswell Incident

Major Virgil Armstrong, UFO expert, mystic, lecturer and author, discusses UFO riddles and shows their significance in our time. He shares research on the Mayan calendar, planetary shifts, new energy configurations, and the Roswell Incident as it relates to each historical period. 88 mins.
VHS: S10218. $29.95.

The Second Coming of Science

Dr. Brian O'Leary, a former astronaut and physicist, investigates the linkage between science and the paranormal, examining psychokinesis, the existence of UFOs, crop circles, free energy and the manifestations of Sai Baba. 90 mins.
VHS: S20166. $29.95.

Strange Harvests 1993

Linda Moultaon Howe is well known for her television appearances on *UFO Report*. Now she investigates in depth the strange killings of animals reported all over the world in 1993. Police are puzzled. All that is certain is that strange moving lights accompanied these bizzare deaths. 60 mins.
VHS: S22971. $29.98.

UFOs and the Alien Presence

Michael Lindemann cites UFO photographs, film clips and eyewitness testimony to authenticate his claims the government has knowingly misled the public about the presence of UFOs. 35 mins.
VHS: S20158. $19.95.

UFOs and the New World Order

Michael Lindemann, an investigative journalist, explores alien presences and discusses his research, claiming the existence of "alien beings" is covered up by a secret government organization, as part of a plan to unleash a New World Order. 60 mins.
VHS: S18042. $24.95.

UFOs and Underground Bases

UFO investigator Bill Hamilton hosts this program, which maintains UFOs and other unexplained phenomena are linked to government sites that reported house underground bases and combine alien and military personnel. 120 mins.
VHS: S20168. $34.95.

UFOs: The Miracle of the Unknown

This is the most comprehensive program ever produced on this interplanetary phenomenon. It features sightings from around the world, expert interviews, eyewitness accounts plus actual photographs of UFOs. There is even the story of a US government cover-up. Two-volume set, 120 mins.
VHS: S23139. $39.95.

UFOs: The Secret Evidence

Michael Hesemann produced this work which tries to validate the existence of UFOs through 44 different film and video clips throughout the world that purport to be various sightings. 110 mins.
VHS: S20167. $49.95.

Undeniable Evidence

Colin Andrews, the British founder of the Circle Phenomenon Research, presents evidence of the authenticity of crop circle phenomena. He showcases the practical features of genuine formations and shots of circles evolving from a single shape to huge symbolic formations. 60 mins.
VHS: S18036. $35.00.

Update on Alien Phenomena

This program offers updated information on crop circles, alien communications, animal metamorphoses, and the facts behind an alleged UFO crash retrieval case. 110 mins.
VHS: S18040. $29.95.

Who's Out There?

Is there intelligent life on other planets? Do they know we exist? Orson Welles narrates this special, which includes interviews with experts, including Dr. Carl Sagan. 55 mins.
VHS: S09254. $39.95.

hollywood studio
ANIMATION

2000-Year-Old Man
This warmly funny, animated feature, starring Carl Reiner and Mel Brooks, explores history from the perspective of a very special old man. It's almost as if the events that shaped today's world were as near as your favorite senior citizen.
VHS: S03917. $14.95.
Leo Salkin, USA, 1974, 24 mins.

Adventures of an American Rabbit
The bravest, most endearing and longest-eared super hero, in one hair-raising escapade after another as he protects America from evil, in enchanting, non-violent animation. 81 mins.
VHS: S08600. $14.95.
Fred Wolf/Nobutaka Nishizawa, USA, 1986, 81 mins.

The Adventures of Popeye, Vol. 2
Seven more adventures, including *Fright to the Finish, Bride and Gloom, Gopher Spinach, Out to Punch, Parlez Voo Woo, A Haul in One, I Don't Care*. Color, 50 mins.
VHS: S04855. $29.95.

Adventures of Roger Ramjet
He's an internationally well-known guy and a flying fool! He swallows his Proton Energy Pill, and has the strength of 20 atom bombs for 20 seconds. He—and only he—can protect law-abiding citizens from dastardly Noodles Romanoff and his evil organization of No-Goods known as N.A.S.T.Y. (National Association of Spies, Traitors and Yahoos). He's Roger Ramjet! 5 complete episodes. 30 mins.
VHS: S06619. $16.96.

The Adventures of Superman
Seven fully-animated adventures of the Man of Steel produced by Max Fleischer. Superman battles Nazi saboteurs, giant gorillas, gold thieves, Bird-Men from beneath the Earth and a clever criminal who puffs off his heists in a "superman" suit. Also an exploding volcano. Action packed. USA, 1942-43, 55 mins.
VHS: S05471. $24.95.

Aesop's Fables Volume 1
Paul Terry cartoons—silent shorts with music added; includes *Up in the Air, Flying Hoofs, Rooster and the Eagle, Wicked City, Red Hot Sands, Hitting the Rails, Runaway Balloon, Fable of the Alley Cat.*
VHS: S08956. $29.95.

Aesop's Fables Volume 2
More Paul Terry animated treasures: *Jungle Sports, Home Sweet Home, Sweet Adeline, Venus of Venice, Puppy Love, Wolf and the Crane, Troubles on the Ark, Cross Country Run.*
VHS: S08957. $29.95.

Aesop's Fables Volume 3
Eight more Paul Terry silent (music added) classics: *In Vaudeville, Picnic, Donkey Tricks, Champion, Sport of Kings, Dissatisfied Cobbler, Rat's Revenge, By Land and Air.*
VHS: S08959. $29.95.

Aesop's Film Fables
Seven silent cartoons with original musical score: *The War Bride* (1922); *In Again—Out Again* (1927); *Fable of the Jolly Rounders* (1923); *Wolf and the Kid* (1921); *Rural Romance* (1924); *Captain Kidder* (1922); and *One Good Turn* (1924). 55 mins.
VHS: S09273. $29.95.

Aladdin
A highly entertaining, Disney animated feature about the epic struggle between Aladdin, an impoverished young boy, and the cruel Jafar, both in love with the Sultan's daughter Princess Jasmine and desperate to gain control of the magic lamp. The fun is provided by Robin Williams' manic and brilliantly inventive turn as the genie inside the lamp. Academy award-winning score by Alan Menken, with prize winning songs by Tim Rice and Howard Ashman.
VHS: S18747. $24.99.
Musker/Clements, USA, 1992, 90 mins.

Aladdin & Jasmine's Moonlight Magic
Disney characters Aladdin, Jasmine and Genie find new adventures in these romantic, magic-laced cartoons. In *Moonlight Madness*, Aladdin entices Jasmine to join him on a date but he gets distracted by the promise of treasure. Then, in *Some Enchanted Genie*, Genie falls in love. 45 mins.
VHS: S27358. $12.99.

Alice in Wonderland
Disney animation based on the Lewis Carroll favorite, wonderfully entertaining! Memory of the Cheshire Cat will remain even after its smile disappears.
VHS: S05322. $26.99.
Laser: CAV. LD74998. $49.99.
Walt Disney, USA, 1951, 75 mins.

Alice of Wonderland in Paris
A psychedelic remixing of Lewis Carroll's classic tale interweaves four separate stories, moving beyond Carroll's original emphasis to involve figures such as the American humorist James Thurber, Eve Titus, Ludwig Bemelmans and Crockett Johnson. Voices by Carl Reiner, Norma Macmillan and Allen Swift. 70 mins.
VHS: S17452. $19.95.

All Dogs Go to Heaven
And some dogs like Charlie visit heaven and head straight back to the land of the living. Burt Reynolds lends his voice and his mannerisms to this animated action adventure about a very bad dog and a very good girl. Other voices are provided by Dom Deluise, Loni Anderson, Melba Moore, Charles Nelson Reilly, Judith Barsi and Vic Tayback as a pit bull known as Carface.
VHS: S12541. $19.98.
Don Bluth, USA/Ireland, 1989, 90 mins.

All This & Tex Avery Too!
This program collects fourteen crazy, weird and distinct works from Tex Avery, whose dramatic use of line, shadow, texture and rhythm made him one of the pioneers of the field. Hypnotic, witty and playful.
Laser: LD70151. $34.98.

Ariel's Undersea Adventures: Whale of a Tale
Two short, animated films from Disney, *Whale of a Tale* and *Urchin*, show the enchanted underwater realm first seen in *The Little Mermaid*. Ariel is joined by Sebastian and Flounder as well as other new, lovable characters in these cartoons. 44 mins.
VHS: S27364. $12.99.

The Aristocats
An animated comedy from Disney, this film has engaging characters, humor and a suspense-laden plot. An heiress leaves her fortune to her cat, Duchess, and her kittens. If only they were out of the way, a certain butler would be a lot wealthier. That's when Thomas O'Malley Cat, a streetwise alley cat, Roquefort, The Detective Mouse, and The Siamese Cat come to the rescue. With the voices of Eva Gabor, Phil Harris, Sterling Holloway, Scatman Crothers, Paul Winchell, Nancy Kulp and others.
VHS: S27539. $26.99.
Wolfgang Reitherman, USA, 1970, 78 mins.

The Art of Tom and Jerry
The explosive wit, energy and exuberance of the cat and mouse team, Tom & Jerry, are repeated in more than 70 cartoons collected in this five-disc set, exploring the full range of their actions, movements and physical humor. 566 mins.
Laser: LD71655. $99.98.

Batman: Mask of the Phantasm
This animated feature promises more bataction, more batfun, more batvillains and even more batlove. Law and order is a dirty business. Maybe that's why saving Gotham City is a task for a man in a mask.
VHS: S20959. $19.98.
Laser: LD72402. $39.98.
Erik Radomski/Bruce Timm, USA, 1994, 76 mins.

Best of Betty Boop
Boop-boop-a-doop! This collection contains *Stop That Noise, Little Nobody, Be Human*, and six other cartoons. USA, 56 mins.
VHS: S02229. $29.95.

Best of George Pal
Before George Pal went on to win five Oscars for Special Effects in the 1950's for such films as *When Worlds Collide, Destination Moon* and *Tom Thumb*, he produced puppet-cartoons for Paramount Pictures. Included here are *Sky Pirates, Captain Kidding* and *Jasper*.
VHS: S00118. $24.95.
George Pal, USA, 1934-, 70 mins.

Best of the Van Beuren Studio
Seven classic pieces of animation by an almost forgotten studio: included are Fox's comic-strip gang—the folks who run the Toonerville Trolley Ride, with Katrinka, The Terrible-Tempered Mr. Bang and the others in *Toonerville Trolley, Toonerville Ahoy,* and *Toonerville Picnic.* Also included are Felix the Cat in *Bold King Cole, Neptune's Nonsense* and *The Goose That Laid the Golden Egg*, as well as the rare *Waif's Welcome.* 50 mins.
VHS: S04858. $29.95.

Best of Warner Brothers Volume 2
Including *Haunted Mouse, Scap Haffy Daffy, Daffy and the Dinosaur, Dover Boys, Yankee Doodle Daffy, Hamateur Night* and *Bars and Stripes.* Color and B&W. USA, 55 mins.
VHS: S01632. $24.95.

Betty Boop Classics
A collection of 10 of the very best Betty Boop cartoons in full color. Betty Boop's outrageous antics and her BOOP-OOP-A-DOOP have made her a cartoon star for more than 50 years.
VHS: S00122. $19.95.
Max Fleischer, USA, 60 mins.

Betty Boop's Dizzy Dozen
Twelve shorts with the witty and seductive siren as Betty Boop is joined by Koko, the Mills Bros. and Singing Sam. Includes *Judge for a Day, One More Chance* and *Betty Minds a Baby.* 90 mins.
VHS: S17847. $24.95.

Boop Oop a Doop
Traces the origins of the animated siren Betty Boop, tracking her metamorphosis from her canine origins into the seductive icon. Uses clips, cartoons and Steve Allen's narration. With musical performances by Cab Calloway and Louis Armstrong. The film also features Popeye's debut and an intimate portrait of the innovative artist Max Fleischer. 74 mins.
VHS: S18026. $19.98.

Bugs
This video refers to one of the superstars of animated cartoons, Mr. Bugs Bunny. Those looking for a video about tiny crawling insects should look elsewhere. This hour-long color collection features seven classic cartoons, including *Gorilla My Dreams, Rabbit Transit, Hare Ribbin'* and *Bugs Bunny and the Three Bears.* USA, 60 mins.
VHS: S06354. $19.95.

Bugs & Daffy—The Wartime Cartoons
Many famous Hollywood personalities served their country in World War II. Some were flesh and blood. Others like Bugs Bunny and Daffy duck were pen and ink but no less patriotic. Leonard Maltin introduces this 11-cartoon collection which includes *Hare Meets Hare, Daffy Gone* and *Gremlins from the Kremlins.* 80 mins.
VHS: S09121. $19.95.
Laser: LD70537. $34.98.

Bugs and Daffy's Carnival of the Animals
All new animation produced, directed and written by Chuck Jones—combined with live action as Bugs and Daffy accompany Michael Tilson Thomas in a performance based on the music of Camille Saint-Saens and the comic poetry of Ogden Nash. 1976, 24 mins.
VHS: S12623. $12.95.

Bugs Bunny Classics
He may have been a stinker but this rabbit did fearlessly promote the consumption of vegetables. Bugs was to carrots what Popeye was to spinach. Spend another hour with your favorite wisecracking bunny as he performs in *Rabbit Punch, Acrobatty Bunny* and *Hare Devil Hare.* 60 mins.
VHS: S09124. $14.95.
Laser: LD70535. $34.98.

Bugs Bunny in King Arthur's Court
Also known as *A Connecticut Rabbit in King Arthur's Court*, this TV special contains all new animation—produced and directed by Chuck Jones. Bugs ends up in King Arthur's (Daffy's) court and is captured by a knight (Elmer) who thinks he's a dragon transformed into a rabbit. Merlin is played by Yosemite Sam. 1977, 24 mins.
VHS: S12624. $12.95.

The Bugs Bunny Mother's Day Special
A special Looney Tunes tribute to the most important folks in the world. After all, it's Mother's Day 365 days a year. 23 mins.
VHS: S15835. $12.95.

The Bugs Bunny Mystery Special
In this hilarious send-up of *Alfred Hitchcock Presents*, Porky Pig is the all-purpose host of this show about the uncompromising detective Elmer Fudd and fugitive Bugs. 24 mins.
VHS: S18149. $12.95.

Bugs Bunny Superstar
Orson Welles narrates this feature-length salute to the animated superstar and carrot fancier, Mr. Bugs Bunny. Animators Chuck Jones, Tex Avery and Bob Clampett are interviewed. Nine of Bugs' best performances are featured. Titles include *I Taw a Putty Tat, The Old Grey Hare* and *What's Cookin' Doc? USA*, 90 mins.
VHS: S06353. $14.95.
Laser: LD70536. $24.98.

Bugs Bunny's 1,001 Rabbit Tales
Feature-length film with Bugs telling tales to Prince Abadaba, the spoiled son of a character played by Yosemite Sam. Also featuring the pin-headed Sultan Sam and Witch Hazel. 74 mins.
VHS: S14614. $14.95.

Bugs Bunny's Bustin' Out All Over
A collection of classic 'toons celebrating Springtime. See Bugs and Elmer when they were teens, Wile E. Coyote finally catch the Road Runner, and much more. From animation legend Chuck Jones. 24 mins.
VHS: S15833. $12.95.

Bugs Bunny's Comedy Classics
This compilation of classic Bugs Bunny capers includes *Easter Yeggs, Racketeer Rabbit, The Hare-Brained Hypnotist, Acrobatty Rabbit, Falling Hare,* and *Haredevil Hare.* Color, 60 mins.
VHS: S13565. $12.98.

Bugs Bunny's Creature Features
Halloween is any time of the year with this collection of animated yuks starring Bugs Bunny, Elmer Fudd and Daffy Duck. Cartoon titles include *Night of the Living Duck, The Duxorcist* and *Invasion of the Bunny Snatchers.* 25 mins.
VHS: S16723. $12.95.

Bugs Bunny's Easter Funnies
Auditions are being held to find out who'll deliver the goodies during the Easter Bunny's illness. Bugs is the likely candidate in this madcap collection of holiday favorites. 50 mins.
VHS: S15834. $12.95.

Bugs Bunny's Hare Raising Tales
45 mins.
VHS: S12625. $12.95.

Bugs Bunny's Lunar Tunes
Bugs must call on his brawn and intelligence to prevent Marvin Martian from blowing up the world. 24 mins.
VHS: S18147. $12.95.

Bugs Bunny's Mad World of Television
Bugs is installed as programming chief and sends his network to the top with his madcap and anarchic shows. 24 mins.
VHS: S18148. $12.95.

Bugs Bunny's Overtures to Disaster
Bugs is cast as a concert maestro who leads the symphony that alternately raises the roof and almost brings down the house. 24 mins.
VHS: S18150. $12.95.

Bugs Bunny's Wild World of Sports
Who's the world's best athlete? You'll catch Olympic fever with the Looney Tunes team, as we check out the many games that cartoon stars play. Great, great animated stuff! USA, color, 24 mins.
VHS: S15415. $12.95.

Bugs Bunny's Zaniest 'Toons
This compilation of classic shorts starring Bugs Bunny and friends includes *Tortoise Bets the Hare, Tortoise Wins by a Hare* and *Rabbit Transit* co-starring Cecil Turtle, and *Hare Trigger, Bugs Bunny Rides Again* and *Buccaneer Bunny* co-starring Yosemite Sam. Color, 60 mins.
VHS: S13566. $12.98.

Bugs Bunny—Hollywood Legend
This compilation of classic shorts contains six episodes from our favorite wise-cracking rabbit, including *Hair-Raising Hare, A Hare Grows in Manhattan,* and *Herr Meets Hare.* Color, 60 mins.
VHS: S13564. $12.98.

Bugs Bunny/Road Runner Movie
This brings together full-length cartoon classics and a string of excerpts from many of Chuck Jones' most original productions with newly added material. Some of the greatest work, such as *Duck Amuck* and *Ali Baba Bunny*, are to be seen here. Definitely for all ages!
VHS: S01781. $14.95.
Chuck Jones, USA, 1979, 98 mins.

Bugs Bunny: All American Hero
History's hysterical when Bugs Bunny relives it in this all-new animated special. A 21-fun salute to the USA. Haw! Haw! USA, color, 24 mins.
VHS: S15413. $12.95.

Bugs Bunny: Cupid Capers
Bugs Bunny fans will love it when Bugs gets bitten by the love bug. The multifaceted Elmer Fudd co-stars as the "Stupid Cupid" who zaps him silly. Buy this one for your sweetie on Valentine's Day! USA, color, 24 mins.
VHS: S15414. $12.95.

Bugs Bunny: Truth or Hare
A new animation collection of hare-raising adventures featuring the screwiest wabbit of them all. Bugs matches wits with Marvin the Martian, Elmer Fudd, Yosemite Sam and the Tasmanian Devil. Cartoon titles include *The Fair Haired Hare, Dr. Devil and Mr. Hare, Wideo Rabbitt* and *Hareway to the Stars.* 33 mins.
VHS: S16717. $12.95.

Bugs vs. Daffy: Battle of the Music Video Stars
Rival video DJs Bugs and Daffy compete for ratings success. Pump up the volume and watch the feathers and fur fly as these two zany, wacky, madcap, loony, anthropomorphized kooks fight to fill the air waves with pretty pictures and easy listenin'. USA, color, 24 mins.
VHS: S15416. $12.95.

Bugs! & Elmer!
The mischievous energy and rakish charm of Bugs and the perennially abused, unfortunately named Elmer Fudd are featured in seven classic cartoons.
Laser: LD70534. $34.98.

Cadillacs and Dinosaurs: "Rogue" and "Dino Drive"
Two episodes from the dinosaur-laden animated series are joined on this video. In the first episode, *Rogue*, a rampaging Tyrannosaurus Rex threatens to turn humans against the dinosaurs. This could upset the delicate ecological balance of the Earth. Then, in *Dino Drive*, Jack and Hannah try to round up a herd of triceratops before they can be harmed by Governor Scharnhorst and her dinosaur-poaching pals. USA, 1993, 46 mins.
VHS: S27553. $9.99.

Cadillacs and Dinosaurs: "Wild Child" and "Pursuit"
In *Wild Child*, Jack and Hannah find a boy with mysterious powers that control dinosaurs. Poachers immediately hope to kidnap this boy in order to trap the unsuspecting giant creatures. In *Pursuit*, Jack is wrongfully accused of a crime. He must clear his name and retrieve a powerful weapon that could spell disaster for dinosaurs. USA, 1993, 46 mins.
VHS: S27554. $9.99.

Cartoon Classics in Color #1
Eight animated delights in color from the 1930's. Included in this collection are *Little Black Sambo* (1935), *Sinbad the Sailor* (1935), *Simple Simon* (1935), and *Ali Baba* (1936) from Ub Iwerks; *Molly Moo-Cow and the Butterflies* (1935), and *The Toonerville Trolley* (1935) from Burt Gillette and Tom Palmer; and *Somewhere in Dreamland* (1936) from Dave Fleischer. USA, 1934-36, 60 mins.
VHS: S05456. $24.95.

Cartoon Classics, Volume 2
Eight gems of art including *Falling Hare* (1943) featuring Bugs Bunny, *Ants in the Plants* (1940) directed by Dave Fleischer, and *Jerky Turkey* (1945) directed by Tex Avery. USA, 60 mins.
VHS: S02231. $24.95.

Cartoon Classics, Volume 3
Six cartoons from the silent era in movies, including two Disney cartoons, *Alice the Toreador* and *The Dinosaur and the Missing Link* (1917) directed by Willis O'Brien, a pioneer of stop-action animation. USA, 55 mins.
VHS: S02226. $24.95.

Cartoon Classics, Volume 4
Eight animated shorts from such masters as Friz Freleng, Max Fleischer, Robert Clampett and the talents of Porky Pig, Farmer Al Falfa, Bosko the Mountie, and a black widow spider who looks like Veronica Lake. Titles include *Porky's Pastry Pirates, Cobweb Hotel, Candy Town, Big Man from the North, The Barnyard Melody* and *Eatin' on the Cuff* or *The Moth Who Came to Dinner*. Various, USA, 1929-42, 55 mins.
VHS: S05457. $24.95.

Cartoon Classics, Volume 5
Eight cartoons from the 1930's, including *April Maze* with Felix the Cat, *Ain't Nature Grand* featuring Bosko, and *Tom Thumb* directed by Ub Iwerks. USA, 60 mins.
VHS: S02232. $24.95.

Cartoon Holidays
Featuring Betty Boop, Rudolph the Rednosed Reindeer, Little Audrey, Hector the Pup and Grampy. These cartoon classics from the Fleischer studios feature beloved characters in full color and animation. Includes: *Betty Boop's Halloween Party, Snow Foolin', Santa's Surprise, Hector's Hectic Life, Rudolph the Rednosed Reindeer* and *Christmas Comes But Once a Year*. 48 mins.
VHS: S09237. $14.95.

Cartoon Moviestars— Starring Bugs Bunny!
This collection of Warner Brothers' favorite rabbit in action contains a lucky seven classic cartoons that provide continuous hilarity. Bugs can be seen in such laugh packed offerings as *Buccaneer Bunny* and *Hare Tonic*. Fun for the whole family and complete strangers as well.
VHS: S08295. $14.95.

Cartoon Moviestars— Starring Tom and Jerry!
They swam with Esther Williams and danced with Gene Kelly. The MGM cartoon cat and mouse team of Tom and Jerry, created by William Hanna and Joe Barbera, won seven Oscars, including one for *Quiet Please*, which is included in this video collection. Also seven more classics including *Mouse Cleaning* and *Jerry and Jumbo*.
VHS: S08294. $14.95.

Cartoonies: Betty Boop
A collection of Betty Boop cartoons. Includes: *Betty Boop's Ups and Downs, Shortin Brad, Hot Air Salesman, Farm Foolery, Betty Boop Limited, Educated Fish, Any Rags*. 47 mins.
VHS: S09233. $14.95.

Cartoonies: Casper the Ghost
Casper the Friendly Ghost in a collection of cartoon classics. Contains: *Friendly Ghost, Ski's the Limit, There's Good Boos Tonight, Stork Market, A Haunting We Will Go,* and *Peeping-Penguins*. 48 mins.
VHS: S09235. $14.95.

Cartoonies: Gabby
The cantankerous cartoon favorite is back with his classic misadventures. Contains: *King for a Day, Fun-shine State, It's a Hap-Hap-Happy Day, Gobs of Fun, All's Well, Win Place or Showboat*. 49 mins.
VHS: S09234. $14.95.

Cartoonies: Little Lulu
Mischief is Little Lulu's specialty, and now she's back in a fun filled program. Contains: *Dog Show Off, Little Brown Jug, Lulu at the Zoo, Big Drip, I'm Just Curious, A-Car-Tune Portrait, Man's Pest Friend*. 49 mins.
VHS: S09236. $14.95.

Cartoons Go to War
Walt Disney and directors Chuck Jones and Frank Capra provided some of the diverse Hollywood talent enlisted by the United States war effort during World War II. Their amazing creations, ranging from characters like Private Snafu and Mr. Hook to the Academy Award winning *Der Fuehrer's Face* are joined on this video.
VHS: S27623. $19.95.
Sharon K. Baker, USA, 1995, 50 mins.

Cartoons That Time Forgot
A historically important, seven-part series on the landmark animation work of Ub Iwerks, the important early Disney collaborator who designed Mickey Mouse and launched the "Silly Symphonies." The program looks at the contributions of the Van Beuren Studios.
Volume 1.
VHS: S18205. $24.95.
Volume 2.
VHS: S18206. $24.95.
Laser: LD72020. $49.99.
Volume 3.
VHS: S18207. $24.95.
Volume 4.
VHS: S18208. $24.95.
Volume 5.
VHS: S18209. $24.95.
Volume 6.
VHS: S18210. $24.95.
Volume 7.
VHS: S18211. $24.95.
The Complete Set.
Laser: LD72287. $124.99.

Casper's Animal Friends
The supernatural wonder Casper finds new friends and animal figures in this imaginative tale of comradeship and bravery. 25 mins.
VHS: S17242. $9.98.

Casper's Fairy Tales
Casper leads his friends through a ghoulish and funny look at Mother Goose tales.
VHS: S17254. $9.98.

Casper's Favorite Days
The Friendly Ghost supervises the fun and spectacle in this collection of stories and tales.
VHS: S17253. $9.98.

Casper's Good Deeds
In four separate ghost stories Casper is called to summon up his supernatural skills and bravery.
VHS: S17255. $9.98.

Casper's Halloween
The world's friendliest ghost stars in this program of four shorts centered around the spectacle and danger of Halloween. 25 mins.
VHS: S17241. $9.98.

Casper's Travels
In these four globetrotting stories, set in England, the South Pole and Mexico, Casper and his pals make new acquaintances. 25 mins.
VHS: S17243. $9.98.

Cats and Mice of Paul Terry
From one of the cinema's pioneer animators, a series of cartoons, all produced during the 1920s, featuring cats and mice who are forever at odds. Included are: *The Wild West, Short Vacation, China Doll, Sunny Italy, Stars of the Circus, Sharpshooter* and *Ship Ahoy*. Silent with music score.
VHS: S05604. $24.95.
Paul Terry, USA, c. 1920, 55 mins.

Chuck Amuck: The Movie
The man behind the madness! Warner Bros. animation legend Chuck Jones takes you on a fun and cartoon-packed tour of his fascinating career. 51 mins.
VHS: S14619. $14.95.

Cinderella
Walt Disney's animated classic feature based on the Charles Perrault fairy tale tells the magical tale of an abused young woman with the only foot in the kingdom to fit a certain glass slipper. With the help of her fairy godmother and a few small animals she dazzles the prince on her night off from household drudgery. With the voices of Ilene Woods, Eleanor Audley, William Phipps and Verna Felton as the magic wand waver.
VHS: S07785. $26.99.
Wilfred Jackson/Clyde Geronimi/Hamilton Luske, USA, 1950, 74 min.

Clutch Cargo
This hysterical and historical collection was culled from television's first animated comic strip. *Clutch Cargo* is also famous for its use of live-action lips superimposed over the mouths of cartoon characters (a process known as "Synchro-Vox"). Join ace pilot Clutch, his kid sidekick Spinner and their dog Paddlefoot as they embark on a series of wacky cliffhanger adventures.
Clutch Cargo: Volume 1.
VHS: S15235. $14.95.
Clutch Cargo: Volume 2.
VHS: S16662. $14.95.

Colonel Bleep
Created in 1956 by Robert Buchanan at his studio in Miami, *Colonel Bleep* was a milestone in television animation—the first original TV cartoon series produced in color. These are the comical adventures of space ranger Bleep and his able assistants, the caveman Scratch and a puppet named Squeek.
Colonel Bleep: Volume 1.
VHS: S15236. $14.95.
Colonel Bleep: Volume 2.
VHS: S16660. $14.95.

Color Adventures of Superman
All color adventures of Superman beautifully animated by the Fleischer studio with the voice of Bud Collyer as Superman. Includes *Superman, The Mechanical Monsters, The Magnetic Telescope, The Japoteurs, The Bulleteers, Jungle Drums* and *The Mummy Strikes*.
VHS: S05474. $24.95.

The Compleat Tex Avery
This five-disc set records the extraordinary range of Tex Avery's greatest works. More than 60 cartoons are reproduced. 540 mins.
Laser: LD71656. $99.98.

Cool McCool: How to Catch a Crook
Eight wacky adventures served up by *Batman* creator Bob Kane featuring Cool McCool, his assistant Breezy, Cool's dad Harry and the Komedy Kops. 60 mins.
VHS: S16937. $14.95.

Cool McCool: Shooting the Breeze
Everyone's favorite cartoon cop, Cool is always one step ahead of disaster in these eight riotous McCool adventures. Also starring The Rattler, Hurricane Harry, Harry McCool and the Komedy Kops. 60 mins.
VHS: S16938. $14.95.

Crusader Rabbit vs. the Pirates
While on vacation, Crusader and his trusty companion, Rags the Tiger, discover a message in a bottle warning of pirates. Join our cartoon heroes as they set sail for Dunkin Island and encounter mean ol' Captain Bilg, scourge of the sea. From Jay Ward, the creator of *Rocky and Bullwinkle*.
VHS: S14684. $12.95.
Jay Ward, USA, 1949, 80 mins.

Crusader Rabbit vs. the State of Texas
While reading the newspaper, Crusader is shocked to discover his jackrabbit relatives in the great state of Texas are being deported. Hopping mad, he enlists the aid of Rags the Tiger in circulating a petition to end this injustice. Along the way they encounter Granite Jaw Jones, Vernon the Vulture and more. From Jay Ward, the creator of *Rocky and Bullwinkle*.
VHS: S14685. $12.95.
Jay Ward, USA, 1949, 60 mins.

Daffy
Daffy Duck stars in this one-hour full-color collection of some of the greatest performances of someone feathered in the history of animation. Titles include *Slightly Daffy, The Upstanding Sitter, Mexican Joyride, Yankee Doodle Daffy* and *Daffy Duck in Hollywood*, plus three more. USA, 60 mins.
VHS: S06355. $14.95.

Daffy Duck's Easter Egg-citement
That screw-loose duck is at it again in this no-holds-barred show of slapstick humor and tongue-twisting lunacy. A crazy salute to Spring unsprung! 24 mins.
VHS: S15836. $12.95.

Daffy Duck's Madcap Mania
45 mins.
VHS: S12626. $12.95.

Daffy Duck's Quackbusters
60% new animation in this feature, including Daffy in *The Duxorcist* and *Night of the Living Duck*. The narrative frame connecting all this involves Daffy's "Ghouls 'R' Us" Agency. 79 mins.
VHS: S14615. $14.95.

Daffy Duck's Thanks for Giving
A animated holiday celebration starring Daffy Duck! See Daffy soar to new heights in *Duck Dodgers and the Return of the 24th-1/2 Century*. Watch him try to survive *The Bitter Half*. Plus even more fun in animation form. 25 mins.
VHS: S16724. $12.95.

Daffy Duck: Tales from the Duckside
Five crazy cartoon capers each starring animation's daffiest duck. "A Masterpiece. Whimsical. Sparkling. Moving. I wept," says the Duck himself. Daffy takes on the roles of a messenger, a stork and Abraham Lincoln in *Wise Quackers, The Impatient Patient, Porky's Pig's Feat* and *Stork Naked*. 33 mins.
VHS: S16718. $12.95.

David Hand's Animaland
Unavailable for over 40 years, this is the first in a series of animated films from the director of Disney's *Bambi* and *Snow White*. A four-volume collection presenting David Hand's complete Animaland and Musical Paintbox series.
Animaland: Volume 1.
VHS: S16647. $14.95.

Dick Deadeye
Based on the drawings of Ronald Searle and the operettas of Gilbert and Sullivan, and directed by Bill Melendez (*The Peanuts*), this is the animated adventure of Dick Deadeye. Join Dick on his quest for the Ultimate Secret while he fends off the evil Pirate King, aided by his sidekicks Nanky and Poo. His mission: to save the Empire. 80 mins.
VHS: S12750. $29.95.

Disney Animation
Your child will delight to these videos of their favorite Disney characters.
Canine Commando Starring Pluto.
VHS: S03046. $14.95.
Here's Donald!
VHS: S03033. $14.95.
Here's Goofy!
VHS: S03034. $14.95.
Here's Mickey!
VHS: S03032. $14.95.
Here's Pluto!
VHS: S03035. $14.95.
Importance of Being Donald.
VHS: S03045. $14.95.
Silly Symphonies.
VHS: S03036. $14.95.
Tale of Two Chipmunks.
VHS: S03048. $14.95.
Winnie the Pooh and a Day for Eeyore.
VHS: S03039. $14.95.
Winnie the Pooh and the Honey Tree.
VHS: S03041. $14.95.
Winnie the Pooh and the Blustery Day.
VHS: S03042. $14.95.
Winnie the Pooh and Tigger Too.
VHS: S03043. $14.95.

Disney Love Tales
The cartoons *Mickey's Delayed Date, Pluto's Heart Throb* and *Mr. Duck Steps Out* show Mickey Mouse, Pluto and Donald Duck experiencing all the joy and humor that love can bring. 25 mins.
VHS: S27361. $12.99.

The Disney Primitive Collection: Alice
Between 1925 and 1927, Disney released a series of silent shorts with the adorable character, Alice. Includes *Alice in the Jungle, Alice Jailbird, Alice Orphan, Alice Rattled by Rats, Alice the Toreador, Alice's Tin Pony, Alice Solves a Puzzle, Alice Chop Suey* and *Alice's Eggplant*. 70 mins.
VHS: S16263. $29.95.

Disney Sing-Alongs
Sing along to classic Disney tunes with these captioned clips from famous Disney cartoons.
Disney's Sing-Along.
VHS: S03038. $14.95.
Disney's Sing-Along Songs: Zip-A-Dee-Doo-Dah.
VHS: S03049. $14.95.
Disney Sing-Along Songs: The Lion King: Circle of Life.
This collection of animated musical numbers contains songs from such mega-blockbusters as *The Lion King*, and the upcoming feature, *Pocahontas*. Kids will treasure this chance to sing songs along with their favorite Disney characters. 30 mins.
VHS: S22984. $14.95.

Disney Sweetheart Stories
Mickey and Minnie Mouse reminisce about the most cherished moments from their animated romance. Donald Duck and Pluto join in the fun. Included are *Mickey's Rival, In Dutch* and *Nifty Nineties*. 23 mins.
VHS: S27360. $12.99.

Disney's Beginnings
Eight early Disney efforts, some from his days in Kansas City from his first company, called Laugh-O-Grams, the remainder done in Hollywood from the series known as Alice in Cartoonland. Includes *Mechanical Cow, Alice Rattled by Rats* and *Great Guns*.
VHS: S00347. $24.95.
Walt Disney, USA, 1920-27, 55 mins.

Donald in Mathmagic Land
In this highly acclaimed film, a curious Donald Duck ventures into a wonderful world of fantasy, discovering that you can have fun with math, fun with fractions and laughs with logic. 27 mins.
VHS: S06593. $14.95.

Dumbo
The animated Disney classic about a baby elephant born with oversize ears. Assisted by his only friend, a mouse named Timothy, Dumbo learns to use his large ears to become the world's only flying elephant.
VHS: Out of print. For rental only.
Laser: LD70959. $49.99.
Walt Disney, USA, 1951, 63 mins.

Early Warner Brothers Cartoons
Eight favorites from the early 1930's, including *Lady Play Your Mandolin, Freddie the Freshman* and *I Love a Parade*. B&W. USA, 1931-32, 55 mins.
VHS: S00387. $24.95.

The Easter Bunny Is Comin' to Town
Fred Astaire narrates this retelling of the grandest Easter traditions. 50 mins.
VHS: S18153. $12.95.

Elmer
Elmer Fudd, the great white hunter with the twisted tongue, stars in this collection of full-color, animated cartoons. Included in this video package are such favorites as *Elmer's Candid Camera, The Wacky Wabbit, What Makes Daffy Duck?, Hare-Brained Hypnotist* and *Good Night Elmer*. USA, 60 mins.
VHS: S06356. $14.95.

Fantasia
The magic of Disney animation is gloriously blended with the music of eight classical pieces conducted by Leopold Stokowski. Relive those memorable moments with dancing mushrooms and hippos, dinosaurs, demons, abstract shapes, centaurs, and a certain sorcerer's apprentice who Walt felt needed a career boost.
VHS: S14755. $24.99.
Walt Disney Productions, USA, 1940, 116 mins.

Fantasy Film Worlds of George Pal
A wonderful tribute to the great genius of animation and special effects, George Pal, tracing the career that won him eight Oscars, with rare film clips and demonstrations of his revolutionary techniques. USA, 1986, 93 mins.
VHS: S04763. $19.95.

Fearless Fortune Hunter
Scrooge McDuck's vast fortune tumbles into the underground home of the Terry Fermies in *Earth Quack!*, touching off an earthshaking caper to recover it. In the second adventure, *Masters of the Djinni*, Scrooge's quest for Aladdin's legendary lamp produces a mystical madcap mess. 44 mins.
VHS: S06594. $14.95.

Felix!
A collection of Felix the Cat cartoons. The works include Felix's stylized debut as a free-wheeling cat in *Feline Follies* (1919), the baseball thriller *Felix Saves the Day* (1922), *Felix in Hollywood* (1923) and the surreal masterpieces *Futuritzy* (1928) and *Felix Woos Whoopee* (1930). "A truculent, resourceful man-cat with a walk that looks like the trudge of a bouncer in a waterfront saloon. One of the most dynamic personalities of the screen" (Vincent Canby). Music score by R.J. Miller. 60 mins.
VHS: S19674. $39.95.
Laser: CAV. LD72082. $39.95.

Fern Gully...The Last Rainforest
An imaginative, animated film that cries out against the destruction of the rain forests. In a secret land a young dreamer named Crysta, the Bettle Boys, a singing lizard and a bat named Batty unite to save their kingdom. With the voices of Robin Williams, Samantha Mathis, Christian Slater, Cheech & Chong, Tim Curry, Jonathan Ward and Grace Zabriskie.
VHS: S16858. $24.98.
Laser: CAV, widescreen. LD71552. $39.98.
Bill Kroyer, USA, 1992, 76 mins.

The First Easter Rabbit
Burl Ives narrates and sings in this delightful story about Stuffy's transformation from child's toy to the first Easter Rabbit. Lyrics by Jules Bass. Music by Maury Laws. 25 mins.
VHS: S18152. $12.95.

Fleischer Color Classics
Eight great cartoon classics from the creator of Betty Boop, including *Dancing on the Moon, Fresh Vegetable Mystery,* and *Rudolph, The Red Nosed Reindeer.*
VHS: S01628. $24.95.
Dave Fleischer, USA, 1934-40, 55 mins.

For Better or Worse
Lynn Johnston's famous, nationally distributed, comic serial, based on the travails of family life as experienced by the Pattersons, is now an animated feature. Three kids and a dog are sure proof that laughter is simply a necessary part of everyday life. 90 mins.
VHS: S21355. $24.95.

Fox Terrytoons
Early animation from the 1930's by Paul Terry and Frank Moser are collected on this video. *Noah's Outing, Grand Uproar, South Pole or Bust, The First Snow, Fox Hunt, Billy Goat's Whiskers, Bug Carnival, Trailer Life* and *Their Last Bean* are the cartoons included.
VHS: S23315. $19.95.

Garfield Christmas Special
Garfield and friends share an old fashioned Christmas down on the farm with good eatin' and great memories of Christmas past.
VHS: S14794. $12.98.

Garfield on the Town
On the way to the vet, Garfield escapes and attempts to survive as a street cat. He discovers his birthplace and family in the inner city. Emmy award winner. 1983, 30 mins.
VHS: S12786. $12.95.

George of the Jungle: Gullible Travels
The tranquility of the Imgwee Gwee Valley is disturbed by the appearance of tycoon Seymour Noodnick, who wants to buy the title "King of the Jungle" from George. What will Bella and Ursula say? Call for Super Chicken when you have an elephant-sized mystery. And Tom Slick races in the Monte Carloff Monster Rally. 1967.
VHS: S15780. $9.98.

George of the Jungle: Jungle Mutants
From Jay Ward, the creator of *Rocky and Bullwinkle,* comes this animated video collection of four classic cartoons, two of which feature a vine-swinging jungle man who hasn't met a tree he hasn't smashed into face first. Also featuring Super Chicken and Tom Slick. With the voices of Bill Scott, June Foray, Paul Frees, and William Conrad. 1967.
VHS: S15778. $9.98.

George of the Jungle: There's No Place Like Jungle
Four more amazing animated episodes starring George of the Jungle and his cartoon pals Shep the Elephant and Ape the, um, ape. Includes a Super Chicken episode and Tom Slick in the Irish Cheapskates. 1967.
VHS: S15779. $9.98.

The Golden Age of Looney Tunes, Vol. 1 (Laser)
The energy and wit of Warner Bros.' golden age of animation is reproduced through this five-boxed set of more than 70 cartoons.
Laser: LD70176. $99.88.

The Golden Age of Looney Tunes, Vol. 2 (Laser)
A continuation of the incredibly popular collection of 70 imaginative Warner Bros. cartoons.
Laser: LD71160. $99.98.

The Golden Age of Looney Tunes, Vol. 3 (Laser)
A wonderful compilation of Warner Bros. animation, this five-disc set features the work of Chuck Jones, Tex Avery, Friz Freleng, Harman-Ising, Frank Tashlin and Bob Clampett, and their enduring characters, Bugs Bunny, Daffy Duck, Elmer Fudd and many others.
Laser: LD71817. $99.98.

Golden Age of Looney Tunes: Vol. 1, 1930s Musicals
The classic cartoons in this collection of musicals include *Smile, Darn Ya, Smile!, Shuffle Off to Buffalo* and *I Love To Singa.*
VHS: S17752. $12.95.

Golden Age of Looney Tunes: Vol. 2, Firsts
This collection gathers the cartoons that made its respective characters famous, containing *The Wild Hare, Daffy Duck and Egghead, A Tale of Two Kitties* and *Life with Feathers.*
VHS: S17753. $12.95.

Golden Age of Looney Tunes: Vol. 3, Tex Avery
This program includes Avery's *Cinderella Meets Fella, Hamateur Night, The Bear's Tale* and *The Crackpot Quail.*
VHS: S17754. $12.95.

Golden Age of Looney Tunes: Vol. 4, Bob Clampett
The flair of Bob Clampett is reproduced in this collection of his best work, including *Wabbit Trouble, Horton Hatches the Egg, A Corny Concerto* and *The Great Piggy Bank Robbery.*
VHS: S17755. $12.95.

Golden Age of Looney Tunes: Vol. 5, Chuck Jones
Devilish wit and amazing colors are the highlights of this collection, including *The Night Watchman, Old Glory, Sniffles Takes a Trip* and *The Aristo-cat.*
VHS: S17756. $12.95.

Golden Age of Looney Tunes: Vol. 6, Friz Freleng
Includes the classics *Rhapsody in Rivets, Pigs in a Polka, Duck Soup to Nuts* and *Hare Trigger.*
VHS: S17757. $12.95.

Golden Age of Looney Tunes: Vol. 8, 1940s Zanies
40s cartoons are on display in this quirky collection, including *Nasty Quacks, The Bashful Buzzard, Daffy Doodles* and *Baby Bottleneck.*
VHS: S17759. $12.95.

Golden Age of Looney Tunes: Vol. 9, Hooray for Hollywood
Top-line drawing, craft and technical innovation highlight this period, including *Daffy Duck in Hollywood, Hollywood Steps Out, What's Cookin' Doc?* and *Slick Hare.*
VHS: S17760. $12.95.

Golden Age of Looney Tunes: Vol. 10, The Art of Bugs
Includes *Tortoise Beats Hare, Rabbit Transit, Old Grey Hare* and *Haredevil Hare.*
VHS: S17761. $12.95.

Guffaw and Order: Looney Tunes Fight Crime
Bugs Bunny, Daffy Duck and Porky Pig are just some of the famous cartoon characters who find themselves on either side of the law in this collection from Looney Tunes' favorite short animated features. Maybe law and order are really just a laughing matter. 99 mins.
Laser: LD72395. $34.98.

The Halloween Tree
Ray Bradbury's classic adventure tale is now a feature length animated film. Four boys try to save their friend's spirit from the ghosts of Halloween past. Mounshroud, a mysterious character spoken by Leonard Nimoy, takes them on a magical journey reaching back 4000 years and encompassing exotic locales from Egypt to Mexico.
VHS: S21754. $19.98.

Happy Birthday Bugs!
The wisecracking Bunny is roasted, or toasted, by such celebrities as Milton Berle, Bill Cosby, Little Richard, Hulk Hogan and Vanna White, among others. Lots of Bugs clips.
VHS: S12860. $14.95.

Hare Beyond Compare: 14 More Bugs Bunny Classics
Warner Brothers' incomparable Bugs Bunny is seen in some of his most endearing short features. This compilation includes such classics as *Big Top Bunny, Mutiny on the Bunny, Bunker Hill Bunny* and many more favorites. 100 mins.
Laser: LD72392. $34.98.

Here Comes Bugs
He's back. An all new release starring that cynical, wise-cracking rabbit, Bugs Bunny. Color, 60 mins.
VHS: S13572. $12.98.

Here Comes Garfield
Garfield and Odie's friskiness lands Odie in the dog pound. It's up to Garfield to break him out. Emmy nominee. 1982, 30 mins.
VHS: S12784. $12.98.

High-Flying Hero
Disney's heroic new adventurer—Launchpad McQuack—finds his courage put to the test in *Hero for Hire* in which the Beagle Boys trick him into performing good deeds that turn out to be crimes, and in *Launchpad's Civil War,* his participation in an annual Civil War pageant explodes into pandemonium. 44 mins.
VHS: S06596. $14.95.

Hoppity Goes to Town
The tranquility of Bugville, which is only 45 inches from Broadway in Manhattan, is threatened by the construction of a new skyscraper, and Hoppity, the grasshopper hero, leads his friends to find a new location for their happy village. One of the great animated Hollywood musicals of all time.
VHS: S00581. $24.95.
Laser: CLV. LD71991. $29.98.
Max Fleischer, USA, 1941, 77 mins.

How Bugs Bunny Won the West
In the lawless frontier communities, Bugs uses his wit and imagination to show how the West was really won. 24 mins.
VHS: S18151. $12.95.

Jay Ward and Bill Scott TV Commercials
Ward and Scott were the brilliant team responsible for *The Rocky and Bullwinkle Show,* with its intriguing mixture of wit and social commentary. These television commercials represent the height of their creative powers. 45 mins. each.
Ward and Scott TV Commercials: Vol. 1.
VHS: S18048. $19.95.
Ward and Scott TV Commercials: Vol. 2.
VHS: S18049. $19.95.

Journey Through Fairyland
Brilliant animation accompanied by original music as well as orchestral masterpieces such as *Flight of the Bumblebees* and *The Nutcracker.* This is intended as an introduction to classical music for both children and adults. Full-length animated feature. 95 mins.
VHS: S09168. $19.98.

Just Plain Daffy
A collection of animated classics all starring one of the first Hollywood ducks to become a star with a temper and speech impediment that didn't work for Walt Disney. Selections include *Hollywood Daffy, Along Came Daffy, Duck Soup to Nuts* and *Daffy Duck Slept Here.* 60 mins.
VHS: S09123. $14.95.

The Ketchup Vampires
Elvira, mistress of the Dark, narrates this animated comic tale of creepy Transylvanians. It mixes Dracula, vegetarianism, a kooky castle and a bunch of bat brats into a laugh-inducing story that is perfect for kids. 90 mins.
VHS: S26365. $24.95.

Koko the Clown
In the 1930's the team of Max and Dave Fleischer were the chief rivals of Disney in animation. Koko the Clown was the star of a series called *Out of the Inkwell,* done between 1915 and 1927. Included are: *Ouija Board, Bubbles* and *Tantalizing Fly.* Musical score.
VHS: S00691. $24.95.
Max Fleischer, USA, 1915-27, 55 mins.

Koko the Clown Cartoons
In ten classic cartoons from 1927 to 1929, the legendary team of Max and Dave Fleischer combine animation and live special effects that easily rival today's animated features. Silent, 70 mins.
VHS: S16502. $19.98.

Koko the Clown, Volume 2
Seven more gems from the Max Fleischer studio, including *Koko in Reverse, Koko's Storm, Koko's Kid, Koko Kills Time, Koko Smokes, Koko's Barnyard* and *Koko's Balloons.* All silent with music track, 50 mins.
VHS: S07481. $24.95.

Krazy Kat: Kokonino County Capers
Krazy Kat's "romantikal" desires for Ignatz the mouse, and Officer Pupp's never-ending quest to catch that rascally rodent are featured in 11 hilarious episodes. 60 mins.
VHS: S16936. $14.95.

The Lion King
Disney's animated feature tells the heart-warming tale of a young lion cub who nearly loses his birthright as king of all that he surveys. Matthew Broderick, Jeremy Irons, James Earl Jones, Robert Guillaume, Richard "Cheech" Marin and Whoopi Goldberg are some of the stars who supply the voices.
VHS: S23053. $26.99.
Laser: Letterboxed, CLV, THX. LD74930. $29.99.
Rob Minkoff/Roger Allers, USA, 1994, 88 mins.

Little Lulu and Friends
A collection of Little Lulu cartoons including *Super Lulu* (47); *A Scout with Gout* (47); *A Lamb in a Jam* (45); *Bored Cuckoo* (48); *Naughty But Nice* (47); *Loose in a Caboose* (47); *Chick and Double Chick* (46).
VHS: S05059. $34.95.

Longitude and Looneytude: 14 Globetrotting Looney Tunes Favorites
With the accent on international flavor, this collection includes Pepe le Peau, Bugs Bunny, Yosemite Sam and Sylvester on some of their foreign travels. It's exotic, mysterious and hilariously funny. 98 mins.
Laser: LD72396. $34.98.

The Looney Looney Looney Bugs Bunny Movie
Featuring the comic antics of Bugs, Porky, Tweety, Sylvester, Pepe Le Peu, and Foghorn Leghorn. Includes *Knighty-Knight Bugs, Birds Anonymous* and much more. 80 mins.
VHS: S14618. $14.95.

Looney Tunes After Dark
Fourteen horror classics, ghoulish wit and supernatural drawing enliven this series, including *Jumpin' Jupiter, Water, Water Every Hare, Bewitched Bunny, Hyde and Hare, The Night of the Living Duck,* and *The Abominable Snow Rabbit.* 99 mins.
Laser: LD71760. $34.98.

Looney Tunes Assorted Nuts
The greatest secondary acts and supporting stars in 16 cult works, including *A Bear for Punishment, Dog Gone South, Mouse Wreckers, A Sheep in the Deep,* and *Strife with Father.* 112 mins.
Laser: LD71762. $34.98.

Looney Tunes Curtain Calls
Bugs Bunny, Daffy Duck, Porky Pig and the gang appear in a series of funny gags and parodies of show business acts and cartoons, including *Rabbit of Seville, One Froggy Evening, Hillbilly Hare, What's Up Doc?,* and *The Scarlet Pumpernickel.* 92 mins.
Laser: LD71763. $34.98.

Looney Tunes Show 1
45 mins.
VHS: S12628. $12.95.

Looney Tunes Show 2
45 mins.
VHS: S12629. $12.95.

Looney Tunes Show 3
45 mins.
VHS: S12630. $12.95.

Looney Tunes: Duck Victory— Daffy Duck
The anarchic wit and rude joys of Daffy Duck are represented in 14 of his films, including *Duck Dodgers in the 24th & 1/2 Century, Duck! Rabbit! Duck!, Muscle Tussle, Don't Axe Me,* and *Duck Amuck.* 98 mins.
Laser: LD71759. $34.98.

Looney Tunes: Ham on Wry
A classic assembly of Porky Pig cartoons, including *Often an Orphan, You Ought to Be in Pictures, The Ducksters, Deduce You Say,* and *The Case of the Stuttering Pig.* 105 mins.
Laser: LD71761. $34.98.

The Lord of the Rings
Ralph Bakshi's interpretation of J.R.R. Tolkien's mystical trilogy, set in Middle Earth, about the different factions in search of the all-powerful rings. Music by Leonard Rosenman. Voices by Christopher Guard, William Squire, Michael Scholes and John Hurt.
VHS: S00767. $14.98.
Ralph Bakshi, USA, 1978, 133 mins.

The Many Adventures of Winnie the Pooh
Only Walt Disney could manage so delightful a screen adaptation of the classic children's book by A.A. Milne. Pooh and his friends Christopher Robin, Tigger, Eeyore, Piglet and others are all here. This original production includes a special "making of" bonus program.
VHS: S27480. $26.99.
Laser: LD75513. $29.99.
Walt Disney, USA, 1977, 83 mins.

Mary Poppins
This beloved Disney film combines brilliant, animated sequences with a delightful story about Julie Andrews as a magical nanny who transforms the lives of the children in her care. With Dick Van Dyke, Glynis Johns, Ed Wynn.
VHS: S01589. $26.99.
Laser: LD71132. $44.99.
Robert Stevenson, USA, 1964, 140 mins.

Max Fleischer Presents Koko the Clown
The fantastic, sublime and common intermingle in nine animated works from Max and Dave Fleischer, covering the years 1915-27, including *Auto Ride, Chinaman, Clown's Little Brother, Koko's Cartoon Factory* and *Perpetual Motion.* 60 mins.
VHS: S17455. $29.95.

Mega Man: 20,000 Leaks Under the Sea
In the first episode on this video, Mega Man and his sidekick Roll and Rush, the robo dog, find themselves lured into an underwater trap. The adventure continues in *The Strange Island of Dr. Wily.* This time, Dr. Wily has a plan involving a remote island that spells disaster for Mega Man. Suitable for ages 8 and up. 45 mins.
VHS: S27557. $9.99.

Mega Man: Robosaur Park
Mega Man and his sidekick Roll and Rush, the robo dog, blast into action in this fully animated series. In the title episode, Mega Man leads the Robo Commandos into action against robotic dinosaurs which have been programmed to attack. In *The Ice Age,* the second episode included on this tape, Ice Man and Dr. Wily hope to start a new ice age. Mega Man is set to foil their evil plan. Great for kids ages 8 and up. 45 mins.
VHS: S27556. $9.99.

Mega Man: The Beginning
Mega Man and his robo dog, Roll and Rush, confront the good-bots pressed into service by the diabolical Dr. Wily. This opening episode of the action-packed children's series could be both the beginning and the end if Mega Man fails. Next, in *Electric Nightmares,* Dr. Wily devises an intriguing plot to turn ordinary appliances against his nemesis, Mega Man. For ages 8 and up. 45 mins.
VHS: S27555. $9.99.

MGM Cartoon Magic
An animated holiday package of Christmas cartoons from the MGM studio. Highlights include Hugh Harman's 1939 Oscar nominated animated short, *Peace on Earth,* and *Alias St. Nick.* Something for the whole family to curl up around the vcr whenever they need a bit of holiday cheer.
VHS: S04979. $14.95.

Mickey and the Beanstalk
Mickey, Donald and Goofy are the hilarious giants destined to confront Willie the Giant in this vivid version of the timeless childhood story. 29 mins.
VHS: S06592. $14.95.

Mickey Loves Minnie
Disney's Mickey and Minnie Mouse join Donald and Daisy Duck, Pluto and Fifi for love, laughter and romance. *Society Dog Show, Donald's Double Trouble* and *The Brave Little Tailor* are included. 25 mins.
VHS: S27359. $12.95.

Muppet Babies: Be My Valentine
Jim Henson's award-winning Muppet Babies lead kids through lessons for making Valentines as the Muppet Babies make some Valentines themselves. Meanwhile, Baby Gonzo is playing Cupid to win Baby Piggy's heart. This animated short is both informative and fun to watch. 25 mins.
VHS: S27362. $12.99.

The Nana and Lil' Puss Puss Show
Together Nana and her Puss take the world by storm. It's like a mixture of Geritol and fur balls. All their wacky crew are here, including The Indian neighbor Soggi, and the cast of Nana's favorite tabloid show, *Hard Edition.* 50 mins.
VHS: S25819. $39.95.

Night of the Sentinels—X-Men
In this action-driven series, X-Men are mutant superheroes forced to combine their extraordinary skills perfected by their mentor, the brilliant scientist Professor Charles Xavier. 44 mins.
VHS: S17682. $12.95.

Original Tom and Jerry: Vol. 1
Tightrope Tricks (33); *Happy Hoboes* (33); *Canduland* (33); *House Cleaning Time* (29); *Feathered Follies* (32); *Ship Ahoy* (30); *Custard Pies* (29); *The Ball Game* (29). Eight classic Van Beuren Studio Tom and Jerry black and white cartoons.
VHS: S05054. $34.95.

Original Tom and Jerry: Vol. 2
Gypped in Egypt (30); *The Jail Brakers* (29); *A Dizzy Day* (33); *Tuning In* (29); *Western Whoopee* (30); *Snow Time* (30); *Venice Vamp* (32); *The Haunted Ship* (30).
VHS: S05055. $34.95.

Original Tom and Jerry: Vol. 3
Barnyard Bunk (32); *Three Little Kittens* (33); *The Cat's Dilemma* (32); *A Fireman's Life* (33); *Hokum Hotel* (32); *Noah Knew His Ark* (30); *In Vaudeville* (27); *Radio Racket* (31).
VHS: S05056. $34.95.

Original Tom and Jerry: Vol. 4
Plane Dumb (32); *Magic Art* (32); *Dixie Days* (30); *Galloping Hooves* (32); *The Lion Tamer* (34); *The Rasslin' Match* (34).
VHS: S05057. $34.95.

Pete's Dragon
Another Disney favorite that combines animation with live action, this time featuring Helen Reddy, Mickey Rooney and Red Buttons, in the heartwarming story of a lonely boy who is befriended by a klutzy dragon.
VHS: S01590. $24.99.
Don Chaffey, USA, 1977, 134 mins.

Pink Panther Follies
A Pink Panther cartoon festival (formerly *A Fly in the Pink*). Color, 60 mins.
VHS: S13570. $12.98.

Pocahontas
Mel Gibson's voice is featured as John Smith in this Disney animated blockbuster. The tale of the noble Native American princess who rescued and married an English colonist has long captivated North Americans. Now this story is updated to highlight some of the less savory aspects of the American conquest, since these themes are handled gently. Featuring the voices of Irene Bedard, Linda Hunt, David Ogden Stiers and the hit song "Colors of the Wind."
VHS: S26928. $26.99.
Mike Gabriel/Eric Goldberg, USA, 1995, 81 mins.

Popeye the Sailor
Three two-reel, full-animation cartoons directed by Fleischer: *Popeye the Sailor Meets Sinbad the Sailor*, *Popeye the Sailor Meets Ali Baba's Forty Thieves* and *Popeye the Sailor and His Wonderful Lamp*.
VHS: S01048. $24.95.
Dave Fleischer, USA, 1936, 54 mins.

Porky
Porky Pig stars in eight animated favorites, including *Kitty Kornered*, *Brother Brat*, *Baby Bottleneck*, *Little Orphan Airdale*, *My Favorite Duck* and *I Haven't Got a Hart*. All the contents of this video concern the exploits of a well adjusted pig with a speech impediment. If you are looking for horny teenagers, b-b-b-beat it, b-b-b-bub. In color. USA, 60 mins.
VHS: S06357. $14.95.

Porky Pig Tales
6 titles: *The Awful Orphan* ('49), *The Pest That Came to Dinner* ('48), *Jumpin Jupiter* ('55), *My Little Duckaroo* ('54), *Dog Collared* ('51) and *China Jones* ('59). 44 mins.
VHS: S12627. $12.95.

Porky Pig: Days of Swine and Roses
The stuttering star of many a Warner Brothers cartoon is back to entertain in five classic animated shorts. "The little ham's never been better," says Bugs Bunny. Titles include *Porky's Party*, *Thumb Fun*, *Porky's Detective Agency* and *Bye, Bye Bluebeard*. 33 mins.
VHS: S16719. $12.95.

Pupettoon Movie
From special-effects wizard George Pal comes this "Fantasia" of puppet animation. Hosted by Gumby and Pokey, *The Pupettoon Movie* features characters like Tubby the Tuba, Jasper in a Jam, hip jazz from Charlie Barnet and Louis Armstrong, and as many as 5,000 individually-carved puppets per short. 80 mins.
VHS: S06541. $12.98.

Reluctant Dragon
One of Disney's best—the story of the undragonlike dragon who'd rather sip tea and sing slaphappy songs until two pals decide to teach him the fine art of ferociousness. Also includes the bonus cartoon *Morris the Midget Moose*. 28 mins.
VHS: S03040. $14.95.

Road Runner & Wile E. Coyote: The Scrapes of Wrath
Join the fun as the popular animated creations of Chuck Jones zoom through the some of the funniest stretches of American cartoon landscape ever drawn. Titles include *Guided Muscle*, *Stop! Look!* and *Hasten!* and *Hopalong Casualty*. 33 mins.
VHS: S16720. $12.95.

The Road Runner vs. Wile E. Coyote: If at First You Don't Succeed
No one tires of watching the endless struggle of the world's most self-assured coyote. Foiling all his schemes, the road runner gets away every time, making it all seem so effortless. 94 mins.
Laser: LD72393. $34.98.

Robin Hood
Walt Disney's feature-length animated cartoon, which tells what really happened in Sherwood Forest, from the point of view of the animals. This great story includes a brilliant collection of endearing characters and songs.
VHS: S02183. $24.99.
Wolfgang Reitherman, USA, 1973, 83 mins.

Rock'a'Doodle
With his family's farm flooded by a terrible storm, young Edmond is convinced that a bedtime story his mother read him is true. To save their farm he must enter the animated world of the storybook and find Chanticleer, a rock & roll rooster who can stop the rain and bring back the sun—but first he'll have to defeat the evil owl Grand Duke.
VHS: S16638. $19.98.
Laser: LD71811. $24.98.
Don Bluth, USA, 1990, 75 mins.

Snow White and the Seven Dwarfs
Walt Disney's masterpiece tells the unforgettable story of a young woman who dreams of meeting Prince Charming but is foiled by a jealous woman. Of course she is helped in her struggle with this evil witch by those charming little people, the seven dwarfs.
VHS: S21316. $26.99.
Walt Disney, USA, 1937, 83 mins.

Speed Racer
The teenage hero-star of the most successful animated TV series, for the first time on video. Courageous, smart, resourceful, Speed Racer has the fastest futuristic car in the world, and has been applauded as a positive role model. "I have simply loved Speed since I first saw him. I was going to marry him. Well, I'm no longer a little girl. I'm 19 and yes, I'm still in love with Speed Racer," wrote one fan to the video manufacturer.
Car with a Brain. 30 mins.
VHS: S11546. $12.98.
Challenge of the Masked Racer. 60 mins.
VHS: S11548. $12.98.
Desperate Racer. 30 mins.
VHS: S11545. $14.98.
Race for Revenge. 60 mins.
VHS: S12739. $19.98.
The Fire Race. Speed Racer is the delightful 1960's animated television series that follows the adventures of a racecar driver, his girlfriend Trixie, a young boy named Spritle and a monkey named Chim Chim. Together they confront a whole range of devious plots. 52 mins.
VHS: S26253. $12.98.
The Great Car Wrestling Match. 30 mins.
VHS: S12740. $14.98.
The Secret Invaders. Once again this group of intrepid adventurers is faced with a compelling plot. This time it concerns secret invaders. 52 mins.
VHS: S26254. $12.98.
The Trick Race. 30 mins.
VHS: S11547. $14.98.

Spiderman
The dual nature of the superhero is explored in these tales set in the present, supporting Spiderman's quest for revenge.
Spiderman: A Firestar Is Born. 30 mins.
VHS: S16943. $14.99.
Spiderman: Curiosity Killed the Spiderman. 30 mins.
VHS: S16941. $14.99.
Spiderman: Dr. Doom, Master of the World. 30 mins.
VHS: S16942. $14.99.
Spiderman: Origin of the Spider-Friends. 30 mins.
VHS: S16944. $14.99.
Spiderman: Revenge of the Green Goblin. 30 mins.
VHS: S16939. $14.99.
Spiderman: Spidey Goes Hollywood. 30 mins.
VHS: S16940. $14.99.

Superman
The 17 original cartoons created by the brilliant animators Max and Dave Fleischer from 1941 to 1943 that subverts the Marvel Comics iconography for a surreal exploration of heroism and identity. Includes the legendary work *Snafuperman*. Transferred from 35mm prints. 150 mins.
VHS: S18259. $24.95.

Superman: The Complete Cartoon Collection
The Man of Steel's best cartoons by the master Max Fleischer are joined on this one video. Seventeen classics tell the story of America's most important superhero. His adventures recall a time when right and wrong were clearly defined and opposing forces. And of course, Superman always did the right thing. 142 mins.
VHS: S21081. $24.95.

Sword in the Stone
The animated version of the King Arthur legend from the studios of Walt Disney, as based on the book by Theodore H. White. "A thorough delight…the songs are bright and singable, the artwork lovely and the plot charming in its twists and turns" (Judith Crist).
VHS: S02182. $26.99.
Laser: CAV. LD74999. $49.99.
Wolfgang Reitherman, USA, 1963, 79 mins.

Sylvester & Tweety: The Best Yeows of Our Lives
Five cartoon frolics from the best known cat-and-bird comedy team on the Warner Brothers Lot. If you tawt you taw a puddy tat, you did. Titles include *Tweet and Sour*, *All a Bir-r-rd* and *Home Tweet Home*. "Purrrrrrrfection—in my humble opinion," says Sylvester. 33 mins.
VHS: S16721. $12.95.

Sylvester and Tweety's Bad Ol' Putty Tat Blues
Tweety seems innocent, but lurking within that bird brain lies a mastermind of deception and escape. While the harmless putty tat tries his best to seem coolly uninterested in Tweety, it's a ruse that lasts only as long as someone is looking. Then he pounces. 100 mins.
Laser: LD72394. $34.98.

Taz-Maniac
Taz is his own worst enemy as he seeks out food and survival in this heady collection of four episodes: *Not a Shadow of a Doubt*, *Food for Thought*, *Gone to Pieces* and *Deer Taz*. 34 mins.
VHS: S19046. $12.95.

Taz-Manimals
The mischievous Taz battles wits with new pets in a rollicking collection of three tales: *The Dog and the Turtle Story* and *Here Kitty Kitty*, Parts I and II. 40 mins.
VHS: S19045. $12.95.

Taz-Tronaut
In this program, Taz, the Looney Tunes character, experiences the power and wonder of space travel in four aeronautical episodes: *Airborne Airhead*, *Taz and the Terodactyl*, *Astro Taz* and *Bottle Cap Blues*. 39 mins.
VHS: S19044. $12.95.

Tex Avery's Screwball Classics
Nobody but nobody made more outrageous cartoons than Tex Avery. Collected on this video are eight of his screwiest, including the hysterical *Who Killed Who?*, *Bad Luck Blackie*, *Symphony in Slang*, and *Swing Shift Cinderella*. 60 mins.
VHS: S07967. $14.95.

Tex Avery's Screwball Classics 3
Tex Avery's style, brimming with anarchy, fantasy, and break-neck action, has led some to characterize the man, who along with Chuck Jones helped develop the Bugs Bunny character, as "a Walt Disney who has read Kafka." This compilation of the acclaimed animator's work includes the wild antics of screwball squirrel, The Hobo Bears, and Sexy Red (this last one sounds especially interesting). 60 mins., color.
VHS: S13555. $12.98.

Tex Avery's Screwball Classics 4
This collection of Tex Avery's looniest 'toons shows off his talents at their best! Visit with two hungry birds who'll do anything for a meal in *What's Buzzin' Buzzard?*, a lovelorn flea finding romance in *What Price Fleadom*; travel to Mars and get a nutty glimpse of *TV of Tomorrow*; and explore the manic mind of a cat obsessed with *The Cuckoo Clock*. Plus: *Blitz Wolf* and *Counterfeit Cat*.
VHS: S15665. $12.95.

Three Caballeros
Donald Duck, Joe Carioca and Panchito are the title characters in this Latin American comedy travelogue that combines animation and live action. Donald goes on a fantasy filled trip to Brazil, Mexico and a special visit with Pablo the Penguin and Little Gauchito and his flying donkey. With Auroir Miranda, Carmen Molina and the voice of Clarence Nash as Donald. 70 mins.
VHS: S07527. $26.99.
Norman Ferguson, USA, 1945, 70 mins.

Tickled Pink
Although this Pink Panther film festival features the short *Tickled Pink*. Color, 60 mins.
VHS: S13569. $12.98.

Tom & Jerry on Parade
No matter where they go, this pair just can't escape each other. Includes: *Cruise Cat*, *His Mouse Friday*, *Tom's Designs on Jerry*, *Push-Button Kitty*, *Pet Peeve*, and *Little School Mouse*.
VHS: S15663. $12.95.

Tom & Jerry Vol. 7
Eight more Tom and Jerry cartoons from the '30's—*The Magic Mummy*, *Runaway Blackie*, *Donkey Tricks*, *Wild Hoose Chase*, *Bring Em Back Half Shot*, *Fisherman's Luck*, *A Close Call*, *Old Hokum Bucket*.
VHS: S06971. $24.99.

Tom & Jerry's Cartoon Cavalcade
An all new collection of Tom & Jerry mayhem, guaranteed to make even the coolest cats howl with laughter! Six hilarious cartoon adventures, including: *Jerry's Cousin*, *Jerry and the Lion*, *Southbound Duckling*, and *Fine Feathered Friend*.
VHS: S15662. $12.95.

Tom & Jerry's Comic Capers
This collection of six classic cartoons features Tom & Jerry and their funniest friends in their wildest misadventures! Includes *Downhearted Duckling*, *Fit to Be Tied*, *Hatch Up Your Troubles*, *Puppy Tale*, *The Flying Sorceress*, and *Polka-Dot Puss*.
VHS: S15660. $12.95.

Tom & Jerry's Festival of Fun
Poor Tom has been hounded by bulldogs, sliced by buzz saws, and blasted by dynamite, just for doing what comes naturally to a cat—chasing a mouse. Six cartoon classics, including: *Tennis Chums*, *Little Quacker*, *Blue Cat Blues*, *The Truce Hurts*, *Touche*, *Pussycat*, and *Sufferin' Cats*.
VHS: S15661. $12.95.

Tom & Jerry's The Night Before Christmas
Tom and Jerry open this colorful Christmas package of four classic cartoons. Includes *The Night Before Christmas*, *Toyland Broadcast*, *The Captain's Christmas* and Tex Avery's *One Ham's Family*. 45 mins.
VHS: S14561. $12.95.

Tom and Jerry: The Movie
These feuding cartoon characters now have their own full-length animated feature. In it, they find they must put aside their differences to help a runaway named Robyn Starling. Sadly, they end up in pet prison, where their ingenuity is sorely tested.
VHS: S22003. $14.98.
Laser: LD75276. $34.98.
Phil Roman, USA, 1992, 84 mins.

A Troll in Central Park
Warner Brothers brings the voices of Dom DeLuise, Cloris Leachman, Hayley Mills and Charles Nelson Reilly to this fantastic animated tale. Dismissed from the kingdom, a troll finds that his only refuge is New York's Central Park. There he befriends a little girl and her skeptical brother.
VHS: S23113. $19.99.
Laser: Widescreen. LD74837. $34.98.
Don Bluth, USA, 1994, 76 mins.

Tweety & Sylvester
Large cats and small birds may not see eye to eye but they sure do work well together in making very funny cartoons. The lovable little Tweety and the never-say-die Sylvester can be seen doing what they do best in this animated collection that includes *Tweety Pie*, *Gruesome Twosome* and *I Taw a Putty Tat*. 60 mins.
VHS: S09122. $14.95.

Ub Iwerks' Famous Fairytales
The animator who was Disney's right-hand man in a collection of priceless animation of some famous fairy tales: *The Headless Horseman*, *Aladdin and His Lamp*, *The King's Tailor*, *Dick Whittington's Cat*, *Mary's Little Lamb*, *Puss in Boots*, and *Jack and the Beanstalk*. Color, 56 mins.
VHS: S04856. $29.95.

Van Beuren Studio, Volume #1
A collection of early animation from the 20s and 30s, including *Custard Pies* (Paul Terry), *Barnyard Melody* (John Foster), *Jungle Fool* (John Foster and Mannie Davies), *Summer Time* (1929, John Foster), *Piano Tuners* (Tom and Jerry, 1932, John Foster & George Rufle) and *Happy Hoboes* (Tom and Jerry, 1933). 55 mins.
VHS: S22009. $14.95.

Van Beuren Studio, Volume #2
A collection of Aesop's fables produced by the Van Beuren animation studio. Includes *A Close Call* (Harry Bailey), *A Romeo Robin* (John Foster & Mannie Rufle), *The Ball Game* (1932, John Foster & George Rufle), *Play Ball*, *Cat's Canary*, *Noah Knew His Ark* and *Cowboy Cabaret*. 57 mins.
VHS: S22010. $14.95.

Van Beuren Studio, Volume #3
The early animations of Paul Terry and Frank Moser. Includes *Noah's Outing*, *Grand Uproar*, *The First Snow*, *Fox Hunt*, *Billy Goat's Whiskers*, *Bug Carnival*, *Trailer Life* and *Their Last Bean*. 55 mins.
VHS: S22011. $14.95.

The Very Best of Tom and Jerry
Watch your favorite dueling cat-and-mouse pair put each other through the paces. Tom usually gets the worst of it. Color, 60 mins.
VHS: S13571. $12.98.

War Time Cartoons
Nine rare animated shorts made for the armed forces by major Hollywood producers. Includes four Private Snafu shorts made at Warner Brothers: *Fighting Tools*, *Rumors*, *The Aleutians*, *Snafurman*, plus five Commandments for Health shorts, featuring Private McGillicuddy, produced by Hugh Harman: *Taking Medicine*, *First Aid*, *Personal Cleanliness*, *Drinking Water*, *Native Food*.
VHS: S06970. $29.95.

Warner Brothers Cartoons
Bugs Bunny, Elmer Fudd, Daffy Duck, Tweety Pie and Caspar the Caveman can be found in this collection of seven animated shorts from the Warner Brothers studio. Titles include *Fresh Hare*, *A Tale of Two Kitties*, *The Wabbit Who Came to Supper* and *Daffy Duck and the Dinosaur*. USA, 1938-53, 54 mins.
VHS: S05475. $24.95.

Will Vinton's Claymation Comedy of Horrors
A freewheeling assembly of spooks and demons populate the strange realm of Will Vinton's world, as the hero, Wilshire Pig, and his reluctant sidekick, Sheldon Snail, search out to discover Dr. Frankenwine's monster. 27 mins.
VHS: S17039. $12.98.

Willie the Operatic Whale
Walt Disney's beloved animated featurette tells the tale of Willie, a singing whale who dreams of performing at the Met. Also included are the Oscar-winning *Ferdinand the Bull* and *Lambert, the Sheepish Lion*. 29 mins.
VHS: S14549. $12.99.

Wince upon a Time: Foolhardy Fairy Tales and Looney Legends
Some of the standards of childhood lore are reconfigured in the Looney Tune mode in *Al-lad-in His Lamp*, *Little Red Rodent Hood*, *Pied Piper Porky* and *Rabbitson Crusoe*. 101 mins.
Laser: LD72397. $34.98.

Wind in the Willows
J. Thaddeus Toad's mad mania for motorcars drives his dear friends Moley, Rat and MacBadger into a frenzy. Disney animation brings this Kenneth Grahame classic to life. Also included are two Disney cartoons, *Motor Mania* starring Goofy and *Trailer Horn* starring Donald Duck and Chip 'n' Dale.
VHS: S01464. $14.95.
Walt Disney, USA, 1982, 47 mins.

Winner by a Hare—Bugs Bunny
The adventures of Bugs Bunny in 14 of his greatest works, including *The Fair Haired Hare*, *Bully for Bugs*, *Captain Hareblower*, *My Bunny Lies over the Sea*, *Box Office Bunny*, and *Rabbit Hood*. 101 mins.
Laser: LD71758. $34.98.

Winnie the Pooh: Making Friends, Learning
Three stories with Pooh, Piglet and Tigger. About "sharing, caring and growing up." Animated. Ages 1-5.
VHS: S24660. $12.99.
Disney Productions, USA, 27 mins.

Wizards
Ralph Bakshi presents this animated futuristic fantasy for adults as a dry run for the *Lord of the Rings* feature he was planning. A cigar-chomping, benevolent geezer with great powers must journey across unfriendly lands to chastise his evil brother and fellow wizard.
VHS: S02910. $19.98.
Ralph Bakshi, USA, 1977, 80 mins.

Woody Woodpecker: Volume 1
This collection of some of Woody's earliest cartoon adventures includes *Woody Woodpecker* (Cracked Nut), *Banquet Busters, Born to Peck* and *The Redwood Sap*. 30 mins.
VHS: S13918. $12.95.

Woody Woodpecker: Volume 2
That wacky bird with the famous laugh is back with another tape filled with animated adventures. Includes *The Coo Coo Bird, Well Oiled, Ace in the Hole* and *Arts and Flowers*. 30 mins.
VHS: S13919. $12.95.

The World According to George
Jay Ward, the creator of *Rocky and Bullwinkle*, tapped into American popular culture with his series *George of the Jungle*, and its support cartoons, *Super Chicken* and *Tom Slick*. They're all represented in this rude collection.
VHS: S15777. $9.98.

Yosemite Sam:
The Good, the Bad and the Ornery!
"Move over Eastwood, yer-a-hoggin' my light," says the rambunctious redhead. This pint-sized, prairie pistolero is not about to back down to any hombre that isn't hand-drawn. See Sam star in such animated shorts as *Mutiny on the Bunny, Sahara Hare, Wild and Wooly Hare* and *Rabbit Every Monday*. 33 mins.
VHS: S16722. $12.95.

INTERNATIONAL & INDEPENDENT ANIMATION

Aardman Animations
A collection from Aardman Animations, the leading animation studio from the UK. The leading short is the Academy Award winning *Creature Comforts*, the Lip Synch Series, and the documentary on the studio, *State of the Art*. 60 mins.
VHS: S17044. $29.95.
Laser: LD71769. $39.95.

Adult Animation
Eight provocative films *For Adults Only*. These naughty hand-drawn and clay-animated pieces have been specially selected to amuse and offend viewers of all tastes. 8 short films, including *The Censor, Desire Pie, Covered in Fleas, Malice in Wonderland, Night on the Town, Wild Times in the Wild Wood, Random Positions* and a special, outrageously funny surprise (information cannot be included in this catalog). 60 mins.
VHS: S13836. $19.95.

Adventures of Prince Achmed
The first animated feature—a landmark of cinema created in Weimar Germany with Lotte Reiniger's unique animation technique of cutout silhouettes. The stories, based on tales from the Arabian Nights, come wonderfully alive in this sensitive and imaginative work. A truly beautiful film that must be seen to be believed. Transferred from an original tinted and toned print.
VHS: S22881. $19.95.
Lotte Reiniger, Germany, 1927, 65 mins.

Alice
A revelation—a feature length film from Jan Svankmajer, one of the world's great animation directors, "a surrealist dream universe as created by one of the few masters of contemporary animation....Rather than illustrating Lewis Carroll's work, the film, in its very structure, aims to represent the essence of surrealism: the marvelous, the cruel, the erotic, the nightmarish, the amoral. Reality is viewed as an inexplicable game: drawers forever refuse to open or they vomit myriad magical objects" (Amos Vogel, *Film Comment*). An international theatrical hit, this masterpiece is the first feature of this great filmmaker.
VHS: S10942. $29.95.
Jan Svankmajer, Great Britain, 1988, 85 mins.

Alice in Wonderland
The long-neglected version by master puppeteer Lou Bunin, this wonderful film combines live-action characters with stop-action puppets in a delightful, unusual, and truly special version of Lewis Carroll's satirical classic. Made in England in 1950, and lost in the wake of the Disney version which came out around the same time, Bunin's *Alice in Wonderland* is notable for its remarkable puppet wizardry. With Carol Marsh as Alice.
VHS: S06599. $39.95.
Lou Bunin, Great Britain, 1950, 80 mins.

Allegro Non Troppo
Bozzetto's cult feature-length parody of Walt Disney's classic *Fantasia* is both a send-up and an imaginative and beautiful film in its own right. But *Allegro* features a Fellini-esque orchestra of old women directed by a mad, boorish conductor; musical passages include Debussy, Ravel, Sibelius, Stravinsky, Dvorak.
VHS: S00035. $19.95.
Bruno Bozzetto, Italy, 1976, 85 mins.

AMIGA Animation: Volume 1
A tape about the diverse applications, multiple purposes and functions of computer animation, as it relates to home use.
VHS: S16981. $19.95.

AMIGA Animation: Volume 2
This second volume features a more advanced look at the area of home computer animation.
VHS: S16982. $24.95.

Animal Farm
Good, straightforward, animated, feature length version of George Orwell's novel. From the largest and most successful animation studio in Britain. This is Britain's only feature length animated film.
VHS: S00054. $29.95.
Laser: LD70835. $39.95.
J. Halas/J. Batchelor, Great Britain, 1955, 73 mins.

An Animated Christmas—
The National Film Board of Canada
A joyous collection of animated Christmas themes, representing some of the best shorts by the NFB of Canada. The collection includes *An Energy Carol, The Great Toy Robbery, Bear's X-Ones* and *An Old Box*. 60 mins.
Laser: LD71938. $39.95.

The Animation Celebration Video Collection, Vol. 1
An entertaining, imaginative mix of works by leading animators, including Paul Vester, Sally Cruikshank, George Griffin, Jane Aaron and Stephen Weston. Includes *Second Class Mail, Sunbeam, It's an OK Life* and *Quest: A Long Ray's Journey*. 90 mins.
VHS: S17041. $39.95.
Laser: LD71772. $49.95.

The Animation Celebration Video Collection, Vol. 2
These cartoons are the best of the Second Los Angeles International Animation Celebration. Included are John Lasseter's *Lady and the Lamp*, Boyo Kenev's *A Crushed World*, Bill Plympton's *25 Ways to Quit Smoking*, work from the ASIFA Children's Film International Animators and shorts from Cuba, Japan and the UK. 90 mins.
VHS: S25826. $39.95.

The Animation Celebration Video Collection, Vol. 3
Once again a number of cartoons, the best of the Third Los Angeles International Animation Celebration, are joined on one video. Included are such works as *The Star Spangled Banner* by Skip Battaglia, Jan Svankmajer's *Light Darkness, Mr. Too* by Bruno Bozzetto and Bill Plympton's *Plymptoons*. Included as well are works from Germany, Italy, the USSR, Czechoslovakia and more.
VHS: S25825. $39.95.

The Animation Celebration Video Collection, Vol. 4
These animated shorts are the best of the Fourth Los Angeles International Animation Celebration. Included are *Dancing* by Bruno Bozzetto, *Office Space* by Beavis and Butthead creator Mike Judge, Corky Quakenbush's *Big Baby* and John Schnall's *Unsavory Avery*. Included are works from the USSR, Japan, Bulgaria and Cuba. 90 mins.
VHS: S25827. $39.95.

Animation Dreams
This magical tapestry of 12 incredible, computer-animated sequences is among the most amazing collection available on video. Human figure animation is a highlight of this imaginative journey where anything is possible—even dolphins fly. John Flommer created the original soundtrack.
VHS: S22418. $9.99.

Animation Festival—
The National Film Board of Canada
On the 50th Anniversary of the NFB of Canada, this collection highlights the best work of Canadian animators, including *The Big Snit, George and Rosemary, Get a Job* and *Strings*. 90 mins.
Laser: LD71937. $49.95.

The Animation Game
Illustration, three-dimensional models and cut-out animation are all explored in this video. Featuring the award-winning animator David Johnson. 15 mins.
VHS: S23498. $49.95.

Animation in the Netherlands
A collection of Dutch animation which looks at the cultural and historical origins of some of the world's leading painters, and at the relationship of art and animation. 30 mins.
VHS: S17053. $19.95.

Animation Legend: Winsor McCay
The Cinematheque Quebecoise discovered important 35mm archival prints of the work of pioneering animator Winsor McCay. The highlights of this program are McCay's first film, *Little Nemo* (1911), which is hand colored; *How a Mosquito Operates* (1912); *Gertie the Dinosaur* (1914); and *The Sinking of the Lusitania* (1918). The program also features fragments of *Gertie on Tour, The Centaurs* and *Flip's Circus*. 100 mins.
VHS: S19675. $39.95.
Laser: CAV. LD72089. $69.95.

Animation of the Apocalypse
Contemporary urban decay...skeletal death spewing fire...a fast-forward meltdown of sex, death, war, and moral decline.... Eight independent visions of doom, despair, and the end of the world—you'll want to be there. Includes *The Beholder, The Fall of the House of Usher, The Side View, I Heard a Fly Buzz When I Died, Loop of Doom, Tearing, Master of Ceremonies* and *Buzz Box*. 60 mins.
VHS: S13835. $19.95.

Animation Propaganda/Education
Four animated lessons that teach you by examples: how to sexually barter with riff-raff to save your grocery store (*Easy Does It*, 1946), how to pollute the surrounding living area by ridding yourself of mosquitos (*The Winged Scourge*, 1954), how not to defecate or urinate in your own fields (*Cleanliness Brings Health*, 1946), and a dentist's office visit with BADUMS and GOODUMS (*Winky the Watchman*, 1951). None of this is made up: these were actual educational films produced to instruct America in better living. 60 mins.
VHS: S09709. $24.95.

Animation Vol. 1: The Beginning
A survey of animation from 1906 to 1927, including *Humorous Phases of Funny Faces, La Rateleur, Fantasmagoria, Mobiliu Fedele, Little Nemo, Revenge of the Kinematograph Cameraman, Professor Bonehead Is Shipwrecked, Gertie the Dinosaur, Dinosaur and the Missing Link, Sinking of the Lusitania, Bobby Bumps Puts a Beanery on the Bum (Out of the Inkwell), Modelling/Bubbles, Laugh-o-Grams, Puss 'n Boots, Alice on the Farm, Small Town Sheriff, Felix in Hollywood, Oswals and the Mechanical Cow*. Various, USA, 1906-1927, 120 mins.
VHS: S04816. $29.95.

Animation Vol. 2
A collection of very early animation including *Dream of a Rarebit Fiend* (1906, 6 mins.); *Gertie* (the true 1914 McKay version, 9 mins.); *Krazy Kat* (1916, 11 mins.); *The Flying House* (1921, 13 mins.); *Surprise* (1923, 8 mins.); *Felix in Fairyland* (1925, 9 mins.); *Alice's Eggplant* (1925, 10 mins.). Total length: 66 mins.
VHS: S08869. $24.95.

Armando Armstrong's
Animation for Fallen Catholics
Nuns on wheels, priests in purgatory, a cola-drinking Christ, a whirling Virgin, heavy guilt, lots of laughs are just a few of the subjects of this irreverent collection which includes such priceless gems as Patti Tauscher's *Alterations* in which the Virgin Mary dances and whirls to the music of a neon jukebox. 10 films on tape, total length: 60 mins.
VHS: S16474. $19.95.

Art and Jazz in America
A four volume series by Faith and John Hubley.
Art and Jazz in America: John and Faith Hubley's Of Men and Demons. Quincy Jones composed the masterful score for this striking animated story about a simple farmer. This farmer confronts nature with a barrage of technical measures. Also included: *Of Stars and Men*, a short film about man and the universe set to music from Bach, Beethoven, Handel, Mozart and Vivaldi. 65 mins.
VHS: S24277. $19.95.
Art and Jazz in America: John and Faith Hubley's The Hole. The title film won an Academy Award. It is about two construction workers debating the fate of the world. Dizzy Gillespie and George Matthews provide the voices for these animated characters. *The Hat* is a similar short animated film featuring Gillespie and Dudley Moore as soldiers patrolling a border. In *Dig* Quincy Jones provides the score while Maureen Stapleton and Jack Warden provide the voices for a fantasy about a boy, his dog and their unique adventure. 58 mins.
VHS: S24278. $19.95.
Art and Jazz in America: John and Faith Hubley's Voyage to Next. The title animated film was nominated for an Academy Award. It features the voices of Maureen Stapleton and Dizzy Gillespie as Mother Earth and Father Time. Gillespie also supplies the music. Five other short films are included: *Tender Game, Eggs, Urbanissmo, Harlem Wednesday* and *Adventures of an* *. Music by Benny Carter, Ella Fitzgerald, Lionel Hampton and others. 51 mins.
VHS: S24279. $19.95.
Art and Jazz in America: The Cosmic Eye. Faith Hubley devised this amazing animated tale about alien musicians who bring a message of peace to the earth. The observations of these creatures yield a variety of perspectives about the nature of our planet. Music by Benny Carter and others. 72 mins.
VHS: S24276. $19.95.

Attack of the Cohl Pumpkins
A collection of early primitives by the pioneer Emile Cohl, including *The Pumpkin Race, The Joyous Microbes, Neo-Impressionist Painter*, and *Bewitched Matches*. 30 mins.
VHS: S05793. $24.95.

Bambi Meets Godzilla and
Other Weird Cartoons
Includes *Betty Boop in Crazy Town*, Max Fleischer creations and many other animated classics. 30 mins.
VHS: S11259. $9.95.

Benny Bear
The first full-length cartoons created from an Amiga computer, this collection of three videos focuses on the Yogi Bear-like creature and his fantastic adventures. 30 mins.
VHS: S17599. $14.95.

Beyond the Mind's Eye
Drawing on the latest in computer animation technology and the music of Jan Hammer, this is a surreal voyage into the mysteries, wonder and beauty of the mind, "the worlds that may exist in alternate dimensions—or only in the minds of the world's leading computer animators."
VHS: S17600. $19.98.

The British Animation Invasion
A variety of animation techniques contribute to this singular, witty collection from the United Kingdom. Everything from light and charming works to dark, macabre imagery is here. Titles include Joanna Quinn's *Body Beautiful*, Bill Mather's *Them* and David Stone's *Jollity Farm*. 90 mins.
VHS: S25824. $39.95.

British Animation Vol. 2
Six rare British animated shorts, including *The Lion* (Animaland), *Platypus* (Animaland), and *Old Manor House* (Bubble and Squeek). 30 mins.
VHS: S08958. $29.95.

Bruno Bozzetto: Animator, Vol. 1
This program looks at the eccentric body of animated and live action pieces by the talented creator of *Allegro Non Troppo*. Includes *Grasshopper, Baby Story, A Man and His World* and *The Sandwich*. 30 mins.
VHS: S17054. $29.95.
Laser: CAV. LD72087. $39.95.

Bruno Bozzetto: Animator, Vol. 2
The creator of *Allegro Non Troppo* has collected a number of his original works on this video. Includes *Moa, Moa; Opera; Ego; Two Castles; Dancing* and more.
VHS: S25820. $39.95.

The Cameraman's Revenge
& Other Fantastic Tales
An anthology of five major animation works from the master Russian artist and filmmaker Wladislaw Starewicz, including *An Insect's Christmas, The Cameraman's Revenge, Frogland, Voice of the Nightingale, The Mascot* and *Winter Carousel*.
VHS: S17860. $39.95.

The Cheese Stands Alone
These animated shorts by Mike Wellens reveal a unique and hilarious comic sense complimented by an innovative style. The nine works include *Au Revoir Mon Frigidaire*, about a man and his lovely refrigerator, and *The Big Fat World of Science*, a spoof of scientific illustration.
VHS: S24395. $24.95.
Mike Wellens, USA, 1994, 87 mins.

Chord Sharp
A 10-minute film which, using innovative animation, tells the story of one street musician's sudden rise to fame.
VHS: S12928. $19.95.
Joachim Kreck, Germany, 1989, 10 mins.

A Christmas Gift
Eight short films animated by the National Film Board of Canada, all reflecting the spirit of the season, including the hilarious *Great Toy Robbery, The Story of Christmas, The Sweater, December Lights, The Energy Carol, An Old Box, The Magic Flute*, and Oscar nominee *The Christmas Cracker*. 65 mins.
VHS: S13342. $29.95.

Classic Shorts Compilation #12:
Winsor McCay
A collection of six short animated films by Winsor McCay, a pioneer in the world of animation. McCay's early style involved delicate line drawings against a plain background; seen today, they still have considerable beauty and charm. This compilation includes *Gertie the Dinosaur* (1911), *Dream* (1922), *Bug Vaudeville* (1912), *Little Nemo* (1911), *The Pet* (1913) and *The Sinking of the Lusitania* (1919).
VHS: S15062. $29.95.
Winsor McKay, 1911-1922, 60 mins.

Classic Shorts Compilation #13:
Lotte Reiniger
Lotte Reiniger was another early pioneer in the development of the animated film. She produced many short films using her technique of animated paper silhouettes. This compilation features five of her animated fairy tales, and a documentary about her work directed by John Isaacs. Includes *Cinderella, The Frog Prince, Hansel and Gretel, Little Chimney Sweep, The Three Wishes*, and *The Art of Lotte Reiniger*. 70 mins.
VHS: S15063. $19.95.

Classic Shorts Compilation #14:
Felix the Cat
Ten rare, early shorts featuring one of the most popular cartoon characters of all time, Felix the Cat. Includes *April Maze* (1930), *Felix All Puzzled* (1936), *Felix Dines and Pines* (1926), *Felix Gets Broadcasted* (1923), *Felix Goes West* (1924), *Felix in Fairyland* (1924), *Felix Turns the Tide* (1924), *Futuritzy* (1928), *Non-Stop Freight* (1927) and *Polly-Tics* (1928). B&W. 65 mins.
VHS: S15064. $29.95.

Classics in Clay
Four claymation shorts are joined on this video. *Good Advice, Fast Food, Bumble-Boogie* and *Jamaica No Problem* combine the best animated clay techniques with humor and insight. USA, 1993, 25 mins.
VHS: S27167. $14.95.

Computer Animation Festival
This compilation features the leading computer animation, technological and aesthetic developments, cutting edge romance, adventure and stylistic experimentation. The program contains 21 award winning shorts created by computer. "Marvelously fluid landscapes [and] fascinating images" (*TV Guide*). 55 mins.
VHS: S18589. $19.95.

Computer Animation Festival
Volume 2.0
Twenty-two award-winning computer animated shorts are collected on this volume. The range of ideas and images is vast, and includes such works as an unseen Peter Gabriel music video, a startling 3-D ride into Devil's Mine, and more.
VHS: S27644. $19.95.
Steven Churchill, USA, 1994, 58 mins.

Computer Animation Magic
A colorful expose on computer graphics, including logos, chrome dinosaurs, a night club piano player. These are just a few samples. 58 mins.
VHS: S13097. $19.98.

Computer Dreams
English actress Amanda Pays (*Max Headroom*) hosts the visually magic world of computer graphics and digital effects. This video anthology contains the work of over 100 artists and demonstrates the latest innovations and advancements. Witness the birth of Nester Sextone, the computer-generated actor. Enjoy the kissing ostriches. Follow the exploits of Captain Power and his digitalized robots.
VHS: S09848. $19.95.
Geoffrey de Valois, 1989, 59 mins.

Crash Corrigan: One More Chance
Sean, the son of a naval pilot, is drawn to excitement and danger, which he pursues through his racing career. When his confidence is shaken by a serious accident, his friends wonder if he can recover for the year's most treacherous race, the Alpine Rally. USA, 1992, 90 mins.
VHS: S18212. $29.95.

Creating Animation on a Computer
Tanya Weinberger, an award-winning animator, explains how she uses computer and video technology to animate her characters. 27 mins.
VHS: S23502. $49.95.

Creative Process: Norman McLaren

A penetrating examination of the art of Norman McLaren, the pioneering filmmaker who made intricate works without the use of cameras and created music without the benefit of instruments. His avant-garde techniques involved direct painting and drawing onto the film strip and music hand carved from a multitude of squiggles. The film draws on previously unviewed footage from McLaren's vaults, including his experimental use of pixilation. *Norman McLaren* is an impressionistic portrait of the artist, distilled from radio and film interviews, artwork, photographs, home movies and various completed and unfinished films. "At last, something new in the art of drawing" (Pablo Picasso). 116 mins.
Laser: LD72230. $69.95.

The Curious Adventures of Mr. Wonderbird

One of cinema's great curiosities, this is the British version of the feature-length animated film by the great French animator Paul Grimault and a result of his collaboration with Jacques Prevert. Both Grimault and Prevert disavowed the film, which Grimault later remade in 1980 as *The King and the Bird*, using about half of this original footage. Nevertheless, in England Peter Ustinov and Claire Bloom lend their voices to this animated fantasy, which begins when an evil king tries to thwart the path of true love. 64 mins.
VHS: S25703. $19.95.

Cut-Out Animation

Cutting out paper figures is only the first step to this type of animation. Award-winning animator David Johnson's group of animated characters show how it is done. 8 mins.
VHS: S23501. $49.95.

Dazzle

Computer wizard James Shiflett brings years of computer programming skill to this brilliant video set to music from leading ambient composer John Serrie. A kaleidoscope of changing imagery is the result, using over two million colors and seemingly endless numbers of patterns and images.
VHS: S27645. $19.95.
John Shiflett, USA, 45 mins.

A Doonesbury Special

From Garry Trudeau's hilarious comic strip comes this animated, Academy Award-winning film by John and Faith Hubley. All the gang from Walden Commune are featured, capturing that unmistakable feeling of the 60's. It's perfect for reminiscing. 26 mins.
VHS: S22868. $19.95.

Dr. Devious: Dance in Cyberspace

The latest trend, previously only available in clubs, is now featured on this video. It's a graphic psychedelic experience for the 1990's. 3-D glasses are included. 45 mins.
VHS: S22045. $24.98.

Dream Tales: The Sacred Ways Collection

In the first of these animated myths, five stories from the Watunna tribe of Venezuela explain the origin of the world and the nature of human sexuality. Then Faith Hubley tells six stories, including one about the Moon Lady, who leads the dead to paradise along the Milky Way.
VHS: S21594. $24.95.
Faith Hubley, USA, 35 mins.

Earthworm Jim: Assault and Battery/Trout!

Peter Puppy is Earthworm Jim's faithful and devoted sidekick. Together with Snott, Earthworm Jim's slurping, mucus-oozing friend, they do battle against Queen Slug-For-A-Butt (whose proper title is really "Queen Pulsating, Bloated, Festering, Sweaty, Puss-Filled, Malformed Slug-For-A-Butt"). This tape also includes interviews with some of the creators and animators of the *Earthworm Jim* series. USA, 1995, 40 mins.
VHS: S27425. $9.98.

Earthworm Jim: Bring Me the Head of Earthworm Jim/Sword of Righteousness

In this first installment of the *Earthworm Jim* series, Jim does battle with Professor Monkey-For-A-Head, the mad scientist with a chimpanzee grafted to his forehead, and with Psy-Crow, the bounty hunter hired by the evil Queen Slug-For-A-Butt to capture Earthworm Jim. Includes interviews with the creators and animators of *Earthworm Jim*. USA, 1995, 40 mins.
VHS: S27423. $9.98.

Earthworm Jim: Conqueror Worm/Day of the Fish

Peter Puppy, Earthworm Jim's faithful and devoted sidekick, appears in *Conqueror Worm* as Monster Dog. Then, in *Day of the Fish*, Jim must do battle against Bob, the world's most cruel and spiteful goldfish, and #4, Bob's "legs". This tape features interviews with the creators and animators of the *Earthworm Jim* series. USA, 1995, 40 mins.
VHS: S27424. $9.98.

Earthworm Jim: The Book of Doom/The Egg Beater

Don't be fooled! While Evil the Cat may look like an innocent, purring Tabby, this scheming feline is really the demon Overlord of the fiery prison colony of a planet known as Heck. No sooner has Jim defeated the felonious kitten, than he must defend the world against Henchrat, a villainous rodent whose only goals in life are to defeat Earthworm Jim and to open his own macrame shop. Yeech. Includes bonus interviews with the creators and animators of *Earthworm Jim*. USA, 1995, 40 mins.
VHS: S27426. $9.98.

Emperor's Nightingale

Full length puppet film notable for puppet design and color, based on the Hans Christian Andersen story. In English.
VHS: S03789. $24.98.
Jiri Trnka, Czechoslovakia, 1948, 67 mins.

The Enchanted Drawing to Tony Sarg's "The First Circus"

This collection showcases 24 of the best animated shorts from the Library of Congress. These works illustrate the first 20 years of this new art form's history. Fragments from Stuart Blackman's live action animation, as well as George Harriman's *Krazy Kat*, are included with the films *The Katzenhammer Kids*, *Bobby Bumps*, *Keeping Up with the Joneses* and *Phables* by Tom Jones. There are also pioneering examples of stop-motion, clay, puppet and cut-out animation. From the *Origins of American Films* series, a joint project of the Library of Congress and Smithsonian Video.
VHS: S21264. $34.95.

Fabulous Adventures of Baron Munchhausen

A masterpiece of animation by Karel Zeman—a fabulous fantasy that mixes live action, antique engravings and animation in a dazzling tour-de-force of fantasy. One of the great works of the cinema. English language version.
VHS: S11474. $29.95.
Karel Zeman, Czechoslovakia, 1965, 75 mins.

Fantastic Planet

Winner of a special Grand Prix, Cannes Film Festival 1973, *Fantastic Planet* is a full length animated fantasy set on the planet of the Draags in a far solar system where humans are kept as pets by a race of huge blue creatures.
VHS: S00432. $29.95.
Rene Laloux, France/Czechoslovakia, 1973, 68 min.

Felix the Cat—Silent—Volume 1

Contains *Felix Wins Out* (1925), *Felix in Fairyland* (1927), *Felix Whoos Whoppie* (1927), *Felix Pines* (1927), *Felix in Hollywood* (1927). 56 mins.
VHS: S11466. $19.95.

Felix the Cat—Silent—Volume 2

Contains *Felix Turns the Tide* (1924), *Felix Switches Witches* (1927), *Forty Winks* (1930), *One Good Turn* (1929), *Felix Busts a Bustle* (1926) and *Outdoor Indoor* (1929). 62 mins.
VHS: S11467. $19.95.

Felix the Cat: Sound and Silent

Twelve Felix the Cat treasures from animator Pat Sullivan, all created from 1928-1930: *Comicalamities*, *With the Cowboys*, *In Dutch*, *Felix Minds the Kid*, *Felix Revolts*, *Tee Time*, *Poly-Tics*, *Forty Winks*, *Outdoor Indore*, *The Oily Bird*, *False Vases* and *Oceantics*.
VHS: S06983. $29.95.
Pat Sullivan, USA, 1928-30, 88 mins.

Films of Paul Glabicki

A collection of four fascinating, intricately constructed shorts from independent filmmaker Paul Glabicki—an artist whose extraordinarily complex recent works are founded on a distinctive graphic style: intricate, hand-drawn geometric animation which is so exact that it looks computer-generated even though Glabicki has drawn these films himself, entirely by hand. Astounding, groundbreaking work from a name to watch in the animation world. Includes *Diagram Film* (1978), *Five Improvisations* (1980), *Film-Wipe-Film* (1984), and *Object Conversation* (1985).
VHS: S15645. $29.95.
Paul Glabicki, USA, 1991, 55 mins.

Follow That Goblin

Produced with claymation technology and featuring a series of brisk, funny musical numbers, *Follow That Goblin* is about a young boy and his sister, trapped in a haunted house, where they befriend Gerbert the Goblin, who's lost the capability to frighten. 28 mins.
VHS: S17040. $12.98.

Fractal Experience

This new dimension of entertainment pairs the mathematical permutations offered by fractal geometry, as realized in computer graphics, with accompaniment from ambient music. 30 mins.
VHS: S22042. $24.98.

Fractal Fantasy: The Art of Mathematics

Fractal Fantasy is an artistic study of unusual areas within a mathematically defined region known as the Mandelbrot Set. The Set was discovered by Dr. Mandelbrot while studying a class of shapes which he labeled Fractals. The unique Fractal images seen in this video are actually enlarged areas along the edge of the Set. Large amounts of mainframe computer time were required to generate these magnified images; over 20 different regions are animated in this 30-minute journey with beautiful color palettes and special effects in a unique merging of art, science, music and mathematics. Fractal images, animation and software by Charles Fitch; music by Michael Strasmich.
VHS: S07322. $29.95.

Fractal Universe

A special program of highlights on fractals, including the Mandelbrot Sets and Julia Sets, dynamical systems, and the frontiers of chaos, serving as an introduction to some of the finest fractal animations to date. The images are accompanied by a variety of unusual electronic soundtracks. 25 mins.
VHS: S11000. $29.95.

Fractasia

In this tape fractal computer-animated imagery is choreographed to classical music by Bach, Wagner and other well-known composers. 32 mins.
VHS: S22043. $24.98.

French Animation Festival

A collection of four short films by the great cinema pioneer Emile Cohl.
VHS: S05180. $29.95.

Future Shock

Specially created visionscapes are accompanied by mesmerizing music. A true "Technopagan" experience. 43 mins.
VHS: S22044. $24.98.

Futuropolis

Steve Segal and Phil Trumbo undercut every conceivable genre in this fresh, invigorating and sharp parody of the near future, as the gritty Lieutenant Cosmo and a band of guerrillas must save the universe from destruction. 30 mins.
VHS: S17055. $19.95.

The Gate to the Mind's Eye

The Mind's Eye series continues with this spectacular example of computer animation. In this episode the collapse, rebirth and future of mankind are all brilliantly visualized. Stunning 3-D imagery, astounding detail and mesmerizing effects are combined in this cybertech fantasy. Directed by Michael Boydstun, 45 mins.
VHS: S23009. $19.95.
Laser: LD74646. $29.95.

The Genesis of Animation, Volume One

Early and rare animated shorts are joined on this video. *Humorous Phases of Funny Faces*, by J. Stuart Blackton, starts off this line-up. Then, works like *The Evils of Alcohol*, *Princess Nicotine*, *Swat The Fly*, *Morpheus Mike*, *Alice the Whaler* and more are included. 55 mins.
VHS: S27485. $19.95.

Gianini and Luzzati: Animators

Italian animators Emmanuele Luzzati and Giulio Gianini collaborate to bring music alive in their unique films. This collection includes the Academy Award-nominated films *The Thieving Magpie* and *Pulcinella*, a film made to the music of Rossini, among others.
VHS: S25831. $39.95.

Greentoons

A collection of ten award-winning shorts which address the issues of environment. Includes *Only the Cat Saw It*, *Oh Dad II*, *Smogging*, *How the Loon* and *Bob the Frog in "Burp"*.
VHS: S16917. $14.95.

Guido Manuli: Animator

Italy's leading underground animator brilliantly interweaves satire and subversive forms and shapes for cutting edge humor. In this dreamy stylized landscapes and outrageous forms, Manuli collides images and movement to spectacular effect. 60 mins.
VHS: S17051. $29.95.
Laser: CAV. LD72091. $49.95.

Heavy Metal

John Candy and Harold Ramis provide the voices for this spellbinding, animated, Heavy Metal-scored feature. Black Sabbath, Blue Oyster Cult, Cheap Trick, DEVO and Stevie Nicks are some of the many performers featured in this fantasy, sci/fi adventure.
VHS: S27756. $22.99.
Laser: LD75579. $39.95.
Gerald Potterton, USA, 1981, 90 mins.

History of the Amiga

This video is about the conception, design and implementation of the Amiga computer and its multiple uses for art, computer graphics and production design.
VHS: S18220. $29.95.

The Hobbit

J.R.R. Tolkien's timeless classic about the struggle between good and evil in a section of the universe known as Middle Earth is retold in animated form. Travel along with Bilbo Baggins and his friends as they search for treasure and adventure and try to avoid a very large dragon. With the voices of Orson Bean, John Huston, Otto Preminger and Richard Boone. Animated.
VHS: S03846. $19.95.
Arthur Rankin, Jr., USA, 78 mins.

Hollywood Salutes Canadian Animation

Seven National Film Board of Canada productions have won Oscars for best animation, and they are included on this special compilation tape: *Every Child*, *The Sand Castle*, *The House That Jack Built*, *Special Delivery*, *The Street* and Norman McLaren's famous *Neighbours*. 57 mins.
VHS: S13340. $29.95.

The Hubley Collection: Volume 1

This is the first in a series of videos bringing together the best short animated films by one of the most famous families in animation history—Faith Hubley and her daughter Emily. These titles are for connoisseurs of animation, and offer challenging and wonderful examples of art and enjoyment. Includes *Enter Life*, *Who Am I?*, *Upside Down* and *Blake Ball*. USA, 36 mins.
VHS: S15396. $39.95.

The Hubley Collection: Volume 2

Award-winning shorts by Faith Hubley examine the relationship of art and science, environment and personal responsibility. The films—*Time of the Angels*; *People, People, People*; *W.O.W. Women of the World*; *Amazonia* and *Yes We Can*—intermingle myth and reality to provoke awareness of the earth and environment. "Faith Hubley has pushed the boundaries of animation beyond their limits and created a work of art that is dazzling to the eye and feeds the spirit" (Robert Redford). 36 mins.
VHS: S19162. $39.95.

The Hubley Collection: Volume 3

Moonbird, *Tall Time Tales*, *Windy City* and *Cloudland* are included in this volume of animation by Faith and John Hubley. It combines two classics with two recent releases, to explore wondrous worlds, magical themes, native art and mythology. 36 mins.
VHS: S21523. $39.95.

Incredible Animation Collection: Vol. 1

A collection of animated shorts from the National Film Board of Canada. Includes *Juke Bar*, *If Only to Be*, *The Cat Came Back*, *Special Delivery* and *Kid Stuff*. 60 mins.
Laser: LD70206. $34.95.

Incredible Animation Collection: Vol. 2

More animation from the National Film Board of Canada: *Every Child* (Eugene Fedorenko), *Real Inside* (John Weldon/David Verrall), *Evolution* (Michael Mills), *Get a Job* (Brad Caslor) and *Cat's Cradle* (Paul Driessen). 60 mins.
Laser: LD70220. $34.95.

Incredible Animation Collection: Vol. 3

Incredible animation from the National Film Board of Canada is presented in this video. *Hot Stuff*, *Log Driver's Waltz*, *The Man Who Stole Dreams*, *No Problem*, *Pies* and *The Awful Fate of Melpominous Jones* are included. 90 mins.
Laser: LD74747. $39.95.

Incredible Manitoba Animation

This collection of animation from Manitoba includes two Academy Award nominees: *The Cat Came Back* and *The Big Snit*. In addition there are *Getting Started*, *The Cat Strikes Back*, *Carried Away* and many more humorous shorts on this great video.
VHS: S25829. $39.95.

The International Tournee of Animation, Vol. 1

14 titles: *Anijam* (Marv Neuland, Canada), *Bottom's Dream* (John Canemaker, USA), *Bitz Butz* (Gil Alkabetz, Israel), *Tony De Peltrie* (National Film Board of Canada), *Sigmund* (Bruno Bozzetto, Italy), *Skywhales* (Austin/Hayes, Great Britain), *Moa Moa* (Bruno Bozzetto, Italy), *Romeo & Juliet* (Dujan Petricic, Yugoslavia), *Jumping* (Osamu Tezuka, Japan), *Conversation Pieces: Early Bird* (Lord/Sproxton, Great Britain), *Incubus* (Guido Manuli, Italy), *Luncheon* (Csaba Varga, Hungary), *Anna & Bella* (Borge Ring, Holland), and *Charade* (Jon Minnis, Canada).
VHS: S17045. $39.95.

The International Tournee of Animation, Vol. 2

16 titles: *The Frog, The Dog & The Devil* (Bob Stenhouse, New Zealand); *Set in Motion* (Jane Aaron, USA); *Success* (Zoltan Lehotay, Hungary); *Garbage In Garbage Out* (Terry Wozniak, USA); *Carnival* (Susan Young, Great Britain); *Baeus* (Bruno Bozzetto, Italy); *Academy Leader Variations*, *A Greek Tragedy* (N. Van Goethem, Belgium); *Plus One, Minus One* (Guido Manuli, Italy); *Your Face* (Bill Plympton, USA); *Break* (G. Bardin, USSR); *Gravity* (F. Rofusz, Hungary); *Augusta Feeds Her Child* (Csaba Varga, Hungary); *Girl's Night Out* (J. Quinn, Great Britain); *Drawing on My Mind* (Bob Kurtz, USA); and *Snookles* (Juliet Stroud, USA).
VHS: S17046. $39.95.

The International Tournee of Animation, Vol. 3

10 titles: *Arnold Escapes from Church* (Craig Bartlett, USA), *Lights Before Dawn* (Sandor Bekesi, Hungary), *Pas a Deux* (Van Dijk/Renault, Holland), *78 Tours* (George Schwizgebel, Switzerland), *When Bats Are Quiet* (Fabio Lignini, Brazil), *Augusta Kneading* (Csaba Varga, Hungary), *Living in a Mobile Home* (Neville Astley, England), *Quiniscopio* (Juan Padron, Cuba), *Technological Threat* (Bill Kroyer, USA), and *The Writer* (Paul Driessen, Holland).
VHS: S17047. $39.95.

The International Tournee of Animation, Vol. 4

18 titles: *All My Relations* (Joanna Priestley, USA), *Animated International Animators Self Portraits*, *The Arnold Waltz* (Craig Bartlett, USA), *Balance* (C. and W. Lauenstein, Germany), *The Bedroom* (Maarten Koopman, Holland), *Cat and Rat* (James Richardson, USA), *The Cow* (Alexander Petrov, USSR), *Gisele Kerozene* (E. Cayo and J. Kounen, France), *Kakania* (Karen Aqua, USA), *Pictures from Memory* (Nedjeljko Dragic, Yugoslavia), *Plymptoons* (Bill Plympton, USA), *A Touch of Deceit* (Michael Gagne, Canada), *Train Gang* (Paul Driessen, Holland), *A Very Very Long Time Ago* (Bill Jarcho and M. Manning, USA), *Vykrutasy* (Garri Bardin, USSR), *Shadrach* (Chris Casady, USA), *Sand Dance* (Richard Quade, USA), and *A Warm Reception in L.A.* (Vincent Cafarelli and Candy Kugel, USA).
VHS: S17042. $39.95.
Laser: LD71770. $49.95.

The International Tournee of Animation, Vol. 5

16 titles: *At One View* (Paul De Nooijer, Holland), *The Big Bang* (Bruno Bozzetto, Italy), *Breakdown* (Klaus Geoggi, Germany), *Capital P* (Stephen Barnes, Canada), *Fast Food Matador* (Vincent Cafarelli and Candy Kugel, USA), *Getting There* (Paul Driessen, Canada), *Grey Wolf & Little Riding Hood* (Garri Bardin, USSR), *I Should See* (Paul De Nooijer, Holland), *Les Saisons Quatre a Quatre* (Daniel Suter, Switzerland), *The Lift* (Alexander Tatarsky, USSR), *Ode to GI Joe* (Gregory Grant, USA), *Oral Hygiene* (David Fain, USA), *Photocopy Cha Cha* (Chel White, USA), *Potato Hunter* (Timothy Hittle, USA), *Push Comes to Shove* (Bill Plympton, USA) and *The Wrong Type* (Candy Guard, Great Britain). 90 mins.
VHS: S25823. $39.95.
Laser: LD71941. $49.95.

The International Tournee of Animation, Vol. 6

14 titles from the 24th Festival: *Get a Haircut* (Mike Smith); *The Stain* (Marjut Rimminen and Christine Roche); *We Love It* (Vincent Cafarelli and Candy Kugel); *The Ride to the Abyss* (Georges Schwizgebel, Studio GDS); *The Square of Light* (Claude Luyet, Studio GDS); *Prehistoric Beast* (excerpt) (Phil Tippett); *The Man Who Yelled* (Mo Willems); *I Think I Was an Alcoholic* (John Callahan); *Gahan Wilson's "Diner"* (Gahan Wilson); *The Billy Nayer Show* (Cory McAbee and Bobby Lurie); *Little Wolf* (An Vrombaut); *The Sandman* (Paul Berry); *Words, Words, Words* (Michaela Pavlatova) and *Mr. Resistor* (Will Vinton Studios). 90 mins.
VHS: S25818. $39.95.

Jan Svankmajer: Alchemist of the Surreal, Program 1

A collection of five animated short films from the world renowned master of animation, Jan Svankmajer (creator of *Alice*). Here Svankmajer employs several different animation styles, including the use of live-action, puppets, life-like sculpted clay figures, and the manipulation of everyday household objects. Among the most recent and sophisticated work from a filmmaker who has already become a legend in the field of animation. Includes *Dimensions of Dialogue*, *The Last Trick*, *Jabberwocky*, *Punch and Judy* and *Et Cetera*.
VHS: S14554. $24.95.
Jan Svankmajer, Czechoslovakia, 1964-1982, 54 mins.

Ladislas Starevitch

Three superb puppet animation films by the great Ladislas Starevitch: *The Mascot* (1934), *Nose to the Wind* (1956, color) and *Winter Carousel* (1958, color).
VHS: S14527. $29.95.
Ladislas Starevitch, France, 60 mins.

Legend of the Forest

Tchaikovsky's Fourth Symphony unifies this animated film, which traces the early history of animation in the U.S. Joined together in dramatic fashion, this collection of vignettes also tells the story of mankind's destruction of nature through relentless expansion driven by the quest for progress. 30 mins.
VHS: S21283. $29.95.
Laser: LD74936. $39.95.

Leonard Maltin's Animation Favorites from the National Film Board of Canada

The popular movie critic from the US picks his favorite animated films from the Canadian Film Board. These include *Begone Dull Care*, *Mindscape*, *The Log Driver's Waltz*, *The Cat Came Back*, *Getting Started*, *The Sweater*, *The Street*, *Pas De Deux* and *Anniversary*.
VHS: S25821. $39.95.

Light Years

An animated, full-length, science fiction adventure with an English screenplay by Isaac Asimov. A mysterious evil force threatens the tranquility of an idyllic world. A brave warrior and his courageous female companion must travel one thousand years into the future to confront the enemy. With the voices of Glenn Close, Christopher Plummer, Jennifer Grey and Penn and Teller.
VHS: S07173. $14.95.
Rene Laloux, France, 1988, 83 mins.

Magic Horse

The first cartoon feature film from the Soviet Union, based on one of the most popular children's folk tales, about a boy who befriends a magical horse. With sound dubbed into English.
VHS: S00798. $29.95.
I. Vano, USSR, 1941, 56 mins.

The Magic Pony

This enchanting animated tale follows a boy who catches a flying horse. Together they overcome the greedy emperor and live happily ever after with a beautiful princess. With voices by Jim Backus.
VHS: S02547. $29.95.
Ivan Ivanov-Vano, Russia, 1977, 80 mins.

The Magic Voyage of Sinbad (Sadko)

The colorful Russian fantasy is about a bearded hero from Novgorod who is on a quest to find the bird of happiness. He apparently isn't particular about the exact color. His isn't Sinbad. A neat ploy to recruit an American audience for '61 release with anglicized cast names. Francis Coppola is credited as a screenwriter?
VHS: S04087. $29.95.
Alexander Ptushko, USSR, 1952

Masters of Animation Volume 1: The North Americans

Animation from the United States, the National Film Board of Canada and Radio Canada/Canadian Independent Animators is examined with a look at themes such as "The Power of Animation", "Exploration of the Medium", and "Excellence in Graphics". The work of Walt Disney, Norman McLaren and Frederick Back, among others, is highlighted. 90 minutes.
VHS: S07613. $29.95.

Masters of Animation Volume 2: The British and The Europeans

Animation from Great Britain, Italy and France is examined with a look at themes such as "Diversity of Style", "Theatricality, Color and the Use of Music", and "New Styles". The work of John Halas, Emanuele Luzzati and Jean-Francois Laguionie, among others, is highlighted. 90 minutes.
VHS: S07614. $29.95.

Masters of Animation Volume 3: The Eastern Europeans

Animation from Russia, Yugoslavia, Poland and Hungry is examined with a look at themes such as the "Use of Folk Tales", "Novel Imagery", "Graphic Arts", and "Central European Humor". The work of Ivanov-Vano, Borivoj Dovnikovic, Witold Giersz and Gyula Macskassy, among others, is highlighted. 120 minutes.
VHS: S07615. $29.95.

Masters of Animation Volume 4: Japanese and the Computer

Animation from Japan and the field of computer animation is examined with a look at themes such as "Visual Poetry", and a first hand look at how computer animation is achieved at the Institute National de l'Audiovisuel in Paris. The work of Renazo Kinoshita, Jean-Charles Hourcade and Carl Rosendahl, among others, is highlighted. 90 minutes.
VHS: S07616. $29.95.

Meet the Feebles

An adult fantasy film, *Meet the Feebles* relates the events that led up to the infamous "Feebles Variety Massacre," the day that rocked the puppet world. The film, directed by Peter Jackson (*Dead Alive, Heavenly Creatures*), who describes it as "a kind of *Roger Rabbit* meets *Brazil*," is set in a contemporary world like ours, with one major difference: there are no human beings. The Feebles' world is entirely populated by puppets—living, breathing, eating puppets with larger-than-life human characteristics and weaknesses…*Meet the Feebles* is a darkly comic satire on greed, lust and jealousy…part satire/soap opera/ musical that is a wildly original feature" (Charles Coleman).
VHS: S26868. $89.95.
Peter Jackson, New Zealand, 1988, 97 mins.

Mind's Eye

A spectacular odyssey through time, your journey begins at the dawn of creation and moves through the rise of man and technology. Travel in the world of abstraction and on into the future with breathtaking computer animation imagery. 40 mins.
VHS: S14596. $19.95.
Laser: CAV. LD72214. $29.95.

Mr. Rossi's Dreams

Further adventures of Mr. Rossi and his faithful dog Harold by *Allegro Non Troppo* animator Bruno Bozzetto. Mr. Rossi pretends he is the king of the jungle, a daring astronaut, Zorro, and many other heroic characters.
VHS: S01721. $39.95.
Bruno Bozzetto, Italy, 1983, 80 mins.

Mr. Rossi's Vacation

From the director of *Allegro Non Troppo*, a delightful animated adventure following the attempts of Mr. Rossi and his dog Harold to take a much needed vacation. One wacky mishap after another involving billy-goats and the abominable snowman.
VHS: S00894. $39.95.
Bruno Bozzetto, Italy, 1983, 82 mins.

The National Film Board of Canada's Animation Festival

This amazing animation resource from North of the border supports a vast array of artists who continue to break ground in this exciting field. It's a great chance to see some of the most intriguing work supported by enlightened government patronage.
VHS: S25830. $39.95.

New British Animation: The Best of Channel 4

The groundbreaking British television program highlights the best English animation, including David Anderson's *Deadtime Story*, the spontaneous *Feet of Song*, *Babylon*, *Black Dog* and *Conversation Pieces*. 60 mins.
VHS: S17050. $29.95.
Laser: CAV. LD72085. $39.95.

On the Comet

Jules Verne's science fiction adventure is brought to life by Czech animator Karel Zeman. Since the early 1950's Zeman has been directing highly imaginative films that combine animation and live action and are marked by his fantastic trick effects. A film for the whole family! English dialog.
VHS: S00958. $24.95.
Karel Zeman, Czechoslovakia, 76 mins.

Outrageous Animation, Vol. 1

Includes *An Inside Job* (Aidan Hickey, Ireland), *Haploid Affair* (Kaminski & Lidster, Canada), *One of Those Days* (Bill Plympton, USA), *The Four Wishes* (Michel Ocelot, France), *Instant Sex* (Bob Godfrey, UK), *Rondino* (Csaba Szorda, Hungary), *Full of Grace* (Nicole Van Goethem, Belgium), *Lupo the Butcher* (Danny Antonucci, Canada), *Striptease* (Bruno Bozzetto, Italy), *Great British Moments* (Peter Mudie, UK), *Love at First Sight* (Pavel Koutsky, Czechoslovakia) and *Vice Versa* (Aleksander Sroczynski, Poland). 60 mins.
VHS: S17043. $29.95.
Laser: LD71771. $39.95.

Outrageous Animation, Vol. 2

Includes *Adam* (J. Ananiades, Greece), *Another Great Moment* (P. Mudie, UK), *The Club* (G. Griffin, USA), *Dialog* (D. Vunak, Yugoslavia), *Eldorado* (B. Bozzetto, Italy), *Erection* (G. Manuli, Italy), *Jac Mac & Rad Boy…Go* (W. Archer, USA), *The Jump* (N. Astley and J. Newitt, UK), *Maxi Cat's Lunch* (Z. Grgic, Yugoslavia), *Mr. Gloom* (B. Kopp, USA), *Observational Hazard* (B. Kopp, USA), *The Prayer* (R. Gvozdanovic, Yugoslavia), *Quad Libet* (G. Van Dijk, Holland), *Royal Flush* (J. McIntyre, USA), *Sweet Dreams Luv* (D. Dames, Holland), *Toilet Bowl* (M. Jones, USA), *You Can't Teach an Old Dog New Tricks* (J. Foray, USA) and *Zwisch* (T. Sivertsen, Norway). 60 mins.
VHS: S17048. $29.95.
Laser: CAV. LD72086. $39.95.

Ovide and the Gang

Winner of the Gemini Award for Best Animated Series, this collection of ten misadventures follows Ovide and his animal friends as they turn their island paradise upside down imitating what they see on television. 120 mins.
VHS: S09590. $39.95.

Paul Driessen: Animator

Eleven imaginative works by the brilliant Dutch-born animator Paul Driessen. His psychedelic work on *Yellow Submarine* and his unique interspersing of the bizarre and ordinary have made him one of the medium's modern masters. 60 mins.
VHS: S18123. $29.95.

Pixar

The Academy Award-winners *Luxo* (1986) and *Tin Toy* (1989) are joined by *Red's Dream* and *Knickknack* in this collection of celebrated animated shorts.
VHS: S25822. $39.95.

Plymptoons

This video offers a kaleidoscopic retrospective of the complete works of Bill Plympton, a surrealist whose use of oblong shapes and angular designs are constantly inventive, witty and surprising. The work includes "Self Portrait," works about the environment and ecology, change and shape alteration, and his "25 Ways to Quit Smoking." 60 mins.
VHS: S16931. $29.95.
Laser: CAV. LD72092. $39.95.

Private S.N.A.F.U.

Seven hilarious episodes of the rarely seen Warner Bros. cartoon figure Private Snafu, that were written by Dr. Seuss (Ted Geisel) and directed by the legendary animator Chuck Jones. Originally intended as an off-center guide to military regulations for enlisted men. 30 mins.
VHS: S17109. $9.95.

Private S.N.A.F.U. Cartoon Festival

A collection of adult-oriented cartoons produced during WWII, intended to teach G.I.'s the finer points of military life.
VHS: S10584. $19.95.

Professor Bunruckle's Guide to Pixilation

Award-winning animator David Johnson's guide to animating people, animals and even inanimate objects is possible using pixilation techniques. The Professor shows how it's done. 16 mins.
VHS: S23499. $49.95.

Puppet Animation

Animated puppet Dennis the Dragon hosts this presentation that highlights the techniques of puppet animation. By award-winning animator David Johnson. 17 mins.
VHS: S23500. $49.95.

Puppet Masters

Three geniuses of animation are represented in this tape: Ladislas Starevich's *The Mascot*, (1934), the surreal tale of a lost dog who enters a world of devilish characters; Jiri Trnka's famous—and wonderful—spoof of Westerns in *Song of the Prairie* (1952); and Ray Harryhausen in one of his charming early works, *King Midas* (1953). Color and B&W, 54 mins.
VHS: S04857. $29.95.

The Quay Brothers: Volume 1

These American twins, who live and work in London, create animation which strikes at the very heart of the human subconscious—their visionary landscapes revealing images so wild you will forget everything you have come to expect from animated films. This tape features two shorts: *Street of Crocodiles* and *The Cabinet of Jan Svankmajer*. "Must rank among the most illustrious of international animated art" (Amos Vogel).
VHS: S14160. $29.95.
Laser: CLV. LD72097. $49.95.
Quay Brothers, USA, 1984/1986, 34 mins.

The Quay Brothers: Volume 2

This tape features three animated shorts by the famous Quay brothers. Their universe of puppet animation, inspired by Czech animator Jan Svankmajer, is one where decaying dolls, primitive machinery, and other found objects interact in an Expressionist world of ultra-reality. They create masterfully bizarre landscapes in *Epic of Gilgamesh*, *Rehearsals of Extinct Anatomies* and *Nocturna Artificiala*. "The loveliest, most hypnotic, most profoundly bizarre films ever made in that particular form" (Terrence Rafferty). 50 mins.
VHS: S14146. $29.95.
Laser: CLV. LD72098. $49.95.

The Rocketship Reel

Sophisticated animation represented by International Rocketship Limited, the award-winning cartoon company located in Vancouver, Canada. An outrageous collection that features *Bambi Meets Godzilla*, *Sing Beast Sing*, *The Butterfly*, *Points*, *Hooray for Sandbox Land*, *Dog Brain*, *Dry Noodles*, *Anijam*, *Black Hula*, *Waddles* and *Lupo the Butcher*. 55 mins.
VHS: S25828. $39.95.
Laser: CAV. LD71496. $34.95.

Scenes from the Surreal

This program collects three short films by Czech animator Jan Svankmajer (*Alice*)—*Darkness of Light Darkness*, *Manly Games* and *Death by Stalinism*—that highlight the individual struggle against social and political repression. On the same program is a documentary, *Jan Svankmajer: The Animator of Prague*, a BBC production by James Marsh that provides a fascinating background into his working methods, using clips from his earlier works and personal discussion on the nature of his bizarre, primal and devastating art. "Disney plus Bunuel = Svankmajer" (Milos Forman). 58 mins.
VHS: S17912. $29.95.

Schimmelstein

This is a claymation satire on the music biz, starring the Jickets. World Music Inc. conspires to defraud the down-home band. There are many odd domestic and corporate scenes.
VHS: S22636. $19.95.
Direct Art, USA, 1985, 25 mins.

Scientific Visualization

Produced by the National Center for Supercomputing Applications, this tape presents the aesthetic highlights of scientific visualization projects of the Center. The projects envision large, mostly three-dimensional Supercomputer data sets of scientific research from astrophysics, chemistry, geophysics and biology. Included are segments about storms, a tornado's complexity modeled by mathematical equations, simulated air flow. 15 mins.
VHS: S10999. $29.95.

The Secret Adventures of Tom Thumb

In this highly acclaimed animated feature the classic tale of Tom Thumb takes a dark, sinister turn more evocative of science fiction and horror films. Through pixilation and 3-D model animation, a world dominated by seedy slums and antiseptic labs emerges. Tom is dragged away from his parents for experimentation. As a result he meets and befriends a group of small creatures who fight together against the tyranny of the "giants."
VHS: S26444. $29.95.
Dave Borthwick, Great Britain, 1994, 57 mins.

Sextoons

A light-hearted look at sex through animation produced by independent filmmakers from 1920 to 1975. Over a dozen films make up this program, utilizing techniques that range from full drawn animation, cut-outs and abstracts to stop-motion clay and pixilation animation. Includes *Buried Treasure*, *Boobs a Lot* (Bernard Ellis); *A Child's Alphabet* (Thomas Spence); *Armchair Inventions* (Gary Moore); *Little Genitalia* (Barry Brilliant); *The Further Adventures of Super Screw*, *Jack in the Fox* (Karl Krogstad); *Hearts and Arrows* (Roy Fridge); *Snow White and the Seven Dwarfs*, *Out of Order*, *Little Ms. Muffet* (Mark Seiderburg); *Seed Reel #1* (Mary Beems); *L'Ombre de la Pomme* (Lapoujade) and *Show Biz* (Algas Nakis). Intended for mature audiences. Color and B&W, 70 mins.
VHS: S17689. $29.95.

A Short Film Festival

Seven short animated films from the legendary animators at the National Film Board of Canada: *Log Driver's Waltz*, *Getting Started*, *Hot Stuff*, *Blowhard*, *The Family That Dwelt Apart*, *Street Musique*, and the hilarious *Lady Fishbourne's Complete Guide to Better Table Manners*. 57 mins.
VHS: S13341. $29.95.

The Soldier's Tale

Conceived and designed by *New Yorker* cartoonist Blechman, *The Soldier's Tale* is a dazzling animation adaptation of a classic Russian folk tale about a soldier tricked by the devil into giving up his violin. The music is by Igor Stravinsky, with voices by Max Von Sydow and Dusan Makavejev. In this version, Blechman makes ingenious use of paints, crayons, color pencil and collages to depict temptation and apocalypse.
VHS: S01228. $79.95.
R.O. Blechman, USA, 1984, 56 mins.

Spike and Mike's Festival of Animation

An exciting compilation of international animated short films which is sure to leave you begging for more. The acclaimed, the depraved and the bizarre—all in one terrific collection.
VHS: S15237. $29.95.
Laser: LD70205. $34.95.

Sword and the Dragon

Beautiful fairytale from Soviet director Alexander Ptushko in which a magic potion and a legendary sword lead a simple farmer into battle against the invading Tugars and their evil leader. Amid galloping hooves and clashing swords, Ilya and his mighty warriors battle to defend their homeland. English dubbed.
VHS: S09194. $19.95.
Alexander Ptushko, USSR, 1960, 81 mins.

Tanka

This prize-winning work by David Lebrun is an animated translation of the Tibetan book of the dead. Tanka means "a thing rolled up." Photographed by Tibetan scroll paintings moving through the 16th and 19th centuries, the program is a cyclical visualizing of ancient gods and demons. "Dazzling and vibrantly colored" (*The Los Angeles Times*). 9 mins.
VHS: S17457. $29.95.

Toccata for Toy Trains

This work by Charles and Roy Eames is an imaginative journey about the function of trains as they travel through a universe of movement, sound, noise and landscapes. Toy trains of various size and shape move from the railyard to the roundhouse to a busy station. On the same program is *Parade* a bright and colorful mosaic of mechanized toys played to a vibrant John Philip Sousa score. 22 mins.
VHS: S19161. $19.95.

Tony Vegas' Acidburn Flashback Tabu

This all-animated collection of award-winning short films features a myriad of styles and ideas. "Aural and visual absorption. Revelation. Animation as drug. Inhale the flaming toxins of graphic hallucinations. Ingest the forbidden fruit. Experience birth, death, rebirth, and the in-between. Breathe. Relax. Dream. Relax. You are welcome here. Tune in and turn on." Timothy Leary calls it "Tripping without drugs." 60 mins.
VHS: S16473. $19.95.

Tribute to Winsor McCay

Born in 1886, Winsor McCay pioneered film animation. Here is a selection of six animated masterpieces from 1909 to 1921, including *Gertie the Dinosaur*, *Bug Vaudeville*, *Flying House* and *Little Nemo*. Musical track.
VHS: S01371. $24.95.
Winsor McCay, USA, 1909, 55 mins.

The Tune

The first animated feature of artist Bill Plympton. A struggling songwriter has 47 minutes to produce a hit song for his tyrannical boss. En route to an important meeting, he winds up in a surreal, strange community called Flooby Nooby, a grotesque landscape of outsized dreamers; a stylized, canine Elvis impersonator; a disfigured cabdriver who sings the blues; and a collection of blissed out surfers. On the same program are the animated shorts *Draw* and *The Making of the Tune*. 80 mins.
VHS: S19061. $59.95.
Laser: LD75488. $39.99.

Vip My Brother Superman

From Bruno Bozzetto, the creator and animator of *Allegro Non Troppo*, comes this eccentric piece about the Vips, modern day inheritors of the superhuman performing a series of legendary adventures. 90 mins.
VHS: S17049. $29.95.
Laser: CAV. LD72094. $49.95.

Wallace and Grommit: A Grand Day Out

Once again the lovable claymation pair first seen in the highly inventive *The Wrong Trousers* find more domestic routine disturbed by an adventure. This film was also nominated for an Oscar. It's witty and superbly animated and will delight all ages.
VHS: S26395. $9.98.
Nick Park, Great Britain, 1990, 30 mins.

Wallace and Grommit: The Wrong Trousers

This Academy Award-winning animation film is an amazingly inventive and entertaining British import. It all begins when an ingenious penguin traps an unsuspecting boob into a pair of automated trousers. The result is a dastardly crime that only a dog can solve.
VHS: S25660. $12.98.
Nick Park, Great Britain, 1994, 30 mins.

Watership Down

Animated version of the Richard Adams novel about the unique world of rabbits features the voices of John Hurt, Ralph Richardson and Zero Mostel.
VHS: S01605. $14.95.
Laser: LD72398. $34.98.
Martin Rosen, Great Britain, 1978, 97 mins.

Weird Cartoons

A wild collection of cartoons and puppetry from the early 1900's through the 1940's, including *Scrub Me Mama with a Boogie Beat*, *Hasher's Delirium*, some of Betty Boop's more bizarre adventures, *Non-Stop Freight*, and many more. USA, 60 mins.
VHS: S01442. $29.95.

Weird Cartoons, Volume 2

A crackling collection of vintage cartoons, everything from the subversive to the sublime, the deranged to the strange, the outrageous to the insane. Featuring Betty Boop, Felix, and rare Max Fleischer. 60 mins.
VHS: S05183. $29.95.

West & Soda

Bruno Bozzetto's (*Allegro Non Troppo*) work is a madcap animated feature that mixes the operatic Westerns of Sergio Leone with the lunatic, freewheeling sensibilities of the Three Stooges, in this grand, flamboyant shoot-em-up. 90 mins.
VHS: S17052. $29.95.
Laser: CAV. LD72093. $49.95.

When the Wind Blows

An enormous success in England, based on the best-selling book by Raymond Briggs, this is the powerful, unforgettable story of the consequences of nuclear war—done entirely in animation. A film of immense power, produced by the creators of *The Yellow Submarine* and featuring the music of David Bowie, Roger Waters, Genesis and Squeeze. England, 1987, 80 mins.
VHS: S06447. $79.95.

Who Framed Roger Rabbit?

The winner of four Academy Awards. A razzle dazzle combination of live action and hilarious animation as private eye Eddie Valiant reluctantly takes on a Toon as a client and learns who is playing patty cake with whom in Los Angeles of the late '40's. With Bob Hoskins, Christopher Lloyd, Joanna Cassidy and the voices of Kathleen Turner as Jessica and Charles Fleischer as Roger. Plus many of your favorite animated friends.
VHS: S10337. $22.99.
Laser: LD71209. $39.99.
Robert Zemeckis, USA, 1988, 104 mins.

Willis O'Brien Primitives

A collection of stop frame shorts by the great animation pioneer, including *Prehistoric Pultry Creation*; *RFD 10,000*, *Dinosaur and the Missing Link*, and excerpts from his feature, *The Lost World*. 60 mins.
VHS: S05792. $29.95.

Works

Stop-motion puppet animations convey post-feminist concerns through wry humor and visual wit in these films. Included are *Rumzababalaars*, in which a Frankenstein woman creates her own destiny; *Psychophony*, which shows girls dancing down into Wall Street; and *Journey to the Afternoon*.
VHS: S22635. $19.95.
Lisa Barnstone, USA, 1990-92, 20 mins.

Works, 1978-79

Terry Mohre, an acclaimed video artist, is revealed in this collection as master of synthesizer and computer animations. There is even a sexy document of a camping trip, where freeze frames assure that nothing goes unseen.
VHS: S22639. $29.95.
Terry Mohre, USA, 1978-1979, 70 mins.

The World's Greatest Animation

Eleven Academy Award winners and five nominees are presented in this collection of innovative animated shorts. Some are profound, others witty and a few are just plain strange. Included are Academy Award winners *Creature Comforts*, *Balance*, *Charade* and *Sundae in New York*. Nine other Oscar winners and five more nominees are included in this great compilation video by the world's most innovative animators. 104 mins.
VHS: S25652. $29.95.
Laser: LD75462. $69.97.

Zi-Zi Pan Pan

This adult animated work uses an exaggerated, clever series of line drawings and movement to pit the superhuman Pan Pan against Nymphomania, a deformed witch with extraordinary powers. 90 mins.
VHS: S16983. $29.95.

japanese ANIMATION

3 x 3 Eyes
The last member of a mysterious group of immortals, Pai relentlessly searches for a natural artifact that will transform her into a human. Moving from Tibet to Tokyo, the 300-year-old seeks out an elderly wise man whose understanding of the strange group could unravel the mystery. English and Japanese with English subtitles. 120 mins.
Laser: LD71944. $39.95.

3 x 3 Eyes Perfect Collection
Pai is the last of a mysterious race of immortals. She seeks an ancient supernatural artifact that can make her human. The young son of a noted archeologist agrees to help, but before he realizes the dangers he will face he finds himself staring down demon worshippers and blood sacrifices. Dubbed in English, 110 min.
VHS: S25064. $19.95.

3 x 3 Eyes, Vol. 1
The first volume of a four-part mini-series adapted from the popular series, focusing on ritual and transcendentalism, peopled with the grotesque and fantastic, set around themes of immortality, ancient curses, demons, arcane powers and crossdressers. In English.
VHS: S17354. $14.95.

3 x 3 Eyes, Vol. 2
In the second installment, Yakumo and Pai are unsuccessful in transforming Pai into regular human form. They're pursued by supernatural monsters eager to take control of Pai's unusual powers. Realizing they have no choice, Yakumo and Pai set off on a new odyssey to protect their friends and larger society.
VHS: S17362. $14.95.

3 x 3 Eyes, Vol. 3
In this episode Pai and Yakumo travel to Hong Kong to unravel the secret of the Statue. 30 mins.
VHS: S17529. $14.95.

3 x 3 Eyes, Vol. 4
The conclusion has Yakumo learning about the mysterious fate of Pai's people, the three-eyed Triclops, and fighting the mad despot seeking control of the Statue to rule the world. 30 mins.
VHS: S17530. $14.95.

8 Man
This is the original cyborg superhero. A ruthless band of drug dealers gun down a promising young cop. The Chief Inspector cannot bear to see him die so he authorizes an experimental operation. A cyborg with an electronic brain results, who then works with Tokyo police to rid the city of violence and crime. Dubbed in English. 91 mins.
VHS: S23289. $89.98.
Laser: LD74964. $39.99.

8 Man After #1
Based on the popular 1960's manga and animated super-hero series, this powerful production introduces a brand new 8 Man in City in Fear. Drug-maddened street gangs called "cyber junkies" are terrorizing the city with their body weapons. Only 8 Man can help. 29 mins.
VHS: S21695. $14.95.

8 Man After #2
This video features five episodes from the 1960's animated sci-fi adventure series. Special agent Brady defied death with the help of Professor Genius. Brady's mind was transmitted to a super robot. As a result, he can battle a host of monstrous space-age creatures such as a gigantic electric eel, an atomic ghost and robot beetles. Anime, dubbed in English. Japan, 1990, 120 mins.
VHS: S24892. $29.95.

8 Man After #3
Daigo the crime lord is overthrown by his cyborg henchmen. These creatures don't want to rule the city but destroy it. Japanese with English subtitles. 29 mins.
VHS: S22408. $14.95.

8 Man After #4
Hazama, the new 8 Man, is closing in on Tony Gleck, the leader of the cyber-junkie criminals. But Tony is looking forward to being found because he wants to install his own brain in 8 Man's super-body, in this graphic, action-animated feature. Japanese with English subtitles.
VHS: S23339. $14.95.

8 Man After: Perfect Collection
Four awesome adventures of the original cyborg cop are joined on this Anime adventure. Brain transplants, cyber junkies, a deadly game of trick or treat, and the mysterious disappearance of 8 Man drive these action-packed episodes. Japanese with English subtitles, 116 mins.
VHS: S25727. $19.98.

801 T.T.S. Airbats: They're Just Plane Crazy!
There is plenty of nudity in this animated adventure about an all-woman flight squadron. As if this premise did not provide enough interest, there is also inter-squadron rivalry, full-scale aerial combat sequences, and even steamy love interests. Japanese with English subtitles, 85 mins.
VHS: S24380. $34.95.

The Abashiri Family
This Anime adventure follows the travails of a comically dysfunctional crime syndicate family. Even though they are prone to mishaps, the Abashiri family is widely respected for their violent ways. Fearing that the sole daughter of the family may not learn the ways of crime, she is sent to a strange finishing school. Unfortunately, few students graduate before an accident befalls them. Japanese with English subtitles, 75 mins.
VHS: S27023. $29.95.

AD Police File #1: Phantom Woman
In Megalopolis Tokyo, two police officers pursue renegade worker androids called Boomers responsible for a series of industrial accidents. One of the female models escapes, carrying the memory of the man who destroyed her. Japanese with English subtitles. 1990. 40 mins.
VHS: S18622. $24.95.

AD Police File #2: The Ripper
Detective Ailis Kara investigates a brutal string of prostitute murders, in the process discovering a frightening pattern of biomechanical replacement. Eventually she meets her principal adversary, who's been injected with the biomechanical implants for surprising reasons. Japanese with English subtitles. 1990. 40 mins.
VHS: S18623. $34.95.

AD Police File #3: The Man Who Bites His Tongue
Critically wounded in a battle with a renegade worker android, officer Billy Fanwold is reborn as an invincible cyborg policeman programmed to kill off the Boomers. Billy must confront his condition and his alienation and loneliness. Japanese with English subtitles. 1990. 40 mins.
VHS: S18624. $34.95.

AD Police Files
In this futuristic animated Japanese series, set in Mega Tokyo 2027, emerging technology has resulted in the birth of Boomers, artificially intelligent androids with the capacity to liberate man from physical labor. Unfortunately, history has shown what happens when technology runs amok. This AD Police Files LD contains three files, The Phantom Woman, The Ripper and The Man Who Bites His Tongue. Japanese with English subtitles. 120 mins.
Laser: LD72333. $39.95.

Adventure Kid, Volume 1
Computer game whiz Norizaku unearths a World War II computer. It contains more than history, however, for buried inside is the spirit of its creator. This creature lusts for vengeance, sparking off an erotic, high-tech adventure. Japanese with English subtitles. 75 mins.
VHS: S23336. $29.95.

Adventure Kid, Volume 2
The king of hell is embarrassed that his own son is the servant of a human, so he sends an agent to bring him home. On earth however, the son is only interested in the beautiful Midori. Even this simple passion is thrown into jeopardy by jealous rivals on all sides. A love potion threatens to turn this story into a sexual sitcom of the strangest sort. Japanese with English subtitles. 40 mins.
VHS: S24246. $29.95.

Ai City (Love City)
At the center of this exciting Anime feature is Kei, an escaped experimental subject with strange powers. The Fraud corporation has a plan for world domination and destruction that only Kei can fully understand. Together with his friends he battles through the streets of New York to ensure the Earth's future and the future of reality as we know it. Japanese with English subtitles, 86 mins.
VHS: S24908. $24.95.

Akai Hayate, Volume 1
The Shinogara are a secret band of ninja who have ruled Japan for 1000 years. Their despotic stranglehold was destroyed when the son of their leader rebelled and murdered his own father. His only chance for escape was to transfer his soul into his sister's body. Now this doubly inhabited entity must evade the vengeance of the Shinogara. Japanese with English subtitles, 60 mins.
VHS: S25024. $29.95.

Akai Hayate, Volume 2
A bitter power struggle divides the Shinogara, the secret organization which has ruled Japan for centuries. Though the rebels must fight in the boardroom, the final clash will occur in the secret headquarters at the base of Mt. Fuji. Hayate, the chief rebel warrior, must overcome being imprisoned in his sister's body and then all questions about the turbulent history of the Shinogara will be answered. Anime, Japanese with English subtitles. 60 mins. Contains episodes 3 & 4 of the Akai Hayate series.
VHS: S26099. $29.95.

Akira
Neo-Tokyo is about to explode. Filled with action and stylized violence, this animated science-fiction feature was based on an equally notorious Japanese graphic (read "comic-book") novel. A gang of motorcycle-riding teenagers, living in post-apocalyptic Neo-Tokyo, must stop one of their own who goes on a rampage after gaining telekinetic powers in a renegade government experiment. 124 minutes.
Akira. English language version.
VHS: S15233. $19.95.
Laser: CAV. LD71555. $124.95.
Akira. Original Japanese with English subtitles.
VHS: S16691. $29.95.
Katsuhiro Otomo, Japan, 1989, 124 mins.

All Purpose Cultural Cat Girl Nuku Nuku, Vol. 1
Inventor Kyusaka transfers the brain of a dead cat into a top-secret android body. In the process, he doesn't lose the family pet but gains a daughter. Though she may appear cute and cuddly, inside lie superhuman strength, advanced android chassis and lightning quick senses, all governed by the reflexes of a domestic feline. This is the first in a series of animated adventures featuring this hybrid heroine. Japanese with English subtitles.
VHS: S23227. $29.95.

All Purpose Cultural Cat Girl Nuku Nuku, Vol. 2
Intrepid cat girl needs all her superhuman abilities to defend her previous master, Ryunosoke, the son of the inventor who crafted her android body. A giant conglomerate is out to gain custody of Ryunosoke because it is run by a ruthless businesswoman, his mother. Cat girl continues to amaze in this second volume of the animated series. Japanese with English subtitles.
VHS: S23228. $29.95.

All Purpose Cultural Cat Girl Nuku Nuku, Vol. 3
Before long cat girl is the number one enemy of Mishima Heavy Industries and its ranks of elite Office Lady Warriors. Mighty Nuku Nuku makes cat play of all their state-of-the-art weaponry. All this fighting still leaves our heroine time for her favorite hobby, chasing small rodents. Japanese with English subtitles.
VHS: S23229. $29.95.

Ambassador Magma
Magma is a golden human rocket that protects the Earth. When an old foe called Goa reawakens, Magma must once again marshall his forces to defend the planet. This first volume of a Japanese animated favorite is comprised of three episodes. Japanese with English subtitles.
VHS: S18697. $29.95.

Ambassador Magma Volume 2: The Two Mamorus/The Government Strategy
In The Two Mamorus, Goa captures Mamoru and dispatches one of his nefarious henchmen to terrorize Atsushi and Junya in their efforts to locate "Earth." In The Government Strategy, the Defense Intelligence Agency tries to anticipate the aliens' next move. Attacked by a creature, Mamoru is aided by "Earth's" innovative rocket-humanoid assistant, Gamu.
VHS: S19711. $24.95.

Ambassador Magma Volume 3
Two episodes of the Japanese superhero are joined in this video. In episode six, The Quintessential Warrior, Mamoru takes his father's advice and follows Kunisaki to the Defense Intelligence Agency, where he learns of a plot to launch a giant tidal wave. Episode seven, Gigantic Task, finds Mamoru abducted while investigating a government installation. Dubbed in English, 60 mins.
VHS: S22904. $29.95.

Ambassador Magma Volume 5
Two episodes of this sci-fi adventure series are included in this volume. In Mother and Her Love Mamoru is startled by an intervening angel who saves his life. In Rage of the Earth Ambassador Magma and Udo are transported back in time to face a tremendous battle. Animated. Dubbed in English. 60 mins.
VHS: S26423. $19.95.

Ambassador Magma Volume 6
Death of Magma and The Planet of Love are the episodes included in this volume of the sci-fi adventure series. First, Ambassador Magma and Udo continue their titanic battle and face an unforseen transformation. Then Mamoru learns the shocking truth about mankind's origin. Animated. Dubbed in English. 60 mins.
VHS: S26424. $19.95.

Angel Cop, Volume 1: Special Security Force
An international terrorist force, The Red May, has targeted Japan, and the Special Security Force is called into action. Angel Cop is the newest member on the team and she will need everything she has to combat this evil cabal. Dubbed in English. 30 mins.
VHS: S26240. $9.95.

Angel Cop, Volume 2: The Disfigured City
The Red May continue to plague Japan. Angel's partner disappears and a trio of psychotic terrorists lose their job by killing terrorists. As Angel tries to figure out this strange turn of events, a super cyborg shows up. Dubbed in English. 30 mins.
VHS: S26241. $9.95.

Angel Cop, Volume 3: The Death Warrant
The Red May leader is in custody and the details of a sinister plot that will destroy Japan are slowly being revealed. Angel tries to maintain a sense of who the good guys and the bad guys are but as the plot thickens it gets more and more difficult to sort out this intriguing conspiracy. Dubbed in English, 30 mins.
VHS: S26379. $9.95.

Angel Cop, Volume 4: Pain
Lucifer is on the rampage forcing the SSF into overtime. They are threatened at every turn and must face yet another danger. The Psychic Hunters have decided that along with terrorists, the SSF must be hunted down and destroyed. Anime. Dubbed in English. 30 mins.
VHS: S26639. $9.95.

Angel Cop, Volume 5
Lucifer, the mad psychic hunter, is determined to finish her job. She wants to kill Angel and the last remaining forces of the SSF. Unfortunately for the SSF, the entire army is also against them in this Anime feature. English dubbed, 30 mins.
VHS: S26766. $9.95.

Angel Cop, Volume 6: Doomsday
Angel must face the fury of the deranged, psychic killer Lucifer on her own. All her comrades are gone and still this desperate struggle leads to ever greater death and destruction. Anime, dubbed in English, 30 mins.
VHS: S27346. $9.95.

Angel of Darkness
The dean calls herself the Angel of Darkness at this allegedly good school. One of the instructors has dug up a monster who demands pretty young women for its unnatural tastes. Atsuko and Sayaka are lovers thrown into this hell. They can only wonder if they will survive. Japanese with English subtitles. 50 mins.
VHS: S22672. $34.95.

Angel of Darkness 2
A teacher maintaining a collection of hungry plants is not the innocent arbiter of educational reform he appears to be. Like his plants, he consumes the life force of other living beings. Insects don't satisfy him, however; he desires beautiful young women. This depiction of inhuman lust is not for the squeamish. Japanese with English subtitles. 45 mins.
VHS: S26246. $29.95.

Angel of Darkness 3
Hiromai lures a group of women who abused her to the lair of the resurrected Professor Shimazakiy. Sexual horror is the result, a dark, nightmarish fantasy. Graphic violence, nudity and sex make this animated feature suitable for adults only. Anime, Japanese with English subtitles, 50 mins.
VHS: S27467. $29.95.

Animeminder
Lum, the alien princess, stars in these animated episodes noted for their silly slapstick and sexy but not sinful situations. She is a big hit in Japan, where her capers have been followed for over 10 years.
VHS: S18652. $24.95.

Arcadia of My Youth
Matsumoto Leiji's tale of Captain Harlock's heroic efforts to be the master of his universe and claim possession of the Earth. Japanese with English subtitles. 1982. 130 mins.
VHS: S18617. $39.95.
Laser: Subtitled. LD74794. $59.95.

Area 88 Act 1: The Blue Skies of Betrayal
Shin had everything—a career as a pilot, a fiance from a powerful company family, and a cheerful outlook, until he was tricked by a friend. Now he must face service defending the Asran nation or buy back his freedom. Japanamation, Japanese with English subtitles. 50 mins.
VHS: S18921. $34.95.
Laser: LD74500. $34.99.

Area 88 Act 2: The Requirements of Wolves
In this second installment of the Japanamation series, Shin's adventures in the protective air force continue. As a mercenary this character presents a chilling look inside the mind of a warrior whose life may be on the line, but whose heart lies elsewhere. Japanese with English subtitles.
VHS: S18922. $34.95.
Laser: LD74501. $34.99.

Area 88 Act 3: Burning Mirage
This animated feature follows the sci-fi adventures of Shin Kazama. Now precariously close to buying out his contract, Shin needs only stay alive a little while longer in the skies above Area 88. However, even if he survives, will he be the same person when he returns to the arms of the beautiful Ryoko? 96 mins. Japanese with English subtitles.
VHS: S18923. $39.95.
Laser: LD74502. $39.99.

Ariel
Ariel is the ultimate female fighting robot, designed by Dr. Kishida to save the Earth from alien invaders. When Dr. Kishida's daughters refuse to pilot her, the battle against alien invaders is left to Aya Kishida. In the end, the fate of the world may rest upon clumsy Aya Kishida's ability to pilot Ariel and fight off the mysterious alien Saber Starblast. Includes two episodes. Japanese with English subtitles. Japan, 1995, 60 mins.
VHS: S27344. $29.95.

Armitage III, Part 1: Electro Blood
Armitage is a cute young police officer posted to Mars in the distant future. She joins Ross to solve the murder case of the "Third Robots". Finding the facts is always her most important objective, but she never expected to find out so much about herself. Japanese with English subtitles, 45 mins.
VHS: S24240. $29.98.
Laser: LD74819. $39.98.

Armitage III, Part 2

In 2179, a cyber girl soldier becomes a deadly weapon dressed in leather. She is Armitage III. This cyborg heroine is searching for Thirds, who, like her, have survived the killing of their kind. Japanese with English subtitles, 45 mins.
VHS: S25680. $24.98.
Laser: LD74993. $34.98.

Armitage III, Part 3

Armitage, the Anime action adventure hero, is a creation with a mission. She wants to find out who she is and why she was created. This desire sparks an adventure which involves the Martian Government Army, a deadly computer and a government conspiracy. Japanese with English subtitles. Japan, 30 mins.
VHS: S27097. $24.98.
Laser: Subtitled/dubbed. LD75450. $34.98.

Armitage III, Part 4: Bit of Love

Armitage and Ross find Dr. Asakura, the developer of the "Third Type" robots. Unfortunately, they cannot learn anything from him because his memory is gone, so they enter into battle blindly. This final episode shows their ultimate confrontation with the Martian Government Army. Japanese with English subtitles. Japan, 1995, 30 mins.
VHS: S27096. $24.98.
Laser: LD75451. $34.98.

Astroboy

Available for the first time in the U.S. is this groundbreaking Japanese serial. Astroboy battles through space and time in 20 exciting episodes, compiled in ten volumes. Japanese with English subtitles.
Astroboy Vol. 1: Birth of Astroboy/The Monster Machine. 30 mins.
VHS: S15960. $24.95.
Astroboy Vol. 2: The Terrible Time Gun/One Million Mammoth Snails. 30 mins.
VHS: S15961. $24.95.
Astroboy Vol. 3: Super Brain/Mystery of the Amless Dam. 30 mins.
VHS: S15962. $24.95.
Astroboy Vol. 4: The Magic Punch Card/The Great Rocket Robbery. 30 mins.
VHS: S15963. $24.95.
Astroboy Vol. 5: Shipwreck in Space/Gift of Zeo. 30 mins.
VHS: S15964. $24.95.
Astroboy Vol. 6: Mystery of the Metal Men/Gangor, the Monster. 30 mins.
VHS: S15965. $24.95.
Astroboy Vol. 7: Brother Jetto/Dogma Palace. 30 mins.
VHS: S15966. $24.95.
Astroboy Vol. 8: The Mad Beltway/Mission at the Middle of the World. 30 mins.
VHS: S15967. $24.95.
Astroboy Vol. 9: The Hooligan Whodunit/Return of Cleopatra. 30 mins.
VHS: S15968. $24.95.
Astroboy Vol. 10: Inca Gold Fever/Hullabaloo Land. 30 mins.
VHS: S15969. $24.95.
Astroboy Vol. 11: Silver Comet/The Robot Olympics. 30 mins.
VHS: S16978. $24.95.
Astroboy Vol. 12: The Three Robotiers/Angel of the Alps. 30 mins.
VHS: S16979. $24.95.

Astroboy 30th Anniversary

On the 30th anniversary of its creation, Astroboy is now available in five volumes, with two episodes per volume. The last volume contains the special episode The Wonderful Christmas Present. 250 mins.
Astroboy: Vol. 1: Vampire Vale/Phoenix Bird.
VHS: S19716. $14.95.
Astroboy: Vol. 2: Cleopatra's Heart/Funnel to the Future.
VHS: S19717. $14.95.
Astroboy: Vol. 3: The Deadly Fires/Astro Boy Goes to School.
VHS: S19718. $14.95.
Astroboy: Vol. 4: General Astro/The Vikings.
VHS: S19719. $14.95.
Astroboy: Vol. 5: Dolphins in Distress/The Wonderful Christmas Present.
VHS: S19720. $14.95.

Astroboy: The Lost Episode, The Beast for 20 Fathoms

Recently this lost episode was found because it had been sent to NBC for dubbing. As a result it exists only in this form and the original Japanese version has been lost. 50 mins.
VHS: S24909. $14.95.

Attack of the Supermonsters

Set in the year 2000, Earth is under siege from the sudden reappearance of deadly, powerful dinosaurs, unleashed from their subterranean caverns by the evil Emperor Tyrannus. Man's only hope for survival is the Gemini Command. 83 mins.
VHS: S17524. $19.99.

Babel II, Part 1: The Awakening

In this Anime adventure a reluctant hero discovers his hidden psychic powers. Now he is "Babel II", a supernatural warrior who must battle an army of ruthless zombies led by Magus. In English. 30 mins.
VHS: S26172. $9.98.

Babel II, Part 2: First Blood

This Anime adventure continues as the war escalates. Powerful alien allies have come to Babel II's aid. He will need their help—the fate of mankind hangs in the balance. In English. 30 mins.
VHS: S26173. $9.98.

Babel II, Part 3: Crossroads

A New York City neighborhood scheduled for demolition is the next site of the ongoing battle. In this Anime adventure, no matter how much Babel II struggles, the fight against evil appears endless. In English. 30 mins.
VHS: S26174. $9.98.

Babel II, Part 4: Final Conflict

The final battle lines have been drawn. In this Anime adventure Babel II faces off against his enemies for a contest of monumental proportions. Only one side can emerge from this bloodbath victorious. In English. 30 mins.
VHS: S26175. $9.98.

Baoh

Baoh is the code name of a genetically engineered parasite. A secret organization made these creature to dominate the world. One of their human guinea pigs has escaped and the organization must find him before he is transformed into an indestructible agent who would may well disturb their plans of conquest. Japanese with English subtitles. 50 mins.
VHS: S24264. $24.95.
Laser: LD74886. $44.95.

Barefoot Gen

Six-year-old Gen miraculously survives the atomic blast of Hiroshima. Though he cannot save his father and siblings, he clings to his wife in his mother in a landscape scarred by the nuclear blast. It's a powerful animated film based on the autobiography of Keiji Nakzawa. Dubbed in English.
VHS: S25890. $29.98.
Masaki Mori, Japan, 80 mins.

Battle Angel

This animated feature tells the story of a beautiful bounty hunter who seeks out some of the most horrible villains imaginable. She manages to work coolly and efficiently because her past was lost, until she must choose between the desires of her employer and the man she loves, her latest assignment for liquidation. Dubbed in English.
VHS: S19413. $34.95.

Battle Royal High School

Hyoudo Riki is a high school student who gets his "kicks" Kung Fu fighting while wearing a tiger mask. Unfortunately, Riki is a dead ringer for Byoudo, Master of the Dark Realm. When the evil Fairy Master notices this, the real Byoudo is called into action, taking possession of Riki and turning his classmates into horrible monsters. On top of all this, sword-happy Space-Time Police Officer Zankan notices all this inter-dimensional commotion and decides to zoom in and settle the score. Now it's up to Riki to save his classmates and his dimension, and this time, it's a matter of life or death. Anime, Japanese with English subtitles. Japan, 1996, 60 mins.
VHS: S27710. $24.95.
Laser: LD75569. $39.95.

Black Magic M-66

A military transport is forced to crash-land in the middle of nowhere, accidentally exposing its cargo. Now two prototype commando robots are on the loose. Heavily armed and incredibly agile, these creations are virtually unstoppable, and their last instructions were to seek out their creator's own daughter! Japanese with English subtitles.
VHS: S16063. $34.95.

The Blade of Kamui

In this exciting sci-fi Anime, a young boy trained in the arts of the Ninja is called upon to exercise all his talents and skill. The Blade of Kamui, which he inherited from his father, will accompany him. It contains both the key to his past and the thread of his destiny. Dubbed in English, 133 mins.
VHS: S25017. $19.99.

Blue Seed Volume 1

Yuzo Takada's Blue Seed is the story of the TAC, a super-secret government organization. The object of the TAC is to combat Aragami, a bizarre race of aliens who have sought to enslave humankind for centuries. Once the source of legends, the Aragami have turned contemporary Japan into a battleground. Anime, Japanese with English subtitles, 60 mins.
VHS: S27022. $29.95.

Blue Seed Volume 2

Teenage Momiji Fujimiya is accidentally impregnated with a "blue seed", the nascent form of the Aragami. Though this has given her psychic powers, she will find herself sacrificed to the Aragami unless she can get help from Mamoru Kusanagi, a servant of the Aragami with supernatural powers of his own, and the T.A.C., the government agency formed to combat the supernatural forces of the Aragami. Anime, Japanese with English subtitles, 60 mins.
VHS: S27461. $29.95.

Blue Seed Volume 3

The story of Momiji Fujimiya, the young Japanese girl who carries an unborn Aragami—a "blue seed"—inside her chest, continues in this Anime series that's been called "...X-Files meets Species....". Anime, Japanese with English subtitles, 60 mins.
VHS: S27686. $29.95.

Blue Sonnet, Volume 1

Take one of the most powerful psychic warriors ever known, and augment her abilities with highly advanced electronics. Thus is born Blue Sonnet, the star of an animated sci-fi feature series. Japanese with English subtitles. Parts 1-3. 90 mins.
VHS: S21833. $29.95.
Laser: CLV. LD75048. $34.95.

Blue Sonnet, Volume 2

With the capture of Lan Komatsuzaki, Talon's plans to conquer the world seem more of a reality than ever before. Locked deep inside the most secure stronghold in Japan, Lan is quickly running out of time. Talon's plans for her are nothing short of satanic: to turn Lan's body into a factory producing an army of super-espers through cloning and artificial insemination. Japanese with English subtitles, 60 mins.
VHS: S23080. $29.95.

Bomber Biker Mecha Pack

Tires burn and fists fly in Shonan Bakusozoku—Bomber Bikers of Shonan. Eguchi Yoosuke is the leader of a high school biker gang and the school's handicrafts club. Between fist fights and fancy needlework, he cuts a strange figure, until you consider the other members of the gang. Madox-01-Metal Skin Panic tell the story of Koji, a teenager who gets trapped in a highly automated personal battle tank. Japanese with English subtitles.
VHS: S23436. $65.00.

Botchon, Parts 1 & 2

A new math teacher arrives at school. In this anime feature he goes on to challenge his students in wholly unexpected ways that surprise both his charges and his superiors with one hilarious situation after another. Japanese with English subtitles. 52 mins.
VHS: S24268. $29.95.

Bounty Dog

Human colonies on the moon are impressive, but they are not invulnerable. Set in the not-so-distant future, the human lunar colonies are threatened by the reemergence of "The Sleeper," an alien life form that could destroy human life on the moon. Strange waves of energy threaten to summon "The Sleeper" unless a member of the Bounty Dog Investigation Unit can put "The Sleeper" back to bed. Anime, dubbed in English, 60 mins.
VHS: S27472. $19.95.

Bubblegum Crash 1: Illegal Army

A gang of mercenaries clad in powered combat suits are robbing banks left and right, and the politically hamstrung AD Police is helpless to stop them. Meanwhile, the vigilante Knight Sabres are on the verge of breaking up! The robberies are a smoke screen to cover up a mysterious voice's master plan to steal Artificial Intelligence Software. Will the Knight Sabres get back together in time? Japanese animation, English subtitles. 45 mins.
VHS: S15954. $34.95.

Bubblegum Crash 2: Geo Climbers

The mystery voice is at it again! Now he is teamed up with the evil Dr. Yuri, and together they plan to capture an advanced Boomer named ADAMA. When the Knight Sabres' resident hot-head, Priss, bumps into ADAMA, Yuri lets loose his gang of Boomer hunters and the chase is on! Japanese animation, English subtitles. 45 mins.
VHS: S15958. $34.95.

Bubblegum Crash 3: Meltdown

The Knight Sabres finally come face to face with the "voice" and are shocked to learn he is an old foe reborn. Unless they can stop him, the nuclear power plant that supplies Mega Tokyo will go up in an explosion of unimaginable force. Japanese animation, English subtitles. 45 mins.
VHS: S15959. $34.95.

Bubblegum Crash LD

In MegaTokyo circa 2034 the Combat Boomers attempt to remake society by stealing top technologies. The Knight Sabers are the only ones who can stop them, but will they forgo this battle to pursue their own careers? Japanese animation, 135 mins.
Laser: LD72387. $49.95.

Bubblegum Crisis

A Japanese animation work which combines cyberpunk, science fiction, outlaw culture, and edgy animation. The story unfolds in MegaToyko, a postmodern Phoenix rising from the ruins of a devastating earthquake. The series concerns the Knight Sabres, a renegade collection of high-tech mercenaries, and their fiendish war against the GEMOM Corporation and the sinister Boomer androids.
Vol. 1: Episodes 1-3.
Laser: LD71832. $64.95.
Vol. 2: Episode 4 and Hurricane Live.
Laser: LD71833. $64.95.
Vol. 3: Episodes 5 and 6.
Laser: LD71834. $64.95.
Vol. 4: Episodes 7 and 8.
Laser: LD71835. $64.95.

Bubblegum Crisis #1 (Dubbed)

In 2032, as MegaTokyo struggles to rebuild from an earthquake, a small band of high tech mercenaries fights a lonely war against the evil Genom corporation. This razor-sharp tale of technology gone wild is set in a cyberpunk future with action, suspense and Rock and Roll. Dubbed in English, 53 mins.
VHS: S22335. $19.95.

Bubblegum Crisis #2 (Dubbed)

The Knight Sabers wage a private war against the sinister Genom Corporation in the futuristic MegaTokyo. A Black Box that controls the USSD satellite weapons system is discovered, forcing all who oppose Genom to run for cover. Japanamation, dubbed in English, 30 mins.
VHS: S22451. $19.95.

Bubblegum Crisis #3 (Dubbed)

Genom Corporation has a new plan for urban renewal in MegaTokyo. It involves combat bomber androids who will terrorize the population to sell their land cheaply. It's all just business for the world's largest corporation. Dubbed in English, 30 mins.
VHS: S22449. $19.95.

Bubblegum Crisis #4 (Dubbed)

After the Knight Sabers' triumph over Genom Corporation, it seems there is time for a little fun. But a mysterious black car, the Griffon, is hunting down bikers in MegaTokyo. When the Griffon tangles with Priss on her new bike, he finds out the true meaning of trouble. Dubbed in English, 40 mins.
VHS: S22450. $19.95.

Bubblegum Crisis I

MegaTokyo was not prepared when the Catastrophic Kanto earthquake hit. With the city up in arms, Bio-Mechanical soldiers (Boomers) have free reign, and are destroying what must slowly be rebuilt. English subtitles.
VHS: S16065. $34.95.

Bubblegum Crisis II: Born to Kill

The GENOM corporation has invented a new line of terror. Three second-generation Boomers are on the rampage, and soon a more recent variation will be unleashed. English subtitles.
VHS: S16066. $29.95.

Bubblegum Crisis III: Blow Up

Brian J. Mason, an executive of GENOM, has deduced the identity of one of the Knight Sabres. Armed with this information and his company's personal armored suits, he has sworn himself to eliminating the vigilantes who have been thwarting his plans for world domination. English subtitles.
VHS: S16067. $24.95.

Bubblegum Crisis IV: Revenge Road

Motorcycle gangs all over MegaTokyo are growing concerned; someone in a death-mobile is systematically hunting them down. With the Juggernaut gaining power with each passing day, the AD Police are helpless to alter the path this vigilante has chosen. English subtitles.
VHS: S16068. $24.95.

Bubblegum Crisis V: Moonlight Rambler

A string of "vampire" killings involves an orbiting space group of Boomers who escaped from an orbiting space colony. When Priss befriends and swears allegiance to one of the renegade Boomers, she puts herself at odds with the rest of the Knight Sabres. English subtitles.
VHS: S16069. $24.95.

Bubblegum Crisis VI: Red Eyes

Priss has become more reticent about her participation in the Knight Sabres, which complicates matters when a group of Knight Sabre impostors wreak havoc on MegaTokyo. English subtitles.
VHS: S16070. $24.95.

Bubblegum Crisis VII: Double Vision

"Vision" (Leika) is one of the most popular singers on the planet, and has an interesting little secret. Not only is she piloting a deadly piece of battle gear, but she is also Irene's sister. English subtitles.
VHS: S16073. $24.95.

Bubblegum Crisis VIII: Scoop Chase

A budding freelance reporter, and daughter of the AD Police Chief, is looking for the one big story that will bring her recognition. English subtitles.
VHS: S16074. $24.95.

Bubblegum Crisis: Collector's Suite

This boxed set of eight Anime episodes tells a story set in MegaTokyo in 2032 AD. The city is struggling to rebuild after a devastating earthquake, but an evil corporation and its androids have other plans. Only a small band of high tech mercenaries can oppose the evil GENOM corporation. Japanese with English subtitles, partial nudity.
VHS: S25717. $190.00.

Burn Up W!—File 1: Skin Dive

The setting is Japan in the near future, and high-tech crime is the way of life. The special SWAT team "Warrior" hits the streets, ready to save the day, on a mission to make the streets safe again. Anime, Japanese with English subtitles, 35 mins.
VHS: S27680. $29.95.

Burn Up!

A futuristic Japanese animated work about two female police officers, computer specialist Remy and sharpshooter Maki, who launch an assault on a corrupt businessman who kidnapped Yuka, a young officer investigating a white slavery ring. This edition features special supplementary materials and footage not contained in the original Japanese release. Japanese with English subtitles.
VHS: S19891. $29.95.

Casshan Robot Hunter, Part 1: Return from the Myth

Civilization stands in ruins as an army of robots enslaves mankind. Only Casshan, a mysterious avenger, is able to defeat these monumental machines. Anime in English. 30 mins.
VHS: S26168. $9.98.

Casshan Robot Hunter, Part 2: Journey to the Past

A new weapon capable of destroying the android army is planned. Casshan must make sure these plans do not fall into the wrong hands. Outnumbered and outgunned, it looks hopeless, but failure is unthinkable. In English. 30 mins.
VHS: S26169. $9.98.

Casshan Robot Hunter, Part 3: Blitz on the Bridge

Armageddon looms; one false move will ensure humankind servitude forever. Casshan is the only hope, but he too is plagued by troubles, his own personal demons. He must meet this internal threat before he can face the final showdown. In English. 30 mins.
VHS: S26170. $9.98.

Casshan Robot Hunter, Part 4: The Reviver

On the verge of the final battle, humankind's secret weapon has been rendered inoperable. Suddenly Casshan is forced to confront an entire army, completely alone. In English. 30 mins.
VHS: S26171. $9.98.

The Castle of Cagliostro

Someone is printing vast amounts of counterfeit money, and the renowned thief, "Wolf", wants the plates. Thus begins this uproarious adventure, with Wolf dragging in tow a samurai warrior and a bumbling shootist-sidekick. Animated. Japanese with English subtitles.
Laser: LD74814. $39.99.
Hayao Miyazaki, Japan, 1991, 100 mins.

Countdown

Two erotic animated shorts, Alimony Hunter and SEEK, are joined on this video. The first of these involves a threesome on the subway where things are not always what they seem. In the second short, a knavish knight rescues a young lady but finds that he is himself in danger of being chained up. Anime with English subtitles, 30 mins.
VHS: S26795. $29.95.

Countdown Continued (Uncut)

This erotic Anime film is based on the hit manga. The first episode is the story of a bride-to-be's last minute lesbian fling; the second, the story of a Samurai Police woman, her perverted giant robot, and a giant walking statue operated by a sex-crazed lunatic power monger. Anime, Japanese with English subtitles, 35 mins.
VHS: S27681. $29.95.

Crimson Wolf

Mysterious deaths befall the members of an archeological team that uncovered the tomb of Genghis Khan. These deaths are connected to an ancient prophecy about three people with Crimson Wolf birthmarks. The fate of the whole world is at stake. Anime, dubbed in English, 60 mins.
VHS: S25068. $29.98.

Crying Freeman, Vol. 1
Yo Hinamura suffers a terrible fate at the hands of the Chinese Mafia. His body becomes the gang's robot-like property, a super assassin, but his mind remains his own. Yo can only cry for the victims of the horrible crimes which he must commit as demanded by his masters. This animated feature faithfully adapts one of Japan's most acclaimed, erotic, romance adventures.
VHS: $20721. $19.98.

Crying Freeman, Vol. 2
Nudity and sexual situations pepper the travails of Freeman, who is now the leader of 108 dragons. Others will stop at nothing to wrest this position of ultimate power from him. 50 mins.
VHS: $21693. $19.98.

Crying Freeman, Vol. 3
Crying Freeman sheds tears when he kills, because of his lingering conscience from a past life. In this episode he takes on the Chinese name of Dragon Sun along with the leadership of a Honk Kong crime syndicate. Before long he is off to Africa combatting rival gangs, while his beloved Tiger Orchid hopes to prove her own fighting spirit by taming a demon spirit that would curse Crying Freeman. Japanese with English subtitles.
VHS: $22907. $19.98.

Crying Freeman, Vol. 4
Two of Freeman's enemies persuade the leader of a religious cult to take over 108 dragons. Then they can attack the entire world. Only Freeman stands in the way. Graphic nudity. Japanese with English subtitles. 50 mins.
VHS: $22407. $19.98.

Crying Freeman, Vol. 5
An abduction in Los Angeles' Chinatown is a trap to bring Crying Freeman within the grasp of an international crime syndicate. This syndicate employs the best ex-commandos and mercenaries from all the world's armies. It's a graphic, action-animated feature. Japanese with English subtitles.
VHS: $23338. $19.98.

Crystal Triangle
Koichiro Kamishiro is on a rather esoteric mission: he seeks the Message of God. The interesting thing is, he's awfully close to finding it. Japanese with English subtitles.
VHS: $16639. $19.95.
Laser: LD74503. $34.95.
Kazuko Tadano, Japan, 1987, 86 mins.

Curse of the Undead Yoma
In this action-laden, animated film, Ninja warriors must battle foes from the dark side, the undead. One lone warrior seeks vengeance for the women and friends he loved, but how can he harm those already dead? In his quest he encounters terrors that are only realizable through animation. Japanese with English subtitles. 90 mins.
VHS: $23872. $29.95.

Cutey Honey
Go Nagai, one of Japan's most innovative creators of Manga and Anime, is now able to bring more action, more gratuitous nudity and more graphic violence in the adventures of Cutey Honey. This female android will transform herself countless times in order to tackle a range of attackers, and each transformation leaves her clothes behind. Japanese with English subtitles. 30 minutes each.
Volume 1.
VHS: $21342. $34.95.
Volume 2.
VHS: $21343. $34.95.

Cutey Honey, Volume 3
Cutey Honey is the ever-changing android Amazon. She's back with a whole new batch of lovely but lethal bodies to use as ruthless villains. This hard-hitting Anime story joins action and nudity in a highly entertaining tale. Japanese with English subtitles. 60 mins.
VHS: $26244. $29.95.

Cyber City Odeo 808: Data 1
Terrorists are holding the city's tallest skyscraper and its 50,000 inhabitants hostage. Cyber Police, criminals fitted with booby trapped collars, must solve this case. Hopefully they can do it within the space of one day or the collar will go off. Japanese with English subtitles, 48 mins.
VHS: $24569. $29.95.

Cyber City Odeo 808: Data 2
One of the Cyber Police has gone back to his evil ways. His ex-con colleagues have 24 hours to uncover a plot that threads through a black market dealing in body parts and brings them face to face with MOLCOS, the military's ultimate killing machine. Japanese with English subtitles, 52 mins.
VHS: $24570. $29.95.

Cyber City Odeo 808: Data 3
Genetic researchers are turning up dead with strange marks on their necks. A victim left a clue scrawled on the wall using his own blood. The trail leads to a cryogenic facility where the undead may simply be frozen. Japanese with English subtitles, 49 mins.
VHS: $24571. $29.95.

Cyber Ninja
This epic fantasy adventure follows Saki, a princess kidnapped amid the turmoil that results from a brutal civil war. Only Cyber Ninja can save her from the Dark Overlord and his evil plans to make her into a human sacrifice. Should the Dark Overlord succeed, he will unleash a hideous tide of evil upon the land.
VHS: $21772. $14.95.
Laser: LD74984. $39.99.

Cybernetics Guardian
In this animated adventure two competing companies vie for the contract a clean up the slums of the futuristic City of Tomorrow. John Stalker and his Guard Suit must face off against the overwhelming Genocyber Killing Machine, and luckily Stalker has a secret that surprises everyone. Japanese with English subtitles. Japan, 1995, 45 mins.
VHS: $27092. $29.95.

Cyborg 009: Legend of the Super Galaxy
Zoa, a powerful space alien, is planning to capture the Vortex, the most powerful force in the universe. Fortunately, the Galaxy Legion, nine invincible cyborgs led by Cyborg 009, are out to stop Zoa and his diabolical plan. Dubbed in English, 130 mins.
VHS: $25020. $19.99.

The Dagger of Kamui
A young boy undertakes a perilous odyssey to track down the ninja responsible for killing his parents, moving from ancient Japan to the mythic American Old West. Japanese with English subtitles. 1985, 132 mins.
VHS: $18618. $39.95.
Laser: LD74662. $59.95.

Dangaio
Tarsan is the unscrupulous space scientist who develops psyonic mecha warriors to sell to the highest bidder. He claims that Mai, Pai, Lamba and Roll are his new creations. They are actually kidnapped victims, stripped of their own identities. This popular animated serial follows the four young mecha warriors on their search to find out who they really are, in three action-packed volumes. Original character design by Haruhiko Mikimoto. Japanese with English subtitles.
Dangaio Part 1. 45 mins.
VHS: $13330. $34.95.
Dangaio Part 2. 45 mins.
VHS: $15956. $34.95.
Dangaio Part 3. 45 mins.
VHS: $15957. $34.95.

Dangaioh: Hyper-Combat Unit
Four psychic warriors, brought together by the mysterious Dr. Tarsan, now form Dangaioh, the world's most powerful combat unit. Together they offer hope to a cosmos terrorized by the tyranny of Captain Garimoth and his evil henchmen. Anime, dubbed in English, 90 mins.
VHS: $27471. $19.95.

Dangard Ace
Contains two programs: Enter Captain Mask, about the meeting between Winstar, the crew at the World Space Institute and Captain Mask; and Down from Mach 2, in which Captain Mask inherits the job of Dangard Ace instructor. 46 mins.
VHS: $18591. $12.98.

Dark Warrior—First Strike
Computer hacker Joe Takami breaks into the Pentagon's computer looking for information on a mysterious girl who's walked into his life. Instead, he finds information on a top-secret government experiment, and now the government wants him dead! Will he be able to evade the government assassins? Anime, Japanese with English subtitles, 60 mins.
VHS: $27685. $29.95.

Deluxe ARIEL 1
ARIEL is the ultimate female fighting robot, designed by Dr. Kishida to save the Earth from alien invaders and their giant, city-stomping monsters. Unable to find any other volunteers, Dr. Kishida shanghais his granddaughters into being the unwilling pilots of ARIEL. Kazumi is the third and youngest pilot on the ARIEL Team. In this episode, she discovers the that the choice between saving the Earth and going on a blind date is more difficult than she expected. Anime, Japanese with English subtitles.
VHS: $27676. $29.95.
Junichi Watanabe, Japan, 1991, 45 mins.

Deluxe ARIEL 2
The aliens have run out of money and are forced to abandon their plans of dominating the Earth. Unfortunately, their humongous starship has run out of gas and is hurtling through space on a crash course with Tokyo. Once again, it's up to female fighting robot ARIEL and her three-sisters team of pilots to save the day. Anime, Japanese with English subtitles.
VHS: $27684. $29.95.
Junichi Watanabe, Japan, 1991, 45 mins.

Demon Beast Invasion, Volume 1
Driven out of their home by ecological disaster, the demon beasts are finally able to return to the Earth. They cannot live in this new atmosphere so they seek out human women to engineer a new species. Only agents Kasu and Muneto stand between them and the women of the world. This erotic Anime adventure is subtitled in English. 48 mins.
VHS: $25980. $29.95.

Demon Beast Invasion, Volume 2
Both Kasu and Tsutomu have been impregnated with a horrifying child by the demon beasts. These incubating creatures threaten not only Muneto for his battle against the invaders. If the demon spawn live the entire world could be lost. This erotic Anime adventure is subtitled in English. 45 mins.
VHS: $25981. $29.95.

Demon Beast Invasion, Volume 4
Kayo's cousin Muneto harbors a powerful force within her soul and this force wants Muneto. Just as this crisis demands attention, the Demon Beast appears at Muneto's family temple. Anime, Japanese with English subtitles.
VHS: $27450. $29.95.
Juki Yohma, Japan, 1991, 45 mins.

Demon Beast Invasion, Volume 5
The Demon Beast has multiplied and has taken over the bodies of several gang members in Hong Kong. Curing them, fortunately, is relatively simple. The only problem is, the cure calls for killing all those possessed. Anime, Japanese with English subtitles.
VHS: $27451. $29.95.
Juki Yohma, Japan, 1991, 45 mins.

Demon Beast Invasion, Volume 6
Even though the Demon Beast is dead, something is killing Muneto's friends. Originally, Muneto meant to get away for a vacation, but between the unexpected deaths and the oddly familiar legend of a girl who falls in love with a monster, she won't get any rest in this Anime adventure. Japanese with English subtitles.
VHS: $27452. $29.95.
Juki Yohma, Japan, 1991, 45 mins.

Demon City Shinjuku
In a devastated Tokyo, the tyrannical Levih Rah plans to conquer the entire planet. Only the beautiful Sayaka Rama and Kyoya, a streetwise teenager, have the courage to face Rah's army of thugs. Animated. Japanese with English subtitles.
VHS: $20473. $19.95.

Detonator Orgun, Part 1
Just before graduation, Tomuru Shindo finds his dreams oddly unsettled by the appearance of alien life forms. This is only a prelude to a plot for worldwide invasion centered on an alien suit of armor. Before long Tomuru is trapped in a struggle beyond his wildest imagination. Japanese animation with English subtitles. 57 mins.
VHS: $21101. $29.95.

Detonator Orgun, Part 2
The soldier Orgun is fighting Tomuru for control of his body, in order to resist the Evoluder invasion. All this intergalactic commotion has drawn other aliens to both sides of the struggle. The fate of the city hangs in the balance. Japanese animation with English subtitles. 49 mins.
VHS: $21102. $29.95.

Detonator Orgun, Part 3
The Evoluder full-scale battle is only three months away, and the Earth forces appear hopelessly bogged down, when suddenly Tomuru unlocks the secret behind the alien technology and, ultimately, their strategy. Can a new software be developed in time? Japanese animation with English subtitles. 53 mins.
VHS: $21103. $29.95.
Laser: CLV. LD75399. $34.99.

Devil Hunter Yohko
An animated horror/comedy about a pre-ordained devil hunter, Yohko Mano, doing battle with the demon forces trying to eliminate her before she makes the transformation into top warrior. Japanese with English subtitles.
VHS: $18064. $29.95.
Laser: CAV, chapter stops. LD74479. $34.95.

Devil Hunter Yohko 2 and 3
When a shrine is destroyed the devil hunter heroine Yohko must get the vengeful spirits out of a number of inanimate objects and animals and back into the grave where they belong. Then Yohko is sent to an alternate dimension where her devil-fighting abilities are stretched to the limit simply in order to stay alive. Only her friends on the other side can bring her back. 65 mins.
VHS: $21704. $34.95.

Devil Hunter Yohko 4-Ever
This special music video clip compilation combines the best from the first three episodes of Yohko's earlier exploits. There are also live action performances by the original vocal cast, giving viewers a behind-the-scenes view of the performers that make it possible. Finally, a new, super-deformed animation sequence concludes this special video offering. 30 mins.
VHS: $21705. $19.95.

Devil Hunter Yohko 5: The Death of Yohko
The bouncy teenage exorcist Yohko will fight against demons even if it means her death. In this episode she makes the ultimate sacrifice and must now contend with demons on their own turf. The indefatigable heroine is not finished yet. Japanese with English subtitles. 50 mins.
VHS: $24227. $29.95.

Devil Hunter Yohko 6: Double Trouble, Double Jeopardy!
The sexy teenage devil hunter finds herself confronted by an unthinkable rival. She is as beautiful, sexy and accomplished as Yohko herself. In fact, she looks exactly like Yohko. It's only a matter for time before their competition leads to an all-out war. Anime, Japanese with English subtitles. Japan, 1995, 45 mins.
VHS: $26439. $29.95.

Devil Hunter Yohko— The Special Edition
In this animated adventure, Yohko finds she must battle the witch who is posing as her high school principal and an incubus who has possessed her best friend. Her principal wants to kill her while the incubus merely hopes to deflower her. Such are the travails of the youngest descendant of a devil-fighting family. Anime, dubbed in English.
VHS: $27020. $19.98.
Tetsuro Aoki, Japan, 1990, 50 mins.

Devilman, Vol. 1
In this animated feature a terrible mask reveals the newly stirring world of demons. They are about to awake and only the pure at heart can stop them. But the strategy is filled with danger as the killer of a demon becomes a demon himself. In this struggle the fate of the entire Earth hangs in the balance. Japanese with English subtitles.
VHS: $18925. $34.95.

Devilman, Vol. 2: Thief of Souls
Ryo and Akira have decoded a frightening secret, the impending invasion of Earth by the Demon World.
VHS: $19710. $34.95.

Dirty Pair Project Eden
This sexy, sci-fi, animated thriller finds Kei and Yuri on the planet Agerna. They must battle an army of mutants in order to foil the scheme of a mad but brilliant genetics expert. In this funny space adventure there is outrageous non-stop action from beginning to end.
VHS: $21755. $19.98.

Dirty Pair: Affair of Nolanda
In this adult Japanese animation work, two clairvoyant female special agents are thrust into a dense, crazy environment that threatens the stability of the planet.
VHS: $17167. $19.98.

Dirty Pair: Flight 005 Conspiracy
Two sexy space sleuths continue their antics in this, the third title from this popular, animated adult series. Now the Dirty Pair must solve a murder mystery involving deadly interplanetary political intrigue. 60 mins.
VHS: $21694. $19.98.

Dog Soldier: Shadows of the Past
When an American scientist carrying a cure for the AIDS virus is kidnapped by a notorious arms merchant, John Kyosuke is called back into action. Japanese animation, English subtitles.
VHS: $16059. $34.95.
Laser: LD74504. $29.99.
Takuji Jizoumoto, Japan, 1989, 45 mins.

Dominion Act I
The Earth of year 2010 is not a friendly place, and when the "Buaku" gang wreak havoc, stern measures are called for. Japanese animation, English subtitles.
VHS: $16056. $34.95.

Dominion Act II
The popular, animated Dominion series continues with this new installment. The Evil Buaku gang attempts another robbery at the hospital, only to be confronted by the Tank Police. Brutal action sequences characterize this sci-fi adventure. Japanese with English subtitles.
VHS: $15953. $34.95.

Dominion Act III
To become complete, Buaku steals a painting of himself valued at $900 million. Now the Red Commandos—a group of ruthless mercenaries led by "Skeleton"—and the Tank Police are in hot pursuit. Japanese animation, English subtitles. 40 mins.
VHS: $16055. $34.95.

Dominion Act IV
Finally, the truth of Buaku's origin is made clear. Could there be something noble in the half-human, half-cyborg blood of this renowned gang leader?
VHS: $16058. $34.95.

Dominion Four Pack
Complete 4 volume set.
VHS: $16697. $119.95.
Laser: LD71818. $69.95.

Dominion II, Vol. 1
In this animated feature an elite anti-terrorist unit, the Tank Police, is desperately trying to preserve order in Newport City. Their zeal frightens many residents, forcing the mayor to rein in their power. Now they must respond to a threat far graver than any they had prepared for. Dubbed in English. 60 mins.
VHS: $23878. $14.95.

Dominion Tank Police, Part I
This program contains Acts I and II of the series. Set in the near-distant future, the world is crippled by a devastating toxic cloud as the ruthless, fanatical Cat Sisters are wreaking havoc. They join forces with the nefarious Buaku Gang, and civilization's only hope is the Tank Police and Mr. Squad Commander Britain. English dubbed.
VHS: $17870. $19.95.

Dominion Tank Police, Part II
Episodes three and four are about the Buaku Gangs that terrorize the Earth. English dubbed.
VHS: $17871. $19.95.

Doomed Megalopolis
Part 1 of a four-hour mini-series that showcased the work of Oz and radically altered the shape of animated horror, Haunted Megalopolis combines the supernatural with stylish decor and imaginative design, "a mind-boggling frenzy of bloodlust and terror." Japanese animation with English subtitles. 60 mins.
VHS: $17743. $19.98.

Doomed Megalopolis 2: The Fall of Tokyo
Kato implants an unwilling victim with his evil seed. A group of men wage a desperate counterattack to Kato's brutal power play. Japanese animation with English subtitles. 50 mins.
VHS: $19487. $19.98.

Doomed Megalopolis 3:
The ancient warrior Masakado is awakened deep below Tokyo's streets and only the combined efforts of science and the supernatural can lay it to rest before Tokyo is destroyed, in this violent Japanese animation program. 47 mins. English language version.
VHS: $20429. $19.98.

Doomed Megalopolis 4: The Battle for Tokyo
Only an animated adult feature from Japan could capture the horror of this tale. Will the extreme violence of this battle save or destroy the futuristic Tokyo of the 21st century? Or is this the last saga to emanate from Megalopolis?
VHS: $20722. $19.98.

Dragon Half
This animated feature tells the unusual story of a teenage girl who is half human and half dragon. She has all kinds of problems as a result, including a vestigial tail and pair of wings. She is in danger because someone wants her skin as a pelt, but this heroine is more interested in affairs of the heart. Japanese with English subtitles. 60 mins.
VHS: $24226. $29.95.

Dragon Knight
This animated feature follows the lewd Dragon Knight on his adventure to free a number of young and exposed damsels in distress. Gold also figures as an object of lust in this funny, action-filled take off of the computer game "Dragon Knight". 40 mins.
VHS: $20691. $34.95.

Dragon Knight— Another Knight on the Town

Lusty Swordsman Takeru has noble intentions, but his aching wanderlust always gets him into trouble. In a village he rescues a small boy who is actually a woman in disguise. Before long he joins forces with her and a cast of lewd characters on an erotic animated adventure. Japanese with English subtitles, 50 mins.
VHS: S25023. $34.95.

Dragon Pink

Set in the world of swordplay and sorcery, this comic animated feature from Ito Yoko follows a slave girl who is transformed by a magical pair of panties into a veritable pussycat. Not everyone is pleased however, and together with her master Santa, she must outwit their wretched foes. Japanese with English subtitles. 35 mins.
VHS: S21144. $29.95.

Dragon Pink 2

This twisted sword, sex and sorcery adventure finds poor Pink getting the raw end of the deal. Bobo is using her for monster bait and paying the bills with her jewelry. When the jewels run out, she is left as collateral. In this uncut version there is plenty of explicit sexual footage. Japanese with English subtitles, 35 mins.
VHS: S25672. $29.95.

Dragon Pink 3

This romping sexual adventure throws the cat-girl Pink into the arms of an overtired Santa. Fortunately, there are wizards, warriors and naked elves, as well as oversexed monsters and lizard girls, to take up the slack. Anime, Japanese with English subtitles. 35 mins.
VHS: S26245. $29.95.

El Hazard, Volume 1

Makoto is an average high school student who magically finds himself transported to another world. The adventure begins when an ancient historic site is uncovered at his school. Then a mysterious girl appears. This is just the beginning of Makoto's travels. Includes the episodes "The War Zone" and "El Hazard." Anime, Japanese with English subtitles, 60 mins.
VHS: S25977. $29.95.
Laser: LD75035. $39.98.

El Hazard, Volume 2

In this animated sci-fi comedy adventure Makoto and his friends find themselves embroiled in war. They have been transferred to a different dimension where the allied nations battle the Bugrom. Staying alive with a few good laughs presents quite a challenge to Makoto and his friends. Japanese with English subtitles, 60 mins.
VHS: S26630. $29.95.
Laser: LD75102. $39.98.

El Hazard, Volume 4

The final chapter of the *El Hazard* series contains episodes 6 and 7, beginning with the destruction of the allied countries and ending with the rescue of Princess Fatora. Anime, Japanese with English subtitles, 75 mins.
VHS: S27692. $29.98.

Elven Bride 1

Elf maiden Milfa decides to marry the very human Kenji. No one in the village is happy about it, and as it turns out, even the bridal pair are less than content with their union because of unforseen anatomical differences. Kenji goes off in search of the ultimate marital aid, leaving Milfa alone and unprotected. Will their marriage—or any of the townspeople—survive the attack of the two-headed dragon? Anime, Japanese with English subtitles. 30 mins.
VHS: S27468. $29.95.

Elven Bride 2

Newlywed elf Milfa must see a gynecologist. It just so happens that the only one available is a well known pervert, M.D. Kenji. Milfa may be able to save the day with a little help from Michiko, a very sexy succubus. Anime, Japanese with English subtitles, 30 mins.
VHS: S27470. $29.95.

End of Summer

This animated feature represents a departure in erotica by concentrating on a simple love story without the usual sci-fi elements. Wataru works in a car restaurant owner whose adopted niece Saotomi eventually comes to love Wataru. Despite the gentle nature of this story its graphic depictions will be preceded by an "Adults Only" warning to alert viewers to its sexual nature. Japanese with English subtitles. 55 mins.
VHS: S20907. $29.95.

End of Summer 2

This video continues the erotic travails of Wataru. He still dreams of Mai and continues to see Satomi, but even these two beauties are not enough. Soon he oversteps the bounds of friendly consolation with his best friend's lovely ex-girlfriend. Japanese with English subtitles, 55 mins.
VHS: S26796. $29.95.

Explorer Woman Ray

Archaeologist Ray Kizuki travels the remote spots of the world to find a templewhich contains a mysterious object that may hold the key to a vanished civilization. 60 mins. Japanese with English subtitles.
VHS: S18427. $34.95.
Laser: LD74505. $34.99.

F3 (Frantic, Frustrated and Female)

In this animated feature the dedicated Hiroe Ogawa tracks down the perfect good feeling found in the "Big O." Together with her friends, she uses all the means she can muster to get in touch with her erotic self. Japanese with English subtitles. 35 mins.
VHS: S21145. $29.95.

F3 (Frantic, Frustrated and Female)— Part 2

It all begins when the lovely young heroine Hiroe confronts a lusty woman biker at the local swimming pool. Soon the biker visits Hiroe at home with two more women friends. The ensuing bedroom antics get so wild even Mom decides to join in. Anime, Japanese with English subtitles, 35 mins.
VHS: S27015. $29.95.

F3 (Frantic, Frustrated and Female)— Part 3

Hiroe Ogawa is already burning with desire when a horny male demon possesses her body. Mayaka hires a professional to help, but the professional called upon has quite a few kinky urges of her own. This film is violent and openly sexual. Anime, Japanese with English subtitles, 35 mins.
VHS: S27466. $29.95.

Fatal Fury

Three young brothers are being trained by their father in martial arts when he is murdered. The brothers continue to train in order to avenge his death, but there is only one way to defeat their enemy. They must learn a secret from their dreaded nemesis. Dubbed in English. 50 mins.
VHS: S23333. $19.95.

Fatal Fury 2: The New Battle

Based on the video games *Neo-Geo, Super Nintendo* and *Sega*, this animated feature contains phenomenal martial arts fight sequences. It's centered on a battered street fighter's recovery from physical and psychic wounds, but then watch out. Dubbed in English, 70 mins.
VHS: S24574. $19.95.

Fatal Fury: The Motion Picture

Whoever wears the "Armor of Mars" is invincible. This suit contains all the powers on which the martial arts are based. One man is seeking the final pieces to the suit. His twin sister fears the worst if he succeeds and she gathers together a group of fighters to stop him. Based on the games Neo-Geo, Super NES and Sega. Anime, dubbed in English. 100 mins.
VHS: S26247. $19.95.

First Loves 1

An erotic Anime contemplation of the magic of first love from the makers of *End of Summer*. It captures all the wonders of first loves. Anime, Japanese with English subtitles, 35 mins.
VHS: S27469. $29.95.

First Loves 2

Kakeru is depressed because his girlfriend has gone away to America. Luckily, a pretty redhead named Rei walks into his life and things finally seem to be looking up for Kakeru. Unfortunately, he discovers that star athlete Doda is after Rei too. Anime, Japanese with English subtitles, 35 mins.
VHS: S27682. $29.95.

Fist of the North Star

Based on the popular graphic novel by Buronson and Tetsuo Hara, this dramatic adventure spawned a successful Japanese television series. This feature-length version has been described as an animated take on what *The Road Warrior* would have been like with Bruce Lee.
VHS: S16698. $19.98.

Gaiking

Two Japanese animated works collected in one program. *Aries Joins the Team* concerns a young baseball player's recruitment to pilot a giant robot; *Right Down the Middle* continues the tale, as the young hero, Aries, learns how to maneuver the robot and deploy its weapons. 46 mins.
VHS: S18595. $12.98.

Galaxy Fraulein Yuna

This comic adventure series follows the travails of teenage Yuna. As if Yuna and her eating-machine sidekick Yuri weren't kept busy enough with cosmic cooking contests, house-destroying wake-up calls and rescuing kidnapped puppies, now they must find out the new girl's secret before it's too late. Home economics classes are just some of the routine daily chores that take on a sinister character after two new students appear. They could be aliens set to get Yuna. Anime, Japanese with English subtitles, 35 mins.
VHS: S27463. $29.95.

Gall Force 1: Eternal Story

A breakaway crew of the Solnoid cruiser Star Leaf must battle for its life, caught in the maelstrom of betrayal and aggressive fire fights in a work containing elements of *Star Wars* and *Alien*. Japanese with English subtitles.
VHS: S17364. $39.95.
Laser: LD74507. $29.99.

Gall Force 2: The Destruction

A continuation of the bloody space battles between the brutal Paranoids and the cunning Solnoids finds ace pilot Lufy, sole survivor of the Starleaf missions. Japanese with English subtitles. 50 mins.
VHS: S19693. $34.95.

Gall Force 3: Stardust War

In this animated feature, a war among the stars could lead to the extinction of two races joined only by their hatred of one another. Both are steadfastly opposed to the notion of peaceful co-existence. The last survivors of the destroyed fleet Lorelei have found hope in a new ally. If they fail to bridge the differences between these two races, all hope is lost. Japanese with English subtitles. 60 mins.
VHS: S21100. $29.95.
Laser: Subtitled. LD74950. $34.99.

Gall Force: Earth Chapter 1

In 2085 the Earth is a wasteland from war, with lethal machines in charge. Sandy Newman and her friends fight for their lives everyday. While searching for underground missiles, they discover a secret sect which worships the Tree of Revival. It may be their only hope. Japanese with English subtitles. 48 mins.
VHS: S22763. $29.95.
Laser: LD75291. $34.98.

Gall Force: Earth Chapter 2

The human forces on Mars are planning a new threat against the survivors on Earth. A plasma cannon that could operate from deep space and still destroy an entire continent is under construction. It might be trained on the base that Sandy and her friends call home, all of Australia. Japanese with English subtitles, 50 mins.
VHS: S22764. $29.95.
Laser: CLV. LD75400. $34.99.

Gall Force: Earth Chapter 3

General MacKenzie plans to invade Earth from Mars. With his superior technology it will be the ultimate battle of man versus computers and robots. Only Sandy Newman can stay ahead of these supercomputing machines. Japanese with English subtitles, 58 mins.
VHS: S22765. $29.95.

Gall Force: New Era 1

After the cyberwar only metropolis cities can support life on planet Earth. These mini-utopias and a new threat from the genetically altered yumans. Fifty years ago a yuman tyrant led a bloody rebellion. Now his descendant, Nova, is ready to try again. If he succeeds it would be the end of mankind. Anime subtitled in Japanese. 50 mins.
VHS: S26251. $29.95.

Gall Force: New Era 2

Mankind is dead. Only six young women have survived the onslaught of the computer Gorn. Catty, an android spawned by another race, understands the terrible destructive nature of humans and saved these women by shooting them out into deep space. Gorn, however, will seek them out by infecting any other computer to ensure the end of mankind. Anime, Japanese with English subtitles. 50 mins.
VHS: S26252. $29.95.
Laser: LD75544. $34.99.

Garaga

Sabotage sends the starship XeBeC hurtling out of control. An emergency landing on a planet filled with dinosaurs and ape-like creatures offers a poor refuge. Slowly, the source of the sabotage is revealed. It involves a powerful general, a ruthless plot and a race of psychics. Anime, Japanese with English subtitles. Japan, 1995, 100 mins.
VHS: S26898. $29.95.

Genesis Survivor Gaiarth: Stage 1

In a devastated, postapocalyptic civilization, artificially intelligent machines are programmed to destroy society. The young hero, Italdel Labard, raised by the aging warlord, may be a link to an earlier time and place. Japanese with English subtitles. 51 mins.
VHS: S18347. $24.95.

Genesis Surviver Gaiarth: Stage 2

In the aftermath of the "Big War," humans and robots struggle to survive amid the ruin and devastation on Gaiarth. After Sahari, Zaxxon and Ital defeat the BeastMaster, they travel to Metro City, where they end up having to battle the dreaded Kampfdraken as well. When the Kampfdraken is defeated, they discover the mysterious egg that it had been guarding, and it soon hatches to reveal Sakuya, an Elf. Japanese with English subtitles.
VHS: S18620. $24.95.
Kitazume Hiroyuki/Aramaki Shinji, Japan, 1993, 46 mins.

Genesis Survivor Gaiarth: Stage 3

Struggling to regain their past, the survivors of a terrible planetary war on Gaiarth find themselves confounded by the remnants of their own technology. Soon Ital, Sahari, Fayk, and Zaxxon must battle to prevent a fate worse than Armageddon. When the Elf Sakuya is kidnapped by the maniacal General, it's up to Sahari, Zaxxon, Ital and their new friend Fayk to rescue her and save Gaiarth from the General's evil plans of world domination. Anime. Japanese with English subtitles.
VHS: S20723. $24.95.
Ooba Hideaki, Japan, 1993, 45 mins.

Genocyber #1: Birth of Genocyber

Based on the Viz comic, this feature combines computer graphics, live action, special effects and cel animation in a story inspired by cyber-punk. Two sisters, each possessing amazing qualities, could be combined to produce an amazing force. Corporate greed will do anything to harbor this power— even destroy world peace. Japanese with English subtitles. 46 mins.
VHS: S21319. $29.95.
Laser: LD74826. $34.99.

Genocyber #2 & #3: Versus Vajuranid

The world is falling apart. While some nations are developing super weapons like the Genocyber, Kuryu enterprises is developing a being to defeat it. Called the Vajuranid, it may be the only living thing that can battle the Genocyber and get away alive. A full length animated adventure. Japanese with English subtitles. 56 mins.
VHS: S21835. $29.95.

Giant Robo, Vol. 1

A nefarious organization known as "Big Fire" attempts to control a powerful energy source to conquer the Earth, waging war through a combined use of physics and giant robots. 55 mins.
VHS: S18341. $24.95.

Giant Robo, Vol. 2

As the Eye of Folger advances toward the last energy source on Earth, all the Experts of Justice are ordered to gather here. This Anime tells the seemingly hopeless tale of their efforts to stop this evil and save the world. Anime, dubbed in English, 45 mins.
VHS: S25726. $14.95.

Giant Robo, Vol. 3: The Twilight of the Superhero

The Eye of Folger resists even the powerful punch of Robo. It could mark the beginning of the end for this animated superhero. Gynrei is also forced to risk her life in battle and, even more worrisome, she finds herself unexpectedly facing her father. Anime, dubbed in English, 45 mins.
VHS: S26239. $14.95.

Giant Robo, Vol. 4: The Truth About Bashtaralle

Daisako is plunged into the icy depths of the Himalayas. Gynrei and Tetsugyu struggle to save him, but as he sleeps in the cold, Daisako dreams. In his dream the origins of Robo stand revealed. Anime. Dubbed in English. 30 mins.
VHS: S26638. $14.95.

Giant Robo, Vol. 5: "Conflict in the Snow Mountains"

Giant Robo joins comrades Daisaku and Gynrei in order to stop the explosion of the Big Balloon. This device absorbs energy so successfully that if it explodes the nearly Earth could be annihilated. Anime, dubbed in English, 45 mins.
VHS: S26767. $14.95.

Giant Robo: The Night the Earth Stood Still

This first volume contains two episodes about the struggle over a new, nearly limitless form of energy. Big Fire inspires a villainous plot and only the young boy Daisaku and Giant Robo can stop them in this sci-fi Anime saga. Dubbed in English, 90 mins.
VHS: S25545. $19.95.

Gigantor

Monstrous robotic juggernauts taking the form of nature's predators battle it out in these violent vignettes spanning the barren landscapes of a future Earth. Japanese with English subtitles.
Gigantor Vol. 1: *Struggle at the South Pole/Battle at the Bottom of the World/String of the Spider.* 25 mins.
VHS: S15970. $19.95.
Gigantor Vol. 2: *Return of the Spider/Spider's Revenge/Secret Valley.* 25 mins.
VHS: S15971. $19.95.
Gigantor Vol. 3: *The Diamond Smugglers/Dangerous Dr. Diamond/Force of Terror.* 75 mins.
VHS: S16700. $19.95.

Gigantor Retrospective 30: Volume 1

Gigantor the animated robot will always defend humanity against any evil anywhere. Two episodes are included in this volume: *World in Danger* and *Badge of Honor*. Saving the world and preserving honor are just two of Gigantor's many specialties. Japanese with English subtitles. 50 mins.
VHS: S21287. $19.95.

Gigantor Retrospective 30: Volume 2

Gigantor battles the incredible Smoke Robots in the first episode of this volume. In the second episode a freezing ray poses a threat that only Gigantor can face. Japanese with English subtitles. 50 mins.
VHS: S21288. $19.95.

Gigantor Retrospective 30: Volume 3

The Magic Multiplier is a grave threat and Gigantor is put to the test battling its terrifying effects. Next, deep underwater lies a submarine base with an array of robotized sea creatures, more spectacular than any living thing. Japanese with English subtitles. 50 mins.
VHS: S21289. $19.95.

Gigantor Retrospective 30: Volume 4

Treasure Mountain is forbidding and alluring at the same time. Gigantor scales its peaks in the first episode of this volume. Then, a mystery missile confounds Gigantor with its explosive dangers. Japanese with English subtitles. 50 mins.
VHS: S21290. $19.95.

Gigantor Retrospective 30: Volume 5

Venomous attacks lie in store for Gigantor in *The Giant Cobra*, while in the second episode, *The Great Hunt*, Gigantor exhibits his great strength and incredible control. Japanese with English subtitles. 50 mins.
VHS: S21291. $19.95.

Gigantor Vol. 2

Jimmy Sparks holds a device that looks like a lunch box, but in actuality it controls a powerful robot called *Gigantor*. With Jimmy's know-how and the robot's great strength they fight crime throughout the world. 120 mins.
Laser: LD74829. $39.95.

Gigantor—30th Annniversary

A lunchbox-shaped device controls the world's most powerful robot, owned by a young boy named Jimmy Sparks. This robot can unleash immense powers and fly effortlessly around the world. Jimmy joins forces with his robot friend to fight crime, leading them on spectacular adventures in exotic locales around the globe. Originally a TV series, these episodes are presented just as they were aired. Dubbed in English, 120 mins.
Laser: LD74608. $39.95.

Girl from Phantasia

Akihiro's amorous intentions are detoured when he is faced with the mischievous Malon and the ruthless magician Rroll, in addition to his annoyed girlfriend Michigo. Based on the Manga series *Fantasia*. Japanese animation with English subtitles. 30 mins.
VHS: S20522. $29.95.

Godmars

An ordinary citizen dedicated to the good of mankind discovers that he is fated to be the source of humanity's destruction in this imaginative Japanamation feature. It's 1999 and aliens are waiting intently for this hero to fulfill his destiny. Fortunately he doesn't believe in giving up. Japanese with English subtitles. 93 mins.
VHS: S22766. $24.95.

Golden Boy 1

Twenty-five-year-old Kintaro has always dreamed of being a computer programmer. When he finds himself quickly climbing the corporate ladder of T.N. Software, a computer software company where Kintaro is the only male employee, he thinks he's hit the jackpot. Unfortunately, when the women find out about Kintaro's programming ideas, he's quickly demoted to office boy. Will Kintaro ever recover? Will he once again be T.N. Software's "Golden Boy"? Anime, Japanese with English subtitles.
VHS: S27713. $24.95.
Laser: LD75571. $39.95.

GoShogun: The Time Etranger, Record of Lodoss War, Volume 3

The GoShogun team has already saved the world and disbanded. Now they are reunited at the deathbed of one of their most taciturn members. After a life of incredible hardship she must battle dark strangers who whisper an evil prophecy. With her team beside her, she will fight to the end. Japanese with English subtitles, 90 mins.
VHS: S25682. $29.95.

Grandizer

In *Robot Back to Action*, the cocky Lance receives a few lessons in humility and must call on Orion's help to battle the Vegans. *Beware the Red Moon* finds the marauders about to launch a surprise attack on Earth as Lance discovers Johnny's actual identity. 46 mins.
VHS: S18594. $12.98.

Great Conquest: The Romance of Three Kingdoms

The true story of Liu Pie, the father of historical China, is at the center of this entrancing animated feature. Pat Morita narrates the story of the man who forged a nation from chaos. Dubbed in English, 110 min.
VHS: S25066. $19.98.

Gunbuster I

Thrill to the adventures of the beautiful space pilot trainee Noriko, whose burning ambition is to continue her father's legacy as a top soldier in the earth Space Force. Two power-packed segments of this popular Japanese animated serial on one tape. From Toshihiro Hirano, the creator of *Iczer-One*.
VHS: S13329. $34.95.

Gunbuster II

Noriko discovers a member of the enemy race for the first time. Meanwhile Kazumi Amano and Freud Jeung try to out-muscle each other with their robots in an effort to develop a mutual admiration society. Japanese animation with English subtitles.
VHS: S16061. $34.95.

Gunbuster III

With Earth's fate all but sealed, our heroes launch a hit-or-miss raid against the invading aliens that is sure to leave only one standing. Japanese animation with English subtitles.
VHS: S16062. $34.95.

Gunsmith Cats #1

Rally Vincent is set to clean up the streets of Chicago. The Windy City will never be the same after this sexy heroine brings her trusty pump-action sidearm into play. Together with her friend Minnie-May, Rally sets the scene for animated erotic action and adventure. Anime, bilingual, Japanese with English subtitles and English dubbed, CAV format.
Laser: LD75439. $39.95.
Takeshi Mori, Japan, 1995, 30 mins.

Gunsmith Cats #1—The Special Edition

Rally Vincent is set to clean up the streets of Chicago. The Windy City will never be the same after this sexy heroine brings her trusty pump-action sidearm into play. Together with her friend Minnie-May, Rally sets the scene for animated erotic action and adventure. This special edition includes the bonus 40-minute *Making of Gunsmith Cats*. Anime in Japanese with English subtitles.
VHS: S27021. $34.95.
Takeshi Mori, Japan, 1995, 70 mins.

Gunsmith Cats #2

The adventures of Rally and her sidekick Minnie May continue with this action-packed thriller. A gun runner named James Washington is claiming someone's trying to kill him, but Rally and Minnie May don't believe his story until he actually turns up dead, shot down outside an ATF safehouse only moments after Rally and Minnie May left. Now they're on the chase after a psychotic Russian and Washington's killer, and the expressways of Chicago, Illinois, may never recover. Anime, Japanese with English subtitles. Japan, 1996, 30 mins.
VHS: S27712. $24.95.
Laser: LD75570. $39.95.

Guy: Awakening of the Devil

Soldier of fortune Guy and his beautiful assistant Raina detect a starship whose passengers have been transformed into mutants. They trace the ship's path to the sinister Prison world, and discover the aliens are the bizarre result of the insane warden's experiments. Japanese with English subtitles. The film is available in two versions, uncut and edited. Note: both versions contain adult content unsuitable for young viewers.
Guy: Awakening of the Devil (Edited).
VHS: S19694. $29.95.
Guy: Awakening of the Devil (Uncut).
VHS: S19690. $29.95.

Guy: Awakening of the Devil and Double Target

This special boxed set is available in two versions, uncut and edited. Note: both versions contain adult content unsuitable for young viewers.
Uncut Version. 75 mins.
VHS: S19692. $39.95.
Edited Version. 70 mins.
VHS: S19695. $39.95.

Guy: Second Target

Guy and Raina destroy an illegal casino before they're drawn into a sinister planet ruled by two power-mad telekinetic tyrants, lovers with phenomenal powers to conjure up monsters. Japanese with English subtitles.
VHS: S19691. $29.95.

The Guyver

The Guyver is a bio-booster armor with an alien design which, when activated on human subjects, transforms them into superhuman warriors of unlimited physical prowess. Animated.
The Guyver: Volume 1.
VHS: Out of print. For rental only.
The Guyver: Volume 2.
VHS: Out of print. For rental only.
The Guyver: Volume 3.
VHS: Out of print. For rental only.
The Guyver: Volume 5.
VHS: S20480. $24.95.

The Guyver: Bio-Booster Armor, Data 1: Genesis of the Guyver

Of three stolen Guyver units, one is accidentally found by a young student. He triggers its mechanism and is magically transformed into the Guyver himself. His life is also altered as he battles the bio-morphic Zoanoids from Chronos, the corporation that invented the Guyver. Anime, dubbed in English, 30 mins.
VHS: S27368. $12.95.

The Guyver: Bio-Booster Armor: Data 2: Battle of the Guyvers

The bio-morphic Zoanoids of Chronos are determined to recover the Guyvers. They send an agent to kidnap Sho, the young student who accidentally triggered the control mechanism of a Guyver, causing he himself to become the Guyver. Unfortunately, the Chronos agent is himself turned into Guyver II, a fighting unit specially trained for combat. This makes the original plan to recover the Guyvers doubly difficult. Anime, dubbed in English, 30 mins.
VHS: S27474. $12.95.

The Guyver: Bio-Booster Armor: Data 3: Mysterious Shadow

Chronos has still not managed to recover the missing Guyver units. Desperate to regain control, they send Commander Gyou and the hyper Zoanoid Zerubus to kidnap Sho's girlfriend and force Sho into a confrontation. Now Sho must once again become the Guyver, a weapon that's half-human, half-machine and all-powerful, and face Gyou, Zerubus and the Mysterious Shadow (better known as Guyver III). Anime, dubbed in English. Japan, 1996, 30 mins.
VHS: S27715. $12.95.

The Guyver: Bio-Booster Armor: Data 4: Attack of the Hyper Zoanoid—Team 5

Our hero, Sho, and his friend Tetsuro have agreed to go public with their information about the evil organization Chronos. Unfortunately, before they can make their move, Commander Gyou returns with an army of five Zoanoids, and Sho knows this is a battle he can't win alone, even as a Guyver. Anime, dubbed in English. Japan, 1996, 31 mins.
VHS: S27717. $12.95.

The Guyver: Out of Control

Sho battles the nefarious Chronos corporation and their biomorphic creatures, the Zoanoids, to save his girlfriend Mizuky Segawa. Japanese with English subtitles.
VHS: S19459. $34.95.

The Guyver: Volume 6

In *Masaki Murakami: Transforming Beastmaster*, Murakami reveals the origins and purpose of the Guyvers. Then in *Aptom's Attack: Reactivate Guyver*, Sho must transform into the Guyver in order to save Mizuky from Aptom. Anime. Dubbed in English. 60 mins.
VHS: S23763. $24.95.

Gynocyber Parts 4 and 5: The Legend of Ark De Grande

After 100 years of war Gynocyber has destroyed human civilization. On the eve of its final battle it mysteriously vanishes, leaving Kuryu's forces alive. In episode five, two lovers arrive in the city of Ark De Grande, but their plans for a new life are interrupted by riots. Could the turmoil be related to the return of Gynocyber? Japanese with English subtitles, 60 mins.
VHS: S23081. $29.95.

Hades Project Zeorymer—Volume 1

Zeorymer is the robot warrior piloted by a genetically engineered pilot called Masato. Realizing that his whole life has been preorchestrated, Masato is consumed by self-doubts even as he must fight the dreaded twin warriors Si Aen and Si Tau. Animation in Japanese with English subtitles. 60 mins.
VHS: S20865. $29.95.

Hades Project Zeorymer—Volume 2

Eight giant robots would rule the world. Zeorymer of the heavens, the most powerful of these robots, must be piloted by a specially engineered human, but this embryo was stolen. Now the pilot awakes and a desperate struggle ensues as enemies emerge to duel with him. The greatest struggle however, may take place in his own psyche, as he grapples with the trauma of his pre-engineered life. Anime with English subtitles. 60 mins.
VHS: S21292. $29.95.

The Hakkenden: Legend of the Dog Warriors, Vol. 1

Eight young warriors struggle to find truth and justice in medieval Japan. Even though they are engaged in war, their dreams and ambitions actually inspire their actions. This story is derived from Bakin Kyokutei's classic novel. Includes the episodes "Kaleidoscope" and "Sacred." Anime, Japanese with English subtitles, 60 mins.
VHS: S25976. $29.95.
Laser: LD75034. $39.98.

The Hakkenden: Legend of the Dog Warriors, Vol. 2

The action-packed adventures of the dog warriors continue in the two episodes joined on this video. Shino and Sosuke learn that they are related. Fortunately this helps cement strong bonds between them because in the next episode they must face horrible accusations. Anime. Japanese with English subtitles, 60 mins.
VHS: S26633. $29.95.
Laser: LD75105. $39.98.

The Hakkenden: Legend of the Dog Warriors, Vol. 3

The dog warriors were brought together by destiny. In the two episodes included on this video they continue their quest and must face the threat of death from crucifixion. Anime adventure. Japanese with English subtitles. 60 mins.
VHS: S26632. $29.95.
Laser: LD75104. $39.98.

The Hakkenden: Legend of the Dog Warriors, Vol. 4

This episode of the Anime series starts off with *The Hakkenden Digest*, a compilation of the first six episodes. In the seventh episode, *Spirits*, the dog warriors learn of their war-filled future. As a bonus, this tape includes a clip of the series' theme song, "Blue Skies." Japanese with English subtitles. Japan, 1995, 45 mins.
VHS: S27095. $29.98.
Laser: LD75452. $34.98.

Hanappe Bazooka

Watch out, E.T. looks like high school slacker Hanappe's dreams of passing his classes and making the local street gang leave him alone may have come true when a pair of pan-dimensional beings step through Hanappe's television and turn his right index finger into the most powerful weapon on Earth. Contains graphic violence, nudity and sex. Anime, Japanese with English subtitles, 55 mins.
VHS: S27459. $29.95.

Harmagedon

From the creator of *Akira*, this futuristic animation work is set in a post-nuclear society as humans defend the Earth from raging psychotic demons and a determined, malevolent space god. Japanese with English subtitles. 132 mins.
VHS: S18745. $39.95.
Laser: LD74508. $49.99.

The Heroic Legend of Arislan, Part 1

An animated Japanese translation of Shakespeare's *Henry IV*, about Daryoon, an exiled officer, who is ordered to secure the safety of the King's son, Prince Arislan. The two come under the influence of the mischievous and eccentric artist Lord Narsus. Japanese with English subtitles
VHS: S19885. $29.95.

The Heroic Legend of Arislan, Part 2

Yoshiki Tanaka, who wrote the popular animation series *Legend of the Galactic Heroes*, also wrote this new, animated adventure feature. It follows a young prince who must battle against an overwhelmingly formidable army that includes a ferocious 12-foot beast. 59 mins.
Japanese with English subtitles.
VHS: S21317. $29.95.
Laser: LD74827. $34.99.
Dubbed in English.
VHS: S21318. $19.95.

The Heroic Legend of Arislan, Parts 3 and 4

The religious fanatics of Lusitania used betrayal and sorcery to destroy Palse's army by burning his forces alive. Prince Arislan escaped, but the Lusitanians have other problems. They must eliminate the fanatic priest Jon Bodan, and his dark powers. Japanese with English subtitles. 60 mins.
VHS: S23335. $29.95.
Laser: CLV. LD75398. $34.99.

Homeroom Affairs, Part 1: "I'll Teach You a Lesson You'll NEVER Forget!"

Tokira Ehara has landed a job at an elite all-girl high school which is populated by very advanced students. In fact, he may learn far more from his students than he could possibly teach them. This sexy animated feature is inspired by the comic characters from *Animal Magazine*. Japanese with English subtitles.
VHS: S26477. $24.95.

Homeroom Affairs, Part 2: "I Was Born Reckless"

Tokira Ehara has resisted the advances of his student Miyako for two months even though they have been living together all that time. This sexy comedy reaches new levels of hilarity when Miyako's ex-boyfriend enters the picture. Based on the comic characters from *Animal Magazine*. Animated. Japanese with English subtitles.
VHS: S26478. $24.95.

The Humanoid

This is story of Dr. Watson and his crowning achievement, Antoinette, a chrome-bodied android. In a vivid portrayal of an ethereal future world filled with endless techno-gadgetry, this intriguing science fiction adventure builds to a music video style climax. Japanese animation, English subtitles. 45 mins.
VHS: S15955. $34.95.

Hurricane Live!

Futuristic animated rock music videos from Japan combined with live-action performance make for a unique concert series. Each tape consists of edited footage from the *Bubblegum Crisis* film series, as well as original animation, accompanied by hard-driving rock music. Japanese lyrics with English subtitles.
Hurricane Live!: Volume 1. 25 mins.
VHS: S16672. $19.95.
Hurricane Live!: Volume 2. 25 mins.
VHS: S16673. $19.95.

Iczelion Acts I & II

Nagisa Kai planned to be a professional wrestler, but unexpectedly became a combat partner of the alien Iczel battleship *Iczelion*. This intense, action-packed anime follows her adventures. Japanese with English subtitles, 60 mins.
VHS: S24700. $34.95.

Iczer 3: Volume 1

Iczer defeated Big Gold and her monstrous army. Though the battle was won, Big Gold left enough of her evil progeny around for another day. These terrible forces have regrouped, and once again, Iczer is called upon to save the Earth, in this exciting animated feature. Japanese with English subtitles. 60 mins.
VHS: S21284. $29.95.

Iczer 3: Volume 2

This anime feature follows Iczer 3 in her lonely battle with Neos Gold. This arch enemy has gotten hold of Iczer 3's power source and has fashioned a special warrior for the fight, an exact duplicate of Iczer 3. Perhaps Nagisa, who suffered so terribly in their last encounter, will come to the rescue after all. Japanese with English subtitles. 60 mins.
VHS: S21285. $29.95.
Laser: CLV. LD75050. $34.95.

Iczer 3: Volume 3

The Queen Fuji arrives at Neo's base and Iczer 1 is there to help, because Iczer 3 has her hands full with Atros, Golem and the newly revived Iczer 2. This anime is loaded with unexpected surprises, including some particularly dirty tricks targeted toward a battle that will decide the fate of the Earth. Japanese with English subtitles. 60 mins.
VHS: S21286. $29.95.
Laser: CLV. LD75397. $34.99.

Iczer-One

The two-volume, four-part set about female warriors fighting an invasion of biomorphic alien creatures. Nagisha, an innocent though gifted fighter, is enlisted by Iczer-One, a mysterious interplanetary warrior, to be her partner. They must confront the equally treacherous Iczer-Two and her Mecha Iczer-Sigma. Japanese with English subtitles.
Vol. 1 (Acts 1 & 2).
VHS: S18107. $24.95.
Vol. 2 (Acts 3 & 4).
VHS: S18169. $24.95.

The Incident in the Bedroom Suburb/ Voice from Heaven

Fearing their neighbors are trying to force them from their home, the Mabuchi family are horrified when their daughter is trapped in the elevator. It seems there is a deep, dark secret that must be concealed at all costs. Animated. Japanese with English subtitles. 52 mins.
VHS: S24271. $29.95.

Iria: Zeiram the Animation, Vol. 1

Zeiram, a hideously powerful monster, is being secretly transported to Earth as a bio-weapon. Iria is a ruthless young bounty hunter with only one thing on her mind—killing the Zeiram, the extra-terrestrial monster who killed her brother. Zeiram's escape spells disaster unless Iria and her streetwise sidekick, Kei, can halt his deadly rampage. Includes Episodes 1 & 2. Anime. Japanese with English subtitles.
VHS: S27343. $29.95.
Tetsurou Amino, Japan, 1995, 60 mins.

Johnny Sokko and His Flying Robot: Episodes 1 and 2

The evil alien Emperor Guillotine is set on world domination. Though Johnny Sokko is a young boy, together with his robot friend he alone can save the world from Emperor Guillotine's terrifying plans. This video includes the first two episodes of the series: *Dracalon, The Great Sea Monster* and *Nucleon, The Magic Globe*.
VHS: S27076. $9.98.

Johnny Sokko and His Flying Robot: Episodes 3 and 4

This tape features the third and fourth episodes of the *Johnny Sokko* series: *Gargoyle Vine, A Space Plant* and *Tyrox, A Strange Monster*.
VHS: S27077. $9.98.

Johnny Sokko and His Flying Robot: Episodes 5 and 6

In *Destroy the Dam* and *The Transformed Humans*, Johnny and his 100-foot tall robot friend once again save the planet from the evil Emperor Guillotine.
VHS: S27078. $9.98.

Johnny Sokko and His Flying Robot: Episodes 7 and 8

The final volume in the *Johnny Sokko* series, this tape features *Dragon, The Ninja Monster* and *The Gigantic Claw*, both of which offer more exciting stories of Johnny and his robot friend.
VHS: S27079. $9.98.

Judge

Most criminals are concerned only with earthly justice, but there is another higher justice. This form is administered by a supernatural being, and there is no appeal. Only an animated feature could capture the terror of this otherworldly retribution. Japanese with English subtitles. 50 mins.
VHS: S21836. $29.95.

Kekkou Kamen Volume 1

This outrageous super heroine wears nothing but her trademark red boots and mask. Miami Takashi is a student in a nightmare academy where Nazi hall monitors oversee the worst types of depravity. She finds that the principal has picked her out for special treatment. Only Kekkou and her amazing body can save this innocent. Animated, Japanese with English subtitles. 55 mins.
VHS: S22673. $29.95.

Kekkou Kamen Volume 2

This continuation of this adult feature series contains more of the same twisted characters from the first volume. Again only Kekkou with her amazing physique stands between utter depravity and the innocent students of this obscene academy. Japanese with English subtitles. 55 mins.
VHS: S22674. $29.95.

Kimagure Orange Road

Kimagure Orange Road is an outstanding example of the unique Japanese "love comedy." It is the story of a teenage love triangle between a boy, Kyosuke, and two girls, the cool Madoka and the bubbly Hikaru. The twist that makes *Orange Road* so outrageous is that Kyosuke and his family are all cursed with psychic powers. Japanese with English subtitles.
Kimagure Orange Road
VHS: S16668. $24.95.
Kimagure Orange Road: Volume 2.
VHS: S16669. $24.95.
Kimagure Orange Road: Volume 3.
VHS: S16670. $24.95.
Kimagure Orange Road: Volume 4.
VHS: S16671. $24.95.
Kimagure Orange Road: Volume 5.
VHS: S17531. $24.95.

Kimagure Orange Road Collector's Suite

This Anime boxed set of five videos follows the comic travails of an indecisive teenager who must choose between the love of two girls. The only problem is that he must not reveal his family's secret. They possess psychic gifts. Japanese with English subtitles.
VHS: S25716. $120.00.

Kishin Heidan, Volume 1

Back in the 40's there was a frightening battle between humans and unknown, otherworldly aliens. In order to fight them and save the earth, Kishin Heidan (The Machine God Troops) were formed. This is the unforgettable beginning of a historical battle. Subtitled. 60 mins.
VHS: S23065. $29.98.
Laser: LD74653. $39.95.

Kishin Heidan, Volume 2

Will the Kishin Corps and Taishi be able to retrieve the odule as they head out to the Kanto Army's Fortress Island? And will they obtain the Kanto Army's Module body as they battle head-to-head on the rail tracks of Manchuria? Subtitled. 60 mins.
VHS: S23066. $29.98.
Laser: LD74654. $39.95.

Kishin Heidan, Volume 3

Panzer Kavalier is the result of an unholy alliance between Nazis and aliens. Kishin Heidan must protect an important scientist facing this outlandish threat. If he cannot stop the Panzer Kavalier far more will be lost than this single life. Japanese with English subtitles, 60 mins.
VHS: S24239. $29.98.
Laser: LD74818. $39.98.

Kishin Heidan, Volume 4

The Kanto Army is pursuing Taishi and his module. This module would crucially enhance the dangerous army. Meanwhile the Nazis attempt to pursue their conquest of the world by using the alien army's frightful technology. Japanese with English subtitles, 60 mins.
VHS: S25677. $29.98.
Laser: LD74990. $39.98.

Kishin—The Symphony

The heart-pounding music of the Kishin Heidan series is performed by the Shinsei Japan Orchestra and the Shinsei Nikkyo Chorus under the direction of Kaoru Wada at the Showa Women's University. Also includes other musical excerpts. Japanese with English subtitles, 60 mins.
VHS: S25678. $29.98.
Laser: LD74991. $39.98.

KOR Whimsical Highways LD Set

Can an indecisive teenager choose between two girls who love him without exposing his family's psychic gifts? There is never a dull moment on whimsical Kimagure Orange Road in this feature length animated film.
Laser: LD74606. $110.00.

La Blue Girl, Volume 1

A secret pact with underworld forces ensured a ninja clan access to great powers. Now the 18-year-old descendent of this clan must struggle to keep these lewd underworld forces at bay. Otherwise both she and her sister could suffer unspeakable consequences. This is a violent, graphic, animated feature. Japanese with English subtitles, 45 mins.
VHS: S25025. $29.95.

La Blue Girl, Volume 2

The Mido family signet case is the prize that will grant power over the world of the Shikima. The Mido girls and their ninja sidekick must battle the Suzuka clan in a veritable sexual endurance test to secure the case. This graphic, animated feature climaxes with the strangest family reunion imaginable. Anime, Japanese with English subtitles.
VHS: S26098. $29.95.

La Blue Girl, Volume 3

In this steamy, violent Anime video, Miko becomes a warrior in order to seek revenge. She must hunt down the Man of a Thousand Faces and find the enchanted sword Zipang. Her father's very life hangs in the balance. Japanese with English subtitles. 45 mins.
VHS: S26900. $29.95.

La Blue Girl, Volume 4

In this sexy Anime adventure series, Miko is subject to a diabolical plot. Danger abounds, especially for Miko's new friend. Japanese with English subtitles. Japan, 1995, 45 mins.
VHS: S27105. $29.95.

La Blue Girl, Volume 5

Miko's supremacy in the underworld is threatened by the appearance of a pretty new girl. This girl is not just beautiful—she is also a Ninja. There is plenty of erotic adventure in this fifth installment of the Anime series. Japanese with English subtitles. Japan, 1995, 45 mins.
VHS: S27106. $29.95.

La Blue Girl, Volume 6

There is more outrageous erotic turmoil in this sixth episode featuring Miko. Miko's nightmares spawn monsters who kidnap her classmates. Even her parents are in peril. The underworld could be invaded by intruders from an even more bizarre realm. Anime, Japanese with English subtitles. Japan, 1995, 45 mins.
VHS: S27107. $29.95.

Legend of Lemnear

Lemnear survives the Dark Lord's devastating legions and emerges as the fabled Champion of Silver. She pledges to avenge her people. Fortunately, her powers are strong enough to change the course of history. That is why the Dark Lord will do anything to possess her. Anime, Japanese with English subtitles. Japan, 1995, 45 mins.
VHS: S26899. $29.95.

Legend of Lyon: Flare 1 & 2

This adults-only, explicit animated feature from Japan follows the exploits of an invading alien army. Swordsmen Zeke and Neris, together with the psychic heroine Flare, are the only ones who stand between a lusty group of intergalactic rampagers and the castle of Lyon. Then the castle becomes host to a malevolent force. Japanese with English subtitles.
VHS: S21732. $29.95.

Legend of the Forest/ Astroboy: The Lost Episode

Tchaikovsky's Fourth Symphony plays over the first of these animated features. It accompanies a convincing and powerful series of vignettes that depict mankind's relentless destruction of nature. The lost *Astroboy* episode is unique. The show's creator ordered it to be destroyed but there was a version of it already waiting at NBC to be dubbed. It is now available on this disc. Dubbed in English. 80 mins.
Laser: LD75055. $39.95.

Lensman

This Japanese, animated, adult, action feature was based upon the popular science-fiction novels of American E.E. "Doc" Smith, which were also the supposed inspiration for *Star Wars*. With several spectacular computer-generated animation sequences. Dubbed in English. Japan, 1984.
VHS: S15409. $29.95.
Laser: CLV. LD72078. $39.95.

Lily C.A.T.

In the 23rd century a starship is sent to explore a newly discovered planet. The journey will take 23 years. Though everything is normal at first, an unseen but hungry alien invades their daily routine. Now their trip becomes a struggle for survival. Dubbed in English. 70 min.
VHS: S25067. $19.98.

Luna Varga Volume 1

Princess Luna summons a dragon to save her ancestral home and gets more than she bargained for. The ferocious creature is frightening enough, but is attached to Luna's most delicate body part. Though the creature can shrink to a vestigial tail, it still ruins the lines of even her most roomy skirts. Marriage may well be out of the question. At least there is plenty of adventure and sexual promise in this animated feature. Anime, Japanese with English subtitles. 60 mins.
VHS: S27016. $29.95.

Luna Varga Volume 2

Young Luna, her dragon Varga and her new prospective boyfriend must travel to Dunbas to save Luna's sister Vena. Together they battle invading demons, a giant sea serpent, a mad magician, a gluttonous general and a corps of shape-changing soldiers. It all makes for a crazy but comic conclusion to this Anime adventure. Japanese with English subtitles. 60 mins.
VHS: S27345. $29.95.

Lupin 3's Greatest Capers

Lupin faces off against a madman with a passion for vintage airplanes and nuclear bombs in the first of these two animated episodes. Then he must battle a robot whose terrorizing actions are wrongly attributed to Lupin himself. Dubbed in English. 50 mins.
VHS: S25065. $19.98.

Lupin 3: Tales of the Wolf

Japanese animation directed by Hayao Miyazaki and adapted from the television series about Wolf, a charismatic and brilliant cat burglar. The episode *Albatross—Wings of Death* has the debonair Wolf matching wits with a deranged billionaire threatening world-wide nuclear destruction. 30 mins.
VHS: S17742. $14.95.

Lupin 3: Tales of the Wolf, Vol. 2

Legendary artist Monkey Punch created the famed characters that star in this animated feature, directed by animator Hayao Miyazaki. Lupin III must fight a gang of ruthless impostors who are using a top secret robot to stage elaborate robberies all over Tokyo.
VHS: S21793. $14.95.

Lupin 3: The Mystery of Mamo

Lupin tries to entrance his beautiful rival Fujiko by pulling off a variety of capers from around the world. Each of these adventures, from Transylvania to Egypt, is associated with eternal life. This animated feature is dubbed in English. 67 mins.
VHS: S25069. $29.98.

Macross II

Eight years have elapsed since the action of *Macross: Do You Remember Love?*, as the descendants of the Zentradi/Meitrandi war have laid down their arms and initiated new relations with Earth. The Zentradi war commands have been suffused into the U.N. Space force, creating a tentative, peaceful co-existence.
Macross II: Volume 1.
VHS: S17003. $24.95.
Macross II: Volume 2.
VHS: S17004. $24.95.
Macross II: Volume 3.
VHS: S17005. $24.95.

Macross II: The Movie

The earth is trapped in a global battle with the Zentradi, alien giants. This animated movie picks up where the wildly popular television series left off, but is 80 years after the relative peace between Earth and Zentradi was achieved. Japanese with English subtitles. 120 mins.
VHS: S26640. $19.95.

Macross Plus

In 2040 A.D., on the colonial planet Eden, the ministry of defense is planning a new defense aircraft to battle alien invaders. Isamu Dyson is the maverick fighter pilot who must test the craft. Complications arrive in the form of an old rival and their former mutual girlfriend. Animation dubbed in English. 40 mins.
VHS: S25544. $14.95.

Macross Plus Volume 1

Anime, Japanese with English subtitles. 40 mins.
VHS: S26236. $24.95.

Macross Plus Volume 2

The sequel to the story of the colonial planet Eden, featuring the adventures of Isamu Dyson. Anime, subtitled.
VHS: S26237. $24.95.

Macross Plus Volume 3

Isamu and Guld are racing to beat the Ghost Fighter. This mysterious ship could destroy the entire Super Nova Project. Anime, Japanese with English subtitles. 40 mins.
VHS: S26238. $24.95.

Macross Plus Volume 4

The pilot-less Valkyrie Ghost X-9 has halted the Stealth Valkyrie trials, and Isamu, Yang and Guld want to get even, even if it's the last thing they ever do. Little do they know that Sharon Apple has taken over the minds of the people of Macross City (starting with Myung) and has decided to use that power to help Ghost X-9 finish Isamu, Yang and Guld off. The final episode in the *Macross Plus* series. Anime, Japanese with English subtitles. Japan, 1996, 40 mins.
VHS: S27716. $24.95.

Mad Bull Vol. 1

John "Sleepy" Estes (aka "Mad Bull") is a New York City cop, patrolling the crime-ridden streets of New York's 34th precinct with his rookie partner, Eddy Diazaburo Ban. In this first episode of the *Mad Bull* series, Eddy struggles with not only the violent forces of gangsters, robbers and drug barons, but also his partner's sometimes unorthodox methods of enforcing law and order. Anime, dubbed in English, 50 mins.
VHS: S27473. $19.95.

Mad Bull Vol. 2: The Manhattan Connection

The adventures of the notorious New York City cop John "Sleepy" Estes (aka "Mad Bull") and his partner, Eddy Diazaburo Ban, continue. When the 34th Precinct's beautiful new female detective turns out to be an old friend of Mad Bull's, she, Mad Bull and Eddy are quickly pulled into a highly dangerous case. Now Mad Bull is forced to play a dangerous game of chance that may end up costing Eddy his life. Anime, dubbed in English. Japan, 1996, 50 mins.
VHS: S27718. $19.95.

MADOX-01

The Army's plans for a new battle tank are thwarted in a budget battle with a civilian contractor turned Robot Exoskeleton. When the first production unit turns up missing, the Army tries everything to debunk the Robot's concept and install their own project. Japanese animation with English subtitles.
VHS: S16071. $24.95.

Magical Twilight

The apprentice witch Chipple must learn the ins and outs of her broom-riding sisters. Soon she sets her sights on Yoshi, but the evil little Irene is also interested in this mortal man. Can he survive the struggle between these two witches?
VHS: S21076. $29.95.

Magical Twilight 2

The teenage witches with lusty appetites, Chipple and Irene, are once again loose in Japan. On a trip to a popular resort they cause trouble over a hunk of a man, leading to a massive train derailment. This human, Tsukasa, is so enticing that soon he is the featured attraction of a resort owner. It's a sexy, comic, animated adventure. Japanese with English subtitles. 35 mins.
VHS: S26440. $29.95.

Magical Twilight 3

Studly Tsukasa and the winsome witch Chipple begin this Anime adventure at a hot springs resort. Tsukasa is continually set upon by the seductive women lurking in the hot tubs. It's a sexy, explicit tale of unquenchable desire. Uncut version, Japanese with English subtitles. 35 mins.
VHS: S27017. $29.95.

Maison Ikkoku: Ronin Blues

Yusaku Godai, a "ronin," a high school graduate who has failed his college entrance exams and must wait another year before trying again. As his new test date nears, his fellow residents at Maison Ikkoku seem intent on preventing him from studying. (And if he fails again, he's going to have to start considering other career options, like—gasp!—vocational school.) Only Kyoko Otonashi, the melancholy new manager of Maison Ikkoku, seems to believe in him. Anime, dubbed in English.
VHS: S27678. $24.95.
Kazuo Yamazaki, Japan, 1996, 60 mins.

Maison Ikkoku: Welcome to Maison Ikkoku

Set at Maison Ikkoku, a boarding house in Japan, this Anime film is based on the best selling story of a clumsy college student who falls in love with the lovely, young widow who manages his apartment building. Though it takes place in Japan, the story proves that love is universal. Dubbed in English, 52 mins.
VHS: S27457. $24.95.

Maps 1 & 2

General Tokishima and his girlfriend are in the midst of a furious battle. Two 60-story spaceships are locked in combat over a defenseless Tokyo. Beautiful Limpura and the ruthless Dye pilot these killer machines and ignore all puny attempts to save the city. Japanese with English subtitles, 60 mins.
VHS: S25674. $29.95.

Maps 3 & 4

Thousands of years ago a race of aliens left behind a great treasure. Only the Mapman can locate the powerful ancient artifact. This continuation of *Maps* has it all: beautiful women, ancient civilizations, evil invaders and stunning battle sequences. Japanese with English subtitles, 60 mins.
VHS: S25675. $29.95.

The Martyr/The Priest of Mt. Kouya

The Martyr by Akutagawa Ryunosuke and *The Priest of Mt. Kouya* by Izuma Kyoya represent great examples of Japanese literature that are now available for everyone in this animated adaptation. The first film tells of a heroic and selfless Christian, while in the second film a priest finds himself entranced by a mysterious beauty. 52 mins. Japanese with English subtitles.
VHS: S24222. $29.95.

MD Geist

Through advanced bio-technology, a race has achieved the age-old quest for the perfect warrior: the Most Dangerous Soldiers. Human in appearance, these creatures are superior in every other way, far too dangerous to be allowed to roam freely. Japanese animation, English subtitles.
VHS: S16703. $19.95.
Laser: LD74511. $34.99.
Hiroshi Negishi, Japan, 1986, 45 mins.

Megami Paradise 1

The Megami Paradise is a world where every woman is a goddess, shielded from the outside world by the purifying Astrostar. It has also long been coveted by the evil Dark Goddesses. Now Lilith, Rurubell, Stasia and Julliana must protect their home and defeat the Dark Goddesses and their followers. Anime, Japanese with English subtitles, 30 mins.
VHS: S27462. $29.95.

Megami Paradise 2

In the Megami Paradise, every woman is a goddess, protected from the corruption and evil of the outside world by the purifying Astrostar and its guardian, the Mother Megami Goddess. As the current Mother Goddess prepares for her final purification ritual before stepping down, the forces of darkness converge on Megami. Now Lilith, a new shrine-maiden candidate, and her friends Rurubell, Stasia and Julliana must protect their home and defeat the Dark Goddesses and their followers before the Megami Paradise is destroyed forever. Anime, Japanese with English subtitles, 35 mins.
VHS: S27629. $29.95.

Megazone 23—Part One

This sci-fi Anime feature follows Shogo, a young rebel who stumbles upon a secret weapon. As he tries to unravel the mystery of this war machine and avenge the death of a friend, political intrigues and government plots rear up. He may very well find the knowledge he seeks, but at what price? Dubbed in English. 80 mins.
VHS: S26380. $29.98.

Mermaid's Scar

Adapted from Rumiko Takahashi's *Rumic World* collection, this clever Japanese animation considers the tale of immortality of those who partake of the mermaid's flesh. Two ageless warriors, the charismatic Yuta and the beautiful Mana, become despondent and undertake a mythic journey through Japan to end their overdue lives. English dubbed. 52 mins.
VHS: S20148. $19.95.

Metal Fighters Miku

By the year 2061, wrestling, perhaps the world's oldest and most universal sport, has also become the world's most popular. Women's Neo Pro-Wrestling brings body slamming into the future with high tech, robot suits. A group of mechanized Amazons soon find themselves facing a new threat, however. Their promoter wants to make them into pop stars. But newcomer Miku just wants to be the greatest wrestler ever. This Anime adventure series is subtitled in English.
Volume 1, Episodes 1, 2 & 3. 90 mins.
VHS: S26270. $24.95.
Volume 2, Episodes 4 & 5. 60 mins.
VHS: S26271. $24.95.
Volume 3, Episodes 6 & 7. 60 mins.
VHS: S26272. $24.95.
Volume 4, Episodes 8 & 9. 60 mins.
VHS: S26273. $24.95.
Volume 5, Episodes 10 & 11. 60 mins.
VHS: S26274. $24.95.
Volume 6, Episodes 12 & 13. 60 mins.
VHS: S26275. $24.95.
Akiyuki Shinbo, Japan, 1994.

Metal Skin Panic Madox-01

In this Anime feature, a prototype battle tank has been lost in Tokyo. Kouji, a teenage boy, finds the fighter and is trapped inside the fully armed machine before he realizes what it can do. All of Tokyo stands by in terror as the army sends other prototypes to retrieve Madox-01. Kouji just wants to see his girlfriend one more time. Dubbed in English.
VHS: S26637. $19.95.

Mighty Space Miners

This sci-fi anime adventure shows a group of miners trapped on an asteroid. Their mission to capture Haley's Comet is thrown off course by unforeseen disaster. Now they must struggle just to stay alive stranded in an unstable deep space environment. Japanese with English subtitles. 60 mins.
VHS: S26438. $29.95.

Moldiver, Volume 1: Metaforce

A young inventor creates the "Mol" unit, which bestows super-human qualities on the wearer. This episode introduces Captain Tokyo, Mirai and the evil Dr. Machinegal and his machine gals. Subtitled. 30 mins.
VHS: S23067. $24.98.
Laser: LD74647. $34.95.

Moldiver, Volume 2: Overzone

The space shuttle that Hiroshi Ozora and his brother Nozomu are on is hijacked by Machinegal, in yet another of his evil plans. Hurry up Moldiver. The second episode of this headliner science fiction comedy is about to blast off. Subtitled. 30 mins.
VHS: S23068. $24.98.
Laser: LD74648. $34.95.

Moldiver, Volume 3: Longing

An ecstatic Mirai goes to the meeting place of the Hachi dog monument. There the Machinegal dolls gather after tracking her Mol reaction, and a tremendous battle ensues over Tokyo. A great action and love comedy series continues. Subtitled. 30 mins.
VHS: S23069. $24.98.
Laser: LD74649. $34.95.

Moldiver, Volume 4: Destruction

Professor Amagi directs the *Yamato* salvage for the upcoming "ZIC Battleship Yamato's 100 Year Celebration." His actual motive is to continue his Godfather's study, "The Ultra Dimension System," which sank with the *Yamato* 100 years before. Subtitled. 30 mins.
VHS: S23070. $24.98.
Laser: LD74650. $34.95.

Moldiver, Volume 5: Intruder

With Hiroshi's efforts the Mol unit is successfully divided into #1 and #2. Mirai comes face-to-face with Machinegal's Superdolls, who plan to stop the project from going forward. Also a mysterious, new and very powerful "Intruder" appears. Subtitled. 30 mins.
VHS: S23071. $24.98.
Laser: LD74651. $34.95.

Moldiver, Volume 6: Verity

The dimension-bound *Sakigaki* continues to speed up in preparation for launch. However, Moldiver III appears, trying to stop the proceedings. Mirai is in her biggest crisis yet. The *Sakigake* and its mission are threatened. Subtitled. 30 mins.
VHS: S23072. $24.98.
Laser: LD74652. $34.95.

Nadia Movie Compilation

Four Japanese animated works distilled from the Nadia collection, which were inspired by Jules Verne's *20,000 Leagues under the Sea*. The collection includes *The Girl on the Eiffel Tower*, *The Little Fugitives*, *The Mysterious Sea Monsters* and *Nautilus to the Rescue*. English and Japanese with English subtitles. 110 mins.
Laser: LD71943. $39.95.

Neo-Tokyo

Three fantastic adventures by Japan's top animation artists including *Labyrinth*, directed by Rin Taro; *The Running Man*, featured on MTV's *Liquid Television*, a cyberpunk thriller; and *The Order to Stop Construction*, a grim sci-fi comedy in which a bureaucrat manages robots deep in the Amazon. 50 mins. English language version.
Laser: LD75031. $34.99.

New Angel

Two high school nerds spot a beautiful new girl at school. When they try to find out more about her, they realize she doesn't really exist. She's a ghost. They try to conjure her with a medium and all hell breaks loose. This uncut version contains explicit sexual footage. Japanese with English subtitles. 50 mins.
VHS: S25673. $29.95.

New Angel 2

This sexy, comic, animated adventure follows the continuing erotic life of Keisuke. After scoring with a ghost, he returns to school where a new rival, a lecherous photographer, and a girl who threatens to jump from the roof compete for his attention. Fortunately, he has three beautiful girls to complicate matters further. Japanese with English subtitles. 35 mins.
VHS: S26441. $29.95.

New Angel 3

This sexy and explicit Anime feature follows the antics of two nerdy guys at a mountain resort. There they are joined by the luscious Keisuke, who is rather combative, and by Naomi, who is not above showing a little skin to get her way. Naomi finds playing tennis without wearing panties can improve her score tremendously. Uncut version, Japanese with English subtitles. 35 mins.
VHS: S27018. $29.95.

New Angel 4

Keisuke is overjoyed when both his and Shizuka's parents leave the country. Things get even better when Shizuka realizes she has accidentally received a suitcase of men's lingerie. This adult Anime film contains sex and nudity. Anime, Japanese with English subtitles. 35 mins.
VHS: S27465. $29.95.

New Cutey Honey Volume 4

Only one woman can stop the evil forces of Panther Zora. Fortunately, Cutey has an entire arsenal of lovely but lethal android bodies. Backed by the psychotic Hayami family, Cutey Honey brings gratuitous violence and sex into a new level of animated fun. Anime, Japanese with English subtitles. 60 mins.
VHS: S27014. $29.95.

New Dominion Tank Police: Volume Two

Leona and her tank Dominion are back in this pair of animated episodes. In both, she must battle the evils of drugs which threaten the citizens of Newport City through chemical means and gang warfare. Includes episode 3, "Limit the Tube Way," and episode 4, "The Chase (Bonaparte in the Mist)." Anime, dubbed in English, 60 mins.
VHS: S26243. $14.95.

New Dominion Tank Police: Volume Three

In Episode 5, *Conflict City*, Leona and Brenten rescue the mayor from a corporate robot, whose identity hints at a disturbing plot. Then in Episode 6, *End the Dreaming*, the tank police are embroiled in a final cataclysmic battle that ends the series. Dubbed in English, 60 mins.
VHS: S26378. $14.95.

Night on the Galactic Railroad

Giovanni is a poor boy who escapes his life of hardship by boarding a mysterious galactic train. This magical and symbol-laden fable is beautifully animated. It is based on the classic 1927 Japanese novel by Miyazawa Kenji. One night while watching the stars in the sky, Giovanni sees a galactic train appear. Together with his friend Campanella, Giovanni follows the train and explores the magical reaches of the Milky Way. Ultimately it is a tale of inner discovery. Anime, Japanese with English subtitles.
VHS: S27453. $29.95.
Gisaburo Sugii, Japan, 1985, 115 mins.

Ninja Scroll

This explicit and violent Anime epic follows a group of Ninjas sent to a village ravaged by an epidemic. There is no disease, only the terror of the Eight Devils of Kimon. They are part of an awful plot that seeks to bring back a despotic ruler. Japanese with English subtitles, partial nudity, 90 mins.
VHS: S25724. $19.95.

Odin: Photon Space Sailor Starlight

In 2099 the futuristic spacecraft *Starlight* and its crew of experienced officers and impetuous young trainees prepare its daring odyssey through unexplored oceans, awaiting danger and excitement in this animation series created by Yoshinobu Nishizaki, author of *Starblazers*. 139 mins. Japanese with English subtitles.
VHS: S18426. $19.95.
Laser: LD74513. $49.99.

Ogre Slayer

As a woman's corpse cools a young boy is born out of her dead body. The result of this unnatural birth is an ogre, destined to kill his own kind in the belief that when all ogres are extinct he will be human. This animated adventure charts his bloody progress. Dubbed in English. 60 mins.
VHS: S26425. $24.95.

Ogre Slayer 2: Grim Fairy Tales

In the first episode, *Chapter of the Ogre Witch*, only the Ogre Slayer can help a mother who has made a terrible mistake. She prayed for a child at an accursed temple inhabited by an ogre. The ogre will ultimately claim any child wished for at this temple. In the second episode, *Chapter of an Ogre's Lament*, the Ogre Slayer travels back to the Meiji Restoration period to battle an ancient monster. Dubbed in English.
VHS: S27091. $24.95.
Yoshio Kato, Japan, 1995, 60 mins.

Oh My Goddess!

Young college freshman Morisato Keiichi finds more than he expected when he dials for dinner. Before long he ends up living with a genuine goddess called Belldandy. Things could get more serious if only he had the courage to stand up to her two sisters, Urd and Skuld. This Anime series leads the character through several racy and bizarre adventures.
Volume 1: Moonlight and Cherry Blossoms.
VHS: S21181. $19.95.
Volume 2: Midsummer Night's Dream.
VHS: S21182. $19.95.
Volume 3: Burning Hearts on the Road.
VHS: S21183. $19.95.
Volume 4: Evergreen Holy Night.
VHS: S21184. $19.95.
Volume 5: For the Goddess of Love.
VHS: S21185. $19.95.

Oh My Goddess! Collector's Suite

It all begins with a call for takeout that accidentally conjures up a beautiful goddess. This Anime boxed set of five videos follows the wacky, sexy, romantic adventures that ensue between this divinity and her ordinary mortal friend. Japanese with English subtitles, partial nudity.
VHS: S25718. $95.00.

Oh My Goddess! Hybrid LD #1

This hybrid Anime laser disc contains the *Oh My Goddess!* episodes *Moonlight and Cherry Blossoms* and *Midsummer Night's Dream*. In the first episode, Keiichi calls for take-out food and gets a Goddess instead. Then, in *Midsummer Night's Dream*, Keiichi can't decide whether to make the moves on a Goddess or not. To make matters worse, Belldandy's sister Goddesses are driving everyone crazy and no one seems to be able to do anything about it. All this and more is in Kousuke Fujishima's *Oh My Goddess!*.
Laser: LD75576. $39.95.
Kousuke Fujishima, Japan, 1993, 58 mins.

Orguss

Set in the year 2062, *Orguss* concerns the struggle and control of the Orbital Elevator between Earth's two superpowers. Whoever takes possession can dictate the world's political and economic structures. Against this backdrop a young fighter pilot has been assigned to destroy the elevator. Animated.
Orguss: Volume 1.
VHS: S16998. $29.95.
Orguss: Volume 2.
VHS: S17001. $24.95.
Orguss: Volume 3.
VHS: S17002. $24.95.
Orguss: Volume 4.
VHS: S18340. $24.95.
Orguss: Volume 5.
VHS: S19697. $24.95.
Orguss: Volume 6.
VHS: S19698. $24.95.
Orguss: Volume 7.
VHS: S20481. $24.95.
Orguss: Volume 8.
VHS: S20482. $24.95.

Orguss 02, Vol. 1

It's been 200 years since the space/time collapse, and a civilization discovers the advanced technology of the Orguss. A fierce battle ensues for world domination as Libera and Zafrim, the two major powers, fight to rule the planet. The two episodes are *The Fool's Choice* and *Where Angles Fear to Tread*.
VHS: S23483. $14.95.

Orguss 02, Vol. 2

Two desperate fighters have been left alone in the middle of a distant inferno. The only problem is, they don't trust each other. If they are going to survive however, they must work together. When one of the two is captured, her new friend in combat comes to her aid. Dubbed in English. 45 mins.
VHS: S25725. $14.95.

Orguss 02, Vol. 3

Episodes five and six of this animated series track the continuing adventures of Naturama. She relies on her psychic powers to help her avoid disaster at the hands of a variety of enemies as she seeks to save the world from the time and space oscillation bomb. Dubbed in English. 45 mins.
VHS: S26377. $14.95.

Otaku No Video

A captivating mock documentary that mixes stylized animation sequences with interviews with hard core fans. The result is a fictionalized history of the Japanese animation studio Gainax. Includes the two episodes *Otaku No Video* and *More Otaku No Video*. Japanese with English subtitles.
VHS: S18348. $39.95.

Outlanders

Johji Manabe's witty science fiction animation work. The plot concerns an unruly band of aliens who are threatening human life, until the daughter of its leader, Princess Kahm, falls for a photojournalist. The daughter wages war against her father's monstrous fleet of elite warriors in an enormous intergalactic space battle. English dubbed. 50 mins.
VHS: S19340. $24.95.

Patlabor 1

In 1999, Tokyo police rely on robots called Labors to patrol the streets. A suicide at the construction site of the Babylon project signals a new crisis. Someone has targeted the Labors with a virus. The Babylon Project tower is the site that must be destroyed in order to stop the virus and save the city. Anime, Japanese with English subtitles. 118 mins.
VHS: S26242. $24.95.

Patlabor 2

In 2002, a United Nations labor team is destroyed. This act sends shockwaves through the military and political power structures of Japan. Police captains Goto and Nagumo do all they can to resist the military takeover, but Nagumo's chief foe is her former teacher and lover, Tsuge. Success ultimately demands betrayal. Anime, Japanese with English subtitles, 120 mins.
VHS: S26765. $29.95.

Phantom Quest Corp., Volume 1

The Phantom Quest Corp. is a ghost busting company in Tokyo. President and CEO Ayaki works with her staff to challenge the supernatural. Includes episodes *Kiss of Fire* and *End of the World*. Japanese with English subtitles, 60 mins.
VHS: S24573. $29.98.
Laser: LD74828. $39.98.

Phantom Quest Corp., Volume 2

Two new episodes detail the adventures of the ghost-busting company Phantom Quest. Ayaka Kisaragi is the CEO who leads her crew on dangerous supernatural battles. Includes episodes *Love Me Tender* and *Lover Come Back to Me*. Anime, Japanese with English subtitles. 60 mins.
VHS: S25679. $29.98.
Laser: LD74992. $39.98.

Planet Busters

On a forgotten planet, a boy, a girl, two bounty hunters and an army of death-dealing robots come together for one wild chase after another. A wild animated feature that leads our heroes on a journey to solve the greatest mystery of the universe. Japan, 80 mins.
VHS: S16643. $29.95.

Plastic Little: The Adventures of Captain Tita

Yietta is a beautiful planet about to free itself after years of indebtedness to the Federation. The entire planet is set to embark upon a promising future in tourism when a plot is uncovered that would jeopardize these plans. Tita, a 17-year-old tomboy, finds herself in the middle of this dastardly plot. Japanese animation with English subtitles. 45 mins.
VHS: S21110. $34.95.

Please Save My Earth, Vol. 1

Alice has always been loved by plants and animals. This unique girl finds herself enmeshed in a fantastic story that starts with the dreams of her classmates. Their dreams involve scientists collecting data about the Earth from a base on the moon. When Alice awakes from the exact same dream, the fantasy takes a dark turn. Anime, dubbed in English. Japan, 1994, 65 mins.
VHS: S27321. $24.95.

Princess Minerva

A tournament for warrior women will reward the winning combatant with enough treasures to make her a princess. Unfortunately Minerva is already a princess but she would rather battle through dangerous adventures. A kidnapping arises to give her exactly the opportunity to set off with a band of lovely warriors. Anime, Japanese with English subtitles, 45 mins.
VHS: S25022. $29.95.

The Professional: Golgo 13

The son of a powerful businessman is brutally assassinated by Duke Togo, a hitman known as Golgo 13, and the father will stop at nothing until he exacts his vengeance. In a perverse reversal, Golgo is now on the run for his life.
VHS: S19486. $19.98.

Project A-ko 1

Imagine an unresolved dispute years in the making, a group of aliens looking for a lost Princess, a power-hungry schoolmate and a truly remarkable soundtrack!
English Language Version.
VHS: S17842. $19.95.
Japanese with English Subtitles.
VHS: S16057. $39.95.
Laser: LD71831. $39.95.

Project A-ko 2: Plot of the Daitokuji Financial Group

In this sci-fi animated thriller the girls have big plans for summer vacation, including A-ko's desire to lose weight and B-ko's intricate designs for the attention of C-ko, who seems intent only on shopping. When B-ko's father uses his daughter's plans for economic espionage, the plot takes on a decidedly sinister character.
Japanese With English subtitles.
VHS: S21111. $29.95.
English Dubbed Version.
VHS: S21320. $19.95.

Project A-ko 3: Cinderella Rhapsody

The girls are rivals once again in this continuation of the animated series *Project A-ko*. Only this time it's over the handsome K. who has the perfect outfit in mind, but it could all be a mistake—at least that's what B-ko hopes. Japanese with English subtitles. 50 mins.
VHS: S21112. $29.95.
Laser: LD74835. $34.99.

Project A-ko 4: Final

The Japanamation adventure continues to an exciting conclusion in this final episode. A hexagram found during an archeological dig is simultaneously discovered on a fleet of spaceships heading towards Earth. This same symbol mysteriously is found on a seductive woman looking for a prospective husband. The connection between these three sightings is the basis for a fun-filled suspense story. 59 mins. Dubbed in English.
VHS: S22767. $19.95.
Japanese with English subtitles.
VHS: S21113. $29.95.

Project A-ko versus Battle 1: Grey Side

C-ko's birthday is interrupted when she is kidnapped from her father's spaceship. Her kidnappers fumble and let her get away, leaving her to be found by A-ko and B-ko. Before they can collect their reward however, C-ko is kidnapped once again in this sci-fi animated feature. Japanese with English subtitles. 54 mins.
VHS: S21114. $29.95.
Laser: C.LV. LD75047. $34.95.

Project A-ko versus Battle 2: Blue Side

The travails of A-ko, B-ko and C-ko continue in this sci-fi animated feature. As they struggle to return to normalcy, a startling fact about C-ko's origins reveals that she may have more in common with her kidnappers than previously believed. Japanese with English subtitles. 52 mins.
VHS: S21115. $29.95.
Laser: LD75292. $34.98.

Ranma 1/2 Collector's Edition: The OVAs, Volume 1

Three complete episodes from the popular Anime series featuring Ranma are included on this video: *Shampoo's Sudden Switch!* *The Curse of the Contrary Jewel; Tendo Family Christmas Scramble* and *Akane vs. Ranma! I'll Be the One to Inherit Mother's Recipes*. Japanese with English subtitles, 90 mins.
VHS: S26854. $34.95.

Ranma 1/2 Collector's Edition: The OVAs, Volume 2

Half guy and half girl, Ranma toughs it out through three episodes of adventures, joined on this single video. Though he is a high school student, this Anime character finds himself/herself enmeshed in battle after battle. Includes the episodes *Stormy Weather Comes to School! Growing Up with Miss Hinako; The One to Carry On, Part One;* and *The One to Carry On, Part Two*. Anime, Japanese with English Subtitles.
VHS: S26897. $34.95.
Junji Nishimura, Japan, 1995, 90 mins.

Ranma 1/2 OVA Series: Faster, Kasumi! Kill! Kill!

First, in *Hell Hath No Fury Like Kasumi Scorned!*, when Happosai goes on another one of his panty raids, he inadvertently frees an oni (the Japanese word for ogre). The oni quickly takes off, possessing person after person in his wake, until he settles inside Kasumi, the eldest Tendo daughter. Then, in *The Two Akanes*, *"Ranma, Look at Me!"*, Ranma and his family visit a hot springs resort where Ranma accidentally knocks over and breaks an ancestral doll which turns out to be cursed. Now the doll's spirit possesses Akane (leaving her spirit trapped inside the doll) and seeks out its revenge on Ranma. Anime, dubbed in English.
VHS: S27677. $29.95.
Junji Nishimura, Japan, 1996, 65 mins.

Ranma 1/2 OVA Series: Like Water for Ranma

Tragedy is imminent as Akane takes over the cooking chores for older sister Kasumi. With the help of mother's recipes what could go wrong? Meanwhile, it looks like it will be head-to-head comedic competition between Ranma and discipline-minded Miss Hinako. A Japanamation feature, dubbed. 60 mins.
VHS: S21838. $34.95.
Laser: LD75519. $39.95.

Ranma 1/2 OVA Series: One Grew Over the Kuno's Nest

In the first episode, *Team Ranma vs. The Legendary Phoenix*, Kuno hopes to defeat Ranma with the Phoenix egg, but it hatches and he finds himself joined with this powerful creature. Then, in *Oh, Cursed Tunnel of Lost Love! Let My Love Be Forever*, Ranma travels to a tunnel of love with legendary amorous influence. Dubbed in English.
VHS: S27090. $29.95.
Junji Nishimura, Japan, 1995, 60 mins.

Ranma 1/2 The Collector's Edition, Volume 1

Three episodes featuring Ranma and his/her sex changing form are joined on this video: *The Strange Stranger from China, School Is No Place for Horsing Around* and *A Sudden Storm of Love...Hey Wait a Minute!*. These stories combine humor, adventure and sexual appeal. Japanese with English subtitles.
VHS: S27151. $34.95.
Tsutomu Shibayama, Japan, 1995, 75 mins.

Ranma 1/2 The Collector's Edition, Volume 3

Now the Anime hit Ranma is available in Japanese with English subtitles. Three complete episodes full of action and humor are included. 75 mins.
VHS: S25681. $34.95.

Ranma 1/2 The Collector's Edition, Volume 5

Three complete TV episodes detailing Ranma's adventures are joined on this volume. Anime dubbed in English, 75 mins.
VHS: S25979. $34.95.

Ranma 1/2 The Collector's Edition, Volume 6

The beautiful animated character Shampoo has decided to wash Ranma out of Akane's memory with a secret memory loss soap. She will then restore Ranma's memory only if he/she meets her price. This premise sets up scenario featuring a series of funny, eventful memories for both Ranma and his/her father. Japanese with English subtitles. 75 mins.
VHS: S26641. $34.95.

Ranma 1/2 The Movie 2 Collector's Edition: Nihao My Concubine

Everyone is wearing a push-up bra and three-inch heels in this animated adventure—even Ranma. It all begins when Ranma is shipwrecked on a desert island. There is a prince on the island who is kidnapping girls in search of the perfect bride, including Akane. Ranma decides to go undercover and comes up against concubine martial arts vixens. Anime, Japanese with English subtitles, 60 mins.
VHS: S27458. $34.95.

Ranma 1/2 The Movie: Big Trouble in Nekonron China

Gender-bending superstar Rumiko Takahashi is at the center of this action/romance animated feature. A strange girl appears at Rumiko's martial arts school with a story of a missing document that promises happiness to whoever holds it. Before long the whole school is off to a prince's castle and lost in adventure. 74 mins.
VHS: S20904. $34.95.

Ranma 1/2, Desperately Seeking Shampoo

In this comic animation work, Shampoo's great-grandmother Cologne endows her with a special brooch that has the capacity to alter people's attitudes and emotions. The brooch transforms love into hate. English dubbed. 52 mins.
VHS: S19892. $34.95.

Ranma 1/2, TV Series Volume 1

Japanese animation from the gifted Rumiko Takahashi. Mr. Tendo, the owner of a martial arts studio, awaits the return of Ranma and his friend Genma. He is shocked to discover the two have been transformed into a girl and panda by an ancient Chinese curse. English dubbed. 52 mins.
VHS: S20149. $29.95.

Ranma 1/2, TV Series Volume 2

Placed under an ancient Chinese curse, Ranma and his friend Genma metamorphose into a girl and panda. Forced to resume their lives, Ranma, under the guise of his female persona, is suddenly the most popular girl in high school, an honor formerly reserved for Akane. English dubbed. 50 mins.
VHS: S20150. $29.95.

Ranma 1/2, TV Series Volume 3

Ranma is transformed into a beautiful young woman when he's placed under an ancient Chinese spell. This complicates not only his day-to-day activities, but his intended marriage to Akane. English dubbed. 50 mins.
VHS: S20151. $29.95.

Ranma 1/2, TV Series Volume 4

Ryogi Hibiki makes his first appearance in this volume of the animated series. This gifted martial arts expert has a poor sense of direction and a grudge against Ranma. It is a combination that leads to a proposed match between the two, which promises to be quite exciting, providing Ryogi can find the agreed-upon place. Dubbed in English. 52 mins.
VHS: S20905. $34.95.

Ranma 1/2, TV Series Volume 5

In this installment of the animated series Akane learns that the gender-bending Ranma is not always a jerk, while Ranma realizes that his problems with Ryoga cannot be solved by bread alone and Ryoga learns to fear the rain. Dubbed in English, 50 mins.
VHS: S20906. $29.95.

Ranma 1/2, TV Series Volume 6

Two episodes, 11 and 12, of this Anime series are joined on this video. Ranma is about to be betrothed to Akane, but Akane is consumed with a martial arts competition. A strange and unforseen competitor appears and throws everyone's plans off kilter. Perhaps if Ranma's beautiful alter ego appears, disaster can be averted. Anime, dubbed in English.
VHS: S24894. $29.95.
Tsutomu Shibayama, Japan, 52 mins.

Ranma 1/2, TV Series Volume 7

Dr. Tofu is under pressure from his mother to marry. Akane has a difficult task cut out for her. She longs for Dr. Tofu, but first she must convince his mother that she would make a good daughter-in-law. Contains episodes 13 and 14. Anime, dubbed in English, 50 mins.
VHS: S24893. $34.95.

Ranma 1/2, TV Series Volume 8

In episode 15, Ranma discovers that turning into a girl gives him some unexpected freedom. Of course he didn't count on a battle that leads either to marriage or, if you're a man, or death, if you're a woman. Then Shampoo decides to get Ranma out of Akane's hair with a secret memory-erasing shampoo. Ranma is soon at the mercy of Shampoo. Can he pay her price to retrieve a forgotten past? Dubbed in English, 50 mins.
VHS: S23082. $29.95.

Ranma 1/2, TV Series Volume 9

Akane still cannot remember Ranma. Ranma can get the shampoo that will restore the memory of Akane if he agrees to hurt female Ranma. Of course, he could also use Ryoga's help. In the next episode, Ranma is plunged into an adventure in China. Dubbed in English. 50 mins.
VHS: S23334. $29.95.

Ranma 1/2: Anything Goes Martial Arts

Rumiko Takahashi continues his animated series of martial arts sex comedies with this the most recent in the Ranma episodes. Ice Princess Azusa hatches a kidnapping scheme that leads to a martial arts figure skating fight to the finish. Dubbed in English. 52 mins.
VHS: S23760. $24.95.

Ranma 1/2: Anything Goes Martial Arts: "Goodbye Girl-Type"

Two episodes of Anime featuring Ranma are joined on this video. The first, *Kuno's House of Gadgets! Guests Check In, But They Don't Check Out*, concerns an ancient curse and a brother/ sister pair noted for their physical prowess. In the second episode, *Goodbye Girl-Type*, Ranma continues his struggle against the brother/sister team, which is made more difficult by complications like an extensive underwear collection. Dubbed in English. 45 mins.
VHS: S26853. $24.95.

Ranma 1/2: Anything Goes Martial Arts: It's Fast or It's Free

First, in *P-Chan Explodes! The Icy Fountain of Love*, the Arts Figure Skating Challenge continues, with Ryoga plotting to break up the team of Ranma and Akane so he can have Akane for himself. Unfortunately, Ryoga instead finds himself skating pairs with Girl-Type Ranma, and skating on very thin ice at that. Then, in *Clash of the Delivery Girls! The Martial Arts Takeout Race*, an old man named Genma shows up on the Tendo doorstep, claiming to be the long-lost father who traded infant Ranma for some fish and two pickles. Now if Ranma wants to remain heir of Anything Goes Martial Arts, Akane has to win the Martial Arts Restaurant Takeout Race. Unfortunately, it seems she's going to be competing against Kaori, Ranma's latest fiancee and the Daikoku School of Martial Arts Restaurant Takeout champion. Anime, Japanese with English subtitles.
VHS: S27679. $29.95.
Koji Sawai, Japan, 1996, 52 mins.

Ranma 1/2: Anything Goes Martial Arts: Tough Cookies

Once again, the half guy, half girl Ranma is trapped in a teenage world made all the more complicated by his mysterious gender instability. Akane wants him to eat her home made cookies, but Kodachi "Black Rose" Kuno has other ideas in mind. Indigestion or scandal could result from this competition for Ranma's attention. Features the episodes *It's a Fine Line Between Pleasure and Pain* and *S.O.S.! The Wrath of Happosai*. Anime, dubbed in English.
VHS: S26896. $24.95.
Tsutomu Shibayama, Japan, 1995, 52 mins.

Ranma 1/2: Chestnuts Roasting on an Open Fire

Ranma is still struggling to become a man again. If that is not enough of a problem, he is also afflicted with "Full Body Cat Tongue," which makes the body so sensitive to heat that even lukewarm water is boiling hot. Only the Phoenix Pill can solve all his troubles and get him out of a job at the infamous Cat Cafe. Anime dubbed in English, 55 mins.
VHS: S26036. $24.95.

Ranma 1/2: Cold Competition

Ranma's affliction, the "Full Body Cat Tongue," makes the body so sensitive to heat that even lukewarm water is boiling hot. In these two episodes he tries to win the Martial Arts Snowman-Carry Race and romance Shampoo all in order to convince Shampoo's great grandmother to give him the Phoenix Pill. Then he could get out of his job at the infamous Cat Cafe. Anime dubbed in English, 52 mins.
VHS: S25978. $24.95.

Ranma 1/2: Fowl Play

It all begins when a young martial arts expert and his father are transformed by falling into a mysterious pool. Now water will make the father into a panda and turn the son into a beautiful woman. Two episodes from this sci-fi adventure series are included here, *The Abduction of Akane* and *Mousse! To Lose Is to Win* Dubbed in English. 60 mins.
VHS: S26426. $24.95.

Ranma 1/2: Ranma and Juliet

In the first segment, *Kissing Is Such Sweet Sorrow! The Taking of Akane's Lips*, Akane is excited about her upcoming stage debut as Juliet until she finds out who's playing Romeo. In *Bathhouse Battle! We're on Some Hot Water Now*, Ranma and Co. set out for a therapeutic bath with disastrous consequences. Anime. Dubbed in English. 52 mins.
VHS: S27320. $24.95.

Ranma 1/2: The Breaking Point

This video contains two Anime episodes of Ranma's adventures: *Ranma Trains on Mt. Terror* and *The Breaking Point! Ryoga's Great Revenge*. Together these stories offer plenty of action between Ranma and his rival, Ryoga. Dubbed in English. 52 mins.
VHS: S26248. $24.95.

Ranma 1/2: The Evil Wakes

Ranma and his/her father are forever having strange comic adventures related to their transformations. Now a series of bad omens portend the arrival of a new, but very ancient foe. Happosai is a lecherous old goat of a demon who also happens to be a martial arts master with important ties to Ranma's father. Dubbed in English. 52 mins.
VHS: S26629. $24.95.

Ranma 1/2: Ukyo Can Cook

Furinkan High School has a new transfer student, Ukyo, who is a spatula-wielding warrior par excellence. But a plot is stewing, as this new student has a grudge against Ranma that extends all the way back to the earliest days of his childhood. Dubbed in English. 52 mins.
VHS: S27456. $24.95.

Raven Tengu Kabuto: The Golden-Eyed Beast

A sinister creation from master technician Buichi Terasawa (*Space Adventure Cobra*) focuses on Kabuto, a fusion of traditional Japanese mythology and outlaw cyberpunk technology. Japanese with English subtitles. 45 mins.
VHS: S18339. $34.95.

Record of Lodoss War, Gift Box

This wide-ranging epic fantasy spans a cosmos peopled by fantastic creatures with great powers. They are engaged in a tremendous struggle, the outcome of which will affect the universe. It's an anime feature series with stunning imagery, compelling characters and gruesome monsters. Japanese with English subtitles. Six volumes.
VHS: S24231. $129.95.
Akinori Nagaoka/Shigeto Makino/Katsuhisa Yamada, et al., Japan, 1990, 355 mins.

Record of Lodoss War, Volume 1 (Episodes 1-3)

Lodoss is cursed by an evil presence that no one could have conceived of in its entirety. As it awakes, six are drawn together to battle against it. Though they scarcely know one another, they are destined to become both heroes and friends. Includes episode 1, *Prologue to the Legend*, episode 2, *Blazing Departure* and episode 3, *The Black Knight*. Anime. Japanese with English subtitles. 80 mins.
VHS: S23765. $29.95.
Akinori Nagaoka/Shigeto Makino/Katsuhisa Yamada, Japan, 1990, 355 mins.

Record of Lodoss War, Volume 2 (Episodes 4 & 5)

Amidst the turmoil accompanying the invasion of Lodoss, intrigues are put in motion. Karla, the "Gray Witch," tries to kidnap the princess, while her ally Kashue is targeted for assassination. Anime. Japanese with English subtitles. 55 mins.
VHS: S23766. $29.95.

Record of Lodoss War, Volume 3 (Episodes 6 & 7)

Karla's plan for Lodoss mystifies everyone. There is no time to ponder her schemes however, because the king of the Holy Knights and the king of the Black Knights are engaged in a duel to the death. Anime. Japanese with English subtitles. 55 mins.
VHS: S23767. $29.95.

Record of Lodoss War, Volume 4 (Episodes 8 & 9)

Though Lodoss is caught up in insoluble turmoil, Karla's motivations become clear at last. Ashram, the king of the Black Knights, makes one last attempt to overcome any obstacle to his dastardly plans. Anime. Japanese with English subtitles. 55 mins.
VHS: S23768. $29.95.

Record of Lodoss War, Volume 5 (Episodes 10 & 11)

At the center of the battle a holy relic emerges that guarantees triumph. The Scepter of Domination is guarded by a formidable force, however: the Shooting Star. Anime. Japanese with English subtitles. 55 mins.
VHS: S23769. $29.95.

Record of Lodoss War, Volume 6 (Episodes 12 & 13)

Battles rage as even more powerful forces are unleashed. The trump card of terror is the dragon Narse. Man battles wizard, and dragon fights dragon in this final clash between good and evil. Anime. Japanese with English subtitles. 55 mins.
VHS: S23770. $29.95.

Rei Rei—Original Version

This adult fantasy animation features Kaguya, a powerful and playful being that can manipulate reality to correspond with her perverse sense of humor. Graphic sex and violence permeate the worlds she creates whether they are based on computer games or parts of the human anatomy. Animation inspired by the graphics of Toshimitsu Shimizu. Japanese with English subtitles. 60 mins.
VHS: S20619. $34.95.

Rei Rei—The Special Edition

The titilating Anime saga of Kaguya, a powerful creature who can manipulate the fabric of reality, has been tamed down for this more presentable edition. Her erotic misadventures are still visible, only everything is no longer fully on display. Now she is naughty, powerful and accessible for wider audiences. Japanese with English subtitles.
VHS: S25021. $29.95.

Renegade Force

A maverick security force enlists a karate champion to operate a powerful, high-tech, armed robot called Magnon. In conjunction with its sister ship, the Magnetta, they battle deadly and sinister aliens for control of the universe. 90 mins.
VHS: S18265. $29.95.

Return of the Dinosaurs

A mysterious comet crash lands on Earth, causing a gravitational pull that plunges the planet back into the prehistoric age and occasions the return of the dinosaurs. When the climate heals the dinosaurs begin dying out and the international community must act to preserve these majestic, astounding animals from certain death. Japanese animation wizard Akira Tsuburaya created this work. 70 mins.
VHS: S17523. $19.99.

RG Veda, Part 1

In this inventive Japanese animated work, set off by some stunning action sequences, the brutal general Taishakuten has murdered the valued Tentei and declared power over the universe. Only one threat remains to his throne, a six-pointed star that rises in the heavens and repositions the world in the golden age. Japanese with English subtitles.
VHS: S19884. $29.95.

RG Veda, Part 2

This animated feature is based on the Hindu story *Rig Veda*. It is prophesied that only the combined strength of six warriors can defeat the tyrannical general who has seized control of the universe. Only five of them have come together. Their quest for the sixth leads them on a dangerous journey into the heart of the tyrant's castle. Japanese with English subtitles. 41 mins.
VHS: S20864. $29.95.
Laser: LD74834. $34.99.

Rhea Gall Force

The Solnoid were annihilated along with their enemies at the battle of Sigma Narse. But their surviving descendants on Earth are about to experience the sad destiny predicted for this once mighty race. World wars have devastated the planet, leaving large killing machines in charge. Only evacuation to Mars base holds any promise for continued survival.
VHS: S21839. $29.95.
Laser: CLV. LD75049. $34.95.

Riding Bean

Got a problem? Call Bean Bandit, the freelance Mr. Fix-all. His latest mission is simple: play chauffeur to a little girl for a few thousand credits. What Bean does not count on is that the assignment looks like a shady kidnapping. If he doesn't play his cards right, he may end up dead! Animated.
Dubbed in English.
VHS: S20752. $19.95.
Japanese with English subtitles.
VHS: S16072. $34.95.

A Roadside Stone, Parts 1 & 2

Goichi is born into a poverty stricken family and must learn to deal with hardship from an early age. Through it all, he diligently struggles to overcome the most severe circumstances. An animated feature. Japanese with English subtitles. 52 mins.
VHS: S24269. $29.95.

Robot Carnival

Showcasing the work of nine top Japanese animators, *Robot Carnival* has been called a cyber-punk *Fantasia*. Each vignette employs the artist's unique vision of robots, a sum which carries the viewer to the past and the future. Japan, 90 mins.
VHS: S16642. $29.95.
Laser: CLV/CAV. LD72079. $39.95.

Robotech

Japanese animation series that blends high tech graphics and movement with science fiction heroism. Two episodes in each volume, 45 minutes each. Dubbed in English.
Vol. 1: Boobytraps.
VHS: S18879. $14.98.
Vol. 2: Space Fold.
VHS: S18880. $14.98.
Vol. 3: Transformation.
VHS: S18881. $14.98.
Vol. 4: Bye Bye Mars.
VHS: S18882. $14.98.
Vol. 5: Miss Macross.
VHS: S18883. $14.98.
Vol. 6: First Contact.
VHS: S18884. $14.98.
Vol. 7: Blue Wand.
VHS: S18885. $14.98.
Vol. 8: Homecoming.
VHS: S18886. $14.98.
Vol. 9: Phantasm.
VHS: S18887. $14.98.
Vol. 10: Bursting Point.
VHS: S18888. $14.98.
Vol. 11: A New Dawn/Battle Hymn.
VHS: S25574. $14.98.
Vol. 12: Reckless/Showdown.
VHS: S25575. $14.98.
Vol. 13: Wedding Bells/The Messenger.
VHS: S25576. $14.98.
Vol. 14: Force of Arms/Reconstruction Blues.
VHS: S25577. $14.98.
Vol. 15: The Robotech Masters/Viva Miriya.
VHS: S25578. $14.98.
Vol. 16: Khyron's Revenge/Broken Heart.
VHS: S25579. $14.98.
Vol. 17: A Rainy Night/Private Time.
VHS: S25580. $14.98.
Vol. 18: Season's Greetings/To the Stars.
VHS: S25581. $14.98.
Vol. 19: Dana's Story/False Start.
VHS: S25582. $14.98.
Vol. 20: Southern Cross/Volunteers.
VHS: S25583. $14.98.
Vol. 21: Half Moon/Danger Zone.
VHS: S25584. $14.98.
Vol. 22: Prelude to Battle/The Trap.
VHS: S25585. $14.98.
Vol. 23: Metal Fire/Star Dust.
VHS: S25586. $14.98.
Vol. 24: Outsiders/Deja Vu.
VHS: S25587. $14.98.
Vol. 25: A New Recruit/Triumvirate.
VHS: S25588. $14.98.
Vol. 26: Clone Chamber/Long Song.
VHS: S25589. $14.98.
Vol. 27: The Hunters/Mind Game.
VHS: S25590. $14.98.
Vol. 28: Dana in Wonderland/Crises Point.
VHS: S25592. $14.98.
Vol. 29: Day Dreamer/Final Nightmare.
VHS: S25593. $14.98.
Vol. 30: The Invid Connection/Catastrophe.
VHS: S25585. $14.98.
Vol. 31: The Invid Invasion/The Lost City.
VHS: S25594. $14.98.
Vol. 32: Lonely Soldier Boy/Survival.
VHS: S25595. $14.98.
Vol. 33: Curtain Call/Hard Time.
VHS: S25596. $14.98.
Vol. 34: Paper Hero/Eulogy.
VHS: S25597. $14.98.
Vol. 35: The Genesis Pit/Enter Marlene.
VHS: S25598. $14.98.
Vol. 36: The Secret Route/The Fortress.
VHS: S25599. $14.98.

Vol. 37: Sandstorms/Annie's Wedding.
VHS: S25600. $14.98.
Vol. 38: Seperate Ways/Metamorphosis.
VHS: S25601. $14.98.
Vol. 39: The Midnight Sun/Ghost Town.
VHS: S25602. $14.98.
Vol. 40: Frostbite/Birthday Blues.
VHS: S25603. $14.98.
Vol. 41: Hired Gun/The Big Apple.
VHS: S25604. $14.98.
Vol. 42: Reflex Point/Dark Finale/Symphony of Light.
VHS: S25605. $14.98.

Robotech II: The Sentinels
This feature film "sequel" to the *Macross* section of Robotech employs restored footage from the original U.S. production of this Japanese adventure series.
VHS: S16659. $19.98.
Laser: CLV/CAV. LD72080. $39.95.

Robotech Perfect Collection
The three latest volumes in the popular, complete Robotech collection feature both the original Japanese versions (Japanese with English subtitles) and the American versions, so that all fans can see and hear the difference. 100 mins. each.
Robotech Perfect Collection: Macross #6.
VHS: S23340. $19.95.
Robotech Perfect Collection: Mospeada #6.
VHS: S23342. $19.95.
Robotech Perfect Collection: Southern Cross #6.
VHS: S23341. $19.95.

Robotech Perfect Collection: Macross #5
This volume in the popular Robotech series includes both the original Japanese version (Japanese with English subtitles) and the American version on each tape. 100 mins.
VHS: S22409. $19.95.

Robotech Perfect Collection: Mospeada
The original series *Genesis Climber: Mospeada* is shown here, using the Japanese episodes with subtitles adapted from the original scripts. In addition, *Robotech* as broadcast on American TV is also presented. Together these action-packed sci-fi animation series show how Japanese popular culture changes when sent to America. Japanese with English subtitles.
VHS: S17353. $19.95.

Robotech Perfect Collection: Mospeada #5
This volume in the popular Robotech series includes both the original Japanese version (Japanese with English subtitles) and the American version on each tape. 100 mins.
VHS: S22411. $19.95.

Robotech Perfect Collection: Southern Cross #5
This volume in the popular Robotech series includes both the original Japanese version (Japanese with English subtitles) and the American version on each tape. 100 mins.
VHS: S22410. $19.95.

Roots Search
A Japanese version of *Alien*, set on a satellite research institute, about an unnatural presence that infiltrates a team of scientists and kills them by getting inside their heads and orchestrating nightmare visions. Japanese with English subtitles.
VHS: S17525. $34.95.
Laser: LD74514. $34.99.

Roujin Z
From the acclaimed director of *Akira* comes this tale of a new and overpowering robot. An elderly invalid is implanted with the Z-001, a robot. It can monitor, bathe, feed, exercise and entertain by linking with Dr.Takazawa's brainwaves. Unfortunately, the Z-001 has some plans of its own. It unexpectedly goes berserk and smashes free of the hospital. The violence it threatens could be linked to a new, advanced military weapon. Now it's up to a young nurse to save the day. Japanese with English subtitles.
VHS: S27455. $29.95.
Katsuhiro Otomo, Japan, 1991, 80 mins.

Rumik World: Fire Tripper
Rumiko Takahashi's *Fire Tripper* concerns the valiant young warrior Suzuko who's thrust 500 years into the past. It's a bleak, violent world of medieval marauders, victimized peasants and heroic rescuers. Japanese with English subtitles.
VHS: S17867. $19.95.
Laser: LD74506. $29.99.

Rumik World: Maris the Chojo
This is the sexy, animated feature that asks the eternal question, "What's a Thanatosian to do?" Maris is broke, and the problems of the world are getting her down. If only she could meet a cute guy. One with money would be even better. Japanese with English subtitles.
VHS: S21837. $19.95.
Laser: LD74510. $39.99.

Rumik World: Mermaid Forest
Yuta, a young, immortal sailor, explores the world in search of his perfect mate, and discovers Mana, the target of the terrifying experiments of Dr. Shina. He races against time to protect her. Japanese with English subtitles.
VHS: S17868. $19.95.
Laser: LD74512. $39.99.

Rumik World: The Laughing Target
A woman scorned wreaks havoc when she returns after 10 years to find her childhood cousin, Yuzuru, whom their parents arranged to marry, involved with another woman, Satomi. Japanese with English subtitles.
VHS: S17869. $19.95.
Laser: LD74509. $34.99.

Rumik World: The Supergal
An unhappy young woman, a Thanatosian, six times stronger than humans, is assigned to rescue the wealthy and charismatic Kogane Maru. Japanese with English subtitles.
VHS: S17528. $34.95.

Rupan III: Legend of the Gold of Babylon
Amazing Babylonian tablets discovered underneath Manhattan set off a desperate search to uncover the true Tower of Babel. A Mafia boss, a beautiful policewomen, a mysterious bad lady and more curious characters compete to find this tower of gold. Japanese with English subtitles. 100 mins.
VHS: S23761. $24.95.
Laser: LD74793. $39.95.

Rupan III: The Fuma Conspiracy
A Japanese wedding celebration is shattered as the bride is kidnapped during a quest for a hidden treasure. Ransom is the key to a hidden treasure. Rupan and Co. set off to find the girl and the gold, but the nefarious Ninjas are right behind them in this action-packed, animated adventure. Japanese with English subtitles. 73 mins.
VHS: S23759. $24.95.
Laser: LD74792. $39.95.

Samurai Showdown
This graphic, animated film tells the story of reincarnated Samurai who seek revenge against the former colleague who betrayed them, leading to their death. As they search for their last lost comrade they face many battles, until finally they must confront their evil nemesis. Dubbed in English. 85 mins.
VHS: S23873. $29.95.

The Secret of Blue Water, Volume 1: The Adventure Begins
Inspired by Jules Verne's classic *20,000 Leagues Under the Sea*, *The Secret of Blue Water* is the story of Jean, a young inventor, his friend Nadia, an orphaned acrobat, and their flight from Lady Grandis, an opportunist intent with her eye on Nadia's amulet. Also known as *Nadia: Parts 1-4*. Anime, dubbed in English.
VHS: S27590. $14.98.
Hideaki Anno, Japan, 1989, 94 mins.

The Secret of Blue Water, Volume 2: The Island Adventure
In this final installment of the Anime story based on *20,000 Leagues Under the Sea*, Jean and Nadia save the world from Gargoyle and his Neo-Atlantean army with the help of Captain Nemo and the crew of *The Nautilus*. Previously released as *Nadia: Parts 5-8*. Anime, dubbed in English.
VHS: S27591. $14.98.
Hideaki Anno, Japan, 1989, 94 mins.

Shonan Bakusozoku
Eguchi Yoosuke is trying to reconcile the two contradictory strands of his nature—the split between the reckless leader of the "Shonan Bakusozoku" biker gang and the class representative of the high school's handicraft club. Japanese with English subtitles. 1986. 52 mins.
VHS: S18619. $34.95.

Shuten Doji 2—The Star Hand Kid
Graphic violence, nudity and sex abound in this erotic horror masterpiece. Jiro tries to solve the mystery of his birth and finds himself locked in struggle with the awesome Oni. Anime, Japanese with English subtitles, 60 mins.
VHS: S27460. $29.95.

Shuten Doji—The Star Hand Kid
A seemingly ordinary high school boy wakes up one day and discovers that he has horns. It seems he was merely raised by his human parents because a giant troll asked them to. Now he is drawn into a world of darkness because his girlfriend has been kidnapped. She is to be the human sacrifice that opens up another dimension that will be the site of humanity's final destruction. Anime, Japanese with English subtitles, 50 mins.
VHS: S27019. $29.95.

Shuten Doji—The Star Hand Kid 3
Jiro and Miyuki's journey through space is disrupted by the oni and their pursuit of the Shuten Doji, sending Miyuki back in time to feudal Japan and Jiro ahead to the space age. Unfortunately, not only do Jiro and Miyuki now have to defeat the oni and find their way back to the present, but Jiro's arrival in the future spells certain doom for the members of the spaceship that he lands upon. Anime, Japanese with English subtitles. Japan, 1996, 50 mins.
VHS: S27711. $29.95.

The Slayers, Volume 1
This Anime fantasy features mercenary swordsman Gourry, mysterious Zelgadis, humanitarian sage Rezo, and cute little Lina, the flamethrowing sorceress. Will Lina and Rezo be able to save the world from Zelgadis's scheme of domination and destruction? Contains episode 1, *ANGRY? Lina's Furious Dragon Slave!*, episode 2, *BAD! Mummy Men Aren't My Type!*, episode 3, *CRASH! Red and White and Suspicious All Over!*, and episode 4, *DASH! Run for It! My Magic Doesn't Work?!*. Japanese with English subtitles.
VHS: S27683. $29.95.
Takashi Watanabe/Makoto Noriza/Osamu Yokota/Masato Sato, Japan, 1995, 100 mins.

Sohryuden Legend of the Dragon Kings, Volume 1
The four Ryudo brothers have strange powers. And these powers are of intense interest to the "old man of Kamurka." He is trying to unravel a secret that promises to grant him great powers. Unfortunately, his mad quest for power threatens the Ryudo brothers and those around them. This Anime adventure is subtitled in English. 97 mins.
VHS: S25982. $29.95.

Sohryuden Legend of the Dragon Kings, Volume 2
The Ryudo brothers' strange powers come from their dragon ancestors. Kamakura plans to ambush them in order to gain control of their powers, by using the brothers' cousin as bait. Only the great powers of the slumbering dragons can defeat this evil old man. This Anime adventure is subtitled in English. 97 mins.
VHS: S25983. $29.95.

Sohryuden Legend of the Dragon Kings, Volume 3
The four Ryudo brothers are descended from dragons. Dr. Tamozawa wants to conduct his twisted medical experiments on these intriguing subjects. The Doctor and his cybernetic Dobermans may well surprise the unsuspecting brothers. Contains episodes 5 and 6. Japanese with English subtitles.
VHS: S27093. $29.95.

Sohryuden Legend of the Dragon Kings, Volume 4
Dr. Tamozawa has discovered the secret of the Ryudo brothers' ancestry. This mad doctor, with the help of his cyborgs, is determined to master their secret by dissecting one of the brothers alive. Contains episode 7, *Revenge of the Four Brothers*, and episode 8, *Rampage of the Iron Dragon*. Anime, Japanese with English subtitles, 97 mins.
VHS: S27454. $29.95.

Sohryuden Legend of the Dragon Kings, Volume 5
Lady L has kidnapped one of the youngest Ryudo brothers for the Mulligan Foundation. Now the brothers must agree to become agents, assassins and saboteurs for the Foundation if they want to see their little brother return unharmed. Contains episode 9, *Storm of the White Dragon King*, and episode 10, *The Brothers' Great Escape*. Anime, Japanese with English subtitles.
VHS: S27673. $29.95.
Yoshiki Tanaka, Japan, 1991, 97 mins.

Sohryuden Legend of the Dragon Kings, Volume 6
The final two episodes in the saga of the Ryudo brothers, four men descended from dragons and endowed with incredible powers of speed, strength and power. Contains episode 11, *The Soaring Blue Dragon King*, and episode 12, *The Four Dragon Kings Take to the Sky*. Anime, Japanese with English subtitles.
VHS: S27674. $29.95.
Yoshiki Tanaka, Japan, 1991, 97 mins.

Sol Bianca
An all-female crew of gold pirates discovers the evil Emperor Batros holds possession of the valuable artifact "Gnosis." Armed with state-of-the-art weaponry and graced with old-fashioned guts, they mount a detailed plan to steal the valuable commodity and dethrone the ruthless despot. Japanese with English subtitles. 60 mins.
VHS: S18333. $39.95.
Laser: CAV, chapter stops. LD74480. $34.95.

Sol Bianca 2
This interstellar anime thriller follows the sexy adventures of the all-woman crew of a pirate spacecraft. Between an infestation of robot worms and a topless ray gun rampage these dynamic pirates provide plenty of gun fights, chase sequences and suspense. Japanese with English subtitles, 60 mins.
VHS: S24379. $29.95.

Space Angel
This animated series, designed by Alex Toth, concerns the cliff-hanging efforts of Scott McCloud, member of the Interplanetary Patrol Force, and his battle to protect the galaxy from cosmic evildoers. A sci-fi adventure that took the "Synchro-Vox" process of superimposing human lips on the mouths of animated characters to the far flung reaches of space.
Space Angel: Volume 1.
VHS: S15238. $14.95.
Space Angel: Volume 2.
VHS: S16664. $14.95.

Space Warriors Baldios
Earth faces doom at the hands of rapacious alien despoilers in this Anime feature. They ruined their own planet and now only one man stands between them and a helpless new environment—the lone warrior Baldios. Dubbed in English, 99 mins.
VHS: S25018. $19.99.

Spacekeeters
In *Aurora Accepts the Challenge*, the young heroine discovers she's the key in preserving the galaxy from the evil Dekos energy. She teams with the cyborg Jesse Dart, her first spacekeeter, to vanquish their enemy. *The Invincible Warrior* reveals Jesse's origins and how he devolved into a cyborg. 46 mins.
VHS: S18592. $12.98.

Spirit of Wonder: Miss China's Ring
Miss China runs a restaurant and boarding house in the late 19th century. Everything seems ideal except for the chronically indebted inventor upstairs and Miss China's mad crush on Jim. Magically, the inventor has finally succeeded in concocting a device that may grant Miss China her greatest wish. Anime, in Japanese with English subtitles.
VHS: S26798. $24.95.
Laser: LD75115. $39.95.
Hongou Mitsuru, Japan, 1992, 45 mins.

Star Blazers
A Japanese animation series about a group of characters engaged in fantastic stories of redemption and order, of "people who live and work beyond the stars." "The best science fiction adventure ever produced."
Tape 1.
VHS: S17800. $19.95.
Tape 2.
VHS: S17801. $19.95.
Tape 3.
VHS: S17802. $19.95.
Tape 4.
VHS: S17803. $19.95.
Tape 5.
VHS: S17804. $19.95.
Tape 6.
VHS: S17805. $19.95.
Tape 7.
VHS: S17806. $19.95.
Tape 8.
VHS: S17807. $19.95.
Tape 9.
VHS: S17808. $19.95.
Tape 10.
VHS: S17809. $19.95.
Tape 11.
VHS: S17810. $19.95.
Tape 12.
VHS: S17811. $19.95.
Tape 13.
VHS: S17812. $19.95.
Tape 14.
VHS: S17813. $19.95.
Tape 15.
VHS: S17814. $19.95.
Tape 16.
VHS: S17815. $19.95.
Tape 17.
VHS: S17816. $19.95.
Tape 18.
VHS: S17817. $19.95.
Tape 19.
VHS: S17818. $19.95.
Tape 20.
VHS: S17819. $19.95.
Tape 21.
VHS: S17820. $19.95.
Tape 22.
VHS: S17821. $19.95.
Tape 23.
VHS: S17822. $19.95.
Tape 24.
VHS: S17823. $19.95.
Tape 25.
VHS: S17824. $19.95.
Tape 26.
VHS: S17825. $19.95.
Tape 27.
VHS: S17826. $19.95.
Tape 28.
VHS: S17827. $19.95.
Tape 29.
VHS: S17828. $19.95.
Tape 30.
VHS: S17829. $19.95.
Tape 31.
VHS: S17830. $19.95.
Tape 32.
VHS: S17831. $19.95.
Tape 33.
VHS: S17832. $19.95.
Tape 34.
VHS: S17833. $19.95.
Tape 35.
VHS: S17834. $19.95.
Tape 36.
VHS: S17835. $19.95.
Tape 37.
VHS: S17836. $19.95.
Tape 38.
VHS: S17837. $19.95.
Tape 39.
VHS: S17838. $19.95.
Tapes 1-13.
VHS: S17839. $259.35.
Tapes 14-26.
VHS: S17840. $259.35.
Tapes 27-39.
VHS: S17841. $259.35.

Starvengers
Who'll Fly Poseidon concerns the invention of the state-of-the-art machine Starvenger and Foul Tip's successful effort to pilot the craft. *Dragon Formation...Switch On* unleashes the all-star battle between the Starvengers fleet and the Pandemonium Empire, in pursuit of the star energizer. 46 mins.
VHS: S18593. $12.98.

Street Fighter II: The Animated Movie
Humanity is under attack in this Anime epic. The not-too-distant future is a dark place where the forces of Shadowlaw attempt to harness psycho power. If they succeed, it could be the end of civilization. Only the legendary Ryu, the greatest street fighter on the planet, can alter the balance of power to favor freedom. Unrated version.
VHS: S26924. $14.95.
Gisaburo Sugii, Japan, 1994, 96 mins.

Sukeban Deka 1
High school convict Saki is being called on by the Feds to infiltrate an evil crime syndicate that poses as an exclusive high school. Armed only with a secret weapon disguised as a yo-yo, will Saki be up to the challenge? This scenario gives her plenty of opportunity to display her fighting and lovemaking abilities. Anime, Japanese with English subtitles, 60 mins.
VHS: S27464. $29.95.

Sukeban Deka 2
Saki is back for more outrageous underground exploits in this animated feature. She went straight from high school to prison. In this second installment of Nobuteru Yuki's *Sukeban Deka*, Saki, a high school convict turned Federal Agent, is putting her life on the line to infiltrate an evil crime syndicate that poses as an exclusive high school. With one flick of her wrist, Saki's secret weapon (disguised as a yo-yo) will leave nothing of her enemies but dust. Anime, Japanese with English subtitles. 60 mins.
VHS: S27630. $29.95.

Super Atoragon
Moments after the United States released the atomic bomb over Hiroshima, two submarines—one American and one Japanese—disappeared forever. Now, over 50 years later, the descendants of the soldiers lost in those submarines are joined together for a special mission: to investigate supernatural phenomena occurring in Antarctica, including the appearance of a strange black cylinder, its fatal companion, a set of deadly rings, and the possible resurrection of the missing submarines. Anime, Japanese with English subtitles. Japan, 1996, 60 mins.
VHS: S27714. $29.95.

The Tale of Genji
Murasaki Shikibu's novel of the Heian era in Japan has been turned into an animated film. It follows the adventures of Genji, the emperor's son, who was made a commoner. His gift for poetry and music ensured he led a truly uncommon life. His loves were legendary for the genuine emotion and depth. 110 mins. Japanese with English subtitles.
VHS: $26250. $29.95.

The Tale of Shunkin/Friendship
In this animated feature, the beautiful, blind harpist Shunkin has been disfigured by her student Sakichi. Ever devoted, Sakichi goes to amazing lengths to preserve the memory of Shunkin's face forever. Japanese with English subtitles. 52 mins.
VHS: $24270. $29.95.

Tank Police Volume 1
This video contains the first two episodes of a sexy, sci-fi Anime sensation. An elite tank squad is set up to bring order to the nearly ruined city of Newport. Leona and Bonepart do everything they can to enforce the law. Unfortunately the dangerous and mercenary Puma sisters will do anything for a price. Dubbed in English, 40 mins.
VHS: $25543. $14.95.

Techno Police
Centinel City has been taken over by criminals. Only a special unit, the Techno Police, can bring back law and order. Before long they realize their struggle is dominated by the fight for survival. Dubbed in English, 80 mins.
VHS: $25019. $19.99.

Tekkaman, the Space Night: Episode 1
In this animation work, set in the year 2037, a brilliant scientist constructs an indestructible space suit, whose possession transforms a brash young space pilot into the superhuman gladiator, Tekkaman, the Space Night. His first mission is defending the earth from an invading band of marauding alien robots. 86 mins.
VHS: $17366. $19.95.

Tekkaman, the Space Night: Episode 2
In this animation about killer alien robots threatening the earth, the young gladiator/warrior, Barry Gallagher, is subjected to a new series of challenges from his foes, who've developed deadlier tools of destruction. 86 mins.
VHS: $17367. $19.95.

Ten Little Gall Force/Scramble Wars
The first program is an example of Super-Deformed, or "SD," a children's variation that replicates the actions of the original characters. Ten Little Gall Force is a series of outtakes from the original series. On the second program, Scramble Wars is an aggressive parody of an elaborate race in the lawless frontier of Gaiarth. Japanese with English subtitles. 1988/92. 70 mins.
VHS: $18621. $34.95.

Tenchi Muyo 1: Ryoko Resurrected
Tenchi, a typical Japanese high school boy, enters into a prohibited area of the mountains where he unknowingly releases a goblin which his forefather trapped 700 years ago. The goblin, a sexy woman, attacks him a month later. Subtitled. 30 mins.
VHS: $23073. $24.98.
Laser: LD74655. $34.95.

Tenchi Muyo 2: Here Comes Ayeka
Ayeka, the crown princess of planet July, is looking for her fiance Yosho, who has been missing since a battle with Rokyo many years ago. As Ayeka approaches Earth she sees Rokyo and attacks. This second episode introduces Ayeka, Sasami and Yosho. Subtitled. 30 mins.
VHS: $23074. $24.98.
Laser: LD74656. $34.95.

Tenchi Muyo 3: Hello Ryo-Ohki
Now we find Tenchi has a blood line with planet Jurai. Ayeka finds unhappy days in Tencho's home as she learns that Yosho is dead and she can't return home without her spaceship. She spends her days recalling memories of Yosho. Subtitled. 30 mins.
VHS: $23075. $24.98.
Laser: LD74657. $34.95.

Tenchi Muyo 4: Miyoshi Falls to the Land of Stars
One of the most wanted space bandits, Kagato, destroys a police squad as he heads toward Earth's solar system. The chief commisioner of the Galaxy Police orders the local police department to pay special attention to him. Subtitled. 30 mins.
VHS: $23076. $24.98.
Laser: LD74658. $34.95.

Tenchi Muyo 5: Kagato Attacks
Ryoko and Ayeka are fighting over Tenchi when Kagato appears. A battle for the magic sword ensues. Ryoko is defeated by Kagato and is put under a spell. Tenchi's grandfather joins the battle, sending Kagato back to his spaceship. Subtitled. 30 mins.
VHS: $23077. $24.98.
Laser: LD74659. $34.95.

Tenchi Muyo 6: We Need Tenchi
Everybody is shocked that Tenchi is dead, so Kagato must die to avenge the murder of Tenchi. Sasami, sad about Tenchi's death, becomes unconscious and begins chanting, disappearing into the tree that is Yoshi's ship. Subtitled. 30 mins.
VHS: $23078. $24.98.
Laser: LD74660. $34.95.

Tenchi Muyo 7: Special: The Night Before Carnival
The Kagato incident is over, but Tenchi has plenty of trouble when five beautiful girls and Ryo-Oh-Ki surround him. An assortment of troubles, everything from small ones to large ones, is in store for him. Subtitled. 30 mins.
VHS: $23079. $24.98.
Laser: LD74661. $39.95.

Tenchi Muyo Episodes 8 & 9
This outrageous continuation of the Tenchi Muyo saga adds intriguing elements to the story. There is a night in the Tenchi household! And what about the secret behind Sasami and Tsunami? Japanese with English subtitles. 60 mins.
VHS: $24572. $29.98.
Laser: LD74825. $39.98.

Tenchi Muyo Episodes 10 & 11
In the episodes I Love Tenchi and Here Is a Goddess Tenchi must struggle to keep his life normal. Naturally it is nearly impossible to do this given the mischievous nature of Ryoko, Sasami and their lovable pet Ryo-Oh-Ki. Japanese with English subtitles, 60 mins.
VHS: $25676. $29.98.
Laser: LD74989. $39.98.

Tenchi Muyo: Mihoshi Special
The beautiful Mihoshi may be scatterbrained but she is also the galaxy's most accomplished police investigator. Recognition of her less visible abilities may well be forthcoming if only she can solve the galaxy's most notorious case. Japanese with English subtitles, 30 mins.
VHS: $24238. $24.98.
Laser: LD74817. $34.98.

Tenchi Muyo: The Magical Girl Pretty Sammy
In the magical world of Juraihime, Tsunami is nominated as the next queen. She hires the magical girl Sasami to help prepare for the royal final exam. There are plenty of hijinks when these two get together—they're sisters after all. Japanese with English subtitles. 45 mins.
VHS: $26631. $29.95.
Laser: LD75103. $39.98.

They Were 11
Moto Hagio's adaptation of his comic strip concerns the actions of a student collection of humans and aliens undergoing their rigorous final exam. They are set adrift inside a derelict spacecraft, when they discover an unaccounted alien presence. Japanese with English subtitles. 45 mins.
VHS: $17798. $39.95.

Those Obnoxious Aliens
The Oni come back to Earth to reclaim it as their own. They offer the planet one chance at a reprieve in a game of tag. Unfortunately, a lazy and lecherous lad is chosen to beat their Princess Lum. This sexy, animated feature is dubbed in English. Two episodes of Urusei Yatsura, the wacky Japanese animated comedy, are included on this videotape. 50 mins.
VHS: $23762. $19.95.

Tobor the 8th Man
With Astroboy and Gigantor, Tobor, the 8th Man is seminal contribution of Japan's giant robot animated works. Constructed around themes of revenge and superhuman efforts, its protagonist is special agent Brady, who's near brain dead condition is restored by the brilliant Professor Genius. His mind is transformed into an electronic brain, Brady is reconstituted into Tobor, the 8th Man, and opens his own detective agency to thwart criminals.
Tobor the 8th Man: Vol. 1. 120 mins.
VHS: $17106. $24.95.
Tobor the 8th Man: Vol. 2. 120 mins.
VHS: $17107. $24.95.
Tobor the 8th Man: Vol. 3. 120 mins.
VHS: $17108. $24.95.
Tobor the 8th Man: Vol. 4. 120 mins.
VHS: $17522. $24.95.

Tokyo Babylon 1
Shinji Nagumo is awfully lucky compared to his fellow skyscraper building friends. Somehow his co-workers succumb to a series of bizzare accidents. A powerful medium is called in to investigate these accidents but he must hurry. Shinji has an enemy that is devising a creature that will destroy this hero's lucky streak permanently. Anime, Japanese with English subtitles, 52 mins.
VHS: $24241. $29.95.

Tokyo Babylon 2
The safety of the subways is violated by the discovery of a number of brutally butchered bodies. Mirei is a psychic who uses her powers to help track the killer, but soon she too is in danger. Only the medium Subaru can solve the mystery of this murderer's identity. Anime, Japanese with English subtitles, 59 mins.
VHS: $24242. $29.95.

Toward the Terra
Earth is just a memory for the inhabitants of a new dystopic world ruthlessly run by computers. These powerful machines engineer all life, and fear the dreaded MU, children branded as different from normal people. They try to hunt out these so-called demons, but now the MU's make a stand for a chance at life. Anime, Japanese with English subtitles. 112 mins.
VHS: $21282. $29.95.
Laser: LD74887. $39.95.

Twilight of the Cockroaches
Mr. Saito is a modern bachelor who loves good food. In turn, Mr. Saito's cockroaches live a very good life and worship him as a god. Memories of hard times when the cockroaches had to scrape and search for food have faded. That is until Saito brings home a new girlfriend who has deadly plans in store for the cockroach kingdom. Original director's cut in letterbox format. Animated. Japanese with English subtitles.
VHS: $16645. $19.95.
Laser: CLV. LD71494. $34.95.
Hiroaki Yoshida, Japan, 1990, 105 mins.

Twin Dolls: Legends of the Heavenly Beasts
Mai and Ai look like a typical pair of teenage sisters. But they are masters of a half dozen martial arts, trained by their grandmother since birth to become professional demon hunters. A green-eyed monster begins to enslave their classmates to quench its unnatural lusts. The sisters must summon all their strength to defeat this demon and its army of sex slaves. Japanese with English subtitles. 50 mins.
VHS: $23337. $34.95.

Twin Dolls II
Mai and Ai are twin dolls who battle an army of demons and a shape-changing incubus in this graphic, sexy anime. Be forewarned, these demons have a voracious, insatiable appetite. Japanese with English subtitles. 50 mins.
VHS: $23869. $34.95.

U-Jin Brand
Two stories: In the first, songwriter Tusujiro idolizes platonically, from afar. What will happen when dreams and reality meet? In the second story, a young girl's fiance is stolen by a rival. Animated. Japanese with English subtitles.
VHS: $20474. $29.95.

The Ultimate Teacher
This animated work boldly mixes science fiction and social critique in the story of a half-cockroach, half-human Ultimate Teacher who declares war against the anti-social gangs that terrorize Emperor High School. Japanese with English subtitles. 60 mins.
VHS: $19437. $34.95.
Laser: LD74516. $34.99.

Ultraman II
Sleek Japanese animation from Akira Tsuburaya and Hiroshi Jinzenji that grafts the pulp and violence of the American superhero onto a Japanese aesthetic, as Ultraman must defend his planet from dark powers that threaten its safety. 86 mins.
VHS: $18590. $19.99.

Ultraman: The Adventure Begins
The story finds three members of the Ultra family protecting the Earth from a mutant creature waging war on it. A co-production of Tsuburuya Productions and Hanna-Barbera. 70 mins.
VHS: $18338. $24.95.

Ultraman: Towards the Future
Ultraman is an intergalactic guard interested in preserving the galaxy. Ultraman has entered the body of astronaut Jack Shindo by fusing with his molecular structure. Jack transforms himself into Ultraman through a special Delta Plasma Pendant. An original English production.

Vol. 1, Episode 1. After a mythic space battle between Ultraman and the Gudis, the mysterious force transmutates into a luminescent green virus and escapes into the Earth's atmosphere, causing infected life forms to mutate into gigantic monsters. Jack Shindo and his alterego Ultraman must save civilization from the invading monsters. 23 mins.
VHS: $18334. $14.95.
Vol. 2, Episode 2. The mysterious Gudis Bacteria has provoked a global warming, melting the polar ice caps, awakening the dormant Gigasaurus. The monster freezes everything in its wake and Ultraman must summon all his strength and resources to defeat the monster. 23 mins.
VHS: $18335. $14.95.
Vol. 3, Episode 3. The Gudis invade the body of Jimmy Martin, who controls a giant Gerukadon that is wreaking havoc on the city. Ultraman and his young friends confront the savage being. 23 mins.
VHS: $18336. $14.95.
Vol. 4, Episode 4. In The Storm Hunter, Jack Shindo and Lloyd Wilder explore a whirlwind that attacked two hunters. They control the force through Aboriginal magic, until a search party attacks the spirit and unleashes its awesome powers and forces Ultraman into an epic struggle. 23 mins.
VHS: $18337. $14.95.
Vol. 5, Episode 5. In The Blast from the Past, the UMA regiments stage a ferocious battle with a mysterious enemy, Barraki. Stanley Haggard is recruited by the UMA to circumvent the monstrous beast. Stanley kidnaps Jean Echo, setting in motion a mammoth conflict between Ultraman and Barraki to protect Jean from the sinister Gudis' forces.
VHS: $19712. $14.95.
Vol. 6, Episode 6. In The Showdown, Ultraman is engaged in his greatest challenge when the Gudis collect enough cells to be born. Strengthed by a violent assault by the armed forces, Gudis descend on the Earth from a volcanic womb. Ultraman prepares for battle.
VHS: $19713. $14.95.
Vol. 7, Episode 7. In The Forest Guardian, the UMA forces have only 24 hours to track down a young girl separated from her mother while she was fleeing a Gazebo monster. Ultraman and the monster engage in an epic battle over a mushroom that paralyzes the monster.
VHS: $19714. $14.95.
Vol. 8, Episode 8. When a crop duster plane is attacked by a colossal mutant creature in The Bitter Harvest, the UMA forces investigate the incident and discover the monster's origins and location. Ultraman must quickly see that only Ultraman can save them from certain destruction.
VHS: $19715. $14.95.
Vol. 9, Episode 9. This classic Japanese television serial from the 1960's is a campy and unforgettable adventure in science fiction hokum. Can you imagine a plant computer symbiot? That's the result of Dr. Krankstein's new breed of organic foliage. Fortunately, Ultraman will save the day. 23 mins.
VHS: $20483. $14.95.
Vol. 10, Episode 10. Japanese television character Ultraman was at the center of a incomparable science fiction serial. Now this 1960's superhero is back. Aliens visiting the Earth are just looking for a good time. Unfortunately Charles doesn't realize this when he falls in love with one of them. Can Ultraman solve this romantic intergalactic mess? 23 mins.
VHS: $20484. $14.95.
Vol. 11, Episode 11. Ultraman is an animated galactic guardian interested in the preservation of the galaxy. In Episode 11, The Survivalists, Jean Echo is kidnapped by a criminal scientist who was presumed killed in an auto accident. Echo is forced to help Norberg attack UMA headquarters, and only Ultraman can stop this plot. Dubbed in English, 23 mins.
VHS: $22906. $14.95.
Vol. 12, Episode 12. Ultraman is a galactic guardian interested in the preservation of the galaxy. In Episode 12 of these animated sci-fi adventures, The Age of Plagues, an underwater earthquake unleashes the creature Kudara from its dwelling on the ocean floor. Dubbed in English. 23 mins.
VHS: $22905. $14.95.
Vol. 13, Episode 13. In this episode, Nemesis, the intergalactic guardian, must find a disk that predicted the chaos currently plaguing the Earth. Like the 1960's live-action television series, this animated feature contains giant monsters and amazing battle scenes. Dubbed in English. 23 mins.
VHS: $23764. $14.95.

Urotsukidoji II: Legend of the Demon Womb
The sinister scientist Dr. Munhihausen orchestrates a desperate plan to overcome the fiendish onslaught of the Overfiend and his brutal army of demons who lay siege to the Earth. The doctor's scientific experiments endow Takeaki with phenomenal powers, setting in motion an epic confrontation. English dubbed. 88 mins.
VHS: $19436. $39.95.
Laser: LD74518. $49.95.

Urotsukidoji III The Movie: Return of the Overfiend
The Overfiend is called out of a 25-year hibernation to greet the arrival of the dreaded Lord of Chaos in Azuma. Rather than the Lord of Chaos himself, it seems the Overfiend's awakening was actually caused by the evolution of a half-breed of demon beasts. Now the Overfiend's only chance of survival is with the help of Amano Jyaku and his sister Megumi. Unfortunately, Munhihausen and Azuma's dictator, Caesar, are ready and waiting to stop Amano. Anime, Japanese with English subtitles.
VHS: $27687. $29.95.
Hideki Takayama, Japan, 1993, 120 mins.

Urotsukidoji III: Return of the Overfiend
Twenty years after the world was ravaged by the destructive monster Nagumo a new order called Demon-Beasts has evolved. Tokyo, under Caesar's rule, has become a battleground for these Demon-Beasts and Caesar's army. These adult animated features contain strong violence and sexual themes.
Urotsukidoji III: Return of the Overfiend, Episode 1. The true Overfiend has forced his birth to occur decades earlier, because he realized that there was an evil being present. Caesar and his cohort Faust anxiously await his demise so that they can rule the world. 60 mins.
VHS: $22057. $29.95.
Urotsukidoji III: Return of the Overfiend, Episode 2. A child has emerged who may be the true Lord of Chaos. Caesar and Faust plan to unite this child with their own creation, Fabrille. Together their powers could defeat the Overfiend. 60 mins.
VHS: $22058. $29.95.
Urotsukidoji III: Return of the Overfiend, Episode 3. The world is in chaos. Caesar takes advantage of this by targeting his nuclear missiles directly at Osaka while Fabrille, in the shape of a giant bird, menaces Tokyo. Humanity's destiny, however, may very well depend not on the power of these great forces, but on the yet unborn child of Caesar's daughter, Alecto. She has been kidnapped by the Demon-Beasts. 50 mins.
VHS: $22059. $29.95.
Urotsukidoji III: Return of the Overfiend, Episode 4. While Caesar pursues his daughter's captors, a new weapon is unveiled—the still unfinished android, Genocidroid. Destiny and a sense of purpose await those who go to meet the Overfiend. 50 mins.
VHS: $22060. $29.95.
Complete Set.
VHS: $22061. $99.95.

Urotsukidoji: Birth of the Overfiend
The story concerns the search for the monstrous Overfiend's origins, as two demons who penetrate Myojin University track down the mysterious force. "Urotsukidoji is exemplary of the darkest and most disturbing side of Japanese animation" (The Village Voice). Japanese with English subtitles.
VHS: $19488. $99.95.

Urotsukidoji: Legend of the Overfiend
The Overfiend, or Chojin, attempts to remake the current world by merging three warring dimensions—the human world, the man beast world and the world of the monster demons. The feature length work was culled from three episodes of Takayama's video series The Wandering Kid. The first animated work to receive an NC-17 rating. Dubbed in English.
VHS: $18441. $39.95.
Laser: LD74517. $49.95.
Hideki Takayama, Japan, 1991, 108 mins.

Urusei Yatsura Movie: Always My Darling
Wily princess Lupica abducts the amazingly handsome Ataru because he is the source for the greatest love potion in the galaxy. His good looks and even his charming personality are just incidental to Lupica's interest. Japanese animation, 77 mins.
VHS: $20724. $24.95.

Urusei Yatsura OVA Series
In this continuation of the crazed antics of the popular animated Japanese characters, Shinobu discovers a mysterious key, constructing a door with Lum and Aratu that propels them through a strange, psychedelic and hypnotic universe, one that predicts their futures. In a parallel plotline, Inaba risks his life to reveal the various destinies of his co-workers at Destiny Production Management. Japanese with English subtitles.
OVA Volume 1.
VHS: $18349. $24.95.
OVA Volume 2.
VHS: $18350. $24.95.
OVA Volume 3.
VHS: $18351. $24.95.
OVA Volume 4.
VHS: $18367. $24.95.
OVA Volume 5.
VHS: $18648. $24.95.
OVA Volume 6.
VHS: $18650. $24.95.

Urusei Yatsura TV Series
A mysterious race of aliens known as Oni arrive to repossess the Earth, with one chance to save the planet. A randomly selected warrior, Ataru, a notorious failure, must defeat their beautiful princess, Lum, at the national sport. In this demented universe, Ataru defeats the princess, setting in motion a surreal sequence of events when Ataru's girlfriend and Lum both believe they are destined to be Ataru's wife. Japanese with English subtitles.
TV Series Volume 1.
VHS: $16980. $24.95.
TV Series Volume 2.
VHS: $17526. $24.95.
TV Series Volume 3.
VHS: $17527. $24.95.

TV Series Volume 4.
VHS: S18352. $24.95.
TV Series Volume 5.
VHS: S18353. $24.95.
TV Series Volume 6.
VHS: S18354. $24.95.
TV Series Volume 7.
VHS: S18646. $24.95.
TV Series Volume 8.
VHS: S18647. $39.95.
TV Series Volume 9.
VHS: S18649. $24.95.
TV Series Volume 10.
VHS: S18651. $24.95.
TV Series Volume 11.
VHS: S18653. $24.95.
TV Series Volume 12.
VHS: S20022. $24.95.
TV Series Volume 13.
VHS: S20725. $24.95.
TV Series Volume 14.
VHS: S20726. $24.95.
TV Series Volume 15.
VHS: S20727. $24.95.
TV Series Volume 16.
VHS: S20728. $24.95.
TV Series Volume 17. This sexy Anime series features the continuing antics of Ataru, Lum and the rest of the gang. In this video they are all off to the beach, which is a perfect setting for the intrigues, misunderstandings and passions that define this wacky comic series. Includes episodes 63-66. Dubbed in English.
VHS: S26636. $24.95.
TV Series Volume 18. Lum's cooking is virtually poisonous, Mendou's arch enemy arrives in Japan, and the Tengu crows think they've found a mate for their princess, Kurama, but they quickly discover he's got a little problem. Follow the continuing adventures of the *Urusei Yatsura* gang as a letter in a bottle sparks a chaotic series of events. Includes episodes 67-70. Anime, Japanese with English subtitles, 100 mins.
VHS: S27655. $24.95.

Urusei Yatsura: Beautiful Dreamer
A witty science fiction adventure for adults that might be described as a Japanese *Carrie*, about an unpopular young woman who wreaks havoc on Lum, the beautiful alien princess, Ataru, the gilded prince, Mendou, the scion of the planet's richest family, and the other students at Tomobiki High who abuse and ignore her. Japanese with English subtitles.
VHS: S17739. $24.95.
Laser: LD74519. $39.99.

Urusei Yatsura: Kanketsuhen (The Final Chapter)
This is the finale to the series of animated adult features that follow the funny, sexy antics of Ataru and Lum. In this installment, Lum's fiancé Lupa appears, as the central protagonists fight to avert the Earth's destruction. Japanese with English subtitles. 90 mins.
VHS: S20731. $24.95.

Urusei Yatsura: Only You
A beautiful alien conjures up an ancient tradition to force the marriage of the young prince, Ataru. As the day approaches, another alien suitor for Ataru's affections subverts her plans and marries him instead, unleashing an intergalactic war between the two space colonies. They discover one of the aliens has a diabolical plan of stockpiling men for devious means. Japanese with English subtitles.
VHS: S17740. $24.95.

Urusei Yatsura: Remember My Love
Ataru is transformed into a pink hippopotamus at a bizarre amusement park by a witch who mistakenly believes she was ostracized by Ataru and Lum. Taking action, things turn increasingly weird and surreal when Lum relentlessly pursues the black magician to return Ataru to his natural state. Japanese with English subtitles. 93 mins.
VHS: S17741. $24.95.

Vampire Hunter D
In the distant future, Earth is plagued by vampires who act as feudal land barons ruling over hopeless pockets of civilization. A beautiful young villager, Doris, promises herself to a passing Vampire Hunter if he can eradicate the evil Count Magnus Lee. 75 mins.
VHS: S16646. $19.98.
Laser: CLV/CAV. LD72081. $39.95.

Vampire Princess Miyu
This sophisticated animation spins a complex tale of Gothic Horror—Japanese style! Join spiritualist Himiko as she hunts down the mysterious Miyu, childlike princess of the Vampires. Is Miyu evil or good? Japanese with English subtitles.
Vampire Princess Miyu: Volume 1. 50 mins.
VHS: S16666. $24.95.
Vampire Princess Miyu: Volume 2. 50 mins.
VHS: S16667. $24.95.

Vampire Princess Miyu Series
Contains volumes 1 and 2.
Laser: LD71511. $64.95.

The Venus Wars
A Japanese animated work about the tensions between the two planets mankind controls, Earth and Venus. Hiro Seno, a motorcyclist on a race team, gets caught in the war between his country and the invading forces of Ishtar. Japanese with English subtitles.
VHS: S18325. $19.95.
Laser: LD74520. $34.99.

Wanna-be's
This Japanese animated work is a witty send up of machismo, focusing on women's wrestling. Eri and Miki must battle the superhuman-like Foxy Ladies. The alternate story concerns the development of a revolutionary though harmful drug that provides uncommon strength. Japanese with English subtitles. 45 mins.
VHS: S17072. $19.95.
Laser: LD74521. $29.99.

Wicked City
This graphic supernatural thriller was a theatrical success and is now available as an adult animated feature. Taki, a human secret agent, accompanied by his shape-shifting counterpart from a parallel dimension, is forced into a life and death struggle. Can they save their two worlds from destruction? 80 mins.
VHS: S21696. $19.98.

A Wind Named Amnesia
In this feature-length, animated, sci-fi adventure, an ill wind has swept away the collective memory of mankind, reducing America to a state of barbarism. One man and woman are spared this fate. Together they seek out those responsible for this horrific turn of events. Japanese with English subtitles. 80 mins.
VHS: S21099. $29.95.
Laser: Subtitled. LD74949. $39.99.

Windaria
A Japanese animation fantasy, this exciting and bittersweet story takes place amid the backdrop of a brutal civil war, *Windaria* is a world destined to be destroyed by love and greed. 95 mins.
VHS: S16644. $29.95.
Laser: LD74961. $39.99.

Wings of Honneamise
This Anime super-epic charts a story of technology, politics, and love with a unique, wry sense of humor. In a future imaginary world ravaged by war and social unrest, desperate measures are in order. Music by Oscar-winning composer Ryuichi Sakamoto. Japanese with English subtitles, partial nudity, 124 mins.
VHS: S25723. $19.95.

The X-Men, The Phoenix Saga: The Dark Shroud
In Part 2, a psychic probe is sweeping the universe. It seems to desire contact with Professor Xavier. Facing this mysterious entity, the X-Men must prevail against The Dark Shroud for the sake of all humanity. 25 mins.
VHS: S25689. $9.95.

The X-Men, The Phoenix Saga: The Sacrifice
Professor Xavier hears psychic calls for help from across the universe. He dispatches the X-Men on a mission that even he doesn't fully understand. In this animated adventure the X-Men must battle to preserve the integrity of the very fabric of space. 25 mins.
VHS: S25690. $9.95.

You're Under Arrest!
It all begins rather badly for a pair of new Highway Patrol Partners. On the way to work, lovely Natsumi is stopped by her equally attractive future partner for a traffic violation. Fortunately, they are both dedicated to getting the Fox, a super traffic offender with a customized vehicle. Anime subtitled and dubbed in English, 52 mins.
VHS: S26006. $19.95.
Laser: LD75036. $39.95.

You're Under Arrest!— Love's Highway Stars
Matchmaking goes awry when Natsumi and Yoriko decide to get involved in their friends' love lives. The pair are afraid that Ken will lose his girlfriend Miyuki to an old high school boyfriend, so the two interfere, with wildly comic results. Anime. Japanese with English subtitles. 25 mins.
VHS: S27323. $19.95.

You're Under Arrest!— On the Road Again
Natsumi is offered the chance to fulfill her dream and become a member of the motorcycle patrol. The only problem is that joining the motorcycle patrol means ending her partnership with Miyuki. Anime. Japanese with English subtitles. 25 mins.
VHS: S27324. $19.95.

You're Under Arrest!— Tokyo Typhoon Rally
The adventures of the loveliest pair of Highway Patrol Partners continue in this consecutive episode. Anime subtitled in English, 25 mins.
VHS: S26007. $19.95.

Zeguy Parts 1 & 2
Miki is a normal teenage girl who inadvertently falls into a parallel universe or cloud world. There she stumbles across a number of odd creatures, but worst of all she learns of an evil plot that spell dooms for both universes. This sexy animated feature is filled with fantasy and action. Japanese with English subtitles, 79 mins.
VHS: S24336. $29.95.
Laser: LD75545. $34.99.

Zenki
Long ago a demon lord was bound to a mountain-dwelling monk. He was called Zenki, the most powerful of the demon lords. Under the monk's instructions, he battled the forces of darkness until he was sealed away for 55 generations. Now his strength is needed once again. Only this time Zenki must work with the descendent of the monk, a teenage school girl. Together they must fight the malevolent god Karma. Animated. Japanese with English subtitles.
Zenki Volume 1. 90 mins.
VHS: S26642. $24.95.
Zenki Volume 2. 60 mins.
VHS: S26643. $24.95.
Zenki Volume 3. 60 mins.
VHS: S26644. $24.95.
Zenki Volume 4. 60 mins.
VHS: S26645. $24.95.
Zenki Volume 5. 60 mins.
VHS: S26646. $24.95.
Zenki Volume 6. 60 mins.
VHS: S26647. $24.95.

Zillion
Champ, Apple and J.J. star in this all-action animated adventure series adapted from the popular Japanese television show. Each volume contains a new installment in the adventures of our high-tech heroes as they try to combat a powerful alien invasion force. Not for children.
Zillion: Volume 1. *They Call Me, J.J.* 25 mins.
VHS: S15239. $14.95.
Zillion: Volume 2. *Hang Fire.* 25 mins.
VHS: S16651. $14.95.
Zillion: Volume 3. *Split Second Chance.* 25 mins.
VHS: S16652. $14.95.
Zillion: Volume 4. *Target: The White Knights.* 25 mins.
VHS: S16653. $14.95.
Zillion: Volume 5. *Judgement Call.* 25 mins.
VHS: S16654. $14.95.

Zillion: Burning Night
The White Knights are back in this outrageous spectacular. J.J., Champ and Apple face their greatest challenge in a bizarre adventure set in a barren frontier town. A special double-episode blending a sci-fi future and the Old West past. 50 mins.
VHS: S16655. $22.95.
Laser: LD74968. $34.99.

Zillion: The Beginning
A stylized, animated work set in the 24th century on the peaceful colony of Maris, which is under siege from the Noza, a brutal warrior class. The colony's only chance for survival is the experimental weapons system Zillion. 65 mins.
VHS: S19689. $19.99.

LARRY JORDAN

H.D. Trilogy
A loving portrait of "H.D."—imagist poet and novelist Hilda Doolittle—a merging of images, Joanna McClure's reading of H.D.'s long poem "Hermetic Definitions" and the traditional music of the Mediterranean by filmmaker Larry Jordan. The three parts of the film, *The Black Oud*, *The Grove* and *Star of Day*, look at Hilda Doolittle through the life of Joanna McClure during the years 1990 through 1992.
VHS: S23210. $29.95.
Larry Jordan, USA, 1994, 115 mins.

Live Short Films by Larry Jordan
Three live action films by filmmaker Larry Jordan which explore the dualities of myth and levels of reality, and one of which is a moving tribute to the American film master Joseph Cornell. In *Visions of a City*, poet Michael McClure emerges from all-reflection imagery of glass shop and car windows, bottles and mirrors, in a dual portrait of both McClure and the city of San Francisco. In *Cornell 1965*, Jordan documents the only film footage which exists of pioneer artist Joseph Cornell—"If you are a Cornell fan, there *isn't* any other film on him." *Magenta Geryon* is a film in three parts: *Adagio* is a nude study of a beautiful woman named Psyche and a nude man called Eros. *In a Summer Garden* explores the mystery roots of the filmmaker's own passion for the world of bright blossoms, the mystical rose, and the ancient gardens of Beardsley and King Arthur. And *Winter Light* is filmed in the dawn hours of California winter and explores the endless permutations of light and illumination as representatives of the Demeter-Persephone myth of the withdrawal of life through the winter months.
VHS: S09419. $59.95.
Larry Jordan, USA, 1977-89, 35 mins.

Rime of the Ancient Mariner
Larry Jordan directed this fully animated film which is narrated by Orson Welles. Using the classic engravings of Gustave Dore and a cut-out style of animation, the film is a powerful spiritual experience as it follows Samuel Taylor Coleridge's long dream of an old mariner (Orson Welles) who kills an albatross and suffers the pains of the damned for it.
VHS: S09418. $59.95.
Larry Jordan, USA, 1977, 42 mins.

The Sacred Art of Tibet/ The Visible Compendium
The Sacred Art of Tibet (1972, 28 mins.) was inspired by a gallery showing of unique Tibetan thankas, religious scroll paintings, rupas and other sacred images and artifacts. Jordan set out to present a visual experience of Tibetan Tantric Buddhism, and the resulting film rises above conventional documentary form to become a beautiful and autonomous work of art in its own right. *The Visible Compendium* (1990, 17 mins.) is an animated film that took two years to make and is one of Jordan's most technically refined works to date. It takes the viewer on a trip through idyllic lands where plants smile, an image of a tiger appears in the sun, and nude women wander about comfortably within an enchanted landscape. A beautiful and densely constructed work, rich in enigmatic and allusive images.
VHS: S14552. $59.95.
Larry Jordan, USA, 1972/90, 45 mins.

Short Animations by Larry Jordan
A program of wonder, discovery, animation magic. In *Duo Concertantes*, Jordan uses 19th century engravings and a cutout animation style to create the "Centennial Exhibition,"—a visual tour-de-force of another time and place; and *Patricia Gives Birth to a Dream by the Doorway* is a series of surreal images within a door frame. *Gymnopedies* uses music by Eric Satie for an intricate sleight-of-mind game dealt by cosmic jesters. *Our Lady of the Spheres* is an animated film-dream journey that juxtaposes delicate 19th century engravings with symbols of the space age. *Moonlight Sonata* is animated to the rhythms of Satie's music as the moon and moonlight are guiding lights for visual interpretation. *Once upon a Time* first presents a haunted castle, and then spirits lead a young man into another world. *Carabosse* forms figures in blue performing a jewel-like opera in black space. *Masquerade* animates hand-engraved cut-outs on a full-color background in a mood-filled evocation of Harlequin.
VHS: S09420. $59.95.
Larry Jordan, USA, 1964-1985, 56 mins.

Sophie's Place
The masterpiece of Larry Jordan's full, hand-painted cut-out animation and the result of five years of work, *Sophie's Place* is an "alchemical autobiography." The film begins in a garden resembling paradise and proceeds to the interior of the Mosque of St. Sophia, then develops into episodes centering around the forms of Sophia—an early Greek and Gnostic embodiment of spiritual wisdom. Filmmaker Stan Brakhage calls Jordan's *Sophie's Place* "the greatest epic animation film ever."
VHS: S09421. $59.95.
Larry Jordan, USA, 1986, 90 mins.

cd-ROMS

Adventure Kid, Vol. 1

Computer whiz Norizaku discovers a World War II-era computer that he thinks will be a fun piece of history to play with. Unfortunately, his curiosity unwittingly releases the encoded spirit of the machine's evil creator, Massago, freed to fulfill his dreams of vengeance against his wife and the army officer who raped her. Anime. Japanese with English subtitles.
   MAC. Req: System 7 or higher. 68020, 68030, 68040, or Power PC CPU and CD ROM drive. 4 MB RAM, 256 color monitor (or better). Quicktime 1.5 or better (included).
   WIN. Req: Windows 3.1 and MS DOS 5.0 or higher. 80386SZ MHz or higher CPU and CD ROM drive. 4MB RAM, SVGA with at least 256 color display. Soundblaster compatible sound card. Quicktime 1.1 or better (included).
   CD-ROM: CD90068. $24.95.
   Japan, 75 mins.

Adventure Pack

Includes the titles *Wayzata World Factbook 1994 Edition*, *Internet Surfer: Getting Started*, *Who Killed Sam Rupert?*, *Quick Art Designer 1*, *Virtual Universe*, *Journey to the Planets*, *SpaceTime and Art*, *Font Pro 3: Designer Type*, *Windsurfing Portfolio CD* and *MusicScapes Professional*.
   DOS. Req: DOS 4.0 or higher; 1 Mb free RAM; hard drive; CD-Rom drive.
   MAC. Req: Mac 7.1 or higher; 1 Mb free RAM; hard drive; CD-Rom drive.
   WIN. Req: Windows 3.1 or higher; 1 Mb free RAM; hard drive; CD-Rom drive.
   CD-ROM: CD90050. $39.00.

All My Hummingbirds Have Alibis

Composer and performer Morton Subotnick presents two breathtaking musical pieces, "All My Hummingbirds Have Alibis" and "Five Scenes from an Imaginary Ballet," written expressly for CD-ROM use. They are combined with images and text by surrealist Max Ernst and commentary from Subotnick.
   MAC. Req: Any Macintosh with color display; System 7; CD-ROM drive; no more than 3.2 Mb available RAM (5 Mb installed); 640x480 resolution (13") color monitor; speakers or headphones if CD-ROM drive is external.
   CD-ROM: CD90027. $39.95.
   Morton Subotnick

Amanda Stories

Kids and parents alike love the mischievous Inigo the Cat and Your Faithful Camel, which are only two of the ten charming stories which *The New York Times* "highly recommended for children". Amanda Goodenough's colorful animations offer lessons about love, friendship and loyalty.
   MAC. Req: Any Macintosh with color display; system 7; CD-ROM drive; no more than 2.2MB available RAM (4MB installed).
   WIN. Req: 25-MHz 486SX or higher processor; MS-DOS 5 or later; 640x480, 16-color display (256-color recommended); 4MB RAM (8MB recommended).
   CD-ROM: CD90006. $59.95.
   Amanda Goodenough, USA

American Heritage: The Civil War

Based on the Pulitzer Prize-winning *American Heritage Picture History of the Civil War* by Bruce Catton, this two-disc CD-ROM package is loaded with information on the American Civil War. Featured are the complete texts of the classic American novels *Uncle Tom's Cabin* and *The Red Badge of Courage*, along with several short stories by author Ambrose Bierce, the works of dozens of other poets and artists, and more. In addition, this CD-ROM features photographs, artwork, maps and video clips, essays on the issues of the time, along with biographies of the people who shaped the era, a look into the military strategies of the Union and the Confederacy, and a game in which the user can experience the Presidency of the United States through the eyes of either Abraham Lincoln or Jefferson Davis.
   MAC. Req: Street date: March 20, 1996. System requirements will be available shortly thereafter.
   WIN. Req: 486 DX 33 or higher, 8Mb of RAM, 8Mb hard drive space, SVGA graphics 640 x 480, 256 color monitor, double speed CD-ROM drive (or faster), MPC compatible sound card, a mouse (or comparable pointing device), Windows version 3.1 or 3.11, and DOS 3.3 or higher.
   CD-ROM: CD90108. $69.95.
   USA

American Poetry: The Nineteenth Century

Over 1,000 poems by nearly 150 poets. Dickinson, Longfellow, Emerson and Poe, among others, are included. Six hours of audio recordings, indexes of all the poets, titles and first lines, biographical notes and photos of 60 poets, extensive annotations and performances by Garrison Keillor, Cynthia Ozick and others.
   MAC. Req: 68030 processor (examples: Performa 575; Quadra; Centris) or better; 7.0 operating system or later; 8 MB RAM; 640x480 color monitor or 13" display; Double-speed CD-ROM drive.
   WIN. Req: 486SX-33 or higher processor; 640x480, 256-color display (accelerator recommended); 8 MB RAM; MPC2-compatible CD-ROM drive; Sound card (16-bit) with speakers or headphones; Windows 3.1 or Windows 95.
   CD-ROM: CD90130. $39.95.

Amnesty Interactive

Sponsored by the human rights watchdog organization Amnesty International, this hybrid CD-ROM gives an overview of human rights and human rights violations, from ancient times through the 20th century. Highlights include the ideas of noted thinkers and political figures, multicultural imagery, art, music, and many other valuable reference materials for teachers and students alike. Features include an atlas of world human rights conditions, stories by former political prisoners, a world music soundtrack and more. Winner of the Interactive Media Festival Award.
   MAC. Req: 68030 processor (examples: Performa 575; Quadra; Centris) or better; 7.0 operating system or later; 8 MB RAM; 640x480 color monitor or 13" display; Double-speed CD-ROM drive.
   WIN. Req: 486SX-25 or higher processor; 640x480, 256-color display; 4MB RAM (8MB recommended); MPC compatible CD-ROM drive; Sound card (8-bit) with speakers or headphones; Microsoft Windows 95.
   CD-ROM: CD90080. $19.95.
   USA

Antonin Dvorak: Symphony No. 9 "From the New World"

The Vienna Philharmonic's audio CD recording of Antonin Dvorak's 1892 symphony, inspired by the vitality of the American people, is accompanied by the entire score, which rolls before you as the music plays (the first of its kind on CD-ROM). Also included is extensive research on the history and social climate of Dvorak's time.
   MAC. Req: Any Macintosh with color display; System 7; CD-ROM drive; no more than 2.2 Mb available RAM (4 Mb installed); speakers or headphones if CD-ROM is external.
   CD-ROM: CD90018. $79.95.
   Robert Winter

Baseball's Greatest Hits

Filled with rare video clips and more than six hours of audio recordings from the greatest moments in baseball, this CD-ROM takes you through more than 60 high points, with box scores of important games, team histories, career statistics, still photos of baseball's greatest players, columns by Pulitzer Prize-winner Red Smith, and introductions by Mel Allen.
   MAC. Req: Any Macintosh with color display; System 7; CD-ROM drive; no more than 2.2 Mb available RAM (4 Mb installed).
   WIN. Req: 25-MHz 486SX or higher processor; MS-DOS 5 or later; 640x480, 256-color display; 4 Mb RAM (8 Mb recommended).
   CD-ROM: CD90043. $59.95.
   Jeff Kisseloff, USA

The Beat Experience: The Red Hot Organization

A portrait of the artists—writers, musicians, poets, filmmakers—who gave birth to the 1950's artistic community. An experience meant to immerse the user in the ethos of the Beat Generation—who and what they were—sexuality, drug use, art. Includes selections from books by Ginsberg, Burroughs, Kerouac; music by Monk, Parker, Davis and Coltrane, and over 50 images from the Whitney exhibition of "Beat Culture and the New America: 1950-1965."
   MAC. Req: 68030 processor (examples: Performa 575; Quadra; Centris) or better; 7.0 operating system or later; 8 MB RAM; 640x480 color monitor or 13" display; Double-speed CD-ROM drive.
   WIN. Req: 486SX-33 or higher processor; 640x480, 256-color display (accelerator recommended); 8 MB RAM; MPC2-compatible CD-ROM drive; Sound card (16-bit) with speakers or headphones; Windows 3.1 or Windows 95.
   CD-ROM: CD90117. $39.95.

Beethoven Lives Upstairs

Based on the popular Classical Kids audio series. This interactive CD (kids can try their hand at playing some of his symphony pieces) features opportunities to learn about Beethoven's life and personality, and to play fun games which supply musical facts. With gorgeous video clips from the live-action film of the same name, this is a seamless blend of historical fact, fiction and imagination.
   WIN. Req: Requires 4MB RAM, 4MB available hard-disk space.
   CD-ROM: CD90109. $901.09.

Beyond the Wall: Stories Behind the Vietnam Wall

Armed Forces Radio D.J. Adrian Cronauer narrates this thought-provoking look at the stories behind the Vietnam Veterans Memorial in Washington, D.C. Veterans' memories and reflections on the war are augmented by newsreel footage, historical photographs, and recordings and newspaper articles about the war and the military buildup that preceded it.
   MAC. Req: System 7.0 or higher; 7.01 system requirement.
   OTHER. Req: Multimedia PC.
   CD-ROM: CD90102. $59.98.

Cartoon Network 'Toon Jam!

Kids create their own music videos with special magic effects and 25 different music themes to choose from. Children can audition for and cast select music for, direct and save their videos and create their own personal film festivals. The delightful *Cartoon Network 'Toon Jam!* is hosted by Moxy, the Cartoon Network host, and features 18 other well-known characters, such as the Jetsons, Yogi Bear, Huckleberry Hound and more. Starring Bobcat Goldthwait as the voice of Moxy. Suitable for ages 4-13 years.
   WIN. Req: 386 SX 25 MHz or better, 4 MB RAM, 2 megs available of hard drive, DOS 6 or later Windows 3.1 or later, single speed CD-ROM drive or better, 16-bit digital sound card, video card display (640 x 480 resolution) with 256 colors, mouse.
   CD-ROM: CD90073. $44.98.

Cinema Volta

Artist and narrator Jim Petrillo looks at the diverse accomplishments and lives of the great electrical inventors of the 19th century juxtaposed with the history of Sicily, Shelley and Byron, James Joyce, the cave paintings of Lascaux, *Frankenstein*, and Petrillo's own childhood. The result is a provocative look at the technology which surrounds us and what we have become—a treat for the eye and mind alike.
   MAC. Req: Any Macintosh with color display; System 7; CD-ROM drive; no more than 4.3MB available RAM (5MB installed); 640x480 resolution (13") color monitor.
   WIN. Req: 486SX-33 or higher processor; 640x480, 256-color display (accelerator recommended); 8MB RAM; MPC2-compatible CD-ROM drive; sound card (16-bit) with speakers or headphones; Windows 3.1 or Windows 95.
   CD-ROM: CD90028. $39.95.
   Jim Petrillo

Comic Book Confidential

This CD-ROM features Ron Mann's critically acclaimed film *Comic Book Confidential* in its entirety and includes over 120 pages of comics by artists such as Stan Lee, William Gaines, Lynda Barry, R. Crumb and Art Spiegelman, as well as biographies of each artist, lists of their published works, and a new introduction by Scott McCloud, author of *Understanding Comics. Comic Book Confidential* spans the history of the comics from the 1930s to the present, and is the only comprehensive documentary of comics and their creators ever made.
   MAC. Req: Any color-capable Macintosh (25-MHz 68030 processor or better recommended): System 7; not more than 6.2MB of available RAM (8MB installed); 13" color monitor; CD-ROM drive.
   WIN. Req: 486SX-33 or higher processor; 640x480, 256-color display (accelerator recommended); 8MB RAM; MPC2-compatible CD-ROM drive; sound card (16-bit) with speakers or headphones; Windows 3.1 or Windows 95.
   CD-ROM: CD90014. $39.95.
   Ron Mann, USA

The Complete Maus

Art Spiegelman won the Pulitzer Prize for his gripping comic book saga of his parents' survival of the Holocaust, *Maus*, in which the Jews are mice and the Nazis are cats. This CD-ROM includes 18 hours with his father, thousands of color sketches, many never seen in public before, and interviews with Spiegelman himself, discussing what went into the making of *Maus*. Each page of the text is linked to historical documents such as maps, prisoners' drawings and photographs.
   MAC. Req: Any color capable Macintosh (25-MHz 68030 processor or better recommended): System 7; not more than 6.2MB of available RAM (8MB installed); 13" color monitor; CD-ROM drive.
   WIN. Req: 486SX-33 or higher processor; 640x480, 256-color display (accelerator recommended); 8MB RAM; MPC2-compatible CD-ROM drive; sound card (16-bit) with speakers or headphones; Windows 3.1 or Windows 95.
   CD-ROM: CD90033. $49.95.
   Art Spiegelman

Countdown (Visual Almanac Series, Vol. 1)

Countdown uses three challenging games to build intuition and math skills, using new approaches to teaching young minds mathematical concepts. Players can increase the difficulty level of problems as they increase their skills.
   MAC. Req: Any Macintosh with color display; System 7; CD-ROM drive; no more than 2.2MB available RAM (4MB installed).
   WIN. Req: 486SX-33 or higher processor; 640x480, 256-color display (accelerator recommended); 8MB RAM; MPC2-compatible CD-ROM drive; sound card (16-bit) with speakers or headphones; Windows 3.1 or Windows 95.
   CD-ROM: CD90010. $29.95.
   M. Nanny & R. Mohl

Criterion Goes to the Movies

Containing clips from the more than 140 films in Voyager's Criterion Collection of laser disc films, this CD-ROM spans from *Some Like It Hot* to *King Kong* to *Blade Runner* to *The Adventures of Baron von Munchausen*. Entries include film credits, essays on the individual films, still photographs of the stars, original theatrical trailers, production photos and more.
   MAC. Req: Any Macintosh with color display; System 7; CD-ROM drive; no more than 3.2MB available RAM (5MB installed); 640x480 resolution (13") color monitor.
   WIN. Req: 25-MHz 486SX or higher processor; MS-DOS 5 or later; 640x480, 256-color display; 4MB RAM (8MB recommended).
   CD-ROM: CD90013. $24.95.

The Day After Trinity: J. Robert Oppenheimer and the Atomic Bomb

Based on the Academy Award-nominated documentary by Jon Else, this hybrid CD-ROM explores the life and mind of J. Robert Oppenheimer, the charismatic yet tragic man who launched the atomic age and the rest of the world into the nuclear age. Featuring rare footage and first person interviews with participants from the first atomic test over 50 years ago in New Mexico, biographical information on all participants, Jon Else's complete film, declassified military and FBI documents, commentary by Else and by historian Michael Renov, a glossary of terms and more.
   MAC. Req: 68030 processor (examples: Performa 575; Quadra; Centris) or better; 7.0 operating system or later; 8 MB RAM; 640x480 color monitor or 13" display; Double-speed CD-ROM drive.
   WIN. Req: 486SX-33 or higher processor; 640x480, 256-color display (accelerator recommended); 8 MB RAM; MPC2-compatible CD-ROM drive; Sound card (16-bit) with speakers or headphones; Windows 3.1 or Windows 95.
   CD-ROM: CD90085. $29.95.
   Jon Else, USA

Dinotopia, Living the Adventure

Dinotopia is set in a series of 10 worlds where humans and dinosaurs coexist. This adventure game features puzzles and games, live actors, puppetry, 3-D animation, enriched graphics and an in-depth story line. This interactive CD teaches the Dinotopia language and allows the opportunity to navigate a submarine, explore new worlds and create musical melodies.
   WIN. Req: MPC 486X33 Mhz or better, 4MB RAM, DOS 3.0 or later/Windows 3.1 or later, Double-speed CD-ROM drive, 16-bit digital sound card and speakers, SVGA video display (640 x 480 resolution) with 256 colors, mouse.
   CD-ROM: CD90071. $69.98.

Eastwood

A retrospective of Clint Eastwood's career as both an actor and director. This two-CD set contains over 200 video and audio clips including dozens of film clips, slide shows, interviews and countless behind-the-scene surprises. Offering hours of entertainment, this set is bound to thrill the Eastwood afficionado as well as the general movie fan.
   WIN. Req: 486DX/66, 8MB RAM, Vesa local-bus or PCi video, 2X ROM drive, 16-bit Windows-compatible sound card.
   CD-ROM: CD90112. $69.98.

Ephemeral Films: 1931-1960

A two-part series capturing tales from the dawn of the American Consumer Age, documenting the revealing, absurd and perverse films of educators, marketers and others. Part 1 is entitled *1931-1945: To New Horizons*, and Part 2 is *1946-1960: You Can't Get There from Here*. Filmmaker Rick Prelinger is a film scholar and anthropologist whose other works include *Call It Home* and *Television Toys*.
   MAC. Req: Any Macintosh with color display; System 7; CD-ROM drive; no more than 2.2MB available RAM (4MB installed).
   WIN. Req: 25-MHz 480SX or higher processor; MS-DOS 5 or later; 640x480, 256-color display; 4MB RAM (8MB recommended).
   CD-ROM: CD90016. $39.95.
   Rick Prelinger, USA

Exotic Japan

An interactive guide to Japanese customs and language with over 150 lessons and quizzes, instructive animations, traditional Japanese games and woodcuts, and information on everything from the bullet train to business cards. Both male and female native Japanese speakers guide you through proper pronunciation as you record and play your own voice speaking Japanese. From Nikki Yokokura, Japanese language professor at McMaster University in Toronto.
   MAC. Req: Macintosh Plus or better (any Mac introduced since 1986) running system 6.0.7 or later; CD-ROM drive; 1.5 Mb of available RAM. If running System 6, must have at least 2 Mb RAM installed; if running System 7, must have at least 3 Mb. Requires speakers or headphones if CD-ROM drive is external.
   WIN. Req: 386SX or higher processor; MS-DOS 3.3 or later; 640x480, 256-color display; 4 Mb RAM.
   CD-ROM: CD90042. $59.95.
   Nikki Yokokura

Explorer Pack

Contains the titles *Tony Quinn's Virtual Galaxy*, *Beyond the Wall of Stars: Quest One of the Taran Trilogy*, *Sound Library Pro*, *World of Motion*, *Loon Magic*, *Matt & Joe's Cool Screen Backgrounds*, *Font Pro 2: Types of Distinction*, *epsPRO 1: Design Elements*, *CD FilmFest: Comedy Classics*, and *Photo Pro Select: The Best of Photo Pro*.
   MAC. Req: Mac 7.1 or higher; 2 Mb free RAM; hard drive; CD-Rom drive.
   WIN. Req: Windows 3.1 or higher; 2 Mb free RAM; hard drive; CD-Rom drive.
   CD-ROM: CD90051. $39.00.

Fellini

Complete information on the Italian master filmmaker, from the script to film's completion: critics' reviews, behind-the-scenes photographs and details of his drawing and music. Contains clips from all 21 of his films, a biography and lists of his national and international awards and prizes.
   WIN. Req: Not available at present.
   CD-ROM: CD90111. $49.99.

The First Emperor of China

This fascinating CD-ROM combines archival film footage of the first days of the excavation of the tomb of the First Emperor of China, Qin Shi Huang Di, with archival materials, a tour through the Qin Museum of Warriors and Horses, over 2,000 slides, and commentary from distinguished scholars to tell the story of this amazing archaeological find. It features a bilingual Chinese/English soundtrack, a glossary of terms, an audio guide to Chinese pronunciation of terms, maps, a timeline, and much more.
   MAC. Req: Any color capable Macintosh (25-MHz 68030 processor or better recommended): System 7; not more than 6.2 Mb of available RAM (8 Mb installed); 13" color monitor; CD-ROM drive.
   CD-ROM: CD90030. $79.95.
   Dr. Ching-chih Chen

First Person: Donald Norman: Defending Human Attributes in the Age of the Machine

Design theorist Donald Norman examines technology in terms of the plight of the human race. Join him as he examines a Macintosh desktop, points out its good points and its bad points, and ties these into the problems humans face by living in the technological age. This so-called "guru of interface design" insists that humanity must come before technology. Thought provoking. From the *First Person* CD-ROM series.

MAC. Req: 68030 processor (examples: Performa 575; Quadra; Centris) or better; 7.0 operating system or later; 8MB RAM; 640x480 color monitor or 13" display; double-speed CD-ROM drive.
WIN. Req: 486SX-33 or higher processor; 640x480, 256-color display (accelerator recommended); 8MB RAM; MPC2-compatible CD-ROM drive; Sound card (16-bit) with speakers or headphones; Windows 3.1 or Windows 95.
CD-ROM: CD90083. $39.95.
USA

First Person: Marvin Minsky, The Society of Mind

Marvin Minsky's theories come to life as he walks, talks and jumps across the page, challenging conventional notions of what makes us tick in a program that combines over 100 minutes of original video, 200 color graphics and 1100 pages of text, including the complete *Society of Mind*. Minsky is the co-founder of the MIT Media Laboratory.

MAC. Req: Any color-capable Macintosh (25-MHz 68030 processor or better recommended); System 7; not more than 6.2MB of available RAM (8MB installed); 13" color monitor; CD-ROM drive.
CD-ROM: CD90001. $49.95.

First Person: Mumia Abu-Jamal: Live from Death Row

Mumia Abu-Jamal is an award-winning Philadelphia journalist who has been on death row since 1982 for the killing of a Philadelphia police officer. Convicted and sentenced under extremely questionable circumstances, Abu-Jamal speaks about the lives and treatment of African-Americans in the United States, the judicial system, life in America's prisons and more. This hybrid CD-ROM features the entire text of Abu-Jamal's autobiography *Live from Death Row*, video and audio interviews with Abu-Jamal, an overview of his life, highlights of his political involvements, other of his writings and more.

MAC. Req: 68030 processor (examples: Performa 575; Quadra; Centris) or better; 7.0 operating system or later; 8 MB RAM; 640x480 color monitor or 13" display; Double-speed CD-ROM drive.
WIN. Req: 486SX-33 or higher processor; 640x480, 256-color display (accelerator recommended); 8 MB RAM; MPC2-compatible CD-ROM drive; Sound card (16-bit) with speakers or headphones; Windows 3.1 or Windows 95.
CD-ROM: CD90084. $29.95.
USA

First Person: Stephen Jay Gould, On Evolution

Best-selling author and evolutionary biologist Stephen Jay Gould tackles evolution and natural history in a lecture delivered for this CD-ROM, in which he poses three intriguing riddles about Charles Darwin. A wealth of additional material includes the best of Gould's published work on the subject and relevant writings by Darwin and other explorers of the Victorian era.

MAC. Req: Any color-capable Macintosh (25-MHz 68030 processor or better recommended); System 7; not more than 6.2MB of available RAM (8MB installed); 13" color monitor; CD-ROM drive.
WIN. Req: 486SX-33 or higher processor; 640x480, 256-color display (accelerator recommended); 8MB RAM; MPC2-compatible CD-ROM drive; sound card (16-bit) with speakers or headphones; Windows 3.1 or Windows 95.
CD-ROM: CD90002. $39.95.

For All Mankind

Between 1968 and 1972, 24 astronauts left Earth for the moon. Culled from 80 hours of interviews, a 79-minute film (complete here) tells the story of the first "extraterrestrial humans." Also included are lunar maps, illustrations, mission histories and astronaut biographies. Hundreds of images from NASA archives.

MAC. Req: 68030 processor (examples: Performa 575; Quadra; Centris) or better; 7.0 operating system or later; 8 MB RAM; 640x480 color monitor or 13" display; Double-speed CD-ROM drive.
WIN. Req: 486SX-33 or higher processor; 640x480, 256-color display (accelerator recommended); 8 MB RAM; MPC2-compatible CD-ROM drive; Sound card (16-bit) with speakers or headphones; Windows 3.1 or Windows 95.
CD-ROM: CD90129. $39.95.

Franz Schubert: "The Trout" Quintet

American music critic and author Alan Rich offers a personal look at "The Trout" Quintet, including the original song "Die Forelle" in both English and German, and the Trout Cookbook.

MAC. Req: Macintosh Plus or better (any Mac produced since 1986) running system 6.0.7 or later; CD-ROM drive; 1.5 Mb of available RAM. If running system 6, must have at least 2MB RAM installed; If running System 7, must have at least 3 Mb. Requires speakers or headphones if CD-ROM drive is external.
CD-ROM: CD90025. $59.95.
Alan Rich, USA

French Pronunciation Tutor

This hybrid CD-ROM simplifies the process of learning French, because it allows students to listen to French as spoken by a native speaker, then record themselves speaking French and compare their speech to that of a native French speaker. This educational CD-ROM features interactive help, hints to explain the finer points of pronunciation, detailed animations of the speech process, interactive exercise screens, pronunciation tests for tracking your progress, audio and video of native speakers and more. From The Learning Company.

MAC. Req: Runs on all Macintosh computers equipped with a CD-ROM drive, a 256-color monitor, 680.30/25MHz or better processor, and System 7. Requires 4 MB of memory. Requires a microphone or MacRecorder.
WIN. Req: System 386 or better; Multimedia PC with CD-ROM drive; Requires 386/25MHz or better; 4 MB RAM, Windows 3.1 or higher, doublespeed CD-ROM drive, Windows compatible sound card, VGA or better, plus a microphone.
CD-ROM: CD90095. $59.98.

German Pronunciation Tutor

This hybrid CD-ROM makes learning German easy because it allows students to listen to German being spoken by a native speaker, record themselves speaking, and then compare the two. This educational CD-ROM features interactive help, hints to explain the finer points of German pronunciation, detailed animations of the speech process, pronunciation tests for tracking your progress in German, video of native speakers and more. From The Learning Company.

MAC. Req: Runs on all Macintosh computers equipped with a CD-ROM drive, a 256-color monitor, 680.30/25MHz or better processor, and System 7. Requires 4 MB of memory. Requires a microphone or MacRecorder.
WIN. Req: System 386 or better; Multimedia PC with CD-ROM drive; Requires 386/25MHz or better, 4 MB RAM, Windows 3.1 or higher, doublespeed CD-ROM drive, Windows compatible sound card, VGA or better, plus a microphone.
CD-ROM: CD90094. $59.98.

Gettysburg Multimedia Battle Simulation

Shelby Foote, noted Civil War Historian, narrates this innovative CD-ROM, which features an historically correct simulation of the battle at Gettysburg. Also featured are video clips from the acclaimed epic *Gettysburg*. This historical simulation can be used in either historical or free play.

WIN. Req: MPC IBM or 100% compatible 386SX/25Mhz, MS Windows 3.1, 4 Megabytes RAM, Double-speed CD-ROM, VGA 256-color graphics, Soundblaster-compatible sound card.
CD-ROM: CD90072. $69.98.

Great Paintings—Renaissance to Impressionism: The Frick Collection

This CD-ROM highlights 138 paintings by 64 different artists from the renowned Frick Collection of New York. Each image features historical background and descriptive information and is displayed in a full-screen format. Includes an online tour of the Frick Collection, sharp, clear images, and more.

MAC. Req: LCII or above (040 CPU or above strongly recommended). 5MB RAM (8-10MB for 16- or 24-bit color). Color Monitor (640 x 480) and 8-bit color (16- or 24-bit color strongly recommended). Double-Speed CD-ROM Drive. System 7.0 or better. Mouse.
WIN. Req: 486/25 or above. 8MB RAM. VGA Monitor (640 x 480) and Video Card running at 256 colors. Double-Speed CD-ROM Drive. Windows 3.1. Windows Compatible Sound Card. Mouse.
CD-ROM: CD90105. $59.95.

Greatest Olympic Moments

Highlights of favorite Summer Olympic stories, from Jesse Owens to Greg Louganis; dozens of QuickTime movies featuring related stories of Olympic history; and anecdotes and historical documentation from each Olympiad, including posters, newspaper articles and rare photos.

MAC. Req: 68030 processor (examples: Performa 575; Quadra; Centris) or better; 7.0 operating system or later; 8 MB RAM; 640x480 color monitor or 13" display; Double-speed CD-ROM drive.
WIN. Req: 486SX-33 or higher processor; 640x480, 256-color display (accelerator recommended); 8 MB RAM; MPC2-compatible CD-ROM drive; Sound card (16-bit) with speakers or headphones; Windows 3.1 or Windows 95.
CD-ROM: CD90123. $39.95.
Bud Greenspan

The Guinness Encyclopedia

This comprehensive, interactive encyclopedia contains articles, illustrations, maps, animations, over 1,000 photographs, more than 30 language samples, and more. *The Guinness Encyclopedia* is thematically arranged, offers in-depth explanations of facts, including animated demonstrations of the way things work, and focuses on such topics as "The Nature of the Universe," "The Human Organism," "Religion and Philosophy," "Language and Literature," "Music and Dance" and "The Countries of the World," among others.

MAC. Req: Mac 7.1 or higher; 1 Mb free RAM; hard drive; CD-Rom drive.
WIN. Req: Windows 3.1 or higher; 1 Mb free RAM; hard drive; CD-Rom drive.
CD-ROM: CD90049. $39.00.
USA

Haight-Ashbury in the Sixties

In the 1960s, San Francisco was a Mecca to the new youth culture. This hybrid CD-ROM takes a look back at the 1960s Haight-Ashbury scene through artwork, articles, photographs, poetry and commentary from Haight-Ashbury's own 1960s counterculture newspaper, *The San Francisco Oracle*. Also included are video clips, text, narration, music and more.

MAC. Req: Not available at present.
OTHER. Req: Multimedia PC.
CD-ROM: CD90089. $54.98.
USA

A Hard Day's Night

The first Beatles' film is interactive and shown in its entirety. Also includes the original script, two short films, clips from the early work of director Richard Lester, an essay on the Beatles and the history of rock n' roll, profiles of the band, cast, and crew, and the movie's original theatrical trailer.

MAC. Req: Any Macintosh with color display; System 7; CD-ROM drive; no more than 3.2MB available RAM (5MB installed).
WIN. Req: Not available at present.
CD-ROM: CD90012. $39.95.
Richard Lester, Great Britain, 1964

How to Read a Film

Film and communication—from technology to theory, politics to personalities, art to business—is explored in this informative and entertaining CD. More than 500 photos, 100 diagrams and animations, and almost one hour of film clips ranging from *Potemkin* (49 edits in one minute and thirty-six seconds) to Altman's *The Player* (one continuous tracking shot lasting 7 minutes and 58 seconds) instruct students and fans to be more film savvy.

MAC. Req: 68030 processor (examples Performa 575; Quadra; Centris) or better; 7.0 operating system or later; 8 MB RAM; 640x480 color monitor or 13" display; Double-speed CD-ROM drive.
WIN. Req: 486SX-33 or higher processor; 640x480, 256 color display; 4MB RAM (8MB recommended); MPC compatible CD-ROM drive; Sound card (8-bit) with speakers or headphones; Microsoft Windows 3.1 or Windows 95.
CD-ROM: CD90122. $39.95.

I Photograph to Remember

I Photograph to Remember is the family memoir of renowned Latin American photographer Pedro Meyer. Narrated by Meyer in both English and Spanish, he documents his parents' last years of life, using the computer as a powerful medium for expression. His photographic work has appeared in more than 125 exhibitions, and is on display in over 20 museums worldwide. His published works include *Espejo de Espinas* (*Mirror of Thorns*).

MAC. Req: Any Macintosh with color display; System 7; CD-ROM drive; no more than 2.2 Mb available RAM (4 Mb installed); 640×480 resolution (13") color monitor; speakers or headphones if CD-ROM drive is external.
WIN. Req: 386SX or higher processor; MS-DOS 3.3 or later; 640x480, 256-color display; 4 Mb RAM.
CD-ROM: CD90031. $39.95.
Pedro Meyer

If Monks Had Macs: A Hearty Stew of Interactive Books, Games, Art

An interactive look at Henry David Thoreau's life and ideas, electronic editions of *Walden*, *The Scarlet Letter* and *JFK Witness* among others, Bruegel's masterpiece "Tower of Babel" examined in detail via the Painting Navigator, and games ranging from an existential art puzzle, a medieval adventure to the Monks' Memory Challenge!

MAC. Req: 68030 processor (examples: Performa 575; Quadra; Centris) or better; 7.0 operating system or later; 8 MB RAM; 640x480 color monitor or 13" display; Double-speed CD-ROM drive.
CD-ROM: CD90131. $34.95.

Igor Stravinsky: The Rite of Spring

This CD-ROM contains the energy and creativity of Igor Stravinsky and invites you to listen to the music of Stravinsky's "The Rite of Spring" as scholar and pianist Robert Winter's commentary on each theme scrolls by. There is also a detailed glossary of musical terms and theory, and a guide to the life and times of Stravinsky.

MAC. Req: Macintosh Plus or better (any Mac produced since 1986) running system 6.0.7 or later; CD-ROM drive; 1.5MB of available RAM; if running system 6, must have at least 2MB RAM installed; if running System 7, must have at least 3MB. Requires speakers or headphones if CD-ROM drive is external.
CD-ROM: CD90021. $79.95.
Robert Winter

Invisible Universe

Dodging Centaurus A, reclining on the Andromeda Galaxy, exploding into the Veil Nebula, Dr. Fiorella Terenzi brings it all to you in this entertaining and informative study of the universe beyond human sight. Dr. Terenzi uses star maps, movies, music and poetry to show you the evolution of stars, black holes, and glimpses of the origins of the universe itself.

MAC. Req: 68030 processor (i.e. Performa 575; Quadra; Centris) or better; 7.0 operating system or later; 8 MB RAM; 640x480 color monitor or 13" display; Double-speed CD-ROM drive.
WIN. Req: 486SX-33 or higher processor; 640x480, 256-color display (accelerator recommended); 8MB RAM; MPC2-compatible CD-ROM drive; Sound card (16-bit) with speakers or headphones; Windows 3.1 or Windows 95.
CD-ROM: CD90128. $39.95.

Jerusalem: An Interactive Pilgrimage to the Holy City

Retrace the Holy City's glorious history, from the New Testament to the present. Discover the shrines, relics, landmarks and people. Explore its spiritual heritage...from the Roman Era, through the Crusades and Islamic periods, to contemporary times. Hundreds of photographs, animations, video and audio clips, and even an interactive game for children. This priceless CD is interesting for all—for the scholar, the pilgrim and the armchair traveller!

MAC. Req: Not available at present.
WIN. Req: Not available at present.
CD-ROM: CD90113. $39.98.

Kon-Tiki

Hundreds of pages of text from Thor Heyerdahl's famous expeditions—the Ra, the Tigris and the Kon-Tiki—are included in this fascinating CD-ROM, with films taken onboard the ocean voyages and at archeological digs. Heyerdahl himself pops up to add explanations, and anecdotes, maps and diagrams contribute as well.

MAC. Req: 68030 processor (examples: Performa 575; Quadra; Centris) or better; 7.0 operating system or later; 8 MB RAM; 640x480 color monitor or 13" display; Double-speed CD-ROM drive.
WIN. Req: 486SX-33 or higher processor; 640x480, 256-color display (accelerator recommended); 8 MB RAM; MPC2-compatible CD-ROM drive; Sound card (16-bit) with speakers or headphones; Windows 3.1 or Windows 95.
CD-ROM: CD90125. $39.95.
Thor Heyerdahl

La Blue Girl, Volume 1

This CD-ROM features episodes 1 and 2 of the story of Miko Mido, an 18-year-old Ninja-in-training. Centuries ago his clan made a deal with the underworld forces, and now those forces are getting a new boss. Miko is suddenly called upon to protect the family business and keep the lustful Shikima away from the humans. Anime, Japanese with English subtitles.

DOS. Req: Windows 3.1 and MS DOS 5.0 or higher; 80386SX MHz or higher CPU and CD ROM drive; 4 Mb RAM; SVGA with at least 256 color display; Soundblaster compatible sound card; Quicktime 1.1 or better (included).
MAC. Req: System 7 or higher; 68030, 68040, or Power PC CPU and CD ROM drive; 4 Mb RAM; 256 color monitor (or better); Quicktime 1.5 or better (included).
WIN. Req: Windows 3.1 and MS DOS 5.0 or higher; 80386SX MHz or higher CPU and CD ROM drive; 4 Mb RAM; SVGA with at least 256 color display; Soundblaster compatible sound card; Quicktime 1.1 or better (included).
CD-ROM: CD90063. $24.95.
90 mins.

Last Chance to See

A spellbinding photographic chronicle of the many species of the world that are on the verge of extinction, including dozens of elephants, egrets, lemurs and more. The CD-ROM includes the entire text of the book *Last Chance to See*, plus over six hours of audio indexed to the text, over 700 photographs, information about each species and its current status, audio segments from the BBC radio series of the book, and more.

MAC. Req: Any Macintosh with color display; System 7; CD-ROM drive; no more than 2.2 Mb available RAM (4 Mb installed); speakers or headphones if CD-ROM drive is external.
WIN. Req: 386SX or higher processor; MS-DOS 3.3 or later; 640x480, 256-color display; 4 Mb RAM.
CD-ROM: CD90037. $59.95.
D. Adams & M. Carwar

Le Louvre: The Palace and Its Paintings

Explore over eight centuries of the Louvre, beginning with the fortress built by Philippe-Auguste and continuing to the Grand Louvre that exists today. This hybrid CD-ROM features over 300 images, more than 200 pages of text, an examination of the museum's artistic and architectural evolution, biographies of artists showcased at the Louvre, and either portraits or self-portraits of artists whose work is on display there. Artwork can be examined through zoom magnification, and is supported by expert commentary, inspiring music, and more.

MAC. Req: System 7.0 or higher; 7.01 system requirement.
OTHER. Req: Multimedia PC.
CD-ROM: CD90100. $49.98.

Leonardo the Inventor

While most people are familiar with Leonardo da Vinci's legacy of paintings and artwork, not everyone is aware that he was also a talented inventor, centuries ahead of his time. This hybrid CD-ROM takes drawing of inventions by da Vinci and animates them, showing what they might have looked like in action, both during da Vinci's lifetime and today. Rated "four mice" by *MacUser*.

MAC. Req: System 7.0 or higher; 7.01 system requirement.
OTHER. Req: Multimedia PC.
CD-ROM: CD90098. $49.98.

Like the Dickens

Includes full text of Dickens's 17 novels and 56 short stories, John Forster's *The Life of Charles Dickens* (numerous editions), and Dickens's obituary in the *London Times*.

WIN. Req: Not available at present.
CD-ROM: CD90115. $39.95.

Ludwig van Beethoven: Symphony No. 9

This CD-ROM contains the energy and creativity of Ludwig van Beethoven and invites you to listen to the music of Beethoven's *Symphony No. 9* as scholar and pianist Robert Winter's commentary on each theme scrolls by. There is also a detailed glossary of musical terms and theory, and a guide to the life and times of Beethoven.

MAC. Req: Macintosh Plus or better (any Mac produced since 1986) running system 6.0.7 or later; CD-ROM drive; 1.5MB of available RAM. If running system 6, must have at least 2MB RAM installed; if running System 7, must have at least 3MB. Requires speakers or headphones if CD-ROM drive is external.
CD-ROM: CD90019. $79.95.
Robert Winter

Making Music

The first true composing space for children. Allows kids to enter notes by painting on the screen, and modify volume, tempo and instrumentation. Lets kids save their compositions, too! Alter melody and rhythm, transpose or change six simple tunes to learn about structure and function. Games involve playing from novice musician to maestro using their own compositions.

MAC. Req: 68030 processor (examples: Performa 575; Quadra; Centris) or better; 7.0 operating system or later; 8 MB RAM; 640x480 color monitor or 13" display; Double-speed CD-ROM drive.
WIN. Req: 486SX-33 or higher processor; 640x480, 256-color display (accelerator recommended); 8 MB RAM; MPC2-compatible CD-ROM drive; Sound card (16-bit) with speakers or headphones; Windows 3.1 or Windows 95.
CD-ROM: CD90126. $39.95.

Masterworks of Japanese Painting: The Etsuko and Joe Price Collection

This CD-ROM features over 1,100 full-color images from the Etsuko and Joe Price collection—outside of Japan, the largest private collection of scrolls and screens from the Edo period. What makes the Edo period remarkable is that during that time, Japan closed its ports to the outside world, allowing Japanese art to grow and flourish without the influence of outsiders. With an introductory movie and in-depth commentary on each image.

MAC. Req: LCII or above (040 CPU or above strongly recommended). 5MB RAM (8-10MB for 16- or 24-bit color). Color Monitor (640 x 480) and 8-bit color (16- or 24-bit color strongly recommended). Double-Speed CD-ROM Drive. System 7.0 or better.
WIN. Req: 486/25 or above. 8MB RAM. VGA Monitor (640 x 480) and Video Card running at 256 colors. Double-Speed CD-ROM Drive. Windows 3.1. Windows Compatible Sound Card. Mouse.
CD-ROM: CD90103. $59.95.

Matisse—Aragon—Prokofiev: An Interactive Adventure in Art

This interactive CD-ROM features over 150 of Matisse's paintings and sculptures, an exploration of the diversity of Matisse's technique, and gives the viewer the opportunity to create a virtual museum. This CD-ROM also includes 60 poems by Aragon, 60 minutes of Prokofiev's music, comprehensive chronologies and extensive bibliographies, and features a complete index. From The Great Artists Collection.

MAC. Req: Apple Macintosh LC or later model with at least 4 MB of RAM for the application. 640 x 480, 256 color graphics. System 7.0 or later. 32-Bit QuickDraw, Quicktime 2.0. Apple-compatible double-speed (300 Kps) CD-ROM drive.
WIN. Req: Multimedia PC. 386sx or better processor, 8 MB of RAM, Double-speed (300 Kps) CD-ROM drive, Microsoft Windows compatible sound card, mouse, Super VGA graphics (640 x 480, 256 colors), Microsoft Windows version 3.1. MS-DOS version 5.0 or later, MS-DOS CD-ROM extensions, stereo headphones or speakers, Minimum 1.5 MB free hard disk space.
CD-ROM: CD90069. $69.98.
Guy Casaril

Modern Art: A Visit to the Foundation of Marguerite & Aimé Maeght

Marguerite and Aimé Maeght had hoped to create an environment architecturally worthy of the greatest works by Joan Miro, Georges Braque, Marc Chagall and other renowned 20th century artists. Works by these and other artists are featured in this hybrid CD-ROM, which takes the user on a guided tour through a detailed presentation of the masterpieces of 20th century art.

MAC. Req: System 7.0 or higher; 7.01 system requirement.
WIN. Req: 4 MB RAM; System 386 or higher; Windows 3.1 or higher; Multimedia PC with CD-ROM drive.
CD-ROM: CD90097. $49.95.

Monet—Verlaine—Debussy: The Impressionist Revolution

This interactive CD-ROM features over 200 of Monet's paintings, including 120 of Monet's "most admired works," an exploration of Monet's inspirational garden Giverny, and allows the opportunity to use Visible Brush Stroke and watch as Monet's works are created before your very eyes. This CD-ROM also includes 60 poems by Verlaine, 74 minutes of Debussy's music, comprehensive chronologies and extensive bibliographies, and features a complete index. From The Great Artists Collection.

MAC. Req: Apple Macintosh LC or later model with at least 4 MB of RAM for the application. 640 x 480, 256 color graphics. System 7.0 or later. 32-Bit QuickDraw, Quicktime 2.0. Apple-compatible double-speed (300 Kps) CD-ROM drive.
WIN. Req: Multimedia PC: 386sx or better processor, 8 MB of RAM, Double-speed (300 Kps) CD-ROM drive, Microsoft Windows compatible sound card, mouse, Super VGA graphics (640 x 480, 256 colors), Microsoft Windows version 3.1. MS-DOS version 5.0 or later, MS-DOS CD-ROM extensions, Stereo headphones or speakers, Minimum 1.5 MB free hard disk space.
CD-ROM: CD90070. $69.98.
Guy Casaril

New Voices New Visions

This compilation CD-ROM contains selections from the 24 winners of a computer art contest. The contest generated over 500 entries from independent artists in 18 different countries. *New Voices New Visions* contains the three grand prize winners, one artist who received an honorable mention, and 21 noteworthy entries.

MAC. Req: 68030 processor (examples: Performa 575; Quadra; Centris) or better; 7.0 operating system or later; 8 MB RAM; 640x480 color monitor or 13" display; Double-speed CD-ROM drive.
CD-ROM: CD90081. $29.95.

Of Mice and Men

Incorporates the text of the novel, 80 photos, six musical numbers from the 1958 Broadway musical, selected Steinbeck correspondence and criticism. The complete text of Jackson J. Benson's *The True Adventures of John Steinbeck, Writer: A Biography* is also included.

MAC. Req: Not available at present.
WIN. Req: Not available at present.
CD-ROM: CD90114. $49.95.

Our Secret Century: Archival Films from the Darker Side of the American Dream, Volumes 1 & 2

This hybrid CD-ROM includes the first two volumes in the 12-part *Our Secret Century: Archival Films from the Darker Side of the American Dream* series. Volume 1: *The Rainbow Is Yours* contains six color films which look at how consumerism and marketing in the 1950s were able to create an American obsession with form and design. Volume 2: *Capitalist Realism* contains three B&W films from the 1930s which borrow heavily from Soviet-style imagery of heroism. These portrayals of workers in corporate films serve to show the human aspects of factory life and mass production. This captivating CD-ROM also includes lectures, supplementary materials, commentary from filmmaker and media archaeologist Rick Prelinger and more.

MAC. Req: A "quadra" or better; Any Macintosh with a CD-ROM drive; At least 8 MB of RAM (5,500K free).
WIN. Req: 486SX-33 or higher processor; 640x480, 256-color display (accelerator recommended); 8 MB RAM; MPC2 compatible CD-ROM drive and sound card with speakers or headphones; Microsoft Windows 3.1; MS-DOS 5.0 or later.
CD-ROM: CD90065. $34.95.
Rick Prelinger, USA, 1995

Our Secret Century: Archival Films from the Darker Side of the American Dream, Volumes 3 & 4

Film scholar and media archaeologist Rick Prelinger continues his exploration of American history and society with the third and fourth installments of his *Our Secret Century: Archival Films from the Darker Side of the American Dream* series. This hybrid CD-ROM begins with Volume 3: *The Behavior Offensive*, an in-depth look at the American post-war mentality and the attempt to instill "family values" into American hearts and homes. The eight films featured document the national crusade of the 1950s for social guidance and social control. In Volume 4: *Menace and Jeopardy*, seven "safety" films warn of the dangers haste and carelessness can cause as they prey on unconscious fears about everyday "risks" Americans encounter at home and on the job.

MAC. Req: A "quadra" or better; Any Macintosh with a CD-ROM drive; At least 8 MB of RAM (5,500K free).
WIN. Req: 486SX-33 or higher processor; 640x480, 256-color display (accelerator recommended); 8 MB RAM; MPC2 compatible CD-ROM drive and sound card with speakers or headphones; Microsoft Windows 3.1; MS-DOS 5.0 or later.
CD-ROM: CD90066. $34.95.
Rick Prelinger, USA, 1995

Our Solar System

Travel on a fully-narrated tour of our solar system—its comets, its asteroids, its planets and their moons—from the torrid world of Venus to the freezing atmosphere of Neptune. Made in cooperation with the Jet Propulsion Laboratory (JPL), the United States Geological Survey and NASA, this hybrid CD-ROM features images never before seen by the general public and is noted for the exceptional quality of its sound and photographs. This "layman's guide to the solar system" includes a space glossary, hundreds of photographs and fascinating facts, music, special effects, and more.

MAC. Req: Any Macintosh computer with 256+ color, Color monitor; XA compatible CD-ROM drive; Macintosh system 6.0.7 or higher with a CD-ROM driver, foreign file access extension.
WIN. Req: IBM PC AT or compatible 80386 or 80486; VGA display or better (minimum 256+ color for acceptable display); DOS 3.3 or higher; Microsoft Windows System 3.0 or higher.
OTHER. Req: Kodak Photo CD, Phillips & Magnavox CD-1, Panasonic 3DO or other Photo CD compatible systems; or TV-Based Players: Sega Saturn, Panasonic 3DO, Phillips CD-i, Kodak Photo CD players and all Photo CD compatible players.
CD-ROM: CD90064. $29.95.
USA, 1995

Painters Painting

Based on the critically acclaimed film by Emile de Antonio, this is a vibrant collective portrait of the legendary figures who powered the tumultuous post-war art scene. Examples of each artist's work, full transcripts of interviews and the 100-minute film are included. Rauschenberg, Rivers, Warhol, Johns, Motherwell, Stella and many more are featured.

MAC. Req: 68030 processor (examples: Performa 575; Quadra; Centris) or better; 7.0 operating system or later; 8 MB RAM; 640x480 color monitor or 13" display; Double-speed CD-ROM drive.
WIN. Req: 486SX-33 or higher processor; 640x480, 256-color display (accelerator recommended); 8 MB RAM; MPC2 compatible CD-ROM drive; Sound card (16-bit) with speakers or headphones; Windows 3.1 or Windows 95.
CD-ROM: CD90118. $39.95.

A Passion for Art: Renoir, Cézanne, Matisse and Dr. Barnes

Explore Dr. Barnes' rarely seen collection of post-impressionist paintings. Paintings by Renoir, Cézanne, Matisse and many other artists are shown in stunning detail, revealing the creativity and passion that went into creating these pieces. These controversial works have been the talk of the art world since the beginning of the 20th century and are now available to be explored and discovered.

MAC. Req: System 7.0 or higher; 7.01 system requirement.
WIN. Req: 4 MB RAM; System 386 or higher; Windows 3.1 or higher; Multimedia PC with CD-ROM drive.
CD-ROM: CD90101. $59.98.

Pathways Through Jerusalem

This hybrid CD-ROM takes the user on a tour of Jerusalem, from the Old City to the more modern East Jerusalem and West Jerusalem. Visit the Western Wall, the Via Delarosa, the Old City's Jewish, Muslim, Christian and Armenian Quarters, the Dome of the Rock and more. View a timeline of 3,000 years of Jerusalem's history or move between eras and watch the face of the city change. Featuring brilliantly crafted video, meticulously re-created historical sites, carefully preserved ruins from the Crusades and more.

MAC. Req: Not available at present.
WIN. Req: Not available at present.
CD-ROM: CD90099. $49.98.

Peter and the Wolf

Classic children's tale of Peter's romp through the meadow is a great CD for the youngest listeners/computer kids. Tony Randall narrates this entertaining look at the symphony, placing the viewer in the concert hall, moving from spectator to participant. Click and explore as kids learn musical phrases; an orchestra pit game allows them to assemble musical phrases in any order they choose. Top-notch visuals and story.

WIN. Req: 4MB RAM, 2MB available hard-disk space.
CD-ROM: CD90110. $49.98.

Photopaedia Vol. 1: 100 Japanese Photographers, 1993

Edited by critic Shuhei Takahashi, this hybrid CD-ROM features over 900 photographs by 100 of the best modern Japanese photographers. Ranging from fashion and advertising to documentary and art, these images represent a wide variety of artistic styles and approaches. Includes a detailed analysis of the work of each photographer, business addresses for all photographers featured in the program, and more.

MAC. Req: Not available at present.
WIN. Req: Not available at present.
CD-ROM: CD90086. $59.95.
Shuhei Takahashi, Japan, 1993

Photopaedia Vol. 2: Faces of Summer by Koichi Inakoshi

This hybrid CD-ROM features over 400 photographs, many never before published, by renowned artist Koichi Inakoshi. Taken during his travels throughout the world, this retrospective collection is full of evocative images of the experiences of his journeys. Also included are accompanying literature, a recent biography of Inakoshi, a critical study of his work, and an autobiographical essay. Edited by noted critic Shuhei Takahashi.

MAC. Req: Not available at present.
WIN. Req: Not available at present.
CD-ROM: CD90087. $59.95.

Photopaedia Vol. 3: Still Lifes by Diane Wesson

British photographer Diane Wesson's still lifes of such familiar objects as stones, feathers, flowers and fruits are highlighted in this hybrid CD-ROM. Over 100 of her images, full of textured transparency, masterfully layered light and delicate composition, are included. This project, edited by Shuhei Takahashi, also includes his essays *Women Photographers* and *History of Photography*.

MAC. Req: Not available at present.
WIN. Req: Not available at present.
CD-ROM: CD90088. $59.95.

Planetary Taxi (Visual Almanac Series, Vol. 2)

Thousands of facts about our solar system come to life in this challenging game of discovery. Find out where a golf ball will fly the farthest, bounce the highest, or freeze the fastest. See the spectacular QuickTime movies of recent NASA missions.

MAC. Req: Any Macintosh with color display; System 7; CD-ROM drive; no more than 2.2MB available RAM (4MB installed).
WIN. Req: 486SX-33 or higher processor; 640x480, 256-color display (accelerator recommended); 8MB RAM; MPC2-compatible CD-ROM drive; sound card (16-bit) with speakers or headphones; Windows 3.1 or Windows 95.
CD-ROM: CD90009. $39.95.
M. Nanny & R. Mohl, USA

Poetry in Motion

Eighteen modern poets, including Helen Adam, Miguel Algarin, Amiri Baraka, Ted Berrigan, Charles Bukowski, William S. Burroughs, John Cage, Jim Carroll, Jayne Cortez, Christopher Dewdney, Kenward Elmslie, Allen Ginsberg, John Giorno, Ed Sanders, Ntozake Shange, Gary Snyder, Tom Waits and Anne Waldman, perform their work and talk about what inspires them. The video is linked with the complete text of each poem so you can read along.

MAC. Req: Any Macintosh with color display; System 7; CD-ROM drive; no more than 2.2MB available RAM (4MB installed).
WIN. Req: 25-MHz 486SX or higher processor; MS-DOS 5 or later; 640x480, 256-color display; 4MB RAM (8MB recommended).
CD-ROM: CD90015. $29.95.
Ron Mann, USA

Poetry in Motion II

Twelve noted authors performs their works and talk about what inspires them. Taking up where *Poetry in Motion* left off, this hybrid CD-ROM includes work by poets Jim Carroll (author of *The Basketball Diaries*), Spalding Gray (author of *Swimming to Cambodia*), Diane di Prima (author of *Memoirs of a Beatnik*), Allen Ginsberg (author of *Howl*), Amiri Baraka, Charles Bukowski, Tom Waits, Cookie Mueller, Anne Waldman, Peter Orlovsky and more. "The readings bring the works alive, revealing intonations a solitary reader might not otherwise notice" (*PC Magazine*).

MAC. Req: 68030 processor (examples: Performa 575; Quadra; Centris) or better; 7.0 operating system or later; 8 MB RAM; 640x480 color monitor or 13" display; Double-speed CD-ROM drive.
WIN. Req: 486SX-33 or higher processor; 640x480, 256-color display (accelerator recommended); 8 MB RAM; MPC2-compatible CD-ROM drive; Sound card (16-bit) with speakers or headphones; Windows 3.1 or Windows 95.
CD-ROM: CD90077. $29.98.
Ron Mann, USA

Portraits of American Presidents

This informative CD-ROM covers more than 200 years of American Presidents, from George Washington to Bill Clinton, and everyone in between. *Portraits of American Presidents* is broken down into three smaller sections: *The Presidents of a New Nation, 1789-1829*, *The Presidents of a National Struggle, 1829-1901* and *The Presidents of a World Power, 1901-Present*. Includes 30 minutes of NBC News footage, more than 300 rare archival photographs and illustrations, commentary by noted scholars, interactive timelines and trivia game challenges to help make learning fun.

WIN. Req: 68030 processor, double speed (recommended), 4 Mb RAM, 3 Mb free hard disk space, EGA or SVGA sound device compatible with Microsoft Windows (recommended), mouse compatible with Microsoft Windows.
CD-ROM: CD90074. $49.95.

Puppet Motel

It's never-ending performance art with Laurie Anderson, the artist known for constantly pushing the boundaries of music, technology and expression. *Puppet Motel* offers the full range of Laurie Anderson's imagination through videos, music, text and excerpts from her recent *Stories from the Nerve Bible* piece. This CD-ROM is the first one to tie directly into World Wide Web and can be used to download new Laurie Anderson videos. Set design by Hsin-Chien Huang.

MAC. Req: 68030 processor (examples: Performa 575; Quadra; Centris) or better; 7.0 operating system or later; 8MB RAM; 640x480 color monitor or 13" display; double-speed CD-ROM drive.
WIN. Req: 486SX-33 or higher processor; 640x480, 256-color display (accelerator recommended); 8MB RAM; MPC2-compatible CD-ROM drive; Sound card (16-bit) with speakers or headphones; Windows 3.1 or Windows 95.
CD-ROM: CD90076. $39.95.
L Anderson & H Huang, USA

Record of Lodoss War, Volume 1

This full-length CD-ROM contains episodes 1-3 of the story of Lodoss, the accursed island. The battle for the future of Lodoss begins as six people are drawn together to save the island from an evil far worse than any of the fires and wars that have ravaged it in the past thousand years. Anime, Japanese with English subtitles.

DOS. Req: Windows 3.1 and MS DOS 5.0 or higher; 80386SX MHz or higher CPU and CD ROM drive; 4 Mb RAM; SVGA with at least 256 color display; Soundblaster compatible sound card; Quicktime 1.1 or better (included).
MAC. Req: System 7 or higher; 68020, 68030, 68040, or Power PC CPU and CD ROM drive; 4 Mb RAM; 256 color monitor (or better); Quicktime 1.5 or better (included).
WIN. Req: Windows 3.1 and MS DOS 5.0 or higher; 80386SX MHz or higher CPU and CD ROM drive; 4 Mb RAM; SVGA with at least 256 color display; Soundblaster compatible sound card; Quicktime 1.1 or better (included).
CD-ROM: CD90062. $24.95.
80 mins.

The Residents: Freak Show

The Residents, based in San Francisco, have created innovative music, videos and performance art since 1972. Their famous quirk is that no one ever sees their faces or learns their true identities, and this is no exception. Animator Jim Ludtke breathes life into The Residents through Tex the Barker, Herman the Human Mole, Harry the Head, Wanda the Worm Woman, Jelly Jack and Benny the Bump, and you peek into their beyond-the-freak-show lives and discover fetishes, fantasies, rituals and tragic secrets.

MAC. Req: Any color-capable Macintosh (25-MHz 68030 processor or better recommended); System 7; not more than 6.2MB of available RAM (8MB installed); 13" color monitor; CD-ROM drive.
WIN. Req: 486SX-33 or higher processor; 640x480, 256-color display (accelerator recommended); 8MB RAM; MPC2-compatible CD-ROM drive; sound card (16-bit) with speakers or headphones; Windows 3.1 or Windows 95.
CD-ROM: CD90032. $39.95.
Jim Ludtke, USA

Richard Strauss: Three Tone Poems

A sweeping, lavish look at Richard Strauss' tribute to Romantic myths and heroes from Russell Steinberg, an author and composer who teaches music at UCLA.

MAC. Req: Macintosh Plus or later (any Mac produced since 1986) running system 6.0.7 or later; CD-ROM drive; 1.5 Mb of available RAM. If running system 6, must have at least 2 Mb RAM installed; if running System 7, must have at least 3 Mb. Requires speakers or headphones if CD-ROM drive is external.
CD-ROM: CD90026. $59.95.
Russell Steinberg, USA

Robert Mapplethorpe: An Overview

An edited overview of the work of controversial photographer Robert Mapplethorpe. While many of the late artist's better known works have not been included, this CD-ROM gives a good introduction to Mapplethorpe's graceful and evocative floral photographs, his insightful celebrity portraits, and some of his less widely known early images. Suitable for all ages.

MAC. Req: 68030 Processor or better. Double-Speed CD-ROM Graphics Card strongly recommended. Double-Speed CD-ROM Drive. System 6.05 or higher with 32-bit QuickDraw (7.0 recommended).
WIN. Req: 8 MB RAM. Microsoft Windows 3.1. 256 Color S-VGA Minimum. 24-bit Graphics Card strongly recommended. Double-Speed CD-ROM Drive.
CD-ROM: CD90104. $59.95.

Rodney's Wonder Window

Artist Rodney Alan Greenblat's 24 hands-on colorful stories include "Probe and Poke Pet Shop", "Data Shorts", "Chip and Peg's Adventures in Shapeland", and more. Children and adults alike will love these interactive episodes in this inventive playland of art and sound.

MAC. Req: Any Macintosh with color display; System 7; CD-ROM drive; 640x480 resolution (13") color monitor; speakers or headphones if CD-ROM drive is external; supports System 6.07.
WIN. Req: 25-MHz 486SX or higher processor; MS-DOS 5 or later; 640x480, 256-color display; 4MB RAM (8MB recommended).
CD-ROM: CD90007. $39.95.

Sacred and Secular: The Aerial Photography of Marilyn Bridges

Photographs of ceremonial places, shot from an altitude of 300 feet, of six featured sites—Egypt, Mexico, Peru, the United States, Greece and Britain. Includes background information about the culture and landscape of each site. Zoom feature allows examination of 100 richly textured B&W photographs in detail, and five guided tours link the photographs thematically. Audio commentary from Marilyn Bridges, the photographer.

MAC. Req: 68030 processor (examples: Performa 575; Quadra; Centris) or better; 7.0 operating system or later; 8 MB RAM; 640x480 color monitor or 13" display; Double-speed CD-ROM drive.
WIN. Req: 486SX-33 or higher processor; 640x480, 256-color display (accelerator recommended); 8 MB RAM; MPC2-compatible CD-ROM drive; Sound card (16-bit) with speakers or headphones; Windows 3.1 or Windows 95.
CD-ROM: CD90121. $39.95.

Salt of the Earth

Features the complete film *Salt of the Earth*, along with the short film *The Hollywood Ten...*. Filmed during the height of the McCarthy Era by blacklisted filmmakers, this film is a moving portrait of the 1951 zinc miners' strike in Silver City, New Mexico. This version includes the original screenplay and notes by Michael Wilson, production photographs, critical and historical essays, reviews of the film, and source materials in English, Spanish, French and German.

MAC. Req: Any color-capable Macintosh (25-MHz 68030 processor or better recommended); System 7; no more than 6.2MB of available RAM (8MB installed); 13" color monitor; CD-ROM drive.
CD-ROM: CD90011. $49.95.
M. Wilson, H. Biberm

Shakespeare's Macbeth

This brilliant edition prepared by UCLA Professor A.R. Braunmuller provides instant annotation, the entire Royal Shakespeare Company performance, clips from Roman Polanski and Orson Welles' film versions or Kurosawa's *Throne of Blood*. The new edition of the play contains 1,500 annotations and a 24,000 word commentary with the RSC in Trevor Nunn's production, with Ian McKellan and Judi Dench as the Macbeths. Includes a gallery of QuickTime clips from other performances of *Macbeth* and concordance and textual analysis.

MAC. Req: 68030 processor (examples: Performa 575; Quadra; Centris) or better; 7.0 operating system or later; 8 MB RAM; 640x480 color monitor or 13" display; double-speed CD-ROM drive.
WIN. Req: 486SX-33 or higher processor; 640x480, 256-color display (accelerator recommended); 8MB RAM; MPC2-compatible CD-ROM drive; sound card (16-bit) with speakers or headphones; Windows 3.1 or Windows 95.
CD-ROM: CD90003. $49.95.

Shining Flower

Available outside of Japan for the first time, *Shining Flower* combines mesmerizing music, rich animations, images from oil paintings and more. This "interactive haiku" aids your mind as it wanders through a metaphorical journey to the Flower, the source of all power and true enlightenment.
MAC. Req: Any Macintosh with color display; System 7; CD-ROM drive; no more than 3.2 Mb available RAM (5 Mb installed).
CD-ROM: CD90029. $39.95.
Japan

A Silly Noisy House

Peggy Weil's children's adventure of secret passageways, a teddy bear's birthday party, magic wands and a piano-playing spider are only a few of the many surprises. Children move from room to room clicking on hundreds of objects to uncover animation, tongue twisters, nursery rhymes, songs and sound effects. For ages three and older; no reading required.
MAC. Req: Any Macintosh with color display; System 7; CD-ROM drive; no more than 2.2MB available RAM (4MB installed).
WIN. Req: 25-MHz 486SX or higher processor; MS-DOS 5 or later; 640x480, 16-color display (256-color recommended); 4MB RAM (8MB recommended).
CD-ROM: CD90005. $59.95.
Peggy Weil

SkyTrip America

Irene Bedard (*Pocahontas*) narrates this interactive look at the United States from the air. Kids control their choice of either a space-age hoverjet, a Wright Brothers-style "sputter-clunker" or a hot air balloon on an adventure through American history and geography. History comes alive when recounted by such pioneers as Christopher Columbus, Mark Twain, Harriet Tubman and Neil Armstrong, and the 3-D graphics and informative video clips give kids a memorable and informative tour of such sites as the Statue of Liberty, Mount Rushmore, the Grand Canyon and the Alamo. Other features include "The Pony Express game," a 3-D Old West Ghost Town, home of the Mining Maze Game" and "Hangman Trivia," and cultural perspectives from celebrities such as pro basketball player Chris Weber, tennis pro Michael Chang and magician Penn Jilette of the infamous combo Penn & Teller. Suitable for children ages 9 & up.
MAC. Req: System hardware: Performa, Centris, Quadra or PowerPC. System software: System 7.0. Memory: 8MB RAM. Monitor: 256 colors. CD-ROM drive: Double speed (2x). Sound card: N/A. Input device: mouse.
WIN. Req: System hardware: 486 33Mhz or faster, Hard Drive. System software: Microsoft Windows 3.1 or Windows 95, MS/PC DOS 3.1. Memory: 8 MB of RAM. Monitor: VGA Monitor (256 colors). CD-ROM drive: Double speed (2x). Sound card: Windows compatible. Input device: mouse. .
CD-ROM: CD90107. $39.95.
USA, 1996

So I've Heard, Vol. 1: Bach and Before

Clips from two millennia of music are accompanied by commentary from American music critic Alan Rich, spanning from ancient Greek rituals to the passionate complexities of Bach and Handel. Also features search tools that will find all references to a particular composer, work, or glossary definition.
MAC. Req: Macintosh Plus or better (any Mac produced since 1986) running system 6.0.7 or later; CD-ROM drive; 1.5MB of available RAM. If running system 6, must have at least 2MB RAM installed; if running System 7, must have at least 3MB. Requires speakers or headphones if CD-ROM drive is external.
CD-ROM: CD90022. $24.95.
Alan Rich, USA

So I've Heard, Vol. 2: The Classical Ideal

American music critic Alan Rich comments on the Eighteenth Century's momentous changes in music, as exemplified by Mozart and Haydn. Special search tools will help you find all references to a particular composer, work, or glossary definition.
MAC. Req: Macintosh Plus or better (any Mac produced since 1986) running system 6.0.7 or later; CD-ROM drive; 1.5MB of available RAM. If running system 6, must have at least 2MB RAM installed; if running System 7, must have at least 3MB. Requires speakers or headphones if CD-ROM drive is external.
CD-ROM: CD90023. $24.95.
Alan Rich, USA

So I've Heard, Vol. 3: Beethoven & Beyond

Clips from the late classical era are accompanied by American music critic Alan Rich's commentaries on the profound impact of Beethoven's masterful compositions. In addition, special search tools help you find all reference to a particular composer, work, or glossary definition.
MAC. Req: Macintosh Plus or better (any Mac produced since 1986) running system 6.0.7 or later; CD-ROM drive; 1.5MB of available RAM. If running system 6, must have at least 2MB RAM installed; if running System 7, must have at least 3MB. Requires speakers or headphones if CD-ROM drive is external. Or, any Macintosh with color display; System 7; CD-ROM drive; 640x480 16-color display; 4MB RAM.
CD-ROM: CD90024. $24.95.
Alan Rich, USA

So I've Heard, Vol. 4: Romantic Heights

Clips of the exquisitely emotional music of the late 19th century are accompanied by American music critic Alan Rich's commentaries. Use special search tools to help you find all references to a particular composer, work, or glossary definition.
MAC. Req: Not available at present.
WIN. Req: Not available at present.
CD-ROM: CD90040. $24.95.
Alan Rich, USA

So I've Heard, Vol. 5: The Stravinsky Impact

The music of the early 20th century and the dawn of a new era in the arts is expounded upon by American music critic and author Alan Rich. Special search tools aid in finding all references to a particular composer, work, or glossary definition.
MAC. Req: Not available at present.
WIN. Req: Not available at present.
CD-ROM: CD90041. $24.95.
Alan Rich, USA

Sound Toys

Part toy, part musical instrument, make music by experimenting with different sounds and visuals. A fusion of wacky and whimsical instruments allows the beginner to compose, record, and save compositions of any length—up to six in one session. Weird and intensely gratifying.
MAC. Req: 68030 processor (examples Performa 575; Quadra; Centris or better). 7.0 operating system or later; 8 MB RAM; 640x480 color monitor or 13" display; Double-speed CD-ROM drive.
WIN. Req: 486SX-33 or higher processor; 640x480, 256-color display (accelerator recommended); 8 MB RAM; MPC2-compatible CD-ROM drive; Sound card (16-bit) with speakers or headphones; Windows 3.1 or Windows 95.
CD-ROM: CD90127. $39.95.

Spanish Pronunciation Tutor

This hybrid CD-ROM aids students either learning Spanish for the first time, or simply fine tuning their Spanish speaking skills. *Spanish Pronunciation Tutor* allows students to listen to Spanish being spoken by a native speaker, record themselves speaking, and then compare the two. This educational CD-ROM features interactive help, hints to explain the finer points of Spanish pronunciation, detailed animations of the speech process, interactive exercise screens, pronunciation tests for tracking your progress, video and audio of native Spanish speakers and more. From The Learning Company.
MAC. Req: Runs on all Macintosh computers equipped with a CD-ROM drive, a 256-color monitor, 680.30/25MHz or better processor, and System 7. Requires 4 MB of memory. Requires a microphone or MacRecorder.
WIN. Req: System 386 or higher; Multimedia PC with CD-ROM drive; Requires 386/25MHz or better, 4 MB RAM, Windows 3.1 or higher, doublespeed CD-ROM drive, Windows compatible sound card, VGA or better, plus a microphone.
CD-ROM: CD90096. $59.98.

Spinal Tap

The CD-ROM companion to Rob Reiner's hilarious rockumentary spoof *This Is Spinal Tap*. This hybrid CD-ROM picks up where the film left off, and is the first CD-ROM to offer three concurrent, synched audio tracks. Includes two audio tracks discussing the making of the film, an hour of QuickTime video that features outtakes, video clips and the working script from the film, a Smart Search feature, 16-bit Dolby sound, commentary from Rob Reiner and more. "Get yourself a copy of this witty, ingenious and deliciously nasty package" (*Premiere Magazine*). Two disc set.
MAC. Req: 68030 processor (examples: Performa 575; Quadra; Centris) or better; 7.0 operating system or later; 8 MB RAM; 640x480 color monitor or 13" display; Double-speed CD-ROM drive.
WIN. Req: 486SX-33 or higher processor; 640x480, 256-color display (accelerator recommended); 8 MB RAM; MPC2-compatible CD-ROM drive; Sound card (16-bit) with speakers or headphones; Windows 3.1 or Windows 95.
CD-ROM: CD90078. $29.95.
Rob Reiner, USA

Stars of the Louvre: 4,000 Years of Greatness

This in-depth tour of the famous Louvre Museum is a stunning and elegant guide to hundreds of the world's most beloved treasures. Over 200 works of art are celebrated here, including works by masters such as Da Vinci, Gericault, Botticelli, Raphael, Van Dyck, Rodin and Reubens. Learn the complete stories behind such masterpieces as the "Mona Lisa," The Raft of the Medusa," the "Seated Scribe," the "Victory of Samothrace" and the "Venus de Milo." State-of-the-art CD-ROM technology allows you to highlight sections of paintings for closer study and to view sculptures from all 360 degrees. A 4,000 year timeline, spanning five of the richest periods of art history, shows the ties between art, politics, and culture. Also included are over three hours of music and two hours of narration, comprehensive biographies of the artists whose works are featured, and a complete index. From *The Great Artists Collection* series.
MAC. Req: Apple Macintosh LC or later model with at least 4 MB of RAM for the application. 640 x 480, 256 color graphics. System 7.0 or later. 32-Bit QuickDraw, Quicktime 2.0. Apple-compatible double-speed (300 Kps) CD-ROM drive.
WIN. Req: 386sx or better processor, 8 MB of RAM, Double-speed (300 Kps) CD-ROM drive, Microsoft Winodws compatible sound card, Super VGA graphics (640 x 480, 256 colors). Microsoft Windows version 3.1. MS-DOS version 5.0 or later, MS-DOS CD-ROM extensions. Stereo headphones or speakers. Minimum 1.5 MB free hard disk space.
OTHER. Req: ONLY available as a PC/MAC Hybrid.
CD-ROM: CD90106. $39.98.
USA/France, 1995

Take Five

The original stress-reduction CD-ROM! This program guides you through four different ways to soothe aching muscles and features 45 video demonstrations of exercises to restore energy and flexibility. Also included is "Visual Vacation", a series of beautiful landscapes to relax your eyes, "Music of the Spheres", an audio program of the surf in the Amazon rain forest, and "The Mind's Eye", a guided imagery program.
MAC. Req: Any Macintosh with color display; System 7; CD-ROM drive; no more than 3.2MB available RAM (5MB installed).
WIN. Req: 486SX-25 or higher processor; 640x480, 256-color display; 4MB RAM (8MB recommended); MPC-compatible CD-ROM drive; sound card (8-bit) with speakers or headphones; Microsoft Windows 3.1 or Windows 95.
CD-ROM: CD90045. $29.95.
Dina Silver, USA

Theatre of the Imagination

During the golden age of radio, Orson Welles was a formidable talent who dazzled listeners with the likes of *War of the Worlds* and *Heart of Darkness*. This hybrid CD-ROM features 15 of Orson Welles' programs from his 1930s and 1940s radio show *Radio Stories by Orson Welles and the Mercury Theatre*. Also featured are program notes and transcripts of every program; over six hours of audio recordings; supplementary articles, videos and clippings on Orson Welles, his programs, and the early history of radio.
MAC. Req: 68030 processor (examples: Performa 575; Quadra; Centris) or better; 7.0 operating system or later; 8 MB RAM; 640x480 color monitor or 13" display; Double-speed CD-ROM drive.
WIN. Req: 486SX-33 or higher processor; 640x480, 256-color display (accelerator recommended); 8 MB RAM; MPC2-compatible CD-ROM drive; Sound card (16-bit) with speakers or headphones; Windows 3.1 or Windows 95.
CD-ROM: CD90079. $29.98.
USA

Think & Talk French

Learn French with the "Berlitz Method," the self-teaching program used by the U.S. foreign service to teach useful words and phrases in record time. This interactive, hybrid CD-ROM allows a phrase to be heard as many times as desired by simply clicking the mouse. Also, record yourself speaking and compare your French to the native speaker's. Includes 50 language lessons, a vocabulary of over 1,000 words, an online, bilingual dictionary and more. From Berlitz.
MAC. Req: System 7.0 or higher; 7.01 system requirement.
OTHER. Req: Multimedia PC.
CD-ROM: CD90090. $199.00.

Think & Talk German

Now the "Berlitz Method," the self-teaching program used by the U.S. foreign service to teach useful words and phrases in record time, is available on CD-ROM. This interactive, hybrid CD-ROM allows a phrase to be heard as many times as desired by simply clicking the mouse. Also, record yourself speaking German and compare your German to that of a native speaker. Includes 50 language lessons, a vocabulary of over 1,000 words, an online, bilingual dictionary, and more. From Berlitz.
MAC. Req: System 7.0 or higher; 7.01 system requirement.
OTHER. Req: Multimedia PC.
CD-ROM: CD90091. $199.00.

Think & Talk Italian

You can learn to speak Italian like a native with the "Berlitz Method," the self-teaching program used by the U.S. foreign service to teach useful words and phrases in record time. This interactive, hybrid CD-ROM allows a phrase to be heard as many times as desired by simply clicking the mouse. Also, record yourself speaking and compare your Italian to that of a native speaker. Includes 50 language lessons, a vocabulary of over 1,000 words, an online, bilingual dictionary, and more. From Berlitz.
MAC. Req: System 7.0 or higher; 7.01 system requirement.
OTHER. Req: Multimedia PC.
CD-ROM: CD90092. $199.00.

Think & Talk Spanish

Learning Spanish will feel effortless with the "Berlitz Method," the self-teaching program used by the U.S. foreign service to teach useful words and phrases in record time. This interactive, hybrid CD-ROM allows a phrase to be heard as many times as desired by simply clicking the mouse. Also, record yourself speaking and compare your Spanish to a native speaker's. Includes 50 language lessons, a vocabulary of over 1,000 words, an online, bilingual dictionary, and more. From Berlitz.
MAC. Req: System 7.0 or higher; 7.01 system requirement.
OTHER. Req: Multimedia PC.
CD-ROM: CD90093. $199.00.

Treasures of the Museum of Natural History

Scientific and anthropological background on 50 of the Museum's greatest treasures, from the Tasmanian wolf to a dinosaur mummy to Margaret Mead. Games, teacher's guide, a 3-D tour of the new Dinosaur Hall and the Hall of African Mammals. Over one hour of historic and descriptive film footage.
MAC. Req: 68030 processor (examples: Performa 575; Quadra; Centris) or better; 7.0 operating system or later; 8 MB RAM; 640x480 color monitor or 13" display; Double-speed CD-ROM drive.
WIN. Req: 486SX-33 or higher processor; 640x480, 256-color display (accelerator recommended); 8 MB RAM; MPC2-compatible CD-ROM drive; Sound card (16-bit) with speakers or headphones; Windows 3.1 or Windows 95.
CD-ROM: CD90124. $39.95.

Trouble Is My Business: The Raymond Chandler Library

Offers the complete Raymond Chandler works, an interactive map of Chandler's L.A., video clips and stills from movies made of his works, some of Chandler's correspondence which relates to his fiction writing. Each book is preceded by a movie still, and searching navigation and printing are easy and evident.
WIN. Req: Not available at present.
CD-ROM: CD90116. $79.98.

Truths & Fictions

This pictorial essay focuses on the work of photographer Pedro Meyer. It is "a journey from documentary to digital photography" as Meyer discusses the methods he uses to compose images and talks about the process through which his works reach completion. "...this disc is truly interactive in a way few multimedia CD-ROMs are: it makes you think" (*USA Today*). This Macintosh CD-ROM features bilingual (English and Spanish) narration, over 2,000 photographs, a "Digital Studio" hosted by Pedro Meyer and more.
MAC. Req: 68030 processor (examples: Performa 575; Quadra; Centris) or better; 7.0 operating system or later; 8 MB RAM; 640x480 color monitor or 13" display; Double-speed CD-ROM drive.
CD-ROM: CD90082. $39.95.
Pedro Meyer

Understanding McLuhan: The Life and Work of Marshall McLuhan

Complete text of McLuhan's *Understanding Media* and *The Gutenberg Galaxy*, a "Probes" section to learn about McLuhan's main theories, an extensive biography, complete audio and text transcript of a McLuhan lecture and video footage of Neil Postman, Camille Paglia and others commenting on McLuhan's theories.
MAC. Req: 68030 processor (examples: Performa 575; Quadra; Centris) or better; 7.0 operating system or later; 8MB RAM; 640x480 color monitor or 13" display; Double-speed CD-ROM drive.
WIN. Req: 486SX-33 or higher processor; 640x480, 256-color display (accelerator recommended); 8 MB RAM; MPC2-compatible CD-ROM drive; Sound card (16-bit) with speakers or headphones; Windows 3.1 or Windows 95.
CD-ROM: CD90119. $39.95.

Urotsukidoji III: Return of the Overfiend 1

The world is ravaged by a savage monster called Nagumo. Now, 20 years later, a new world order has evolved and is headed by the Demon Beasts. Tokyo and its ruler, Caesar, are at constant war with the Demon Beasts. Elsewhere in the story, the Overfiend is born decades earlier than he is supposed to be because he becomes aware of an evil presence. Anime. In English.
MAC. Req: System 7 or higher. 68020, 68030, 68040, or Power PC CPU and CD ROM drive. 4 MB RAM, 256 color monitor (or better). Quicktime 1.5 or better (included).
WIN. Req: Windows 3.1 and MS DOS 5.0 or higher. 80386SZ MHz or higher CPU and CD ROM drive. 4MB RAM, SVGA with at least 256 color display. Soundblaster compatible sound card. Quicktime 1.1 or better (included).
CD-ROM: CD90067. $24.95.
Japan, 60 mins.

Using Macromedia Director

The complete guide to version 3.1.3 of Director, the bestselling guide to the graphics authoring tool. A comprehensive source for new authors and seasoned professionals alike, this CD-ROM offers over 80 movies (in both QuickTime and Director formats), Lingo scripts, and more.
MAC. Req: Macintosh Plus or better (any Mac produced since 1986) running system 6.0.7 or later; CD-ROM drive; 1.5 Mb of available RAM. If running system 6, must have at least 2 Mb RAM installed; if running system 7, must have at least 3 Mb. Or, any Macintosh with color display; System 7; CD-ROM drive.
CD-ROM: CD90046. $49.95.
T. Bove & C. Rhodes

Van Gogh: Starry Night: A History of Matter and a Matter of History

This hybrid CD-ROM's foundation is Vincent Van Gogh's famous painting "Starry Night." Research done at UCLA's Griffith Observatory determined that the painting was most probably a representation of the pre-dawn sky over Saint Rémy on June 19, 1889. Art history professor Albert Boime used that information as a starting point to create a CD-ROM that features audio, over 200 images, Van Gogh's personal correspondence, illustrations, photographs and more.
MAC. Req: 68030 processor (examples: Performa 575; Quadra; Centris) or better; 7.0 operating system or later; 8 MB RAM; 640x480 color monitor or 13" display; Double-speed CD-ROM drive.
WIN. Req: 486SX-33 or higher processor; 640x480, 256-color display (accelerator recommended); 8 MB RAM; MPC2-compatible CD-ROM drive; Sound card (16-bit) with speakers or headphones; Windows 3.1 or Windows 95.
CD-ROM: CD90075. $39.98.
Albert Boime, USA

The Visual Almanac Complete

The complete package includes the same videodisc found in the original *Almanac*, featuring 7,000 image resources, a full hour of sound, and both still images and motion video. Also included is a 200-page guide which explains the contents of both the video and software, and suggests activities for classroom use. The updated software includes a data-management system for finding images based on key words, lets you manipulate and present sounds and images, and includes a list of suggested classroom activities.
MAC. Req: Macintosh Plus or better (any Mac produced since 1986) running system 6.0.7 or later; CD-ROM drive; 1.5 Mb of available RAM. If running system 6, must have at least 2 Mb RAM installed; if running System 7, must have at least 3 Mb. Multiple configurations or special requirements possible; supports System 6.0.7.
CD-ROM: CD90044. $149.95.
USA, 1994

The Visual Almanac Upgrade

Originally released in 1990, *The Visual Almanac* has become an essential teaching and learning tool in classrooms across the country, perfect for all disciplines and grade levels. This update makes *The Visual Almanac* compatible with today's improved Macintosh hardware and software, and includes a data-management system that finds and organizes according to key words, sample compositions, suggested classroom activities and HyperCard 2.1.
MAC. Req: Macintosh Plus or better (any Mac produced since 1986) running system 6.0.7 or later; CD-ROM drive; 1.5MB of available RAM. If running system 6, must have at least 2MB RAM installed; if running System 7, must have at least 3MB. Multiple configurations or special requirements possible; supports System 6.0.7.
CD-ROM: CD90035. $49.95.
USA, 1994

Who Built America? Education Edition

This edition of *Who Built America?* features five copies of the CD-ROM along with specially prepared Expanded Book editions of five works of the period, an extensive teaching guide, lesson plans, student activities, and suggestions for uses across the curriculum. This program is suitable for students grades 9 through college and allows them access to thousands of primary sources, including original diaries, letters, photographs, archival audio and oral histories and films.
MAC. Req: Any color-capable Macintosh (25-MHz 68030 processor or better recommended); System 7; not more than 6.2 Mb of available RAM (8 Mb installed); 13" color monitor; CD-ROM drive. Or, all Powerbooks and Duos, and all desktop Macintoshes driving 13" monitors; 1.5 Mb of available RAM. If running system 6.0.7 or 6.0.8, must have at least 2 Mb RAM installed; if running System 7, must have at least 3 Mb installed.
CD-ROM: CD90034. $350.00.
R. Rosenzweig, S. Br, USA

Who Built America? American Social History Project

Based on a definitive two-volume history, authors Roy Rosenzweig and Steve Brier have extended their text with thousands of source documents—audio, video and text. Read 20 years of a Norwegian immigrant's poignant letters home, listen to a young boy's account of a lynching in rural Florida in 1902 or to William Jennings Bryan's famous "Cross of God" speech. Thousands of historical documents including pictures, letters, photographs, archival audio and films, graphs, games and quizzes, the world's first crossword puzzle, and extensive research tools including search, index and notebook.
MAC. Req: Color capable, 25-MHz or better, 13" monitor, CD-ROM drive.
CD-ROM: CD90004. $99.95.

With Open Eyes: Images from the Art Institute of Chicago

Includes a laserdisc and Mac software, designed especially for young students, to offer an entertaining introduction to the world of art. This program includes over 200 works of art selected from the Art Institute of Chicago's collection and each is accompanied by music, sound effects, poetry and spoken information about the work, allowing pre-readers to explore artworks independently. Also includes jigsaw puzzles, connect the dots, hide and seek games, magnified details and more.

MAC. Req: 68030 processor (examples: Performa 575; Quadra; Centris) or better; 7.0 operating system or later; 8MB RAM; 640x480 color monitor or 13" display; double-speed CD-ROM drive.

WIN. Req: 486SX-33 or higher processor; 640x480, 256-color display (accelerator recommended); 8MB RAM; MPC2-compatible CD-ROM drive; sound card (16-bit) with speakers or headphones; Windows 3.1 or Windows 95.

CD-ROM: CD90036. $39.95.

Wolfgang Amadeus Mozart: The "Dissonant" Quartet

This CD-ROM contains the energy and creativity of Wolfgang Amadeus Mozart and invites you to listen to the music of Mozart's "Dissonant" Quartet as scholar and pianist Robert Winter's commentary on each theme scrolls by. There is also a detailed glossary of musical terms and theory, and a guide to the life and times of Mozart.

MAC. Req: Macintosh Plus or better (any Mac produced since 1986) running system 6.0.7 or later; CD-ROM drive; 1.5MB of available RAM. If running system 6, must have at least 2MB RAM installed; if running System 7, must have at least 3MB. Requires speakers or headphones if CD-ROM drive is external.

CD-ROM: CD90020. $59.95.

Robert Winter

A World Alive

James Earl Jones narrates this interactive documentary which covers everything from the humpback whale to leaf-cutter ants to the Pacific Ocean to Northern elephant seals. The documentary is linked to an interactive program that showcases the more than 100 species featured in the movie.

MAC. Req: Any Macintosh with color display; System 7; CD-ROM drive; no more than 2.2MB available RAM (4MB installed).

WIN. Req: 486SX-25 or higher processor; 640x480, 256-color display; 4MB RAM (8MB recommended); MPC-compatible CD-ROM drive; sound card (8-bit) with speakers or headphones; Microsoft Windows 3.1 or Windows 95.

CD-ROM: CD90008. $39.95.

39 mins.

Writing Women's Lives: Interviews with Eight Accomplished Writers

Isabel Allende, Harriet Doerr, June Jordan, Doris Lessing, Bharati Mukherjee, Mona Simpson, Gloria Steinem and Amy Tan speak about their creative processes. Samples from each author's body of work (including a chapter of Tan's *Joy Luck Club*) and a full length documentary, originally aired on PBS, are included.

MAC. Req: 68030 processor (examples: Performa 575; Quadra; Centris) or better; 7.0 operating system or later; 8 MB RAM; 640x480 color monitor or 13" display; Double-speed CD-ROM drive.

WIN. Req: 486SX-33 or higher processor; 640x480, 256-color display (accelerator recommended); 8 MB RAM; MPC2-compatible CD-ROM drive; Sound card (16-bit) with speakers or headphones; Windows 3.1 or Windows 95.

CD-ROM: CD90120. $39.95.

short film INDEX

director INDEX

title INDEX

D

J

indexes 505

ORDER TOLL FREE 1-800-331-6197

FACETS VIDEO ORDER FORM

QTY	ORDER NO.	TITLE	UNIT PRICE	TOTAL PRICE

If ordering CD-ROM please specify platform.

SHIP TO:

NAME _____

ORGANIZATION _____

STREET _____

CITY _____ STATE _____ ZIP _____

PHONE (____) _____ EVE (____) _____

SUBTOTAL _____

8.75% SALES TAX ON
DELIVERIES WITHIN ILLINOIS _____

SHIPPING & HANDLING: $4.75 MINIMUM
(SEE LEFT COLUMN TO CALCULATE) _____

FACETS COMPLETE
VIDEO CATALOG: $11.95 _____

TOTAL AMOUNT ENCLOSED _____

Thank You for Your Order!

CT14

ORDER TOLL FREE 1-800-331-6197

FACETS VIDEO ORDER FORM

QTY	ORDER NO.	TITLE	UNIT PRICE	TOTAL PRICE

If ordering CD-ROM please specify platform.

SHIP TO:

NAME _____

ORGANIZATION _____

STREET _____

CITY _____ STATE _____ ZIP _____

PHONE (____) _____ EVE (____) _____

SUBTOTAL _____

8.75% SALES TAX ON
DELIVERIES WITHIN ILLINOIS _____

SHIPPING & HANDLING: $4.75 MINIMUM
(SEE LEFT COLUMN TO CALCULATE) _____

FACETS COMPLETE
VIDEO CATALOG: $11.95 _____

TOTAL AMOUNT ENCLOSED _____

Thank You for Your Order!

CT14